*The
Bedford
Introduction
to Drama*

The Bedford Introduction to Drama

FOURTH EDITION

Lee A. Jacobus
University of Connecticut

BEDFORD / ST. MARTIN'S   BOSTON ◆ NEW YORK

This book is dedicated to David Krause.

For Bedford/St.Martin's
Developmental Editor: Maura Shea
Production Editor: Bridget Leahy
Production Supervisor: Dennis Conroy
Director of Marketing: Karen Melton
Editorial Assistant: Tracey Lynne Finch
Production Assistant: Thomas Crehan
Copyeditor: Rosemary Winfield
Text Design: Claire Seng-Niemoeller
Cover Design: Hannus Design Associates
Cover Photo: From the Cottesloe Theatre/Royal National Theatre (London) 1997
   production of *Othello*. Photograph by Donald Cooper/Photostage.
Composition: Stratford Publishing Services
Printing and Binding: RR Donnelley & Sons Company

President: Charles H. Christensen
Editorial Director: Joan E. Feinberg
Editor in Chief: Karen S. Henry
Director of Editing, Design, and Production: Marcia Cohen
Managing Editor: Elizabeth M. Schaaf

Library of Congress Control Number: 00–103098

Acknowledgments

Greek Drama

Figure 1. The Theater of Epidauros, Greece. CORBIS/Michael Nicholson.
Figure 2. Theater at Epidauros from *The Theatre of Dionysus in Athens* by Arthur Wallace Pickard-Cambridge.
   Reprinted by permission of Oxford University Press.

Preface for Instructors

In its fourth edition, *The Bedford Introduction to Drama* remains first and foremost the most comprehensive anthology available: a collection of fifty-two important plays that have shaped dramatic literature from the time of the early Greek dramatists to the present. The book incorporates a number of features that distinguish it from other introductions to drama. Most notably it presents four major playwrights in greater than usual depth — with three plays by William Shakespeare and two each by Sophocles, Henrik Ibsen, and Tennessee Williams. Ninety-one commentaries by playwrights, directors, actors, reviewers, and critics, three cultural casebooks, thorough biographical and critical introductions, brief performance histories, and photographs of landmark productions accompany these and all the plays in the book and offer drama students a unique opportunity to study and write about major figures in the development of drama.

Even when it appears most timeless, all drama (like, of course, all literature) is a product of language, an era, and a complex range of political, social, and ethnic influences. *The Bedford Introduction to Drama* offers a succinct but thorough history of Western drama. A general introduction gives an overview of the great ages of drama, the major genres and elements, and the cultural value of drama. Throughout the book, introductions to significant periods of drama, the playwrights, and the plays focus on the cultural contexts of the works and on their stage history. Timelines following the introduction to each dramatic period present important developments in theater history in their appropriate political, social, and cultural contexts.

The Bedford Introduction to Drama is also a complete resource book for the beginning student of drama. In the general introduction, a discussion of the elements of drama defines the important terms and concepts and demonstrates these concepts in action, drawing its examples from Lady Gregory's one-act play, *The Rising of the Moon*. Nearly every play is accompanied by one or more striking theater photographs, and the plays by playwrights treated in depth are illustrated by photo essays often featuring more than one production to help students understand the plays as texts to be interpreted through performance.

Writing about Drama, the first appendix, shows students possible approaches to commenting on dramatic literature and points the way to developing ideas that can result in probing critical essays. From prewriting to outlining and drafting, the process of writing about drama is illustrated by reference to

Lady Gregory's play, and a sample essay on the play provides one example of drama criticism. Especially useful for assignments involving attendance at theater productions, the section on How to Write a Review analyzes professional reviews and offers suggestions for students writing reviews. The second appendix, the Glossary of Dramatic Terms, defines concepts and terms clearly and concisely. When these terms are first introduced and defined in the text, they appear in small capital letters.

The Selected Bibliography, a third appendix, includes a list of reference works for the major periods of drama, the playwrights, and the plays by the four playwrights treated in depth. The cited general references, histories, biographies, critical studies, journal articles, reviews, and collections of plays are especially useful for research in drama.

While the book presents the plays as texts to be read, a fourth appendix, the Selected List of Film, Video, and Audiocassette Resources, reinforces the element of performance. This list, accompanied by a list of distributors, can help instructors and students find an illuminating treatment of the plays in performance.

New to This Edition
New Plays and Commentaries

Fifteen plays are new to this edition; among them are William Shakespeare's *Othello*, Pedro Calderón de la Barca's *Life Is a Dream*, Bernard Shaw's *Mrs. Warren's Profession*, John Millington Synge's *The Playboy of the Western World*, Eugène Ionesco's *The Lesson*, Caryl Churchill's *Cloud Nine*, Martin McDonagh's *The Beauty Queen of Leenane*, and Paula Vogel's *How I Learned to Drive*. Also new to this edition are thirty-one of ninety-one commentaries that provide a variety of ways for students to think about a play — from the perspective of a critic, a reviewer, an actor, a director, and a playwright.

The fourth edition continues the tradition of offering a strong representation of multicultural and women playwrights and representing them with their most significant works, including *The Rover* by Aphra Behn, *Trifles* by Susan Glaspell, *A Raisin in the Sun* by Lorraine Hansberry, *The Strong Breed* by Wole Soyinka, *Zoot Suit* by Luis Valdez, *Cloud Nine* by Caryl Churchill, *'night, Mother* by Marsha Norman, *Fences* by August Wilson, *M. Butterfly* by David Henry Hwang, *The Death of the Last Black Man in the Whole Entire World* by Suzan-Lori Parks, *"Art"* by Yasmina Reza, and *How I Learned to Drive* by Paula Vogel.

New Cultural Casebooks

Three new cultural casebooks on "The Issue of Race and *Othello*," "The 'Woman Question' in Late Nineteenth-Century Drama," and "The Abbey Theatre and the Irish Literary Renaissance" enable students to think critically about a play or group of plays through a focused study of important cultural contexts. Each casebook comprises an introduction to the topic followed by selected documents, including journal entries, letters, newspaper accounts, and essays. The documents are accompanied by visual materials that illuminate the subject.

More Performance Photographs and Enhanced Design

Significantly more theater photographs (fifty-two are new) of important productions help students visualize the plays in performance. Illuminating theater diagrams and photographs have been added to the historical introductions. New portraits accompany each playwright who is represented by multiple plays. The new larger trim size and opaque paper enhance the quality of the reproductions.

Companion Web Site and Video Library

The new companion Web site at www.bedfordstmartins.com/jacobus helps students succeed in the course with study questions, writing suggestions, and Web assignments to accompany each play; annotated research links for the plays and playwrights in the book; and links to online reviews, important repertory theaters around the country, and internship opportunities. Sample syllabi and assignment ideas are offered for instructors.

A selection of videotapes of plays in the book is available from the Bedford/St. Martin's video library to qualified adopters.

Compact Edition

The Bedford Introduction to Drama, Fourth Edition, is also available in a compact edition containing twenty-six plays, fifty-one commentaries, and one cultural casebook on "The Issue of Race and *Othello*." The compact edition retains all of the longer book's editorial features for those who want a smaller, less expensive anthology.

Acknowledgments

First, I would like to thank those who offered their advice on what to include in the first edition of this book: Jeff Glauner, Park College; Susan Smith, University of Pittsburgh; and Jordan Miller, University of Rhode Island. Second, I am grateful to those who read the introductions and commentaries in the first edition and who gave me the advantage of their knowledge and wisdom. G. Jennifer Wilson, University of California, Los Angeles; William Carroll, Boston University; Ronald Bryden, Graduate Centre for the Study of Drama, University of Toronto; Robert Dial, University of Akron; Jonnie Guerra, Mount Vernon College; and John Timpane, Lafayette College, were all unhesitating in offering suggestions and improvements.

For the second edition, experts in specific historical periods examined the introductions for accuracy and comprehensiveness. Each of the introductions was revised with their suggestions in mind. These reviewers were Michael Cadden, Princeton University; Mary Coogan, University of Colorado, Boulder; Anthony Graham-White, University of Illinois, Chicago; C. Fenno Hoffman; Robert D. Hume, Pennsylvania State University; Paul G. Reeve, University of Houston, University Park; Laurence Senelick, Tufts University; and Timothy Wiles, Indiana University, Bloomington.

I am also grateful to Keith Hull of the University of Wyoming for the warmth of his response to the book. Especially helpful in preparing the second edition were Elias Abdou, Community College of Allegheny, Pittsburgh; Robert E. Aldridge, Kirkwood Community College; Katya Amato, Portland State University; Keith Appler, University of Illinois, Urbana; Nora Bicki, University of Illinois, Champaign; Reverend Doctor Nadean Bishop, Eastern Michigan University; François Bonneville, State University of New York, Albany; Michael Boudreau, University of Illinois, Urbana; David Bratt, Winona State University; Marianne Cooley, University of Houston, University Park; Walter Creed, University of Hawaii, Manoa; Mary Beth Culp, Marymount

College; Merilee Cunningham, University of Houston; Joan D'Antoni, University of Louisville; Wayne G. Deahl, Eastern Wyoming College; Charlotte Doctor, Los Angeles Pierce College; Janet Dow, Western Connecticut State University; Jerry D. Eisenhour, Eastern Illinois University; Fred M. Fetrow, United States Naval Academy; Jane E. Fisher, Canisius College; Charles Frey, University of Washington; Robert W. Funk, Eastern Illinois University; Stephen R. Grecco, Pennsylvania State University; L. W. Harrison, Santa Rosa Junior College; Dave Hartley, Central Florida Community College; Andrew Jay Hoffman, Central Connecticut State University; Claudia L. Johnson, Marquette University; Ellen Redding Kaler, University of Kansas; Harvey Kassebaum, Cuyahoga Community College; Dorothy Louise, Franklin and Marshall College; Annette McGregor, Purdue University; Jack Mahoney, Vincennes University; James Marlow, Southeastern Massachusetts University; Christy Minadeo, Eastern Michigan University; Carol A. Moore, Louisiana State University; Roark Mulligan, University of Oregon; Eric Pederson, Butler County Community College; M. Bernice Pepke, Manatee Community College; Patrick Quade, Saint Olaf College; Carol Replogle, Loyola University, Chicago; William Reynolds, Hope College; Mark Rocha, California State University, Northridge; Matthew C. Roudane, Georgia State University; Dolores J. Sarafinski, Gannon University; Carol Scklenica, Marquette University; Rodney Simard, California State University, San Bernardino; James Stephens, Marquette University; Jeannie B. Thomas, University of Oregon; Gregory Ulmer, Kearney State College; Susan Vick, Worcester Polytechnic Institute; Linda Wells, Boston University; Keith Welsh, Webster University; Virginia West, Franklin and Marshall College; Paul Wood, Villanova University; and J. S. Wszalek, James Madison University.

For the third edition, Samuel Abel of Dartmouth College reviewed the historical material for accuracy and offered a number of very useful suggestions that I incorporated into the text. I am grateful for his help and for the response of those who offered suggestions and advice for improving the book, especially Cora Agatucci, Central Oregon Community College; Joan D'Antoni, University of Louisville; Harold J. Baxter, Trinity International University; Irene Blakely, Northland College; Cynthia Bowers, Loyola University, Chicago; Jody D. Brown, Ferrum College; Mark Browning, Johnson County Community College; William D. Buckley, Indiana University NW; William J. Campbell, SUNY College of Technology at Delhi; Heather S. Collins, Mott Community College; Ruth Contrell, New Mexico State University; Kenneth Cox, Oklahoma State University; Judith P. Cronk, Oklahoma State University; Marsha Cummins, Bronx Community College; James D. Cunningham, Florida Southern College; Tom DeSpain, Chemeketa Community College; Dexter Roger Dixon, University of Arkansas; Nancy Eddy, Indiana University–Purdue University at Indianapolis; Tom Empy, Casper College; Shawn Paul Evans, University of Tennessee at Chattanooga; Harry Feiner, Queens College; Monika Fischer, University of Oregon; James Fisher, Wabash College; Kay Forston, Phillips University; John E. Hallwas, Western Illinois University; Wilma Hahn Hasse, Mitchell University; David Henry, El Paso Community College; Kirsten F. Herdd, Eastern Michigan University; D. E. Jukes, Community College of Allegheny County; E. Kahn, Lehigh University; Jackson Kesler, Western Kentucky University; Lawrence Kinsman, New Hampshire College; Terry A. Klenk,

Santa Fe Community College; Marcia K. Morrison, Genesee Community College; Eva Patton, Fordham University; Richard Pettergill, University of Illinois at Chicago; David Pinner, Colgate University; Joseph Rice, University of Cincinnati; Deborah A. Ring, Case Western Reserve University; Hans H. Rudnick, Southern Illinois University; Samuel Schuman, University of North Carolina; William O. Scott, University of Kansas; Rita Smilkstein, North Seattle Community College; Gerald F. Snelson, Frostburg State University; N. J. Stanley, Agnes Scott College; Catherine Stevenson, University of Hartford; John S. Terhes, Chemeketa Community College; Charles Trainor, Siena College; Anita J. Turpin, Roanoke College; Joy Walsh, Butler County Community College; Gladdy White, Notre Dame College; Celeste Wiggins, Ursuline College; Salaam Yousif, California State University; and Ruth Zielke, Concordia College.

For the fourth edition, I am grateful to those who offered suggestions and advice for improving the book, especially David Adamson, University of North Carolina, Chapel Hill; Joan Angelis, Woodbury University; Karen C. Blansfield, University of North Carolina, Chapel Hill; Stephen F. Bloom, Emmanuel College; Cathy A. Brookshire, James Madison University; Barbara Clayton, University of Wisconsin, Madison; John J. Conlon, University of Massachusetts, Boston; Heath A. Diehl, Bowling Green State University; Richard Donnelly, University of Notre Dame; Joseph Fahey, Ohio State University; John E. R. Friedenberg, Wake Forest University; Stanton B. Garner Jr., University of Tennessee; Anthony Graham-White, University of Illinois at Chicago; Leigh Harbin, Angelo State University; Jim Hauser, William Patterson University; Don Haynes, Robert Morris College; Gregory Kable, University of North Carolina, Chapel Hill; Theresa M. Kenosa, Lincoln Land Community College; Sonya Lancaster, University of Kansas; Charlotte Langford, Pima Community College; Sandee McGlaun, Ohio State University; Deborah Montuori, Shippensburg University; Joan Navarre, Marquette University; Susan Sanders, Northern Essex Community College; Helen Scheck, University of Albany; Joel Shatzky, SUNY College at Cortland; Michelle L. Stie, University of Kansas; James Symmons, Pennsylvania State University, Media; George Wead, James Madison University; Janet S. Wolf, SUNY College at Cortland; and Tom Zimmerman, Washtenaw Community College.

I am indebted to many talented people who, were they in a drama, could constitute a crowd scene, and yet each played an indispensable solo role in making this book a reality. Martha Friedman did the photo research and secured permissions in outstanding fashion. Virginia Creedon cleared the text permissions in record time. Ed Kahn researched performance histories and located many commentaries. Julie Parker assisted him. Valerie Smith updated the Selected Bibliography and, with Amanda Nelson, wrote the study questions, writing suggestions, and Web assignments for the Web site. Joanne Diaz expanded and updated the timelines, updated the list of audiovisual materials, and checked controversial dates and facts throughout the book. Jon Rossini of Duke University provided the excellent gloss notes for the phrases of Calò dialect in Luis Valdez's *Zoot Suit*.

A number of colleagues at the University of Connecticut were generous with their time — both in talking about the plays they love and teach and in talking about how they should be presented in a text such as this. Among them are Thomas Jambeck, Jack Manning, and Brenda Murphy, all of whom teach drama regularly. I also wish to thank Regina Barreca and Michael Meyer, with whom my discussions of literature have been an ongoing delight for more than a decade.

I owe a very special debt of gratitude to the people at Bedford/St. Martin's who worked behind the scenes to produce this book. In preparation for this revision, editorial assistants Amanda Bristow and Nicole Simonsen contacted users of earlier editions, solicited their suggestions and opinions, and collated their responses. Tracey Finch provided invaluable editorial assistance throughout the book's development, including numerous hours of library research and profoundly helpful manuscript preparation. The production editor, Bridget Leahy, who worked on earlier versions of this book, kept the production on schedule and made the process seem effortless. Production supervisor Dennis Conroy and managing editor Elizabeth Schaaf watched over the project carefully, keeping everything going smoothly throughout. Thomas Crehan, production assistant, helped meet the deadlines. The copyeditor, Rosemary Winfield; the book's designer, Claire Seng-Niemoeller; and proofreaders Janet Cocker and Jocelyn Hummelsine all worked together to make the book both accurate and pleasant to read. Art director Donna Dennison and junior designer Zenobia Rivetna made the cover dynamic and inviting. Project manager/copywriter Pelle Cass oversaw the design, production, and distribution of the brochure. Web master Jen Lesar took care in the design and production of the web site, one of the special features of this edition.

As always, I owe an immense debt of gratitude to the guidance and intelligence of the publishers, Charles Christensen and Joan Feinberg, who stand not just as pillars of publishing but as staunch friends for whom this book has a special meaning. They are smart, imaginative, and inspirational. Karen Henry, my editor for the first three editions of this book, has become a standard-bearer but is also a person of warmth, with an affection for the art of drama and a passion for getting it right. She kept her hand in this edition and remains a beacon for my work. Finally, I must single out my current editor, Maura Shea, who is the most amazing "go-to" editor I have worked with. She worked closely with me on every stage of this project, from selection of photos to selection of plays, from innovations in design to development of casebooks. Her enthusiasm and her intelligence in relation to the development of drama have been powerful elements in making this edition new and vigorous. She has my total respect and admiration because she represents everything that the term *editorial excellence* implies.

Lee A. Jacobus
University of Connecticut, Storrs

Contents

Introduction:
Thinking about Drama   1

Lady Gregory   21

Drama in the Early and Mid-Twentieth Century   888

John Millington Synge   899
THE PLAYBOY OF THE WESTERN WORLD   900

COMMENTARY ON SYNGE

Appendices

*The
Bedford
Introduction
to Drama*

Introduction: Thinking about Drama

What Is Drama?

DRAMA is the art of representing for the pleasure of others events that happened or that we imagine happening. The primary ingredients of drama are characters, represented by players; action, described by gestures and movement; thought, implied by dialogue, words, and action; spectacle, represented by scenery, music, and costume; and, finally, audiences, who respond to this complex mixture.

When we are in the theater, we see the actors, hear the lines, are aware of the setting, and sense the theatrical community of which we are a part. Even when reading a play, we should imagine actors speaking lines and visualize a setting in which those lines are spoken. Drama is an experience in which we participate on many levels simultaneously. On one level, we may believe that what we see is really happening; on another level, we know it is only make-believe. On one level we may be amused, but on another level we realize that serious statements about our society are being made. Drama both entertains and instructs.

When Aristotle wrote about drama in the *Poetics,* a work providing one of the earliest and most influential theories of drama, he began by explaining it as the imitation of an action (MIMESIS). Those analyzing his work have interpreted this statement in several ways. One interpretation is that drama imitates life. On the surface, such an observation may seem simple, even obvious. But on reflection we begin to find complex significance in his comment. The drama of the Greeks, for example, with its intense mythic structure, its formidable speeches, and its profound actions, often seems larger than life or other than life. Yet we recognize characters saying words that we ourselves are capable of saying, doing things that we ourselves might do. The great Greek tragedies are certainly lifelike and certainly offer literary mirrors in which we can examine human nature. And the same is true of Greek comedies.

The relationship between drama and life has always been subtle and complex. In some plays, such as Luigi Pirandello's *Six Characters in Search of an Author,* it is one of the central issues. We begin our reading or viewing of most plays knowing that the dramatic experience is not absolutely real in the sense that, for example, the actor playing Hamlet does not truly die or truly see a ghost or truly frighten his mother. The play imitates those imagined actions, but when done properly it is realistic enough to make us fear, if only for a moment, that they could be real.

We see significance in the actions Hamlet imitates; his actions help us live our own lives more deeply, more intensely, because they give us insight into the possibilities of life. We are all restricted to living this life as ourselves; drama is one art form that helps us realize the potential of life, for both the good and the bad. In an important sense, we can share the experience of a character such as Hamlet when he soliloquizes over the question of whether it is better to die than to live in a world filled with sin and crime.

Drama and Ritual

Such imaginative participation is only a part of what we derive from drama. In its origins, drama may have evolved from ancient Egyptian and Greek rituals, ceremonies that were performed the same way again and again and were thought to have a propitious effect on the relationship between the people and their gods.

In ancient Egypt some religious rituals evolved into repeated passion plays, such as those celebrating Isis and Osiris at the festivals of Heb-Seb in Abydos some three thousand years ago. Greek drama was first performed during yearly religious celebrations dedicated to the god Dionysus. The early Greek playwrights, such as Sophocles in *Oedipus Rex* and *Antigone,* emphasized the interaction between the will of the gods and the will of human beings, often pitting the truths of men and women against the truths of the gods.

The rebirth of drama in the Middle Ages — after the fall of Rome and the loss of classical artistic traditions — took place first in monasteries, then later in the cathedrals of Europe. It evolved from medieval religious ceremonies that helped the faithful understand more about their own moral predicament. *Everyman,* a late play in the medieval theater (it was written about 1500), concerns itself with the central issue of reward and punishment after this life because the soul is immortal.

Drama: The Illusion of Reality

From the beginning, drama has had the capacity to hold up an illusion of reality like the reflection in a mirror: we take the reality for granted while recognizing that it is nonetheless illusory. As we have seen, Aristotle described DRAMATIC ILLUSION as an imitation of an action. But unlike the reflection in a mirror, the action of most drama is not drawn from our actual experience of life but from our potential or imagined experience. In the great Greek drama, the illusion includes the narratives of ancient myths that were thought to offer profound illumination. The interpretation of the myths by the Greek playwrights over a two-hundred-year period helped the Greek people participate in the myths, understand them, and apply their values to their daily lives.

Different ages have had different approaches to representing reality onstage. Greek actors spoke in verse and wore masks. The staging consisted of very little setting and no special costumes except for some comedies and satyr plays. Medieval drama was sometimes acted on pushwagons and carts, but the special machinery developed to suggest hellfire and the presence of devils was said to be so realistic as to be frightening. Elizabethan audiences were accustomed to actors who spoke directly to the crowds at their feet near the apron of the stage. All Elizabethan plays were done in essentially contemporary clothing, often with no more scenery than the suggestion of it in the spoken descriptions of the players. The actors recited their lines in verse, except when the author had a particular reason to use prose — for example, to imply that the speaker was of low social station. Yet Elizabethans reported that their theater was much like life itself.

In Shakespeare's *A Midsummer Night's Dream,* fairies, enchantments, an ass's head on the shoulders of a man — all these are presented as illusions, and we accept them. They inform the audience — in Shakespeare's day and in modern times — not by showing us ourselves in a mirror but by demonstrating that even fantastic realities have significance for us.

Certainly *A Midsummer Night's Dream* gives us insight into the profound range of human emotions. We learn about the pains of rejection when we see Helena longing for Demetrius, who in turn longs for Hermia. We learn about jealousy and possessiveness when we see Oberon cast a spell on his wife, Titania, over a dispute concerning a changeling. And we learn, too, about the worldly ambitions of the "rude mechanicals" who themselves put on a play whose reality they fear might frighten their audience. They solve the problem by reminding their audience that it is only a play and that they need not fear that reality will spoil their pleasure.

In modern drama the dramatic illusion of reality includes not just the shape of an action, the events, and the characters but also the details of everyday life. When the action changes locale, the setting changes as well. Some contemporary playwrights make an effort to re-create a reality close to the one we live in. Some modern plays, like August Wilson's *Fences,* make a precise representation of reality a primary purpose, shaping the tone of the language to reflect the way modern people speak, re-creating contemporary reality in the setting, language, and other elements of the drama.

But describing a play as an illusion of reality in no way means that it represents the precise reality that we take for granted in our everyday experience. Rather, drama ranges widely and explores multiple realities, some of which may seem very close to our own and some of which may seem improbably removed from our everyday experience.

Seeing a Play Onstage

For an audience, drama is one of the most powerful artistic experiences. When we speak about participating in drama, we mean that as a member of the audience we become a part of the action that unfolds. This is a mysterious phenomenon.

When we see a play today, we are usually seated in a darkened theater looking at a lighted stage. In ages past, this contrast was not the norm. Greek plays took place outdoors during the morning and the afternoon; most Elizabethan plays were staged outdoors in the afternoon; in the Renaissance, some plays began to be staged indoors with ingenious systems of lighting that involved candles and reflectors. In the early nineteenth century most theaters used gaslight onstage; electricity took over in the later part of the century, and its use has grown increasingly complex. In most large theaters today computerized lighting boards have replaced Renaissance candles.

Sitting in the darkness has made the experience of seeing Greek and Elizabethan plays much different for us than it was for the original audiences. We do not worry about being seen by the "right people" or about studying the quality of the audience, as people did during the Restoration in the late seventeenth century. The darkness isolates us from all except those who sit adjacent to us. Yet we instantly respond when others in the audience laugh, when they gasp, when they shift restlessly. We recognize in those moments that we are part of a larger community drawn together by theater and that we are all involved in the dramatic experience.

Theaters and Their Effect

Different kinds of theaters make differing demands on actors and audiences. Despite its huge size, the open ARENA style theater of the early Greeks brought the audience into a special kind of intimacy with the actors. The players came very close to the first rows of seats, and the acoustics permitted even a whisper onstage to be audible in the far seats. The Greek theater also imparted a sense of formality to the occasion of drama. For one thing, its regularity and circularity was accompanied by a relatively rigid seating plan. The officials and nobility sat in special seats. Then each section of the theater was given over to specific families, with the edges of the seating area devoted to travelers and strangers to the town. One knew one's place in the Greek theater. Its regularity gave the community a sense of order.

Medieval theater also gave its audiences a sense of community, both when it used playing areas called *mansions* inside and outside the churches and when it used wagons wheeled about in processions in the streets or outside the city walls. That the medieval theater repeated the same cycles of plays again and again for about two hundred years, to the delight of many European communities, tells us something about the stability of those communities. Their drama was integrated with their religion, and both helped them express their sense of belonging to the church and the community.

In some medieval performances the actors came into the audience, breaking the sense of distance or the illusion of separation. It is difficult for us to know how much participation and involvement in the action the medieval audience felt. Modern audiences have responded very well to productions of medieval plays such as *The Second Shepherds' Play, Noah's Flood,* and *Everyman,* and we have every reason to think that medieval audiences enjoyed their dramas immensely. The guilds that performed them took pride in making their plays as exciting and involving as possible.

The Elizabethan playhouse was a wooden structure providing an enclosed space around a courtyard open to the sky. A covered stage thrust into the courtyard. As in the Greek theater, the audience was arranged somewhat by social station. Around the stage, which was about five feet off the ground, stood the groundlings, those who paid least for their entrance. Then in covered galleries in the building itself sat patrons who paid extra for a seat. The effect of the enclosed structure was of a small, contained world. Actors were in the habit of speaking directly to members of the audience, and the audience rarely kept a polite silence. It was a busy, humming theater that generated intimacy and involvement between actors and audience.

The proscenium stage of the nineteenth and twentieth centuries distanced the audience from the play, providing a clear frame (the PROSCENIUM) behind which the performers acted out their scenes. This detachment was especially effective for plays that demanded a high degree of realism because the effect of the proscenium is to make the audience feel that it is witnessing the action as a silent observer, looking in as if through an imaginary fourth wall on a living room or other intimate space in which the action takes place. The proscenium arch gives the illusion that the actors are in a world of their own, unaware of the audience's presence.

In the twentieth century some of the virtues of the Greek arena theater, or THEATER IN THE ROUND, were rediscovered. In an effort to close the distance between audience and players, Antonin Artaud, the French actor and director, developed in the 1920s and 1930s a concept called the *theater of cruelty*. Using theater in the round, Artaud robbed the audience of the comfort of watching a distant stage and pressed his actors into the space of the viewers. His purpose was to force theatergoers to deal with the primary issues of the drama by stripping them of the security of darkness and anonymity. Theaters in Russia and Britain developed similar spaces in the 1930s and 1940s, and since the 1950s the Arena Theater in Washington, D.C., and the Circle in the Square in New York have continued the tradition.

Twenty-first-century theater is eclectic. It uses thrust, arena, proscenium, and every other kind of stage already described. Some contemporary theater also converts nontheatrical space, such as warehouses or city streets, into space for performance.

Reading a Play

Reading a play is a different experience from seeing it enacted. For one thing, readers do not have the benefit of the interpretations made by a director, actors, and scene designers in presenting a performance. These interpretations are all critical judgments based on a director's ideas of how the play should be presented and on actors' insights into the meaning of the play.

A reading of a play produces an interpretation that remains in our heads and is not translated to the stage. The dramatic effect of the staging is lost to us unless we make a genuine effort to visualize it and to understand its contribution to the dramatic experience. For a fuller experience of the drama when reading plays, one should keep in mind the historical period and the conventions of staging that are appropriate to the period and that are specified by the playwright.

Some plays were prepared by their authors for reading as well as for staging, as evident in plays whose stage directions supply information that would be unavailable to an audience, such as the color of the characters' eyes, characters' secret motives, and other such details. Occasionally, stage directions, such as those of Bernard Shaw and Tennessee Williams, are written in a poetic prose that can be appreciated only by a reader.

It is not a certainty that seeing a play will produce an experience more "true" to the play's meaning than reading it. Every act of reading silently or speaking the lines aloud is an act of interpretation. No one can say which is the best interpretation. Each has its own merits, and the ideal is probably to read and see any play.

The Great Ages of Drama

Certain historical periods have produced great plays and great playwrights, although why some periods generate more dramatic activity than others is still a matter of conjecture for scholars examining the social, historical, and religious conditions of the times. Each of the great ages of drama has affected the way plays are written, acted, and staged in successive ages. In every age, drama borrows important elements from each earlier period.

Greek Drama

The Greeks of the fifth century B.C. are credited with the first masterful dramatic age, which lasted from the birth of Aeschylus (c. 525 B.C.) to the death of Aristophanes (c. 385 B.C.). Their theaters were supported by public funds, and the playwrights competed for prizes during the great festivals of Dionysus. Sometimes as many as ten to fifteen thousand people sat in the theaters and watched with a sense of delight and awe as the actors played out their tales.

Theater was extremely important to the Greeks as a way of interpreting their relationships with their gods and of reinforcing their sense of community. The fifth-century B.C. audience, mostly wealthy citizens, came early in the morning and spent the entire day in the theater. Drama for the Greeks was not mere escapism or entertainment, not a frill or a luxury. Connected as it was with religious festivals, it was a cultural necessity.

Sophocles' plays *Oedipus Rex* and *Antigone* are examples of the powerful tragedies that have transfixed audiences for centuries. Euripides, slightly younger than Sophocles, was also a prize-winning tragedian. His *Trojan Women, Alcestis, Medea, Bacchae,* and *Elektra* [*Electra*] are still performed and still exert an influence on today's drama. The same is true of Aeschylus, who was slightly older than both and whose *Agamemnon, The Libation Bearers, The Eumenides* (known collectively as the *Oresteia*), and *Prometheus Bound* have all been among the most lasting of plays.

In addition to such great tragedians, the Greeks also produced the important comedians Aristophanes and Menander (late fourth century B.C.), whose work has been plundered for plays as diverse as a Shakespeare comedy and a Broadway musical. Aristophanes' *Lysistrata,* in which the Athenian and Spartan women agree to withhold sex from their husbands until the men promise to stop making war, is a powerful social comedy. Menander produced a more subtle type of comedy that made the culture laugh at itself. Both styles of comedy are the staple of popular entertainment even today. Menander's social comedies were the basis of the comedy of manners, in which society's ways of behavior are criticized. The comedy of manners is exemplified in William Congreve's eighteenth-century *The Way of the World* and Molière's *The Misanthrope.*

Roman Drama

The Romans became aware of Greek drama in the third century B.C. and began to import Greek actors and playwrights. Because of many social and cultural differences between the societies, however, drama never took a central role in the life of the average Roman. Seneca, who is now viewed as Rome's most important tragedian, almost certainly wrote his plays to be read rather than to be seen onstage.

Roman comedy produced two great playwrights, Plautus and Terence, who helped develop the STOCK (or type) CHARACTER, such as the skinflint or the prude. Plautus was the great Roman comedian in the tradition of Menander's comedy of manners. Plautus's best-known plays are *The Braggart Warrior* and

The Twin Menaechmi; and during the Renaissance, when all European school-children read Latin, his works were favorites.

Terence's work was praised during the Middle Ages and the Renaissance as being smoother, more elegant, and more polished and refined than Plautus's. In his own age Terence was less admired by the general populace but more admired by connoisseurs of drama. His best-known plays — *The Woman of Andros, Phormio,* and *The Brothers* — are rarely performed today.

Drama took its place beside many other forms of entertainment in Roman culture — sports events, gladiator battles to the death, chariot races, the slaughter of wild beasts, and sacrifices of Christians and others to animals. The Roman public, when it did attend plays, enjoyed farces and relatively coarse humor. The audiences for Plautus and Terence, aristocratic in taste, may not have represented the cross-section of the community that was typical of Greek audiences.

Medieval Drama

After the fall of Rome and the spread of the Goths and Visigoths across southern Europe in the fifth century, Europe experienced a total breakdown of the strong central government Rome had provided. When Rome fell, Greek and Roman culture virtually disappeared. The great classical texts went largely unread until the end of the medieval period in the fourteenth and fifteenth centuries; however, expressions of culture, including art forms such as drama, did not entirely disappear. During the medieval period the church's power and influence grew extensively, and it tried to fill the gap left by the demise of the Roman empire. The church became a focus of both religious and secular activity for people all over Europe.

After almost five centuries of relative inactivity, European drama was reborn in religious ceremonies in monasteries. It moved inside churches, then out of doors by the twelfth century, perhaps because its own demands outgrew its circumstances. Drama had become more than an adjunct of the religious ceremonies that had spawned it.

One reason that the medieval European communities regarded their drama so highly is that it expressed many of their concerns and values. The age was highly religious; in addition, the people who produced the plays were members of guilds whose personal pride was represented in their work. Their plays came to be called MYSTERY PLAYS because the trade that each guild represented was a special skill — a mystery to the average person. Of course, the pun on religious mystery was understood by most audiences.   ·

Many of these plays told stories drawn from the Bible. The tales of Noah's Ark, Abraham and Isaac, and Samson and Delilah all had dramatic potential, and the mystery plays capitalized on that potential, as did plays on the life and crucifixion of Christ. Among mystery plays, *The Second Shepherds' Play* and *Abraham and Isaac* are still performed regularly.

Most mystery plays were gathered into groups of plays called CYCLES dramatizing incidents from the Bible, among other sources. They were usually performed outdoors, at times on movable wagons that doubled as stages. The audience either moved from wagon to wagon to see each play in a cycle, or the wagons moved among the audience.

By the fifteenth and sixteenth centuries, another form of play developed that was not associated with cycles or with the guilds. These were the MORALITY

PLAYS, and their purpose was to touch on larger contemporary issues that had a moral overtone. *Everyman*, the best known of the morality plays, was performed in many nations in various languages.

Renaissance Drama   The revival of learning in the Renaissance, beginning in Italy in the fourteenth century, had considerable effect on drama because classical Greek and Roman plays were discovered and studied. In the academies in Italy, some experiments in re-creating Greek and Roman plays introduced music into drama. New theaters, such as Teatro Olympico in Vicenza (1579), were built to produce these plays; they allow us to see how the Renaissance reconceived the classical stage. Some of these experiments developed into modern opera. The late medieval traditions of the Italian theater's COMMEDIA DELL'ARTE, a stylized improvisational slapstick comedy performed by actors' guilds, began to move outside Italy into other European nations. The commedia's stock characters, Harlequins and Pulcinellas, began to appear in many countries in Europe.

Elizabethan and Jacobean (named for King James I, who succeeded Elizabeth and reigned from 1603 to 1625) drama developed most fully during the fifty years from approximately 1590 to 1640. Audiences poured into the playhouses eager for plays about history and for the great tragedies of Christopher Marlowe, such as *Doctor Faustus,* and of Shakespeare, including *Macbeth, Hamlet, Othello, Julius Caesar,* and *King Lear.* But there were others as well: Middleton and Rowley's *The Changeling,* Cyril Tourneur's *Revenger's Tragedy,* and John Webster's *The White Devil* and his sensational *The Duchess of Malfi.*

The great comedies of the age came mostly from the pen of William Shakespeare: *A Midsummer Night's Dream, The Comedy of Errors, As You Like It, Much Ado about Nothing, The Taming of the Shrew,* and *Twelfth Night.* Many of these plays derived from Italian originals, usually novellas or popular poems and sometimes comedies. But Shakespeare, of course, elevated and vastly improved everything he borrowed.

Ben Jonson, a playwright who was significantly influenced by the classical writers, was also well represented on the Elizabethan stage, with *Volpone, The Alchemist, Everyman in His Humour, Bartholomew Fair,* and other durable comedies. Jonson is also important for his contributions to the MASQUE, an aristocratic entertainment that featured music, dance, and fantastic costuming. His *Masque of Blacknesse* was performed in the royal court with the queen as a performer.

The Elizabethan stage sometimes grew bloody, with playwrights and audiences showing a passion for tragedies that, like *Hamlet,* centered on revenge and often ended with most of the characters meeting a premature death. Elizabethan plays also show considerable variety, with many plays detailing the history of English kings and, therefore, the history of England. It was a theater of powerful effect, and contemporary diaries indicate that the audiences delighted in it. Theaters also flourished in Spain in this period, producing Lope de Vega (1562–1635), who may have written as many as seventeen hundred plays.

Vega's immediate successor, Pedro Calderón de la Barca (1600–1681), is sometimes considered to be more polished in style, but also more stiffly aristocratic in appeal. He wrote fewer plays than Vega, but still produced an amazing body of work. He is said to have written at least 111 dramas and seventy or eighty *auto sacramentales,* the Spanish equivalent of religious morality plays designed for special religious ceremonies. Calderón is best known for *La vida es sueño (Life Is a Dream),* which is still performed today.

Theaters in Shakespeare's day were built outside city limits in seamy neighborhoods near brothels and bear-baiting pits, where chained bears were set upon by large dogs for the crowd's amusement. Happily, the theaters' business was good; the plays were constructed of remarkable language that seems to have fascinated all social classes, since all flocked to the theater by the thousands.

Late Seventeenth- and Eighteenth-Century Drama

After the Puritan reign in England from 1642 (when the theaters were closed) to 1660, during which dramatic productions were almost nonexistent, the theater was suddenly revived. In 1660 Prince Charles, sent to France by his father during the English Civil War, was invited back to be king, thus beginning what was known in England as the Restoration. It was a gay, exciting period in stark contrast to the gray Puritan era. During the period new indoor theaters modeled on those in France were built, and a new generation of actors and actresses (women took part in plays for the first time in England) came forth to participate in the dramatic revival.

Since the mid-1600s, French writers, interpreting Aristotle's description of Greek drama, had leaned toward development of a classical theater, which was supposed to observe the "unities" of time, place, and action: a play had one plot and one setting and covered the action of one day. In 1637 Pierre Corneille wrote *Le Cid,* using relatively modern Spanish history as his theme and following certain classical techniques. Jean-Baptiste Racine was Corneille's successor, and his plays became even more classical by centering on classical topics. His work includes *Andromache, Britannicus,* and, possibly his best play, *Phaedra.* Racine retired from the stage at the end of the century, but he left a powerful legacy of classicism that reached well into the eighteenth century.

Molière, an actor and producer, was the best comedian of seventeenth-century France. Among his plays, *The Misanthrope* and several others are still produced regularly in the West. Molière was classical in his way, borrowing ancient comedy's technique of using type, or stock, characters in his social satires.

Among the important playwrights of the new generation were Aphra Behn, the first professional English female writer, whose play *The Rover* was one of the most popular plays of the late seventeenth century, and William Congreve, whose best-known play, *The Way of the World,* is often still produced. The latter is a lively comedy that aimed to chasten as well as entertain Congreve's audiences.

The eighteenth century saw the tradition of the comedy of manners continued in Richard Brinsley Sheridan's *School for Scandal* and Oliver Goldsmith's *She Stoops to Conquer.* The drama of this period focuses on social manners, and much of it is SATIRE — that is, drama that offers mild criticism of society and holds society up to comic ridicule. But underlying that ridicule is the relatively noble motive of reforming society. We can see some of that motive at work in the plays of Molière and Congreve.

During much of the eighteenth century, theater in France centered on the court and was controlled by a small coterie of snobbish people. The situation in England was not quite the same, although the audiences were snobbish and socially conscious. They went to the theater to be seen, and they often went in claques — groups of like-minded patrons who applauded or booed together to express their views. Theater was important, but attendance at it was like a material possession, something to be displayed for others to admire.

Nineteenth-Century Drama through the Turn of the Century

English playwrights alone produced more than thirty thousand plays during the nineteenth century. Most of the plays were sentimental, melodramatic, and dominated by a few very powerful actors, stars who often overwhelmed the works written for them. The audiences were quite different from those of the seventeenth and eighteenth centuries. The upwardly mobile urban middle classes and the moneyed factory and mill owners who had benefited economically from the industrial revolution demanded a drama that would entertain them.

The new audiences were not especially well educated, nor were they interested in plays that were intellectually demanding. Instead, they wanted escapist and sentimental entertainment that was easy to respond to and did not challenge their basic values. Revivals of old plays and adaptations of Shakespeare were also common in the age, with great stars like Edmund Kean, Sir Henry Irving, Edwin Forrest, Edwin Booth, and William Macready using the plays as platforms for overwhelming, and sometimes overbearing, performances. Thrillers were especially popular, as were historical plays and melodramatic plays featuring a helpless heroine.

As an antidote to such a diet, the new Realist movement in literature, marked by the achievements of French novelists Émile Zola and Gustave Flaubert, finally struck the stage in the 1870s and 1880s in plays by August Strindberg and Henrik Ibsen. Revolutionizing Western drama, these Scandinavians forced their audiences to pay attention to important issues and deeper psychological concerns than earlier audiences had done.

Strindberg's *Miss Julie,* a psychological study, challenged social complacency based on class and social differences. Ibsen's *A Doll House* was a blow struck for feminism, but it did not amuse all audiences. Some were horrified at the thought that Nora Helmer was to be taken as seriously as her husband. Such a view was heretical, but it was also thrilling for a newly awakened European conscience. Those intellectuals and writers who responded positively to Ibsen, including Bernard Shaw, acted as the new conscience and began a move that soon transformed drama. Feminism is also a theme, but perhaps less directly, of Ibsen's *Hedda Gabler,* the story of a woman whose frustration at being cast into an inferior role contributes toward a destructive — and ultimately self-destructive — impulse. Both plays are acted in a physical setting that seems to be as ordinary as a nineteenth-century sitting room, with characters as small — and yet as large — as the people who watched them.

The Russian Anton Chekhov's plays *Three Sisters, Uncle Vanya,* and *The Cherry Orchard,* written at the turn of the twentieth century, are realistic as well, but they are also patient examinations of character rather than primarily problem plays — like Ibsen's successful dramas *Ghosts* and *The Master Builder.* Chekhov is aware of social change in Russia, especially the changes that revealed a hitherto repressed class of peasants evolving into landowners and merchants. *The Cherry Orchard* is suffused with an overpowering sense of inevitability through which Chekhov depicts the conflict between the necessity for change and a nostalgia for the past. The comedies of Oscar Wilde, such as *Lady Windermere's Fan* and *The Importance of Being Ernest,* poked fun at the foibles of the upper classes. Amusing as they are, their satirical quality constitutes social criticism.

These plays introduced a modern realism of a kind that was rare in earlier drama. Melodrama of the nineteenth century was especially satisfying to mass audiences because the good characters were very good, the bad characters were very bad, and justice was meted out at the end. But it is difficult in Chekhov to be sure who the heroes and villains are. Nothing is as clear-cut in these plays as it is in popular melodramas. Instead, Chekhov's plays are as complicated as life itself. Such difficulties of distinction have become the norm of the most important drama of the twentieth century.

Drama in the Early and Mid-Twentieth Century

The drama of the early twentieth century nurtured the seeds of nineteenth-century realism into bloom, but sometimes this drama experimented with audience expectations. Eugene O'Neill's *Desire under the Elms* is a tragedy that features the ordinary citizen rather than the noble. This play focuses on New England farmers as tragic characters. Arthur Miller's *Death of a Salesman* invokes a sense of dreadful inevitability within the world of the commercial salesman, the ordinary man. As in many other twentieth-century tragedies, the point is that the life of the ordinary man can be as tragic as Oedipus's life.

Luigi Pirandello experiments with reality in *Six Characters in Search of an Author,* a play that has a distinctly absurd quality, since it expects us to accept the notion that the characters on the stage are waiting for an author to put them into a play. Pirandello plays with our sense of illusion and of expectation and realism to such an extent that he forces us to reexamine our concepts of reality.

Bertolt Brecht's *Mother Courage,* an example of what the playwright called EPIC DRAMA, explores war from a complex series of viewpoints. On the one hand Courage is a powerful figure who has been seen as a model of endurance, but Brecht also wanted his audience to see that Courage brings on much of her own suffering by trying to profit from war. The sole act of self-sacrifice in the play comes at the end, when Kattrin beats her drum to warn villagers of the approach of a destroying army. Brecht produced the play early in World War II as a protest. Playwrights around the world responded to events such as World War I, the Communist revolution, and the Great Depression by writing plays that no longer permitted audiences to sit comfortably and securely in darkened theaters. Brecht and other playwrights instead came out to get their audiences, to make them feel and think, to make them realize their true condition.

Samuel Beckett's dramatic career began with *Waiting for Godot,* which audiences interpreted as an examination of humans' eternal vigilance for the revelation of God or of some transcendent meaning in their lives. In the play, Godot never comes, yet the characters do not give up hope. *Endgame*'s characters seem to be awaiting the end of the world: in the 1950s the shadow of nuclear extinction cast by the cold war dominated most people's imagination.

Tennessee Williams examines a physically and psychically frail young woman's withdrawal from life in *The Glass Menagerie.* The play derives from personal experience: Williams's sister was such a woman. Personal experience may also inform his *Cat on a Hot Tin Roof,* which portrays themes of homosexuality and marital sexual tension — themes that were not openly discussed in contemporary American theater except in veiled mythic terms, in the manner, for example, of O'Neill's *Desire under the Elms.*

Nigerian playwright Wole Soyinka, who won the Nobel Prize for literature in 1986, portrays the complex intersection of a person's past and the present in his play *The Strong Breed,* set in an African village reminiscent of the Greek *polis.* Indeed, he has experimented with Greek tragic forms in *The Bacchae of Euripides,* which is also set in Africa. Soyinka's insights into the nature of culture and drama provide us with a new way of reflecting on drama's power in our lives.

Modern dramatists from the turn of the century to the Korean War explored in many different directions and developed new approaches to themes of dramatic illusion as well as to questions concerning the relationship of an audience to the stage and the players.

Contemporary Drama

As we begin the twenty-first century, the stage is vibrant. Although the commercial theaters in England and America are beset by high costs, they are producing remarkable plays. In Latin America, Germany, and France, the theater is active and exciting. Poland produced unusual experimental drama in the 1960s that is still performed today. The former Soviet Union, too, produced a number of plays that have been given a worldwide currency.

The hallmark of many of these plays has been experimentalism. Caryl Churchill's *Cloud Nine* confounds expectations by having a wife played by a man, a black servant played by a white, and a son, Edward, played by a woman. Because the play is about colonial exploitation, these experiments heighten the audience's awareness of central themes.

Sam Shepard, well known as an actor, was for many years among the most experimental playwrights living in New York's Greenwich Village. *True West* begins as a relatively straightforward play about Austin and Lee, two brothers, but quickly reveals the drama that lies beneath the surface. Lee has arrived to steal his mother's television set but ends by stealing something of his brother's personality.

In *'night, Mother,* Marsha Norman portrays two women whose lives are constricted, limited, and painful. Thelma, the mother, is desperately trying to keep Jessie, her daughter, from committing suicide. The structure of the play is traditional, but the material is highly controversial. The people in these modern plays have been given a bad deal and have given themselves a bad deal, and the drama compels us both to examine characters from whom we might otherwise turn away and to confront what those characters represent in our own lives.

Not all modern theater is experimental, however. August Wilson's *Fences* shows us the pain of life at the lower end of the economic ladder and in a form that is recognizably realistic and plausible. The play is set in the 1950s and focuses on Troy Maxon, a black man, and his relationship with his son and his wife. Tenement life is one subject of the play, but the most important subject is the courage it takes to keep going after tasting defeat. The entire drama develops within the bounds of conventional nineteenth-century realism.

Suzan-Lori Parks is a highly experimental playwright, generally forsaking the structure of the conventional realistic drama. Her *The Death of the Last*

Black Man in the Whole Entire World, like its title, is blissfully excessive. She employs some of Brecht's techniques by structuring the play in "panels"— brief, intense scenes that connect imaginatively. Tony Kushner employs similar techniques in *Angels in America.* Its brilliantly staged scenes are filled with emotional intensity and the audience is carried on waves of imaginative speculation on America's history as well as on America's present. Anna Deavere Smith brings an interesting experimentation to a logical conclusion: she writes and performs her work, assuming the parts of multiple characters of every race and gender. Her *Twilight in Los Angeles: 1992,* an example of PERFORMANCE ART, is a form of drama becoming popular in many parts of the world. Laurie Anderson, Karen Finley, and Eric Bogosian are a few of the best-known performance artists. Experimentation is probably at the heart of the work of many playwrights, although it still does not please mainstream audiences on the scale of traditional drama.

The most celebrated of contemporary playwrights seem to mix experimental and conventional dramatic techniques. Martin McDonagh, a young Irish playwright, examines the past in plays such as *The Beauty Queen of Leenane* and *The Cripple of Inishmaan,* both set in mid-twentieth century Ireland. He successfully combines the techniques of John Millington Synge with the melodramatic techniques of an even earlier Irish playwright, Dion Boucicault, who was popular in the 1860s. Yasmina Reza, author of *Art,* has characters speak directly to the audience while remaining engaged in the action, which takes place in one extended act of several scenes. Paula Vogel's plays frequently interrupt the dramatic action with asides, but they are also imaginatively structured so that time feels fluid and the action moves in emotionally significant sweeps. *The Baltimore Waltz,* derived from Vogel's experience of watching her brother die of AIDS, brings humor to a tragic situation. Similarly, *How I Learned to Drive,* which sensitively treats the subject of sexual molestation in families, also has comic moments. In *Cloud Tectonics,* José Rivera, one of the more experimental of contemporary dramatists, plays with time and reality in ways that surprise and excite audiences. The theater in our time experiments with a wide range of techniques to which audiences respond positively.

Genres of Drama
Tragedy

Drama since the great age of the Greeks has taken several different forms. As we have seen, tragedies were one genre that pleased Greek audiences, and comedies pleased the Romans. In later ages, a blend of the comic and the tragic produced a hybrid genre: tragicomedy. In our time, unless a play is modeled on the Greek or Shakespearean tragedies, as is O'Neill's *Desire under the Elms,* it is usually considered tragicomic rather than tragic. Our age still enjoys the kind of comedy that people laugh at, although most plays that are strictly comedy are frothy, temporarily entertaining, and not lasting.

TRAGEDY demands a specific worldview. Aristotle, in his *Poetics,* points out that the tragic hero or heroine should be noble of birth, perhaps a king like Oedipus or a princess like Antigone. This has often been interpreted to mean that the tragic hero or heroine should be more magnanimous, more daring, larger in spirit than the average person.

Modern tragedies have rediscovered tragic principles, and while O'Neill and Miller rely on Aristotle's precepts, they have shown that in a modern society shorn of the distinctions between noble and peasant it is possible for audiences to see the greatness in all classes. This has given us a new way of orienting ourselves to the concept of fate; to HAMARTIA, the wrong act that leads people to a tragic end; and to the hero's or heroine's relationship to the social order.

Aristotle suggested that plot was the heart and soul of tragedy and that character came second. But most older tragedies take the name of the tragic hero or heroine as their title; this signifies the importance that dramatists invested in their tragic characters. Yet they also heeded Aristotle's stipulation that tragic action should have one plot rather than the double or triple plots that often characterize comedies. (Shakespeare was soundly criticized in the eighteenth century for breaking this rule in his tragedies.) And they paid attention to the concept of PERIPETEIA, which specifies that the progress of the tragic characters sometimes leads them to a reversal: they get what they want, but what they want turns out to be destructive. Aristotle especially valued a plot in which the reversal takes place simultaneously with the recognition of the truth, or the shift from ignorance to awareness, as it does in Sophocles' *Oedipus Rex*.

Playwrights in the seventeenth and eighteenth centuries in France were especially interested in following classical precepts. They were certain that Greek tragedy and Roman comedy were the epitome of excellence in drama. They interpreted Aristotle's discussion of dramatic integrity to be a set of rules governing dramatic form. These became known as the dramatic UNITIES specifying one plot, a single action that takes place in one day in a single setting. The neoclassical reinterpretation of the unities was probably much stricter than Aristotle intended.

Comedy

Two kinds of comedy developed among the ancient Greeks: OLD COMEDY, which resembles FARCE (light drama characterized by broad satirical comedy and an improbable plot) and often pokes fun at individuals with social and political power, and NEW COMEDY, which is a more refined commentary on the condition of society.

Old Comedy survives in the masterful works of Aristophanes, such as *Lysistrata,* while New Comedy hearkens back to the lost plays of Menander and resurfaces in plays such as Molière's *The Misanthrope.* Molière uses humor but mixes it with a serious level of social commentary. Modern COMEDY OF MANNERS studies and sometimes ridicules modern society as in Oscar Wilde's *The Importance of Being Earnest.*

Comedy is not always funny. Chekhov thought *The Cherry Orchard* was a comedy, while his producer, the great Konstantin Stanislavsky, who trained actors to interpret his lines and who acted in other Chekhov plays, thought it was a tragedy. The argument may have centered on the ultimate effect of the play on its audiences, but it may also have centered on the question of laughter. There are laughs in *The Cherry Orchard,* but they usually come at the expense of a character or a social group. This is true, as well, of Samuel Beckett's *Endgame.* We may laugh, but we also know that the play is at heart very serious.

Tragicomedy

Since the early seventeenth century, serious plays have been called TRAGICOMEDIES when they do not adhere strictly to the structure of tragedy, which emphasizes the nobility of the hero or heroine, fate, the wrong action of the hero or heroine, and a resolution that includes death, exile, or a similar end.

Many serious plays have these qualities, but they also have some of the qualities of comedy: a commentary on society, raucous behavior that draws laughs, and a relatively happy ending. Yet their darkness is such that we can hardly feel comfortable regarding them as comedies.

Plays such as Sam Shepard's *True West* and Lorraine Hansberry's *A Raisin in the Sun* can be considered tragicomedy. Indeed, the modern temperament has especially relied on the mixture of comic and tragic elements for its most serious plays. Eugene O'Neill, Tennessee Williams, Harold Pinter, Marsha Norman, and Caryl Churchill have all been masters of tragicomedy.

In contemporary drama tragicomedy takes several forms. One is the play whose seriousness is relieved by comic moments; another is a play whose comic structure absorbs a tragic moment and continues to express affirmation. Yet another is the dark comedy whose sardonic humor leaves us wondering how we can laugh at something that is ultimately frightening. This is the case with some absurdist comedies, which insist that there is no meaning in events other than the meaning we invent for ourselves. Pinter's *Betrayal* and Beckett's *Endgame* are such plays. They are funny yet sardonic, and when we laugh we do so uneasily.

Other genres of drama exist, although they are generally versions of tragedy, comedy, and tragicomedy. Improvisational theater, in which actors use no scripts and may switch roles at any moment, defies generic description. Musical comedies and operas are dramatic entertainments that have established their own genres related in some ways to the standard genres of drama.

Genre distinctions are useful primarily because they establish expectations in the minds of audiences with theatrical experience. Tragedies and comedies make different demands on an audience. According to Marsha Norman's explanation of the "rules" of drama, you have to know in a play just what is at stake. Understanding the principles that have developed over the centuries to create the genres of drama helps us know what is at stake.

Elements of Drama

All plays share some basic elements with which playwrights and producers work: plots, characters, settings, dialogue, movement, and themes. In addition, many modern plays pay close attention to lighting, costuming, and props. When we respond to a play, we observe the elements of drama in action together, and the total experience is rich, complex, and subtle. Occasionally, we respond primarily to an individual element — the theme or characterization, for instance — but that is rare. Our awareness of the elements of drama is most useful when we are thinking analytically about a play and the way it affects us.

For the sake of discussion, we will consider the way the basic elements of drama function in Lady Gregory's one-act play *The Rising of the Moon* (which follows this section). It has all the elements we expect from drama, and it is both a brief and a very successful play.

Plot

PLOT is a term for the action of a drama. Plot implies that the ACTION has a shape and form that will ultimately prove satisfying to the audience. Generally, a carefully plotted play begins with EXPOSITION, an explanation of what happened before the play began and of how the characters arrived at their present situation. The play then continues, using SUSPENSE to build tension in the audience and in the characters and to develop further the pattern of RISING ACTION. The audience wonders what is going to happen, sees the characters set in motion, and then watches as certain questions implied by the drama are answered one by one. The action achieves its greatest tension as it moves to a point of CLIMAX, when a revelation is experienced, usually by the chief characters. Once the climax has been reached, the plot continues, sometimes very briefly, in a pattern of FALLING ACTION as the drama reaches its conclusion and the characters understand their circumstances and themselves better than they did at the beginning of the play.

The function of plot is to give action a form that helps us understand elements of the drama in relation to one another. Plays can have several interrelated plots or only one. Lady Gregory's *The Rising of the Moon* has one very simple plot: a police sergeant is sent out with two policemen to make sure a political rebel does not escape from the area. The effect of the single plot is that the entire play focuses intensely on the interaction between the rebel, disguised as a ballad singer, and the sergeant. The sergeant meets the rebel, listens to him sing ballads, and then recognizes in him certain qualities they share. The audience wonders if a reward of one hundred pounds will encourage the sergeant to arrest the ballad singer or if, instead, the ballad singer's sense that his cause is just will convince the sergeant to let him go. The climax of the action occurs when the sergeant's two policemen return, as the ballad singer hides behind a barrel, and ask if the sergeant has seen any signs of the rebel. Not until that moment does the audience know for sure what the sergeant will do. When he gives his answer, the falling action begins.

Plots depend on CONFLICT between characters, and in *The Rising of the Moon* the conflict is very deep. It is built into the characters themselves, but it is also part of the institution of law that the sergeant serves and the ongoing struggle for justice that the ballad singer serves. This conflict, still evident today, was a very significant national issue in Ireland when the play was first produced in Dublin in 1907.

Lady Gregory works subtly with the conflict between the sergeant and the ballad singer, showing that although they are on completely opposite sides of the law — and of the important political issues — they are more alike than they are different. The ballad singer begins to sing the "Granuaile," a revolutionary song about England's unlawful dominance over Ireland through seven centuries; when he leaves out a line, the sergeant supplies it. In that action the sergeant reveals that, although he is paid by the English to keep law and order, his roots lie with the Irish people. By his knowledge of the revolutionary songs he reveals his sympathies.

Characterization

Lady Gregory has effectively joined CHARACTER and conflict in *The Rising of the Moon*: as the conflict is revealed, the characters of the sergeant and the ballad singer are also revealed. At first the sergeant seems eager to get the reward, and he acts bossy with Policeman X and Policeman B. And when he first meets the ballad singer he seems demanding and policemanlike. It is only when he begins to sense who the ballad singer really is that he changes and reveals a deep, sympathetic streak.

Lady Gregory, in a note to the play, said that in Ireland when the play was first produced, those who wanted Ireland to become part of England were incensed to see a policeman portrayed so as to show his sympathies with rebels. Those who wished Ireland to become a separate nation from England were equally shocked to see a policeman portrayed so sympathetically.

The sergeant and the ballad singer are both major characters in the play, but it is not clear that either is the villain or the hero. When the play begins, the sergeant seems to be the hero because he represents the law and the ballad singer appears to be the villain because he has escaped from prison. But as the action develops, those characterizations change. What replaces them is an awareness of the complications that underlie the relationship between the law and the lawbreaker in some circumstances. This is part of the point of Lady Gregory's play.

Lady Gregory has given a very detailed portrait of both main characters, although in a one-act play she does not have enough space to be absolutely thorough in developing them. Yet we get an understanding of the personal ambitions of each character, and we understand both their relationship to Ireland and their particular allegiances as individuals. They speak with each other in enough detail to show that they understand each other, and when the ballad singer hides behind the barrel at the approach of the other two policemen, he indicates that he trusts the sergeant not to reveal him.

Policeman X and Policeman B are only sketched in. Yet their presence is important. It is with them that the sergeant reveals his official personality, and it is their presence at the end that represents the most important threat to the security of the ballad singer. We know, though, little or nothing about them personally. They are characters who are functionaries, a little like Rosencrantz and Guildenstern in *Hamlet,* but without the differentiating characterizations that Shakespeare was able to give minor players in his full-length play.

The plays in this collection have some of the most remarkable characters ever created in literature. Tragedy usually demands complex characters, such as Oedipus, Antigone, Medea, Hamlet, and Willy Loman. We come to know them through their own words, through their interaction with other characters, through their expression of feelings, through their decisions, and through their presence onstage depicted in movement and gesture.

Characters in tragicomedies are individualized and complexly portrayed, such as Madame Ranevskaya in *The Cherry Orchard,* Hedda Gabler, Miss Julie, and Nora Helmer in *A Doll House.* But just as effective in certain kinds of drama are characters drawn as types, such as Alceste, the misanthrope in Molière's play, and Everyman in medieval drama.

In many plays we see that the entire shape of the action derives from the characters, from their strengths and weaknesses. In such plays we do not feel that the action lies outside the characters and that they must live through an arbitrary sequence of events. Instead we feel that they create their own opportunities and problems.

Setting

The SETTING of a play includes many things. First, it refers to the time and place in which the action occurs. Second, it refers to the scenery, the physical elements that appear onstage to vivify the author's stage directions. In Lady Gregory's play, we have a dock with barrels to suggest the locale and darkness to suggest night. These are important details that influence the emotional reaction of the audience.

Some plays make use of very elaborate settings, as does August Wilson's *Fences,* which is produced with a detailed tenement backyard onstage. Others make use of simple settings, such as the empty stage of Pirandello's *Six Characters in Search of an Author.*

Lady Gregory's setting derives from her inspiration for the play. She visited the quays — places where boats dock and leave with goods — as a young girl and imagined how someone might escape from the nearby prison and make his getaway "under a load of kelp" in one of the ships. The quay represents the meeting of the land and water, and it represents the getaway, the possibility of freedom. The barrel is a symbol of trade, and the sergeant and the ballad singer sit on its top and trade the words of a revolutionary song with each other.

The title of the play refers to another element of the setting: the moonlight. The night protects the ballad singer, and it permits the sergeant to bend his sworn principles a bit. The rising of the moon, as a rebel song suggests, signifies a change in society, the time when "the small shall rise up and the big shall fall down." Lady Gregory uses these elements in the play in a very effective way, interrelating them so that their significance becomes increasingly apparent as the play progresses.

Dialogue

Plays depend for their unfolding on dialogue. The DIALOGUE is the verbal exchanges between the characters. Since there is no description or commentary on the action, as there is in most novels, the dialogue must tell the whole story. Fine playwrights have developed ways of revealing character, advancing action, and introducing themes by a highly efficient use of dialogue.

Dialogue is spoken by one character to another, who then responds. But sometimes, as in Shakespeare's *Hamlet,* a character delivers a SOLILOQUY, in which he or she speaks onstage to him- or herself. Ordinarily, such speeches take on importance because they are thought to be especially true. Characters, when they speak to each other, may well wish to deceive, but generally when they speak to themselves, they have no reason to say anything but the truth.

In *The Rising of the Moon* Lady Gregory has written an unusual form of dialogue that reveals a regional way of speech. Lady Gregory was Anglo-Irish, but she lived in the west of Ireland and was familiar with the speech patterns that the characters in this play would have used. She has been recognized for her ability to re-create the speech of the rural Irish, and passages such as the following are meant to reveal the peculiarities of the rhythms and syntax of English as it was spoken in Ireland at the turn of the century:

SERGEANT: Is he as bad as that?
MAN: He is then.
SERGEANT: Do you tell me so?

Lady Gregory makes a considerable effort to create dialogue that is rich in local color as well as in spirit. John Millington Synge, another Irish playwright, whose dialogue in *Playboy of the Western World* is also an effort to re-create the sounds and rhythms of rural Irish speech, once said: "In a good play every speech should be as fully flavored as a nut or apple, and such speeches cannot be written by anyone who works among people who have shut their lips on poetry." Lady Gregory, who produced the plays of Synge at the Abbey Theatre in Dublin, would certainly agree, as her dialogue in *The Rising of the Moon* amply shows.

Music

Lady Gregory introduces another dramatic element: music. In *The Rising of the Moon* the music is integral to the plot because it allows the ballad singer, by omitting a line of a rebel song, gradually to expose the sergeant's sympathies with the rebel cause. The sergeant is at first mindful of his duty and insists that the balladeer stop, but eventually he is captivated by the music. As the ballad singer continues, he sings a song containing the title of the play, and the audience or reader realizes that the title exposes the play's rebel sympathies.

Movement

We as readers or witnesses are energized by the movement of the characters in a play. As we read, stage directions inform us where the characters are, when they move, how they move, and perhaps even what the significance of their movement is. In modern plays the author may give many directions for the action; in earlier plays stage directions are few and often supplemented by those of a modern editor. In performance the movements that you see may well have been invented by the director, although the text of a play often requires certain actions, as in the ghost scene and final dueling scene in *Hamlet*. In some kinds of drama, such as musical comedy and Greek drama, part of the action may be danced.

Lady Gregory moves the ballad singer and the sergeant in telling ways. They move physically closer to one another as they become closer in their thinking. Their movement seems to pivot around the barrel, and in one of the most charming moments of the play, they meet each other's eyes when the ballad singer sits on the barrel and comments on the way the sergeant is pacing back and forth. They then both sit on the barrel, facing in opposite directions, and share a pipe between them, almost as a peace offering.

Theme

The theme of a play is its message, its central concerns — in short, what it is about. It is by no means a simple thing to decide what the theme of a play is, and many plays contain several rather than just a single theme. Often, the search for a theme tempts us to oversimplify and to reduce a complex play to a relatively simple catchphrase.

Sophocles' *Antigone* focuses on the conflict between human law and the law of the gods when following both sets of laws seems to be impossible. Antigone wishes to honor the gods by burying her brother, but the law of Kreon decrees that he shall have no burial, since her brother is technically a traitor to the state. Similar themes are present in other Greek plays. *Hamlet* has many themes. On a very elementary level, the main theme of *Hamlet* is revenge. This is played out in the obligation of a son to avenge the murder of a father, even when the murderer is a kinsman. Another theme centers on corruption in the state of Denmark.

Lady Gregory's play has revolution as one theme. The rising of the moon is a sign for "the rising" or revolution of the people against their English oppressors. The sergeant is an especially English emblem of oppression because the police were established by an Englishman, Robert Peele. At one point the balladeer suggests a song, "The Peeler and the Goat," but rejects it because in slang a peeler is a policeman.

Another important theme in *The Rising of the Moon* is that of unity among the Irish people. The sergeant seems to be at an opposite pole from the ballad singer when the play opens. He is posting signs announcing a reward that he could well use, since he is a family man. But as the play proceeds, the sergeant moves closer in thought to the Irish people, represented by the rebel, the ballad singer.

If concerned that readers and viewers will miss their thematic intentions, playwrights sometimes reveal these in one or two speeches. Usually, a careful reader or viewer has already divined the theme, and the speeches are intrusive. But Lady Gregory is able to introduce thematic material in certain moments of dialogue, as in this comment by the sergeant, revealing that the police are necessary to prevent a revolution:

> SERGEANT: Well, we have to do our duty in the force. Haven't we the whole country depending on us to keep law and order? It's those that are down would be up and those that are up would be down, if it wasn't for us.

But the thematic material in *The Rising of the Moon* is spread evenly throughout, as is the case in most good plays.

In every play, the elements of drama will work differently, sometimes giving us the feeling that character is dominant over theme, or plot over character, or setting over both. Ordinarily, critics feel that character, plot, and theme are the most important elements of drama, while setting, dialogue, music, and movement come next. But in the best of dramas each has its importance and each balances the others. The plays in this collection strive for that harmony; most achieve it memorably.

Lady Gregory

Isabella Augusta Persse (1852–1932) was born in the west of Ireland. Her family was known as "ascendancy stock"— that is, it was educated, wealthy, and Protestant living in a land that was largely uneducated, poverty-ridden, and Roman Catholic. A gulf existed between the rich ascendancy families, who lived in great houses with considerable style, partaking in lavish hunts and balls, and the impoverished Irish, who lived in one-room straw-roofed homes and worked the soil with primitive tools.

Lady Gregory took a strong interest in the Irish language, stimulated in part by a nurse who often spoke the language to her when she was a child. Her nurse was an important source of Irish folklore and a contact with the people who lived in the modest cottages around her family estate. It was extraordinary for any wealthy Protestant to pay attention to the language or the life of the poor laborers of the west of Ireland. Yet these are the very people who figure most importantly in the plays that Lady Gregory wrote in later life.

Isabella Persse met Sir William Gregory when she was on a family trip to Nice and Rome. They were actually neighbors in Ireland, but only slightly acquainted. He was also of Irish ascendancy stock and had been a governor of Ceylon. They were married the following year, when she was twenty-eight and he was sixty-three. Their marriage was apparently quite successful, and in 1881, their son, Robert Gregory, was born. They used the family home, Coole Park, as a retreat for short periods, but most of their time was spent traveling and living in London, where Sir William was a trustee of the National Gallery of Art. W. B. Yeats, Bernard Shaw, and numerous other important literary figures spent time in Coole Park and its beautiful great house in the early part of the twentieth century.

Lady Gregory led a relatively conventional life until Sir William Gregory died in 1892. According to the laws of that time, the estate passed to her son, so she anticipated a life of relatively modest circumstances. In the process of finishing Sir William's memoirs, she found herself to be a gifted writer. She used some of her spare time to learn Irish well enough to talk with the old cottagers in the hills, where she went to gather folklore and old songs. Although W. B. Yeats and others had collected volumes of Irish stories and poems, they did not know Irish well enough to authenticate what they heard. Lady Gregory published her Kiltartan tales (she had dubbed her neighborhood Kiltartan) as a way of preserving the rapidly disappearing myths and stories that were still told around the hearth as a matter of course in rural Ireland.

She was already an accomplished writer when she met W. B. Yeats in 1894. Their meeting was of immense importance for the history of drama, since they decided to forge their complementary talents and abilities to create an Irish theater. Their discussions included certain Irish neighbors, among them Edward Martyn, a Catholic whose early plays were very successful. They also talked with Dr. Douglas Hyde, a mythographer and linguist and the first president of modern Ireland. Another neighbor who took part, the flamboyant George Moore, was a well-established novelist and playwright.

The group's first plays — Yeats's *The Countess Cathleen* and Martyn's *The Heather Field* — were performed on May 8 and 9, 1899, under the auspices of the Irish Literary Theatre in Dublin at the Ancient Concert Rooms. Dedicated to producing plays by Irish playwrights on Irish themes, the Irish Literary Theatre became an immediate success. The greatest problem the founders faced was finding more plays. Lady Gregory tried her own hand and discovered herself, at age fifty, to be a playwright.

Her ear for people's speech was unusually good — good enough that she was able to give the great poet Yeats lessons in dialogue and to help him prepare his own plays for the stage. She collaborated with Yeats on *The Pot of Broth* in 1902, the year she wrote her first plays, *The Jackdaw* and *A Losing Game*. Her first produced play, *Twenty-Five*, was put on in 1903. By 1904 the group had rented the historic Abbey Theatre. Some of her plays were quite popular and were successful even in later revivals: *Spreading the News* (1904); *Kincora* and *The White Cockade* (1905); and *Hyacinth Halvey, The Doctor in Spite of Himself, The Gaol Gate,* and *The Canavans* (all 1906). In the next year, there were troubles at the Abbey over John Millington Synge's *Playboy of the Western World*. The middle-class audience resented the portrait of the Irish peasants as people who would celebrate a self-confessed father-killer, even though he had not actually done the "gallous deed." Lady Gregory faced down a rioting audience who were protesting what she felt was excellent drama.

In 1918 her son, a World War I pilot, was shot down over Italy. The years that followed were to some extent years of struggle. Lady Gregory managed the Abbey Theatre, directed its affairs, and developed new playwrights, among them Sean O'Casey. During the Irish Civil War (1920–1922), she was physically threatened, and eventually her family home, Roxborough, was burned. In 1926, after discovering that she had cancer, she made arrangements to sell Coole Park to the government with the agreement that she could remain there for life. She died in 1932, the writer of a large number of satisfying plays and the prime mover in developing one of the century's most important literary theaters.

THE RISING
OF THE MOON

One of Lady Gregory's shortest but most popular plays, *The Rising of the Moon* is openly political in its themes. Lady Gregory had been writing plays only a short time, and she had been directing the Irish Literary Theatre when it became the Abbey Theatre Company and produced this play in 1907. Her interest in Irish politics developed, she said, when she was going through the papers of a distant relative of her husband. That man had been in the Castle, the offices of the English authorities given the task of ruling Ireland from Dublin. She said that the underhanded dealings revealed in those papers convinced her that Ireland should be a nation apart from England if justice were ever to be done.

In 1907 the question of union with England or separation and nationhood was on everyone's lips. Ireland was calm, and the people in Dublin were relatively prosperous and by no means readying for a fight or a revolution. Yet there had been a tradition of risings against the English dating back to the Elizabethan age and earlier. In 1907 the average Irish person believed that revolution was a thing of the past; actually, it was less than ten years in the future. Certain organizations had been developing, notably the widespread Gaelic League and the less-known Sinn Féin (We Ourselves), to promote Irish lore, language, and culture. English was the dominant language in Ireland, since it was the language of commerce, but it tended to obliterate the Irish culture. Lady Gregory's work with the Abbey Theatre, which was making one of the age's most important contributions to Irish culture, thus coincided with growing interest in the rest of Ireland in rediscovering its literary past.

The title *The Rising of the Moon* comes from a popular old rebel song that pointed to the rising of the moon as the signal for the rising of peoples against oppression. The main characters of the play represent the two opposing forces in Ireland: freedom and independence, personified by the ballad singer ("a Ragged Man"); and law and order, represented by the sergeant. The ballad singer is aligned with those who want to change the social structure of Ireland so that the people now on the bottom will be on top. The sergeant's job is to preserve the status quo and avoid such a turning of the tables.

In an important way, the sergeant and the ballad singer represent the two alternatives that face the modern Irish — now as in the past. One alternative is to accept the power of the English and be in their pay, like the sergeant; one would then be well fed and capable of supporting a family. The other alternative is to follow the revolutionary path of the ballad singer and risk prison, scorn, and impoverishment. The ballad singer is a ragged man because he has been totally reduced in circumstances by his political choices.

For Lady Gregory, this play was a serious political statement. She and W. B. Yeats — both aristocratic Protestant Irish — were sympathetic to the Irish revolutionary causes. They each wrote plays that struck a revolutionary note during this period. Neither truly expected a revolution; when the Easter Uprising of 1916 was put down with considerable loss of life and immense destruction of central Dublin, Yeats lamented that his plays may have sent some young men to their deaths.

It is possible that if either Yeats or Lady Gregory had thought there would be a revolution they would not have written such plays. They opposed violence, but it was clear to some that violence was the only means by which Ireland would be made into a separate nation.

The success of *The Rising of the Moon* lies in Lady Gregory's exceptional ear for dialogue. She captures the way people speak, and she also manages to draw the characters of the sergeant and ballad singer so as to gain our sympathies for both. In a remarkably economic fashion she dramatizes the problem of politics in Ireland, characterizing the two polarities and revealing some of the complexities that face anyone who tries to understand them.

Lady Gregory (1852–1932)
THE RISING OF THE MOON

1907

Persons

SERGEANT   POLICEMAN B
POLICEMAN X   A RAGGED MAN

Scene: *Side of a quay in a seaport town. Some posts and chains. A large barrel. Enter three policemen. Moonlight.*

(*Sergeant, who is older than the others, crosses the stage to right and looks down steps. The others put down a pastepot and unroll a bundle of placards.*)

POLICEMAN B: I think this would be a good place to put up a notice. (*He points to barrel.*)

POLICEMAN X: Better ask him. (*Calls to Sergeant.*) Will this be a good place for a placard?

(*No answer.*)

POLICEMAN B: Will we put up a notice here on the barrel?

(*No answer.*)

SERGEANT: There's a flight of steps here that leads to the water. This is a place that should be minded well. If he got down here, his friends might have a boat to meet him; they might send it in here from outside.

POLICEMAN B: Would the barrel be a good place to put a notice up?

SERGEANT: It might; you can put it there.

(*They paste the notice up.*)

SERGEANT (*reading it*): Dark hair — dark eyes, smooth face, height five feet five — there's not much to take hold of in that — It's a pity I had no chance of seeing him before he broke out of jail. They say he's a wonder, that it's he makes all the plans for the whole organization. There isn't another man in Ireland would have broken jail the way he did. He must have some friends among the jailers.

POLICEMAN B: A hundred pounds is little enough for the Government to offer for him. You may be sure any man in the force that takes him will get promotion.

SERGEANT: I'll mind this place myself. I wouldn't wonder at all if he came this way. He might come slipping along there (*points to side of quay*), and his friends might be waiting for him there (*points down steps*), and once he got away it's little chance we'd have of finding him; it's maybe under a load of kelp he'd be in a fishing boat, and not one to help a married man that wants it to the reward.

POLICEMAN X: And if we get him itself, nothing but abuse on our heads for it from the people, and maybe from our own relations.

SERGEANT: Well, we have to do our duty in the force. Haven't we the whole country depending on us to keep law and order? It's those that are down would be up and those that are up would be down, if it wasn't for us. Well, hurry on, you have plenty of other places to placard yet, and come back here then to me. You can take the lantern. Don't be too long now. It's very lonesome here with nothing but the moon.

POLICEMAN B: It's a pity we can't stop with you. The Government should have brought more police into the town, with *him* in jail, and at assize° time too. Well, good luck to your watch.

(*They go out.*)

SERGEANT (*walks up and down once or twice and looks at placard*): A hundred pounds and promotion sure. There must be a great deal of spending in a hundred pounds. It's a pity some honest man not to be better of that.

(*A Ragged Man appears at left and tries to slip past. Sergeant suddenly turns.*)

SERGEANT: Where are you going?

MAN: I'm a poor ballad-singer, your honor. I thought to sell some of these (*holds out bundle of ballads*) to the sailors.

(*He goes on.*)

SERGEANT: Stop! Didn't I tell you to stop? You can't go on there.

MAN: Oh, very well. It's a hard thing to be poor. All the world's against the poor!

SERGEANT: Who are you?

MAN: You'd be as wise as myself if I told you, but I don't mind. I'm one Jimmy Walsh, a ballad-singer.

SERGEANT: Jimmy Walsh? I don't know that name.

MAN: Ah, sure, they know it well enough in Ennis. Were you ever in Ennis, sergeant?

SERGEANT: What brought you here?

MAN: Sure, it's to the assizes I came, thinking I might make a few shillings here or there. It's in the one train with the judges I came.

SERGEANT: Well, if you came so far, you may as well go farther, for you'll walk out of this.

MAN: I will, I will; I'll just go on where I was going.

(*Goes toward steps.*)

SERGEANT: Come back from those steps; no one has leave to pass down them tonight.

MAN: I'll just sit on the top of the steps till I see will some sailor buy a ballad off me that would give me my supper. They do be late going back to the ship. It's often I saw them in Cork carried down the quay in a handcart.

SERGEANT: Move on, I tell you. I won't have anyone lingering about the quay tonight.

MAN: Well, I'll go. It's the poor have the hard life! Maybe yourself might like one, sergeant. Here's a good sheet now. (*Turns one over.*) "Content and a pipe"— that's not much. "The Peeler and the goat"— you wouldn't like that. "Johnny Hart"— that's a lovely song.

SERGEANT: Move on.

MAN: Ah, wait till you hear it. (*Sings.*)

assize: Judicial inquest.

There was a rich farmer's daughter lived near the town of Ross;
She courted a Highland soldier, his name was Johnny Hart;
Says the mother to her daughter, "I'll go distracted mad
If you marry that Highland soldier dressed up in Highland plaid."

SERGEANT: Stop that noise.

(*Man wraps up his ballads and shuffles toward the steps.*)

SERGEANT: Where are you going?

MAN: Sure you told me to be going, and I am going.

SERGEANT: Don't be a fool. I didn't tell you to go that way; I told you to go back to the town.

MAN: Back to the town, is it?

SERGEANT (*taking him by the shoulder and shoving him before him*): Here, I'll show you the way. Be off with you. What are you stopping for?

MAN (*who has been keeping his eye on the notice, points to it*): I think I know what you're waiting for, sergeant.

SERGEANT: What's that to you?

MAN: And I know well the man you're waiting for — I know him well — I'll be going.

(*He shuffles on.*)

SERGEANT: You know him? Come back here. What sort is he?

MAN: Come back is it, sergeant? Do you want to have me killed?

SERGEANT: Why do you say that?

MAN: Never mind. I'm going. I wouldn't be in your shoes if the reward was ten times as much. (*Goes on off stage to left.*) Not if it was ten times as much.

SERGEANT (*rushing after him*): Come back here, come back. (*Drags him back.*) What sort is he? Where did you see him?

MAN: I saw him in my own place, in the County Clare. I tell you you wouldn't like to be looking at him. You'd be afraid to be in the one place with him. There isn't a weapon he doesn't know the use of, and as to strength, his muscles are as hard as that board (*slaps barrel*).

SERGEANT: Is he as bad as that?

MAN: He is then.

SERGEANT: Do you tell me so?

MAN: There was a poor man in our place, a sergeant from Ballyvaughan. — It was with a lump of stone he did it.

SERGEANT: I never heard of that.

MAN: And you wouldn't, sergeant. It's not everything that happens gets into the papers. And there was a policeman in plain clothes, too. . . . It is in Limerick he was. . . . It was after the time of the attack on the police barrack at Kilmallock. . . . Moonlight . . . just like this . . . waterside. . . . Nothing was known for certain.

SERGEANT: Do you say so? It's a terrible county to belong to.

MAN: That's so, indeed! You might be standing there, looking out that way, thinking you saw him coming up this side of the quay (*points*), and he might be coming up this other side (*points*), and he'd be on you before you knew where you were.

SERGEANT: It's a whole troop of police they ought to put here to stop a man like that.

MAN: But if you'd like me to stop with you, I could be looking down this side. I could be sitting up here on this barrel.

SERGEANT: And you know him well, too?

MAN: I'd know him a mile off, sergeant.

SERGEANT: But you wouldn't want to share the reward?

MAN: Is it a poor man like me, that has to be going the roads and singing in fairs, to have the name on him that he took a reward? But you don't want me. I'll be safer in the town.

SERGEANT: Well, you can stop.

MAN (*getting up on barrel*): All right, sergeant. I wonder, now, you're not tired out, sergeant, walking up and down the way you are.

SERGEANT: If I'm tired I'm used to it.

MAN: You might have hard work before you tonight yet. Take it easy while you can. There's plenty of room up here on the barrel, and you see farther when you're higher up.

SERGEANT: Maybe so. (*Gets up beside him on barrel, facing right. They sit back to back, looking different ways.*) You made me feel a bit queer with the way you talked.

MAN: Give me a match, sergeant (*he gives it and man lights pipe*); take a draw yourself? It'll quiet you. Wait now till I give you a light, but you needn't turn round. Don't take your eye off the quay for the life of you.

SERGEANT: Never fear, I won't. (*Lights pipe. They both smoke.*) Indeed it's a hard thing to be in the force, out at night and no thanks for it, for all the danger we're in. And it's little we get but abuse from the people, and no choice but to obey our orders, and never asked when a man is sent into danger, if you are a married man with a family.

MAN (*sings*): As through the hills I walked to view the hills and shamrock plain,

I stood awhile where nature smiles to view the rocks and streams,

On a matron fair I fixed my eyes beneath a fertile vale,

And she sang her song it was on the wrong of poor old Granuaile.

SERGEANT: Stop that; that's no song to be singing in these times.

MAN: Ah, sergeant, I was only singing to keep my heart up. It sinks when I think of him. To think of us two sitting here, and he creeping up the quay, maybe, to get to us.

SERGEANT: Are you keeping a good lookout?

MAN: I am; and for no reward too. Amn't I the foolish man? But when I saw a man in trouble, I never could help trying to get him out of it. What's that? Did something hit me?

(*Rubs his heart.*)

SERGEANT (*patting him on the shoulder*): You will get your reward in heaven.

MAN: I know that, I know that, sergeant, but life is precious.

SERGEANT: Well, you can sing if it gives you more courage.

MAN (*sings*): Her head was bare, her hands and feet with iron bands were bound,

Her pensive strain and plaintive wail mingles with the evening gale,

And the song she sang with mournful air, I am old Granuaile.

Her lips so sweet that monarchs kissed . . .

SERGEANT: That's not it. . . . "Her gown she wore was stained with gore." . . . That's it — you missed that.

MAN: You're right, sergeant, so it is; I missed it. (*Repeats line.*) But to think of a man like you knowing a song like that.

SERGEANT: There's many a thing a man might know and might not have any wish for.

MAN: Now, I daresay, sergeant, in your youth, you used to be sitting up on a wall, the way you are sitting up on this barrel now, and the other lads beside you, and you singing "Granuaile"? . . .

SERGEANT: I did then.

MAN: And the "Shan Van Vocht"? . . .

SERGEANT: I did then.

MAN: And the "Green on the Cape"?

SERGEANT: That was one of them.

MAN: And maybe the man you are watching for tonight used to be sitting on the wall, when he was young, and singing those same songs. . . . It's a queer world. . . .

SERGEANT: Whisht! . . . I think I see something coming. . . . It's only a dog.

MAN: And isn't it a queer world? . . . Maybe it's one of the boys you used to be singing with that time you will be arresting today or tomorrow, and sending into the dock. . . .

SERGEANT: That's true indeed.

MAN: And maybe one night, after you had been singing, if the other boys had told you some plan they had, some plan to free the country, you might have joined with them . . . and maybe it is you might be in trouble now.

SERGEANT: Well, who knows but I might? I had a great spirit in those days.

MAN: It's a queer world, sergeant, and it's little any mother knows when she sees her child creeping on the floor what might happen to it before it has gone through its life, or who will be who in the end.

SERGEANT: That's a queer thought now, and a true thought. Wait now till I think it out. . . . If it wasn't for the sense I have, and for my wife and family, and for me joining the force the time I did, it might be myself now would be after breaking jail and hiding in the dark, and it might be him that's hiding in the dark and that got out of jail would be sitting up here where I am on this barrel. . . . And it might be myself would be creeping up trying to make my escape from himself, and it might be himself would be keeping the law, and myself would be breaking it, and myself would be trying to put a bullet in his head, or to take up a lump of stone the way you said he did . . . no, that myself did. . . . Oh! (*Gasps. After a pause.*) What's that? (*Grasps man's arm.*)

MAN (*jumps off barrel and listens, looking out over water*): It's nothing, sergeant.

SERGEANT: I thought it might be a boat. I had a notion there might be friends of his coming about the quays with a boat.

MAN: Sergeant, I am thinking it was with the people you were, and not with the law you were, when you were a young man.

SERGEANT: Well, if I was foolish then, that time's gone.

MAN: Maybe, sergeant, it comes into your head sometimes, in spite of your belt and your tunic, that it might have been as well for you to have followed Granuaile.

SERGEANT: It's no business of yours what I think.

MAN: Maybe, sergeant, you'll be on the side of the country yet.

SERGEANT (*gets off barrel*): Don't talk to me like that. I have my duties and I know them. (*Looks round.*) That was a boat; I hear the oars.

(*Goes to the steps and looks down.*)

MAN (*sings*): O, then, tell me, Shawn O'Farrell,
    Where the gathering is to be.
  In the old spot by the river
    Right well known to you and me!

SERGEANT: Stop that! Stop that, I tell you!

MAN (*sings louder*): One word more, for signal token,
    Whistle up the marching tune,
  With your pike upon your shoulder,
    At the Rising of the Moon.

SERGEANT: If you don't stop that, I'll arrest you.

(*A whistle from below answers, repeating the air.*)

SERGEANT: That's a signal. (*Stands between him and steps.*) You must not pass this way. . . . Step farther back. . . . Who are you? You are no ballad-singer.

MAN: You needn't ask who I am; that placard will tell you. (*Points to placard.*)

SERGEANT: You are the man I am looking for.

MAN (*takes off hat and wig. Sergeant seizes them*): I am. There's a hundred pounds on my head. There is a friend of mine below in a boat. He knows a safe place to bring me to.

SERGEANT (*looking still at hat and wig*): It's a pity! It's a pity. You deceived me. You deceived me well.

MAN: I am a friend of Granuaile. There is a hundred pounds on my head.

SERGEANT: It's a pity, it's a pity!

MAN: Will you let me pass, or must I make you let me?

SERGEANT: I am in the force. I will not let you pass.

MAN: I thought to do it with my tongue. (*Puts hand in breast.*) What is that?

VOICE OF POLICEMAN X (*outside*): Here, this is where we left him.

SERGEANT: It's my comrades coming.

MAN: You won't betray me . . . the friend of Granuaile. (*Slips behind barrel.*)

VOICE OF POLICEMAN B: That was the last of the placards.

POLICEMAN X (*as they come in*): If he makes his escape it won't be unknown he'll make it.

(*Sergeant puts hat and wig behind his back.*)

POLICEMAN B: Did anyone come this way?

SERGEANT (*after a pause*): No one.

POLICEMAN B: No one at all?

SERGEANT: No one at all.

POLICEMAN B: We had no orders to go back to the station; we can stop along with you.

SERGEANT: I don't want you. There is nothing for you to do here.

POLICEMAN B: You bade us to come back here and keep watch with you.

SERGEANT: I'd sooner be alone. Would any man come this way and you making all that talk? It is better the place to be quiet.

POLICEMAN B: Well, we'll leave you the lantern anyhow.

(*Hands it to him.*)

SERGEANT: I don't want it. Bring it with you.

POLICEMAN B: You might want it. There are clouds coming up and you have the darkness of the night before you yet. I'll leave it over here on the barrel. (*Goes to barrel.*)

SERGEANT: Bring it with you, I tell you. No more talk.

POLICEMAN B: Well, I thought it might be a comfort to you. I often think when I have it in my hand and can be flashing it about into every dark corner (*doing so*) that it's the same as being beside the fire at home, and the bits of bogwood blazing up now and again.

(*Flashes it about, now on the barrel, now on Sergeant.*)

SERGEANT (*furious*): Be off the two of you, yourselves and your lantern!

(*They go out. Man comes from behind barrel. He and Sergeant stand looking at one another.*)

SERGEANT: What are you waiting for?

MAN: For my hat, of course, and my wig. You wouldn't wish me to get my death of cold?

(*Sergeant gives them.*)

MAN (*going toward steps*): Well, good night, comrade, and thank you. You did me a good turn tonight, and I'm obliged to you. Maybe I'll be able to do as much for you when the small rise up and the big fall down . . . when we all change places at the Rising (*waves his hand and disappears*) of the Moon.

SERGEANT (*turning his back to audience and reading placard*): A hundred pounds reward! A hundred pounds! (*Turns toward audience.*) I wonder, now, am I as great a fool as I think I am?

Greek Drama

Origins of Greek Drama

Because our historical knowledge of Greek drama is limited by the available contemporary commentaries and by partial archaeological remains — in the form of ruined theaters — we do not know when Greek theater began or what its original impulses were. Our best information points to 534 B.C. as the beginning of the formal competitions among playwrights for coveted prizes that continued to be awarded for several centuries. Thespis, credited as the first tragedy writer, seems to have changed the nature of the form by stepping out of the chorus and taking a solo part. But the origin of *tragedy*, which translates in Greek as "goat-song" or "song for the sacrificial goat," is obscure. One theory is that tragedy may have developed from the rites of rural cults that sacrificed a she-goat at some Dionysian festivals or from masked animal dances at certain cult celebrations.

One source that may well have influenced the Greeks was the Egyptian civilization of the first millennium B.C. Egyptian culture was fully formed, brilliant, and complex. And while Egyptologists do not credit it with having a formal theater, certain ceremonies, repeated annually at major festivals, seem to have counterparts in later Greek rituals and drama. The most important and most impressive Egyptian ritual, described by some scholars as a passion play, concerned the dramatic story of Isis and Osiris and the treachery of Osiris's brother Set.

The closest Greek counterpart to Osiris was DIONYSUS, who inspired orgiastic celebrations that found their way into early Greek drama. Dionysus was an agricultural deity, the Greek god of wine and the symbol of life-giving power. In several myths he, like Osiris, was ritually killed and dismembered and his parts scattered through the land. These myths paralleled the agricultural cycle of death and disintegration during the winter, followed by cultivation and rebirth in the spring, and reinforced the Greeks' understanding of the meaning of birth, life, and death.

Drama developed in ancient Greece in close connection with the Dionysia, religious celebrations dedicated to Dionysus. Four Dionysiac celebrations were held each winter in Athens beginning at the grape harvest and culminating during the first wine tastings: the Rural Dionysia in December, the Lenaia in January, the Anthesteria in February, and the City Dionysia in March. Except for the Anthesteria, the festivals featured drama contests among playwrights, and some of the works performed in those competitions have endured through the centuries. Theories that connect the origins of drama with religion hypothesize that one function of the religious festivals within which the drama competitions took place was the ritual attempt to guarantee fertility and the growth of the crops, on which the society depended.

The CITY DIONYSIA, the most lavish of the festivals, lasted from five to seven days. It was open to non-Athenians and therefore offered Athenians the opportunity to show off their wealth, their glorious history, and their heroes, who were often honored in parades the day before the plays began. There is some question about what was presented on each day. Two days were probably taken up with dithyrambic contests among the ten tribes of Athens. Generally each tribe presented two choruses — one of men and one of boys — each singing a narrative lyric called a DITHYRAMB. A prize was awarded the best performers. Three days were devoted to contests among tragedians, most of whom worked for half the year on three tragedies and a SATYR PLAY, an erotic piece of comic relief that ended the day's performance. A tragedian's three plays sometimes shared related themes or myths, but often they did not. The tragedians wrote the plays, trained and rehearsed the actors, composed music, and created setting, dances, costumes, and masks. After 486 B.C. the first comedy competition was held, when five and later three comedies were also presented during the festival. The performances were paid for by wealthy Athenians as part of their civic duty. The great Greek plays thus were not commercial enterprises but an important part of civic and religious festivals.

Judges chosen by lottery awarded prizes, usually basing their decisions on the merits of the dramas. First prize went to the tragedian whose four plays were most powerful and most beautifully conceived.

The Greeks and Their Gods

The great achievement of Greek religion was the humanizing of their gods. Apollo, Zeus, Aphrodite, Athena, and Bacchus had recognizable emotions and pleasures. The Greeks built temples to their gods and made offerings at appropriate times to avoid catastrophe and bad luck. But the Greeks had no official religious text, no system of religious belief that they all followed, and few ethical teachings derived from religion. The impression we have today is that Greeks' efforts to define and know the gods were shaped by great artists such as Phidias, who sculpted Zeus at Olympia; Homer, who portrayed the gods in *The Iliad* and *The Odyssey;* and the great Greek playwrights, who sometimes revealed the actions of the gods. Our present knowledge of Greek gods resides in the literary and artistic remains of Greek culture.

Fortunately for us, most Greek drama was associated with important celebrations designed to honor Greek gods. We would not, however, call this drama religious in nature — as we characterize the medieval drama designated to celebrate Christian holidays. What we learn from Greek drama is that the gods can favor individual humans for reasons of their own. And likewise, the gods can choose to punish individual humans. To some extent Greek drama is designed to explain the divine approach to favor and disfavor.

The Greek Stage

At the center of the Greek theater was the ORCHESTRA, where the chorus sang and danced (*orches* is derived from the Greek for "dancing place"). The audience, sometimes numbering fifteen thousand, sat in rising rows on three sides of the orchestra. The steep sides of a hill formed a natural amphitheater for Greek audiences. Eventually, on the rim of the orchestra, an oblong building called the SKENE, or scene house, developed as a space for the actors and a background for the action. The term PROSKENION was sometimes used to refer to a raised stage added in later times in front of the *skene* where the actors performed. The theater at Epidaurus (Figures 1 and 2) was a model for the Greek theater plan.

Greek theaters were widely dispersed from Greece to present-day Turkey, to Sicily, and even to southern France. Wherever the Greeks developed new colonies and city-states, they built theaters. In many of the surviving theaters the acoustics are so fine that a human voice onstage can be heard from any seat in the theater.

Perhaps the most spectacular theatrical device used by the Greek playwrights, the MEKANE ("machine"), was implemented onstage by means of elaborate booms or derricks. Actors were lowered onto the stage to enact the roles of Olympian gods intervening in the affairs of humans. Some commentators, such as Aristotle (384–322 B.C.), felt that the *mekane* should be used only if the intercession of deities was in keeping with the character of the play. The last of the great Greek tragedians, Euripides (c. 485–c. 406 B.C.), used the device in almost half of his tragedies. In *Medea* Euripides uses the *mekane* to lift Medea to the roof of the *skene* and into her dragon chariot as a means of resolving the play's conflict. At the end of the play Medea is beyond her persecutors' reach and is headed for safety in another country. Modern dramatists use a version of this, called *deus ex machina*, literally, "the god from the machine," when they rescue characters at the last moment by improbable accidents or strokes of luck. Usually, these are unsatisfying means of solving dramatic problems.

Genres of Greek Drama
Tragedy

Greek tragedy focused on a person of noble birth who in some cases had risen to a great height and then fell precipitately. Tragedies showed humans at the mercy of MOIRA, their fate, which they only partly understood. One objective of Greek drama was to have the audience experience a CATHARSIS, which Aristotle describes as a purging or purifying of the emotions of pity and fear. According to the Greeks, these are emotions that a person associates with the fall of someone in a high social station, such as a king or queen. A central character, or PROTAGONIST, of noble birth was therefore an essential element for the playwright striving to evoke catharsis in an audience. Twentieth-century experiments with tragic figures who are ordinary people, such as Arthur Miller's *Death of a Salesman*, as masterful as they are, would not have made sense to the Greeks. For the Greeks, tragedy could befall only the great.

The modern critic Kenneth Burke identified a pattern for Greek tragedies. The tragic figure — for whom the play is usually named — experiences three stages of development: purpose, passion, and perception. The play begins with a purpose, such as finding the source of the plague in *Oedipus Rex*. Then, as the path becomes tangled and events unfold, the tragic figure begins an

Figure 1. The theater at Epidaurus, Greece, looking east. This is the best preserved (and now restored) Greek theater. Built in the fourth century B.C. by Polykleitos the Younger and approximately 124 feet in diameter, it seats twelve thousand people and remains in use today with excellent acoustics.

Figure 2. Theater at Epidaurus.

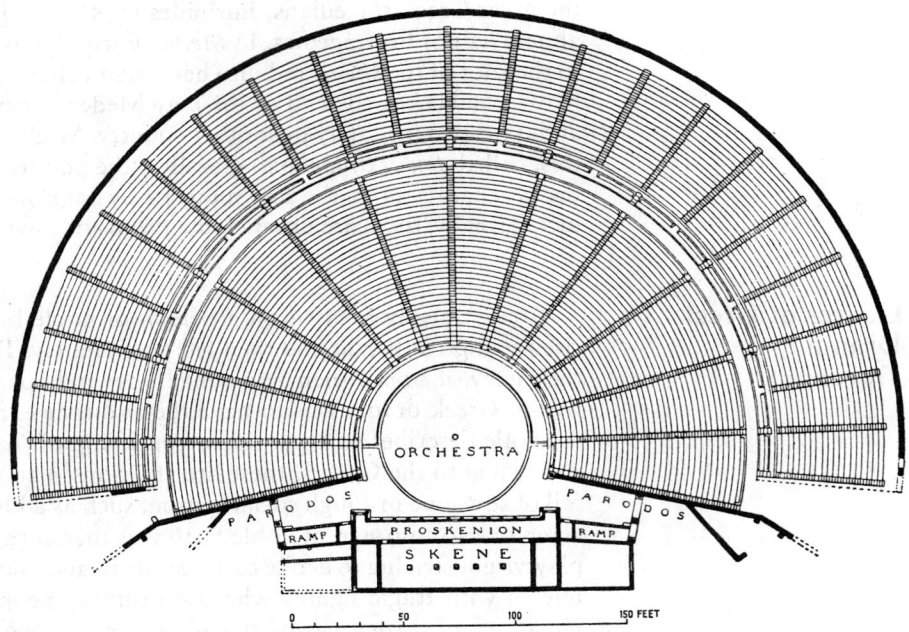

extensive process of soul-searching and suffers an inner agony — the passion. The perception of the truth involves a fate that the tragic figure would rather not face. It might be death or, as in *Oedipus Rex,* exile. It always involves separation from the human community. For the Greeks, that was the greatest punishment.

According to Aristotle, the tragic hero's perception of the truth was the most intense moment in the drama. He called it ANAGNORISIS, or recognition. When it came at the same moment that the tragic figure's fortunes reversed — the PERIPETEIA — Aristotle felt that the tragedy was most fulfilling for the audience. This is the case in *Oedipus Rex*. Aristotle's comments in his *Poetics* on the structure and effect of *Oedipus Rex* remain the most significant critical observations made by a contemporary on Greek theater. (See the excerpt from the *Poetics* on page 94.)

The Structure of Greek Tragedies. The earliest tragedies seem to have developed from the emotional, intense dithyrambs sung by Athenian choruses. The CHORUS in most tragedies numbered twelve or fifteen men. They usually represented the citizenry in the drama. They dressed simply, and their song was sometimes sung in unison, sometimes delivered by the chorus leader. Originally, there were no actors separate from the chorus.

According to legend, Thespis (sixth century B.C.) was the first actor — the first to step from the chorus to act in dialogue with it — thus creating the AGON, or dramatic confrontation. He won the first prize for tragedy in 532 B.C. As the only actor, he took several parts, wearing MASKS to distinguish the different characters. One actor was the norm in tragedies until Aeschylus (525–456 B.C.), the first important Greek tragedian whose work survives, introduced a second actor, and then Sophocles (c. 496–c. 406 B.C.) added a third. (Only comedy used more: four actors.)

Like the actors, the members of the chorus wore masks. At first the masks were simple, but they became more ornate, often trimmed with hair and decorated with details that established the gender, age, or station of each character. The chorus and all the actors were male.

Eventually the structure of the plays became elaborated into a series of alternations between the characters' dialogue and the choral odes, with each speaking part developing the action or responding to it. Often crucial information furthering the action came from the mouth of a messenger, as in *Oedipus Rex*. The tragedies were structured in three parts: the PROLOGUE established the conflict; the episodes or agons developed the dramatic relationships between characters; and the EXODOS concluded the action. Between these sections the chorus performed different songs: PARODOS while moving onto the stage and STASIMA while standing still. In some plays the chorus sang choral ODES called the STROPHE as it moved from right to left. It sang the ANTISTROPHE while moving back to the right. The actors' episodes consisted of dialogue with each other and with the chorus. The scholar Bernhard Zimmerman has plotted the structure of *Oedipus Rex* in this fashion:

Prologue: Dialogue with Oedipus, the Priests, and Kreon establishing that the plague afflicting Thebes will cease when Laios's murderer is found.

Parodos: The opening hymn of the Chorus appealing to the gods.

First Episode: Oedipus seeks the murderer; Teiresias says it is Oedipus.

First Stasimon: The Chorus supports Oedipus, disbelieving Teiresias.

Second Episode: Oedipus accuses Kreon of being in league with Teiresias and the real murderer. Iokaste pleads for Kreon and tells the oracle of Oedipus's birth and of the death of Laios at the fork of a road. Oedipus sends for the eyewitness of the murder.

Second Stasimon: The Chorus, in a song, grows agitated for Oedipus.

Third Episode: The messenger from Oedipus's "hometown" tells him that his adoptive father has died and is not his real father. Iokaste guesses the truth and Oedipus becomes deeply worried.

Third Stasimon: The Chorus delivers a reassuring, hopeful song.

Fourth Episode: Oedipus, the Shepherd, and the Messenger confront the facts and Oedipus experiences the turning point of the play: he realizes he is the murderer he seeks.

Fourth Stasimon: The Chorus sings of the illusion of human happiness.

Exodos: Iokaste kills herself; Oedipus puts out his eyes; the Chorus and Kreon try to decide the best future action.

As this brief structural outline of *Oedipus Rex* demonstrates, the chorus assumed an important part in the tragedies. In Aeschylus's *Agamemnon* it represents the elders of the community. In Sophocles' *Oedipus Rex* it is a group of concerned citizens who give Oedipus advice and make demands on him. In *Antigone* the chorus consists of men loyal to the state. In Euripides' *Medea* the chorus is a group of the important women of Corinth.

Satyr Plays

The drama competitions held regularly from 534 B.C. consisted usually of the work of three playwrights who each produced three tragedies and one satyr play, a form of comic relief. In a satyr play, the chorus dressed as satyrs, comic half-beast, half-man figures who cavorted with a PHALLUS, a mock penis, and engaged in riotous, almost slapstick antics. The characters were not psychologically developed, as they were in tragedy; the situations were not socially instructive, as they were in comedy. Rough-hewn and lighthearted, the satyr plays may have been a necessary antidote to the intensity of the tragedies.

Only one satyr play survives, perhaps an indication that the form was not as highly valued as tragedy. In Euripides' *Cyclops,* based on Odysseus's confrontation with the one-eyed giant who dined on a number of his men, Odysseus outwits the giant with the aid of a well-filled wineskin. The powers of Bacchus (Dionysus) are often alluded to, and drunkenness is a prime ingredient. The play is witty, entertaining, and brief. It might well have been the perfect way to end an otherwise serious drama festival.

Comedy

No coherent Greek theories on comedy have come down to us. (Aristotle is said to have written a lost treatise on comedy.) In the *Poetics,* Aristotle points out that comedy shows people from a lower social order than the nobility, who are the main figures in tragedy.

The two greatest Greek comic writers were Aristophanes (c. 448–c. 385 B.C.), whose *Lysistrata* appears in this collection, and Menander (c. 342–c. 291 B.C.). The first was a master of OLD COMEDY (which lasted from c. 486 to c. 400 B.C.), in which individuals — sometimes well known to the audience — could be attacked personally. The nature of the humor was often ribald, coarse, and brassy, but, according to Aristotle, it was not vicious. Physical devices onstage, such as the erect phalluses beneath the men's garments in *Lysistrata*, accompanied ribald lines, and Athenian audiences were mightily entertained. Comedy appears to have provided release, but for entirely different emotions than those evoked by tragedy.

The Old Comedy of Aristophanes concentrated on buffoonery and farce. Although we know little about it, a form known as MIDDLE COMEDY seems to have flourished from approximately 400 to 320 B.C. Our evidence is from statuettes of players that indicate a more realistic portrayal of character and thus a less broad and grotesque form of comedy than in some of the plays of Aristophanes. The NEW COMEDY of Menander and others whose work is now lost provided a less ribald humor that centered on the shortcomings of the middle classes. Although Menander enjoyed a great reputation in his own time and was highly regarded by Roman playwrights much later, very little of his work has survived. He is said to have written a few more than one hundred plays, but only one, *The Grouch,* survives intact. Twenty-three of his plays existed in a manuscript in Constantinople in the sixteenth century, but nothing of that volume seems to have survived. We know a number of titles, such as *The Lady from Andros, The Flatterer,* and *The Suspicious Man.* And we know that the Romans pilfered liberally from his plays. Beyond that we know little.

Menander's New Comedy concentrated on social manners. Instead of attacking individuals, as Aristophanes frequently did, Menander was more likely to attack a vice, such as vanity, or to portray the foibles of a social class. He aimed at his own middle class and established the pattern of parents or guardians struggling, usually over the issue of marriage, against the wishes of their children. The children ordinarily foil their parents' wishes, frequently with the help of an acerbic slave who provides the comedy with most of its humor. This pattern has proved so durable that it is used virtually every day in modern situation comedies on television.

Both Old and New Comedy have influenced theater from the time of the Greeks to the present. The nineteenth-century comedy of Oscar Wilde (in this collection) is an example of New Comedy, while the Marx Brothers' movies are examples of Old Comedy.

The Great Age of Greek Drama

The fifth century B.C. was not only the great creative age of Athenian theater but also the age of Athenian power in Greek politics. By the beginning of the century, Greece dominated trade in the Mediterranean and therefore in many of the major civilized urban centers of the world. The most important threat to Greek power came from the Persians, living to the east. After the Persians attacked in 490, Greek city-states such as Athens formed the Delian League to defend themselves, pouring their funds into the treasury at Delos. When the Persians threatened again in 483 B.C., Themistocles (525?–460? B.C.), Athenian soldier and statesman, realized he could not win a battle on land. By skillful political moves he managed to create a powerful navy. When the Persians attacked Athens in 480 B.C., Themistocles left a small rear guard to defend the Acropolis, the city's religious fortress. The Persians took the fortress, burned everything, and were lured by a clever ruse to Salamis, where they thought that a puny Athenian navy was making a getaway. Once the Persians set sail for

Salamis, Themistocles turned on them and revealed a powerful fighting force that defeated the Persians once and for all.

In the years immediately following, Athens overstated its role in the Persian defeat and assumed an air of imperial importance. It appropriated the gold in the Delian League treasury, using it to rebuild the Acropolis beginning in 448 B.C. The great Greek general and leader Pericles (495?–429? B.C.) chose his friend Phidias to supervise the construction of the Parthenon and the other main buildings that are on the Acropolis even today. The threat of Athenian domination seems to have triggered the Peloponnesian Wars (432–406 B.C.), which pitted the Spartan alliance against the Athenian alliance. Athens eventually lost the war and its democratic government.

The events of these years — dominated by interminable wars, threats of a return to tyranny, cultural instability — are coterminous with the great flourishing of Greek art, drama, and philosophy. The geniuses of Greek drama cluster in the period dating from the birth of Aeschylus (c. 525 B.C.) to the death of the philosopher Socrates (399 B.C.). Aeschylus wrote *The Persians* (472 B.C.); *Seven against Thebes* (467 B.C.); and the *Oresteia* (458 B.C.), a trilogy centering on Orestes and consisting of *Agamemnon, The Libation Bearers,* and *The Eumenides. The Suppliants* and *Prometheus Bound* are of uncertain dates.

Aeschylus's introduction of a second actor made it possible to intensify the dramatic value of each *agon,* the confrontation between ANTAGONISTS. He is also notable for giving minor characters, such as the watchman who opens *Agamemnon,* both dimension and depth. Aeschylus's *Oresteia,* the only surviving trilogy, tells of the death of Agamemnon and the efforts of his son Orestes to avenge that death.

Sophocles (c. 496–c. 406 B.C.) and Euripides (c. 485–406 B.C.) learned from Aeschylus and from each other since they were all sometimes rivals. In addition to *Oedipus Rex* (c. 429 B.C.), Sophocles is known today for *Ajax* (c. 442 B.C.), *Philoctetes* (c. 409 B.C.), *Oedipus at Colonus* (406 B.C.), and *Electra* (date uncertain).

Euripides, the last of the great tragedians, may have written as many as ninety-two plays. Of the nineteen that survive, the best known are *Alcestis* (438 B.C.), *Medea* (431 B.C.), *Electra* (date uncertain), *The Trojan Women* (415 B.C.), and *The Bacchae* (produced in 405 B.C.). He is especially noteworthy for his portrayal of women and for his experimental approach to theater.

These three tragedians, along with Aristophanes, provide us with insight into the Greek dramatic imagination. They also reveal something of our common humanity, since their achievement — lost though it was for many centuries — shapes our current dramatic practice. The Greeks give us not only the beginnings of drama but the basis of drama. We build on it today whenever a play is written, whenever we witness a play.

Greek Drama Timeline

DATE	THEATER	POLITICAL	SOCIAL/CULTURAL
1000–800 B.C.			Classic paganism is in full bloom in Greece. Temple of Hera, oldest surviving temple in Olympia, Greece, is built. **9th c.:** Age of the Homeric epic; *The Illiad, The Odyssey*
800–700		First Messenian War: Sparta gains power in Greece.	Choral and dramatic music develops. Hesiod, poet whose *Works and Days* classified the five ages of mankind: Golden (peaceful), Silver (less happy), Bronze (art and warfare), Heroic (Trojan War), and Iron (the present) **776:** First Olympian festival (predecessor of the modern Olympic games). Only one event is featured: a footrace of approximately 200 meters.
700–600		First written laws of Athens are recorded by Draco.	Sappho of Lesbos, Greek poet Archilochus, Greek lyricist and author of fables Construction of the Acropolis begins in Athens.
600–500	**534:** First contest for best tragedy is held in Athens as part of the annual City Dionysia, a major religious festival. The winning playwright (and actor) is Thespis. **c. 501:** Satyr plays are added to the City Dionysia play competition. Each playwright now has to present a trilogy of tragedies and a satyr play.	**594:** Solon's law allows for the Council of Four Hundred and various reforms pertaining to land ownership and civil liberties. **c. 525–459:** Themistocles, Athenian statesman and naval commander, builds a Greek navy and fortifications. **525–405:** Persians conquer Egypt.	The influence of the oracle at Delphi and its priestess is at its height. The theater of Delphi is built. **c. 582–507:** Pythagoras, philosopher, mathematician, and musical theorist Public libraries in Athens **c. 563–483:** Siddartha, founder of Buddhism, begins his religious journey in 534. **c. 520–438:** Pindar, Greek musician and poet
500–400	**487–486:** Comedy is introduced as a dramatic form in the City Dionysia. **c. 471:** Aeschylus introduces the second actor in the performance of tragedy at the City Dionysia.	**500–449:** Persian Wars **494:** King Darius of Persia annexes all of Greece. **490:** Athenians defeat the Persians in the Battle of Marathon.	**c. 460–370:** Hippocrates, Greek physician who did much to separate medicine from superstition. **485–424:** Herodotus, a Greek historian, writes the history of the Persian Wars.

Greek Drama Timeline *(continued)*

DATE	THEATER	POLITICAL	SOCIAL/CULTURAL
500–400 B.C. (continued)	c. 468: Sophocles is credited with introducing the third actor in the performance of tragedies at the City Dionysia. 458: First performance of Aeschylus's trilogy the *Oresteia* at the City Dionysia 458: *Skene,* or scene house, is introduced in Greek theater. c. 441: First performance of Sophocles' *Antigone* at the City Dionysia c. 430–425: First performance of Sophocles' *Oedipus Rex* at the City Dionysia 411: First performance of Aristophanes' *Lysistrata*	480: At the Battle of Thermopylae, the Spartans defeat the Persians. 479: Xerxes, son of Darius, returns to Persia; the Persian Wars end. 462–429: Periclean Athens 431: The Peloponnesian War begins; Athens is defeated in 404. Thucydides records the events in his history *The Peloponnesian War.*	460–370: Democritus, Greek philosopher who believed that all living things are composed of atoms 438: The Parthenon is completed.
400–300	400–c. 320: Era of Middle Comedy, which concentrates on more accurately portraying daily life rather than the more fantastic plots of Old Comedy (Aristophanes) 336–300: Era of New Comedy. Menander and others move further away from Aristophanes; stock characters are common. 335–323: Aristotle writes *Poetics.*	395: The Corinthian War begins. Athens joins with Corinth, Thebes, and Argos to attack Sparta. Athens emerges from the ten-year war as a partially restored power. 332: Alexander the Great conquers Egypt. 321: Alexander the Great dies of a fever at age thirty-three. His successors divide the empire into Macedon, Egypt, and the Seleucid empire.	399: Socrates is tried and executed for corrupting the youth of Athens. 373: Plato writes *Republic.* 340–271: Epicurus, Greek philosopher who believed in pleasure, spontaneity, and freedom of will 320–330: Hellenistic period of Greek art 307: The museum and library of Alexandria are begun under Ptolemy Soter.
300–100	277: Artists of Dionysis, a performing artists' guild, is formed.		275–195: Eratosthenes, Greek scientist, suggests that the earth moves around the sun and makes close estimates of the earth's circumference.
100 B.C.–300 A.D.		100 B.C.–1 A.D.: Alexandria is the Mediterranean center of culture and commerce.	
300–400 A.D.			346–395: The Roman emperor Theodosius forbids the celebration of Olympic games in Greece.

Aeschylus

Very little is known for certain about the life of Aeschylus (c. 525–456 B.C.) despite a first attempt at a biographical sketch in 300 B.C. What is known is that he was born in Eleusis near Athens at a time that marked Athens's beginning as an important power in Greece and as the cradle of Western art and thought. When Aeschylus was born, Athens was under the control of tyrants, a control that ended in 510 to 508 B.C.; when he died, Athens was a democracy and one of the strongest states in the Greek confederation. The great threat to Athens's security came from the Persians, powerful Eastern warriors whose aim was the destruction of Greek economic power. Of the three great playwrights who lived in these times, Aeschylus is the only one who actually went to war against the Persians.

The records reveal that in 490 B.C. Aeschylus fought at the battle of Marathon, in which his brother was killed. The Persians were defeated at Marathon, and their king, Darius, died shortly thereafter. For ten years the Athenians enjoyed an uneasy peace, but in 480 B.C. the Persians returned under King Xerxes with a powerful fleet and army. Aeschylus fought at Salamis and probably also at a later victory in Plataea.

He seems to have been writing tragedies for fifteen years before his first victory in the drama competitions. He began competing in 499 to 496 B.C.; he won his first victory in 484 B.C. Aeschylus went on to win a total of thirteen competitions with thirteen tetralogies: groups of three tragedies and a satyr play. He may have written as many as ninety plays; the titles of eighty-three have come down to us, with seven plays and many fragments surviving. *Agamemnon* is the first play in the *Oresteia,* the only surviving trilogy of Greek tragedies that we know were produced together. Sophocles' Oedipus plays were, by contrast, composed over a long period of time and never performed as a trilogy until recent times.

Many efforts have been made to connect Aeschylus's plays to his life and times, but on the whole such efforts have been unprofitable. Clearly, though, he wrote some plays that spoke to the times, such as *The Persians* (472 B.C.), undoubtedly inspired by Athenian success in the Persian Wars. He also wrote plays associated with specific places, as in *The Women of Aetna,* produced in Sicily near Mount Aetna. *The Persians* won first prize, and its expenses were paid for by Athens's ruler, Pericles, who, after the battle of Salamis, rebuilt the Acropolis with the Parthenon and the other important buildings, such as the Erectheum, that still stand there.

Aeschylus is sometimes credited with a rough and powerful style expressed in a language that sometimes forced him to make up new words. The power of his language is always remarked on by those who know his Greek original, and his translators have often been poets in their own right. By contrast, the younger Sophocles uses a language that is smoother, more lyrical, and more graceful. Some critics have asserted that the younger playwrights profited from Aeschylus's development of tragic style.

Aeschylus died at age sixty-eight in Gela, Sicily, where he spent time at the request of a friendly tyrant, Hieron. The story surrounding Aeschylus's death has been told many times and is probably only legend. It was said that an eagle grasping a tortoise flew high into the air and accidentally dropped the tortoise on Aeschylus's head, killing him. His death came at the height of the development of Greek tragedy.

AGAMEMNON

Agamemnon is the first play in the *Oresteia*, the only extant trilogy of Greek tragedies. The trilogy was performed in 458 B.C., winning first prize in the competition. As its name implies, it concerns the fate of Orestes, son of Agamemnon, even though Orestes is not present during *Agamemnon*. He does not enter until *The Libation Bearers* but becomes the center of the action in the third play, *The Eumenides*. As many commentators have observed, the three plays are in essence three acts of one larger play.

Lying behind the action of the three plays is a memory of the horror that has befallen the House of Atreus, the family to which Agamemnon and Aegisthus and Orestes belong. Centuries before Aeschylus, Homer had told part of the story, which was a myth of significant proportions by the time Aeschylus dramatized it. It is recounted by Aegisthus near the end of *Agamemnon* (lines 1731–1766), although he omits at least one important detail. Pelops, son of Tantalus, had two sons: Atreus and Thyestes. The legend has several forms, but in essence Atreus and Thyestes have a falling out over the throne of their father. In addition Atreus suspects that Thyestes has slept with his wife. With Atreus in control of the kingdom, Thyestes is invited to return for a reconciliation, but Atreus plans a fearful revenge. Pretending to prepare a feast of slaughtered animals, Atreus serves Thyestes his own two children chopped into a stew. Once he has eaten, Thyestes is shown the heads, hands, and feet of his children and vomits. He then flees into exile with his remaining infant son, Aegisthus.

Atreus's sons were Menelaus, who led the Greeks to Troy to regain his errant wife, Helen; and Agamemnon, who returned victorious from Troy. Agamemnon's children were Iphigenia, Electra (who figures in *The Libation Bearers*), and Orestes. The *Oresteia*, then, works out the curse on the house of Atreus.

Agamemnon reveals several forceful characters. Clytemnestra, the wife of Agamemnon, presents herself as a faithful, long-suffering wife waiting patiently for her husband's return from war. However, the Chorus, composed of older men, knows that she has taken a lover, Aegisthus. Clytemnestra faces up to the rumors of her infidelity when Agamemnon returns, daring anyone to contradict her. Secretly, though, she plans (with the help of Aegisthus) to kill Agamemnon. Her discovery that her husband is returning with a female slave, the prophetess Cassandra, as his concubine gives her further motivation. When she confesses to the murder of Agamemnon and Cassandra, she tells the Chorus that she is exacting revenge against Agamemnon for sacrificing their daughter Iphigenia in order to get a favorable wind to sail to Troy. Later, Aegisthus justifies his role in the killing as revenge against the crimes of Agamemnon's father, Atreus.

To ensnare Agamemnon, Clytemnestra has woven an intricate web — the image of the spider is invoked in the play. She is warned of his return by the pillars of fire that are set from Troy to Greece as Agamemnon returns, so she is prepared. She produces a richly woven purple cloth — the equivalent of what we call a red carpet — on which she expects Agamemnon to walk into the palace. Knowing that to do so could offend the gods, he at first refuses. Ultimately he yields to her entreaties and enters the palace, leaving Cassandra outside to prophesy his death — and hers — to the unbelieving Chorus. Inside, Clytemnestra continues the pattern by winding a regal cloak about Agamemnon as he is in the bath, disabling him so that she is able to stab him mortally.

Throughout, *Agamemnon* emphasizes issues of gender. Often the Chorus comments on Clytemnestra's speaking with the authority of a man. The invocation of the god Apollo throughout the trilogy has been taken to imply an important cultural shift that Aeschylus recognizes. Is he referring to a distant past in which female deities were dominant but then were replaced by masculine deities? Such speculation is impossible to verify (see Lois Spatz's commentary on p. 63), but it is clear that the women in the *Oresteia* are powerful in their presence, demanding in their actions, and insistent in their demand for justice. *Agamemnon* ends with Clytemnestra facing down an angry and mistrustful Chorus and with Aegisthus claiming the throne and governing as a tyrant.

Agamemnon in Performance

The first production of Aeschylus's trilogy in 458 B.C. won first prize in the drama competitions. Although tragedies were not usually revived, it seems that this trilogy was played again at Greek festivals some few years after Aeschylus's death in 456 B.C. Unfortunately, after the demise of the Greek festivals, Aeschylus was not performed again until the sixteenth century. Early in the twentieth century the *Oresteia* was produced in Greek in the United States to a limited but enthusiastic audience. Harvard University produced *Agamemnon* in 1906, using all male actors, who spoke the lines in Greek. Max Reinhardt produced the trilogy in Berlin in 1915, but problems with the size of the theater and the nature of the stage resulted in an unsuccessful production. In 1968 the Minnesota Theater Company adapted the trilogy as *The House of Atreus*, directed by Tyrone Guthrie, taking it to Broadway at the Billy Rose Theater. Beginning in 1977 in New York, Andrei Serban experimented with performing Agamemnon in a mixture of English and Greek because, as he said, "Greek sounds have the power to catch the real emotional experience of the text." Serban produced the play at the Vivian Beaumont Theatre in Lincoln Center, New York. The high-tech staging, with exposed metal mesh floors and walls, created powerful effects. The Royal Shakespeare Company in 1980 put together an eleven-hour sequence of plays of Aeschylus, Euripides, and Sophocles on the fall of Troy, calling it *The Greeks*; it was successful both in England and abroad. The National Theatre in London produced the *Oresteia* in 1981 to considerable acclaim. Interestingly, the reviews of that production describe *Agamemnon* as having been eclipsed in dramatic importance by *The Libation Bearers*, which "becomes the great dramatic moment of the trilogy." Combining Euripides' *Iphigenia in Aulis* with the trilogy, the French Théâtre du Soleil performed *Les Atrides* in Paris, Montreal, and New York in 1992. Ariane Mnouchkine directed and conceived the production (in French with simultaneous translation), using only five actors. Paul Nadler compared *Les Atrides* with bullfights, which "deal with killers and victims acting out their fates upon fields of honor."

Aeschylus (*c. 525–456 B.C.*)

AGAMEMNON

458 B.C.

TRANSLATED BY DAVID GREENE AND WENDY DONIGER O'FLAHERTY

Dramatis Personae

SENTRY
CHORUS, *old men of Argos left behind after the Argives went to Troy*
CLYTEMNESTRA, *queen of Argos in the absence of King Agamemnon at Troy*
HERALD *from the Greek army*
KING AGAMEMNON
CASSANDRA, *princess of Troy, daughter of King Priam*
AEGISTHUS

SENTRY: You gods, release me.
    Crouched like a dog, I watch always, all year long,
    on the tower of the sons of Atreus.
    I have come to know the nightly gathering of the
      stars
    and those radiant dynasts of the firmament that lead
5   them.
    They bring winter and summer to men.
    Now I watch for a flaming light,
    the beacon fire, the tell-tale witness that Troy is
      captured.
    Such are my orders, orders from a hopeful queen
10   who thinks with the mind of a man.
    I have a bed here, soaked with dew, always shifting.
    But no dreams. Fear is my visitor, not sleep.
    I cannot close my eyes for fear.
    Sometimes I whistle or hum;
15   the tunes are my drug against my sleepiness.
    But then the sorrow comes.
    This house is in bitter trouble.
    Once it was well governed; not now.
    Still, may the fire of good news light the darkness
20   to be the lucky release from our troubles.

    The beacon! Day out of night!
    The dances everywhere in Argos!
    Thanks, good beacon!

My lady, Agamemnon's wife, get out of bed!
Cry aloud a blessing on this beacon,   25
since Troy is surely captured.
I will myself begin the dance, for I'll score to myself,
    too,
the winning dice that the beacon threw for my
    master.
Oh, that I could touch with this hand of mine
the hand that I love, my lord's.   30
As for the rest, I haven't a word;
a great ox stands on my tongue.
If the house itself had a voice to speak,
it would tell the clearest story.
I choose to speak to those who understand;   35
for the others, I am all forgetfulness.
CHORUS: This is the tenth year
since they launched from this land
the Greek fleet of a thousand ships
to help right wrongs done.   40
They launched it, King Menelaus,
great plaintiff against Priam,
and Agamemnon his brother;
twin the yoke joining them in honor and throne,
twin their shared grace of God.   45

From their hearts the great war cry;
they screamed like eagles,
that wheel and wheel high above their eyries,
driven by the oarage of their wings,
in lonely agony for the loss of their nestlings,   50
and all the watchful care they had spent guarding
    them.

But One yet higher up, some Apollo or Pan or
    Zeus,°

---

52. **Apollo or Pan or Zeus:** Greek gods with the power to avenge crimes.

hears the shrill-voiced sorrow of these settlers in his
    kingdom
and sends on the evildoers
55   the Fury that brings punishment, however late.
So a Lord greater than the kings, Zeus god of guest-
    friends,
sends the sons of Atreus on Alexander;°
in this quarrel over a woman of many men,
he would lay upon Greeks and Trojans alike
60   many wrestlings where the limbs grow heavy
and the knee is pressed into the dust
and the spear is shattered in the first rites of
    engagement.
Yet it is now as it is.
Fulfillment moves toward what is fated.
And not with burnt offerings nor with pouring on
65   of wine
nor sacrifice to the gods below
will you assuage that stubborn anger.

But we, dishonored for the ancientness of our flesh,
were left behind then when the army went;
we remain, propping on staffs a strength like a
70   child's.
For the child's marrow, too, leaps within his breast
but is only the match of an old man's;
the god of war is not there either.
And the overold, the leafage already withering,
walks his three-footed way,° no stronger than a
75   child;
wanders, a dream in the daylight.

You, daughter of Tyndareus, Queen Clytemnestra,
What's the matter? What's the news? What have
    you heard?
What message do you trust, that you order sacrifices
80   at all the altars?
Of all the gods that hold our city,
of those above and those beneath the earth,
of those at the doorpost and those at the
    marketplace,
the altars blaze with offerings.
85   Here one torch sends its flames to the sky,
and another raises its light,
charmed by the soft, guileless urgings of pure
    streams of oil
drawn from the depth of the royal store.
Tell us what you can and what may be said
90   about all these things.
Cure this care that now broods darkly on our
    minds.
But then hope, shining out of the sacrifice,

turns away the insatiable thoughts that might
    otherwise
eat out the heart in sorrow.

It is mine to declare the omens of victory   95
given to princely men on the journey.
For by God's grace, old age, which grows with life,
    my life,
still breathes on my lips persuasion,
the strength of song.
I tell how the princes of the Achaeans,   100
twin-throned, single-hearted
lords of the youth of Greece,
were sent against the land of Troy
with spear in hand to exact vengeance.
The furious omen-birds° sent them,   105
one black eagle, one white-tail,
the kings of birds to the kings of the ships.
Near the palace they came on the spear-striking
    side,
perched where all could see them
as they fed on the womb's gravid load of leverets,°   110
mother and all, pulled down in the hare's last
    course.
Cry sorrow, sorrow, but let the good prevail.

Yet the honest prophet of the army saw
the two sons of Atreus,
twin in military spirit,   115
and knew the princely leaders and hare-
    devourers —
knew that they were one and the same.
And so he declared in his prophecy,
"In time, this journey will capture Troy, Priam's°
    city;
and all the communal herds that graze before her
    towers   120
shall Fate give violently to plunder.
I only pray that no anger from the God will cast a
    cloud
upon this army forged from before to be
a great iron bit in the mouth of Troy.
For Queen Artemis° is full of pity out of jealousy   125
against those winged hounds of her father
who devour in sacrifice
the unhappy cowering mother with her brood
before they come to birth.
She hates the eagles' feast.   130
Cry sorrow, sorrow, but let the good prevail.

---

57. Alexander: Also known as Paris, Alexander was the son of King Priam and Queen Hecuba of Troy. He carried off Helen, the wife of Greek commander Menelaus (Agamemnon's brother), and this action caused the Trojan War. **75. three-footed way:** Walking with a cane or staff.

105. omen-birds: Eagles, thought to be messengers of the gods. **110. leverets:** Young hares. **119. Priam:** King of Troy at the time of the Trojan War. **125. Artemis:** Greek goddess, who was the daughter of Zeus and sister of Apollo. Artemis was the protector of young animals. Angered at the slaughter of the leverets, she caused contrary winds to prevent the Greeks from sailing for Troy. Agamemnon was forced to sacrifice his daughter Iphigeneia to appease Artemis and secure favorable winds.

Yes, she is kindly, that beautiful one,
to cubs, scarcely crawling, of savage lions,
and she finds her delight in all the breast-loving
    infants
135   of wild things of the field.
Yet she grants fulfillment of what the omens imply:
grant, Lady, favorable fulfillment, and void the
    other.
I call on Apollo the Healer
to keep her from setting against the Greeks
140   those contrary winds, winds that hold ships,
staying winds, winds that stop sailing altogether.
She might do this in eagerness for a different
    sacrifice,
one that is lawless and horrible,
a trueborn craftsman of quarrels,
145   that has no awe of a husband.
For full of terrors it lurks,
house keeping, crafty, long-memoried,
an anger that punishes child-slaughter."

Such were the prophecies of Calchas's° voice,
150   mingled with the good things,
and all predicted for our royal house
from omens on the way.
In harmony with these,
cry sorrow, sorrow, but let the good prevail.

155   Zeus, whoever he is,
if it is dear to him to be so called,
this is how I call him.
I have thrown all into the scale,
but cannot find his likeness —
160   there is only Zeus,
if I must cast my burden of vain care from the heart
in honest truth.

Not he that once was great,
swelling with daring, challenging all comers,
165   shall even be spoken of, for he is of the past.
And he that came after him
has had his three falls wrestling,
and is gone.
But whoever sings to Zeus
170   the victory song from a full heart,
he shall win all that his heart desires.

Zeus it is that has made man's road;
he it is who has laid down the rule
that understanding comes through suffering.
175   Instead of sleep, there drips before the heart
the recollected sorrow of past pain.
It is against our wills that we become wise.
Forced indeed upon us is the grace of our gods
that sit on their solemn thrones.

So on that day, the old leader of the Greek ships,   180
faulting no prophet, caught his breath at his sudden
    calamity,
when the Greek host was burdened
with ships halted and empty holds,
as they held the coast over against Chalcis,°
at Aulis° where the tides roar to and fro.   185

The hurricane that came from Strymon,°
breeding deadly delays, starvation, lost anchorages,
driving crews to aimless wanderings,
sparing neither ships nor cables,
wore down the flower of the Argives,   190
doubling their time with enforced lingering.
So when the prophet's voice rang out,
proclaiming to the princes another cure for the
    bitter storm,
a cure yet heavier to bear,
he backed his prophecies with Artemis's name,   195
and the twin sons of Atreus beat the ground with
    their staves
and could not hold back their tears.
Then the old king spoke and said,
"Heavy indeed my fate if I disobey,
but heavy, too, if I must butcher my child,   200
the glory of my house, polluting a father's hands
with streams of a virgin's blood beside the altar.
Which of these two things is without evil?
How shall I become a deserter of my fleet and fail
    my allies?
There is sacred law on their side, that they
    passionately covet   205
a virgin's blood as sacrifice to quell the winds.
May it turn out well."

When he put on the harness of Necessity,
his spirit veered in a breath of change —
to impiety, to unholiness, to desecration,   210
and from it he drew audacity for his heart
to stop at nothing.
For indeed there is a wretched distraction of the
    wits,
a primal source of ruin,
that puts recklessness in man's mind   215
and counsels ugliness.
So he dared to become his daughter's sacrificer
to aid the war waged for a woman —
first rites of deliverance for the ships.
Her prayers, and her cries of "Father," and her
    maiden life   220
they set at nothing, those military umpires.
Her father ordered his servants to lift her
carefully over the altar

---

149. **Calchas:** A prophet who accompanied the Greek army to
Troy.

184. **Chalcis:** City in Asia Minor across the straits from
Aulis, where the Greeks were detained by contrary winds.
185. **Aulis:** City where the Greek fleet collected before sailing to
Troy.   186. **Strymon:** River in Asia Minor across from Aulis.

after the prayer, swooning, her clothes all round her,
225 like a young goat,
and with a gag on her beautiful lips
to restrain the cry that would curse his house.
Constrained to voicelessness by the violence of the
bit,
she slipped to the ground her saffron robes,
and with darting, pitiful eyes struck each of her
230 sacrificers.
She stood out, like a figure in a picture, struggling
to speak,
for often she had sung in her father's hospitable halls,
and with pure maiden voice lovingly honored
her beloved father's victory hymn,
235 with its triple libation to bring good luck.
What happened after that I neither saw nor tell.
But Calchas's divining art bore fruit;
the scales of justice have come down and brought,
with suffering, understanding.
240 You will learn the future when it happens.
Till then, let it be.
To do otherwise is to have sorrow before you need.
For it will come clear with the dawn's light.

(*Enter Clytemnestra.*)

But at the end of all this let there be good fortune.
245 Surely that is the wish of this (*turning to the queen*)
our sole and closest bulwark against trouble in
Argos.
I have come, Queen Clytemnestra, to pay you my
respects;
for it is right, in the absence of the prince,
to honor the wife of the man whose throne is empty.
250 I would be glad to know
if you are sure of good tidings or not.
Is it in the hope of happy news
that you are ordering sacrifice?
But I won't resent it if you must be silent.
255 CLYTEMNESTRA: As the proverb goes,
"May dawn be the dawn of good news
as she comes from her mother night"—
you shall learn of a joy greater than you hope.
For the Argives have captured Priam's city.
CHORUS: What? I cannot believe you; I cannot
260 understand.
CLYTEMNESTRA: Troy is the Greeks' city now. Are my
words clear?
CHORUS: Joy steals over me, and calls out tears, too.
CLYTEMNESTRA: Your eyes proclaim you a subject true
and loyal.
CHORUS: What makes you trust the news? Have you
proof of it?
CLYTEMNESTRA: I have, of course — unless the gods
265 deceived me.
CHORUS: Dream visions? Do you believe in them?
CLYTEMNESTRA: No sleeping mind for me, no, nor its
fancies.
CHORUS: Have flying rumors bloated you?
CLYTEMNESTRA: As if I were a child, you taunt me.

CHORUS: But when was it that the city was sacked? 270
CLYTEMNESTRA: In this last night that brought this
dawn to birth.
CHORUS: What messenger can be as quick as that?
CLYTEMNESTRA: The god of fire, sending his brilliant
glow from Mount Ida.
Beacon sent beacon here with courier fires,
Ida to the crag of Hermes in Lemnos;° 275
then from that island a third flame sent on
was welcomed by the heights of Athos that belong
to Zeus;
and high, spanning the sea's back,
the strength of the escorting flame went joyously
onward.
The pine fire sent its golden blaze, almost a sun, 280
to the watchtowers of Macistus.
He didn't hesitate nor carelessly succumb to sleep,
but passed his share of the message,
and from afar, over the streams of Euripus,
he gave to the sentries of Messapion 285
the sign that the beacon's light had traveled to him.
They in their turn lit up and sent the message
farther,
firing a great heap of ancient gorse.
Still strong, the beacon's light never flagged,
but leapt over the plain of Asopus like a radiant
moon, 290
to Mount Cithaeron, and there awakened
another relay of traveling fire.
The guard station did not refuse the far-escorted
flame;
it kindled more than was ordered, and launched its
light
over the Gorgon lake; and coming to 295
the goat-haunted mountain,
urged the watchman not to scant the ordinance of
fire.
They lit a huge beard of flame that burnt
ungrudgingly,
and sent it over the Saronic gulf, now become its
mirror,
beyond the headland, till it struck the heights of
Arachnus, 300
our neighboring sentry post here, and then again
struck right here on this roof of the sons of
Atreus —
this fire that is the grandchild of that fire on Mount
Ida.
Such were the courses of the torchbearers,
one from the other in relays, 305
and victor is he that ran first and last.
Such proof I have and such confirmation,
sent me out of Troy by my man.

273–75. **Mount Ida . . . Lemnos:** Mountain in Asia Minor
southeast of Troy from which the gods could view the battles.
The place names that follow trace the course of beacon fires set
to bring the news of the Greek victory from Troy to Greece.

CHORUS: My lady, to the gods once again
310   I shall give my prayer of thanks,
    but I would like you to tell me all this again,
    that I might hear the words and marvel at them
    from beginning to end.
CLYTEMNESTRA: Troy is captured; this is the day; the
        Greeks hold it.
315   Within that city there rings out
    a volume of cries that do not mingle.
    This is how I see it.
    Mix oil and vinegar in the same jar
    and you could not call them friends;
320   they will not be at one.
    So in Troy you might hear two sorts of crying:
    the conquered and the conquerors.
    The act is single, the meaning double.
    Here are these:
325   throwing themselves on the dead bodies
    of husbands and brothers,
    children on the bodies of their fathers,
    all sorrowing for the destiny of their dead,
    they cry from throats no longer free.
330   Then there are the others:
    roving all night after the fight
    sets them down hungry to breakfast
    on such foods as the city has;
    they all share, no rank or place assigned,
335   but as each has got the luck of the draw.
    They are already living in Troy's captured houses,
    free of the frost beneath the sky, free of the dews.
    They will sleep all night long without a guard,
    like happy men.
    If they revere the gods of that city in that captured
340   land,
    if they revere the gods' sacred places,
    they who are conquerors will not be reconquered.
    Only let no lust seize the army first,
    let no greed conquer them,
345   to make them ravish what they should not.
    They must still make the home voyage safely,
    travel the other leg of the double track.
    But even if the army came through offenseless
    in the sight of the gods,
350   the wrong done to the dead may yet awaken,
    seeking to contrive some sudden mischief.
    This is what you hear from me, a woman.
    But may the good prevail for all to see, past dispute.
    Of the many good things I might have,
355   this is what I would choose.
CHORUS: My lady, you talk wisely, like a sensible man.
    I have learned from you your convincing proofs,
    and now again I prepare to greet the gods.
    Surely we should thank them for what they have
        done for us.
360   O Zeus the king, and friendly night,
    that has endowed us with great glory,
    you that have cast upon the towers of Troy
    a close-fitting mesh so that no one young or old
    can overleap the great net of slavery,

the all-catching trap of ruin —   365
great Zeus of guest-friends I revere.
He has done all this. He has forever bent his bow
against Alexander, that no bolt should fail,
neither missing the mark nor scaling the stars.
They can say, "It is the stroke of Zeus";   370
the track of it is clear to see.
Zeus has acted as he has determined.
Someone has said,
"The gods do not deign to take heed of mortals
who trample underfoot the grace of holiness."   375
But he that said that had no piety in him.
The recklessness stands revealed
of those who breathe war beyond justice.
It is a recklessness that breeds consequences
when houses are overcrammed   380
beyond the measure of the best.
So I escape harm, let but a sufficiency be mine,
with abundance of good judgment.
For wealth gives no defense
for the man insolent with gorging,   385
who kicks the great altar of justice
to where none can see it.
Wretched persuasion,
intolerable child of forecounseling ruin,
drives him on violently.   390
And all cure is vain. It is not hidden, no —
the mischief shines, a lamp of evil light.
The black grain in Paris° shows through the test,
like base copper rubbed bare with use.
He has been like a child that chases a bird;   395
he has brought on this city an intolerable infection,
and no one of the gods will hear his prayer —
rather, pull down the unjust man
conversant with such things.
Such a one is Paris, who came   400
to the house of the sons of Atreus
and stained with shame the table of his host
by the theft of that host's wife.
She has left to her fellow citizens
the clanging of shields, the arming of sailors,
    ambushes.   405
To Ilium she has brought ruin instead of dowry.
Her daring defying all limits,
she darted quickly through the gates.
And many a groan there was
among those that spoke for the palace: 410
"Ah me, ah me, for the house, the house and the
    princes.
Ah me for the bed and the tracks of the love of men
    on it."
There one can see the silence —
dishonored, unreviling, inexorable —
of him that sits apart.   415
Through yearning for the one gone over the sea,
a ghost will seem to rule the house.

393. Paris: A prince of Troy, Paris abducted Helen of Greece, thus defying Zeus's law of hospitality.

The grace of beautiful statues is hateful to the man.
Their eyes are empty, and before them
420 all passionate love falls dead.
Fancies haunt him in dreams persuasively;
theirs is a grace without substance.
Unsubstantial it is, when one sees,
and dreaming reaches to the touch,
and the phantom is gone, quickly slipping through
425   his hands,
as it follows the winged paths of sleep.
Such are the sorrows at home at the hearth;
but there are worse than these for all,
for those who joined the fleet and left the land of
    Greece.
430 In the house of every one of these
preeminent there is grief that reaches the heart.
They know whom they have sent forth, but instead
    of men
there come home urns and ashes to each house.
The war god is a money changer;
435 men's bodies are his money.
He holds the scales in the battle of the spear.
From Ilium he sends back to those who loved them
the scrapings of dust made heavy with their tears;
he loads the elegant urns with the dust that was
    once a man.
440 They mourn this man as they praise him —
how skilled he was in the fight — and another —
how gallantly he fell in his blood —
for another man's woman.
That is what they whisper and snarl;
445 and pain creeps about, full of ill will
toward the plaintiffs, the sons of Atreus.
But those others keep to their graves in all their
    beauty,
where they were, around the walls of Troy.
The enemy land that they have taken at last
450 has taken them, hidden them in itself.
The malicious speech of citizens is hard to bear;
it is the equal of a public curse.
And still I am troubled, lest I come to hear
something hidden in dark night.

455 For watchful are the gods' eyes
for those that kill by the thousands.
The black Furies reduce to dim nothingness
the man whose success has no justice in it,
wear him down, reversing his life's fortune.
460 And when he is among those we cannot see,
there is no help for him.
To be too well spoken of is heavy indeed.
For the thunderbolt is hurled from the eyes of Zeus.
May I not be a city-sacker, nor yet look upon my
    own life,
465 captured by others.
Swift is the rumor coursing through the city,
spurred by the fire of good tidings.
But whether it is true, who knows, or whether
somehow the gods deceive us.

Who is there so childish, so maimed of wit, 470
that the messages of fire should kindle his heart
only to sicken later when the news changes?
It is like the mettle of a woman's spirit
to praise the gracious gift before it is certainly there.
The limits of a woman's belief can be 475
as easily and quickly crossed
as cattle graze across a boundary.
But quickly, too, dies the report
a woman utters.
Soon we shall know about the lights from the
    beacons 480
and all the exchange of watch fires:
whether they are true or whether, like dreams,
a light of joy has stolen upon us and cheated our
    minds.
Here I see the herald coming from the shore,
shaded with twigs of olive. 485
The thirsty dust, twin sister of mud across the
    boundary,
is my witness; it witnesses to me that he has a *real*
    voice,
and so his testimony is not one of the smoky fire
of some wood on the hillside.
He will rather speak out and tell us to be glad, 490
or — God forbid it is the contrary message.
There *have* been good things that have shown
    through;
grant that this is their consummation.
Whoever prays anything else for this city,
I would he might reap the fruit of his mistaken
    thoughts. 495

(*Enter a herald.*)

HERALD: O my fathers' earth, Argos, Argos,
ten long years and I have come to you;
so many shipwrecked hopes, and one a winner.
I never dreamed that I would have for my share in
    death
a piece of dearest Argive land. 500
Now welcome earth, welcome the light of sun,
and Zeus supreme lord; and the Pythian King,°
no longer shooting his arrows against us;
you were harsh enough along Scamander's banks,
but now you are different, now you are savior and
    healer, 505
King Apollo. My greetings to all the gods in
    assembly.
My greeting to my patron god, Hermes, dear herald,
whom all heralds worship.
My greetings to the heroes that sent us out
and kindly welcome back what's left of us after the
    fight. 510
Hail, royal halls, roofs I have loved,
hail, holy seats and you divinities that face the
    sunlight.

---

502. **Pythian King:** The god Apollo.

Receive now with faces bright in joy —
if ever you did in days gone by —
515 now receive the king in glory after so long.
He comes and brings light after night's darkness,
a light to you and to all these —
King Agamemnon.
Give him true welcome; truly it belongs to him,
the king who dug down Troy with the spade of
520   God's justice,
made plowland of Troy;
and the seed has perished from all their country.
Their altars and the shrines of their gods are gone.
Such a yoking chain has he cast on Troy,
525 the king, Atreus's son, the old and happy man.
And now he comes here, most worthy of all
that now live and die.
Neither Paris nor the city that supports him
can boast that they have done more than they have
    paid for.
530 He was condemned for rape and theft —
lost what he carried off.
He has reaped for harvest
the utter ruin of his father's house.
And doubly have the sons of Priam paid for their
    offenses.
CHORUS: Herald of the Argive army, joy on your
535   homecoming!
HERALD: Joy, indeed. If the gods should end my life
    now,
    I'd not deny them.
CHORUS: Has the love of your lost homeland tortured
    you so?
HERALD: Yes; the tears you see are tears of joy.
CHORUS: That disease had its pleasure for you, all the
540   same.
HERALD: What disease? What should I understand by
    that?
CHORUS: Love's stroke. But you got love for the love
    you gave.
HERALD: You mean this land has missed the army as
    we missed you?
CHORUS: We were faint and weak and so have groaned
    for you.
HERALD: Why so uneasy? What horror was in your
545   mind?
CHORUS: I say nothing and am safe — a long, long
    silence.
HERALD: How could that be? Your king was away; did
    you fear others?
CHORUS: As you said just now, I would have welcomed
    death.
HERALD: It *has* been a success. Of course, in the length
    of time,
550 one must say some things have gone well, some ill.
Who except the gods lives the whole span of his life
without trouble?
Yes, if I were to speak of the hard work
and the bad quarters,
555 the narrow gangways and the hard beds,

there's plenty to complain about.
Then there were the troubles on land,
disgusting things, too.
Our beds were under the enemy's walls.
Rain from the sky and dew from the grass soaked us 560
and kept rotting our clothing
and bred lice in our hair.
I could talk about the winter, which killed the birds;
Mount Ida and its snow made that intolerable.
And then there was the heat, 565
when the sea fell on its noontide bed and slept.
Not a breath of wind, not a stir on the waves —
Oh, why should I still feel pain for all this?
It's over, isn't it, all the trouble?
It's over indeed, for them, too, the dead; 570
they'll never have to trouble about getting up again.
Why should I reckon up the numbers of those who
    are gone?
Why should the living grieve because
fortune turned against us?
I'm ready to say a long goodbye to all that's
    happened. 575
For us that are left of the Greek army,
the gain certainly wins out,
and the bad side of things doesn't weigh it down.
So, those of us who have sped over land and sea
can stand facing the sunlight and make our boast: 580
"There was a day when the Argive army took Troy.
They have nailed the spoils of it
on the homes of the gods throughout Greece
to be a glory forever and ever."
When they hear this, men must praise 585
the city and its generals.
We shall also honor the grace of God
who brought it to pass.
That's my whole speech.
CHORUS: What you say wins me over; I admit it. 590
To be ready to learn is what makes a young man
out of an old one.
But it is this house and Clytemnestra
that the news most concerns,
though I, too, am the richer for it. 595
CLYTEMNESTRA: I rejoiced long ago,
and raised the cry of joy over the news,
when first the fire came as my messenger in the
    night,
telling of Troy's capture and destruction.
That was when everyone found fault with me: 600
"Is it beacon fires that convince you
that Troy has now been sacked?
How like a woman's heart to be so lifted up."
In rumors such as these I appeared
to have gone astray in my wits. 605
But yet I made the sacrifices,
and following this "woman's fashion"
they all raised the chant, now here, now there,
throughout the city,
the songs of blessing at the gods' shrines, 610
and there they lulled to sleep

the sweet-smelling sacrificial fires.
Why *now* should I depend on you to tell me more?
I shall learn the whole story from my lord himself.
615 How shall I make best haste to receive him home,
my honored husband?
What sweeter day for a wife's eye to see
than when she opens the doors to her man
coming from the army,
620 when the gods have brought him safely back to her?
Tell my husband this:
bid him come as quick as he can,
the city's darling.
And when he comes may he find his wife
625 true as he left her,
the watchdog of his house,
devoted to him, enemy to his enemies,
the same always and ever.
I never broke the seal
630 in all those years.
I know of no pleasure with another man
nor any talk or evil gossip against me,
anymore than I know how to dip this blade
to temper it.
635 Such is my boast, so full of truth
that even a well-bred wife
need not blush to utter it.
                    (*Exit Clytemnestra.*)
CHORUS: She has spoken very suitably
for those who understand her.
640 But tell me, Herald,
what of Menelaus?
Was he among the returning army?
Is he safe among you?
And will he come back home again, our dear
prince?
645 HERALD: I don't know how to put a fair face on lies:
my friends would only have good of it
for a short time anyway.
CHORUS: Why can't you tell news that is both good
and true?
When you separate them, you can't get away with
it.
HERALD: Then — the man has vanished from the
650 Greek army,
he and his ship. *That* is not a lie.
CHORUS: Did you see him set forth from Ilium on his
own?
Or did some storm that struck you all together
snatch him away?
655 HERALD: You've hit it exactly;
in a few words you've covered a long, sad story.
CHORUS: What do the rest of his shipmates think?
Do they say he's alive or dead?
HERALD: No one knows how to tell the news clearly —
660 except the sun, there, that gives life to the world.
CHORUS: What do you mean? Was there a storm
that came upon the fleet by the gods' anger
and then ended?
HERALD: A day of good news — one should not infect it

with the tongue of bad news.   665
The honor due to the two kinds of gods
is separate.
When a messenger with a gloomy face bears cursed
news
of an army's downfall,
there is one common injury which is public,   670
and then, besides, many a man is banned from his
home;
this is the double lash that the god of war loves,
a two-speared ruin, a bloody pair.
When, I say, a messenger is loaded with such
calamities,
he must sing his news as his hymn to the Furies.   675
But when the saving messenger of good news
comes to a city that rejoices in well-being
— how should I mingle good with bad
in telling you of this storm
which surely did proceed from the gods' anger   680
against the Greeks?
For fire and sea, those two oldest and deepest of
enemies,
swore a conspiracy and pledged their common
allegiance
to destroy the wretched Greek army.
In the night, waves lashed by the storm   685
arose to plague us.
For the Thracian winds battered ship on ship.
Butting one another savagely
in the hurricane and sheets of hail,
they sank from sight, as our evil shepherd   690
drove us here and there.
When the clear light of the day came back,
we saw the sea blooming,
and its flowers were dead Greeks and wrecks.
For ourselves and our boat, we went unharmed;   695
some god stole us through it or begged us off;
he must have steered us himself,
for no man touched the steering oar.
Luck chose to become our savior, and sat on our
ship,
so that we missed the driving waves when we were
at anchor,   700
nor were driven aground on the rugged land.
Afterward, when we had escaped our watery hell,
in the white light of day, we hardly dared to trust
our luck;
and in our own thoughts we were constantly
shepherds of some new calamity,   705
seeing how the fleet had been pounded and ground
to pieces.
Now, if any of them still breathes,
they speak of us as lost; of course they do.
We have much the same idea about them.
Let it turn out well. For Menelaus,   710
in all likelihood you may expect him back.
For if the beams of the sun discover him living and
seeing,
through the workings of God —

for surely God will not yet blot out
715   the whole family —
there is some hope that he'll come home again.
This is really the truth that you have heard.

(Exit herald.)

CHORUS: Who can have named her so,
with such truth, utterly?
720   Could it be someone we cannot see,
with foreknowledge of destiny,
that used his tongue in harmony with fortune?
She was called Helen,°
the bride won by the spear, sought in strife.
725   Helen means death, and death indeed she was,
death to ships and men and city
as she sailed out of the delicate fabrics of her
      curtained room,
fanned by the breeze of giant Zephyr;°
and the man-swarm of shield-bearing hunters
730   came on the track of her,
the vanished track of the oar blades
which beached on the ever-green shores of Simoeis
on the heels of their bloody quarrel.

To Ilium it drove her,
735   the wrath that brings fulfillment,
and again the word proved true, that equates
marriage and mourning,
for the wrath exacted vengeance at the last
for the guest-table dishonored at the hearth shared
      by Zeus.
740   Wrath punished as victims those men,
the new marriage kinsmen,
who on that day must celebrate,
sing out of full throats
the hymn that honored the bride.
745   Perhaps that ancient city of Priam
has learned another tune now,
a tuneful dirge that calls him
Paris the dismally bedded;
the city has endured the ruin of its life,
750   the voice of countless lamentations,
through the wretched bloodletting of its citizens.
Once on a time there was a man
who raised a lion cub in his home.
It was a little thing, starved of milk,
755   still a suckling, still in the first rituals of its life,
gentle, a friend of children,
and a delight to the old.
Many a time it lay in their arms,
like a young baby;
760   its face was bright as it fawned on the hand
at the dictates of its belly's needs.
But time passed, and it showed
what disposition it had from its breeding;

723. **Helen:** Daughter of Zeus and Leda, a mortal woman, Helen was the wife of the Greek commander Menelaus before she was abducted by Paris and brought to Troy.   728. **Zephyr:** God of the west wind.

it requited the grace of those that brought it up
by horrid slaughtering of their sheep,   765
an unbidden dinner guest.
And the house was confused and befouled with
      blood;
an evil it was that the servants couldn't fight,
a very murderous mischief.   770
God reared the lion in the house to become
an additional priest of ruin.
But on that first day — as I tell the story —
she came to the city of Ilium
a spirit of windless calm,
the delicate glory of wealth,   775
the soft arrow darting from her eyes,
the flower of love that bites the heart.
Then she changed direction, and brought
a bitter ending to the marriage,
hastening to the daughters of Priam   780
to sit with them and live with them
to their ruin.
Zeus, the god of guests, brought her there,
a Fury to make wives weep.
There is an old saying among men, first spoken long
      ago,   785
that a man's great prosperity, when perfected,
gives birth and doesn't die childless,
but from that good fortune in true descent
there grows an ever-greedy misery.
In this, my mind is different from others'.   790
No, I say, it is the wicked deed
that breeds more wickedness, and like to its own
      kind.
For the house that is straight-dealing and just
is fated always to have good children.
The ancient deed of sacrilege always breeds a young
      one,   795
full of disaster for man, now or then,
when comes the dawn appointed for its birth.
A spirit but a clansman —
one cannot war against him nor fight him —
he is a thing unholy,   800
a daring, a black ruin to the halls,
and very like his parents.
For justice shines in houses grimed with smoke,
and she honors the good man.
And those gilded palaces where hands are dirty   805
she leaves, averting her eyes;
she goes to what is clean,
for she doesn't honor power
whose coinage is misstamped by the praise of the
      rich.
And she guides everything to its due end.   810

(Enter Agamemnon and Cassandra.)

My lord, conqueror of Troy, descendant of Atreus,
how shall I greet you, how do you reverence,
neither exceeding nor scanting due measure of
      praise?
Many men, indeed, who transgress justice,

815　honor appearance over reality.
　　　Everyone is ready to cry over the unfortunate,
　　　but the bite of that sorrow doesn't reach the heart.
　　　So, too, there are those that seem to share joy,
　　　yet the faces that they force have no laughter in
　　　　them.
820　When one is a good judge of stock,
　　　one doesn't miss the meaning of the man's eyes,
　　　fawning in watery friendship
　　　when they seem all loyalty.
　　　In the days when you led the expedition from
　　　　Greece,
825　for Helen's sake,
　　　I saw you painted in ugly colors —
　　　I will not hide that from you —
　　　as one who had an unskillful hand
　　　on the rudder of his wits
830　when you tried to win back through men's dying
　　　a willing whore.
　　　But now from the depth of my heart, in true
　　　　friendship,
　　　I say, May the work be kind to those who did it so
　　　　well.
　　　In time you shall know by enquiry
835　which of your citizens that stayed here at home
　　　dealt justly, and which did wrong.
　　　AGAMEMNON: First Argos and my country's gods,
　　　I must address you; you and I are coauthors
　　　of my home return and the justice
840　I exacted from Priam's city.
　　　The causes were not spoken aloud,
　　　but the gods heard them
　　　and cast their votes with no opposing voices
　　　into the bloody urn: for Ilium's destruction
845　and the deaths of men.
　　　To the other urn nothing drew near
　　　but the shadowy hope of a hand;
　　　there was no filling that urn.
　　　You can still see the smoke from the city's capture.
850　The hot blasts of ruin live there yet,
　　　but there is ash, too, dying
　　　as it sends into the air its breaths fattened on rich
　　　　things.
　　　For all of this we should pay our gods
　　　much-remembering thanks.
855　We have taken vengeance for insolent robbery.
　　　And for the sake of a woman a city has been leveled
　　　by the biting beast of Argos, the colt,
　　　the shield-bearing host,
　　　that made its leap about the time of the setting
　　　　Pleiades.
860　A ravening lion leaped over the wall
　　　and licked its fill of royal blood.
　　　So far my prelude stretches; that's for the gods.
　　　What you've said of your feelings, I've heard and
　　　　remember.
　　　I say the same. You have me as your advocate.
865　In very few men is it native
　　　to admire a successful friend without envying him.

For the poison of malice, settling on the heart,
doubles its weight in one who is stricken with envy.
He suffers under the load of his own troubles,
and groans to see the prosperity of the other man.　870
I know of what I speak; I very well understand
the glassy mirror of comradeship, that shadow of a
　shade,
which those prove to be who seemed my truest
　friends.
Only Odysseus,° who joined the fleet unwillingly,
once he was yoked was for me a ready trace horse.　875
Even as I speak of him, I do not know
if I speak of the dead or the living.
For other matters, we will set up public meetings
and take counsel in full assembly.
What is now well shall remain well; we shall see to
　it.　880
But where there is need for healing medicines,
we will try by surgery or cautery°
intelligently to avert the disease.
Now I will go in, into my halls, my hearth, my
　home,
and there I will first greet the gods　885
who sent me forth and brought me back again.
Victory has followed us;
let her be ours still, constantly!

(Enter Clytemnestra.)

CLYTEMNESTRA: You citizens, elders of Argos,
I will not be ashamed of speaking to you　890
of how I love my husband.
Modest inhibition is something
that dies away in human dealings.
I will tell of how wretched my life has been
while this man was in Troy —　895
at first hand I will tell it; it has been *my* life.
First, that a woman should sit in her house,
lonely without her male,
is something terrifying.
She hears so many hateful rumors;　900
here's one has come, and then another,
announcing a greater disaster still,
mouthing the ruin of the house.
If this man here had had as many wounds
as streams of rumor would have it,　905
he would have had more holes in him than a net.
If he had died, as his deaths multiplied in stories of
　him,
he must have had three bodies, like Geryon;
he would have boasted of taking a triple
shroud of earth to himself.　910
It was because of these hateful reports
that others, not I, have loosened many a cord
as it tightened round my neck.

---

874. Odysseus: Throughout the *Iliad,* Homer's story of the Trojan war, Odysseus is a brave soldier. He gives wise, even wily advice to the Greeks.　**882. cautery:** The process of burning with a hot iron in order to heal.

915 And that is why your son
doesn't stand beside me as he should,
the proof of our trust, mine to you, yours to me,
our Orestes.
Do not wonder at this; a loyal ally keeps him safe,
Strophius the Phocian.°
920 He spoke to me of twin troubles:
your danger at Ilium, and then that here, too,
the anarchy of the people's voices
might overturn good counsel.
Indeed, it is inbred in men
925 to kick the man that's down.
That's the advice of Strophius, and there's no deceit
in it.
For my own part, the gushing springs of my grief
have dried up;
there's not a drop left.
930 My eyes are in pain from late watching,
weeping for the beacons that should tell of you,
but never called for firing.
In my dreams, I have started up,
roused by the light strokes of the gnat's flight;
935 I have seen so much more happen to you
than could be contained within the time
with which I shared my sleep.
But now I have come through all this;
my heart is free of sorrow;
940 and so I can describe this man of mine —
a watchdog of the house,
the saving forestay of the ship,
the rooted pillar of the towering roof,
the single child of a father,
the land seen by sailors when they had given over
945 hope,
the fairest day to see after the storm,
the springwater stream for the thirsty traveler.
It is sweet indeed to escape the harsh stroke of
necessity.
Such terms of address would, I think, belong to him.
950 But let no one be jealous.
Many, indeed, were the evils we endured before.
Now, dear heart,
step from the carriage, but do not place on earth,
my king,
this foot that trod Troy to destruction.
955 Servants, to whom I have commanded the task
of strewing his path to the house with tapestries —
let his way lie straight before him strewn with purple,
that justice may guide him to the home he never
hoped for.
Everything else earned by fate
960 an unsleeping mind, with the help of the gods,
will arrange justly.

AGAMEMNON: Daughter of Leda,° guardian of my house,

919. Strophius the Phocian: A family friend with whom Orestes stayed at the time of Agamemnon's murder. **962. Leda:** Mother of Clytemnestra by her husband, Tyndareus, and of Helen by Zeus, who approached Leda in the form of a swan.

your speech is a good fit for my absence:
both have stretched out long.
But to praise me in due fashion   965
is an honor that others should give.
Besides, do not make much of me in this woman's
fashion,
nor grovel and gape flatteringly, like some foreigner,
nor strew my path with garments that would make it
an object of ill will;   970
it is the gods one should honor with such things.
For one who is mortal, for me certainly,
to walk on subtly woven beauties like these
cannot be without fear.
I tell you, honor me as man, not god.   975
Footmats and embroideries — they sound
differently,
they are different.
Not to be presumptuous
is the greatest gift the gods can give you.
It's only when a life has ended, and ended well,   980
that one dare say, "Well done."
I would be cheerful if my life
were like this in everything.

CLYTEMNESTRA: Then tell me this, and let it be your
own true judgment.

AGAMEMNON: Be sure, I will not falsify that judgment. 985

CLYTEMNESTRA: Was it through fear of the gods
that you made this vow?

AGAMEMNON: I said, if any man ever did, what I knew
would happen.

CLYTEMNESTRA: And what of Priam, if he had
conquered as you have?

AGAMEMNON: He would certainly have trodden on the
tapestry.   990

CLYTEMNESTRA: Don't be ashamed, then, of human
reproach.

AGAMEMNON: Yes, but the ill repute of the people's
voices
has a great power.

CLYTEMNESTRA: He that is not envied is also not
admired.

AGAMEMNON: A woman should not long so for a fight.   995

CLYTEMNESTRA: In those that win, yielding is graceful.

AGAMEMNON: Do you set such store on victory in this
dispute?

CLYTEMNESTRA: Let me have my way. You are the victor
if you yield readily.

AGAMEMNON: Well, if you will — here, someone undo
my sandals,   1000
that are like slaves for the treading of my foot.
And as I walk upon these lovely cloths,
I pray against the envious eye of the gods
lest from afar it strike me.
It's a great shame to spoil a house's wealth,   1005
these weavings so dear in price, with the dirt of
treading feet.
Enough of this.
Bring in this stranger here, and use her kindly.
The god looks from afar with approval

1010   on the merciful conqueror.
        No one chooses to become a slave.
        This woman is the very flower, picked out
        from the spoils of war;
        as a gift from the army to me, she followed me.
1015   Well, since I've been subdued to listen to you,
        I will go into my house, treading on purple.
        CLYTEMNESTRA: There is a sea — and who shall drain
            it dry? —
        nourishing a spring, always new, an abundance of
            purple
        to be bought with silver for the dyeing of garments.
1020   This house, my lord, has store enough of it,
        thanks be to the gods.
        This house does not know poverty.
        I would have vowed the treading of many garments,
        had I been so ordered by the shrines of the oracles,
1025   to win the safe return of your life.
        When the root is there, the leaf comes to the house,
        and stretches its shade against the dog star's heat.
        And when you came to this house and hearth of
            yours,
        it meant what heat means in the winter time.
1030   And when Zeus makes wine from the bitter grape,
        it is still cool within the house,
        when its perfected lord paces through the halls.
        Zeus, Zeus, that brings all to perfection,
        perfect my prayer.
1035   Bring to perfection all you have to do.
        CHORUS: Why this fluttering, insistent terror
        that keeps guard before my heart?
        Is the song prophetic
        that rises unhired and unbidden?
1040   My grounded mind has no confidence to dismiss it
        like an obscure nightmare.
        Time has grown old since the boats,
        their hawsers all thrown out along the sands,
        set out to Ilium.
1045   With my eyes I am my own witness
        to their homecoming.
        But nonetheless, my spirit within me
        drones this tune of the Furies,
        accompanied by no lyre,
1050   a song taught by none but itself.
        It has none of the dear confidence of hope.
        Not for nothing is the boding of my entrails,
        the whirling of my heart, harmonized with
        eddies of my mind that will surely bring fulfillment.
1055   But I pray that what I expect may fall away,
        a lie, into unfulfillment.
        There is no limit in health;
        it is insatiable.
        For disease is its next-door neighbor;
1060   there is but a single wall between them.
        A man's destiny, facing straight ahead,
        often crashes on the hidden reef.
        Yet, if beforehand in prudent fear,
        he casts overboard part of what he owns
1065   with the derrick of good measure,

his whole house does not sink utterly,
though overloaded to overflowing,
nor does the frame of the ship sink.
Many times the generous gifts of Zeus,
and those of the furrows yearly tilled,   1070
banish the disease of hunger.
But the black blood of a man,
when once it has fallen to the earth in his death,
who shall conjure it back again with any
    incantation?
Did not Zeus, for the safety of the world,   1075
stop the wizard who would raise the dead?
If there were no fates appointed by the gods
which checked other fates from having overmuch,
my heart would have outstripped my tongue
and poured this out.   1080
But now in the dark it mutters, in heart-anguish,
with never a hope of spinning out of my burning
    mind
what is right for this moment.
CLYTEMNESTRA: In with you too, now, Cassandra,
since Zeus (you cannot be angry with Zeus)   1085
has made you a sharer in the sacrifices in our
    house,
standing near the altar with many slaves that we
    own.
Get down from that carriage;
none of your high spirit of pride.
They say that Heracles, Alcmene's son,°   1090
was sold and forced to eat the bread of slavery.
If then the necessity of fate's scales
has forced this on you,
you should be very grateful for masters anciently
    rich.
Those who have reaped a harvest they never
    expected   1095
are always excessive in harshness toward their
    slaves.
From us you will have all the usual treatment.
CHORUS: She has finished; it is to you she spoke,
and what she says is clear enough.
You are taken, a quarry in fate's net;   1100
obey her, then —
though I will understand if you don't.
CLYTEMNESTRA: If she has anything besides her
    swallow twitterings,
a barbaric speech that no one knows,
I'll try to persuade her within her understanding.   1105
CHORUS: Follow her. What she says is the best there is
    for you;
leave the carriage; obey her.
CLYTEMNESTRA: I have no time to waste here with her
    outside the palace.
The sheep stand ready for slaughter   1110
in front of the hearth at the center of the house.

1090. Heracles, Alcmene's son: Heracles was a popular Greek
hero. According to legend, he was sold into slavery to
Omphale, Queen of Lydia.

(*To Cassandra.*)

You, if you're going to do anything that I tell you,
    do it quickly.
But if you disobey because you don't take in my
    words —

(*To Chorus.*)

1115   Here, you!
    Don't speak to her any more; use your hands;
    that's all these foreigners understand.
CHORUS: I think the woman needs a good interpreter;
    she looks like a wild thing newly caught.
CLYTEMNESTRA: She's crazy; she hears only her
1120   distraught mind.
    Of course she does, she that has left her newly
        captured city,
    come here not yet knowing how to wear the curb bit,
    till she's frothed out her spirit in blood.
    I won't throw any more words at her to be belittled.

                            (*Exit Clytemnestra.*)
1125
CHORUS: I pity her, and so I won't be angry.
    Come, you poor girl, desert your place in the
        carriage;
    yield to what must be; wear your yoke for the first
        time.
CASSANDRA: Oh! Oh! Oh! Oh, the land!
    Lord Apollo! Lord Apollo!
1130 CHORUS: Why do you raise such dismal cries to
        Apollo?
    He is no god for the singer of dirges.
CASSANDRA: Oh! Oh! Oh! Oh, the land!
    Lord Apollo! Lord Apollo!
1135 CHORUS: Again she calls with her ill omens
    upon the god who has no suitable place
    at scenes of mourning.
CASSANDRA: Lord Apollo! Lord Apollo! God of the
        streets,
    god of destruction! Now again, god of my
        destruction,
    and so easily.
1140 CHORUS: She seems to me about to prophesy her own
        misfortunes.
    The gift of prophecy still sticks
    even though the mind is now a slave's.
CASSANDRA: Lord Apollo! Lord Apollo!
1145   God of my destruction! God of the streets!
    Through what streets have you led me now,
    to what house?
CHORUS: To that of the sons of Atreus. If you don't
        know that,
    that I can tell you. And you won't say it's a lie.
1150 CASSANDRA: Yes, to a house the gods hate;
    it has been witness of so many
    murders of kin, butcheries,
    bowl full of man's blood, ground soaked in shed
        blood.
CHORUS: The stranger has a nose as keen as a hound;
1155   she's on the trail of a murder and will find it.

CASSANDRA: What convinces me are the witnesses —
    the children, the babies screaming of their cut
        throats,
    of their flesh roasted and eaten by their father.
CHORUS: We have heard of your fame as a prophet;
    but we need no foretellers here.   1160
CASSANDRA: Oh, what does she plan?
    What is the great new grief?
    It is a great evil against the house
    that she is planning.
    It is unbearable for its friends, uncurable.   1165
    Defense stands aloof and keeps away.
CHORUS: These last foretellings are quite beyond my
        understanding;
    the others I know — indeed the whole city cries
        them aloud.
CASSANDRA: Oh, you wretched woman,
    is this what you bring to consummation?   1170
    You have cleaned him in the bath
    till his skin shined,
    the husband to share your bed.
    And how shall I tell the consummation?
    It would be quick: the line of clutching hands,   1175
    stretching out, one hooked to another.
CHORUS: I don't understand that yet;
    you spoke riddles before,
    but now what baffles me is the dimness
    of what comes from the gods in words.   1180
CASSANDRA: Oh! Oh! Oh! What is this that appears?
    A net, a net of death. Can it be so?
    But the meshes are the bedfellow, the accomplice in
        murder.
    Let the pack that ravens insatiate against the family
    bay for a sacrifice that merits death by stoning. 1185
CHORUS: What Fury is this you bid raise its cries
    against the house?
    I find no cleaning in your words.
    To my heart rush back the blood drops of yellowing
        stain,
    as when the eyes grow dim at the setting of a life's
        day,   1190
    a man falling by the point of a spear.
    And destruction comes quick.
CASSANDRA: Look at that! Look at that!
    Keep away the bull from the cow!
    She will take him in the folds of the robe   1195
    with the trick of the black horn.
    She strikes! He falls! He falls
    in the water of the bath.
    That is his end, I tell you,
    a treacherous murder in a cauldron.
CHORUS: I will not boast of being a keen judge of   1200
        prophecy,
    but this certainly looks like something evil.
    Anyway, what good word ever came to mankind
    from the prophets?
    It is through evils that the wordy tricks of the
        prophets   1205
    bring terrors for us to understand.

CASSANDRA: Oh, the ill boding of my own sad fate!
  For it is my own suffering, on top of his,
  that my tongue spills out.

(*To the god.*)

1210   Where is this you have brought me to in my
       sorrow?
     For nothing but to share his death; what else?
   CHORUS: You are someone god-possessed;
     the god carries you along.
     It is for yourself you cry out this tuneless tune.
1215   Like the brown nightingale,° that can never have
       enough of song,
     as she cries "Itys! Itys!" for her life rich in sorrows,
     and her mind loves pity for herself.
   CASSANDRA: Oh! The life of the shrill-voiced
       nightingale!
1220   The gods covered *her* with a feathered body;
     I tell you, they gave her a *sweet* life,
     and her cries are not cries of sorrow.

1214–21. Like the brown nightingale: The chorus alludes to the story of Philomela, who was raped by her brother-in-law, Tereus. Although her tongue was cut out to prevent her from telling anyone of the crime, Philomela sent her sister a piece of embroidery that revealed all. The sisters took their revenge on Tereus by tricking him into eating his son, Itys. According to some accounts, the gods turned Philomela into a nightingale.

   But what remains for me
     is the splitting of the flesh with the two-edged spear.
   CHORUS: Where do they come from, these rushes   1225
     of useless agony carried by the god?
     You make music that is a mixture,
     ugly cries of terror and high-pitched melodies.
     Where did you get the milestones of evil words
     that mark your prophetic journey?   1230
   CASSANDRA: The marriage! The marriage of Paris,
     deadly to those who loved him.
     Scamander, river that my fathers drank of,
     in that time I was raised on your shores;
     but now around the banks of Cocytus and Acheron,°   1235
     the rivers of death, I am likely to prophesy,
     and soon.
   CHORUS: What is this word you have spoken all too
       clearly?
     A newborn child could understand.
     The bite of murder has pierced me   1240
     as you whimper at your painful fortune.
     It is a heartbreak to hear you.
   CASSANDRA: The agony, agony of the city utterly
       ruined.
     The sacrifices that my father made before the walls,
     the multiplied slaughter of cattle and woolly sheep.

1234. Cocytus and Acheron: Rivers flowing together at the entrance to the kingdom of death.

A scene from the American Repertory Theatre's 1994 production of the *Oresteia*, directed by François Rochaix.

1245 None of it helped; it was no cure.
The city suffered as it was fated to suffer.
And I shall soon be thrown on the ground
in my own warm blood.
CHORUS: What you say now follows what you said
before.
Some malevolent god who falls on you with fearful
1250 weight
makes you a singer of these deadly mournful things.
But as for the end — I am at a loss.
CASSANDRA: Now my prophecy shall no longer peer
from behind veils
like a newly married bride.
1255 No, it will rush on, a wind brightly blowing
into the sun's rising,
to send disaster surging like a wave to meet the
sunbeams,
a disaster yet greater than this.
I will not school you in riddles any longer.
1260 And do you be my witness that my nose is keen
and my tracking by shortcuts
on the path of crimes committed long ago.
Never do they leave the house,
that chorus that sings in ugly harmony.
1265 For their speech is of evil.
The revelers have drunk, to whet their courage more,
man's blood, and so they abide in the house,
and none shall expel them: they are the Furies,
that attend on the murder of kin.
1270 The song they sing as they beleaguer the house
is the song of the primal destruction,
when the mind is blinded.
And each of the Furies has spat in disgust
on the brother's bed that hates its violator.
1275 Hah! Am I an archer that missed,
or have I hit the mark?
Or am I a false prophet
that raps on doors and babbles?
Be my witness, you, but first make your sworn oath
1280 that I know the story of the ancient sins
of this house.
CHORUS: How would such an oath, even plighted in all
honesty,
serve as any kind of cure?
True, I do wonder at you,
that you, reared beyond the sea and speaking a
1285 strange tongue
should talk of these things as if you had been there.
CASSANDRA: It was Apollo the prophet
that charged me with the office of prophecy.
CHORUS: He fell in love with you?
1290 Is that possible for a god?
CASSANDRA: Till now I was ashamed to speak of it.
CHORUS: As long as things go well, one has one's
delicacy.
CASSANDRA: He was a wrestler, that breathed his grace
into me.
CHORUS: Did you come to the breeding of children,
1295 like other couples?

CASSANDRA: I promised the god and cheated him.
CHORUS: Had you already got your gift of prophecy?
CASSANDRA: Oh yes, I used to tell my countrymen
all that would happen.
CHORUS: How did you escape the god's anger?   1300
CASSANDRA: Since my offense against him,
no one believed a word of mine.
CHORUS: Ah, but to us right now, you seem to
prophesy truly.
CASSANDRA: Oh, oh, my agony! There it is again!
The fearful pain of true prophecy   1305
that twists me, that drives me wild;
and it is still only prelude.
Look! Look! You see them! The young ones,
sitting on the house like dream phantoms.
They are the likenesses of those children dead and
gone,   1310
killed by those they loved;
their hands are full of meat, their own flesh.
You can see it clearly; they carry the pitiful load
of their guts, and their father has tasted them.
I tell you, there is punishment for this,   1315
and someone is plotting it,
a lion, but a coward, that wallows, a housekeeper
in the bed of the returning lord —
O mine, my lord — for I must bear the yoke of
slavery.
The captain of the ships, the sacker of Ilium,   1320
he knows not what tongue is licking him,
the tongue of the hateful bitch, her ears pricked,
like a secret blind vengeance,
that will work out his evil fate.
So far her daring reaches: 1325
the woman will murder the man.
She is — what shall I call her and be right?
this monstrous, biting creature.
A snake with poison at both ends;
some Scylla° living in the rocks, death to sailors;   1330
some murderous, raging mother of hell;
some truceless god of war;
a war she has declared upon her loved ones!
So let her cry her war cry,
whose daring knows no limit,   1335
as at the moment when the battle turns.
Yet she seems to rejoice that he has come safe home.
It is all one to me, if you do not believe any of this;
what difference?
It is to be and will come.   1340
Soon you will stand here and say of me, in pity,
she was too true a prophet.
CHORUS: The feast of Thyestes, and the flesh of the
children,
I understand and shudder; fear is on me
as I hear the truth, and no mere likenesses.   1345

1330. Scylla: A sea monster living in a cave opposite the
whirlpool, Charybdis. Ships could not escape the double
threat.

But for the rest I heard from you,
I have fallen off the course and run wide.
CASSANDRA: I tell you, you will live to see
   Agamemnon's death.
CHORUS: Wretched girl, hold your tongue in piety.
CASSANDRA: No, no holy god of healing presides over
1350   this story.
CHORUS: True, if what you say is so; but God forbid it
   should be.
CASSANDRA: You are all for God forbidding;
   but their job is killing.
CHORUS: What man is he that furnishes this grief?
CASSANDRA: You have surely fallen astray of my
1355   prophecies.
CHORUS: Yes, for I do not understand how the plotter
   will make his plan work.
CASSANDRA: Yet I know Greek rather too well.
CHORUS: So does the Delphic oracle;° but it's hard to
   understand,
1360   all the same.
CASSANDRA: Oh! It attacks me like fire!
   Oh! Oh! O god! O Lycian Apollo!
   There she is, the lioness, two-footed bedfellow of
      the wolf,
   in the absence of the true-bred lion.
1365   She will kill me. Like one that brews a potion,
   She will put my reward, too, in the drink.
   She cries her glee in triumph, as she whets the knife
   for a man, to pay him in murder for bringing me
      here.

(*She starts tearing off her robe and garlands.*)

   Why should I have these mockeries about me,
1370   this staff, the prophet's garlands round my neck?
   Before I die myself, I shall at least destroy you.
   Go; you shall be no more. Lie on the ground as you
      fall.
   Thus I requite you.
   Enrich some other girl with blinded madness,
1375   some other girl than me.
   Look, Apollo himself undoes his prophetess
   of her prophetic mantle; he has watched me
   laughed to scorn even in this trumpery,
   laughed at by friends turned foes,
1380   with never a quiver in the scale — what hollowness!
   Ill-treated like a wandering beggar priest,
   in misery half-starved to death, I still endured.
   But now the prophet has unmade the prophet
   and brought me here to meet my chance death.
1385   No father's altar, but a chopping block, waits for me,
   to be warmed with my blood as I am butchered,
   the preliminary victim. Yet, all the same, I shall not
      die
   dishonored by the gods.

But another will come° to take vengeance for me;
he will kill the mother in whom he was seeded,   1390
and will avenge his father.
A wanderer outcast, grown alien to this land,
who will return from exile
to put a coping stone of ruin for those he loved,
for he has sworn a great oath by the gods   1395
that his father's corpse shall bring him home again.
Why do I go on this way, crying, full of self-pity? —
now that I have seen Troy's ruin, as I saw it,
now as Troy's conquerors come off in the god's
      judgment,
as I see them now.   1400
I will go and face it; I will face my death.
These gates before me here, I call you now by name:
the gates of death.
But I pray that the stroke that reaches me
may be a mortal stroke,   1405
that without struggle, as the blood runs freely,
in easy death I may close these eyes of mine.
CHORUS: You are a woman that has suffered much,
   and have understood much; and you have said
      much.
   But if you truly know your fate,   1410
   why do you walk up to the altar steadfastly,
   like an ox?
CASSANDRA: There is no escape, my friends; the time is
   full.
CHORUS: Yet the latest moment has a special value.
CASSANDRA: This day has come; there is little I would
   gain by flight.   1415
CHORUS: How courageous and steadfast!
CASSANDRA: No one who's happy hears these
   compliments.
CHORUS: But death, if fame comes with it,
   comes still with grace to those that must die
      anyway.
CASSANDRA: I weep for you, father, and for your noble
   children.   1420

(*She recoils.*)

CHORUS: What is it? What is the fear that turns you
   back?

(*Cassandra shudders.*)

CHORUS: What made you shudder?
   Is it something in your mind that disgusts you?
CASSANDRA: The house! It reeks of murder, of dripping
   blood!
CHORUS: What? It's just the blood of sacrificed
   animals.   1425
CASSANDRA: No, it is just like the smell of a grave.
CHORUS: It is no delicate Syrian incense in the house
   that you speak of.

1359. Delphic oracle: The chief oracle of ancient Greece, presided over by Apollo. The utterings of the oracle were ambiguous and had to be interpreted.

1389. another will come: Reference to Orestes, who avenges his father's murder in the second part of Aeschylus's trilogy.

CASSANDRA: Still — I will go into the house,
to mourn with cries my own and Agamemnon's
1430   deaths.
I have enough of life.
My friends, I'm not scared
like a bird startled at a bush
in empty terror.
1435   When I die, you will be my witness to this,
when a woman dies to match my woman's death,
when a man falls to match that other man,
whose wife was his assassin.
This friendly office I lay on you, as I die now.
1440   CHORUS: Poor girl, I pity you for your death,
that the god predicted.
CASSANDRA: I have one more speech to make,
or shall I call it a dirge, just for myself.
As I face this last sunlight,
1445   I call on those who shall be my avengers
to make my enemies pay for *my* murder too,
only a dead slave, such an easy victory.
Men's fortunes, when they are good,
one might say of them, "They are like shadows only."
1450   When they're bad, a wet sponge
with one stroke wipes it all out.
The first truth has my pity, far more than the second.
                              (*Exit Cassandra.*)
CHORUS: To be successful is to be endlessly hungry for
more;
all men are so.
There is no one who banishes good fortune from his
1455   house,
so long as fingers point at it.
No man says, "Do not come here again, good
fortune."
Here is this king, to whom the blessed gods granted
the sacking of Priam's city;
he came home with all the honors that the gods
1460   gave him.
But now, if he shall pay for the blood of the past
and dying render the price of others' deaths,
who that hears this and must die himself
dare boast that a man may be born
1465   to live a whole life unharmed?
AGAMEMNON (*from within*): I've been hit! I am hurt to
death.
CHORUS: Hush! Who is it that cries out, hurt to death?
AGAMEMNON: I'm hit again!
CHORUS: It is the king crying out; I think all is over.
1470   But let us plan safety for ourselves — if we can.
1. My vote is to cry, Help! to the citizens
to come to the palace.
2. Yes, and at once, I think,
to catch them red-handed with dripping sword.
3. I think you're right; at least we should do
1475   something.
It certainly isn't the moment for hesitation.
4. But we can see. This is a kind of first act;
it looks like the beginning of a tyranny.
5. Yes, it does — because we're wasting time.
1480   Their hands don't sleep, and they trample underfoot

the good reputation of delay.
6. I really do not know what would be best.
Those who do the deed of course find it easy to plan.
7. Yes, I am with you. Anyhow,
one cannot by talking bring the dead to life again.   1485
8. Are we then, in order to stretch our own lives,
to yield to a government that shames our royal
house?
9. No, that is awful. Death is better than that.
Death is better than subjection to a tyranny.
10. Is the evidence of the cries good enough?   1490
Are we right to predict that the man is dead?
11. Yes, one must know before one gets angry.
Knowing the truth is very far from guessing.
12. I have the support of many voices among you:
that we should be told clearly how it is with
Agamemnon.   1495

(*Enter Clytemnestra.*)

CLYTEMNESTRA: Till now I have said much to meet the
occasion,
but now I will not be ashamed to say the opposite.
How could one, rendering hate to those who hated
but looked like loved ones,
hedge the trap about with sides too high to be leapt
over?   1500
This was my day of trial; I have thought of it
enough and long enough, a trial of an old quarrel
years and years old.
Now I stand here where I have struck him.
He is dead, and the sequence ended.   1505
This is how I managed — I will not disavow it —
that he should not escape, nor defend himself from
death.
I threw about him an encompassing net,
as it might be for fish, all-entangling,
an evil wealth of cloak.   1510
I struck him twice. He gave two groans,
and his body went limp;
as he lay there, I gave him a third,
in honor of the Zeus that keeps the dead
securely in the underworld.   1515
This was my grace and prayer for him.
So, as he lay there, he gasped out his spirit,
choking, poured out a sharp stream of his blood
and struck me with the dark bloody shower.
I rejoiced as much as the new-sown earth   1520
rejoices in the glad rain of Zeus,
when the buds strike in earth's womb.
So it is, you old men of Argos here;
be glad, if you can. I triumph in it.
If it were right to pour libations   1525
on a dead man's body, I would have done so to him,
and more than justly done so.
Here's a bowl of horrors, cursed horrors,
that he filled within our house,
and then he came and drank it off himself.   1530
CHORUS: I wonder at your tongue, how boldly it wags,
that you should boast like this over a dead husband.
CLYTEMNESTRA: You try me out as if I were

a woman that cannot think.
1535 But my heart doesn't tremble,
and I speak to you who know;
whether you wish to praise or blame me is all one
      to me.
Here is Agamemnon, my husband, now a corpse —
his death the work of this right hand of mine,
1540 an efficient craftsman.
That is how *that* is.
  CHORUS: Woman, what evil thing have you eaten
    that grows in the earth,
    what draught have you tasted that comes from the
      salt sea,
1545 that you have taken upon you so horrible a sacrifice
    and the curse of the people's voice?
    You have cast away, you have torn apart,
    and you shall be cast and torn away from the city,
    a monstrous object of hate to the citizens.
  CLYTEMNESTRA: Now it's against me that you proclaim
1550   banishment,
    that the hatred and curses of the citizens shall be
      mine,
    but in the old days you brought nothing against
      that man,
    who, with all the indifference of one whose pastures
      are full
1555 of teeming flocks, rich in wool,
    had no care for the death of a lamb.
    He sacrificed his own daughter,
    dearest pain of my womb,
    to charm the contrariness of Thracian winds.
    For this, should you not have banished him,
1560 payment for his polluting wickedness?
    No, you are a careful hearer and harsh judge
    only of *my* acts.
    Threaten away! I tell you now, if once you
      conquer me
    in a fair fight, I'll be your subject;
1565 but if God gives another outcome,
    you will get an education in discretion
    and learn it thoroughly, though the knowledge
      comes very late.
  CHORUS: You think big thoughts, and you scream
      proud defiance,
1570 as though the bloody smear of your success
    had maddened your mind.
    The smear of blood — I can see it in your eyes.
    But still you must pay stroke for stroke,
    with no friend to take your part.
  CLYTEMNESTRA: You may now hear the solemn
1575   swearing of my oath:
    By the justice due to my child, and now perfected,
    by the Spirit of Destruction and the Fury,
    in whose honor I cut this man's throat,
    my hope treads not within the hall of Fear
1580 so long as Aegisthus lights the hearth fire for me,
    my loyal friend, as he has always been,
    shield for my daring — no small one.
    There lies Agamemnon, this girl's seducer —
    he was the darling of all the women of Troy —

and there she is, our prophet, prisoner of war,   1585
    that shared his bed, a faithful whore
    that spoke her auguries for him, and knew as well
    the rubbing of the sailors' benches.
    Both have suffered as they deserved.
    He died as I said, and she has sung her swan song in
      death,   1590
    and lies with him, her lover.
    But to me she has brought an additional side dish
    to *my* pleasure in bed.
  CHORUS: What day of doom may I look for soon,
    one with not too much pain, not too long
      bedridden,   1595
    that shall bring me the sleep that has no ending,
    now that my kindest of guardians has been
      overcome,
    suffering so much at a woman's hands.
    By a woman his life has perished.
    Curse on you, crazy Helen, that were the single
      murderess   1600
    of all those lives, those many lives,
    lost under Troy's walls;
    now you have made the fulfillment,
    the fine flowering, of whatever it was,
    that quarrel within the house   1605
    built to bring a man to misery.
    You have perfected it,
    through bloodshed that cannot be washed out.
  CLYTEMNESTRA: Do not pray for your end in death
    because of the burden of your grief in this,   1610
    nor turn your anger against Helen,
    as the man-killer who destroyed
    those many lives of the Greeks,
    and brought into being an incurable pain.
  CHORUS: Spirit that attacks the house of the sons of
      Atreus,   1615
    you master me to the breaking of my heart;
    your power is wielded by two women of like soul.
    And now you stand like an evil raven,
    and croak over the dead a lawless hymn of victory.
  CLYTEMNESTRA: Now indeed you have made right   1620
    the judgment of your mouth,
    as you name the thrice-glutted spirit of this race.
    It is through him that the love of blood-licking
    is nourished in the belly,
    and before the old wound has healed,   1625
    new pus comes.
  CHORUS: Yes, the one you name is indeed great,
    the spirit whose anger lies heavy on this house.
    And the tale you have to tell is evil;
    it has an endless appetite for the events of blind
      madness.   1630
    But surely these are through Zeus,
    who is cause of all, who brings all to pass.
    For what is there that is fulfilled for man,
    except through Zeus?
    What is there of all this   1635
    that is not of God's accomplishment?
    O my king, my king,
    how shall I sorrow for you?

1640

What shall I say from a heart that loves you?
You lie there in that spider's web,
gasping out your life in an unholy death.
Oh, oh! Conquered by deadly treachery,
to fall to such an ignoble bed
by a wife's hand and a double-edged blade.

1645

CLYTEMNESTRA: You cry aloud on this as *my* work;
but do not call me Agamemnon's wife.
No, it is the old, bitter, Evil Genius
of Atreus, giver of the cruel feast,
that has likened himself to the wife of this dead man

1650

and has paid him off, sacrificing a full-grown victim
in fulfillment for those young children.

CHORUS: But who will bear you witness
that you are guiltless of the murder?
How, how so? It is true, there may be,

1655

on his father's side, the Evil Genius to help you.
And the black god of war presses on
through tides of kindred blood
to the place of his advance,
where he pays just requital

1660

for the congealed fragments of the eaten children.
O my king, my king,
how shall I sorrow for you?
What shall I say from a heart that loves you?
You lie there in that spider's web,

1665

gasping out your life in an unholy death.
Oh, oh! Conquered by deadly treachery,
to fall to such an ignoble bed
by a wife's hand and a double-edged blade.

CLYTEMNESTRA: Did *he* not also lay upon the house

1670

a treacherous destruction?
The victim, my daughter, raised from his loins,
Iphigeneia, whom I mourn for.
What he did is what he suffered for.
Let him not boast of anything in the house of death,

1675

for he paid for what he had done
with death by the mischief of the sword.

CHORUS: I am all bewildered about what road to take
as the house falls;
my wits are deserted by their skillful carefulness.

1680

I fear the crash of the bloody torrent of rain
that will shake the house to its foundation.
Now it is a shower no longer.
Fate is whetting its justice on other whetstones
for another deed of injury.

1685

Earth, Earth, would you had received me
before I lived to see him in his lowly couch
in a silver-sided bath.
Who shall bury him? Who shall keen him?
Will you dare to do this, to make lament for him,

1690

you who killed him, your husband?
Will you accomplish for his soul a grace no grace
as thanks for his great deeds?
Who shall stand at the grave and chant
a praise of the hero

1695

with tears in the eye and truthful sorrow at heart?

CLYTEMNESTRA: The care of that concerns you not at all.
It is by our hand that he fell, that he died,
and we shall bury him

with no cries of mourning from this house.
But his daughter Iphigeneia, as is right,

1700

will welcome her father by the swift-flowing passage
over the River of Sorrows
and throw her arms around him and kiss him.

CHORUS: This is but the exchange of insult for insult;
it is hard to judge the issue of such a fight.

1705

The pirate plunders the pirate,
the killer pays for the killing.
Still there remains, as long as Zeus remains on his
throne,
the rule that he who has acted shall suffer accordingly.
That is the divine law.

1710

Who shall expel from the house the brood of curses?
The whole race is welded to destruction.

CLYTEMNESTRA: In what you say now, the prophecy
has become truth.
For my part, I am willing to make a sworn compact
with the evil spirit of this house

1715

to be satisfied with things as they are, however bad,
on condition that he, in the days to come,
may go from our house and wear out some other
breed
with murders of one another in the family.
I will be utterly content with a small part of wealth,

1720

if I can banish from these halls
the madness of mutual bloodletting.

(Enter Aegisthus.)

AEGISTHUS: O happy light, day of justified revenge!
Now I will say that the gods
in watchfulness so high above the earth

1725

still bear an eye on the sorrows of mortals to avenge
them.
Now I take pleasure to have seen this man
lying here in the robes that were
the nets of the Furies for him,
paying for the plots his father's hand contrived.

1730

For Atreus, ruler of this land, was this man's father,
and his brother Thyestes was my father.
Both were Pelops's sons; this is the plain story.
The two of them were in dispute about the throne,
and Atreus banished my father from city and home.

1735

The unlucky Thyestes later returned,
a suppliant at Atreus's hearth, and found safety
there —
I mean for his own part, for he did not die
nor stained his fatherland with blood.
But the vile Atreus, father of the dead man here,

1740

with show of eagerness rather than love,
gave my father a banquet of welcome.
He pretended to celebrate a day of feasting
on flesh slaughtered for meat,
in all hospitality,

1745

but the meat he gave my father was his own
children's.
The feet and the ends of the fingers he put apart and
hid,
as the guests sat man by man at separate tables.
So Thyestes in ignorance ate the other parts,

1750 a meal that brought a curse, as you see, on all the race.
Later, when he discovered what awful act he had committed,
he moaned aloud, recoiled, and vomited up the bloody mess.
"A doom intolerable will overtake," he said,
"the house of Pelops."
1755 He kicked the dinner over to back the oath,
crying, "So perish every one of all your breed."
That is why you can see this man fallen dead here,
and I am justly the one who stitched together his murder.
I was the third son, and while I was still in swaddling clothes
1760 he drove me out along with my luckless father.
But when I grew to manhood, justice brought me back.
And so I laid my hand on him, though not face to face;
mine was the whole contriving of the evil plot.
So glorious the result,
1765 that now I would welcome death itself,
having seen him in the traps of justice.
CHORUS: Aegisthus, I do not respect insolence
at the moment of calamity.
Do you say that with aforethought you killed Agamemnon,
1770 that you alone planned this miserable murder?
In that case, I do not think your life will escape
the justice of the public curse, the stoning.
That's what I think.
AEGISTHUS: Do you talk back to me, you who sit at the lower oar,
1775 when we are in possession of the upper deck?
You will find out, despite your age,
how uncomfortable such learning is for an old man,
when discretion is the lesson set.
Chains in old age and hunger's pangs
1780 are the very sharpest healing prophets of the mind.
Don't you see this when you see?
Kick not against the pricks, lest your own striking hurt you.
CHORUS: Woman, you who were his housekeeper
and at the same time sullied his bed,
did you plot his death when the victors were newly home
1785 and he had been their general?
AEGISTHUS: These words of yours are true progenitors of sorrows.
Yours is a tongue the opposite of Orpheus's:
he led all things his captive through the joy of his own voice,
but you with silly yappings arouse others to lead
1790 *you* captive.
Once you are mastered, you'll be a tamer animal.
CHORUS: I suppose you'll be the sovereign of the Argives,
you, who when you plotted this man's murder
didn't dare to do the deed with your own hand.

AEGISTHUS: Well, no. The treachery was a woman's part,
1795 clearly so. I would be suspected as his old enemy.
But his wealth will give me a base to rule the citizens,
and the disobedient man I will yoke in heavy chains;
he will not be, I assure you, like a full-fed young trace horse.
No, unwelcome hunger and a dark cell
1800 will see him through into submission.
CHORUS: Why didn't you kill him yourself, with your cowardly soul?
No, your partner, the woman, did the killing,
to be the pollution of the land and of the gods of the land.
But I tell you, Orestes still sees the light of day,
1805 that he may come home, and with good luck on his side
be conquerer and the death of both of you.
AEGISTHUS: Since you're resolved to act and talk like this,
you'll soon know —
here, my bodyguards, this is your work, right here.
1810 CHORUS: Here, let each one of you be ready, hand on sword hilt.
AEGISTHUS: I, too, hold the hilt of my sword.
I will face my death.
CHORUS: You talk of death; I welcome it. But I will try my chances.
1815 CLYTEMNESTRA: No, dearest, no. Let us do no further evils.
Those that there are, are many, a bloody harvest;
we have a good store of calamity.
No, no bloodletting.
Good old men, off with you to your houses.
1820 Yield to what must be, before you suffer.
What we did had to be done.
If this should be all of troubles, I would gladly welcome it,
though struck with misfortune
by the heavy hoof of the evil spirit.
1825 That is a woman's word, if anyone should think it worth heeding.
AEGISTHUS: No, but to have them letting their tongues blossom in insolence, to throw their empty threats about —
"That they would try their chances"—
1830 You lack all brains, so to abuse your master.
CHORUS: It does not fit an Argive to fawn on a villain.
AEGISTHUS: I will get even with you in the days to come.
CHORUS: Not if the Spirit brings Orestes home.
AEGISTHUS: I know the diet of exiles is rich in hope.
1835 CHORUS: Yes, do things, grow fat, pollute justice — while you can.
AEGISTHUS: You know you will pay me for your foolishness.
CHORUS: Boast, do; be bold — a cock beside your hen.
CLYTEMNESTRA: Do not pay heed to their vain yappings. I
and you together will make all things well,
1840 for we are masters of this house.

COMMENTARIES

Albrecht Dihle (b. 1923)
ORESTES AND THE GODS   *1991*

TRANSLATED BY CLARE KROJZL

Dihle, in his A History of Greek Literature, *takes up the role of the old and the new gods in the* Oresteia. *In Dihle's view the question of interpretation of the will of the gods and of the law becomes central to the drama.*

The act of vengeance perpetrated by Orestes[1] is by the express orders of the god Apollo, but the deed draws the attention of other deities responsible for the sanctity of the bond between mother and child. These, the Erinyes or Furies (goddesses of curses), hound the matricide mercilessly from one town to the next. He finds only fleeting refuge with Apollo in the temple at Delphi. The third play in the trilogy, *The Eumenides,* resolves this apparently hopeless conflict. A legal battle is fought out at the Areopagus, the time-honored murder court of the city of Athens, which convenes under the aegis of the goddess Athena. Apollo, representing the new order established by the Olympian gods, defends the deed of Orestes by pointing out the necessity of punishing the murder of a husband and king. The Erinyes, on the other hand, invoke the earlier order, calling for the expiation of matricide. The Areopagus dismisses the case against Orestes, at the same time mollifying the Erinyes by introducing their cult into Athens, where they are henceforth to dwell as *The Eumenides,* the gracious bestowers of blessings.

Aeschylus's theological interpretation of myth is based on a firm belief in the essential justice of the divine order of the universe. The idea of this justice making the gods into defenders of law and order among humankind had already been put forward by Hesiod, and later with a heightened sense of political responsibility by Solon. The notion that the actions of gods and heroes related in myth ought to correspond to the moral standards of his own day had moreover been the most important motif in the mythical interpretations of Pindar. What was new about Aeschylus's conception is that the law established by Zeus was more than a body of fixed rules whose observance was watched over by the gods with a system of reward and punishment. Instead, it was seen as a vital force constantly proving itself in ever new manifestations, and even able to resolve conflict which seemed hopeless from the human viewpoint. Apollo's claim is as valid as that of the Erinyes, so that Orestes, who must satisfy both, seems bound to be destroyed by this dilemma, as two divine powers conduct a mutual conflict with each other through his action and suffering, without releasing him from his moral responsibility. The trial instigated by Athena, the motherless daughter of Zeus, allows the dynamic nature of his law to manifest itself clearly, thereby resolving a unique, unforeseeable conflict

---

[1]To avenge the murder of his father, Agamemnon.

through a decision that is specific to the situation, but also creates a new order, while at the same time reconciling two equally valid claims that had seemed to be hopelessly at odds. Nevertheless, it is in human action, carried out with a consciousness of responsibility, that this conflict between divine powers is acted out and resolved. Were it not for human beings, as is demonstrated using the metaphor of the court of Athenian citizens, the law of Zeus would have no scope in which to unfold. Human dignity consists in becoming the necessary partner of the gods, and in the right order of human society matching the divine order as closely as possible.

Lois Spatz (b. 1940)
ORESTEIA: TRILOGY PRESERVED   *1982*

In her examination of Aeschylus, Lois Spatz discusses how he conceived of the three plays of the Oresteia *as a unified whole. She also provides some of the key background information that most of the original Greek audience would have known. Spatz connects the plays to events of the time in Athens, so we can better understand* Agamemnon *in the context of history and the other two plays to which it is linked.*

The *Oresteia* won first prize at the Great Dionysia of 458 B.C., just two years before Aeschylus's death. The three tragedies, *Agamemnon, The Libation Bearers (Choephoroi),* and *The Eumenides,* were presented in a sequence which concluded with a lost satyr play, *Proteus,* about the wanderings of Agamemnon's brother, Menelaus. Modern readers often study *Agamemnon* alone, although it is extremely difficult to follow and does not resolve the dramatic questions it raises, but the ancient spectators would have considered the drama as a first act in a larger whole. The trilogy is composed so that the *Agamemnon* and *The Libation Bearers* define a conflict which can only be resolved by a third and different action. *Agamemnon,* taken alone, seems an obscure play, for the extreme complexity of image, diction, and action is a dramatic device which conveys the moral, emotional, and political confusion of the initial situation. In the second play, where the next generation of characters better understand their positions and motivations, the action is clearer. In *The Eumenides,* Aeschylus illuminates the issues underlying the action and resolves them.

Because one must study the parts together to appreciate the whole, the trilogy will be treated as a single play. Although Aeschylus begins his drama *in medias res,* as Agamemnon is about to return from Troy, the audience was familiar with the stories concerning the crimes of Agamemnon's father, Atreus. Therefore, it would have suspected with increasing dread some relationship between the events of the present generation and the horrors of the past, which the poet does not mention directly until the last third of the play, when the curse on the House of Atreus becomes a central theme of the trilogy. Atreus was head of the house and ruler of Argos when Thyestes, his brother, raped his wife and attempted to steal his property and power. First Atreus exiled his brother, but judging that penalty inadequate, he invited him home and cooked and served Thyestes' children to him at a feast celebrating the reunion. When Thyestes discovered he had eaten his own sons, he cursed Atreus, promising revenge, and left Argos with his one remaining son, Aegisthus.

The curse arising from this horrible act brought misfortune to the next generation. Atreus's sons, Agamemnon and Menelaus, had married sisters, Clytemnestra and Helen, respectively. Helen, the most beautiful woman in Greece, was seduced and stolen away from the hearth of the House of Atreus by their guest, Paris (Alexander), son of King Priam of Troy. Paris's adultery was a violation of the sacred relationship between guest and host protected by Zeus Xenios ("Guest-Friend"). Therefore, the Argives considered it a serious crime demanding revenge, and launched the Trojan War, subject of the *Iliad* and epic cycle.

The Greek warriors who had sworn to support Menelaus met at Aulis under the leadership of Agamemnon, elder brother of the wronged husband and most powerful king in Greece. When rough seas prevented the fleet's passage to Troy, the priest Calchas informed Agamemnon that he must sacrifice his daughter, Iphigenia, to the goddess Artemis in order to calm the winds. Agamemnon, confident of the justice of the war and fearful of his restive troops, decided to slaughter Iphigenia so that the expedition could set sail.

Aeschylus begins his drama just as the Argives receive the news that Agamemnon has defeated Troy. The audience would know, however, from such sources as the *Odyssey,* the return stories of the cycle, and the *Oresteia* by the lyric poet Stesichorus, that, during these ten years of war, Clytemnestra had sent her son Orestes away and taken Aegisthus as a lover, and that the Greek soldiers in Troy had committed crimes which were punished on the return voyages. Aeschylus's gradual and sparing presentation of this background increases the mystery surrounding the events of the play itself.

Act I and Act II are both return and revenge stories. In *Agamemnon* several characters in sequence, the watchman, citizen/chorus, Queen Clytemnestra, and the herald, express hope and anxiety about the general's experiences in the Trojan War and his safe victorious return. Tension builds because the expectation of victory as the just punishment of Troy is constantly undercut by suggestions that the general and his men have themselves committed atrocities to insure victory. In fact, the Greek fleet has already been punished, destroyed by a god-sent storm at sea. At the mid-point in the drama, Agamemnon enters in triumph with his war prize, Cassandra, and is welcomed with Eastern pomp by his queen, Clytemnestra, who entices him to enter the palace on a luxurious tapestry. This greeting initiates the revenge story. After Agamemnon's entrance into the palace, Cassandra, the Trojan priestess of Apollo, predicts his murder and hers and relates it to the bloody history of the House of Atreus. Then Clytemnestra murders Agamemnon and his mistress and justifies her deed to the citizens as divine retribution for his sacrifice of their daughter, Iphigenia. Aegisthus, Clytemnestra's lover, later explains that history more precisely, justifying his part in Agamemnon's death as revenge for his uncle Atreus's slaughter of his brothers. Thus, the cycle of revenge as punishment which demands further revenge is clearly established by the end of the play. It is equally clear that Clytemnestra's act of revenge cannot break the cycle. She and her lover plan to replace Agamemnon as rulers of Argos, but they respond with threats of violence to the chorus's protests against their tyranny. *Agamemnon* ends with the chorus cowed for the moment, but predicting that Orestes, Agamemnon's son, sent away by Clytemnestra, will someday return to avenge the death of his father and assume his rightful place as head of the family and ruler of the state.

Act II, *The Libation Bearers,* also exhibits the return and revenge patterns, in dramatizing the murder of Agamemnon's murderers. First Orestes returns, fulfilling the hopes of his sister, Electra, and the chorus of household slaves, captives from Troy loyal to their conqueror, Agamemnon. Orestes later learns that his return has also fulfilled the nightmares of his mother, Clytemnestra. He enters, not as a conquering hero like his father, to be warmly welcomed and then duped, but as an exile in disguise, announcing his own death in order to deceive his mother and her lover. He has been spurred on by Apollo's demand that he avenge his father's death or suffer dire punishments, but he also acts from private motives as son, disinherited heir, and legitimate ruler of Argos. After praying with his sister and the chorus at the tomb of Agamemnon to invoke the aid of the gods and the powerful dead, he tricks Clytemnestra, kills Aegisthus, and then confronts his mother again. She tries to dissuade him, but he leads her into the house for the slaughter. When Orestes afterwards proclaims the justice of the matricide to the satisfied chorus, he does not gloat, as his mother before him did, for he recognizes that his deed was a crime as well as a necessity. He confesses that his pollution is a danger to himself and his community and prepares to leave Argos to be purified of blood guilt by Apollo. As he announces his plans, however, madness overtakes him; he seems to see the very Furies (Erinyes) from Hell descending on him to avenge his matricide. The chorus is puzzled that this act has not ended the chain of reciprocal revenge in the House of Atreus, but sends him forward to Apollo with prayers for success.

Act III, *The Eumenides,* introduces a new story pattern, "suppliant received"; a new setting, the shrines of the gods in Delphi and Athens; and new characters, the gods themselves — Apollo, the Furies, and Athena. The play begins at the shrine of Apollo in Delphi, where Orestes has arrived as a suppliant begging asylum from the Furies and release from blood guilt. Although Apollo has temporarily drugged the Furies into sleep, he cannot permanently protect Orestes from their vengeance. The god directs the matricide to the shrine of Athena in the Acropolis of Athens, where the goddess will release him from the curse. Once Orestes has fled, the ghost of Clytemnestra angrily arouses the sleeping Furies and sends them to track their prey. Orestes arrives in Athens and clings to the goddess's shrine, but the Furies enter soon after and threaten to destroy him. Athena returns just in time, and after questioning Orestes and the chorus of Furies, she decides the conflict is too important for her to resolve alone. Instead, she establishes a homicide court (modeled on the murder trials of the Court of the Areopagus) where citizen-judges (dicasts) will hear arguments for both sides and decide between them. The two present their cases, with Apollo supporting Orestes' plea. When the jury's vote is equally split, Orestes is set free by Athena's order. Before he returns home, he thanks Apollo, Athena, and the court, promising eternal peace between Argos and Athens and wishing the city prosperity and victory forever. The Furies, incensed by the verdict, call down curses on Athens, but Athena persuades them to become honored participants in the new procedure, ever punishing injustice, but showering blessings on the good as well. When they accept her offer, they exchange their loathsome black garments for the red robes of metics (foreign residents in Athens), a visible sign of their transformation from Furies to Eumenides ("Kindly Ones"). The trilogy ends with a torchlight procession, similar to the Panathenaic Festival, in which the citizens escort the goddesses to their new home, a hallowed cave at the foot of the Acropolis.

It is a long way from the polluted House of Atreus in Argos, whose bloody Furies roost like metics on the roof (*L.B.,* 1023), to the clear bright light of Athens, with its court system, public festivals, rites of Apollo, and the patronage of Zeus's daughter, Athena. Aeschylus has chosen a primitive myth about a blood-vendetta which extends for generations and includes cannibalism and child sacrifice. But he has dramatized the saga in a way which makes it relevant to his fifth-century audience. In none of the earlier versions of the story (i.e., *Odyssey, Cypria, Nostoi,* Stesichorus's *Oresteia*) was Orestes freed by a verdict of the Court of the Areopagus in Athens. Aeschylus originated this resolution so that he could trace the development of human justice — from the blood-vendetta carried out by the family with the support of the Furies who automatically avenge kindred bloodshed, through the purification rituals performed at the shrines of Apollo, to its culmination in the state court system, established by Athena with Zeus's blessing.[1] In dramatizing the progress of justice from vendetta to trial, he is also tracing the evolution of social institutions, from family and clan united by kindred blood, through cult united by ritual and a common patron, up to its perfection in the democratic polls, exemplified by Athens, where the families were ruled by law, the gods supported the new institutions, and the citizens united into a harmonious and effective whole.[2] No Athenian could sit unmoved while Athena voted like a citizen according to the procedures established in mythic time, but still in effect in 458 B.C. Nor could he watch without pride the imitation of his great Panathenaic Festival and the respectful acceptance of the dread Furies as metics in his own state. Thus would the contemporary Athenian recognize the ideals and glory of his city in the resolution of the myth.

But if this resolution represents the culmination of human progress, at least two problems disturbed the polls in 458. The Court of the Areopagus (the aristocratic body of ex-archons which once functioned as supreme overseer of the laws of the land) had recently been a target of the democratic reform. In 462, Ephialtes and Pericles carried through the Assembly an act which removed the court's right to interfere with democratic legislation and reduced its jurisdiction to cases of premeditated murder. The aristocrats were incensed and Ephialtes himself was assassinated. Although Aeschylus's own position on this democratic reform cannot be determined with certainty, in *The Eumenides* the court's function as a tribunal for murder is given a divine validation. Ephialtes and Pericles had also favored challenging Spartan hegemony in Greece by allying with Argos, Sparta's main rival in the Peloponnese. In 461, the leader of the aristocrats, Cimon, was ostracized and the alliance with Argos approved. This change, which also produced fierce debate in the ensuing years, received attention from Aeschylus in the *Oresteia*. Orestes is clearly a political representative of Argos who allies himself with Athens, seemingly with Aeschylus's approval.[3]

[1]For a different opinion of Apollo's place, see George Derwent Thomson, *Aeschylus and Athens: A Study in the Social Origins of Drama,* 2nd ed. (London: Lawrence & Wishart, 1967), pp. 259–61, and R. P. Winnington-Ingram, "The Role of Apollo in the Oresteia," *Classical Review* 47 (1933): 97–104. On the relation of purification to the laws on homicide, see D. M. MacDowell, *Athenian Homicide Law in the Age of the Orators* (Manchester: University of Manchester Press, 1963), pp. 4–5, 141–50.

[2]The family remained important, however, even in the legal prosecution for homicide, as MacDowell points out (*Athenian Homicide,* pp. 8–30). For a study of this evolution, see Richard Kuhns, *The House, the City, and the Judge: The Growth of Moral Awareness in the "Oresteia"* (Indianapolis: Bobbs-Merrill, 1962). George Thomson also traces the development from tribe to state and its influence on the form and ideas of drama, and on the *Oresteia* in particular (*Aeschylus,* pp. 229–78).

[3]The debate about Aeschylus's position on the reforms is summarized by Anthony J. Podlecki in *The Political Background of Aeschylean Tragedy* (Ann Arbor: U of Michigan P, 1966), pp. 81–92.

It is not as important to label Aeschylus an aristocrat or radical as it is to recognize in the entire trilogy a paradigm for necessary compromise between disparate elements in the state.[4] If political vendettas are not controlled, there can be no civil order and consequently no peace and prosperity. Traditional groups like the Furies must be reconciled to the new system, treated with honor, and allowed to serve the state so that they can preserve for themselves and the community whichever of their principles remain valuable. Athena, establishing the Court of the Areopagus, defines its functions in words which echo the Furies' defense of their grim penalties:

> Here the reverence
> of citizens, their fear and kindred do-no-wrong
> shall hold by day and in the blessing of night alike
> all while the people do not muddy their own laws
> with foul infusions. But if bright water you stain
> with mud, you nevermore will find it fit to drink.
> No anarchy, no rule of a single master. Thus
> I advise my citizens to govern and to grace,
> and not to cast fear utterly from your city. What
> man who fears nothing at all is ever righteous? Such
> be your just terrors, and you may deserve and have
> salvation for your citadel, your land's defence
> such as is nowhere else found among men . . .
> (*The Eumenides*, 11. 690–702)[5]

Her admonitions provide not only an eternal definition of good government, but also a timely warning to a population recently embroiled in civil strife.

---

[4]A forceful spokesman for this view is E. R. Dodds, "Morals and Politics," from *The Ancient Concept of Progress and Other Essays* (Oxford UP, 1973), pp. 54–62.

[5]I have used the translation of Richmond Lattimore which appears in *The Complete Greek Tragedies: Aeschylus I* (New York, n.d.).

Sophocles

Sophocles (c. 496–c. 406 B.C.) won more prizes than any other tragedian in the Greek drama competitions, and he never came in lower than second place. His first victory was against the grand old master Aeschylus in 468 B.C. Sophocles' last plays, which he wrote in his eighties, were among his greatest. We have fragments of some ninety plays or poems and seven complete tragedies, while records suggest that his output numbered something over a hundred twenty plays.

Sophocles lived in interesting times. He would have recalled the first defeat of the Persians in 490 B.C., when the news came by a messenger who had run twenty-six miles from Marathon to Athens. In his adolescence, Athens achieved its astonishing and decisive victory over the Persians at Salamis. His popularity as a tragedian and as a statesman coincided with the development of an imperial attitude in Athens. Athenian society honored the greatness of men like Aeschylus, Sophocles, Euripides, the historian Herodotus, and all the politicians and artists that Pericles drew to Athens for its rebuilding. It was a golden age shadowed by war.

Sophocles was both sociable and religious, serving as the priest of several religious cults. He was also a man of action, popular enough to be elected as one of Athens's twelve generals; he participated with Pericles in the Samian War (440–439 B.C.). His plays — especially *Antigone* (441 B.C.), which preceded his election to generalship — often have deep political concerns. One of his primary themes concerns the relation of the individual to the *polis,* the state itself. Since the Greeks valued the individual and at the same time regarded the *polis* as a sacred bulwark against a return to barbarism, conflicts between the individual and the *polis* were immensely painful.

When Sophocles began writing, he broke with an old tradition. From the time of Thespis (mid-sixth century B.C.), each playwright acted in his own plays. Aeschylus probably did so, but it is on record that Sophocles' voice was not strong enough to permit him to take a part in his plays. He played the lyre well enough to appear onstage, and he participated in a game of ball in one of his plays, but he did not appear as an actor. He also introduced innovations in the structure of his plays by changing the size of the chorus to fifteen and by adding painted scenery, more props, and a third actor to the two that Aeschylus and other tragedians had used. Sophocles wrote some of his plays with specific actors in mind, much as Shakespeare, Molière, and many other first-rank playwrights have done.

Sophocles was versed in the epics of Homer. Some of his plays derive from the *Iliad* or the *Odyssey,* although Sophocles always adapted the material of others to his own purposes. His nickname was the Attic Bee because he could investigate wonderful pieces of literature and always return with a useful idea. The approach he took to the structure of the play, measuring the effect of the rising action of complication and then ensuring that the moment of recognition occurred at the same time the falling action began, was recognized as a supremely elegant skill. Nowhere is this illustrated with more completeness than in *Oedipus Rex.*

Bust of Sophocles. The
Capitoline Museum, Rome.

The plays of Aeschylus, powerful though they are, do not have the same delicacy of construction as do Sophocles'. They are forceful but, in terms of structure, somewhat simpler. The structure of the plays of Euripides, Sophocles' successor, was never as fully worked out; and when Aristotle discussed the nature of tragedy in his *Poetics*, it was to Sophocles he turned for a model, not to the other two master playwrights of the genre.

Besides the Oedipus plays, Sophocles' other surviving plays are *Philoctetes*, *Ajax*, *Trachiniae*, and *Elektra*.

OEDIPUS REX

Oedipus Rex is one of three plays by Sophocles that treat the fate of Oedipus and his children. The plays were written over a period of thirty years: *Antigone* (first produced in 441 B.C.), *Oedipus Rex* (produced approximately fifteen years later, between 430 and 427 B.C.), and *Oedipus at Colonus* (produced in 401 B.C., after Sophocles' death). When these plays are produced together today, they are usually given in an order that follows the events of Oedipus's and Antigone's lives — *Oedipus Rex, Oedipus at Colonus,* and *Antigone* — almost like the trilogies that Athenian audiences often viewed in the early years of the drama competitions. In fact, they were never a unified trilogy, and one of Sophocles' distinctions is that he did not present as trilogies plays that were thematically related, as poets before him had done.

The original narratives of the Oedipus plays were known to Sophocles' audience — with the possible exception of the story of Antigone — and one of the special pleasures for the audience watching the action of *Oedipus Rex* was that they knew the outcome. They watched for the steps, the choices, that led Oedipus to his fate.

Oedipus Rex is the story of a noble man who seeks knowledge that in the end destroys him. His greatness is measured in part by the fact that the gods have prophesied his fate: the gods do not take interest in insignificant men. Before the action of the play begins, Oedipus has set out to discover whether he is truly the son of Polybos and Merope, the people who have reared him. He learns from the oracle of Apollo at Delphi, the most powerful interpreter of the voice and the will of the gods, that he will kill his father and marry his mother. His response is overwhelmingly human: he has seen his *moira,* his fate, and he cannot accept it. His reaction is to do everything he can, including leaving his homeland as quickly as possible, to avoid the possibility of killing Polybos and marrying Merope.

The Greek audience would have known that Oedipus was a descendant of Kadmos, founder of Thebes, who had sown the dragon teeth that produced the Spartoi (the sown men). Legend determined that the rulership of Thebes would be in dispute, with fraternal rivalry resembling that of the Spartoi, who fought and killed each other. This bloody legacy follows Oedipus, but it also reaches into all the plays of the trilogy. For example, in *Antigone* we learn that Antigone's brothers Polyneices and Eteocles killed each other in the shadow of the city walls. Thus, the fate Oedipus attempts to avoid actually dooms most of the characters in the three plays, including his true father, Laios, and his daughter Antigone.

Sophocles develops the drama in terms of IRONY — the disjunction between what seems to be true and what is true. Knowing the outcome of the action, the audience savors the ironic moments from the beginning of the play to the end. Oedipus flees his homeland to avoid fulfilling the prophecy, only to run headlong into the fate foretold by the oracle. He unwittingly returns to his original home, Thebes, and to his parents, murdering Laios, his true father, at a crossroads on the way and marrying Iokaste, his true mother, and becoming king of Thebes. The blind seer Teiresias warns Oedipus not to pursue the truth, but, in human fashion, Oedipus refuses to heed Teiresias's warnings. When the complete truth becomes clear to Oedipus, he physically blinds himself in horror and expiation. Like the blind Teiresias, Oedipus must now look inward for the truth, without the distractions of surface experiences.

The belief that the moral health of the ruler directly affected the security of the *polis* was widespread in Athenian Greece. Indeed, the Athenians regarded their state as fragile — like a human being whose health, physical and moral, could change suddenly. Because the Greeks were concerned for the well-being of their state, the *polis* often figures in the tragedies. The Sophoclean Oedipus trilogy is usually called the Theban plays, a nomenclature that reminds us that the story of Oedipus can be read as the story of an individual or as the story of a state.

Oedipus Rex examines the tension between and interdependence of the individual and the state. The agricultural and ritual basis of the Dionysian festivals — in which Greek drama developed — underscores the importance the Greeks attached to the individual's dependence on the state that feeds him and on the proper ways of doing things. This could be planting and harvesting or worshiping the gods or living as part of a political entity.

The underlying conflict in the play is political. The political relationship of human beings to the gods, the arbiters of their fate, is dramatized in Oedipus's relationship with the seer Teiresias. If he had his way, Oedipus might disregard Teiresias entirely. But Oedipus cannot command everything, even as ruler. His incomplete knowledge, despite his wisdom, is symptomatic of the limitations of every individual.

The contrast of Oedipus and Kreon, Iokaste's brother, is one of political style. Oedipus is a fully developed character who reveals himself as sympathetic but willful. He acts on his misunderstanding of the prophecy without reconsulting the oracle. He marries Iokaste and blinds himself without reconsulting the oracle. Kreon, who is much less complicated, never acts without consulting the oracle and thoughtfully reflecting on the oracle's message. Oedipus sometimes behaves tyrannically, and he appears eager for power. Kreon takes power only when forced to do so.

The depth of Sophocles' character development was unmatched, except by his contemporary Euripides, for almost two thousand years. Sophocles' drama is one of psychological development. His audiences saw Oedipus as a model for human greatness but also as a model for the human capacity to fall from a great height. The play is about the limits of human knowledge; it is also about the limits and frailty of human happiness.

Oedipus Rex in Performance

Oedipus Rex has enjoyed great popularity since its first performance. The Greeks, who originally restricted their plays to one performance, eventually began to revive plays of the masters. *Oedipus* was one of the most popular. In modern times, performance has been almost constant since the seventeenth century. Great dramatists have produced it in their own adaptations — Corneille (1659), John Dryden (1679), Voltaire (1718), William Butler Yeats (1923), and Jean Cocteau (1931) — proving the durability of the themes and the adaptability of the play. The early American performances (beginning in 1881) were in Greek but soon gave way to English. Modern versions have been both very traditional, such as those developed by the Royal Shakespeare Company in the 1970s, and experimental, such as that of Peter Brook (1968). Brook's production began with a huge golden cube reflecting brilliant light like the sun and ended with the ritual unveiling of a giant phallus. John Gielgud played Oedipus and Irene Worth, all in black, played Iokaste. Currently, Greek companies perform the play regularly in the theater of Dionysus in Athens as well as in Epidaurus and elsewhere.

Sophocles *(c. 496–c. 406 B.C.)*

OEDIPUS REX
TRANSLATED BY DUDLEY FITTS AND ROBERT FITZGERALD

c. 430 B.C.

Characters

OEDIPUS, *King of Thebes, supposed son of Polybos and Merope, King and Queen of Corinth*

IOKASTE, *wife of Oedipus and widow of the late King Laios*

KREON, *brother of Iokaste, a prince of Thebes*

TEIRESIAS, *a blind seer who serves Apollo*

PRIEST

MESSENGER, *from Corinth*

SHEPHERD, *former servant of Laios*

SECOND MESSENGER, *from the palace*

CHORUS OF THEBAN ELDERS

CHORAGOS, *leader of the Chorus*

ANTIGONE *and* ISMENE, *young daughters of Oedipus and Iokaste. They appear in the Exodos but do not speak.*

SUPPLIANTS, GUARDS, SERVANTS

The Scene: *Before the palace of Oedipus, King of Thebes. A central door and two lateral doors open onto a platform which runs the length of the facade. On the platform, right and left, are altars; and three steps lead down into the orchestra, or chorus-ground. At the beginning of the action these steps are crowded by suppliants who have brought branches and chaplets of olive leaves and who sit in various attitudes of despair. Oedipus enters.*

PROLOGUE°

OEDIPUS: My children, generations of the living
    In the line of Kadmos,° nursed at his ancient hearth:
    Why have you strewn yourselves before these altars
    In supplication, with your boughs and garlands?
5   The breath of incense rises from the city
    With a sound of prayer and lamentation.
                        Children,
    I would not have you speak through messengers,
    And therefore I have come myself to hear you —
    I, Oedipus, who bear the famous name.
    (*To a Priest.*) You, there, since you are eldest in the
10   company,
    Speak for them all, tell me what preys upon you,
    Whether you come in dread, or crave some blessing:

Prologue: Portion of the play explaining the background and current action. **2. Kadmos:** Founder of Thebes.

Tell me, and never doubt that I will help you
    In every way I can; I should be heartless
    Were I not moved to find you suppliant here.   15
PRIEST: Great Oedipus, O powerful king of Thebes!
    You see how all the ages of our people
    Cling to your altar steps: here are boys
    Who can barely stand alone, and here are priests
    By weight of age, as I am a priest of God,   20
    And young men chosen from those yet unmarried;
    As for the others, all that multitude,
    They wait with olive chaplets in the squares,
    At the two shrines of Pallas,° and where Apollo°
    Speaks in the glowing embers.
                      Your own eyes   25
    Must tell you: Thebes is tossed on a murdering sea
    And can not lift her head from the death surge.
    A rust consumes the buds and fruits of the earth;
    The herds are sick; children die unborn,
    And labor is vain. The god of plague and pyre   30
    Raids like detestable lightning through the city,
    And all the house of Kadmos is laid waste,
    All emptied, and all darkened: Death alone
    Battens upon the misery of Thebes.

You are not one of the immortal gods, we know;   35
    Yet we have come to you to make our prayer
    As to the man surest in mortal ways
    And wisest in the ways of God. You saved us
    From the Sphinx,° that flinty singer, and the tribute
    We paid to her so long; yet you were never   40
    Better informed than we, nor could we teach you:
    A god's touch, it seems, enabled you to help us.

Therefore, O mighty power, we turn to you:
    Find us our safety, find us a remedy,
    Whether by counsel of the gods or of men.   45
    A king of wisdom tested in the past
    Can act in a time of troubles, and act well.
    Noblest of men, restore
    Life to your city! Think how all men call you
    Liberator for your boldness long ago;   50
    Ah, when your years of kingship are remembered,

24. Pallas: Pallas Athene, daughter of Zeus and goddess of wisdom. **Apollo:** Son of Zeus and god of the sun, of light and truth. **39. Sphinx:** A winged monster with the body of a lion and the face of a woman, the Sphinx had tormented Thebes with her riddle, killing those who could not solve it. When Oedipus solved the riddle, the Sphinx killed herself.

Let them not say *We rose, but later fell* —
Keep the State from going down in the storm!
Once, years ago, with happy augury,
55 You brought us fortune; be the same again!
No man questions your power to rule the land:
But rule over men, not over a dead city!
Ships are only hulls, high walls are nothing,
When no life moves in the empty passageways.

60 OEDIPUS: Poor children! You may be sure I know
All that you longed for in your coming here.
I know that you are deathly sick; and yet,
Sick as you are, not one is as sick as I.
Each of you suffers in himself alone
65 His anguish, not another's; but my spirit
Groans for the city, for myself, for you.

I was not sleeping, you are not waking me.
No, I have been in tears for a long while
And in my restless thought walked many ways.
70 In all my search I found one remedy,
And I have adopted it: I have sent Kreon,
Son of Menoikeus, brother of the queen,
To Delphi,° Apollo's place of revelation,
To learn there, if he can,
75 What act or pledge of mine may save the city.
I have counted the days, and now, this very day,
I am troubled, for he has overstayed his time.
What is he doing? He has been gone too long.
Yet whenever he comes back, I should do ill
80 Not to take any action the god orders.

PRIEST: It is a timely promise. At this instant
They tell me Kreon is here.

OEDIPUS: O Lord Apollo!
May his news be fair as his face is radiant!

PRIEST: Good news, I gather! he is crowned with bay,
The chaplet is thick with berries.

85 OEDIPUS: We shall soon know;
He is near enough to hear us now.   (*Enter Kreon.*)
    O prince:
Brother: son of Menoikeus:
What answer do you bring us from the god?

KREON: A strong one. I can tell you, great afflictions
90 Will turn out well, if they are taken well.

OEDIPUS: What was the oracle? These vague words
Leave me still hanging between hope and fear.

KREON: Is it your pleasure to hear me with all these
Gathered around us? I am prepared to speak,
But should we not go in?

95 OEDIPUS: Speak to them all,
It is for them I suffer, more than for myself.

KREON: Then I will tell you what I heard at Delphi.
In plain words
The god commands us to expel from the land of
    Thebes
100 An old defilement we are sheltering.

73. **Delphi:** Site of the oracle, source of religious authority and prophecy, under the protection of Apollo.

It is a deathly thing, beyond cure;
We must not let it feed upon us longer.

OEDIPUS: What defilement? How shall we rid ourselves
of it?

KREON: By exile or death, blood for blood. It was
Murder that brought the plague-wind on the city.   105

OEDIPUS: Murder of whom? Surely the god has named
him?

KREON: My Lord: Laios once ruled this land,
Before you came to govern us.

OEDIPUS: I know;
I learned of him from others; I never saw him.

KREON: He was murdered; and Apollo commands us
now   110
To take revenge upon whoever killed him.

OEDIPUS: Upon whom? Where are they? Where shall
we find a clue
To solve that crime, after so many years?

KREON: Here in this land, he said. Search reveals
Things that escape an inattentive man.   115

OEDIPUS: Tell me: Was Laios murdered in his house,
Or in the fields, or in some foreign country?

KREON: He said he planned to make a pilgrimage.
He did not come home again.

OEDIPUS: And was there no one,
No witness, no companion, to tell what happened?   120

KREON: They were all killed but one, and he got away
So frightened that he could remember one thing
only.

OEDIPUS: What was that one thing? One may be the
key
To everything, if we resolve to use it.

KREON: He said that a band of highwaymen attacked
them,   125
Outnumbered them, and overwhelmed the king.

OEDIPUS: Strange, that a highwayman should be so
daring —
Unless some faction here bribed him to do it.

KREON: We thought of that. But after Laios' death
New troubles arose and we had no avenger.   130

OEDIPUS: What troubles could prevent your hunting
down the killers?

KREON: The riddling Sphinx's song
Made us deaf to all mysteries but her own.

OEDIPUS: Then once more I must bring what is dark to
light.
It is most fitting that Apollo shows,   135
As you do, this compunction for the dead.
You shall see how I stand by you, as I should,
Avenging this country and the god as well,
And not as though it were for some distant friend,
But for my own sake, to be rid of evil.   140
Whoever killed King Laios might — who knows? —
Lay violent hands even on me — and soon.
I act for the murdered king in my own interest.

Come, then, my children: leave the altar steps,
Lift up your olive boughs!
                    One of you go   145

And summon the people of Kadmos to gather here.
I will do all that I can; you may tell them that.

(Exit a Page.)

So, with the help of God,
We shall be saved — or else indeed we are lost.

150 PRIEST: Let us rise, children. It was for this we came,
And now the king has promised it.
Phoibos° has sent us an oracle; may he descend
Himself to save us and drive out the plague.

*(Exeunt° Oedipus and Kreon into the palace by the
central door. The Priest and the Suppliants disperse right
and left. After a short pause the Chorus enters the orchestra.)*

PARADOS° • *Strophe° 1*

CHORUS: What is God singing in his profound
   Delphi of gold and shadow?
   What oracle for Thebes, the Sunwhipped city?
   Fear unjoints me, the roots of my heart tremble.
   Now I remember, O Healer, your power, and
5   wonder:
   Will you send doom like a sudden cloud, or weave it
   Like nightfall of the past?
   Speak to me, tell me, O
   Child of golden Hope, immortal Voice.

Antistrophe° 1

   Let me pray to Athene, the immortal daughter of
10   Zeus,
   And to Artemis° her sister
   Who keeps her famous throne in the market ring,
   And to Apollo, archer from distant heaven —
   O gods, descend! Like three streams leap against
15   The fires of our grief, the fires of darkness;
   Be swift to bring us rest!
   As in the old time from the brilliant house
   Of air you stepped to save us, come again!

Strophe 2

   Now our afflictions have no end,
20   Now all our stricken host lies down
   And no man fights off death with his mind;
   The noble plowland bears no grain,
   And groaning mothers can not bear —
   See, how our lives like birds take wing,

Like sparks that fly when a fire soars,   25
To the shore of the god of evening.

Antistrophe 2

   The plague burns on, it is pitiless,
   Though pallid children laden with death
   Lie unwept in the stony ways,
   And old gray women by every path   30
   Flock to the strand about the altars
   There to strike their breasts and cry
   Worship of Phoibos in wailing prayers:
   Be kind, God's golden child!

Strophe 3

   There are no swords in this attack by fire,   35
   No shields, but we are ringed with cries.
   Send the besieger plunging from our homes
   Into the vast sea-room of the Atlantic
   Or into the waves that foam eastward of Thrace —
   For the day ravages what the night spares —   40
   Destroy our enemy, lord of the thunder!
   Let him be riven by lightning from heaven!

Antistrophe 3

   Phoibos Apollo, stretch the sun's bowstring,
   That golden cord, until it sing for us,
   Flashing arrows in heaven!
                                       Artemis, Huntress,   45
   Race with flaring lights upon our mountains!
   O scarlet god,° O golden-banded brow,
   O Theban Bacchos in a storm of Maenads,°

(Enter Oedipus, center.)

   Whirl upon Death, that all the Undying hate!
   Come with blinding torches, come in joy!   50

SCENE 1

OEDIPUS: Is this your prayer? It may be answered.
   Come,
   Listen to me, act as the crisis demands,
   And you shall have relief from all these evils.

   Until now I was a stranger to this tale,
   As I had been a stranger to the crime.   5
   Could I track down the murderer without a clue?
   But now, friends,
   As one who became a citizen after the murder,

---

152. Phoibos: Apollo.   **154.** [S.D.] *Exeunt:* Latin for "they go
out."   **Parados:** The song or ode chanted by the Chorus on
their entry.   **Strophe:** Song sung by the Chorus as they danced
from stage right to stage left.   **Antistrophe:** Song sung by the
Chorus following the Strophe, as they danced back from stage
left to stage right.   **11. Artemis:** The huntress, daughter of
Zeus, twin sister of Apollo.

47. scarlet god: Bacchus, god of wine and revelry; also called
Dionysus.   **48. Maenads:** Female worshipers of Bacchus
(Dionysus).

I make this proclamation to all Thebans:
If any man knows by whose hand Laios, son of
10   Labdakos,
Met his death, I direct that man to tell me everything,
No matter what he fears for having so long
    withheld it.
Let it stand as promised that no further trouble
Will come to him, but he may leave the land in safety.
Moreover: If anyone knows the murderer to be
15   foreign,
Let him not keep silent: he shall have his reward
    from me.
However, if he does conceal it; if any man
Fearing for his friend or for himself disobeys this
    edict,
Hear what I propose to do:

20   I solemnly forbid the people of this country,
Where power and throne are mine, ever to receive
    that man
Or speak to him, no matter who he is, or let him
Join in sacrifice, lustration, or in prayer.
I decree that he be driven from every house,
25   Being, as he is, corruption itself to us: the Delphic
Voice of Apollo has pronounced this revelation.
Thus I associate myself with the oracle
And take the side of the murdered king.

As for the criminal, I pray to God —
30   Whether it be a lurking thief, or one of a number —
I pray that that man's life be consumed in evil and
    wretchedness.
And as for me, this curse applies no less
If it should turn out that the culprit is my guest here,
Sharing my hearth.
             You have heard the penalty.
35   I lay it on you now to attend to this
For my sake, for Apollo's, for the sick
Sterile city that heaven has abandoned.
Suppose the oracle had given you no command:
Should this defilement go uncleansed for ever?
40   You should have found the murderer: your king,
A noble king, had been destroyed!
                 Now I,
Having the power that he held before me,
Having his bed, begetting children there
Upon his wife, as he would have, had he lived —
45   Their son would have been my children's brother,
If Laios had had luck in fatherhood!
(And now his bad fortune has struck him down) —
I say I take the son's part, just as though
I were his son, to press the fight for him
50   And see it won! I'll find the hand that brought
Death to Labdakos' and Polydoros' child,
Heir of Kadmos' and Agenor's line.°

51–52. **Labdakos, Polydoros, Kadmos, and Agenor:** Father,
grandfather, great-grandfather, and great-great-grandfather of
Laios.

And as for those who fail me,
May the gods deny them the fruit of the earth,
Fruit of the womb, and may they rot utterly!   55
Let them be wretched as we are wretched, and
    worse!

For you, for loyal Thebans, and for all
Who find my actions right, I pray the favor
Of justice, and of all the immortal gods.
CHORAGOS: Since I am under oath, my lord, I swear   60
   I did not do the murder, I can not name
The murderer. Phoibos ordained the search;
Why did he not say who the culprit was?
OEDIPUS: An honest question. But no man in the world
Can make the gods do more than the gods will.   65
CHORAGOS: There is an alternative, I think —
OEDIPUS: Tell me.
   Any or all, you must not fail to tell me.
CHORAGOS: A lord clairvoyant to the lord Apollo,
As we all know, is the skilled Teiresias.
One might learn much about this from him, Oedipus.   70
OEDIPUS: I am not wasting time:
   Kreon spoke of this, and I have sent for him —
   Twice, in fact; it is strange that he is not here.
CHORAGOS: The other matter — that old report —
    seems useless.
OEDIPUS: What was that? I am interested in all reports.   75
CHORAGOS: The king was said to have been killed by
    highwaymen.
OEDIPUS: I know. But we have no witnesses to that.
CHORAGOS: If the killer can feel a particle of dread,
   Your curse will bring him out of hiding!
OEDIPUS: No.
   The man who dared that act will fear no curse.   80

(*Enter the blind seer Teiresias, led by a Page.*)

CHORAGOS: But there is one man who may detect the
    criminal.
   This is Teiresias, this is the holy prophet
   In whom, alone of all men, truth was born.
OEDIPUS: Teiresias: seer: student of mysteries,
   Of all that's taught and all that no man tells,   85
   Secrets of Heaven and secrets of the earth:
   Blind though you are, you know the city lies
   Sick with plague; and from this plague, my lord,
   We find that you alone can guard or save us.

Possibly you did not hear the messengers?   90
Apollo, when we sent to him,
Sent us back word that this great pestilence
Would lift, but only if we established clearly
The identity of those who murdered Laios.
They must be killed or exiled.
                 Can you use   95
Birdflight° or any art of divination
To purify yourself, and Thebes, and me

96. **Birdflight:** Prophets used the flight of birds to predict the
future.

From this contagion? We are in your hands.
There is no fairer duty
100   Than that of helping others in distress.
  Teiresias: How dreadful knowledge of the truth can be
When there's no help in truth! I knew this well,
But did not act on it; else I should not have come.
  Oedipus: What is troubling you? Why are your eyes so
cold?
105 Teiresias: Let me go home. Bear your own fate, and I'll
Bear mine. It is better so: trust what I say.
  Oedipus: What you say is ungracious and unhelpful
To your native country. Do not refuse to speak.
  Teiresias: When it comes to speech, your own is
neither temperate
110 Nor opportune. I wish to be more prudent.
  Oedipus: In God's name, we all beg you —
                        You are all ignorant.
No; I will never tell you what I know.
Now it is my misery; then, it would be yours.
  Oedipus: What! You do know something, and will not
tell us?
115 You would betray us all and wreck the State?
  Teiresias: I do not intend to torture myself, or you.
Why persist in asking? You will not persuade me.

Oedipus: What a wicked old man you are! You'd try a
stone's
Patience! Out with it! Have you no feeling at all?
  Teiresias: You call me unfeeling. If you could only see   120
The nature of your own feelings . . .
  Oedipus: Why,
Who would not feel as I do? Who could endure
Your arrogance toward the city?
  Teiresias: What does it matter?
Whether I speak or not, it is bound to come.
  Oedipus: Then, if "it" is bound to come, you are
bound to tell me.   125
  Teiresias: No, I will not go on. Rage as you please.
  Oedipus: Rage? Why not!
                    And I'll tell you what I think:
You planned it, you had it done, you all but
Killed him with your own hands: if you had eyes,
I'd say the crime was yours, and yours alone.   130
  Teiresias: So? I charge you, then,
Abide by the proclamation you have made:
From this day forth
Never speak again to these men or to me;
You yourself are the pollution of this country.   135
  Oedipus: You dare say that! Can you possibly think
you have
Some way of going free, after such insolence?
  Teiresias: I have gone free. It is the truth sustains me.
  Oedipus: Who taught you shamelessness? It was not
your craft.
  Teiresias: You did. You made me speak. I did not
want to.   140
  Oedipus: Speak what? Let me hear it again more
clearly.
  Teiresias: Was it not clear before? Are you tempting
me?
  Oedipus: I did not understand it. Say it again.
  Teiresias: I say that you are the murderer whom you
seek.
  Oedipus: Now twice you have spat out infamy.
You'll pay for it!   145
  Teiresias: Would you care for more? Do you wish to
be really angry?
  Oedipus: Say what you will. Whatever you say is
worthless.
  Teiresias: I say you live in hideous shame with those
Most dear to you. You can not see the evil.
  Oedipus: Can you go on babbling like this for ever?   150
  Teiresias: I can, if there is power in truth.
  Oedipus: There is:
But not for you, not for you,
You sightless, witless, senseless, mad old man!
  Teiresias: You are the madman. There is no one here
Who will not curse you soon, as you curse me.   155
  Oedipus: You child of total night! I would not touch
you;
Neither would any man who sees the sun.
  Teiresias: True: it is not from you my fate will come.
That lies within Apollo's competence,
As it is his concern.

FAR LEFT: Le Clanche Du Rand
as Iokaste in Donald Sutherland
and Robert Loper's production
of *Oedipus Rex* at the 1975
Oregon Shakespeare Festival in
Ashland. RIGHT: Philip L. Jones
as the Shepherd. (Photos by
Henry S. Kranzler.) BELOW:
Franz Mertz's design for a 1952
production of *Oedipus Rex*
directed by G. R. Sellner at
Darmstadt Landestheater.

160 OEDIPUS: Tell me, who made
These fine discoveries? Kreon? or someone else?
TEIRESIAS: Kreon is no threat. You weave your own
doom.
OEDIPUS: Wealth, power, craft of statemanship!
Kingly position, everywhere admired!
165 What savage envy is stored up against these,
If Kreon, whom I trusted, Kreon my friend,
For this great office which the city once
Put in my hands unsought — if for this power
Kreon desires in secret to destroy me!

170 He has bought this decrepit fortune-teller, this
Collector of dirty pennies, this prophet fraud —
Why, he is no more clairvoyant than I am!
Tell us:
Has your mystic mummery ever approached the
truth?
When that hellcat the Sphinx was performing here,
175 What help were you to these people?
Her magic was not for the first man who came along:
It demanded a real exorcist. Your birds —
What good were they? or the gods, for the matter of
that?
But I came by,
180 Oedipus, the simple man, who knows nothing —
I thought it out for myself, no birds helped me!
And this is the man you think you can destroy,
That you may be close to Kreon when he's king!
Well, you and your friend Kreon, it seems to me,
185 Will suffer most. If you were not an old man,
You would have paid already for your plot.
CHORAGOS: We can not see that his words or yours
Have been spoken except in anger, Oedipus,
And of anger we have no need. How to accomplish
190 The god's will best: that is what most concerns us.
TEIRESIAS: You are a king. But where argument's
concerned
I am your man, as much a king as you.
I am not your servant, but Apollo's.
I have no need of Kreon or Kreon's name.

195 Listen to me. You mock my blindness, do you?
But I say that you, with both your eyes, are blind:
You can not see the wretchedness of your life,
Nor in whose house you live, no, nor with whom.
Who are your father and mother? Can you tell me?
200 You do not even know the blind wrongs
That you have done them, on earth and in the world
below.
But the double lash of your parents' curse will whip
you
Out of this land some day, with only night
Upon your precious eyes.
205 Your cries then — where will they not be heard?
What fastness of Kithairon° will not echo them?

206. **Kithairon:** The mountain where Oedipus was abandoned
as an infant.

And that bridal-descant of yours — you'll know it
then,
The song they sang when you came here to Thebes
And found your misguided berthing.
All this, and more, that you can not guess at now, 210
Will bring you to yourself among your children.

Be angry, then. Curse Kreon. Curse my words.
I tell you, no man that walks upon the earth
Shall be rooted out more horribly than you.
OEDIPUS: Am I to bear this from him? — Damnation 215
Take you! Out of this place! Out of my sight!
TEIRESIAS: I would not have come at all if you had not
asked me.
OEDIPUS: Could I have told that you'd talk nonsense,
that
You'd come here to make a fool of yourself, and of
me?
TEIRESIAS: A fool? Your parents thought me sane
enough. 220
OEDIPUS: My parents again! — Wait: who were my
parents?
TEIRESIAS: This day will give you a father, and break
your heart.
OEDIPUS: Your infantile riddles! Your damned
abracadabra!
TEIRESIAS: You were a great man once at solving riddles.
OEDIPUS: Mock me with that if you like; you will find
it true. 225
TEIRESIAS: It was true enough. It brought about your
ruin.
OEDIPUS: But if it saved this town?
TEIRESIAS (to the Page): Boy, give me your hand.
OEDIPUS: Yes, boy; lead him away.
— While you are here
We can do nothing. Go; leave us in peace. 230
TEIRESIAS: I will go when I have said what I have to say.
How can you hurt me? And I tell you again:
The man you have been looking for all this time,
The damned man, the murderer of Laios,
That man is in Thebes. To your mind he is
foreign-born,
But it will soon be shown that he is a Theban, 235
A revelation that will fail to please.
A blind man,
Who has his eyes now; a penniless man, who is rich
now;
And he will go tapping the strange earth with his staff.
To the children with whom he lives now he will be 240
Brother and father — the very same; to her
Who bore him, son and husband — the very same
Who came to his father's bed, wet with his father's
blood.
Enough. Go think that over.
If later you find error in what I have said, 245
You may say that I have no skill in prophecy.

(*Exit Teiresias, led by his Page.*
Oedipus goes into the palace.)

ODE° 1 • Strophe 1

CHORUS: The Delphic stone of prophecies
    Remembers ancient regicide
    And a still bloody hand.
    That killer's hour of flight has come.
5   He must be stronger than riderless
    Coursers of untiring wind,
    For the son of Zeus° armed with his father's thunder
    Leaps in lightning after him;
    And the Furies° hold his track, the sad Furies.

Ode: Song sung by the Chorus. **7. son of Zeus:** Apollo.
9. Furies: Spirits called on to avenge crimes, especially against kin.

Antistrophe 1

Holy Parnassos'° peak of snow   10
    Flashes and blinds that secret man,
    That all shall hunt him down:
    Though he may roam the forest shade
    Like a bull gone wild from pasture
    To rage through glooms of stone.   15
    Doom comes down on him; flight will not avail him;
    For the world's heart calls him desolate,
    And the immortal voices follow, for ever follow.

10. Parnassos: Mountain sacred to Apollo.

Josef Svoboda's stage design
for M. Machacek's 1963
production of *Oedipus Rex*
in Prague.

Strope 2

But now a wilder thing is heard
From the old man skilled at hearing Fate in the
20 wing-beat of a bird.
Bewildered as a blown bird, my soul hovers and can
  not find
Foothold in this debate, or any reason or rest of
  mind.
But no man ever brought — none can bring
Proof of strife between Thebes' royal house,
25 Labdakos' line, and the son of Polybos;°
And never until now has any man brought word
Of Laios' dark death staining Oedipus the King.

Antistrophe 2

Divine Zeus and Apollo hold
Perfect intelligence alone of all tales ever told;
And well though this diviner works, he works in his
30 own night;
No man can judge that rough unknown or trust in
  second sight,
For wisdom changes hands among the wise.
Shall I believe my great lord criminal
At a raging word that a blind old man let fall?
I saw him, when the carrion woman° faced him of
35 old,
Prove his heroic mind. These evil words are lies.

SCENE 2

KREON: Men of Thebes:
 I am told that heavy accusations
 Have been brought against me by King Oedipus.

 I am not the kind of man to bear this tamely.

5 If in these present difficulties
 He holds me accountable for any harm to him
 Through anything I have said or done — why, then,
 I do not value life in this dishonor.
 It is not as though this rumor touched upon
10 Some private indiscretion. The matter is grave.
 The fact is that I am being called disloyal
 To the State, to my fellow citizens, to my friends.
CHORAGOS: He may have spoken in anger, not from his
  mind.
KREON: But did you not hear him say I was the one
15 Who seduced the old prophet into lying?
CHORAGOS: The thing was said; I do not know how
  seriously.
KREON: But you were watching him! Were his eyes
  steady?

25. Polybos: King who adopted Oedipus. **35. woman:** The
Sphinx.

Did he look like a man in his right mind?
CHORAGOS: I do not know.
 I can not judge the behavior of great men.
 But here is the king himself.

(*Enter Oedipus.*)

OEDIPUS: So you dared come back. 20
 Why? How brazen of you to come to my house,
 You murderer!
     Do you think I do not know
 That you plotted to kill me, plotted to steal my
  throne?
 Tell me, in God's name: am I coward, a fool,
 That you should dream you could accomplish this? 25
 A fool who could not see your slippery game?
 A coward, not to fight back when I saw it?
 You are the fool, Kreon, are you not? hoping
 Without support or friends to get a throne?
 Thrones may be won or bought: you could do
  neither. 30
KREON: Now listen to me. You have talked; let me talk,
  too.
 You can not judge unless you know the facts.
OEDIPUS: You speak well: there is one fact; but I find it
  hard
 To learn from the deadliest enemy I have.
KREON: That above all I must dispute with you. 35
OEDIPUS: That above all I will not hear you deny.
KREON: If you think there is anything good in being
  stubborn
 Against all reason, then I say you are wrong.
OEDIPUS: If you think a man can sin against his own
  kind
 And not be punished for it, I say you are mad. 40
KREON: I agree. But tell me: what have I done to
  you?
OEDIPUS: You advised me to send for that wizard,
  did you not?
KREON: I did. I should do it again.
OEDIPUS: Very well. Now tell me:
 How long has it been since Laios —
KREON: What of Laios?
OEDIPUS: Since he vanished in that onset by the road? 45
KREON: It was long ago, a long time.
OEDIPUS: And this prophet,
 Was he practicing here then?
KREON: He was; and with honor,
  as now.
OEDIPUS: Did he speak of me at that time?
KREON: He never did,
 At least, not when I was present.
OEDIPUS: But . . . the enquiry?
 I suppose you held one?
KREON: We did, but we learned nothing. 50
OEDIPUS: Why did the prophet not speak against me
  then?
KREON: I do not know; and I am the kind of man
 Who holds his tongue when he has no facts to
  go on.

OEDIPUS: There's one fact that you know, and you
  could tell it.
KREON: What fact is that? If I know it, you shall
55 have it.
OEDIPUS: If he were not involved with you, he could
  not say
 That it was I who murdered Laios.
KREON: If he says that, you are the one that knows
  it! —
 But now it is my turn to question you.
60 OEDIPUS: Put your questions. I am no murderer.
KREON: First, then: You married my sister?
OEDIPUS: I married your sister.
KREON: And you rule the kingdom equally with her?
OEDIPUS: Everything that she wants she has from me.
KREON: And I am the third, equal to both of you?
65 OEDIPUS: That is why I call you a bad friend.
KREON: No. Reason it out, as I have done.
 Think of this first: would any sane man prefer
 Power, with all a king's anxieties,
 To that same power and the grace of sleep?
70 Certainly not I.
 I have never longed for the king's power — only his
  rights.
 Would any wise man differ from me in this?
 As matters stand, I have my way in everything
 With your consent, and no responsibilities.
75 If I were king, I should be a slave to policy.
 How could I desire a scepter more
 Than what is now mine — untroubled influence?
 No, I have not gone mad; I need no honors,
 Except those with the perquisites I have now.
80 I am welcome everywhere; every man salutes me,
 And those who want your favor seek my ear,
 Since I know how to manage what they ask.
 Should I exchange this ease for that anxiety?
 Besides, no sober mind is treasonable.
85 I hate anarchy
 And never would deal with any man who likes it.
 Test what I have said. Go to the priestess
 At Delphi, ask if I quoted her correctly.
 And as for this other thing: if I am found
90 Guilty of treason with Teiresias,
 Then sentence me to death. You have my word
 It is a sentence I should cast my vote for —
 But not without evidence!
        You do wrong
 When you take good men for bad, bad men for
  good.
95 A true friend thrown aside — why, life itself
 Is not more precious!
      In time you will know this well:
 For time, and time alone, will show the just man,
 Though scoundrels are discovered in a day.
CHORAGOS: This is well said, and a prudent man
  would ponder it.
100 Judgments too quickly formed are dangerous.
OEDIPUS: But is he not quick in his duplicity?
 And shall I not be quick to parry him?

Would you have me stand still, hold my peace,
 and let
This man win everything, through my inaction?
KREON: And you want — what is it, then? To banish
 me?   105
OEDIPUS: No, not exile. It is your death I want,
 So that all the world may see what treason means.
KREON: You will persist, then? You will not believe
 me?
OEDIPUS: How can I believe you?
KREON: Then you are a fool.
OEDIPUS: To save myself?
KREON: In justice, think of me.   110
OEDIPUS: You are evil incarnate.
KREON: But suppose that you are wrong?
OEDIPUS: Still I must rule.
KREON: But not if you rule badly.
OEDIPUS: O city, city!
KREON: It is my city, too!
CHORAGOS: Now, my lords, be still. I see the queen,
 Iokaste, coming from her palace chambers;   115
 And it is time she came, for the sake of you both.
 This dreadful quarrel can be resolved through her.

(*Enter Iokaste.*)

IOKASTE: Poor foolish men, what wicked din is this?
 With Thebes sick to death, is it not shameful
 That you should take some private quarrel up? 120
 (*To Oedipus.*) Come into the house.
       — And you, Kreon, go now:
 Let us have no more of this tumult over nothing.
KREON: Nothing? No, sister: what your husband plans
 for me
 Is one of two great evils: exile or death.
OEDIPUS: He is right.
     Why, woman I have caught him squarely 125
 Plotting against my life.
KREON: No! Let me die
 Accurst if ever I have wished you harm!
IOKASTE: Ah, believe it, Oedipus!
 In the name of the gods, respect this oath of his
 For my sake, for the sake of these people here! 130

Strophe 1

CHORAGOS: Open your mind to her, my lord. Be ruled
  by her, I beg you!
OEDIPUS: What would you have me do?
CHORAGOS: Respect Kreon's word. He has never
  spoken like a fool,
 And now he has sworn an oath.
OEDIPUS: You know what you ask?
CHORAGOS: I do.
OEDIPUS: Speak on, then.
CHORAGOS: A friend so sworn should not be baited so, 135
 In blind malice, and without final proof.
OEDIPUS: You are aware, I hope, that what you say
 Means death for me, or exile at the least.

Strophe 2

CHORAGOS: No, I swear by Helios, first in heaven!
140   May I die friendless and accurst,
      The worst of deaths, if ever I meant that!
      It is the withering fields
          That hurt my sick heart:
      Must we bear all these ills,
145   And now your bad blood as well?
OEDIPUS: Then let him go. And let me die, if I must,
      Or be driven by him in shame from the land of
          Thebes.
      It is your unhappiness, and not his talk,
      That touches me.
              As for him —
150   Wherever he goes, hatred will follow him.
KREON: Ugly in yielding, as you were ugly in rage!
      Natures like yours chiefly torment themselves.
OEDIPUS: Can you not go? Can you not leave me?
KREON: I can.
      You do not know me; but the city knows me,
155   And in its eyes I am just, if not in yours.
                                      (*Exit Kreon.*)

Antistrophe 1

CHORAGOS: Lady Iokaste, did you not ask the King to
          go to his chambers?
IOKASTE: First tell me what has happened.
CHORAGOS: There was suspicion without evidence; yet
          it rankled
      As even false charges will.
IOKASTE: On both sides?
CHORAGOS: On both.
160 IOKASTE: But what was said?
CHORAGOS: Oh let it rest, let it be done with!
      Have we not suffered enough?
OEDIPUS: You see to what your decency has brought
          you:
      You have made difficulties where my heart saw
          none.

Antistrophe 2

CHORAGOS: Oedipus, it is not once only I have told
165   you —
      You must know I should count myself
          unwise
      To the point of madness, should I now forsake
          you —
          You, under whose hand,
              In the storm of another time,
170   Our dear land sailed out free.
      But now stand fast at the helm!
IOKASTE: In God's name, Oedipus, inform your wife as
          well:
      Why are you so set in this hard anger?

OEDIPUS: I will tell you, for none of these men deserves
      My confidence as you do. It is Kreon's work,   175
      His treachery, his plotting against me.
IOKASTE: Go on, if you can make this clear to me.
OEDIPUS: He charges me with the murder of Laios.
IOKASTE: Has he some knowledge? Or does he speak
          from hearsay?
OEDIPUS: He would not commit himself to such a
          charge,   180
      But he has brought in that damnable soothsayer
      To tell his story.
IOKASTE: Set your mind at rest.
      If it is a question of soothsayers, I tell you
      That you will find no man whose craft gives
          knowledge
      Of the unknowable.
                      Here is my proof: 185
      An oracle was reported to Laios once
      (I will not say from Phoibos himself, but from
      His appointed ministers, at any rate)
      That his doom would be death at the hands of his
          own son —
      His son, born of his flesh and of mine!   190

      Now, you remember the story: Laios was killed
      By marauding strangers where three highways meet;
      But his child had not been three days in this world
      Before the king had pierced the baby's ankles
      And left him to die on a lonely mountainside.   195

      Thus, Apollo never caused that child
      To kill his father, and it was not Laios' fate
      To die at the hands of his son, as he had feared.
      This is what prophets and prophecies are worth!
      Have no dread of them.
                      It is God himself   200
      Who can show us what he wills, in his own way.
OEDIPUS: How strange a shadowy memory crossed my
          mind,
      Just now while you were speaking; it chilled my
          heart.
IOKASTE: What do you mean? What memory do you
          speak of?
OEDIPUS: If I understand you, Laios was killed   205
      At a place where three roads meet.
IOKASTE: So it was said;
      We have no later story.
OEDIPUS: Where did it happen?
IOKASTE: Phokis, it is called: at a place where the
          Theban Way
      Divides into the roads toward Delphi and Daulia.
OEDIPUS: When?
IOKASTE: We had the news not long before you came 210
      And proved the right to your succession here.
OEDIPUS: Ah, what net has God been weaving for me?
IOKASTE: Oedipus! Why does this trouble you?
OEDIPUS: Do not ask me yet.
      First, tell me how Laios looked, and tell me
      How old he was.

215 IOKASTE: He was tall, his hair just touched
       With white; his form was not unlike your own.
     OEDIPUS: I think that I myself may be accurst
       By my own ignorant edict.
     IOKASTE: You speak strangely.
       It makes me tremble to look at you, my king.
220 OEDIPUS: I am not sure that the blind man can not see.
       But I should know better if you were to tell me —
     IOKASTE: Anything — though I dread to hear you ask
       it.
     OEDIPUS: Was the king lightly escorted, or did he ride
       With a large company, as a ruler should?
     IOKASTE: There were five men with him in all: one was
225   a herald;
       And a single chariot, which he was driving.
     OEDIPUS: Alas, that makes it plain enough!
                                          But who —
       Who told you how it happened?
     IOKASTE: A household servant,
       The only one to escape.
     OEDIPUS: And is he still
       A servant of ours?
230 IOKASTE: No; for when he came back at last
       And found you enthroned in the place of the dead
         king,
       He came to me, touched my hand with his, and
         begged
       That I would send him away to the frontier district
       Where only the shepherds go —
235   As far away from the city as I could send him.
       I granted his prayer; for although the man was a
         slave,
       He had earned more than this favor at my hands.
     OEDIPUS: Can he be called back quickly?
     IOKASTE: Easily.
       But why?
240 OEDIPUS: I have taken too much upon myself
       Without enquiry; therefore I wish to consult him.
     IOKASTE: Then he shall come.
                                   But am I not one also
       To whom you might confide these fears of yours?
     OEDIPUS: That is your right; it will not be denied you,
245   Now least of all; for I have reached a pitch
       Of wild foreboding. Is there anyone
       To whom I should sooner speak?

       Polybos of Corinth is my father.
       My mother is a Dorian: Merope.
250   I grew up chief among the men of Corinth
       Until a strange thing happened —
       Not worth my passion, it may be, but strange.
       At a feast, a drunken man maundering in his cups
       Cries out that I am not my father's son!
255   I contained myself that night, though I felt anger
       And a sinking heart. The next day I visited
       My father and mother, and questioned them. They
         stormed,
       Calling it all the slanderous rant of a fool;
       And this relieved me. Yet the suspicion

Remained always aching in my mind;   260
I knew there was talk; I could not rest;
And finally, saying nothing to my parents,
I went to the shrine at Delphi.

The god dismissed my question without reply;
He spoke of other things.
                           Some were clear,   265
Full of wretchedness, dreadful, unbearable:
As, that I should lie with my own mother, breed
Children from whom all men would turn their
    eyes;
And that I should be my father's murderer.

I heard all this, and fled. And from that day   270
Corinth to me was only in the stars
Descending in that quarter of the sky,
As I wandered farther and farther on my way
To a land where I should never see the evil
Sung by the oracle. And I came to this country   275
Where, so you say, King Laios was killed.

I will tell you all that happened there, my lady.
There were three highways
Coming together at a place I passed;
And there a herald came towards me, and a chariot   280
Drawn by horses, with a man such as you describe
Seated in it. The groom leading the horses
Forced me off the road at his lord's command;
But as this charioteer lurched over towards me
I struck him in my rage. The old man saw me   285
And brought his double goad down upon my head
As I came abreast.
                   He was paid back, and more!
Swinging my club in this right hand I knocked him
Out of his car, and he rolled on the ground.
                                   I killed him.

I killed them all.   290
Now if that stranger and Laios were — kin,
Where is a man more miserable than I?
More hated by the gods? Citizen and alien alike
Must never shelter me or speak to me —
I must be shunned by all.
                          And I myself   295
Pronounced this malediction upon myself!

Think of it: I have touched you with these hands,
These hands that killed your husband. What
    defilement!

Am I all evil, then? It must be so,
Since I must flee from Thebes, yet never again   300
See my own countrymen, my own country,
For fear of joining my mother in marriage
And killing Polybos, my father.
                                Ah,
If I was created so, born to this fate,
Who could deny the savagery of God?   305

O holy majesty of heavenly powers!
May I never see that day! Never!
Rather let me vanish from the race of men
Than know the abomination destined me!

310 CHORAGOS: We too, my lord, have felt dismay at this.
But there is hope: you have yet to hear the shepherd.
OEDIPUS: Indeed, I fear no other hope is left me.
IOKASTE: What do you hope from him when he comes?
OEDIPUS: This much:
If his account of the murder tallies with yours,
Then I am cleared.
315 IOKASTE: What was it that I said
Of such importance?
OEDIPUS: Why, "marauders," you said,
Killed the king, according to this man's story.
If he maintains that still, if there were several,
Clearly the guilt is not mine: I was alone.
320 But if he says one man, singlehanded, did it,
Then the evidence all points to me.
IOKASTE: You may be sure that he said there were
              several;
And can he call back that story now? He can not.
The whole city heard it as plainly as I.
325 But suppose he alters some detail of it:
He can not ever show that Laios' death
Fulfilled the oracle: for Apollo said
My child was doomed to kill him; and my child —
Poor baby! — it was my child that died first.

330 No. From now on, where oracles are concerned,
I would not waste a second thought on any.
OEDIPUS: You may be right.
                                 But come: let someone go
For the shepherd at once. This matter must be
              settled.
IOKASTE: I will send for him.
335 I would not wish to cross you in anything,
And surely not in this. — Let us go in.
                    (*Exeunt into the palace.*)

ODE 2 • *Strophe 1*

CHORUS: Let me be reverent in the ways of right,
    Lowly the paths I journey on;
    Let all my words and actions keep
    The laws of the pure universe
5   From highest Heaven handed down.
    For Heaven is their bright nurse,
    Those generations of the realms of light;
    Ah, never of mortal kind were they begot,
    Nor are they slaves of memory, lost in sleep:
10   Their Father is greater than Time, and ages not.

Antistrophe 1

    The tyrant is a child of Pride
    Who drinks from his great sickening cup

    Recklessness and vanity,
    Until from his high crest headlong
    He plummets to the dust of hope.   15
    That strong man is not strong.
    But let no fair ambition be denied;
    May God protect the wrestler for the State
    In government, in comely policy,
    Who will fear God, and on his ordinance wait.   20

Strophe 2

    Haughtiness and the high hand of disdain
    Tempt and outrage God's holy law;
    And any mortal who dares hold
    No immortal Power in awe
    Will be caught up in a net of pain: 25
    The price for which his levity is sold.
    Let each man take due earnings, then,
    And keep his hands from holy things,
    And from blasphemy stand apart —
    Else the crackling blast of heaven   30
    Blows on his head, and on his desperate heart.
    Though fools will honor impious men,
    In their cities no tragic poet sings.

Antistrophe 2

    Shall we lose faith in Delphi's obscurities,
    We who have heard the world's core   35
    Discredited, and the sacred wood
    Of Zeus at Elis praised no more?
    The deeds and the strange prophecies
    Must make a pattern yet to be understood.
    Zeus, if indeed you are lord of all,   40
    Throned in light over night and day,
    Mirror this in your endless mind:
    Our masters call the oracle
    Words on the wind, and the Delphic vision blind!
    Their hearts no longer know Apollo,   45
    And reverence for the gods has died away.

SCENE 3

(*Enter Iokaste.*)

IOKASTE: Princes of Thebes, it has occurred to me
    To visit the altars of the gods, bearing
    These branches as a suppliant, and this incense.
    Our king is not himself: his noble soul
    Is overwrought with fantasies of dread,   5
    Else he would consider
    The new prophecies in the light of the old.
    He will listen to any voice that speaks disaster,
    And my advice goes for nothing. (*She approaches
        the altar, right.*)
                  To you, then, Apollo,

10 Lycean lord, since you are nearest, I turn in prayer
Receive these offerings, and grant us deliverance
From defilement. Our hearts are heavy with fear
When we see our leader distracted, as helpless
        sailors
Are terrified by the confusion of their helmsman.

(*Enter Messenger.*)

15 MESSENGER: Friends, no doubt you can direct me:
Where shall I find the house of Oedipus,
Or, better still, where is the king himself?
CHORAGOS: It is this very place, stranger; he is inside.
This is his wife and mother of his children.
20 MESSENGER: I wish her happiness in a happy house,
Blest in all the fulfillment of her marriage.
IOKASTE: I wish as much for you: your courtesy
Deserves a like good fortune. But now, tell me:
Why have you come? What have you to say to us?
MESSENGER: Good news, my lady, for your house and
25   your husband.
IOKASTE: What news? Who sent you here?
MESSENGER: I am from Corinth.
The news I bring ought to mean joy for you,
Though it may be you will find some grief in it.
IOKASTE: What is it? How can it touch us in both
        ways?
MESSENGER: The word is that the people of the
30   Isthmus
Intend to call Oedipus to be their king.
IOKASTE: But old King Polybos — is he not reigning
        still?
MESSENGER: No. Death holds him in his sepulchre.
IOKASTE: What are you saying? Polybos is dead?
MESSENGER: If I am not telling the truth, may I die
35   myself.
IOKASTE (*to a Maidservant*): Go in, go quickly; tell this
        to your master.
O riddlers of God's will, where are you now!
This was the man whom Oedipus, long ago,
Feared so, fled so, in dread of destroying him —
40 But it was another fate by which he died.

(*Enter Oedipus, center.*)

OEDIPUS: Dearest Iokaste, why have you sent for me?
IOKASTE: Listen to what this man says, and then tell
        me
What has become of the solemn prophecies.
OEDIPUS: Who is this man? What is his news for me?
IOKASTE: He has come from Corinth to announce your
45   father's death!
OEDIPUS: Is it true, stranger? Tell me in your own
        words.
MESSENGER: I can not say it more clearly: the king is
        dead.
OEDIPUS: Was it by treason? Or by an attack of
        illness?
MESSENGER: A little thing brings old men to their rest.
OEDIPUS: It was sickness, then?
50 MESSENGER: Yes, and his many years.

OEDIPUS: Ah!
Why should a man respect the Pythian hearth,° or
Give heed to the birds that jangle above his head?
They prophesied that I should kill Polybos,
Kill my own father; but he is dead and buried,   55
And I am here — I never touched him, never,
Unless he died of grief for my departure,
And thus, in a sense, through me. No. Polybos
Has packed the oracles off with him underground.
They are empty words.
IOKASTE: Had I not told you so?   60
OEDIPUS: You had; it was my faint heart that betrayed
        me.
IOKASTE: From now on never think of those things
        again.
OEDIPUS: And yet — must I not fear my mother's bed?
IOKASTE: Why should anyone in this world be afraid
Since Fate rules us and nothing can be foreseen?   65
A man should live only for the present day.

Have no more fear of sleeping with your mother:
How many men, in dreams, have lain with their
        mothers!
No reasonable man is troubled by such things.
OEDIPUS: That is true, only —   70
If only my mother were not still alive!
But she is alive. I can not help my dread.
IOKASTE: Yet this news of your father's death is
        wonderful.
OEDIPUS: Wonderful. But I fear the living woman.
MESSENGER: Tell me, who is this woman that you fear?   75
OEDIPUS: It is Merope, man; the wife of King Polybos.
MESSENGER: Merope? Why should you be afraid of
        her?
OEDIPUS: An oracle of the gods, a dreadful saying.
MESSENGER: Can you tell me about it or are you sworn
        to silence?
OEDIPUS: I can tell you, and I will.   80
Apollo said through his prophet that I was the man
Who should marry his own mother, shed his father's
        blood
With his own hands. And so, for all these years
I have kept clear of Corinth, and no harm has
        come —
Though it would have been sweet to see my parents
        again.   85
MESSENGER: And is this the fear that drove you out of
        Corinth?
OEDIPUS: Would you have me kill my father?
MESSENGER: As for that
You must be reassured by the news I gave you.
OEDIPUS: If you could reassure me, I would reward
        you.
MESSENGER: I had that in mind, I will confess: I
        thought   90
I could count on you when you returned to Corinth.
OEDIPUS: No: I will never go near my parents again.

52. Pythian hearth: Delphi.

MESSENGER: Ah, son, you still do not know what you
    are doing —
OEDIPUS: What do you mean? In the name of God tell
    me!
MESSENGER: — If these are your reasons for not going
95   home.
OEDIPUS: I tell you, I fear the oracle may come true.
MESSENGER: And guilt may come upon you through
    your parents?
OEDIPUS: That is the dread that is always in my heart.
MESSENGER: Can you not see that all your fears are
    groundless?
100 OEDIPUS: Groundless? Am I not my parents' son?
MESSENGER: Polybos was not your father.
OEDIPUS: Not my father?
MESSENGER: No more your father than the man
    speaking to you.
OEDIPUS: But you are nothing to me!
MESSENGER: Neither was he.
OEDIPUS: Then why did he call me son?
MESSENGER: I will tell you:
105   Long ago he had you from my hands, as a gift.
OEDIPUS: Then how could he love me so, if I was not
    his?
MESSENGER: He had no children, and his heart turned
    to you.
OEDIPUS: What of you? Did you buy me? Did you find
    me by chance?
MESSENGER: I came upon you in the woody vales of
    Kithairon.
OEDIPUS: And what were you doing there?
110 MESSENGER: Tending my flocks.
OEDIPUS: A wandering shepherd?
MESSENGER: But your savior, son, that day.
OEDIPUS: From what did you save me?
MESSENGER: Your ankles should tell you that.
OEDIPUS: Ah, stranger, why do you speak of that
    childhood pain?
MESSENGER: I pulled the skewer that pinned your feet
    together.
OEDIPUS: I have had the mark as long as I can
115   remember.
MESSENGER: That was why you were given the name°
    you bear.
OEDIPUS: God! Was it my father or my mother who
    did it?
    Tell me!
MESSENGER: I do not know. The man who gave you
    to me
    Can tell you better than I.
120 OEDIPUS: It was not you that found me, but another?
MESSENGER: It was another shepherd gave you to me.
OEDIPUS: Who was he? Can you tell me who he was?
MESSENGER: I think he was said to be one of Laios'
    people.
OEDIPUS: You mean the Laios who was king here years
    ago?

---

116. name: "Oedipus" literally means swollen foot.

MESSENGER: Yes; King Laios; and the man was one of
    his herdsmen.   125
OEDIPUS: Is he still alive? Can I see him?
MESSENGER: These men here
    Know best about such things.
OEDIPUS: Does anyone here
    Know this shepherd that he is talking about?
    Have you seen him in the fields, or in the town?
    If you have, tell me. It is time things were made
    plain.   130
CHORAGOS: I think the man he means is that same
    shepherd
    You have already asked to see. Iokaste perhaps
    Could tell you something.
OEDIPUS: Do you know anything
    About him, Lady? Is he the man we have
    summoned?
    Is that the man this shepherd means?
IOKASTE: Why think of him? 135
    Forget this herdsman. Forget it all.
    This talk is a waste of time.
OEDIPUS: How can you say that,
    When the clues to my true birth are in my hands?
IOKASTE: For God's love, let us have no more
    questioning!
    Is your life nothing to you?   140
    My own is pain enough for me to bear.
OEDIPUS: You need not worry. Suppose my mother a
    slave,
    And born of slaves: no baseness can touch you.
IOKASTE: Listen to me, I beg you: do not do this thing!
OEDIPUS: I will not listen; the truth must be made
    known.   145
IOKASTE: Everything that I say is for your own good!
OEDIPUS: My own good
    Snaps my patience, then; I want none of it.
IOKASTE: You are fatally wrong! May you never learn
    who you are!
OEDIPUS: Go, one of you, and bring the shepherd here.
    Let us leave this woman to brag of her royal name. 150
IOKASTE: Ah, miserable!
    That is the only word I have for you now.
    That is the only word I can ever have.
                          (*Exit into the palace.*)
CHORAGOS: Why has she left us, Oedipus? Why has
    she gone
    In such a passion of sorrow? I fear this silence: 155
    Something dreadful may come of it.
OEDIPUS: Let it come!
    However base my birth, I must know about it.
    The Queen, like a woman, is perhaps ashamed
    To think of my low origin. But I
    Am a child of Luck, I can not be dishonored. 160
    Luck is my mother; the passing months, my
    brothers,
    Have seen me rich and poor.
                          If this is so,
    How could I wish that I were someone else?
    How could I not be glad to know my birth?

ODE 3 • *Strophe*

CHORUS: If ever the coming time were known
   To my heart's pondering,
   Kithairon, now by Heaven I see the torches
   At the festival of the next full moon
5   And see the dance, and hear the choir sing
   A grace to your gentle shade:
   Mountain where Oedipus was found,
   O mountain guard of a noble race!
   May the god° who heals us lend his aid,
10 And let that glory come to pass
   For our king's cradling-ground.

Antistrophe

   Of the nymphs that flower beyond the years,
   Who bore you,° royal child,
   To Pan° of the hills or the timberline Apollo,
15 Cold in delight where the upland clears,
   Or Hermes° for whom Kyllene's° heights are piled?
   Or flushed as evening cloud,
   Great Dionysos,° roamer of mountains,
   He — was it he who found you there,
20 And caught you up in his own proud
   Arms from the sweet god-ravisher
   Who laughed by the Muses'° fountains?

SCENE 4

OEDIPUS: Sirs: though I do not know the man,
   I think I see him coming, this shepherd we want:
   He is old, like our friend here, and the men
   Bringing him seem to be servants of my house.
5   But you can tell, if you have ever seen him.

(*Enter Shepherd escorted by Servants.*)

CHORAGOS: I know him, he was Laios' man. You can
   trust him.
OEDIPUS: Tell me first, you from Corinth: is this the
   shepherd
   We were discussing?
MESSENGER: This is the very man.
OEDIPUS (*to Shepherd*): Come here. No, look at me.
   You must answer
10 Everything I ask. — You belonged to Laios?

---

9. **god:** Apollo.   13. **Who bore you:** The Chorus is asking if
Oedipus is the son of an immortal nymph and a god: Pan,
Apollo, Hermes, or Dionysus.   14. **Pan:** God of nature,
forests, flocks, and shepherds, depicted as half-man and half-
goat.   16. **Hermes:** Son of Zeus, messenger of the gods.
Kyllene: Mountain reputed to be the birthplace of Hermes; also
the center of a cult to Hermes.   18. **Dionysos:** (Dionysus) God
of wine around whom wild, orgiastic rituals developed; also
called Bacchus.   22. **Muses:** Nine sister goddesses who presided over poetry and music, art and sciences.

SHEPHERD: Yes: born his slave, brought up in his
   house.
OEDIPUS: Tell me: what kind of work did you do for
   him?
SHEPHERD: I was a shepherd of his, most of my life.
OEDIPUS: Where mainly did you go for pasturage?
SHEPHERD: Sometimes Kithairon, sometimes the hills
   near-by.   15
OEDIPUS: Do you remember ever seeing this man out
   there?
SHEPHERD: What would he be doing there? This man?
OEDIPUS: This man standing here. Have you ever seen
   him before?
SHEPHERD: No. At least, not to my recollection.
MESSENGER: And that is not strange, my lord. But I'll
   refresh   20
   His memory: he must remember when we two
   Spent three whole seasons together, March to
   September,
   On Kithairon or thereabouts. He had two flocks;
   I had one. Each autumn I'd drive mine home
   And he would go back with his to Laios'
   sheepfold. —   25
   Is this not true, just as I have described it?
SHEPHERD: True, yes; but it was all so long ago.
MESSENGER: Well, then: do you remember, back in
   those days,
   That you gave me a baby boy to bring up as my
   own?
SHEPHERD: What if I did? What are you trying to say? 30
MESSENGER: King Oedipus was once that little child.
SHEPHERD: Damn you, hold your tongue!
OEDIPUS: No more of that!
   It is your tongue needs watching, not this man's.
SHEPHERD: My king, my master, what is it I have done
   wrong?
OEDIPUS: You have not answered his question about
   the boy.   35
SHEPHERD: He does not know . . . He is only making
   trouble . . .
OEDIPUS: Come, speak plainly, or it will go hard with
   you.
SHEPHERD: In God's name, do not torture an old man!
OEDIPUS: Come here, one of you; bind his arms behind
   him.
SHEPHERD: Unhappy king! What more do you wish to
   learn?   40
OEDIPUS: Did you give this man the child he speaks of?
SHEPHERD: I did.
   And I would to God I had died that very day.
OEDIPUS: You will die now unless you speak the truth.
SHEPHERD: Yet if I speak the truth, I am worse than
   dead.
OEDIPUS (*to Attendant*): He intends to draw it out,
   apparently —   45
SHEPHERD: No! I have told you already that I gave him
   the boy.
OEDIPUS: Where did you get him? From your house?
   From somewhere else?

The Shepherd (Oliver Cliff) tells Oedipus (Kenneth Welsh) the truth about his birth in the Guthrie Theater Company's 1973 production directed by Michael Langham.

SHEPHERD: Not from mine, no. A man gave him
    to me.
OEDIPUS: Is that man here? Whose house did he
    belong to?
SHEPHERD: For God's love, my king, do not ask me any
50   more!
OEDIPUS: You are a dead man if I have to ask you
    again.
SHEPHERD: Then . . . Then the child was from the
    palace of Laios.
OEDIPUS: A slave child? or a child of his own line?
SHEPHERD: Ah, I am on the brink of dreadful speech!
55 OEDIPUS: And I of dreadful hearing. Yet I must hear.
SHEPHERD: If you must be told, then . . .
                    They said it was Laios' child;
    But it is your wife who can tell you about that.
OEDIPUS: My wife — Did she give it to you?
SHEPHERD: My lord, she did.
OEDIPUS: Do you know why?
SHEPHERD: I was told to get rid of it.
OEDIPUS: Oh heartless mother!
60 SHEPHERD: But in dread of prophecies . . .
OEDIPUS: Tell me.
SHEPHERD: It was said that the boy would kill
    his own father.
OEDIPUS: Then why did you give him over to this old
    man?
SHEPHERD: I pitied the baby, my king,
    And I thought that this man would take him far
    away
    To his own country.
65   He saved him — but for what a fate!
    For if you are what this man says you are,
    No man living is more wretched than Oedipus.
OEDIPUS: Ah God!
    It was true!
        All the prophecies!
                   — Now,
70 O Light, may I look on you for the last time!
I, Oedipus,
Oedipus, damned in his birth, in his marriage
    damned,
Damned in the blood he shed with his own hand!

(*He rushes into the palace.*)

ODE 4 • *Strophe 1*

CHORUS: Alas for the seed of men.
    What measure shall I give these generations
    That breathe on the void and are void
    And exist and do not exist?
5   Who bears more weight of joy
    Than mass of sunlight shifting in images,
    Or who shall make his thought stay on
    That down time drifts away?
    Your splendor is all fallen.
10   O naked brow of wrath and tears,

O change of Oedipus!
I who saw your days call no man blest —
Your great days like ghosts gone.

Antistrophe 1

That mind was a strong bow.
Deep, how deep you drew it then, hard archer,   15
At a dim fearful range,
And brought dear glory down!
You overcame the stranger° —
The virgin with her hooking lion claws —
And though death sang, stood like a tower   20
To make pale Thebes take heart.
Fortress against our sorrow!
True king, giver of laws,
Majestic Oedipus!
No prince in Thebes had ever such renown,   25
No prince won such grace of power.

Strophe 2

And now of all men ever known
Most pitiful is this man's story:
His fortunes are most changed; his state
Fallen to a low slave's   30
Ground under bitter fate.
O Oedipus, most royal one!
The great door° that expelled you to the light
Gave at night — ah, gave night to your glory:
As to the father, to the fathering son.   35
All understood too late.
How could that queen whom Laios won,
The garden that he harrowed at his height,
Be silent when that act was done?

Antistrophe 2

But all eyes fail before time's eye,   40
All actions come to justice there.
Though never willed, though far down the deep
    past,
Your bed, your dread sirings,
Are brought to book at last.
Child by Laios doomed to die,   45
Then doomed to lose that fortunate little death,
Would God you never took breath in this air
That with my wailing lips I take to cry:
For I weep the world's outcast.
I was blind, and now I can tell why:
Asleep, for you had given ease of breath
To Thebes, while the false years went by.   50

18. stranger: The Sphinx.   **33. door:** Iokaste's womb.

EXODOS°

(*Enter, from the palace, Second Messenger.*)

SECOND MESSENGER: Elders of Thebes, most honored
      in this land,
   What horrors are yours to see and hear, what
      weight
   Of sorrow to be endured, if, true to your birth,
   You venerate the line of Labdakos!
5   I think neither Istros nor Phasis, those great rivers,
   Could purify this place of all the evil
   It shelters now, or soon must bring to light —
   Evil not done unconsciously, but willed.

   The greatest griefs are those we cause ourselves.
CHORAGOS: Surely, friend, we have grief enough
10   already;
   What new sorrow do you mean?
SECOND MESSENGER: The queen is dead.
CHORAGOS: O miserable queen! But at whose hand?
SECOND MESSENGER: Her own.
   The full horror of what happened you can not
      know,
   For you did not see it; but I, who did, will tell you
15   As clearly as I can how she met her death.

   When she had left us,
   In passionate silence, passing through the court,
   She ran to her apartment in the house,
   Her hair clutched by the fingers of both hands.
   She closed the doors behind her; then, by that bed
20   Where long ago the fatal son was conceived —
   That son who should bring about his father's
      death —
   We heard her call upon Laios, dead so many years,
   And heard her wail for the double fruit of her
      marriage,
25   A husband by her husband, children by her child.

   Exactly how she died I do not know:
   For Oedipus burst in moaning and would not let us
   Keep vigil to the end: it was by him
   As he stormed about the room that our eyes were
      caught.
   From one to another of us he went, begging a
30   sword,
   Hunting the wife who was not his wife, the mother
   Whose womb had carried his own children and
      himself.
   I do not know: it was none of us aided him,
   But surely one of the gods was in control!
35   For with a dreadful cry
   He hurled his weight, as though wrenched out of
      himself,
   At the twin doors: the bolts gave, and he rushed in.
   And there we saw her hanging, her body swaying

Exodos: Final scene.

From the cruel cord she had noosed about her neck.
A great sob broke from him, heartbreaking to hear,   40
As he loosed the rope and lowered her to the
   ground.

I would blot out from my mind what happened
   next!
For the king ripped from her gown the golden
   brooches
That were her ornament, and raised them, and
   plunged them down
Straight into his own eyeballs, crying, "No more,   45
No more shall you look on the misery about me,
The horrors of my own doing! Too long you have
   known
The faces of those whom I should never have seen,
Too long been blind to those for whom I was
   searching!
From this hour, go in darkness!" And as he spoke,   50
He struck at his eyes — not once, but many times;
And the blood spattered his beard,
Bursting from his ruined sockets like red hail.

So from the unhappiness of two this evil has sprung,
A curse on the man and woman alike. The old   55
Happiness of the house of Labdakos
Was happiness enough: where is it today?
It is all wailing and ruin, disgrace, death — all
The misery of mankind that has a name —
And it is wholly and for ever theirs.   60
CHORAGOS: Is he in agony still? Is there no rest for
   him?
SECOND MESSENGER: He is calling for someone to open
      the doors wide
   So that all the children of Kadmos may look upon
   His father's murderer, his mother's — no,
   I can not say it!
                  And then he will leave Thebes,   65
   Self-exiled, in order that the curse
   Which he himself pronounced may depart from the
      house.
   He is weak, and there is none to lead him,
   So terrible is his suffering.
                        But you will see:
   Look, the doors are opening; in a moment   70
   You will see a thing that would crush a heart of
      stone.

(*The central door is opened; Oedipus, blinded, is led in.*)

CHORAGOS: Dreadful indeed for men to see.
   Never have my own eyes
   Looked on a sight so full of fear.

   Oedipus!   75
   What madness came upon you, what demon
   Leaped on your life with heavier
   Punishment than a mortal man can bear?
   No: I can not even
   Look at you, poor ruined one.   80

And I would speak, question, ponder,
If I were able. No.
You make me shudder.
OEDIPUS: God. God.
85   Is there a sorrow greater?
Where shall I find harbor in this world?
My voice is hurled far on a dark wind.
What has God done to me?
CHORAGOS: Too terrible to think of, or to see.

Strophe 1

90   OEDIPUS: O cloud of night,
Never to be turned away: night coming on,
I can not tell how: night like a shroud!
My fair winds brought me here.
                                    O God. Again
The pain of the spikes where I had sight,
95   The flooding pain
Of memory, never to be gouged out.
CHORAGOS: This is not strange.
You suffer it all twice over, remorse in pain,
Pain in remorse.

Antistrophe 1

100 OEDIPUS: Ah dear friend
Are you faithful even yet, you alone?
Are you still standing near me, will you stay here,
Patient, to care for the blind?
                                    The blind man!
Yet even blind I know who it is attends me,
105   By the voice's tone —
Though my new darkness hide the comforter.
CHORAGOS: Oh fearful act!
What god was it drove you to rake black
Night across your eyes?

Strophe 2

110 OEDIPUS: Apollo. Apollo. Dear
Children, the god was Apollo.
He brought my sick, sick fate upon me.
But the blinding hand was my own!
How could I bear to see
115   When all my sight was horror everywhere?
CHORAGOS: Everywhere; that is true.
OEDIPUS: And now what is left?
Images? Love? A greeting even,
Sweet to the senses? Is there anything?
120   Ah, no, friends: lead me away.
Lead me away from Thebes.
                                    Lead the great wreck
And hell of Oedipus, whom the gods hate.
CHORAGOS: Your misery, you are not blind to that.
Would God you had never found it out!

Antistrophe 2

OEDIPUS: Death take the man who unbound   125
My feet on that hillside
And delivered me from death to life! What life?
If only I had died,
This weight of monstrous doom
Could not have dragged me and my darlings down.   130
CHORAGOS: I would have wished the same.
OEDIPUS: Oh never to have come here
With my father's blood upon me! Never
To have been the man they call his mother's husband!
Oh accurst! Oh child of evil,   135
To have entered that wretched bed —
                                    the selfsame one!
More primal than sin itself, this fell to me.
CHORAGOS: I do not know what words to offer you.
You were better dead than alive and blind.
OEDIPUS: Do not counsel me any more. This
          punishment   140
That I have laid upon myself is just.
If I had eyes,
I do not know how I could bear the sight
Of my father, when I came to the house of Death,
Or my mother: for I have sinned against them both 145
So vilely that I could not make my peace
By strangling my own life.
                          Or do you think my children,
Born as they were born, would be sweet to my eyes?
Ah never, never! Nor this town with its high walls,
Nor the holy images of the gods.
                                    For I,   150
Thrice miserable! — Oedipus, noblest of all the line
Of Kadmos, have condemned myself to enjoy
These things no more, by my own malediction
Expelling that man whom the gods declared
To be a defilement in the house of Laios.   155
After exposing the rankness of my own guilt,
How could I look men frankly in the eyes?
No, I swear it,
If I could have stifled my hearing at its source,
I would have done it and made all this body   160
A tight cell of misery, blank to light and sound:
So I should have been safe in my dark mind
Beyond external evil.
                          Ah Kithairon!
Why did you shelter me? When I was cast upon you,
Why did I not die? Then I should never   165
Have shown the world my execrable birth.

Ah Polybos! Corinth, city that I believed
The ancient seat of my ancestors: how fair
I seemed, your child! And all the while this evil
Was cancerous within me!
                                    For I am sick   170
In my own being, sick in my origin.
O three roads, dark ravine, woodland and way
Where three roads met; you, drinking my father's
          blood,

My own blood, spilled by my own hand: can you
    remember
175 The unspeakable things I did there, and the things
I went on from there to do?
                O marriage, marriage!
The act that engendered me, and again the act
Performed by the son in the same bed —
                      Ah, the net
Of incest, mingling fathers, brothers, sons,
180 With brides, wives, mothers: the last evil
That can be known by men: no tongue can say
How evil!
        No. For the love of God, conceal me
Somewhere far from Thebes; or kill me; or hurl me
Into the sea, away from men's eyes for ever.

185 Come, lead me. You need nor fear to touch me.
Of all men, I alone can bear this guilt.

(*Enter Kreon.*)

CHORAGOS: Kreon is here now. As to what you ask,
He may decide the course to take. He only
Is left to protect the city in your place.
OEDIPUS: Alas, how can I speak to him? What right
190   have I
To beg his courtesy whom I have deeply wronged?
KREON: I have not come to mock you, Oedipus,
Or to reproach you, either.
(*To Attendants.*)   — You, standing there:
If you have lost all respect for man's dignity,
195 At least respect the flame of Lord Helios:°
Do not allow this pollution to show itself
Openly here, an affront to the earth
And Heaven's rain and the light of day. No, take
    him
Into the house as quickly as you can.
200 For it is proper
That only the close kindred see his grief.
OEDIPUS: I pray you in God's name, since your
    courtesy
Ignores my dark expectation, visiting
With mercy this man of all men most execrable:
205 Give me what I ask — for your good, not for mine.
KREON: And what is it that you turn to me begging for?
OEDIPUS: Drive me out of this country as quickly as
    may be
To a place where no human voice can ever greet
    me.
KREON: I should have done that before now — only,
210 God's will had not been wholly revealed to me.
OEDIPUS: But his command is plain: the parricide
Must be destroyed. I am that evil man.
KREON: That is the sense of it, yes; but as things are,
We had best discover clearly what is to be done.
215 OEDIPUS: You would learn more about a man like me?
KREON: You are ready now to listen to the god.

195. Lord Helios: The sun god.

OEDIPUS: I will listen. But it is to you
That I must turn for help. I beg you, hear me.

The woman is there —
Give her whatever funeral you think proper: 220
She is your sister.
             — But let me go, Kreon!
Let me purge my father's Thebes of the pollution
Of my living here, and go out to the wild hills,
To Kithairon, that has won such fame with me,
The tomb my mother and father appointed for me,   225
And let me die there, as they willed I should.
And yet I know
Death will not ever come to me through sickness
Or in any natural way: I have been preserved
For some unthinkable fate. But let that be.   230

As for my sons, you need not care for them.
They are men, they will find some way to live.
But my poor daughters, who have shared my table,
Who never before have been parted from their
    father —
Take care of them, Kreon; do this for me.   235

And will you let me touch them with my hands
A last time, and let us weep together?
Be kind, my lord,
Great prince, be kind!
                Could I but touch them,
They would be mine again, as when I had my eyes.   240

(*Enter Antigone and Ismene, attended.*)

Ah, God!
Is it my dearest children I hear weeping?
Has Kreon pitied me and sent my daughters?
KREON: Yes, Oedipus: I knew that they were dear to
    you
In the old days, and know you must love them still.   245
OEDIPUS: May God bless you for this — and be a
    friendlier
Guardian to you than he has been to me!

Children, where are you?
Come quickly to my hands: they are your
    brother's —
Hands that have brought your father's once clear
    eyes   250
To this way of seeing —
                Ah dearest ones,
I had neither sight nor knowledge then, your father
By the woman who was the source of his own life!
And I weep for you — having no strength to see
    you —,
I weep for you when I think of the bitterness   255
That men will visit upon you all your lives.
What homes, what festivals can you attend
Without being forced to depart again in tears?
And when you come to marriageable age,

260 Where is the man, my daughters, who would dare
Risk the bane that lies on all my children?
Is there any evil wanting? Your father killed
His father; sowed the womb of her who bore him;
Engendered you at the fount of his own existence!
That is what they will say of you.

265   Then, whom
Can you ever marry? There are no bridegrooms for
   you,
And your lives must wither away in sterile
   dreaming.

O Kreon, son of Menoikeus!
You are the only father my daughters have,
270 Since we, their parents, are both of us gone for ever.
They are your own blood: you will not let them
Fall into beggary and loneliness;
You will keep them from the miseries that are mine!
Take pity on them; see, they are only children,
275 Friendless except for you. Promise me this,
Great prince, and give me your hand in token of it.

(Kreon clasps his right hand.)

Children:
I could say much, if you could understand me,
But as it is, I have only this prayer for you:
280 Live where you can, be as happy as you can —
Happier, please God, than God has made your
   father.
KREON: Enough. You have wept enough. Now go
   within.

OEDIPUS: I must, but it is hard.
KREON: Time eases all things.
OEDIPUS: You know my mind, then?
KREON: Say what you desire.
OEDIPUS: Send me from Thebes!
KREON: God grant that I may!   285
OEDIPUS: But since God hates me . . .
KREON: No, he will grant your wish.
OEDIPUS: You promise?
KREON: I can not speak beyond my knowledge.
OEDIPUS: Then lead me in.
KREON: Come now, and leave your children.   290
OEDIPUS: No! Do not take them from me!
KREON: Think no longer
That you are in command here, but rather think
How, when you were, you served your own
   destruction.

*(Exeunt into the house all but
the Chorus; the Choragos
chants directly to the audience.)*

CHORAGOS: Men of Thebes: look upon Oedipus.

This is the king who solved the famous riddle   295
And towered up, most powerful of men.
No mortal eyes but looked on him with envy,
Yet in the end ruin swept over him.

Let every man in mankind's frailty
Consider his last day; and let none   300
Presume on his good fortune until he find
Life, at his death, a memory without pain.

COMMENTARIES

Critical comment on the plays of Sophocles has been rich and various and has spanned the centuries. We are especially fortunate to have a commentary from the great age of Greek thought a century after Sophocles himself flourished. In *Oedipus Rex* Sophocles gave the philosopher Aristotle a perfect drama on which to build a theory of tragedy, and Aristotle's observations have remained the most influential comments made on drama in the West. In some ways they have established the function, limits, and purposes of drama. In the twentieth century, for instance, when Bertolt Brecht tried to create a new theory of the drama, he specifically described his ideas as an alternative to Aristotelian notions.

Although not a critic, Sigmund Freud saw in the Oedipus myth as interpreted by Sophocles a basic psychological phenomenon experienced by all people in their infancy. This "Oedipus complex" is now well established in psychology and in the popular imagination.

The extraordinary range of commentary on the Oedipus story is demonstrated nowhere more amazingly than in Claude Lévi-Strauss's structural reading of the myth, both in Sophocles' version and in other versions. Lévi-Strauss shows that a pattern emerges when certain actions in the play are placed side by side. If he is correct, his theory offers a way to interpret myths and to see why they were valued so highly by the Greeks in their drama.

Aristotle (384–322 B.C.)

POETICS: COMEDY AND EPIC AND TRAGEDY   *c. 334–323 B.C.*

TRANSLATED BY GERALD F. ELSE

Aristotle was Plato's most brilliant student and the heir of his teaching mantle. He remained with Plato for twenty years and then began his own school, called the Lyceum. His extant work consists mainly of his lectures, which were recorded by his students and carefully preserved. Called his treatises, they have greatly influenced later thought and deal with almost every branch of philosophy, science, and the arts. His Poetics remains, more than two thousand years later, a document of immense importance for literary criticism. Although sometimes ambiguous, difficult, and unfinished, it provides insight into the theoretical basis of Greek tragedy and comedy, and it helps us see that the drama was significant enough in intellectual life to warrant an examination by the best Greek minds.

Comedy

Comedy is, as we said it was, an imitation of persons who are inferior; not, however, going all the way to full villainy, but imitating the ugly, of which the ludicrous is one part. The ludicrous, that is, is a failing or a piece of ugliness which causes no pain or destruction; thus, to go on farther, the comic mask° is something ugly and distorted but painless.

Now the stages of development of tragedy, and the men who were responsible for them, have not escaped notice but comedy did escape notice in the beginning because it was not taken seriously. (In fact it was late in its history that the presiding magistrate officially "granted a chorus" to the comic poets; until then they were volunteers.) Thus comedy already possessed certain defining characteristics when the first "comic poets," so-called, appear in the record. Who gave it masks, or prologues, or troupes of actors and all that sort of thing is not known. The composing of plots came originally from Sicily; of the Athenian poets, Crates° was the first to abandon the lampooning mode and compose arguments, that is, plots, of a general nature.

---

the comic mask: Actors in Greek drama wore masks behind which they spoke their lines. The masks were made individually for each character.

Crates: Greek actor and playwright (fl. 470 B.C.), credited by Aristotle with developing Greek comedy into a fully plotted, credible form. Aristophanes (c. 448–c. 385 B.C.), another Greek comic playwright, says that Crates was the first to portray a drunkard onstage.

Epic and Tragedy

Well, then, epic poetry followed in the wake of tragedy up to the point of being a (1) good-sized (2) imitation (3) in verse (4) of people who are to be taken seriously; but in its having its verse unmixed with any other and being narrative in character, there they differ. Further, so far as its length is concerned, tragedy tries as hard as it can to exist during a single daylight period, or to vary but little, while the epic is not limited in its time and so differs in that respect. Yet originally they used to do this in tragedies just as much as they did in epic poems.

The constituent elements are partly identical and partly limited to tragedy. Hence anybody who knows about good and bad tragedy knows about epic also; for the elements that the epic possesses appertain to tragedy as well, but those of tragedy are not all found in the epic.

Tragedy and Its Six Constituent Elements

Our discussions of imitative poetry in hexameters,° and of comedy, will come later; at present let us deal with tragedy, recovering from what has been said so far the definition of its essential nature, as it was in development. Tragedy, then, is a process of imitating an action which has serious implications, is complete, and possesses magnitude; by means of language which has been made sensuously attractive, with each of its varieties found separately in the parts; enacted by the persons themselves and not presented through narrative; through a course of pity and fear completing the purification of tragic acts which have those emotional characteristics. By "language made sensuously attractive" I mean language that has rhythm and melody, and by "its varieties found separately" I mean the fact that certain parts of the play are carried on through spoken verses alone and others the other way around, through song.

Now first of all, since they perform the imitation through action (by acting it), the adornment of their visual appearance will perforce constitute some part of the making of tragedy; and song-composition and verbal expression also, for those are the media in which they perform the imitation. By "verbal expression" I mean the actual composition of the verses, and by "song-composition" something whose meaning is entirely clear.

Next, since it is an imitation of an action and is enacted by certain people who are performing the action, and since those people must necessarily have certain traits both of character and thought (for it is thanks to these two factors that we speak of people's actions also as having a defined character, and it is in accordance with their actions that all either succeed or fail); and since the imitation of the action is the plot, for by "plot" I mean here the structuring of the events, and by the "characters" that in accordance with which we say that the persons who are acting have a defined moral character, and by "thought" all the passages in which they attempt to prove some thesis or set forth an opinion — it follows of necessity, then, that tragedy as a whole has just six constituent elements, in relation to the essence that makes it a distinct species; and they are plot, characters, verbal expression, thought, visual adornment, and song-composition. For the elements by which they imitate are two (i.e., verbal expression and song-composition), the manner in

---

hexameters: The first known metrical form for classical verse. Each line had six metrical feet, some of which were prescribed in advance. It is the meter used for epic poetry and for poetry designed to teach a lesson. The form has sometimes been used in comparatively modern poetry but rarely with success except in French.

which they imitate is one (visual adornment), the things they imitate are three (plot, characters, thought), and there is nothing more beyond these. These then are the constituent forms they use.

The Relative Importance of the Six Elements

The greatest of these elements is the structuring of the incidents. For tragedy is an imitation not of men but of a life, an action, and they have moral quality in accordance with their characters but are happy or unhappy in accordance with their actions; hence they are not active in order to imitate their characters, but they include the characters along with the actions for the sake of the latter. Thus the structure of events, the plot, is the goal of tragedy, and the goal is the greatest thing of all.

Again: a tragedy cannot exist without a plot, but it can without characters: thus the tragedies of most of our modern poets are devoid of character, and in general many poets are like that; so also with the relationship between Zeuxis and Polygnotus,° among the painters: Polygnotus is a good portrayer of character, while Zeuxis's painting has no dimension of character at all.

Again: if one strings end to end speeches that are expressive of character and carefully worked in thought and expression, he still will not achieve the result which we said was the aim of tragedy; the job will be done much better by a tragedy that is more deficient in these other respects but has a plot, a structure of events. It is much the same case as with painting: the most beautiful pigments smeared on at random will not give as much pleasure as a black-and-white outline picture. Besides, the most powerful means tragedy has for swaying our feelings, namely the peripeties and recognitions,° are elements of plot.

Again: an indicative sign is that those who are beginning a poetic career manage to hit the mark in verbal expression and character portrayal sooner than they do in plot construction; and the same is true of practically all the earliest poets.

So plot is the basic principle, the heart and soul, as it were, of tragedy, and the characters come second: [. . .] it is the imitation of an action and imitates the persons primarily for the sake of their action.

Third in rank is thought. This is the ability to state the issues and appropriate points pertaining to a given topic, an ability which springs from the arts of politics and rhetoric; in fact the earlier poets made their characters talk "politically," the present-day poets rhetorically. But "character" is that kind of utterance which clearly reveals the bent of a man's moral choice (hence there is no character in that class of utterances in which there is nothing at all that the speaker is choosing or rejecting), while "thought" is the passages in which they try to prove that something is so or not so, or state some general principle.

Fourth is the verbal expression of the speeches. I mean by this the same thing that was said earlier, that the "verbal expression" is the conveyance of thought through language: a statement which has the same meaning whether one says "verses" or "speeches."

Zeuxis and Polygnotus: Zeuxis (fl. 420–390 B.C.) developed a method of painting in which the figures were rounded and apparently three-dimensional. Thus, he was an illusionistic painter, imitating life in a realistic style. Polygnotus (c. 470–440 B.C.) was famous as a painter, and his works were on the Acropolis as well as at Delphi. His draftsmanship was especially praised.

peripeties and recognitions: The turning about of fortune and the recognition on the part of the tragic hero of the truth. This is, for Aristotle, a critical moment in the drama, especially if both events happen simultaneously, as they do in *Oedipus Rex*. It is quite possible for these moments to happen apart from one another.

The song-composition of the remaining parts is the greatest of the sensuous attractions, and the visual adornment of the dramatic persons can have a strong emotional effect but is the least artistic element, the least connected with the poetic art; in fact the force of tragedy can be felt even without benefit of public performance and actors, while for the production of the visual effect the property man's art is even more decisive than that of the poets.

General Principles of the Tragic Plot

With these distinctions out of the way, let us next discuss what the structuring of the events should be like, since this is both the basic and the most important element in the tragic art. We have established, then, that tragedy is an imitation of an action which is complete and whole and has some magnitude (for there is also such a thing as a whole that has no magnitude). "Whole" is that which has beginning, middle, and end. "Beginning" is that which does not necessarily follow on something else, but after it something else naturally is or happens; "end," the other way around, is that which naturally follows on something else, either necessarily or for the most part, but nothing else after it; and "middle" that which naturally follows on something else and something else on it. So, then, well constructed plots should neither begin nor end at any chance point but follow the guidelines just laid down.

Furthermore, since the beautiful, whether a living creature or anything that is composed of parts, should not only have these in a fixed order to one another but also possess a definite size which does not depend on chance — for beauty depends on size and order; hence neither can a very tiny creature turn out to be beautiful (since our perception of it grows blurred as it approaches the period of imperceptibility) nor an excessively huge one (for then it cannot all be perceived at once and so its unity and wholeness are lost), if for example there were a creature a thousand miles long — so, just as in the case of living creatures they must have some size, but one that can be taken in a single view, so with plots: they should have length, but such that they are easy to remember. As to a limit of the length, the one is determined by the tragic competitions and the ordinary span of attention. (If they had to compete with a hundred tragedies they would compete by the water clock, as they say used to be done [?].) But the limit fixed by the very nature of the case is: the longer the plot, up to the point of still being perspicuous as a whole, the finer it is so far as size is concerned; or to put it in general terms, the length in which, with things happening in unbroken sequence, a shift takes place either probably or necessarily from bad to good fortune or from good to bad — that is an acceptable norm of length.

But a plot is not unified, as some people think, simply because it has to do with a single person. A large, indeed an indefinite number of things can happen to a given individual, some of which go to constitute no unified event; and in the same way there can be many acts of a given individual from which no single action emerges. Hence it seems clear that those poets are wrong who have composed *Heracleïds,* *Theseïds,* and the like. They think that since Heracles was a single person it follows that the plot will be single too. But Homer, superior as he is in all other respects, appears to have grasped this point well also, thanks either to art or nature, for in composing an *Odyssey* he did not incorporate into it everything that happened to the hero, for example how he was wounded on Mt. Parnassus° or how he

---

Mt. Parnassus: A mountain in central Greece traditionally sacred to Apollo. In legend, Odysseus was wounded there, but the point Aristotle is making is that the writer of epics need not include every detail of his hero's life in a given work. Homer, in writing the *Odyssey,* was working with a hero, Odysseus, whose story had been legendary long before he began writing.

feigned madness at the muster, neither of which events, by happening, made it at all necessary or probable that the other should happen. Instead, he composed the *Odyssey* — and the *Iliad* similarly — around a unified action of the kind we have been talking about.

A poetic imitation, then, ought to be unified in the same way as a single imitation in any other mimetic field, by having a single object: since the plot is an imitation of an action, the latter ought to be both unified and complete, and the component events ought to be so firmly compacted that if any one of them is shifted to another place, or removed, the whole is loosened up and dislocated; for an element whose addition or subtraction makes no perceptible extra difference is not really a part of the whole.

From what has been said it is also clear that the poet's job is not to report what has happened but what is likely to happen: that is, what is capable of happening according to the rule of probability or necessity. Thus the difference between the historian and the poet is not in their utterances being in verse or prose (it would be quite possible for Herodotus's work to be translated into verse, and it would not be any the less a history with verse than it is without it); the difference lies in the fact that the historian speaks of what has happened, the poet of the kind of thing that *can* happen. Hence also poetry is a more philosophical and serious business than history; for poetry speaks more of universals, history of particulars. "Universal" in this case is what kind of person is likely to do or say certain kinds of things, according to probability or necessity; that is what poetry aims at, although it gives its persons particular names afterward; while the "particular" is what Alcibiades did or what happened to him.

In the field of comedy this point has been grasped: our comic poets construct their plots on the basis of general probabilities and then assign names to the persons quite arbitrarily, instead of dealing with individuals as the old iambic poets° did. But in tragedy they still cling to the historically given names. The reason is that what is possible is persuasive; so what has not happened we are not yet ready to believe is possible, while what has happened is, we feel, obviously possible: for it would not have happened if it were impossible. Nevertheless, it is a fact that even in our tragedies, in some cases only one or two of the names are traditional, the rest being invented, and in some others none at all. It is so, for example, in Agathon's *Antheus* — the names in it are as fictional as the events — and it gives no less pleasure because of that. Hence the poets ought not to cling at all costs to the traditional plots, around which our tragedies are constructed. And in fact it is absurd to go searching for this kind of authentication, since even the familiar names are familiar to only a few in the audience and yet give the same kind of pleasure to all.

So from these considerations it is evident that the poet should be a maker of his plots more than of his verses, insofar as he is a poet by virtue of his imitations and what he imitates is actions. Hence even if it happens that he puts something that has actually taken place into poetry, he is none the less a poet; for there is nothing to prevent some of the things that have happened from being the kind of things that can happen, and that is the sense in which he is their maker.

old iambic poets: Aristotle may be referring to Archilochus (fl. 650 B.C.) and the iambic style he developed. The iamb is a metrical foot of two syllables, a short and a long syllable, and was the most popular metrical style before the time of Aristotle. "Dealing with individuals" implies using figures already known to the audience rather than figures whose names can be arbitrarily assigned because no one knows who they are.

*Simple and Complex
Plots*

Among simple plots and actions the episodic are the worst. By "episodic" plot I mean one in which there is no probability or necessity for the order in which the episodes follow one another. Such structures are composed by the bad poets because they are bad poets, but by the good poets because of the actors: in composing contest pieces for them, and stretching out the plot beyond its capacity, they are forced frequently to dislocate the sequence.

Furthermore, since the tragic imitation is not only of a complete action but also of events that are fearful and pathetic,° and these come about best when they come about contrary to one's expectation yet logically, one following from the other; that way they will be more productive of wonder than if they happen merely at random, by chance — because even among chance occurrences the ones people consider most marvelous are those that seem to have come about as if on purpose: for example the way the statue of Mitys at Argos killed the man who had been the cause of Mitys's death, by falling on him while he was attending the festival; it stands to reason, people think, that such things don't happen by chance — so plots of that sort cannot fail to be artistically superior.

Some plots are simple, others are complex; indeed the actions of which the plots are imitations already fall into these two categories. By "simple" action I mean one the development of which being continuous and unified in the manner stated above, the reversal comes without peripety or recognition, and by "complex" action one in which the reversal is continuous but with recognition or peripety or both. And these developments must grow out of the very structure of the plot itself, in such a way that on the basis of what has happened previously this particular outcome follows either by necessity or in accordance with probability; for there is a great difference in whether these events happen because of those or merely after them.

"Peripety" is a shift of what is being undertaken to the opposite in the way previously stated, and that in accordance with probability or necessity as we have just been saying; as for example in the *Oedipus* the man who has come, thinking that he will reassure Oedipus, that is, relieve him of his fear with respect to his mother, by revealing who he once was, brings about the opposite; and in the *Lynceus,* as he (Lynceus) is being led away with every prospect of being executed, and Danaus pursuing him with every prospect of doing the executing, it comes about as a result of the other things that have happened in the play that *he* is executed and Lynceus is saved. And "recognition" is, as indeed the name indicates, a shift from ignorance to awareness, pointing in the direction either of close blood ties or of hostility, of people who have previously been in a clearly marked state of happiness or unhappiness.

The finest recognition is one that happens at the same time as a peripety, as is the case with the one in the *Oedipus.* Naturally, there are also other kinds of recognition: it is possible for one to take place in the prescribed manner in relation to inanimate objects and chance occurrences, and it is possible to recognize whether a person has acted or not acted. But the form that is most integrally a part of the plot, the action, is the one aforesaid; for that kind of recognition combined with peripety will excite either pity or fear (and these are the kinds of action of which tragedy is

---

fearful and pathetic: Aristotle said that tragedy should evoke two emotions: terror and pity. The terror results from our realizing that what is happening to the hero might just as easily happen to us; the pity results from our human sympathy with a fellow sufferer. Therefore, the fearful and pathetic represent significant emotions appropriate to our witnessing drama.

an imitation according to our definition), because both good and bad fortune will also be most likely to follow that kind of event. Since, further, the recognition is a recognition of persons, some are of one person by the other one only (when it is already known who the "other one" is), but sometimes it is necessary for both persons to go through a recognition, as for example Iphigenia is recognized by her brother° through the sending of the letter, but of him by Iphigenia another recognition is required.

These then are two elements of plot: peripety and recognition; third is the *pathos*. Of these, peripety and recognition have been discussed; a *pathos* is a destructive or painful act, such as deaths on stage, paroxysms of pain, woundings, and all that sort of thing.

Sigmund Freud (1856–1939)
THE OEDIPUS COMPLEX   *1900–1930*°

TRANSLATED BY JAMES STRACHEY

Sigmund Freud is the most celebrated psychiatrist of the twentieth century and the father of psychoanalytic theory. His researches into the unconscious changed the way we think about the human mind, and his explorations into the symbolic meaning of dreams have been widely regarded as a breakthrough in connecting the meaning of world myth to personal life.

In his Interpretation of Dreams *he turned to Sophocles' drama and developed his theories of the Oedipus complex: the desire to kill one parent and marry the other may be rooted in the deepest natural psychological development of the individual. The following passage provides insight not only into a psychological state that all humans may share but also into the way in which a man of Freud's temperament read and interpreted a great piece of literature. Like Sophocles himself, Freud believed that the myth underlying* Oedipus Rex *has a meaning and importance for all human beings.*

In my experience, which is already extensive, the chief part in the mental lives of all children who later become psychoneurotics is played by their parents. Being in love with the one parent and hating the other are among the essential constituents of the stock of psychical impulses which is formed at that time and which is of such importance in determining the symptoms of the later neurosis. It is not my belief, however, that psychoneurotics differ sharply in this respect from other human beings who remain normal — that they are able, that is, to create something absolutely new and peculiar to themselves. It is far more probable — and this is confirmed by occasional observations on normal children — that they are only distinguished by exhibiting on a magnified scale feelings of love and hatred to their parents which occur less obviously and less intensely in the minds of most children.

---

her brother: Orestes is Iphigenia's brother. Aristotle may be referring to a lost play.
1900–1930: *Interpretation of Dreams* was first published in 1900 and updated regularly by Freud through eight editions. This passage is taken from the eighth edition, published in 1930.

This discovery is confirmed by a legend that has come down to us from classical antiquity: a legend whose profound and universal power to move can only be understood if the hypothesis I have put forward in regard to the psychology of children has an equally universal validity. What I have in mind is the legend of King Oedipus and Sophocles' drama which bears his name.

Oedipus, son of Laïus, King of Thebes, and of Jocasta, was exposed [to the elements and left to die] as an infant because an oracle had warned Laïus that the still unborn child would be his father's murderer. The child was rescued and grew up as a prince in an alien court, until, in doubts as to his origin, he too questioned the oracle and was warned to avoid his home since he was destined to murder his father and take his mother in marriage. On the road leading away from what he believed was his home, he met King Laïus and slew him in a sudden quarrel. He came next to Thebes and solved the riddle set him by the Sphinx who barred his way. Out of gratitude the Thebans made him their king and gave him Jocasta's hand in marriage. He reigned long in peace and honor, and she who, unknown to him, was his mother bore him two sons and two daughters. Then at last a plague broke out and the Thebans made inquiry once more of the oracle. It is at this point that Sophocles' tragedy opens. The messengers bring back the reply that the plague will cease when the murderer of Laïus has been driven from the land.

> But he, where is he? Where shall now be read
> The fading record of this ancient guilt?[1]

The action of the play consists in nothing other than the process of revealing, with cunning delays and ever-mounting excitement — a process that can be likened to the work of a psychoanalysis — that Oedipus himself is the murderer of Laïus, but further that he is the son of the murdered man and of Jocasta. Appalled at the abomination which he has unwittingly perpetrated, Oedipus blinds himself and forsakes his home. The oracle has been fulfilled.

Oedipus Rex is what is known as a tragedy of destiny. Its tragic effect is said to lie in the contrast between the supreme will of the gods and the vain attempts of mankind to escape the evil that threatens them. The lesson which, it is said, the deeply moved spectator should learn from the tragedy is submission to the divine will and realization of his own impotence. Modern dramatists have accordingly tried to achieve a similar tragic effect by weaving the same contrast into a plot invented by themselves. But the spectators have looked on unmoved while a curse or an oracle was fulfilled in spite of all the efforts of some innocent man: later tragedies of destiny have failed in their effect.

If *Oedipus Rex* moves a modern audience no less than it did the contemporary Greek one, the explanation can only be that its effect does not lie in the contrast between destiny and human will, but is to be looked for in the particular nature of the material on which that contrast is exemplified. There must be something which makes a voice within us ready to recognize the compelling force of destiny in the *Oedipus,* while we can dismiss as merely arbitrary such dispositions as are laid down in [Grillparzer's] *Die Ahnfrau* or other modern tragedies of destiny. And a factor of this kind is in fact involved in the story of King Oedipus. His destiny

---

[1]Lewis Campbell's translation (1883), lines 108ff [Dudley Fitts and Robert Fitzgerald, *Sophocles: The Oedipus Cycle, an English Version* (Harcourt Brace & Company, 1949), Prologue, lines 112–13].

moves us only because it might have been ours — because the oracle laid the same curse upon us before our birth as upon him. It is the fate of all of us, perhaps, to direct our first sexual impulse toward our mother and our first hatred and our first murderous wish against our father. Our dreams convince us that that is so. King Oedipus, who slew his father Laïus and married his mother Jocasta, merely shows us the fulfillment of our own childhood wishes. But, more fortunate than he, we have meanwhile succeeded, in so far as we have not become psychoneurotics, in detaching our sexual impulses from our mothers and in forgetting our jealousy of our fathers. Here is one in whom these primeval wishes of our childhood have been fulfilled, and we shrink back from him with the whole force of the repression by which those wishes have since that time been held down within us. While the poet, as he unravels the past, brings to light the guilt of Oedipus, he is at the same time compelling us to recognize our own inner minds, in which those same impulses, though suppressed, are still to be found. The contrast with which the closing Chorus leaves us confronted —

> . . . Fix on Oedipus your eyes,
> Who resolved the dark enigma, noblest champion and most wise.
> Like a star his envied fortune mounted beaming far and wide:
> Now he sinks in seas of anguish, whelmed beneath a raging tide . . .[2]

— strikes as a warning at ourselves and our pride, at us who since our childhood have grown so wise and so mighty in our own eyes. Like Oedipus, we live in ignorance of these wishes, repugnant to morality, which have been forced upon us by Nature, and after their revelation we may all of us well seek to close our eyes to the scenes of our childhood.[3]

There is an unmistakable indication in the text of Sophocles' tragedy itself that the legend of Oedipus sprang from some primeval dream material which had as its content the distressing disturbance of a child's relation to his parents owing to the first stirrings of sexuality. At a point when Oedipus, though he is not yet enlightened, has begun to feel troubled by his recollection of the oracle, Jocasta consoles him by referring to a dream which many people dream, though, as she thinks, it has no meaning:

> Many a man ere now in dreams hath lain
> With her who bare him. He hath least annoy
> Who with such omens troubleth not his mind.[4]

Today, just as then, many men dream of having sexual relations with their mothers, and speak of the fact with indignation and astonishment. It is clearly the key to the tragedy and the complement to the dream of the dreamer's father being dead. The story of Oedipus is the reaction of the imagination to these two typical dreams.

---

[2]Lewis Campbell's translation, lines 1524ff [Fitts and Fitzgerald, antistrophe 2, lines 292–96].

[3][*Footnote added by Freud in 1914 edition.*] None of the findings of psychoanalytic research has provoked such embittered denials, such fierce opposition — or such amusing contortions — on the part of critics as this indication of the childhood impulses toward incest which persist in the unconscious. An attempt has even been made recently to make out, in the face of all experience, that the incest should only be taken as "symbolic."— Ferenczi (1912) has proposed an ingenious "overinterpretation" of the Oedipus myth, based on a passage in one of Schopenhauer's letters. [*Added 1919.*] Later studies have shown that the "Oedipus complex," which was touched upon for the first time in the above paragraphs in the *Interpretation of Dreams*, throws a light of undreamt-of importance on the history of the human race and the evolution of religion and morality.

[4]Lewis Campbell's translation, lines 982ff [Fitts and Fitzgerald, scene 3, lines 67–69].

And just as these dreams, when dreamt by adults, are accompanied by feelings of repulsion, so too the legend must include horror and self-punishment. Its further modification originates once again in a misconceived secondary revision of the material, which has sought to exploit it for theological purposes. . . . The attempt to harmonize divine omnipotence with human responsibility must naturally fail in connection with this subject matter just as with any other.

Claude Lévi-Strauss (b. 1908)
FROM THE STRUCTURAL STUDY OF MYTH   1955

Claude Lévi-Strauss is one of a handful of modern anthropologists whose interests span the range of thought, culture, and understanding. His work has been of immense influence on French intellectual life and, by extension, on the intellectual life of modern times. His works include Triste Tropiques *(translated as* A World on the Wane*), about his own experiences as an anthropologist;* Structural Anthropology, *about the ways in which the study of anthropology implies a study of the structure of thought; and* Mythologies, *a four-volume summation of his thought. The excerpt that follows is structuralist in scope in that it attempts to understand the myth of Oedipus by examining the patterns of repetition in the original narrative. By setting up a grid, Lévi-Strauss begins to sort out the implications of the myth and to seek a meaning that is not necessarily apparent in the chronological order of the narrative. He examines the myth diachronically — across the lines of time — and thereby sees a new range of implications, which he treats as the structural implications of the myth. His reading is complex, suggesting that the Oedipus myth is a vegetation myth explaining the origins of mankind. Lévi-Strauss gives us a new way to interpret the significance of literary myths.*

The time has come to give a concrete example of the method we propose. We will use the Oedipus myth which has the advantage of being well known to everybody and for which no preliminary explanation is therefore needed. By doing so, I am well aware that the Oedipus myth has only reached us under late forms and through literary transfigurations concerned more with esthetic and moral preoccupations than with religious or ritual ones, whatever these may have been. But as will be shown later, this apparently unsatisfactory situation will strengthen our demonstration rather than weaken it.

The myth will be treated as would be an orchestra score perversely presented as a unilinear series and where our task is to reestablish the correct disposition. As if, for instance, we were confronted with a sequence of the type: 1,2,4,7,8,2,3,4,6,8,1,4,5,7,8,1,2,5,7,3,4,5,6,8 . . . , the assignment being to put all the 1's together, all the 2's, the 3's, etc.; the result is a chart:

$$
\begin{array}{cccccc}
1 & 2 & 4 & & 7 & 8 \\
 & 2 & 3 & 4 & 6 & 8 \\
1 & & 4 & 5 & 7 & 8 \\
1 & 2 & & 5 & 7 & \\
 & 3 & 4 & 5 & & \\
 & & & 6 & & 8 \\
\end{array}
$$

We will attempt to perform the same kind of operation on the Oedipus myth, trying out several dispositions. [. . .] Let us suppose, for the sake of argument, that the best arrangement is the following (although it might certainly be improved by the help of a specialist in Greek mythology):

Kadmos seeks his sister Europa ravished by Zeus.		Kadmos kills the dragon.	
	The Spartoi kill each other.		Labdacos (Laios's father) = *lame* (?).
	Oedipus kills his father Laios.		Laios (Oedipus's father) = *left-sided* (?).
		Oedipus kills the Sphinx.	
Oedipus marries his mother Jocasta.			
	Eteocles kills his brother Polyneices.		Oedipus = *swollen-foot* (?).
Antigone buries her brother Polyneices despite prohibition.			

Thus, we find ourselves confronted with four vertical columns each of which includes several relations belonging to the same bundle. Were we to *tell* the myth, we would disregard the columns and read the rows from left to right and from top to bottom. But if we want to *understand* the myth, then we will have to disregard one half of the diachronic° dimension (top to bottom) and read from left to right, column after column, each one being considered as a unit.

All the relations belonging to the same column exhibit one common feature which it is our task to unravel. For instance, all the events grouped in the first column on the left have something to do with blood relations which are overemphasized, i.e., are subject to a more intimate treatment than they should be. Let us say, then, that the first column has as its common feature the *overrating of blood relations*. It is obvious that the second column expresses the same thing, but inverted: *underrating of blood relations*. The third column refers to monsters being slain. As

diachronic: Not ordered linearly in time but through time.

to the fourth, a word of clarification is needed. The remarkable connotation of the surnames in Oedipus's father-line has often been noticed. However, linguists usually disregard it, since to them the only way to define the meaning of a term is to investigate all the contexts in which it appears, and personal names, precisely because they are used as such, are not accompanied by any context. With the method we propose to follow the objection disappears since the myth itself provides its own context. The meaningful fact is no longer to be looked for in the eventual sense of each name, but in the fact that all the names have a common feature: i.e., that they may eventually mean something and that all these hypothetical meanings (which may well remain hypothetical) exhibit a common feature, namely they refer to *difficulties to walk and to behave straight.*

What is then the relationship between the two columns on the right? Column three refers to monsters. The dragon is a chthonian° being which has to be killed in order that mankind be born from the earth; the Sphinx is a monster unwilling to permit men to live. The last unit reproduces the first one which has to do with the *autochthonous*° origin of mankind. Since the monsters are overcome by men, we may thus say that the common feature of the third column is *the denial of the autochthonous origin of man.*

This immediately helps us to understand the meaning of the fourth column. In mythology it is a universal character of men born from the earth that at the moment they emerge from the depth, they either cannot walk or do it clumsily. This is the case of the chthonian beings in the mythology of the Pueblo: Masauwu, who leads the emergence, and the chthonian Shumaikoli are lame ("bleeding-foot," "sore-foot"). The same happens to the Koskimo of the Kwakiutl after they have been swallowed by the chthonian monster, Tsiakish: when they returned to the surface of the earth "they limped forward or tripped sideways." Then the common feature of the fourth column is: *the persistence of the autochthonous origin of man.* It follows that column four is to column three as column one is to column two. The inability to connect two kinds of relationships is overcome (or rather replaced) by the positive statement that contradictory relationships are identical inasmuch as they are both self-contradictory in a similar way. Although this is still a provisional formulation of the structure of mythical thought, it is sufficient at this stage.

Turning back to the Oedipus myth, we may now see what it means. The myth has to do with the inability, for a culture which holds the belief that mankind is autochthonous [. . .] to find a satisfactory transition between this theory and the knowledge that human beings are actually born from the union of man and woman. Although the problem obviously cannot be solved, the Oedipus myth provides a kind of logical tool which, to phrase it coarsely, replaces the original problem: born from one or born from two? born from different or born from same? By a correlation of this type, the overrating of blood relations is to the underrating of blood relations as the attempt to escape autochthony is to the impossibility to succeed in it. Although experience contradicts theory, social life verifies the cosmology by its similarity of structure. Hence cosmology is true.

Two remarks should be made at this stage.

In order to interpret the myth, we were able to leave aside a point which has until now worried the specialists, namely, that in the earlier (Homeric) versions of

---

chthonian: From the underworld.
autochthonous: Native, aboriginal; in this case, born of the earth.

the Oedipus myth, some basic elements are lacking, such as Jocasta killing herself and Oedipus piercing his own eyes. These events do not alter the substance of the myth although they can easily be integrated, the first one as a new case of auto-destruction (column three) while the second is another case of crippledness (column four). At the same time there is something significant in these additions since the shift from foot to head is to be correlated with the shift from: autochthonous origin negated to: self-destruction.

Thus, our method eliminates a problem which has been so far one of the main obstacles to the progress of mythological studies, namely, the quest for the *true* version, or the *earlier* one. On the contrary, we define the myth as consisting of all its versions; to put it otherwise: a myth remains the same as long as it is felt as such. A striking example is offered by the fact that our interpretation may take into account, and is certainly applicable to, the Freudian use of the Oedipus myth. Although the Freudian problem has ceased to be that of autochthony *versus* bisexual reproduction, it is still the problem of understanding how *one* can be born from *two*: how is it that we do not have only one procreator, but a mother plus a father? Therefore, not only Sophocles, but Freud himself, should be included among the recorded versions of the Oedipus myth on a par with earlier or seemingly more "authentic" versions.

ANTIGONE

Antigone was Sophocles' thirty-second play, produced in March 441 B.C., when he was in his mid-fifties. It draws a powerful response from its audience partly because it portrays the conflict between two proud, willful people: Antigone, a daughter of Oedipus and Iokaste, and Kreon, Iokaste's brother and the king of Thebes. Its original success was due in part to its portrayal of the individual's struggle against a tyrannical king. After enjoying thirty years of peace with its archrival Sparta, Athens was moving slowly toward war; and the memory of previous tyrants — both good, like Peisistratus, and bad, like his son Hippias — remained in the minds of Sophocles' audience.

It has never been easy to determine which of the two main characters is correct. Kreon's portrayal as a tyrant content to take up the state as his private property tells us that he is not to be fully trusted. At the same time, Antigone knows that the social mores of Thebes imply that a citizen must obey the ruler. Antigone's great courage makes the audience feel sympathy and admiration for her. She is a martyr to her beliefs, an ancient Joan of Arc.

The main conflict in *Antigone* centers on a distinction between law and justice, the conflict between a human law and a higher law. Kreon, the uncle of Antigone and Ismene, has made a decree: Polyneices, the brother of Antigone and Ismene, was guilty not only of killing his brother Eteocles but also of attacking the state and, like all traitors, will be denied a proper burial. When the action of the play begins, Antigone is determined to give her brother the burial that ancient tradition and her religious beliefs demand.

The opening dialogue with Ismene clarifies the important distinction between human law and the higher law on which Antigone says she must act. Ismene declares simply that she cannot go against the law of the citizens. Kreon has been willful in establishing the law, but it is nonetheless the law. Antigone, knowing full well the consequences of defying Kreon, nonetheless acts on her principles.

The complex conflict between Antigone and Kreon occurs on the level of citizen and ruler and is affected on the personal level by the relationship between Haimon, Kreon's son, and his intended bride, Antigone. The antagonism between Kreon and Haimon begins slowly, as Haimon appears to yield to the will of his father, but culminates in Haimon's ultimate rejection of his father by choosing to join Antigone in death.

When Teiresias reveals a prophecy of death and punishment and begs Kreon, for the sake of the suffering Thebes, to rescind his decree and give Polyneices a proper burial, Kreon willfully continues to heed his own declarations rather than oracular wisdom or the pleas of others.

By the time Kreon accepts Teiresias's prophecy, it is too late: he has lost his son, and his wife has killed herself. Power not only has corrupted Kreon but also has taken from him the people about whom he cared most. He emerges as an unyielding tyrant, guilty of making some of the same mistakes that haunted Oedipus.

Antigone emerges as a heroine who presses forward in the full conviction that she is right. She must honor her dead brother at all costs. Even if she must break the law of the state, she must answer to what she regards as a higher law. As she says early in the play, she has "dared the crime of piety." Yet she has within her the complexity of all humans: she in one sense acts in the knowledge that she is right but in another dares Kreon to punish her. She challenges Kreon so boldly that her every move forces the proud Kreon to harden his position and set in motion the ultimate tragedy — the loss of all he holds dear. This is yet one more tragic irony in the Theban trilogy.

Antigone in Performance

Since the eighteenth century *Antigone* has been produced in Europe and the Western Hemisphere in more or less its original form and in various adaptations and rewritings. Jean Cocteau combined his version with music by Arthur Honegger in 1930. It was rewritten and produced by Walter Hasenclever in 1917 as a protest against the First World War and then in 1944 by Jean Anouilh as a protest against Nazi occupation of Paris during World War II (see the excerpt on p. 127). The Royal Shakespeare Company produced *Antigone* along with all the surviving Greek tragedies in 1980. Bertolt Brecht's production of *Antigone* in 1948 introduced a Gestapo officer and Nazi brutality. Athol Fugard's *The Island* (1973) features a remarkable production of *Antigone* as a play within a play, produced by convicts in a South African island jail as a Christmas entertainment for their jailers and specially invited white guests. Fugard found, as have so many other adapters and producers, that the political power of *Antigone* leaps out for virtually all contemporary audiences. Janusz Glowacki, a Polish playwright, produced *Antigone in New York* at the Arena

Stage in Washington in March 1993. Inspired by both Sophocles and Beckett, it is set in Tompkins Square Park in New York. The action centers on a homeless Puerto Rican woman's efforts to bury a homeless man in the park. The action of the play demonstrates the durability of *Antigone*'s basic concept — that a decent burial is an essential vestige of humanity.

Sophocles (*c. 496–c. 406 B.C.*)

ANTIGONE
TRANSLATED BY DUDLEY FITTS AND ROBERT FITZGERALD

441 B.C.

Characters

ANTIGONE, } *daughters of Oedipus*
ISMENE,
EURYDICE, *wife of Kreon*
KREON, *King of Thebes*
HAIMON, *son of Kreon*
TEIRESIAS, *a blind seer*
A SENTRY
A MESSENGER
CHORUS

Scene: *Before the palace of Kreon, King of Thebes. A central double door, and two lateral doors. A platform extends the length of the facade, and from this platform three steps lead down into the orchestra, or chorus-ground.*

Time: *Dawn of the day after the repulse of the Argive army from the assault on Thebes.*

PROLOGUE°

(*Antigone and Ismene enter from the central door of the palace.*)

ANTIGONE: Ismene, dear sister,
   You would think that we had already suffered enough
   For the curse on Oedipus.°

Prologue: Portion of the play explaining the background and current action.   **3. curse on Oedipus:** Oedipus, king of Thebes and the father of Antigone and Ismene, was abandoned by his parents as an infant after the oracle foretold that he would one day kill his father and marry his mother. Rescued by a shepherd and raised by the king of Corinth, Oedipus returned years later to Thebes and unknowingly lived out the oracle's prophecy by killing Laios and marrying Iokaste. After his two sons, Eteocles and Polyneices, killed each other in combat, the throne went to Kreon, Iokaste's brother.

                        I cannot imagine any grief
   That you and I have not gone through. And now —   5
   Have they told you of the new decree of our King
      Kreon?
ISMENE: I have heard nothing: I know
   That two sisters lost two brothers, a double death
   In a single hour; and I know that the Argive army
   Fled in the night; but beyond this, nothing.   10
ANTIGONE: I thought so. And that is why I wanted
      you
   To come out here with me. There is something we
      must do.
ISMENE: Why do you speak so strangely?
ANTIGONE: Listen, Ismene:
   Kreon buried our brother Eteocles   15
   With military honors, gave him a soldier's funeral,
   And it was right that he should; but Polyneices,
   Who fought as bravely and died as miserably, —
   They say that Kreon has sworn
   No one shall bury him, no one mourn for him,   20
   But his body must lie in the fields, a sweet treasure
   For carrion birds to find as they search for food.
   That is what they say, and our good Kreon is
      coming here
   To announce it publicly; and the penalty —
   Stoning to death in the public square!
                                There it is,   25
   And now you can prove what you are:
   A true sister, or a traitor to your family.
ISMENE: Antigone, you are mad! What could I possibly
      do?
ANTIGONE: You must decide whether you will help me
      or not.
ISMENE: I do not understand you. Help you in what?   30
ANTIGONE: Ismene, I am going to bury him. Will you
      come?
ISMENE: Bury him! You have just said the new law
      forbids it.
ANTIGONE: He is my brother. And he is your brother,
      too.

ISMENE: But think of the danger! Think what Kreon
    will do!
ANTIGONE: Kreon is not strong enough to stand in my
35   way.
ISMENE: Ah sister!
    Oedipus died, everyone hating him
    For what his own search brought to light, his eyes
    Ripped out by his own hand; and Iocaste died,
40   His mother and wife at once: she twisted the cords
    That strangled her life; and our two brothers died,
    Each killed by the other's sword. And we are left:
    But oh, Antigone,
    Think how much more terrible than these
    Our own death would be if we should go against
45   Kreon
    And do what he has forbidden! We are only
        women,
    We cannot fight with men, Antigone!
    The law is strong, we must give in to the law
    In this thing, and in worse. I beg the Dead
50   To forgive me, but I am helpless: I must yield
    To those in authority. And I think it is dangerous
        business
    To be always meddling.
ANTIGONE: If that is what you think,
    I should not want you, even if you asked to come.
    You have made your choice, you can be what you
        want to be.
55   But I will bury him; and if I must die,
    I say that this crime is holy: I shall lie down
    With him in death, and I shall be as dear
    To him as he to me.
                    It is the dead,
    Not the living, who make the longest demands:
    We die for ever . . .
60   You may do as you like,
    Since apparently the laws of the gods mean nothing
        to you.
ISMENE: They mean a great deal to me; but I have no
        strength
    To break laws that were made for the public good.
ANTIGONE: That must be your excuse, I suppose. But as
        for me,
    I will bury the brother I love.
65 ISMENE: Antigone,
    I am so afraid for you!
ANTIGONE: You need not be:
    You have yourself to consider, after all.
ISMENE: But no one must hear of this, you must tell no
        one!
    I will keep it a secret, I promise!
ANTIGONE: O tell it! Tell everyone!
70   Think how they'll hate you when it all comes out
    If they learn that you knew about it all the time!
ISMENE: So fiery! You should be cold with fear.
ANTIGONE: Perhaps. But I am doing only what I must.
ISMENE: But can you do it? I say that you cannot.
75 ANTIGONE: Very well: when my strength gives out,
    I shall do no more.

ISMENE: Impossible things should not be tried at all.
ANTIGONE: Go away, Ismene:
    I shall be hating you soon, and the dead will too,
    For your words are hateful. Leave me my foolish
        plan: 80
    I am not afraid of the danger; if it means death,
    It will not be the worst of deaths — death without
        honor.
ISMENE: Go then, if you feel that you must.
    You are unwise,
    But a loyal friend indeed to those who love you.   85

(*Exit into the palace. Antigone goes off, left. Enter the
Chorus.*)

PARODOS° • *Strophe° 1*

CHORUS: Now the long blade of the sun, lying
    Level east to west, touches with glory
    Thebes of the Seven Gates. Open, unlidded
    Eye of golden day! O marching light
    Across the eddy and rush of Dirce's stream,°   5
    Striking the white shields of the enemy
    Thrown headlong backward from the blaze of
        morning!
CHORAGOS:° Polyneices their commander
    Roused them with windy phrases,
    He the wild eagle screaming   10
    Insults above our land,
    His wings their shields of snow,
    His crest their marshalled helms.

Antistrophe° 1

CHORUS: Against our seven gates in a yawning ring
    The famished spears came onward in the night;   15
    But before his jaws were sated with our blood,
    Or pinefire took the garland of our towers,
    He was thrown back, and as he turned, great
        Thebes —
    No tender victim for his noisy power —
    Rose like a dragon behind him, shouting war.   20
CHORAGOS: For God hates utterly
    The bray of bragging tongues;
    And when he beheld their smiling,
    Their swagger of golden helms,
    The frown of his thunder blasted   25
    Their first man from our walls.

Parodos: The song or ode chanted by the Chorus on its entry.
Strophe: Song sung by the Chorus as it danced from stage right
to stage left.   **5. Dirce's stream:** River near Thebes.   **8. Choragos:** Leader of the Chorus.   **Antistrophe:** Song sung by the
Chorus following the Strophe, as it danced back from stage left
to stage right.

Antigone (Martha Henry)
reassures Ismene in the
Repertory Theatre of Lincoln
Center production of *Antigone*
at the Vivian Beaumont
Theatre, directed by John
Hirsch in 1971.

Strophe 2

CHORUS: We heard his shout of triumph high in the air
        Turn to a scream; far out in a flaming arc
        He fell with his windy torch, and the earth struck
        him.
30   And others storming in fury no less than his
        Found shock of death in the dusty joy of battle.
CHORAGOS: Seven captains at seven gates
        Yielded their clanging arms to the god
        That bends the battle-line and breaks it.
35   These two only, brothers in blood,

Face to face in matchless rage,
Mirroring each the other's death
Clashed in long combat.

Antistrophe 2

CHORUS: But now in the beautiful morning of victory
        Let Thebes of the many chariots sing for joy!   40
        With hearts for dancing we'll take leave of war:
        Our temples shall be sweet with hymns of praise,
        And the long nights shall echo with our chorus.

SCENE 1

CHORAGOS: But now at last our new King is coming:
    Kreon of Thebes, Menoikeus' son.
    In this auspicious dawn of his reign
    What are the new complexities
5   That shifting Fate has woven for him?
    What is his counsel? Why has he summoned
    The old men to hear him?

(*Enter Kreon from the palace, center. He addresses the
Chorus from the top step.*)

KREON: Gentlemen: I have the honor to inform you that
    our Ship of State, which recent storms have threat-
10 ened to destroy, has come safely to harbor at last,
    guided by the merciful wisdom of Heaven. I have
    summoned you here this morning because I know
    that I can depend upon you: your devotion to King
    Laios was absolute; you never hesitated in your duty
15 to our late ruler Oedipus; and when Oedipus died,
your loyalty was transferred to his children. Unfortunately, as you know, his two sons, the princes Eteocles and Polyneices, have killed each other in battle;
and I, as the next in blood, have succeeded to the full
power of the throne.   20

I am aware, of course, that no Ruler can expect
complete loyalty from his subjects until he has been
tested in office. Nevertheless, I say to you at the very
outset that I have nothing but contempt for the kind
of Governor who is afraid, for whatever reason, to   25
follow the course that he knows is best for the State;
and as for the man who sets private friendship above
the public welfare, — I have no use for him, either. I
call God to witness that if I saw my country headed
for ruin, I should not be afraid to speak out plainly;   30
and I need hardly remind you that I would never
have any dealings with an enemy of the people. No
one values friendship more highly than I; but we
must remember that friends made at the risk of
wrecking our Ship are not real friends at all.   35

Kreon (Philip Bosco), Antigone, and Haimon (David Birney).

These are my principles, at any rate, and that is
why I have made the following decision concerning
the sons of Oedipus: Eteocles, who died as a man
should die, fighting for his country, is to be buried
40 with full military honors, with all the ceremony that
is usual when the greatest heroes die; but his brother
Polyneices, who broke his exile to come back with
fire and sword against his native city and the shrines
of his fathers' gods, whose one idea was to spill
45 the blood of his blood and sell his own people into
slavery — Polyneices, I say, is to have no burial: no
man is to touch him or say the least prayer for
him; he shall lie on the plain, unburied; and the birds
and the scavenging dogs can do with him whatever
50 they like.
　　This is my command, and you can see the wisdom
behind it. As long as I am King, no traitor is going to
be honored with the loyal man. But whoever shows
by word and deed that he is on the side of the
55 State, — he shall have my respect while he is living
and my reverence when he is dead.

CHORAGOS: If that is your will, Kreon son of
　　Menoikeus,
　　You have the right to enforce it: we are yours.

KREON: That is my will. Take care that you do your
　　part.

CHORAGOS: We are old men: let the younger ones carry
60 　　it out.

KREON: I do not mean that: the sentries have been
　　appointed.

CHORAGOS: Then what is it that you would have us do?

KREON: You will give no support to whoever breaks
　　this law.

CHORAGOS: Only a crazy man is in love with death!

65 KREON: And death it is; yet money talks, and the wisest
　　Have sometimes been known to count a few coins
　　too many.

(*Enter Sentry from left.*)

SENTRY: I'll not say that I'm out of breath from running,
　　King, because every time I stopped to think about
　　what I have to tell you, I felt like going back. And all
70 　　the time a voice kept saying, "You fool, don't you
　　know you're walking straight into trouble?"; and
　　then another voice: "Yes, but if you let somebody
　　else get the news to Kreon first, it will be even worse
　　than that for you!" But good sense won out, at least I
75 　　hope it was good sense, and here I am with a story
　　that makes no sense at all; but I'll tell it anyhow,
　　because, as they say, what's going to happen's going
　　to happen and —

KREON: Come to the point. What have you to say?

80 SENTRY: I did not do it. I did not see who did it.
　　You must not punish me for what someone else has
　　done.

KREON: A comprehensive defense! More effective,
　　perhaps,
　　If I knew its purpose. Come: what is it?

SENTRY: A dreadful thing . . . I don't know how to put
　　it —

KREON: Out with it!

SENTRY: 　　　　　　Well, then;　　　　　　　　85
　　The dead man —
　　　　　　　　Polyneices —

(*Pause. The Sentry is overcome, fumbles for words.
Kreon waits impassively.*)

　　　　　　　　　　　out there —
　　　　　　　　　　　　　someone, —
　　New dust on the slimy flesh!

(*Pause. No sign from Kreon.*)

　　Someone has given it burial that way, and
　　Gone . . .

(*Long pause. Kreon finally speaks with deadly control.*)

KREON: And the man who dared do this?

SENTRY: 　　　　　　　　　　I swear I
　　Do not know! You must believe me!
　　　　　　　　　　　　Listen:　　　　90
　　The ground was dry, not a sign of digging, no,
　　Not a wheeltrack in the dust, no trace of anyone.
　　It was when they relieved us this morning: and one
　　　of them,
　　The corporal, pointed to it.
　　　　　　　There it was,
　　The strangest —
　　　　　　Look:　　　　　　　　　　95
　　The body, just mounded over with light dust: you
　　　see?
　　Not buried really, but as if they'd covered it
　　Just enough for the ghost's peace. And no sign
　　Of dogs or any wild animal that had been there.

　　And then what a scene there was! Every man of us　100
　　Accusing the other: we all proved the other man
　　　did it.
　　We all had proof that we could not have done it.
　　We were ready to take hot iron in our hands,
　　Walk through fire, swear by all the gods,
　　It was not I!　　　　　　　　　　105
　　I do not know who it was, but it was not I!

(*Kreon's rage has been mounting steadily, but the Sentry
is too intent upon his story to notice it.*)

　　And then, when this came to nothing, someone said
　　A thing that silenced us and made us stare
　　Down at the ground: you had to be told the news,
　　And one of us had to do it! We threw the dice,　　110
　　And the bad luck fell to me. So here I am,
　　No happier to be here than you are to have me:
　　Nobody likes the man who brings bad news.

CHORAGOS: I have been wondering, King: can it be that
　　the gods have done this?

KREON (*furiously*): Stop!　　　　　　　　　115
　　Must you doddering wrecks

Go out of your heads entirely? "The gods"!
Intolerable!
The gods favor this corpse? Why? How had he
    served them?
120 Tried to loot their temples, burn their images,
Yes, and the whole State, and its laws with it!
Is it your senile opinion that the gods love to honor
    bad men?
A pious thought! —
                   No, from the very beginning
There have been those who have whispered
    together,
125 Stiff-necked anarchists, putting their heads together,
Scheming against me in alleys. These are the men,
And they have bribed my own guard to do this
    thing.
(*Sententiously.*) Money!
There's nothing in the world so demoralizing as
    money.
130 Down go your cities,
Homes gone, men gone, honest hearts corrupted,
Crookedness of all kinds, and all for money!
(*To Sentry.*)   But you —
I swear by God and by the throne of God,
The man who has done this thing shall pay for it!
135 Find that man, bring him here to me, or your death
Will be the least of your problems: I'll string you up
Alive, and there will be certain ways to make you
Discover your employer before you die;
And the process may teach you a lesson you seem to
    have missed:
140 The dearest profit is sometimes all too dear:
That depends on the source. Do you understand
    me?
A fortune won is often misfortune.
SENTRY: King, may I speak?
KREON: Your very voice distresses me.
SENTRY: Are you sure that it is my voice, and not your
    conscience?
145 KREON: By God, he wants to analyze me now!
SENTRY: It is not what I say, but what has been done,
    that hurts you.
KREON: You talk too much.
SENTRY: Maybe; but I've done nothing.
KREON: Sold your soul for some silver: that's all you've
    done.
SENTRY: How dreadful it is when the right judge judges
    wrong!
150 KREON: Your figures of speech
May entertain you now; but unless you bring me the
    man,
You will get little profit from them in the end.
                        (*Exit Kreon into the palace.*)
SENTRY: "Bring me the man"— !
I'd like nothing better than bringing him the man!
But bring him or not, you have seen the last of me
155   here.
At any rate, I am safe!   (*Exit Sentry.*)

ODE° 1 • *Strophe 1*

CHORUS: Numberless are the world's wonders, but
        none
    More wonderful than man; the stormgray sea
    Yields to his prows, the huge crests bear him high;
    Earth, holy and inexhaustible, is graven
    With shining furrows where his plows have gone   5
    Year after year, the timeless labor of stallions.

Antistrophe 1

    The lightboned birds and beasts that cling to cover,
    The lithe fish lighting their reaches of dim water,
    All are taken, tamed in the net of his mind;
    The lion on the hill, the wild horse windy-maned,   10
    Resign to him; and his blunt yoke has broken
    The sultry shoulders of the mountain bull.

Strophe 2

    Words also, and thought as rapid as air,
    He fashions to his good use; statecraft is his
    And his the skill that deflects the arrows of snow,   15
    The spears of winter rain: from every wind
    He has made himself secure — from all but one:
    In the late wind of death he cannot stand.

Antistrophe 2

    O clear intelligence, force beyond all measure!
    O fate of man, working both good and evil!   20
    When the laws are kept, how proudly his city stands!
    When the laws are broken, what of his city then?
    Never may the anarchic man find rest at my hearth,
    Never be it said that my thoughts are his thoughts.

SCENE 2

(*Reenter Sentry leading Antigone.*)

CHORAGOS: What does this mean? Surely this captive
        woman
    Is the Princess, Antigone. Why should she be taken?
SENTRY: Here is the one who did it! We caught her
    In the very act of burying him. — Where is Kreon?
CHORAGOS: Just coming from the house.

(*Enter Kreon, center.*)

KREON: What has happened?   5
    Why have you come back so soon?
SENTRY (*expansively*):   O King,

Ode: Song sung by the Chorus.

A man should never be too sure of anything:
I would have sworn
That you'd not see me here again: your anger
Frightened me so, and the things you threatened me
10   with;
But how could I tell then
That I'd be able to solve the case so soon?
No dice-throwing this time: I was only too glad to
     come!
Here is this woman. She is the guilty one:
15   We found her trying to bury him.
Take her, then; question her; judge her as you will.
I am through with the whole thing now, and glad of
     it.
KREON: But this is Antigone! Why have you brought
     her here?
SENTRY: She was burying him, I tell you!
KREON (*severely*):   Is this the truth?
20 SENTRY: I saw her with my own eyes. Can I say more?
KREON: The details: come, tell me quickly!
SENTRY: It was like this:
After those terrible threats of yours, King,
We went back and brushed the dust away from the
     body.
The flesh was soft by now, and stinking,
25   So we sat on a hill to windward and kept guard.
No napping this time! We kept each other awake.
But nothing happened until the white round sun
Whirled in the center of the round sky over us:
Then, suddenly,
A storm of dust roared up from the earth, and the
30   sky
Went out, the plain vanished with all its trees
In the stinging dark. We closed our eyes and
     endured it.
The whirlwind lasted a long time, but it passed;
And then we looked, and there was Antigone!
35 I have seen
A mother bird come back to a stripped nest, heard
Her crying bitterly a broken note or two
For the young ones stolen. Just so, when this girl
Found the bare corpse, and all her love's work
     wasted,
40 She wept, and cried on heaven to damn the hands
That had done this thing.
                         And then she brought more dust
And sprinkled wine three times for her brother's
     ghost.
We ran and took her at once. She was not afraid,
Not even when we charged her with what she had
     done.
She denied nothing.
                    And this was a comfort to me,
45 And some uneasiness: for it is a good thing
To escape from death, but it is no great pleasure
To bring death to a friend.
                             Yet I always say
There is nothing so comfortable as your own safe
     skin!

KREON (*slowly, dangerously*): And you, Antigone,   50
You with your head hanging, — do you confess this
     thing?
ANTIGONE: I do. I deny nothing.
KREON (*to Sentry*):   You may go.
                                        (*Exit Sentry.*)
(*To Antigone.*) Tell me, tell me briefly:
Had you heard my proclamation touching this
     matter?
ANTIGONE: It was public. Could I help hearing it?   55
KREON: And yet you dared defy the law.
ANTIGONE: I dared.
It was not God's proclamation. That final Justice
That rules the world below makes no such laws.

Your edict, King, was strong,
But all your strength is weakness itself against   60
The immortal unrecorded laws of God.
They are not merely now: they were, and shall be,
Operative for ever, beyond man utterly.

I knew I must die, even without your decree:
I am only mortal. And if I must die   65
Now, before it is my time to die,
Surely this is no hardship: can anyone
Living, as I live, with evil all about me,
Think Death less than a friend? This death of mine
Is of no importance; but if I had left my brother   70
Lying in death unburied, I should have suffered.
Now I do not.
             You smile at me. Ah Kreon,
Think me a fool, if you like; but it may well be
That a fool convicts me of folly.
CHORAGOS: Like father, like daughter: both headstrong,
     deaf to reason!   75
She has never learned to yield.
KREON: She has much to learn.
The inflexible heart breaks first, the toughest iron
Cracks first, and the wildest horses bend their necks
At the pull of the smallest curb.
                                  Pride? In a slave?
This girl is guilty of a double insolence,   80
Breaking the given laws and boasting of it.
Who is the man here,
She or I, if this crime goes unpunished?
Sister's child, or more than sister's child,
Or closer yet in blood — she and her sister   85
Win bitter death for this!
(*To Servants.*)   Go, some of you,
Arrest Ismene. I accuse her equally.
Bring her: you will find her sniffling in the house
     there.

Her mind's a traitor: crimes kept in the dark
Cry for light, and the guardian brain shudders;   90
But how much worse than this
Is brazen boasting of barefaced anarchy!
ANTIGONE: Kreon, what more do you want than my
     death?

TOP: Kreon (F. Murray
Abraham) in a scene from the
1982 New York Shakespeare
Festival production directed by
Joseph Chaikin. RIGHT:
Antigone (Lisa Banes)
steadfastly admitting her guilt.

The Chorus urges Kreon to change his decree before it is too late.

KREON: Nothing.
    That gives me everything.
ANTIGONE: Then I beg you: kill me.
95   This talking is a great weariness: your words
    Are distasteful to me, and I am sure that mine
    Seem so to you. And yet they should not seem so:
    I should have praise and honor for what I have
        done.
    All these men here would praise me
100 Were their lips not frozen shut with fear of you.
    (*Bitterly.*) Ah the good fortune of kings,
    Licensed to say and do whatever they please!
KREON: You are alone here in that opinion.
ANTIGONE: No, they are with me. But they keep their
        tongues in leash.
105 KREON: Maybe. But you are guilty, and they are not.
ANTIGONE: There is no guilt in reverence for the dead.
KREON: But Eteocles — was he not your brother too?

ANTIGONE: My brother too.
KREON: And you insult his memory?
ANTIGONE (*softly*): The dead man would not say that I
        insult it.
KREON: He would: for you honor a traitor as much as
        him.   110
ANTIGONE: His own brother, traitor or not, and equal
        in blood.
KREON: He made war on his country. Eteocles defended
        it.
ANTIGONE: Nevertheless, there are honors due all the
        dead.
KREON: But not the same for the wicked as for the
        just.
ANTIGONE: Ah Kreon, Kreon,   115
    Which of us can say what the gods hold wicked?
KREON: An enemy is an enemy, even dead.
ANTIGONE: It is my nature to join in love, not hate.

KREON (*finally losing patience*): Go join them then; if
    you must have your love,
120   Find it in hell!
CHORAGOS: But see, Ismene comes:

(*Enter Ismene, guarded.*)

    Those tears are sisterly, the cloud
    That shadows her eyes rains down gentle sorrow.
KREON: You too, Ismene,
125   Snake in my ordered house, sucking my blood
    Stealthily — and all the time I never knew
    That these two sisters were aiming at my throne!
                             Ismene,
    Do you confess your share in this crime, or deny it?
    Answer me.
130 ISMENE: Yes, if she will let me say so. I am guilty.
    ANTIGONE (*coldly*): No, Ismene. You have no right to
        say so.
    You would not help me, and I will not have you
        help me.
    ISMENE: But now I know what you meant; and I am
        here
    To join you, to take my share of punishment.
    ANTIGONE: The dead man and the gods who rule the
135   dead
    Know whose act this was. Words are not friends.
    ISMENE: Do you refuse me, Antigone? I want to die
        with you:
    I too have a duty that I must discharge to the dead.
    ANTIGONE: You shall not lessen my death by sharing it.
140 ISMENE: What do I care for life when you are dead?
    ANTIGONE: Ask Kreon. You're always hanging on his
        opinions.
    ISMENE: You are laughing at me. Why, Antigone?
    ANTIGONE: It's a joyless laughter, Ismene.
    ISMENE: But can I do nothing?
    ANTIGONE: Yes. Save yourself. I shall not envy you.
    There are those who will praise you; I shall have
145   honor, too.
    ISMENE: But we are equally guilty!
    ANTIGONE: No more, Ismene.
    You are alive, but I belong to Death.
    KREON (*to the Chorus*): Gentlemen, I beg you to
        observe these girls:
    One has just now lost her mind; the other,
150   It seems, has never had a mind at all.
    ISMENE: Grief teaches the steadiest minds to waver,
        King.
    KREON: Yours certainly did, when you assumed guilt
        with the guilty!
    ISMENE: But how could I go on living without her?
    KREON: You are.
    She is already dead.
    ISMENE: But your own son's bride!
    KREON: There are places enough for him to push his
155   plow.
    I want no wicked women for my sons!
    ISMENE: O dearest Haimon, how your father wrongs
    you!

KREON: I've had enough of your childish talk of
    marriage!
CHORAGOS: Do you really intend to steal this girl from
    your son?
KREON: No; Death will do that for me.
CHORAGOS: Then she must die? 160
KREON (*ironically*): You dazzle me.
                  — But enough of this talk!
    (*To Guards.*) You, there, take them away and guard
    them well:
    For they are but women, and even brave men run
    When they see Death coming.
          (*Exeunt° Ismene, Antigone, and Guards.*)

ODE 2 • *Strophe 1*

CHORUS: Fortunate is the man who has never tasted
    God's vengeance!
Where once the anger of heaven has struck, that
    house is shaken
For ever: damnation rises behind each child
Like a wave cresting out of the black northeast,
When the long darkness under sea roars up   5
And bursts drumming death upon the windwhipped
    sand.

Antistrophe 1

I have seen this gathering sorrow from time long
    past
Loom upon Oedipus' children: generation from
    generation
Takes the compulsive rage of the enemy god.
So lately this last flower of Oedipus' line   10
Drank the sunlight! but now a passionate word
And a handful of dust have closed up all its beauty.

Strophe 2

What mortal arrogance
Transcends the wrath of Zeus?
Sleep cannot lull him nor the effortless long months 15
Of the timeless gods: but he is young for ever,
And his house is the shining day of high Olympos.
    All that is and shall be,
    And all the past, is his.
No pride on earth is free of the curse of heaven. 20

Antistrophe 2

The straying dreams of men
    May bring them ghosts of joy:
But as they drowse, the waking embers burn them;

165. [S.D.] *Exeunt:* Latin for "they go out."

25 Or they walk with fixed eyes, as blind men walk.
But the ancient wisdom speaks for our own time:
    Fate works most for woe
    With Folly's fairest show.
Man's little pleasure is the spring of sorrow.

SCENE 3

CHORAGOS: But here is Haimon, King, the last of all
    your sons.
    Is it grief for Antigone that brings him here,
    And bitterness at being robbed of his bride?

(*Enter Haimon.*)

KREON: We shall soon see, and no need of diviners.
                                                    — Son,
5   You have heard my final judgment on that girl:
    Have you come here hating me, or have you come
    With deference and with love, whatever I do?
HAIMON: I am your son, father. You are my guide.
    You make things clear for me, and I obey you.
    No marriage means more to me than your
10   continuing wisdom.
KREON: Good. That is the way to behave: subordinate
    Everything else, my son, to your father's will.
    This is what a man prays for, that he may get
    Sons attentive and dutiful in his house,
15   Each one hating his father's enemies,
    Honoring his father's friends. But if his sons
    Fail him, if they turn out unprofitably,
    What has he fathered but trouble for himself
    And amusement for the malicious?
                                    So you are right
20   Not to lose your head over this woman.
    Your pleasure with her would soon grow cold,
        Haimon,
    And then you'd have a hellcat in bed and
        elsewhere.
    Let her find her husband in Hell!
    Of all the people in this city, only she
25   Has had contempt for my law and broken it.

    Do you want me to show myself weak before the
        people?
    Or to break my sworn word? No, and I will not.
    The woman dies.
    I suppose she'll plead "family ties." Well, let her.
30   If I permit my own family to rebel,
    How shall I earn the world's obedience?
    Show me the man who keeps his house in hand,
    He's fit for public authority.
                            I'll have no dealings
    With lawbreakers, critics of the government:
35   Whoever is chosen to govern should be obeyed —
    Must be obeyed, in all things, great and small,
    Just and unjust! O Haimon,
    The man who knows how to obey, and that man
        only,

Knows how to give commands when the time
    comes.
You can depend on him, no matter how fast   40
The spears come: he's a good soldier, he'll stick it
    out.
Anarchy, anarchy! Show me a greater evil!
This is why cities tumble and the great houses rain
    down,
This is what scatters armies!
No, no: good lives are made so by discipline.   45
We keep the laws then, and the lawmakers,
And no woman shall seduce us. If we must lose,
Let's lose to a man, at least! Is a woman stronger
    than we?
CHORAGOS: Unless time has rusted my wits,
    What you say, King, is said with point and dignity.   50
HAIMON (*boyishly earnest*): Father:
    Reason is God's crowning gift to man, and you are
        right
    To warn me against losing mine. I cannot say —
    I hope that I shall never want to say! — that you
    Have reasoned badly. Yet there are other men   55
    Who can reason, too; and their opinions might be
        helpful.
    You are not in a position to know everything
    That people say or do, or what they feel:
    Your temper terrifies — everyone
    Will tell you only what you like to hear.   60
    But I, at any rate, can listen; and I have heard them
    Muttering and whispering in the dark about this girl.
    They say no woman has ever, so unreasonably,
    Died so shameful a death for a generous act:
    "She covered her brother's body. Is this indecent?   65
    She kept him from dogs and vultures. Is this a
        crime?
    Death? — She should have all the honor that we can
        give her!"

    This is the way they talk out there in the city.
    You must believe me:
    Nothing is closer to me than your happiness.   70
    What could be closer? Must not any son
    Value his father's fortune as his father does his?
    I beg you, do not be unchangeable:
    Do not believe that you alone can be right.
    The man who thinks that,   75
    The man who maintains that only he has the power
    To reason correctly, the gift to speak, the soul —
    A man like that, when you know him, turns out
        empty.
    It is not reason never to yield to reason!

    In flood time you can see how some trees bend,   80
    And because they bend, even their twigs are safe,
    While stubborn trees are torn up, roots and all.
    And the same thing happens in sailing:
    Make your sheet fast, never slacken, — and over
        you go,
    Head over heels and under: and there's your voyage.   85

Forget you are angry! Let yourself be moved!
I know I am young; but please let me say this:
The ideal condition
Would be, I admit, that men should be right by
       instinct;
90 But since we are all too likely to go astray,
The reasonable thing is to learn from those who can
       teach.
CHORAGOS: You will do well to listen to him, King,
If what he says is sensible. And you, Haimon,
Must listen to your father. — Both speak well.
KREON: You consider it right for a man of my years
95   and experience
To go to school to a boy?
HAIMON: It is not right
If I am wrong. But if I am young, and right,
What does my age matter?
KREON: You think it right to stand up for an anarchist?
100 HAIMON: Not at all. I pay no respect to criminals.
KREON: Then she is not a criminal?
HAIMON: The City would deny it, to a man.
KREON: And the City proposes to teach me how to rule?
HAIMON: Ah. Who is it that's talking like a boy now?
KREON: My voice is the one voice giving orders in this
105   City!
HAIMON: It is no City if it takes orders from one voice.
KREON: The State is the King!
HAIMON: Yes, if the State is a desert.

(*Pause.*)

KREON: This boy, it seems, has sold out to a woman.
HAIMON: If you are a woman: my concern is only for
       you.
KREON: So? Your "concern"! In a public brawl with
110   your father!
HAIMON: How about you, in a public brawl with
       justice?
KREON: With justice, when all that I do is within my
       rights?
HAIMON: You have no right to trample on God's right.
KREON (*completely out of control*): Fool, adolescent
       fool! Taken in by a woman!
115 HAIMON: You'll never see me taken in by anything vile.
KREON: Every word you say is for her!
HAIMON (*quietly, darkly*):   And for you.
And for me. And for the gods under the earth.
KREON: You'll never marry her while she lives.
HAIMON: Then she must die. — But her death will
       cause another.
120 KREON: Another?
       Have you lost your senses? Is this an open threat?
HAIMON: There is no threat in speaking to emptiness.
KREON: I swear you'll regret this superior tone of
       yours!
You are the empty one!
HAIMON: If you were not my father,
125 I'd say you were perverse.
KREON: You girl-struck fool, don't play at words with
       me!

HAIMON: I am sorry. You prefer silence.
KREON: Now, by God —
I swear, by all the gods in heaven above us,
You'll watch it, I swear you shall!
(*To the Servants.*)   Bring her out!
Bring the woman out! Let her die before his eyes!   130
Here, this instant, with her bridegroom beside her!
HAIMON: Not here, no; she will not die here, King.
And you will never see my face again.
Go on raving as long as you've a friend to endure
       you.   (*Exit Haimon.*)
CHORAGOS: Gone, gone.   135
Kreon, a young man in a rage is dangerous!
KREON: Let him do, or dream to do, more than a man
       can.
He shall not save these girls from death.
CHORAGOS: These girls?
You have sentenced them both?
KREON: No, you are right.
I will not kill the one whose hands are clean.   140
CHORAGOS: But Antigone?
KREON (*somberly*):   I will carry her far away
Out there in the wilderness, and lock her
Living in a vault of stone. She shall have food,
As the custom is, to absolve the State of her death.
And there let her pray to the gods of hell: 145
They are her only gods:
Perhaps they will show her an escape from death,
Or she may learn,
                    though late,
That piety shown the dead is pity in vain.
                                    (*Exit Kreon.*)

ODE 3 • *Strophe*

CHORUS: Love, unconquerable
Waster of rich men, keeper
Of warm lights and all-night vigil
In the soft face of a girl:
Sea-wanderer, forest-visitor!   5
Even the pure Immortals cannot escape you,
And mortal man, in his one day's dusk,
Trembles before your glory.

Antistrophe

Surely you swerve upon ruin
The just man's consenting heart,   10
As here you have made bright anger
Strike between father and son —
And none has conquered but Love!
A girl's glance working the will of heaven:
Pleasure to her alone who mocks us,   15
Merciless Aphrodite.°

16. Aphrodite: Goddess of love and beauty.

SCENE 4

CHORAGOS (*as Antigone enters guarded*): But I can no
      longer stand in awe of this,
   Nor, seeing what I see, keep back my tears.
   Here is Antigone, passing to that chamber
   Where all find sleep at last.

Strophe 1

5 ANTIGONE: Look upon me, friends, and pity me
      Turning back at the night's edge to say
      Good-by to the sun that shines for me no longer;
      Now sleepy Death
      Summons me down to Acheron,° that cold shore:
10   There is no bridesong there, nor any music.
   CHORUS: Yet not unpraised, not without a kind of
      honor,
      You walk at last into the underworld
      Untouched by sickness, broken by no sword.
      What woman has ever found your way to death?

Antistrophe 1

15 ANTIGONE: How often I have heard the story of Niobe,°
      Tantalos' wretched daughter, how the stone
      Clung fast about her, ivy-close: and they say
      The rain falls endlessly
      And sifting soft snow; her tears are never done.
20   I feel the loneliness of her death in mine.
   CHORUS: But she was born of heaven, and you
      Are woman, woman-born. If her death is yours,
      A mortal woman's, is this not for you
      Glory in our world and in the world beyond?

Strophe 2

25 ANTIGONE: You laugh at me. Ah, friends, friends,
      Can you not wait until I am dead? O Thebes,
      O men many-charioted, in love with Fortune,
      Dear springs of Dirce, sacred Theban grove,
      Be witnesses for me, denied all pity,
30   Unjustly judged! and think a word of love
      For her whose path turns
      Under dark earth, where there are no more tears.
   CHORUS: You have passed beyond human daring and
      come at last
      Into a place of stone where Justice sits.
35   I cannot tell
      What shape of your father's guilt appears in this.

---

9. Acheron: River in Hades, domain of the dead.   **15. Niobe:**
When Niobe's many children (up to twenty in some accounts)
were slain in punishment for their mother's boastfulness, Niobe
was turned into a stone on Mount Sipylus. Her tears became
the mountain's streams.

Antistrophe 2

ANTIGONE: You have touched it at last: that bridal bed
   Unspeakable, horror of son and mother mingling:
   Their crime, infection of all our family!
   O Oedipus, father and brother!   40
   Your marriage strikes from the grave to murder
      mine.
   I have been a stranger here in my own land:
   All my life
   The blasphemy of my birth has followed me.
CHORUS: Reverence is a virtue, but strength   45
   Lives in established law: that must prevail.
   You have made your choice,
   Your death is the doing of your conscious hand.

Epode°

ANTIGONE: Then let me go, since all your words are
      bitter,
   And the very light of the sun is cold to me.   50
   Lead me to my vigil, where I must have
   Neither love nor lamentation; no song, but silence.

(*Kreon interrupts impatiently.*)

KREON: If dirges and planned lamentations could put
      off death,
   Men would be singing for ever.
   (*To the Servants.*)   Take her, go!
   You know your orders: take her to the vault   55
   And leave her alone there. And if she lives or dies,
   That's her affair, not ours: our hands are clean.
ANTIGONE: O tomb, vaulted bride-bed in eternal rock,
   Soon I shall be with my own again
   Where Persephone° welcomes the thin ghosts
      underground: 60
   And I shall see my father again, and you, mother,
   And dearest Polyneices —
                         dearest indeed
   To me, since it was my hand
   That washed him clean and poured the ritual wine:
   And my reward is death before my time!   65

   And yet, as men's hearts know, I have done no
      wrong,
   I have not sinned before God. Or if I have,
   I shall know the truth in death. But if the guilt
   Lies upon Kreon who judged me, then, I pray,
   May his punishment equal my own.
CHORAGOS: O passionate heart,   70
   Unyielding, tormented still by the same winds!
KREON: Her guards shall have good cause to regret
      their delaying.
ANTIGONE: Ah! That voice is like the voice of death!

Epode: Song sung by the Chorus while standing still after
singing the strophe and antistrophe.   **60. Persephone:** Abducted by Pluto, god of the underworld, to be his queen.

KREON: I can give you no reason to think you are
         mistaken.

75 ANTIGONE: Thebes, and you my fathers' gods,
         And rulers of Thebes, you see me now, the last
         Unhappy daughter of a line of kings,
         Your kings, led away to death. You will remember
         What things I suffer, and at what men's hands,

80   Because I would not transgress the laws of heaven.
         (*To the Guards, simply.*) Come: let us wait no
             longer.   (*Exit Antigone, left, guarded.*)

ODE 4 • Strophe 1

CHORUS: All Danae's beauty was locked away
         In a brazen cell where the sunlight could not come:
         A small room still as any grave, enclosed her.
         Yet she was a princess too,

5   And Zeus in a rain of gold poured love upon her.°
         O child, child,
         No power in wealth or war
         Or tough sea-blackened ships
         Can prevail against untiring Destiny!

Antistrophe 1

10   And Dryas's son° also, that furious king,
         Bore the god's prisoning anger for his pride:
         Sealed up by Dionysos in deaf stone,
         His madness died among echoes.
         So at the last he learned what dreadful power

15   His tongue had mocked:
         For he had profaned the revels,
         And fired the wrath of the nine
         Implacable Sisters° that love the sound of the flute.

Strophe 2

20   And old men tell a half-remembered tale
         Of horror° where a dark ledge splits the sea
         And a double surf beats on the gray shores:
         How a king's new woman, sick
         With hatred for the queen he had imprisoned,
         Ripped out his two sons' eyes with her bloody
             hands

1–5. All Danae's beauty . . . poured love upon her: Locked
away to prevent the fulfillment of a prophecy that she would
bear a son who would kill her father, Danae was nonetheless
impregnated by Zeus, who came to her in a shower of gold.
The prophecy was fulfilled by the son that came of their union.
10. Dryas's son: King Lycurgus of Thrace, whom Dionysus,
god of wine, caused to be stricken with madness.   **18. Sisters:**
The Muses, nine sister goddesses who presided over poetry and
music, arts and sciences.   **19–20. half-remembered tale of horror:** The second wife of King Phineas blinded the sons of his
first wife, Cleopatra, whom Phineas had imprisoned in a cave.

While grinning Ares° watched the shuttle plunge   25
Four times: four blind wounds crying for revenge,

Antistrophe 2

Crying, tears and blood mingled. — Piteously born,
Those sons whose mother was of heavenly birth!
Her father was the god of the North Wind
And she was cradled by gales,   30
She raced with young colts on the glittering hills
And walked untrammeled in the open light:
But in her marriage deathless Fate found means
To build a tomb like yours for all her joy.

SCENE 5

(*Enter blind Teiresias, led by a boy. The opening speeches
of Teiresias should be in singsong contrast to the realistic lines of Kreon.*)

TEIRESIAS: This is the way the blind man comes,
         Princes, Princes,
         Lockstep, two heads lit by the eyes of one.
KREON: What new thing have you to tell us, old
         Teiresias?
TEIRESIAS: I have much to tell you: listen to the prophet,
         Kreon.
KREON: I am not aware that I have ever failed to listen.   5
TEIRESIAS: Then you have done wisely, King, and ruled
         well.
KREON: I admit my debt to you. But what have you to
         say?
TEIRESIAS: This, Kreon: you stand once more on the
         edge of fate.
KREON: What do you mean? Your words are a kind of
         dread.
TEIRESIAS: Listen, Kreon: 10
         I was sitting in my chair of augury, at the place
         Where the birds gather about me. They were all a-
             chatter,
         As is their habit, when suddenly I heard
         A strange note in their jangling, a scream, a
         Whirring fury; I knew that they were fighting,   15
         Tearing each other, dying
         In a whirlwind of wings clashing. And I was afraid.
         I began the rites of burnt-offering at the altar
         But Hephaistos° failed me: instead of bright flame,
         There was only the sputtering slime of the fat
             thigh-flesh
         Melting: the entrails dissolved in gray smoke,   20
         The bare bone burst from the welter. And no blaze!

         This was a sign from heaven. My boy described it,
         Seeing for me as I see for others.
         I tell you, Kreon, you yourself have brought   25

25. Ares: God of war.   **19. Hephaistos:** God of fire.

This new calamity upon us. Our hearths and altars
Are stained with the corruption of dogs and carrion
    birds
That glut themselves on the corpse of Oedipus's son.
The gods are deaf when we pray to them, their fire
30 Recoils from our offering, their birds of omen
Have no cry of comfort, for they are gorged
With the thick blood of the dead.
                                    O my son,
These are no trifles! Think: all men make mistakes,
But a good man yields when he knows his course is
    wrong,
35 And repairs the evil. The only crime is pride.

Give in to the dead man, then: do not fight with a
    corpse —
What glory is it to kill a man who is dead?
Think, I beg you:
It is for your own good that I speak as I do.
40 You should be able to yield for your own good.
KREON: It seems that prophets have made me their
    especial province.
All my life long
I have been a kind of butt for the dull arrows
Of doddering fortune-tellers!
                            No, Teiresias:
45 If your birds — if the great eagles of God himself
Should carry him stinking bit by bit to heaven,
I would not yield. I am not afraid of pollution:
No man can defile the gods.
                            Do what you will,
Go into business, make money, speculate
50 In India gold or that synthetic gold from Sardis,
Get rich otherwise than by my consent to bury him.
Teiresias, it is a sorry thing when a wise man
Sells his wisdom, lets out his words for hire!
TEIRESIAS: Ah Kreon! Is there no man left in the
    world —
KREON: To do what? — Come, let's have the
55   aphorism!
TEIRESIAS: No man who knows that wisdom outweighs
    any wealth?
KREON: As surely as bribes are baser than any
    baseness.
TEIRESIAS: You are sick, Kreon! You are deathly sick!
KREON: As you say: it is not my place to challenge a
    prophet.
60 TEIRESIAS: Yet you have said my prophecy is for sale.
KREON: The generation of prophets has always loved
    gold.
TEIRESIAS: The generation of kings has always loved
    brass.
KREON: You forget yourself! You are speaking to your
    King.
TEIRESIAS: I know it. You are a king because of me.
65 KREON: You have a certain skill; but you have sold out.
TEIRESIAS: King, you will drive me to words that —
KREON: Say them, say them!

Only remember: I will not pay you for them.
TEIRESIAS: No, you will find them too costly.
KREON: No doubt. Speak:
Whatever you say, you will not change my will.
TEIRESIAS: Then take this, and take it to heart!   70
The time is not far off when you shall pay back
Corpse for corpse, flesh of your own flesh.
You have thrust the child of this world into living
    night,
You have kept from the gods below the child that is
    theirs:
The one in a grave before her death, the other,   75
Dead, denied the grave. This is your crime:
And the Furies° and the dark gods of Hell
Are swift with terrible punishment for you.

Do you want to buy me now, Kreon?

                                    Not many days,
And your house will be full of men and women
    weeping,   80
And curses will be hurled at you from far
Cities grieving for sons unburied, left to rot
Before the walls of Thebes.

These are my arrows, Kreon: they are all for you.

(To Boy.) But come, child: lead me home.   85
Let him waste his fine anger upon younger men.
Maybe he will learn at last
To control a wiser tongue in a better head.
                                    (Exit Teiresias.)
CHORAGOS: The old man has gone, King, but his
    words
Remain to plague us. I am old, too,   90
But I cannot remember that he was ever false.
KREON: That is true. . . . It troubles me.
Oh it is hard to give in! but it is worse
To risk everything for stubborn pride.
CHORAGOS: Kreon: take my advice.
KREON: What shall I do?   95
CHORAGOS: Go quickly: free Antigone from her vault
And build a tomb for the body of Polyneices.
KREON: You would have me do this!
CHORAGOS: Kreon, yes!
And it must be done at once: God moves
Swiftly to cancel the folly of stubborn men.   100
KREON: It is hard to deny the heart! But I
Will do it: I will not fight with destiny.
CHORAGOS: You must go yourself, you cannot leave it
    to others.
KREON: I will go.
                — Bring axes, servants:
Come with me to the tomb. I buried her, I   105

77. **Furies:** Spirits called on to avenge crimes, especially those
against kin.

Will set her free.
                            Oh quickly!
My mind misgives —
The laws of the gods are mighty, and a man must
    serve them
To the last day of his life!   (*Exit Kreon.*)

PAEAN° • *Strophe 1*

CHORAGOS: God of many names
CHORUS: O Iacchos
                                              son
    of Kadmeian Semele
                          O born of the Thunder!
    Guardian of the West
                            Regent
    of Eleusis' plain
                      O Prince of maenad Thebes
5   and the Dragon Field by rippling Ismenos:°

Antistrophe 1

CHORAGOS: God of many names
CHORUS: the flame of torches
    flares on our hills
                        the nymphs of Iacchos
    dance at the spring of Castalia:°
    from the vine-close mountain
                                  come ah come in ivy:
10 *Evohe evohe!*° sings through the streets of Thebes

Strophe 2

CHORAGOS: God of many names
CHORUS: Iacchos of Thebes
    heavenly Child
                    of Semele bride of the Thunderer!
    The shadow of plague is upon us:
                                      come
    with clement feet
                        oh come from Parnasos
    down the long slopes
                          across the lamenting water
15

Paean: A song of praise or prayer.   **1–5. God of many names . . .
rippling Ismenos:** The following is a litany of names for Dionysus (Iacchos): he was son of Zeus ("Thunder") and Semele;
he was honored in secret rites at Eleusis; and he was worshiped
by the Maenads of Thebes. Kadmos, Semele's father, sowed
dragon's teeth in a field beside the river Ismenos from which
sprang warriors who became the first Thebans.   **8. spring of
Castalia:** A spring on Mount Parnassus used by priestesses of
Dionysus in rites of purification.   **10.** *Evohe evohe!:* Cry of the
Maenads to Dionysus.

Antistrophe 2

CHORAGOS: Io Fire! Chorister of the throbbing stars!
    O purest among the voices of the night!
    Thou son of God, blaze for us!
CHORUS: Come with choric rapture of circling Maenads
    Who cry *Io Iacche!*°
                      God of many names!   20

EXODOS°

(*Enter Messenger from left.*)

MESSENGER: Men of the line of Kadmos, you who live
    Near Amphion's citadel,°
                              I cannot say
    Of any condition of human life "This is fixed,
    This is clearly good, or bad." Fate raises up,
    And Fate casts down the happy and unhappy alike: 5
    No man can foretell his Fate.
                                  Take the case of Kreon:
    Kreon was happy once, as I count happiness:
    Victorious in battle, sole governor of the land,
    Fortunate father of children nobly born.
    And now it has all gone from him! Who can say   10
    That a man is still alive when his life's joy fails?
    He is a walking dead man. Grant him rich,
    Let him live like a king in his great house:
    If his pleasure is gone, I would not give
    So much as the shadow of smoke for all he owns.   15
CHORAGOS: Your words hint at sorrow: what is your
    news for us?
MESSENGER: They are dead. The living are guilty of
    their death.
CHORAGOS: Who is guilty? Who is dead? Speak!
MESSENGER: Haimon.
    Haimon is dead; and the hand that killed him
    Is his own hand.
CHORAGOS: His father's? or his own?   20
MESSENGER: His own, driven mad by the murder his
    father had done.
CHORAGOS: Teiresias, Teiresias, how clearly you saw it
    all!
MESSENGER: This is my news: you must draw what
    conclusions you can from it.
CHORAGOS: But look: Eurydice, our Queen:
    Has she overheard us?   25

(*Enter Eurydice from the palace, center.*)

EURYDICE: I have heard something, friends:
    As I was unlocking the gate of Pallas'° shrine,
    For I needed her help today, I heard a voice
    Telling of some new sorrow. And I fainted

20. *Io Iacche!:* Ritual cry.   **Exodos:** Final scene.   **2. Amphion's citadel:** A name for Thebes.   **27. Pallas:** Pallas Athene,
goddess of wisdom.

30   There at the temple with all my maidens about me.
      But speak again: whatever it is, I can bear it:
      Grief and I are no strangers.
    MESSENGER: Dearest Lady,
      I will tell you plainly all that I have seen.
35   I shall not try to comfort you: what is the use,
      Since comfort could lie only in what is not true?
      The truth is always best.
                  I went with Kreon
      To the outer plain where Polyneices was lying,
      No friend to pity him, his body shredded by dogs.
      We made our prayers in that place to Hecate
      And Pluto,° that they would be merciful. And we
40   bathed
      The corpse with holy water, and we brought
      Fresh-broken branches to burn what was left of it,
      And upon the urn we heaped up a towering barrow
      Of the earth of his own land.
                When we were done, we ran
      To the vault where Antigone lay on her couch of
45   stone.
      One of the servants had gone ahead,
      And while he was yet far off he heard a voice
      Grieving within the chamber, and he came back
      And told Kreon. And as the King went closer,
50   The air was full of wailing, the words lost,
      And he begged us to make all haste. "Am I a
      prophet?"
      He said, weeping, "And must I walk this road,
      The saddest of all that I have gone before?
      My son's voice calls me on. Oh quickly, quickly!
55   Look through the crevice there, and tell me
      If it is Haimon, or some deception of the gods!"

      We obeyed; and in the cavern's farthest corner
      We saw her lying:
      She had made a noose of her fine linen veil
60   And hanged herself. Haimon lay beside her,
      His arms about her waist, lamenting her,
      His love lost under ground, crying out
      That his father had stolen her away from him.

      When Kreon saw him the tears rushed to his eyes
      And he called to him: "What have you done, child?
65   speak to me.
      What are you thinking that makes your eyes so
      strange?
      O my son, my son, I come to you on my knees!"
      But Haimon spat in his face. He said not a word,
      Staring —
              And suddenly drew his sword
      And lunged. Kreon shrank back, the blade missed;
70   and the boy,
      Desperate against himself, drove it half its length
      Into his own side, and fell. And as he died
      He gathered Antigone close in his arms again,

39–40. Hecate and Pluto: Goddess of witchcraft and sorcery
and King of Hades, the underworld.

Choking, his blood bright red on her white cheek.
    And now he lies dead with the dead, and she is his   75
    At last, his bride in the house of the dead.
               (*Exit Eurydice into the palace.*)
CHORAGOS: She has left us without a word. What can
    this mean?
MESSENGER: It troubles me, too; yet she knows what is
    best,
    Her grief is too great for public lamentation,
    And doubtless she has gone to her chamber to weep   80
    For her dead son, leading her maidens in his dirge.

(*Pause.*)

CHORAGOS: It may be so: but I fear this deep silence.
MESSENGER: I will see what she is doing. I will go in.
             (*Exit Messenger into the palace.*)

(*Enter Kreon with attendants, bearing Haimon's body.*)

CHORAGOS: But here is the king himself: oh look at
    him,
    Bearing his own damnation in his arms.   85
KREON: Nothing you say can touch me any more.
    My own blind heart has brought me
    From darkness to final darkness. Here you see
    The father murdering, the murdered son —
    And all my civic wisdom!   90

    Haimon my son, so young, so young to die,
    I was the fool, not you; and you died for me.
CHORAGOS: That is the truth; but you were late in
    learning it.
KREON: This truth is hard to bear. Surely a god
    Has crushed me beneath the hugest weight of
    heaven,
     95
    And driven me headlong a barbaric way
    To trample out the thing I held most dear.

    The pains that men will take to come to pain!

(*Enter Messenger from the palace.*)

MESSENGER: The burden you carry in your hands is
    heavy,
    But it is not all: you will find more in your house.   100
KREON: What burden worse than this shall I find there?
MESSENGER: The Queen is dead.
KREON: O port of death, deaf world,
    Is there no pity for me? And you, Angel of evil,
    I was dead, and your words are death again.   105
    Is it true, boy? Can it be true?
    Is my wife dead? Has death bred death?
MESSENGER: You can see for yourself.

(*The doors are opened and the body of Eurydice is disclosed within.*)

KREON: Oh pity!
    All true, all true, and more than I can bear!   110
    O my wife, my son!
MESSENGER: She stood before the altar, and her heart
    Welcomed the knife her own hand guided,

And a great cry burst from her lips for Megareus°
    dead,
115   And for Haimon dead, her sons; and her last breath
    Was a curse for their father, the murderer of her sons.
    And she fell, and the dark flowed in through her
        closing eyes.
KREON: O God, I am sick with fear.
    Are there no swords here? Has no one a blow for
        me?
MESSENGER: Her curse is upon you for the deaths of
120   both.
KREON: It is right that it should be. I alone am guilty.
    I know it, and I say it. Lead me in,
    Quickly, friends.
    I have neither life nor substance. Lead me in.
CHORAGOS: You are right, if there can be right in so
125   much wrong.
    The briefest way is best in a world of sorrow.

114. **Megareus:** Son of Kreon and brother of Haimon,
Megareus sacrificed himself in the unsuccessful attack upon
Thebes, believing that his death was necessary to save Thebes.

KREON: Let it come,
    Let death come quickly, and be kind to me.
    I would not ever see the sun again.
CHORAGOS: All that will come when it will; but we,
        meanwhile,   130
    Have much to do. Leave the future to itself.
KREON: All my heart was in that prayer!
CHORAGOS: Then do not pray any more: the sky is deaf.
KREON: Lead me away. I have been rash and foolish.
    I have killed my son and my wife.   135
    I look for comfort; my comfort lies here dead.
    Whatever my hands have touched has come to
        nothing.
    Fate has brought all my pride to a thought of dust.

(*As Kreon is being led into the house, the Choragos
advances and speaks directly to the audience.*)

CHORAGOS: There is no happiness where there is no
        wisdom;
    No wisdom but in submission to the gods.   140
    Big words are always punished,
    And proud men in old age learn to be wise.

COMMENTARIES

    Oliver Taplin's emphasis on the audience's emotional state during the per-
formance of a Greek tragedy brings us back to the seminal comments of Aristotle. Tragedies were noted for their capacity to invoke pity and fear in the
audience. Taplin helps us understand how an audience's emotional response
can clarify our critical view of tragedy.
    Jean Anouilh, a major French playwright in the mid-twentieth century,
wrote a version of *Antigone* during the Nazi occupation of Paris and much of
France. The political content of the play takes on interesting meaning in light
of his experience. The excerpt that appears here offers a modern interpretation
of the struggle between Antigone and Kreon.

Oliver Taplin (*b. 1943*)
EMOTION AND MEANING IN GREEK TRAGEDY   *1983*

    *Scholar Oliver Taplin focuses on one of Aristotle's concerns in his commentary
on tragedy: the emotions aroused by drama. Taplin explores the argument that
devalues an emotional response to tragedy, and then he considers the proposition
that "tragedy is essentially the emotional experience of its audience."*

It seems to me, then, that Gorgias° is right that tragedy is essentially the *emotional experience of its audience.* Whatever it tells us about the world is conveyed by means of these emotions. Plato agreed with Gorgias in this, but he disapproved of the process and regarded it as harmful. Aristotle agreed with him too, but, contrary to Plato, regarded it as beneficial and salutary. Plato's objection was that such emotions are not the province of the highest part of the soul, the intellectual part. This is the forefather of the error made by so many later critics who have not acknowledged the centrality of emotion in the communication of tragedy. They think that if tragedy is essentially an emotional experience, it must be *solely* that; and they think this because they assume that strong emotion is necessarily in opposition to thought, that the psychic activities are mutually exclusive. But is this right? Understanding, reason, learning, moral discrimination; these things are not, in my experience, incompatible with emotion (nor presumably in the experience of Gorgias and Aristotle): What is incompatible is cold insensibility. Whether or not emotion is inimical to such intellectual processes depends on the *circumstances in which it is aroused.*

The characteristic tragic emotions — pity, horror, fascination, indignation, and so forth — are felt in many other situations besides in the theater. Above all we suffer them in the face of the misfortunes of real life, of course. What distinguishes the experience of a great tragedy? For one thing, as already remarked, we feel for the fortunes of people who have no direct personal relation to us: While this does not decrease the intensity of the emotion, it affords us some distance and perspective. We can feel and at the same time observe from outside. But does this distinguish tragedy from other "contrived" emotional experiences (most of them tending to the anti-intellectual), for example an animal hunt, a football match, an encounter group, reading a thriller, or watching a horror movie? Well, the experience of tragedy is by no means a random series of sensations. Our emotional involvement has perspective and context at the same time, and not just in retrospect. Thus the events of the tragedy are in an ordered *sequence,* a sequence which gives shape and comprehensibility to what we feel. And, most important of all, the affairs of the characters which move us are given a moral setting which is argued and explored in the play. They act and suffer within situations of moral conflict, or social, intellectual, and theological conflict. The quality of the tragedy depends *both* on its power to arouse our emotions *and* on the setting of those emotions in a sequence of moral and intellectual complications which is set out and examined. Tragedy evokes our feelings for others, like much else; but it is distinguished by the order and significance it imparts to suffering. So if the audience is not moved, then the tragedy, however intellectual, is a total failure: If its passions are aroused, but in a thoughtless, amorphous way, then it is merely a bad tragedy, sensational, melodramatic.

Thus it is that our emotions in the theater, far from driving out thought and meaning, are indivisible from them: They are simultaneous and mutually dependent. The experience of tragedy can achieve this coherence in a way that the emotional experiences of real life generally cannot because they are too close, too cluttered with detail and partiality, to be seen in perspective. Tragedy makes us feel that we understand life in its tragic aspects. We have the sense that we can better sympathize with and cope with suffering, misfortune, and waste. It is this sense of understanding (not isolated pearls of wisdom) that is the "message" of a tragedy,

Gorgias: Greek orator and rhetorician (c. 483–376 B.C.).

that the great playwright imparts. This is well put in T. S. Eliot's essay "Shakespeare and the Stoicism of Seneca," where he argues that it is the quality of the emotional expression rather than the quality of the philosophy which makes literature great, which makes it "strong, true and informative . . . useful and beneficial in the sense in which poetry is useful and beneficial." "All great poetry," Eliot° writes, "gives the illusion of a view of life . . . for every precise emotion tends towards intellectual formulation."

T. S. Eliot: Poet and critic (1888–1965).

Jean Anouilh (1910–1987)
FROM *ANTIGONE*   *1942*

TRANSLATED BY LEWIS GALANTIÈRE

Jean Anouilh began writing plays in 1931. Some of his best-known works, in addition to Antigone, *are* Eurydice *(1941),* Orestes *(1942),* Medea *(1946),* Ring Round the Moon *(1947),* The Waltz of the Toreadors *(1951), and* The Lark *(1952), which is about Joan of Arc. Anouilh wrote* Antigone *in 1942 in occupied Paris and produced it with his wife in the title role in February 1944, when the Nazis controlled most of Europe. Kreon (spelled Creon in this excerpt) is more willing to compromise in Anouilh's version of the play, and for that reason some critics saw the play as pro-Nazi. But Anouilh's sympathies were with Antigone, who represented the anti-Nazi view of the Parisian Resistance. Throughout its early run, the play was an inspiration to the patriotic French.*

This excerpt begins when Ismene returns to accept some of the responsibility for Polyneices' burial and continues through the confrontation of Haimon (Haemon in this excerpt) and Kreon to the end of the play.

(*Ismene enters through arch.*)

ISMENE (*distraught*): Antigone!
ANTIGONE (*turns to Ismene*): You, too? What do you want?
ISMENE: Oh, forgive me, Antigone. I've come back. I'll be brave. I'll go with you now.
ANTIGONE: Where will you go with me?
ISMENE (*to Creon*): Creon! If you kill her, you'll have to kill me too.
ANTIGONE: Oh, no, Ismene. Not a bit of it. I die alone. You don't think I'm going to let you die with me after what I've been through? You don't deserve it.
ISMENE: If you die, I don't want to live. I don't want to be left behind, alone.
ANTIGONE: You chose life and I chose death. Now stop blubbering. You had your chance to come with me in the black night, creeping on your hands and knees. You had your chance to claw up the earth with your nails, as I did; to get yourself caught like a thief, as I did. And you refused it.
ISMENE: Not anymore. I'll do it alone tonight.
ANTIGONE (*turns round toward Creon*): You hear that, Creon? The thing is catching! Who knows but that lots of people will catch the disease from me! What are you waiting for? Call in your guards! Come on, Creon! Show a little courage! It only hurts for a minute! Come on, cook!
CREON (*turns toward arch and calls*): Guard!

(*Guards enter through arch.*)

ANTIGONE (*in a great cry of relief*): At last, Creon!

(*Chorus enters through left arch.*)

CREON (*to the Guards*): Take her away! (*Creon goes up on top step.*)

(*Guards grasp Antigone by her arms, turn and hustle her toward the arch, right, and exeunt.° Ismene mimes horror, backs away toward the arch, left, then turns and runs out through the arch. A long pause, as Creon moves slowly downstage.*)

CHORUS (*Behind Creon. Speaks in a deliberate voice*): You are out of your mind, Creon. What have you done?

CREON (*his back to Chorus*): She had to die.

CHORUS: You must not let Antigone die. We shall carry the scar of her death for centuries.

CREON: She insisted. No man on earth was strong enough to dissuade her. Death was her purpose, whether she knew it or not. Polynices was a mere pretext. When she had to give up that pretext, she found another one — that life and happiness were tawdry things and not worth possessing. She was bent upon only one thing: to reject life and to die.

CHORUS: She is a mere child, Creon.

CREON: What do you want me to do for her? Condemn her to live?

HAEMON (*calls from offstage*): Father! (*Haemon enters through arch, right. Creon turns toward him.*)

CREON: Haemon, forget Antigone. Forget her, my dearest boy.

HAEMON: How can you talk like that?

CREON (*grasps Haemon by the hands*): I did everything I could to save her, Haemon. I used every argument. I swear I did. The girl doesn't love you. She could have gone on living for you; but she refused. She wanted it this way; she wanted to die.

HAEMON: Father! The guards are dragging Antigone away! You've got to stop them! (*He breaks away from Creon.*)

CREON (*looks away from Haemon*): I can't stop them. It's too late. Antigone has spoken. The story is all over Thebes. I cannot save her now.

CHORUS: Creon, you must find a way. Lock her up. Say that she has gone out of her mind.

CREON: Everybody will know it isn't so. The nation will say that I am making an exception of her because my son loves her. I cannot.

CHORUS: You can still gain time and get her out of Thebes.

CREON: The mob already knows the truth. It is howling for her blood. I can do nothing.

HAEMON: But, Father, you are master in Thebes!

CREON: I am master under the law. Not above the law.

HAEMON: You cannot let Antigone be taken from me. I am your son!

CREON: I cannot do anything else, my poor boy. She must die and you must live.

HAEMON: Live, you say! Live a life without Antigone? A life in which I am to go on admiring you as you busy yourself about your kingdom, make your persuasive speeches, strike your attitudes? Not without Antigone. I love Antigone. I will not live without Antigone!

CREON: Haemon — you will have to resign yourself to life without Antigone. (*He moves to left of Haemon.*) Sooner or later there comes a day of sorrow in each man's life when he must cease to be a child and take up the burden of manhood. That day has come for you.

HAEMON (*backs away a step*): That giant strength, that courage. That massive god who used to pick me up in his arms and shelter me from shadows and monsters — was that you, Father? Was it of you I stood in awe? Was that man you?

CREON: For God's sake, Haemon, do not judge me! Not you, too!

HAEMON (*pleading now*): This is all a bad dream, Father. You are not yourself. It isn't true that we have been backed up against a wall, forced to surrender. We don't have to say *yes* to this terrible thing. You are still king. You are still the father I revered.

exeunt: Latin for "they go out."

You have no right to desert me, to shrink into nothingness. The world will be too bare, I shall be too alone in the world, if you force me to disown you.

CREON: The world *is* bare, Haemon, and you *are* alone. You must cease to think your father all-powerful. Look straight at me. See your father as he is. That is what it means to grow up and be a man.

HAEMON (*stares at Creon for a moment*): I tell you that I will not live without Antigone. (*Turns and goes quickly out through arch.*)

CHORUS: Creon, the boy will go mad.

CREON: Poor boy! He loves her.

CHORUS: Creon, the boy is wounded to death.

CREON: We are all wounded to death.

(*First Guard enters through arch, right, followed by Second and Third Guards pulling Antigone along with them.*)

FIRST GUARD: Sir, the people are crowding into the palace!

ANTIGONE: Creon, I don't want to see their faces. I don't want to hear them howl. You are going to kill me; let that be enough. I want to be alone until it is over.

CREON: Empty the palace! Guards at the gates!

(*Creon quickly crosses toward the arch; exit. Two Guards release Antigone; exeunt behind Creon. Chorus goes out through arch, left. The lighting dims so that only the area about the table is lighted. The cyclorama° is covered with a dark blue color. The scene is intended to suggest a prison cell, filled with shadows and dimly lit. Antigone moves to stool and sits. The First Guard stands upstage. He watches Antigone, and as she sits, he begins pacing slowly downstage, then upstage. A pause.*)

ANTIGONE (*turns and looks at the Guard*): It's you, is it?

GUARD: What do you mean, me?

ANTIGONE: The last human face that I shall see. (*A pause as they look at each other, then Guard paces upstage, turns, and crosses behind table.*) Was it you that arrested me this morning?

GUARD: Yes, that was me.

ANTIGONE: You hurt me. There was no need for you to hurt me. Did I act as if I was trying to escape?

GUARD: Come on now, Miss. It was my business to bring you in. I did it. (*A pause. He paces to and fro upstage. Only the sound of his boots is heard.*)

ANTIGONE: How old are you?

GUARD: Thirty-nine.

ANTIGONE: Have you any children?

GUARD: Yes. Two.

ANTIGONE: Do you love your children?

GUARD: What's that got to do with you? (*A pause. He paces upstage and downstage.*)

ANTIGONE: How long have you been in the Guard?

GUARD: Since the war. I was in the army. Sergeant. Then I joined the Guard.

ANTIGONE: Does one have to have been an army sergeant to get into the Guard?

GUARD: Supposed to be. Either that or on special detail. But when they make you a guard, you lose your stripes.

ANTIGONE (*murmurs*): I see.

GUARD: Yes. Of course, if you're a guard, everybody knows you're something special; they know you're an old N.C.O.° Take pay, for instance. When you're a guard you get your pay, and on top of that you get six months' extra pay, to make sure you don't lose anything by not being a sergeant anymore. And of course you do better than that. You get a house, coal, rations, extras for the wife and kids. If you've got two kids, like me, you draw better than a sergeant.

ANTIGONE (*barely audible*): I see.

---

cyclorama: Curved cloth or wall forming the back of many modern stage settings.
N.C.O.: Noncommissioned officer, usually of a subordinate rank such as sergeant.

GUARD: That's why sergeants, now, they don't like guards. Maybe you noticed they try to make out they're better than us? Promotion, that's what it is. In the army, any-body can get promoted. All you need is good conduct. Now in the Guard, it's slow, and you have to know your business — like how to make out a report and the like of that. But when you're an N.C.O. in the Guard, you've got something that even a sergeant major ain't got. For instance —

ANTIGONE (*breaking him off*): Listen.

GUARD: Yes, Miss.

ANTIGONE: I'm going to die soon.

(*The Guard looks at her for a moment, then turns and moves away.*)

GUARD: For instance, people have a lot of respect for guards, they have. A guard may be a soldier, but he's kind of in the civil service, too.

ANTIGONE: Do you think it hurts to die?

GUARD: How would I know? Of course, if somebody sticks a saber in your guts and turns it round, it hurts.

ANTIGONE: How are they going to put me to death?

GUARD: Well, I'll tell you. I heard the proclamation all right. Wait a minute. How did it go now? (*He stares into space and recites from memory.*) "In order that our fair city shall not be pol-luted with her sinful blood, she shall be im-mured — immured." That means, they shove you in a cave and wall up the cave.

ANTIGONE: Alive?

GUARD: Yes. . . . (*He moves away a few steps.*)

ANTIGONE (*murmurs*): O tomb! O bridal bed! Alone! (*Antigone sits there, a tiny figure in the middle of the stage. You would say she felt a little chilly. She wraps her arms round herself.*)

GUARD: Yes! Outside the southeast gate of the town. In the Cave of Hades. In broad daylight. Some detail, eh, for them that's on the job! First they thought maybe it was a job for the army. Now it looks like it's going to be the Guard. There's an outfit for you! Nothing the Guard can't do. No wonder the army's jealous.

ANTIGONE: A pair of animals.

GUARD: What do you mean, a pair of animals?

ANTIGONE: When the winds blow cold, all they need do is to press close against one another. I am all alone.

GUARD: Is there anything you want? I can send out for it, you know.

ANTIGONE: You are very kind. (*A pause. Antigone looks up at the Guard.*) Yes, there is something I want. I want you to give someone a letter from me, when I am dead.

GUARD: How's that again? A letter?

ANTIGONE: Yes, I want to write a letter; and I want you to give it to someone for me.

GUARD (*straightens up*): Now, wait a minute. Take it easy. It's as much as my job is worth to go handing out letters from prisoners.

ANTIGONE (*removes a ring from her finger and holds it out toward him*): I'll give you this ring if you will do it.

GUARD: Is it gold? (*He takes the ring from her.*)

ANTIGONE: Yes, it is gold.

GUARD (*shakes his head*): Uh-uh. No can do. Suppose they go through my pockets. I might get six months for a thing like that. (*He stares at the ring, then glances off right to make sure that he is not being watched.*) Listen, tell you what I'll do. You tell me what you want to say, and I'll write it down in my book. Then, afterwards, I'll tear out the pages and give them to the party, see? If it's in my handwriting, it's all right.

ANTIGONE (*winces*): In your handwriting? (*She shudders slightly.*) No. That would be awful. The poor darling! In your handwriting.

GUARD (*offers back the ring*): O.K. It's no skin off my nose.

ANTIGONE (*quickly*): Of course, of course. No, keep the ring. But hurry. Time is getting short. Where is your notebook? (*The Guard pockets the ring, takes his notebook and pencil from his pocket, puts his foot up on chair, and rests the notebook on his knee, licks his pencil.*) Ready? (*He nods.*) Write, now. "My darling . . ."

GUARD *(writes as he mutters)*: The boyfriend, eh?

ANTIGONE: "My darling. I wanted to die, and perhaps you will not love me anymore . . ."

GUARD *(mutters as he writes)*: ". . . will not love me anymore."

ANTIGONE: "Creon was right. It is terrible to die."

GUARD *(repeats as he writes)*: ". . . terrible to die."

ANTIGONE: "And I don't even know what I am dying for. I am afraid . . ."

GUARD *(looks at her)*: Wait a minute! How fast do you think I can write?

ANTIGONE *(takes hold of herself)*: Where are you?

GUARD *(reads from his notebook)*: "And I don't even know what I am dying for."

ANTIGONE: No. Scratch that out. Nobody must know that. They have no right to know. It's as if they saw me naked and touched me, after I was dead. Scratch it all out. Just write: "Forgive me."

GUARD *(looks at Antigone)*: I cut out everything you said there at the end, and I put down, "Forgive me"?

ANTIGONE: Yes. "Forgive me, my darling. You would all have been so happy except for Antigone. I love you."

GUARD *(finishes the letter)*: ". . . I love you." *(He looks at her.)* Is that all?

ANTIGONE: That's all.

GUARD *(straightens up, looks at notebook)*: Damn funny letter.

ANTIGONE: I know.

GUARD *(looks at her)*: Who is it to? *(A sudden roll of drums begins and continues until after Antigone's exit. The First Guard pockets the notebook and shouts at Antigone.)* O.K. That's enough out of you! Come on!

(At the sound of the drum roll, Second and Third Guards enter through the arch. Antigone rises. Guards seize her and exeunt with her. The lighting moves up to suggest late afternoon. Chorus enters.)

CHORUS: And now it is Creon's turn.

(Messenger runs through the arch, right.)

MESSENGER: The Queen . . . the Queen! Where is the Queen?

CHORUS: What do you want with the Queen? What have you to tell the Queen?

MESSENGER: News to break her heart. Antigone had just been thrust into the cave. They hadn't finished heaving the last block of stone into place when Creon and the rest heard a sudden moaning from the tomb. A hush fell over us all, for it was not the voice of Antigone. It was Haemon's voice that came forth from the tomb. Everybody looked at Creon; and he howled like a man demented: "Take away the stones! Take away the stones!" The slaves leaped at the wall of stones, and Creon worked with them, sweating and tearing at the blocks with his bleeding hands. Finally a narrow opening was forced, and into it slipped the smallest guard.

Antigone had hanged herself by the cord of her robe, by the red and golden twisted cord of her robe. The cord was round her neck like a child's collar. Haemon was on his knees, holding her in his arms and moaning, his face buried in her robe. More stones were removed, and Creon went into the tomb. He tried to raise Haemon to his feet. I could hear him begging Haemon to rise to his feet. Haemon was deaf to his father's voice, till suddenly he stood up of his own accord, his eyes dark and burning. Anguish was in his face, but it was the face of a little boy. He stared at his father. Then suddenly he struck him — hard; and he drew his sword. Creon leaped out of range. Haemon went on staring at him, his eyes full of contempt — a glance that was like a knife, and that Creon couldn't escape. The King stood trembling in the far corner of the tomb, and Haemon went on staring. Then, without a word, he stabbed himself and lay down beside Antigone, embracing her in a great pool of blood.

(A pause as Creon and Page enter through arch on the Messenger's last words. Chorus and the Messenger both turn to look at Creon; then exit the Messenger through curtain.)

CREON: I have had them laid out side by side. They are together at last, and at peace. Two lovers on the morrow of their bridal. Their work is done.

CHORUS: But not yours, Creon. You have still one thing to learn. Eurydice, the Queen, your wife —

CREON: A good woman. Always busy with her garden, her preserves, her sweaters — those sweaters she never stopped knitting for the poor. Strange, how the poor never stop needing sweaters. One would almost think that was all they needed.

CHORUS: The poor in Thebes are going to be cold this winter, Creon. When the Queen was told of her son's death, she waited carefully until she had finished her row, then put down her knitting calmly — as she did everything. She went up to her room, her lavender-scented room, with its embroidered doilies and its pictures framed in plush; and there, Creon, she cut her throat. She is laid out now in one of those two old-fashioned twin beds, exactly where you went to her one night when she was still a maiden. Her smile is still the same, scarcely a shade more melancholy. And if it were not for that great red blot on the bed linen by her neck, one might think she was asleep.

CREON (*in a dull voice*): She, too. They are all asleep. (*Pause.*) It must be good to sleep.

CHORUS: And now you are alone, Creon.

CREON: Yes, all alone. (*To Page.*) My lad.

PAGE: Sir?

CREON: Listen to me. They don't know it, but the truth is, the work is there to be done, and a man can't fold his arms and refuse to do it. They say it's dirty work. But if we didn't do it, who would?

PAGE: I don't know, sir.

CREON: Of course you don't. You'll be lucky if you never find out. In a hurry to grow up, aren't you?

PAGE: Oh, yes, sir.

CREON: I shouldn't be if I were you. Never grow up if you can help it. (*He is lost in thought as the hour chimes.*) What time is it?

PAGE: Five o clock, sir.

CREON: What have we on at five o'clock?

PAGE: Cabinet meeting, sir.

CREON: Cabinet meeting. Then we had better go along to it.

(*Exeunt Creon and Page slowly through arch, left, and Chorus moves downstage.*)

CHORUS: And there we are. It is quite true that if it had not been for Antigone they would all have been at peace. But that is over now. And they are all at peace. All those who were meant to die have died: those who believed one thing, those who believed the contrary thing, and even those who believed nothing at all, yet were caught up in the web without knowing why. All dead: stiff, useless, rotting. And those who have survived will now begin quietly to forget the dead: they won't remember who was who or which was which. It is all over. Antigone is calm tonight, and we shall never know the name of the fever that consumed her. She has played her part.

(*Three Guards enter, resume their places on steps as at the rise of the curtain, and begin to play cards.*)

A great melancholy wave of peace now settles down upon Thebes, upon the empty palace, upon Creon, who can now begin to wait for his own death. Only the guards are left, and none of this matters to them. It's no skin off their noses. They go on playing cards.

(*Chorus walks toward the arch, left, as the curtain falls.*)

Euripides

Euripides (c. 485–c. 406 B.C.), last of the great Greek tragedians, did not enjoy the personal popularity accorded Aeschylus and Sophocles, possibly because his work criticized Athenian politics and society. Moreover, he was not highly regarded because he broke away from the formality of language and theme of his predecessors.

Euripides was raised in Salamis, the island from which the Greeks decisively defeated the Persians in 480 B.C. This victory heralded the Periclean Age (c. 460–404 B.C.), when Athens enjoyed its greatest power. During that time, however, the Athenians spent almost three decades fighting the Peloponnesian Wars (431–404 B.C.), which drained their energies and treasury. Eventually, they were forced to relinquish their dominance to Sparta. In such an environment, the officials and patriots of Athens were not happy with the work of someone who reminded them of their mistakes and questioned their values.

Euripides is especially noted for shifting the focus of dramatic events from the gods to humans. He valued individual human beings and the working of their wills. Influenced by the teaching of the Sophists, wandering professors who taught argument and philosophy, he agreed with Protagoras's principle "Man is the measure of all things." The ancients sometimes referred to Euripides as the philosopher of the stage.

One aspect of his dramatic critique of Greek culture was an unusual emphasis on women. Medea is the first thoroughly developed female character in Greek drama. She is treated as an independent woman, not as Jason's wife or as someone's mother. She is herself. Athenians, intolerant of foreigners and women, felt both groups to be inferior to Greek aristocratic men. It is no wonder that of the twenty plays Euripides produced at the feasts of Dionysus only five won prizes.

Of his ninety-two plays, eighteen survive — more than twice as many as survive from any other Greek tragedian: *Alcestis* (438), *Medea* (431), *Hippolytus* (428), *Andromache* (426?), *Cyclops* (c. 423), *The Children of Heracles* (c. 430), *Heracles* (c. 417), *The Suppliants* (c. 422), *Hecuba* (c. 424), *The Trojan Women* (415), *Electra* (c. 417), *Iphigenia in Taurus* (c. 412), *Helen* (412), *Ion* (c. 411), *The Phoenician Women* (c. 412–408), *Orestes* (408), *The Bacchae* (405), and *Iphigenia in Aulis* (405). Another play, *Rhesus*, long attributed to Euripides, is now thought to have been written by an anonymous fourth-century B.C. playwright. Ten of Euripides' remaining plays place women at their center.

Euripides continued Aeschylus's innovations in his use of the *skene*. Instead of representing the front of a palace, the *skene* in Euripides' plays sometimes represented a peasant's hut, a rural shrine, or other common structure. He was interested in theatrical devices, especially machines that gave him the opportunity to achieve dramatic effects. He often used the *mekane* — a crane or derrick that lifted actors in or out of the play — to resolve his dramas when his characters found themselves in impossible situations. His choral odes, although beautiful, are sometimes considered detachable from the episodes of dramatic action. Moreover, his dialogue is more colloquial — closer to everyday speech — than is the dialogue found in other Greek tragedies. All these deviations from the dramatic norm emphasize the humanity in his plays and elevate human values over those of the gods.

Eighteen months before his death, Euripides left Athens for the court of King Archelaus in Macedon. His departure may have signaled his dissatisfaction with the politics of Athens, or it may have been prompted by the indifference of Athens to his talents. In any event, his works were performed long after his death, and, ironically, his posthumous popularity dwarfed that of the other tragic playwrights.

MEDEA

Although *Medea* won only last prize at the City Dionysia festival in 431 B.C., behind works by Euphorion, son of Aeschylus, and Sophocles, the play's emotional dimension and Medea's depth of feeling have made her one of the most impressive characters in dramatic fiction.

In his first play, *The Daughters of Pelias* (454 B.C.), Euripides treated part of the well-known legend of Jason and Medea. On the order of his enemy, King Pelias of Iolcus, Jason sailed with the Argonauts to Colchis. There, with the help of Medea's witchcraft, he retrieved the Golden Fleece. Medea returned with Jason to Iolcus, where she convinced Pelias's daughters that they could restore their father's youth if they cut him into pieces and boiled the pieces with magic herbs, as she had done with a ram. When the daughters tried it, however, the treacherous Medea gave them impotent herbs and Pelias died. Jason's Argonauts captured Iolcus, and Medea and Jason escaped to Corinth.

Euripides continued the tale in *Medea*. When the play opens, Jason and Medea are in exile in Corinth. Jason has decided to marry King Creon's daughter Glauke, supposedly to guarantee the safety of the children he has had with Medea. Considering all the sacrifices she has made for Jason, Medea feels betrayed and cast aside for a younger woman. Medea's situation is painful. The Chorus recognizes the legality of Jason's decision to put aside his wife in favor of a younger woman. His motives might be interpreted as plausible and perhaps noble. Medea is Asiatic, a foreigner. By marrying Glauke, Jason will impart noble status on his and Medea's children. By law he can maintain Medea as a concubine along with his wife. Medea knows this, but she rejects Jason's explanations. He assumes that she is merely sexually jealous of Glauke.

The themes of this tragedy are certainly accessible to modern audiences. As the critic G.M.A. Grube has pointed out, "The tragedy of *Medea* — of Love turning to hatred when betrayed, until the woman's whole soul is dominated by a lust for vengeance that overpowers even maternal love — is one which no modern reader should, in its essentials, find difficult to make his own." The modern audience, however, may take pause at Medea's revenge. She plans not only to rid Jason of his young bride but to kill Creon as well. And her vengeance does not stop there: she determines to kill those whom Jason most loves — their two sons.

Exploring Medea's feelings and her awareness of the gravity of her actions sets Euripides' work apart from that of other Greek tragedians. His sympathy for the many tragic heroines he created marks his work from beginning to end. Unlike other playwrights working with the Medea legend, Euripides saves Medea from the punishment of Jason and the people of Corinth. To do this, he uses the *mekane,* in the form of the dragon chariot that lifts her above the *skene* beyond Jason's reach at the end of the play. She leaves him in an agony of grief.

Medea in Performance

Medea has one of the longest and most active production histories in all of drama. Not only did Alexander the Great produce the play in the fourth century, but the Roman playwright Seneca wrote his own version (A.D. 60), with a much less sympathetic Medea. Seneca's Jason is a reasonable man unfairly wronged by a witch. French and English productions and adaptations began in 1553 and have continued to the present. The French playwright Corneille wrote his version in 1634, and an English version of 1756 portrays Medea as insane.

Important modern productions began in the early twentieth century. The American actress Margaret Anglin was a sensation in the 1918 production, which established her as the greatest Medea up to her time. Hans Henny Jahnne adapted *Medea* for a production in Berlin in 1926. According to a review written at the time, Medea was portrayed by an older black actress whose magic potions kept Jason young while she aged. The poisoned robe Medea gave to her young rival had the power to turn the princess into an elderly woman "who gradually [grew] older and older and [decayed] into death and decomposition."

Judith Anderson made the role hers in 1947, in a version by the American poet Robinson Jeffers that played for almost a decade. In the 1982 production with John Gielgud as Jason and Zoë Caldwell as Medea, a much older Judith Anderson played the nurse and received extraordinary reviews. In 1974 Greek actress Irene Papas starred in New York in a colloquial English version. Important productions were staged in Russia in the 1960s. Countee Cullen very successfully produced the play in 1959 with a black Medea. In 1986, an all-male Kabuki version of *Medea* was presented at the Delacorte Theater in Central Park by the Japanese Toho Company under the direction of Yukio Ninagawa. A critic from the *New York Times* described the director's intentions: "Yukio Ninagawa, known for his productions of classical theater as avant-garde spectacle, aims in his work to create a universal theater that fuses the traditions of Japanese and Western culture in an expressive style of its own" (Jennifer Dunning, *New York Times,* Aug. 31, 1986). A *Boston Globe* critic praised the power of the Kabuki production: "This was a Medea of stunning theatrical imagery. Classical Corinthian order was gradually and relentlessly replaced by savage revenge and blood-stained chaos" (Lyn Gardner, *Boston Globe,* Aug. 29, 1986). In April 1994 Diana Rigg was Medea in a production highly praised in both London and New York. She was seen as commanding and powerful in the part, played starkly and simply.

Euripides (c. 485–406 B.C.)

MEDEA

TRANSLATED BY PAUL ROCHE

Characters

NURSE
TUTOR *to Medea's sons*
MEDEA, *Asiatic princess*
CHORUS *of Corinthian women*
CREON, *King of Corinth*
JASON, *husband of Medea*
AEGEUS, *King of Athens*
MESSENGER
TWO BOYS, *sons of Medea*
HANDMAIDS *of Medea*
ATTENDANTS AND GUARDS *for Creon and Aegeus*

Time and Setting: *It is midmorning outside Jason's house in Corinth. Ten years have passed since the Argonauts sailed home after finding the Golden Fleece. During that time, Jason and Medea [the Asian bride he brought back with him] have been living modestly in Corinth: models of an unassailable married life of devotion to each other and their children. But the news has just broken that Jason is to marry the daughter of the King of Corinth. [The exit on stage left leads to the town and royal palace, that on the right to the country.]*

[*Enter the Nurse from the house. She is an old woman who has looked after Medea from babyhood. Her face, the only part of her showing from the dark, heavy clothes that envelop her, is puckered with age and distress.*]

PROLOGUE°

NURSE: Why did the winged oars of the Argo°
    ever weave between those gnashing blue
    fjords towards the land of Colchis?
        Why did the pines in the dells of Pelion°
5   ever fall to the axe and fill
    the rowing hands of heroes sent by Pelias°
    to fetch the Golden Fleece?
        My mistress, Medea, then

never would have sailed to Iolcus° with its towers
or been struck to the heart with love of Jason.   10
    She never would have baited Pelias' daughters
to the murder of their father°
and be living here in Corinth° now
with her husband and her children . . .
    Ah, she has merited this city's good opinion,   15
exile though she came,
and was in everything Jason's perfect foil,
being in marriage that saving thing:
a wife who does not go against her man.

[*With a despairing glance toward the house.*]

    Now everything has turned to hate,   20
her passion to a plague.
    Jason has betrayed his sons and her,
takes to bed a royal bride
Creon's daughter — the king of Corinth's.
    Medea, spurned and desolate,   25
breaks out in oaths,
invokes the solemnest vows,
calls the gods to witness
how Jason has rewarded her.
    She does not eat,   30
lies prostrate, slumped in anguish,
wastes away in day-long tears.
    Ever since she heard of Jason's perfidy
she has not raised her eyes
or looked up from the floor.   35
    She might be a rock or wave of the sea,
for all she heeds of sympathy from friends,
except sometimes to tilt her pale head away
and moan to herself about her father —
whom she loved —   40
and her country and the home she sacrificed°
to journey here

[Prologue: Portion of the play explaining the background and current action. (The editor's notes are in brackets.)]   **1. Argo:** The ship in which Jason and his companions sailed on the quest for the Golden Fleece.   **4. Pelion:** A mountain in northern Greece.   **6. Pelias:** When Jason came to claim the kingdom of Iolcus, from which Pelias had expelled Jason's father, Pelias sent Jason to get the Golden Fleece.

9. Iolcus: Town from which the Argonauts sailed.   **11–12. She never . . . murder of their father:** Medea, a sorceress by reputation, tricked Pelias's daughters into cutting their father into pieces and boiling them, on the pretext that this would magically restore him to youth. This was her revenge on Pelias, who had murdered Jason's father, Aeson, during Jason's absence on the quest for the Golden Fleece, which was successful.   **13. be living here in Corinth:** Expelled from the kingdom [of Iolcus], Jason and Medea took refuge in Corinth, a wealthy city and rival of Athens, located on the isthmus between the Peloponnese and Attica.   **41. home she sacrificed:** Medea had helped Jason take the Golden Fleece away from her own father's kingdom.

with a man — oh — who so disdains her now.
      Yes, now she knows
45 at a terrible first hand
what it is to miss one's native land.

[*She pauses; almost whispers the next words.*]

      She hates her sons.
      Takes no pleasure in their sight.
      I dread to think
50 of what is hatching in her mind.
      She is a fierce spirit:
takes no insult lying down.
      I know her well. She frightens me:°
a dangerous woman, and
55 anyone who crosses her
will not easily sing a song of triumph.
      But here come the boys after their run:
suspecting nothing of a mother's tragedy . . .
      Oh, it is true —
60 unhappy thoughts and youth never go together.

[*Enter Tutor with Two Boys, aged about eight and ten.
Tutor is an old man, dressed loosely in an ochercolored
cloak. The boys are squeezed into shorts and have close-
fitting woolen caps on their heads. They hang about in
the background, laughing and talking, while the old
man advances.*]

TUTOR [*with a half-teasing familiarity*]:   Ah, Nurse!
      Faithful old appendage of my Lady's home,
what are you doing here all forlorn,
standing moaning to yourself outside the gates?
65   Does Medea really want to be left alone?
NURSE: Ah, dogged old pedagogue of Jason's sons,
when a master's fortunes are struck down
the heart of a faithful slave is stricken too.
      I am plunged in such a depth of grief
70 I came out here to tell the earth and sky
      Medea's catastrophe.
TUTOR: What! Has the poor woman not stopped her
      crying yet?
NURSE: Stopped! You amaze me.
      Her ordeal, far from halfway done,
75   hardly has begun.
TUTOR: Poor innocent fool — to be quite frank about
            our mistress —
      she knows little of the latest blow.
NURSE: Latest? What's that, old man?
      Don't keep it from me.
80 TUTOR: Nothing, nothing . . . I'm sorry I even spoke.
NURSE: Come now, we're both slaves here, are we not?
      By your own gray beard, do not hold it back . . .

53. She frightens me: [The translator notes that he has omitted
four lines bracketed by many editors as doubtful (lines 40–43
in the original Greek text).] Dramatically, they are certainly a
mistake: "*I am frightened she will slip / into the palace
unawares, / and in the nuptial bedroom / ram a sharp knife into
Jason's side, / or even kill the King as well as bridegroom / and
get herself a far worse doom.*"

I can keep a secret if I must.
TUTOR: Well, I'd gone to where the old dice-players sit,
      near Pirene's sacred fountain,   85
and there I overheard (pretending not to listen)
someone say:
      "Creon, this country's king,
is making plans to drive these boys from Corinth —
      their mother too"—   90
I don't know if the story's true.
      I hope that it is not.
NURSE: No, surely no?
      Jason would not let his sons be treated so,
however far he's parted from their mother.   95
TUTOR [*grimly*]: Old loves are left behind by new.
      That man is not this house's friend.
NURSE: We're all finished, then —
      if we ship this second wave
before we've bailed the first.   100
TUTOR: Now listen —
      this is not the time to let our mistress know.
Just keep quiet about it — not a word.
NURSE [*with an anguished glance over her shoulder, in
      a whisper*]: Poor little boys,
do you hear how much your father's worth to you?   105
      I wish he were . . .

[*Checks herself.*]

no, not dead, he is my master still . . .
but, oh, what an enemy he's proved
to those he should have loved!
TUTOR: What human being is not?   110
      Is this news to you,
that every person's dearest neighbor is himself:
some rightly so, some out of greed and selfishness.
      This father does not love his sons, but —
his new wedding bed.   115
NURSE: Come along, boys, into the house.
      Everything is going to be all right.

[*Dropping her voice.*]

      Keep them away as much as you can.
      Do not let them near their mother
so long as she is in this deadly mood.   120
      Already I have caught her eyes on them:
the eyes of a mad bull.
      There's something she is plotting
and her fury won't lie down — this I know —
until the lightning strikes and someone's felled.   125
      Let us hope it's enemies, not friends.

[*A long-drawn-out sob — Medea's — is heard from the
house.*]°

MEDEA: I am so unhappy — oh!
      the misery of it! I wish I were dead.

126. The next 116 lines in the Greek [to the end of the Parodos]
are cast in a different meter, which [the translator] transposed
into the nearest English equivalent.

NURSE [*hustling the children toward the door*]:
    Listen — there . . . poor children, your mother,
130   Raking her heart up, raking her rage.
    Quick, inside: into the house.
    Don't come anywhere near her sight.
    Don't approach. Beware, watch out
    For her savage mood, destructive spleen:
135   Yes and her implacable will.
    Off with you now; hurry inside.
    Soon, I know, her fury will flare
    Out from the slowly gathering cloud.
    What will she perpetrate then, I fear —
140   Proud, importunate willful soul —
        So bitterly spurned.

                [*Exeunt° Tutor and Boys.*]

[*A long-suppressed shout is heard from inside: Medea's voice.*]

MEDEA: Oh, what misery! Oh, what pain!
    Cursed sons, and a mother for cursing!
    Death take you all — you and your father:
145   The whole house wither.
NURSE [*sobbing*]: Oh, how it grieves me!
    Why make the sons
        share in their father's
    Guilt? Oh, why
150   should *they* be hated?
    Poor young children, your danger appals me.
    Ruthless is the temper of royalty:
    Often commanding, seldom commanded;
    Terribly slow to forgive and forget.
155   How much better to live among equals.
    I want no part of greatness and glory:
    Let me decline in a safe old age.
    The very name of the "middle way"
    Has health in it: is best for man.
160   Good never comes from overreaching,
    And when it provokes the gods, it destroys
        All the more thoroughly.

PARODOS OR ENTRY SONG

[*The Chorus of Corinthian women enters, full of apprehension and concern for Medea.*]

CHORUS: I heard her voice, I heard her shout,
    It was the most unhappy
    Woman from Colchis — far from calm yet —
    But tell me, old Nurse.
5   From the porch of the house, it moaned outside.
    O women, I cannot delight
    In the pain of Jason's house:
    A house I have loved very well.
NURSE: House there is none: life of it gone.
10   The master is had . . . by a princess's bed.

[**141.** (s.d.) *Exeunt:* Latin for "they go out."]

The mistress in her boudoir pines.
    There are no words her friends can find
    To touch her disconsolate heart.
MEDEA [*in another spasm*]: Ahhh!
    Cleave my brain with a flash from the sky.   15
    What good is left for me in living?
    Alas! Alas! Come Death, unloose
        My life from a life I loathe.

[*Strophe*]°

CHORUS: Listen, O Zeus and Earth and Light
    To the stricken tune of this plangent° wife.   20
    And you, loveless lady,
    What yearning for love on a bed of delight
    Could make you hurry to death, the night?
        Pray not for that.
    If your husband has gone to adore   25
    A new bride in his bed, why, this
    Has often happened before.
    Do not harrow your soul. For Zeus
    Will succor your cause. What use
    To lessen your life with grief   30
    For a lost lord?
MEDEA [*from inside*]: O mighty Themis,° and
        Artemis,° Queen,
    For all the fine vows I bound him with,
    See what my hated husband has done.
    Grant me to watch him, at last, with his bride,   35
    Palace and all, crumble in ruin.
    How dare they do to me what they have done!
    O Father, my country, the land I abandoned,
        Flagrantly killing my brother.°
NURSE: Hear what she says   40
    with her cry from the heart
    To Themis and Zeus:
        (goddess of rights
    And he whom mankind
        makes keeper of vows.)   45
    Certainly soon
    in no small way
    Her fury will play itself out.

[*Antistrophe*]°

CHORUS: If she would come out and, face to face,
    Listen to what we have to say,   50
    She might let go

[**Strophe:** Song sung by the Chorus as it danced from stage right to stage left.]   **20. plangent:** Lamenting.   **32. Themis:** Justice. **Artemis:** Guardian of women. Called Diana by the Romans. **39. killing my brother:** Medea slew her brother Absyrtus when she escaped with Jason and tossed him piecemeal over the side of the ship, knowing that their pursuers would stop to pick the pieces up.   [**Antistrophe:** Song sung by the Chorus following the Strophe, as it danced back from stage left to stage right.]

This rampant anger, spite of soul.
I hope I never fail my friends.
So go, Nurse, entice her to come:
55   Say we are *with* her: we are her friends.
Hurry, before she does any harm
    To those inside . . .
Grief can swell to enormity.
NURSE [*walking to the door*]: I'll do my best, but am
60   afraid I
May *not* be able to persuade My Lady; and yet
    I am glad to shoulder the burden;
Although she glares with a bull-mad gaze
(Or is it a lioness with her whelps)
65   When anyone comes or speaks or helps.

[*She turns at the door.*]

    Oh, botchers and blunderers! Yes,
That's what they were, those artists of old:
Makers of music for life and joy,
For grand celebrations and groaning boards;
70   But, oh, nothing for sorrow and pain:
No music or song on hand-plucked lyre
    For the thing that brings death
And terrible endings to many a home.

    Oh, what a blessing is missed
75   by having no music for this!
    What a waste of it, then
            by singing in vain,
    When fullness at feasts
            is its own joy and gain.

[*Exit Nurse into the house.*]

80   CHORUS: Deep is her sobbing from depths of pain:
    Shrill the news her suffering brings
    Of marriage betrayed, a love gone wrong.
        Outraged, she
            importunate prays
    To Themis, the daughter of Zeus:
85   Keeper of vows, who sailed her through
        Those dangerous straits and the night
    To Hellas° across the salt of the sea.

FIRST EPISODE

[*Medea enters from the house, colorfully, even opulently, dressed. She is wan and her eyes are red with weeping, but she is surprisingly calm and in control.*]

MEDEA: Women of Corinth, be indulgent, please:
    I have obeyed you and come out.
        The charge of aloofness — as I know too well —
    is something often leveled
5   at both the retiring and the busy man.
        He who chooses a quiet life
    has this alleged against him too:

87. **Hellas:** Greece.

laziness and lack of spirit.
    Yes, public opinion has most shallow eyes.
    People hate at sight   10
a harmless human being,
knowing nothing of the real man.
    I agree, of course,
that a foreigner should conform,
adapt to his society . . .   15
and a citizen is censurable no less
when too self-centered or uncouth
to avoid offending his companions.
    Nevertheless, I . . .

[*She breaks off with a pang.*]

    I . . . out of a clear sky   20
have been struck a blow that breaks my heart.
    My friends, it is over.
    I want to die.
    Life has lost all point.
    The man who was my life   25
— and he knows it too —
has become for me beneath contempt.

[*She surveys the women.*]

    Of all the creatures that can feel and think,
we women are the worst-treated things alive.
    To begin with,   30
we bid the highest price in dowries
just to buy some man
to be dictator of our bodies . . .
    How that compounds the wrong!
    Then there is the terrifying risk: 35
Shall we get a good man or a bad?
    Divorce is a disgrace
(at least for women),
to repudiate the man, not possible.
    So, plunged into habits new to her,   40
conventions she has never known at home,
she has to guess like some clairvoyant
how to handle the man who shares her bed.
    And if we learn our lesson well
in this exacting role,   45
and our husband does not kick against the marriage
        yoke,
oh, ours is an enviable life!
    Otherwise, we are better dead.
    When a man gets bored with wife and home,
he simply roams abroad,   50
relieves the tedium of his spirit:
turns to a friend or finds his cronies.
    We women, on the other hand,
turn only to a single man.
    We live safe at home, they say.   55
They do battle with the spear.
    How superficial!
I had rather stand my ground three times among the
        shields
than face a childbirth once.
    Anyway,   60

your case and mine are not the same.
        You have your city.
        You have your father's home.
Life offers you the sweet fellowship of friends.
65   I am alone,
without a city, wronged by a husband,
uprooted from a foreign land.
        I have no mother, brother, cousin;
am without a haven from this storm.
70   So, please, I ask you this:
if I can find a way to pay my husband back —
your silence.
        Woman, on the whole, is a timid thing:
the din of war, the flash of steel, unnerves her;
75   but, wronged in love,
there is no heart more murderous.
LEADER: As you wish, Medea.
        You have a score to settle with your lord.
        I do not wonder that you smart . . .
80   But, look, I see Creon coming:
this country's king —
bristling, I dare say, with new decisions.

[*Enter Creon with attendants. He is a bearded man of about sixty, royally but modestly dressed. His face wears a look of troubled resolution.*]

CREON: Go, Medea. Remove yourself.
        Get packing from this land.
85   I order you —
you with your black-faced fury
lowering against your lord.
        And take your brace of offspring with you;
no dallying either.
90   I am here to see this order done,
and until I've pushed you out and over the border,
I'll not go home.
MEDEA: So.
        I am lost — crushed utterly.
95   My enemies let out the sail,
while I have no place to disembark from doom.
        Nevertheless, hard-pressed as I am,
I ask you this:
For what reason, Creon, do you drive me out?
100 CREON: Fear:
no need to camouflage the fact;
I am afraid you'll deal my child some lethal
        blow . . .
and many things conspire to make me fear.
        You are a woman of some knowledge,
105 versed in many an unsavory skill.
        Your husband's gone:
your soul is raw with loss of love . . .
and now it is reported that you threaten me:
mean to hurt the father of the bride
110 and of course the bride and groom.
        That is what I want to guard against —
an accident.
        Madam, better to be hated now by you
than soften and pay later with regrets.

MEDEA [*exchanging a look with the Chorus*]:
        Heaven help me!   115
My reputation is a curse:
This is not the only time it has done me lasting
        harm.
        Oh, let the perspicacious man
keep his children from enlightenment —
above the general run.   120
        It will earn them only
the sneer of uselessness
and the spiteful jealousy of fellow men.
        Bring education to the dolt
and, far from being accounted wise,   125
you will yourself be cast as dolt.
        Outshine a pundit of established fame
and you become a byword of distaste.
        This precisely
is what I have to face.   130
        Because I have a little knowledge,
some are filled with jealousy,
others think me secretive, and crazy.

        In point of fact, my knowledge
does not amount to much.   135

[*She turns upon Creon eyes pathetic with innocence.*]

        But now I frighten *you*:
do you think I'll strike some death-knell on your
        house?
        No, no: I am not like that.
        Creon, forget your fear:
I have no criminal intent against a king.   140
        For how have *you* wronged me?
        You simply gave your virgin child
to a suitor of your bent.
        No, it is my husband that I hate.
        You, I think, have acted prudently   145
and even now I don't begrudge your enterprise
        success.
        Marry them both and blessings on you,
only let me go on living in this land.
        Ill-used though I am, I shall keep quiet:
I am overruled.   150
CREON: Reassuring talk,
        but it chills me to the marrow.
        What are you really hatching in your mind?
        I trust you, Madam,
less even than I did before.   155
        The impassioned woman,
like the impassioned man,
is easier to watch than the crafty and the quiet.
        So, leave, I say, at once,
and no speeches, please.   160
        My mind's made up.
        You are dangerous.
        All your cleverness
shall not keep you here.
MEDEA: Please, I beg you — on my knees —   165
        by your fresh young daughter-bride . . .

CREON: You waste your words.
    I am adamant.
MEDEA: Will you expel me —
170   heedless of my prayers?
CREON: I will. For I love you less
    than I love my home.
MEDEA: Ah, home! My own beloved country.
    What memories crowd upon me now!
175 CREON: Exactly: next to my own children,
    my country is *my* dearest love as well.
MEDEA: Love, did you say?
    It is a mighty curse.
CREON: In my opinion . . . that depends . . .
180 MEDEA: O Zeus, remember
    the author of this crime.
CREON: Go away — you poor deluded thing —
    rid me of my troubles.
MEDEA: The troubles are all mine:
185   I have a glut of them.
CREON [*turning on his heel*]: I'll call the servants:
    They'll put you out by force.
MEDEA [*clinging to him*]: No, not that . . . Creon,
    I have something else . . .
190 CREON: You seem determined, Madam,
    to make a nuisance of yourself.
MEDEA: No, I'll go into banishment . . .
    That is not what I beg you now.
CREON: Then, why not *go*, and let this land be rid of
    you?
195 MEDEA: Just let me stay this single day
    to arrange my exodus from here
    and make provision for my little sons —
    whose father cannot bring himself to care.
    Be kind to them.
200   You are a father too:
    you know what kindly feelings are.
    As for me,
    it means nothing to me
    whether I stay or go.
205   It's them I shed my tears for:
    their lot is hard.
CREON [*after a tussle with himself*]:
    My soul is not tyrannical enough.
    My heart has often let me down . . .
    So now, Medea,
210 though I know I take a false step:
    have it your own way.
    But let me warn you solemnly,
    if tomorrow's holy light
    sees you and your two children
215 still inside the borders of this realm,
    you die.
    Every word of this I mean.
    Now, stay if you must; but one day only . . .
    not long enough for you to perpetrate anything I
    dread.
        [*Exit Creon.*]
220 CHORUS: Ill-starred woman,
    Oh, what a nightmare of anguish is on you!

Whom will you turn to? Where will you turn?
What country, what stranger, what home for a
    haven?
    Who will receive you?
God has certainly steered you —   225
Oh, my poor Medea —
Into a sea-race of sorrows.
MEDEA [*turning on them with the gleam of revenge*]:
    In the center of disasters, yes,
    but all is far from lost — make no mistake —
    a test awaits the newlyweds,   230
    no little ordeal for the happy pair.

[*With a laugh of derision.*]

    Do you think I ever would have toadied to this
        man
    if nothing could be got from it, no gain, no tool?
    No, not one syllable,
    not a touch with my little finger.   235
    The fool!
    He could have scotched me with one stroke,
    flung me out;
    instead he lets me stay one extra day,
    to make three enemies three corpses: 240
    ha! father, daughter, and my husband.

[*She leans toward the Chorus.*]

    Friends,
    I can think of several ways to bring their death
        about.
    Which one shall I choose?
    Shall I set their house of honeymoon alight,   245
    or creep into the nuptial bower
    and plunge a sharp knife through their vitals?
    One thing makes me pause:
    if I am caught entering the palace, or red-handed,
    I die . . . and give my enemies the last laugh.   250
    No, there is a surer way,
    one more direct;
    for which I have a natural bent:
    death by poison.
    Yes, that is it.   255

[*She walks, thinking.*]

    Well, suppose they are dead:
    will any city take me in,
    will any man afford me home in a country safe for
        living
    and shield me from reprisals?
    No, there is none.   260
    I must postpone it, therefore, for a while
    until some tower of strength appears for me;
    then, through trickery and stealth,
    I shall proceed with death by poison.
    What if I'm forced to go before it's done?   265
    Ah, then I shall seize a sword,
    face certain death,
    and with my own hands run them through.
    I shall not shrink from such a step,

270 by Hecate,° no: the goddess who abides
in the shrine of my inner hearth —
the one I reverence most of all the gods
and have chosen to abet me.
Nobody breaks my heart —
275 with impunity.
Their wedding I'll reduce
to agony and grief:
agony for having met and married,
and grief for having banished me.
280 Good!
Use your magic to the hilt.
Plot, Medea, devise your recipes:
advance to the deadly act that tests your courage.
See your present plight:
285 laughed at by the seed of Sisyphus°
because of Jason's match?
Never.
Your father was a king:
his father, Helios the Sun . . .
290 be aware of *that*.
Besides, you are a born woman:
feeble when it comes to the sublime,
marvelously inventive over crime.

FIRST CHORAL ODE°

[*The Chorus sings an ode about the topsy-turvy changing standards of the world. Out of the turmoil will come
a new importance for women, and a new reverence.
Meanwhile, Medea is a harbinger of female independence and vitality.*]

[*Strophe 1*]

Back to their fountains
the sacred rivers are falling;
The cosmos and all morality
turning to chaos.
5 The mind of a man is nothing but fraud
and his faith in the gods a delusion.
One day the story will change:
then shall the glory
of women resound,
10 And reverence will come to the race of woman,
Reversing at last the sad
reputation of ladies.

270. Hecate: Identified with Artemis, and sometimes called
Persephone (Roman name Proserpina), she was supposed to
preside over magic and witchcraft. [**285. seed of Sisyphus:**
Sisyphus, a king of Corinth, was punished in the otherworld by
being made to roll a boulder up a hill. As it approached the top,
the boulder would roll back down, creating a never-ending
task. To be a descendant of Sisyphus was considered a disgrace
by the ancients.] [**Ode:** Song sung by the Chorus.]

[*Antistrophe 1*]

The ballads of ages gone by
that harped on the falseness
Of women, will cease to be sung . . . 15
If only Apollo,
Prince of the lyric, had put
in *our* hearts the invention
Of music and songs for the lyre
Wouldn't I then have raised 20
up a feminine paean
To answer the epic of men?
Time in the roll of the ages has much to unfold
Of the fortunes of women no less
than the fortunes of men. 25

[*Strophe 2*]

So you, Medea, sailing away
from your father's house,
Threading a passage with heart on fire
through the jowls of the Euxine
Cliffs° to inhabit a strange 30
land where your bed is empty of man
(The lover you lost, O heartbroken lady!)
Now are chased from the realm,
shamed and banned.

[*Antistrophe 2*]

The joy of a bond is gone; 35
and wide of the world of Hellas,
All shame has flown —
high in the sky and away.
Bereft of a fatherly home,
Where can you sail for a haven against 40
The storm, unfortunate woman —
Your bed
Royally quelled by another
who queens it in your home?

SECOND EPISODE

[*Jason enters from the road that leads to the palace. He
is a young-looking man, dressed in the swash-buckling
cloak and plumed helmet of a captain in the King's
Guards.*]

JASON [*embarrassed and exasperated*]:
So . . . this is not the first time
I have seen irrevocable damage done
by a barbarous rage.
You could have stayed here,

29–30. Euxine Cliffs: On the Black Sea.

5   in this land, in this house,
had you submitted quietly to your ruler's plans.
        Instead, you ranted like a lunatic . . .
so now are banished.
        To me your tirade does not mean a thing:
10   go on declaiming what a monster Jason is.
        But when it comes to royalty,
the princess and the king,
count yourself lucky to be only banished.
        I have tried continuously to calm things down;
15   for I should like you to remain.
        But you, Madam,
obstinate in folly,
have continuously reviled our royalty,
And so you are banished.
20   Yet, in spite of everything, I come, Medea,
patient to the last with someone I am fond of,
to do what I can to help.
        You and the children
need not leave the country penniless
25   and unprovided for . . .
exile drags with it a chain of troubles.
        And hate me though you may,
I cannot bring myself to wish you harm.
MEDEA: You criminal —
30   an epithet too good for you . . . such inhumanity . . .
so you come to me, do you,
you byword of aversion both in heaven and on earth,°
to me your own worst enemy?
        This is not courage.
35   This is not being brave:
to look a victim in the eyes whom you've betrayed —
somebody you loved —
        This is a disease,
and the foulest that a man can have:
40   you are shameless.

[*With the thinnest of smiles.*]

        But you have done well to come:
I can unload some venom from my heart
and you can smart to hear it.
        To begin at the beginning,
45   yes, first things first:
        I saved your life —
as every son of Greece who stepped on board the
        Argo knows.
        You were sent to yoke
the fire-breathing bulls
50   and sow the plot of death.
        Yes, I saved you, lit up life for you,
when I slew the guardian of the Golden Fleece,
that giant snake which hugged it, sleepless,
coil on coil.
55   I deserted my own father and my home
to come away with you to Iolcus by Mount Pelion,
full of zeal and very little sense.

32. Editors bracket this line as doubtful.

        King Pelias, I killed,
a most horrid death —
perpetrated through his daughters —   60
and overturned their home.
        All this for you,
I even bore you sons — you most reprobate man —
just to be discarded for a new bride.
        Had you been childless,   65
this craving for another bedmate
might have been forgiven.
        But no: all faith in vows is shattered.
I am baffled:
        Do you suppose the gods of old no longer rule?   70
Or is it that mankind
now has different principles —
because your every vow to me, I'm sure you know,
is null and void.
        Curse this right hand of mine,   75
so often held by yours;
and these knees of mine —
sullied to no purpose
by the grasp of a rotten man.
        You turned my hopes to lies.   80
        Come now, tell me frankly —
as if we were two friends,
as if you really were prepared to help
(and I hope the question makes you feel ashamed) —
where do I go from here?   85

[*With a bitter laugh.*]

        Home to my father, perhaps,
and my native land,
both of whom I sacrificed for *you*?
        Or to the poor deprived daughters of Pelias?
They would be overjoyed to entertain   90
their father's murderer.
        Yes: this is how things stand.
        Among my own friends
I am an execrated woman.
        There was no call for me to hurt *them*,   95
but now I have a death-feud on my hands —
and all for you.
        What a reward!
        What a heroine you have made me
among the daughters of Hellas!   100
        Lucky Medea, having *you*:
such a wonderful husband . . . and so loyal!
        I leave this land displaced, expelled,
deprived of friends,
only my children with me, and alone.   105
        What a charming record for our new bridegroom
        this:
"His own sons and the wife who saved him
are wayside beggars."

[*She breaks off and looks upward.*]

        O Zeus, what made you give us
clear signs for telling   110

mere glitter from true gold,
but when we need to know
the base metal of a man
no stamp upon his flesh for telling counterfeit?

115 LEADER: How frightening is resentment
how difficult to cure,
When lovers hurl past love
at one another's hate.

JASON: I'll have to choose my words
120 with no uncommon skill, it seems . . .
like a good sailor riding out a storm,
if I am to sail close-sheeted, Madam,
through your lashing, dangerous tongue.

[*Folding his arms.*]

So, you pile up what you did for me
125 into pinnacles of grace.
Well, as far as I am concerned,
it was Aphrodite° and no one else in heaven or earth
who saved me on my voyage.
Your cleverness played a part, of course,
130 but I could underline, if I wanted to be ungenerous,
how it was infatuation, sheer shooting passion,
that drove you to save my life.
I shall not stress the point.
After all, your service did no harm.
135 But this I shall maintain:
that what you gained by saving me
was far more than you gave.

[*Holds up a hand to stop Medea from interrupting.*]

In the first place,
you have a home in Hellas
140 instead of some barbarian land.
You have known justice:
the benefit of laws which never yield to might;
have had your talents recognized all over Greece
and won renown.
145 For, were you living at the world's ends,
your name would not be known . . .
Oh, to me, houses crammed with gold,
and a sweeter song than Orpheus sang,
are nothing with no name.
150 But, enough discussion of my dangerous voyage:
an argument which *you* provoked.
Now to your vindictive challenge
of my royal marriage.
I'll show you, first, it was an act of common sense,
155 secondly, unselfish,
and, finally, a mark of my devotion
to you and all my family.

[*Medea gives a gasp of incredulity.*]

No, be still.
When I came here from the land of Iolcus,
160 frustrations crowding on my trail,
could I, a wretched fugitive,

have hit upon a greater stroke of luck
than marriage to the daughter of the king?
It was not — which cuts you to the quick —
that I was tired of your attractions   165
and smitten with a longing for a new wife;
still less that I was out to multiply my offspring
(I am quite satisfied with the sons we have);
no, it was simply that I wanted above all
to let us live in comfort, not be poor . . .   170
I know too well
how the pauper is avoided by his friends.
I wanted our children to be reared
in a manner worthy of my ancestry,
and, begetting others, brothers for your sons,   175
knit them all together
into one close and happy family.
What point was there for *you* to have more
children?
My intention was — and it seemed real gain —
to help the ones I have,   180
through those I hope to have.
Was this such a wicked plan?
You would not say so,
except through jealousy — that stinging jealousy of
bed.
You women are all the same.   185
If your love life goes all right,
everything is fine;
but once crossed in bed,
the liveliest and best that life can offer
might as well be wormwood.   190
What we poor males really need
is a way of having babies on our own —
no females, please.
Then the world would be
completely trouble free.   195

LEADER [*sternly*]: Jason, this speech of yours is
plausible,
But say what you like, it is not right
To sacrifice your wife.

MEDEA [*with cold disdain*]:
My outlook must be very different, then, from
others.
To my mind a hypocrite who is too glib   200
only multiplies the danger that it puts him in:
the more he glozes° falsehood with his tongue,
the more confident and rash he grows.
He ends by not being very clever.
So, you, toward me —   205
you'd better drop your specious pleading.
One simple observation
lays the whole thing flat:
were you not a coward, it was your duty
to convince *me*; not go sneaking off to marry. 210

JASON: And you would have welcomed the suggestion,
I am sure.
Why, even now you can't contain your blazing rage.

---

127. Aphrodite: Goddess of love, called Venus by the Romans.

202. glozes: Glosses over.

MEDEA: *That* was not what governed you:
    you felt your glory tarnished by an aging oriental
        wife.
215 JASON: Please, please believe me:
    it was nothing to do with women —
    my desire to make this match —
    but as I have already said
    to safeguard you and rear young princes
220   to be brothers to my sons . . .
    so make our family solid.
MEDEA [*with a bitter laugh*]:
    Haha! Solid happiness on the grave of love;
    Prosperity with a secret sting . . .
    O you gods — not for me — ever.
225 JASON [*earnestly*]: Please change your prayer to this
    and make it reasonable:
        "May success not seem to me sad failure,
    nor good fortune ever a disaster."
MEDEA: You go on mocking me: *you* have roof and
        shelter.
230   I am deserted, flying for my life, alone.
JASON: *You* chose it. Blame no one else.
MEDEA: Did I? I was the one who wed and then
        betrayed?
JASON: No: you just swore a heap of filthy curses on
        the king.
MEDEA: Yes, and you shall find that *I* am the curse
235   that Fate has made to haunt you.
JASON: There's no point in talking any more with
        you.

[*Preparing to go.*]

    Anything that you or the children want in exile,
    let me know; I'd gladly furnish it,
    or send letters of introduction for you
240   to friends abroad who will be kind.
        To turn this offer down, Medea,
    is nothing short of madness.
        Forget your feelings of resentment:
    let yourself be helped.
MEDEA [*spitting out the words*]:
245   Not your friends, not your things:
    I would not touch anything of yours —
    how dare you offer it!
        The presents of the wicked are pure poison.
JASON [*flinging his cloak about him*]:
    In that case, heaven be my witness:
250   all my design to help you and your sons
    is thwarted by your preference for evil.
        Your self-will cuts you off.
    Suffer then accordingly.

[*He begins to go.*]

MEDEA: Go then. Don't waste your passion here:
255   go to the fresh young virgin you can't wait for . . .
        Have her.
            [*As Jason exits, furious and embarrassed.*]
        And God grant
    the match you make, you'll long to have unmade.

SECOND CHORAL ODE

[*The women of the Chorus, appalled by what has happened to Medea, speak of the dangers of love and the
sufferings of exile.*]

[*Strophe 1*]

    Love is a dangerous thing:
    Loving without any limit.
    Discredit and loss it can bring . . .
    But, oh, if the goddess should visit
    A love that is modest and right,   5
    No god is so exquisite.
    Great lady, aim not at me
    Your gold and infallibly
    Passion-tipped, poisoned delight.

[*Antistrophe 1*]

    Stay me with innocent living;   10
    Most beautiful gift of the gods.
    Never let Cypris° the fierce
    Queen of desire propel
    My heart to a dissolute lust
    From old to a new and another   15
    Bed and a dissonant longing,
    But test with a sweet eye for peace
    The love-bonds of reverent women.

[*Strophe 2*]

    O my country, my home, never let
    Me lose my state and my city —   20
    Living that desperate loss
    so helpless and hard, without pity.
    Death: I would bargain with death,
    To die such a day to a finish.
    For nothing is like the sorrow   25
    Or supersedes the sadness
    Of losing your native land.

[*Antistrophe 2*]

LEADER: The thing is before my eyes.
    Learned from no rumor or lies:
    Medea without city or friends
    Nowhere where pity extends —   30
    Oh, how you must suffer! . . .
    Let a man rot in a charmless lot
    If he never unshutters his heart
    To the cleansing esteem of another.   35
    He'll not be my friend: no, never.

12. Cypris: Aphrodite, goddess of love.

THIRD EPISODE

[*Enter Aegeus from the country. He is a man in his early middle years and dressed in traveling clothes. His open features — kindly but unimaginative — seem preoccupied. In his retinue are Noblemen and Servants.*]

AEGEUS [*stretching out his hands*]:
    Medea, all health and happiness . . .
    and one can say a fairer thing when greeting friends?
MEDEA [*wanly*]: Health and happiness to you, good Aegeus,
    wise Panidon's son . . . But where do you stem from?
AEGEUS: I have just left Apollo's ancient oracle at
5   Delphi.
MEDEA: What — a pilgrim there — the nub of the
        world of prophecy?
AEGEUS: I went to ask for progeny — for a fruitful seed.
MEDEA [*suddenly interested*]:
    In the name of heaven! Have you been childless all
        this time?
10 AEGEUS: Childless, yes — by some design of heaven.
MEDEA: But with a wife . . . or have you never married?
AEGEUS: I am married. Yes, I have a wife who shares
        my bed.
MEDEA: And what did Apollo say about your having
        children?
AEGEUS: Something far too deep for me, a mere mortal,
        to unravel.
15 MEDEA: Am I allowed to know the god's reply?
AEGEUS: Certainly. It would take a mind like yours to
        fathom.
MEDEA: Tell me . . . what did he say . . . since you are
        allowed?
AEGEUS: Why, just this:
        "Do not unstopper the wine-skin till . . ."°
MEDEA: Till you've done something — been
20   somewhere — special?
AEGEUS [*baffled*]: Until I'm back at home again.
MEDEA: Then why did you sail in here?
AEGEUS: There is a man called Pittheus, king of
        Troezen . . .
MEDEA: Yes, a son of Pelops: a very pious man, they
        say.
25 AEGEUS: I want to ask his help about this oracle.
MEDEA: Yes, a clever man, and an expert in such
        things.
AEGEUS: And of all my old battle cronies, my favorite.
MEDEA: Well, I hope that all your dreams come true.
AEGEUS: Medea, you look so pale, so sad. What is it?
MEDEA: My husband, Aegeus: he is the world's most
30   wicked man.
AEGEUS: You don't say? . . . Come, tell me all about
        your troubles.
MEDEA: He's set up a mistress to queen it in my home.
AEGEUS: Dear me! Would he really do a thing like that?

---

19. "**Do not . . . wine-skin**": Probably "Do not have sexual intercourse."

MEDEA: Yes, yes . . . And I am deposed — the one he
        loved.
AEGEUS: Did he fall in love . . . or is he just tired of *you*?   35
MEDEA: In love — Ha — head over heels . . .
        flinging all fidelity to the winds.
AEGEUS: Let him get on with it . . . since he's as wicked
        as you say he is.
MEDEA: But it was with royalty he fell in love:
        a king's daughter.
AEGEUS: Eh? What king's daughter? Please go on.   40
MEDEA: Creon's, king of Corinth.
AEGEUS: In that case, Madam, it *is* serious.
        You have my sympathies.
MEDEA: It is the end. What is more, I am being
        banished.
AEGEUS: Banished? This is indeed a crowning blow —   45
        but by whom?
MEDEA: Creon: he wants to banish me from Corinth.
AEGEUS: And Jason agrees? I find that monstrous.
MEDEA [*with fierce irony*]: Oh, he says he doesn't —
        but he'll bear it bravely.   50

[*On her knees.*]

    Aegeus, I beg you,
by your beard,
by these knees of yours I clasp,
pity me, pity my unhappiness.
    Do not see me banished and alone,   55
let me come to Athens, shelter me,
accept me in your home.
    The gods will pay you back,
give you the children you so long to have,
surround your death with happiness.   60
    You do not guess how Providence has blessed
        you, meeting me.
    I mean to end your childlessness
and make your seed bear sons.

[*Almost in a whisper.*]

    I promise it. I know the drugs.
AEGEUS [*impressed*]: Medea, many reasons make me
        ready   65
to acquiesce in your request,
not least of all the gods;
then because you've given me — a promise:
promise of children . . .
oh, left to myself, I had all but given up.   70

[*Gently raising her.*]

    My proposition, then is this:
get yourself to Athens
and there, as is incumbent on me,
I shall do my utmost to protect you.
    However, I must tell you clearly,   75
I cannot take you with me out of Corinth,
but if you reach my palace on your own,
there you shall have full sanctuary
and to no one shall I give you up.
    So, by your own means you must leave this land: 80

I cannot risk offending the Corinthians —
who are also friends of mine.
MEDEA: As you say . . . but . . .
    if only you could promise it on oath,
85   it would make it all so . . . settled between us.
AEGEUS: Do you not trust me? What is the matter
        now?
MEDEA [*glancing nervously over her shoulders*]:
        I do trust you . . . but . . .
    but I have my enemies.
    It isn't only Creon,
90   there is the house of Pelias too:
    They'll want to prize me from your territories.
        If you are bound by oath
    you will not give me up.
    But if you have only made a promise,
95   not sworn it to the gods,
    there is always the chance that sheer diplomacy
    will win you to their wishes.
        I have no weapons on my side,
    on theirs is wealth and all the weight of royalty.
100 AEGEUS: You are very provident, Medea.
        However, if that is what you want,
    I shall not go against it.
        In point of fact,
    to swear an oath protects me too:
105   I can counter those who wish you ill
    with a clear excuse;
    and you of course, are well secured.
        So, name your deities.
MEDEA [*in crystal-cold syllables*]:
    Swear by the Earth on which you tread.
110   Swear by the Sun, my father's father dread.
    Swear by every god and godhead.
AEGEUS: Yes, but what to do or not to do? Please say.
MEDEA: Never yourself to drive me from your land,
    and if an enemy of mine tries to drag me off,
115   never while you live to let me go.
AEGEUS: I swear by the Earth and sacred light of the
        Sun
    to abide by the words you have just pronounced.
MEDEA [*relentlessly*]:
    Good . . . but if you break your word — what
        penalty?
AEGEUS: The penalty for sacrilege.

[*They clasp hands in silence.*]

120 MEDEA: Go now and be glad. All is well.
    I shall come to Athens as quickly as I can,
    but first I have some work to do, to carry out a plan.

[*As Aegeus is leaving.*]

LEADER: We hope that Hermes, master of journeys,
    Will hasten you home safely to Athens:
125   Home to the hope of your heart's desire,
        For, Aegeus, you are
        A most magnanimous man.
MEDEA [*wheels round and faces the Chorus*]:
    O Zeus and lady daughter, Justice,

O resplendent Sun!
And you my friends,
    At last we are on the road to vengeance   130
and to our song of triumph. At last there is hope:
we shall see my enemies put down.
    At the very point my plot could founder,
this man opens up a port, an anchorage.   135
    So to Athens I shall go
and moor to her fast towers

[*She beckons the women closer.*]

    Now I can unfold to you my whole design:
there is nothing sweet in it, as you will see.
    I send a servant of my house to Jason   140
asking him to come to me.
    He arrives
I tell him in the softest accents;
how I now agree;
how it all seems for the best: 145
his royal marriage, his sacrifice of me;
everything that he has planned is for the best.
    But I ask him to let my children stay . . .
with no intention — you understand —
of leaving any child of mine in a hostile place   150
for those who hate me to maltreat.
    No, this is just a device
for murdering the daughter of the king.
    I send them there with presents in their hands,
presents for the bride — as a kind of plea   155
against their banishment —
yes, a gown of gossamer and a diadem made of
        beaten gold.
    If she takes this finery and puts it on,
the girl will die in agony
and anyone who touches her;   160
so deadly are the poisons I shall steep the presents in.
    But now my whole tone changes:
a sob of pain for the next thing I must do.
    I kill my sons — my own —
no one shall snatch them from me.   165
    And when I have desolated Jason's house beyond
        recall,
I shall escape from here:
fly from the murder of my little ones,
my mission done.
    People that one hates, my friends,   170
must never have the last laugh.
    Well, so be it.
    What good is life to me?
    I have no father, home, defense from danger.
    Oh, the mistake I made was when I left his house,   175
trusting the word of a man from Greece . . .
but he is going to pay the price.
    Never again alive
shall he see the sons he had by me,
nor any child by this new bride of his —   180
poor girl, who has to die a wretched death,
poisoned by me.
    Let no man think me insignificant or weak:

185   I am no meek martyr, no — quite the contrary —
         relentless an enemy I make;
             though kind enough to friends.
                 Such is the genius of my life.
     LEADER [*imploringly*]:
             Though you have shared all this in confidence with
                 us, Medea,
         and though I long to be of help,
190   we must uphold the laws of life:
         and so I say to you: "You must not do it."
     MEDEA: There is no other way.
             And though I understand your sentiments,
             you have not been through my agony.
195 LEADER: But, my lady, to kill your own two sons. . . ?
     MEDEA: It is the supreme way to hurt my husband.
     LEADER: And it makes you the most desolate of
                 women.
     MEDEA: Be that as it may.
             Argument is now superfluous.

     [*She turns to the Nurse, who has entered during the pre-
     vious dialogue.*]

200   Nurse, when I need real loyalty
         you are the one I always turn to.
             Go now and fetch Jason here.
             But as you are a woman
         and a faithful servant of this house,
205   whisper no syllable of what I plan.

                             [*Exit Nurse, dragging her feet.*]

THIRD CHORAL ODE

[*The Women of Corinth desperately try to move Medea
from her purpose. Does she imagine Athens, that
blessed land, will welcome a murderess? Surely, she herself will flinch from the cold-blooded killing of her
sons?*]

[*Strophe 1*]

         The people of Athens are blest through the ages,
             Seeds of the all-hallowed gods,
         Born on a soil unravaged and holy,
             They feed on the wide
5   Bright pastures of knowledge.
         Lightly they walk through the crystal air
         In a land where Harmonia,
             Goldenly fair,
         Once gave birth, they say, to the nine
10   Muses, the pure
                 Maids of Pieria.°

7–11. where Harmonia . . . Maids of Pieria: Harmonia, the
balance of nature, and the genius of the people resulted in the
cultivation of the arts. Pieria was a holy fountain in Boetia
where the nine Muses were supposed to live.

[*Antistrophe 1*]

         And out of the sweetly flowing currents
             Of Cephisus,° they declare,
             Aphrodite sprinkles the land
         And fragrantly breathes   15
             Delicate breezes.
         Forever she sheds from the stream of her hair,
             Plaited with roses,
         Scented petals; and sends the Loves — the Erotes —
         To preside with Wisdom over the heart   20
             And together prepare
             The glories of art.

[*Strophe 2*]

         How then shall a glorious city,
             City of sacred rivers,
             Host of the salutary guest,   25
         Kindly take to the killer of children,
         Harbor among them a murderess?
         Think of how you are stabbing your sons.
         Think, too, of the blood you assume.
         Do not, please, we beg by your knees,   30
         By everything and every means —
             Murder your children.

[*Antistrophe 2*]

         Where, when, will you find the mind,
             The hand or the callous heart
             Hardened enough to strike   35
         These, yours — oh, heartless enough? —
         How then will you see through your gaze
         Swollen with tears as you sight your aim?
         No, no, when your little ones kneel
         Crying for mercy, you will not   40
         Find the nerve, never be able,
             To bloody your hands.

FOURTH EPISODE

[*Jason enters with the Nurse behind him. On his face is
written apprehension mixed with hope; on hers, despair.*]

JASON: I have come, Medea, because you asked me.
             I put myself at your disposal
         even though you are against me.
             What, Madam, can I do for you?
MEDEA [*in a small, contrite voice*]:
             Jason please forgive me for all the things I said.   5
             Bear lightly with my outbursts, will you,
         if only in remembrance of our great love together.
             I have been arguing with myself,

13. Cephisus: An Athenian river.

have taxed myself severely.
10 "You raving fool," I said,
"To antagonize those who want to do you good,
setting yourself against your rulers and your husband.
  His royal marriage
and his design to bring up brothers for your sons
15 does you the greatest service that he could.
  Why not calm yourself?
  Are *you* suffering because the gods are good?
  Have you no children of your own?
  And are you not aware
20 you came as fugitive with not too many friends?"
  Such reflections made me realize
I have been out of my mind, hysterical.
  Now I thank you.
  Now I am convinced
25 that in securing us this benefit
you are the wise one, *I* the fool —
I who should have been your ally
and encouraged you.
  Yes, I should have been at hand to help,
30 decked the bed, dressed the bride —
and been glad to do it . . .
  But we women —
well, we are what we are: let's leave it at that!
  Do not copy us in our perverseness
35 or try to get your own back, giving tit for tat.
  I ask your pardon.
  I admit to being wrong.
  I've thought better of it now.

[*With an upsurge of put-on happiness.*]

  Children, children, come out here,
40 out of the house.

[*The two Boys appear with their Tutor.*]

  Come greet your father, hug him, join with me
in loving, not resenting him.
  Your mother's rancor's over.
  There's peace between us: the fighting's done.
45 Come, take his hand.

[*As the children run into their father's arms.*]

  O God, what a presentiment!
  What an image looming in the dark!
JASON: My sons, my sons,°
  if only you could go on living, go on loving,
  with your arms stretched out like that to me
50   forever . . .
MEDEA [*choking*]: It breaks my heart;
  I am far too prone to tears, too full of tears . . .
  it is the sudden ending of my quarrel with your father
  which makes them flow.

48. To my mind there is no doubt that this line and half the
next (in the Greek) go to Jason, and not Medea as the manuscripts and editors have it. Otherwise, Medea's remark in 93
[930] makes no sense. The attempt to have it correspond to
Jason's wish in 72 [916] does not work. [Translator's note.]

A sight so touching . . .   55
  it overflows.
LEADER: My eyes, too, are stinging,
  but may this be the worst that is to come.
JASON [*gently releasing the Boys*]: I praise you now,
      Medea,
  and I did not blame you then.   60
  It is natural for a woman to be enraged
when her husband goes off making second marriages.
  But now
  you are in a better frame of mind
and, even if it took a little time,   65
realize the good points of this plan . . .
  the decision is a level-headed woman's.

[*Turning to the children.*]

  As for you, my boys,
  your father has been far from idle
and, heaven willing, he has made   70
good settlements for you.
  In time I shouldn't wonder
if you were not first citizens in Corinth —
along with your new brothers.

[*Laying his hands on their shoulders.*]

  Grow up now fine fellows.   75
  Your father and a kindly providence
  have the rest in hand.
  How I look toward the time
when you will be two strapping grown young men,
trampling down my enemies.   80

[*Medea has averted her head and is sobbing. Her feelings, though genuine, are being used by her to further
her next move.*]

  But, Medea, what is this —
these dewy eyes, these tears;
your white face turned away
as if my words struck pain, not joy?
MEDEA: It is nothing.   85
  I was just thinking of our sons.
JASON: Well, be of good heart now:
  I shall see them through.
MEDEA: I will do my best . . . it isn't that I don't believe
      you,
  but you know how women weep.   90
JASON: I know, but don't be sad for *them* . . . why
      should you?
MEDEA [*watching the tender look on Jason's face*]:
  I am their mother.
  When you prayed just now
for a long life for your sons,
a sudden sadness whispered: "Will this be?"   95
  Well, that's one item only
of what I had to say.
  The other thing is this:
  Since the king has set his mind
on sending me away from Corinth,   100
and since I've come to recognize that this is best

Tokusaburo Arashi as Medea
with her two sons in a
Japanese version of *Medea*
performed at the National
Theatre in London, September
24, 1987.

(for I'd only be an obstacle to you,
living with the royal family here —
who think I am a menace to their house),
105   I shall take myself away, go into banishment.
        But the children, please, I should like *them*
to grow up under your own hand.
        Persuade Creon to let them stay.
JASON [*taken off his guard, but flattered*]:
        I — I am not certain that I can:
110   it'll take a little trying.
MEDEA: But you could ask your wife to beg her father
        to let the two boys stay.
JASON [*reflecting*]: Why not? I think I can get her to
           agree.
MEDEA: Of course you can:
115   if she's the slightest bit like any woman.
        And here *I* can play a useful part.
        I shall send her a present

more ravishingly beautiful, believe me,
than anything this age has seen:
a gown of gossamer and a diadem of beaten gold.   120
    These the boys shall carry them to her.

[*She claps her hands and two Maids appear.*]

    Go quickly, one of you,
and bring the gorgeous presents here.

[*One of the Maids hurries into the house.*]

    What a double delight
    What a shower of happiness for her   125
to have you for a hero husband
and now these treasures which were handed down
by my father's father — the glorious Sun.

[*The Maid comes back with two boxes. Medea turns to
the Boys.*]

Boys, take hold of this wedding gift.
130   Carry it to the happy princess-bride.
        Place it in her hands.
        It is not the kind of present she'll despise.
JASON [*as the Boys step forward*]:
        You foolish woman — why empty your hands?
        Do you think a royal wardrobe is in want,
135   or a palace short of gold?
        Keep these things. Don't give them up.
        If my wife values me at all,
        my mere wish will have more weight than *things,*
        I'm sure of that.
MEDEA [*with an onrush of conviction*]: Do not deny
140   me.
        Even the gods, they say, succumb to gifts,
        and gold is stronger than the strongest wits.
        She is lucky, *she* is blessed, *she* increases.
        This exile I would barter for my babies
145   not just with gold but with my life.

[*Forcing the boxes into the Boys' hands.*]

        Go, my sons, into the halls of wealth;
        down on your knees and beg her —
        this new wife of your father's, and my mistress —
        to let you stay in Corinth.
150   Most important of all,
        see that she takes the precious things
        into her own hands.

[*Packing them off.*]

        Quick, now, go. Success be yours.
        Come and tell me the good news.
155   Your mother waits with all ears.

[*Exeunt the Boys with their Tutor, followed by Jason.*]

FOURTH CHORAL ODE

[*The multimurders are imminent. Woe to the victims!
Woe to the murderess!*]

[*Strophe 1*]

Now has the last hope gone of the children living,
Gone and forever: they walk already to murder.
The bride is taking the golden diadem,
        Is taking the poison and doom.
5   Over her yellow hair her hands are fitting
        The decorated dying.

[*Antistrophe 1*]

The gorgeousness of the gossamer gown will win,
And the beaten gold of the diadem embrace her.
The bride is decked and ready to meet the dead.
        The trap is lethally set:
10   Doomed miserable woman, doomed to fall in —
        Ineluctably caught by Fate.

[*Strophe 2*]

And you who are groomed for a murder:
        Son-in-law of a king,
        Jason unsuspecting —   15
Are to bring on your sons a demise, and a death
On your bride of a hideous kind.
        Unhappy man, how far
        You are falling.

[*Antistrophe 2*]

And you the unenviable mother,   20
        How I weep for your pain!
        Killer of children for
A vengeance of love that has gone, betrayed
By your man for another
Bride whom he sleeps beside   25
        In his wrong.

FIFTH EPISODE

[*The Tutor hurries in from the palace with the two Boys.*]

TUTOR [*breathless with excitement*]: My lady, your
        boys —
        they won't be banished.
        And the princess, the bride —
        with her own hands —
        she took your presents, oh, so gladly . . .   5
        Now the children's danger is over!

[*Baffled by Medea's grim reaction.*]

        Well I never! Isn't this good news?
        What so transfixes you?

[*Medea draws in her breath in a muffled cry of pain.*]

TUTOR: What I hear is out of tune with what I say.

[*Medea sighs deeply.*]

TUTOR: I thought I brought good news.   10
        What kind of news, I wonder, have I brought?
MEDEA: What you have brought, you have brought:
        the fault is not with you.
TUTOR: Why, my Lady, these shuttered eyes:
        these tears falling.   15
MEDEA: Oh, I am pressed, old friend — hard pressed:
        the gods and my own evil counsels.
TUTOR: Courage, dear mistress:
        Your sons will always bring you home.
MEDEA [*in a kind of trance*]:
        Home? . . . First I must send others there . . . Mercy! 20
TUTOR: You are not the only mother to be severed from
        her sons.
        We have to bear our own humanity — humanely.
MEDEA [*pressing his hand*]:
        I shall try . . . Now go inside
        and see to what the children need today.
                        [*Exit Tutor, worried.*]

MEDEA [*throwing out her arms toward the two Boys*]: My sons, my sons,
you will have a city and a home
far from me.
I shall be left lonely,
and you will live without your mother always.
For I must go in exile to another land:
never have my joy in you,
or see your bright young progress;
never deck your brides, your marriage beds,
or light you radiant to your wedding day.

[*The Boys are now in her arms.*]

Oh, what a blight my ruthlessness has been!
How useless, little ones,
my nursing all your growing up!
How useless all the cares endured:
the wearying solicitudes,
the shooting agony of giving you your lives.
And now, how miserably have dwindled
my innumerable dreams of you:
your loving comfort when I'm old,
your own hands dressing me when I am dead —
a passing every person might desire.
Such sweet fancy vanishes
and, wrenched from you instead,
I shall drag my sad life out alone.

[*She cups their faces in her hands in turn.*]

Your own dear eyes shall miss forever
your poor mother's face —
your way of life and hers utterly apart.
Oh, children
do you let those eyes now stare their fill,
and your last smiles linger to the last?

[*She turns to the Chorus, panting.*]

O–h! What shall I do?
My heart dissolves
when I gaze into their bright irises . . .
No, I cannot do it.
Goodbye to my determination.
I shall take my boys away with me.
Why damage *them* in trying to hurt their father,
and only hurt myself twice over?
No, I cannot.
Goodbye to my decisions.

[*A pause, then she suddenly breaks away from the Boys.*]

What — what undermines me now?
Do I really mean to let my enemies go,
to laugh at me?
Steel yourself, Medea:
away with this cowardice, these arguments that melt.

[*Almost pushing them.*]

Go, Boys, into the house.

[*She turns to the Chorus grimly.*]

Anyone whose conscience will not let him stay
let him look to it: avoid my sacrifice . . .
this hand of mine shall never falter.

[*Another spasm of emotion grips her, and she runs to the Boys as they reach the door.*]

No, no! Stop me, my heart:
we must not do this thing.
Let them go, you stricken woman,
spare your sons.
Let them live with you in Athens:
they will be your joy.

[*Throwing her arms round them again.*]

Ah! Not by all the haunting spirits of the underworld,
shall I leave my children for my enemies to trample down.
No, never.°

[*With a sharp realization.*]

But — they have to die —
the whole thing is settled anyway . . .
Yes . . . the diadem is on her head . . .
the royal bride at this moment rots,
dying in her gown — I know it.

[*She turns to the Chorus as if to explain her second impulsive embrace.*]

You see: the path I have to tread
is unutterably sad,
but the one I set these children on
is sadder still . . .
Therefore I desire to speak with them.

[*Seizing their hands.*]

Give me your right hands to kiss,
each of you, my little ones —
give them to your mother.

[*Covering their hands, their faces, their bodies, in kisses.*]

How adorable — this hand — and this . . .
These lips — how very much adored!
And this face and form of childhood's
ingenuous nobility . . . how I bless you both . . .
not here — beyond . . .
every blessing here your father has despoiled.
So sweet . . . the mere touch of you:
the bloom of children's skin—so soft . . .
their breath — a perfect balm.

[*Gently releasing them; then almost savagely turning her back.*]

---

82. [Translator has followed] editors [who] omit lines 1062 and 1063 [of the Greek text] as a melodramatic interpolation: *"But they have to die, and since they must, / let it be by the hands of her who gave them life."*

105 Go, go . . . I cannot look at you.
    I am in an agony, and lost.

[*The two Boys, weeping, hurry into the house.*]

    The evil that I do, I understand full well,
    But a passion drives me greater than my will.
        Passion is the curse of man:
110   It wreaks the greatest ill.

FIFTH CHORAL ODE

[*If there can be a feminine philosophy of parenthood, is its honest judgment likely to be that children are worth it after all?*]

    So often before
    Have I gone toward concepts far too tenuous
    And come upon questions far too deep
    For the race of woman to try to unravel.
5   Nevertheless, even we women
    Have a muse of our own, that ushers us in.
    (Though, alas, not all) to the world of wisdom.
    Perhaps you might find it one in a thousand.
    It serves to inspire the talent of ladies,
10   And makes me able now to proclaim
    That people without the function of parent
    Are happier than begetters of offspring.
    The childless man has no way of telling
    Whether he misses a curse or a blessing.
15   Nevertheless, the childless person
    Certainly misses many a burden.
    I mark how the man with children growing
    Sweetly at home is worn with worrying:
    How to make sure they are properly fed,
20   How to leave them a livelihood.
    And then after all to be in the dark:
    Were all the worries worth it or not?
    Were they a worthy or worthless lot?

    But now let me tell
25   Of the worst and saddest trait of all.
    Suppose the children have quite a good life,
    Reach their teenhood honest and fine,
    What if a fate like Death the cruel
    Carries them downward body and soul?
30   What is the use if after all
    (On top of all those other ones)
    The gods let loose this grief as well . . .
    Just for the joy of having sons?

SIXTH EPISODE

[*Medea has been sitting during the Chorus. Now she leaps up as she catches sight of a man lunging breathlessly toward them from the street: the Messenger.*]

MEDEA: Somebody with news at last, my friends,
    And from the right direction.

    Yes, I see him:
one of Jason's men — panting as he hurries —
    With some tremendous news of bad.   5

[*The Messenger — an official of the Bride's house — bursts in: hardly able to get his words out.*]

MESSENGER: Run, Medea, run!
    What — you have done . . . is . . . too
        unthinkable . . .
too awful . . .
    Seize whatever means you can . . .
sailing boat or chariot . . . Escape!   10
MEDEA: Run? Escape? Is it then so vital?
MESSENGER: Dead . . . They are this minute dead . . .
    the princess royal with her father —
    and through your poisons.
MEDEA: What a pretty word you bring —   15
    my benefactor, my friend forever!
MESSENGER [*recoiling*]: What are you saying, Madam?
    Are you in your right mind — not unhinged?
    A king's home a charnel house —
and you rejoice? . . . Are you not afraid?   20
MEDEA: I have my ready answer too,
    so don't be hasty, friend,
    but tell me how they perished.
    An appalling death
    would give me double joy.   25
MESSENGER [*supports himself against a pillar as he
        begins to recollect an agonizing experience*]:
    We were so pleased to see your brace of boys
    come hand in hand to the bride's house with their
        father:
for your ordeal had upset us servants greatly.
    The rumor went racing through the house
that all was well again between your husband and
        yourself.   30
    Some of us kissed the children's hands,
kissed their golden tops;
and I in my enthusiasm even followed them
to the women's wing.
    There, the mistress —   35
I mean the one we have to honor now —
had eyes so taken up with Jason
she did not even see at first
the two boys hand in hand.
    But when she did,   40
a veil of scorn dropped over her eyes,
she turned her lovely face away,
bristling at your sons' intrusion.
    Your husband then began to woo her
from her petulance and girlish tantrums, saying: 45
    "You must not hate your friends.
    Stop being hurt and turn your head around.
    Consider yours your husband's loved ones.
    Come, won't you take their presents
and beseech your father   50
to let these boys off banishment — just for me?"

[*Pauses and sits down hopelessly on a step.*]

When she saw how exquisite the presents were,
far from holding out on him,
there was nothing she withheld:
55   but gave in completely to her groom.
        And hardly had your husband and your children
left the house
when she took the gorgeous robe and put it on,
and placed the golden circlet on her curls,
60   arranging the ringlets in the brightness of a mirror
and smiling at her own dead image there.
        Then rising from her stool
she minced off through the halls
on dainty milk white toes,
65   wildly pleased with what she had received,
over and over again
running her eyes down the clear sweep to her heels.
        But all at once
a hideous spectacle took place.
70   Her color changed. She tottered back;
shuddered in every limb; was able just in time
to fall into a chair and not upon the floor.
        An old woman there, attending her,
thinking that perhaps the fierce possession of Pan°
75   or some other power was on her,
broke into a chant of wonder,
then saw the white froth spuming at her lips,
her eyeballs bulging all askew,
her skin quite leached of blood,
80   and changed her chanting to a yelp:
a wail of horror.
        A maid went dashing to the palace for her father,
another went to tell the fresh-wed groom
what was happening to his bride.
85   The whole house rang with footsteps running.
        It took no longer than a sprinter takes
to go the hundred yards,
before the poor girl lay unconscious with her eyelids
        shut.
        Then suddenly she rallied
90   and gave a curdling shriek,
fighting off a double nightmare.

[*He pauses, gulps, takes a deep breath.*]

        The golden diadem that clasped her head
burst into a voracious and uncanny flow of fire,
while the robe of gossamer your children gave her
95   began to eat her tender flesh away.
        Streaming with flame,
she leapt up from her chair and fled,
tossing her mane of hair from side to side,
in a frantic bid to shake the diadem off.
100   But its grip was adamant
and the golden circlet held.
        The more she tossed,
the more the fire flowed,
till, overwhelmed with pain,

she sank down to the floor —   105
unrecognizable to all except her father —
her calm regard grotesquely twisted,
her sweet symmetry all shattered;
and from the crown of her head in molten clots
fire and blood dripped down together.   110
        The flesh curdled off her bones
like the teardrops congealing out of pines,
inexplicably dissolved by those ravening venoms.
        It was curious and horrible to see.
        No one dared to touch her body: 115
the warning was too obvious.
        But her father, unawares, poor man,
rushed headlong through the room,
flung himself lamenting on the body,
hugged and kissed it, sobbing out: 120
"My stricken darling,
what evil power has done this to you,
who has made you dead
and left me, like some ancient tombstone, derelict?
O gods! . . . let me die with you, my daughter."   125
        But . . . but when he stopped . . .
from these outpourings —
these melancholy sobs . . .
and tried to lift his aged carcass up,
he found himself stuck fast —   130
clamped to the flimsy robe
like ivy to a laurel bole.
        A ghastly wrestling match ensued.
        He would try to raise a knee,
she would drag him back;   135
and when he took to force,
his own decrepit flesh
pulled off from the bone.
        At last, exhausted,
pathetically unable   140
to lift himself above the shambles,
he gave his spirit up.
        There they lie, corpse by corpse,
father and young daughter —
fit objects for our tears.   145

[*He rises, swaying.*]

        To you, Medea . . . from me . . .
there are no words to say.
        Retribution? You yourself will know
the best escape . . .
though in my esteem — and not just for today —   150
the whole of life is shadow,
and I would even say:
the people who know best or seem to know,
the subtlest professors,
are the very ones who pay the dearest price.   155

[*Flinging his cloak about him.*]

        A happy human being? Ha, there's no such
        thing . . .
more prosperity, more success in one maybe:
but happier? . . . It does not make one happy.
                                    [*Exit Messenger.*]

---

74. **Pan:** The god of wild nature was supposed to be the cause
of seizures and sudden madness. Hence our word *panic*.

LEADER: Justice personified this day
160   has brought on Jason's head
     — oh, we have seen it! —
     the richest retribution.
       But it is you we weep for,
     poor blighted child of Creon,
165   walking through the gates of death
     because you married Jason.
MEDEA [*in clear, cold tones*]:
       Now, friends, to complete this mission with
         dispatch:
     to slay my children and hurry from this land.
     I must not dawdle and betray my sons
170   to much more savage hands than mine to kill.
       There's no way out. They have to die.
       And since they must,
     let me be the one to cut them down:
     the very one who gave them life!

[*She begins her walk to the door, almost like a sleep-walker, talking to herself.*]

175   Yes, heart, be steel.
       Why vacillate?
       The act is . . .
     necessary as it is cruel and hard.
       Come, reluctant hand,
180   grip the sword — grip it, Medea:
     cross your borderline of lifelong pain.
       Away this flinching!
       Away this longing:
     consign to oblivion the love you had for them —
185   the children of your flesh.
       Even when you kill them they are dear . . .
     oh, my sons! . . . I am in despair, despair.

[*Medea, with the Nurse mutely following in tears, passes into the house.*]

SIXTH CHORAL ODE

[*The women pray desperately for something to stop the imminent murder.*]

[*Strophe*]

       Come Earth, come sunshafts of the Sun,
       Behold this woman and withhold her
       From her laying scarlet fingers
       On the children of her blood.
5   Gold of your gold are they begotten:
       Heinous is to spill this holy
       Ichor in the blood of mortals.
       Curb her, stop her, godborn Light, oh,
       Keep this house from murder! Keep it
10   Never haunted by the Furies.°

---

10. Furies: Ministers of the vengeance of the gods, employed in punishing the guilty on earth as well as in the underworld.

[*Antistrophe*]

       Were those birth pangs wasted bearing:
       Children's birth pangs wasted birth?
       You, my lady, after sailing
       Safe between the dark blue clashing
       Gorges, will you hug a rankling   15
       Hatred to your heart, a loathsome
       Rage for murder and revenge?
       Those that spill the blood of family
       Stain themselves with heaven's anger,
       Haunt their homes with doom forever.   20

SEVENTH EPISODE *or* DENOUEMENT

[*Cries are heard from inside the house.*]

FIRST WOMAN: A shout — listen — a shout from the
     boys.
FIRST BOY: O–h! What can we do? . . .
     Our mother is on us!
SECOND BOY: Brother, brother! . . . We're going to be
     killed.
SECOND WOMAN: That murderous relentless woman!   5
THIRD WOMAN: Shall we break in, snatch them from
     death?
FIRST BOY: Yes, by heaven . . . save us . . . help!
SECOND BOY: We're trapped, cornered . . . now . . . by
     her sword.

[*As the Chorus beat on the barred doors, there are groans and cries, and presently a trickle of blood oozes from under the doors. The women watch it, fascinated.*]

CHORUS: Woman of stone, heart of iron,
     Disconsolate woman, ready to kill   10
     The seed of your hands with the hand that tilled.
     One other only, one have I known
     Murderously handle the fruit of her womb:
     Ino the maniac, god-driven one,
     Whom Zeus's wife drove out to roam —°   15
     Desperate woman goaded to slaughter
     The sons of her flesh, clean against nature.
     She pitched from the precipice into the sea,
     Fell where her foot fell into the ocean,
     Dashing two infants to death with her own.   20
     What ghastlier thing is left to be known?

     Women, O women, in love and in pangs,
     What ruin you've brought on us human beings!

[*Jason, breathless, his face twisted with hatred, bursts in with a troop of servants.*]

14–15. Ino the maniac . . . out to roam: Ino, a daughter of Cadmus and Harmonia, tried to destroy her two stepchildren so that her own two children might ascend the throne. Pursued, in turn, by their father, her husband Athamas, she leapt into the sea with her two boys. [The account given here] is Euripides' version.

Diana Rigg as Medea in the
National Theatre's 1995
production of Euripides'
play.

JASON: You women standing here outside this house,
25   is that she-ravager, Medea, still at home,
    or has she fled?

[*He waits for a reply, but the women cower before the
door.*]

    Deep down in the earth let that woman hide,
    or wing into the highest alcoves of the sky,
    before she ever saves herself from justice by this
        royal house.
30   Does she think that she can kill
    a princess and a country's king
    and vanish with impunity?

[*He strides toward the door.*]

    But it is my sons, not her, I fear for.
    She, she shall be repaid
35   through her victims.
    I have come to save my children's lives
    from some enormous retribution by the family of
        the dead
    for those enormities their mother did.
LEADER: Jason, you poor optimistic man,
40   you still don't know the evils that have come —
    or you would not say what you have said.
JASON: What? Does she mean to kill me too?
LEADER: Your sons are dead: murdered by their mother.
JASON [*reeling*]: What — did — you — say?
45   Oh, woman — my own wife — you kill me too.
LEADER [*as the women form an avenue to the door,
    and Jason sees for the first time the blood
    beginning to trickle down the steps*]:
    Yes. Your children.
    You cannot think of them as being alive.
JASON [*limply*]:
    Where did she kill them . . . here . . . outside,
    or was it in the house?
50 LEADER: Force these doors
    and you will see your children in their blood.

JASON [*drawing his sword in a frenzy*]: Servants, on the
    double,
    break these bolts,
    force the hinges: let me see
    the double homicide,   55
    the murdered dead . . . and the murderess to die.

[*There is a rumbling sound, and out of a cloud above
the house Medea appears in a chariot drawn by dragons. By her side are the dead bodies of the two Boys.*]

MEDEA [*in triumphant disdain*]:
    Why this battering, this beating at the doors?
    Are you looking for their bodies —
    and for me who did this thing?
    Save yourself the trouble.   60
    If there's anything you want, then ask.
    But me you shall not lay a hand upon.
    This chariot, the Sun
    — my father's father — gave me
    to keep me safe against my enemies.   65
JASON [*hissing with revulsion*]:
    You miserable, mephitic° woman!
    Beyond abhorrence —
    by me, the gods, the rest of men —
    you could put your own sons to the sword,
    the sons you bore,   70
    and kill me too with childlessness . . .
    Yet still look upon the sun, see the earth . . .
    Be damned! . . .
    At last I understand
    what I never understood before,   75
    when I took you from your foreign home to live in
        Greece,
    the sheer wickedness of you,
    the treachery to your father and the land that reared
        you.
    You are possessed

[**66. mephitic:** Foul-smelling.]

156

80   and the gods have unleashed the fiend in you on *me;*
        on your own brother, too, cut down in his home
        before you came aboard the sweet ship *Argo*'s hull.
                Your work already had begun.
                You married me, bore my sons,
85   and murdered them through jealousy of love.
                No woman in the whole of Hellas
        would have dared so much;
        yet you were the one I married,
        not a girl from Greece.
90   Oh, I married a tigress,
        not a woman, not a wife,
        and yoked myself to a hater and destroyer:
        to a viciousness more fierce than any Tuscan Scylla.°

[*Turning away from the door in a gesture of helplessness.*]

        But why go on?
95   A million accusations would not make you wince:
        you are shameless through and through . . .
        you — you bloodstained ogress, infanticide . . .
                Hell take you!
        Leave me to mourn my destiny of pain:
100   my fresh young wedding without joy,
        my sons begot and reared and lost —
        never to be seen alive again.

MEDEA [*with acid imperiousness from the chariot*]:
        How tediously I could rebut you point by point!
                Zeus the Father knows
105   exactly what you got from me
        and how you then behaved.
                I would not let you or your royal princess
        set our wedded life aside,
        make me cheap,
110   so that you could live in bliss;
        or let that match-arranger, Creon,
        dismiss me from the land without a fight.
                So, call me a tigress if you like,
        or a Scylla haunting the Tyrrhenian shore,
115   I have done what I ought:
        broken your own heart to the core.

JASON [*wheeling round to face her*]:
        You are in agony too:
        you share my broken life.

MEDEA: It is worth the suffering
120   since *you* cannot scoff.

JASON: Poor children, what a monster
                fate gave you for a mother!

MEDEA: Poor sons, what a disaster
                your selfish father was!

125 JASON: It was not *his* right hand
                that killed and struck them down.

MEDEA: No, it was his pride
                the lust of his new love.

JASON: You think it right to murder
130   just for a thwarted bed.

MEDEA: And do you think that a thwarted bed
                is trifling to a woman?

JASON: A modest woman, yes:
                to you the world's worst crime.

MEDEA [*pointing at the dead children*]:
        See, they are no more;   135
                I can hurt you too.

JASON: They'll live, I think,
                in your tormented brain.

MEDEA: The gods know who began
                this whole calamity.   140

JASON: Yes, the gods know well
                your pernicious heart.

MEDEA: Hate then: I spurn
                the wormwood from your lips.

JASON: As I do yours; so let us   145
                be rid of one another.

MEDEA: Yes, but on what terms?
                That's also what *I* want.

JASON: Let me have the boys —
                to mourn and bury them.   150

MEDEA: Never!
        My own hands shall bury them, they shall be carried
        to the sanctuary of Hera on the Cape,
        where no enemy shall ever do them harm
        or violate their sepulchre.   155
                Here in Corinth, the land of Sisyphus,
        I shall inaugurate a solemn festival°
        with rites in perpetuity
        to exorcise this murder.
                I myself shall go to Athens, land of Erechtheus, 160
        to live with Aegeus, Pandion's son . . .
        you to a paltry death that fits you well:
        your skull smashed by a fragment of the *Argo*'s hull:
        ironic ending to the saga of your love for me.

THE EXODOS°

[*As the Chorus begin to form for the exodos march, the
meter changes. Jason strides into the middle of the arena.*]

JASON: Murder is punished, and you'll be destroyed
                by the avenging phantoms of your children.

MEDEA: What power or divine one is ready to hear
                you:
        perjurer, liar, treacherous guest?

JASON: Vile, vile, murderess of little ones!   5

MEDEA: Go — go and bury your bride.

JASON: Broken I go: bereft of two sons.

MEDEA: You bemoan too soon: wait till you're old.

JASON: Dearest children!

MEDEA: Dear to their mother.   10

JASON: And so she slew them.

MEDEA: To get at your heart.

JASON: You did! You did! How I long to press
        my little children's lips to mine!

---

93. **Tuscan Scylla:** A monster that inhabited the straits between
Italy and Sicily and snatched sailors off passing ships and
devoured them.

157. **solemn festival:** Similar ceremonies were still performed at
Corinth in Euripides' time.   [**Exodos:** Final scene.]

15 MEDEA: Now you are longing, now you call;
        you utterly turned from them before.
    JASON: For the love of the gods, allow me this:
        to stroke my children's tender skin.
    MEDEA: No, you shall not: you waste your words.
    JASON [*flinging out his arms*]: Zeus, do you hear how
20   I'm at bay,
        Dismissed by this ogress, odious woman,
        Tigress besmirched with the blood of her young?
        So I mourn and call on the gods while I may,
        On the powers to witness how you have slain
25   My children, and now prevent my hands
        From touching them, dead, interring their clay.
        I'd rather they'd never been born to me
        Than have lived to see you destroy them this day.

[*Before the end of these words, Medea, with a cold, vindictive smile, has moved off in the chariot. Jason staggers out of the arena.*]

ENVOI°

CHORUS: Wide is the range of Zeus on Olympus.
        Wide the surprise which the gods can bring:
        What was expected is never perfected,
        What was not, finds a way opened up . . .
        So ended this terrible thing.   5

[**Envoi:** Concluding remarks.]

COMMENTARY

John Simon (b. 1925)
REVIEW OF *MEDEA*   1994

Critic John Simon's review of Medea *focuses on the problems the play presents
for modern production and how the director handled them. He is especially interested in the problem, as he views it, of the chorus, reminding us that this modern
production reduced the original number from fifteen to three women. However, he
also has useful commentary on the dramatic setting and the music and sounds,
which help us understand how the play was staged.*

"One must be absolutely modern. This is what Euripides was, as he still is,"
writes our premier classical scholar, Bernard Knox (with an acknowledged assist
from Rimbaud), in his absorbing new book, *Backing Into the Future.* In a letter of
May 17, 1948, our still undervalued poet-playwright Robinson Jeffers, who wrote
his version of *Medea,* declares, "There is much in any Greek play that would seem
dull or absurd to anyone but a classical scholar." Which statement is true? Both.

Any new production of *Medea* must come to grips with the fact that although
Euripides speaks as one of us, much of his technique strikes us as dated, though less
so than that of his fellow Greek dramatists. This *Medea,* originally produced at London's Almeida Theatre, has many features to its credit, most notably that its director,
Jonathan Kent, is aware of this *aporia* (as the Greek would call it) or hot potato (as
we would): Euripides today is both necessary and impossible. So Kent pawkily tries
to steer a course between these infernal Symplegades (or a rock and a hard place).

The first and worst problem a director of a Greek drama now faces is what to do
with the chorus. In the case of *Medea,* Jeffers reduced it to three women, as Grill-

parzer did before him; Anouilh, in his version, eliminated it altogether. Kent, too, retains three women, but then what? How should they look? Since Paul Brown's costumes here are modern, but with classical Greek overtones, Kent picked something resembling contemporary Greek folk dress, but with distinct echoes of a Melina Mercouri movie. It doesn't look quite right, but what would? Next, how to explain the chorus's very presence? "It is hard to imagine fifteen women standing by while a mother murders her children," wrote Moses Hadas, the late, great classicist. *Three* women standing by doesn't make it much easier. For this, Kent has no solution. But by assigning the roles to three actresses of very different ages and types (the eldest coming across like a man), he achieves a nice, stylized effect — something like the Three Ages of Woman.

The Greek chorus sang and danced; so Kent lets his women do some singing and dancing. For the former, they are usually backed up by an invisible choir, which makes for a bizarre but not uninteresting effect. The dancing, such as it is, is pretty ludicrous, but one admires Kent's guts for risking it at all. And there isn't much of it.

The next problem is what kind of decor to use, other than the standard all-purpose Greek-drama set (Woolworth Hellenic), of which everyone is heartily sick. With the help of his set designer, Peter J. Davison, Kent came up with an imposingly monumental solution, which, along with the scenery for the current *Carousel,* raises the troubling possibility that British set design has way outstripped ours. What we get makes scant sense architecturally but is fiercely theatrical. Two tall, asymmetrical facades intersect at right angles; they are seemingly made of large square bronze sheets, artfully imbricated, with rivets displayed. In the lesser facade, stage right, is an empty doorway revealing some mighty girders. The main facade has, among other things, a picture window that sometimes lights up to reveal, say, Medea a shut-in in her palace, or hovering over her slain children, something the Greeks would never have shown. There is also a functioning, likewise square, onstage well. And in the end, the set does something sensational that you have to see for yourself.

Jonathan Dove's music is, in the spirit of the show, neither modern nor antiquarian, sometimes haunting and sometimes, alas, banal. More interesting sounds are produced by carefully calibrated bangings on the walls. The acting, by a low-profile British cast (save for the star, about whom more anon), is generally solid, distinguished by elocution American actors should envy. The diction of John Turner (Creon) — a tall, imposing man in a fuzzy black greatcoat for which numerous sheep must have been left shivering — is so good I felt virtually impaled by his consonants. I liked Tim Oliver Woodward's Jason, a fellow with one foot in tragedy, the other in trashiness, paltry one moment and deeply pitiable the next.

Diana Rigg's Medea is seldom absolutely right, but always hugely watchable. She, I think, suffers most from the directorial ambivalence: One moment a Mycenean lioness, she turns Mayfair hostess in a twinkling, her tigerish stalking yielding too readily to a kittenish purr. With her back frequently against the wall, her regal figure and darting eyes, she looks part caryatid, part Fury. In this she is superbly abetted by Wayne Dowdeswell's lighting, which uses horizontal and diagonal shafts of light to mesmeric or hallucinatory effect.

And yet Miss Rigg's disciplined and highly cultivated tones, and her fine sense of humor (which she has manifestly been urged to indulge), have a way of making this a thoroughly modern Medea, one eliciting too many knowingly deliberate laughs. Miss Rigg is, rightly, more sensual than her New York predecessors in the role,

Judith Anderson and Zoë Caldwell, but they were, rightly, more terrifying. And for all that she looks sexy in red and marmoreal in discreetly blood-spattered white, she seems, like those others, a bit overmature for the role.

All in all, this is a production that deserves to be seen — as well as heard, in Alistair Elliot's wonderfully colloquial yet not unpoetic translation — even if its split personality militates against full impact. It is rich in ideas in its every aspect, including Miss Rigg's performance, and ideas, even intermittently misguided ones, are precious in our theater so habitually short on thought.

Aristophanes

The best known of the Greek comic playwrights, Aristophanes (c. 448–c. 385 B.C.) lived through some of the most difficult times in Athenian history. He watched Athenian democracy fade and decay as factionalism and war took their toll on the strength of the city-state. By the time he died, Athens was caught up in a fierce struggle between supporters of democracy and supporters of oligarchy, government by a small group of leaders.

Aristophanes' plays are democratic in that they appealed to sophisticated and unsophisticated theatergoers alike. Skilled at complex wordplay, he also enjoyed spirited and rowdy comedy. Since his plays were often sharply critical of Athenian policies, his ability to make people laugh was essential to conveying his message. He was a practitioner of what we now call Old Comedy, an irreverent form that ridiculed and insulted prominent people and important institutions. By Aristophanes' time, Old Comedy had become fiercely satirical, especially concerning political matters. Because Aristophanes held strong opinions, he found satire an ideal form for his talents.

Of his more than thirty known plays, only eleven survive. They come from three main periods in his life, beginning, according to legend, when he was a young man, in 427 B.C. *The Acharnians* (425 B.C.), from his first period, focuses on the theme of peace. Dicaeopolis (whose name means "honest" or "good citizen") decides to make a separate peace after the Spartans have ravaged the Acharnian vineyards. The Acharnians vow revenge, but Dicaeopolis explains that peace must begin as an individual decision. Aristophanes saw war as a corporate venture; peacemaking was easier for an individual than for a group or a nation.

The Acharnians was followed by *The Peace* in 421 B.C., just before Sparta and Athens signed a treaty, and it seems clearly to have been written in support of the Athenian peace party, whose power had been growing from the time of *The Acharnians* and whose cause had been aided by that play.

His second period was also dominated by the problems of war. Athens's ill-fated expedition to Sicily in violation of the Treaty of Nicias lies thematically beneath the surface of *The Birds* (414 B.C.), in which some citizens build Cloud-Cuckoo-Land to come between the world of humans and the world of the gods. *Lysistrata* (411 B.C.) is also from this period; its frank antiwar theme is related to the Sicilian wars and to the ultimately devastating Peloponnesian Wars. These were wars fought by Greek city-states in the areas south of Athens, the Peloponneus. The states had voluntarily contributed money to arm and support Athens against the Persians in 480 B.C. — resulting in the Athenian victory at Salamis. The states later became angry when Pericles, the Athenian leader, demanded that they continue giving contributions, much of which he used to fund the rebuilding of the Akropolis and other civic projects in Athens.

The other Greek city-states felt that Athens was becoming imperialistic and was overreaching itself. War broke out between the city-states in 431 B.C. and lasted for nearly thirty years. These struggles and the difficulties of conducting a costly, long-distance war in Sicily combined eventually to exhaust the Athenian resources of men and funds. Soundly defeated in 405 B.C., Athens surrendered to Sparta in 404. Aristophanes lived to see the Spartan ships at rest in the harbors of Athens's chief port, the Piraeus. And he saw, too, the destruction of the walls of the city, leaving it essentially defenseless.

Aristophanes' third and final period, from 393 B.C. to his death, includes *The Ecclesiazusae* (c. 392 B.C.) (translated as "The Women in Government"), in which women dress as men, find their way into parliament, and pass a new constitution. It is a highly topical play that points to the current situation in Athens and the people's general discontent and anxiety. The last part of *The Plutus,* written five years later, is an allegory about the god of wealth, who is eventually encouraged to make the just wealthy and the unjust poor.

Among the best known of Aristophanes' plays are several whose names refer to the disguises or costumes of the chorus, among them *The Knights, The Wasps,* and *The Frogs. The Frogs* (405 B.C.) is especially interesting for its focus on literary issues. It features a contest in the underworld between Aeschylus, who had been dead more than fifty years, and Euripides, who had just died at a relatively young age. Aristophanes uses the contest to make many enlightening comments about Greek tragedy and the skills of the two authors.

Even in his last period Aristophanes was an innovative force in theater. His last surviving play virtually does away with the chorus as an important character in the action. His later plays resemble modern comedies partly because the chorus does not intrude in the action. His genius helped shape later developments in comedy.

Lysistrata

At the time *Lysistrata* was written (411 B.C.), Athens had had a steady diet of war for more than twenty years. Political groups were actively trying to persuade Athenian leaders to discontinue the policies that had alienated Athens from the other city-states that were once its supporters in the Delian League, the group that had funded Athens's struggle against the Persian threat. Aristophanes opposed the imperialist attitudes that conflicted with the democratic spirit of only a generation earlier.

Lysistrata makes it clear that war is the central business of the nation at that time. No sooner is one campaign ended than another begins. The men encountered by the heroine Lysistrata (whose name means "disband the army") on the Acropolis — men who guard the national security and the national treasury — are old and decrepit. The young men are in the field. As Kalonike tells Lysistrata, her man has been away for five months. Such separations were common, and these women are fed up. Lysistrata has gathered the discontented women together to propose a scheme to bring peace and negotiate a treaty.

The scheme is preposterous, but, typical of Old Comedy, its very outrageousness is its source of strength. In time, the idea begins to seem almost reasonable: Lysistrata asks the women to refuse to engage in sex with their husbands until the men stop making war. The women also seize the Acropolis and hold the treasury hostage. Without the national treasury there can be no war. And because they are confident of getting the support of the larger community of women in other nations — who suffer as they do — they do not fear the consequences of their acts.

In amusing scenes generated by this situation Aristophanes pokes fun at both sexes. We hear the gossipy conversation of the women, all of whom arrive late to Lysistrata's meeting. The men are dependent, helpless, ineffectual, and cannot resist the takeover. When the truth begins to settle in, the men solicit their wives' attention with enormous erections protruding beneath their gowns, one example of the exaggerated visual humor Aristophanes counted on. The double meanings in the conversations are also a great source of humor.

The wonderful scene (3) between Myrrhine and her husband Kinesias is predicated on the agony of the husband whose wife constantly promises, and then reneges, to build his sexual excitement to a fever pitch. It is no wonder that Lysistrata can eventually bring the men to sign any treaties she wants.

This heterosexual hilarity is also balanced by a number of homosexual allusions. Kleisthenes, possibly a bisexual Athenian, stands ready to relieve some of the men's sexual discomfort, while Lysistrata admits that if the men do not capitulate, the women will have to satisfy their own needs. Such frankness is typical of Athenian comedy.

Women dominate the action of the play, although we must remember that male actors played women's roles. The women see the stupidity and waste of the war and devise a plan that will end it. Observing that they are the ones who suffer most from the effects of war, the women also note that they pay their taxes in babies. The suffering of women had been a major theme in the tragedies of Euripides, and everyone in Aristophanes' audience would have understood Lysistrata's motivation. The idea that a woman should keep her place is expressed by several characters. And since Athenian audiences would have agreed that women should not meddle in war or government, Aristophanes offered them a fantasy that challenged them on many levels.

Aristophanes praises Lysistrata's ingenuity and her perseverance. When the other women want to give up the plan because of their own sexual needs, she holds firm. She demands that they stand by their resolve. The picture of a strong, independent, intelligent, and capable woman obviously pleased the Athenians because they permitted this play to be performed more than once — an unusual practice. Lysistrata became a recognizable and admirable character in Athenian life.

The following translation of *Lysistrata* has several interesting features. It is comprised of scenes, a division not made in the original Greek. The strophe and antistrophe are speeches given by the chorus, probably moving first in one direction and then in the opposite. Instead of having a chorus of elders, as in *Antigone*, Aristophanes uses two choruses — one of men and one of women — that are truly representative of the people: they are as divided and antagonistic as Sophocles' chorus is united and wise. The KORYPHAIOS (leader) of the men's chorus speaks alone, often in opposition to the koryphaios of the women's chorus.

The rhyming patterns of some of the songs are approximated in English, and the sense of dialect is maintained in the speech of Lampito, who represents a kind of country bumpkin. She is very muscular from the workouts that she and all other Spartans engaged in; Aristophanes reveals certain Athenian prejudices toward the Spartans in the scene where Lampito is taunted for her physique.

Lysistrata in Performance

Lysistrata has enjoyed and still enjoys numerous productions, both on college and commercial stages. Because it is a bawdy play, it has sometimes run into trouble. In 1932 the New York police shut down a performance and sent out a warrant for the arrest of "Arthur" Aristophanes. In 1959 Dudley Fitts's translation (used here) was performed at the Phoenix Theater in New York with "women . . . wearing simulated breasts, tipped with sequins, and the ruttish old men stripped down to union suits." Hunter College's 1968 production used rock music, hippie beads, and headbands. Less controversial productions include the first modern version, by Maurice Donnay in Paris (1892), in which Lysistrata takes a general as a lover. The Moscow Art Theater produced a highly acclaimed version in 1923 and brought it to the United States in 1925. That version, modified by Gilbert Seldes (published in book form with illustrations by Picasso), was produced throughout the 1930s. All-black versions of the play have been staged several times since 1938. *Lysistrata* ranks among the favorites of classical drama.

Aristophanes c. 448–c. 385 B.C.)

LYSISTRATA   *411 B.C.*
TRANSLATED BY DUDLEY FITTS

Persons Represented

LYSISTRATA, ⎫
KALONIKE, ⎬ *Athenian women*
MYRRHINE, ⎭
LAMPITO, *a Spartan woman*
CHORUS
COMMISSIONER
KINESIAS, *husband of Myrrhine*
SPARTAN HERALD
SPARTAN AMBASSADOR
A SENTRY
[BABY SON OF KENESIAS
STRATYLLIS
SPARTANS
ATHENIANS]

Scene: *Athens. First, a public square; later, beneath the walls of the Akropolis;° later, a courtyard within the Akropolis.*

Akropolis: Fortress of Athens, sacred to the goddess Athena.

PROLOGUE°

(*Athens; a public square; early morning; Lysistrata alone.*)

LYSISTRATA: If someone had invited them to a
          festival —
     of Bacchos,° say; or to Pan's° shrine, or to
          Aphrodite's°
     over at Kolias — , you couldn't get through the
          streets,
     what with the drums and the dancing. But now,
     not a woman in sight!
                    Except — oh, yes!   5

(*Enter Kalonike.*)

Prologue: Portion of the play explaining the background and current action.   **2. Bacchos:** (Bacchus) God of wine and the object of wild, orgiastic ritual and celebration; also called Dionysus.   **Pan:** God of nature, forests, flocks, and shepherds, depicted as half-man and half-goat. Pan was considered playful and lecherous.   **Aphrodite:** Goddess of love.

Here's one of my neighbors, at last. Good
    morning, Kalonike.
KALONIKE: Good morning, Lysistrata.
                                       Darling,
    don't frown so! You'll ruin your face!
LYSISTRATA: Never mind my face.
    Kalonike,
    the way we women behave! Really, I don't blame
10   the men
    for what they say about us.
KALONIKE: No; I imagine they're right.
LYSISTRATA: For example: I call a meeting
    to think out a most important matter — and
    what happens?
    The women all stay in bed!
KALONIKE: Oh, they'll be along.
15   It's hard to get away, you know: a husband, a cook,
    a child . . . Home life can be *so* demanding!
LYSISTRATA: What I have in mind is even more
    demanding.
KALONIKE: Tell me: what is it?
LYSISTRATA: It's big.
KALONIKE: Goodness! *How* big?
LYSISTRATA: Big enough for all of us.
KALONIKE: But we're not all here!
LYSISTRATA: We would be, if *that's* what was up!
20   No, Kalonike,
    this is something I've been turning over for nights,
    long sleepless nights.
KALONIKE: It must be getting worn down, then,
    if you've spent so much time on it.
LYSISTRATA: Worn down or not,
    it comes to this: Only we women can save Greece!
KALONIKE: Only we women? Poor Greece!
25 LYSISTRATA: Just the same,
    it's up to us. First, we must liquidate
    the Peloponnesians —
KALONIKE: Fun, fun!
LYSISTRATA: — and then the Boiotians.°
KALONIKE: Oh! But not those heavenly eels!
LYSISTRATA: You needn't worry.
    I'm not talking about eels. — But here's the point:
30   If we can get the women from those places —
    all those Boiotians and Peloponnesians —
    to join us women here, why, we can save all Greece!
KALONIKE: But dearest Lysistrata!
    How can women do a thing so austere, so
35   political? We belong at home. Our only armor's
    our perfumes, our saffron dresses and
    our pretty little shoes!
LYSISTRATA: Exactly. Those
    transparent dresses, the saffron, the perfume, those
    pretty shoes —
KALONIKE: Oh?
LYSISTRATA: Not a single man would lift
    his spear —

---

27. Boiotians: Crude-mannered inhabitants of Boiotia, which
was noted for its seafood.

KALONIKE: I'll send my dress to the dyer's tomorrow!
LYSISTRATA: — or grab a shield —
KALONIKE: The sweetest little negligee —   40
LYSISTRATA: — or haul out his sword.
KALONIKE: I know where
    I can buy the dreamiest sandals!
LYSISTRATA: Well, so you see. Now, shouldn't
    the women have come?
KALONIKE: Come? They should have *flown*!
LYSISTRATA: Athenians are always late.
                      But imagine!
    There's no one here from the South Shore, or from
    Salamis.   45
KALONIKE: Things are hard over in Salamis, I swear.
    They have to get going at dawn.
LYSISTRATA: And nobody from Acharnai.
    I thought they'd be here hours ago.
KALONIKE: Well, you'll get
    that awful Theagenes woman: she'll be
    a sheet or so in the wind.
                       But look!   50
    Someone at last! Can you see who they are?

(*Enter Myrrhine and other women.*)

LYSISTRATA: They're from Anagyros.
KALONIKE: They certainly are.
    You'd know them anywhere, by the scent.
MYRRHINE: Sorry to be late, Lysistrata.
                      Oh come,
    don't scowl so. Say something!
LYSISTRATA: My dear Myrrhine,   55
    what is there to say? After all,
    you've been pretty casual about the whole thing.
MYRRHINE: Couldn't find
    my girdle in the dark, that's all.
                  But what *is*
    "the whole thing"?
KALONIKE: No, we've got to wait
    for those Boiotians and Peloponnesians.   60
LYSISTRATA: That's more like it. — But, look!
    Here's Lampito!

(*Enter Lampito with women from Sparta.*)

LYSISTRATA: Darling Lampito,
    how pretty you are today! What a nice color!
    Goodness, you look as though you could strangle a
    bull!   65
LAMPITO: Ah think Ah could! It's the work-out
    in the gym every day; and, of co'se that dance of ahs
    where y' kick yo' own tail.
KALONIKE: What an adorable figure!
LAMPITO: Lawdy, when y' touch me lahk that,
    Ah feel lahk a heifer at the altar!
LYSISTRATA: And this young lady?   70
    Where is she from?
LAMPITO: Boiotia. Social-Register type.
LYSISTRATA: Ah. "Boiotia of the fertile plain."
KALONIKE: And if you look,
    you'll find the fertile plain has just been mowed.

LYSISTRATA: And this lady?
LAMPITO: Hagh, wahd, handsome.
75   She comes from Korinth.
KALONIKE: High and wide's the word for it.
LAMPITO: Which one of you
    called this heah meeting, and why?
LYSISTRATA: I did.
LAMPITO: Well, then, tell us:
    What's up?
MYRRHINE: Yes, darling, what *is* on your mind, after
                                                            all?
LYSISTRATA: I'll tell you. — But first, one little question.
MYRRHINE: Well?
LYSISTRATA: It's your husbands. Fathers of your
80   children. Doesn't it bother you
    that they're always off with the Army? I'll stake my
        life,
    not one of you has a man in the house this minute!
KALONIKE: Mine's been in Thrace the last five months,
        keeping an eye
    on that General.
MYRRHINE: Mine's been in Pylos for seven.
LAMPITO: And mahn,
85   whenever he gets a *dis*charge, he goes raht back
    with that li'l ole shield of his, and enlists again!
LYSISTRATA: And not the ghost of a lover to be found!
    From the very day the war began —
                                    those Milesians!
    I could skin them alive!
                            — I've not seen so much, even,
90   as one of those leather consolation prizes. —
    But there! What's important is: If I've found a way
    to end the war, are you with me?
MYRRHINE: I should *say* so!
    Even if I have to pawn my best dress and
    drink up the proceeds.
KALONIKE: Me, too! Even if they split me
    right up the middle, like a flounder.
95 LAMPITO: Ah'm shorely with you.
    Ah'd crawl up Taygetos° on mah knees
    if that'd bring peace.
LYSISTRATA: All right, then; here it is:
    Women! Sisters!
    If we really want our men to make peace,
    we must be ready to give up —
100 MYRRHINE: Give up what?
    Quick, tell us!
LYSISTRATA: But *will* you?
MYRRHINE: We will, even if it kills us.
LYSISTRATA: Then we must give up going to bed with
    our men.

(*Long silence.*)

    Oh? So now you're sorry? Won't look at me?
    Doubtful? Pale? All teary-eyed?
                            But come: be frank with me.
    Will you do it, or not? Well? Will you do it?

96. **Taygetos:** A mountain range.

MYRRHINE: I couldn't. No. 105
    Let the war go on.
KALONIKE: Nor I. Let the war go on.
LYSISTRATA: You, you little flounder,
    ready to be split up the middle?
KALONIKE: Lysistrata, no!
    I'd walk through fire for you — you *know* I
        would! — but don't
    ask us to give up *that*! Why, there's nothing like it! 110
LYSISTRATA: And you?
BOIOTIAN: No. I must say *I'd* rather walk
    through fire.
LYSISTRATA: What an utterly perverted sex we women
    are!
    No wonder poets write tragedies about us.
    There's only one thing we can think of.
                                    But you from Sparta:
    if you stand by me, we may win yet! Will you? 115
    It means so much!
LAMPITO: Ah sweah, it means *too* much!
    By the Two Goddesses,° it does! Asking a girl
    to sleep — Heaven knows how long! — in a great
        big bed
    with nobody there but herself! But Ah'll stay with
        you!
    Peace comes first!
LYSISTRATA: Spoken like a true Spartan! 120
KALONIKE: But if —
            oh dear!
                    — if we give up what you tell us to,
    will there *be* any peace?
LYSISTRATA: Why, mercy, of course there will!
    We'll just sit snug in our very thinnest gowns,
    perfumed and powdered from top to bottom, and
        those men
    simply won't stand still! And when we say No, 125
    they'll go out of their minds! And there's your peace.
    You can take my word for it.
LAMPITO: Ah seem to remember
    that Colonel Menelaos threw his sword away
    when he saw Helen's breast all bare.°
KALONIKE: But, goodness me!
    What if they just get up and leave us?
LYSISTRATA: In that case 130
    we'll have to fall back on ourselves, I suppose.
    But they won't.
KALONIKE: I must say that's not much help. But
    what if they drag us into the bedroom?
LYSISTRATA: Hang on to the door.
KALONIKE: What if they slap us?
LYSISTRATA: If they do, you'd better give in.
    But be sulky about it. Do I have to teach you how? 135

117. **Two Goddesses:** A woman's oath referring to Demeter, the earth goddess, and her daughter Persephone, who was associated with seasonal cycles of fertility. **128–29. Colonel Menelaos . . . Helen's breast:** Helen, wife of King Menelaos of Sparta, was abducted by Paris and taken to Troy. The incident led to the Trojan War.

You know there's no fun for men when they have to
  force you.
There are millions of ways of getting them to see
  reason.
Don't you worry: a man
doesn't like it unless the girl cooperates.
140 KALONIKE: I suppose so. Oh, all right. We'll go along.
LAMPITO: Ah imagine us Spahtans can arrange a peace.
  But you
Athenians! Why, you're just war-mongerers!
LYSISTRATA: Leave that to me.
I know how to make them listen.
LAMPITO: Ah don't see how.
After all, they've got their boats; and there's lots of
  money
piled up in the Akropolis.
145 LYSISTRATA: The Akropolis? Darling,
we're taking over the Akropolis today!
That's the older women's job. All the rest of us
are going to the Citadel to sacrifice — you
  understand me?
And once there, we're in for good!
LAMPITO: Whee! Up the rebels!
Ah can see you're a good strate*egist*.
150 LYSISTRATA: Well, then, Lampito,
what we have to do now is take a solemn oath.
LAMPITO: Say it. We'll sweah.
LYSISTRATA: This is it.
  — But where's our Inner Guard?
                — Look. Guard: you see this shield?
Put it down here. Now bring me the victim's
  entrails.
KALONIKE: But the oath?
LYSISTRATA: You remember how in Aischylos'
155   *Seven*°
they killed a sheep and swore on a shield? Well, then?
KALONIKE: But I don't see how you can swear for
  peace on a shield.
LYSISTRATA: What else do you suggest?
KALONIKE: Why not a white horse?
We could swear by that.
LYSISTRATA: And where will you get a white horse?
KALONIKE: I never thought of that. *What* can we do?
160 LYSISTRATA: I have it!
Let's set this big black wine-bowl on the ground
and pour in a gallon or so of Thasian,° and swear
not to add one drop of water.
LAMPITO: Ah lahk *that* oath!
LYSISTRATA: Bring the bowl and the wine-jug.
KALONIKE: Oh, what a simply *huge* one!
LYSISTRATA: Set it down. Girls, place your hands on the
165   gift-offering.
O Goddess of Persuasion! And thou, O Loving-cup:
Look upon this our sacrifice, and
be gracious!

155. ***Seven:*** Aeschylus's *Seven against Thebes,* which deals with
the war between the sons of Oedipus for the throne of Thebes.
162. **Thasian:** Wine from Thasos.

KALONIKE: See the blood spill out. How red and pretty
  it is!
LAMPITO: And Ah must say it smells good.
MYRRHINE: Let me swear first! 170
KALONIKE: No, by Aphrodite, we'll match for it!
LYSISTRATA: Lampito: all of you women: come, touch
  the bowl,
and repeat after me — remember, this is an oath — :
  I WILL HAVE NOTHING TO DO WITH MY
  HUSBAND OR MY LOVER
KALONIKE: *I will have nothing to do with my husband*
  or my lover   175
LYSISTRATA: THOUGH HE COME TO ME IN
  PITIABLE CONDITION
KALONIKE: *Though he come to me in pitiable condition*
  (Oh Lysistrata! This is killing me!)
LYSISTRATA: IN MY HOUSE I WILL BE
  UNTOUCHABLE
KALONIKE: *In my house I will be untouchable*   180
LYSISTRATA: IN MY THINNEST SAFFRON SILK
KALONIKE: *In my thinnest saffron silk*
LYSISTRATA: AND MAKE HIM LONG FOR ME.
KALONIKE: *And make him long for me.*
LYSISTRATA: I WILL NOT GIVE MYSELF   185
KALONIKE: *I will not give myself*
LYSISTRATA: AND IF HE CONSTRAINS ME
KALONIKE: *And if he constrains me*
LYSISTRATA: I WILL BE COLD AS ICE AND NEVER
  MOVE
KALONIKE: *I will be cold as ice and never move*   190
LYSISTRATA: I WILL NOT LIFT MY SLIPPERS
  TOWARD THE CEILING
KALONIKE: *I will not lift my slippers toward the ceiling*
LYSISTRATA: OR CROUCH ON ALL FOURS LIKE
  THE LIONESS IN THE CARVING
KALONIKE: *Or crouch on all fours like the lioness in*
  the carving
LYSISTRATA: AND IF I KEEP THIS OATH LET ME
  DRINK FROM THIS BOWL   195
KALONIKE: *And if I keep this oath let me drink from*
  this bowl
LYSISTRATA: IF NOT, LET MY OWN BOWL BE
  FILLED WITH WATER.
KALONIKE: *If not, let my own bowl be filled with*
  water.
LYSISTRATA: You have all sworn?
MYRRHINE: We have.
LYSISTRATA: Then thus
I sacrifice the victim.

(*Drinks largely.*)

KALONIKE: Save some for us!   200
Here's to you, darling, and to you, and to you!

(*Loud cries offstage.*)

LAMPITO: What's all *that* whoozy-goozy?
LYSISTRATA: Just what I told you.
The older women have taken the Akropolis.
Now you, Lampito,

205 rush back to Sparta. We'll take care of things here.
          Leave
these girls here for hostages.
                              The rest of you,
up to the Citadel: and mind you push in the bolts.
KALONIKE: But the men? Won't they be after us?
LYSISTRATA: Just you leave
210 the men to me. There's not fire enough in the world,
or threats either, to make me open these doors
except on my own terms.
KALONIKE: I hope not, by Aphrodite!
After all,
we've got a reputation for bitchiness to live up to.
                                        (*Exeunt.*°)

PARODOS:°
CHORAL EPISODE

(*The hillside just under the Akropolis. Enter Chorus of
Old Men with burning torches and braziers; much puffing and coughing.*)

KORYPHAIOS(man):° Forward march, Drakes, old friend:
          never you mind
     that damn big log banging hell down on your back.

Strophe° 1

CHORUS(men): There's this to be said for longevity:
     You see things you thought that you'd never see.
5   Look, Strymodoros, who would have thought it?
     We've caught it —
                    the New Femininity!
     The wives of our bosom, our board, our bed —
     Now, by the gods, they've gone ahead
     And taken the Citadel (Heaven knows why!),
10   Profanèd the sacred statuar-y,
                         And barred the doors,
                         The subversive whores!
KORYPHAIOS(m): Shake a leg there, Philurgos, man: the
          Akropolis or bust!
     Put the kindling around here. We'll build one
          almighty big
15   bonfire for the whole bunch of bitches, every last one;
     and the first we fry will be old Lykon's woman.

Antistrophe° 1

CHORUS(m): They're not going to give me the old horse-
          laugh!

---

213. [S.D.] *Exeunt:* Latin for "they go out."   **Parodos:** The song
or ode chanted by the Chorus on their entry.   **1. Koryphaios:**
Leader of the Chorus; also called *Choragos.* There are two
Choruses and two Koryphaioi, one male and one female.
Strophe: Song sung by the Chorus as it danced from stage right
to stage left.   **Antistrophe:** Song sung by the Chorus following
the Strophe, as it danced back from stage left to stage right.

No, by Demeter, they won't pull this off!
     Think of Kleomenes: even he
     Didn't go free
               till he brought me his stuff.   20
A good man he was, all stinking and shaggy,
Bare as an eel except for the bag he
Covered his rear with. God, what a mess!
Never a bath in six years, I'd guess.
                    Pure Sparta, man!   25
                    He also ran.
KORYPHAIOS(m): That was a siege, friends! Seventeen
     ranks strong
we slept at the Gate. And shall we not do as much
against these women, whom God and Euripides hate?
If we don't, I'll turn in my medals from Marathon.   30

Strophe 2

CHORUS(m): Onward and upward! A little push,
     And we're there.
Ouch, my shoulders! I could wish
     For a pair
Of good strong oxen. Keep your eye   35
     On the fire there, it mustn't die.
          Akh! Akh!
     The smoke would make a cadaver cough!

Antistrophe 2

Holy Herakles, a hot spark
     Bit my eye!   40
Damn this hellfire, damn this work!
     So say I.
Onward and upward just the same.
(Laches, remember the Goddess: for shame!)
          Akh! Akh!   45
The smoke would make a cadaver cough!
KORYPHAIOS(m): At last (and let us give suitable thanks
     to God
for his infinite mercies) I have managed to bring
my personal flame to the common goal. It breathes,
     it lives.
Now, gentlemen, let us consider. Shall we insert   50
the torch, say, into the brazier, and thus extract
a kindling brand? And shall we then, do you think,
push on to the gate like valiant sheep? On the whole
     yes.
But I would have you consider this, too: if they —
I refer to the women — should refuse to open,   55
what then? Do we set the doors afire
and smoke them out? At ease, men. Meditate.
Akh, the smoke! Woof! What we really need
is the loan of a general or two from the Samos
     Command.°
At least we've got this lumber off our backs.   60
That's something. And now let's look to our fire.

---

59. **Samos Command:** Headquarters of the Athenian military.

O Pot, brave Brazier, touch my torch with flame!
Victory, Goddess, I invoke thy name!
Strike down these paradigms of female pride
65 And we shall hang our trophies up inside.

(*Enter Chorus of Old Women on the walls of the Akropolis, carrying jars of water.*)

KORYPHAIOS(woman): Smoke, girls, smoke! There's smoke
    all over the place!
Probably fire, too. Hurry, girls! Fire! Fire!

Strophe 1

CHORUS(women): Nikodike, run!
    Or Kalyke's done
70 To a turn, and poor Kritylla's
    Smoked like a ham.
          Damn
These old men! Are we too late?
I nearly died down at the place
Where we fill our jars:
75   Slaves pushing and jostling —
    Such a hustling
I never saw in all my days.

Antistrophe 1

But here's water at last.
Haste, sisters, haste!
80 Slosh it on them, slosh it down,
The silly old wrecks!
          Sex
Almighty! What they want's
A hot bath? Good. Send one down.
Athena of Athens town,
85   Trito-born!° Helm of Gold!
    Cripple the old
Firemen! Help us help them drown!

(*The old men capture a woman, Stratyllis.*)

STRATYLLIS: Let me go! Let me go!
KORYPHAIOS(w):   You walking corpses,
    have you no shame?
KORYPHAIOS(m):   I wouldn't have believed it!
90 An army of women in the Akropolis!
KORYPHAIOS(w): So we scare you, do we? Grandpa,
    you've seen
    only our pickets yet!
KORYPHAIOS(m):   Hey, Phaidrias!
Help me with the necks of these jabbering hens!
KORYPHAIOS(w): Down with your pots, girls! We'll need
    both hands
    if these antiques attack us!
95 KORYPHAIOS(m):   Want your face kicked in?
KORYPHAIOS(w): Want your balls chewed off?

85. **Trito-born:** Athena, goddess of wisdom, was said to have been born near Lake Tritonis in Libya.

KORYPHAIOS(m):   Look out! I've got a stick!
KORYPHAIOS(w): You lay a half-inch of your stick on
    Stratyllis,
    and you'll never stick again!
KORYPHAIOS(m): Fall apart!
KORYPHAIOS(w):   I'll spit up your guts!
KORYPHAIOS(m):   Euripides! Master!
How well you knew women!
KORYPHAIOS(w):   Listen to him, Rhodippe, 100
    up with the pots!
KORYPHAIOS(m):   Demolition of God,
    what good are your pots?
KORYPHAIOS(w):   You refugee from the tomb,
    what good is your fire?
KORYPHAIOS(m):   Good enough to make a pyre
    to barbecue you!
KORYPHAIOS(w):   We'll squizzle your kindling!
KORYPHAIOS(m): You think so?
KORYPHAIOS(w):   Yah! Just hang around a while! 105
KORYPHAIOS(m): Want a touch of my torch?
KORYPHAIOS(w):   It needs a good soaping.
KORYPHAIOS(m): How about you?
KORYPHAIOS(w):   Soap for a senile bridegroom!
KORYPHAIOS(m): Senile? Hold your trap
KORYPHAIOS(w):   Just *you* try to hold it!
KORYPHAIOS(m): The yammer of women!
KORYPHAIOS(w):   Oh is that so?
You're not in the jury room now, you know. 110
KORYPHAIOS(m): Gentlemen, I beg you, burn off that
    woman's hair!
KORYPHAIOS(w): Let it come down!

(*They empty their pots on the men.*)

KORYPHAIOS(m): What a way to drown!
KORYPHAIOS(w):   Hot, hey?
KORYPHAIOS(m):   Say, enough!
KORYPHAIOS(w): Dandruff
    needs watering. I'll make you 115
    nice and fresh.
KORYPHAIOS(m):   For God's sake, you,
    hold off!

SCENE 1

(*Enter a Commissioner accompanied by four constables.*)

COMMISSIONER: These degenerate women! What a
    racket of little drums,
what a yapping for Adonis° on every house-top!
It's like the time in the Assembly when I was listening
to a speech — out of order, as usual — by that fool
Demostratos,° all about troops for Sicily,° 5
that kind of nonsense —
          and there was his wife

2. **Adonis:** Fertility god, loved by Aphrodite.   5. **Demostratos:** Athenian orator and politician.   **Sicily:** Reference to the Sicilian Expedition (415–413 B.C.) in which Athens was decisively defeated.

trotting around in circles howling
Alas for Adonis! —
            and Demostratos insisting
we must draft every last Zakynthian that can walk —
10   and his wife up there on the roof,
drunk as an owl, yowling
Oh weep for Adonis! —
            and that damned ox Demostratos
mooing away through the rumpus. That's what we
    get
for putting up with this wretched woman-business!
KORYPHAIOS⁽ᵐ⁾: Sir, you haven't heard the half of it.
15   They laughed at us!
Insulted us! They took pitchers of water
and nearly drowned us! We're still wringing out our
    clothes,
for all the world like unhousebroken brats.
COMMISSIONER: Serves you right, by Poseidon!
20   Whose fault is it if these women-folk of ours
get out of hand? We coddle them,
we teach them to be wasteful and loose. You'll see a
    husband
go into a jeweler's. "Look," he'll say,
"jeweler," he'll say, "you remember that gold choker
you made for my wife? Well, she went to a dance
25   last night
and broke the clasp. Now, I've got to go to Salamis,
and can't be bothered. Run over to my house tonight,
will you, and see if you can put it together for her."
Or another one
30   goes to a cobbler — a good strong workman, too,
with an awl that was never meant for child's play.
    "Here,"
he'll tell him, "one of my wife's shoes is pinching
her little toe. Could you come up about noon
and stretch it out for her?"
                    Well, what do you expect?
35   Look at me, for example, I'm a Public Officer,
and it's one of my duties to pay off the sailors.
And where's the money? Up there in the Akropolis!
And those blasted women slam the door in my face!
But what are we waiting for?
                    — Look here, constable,
40   stop sniffing around for a tavern, and get us
some crowbars. We'll force their gates! As a matter
    of fact,
I'll do a little forcing myself.

(*Enter Lysistrata, above, with Myrrhine, Kalonike, and
the Boiotian.*)

LYSISTRATA: No need of forcing.
Here I am, of my own accord. And all this talk
about locked doors — ! We don't need locked doors,
45   but just the least bit of common sense.
COMMISSIONER: Is that so, ma'am!
                    — Where's my constable?
                    — Constable,
arrest that woman, and tie her hands behind her.
LYSISTRATA: If he touches me, I swear by Artemis

there'll be one scamp dropped from the public pay-
    roll tomorrow!
COMMISSIONER: Well, constable? You're not afraid, I
    suppose? Grab her,   50
two of you, around the middle!
KALONIKE: No, by Pandrosos!°
Lay a hand on her, and I'll jump on you so hard
your guts will come out the back door!
COMMISSIONER: That's what *you* think!
Where's the sergeant? — Here, you: tie up that
    trollop first,
the one with the pretty talk!
MYRRHINE: By the Moon-Goddess,°   55
just try! They'll have to scoop you up with a spoon!
COMMISSIONER: Another one!
                    Officer, seize that woman!
                    I swear
I'll put an end to this riot!
BOIOTIAN: By the Taurian,°
one inch closer, you'll be one screaming bald-head!
COMMISSIONER: Lord, what a mess! And my
    constables seem ineffective.   60
But — women get the best of us? By God, no!
                    — Skythians!°
Close ranks and forward march!
LYSISTRATA: "Forward," indeed!
By the Two Goddesses, what's the sense in *that*?
They're up against four companies of women
armed from top to bottom.
COMMISSIONER: Forward, my Skythians!   65
LYSISTRATA: Forward, yourselves, dear comrades!
You grainlettucebeanseedmarket girls!
You garlicandonionbreadbakery girls!
Give it to 'em! Knock 'em down! Scratch 'em!
Tell 'em what you think of 'em!

(*General melee, the Skythians yield.*)

                    — Ah, that's enough!   70
Sound a retreat: good soldiers don't rob the dead.
COMMISSIONER: A nice day *this* has been for the
    police!
LYSISTRATA: Well, there you are. — Did you really
    think we women
would be driven like slaves? Maybe now you'll admit
that a woman knows something about spirit.
COMMISSIONER: Spirit enough,   75
especially spirits in bottles! Dear Lord Apollo!
KORYPHAIOS⁽ᵐ⁾: Your Honor, there's no use talking to
    them. Words
mean nothing whatever to wild animals like these.
Think of the sousing they gave us! and the water
was not, I believe, of the purest.   80

51. Pandrosos: A woman's oath referring to one of the daughters of the founder of Athens.   **55. Moon-Goddess:** Artemis,
goddess of the hunt and of fertility, daughter of Zeus.
58. Taurian: Reference to Artemis, who was said to have been
worshiped in a cult at Taurica Chersonesos.   **61. Skythians:**
Athenian archers.

KORYPHAIOS[w]: You shouldn't have come after us. And
    if you try it again,
you'll be one eye short! — Although, as a matter of
    fact,
what I like best is just to stay at home and read,
like a sweet little bride: never hurting a soul, no,
85 never going out. But if you *must* shake hornets' nests,
look out for the hornets.

Strophe 1

CHORUS[m]: Of all the beasts that God hath wrought
    What monster's worse than woman?
Who shall encompass with his thought
90   Their guile unending? No man.

They've seized the Heights, the Rock, the Shrine —
    But to what end? I wot not.
Sure there's some clue to their design!
    Have you the key? I thought not.
KORYPHAIOS[m]: We might question them, I suppose.
95   But I warn you, sir,
don't believe anything you hear! It would be un-
    Athenian
not to get to the bottom of this plot.
COMMISSIONER: Very well.
My first question is this: Why, so help you God,
did you bar the gates of the Akropolis?
LYSISTRATA: Why?
100 To keep the money, of course. No money, no war.
COMMISSIONER: You think that money's the cause of
    war?
LYSISTRATA: I do.
Money brought about that Peisandros° business
and all the other attacks on the State. Well and good!
They'll not get another cent here!
105 COMMISSIONER: And what will you do?
LYSISTRATA: What a question! From now on, we intend
    to control the Treasury.
COMMISSIONER: Control the Treasury!
LYSISTRATA: Why not? Does that seem strange?
    After all,
we control our household budgets.
COMMISSIONER: But that's different!
LYSISTRATA: "Different"? What do you mean?
110 COMMISSIONER: I mean simply this:
it's the Treasury that pays for National Defense.
LYSISTRATA: Unnecessary. We propose to abolish war.
COMMISSIONER: Good God. — And National
    Security?
LYSISTRATA: Leave that to us.
COMMISSIONER: You?
LYSISTRATA: Us.
COMMISSIONER: We're done for, then!
115 LYSISTRATA: Never mind.

103. Peisandros: A politician who plotted against the Athenian
democracy.

We women will save you in spite of yourselves.
COMMISSIONER: What nonsense!
LYSISTRATA: If you like. But you must accept it, like it
    or not.
COMMISSIONER: Why, this is downright subversion!
LYSISTRATA: Maybe it is.
    But we're going to save you, Judge.
COMMISSIONER: I don't *want* to be saved.
LYSISTRATA: Tut. The death-wish. All the more reason. 120
COMMISSIONER: But the idea of women bothering
    themselves about peace and war!
LYSISTRATA: Will you listen to me?
COMMISSIONER: Yes. But be brief, or I'll —
LYSISTRATA: This is no time for stupid threats.
COMMISSIONER: By the gods,
    I can't stand any more!
AN OLD WOMAN: Can't stand? Well, well.
COMMISSIONER: That's enough out of you, you old
    buzzard!   125
    Now, Lysistrata: tell me what you're thinking.
LYSISTRATA: Glad to.
             Ever since this war began
We women have been watching you men, agreeing
    with you,
keeping our thoughts to ourselves. That doesn't mean
we were happy: we weren't, for we saw how things
    were going;   130
but we'd listen to you at dinner
arguing this way and that.
           — Oh you, and your big
Top Secrets! —
           And then we'd grin like little patriots
(though goodness knows we didn't feel like
    grinning) and ask you:
"Dear, did the Armistice come up in Assembly
    today?"   135
And you'd say, "None of your business! Pipe
    down!" you'd say.
And so we would.
AN OLD WOMAN: *I* wouldn't have, by God!
COMMISSIONER: You'd have taken a beating, then!
                    — Go on.
LYSISTRATA: Well, we'd be quiet. But then, you know,
    all at once
you men would think up something worse than ever. 140
Even *I* could see it was fatal. And, "Darling," I'd say,
"have you gone completely mad?" And my husband
    would look at me
and say, "Wife, you've got your weaving to attend
    to.
Mind your tongue, if you don't want a slap.
'War's a man's affair!' "°   145
COMMISSIONER: Good words, and well pronounced.
LYSISTRATA: You're a fool if you think so.
           It was hard enough
to put up with all this banquet-hall strategy.

144–45. 'War's a man's affair!': Quoted from Homer's *Iliad*,
VI, 492, Hector's farewell to his wife, Andromache.

But then we'd hear you out in the public square:
150 "Nobody left for the draft-quota here in Athens?"
     you'd say; and, "No," someone else would say, "not
        a man!"
     And so we women decided to rescue Greece.
     You might as well listen to us now: you'll have to,
        later.
COMMISSIONER: *You* rescue Greece? Absurd.
LYSISTRATA: You're the absurd one.
COMMISSIONER: You expect me to take orders from a
        woman?
155   I'd die first!
LYSISTRATA: Heavens, if that's what's bothering you,
        take my veil,
     here, and wrap it around your poor head.
KALONIKE: Yes
     and you can have my market-basket, too.
     Go home, tighten your girdle, do the washing, mind
160 your beans! "War's
     a woman's affair!"
KORYPHAIOS⁽ʷ⁾:   Ground pitchers! Close ranks!

Antistrophe

CHORUS⁽ʷ⁾: This is a dance that I know well,
        My knees shall never yield.
     Wobble and creak I may, but still
165   I'll keep the well-fought field.
     Valor and grace march on before,
        Love prods us from behind.
     Our slogan is EXCELSIOR,
        Our watchword SAVE MANKIND.
KORYPHAIOS⁽ʷ⁾: Women, remember your grandmothers!
170   Remember
     that little old mother of yours, what a stinger she
        was!
     On, on, never slacken. There's a strong wind astern!
LYSISTRATA: O Eros of delight! O Aphrodite! Kyprian!°
     If ever desire has drenched our breasts or dreamed
     in our thighs, let it work so now on the men of
175   Hellas°
     that they shall tail us through the land, slaves, slaves
     to Woman, Breaker of Armies!
COMMISSIONER: And if we do?
LYSISTRATA: Well, for one thing, we shan't have to
        watch you
     going to market, a spear in one hand, and heaven
        knows
     what in the other.
180 KALONIKE: Nicely said, by Aphrodite!
LYSISTRATA: As things stand now, you're neither men
        nor women.

---

173. Kyprian: Reference to Aphrodite's association with Cyprus (Kyprus), a place sacred to her and a center for her worship.
175. Hellas: Greece.

Armor clanking with kitchen pans and pots —
     You sound like a pack of Korybantes!°
COMMISSIONER: A man must do what a man must do.
LYSISTRATA: So I'm told.
     But to see a General, complete with Gorgon-shield, 185
     jingling along the dock to buy a couple of herrings!
KALONIKE: *I* saw a Captain the other day — lovely
        fellow he was,
     nice curly hair — sitting on his horse; and — can
        you believe it? —
     he'd just bought some soup, and was pouring it into
        his helmet!
     And there was a soldier from Thrace   190
     swishing his lance like something out of Euripides,
     and the poor fruit-store woman got so scared
     that she ran away and let him have his figs free!
COMMISSIONER: All this is beside the point.
                         Will you be so kind
     as to tell me how you mean to save Greece?
LYSISTRATA: Of course. 195
     Nothing could be simpler.
COMMISSIONER: I assure you, I'm all ears.
LYSISTRATA: Do you know anything about weaving?
     Say the yarn gets tangled: we thread it
     this way and that through the skein, up and down,
     until it's free. And it's like that with war.   200
     We'll send our envoys
     up and down, this way and that, all over Greece,
     until it's finished.
COMMISSIONER: Yarn? Thread? Skein?
     Are you out of your mind? I tell you,
     war is a serious business.
LYSISTRATA: So serious   205
     that I'd like to go on talking about weaving.
COMMISSIONER: All right. Go ahead.
LYSISTRATA: The first thing we have to do
     is to wash our yarn, get the dirt out of it.
     You see? Isn't there too much dirt here in Athens?
     You must wash those men away.
                         Then our spoiled wool —   210
     that's like your job-hunters, out for a life
     of no work and big pay. Back to the basket,
     citizens or not, allies or not,
     or friendly immigrants.
                         And your colonies?
     Hanks of wool lost in various places. Pull them   215
     together, weave them into one great whole,
     and our voters are clothed for ever.
COMMISSIONER: It would take a woman
     to reduce state questions to a matter of carding and
        weaving.
LYSISTRATA: You fool! Who were the mothers whose
        sons sailed off
     to fight for Athens in Sicily?

---

183. Korybantes: Priestesses of Cybele, a fertility goddess, who was celebrated in frenzied rituals accompanied by the beating of cymbals.

220 COMMISSIONER: Enough!
    I beg you, do not call back those memories.
    LYSISTRATA: And then,
    instead of the love that every woman needs,
    we have only our single beds, where we can
        dream
    of our husbands off with the Army.
                                    Bad enough for wives!
225 But what about our girls, getting older every day,
    and older, and no kisses?
    COMMISSIONER: Men get older, too.
    LYSISTRATA: Not in the same sense.
                            A soldier's discharged,
    and he may be bald and toothless, yet he'll find
    a pretty young thing to go to bed with.
                                    But a woman!
230 Her beauty is gone with the first gray hair.
    She can spend her time
    consulting the oracles and the fortune-tellers,
    but they'll never send her a husband.
    COMMISSIONER: Still, if a man can rise to the
        occasion —
235 LYSISTRATA: Rise? Rise, yourself!

(*Furiously.*)

    Go invest in a coffin!
                        You've money enough.
                                    I'll bake you
    a cake for the Underworld.
                        And here's your funeral wreath!

(*She pours water upon him.*)

MYRRHINE: And here's another!

(*More water.*)

KALONIKE: And here's
    my contribution!

(*More water.*)

LYSISTRATA: What are you waiting for?
    All aboard Styx Ferry!
                        Charon's° calling for you!
240 It's sailing-time: don't disrupt the schedule!
    COMMISSIONER: The insolence of women! And
        to me!
    No, by God, I'll go back to town and show
    the rest of the Commission what might happen to
        them.   (*Exit Commissioner.*)
    LYSISTRATA: Really, I suppose we should have laid out
245   his corpse
    on the doorstep, in the usual way.
                                    But never mind.
    We'll give him the rites of the dead tomorrow
        morning.

        (*Exit Lysistrata with Myrrhine and Kalonike.*)

240. **Charon:** The god who ferried the souls of the newly dead
across the river Styx to Hades.

PARABASIS:°
CHORAL EPISODE • *Ode*° *1*

KORYPHAIOS(m): Sons of Liberty, awake! The day of
    glory is at hand.
CHORUS(m): I smell tyranny afoot, I smell it rising from
    the land.
    I scent a trace of Hippias,° I sniff upon the breeze
    A dismal Spartan hogo that suggests King
        Kleisthenes.°
    Strip, strip for action, brothers!   5
    Our wives, aunts, sisters, mothers
    Have sold us out: the streets are full of godless
        female rages.
    Shall we stand by and let our women confiscate our
        wages?
                                    [Epirrhema° 1]
KORYPHAIOS(m): Gentlemen, it's a disgrace to Athens, a
    disgrace
    to all that Athens stands for, if we allow these
        grandmas   10
    to jabber about spears and shields and making
        friends
    with the Spartans. What's a Spartan? Give me a
        wild wolf
    any day. No. They want the Tyranny back, I
        suppose.
    Are we going to take that? No. Let us look like
    the innocent serpent, but be the flower under it,   15
    as the poet sings. And just to begin with,
    I propose to poke a number of teeth
    down the gullet of that harridan over there.

Antode° 1

KORYPHAIOS(w): Oh, is that so? When you get home,
    your own mamma won't know you!
CHORUS(w): Who do you think we are, you senile
    bravos? Well, I'll show you.   20
    I bore the sacred vessels in my eighth year,° and at ten
    I was pounding out the barley for Athena Goddess;°
        then

Parabasis: Section of the play in which the author presented his
own views through the Koryphaios directly to the audience.
The parabasis in *Lysistrata* is shorter than those in Aristophanes' other works and unusual in that the Koryphaios does not
speak directly for the author. **Ode:** Song sung by the Chorus.
3. **Hippias:** An Athenian tyrant. 4. **Kleisthenes:** A bisexual
Athenian. **Epirrhema:** A part of the parabasis spoken by the
Koryphaios following an ode delivered by his or her half of the
Chorus. **Antode:** Lyric song sung by half of the Chorus in
response to the Ode sung by the other half. 21. **eighth year:**
Young girls between the ages of seven and eleven served in the
temple of Athena in the Akropolis. 22. **pounding out the barley for Athena Goddess:** At age ten a girl could be chosen to
grind the sacred grain of Athena.

They made me Little Bear
At the Brauronian Fair;°
25   I'd held the Holy Basket° by the time I was of age,
The Blessed Dry Figs had adorned my plump
decolletage.

[Antepirrhema° 1]

KORYPHAIOS⁽ʷ⁾: A "disgrace to Athens," and I, just at
the moment
I'm giving Athens the best advice she ever had?
Don't I pay taxes to the State? Yes, I pay them
30   in baby boys. And what do you contribute,
you impotent horrors? Nothing but waste: all
our Treasury,° dating back to the Persian Wars,
gone! rifled! And not a penny out of your pockets!
Well, then? Can you cough up an answer to that?
35   Look out for your own gullet, or you'll get a crack
from this old brogan that'll make your teeth see
stars!

Ode 2

CHORUS⁽ᵐ⁾: Oh insolence!
Am I unmanned?
Incontinence!
40   Shall my scarred hand
Strike never a blow
To curb this flow-
ing female curse?

Leipsydrion!°
45   Shall I betray
The laurels won
On that great day?
Come, shake a leg,
Shed old age, beg
50   The years reverse!

[Epirrhema 2]

KORYPHAIOS⁽ᵐ⁾: Give them an inch, and we're done
for! We'll have them
launching boats next and planning naval
strategy,
sailing down on us like so many Artemisias.
Or maybe they have ideas about the cavalry.
55   That's fair enough, women are certainly good
in the saddle. Just look at Mikon's paintings,
all those Amazons wrestling with all those men!
On the whole, a straitjacket's their best uniform.

---

24. Brauronian Fair: A ritual in the cult of Artemis, who is
associated with wild beasts, in which young girls dressed up as
bears and danced for the goddess.   **25. Holy Basket:** In one
ritual to Athena, young girls carried baskets of objects sacred to
the goddess.   **Antepirrhema:** The speech delivered by the second Koryphaios after the second half of the Chorus had sung
an ode.   **32. Treasury:** Athenian politicians were raiding the
funds that were collected by Athens to finance a war against
Persia.   **44. Leipsydrion:** A place where Athenian patriots had
heroically fought.

Antode 2

CHORUS⁽ʷ⁾: Tangle with me,
And you'll get cramps.   60
Ferocity
's no use now, Gramps!
By the Two,
I'll get through
To you wrecks yet!   65

I'll scramble your eggs,
I'll burn your beans,
With my two legs.
You'll see such scenes
As never yet   70
Your two eyes met.
A curse? You bet!

[Antepirrhema 2]

KORYPHAIOS⁽ʷ⁾: If Lampito stands by me, and that
delicious Theban girl,
Ismenia — what good are *you*? You and your
seven
Resolutions! Resolutions? Rationing Boiotian eels   75
and making our girls go without them at Hekate's°
Feast!
That was statesmanship! And we'll have to put up
with it
and all the rest of your decrepit legislation
until some patriot — God give him strength! —
grabs you by the neck and kicks you off the Rock.   80

SCENE 2

(*Reenter Lysistrata and her lieutenants.*)

KORYPHAIOS⁽ʷ⁾ (*tragic tone*): Great Queen, fair
Architect of our emprise,
Why lookst thou on us with foreboding eyes?
LYSISTRATA: The behavior of these idiotic women!
There's something about the female temperament
that I can't bear!
KORYPHAIOS⁽ʷ⁾:   What in the world do you mean?   5
LYSISTRATA: Exactly what I say.
KORYPHAIOS⁽ʷ⁾: What dreadful thing has happened?
Come, tell us: we're all your friends.
LYSISTRATA: It isn't easy
to say it; yet, God knows, we can't hush it up.
KORYPHAIOS⁽ʷ⁾: Well, then? Out with it!
LYSISTRATA: To put it bluntly,   10
we're dying to get laid.
KORYPHAIOS⁽ʷ⁾:   Almighty God!
LYSISTRATA: Why bring God into it? — No, it's just as
I say.
I can't manage them any longer: they've gone
man-crazy,

---

76. Hekate: Patron of successful wars, object of a Boiotian cult
(later associated with sorcery).

they're all trying to get out.
                              Why, look:

15 one of them was sneaking out the back door
over there by Pan's cave; another
was sliding down the walls with rope and tackle;
another was climbing aboard a sparrow, ready to
   take off
for the nearest brothel — I dragged *her* back by the
   hair!
They're all finding some reason to leave.

20   Look there!
There goes another one.
                        — Just a minute, you!
Where are you off to so fast?
FIRST WOMAN: I've got to get home.
I've a lot of Milesian wool, and the worms are
   spoiling it.
LYSISTRATA: Oh bother you and your worms! Get back
   inside!
25 FIRST WOMAN: I'll be back right away, I swear I will.
I just want to get it stretched out on my bed.
LYSISTRATA: You'll do no such thing. You'll stay
   right here.
FIRST WOMAN: And my wool?
You want it ruined?
LYSISTRATA: Yes, for all I care.
SECOND WOMAN: Oh dear! My lovely new flax from
   Amorgos —
I left it at home, all uncarded!
30 LYSISTRATA: Another one!
And all she wants is someone to card her flax.
Get back in there!
SECOND WOMAN: But I swear by the Moon-Goddess
the minute I get it done, I'll be back!
LYSISTRATA: I say No.
If you, why not all the other women as well?
THIRD WOMAN: O Lady Eileithyia!° Radiant goddess!
35   Thou
intercessor for women in childbirth! Stay, I pray thee,
oh stay this parturition. Shall I pollute
a sacred spot?°
LYSISTRATA: And what's the matter with *you*?
THIRD WOMAN: I'm having a baby — any minute now.
LYSISTRATA: But you weren't pregnant yesterday.
40 THIRD WOMAN: Well, I am today.
Let me go home for a midwife, Lysistrata:
there's not much time.
LYSISTRATA: I never heard such nonsense.
What's that bulging under your cloak?
THIRD WOMAN: A little baby boy.
LYSISTRATA: It certainly isn't. But it's something hollow,
45 like a basin or — Why, it's the helmet of Athena!
And you said you were having a baby.
THIRD WOMAN: Well, I am! So there!

---

35. **Eileithyia:** Goddess of childbirth.   **37–38. pollute a sacred spot:** Giving birth on the Akropolis was forbidden because it was sacred ground.

LYSISTRATA: Then why the helmet?
THIRD WOMAN: I was afraid that my pains
might begin here in the Akropolis; and I wanted
to drop my chick into it, just as the dear doves do.
LYSISTRATA: Lies! Evasions! — But at least one thing's
   clear: 50
you can't leave the place before your purification.°
THIRD WOMAN: But I can't stay here in the Akropolis!
   Last night I dreamed
of the Snake.
FIRST WOMAN: And those horrible owls, the noise they
   make!
I can't get a bit of sleep; I'm just about dead.
LYSISTRATA: You useless girls, that's enough: Let's have
   no more lying.   55
Of course you want your men. But don't you imagine
that they want you just as much? I'll give you my
   word,
their nights must be pretty hard.
                           Just stick it out!
A little patience, that's all, and our battle's won.
I have heard an Oracle. Should you like to hear it?   60
FIRST WOMAN: An Oracle? Yes, tell us!
LYSISTRATA: Here is what it says:
WHEN SWALLOWS SHALL THE HOOPOE SHUN
   AND SPURN HIS HOT DESIRE,
ZEUS WILL PERFECT WHAT THEY'VE BEGUN
   AND SET THE LOWER HIGHER.   65
FIRST WOMAN: Does that mean we'll be on top?
LYSISTRATA: BUT IF THE SWALLOWS SHALL FALL
   OUT
   AND TAKE THE HOOPOE'S BAIT,
A CURSE MUST MARK THEIR HOUR OF
   DOUBT,
   INFAMY SEAL THEIR FATE.   70
THIRD WOMAN: I swear, *that* Oracle's all too clear.
FIRST WOMAN: Oh the dear gods!
LYSISTRATA: Let's not be downhearted, girls. Back to
   our places!
The god has spoken. How can we possibly fail him?

     (*Exit Lysistrata with the dissident women.*)

CHORAL EPISODE • *Strophe*

CHORUS⁽ᵐ⁾: I know a little story that I learned way
   back in school
Goes like this:
Once upon a time there was a young man — and no
   fool —
Named Melanion; and his
One aversion was marriage. He loathed the very
   thought.   5
So he ran off to the hills, and in a special grot
Raised a dog, and spent his days
Hunting rabbits. And it says

---

51. **purification:** A ritual cleansing of a woman after childbirth.

That he never never never did come home.
10   It might be called a refuge *from* the womb.
All right,
　　　all right,
　　　　　all right!
We're as bright as young Melanion, and we hate the
　　　very sight
Of you women!
A MAN: How about a kiss, old lady?
15   A WOMAN: Here's an onion for your eye!
A MAN: A kick in the guts, then?
A WOMAN: Try, old bristle-tail, just try!
A MAN: Yet they say Myronides
　　　On hands and knees
20   Looked just as shaggy fore and aft as I!

Antistrophe

CHORUS[w]: Well, *I* know a little story, and it's just as
　　　good as yours.
　　　Goes like this:
Once there was a man named Timon — a rough
　　　diamond, of course,
And that whiskery face of his
Looked like murder in the shrubbery. By God, he
25   　　　was a son
Of the Furies, let me tell you! And what did he do
　　　but run
From the world and all its ways,
Cursing mankind! And it says
That his choicest execrations as of then
30   Were leveled almost wholly at *old* men.
All right,
　　　all right,
　　　　　all right!
But there's one thing about Timon: he could always
　　　stand the sight
of us women.
A WOMAN: How about a crack in the jaw, Pop?
35   A MAN: I can take it, Ma — no fear!
A WOMAN: How about a kick in the face?
A MAN: You'd reveal your old caboose?
A WOMAN: What I'd show,
　　　I'll have you know,
40   Is an instrument you're too far gone to use.

SCENE 3

(*Reenter Lysistrata.*)

LYSISTRATA: Oh, quick, girls, quick! Come here!
A WOMAN:　　　　　　　　　　　　　What is it?
LYSISTRATA:　　　　　　　　　　　　　A man.
A man simply bulging with love.
　　　　　　　　　　　O Kyprian Queen,°
O Paphian, O Kythereian! Hear us and aid us!

2. Kyprian Queen: Aphrodite.

A WOMAN: Where is this enemy?
LYSISTRATA:　　　　　Over there, by Demeter's shrine.
A WOMAN: Damned if he isn't. But who *is* he?
MYRRHINE:　　　　　　　　　My husband.　5
Kinesias.
LYSISTRATA: Oh then, get busy! Tease him! Undermine
　　　him!
Wreck him! Give him everything — kissing, tickling,
　　　nudging,
whatever you generally torture him with — : give
　　　him everything
except what we swore on the wine we would not
　　　give.
MYRRHINE: Trust me.
LYSISTRATA:　　　I do. But I'll help you get him started.　10
The rest of you women, stay back.

(*Enter Kinesias.*)

KINESIAS:　　　　　　　　Oh God! Oh my God!
I'm stiff from lack of exercise. All I can do to stand
　　　up.
LYSISTRATA: Halt! Who are you, approaching our lines?
KINESIAS: Me? I.
LYSISTRATA: A man?
KINESIAS:　　　　You have eyes, haven't you?
LYSISTRATA:　　　　　　　　　　Go away.　15
KINESIAS: Who says so?
LYSISTRATA:　　　　Officer of the Day.
KINESIAS:　　　　　　　　Officer, I beg you,
　　　by all the gods at once, bring Myrrhine out.
LYSISTRATA: Myrrhine? And who, my good sir, are
　　　you?
KINESIAS: Kinesias. Last name's Pennison. Her husband.
LYSISTRATA: Oh, of course. I beg your pardon. We're
　　　glad to see you.　　　　　　　　　　　20
We've heard so much about you. Dearest Myrrhine
is always talking about Kinesias — never nibbles an
　　　egg
or an apple without saying
"Here's to Kinesias!"
KINESIAS:　　　　Do you really mean it?
LYSISTRATA:　　　　　　　　　I do.
When we're discussing men, she always says　25
"Well, after all, there's nobody like Kinesias!"
KINESIAS: Good God. — Well, then, please send her
　　　down here.
LYSISTRATA: And what do *I* get out of it?
KINESIAS:　　　　　　　　A standing promise.
LYSISTRATA: I'll take it up with her.
　　　　　　　　　　　(*Exit Lysistrata.*)
KINESIAS:　　　　　　　　But be quick about it!
Lord, what's life without a wife? Can't eat. Can't
　　　sleep.　　　　　　　　　　　　　　30
Every time I go home, the place is so empty, so
insufferably sad. Love's killing me, Oh,
hurry!

(*Enter Manes, a slave, with Kinesias's baby; the voice of
Myrrhine is heard offstage.*)

MYRRHINE: But of course I love him! Adore him —
                                                          But no,
        he hates love. No. I won't go down.

(Enter Myrrhine, above.)

KINESIAS: Myrrhine!
35   Darlingest Myrrhinette! Come down quick!
MYRRHINE: Certainly not.
KINESIAS: Not? But why, Myrrhine?
MYRRHINE: Why? You don't need me.
KINESIAS: Need you? My God, *look* at me!
MYRRHINE: So long!

(Turns to go.)

KINESIAS: Myrrhine, Myrrhine, Myrrhine!
        If not for my sake, for our child!

(Pinches Baby.)

                                — All right, you: pipe up!
BABY: Mummie! Mummie! Mummie!
40 KINESIAS: You hear that?
        Pitiful, I call it. Six days now
        with never a bath; no food; enough to break your
            heart!
MYRRHINE: My darlingest child! What a father *you*
        acquired!
KINESIAS: At least come down for his sake.
MYRRHINE: I suppose I must.
45   Oh, this mother business!   *(Exit.)*
KINESIAS: How pretty she is! And younger!
        The harder she treats me, the more bothered I get.

(Myrrhine enters, below.)

MYRRHINE: Dearest child,
        you're as sweet as your father's horrid. Give me a kiss.
KINESIAS: Now don't you see how wrong it was to get
        involved
50   in this scheming League of women? It's bad
        for us both.
MYRRHINE: Keep your hands to yourself!
KINESIAS: But our house
        going to rack and ruin?
MYRRHINE: *I* don't care.
KINESIAS: And your knitting
        all torn to pieces by the chickens? Don't you care?
MYRRHINE: Not at all.
55 KINESIAS: And our debt to Aphrodite?
        Oh, *won't* you come back?
MYRRHINE: No. — At least, not until you men
        make a treaty and stop this war.
KINESIAS: Why, I suppose
        that might be arranged.
MYRRHINE: Oh? Well, I suppose
        I might come down then. But meanwhile,
        I've sworn not to.
60 KINESIAS: Don't worry. — Now let's have fun.
MYRRHINE: No! Stop it! I said no!
                                — Although, of course,
        I *do* love you.

KINESIAS: I know you do. Darling Myrrhine:
        come, shall we?
MYRRHINE: Are you out of your mind? In front of the
        child?
KINESIAS: Take him home, Manes.
                                (Exit Manes with Baby.)
                                There. He's gone.
                                            Come on!
        There's nothing to stop us now.
MYRRHINE: You devil! But where? 65
KINESIAS: In Pan's cave. What could be snugger than
        that?
MYRRHINE: But my purification before I go back to the
        Citadel?
KINESIAS: Wash in the Klepsydra.°
MYRRHINE: And my oath?
KINESIAS: Leave the oath to me.
        After all, I'm the man.
MYRRHINE: Well . . . if you say so.
                                I'll go find a bed.
KINESIAS: Oh, bother a bed! The ground's good
        enough for me.   70
MYRRHINE: No. You're a bad man, but you deserve
        something better than dirt.   *(Exit Myrrhine.)*
KINESIAS: What a love she is! And how thoughtful!

(Reenter Myrrhine.)

MYRRHINE: Here's your bed.
        Now let me get my clothes off.
                                But, good horrors!
        We haven't a mattress.
KINESIAS: Oh, forget the mattress!
MYRRHINE: No.
        Just lying on blankets? Too sordid.
KINESIAS: Give me a kiss. 75
MYRRHINE: Just a second.   *(Exit Myrrhine.)*
KINESIAS: I swear, I'll explode!

(Reenter Myrrhine.)

MYRRHINE: Here's your mattress.
        I'll just take my dress off.
                                But look —
        where's our pillow?
KINESIAS: I don't *need* a pillow!
MYRRHINE: Well, *I* do.
                                (Exit Myrrhine.)
KINESIAS: I don't suppose even Herakles°
        would stand for this!

(Reenter Myrrhine.)

MYRRHINE: There we are. Ups-a-daisy! 80
KINESIAS: So we are. Well, come to bed.
MYRRHINE: But I wonder:
        is everything ready now?
KINESIAS: I can swear to that. Come, darling!

---

68. **Klepsydra:** A water clock beneath the walls of the Akropolis. Kinesias's suggestion borders on blasphemy.   79. **Herakles:** Greek hero (Hercules) known for his Twelve Labors.

MYRRHINE: Just getting out of my girdle.
                                            But remember, now,
    what you promised about the treaty.
KINESIAS: Yes, yes, yes!
MYRRHINE: But no coverlet!
85 KINESIAS: Damn it, I'll be your coverlet!
MYRRHINE: Be right back.   (*Exit Myrrhine.*)
KINESIAS: This girl and her coverlets
    will be the death of me.

(*Reenter Myrrhine.*)

MYRRHINE: Here we are. Up you go!
KINESIAS: Up? I've been up for ages.
MYRRHINE: Some perfume?
KINESIAS: No, by Apollo!
MYRRHINE: Yes, by Aphrodite!
90   I don't care whether you want it or not.
                                            (*Exit Myrrhine.*)
KINESIAS: For love's sake, hurry!

(*Reenter Myrrhine.*)

MYRRHINE: Here, in your hand. Rub it right in.
KINESIAS: Never cared for perfume.
    And this is particularly strong. Still, here goes.
MYRRHINE: What a nitwit I am! I brought you the
    Rhodian bottle.
95 KINESIAS: Forget it. You just wait here.
MYRRHINE: No trouble at all. You just wait here.
                                            (*Exit Myrrhine.*)
KINESIAS: God damn the man who invented perfume!

(*Reenter Myrrhine.*)

MYRRHINE: At last! The right bottle!
KINESIAS: I've got the rightest bottle of all,
    and it's right here waiting for you.
    Darling, forget everything else. Do come to bed.
MYRRHINE: Just let me get my shoes off.
100   — And, by the way,
    you'll vote for the treaty?
KINESIAS: I'll think about it.
                                            (*Myrrhine runs away.*)
    There! That's done it! The damned woman,
    she gets me all bothered, she half kills me,
    and off she runs! What'll I do? Where
    can I get laid?
105   — And you, little prodding pal,
    who's going to take care of *you?* No, you and I
    had better get down to old Foxdog's Nursing Clinic.
CHORUS[m]: Alas for the woes of man, alas
        Specifically for you.
110 She's brought you to a pretty pass:
        What are you going to do?
    Split, heart! Sag, flesh! Proud spirit, crack!
    Myrrhine's got you on your back.
KINESIAS: The agony, the protraction!
KORYPHAIOS[m]:   Friend,
115   What woman's worth a damn?
    They bitch us all, world without end.
KINESIAS: Yet they're so damned sweet, man!

KORYPHAIOS[m]: Calamitous, that's what I say.
    You should have learned that much today.
CHORUS[m]: O blessed Zeus, roll womankind   120
    Up into one great ball;
    Blast them aloft on a high wind,
        And once there, let them fall.
    Down, down they'll come, the pretty dears,
    And split themselves on our thick spears.   125
                                            (*Exit Kinesias.*)

SCENE 4

(*Enter a Spartan Herald.*)

HERALD: Gentlemen, Ah beg you will be so kind
    as to direct me to the Central Committee.
    Ah have a communication.

(*Reenter Commissioner.*)

COMMISSIONER: Are you a man,
    or a fertility symbol?
HERALD: Ah refuse to answer that question!
    Ah'm a certified herald from Spahta, and Ah've come   5
    to talk about an ahmistice.
COMMISSIONER: Then why
    that spear under your cloak?
HERALD: Ah have no speah!
COMMISSIONER: You don't walk naturally, with your
        tunic
    poked out so. You have a tumor, maybe,
    or a hernia?
HERALD: You lost yo' mahnd, man?
COMMISSIONER: Well,   10
    something's up, I can see that. And I don't like it.
HERALD: Colonel, Ah resent this.
COMMISSIONER: So I see. But what *is* it?
HERALD: A staff
    with a message from Spahta.
COMMISSIONER: Oh, I know about those staffs.
    Well, then, man, speak out: How are things in Sparta?
HERALD: Hahd, Colonel, hahd! We're at a standstill.   15
    Cain't seem to think of anything but women.
COMMISSIONER: How curious! Tell me, do you
        Spartans think
    that maybe Pan's to blame?
HERALD: Pan? No, Lampito and her little naked friends.
    They won't let a man come nigh them.   20
COMMISSIONER: How are you handling it?
HERALD: Losing our mahnds,
    if y' want to know, and walking around hunched over
    lahk men carrying candles in a gale.
    The women have swohn they'll have nothing to do
        with us
    until we get a treaty.
COMMISSIONER: Yes. I know.   25
    It's a general uprising, sir, in all parts of Greece.
    But as for the answer —
                                    Sir: go back to Sparta
    and have them send us your Armistice Commission.

Geraldine James (far left) is Lysistrata in the Old Vic Theatre production in London, 1993.

I'll arrange things in Athens.
                              And I may say
30   that my standing is good enough to make them listen.
     HERALD: A man after mah own haht! Seh, Ah thank
          you.   (*Exit Herald.*)

CHORAL EPISODE • *Strophe*

CHORUS(m): Oh these women! Where will you find
     A slavering beast that's more unkind?
          Where's a hotter fire?
     Give me a panther, any day.
5   He's not so merciless as they,
          And panthers don't conspire.

Antistrophe

CHORUS(w): We may be hard, you silly old ass,
     But who brought you to this stupid pass?
          You're the ones to blame.
10   Fighting with us, your oldest friends,
     Simply to serve your selfish ends —
          Really, you have no shame!
KORYPHAIOS(m): No, I'm through with women for ever.

KORYPHAIOS(w):   If you say so.
     Still, you might put some clothes on. You look too
          absurd
     standing around naked. Come, get into this cloak.   15
KORYPHAIOS(m): Thank you; you're right. I merely took
          it off
     because I was in such a temper.
KORYPHAIOS(w):   That's much better.
     Now you resemble a man again.
                         Why have you been so horrid?
     And look: there's some sort of insect in your eye.
     Shall I take it out?
KORYPHAIOS(m):   An insect, is it? So that's   20
     what's been bothering me. Lord, yes: take it out!
KORYPHAIOS(w): You might be more polite.
                              — But, heavens!
     What an enormous mosquito!
KORYPHAIOS(m):   You've saved my life.
     That mosquito was drilling an artesian well
     in my left eye.
KORYPHAIOS(w):   Let me wipe   25
     those tears away. — And now: one little kiss?
KORYPHAIOS(m): No, no kisses.
KORYPHAIOS(w): You're so difficult.
KORYPHAIOS(m): You impossible women! How you do
          get around us!

30   The poet was right: Can't live with you, or without
          you.
      But let's be friends.
      And to celebrate, you might join us in an Ode.

Strophe 1

CHORUS(m and w): Let it never be said
          That my tongue is malicious:
35   Both by word and by deed
      I would set an example that's noble and gracious.
          We've had sorrow and care
          Till we're sick of the tune.
          Is there anyone here
40   Who would like a small loan?
              My purse is crammed,
              As you'll soon find;
      And you needn't pay me back if the Peace gets signed.

Strophe 2

          I've invited to lunch
45   Some Karystian rips° —
          An esurient bunch,
      But I've ordered a menu to water their lips.
          I can still make soup
          And slaughter a pig.
50   You're all coming, I hope?
          But a bath first, I beg!
              Walk right up
              As though you owned the place,
      And you'll get the front door slammed to in your face.

SCENE 5

(*Enter Spartan Ambassador, with entourage.*)

KORYPHAIOS(m): The Commission has arrived from
          Sparta.
              How oddly they're walking!
                      Gentlemen, welcome to Athens!
      How is life in Lakonia?
AMBASSADOR: Need we discuss that?
      Simply use your eyes.
CHORUS(m):   The poor man's right:
                      What a sight!
5   AMBASSADOR: Words fail me.
      But come, gentlemen, call in your Commissioners,
      and let's get down to a Peace.
CHORAGOS(m):   The state we're in! Can't bear
      a stitch below the waist. It's a kind of pelvic
      paralysis.

45. **Karystian rips:** The Karystians were allies of Athens but
were scorned for their primitive ways and loose morals.

COMMISSIONER: Won't somebody call Lysistrata? —
                          Gentlemen,
      we're no better off than you.
AMBASSADOR: So I see.   10
A SPARTAN: Seh, do y'all feel a certain strain early in the
          morning?
AN ATHENIAN: I do, sir. It's worse than a strain.
      A few more days, and there's nothing for us but
          Kleisthenes,
      that broken blossom.
CHORAGOS(m):   But you'd better get dressed again.
      You know these people going around Athens with
          chisels   15
      looking for statues of Hermes.°
ATHENIAN: Sir, you are right.
SPARTAN: He certainly is! Ah'll put mah own clothes
          back on.

(*Enter Athenian Commissioners.*)

COMMISSIONER: Gentlemen from Sparta, welcome.
      This is a sorry business.
SPARTAN (*to one of his own group*): Colonel, we got
          dressed just in time. Ah sweah,
      if they'd seen us the way we were, there'd have been
          a new wah   20
      between the states.
COMMISSIONER: Shall we call the meeting to order?
                      Now, Lakonians,
      what's your proposal?
AMBASSADOR: We propose to consider peace.
COMMISSIONER: Good. That's on our minds, too.
                      — Summon Lysistrata.
      We'll never get anywhere without her.
AMBASSADOR: Lysistrata? 25
      Summon Lysis-*any*body! Only, summon!
KORYPHAIOS(m):   No need to summon:
      here she is, herself.

(*Enter Lysistrata.*)

COMMISSIONER: Lysistrata! Lion of women!
      This is your hour to be
      hard and yielding, outspoken and shy, austere and
          gentle. You see here   30
      the best brains of Hellas (confused, I admit,
      by your devious charming) met as one man
      to turn the future over to you.
LYSISTRATA: That's fair enough,
      unless you men take it into your heads
      to turn to each other instead of to us. But I'd know 35
      soon enough if you did.
                      — Where is Reconciliation?
      Go, some of you: bring her here.
                      (*Exeunt two women.*)

16. **statues of Hermes:** The usual representation of Hermes was
with an erect phallus. Statues of Hermes were scattered
throughout Athens and were attacked by vandals just before
the Sicilian Expedition.

And now, women,
lead the Spartan delegates to me: not roughly
or insultingly, as our men handle them, but gently,
40   politely, as ladies should. Take them by the hand,
or by anything else if they won't give you their hands.

(*The Spartans are escorted over.*)

There. — The Athenians next, by any convenient
handle.

(*The Athenians are escorted.*)

Stand there, please. — Now, all of you, listen to me.

(*During the following speech the two women reenter,
carrying an enormous statue of a naked girl; this is
Reconciliation.*)

I'm only a woman, I know; but I've a mind,
45   and, I think, not a bad one: I owe it to my father
and to listening to the local politicians.
So much for that.
                    Now, gentlemen,
since I have you here, I intend to give you a scolding.
We are all Greeks.
50   Must I remind you of Thermopylai,° of Olympia,
of Delphoi? names deep in all our hearts?
Are they not a common heritage?
                            Yet you men
go raiding through the country from both sides,
Greek killing Greek, storming down Greek cities —
55   and all the time the Barbarian across the sea
is waiting for his chance!
                        — That's my first point.
AN ATHENIAN: Lord! I can hardly contain myself.
LYSISTRATA: As for you Spartans:
Was it so long ago that Perikleides°
came here to beg our help? I can see him still,
his gray face, his sombre gown. And what did he
60   want?
An army from Athens. All Messene
was hot at your heels, and the sea-god splitting your
land.
Well, Kimon and his men,
four thousand strong, marched out and saved all
Sparta.
And what thanks do we get? You come back to
65   murder us.
AN ATHENIAN: They're aggressors, Lysistrata!
A SPARTAN: Ah admit it.
When Ah look at those laigs, Ah sweah Ah'll
aggress mahself!

---

50. **Thermopylai:** A narrow pass where, in 480 B.C., an army
of three hundred Spartans held out for three days against a superior Persian force.   58. **Perikleides:** Spartan ambassador to
Athens who successfully urged Athenians to aid Sparta in
quelling a rebellion.

LYSISTRATA: And you, Athenians: do you think you're
blameless?
Remember that bad time when we were helpless,
and an army came from Sparta,   70
and that was the end of the Thessalian menace,
the end of Hippias and his allies.
                            And that was Sparta,
and only Sparta; but for Sparta, we'd be
cringing slaves today, not free Athenians.

(*From this point, the male responses are less to Lysistrata
than to the statue.*)

A SPARTAN: A well shaped speech.
AN ATHENIAN: Certainly it has its points.   75
LYSISTRATA: Why are we fighting each other? With all
this history
of favors given and taken, what stands in the way
of making peace?
AMBASSADOR: Spahta is ready, ma'am,
so long as we get that place back.
LYSISTRATA: What place, man?
AMBASSADOR: Ah refer to Pylos.
COMMISSIONER: Not a chance, by God!   80
LYSISTRATA: Give it to them, friend.
COMMISSIONER: But — what shall we have to bargain
with?
LYSISTRATA: Demand something in exchange.
COMMISSIONER: Good idea. — Well, then:
Cockeville first, and the Happy Hills, and the country
between the Legs of Megara.
AMBASSADOR: Mah government objects.   85
LYSISTRATA: Overruled. Why fuss about a pair of legs?

(*General assent. The statue is removed.*)

AN ATHENIAN: I want to get out of these clothes and
start my plowing.
A SPARTAN: Ah'll fertilize mahn first, by the Heavenly
Twins!
LYSISTRATA: And so you shall,
once you've made peace. If you are serious,   90
go, both of you, and talk with your allies.
COMMISSIONER: Too much talk already. No, we'll
stand together.
We've only one end in view. All that we want
is our women; and I speak for our allies.
AMBASSADOR: Mah government concurs.
AN ATHENIAN: So does Karystos.   95
LYSISTRATA: Good. — But before you come inside
to join your wives at supper, you must perform
the usual lustration. Then we'll open
our baskets for you, and all that we have is yours.
But you must promise upright good behavior   100
from this day on. Then each man home with his
woman!
AN ATHENIAN: Let's get it over with.
A SPARTAN: Lead on. Ah follow.
AN ATHENIAN: Quick as a cat can wink!
                            (*Exeunt all but the Choruses.*)

Antistrophe 1

CHORUS(w): Embroideries and
105   Twinkling ornaments and
          Pretty dresses — I hand
     Them all over to you, and with never a qualm.
          They'll be nice for your daughters
               On festival days
110   When the girls bring the Goddess
          The ritual prize.
          Come in, one and all:
          Take what you will.
     I've nothing here so tightly corked that you can't
               make it spill.

Antistrophe 2

115   You may search my house
          But you'll not find
          The least thing of use,
     Unless your two eyes are keener than mine.
          Your numberless brats
120   Are half starved? and your slaves?
          Courage, grandpa! I've lots
          Of grain left, and big loaves.
          I'll fill your guts,
          I'll go the whole hog;
     But if you come too close to me, remember: 'ware
125   the dog!   (*Exeunt Choruses.*)

EXODOS°

(*A Drunken Citizen enters, approaches the gate, and is halted by a sentry.*)

CITIZEN: Open. The. Door.
SENTRY: Now, friend, just shove along!
     — So you want to sit down. If it weren't such an old
          joke,
     I'd tickle your tail with this torch. Just the sort of
          gag
     this audience appreciates.
CITIZEN: I. Stay. Right. Here.
5 SENTRY: Get away from there, or I'll scalp you!
          The gentlemen from Sparta
     are just coming back from dinner.

(*Exit Citizen; the general company reenters; the two Choruses now represent Spartans and Athenians.*)

A SPARTAN: Ah must say,
     Ah never tasted better grub.
AN ATHENIAN: And those Lakonians!
     They're gentlemen, by the Lord! Just goes to show,
     a drink to the wise is sufficient.

Exodos: Final scene.

COMMISSIONER: And why not?   10
     A sober man's an ass.
     Men of Athens, mark my words: the only efficient
     Ambassador's a drunk Ambassador. Is that clear?
     Look: we go to Sparta,
     and when we get there we're dead sober. The result?   15
     Everyone cackling at everyone else. They make
          speeches;
     and even if we understand, we get it all wrong
     when we file our reports in Athens. But today — !
     Everybody's happy. Couldn't tell the difference
     between *Drink to Me Only* and   20
     The Star-Spangled Athens.
                    What's a few lies,
     washed down in good strong drink?

(*Reenter the Drunken Citizen.*)

SENTRY: God almighty,
     he's back again!
CITIZEN: I. Resume. My. Place.
A SPARTAN (*to an Athenian*): Ah beg yo', seh,
     take yo' instrument in yo' hand and play for us.   25
     Ah'm told
     yo' understand the in*tric*acies of the floot?
     Ah'd lahk to execute a song and dance
     in honor of Athens,
                    and, of cohse, of Spahta.
CITIZEN: Toot. On. Your. Flute.   30

(*The following song is a solo — an aria — accompanied by the flute. The Chorus of Spartans begins a slow dance.*)

A SPARTAN: O Memory,
     Let the Muse speak once more
     In my young voice. Sing glory.
     Sing Artemision's shore,
     Where Athens fluttered the Persians. *Alalai,°*   35
     Sing glory, that great
     Victory! Sing also
     Our Leonidas and his men,
     Those wild boars, sweat and blood
     Down in a red drench. Then, then   40
     The barbarians broke, though they had stood
     Numberless as the sands before!

     O Artemis,
     Virgin Goddess, whose darts
     Flash in our forests: approve   45
     This pact of peace and join our hearts,
     From this day on, in love.
     Huntress, descend!
LYSISTRATA: All that will come in time.
                    But now, Lakonians,
     take home your wives. Athenians, take yours.   50
     Each man be kind to his woman; and you, women

35. *Alalai:* War cry.

be equally kind. Never again, pray God,
shall we lose our way in such madness.
KORYPHAIOS(Athenian):   And now let's dance our joy.

(*From this point the dance becomes general.*)

CHORUS(Athenian): Dance, you Graces
                                    Artemis, dance
                Dance, Phoibos,° Lord of dancing
55   Dance,
                In a scurry of Maenads,° Lord Dionysos
                                Dance, Zeus Thunderer
                        Dance, Lady Hera°
                Queen of the sky
                        Dance, dance, all you gods
                Dance witness everlasting of our pact
60   *Evohi Evohe*°
                Dance for the dearest
                            the Bringer of Peace
                Deathless Aphrodite!
COMMISSIONER: Now let us have another song from
        Sparta.
CHORUS(Spartan): From Taygetos, from Taygetos,
65   Lakonian Muse, come down.

---

55. Phoibos: Apollo, god of the sun.   **56. Maenads:** Female
worshipers of Bacchus (Dionysus).   **57. Hera:** Wife of Zeus.
60. *Evohi Evohe*: "Come forth! Come forth!" An orgiastic cry
associated with rituals of Bacchus.

Sing to the Lord Apollo
    Who rules Amyklai Town.

Sing Athena of the House of Brass!°
Sing Leda's Twins,° that chivalry
    Resplendent on the shore   70
Of our Eurotas; sing the girls
    That dance along before:
Sparkling in dust their gleaming feet,
    Their hair a Bacchant fire,
And Leda's daughter, thyrsos° raised,   75
    Leads their triumphant choir.

CHORUS(S and A): *Evohe!*
                        Evohai!
                            Evohe!
                                We pass
            Dancing
                    dancing
                            to greet
    Athena of the House of Brass.

---

68. House of Brass: Temple to Athena on the Akropolis of
Sparta.   **69. Leda's Twins:** Leda, raped by Zeus, bore quadru-
plets, two daughters (one of whom was Helen) and two sons.
75. thyrsos: A staff twined with ivy and carried by Bacchus and
his followers.

COMMENTARY

Brooks Atkinson (1894–1984)
REVIEW OF *LYSISTRATA*   *1930*

This 1930 review of Lysistrata *by the then-reigning* New York Times *reviewer
reminds us that the play is racy enough that "members of the constabulary" needed
to view it to be sure it would not offend the public's sensibilities. Atkinson's review
captures the lively sense of fun manifest in producer Norman Bel Geddes's comedic
romp.*

On second thought, the *Lysistrata,* which was put on at the Forty-fourth Street
last evening, does not come direct from Athens. Between Aristophanes and us
stands Norman Bel Geddes, scene designer extraordinary, who produced this version for the Philadelphia Theatre Association several weeks ago, and whose bountiful scenery now sweeps up toward the flies in a Broadway playhouse. He has
designed a magnificent production, imaginative, free, sculptural and colorful, and

the concluding bacchanal, when viewed from the rear of the auditorium, is a memorable flow of color and motion.

If *Lysistrata* were *Antigone* or *Electra,* this spacious edifice would be a masterful scene conception for the dignity of groupings and the declamation of Greek tragedy. But *Lysistrata* is horseplay, broader than a Second Avenue burlesque, full of rough-and-tumble, full of bawdry. The comic spirit could dance more freely if Mr. Geddes had spared the picture somewhat and tightened the performance. When he has experienced actors at his command — Violet Kemble Cooper, Ernest Truex, Sydney Greenstreet — Aristophanes triumphs over magnificence of scenery, for good actors know the craft of expression. But the pictorial quality of this *Lysistrata* is no unmixed dispensation for the younger actors. When the performance begins to sprawl, as it still does despite considerable cutting, you suspect that Mr. Geddes's setting is more on the side of the tragedians than the mountebanks.

But that is counsel of perfection, and *Lysistrata* is too hearty a comedy to be stared out of countenance by a promethean artist. Gilbert Seldes has written an English adaptation colloquial enough to be relished, and the sheer artlessness of the slapstick episodes makes them palatable and enjoyable even for the sciolists of Broadway. As everyone must know by this time, *Lysistrata* is the story of the women of Greece who plot to conclude a tedious and ruinous interstate war by abstaining from love until their menfolk have made peace. Soldiers denied the consolations of domesticity grew less Martian and more reasonable politically. [. . .]

Members of the constabulary were present last evening to safeguard the morals of Broadway art patrons. Although the police listened to some of the raciest conversation to be heard outside the marts of commerce, they will be relieved to know that it is tamer than what members of the Philadelphia Theatre Association heard when *Lysistrata* opened in that well-bred metropolis. [. . .]

Although *Lysistrata* is a robust comedy, it is not sophisticated. Instead of cracking jokes, it pummels and grimaces, or splashes jars of water on a parcel of feeble old men. And, although the pace of the performance is slow and uneven, and lacking rhythm, it is a tempo not unsuited to the festival quality of the humors.

Those who expect a neat, brisk show will be disappointed. But those who still like to snort over the earthy japery of elementary comedy will find that the congenial version of *Lysistrata* has laughing matter of rare quality.

Roman Drama

Roman drama has several sources, not all of them well understood. The first and most literary is Greek drama, but among the more curious are the indigenous sources, which are especially difficult to trace. One such source might be the Etruscans, members of an old and obscure civilization in northern Italy that reached its height in the sixth century B.C. and that the Romans eventually absorbed. The Etruscans had developed an improvised song and dance that was very entertaining. The town of Atella provided another indigenous comic tradition known as the ATELLAN FARCE, a very broad and sometimes coarse popular comedy. Such entertainments may have been acted in open spaces or at fairs, probably not on a stage at first.

The Atellan farce is especially interesting for developments in later Roman drama and world drama. The characters in this farce seem to have been STOCK CHARACTERS, characters who are always recognizable and whose antics are predictable. The most common in the Atellan farce are Maccus the clown; Bucco the stupid, and probably fat, clown; Pappus, the foolish or stubborn old man; and the hunchbacked, wily slave Dossennus. At first these pieces of drama were improvised to a repeatable pattern, often involving a master who tries to get his slave to do his bidding but who somehow ends up being made to look the fool by the cunning slave. When the farces began to develop in Rome, they were written down and played onstage.

The concept of the stock character is associated with the masters of Roman comedy, Plautus and Terence, who often adapted Greek plays and made them their own. The braggart warrior (*miles gloriosus*), a stock character on the Roman stage, reappears in modern plays. The miser has been a mainstay in literature since Roman times and probably is best known today as Scrooge in Dickens's *A Christmas Carol* and as *The Miser* of Molière. The parasite was Roman in origin and can be seen today in numerous television situation comedies. Another Roman invention is the use of identical twins for comic effect. Because it permitted a wide range of comic misunderstandings, this device has been used by many playwrights, including Shakespeare in *The Comedy of Errors*. The Roman use of masks made the twins device much easier to employ than it would be in today's productions.

The Greek Influence

According to legend, in 240 B.C., a slave, Livius Andronicus, presented performances of his Latin translations of a Greek tragedy and a Greek comedy, giving the Romans their first real taste of Greek drama and literature. Livius soon earned his freedom, and his literary career became so firmly established that his translations from the Greek were those read in Rome for more than two hundred years. His translation of the *Odyssey* was the standard text through the time of Cicero (first century B.C.).

Roman comedy derived primarily from the New Comedy of Menander, although it could, like Aristophanes' Old Comedy, sometimes be risqué. Comedy was the most well attended and the most performed of Rome's drama. That is not to say that the Romans produced no tragedies. They did, and the influence of Roman tragedy has been as long-lasting as that of comedy. Still, the Roman people preferred to laugh rather than to feel the pity and terror of tragic emotion.

Just as the Greek plays developed in connection with festivals, the Roman plays became associated with games held several times a year. During the games, performances were offered on an average of five to eleven days. The Megalesian Games took place in early April, in honor of the Great Mother, the goddess Cybele, whose temple stood on the Palatine Hill. In late April the Floral Games were held in front of the temple of Flora on the Aventine Hill. The most important were the Roman Games in September and the Plebeian Games in November.

The Greek drama competitions had no counterpart among the Romans, for whom drama was not the primary entertainment during the festivals. Roman playwrights and actors were hired to put on performances to entertain and divert the impatient audiences who could choose among a variety of spectacles, including gladiator fights, chariot races, and animal baiting. The producer had to please the audience or lose his chance to supply more entertainment.

Roman comedies were sometimes revisions or amalgamations of Greek plays. The themes and characters of Roman tragedies also derived from Greek originals. Figuring often in Roman tragedies was the Trojan War; its characters were reworked into new situations and their agonies reinterpreted.

For costumes the actors wore the Greek tunic (called a CHITON) and a long white cloak or mantle called the PALLIUM. Like the Greeks, the Romans wore low shoes, called the SOCK, for comedy, and shoes with an elevated sole, the BUSKIN, for tragedy. For plays that had a totally Roman setting and narrative, the actors wore the Roman toga. Eventually, Roman actors used traditional Greek masks that immediately identified the characters for the audience. (The question of whether the earliest Roman actors wore masks as well has not been resolved.) The younger Roman characters wore black wigs, older characters wore white wigs, and characters representing slaves wore red wigs.

One of the most intriguing questions concerning Roman plays is the importance of music in the drama. In Greek plays the chorus took most of the responsibility for the music, but in Roman drama actors may have sung their lines, so the Roman plays may have resembled musical comedies. The dialogue in some comedies introduces an interlude of flute playing, indicating that there were times with no actor onstage, no spoken words, and no mimed action, but only a musician to entertain the audience.

The Roman Stage

In the third century B.C. the Romans began building wooden stages that could be taken down quickly and moved as necessary. Eventually, they built stone theaters following Greek plans but varying from the Greek model in a number of·important respects. They were built on flat ground, rather than on the hillsides as were the Greek theaters. The influence of the Romans' early wooden stage remained in the permanent buildings in several ways. The Roman stage was elevated, and since there was little or no chorus, the orchestra, in which the chorus moved from place to place, was no longer needed. The SCAENA, or background, against which the action took place, was often three stories tall and was proportionally longer than the Greek *skene* (as in Figure 3). This wide but shallow stage was exploited by the playwrights, who often set their plays on a street with various houses, temples, and other buildings along it.

The space in front of the *scaena* was known as the PROSCAENA, from which the PROSCENIUM ARCH, which frames the stage and separates the actors from the audience, developed much later in the Renaissance. The action took place on

Figure 3. Roman theater at Sabratha, Libya. With the *frons scaena* still in good shape, this photograph shows how the Romans modified the basic Greek design.

Figure 4. Theater of Marcellus.

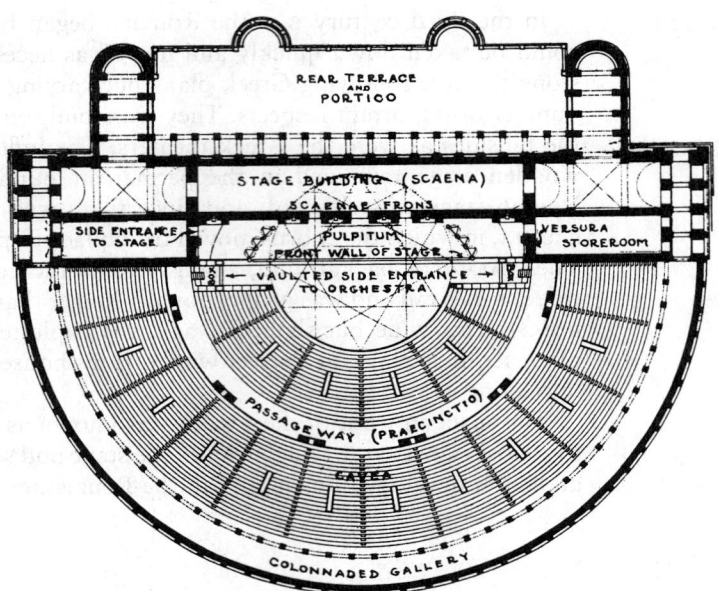

REAR TERRACE AND PORTICO

STAGE BUILDING (SCAENA)

SCAENAE FRONS

SIDE ENTRANCE TO STAGE

PULPITUM
FRONT WALL OF STAGE

VERSURA STOREROOM

VAULTED SIDE ENTRANCE TO ORCHESTRA

PASSAGE WAY (PRAECINCTIO)

CAVEA

COLONNADED GALLERY

the *pulpitum*, behind the *proscaena*. The potential for the proscenium arch is evident in the plan of the Theater of Marcellus (Figure 4), where the sections to the left and the right of the stage (*pulpitum*) already indicate a separation from the audience.

As in the plan of the Theater of Marcellus, the *frons scaena* (the front wall, or façade) usually had three doors (some had only two), which were ordinarily established as doors of separate buildings, sometimes a temple and the others the homes of chief characters. These doors were active "participants" in the drama; it has been said that the most common line heard in a Roman play is a statement that the door is opening and someone is coming in. The standard Roman play takes great care to justify the entrances and exits of its characters, which may indicate that Roman audiences expected more realism in their comedies than did their Greek counterparts.

The *frons scaena*, the front of the theater, not only was several stories high but also was much more architecturally developed than the *skene* of the Greek theater. The typical Roman architectural devices of multiple arches, columns, and pilasters decorated the *scaena*, giving it a stately appearance. Like the Greek theater, the Roman theater used machinery that permitted actors to be moved through the air and to make entrances from the heavens.

The greatest of the Roman dramatists, Plautus and Terence, would have had their plays produced originally on early wooden stages or on Greek stages. The characteristic Roman theater was not created until the period of the empire, more than a hundred years after their deaths. By that time Seneca could have seen his plays produced in the Roman theater, but they may not ever have been produced in Roman times. His plays may have been closet dramas, designed only to be read.

Roman Drama Timeline

DATE	THEATER	POLITICAL	SOCIAL/CULTURAL
800–600 B.C.			**753:** Rome is founded.
600–500			**6th c.:** The Circus Maximus is constructed for chariot races and athletic contests. **509–527:** Roman Republic
500–400			**450:** Roman law is codified in the Twelve Tables.
400–300		**390:** Rome is rebuilt after a Gallic invasion.	
300–200	**3rd c.:** Atellan farce, lively improvised scenarios based on domestic life, is imported from southern Italy to Rome. **240:** Ludi Romani, a festival in honor of Jupiter, incorporates comedy and tragedy for the first time. The festival, established by the elder Tarquin, Etruscan ruler of Rome, already included chariot races, boxing matches, and other popular entertainments. The plays performed at the festival in 240 are probably translations or imitations of Greek plays. **205–184:** Titus Maccius Plautus writes his plays, including *The Twin Menaechmi*.	**272:** Rome conquers central and southern Italy. **264–241:** First Punic War with Carthage **222:** Rome conquers northern Italy. **218–201:** Second Punic War	**c. 300:** Roman consul Appius Claudius Crassus builds the Appian Way, which stretches from Rome to Capua. **287:** Full equality between plebeians and patricians in Rome
200–100	**160:** Publius Terentius Afer (Terence) writes *The Brothers*. **c. 126–c. 62:** Roscius, a popular Roman actor	**195:** Cato the Elder becomes consul and initiates many reforms in urban development and government representation. **149–146:** The Third Punic War. Rome destroys Carthage and Corinth and conquers Greece. **133:** Tiberius Gracchus, Roman reformer, is murdered at the instigation of the Senate.	**186:** Wild animals are exhibited at the Circus Maximus. Contests between wild animals and humans begin shortly hereafter. **106–43:** Cicero, Roman orator **105:** Gladiatorial contests become part of state festivals.

DATE	THEATER	POLITICAL	SOCIAL/CULTURAL
100 B.C.–1 A.D.	**1st c.:** Theaters are built throughout the Roman empire. **90:** Vitruvius writes *De Architectura*, a treatise on Roman architecture that discusses theater architecture in Greece and Rome. **55:** The first permanent stone theater is built in Rome. **4 B.C.–A.D. 65:** Seneca. Dates for his plays, including *Medea*, are unknown. Seneca commits suicide after suffering a decline in power and influence.	**69** B.C.: Cleopatra born. She reigns as queen of Egypt from 51 to 49 and from 48 to her death in 30. **60:** First Triumvirate (Pompey, Crassus, and Julius Caesar) rules Rome. **47:** Herod is appointed King of Judea. **45:** Julius Caesar is declared dictator by Roman Senate. **44:** On the Ides of March Caesar is assassinated. **43–28:** The Second Triumvirate (Antony, Lepidus, and Octavius) rules Rome. **27** B.C.–A.D. **476:** Roman empire **27:** Gaius Octavius, Julius Caesar's grand-nephew, becomes the first emperor of the Roman empire, assuming the name Augustus.	**87–54:** Catullus, Roman poet **70–19:** Virgil (P. Virgilius Maro), poet and author of the *Aeneid* **47:** The library of Ptolemy in Alexandria destroyed by fire; many valuable manuscripts and works of art are lost. **46:** Julius Caesar stages the first *naumachia* (mock sea battle). **43** B.C.–A.D. **17:** Ovid (Publius Ovidius Naso), poet and author of the *Metamorphoses* **22:** Roman pantomime, a predecessor of modern ballet, is introduced by Pylades and Bathyllus. **19:** Horace (65–8 B.C.) writes *Ars Poetica*. **4:** Birth of Jesus
1–100		**14:** Augustus dies, and his stepson Tiberius becomes emperor. **37:** Tiberius's grand-nephew Gaius Caesar (Caligula) is named emperor. **41:** Caligula is assassinated by his own guards; his wife and young daughter are also murdered. Caligula's uncle Claudius is named emperor. **54:** Claudius is allegedly poisoned by his wife, Julia Agrippina. Claudius's stepson Nero is named emperor. **68:** Nero commits suicide. **69:** Vespasian is named emperor. He is succeeded by his son Titus.	**c. 30:** Crucifixion of Jesus **64:** Much of Rome is destroyed by fire. Nero blames the fire on Rome's increasing Christian population and initiates the first large-scale persecution of Christians in Rome. **79:** Mount Vesuvius erupts, destroying Pompeii. **80:** The Colosseum is completed.

Roman Drama Timeline *(continued)*

DATE	THEATER	POLITICAL	SOCIAL/CULTURAL
100–200	**197–202:** Tertullian writes *De Spectaculis*, denouncing the theater as anti-Christian.	**117:** Hadrian becomes emperor. **120:** Hadrian commissions the building of the Pantheon ("the place of all gods"). **122–126:** Hadrian's Wall is extended across Great Britain. **138:** Hadrian dies and is succeeded by Antonius Pius and then by Marcus Aurelius.	**c. 130–200:** Galen, Roman physicist and pioneer in anatomy and physiology **164–180:** A devastating plague sweeps the Roman empire.
200–300	**c. 300:** Records of earliest religious plays.	Roman citizenship given to every freeborn subject in the empire. Under Roman rule, Carthage regains prominence as a center of culture and commerce. **220:** Goths invade the Balkan Peninsula and Asia Minor. **257:** Goths invade the Black Sea provinces.	
300–400		**313:** Edict of Milan. Emperor Constantine establishes toleration of Christianity. **331:** Emperor Constantine moves the Roman capital from Rome to Constantinople. **360:** Huns invade Europe.	**354–430:** St. Augustine, author of the influential *City of God* and *Confessions* **c. 360:** Scrolls begin to be replaced by books.
400–500		**401–403:** Visigoths invade Italy. **410:** Alaric, king of Visigoths, sacks Rome.	**c. 400:** In part because of the rise of Christianity, state festivals honoring pagan gods cease in Rome. **404:** Gladiatorial contests are abolished. **c. 410:** Experiments with alchemy begin. **523:** Wild animal contests are abolished.

Roman Dramatists
Plautus

All surviving Roman comedy shows the influence of Greek originals. Plautus (254–184 B.C.) is among Rome's most famous playwrights and may have been a member of a troupe that performed Atellan comedy. His middle name is Maccius (a form of Maccus, the clown of the farces), possibly alluding to the role he had habitually played. Tradition has it that he was in the theater for a good while before he began writing comedies. His first plays date from 205 B.C., about thirty-five years after Livius introduced Greek drama to the Romans. No one knows how many plays he wrote, and it has been common to assign many unauthenticated titles to him. About twenty-one plays exist that are thought to be his, the most famous of which are *Amphitryon*, *The Pot of Gold*, *The Captives*, *Curculio*, *The Braggart Warrior*, *The Rope*, and *The Twin Menaechmi*.

The last play is probably the best-known Roman comedy. It features Menaechmus from Syracuse, who goes to Epidamnus searching for his lost twin. There he meets people who mistake him for his brother: a cook; a prostitute; Sponge, a typical parasite; and even his brother's wife and father-in-law. The comedy uses all the confusions inherent in mistaken identity.

Plautus (254–184 B.C.)

FROM *THE TWIN MENAECHMI*   *c. 205–184 B.C.*

TRANSLATED BY LIONEL CASSON

The Twin Menaechmi was the first ancient play to be translated into a modern language and put on the stage (1486 in Italy). It has been adapted by numerous modern playwrights, including Shakespeare in *The Comedy of Errors* and, more recently, Rodgers and Hart in *The Boys from Syracuse* (1938), a musical that ran on Broadway for 235 performances. *Boys* has been revived numerous times and is still a popular summer theater play. The following scene from the beginning of act III of *The Twin Menaechmi* shows the parasite Sponge mistaking the identity of Menaechmus of Syracuse for that of his friend Menaechmus of Epidamnus. They have a great go-around over a dress in a typical mixup of the kind that originated with Roman comedies and has been popular in farces and comedies ever since.

ACT III

SPONGE: I'm over thirty now, and never have I ever in all those years pulled a more damned fool stunt than the one I pulled today: There was this town meeting, and *I* had to dive in and come up right in the middle of it. While I'm standing there with my mouth open, Menaechmus sneaks off on me. I'll bet he's gone to his girlfriend. Perfectly willing to leave me behind, too!

(*Paces up and down a few times, shaking his head bitterly. Then, in a rage.*) Damn, damn, damn the fellow who first figured out town meetings! All they do is keep a busy man away from his business. Why don't people pick a panel of men of leisure for this kind of thing? Hold a roll call at each meeting and whoever doesn't answer gets fined on the spot. There are plenty of persons around who need only one meal a day; they don't have business hours to keep because they don't go after dinner invitations or give them out. They're the ones to fuss with town meetings and town elections. If that's how things were run, I wouldn't have lost my lunch today. He sure wanted me along, didn't he? I'll go in, anyway. There's still hope of leftovers to soothe my soul. (*He is about to go up to the door when it suddenly swings open and Menaechmus of Syracuse appears, standing on the threshold with a garland, a little askew, on his head; he is holding the dress and listening to Lovey who is chattering at him from inside. Sponge quickly backs off into a corner.*) What's this I see? Menaechmus — and he's leaving, garland and all! The table's been cleared! I sure came in time — in time to walk him home. Well, I'll watch what his game is, and then I'll go and have a word with him.

MENAECHMUS OF SYRACUSE (*to Lovey inside*): Take it easy, will you! I'll have it back to you today in plenty of time, altered and trimmed to perfection. (*Slyly.*) Believe me, you'll say it's not your dress; you won't know it any more.

SPONGE (*to the audience*): He's bringing the dress to the dressmaker. The dining's done, the drinks are down — and Sponge spent the lunch hour outside. God damn it I'm not the man I think I am if I don't get even with him for this, but really even. You just watch. I'll give it to him, I will.

MENAECHMUS OF SYRACUSE (*closing the door and walking downstage; to the audience, jubilantly*): Good god, no one ever expected less — and got more blessings from heaven in one day than me. I dined, I wined, I wenched, and (*holding up the dress*) made off with this to which, from this moment on, she hereby forfeits all right, title, and interest.

SPONGE (*straining his ears, to the audience*): I can't make out what he's saying from back here. Is that full-belly talking about me and my right title and interest?

MENAECHMUS OF SYRACUSE (*to the audience*): She said I stole it from my wife and gave it to her. I saw she was mistaking me for someone else, so I promptly played it as if she and I were having a hot and heavy affair and began to yes her; I agreed right down the line to everything she said. Well, to make a long story short, I never had it so good for so little.

SPONGE (*clenching his fists, to the audience*): I'm going up to him. I'm itching to give him the works. (*Leaves his corner and strides belligerently toward Menaechmus.*)

MENAECHMUS OF SYRACUSE (*to the audience*): Someone coming up to me. Wonder who it is?

SPONGE (*roaring*): Well! You featherweight, you filth, you slime, you disgrace to the human race, you double-crossing good-for-nothing! What did I ever do to you that you had to ruin my life? You sure gave me the slip downtown a little while ago! You killed off the day all right — and held the funeral feast without me. Me who was coheir under the will! Where do you come off to do a thing like that!

MENAECHMUS OF SYRACUSE (*too pleased with life to lose his temper*): Mister, will you please tell me what business you and I have that gives you the right to use language like that to a stranger here, someone you never saw in your life? You hand me that talk and I'll hand you something you won't like.

SPONGE (*dancing with rage*): God damn it, you already have! I know god damned well you have!

MENAECHMUS OF SYRACUSE (*amused and curious*): What's your name, mister?

SPONGE (*as before*): Still making jokes, eh? As if you don't know my name!

MENAECHMUS OF SYRACUSE: So help me, so far as I know, I never heard of you or saw you till this minute. But I know one thing for sure: whoever you are, you'd better behave yourself and stop bothering me.

SPONGE (*taken aback for a minute*): Menaechmus! Wake up!

MENAECHMUS OF SYRACUSE (*genially*): Believe me, to the best of my knowledge, I am awake.

SPONGE: You don't know me?

MENAECHMUS OF SYRACUSE (*as before*): If I did, I wouldn't say I didn't.

SPONGE (*incredulously*): You don't know your own parasite?

MENAECHMUS OF SYRACUSE: Mister, it looks to me as if you've got bats in your belfry.

SPONGE (*shaken, but not convinced*): Tell me this: Didn't you steal that dress there from your wife today and give it to Lovey?

MENAECHMUS OF SYRACUSE: Good god, no! I don't have a wife, I never gave anything to any Lovey, and I never stole any dress. Are you in your right mind?

SPONGE (*aside, groaning*): A dead loss, the whole affair. (*To Menaechmus.*) But you came out of your house wearing the dress! I saw you myself!

MENAECHMUS OF SYRACUSE (*exploding*): Damn you! You think everybody's a pervert just because you are? I was wearing this dress? Is that what you're telling me?

SPONGE: I most certainly am.

MENAECHMUS OF SYRACUSE: Now you go straight to the one place fit for you! No — get yourself to the lunatic asylum; you're stark-raving mad.

SPONGE (*venomously*): God damn it, there's one thing nobody in the world is going to stop me from doing: I'm telling the whole story, exactly what happened, to your wife this minute. All these insults are going to boomerang back on your own head. Believe you me, you'll pay for eating that whole lunch yourself. (*Dashes into the house of Menaechmus of Epidamnus.*)

MENAECHMUS OF SYRACUSE (*throwing his arms wide, to the audience*): What's going on here? Must everyone I lay eyes on play games with me this way? Wait — I hear the door.

(*The door of Lovey's house opens, and one of her maids comes out holding a bracelet. She walks over to Menaechmus and, as he looks on blankly, hands it to him.*)

MAID: Menaechmus, Lovey says would you please do her a big favor and drop this at the jeweler's on your way? She wants you to give him an ounce of gold and have him make the whole bracelet over.

MENAECHMUS OF SYRACUSE (*with alacrity*): Tell her I'll not only take care of this but anything else she wants taken care of. Anything at all. (*He takes the piece and examines it absorbedly.*)

MAID (*watching him curiously, in surprise*): Don't you know what bracelet it is?

MENAECHMUS OF SYRACUSE: Frankly no — except that it's gold.

MAID: It's the one you told us you stole from your wife's jewel box when nobody was looking.

MENAECHMUS OF SYRACUSE (*forgetting himself, in high dudgeon*): I never did anything of the kind!

MAID: You mean you don't remember it? Well, if that's the case, you give it right back!

MENAECHMUS OF SYRACUSE (*after a few seconds of highly histrionic deep thought*): Wait a second. No, I *do* remember it. Of course — this is the one I gave her. Oh, and there's something else: Where are the armlets I gave her at the same time?

MAID (*puzzled*): You never gave her any armlets.

MENAECHMUS OF SYRACUSE (*quickly*): Right you are. This was all I gave her.

MAID: Shall I tell her you'll take care of it?

MENAECHMUS OF SYRACUSE: By all means, tell her. I'll take care of it, all right. I'll see she gets it back the same time she gets the dress back.

MAID (*going up to him and stroking his cheek*): Menaechmus dear, will you do me a favor too? Will you have some earrings made for me? Drop earrings, please; ten grams of gold in each. (*Meaningfully.*) It'll make me *so* glad to see you every time you come to the house.

MENAECHMUS OF SYRACUSE: Sure. (*With elaborate carelessness.*) Just give me the gold. I'll pay for the labor myself.

MAID: Please, you pay for the gold too. I'll make it up to you afterward.

MENAECHMUS OF SYRACUSE: No, you pay for the gold. I'll make it up to *you* afterward. Double.

MAID: I don't have the money.

MENAECHMUS OF SYRACUSE (*with a great air of magnanimity*): Well, any time you get it, you just let me have it.

MAID (*turning to go*): I'm going in now. Anything I can do for you?

MENAECHMUS OF SYRACUSE: Yes. Tell her I'll see to both things — (*sotto voce, to the audience*) that they get sold as quickly as possible for whatever they'll bring. (*As the maid starts walking toward the door.*) Has she gone in yet? (*Hearing a slam.*) Ah, she's in, the door's closed. (*Jubilantly.*) The lord loves me! I've had a helping hand from heaven! (*Suddenly looks about warily.*) But why hang around when I have the time and chance to get away from this (*jerking his thumb at Lovey's house*) pimping parlor here? Menaechmus! Get a move on, hit the road, forward march! I'll take off this garland and toss it to the left here (*doing so*). Then, if anyone tries to follow me, he'll think I went that way. Now I'll go and see if I can find my servant. I want to let him know all the blessings from heaven I've had.

(*He races off, stage right. The stage is now empty.*)

Terence

Terence (c. 190–159 B.C.) is said to have been a North African slave brought to Rome, where his master realized he was unusually intelligent and gifted. After he was freed, Terence took his place in Roman literary life and produced a body of six plays, all of which still exist: *The Woman of Andros, The Self-Tormentor, The Eunuch, Phormio, The Mother-in-Law,* and *The Brothers.* Terence's plays are notable for including a subplot or secondary action — carefully — and for avoiding the technique of addressing the audience directly.

The Romans preferred Plautus's broad farcical humor to Terence's more carefully plotted, elegantly styled plays. Terence borrowed liberally from Greek sources, often more than one for each of his plays, to develop unusually complicated plots. A manager or producer worked with him on all his plays, and the musician who worked with him was a slave, Flaccus. Terence's productive life was relatively short. He died on a trip to Greece, apparently worrying over a piece of missing luggage said to have contained new plays.

Terence's situation was unusual: he had two wealthy Roman patrons who were interested in seeing the best Greek comedy brought to the Romans. Consequently, they paid for his productions and gave him more support than the average comic playwright could have expected. Terence's dramatic skills developed considerably from the beginning to the end of his work, contrasting sharply with the repetitive nature of Plautus's work. Terence was more than a translator, but he wrote at a time when Romans were interested in emulating the Greeks, and his fidelity to Greek originals was one of his strongest recommendations.

Terence (*c. 190–159 B.C.*)

FROM *THE BROTHERS*   160 B.C.

TRANSLATED BY ROBERT GRAVES

The ending of *The Brothers,* generally recognized as Terence's masterpiece and certainly the most influential of his plays, has Demea planning a reversal on his brother, Micio. Micio is a good, easygoing bachelor who wishes well for others. Demea has been a stern father to one of his sons, Ctesipho, and has tried to steer him in a direction other than the one Ctesipho wants to follow. Demea has entrusted the upbringing of his second son, Aeschinus, to his lenient brother, Micio. Both sons deceive both brothers and end up with the women they want rather than the women the brothers want for them. Meanwhile, Demea gives up and turns the tables on Micio, engineering his brother's marriage to Aeschinus's mother-in-law. In the process of all this, Demea decides to adopt the gentle, easygoing ways of his brother and to forsake his former stern behavior.

This play was adapted often in the seventeenth century by Marston, Beaumont and Fletcher, and others. Molière relied on it for his *School for Wives*. At least five plays were adapted from it for the eighteenth-century English stage.

FROM ACT V

MICIO (*to Syrus, within*): My brother ordered it,° say ye! Where is he? . . . Hah, Brother, was it you who ordered this?

DEMEA: Yes, that I did! And in this and all things else I'm ready to do whatever may conduce to the uniting, serving, helping, and the joining together of both families.

AESCHINUS (*to Micio*): Pray, Sir, let it be so!

MICIO: Well, I've nothing to say against it.

DEMEA: Truth, 'tis no more than we are obliged to do. For first, she's your son's mother-in-law . . .

MICIO: What then?

DEMEA: A very virtuous and modest woman . . .

MICIO: So they say indeed.

DEMEA: Not weighed down by years . . .

MICIO: Not yet.

DEMEA: But past child-bearing: a lonesome woman whom nobody esteems . . .

MICIO (*aside*): What the Devil is he at?

DEMEA: . . . Therefore you ought to marry her; and you Aeschinus, should do what you can to bring this about.

MICIO: Who? I marry?

DEMEA: Yes, you.

MICIO: I, prithee?

DEMEA: Yes, you I say.

MICIO: Pho, you are fooling us, surely?

DEMEA (*to Aeschinus*): If thou hast any life in thee, persuade him to it.

AESCHINUS: Dear Father . . .

MICIO (*interrupting*): Blockhead! Dost thou take in earnest what he says?

DEMEA: 'Tis in vain to refuse; it can't be avoided.

MICIO: Pho, you are in your dotage!

AESCHINUS: Good Sir, let me win this one favor.

MICIO (*angrily*): Art out of thy wits, let me alone!

DEMEA: Come, come! Hearken for once to what your son says.

MICIO: Haven't ye played the fool enough yet? Shall I at threescore and five marry an old woman who's ready to drop into the grave? This is your wise counsel, is it?

AESCHINUS: Pray, Sir, do; I've promised you shall.

MICIO: You promised, with a mischief! Promise for thyself, thou chit!

DEMEA: Fie, fie! What if he had begged a greater favor from you?

MICIO: As if there were any greater favor than this!

DEMEA: Pray grant his request.

AESCHINUS: Good Sir, be not so hard-hearted.

DEMEA: Pho, promise him for once!

MICIO: Will ye never leave baiting me?

My brother ordered it: Demea ordered the breaking down of a wall to allow the two families to communicate. In this way Demea imitates the good-naturedness of his brother, Micio, and traps him into marrying Aeschinus's mother-in-law.

AESCHINUS: Not till I've prevailed, Sir.

MICIO: Truth, this is downright forcing a man.

DEMEA: Come, Micio, be good-natured and consent.

MICIO: Though this be the most damned, foolish, ridiculous whim, and the most averse to my nature that could possibly be, yet since you are so extremely set upon it, I'll humor ye for once.

AESCHINUS: That is excellent, I'm obliged to ye beyond measure.

DEMEA (*aside*): Well, what's next? . . . What shall I say next? This is as I'd have it. . . . What's more to be done?

(*To Micio.*)

Ho! There's Hegio our poor kinsman, and nearest relation; in truth, we ought in conscience to do something for him.

MICIO: What, pray?

DEMEA: There's a small plot of land in the suburbs, which you farm out — pray let's give him that to live on.

MICIO: A small one, say ye?

DEMEA: Though it were a great one, you might yet give it to him. He has been as good as a father to Pamphila; he's a very honest man, our kinsman, and you couldn't bestow it better. Besides, Brother, there's a certain proverb (none of my own, I assure you) which you so well and wisely made use of: "That age has always this ill effect of making us more worldly, as well as wiser." We should do well to avoid this scandal. 'Tis a true proverb, Brother, and ought to be held in mind.

MICIO: What's all this? . . . Well, so let it be, if he has need of it.

AESCHINUS: Brave Father, I vow!

DEMEA: Now you are my true brother, both in body and soul.

MICIO: I'm glad of it.

DEMEA (*aside, laughing*): I've stabbed him with his own weapons, i'fack!

(*Enter Syrus, with a pick-axe upon his shoulders.*)

SYRUS (*to Demea*): The job is done as ye ordered, Sir.

DEMEA: Thou art an honest lad. . . . And upon my conscience I think Syrus deserves his freedom.

MICIO: He, his freedom? For what exploit?

DEMEA: O, for a thousand.

SYRUS: O dear Mr. Demea, you are a rare gentleman, edad you are! You know I've looked after the young gentlemen from their cradles. I taught them, advised them, and instructed them all I possibly could.

DEMEA: Nothing more evident! Nay, more than that, he catered for them, pimped for them, and in the morning took care of a debauchee for them. These are no ordinary accomplishments, I can assure ye.

SYRUS: Your worship's very merry.

DEMEA: Besides, he was prime mover in buying this music-girl. It was he who managed the whole intrigue, and 'tis no more than justice to reward him, as an encouragement to others! In short, Aeschinus desires the same thing.

MICIO (*to Aeschinus*): Do you desire it too?

AESCHINUS: Yes, if you please, Sir.

MICIO: Since 'tis so, come hither, Syrus! Thou art a free man.

(*Syrus kneels down, Micio lays his hand on his head, and after that gives him a cuff on the ear.*)

SYRUS (*rising up*): Generously done! A thousand thanks to ye all, and to you, Mr. Demea.

DEMEA: I'm well satisfied.

AESCHINUS: And I too.

SYRUS: I won't question it, Sir. But I wish heartily my joy were more complete, that my poor spouse Phrygia might be made as free as I am.

DEMEA: Truth, she's a mighty good woman.

SYRUS: And your grandson's first foster-mother, too.

DEMEA: Faith, in good earnest, if for that, she deserves her freedom before any woman in the world.

MICIO: What! For that simple service?

DEMEA: Yes, indeed! In fine, I'll pay for her freedom myself.

SYRUS: God's blessing light upon your worship, and grant all your wishes.

MICIO: Syrus, thou hast made a good day's work of it.

DEMEA: Besides, Brother, it would be a deed of charity to lend him a little money to set up in business that he may face the world without fear. I undertake that he'll soon repay it.

MICIO: Not a penny-piece!

AESCHINUS: He's a very honest fellow, Sir.

SYRUS: Upon my word, I'll repay you the loan. Do but trust me!

AESCHINUS: Pray do, Sir.

MICIO: I'll consider the matter with care.

DEMEA: He shall pay ye, I'll see to that.

SYRUS (*to Demea*): Egad, you're the best man alive.

AESCHINUS: And the pleasantest in the world.

MICIO: What's the meaning of this, Brother? How comes this sudden change of humor? Why this gallant squandering and profusion?

DEMEA: I'll tell ye, Brother. These sons of yours don't reckon you a sweet-natured and pleasant man because you live as you should and do what is just and reasonable, but because you fawn upon them, cocker them up, and give them what they'll spend. Now, son Aeschinus, if you are dissatisfied with my course of life, because I wouldn't indulge you in all things, right or wrong, then I'll not trouble my head with you any further. Be free to squander, buy mistresses, and do what you will! But if you wish me to advise ye, and set ye up, and help ye too in matters of which your youth can give ye but little understanding — matters of which you are over-fond, and don't well consider — see, here I'm ready to stand by you.

AESCHINUS: Dear Sir, we commit ourselves wholly to your charge; for you know what's fitting to be done far better than we . . . But what will ye do for my brother Ctesipho?

DEMEA: Why, let him take the music-girl; and so bid adieu to general wenching.

AESCHINUS: That's very reasonable. (*To the spectators.*) Gentlemen, your favor!

(*Exeunt° all.*)

[S.D.] *Exeunt:* Latin for "they go out."

Seneca

The surviving Roman plays come from just three hands: Plautus, Terence, and Seneca (4 B.C.–A.D. 65). The comedies of Plautus are raucous, broad, and farcical; those of Terence are polished and carefully structured. Seneca wrote tragedies that were well known to Elizabethans such as Marlowe and Shakespeare, and it is clear that the Elizabethan Age found SENECAN TRAGEDY to be peculiarly suited to its own temperament.

Senecan tragedies were based on either Greek or Roman themes and included murder, bloodthirsty actions (many of which did not occur on stage but were only described), horror of various kinds, ghosts, and long, bombastic speeches. Signs of Senecan influence can be seen in Elizabethan drama, with its taste for many of these devices; plays like *Hamlet* are notable for ending in a pool of blood, with most of the actors lying dead onstage. The theme of revenge was also prized by Seneca and, later, by the Elizabethans.

Not a professional theater person, Seneca was wealthy and learned, a philosopher active in the government of Emperor Nero's Rome. His plays, most of which were adapted from Euripides, were probably written only to be read, as was common at his time, or perhaps recited, although there is no record of their having been performed. The Roman people thirsted for mime and farce but had much less taste for serious plays.

Ten plays attributed to Seneca exist, nine of which are surely his and one of which is only possibly his. His most famous are *Mad Hercules, The Phoenician Women, Medea, Phaedra, Agamemnon, Thyestes,* and *The Trojan Women.*

Seneca *(4 B.C.–A.D. 65)*

FROM *THYESTES*

TRANSLATED BY ELLA ISABEL HARRIS

Thyestes, probably adapted from the *Oresteia* of Aeschylus, influenced a number of Elizabethan revenge tragedies, such as Shakespeare's *Hamlet.* The story is gruesome even by modern standards. Thyestes seduces his brother Atreus's wife, and Atreus banishes him. When Atreus summons Thyestes to Atreus's home, he goes suspiciously, hoping to be able to see his children. The banquet Atreus holds for Thyestes seems to signal reconciliation between the brothers. But when it is over, Atreus brings in the heads of Thyestes' children, revealing that Thyestes has just eaten their bodies in the feast.

The second scene from act V — before Thyestes is told about the meal he has eaten — follows in its entirety. It shows Thyestes wrestling with himself in a passion of uncertainty. Thyestes' soliloquy is a psychological study of the effects of grief, care, uncertainty, and fear. Seneca's plays have many such soliloquies, and their revelations of complex emotional states deeply impressed the age of Shakespeare.

ACT V • Scene II

(Thyestes sits alone at the banquet table, half overcome with wine; he tries to sing and be gay, but some premonition of evil weighs upon him.)

THYESTES (*to himself*): By long grief dulled, put by thy cares, my heart,
    Let fear and sorrow fly and bitter need,
    Companion of thy timorous banishment,
    And shame, hard burden of afflicted souls.
    Whence thou has fallen profits more to know
    Than whither; great is he who with firm step
    Moves on the plain when fallen from the height;
    He who, oppressed by sorrows numberless
    And driven from his realm, with unbent neck
    Carries his burdens, not degenerate
    Or conquered, who stands firm beneath the weight
    Of all his burdens, he is great indeed.
    Now scatter all the clouds of bitter fate,
    Put by all signs of thy unhappy days,
    In happy fortunes show a happy face,
    Forget the old Thyestes. Ah, this vice
    Still follows misery: never to trust

In happy days; though better fortunes come,
Those who have borne afflictions find it hard
To joy in better days. What holds me back,
Forbids me celebrate the festal tide?
What cause of grief, arising causelessly,
Bids me to weep? What art thou that forbids
That I should crown my head with festal wreath?
It does forbid, forbid! Upon my head
The roses languish, and my hair that drips
With ointment rises as with sudden fear,
My face is wet with showers of tears that fall
Unwillingly, and groans break off my song.
Grief loves accustomed tears, the wretched feel
That they must weep. I would be glad to make
Most bitter lamentation, and to wail,
And rend this robe with Tyrian purple dyed.
My mind gives warning of some coming grief,
Presages future ills. The storm that smites
When all the sea is calm weighs heavily
Upon the sailor. Fool! What grief, what storm,
Dost thou conceive? Believe thy brother now.
Be what it may, thou fearest now too late,
Or causelessly. I do not wish to be
Unhappy, but vague terror smites my breast.
No cause is evident and yet my eyes
O'erflow with sudden tears. What can it be,
Or grief, or fear? Or has great pleasure tears?

The surviving Roman plays offer enough variety to give us an idea of what the drama achieved. Like so much of Roman culture, Roman drama rested in the shadow of Greek accomplishments. The Romans were responsible for maintaining the Greek texts, allowing us to see a great deal of their work. Although it may be true that much of the Roman drama that was produced no longer exists, what survives shows variety and high quality.

Medieval Drama

The Role of the Church

The medieval period in Europe (A.D. 476–1500) began with the collapse of Rome, a calamity of such magnitude that the years between then and the beginning of the Crusades in 1095 have been traditionally, if erroneously, called the Dark Ages. Historians used this term to refer to their lack of knowledge about a time in which no great central powers organized society or established patterns of behavior and standards in the arts.

Drama, or at least records of it, all but disappeared. The major institution to profit from the fall of the Roman empire was the Roman Catholic Church, which in the ninth and tenth centuries enjoyed considerable power and influence. Many bishops considered drama a godless activity, a distraction from the piety that the church demanded of its members. During the great age of cathedral building and the great ages of religious painting and religious music — from the seventh century to the thirteenth — drama was not officially approved. Therefore, it is a striking irony that the rebirth of drama in the Western world should have taken place in the heart of the monasteries, developing slowly and inconspicuously until it outgrew its beginnings.

The Church may well have intended nothing more than the simple dramatization of its message. Or it is possible that the people may have craved drama, and the Church's response could have been an attempt to answer their needs. In either event, the Church could never have foreseen the outcome of adding a few moments of drama to the liturgy, the church services. LITURGICAL DRAMA began in the ninth century with TROPES, or embellishments, which were sung during parts of the Mass (the public celebration of the Eucharist). The earliest known example of a trope, called the QUEM QUAERITIS ("Whom seek ye?"), grew out of the Easter Mass and was sung in a monastic settlement in Switzerland called St. Gall:

ANGEL: Whom seek ye in the sepulchre, O ye Christians?
THREE MARYS: Jesus of Nazareth, who was crucified, O ye Angels.
ANGEL: He is not here; he is risen as he has foretold.
    Go, announce that he is risen from the sepulchre.

Some scholars think that in its earliest form this trope was sung by four monks in a dialogue pattern, three monks representing the three Marys at Christ's tomb and the other representing the angel. Tropes like the *Quem Quaeritis* evolved over the years to include a number of participants — monks, nuns, and choirboys in different communities — as the tropes spread from church to church throughout the Continent. These dramatic interpolations never became dramas separate from the Mass itself, although their success and popularity led to experiments with other dramatic sequences centering on moments in the Mass and in the life of Christ. The actors in these pieces did not think of themselves as specialists or professionals; they were simply monks or nuns who belonged to the church. The churchgoers obviously enjoyed the tropes, and more were created, despite the Church's official position on drama.

In the tenth century a nun called Hrotsvitha entertained herself and her fellow nuns with imitations of the Latin dramatist Terence. Although her own subject matter was holy in nature, she realized that Terence was an amusing comic writer with a polished style. She referred to herself as "the strong voice of Gandersheim," her community in Saxony, and said that she had "not hesitated to imitate in my writings a poet whose works are so widely read, my object being to glorify, within the limits of my poor talent, the laudable chastity of Christian virgins." Her plays are very short moral tales, often illustrating moments in the lives of Christian martyred women. As far as is known, these plays do not seem to have gone beyond the nuns' walls; therefore, they had little effect on the drama developing in the period.

Once dramatic scenes were added that took the action outside of the liturgy, it was not long before dramas were being staged outside the church. The Anglo-Norman drama *Adam,* dating from the twelfth century, has explicit stage directions establishing its setting outside the church. The play is to be staged on the west side of the church with a platform extending from the steps. The characters of Adam, Eve, God (called Figura), and the Devil and his assistants are given costumes and extensive dialogue. The dramatic detail in this play implies a considerable development of plot and action, which, despite its theological matter, is plainly too elaborate to be contained within the service of the Mass.

Miracle Plays

Once outside the church, the drama flourished and soon became independent, although its themes continued to be religious and its services were connected with religious festivals. In 1264 Pope Urban IV added to the religious calendar a new, important feast: Corpus Christi, celebrated beginning on the first Thursday after Trinity Sunday, about two months after Easter. The purpose of the feast was to celebrate the doctrine declaring that the body of Christ was real and present in the Host (consecrated bread or wafer) taken by the faithful in the sacrament of Communion.

At first the feast of Corpus Christi was localized in Liège, Belgium. But in the fourteenth and fifteenth centuries it spread through papal decree and became one of the chief feasts of the church. Among other things, it featured a procession and pageant in which the Host was displayed publicly through the streets of a town. Because of the importance and excitement of this feast, entire communities took part in the celebration.

MIRACLE PLAYS on the subject of miracles performed by saints developed late in the twelfth century in both England and on the Continent. Typically, these plays focused on the Virgin Mary and St. Nicholas, both of whom had strong followings (sometimes described as cults) during the medieval period. Mary is often portrayed as helping those in need and danger — often at the last minute. Some of those she saved may have seemed unsavory sinners to a pious audience, but the point was that the saint saved all who truly wished to be saved.

Although they quickly became public entertainments removed from the church building and were popular as Corpus Christi entertainments throughout the fifteenth century, few miracle plays survive in English because King Henry VIII banned them in the middle of the sixteenth century during his reformation of the Church. As a result, they were not performed or preserved.

The craft guilds, professional organizations of workers involved in the same trade — carpenters, wool merchants, and so on — soon began competing with each other in producing plays that could be performed during the feast of Corpus Christi. Most of their plays derived from Bible stories and the life of Christ. Religious guilds, such as the Confrerie of the Passion, produced plays in Paris and elsewhere on the Continent. Because the Bible is silent on many details of Christ's life, some plays invented new material and illuminated dark areas, thereby satisfying the intense curiosity medieval Christians had about events the Bible omitted.

Mystery Plays

The Church did not ignore drama after it left the church buildings. Since the plays had religious subject matter and could be used to teach the Bible and to model Christian behavior, they remained of considerable value to the Church.

First performed by the clergy, these religious plays dramatized the mystery of Christ's Passion. Later the plays were produced by members of craft guilds, and they became known as CRAFT or MYSTERY PLAYS. Beginning in the medieval period, the word *mystery* was used to describe a skill or trade known only to a few who apprenticed and mastered its special techniques; it also referred to religious mysteries.

By the fifteenth century, mystery plays and the feast of Corpus Christi were popular almost everywhere in Europe, and in England certain towns produced exceptionally elaborate cycles with unusually complex and ambitious plays. The CYCLES were groups of plays numbering from twenty-four to forty-eight. Four cycles have been preserved: the Chester, York, Towneley (Wakefield), and N-Town cycles, named for their towns of origin. N-Town plays were a generic version of plays that any town could take and use as its own, although the plays were probably written near Lincoln.

The plays were performed again and again during annual holidays and feasts, and the texts were carefully preserved. Some of the plays, such as *The Fall of Lucifer,* are very short. Others are more elaborate in length and complexity and resemble modern plays: *Noah,* from the Wakefield Cycle, which has been produced regularly in recent history; *The Slaughter of Innocents;* and *The Second Shepherds' Play,* one of the most entertaining mystery plays.

The producers of the plays often had a sense of appropriateness in their choice of subjects. For example, the Water-Drawers guild sponsored *Noah's Flood,* the Butchers (because they sold "flesh") *Temptation, The Woman Taken in Adultery,* and the Shipwrights *The Building of the Ark.*

Among the best-known mystery plays is the somewhat farcical *The Second Shepherds' Play,* which is both funny and serious. It tells of a crafty shepherd named Mak who steals a lamb from his fellow shepherds and takes it home. His wife, Gill, then places it in a cradle and pretends it is her baby. Eventually the shepherds — who suspect Mak from the first — smoke out the fraud and give Mak a blanket-tossing for their trouble. But after they do so, they see a star in the heavens and turn their attention to the birth of baby Jesus, the Lamb of God. They join the Magi and come to pay homage to the Christ Child.

The easy way in which the profane elements of everyday life coexisted with the sacred in medieval times has long interested scholars. *The Second Shepherds' Play* virtually breaks into two parts, the first dedicated to the wickedness of Mak and Gill and the horseplay of the shepherds. But once Mak has had his due reward, the play alters in tone and the sense of devotion to Christian teachings becomes uppermost. The fact that the mystery plays moved away from liturgical Latin and to the vernacular (local) language made such a juxtaposition of sacred and profane much more possible.

The dominance of the guilds in producing mystery plays suggests that guilds enjoyed increasing political power and authority. The guilds grew stronger and more influential — probably at the expense of the Church. Some historians have seen this development as crucial to the growing secularization of the Middle Ages.

Morality Plays

MORALITY PLAYS were never part of any cycle but developed independently as moral tales in the late fourteenth or early fifteenth century on the Continent and in England. They do not illustrate moments in the Bible, nor do they describe the life of Christ or the saints. Instead, they describe the lives of people facing the temptations of the world. The plays are careful to present a warning to the unwary that their souls are always in peril, that the devil is on constant watch, and that people must behave properly if they are to be saved.

One feature of morality plays is their reliance on ALLEGORY, a favorite medieval device. Allegory is the technique of giving abstract ideas or values a physical representation. In morality plays, abstractions such as goodness became characters in the drama. In modern times we sometimes use allegory in art, as when we represent justice as a blindfolded woman. Allegorically, justice should act impartially because she does not "see" any distinctions, such as those of rank or privilege, that characterize most people standing before a judge.

The use of allegory permitted medieval dramatists to personify abstract values such as sloth, greed, daintiness, vanity, strength, and hope by making them characters and placing them onstage in action. The dramatist specified symbols, clothing, and gestures appropriate to these abstract figures, thus helping the audience recognize the ideas the characters represented. The use of allegory was an extremely durable technique that was already established in medieval painting, printed books, and books of emblems, in which, for example, sloth would be shown as a man reclining lazily on a bed or greed would be represented as overwhelmingly fat and vanity as a figure completely absorbed in a mirror.

The central problem in the morality play was the salvation of human beings, represented by an individual's struggle to avoid sin and damnation and achieve salvation in the otherworld. As in *Everyman* (c. 1495), a late-medieval play that is the best known of the morality plays, the subjects were usually abstract battles between certain vices and specific virtues for the possession of the human soul, a theme repeated in the Elizabethan age in Marlowe's *Doctor Faustus*.

In many ways the morality play was a dramatized sermon designed to teach a moral lesson. Marked by high seriousness, it was nevertheless entertaining. Using allegory to represent abstract qualities allowed the didactic playwrights to draw clear-cut lines of moral force: Satan was always bad; angels were always good. The allegories were clear, direct, and apparent to all who witnessed the plays.

We do not have much knowledge of the origins of morality plays. Many of them are lost, but some that remain are occasionally performed: *The Pride of Life,* the earliest extant morality play; *The Castle of Perseverance; Wisdom; Mankind;* and *Everyman* are the best known. They all enjoyed a remarkable popularity in the latter part of the medieval period, all the way up to the early Renaissance.

The Medieval Stage

Relatively little commentary survives about the conventions of medieval staging, and some of it is contradictory. We know that in the earliest years — after the tropes developed into full-blown religious scenes acted inside the cathedrals — certain sections of the church were devoted to specific short plays. These areas of the church became known as MANSIONS; each mansion represented a building or physical place known to the audience. The audience moved from one mansion to another, seeing play after play, absorbing the dramatic representation of the events, characters, and locale associated with each mansion.

The tradition of moving from mansion to mansion inside the church carried over into the performances that took place later outside the church. Instead of mansions, wagons with raised stages provided the playing areas. Usually, the wagons remained stationary and the audience moved from one to another. During the guild cycles the pageants would move; the performers would give their plays at several locales so that many people could see them.

According to medieval descriptions, drawings, and reconstructions, a PAGEANT CART could also be simply a flat surface drawn on wheels that had a wagon next to it; these structures touched on their long side. In some cases a figure could descend from an upper area as if from the clouds, or actors could descend from the pageants onto the audience's level to enact a descent into an underworld. The stage was, then, a raised platform visible to the audience below (Figure 5).

A curtain concealed a space, usually inside or below the wagon, for changing costumes. The actors used costumes and props, sometimes very elaborate and expensive, in an effort to make the drama more impressive. Indeed, between the thirteenth and the sixteenth centuries, a number of theatrical effects were developed to please a large audience. For instance, in the morality and mystery plays the devils were often portrayed as frightening, grotesque, and sometimes even comic figures. They became crowd pleasers. A sensational element was developed in some of the plays in the craft cycles, especially those about the lives of the saints and martyrs, in which there were plenty of chances to portray horrifying tortures.

The prop that seems to have pleased the most audiences was a complex machine known as the MOUTH OF HELL or "Hell mouth," usually a large fish-shaped orifice from which smoke and explosions, fueled by gunpowder, belched constantly. The devils took great delight in stuffing their victims into these maws. According to a contemporary account, one of the machines required seventeen men to operate.

The level of realism achieved by medieval plays was at times startling. In addition to visual realism, medieval plays involved a psychological level of participation on the part of both audience and actor. Sometimes they demanded

Figure 5. Pageant wagon

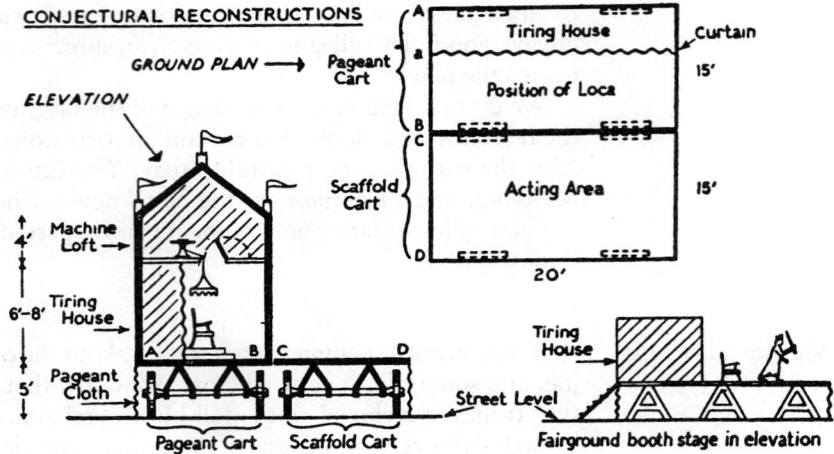

that the actors suffer in accord with the characters they played. Some records attest to characters playing Christ on the cross having to be revived after their hearts stopped, and at least one Judas apparently was hanged just a little too long and had to be resuscitated.

The Actors

In the early days of liturgical drama, the actors in the tropes were monks and choirboys, and in the mystery plays they were drawn from the guilds. At first all the actors were male, but records show that eventually women took important roles.

The demands of more sophisticated plays encouraged the development of a kind of professionalism, although it seems unlikely that players in the cycles could have supported themselves exclusively on their earnings. Special skills became essential for the design and operation of complex stage machines and for the performance of acrobatics that were expected of certain characters, such as devils. As actors developed facility in delivering lines and as writers found ways to incorporate more challenging elements in their plays, a professionalism no doubt arose, even if actors and writers had few opportunities to earn a living on the stage.

By the second half of the sixteenth century, the early Renaissance, groups of wandering actors were producing highly demanding and sophisticated plays, and writers such as Shakespeare were able to join them and make a living. When these professionals secured their own theaters, they had no problems filling them with good drama, with actors, and with an audience.

Dramatic techniques developed in the medieval period were put to good use in the Renaissance theater. For example, the colorful and dramatic devil characters that stalked the mystery plays were transformed into sophisticated villains in Elizabethan drama. The devil Mephistopheles (Mephistophilis) behaves like a smooth Tudor lawyer in Marlowe's *Doctor Faustus;* Iago in *Othello* is suspected of having cloven hooves. Perhaps one important difference is that the Elizabethan devil-villains are truly frightening, since they are so recognizably human in their villainy.

Medieval Drama Timeline

DATE	THEATER	POLITICAL	SOCIAL/CULTURAL
400–500		**476:** The fall of Rome and beginning of the Dark Ages **483–565:** Byzantine Emperor Justinian, author of the Code of Civil Laws	**480–524:** Boëthius, Roman scholar, philosopher, and theologian, is executed for treason.
500–600	**500–1000:** Traveling performers proliferate in Europe.		**570–632:** Muhammed, founder of Islam **590–594:** Devastating plague spreads through Europe and kills half the population.
600–700		Persians take Damascus and Jerusalem.	**636:** Anglo-Saxons are introduced to Christianity. **695:** Jews are persecuted in Spain.
700–800		**768–814:** Charlemagne reigns in France and is crowned Holy Roman Emperor in 800 by Pope Leo III in Rome on Christmas Day. **792:** Beginning of the Viking era in Britain	**c. 710:** Buddhist monasteries in Japan become centers of civilization. **787:** The Council of Nicaea officially rejects iconoclasm.
800–900	**9th c.:** Beginnings of liturgical drama	**843:** Treaty of Verdun divides the Holy Roman Empire into German, French, and Italian kingdoms. **850:** Rurik, a Northman, becomes ruler of Kiev, an important Russian trading post. Trade begins with Constantinople, which remains a commercial and cultural center throughout the Dark Ages.	**c. 800–1000:** *Beowulf,* one of the first long poems written in English **855:** Earliest known attempts at polyphonic music **863:** Cyril and Methodius invent a Slavic alphabet called Cyrillic.
900–1000	**c. 900:** Farces make their first appearance since classical times. **925:** Earliest extant Easter trope **965–975:** Compilation of the *Regularis Concordia* (Monastic Agreement) by Ethelwood, bishop of Winchester, England. The *Regularis Concordia* contains the text of the earliest extant playlet in Europe, with directions for its performance.		**c. 900:** The beginnings of the famous Arabian tales called *A Thousand and One Nights*

207

Medieval Drama Timeline (continued)

DATE	THEATER	POLITICAL	SOCIAL/CULTURAL
900–1000 (continued)	**970:** Plays of Hrosvitha, a German nun and the first known female playwright. The six plays are modeled on the comedies of Terence but deal with serious religious matters.	**1000:** Leif Ericson, possibly the first European to venture to North America	**975:** Arabic arithmetical notation is brought to Europe by the Arabs. **980–1037:** Avicenna (Ibn Sina), Arab physician and philosopher **990:** Development of systemic musical notation.
1000–1100		**1066:** The Normans conquer Britain. **1086:** Compilation of the *Domesday Book,* a survey of the British economy, population, and land ownership at that time **1096–1099:** First Crusade. Crusaders take Jerusalem from the Arabs.	**1054:** The Great Schism separates Eastern and Western Churches in Europe. **1079–1142:** Peter Abelard, French theologian and philosopher
1100–1200	**12th c.:** Religious plays are first performed outside churches.	**1109–1113:** Anglo-French War **1147–1149:** Second Crusade. Crusaders lose Jerusalem to the Arabs. **1167–1227:** Genghis Khan, founder of Mongol empire **1189-1193:** Third Crusade. Crusaders fail to recapture Jerusalem.	**c. 1125:** Beginnings of French troubadour and trouvère music **1133–1855:** St. Bartholomew's Fair, London, England **1167:** Oxford University is founded.
1200–1300	**1250:** *Easter Play of Muri,* beginnings of German drama **1276–1277:** French poet Adam de la Halle writes *The Play of the Greenwood,* the oldest extant medieval secular drama.	**1202–1204:** Fourth Crusade. Crusaders seize Constantinople. **1212:** Children's Crusade. Thousands of children are sent as crusaders to Jerusalem; most die or are sold as slaves. **1215:** King John of England signs the Magna Carta, guaranteeing habeas corpus, trial by jury, and restrictions on the power of the king. **1224–1227:** Anglo-French War **1228:** Sixth Crusade **1248:** Seventh Crusade	**c. 1202:** Court jesters appear at European courts. **1225:** Guillaume de Lorris writes *Roman de la Rose,* a story of courtly wooing. **1225–1274:** Thomas Aquinas, important Scholastic philosopher **1254–1324:** Marco Polo, Venetian traveler whose accounts of life in China became famous in the West **1264:** First celebration of the feast of Corpus Christi **c. 1282:** Florence emerges as the leading European city of commerce and finance.

DATE	THEATER	POLITICAL	SOCIAL/CULTURAL
1300–1400	**14th c.:** Beginnings of *noh* drama in Japan **c. 1375:** *The Second Shepherds' Play,* part of the English Wakefield Cycle **1398–1548:** Confrérie de la Passion at Paris performs religious plays.	**1337:** Hundred Years War begins.	**c. 1302:** Dante's *Divine Comedy* **1304–1374:** Petrarch, Italian poet **1347–1351:** The Black Death kills approximately 75 million people throughout Europe. **1360–1400:** *Piers Plowman* and *Sir Gawain and the Green Knight*: achievements of Middle English literature **1387:** Chaucer's *Canterbury Tales*
1400–1500	**c. 1425:** *The Castle of Perseverance,* English morality play **1429:** Plautus's plays are rediscovered in Italy. **c. 1470:** *Pierre Patheline,* most renowned of medieval French farces **1490:** *Corpus Christi* play of Eger, Bohemia **c. 1495:** *Everyman,* best-known English morality play	**1429:** Joan of Arc's troops resist the British siege of Orleans, an important turning point in the Hundred Years War. **1431:** Joan of Arc is captured and burned as a heretic. **1453:** France wins the Hundred Years War and becomes an important continental power. England abandons the Continent to develop its naval forces. **1481:** Spanish Inquisition **1482–1485:** Reign of Richard III. Richard maintains a company of actors at court, which tours surrounding towns when not needed by His Majesty. **1485–1509:** Reign of Henry VII, first of the Tudor rulers. Like Richard III, Henry maintains a company of actors.	**1400–1455:** Fra Angelico, Italian painter **c. 1406–1469:** Fra Lippo Lippi, Italian painter best known for his frescoes **c. 1430:** Modern English develops from Middle English. **c. 1450:** Gutenberg invents movable type. **1485:** Sir Thomas Malory publishes *Le Morte Darthur,* one of the first books printed in England. **1492:** Columbus sets sail across the Atlantic.
1500–1600	**1527:** Henry VII builds a House of Revels in which to stage court entertainments. **1548:** Production of plays is forbidden in Paris. **1558:** Elizabeth I forbids performance of all religious plays.	**1509–1547:** Reign of Henry VII **1534:** Henry VII breaks with the Roman Catholic Church. Drama is used as a political instrument to attack or defend opposing viewpoints. **1558–1603:** Reign of Elizabeth I	**1509:** Pope Clement V resides at Avignon, beginning the Babylonian Captivity, during which Rome is not the papal seat. **1545–1563:** The Council of Trent is convened by the Catholic Church to solidify its control over expressions of Church doctrine. Medieval religious plays are deemed provocative and controversial.

Hrosvitha

The German nun Hrosvitha (also Hroswitha, Roswitha, Hrotsvit, and Hrotsuit) belonged to the Benedictine convent in Gandersheim, founded in 852. Her name translates to "strong voice," a term she uses to describe herself in her writing. Her voice is that of a learned woman, and today it can be heard as a feminist voice in a time and society that were unquestioningly patriarchal.

Hrosvitha is considered not only the earliest German woman poet but the first woman dramatist in Europe. A Saxon noblewoman, she entered the convent c. 959, living with nuns who were themselves of noble birth. The abbey was under the protection of Otto I (912–973), who united a powerful Germany and produced a long-lasting period of peace and development. Otto became the Holy Roman Emperor on February 13, 962. His rule, dubbed the Ottonian Renaissance, favored religion, learning, the arts, and music.

During this period, the abbey at Gandersheim was obligated not to the Church but to the king himself, and Otto eventually released it from his direct governance, permitting it to maintain a law court and to coin money. While such political issues may not have affected Hrosvitha, the fact that the period was one of learning and scholarship was of great importance. Hrosvitha was educated in the liberal arts, beginning with the quadrivium (geometry, arithmetic, music, and astronomy) and continuing with the trivium (grammar, rhetoric, and logic). Her studies were conducted in Latin, the language she used to write her plays. Her education was comparable to that of liberally educated men and of the nuns who lived with her.

Hrosvitha's work is deeply rooted in her religious beliefs. Her religious order meditated on the drama of the lives of Christian saints and especially on their often spectacular martyrdoms. The abbey gave its inhabitants a life of contemplation, removed from the world. But it is also clear that the nuns had the talent, education, and opportunities to write religious tracts and, in the case of Hrosvitha, religious drama. The question of whether Hrosvitha's six plays were actually produced is not settled.

Hrosvitha wrote six plays and several other prose and poetic works. The plays reject the temptations of the world in the name of Christ. In *Gallicanus* the title character is promised the hand of Constantia if he wins a specific battle, but Constantia, daughter of the Christian emperor Constantine, has taken a vow of chastity. Eventually, with the aid of saints, Gallicanus converts to Christianity and becomes a martyr. The conversion of an important Roman is the theme of *Callimachus,* and the conversion theme dominates *Paphnutius* and *Abraham. Sapientia* also emphasizes martyrdom. Sapienta's three daughters, whose names translate as Faith, Hope, and Charity, offer a threat to the stability of Emperor Hadrian's rule. They are tortured brutally but survive without pain until Hadrian beheads them. Eventually Sapientia joins her daughters in heavenly bliss, inspiring the local women who have witnessed the events.

DULCITIUS

Dulcitius is probably the second of Hrosvitha's plays. It was rediscovered in 1494 in an eleventh-century manuscript along with her other dramatic works. Its first printing was in 1501 in an edition with woodcuts by Albrecht Dürer, indicating its importance at the time. The play is plainly didactic and was designed to teach a lesson rather than merely to entertain. The lesson, as in all her plays, is a moral one, urging listeners or readers to live a life of purity and virtue to celebrate the greatness of God. In this sense, Hrosvitha wrote in the medieval literary tradition of Europe. Her plays are fascinating to the modern reader, however, because she purposely emulated the techniques of the Roman playwright Terence.

She chose Terence as her model because his texts were used in education and therefore widely known in Europe. Moreover, they were amusing comedies written with such great style that they were models of elocution. Hrosvitha admits to imitating Terence, but her motives were subversive. She wished to use the eloquent style of Terence not to entertain her audience with secular amusement and charming courtesans but to honor the virtue of chaste virgins who praised God and Christian virtues.

Dulcitius, a jail governor, lusts after the three virgins Agape, Chionia, and Hirenia (Love, Purity, and Peace). Hrosvitha emphasizes his power, but all his worldly power comes to nothing in the face of the virgins' beliefs. In this sense, Hrosvitha celebrates how the apparent weakness of females in her own society can confound the apparent strength of males. Despite his position and power, Dulcitius's lust cannot be satisfied.

Moreover, the three virgins are problematic not only to Dulcitius but to Emperor Diocletian as well. When Agape tells Diocletian that it is dangerous to offend almighty God, Diocletian asks: "Dangerous to whom?" She responds, "To you and to the state you rule." Hrosvitha therefore not only establishes the power of the virgins but of the Christian religion. Astonishingly, this "new-fangled religion" threatens Rome itself, which is why Diocletian persecuted Christians so brutally during his reign.

The play's short lines, quick realistic dialogue, and carefully focused interaction are recognizably like Terence's. The present translation uses virgules (/) to indicate the end of lines as they were printed in the original Latin. The broad farcical humor of the "miraculous" scene in which Dulcitius embraces pots and pans in the kitchen thinking they are the three virgins — a scene performed while the virgins watch through the crack in the door — is also in the tradition of Roman comedy.

Despite the three virgins' ultimate martyrdom, the play is a comedy. The soldiers and Dulcitius will end up in "Tartarus," while the virgins "will enter the heavenly bridal chamber of the Eternal King." For the devout canonness Hrosvitha, no ending could be happier.

Dulcitius in
Performance

In the opinion of most scholars, the plays of Hrosvitha were not produced but instead read as CLOSET DRAMA. On the other hand, comic scenes such as the one in which Dulcitius blackens his face against the pots and pans have led some theater historians to speculate that the plays were performed by the nuns themselves in the abbey. In any event, *Dulcitius* would not have had a public audience and may not have influenced other medieval drama. It is, however, a remarkable moment in the history of drama. As Hrosvitha tells us: "I, the strong voice of Gandersheim, have not hesitated to imitate in my writings a poet whose works are so widely read, my object being to glorify, within the limits of my poor talent, the laudable chastity of Christian virgins in that self-same form of composition which has been used to describe the shameless acts of licentious women."

Hrosvitha (c. 935–1000)

DULCITIUS
THE MARTYRDOM OF THE HOLY VIRGINS AGAPE, CHIONIA, AND HIRENA

c. 965

TRANSLATED BY K. M. WILSON

[Characters

DIOCLETIAN	
AGAPE	WIFE (OF DULCITIUS)
CHIONIA	SISSINUS
HIRENA	SOLDIERS
DULCITIUS	GUARDS]

The martyrdom of the holy virgins° Agape, Chionia, and Hirena, whom, in the silence of the night, Governor Dulcitius secretly visited, desiring to delight in their embrace. But as soon as he entered, / he became demented / and kissed and hugged the pots and pans, mistaking them for the girls until his face and his clothes were soiled with disgusting black dirt. Afterward Count Sissinus, acting on orders, / was given the girls so he might put them to tortures. / He, too, was deluded miraculously / but finally ordered that Agape and Chionia be burnt and Hirena be slain by an arrow.

DIOCLETIAN: The renown of your free and noble descent / and the brightness of your beauty demand / that you be married to one of the foremost men of my court. This will be done according to our command if you deny Christ° and comply by bringing offerings to our gods.° 5

The martyrdom of the holy virgins: The martyrdom of the three virgins occurred in 290 during Diocletian's persecution of the Christians in Thessalonica.   **5. deny Christ:** Deny the vow of virginity they made in the name of Christ.   **6. our gods:** Gods acknowledged by the Roman empire.

AGAPE: Be free of care, / don't trouble yourself to prepare our wedding / because we cannot be compelled under any duress / to betray Christ's holy name, which we must confess, / nor to stain our virginity. 10
DIOCLETIAN: What madness possesses you? What rage drives you three? /
AGAPE: What signs of our madness do you see? /
DIOCLETIAN: An obvious and great display. /
AGAPE: In what way? / 15
DIOCLETIAN: Chiefly in that renouncing the practices of ancient religion / you follow the useless, new-fangled ways of the Christian superstition. /
AGAPE: Heedlessly you offend the majesty of the omnipotent God. That is dangerous . . . 20
DIOCLETIAN: Dangerous to whom?
AGAPE: To you and to the state you rule. /
DIOCLETIAN: She is mad; remove the fool! /
CHIONIA: My sister is not mad; she rightly reprehended your folly. 25
DIOCLETIAN: She rages even more madly; remove her from our sight and arraign the third girl. /
HIRENA: You will find the third, too, a rebel / and resisting you forever. /
DIOCLETIAN: Hirena, although you are younger in birth, / be greater in worth! / 30
HIRENA: Show me, I pray, how?
DIOCLETIAN: Bow your neck to the gods, set an example for your sisters, and be the cause for their freedom!
HIRENA: Let those worship idols, Sire, / who wish to incur God's ire. / But I won't defile my head, anointed 35

with royal unguent by debasing myself at the idols' feet.

40 DIOCLETIAN: The worship of gods brings no dishonor / but great honor. /

HIRENA: And what dishonor is more disgraceful, / what disgrace is any more shameful / than when a slave is venerated as a master?

DIOCLETIAN: I don't ask you to worship slaves / but the 45 mighty gods of princes and greats. /

HIRENA: Is he not anyone's slave / who, for a price, is up for sale? /

DIOCLETIAN: For her speech so brazen, / to the tortures she must be taken. /

50 HIRENA: This is just what we hope for, this is what we desire, / that for the love of Christ through tortures we may expire. /

DIOCLETIAN: Let these insolent girls / who defy our decrees and words / be put in chains and kept in the 55 squalor of prison until Governor Dulcitius can examine them.

DULCITIUS: Bring forth, soldiers, the girls whom you hold sequestered. /

SOLDIERS: Here they are whom you requested. /

60 DULCITIUS: Wonderful, indeed, how beautiful, how graceful, how admirable these little girls are!

SOLDIERS: Yes, they are perfectly lovely.

DULCITIUS: I am captivated by their beauty.

SOLDIERS: That is understandable.

65 DULCITIUS: To draw them to my heart, I am eager. /

SOLDIERS: Your success will be meager. /

DULCITIUS: Why?

SOLDIERS: Because they are firm in faith.

DULCITIUS: What if I sway them by flattery? /

70 SOLDIERS: They will despise it utterly. /

DULCITIUS: What if with tortures I frighten them? /

SOLDIERS: Little will it matter to them. /

DULCITIUS: Then what should be done, I wonder? /

SOLDIERS: Carefully you should ponder. /

75 DULCITIUS: Place them under guard in the inner room of the pantry, where they keep the servants' pots. /

SOLDIERS: Why in that particular spot? /

DULCITIUS: So that I may visit them often at my leisure. /

SOLDIERS: At your pleasure. /

80 DULCITIUS: What do the captives do at this time of night? /

SOLDIERS: Hymns they recite. /

DULCITIUS: Let us go near. /

SOLDIERS: From afar we hear their tinkling little voices 85 clear. /

DULCITIUS: Stand guard before the door with your lantern / but I will enter / and satisfy myself in their longed-for embrace. /

SOLDIERS: Enter. We will guard this place. /

90 AGAPE: What is that noise outside the door? /

HIRENA: That wretched Dulcitius coming to the fore. /

CHIONIA: May God protect us!

AGAPE: Amen.

CHIONIA: What is the meaning of this clash of the pots and the pans?   95

HIRENA: I will check. / Come here, please, and look through the crack! /

AGAPE: What is going on?

HIRENA: Look, the fool, the madman base, / he thinks he is enjoying our embrace. /   100

AGAPE: What is he doing?

HIRENA: Into his lap he pulls the utensils, / he embraces the pots and the pans, giving them tender kisses. /

CHIONIA: Ridiculous!

HIRENA: His face, his hands, his clothes, are so soiled, so 105 filthy, that with all the soot that clings to him, he looks like an Ethiopian.

AGAPE: It is only right that he should appear in body the way he is in his mind: possessed by the Devil.

HIRENA: Wait! He prepares to leave. Let us watch how 110 he is greeted, / and how he is treated / by the soldiers who wait for him.

SOLDIERS: Who is coming out? / A demon without doubt. / Or rather, the Devil himself is he; / let us flee! /

DULCITIUS: Soldiers, where are you taking yourselves 115 in flight? / Stay! Wait! Escort me home with your light! /

SOLDIERS: The voice is our master's tone / but the look the Devil's own. / Let us not stay! / Let us run away; the apparition will slay us! /   120

DULCITIUS: I will go to the palace and complain, / and reveal to the whole court the insults I had to sustain. /

DULCITIUS: Guards, let me into the palace; / I must have a private audience. /

GUARDS: Who is this vile and detestable monster cov- 125 ered in torn and despicable rags? Let us beat him, / from the steps let us sweep him; / he must not be allowed to enter.

DULCITIUS: Alas, alas, what has happened? Am I not dressed in splendid garments? Don't I look neat and 130 clean? / Yet anyone who looks at my mien / loathes me as a foul monster. To my wife I shall return, / and from her learn / what has happened. But there is my spouse, / with disheveled hair she leaves the house, / and the whole household follows her in tears.   135

WIFE: Alas, alas, my Lord Dulcitius, what has happened to you? / You are not sane; the Christians have made a laughing stock out of you. /

DULCITIUS: Now I know at last. I owe this mockery to their witchcraft.   140

WIFE: What upsets me so, what makes me more sad, is that you were ignorant of all that happened to you.

DULCITIUS: I command that those insolent girls be led forth, / and that they be publicly stripped of all their clothes, / so that they experience similar mockery in 145 retaliation for ours.

SOLDIERS: We labor in vain; / we sweat without gain. / Behold, their garments stick to their virginal bodies like skin, / and he who urged us to strip them snores in his seat, / and he cannot be awakened from his   150 sleep. / Let us go to the Emperor and report what has happened.

DIOCLETIAN: It grieves me very much / to hear that Governor Dulcitius has been so greatly deluded, / so greatly
155 insulted, / so utterly humiliated. / But these vile young women shall not boast with impunity of having made a mockery of our gods and those who worship them. I shall direct Count Sissinus to take due vengeance.

SISSINUS: Soldiers, where are those insolent girls who
160 are to be tortured?
SOLDIERS: They are kept in prison.
SISSINUS: Leave Hirena there, / bring the others here. /
SOLDIERS: Why do you except the one?
SISSINUS: Sparing her youth. Perchance, she may be con-
165 verted easier, if she is not intimidated by her sisters' presence. /
SOLDIERS: That makes sense. /

SOLDIERS: Here are the girls whose presence you re-
quested.
170 SISSINUS: Agape and Chionia, give heed, / and to my council accede! /
AGAPE: We will not give heed. /
SISSINUS: Bring offerings to the gods.
AGAPE: We bring offerings of praise forever / to the true
175 Father eternal, / and to His Son co-eternal, / and also to the Holy Spirit.
SISSINUS: This is not what I bid, / but on pain of penalty prohibit. /
AGAPE: You cannot prohibit it; neither shall we ever sac-
180 rifice to demons.
SISSINUS: Cease this hardness of heart, and make your offerings. But if you persist, / then I shall insist / that you be killed according to the Emperor's orders.
CHIONIA: It is only proper that you should obey the
185 orders of your Emperor, whose decrees we disdain, as you know. For if you wait and try to spare us, then you could be rightfully killed.
SISSINUS: Soldiers, do not delay, / take these blasphem-ing girls away, / and throw them alive into the flames.
190 SOLDIERS: We shall instantly build the pyre you asked for, and we will cast these girls into the raging fire, and thus we'll put an end to these insults at last. /
AGAPE: O Lord, nothing is impossible for Thee; / even the fire forgets its nature and obeys Thee; / but we are
195 weary of delay; / therefore, dissolve the earthly bonds that hold our souls, we pray, / so that as our earthly bodies die, / our souls may sing your praise in Heaven.
SOLDIERS: Oh, marvel, oh stupendous miracle! Behold their souls are no longer bound to their bodies, / yet
200 no traces of injury can be found; neither their hair, nor their clothes are burnt by the fire, / and their bodies are not at all harmed by the pyre. /
SISSINUS: Bring forth Hirena.

SOLDIERS: Here she is.
205 SISSINUS: Hirena, tremble at the deaths of your sisters and fear to perish according to their example.

HIRENA: I hope to follow their example and expire, / so with them in Heaven eternal joy I may acquire. /
SISSINUS: Give in, give in to my persuasion. /
HIRENA: I will never yield to evil persuasion. /   210
SISSINUS: If you don't yield, I shall not give you a quick and easy death, but multiply your sufferings.
HIRENA: The more cruelly I'll be tortured, / the more gloriously I'll be exalted. /
SISSINUS: You fear no tortures, no pain? / What you   215
abhor, I shall ordain. /
HIRENA: Whatever punishment you design, / I will escape with help Divine. /
SISSINUS: To a brothel you will be consigned, / where your body will be shamefully defiled. /   220
HIRENA: It is better that the body be dirtied with any stain than that the soul be polluted with idolatry.
SISSINUS: If you are so polluted in the company of har-lots, you can no longer be counted among the vir-ginal choir.   225
HIRENA: Lust deserves punishment, but forced compli-ance the crown. With neither is one considered guilty, / unless the soul consents freely. /
SISSINUS: In vain have I spared her, in vain have I pitied her youth.   230
SOLDIERS: We knew this before; / for on no possible score / can she be moved to adore our gods, nor can she be broken by terror.
SISSINUS: I shall spare her no longer. /
SOLDIERS: Rightly you ponder. /   235
SISSINUS: Seize her without mercy, / drag her with cru-elty, / and take her in dishonor to the brothel. /
HIRENA: They will not do it. /
SISSINUS: Who can prohibit it? /
HIRENA: He whose foresight rules the world. /   240
SISSINUS: I shall see . . . /
HIRENA: Sooner than you wish, it will be. /
SISSINUS: Soldiers, be not afraid / of what this blas-pheming girl has said. /
SOLDIERS: We are not afraid, / but eagerly follow what   245
you bade. /

SISSINUS: Who are those approaching? How similar they are to the men / to whom we gave Hirena just then. / They are the same. Why are you returning so fast? / Why so out of breath, I ask? /   250
SOLDIERS: You are the one for whom we look. /
SISSINUS: Where is she whom you just took? /
SOLDIERS: On the peak of the mountain.
SISSINUS: Which one?
SOLDIERS: The one close by.   255
SISSINUS: Oh you idiots, dull and blind. / You have com-pletely lost your mind! /
SOLDIERS: Why do you accuse us, / why do you abuse us, / why do you threaten us with menacing voice and face?
SISSINUS: May the gods destroy you!   260
SOLDIERS: What have we committed? What harm have we done? How have we transgressed against your orders?
SISSINUS: Have I not given the orders that you should take that rebel against the gods to a brothel?   265

SOLDIERS: Yes, so you did command, / and we were eager to fulfill your demand, / but two strangers intercepted us / saying that you sent them to us / to lead Hirena to the mountain's peak.

270 SISSINUS: That's new to me. /

SOLDIERS: We can see. /

SISSINUS: What were they like? /

SOLDIERS: Splendidly dressed and an awe-inspiring sight. /

275 SISSINUS: Did you follow? /

SOLDIERS: We did so. /

SISSINUS: What did they do? /

SOLDIERS: They placed themselves on Hirena's left and right, / and told us to be forthright / and not to hide

280 from you what happened.

SISSINUS: I see a sole recourse, / that I should mount my horse / and seek out those who so freely made sport with us.

SISSINUS: Hmm, I don't know what to do. I am bewil-

285 dered by the witchcraft of these Christians. I keep going around the mountain and keep finding this track / but I neither know how to proceed nor how to find my way back. /

SOLDIERS: We are all deluded by some intrigue; / we are afflicted with a great fatigue; / if you allow this 290 insane person to stay alive, / then neither you nor we shall survive. /

SISSINUS: Anyone among you, / I don't care which, string a bow, and shoot an arrow, and kill that witch! / 295

SOLDIERS: Rightly so. /

HIRENA: Wretched Sissinus, blush for shame, and proclaim your miserable defeat because without the help of weapons, you cannot overcome a tender little virgin as your foe. / 300

SISSINUS: Whatever the shame that may be mine, I will bear it more easily now because I know for certain that you will die.

HIRENA: This is the greatest joy I can conceive, / but for you this is a cause to grieve, / because you shall 305 be damned in Tartarus° for your cruelty, / while I shall receive the martyr's palm and the crown of virginity; / thus I will enter the heavenly bridal chamber of the Eternal King, to whom are all honor and glory in all eternity. / 310

306. **Tartarus:** Hell.

COMMENTARIES

Marla Carlson
READING HROTSVIT'S TORMENTED BODIES   *1998*

In this excerpt from an article that appeared in Theatre Journal, *Marla Carlson reminds us in this brief treatment of* Dulcitius *that the question of physical beauty can be interpreted in several different ways. In the world of Hrosvitha, the pagan emphasis on the physical body must always be seen in relation to the Christian emphasis on the soul. Carlson sees a gender connection between the two.*

In *The Martyrdom of the Holy Virgins Agape, Chionia, and Hirena,* beauty is a transparent sign of virtue. The play (also known as *Dulcitius*) begins with an ironic contrast: the pagan Emperor Diocletian manifests the rage and madness he attributes to the virgins, while they remain impassive. The girls' bodies function as foci of desire but are themselves free from desire. By contrast, the non-Christian men are represented as desiring subjects, which also means they are *subject* to their bodies. Diocletian wants to direct the disposal of the girls in marriage. Governor Dulcitius wants to use and possess them himself, and his desire produces his downfall. After he is blackened in the kitchen by making love to the pots and pans he mistakes for the virgins, Agape observes that now Dulcitius's body corresponds to his mind. On the other side of the balance, although the physical beauty of the girls is a visible manifestation of their virtue, pagan interpreters misread it as a sign of commodity exchange value, beginning with Diocletian's demand that the girls bring offerings to the Roman gods *in order* to be married well (the last thing they'd want!). But while the signs can be misread, Christian virtue cannot be *degraded*. When Dulcitius orders Agape, Chionia, and Hirena stripped for display, their clothes magically adhere to their bodies and cannot be removed. Hirena is threatened with sexual degradation in a brothel and retorts: "Lust deserves punishment, but forced compliance the crown; neither is one considered guilty, / unless the soul consents freely." All the same, God prevents her body from being defiled, and although Agape and Chionia are thrown into a fire and their souls depart at once, their physical bodies remain unharmed. Death is not a sign of pagan power but of God's grace, and at the final Resurrection, the martyr's beautiful body will again serve as the proper sign of the pure soul. In this play, the body — and in particular, its sexual properties — focuses the conflict between Christian female and pagan male.

Sue-Ellen Case (b. 1942)
RE-VIEWING HROTSVIT   *1983*

Sue-Ellen Case not only examines the plays of Hrosvitha but actually produced them. She discusses the feminist issues in the plays and explains the symmetry between Hrosvitha's six plays and the six plays of Terence. She demonstrates the significance of the plays of Hrosvitha for a modern audience.

The Plays

Hrotsvit wrote six plays in response to the six plays of Terence. Her project was to change the roles for women on the stage from negative ones to positive ones. However, critics have traditionally ignored this feminist aspect of her project and concentrated on the Christian context for it. A. Daniel Frankforter, in his article "Sexism and the Search for Thematic Structure of the Plays of Hroswitha of Gandersheim," characterizes the critics' misapprehension of Hrotsvit as stemming from "an asexual (male) perspective" which regards Hrotsvit as "a monk of generation" whose "sex is assumed to have little or no significance . . . her choice of women as chief characters is not seen as crucial to interpretation," and therefore "she emerges as a minor eulogist of ordinary Christian heroes."[1] Frankforter opposes this sexist perspective and finds that if Hrotsvit's project is seen as a revision of the roles for women "what emerges from the six plays . . . is a systematic exploration of each of the opportunities for female integrity possible in the social roles permitted women in Hroswitha's world."[2]

A brief description of roles of women in three of Terence's plays elicits some of the basic roles and attendant social issues Hrotsvit revised. *The Girl from Andros* never appears onstage, though her offstage screams during labor are used for comic development of the plot. Only two women appear onstage: a "sloppy drunken

---

[1]A. Daniel Frankforter, "Sexism and the Search for Thematic Structure of the Plays of Hroswitha of Gandersheim," *International Journal of Women's Studies*, vol. 2, no. 3, p. 225.
[2]Frankforter, p. 226.

slut" who is a midwife from Lesbos and a slave girl who is frightened and manipulated by her witty male counterpart, the slave Davus.[3] This Imperial Comedy centers on the relationship between father and son in which women are assets (ingenues from good families) or liabilities (mercenary courtesans) in the son's economy of obedience to his father and the patriarchal social order. *The Self Tormentor* uses the traditional double plot, centering on two father/son relationships. The double plot engineers male rivalry for the possession of women, completing the portrait of patriarchal economy. Luce Irigaray, a pioneer in feminist theories of morphology, described women's position within this economy: "woman is traditionally use-value for man, exchange value among men. Merchandise, then . . . she is never anything more than the scene of more or less rival exchange between two men."[4] In this play, an interesting piece of women's social history emerges to push the plot to its happy ending. One of the fathers had ordered his wife to kill their baby if it were a girl. The wife did not obey (an act perceived as cowardice and infidelity), and now the girl can be used as marriage material to solve the rivalry between the two sons and reconcile them both with their father's wishes.

The Eunuch was Terence's most popular play in Rome. The central issue in the play is one central to several plays by Hrotsvit — rape. A young man sees a girl cross the marketplace (an apt setting) and falls in love with her because of her beauty. In order to gain entrance to her house, he disguises himself as a eunuch and rapes her. The girl's response is never staged, but it is reported that she sits in torn garments and weeps. Nevertheless, because of his love for her, the young man's crime is forgiven, and he gains the girl in marriage. From these three plays, one can summarize the Classical inheritance Hrotsvit received for women on the stage: they are relatively invisible, their responses are rarely dramatized and most often reported by men, they are manipulated as use value among men in the plot situation, and their best possible ending is marriage — with or without consent.

The most striking difference between the plays of Hrotsvit and those of Terence is that in her plays women are at the center of the action and it is their response to male aggression which determines the development of the plot. Hrotsvit places her heroines in the context of objectification, use, and violence but offers them an alternative. The play *Dulcitius* opens with three young women before the Emperor Diocletian and his soldiers. Diocletian declares the patriarchal edict: "The pure and famous race to which you belong and your own rare beauty make it fitting that you should be wedded to the highest in the court." Beauty and high station are the trap of objectification. In spite of the rank and military power which confronts these young girls, they resist, answering that they have vowed to live in chastity. Angered, the emperor sends them to prison and to the charge of Governor Dulcitius. Dulcitius wants them because of their beauty, but the guards tell him they will resist seduction. He responds "Then I shall woo in another fashion — with torture!" The latent relationship in such a patriarchal society between desire and dominance becomes literal. The stage setting reveals the passive position of the women as prisoners and sets up the alliance between desire and privilege in the role of the Governor. However, the internal power of the women's wishes overcomes

---

[3]Constance Carrier and Douglass Parker, *The Complete Comedies of Terence* (New Brunswick: Rutgers University Press, 1974), p. 21.

[4]Luce Irigaray, "This Sex Which Is Not One," in *New French Feminisms* (New York: Schocken Books, 1981), p. 105.

this material one. A spell overcomes Dulcitius as he enters to rape them, and he makes love to pots and pans, thinking they are the women. Hrotsvit has given a stage metaphor to the objectification of women, as objects are substituted for women, particularly objects associated with their domestic labor. The women watch Dulcitius and giggle. In their laughter and his foolishness as a result of their spell-binding power, the women dominate the rapist. The male dramatic perspective has been reversed.

The play *Callimachus* also centers on rape. In the opening scenes, Callimachus tells Drusiana he loves her because of her beauty. Her response is one of incomprehension: "My beauty? What is my beauty to you?" From a woman's point of view, this is a deep, provocative question, but Callimachus answers it in terms of patriarchal economy: "But little now . . . I hope it might be much before long." Drusiana persists in her refusal, telling Callimachus that even though she is married, she has taken the vow of chastity. He responds that he will use all of his skill and strength to trap her — the motor of Classical plots. Instead, Drusiana asks Christ to help her to die, so she may escape her dilemma. Christ complies with her wish immediately. Women have the power to petition and to succeed. Undaunted by her death, Callimachus enters her tomb to rape the corpse. Hrotsvit has dramatized the essence of the passive victim and of the objectification of patriarchal desire. Unlike Terence, who ultimately resolves it as natural, she has staged it as perverse. Callimachus is killed by a heavenly serpent before he can complete the act (nature is on the side of the heroine) and is later resurrected (along with Drusiana) and converted to her world view. In other words, the plot moves in her direction and is moved by her resolve.

The alternative to patriarchal possession is characterized by Hrotsvit as the vow of chastity. Later periods have regarded this vow as ultimate repression rather than as a declaration of independence. Yet Hrotsvit's solution answers a question posed by Irigaray "What if the goods refuse to go to market? What if they maintained among themselves another kind of trade?"[5] Chastity was the choice available to women to remain outside the patriarchal order of desire. In the case of a nun such as Hrotsvit, the removal into a women's community (perhaps the first separatist collectives) brought the opportunity to be educated and to be an educator. Hrotsvit was what Frankforter calls a "career nun."[6] Given her collective context, Hrotsvit may have been the first woman playwright to write for a community of women. Thus, in writing from a woman's point of view for women to watch, she is involved in an entirely new dramatic dynamic. Yet her identity as a nun has traditionally been cited as the cause of elements of suppression rather than liberation in her works. The patriarchal bias of Freudian analysis perceived her profession as oppression. Rosamond Gilder formulated the case simply: "Hrotsvit gives expression to a vein of sadism which is also associated with certain acts of repression." Gilder elaborates on the psychological mechanism: "Hrotsvit obtained a certain release for her emotional suppressions by elaborating these pictures of carnal dangers and the pitfalls of the flesh."[7] Such a Freudian analysis assigns the responsibility for the victimization of women in the plays to Hrotsvit's repressed sexuality and its resultant fantasies rather than to the patriarchal society in which her characters

[5]Irigaray, p. 110.
[6]Frankforter, p. 226.
[7]Rosamond Gilder, *Enter the Actress* (London: Harrap and Co., 1931), pp. 34–35.

were situated. Perhaps the easiest refutation of such an assertion lies in the fact that Hrotsvit did not invent her own plots. Instead, she worked from materials which were considered historical in her time. For example, the martyrdom and rape of the young women in *Dulcitius* was taken from *The Acts of Christian Martyrs*. The story was recorded in the fourth century, based on historical edicts of Diocletian and records of the trial and punishment of the women. Hrotsvit's project was to dramatize the violence against women recorded in these histories and was in no way to record her own fantasies.

Feminine Morphology and Paphnutius

Since this essay is meant to be merely an exploration of the application of feminist critical technique to the work and role of Hrotsvit, this section will illustrate the application of only one feminist theory of form to a single play — *Paphnutius*. The theory is derived from essays by Irigaray, Hélène Cixous (whose work "The Laugh of the Medusa" is now a classic in feminist studies), and Jane Gallop's book on feminism and psychoanalysis.[8] The source of their ideas lies in a feminist reading of the works of Derrida, Lacan, and Foucault. The basic assumption of these authors is that the dominant cultural form is phallocentrism. This means two things: that the dominant form is organized around a concept of centrality and that the phallus is at the center of all dominant morphology. Because of its centric location, the phallus determines a form based upon phallic privilege, phallic exhibition, and a phallic desire to possess. Therefore, the phallocentric form is both clear (exhibited, as in linear, logical development) and closed (self-possessed — as in beginning, middle, and end).

The alternative form found in women's work is described as contiguous. Irigaray describes it as a "nearness," a form "constantly in the process of weaving itself . . . embracing words and yet casting them off," concerned not with clarity, but with what is "touched upon" (p. 103). Cixous calls it "working the in-between" (p. 254), while Gallop describes it as "the register of touching, nearness, presence, immediacy, contact" (p. 30). It can be elliptical rather than illustrative, fragmentary rather than whole, ambiguous rather than clear, and interrupted rather than complete. The stage society within such a form could never be the plain patriarchy of Terence, with its clear line of power from father to son. Rather, it is a complex society of subtle dependencies which manifest themselves in resonances of one another's changes.

This sense of contiguity is the organizing principle, as well as the subject of the opening scene of the play *Paphnutius*. The play opens on the sadness of Father Paphnutius. When asked by his disciples about its cause, he launches into a medieval discourse on the world as harmonic, proceeding from an explanation of the quadrivium, through a Boethian discussion of music to the organizing principle of concord and discord. The organization of all things is contiguous. Paphnutius describes its residence in "not only, as I have told you, in the combination of body and soul, and in the utterance of the voice, now high, now low, but even in the pulsation of the veins and in the proportion of our members." As the scene proceeds, the disciples ask Paphnutius about his sadness. He replies that it is because of the

---

[8]Hélène Cixous, "The Laugh of the Medusa," in Irigaray, *New French Feminisms;* and Jane Gallop, *The Daughter's Seduction: Feminism and Psychoanalysis* (Ithaca: Cornell University Press, 1982).

whore Thais. The rest of the play is concerned with his work to change her relationship to her own sexuality, her residency in a convent in which she practices self-mortification, and Paphnutius's concluding vision of her transfiguration.

The "contempt with which the learned musical Prologue was regarded for over half a century" originated in an assessment of the Scholastic discourse as mediocre medieval philosophy.[9] The "modern disparagement of the Prologue" rests on the perception that it does not work in the overall construction of the drama.[10] There seems to be no connection between the ideas of music and nature, and the sadness in Paphnutius caused by the whore Thais. The ideas in the prologue seem to be abandoned as the story of Thais unfolds. Yet if one replaces the phallocentric model of form with one of contiguity, the play seems to be tightly constructed. Hrotsvit has begun her play with an exposition of the contiguous dependency among parts of the world. A monk in a distant monastery, who has never seen the whore Thais, can find no peace until the concord between her understanding and her sexuality is restored. The inner dynamics of Thais's personality "touches upon" the surrounding world in which she lives. Paphnutius can find no peace until he has removed this woman from the colonized use of her body in the city to her own repossession of it within a convent. Hrotsvit has merely used the most basic ideas in Scholastic discourse to set up her dramatic situation — to provide the intellectual environment for the personal story. Hrotsvit makes no linear transition from the opening scene to the story because her world is contiguous. Her short scenes suggest rather than explicate, "touch upon" each other rather than develop. In this play, she has replaced the objectified, patriarchal intercourse between men and women which she dramatizes in her Roman settings, with the contiguous resonances of sexual concord which exist between Thais and Paphnutius. When the play is approached from a feminist, rather than phallocentric model of form, it seems a masterpiece rather than a mediocre medieval morality story.

Performance

Hrotsvit's plays were not collected for circulation until the sixteenth century. They were not translated into modern Romance languages until the mid-nineteenth century and not into English until the twentieth century. The relative unavailability of her texts made production before the twentieth century improbable. Yet in the twentieth century, it is important to note that productions of her plays were often by women or in times in which women's issues were important to the theater world. A good example of the latter condition is the production history of Hrotsvit's work in London. The first major production of *Paphnutius* was directed by Edith Craig (daughter of Ellen Terry and sister of Gordon) in London in 1914. The production was by the Pioneer Players, a group founded and directed by Edith Craig, with Ellen Terry playing the role of the abbess in the convent in which Thais was confined. The translation was done by Christopher St. John, a *nom de plume* (indicative practice) for Christabel Marshall. Marshall had recently adapted the suffragette play *How the Vote Was Won* in 1909 and the play *The First Actress* in 1911 — an indication that her interest in the text of Hrotsvit probably came from an interest in a woman playwright. Indeed, there was a movement in London the-

---

[9]David Chamberlain, "Musical Learning and Dramatic Action in Hrotsvit's *Pafnutius*," *Studies in Philology*. Fall 1980, p. 319.
[10]Ibid.

ater at that time to be concerned with women's issues — particularly the vote. In 1908, actresses had formed a franchise league to support the suffrage movement, which produced plays about the vote and satires of male chauvinism.[11] The English women did not get the vote until 1928, and the decade of the 1920s was filled with the issue. Within this context, the 1920 production of *Callimachus* at the Art Theatre, the 1924 production of *Paphnutius* at the Maddermarket Theatre, the founding of the Roswitha club in 1926, the new translations by St. John, Waley and Tillyard during the decade, and the cessation of Hrotsvit productions after that decade can be easily understood.

My production of her works in 1982 came as a result of teaching a class on women and theater and becoming familiar with all of the new productions and critical studies evolving from the works of women playwrights and women's theater groups. The first problem in producing Hrotsvit is the obscurity of her name and play titles. The second is the short playing time of her texts. I decided to solve both problems by directing three plays in one evening and creating a title which might attract the Seattle women's community by identifying the plays according to the social roles of their three heroines: "The Virgin (*Dulcitius*), The Whore (*Paphnutius*), and The Desperate One" (*Callimachus*). My choice of production concept was determined by my goal of producing the first woman playwright. In order to emphasize her historical role, I decided to direct the play as a period piece. This introduces another set of difficulties, since the theater has no tradition of staging plays from the early Middle Ages and hence no concept of costumes, sets, or playing style. We took the costumes from mosaics and illuminations around the period and decided on flats, imitating the two-dimensional painting style of the time, with edifices found in Ottonian manuscript illuminations. The playing style was a combination of a classical sense of formal blocking and gestures, combined with intense, personal purpose. A projection screen rose from the back of a steeply raked stage and a processional ramp ran from the front of the stage through the center of the audience. This combination created the feeling of the space in a cathedral. The elevated ramp gave the Saints elevation and dominance. Between the plays, early medieval music was performed. All this allowed a style to emerge which was both an imitation of classical formality and liturgical ceremony.

The context of Christianity and its trappings often created an audience response which was marked in its silent reverence. People seemed afraid to wiggle or whisper. At other times, this same sense turned into an active irreverence, manifested by laughter and something close to jeering. Contemporary staging of a Christian play is complicated to understand. Shakespeare productions have prepared an audience for the Elizabethan world of superstition, and Greek plays have prepared them for the world of pagan mythology, but the relative absence of medieval productions leaves the world of medieval Christianity to be understood by personal opinions about Christianity rather than the sense of it as a historical world view. Thus, for some feminists, the Christianity was seen as offensive and patriarchal. Particularly in these times of the Moral Majority, Hrotsvit's plays seemed to them to be written by an "Uncle Tom" trapped by male values. Many audience members laughed hysterically at the miracles, the voice of God, and the resurrections — seeing them not as stage conventions but as bygone beliefs. Christopher St. John records a similar

[11]Michelene Wandor, *Understudies: Theatre and Sexual Politics* (London: Eyre Methuen, 1981), p. 10.

reaction to the plays in their early London productions, citing a scene in *Callimachus* "Drusiana's prayer that she might die rather than yield to Callimachus was greeted with shouts of laughter" (p. 159). I think the only solution to this problem lies not in the staging concept of such scenes, but in establishing a familiarity with the playwright and her conventions through productions and an acquaintance with her texts in theater history and criticism classes.

For the actors, this problem translates into ways for them to individually understand the dilemma of their characters. The women identified instances of martyrdom and conviction which meant something to them. These ranged from pictures of concentration camp women, which some of the Jewish women brought to rehearsal, to stories of guerrillas in El Salvador or instances of rape victims who resisted. They did not focus so much on religious experiences, as on sexual ones, political ones, or psychological approaches to their own fears and strengths. The men in the cast resisted identifying with the male aggression and cruelty portrayed by many of the characters. When asked to torment one of the young virgins in a flirtatious manner, they insisted they didn't know how. This identification came slowly, through memories of teasing girls in grade school, to early experiences of seduction and sexual aggression. For the men playing Saints, the problem was in giving focus to the women onstage and learning how to respond to the power of the women in a realistic fashion. This involved investigating their own fears of women's power.

For the actors, one of the most difficult aspects of Hrotsvit's work was her contiguous sense of form and her compressed, almost fragmentary sense of a scene. Characters have extremely short speeches of only one or two sentences, compressed into scenes of relatively scant dialogue and often no physical action. Fortunately, recent productions of plays by such authors as Beckett and Kroetz provided the actors with some experience in this style. The method which seemed most useful was to play the entire scene by improvising a long, literal development of its situation and then compress it moment by moment until it played in Hrotsvit's form. One fortunate consequence of this playing style is that the concentration and deliberation required by the actor, made him or her oblivious to the sometimes raucous audience response.

Finally, the response of the critics illustrated an interesting aspect of viewing the plays. Almost all announcements and reviews of the plays included the words "rape" and "necrophilia" in their titles. One critic pointed out that these plays should make contemporary audiences feel less defensive about violence on TV, since it was already popular in the early Middle Ages. The titles are surprising, since neither the rapes nor the necrophilia ever occur. They are the intentions of the male characters but are foiled by heavenly intervention. The preoccupation by critics with these intentions might suggest that they were watching the male characters more than the females, even though it was not the focus of the text nor of the blocking. In fact, given the staging of resurrections and other such miracles, these dramatic intentions seemed minor parts of the staging. Yet they were the focus of critical reviews. This critical reception points out the necessity for a re-viewing of Hrotsvit from a feminist point of view and underlines the sense that her position and its implications in the world of theater is still long overdue.

EVERYMAN

This late medieval play may have origins in northern Europe. A Flemish play, *Elckerlijk* ("Everyman"), dates from c. 1495, and the question of whether the English *Everyman* was translated from it or whether it is a translation of *Everyman* has not been settled. Both plays may have had a common origin in an unknown play. The English *Everyman* was produced frequently in the early years of the sixteenth century. Its drama was largely theological; its purpose, to reform the audience. One indication that entertainment was not the primary goal of this morality play is its lack of the comic moments found in other plays, such as *The Second Shepherds' Play*.

The author of the play may have been a priest. This assumption has long been common because the play has much theological content and offers a moral message of the kind one might expect to hear from the pulpit. The theme of the play is fundamental: the inevitability of death. And for that reason, in part, the play continues to have a universal appeal. Modern productions may not give the audience a suitable medieval chill, but the message of the play is still relevant for everyone.

The medieval reliance on allegory is apparent in the naming of the characters in *Everyman*: Death, Kindred, Cousin, Goods, Knowledge, Strength, Beauty, and Everyman himself. Each character does not just stand for a specific quality; he or she *is* that quality. The allegorical way of thinking derived from the medieval faith that everything in the world had a moral meaning. Morality plays depended on this belief and always articulated setting, characters, and circumstances in terms of their moral value. This was in keeping with the medieval belief that the soul was always in jeopardy and that life was a test of one's moral condition. When Everyman meets a character, the most important information about his or her moral value is communicated instantly in the name of the character. Characters in allegorical plays also reveal themselves through their costumes and props. The character Good Deeds is simply good deeds: there is no need for psychological development because the medieval audience had a full understanding of what good deeds meant and how Good Deeds as a character would behave.

The structure of *Everyman* resembles a journey. Everyman undertakes to see who among all his acquaintances will accompany him on his most important trip: to the grave and the judgment of God Almighty. Seeing life as a journey — or as part of a journey — was especially natural for the medieval mind, which had as models the popular and costly religious pilgrimages to holy shrines and to the Holy Land itself. If life on earth is only part of the journey of the soul, then the morality play helps to put it into clear perspective. This life is not, the play tells us, the most important part of the soul's existence.

At its core, *Everyman* has a profound commercial metaphor: Everyman is called to square accounts with God. The metaphor of accounting appears early in the play, when Everyman talks about his accounts and reckonings as if they appeared in a book that should go with him to heaven. His life will be examined, and if he is found wanting, he will go into the fires of hell. If he has lived profitably from a moral viewpoint, he will enjoy life everlasting. The language of the play is heavily loaded with accounting metaphors that identify it as the product of a society quite unlike that of the Greeks or the Romans. Such metaphors suggest that *Everyman* directs its message to middle-class merchants for whom accounting was a significant concept.

Like many sermons, *Everyman* imparts a lesson that its auditors were expected to heed. Hence the key points of the play are repeated at the end by the Doctor. For moderns, didactic plays are sometimes tedious. For the medieval mind, they represented delightful ways of learning important messages.

Everyman in Performance

Very little is known about early productions of *Everyman*. It was produced in Holland and England for seventy-five years beginning in the mid-fifteenth century. The play disappeared from the stage for centuries, finally resurfacing in 1901 in a production under the auspices of the Elizabethan Stage Society in London, directed by William Poel. Poel designed the costumes and set, directed, and played at first the part of Death, and then when he got older, the part of God. Poel produced *Everyman* many times over the next fifteen years.

The 1901 production was followed by a 1902 revival in New York starring Edith Wynne Matthison and produced by Ben Greet, marking the play's first American performance. Greet continued producing *Everyman* for the next thirty-five years in both England and America.

After seeing Poel's production, Max Reinhardt, the legendary German director, decided to produce *Everyman* in Germany. The Austrian poet and playwright Hugo von Hofmannsthal wrote a new German adaptation, *Jedermann,* for Reinhardt. The adaptation features Everyman as a wealthy burgher, and central to the play is an ornate banquet scene in which Death appears. Hofmannsthal's German adaptation marked a shift in emphasis from the simpler and more personal English *Everyman* to the spectacular *Jedermann* that concentrates on a wealthy man's lustful life and his attempts to get into heaven. *Jedermann* was first produced in Berlin on December 1, 1911. In 1913 Reinhardt produced the play in Salzburg, Austria, at the Salzburg Cathedral square, and except for the years of World War II, Reinhardt's version of *Jedermann* has been performed regularly at the annual Salzburg Festival. The critic Brooks Atkinson found Reinhardt's production "nothing short of miraculous." In a review of Reinhardt's 1927 production, the critic Gilbert Gabriel found *Jedermann,* "crammed with splendors for the eye, largesse of bells and uplifting voices for the ear." A reviewer at the 1936 Salzburg Festival production of *Jedermann* wrote that the play "has everything but simplicity."

The popularity of the Reinhardt productions of *Jedermann* paved the way for numerous productions of *Everyman* over the years. In 1936, during the Great Depression in the United States, the WPA (Works Progress Administration) held special Sunday church performances of *Everyman*. Other notable productions include a 1941 *Everyman* in New York performed by refugee actors from Europe, and a 1955 tour with college casts in New England and California. In 1922 a new English adaptation of the German *Jedermann* by Sir

John Martin-Harvey was presented at Stratford-on-Avon. This production toured to London and New York in 1923. In 1936 Sir John's adaptation was performed at the Hollywood Bowl in California with Peggy Wood and Lionel Braham. Long popular with college and community groups, the play continues to be performed around the world.

Anonymous

EVERYMAN   *c. 1495*

EDITED BY A. C. CAWLEY

Characters

GOD	KNOWLEDGE
MESSENGER	CONFESSION
DEATH	BEAUTY
EVERYMAN	STRENGTH
FELLOWSHIP	DISCRETION
KINDRED	FIVE WITS
COUSIN	ANGEL
GOODS	DOCTOR
GOOD DEEDS	

Here beginneth a treatise how the high Father of Heaven sendeth Death to summon every creature to come and give account of their lives in this world, and is in manner of a moral play.

MESSENGER: I pray you all give your audience,
 And hear this matter with reverence,
 By figure° a moral play:
 The *Summoning of Everyman* called it is,
5 That of our lives and ending shows
 How transitory we be all day.°
 This matter is wondrous precious,
 But the intent of it is more gracious,
 And sweet to bear away.
10 The story saith: Man, in the beginning
 Look well, and take good heed to the ending,
 Be you never so gay!
 Ye think sin in the beginning full sweet,
 Which in the end causeth the soul to weep,
15 When the body lieth in clay.
 Here shall you see how Fellowship and Jollity,
 Both Strength, Pleasure, and Beauty,
 Will fade from thee as flower in May;
 For ye shall hear how our Heaven King
20 Calleth Everyman to a general reckoning:
 Give audience, and hear what he doth say.

                                                              (*Exit.*)

(*God speaketh.*)

GOD: I perceive, here in my majesty,
 How that all creatures be to me unkind,°
 Living without dread in worldly prosperity:
 Of ghostly sight° the people be so blind,   25
 Drowned in sin, they know me not for their God;
 In worldly riches is all their mind,
 They fear not my righteousness, the sharp rod.
 My law that I showed, when I for them died,
 They forget clean, and shedding of my blood red;   30
 I hanged between two, it cannot be denied;
 To get them life I suffered to be dead;
 I healed their feet, with thorns hurt was my head.
 I could do no more than I did, truly;
 And now I see the people do clean forsake me: 35
 They use the seven deadly sins damnable,
 As pride, covetise, wrath, and lechery
 Now in the world be made commendable;
 And thus they leave of angels the heavenly
   company.
 Every man liveth so after his own pleasure,   40
 And yet of their life they be nothing sure:
 I see the more that I them forbear
 The worse they be from year to year.
 All that liveth appaireth° fast;
 Therefore I will, in all the haste,   45
 Have a reckoning of every man's person;
 For, and° I leave the people thus alone
 In their life and wicked tempests,
 Verily they will become much worse than beasts;
 For now one would by envy another up eat;   50
 Charity they do all clean forget.
 I hoped well that every man
 In my glory should make his mansion,
 And thereto I had them all elect;
 But now I see, like traitors deject,°   55

---

3. By figure: In form.   **6. all day:** Always.

23. unkind: Ungrateful.   **25. ghostly sight:** Spiritual vision.
44. appaireth: Degenerates.   **47. and:** If.   **55. deject:** Abject.

They thank me not for the pleasure that I to them
    meant,
Nor yet for their being that I them have lent.
I proffered the people great multitude of mercy,
And few there be that asketh it heartily.
60 They be so cumbered with worldly riches
That needs on them I must do justice,
On every man living without fear.
Where art thou, Death, thou mighty messenger?

(Enter Death.)

DEATH: Almighty God, I am here at your will,
65   Your commandment to fulfill.
GOD: Go thou to Everyman,
    And show him, in my name,
    A pilgrimage he must on him take,
    Which he in no wise may escape;
70   And that he bring with him a sure reckoning
    Without delay or any tarrying.
              (God withdraws.)
DEATH: Lord, I will in the world go run overall,
    And cruelly outsearch both great and small;
    Every man will I beset that liveth beastly
75   Out of God's laws, and dreadeth not folly.
    He that loveth riches I will strike with my dart,
    His sight to blind, and from heaven to depart° —
    Except that alms be his good friend —
    In hell for to dwell, world without end.
80   Lo, yonder I see Everyman walking.
    Full little he thinketh on my coming;
    His mind is on fleshly lusts and his treasure,
    And great pain it shall cause him to endure
    Before the Lord, Heaven King.

(Enter Everyman.)

85 Everyman, stand still! Whither art thou going
    Thus gaily? Hast thou thy Maker forget?
EVERYMAN: Why askest thou?
    Wouldest thou wit?°
DEATH: Yea, sir; I will show you:
90   In great haste I am sent to thee
    From God out of his majesty.
EVERYMAN: What, sent to me?
DEATH: Yea, certainly.
    Though thou have forget him here,
95   He thinketh on thee in the heavenly sphere,
    As, ere we depart, thou shalt know.
EVERYMAN: What desireth God of me?
DEATH: That shall I show thee:
    A reckoning he will needs have
100   Without any longer respite.
EVERYMAN: To give a reckoning longer leisure I crave;
    This blind matter troubleth my wit.
DEATH: On thee thou must take a long journey;
    Therefore thy book of count° with thee thou
        bring,

For turn° again thou cannot by no way.   105
And look thou be sure of thy reckoning,
For before God thou shalt answer, and show
Thy many bad deeds, and good but a few;
How thou hast spent thy life, and in what wise,
Before the chief Lord of paradise.   110
Have ado that we were in that way,°
For, wit thou well, thou shalt make none attorney.°
EVERYMAN: Full unready I am such reckoning to give.
    I know thee not. What messenger art thou?
DEATH: I am Death, that no man dreadeth,°   115
    For every man I rest,° and no man spareth;
    For it is God's commandment
    That all to me should be obedient.
EVERYMAN: O Death, thou comest when I had thee
    least in mind!
    In thy power it lieth me to save;   120
    Yet of my good° will I give thee, if thou will be kind:
    Yea, a thousand pound shalt thou have,
    And defer this matter till another day.
DEATH: Everyman, it may not be, by no way.
    I set not by gold, silver, nor riches,   125
    Ne by pope, emperor, king, duke, ne princes;
    For, and I would receive gifts great,
    All the world I might get;
    But my custom is clean contrary.
    I give thee no respite. Come hence, and not tarry.   130
EVERYMAN: Alas, shall I have no longer respite?
    I may say Death giveth no warning!
    To think on thee, it maketh my heart sick,
    For all unready is my book of reckoning.
    But twelve year and I might have abiding,°   135
    My counting-book I would make so clear
    That my reckoning I should not need to fear.
    Wherefore, Death, I pray thee, for God's mercy,
    Spare me till I be provided of remedy.
DEATH: Thee availeth not to cry, weep, and pray;   140
    But haste thee lightly that thou were gone that
      journey,°
    And prove thy friends if thou can;
    For, wit thou well, the tide abideth no man,
    And in the world each living creature
    For Adam's sin must die of nature.°   145
EVERYMAN: Death, if I should this pilgrimage take,
    And my reckoning surely make,
    Show me, for saint charity,°
    Should I not come again shortly?
DEATH: No, Everyman; and thou be once there,   150
    Thou mayst never more come here,
    Trust me verily.

---

105. turn: Return.   111. Have ado . . . that way: Let us see about making that journey.   112. none attorney: No one [your] advocate.   115. no man dreadeth: Fears no man.   116. rest: Arrest.   121. good: Goods.   135. But twelve year . . . abiding: If I could stay for just twelve more years.   141. But haste thee . . . that journey: But set off quickly on your journey.   145. of nature: In the course of nature.   148. for saint charity: In the name of holy charity.

---

77. depart: Separate.   88. wit: Know.   104. count: Account.

EVERYMAN: O gracious God in the high seat celestial,
    Have mercy on me in this most need!
155   Shall I have no company from this vale terrestrial
    Of mine acquaintance, that way me to lead?
DEATH: Yea, if any be so hardy
    That would go with thee and bear thee company.
    Hie thee that thou were gone to God's magnificence,
160   Thy reckoning to give before his presence.
    What, weenest° thou thy life is given thee,
    And thy worldly goods also?
EVERYMAN: I had wend° so, verily.
DEATH: Nay, nay; it was but lent thee;
165   For as soon as thou art go,
    Another a while shall have it, and then go therefro,
    Even as thou has done.
    Everyman, thou art mad! Thou hast thy wits five,
    And here on earth will not amend thy life;
170   For suddenly I do come.
EVERYMAN: O wretched caitiff,° whither shall I flee,
    That I might scape this endless sorrow?
    Now, gentle Death, spare me till to-morrow,
    That I may amend me
175   With good advisement.
DEATH: Nay, thereto I will not consent,
    Nor no man will I respite;
    But to the heart suddenly I shall smite
    Without any advisement.
180   And now out of thy sight I will me hie;
    See thou make thee ready shortly,
    For thou mayst say this is the day
    That no man living may scape away.

                              (*Exit Death.*)
EVERYMAN: Alas, I may well weep with sighs deep!
185   Now have I no manner of company
    To help me in my journey, and me to keep;
    And also my writing is full unready,
    How shall I do now for to excuse me?
    I would to God I had never be get!°
190   To my soul a full great profit it had be;
    For now I fear pains huge and great.
    The time passeth. Lord, help, that all wrought!
    For though I mourn it availeth nought.
    The day passeth, and is almost ago;°
195   I wot not well what for to do.
    To whom were I best my complaint to make?
    What and I to Fellowship thereof spake,
    And showed him of this sudden chance?
    For in him is all mine affiance;°
200   We have in the world so many a day
    Be good friends in sport and play.
    I see him yonder, certainly.
    I trust that he will bear me company;
    Therefore to him will I speak to ease my sorrow.
205   Well met, good Fellowship, and good morrow!

---

161. weenest: Suppose. 163. wend: Supposed. 171. caitiff:
Captive. 189. be get: Been born. 194. ago: Gone. 199. af-
fiance: Trust.

(*Fellowship speaketh.*)

FELLOWSHIP: Everyman, good morrow, by this day!
    Sir, why lookest thou so piteously?
    If any thing be amiss, I pray thee me say,
    That I may help to remedy.
EVERYMAN: Yea, good Fellowship, yea;   210
    I am in great jeopardy.
FELLOWSHIP: My true friend, show to me your mind;
    I will not forsake thee to my life's end,
    In the way of good company.
EVERYMAN: That was well spoken, and lovingly.   215
FELLOWSHIP: Sir, I must needs know your heaviness;°
    I have pity to see you in any distress.
    If any have you wronged, ye shall revenged be,
    Though I on the ground be slain for thee —
    Though that I know before that I should die.   220
EVERYMAN: Verily, Fellowship, gramercy.°
FELLOWSHIP: Tush! by thy thanks I set not a straw.
    Show me your grief, and say no more.
EVERYMAN: If I my heart should to you break,°
    And then you to turn your mind from me,   225
    And would not me comfort when ye hear me speak,
    Then should I ten times sorrier be.
FELLOWSHIP: Sir, I say as I will do indeed.
EVERYMAN: Then be you a good friend at need:
    I have found you true herebefore.   230
FELLOWSHIP: And so ye shall evermore;
    For, in faith, and thou go to hell,
    I will not forsake thee by the way.
EVERYMAN: Ye speak like a good friend; I believe you
    well.
    I shall deserve° it, and I may.   235
FELLOWSHIP: I speak of no deserving, by this day!
    For he that will say, and nothing do,
    Is not worthy with good company to go;
    Therefore show me the grief of your mind,
    As to your friend most loving and kind.   240
EVERYMAN: I shall show you how it is:
    Commanded I am to go a journey,
    A long way, hard and dangerous,
    And give a strait count, without delay,
    Before the high Judge, Adonai.°   245
    Wherefore, I pray you, bear me company,
    As ye have promised, in this journey.
FELLOWSHIP: That is matter indeed.° Promise is duty;
    But, and I should take such a voyage on me,
    I know it well, it should be to my pain;   250
    Also it maketh me afeard, certain.
    But let us take counsel here as well as we can,
    For your words would fear a strong man.
EVERYMAN: Why, ye said if I had need
    Ye would me never forsake, quick ne dead,   255
    Though it were to hell, truly.

---

216. heaviness: Sorrow. 221. gramercy: Thanks. 224. break:
Open. 235. deserve: Repay. 245. Adonai: Hebrew name for
God. 248. That is matter indeed: That is a good reason
indeed [for asking me].

FELLOWSHIP: So I said, certainly,
    But such pleasures be set aside, the sooth to say;
    And also, if we took such a journey,
260   When should we come again?
EVERYMAN: Nay, never again, till the day of doom.
FELLOWSHIP: In faith, then will not I come there!
    Who hath you these tidings brought?
EVERYMAN: Indeed, Death was with me here.
265 FELLOWSHIP: Now, by God that all hath bought,°
    If Death were the messenger,
    For no man that is living to-day
    I will not go that loath journey —
    Not for the father that begat me!
270 EVERYMAN: Ye promised otherwise, pardie.°
FELLOWSHIP: I wot well I said so, truly;
    And yet if thou wilt eat, and drink, and make good
      cheer,
    Or haunt to women the lusty company,°
    I would not forsake you while the day is clear,°
275   Trust me verily.
EVERYMAN: Yea, thereto ye would be ready!
    To go to mirth, solace, and play,
    Your mind will sooner apply,
    Than to bear me company in my long journey.
280 FELLOWSHIP: Now, in good faith, I will not that way.
    But and thou will murder, or any man kill,
    In that I will help thee with a good will.
EVERYMAN: O, that is a simple advice indeed.
    Gentle fellow, help me in my necessity!
285   We have loved long, and now I need;
    And now, gentle Fellowship, remember me.
FELLOWSHIP: Whether ye have loved me or no,
    By Saint John, I will not with thee go.
EVERYMAN: Yet, I pray thee, take the labor, and do so
      much for me
290   To bring me forward, for saint charity,
    And comfort me till I come without the town.
FELLOWSHIP: Nay, and thou would give me a new gown,
    I will not a foot with thee go;
    But, and thou had tarried, I would not have left
      thee so.
295   And as now God speed thee in thy journey,
    For from thee I will depart as fast as I may.
EVERYMAN: Whither away, Fellowship? Will thou
      forsake me?
FELLOWSHIP: Yea, by my fay!° To God I betake° thee.
EVERYMAN: Farewell, good Fellowship; for thee my
      heart is sore.
300   Adieu for ever! I shall see thee no more.
FELLOWSHIP: In faith, Everyman, farewell now at the
      ending;
    For you I will remember that parting is mourning.
                        (*Exit Fellowship.*)

EVERYMAN: Alack! shall we thus depart° indeed —
    Ah, Lady, help! — without any more comfort?
    Lo, Fellowship forsaketh me in my most need.   305
    For help in this world whither shall I resort?
    Fellowship herebefore with me would merry make,
    And now little sorrow for me doth he take.
    It is said, "In prosperity men friends may find,
    Which in adversity be full unkind."   310
    Now whither for succor shall I flee,
    Sith° that Fellowship hath forsaken me?
    To my kinsmen I will, truly,
    Praying them to help me in my necessity;
    I believe that they will do so,   315
    For kind will creep where it may not go.°
    I will go say,° for yonder I see them.
    Where be ye now, my friends and kinsmen?

(*Enter Kindred and Cousin.*)

KINDRED: Here be we now at your commandment.
    Cousin, I pray you show us your intent   320
    In any wise, and do not spare.
COUSIN: Yea, Everyman, and to us declare
    If ye be disposed to go anywhither;
    For, wit you well, we will live and die together.
KINDRED: In wealth and woe we will with you hold,   325
    For over his kin a man may be bold.°
EVERYMAN: Gramercy, my friends and kinsmen kind.
    Now shall I show you the grief of my mind:
    I was commanded by a messenger,
    That is a high king's chief officer;   330
    He bade me go a pilgrimage, to my pain,
    And I know well I shall never come again;
    Also I must give a reckoning strait,
    For I have a great enemy° that hath me in wait,°
    Which intendeth me for to hinder.   335
KINDRED: What account is that which ye must render?
    That would I know.
EVERYMAN: Of all my works I must show
    How I have lived and my days spent;
    Also of ill deeds that I have used   340
    In my time, sith life was me lent;
    And of all virtues that I have refused.
    Therefore, I pray you, go thither with me
    To help to make mine account, for saint charity.
COUSIN: What, to go thither? Is that the matter?   345
    Nay, Everyman, I had liefer fast bread and water°
    All this five year and more.
EVERYMAN: Alas, that ever I was bore!
    For now shall I never be merry,
    If that you forsake me.   350

---

265. **bought:** Redeemed.   **270. pardie:** By God.   **273. haunt to women the lusty company:** Frequent the lively company of women.   **274. while the day is clear:** Until daybreak.   **298. fay:** Faith.   **betake:** Commend.

303. depart: Part.   **312. Sith:** Since.   **316. for kind will creep where it may not go:** For kinship will creep where it cannot walk; i.e., blood is thicker than water.   **317. say:** Essay, try.   **326. For over his kin . . . may be bold:** For a man may be sure of his kinsfolk.   **334. enemy:** Devil.   **hath me in wait:** Has me under observation.   **346. liefer fast bread and water:** Rather fast on bread and water.

KINDRED: Ah, sir, what ye be a merry man!
    Take good heart to you, and make no moan.
    But one thing I warn you, by Saint Anne —
    As for me, ye shall go alone.
355 EVERYMAN: My Cousin, will you not with me go?
    COUSIN: No, by our Lady! I have the cramp in my toe.
    Trust not to me, for, so God me speed,
    I will deceive you in your most need.
    KINDRED: It availeth not us to tice.°
360   Ye shall have my maid with all my heart;
    She loveth to go to feasts, there to be nice,°
    And to dance, and abroad to start:
    I will give her leave to help you in that journey,
    If that you and she may agree.
    EVERYMAN: Now show me the very effect° of your
365   mind:
    Will you go with me, or abide behind?
    KINDRED: Abide behind? Yea, that will I, and I may!
    Therefore farewell till another day.
                    (*Exit Kindred.*)
    EVERYMAN: How should I be merry or glad?
370   For fair promises men to me make,
    But when I have most need they me forsake.
    I am deceived; that maketh me sad.
    COUSIN: Cousin Everyman, farewell now,
    For verily I will not go with you.
375   Also of mine own an unready reckoning
    I have to account; therefore I make tarrying.
    Now God keep thee, for now I go.
                    (*Exit Cousin.*)
    EVERYMAN: Ah, Jesus, is all come hereto?
    Lo, fair words maketh fools fain;°
380   They promise, and nothing will do, certain.
    My kinsmen promised me faithfully
    For to abide with me steadfastly,
    And now fast away do they flee:
    Even so Fellowship promised me.
385   What friend were best me of to provide?°
    I lose my time here longer to abide.
    Yet in my mind a thing there is:
    All my life I have loved riches;
    If that my Good° now help me might,
390   He would make my heart full light.
    I will speak to him in this distress —
    Where art thou, my Goods and riches?

(*Goods speaks from a corner.*)

GOODS: Who calleth me? Everyman? What! hast thou
    haste?
    I lie here in corners, trussed and piled so high,
395   And in chests I am locked so fast,
    Also sacked in bags. Thou mayst see with shine eye
    I cannot stir; in packs low I lie.
    What would ye have? Lightly° me say.

EVERYMAN: Come hither, Good, in all the haste thou
    may,
    For of counsel I must desire thee.   400
GOODS: Sir, and ye in the world have sorrow or
    adversity,
    That can I help you to remedy shortly.
EVERYMAN: It is another disease that grieveth me;
    In this world it is not, I tell thee so.
    I am sent for, another way to go,   405
    To give a strait count general
    Before the highest Jupiter of all;
    And all my life I have had joy and pleasure in thee,
    Therefore, I pray thee, go with me;
    For, peradventure, thou mayst before God
    Almighty   410
    My reckoning help to clean and purify;
    For it is said ever among
    That money maketh all right that is wrong.
GOODS: Nay, Everyman, I sing another song.
    I follow no man in such voyages;   415
    For, and I went with thee,
    Thou shouldst fare much the worse for me;
    For because on me thou did set thy mind,
    Thy reckoning I have made blotted and blind,
    That shine account thou cannot make truly;   420
    And that hast thou for the love of me.
EVERYMAN: That would grieve me full sore,
    When I should come to that fearful answer.
    Up, let us go thither together.
GOODS: Nay, not so! I am too brittle, I may not
    endure;   425
    I will follow no man one foot, be ye sure.
EVERYMAN: Alas, I have thee loved, and had great
    pleasure
    All my life-days on good and treasure.
GOODS: That is to thy damnation, without leasing,°
    For my love is contrary to the love everlasting;   430
    But if thou had me loved moderately during,
    As to the poor to give part of me,
    Then shouldst thou not in this dolor be,
    Nor in this great sorrow and care.
EVERYMAN: Lo, now was I deceived ere I was ware, 435
    And all I may wite° misspending of time.
GOODS: What, weenest thou that I am thine?
EVERYMAN: I had wend so.
GOODS: Nay, Everyman, I say no.
    As for a while I was lent thee;   440
    A season thou hast had me in prosperity.
    My condition is man's soul to kill;
    If I save one, a thousand I do spill.°
    Weenest thou that I will follow thee?
    Nay, not from this world, verily.   445
EVERYMAN: I had wend otherwise.
GOODS: Therefore to thy soul Good is a thief;
    For when thou art dead, this is my guise —

---

359. tice: Entice.   **361. nice:** Wanton.   **365. effect:** Tenor.
379. fain: Glad.   **385. me of to provide:** To provide myself with.
389. Good: Goods.   **398. Lightly:** Quickly.

429. without leasing: Without a lie, i.e., truly.   **436. wite:** Blame.
443. spill: Ruin.

Another to deceive in this same wise
450   As I have done thee, and all to his soul's reprief.°
EVERYMAN: O false Good, cursed may thou be,
    Thou traitor to God, that hast deceived me
    And caught me in thy snare!
GOODS: Marry, thou brought thyself in care,
455   Whereof I am glad;
    I must needs laugh, I cannot be sad.
EVERYMAN: Ah, Good, thou hast had long my heartly
        love;
    I gave thee that which should be the Lord's above.
    But wilt thou not go with me indeed?
460   I pray thee truth to say.
GOODS: No, so God me speed!
    Therefore farewell, and have good day.

                                                     (Exit Goods.)

EVERYMAN: O, to whom shall I make my moan
    For to go with me in that heavy journey?
465   First Fellowship said he would with me gone;
    His words were very pleasant and gay,
    But afterward he left me alone.
    Then spake I to my kinsmen, all in despair,
    And also they gave me words fair;
470   They lacked no fair speaking,
    But all forsook me in the ending.
    Then went I to my Goods, that I loved best,
    In hope to have comfort, but there had I least;
    For my Goods sharply did me tell
475   That he bringeth many into hell.
    Then of myself I was ashamed,
    And so I am worthy to be blamed;
    Thus may I well myself hate.
    Of whom shall I now counsel take?
480   I think that I shall never speed
    Till that I go to my Good Deed.
    But, alas, she is so weak
    That she can neither go nor speak;
    Yet will I venture on her now.
485   My Good Deeds, where be you?

(Good Deeds speaks from the ground.)

GOOD DEEDS: Here I lie, cold in the ground;
    Thy sins hath me sore bound,
    That I cannot stir.
EVERYMAN: O Good Deeds, I stand in fear!
490   I must you pray of counsel,
    For help now should come right well.°
GOOD DEEDS: Everyman, I have understanding
    That ye be summoned account to make
    Before Messias, of Jerusalem King;
    And you do by me,° that journey with you will I
495   take.
EVERYMAN: Therefore I come to you, my moan to
        make;
    I pray you that ye will go with me.

GOOD DEEDS: I would full fain, but I cannot stand,
        verily.
EVERYMAN: Why, is there anything on you fall?
GOOD DEEDS: Yea, sir, I may thank you of° all;   500
    If ye had perfectly cheered me,
    Your book of count full ready had be.
    Look, the books of your works and deeds eke!°
    Behold how they lie under the feet,
    To your soul's heaviness.   505
EVERYMAN: Our Lord Jesus help me!
    For one letter here I cannot see.
GOOD DEEDS: There is a blind reckoning in time of
        distress.
EVERYMAN: Good Deeds, I pray you help me in this
        need,
    Or else I am for ever damned indeed;   510
    Therefore help me to make reckoning
    Before the Redeemer of all thing,
    That King is, and was, and ever shall.
GOOD DEEDS: Everyman, I am sorry of your fall,
    And fain would I help you, and I were able.   515
EVERYMAN: Good Deeds, your counsel I pray you
        give me.
GOOD DEEDS: That shall I do verily;
    Though that on my feet I may not go,
    I have a sister that shall with you also,
    Called Knowledge, which shall with you abide,   520
    To help you to make that dreadful reckoning.

(Enter Knowledge.)

KNOWLEDGE: Everyman, I will go with thee, and be thy
        guide,
    In thy most need to go by thy side.
EVERYMAN: In good condition I am now in every
        thing,
    And am wholly content with this good thing,   525
    Thanked be God my creator.
GOOD DEEDS: And when she hath brought you there
    Where thou shalt heal thee of thy smart,
    Then go you with your reckoning and your Good
        Deeds together,
    For to make you joyful at heart   530
    Before the blessed Trinity.
EVERYMAN: My Good Deeds, gramercy!
    I am well content, certainly,
    With your words sweet.
KNOWLEDGE: Now go we together lovingly   535
    To Confession, that cleansing river.
EVERYMAN: For joy I weep; I would we were there!
    But, I pray you, give me cognition
    Where dwelleth that holy man, Confession.
KNOWLEDGE: In the house of salvation: 540
    We shall find him in that place,
    That shall us comfort, by God's grace.

(Knowledge takes Everyman to Confession.)

---

450. reprief: Shame.   **491. should come right well:** Would be
very welcome.   **495. by me:** As I advise.

500. of: For.   **503. eke:** Also.

Lo, this is Confession. Kneel down and ask mercy,
For he is in good conceit° with God Almighty.
EVERYMAN: O glorious fountain, that all uncleanness
545   doth clarify,
Wash from me the spots of vice unclean,
That on me no sin may be seen.
I come with Knowledge for my redemption,
Redempt with heart° and full contrition;
550   For I am commanded a pilgrimage to take,
And great accounts before God to make.
Now I pray you, Shrift, mother of salvation,
Help my Good Deeds for my piteous exclamation.
CONFESSION: I know your sorrow well, Everyman.
555   Because with Knowledge ye come to me,
I will you comfort as well as I can,
And a precious jewel I will give thee,
Called penance, voider of adversity;
Therewith shall your body chastised be,
560   With abstinence and perseverance in God's service.
Here shall you receive that scourge of me,
Which is penance strong that ye must endure,
To remember thy Savior was scourged for thee
With sharp scourges, and suffered it patiently;
565   So must thou, ere thou scape that painful pilgrimage.
Knowledge, keep him in this voyage,
And by that time Good Deeds will be with thee.
But in any wise be siker° of mercy,
For your time draweth fast; and° ye will saved be,
570   Ask God mercy, and he will grant truly.
When with the scourge of penance man doth him
    bind,
The oil of forgiveness then shall he find.
EVERYMAN: Thanked be God for his gracious work!
For now I will my penance begin;
575   This hath rejoiced and lighted my heart,
Though the knots be painful and hard within.
KNOWLEDGE: Everyman, look your penance that ye
    fulfill,
What pain that ever it to you be;
And Knowledge shall give you counsel at will
580   How your account ye shall make clearly.
EVERYMAN: O eternal God, O heavenly figure,
O way of righteousness, O goodly vision,
Which descended down in a virgin pure
Because he would every man redeem,
585   Which Adam forfeited by his disobedience:
O blessed Godhead, elect and high divine,
Forgive my grievous offense;
Here I cry thee mercy in this presence.°
O ghostly treasure, O ransomer and redeemer,
590   Of all the world hope and conductor,
Mirror of joy, and founder of mercy,
Which enlumineth heaven and earth thereby,
Hear my clamorous complaint, though it late be;

Receive my prayers, of thy benignity;
Though I be a sinner most abominable,   595
Yet let my name be written in Moses' table.°
O Mary, pray to the Maker of all thing,
Me for to help at my ending;
And save me from the power of my enemy,
For Death assaileth me strongly.   600
And, Lady, that I may by mean of thy prayer
Of your Son's glory to be partner,
By the means of his passion, I it crave;
I beseech you help my soul to save.
Knowledge, give me the scourge of penance;   605
My flesh therewith shall give acquittance:°
I will now begin, if God give me grace.
KNOWLEDGE: Everyman, God give you time and space!
Thus I bequeath you in the hands of our Saviour;
Now may you make your reckoning sure.   610
EVERYMAN: In the name of the Holy Trinity,
My body sore punished shall be:
Take this, body, for the sin of the flesh!

(*Scourges himself.*)

Also° thou delightest to go gay and fresh,
And in the way of damnation thou did me bring,   615
Therefore suffer now strokes and punishing.
Now of penance I will wade the water clear,
To save me from purgatory, that sharp fire.

(*Good Deeds rises from the ground.*)

GOOD DEEDS: I thank God, now I can walk and go,
And am delivered of my sickness and woe.   620
Therefore with Everyman I will go, and not spare;
His good works I will help him to declare.
KNOWLEDGE: Now, Everyman, be merry and glad!
Your Good Deeds cometh now; ye may not be sad.
Now is your Good Deeds whole and sound,   625
Going upright upon the ground.
EVERYMAN: My heart is light, and shall be evermore;
Now will I smite° faster than I did before.
GOOD DEEDS: Everyman, pilgrim, my special friend,
Blessed be thou without end;   630
For thee is preparate the eternal glory.
Ye have me made whole and sound,
Therefore I will bide by thee in every stound.°
EVERYMAN: Welcome, my Good Deeds; now I hear thy
    voice,
I weep for very sweetness of love.   635
KNOWLEDGE: Be no more sad, but ever rejoice;
God seeth thy living in his throne above.
Put on this garment to thy behoof,°

---

544. **conceit:** Esteem. 549. **heart:** Heartfelt. 568. **siker:**
Sure. 569. **and:** If. 588. **in this presence:** In the presence of
this company.

596. **Moses' table:** Medieval theologians regarded the two
tablets given to Moses on Mount Sinai as symbols of baptism
and penance. Thus Everyman is asking to be numbered among
those who have escaped damnation by doing penance for their
sins. 606. **acquittance:** Satisfaction (as part of the sacrament
of penance). 614. **Also:** As. 628. **smite:** Strike. 633. **stound:**
Trial. 638. **behoof:** Advantage.

640 Which is wet with your tears,
Or else before God you may it miss,
When ye to your journey's end come shall.
EVERYMAN: Gentle Knowledge, what do ye it call?
KNOWLEDGE: It is a garment of sorrow:
From pain it will you borrow;°
645 Contrition it is,
That geteth forgiveness;
It pleaseth God passing well.
GOOD DEEDS: Everyman, will you wear it for your
heal?°
EVERYMAN: Now blessed be Jesu, Mary's Son,
650 For now have I on true contrition.
And let us go now without tarrying;
Good Deeds, have we clear our reckoning?
GOOD DEEDS: Yea, indeed, I have it here.
EVERYMAN: Then I trust we need not fear;
655 Now, friends, let us not part in twain.
KNOWLEDGE: Nay, Everyman, that will we not, certain.
GOOD DEEDS: Yet must thou lead with thee
Three persons of great might.
EVERYMAN: Who should they be?
660 GOOD DEEDS: Discretion and Strength they hight,°
And thy Beauty may not abide behind.
KNOWLEDGE: Also ye must call to mind
Your Five Wits as for your counsellors.
GOOD DEEDS: You must have them ready at all hours.
665 EVERYMAN: How shall I get them hither?
KNOWLEDGE: You must call them all together,
And they will hear you incontinent.°
EVERYMAN: My friends, come hither and be present,
Discretion, Strength, my Five Wits, and Beauty.

(*Enter Beauty, Strength, Discretion, and Five Wits.*)

670 BEAUTY: Here at your will we be all ready.
What will ye that we should do?
GOOD DEEDS: That ye would with Everyman go,
And help him in his pilgrimage.
Advise you, will ye with him or not in that voyage?
675 STRENGTH: We will bring him all thither,
To his help and comfort, ye may believe me.
DISCRETION: So will we go with him all together.
EVERYMAN: Almighty God, lofed° may thou be!
I give thee laud that I have hither brought
Strength, Discretion, Beauty, and Five Wits. Lack I
680 nought.
And my Good Deeds, with Knowledge clear,
All be in my company at my will here;
I desire no more to my business.
STRENGTH: And I, Strength, will by you stand in
distress,
685 Though thou would in battle fight on the ground.
FIVE WITS: And though it were through the world
round,
We will not depart for sweet ne sour.

BEAUTY: No more will I unto death's hour,
Whatsoever thereof befall.
DISCRETION: Everyman, advise you first of all;   690
Go with a good advisement and deliberation.
We all give you virtuous monition°
That all shall be well.
EVERYMAN: My friends, harken what I will tell:
I pray God reward you in his heavenly sphere.   695
Now harken, all that be here,
For I will make my testament
Here before you all present:
In alms half my good I will give with my hands twain
In the way of charity, with good intent,   700
And the other half still shall remain
In queth,° to be returned there it ought to be.°
This I do in despite of the fiend of hell,
To go quit out of his peril°
Ever after and this day.   705
KNOWLEDGE: Everyman, harken what I say:
Go to priesthood, I you advise,
And receive of him in any wise°
The holy sacrament and ointment together.
Then shortly see ye turn again hither;   710
We will all abide you here.
FIVE WITS: Yea, Everyman, hie you that ye ready were.
There is no emperor, king, duke, ne baron,
That of God hath commission
As hath the least priest in the world being;   715
For of the blessed sacraments pure and benign
He beareth the keys, and thereof hath the cure°
For man's redemption — it is ever sure —
Which God for our soul's medicine
Gave us out of his heart with great pine.°   720
Here in this transitory life, for thee and me,
The blessed sacraments seven there be:
Baptism, confirmation, with priesthood good,
And the sacrament of God's precious flesh and blood,
Marriage, the holy extreme unction, and penance;   725
These seven be good to have in remembrance,
Gracious sacraments of high divinity.
EVERYMAN: Fain would I receive that holy body,
And meekly to my ghostly father I will go.
FIVE WITS: Everyman, that is the best that ye can do. 730
God will you to salvation bring,
For priesthood exceedeth all other thing:
To us Holy Scripture they do teach,
And converteth man from sin heaven to reach;
God hath to them more power given   735
Than to any angel that is in heaven.
With five words° he may consecrate,

---

644. **borrow:** Release.   648. **heal:** Salvation.   660. **hight:** Are called.   667. **incontinent:** Immediately.   678. **lofed:** Praised.

692. **monition:** Forewarning.   702. **queth:** Bequest.   **returned there it ought to be:** This line probably refers to restitution, that is, the restoration to its proper owner of unlawfully acquired property.   704. **quit out of his peril:** Free out of his power.   708. **in any wise:** Without fail.   717. **cure:** Charge.   720. **pine:** Suffering.   737. **five words:** *Hoc est enim Corpus meum* ("For this is my body," the words of the consecration of the body of Christ at Mass).

Scene from the Guthrie Theater
production of *Everyman,* directed by
Robert Benedetti.

God's body in flesh and blood to make,
And handleth his Maker between his hands.
740   The priest bindeth and unbindeth all bands,
Both in earth and in heaven.
Thou ministers all the sacraments seven;
Though we kissed thy feet, thou were worthy;
Thou art surgeon that cureth sin deadly:
745   No remedy we find under God
But all only priesthood.°
Everyman, God gave priests that dignity,

746. But all only priesthood: Except only from the priesthood.

And setteth them in his stead among us to be;
Thus be they above angels in degree.

(*Everyman goes to the priest to receive the last sacraments.*)

KNOWLEDGE: If priests be good, it is so, surely.   750
But when Jesus hanged on the cross with great
   smart,
There he gave out of his blessed heart
The same sacrament in great torment:
He sold them not to us, that Lord omnipotent.
Therefore Saint Peter the apostle doth say   755
That Jesu's curse hath all they

Which God their Savior do buy or sell,
Or they for any money do take or tell.°
Sinful priests giveth the sinners example bad;
Their children sitteth by other men's fires, I have
760   heard;
And some haunteth women's company
With unclean life, as lusts of lechery:
These be with sin made blind.
FIVE WITS: I trust to God no such may we find;
765   Therefore let us priesthood honor,
And follow their doctrine for our souls' succor.
We be their sheep, and they shepherds be
By whom we all be kept in surety.
Peace, for yonder I see Everyman come,
770   Which hath made true satisfaction.
GOOD DEEDS: Methink it is he indeed.

(*Reenter Everyman.*)

EVERYMAN: Now Jesu be your alder speed!°
I have received the sacrament for my redemption,
And then mine extreme unction:
775   Blessed be all they that counselled me to take it!
And now, friends, let us go without longer respite;
I thank God that ye have tarried so long.
Now set each of you on this rood° your hand,
And shortly follow me:
780   I go before there I would be; God be our guide!
STRENGTH: Everyman, we will not from you go
Till ye have done this voyage long.
DISCRETION: I, Discretion, will bide by you also.
KNOWLEDGE: And though this pilgrimage be never so
strong,°
785   I will never part you fro.
STRENGTH: Everyman, I will be as sure by thee
As ever I did by Judas Maccabee.°

(*Everyman comes to his grave.*)

EVERYMAN: Alas, I am so faint I may not stand;
My limbs under me doth fold.
790   Friends, let us not turn again to this land,
Not for all the world's gold;
For into this cave must I creep
And turn to earth, and there to sleep.
BEAUTY: What, into this grave? Alas!
795   EVERYMAN: Yea, there shall ye consume, more and less.
BEAUTY: And what, should I smother here?
EVERYMAN: Yea, by my faith, and never more appear.
In this world live no more we shall,
But in heaven before the highest Lord of all.

BEAUTY: I cross out all this;° adieu, by Saint John!   800
I take my cap in my lap,° and am gone.
EVERYMAN: What, Beauty, whither will ye?
BEAUTY: Peace, I am deaf; I look not behind me,
Not and thou wouldest give me all the gold in thy
chest.   (*Exit Beauty.*)
EVERYMAN: Alas, whereto may I trust?   805
Beauty goeth fast away from me;
She promised with me to live and die.
STRENGTH: Everyman, I will thee also forsake and
deny;
Thy game liketh° me not at all.
EVERYMAN: Why, then, ye will forsake me all?   810
Sweet Strength, tarry a little space.
STRENGTH: Nay, sir, by the rood of grace!
I will hie me from thee fast,
Though thou weep till thy heart to-brast.°
EVERYMAN: Ye would ever bide by me, ye said.   815
STRENGTH: Yea, I have you far enough conveyed.
Ye be old enough, I understand,
Your pilgrimage to take on hand;
I repent me that I hither came.
EVERYMAN: Strength, you to displease I am to blame;   820
Yet promise is debt, this ye well wot.
STRENGTH: In faith, I care not.
Thou art but a fool to complain;
You spend your speech and waste your brain.
Go thrust thee into the ground!   (*Exit Strength.*) 825
EVERYMAN: I had wend surer I should you have found.
He that trusteth in his Strength
She him deceiveth at the length.
Both Strength and Beauty forsaketh me;
Yet they promised me fair and lovingly.   830
DISCRETION: Everyman, I will after Strength be gone;
As for me, I will leave you alone.
EVERYMAN: Why, Discretion, will ye forsake me?
DISCRETION: Yea, in faith, I will go from thee,
For when Strength goeth before   835
I follow after evermore.
EVERYMAN: Yet, I pray thee, for the love of the Trinity,
Look in my grave once piteously.
DISCRETION: Nay, so nigh will I not come;
Farewell, every one!   (*Exit Discretion.*)   840
EVERYMAN: O, all thing faileth, save God alone —
Beauty, Strength, and Discretion;
For when Death bloweth his blast,
They all run from me full fast.
FIVE WITS: Everyman, my leave now of thee I take;   845
I will follow the other, for here I thee forsake.
EVERYMAN: Alas, then may I wail and weep,
For I took you for my best friend.
FIVE WITS: I will no longer thee keep;
Now farewell, and there an end.   850
(*Exit Five Wits.*)

755–58. **Therefore Saint Peter . . . do take or tell:** Reference to the sin of simony, the selling of church offices or benefits.   **tell:** Count out, i.e., sell.   772. **your alder speed:** The helper of you all.   778. **rood:** Cross.   784. **strong:** Grievous.   787. **Judas Maccabee:** Judas Maccabeus, who overcame Syrian domination and won religious freedom for the Jews in 165 B.C., believed that his strength came not from worldly might but from heaven (1 Maccabees 3:19).

800. **I cross out all this:** I cancel all this, i.e., my promise to stay with you.   801. **I take my cap in my lap:** Doff my cap [so low that it comes] into my lap.   809. **liketh:** Pleases.   814. **brast:** Break.

EVERYMAN: O Jesu, help! All hath forsaken me.
GOOD DEEDS: Nay, Everyman; I will bide with thee.
   I will not forsake thee indeed;
   Thou shalt find me a good friend at need.
EVERYMAN: Gramercy, Good Deeds! Now may I true
855   friends see.
   They have forsaken me, every one;
   I loved them better than my Good Deeds alone.
   Knowledge, will ye forsake me also?
KNOWLEDGE: Yea, Everyman, when ye to Death shall
     go;
860   But not yet, for no manner of danger.
EVERYMAN: Gramercy, Knowledge, with all my heart.
KNOWLEDGE: Nay, yet I will not from hence depart
   Till I see where ye shall become.
EVERYMAN: Methink, alas, that I must be gone
865   To make my reckoning and my debts pay,
   For I see my time is nigh spent away.
   Take example, all ye that this do hear or see,
   How they that I loved best do forsake me,
   Except my Good Deeds that bideth truly.
870 GOOD DEEDS: All earthly things is but vanity:
   Beauty, Strength, and Discretion do man forsake,
   Foolish friends, and kinsmen, that fair spake —
   All fleeth save Good Deeds, and that am I.
EVERYMAN: Have mercy on me, God most mighty;
   And stand by me, thou mother and maid, holy
875   Mary.
GOOD DEEDS: Fear not; I will speak for thee.
EVERYMAN: Here I cry God mercy.
GOOD DEEDS: Short our end, and minish our pain;
   Let us go and never come again.
880 EVERYMAN: Into thy hands, Lord, my soul I
     commend;
   Receive it, Lord, that it be not lost.
   As thou me boughtest, so me defend,
   And save me from the fiend's boast,
   That I may appear with that blessed host
885   That shall be saved at the day of doom.
   In manus tuas, of mights most
   For ever, *commendo spiritum meum.*°

(*He sinks into his grave.*)

KNOWLEDGE: Now hath he suffered that we all shall
     endure;
   The Good Deeds shall make all sure.
   Now hath he made ending;   890
   Methinketh that I hear angels sing,
   And make great joy and melody
   Where Everyman's soul received shall be.
ANGEL: Come, excellent elect spouse, to Jesu!
   Hereabove thou shalt go   895
   Because of thy singular virtue.
   Now the soul is taken the body fro,
   Thy reckoning is crystal-clear.
   Now shalt thou into the heavenly sphere,
   Unto the which all ye shall come   900
   That liveth well before the day of doom.

(*Enter Doctor.*)

DOCTOR: This moral men may have in mind.
   Ye hearers, take it of worth, old and young,
   And forsake Pride, for he deceiveth you in the end;
   And remember Beauty, Five Wits, Strength, and
     Discretion,   905
   They all at the last do every man forsake,
   Save his Good Deeds there doth he take.
   But beware, for and they be small
   Before God, he hath no help at all;
   None excuse may be there for every man.   910
   Alas, how shall he do then?
   For after death amends may no man make,
   For then mercy and pity doth him forsake.
   If his reckoning be not clear when he doth come,
   God will say: *"Ite, maledicti, in ignem eternum."*°   915
   And he that hath his account whole and sound,
   High in heaven he shall be crowned;
   Unto which place God bring us all thither,
   That we may live body and soul together.
   Thereto help the Trinity!   920
   Amen, say ye, for saint charity.

Thus endeth this moral play of Everyman.

886–87. *In manus tuas . . . commendo spiritum meum:* Into your hands, most mighty One for ever, I commend my spirit.

915. *"Ite, maledicti, in ignem eternum":* Depart, ye cursed, into everlasting fire.

Renaissance Drama

Italian Drama

The period following the Middle Ages in Europe, from about the fourteenth to the seventeenth centuries, is known as the *Renaissance*, a term meaning "rebirth." In this period a shift away from medieval values and culture was motivated by a revival of classical learning; advances in physics, astronomy, and the biological sciences; the exploration of the "new world" of the Americas; and political and economic developments. This shift was not abrupt, however; it was gradual, like a thaw. It began in the south, in Italy, in the late 1300s and moved northward through the activities of scholars, travelers, performers, and writers, until it reached England sometime late in the 1400s.

The Renaissance built on medieval culture and at the same time developed a secular understanding of the individual in society that eventually transformed this culture, long dominated by the Roman Catholic Church in many spheres — artistic, intellectual, and political, as well as spiritual. The transformation was influenced by the work of great writers, scholars, philosophers, and scientists such as Desiderius Erasmus (1466?–1536), Niccolò Machiavelli (1469–1527), Nicolaus Copernicus (1473–1543), Francis Bacon (1561–1626), and Galileo Galilei (1564–1642). In addition, the rise in power of the guilds and the increase in wealth of the successful Italian trading states, which produced large and influential families in cities such as Florence, Venice, Milan, and Genoa, contributed to the erosion of the Church's power.

Italian scholars, following classical models, had begun in the last decades of the fourteenth century to center their studies on human achievements. Such studies, known as the humanities, became the chief concern of the most innovative thinkers of the day. Their interests were well served by the rediscovery of ancient Greek philosophical and scientific texts. Although ancient texts had been preserved in monasteries for centuries, knowledge of them was restricted. A new demand for classical texts, fed by the humanists' focus on ancient models as the source of wisdom and by their return to a liberal arts curriculum established by the Greeks, led to the wide dissemination of the works of Plato, Aristotle, Cicero, and important Greek dramatists during the Renaissance. The achievement of the ancients was an inspiration to Renaissance writers and reaffirmed their conviction that a study of the humanities was the key to transforming the old medieval attitudes into a new, dynamic worldview.

Vitruvius and the Rediscovery of Roman Design

Most medieval Italian theater depended on portable stages, but it was clear in the last decades of the fourteenth century that to present the newly rediscovered Roman or Greek plays, something more closely resembling the original Greek theater would be necessary. Fortunately, *The Ten Books of Architecture* (written c. 16–13 B.C.) of the great Roman architect Vitruvius (first century B.C.) was rediscovered in a manuscript in the monastery of St. Gall. It included detailed plans for the Greek-inspired Roman theater.

Using Vitruvius's designs, the Italians began building stages that were raised platforms with a FRONS SCAENA, the flat front wall used in the Roman theater. The earliest Italian woodcuts show the stages to be relatively simple with pillars supporting a roof or cover. Curtains stretched between the pillars permitted the actors to enter and exit. Usually, three "doors" with names over each indicated the houses of specific characters.

The study of Roman architecture eventually produced, in 1584, one of the wonders of the Renaissance, the Olympic Theater (Teatro Olimpico) in Vicenza, designed by the great Renaissance architect Andrea Palladio (1508–1580), whose interpretation of Roman architecture was so compelling that it influenced architecture all over the world (Figure 6). The Olympic Theater, which has been preserved and is still used for performances, has an orchestra, a semicircular seating area, and a multistory frons scaena. But it also has several vistas of streets constructed in three-dimensional forced perspective running backward from the frons scaena.

The Olympic Theater was built with an essentially conservative design that worked well for Roman plays but not for Renaissance plays. It did not inspire new theater designs. In newer theaters, Italian plays had begun to use scenery and painted backdrops that could be changed to suggest a change in location of the action. Carefully painted backdrops were also effective in increasing illusion: one backdrop could immediately locate an action on a city street, while another could help shift the audience imaginatively to a woodland scene. These innovations proved difficult in the Olympic Theater.

The theory of vanishing-point perspective developed by the architect Filippo Brunelleschi (1377–1446) and published by Leon Battista Alberti in *On Painting* in 1435 helped revolutionize the design of flat theatrical backdrops. Earlier Renaissance painters had had no way to establish a firm sense of perspective on a flat surface, so all three-dimensional objects appeared flat; all space in a landscape or cityscape seemed shortened and unreal. The use of a single vanishing point — in which lines were lightly drawn from the edges of the canvas (or theatrical backdrop) so that they met in a single point in the center — made it possible to show buildings, trees, and figures in their proper proportion to one another (Figure 7). For the first time, Renaissance painters could achieve lifelike illusions on a flat surface. On the other hand, three-dimensional scenery was possible in the Olympic Theater — as well as some others — at this time, and the illusion of reality was thus intensified.

The designer Sebastiano Serlio (1475–1554) used the vanishing-point technique, intensified by receding lines of tiles in the floor and on the painted

ABOVE: Figure 6. Designed by Andrea Palladio, the Teatro Olimpico (begun 1579) in Vicenza, Italy, was the first indoor theater of the Renaissance. The scaena's openings produced an illusion of depth. RIGHT: Figure 7. Perspective setting designed by Baldassare Peruzzi (1481–1536).

backdrop. Serlio established all-purpose settings for comedy, tragedy, and satire. The rigidity of the backdrops for comedy and tragedy — both used a piazza, a small town square, ringed by stone buildings — restricted their use. But the setting for satire was rustic: trees, bushes, a couple of cottages. Until the nineteenth century, European theaters were equipped with sets of backdrops and wingpieces derived from his designs.

The most important and long-lasting development of Italian theater design in the mid-1500s was the PROSCENIUM ARCH, a "frame" that surrounds the stage, permitting the audience to look in on the scene, whether in a room or in a town square. The arch lent a finished touch to the theater, separating the action from the audience and distancing the actors. The proscenium arch is common in most theaters today.

Commedia dell'Arte

Renaissance Italy had two traditions of theater. *Commedia erudita* was learned, almost scholarly, in its interests in Roman staging and Roman plays. COMMEDIA DELL'ARTE was less reverent, more slapstick, and generally more popular. It is difficult, however, to say which was more influential on literature over the years. Each made its contribution.

In terms of acting and storytelling, the influence of the commedia dell'arte is almost unparalleled. The term means "comedy performed by professionals." The actors usually had grown up in performing families that made their living touring the countryside, performing at fairs and on feast days. From the early Renaissance through the eighteenth century, the commedia dell'arte entertained all of Europe and influenced comic theater in every nation.

The essence of commedia dell'arte was improvised scripts. A general narrative outline served as a basis, but the speeches were improvised to a degree (with some reliance on set elements and on experience with performing the same role many times). The principal characters were types who soon became familiar all over Europe: Pantalone, the often magisterial but miserly old man; Arlecchino (Harlequin), the cunning clown. Pulcinella, the Punch of Punch and Judy, and Columbina, the innocent *zanni,* began as clowns. They joined a host of other STOCK CHARACTERS such as pedantic lawyers, a braggart captain, and a serving maid. Certain versions of general characters — such as Arlecchino,

who began as a simple *zanno* — became famous and were copied in many countries. When Volpone calls Mosca a "zany" near the end of Ben Jonson's *Volpone,* he reminds his audience that his characters are indebted to the *zanni* in commedia dell'arte. Knowing who the characters were even before the play began was a convenience that Renaissance audiences enjoyed.

The youthful lovers in the commedia did not require masks, but the old men, the *zanni,* and other characters all had masks that identified them and made them look, to modern eyes, rather grotesque. These masks survive today in the carnival, in Venice, where the commedia began. Stock characters thrive in popular comedies everywhere. Molière and, much later, Bernard Shaw depended on them. To a large extent, one of comedy's greatest sources of energy lies in the delight that audiences have always taken in stock characters. Today hardly a situation comedy on television could survive without them.

The staging of commedia dell'arte was simple. It often took place in open air, but sometimes indoors in a more formal theatrical setting. Sometimes performers dispensed with the stage altogether and worked in marketplaces. Their scenarios were farcical crowd pleasers filled with buffoonery. They were based on the LAZZO and the BURLA. The *burla* was the general plot for any given performance. *Lazzi* were comic routines something like Abbott and Costello's "Who's on First?" skit. Abbott and Costello developed their routine for burlesque, a form of comedy popular in the first half of the twentieth century centering on broad gags, routines, and running jokes. *Lazzi* were carefully planned to seem to be spontaneous interruptions of the action. Chevy Chase's trademark pratfall as he enters a scene is a descendant of the sixteenth-century *lazzo.*

Elizabethan Drama

The reign of Queen Elizabeth I (1558–1603) is known as the Elizabethan age in England — a period of discovery and prosperity as well as a period of great achievement in the arts, especially drama. Sir Francis Drake and Sir Walter Raleigh adventured across the Atlantic Ocean to the "New World," and England secured its economic future by defeating the invasion attempt of the Spanish Armada in 1588. England had become Protestant in the 1530s — one reason Catholic Spain felt it needed to subdue the nation.

Elizabethan England, especially after the defeat of the Armada, produced one of the great ages of drama, rivaling the great age of Greece. During this period, playwrights such as Thomas Kyd (1558–1594), Christopher Marlowe (1564–1593), William Shakespeare (1564–1616), Ben Jonson (1572–1637), John Marston (1576–1634), John Fletcher (1579–1625), John Webster (1580?–1625?), Thomas Middleton (1580?–1627), and John Ford (1586–1639) drew crowds by the thousands.

That the Elizabethans enjoyed plays with a moral basis is plain from the fact that so much of the great drama of the late 1500s and early 1600s is moral in character. Still, early Elizabethan plays were less obviously moralistic than the then-popular morality plays. They did not aim specifically to teach a moral lesson, although there are many lessons to be learned from Shakespeare and his contemporaries.

During Shakespeare's youth wandering players put on a number of plays from REPERTORY, their stock of perhaps a dozen current plays they could perform. How many players there were or what their source of plays was, we do not know. Much of what we know comes directly from *Hamlet* and the appearance of the players who perform Hamlet's "Mouse-trap." What we learn there tells us that dramatic styles had developed in the English country-side and that theater was thriving.

The First Professional Companies

Although professional players' groups had long been licensed to perform in France and Italy, until the 1570s professional actors — those who had no other trade — did not enjoy favor in England. Such people could be arrested for vagrancy. The law, however, changed, and actors with royal patronage were permitted to perform. The history of theater changed, too. In 1576 James Burbage (father of the famous star of Shakespeare's plays, Richard Burbage) built the first building made specially for plays in England. It was called The Theatre.

Soon there were other theaters: the Swan, the Globe (Figure 8), the Rose, the Fortune, the Hope. The Globe was large enough to accommodate two to three thousand people. Because these theaters were open-air, they could not be used in winter, but all were extraordinarily successful. Shakespeare, who was part owner of the Globe and, later, of the second indoor Blackfriars Theatre, received money from admission fees and from his role as chief playwright. He became rich enough to retire in splendid style to Stratford, his hometown. Few other Elizabethan actors and playwrights had as much of a financial stake in their work as did Shakespeare.

The Elizabethan Theater

The design of the Elizabethan theater is a matter of some speculation. Many of the plays popular before the theaters were built were performed in a square inn yard, with a balcony above. The audience looked out their windows or stood in the yard. One location of the earliest English drama is the Inns of Court, essentially a college for law students in London, where students staged plays. The audience there would have been learned, bright, and imaginative. Indeed, the first English tragedy, *Gorboduc*, by Thomas Sackville and Thomas Norton, was played indoors at the Inner Temple, one of the Inns of Court, in 1562, before Marlowe and Shakespeare were born.

The shape of the early theaters was often octagonal or circular, like the bear pits in which bears, tied to stakes, were baited by dogs for the amusement of the audience. The stage was raised about five feet from the ground with levels of seating in several galleries. Approximately half the area over the stage was roofed and contained machinery to lower actors from the "heavens"; it was painted blue with stars to simulate the sky. Some stages were approximately twenty-five by forty feet. Doors or curtained openings at the back of the stage served for entrances and exits, and at the back of the stage was a special room for costume changes. The stage may have contained a section that was nor-mally curtained but that opened to reveal an interior, such as a bedroom. The existence of this feature is, however, in considerable dispute.

The Elizabethan Audience

The entrance fee to the theaters was a penny, probably the equivalent of five to ten dollars in today's money. For another penny one could take a seat, prob-ably on a bench, in one of the upper galleries. In some theaters more private spaces were available as well. A great many playgoers were satisfied to stand

Figure 8. A conjectural
reconstruction of the Globe
Theatre, 1599 to 1613.

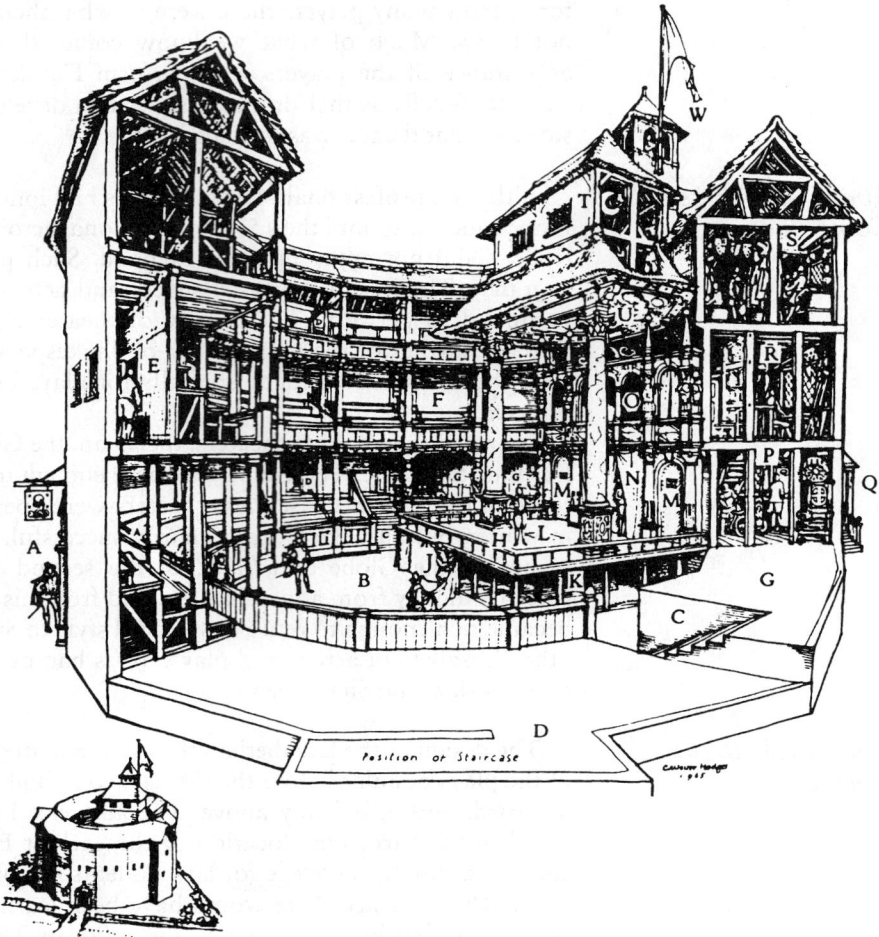

Position of Staircase

A   Main entrance
B   The yard
C   Entrances to lowest gallery
D   Position of entrances to staircase and
    upper galleries
E   Corridor serving the different sections
    of the middle gallery
F   Middle gallery ("Twopenny Rooms")
G   Position of "Gentlemen's Rooms" or
    "Lords' Rooms"
H   The stage
J   The hanging being put up round the
    stage
K   The "hell" under the stage

L   The stage trap leading down to the hell
M   Stage doors
N   Curtained "place behind the stage"
O   Gallery above the stage, used as required
    sometimes by musicians, sometimes by
    spectators, and often as part of the play
P   Backstage area (the tiring-house)
Q   Tiring-house door
R   Dressing-rooms
S   Wardrobe and storage
T   The hut housing the machine for lower-
    ing enthroned gods, etc., to the stage
U   The "heavens"
W   Hoisting the playhouse flag

around the stage and were thus nicknamed "groundlings." Hamlet calls them the "understanding gentlemen of the ground." The more academic playwrights, Marlowe and Jonson, used the term to mean those who would not perfectly understand the significance of the plays.

Shakespeare and other Elizabethan playwrights expected a widely diverse audience — from coarse to extraordinarily polished. Shakespeare had the gift, as did Marlowe and even Jonson in his comedies, to appeal to them all. Shakespeare's plays were given in public playhouses open to everyone. They were also given in university theaters, as in the case of *Macbeth;* in indoor private theaters; and in royal command performances. Shakespeare's universality reveals itself in his appeal to many different kinds of people.

Female Characters on the English Stage

Because the theater was considered to be morally questionable, women were not allowed to act on English stages. Boys and young men filled the parts of young female characters such as Juliet, Desdemona, and Ophelia. No contemporary commentator makes any complaint about having to put up with a boy playing the part of Juliet or any of Shakespeare's other love interests, such as Desdemona in *Othello,* Ophelia in *Hamlet,* or even Queen Cleopatra. Older women, such as the Nurse in *Romeo and Juliet,* were played by some of the gifted male character actors of the company.

The Masque

The Elizabethan MASQUE was a special entertainment of royalty. It was a celebration that included a rudimentary plot, a great deal of singing and dancing, and magnificent costumes and lighting. Masques were usually performed only once, often to celebrate a royal marriage. Masque audiences participated in the dances and were usually delighted by complex machinery that lifted or lowered characters from the skies. The masque was devised in Italy in the 1570s by Count Giovanni Bardi, founder of the Florentine Camerata, a Renaissance group of theatergoers sponsored by Lorenzo de' Medici.

The geniuses of the masque are generally considered to have been Ben Jonson and Inigo Jones. Jones was the architect whose Banqueting Hall at Whitehall in London, which still stands, provided the setting for most of the great masques of the seventeenth century. Jonson and Jones worked together from 1605 to 1631 to produce a remarkable body of masques that today resemble the bones of a dinosaur: what we read on the page suggests in only the vaguest way what the presentation must have been like when the masques were mounted.

Because of the expenses of costuming and staging, most masques were too costly to be produced more than once. The royal exchequer was frequently burdened in Queen Elizabeth's time; more so after King James took the throne in 1603. Masque costumes were impressive, the scenery astounding, and the effects amazing. In all of this, the words — which are, after all, at the center of Shakespeare's plays as well as other plays of the period — were of least account. As a result of the emphasis on the machinery and designs — the work of Inigo Jones — Jonson abandoned his partnership in a huff, complaining that he could not compete with the scene painters and carpenters.

The value placed on spectacle in the masques tells us something about the taste of the aristocrats, who enjoyed sumptuous foods, clothes, and amusements. Eventually, audiences of the public theaters hungered for spectacle, too.

Their appetite was satisfied by masques inserted in the plays of Marston, Webster, and Shakespeare, whose masque in *The Tempest* is a delightful short tribute to the genre. An added device for achieving spectacular effects onstage was huge storm machines installed in the Globe. Some say that one reason Shakespeare wrote *The Tempest* was to take advantage of the new equipment. Foreign visitors described London theaters as gorgeous places of entertainment far surpassing their own. The quest for more intense spectacle eventually led to disaster in one theater. The Globe actually burned down in 1613 because a cannon in the roof above the stage misfired and brought the house down in real flames.

The royal demand for masques was unaffected. As Francis Bacon said in his essay "On Masques" (1625), "These things are but toys to come amongst such serious observations. But yet, since princes will have such things, it is better they should be graced with elegancy than daubed with cost. Dancing to song is a thing of great state and pleasure."

Spanish Drama

The Spanish developed, independently, a corral, or open theatrical space, resembling the Elizabethan inn yard, in which they produced plays. This development may have been an accident of architecture — because of the widespread need for inns and for places to store horses — that permitted the symmetry of growth of the English Elizabethan and the Spanish Golden Age theaters.

The most important playwright of the Spanish theater was Lope de Vega (1562–1635), who is said to have written twelve hundred plays (seven hundred fifty survive). Many of them are relatively brief, and some resemble the scenarios for the commedia dell'arte. A good number, though, are full-length and impressive works, such as *The Sheep Well, The King, The Greatest Alcalde,* and *The Gardener's Dog.* Pedro Calderón de la Barca (1600–1681) became, on Lope de Vega's death, the reigning Spanish playwright. His *Life Is a Dream* is performed regularly throughout the world. Calderón became a priest in 1651 and wrote religious plays that on rare occasions got him into trouble with the Inquisition, an agency of the church that searched out and punished heresy. He was especially imaginative in his use of stage machinery and especially gifted in producing philosophical and poetic dialogue.

Renaissance Drama Timeline

DATE	THEATER	POLITICAL	SOCIAL/CULTURAL
1300–1400	**1377–1446:** Filippo Brunelleschi, an Italian architect, develops vanishing-point perspective, which allows theatrical scenery to be drawn in realistic proportions.		**1348–1353:** Boccaccio's *Decameron* becomes a model for Italian prose. **c. 1386–1466:** Donatello, Italian painter and major innovator in Renaissance sculpture
1400–1500	**1414:** Rediscovery of Vitruvius's *De Architectura* (90 B.C.) in Italy. After its publication in 1486, the treatise significantly influences the development of staging practices.		**1450:** Florence under the Medici family becomes the center of Renaissance and humanism. **1452–1519:** Leonardo da Vinci, brilliant inventor, architect, musician, and artist **1469–1527:** Niccolò Machiavelli, who writes the political treatise *The Prince* in 1513 and the comedy *Mandragola* between 1513 and 1520 **1473–1543:** Nicolaus Copernicus, founder of modern astronomy
	1495: The Dutch morality play *Elckerlijk* by Peter Dorland van Diest becomes the prototype for the English *Everyman*.	**1494:** The Parliament of Drogheda marks the subservience of Ireland to England.	**1496:** Henry VII commissions Venetian navigator John Cabot (1450–1498) to discover a new trade route to Asia. **1497:** Cabot reaches the east coast of North America. **1497:** Vasco de Gama (c. 1469–1524) rounds the Cape of Good Hope.
1500–1600		**1503:** James IV of Scotland marries Margaret Tudor, daughter of Henry VII.	**1507:** Pope Julius II announces the sale of indulgences to finance the rebuilding of St. Peter's Basilica in Rome. **1509–1564:** John Calvin, Swiss reformer
	1508: Vernacular drama begins in Italy with Ludovico Ariosto's *The Casket*. **1508:** The Hôtel de Bourgogne, a permanent theater building, opens in Paris.		**c. 1509:** A massive slave trade begins in the New World. **1512:** Copernicus's *Commentariolus* states that the earth and other planets turn around the sun. **1514–1564:** Andreas Vesalius, Dutch physician, founder of modern anatomy **1516–1547:** Henry Howard, Earl of Surrey, English poet
	1512: The word *masque* is first used to denote a poetic drama.	**1517:** Martin Luther protests the sale of indulgences by posting his 95 theses on a church door in Wittenberg, Germany, thus launching the Protestant Reformation in Germany.	**1519:** Hernando Cortés enters Tenochtitlán, capital of Mexico; is received by Montezuma, the Aztec ruler; and assumes control of Mexico in 1521.

Renaissance Drama Timeline (continued)

DATE	THEATER	POLITICAL	SOCIAL/CULTURAL
1500–1600 (continued)	**1550–1650:** Golden Age of Spanish drama. The two principal playwrights are Lope de Vega (1562–1635) and Pedro Calderón de la Barca (1600–1681). **1558–1594:** Playwright Thomas Kyd, author of *The Spanish Tragedy* (c. 1587) **1562:** The First English tragedy, *Gorboduc*, is performed at the Inns of Court. **1564–1593:** Christopher Marlowe, author of *Doctor Faustus* (c. 1588), *Tamburlaine* (1590), and *Edward II* (c. 1592) **1564–1616:** William Shakespeare **c. 1568:** Formation of the Italian commedia dell'arte company I Gelosi **1572–1637:** Playwright Ben Jonson, author of *Volpone* (1605) and *Bartholomew Fair* (1614) **1574:** The Earl of Leicester's Men, the first important acting troupe in London, is licensed. **1575:** *Gammer Gurton's Needle*, early English farce, author unknown **1576:** James Burbage builds The Theatre for the public performance of plays. Blackfriars, London's first private theater, is also built. **1577:** John Northbrooke publishes *A Treatise against Dicing, Dancing, Plays, and Interludes*, one of several tracts attacking the growing professional theater. **1580–1627:** Playwright Thomas Middleton, author of *A Chaste Maid in Cheapside* (1630) and *The Changeling* (with William Rowley, 1622)	**1534:** Henry VIII (reigned 1509–1547) breaks with the Roman Catholic Church. **1535:** Henry VIII's Act of Supremacy names him head of the Church of England. Sir Thomas More is executed after refusing to comply with the Act. **1547:** Ivan IV (the Terrible) becomes czar of Russia. Moscow is destroyed by fire in the same year. **1553–1558:** Reign of Mary I of England. The country returns temporarily to Catholicism. **1558–1603:** Reign of Elizabeth I in England. Protestantism becomes the religion of the realm. England emerges as a world power. **1570:** Japan opens the port of Nagasaki to trade with the West. **1572:** At the Saint Bartholomew's Day Massacre in France, thousands of Protestants are killed.	**1522:** Luther translates the New Testament into German and translates the Old Testament in 1534. **1547–1616:** Miguel de Cervantes, author of the novel *Don Quixote* and many plays **c. 1552–1599:** Edmund Spenser, English poet, author of *Faerie Queene* **1554–1586:** Sir Philip Sidney, poet and soldier, author of *An Apology for Poetry* **1561–1626:** Francis Bacon, English philosopher and statesman **1564–1642:** Galileo Galilei, Italian astronomer **1571–1630:** Johannes Kepler, German astronomer. His laws accurately describe the revolutions of the planets around the sun. **1572–1631:** John Donne, English metaphysic poet **1577:** *Chronicles of England, Scotland and Ireland* is published by Raphael Holinshed and provides Shakespeare with information for his historical plays. **1580:** Sir Francis Drake, first Englishman to circumnavigate the globe

Renaissance Drama Timeline (continued)

DATE	THEATER	POLITICAL	SOCIAL/CULTURAL
1500–1600 (continued)	**1584:** Completion of the Teatro Olimpico in Vicenza, Italy, designed by architect Andrea Palladio (1508–1580). **1586?–c. 1640:** Playwright John Ford, author of *'Tis Pity She's a Whore* (1633) **1593:** London theaters are closed because of a plague and open again in 1594. **1595–1596:** Shakespeare's comedy *A Midsummer Night's Dream* **1599:** The Globe Theatre is built in London.	**1587:** The Catholic Mary Stuart, queen of Scotland, is executed in England. **1587–1649:** John Winthrop, first governor of the Massachusetts Bay Colony **1588:** The English fleet defeats the Spanish Armada. **1589:** Henry IV of France, first of the Bourbon line **1589:** Russian czar Boris Godunov separates Moscow's church from that in Constantinople. **1595:** The Dutch begin to colonize the East Indies. **1598:** The Edict of Nantes grants French Huguenots freedom of worship, but is revoked in 1685.	**1583:** Sir Philip Sydney's *Defence of Poesy* argues for literature's importance in teaching morality and virtue. **1596–1650:** René Descartes, French philosopher, mathematician, and scientist
1600–1700	**1600–1601:** Shakespeare's *Hamlet* **1611–1612:** Shakespeare's *The Tempest* **1613:** Fire destroys the Globe Theatre. **1633:** The Oberammergau Passion play is first performed in Germany. **1642:** The English Parliament closes the theaters.	**1603:** Death of Elizabeth I. James VI of Scotland, son of Mary Stuart, becomes James I of England. **1605:** The Gunpowder Plot, an attempt to blow up the English Parliament and James I, is uncovered. **1618–1648:** The Thirty Years War is initiated by a Protestant revolt in Bohemia against the authority of the Holy Roman emperor. **1625:** Death of James I. His son becomes Charles I of England. **1630:** John Winthrop founds Boston. **1642:** Civil war begins in England. **1643:** Louis XIV becomes king of France at age four. **1649:** Charles I is beheaded in England, beginning the Commonwealth and Protectorate. **1648:** The Treaty of Westphalia ends the Thirty Years War.	**1600:** Dutch opticians invent the telescope. **1602:** The Dutch East India Company is established to trade with the Far East. **1606–1669:** Rembrandt van Rijn, greatest master of the Dutch school of painting **1607:** Jamestown, Virginia, the first permanent settlement across the Atlantic, is founded. **1608–1674:** John Milton, English poet, author of *Paradise Lost* **1611:** The King James Bible is published. **1619:** The first slaves from Africa arrive in Virginia. **1620:** The Pilgrims land at Plymouth Rock, Massachusetts. **1626:** Peter Minuit purchases Manhattan Island from native Indian chiefs. **1632–1704:** John Locke, English philosopher, founder of empiricism

Christopher Marlowe

Christopher Marlowe (1564–1593) was born two months before William Shakespeare and in somewhat similar social circumstances. Marlowe's father was a shoemaker; Shakespeare's a glovemaker. But unlike Shakespeare, Marlowe won a scholarship to Cambridge, where he remained six years and began his career as a playwright. His first play, *Tamburlaine,* was finished before he left the university. When it was performed in London it had the benefit of Edward Alleyn, the finest actor of his time, playing the title role.

The son-in-law of Philip Henslowe, who owned the Rose, the Fortune, and the Hope theaters in London, Alleyn was a rhetorical actor with a commanding voice and gestures. His style was perfect for declaiming what Ben Jonson called Marlowe's "Mighty line": his IAMBIC PENTAMETER BLANK VERSE, which moves in stately rhythms and which dominated the Elizabethan stage. Marlowe's blank verse, especially in the emotional moments of Faustus's career — as in his invocation of the devils in act I, scene III — resonates and rolls from the tongue in mighty billows. It has a virtually incantatory effect on the listener, and in a London theater of the time, as spoken by Edward Alleyn, it must have been mesmerizing.

Marlowe also had considerable success as a poet and as a translator of the classics. His version of Ovid's *Amores* is very lively, and his long poem *Hero and Leander* is a dynamic contribution to the poetry of Renaissance humanism. It shows his affection for the classics in a form that Shakespeare also employed: the longer narrative poem.

Marlowe's university scholarship was intended for those studying for the ministry, but instead of entering the ministry, he went up to London in 1587. Some of his friends revealed that his beliefs were close to those of atheism, a charge that in his time could have resulted in death. Fortunately, when he applied for his master's degree and was on the verge of having it denied, Queen Elizabeth intervened on his behalf. Her involvement has made subsequent generations think that he must have been a spy on her behalf during at least some of the time he was in Catholic sections of France.

Partly as a result of his connection with Elizabeth, Marlowe has often been portrayed as a romantic swashbuckler in the heart of complex intrigues. He was also well known to most of the literary people of London: Shakespeare, Sir Walter Raleigh, Francis Bacon, Thomas Kyd, and Thomas Harriot (an astronomer and writer) were all close associates. They and Marlowe were also acquainted with the remarkable magician Dr. John Dee. As members of a group dubbed the School of Night, they met privately to discuss ideas of the occult, alchemy, and skeptic philosophy — subjects that could not easily be talked about in the open.

Marlowe's first play was *Tamburlaine* (1587; in two parts), followed by *The Jew of Malta* (1589) and *Edward the Second* (1592). They are all powerful plays that feature a great tragic character. *The Massacre at Paris* (1593) is based on the St. Bartholomew Day's Massacre in 1573, when some thirty thousand Huguenots — French Protestants — were killed by Catholics in Paris. Marlowe's knowledge of the details of the events seems to have been considerable, although the play itself is not as powerful as his earlier tragedies. *Dido, Queen of Carthage* (1593; with Thomas Nashe) is a typical kind of collaboration of the period. None of these plays, good as they are, come to the level of *Doctor Faustus*, which stands as one of the greatest plays of the Elizabethan age.

Apparently quick to anger, Marlowe was involved in one murder before he himself was murdered over a bar bill at the inn of the Widow Bull in Deptford. He was drinking with an acquaintance, Ingram Frizer, who worked for the great Walsingham family, a patron of Marlowe's. During an argument Marlowe grabbed Frizer from behind, but Frizer broke free and stabbed Marlowe, who died instantly. At the time of Marlowe's death Shakespeare was just beginning his career as a playwright.

DOCTOR FAUSTUS

Doctor Faustus was probably written between 1588 and 1593, shortly before Marlowe died. There is a record of its being readied for the press in 1601, but if that version was printed, no copies survive. The first printed version, now called the A-text, is from 1604; an amplified version, called the B-text, came out in 1616. Neither had been supervised by Marlowe, and to make things more complicated, records indicate that Henslowe paid two writers a substantial sum to add to the original text. What the additions were or what the original text was, we probably will never know.

Current scholarship leads us to believe that the 1616 text, printed here, is actually closer to the original acting version than the 1604 text was. The breaking of the text into five acts and their scenes is a modern convention, as is the supplying of most of the stage directions. The five-act pattern common in classical plays is natural to Elizabethan plays as well.

The influence of the medieval stage is readily apparent in *Doctor Faustus*. The emphasis on the devils, the seven deadly sins, and the terrifying vision of hell in act V is reminiscent of the devils of the mystery plays and their reliance on frightening hell's mouth props. The allusion to medieval theater's tradition of the mansion in Mephistophilis's speech in act V also echoes the basic message of the morality plays:

> Ay, Faustus, now thou hast no hope of heaven;
> Therefore despair. Think only upon hell,
> For that must be thy mansion, there to dwell.

Doctor Faustus differs from the morality plays in one very important way, though. We are never led to think that Faustus would have lived a better or more interesting life if he had restrained his ambition. Faustus is a hero, especially of the romantic sort that strove to achieve great things and challenge the gods. The Elizabethans admired Faustus much more than they condemned him, no matter what moral tags Marlowe might have put in the play to satisfy society's official view of itself.

Among the sources of the play are a medieval folklore tradition connected with the wizard who sold his soul to the devil for greater powers and a German book called *Historia von D. Johan Fausten,* published in 1587. Marlowe may have seen the book or, more likely, may have seen an English translation in 1592 called *The History of the damnable life, and deserved death of Doctor John Faustus.* In either event, the Faust legend goes back to the early medieval period and could have reached Marlowe in any number of ways.

Doctor Faustus is one of the earliest English tragedies. Its hero is in many ways larger than life, and while not a member of the nobility, he is at ease with royalty and clearly superior in intellectual abilities. The richness of the psychological portrayal of Faustus — as well as of Wagner and Mephistophilis — elevates the play from the best earlier efforts of English and European dramatists. Faustus represents an interesting tradition: the University of Wittenberg produced the most important Protestant of the sixteenth century, Martin Luther. His daring — comparable in some ways to Faustus's overreaching — led to the Reformation, one of the most cataclysmic changes in European thought in the Renaissance. Hamlet is also a student at Wittenberg, a fact that gives us insight into the Elizabethan imagination. Wittenberg to the Elizabethans meant fierce intellectual energy and daring.

As in the case of many of Shakespeare's tragedies, *Doctor Faustus* has interludes of comic relief, with the horse coursers who are bilked by Faustus and with other clowns and mechanicals who wonder openly about the terrifying skills of the magician. This linking of magic and comic has annoyed some critics who have agreed with Aristotle that such a mixture is problematic and tends to diffuse the effect of the drama. Actually, in performance the comic scenes are in no way a dilution of effect. They tend to buoy the energy of the play and help us focus anew on the insatiable Faustus.

But *Doctor Faustus* has a modern twist that takes it out of the medieval mold. The Renaissance was a period of expansion, especially the expansion of knowledge. Astronomy was symbolic of the new age: Telescopes were beginning to give Europeans a sense of the vastness and complexity of the universe. When Faustus asks information of Mephistophilis, he begins with questions about the planets and the universe, knowledge of which had long been thought to be somehow secret. Mastering that knowledge was symbolic of mastering the knowledge of the innermost workings of science.

Faustus's quest for knowledge became for some people a Renaissance theme. The magicians referred to in the text, such as Roger Bacon and Cornelius Agrippa, were genuine. Their work was read throughout Europe, and the kinds of magic actions that Faustus aspires to were thought possible. The Elizabethans definitely believed in the presence of spirits, of ghosts, of intervention through witches of the otherworld. *Doctor Faustus* fed the contemporary interest in the occult. Faustus quests for forbidden knowledge; he must sell his soul to the devil to acquire it. His lust for knowledge — he says at the outset that he has dominated all the world of learning available to him — is without bounds.

Many of Marlowe's audience would have seen in Doctor Faustus an allusion to the magus John Dee, who cast the horoscope of Queen Elizabeth. Marlowe knew Dee, on whom the description of Faustus is based. Known throughout Europe for his almost supernormal intellectual capacity, Dee was learned in many sciences. His introduction to the first English edition of Euclid's *Geometry* made him not only respected in Europe but eventually known throughout the New World. Dee's version of Euclid was used at Harvard until the late 1700s. Because Dee was a wizard, his house at Mortlake was attacked and burned to the ground by frightened peasants while he was abroad. With his house went one of the most impressive personal libraries in Europe.

Faustus was willing to seek forbidden knowledge — in the way Adam and Eve did — at all costs, in full awareness that he risked the loss of his soul. And while Marlowe condemns Faustus to hell and does not save him at the end, we have the feeling — as did Elizabethans — that there is something grand and heroic about Faustus's risk taking. He fails, yes, but he does so in a way that makes mediocre citizens who would never have had his imagination or daring seem pallid and weak. We find ourselves involved in Faustus's struggle.

Dr. Faustus in Performance

Marlowe may not have seen *Doctor Faustus* performed. There are no performance records until 1594, when Philip Henslowe and the Royal Admiral's Men produced the play. Productions were frequent until 1598, and Henslowe's records indicate that the play was extremely popular. The great actor Edward Alleyn portrayed Faustus. Along with several reissuings of printed versions of the play, productions seem to have continued into the early part of the 1600s, when a number of writers were hired at different times to add lines to the original text. After the Restoration in 1660 and the reopening of the theaters, *Doctor Faustus* was again played frequently, with Thomas Betterton in the title role. In the eighteenth century the play was sometimes staged as a farce and in some cases reduced to a puppet show. In the nineteenth century, however, audiences were given the chance to see the play as a serious tragedy, with Sir Henry Irving, one of the greatest of the nineteenth-century actors, performing in London at the Lyceum Theatre in 1885. Twentieth-century performances included a number of amateur productions, including one during wartime by the great director Peter Brook in 1942.

Orson Welles performed the title role in a Works Progress Administration production in New York; reviews were mixed. Welles, himself a magician, emphasized the magical elements so that trapdoors and special effects became great moments of entertainment. The Phoenix Theatre's 1964 production in New York continued that tradition, with fireworks accompanying the entrance of the "hot whore." That production emphasized the blackness of the play, with dark sets and glittering dark costumes. At the end of the play, Faustus was faced with the yawning pit of hellfire. Productions of the play were also popular in Germany in the first half of the twentieth century. In his novel *Doctor Faustus*, Thomas Mann saw in the play a metaphor for Germany's having sold its soul to Hitler.

Christopher Marlowe (1564–1593)
THE TRAGICAL HISTORY OF THE LIFE AND DEATH OF DOCTOR FAUSTUS   *c. 1593*

The Players

THE CHORUS
DOCTOR FAUSTUS
WAGNER, *his student and servant*
VALDES
CORNELIUS
THREE SCHOLARS
AN OLD MAN

POPE ADRIAN
RAYMOND, *King of Hungary*
BRUNO, *the rival Pope*
TWO CARDINALS
THE ARCHBISHOP OF RHEIMS
CHARLES V, *Emperor of Germany*
MARTINO
FREDERICK   } *Gentlemen of the Emperor's court*
BENVOLIO
BEELZEBUB
DUKE OF SAXONY
DUKE OF ANHOLT
DUCHESS OF ANHOLT
ROBIN, *the clown, a hostler*
DICK
A VINTNER
A HORSE-COURSER
A CARTER
HOSTESS

GOOD ANGEL
BAD ANGEL
LUCIFER
MEPHISTOPHILIS
PRIDE
COVETOUSNESS
ENVY
WRATH   } *The Seven Deadly Sins*
GLUTTONY
SLOTH
LECHERY
ALEXANDER, THE GREAT
HIS PARAMOUR
DARIUS, *King of Persia*
HELEN OF TROY
TWO CUPIDS
DEVILS, BISHOPS, MONKS, FRIARS, SOLDIERS

Note: Material in brackets has been added by the editor.

The Scene: *Wittenberg, Rome, the Emperor's court at Innsbruck, court of the Duke of Anholt, and the neighboring countryside.*

PROLOGUE

(Enter Chorus.)

CHORUS: Not marching in the fields of Trasimene
    Where Mars° did mate° the warlike Carthagens,°
    Nor sporting in the dalliance of love
    In courts of kings where state° is overturned,
    Nor in the pomp of proud audacious deeds   5
    Intends our muse to vaunt his heavenly verse.
    Only this, gentles: we must now perform
    The form of Faustus' fortunes, good or bad.
    And now to patient judgments we appeal,
    And speak for Faustus in his infancy.   10
    Now is he born, of parents base of stock,
    In Germany, within a town called Rhode.
    At riper years to Wittenberg he went,
    Whereas his kinsmen chiefly brought him up.
    So much he profits in divinity,   15
    The fruitful plot of scholarism graced,°
    That shortly he was graced with doctor's name,
    Excelling all whose sweet delight disputes°
    In th'heavenly matters of theology,
    Till swoll'n with cunning of a self-conceit,   20
    His waxen wings did mount above his reach,
    And melting,° heavens conspired his overthrow;
    For, falling to a devilish exercise
    And glutted now with learning's golden gifts,
    He surfeits upon cursèd necromancy.   25
    Nothing so sweet as magic is to him,
    Which he prefers before his chiefest bliss;
    And this the man that in his study sits.

Prologue. **1–2. Trasimene . . . Carthagens:** Perhaps an allusion to a lost play about the Carthaginian Hannibal, who achieved one of his greatest victories at Lake Trasimene in 217 B.C. **2. Mars:** Roman god of war. **mate:** Rival, meet in battle. **4. state:** Government. **16. fruitful plot . . . graced:** Adorned the university. **18. whose sweet delight disputes:** Who takes pleasure in disputing. **21–22. waxen wings . . . melting:** Metaphor referring to Icarus's attempt to fly with waxen wings, which melted when he ignored his father's warning and flew too near the sun.

ACT I • *Scene 1*

(*Faustus in his study.*)

FAUSTUS: Settle thy studies, Faustus, and begin
    To sound the depth of that thou wilt profess.
    Having commenced,° be a divine in show;
    Yet level° at the end of every art,
5   And live and die in Aristotle's works.
    Sweet Analytics, 'tis thou hast ravished me!
    Bene' disserere est finis logices.°
    Is to dispute well logic's chiefest end?
    Affords this art no greater miracle?
10   Then read no more; thou hast attained that end.
    A greater subject fitteth Faustus' wit!
    Bid *On cay mae on*° farewell, Galen° come.
    Seeing *ubi desinit philosophus ibi incipit medicus,°*
    Be a physician, Faustus; heap up gold,
15   And be eternized for some wondrous cure.
    Summum bonum medicinae sanitas.°
    The end of physic is our body's health.
    Why, Faustus, hast thou not attained that end?
    Is not thy common talk sound aphorisms?
20   Are not thy bills° hung up as monuments,
    Whereby whole cities have escaped the plague,
    And divers desperate maladies been cured?
    Yet art thou still but Faustus and a man.
    Couldst thou make men to live eternally,
25   Or, being dead, raise them to life again,
    Then this profession were to be esteemed.
    Physic, farewell! Where is Justinian?°
    Si una eademque res legatus duobus,   [*He reads.*]
    Alter rem, alter valorem rei, etc.°
30   A petty case of paltry legacies!
    Exhaereditare filium non potest pater nisi° —
                                             [*He reads.*]
    Such is the subject of the Institute
    And universal body of the law.
    This study fits a mercenary drudge
35   Who aims at nothing but external trash,
    Too servile and illiberal for me.

When all is done, divinity is best.
Jerome's Bible,° Faustus, view it well:
Stipendium peccati mors est.° Ha! *Stipendium, etc.*
                              [*He reads.*]
The reward of sin is death. That's hard.   40
Si pecasse negamus, fallimur   [*He reads.*]
Et nulla est in nobis veritas.°
If we say that we have no sin,
We deceive ourselves, and there's no truth in us.
Why then belike we must sin,   45
And so consequently die.
Ay, we must die an everlasting death.
What doctrine call you this? *Che serà, serà:*
What will be, shall be! Divinity, adieu!
These metaphysics of magicians,   50
And necromantic books are heavenly.
Lines, circles, signs, letters, and characters —
Ay, these are those that Faustus most desires.
O, what a world of profit and delight,
Of power, of honor, of omnipotence   55
Is promised to the studious artisan!
All things that move between the quiet poles
Shall be at my command. Emperors and kings
Are but obeyed in their several provinces,
Nor can they raise the wind or rend the clouds,   60
But his dominion that exceeds in this
Stretcheth as far as doth the mind of man.
A sound magician is a demi-god.
Here try thy brains to get a deity!
Wagner!

(*Enter Wagner.*)

        Commend me to my dearest friends,   65
The German Valdes and Cornelius;
Request them earnestly to visit me.
WAGNER: I will sir.
                                    (*Exit.*)
FAUSTUS: Their conference will be a greater help to me
Than all my labors, plod I ne'er so fast.   70

(*Enter the Good Angel and the Evil Angel.*)

GOOD ANGEL: O, Faustus, lay that damnèd book aside,
    And gaze not on it, lest it tempt thy soul
    And heap God's heavy wrath upon thy head.
    Read, read the Scriptures. That is blasphemy.
BAD ANGEL: Go forward, Faustus, in that famous art   75
    Wherein all nature's treasury is contained.
    Be thou on earth as Jove is in the sky,
    Lord and commander of these elements.
                            (*Exeunt*° Angels.)
FAUSTUS: How am I glutted with conceit° of this!
    Shall I make spirits fetch me what I please,   80

I, I. 3. **commenced:** Taken a degree.   **4. level:** Aim.   **7. *Bene'
disserere est finis logices:*** The end of logic is to dispute well. A
tenet of the anti-Aristotelian system introduced at Cambridge
when Marlowe was a student there.   **12. *On cay mae on:***
From Aristotle, being or not being.   **Galen:** Greek physician
regarded throughout the Middle Ages as a medical authority.
13. *ubi desinit philosophus ibi incipit medicus:* Where the
philosopher stops, the doctor begins.   **16. *Summum . . . sani-
tas:*** Health is the highest good of the practice of medicine.
20. bills: Medical prescriptions.   **27. Justinian:** Roman
emperor of Constantinople (527–565), responsible for assembling the Roman law and renowned throughout the Middle
Ages as a jurist.   **28–29. *Si . . . rei, etc.:*** If the same object is
willed to two persons, let one have the thing itself and the other
its value, etc. This is an incorrect version of one of Justinian's
rules.   **31. *Exhaereditare . . . nisi —*:** The father cannot dis-
inherit the son except — ; another of Justinian's rules roughly
paraphrased.

38. Jerome's Bible: St. Jerome's Vulgate [Latin] translation of
the Bible.   **39. *Stipendium . . . est:*** Translated in line 40
(Rom. 6:23).   **41–42. *Si . . . veritas:*** Translated in lines 43–44
(1 John 1:8).   **78. [S.D.] *Exeunt:*** Latin for "they go out."
79. conceit: The conception of attaining.

Resolve me of° all ambiguities,
Perform what desperate enterprise I will?
I'll have them fly to India for gold,
Ransack the ocean for orient pearl,
85 And search all corners of the new-found world
For pleasant fruits and princely delicates.
I'll have them read me strange philosophy
And tell the secrets of all foreign kings;
I'll have them wall all Germany with brass
90 And make swift Rhine circle fair Wittenberg.°
I'll have them fill the public schools with silk
Wherewith the students shall be bravely clad.
I'll levy soldiers with the coin they bring
And chase the Prince of Parma from our land
95 And reign sole king of all the provinces.°
Yea, stranger engines for the brunt of war
Than was the fiery keel at Antwerp's bridge°
I'll make my servile spirits to invent.
Come, German Valdes and Cornelius,
                                         [He calls within.]
100 And make me blessed with your sage conference!

(Enter Valdes and Cornelius.)

Valdes, sweet Valdes, and Cornelius,
Know that your words have won me at the last
To practice magic and concealed arts;
Yet not your words only, but mine own fantasy
105 That will receive no object, for my head
But ruminates on necromantic skill.
Philosophy is odious and obscure;
Both law and physic are for petty wits;
Divinity is basest of the three,
110 Unpleasant, harsh, contemptible and vile.
'Tis, magic, magic, that hath ravished me.
Then, gentle friends, aid me in this attempt,
And I, that have with subtle syllogisms
Gravelled° the pastors of the German church,
115 And made the flowering pride of Wittenberg
Swarm to my problems° as th'infernal spirits
On sweet Musaeus° when he came to hell,
Will be as cunning as Agrippa was,
Whose shadows° made all Europe honor him.
VALDES: Faustus, these books, thy wit, and our
120   experience
Shall make all nations to canonize us.
As Indian Moors° obey their Spanish lords,

So shall the spirits of every element
Be always serviceable to us three.
Like lions shall they guard us when we please,   125
Like Almain rutters° with their horsemen's staves
Or Lapland giants trotting by our sides,
Sometimes like women or unwedded maids,
Shadowing° more beauty in their airy brows
Than in the white breasts of the queen of love.   130
From Venice shall they drag huge argosies,
And from America the golden fleece
That yearly stuffs old Philip's treasury,
If learnèd Faustus will be resolute.
FAUSTUS: Valdes, as resolute am I in this   135
As thou to live; therefore object it not.
CORNELIUS: The miracles that magic will perform
Will make thee vow to study nothing else.
He that is grounded in astrology,
Enriched with tongues,° well seen in minerals,   140
Hath all the principles magic doth require.
Then doubt not, Faustus, but to be renowned
And more frequented for this mystery
Than heretofore the Delphian oracle.°
The spirits tell me they can dry the sea   145
And fetch the treasure of all foreign wracks,
Yea, all the wealth that our forefathers hid
Within the massy entrails of the earth.
Then tell me, Faustus, what shall we three want?
FAUSTUS: Nothing, Cornelius. O, this cheers my soul! 150
Come, show me some demonstrations magical,
That I may conjure in some lusty grove
And have these joys in full possession.
VALDES: Then haste thee to some solitary grove,
And bear wise Bacon's and Abanus' works,°   155
The Hebrew Psalter, and New Testament;
And whatsoever else is requisite
We will inform thee ere our conference cease.
CORNELIUS: Valdes, first let him know the words of
    art,
And then, all other ceremonies learned,   160
Faustus may try his cunning by himself.
VALDES: First I'll instruct thee in the rudiments,
And then wilt thou be perfecter than I.
FAUSTUS: Then come and dine with me, and after meat
We'll canvass every quiddity° thereof,   165
For ere I sleep I'll try what I can do.
This night I'll conjure, though I die therefore.
                                         (Exeunt.)

81. Resolve me of: Explain to me.   **90. Rhine . . . Wittenberg:** Wittenberg is actually on the Elbe River, not the Rhine.   **95. provinces:** The Netherlands.   **97. fiery . . . bridge:** In April 1584 the Dutch used a fireship to destroy a bridge built across a river by the Prince of Parma in an attempt to blockade Antwerp.   **114. Gravelled:** Puzzled and amazed.   **116. problems:** Public disputations.   **117. Musaeus:** A semimythical Greek poet. Following Virgil, Marlowe has him visit hell like the mythical Orpheus.   **118–19. Agrippa . . . shadows:** Cornelius Agrippa (1486?–1535), a German physician and student of the occult, was said to have power to raise spirits (shadows) from the dead.   **122. Indian Moors:** American Indians.

126. Almain rutters: German cavalry.   **129. Shadowing:** Harboring, sheltering.   **140. Enriched with tongues:** Fluent in Latin, the language used for communicating with spirits.   **144. Delphian oracle:** The high priest of Apollo at Delphi who had power to foretell the future. [An oracle is the response of a god to a question asked by one who worships the god. The Delphic Oracle was the chief oracle of Greece, presided over by Apollo.]   **155. Bacon's . . . works:** Roger Bacon (1214?–1294) and Pietro D'Abano (1250–1316) were famous in the Middle Ages for their feats of magic.   **165. quiddity:** Essential element (a term from scholastic logic).

Scene II

(*Enter two Scholars.*)

FIRST SCHOLAR: I wonder what's become of Faustus, that
was wont to make our schools ring with *sic probo.*°

(*Enter Wagner.*)

SECOND SCHOLAR: That shall we presently know; here
comes his boy.

5   FIRST SCHOLAR: How now sirrah! Where's thy master?
WAGNER: God in heaven knows.
SECOND SCHOLAR: Why, dost not thou know then?
WAGNER: Yes, I know, but that follows not.
FIRST SCHOLAR: Go to, sirrah! Leave your jesting and
10   tell us where he is.
WAGNER: That follows not by force of argument, which
you, being licentiates,° should stand upon; therefore
acknowledge your error and be attentive.
SECOND SCHOLAR: Then you will not tell us?
15 WAGNER: You are deceived, for I will tell you. Yet if you
were not dunces, you would never ask me such a
question. For is he not *corpus naturale*, and is not
that *mobile?*° Then wherefore should you ask such a
question? But that I am by nature phlegmatic, slow
20   to wrath, and prone to lechery — to love, I would
say — it were not for you to come within forty foot
of the place of execution, although I do not doubt
but to see you both hanged the next sessions. Thus
having triumphed over you, I will set my counte-
25   nance like a precisian° and begin to speak thus:
Truly, my dear brethren, my master is within at dinner with Valdes and Cornelius, as this wine, if it
could speak, would inform your worships. And so,
the Lord bless you, preserve you, and keep you, my
30   dear brethren.

(*Exit.*)

FIRST SCHOLAR: O Faustus, then I fear that which I
have long suspected.
That thou art fall'n into that damnèd art
For which they two are infamous through the
world.
SECOND SCHOLAR: Were he a stranger, not allied
to me,
35   The danger of his soul would make me mourn.
But come, let us go and inform the rector.°
It may be his grave counsel may reclaim him.
FIRST SCHOLAR: I fear me nothing will reclaim
him now.
SECOND SCHOLAR: Yet let us see what we
can do.

(*Exeunt.*)

I, II. 2. *sic probo*: Thus I prove (used in scholastic argument).
12. licentiates: Holders of university degrees.   **17–18.** *corpus
naturale . . . mobile*: The subject matter of physics, in scholastic terms, was *corpus naturale seu mobile* (natural body in
motion).   **25. precisian**: Puritan.   **36. rector**: Head of the university.

Scene III

(*Thunder. Enter [above] Lucifer and four Devils. Enter
Faustus to conjure.*)

FAUSTUS: Now that the gloomy shadow of the night,
Longing to view Orion's drizzling look,
Leaps from th'Antarctic world unto the sky
And dims the welkin° with her pitchy breath,
Faustus begin thine incantations,   5
And try if devils will obey thy hest,
Seeing thou hast prayed and sacrificed to them.
Within this circle is Jehovah's name,
Forward and backward anagrammatized,
Th'abbreviated names of holy saints,   10
Figures of every adjunct to the heavens,
And characters of signs and erring° stars,
By which the spirits are enforced to rise.
Then fear not, Faustus, to be resolute,
And try the utmost magic can perform.   15

(*Thunder.*)

*Sint mihi Dei Acherontis propitii! Valeat numen tri-
plex Jehovae. Ignei, aerii, aquatani spiritus, salvete!
Orientis princeps, Beelzebub, inferni ardentis monar-
cha, et Demogorgon, propitiamus vos, ut appareat et
surgat Mephistophilis. Quid tu moraris? Per Jehovam*   20
*Gehennam, et consecratam aquam quam nunc spargo,
signumque crucis quod nunc facto, et per vota nostra,
ipse nunc surgat nobis dicatus Mephistophilis.*°

(*Enter [Mephistophilis,] a Devil.*)

I charge thee to return and change thy shape;
Thou art too ugly to attend on me.   25
Go, and return an old Franciscan friar;
That holy shape becomes a devil best.

(*Exit Devil.*)

I see there's virtue in my heavenly words.
Who would not be proficient in this art?
How pliant is this Mephistophilis,   30
Full of obedience and humility.
Such is the force of magic and my spells.
Now Faustus, thou art conjurer laureate,
That canst command great Mephistophilis.
Quin redis Mephistophilis fratris imagine.°   35

(*Enter Mephistophilis [dressed like a Franciscan friar].*)

MEPHISTOPHILIS: Now Faustus, what wouldst thou
have me do?

I, III. **4. welkin**: Sky.   **12. erring**: Wandering.   **16–23.** *Sint . . .
Mephistophilis*: May the gods of Aceron be propitious to me.
Let the triple name of Jehova [the trinity] be gone. Hail spirits
of fire, air, and water. Prince of the East, Beelzebub, monarch of
burning hell, and Demogorgon, we petition you that Mephistophilis may appear and rise. Why do you linger? By Jehova,
Gehenna, and the holy water which I now sprinkle and the sign
of the cross which I now make and by our vows, let Mephistophilis himself now rise to serve us.   **35.** *Quin . . . imagine*: Return, Mephistophilis, in the shape of a friar.

FAUSTUS: I charge thee wait upon me whilst I live,
    To do whatever Faustus shall command,
    Be it to make the moon drop from her sphere
40 Or the ocean to overwhelm the world.
MEPHISTOPHILIS: I am a servant to great Lucifer
    And may not follow thee without his leave.
    No more than he commands must we perform.
FAUSTUS: Did not he charge thee to appear to me?
MEPHISTOPHILIS: No, I came hither of mine own
45   accord.
FAUSTUS: Did not my conjuring speeches raise thee?
    Speak.
MEPHISTOPHILIS: That was the cause, but yet *per
    accidens,*°
    For when we hear one rack the name of God,
    Abjure the Scriptures and his Savior Christ,
50 We fly in hope to get his glorious soul;
    Nor will we come unless he use such means
    Whereby he is in danger to be damned.
    Therefore the shortest cut for conjuring
    Is stoutly to abjure the Trinity
55 And pray devoutly to the prince of hell.
FAUSTUS: So Faustus hath
    Already done, and holds this principle:
    There is no chief but only Beelzebub,
    To whom Faustus doth dedicate himself.
60 This word "damnation" terrifies not me,
    For I confound hell in Elysium.
    My ghost° be with the old philosophers!
    But leaving these vain trifles of men's souls,
    Tell me what is that Lucifer thy lord?
MEPHISTOPHILIS: Arch-regent and commander of all
65   spirits.
FAUSTUS: Was not that Lucifer an angel once?
MEPHISTOPHILIS: Yes Faustus, and most dearly loved
    of God.
FAUSTUS: How comes it then that he is prince of devils?
MEPHISTOPHILIS: O, by aspiring pride and insolence,
70 For which God threw him from the face of heaven.
FAUSTUS: And what are you that live with Lucifer?
MEPHISTOPHILIS: Unhappy spirits that fell with
    Lucifer,
    Conspired against our God with Lucifer,
    And are for ever damned with Lucifer.
FAUSTUS: Where are you damned?
75 MEPHISTOPHILIS: In hell.
FAUSTUS: How comes it then that thou art out of hell?
MEPHISTOPHILIS: Why this is hell, nor am I out of it.
    Think'st thou that I who saw the face of God
    And tasted the eternal joys of heaven
80 Am not tormented with ten thousand hells
    In being deprived of everlasting bliss?
    O Faustus, leave these frivolous demands
    Which strike a terror to my fainting soul.
FAUSTUS: What, is great Mephistophilis so passionate
85   For being deprivèd of the joys of heaven?

Learn thou of Faustus' manly fortitude,
    And scorn those joys thou never shalt possess.
    Go bear these tidings to great Lucifer:
    Seeing Faustus hath incurred eternal death
    By desperate thoughts against Jove's deity,   90
    Say he surrenders up to him his soul,
    So he will spare him four and twenty years,
    Letting him live in all voluptuousness,
    Having thee ever to attend on me,
    To give me whatsoever I shall ask,   95
    To tell me whatsoever I demand,
    To slay mine enemies, and aid my friends,
    And always be obedient to my will.
    Go, and return to mighty Lucifer,
    And meet me in my study at midnight,   100
    And then resolve me of thy master's mind.
MEPHISTOPHILIS: I will, Faustus.

                                            (*Exit.*)

FAUSTUS: Had I as many souls as there be stars,
    I'd give them all for Mephistophilis.
    By him I'll be great emperor of the world,   105
    And make a bridge thorough the moving air,
    To pass the ocean with a band of men.
    I'll join the hills that bind° the Afric shore,
    And make that country continent to Spain,
    And both contributory to my crown.   110
    The Emperor shall not live but by my leave,
    Nor any potentate of Germany.
    Now that I have obtained what I desire,
    I'll live in speculation of this art
    Till Mephistophilis return again.   115

                                            (*Exit.*)

Scene IV

(*Enter Wagner and* [*Robin,*] *the Clown.*)

WAGNER: Come hither, sirrah boy.
ROBIN: Boy! O disgrace to my person. Zounds, boy in
    your face! You have seen many boys with such
    pickedevants,° I am sure.
WAGNER: Sirrah, hast thou no comings in?°   5
ROBIN: Yes, and goings out too, you may see, sir.
WAGNER: Alas, poor slave! See how poverty jests in his
    nakedness. I know the villain's out of service, and so
    hungry that I know he would give his soul to the
    devil for a shoulder of mutton, though it were blood-   10
    raw.
ROBIN: Not so neither. I had need to have it well
    roasted, and good sauce to it, if I pay so dear, I can
    tell you.
WAGNER: Sirrah, wilt thou be my man and wait on me,   15
    and I will make thee go like *Qui mihi discipulus?*°

---

47. cause . . . *per accidens:* The terms are from scholastic logic.
62. ghost: Spirit.

108. bind: Enclose. **I, IV. 4. pickedevants:** Pointed beards.
5. comings in: Earnings. **16. *Qui mihi discipulus:*** Who is my
disciple (the opening words of a Latin poem by William Lyly,
well known to Elizabethan schoolboys).

ROBIN: What, in verse?

WAGNER: No slave; in beaten° silk and staves-acre.°

ROBIN: Staves-acre? That's good to kill vermin. Then,
20   belike, if I serve you I shall be lousy.

WAGNER: Why, so thou shalt be, whether thou dost it or
        no; for, sirrah, if thou dost not presently bind thyself
        to me for seven years, I'll turn all the lice about thee
        into familiars° and make them tear thee in pieces.

25 ROBIN: Nay sir, you may save yourself a labor, for they
        are as familiar with me as if they paid for their meat
        and drink, I can tell you.

WAGNER: Well, sirrah, leave your jesting and take these
        guilders.

30 ROBIN: Yes, marry sir, and I thank you too.

WAGNER: So, now thou art to be at an hour's warning,
        whensoever and wheresoever the devil shall fetch
        thee.

ROBIN: Here, take your guilders again. I'll none of 'em.

35 WAGNER: Not I. Thou art pressed.° Prepare thyself, for I
        will presently raise up two devils to carry thee away.
        Banio! Belcher!

ROBIN: Belcher? And Belcher come here, I'll belch him. I
        am not afraid of a devil.

(*Enter two Devils.*)

40 WAGNER: How now, sir? Will you serve me now?

ROBIN: Ay, good Wagner; take away the devil then.

WAGNER: Spirits away! Now, sirrah, follow me.
                                        [*Exeunt Devils.*]

ROBIN: I will sir. But hark you, master, will you teach me
        this conjuring occupation?

45 WAGNER: Ay, sirrah. I'll teach thee to turn thyself to a
        dog, or a cat, or a mouse, or a rat, or any thing.

ROBIN: A dog, or a cat, or a mouse, or a rat! O brave
        Wagner!

WAGNER: Villain, call me Master Wagner, and see that
50   you walk attentively, and let your right eye be always
        diametrally° fixed upon my left heel, that thou may'st
        quasi vestigial nostras insistere.°

ROBIN: Well, sir, I warrant you.

                                        (*Exeunt.*)

ACT II • *Scene* I

(*Enter Faustus in his Study.*)

FAUSTUS: Now Faustus must thou needs be damned,
        And canst thou not be saved.
        What boots° it then to think on God or heaven?
        Away with such vain fancies, and despair;
5   Despair in God, and trust in Beelzebub.
        Now go not backward; Faustus, be resolute.

Why waver'st thou? O, something soundeth in mine
        ear:
"Abjure this magic; turn to God again."
Ay, and Faustus will turn to God again!
To God? He loves thee not.   10
The God thou serv'st is thine own appetite,
Wherein is fixed the love of Beelzebub.
To him I'll build an altar and a church,
And offer lukewarm blood of new-born babes.

(*Enter the two Angels.*)

BAD ANGEL: Go forward, Faustus, in that famous art.   15

GOOD ANGEL: Sweet Faustus, leave that execrable art.

FAUSTUS: Contrition, prayer, repentance — what of
        these?

GOOD ANGEL: O, they are means to bring thee unto
        heaven.

BAD ANGEL: Rather illusions, fruits of lunacy,
        That make men foolish that do use them most.   20

GOOD ANGEL: Sweet Faustus, think of heaven and
        heavenly things.

BAD ANGEL: No Faustus, think of honor and wealth.
                                        (*Exeunt Angels.*)

FAUSTUS: Wealth? Why, the signory of Emden° shall be
        mine.
        When Mephistophilis shall stand by me,
        What power can hurt me? Faustus thou art safe.   25
        Cast no more doubts. Mephistophilis, come
        And bring glad tidings from great Lucifer.
        Is't not midnight? Come, Mephistophilis.
        Veni,° *veni, Mephistophile.*

(*Enter Mephistophilis.*)

        Now tell me what saith Lucifer, thy lord?   30

MEPHISTOPHILIS: That I shall wait on Faustus whilst
        he lives,
        So he will buy my service with his soul.

FAUSTUS: Already Faustus hath hazarded that for thee.

MEPHISTOPHILIS: But now thou must bequeath it
        solemnly
        And write a deed of gift with thine own blood,   35
        For that security craves great Lucifer.
        If thou deny it, I must back to hell.

FAUSTUS: Stay, Mephistophilis! Tell me what good
        Will my soul do thy lord.

MEPHISTOPHILIS: Enlarge his kingdom.

FAUSTUS: Is that the reason why he tempts us thus?   40

MEPHISTOPHILIS: *Solamen miseris socios habuisse
        doloris.*°

FAUSTUS: Why, have you any pain that torture others?

MEPHISTOPHILIS: As great as have the human souls of
        men.
        But tell me, Faustus, shall I have thy soul?

---

18. beaten: Embroidered with metal.   **staves-acre:** A plant used for killing vermin.   **24. familiars:** Attendant evil spirits.   **35. pressed:** Enlisted into service in exchange for money.   **51. diametrally:** In a straight line.   **52. *quasi . . . insistere:*** As if to walk in our tracks.   **II, I. 3. boots:** Avails.

23. Emden: The chief city of East Friesland near the mouth of the river Ems, which had considerable trade relations with Elizabethan England.   **29. *Veni:*** Come.   **41. *Solamen . . . doloris:*** It is a consolation in misery to have a fellow sufferer.

45   And I will be thy slave and wait on thee
      And give thee more than thou hast wit to ask.
FAUSTUS: Ay, Mephistophilis, I'll give it him.
MEPHISTOPHILIS: Then Faustus, stab thy arm
      courageously,
      And bind thy soul that at some certain day
50   Great Lucifer may claim it as his own,
      And then be thou as great as Lucifer.
FAUSTUS: [*stabbing his arm*] Lo, Mephistophilis, for
      love of thee,
      I cut mine arm, and with my proper° blood
      Assure my soul to be great Lucifer's,
55   Chief lord and regent of perpetual night.
      View here this blood that trickles from mine arm,
      And let it be propitious for my wish.
MEPHISTOPHILIS: But Faustus,
      Write it in manner of a deed of gift.
60   FAUSTUS: Ay, so I do. [*He writes.*] But Mephistophilis,
      My blood congeals, and I can write no more.
MEPHISTOPHILIS: I'll fetch thee fire to dissolve it
      straight.
                                              (*Exit.*)
FAUSTUS: What might the staying of my blood portend?
      Is it unwilling I should write this bill?
65   Why streams it not that I may write afresh?
      "Faustus gives to thee his soul." Ah, there it stayed.
      Why shouldst thou not? Is not thy soul thine own?
      Then write again: "Faustus gives to thee his soul."

(*Enter Mephistophilis with the chafer of fire.*)

MEPHISTOPHILIS: See Faustus, here is fire. Set it on.°
70   FAUSTUS: So. Now the blood begins to clear again.
      Now will I make an end immediately.
                                          [*He writes.*]
MEPHISTOPHILIS: [*Aside.*] What will not I do to obtain
      his soul?
FAUSTUS: *Consummatum est;*° this bill is ended,
      And Faustus hath bequeathed his soul to Lucifer.
75   But what is this inscription on mine arm?
      Homo fuge!° Whither should I fly?
      If unto God, he'll throw me down to hell.
      My senses are deceived; here's nothing writ.
      O yes, I see it plain. Even here is writ
80   *Homo fuge!* Yet shall not Faustus fly.
MEPHISTOPHILIS: [*Aside.*] I'll fetch him somewhat to
      delight his mind.
                                              (*Exit.*)

(*Enter Devils, giving crowns and rich apparel to Faustus. They dance and then depart. Enter Mephistophilis.*)

FAUSTUS: What means this show? Speak Mephistophilis.
MEPHISTOPHILIS: Nothing, Faustus, but to delight thy
      mind
      And let thee see what magic can perform.

FAUSTUS: But may I raise such spirits when I please?   85
MEPHISTOPHILIS: Ay Faustus, and do greater things
      than these.
FAUSTUS: Then, Mephistophilis, receive this scroll,
      A deed of gift of body and of soul,
      But yet conditionally that thou perform
      All covenants and articles between us both.   90
MEPHISTOPHILIS: Faustus, I swear by hell and Lucifer
      To effect all promises between us made.
FAUSTUS: Then hear me read it Mephistophilis.
      On these conditions following:
      First, that Faustus may be a spirit in form and sub-   95
      stance;
      Secondly, that Mephistophilis shall be his servant and
      be at his command;
      Thirdly, that Mephistophilis shall do for him and
      bring him whatsoever;   100
      Fourthly, that he shall be in his chamber or house
      invisible;
      Lastly, that he shall appear to the said John Faustus
      at all times, in what form or shape soever he please: I,
      John Faustus, of Wittenberg, doctor, by these pres-   105
      ents, do give both body and soul to Lucifer, Prince of
      the East, and his minister, Mephistophilis; and fur-
      thermore grant unto them that four and twenty years
      being expired, the articles above written inviolate,
      full power to fetch or carry the said John Faustus,   110
      body and soul, flesh, blood, or goods, into their habi-
      tation wheresoever.
                          By me, John Faustus.
MEPHISTOPHILIS: Speak Faustus. Do you deliver this as
      your deed?
FAUSTUS: Ay, take it, and the devil give thee good of it.   115
MEPHISTOPHILIS: So now, Faustus, ask me what thou
      wilt.
FAUSTUS: First will I question with thee about hell.
      Tell me, where is the place that men call hell?
MEPHISTOPHILIS: Under the heavens.
FAUSTUS: Ay, so are all things else. But whereabouts?   120
MEPHISTOPHILIS: Within the bowels of these elements,
      Where we are tortured and remain for ever.
      Hell hath no limits, nor is circumscribed
      In one self place, but where we are is hell,
      And where hell is, there must we ever be.   125
      And, to be short, when all the world dissolves
      And every creature shall be purified,
      All places shall be hell that is not heaven.
FAUSTUS: I think hell's a fable.
MEPHISTOPHILIS: Ay, think so still, till experience
      change thy mind.   130
FAUSTUS: Why, dost thou think that Faustus shall be
      damned?
MEPHISTOPHILIS: Ay, of necessity, for here's the scroll
      In which thou hast given thy soul to Lucifer.
FAUSTUS: Ay, and body too. But what of that?
      Think'st thou that Faustus is so fond° to imagine   135

---

53. proper: Own.   **69. Set it on:** Set the dish of blood on the
fire.   **73.** *Consummatum est:* It is completed (the words of Jesus
at his Crucifixion; John 19:30).   **76.** *Homo fuge:* Fly, man.

135. fond: Foolish.

That after this life there is any pain?
No, these are trifles and mere old wives' tales.
MEPHISTOPHILIS: But I am an instance to prove the
    contrary,
For I tell thee I am damned and now in hell.
FAUSTUS: Nay, and this be hell, I'll willingly be
140   damned.
What? Sleeping, eating, walking and disputing?
But, leaving off this, let me have a wife,
The fairest maid in Germany,
For I am wanton and lascivious,
145 And cannot live without a wife.
MEPHISTOPHILIS: I prithee, Faustus, talk not of a wife.
FAUSTUS: Nay, sweet Mephistophilis, fetch me one, for
    I will have one.
MEPHISTOPHILIS: Well, Faustus, thou shalt have a
    wife.
Sit there till I come.   [*Exit.*]

(*Enter [Mephistophilis] with a Devil dressed like a
woman, with fireworks.*)

150 FAUSTUS: What sight is this?
MEPHISTOPHILIS: Now Faustus, how dost thou like thy
    wife?
FAUSTUS: Here's a hot whore indeed! No, I'll no wife.
MEPHISTOPHILIS: Marriage is but a ceremonial toy,
And if thou lovest me, think no more of it.
155 I'll cull thee out the fairest courtesans
And bring them every morning to thy bed.
She whom thine eye shall like, thy heart shall have,
Were she as chaste as was Penelope,°
As wise as Saba,° or as beautiful
160 As was bright Lucifer before his fall.
Hold; take this book; peruse it thoroughly.
The iterating of these lines brings gold;
The framing of this circle on the ground
Brings thunder, whirlwinds, storm and lightning.
165 Pronounce this thrice devoutly to thyself,
And men in harness° shall appear to thee,
Ready to execute what thou command'st.
FAUSTUS: Thanks, Mephistophilis, for this sweet book.
This will I keep as chary as my life.

                            (*Exeunt.*)

Scene II

(*Enter Faustus in his study and Mephistophilis.*)

FAUSTUS: When I behold the heavens, then I repent
And curse thee, wicked Mephistophilis,
Because thou hast deprived me of those joys.
MEPHISTOPHILIS: 'Twas thine own seeking, Faustus;
    thank thyself.
5 But think'st thou heaven is such a glorious thing?

158. **Penelope:** The faithful wife of Ulysses in Homer's
Odyssey. 159. **Saba:** The Queen of Sheba. 166. **harness:**
Armor.

I tell thee, Faustus, 'tis not half so fair
As thou, or any man that breathes on earth.
FAUSTUS: How prov'st thou that?
MEPHISTOPHILIS: 'Twas made for man; then he's more
    excellent.
FAUSTUS: If heaven was made for man, 'twas made for
    me.   10
I will renounce this magic and repent.

(*Enter the two Angels.*)

GOOD ANGEL: Faustus repent; yet God will pity thee.
BAD ANGEL: Thou art a spirit;° God cannot pity thee.
FAUSTUS: Who buzzeth in mine ears I am a spirit?
Be I a devil, yet God may pity me;   15
Yea, God will pity me if I repent.
BAD ANGEL: Ay, but Faustus never shall repent.
                     (*Exeunt angels.*)
FAUSTUS: My heart is hardened; I cannot repent.
Scarce can I name salvation, faith, or heaven,
But fearful echoes thunder in mine ears: 20
"Faustus, thou art damned!" Then swords and
    knives,
Poison, guns, halters, and envenomed steel
Are laid before me to dispatch myself;
And long ere this I should have done the deed,
Had not sweet pleasure conquered deep despair. 25
Have not I made blind Homer sing to me
Of Alexander's love and Oenone's death?°
And hath not he, that built the walls of Thebes
With ravishing sound of his melodious harp,°
Made music with my Mephistophilis?   30
Why should I die then, or basely despair?
I am resolved; Faustus shall not repent.
Come, Mephistophilis, let us dispute again
And reason of divine astrology.
Speak; are there many spheres above the moon? 35
Are all celestial bodies but one globe,
As is the substance of this centric earth?
MEPHISTOPHILIS: As are the elements, such are the
    heavens,
Even from the moon unto the empyreal orb,
Mutually folded in each others' spheres,   40
And jointly move upon one axle-tree.
Whose terminè° is termed the world's wide pole;
Nor are the names of Saturn, Mars, or Jupiter
Feigned, but are erring stars.°
FAUSTUS: But have they all
One motion, both *situ et tempore?*°   45

II, ɪɪ. 13. spirit: Devil. **27. Alexander's . . . death:** Paris (also
called Alexander) loved the nymph Oenone when he lived as a
shepherd on Mt. Ida. Oenone died of a broken heart when he
left her. **28–29. he . . . harp:** Amphion, son of Zeus and
Antiope, caused stones to move and the walls of Thebes to be
built simply by playing on the lyre given to him by Hermes.
42. terminè: Limit. **44. erring stars:** Planets. **45. *situ et tempore:*** In position (direction of movement) and in the time they
take to revolve about the earth.

MEPHISTOPHILIS: All move from east to west in four and twenty hours upon the poles of the world, but differ in their motions upon the poles of the zodiac.

FAUSTUS: These slender questions Wagner can decide.
50   Hath Mephistophilis no greater skill?
     Who knows not the double motion of the planets?
     That the first is finished in a natural day?
     The second thus? Saturn in thirty years?
     Jupiter in twelve; Mars in four; the sun, Venus and
55   Mercury in a year, the moon in twenty eight days.
     These are freshmen's suppositions. But tell me hath
     every sphere a dominion or *intelligentia?*°

MEPHISTOPHILIS: Ay.

FAUSTUS: How many heavens or spheres are there?
60   MEPHISTOPHILIS: Nine — the seven planets, the firmament, and the empyreal heaven.

FAUSTUS: But is there not *coelum igneum, et crystallinum?*°

MEPHISTOPHILIS: No, Faustus, they be but fables.
65   FAUSTUS: Resolve me then in this one question: why are not conjunctions, oppositions, aspects, eclipses° all at one time, but in some years we have more, in some less?

MEPHISTOPHILIS: *Per inaequalem motum respectu*
70   *totius.*°

FAUSTUS: Well, I am answered. Now tell me who made the world.

MEPHISTOPHILIS: I will not.

FAUSTUS: Sweet Mephistophilis, tell me.
75   MEPHISTOPHILIS: Move me not, Faustus.

FAUSTUS: Villain, have not I bound thee to tell me any thing?

MEPHISTOPHILIS: Ay, that is not against our kingdom. This is. Thou art damned. Think thou of hell.

FAUSTUS: Think, Faustus, upon God that made the
80   world.

MEPHISTOPHILIS: Remember this.
                                             (*Exit.*)

FAUSTUS: Ay, go accursèd spirit to ugly hell.
     'Tis thou hast damned distressèd Faustus' soul.
     Is't not too late?

(*Enter the two Angels.*)

85   BAD ANGEL: Too late.

GOOD ANGEL: Never too late, if Faustus will repent.

BAD ANGEL: If thou repent, devils will tear thee in pieces.

GOOD ANGEL: Repent, and they shall never raze thy skin.
                                      (*Exeunt Angels.*)

FAUSTUS: O Christ, my Savior, my Savior,
     Help to save distressèd Faustus' soul.   90

(*Enter Lucifer, Beelzebub, and Mephistophilis.*)

LUCIFER: Christ cannot save thy soul, for he is just.
     There's none but I have interest in the same.

FAUSTUS: O, what art thou that look'st so terribly?

LUCIFER: I am Lucifer,
     And this is my companion prince in hell.   95

FAUSTUS: O, Faustus, they are come to fetch thy soul.

BEELZEBUB: We are come to tell thee thou dost injure us.

LUCIFER: Thou call'st on Christ, contrary to thy promise.

BEELZEBUB: Thou shouldst not think on God.

LUCIFER: Think on the devil.   100

BEELZEBUB: And his dam too.

FAUSTUS: Nor will I henceforth. Pardon me in this,
     And Faustus vows never to look to heaven,
     Never to name God, or to pray to him,
     To burn his Scriptures, slay his ministers,   105
     And make my spirits pull his churches down.

LUCIFER: So shalt thou show thyself an obedient servant,
     And we will highly gratify thee for it.

BEELZEBUB: Faustus, we are come from hell in person to show thee some pastime. Sit down, and thou shalt 110 behold the Seven Deadly Sins appear to thee in their own proper shapes and likeness.

FAUSTUS: That sight will be as pleasant to me as Paradise was to Adam the first day of his creation.

LUCIFER: Talk not of Paradise or creation, but mark the 115 show. Go, Mephistophilis, fetch them in.
                                  [*Exit Mephistophilis.*]

(*Enter the Seven Deadly Sins, [with Mephistophilis, led by a Piper*].)

BEELZEBUB: Now Faustus, question them of their names and dispositions.

FAUSTUS: That shall I soon. What art thou, the first?

PRIDE: I am Pride. I disdain to have any parents. I am 120 like to Ovid's flea:° I can creep into every corner of a wench. Sometimes, like a periwig, I sit upon her brow. Next, like a necklace, I hang about her neck. Then, like a fan of feathers, I kiss her lips, and then, turning myself to a wrought smock, do what I list. 125 But fie, what a smell is here! I'll not speak another word unless the ground be perfumed and covered with cloth of Arras.°

FAUSTUS: Thou art a proud knave indeed. What art thou, the second?   130

COVETOUSNESS: I am Covetousness, begotten of an old churl in a leather bag, and might I now obtain my wish, this house, you and all, should turn to gold, that I might lock you safe into my chest. O my sweet gold!

---

57. **dominion or *intelligentia*:** Governing angel.   62–63. **coelum . . . crystallinum:** The fiery heaven and crystalline sphere of Ptolemaic astronomy.   66. **conjunctions:** Seeming proximities of heavenly bodies.   **oppositions:** Divergences of heavenly bodies.   **aspects:** Any other relations of such bodies to one another.   **eclipses:** The blottings out of one heavenly body by another.   69–70. **Per . . . totius:** By their unequal movements in respect to the whole (i.e., the different speeds of the various planets within the total cosmos).

121. **Ovid's flea:** The medieval poem *Carmine de Pulice* (Poem of the Flea) was generally attributed to Ovid.   128. **cloth of Arras:** Flemish cloth used generally for tapestries.

Emry James (l.) as Mephostophilis
and Ian McKellen as Doctor
Faustus in the 1974 Royal
Shakespeare Company's
production of Marlowe's play.

135 FAUSTUS: And what art thou, the third?
ENVY: I am Envy, begotten of a chimney-sweeper and an
    oyster-wife. I cannot read and therefore wish all
    books burned. I am lean with seeing others eat. O,
    that there would come a famine over all the world,
140 that all might die, and I live alone; then thou shouldst
    see how fat I'd be. But must thou sit and I stand?
    Come down, with a vengeance.
FAUSTUS: Out envious wretch! But what are thou, the
    fourth?
145 WRATH: I am Wrath. I had neither father nor mother. I
    leaped out of a lion's mouth when I was scarce an
    hour old, and ever since have run up and down the
    world with this case of rapiers, wounding myself
    when I could get none to fight withal. I was born in
150 hell, and look to it, for some of you shall be my
    father.
FAUSTUS: And what are you, the fifth?
GLUTTONY: I am Gluttony. My parents are all dead, and
    the devil a penny they have left me but a small pen-
155 sion, and that buys me thirty meals a day and ten
    bevers° — a small trifle to suffice nature. I come of a
    royal pedigree. My father was a gammon of bacon,
    and my mother was a hogshead of claret wine. My
    godfathers were these: Peter Pickled-herring and
160 Martin Martlemas-beef.° But my godmother, O, she

was a jolly gentlewoman, and well beloved in every
good town and city; her name was Mistress Margery
March-beer.° Now Faustus, thou hast heard all my
progeny; wilt thou bid me to a supper.
FAUSTUS: Not I. Thou wilt eat up all my victuals.   165
GLUTTONY: Then the devil choke thee.
FAUSTUS: Choke thyself, glutton. What art thou, the
    sixth?
SLOTH: Heigh ho! I am Sloth. I was begotten on a sunny
    bank, where I have lain ever since, and you have done 170
    me great injury to bring me from thence. Let me be
    carried thither again by Gluttony and Lechery. Heigh
    ho! I'll not speak a word more for a king's ransom.
FAUSTUS: And what are you Mistress Minx, the seventh
    and last?   175
LECHERY: Who, I, sir? I am one that loves an inch of raw
    mutton° better than an ell of fried stockfish,° and the
    first letter of my name begins with lechery.
LUCIFER: Away to hell! Away! On piper!
    (*Exeunt the seven Sins [and the Piper].*)
FAUSTUS: O, how this sight doth delight my soul!   180
LUCIFER: But Faustus, in hell is all manner of delight.
FAUSTUS: O, might I see hell and return again safe, how
    happy were I then!
LUCIFER: Faustus, thou shalt. At midnight I will send
    for thee. Meanwhile peruse this book and view it   185

---

156. bevers: Light snacks taken between regular meals.
160. Martlemas-beef: Salted meat hung for the winter on Mar-
tinmas, November 11.

163. March-beer: A fine ale made in the springtime and aged
for two years before being drunk.   **176–177. raw mutton:**
Common slang for "whore."   **177. stockfish:** Dried codfish.

thoroughly, and thou shalt turn thyself into what
shape thou wilt.
FAUSTUS: Thanks, mighty Lucifer.
This will I keep as chary as my life.
190 LUCIFER: Now Faustus, farewell.
FAUSTUS: Farewell, great Lucifer. Come, Mephistophilis.
(*Exeunt, several ways.*)

Scene III

(*Enter the Clown,* [*Robin, holding a book*].)

ROBIN: What, Dick, look to the horses there till I come
again. I have gotten one of Doctor Faustus' conjuring
books, and now we'll have such knavery as't passes.

(*Enter Dick.*)

DICK: What, Robin, you must come away and walk the
5   horses.
ROBIN: I walk the horses? I scorn't, 'faith. I have other
matters in hand. Let the horses walk themselves and
they will. [*He reads.*] *A per se a; t, h, e, the; o per se o;
deny orgon, gorgon.* Keep further from me, O thou
10   illiterate and unlearned hostler.
DICK: 'Snails,° what hast thou got there? A book? Why,
thou canst not tell ne'er a word on't.
ROBIN: That thou shalt see presently. Keep out of the
circle, I say, lest I send you into the hostry with a
15   vengeance.
DICK: That's like, 'faith. You had best leave your foolery, for an my master come, he'll conjure you, 'faith.
ROBIN: My master conjure me? I'll tell thee what: an my
master come here, I'll clap as fair a pair of horns°
20   on's head as e'er thou sawest in thy life.
DICK: Thou needst not do that, for my mistress hath
done it.
ROBIN: Ay, there be of us here that have waded as deep
into matters as other men, if they were disposed to
25   talk.
DICK: A plague take you! I thought you did not sneak up
and down after her for nothing. But I prithee, tell me
in good sadness,° Robin, is that a conjuring book?
ROBIN: Do but speak what thou'lt have me to do, and
30   I'll do't. If thou'lt dance naked, put off thy clothes
and I'll conjure thee about presently. Or if thou'lt go
but to the tavern with me, I'll give thee white wine,
red wine, claret wine, sack, muscadine, malmesey
and whippincrust.° Hold belly, hold, and we'll not
35   pay one penny for it.
DICK: O brave! Prithee let's to it presently, for I am as
dry as a dog.
ROBIN: Come then, let's away.
(*Exeunt.*)

II, III. 11. '**Snails:** By God's nails.   **19. horns:** The common sign
of a cuckold.   **28. sadness:** Seriousness.   **34. whippincrust:**
Possibly a corruption of "hippocras," a highly spiced and
sugared wine.

ACT III • *Prologue*

(*Enter the Chorus.*)

CHORUS: Learnèd Faustus,
To find the secrets of astronomy
Graven in the book of Jove's high firmament,
Did mount him up to scale Olympus' top,
Where, sitting in a chariot burning bright   5
Drawn by the strength of yokèd dragons' necks,
He views the clouds, the planets, and the stars,
The tropics, zones, and quarters of the sky,
From the bright circle of the hornèd moon
Even to the height of *Primum Mobile.*°   10
And whirling round with this circumference,
Within the concave compass of the pole,
From east to west his dragons swiftly glide
And in eight days did bring him home again.
Not long he stayed within his quiet house   15
To rest his bones after his weary toil,
But new exploits do hale him out again,
And mounted then upon a dragon's back,
That with his wings did part the subtle air,
He now is gone to prove cosmography,°   20
That measures coasts and kingdoms of the earth,
And, as I guess, will first arrive at Rome
To see the Pope and manner of his court
And take some part of holy Peter's feast,
The which this day is highly solemnized.   25
(*Exit.*)

Scene I

(*Enter Faustus and Mephistophilis.*)

FAUSTUS: Having now, my good Mephistophilis,
Passed with delight the stately town of Trier,
Environed round with airy mountain tops,
With walls of flint, and deep entrenchèd lakes,°
Not to be won by any conquering prince;   5
From Paris next, coasting the realm of France,
We saw the river Main fall into Rhine,
Whose banks are set with groves of fruitful vines;
Then up to Naples, rich Campania,
Whose buildings fair and gorgeous to the eye,   10
The streets straight forth and paved with finest brick,
Quarters the town in four equivalents.
There saw we learnèd Maro's° golden tomb,
The way he cut, an English mile in length,
Through a rock of stone in one night's space.°   15

III, Prologue. 10. *Primum Mobile:* In Ptolemaic astronomy
the outermost sphere of creation, which moves the other
nine spheres.   **20. prove cosmography:** Explore the universe.
III, I. 4. entrenchèd lakes: Castle moats.   **13. Maro:** Virgil.
14–15. way . . . space: A tunnel between the bays of Naples
and Baiae, through Mt. Posilipo, was said to have been cut by
Virgil (regarded as a magician in the Middle Ages) by supernatural art.

From thence to Venice, Padua, and the rest,
In midst of which a sumptuous temple stands,
That threats the stars with her aspiring top,
Whose frame is paved with sundry colored stones,
20   And roofed aloft with curious work in gold.°
Thus hitherto hath Faustus spent his time.
But tell me now, what resting-place is this?
Hast thou, as erst I did command,
Conducted me within the walls of Rome?
MEPHISTOPHILIS: I have, my Faustus, and for proof
25   thereof
This is the goodly palace of the Pope;
And 'cause we are no common guests,
I choose his privy chamber for our use.
FAUSTUS: I hope his holiness will bid us welcome.
MEPHISTOPHILIS: All's one, for we'll be bold with his
30   venison.
But now, my Faustus, that thou may'st perceive
What Rome contains for to delight thine eyes,
Know that this city stands upon seven hills
That underprop the groundwork of the same.
35   Just through the midst runs flowing Tiber's stream,
With winding banks that cut it in two parts,
Over the which four stately bridges lean,
That make safe passage to each part of Rome.
Upon the bridge called Ponte Angelo
40   Erected is a castle passing strong,
Where thou shalt see such store of ordinance
As that the double cannons, forged of brass,
Do match the number of the days contained
Within the compass of one complete year;
45   Beside the gates and high pyramidès
That Julius Caesar brought from Africa.°
FAUSTUS: Now, by the kingdoms of infernal rule,
Of Styx, of Acheron, and the fiery lake
Of ever-burning Phlegethon, I swear
50   That I do long to see the monuments
And situation of bright-splendent Rome.
Come, therefore, let's away.
MEPHISTOPHILIS: Nay, stay my Faustus. I know you'd
see the Pope
And take some part of holy Peter's feast,
55   The which, in state and high solemnity,
This day is held through Rome and Italy
In honor of the Pope's triumphant victory.
FAUSTUS: Sweet Mephistophilis, thou pleasest me.
Whilst I am here on earth, let me be cloyed
60   With all things that delight the heart of man.
My four and twenty years of liberty
I'll spend in pleasure and in dalliance,
That Faustus' name, whilst this bright frame doth
stand,
May be admirèd through the furthest land.

MEPHISTOPHILIS: 'Tis well said, Faustus. Come then,
stand by me   65
And thou shalt see them come immediately.
FAUSTUS: Nay, stay, my gentle Mephistophilis,
And grant me my request, and then I go.
Thou know'st within the compass of eight days
We viewed the face of heaven, of earth, and hell.   70
So high our dragons soared into the air,
That looking down, the earth appeared to me
No bigger than my hand in quantity.
There did we view the kingdoms of the world,
And what might please mine eye I there beheld.   75
Then in this show let me an actor be,
That this proud Pope may Faustus' cunning see.
MEPHISTOPHILIS: Let it be so, my Faustus. But, first stay
And view their triumphs° as they pass this way,
And then devise what best contents thy mind   80
By cunning in thine art to cross the Pope
Or dash the pride of this solemnity,
To make his monks and abbots stand like apes
And point like antics at his triple crown,
To beat the beads about the friars' pates   85
Or clap huge horns upon the cardinals' heads,
Or any villainy thou canst devise,
And I'll perform it, Faustus. Hark, they come.
This day shall make thee be admired in Rome.

(*Enter the Cardinals and Bishops, some bearing crosiers,
some the pillars; Monks and Friars singing their procession. Then the Pope, and Raymond, King of Hungary,
with Bruno, led in chains.*)

POPE: Cast down our footstool.
RAYMOND: Saxon Bruno, stoop,   90
Whilst on thy back his holiness ascends
Saint Peter's chair and state pontifical.
BRUNO: Proud Lucifer, that state belongs to me,
But thus I fall to Peter, not to thee.
POPE: To me and Peter shalt thou groveling lie   95
And crouch before the papal dignity.
Sound trumpets then, for thus Saint Peter's heir
From Bruno's back ascends Saint Peter's chair.

(*A flourish while he ascends.*)

Thus, as the gods creep on with feet of wool
Long ere with iron hands they punish men,   100
So shall our sleeping vengeance now arise
And smite with death thy hated enterprise.
Lord Cardinals of France and Padua,
Go forthwith to our holy consistory,
And read amongst the Statutes Decretal°   105
What, by the holy council held at Trent,°
The sacred synod hath decreed for him
That doth assume the papal government

17–20. **In midst . . . gold:** St. Mark's cathedral in Venice.
45–46. **gates . . . Africa:** Before the gates of St. Peter's there still
stands the obelisk that was brought to Rome from Heliopolis
by the Emperor Caligula in the first century A.D.

79. **triumphs:** Spectacular displays. 105. **Statutes Decretal:**
Papal decrees concerning religious doctrine or ecclesiastical law.
106. **council . . . Trent:** The Council of Trent, held by the
Church from 1545 to 1563.

Without election and a true consent.
110   Away, and bring us word with speed.
FIRST CARDINAL: We go my Lord.
                                    (*Exeunt Cardinals.*)
POPE: Lord Raymond.   [*They talk apart.*]
FAUSTUS: Go, haste thee, gentle Mephistophilis,
       Follow the cardinals to the consistory,
115   And as they turn their superstitious books,
       Strike them with sloth and drowsy idleness,
       And make them sleep so sound that in their shapes
       Thyself and I may parley with this Pope,
       This proud confronter of the Emperor,
120   And in despite of all his holiness
       Restore this Bruno to his liberty
       And bear him to the states of Germany.
MEPHISTOPHILIS: Faustus, I go.
FAUSTUS: Dispatch it soon.
125   The Pope shall curse that Faustus came to Rome.
                    (*Exeunt Faustus and Mephistophilis.*)
BRUNO: Pope Adrian,° let me have some right of law.
       I was elected by the Emperor.
POPE: We will depose the Emperor for that deed
       And curse the people that submit to him.
130   Both he and thou shalt stand excommunicate
       And interdict from church's privilege
       And all society of holy men.
       He grows too proud in his authority,
       Lifting his lofty head above the clouds,
135   And like a steeple overpeers the church.
       But we'll pull down his haughty insolence,
       And as Pope Alexander, our progenitor,
       Trod on the neck of German Frederick,°
       Adding this golden sentence to our praise,
140   "That Peter's heirs should tread on emperors
       And walk upon the dreadful adder's back,
       Treading the lion and the dragon down
       And fearless spurn the killing basilisk,"°
       So will we quell that haughty schismatic,
145   And by authority apostolical
       Depose him from his regal government.
BRUNO: Pope Julius swore to princely Sigismond,°
       For him and the succeeding popes of Rome,
       To hold the emperors their lawful lords.
150 POPE: Pope Julius did abuse the church's rites,
       And therefore none of his decrees can stand.

126. **Pope Adrian:** Marlowe perhaps means Pope Hadrian IV (1154–1159), who tried to assert his authority over Frederick Barbarossa, the Holy Roman Emperor. What historicity there may be in these scenes at the papal court is badly confused. 137–138. **Pope Alexander . . . Frederick:** Pope Alexander III (1159–1181), successor to Hadrian IV, continued the struggle against Barbarossa, forcing him to acknowledge the papal supremacy at Canossa. 143. **basilisk:** A mythical monster with power to kill by its looks. 147. **Pope Julius . . . Sigismond:** None of the three popes named Julius was contemporary with the Emperor Sigismund (1368–1437). Sigismund did, however, in 1414 summon the Council of Constance, which sought to end the Great Schism (1378–1417), during which the papacy in Rome was challenged by a line of popes in Avignon.

Is not all power on earth bestowed on us?
And therefore, though we would, we cannot err.
Behold this silver belt, whereto is fixed
Seven golden keys fast sealed with seven seals   155
In token of our sevenfold power from heaven,
To bind or loose, lock fast, condemn or judge,
Resign, or seal, or whatso pleaseth us.
Then he and thou and all the world shall stoop,
Or be assurèd of our dreadful curse   160
To light as heavy as the pains of hell.

(*Enter Faustus and Mephistophilis, like the Cardinals.*)

MEPHISTOPHILIS: Now tell me, Faustus, are we not
       fitted well?
FAUSTUS: Yes, Mephistophilis, and two such cardinals
       Ne'er served a holy pope as we shall do.
       But whilst they sleep within the consistory,   165
       Let us salute his reverend fatherhood.
RAYMOND: Behold, my lord, the cardinals are
       returned.
POPE: Welcome, grave fathers. Answer presently:
       What have our holy council there decreed
       Concerning Bruno and the Emperor,   170
       In quittance of their late conspiracy
       Against our state and papal dignity?
FAUSTUS: Most sacred patron of the church of Rome,
       By full consent of all the synod
       Of priests and prelates it is thus decreed: 175
       That Bruno and the German Emperor
       Be held as Lollards° and bold schismatics
       And proud disturbers of the church's peace.
       And if that Bruno by his own assent,
       Without enforcement of the German peers,   180
       Did seek to wear the triple diadem
       And by your death to climb Saint Peter's chair,
       The Statutes Decretal have thus decreed:
       He shall be straight condemned of heresy
       And on a pile of fagots burned to death.   185
POPE: It is enough. Here, take him to your charge,
       And bear him straight to Ponte Angelo,
       And in the strongest tower enclose him fast.
       Tomorrow, sitting in our consistory
       With all our college of grave cardinals,   190
       We will determine of his life or death.
       Here, take his triple crown along with you,
       And leave it in the church's treasury.
       Make haste again, my good lord cardinals,
       And take our blessing apostolical.   195
MEPHISTOPHILIS: So, so. Was never devil thus blessed
       before.
FAUSTUS: Away, sweet Mephistophilis, be gone.
       The cardinals will be plagued for this anon.

(*Exeunt Faustus and Mephistophilis* [*with Bruno*].)

POPE: Go presently and bring a banquet forth,
       That we may solemnize Saint Peter's feast,   200

177. **Lollards:** Followers of John Wyclif (1320?–1384), the English reformer.

And with Lord Raymond, King of Hungary,
Drink to our late and happy victory.   (*Exeunt.*)

Scene II

(*A sennet* [*is sounded*] *while the banquet is brought in; and then enter Faustus and Mephistophilis in their own shapes.*)

MEPHISTOPHILIS: Now, Faustus, come, prepare thyself
　　for mirth.
　　The sleepy cardinals are hard at hand
　　To censure Bruno, that is posted hence,
　　And on a proud-paced steed, as swift as thought,
5　　Flies o'er the Alps to fruitful Germany,
　　There to salute the woeful Emperor.
FAUSTUS: The Pope will curse them for their sloth
　　today,
　　That slept both Bruno and his crown away.
　　But now, that Faustus may delight his mind
10　And by their folly make some merriment,
　　Sweet Mephistophilis, so charm me here
　　That I may walk invisible to all
　　And do whate'er I please unseen of any.
MEPHISTOPHILIS: Faustus, thou shalt. Then kneel down
　　presently:
15　　*Whilst on thy head I lay my hand*
　　　And charm thee with this magic wand.
　　　First wear this girdle; then appear
　　　Invisible to all are here.
　　　The planets seven, the gloomy air,
20　　*Hell and the Furies'*° *forkèd hair,*
　　　Pluto's blue fire, and Hecate's tree,°
　　　With magic spells so compass thee
　　　That no eye may thy body see.
　　So Faustus. Now, for all their holiness,
25　　Do what thou wilt, thou shalt not be discerned.
FAUSTUS: Thanks, Mephistophilis. Now friars take heed
　　Lest Faustus make your shaven crowns to bleed.
MEPHISTOPHILIS: Faustus, no more. See where the
　　cardinals come.

(*Enter Pope and all the Lords. Enter the Cardinals with a book.*)

POPE: Welcome, lord cardinals. Come, sit down.
30　Lord Raymond, take your seat. Friars attend,
　　And see that all things be in readiness,
　　As best beseems this solemn festival.
FIRST CARDINAL: First, may it please your sacred
　　holiness
　　To view the sentence of the reverend synod
35　Concerning Bruno and the Emperor?
POPE: What needs this question? Did I not tell you
　　Tomorrow we would sit i' th' consistory

And there determine of his punishment?
You brought us word even now; it was decreed
That Bruno and the cursèd Emperor   40
Were by the holy council both condemned
For loathèd Lollards and base schismatics.
Then wherefore would you have me view that
　　book?
FIRST CARDINAL: Your grace mistakes. You gave us no
　　such charge.
RAYMOND: Deny it not. We all are witnesses   45
That Bruno here was late delivered you,
With his rich triple crown to be reserved
And put into the church's treasury.
BOTH CARDINALS: By holy Paul, we saw them not.
POPE: By Peter, you shall die   50
Unless you bring them forth immediately.
Hale them to prison. Lade their limbs with
　　gyves.°
False prelates, for this hateful treachery
Cursed be your souls to hellish misery.

　　　[*Exeunt the two Cardinals with Attendants.*]

FAUSTUS: So, they are safe. Now, Faustus, to the
　　feast.   55
　　The Pope had never such a frolic guest.
POPE: Lord Archbishop of Rheims, sit down with us.
ARCHBISHOP: I thank your holiness.
FAUSTUS: Fall to. The devil choke you an you spare.°
POPE: Who's that spoke? Friars look about.   60
FRIAR: Here's nobody, if it like your holiness.
POPE: Lord Raymond, pray fall to. I am beholding
　　To the Bishop of Milan for this so rare a present.
FAUSTUS: I thank you, sir.   [*He snatches the dish.*]
POPE: How now? Who snatched the meat from me?   65
　　Villains, why speak you not?
　　My good Lord Archbishop, here's a most dainty
　　dish
　　Was sent me from a cardinal in France.
FAUSTUS: I'll have that too.   [*He snatches the dish.*]
POPE: What Lollards do attend our holiness,   70
　　That we receive such great indignity?
　　Fetch me some wine.
FAUSTUS: Ay, pray do, for Faustus is a-dry.
POPE: Lord Raymond, I drink unto your grace.
FAUSTUS: I pledge your grace.   [*He snatches the cup.*]　75
POPE: My wine gone too? Ye lubbers, look about
　　And find the man that doth this villainy,
　　Or by our sanctitude, you all shall die.
　　I pray, my lords, have patience at this
　　Troublesome banquet.   80
ARCHBISHOP: Please it your holiness, I think it be some
　　ghost crept out of purgatory, and now is come unto
　　your holiness for his pardon.
POPE: It may be so.
　　Go then, command our priests to sing a dirge   85

III, II. 20. *Furies:* Spirits called on to avenge crimes, especially crimes against kin.   21. *Hecate's tree:* Hecate is the goddess of witchcraft.

52. Lade . . . gyves: Shackle their limbs.   59. an you spare: If you hold back.

To lay the fury of this same troublesome ghost.
                                    [*Exit an attendant.*]
Once again, my lord, fall to.
                        (*The Pope crosseth himself.*)
FAUSTUS: How now?
   Must every bit be spiced with a cross?
90   Nay then, take that.   [*He strikes the Pope.*]
POPE: O I am slain. Help me, my lords.
   O come and help to bear my body hence.
   Damned be this soul for ever for this deed.

                    (*Exeunt the Pope and his train.*)

MEPHISTOPHILIS: Now, Faustus, what will you do now?
95   For I can tell you you'll be cursed with bell, book,
   and candle.°
FAUSTUS: Bell, book, and candle; candle, book, and bell,
   Forward and backward, to curse Faustus to hell.

(*Enter the Friars with bell, book, and candle for the dirge.*)

FIRST FRIAR: Come, brethren, let's about our business
100   with good devotion.   [*They chant.*]
      *Cursed be he that stole his holiness' meat from
      the table.*
         Maledicat Dominus!°
      *Cursed be he that struck his holiness a blow on
      the face.*
         Maledicat Dominus!
      *Cursed be he that struck Friar Sandelo a blow on
105   the pate.*
         Maledicat Dominus!
      Cursed be he that disturbeth our holy dirge.
         Maledicat Dominus!
      Cursed be he that took away his holiness's wine.
110   *Maledicat Dominus! Et omnes sancti.*°
      Amen.

([*Faustus and Mephistophilis*] *beat the Friars, fling fireworks among them, and exeunt.*)

Scene III

(*Enter* [*Robin,*] *the clown, and Dick, with a cup.*)

DICK: Sirrah Robin, we were best look that your devil
   can answer the stealing of this same cup, for the vintner's boy follows us at the hard heels.
ROBIN: 'Tis no matter. Let him come. An he follow us,
5   I'll so conjure him as he was never conjured in his
   life, I warrant him. Let me see the cup.

(*Enter Vintner.*)

DICK: Here 'tis. Yonder he comes. Now, Robin, now or
   never show thy cunning.

95–96. bell, book, and candle: Used traditionally in the rite of excommunication.   102. *Maledicat Dominus:* May the Lord curse him.   110. *Et omnes sancti:* And all the saints.

VINTNER: O, are you here? I am glad I have found you.
   You are a couple of fine companions. Pray, where's   10
   the cup you stole from the tavern?
ROBIN: How, how? We steal a cup? Take heed what you
   say. We look not like cup stealers, I can tell you.
VINTNER: Never deny's, for I know you have it, and I'll
   search you.   15
ROBIN: Search me? Ay, and spare not. Hold the cup, Dick.
   [*Aside to Dick.*] Come, come, search me, search me.

[*The Vintner searches Robin.*]

VINTNER: [*to Dick*] Come on, sirrah, let me search you
   now.
DICK: Ay, ay, do, do. Hold the cup, Robin. [*Aside to*   20
   Robin.] I fear not your searching. We scorn to steal
   your cups, I can tell you.

[*The Vintner searches Dick.*]

VINTNER: Never outface me for the matter, for sure the
   cup is between you two.
ROBIN: Nay, there you lie. 'Tis beyond us both.   25
VINTNER: A plague take you! I thought 'twas your knavery to take it away. Come, give it me again.
ROBIN: Ay, much. When? Can you tell? Dick, make me
   a circle, and stand close at my back, and stir not for
   thy life. Vintner, you shall have your cup anon. Say   30
   nothing, Dick, *O per se, O Demogorgon, Belcher*
   and Mephistophilis.

(*Enter Mephistophilis.* [*Exit the Vintner, in fright.*])

MEPHISTOPHILIS: Monarch of hell, under whose black
      survey
   Great potentates do kneel with awful fear,
   Upon whose altars thousand souls do lie,   35
   How am I vexèd by these villains' charms!
   From Constantinople have they brought me now,
   Only for pleasure of these damnèd slaves.
ROBIN: By Lady, sir, you have had a shrewd journey of
   it. Will it please you to take a shoulder of mutton to   40
   supper and a tester° in your purse, and go back again?
DICK: Ay, I pray you heartily, sir, for we called you but in
   jest, I promise you.
MEPHISTOPHILIS: To purge the rashness of this cursèd
      deed,
   First be thou turnèd to this ugly shape,   45
   For apish deeds transformèd to an ape.
ROBIN: O brave, an ape! I pray sir, let me have the carrying of him about to show some tricks.
MEPHISTOPHILIS: And so thou shalt. Be thou transformed to a dog, and carry him upon thy back. Away,   50
   be gone!
ROBIN: A dog? That's excellent. Let the maids look well
   to their porridge pots, for I'll into the kitchen presently. Come, Dick, come.

                (*Exeunt* [*Robin and Dick,*] *the two clowns.*)

III, III. 41. tester: Sixpence.

55 MEPHISTOPHILIS: Now with the flames of everburning
    fire,
    I'll wing myself and forthwith fly amain
    Unto my Faustus, to the great Turk's court.

                                (*Exit.*)

ACT IV • *Prologue*

(*Enter Chorus.*)

CHORUS: When Faustus had with pleasure ta'en the
    view
    Of rarest things and royal courts of kings,
    He stayed his course and so returnèd home;
    Where such as bare his absence but with grief —
5   I mean his friends and nearest companions —
    Did gratulate his safety with kind words,
    And in their conference of what befell,
    Touching his journey through the world and air,
    They put forth questions of astrology,
10   Which Faustus answered with such learnèd skill
    As they admired and wondered at his wit.
    Now is his fame spread forth in every land.
    Amongst the rest, the Emperor is one —
    Carolus the fifth° — at whose palace now
15   Faustus is feasted 'mongst his noblemen.
    What there he did in trial of his art
    I leave untold, your eyes shall see performed.

                                (*Exit.*)

Scene I

(*Enter Martino and Frederick, at several doors.*)

MARTINO: What ho, officers, gentlemen,
    Hie to the presences° to attend the Emperor.
    Good Frederick, see the rooms be voided
      straight;
    His majesty is coming to the hall.
5   Go back, and see the state° in readiness.
FREDERICK: But where is Bruno, our elected Pope,
    That on a fury's back came post from Rome?
    Will not his grace consort the Emperor?
MARTINO: O yes, and with him comes the German
      conjurer,
10   The learnèd Faustus, fame of Wittenberg,
    The wonder of the world for magic art;
    And he intends to show great Carolus
    The race of all his stout progenitors,
    And bring in presence of his majesty
15   The royal shapes and warlike semblances
    Of Alexander° and his beauteous paramour.

IV, Prologue. **14. Carolus the fifth:** Charles V, King of Spain
(as Charles I from 1516 to 1556) and Holy Roman Emperor
from 1519 to 1556.   **IV, I. 2. presences:** Emperor's chamber.
5. state: Throne.   **16. Alexander:** Alexander the Great.

FREDERICK: Where is Benvolio?
MARTINO: Fast asleep, I warrant you.
    He took his rouse with stoups° of Rhenish wine
    So kindly yesternight to Bruno's health   20
    That all this day the sluggard keeps his bed.
FREDERICK: See, see, his window's ope. We'll call to
    him.
MARTINO: What ho, Benvolio!

(*Enter Benvolio above at a window, in his nightcap, buttoning.*)

BENVOLIO: What a devil ail you two?
MARTINO: Speak softly, sir, lest the devil hear you,   25
    For Faustus at the court is late arrived,
    And at his heels a thousand furies wait
    To accomplish whatsoever the doctor please.
BENVOLIO: What of this?
MARTINO: Come, leave thy chamber first, and thou
      shalt see   30
    This conjurer perform such rare exploits
    Before the Pope° and royal Emperor
    As never yet was seen in Germany.
BENVOLIO: Has not the Pope enough of conjuring yet?
    He was upon the devil's back late enough,   35
    And if he be so far in love with him,
    I would he would post with him to Rome again.
FREDERICK: Speak, wilt thou come and see this sport?
BENVOLIO: Not I.
MARTINO: Wilt thou stand in thy window and see it
    then?   40
BENVOLIO: Ay, and I fall not asleep i' th' meantime.
MARTINO: The Emperor is at hand, who comes to see
    What wonders by black spells may compassed be.
BENVOLIO: Well, go you attend the Emperor. I am con-
    tent for this once to thrust my head out at a window, 45
    for they say if a man be drunk overnight the devil
    cannot hurt him in the morning. If that be true, I
    have a charm in my head shall control him as well as
    the conjurer, I warrant you.

(*Exit [Frederick, with Martino. Benvolio remains at the
window above].*)

Scene II

(*A sennet [is sounded. Enter] Charles, the German Emperor, Bruno, [the Duke of] Saxony, Faustus, Mephistophilis, Frederick, Martino, and Attendants.*)

EMPEROR: Wonder of men, renowned magician,
    Thrice-learnèd Faustus, welcome to our court.
    This deed of thine, in setting Bruno free
    From his and our professèd enemy,
    Shall add more excellence unto thine art   5

19. took . . . stoups: Had a drinking bout with brimming gob-
lets.   **32. the Pope:** Bruno.

Than if by powerful necromantic spells
Thou couldst command the world's obedience.
Forever be beloved of Carolus,
And if this Bruno thou hast late redeemed°
10   In peace possess the triple diadem
And sit in Peter's chair despite of chance,
Thou shalt be famous through all Italy
And honored of the German Emperor.
FAUSTUS: These gracious words, most royal Carolus,
15   Shall make poor Faustus to his utmost power
Both love and serve the German Emperor
And lay his life at holy Bruno's feet.
For proof whereof, if so your grace be pleased,
The doctor stands prepared by power of art
20   To cast his magic charms that shall pierce through
The ebon gates of ever-burning hell,
And hale the stubborn Furies from their caves
To compass whatsoe'er your grace commands.
BENVOLIO: [above] Blood, he speaks terribly, but for all
25   that, I do not greatly believe him. He looks as like a
conjurer as the Pope° to a costermonger.°
EMPEROR: Then, Faustus, as thou late did'st promise us,
We would behold that famous conqueror,
Great Alexander, and his paramour
30   In their true shapes and state majestical,
That we may wonder at their excellence.
FAUSTUS: Your majesty shall see them presently.
Mephistophilis, away,
And with a solemn noise of trumpets' sound
35   Present before this royal Emperor,
Great Alexander and his beauteous paramour.
MEPHISTOPHILIS: Faustus, I will.
                                                              [Exit.]
BENVOLIO: Well, master doctor, an your devils come not
away quickly, you shall have me asleep presently.
40   Zounds, I could eat myself for anger to think I have
been such an ass all this while, to stand gaping after
the devil's governor and can see nothing.
FAUSTUS: I'll make you feel something anon, if my art
fail me not
My lord, I must forewarn your majesty
45   That when my spirits present the royal shapes
Of Alexander and his paramour,
Your grace demand no questions of the king,
But in dumb silence let them come and go.
EMPEROR: Be it as Faustus please; we are content.
50   BENVOLIO: Ay, ay, and I am content too. And thou bring
Alexander and his paramour before the Emperor, I'll
be Actaeon and turn myself to a stag.
FAUSTUS: And I'll play Diana and send you the horns
presently.

([A] sennet [is sounded]. Enter at one [door] the Emperor Alexander, at the other Darius.° They meet [in

combat]. Darius is thrown down; Alexander kills him,
takes off his crown, and, offering to go out, his paramour meets him. He embraceth her and sets Darius'
crown upon her head; and coming back, both salute the
Emperor, who, leaving his state, offers to embrace them,
which Faustus seeing, suddenly stays him. Then trumpets cease and music sounds.)

My gracious lord, you do forget yourself.
These are but shadows, not substantial.   55
EMPEROR: O pardon me. My thoughts are so ravishèd
With sight of this renownèd emperor,
That in mine arms I would have compassed him.
But, Faustus, since I may not speak to them,
To satisfy my longing thoughts at full,   60
Let me this tell thee: I have heard it said
That this fair lady, whilst she lived on earth,
Had on her neck a little wart or mole;
How may I prove that saying to be true?
FAUSTUS: Your majesty may boldly go and see.   65
EMPEROR: Faustus, I see it plain,
And in this sight thou better pleasest me
Than if I gained another monarchy.
FAUSTUS: Away! Be gone!
                                             (Exit show.)
See, see, my gracious lord, what strange beast is yon,   70
that thrusts his head out at window?
EMPEROR: O wondrous sight! See, Duke of Saxony,
Two spreading horns most strangely fastenèd
Upon the head of young Benvolio.
SAXONY: What? Is he asleep or dead?   75
FAUSTUS: He sleeps, my lord, but dreams not of his
horns.
EMPEROR: This sport is excellent. We'll call and wake
him.
What ho, Benvolio!
BENVOLIO: A plague upon you! Let me sleep a while.
EMPEROR: I blame thee not to sleep much, having such a   80
head of thine own.
SAXONY: Look up, Benvolio; 'tis the Emperor calls.
BENVOLIO: The Emperor? Where? O zounds, my head!
EMPEROR: Nay, and thy horns hold, 'tis no matter for
thy head, for that's armed sufficiently.   85
FAUSTUS: Why, how now, sir knight! What, hanged by the
horns? This is most horrible. Fie, fie, pull in your head
for shame. Let not all the world wonder at you.
BENVOLIO: Zounds, doctor, is this your villainy?
FAUSTUS: O say not so, sir. The doctor has no skill,   90
No art, no cunning, to present these lords
Or bring before this royal Emperor
The mighty monarch, warlike Alexander.
If Faustus do it, you are straight resolved
In bold Actaeon's shape to turn a stag.   95
And therefore, my lord, so please your majesty,
I'll raise a kennel of hounds shall hunt him so
As all his footmanship shall scarce prevail
To keep his carcass from their bloody fangs
Ho, Belimote, Argiron, Asterote!   100
BENVOLIO: Hold, hold! Zounds, he'll raise up a kennel of

IV, II. 9. **redeemed:** Rescued.   **26. the Pope:** Bruno. **Costermonger:** Fruit vendor; a term of contempt.   **53. [S.D.] Darius:**
King Darius III of Persia (336–330 B.C.), defeated at Granicus
in 334 B.C. by the Greeks under Alexander the Great.

devils, I think, anon. Good, my lord, entreat for me.
'Sblood, I am never able to endure these torments.
EMPEROR: Then, good master doctor,
105   Let me entreat you to remove his horns.
    He has done penance now sufficiently.
FAUSTUS: My gracious lord, not so much for injury done
    to me, as to delight your majesty with some mirth,
    hath Faustus justly requited this injurious° knight;
110   which being all I desire, I am content to remove his
    horns. Mephistophilis, transform him.

                    [*Mephistophilis removes the horns.*]

    And hereafter, sir, look you speak; well of scholars.
BENVOLIO: [*aside.*] Speak well of ye? 'Sblood, and schol-
    ars be such cuckold makers to clap horns of honest
115   men's heads o' this order, I'll ne'er trust smooth faces
    and small ruffs° more. But an I be not revenged for
    this, would I might be turned to a gaping oyster and
    drink nothing but salt water.
                                    [*Exit Benvolio above.*]
EMPEROR: Come, Faustus. While the Emperor lives,
120   In recompense of this thy high desert,
    Thou shalt command the state of Germany
    And live beloved of mighty Carolus.
                                    (*Exeunt.*)

Scene III

(*Enter Benvolio, Martino, Frederick, and Soldiers.*)

MARTINO: Nay, sweet Benvolio, let us sway thy
    thoughts
    From this attempt against the conjurer.
BENVOLIO: Away! You love me not to urge me thus.
    Shall I let slip so great an injury,
5   When every servile groom jests at my wrongs
    And in their rustic gambols proudly say,
    "Benvolio's head was graced with horns today"?
    O, may these eyelids never close again
    Till with my sword I have that conjurer slain.
10   If you will aid me in this enterprise,
    Then draw your weapons and be resolute.
    If not, depart. Here will Benvolio die,
    But Faustus' death shall quit° my infamy.
FREDERICK: Nay, we will stay with thee, betide what
    may,
15   And kill that doctor if he come this way.
BENVOLIO: Then, gentle Frederick, hie thee to the grove,
    And place our servants and our followers
    Close in an ambush there behind the trees.
    By this, I know, the conjurer is near.
20   I saw him kneel and kiss the Emperor's hand
    And take his leave, laden with rich rewards.
    Then, soldiers, boldly fight. If Faustus die,
    Take you the wealth; leave us the victory.

109. **injurious:** Insulting.   116. **small ruffs:** Academic gowns.
IV, III. 13. **quit:** Pay for.

FREDERICK: Come, soldiers. Follow me unto the grove.
    Who kills him shall have gold and endless love.   25

                    (*Exit Frederick with the Soldiers.*)

BENVOLIO: My head is lighter than it was by th'horns,
    But yet my heart's more ponderous than my head
    And pants until I see that conjurer dead.
MARTINO: Where shall we place ourselves, Benvolio?
BENVOLIO: Here will we stay to bide the first assault.   30
    O, were that damnèd hell-hound but in place,
    Thou soon shouldst see me quit my foul disgrace.

(*Enter Frederick.*)

FREDERICK: Close, close, the conjurer is at hand
    And all alone comes walking in his gown.
    Be ready then, and strike the peasant down.   35
BENVOLIO: Mine be that honor then. Now, sword,
    strike home.
    For horns he gave I'll have his head anon.

(*Enter Faustus with the false head.*)

MARTINO: See, see, he comes.
BENVOLIO: No words! This blow ends all.
    Hell take his soul; his body thus must fall.
                                    [*He stabs Faustus.*]
FAUSTUS: [*falling*] Oh!   40
FREDERICK: Groan you, master doctor?
BENVOLIO: Break may his heart with groans! Dear
    Frederick, see,
    Thus will I end his griefs immediately.
MARTINO: Strike with a willing hand. His head is off.

[*Benvolio strikes off Faustus' false head.*]

BENVOLIO: The devil's dead. The Furies now may
    laugh.   45
FREDERICK: Was this that stern aspèct, that awful
    frown,
    Made the grim monarch of infernal spirits
    Tremble and quake at his commanding charms?
MARTINO: Was this that damnèd head whose heart
    conspired
    Benvolio's shame before the Emperor?   50
BENVOLIO: Ay, that's the head, and here the body lies,
    Justly rewarded for his villainies.
FREDERICK: Come, let's devise how we may add more
    shame
    To the black scandal of his hated name.
BENVOLIO: First, on his head, in quittance of my
    wrongs,   55
    I'll nail huge forkèd horns and let them hang
    Within the window where he yoked° me first,
    That all the world may see my just revenge.
MARTINO: What use shall we put his beard to?
BENVOLIO: We'll sell it to a chimney-sweeper. It will   60
    wear out ten birchen brooms, I warrant you.
FREDERICK: What shall eyes do?

57. **yoked:** Placed the horns on.

BENVOLIO: We'll put out his eyes, and they shall serve
    for buttons to his lips to keep his tongue from catch-
65   ing cold.
MARTINO: An excellent policy! And now, sirs, having
    divided him, what shall the body do?

[*Faustus rises.*]

BENVOLIO: Zounds, the devil's alive again.
FREDERICK: Give him his head, for God's sake.
FAUSTUS: Nay, keep it. Faustus will have heads and
70   hands,
    Ay, all your hearts, to recompense this deed.
    Knew you not, traitors, I was limited
    For four-and-twenty years to breathe on earth?
    And had you cut my body with your swords,
75   Or hewed this flesh and bones as small as sand,
    Yet in a minute had my spirit returned,
    And I had breathed a man made free from harm.
    But wherefore do I dally my revenge?
    Asteroth, Belimoth, Mephistophilis!

(*Enter Mephistophilis and other Devils.*)

80   Go, horse these traitors on your fiery backs,
    And mount aloft with them as high as heaven;
    Thence pitch them headlong to the lowest hell.
    Yet stay. The world shall see their misery,
    And hell shall after plague their treachery.
85   Go, Belimoth, and take this caitiff° hence
    And hurl him in some lake of mud and dirt.
    Take thou this other; drag him through the woods
    Amongst the pricking thorns and sharpest briars,
    Whilst with my gentle Mephistophilis
90   This traitor flies unto some steepy rock
    That, rolling down, may break the villain's bones
    As he intended to dismember me.
    Fly hence. Dispatch my charge immediately.
FREDERICK: Pity us, gentle Faustus. Save our lives.
FAUSTUS: Away!
95 FREDERICK: He must needs go that the devil drives.

(*Exeunt Spirits with the Knights.*)

(*Enter the ambushed Soldiers.*)

FIRST SOLDIER: Come, sirs, prepare yourselves in
    readiness.
    Make haste to help these noble gentlemen;
    I heard them parley with the conjurer.
SECOND SOLDIER: See where he comes. Dispatch and
    kill the slave.
100 FAUSTUS: What's here? An ambush to betray my life?
    Then, Faustus, try thy skill. Base peasants, stand,
    For lo, these trees remove at my command
    And stand as bulwarks 'twixt yourselves and me,
    To shield me from your hated treachery.
105   Yet to encounter this your weak attempt,
    Behold an army comes incontinent.°

85. **caitiff:** Despicable wretch.   106. **incontinent:** At once.

(*Faustus strikes the door, and enter a Devil playing on a drum, after him another bearing an ensign, and divers with weapons, Mephistophilis with fireworks. They set upon the Soldiers and drive them out. [Exit Faustus.]*)

Scene IV

(*Enter at several doors Benvolio, Frederick, and Martino, their heads and faces bloody and besmeared with mud and dirt, all having horns on their heads.*)

MARTINO: What ho, Benvolio!
BENVOLIO: Here! What, Frederick, ho!
FREDERICK: O help me, gentle friend. Where is Martino?
MARTINO: Dear Frederick, here,
    Half smothered in a lake of mud and dirt,   5
    Through which the Furies dragged me by the heels.
FREDERICK: Martino, see! Benvolio's horns again.
MARTINO: O misery! How now, Benvolio?
BENVOLIO: Defend me, heaven. Shall I be haunted° still?
MARTINO: Nay, fear not man; we have not power to kill. 10
BENVOLIO: My friends transformèd thus! O hellish
    spite!
    Your heads are all set with horns.
FREDERICK: You hit it right.
    It is your own you mean. Feel on your head.
BENVOLIO: Zounds, horns again!
MARTINO: Nay, chafe not man. We all are sped.°   15
BENVOLIO: What devil attends this damned magician,
    That, spite of spite, our wrongs are doublèd?
FREDERICK: What may we do, that we may hide our
    shames?
BENVOLIO: If we should follow him to work revenge,
    He'd join long asses' ears to these huge horns,   20
    And make us laughing-stocks to all the world.
MARTINO: What shall we then do, dear Benvolio?
BENVOLIO: I have a castle joining near these woods,
    And thither we'll repair and live obscure
    Till time shall alter these our brutish shapes.   25
    Sith black disgrace hath thus eclipsed our fame,
    We'll rather die with grief than live with shame.
                        (*Exeunt omnes.°*)

Scene V°

(*Enter Faustus and Mephistophilis.*)

FAUSTUS: Now, Mephistophilis, the restless course
    That time doth run with calm and silent foot,
    Shortening my days and thread of vital life,
    Calls for the payment of my latest years.

IV, IV. 9. haunted: (1) Bewitched; (2) hunted, pursued (since he is a stag).   **15. sped:** provided (with horns).   **27. [s.d.] Exeunt omnes:** Latin for "All go out."   **IV, v.** The first eleven lines of this scene do not appear in all versions of the play, but they provide a transition to the Horse-Courser episode and remind readers of Faustus's impending tragedy.

5   Therefore, sweet Mephistophilis, let us
      Make haste to Wittenberg.
MEPHISTOPHILIS: What, will you go on horseback, or
      on foot?
FAUSTUS: Nay, till I am past this fair and pleasant
      green,
      I'll walk on foot.

                                    [*Exit Mephistophilis.*]

(*Enter a Horse-Courser.°*)

10 HORSE-COURSER: I have been all this day seeking one
      Master Fustian.° Mass, see where he is. God save you,
      master doctor.
FAUSTUS: What, horse-courser! You are well met.
HORSE-COURSER: I beseech your worship, accept of
15   these forty dollars.
FAUSTUS: Friend, thou canst not buy so good a horse for
      so small a price. I have no great need to sell him, but
      if thou likest him for ten dollars more, take him,
      because I see thou hast a good mind to him.
20 HORSE-COURSER: I beseech you, sir, accept of this. I am
      a very poor man and have lost very much of late by
      horse-flesh, and this bargain will set me up again.
FAUSTUS: Well, I will not stand with thee.° Give me the
      money.

[*The Horse-Courser gives Faustus money.*]

25   Now, sirrah, I must tell you that you may ride him
      o'er hedge and ditch, and spare him not. But, do you
      hear? In any case, ride him not into the water.
HORSE-COURSER: How sir? Not into the water? Why,
      will he not drink of all waters?°
30 FAUSTUS: Yes, he will drink of all waters, but ride him
      not into the water — o'er hedge and ditch, or where
      thou wilt, but not into the water. Go, bid the hostler
      deliver him unto you, and remember what I say.
HORSE-COURSER: I warrant you, sir. O joyful day!
35   Now am I a man made forever.

                                          (*Exit.*)

FAUSTUS: What art thou, Faustus, but a man
      condemned to die?
      Thy fatal time draws to a final end.
      Despair doth drive distrust into my thoughts.
      Confound these passions with a quiet sleep.
40   Tush! Christ did call the thief upon the cross;
      Then rest thee, Faustus, quiet in conceit.°

(*He sits to sleep [in his chair].*)

(*Enter the Horse-Courser, wet.*)

HORSE-COURSER: O what a cozening doctor was this? I
      riding my horse into the water, thinking some hidden
      mystery° had been in the horse, I had nothing under

me but a little straw and had much ado to escape   45
drowning. Well, I'll go rouse him and make him give
me my forty dollars again. Ho, sirrah doctor, you
cozening scab!° Master doctor, awake and rise, and
give me my money again, for your horse is turned to
a bottle° of hay. Master doctor!   50

(*He [tries to wake Faustus, and in doing so] pulls off
his leg.*)

Alas, I am undone! What shall I do? I have pulled off
his leg.

[*Faustus awakes.*]

FAUSTUS: O, help, help! The villain hath murdered me.
HORSE-COURSER: Murder or not murder, now he has
      but one leg, I'll outrun him and cast this leg into   55
      some ditch or other.
FAUSTUS: Stop him, stop him, stop him! Ha, ha, ha,
      Faustus hath his leg again, and the horse-courser a
      bundle of hay for his forty dollars.

(*Enter Wagner.*)

How now, Wagner, what news with thee?   60
WAGNER: If it please you, the Duke of Anholt doth
      earnestly entreat your company and hath sent some
      of his men to attend you with provision fit for your
      journey.
FAUSTUS: The Duke of Anholt's an honorable gentle-   65
      man, and one to whom I must be no niggard of my
      cunning. Come away.

                                    (*Exeunt.*)

Scene VI

(*Enter [Robin, the] Clown, Dick, [the] Horse-Courser,
and a Carter.°*)

CARTER: Come, my masters, I'll bring you to the best
      beer in Europe. What ho, hostess! Where be these
      whores?

(*Enter Hostess.*)

HOSTESS: How now, what lack you? What, my old
      guests, welcome.   5
ROBIN: Sirrah, Dick, dost thou know why I stand so
      mute?
DICK: No, Robin; why is't?
ROBIN: I am eighteen pence on the score.° But say noth-
      ing, see if she have forgotten me.   10
HOSTESS: Who's this that stands so solemnly by himself?
      What, my old guest?
ROBIN: O hostess, how do you? I hope my score stands
      still.°

---

9. [S.D.] *Horse-Courser:* One who deals in horses.   11. **Fustian:** The perversion of Faustus's name is a deliberate attempt at
humor.   23. **stand with thee:** Bargain.   29. **drink . . . waters:**
Be ready for anything (a common proverb of the time).
41. **conceit:** Thoughts.   44. **mystery:** Quality.

48. **cozening scab:** Deceitful, contemptible rascal.   50. **bottle:**
Bundle.   IV, VI. [S.D.] *Carter:* A person who drives a cart.
9. **on the score:** In debt.   13–14. **stands still:** Does not go
higher.

15 HOSTESS: Ay, there's no doubt of that, for methinks you
        make no haste to wipe it out.
    DICK: Why, hostess, I say, fetch us some beer.
    HOSTESS: You shall presently. Look up into th'hall
        there, ho!
                                                    (*Exit.*)
20 DICK: Come, sirs, what shall we do now till mine hostess
        come?
    CARTER: Marry, sir, I'll tell you the bravest tale how a
        conjurer served me. You know Doctor Fauster?
    HORSE-COURSER: Ay, a plague take him. Here's some
25   on's have cause to know him. Did he conjure thee
        too?
    CARTER: I'll tell you how he served me. As I was going to
        Wittenberg t'other day with a load of hay, he met me
        and asked me what he should give me for as much
30   hay as he could eat. Now, sir, I thinking that a little
        would serve his turn, bade him take as much as he
        would for three farthings. So he presently gave me
        my money and fell to eating; and as I am a cursen°
        man, he never left eating till he had eat up all my load
35   of hay.
    ALL: O monstrous! Eat a whole load of hay!
    ROBIN: Yes, yes, that may be, for I have heard of one
        that has eat a load of logs.
    HORSE-COURSER: Now, sirs, you shall hear how villain-
40   ously he served me. I went to him yesterday to buy a
        horse of him, and he would by no means sell him
        under forty dollars. So, sir, because I knew him to be
        such a horse as would run over hedge and ditch and
        never tire, I gave him his money. So when I had my
45   horse, Doctor Fauster bade me ride him night and
        day and spare him no time; but, quoth he, in any case
        ride him not into the water. Now sir, I thinking the
        horse had had some rare quality that he would not
        have me know of, what did I but rid him into a
50   great river, and when I came just in the midst, my
        horse vanished away, and I sat straddling upon a
        bottle of hay.
    ALL: O brave doctor!
    HORSE-COURSER: But you shall hear how bravely I
55   served him for it. I went me home to his house, and
        there I found him asleep. I kept a hallooing and
        whooping in his ears, but all could not wake him. I
        seeing that took him by the leg and never rested
        pulling till I had pulled me his leg quite off, and now
60   'tis at home in mine hostry.
    ROBIN: And has the doctor but one leg then? That's
        excellent, for one of his devils turned me into the
        likeness of an ape's face.
    CARTER: Some more drink, hostess.
65 ROBIN: Hark you, we'll into another room and drink a
        while, and then we'll go seek out the doctor.
                                                    (*Exeunt.*)

Scene VII

(*Enter the Duke of Anholt, his Duchess, Faustus, and
Mephistophilis,* [*Servants and Attendants*].)

DUKE: Thanks, master doctor, for these pleasant sights.
    Nor know I how sufficiently to recompense your
    great deserts° in erecting that enchanted castle in the
    air, the sight whereof so delighted me, as nothing in
    the world could please me more.   5
FAUSTUS: I do think myself, my good lord, highly recom-
    pensed in that it pleaseth your grace to think but well
    of that which Faustus hath performed. But, gracious
    lady, it may be that you have taken no pleasure in
    those sights. Therefore, I pray you, tell me what is the 10
    thing you most desire to have; be it in the world, it
    shall be yours. I have heard that great-bellied women
    do long for things are rare and dainty.
DUCHESS: True, master doctor, and since I find you so
    kind, I will make known unto you what my heart   15
    desires to have. And were it now summer, as it is Jan-
    uary, a dead time of the winter, I would request no
    better meat than a dish of ripe grapes.
FAUSTUS: This is but a small matter. Go, Mephistophilis,
    away!   20
                            (*Exit Mephistophilis.*)
    Madam I will do more than this for your content.

(*Enter Mephistophilis again with the grapes.*)

    Here; now taste ye these. They should be good, for
    they come from a far country, I can tell you.
DUKE: This makes me wonder more than all the rest,
    that at this time of year, when every tree is barren of 25
    his fruit, from whence you had these ripe grapes.
FAUSTUS: Please it, your grace, the year is divided into
    two circles over the whole world, so that when it
    is winter with us, in the contrary circle it is like-
    wise summer with them, as in India, Saba,° and such   30
    countries that lie far east, where they have fruit twice
    a year. From whence, by means of a swift spirit that I
    have, I had these grapes brought, as you see.
DUCHESS: And trust me, they are the sweetest grapes
    that e'er I tasted.   35

(*The Clown*[*s, Robin, Dick, the Carter, and the Horse-
Courser,*] *bounce at the gate within.*)

DUKE: What rude disturbers have we at the gate?
    Go, pacify their fury. Set it ope,
    And then demand of them what they would have.
                                    [*Exit a Servant.*]

(*They knock again and call out to talk with Faustus.*)

[*Enter Servant to them.*]

SERVANT: Why, how now, masters, what a coil° is there?
    What is the reason you disturb the duke.   40

---

33. **cursen:** Christened.

IV, VII. **3. deserts:** Good deeds.   **30. Saba:** Sheba.   **39. coil:**
Disturbance.

DICK: We have no reason for it; therefore a fig for him.
SERVANT: What, saucy varlets,° dare you be so bold?
HORSE-COURSER: I hope, sir, we have wit enough to be
more bold than welcome.
45 SERVANT: It appears so. Pray be bold elsewhere,
And trouble not the duke.
DUKE: What would they have?
SERVANT: They all cry out to speak with Doctor Faustus.
CARTER: Ay, and we will speak with him.
DUKE: Will you, sir? Commit the rascals.
50 DICK: Commit with us! He were as good commit with
his father as commit with us.
FAUSTUS: I do beseech your grace, let them come in;
They are good subject for a merriment.
DUKE: Do as thou wilt, Faustus. I give thee leave.
FAUSTUS: I thank your grace.

(Enter Robin, Dick, Carter, and Horse-Courser.)

55   Why, how now, my good friends?
'Faith you are too outrageous,° but come near;
I have procured your pardons. Welcome all!
ROBIN: Nay, sir, we will be welcome for our money, and
we will pay for what we take. What ho! Give's half a
60   dozen of beer here, and be hanged.
FAUSTUS: Nay, hark you; can you tell me where you are?
CARTER: Ay, marry can I: we are under heaven.
SERVANT: Ay, but sir sauce-box, know you in what
place?
HORSE-COURSER: Ay, ay, the house is good enough to
65   drink in. Zounds, fill us some beer, or we'll break all
the barrels in the house and dash out all your brains
with your bottles.
FAUSTUS: Be not so furious. Come, you shall have beer.
My lord, beseech you give me leave a while:
70   I'll gage my credit, 'twill content your grace.
DUKE: With all my heart, kind doctor. Please thyself;
Our servants and our court's at thy command.
FAUSTUS: I humbly thank your grace. Then fetch some
beer.
HORSE-COURSER: Ay, marry, there spake a doctor
indeed, and 'faith,
75   I'll drink a health to thy wooden leg for that word.
FAUSTUS: My wooden leg? What dost thou mean by
that?
CARTER: Ha, ha, ha! Dost hear him, Dick? He has
forgot his leg.
HORSE-COURSER: Ay, ay, he does not stand much°
upon that.
FAUSTUS: No, faith; not much upon a wooden leg.
80 CARTER: Good lord, that flesh and blood should be so
frail with your worship! Do not you remember a
horse-courser you sold a horse to?
FAUSTUS: Yes, I remember I sold one a horse.
CARTER: And do you remember you bid he should not
85   ride into the water?

FAUSTUS: Yes, I do very well remember that.
CARTER: And do you remember nothing of your leg?
FAUSTUS: No, in good sooth.
CARTER: Then, I pray, remember your courtesy.°
FAUSTUS: I thank you, sir.   90
CARTER: 'Tis not so much worth. I pray you, tell me one
thing.
FAUSTUS: What's that?
CARTER: Be both your legs bedfellows every night to-
gether?   95
FAUSTUS: Wouldst thou make a Colossus° of me, that
thou askest me such questions?
CARTER: No, truly, sir. I would make nothing of you, but
I would fain know that.

(Enter Hostess with drink.)

FAUSTUS: Then, I assure thee, certainly they are.   100
CARTER: I thank you; I am fully satisfied.
FAUSTUS: But wherefore dost thou ask?
CARTER: For nothing, sir. But methinks you should have
a wooden bedfellow of one of 'em.
HORSE-COURSER: Why, do you hear, sir; did not I pull 105
off one of your legs when you were asleep?
FAUSTUS: But I have it again, now I am awake. Look you
here, sir.
ALL: O horrible! Had the doctor three legs?
CARTER: Do you remember, sir, how you cozened me   110
and ate up my load of —

(Faustus charms him dumb.)

DICK: Do you remember how you made me wear an
ape's —

[Faustus charms him dumb.]

HORSE-COURSER: You whoreson conjuring scab, do you
remember how you cozened me with a ho —   115

[Faustus charms him dumb.]

ROBIN: Ha' you forgotten me? You think to carry it
away° with your *hey-pass* and *re-pass;* do you remember the dog's fa —

[Faustus charms him dumb.]   *(Exeunt Clowns.)*

HOSTESS: Who pays for the ale? Hear you, master doctor, now you have sent away my guests, I pray who   120
shall pay me for my a —

[Faustus charms her dumb.]   *(Exit Hostess.)*

DUCHESS: My lord,
We are much beholding to this learnèd man.
DUKE: So are we, madam, which we will recompense
With all the love and kindness that we may.   125
His artful sport drives all sad thoughts away.
                                        (Exeunt.)

---

42. varlets: Knaves, rascals. **56. outrageous:** violent.
78. stand much: Make much of (with a quibble).

89. courtesy: Curtsy, or leg. **96. Colossus:** A giant statue said
to have stood with its legs astride at the entrance to the ancient
harbor of Rhodes. **116–17. carry it away:** Come off best.

ACT V • Scene 1

(*Thunder and lightning. Enter Devils with covered dishes. Mephistophilis leads them into Faustus' study. Then enter Wagner.*)

WAGNER: I think my master means to die shortly.
He has made his will and given me his wealth,
His house, his goods, and store of golden plate,
Besides two thousand ducats ready coined.
5   I wonder what he means. If death were nigh,
He would not frolic thus. He's now at supper
With the scholars, where there's such belly-cheer
As Wagner in his life ne'er saw the like.
And see where they come; belike the feast is done.
                                        (*Exit.*)

(*Enter Faustus, Mephistophilis, and two or three Scholars.*)

10 FIRST SCHOLAR: Master Doctor Faustus, since our conference about fair ladies, which was the beautifulest
in all the world, we have determined with ourselves
that Helen of Greece was the admirablest lady that
ever lived. Therefore, master doctor, if you will do us
15 so much favor as to let us see that peerless dame of
Greece, whom all the world admires for majesty, we
should think ourselves much beholding unto you.
FAUSTUS: Gentlemen,
For that I know your friendship is unfeigned,
20 And Faustus' custom is not to deny
The just requests of those that wish him well,
You shall behold that peerless dame of Greece,
No otherwise for pomp and majesty
Than when Sir Paris crossed the seas with her
25 And brought the spoils to rich Dardania.°
Be silent then, for danger is in words.

(*Music sounds. Mephistophilis brings in Helen; she passeth over the stage.*)

SECOND SCHOLAR: Was this fair Helen, whose admirèd
    worth
Made Greece with ten years' war afflict poor Troy?
Too simple is my wit to tell her praise,
30 Whom all the world admires for majesty.
THIRD SCHOLAR: No marvel though the angry Greeks
    pursued
With ten years' war the rape of such a queen,
Whose heavenly beauty passeth all compare.
FIRST SCHOLAR: Since we have seen the pride of
    nature's works
35 And only paragon of excellence,
We'll take our leaves and for this blessèd sight
Happy and blest be Faustus evermore.
FAUSTUS: Gentlemen, farewell; the same wish I to you.
                                        (*Exeunt Scholars.*)

(*Enter an Old Man.*)

OLD MAN: O gentle Faustus, leave this damnèd art,
This magic that will charm thy soul to hell   40
And quite bereave thee of salvation.
Though thou hast now offended like a man,
Do not persevere in it like a devil.
Yet, yet, thou hast an amiable° soul,
If sin by custom grow not into nature.   45
Then, Faustus, will repentance come too late;
Then thou art banished from the sight of heaven.
No mortal can express the pains of hell.
It may be this my exhortation
Seems harsh and all unpleasant; let it not,   50
For, gentle son, I speak it not in wrath
Or envy of° thee, but in tender love
And pity of thy future misery.
And so have hope that this my kind rebuke,
Checking° thy body, may amend thy soul.   55
FAUSTUS: Where art thou, Faustus? Wretch, what hast
    thou done?
Damned art thou, Faustus, damned; despair and die!
Hell claims his right, and with a roaring voice
Says, "Faustus, come; thine hour is almost come";
And Faustus now will come to do thee right.   60

(*Mephistophilis gives him a dagger.*)

OLD MAN: O stay, good Faustus, stay thy desperate
    steps.
I see an angel hovers o'er thy head,
And with a vial full of precious grace
Offers to pour the same into thy soul.
Then call for mercy and avoid despair.   65
FAUSTUS: Ah, my sweet friend, I feel thy words
To comfort my distressèd soul.
Leave me a while to ponder on my sins.
OLD MAN: Faustus, I leave thee, but with grief of heart,
Fearing the enemy of thy hapless soul.   70
                                        (*Exit.*)
FAUSTUS: Accursèd Faustus, where is mercy now?
I do repent, and yet I do despair.
Hell strives with grace for conquest in my breast.
What shall I do to shun the snares of death?
MEPHISTOPHILIS: Thou traitor, Faustus, I arrest thy
    soul   75
For disobedience to my sovereign lord.
Revolt, or I'll in piecemeal tear thy flesh.
FAUSTUS: I do repent I e'er offended him.
Sweet Mephistophilis, entreat thy lord
To pardon my unjust presumption,   80
And with my blood again I will confirm
The former vow I made to Lucifer.
MEPHISTOPHILIS: Do it then, Faustus, with unfeignèd°
    heart,
Lest greater dangers do attend thy drift.°

V, I. 22–25. **peerless dame . . . Dardania:** The Greek Helen (the "peerless dame"), wife of Menelaus, was carried off to Troy (Dardania) by Paris, sparking the Trojan War.

44. **amiable:** Worthy of divine love or grace.   52. **envy of:** Ill will toward.   55. **Checking:** Admonishing.   83. **unfeignèd:** Honest.   84. **drift:** Purpose.

[*Faustus stabs his arm and writes on a paper with his blood.*]

FAUSTUS: Torment, sweet friend, that base and agèd
85   man
    That durst dissuade me from thy Lucifer,
    With greatest torment that our hell affords.
MEPHISTOPHILIS: His faith is great; I cannot touch his
    soul,
    But what I may afflict his body with
90   I will attempt, which is but little worth.
FAUSTUS: One thing, good servant, let me crave of
    thee
    To glut the longing of my heart's desire —
    That I may have unto my paramour
    That heavenly Helen which I saw of late,
95   Whose sweet embracings may extinguish clear
    Those thoughts that do dissuade me from my vow,
    And keep mine oath I made to Lucifer.
MEPHISTOPHILIS: This, or what else my Faustus shall
    desire,
    Shall be performed in twinkling of an eye.

(*Enter Helen again, passing over* [*the stage*] *between two Cupids.*)

FAUSTUS: Was this the face that launched a thousand
100   ships
    And burnt the topless towers of Ilium?
    Sweet Helen, make me immortal with a kiss.

[*She kisses him.*]

    Her lips suck forth my soul. See where it flies!
    Come, Helen, come, give me my soul again.
105   Here will I dwell, for heaven is in these lips,
    And all is dross that is not Helena.

[*Enter the Old Man.*]

    I will be Paris, and for love of thee
    Instead of Troy shall Wittenberg be sacked;
    And I will combat with weak Menelaus°
110   And wear thy colors on my plumèd crest.
    Yea, I will wound Achilles° in the heel
    And then return to Helen for a kiss.
    O, thou art fairer than the evening's air,
    Clad in the beauty of a thousand stars.
115   Brighter art thou than flaming Jupiter°
    When he appeared to hapless Semele,°
    More lovely than the monarch of the sky
    In wanton Arethusa's azured arms,°
    And none but thou shalt be my paramour.

            (*Exeunt* [*all but the Old Man*].)

109. Menelaus: The husband of Helen of Troy.   **111. Achilles:** The Greek hero of the Trojan war, wounded in the heel by Paris.   **115. Jupiter:** Zeus.   **116. Semele:** The daughter of Cadmus and Harmonia who bore Zeus the child, Dionysus. **117–18. monarch . . . arms:** Arethusa was a nymph, one of the Nereids, who governed a fountain on the isle of Ortygia near Syracuse.

OLD MAN: Accursèd Faustus, miserable man,   120
    That from thy soul exclud'st the grace of heaven
    And fliest the throne of his tribunal seat!

(*Enter the Devils.*)

    Satan begins to sift me with his pride.
    As in this furnace God shall try my faith,
    My faith, vile hell, shall triumph over thee.   125
    Ambitious fiends, see how the heavens smiles
    At your repulse and laughs your state° to scorn.
    Hence hell, for hence I fly unto my God.

                      (*Exeunt.*)

Scene II

(*Thunder. Enter* [*above*] *Lucifer, Beelzebub, and Mephistophilis.*)

LUCIFER: Thus from infernal Dis° do we ascend
    To view the subjects of our monarchy,
    Those souls which sin seals the black sons of hell,
    'Mong which as chief, Faustus, we come to thee,
    Bringing with us lasting damnation   5
    To wait upon thy soul. The time is come
    Which makes it forfeit.
MEPHISTOPHILIS: And this gloomy night,
    Here in this room will wretched Faustus be.
BEELZEBUB: And here we'll stay
    To mark him how he doth demean himself.   10
MEPHISTOPHILIS: How should he, but in desperate
    lunacy?
    Fond worldling, now his heart-blood dries with
    grief;
    His conscience kills it, and his laboring brain
    Begets a world of idle fantasies
    To over-reach the devil. But all in vain;   15
    His store of pleasures must be sauced° with pain.
    He and his servant, Wagner, are at hand.
    Both come from drawing Faustus' latest will.
    See where they come.

(*Enter Faustus and Wagner.*)

FAUSTUS: Say, Wagner, thou has perused my will;   20
    How dost thou like it?
WAGNER: Sir, so wondrous well
    As in all humble duty I do yield
    My life and lasting service for your love.

(*Enter the Scholars.*)

FAUSTUS: Gramercies,° Wagner. Welcome, gentlemen.
                      [*Exit Wagner.*]
FIRST SCHOLAR: Now, worthy Faustus, methinks your   25
    looks are changed.
FAUSTUS: Ah, gentlemen!

127. state: Royal power.   **V, II. 1. Dis:** Hades, or hell. **16. sauced:** Paid for.   **24. Gramercies:** Thanks.

SECOND SCHOLAR: What ails Faustus?

FAUSTUS: Ah, my sweet chamber-fellow, had I lived with
30   thee, then had I lived still, but now must die eternally.
Look, sirs; comes he not? Comes he not?

FIRST SCHOLAR: O my dear Faustus, what imports this
fear?

SECOND SCHOLAR: Is all our pleasure turned to melan-
35   choly?

THIRD SCHOLAR: He is not well with being over-solitary.

SECOND SCHOLAR: If it be so, we'll have physicians, and
Faustus shall be cured.

THIRD SCHOLAR: 'Tis but a surfeit sir; fear nothing.

40   FAUSTUS: A surfeit of deadly sin that hath damned both
body and soul.

SECOND SCHOLAR: Yet Faustus, look up to heaven, and
remember mercy is infinite.

FAUSTUS: But Faustus' offence can ne'er be pardoned.
45   The serpent that tempted Eve may be saved, but not
Faustus. Ah gentlemen, hear me with patience and
tremble not at my speeches. Though my heart pants
and quivers to remember that I have been a student
here these thirty years, O, would I had never seen
50   Wittenberg, never read book. And what wonders I
have done, all Germany can witness — yea, all the
world — for which Faustus hath lost both Germany
and the world, yea heaven itself, heaven the seat of
God, the throne of the blessed, the kingdom of joy,
55   and must remain in hell for ever. Hell, ah hell for
ever! Sweet friends, what shall become of Faustus,
being in hell for ever?

SECOND SCHOLAR: Yet Faustus, call on God.

FAUSTUS: On God, whom Faustus hath abjured? On
60   God, whom Faustus hath blasphemed? Ah, my God,
I would weep, but the devil draws in my tears. Gush
forth blood instead of tears, yea life and soul. O, he
stays my tongue! I would lift up my hands, but see,
they hold 'em; they hold 'em.

65   ALL: Who, Faustus?

FAUSTUS: Why, Lucifer and Mephistophilis. Ah, gentlemen, I gave them my soul for my cunning.

ALL: God forbid!

FAUSTUS: God forbade it indeed, but Faustus hath done
70   it. For the vain pleasure of four and twenty years
hath Faustus lost eternal joy and felicity. I writ them
a bill with mine own blood. The date is expired. This
is the time, and he will fetch me.

FIRST SCHOLAR: Why did not Faustus tell us of this
75   before, that divines might have prayed for thee?

FAUSTUS: Oft have I thought to have done so, but the
devil threatened to tear me in pieces if I named God,
to fetch me, body and soul, if I once gave ear to divinity. And now 'tis too late. Gentlemen away, lest you
80   perish with me.

SECOND SCHOLAR: O, what may we do to save Faustus?

FAUSTUS: Talk not of me, but save yourselves and depart.

THIRD SCHOLAR: God will strengthen me; I will stay
85   with Faustus.

FIRST SCHOLAR: Tempt not God, sweet friend, but let us
into the next room and there pray for him.

FAUSTUS: Ay, pray for me, pray for me; and what noise
soever you hear, come not unto me, for nothing can
rescue me.   90

SECOND SCHOLAR: Pray thou, and we will pray that God
may have mercy upon thee.

FAUSTUS: Gentlemen, farewell. If I live till morning, I'll
visit you; if not, Faustus is gone to hell.

ALL: Faustus, farewell.   95

(*Exeunt Scholars.*)

MEPHISTOPHILIS: [*above*] Ay, Faustus, now thou hast
no hope of heaven;
Therefore despair. Think only upon hell,
For that must be thy mansion, there to dwell.

FAUSTUS: O thou bewitching fiend, 'twas thy
temptation
Hath robbed me of eternal happiness.   100

MEPHISTOPHILIS: I do confess it, Faustus, and rejoice.
'Twas I, that when thou wert i' the way to heaven,
Damned up thy passage. When thou took'st the
book
To view the Scriptures, then I turned the leaves
And led thine eye.   105
What, weep'st thou? 'Tis too late. Despair!
Farewell!
Fools that will laugh on earth must weep in hell.

(*Exit.*)

(*Enter the Good Angel and the Bad Angel at several
doors.*)

GOOD ANGEL: Ah, Faustus, if thou hadst given ear to
me,
Innumerable joys had followed thee;
But thou didst love the world.

BAD ANGEL: Gave ear to me,   110
And now must taste hell's pains perpetually.

GOOD ANGEL: O what will all thy riches, pleasures,
pomps
Avail thee now?

BAD ANGEL: Nothing but vex thee more,
To want in hell, that had on earth such store.

(*Music while the throne descends.*)

GOOD ANGEL: O, thou hast lost celestial happiness,   115
Pleasures unspeakable, bliss without end.
Hadst thou affected sweet divinity,
Hell or the devil had had no power on thee.
Hadst thou kept on that way, Faustus, behold
In what resplendent glory thou hadst sat   120
In yonder throne, like those bright shining saints,
And triumphed over hell. That hast thou lost,
And now, poor soul, must thy good angel leave thee.

[*The throne ascends.*]

The jaws of hell are open to receive thee.

(*Exit.*)

(*Hell is discovered.*)

BAD ANGEL: Now, Faustus, let thine eyes with horror
125   stare
    Into that vast perpetual torture-house.
    There are the Furies tossing damnèd souls
    On burning forks; their bodies boil in lead.
    There are live quarters broiling on the coals,
130   That ne'er can die. This ever-burning chair
    Is for o'er-tortured souls to rest them in.
    These that are fed with sops of flaming fire
    Were gluttons and loved only delicates
    And laughed to see the poor starve at their gates.
135   But yet all these are nothing; thou shalt see
    Ten thousand tortures that more horrid be.
FAUSTUS: O, I have seen enough to torture me.
BAD ANGEL: Nay, thou must feel them, taste the smart
    of all.
    He that loves pleasure must for pleasure fall.
140   And so I leave thee, Faustus, till anon;
    Then wilt thou tumble in confusion.

([*Hell disappears.*] *The clock strikes eleven.*)

FAUSTUS: Ah Faustus,
    Now hast thou but one bare hour to live,
    And then thou must be damned perpetually.
145   Stand still, you ever-moving spheres of heaven,
    That time may cease and midnight never come.
    Fair nature's eye, rise, rise again, and make
    Perpetual day; or let this hour be but
    A year, a month, a week, a natural day,
150   That Faustus may repent and save his soul.
    O lente, lente currite noctis equi!°
    The stars move still; time runs; the clock will
    strike;
    The devil will come, and Faustus must be
    damned.
    O, I'll leap up to my God! Who pulls me down?
    See, see, where Christ's blood streams in the
155   firmament!
    One drop would save my soul, half a drop! Ah, my
    Christ!
    Rend not my heart for naming of my Christ!
    Yet will I call on him. O, spare me, Lucifer!
    Where is it now? 'Tis gone. And see where God
160   Stretcheth out his arm and bends his ireful brows.
    Mountains and hills, come, come, and fall on me,
    And hide me from the heavy wrath of God.
    No, no!
    Then will I headlong run into the earth.
165   Earth, gape! O no, it will not harbor me!
    You stars that reigned at my nativity,
    Whose influence hath allotted death and hell.
    Now draw up Faustus like a foggy mist
    Into the entrails of yon laboring cloud,
170   That when you vomit forth into the air,

    My limbs may issue from your smoky mouths,
    So that my soul may but ascend to heaven.
(*The watch strikes.*)
    Ah, half the hour is past; 'twill all be past anon.
    O God,
    If thou wilt not have mercy on my soul,
    Yet for Christ's sake, whose blood hath ransomed 175
    me,
    Impose some end to my incessant pain.
    Let Faustus live in hell a thousand years,
    A hundred thousand, and at last be saved.
    O, no end is limited to damnèd souls. 180
    Why wert thou not a creature wanting soul?
    Or why is this immortal that thou hast?
    Ah, Pythagoras' *metempsychosis*,° were that
    true,
    This soul should fly from me and I be changed
    Into some brutish beast. All beasts are happy, 185
    For, when they die
    Their souls are soon dissolved in elements,
    But mine must live still to be plagued in hell.
    Cursed be the parents that engendered me!
    No, Faustus, curse thyself, curse Lucifer 190
    That hath deprived thee of the joys of heaven.
(*The clock strikes twelve.*)
    O, it strikes, it strikes! Now, body, turn to air,
    Or Lucifer will bear thee quick° to hell.
    O soul, be changed to little water-drops,
    And fall into the ocean, ne'er be found! 195
(*Thunder, and enter the Devils.*)
    My God, my God, look not so fierce on me!
    Adders and serpents, let me breathe a while!
    Ugly hell, gape not! Come not, Lucifer!
    I'll burn my books! Ah, Mephistophilis!
              (*Exeunt* [*Faustus and Devils*].)

Scene III

(*Enter the Scholars.*)

FIRST SCHOLAR: Come, gentlemen, let us go visit
    Faustus,
    For such a dreadful night was never seen
    Since first the world's creation did begin.
    Such fearful shrieks and cries were never heard.
    Pray heaven the doctor have escaped the danger. 5
SECOND SCHOLAR: O help us, heaven! See, here are
    Faustus' limbs,
    All torn asunder by the hand of death.

---

151. *O . . . equi:* O slowly, slowly; run you horses of night (adapted from Ovid's *Amores*).

183. *metempsychosis:* Belief in the transmigration of souls, associated with the Greek philosopher Pythagoras of Samos. **193.** *quick:* Alive.

THIRD SCHOLAR: The devils whom Faustus served
    have torn him thus;
    For 'twixt the hours of twelve and one, methought
10   I heard him shriek and call aloud for help,
    At which self time the house seemed all on fire
    With dreadful horror of these damnèd fiends.
SECOND SCHOLAR: Well, gentlemen, though Faustus'
    end be such
    As every Christian heart laments to think on,
15   Yet for he was a scholar, once admired
    For wondrous knowledge in our German schools,
    We'll give his mangled limbs due burial;
    And all the students clothed in mourning black,
    Shall wait upon° his heavy° funeral.

                         (*Exeunt.*)

V, III. 19. **wait upon:** Be present at.   **heavy:** Sorrowful.

EPILOGUE

(*Enter Chorus.*)

CHORUS: Cut is the branch that might have grown full
    straight,
    And burnèd is Apollo's laurel bough
    That sometime grew within this learnèd man.
    Faustus is gone. Regard his hellish fall,
    Whose fiendful fortune may exhort the wise   5
    Only to wonder at unlawful things,
    Whose deepness doth entice such forward wits
    To practice more than heavenly power permits.

                         [*Exit.*]

    Terminat hora diem; terminat author opus.°

Epilogue. 9. *Terminat . . . opus:* The hour ends the day; the author ends his work.

COMMENTARY

Ernst Honigmann (*b. 1927*)
FROM *TEN PROBLEMS IN* DOCTOR FAUSTUS   *1991*

> *Honigmann, a distinguished critic of Shakespeare and Renaissance drama, raises certain questions about first the "togetherness" of Faustus and Mephistophilis and then the rationality of Faustus. If Faustus is a champion of the rational, why does he behave as he does in the face of a self-confessed devil? Some of Honigmann's observations are dependent on either the A-text or the B-text, the two earliest printings of the play. But whichever text one consults, the problems he sees are intriguing.*

How much genuine fellow-feeling is there in this strange relationship? Quite apart from the fact that they both enjoy the same jokes, they address each other affectionately as "my Faustus" and "my Mephostophilis," and Mephostophilis even speaks of "my Faustus" in the latter's absence.

> I'll wing myself and forthwith fly amain
> Unto my Faustus to the great Turk's court.   (B 1179)

If something close to tenderness seems at times to bind them together, let us remember that there is a connection between loving a person and thinking that you own him (or her). True, we note some dramatic irony as well, as when Faustus addresses "my good Mephostophilis" (A 822); and it suits both of them to get on together, so they call each other "sweet Mephostophilis," "sweet friend" and the like (A 696,

1342), to oil the relationship. Yet since they also rage against each other every so often it has the dynamics of a very human relationship — including deception and (on Faustus' part) some self-deception. Mephostophilis, indeed, insofar as he was once an angel and fell with Lucifer, assumes a kind of "older brother" stance in answering Faustus' questions about heaven and hell; he has been through it all himself, he understands Faustus' point of view — does that not beget fellow-feeling? And perhaps even affection? Ben Jonson remembered Faustus and Mephostophilis when he created Volpone and Mosca, including the delicious twist that the servant plans to outwit his master — yet Jonson's rogues strike me as a colder pair, their relationship as largely professional, whereas Faustus and Mephostophilis also interact unprofessionally. Mephostophilis risks losing Faustus' soul by speaking too honestly:

> FAUSTUS: And what are you that live with Lucifer?
> MEPHOST: Unhappy spirits that live with Lucifer,
>   Conspired against our God with Lucifer,
>   And are for ever damned with Lucifer.   (A 314)

We are encouraged to think of Faustus and Mephostophilis as very close — though exactly how close remains a mystery. When they play their pranks on the Pope and others they may even hug or slap each other with delight — or, alternatively, Mephostophilis may signal to us, grimacing, that he has to humour a childish master. The *togetherness* of Faustus and Mephostophilis, in short, has been an issue throughout the play, and probably one that should not be resolved until Faustus' very last utterance, the moment of truth: "ah, Mephostophilis!"

I must not pretend, however, that this central relationship is identical in the two texts — far from it. Two passages in the B-text, not found in A, stress the distance between the two principals, the malignancy of Mephostophilis and his delight in destroying Faustus. These passages, both placed just before the end, suggest that in the B-text Mephostophilis savors his victim's death-agony. First the devils ascend from hell to "mark [Faustus] how he doth demean himself." How should he, exclaims Mephostophilis —

> How should he, but in desperate lunacy?
> Fond worldling, now his heart-blood dries with grief,
> His conscience kills it, and his labouring brain
> Begets a world of idle fantasies
> To overreach the devil — but all in vain.
> His store of pleasures must be sauced with pain.   (B 1906)

All fellow-feeling has vanished. And when the scholars depart, leaving Faustus to his final meditations, Mephostophilis turns on him gleefully —

> MEPHOST: Ay, Faustus, now hast thou no hope of heaven,
>   Therefore despair, think only upon hell!
>   For that must be thy mansion, there to dwell.
> FAUSTUS: O thou bewitching fiend, 'twas thy temptation
>   Hath robbed me of eternal happiness.
> MEPHOST: I do confess it, Faustus, and rejoice . . .   (B 1983)

It makes a difference, too, that in the B-text Mephostophilis remains onstage during Faustus' interview with the scholars, and that in the B-text Mephostophilis "brings in" Helen of Troy, the first time she appears — presumably like a ringmaster or auctioneer, pointing out her special attractions. (Not so in the *Faust-book,* where Faustus tells his friends that he will "bring her into your presence personally": ch. 45.) The Mephostophilis of the A-text has a subtler relationship with Faustus, less devilish, more human.

Mephostophilis, I said, risks losing Faustus' soul by speaking too honestly. Here is another "theological" problem, for which I see no easy solution. Many a rationalist has thought, before and after Marlowe, "I am aware of no convincing evidence for the existence of God, therefore I shall behave as if there is no God." Yet is it rational to go on denying God when you are talking to a self-confessed devil? And when the devil appears to be unshakeable in the conviction that God exists?

> FAUSTUS: Was not that Lucifer an angel once?
> MEPHOST: Yes, Faustus, and most dearly loved of God.   (A 309)

Put the case that *one* of the supernatural beings of the Christo-Hebraic tradition incontrovertibly exists — good angel, bad angel, Lucifer — then there is an inherent likelihood that God "exists" as well. And if a hostile witness, such as Mephostophilis, assures Faustus that God exists, how can a rational man turn his back on God? make war on the Omnipotent? and choose Hell instead? —

> FAUSTUS: Come, I think hell's a fable.
> MEPHOST: Ay, think so still, till experience change thy mind!   (A 574)

Could it be that Faustus is a very confused doctor of divinity? or is Marlowe a very confused dramatist? or am I guilty now of trying to "over-explain"?

Some critics have argued that Faustus deteriorates intellectually in the course of the play, like Milton's Satan, as witnessed by his childish activities in the middle scenes. Alternatively, Chorus' opening statement

> So much he profits in divinity
> That shortly he was graced with doctor's name,
> Excelling all, and sweetly can dispute . . .   (B 16)

may refer to the past, not to Faustus as he now is —

> For, falling to a devilish exercise
> And glutted now with learning's golden gifts
> He surfeits upon cursed necromancy.   (B 23)

Theologians sometimes talk of a "fall before the Fall" (Milton appears to allude to this in Eve's dream before the Fall). Marlowe's Faustus, perhaps, should be seen as fallen, or devil-possessed, before he signs his formal pact — therefore intellectually impaired from the play's beginning. I prefer this explanation because he behaves irrationally from the beginning, already believing in spirits, and Lucifer, but not in God. Marlowe allows us to think of Faustus as something other than the ideal theologian by inserting implicit stage directions in the speech in his study. "Bid *on kai me on* farewell; Galen, come," "Physic farewell; where is Justinian?", "divinity, adieu"— does Faustus simply pick up one book after another? or should he hurl them away, frustrated, with each sarcastic "adieu" and "farewell"? A frightening impulsiveness, breaking out during this first meditation, could help to reconcile us to Faustus' perplexing irrationality. The *Faust-book* offered this possibility: Dr. Faustus "fell into such fantasies and deep cogitations, that . . . sometime he would *throw the Scripture from him*" (ch. I).

William Shakespeare

Despite the fact that Shakespeare wrote some thirty-seven plays, owned part of his theatrical company, acted in plays, and retired a relatively wealthy man in the city of his birth, there is much we do not know about him. His father was a glovemaker with pretensions to being a gentleman; Shakespeare himself had his coat of arms placed on his home, New Place, purchased in part because it was one of the grandest buildings in Stratford. Church records indicate that he was born in April 1564 and died in April 1616, after having been retired from the stage for two or three years. We know that he married Anne Hathaway in 1582, when he was eighteen and she twenty-six; that he had a daughter Susanna and twins, Judith and Hamnet; and that Hamnet, his only son, died at age eleven. He has no direct descendants today.

We know very little about his education. We assume that he went to the local grammar school, since as the son of a burgess he was eligible to attend for free. If he did so, he would have received a very strong education based on rhetoric, logic, and classical literature. He would have been exposed to the

The engraving by Martin Droeshout of William Shakespeare appeared in the First Folio Edition, published in 1623.

comedies of Plautus, the tragedies of Seneca, and the poetry of Virgil, Ovid, and a host of other, lesser writers.

A rumor has persisted that he spent some time as a Latin teacher. No evidence exists to suggest that Shakespeare went to a university, although his general learning and knowledge are so extraordinary and broad that generations of scholars have assumed that he may have also gone to the Inns of Court to study law. This cannot be proved, though; thus, some people claim that another person, with considerable university education, must have written his plays. However, no one in the Elizabethan theater had an education of the sort often proposed for Shakespeare. Marlowe and Ben Jonson were the most learned of Elizabethan playwrights, but their work is quite different in character and feeling from that of Shakespeare.

One recent theory about Shakespeare's early years suggests that before going to London to work in theater he belonged to a wandering company of actors much like those who appear in *Hamlet*. It is an ingenious theory and has much to recommend it, among which is explaining how Shakespeare could take the spotlight so quickly as to arouse the anger of more experienced London writers.

Shakespeare did not begin his career writing for the stage but, in the more conventional approach for the age, as a poet. He sought the support of an aristocratic patron, the earl of Southampton. Like many wealthy and polished young courtiers, Southampton felt it a pleasant ornament to sponsor a poet whose works would be dedicated to him. Shakespeare wrote sonnets apparently with Southampton in mind, and, hoping for preferment, the long narrative poems *Venus and Adonis, The Rape of Lucrece*, and *The Phoenix and the Turtle*. However, Southampton eventually decided to become the patron of another poet, John Florio, an Italian who had translated Michel de Montaigne's *Essays*.

Shakespeare's response was to turn to the stage. His first plays were a considerable success: *King Henry VI* in three parts — three full-length plays. Satisfying London's taste for plays that told the history of England's tangled political past, Shakespeare won considerable renown with a lengthy series of plays ranging from *Richard II* through the two parts of *King Henry IV* to *Henry V*. Audiences were delighted; competing playwrights envied him his triumphs. Francis Meres's famous book of the period, *Palladis Tamia: Wit's Treasury*, cites Shakespeare as modern Plautus and Seneca, the best in both comedy and tragedy. Meres says that by 1598 Shakespeare was known for a dozen plays. That his success was firm by this time is demonstrated by his having purchased his large house, New Place, in Stratford in 1597. He could not have done this without financial security.

In the next few years Shakespeare made a number of interesting purchases of property in Stratford; he also made deals with his own theater company to secure the rights to perform in London. These arrangements produced legal records that give us some of the clearest information we have concerning Shakespeare's activities during this period. His company was called the Lord Chamberlain's Men while Queen Elizabeth was alive but was renamed the King's Men by King James in the spring of 1603, less than two months after Elizabeth died. As the King's Men, Shakespeare's company had considerable power and success. Its audience sometimes included King James, as in the first performance of *Macbeth*.

Shakespeare was successful as a writer of histories, comedies, and tragedies. He also wrote in another genre, known as romance. These plays share elements with both comedies and tragedies, and they often depend on supernatural or improbable elements. *Cymbeline, The Winter's Tale,* and *The Tempest* are the best known of Shakespeare's romances. They are late works and have a fascinating complexity.

When Shakespeare died on April 23, 1616, he was buried as a gentleman in the church in which he had been baptized in Stratford-upon-Avon. His will left most of his money and possessions to his two daughters, Judith and Susanna.

A MIDSUMMER NIGHT'S DREAM

A Midsummer Night's Dream (1595–1596) is an early comedy and one of Shakespeare's most beloved works. It is also one of his most imaginative plays, introducing us to the world of fairies and the realm of dreams. Romantic painters, such as Fuseli, have long found in this play a rich store of images that stretch far beyond the limits of the real world of everyday experience.

For Shakespeare the fun of the play is in showing how the world of the fairies intersects with the world of real people, and we can interpret the play as a hint of what would happen if the world of dreams were to cross the world of real experience. The fact that these worlds are more alike than they are different gives Shakespeare the comic basis on which to work. He also finds some new and amusing ways to interpret the device of mistaken identities.

The play is set in Athens, with Duke Theseus about to wed Hippolyta, the queen of the Amazons. Helena and Hermia are young women in love with Demetrius and Lysander, respectively. Demetrius, however, wants to marry Hermia and has the blessing of Hermia's father. Hermia's refusal to follow her father's wishes drives her into the woods, where she is followed by both young men and Helena, who does not want to lose Demetrius.

The four young people find themselves in the world of the fairies, although the humans cannot see the fairies. Puck, an impish sprite, is ordered by Oberon, king of the fairies, to put the juice of a certain flower in Demetrius's eyes so that he will fall in love with Helena. When Puck puts it in Lysander's eyes instead, the plot backfires: Lysander is suddenly in love with Helena, and Hermia is confounded. Oberon has Puck place the same juice in the eyes of Titania, the queen of the fairies, causing her to fall in love with the first creature she sees when she awakes.

That creature is Bottom, the "rude mechanical" (ignorant artisan) whose head has been transformed into an ass's head. Such a trick opens up possibilities for wonderful comic elements. The richness of the illusions that operate onstage constantly draws us to the question of how we ever can know the truth of our own experiences, especially when some of them are dreams whose imaginative power is occasionally overwhelming.

Shakespeare plays here with some of the Aristotelian conventions of the drama, especially Aristotle's view that drama imitates life. One of the great comic devices in *A Midsummer Night's Dream* is the play within a play that Bottom, Quince, Snug, Flute, and Starveling are to put on before Theseus and Hippolyta. They tell the story of Pyramus and Thisby, lovers who lose each other because they misinterpret signs. It is "Merry and tragical! Tedious and brief!" But it is also a wonderful parody of what playwrights — including Shakespeare — often do when operating in the Aristotelian mode. The aim of the play is realism, yet the players are naive and inexperienced in drama; they do their best constantly to remind the audience that it is only a play.

The comic ineptness of the rude mechanicals' play needs no disclaimers of this sort, and the immediate audience — Theseus, Hippolyta, Demetrius, Helena, Lysander, and Hermia — is amused by the ardor of the players. The audience in the theater is also mightily amused at the antics of the mechanicals, which on the surface are simply funny and a wonderful pastiche of artless play-acting.

Beneath the surface, something more serious is going on. Shakespeare is commenting on the entire function of drama in our lives. He constantly reminds us in this play that we are watching an illusion, even an illusion within an illusion, but he also convinces us that illusions teach us a great deal about reality. The real-world setting of *A Midsummer Night's Dream* — Athens — is quite improbable. The mechanicals all have obviously English names and are out of place in an Athenian pastoral setting. The play on the level of Athens is pure fantasy, with even more fantastic goings-on at the level of the fairy world. But fantasy nourishes us. It helps us interpret our own experiences by permitting us to distance ourselves from them and reflect on how they affect others, one of the deepest functions of drama.

As in most comedies, everything turns out exceptionally well. A multiple marriage, one of the delightful conventions of many comedies, ends the drama, and virtually everyone receives what she or he wanted. We are left with a sense of satisfaction because we, too, get our wish about how things should turn out. Puck, one of the greatest of Shakespeare's characters, turns out to be sympathetic and human in his feelings about people. And Bottom, a clown whose origins are certainly Greek and Roman, endears us to him with his generosity and caring toward others. Shakespeare promotes a remarkably warm view of humanity in this play, leaving us with a sense of delight and a glow that is rare even in comedy.

A Midsummer Night's Dream in Performance

A Midsummer Night's Dream has attracted many great directors in modern times, although in the late seventeenth and eighteenth centuries the play was adapted essentially as a vehicle for presenting the world of the fairies. It even became an opera in 1692. Ludwig Tieck engaged Mendelssohn to write incidental music for the play in Berlin in 1843; their production was for many years the most influential post-Shakespearean adaptation. Beerbohm Tree's 1900 production in London's Savoy Theatre included real rabbits and many other highly realistic details; eventually it played to more than 220,000 patrons. After numerous adaptations it was produced by Granville Barker in London from 1912 to 1914 in its original text, and in New York in 1915. The Old Vic's 1954 production was so lavish that it was staged at the Metropolitan Opera House in New York. Peter Brook played down the fairies and explored the play as a study of love. His 1970 production is well remembered for his having placed Oberon and Puck on trapezes set against a stark white background. He also used some costumes and other elements of commedia dell'arte to spark the comedy. (See Barnes's review of the Brook production on p. 322.) The American Repertory Theatre's 1986 Boston production (see photos on pp. 294–95) reflects the approach to staging that the Royal Shakespeare Company has taken in recent years. The themes of love and transformation inspire the players in a way that shows off the brilliance of the play.

   A Midsummer's Night Dream has been filmed several times. In 1935 both James Cagney and Mickey Rooney starred in a version that has some charm. In 1968 the Royal Shakespeare Company with Diana Rigg produced a somewhat less interesting film. The most recent version with Kevin Kline, Michelle Pfeiffer, and Stanley Tucci was produced to generally good reviews in 1999.

William Shakespeare (1564–1616)
A MIDSUMMER NIGHT'S DREAM   *c. 1596*

[Dramatis Personae

THESEUS, *Duke of Athens*
EGEUS, *father to Hermia*
LYSANDER, }
DEMETRIUS, }   *in love with Hermia*
PHILOSTRATE, *Master of the Revels to Theseus*

QUINCE, *a carpenter*
SNUG, *a joiner*
BOTTOM, *a weaver*
FLUTE, *a bellows-mender*
SNOUT, *a tinker*
STARVELING, *a tailor*

HIPPOLYTA, *Queen of the Amazons, betrothed to Theseus*
HERMIA, *daughter to Egeus, in love with Lysander*

Note: The text of *A Midsummer Night's Dream* has come down to us in different versions — such as the first quarto, the second quarto, and the first Folio. The copy of the text used here is largely drawn from the first quarto. Passages enclosed in square brackets are taken from one of the other versions.

HELENA, *in love with Demetrius*
OBERON, *King of the Fairies*
TITANIA, *Queen of the Fairies*
PUCK, *or Robin Goodfellow*
PEASEBLOSSOM, }
COBWEB, }
MOTH, }   *fairies*
MUSTARDSEED, }
Other FAIRIES *attending their king and queen*
ATTENDANTS *on Theseus and Hippolyta*

Scene: *Athens, and a wood near it.*]

{*ACT I* • *Scene 1*}°

(*Enter Theseus, Hippolyta, [Philostrate,] with others.*)

THESEUS: Now, fair Hippolyta, our nuptial hour
   Draws on apace. Four happy days bring in
   Another moon; but, O, methinks, how slow

I, I. Location: The palace of Theseus.

This old moon wanes! She lingers° my desires
5   Like to a step-dame° or a dowager°
Long withering out a young man's revenue.
HIPPOLYTA: Four days will quickly steep themselves in
     night,
Four nights will quickly dream away the time;
And then the moon, like to a silver bow
10   New-bent in heaven, shall behold the night
Of our solemnities.
THESEUS: Go, Philostrate,
Stir up the Athenian youth to merriments,
Awake the pert and nimble spirit of mirth,
Turn melancholy forth to funerals;
15   The pale companion° is not for our pomp.°
                              [*Exit Philostrate.*]
Hippolyta, I woo'd thee with my sword,°
And won thy love doing thee injuries;
But I will wed thee in another key,
With pomp, with triumph,° and with reveling.

(*Enter Egeus and his daughter Hermia, and Lysander,
and Demetrius.*)

20   EGEUS: Happy be Theseus, our renowned Duke!
THESEUS: Thanks, good Egeus. What's the news with
     thee?
EGEUS: Full of vexation come I, with complaint
Against my child, my daughter Hermia.
Stand forth, Demetrius. My noble lord,
25   This man hath my consent to marry her.
Stand forth, Lysander. And, my gracious Duke,
This man hath bewitch'd the bosom of my child.
Thou, thou, Lysander, thou hast given her rhymes
And interchang'd love tokens with my child.
30   Thou hast by moonlight at her window sung
With feigning voice verses of feigning° love,
And stol'n the impression of her fantasy,°
With bracelets of thy hair, rings, gauds,° conceits,°
Knacks,° trifles, nosegays, sweetmeats —
     messengers
35   Of strong prevailment in unhardened youth.
With cunning hast thou filch'd my daughter's heart,
Turn'd her obedience, which is due to me,
To stubborn harshness. And, my gracious Duke,
Be it so she will not here before your Grace
40   Consent to marry with Demetrius,
I beg the ancient privilege of Athens:
As she is mine, I may dispose of her,

4. lingers: Lengthens, protects.   **5. step-dame:** Stepmother.
dowager: Widow with a jointure or dower [an estate or title
from her deceased husband].   **15. companion:** Fellow.
pomp: Ceremonial magnificence.   **16. with my sword:** In a
military engagement against the Amazons, when Hippolyta
was taken captive.   **19. triumph:** Public festivity.   **31. feigning:** (1) Counterfeiting, (2) faining, desirous.   **32. And . . .
fantasy:** And made her fall in love with you (imprinting your
image on her imagination) by stealthy and dishonest means.
33. gauds: Playthings.   **conceits:** Fanciful trifles.   **34. Knacks:**
Knickknacks.

Which shall be either to this gentleman
Or to her death, according to our law
Immediately° provided in that case.   45
THESEUS: What say you, Hermia? Be advis'd, fair maid.
To you your father should be as a god —
One that compos'd your beauties, yea, and one
To whom you are but as a form in wax
By him imprinted and within his power   50
To leave° the figure or disfigure° it.
Demetrius is a worthy gentleman.
HERMIA: So is Lysander.
THESEUS: In himself he is;
But in this kind,° wanting° your father's voice,°
The other must be held the worthier.   55
HERMIA: I would my father look'd but with my eyes.
THESEUS: Rather your eyes must with his judgment look.
HERMIA: I do entreat your Grace to pardon me.
I know not by what power I am made bold,
Nor how it may concern° my modesty,   60
In such a presence here to plead my thoughts;
But I beseech your Grace that I may know
The worst that may befall me in this case,
If I refuse to wed Demetrius.
THESEUS: Either to die the death, or to abjure   65
Forever the society of men.
Therefore, fair Hermia, question your desires,
Know of your youth, examine well your blood,°
Whether, if you yield not to your father's choice,
You can endure the livery° of a nun,   70
For aye° to be in shady cloister mew'd,°
To live a barren sister all your life,
Chanting faint hymns to the cold fruitless moon.
Thrice blessed they that master so their blood
To undergo such maiden pilgrimage,   75
But earthlier happy° is the rose distill'd,
Than that which withering on the virgin thorn
Grows, lives, and dies in single blessedness.
HERMIA: So will I grow, so live, so die, my lord,
Ere I will yield my virgin patent° up   80
Unto his lordship, whose unwished yoke
My soul consents not to give sovereignty.
THESEUS: Take time to pause; and, by the next new
     moon —
The sealing-day betwixt my love and me
For everlasting bond of fellowship —   85
Upon that day either prepare to die
For disobedience to your father's will,
Or° else to wed Demetrius, as he would,
Or on Diana's altar° to protest°
For aye austerity and single life.   90

45. Immediately: Expressly.   **51. leave:** Leave unaltered.   **disfigure:** Obliterate.   **54. kind:** Respect.   **wanting:** Lacking
voice: Approval.   **60. concern:** Befit.   **68. blood:** Passions.
70. livery: Habit.   **71. aye:** Ever.   **mew'd:** Shut in (said of a
hawk, poultry, etc.).   **76. earthlier happy:** Happier as respects
this world.   **80. patent:** Privilege.   **88. Or:** Either.   **89. Diana's altar:** Diana was a virgin goddess.   **protest:** Vow.

DEMETRIUS: Relent, sweet Hermia, and, Lysander, yield
   Thy crazed° title to my certain right.
LYSANDER: You have her father's love, Demetrius;
   Let me have Hermia's. Do you marry him.
95 EGEUS: Scornful Lysander! True, he hath my love,
   And what is mine my love shall render him.
   And she is mine, and all my right of her
   I do estate unto° Demetrius.
LYSANDER: I am, my lord, as well deriv'd° as he,
100 As well possess'd;° my love is more than his;
   My fortunes every way as fairly° rank'd,
   If not with vantage,° as Demetrius';
   And, which is more than all these boasts can be,
   I am belov'd of beauteous Hermia.
105 Why should not I then prosecute my right?
   Demetrius, I'll avouch it to his head,°
   Made love to Nedar's daughter, Helena,
   And won her soul; and she, sweet lady, dotes,
   Devoutly dotes, dotes in idolatry,
110 Upon this spotted° and inconstant man.
THESEUS: I must confess that I have heard so much,
   And with Demetrius thought to have spoke thereof;
   But, being over-full of self-affairs,
   My mind did lose it. But, Demetrius, come,
115 And come, Egeus, you shall go with me;
   I have some private schooling for you both.
   For you, fair Hermia, look you arm° yourself
   To fit your fancies° to your father's will;
   Or else the law of Athens yields you up —
120 Which by no means we may extenuate° —
   To death, or to a vow of single life.
   Come, my Hippolyta. What cheer, my love?
   Demetrius and Egeus, go° along.
   I must employ you in some business
125 Against° our nuptial, and confer with you
   Of something nearly that° concerns yourselves.
EGEUS: With duty and desire we follow you.

       (*Exeunt*° [*all but Lysander and Hermia*].)

LYSANDER: How now, my love, why is your cheek so
   pale?
   How chance the roses there do fade so fast?
130 HERMIA: Belike° for want of rain, which I could well
   Beteem° them from the tempest of my eyes.
LYSANDER: Ay me! For aught that I could ever read,
   Could ever hear by tale or history,
   The course of true love never did run smooth;
135 But either it was different in blood° —

HERMIA: O cross,° too high to be enthrall'd to low!
LYSANDER: Or else misgraffed° in respect of years —
HERMIA: O spite, too old to be engag'd to young!
LYSANDER: Or else it stood upon the choice of
   friends° —
HERMIA: O hell, to choose love by another's eyes!   140
LYSANDER: Or, if there were a sympathy in choice,
   War, death, or sickness did lay siege to it,
   Making it momentany° as a sound,
   Swift as a shadow, short as any dream,
   Brief as the lightning in the collied° night,   145
   That, in a spleen,° unfolds° both heaven and earth,
   And ere a man hath power to say "Behold!"
   The jaws of darkness do devour it up.
   So quick° bright things come to confusion.°
HERMIA: If then true lovers have been ever cross'd,°   150
   It stands as an edict in destiny.
   Then let us teach our trial patience,°
   Because it is a customary cross,
   As due to love as thoughts and dreams and sighs,
   Wishes and tears, poor fancy's° followers.   155
LYSANDER: A good persuasion. Therefore, hear me,
   Hermia.
   I have a widow aunt, a dowager
   Of great revenue, and she hath no child.
   From Athens is her house remote seven leagues;
   And she respects° me as her only son.   160
   There, gentle Hermia, may I marry thee,
   And to that place the sharp Athenian law
   Cannot pursue us. If thou lovest me, then,
   Steal forth thy father's house tomorrow night;
   And in the wood, a league without the town,   165
   Where I did meet thee once with Helena
   To do observance to a morn of May,°
   There will I stay for thee.
HERMIA: My good Lysander!
   I swear to thee, by Cupid's strongest bow,
   By his best arrow with the golden head,°   170
   By the simplicity° of Venus' doves,°
   By that which knitteth souls and prospers loves,
   And by that fire which burn'd the Carthage queen,
   When the false Troyan° under sail was seen,

---

92. **crazed:** Cracked, unsound.   98. **estate unto:** Settle or bestow upon.   99. **deriv'd:** Descended, i.e., "as well born."   100. **possess'd:** Endowed with wealth.   101. **fairly:** Handsomely.   102. **vantage:** Superiority.   106. **head:** Face.   110. **spotted:** Morally stained.   117. **look you arm:** Take care you prepare.   118. **fancies:** Likings, thoughts of love.   120. **extenuate:** Mitigate.   123. **go:** Come.   125. **Against:** In preparation for.   126. **nearly that:** That closely.   127. [s.d.] *Exeunt:* Latin for "they go out."   130. **Belike:** Very likely.   131. **Beteem:** Grant, afford.   135. **blood:** Hereditary station.

136. **cross:** Vexation.   137. **misgraffed:** Ill grafted, badly matched.   139. **friends:** Relatives.   143. **momentany:** Lasting but a moment.   145. **collied:** Blackened (as with coal dust), darkened.   146. **in a spleen:** In a swift impulse in a violent flash. **unfolds:** Discloses.   149. **quick:** Quickly; or, perhaps, living, alive. **confusion:** Ruin.   150. **ever cross'd:** Always thwarted.   152. **teach . . . patience:** Teach ourselves patience in this trial.   155. **fancy's:** Amorous passion's.   160. **respects:** Regards.   167. **do . . . May:** Perform the ceremonies of May Day.   170. **best arrow . . . golden head:** Cupid's best gold-pointed arrows were supposed to induce love, his blunt leaden arrows aversion.   171. **simplicity:** Innocence. **doves:** Those that drew Venus's chariot.   173–74. **by that fire . . . false Troyan:** Dido, Queen of Carthage, immolated herself on a funeral pyre after having been deserted by the Trojan hero Aeneas.

175　　By all the vows that ever men have broke,
　　　　In number more than ever women spoke,
　　　　In that same place thou hast appointed me
　　　　Tomorrow truly will I meet with thee.
　　LYSANDER: Keep promise, love. Look, here comes
　　　　Helena.

(*Enter Helena.*)

180　HERMIA: God speed fair° Helena, whither away?
　　HELENA: Call you me fair? That fair again unsay.
　　　　Demetrius loves your fair.° O happy fair!°
　　　　Your eyes are lodestars,° and your tongue's sweet air°
　　　　More tuneable° than lark to shepherd's ear
185　　When wheat is green, when hawthorn buds appear.
　　　　Sickness is catching. O, were favor° so,
　　　　Yours would I catch, fair Hermia, ere I go;
　　　　My ear should catch your voice, my eye your eye,
　　　　My tongue should catch your tongue's sweet melody.
190　　Were the world mine, Demetrius being bated,°
　　　　The rest I'd give to be to you translated.°
　　　　O, teach me how you look, and with what art
　　　　You sway the motion° of Demetrius' heart.
　　HERMIA: I frown upon him, yet he loves me still.
　　HELENA: O that your frowns would teach my smiles
195　　　　such skill!
　　HERMIA: I give him curses, yet he gives me love.
　　HELENA: O that my prayers could such affection°
　　　　move!°
　　HERMIA: The more I hate, the more he follows me.
　　HELENA: The more I love, the more he hateth me.
200　HERMIA: His folly, Helena, is no fault of mine.
　　HELENA: None, but your beauty. Would that fault were
　　　　mine!
　　HERMIA: Take comfort. He no more shall see my face.
　　　　Lysander and myself will fly this place.
　　　　Before the time I did Lysander see,
205　　Seem'd Athens as a paradise to me.
　　　　O, then, what graces in my love do dwell,
　　　　That he hath turn'd a heaven unto a hell!
　　LYSANDER: Helen, to you our minds we will unfold.
　　　　Tomorrow night, when Phoebe° doth behold
210　　Her silver visage in the wat'ry glass,°
　　　　Decking with liquid pearl the bladed grass,
　　　　A time that lovers' flights doth still° conceal,
　　　　Through Athens' gates have we devis'd to steal.
　　HERMIA: And in the wood, where often you and I
215　　Upon faint° primrose beds were wont to lie,
　　　　Emptying our bosoms of their counsel° sweet,

There my Lysander and myself shall meet;
And thence from Athens turn away our eyes,
To seek new friends and stranger companies.
Farewell, sweet playfellow. Pray thou for us,　　220
And good luck grant thee thy Demetrius!
Keep word, Lysander. We must starve our sight
From lovers' food till morrow deep midnight.
LYSANDER: I will, my Hermia.　　　　(*Exit Hermia.*)
　　　　　　　　Helena, adieu.
As you on him, Demetrius dote on you!　　225
　　　　　　　　(*Exit Lysander.*)
HELENA: How happy some o'er other some can be!°
　　Through Athens I am thought as fair as she.
　　But what of that? Demetrius thinks not so;
　　He will not know what all but he do know.
　　And as he errs, doting on Hermia's eyes,　　230
　　So I, admiring of° his qualities.
　　Things base and vile, holding no quantity,°
　　Love can transpose to form and dignity.
　　Love looks not with the eyes, but with the mind,
　　And therefore is wing'd Cupid painted blind.　　235
　　Nor hath Love's mind of any judgment taste;°
　　Wings, and no eyes, figure° unheedy haste.
　　And therefore is Love said to be a child,
　　Because in choice he is so oft beguil'd.
　　As waggish boys in game° themselves forswear,　　240
　　So the boy Love is perjur'd everywhere.
　　For ere Demetrius look'd on Hermia's eyne,°
　　He hail'd down oaths that he was only mine;
　　And when this hail some heat from Hermia felt,
　　So he dissolv'd, and show'rs of oaths did melt.　　245
　　I will go tell him of fair Hermia's flight.
　　Then to the wood will he tomorrow night
　　Pursue her; and for this intelligence°
　　If I have thanks, it is a dear° expense.°
　　But herein mean I to enrich my pain,　　250
　　To have his sight thither and back again.　　(*Exit.*)

{*Scene II*}°

(*Enter Quince the Carpenter, and Snug the Joiner, and
Bottom the Weaver, and Flute the Bellows-Mender, and
Snout the Tinker, and Starveling the Tailor.*)

QUINCE: Is all our company here?
BOTTOM: You were best to call them generally,° man by
　　man, according to the scrip.°

---

180. **fair:** Fair-complexioned (generally regarded by the Elizabethans as more beautiful than dark-complexioned). **182. your
fair:** Your beauty (even though Hermia is dark-complexioned).
happy fair: Lucky fair one. **183. lodestars:** Guiding stars.
air: Music. **184. tuneable:** Tuneful, melodious. **186. favor:**
Appearance, looks. **190. bated:** Excepted. **191. translated:**
Transformed. **193. motion:** Impulse. **197. affection:** Passion.
move: Arouse. **209. Phoebe:** Diana, the moon. **210. glass:**
Mirror. **212. still:** Always. **215. faint:** Pale. **216. counsel:**
Secret thought.

226. **o'er . . . can be:** Can be in comparison to some others.
231. **admiring of:** Wondering at. 232. **holding no quantity:**
Unsubstantial, unshapely. 236. **Nor . . . taste:** Nor has Love,
which dwells in the fancy or imagination, any *taste* or least
bit of judgment or reason. 237. **figure:** Are a symbol of.
240. **game:** Sport, jest. 242. **eyne:** Eyes (old form of plural).
248. **intelligence:** Information. 249. **dear:** Costly. **a dear
expense:** A trouble worth taking. I, II. **Location:** Athens.
Quince's house(?). 2. **generally:** Bottom's blunder for *individually.* 3. **scrip:** Script, written list.

QUINCE: Here is the scroll of every man's name which is
    thought fit, through all Athens, to play in our in-
    terlude before the Duke and the Duchess on his
    wedding-day at night.

BOTTOM: First, good Peter Quince, say what the play
    treats on, then read the names of the actors, and so
    grow to° a point.

QUINCE: Marry,° our play is "The most lamentable com-
    edy and most cruel death of Pyramus and Thisby."

BOTTOM: A very good piece of work, I assure you, and a
    merry. Now, good Peter Quince, call forth your
    actors by the scroll. Masters, spread yourselves.

QUINCE: Answer as I call you. Nick Bottom, the weaver.

BOTTOM: Ready. Name what part I am for, and proceed.

QUINCE: You, Nick Bottom, are set down for Pyramus.

BOTTOM: What is Pyramus? A lover, or a tyrant?

QUINCE: A lover, that kills himself most gallant for love.

BOTTOM: That will ask some tears in the true perform-
    ing of it. If I do it, let the audience look to their eyes.
    I will move storms; I will condole° in some measure.
    To the rest — yet my chief humor° is for a tyrant. I
    could play Ercles° rarely, or a part to tear a cat° in, to
    make all split.°

    "The raging rocks
    And shivering shocks
    Shall break the locks
       Of prison gates;
    And Phibbus' car°
    Shall shine from far
    And make and mar
       The foolish Fates."

    This was lofty! Now name the rest of the players. This
    is Ercles' vein, a tyrant's vein. A lover is more con-
    doling.

QUINCE: Francis Flute, the bellows-mender.

FLUTE: Here, Peter Quince.

QUINCE: Flute, you must take Thisby on you.

FLUTE: What is Thisby? A wand'ring knight?

QUINCE: It is the lady that Pyramus must love.

FLUTE: Nay, faith, let not me play a woman. I have a
    beard coming.

QUINCE: That's all one.° You shall play it in a mask, and
    you may speak as small° as you will.

BOTTOM: An° I may hide my face, let me play Thisby
    too. I'll speak in a monstrous little voice, "Thisne,
    Thisne!" "Ah Pyramus, my lover dear! Thy Thisby
    dear, and lady dear!"

QUINCE: No, no; you must play Pyramus; and, Flute,
    you Thisby.

BOTTOM: Well, proceed.

QUINCE: Robin Starveling, the tailor.

STARVELING: Here, Peter Quince.

QUINCE: Robin Starveling, you must play Thisby's
    mother. Tom Snout, the tinker.

SNOUT: Here, Peter Quince.

QUINCE: You, Pyramus' father; myself, Thisby's father;
    Snug, the joiner, you, the lion's part; and I hope here
    is a play fitted.

SNUG: Have you the lion's part written? Pray you, if it
    be, give it me, for I am slow of study.

QUINCE: You may do it extempore, for it is nothing but
    roaring.

BOTTOM: Let me play the lion too. I will roar that I will
    do any man's heart good to hear me. I will roar that I
    will make the Duke say, "Let him roar again, let him
    roar again."

QUINCE: An you should do it too terribly, you would
    fright the Duchess and the ladies, that they would
    shriek; and that were enough to hang us all.

ALL: That would hang us, every mother's son.

BOTTOM: I grant you, friends, if you should fright the
    ladies out of their wits, they would have no more dis-
    cretion but to hang us; but I will aggravate° my voice
    so that I will roar you° as gently as any sucking dove;
    I will roar you an 'twere any nightingale.

QUINCE: You can play no part but Pyramus; for Pyra-
    mus is a sweet-fac'd man, a proper° man as one shall
    see in a summer's day, a most lovely gentleman-like
    man. Therefore you must needs play Pyramus.

BOTTOM: Well, I will undertake it. What beard were I
    best to play it in?

QUINCE: Why, what you will.

BOTTOM: I will discharge° it in either your° straw-color
    beard, your orange-tawny beard, your purple-in-
    grain° beard, or your French-crown-color° beard,
    your perfect yellow.

QUINCE: Some of your French crowns° have no hair at
    all, and then you will play barefac'd. But, masters,
    here are your parts. [*He distributes parts.*] And I am
    to entreat you, request you, and desire you, to con°
    them by tomorrow night; and meet me in the palace
    wood, a mile without the town, by moonlight. There
    will we rehearse; for if we meet in the city, we shall be
    dogg'd with company, and our devices° known. In
    the meantime I will draw a bill° of properties, such as
    our play wants. I pray you, fail me not.

BOTTOM: We will meet, and there we may rehearse most
    obscenely° and courageously. Take pains, be perfect;°
    adieu.

---

10. grow to: Come to.   **11. Marry:** A mild oath, originally the name of the Virgin Mary.   **23. condole:** Lament, arouse pity. **24. humor:** Inclination, whim.   **25. Ercles:** Hercules (the tradition of ranting came from Seneca's *Hercules Furens*).   **tear a cat:** Rant.   **26. make all split:** Cause a stir, bring the house down.   **31. Phibbus' car:** Phoebus's, the sun-god's, chariot. **45. That's all one:** It makes no difference.   **46. small:** High-pitched.   **47. An:** If.

76. aggravate: Bottom's blunder for *diminish*.   **77. roar you:** Roar for you.   **80. proper:** Handsome.   **86. discharge:** Perform.   **your:** I.e., you know the kind I mean.   **87–88. purple-in-grain:** Dyed a very deep red (from *grain*, the name applied to the dried insect used to make the dye).   **88. French-crown-color:** Color of a French crown, a gold coin.   **90. crowns:** Heads bald from syphilis, the "French disease."   **93. con:** Learn by heart.   **97. devices:** Plans.   **98. bill:** List.   **101. obscenely:** An unintentionally funny blunder, whatever Bottom meant to say.   **perfect:** Letter-perfect in memorizing your parts.

QUINCE: At the Duke's oak we meet.
BOTTOM: Enough. Hold, or cut bow-strings.°

(*Exeunt.*)

{*ACT II • Scene 1*}°

(*Enter a Fairy at one door, and Robin Goodfellow [Puck] at another.*)

PUCK: How now, spirit! Whither wander you?
FAIRY: Over hill, over dale,
   Thorough° bush, thorough brier,
   Over park, over pale,°
5   Thorough flood, thorough fire,
   I do wander every where,
   Swifter than the moon's sphere;
   And I serve the Fairy Queen,
   To dew her orbs° upon the green.
10   The cowslips tall her pensioners° be.
   In their gold coats spots you see;
   Those be rubies, fairy favors,°
   In those freckles live their savors.°
   I must go seek some dewdrops here
15   And hang a pearl in every cowslip's ear.
   Farewell, thou lob° of spirits; I'll be gone.
   Our Queen and all her elves come here anon.°
PUCK: The King doth keep his revels here tonight.
   Take heed the Queen come not within his sight.
20   For Oberon is passing fell° and wrath,°
   Because that she as her attendant hath
   A lovely boy, stolen from an Indian king;
   She never had so sweet a changeling.°
   And jealous Oberon would have the child
25   Knight of his train, to trace° the forests wild.
   But she perforce° withholds the loved boy,
   Crowns him with flowers and makes him all her joy.
   And now they never meet in grove or green,
   By fountain° clear, or spangled starlight sheen,
30   But they do square,° that all their elves for fear
   Creep into acorn-cups and hide them there.
FAIRY: Either I mistake your shape and making quite,
   Or else you are that shrewd° and knavish sprite°
   Call'd Robin Goodfellow. Are not you he
35   That frights the maidens of the villagery,
   Skim milk, and sometimes labor in the quern,°
   And bootless° make the breathless huswife churn,

And sometime make the drink to bear no barm,°
Mislead night-wanderers, laughing at their harm?
Those that Hobgoblin call you and sweet Puck, 40
You do their work, and they shall have good luck.
Are you not he?
PUCK: Thou speakest aright;
   I am that merry wanderer of the night.
   I jest to Oberon and make him smile
   When I a fat and bean-fed horse beguile, 45
   Neighing in likeness of a filly foal;
   And sometime lurk I in a gossip's° bowl,
   In very likeness of a roasted crab,°
   And when she drinks, against her lips I bob
   And on her withered dewlap° pour the ale. 50
   The wisest aunt,° telling the saddest° tale,
   Sometime for three-foot stool mistaketh me;
   Then slip I from her bum, down topples she,
   And "tailor"° cries, and falls into a cough;
   And then the whole quire° hold their hips and
      laugh, 55
   And waxen° in their mirth and neeze° and swear
   A merrier hour was never wasted there.
   But, room, fairy! Here comes Oberon.
FAIRY: And here my mistress. Would that he were
   gone!

(*Enter [Oberon] the King of Fairies at one door, with his train; and [Titania] the Queen at another, with hers.*)

OBERON: Ill met by moonlight, proud Titania. 60
TITANIA: What, jealous Oberon? Fairies, skip hence.
   I have forsworn his bed and company.
OBERON: Tarry, rash wanton.° Am not I thy lord?
TITANIA: Then I must be thy lady; but I know
   When thou hast stolen away from fairy land, 65
   And in the shape of Corin° sat all day,
   Playing on pipes of corn° and versing love
   To amorous Phillida.° Why art thou here,
   Come from the farthest steep° of India,
   But that, forsooth, the bouncing Amazon, 70
   Your buskin'd° mistress and your warrior love,
   To Theseus must be wedded, and you come
   To give their bed joy and prosperity.
OBERON: How canst thou thus for shame, Titania,
   Glance at my credit with Hippolyta,° 75
   Knowing I know thy love to Theseus?
   Didst not thou lead him through the glimmering
   night

---

104. Hold . . . bow-strings: An archer's expression not definitely explained, but probably meaning here "keep your promises, or give up the play." **II, 1. Location:** A wood near Athens. **3. Thorough:** Through. **4. pale:** Enclosure. **9. orbs:** Circles, i.e., fairy rings. **10. pensioners:** Retainers, members of the royal bodyguard. **12. favors:** Love tokens. **13. savors:** Sweet smells. **16. lob:** Country bumpkin. **17. anon:** At once. **20. passing fell:** Exceedingly angry. **wrath:** Wrathful. **23. changeling:** Child exchanged for another by the fairies. **25. trace:** Range through. **26. perforce:** Forcibly. **29. fountain:** Spring. **30. square:** Quarrel. **33. shrewd:** Mischievous. **sprite:** Spirit. **36. quern:** Handmill. **37. bootless:** In vain.

38. barm: Yeast, head on the ale. **47. gossip's:** Old woman's. **48. crab:** Crab apple. **50. dewlap:** Loose skin on neck. **51. aunt:** Old woman. **saddest:** Most serious. **54. tailor:** Possibly because she ends up sitting cross-legged on the floor, looking like a tailor. **55. quire:** Company. **56. waxen:** Increase. **neeze:** Sneeze. **63. wanton:** Headstrong creature. **66, 68. Corin, Phillida:** Conventional names of pastoral lovers. **67. corn:** Here, oat stalks. **69. steep:** Mountain range. **71. buskin'd:** Wearing half-boots called buskins. **75. Glance . . . Hippolyta:** Make insinuations about my favored relationship with Hippolyta.

From Perigenia,° whom he ravished?
And make him with fair Aegles° break his faith,
80   With Ariadne° and Antiopa?°
TITANIA: These are the forgeries of jealousy;
And never, since the middle summer's spring,°
Met we on hill, in dale, forest, or mead,
By paved° fountain or by rushy° brook,
85   Or in° the beached margent° of the sea,
To dance our ringlets° to the whistling wind,
But with thy brawls thou hast disturb'd our sport.
Therefore the winds, piping to us in vain,
As in revenge, have suck'd up from the sea
90   Contagious° fogs; which falling in the land
Hath every pelting° river made so proud
That they have overborne their continents.°
The ox hath therefore stretch'd his yoke in vain,
The ploughman lost his sweat, and the green corn°
95   Hath rotted ere his youth attain'd a beard;
The fold° stands empty in the drowned field,
And crows are fatted with the murrion° flock;
The nine men's morris° is fill'd up with mud,
And the quaint mazes° in the wanton° green
100   For lack of tread are undistinguishable.
The human mortals want° their winter° here;
No night is now with hymn or carol bless'd.
Therefore° the moon, the governess of floods,
Pale in her anger, washes all the air,
105   That rheumatic diseases° do abound.
And thorough this distemperature° we see
The seasons alter: hoary-headed frosts
Fall in the fresh lap of the crimson rose,
And on old Hiems'° thin and icy crown
110   An odorous chaplet of sweet summer buds
Is, as in mockery, set. The spring, the summer,

The childing° autumn, angry winter, change
Their wonted liveries,° and the mazed° world,
By their increase,° now knows not which is which.
And this same progeny of evils comes   115
From our debate,° from our dissension;
We are their parents and original.°
OBERON: Do you amend it then; it lies in you.
Why should Titania cross her Oberon?
I do but beg a little changeling boy,   120
To be my henchman.°
TITANIA: Set your heart at rest.
The fairy land buys not the child of me.
His mother was a vot'ress° of my order,
And, in the spiced Indian air, by night,
Full often hath she gossip'd by my side,   125
And sat with me on Neptune's yellow sands,
Marking th' embarked traders° on the flood,°
When we have laugh'd to see the sails conceive
And grow big-bellied with the wanton° wind;
Which she, with pretty and with swimming gait,   130
Following — her womb then rich with my young
squire —
Would imitate, and sail upon the land
To fetch me trifles, and return again,
As from a voyage, rich with merchandise.
But she, being mortal, of that boy did die;   135
And for her sake do I rear up her boy,
And for her sake I will not part with him.
OBERON: How long within this wood intend you stay?
TITANIA: Perchance till after Theseus' wedding-day°
If you will patiently dance in our round°   140
And see our moonlight revels, go with us;
If not, shun me, and I will spare° your haunts.
OBERON: Give me that boy, and I will go with thee.
TITANIA: Not for thy fairy kingdom. Fairies, away!
We shall chide downright, if I longer stay.   145

(*Exeunt [Titania with her train].*)

OBERON: Well, go thy way. Thou shalt not from° this
grove
Till I torment thee for this injury.
My gentle Puck, come hither. Thou rememb'rest
Since° once I sat upon a promontory,
And heard a mermaid on a dolphin's back   150
Uttering such dulcet and harmonious breath°
That the rude sea grew civil at her song
And certain stars shot madly from their spheres,
To hear the sea-maid's music.
PUCK: I remember.
OBERON: That very time I saw, but thou couldst not,   155

---

78. Perigenia: Perigouna, one of Theseus's conquests. (This and the following women are named in Thomas North's translation of Plutarch's *Life of Theseus*.) **79. Aegles:** Aegle, for whom Theseus deserted Ariadne according to some accounts. **80. Ariadne:** The daughter of Minos, King of Crete, who helped Theseus escape the labyrinth after killing the Minotaur; later she was abandoned by Theseus. **Antiopa:** Queen of the Amazons and wife of Theseus; elsewhere identified with Hippolyta, but here thought of as a separate woman. **82. middle summer's spring:** Beginning of midsummer. **84. paved:** With pebbled bottom. **rushy:** Bordered with rushes. **85. in:** On. **margent:** Edge, border. **86. ringlets:** Dances in a ring. (See *orbs* in line 9.) **90. Contagious:** Noxious. **91. pelting:** Paltry; or striking, moving forcefully. **92. continents:** Banks that contain them. **94. corn:** Grain of any kind. **96. fold:** Pen for sheep or cattle. **97. murrion:** Having died of the murrain, plague. **98. nine men's morris:** Portion of the village green marked out in a square for a game played with nine pebbles or pegs. **99. quaint mazes:** Intricate paths marked out on the village green to be followed rapidly on foot as a kind of contest. **wanton:** Luxuriant. **101. want:** Lack. **winter:** Regular winter season; or proper observances of winter, such as the *hymn or carol* in the next line (?). **103. Therefore:** I.e., as a result of our quarrel. **105. rheumatic diseases:** Colds, flu, and other respiratory infections. **106. distemperature:** Disturbance in nature. **109. Hiems:** The winter god.

112. childing: Fruitful, pregnant. **113. wonted liveries:** Usual apparel. **mazed:** Bewildered. **114. their increase:** Their yield, what they produce. **116. debate:** Quarrel. **117. original:** Origin. **121. henchman:** Attendant, page. **123. vot'ress:** Female votary; devotee, worshiper. **127. traders:** Trading vessels. **flood:** Flood tide. **129. wanton:** Sportive. **140. round:** Circular dance. **142. spare:** Shun. **146. from:** Go from. **149. Since:** When. **151. breath:** Voice, song.

Flying between the cold moon and the earth,
Cupid all° arm'd. A certain aim he took
At a fair vestal° throned by the west,
And loos'd his love-shaft smartly from his bow,
160 As° it should pierce a hundred thousand hearts;
But I might° see young Cupid's fiery shaft
Quench'd in the chaste beams of the wat'ry moon,
And the imperial vot'ress passed on,
In maiden meditation, fancy-free.°
165 Yet mark'd I where the bolt of Cupid fell:
It fell upon a little western flower,
Before milk-white, now purple with love's wound,
And maidens call it love-in-idleness.°
Fetch me that flow'r; the herb I showed thee once.
170 The juice of it on sleeping eyelids laid
Will make or man or° woman madly dote
Upon the next live creature that it sees.
Fetch me this herb, and be thou here again
Ere the leviathan° can swim a league.
175 PUCK: I'll put a girdle round about the earth
In forty° minutes.   [*Exit.*]
OBERON: Having once this juice,
I'll watch Titania when she is asleep,
And drop the liquor of it in her eyes.
The next thing then she waking looks upon,
180 Be it on lion, bear, or wolf, or bull,
On meddling monkey, or on busy ape,
She shall pursue it with the soul of love.
And ere I take this charm from off her sight,
As I can take it with another herb,
185 I'll make her render up her page to me.
But who comes here? I am invisible,
And I will overhear their conference.

(*Enter Demetrius, Helena following him.*)

DEMETRIUS: I love thee not, therefore pursue me not.
Where is Lysander and fair Hermia?
190 The one I'll slay, the other slayeth me.
Thou told'st me they were stol'n unto this wood;
And here am I, and wode° within this wood,
Because I cannot meet my Hermia.
Hence, get thee gone, and follow me no more.
195 HELENA: You draw me, you hard-hearted adamant;°
But yet you draw not iron, for my heart
Is true as steel. Leave° you your power to draw,
And I shall have no power to follow you.

DEMETRIUS: Do I entice you? Do I speak you fair?°
Or, rather, do I not in plainest truth   200
Tell you I do not nor I cannot love you?
HELENA: And even for that do I love you the more.
I am your spaniel; and, Demetrius,
The more you beat me, I will fawn on you.
Use me but as your spaniel, spurn me, strike me,   205
Neglect me, lose me; only give me leave,
Unworthy as I am, to follow you.
What worser place can I beg in your love —
And yet a place of high respect with me —
Than to be used as you use your dog?   210
DEMETRIUS: Tempt not too much the hatred of my
    spirit,
For I am sick when I do look on thee.
HELENA: And I am sick when I look not on you.
DEMETRIUS: You do impeach° your modesty too much
To leave the city and commit yourself   215
Into the hands of one that loves you not,
To trust the opportunity of night
And the ill counsel of a desert° place
With the rich worth of your virginity.
HELENA: Your virtue° is my privilege.° For that° 220
It is not night when I do see your face,
Therefore I think I am not in the night;
Nor doth this wood lack worlds of company,
For you in my respect° are all the world.
Then how can it be said I am alone,   225
When all the world is here to look on me?
DEMETRIUS: I'll run from thee and hide me in the
    brakes,°
And leave thee to the mercy of wild beasts.
HELENA: The wildest hath not such a heart as you.
Run when you will, the story shall be chang'd: 230
Apollo flies and Daphne holds the chase,°
The dove pursues the griffin,° the mild hind°
Makes speed to catch the tiger — bootless° speed,
When cowardice pursues and valor flies.
DEMETRIUS: I will not stay° thy questions.° Let me go! 235
Or if thou follow me, do not believe
But I shall do thee mischief in the wood.
HELENA: Ay, in the temple, in the town, the field,
You do me mischief. Fie, Demetrius!
Your wrongs do set a scandal on my sex.   240
We cannot fight for love, as men may do;
We should be woo'd and were not made to woo.
                                    [*Exit Demetrius.*]

---

157. all: Fully.   **158. vestal:** Vestal virgin (contains a complimentary allusion to Queen Elizabeth as a votaress of Diana and probably refers to an actual entertainment in her honor at Elvetham in 1591).   **160. As:** As if.   **161. might:** Could.   **164. fancy-free:** Free of love's spell.   **168. love-in-idleness:** Pansy, heartsease.   **171. or . . . or:** Either . . . or.   **174. leviathan:** Sea monster, whale.   **176. forty:** Used indefinitely.   **192. wode:** Mad (pronounced "wood" and often spelled so).   **195. adamant:** Lodestone, magnet (with pun on *hard-hearted,* since adamant was also thought to be the hardest of all stones and was confused with the diamond).   **197. Leave:** Give up.

199. fair: Courteously.   **214. impeach:** Call into question.   **218. desert:** Deserted.   **220. virtue:** Goodness or power to attract.   **privilege:** Safeguard, warrant.   **For that:** Because.   **224. in my respect:** As far as I am concerned.   **227. brakes:** Thickets.   **231. Apollo . . . chase:** In the ancient myth, Daphne fled from Apollo and was saved from rape by being transformed into a laurel tree; here it is the female who *holds the chase,* or pursues, instead of the male.   **232. griffin:** A fabulous monster with the head of an eagle and the body of a lion.   **hind:** Female deer.   **233. bootless:** Fruitless.   **235. stay:** Wait for.   **questions:** Talk or argument.

I'll follow thee and make a heaven of hell,
To die upon° the hand I love so well.   [*Exit.*]
OBERON: Fare thee well, nymph. Ere he do leave this
245   grove,
Thou shalt fly him and he shall seek thy love.

(*Enter Puck.*)

Hast thou the flower there? Welcome, wanderer.
PUCK: Ay, there it is.   [*Offers the flower.*]
OBERON: I pray thee, give it me.
I know a bank where the wild thyme blows,°
250 Where oxlips° and the nodding violet grows,
Quite over-canopied with luscious woodbine,°
With sweet musk-roses° and with eglantine.°
There sleeps Titania sometime of the night
Lull'd in these flowers with dances and delight;
255 And there the snake throws° her enamel'd skin,
Weed° wide enough to wrap a fairy in.
And with the juice of this I'll streak° her eyes,
And make her full of hateful fantasies.
Take thou some of it, and seek through this grove.
                    [*Gives some love-juice.*]
260 A sweet Athenian lady is in love
With a disdainful youth. Anoint his eyes,
But do it when the next thing he espies
May be the lady. Thou shalt know the man
By the Athenian garments he hath on.
265 Effect it with some care, that he may prove
More fond on° her than she upon her love;
And look thou meet me ere the first cock crow.
PUCK: Fear not, my lord, your servant shall do so.
                        (*Exeunt.*)

{*Scene II*}°

(*Enter Titania, Queen of Fairies, with her train.*)

TITANIA: Come, now a roundel° and a fairy song;
Then, for the third part of a minute, hence —
Some to kill cankers° in the musk-rose buds,
Some war with rere-mice° for their leathern wings,
5 To make my small elves coats, and some keep back
The clamorous owl, that nightly hoots and wonders
At our quaint° spirits. Sing me now asleep.
Then to your offices and let me rest.

(*Fairies sing.*)

FIRST FAIRY: You spotted snakes with double° tongue,
10   Thorny hedgehogs, be not seen;

Newts° and blindworms, do no wrong,
Come not near our fairy queen.
[*Chorus.*] Philomel,° with melody
Sing in our sweet lullaby;
Lulla, lulla, lullaby, lulla, lulla, lullaby.   15
Never harm,
Nor spell nor charm,
Come our lovely lady nigh.
So, good night, with lullaby.
FIRST FAIRY: Weaving spiders, come not here;   20
Hence, you long-legg'd spinners, hence!
Beetles black, approach not near;
Worm nor snail, do no offense.
[*Chorus.*] Philomel, with melody, etc.
SECOND FAIRY: Hence, away! Now all is well.   25
One aloof stand sentinel.
        [*Exeunt Fairies. Titania sleeps.*]

(*Enter Oberon [and squeezes the flower on Titania's eyelids].*)

OBERON: What thou seest when thou dost wake,
Do it for thy true-love take;
Love and languish for his sake.
Be it ounce,° or cat, or bear,   30
Pard,° or boar with bristled hair,
In thy eye that shall appear
When thou wak'st, it is thy dear
Wake when some vile thing is near.   [*Exit.*]

(*Enter Lysander and Hermia.*)

LYSANDER: Fair love, you faint with wand'ring in the
        wood;   35
And to speak troth,° I have forgot our way.
We'll rest us, Hermia, if you think it good,
And tarry for the comfort of the day.
HERMIA: Be 't so, Lysander. Find you out a bed,
For I upon this bank will rest my head.   40
LYSANDER: One turf shall serve as pillow for us both,
One heart, one bed, two bosoms, and one troth.°
HERMIA: Nay, good Lysander; for my sake, my dear,
Lie further off yet, do not lie so near.
LYSANDER: O, take the sense, sweet, of my
        innocence!°   45
Love takes the meaning in love's conference.°
I mean, that my heart unto yours is knit
So that but one heart we can make of it;
Two bosoms interchained with an oath —
So then two bosoms and a single troth.   50

---

244. upon: By. **249. blows:** Blooms. **250. oxlips:** Flowers
resembling cow-slip and primrose. **251. woodbine:** Honeysuckle. **252. musk-roses:** A kind of large, sweet-scented rose.
eglantine: Sweetbriar, another kind of rose. **255. throws:**
Sloughs off, sheds. **256. Weed:** Garment. **257. streak:** Anoint,
touch gently. **266. fond on:** Doting on. **II, I. Location:** The
wood. **1. roundel:** Dance in a ring. **3. cankers:** Cankerworms.
4. rere-mice: Bats. **7. quaint:** Dainty. **9. double:** Forked.

11. Newts: water lizards (considered poisonous, as were blindworms — small snakes with tiny eyes — and spiders).
13. Philomel: The nightingale. (Philomela, daughter of King
Pandion, was transformed into a nightingale, according to
Ovid's *Metamorphoses,* after she had been raped by her sister
Procne's husband, Tereus.) **30. ounce:** Lynx. **31. Pard:**
Leopard. **36. troth:** Truth. **42. troth:** Faith, troth-plight.
45. take . . . innocence: Interpret my intention as innocent.
46. Love . . . conference: When lovers confer, love teaches each
lover to interpret the other's meaning lovingly.

NEAR RIGHT: Oberon instructing Puck in the power of the "little western flower" in the American Repertory Theatre's 1986 production. CENTER: Oberon with Titania upon his shoulder. FAR RIGHT: The rude mechanicals: Moonshine with Lion. BELOW: Kevin Kline, Bottom, and Michelle Pfeiffer, Titania, in a touching moment from the 1999 film, *William Shakespeare's A Midsummer Night's Dream,* directed by Michael Hoffman.

Then by your side no bed-room me deny,
For lying so, Hermia, I do not lie.°
HERMIA: Lysander riddles very prettily.
Now much beshrew° my manners and my pride
55 If Hermia meant to say Lysander lied.
But, gentle friend, for love and courtesy
Lie further off, in human° modesty;
Such separation as may well be said
Becomes a virtuous bachelor and a maid,
60 So far be distant; and, good night, sweet friend.
Thy love ne'er alter till thy sweet life end!
LYSANDER: Amen, amen, to that fair prayer, say I,
And then end life when I end loyalty!
Here is my bed. Sleep give thee all his rest!
HERMIA: With half that wish the wisher's eyes be
65 press'd!°
[*They sleep, separated by a short distance.*]

(*Enter Puck.*)

52. lie: Tell a falsehood (with a riddling pun on *lie*, recline).
54. beshrew: Curse (but mildly meant).   57. human: Courteous.   65. With . . . press'd: May we share your wish, so that
your eyes too are *press'd*, closed, in sleep.

PUCK: Through the forest have I gone,
But Athenian found I none
On whose eyes I might approve°
This flower's force in stirring love.
Night and silence. — Who is here?   70
Weeds of Athens he doth wear.
This is he, my master said,
Despised the Athenian maid;
And here the maiden, sleeping sound,
On the dank and dirty ground.   75
Pretty soul! She durst not lie
Near this lack-love, this kill-courtesy.
Churl, upon thy eyes I throw
All the power this charm doth owe.°
                              [*Applies the love-juice.*]
When thou wak'st, let love forbid   80
Sleep his seat on thy eyelid.
So awake when I am gone,
For I must now to Oberon.   (*Exit.*)

(*Enter Demetrius and Helena, running.*)

68. approve: Test.   79. owe: Own.

HELENA: Stay, though thou kill me, sweet Demetrius.
DEMETRIUS: I charge thee, hence, and do not haunt me
85   thus.
HELENA: O, wilt thou darkling° leave me? Do not so.
DEMETRIUS: Stay, on thy peril!° I alone will go.
                                                    [*Exit.*]
HELENA: O, I am out of breath in this fond° chase!
        The more my prayer, the lesser is my grace.°
90   Happy is Hermia, wheresoe'er she lies,°
        For she hath blessed and attractive eyes.
        How came her eyes so bright? Not with salt
            tears;
        If so, my eyes are oft'ner wash'd than hers.
        No, no, I am as ugly as a bear;
95   For beasts that meet me run away for fear.
        Therefore no marvel though Demetrius
        Do, as a monster, fly my presence thus.
        What wicked and dissembling glass of mine
        Made me compare with Hermia's sphery eyne?°
100   But who is here? Lysander, on the ground?
        Dead, or asleep? I see no blood, no wound.
        Lysander, if you live, good sir, awake.
LYSANDER [*awaking*]: And run through fire I will for
            thy sweet sake.
        Transparent° Helena! Nature shows art,
105   That through thy bosom makes me see thy heart.
        Where is Demetrius? O, how fit a word
        Is that vile name to perish on my sword!
HELENA: Do not say so, Lysander, say not so.
        What though he love your Hermia? Lord, what
            though?
110   Yet Hermia still loves you. Then be content.
LYSANDER: Content with Hermia? No! I do repent
        The tedious minutes I with her have spent.
        Not Hermia but Helena I love.
        Who will not change a raven for a dove?
115   The will of man is by his reason sway'd,
        And reason says you are the worthier maid.
        Things growing are not ripe until their season;
        So I, being young, till now ripe not° to reason.
        And touching° now the point° of human skill,°
120   Reason becomes the marshal to my will
        And leads me to your eyes, where I o'erlook°
        Love's stories written in love's richest book.
HELENA: Wherefore was I to this keen mockery born?
        When at your hands did I deserve this scorn?
125   Is 't not enough, is 't not enough, young man,
        That I did never, no, nor never can,
        Deserve a sweet look from Demetrius' eye,
        But you must flout my insufficiency?

Good troth,° you do me wrong, good sooth,° you do,
In such disdainful manner me to woo.   130
But fare you well. Perforce I must confess
I thought you lord of° more true gentleness.
O, that a lady, of° one man refus'd,
Should of another therefore be abus'd!°   (*Exit.*)
LYSANDER: She sees not Hermia. Hermia, sleep thou
        there,   135
And never mayst thou come Lysander near!
For as a surfeit of the sweetest things
The deepest loathing to the stomach brings,
Or as the heresies that men do leave
Are hated most of those they did deceive,   140
So thou, my surfeit and my heresy,
Of all be hated, but the most of me!
And, all my powers, address your love and might
To honor Helen and to be her knight!   (*Exit.*)
HERMIA [*awaking*]: Help me, Lysander, help me! Do
        thy best   145
To pluck this crawling serpent from my breast!
Ay me, for pity! What a dream was here!
Lysander, look how I do quake with fear.
Methought a serpent eat° my heart away,
And you sat smiling at his cruel prey.°   150
Lysander! What, remov'd? Lysander! Lord!
What, out of hearing? Grone? No sound, no word?
Alack, where are you? Speak, an if you hear,
Speak, of all loves!° I swoon almost with fear.
No? Then I well perceive you are not nigh.   155
Either death, or you, I'll find immediately.
        (*Exit.* [*Manet*° *Titania lying asleep.*])

{*ACT III • Scene 1*}°

(*Enter the Clowns* [*Quince, Snug, Bottom, Flute, Snout, and Starveling*].)

BOTTOM: Are we all met?
QUINCE: Pat, pat; and here's a marvailes° convenient
    place for our rehearsal. This green plot shall be our
    stage, this hawthorn brake° our tiring-house,° and
    we will do it in action as we will do it before the   5
    Duke.
BOTTOM: Peter Quince?
QUINCE: What sayest thou, bully° Bottom?
BOTTOM: There are things in this comedy of Pyramus
    and Thisby that will never please. First, Pyramus   10
    must draw a sword to kill himself, which the ladies
    cannot abide. How answer you that?

86. darkling: In the dark.   **87. on thy peril:** On pain of danger to you if you don't obey me and stay.   **88. fond:** Doting.
89. my grace: The favor I obtain.   **90. lies:** Dwells.
99. sphery eyne: Eyes as bright as stars in their spheres.
104. Transparent: (1) Radiant; (2) able to be seen through.
118. ripe not: (Am) not ripened.   **119. touching:** Reaching.
point: Summit.   **skill:** Judgment.   **121. o'erlook:** Read.

129. Good troth, good sooth: Indeed, truly.   **132. lord of:** Possessor of.   **gentleness:** Courtesy.   **133. of:** By.   **134. abus'd:** Ill treated.   **149. eat:** Ate (pronounced "et").   **150. prey:** Act of preying.   **154. of all loves:** For all love's sake.   **156. [S.D.]** *Manet:* Latin for "she remains."   **III, I. Location:** Scene continues.   **2. marvailes:** Marvelous.   **4. brake:** Thicket.   **tiring-house:** Attiring area, hence backstage.   **8. bully:** Worthy, jolly, fine fellow.

SNOUT: By 'r lakin,° a parlous° fear.

STARVELING: I believe we must leave the killing out,
15   when all is done.°

BOTTOM: Not a whit. I have a device to make all well.
Write me° a prologue; and let the prologue seem to
say, we will do no harm with our swords and that
Pyramus is not kill'd indeed; and, for the more better
20   assurance, tell them that I Pyramus am not Pyramus,
but Bottom the weaver. This will put them out of
fear.

QUINCE: Well, we will have such a prologue, and it shall
be written in eight and six.°

25 BOTTOM: No, make it two more; let it be written in eight
and eight.

SNOUT: Will not the ladies be afeard of the lion?

STARVELING: I fear it, I promise you.

BOTTOM: Masters, you ought to consider with your-
30   selves, to bring in — God shield us! — a lion among
ladies,° is a most dreadful thing. For there is not a
more fearful° wild-fowl than your lion living; and we
ought to look to 't.

SNOUT: Therefore another prologue must tell he is not a
35   lion.

BOTTOM: Nay, you must name his name, and half his
face must be seen through the lion's neck, and he
himself must speak through, saying thus, or to the
same defect:° "Ladies"— or "Fair ladies — I would
40   wish you"— or "I would request you"— or "I
would entreat you — not to fear, not to tremble;
my life for yours.° If you think I come hither as a
lion, it were pity of my life.° No, I am no such thing,
I am a man as other men are." And there indeed let
45   him name his name, and tell them plainly he is Snug
the joiner.

QUINCE: Well, it shall be so. But there is two hard
things: that is, to bring the moonlight into a chamber; for, you know, Pyramus and Thisby meet by
50   moonlight.

SNOUT: Doth the moon shine that night we play our play?

BOTTOM: A calendar, a calendar! Look in the almanac.
Find out moonshine, find out moonshine.

                             [*They consult an almanac.*]

QUINCE: Yes, it doth shine that night.

55 BOTTOM: Why then may you leave a casement of the
great chamber window, where we play, open, and the
moon may shine in at the casement.

QUINCE: Ay; or else one must come in with a bush of
thorns° and a lantern, and say he comes to disfigure,°
or to present,° the person of Moonshine. Then there 60
is another thing: we must have a wall in the great
chamber; for Pyramus and Thisby, says the story, did
talk through the chink of a wall.

SNOUT: You can never bring in a wall. What say you,
Bottom? 65

BOTTOM: Some man or other must present Wall. And
let him have some plaster, or some loam, or some
rough-cast° about him, to signify wall; and let him
hold his fingers thus, and through that cranny shall
Pyramus and Thisby whisper. 70

QUINCE: If that may be, then all is well. Come, sit down,
every mother's son, and rehearse your parts. Pyramus, you begin. When you have spoken your speech,
enter into that brake, and so every one according to
his cue. 75

(*Enter Robin* [*Puck*].)

PUCK: What hempen° home-spuns have we swagg'ring
    here,
    So near the cradle of the Fairy Queen?
    What, a play toward?° I'll be an auditor;°
    An actor too perhaps, if I see cause.

QUINCE: Speak, Pyramus. Thisby, stand forth. 80

BOTTOM: "Thisby, the flowers of odious savors
    sweet,"—

QUINCE: Odors, odors.

BOTTOM: —"Odors savors sweet;
    So hath thy breath, my dearest Thisby dear.
    But hark, a voice! Stay thou but here awhile, 85
    And by and by I will to thee appear."   (*Exit.*)

PUCK: A stranger Pyramus than e'er played here.°
                                    [*Exit.*]

FLUTE: Must I speak now?

QUINCE: Ay, marry, must you; for you must understand
he goes but to see a noise that he heard, and is to 90
come again.

FLUTE: "Most radiant Pyramus, most lily-white of hue,
    Of color like the red rose on triumphant brier,
    Most brisky juvenal° and eke° most lovely Jew,°
    As true as truest horse that yet would never tire. 95
    I'll meet thee, Pyramus, at Ninny's tomb."

QUINCE: "Ninus'° tomb," man. Why, you must not speak
that yet. That you answer to Pyramus. You speak all

---

13. By 'r lakin: By our ladykin, the Virgin Mary.   **parlous:** Perilous.   **15. when all is done:** When all is said and done.
17. Write me: Write at my suggestion.   **24. eight and six:** Alternate lines of eight and six syllables, a common ballad measure.
30–31. lion among ladies: A contemporary pamphlet tells how
at the christening in 1594 of Prince Henry, eldest son of King
James VI of Scotland, later James I of England, a "blackmoor"
instead of a lion drew the triumphal chariot, since the lion's
presence might have "brought some fear to the nearest."
32. fearful: Fear-inspiring.   **39. defect:** Bottom's blunder for
effect.   **42. my life for yours:** I pledge my life to make your
lives safe.   **43. it were . . . life:** My life would be endangered.

58–59. bush of thorns: Bundle of thornbush faggots (part of
the accoutrements of the man in the moon, according to the
popular notions of the time, along with his lantern and his dog).
59. disfigure: Quince's blunder for *prefigure.* **60. present:**
Represent.   **68. rough-cast:** A mixture of lime and gravel used
to plaster the outside of buildings. **76. hempen:** Made of
hemp, a rough fiber.   **78. toward:** About to take place. **auditor:** One who listens, i.e., part of the audience. **87. here:** In
this theater (?). **94. brisky juvenal:** Brisk youth. **eke:** Also.
Jew: Probably an absurd repetition of the first syllable of *juvenal.* **97. Ninus:** Mythical founder of Nineveh (whose wife,
Semiramis, was supposed to have built the walls of Babylon
where the story of Pyramus and Thisby takes place).

100 your part at once, cues and all. Pyramus enter. Your
cue is past; it is, "never tire."
FLUTE: O —"As true as truest horse, that yet would
never tire."

[Enter Puck, and Bottom as Pyramus with the ass head.]°

BOTTOM: "If I were fair,° Thisby, I were° only thine."
QUINCE: O monstrous! O strange! We are haunted.
Pray, masters! Fly, masters! Help!

[Exeunt Quince, Snug, Flute, Snout, and Starveling.]

105 PUCK: I'll follow you, I'll lead you about a round,°
Through bog, through bush, through brake,
through brier.
Sometime a horse I'll be, sometime a hound,
A hog, a headless bear, sometime a fire,°
And neigh, and bark, and grunt, and roar, and burn,
110 Like horse, hound, hog, bear, fire, at every turn.
(Exit.)

BOTTOM: Why do they run away? This is a knavery of
them to make me afeard.

(Enter Snout.)

SNOUT: O Bottom, thou art chang'd! What do I see on
thee?
115 BOTTOM: What do you see? You see an ass-head of your
own, do you?   *[Exit Snout.]*

(Enter Quince.)

QUINCE: Bless thee, Bottom, bless thee! Thou art translated.°   *(Exit.)*
BOTTOM: I see their knavery. This is to make an ass of
120 me, to fright me, if they could. But I will not stir from
this place, do what they can. I will walk up and down
here, and I will sing, that they shall hear I am not
afraid.   *[Sings.]*
The woosel cock° so black of hue,
125 With orange-tawny bill,
The throstle° with his note so true,
The wren with little quill° —
TITANIA [*awaking*]: What angel wakes me from my
flow'ry bed?
130 BOTTOM [*sings*]: The finch, the sparrow, and the lark,
The plain-song° cuckoo grey,
Whose note full many a man doth mark,
And dares not answer nay° —
For, indeed, who would set his wit to so foolish a
bird? Who would give a bird the lie,° though he cry
135 "cuckoo" never so?°

101. [s.d.] **with the ass head**: This stage direction, taken from
the Folio, presumably refers to a standard stage property.
102. **fair**: Handsome. **were**: Would be. 105. **about a round**:
Roundabout. 108. **fire**: Will-o'-the-wisp. 117–18. **translated**:
Transformed. 124. **woosel cock**: Male ousel or ouzel, black-
bird. 126. **throstle**: Song thrush. 127. **quill**: Literally, a reed
pipe; hence, the bird's piping song. 130. **plain-song**: Singing
a melody without variations. 132. **dares . . . nay**: Cannot
deny that he is a cuckold. 134. **give . . . lie**: Call the bird a
liar. 135. **never so**: Ever so much.

TITANIA: I pray thee, gentle mortal, sing again.
Mine ear is much enamored of thy note;
So is mine eye enthralled to thy shape;
And thy fair virtue's force° perforce doth move me
140 On the first view to say, to swear, I love thee.
BOTTOM: Methinks, mistress, you should have little rea-
son for that. And yet, to say the truth, reason and
love keep little company together nowadays. The
more the pity that some honest neighbors will not
make them friends. Nay, I can gleek° upon occasion. 145
TITANIA: Thou art as wise as thou art beautiful.
BOTTOM: Not so, neither. But if I had wit enough to get
out of this wood, I have enough to serve mine own
turn.°
TITANIA: Out of this wood do not desire to go. 150
Thou shalt remain here, whether thou wilt or no.
I am a spirit of no common rate.°
The summer still° doth tend upon my state;°
And I do love thee. Therefore, go with me.
I'll give thee fairies to attend on thee, 155
And they shall fetch thee jewels from the deep,
And sing while thou on pressed flowers dost sleep.
And I will purge thy mortal grossness so
That thou shalt like an airy spirit go.
Peaseblossom, Cobweb, Moth,° and Mustard-
seed! 160

*(Enter four Fairies [Peaseblossom, Cobweb, Moth, and
Mustardseed].)*

PEASEBLOSSOM: Ready.
COBWEB: And I.
MOTH: And I
MUSTARDSEED: And I.
ALL: Where shall we go?
TITANIA: Be kind and courteous to this gentleman.
Hop in his walks and gambol in his eyes;
Feed him with apricocks and dewberries, 165
With purple grapes, green figs, and mulberries;
The honey-bags steal from the humble-bees,
And for night-tapers crop their waxen thighs
And light them at the fiery glow-worm's eyes,
To have my love to bed and to arise; 170
And pluck the wings from painted butterflies
To fan the moonbeams from his sleeping eyes.
Nod to him, elves, and do him courtesies.
PEASEBLOSSOM: Hail, mortal!
COBWEB: Hail! 175
MOTH: Hail!
MUSTARDSEED: Hail!
BOTTOM: I cry your worship's mercy, heartily. I beseech
your worship's name.

139. **thy . . . force**: The power of your beauty. 145. **gleek**:
Scoff, jest. 148–49. **serve . . . turn**: Answer my purpose.
152. **rate**: Rank, value. 153. **still**: Ever always. **doth . . .
state**: Waits upon me as part of my royal retinue. 160. **Moth**:
Mote, speck. (The two words *moth* and *mote* were pronounced
alike.)

180   COBWEB: Cobweb.
       BOTTOM: I shall desire you of more acquaintance, good
          Master Cobweb. If I cut my finger, I shall make bold
          with you.° Your name, honest gentleman?
       PEASEBLOSSOM: Peaseblossom.
185   BOTTOM: I pray you, commend me to Mistress Squash,°
          your mother, and to Master Peascod,° your father.
          Good Master Peaseblossom, I shall desire you of more
          acquaintance too. Your name, I beseech you, sir?
       MUSTARDSEED: Mustardseed.
190   BOTTOM: Good Master Mustardseed, I know your pa-
          tience° well. That same cowardly, giant-like ox-beef
          hath devour'd many a gentleman of your house. I
          promise you your kindred hath made my eyes water
          ere now. I desire you of more acquaintance, good
195   Master Mustardseed.
       TITANIA: Come wait upon him; lead him to my bower.
          The moon methinks looks with a wat'ry eye;
          And when she weeps,° weeps every little flower,
          Lamenting some enforced° chastity.
200   Tie up my lover's tongue, bring him silently.
                                                    (*Exeunt.*)

       {*Scene II*}°

       (*Enter* [*Oberon,*] *King of Fairies.*)

       OBERON: I wonder if Titania be awak'd;
          Then, what it was that next came in her eye,
          Which she must dote on in extremity.

       ([*Enter*] *Robin Goodfellow* [*Puck*].)

          Here comes my messenger. How now, mad spirit?
5   What night-rule° now about this haunted° grove?
       PUCK: My mistress with a monster is in love.
          Near to her close° and consecrated bower,
          While she was in her dull° and sleeping hour,
          A crew of patches,° rude mechanicals,°
10   That work for bread upon Athenian stalls,
          Were met together to rehearse a play
          Intended for great Theseus' nuptial day.
          The shallowest thick-skin of that barren sort,°
          Who Pyramus presented,° in their sport
15   Forsook his scene° and ent'red in a brake.
          When I did him at this advantage take,
          An ass's nole° I fixed on his head.

182–83. **If . . . you:** Cobwebs were used to stanch bleeding.
185. **Squash:** Unripe pea pod.   186. **Peascod:** Ripe pea pod.
190–91. **your patience:** What you have endured.   198. **she
weeps:** I.e., she causes dew.   199. **enforced:** Forced, violated; or, possibly, constrained (since Titania at this moment is
hardly concerned about chastity).   **III, ii. Location:** The
wood.   5. **night-rule:** Diversion for the night.   **haunted:**
Much frequented.   7. **close:** Secret, private.   8. **dull:** Drowsy.
9. **patches:** Clowns, fools.   **rude mechanicals:** Ignorant artisans.   13. **barren sort:** Stupid company or crew.   14. **presented:** Acted.   15. **scene:** Playing area.   17. **nole:** Noddle,
head.

          Anon his Thisby must be answered,
          And forth my mimic° comes. When they him spy,
          As wild geese that the creeping fowler eye,   20
          Or russet-pared choughs,° many in sort,°
          Rising and cawing at the gun's report,
          Sever° themselves and madly sweep the sky,
          So, at his sight, away his fellows fly;
          And, at our stamp, here o'er and o'er one falls;   25
          He murder cries and help from Athens calls.
          Their sense thus weak, lost with their fears thus
             strong,
          Made senseless things begin to do them wrong,
          For briers and thorns at their apparel snatch;
          Some, sleeves — some, hats; from yielders all things
             catch.   30
          I led them on in this distracted fear
          And left sweet Pyramus translated there,
          When in that moment, so it came to pass,
          Titania wak'd and straightway lov'd an ass.
       OBERON: This falls out better than I could devise.   35
          But hast thou yet latch'd° the Athenian's eyes
          With the love-juice, as I did bid thee do?
       PUCK: I took him sleeping — that is finish'd too —
          And the Athenian woman by his side,
          That, when he wak'd, of force° she must be ey'd.   40

       (*Enter Demetrius and Hermia.*)

       OBERON: Stand close. This is the same Athenian.
       PUCK: This is the woman, but not this the man.
                                          [*They stand aside.*]
       DEMETRIUS: O, why rebuke you him that loves you so?
          Lay breath so bitter on your bitter foe.
       HERMIA: Now I but chide; but I should use thee worse,   45
          For thou, I fear, hast given me cause to curse.
          If thou hast slain Lysander in his sleep,
          Being o'er shoes in blood, plunge in the deep,
          And kill me too.
          The sun was not so true unto the day   50
          As he to me. Would he have stolen away
          From sleeping Hermia? I'll believe as soon
          This whole° earth may be bor'd and that the moon
          May through the center creep and so displease
          Her brother's° noontide with th' Antipodes.°   55
          It cannot be but thou has murd'red him;
          So should a murderer look, so dead,° so grim.
       DEMETRIUS: So should the murdered look, and so
             should I,
          Pierc'd through the heart with your stern cruelty.
          Yet you, the murderer, look as bright, as clear,   60
          As yonder Venus in her glimmering sphere.
       HERMIA: What's this to my Lysander? Where is he?
          Ah, good Demetrius, wilt thou give him me?

19. **mimic:** Burlesque actor.   21. **russet-paled choughs:** Gray-
headed jackdaws.   **in sort:** In a flock.   23. **Sever:** Scatter.
36. **latch'd:** Moistened, anointed.   40. **of force:** Perforce.
53. **whole:** Solid.   55. **Her brother's:** I.e., the sun's.   **th' Antipodes:** The people on the opposite side of the earth.   57. **dead:**
Deadly, or deathly pale.

DEMETRIUS: I had rather give his carcass to my hounds.
HERMIA: Out dog! Out cur! Thou driv'st me past the
65   bounds
    Of maiden's patience. Hast thou slain him, then?
    Henceforth be never numb'red among men!
    O, once tell true, tell true, even for my sake!
    Durst thou have look'd upon him being awake,
70   And hast thou kill'd him sleeping? O brave touch!°
    Could not a worm,° an adder, do so much?
    An adder did it, for with doubler tongue
    Than thine, thou serpent, never adder stung.
DEMETRIUS: You spend your passion° on a mispris'd
    mood.°
75   I am not guilty of Lysander's blood,
    Nor is he dead, for aught that I can tell.
HERMIA: I pray thee, tell me then that he is well.
DEMETRIUS: An if I could, what should I get
    therefore?
HERMIA: A privilege never to see me more.
80   And from thy hated presence part I so.
    See me no more, whether he be dead or no.
                  (*Exit.*)
DEMETRIUS: There is no following her in this fierce
    vein.
    Here therefore for a while I will remain.
    So sorrow's heaviness doth heavier° grow
85   For debt that bankrupt° sleep doth sorrow owe;
    Which now in some slight measure it will pay,
    If for his tender here I make some stay.°
            (*Lie down* [*and sleep*].)
OBERON: What hast thou done? Thou hast mistaken
    quite
    And laid the love-juice on some true-love's sight.
90   Of thy misprision° must perforce ensue
    Some true love turn'd and not a false turn'd true.
PUCK: Then fate o'er-rules, that, one man holding
    troth,°
    A million fail, confounding oath on oath.°
OBERON: About the wood go swifter than the wind,
95   And Helena of Athens look thou find.
    All fancy-sick° she is and pale of cheer°
    With sighs of love, that cost the fresh blood° dear.
    By some illusion see thou bring her here.
    I'll charm his eyes against she do appear.°

---

70. brave touch: Noble exploit (said ironically).   **71. worm:**
Serpent.   **74. passion:** Violent feelings.   **mispris'd mood:**
Anger based on misconception.   **84. heavier:** (1) Harder to
bear, (2) drowsier.   **85. bankrupt:** Demetrius is saying that
his sleepiness adds to the weariness caused by sorrow.
86–87. Which . . . stay: To a small extent I will be able to "pay
back" and hence find some relief from sorrow, if I pause here
a while (*make some stay*) while sleep "tenders" or offers itself
by way of paying the debt owed to sorrow.   **90. misprision:**
Mistake.   **92. troth:** Faith.   **93. confounding . . . oath:** Inval-
idating one oath with another.   **96. fancy-sick:** Lovesick.
cheer: Face.   **97. sighs . . . blood:** An allusion to the physio-
logical theory that each sigh costs the heart a drop of blood.
99. against . . . appear: In anticipation of her coming.

PUCK: I go, I go; look how I go   100
    Swifter than arrow from the Tartar's bow.°
                  [*Exit.*]
OBERON: Flower of this purple dye,
    Hit with Cupid's archery.
    Sink in angle of his eye.
      [*Applies love-juice to Demetrius' eyes.*]
    When his love he doth espy,   105
    Let her shine as gloriously
    As the Venus of the sky.
    When thou wak'st, if she be by,
    Beg of her for remedy.

(*Enter Puck.*)

PUCK: Captain of our fairy band,   110
    Helena is here at hand,
    And the youth, mistook by me,
    Pleading for a lover's fee.°
    Shall we their fond pageant° see?
    Lord, what fools these mortals be!   115
OBERON: Stand aside. The noise they make
    Will cause Demetrius to awake.
PUCK: Then will two at once woo one;
    That must needs be sport alone;°
    And those things do best please me   120
    That befall prepost'rously.°
              [*They stand aside.*]

(*Enter Lysander and Helena.*)

LYSANDER: Why should you think that I should woo in
    scorn?
    Scorn and derision never come in tears.
    Look when° I vow, I weep; and vows so born,
    In their nativity all truth appears.°   125
    How can these things in me seem scorn to you,
    Bearing the badge° of faith, to prove them true?
HELENA: You do advance° your cunning more and
    more.
    When truth kills truth,° O devilish-holy fray!
    These vows are Hermia's. Will you give her o'er?   130
    Weigh oath with oath, and you will nothing weigh.
    Your vows to her and me, put in two scales
    Will even weigh, and both as light as tales.°
LYSANDER: I had no judgment when to her I swore.
HELENA: Nor none, in my mind, now you give her o'er.   135
LYSANDER: Demetrius loves her, and he loves not you.
DEMETRIUS [*awaking*]: O Helen, goddess, nymph,
    perfect, divine!
    To what, my love, shall I compare thine eyne?

---

101. Tartar's bow: Tartars were famed for their skill with the
bow.   **113. fee:** Privilege, reward.   **114. fond pageant:** Foolish exhibition.   **119. alone:** Unequaled.   **121. prepost'rously:**
Out of the natural order.   **124. Look when:** Whenever.
124–25. vows . . . appears: Vows made by one who is weeping
give evidence thereby of their sincerity.   **127. badge:** Identifying device such as that worn on servants' livery.   **128. advance:** Carry forward, display.   **129. truth kills truth:** One of
Lysander's vows must invalidate the other.   **133. tales:** Lies.

Crystal is muddy. O, how ripe in show°
140   Thy lips, those kissing cherries, tempting grow!
That pure congealed white, high Taurus'° snow,
Fann'd with the eastern wind, turns to a crow°
When thou hold'st up thy hand. O, let me kiss
This princess of pure white, this seal° of bliss!
145   HELENA: O spite! O hell! I see you all are bent
To set against me for your merriment.
If you were civil and knew courtesy,
You would not do me thus much injury.
Can you not hate me, as I know you do,
150   But you must join in souls to mock me too?
If you were men, as men you are in show,
You would not use a gentle lady so —
To vow, and swear, and superpraise° my parts,°
When I am sure you hate me with your hearts.
155   You both are rivals, and love Hermia;
And now both rivals, to mock Helena.
A trim° exploit, a manly enterprise,
To conjure tears up in a poor maid's eyes
With your derision! None of noble sort
160   Would so offend a virgin and extort°
A poor soul's patience, all to make you sport.
LYSANDER: You are unkind, Demetrius. Be not so;
For you love Hermia; this you know I know.
And here, with all good will, with all my heart,
165   In Hermia's love I yield you up my part;
And yours of Helena to me bequeath,
Whom I do love and will do till my death.
HELENA: Never did mockers waste more idle breath.
DEMETRIUS: Lysander, keep thy Hermia; I will none.°
170   If e'er I lov'd her, all that love is gone.
My heart to her but as guest-wise sojourn'd,
And now to Helen is it home return'd,
There to remain.
LYSANDER: Helen, it is not so.
DEMETRIUS: Disparage not the faith thou dost not know,
175   Lest, to thy peril, thou aby° it dear.
Look where thy love comes; yonder is thy dear.

(*Enter Hermia.*)

HERMIA: Dark night, that from the eye his° function
        takes,
The ear more quick of apprehension makes;
Wherein it doth impair the seeing sense,
180   It pays the hearing double recompense.
Thou art not by mine eye, Lysander, found;
Mine ear, I thank it, brought me to thy sound.
But why unkindly didst thou leave me so?
LYSANDER: Why should he stay, whom love doth press
        to go?

HERMIA: What love could press Lysander from my
        side?   185
LYSANDER: Lysander's love, that would not let him
        bide,
Fair Helena, who more engilds the night
Than all yon fiery oes° and eyes of light.
Why seek'st thou me? Could not this make thee
        know,
The hate I bear thee made me leave thee so?   190
HERMIA: You speak not as you think. It cannot be.
HELENA: Lo, she is one of this confederacy!
Now I perceive they have conjoin'd all three
To fashion this false sport, in spite of me.°
Injurious Hermia, most ungrateful maid!   195
Have you conspir'd, have you with these contriv'd°
To bait° me with this foul derision?
Is all the counsel° that we two have shar'd,
The sisters' vows, the hours that we have spent,
When we have chid the hasty-footed time   200
For parting us — O, is all forgot?
All school-days friendship, childhood innocence?
We, Hermia, like two artificial° gods,
Have with our needles created both one flower,
Both on one sampler, sitting on one cushion,   205
Both warbling of one song, both in one key,
As if our hands, our sides, voices, and minds
Had been incorporate. So we grew together,
Like to a double cherry, seeming parted,
But yet an union in partition;   210
Two lovely° berries molded on one stem;
So, with two seeming bodies, but one heart;
Two of the first, like coats in heraldry,
Due but to one and crowned with one crest.°
And will you rent° our ancient love asunder,   215
To join with men in scorning your poor friend?
It is not friendly, 'tis not maidenly.
Our sex, as well as I, may chide you for it,
Though I alone do feel the injury.
HERMIA: I am amazed at your passionate words.   220
I scorn you not. It seems that you scorn me.
HELENA: Have you not set Lysander, as in scorn,
To follow me and praise my eyes and face?
And made your other love, Demetrius,
Who even but now did spurn me with his foot,   225
To call me goddess, nymph, divine and rare,
Precious, celestial? Wherefore speaks he this
To her he hates? And wherefore doth Lysander
Deny your love, so rich within his soul,
And tender° me, forsooth, affection,   230
But by your setting on, by your consent?

---

188. **oes:** Circles, orbs, stars.   194. **in spite of me:** To vex me.   196. **contriv'd:** Plotted.   197. **bait:** Torment, as one sets on dogs to bait a bear.   198. **counsel:** Confidential talk. 203. **artificial:** Skilled in art or creation.   211. **lovely:** Loving. 213–14. **Two . . . crest:** We have two separate bodies, just as a coat of arms in heraldry can be represented twice on a shield but surmounted by a single crest.   215. **rent:** Rend.   230. **tender:** Offer.

---

139. **show:** Appearance.   141. **Taurus:** A lofty mountain range in Asia Minor.   142. **turns to a crow:** Seems black by contrast.   144. **seal:** Pledge.   153. **superpraise:** Overpraise. **parts:** Qualities.   157. **trim:** Pretty, fine (said ironically). 160. **extort:** Twist, torture.   169. **will none:** Wish none of her. 175. **aby:** Pay for.   177. **his:** Its.

What though I be not so in grace° as you,
So hung upon with love, so fortunate,
But miserable most, to love unlov'd?
235   This you should pity rather than despise.
HERMIA: I understand not what you mean by this.
HELENA: Ay, do! Persever, counterfeit sad° looks,
   Make mouths° upon° me when I turn my back,
   Wink each at other, hold the sweet jest up.
240   This sport, well carried,° shall be chronicled.
   If you have any pity, grace, or manners,
   You would not make me such an argument.°
   But fare ye well. 'Tis partly my own fault,
   Which death, or absence, soon shall remedy.
245 LYSANDER: Stay, gentle Helena; hear my excuse,
   My love, my life, my soul, fair Helena!
HELENA: O excellent!
HERMIA: Sweet, do not scorn her so.
DEMETRIUS: If she cannot entreat,° I can compel.
LYSANDER: Thou canst compel no more than she
      entreat.
   Thy threats have no more strength than her weak
250   prayers.
   Helen, I love thee, by my life, I do!
   I swear by that which I will lose for thee,
   To prove him false that says I love thee not.
DEMETRIUS: I say I love thee more than he can do.
255 LYSANDER: If thou say so, withdraw, and prove it too.
DEMETRIUS: Quick, come!
HERMIA: Lysander, whereto tends all this?
LYSANDER: Away, you Ethiope!°
      [He tries to break away from Hermia.]
DEMETRIUS: No, no; he'll
   Seem to break loose; take on as you would follow,
   But yet come not. You are a tame man, go!
LYSANDER: Hang off,° thou cat, thou burr! Vile thing,
260   let loose,
   Or I will shake thee from me like a serpent!
HERMIA: Why are you grown so rude? What change is
      this,
   Sweet love?
LYSANDER: Thy love? Out, tawny Tartar, out!
   Out, loathed med'cine!° O hated potion, hence!
HERMIA: Do you not jest?
265 HELENA: Yes, sooth,° and so do you.
LYSANDER: Demetrius, I will keep my word with thee.
DEMETRIUS: I would I had your bond, for I perceive
   A weak bond° holds you. I'll not trust your word.
LYSANDER: What, should I hurt her, strike her, kill her
      dead?
270   Although I hate her, I'll not harm her so.

HERMIA: What, can you do me greater harm than hate?
   Hate me? Wherefore? O me, what news,° my love?
   Am not I Hermia? Are not you Lysander?
   I am as fair now as I was erewhile.°
   Since night you lov'd me; yet since night you left me.   275
   Why, then you left me — O, the gods forbid! —
   In earnest, shall I say?
LYSANDER: Ay, by my life!
   And never did desire to see thee more.
   Therefore be out of hope, of question, of doubt;
   Be certain, nothing truer. 'Tis no jest   280
   That I do hate thee and love Helena.
HERMIA: O me! You juggler! You cankerblossom!°
   You thief of love! What, have you come by night
   And stol'n my love's heart from him?
HELENA: Fine, i' faith!
   Have you no modesty, no maiden shame,   285
   No touch of bashfulness? What, will you tear
   Impatient answers from my gentle tongue?
   Fie, fie! You counterfeit, you puppet,° you!
HERMIA: Puppet? Why so? Ay, that way goes the game.
   Now I perceive that she hath made compare   290
   Between our statures; she hath urg'd her height,
   And with her personage, her tall personage,
   Her height, forsooth, she hath prevail'd with him.
   And are you grown so high in his esteem,
   Because I am so dwarfish and so low?   295
   How low am I, thou painted maypole? Speak!
   How low am I? I am not yet so low
   But that my nails can reach unto thine eyes.
      [She flails at Helena but is restrained.]
HELENA: I pray you, though you mock me, gentlemen,
   Let her not hurt me. I was never curst;°   300
   I have no gift at all in shrewishness;
   I am a right° maid for my cowardice.
   Let her not strike me. You perhaps may think,
   Because she is something° lower than myself,
   That I can match her.
HERMIA: Lower! Hark, again!   305
HELENA: Good Hermia, do not be so bitter with me.
   I evermore did love you, Hermia,
   Did ever keep your counsels, never wrong'd you;
   Save that, in love unto Demetrius,
   I told him of your stealth° unto this wood.   310
   He followed you; for love I followed him.
   But he hath chid me hence and threat'ned me
   To strike me, spurn me, nay, to kill me too.
   And now, so° you will let me quiet go,
   To Athens will I bear my folly back   315
   And follow you no further. Let me go.
   You see how simple and how fond° I am.
HERMIA: Why, get you gone. Who is 't that hinders you?

---

232. **grace:** Favor.   237. **sad:** Grave, serious.   238. **mouths:**
Maws, faces, grimaces.   **upon:** At.   240. **carried:** Managed.
242. **argument:** Subject for a jest.   248. **entreat:** Succeed by
entreaty.   257. **Ethiope:** Referring to Hermia's relatively dark
hair and complexion; see also *tawny Tartar* six lines later.
260. **Hang off:** Let go.   264. **med'cine:** Poison.   265. **sooth:**
Truly.   268. **weak bond:** Hermia's arm (with a pun on *bond*,
oath, in the previous line).

272. **what news:** What is the matter.   274. **erewhile:** Just now.
282. **cankerblossom:** Worm that destroys the flower bud (?).
288. **puppet:** (1) Counterfeit, (2) dwarfish woman (in reference to Hermia's smaller stature).   300. **curst:** Shrewish.
302. **right:** True.   304. **something:** Somewhat.   310. **stealth:**
Stealing away.   314. **so:** If only.   317. **fond:** Foolish.

HELENA: A foolish heart, that I leave here behind.
HERMIA: What, with Lysander?
320 HELENA: With Demetrius.
LYSANDER: Be not afraid; she shall not harm thee,
    Helena.
DEMETRIUS: No, sir, she shall not, though you take her
    part.
HELENA: O, when she is angry, she is keen and
    shrewd!°
    She was a vixen when she went to school;
325   And though she be but little, she is fierce.
HERMIA: "Little" again! Nothing but "low" and
    "little"!
    Why will you suffer her to flout me thus?
    Let me come to her.
LYSANDER: Get you gone, you dwarf!
    You minimus,° of hind'ring knot-grass° made!
    You bead, you acorn!
330 DEMETRIUS: You are too officious
    In her behalf that scorns your services.
    Let her alone. Speak not of Helena;
    Take not her part. For, if thou dost intend°
    Never so little show of love to her,
    Thou shalt aby° it.
335 LYSANDER: Now she holds me not;
    Now follow, if thou dar'st, to try whose right,
    Of thine or mine, is most in Helena.   [*Exit.*]
DEMETRIUS: Follow? Nay, I'll go with thee, cheek by
    jowl.°

                    [*Exit, following Lysander.*]

HERMIA: You, mistress, all this coil° is 'long of° you.
    Nay, go not back.°
340 HELENA: I will not trust you, I,
    Nor longer stay in your curst company.
    Your hands than mine are quicker for a fray;
    My legs are longer, though, to run away.   [*Exit.*]
HERMIA: I am amaz'd, and know not what to say.
                                        (*Exit.*)
345 OBERON: This is thy negligence. Still thou mistak'st,
    Or else committ'st thy knaveries willfully.
PUCK: Believe me, king of shadows, I mistook.
    Did not you tell me I should know the man
    By the Athenian garments he had on?
350   And so far blameless proves my enterprise
    That I have 'nointed an Athenian's eyes;
    And so far am I glad it so did sort°
    As this their jangling I esteem a sport.
OBERON: Thou see'st these lovers seek a place to fight.
355   Hie therefore, Robin, overcast the night;
    The starry welkin° cover thou anon

With drooping fog as black as Acheron,°
And lead these testy rivals so astray
As° one come not within another's way.
Like to Lysander sometime frame thy tongue,   360
Then stir Demetrius up with bitter wrong;°
And sometime rail thou like Demetrius.
And from each other look thou lead them thus,
Till o'er their brows death-counterfeiting sleep
With leaden legs and batty° wings doth creep.   365
Then crush this herb° into Lysander's eye,
                                    [*Gives herb.*]
Whose liquor hath this virtuous° property,
To take from thence all error with his° might
And make his eyeballs roll with wonted° sight.
When they next wake, all this derision°   370
Shall seem a dream and fruitless vision,
And back to Athens shall the lovers wend
With league whose date° till death shall never end.
Whiles I in this affair do thee employ,
I'll to my queen and beg her Indian boy;   375
And then I will her charmed eye release
From monster's view, and all things shall be peace.
PUCK: My fairy lord, this must be done with haste,
For night's swift dragons° cut the clouds full fast,
And yonder shines Aurora's harbinger,°   380
At whose approach, ghosts, wand'ring here and
    there,
Troop home to churchyards. Damned spirits all,
That in crossways and floods have burial,°
Already to their wormy beds are gone.
For fear lest day should look their shames upon,   385
They willfully themselves exile from light
And must for aye° consort with black-brow'd night.
OBERON: But we are spirits of another sort.
I with the Morning's love° have oft made sport,
And, like a forester,° the groves may tread   390
Even till the eastern gate, all fiery-red,
Opening on Neptune with fair blessed beams,
Turns into yellow gold his salt green streams.
But, notwithstanding, haste; make no delay.
We may effect this business yet ere day.   [*Exit.*] 395
PUCK: Up and down, up and down,
    I will lead them up and down.
    I am fear'd in field and town.

---

323. **shrewd:** Shrewish.   329. **minimus:** Diminutive creature.
knot-grass: A weed, an infusion of which was thought to stunt
the growth.   333. **intend:** Give sign of.   335. **aby:** Pay for.
338. **cheek by jowl:** Side by side.   339. **coil:** Turmoil, dissension. **'long of:** On account of.   340. **go not back:** Don't retreat. (Hermia is again proposing a fight.)   352. **sort:** Turn out.
356. **welkin:** Sky.

357. **Acheron:** River of Hades (here representing Hades itself).   359. **As:** That.   361. **wrong:** Insults.   365. **batty:** Bat-
like.   366. **this herb:** The antidote (mentioned in II, I, 184)
to love-in-idleness.   367. **virtuous:** Efficacious.   368. **his:** Its.
369. **wonted:** Accustomed.   370. **derision:** Laughable business.   373. **date:** Term of existence.   379. **dragons:** Supposed
to be yoked to the car of the goddess of night.   380. **Aurora's
harbinger:** The morning star, precursor of dawn.   383. **crossways . . . burial:** Those who had committed suicide were buried
at crossways, with a stake driven through them; those
drowned, i.e., buried in floods or great waters, were condemned to wander disconsolate for want of burial rites.
387. **for aye:** Forever.   389. **Morning's love:** Cephalus, a beautiful youth beloved by Aurora; or perhaps the goddess of the
dawn herself.   390. **forester:** Keeper of a royal forest.

Goblin, lead them up and down.
400   Here comes one.

(*Enter Lysander.*)

LYSANDER: Where art thou, proud Demetrius? Speak
   thou now.
PUCK [*mimicking Demetrius*]: Here, villain, drawn°
   and ready. Where art thou?
LYSANDER: I will be with thee straight.°
PUCK: Follow me, then,
   To plainer° ground.
             [*Lysander wanders about, following the voice.*]°

(*Enter Demetrius.*)

DEMETRIUS: Lysander! Speak again!

---

402. drawn: With drawn sword.   **403. straight:** Immediately.
404. plainer: Smoother.   **404.** [S.D.] *Lysander wanders about:*
It is not clearly necessary that Lysander exit at this point; neither exit nor reentrance is indicated in the early texts.

Thou runaway, thou coward, art thou fled?   405
Speak! In some bush? Where dost thou hide thy
   head?
PUCK [*mimicking Lysander*]: Thou coward, art thou
   bragging to the stars,
Telling the bushes that thou look'st for wars,
And wilt not come? Come, recreant;° come, thou
   child,
I'll whip thee with a rod. He is defil'd   410
That draws a sword on thee.
DEMETRIUS: Yea, art thou there?
PUCK: Follow my voice. We'll try° no manhood here.
                                             (*Exeunt.*)

[*Lysander returns.*]

LYSANDER: He goes before me and still dares me on.
   When I come where he calls, then he is gone.
   The villain is much lighter-heel'd than I.   415

---

409. recreant: Cowardly wretch.   **412. try:** Test.

RIGHT: Elizabeth McGovern as Helena in the 1987 New York Shakespeare festival production of *A Midsummer Night's Dream*, directed by A. J. Antoon.
LEFT: F. Murray Abraham (left) as Bottom, playing Pyramus.

I followed fast, but faster he did fly,
That fallen am I in dark uneven way,
And here will rest me. [*Lies down.*] Come, thou
   gentle day!
For if but once thou show me thy gray light,
420   I'll find Demetrius and revenge this spite.   [*Sleeps.*]

   ([*Enter*] *Robin* [*Puck*] *and Demetrius.*)

PUCK: Ho, ho, ho! Coward, why com'st thou not?
DEMETRIUS: Abide me, if thou dar'st; for well I wot°
   Thou runn'st before me, shifting every place,
   And dar'st not stand nor look me in the face.
   Where art thou now?
425   PUCK: Come hither. I am here.
DEMETRIUS: Nay, then, thou mock'st me. Thou shalt
   buy° this dear,°
   If ever I thy face by daylight see.
   Now, go thy way. Faintness constraineth me
   To measure out my length on this cold bed.
430   By day's approach look to be visited.
               [*Lies down and sleeps.*]

   (*Enter Helena.*)

HELENA: O weary night, O long and tedious night,
   Abate° thy hours! Shine, comforts, from the east,

422. wot: Know. **426. buy:** Pay for. **dear:** Dearly.
432. Abate: Lessen, shorten.

That I may back to Athens by daylight,
From these that my poor company detest;
And sleep, that sometimes shuts up sorrow's eye,   435
Steal me awhile from mine own company.
           [*Lies down and*] *sleep*[*s*].
PUCK: Yet but three? Come one more;
   Two of both kinds makes up four.
   Here she comes, curst and sad.
   Cupid is a knavish lad,   440
   Thus to make poor females mad.

[*Enter Hermia.*]

HERMIA: Never so weary, never so in woe,
   Bedabbled with the dew and torn with briers,
   I can no further crawl, no further go;
   My legs can keep no pace with my desires.   445
   Here will I rest me till the break of day.
   Heavens shield Lysander, if they mean a fray!
           [*Lies down and sleeps.*]
PUCK: On the ground
   Sleep sound.
   I'll apply   450
   To your eye,
Gentle lover, remedy.
       [*Squeezing the juice on Lysander's eyes.*]
   When thou wak'st,
   Thou tak'st
   True delight   455

In the sight
Of thy former lady's eye;
And the country proverb known,
That every man should take his own,
460   In your waking shall be shown:
Jack shall have Jill;
Nought shall go ill;
The man shall have his mare again, and all shall be
well.   [*Exit. Manent the four lovers.*]

{*ACT IV* • *Scene 1*}°

(*Enter* [*Titania,*] *Queen of Fairies, and* [*Bottom the*]
Clown, and Fairies; and [*Oberon,*] *the King, behind
them.*)

TITANIA: Come, sit thee down upon this flow'ry bed,
While I thy amiable° cheeks do coy,°
And stick musk-roses in thy sleek smooth head,
And kiss thy fair large ears, my gentle joy.
                                        [*They recline.*]
5   BOTTOM: Where's Peaseblossom?
PEASEBLOSSOM: Ready.
BOTTOM: Scratch my head, Peaseblossom. Where's
Mounsieur Cobweb?
COBWEB: Ready.
10   BOTTOM: Mounsieur Cobweb, good mounsieur, get you
your weapons in your hand, and kill me a red-hipp'd
humble-bee on the top of a thistle; and, good mounsieur, bring me the honey-bag. Do not fret yourself
too much in the action, mounsieur; and, good moun-
15   sieur, have a care the honey-bag break not; I would
be loath to have you overflown with a honey-bag,
signior. Where's Mounsieur Mustardseed?
MUSTARDSEED: Ready.
BOTTOM: Give me your neaf,° Mounsieur Mustardseed.
20   Pray you, leave your curtsy,° good mounsieur.
MUSTARDSEED: What's your will?
BOTTOM: Nothing, good mounsieur, but to help Cav-
alery° Cobweb° to scratch. I must to the barber's,
mounsieur; for methinks I am marvailes hairy about
25   the face; and I am such a tender ass, if my hair do but
tickle me, I must scratch.
TITANIA: What, wilt thou hear some music, my sweet
love?
BOTTOM: I have a reasonable good ear in music. Let's
30   have the tongs and the bones.°
                            [*Music: tongs, rural music.*]°

TITANIA: Or say, sweet love, what thou desirest to eat.
BOTTOM: Truly, a peck of provender. I could munch your
good dry oats. Methinks I have a great desire to a
bottle° of hay. Good hay, sweet hay, hath no fellow.°
TITANIA: I have a venturous fairy that shall seek   35
The squirrel's hoard, and fetch thee new nuts.
BOTTOM: I had rather have a handful or two of dried
peas. But, I pray you, let none of your people stir me.
I have an exposition° of sleep come upon me.
TITANIA: Sleep thou, and I will wind thee in my arms.   40
Fairies, be gone, and be all ways° away.
                                        [*Exeunt fairies.*]
So doth the woodbine the sweet honeysuckle
Gently entwist; the female ivy so
Enrings the barky fingers of the elm.
Oh, how I love thee! How I dote on thee!   45
                                        [*They sleep.*]

(*Enter Robin Goodfellow* [*Puck*].)

OBERON [*advancing*]: Welcome, good Robin. See'st
thou this sweet sight?
Her dotage now I do begin to pity.
For, meeting her of late behind the wood,
Seeking sweet favors° for this hateful fool,
I did upbraid her and fall out with her.   50
For she his hairy temples then had rounded
With coronet of fresh and fragrant flowers;
And that same dew, which sometime° on the buds
Was wont to swell like round and orient pearls,°
Stood now within the pretty flouriets'° eyes   55
Like tears that did their own disgrace bewail.
When I had at my pleasure taunted her,
And she in mild terms begg'd my patience,
I then did ask of her her changeling child;
Which straight she gave me, and her fairy sent   60
To bear him to my bower in fairy land.
And, now I have the boy, I will undo
This hateful imperfection of her eyes.
And, gentle Puck, take this transformed scalp
From off the head of this Athenian swain,   65
That, he awaking when the other° do,
May all to Athens back again repair,
And think no more of this night's accidents
But as the fierce vexation of a dream.
But first I will release the Fairy Queen.   70
[*Squeezes juice in her eyes.*]
Be as thou wast wont to be;
See as thou wast wont to see.
Dian's bud° o'er Cupid's flower

IV, I. **Location:** Scene continues. The four lovers are still asleep
onstage. **2. amiable:** Lovely. **coy:** Caress. **19. neaf:** Fist.
20. leave your curtsy: Put on your hat. **22–23. Cavalery:** Cav-
alièr. Form of address for a gentleman. **23. Cobweb:** Seemingly an error, since Cobweb has been sent to bring honey while
Peaseblossom has been asked to scratch. **30. tongs . . . bones:**
Instruments for rustic music. (The tongs were played like a triangle, whereas the bones were held between the fingers and
used as clappers.) [s.d.] *Music . . . music:* This stage direction is added from the Folio.

34. bottle: Bundle. **fellow:** Equal. **39. exposition:** Bottom's word for *disposition.* **41. all ways:** In all directions.
49. favors: I.e., gifts of flowers. **53. sometime:** Formerly.
54. orient pearls: The most beautiful of all pearls, those coming
from the Orient. **55. flouriets':** Flowerets'. **66. other:** Others. **73. Dian's bud:** Perhaps the flower of the *agnus castus* or
chaste-tree, supposed to preserve chastity; or perhaps referring
simply to Oberon's herb by which he can undo the effects of
"Cupid's flower," the love-in-idleness of II, I, 165–68.

Hath such force and blessed power.
75 Now, my Titania, wake you, my sweet queen.
TITANIA [*waking*]: My Oberon! What visions have I
        seen!
    Methought I was enamor'd of an ass.
OBERON: There lies your love.
TITANIA: How came these things to pass?
    O, how mine eyes do loathe his visage now!
80 OBERON: Silence awhile. Robin, take off this head.
    Titania, music call, and strike more dead
    Than common sleep of all these five° the sense.
TITANIA: Music, ho! Music, such as charmeth sleep!
                                        [*Music.*]
PUCK [*removing the ass's head*]: Now, when thou
        wak'st, with thine own fool's eyes peep.
OBERON: Sound, music! Come, my queen, take hands
85   with me,
    And rock the ground whereon these sleepers be.
                                        [*Dance.*]
    Now thou and I are new in amity,
    And will tomorrow midnight solemnly°
    Dance in Duke Theseus' house triumphantly
90 And bless it to all fair prosperity.
    There shall the pairs of faithful lovers be
    Wedded, with Theseus, all in jollity.
PUCK: Fairy King, attend, and mark:
    I do hear the morning lark.
95 OBERON: Then, my queen, in silence sad,°
    Trip we after night's shade.
    We the globe can compass soon,
    Swifter than the wand'ring moon.
TITANIA: Come, my lord, and in our flight
100   Tell me how it came this night
    That I sleeping here was found
    With these mortals on the ground.   (*Exeunt.*)
                                        (*Wind horn* [*within*].)

(*Enter Theseus and all his train;* [*Hippolyta, Egeus*].)

THESEUS: Go, one of you, find out the forester,
    For now our observation° is perform'd;
105 And since we have the vaward° of the day,
    My love shall hear the music of my hounds.
    Uncouple in the western valley; let them go.
    Dispatch, I say, and find the forester.
                                [*Exit an Attendant.*]
    We will, fair queen, up to the mountain's top
110 And mark the musical confusion
    Of hounds and echo in conjunction.
HIPPOLYTA: I was with Hercules and Cadmus° once,
    When in a wood of Crete they bay'd° the bear
    With hounds of Sparta.° Never did I hear

Such gallant chiding; for, besides the groves,   115
    The skies, the fountains, every region near
    Seem'd all one mutual cry. I never heard
    So musical a discord, such sweet thunder.
THESEUS: My hounds are bred out of the Spartan kind,
    So flew'd,° so sanded;° and their heads are hung   120
    With ears that sweep away the morning dew;
    Crook-knee'd, and dewlapp'd° like Thessalian bulls;
    Slow in pursuit, but match'd in mouth like bells,
    Each under each.° A cry° more tuneable°
    Was never holla'd to, nor cheer'd with horn,   125
    In Crete, in Sparta, nor in Thessaly.
    Judge when you hear. [*Sees the sleepers.*] But, soft!
        What nymphs are these?
EGEUS: My lord, this' my daughter here asleep;
    And this, Lysander; this Demetrius is;
    This Helena, old Nedar's Helena.   130
    I wonder of their being here together.
THESEUS: No doubt they rose up early to observe
    The rite of May, and, hearing our intent,
    Came here in grace of our solemnity.°
    But speak, Egeus. Is not this the day   135
    That Hermia should give answer of her choice?
EGEUS: It is, my lord.
THESEUS: Go, bid the huntsmen wake them with their
        horns.
                                    [*Exit an Attendant.*]
(*Shout within. Wind horns. They all start up.*)

    Good morrow, friends. Saint Valentine° is past.
    Begin these wood-birds but to couple now?   140
LYSANDER: Pardon, my lord.   [*They kneel.*]
THESEUS: I pray you all, stand up.
    I know you two are rival enemies;
    How comes this gentle concord in the world,
    That hatred is so far from jealousy
    To sleep by hate and fear no enmity?   145
LYSANDER: My lord, I shall reply amazedly,
    Half sleep, half waking; but as yet, I swear,
    I cannot truly say how I came here.
    But, as I think — for truly would I speak,
    And now I do bethink me, so it is —   150
    I came with Hermia hither. Our intent
    Was to be gone from Athens, where° we might,
    Without° the peril of the Athenian law —
EGEUS: Enough, enough, my lord; you have enough.
    I beg the law, the law, upon his head.   155
    They would have stol'n away; they would, Demetrius,

---

82. these five: I.e., the four lovers and Bottom.   **88. solemnly:** Ceremoniously.   **95. sad:** Sober.   **104. observation:** Observance to a morn of May (I, I, 167).   **105. vaward:** Vanguard, i.e., earliest part.   **112. Cadmus:** Mythical founder of Thebes. (This story about him is unknown.)   **113. bay'd:** Brought to bay.   **114. hounds of Sparta:** Breed famous in antiquity for their hunting skill.

120. So flew'd: Similarly having large hanging chaps or fleshy covering of the jaw.   **sanded:** Of sandy color.   **122. dewlapp'd:** Having pendulous folds of skin under the neck.   **123–24. match'd . . . under each:** Harmoniously matched in their various cries like a set of bells, from treble down to bass.   **124. cry:** Pack of hounds.   **tuneable:** Well tuned, melodious.   **134. solemnity:** Observance of these same rites of May.   **139. Saint Valentine:** Birds were supposed to choose their mates on St. Valentine's Day.   **152. where:** Wherever; or to where.   **153. Without:** Outside of, beyond.

Thereby to have defeated you and me,
You of your wife and me of my consent,
Of my consent that she should be your wife.
DEMETRIUS: My lord, fair Helen told me of their
160   stealth,
Of this their purpose hither to this wood,
And I in fury hither followed them,
Fair Helena in fancy following me.
But, my good lord, I wot not by what power —
165 But by some power it is — my love to Hermia,
Melted as the snow, seems to me now
As the remembrance of an idle gaud.°
Which in my childhood I did dote upon;
And all the faith, the virtue of my heart,
170 The object and the pleasure of mine eye,
Is only Helena. To her, my lord,
Was I betroth'd ere I saw Hermia,
But like a sickness did I loathe this food;
But, as in health, come to my natural taste,
175 Now I do wish it, love it, long for it,
And will for evermore be true to it.
THESEUS: Fair lovers, you are fortunately met.
Of this discourse we more will hear anon.
Egeus, I will overbear your will;
180 For in the temple, by and by, with us
These couples shall eternally be knit.
And, for° the morning now is something° worn,
Our purpos'd hunting shall be set aside.
Away with us to Athens. Three and three,
185 We'll hold a feast in great solemnity.
Come, Hippolyta.

       [*Exeunt Theseus, Hippolyta, Egeus, and train.*]

DEMETRIUS: These things seem small and
    undistinguishable,
Like far-off mountains turned into clouds.
HERMIA: Methinks I see these things with parted° eye,
When every thing seems double.
190 HELENA: So methinks;
And I have found Demetrius like a jewel,
Mine own, and not mine own.°
DEMETRIUS: Are you sure
That we are awake? It seems to me
That yet we sleep, we dream. Do not you think
195 The Duke was here, and bid us follow him?
HERMIA: Yea, and my father.
HELENA: And Hippolyta.
LYSANDER: And he did bid us follow to the temple.
DEMETRIUS: Why, then, we are awake. Let's follow
    him,
And by the way let us recount our dreams.
                           [*Exeunt.*]

BOTTOM [*awaking*]: When my cue comes, call me, and 200
I will answer. My next is, "Most fair Pyramus."
Heigh-ho! Peter Quince! Flute, the bellows-mender!
Snout, the tinker! Starveling! God's my life, stol'n
hence, and left me asleep! I have had a most rare
vision. I have had a dream, past the wit of man to say 205
what dream it was. Man is but an ass, if he go about°
to expound this dream. Methought I was — there is
no man can tell what. Methought I was — and methought I had — but man is but a patch'd° fool, if he
will offer° to say what me-thought I had. The eye of 210
man hath not heard, the ear of man hath not seen,
man's hand is not able to taste, his tongue to conceive, nor his heart to report, what my dream was. I
will get Peter Quince to write a ballad of this dream.
It shall be call'd "Bottom's Dream," because it hath 215
no bottom; and I will sing it in the latter end of a
play, before the Duke. Peradventure, to make it the
more gracious, I shall sing it at her° death.   [*Exit.*]

{*Scene II*}°

(*Enter Quince, Flute, [Snout, and Starveling].*)

QUINCE: Have you sent to Bottom's house? Is he come
home yet?
STARVELING: He cannot be heard of. Out of doubt he is
transported.°
FLUTE: If he come not, then the play is marr'd. It goes 5
not forward, doth it?
QUINCE: It is not possible. You have not a man in all
Athens able to discharge° Pyramus but he.
FLUTE: No, he hath simply the best wit of any handicraft
man in Athens. 10
QUINCE: Yea, and the best person too; and he is a very
paramour for a sweet voice.
FLUTE: You must say "paragon." A paramour is, God
bless us, a thing of naught.

(*Enter Snug the Joiner.*)

SNUG: Masters, the Duke is coming from the temple, 15
and there is two or three lords and ladies more married. If our sport had gone forward, we had all been
made men.
FLUTE: O sweet bully Bottom! Thus hath he lost sixpence a day° during his life; he could not have scap'd 20
sixpence a day. An the Duke had not given him sixpence a day for playing Pyramus, I'll be hang'd. He
would have deserv'd it. Sixpence a day in Pyramus,
or nothing.

(*Enter Bottom.*)

---

167. idle gaud: Worthless trinket. **182. for:** Since. **something:** Somewhat. **189. parted:** Improperly focused. **191–92. like . . . not mine own:** Like a jewel that one finds by chance and therefore possesses but cannot certainly consider one's own property.

206. go about: Attempt. **209. patch'd:** Wearing motley, i.e., a dress of various colors. **210. offer:** Venture. **218. her:** Thisby's (?). **IV, II. Location:** Athens, Quince's house (?). **4. transported:** Carried off by fairies; or, possibly, transformed. **8. discharge:** Perform. **19–20. sixpence a day:** As a royal pension.

Stage model of the set for Max Reinhardt's 1913 production of *A Midsummer Night's Dream* at the Deutsches Theater in Berlin. The design called for an entire forest to be built on a stage that revolved as the action shifted.

25 BOTTOM: Where are these lads? Where are these hearts?°
QUINCE: Bottom! O most courageous day! O most happy hour!
BOTTOM: Masters, I am to discourse wonders.° But ask me not what; for if I tell you, I am no true Athenian. I
30 will tell you everything, right as it fell out.
QUINCE: Let us hear, sweet Bottom.
BOTTOM: Not a word of° me. All that I will tell you is, that the Duke hath din'd. Get your apparel together, good strings° to your beards, new ribands° to
35 your pumps, meet presently° at the palace, every man look o'er his part; for the short and the long is, our play is preferr'd.° In any case, let Thisby have clean linen; and let not him that plays the lion pare his nails, for they shall hang out for the lion's claws. And,
40 most dear actors, eat no onions nor garlic, for we are to utter sweet breath; and I do not doubt but to hear them say, it is a sweet comedy. No more words. Away! go, away!   [*Exeunt.*]

25. hearts: Good fellows.   **28. am . . . wonders:** Have wonders to relate.   **32. of:** Out of.   **34. strings:** To attach the beards. **ribands:** Ribbons.   **35. presently:** Immediately.   **37. preferr'd:** Selected for consideration.

{*ACT V* • *Scene 1*}°

(*Enter Theseus, Hippolyta, and Philostrate, [Lords, and Attendants].*)

HIPPOLYTA: 'Tis strange, my Theseus, that° these lovers speak of.
THESEUS: More strange than true. I never may° believe
   These antic° fables, nor these fairy toys.°
   Lovers and madmen have such seething brains
   Such shaping fantasies,° that apprehend   5
   More than cool reason ever comprehends.
   The lunatic, the lover, and the poet
   Are of imagination all compact.°
   One sees more devils than vast hell can hold;
   That is the madman. The lover, all as frantic,   10
   Sees Helen's° beauty in a brow of Egypt.°
   The poet's eye, in a fine frenzy rolling,

V, i. Location: Athens. The palace of Theseus.   **1. that:** That which.   **2. may:** Can.   **3. antic:** Strange, grotesque (with additional punning sense of *antique,* ancient).   **fairy toys:** Trifling stories about fairies.   **5. fantasies:** Imaginations. **8. compact:** Formed, composed.   **11. Helen's:** Of Helen of Troy, pattern of beauty.   **brow of Egypt:** Face of a gypsy.

Doth glance from heaven to earth, from earth to
    heaven;
And as imagination bodies forth
15   The forms of things unknown, the poet's pen
Turns them to shapes and gives to airy nothing
A local habitation and a name.
Such tricks hath strong imagination
That, if it would but apprehend some joy,
20   It comprehends some bringer° of that joy;
Or in the night, imagining some fear,°
How easy is a bush suppos'd a bear!
HIPPOLYTA: But all the story of the night told over,
And all their minds transfigur'd so together,
25   More witnesseth than fancy's images°
And grows to something of great constancy;°
But, howsoever,° strange and admirable.°

(*Enter lovers: Lysander, Demetrius, Hermia, and Helena.*)

THESEUS: Here come the lovers, full of joy and mirth.
Joy, gentle friends! Joy and fresh days of love
Accompany your hearts!
30   LYSANDER: More than to us
Wait in your royal walks, your board, your bed!
THESEUS: Come now, what masques, what dances shall
    we have,
To wear away this long age of three hours
Between our after-supper and bed-time?
35   Where is our usual manager of mirth?
What revels are in hand? Is there no play,
To ease the anguish of a torturing hour?
Call Philostrate.
PHILOSTRATE: Here, mighty Theseus.
THESEUS: Say, what abridgement° have you for this
    evening?
40   What masque? What music? How shall we beguile
The lazy time, if not with some delight?
PHILOSTRATE: There is a brief° how many sports are
    ripe.
Make choice of which your Highness will see first.
                               [*Giving a paper.*]
THESEUS [*reads*]: "The battle with the Centaurs,° to be
    sung
45   By an Athenian eunuch to the harp."
We'll none of that. That have I told my love,
In glory of my kinsman° Hercules.

[*Reads.*] "The riot of the tipsy Bacchanals,
Tearing the Thracian singer in their rage."°
That is an old device; and it was play'd   50
When I from Thebes came last a conqueror.
[*Reads.*] "The thrice three Muses mourning for the
    death
Of Learning, late deceas'd in beggary."°
That is some satire, keen and critical,
Not sorting with° a nuptial ceremony.   55
[*Reads.*] "A tedious brief scene of young Pyramus
And his love Thisby; very tragical mirth."
Merry and tragical? Tedious and brief?
That is, hot ice and wondrous strange° snow.
How shall we find the concord of this discord?   60
PHILOSTRATE: A play there is, my lord, some ten words
    long,
Which is as brief as I have known a play;
But by ten words, my lord, it is too long,
Which makes it tedious. For in all the play
There is not one word apt, one player fitted.   65
And tragical, my noble lord, it is,
For Pyramus therein doth kill himself.
Which, when I saw rehears'd, I must confess,
Made mine eyes water, but more merry tears
The passion of loud laughter never shed.   70
THESEUS: What are they that do play it?
PHILOSTRATE: Hard-handed men that work in Athens
    here,
Which never labor'd in their minds till now,
And now have toil'd° their unbreathed° memories
With this same play, against° your nuptial.   75
THESEUS: And we will hear it.
PHILOSTRATE: No, my noble lord,
It is not for you. I have heard it over,
And it is nothing, nothing in the world;
Unless you can find sport in their intents,
Extremely stretch'd° and conn'd° with cruel pain,   80
To do you service.
THESEUS: I will hear that play;
For never anything can be amiss'
When simpleness and duty tender it.
Go, bring them in; and take your places, ladies.

           [*Philostrate goes to summon the players.*]

HIPPOLYTA: I love not to see wretchedness o'ercharg'd°   85
And duty in his service° perishing.
THESEUS: Why, gentle sweet, you shall see no such thing.

---

20. **bringer:** Source.   **21. fear:** Object of fear.   **25. More . . . images:** Testifies to something more substantial than mere imaginings.   **26. constancy:** Certainty.   **27. howsoever:** In any case.   **admirable:** A source of wonder.   **39. abridgement:** Pastime (to abridge or shorten the evening).   **42. brief:** Short written statement, list.   **44. "battle . . . Centaurs":** Probably refers to the battle of the Centaurs and the Lapithae, when the Centaurs attempted to carry off Hippodamia, bride of Theseus's friend Pirothous.   **47. kinsman:** Plutarch's *Life of Theseus* states that Hercules and Theseus were near-kinsmen. Theseus is referring to a version of the battle of the Centaurs in which Hercules was said to be present.

48–49. "The riot . . . rage": This was the story of the death of Orpheus, as told in *Metamorphoses*.   **52–53. "The thrice . . . beggary":** Possibly an allusion to Spenser's *Teares of the Muses* (1591), though "satires" deploring the neglect of learning and the creative arts were common-place.   **55. sorting with:** Befitting.   **59. strange:** Seemingly an error for some adjective that would contrast with *snow*, just as *hot* contrasts with *ice*.   **74. toil'd:** Taxed.   **unbreathed:** Unexercised.   **75. against:** In preparation for.   **80. stretch'd:** Strained.   **conn'd:** Memorized.   **85. wretchedness o'ercharg'd:** Incompetence overburdened.   **86. his service:** Its attempt to serve.

HIPPOLYTA: He says they can do nothing in this kind.°
THESEUS: The kinder we, to give them thanks for
    nothing.
90   Our sport shall be to take what they mistake;
      And what poor duty cannot do, noble respect
      Takes it in might, not merit.°
      Where I have come, great clerks° have purposed
      To greet me with premeditated welcomes;
95   Where I have seen them shiver and look pale,
      Make periods in the midst of sentences,
      Throttle their practic'd accent° in their fears,
      And in conclusion dumbly have broke off,
      Not paying me a welcome. Trust me, sweet,
100   Out of this silence yet I pick'd a welcome;
      And in the modesty of fearful duty
      I read as much as from the rattling tongue
      Of saucy and audacious eloquence.
      Love, therefore, and tongue-tied simplicity
105   In least° speak most, to my capacity.°

[*Philostrate returns.*]

PHILOSTRATE: So please your Grace, the Prologue° is
    address'd.°
THESEUS: Let him approach.   [*Flourish of trumpets.*]

(*Enter the Prologue* [*Quince*].)

PROLOGUE: If we offend, it is with our good will.
    That you should think, we come not to offend,
110   But with good will. To show our simple skill,
      That is the true beginning of our end.
      Consider, then, we come but in despite.
      We do not come, as minding° to content you,
      Our true intent is. All for your delight
115   We are not here. That you should here repent you,
      The actors are at hand; and, by their show,
      You shall know all that you are like to know.
THESEUS: This fellow doth not stand upon points.°
LYSANDER: He hath rid his prologue like a rough° colt;
120   he knows not the stop.° A good moral, my lord: it is
      not enough to speak, but to speak true.
HIPPOLYTA: Indeed he hath play'd on his prologue like
    a child on a recorder;° a sound, but not in gov-
    ernment.°
125 THESEUS: His speech was like a tangled chain, nothing°
      impair'd, but all disorder'd. Who is next?

---

88. **kind:** Kind of thing.   92. **Takes . . . merit:** Values it for the
effort made rather than for the excellence achieved.
93. **clerks:** Learned men.   97. **practic'd accent:** Rehearsed
speech; or usual way of speaking.   105. **least:** Saying least.
to my capacity: In my judgment and understanding.
106. **Prologue:** Speaker of the prologue.   **address'd:** Ready.
113. **minding:** Intending.   118. **stand upon points:** (1) Heed
niceties or small points, (2) pay attention to punctuation in his
reading. (The humor of Quince's speech is in the blunders of its
punctuation.)   119. **rough:** Unbroken.   120. **stop:** (1) The
stopping of a colt by reining it in, (2) punctuation mark.
123. **recorder:** A wind instrument like a flute.   123–24. **government:** Control.   125. **nothing:** Not at all.

(*Enter Pyramus and Thisby, and Wall, and Moonshine,
and Lion.*)

PROLOGUE: Gentles, perchance you wonder at this
    show;
    But wonder on, till truth make all things plain.
    This man is Pyramus, if you would know;
    This beauteous lady Thisby is certain.   130
    This man, with lime and rough-cast, doth present
    Wall, that vile Wall which did these lovers sunder;
    And through Wall's chink, poor souls, they are
        content
    To whisper. At the which let no man wonder.
    This man, with lantern, dog, and bush of thorn,   135
    Presenteth Moonshine; for, if you will know,
    By moonshine did these lovers think no scorn°
    To meet at Ninus' tomb, there, there to woo.
    This grisly beast, which Lion hight° by name,
    The trusty Thisby, coming first by night,   140
    Did scare away, or rather did affright;
    And, as she fled, her mantle she did fall,°
    Which Lion vile with bloody mouth did stain.
    Anon comes Pyramus, sweet youth and tall,°
    And finds his trusty Thisby's mantle slain;   145
    Whereat, with blade, with bloody blameful blade,
    He bravely broach'd° his boiling bloody breast.
    And Thisby, tarrying in mulberry shade,
    His dagger drew, and died. For all the rest,
    Let Lion, Moonshine, Wall, and lovers twain   150
    At large° discourse, while here they do remain.

            (*Exeunt Lion, Thisby, and Moonshine.*)

THESEUS: I wonder if the lion be to speak.
DEMETRIUS: No wonder, my lord. One lion may, when
    many asses do.
WALL: In this same interlude it doth befall   155
    That I, one Snout by name, present a wall;
    And such a wall, as I would have you think,
    That had in it a crannied hole or chink,
    Through which the lovers, Pyramus and Thisby,
    Did whisper often very secretly.   160
    This loam, this rough-cast, and this stone doth show
    That I am that same wall; the truth is so.
    And this the cranny is, right and sinister,°
    Through which the fearful lovers are to whisper.
THESEUS: Would you desire lime and hair to speak better?   165
DEMETRIUS: It is the wittiest partition° that ever I heard
    discourse, my lord.

[*Pyramus comes forward.*]

THESEUS: Pyramus draws near the wall. Silence!

---

137. **think no scorn:** Think it no disgraceful matter.
139. **hight:** Is called.   142. **fall:** Let fall.   144. **tall:** Courageous.   147. **broach'd:** Stabbed.   151. **At large:** In full, at
length.   163. **right and sinister:** The right side of it and the
left (sinister); or running from right to left, horizontally.
166. **partition:** (1) Wall, (2) section of a learned treatise or
oration.

PYRAMUS: O grim-look'd° night! O night with hue so
　　black!
170　O night, which ever art when day is not!
　　O night, O night! Alack, alack, alack,
　　I fear my Thisby's promise is forgot.
　　And thou, O wall, O sweet, O lovely wall,
　　That stand'st between her father's ground and mine,
175　Thou wall, O wall, O sweet and lovely wall,
　　Show me thy chink, to blink through with mine eyne!

　　　　　　　　　　　　　[*Wall holds up his fingers.*]

　　Thanks, courteous wall. Jove shield thee well for
　　　this!
　　But what see I? No Thisby do I see.
　　O wicked wall, through whom I see no bliss!
180　Curs'd be thy stones for thus deceiving me!
THESEUS: The wall, methinks, being sensible,° should
　　curse again.
PYRAMUS: No, in truth, sir, he should not. "Deceiving
　　me" is Thisby's cue: she is to enter now, and I am to
185　spy her through the wall. You shall see, it will fall pat
　　as I told you. Yonder she comes.

　　　(*Enter Thisby.*)

THISBY: O wall, full often hast thou heard my moans,
　　For parting my fair Pyramus and me.
　　My cherry lips have often kiss'd thy stones,
190　Thy stones with lime and hair knit up in thee.
PYRAMUS: I see a voice. Now will I to the chink,
　　To spy an° I can hear my Thisby's face.
　　Thisby!
THISBY: My love! Thou art my love, I think.
PYRAMUS: Think what thou wilt, I am thy lover's
195　　grace;°
　　And, like Limander° am I trusty still.
THISBY: And I like Helen,° till the Fates me kill.
PYRAMUS: Not Shafalus° to Procrus° was so true.
THISBY: As Shafalus to Procrus, I to you.
200 PYRAMUS: O, kiss me through the hole of this vile wall!
THISBY: I kiss the wall's hole, not your lips at all.
PYRAMUS: Wilt thou at Ninny's tomb meet me
　　straightway?
THISBY: 'Tide° life, 'tide death, I come without delay.

　　　　　　　　[*Exeunt Pyramus and Thisby.*]

WALL: Thus have I, Wall, my part discharged so;
205　And, being done, thus Wall away doth go.　　[*Exit.*]
THESEUS: Now is the mural down between the two
　　neighbors.
DEMETRIUS: No remedy, my lord, when walls are so
　　willful to hear° without warning.°
210 HIPPOLYTA: This is the silliest stuff that ever I heard.

---

169. grim-look'd: Grim-looking.　**181. sensible:** Capable of feeling.　**192. an:** If.　**195. lover's grace:** Gracious lover.　**196. Li-
mander:** Blunder for *Leander*.　**197. Helen:** Blunder for *Hero*.
198. Shafalus, Procrus: Blunders for *Cephalus* and *Procris*, also
famous lovers.　**203. 'Tide:** Betide, come.　**209. to hear:** As to
hear.　**without warning:** Without warning the parents.

THESEUS: The best in this kind° are but shadows;° and
　　the worst are no worse, if imagination amend them.
HIPPOLYTA: It must be your imagination then, and not
　　theirs.
THESEUS: If we imagine no worse of them than they of　215
　　themselves, they may pass for excellent men. Here
　　come two noble beasts in, a man and a lion.

　　　(*Enter Lion and Moonshine.*)

LION: You, ladies, you, whose gentle hearts do fear
　　The smallest monstrous mouse that creeps on floor,
　　May now perchance both quake and tremble here,　220
　　When lion rough in wildest rage doth roar.
　　Then know that I, as Snug the joiner, am
　　A lion fell,° nor else no lion's dam;
　　For, if I should as lion come in strife
　　Into this place, 'twere pity on my life.　　　225
THESEUS: A very gentle beast, and of a good conscience.
DEMETRIUS: The very best at a beast, my lord, that e'er I
　　saw.
LYSANDER: This lion is a very fox for his valor.°
THESEUS: True; and a goose for his discretion.°　　230
DEMETRIUS: Not so, my lord; for his valor cannot carry
　　his discretion; and the fox carries the goose.
THESEUS: His discretion, I am sure, cannot carry his
　　valor, for the goose carries not the fox. It is well.
　　Leave it to his discretion, and let us listen to the　235
　　moon.
MOON: This lanthorn° doth the horned moon present —
DEMETRIUS: He should have worn the horns on his
　　head.°
THESEUS: He is no crescent, and his horns are invisible　240
　　within the circumference.
MOON: This lanthorn doth the horned moon present;
　　Myself the man i' th' moon do seem to be.
THESEUS: This is the greatest error of all the rest. The
　　man should be put into the lanthorn. How is it else　245
　　the man i' th' moon?
DEMETRIUS: He dares not come there for the° candle;
　　for, you see, it is already in snuff.°
HIPPOLYTA: I am aweary of this moon. Would he would
　　change!　　　　　　　　　　　　　　　250
THESEUS: It appears, by his small light of discretion, that
　　he is in the wane; but yet, in courtesy, in all reason,
　　we must stay the time.
LYSANDER: Proceed, Moon.

---

211. in this kind: Of this sort.　**shadows:** Likenesses, representations.　**223. lion fell:** Fierce lion (with a play on the idea of
lion skin).　**229. is . . . valor:** His valor consists of craftiness
and discretion.　**230. goose . . . discretion:** As discreet as a
goose, that is, more foolish than discreet.　**237. lanthorn:** This
original spelling may suggest a play on the *horn* of which
lanterns were made and also on a cuckold's horns; but the
spelling *lanthorn* is not used consistently for comic effect in this
play or elsewhere. In V, I, 135, for example, the word is *lantern*
in the original.　**238–39. on his head:** As a sign of cuckoldry.
247. for the: Because of the.　**248. in snuff:** (1) Offended,
(2) in need of snuffing.

255   MOON: All that I have to say is to tell you that the lanthorn is the moon, I, the man in the moon, this thorn-
bush my thorn-bush, and this dog my dog.

DEMETRIUS: Why, all these should be in the lanthorn;
for all these are in the moon. But silence! Here comes

260   Thisby.

(Enter Thisby.)

THISBY: This is old Ninny's tomb. Where is my love?
LION [*roaring*]: Oh —   [*Thisby runs off.*]
DEMETRIUS: Well roar'd, Lion.
THESEUS: Well run, Thisby.

265   HIPPOLYTA: Well shone, Moon. Truly, the moon shines
with a good grace.

        [*The Lion shakes Thisby's mantle, and exit.*]

THESEUS: Well mous'd,° Lion.
DEMETRIUS: And then came Pyramus.
LYSANDER: And so the lion vanish'd.

(Enter Pyramus.)

PYRAMUS: Sweet Moon, I thank thee for thy sunny
270   beams;
I thank thee, Moon, for shining now so bright;
For, by thy gracious, golden, glittering gleams,
I trust to take of truest Thisby sight.
    But stay, O spite!
275   But mark, poor knight,
What dreadful dole° is here!
    Eyes, do you see?
    How can it be?
O dainty duck! O dear!
280   Thy mantle good,
    What, stain'd with blood!
Approach, ye Furies fell!°
    O Fates, come, come,
    Cut thread and thrum;°
285   Quail,° crush, conclude, and quell!°
THESEUS: This passion, and the death of a dear friend,
would go near to make a man look sad.°
HIPPOLYTA: Beshrew my heart, but I pity the man.
PYRAMUS: O wherefore, Nature, didst thou lions frame?
290   Since lion vile hath here deflow'r'd my dear,
Which is — no, no — which was the fairest dame
That liv'd, that lov'd, that lik'd, that look'd with
      cheer.°
    Come, tears, confound,
    Out, sword, and wound
295   The pap of Pyramus;
    Ay, that left pap,
    Where heart doth hop.   [*Stabs himself.*]
Thus die I, thus, thus, thus.

---

267. **mous'd:** Shaken.   276. **dole:** Grievous event.   282. **fell:** Fierce.   284. **thread and thrum:** The warp in weaving and the loose end of the warp.   285. **Quail:** Overpower.   **quell:** Kill, destroy.   286–87. **This . . . sad:** If one had other reason to grieve, one might be sad, but not from this absurd portrayal of passion.   292. **cheer:** Countenance.

    Now am I dead,
    Now am I fled;   300
My soul is in the sky.
    Tongue, lose thy light;
    Moon, take thy flight.   [*Exit Moonshine.*]
Now die, die, die, die, die.   [*Dies.*]
DEMETRIUS: No die, but an ace,° for him; for he is but   305
one.°
LYSANDER: Less than an ace, man; for he is dead, he is
nothing.
THESEUS: With the help of a surgeon he might yet
recover, and yet prove an ass.°   310
HIPPOLYTA: How chance Moonshine is gone before
Thisby comes back and finds her lover?
THESEUS: She will find him by starlight. Here she comes;
and her passion ends the play.

[*Enter Thisby.*]

HIPPOLYTA: Methinks she should not use a long one for   315
such a Pyramus. I hope she will be brief.
DEMETRIUS: A mote will turn the balance, which Pyra-
mus, which° Thisby, is the better: he for a man God
warr'nt us; she for a woman, God bless us.
LYSANDER: She hath spied him already with those sweet   320
eyes.
DEMETRIUS: And thus she means,° videlicet:°
THISBY: Asleep, my love?
    What, dead, my dove?
    O Pyramus, arise!   325
    Speak, speak. Quite dumb?
Dead, dead? A tomb
Must cover thy sweet eyes.
    These lily lips,
    This cherry nose,   330
These yellow cowslip cheeks,
    Are gone, are gone!
    Lovers, make moan.
His eyes were green as leeks.
    O Sisters Three,°   335
    Come, come to me,
With hands as pale as milk;
    Lay them in gore,
    Since you have shore°
With shears his thread of silk.   340
    Tongue, not a word.
    Come, trusty sword,
Come, blade, my breast imbrue!°   [*Stabs herself.*]
    And farewell, friends.
    Thus Thisby ends.   345
Adieu, adieu, adieu.   [*Dies.*]

---

305. **ace:** The side of the die featuring the single pip, or spot. (The pun is on *die* as a singular of *dice*; Bottom's performance is not worth a whole *die* but rather one single face of it, one small portion.)   306. **one:** (1) An individual person, (2) unique.   310. **ass:** With a pun on *ace*.   317–18. **which . . . which:** Whether . . . or.   322. **means:** Moans, laments.   **videlicet:** To wit.   335. **Sisters Three:** The Fates.   339. **shore:** Shorn.   343. **imbrue:** Stain with blood.

THESEUS: Moonshine and Lion are left to bury the dead.
DEMETRIUS: Ay, and Wall too.
BOTTOM [*starting up*]: No, I assure you; the wall is
350   down that parted their fathers. Will it please you to
see the epilogue, or to hear a Bergomask dance° between two of our company?
THESEUS: No epilogue, I pray you; for your play needs
no excuse. Never excuse; for when the players are all
355   dead, there need none to be blam'd. Marry, if he that
writ it had play'd Pyramus and hang'd himself in
Thisby's garter, it would have been a fine tragedy;
and so it is, truly, and very notably discharg'd. But,
come, your Bergomask. Let your epilogue alone.
                                               [*A dance.*]
360   The iron tongue of midnight hath told° twelve.
Lovers, to bed; 'tis almost fairy time.
I fear we shall outsleep the coming morn
As much as we this night have overwatch'd.°
This palpable-gross° play hath well beguil'd
365   The heavy° gait of night. Sweet friends, to bed.
A fortnight hold we this solemnity,
In nightly revels and new jollity.   (*Exeunt.*)

(*Enter Puck*)

PUCK: Now the hungry lion roars,
        And the wolf behowls the moon;
370   Whilst the heavy ploughman snores,
        All with weary task fordone.°
Now the wasted brands° do glow,
        Whilst the screech-owl, screeching loud,
Puts the wretch that lies in woe
375   In remembrance of a shroud.
Now it is the time of night
        That the graves, all gaping wide,
Every one lets forth his sprite,°
        In the churchway paths to glide.
380   And we fairies, that do run
        By the triple Hecate's° team
From the presence of the sun,
        Following darkness like a dream,
Now are frolic.° Not a mouse
385   Shall disturb this hallowed house.
I am sent with broom before,
To sweep the dust behind° the door.

(*Enter [Oberon and Titania,] King and Queen of Fairies,
with all their train.*)

OBERON: Through the house give glimmering light,
        By the dead and drowsy fire;
Every elf and fairy sprite   390
        Hop as light as bird from brier;
And this ditty, after me,
Sing, and dance it trippingly.
TITANIA: First, rehearse your song by rote,
To each word a warbling note,   395
Hand in hand, with fairy grace,
Will we sing, and bless this place.

                                           [*Song and dance.*]

OBERON: Now, until the break of day,
Through this house each fairy stray.
To the best bride-bed will we,   400
Which by us shall blessed be;
And the issue there create°
Ever shall be fortunate.
So shall all the couples three
Ever true in loving be;   405
And the blots of Nature's hand
Shall not in their issue stand;
Never mole, hare lip, nor scar,
Nor mark prodigious,° such as are
Despised in nativity,   410
Shall upon their children be.
With this field-dew consecrate,°
Every fairy take his gait,°
And each several° chamber bless,
Through this palace, with sweet peace;   415
And the owner of it blest
Ever shall in safety rest.
Trip away; make no stay;
Meet me all by break of day.

                    (*Exeunt [Oberon, Titania, and train].*)

PUCK: If we shadows have offended,   420
Think but this, and all is mended,
That you have but slumb'red here°
While these visions did appear.
And this weak and idle theme,
No more yielding but° a dream,   425
Gentles, do not reprehend.
If you pardon, we will mend.
And, as I am an honest Puck,
If we have unearned luck
Now to scape the serpent's tongue,°   430
We will make amends ere long;
Else the Puck a liar call.
So, good night unto you all.
Give me your hands,° if we be friends,
And Robin shall restore amends.   [*Exit.*]   435

---

351. Bergomask dance: A rustic dance named for Bergamo, a province in the state of Venice. **360. told:** Counted, struck ("tolled"). **363. overwatch'd:** Stayed up too late. **364. palpable-gross:** Obviously crude. **365. heavy:** Drowsy, dull. **371. fordone:** Exhausted. **372. wasted brands:** Burned-out logs. **378. Every . . . sprite:** Every grave lets forth its ghost. **381. triple Hecate's:** Hecate ruled in three capacities: as Luna or Cynthia in heaven, as Diana on earth, and as Proserpina in hell. **384. frolic:** Merry. **387. behind:** From behind. (Robin Goodfellow was a household spirit who helped good housemaids and punished lazy ones.)

402. create: Created. **409. prodigious:** Monstrous, unnatural. **412. consecrate:** Consecrated. **413. take his gait:** Go his way. **414. several:** Separate. **422. That . . . here:** That it is a "midsummer night's dream." **425. No . . . but:** Yielding no more than. **430. serpent's tongue:** Hissing. **434. Give . . . hands:** Applaud.

COMMENTARIES

Some of the finest critical commentary ever written has been devoted to the works of Shakespeare. From the seventeenth century to the present, critics have taken a considerable interest in the nuances of his work.

In the commentary on *A Midsummer Night's Dream* we find a wide range of responses to the work. Enid Welsford's comments are in a special context, that of the court masque, the rich entertainments that were designed to please royalty. As Welsford explains, *A Midsummer Night's Dream* has many elements of the masque.

In a more specifically feminist observation, critic Linda Bamber shows how assumptions regarding power in a male-female relationship affect our interpretation of the play.

Peter Brook, one of the most notable contemporary directors of Shakespeare and the producer of a landmark production of *A Midsummer Night's Dream* (1970), gives us a director's view of the play. He centers the discussion on love, which in many forms is at the heart of the play. See the review of his production on page 319.

Clive Barnes's review gives us a clear sense of the visual and kinetic details that made Peter Brook's *A Midsummer Night's Dream* one of the most memorable modern stagings of Shakespeare. The use of juggling, acrobats, and trapezes energized the production and underscored the youthful vitality of the characters.

Contemporary reviews of Shakespeare's plays take a very different approach to the plays than do critical studies. The reviewers are concerned first with the actors and their interpretation of the drama. They are then concerned with the director's insights and sense of pacing. In addition to focusing on the title roles, critics also aim to communicate a sense of the dynamics of the production as a whole. Peter Brook's production of *A Midsummer Night's Dream,* for example, was perhaps most startling for its all-white set and backdrop, and for the marvelous scenes staged with principal actors lolling on simple white swings. Critics can give us insight into the staging of the work and the ways in which the staging imparts meaning to the drama.

Enid Welsford (1892–1981)
MASQUE ELEMENTS IN *A MIDSUMMER NIGHT'S DREAM*

1927

Enid Welsford examines A Midsummer Night's Dream *from the point of view of its masquelike qualities. Shakespeare's* The Tempest *includes a masque and has certain scenic qualities that link it to that tradition, and so does* A Midsummer Night's Dream. *Its fantastic costumes and remarkable fairy population could be*

315

considered part of the antimasque, a parody of the masque itself. The antimasque often involved masquers dressed in grotesque animal costumes, making a loud racket, and dancing in erratic and fantastic gestures. Meant originally as a contrast to the magnificence of the masque, the antimasque became a favorite of the less conservative masquers.

The only character study in *A Midsummer Night's Dream* is to be found in the portrayal of Bottom, Theseus, and perhaps Hippolyta. Even in drawing these characters Shakespeare was evidently influenced by the memory of pageants, complimentary speeches, and entertainments addressed by townspeople and humble folk to the Queen or to the nobility. A glance through Nichols's *Public Progresses* shows what innumerable lengthy speeches, what innumerable disguisings and shows, Elizabeth was obliged to bear with gracious demeanor. Her experiences were similar to those of Theseus:

> Where I have come, great clerks have purposed
> To greet me with premeditated welcomes;
> Where I have seen them shiver and look pale,
> Make periods in the midst of sentences,
> Throttle their practic'd accent in their fears,
> And, in conclusion, dumbly have broke off,
> Not paying me a welcome.

One Sunday afternoon, at Kenilworth Castle, Elizabeth and her court whiled away the time by watching the countrypeople at a Brideale and Morris Dance. Their amused kindly tolerance is just that of Theseus and the lovers toward the Athenian workmen. So that even in the most solid and dramatic parts of his play Shakespeare is only giving an idealized version of courtly and country revels and of the people that played a part in them.

In *A Midsummer Night's Dream* Bottom and his companions serve the same purpose as the antimasque in the courtly revels. It is true that Shakespeare's play was written before Ben Jonson had elaborated and defined the antimasque, but from the first grotesque dances were popular, and the principle of contrast was always latent in the masque. There is, however, a great difference between Jonson's and Shakespeare's management of foil and relief. In the antimasque the transition is sudden and the contrast complete, a method of composition effective enough in spectacle and ballet. But in a play, as Shakespeare well knew, the greatest beauty is gained through contrast when the difference is not obvious and striking, but rises out of a deep though unobtrusive resemblance. This could not be better illustrated than by the picture of Titania winding the ass-headed Bottom in her arms. Why is it that this is a pleasing picture, why is it that the rude mechanicals do not, as a matter of fact, disturb or sully Titania's "close and consecrated bower"? Malvolio° in Bottom's place would be repellent, yet Malvolio, regarded superficially, is less violently contrasted to the Fairy Queen than is Nick Bottom. Bottom with his ass's head is grotesquely hideous, and in ordinary life he is crude, raw, and very stupid. We have no reason to suppose that Malvolio was anything but a well-set-up, proper-looking man, spruce, well dressed, the perfect family butler. His mentality too is of a distinctly higher order than Bottom's. He fills a responsible position with

Malvolio: A character in Shakespeare's *Twelfth Night.*

credit, he follows a reasoned line of conduct, he thinks nobly of the soul. Two things alone he lacks (and that is why no self-respecting fey could ever kiss him) — humor and imagination. Malvolio is, therefore, the only character who cannot be included in the final harmony of *Twelfth Night*. Bottom and his fellows did perhaps lack humor (though the interview with the fairies suggests that Bottom had a smack of it), but in its place they possessed unreason. Imagination they did have, of the most simple, primal, childlike kind. It is their artistic ambition that lifts them out of the humdrum world and turns them into Midsummer Dreamers, and we have seen how cunningly Shakespeare extracts from their very stupidity romance and moonshine. But, indeed, grotesqueness and stupidity (of a certain kind) have a kinship with beauty. For these qualities usually imply a measure of spiritual freedom, they lead to at least a temporary relief from the tyranny of reason and from the pressure of the external world. In *A Midsummer Night's Dream* the dominance of the Lord of Misrule is not marked by coarse parody, but by the partial repeal of the laws of cause and effect. By delicate beauty, gentle mockery, and simple romantic foolishness our freedom is gained.

Linda Bamber (b. 1945)
ON *A MIDSUMMER NIGHT'S DREAM*   *1982*

The question of masculine and feminine is central to A Midsummer Night's Dream. *Much of the action is precipitated by a power struggle between Titania and Oberon, and the young Athenians who rush off to the woods are there because a father has decided to oppose the will of his daughter regarding her marriage. Linda Bamber is a feminist critic interested in examining the centers of power in the play, particularly with an eye for what we accept as the natural order of relationships. She shows that the action of the comedy is essentially tied into questions of gender, which begin to become questions of genre.*

The best example [in Shakespeare] of the relationship between male dominance and the status quo comes in *A Midsummer Night's Dream,* which begins with a rebellion of the feminine against the power of masculine authority. Hermia refuses the man both Aegeus and Theseus order her to marry; her refusal sends us off into the forest, beyond the power of the father and the masculine state. Once in the forest, of course, we find the social situation metaphorically repeated in this world of imagination and nature. The fairy king, Oberon, rules the forest. His rule, too, is troubled by the rebellion of the feminine. Titania has refused to give him her page, the child of a human friend who died in childbirth. But by the end of the story Titania is conquered, the child relinquished, and order restored. Even here the comic upheavals, whether we see them as May games or bad dreams, are associated with an uprising of women. David P. Young has pointed out how firmly this play connects order with masculine dominance and the disruption of order with the rebellion of the feminine:

> It is appropriate that Theseus, as representative of daylight and right reason, should have subdued his bride-to-be to the rule of his masculine will. That is the natural order of

things. It is equally appropriate that Oberon, as king of darkness and fantasy, should have lost control of his wife, and that the corresponding natural disorder described by Titania should ensue.[1]

The natural order, the status quo, is for men to rule women. When they fail to do so, we have the exceptional situation, the festive, disruptive, disorderly moment of comedy.

A Midsummer Night's Dream is actually an anomaly among the festive comedies. It is unusual for the forces of the green world to be directed, as they are here, by a masculine figure. Because the green world here is a partial reproduction of the social world, the feminine is reduced to a kind of first cause of the action while a masculine power directs it. In the other festive comedies the feminine Other presides. She does not *command* the forces of the alternative world, as Oberon does, but since she acts in harmony with these forces her will and desire often prevail.

Where are we to bestow our sympathies? On the forces that make for the disruption of the status quo and therefore for the plot? Or on the force that asserts itself against the disruption and reestablishes a workable social order? Of course we cannot choose. We can only say that in comedy we owe our holiday to such forces as the tendency of the feminine to rebel, whereas to the successful reassertion of masculine power we owe our everyday order. Shakespearean comedy endorses both sides. Holiday is, of course, the subject and the analogue of each play; but the plays always end in a return to everyday life. The optimistic reading of Shakespearean comedy says that everyday life is clarified and enriched by our holiday from it; according to the pessimistic reading the temporary subversion of the social order has revealed how much that order excludes, how high a price we pay for it. But whether our return to everyday life is a comfortable one or not, the return itself is the inevitable conclusion to the journey out.

Does this make the comedies sexist? Is the association of women with the disruption of the social order an unconscious and insulting projection? It seems to begin as such; but as the form of Shakespearean comedy develops, the Otherness of the feminine develops into as powerful a force in the drama as the social authority of the masculine Self. For the feminine in Shakespearean comedy begins as a shrew but develops into a comic heroine. The shrew's rebellion directly challenges masculine authority, whereas the comic heroine merely presides over areas of experience to which masculine authority is irrelevant. But the shrew is essentially powerless against the social system, whereas the comic heroine is in alliance with forces that can never be finally overcome. The shrew is defeated by the superior strength, physical and social, of a man, or by women who support the status quo. She provokes a battle of the sexes, and the outcome of this battle, from Shakespeare's point of view, is inevitable. The comic heroine, on the other hand, does not fight the system but merely surfaces, again and again, when and where the social system is temporarily subverted. The comic heroine does not actively resist the social and political hegemony° of the men, but as an irresistible version of the Other she successfully competes for our favor with the (masculine) representatives of the social Self. The development of the feminine from the shrew to the comic heroine indicates a certain consciousness on the author's part of sexual politics; and it indicates

---

[1]David P. Young, *Something of Great Constancy* (New Haven, CT: Yale UP, 1966), 183.
hegemony: Overriding authority.

a desire, at least, to create conditions of sexual equality within the drama even while reflecting the unequal conditions of men and women in the society at large.

Peter Brook (b. 1925)
THE PLAY IS THE MESSAGE . . .   *1987*

When a distinguished director becomes a critic, we have the opportunity to understand a play from the point of view of one who has to make the play work in front of an audience. Brook's production of A Midsummer Night's Dream *was a sensation in England and the United States in 1970. It featured absolutely white lighting, white sets, and actors in swings. Brook had analyzed the play in such a fashion that he saw love as its constant concern, "constantly repeated." He concluded that to present the play, the players must embody the concept of love. They must bring to the play their own realization of the play's themes — even to the point of seeing theater anew, like the mechanicals "who are touching an extraordinary world with the tips of their fingers, a world which transcends their daily experience and which fills them with wonder"— the effect of the love they bring to their task.*

People have often asked me: "What is the theme of *A Midsummer Night's Dream?*" There is only one answer to that question, the same as one would give regarding a cup. The quality of a cup is its cupness. I say this by way of introduction, to show that if I lay so much stress on the dangers involved in trying to define the themes of the *Dream* it is because too many productions, too many attempts at visual interpretation are based on preconceived ideas, as if these had to be illustrated in some way. In my opinion we should first of all try to rediscover the play as a living thing; then we shall be able to analyze our discoveries. Once I have finished working on the play, I can begin to produce my theories. It was fortunate that I did not attempt to do so earlier because the play would not have yielded up its secrets.

At the center of the *Dream*, constantly repeated, we find the word "love." Everything comes back to this, even the structure of the play, even its music. The quality the play demands from its performers is to build up an atmosphere of love during the performance itself, so that this abstract idea — for the word "love" is in itself a complete abstraction — may become palpable. The play presents us with forms of love which become less and less blurred as it goes on. "Love" soon begins to resound like a musical scale and little by little we are introduced to its various modes and tones.

Love is, of course, a theme which touches all men. No one, not even the most hardened, the coldest, or the most despairing, is insensitive to it, even if he does not know what love is. Either his practical experience confirms its existence or he suffers from its absence, which is another way of recognizing that it exists. At every moment the play touches something which concerns everyone.

As this is theater, there must be conflicts, so this play about love is also a play about the opposite of love, love and its opposite force. We are brought to realize that love, liberty, and imagination are closely connected. Right at the beginning of the play, for example, the father in a long speech tries to obstruct his daughter's love and we are surprised that such a character, apparently a secondary role, should have so long a speech — until we discover the real importance of his words. What he says not only reflects a generation gap (a father opposing his daughter's love because he had intended her for someone else), it also explains the reasons for his feeling of suspicion toward the young man whom his daughter loves. He describes him as an individual prone to fantasy, led by his imagination — an unpardonable weakness in the father's eyes.

From this starting point we see, as in any of Shakespeare's plays, a confrontation. Here it is between love and its opposing qualities, between fantasy and solid common sense — caught in an endless series of mirrors. As usual, Shakespeare confuses the issue. If we asked someone's opinion on the father's point of view, he might say, for example, that "The father is in the wrong because he is against freedom of the imagination," a very widespread attitude today.

In this way, for most present-day audiences, the girl's father comes over as the classical father figure who misunderstands young people and their flights of fancy. But later on, we discover surprisingly that he is right, because the imaginative world in which this lover lives causes him to behave in a quite disgusting way toward the very same daughter: as soon as a drop of liquid falls into his eyes, acting as a drug which liberates natural tendencies, he not only jilts her but his love is transformed into violent hate. He uses words which might well be borrowed from *Measure for Measure,* denouncing the girl with the kind of vehemence that, in the Middle Ages, led people to burn one another at the stake. Yet at the end of the play we are once more in agreement with the Duke, who rejects the father in the name of love. The young man has now been transformed.

So we observe this game of love in a psychological and metaphysical context; we hear Titania's assertion that the opposition between herself and Oberon is fundamental, primordial. But Oberon's acts deny this, for he perceives that within their opposition a reconciliation is possible.

The play covers an extraordinarily broad range of universal forces and feelings in a mythical world, which suddenly changes, in the last part, into high society. We find ourselves back in the very real palace: and the same Shakespeare who, a few pages earlier, offered us a scene of pure fantasy between Titania and Oberon, where it would be absurd to ask prosaic questions like "Where does Oberon live?" or "When describing a queen like Titania did Shakespeare wish to express political ideas?," now takes us into a precise social environment. We are present at the meeting point of two worlds, that of the workmen and the court, the world of wealth and elegance, and alleged sensitivity, the world of people who have had the leisure to cultivate fine sentiments and are now shown as insensitive and even disgusting in their superior attitude toward the poor.

At the beginning of the court scene we see our former heroes, who have spent the entire play involved in the theme of love, and would no doubt be quite capable of giving academic lectures on the subject, suddenly finding themselves plunged into a context which has apparently nothing to do with love (with their own love, since all their problems have been solved). Now they are in the context of a relationship with each other and with another social class, and they are at a loss. They do not realize that here too scorn eliminates love.

We see how well Shakespeare has situated everything. Athens in the *Dream* resembles our Athens in the sixties: the workmen, as they state in the first scene, are very much afraid of the authorities; if they commit the slightest error they will be

hanged, and there is nothing comical about that. Indeed, they risk hanging as soon
as they shed their anonymity. At the same time they are irresistibly attracted by the
carrot of "sixpence a day" which will enable them to escape poverty. Yet their real
motive is neither glory nor adventure nor money (that is made very clear and
should guide the actors who perform this scene). Those simple men who have only
ever worked with their hands apply to the use of the imagination exactly the same
quality of love which traditionally underlies the relationship between a craftsman
and his tools. That is what gives these scenes both their strength and their comic
quality. These craftsmen make efforts which are grotesque in one sense because
they push awkwardness to its limit, but at another level they set themselves to their
task with such love that the meaning of their clumsy efforts changes before our
eyes.

The spectators can easily decide to adopt the same attitude as the courtiers: to
find all this quite simply ridiculous; to laugh with the complacency of people who
quite confidently mock the efforts of others. Yet the audience is invited to take a
step back: to feel it cannot quite identify with the court, with people who are too
grand and too unkind. Little by little, we come to see that the craftsmen, who
behave with little understanding but who approach their new job with love, are
discovering theater — an imaginary world for them, toward which they instinctively feel great respect. In fact, the "mechanicals" scene is often misinterpreted
because the actors forget to look at theater through innocent eyes, they take a professional actor's views of good or bad acting, and in so doing they diminish the
mystery and the sense of magic felt by these amateurs, who are touching an extraordinary world with the tips of their fingers, a world which transcends their daily
experience and which fills them with wonder.

We see this quite clearly in the part of the boy who plays the girl, Thisby. At first
sight this tough lad is irresistibly absurd, but by degrees, through his love for what
he is doing, we discover what more is involved. In our production, the actor playing the part is a professional plumber, who only took to acting a short while ago.
He well understands what is involved, what it means to feel this nameless and
shapeless kind of love. This boy, himself new to theater, acts the part of someone
who is new to theater. Through his conviction and his identification we discover
that these awkward craftsmen, without knowing it, are teaching us a lesson — or it
might be preferable to say that a lesson is being taught us through them. These
craftsmen are able to make the connection between love for their trade and for a
completely different task, whereas the courtiers are not capable of linking the love
about which they talk so well with their simple role as spectators.

Nonetheless, little by little the courtiers become involved, even touched by the
play within the play, and if one follows very closely what is there in the text we see
that for a moment the situation is completely transformed. One of the central
images of the play is a wall, which, at a given moment, vanishes. Its disappearance,
to which Bottom draws our attention, is caused by an act of love. Shakespeare is
showing us how love can pervade a situation and act as a transforming force.

The *Dream* touches lightly on the fundamental question of the transformations
which may occur if certain things are better understood. It requires us to reflect on
the nature of love. All the landscapes of love are thrown into relief, and we are
given a particular social context through which the other situations can be measured. Through the subtlety of its language the play removes all kinds of barriers. It
is therefore not a play which provokes resistance, or creates disturbance in the

usual sense. Rival politicians could sit side by side at a performance of *A Midsummer Night's Dream* and each leave with the impression that the play fits his point of view perfectly. But if they give it a fine, sensitive attention they cannot fail to perceive a world just like their own, more and more riddled with contradictions and, like their own, waiting for that mysterious force, love, without which harmony will never return.

Clive Barnes (b. 1927)
REVIEW OF *A MIDSUMMER NIGHT'S DREAM*   1970

Clive Barnes's review credits the Peter Brook production of A Midsummer Night's Dream *as a landmark. Audiences in Stratford, London, New York, and elsewhere agreed. Brook (b. 1925) emphasized the dramatic spectacle — the sets, costumes, and action — in such a way as to reveal new depths of emotion. The playfulness of the jugglers, acrobats, and those on the trapezes emphasized the joy and youth of the main characters.*

Once in a while, once in a very rare while, a theatrical production arrives that is going to be talked about as long as there is a theater, a production that, for good or ill, is going to exert a major influence on the contemporary stage. Such a production is Peter Brook's staging of Shakespeare's *A Midsummer Night's Dream*, which the Royal Shakespeare Company introduced here tonight.

It is a magnificent production, the most important work yet of the world's most imaginative and inventive director. If Peter Brook had done nothing else but this "Dream" he would have deserved a place in theater history,

Brook has approached the play with a radiant innocence. He has treated the script as if it had just been written and sent to him through the mail. He has staged it with no reference to the past, no reverence for tradition.

He has stripped the play down, asked exactly what it is about. He has forgotten gossamer fairies, sequined eyelids, gauzy veils, and whole forests of Beerbohm-trees.

He sees the play for what it is — an allegory of sensual love, and a magic playground of lost innocence and hidden fears. Love in Shakespeare comes as suddenly as death, and when Shakespeare's people love they are all but consumed with sexual passion.

Brook's first concern is to enchant us — to reveal this magic playground. He has conceived the production as a box of theatrical miracles. It takes place in a pure-white setting. The stage is walled in on three sides and the floor is also white. Ladders lead up the walls and on the top are scaffolds and rostrums from which actors can look down on the playing area like spectators at a bullfight.

The fairy characters — Oberon, Titania, and Puck — are made into acrobats and jugglers. They swing in on trapezes, they amaze us with juggling tricks, Tarzan-like swings across the stage, all the sad deftness of clowns.

Shakespeare's quartet of mingled lovers, now mod kids humming love songs to loosely strummed guitars, are lost in the Venetian woods. The trees are vast metal coils thrown down from the walls on fishing rods, and moving in on unwary lovers like spiraling metallic tendrils. And in this wood of animal desire the noises are not the friendly warblings of fairyland, but the grunts and groans of some primeval jungle.

Sex and sexuality are vital in the play. Oberon and Titania, even when quarreling, kiss with hasty, hungry passion — no shining moon for them — and the lovers seem to be journeying through some inner landscape of their own desires toward maturity.

The sexual relationships — with the wittiest use of phallic symbolism the stage can have ever seen — is stressed between Titania and her Bottom. Yet the carnality of the piece is seen with affectionate tolerance rather than the bitterness the playwright shows in *Troilus and Cressida,* and this tolerance, even playfulness, suffuses the production.

Brook is a magician and he gives us new eyes. Here, for reasons admirably supported by the text, he has Theseus and Hippolyta (that previously rather dull royal couple whose wedding provides the framework for the play) played by the same actors as play Oberon and Titania. At once the play takes on a new and personal dimension. The fairies take on a new humanity, and these human princelings, once so uninteresting, are now endowed with a different mystery, and the gentle, almost sad note on which the play ends has a feeling of human comprehension and godlike compassion to it. It is most moving.

Two other characters take on dual assignments. Philostrate, that court master of ceremonies for Theseus, is also, naturally enough, Puck, and, rather more puzzlingly, Egeus, the angry father of Hermia, whose opposition to her marriage sets off the action, is also Peter Quince, one of the mechanicals. Presumably the purpose is to bring the play within the play more closely into the main structure, for just as Egeus initiates the real action, so Quince initiates the inner play. But it savors of a literary rather than dramatic device.

Puck is the key figure in this version. Looking like a more than usually perky Picasso clown, he bounces through the action with happy amiability, the model of toleration. John Kane plays him delightfully, performing his tricks with a true circus expertise and acting with unaffected delight.

The Theseus/Oberon and Hippolyta/Titania of Alan Howard and Sara Kestelman are special pleasures, and the mechanicals with the terrible tragedy of *Pyramus and Thisbe* are the best I have ever seen, with David Waller's virile Bottom particularly splendid.

But the star of this dream is Peter Brook himself, with his ideas, his theories, and above all his practices. Of course he is helped — first by the samite-white pleasure palace devised by his Los Angeles–based designer, Sally Jacobs, and the richly evocative music and sound score provided by Richard Peaslee. But Mr. Brook is the genius architect of our most substantial pleasure.

He makes it all so fresh and so much fun. After a riotously funny and bawdy courtship of Titania by Bottom, the two leave the stage to, of all wonderful things, Mendelssohn's Wedding March, and all hell breaks loose, with confetti, paper streamers, and Oberon himself flying in urbane mockery across the stage.

And Brook uses everything to hand — he is defiantly eclectic. It is as though he is challenging the world, by saying that there is no such thing as Shakespearean style. If it suits his purpose he will use a little kathakali, a pop song, sparklers borrowed from a toyshop, dramatic candles borrowed from Grotowski. It is all splendid grist to his splendid mill. Shakespeare can be fun, Shakespeare can be immediate, Shakespeare can most richly live.

HAMLET

Hamlet (1600–1601), Shakespeare's boldest, most profound play, is a landmark in the poet's work. It coincides with the new century and the uncertainties of the last years of the old regime, brought to an end by the death of Queen Elizabeth in 1603. Until the very moment of her death, the succession was in doubt, but at her death she indicated that her cousin James of Scotland would take the throne. The new age was in many ways more complicated, more ambiguous, and more democratic than the old. It was also more dangerous because it was more uncertain.

Hamlet returns to a Denmark and a court that he hardly recognizes, to a mother newly wed to his uncle and in many ways not the woman he remembers, and, finally, to a ghostly father who will not rest until the crimes against him are avenged. Like Marlowe's Faustus, Hamlet was a scholar at the University of Wittenberg, where he presumably had studied theology and therefore had a special knowledge of the world of the spirits. Perhaps he studied medicine and law as well. He gives evidence of knowing literature and having a taste for theater, and he is a ready hand with weapons when necessary.

Hamlet is also a melancholic. To the Elizabethan, *melancholic* did not mean depressed, although Hamlet dresses in black and still mourns for his father, even against the wishes of his uncle. The melancholic, rather, was introspective, thoughtful, perhaps world-weary, and possibly a touch sardonic. Above all things, he was an intellectual, a person of wide-ranging knowledge and intelligence, a reliable commentator with a probing mind.

Hamlet's broad intelligence and the penetrating introspection revealed in his soliloquies, such as his famous "To be, or not to be" meditation on suicide, make him a character with more psychological dimension, more "soul," than many people we know in life. In this sense the play is thoroughly modern; it satisfies our modern need to know the interior lives of characters who engage us onstage. Hamlet's range of feeling, his range of felt and expressed emotion, is impressive to any audience.

Hamlet is a revenge tragedy, a type of play that was especially appealing to the Elizabethans. Thomas Kyd's *The Spanish Tragedy* and John Marston's *Antonio's Revenge* are two examples of successful Elizabethan revenge tragedies. Shakespeare had written an earlier play that could be termed a revenge tragedy, *Titus Andronicus*, in 1594. Below are some characteristics of the revenge tragedy.

The revenge of a relative's murder or rape

The revenge of a father by a son or vice versa

The appearance of a ghost

The hesitancy or delay of the hero

Tricks or devices to achieve revenge

The use of real or pretended insanity

Suicide

Political intrigue in a court

An able, scheming villain who is a ruler above the law

Philosophical soliloquies

Sensational use of horror (murder and gore onstage)

All these elements are present in *Hamlet*. But the play has other important qualities as well. The minor characters are developed in unexpected ways. Ophelia, the innocent, loving woman, becomes a touching figure in her own right. Unable to understand the nature of evil in the Danish court and driven to insanity by Hamlet's rejection of her and by her father's murder, she permits herself to sink to a watery death in a stream. Audiences are moved by her songs, her insane ramblings, and her devotion to her father as well as to Hamlet.

Characters such as Gertrude, Hamlet's mother, reveal a richness of psychology that sometimes startles us. Polonius, Ophelia's father, is virtually a stock character — the old, foolish philosopher — but he takes on special significance when he urges Ophelia to spy for him and when he ultimately dies at the hand of Hamlet. As Hamlet says, it was an unnecessary death for a "wretched, rash, intruding fool." But Polonius's son, Laertes, loved his father, and when Laertes returns grief-stricken, he does not hesitate a moment to get his revenge.

Hamlet's hesitancy is linked with his reputation as a melancholic. Because he thinks things through so deeply, he does not act instantly, as does Laertes. Even when the ghost reveals himself as his father and tells him that he has been murdered and must be avenged, Hamlet fears that the apparition might be a dangerous fakery of the devil to lure him to murder.

But Hamlet shows that he can act swiftly — indeed, rashly. His killing of Polonius is a rash act. He thinks the man behind the tapestry in his mother's bedroom is his uncle, since no other man but her husband has any right to be there. When Hamlet is sent to England with Rosencrantz and Guildenstern, he quickly senses a plot, undoes it, leaps aboard a pirate ship, and negotiates his way home with alacrity. This is not the work of a man who cannot act. In the graveyard scene he acts just as impulsively as Laertes would when he leaps into Ophelia's grave.

Hamlet's talents exhibited in his welcoming of the players in act II show him to be an experienced theatergoer, one with some skills onstage. He is also an expert writer; his additions to *The Murder of Gonzago* convert that imaginary play into a "mousetrap" baited to catch the murderer of his father. In early Renaissance paintings the mousetrap is a symbol for Jesus Christ, who catches the devil. The allusion would not have been lost on the Elizabethan audience, who would have seen Hamlet's psychological approach as being quite reasonable.

Emotions are of great importance to Hamlet. He feels deeply and he watches others to see what their feelings are. He knows that their demeanor may not reveal them as they are, so he must learn to be a careful student of behavior. As he tells his mother, "I know not 'seems.'" What seems is only what is apparent; his procedure is always to penetrate the surfaces of things to know their reality, which is why he uses drama as an instrument to penetrate psychological surfaces.

Hamlet in Performance

Richard Burbage played Hamlet in its original production, which was probably in 1601 but may have been in 1600. He continued playing the part into advanced age. *Hamlet* was staged on an English ship off the coast of Africa in 1607. The first American production was in 1759. When one thinks of productions of the play, one thinks of the great actors who played the role. Their names read like a *Who's Who* of acting: David Garrick (1717–1779), Edmund Kean (1789–1833), William Charles Macready (1793–1873), and Sir Henry Irving (1838–1905) were all identified with the role.

In the twentieth century the two most dominating Hamlets were John Gielgud and Laurence Olivier, who both acted for the Old Vic Theatre. To interpret the part, Olivier studied psychoanalyst Ernest Jones's essay on Hamlet's Oedipus complex. Jones was a disciple of Freud, who discussed Hamlet in his *Interpretation of Dreams* (see Freud's commentary on p. 384). Paul Scofield, in Peter Brook's 1955 production, found the part so challenging that he said playing it "feels like trespassing." Christopher Plummer, Derek Jacobi, and Jonathan Pryce have played the part to acclaim from the 1950s to recent times. Richard Burton also played Hamlet in New York in 1964. Michael Pennington's version for the Royal Shakespeare Company's 1980 production (see photos on p. 358) was well received by both critics and audiences. Pennington felt that the part tested not only one's skill but also one's character. He said, "When things go well you could do three performances a day and still be the last to leave the party, and at other times the part shakes you like a rat."

The major productions in the 1980s alone were astonishingly numerous: Christopher Walken for the American Shakespeare Festival in Stratford, Connecticut (1982); Roger Rees for the Royal Shakespeare Company in Stratford, England (1984); Kevin Kline for the New York Shakespeare Festival (1986); Ingmar Bergman's acclaimed production in Swedish (1988) in Sweden and New York; Daniel Day-Lewis for the National Theatre in London (1989); Austin Pendleton for the Riverside Shakespeare Company in New York (1989).

Franco Zeffirelli cast Mel Gibson in his 1990 film, which presents a credible Hamlet capable of deep emotional outburst. The setting of the film is lavish, and the interaction between Hamlet and Gertrude has a special psychological valence. *Hamlet* had a banner year in 1995 when Liam Neeson played the Danish prince in London and New York to considerable acclaim. That production was marked by a careful deemphasis of the great soliloquies. Ralph Fiennes, in the wake of a film success in *Schindler's List,* played in Edwardian clothes on Broadway, using madness as "a way of acting out." Keanu Reeves, another film actor, performed the part at the Manitoba Theater Center in Winnipeg, Canada. One critic said of Reeves's performance, "His hairstyle changed with his moods." Robert Wilson, known for massive semioperatic productions, played entirely alone, in a production premiered in Houston called *Hamlet: A Monologue.* On his deathbed Hamlet relives his story in flashbacks; he provides critical speeches of other characters himself. Among his efforts at Shakespeare, Kenneth Branagh took the title role in a lavish production of *Hamlet* in 1996. His richly produced Shakespeare films continue to be box office and critical successes. There is no end in sight for creative interpretations of this great play.

Hamlet has been the dream role not only of great actors but of great actresses as well. Sarah Bernhardt played Hamlet in the late nineteenth century, and Eva Le Gallienne, Siobhan McKenna, and Judith Anderson took on the part in the twentieth century. *Hamlet* has also given rise to numerous spin-offs, the best of which is Tom Stoppard's *Rosencrantz and Guildenstern Are Dead* (1967). Heiner Müller's *Hamlet-machine* (1977) is a respected avant-garde version of the play. Lee Blessing's *Fortinbras* (1991) is also an innovative retelling of the play from the point of view of a minor character — except that this character becomes the king. Blessing's success suggests that *Hamlet* is rich enough and inspiring enough to generate numerous further redactions and interpretations.

William Shakespeare (1564–1616)
HAMLET, PRINCE OF DENMARK   *c. 1600*

[Dramatis Personae

CLAUDIUS, *King of Denmark*
HAMLET, *son to the late King Hamlet, and nephew to the present King*
POLONIUS, *Lord Chamberlain*
HORATIO, *friend to Hamlet*
LAERTES, *son to Polonius*
VOLTIMAND,
CORNELIUS,
ROSENCRANTZ,   } *courtiers*
GUILDENSTERN,
OSRIC,
GENTLEMAN,
PRIEST, OR DOCTOR OF DIVINITY
MARCELLUS,   } *officers*
BERNARDO,
FRANCISCO, *a solider*
REYNALDO, *servant to Polonius*
PLAYERS
TWO CLOWNS, *grave-diggers*
FORTINBRAS, *Prince of Norway*
CAPTAIN
ENGLISH AMBASSADORS

GERTRUDE, *Queen of Denmark, mother to Hamlet*
OPHELIA, *daughter to Polonius*

LORDS, LADIES, OFFICERS, SOLDIERS, SAILORS,
    MESSENGERS, AND OTHER ATTENDANTS
GHOST *of Hamlet's father*

Scene: *Denmark.*]

Note: The text of *Hamlet* has come down to us in different versions — such as the first quarto, the second quarto, and the first Folio. The copy of the text used here is largely drawn from the second quarto. Passages enclosed in square brackets are taken from one of the other versions, in most cases the first Folio.

{*ACT I* • *Scene 1*}°

(*Enter Bernardo and Francisco, two sentinels, [meeting].*)

BERNARDO: Who's there?
FRANCISCO: Nay, answer me.° Stand and unfold
    yourself.
BERNARDO: Long live the King!
FRANCISCO: Bernardo?
BERNARDO: He.   5
FRANCISCO: You come most carefully upon your hour.
BERNARDO: 'Tis now struck twelve. Get thee to bed,
    Francisco.
FRANCISCO: For this relief much thanks. 'Tis bitter
    cold,
    And I am sick at heart.
BERNARDO: Have you had quiet guard?
FRANCISCO: Not a mouse stirring.   10
BERNARDO: Well, good night.
    If you do meet Horatio and Marcellus,
    The rivals° of my watch, bid them make haste.

(*Enter Horatio and Marcellus.*)

FRANCISCO: I think I hear them. Stand, ho! Who is
    there?
HORATIO: Friends to this ground.
MARCELLUS: And liegemen to the Dane.°   15
FRANCISCO: Give you° good night.
MARCELLUS: O, farewell, honest soldier.
    Who hath relieved you?
FRANCISCO: Bernardo hath my place.
    Give you good night.   (*Exit Francisco.*)

I, I. Location: Elsinore castle. A guard platform.   **2. me:** Francisco emphasizes that *he* is the sentry currently on watch. **13. rivals:** Partners.   **15. liegemen to the Dane:** Men sworn to serve the Danish king.   **16. Give you:** God give you.

MARCELLUS: Holla, Bernardo!
BERNARDO: Say,
     What, is Horatio there?
HORATIO: A piece of him.
BERNARDO: Welcome, Horatio. Welcome, good
20   Marcellus.
HORATIO: What, has this thing appear'd again tonight?
BERNARDO: I have seen nothing.
MARCELLUS: Horatio says 'tis but our fantasy,
     And will not let belief take hold of him
25   Touching this dreaded sight, twice seen of us.
     Therefore I have entreated him along
     With us to watch the minutes of this night,
     That if again this apparition come
     He may approve° our eyes and speak to it.
HORATIO: Tush, tush, 'twill not appear.
30 BERNARDO: Sit down awhile,
     And let us once again assail your ears,
     That are so fortified against our story,
     What we have two nights seen.
HORATIO: Well, sit we down,
     And let us hear Bernardo speak of this.
35 BERNARDO: Last night of all,
     When yond same star that's westward from the pole°
     Had made his° course t' illume that part of heaven
     Where now it burns, Marcellus and myself,
     The bell then beating one —

(Enter Ghost.)

MARCELLUS: Peace, break thee off! Look where it
40   comes again!
BERNARDO: In the same figure, like the King that's dead.
MARCELLUS: Thou art a scholar.° Speak to it, Horatio.
BERNARDO: Looks 'a° not like the King? Mark it,
          Horatio.
HORATIO: Most like. It harrows me with fear and
          wonder.
BERNARDO: It would be spoke to.
45 MARCELLUS: Speak to it,° Horatio.
HORATIO: What art thou that usurp'st this time of
          night,
     Together with that fair and warlike form
     In which the majesty of buried Denmark°
     Did sometimes° march? By heaven I charge thee
          speak!
MARCELLUS: It is offended.
50 BERNARDO: See, it stalks away.
HORATIO: Stay! Speak, speak. I charge thee, speak.
                              (Exit Ghost.)
MARCELLUS: 'Tis gone, and will not answer.
BERNARDO: How now, Horatio? You tremble and look
          pale.

---

29. **approve:** Corroborate.   36. **pole:** Polestar.   37. **his:** Its.
42. **scholar:** One learned in Latin and able to address spirits.
43. **'a:** He.   45. **It . . . it:** A ghost could not speak until spoken
to.   48. **buried Denmark:** The buried king of Denmark.
49. **sometimes:** Formerly.

Is not this something more than fantasy?
     What think you on 't?   55
HORATIO: Before my God, I might not this believe
     Without the sensible° and true avouch
     Of mine own eyes.
MARCELLUS: Is it not like the King?
HORATIO: As thou art to thyself.
     Such was the very armor he had on   60
     When he the ambitious Norway° combated.
     So frown'd he once when, in an angry parle,°
     He smote the sledded° Polacks° on the ice.
     'Tis strange.
MARCELLUS: Thus twice before, and jump° at this dead
          hour,   65
     With martial stalk hath he gone by our watch.
HORATIO: In what particular thought to work I know
          not,
     But, in the gross and scope° of mine opinion,
     This bodes some strange eruption to our state.
MARCELLUS: Good now,° sit down, and tell me, he that
          knows,   70
     Why this same strict and most observant watch
     So nightly toils° the subject° of the land,
     And why such daily cast° of brazen cannon,
     And foreign mart° for implements of war,
     Why such impress° of shipwrights, whose sore task   75
     Does not divide the Sunday from the week.
     What might be toward,° that this sweaty haste
     Doth make the night joint-laborer with the day?
     Who is 't that can inform me?
HORATIO: That can I,
     At least, the whisper goes so. Our last king,   80
     Whose image even but now appear'd to us,
     Was, as you know, by Fortinbras of Norway,
     Thereto prick'd on° by a most emulate° pride,
     Dar'd to the combat; in which our valiant
          Hamlet —
     For so this side of our known world esteem'd
          him —   85
     Did slay this Fortinbras; who, by a seal'd compact,
     Well ratified by law and heraldry,
     Did forfeit, with his life, all those his lands
     Which he stood seiz'd° of, to the conqueror;
     Against the° which a moi'ty competent°   90
     Was gaged° by our king, which had return'd
     To the inheritance of Fortinbras

---

57. **sensible:** Confirmed by the senses.   61. **Norway:** King of
Norway.   62. **parle:** Parley.   63. **sledded:** Traveling on sleds.
Polacks: Poles.   65. **jump:** Exactly.   68. **gross and scope:**
General view.   70. **Good now:** An expression denoting entreaty or expostulation.   72. **toils:** Causes to toil.   **subject:**
Subjects.   73. **cast:** Casting.   74. **mart:** Buying and selling.
75. **impress:** Impressment, conscription.   77. **toward:** In
preparation.   83. **prick'd on:** Incited.   **emulate:** Ambitious.
89. **seiz'd:** Possessed.   90. **Against the:** In return for. . . .
moi'ty competent: Sufficient portion.   91. **gaged:** Engaged,
pledged.

Had he been vanquisher, as, by the same comart°
And carriage° of the article design'd,
His fell to Hamlet. Now, sir, young Fortinbras,
Of unimproved° mettle hot and full,
Hath in the skirts° of Norway here and there
Shark'd up° a list of lawless resolutes°
For food and diet° to some enterprise
That hath a stomach° in 't, which is no other —
As it doth well appear unto our state —
But to recover of us, by strong hand
And terms compulsatory, those foresaid lands
So by his father lost. And this, I take it,
Is the main motive of our preparations,
The source of this our watch, and the chief head°
Of this post-haste and romage° in the land.
BERNARDO: I think it be no other but e'en so.
Well may it sort° that this portentous figure
Comes armed through our watch so like the King
That was and is the question of these wars.
HORATIO: A mote° it is to trouble the mind's eye.
In the most high and palmy° state of Rome,
A little ere the mightiest Julius fell,
The graves stood tenantless and the sheeted° dead
Did squeak and gibber in the Roman streets;
As° stars with trains of fire and dews of blood,
Disasters° in the sun; and the moist star°
Upon whose influence Neptune's° empire stands°
Was sick almost to doomsday° with eclipse.
And even the like precurse° of fear'd events,
As harbingers° preceding still° the fates
And prologue to the omen° coming on,
Have heaven and earth together demonstrated
Unto our climatures° and countrymen.

(*Enter Ghost.*)

But soft, behold! Lo where it comes again!
I'll cross° it, though it blast me. Stay, illusion!
If thou hast any sound, or use of voice,
Speak to me!   (*It spreads his arms.*)
If there be any good thing to be done
That may to thee do ease and grace to me,

Speak to me!
If thou art privy to thy country's fate,
Which, happily,° foreknowing may avoid,
O, speak!
Or if thou hast uphoarded in thy life
Extorted treasure in the womb of earth,
For which, they say, you spirits oft walk in death,
                    (*The cock crows.*)
Speak of it. Stay, and speak! Stop it, Marcellus.
MARCELLUS: Shall I strike at it with my partisan?°
HORATIO: Do, if it will not stand.   [*They strike at it.*]
BERNARDO: 'Tis here!
HORATIO: 'Tis here!
MARCELLUS: 'Tis gone.   [*Exit Ghost.*]
We do it wrong, being so majestical,
To offer it the show of violence;
For it is, as the air, invulnerable,
And our vain blows malicious mockery.
BERNARDO: It was about to speak when the cock
crew.
HORATIO: And then it started like a guilty thing
Upon a fearful summons. I have heard,
The cock, that is the trumpet to the morn,
Doth with his lofty and shrill-sounding throat
Awake the god of day, and, at his warning,
Whether in sea or fire, in earth or air,
Th' extravagant and erring° spirit hies
To his confine; and of the truth herein
This present object made probation.°
MARCELLUS: It faded on the crowing of the cock.
Some say that ever 'gainst° that season comes
Wherein our Savior's birth is celebrated,
The bird of dawning singeth all night long,
And then, they say, no spirit dare stir abroad;
The nights are wholesome, then no planets
strike,°
No fairy takes,° nor witch hath power to charm,
So hallowed and so gracious° is that time.
HORATIO: So have I heard and do in part believe it.
But, look, the morn, in russet mantle clad,
Walks o'er the dew of yon high eastward hill.
Break we our watch up, and by my advice
Let us impart what we have seen tonight
Unto young Hamlet; for, upon my life,
This spirit, dumb to us, will speak to him.
Do you consent we shall acquaint him with it,
As needful in our loves, fitting our duty?
MARCELLUS: Let's do 't, I pray, and I this morning
know
Where we shall find him most conveniently.
                    (*Exeunt.*)°

93. **comart:** Joint bargain (?).   94. **carriage:** Import, bearing.
96. **unimproved:** Not turned to account (?) or untested (?).
97. **skirts:** Outlying regions, outskirts.   98. **Shark'd up:** Got
together in haphazard fashion. **resolutes:** Desperadoes.
99. **food and diet:** No pay but their keep.   100. **stomach:**
Relish of danger.   106. **head:** Source.   107. **romage:**
Bustle, commotion.   109. **sort:** Suit.   112. **mote:** Speck of
dust.   113. **palmy:** Flourishing.   115. **sheeted:** Shrouded.
117. **As:** This abrupt transition suggests that matter is possibly
omitted between lines 116 and 117.   118. **Disasters:** Unfavorable signs of aspects. **moist star:** Moon, governing
tides.   119. **Neptune:** God of the sea. **stands:** Depends.
120. **sick . . . doomsday:** See Matt. 24:29 and Rev. 6:12.
121. **precurse:** Heralding, foreshadowing.   122. **harbingers:**
Forerunners. **still:** Continually.   123. **omen:** Calamitous
event.   125. **climatures:** Regions.   127. **cross:** Meet, face
directly.

134. **happily:** Haply, perchance.   140. **partisan:** Long-handled
spear.   154. **extravagant and erring:** Wandering. (The words
have similar meaning.)   156. **probation:** Proof.   158. **'gainst:**
Just before.   162. **strike:** Exert evil influence.   163. **takes:**
Bewitches.   164. **gracious:** Full of goodness.   175. [s.d.]
Exeunt: Latin for "they go out."

{*Scene II*}°

(*Flourish. Enter Claudius, King of Denmark, Gertrude the Queen, Councilors, Polonius and his son Laertes, Hamlet, cum aliis*° [*including Voltimand and Cornelius*].)

KING: Though yet of Hamlet our dear brother's death
    The memory be green, and that it us befitted
    To bear our hearts in grief and our whole kingdom
    To be contracted in one brow of woe,
5   Yet so far hath discretion fought with nature
    That we with wisest sorrow think on him,
    Together with remembrance of ourselves.
    Therefore our sometime sister, now our queen,
    Th' imperial jointress° to this warlike state,
10 Have we, as 'twere with a defeated joy —
    With an auspicious and a dropping eye,
    With mirth in funeral and with dirge in marriage,
    In equal scale weighing delight and dole —
    Taken to wife. Nor have we herein barr'd
15 Your better wisdoms, which have freely gone
    With this affair along. For all, our thanks.
    Now follows that you know° young Fortinbras,
    Holding a weak supposal° of our worth,
    Or thinking by our late dear brother's death
20 Our state to be disjoint and out of frame,
    Colleagued with° this dream of his advantage,°
    He hath not fail'd to pester us with message
    Importing° the surrender of those lands
    Lost by his father, with all bands° of law,
25 To our most valiant brother. So much for him.
    Now for ourself and for this time of meeting.
    Thus much the business is: we have here writ
    To Norway, uncle of young Fortinbras —
    Who, impotent and bed-rid, scarcely hears
30 Of this his nephew's purpose — to suppress
    His° further gait° herein, in that the levies,
    The lists, and full proportions are all made
    Out of his subject;° and we here dispatch
    You, good Cornelius, and you, Voltimand,
35 For bearers of this greeting to old Norway,
    Giving to you no further personal power
    To business with the King, more than the scope
    Of these delated° articles allow.   [*Gives a paper.*]
    Farewell, and let your haste commend your duty.
    CORNELIUS, VOLTIMAND: In that, and all things, will
40   we show our duty.
    KING: We doubt it nothing. Heartily farewell.

        [*Exit Voltimand and Cornelius.*]

And now, Laertes, what's the news with you?
    You told us of some suit; what is 't, Laertes?
    You cannot speak of reason to the Dane°
    And lose your voice.° What wouldst thou beg,
        Laertes,   45
    That shall not be my offer, not thy asking?
    The head is not more native° to the heart,
    The hand more instrumental° to the mouth,
    Than is the throne of Denmark to thy father.
    What wouldst thou have, Laertes?
LAERTES: My dread lord,   50
    Your leave and favor to return to France,
    From whence though willingly I came to Denmark
    To show my duty in your coronation,
    Yet now I must confess, that duty done,
    My thoughts and wishes bend again toward France   55
    And bow them to your gracious leave and pardon.°
KING: Have you your father's leave? What says
        Polonius?
POLONIUS: H'ath, my lord, wrung from me my slow
        leave
    By laborsome petition, and at last
    Upon his will I seal'd my hard° consent.   60
    I do beseech you, give him leave to go.
KING: Take thy fair hour, Laertes. Time be thine,
    And thy best graces spend it at thy will!
    But now, my cousin° Hamlet, and my son —
HAMLET: A little more than kin, and less than kind.°   65
KING: How is it that the clouds still hang on you?
HAMLET: Not so, my lord. I am too much in the sun.°
QUEEN: Good Hamlet, cast thy righted color off,
    And let thine eye look like a friend on Denmark.
    Do not forever with thy veiled° lids   70
    Seek for thy noble father in the dust.
    Thou know'st 'tis common,° all that lives must die,
    Passing through nature to eternity.
HAMLET: Ay, madam, it is common.
QUEEN: If it be,
    Why seems it so particular with thee?   75
HAMLET: Seems, madam! Nay, it is. I know not "seems."
    'Tis not alone my inky cloak, good mother,
    Nor customary suits of solemn black,
    Nor windy suspiration of forc'd breath,
    No, nor the fruitful° river in the eye,   80
    Nor the dejected havior of the visage,

I, II. Location: The castle.   [S.D.] *cum aliis*: With others.
9. jointress: Woman possessed of a joint tenancy of an estate.
17. know: Be informed (that).   18. weak supposal: Low estimate.   21. Colleagued with: Joined to, allied with.   dream . . . advantage: Illusory hope of success.   23. Importing: Pertaining to.   24. bands: Contracts.   31. His: Fortinbras's.   gait: Proceeding.   31–33. in that . . . subject: Since the levying of troops and supplies is drawn entirely from the King of Norway's own subjects.   38. delated: Detailed. (Variant of *dilated*.)

44. the Dane: The Danish king.   45. lose your voice: Waste your speech.   47. native: Closely connected, related.   48. instrumental: Serviceable.   56. leave and pardon: Permission to depart.   60. hard: Reluctant.   64. cousin: Any kin not of the immediate family.   65. A little . . . kind: Closer than an ordinary nephew (since I am stepson), and yet more separated in natural feeling (with pun on *kind*, meaning affectionate and natural, lawful). This line is often read as an aside, but it need not be.   67. sun: The sunshine of the King's royal favor (with pun on *son*).   70. veiled: Downcast.   72. common: Of universal occurrence. (But Hamlet plays on the sense of *vulgar* in line 74.)   80. fruitful: Abundant.

Together with all forms, moods, shapes of grief,
That can denote me truly. These indeed seem,
For they are actions that a man might play.
85 But I have that within which passes show;
These but the trappings and the suits of woe.
KING: 'Tis sweet and commendable in your nature,
    Hamlet,
To give these mourning duties to your father.
But you must know your father lost a father,
90 That father lost, lost his, and the survivor bound
In filial obligation for some term
To do obsequious° sorrow. But to persever°
In obstinate condolement° is a course
Of impious stubbornness. 'Tis unmanly grief.
95 It shows a will most incorrect to heaven,
A heart unfortified, a mind impatient,
An understanding simple and unschool'd.
For what we know must be and is as common
As any the most vulgar thing to sense,°
100 Why should we in our peevish opposition
Take it to heart? Fie, 'tis a fault to heaven,
A fault against the dead, a fault to nature,
To reason most absurd, whose common theme
Is death of fathers, and who still hath cried,
105 From the first corse° till he that died today,
"This must be so." We pray you, throw to earth
This unprevailing° woe, and think of us
As of a father; for let the world take note,
You are the most immediate° to our throne,
110 And with no less nobility of love
Than that which dearest father bears his son
Do I impart toward you. For your intent
In going back to school in Wittenberg,°
It is most retrograde° to our desire,
115 And we beseech you, bend you° to remain
Here in the cheer and comfort of our eye,
Our chiefest courtier, cousin, and our son.
QUEEN: Let not thy mother lose her prayers, Hamlet.
I pray thee stay with us, go not to Wittenberg.
120 HAMLET: I shall in all my best obey you, madam.
KING: Why, 'tis a loving and a fair reply.
Be as ourself in Denmark. Madam, come.
This gentle and unforc'd accord of Hamlet
Sits smiling to my heart, in grace whereof
125 No jocund° health that Denmark drinks today
But the great cannon to the clouds shall tell,
And the King's rouse° the heaven shall bruit again,°
Respeaking earthly thunder.° Come away.

(*Flourish. Exeunt all but Hamlet.*)

HAMLET: O, that this too too sullied° flesh would melt,
Thaw, and resolve itself into a dew!   130
Or that the Everlasting had not fix'd
His canon° 'gainst self-slaughter! O God, God,
How weary, stale, flat, and unprofitable
Seem to me all the uses of this world!
Fie on 't, ah, fie! 'Tis an unweeded garden   135
That grows to seed. Things rank and gross in
    nature
Possess it merely.° That it should come to this!
But two months dead — nay, not so much, not two.
So excellent a king, that was to° this
Hyperion° to a satyr; so loving to my mother   140
That he might not beteem° the winds of heaven
Visit her face too roughly. Heaven and earth,
Must I remember? Why, she would hang on him
As if increase of appetite had grown
By what it fed on, and yet, within a month —   145
Let me not think on 't. Frailty, thy name is
    woman! —
A little month, or ere those shoes were old
With which she followed my poor father's body,
Like Niobe,° all tears, why she, even she —
O God, a beast, that wants discourse of reason,°   150
Would have mourn'd longer — married with my
    uncle,
My father's brother, but no more like my father
Than I to Hercules. Within a month,
Ere yet the salt of most unrighteous tears
Had left the flushing in her galled° eyes,   155
She married. O, most wicked speed, to post
With such dexterity to incestuous° sheets!
It is not nor it cannot come to good.
But break, my heart, for I must hold my tongue.

(*Enter Horatio, Marcellus, and Bernardo.*)

HORATIO: Hail to your lordship!
HAMLET: I am glad to see you well.   160
    Horatio! — or I do forget myself.
HORATIO: The same, my lord, and your poor servant
    ever.
HAMLET: Sir, my good friend; I'll change° that name
    with you.
    And what make° you from Wittenberg, Horatio?
    Marcellus?   165

---

92. **obsequious:** Suited to obsequies or funerals. **persever:** Persevere. 93. **condolement:** Sorrowing. 99. **As . . . sense:** As the most ordinary experience. 105. **corse:** Corpse. 107. **unprevailing:** Unavailing. 109. **most immediate:** Next in succession. 113. **Wittenberg:** Famous German university founded in 1502. 114. **retrograde:** Contrary. 115. **bend you:** Incline yourself. 125. **jocund:** Merry. 127. **rouse:** Draft of liquor. **bruit again:** Loudly echo. 128. **thunder:** Of trumpet and kettledrum sounded when the King drinks, see I, IV, 8–12.

129. **sullied:** Defiled. (The early quartos read *sallied,* the Folio *solid.*) 132. **canon:** Law. 137. **merely:** Completely. 139. **to:** In comparison to. 140. **Hyperion:** Titan sun-god, father of Helios. 141. **beteem:** Allow. 149. **Niobe:** Tantalus's daughter, Queen of Thebes, who boasted that she had more sons and daughters than Leto; for this, Apollo and Artemis, children of Leto, slew her fourteen children. She was turned by Zeus into a stone that continually dropped tears. 150. **wants . . . reason:** Lacks the faculty of reason. 155. **galled:** Irritated, inflamed. 157. **incestuous:** In Shakespeare's day, the marriage of a man like Claudius to his deceased brother's wife was considered incestuous. 163. **change:** Exchange (i.e., the name of friend). 164. **make:** Do.

MARCELLUS: My good lord.
HAMLET: I am very glad to see you. [*To Bernardo.*]
　　Good even, sir. —
　　But what, in faith, make you from Wittenberg?
HORATIO: A truant disposition, good my lord.
170　HAMLET: I would not hear your enemy say so,
　　Nor shall you do my ear that violence
　　To make it truster of your own report
　　Against yourself. I know you are no truant.
　　But what is your affair in Elsinore?
175　We'll teach you to drink deep ere you depart.
HORATIO: My lord, I came to see your father's
　　funeral.
HAMLET: I prithee do not mock me, fellow student;
　　I think it was to see my mother's wedding.
HORATIO: Indeed, my lord, it followed hard° upon.
HAMLET: Thrift, thrift, Horatio! The funeral bak'd
180　meats
　　Did coldly furnish forth the marriage tables.
　　Would I had met my dearest° foe in heaven
　　Or° ever I had seen that day, Horatio!
　　My father! — Methinks I see my father.
HORATIO: Where, my lord?
185　HAMLET:　　　　　　　　In my mind's eye, Horatio.
HORATIO: I saw him once. 'A° was a goodly king.
HAMLET: 'A was a man, take him for all in all,
　　I shall not look upon his like again.
HORATIO: My lord, I think I saw him yesternight.
190　HAMLET: Saw? Who?
HORATIO: My lord, the King your father.
HAMLET:　　　　　　　　　The King my father?
HORATIO: Season your admiration° for a while
　　With an attent° ear, till I may deliver,
　　Upon the witness of these gentlemen,
　　This marvel to you.
195　HAMLET:　　　　　　　For God's love, let me hear!
HORATIO: Two nights together had these gentlemen,
　　Marcellus and Bernardo, on their watch,
　　In the dead waste and middle of the night,
　　Been thus encount'red. A figure like your father,
200　Armed at point° exactly, cap-a-pe,°
　　Appears before them, and with solemn march
　　Goes slow and stately by them. Thrice he walk'd
　　By their oppress'd and fear-surprised eyes
　　Within his truncheon's° length, whilst they,
　　distill'd
205　Almost to jelly with the act° of fear,
　　Stand dumb and speak not to him. This to me
　　In dreadful secrecy impart they did,
　　And I with them the third night kept the watch,
　　Where, as they had delivered, both in time,
210　Form of the thing, each word made true and good,

179. **hard:** Close.　182. **dearest:** Direst.　183. **or:** Ere, before.
186. **'A:** He.　192. **Season your admiration:** Restrain your
astonishment.　193. **attent:** Attentive.　200. **at point:** Completely.　**cap-a-pe:** From head to foot.　204. **truncheon:** Officer's staff.　205. **act:** Action, operation.

The apparition comes. I knew your father;
　These hands are not more like.
HAMLET:　　　　　　　　But where was this?
MARCELLUS: My lord, upon the platform where we
　watch.
HAMLET: Did you not speak to it?
HORATIO:　　　　　　　　My lord, I did,
　But answer made it none. Yet once methought　215
　It lifted up it° head and did address
　Itself to motion, like as it would speak;
　But even then the morning cock crew loud,
　And at the sound it shrunk in haste away,
　And vanish'd from our sight.
HAMLET:　　　　　　　　'Tis very strange.　220
HORATIO: As I do live, my honor'd lord, 'tis true,
　And we did think it writ down in our duty
　To let you know of it.
HAMLET: Indeed, indeed, sirs. But this troubles me.
　Hold you the watch tonight?
ALL:　　　　　　　　We do, my lord.　225
HAMLET: Arm'd, say you?
ALL: Arm'd, my lord.
HAMLET: From top to toe?
ALL:　　　　　　　My lord, from head to foot.
HAMLET: Then saw you not his face?
HORATIO: O, yes, my lord. He wore his beaver° up.　230
HAMLET: What, looked he frowningly?
HORATIO:　　　　　　　　A countenance more
　In sorrow than in anger.
HAMLET:　　　　　　　Pale or red?
HORATIO: Nay, very pale.
HAMLET:　　　　　　　And fix'd his eyes upon you?
HORATIO: Most constantly.
HAMLET:　　　　　　　I would I had been there.
HORATIO: It would have much amaz'd you.　235
HAMLET: Very like, very like. Stay'd it long?
HORATIO: While one with moderate haste might tell° a
　hundred.
MARCELLUS, BERNARDO: Longer, longer.
HORATIO: Not when I saw 't.
HAMLET:　　　　　　　His beard was grizzl'd, — no?
HORATIO: It was, as I have seen it in his life,　240
　A sable silver'd.°
HAMLET:　　　　　　I will watch tonight.
　Perchance 'twill walk again.
HORATIO:　　　　　　　　I warr'nt it will.
HAMLET: If it assume my noble father's person,
　I'll speak to it, though hell itself should gape
　And bid me hold my peace. I pray you all,　245
　If you have hitherto conceal'd this sight,
　Let it be tenable° in your silence still,
　And whatsomever else shall hap tonight,
　Give it an understanding, but no tongue.
　I will requite your loves. So, fare you well.　250

216. **it:** Its.　230. **beaver:** Visor on the helmet.　237. **tell:**
Count.　241. **sable silver'd:** Black mixed with white.
247. **tenable:** Held tightly.

Upon the platform, 'twixt eleven and twelve,
I'll visit you.
ALL: Our duty to your honor.
HAMLET: Your loves, as mine to you. Farewell.
                        (*Exeunt* [*all but Hamlet*].)
My father's spirit in arms! All is not well.
I doubt° some foul play. Would the night were
255   come!
Till then sit still, my soul. Foul deeds will rise,
Though all the earth o'erwhelm them, to men's eyes.
                                        (*Exit.*)

{*Scene III*}°

(*Enter Laertes and Ophelia, his sister.*)

LAERTES: My necessaries are embark'd. Farewell.
    And, sister, as the winds give benefit
    And convoy is assistant,° do not sleep
    But let me hear from you.
OPHELIA: Do you doubt that?
5 LAERTES: For Hamlet, and the trifling of his favor,
    Hold it a fashion and a toy in blood,°
    A violet in the youth of primy° nature,
    Forward,° not permanent, sweet, not lasting,
    The perfume and suppliance° of a minute —
    No more.
OPHELIA: No more but so?
10 LAERTES: Think it no more.
    For nature crescent° does not grow alone
    In thews° and bulk, but, as this temple° waxes,
    The inward service of the mind and soul
    Grows wide withal.° Perhaps he loves you now,
15 And now no soil° nor cautel° doth besmirch
    The virtue of his will;° but you must fear,
    His greatness weigh'd,° his will is not his own.
    [For he himself is subject to his birth.]
    He may not, as unvalued persons do,
20 Carve° for himself; for on his choice depends
    The safety and health of this whole state,
    And therefore must his choice be circumscrib'd
    Unto the voice and yielding° of that body
    Whereof he is the head. Then if he says he loves
        you,
25 It fits your wisdom so far to believe it
    As he in his particular act and place
    May give his saying deed,° which is no further

Than the main voice of Denmark goes withal.
Then weigh what loss your honor may sustain
If with too credent° ear you list° his songs,   30
Or lose your heart, or your chaste treasure open
To his unmaster'd importunity.
Fear it, Ophelia, fear it, my dear sister,
And keep you in the rear of your affection,
Out of the shot° and danger of desire.   35
The chariest° maid is prodigal enough
If she unmask her beauty to the moon.
Virtue itself scapes not calumnious strokes.
The canker galls° the infants of the spring
Too oft before their buttons° be disclos'd,°   40
And in the morn and liquid dew° of youth
Contagious blastments° are most imminent.
Be wary then; best safety lies in fear.
Youth to itself rebels, though none else near.
OPHELIA: I shall the effect of this good lesson keep   45
    As watchman to my heart. But, good my brother,
    Do not, as some ungracious pastors do,
    Show me the steep and thorny way to heaven,
    Whiles, like a puff'd° and reckless libertine,
    Himself the primrose path of dalliance treads,   50
    And recks° not his own rede.°

(*Enter Polonius.*)

LAERTES: O, fear me not.
    I stay too long. But here my father comes.
    A double blessing is a double° grace;
    Occasion° smiles upon a second leave.
POLONIUS: Yet here, Laertes? Aboard, aboard, for
        shame!   55
    The wind sits in the shoulder of your sail,
    And you are stay'd for. There — my blessing with
        thee!
    And these few precepts in thy memory
    Look thou character.° Give thy thoughts no tongue
    Nor any unproportion'd thought his° act.   60
    Be thou familiar,° but by no means vulgar.°
    Those friends thou hast, and their adoption tried,°
    Grapple them to thy soul with hoops of steel,
    But do not dull thy palm with entertainment
    Of each new-hatch'd, unfledg'd courage.° Beware   65
    Of entrance to a quarrel, but, being in,
    Bear't that° th' opposed may beware of thee.
    Give every man thy ear, but few thy voice;
    Take each man's censure,° but reserve thy judgment.

---

255. **doubt:** Suspect.   **I, III. Location:** Polonius's chambers.
3. **convoy is assistant:** Means of conveyance are available.
6. **toy in blood:** Passing amorous fancy.   7. **primy:** In its prime,
springtime.   8. **Forward:** Precocious.   9. **suppliance:** Supply,
filler.   11. **crescent:** Growing, waxing.   12. **thews:** Bodily
strength.   **temple:** Body.   14. **Grows wide withal:** Grows
along with it.   15. **soil:** Blemish.   **cautel:** Deceit.   16. **will:**
Desire.   17. **greatness weigh'd:** High position considered.
20. **Carve:** Choose pleasure.   23. **voice and yielding:** Assent,
approval.   27. **deed:** Effect.

30. **credent:** Credulous.   **list:** Listen to.   35. **shot:** Range.
36. **chariest:** Most scrupulously modest.   39. **canker galls:**
Cankerworm   destroys.   40. **buttons:** Buds.   **disclos'd:**
Opened.   41. **liquid dew:** Time when dew is fresh.   42. **blast-
ments:** Blights.   49. **puff'd:** Bloated.   51. **recks:** Heeds.
rede: Counsel.   53. **double:** I.e., Laertes has already bidden his
father good-bye.   54. **Occasion:** Opportunity.   59. **character:**
Inscribe.   60. **his:** Its.   61. **familiar:** Sociable.   **vulgar:** Common.   62. **tried:** Tested.   65. **courage:** Young man of spirit.
67. **Bear't that:** Manage it so that.   69. **censure:** Opinion,
judgment.

70 Costly thy habit as thy purse can buy,
    But not express'd in fancy; rich, not gaudy,
    For the apparel oft proclaims the man,
    And they in France of the best rank and station
    Are of a most select and generous chief° in that.
75 Neither a borrower nor a lender be,
    For loan oft loses both itself and friend,
    And borrowing dulleth edge of husbandry.°
    This above all: to thine own self be true,
    And it must follow, as the night the day,
80 Thou canst not then be false to any man.
    Farewell. My blessing season° this in thee!
LAERTES: Most humbly do I take my leave, my lord.
POLONIUS: The time invests° you. Go, your servants
    tend.°
LAERTES: Farewell, Ophelia, and remember well
85 What I have said to you.
OPHELIA: 'Tis in my memory lock'd,
    And you yourself shall keep the key of it.
LAERTES: Farewell.   (Exit Laertes.)
POLONIUS: What is 't, Ophelia, he hath said to you?
OPHELIA: So please you, something touching the Lord
90   Hamlet.
POLONIUS: Marry,° well bethought.
    'Tis told me he hath very oft of late
    Given private time to you, and you yourself
    Have of your audience been most free and
        bounteous.
95 If it be so — as so 'tis put on° me,
    And that in way of caution — I must tell you
    You do not understand yourself so clearly
    As it behooves my daughter and your honor.
    What is between you? Give me up the truth.
OPHELIA: He hath, my lord, of late made many
100   tenders°
    Of his affection to me.
POLONIUS: Affection? Pooh! You speak like a green
        girl,
    Unsifted° in such perilous circumstance.
    Do you believe his tenders, as you call them?
105 OPHELIA: I do not know, my lord, what I should think.
POLONIUS: Marry, I will teach you. Think yourself a
        baby
    That you have ta'en these tenders° for true pay,
    Which are not sterling.° Tender° yourself more
        dearly,
    Or — not to crack the wind° of the poor phrase,
110   Running it thus — you'll tender me a fool.°

OPHELIA: My lord, he hath importun'd me with
        love
    In honorable fashion.
POLONIUS: Ay, fashion° you may call it. Go to, go to.
OPHELIA: And hath given countenance° to his speech,
        my lord,
    With almost all the holy vows of heaven.   115
POLONIUS: Ay, springes° to catch woodcocks.° I do
        know,
    When the blood burns, how prodigal the soul
    Lends the tongue vows. These blazes,
        daughter,
    Giving more light than heat, extinct in both
    Even in their promise, as it is a-making,   120
    You must not take for fire. From this time
    Be something scanter of your maiden presence.
    Set your entreatments° at a higher rate
    Than a command to parle.° For Lord Hamlet,
    Believe so much in him° that he is young,   125
    And with a larger tether may he walk
    Than may be given you. In few,° Ophelia,
    Do not believe his vows, for they are brokers,°
    Not of that dye° which their investments° show,
    But mere implorators° of unholy suits,   130
    Breathing° like sanctified and pious bawds,
    The better to beguile. This is for all:
    I would not, in plain terms, from this time forth
    Have you so slander° any moment leisure
    As to give words or talk with the Lord Hamlet.   135
    Look to 't, I charge you. Come your ways.
OPHELIA: I shall obey, my lord.   (Exeunt.)

{Scene IV}°

(Enter Hamlet, Horatio, and Marcellus.)

HAMLET: The air bites shrewdly; it is very cold.
HORATIO: It is a nipping and an eager air.
HAMLET: What hour now?
HORATIO: I think it lacks of twelve.
MARCELLUS: No, it is struck.
HORATIO: Indeed? I heard it not.
    It then draws near the season   5
    Wherein the spirit held his wont to walk.

---

74. generous chief: Noble eminence (?).   77. husbandry:
Thrift.   81. season: Mature.   83. invests: Besieges. . . . tend:
Attend, wait.   91. Marry: By the Virgin Mary (a mild oath).
95. put on: Impressed on, told to.   100. tenders: Offers.
103. Unsifted: Untried.   107. tenders: With added meaning
here of *promises to pay*.   108. sterling: Legal currency. Tender: Hold.   109. crack the wind: Run it until it is broken,
winded.   110. tender me a fool: (1) Show yourself to me as a
fool, (2) show me up as a fool, (3) present me with a grandchild
(*fool* was a term of endearment for a child).

113. fashion: Mere form, pretense.   114. countenance: Credit,
support.   116. springes: Snares. woodcocks: Birds easily
caught; here used to connote gullibility.   123. entreatments:
Negotiations for surrender (a military term).   124. parle: Discuss terms with the enemy. (Polonius urges his daughter, in
the metaphor of military language, not to meet with Hamlet
and consider giving in to him merely because he requests an
interview.)   125. so . . . him: This much concerning him.
127. In few: Briefly.   128. brokers: Go-betweens, procurers.
129. dye: Color or sort. investments: Clothes (i.e., they are
not what they seem).   130. mere implorators: Out-and-
out solicitors.   131. Breathing: Speaking.   134. slander:
Bring disgrace or reproach upon.   I, IV. Location: The guard
platform.

(*A flourish of trumpets, and two pieces° go off*
[*within*].)

What does this mean, my lord?
HAMLET: The King doth wake° tonight and takes his
rouse,°
Keeps wassail,° and the swagg'ring up-spring° reels;
10 And as he drains his draughts of Rhenish° down,
The kettle-drum and trumpet thus bray out
The triumph of his pledge.°
HORATIO: Is it a custom?
HAMLET: Ay, marry, is 't,
But to my mind, though I am native here
15 And to the manner° born, it is a custom
More honor'd in the breach than the observance.°
This heavy-headed revel east and west°
Makes us traduc'd and tax'd of° other nations.
They clepe° us drunkards, and with swinish phrase°
20 Soil our addition;° and indeed it takes
From our achievements, though perform'd at
height,°
The pith and marrow of our attribute.
So, oft it chances in particular men,
That for some vicious mole of nature° in them,
25 As in their birth — wherein they are not guilty,
Since nature cannot choose his° origin —
By the o'ergrowth of some complexion,°
Oft breaking down the pales° and forts of reason,
Or by some habit that too much o'er-leavens°
30 The form of plausive° manners, that these men,
Carrying, I say, the stamp of one defect,
Being nature's livery,° or fortune's star,°
Their virtues else, be they as pure as grace,
As infinite as man may undergo,
35 Shall in the general censure take corruption
From that particular fault. The dram of eale°
Doth all the noble substance of a doubt°
To his own scandal.°

(*Enter Ghost.*)

HORATIO: Look, my lord, it comes!
HAMLET: Angels and ministers of grace defend us!
Be thou a spirit of health° or goblin damn'd,   40
Bring with thee airs from heaven or blasts from
hell,
Be thy intents wicked or charitable,
Thou com'st in such a questionable° shape
That I will speak to thee. I'll call thee Hamlet,
King, father, royal Dane. O, answer me!   45
Let me not burst in ignorance, but tell
Why thy canoniz'd° bones, hearsed° in death,
Have burst their cerements;° why the sepulcher
Wherein we saw thee quietly interr'd
Hath op'd his ponderous and marble jaws   50
To cast thee up again. What may this mean,
That thou, dead corse, again in complete steel
Revisits thus the glimpses of the moon,°
Making night hideous, and we fools of nature°
So horridly to shake our disposition   55
With thoughts beyond the reaches of our souls?
Say, why is this? Wherefore? What should we do?
([*Ghost*] *beckons* [*Hamlet*].)
HORATIO: It beckons you to go away with it,
As if it some impartment° did desire
To you alone.
MARCELLUS: Look with what courteous action   60
It waves you to a more removed ground.
But do not go with it.
HORATIO: No, by no means.
HAMLET: It will not speak. Then I will follow it.
HORATIO: Do not, my lord.
HAMLET: Why, what should be the fear?
I do not set my life at a pin's fee,°   65
And for my soul, what can it do to that,
Being a thing immortal as itself?
It waves me forth again. I'll follow it.
HORATIO: What if it tempt you toward the flood, my
lord
Or to the dreadful summit of the cliff   70
That beetles o'er° his° base into the sea,
And there assume some other horrible form
Which might deprive your sovereignty of reason,°
And draw you into madness? Think of it.
The very place puts toys of desperation,°   75
Without more motive, into every brain
That looks so many fathoms to the sea
And hears it roar beneath.
HAMLET: It waves me still.
Go on, I'll follow thee.

---

6. [S.D.] *pieces*: I.e., of ordnance, cannon.   **8. wake**: Stay awake
and hold revel.   **rouse**: Carouse, drinking bout.   **9. wassail**:
Carousal.   **up-spring**: Wild German dance.   **10. Rhenish**:
Rhine wine.   **12. triumph . . . pledge**: His feat in draining the
wine in a single draft.   **15. manner**: Custom (of drinking).
16. More . . . observance: Better neglected than followed.
17. east and west: I.e., everywhere.   **18. tax'd of**: Censured by.
19. clepe: Call.   **with swinish phrase**: By calling us swine.
20. addition: Reputation.   **21. at height**: Outstandingly.
24. mole of nature: Natural blemish in one's constitution.
26. his: Its.   **27. complexion**: Humor (i.e., one of the four
humors or fluids thought to determine temperament).
28. pales: Palings, fences (as of a fortification).   **29. o'er-
leavens**: Induces a change throughout (as yeast works in dough).
30. plausive: Pleasing.   **32. nature's livery**: Endowment from
nature.   **fortune's star**: Mark placed by fortune.   **36. dram of
eale**: Small amount of evil (?).   **37. of a doubt**: A famous crux,
sometimes emended to *oft about or often dout*, i.e., often erase
or do out, or to *antidote*, counteract.   **38. To . . . scandal**: To
the disgrace of the whole enterprise.

40. of health: Of spiritual good.   **43. questionable**: Inviting
question or conversation.   **47. canoniz'd**: Buried according to
the canons of the church.   **hearsed**: Coffined.   **48. cerements**:
Grave-clothes.   **53. glimpses of the moon**: Earth by night.
54. fools of nature: Mere men, limited to natural knowledge.
59. impartment: Communication.   **65. fee**: Value.   **71. beetles
o'er**: Overhangs threateningly.   **his**: Its.   **73. deprive . . . reason**: Take away the rule of reason over your mind.   **75. toys of
desperation**: Fancies of desperate acts, i.e., suicide.

MARCELLUS: You shall not go, my lord.
                                        [*They try to stop him.*]
80 HAMLET: Hold off your hands!
HORATIO: Be rul'd, you shall not go.
HAMLET: My fate cries out,
   And makes each petty artery° in this body
   As hardy as the Nemean lion's° nerve.°
   Still am I call'd. Unhand me, gentlemen.
85 By heaven, I'll make a ghost of him that lets° me!
   I say, away! Go on. I'll follow thee.
                              (*Exeunt Ghost and Hamlet.*)
HORATIO: He waxes desperate with imagination.
MARCELLUS: Let's follow. 'Tis not fit thus to obey him.
HORATIO: Have after. To what issue° will this come?
MARCELLUS: Something is rotten in the state of
90   Denmark.
HORATIO: Heaven will direct it.°
MARCELLUS: Nay, let's follow him. (*Exeunt.*)

{*Scene V*}°

(*Enter Ghost and Hamlet.*)

HAMLET: Whither wilt thou lead me? Speak. I'll go no
      further.
GHOST: Mark me.
HAMLET: I will.
GHOST: My hour is almost come,
   When I to sulph'rous and tormenting flames
   Must render up myself.
HAMLET: Alas, poor ghost!
5 GHOST: Pity me not, but lend thy serious hearing
   To what I shall unfold.
HAMLET: Speak. I am bound to hear.
GHOST: So art thou to revenge, when thou shalt hear.
HAMLET: What?
10 GHOST: I am thy father's spirit,
   Doom'd for a certain term to walk the night,
   And for the day confin'd to fast° in fires,
   Till the foul crimes° done in my days of nature
   Are burnt and purg'd away. But that° I am forbid
15 To tell the secrets of my prison-house,
   I could a tale unfold whose lightest word
   Would harrow up thy soul, freeze thy young blood,
   Make thy two eyes, like stars, start from their
      spheres,°
   Thy knotted and combined locks° to part,
20 And each particular hair to stand an end,°

Like quills upon the fearful porpentine.°
But this eternal blazon° must not be
To ears of flesh and blood. List, list, O, list!
If thou didst ever thy dear father love —
HAMLET: O God!   25
GHOST: Revenge his foul and most unnatural murder.
HAMLET: Murder?
GHOST: Murder most foul, as in the best it is,
   But this most foul, strange, and unnatural.
HAMLET: Haste me to know 't, that I, with wings as
      swift   30
   As meditation or the thoughts of love,
   May sweep to my revenge.
GHOST: I find thee apt;
   And duller shouldst thou be than the fat weed
   That roots itself in ease on Lethe° wharf,°
   Wouldst thou not stir in this. Now, Hamlet, hear.   35
   'Tis given out that, sleeping in my orchard,
   A serpent stung me. So the whole ear of Denmark
   Is by a forged process° of my death
   Rankly abus'd.° But know, thou noble youth,
   The serpent that did sting thy father's life   40
   Now wears his crown.
HAMLET: O my prophetic soul!
   My uncle!
GHOST: Ay, that incestuous, that adulterate° beast,
   With witchcraft of his wits, with traitorous gifts —
   O wicked wit and gifts, that have the power   45
   So to seduce! — won to his shameful lust
   The will of my most seeming-virtuous queen.
   O Hamlet, what a falling-off was there!
   From me, whose love was of that dignity
   That it went hand in hand even with the vow   50
   I made to her in marriage, and to decline
   Upon a wretch whose natural gifts were poor
   To those of mine!
   But virtue, as it never will be moved,
   Though lewdness court it in a shape of heaven,°   55
   So lust, though to a radiant angel link'd,
   Will sate itself in a celestial bed,
   And prey on garbage.
   But, soft, methinks I scent the morning air.
   Brief let me be. Sleeping within my orchard,   60
   My custom always of the afternoon,
   Upon my secure° hour thy uncle stole,
   With juice of cursed hebona° in a vial,
   And in the porches of my ears did pour
   The leprous° distillment, whose effect   65
   Holds such an enmity with blood of man

---

82. artery: Sinew.   83. Nemean lion: One of the monsters slain by Hercules in his twelve labors.   nerve: Sinew 85. lets: Hinders.   89. issue: Outcome.   91. it: The outcome.   I, v. Location: The battlements of the castle.   12. fast: Do penance.   13. crimes: Sins.   14. But that: Were it not that.   18. spheres: Eye sockets, here compared to the orbits or transparent revolving spheres in which, according to Ptolemaic astronomy, the heavenly bodies were fixed.   19. knotted . . . locks: Hair neatly arranged and confined.   20. an end: On end.

21. fearful porpentine: Frightened porcupine.   22. eternal blazon: Revelation of the secrets of eternity.   34. Lethe: The river of forgetfulness in Hades.   wharf: Bank.   38. forged process: Falsified account.   39. abus'd: Deceived.   43. adulterate: Adulterous.   55. shape of heaven: Heavenly form.   62. secure: Confident, unsuspicious.   63. hebona: Poison. (The word seems to be a form of *ebony*, though it is thought perhaps to be related to *henbane*, a poison, or to *ebenus*, yew.)   65. leprous: Causing leprosy-like disfigurement.

That swift as quicksilver it courses through
The natural gates and alleys of the body,
And with a sudden vigor it doth posset°
70 And curd, like eager° droppings into milk,
The thin and wholesome blood. So did it mine,
And a most instant tetter° bark'd° about,
Most lazar-like,° with vile and loathsome crust,
All my smooth body.
75 Thus was I, sleeping, by a brother's hand
Of life, of crown, of queen, at once dispatch'd,°
Cut off even in the blossoms of my sin,
Unhous'led,° disappointed,° unanel'd,°
No reck'ning made, but sent to my account
80 With all my imperfections on my head.
O, horrible! O, horrible, most horrible!
If thou hast nature° in thee, bear it not.
Let not the royal bed of Denmark be
A couch for luxury° and damned incest.
85 But, howsomever thou pursues this act,
Taint not thy mind, nor let thy soul contrive
Against thy mother aught. Leave her to heaven
And to those thorns that in her bosom lodge,
To prick and sting her. Fare thee well at once.
90 The glow-worm shows the matin° to be near,
And 'gins to pale his uneffectual fire.°
Adieu, adieu, adieu! Remember me.   [*Exit.*]
HAMLET: O all you host of heaven! O earth! What
    else?
And shall I couple° hell? O fie! Hold, hold, my
    heart,
95 And you, my sinews, grow not instant old,
But bear me stiffly up. Remember thee!
Ay, thou poor ghost, whiles memory holds a seat
In this distracted globe.° Remember thee!
Yea, from the table° of my memory
100 I'll wipe away all trivial fond° records,
All saws° of books, all forms,° all pressures° past
That youth and observation copied there,
And thy commandment all alone shall live
Within the book and volume of my brain,
105 Unmix'd with baser matter. Yes, by heaven!
O most pernicious woman!
O villain, villain, smiling, damned villain!
My tables — meet it is I set it down,
That one may smile, and smile, and be a villain.
110 At least I am sure it may be so in Denmark.
                                          [*Writing.*]

So, uncle, there you are. Now to my word;
It is "Adieu, adieu! Remember me."
I have sworn 't.

(*Enter Horatio and Marcellus.*)

HORATIO: My lord, my lord!
MARCELLUS: Lord Hamlet!
HORATIO: Heavens secure him!
HAMLET: So be it!   115
MARCELLUS: Illo, ho, ho, my lord!
HAMLET: Hillo, ho, ho,° boy! Come, bird, come.
MARCELLUS: How is 't, my noble lord?
HORATIO: What news, my lord?
HAMLET: O, wonderful!
HORATIO: Good my lord, tell it.
HAMLET: No, you will reveal it.   120
HORATIO: Not I, my lord, by heaven.
MARCELLUS: Nor I, my lord.
HAMLET: How say you, then, would heart of man once
    think it?
But you'll be secret?
HORATIO, MARCELLUS: Ay, by heaven, my lord.
HAMLET: There's never a villain dwelling in all
    Denmark
But he's an arrant° knave.   125
HORATIO: There needs no ghost, my lord, come from
    the grave
To tell us this.
HAMLET: Why, right, you are in the right.
And so, without more circumstance° at all,
I hold it fit that we shake hands and part,
You, as your business and desire shall point you —   130
For every man hath business and desire,
Such as it is — and for my own poor part,
Look you, I'll go pray.
HORATIO: These are but wild and whirling words, my
    lord.
HAMLET: I am sorry they offend you, heartily;   135
Yes, faith, heartily.
HORATIO: There's no offense, my lord.
HAMLET: Yes, by Saint Patrick,° but there is, Horatio,
And much offense too. Touching this vision here,
It is an honest° ghost, that let me tell you.
For your desire to know what is between us,   140
O'ermaster 't as you may. And now, good friends
As you are friends, scholars, and soldiers,
Give me one poor request.
HORATIO: What is 't, my lord? We will.
HAMLET: Never make known what you have seen
    tonight.   145
HORATIO, MARCELLUS: My lord, we will not.

---

69. **posset:** Coagulate, curdle.   70. **eager:** Sour, acid.   72. **tetter:** Eruption of scabs.   **bark'd:** Covered with a rough covering, like bark on a tree.   73. **lazar-like:** Leper-like.   76. **dispatch'd:** Suddenly deprived.   78. **Unhous'led:** Without having received the sacrament [of Holy Communion].   **disappointed:** Unready (spiritually) for the last journey.   **unanel'd:** Without having received extreme unction.   82. **nature:** The promptings of a son.   84. **luxury:** Lechery.   90. **matin:** Morning.   91. **uneffectual fire:** Cold light.   94. **couple:** Add.   98. **globe:** Head.   99. **table:** Writing tablet.   100. **fond:** Foolish.   101. **saws:** Wise sayings.   **forms:** Images.   **pressures:** Impressions stamped.

117. **Hillo, ho, ho:** A falconer's call to a hawk in air. Hamlet is playing upon Marcellus's *Illo,* i.e., *halloo.*   125. **arrant:** Thoroughgoing.   128. **circumstance:** Ceremony.   137. **Saint Patrick:** The keeper of purgatory and patron saint of all blunders and confusion.   139. **honest:** I.e., a real ghost and not an evil spirit.

HAMLET: Nay, but swear 't.
HORATIO: In faith,
  My lord, not I.
MARCELLUS: Nor I, my lord, in faith.
HAMLET: Upon my sword.°   [Holds out his sword.]
MARCELLUS: We have sworn, my lord, already.
HAMLET: Indeed, upon my sword, indeed.
                          (Ghost cries under the stage.)
150 GHOST: Swear.
HAMLET: Ha, ha, boy, say'st thou so? Art thou there,
        truepenny?°
     Come on, you hear this fellow in the cellarage.
     Consent to swear.
HORATIO: Propose the oath, my lord.
HAMLET: Never to speak of this that you have seen,
155   Swear by my sword.
GHOST [beneath]: Swear.
HAMLET: Hic et ubique?° Then we'll shift our ground.
                          [He moves to another spot.]
     Come hither, gentlemen,
     And lay your hands again upon my sword.
160   Swear by my sword
     Never to speak of this that you have heard.
GHOST [beneath]: Swear by his sword.
HAMLET: Well said, old mole! Canst work i' th' earth
        so fast?
     A worthy pioner!° Once more remove, good friends.
                          [Moves again.]
HORATIO: O day and night, but this is wondrous
165   strange!
HAMLET: And therefore as a stranger give it welcome.
     There are more things in heaven and earth, Horatio,
     Than are dreamt of in your philosophy.°
     But come;
170   Here, as before, never, so help you mercy,
     How strange or odd soe'er I bear myself —
     As I perchance hereafter shall think meet
     To put an antic° disposition on —
     That you, at such times seeing me, never shall,
175   With arms encumb'red° thus, or this headshake,
     Or by pronouncing of some doubtful phrase,
     As "Well, well, we know," or "We could, an if° we
        would,"
     Or "If we list° to speak," or "There be, an if they
        might,"
     Or such ambiguous giving out,° to note°
180   That you know aught of me — this do swear,
     So grace and mercy at your most need help you.
GHOST [beneath]: Swear.   [They swear.]

HAMLET: Rest, rest, perturbed spirit! So, gentlemen,
     With all my love I do commend me to you;
     And what so poor a man as Hamlet is   185
     May do, t' express his love and friending to you,
     God willing, shall not lack. Let us go in together,
     And still° your fingers on your lips, I pray.
     The time is out of joint. O cursed spite,
     That ever I was born to set it right!   190
                          [They wait for him to leave first.]
     Nay, come, let's go together.   (Exeunt.)

{ACT II • Scene 1}°

(Enter old Polonius, with his man [Reynaldo].)

POLONIUS: Give him this money and these notes,
        Reynaldo.
REYNALDO: I will, my lord.
POLONIUS: You shall do marvel's° wisely, good
        Reynaldo,
     Before you visit him, to make inquire
     Of his behavior.
REYNALDO: My lord, I did intend it.   5
POLONIUS: Marry, well said, very well said. Look you,
        sir,
     Inquire me first what Danskers° are in Paris,
     And how, and who, what means,° and where they
        keep,°
     What company, at what expense; and finding
     By this encompassment° and drift° of question   10
     That they do know my son, come you more nearer
     Than your particular demands will touch it.°
     Take° you, as 'twere, some distant knowledge of him,
     As thus, "I know his father and his friends,
     And in part him." Do you mark this, Reynaldo?   15
REYNALDO: Ay, very well, my lord.
POLONIUS: "And in part him, but," you may say, "not
        well.
     But, if 't be he I mean, he's very wild,
     Addicted so and so," and there put on° him
     What forgeries° you please — marry, none so rank   20
     As may dishonor, him take heed of that,
     But, sir, such wanton,° wild, and usual slips,
     As are companions noted and most known
     To youth and liberty.
REYNALDO: As gaming, my lord.
POLONIUS: Ay, or drinking, fencing, swearing,   25
     Quarreling, drabbing° — you may go so far.

---

148. sword: The hilt in the form of a cross.   151. truepenny:
Honest old fellow.   157. Hic et ubique: Here and everywhere
(Latin).   164. pioner: Pioneer, digger, miner.   168. your philosophy: This subject called "natural philosophy" or "science"
that people talk about.   173. antic: Fantastic.   175. encumb-
b'red: Folded or entwined.   177. an if: If.   178. list: Were
inclined.   179. giving out: Profession of knowledge.   note:
Give a sign, indicate.

188. still: Always. II, i. Location: Polonius's chambers.
3. marvel's: Marvelous(ly). 7. Danskers: Danes. 8. what
means: What wealth (they have). keep: Dwell. 10. encom-
passment: Roundabout talking. drift: Gradual approach or
course. 11–12. come . . . it: You will find out more this
way than by asking pointed questions (particular demands).
13. Take: Assume, pretend. 19. put on: Impute to. 20. forgeries: Invented tales. 22. wanton: Sportive, unrestrained.
26. drabbing: Whoring.

REYNALDO: My lord, that would dishonor him.
POLONIUS: Faith, no, as you may season° it in the
    charge.
    You must not put another scandal on him
30   That he is open to incontinency;°
    That's not my meaning. But breathe his faults so
      quaintly°
    That they may seem the taints of liberty,°
    The flash and outbreak of a fiery mind,
    A savageness in unreclaimed° blood,
    Of general assault.°
35 REYNALDO: But, my good lord —
POLONIUS: Wherefore should you do this?
REYNALDO: Ay, my lord,
    I would know that.
POLONIUS: Marry, sir, here's my drift,
    And, I believe, it is a fetch of wit.°
    You laying these slight sullies on my son,
40   As 'twere a thing a little soil'd i' th' working,°
    Mark you,
    Your party in converse,° him you would
      sound,°
    Having ever° seen in the prenominate crimes°
    The youth you breathe° of guilty, be assur'd
45   He closes with you in this consequence:°
    "Good sir," or so, or "friend," or "gentleman,"
    According to the phrase or the addition°
    Of man and country.
REYNALDO: Very good, my lord.
POLONIUS: And then, sir, does 'a this —'a does — what
    was I about to say?
50   By the mass, I was about to say something.
    Where did I leave?
REYNALDO: At "closes in the consequence."
POLONIUS: At "closes in the consequence," ay,
    marry.
    He closes thus: "I know the gentleman;
    I saw him yesterday, or th' other day,
    Or then, or then, with such, or such, and, as you
55   say,
    There was 'a gaming, there o'ertook in 's rouse,°
    There falling out° at tennis," or perchance,
    "I saw him enter such a house of sale,"
    Videlicet,° a brothel, or so forth. See you now,
60   Your bait of falsehood takes this carp° of truth;
    And thus do we of wisdom and of reach,°

With windlasses° and with assays of bias,°
By indirections find directions° out.
So by my former lecture and advice
Shall you my son. You have me, have you not?   65
REYNALDO: My lord, I have.
POLONIUS: God buy ye; fare ye well.
REYNALDO: Good my lord.
POLONIUS: Observe his inclination in yourself.°
REYNALDO: I shall, my lord.
POLONIUS: And let him ply° his music.
REYNALDO: Well, my lord.   70
POLONIUS: Farewell.   (*Exit Reynaldo.*)

(*Enter Ophelia.*)

        How now, Ophelia, what's the matter?
OPHELIA: O, my lord, my lord, I have been so
    affrighted!
POLONIUS: With what, i' th' name of God?
OPHELIA: My lord, as I was sewing in my closet,°
    Lord Hamlet, with his doublet° all unbrac'd,°   75
    No hat upon his head, his stockings fouled,
    Ungart'red, and down-gyved to his ankle,°
    Pale as his shirt, his knees knocking each other,
    And with a look so piteous in purport
    As if he had been loosed out of hell   80
    To speak of horrors — he comes before me.
POLONIUS: Mad for thy love?
OPHELIA: My lord, I do not know,
    But truly I do fear it.
POLONIUS: What said he?
OPHELIA: He took me by the wrist and held me hard.
    Then goes he to the length of all his arm,   85
    And, with his other hand thus o'er his brow
    He falls to such perusal of my face
    As 'a would draw it. Long stay'd he so.
    At last, a little shaking of mine arm
    And thrice his head thus waving up and down,   90
    He rais'd a sigh so piteous and profound
    As it did seem to shatter all his bulk°
    And end his being. That done, he lets me go,
    And, with his head over his shoulder turn'd,
    He seem'd to find his way without his eyes,   95
    For out o' doors he went without their helps,
    And, to the last, bended their light on me.
POLONIUS: Come, go with me. I will go seek the King.
    This is the very ecstasy° of love
    Whose violent property° fordoes° itself   100

---

28. season: Temper, soften. **30. incontinency:** Habitual loose behavior. **31. quaintly:** Delicately, ingeniously. **32. taints of liberty:** Faults resulting from freedom. **34. unreclaimed:** Untamed. **35. general assault:** Tendency that assails all unrestrained youth. **38. fetch of wit:** Clever trick. **40. soil'd i' th' working:** Shopworn. **42. converse:** Conversation. **sound:** Sound out. **43. Having ever:** If he has ever. **prenominated crimes:** Before-mentioned offenses. **44. breathe:** Speak. **45. closes . . . consequence:** Follows your lead in some fashion as follows. **47. addition:** Title. **56. o'ertook in 's rouse:** Overcome by drink. **57. falling out:** Quarreling. **59. Videlicet:** Namely. **60. carp:** A fish. **61. reach:** Capacity, ability.

62. windlasses: Circuitous paths (literally, circuits made to head off the game in hunting). **assays of bias:** Attempts through indirection (like the curving path of the bowling ball, which is biased or weighted to one side). **63. directions:** The way things really are. **68. in yourself:** In your own person (as well as by asking questions). **70. let him ply:** See that he continues to study. **74. closet:** Private chamber. **75. doublet:** Close-fitting jacket. **unbrac'd:** Unfastened. **77. down-gyved to his ankle:** Fallen to the ankles (like gyves or fetters). **92. bulk:** Body. **99. ecstasy:** Madness. **100. property:** Nature. **fordoes:** Destroys.

And leads the will to desperate undertakings
As oft as any passion under heaven
That does afflict our natures. I am sorry.
What, have you given him any hard words of late?
OPHELIA: No, my good lord, but, as you did
105   command,
I did repel his letters and denied
His access to me.
POLONIUS: That hath made him mad.
I am sorry that with better heed and judgment
I had not quoted° him. I fear'd he did but trifle
And meant to wrack thee; but, beshrew my
110   jealousy!°
By heaven, it is as proper to our age°
To cast beyond° ourselves in our opinions
As it is common for the younger sort
To lack discretion. Come, go we to the King.
This must be known, which, being kept close,°
115   might move
More grief to hide than hate to utter love.°
Come.   (*Exeunt.*)

{*Scene II*}°

(*Flourish. Enter King and Queen, Rosencrantz, and Guildenstern [with others].*)

KING: Welcome, dear Rosencrantz and Guildenstern.
Moreover that° we much did long to see you,
The need we have to use you did provoke
Our hasty sending. Something have you heard
5   Of Hamlet's transformation — so call it,
Sith° nor th' exterior nor° the inward man
Resembles that° it was. What it should be,
More than his father's death, that thus hath put him
So much from th' understanding of himself,
10 I cannot dream of. I entreat you both
That, being of so young days° brought up with him,
And sith so neighbor'd to his youth and havior,
That you vouchsafe your rest° here in our court
Some little time, so by your companies
15 To draw him on to pleasures, and to gather
So much as from occasion you may glean,
Whether aught to us unknown afflicts him thus,
That, open'd,° lies within our remedy.
QUEEN: Good gentlemen, he hath much talk'd of you
20 And sure I am two men there is not living

To whom he more adheres. If it will please you
To show us so much gentry° and good will
As to expend your time with us awhile
For the supply and profit° of our hope,
Your visitation shall receive such thanks   25
As fits a king's remembrance.
ROSENCRANTZ: Both your Majesties
Might, by the sovereign power you have of us,
Put your dread pleasures more into command
Than to entreaty.
GUILDENSTERN: But we both obey,
And here give up ourselves in the full bent°   30
To lay our service freely at your feet,
To be commanded.
KING: Thanks, Rosencrantz and gentle Guildenstern.
QUEEN: Thanks, Guildenstern and gentle Rosencrantz.
And I beseech you instantly to visit   35
My too much changed son. Go, some of you,
And bring these gentlemen where Hamlet is.
GUILDENSTERN: Heavens make our presence and our
    practices
Pleasant and helpful to him!
QUEEN: Ay, amen!
    (*Exeunt Rosencrantz and Guildenstern
    [with some Attendants].*)

(*Enter Polonius.*)

POLONIUS: Th' ambassadors from Norway, my good
    lord,   40
Are joyfully return'd.
KING: Thou still° hast been the father of good news.
POLONIUS: Have I, my lord? I assure my good liege
I hold my duty, as I hold my soul,
Both to my God and to my gracious king;   45
And I do think, or else this brain of mine
Hunts not the trail of policy so sure
As it hath us'd to do, that I have found
The very cause of Hamlet's lunacy.
KING: O, speak of that! That do I long to hear.   50
POLONIUS: Give first admittance to th' ambassadors.
My news shall be the fruit° to that great feast.
KING: Thyself do grace to them, and bring them in.
                      (*Exit Polonius.*)
He tells me, my dear Gertrude, he hath found
The head and source of all your son's distemper.   55
QUEEN: I doubt° it is no other but the main,°
His father's death, and our o'erhasty marriage.

(*Enter Ambassadors [Voltimand and Cornelius, with
Polonius].*)

KING: Well, we shall sift him. — Welcome, my good
    friends!
Say, Voltimand, what from our brother Norway?

---

109. **quoted:** Observed.   110. **beshrew my jealousy:** A plague upon my suspicious nature.   111. **proper . . . age:** Characteristic of us (old) men.   112. **cast beyond:** Overshoot, miscalculate. 115. **close:** Secret. 115–16. **might . . . love:** Might cause more grief (to others) by hiding the knowledge of Hamlet's strange behavior to Ophelia than hatred by telling it. **II, II. Location:** The castle. 2. **Moreover that:** Besides the fact that. 6. **Sith:** Since. **nor . . . nor:** Neither . . . nor. 7. **that:** What. 11. **of . . . days:** From such early youth. 13. **vouchsafe your rest:** Please to stay. 18. **open'd:** Revealed.

22. **gentry:** Courtesy. 24. **supply and profit:** Aid and successful outcome. 30. **in . . . bent:** To the utmost degree of our capacity. 42. **still:** Always. 52. **fruit:** Dessert. 56. **doubt:** Fear, suspect. **main:** Chief point, principal concern.

60   VOLTIMAND: Most fair return of greetings and desires.
          Upon our first,° he sent out to suppress
          His nephew's levies, which to him appear'd
          To be a preparation 'gainst the Polack,
          But, better look'd into, he truly found
65   It was against your Highness. Whereat griev'd
          That so his sickness, age, and impotence
          Was falsely borne in hand,° sends out arrests
          On Fortinbras, which he, in brief, obeys,
          Receives rebuke from Norway, and in fine°
70   Makes vow before his uncle never more
          To give th' assay° of arms against your Majesty.
          Whereon old Norway, overcome with joy,
          Gives him three score thousand crowns in annual
               fee,
          And his commission to employ those soldiers,
75   So levied as before, against the Polack,
          With an entreaty, herein further shown,
                                          [*Giving a paper.*]
          That it might please you to give quiet pass
          Through your dominions for this enterprise,
          On such regards of safety and allowance°
          As therein are set down.
80   KING: It likes° us well;
          And at our more consider'd° time we'll read,
          Answer, and think upon this business.
          Meantime we thank you for your well-took labor.
          Go to your rest; at night we'll feast together.
          Most welcome home!   (*Exeunt Ambassadors.*)
85   POLONIUS: This business is well ended.
          My liege, and madam, to expostulate°
          What majesty should be, what duty is,
          Why day is day, night night, and time is time,
          Were nothing but to waste night, day, and time.
90   Therefore, since brevity is the soul of wit,°
          And tediousness the limbs and outward flourishes,
          I will be brief. Your noble son is mad.
          Mad call I it, for, to define true madness,
          What is 't but to be nothing else but mad?
          But let that go.
95   QUEEN: More matter, with less art.
     POLONIUS: Madam, I swear I use no art at all.
          That he is mad, 'tis true; 'tis true 'tis pity,
          And pity 'tis 'tis true — a foolish figure,°
          But farewell it, for I will use no art.
100   Mad let us grant him, then, and now remains
          That we find out the cause of this effect,
          Or rather say, the cause of this defect,
          For this effect defective comes by cause.°

          Thus it remains, and the remainder thus.
          Perpend.°   105
          I have a daughter — have while she is mine —
          Who, in her duty and obedience, mark,
          Hath given me this. Now gather, and surmise.
          [*Reads the letter.*] "To the celestial and my soul's
               idol,
          the most beautified Ophelia"—   110
          That's an ill phrase, a vile phrase; "beautified" is a
               vile
          phrase. But you shall hear. Thus: [*Reads.*]
          "In her excellent white bosom, these, etc."
     QUEEN: Came this from Hamlet to her?
     POLONIUS: Good madam, stay awhile; I will be
          faithful.   115
                                              [*Reads.*]
          "Doubt° thou the stars are fire,
               Doubt that the sun doth move,
          Doubt truth to be a liar,
               But never doubt I love.
          O dear Ophelia, I am ill at these numbers.° I have   120
          not art to reckon° my groans. But that I love thee
          best, O most best, believe it. Adieu.
               Thine evermore, most dear lady, whilst this
                    machine° is to him, Hamlet."
          This in obedience hath my daughter shown me,   125
          And, more above,° hath his solicitings,
          As they fell out° by time, by means, and place,
          All given to mine ear.
     KING: But how hath she
          Receiv'd his love?
     POLONIUS: What do you think of me?
     KING: As of a man faithful and honorable.   130
     POLONIUS: I would fain prove so. But what might you
          think,
          When I had seen this hot love on the wing —
          As I perceiv'd it, I must tell you that,
          Before my daughter told me — what might you,
          Or my dear Majesty your Queen here, think,   135
          If I had play'd the desk or table-book,°
          Or given my heart a winking,° mute and dumb,
          Or look'd upon this love with idle sight?°
          What might you think? No, I went round° to work,
          And my young mistress thus I did bespeak:°   140
          "Lord Hamlet is a prince, out of thy star;°
          This must not be." And then I prescripts gave her,
          That she should lock herself from his resort,
          Admit no messengers, receive no tokens.

---

61. Upon our first: At our first words on the business.
67. borne in hand: Deluded, taken advantage of.   **69. in fine:**
In the end.   **71. assay:** Trial.   **79. On . . . allowance:** With such
pledges of safety and provisos.   **80. likes:** Pleases.   **81. consider'd:** Suitable for deliberation.   **86. expostulate:** Expound.
90. wit: Sound sense or judgment.   **98. figure:** Figure of speech.
103. For . . . cause: I.e., for this defective behavior, this madness has a cause.

105. Perpend: Consider.   **116. Doubt:** Suspect, question.
120. ill . . . numbers: Unskilled at writing verses.   **121. reckon:**
(1) Count, (2) number metrically, scan.   **124. machine:** Body.
126. more above: Moreover.   **127. fell out:** Occurred.
136. play'd . . . table-book: Remained shut up, concealing the
information.   **137. winking:** Closing of the eyes.   **138. with
idle sight:** Complacently or uncomprehendingly.   **139. round:**
Roundly, plainly.   **140. bespeak:** Address.   **141. out of thy
star:** Above your sphere, position.

145   Which done, she took the fruits of my advice;
       And he, repelled — a short tale to make —
       Fell into a sadness, then into a fast,
       Thence to a watch,° thence into a weakness,
       Thence to a lightness,° and, by this declension,°
150   Into the madness wherein now he raves,
       And all we mourn for.
       KING: Do you think this?
       QUEEN: It may be, very like.
       POLONIUS: Hath there been such a time — I would fain
       know that —
       That I have positively said "'Tis so,"
       When it prov'd otherwise?
155   KING: Not that I know.
       POLONIUS [*pointing to his head and shoulder*]: Take
       this from this, if this be otherwise.
       If circumstances lead me, I will find
       Where truth is hid, though it were hid indeed
       Within the center.°
       KING: How may we try it further?
       POLONIUS: You know, sometimes he walks four hours
160   together
       Here in the lobby.
       QUEEN: So he does indeed.
       POLONIUS: At such a time I'll loose my daughter to
       him.
       Be you and I behind an arras° then.
       Mark the encounter. If he love her not
165   And be not from his reason fall'n thereon,°
       Let me be no assistant for a state,
       But keep a farm and carters.
       KING: We will try it.

       (*Enter Hamlet [reading on a book].*)

       QUEEN: But look where sadly the poor wretch comes
       reading.
       POLONIUS: Away, I do beseech you both, away.
       I'll board° him presently.

       (*Exeunt King and Queen [with Attendants].*)

170   O, give me leave.
       How does my good Lord Hamlet?
       HAMLET: Well, God-a-mercy.°
       POLONIUS: Do you know me, my lord?
       HAMLET: Excellent well. You are a fishmonger.°
175   POLONIUS: Not I, my lord.
       HAMLET: Then I would you were so honest a man.
       POLONIUS: Honest, my lord?
       HAMLET: Ay, sir. To be honest, as this world goes, is to
       be one man pick'd out of ten thousand.

POLONIUS: That's very true, my lord.   180
HAMLET: For if the sun breed maggots in a dead dog, be-
    ing a good kissing carrion° — Have you a daughter?
POLONIUS: I have, my lord.
HAMLET: Let her not walk i' th' sun.° Conception° is a
    blessing, but as your daughter may conceive, friend,   185
    look to 't.
POLONIUS [*aside*]: How say you by that? Still harping on
    my daughter. Yet he knew me not at first; 'a said I
    was a fishmonger. 'A is far gone. And truly in my
    youth I suff'red much extremity for love, very near   190
    this. I'll speak to him again. — What do you read,
    my lord?
HAMLET: Words, words, words.
POLONIUS: What is the matter,° my lord?
HAMLET: Between who?   195
POLONIUS: I mean, the matter that you read, my lord.
HAMLET: Slanders, sir, for the satirical rogue says here
    that old men have gray beards, that their faces are
    wrinkled, their eyes purging° thick amber and plum-
    tree gum, and that they have a plentiful lack of wit,   200
    together with most weak hams. All which, sir, though
    I most powerfully and potently believe, yet I hold it
    not honesty° to have it thus set down, for you your-
    self, sir, shall grow old as I am, if like a crab you
    could go backward.   205
POLONIUS [*aside*]: Though this be madness, yet there is
    method in 't. — Will you walk out of the air, my lord?
HAMLET: Into my grave.
POLONIUS: Indeed, that's out of the air. [*Aside.*] How
    pregnant° sometimes his replies are! A happiness°   210
    that often madness hits on, which reason and sanity
    could not so prosperously° be deliver'd of. I will
    leave him, [and suddenly contrive the means of meet-
    ing between him] and my daughter. — My honorable
    lord, I will most humbly take my leave of you.   215
HAMLET: You cannot, sir, take from me any thing that I
    will more willingly part withal — except my life,
    except my life, except my life.

(*Enter Guildenstern and Rosencrantz.*)

POLONIUS: Fare you well, my lord.
HAMLET: These tedious old fools!°   220
POLONIUS: You go to seek the Lord Hamlet; there he is.
ROSENCRANTZ [*to Polonius*]: God save you, sir!
                                            [*Exit Polonius.*]

GUILDENSTERN: My honor'd lord!
ROSENCRANTZ: My most dear lord!

---

148. watch: State of sleeplessness.   149. lightness: Light-head-
edness. declension: Decline, deterioration.   159. center:
Middle point of the earth (which is also the center of the Ptolemaic universe).   163. arras: Hanging, tapestry.   165. thereon:
On that account.   170. board: Accost.   172. God-a-mercy:
Thank you.   174. fishmonger: Fish merchant (with connotation of *bawd, procurer*[?]).

182. good kissing carrion: A good piece of flesh for kissing,
or for the sun to kiss.   184. i' th' sun: With additional implication of the sunshine of princely favors. Conception:
(1) Understanding, (2) pregnancy.   194. matter: Substance
(but Hamlet plays on the sense of *basis for a dispute*).   199. purging: Discharging.   203. honesty: Decency.   210. pregnant:
Full of meaning. happiness: Felicity of expression.   212. pros-
perously: Successfully.   220. old fools: I.e., old men like
Polonius.

225 HAMLET: My excellent good friends! How dost thou,
      Guildenstern? Ah, Rosencrantz! Good lads, how do
      you both?
    ROSENCRANTZ: As the indifferent° children of the earth.
    GUILDENSTERN: Happy in that we are not over-happy.
230   On Fortune's cap we are not the very button.
    HAMLET: Nor the soles of her shoe?
    ROSENCRANTZ: Neither, my lord.
    HAMLET: Then you live about her waist, or in the middle
      of her favors?
235 GUILDENSTERN: Faith, her privates° we.
    HAMLET: In the secret parts of Fortune? O, most true;
      she is a strumpet.° What news?
    ROSENCRANTZ: None, my lord, but the world's grown
      honest.
240 HAMLET: Then is doomsday near. But your news is not
      true. [Let me question more in particular. What have
      you, my good friends, deserv'd at the hands of For-
      tune that she sends you to prison hither?
    GUILDENSTERN: Prison, my lord?
245 HAMLET: Denmark's a prison.
    ROSENCRANTZ: Then is the world one.
    HAMLET: A goodly one, in which there are many con-
      fines,° wards,° and dungeons, Denmark being one o'
      th' worst.
250 ROSENCRANTZ: We think not so, my lord.
    HAMLET: Why then 'tis none to you, for there is nothing
      either good or bad but thinking makes it so. To me it
      is a prison.
    ROSENCRANTZ: Why then, your ambition makes it one.
255   'Tis too narrow for your mind.
    HAMLET: O God, I could be bounded in a nutshell and
      count myself a king of infinite space, were it not that
      I have bad dreams.
    GUILDENSTERN: Which dreams indeed are ambition, for
260   the very substance of the ambitious° is merely the
      shadow of a dream.
    HAMLET: A dream itself is but a shadow.
    ROSENCRANTZ: Truly, and I hold ambition of so airy and
      light a quality that it is but a shadow's shadow.
265 HAMLET: Then are our beggars bodies,° and our mon-
      archs and outstretch'd° heroes the beggars' shadows.
      Shall we to th' court? For, by my fay,° I cannot
      reason.
    ROSENCRANTZ, GUILDENSTERN: We'll wait upon° you.
270 HAMLET: No such matter. I will not sort° you with the
      rest of my servants, for, to speak to you like an hon-

est man, I am most dreadfully attended.°] But, in the
beaten way° of friendship, what make° you at Elsinore?
ROSENCRANTZ: To visit you, my lord, no other occasion. 275
HAMLET: Beggar that I am, I am even poor in thanks;
  but I thank you, and sure, dear friends, my thanks
  are too dear a halfpenny.° Were you not sent for? Is it
  your own inclining? Is it a free visitation? Come,
  come, deal justly with me. Come, come; nay, speak. 280
GUILDENSTERN: What should we say, my lord?
HAMLET: Why, anything, but to th' purpose. You were
  sent for; and there is a kind of confession in your
  looks which your modesties have not craft enough to
  color. I know the good King and Queen have sent for 285
  you.
ROSENCRANTZ: To what end, my lord?
HAMLET: That you must teach me. But let me conjure°
  you, by the rights of our fellowship, by the consonancy of our youth,° by the obligation of our ever- 290
  preserv'd love, and by what more dear a better
  proposer° could charge° you withal, be even° and
  direct with me, whether you were sent for, or no?
ROSENCRANTZ [aside to Guildenstern]: What say you?
HAMLET [aside]: Nay then, I have an eye of° you. — If 295
  you love me, hold not off.
GUILDENSTERN: My lord, we were sent for.
HAMLET: I will tell you why; so shall my anticipation
  prevent your discovery,° and your secrecy to the King
  and Queen molt no feather.° I have of late — but 300
  wherefore I know not — lost all my mirth, forgone
  all custom of exercises; and indeed it goes so heavily
  with my disposition that this goodly frame, the earth,
  seems to me a sterile promontory; this most excellent
  canopy, the air, look you, this brave° o'erhanging fir- 305
  mament, this majestical roof fretted° with golden
  fire, why, it appeareth nothing to me but a foul and
  pestilent congregation of vapors. What a piece of
  work is a man! How noble in reason, how infinite in
  faculties, in form and moving how express° and ad- 310
  mirable, in action how like an angel, in apprehension
  how like a god! The beauty of the world, the paragon
  of animals! And yet, to me, what is this quintessence°
  of dust? Man delights not me — no, nor woman neither, though by your smiling you seem to say so. 315

228. **indifferent:** Ordinary.   235. **privates:** Close acquaintances (with sexual pun on *private parts*).   237. **strumpet:**
Prostitute (a common epithet for indiscriminate Fortune, see
line 497 p. 347).   247–48. **confines:** Places of confinement.
248. **wards:** Cells.   260. **the very . . . ambitious:** That seemingly very substantial thing which the ambitious pursue.
265. **bodies:** Solid substances rather than shadows (since beggars are not ambitious).   266. **outstretch'd:** (1) Far-reaching
in their ambition, (2) elongated as shadows.   267. **fay:** Faith.
269. **wait upon:** Accompany, attend.   270. **sort:** Class, associate.

272. **dreadfully attended:** Waited upon in slovenly fashion.
273. **beaten way:** Familiar path.   **make:** Do.   278. **dear a
halfpenny:** Expensive at the price of a halfpenny, i.e., of little
worth.   288. **conjure:** Adjure, entreat.   289–90. **consonancy
of our youth:** The fact that we are of the same age.
291–92. **better proposer:** More skillful propounder.
292. **charge:** Urge.   **even:** Straight, honest.   295. **of:** On.
299. **prevent your discovery:** Forestall your disclosure.
300. **molt no feather:** Not diminish in the least.   305. **brave:**
Splendid.   306. **fretted:** Adorned (with fret-work, as in a
vaulted ceiling).   310. **express:** Well-framed (?), exact (?).
313. **quintessence:** The fifth essence of ancient philosophy,
beyond earth, water, air, and fire, supposed to be the substance
of the heavenly bodies and to be latent in all things.

ROSENCRANTZ: My lord, there was no such stuff in my thoughts.

HAMLET: Why did you laugh then, when I said "man delights not me"?

320 ROSENCRANTZ: To think, my lord, if you delight not in man, what lenten entertainment° the players shall receive from you. We coted° them on the way, and hither are they coming, to offer you service.

HAMLET: He that plays the king shall be welcome; his
325 Majesty shall have tribute of me. The adventurous knight shall use his foil and target,° the lover shall not sigh gratis, the humorous man° shall end his part in peace, [the clown shall make those laugh whose lungs are tickle o' th' sere°], and the lady shall say her
330 mind freely, or the blank verse shall halt° for 't. What players are they?

ROSENCRANTZ: Even those you were wont to take such delight in, the tragedians of the city.

HAMLET: How chances it they travel? Their residence,° both in reputation and profit, was better both ways. 335

ROSENCRANTZ: I think their inhibition° comes by the means of the innovation.°

HAMLET: Do they hold the same estimation they did when I was in the city? Are they so follow'd?

ROSENCRANTZ: No, indeed, are they not. 340

[HAMLET: How comes it? Do they grow rusty?

ROSENCRANTZ: Nay, their endeavor keeps in the wonted° pace. But there is, sir, an aery° of children, little eyases,° that cry out on the top of question,° and are most tyrannically° clapp'd for 't. These are 345 now the fashion, and so berattle° the common stages° — so they call them — that many wearing

---

321. lenten entertainment: Meager reception (appropriate to Lent). **322. coted:** Overtook and passed beyond. **326. foil and target:** Sword and shield. **327. humorous man:** Eccentric character, dominated by one trait or "humor." **329. tickle o' th' sere:** Easy on the trigger, ready to laugh easily. (*Sere* is part of a gunlock.) **330. halt:** Limp.

334. residence: Remaining in one place, i.e., in the city. **336. inhibition:** Formal prohibition (from acting plays in the city). **337. innovation:** I.e., the new fashion in satirical plays performed by boy actors in the "private" theaters; or possibly a political uprising; or the strict limitations set on the theater in London in 1600. **343. wonted:** Usual. **aery:** Nest. **344. eyases:** Young hawks. **cry . . . question:** Speak shrilly, dominating the controversy (in decrying the public theaters). **345. tyrannically:** Outrageous. **346. berattle:** Berate. **346–47. common stages:** Public theaters.

LEFT: Hamlet returns to Denmark. Left to right, Voltemand (Jeremy Geidt), Gertrude (Christine Estabrook), Claudius (Mark Metcalf), Hamlet (Mark Rylance), and Laertes (Derek Smith) in the 1991 American Repertory Theatre production of *Hamlet*, directed by Ron Daniels. RIGHT: The dumb-show sequence with Candy Buckley as the Player Queen.

rapiers° are afraid of goose-quills° and dare scarce come thither.

350 HAMLET: What, are they children? Who maintains 'em? How are they escoted?° Will they pursue the quality° no longer than they can sing?° Will they not say afterwards, if they should grow themselves to common° players — as it is most like, if their means are
355 no better — their writers do them wrong, to make them exclaim against their own succession?°

ROSENCRANTZ: Faith, there has been much to do° on both sides, and the nation holds it no sin to tarre° them to controversy. There was, for a while, no
360 money bid for argument° unless the poet and the player went to cuffs in the question.°

HAMLET: Is 't possible?

GUILDENSTERN: O, there has been much throwing about of brains.

365 HAMLET: Do the boys carry it away?°

ROSENCRANTZ: Ay, that they do, my lord — Hercules and his load° too.°]

HAMLET: It is not very strange, for my uncle is King of Denmark, and those that would make mouths° at him while my father liv'd, give twenty, forty, fifty, a 370 hundred ducats° apiece for his picture in little.° 'Sblood,° there is something in this more than natural, if philosophy could find it out.

(*A flourish* [*of trumpets within*].)

GUILDENSTERN: There are the players.

HAMLET: Gentlemen, you are welcome to Elsinore. Your 375 hands, come then. Th' appurtenance of welcome is fashion and ceremony. Let me comply° with you in this garb,° lest my extent° to the players, which, I tell you, must show fairly outwards,° should more appear like entertainment° than yours. You are welcome. 380 But my uncle-father and aunt-mother are deceiv'd.

347–48. many wearing rapiers: Many men of fashion, who were afraid to patronize the common players for fear of being satirized by the poets who wrote for the children.   **348. goose-quills:** Pens of satirists.   **351. escoted:** Maintained.   **quality:** (Acting) profession.   **352. no longer . . . sing:** Only until their voices change.   **353–54. common:** Regular, adult.   **356. succession:** Future careers.   **357. to do:** Ado.   **358. tarre:** Set on (as dogs).   **360. argument:** Plot for a play.   **361. went . . . question:** Came to blows in the play itself.   **365. carry it away:** Win the day.

366–67. Hercules . . . load: Thought to be an allusion to the sign of the Globe Theatre, which was Hercules bearing the world on his shoulder.   **341–67. How . . . load too:** The passage, omitted from the early quartos, alludes to the so-called War of the Theatres, 1599–1602, the rivalry between the children companies and the adult actors.   **369. mouths:** Faces.   **371. ducats:** Gold coins.   **in little:** In miniature.   **372. 'Sblood:** By His (God's, Christ's) blood.   **377. comply:** Observe the formalities of courtesy.   **378. garb:** Manner.   **my extent:** The extent of my showing courtesy.   **379. show fairly outwards:** Look cordial to outward appearances.   **380. entertainment:** A (warm) reception.

GUILDENSTERN: In what, my dear lord?

HAMLET: I am but mad north-north-west.° When the wind is southerly I know a hawk from a handsaw.°

(Enter Polonius.)

385 POLONIUS: Well be with you, gentlemen!

HAMLET: Hark you, Guildenstern, and you too; at each ear a hearer. That great baby you see there is not yet out of his swaddling-clouts.°

ROSENCRANTZ: Happily° he is the second time come to
390   them; for they say an old man is twice a child.

HAMLET: I will prophesy he comes to tell me of the players; mark it. — You say right, sir, o' Monday morning, 'twas then indeed.

POLONIUS: My lord, I have news to tell you.

395 HAMLET: My lord, I have news to tell you. When Roscius° was an actor in Rome —

POLONIUS: The actors are come hither, my lord.

HAMLET: Buzz,° buzz!

POLONIUS: Upon my honor —

400 HAMLET: Then came each actor on his ass —

POLONIUS: The best actors in the world, either for tragedy, comedy, history, pastoral, pastoral-comical, historical-pastoral, tragical-historical, tragical-comical-historical-pastoral, scene individable,° or poem
405   unlimited.° Seneca° cannot be too heavy, nor Plautus° too light. For the law of writ and the liberty,° these are the only men.

HAMLET: O Jephthah, judge of Israel,° what a treasure hadst thou!

410 POLONIUS: What a treasure had he, my lord?

HAMLET: Why,

"One fair daughter, and no more,
The which he loved passing° well."

POLONIUS [*aside*]: Still on my daughter.

415 HAMLET: Am I not i' th' right, old Jephthah?

POLONIUS: If you call me Jephthah, my lord, I have a daughter that I love passing well.

HAMLET: Nay, that follows not.

POLONIUS: What follows, then, my lord?

420 HAMLET: Why,

"As by lot, God wot,"°
and then, you know,

---

383. **north-north-west:** Only partly, at times. 384. **hawk, handsaw:** Mattock (or *hack*) and a carpenter's cutting tool respectively; also birds, with a play on *hernshaw* or heron. 388. **swaddling-clouts:** Cloths in which to wrap a newborn baby. 389. **Happily:** Haply, perhaps. 396. **Roscius:** A famous Roman actor who died in 62 B.C. 398. **Buzz:** An interjection used to denote stale news. 404. **scene individable:** A play observing the unity of place. 404–05. **poem unlimited:** A play disregarding the unities of time and place. 405. **Seneca:** Writer of Latin tragedies. 405–06. **Plautus:** Writer of Latin comedy. 406. **law . . . liberty:** Dramatic composition both according to rules and without rules, i.e., "classical" and "romantic" dramas. 408. **Jephthah . . . Israel:** Jephthah had to sacrifice his daughter; see Judges 11. Hamlet goes on to quote from a ballad on the theme. 413. **passing:** Surpassingly. 421. **wot:** Knows.

"It came to pass, as most like° it was."

The first row° of the pious chanson° will show you more, for look where my abridgement° comes.   425

(Enter the Players.)

You are welcome, masters; welcome, all. I am glad to see thee well. Welcome, good friends. O, old friend! Why, thy face is valanc'd° since I saw thee last. Com'st thou to beard° me in Denmark? What, my young lady° and mistress? By 'r lady, your ladyship is   430
nearer to heaven than when I saw you last, by the altitude of a chopine.° Pray God your voice, like a piece of uncurrent° gold, be not crack'd within the ring.° Masters, you are all welcome. We'll e'en to 't like French falconers, fly at anything we see. We'll   435
have a speech straight.° Come, give us a taste of your quality; come, a passionate speech.

FIRST PLAYER: What speech, my good lord?

HAMLET: I heard thee speak me a speech once, but it was never acted, or, if it was, not above once, for the   440
play, I remember, pleas'd not the million; 'twas caviary to the general.° But it was — as I receiv'd it, and others, whose judgments in such matters cried in the top of° mine — an excellent play, well digested in the scenes, set down with as much modesty as   445
cunning.° I remember one said there were no sallets° in the lines to make the matter savory, nor no matter in the phrase that might indict° the author of affectation, but call'd it an honest method, as wholesome as sweet, and by very much more handsome than fine.   450
One speech in 't I chiefly lov'd: 'twas Aeneas' tale to Dido, and thereabout of it especially when he speaks of Priam's slaughter.° If it live in your memory, begin at this line: let me see, let me see —

"The rugged Pyrrhus,° like th' Hyrcanian beast"° —   455

'Tis not so. It begins with Pyrrhus:

"The rugged Pyrrhus, he whose sable° arms,

---

423. **like:** Likely, probable. 424. **row:** Stanza. **chanson:** Ballad, song. 425. **my abridgement:** Something that cuts short my conversation; also, a diversion. 428. **valanc'd:** Fringed (with a beard). 429. **beard:** Confront (with obvious pun). 430. **young lady:** Boy playing women's parts. 432. **chopine:** Thick-soled shoe of Italian fashion. 433. **uncurrent:** Not passable as lawful coinage. 433–34. **crack'd . . . ring:** Changed from adolescent to male voice, no longer suitable for women's roles. (Coins featured rings enclosing the sovereign's head; if the coin was cracked within this ring, it was unfit for currency.) 436. **straight:** At once. 442. **caviary to the general:** Caviar to the multitude, i.e., a choice dish too elegant for coarse tastes. 443–44. **cried in the top of:** Spoke with greater authority than. 446. **cunning:** Skill. **sallets:** Salad, i.e., spicy improprieties. 448. **indict:** Convict. 450. **fine:** Elaborately ornamented, showy. 453. **Priam's slaughter:** The slaying of the ruler of Troy, when the Greeks finally took the city. 455. **Pyrrhus:** A Greek hero in the Trojan War, also known as Neoptolemus, son of Achilles. **Hyrcanian beast:** I.e., the tiger. (See Virgil, *Aeneid*, IV, 266; compare the whole speech with Marlowe's *Dido Queen of Carthage*, II, I, 214 ff.) 457. **sable:** Black (for reasons of camouflage during the episode of the Trojan horse).

Black as his purpose, did the night resemble
When he lay couched in the ominous horse,°
460 Hath now this dread and black complexion smear'd
With heraldry more dismal.° Head to foot
Now is he total gules,° horridly trick'd°
With blood of fathers, mothers, daughters, sons,
Bak'd and impasted° with the parching streets,°
465 That lend a tyrannous and a damned light
To their lord's° murder. Roasted in wrath and fire,
And thus o'er-sized° with coagulate gore,
With eyes like carbuncles, the hellish Pyrrhus
Old grandsire Priam seeks."
470 So proceed you.

POLONIUS: 'Fore God, my lord, well spoken, with good
accent and good discretion.

FIRST PLAYER: "Anon he finds him
Striking too short at Greeks. His antique sword,
Rebellious to his arm, lies where it falls,
475 Repugnant° to command. Unequal match'd,
Pyrrhus at Priam drives, in rage strikes wide,
But with the whiff and wind of his fell° sword
Th' unnerved father falls. [Then senseless Ilium,°]
Seeming to feel this blow, with flaming top
480 Stoops to his° base, and with a hideous crash
Takes prisoner Pyrrhus' ear. For, lo! His sword,
Which was declining on the milky head
Of reverend Priam, seem'd i' th' air to stick.
So as a painted° tyrant Pyrrhus stood,
485 And, like a neutral to his will and matter,°
Did nothing.
But, as we often see, against° some storm,
A silence in the heavens, the rack° stand still,
The bold winds speechless, and the orb below
490 As hush as death, anon the dreadful thunder
Doth rend the region,° so, after Pyrrhus' pause,
Aroused vengeance sets him new a-work,
And never did the Cyclops'° hammers fall
On Mars's armor forg'd for proof eterne°
495 With less remorse than Pyrrhus' bleeding sword
Now falls on Priam.
Out, out, thou strumpet Fortune! All you gods,
In general synod,° take away her power!
Break all the spokes and fellies° from her wheel,

And bowl the round nave° down the hill of
heaven,   500
As low as to the fiends!"

POLONIUS: This is too long.

HAMLET: It shall to the barber's with your beard. —
Prithee say on. He's for a jig° or a tale of bawdry, or
he sleeps. Say on, come to Hecuba.°   505

FIRST PLAYER: "But who, ah woe! had seen the
mobled° queen"—

HAMLET: "The mobled queen?"

POLONIUS: That's good. "Mobled queen" is good.

FIRST PLAYER: "Run barefoot up and down, threat'ning
the flames
With bisson rheum,° a clout° upon that head   510
Where late the diadem stood, and for a robe,
About her lank and all o'er-teemed° loins,
A blanket, in the alarm of fear caught up —
Who this had seen, with tongue in venom steep'd,
'Gainst Fortune's state° would treason have
pronounc'd.°   515
But if the gods themselves did see her then
When she saw Pyrrhus make malicious sport
In mincing with his sword her husband's limbs,
The instant burst of clamor that she made,
Unless things mortal move them not at all,   520
Would have made milch° the burning eyes of
heaven,
And passion in the gods."

POLONIUS: Look whe'er° he has not turn'd his color and
has tears in 's eyes. Prithee, no more.

HAMLET: 'Tis well; I'll have thee speak out the rest of   525
this soon. Good my lord, will you see the players well
bestow'd?° Do you hear, let them be well us'd, for
they are the abstract° and brief chronicles of the
time. After your death you were better have a bad
epitaph than their ill report while you live.   530

POLONIUS: My lord, I will use them according to their
desert.

HAMLET: God's bodkin,° man, much better! Use every
man after his desert, and who shall scape whipping?
Use them after your own honor and dignity. The less   535
they deserve, the more merit is in your bounty. Take
them in.

POLONIUS: Come, sirs.

HAMLET: Follow him, friends. We'll hear a play tomorrow. [*As they start to leave, Hamlet detains the First*   540
Player.] Dost thou hear me, old friend? Can you play
the Murder of Gonzago?

FIRST PLAYER: Ay, my lord.

---

459. **ominous horse:** Trojan horse, by which the Greeks gained access to Troy.   461. **dismal:** Ill-omened.   462. **gules:** Red (a heraldic term).   **trick'd:** Adorned, decorated.   464. **impasted:** Crusted, like a thick paste.   **with . . . streets:** By the parching heat of the streets (because of the fires everywhere).   466. **their lord's:** Priam's.   467. **o'er-sized:** Covered as with size or glue.   475. **Repugnant:** Disobedient, resistant.   477. **fell:** Cruel.   478. **senseless Ilium:** Insensate Troy.   480. **his:** Its.   484. **painted:** Painted in a picture.   485. **like . . . matter:** As though poised indecisively between his intention and its fulfillment.   487. **against:** Just before.   488. **rack:** Mass of clouds.   491. **region:** Sky.   493. **Cyclops:** Giant armor makers in the smithy of Vulcan.   494. **proof eterne:** Eternal resistance to assault.   498. **synod:** Assembly.   499. **fellies:** Pieces of wood forming the rim of a wheel.

500. **nave:** Hub.   504. **jig:** Comic song and dance often given at the end of a play.   505. **Hecuba:** Wife of Priam.   506. **mobled:** Muffled.   510. **bisson rheum:** Blinding tears.   **clout:** Cloth.   512. **o'er-teemed:** Worn out with bearing children.   515. **state:** Rule, managing.   **pronounc'd:** Proclaimed.   521. **milch:** Milky moist with tears.   523. **whe'er:** Whether.   527. **bestow'd:** Lodged.   528. **abstract:** Summary account.   533. **God's bodkin:** By God's (Christ's) little body, *bodykin* (not to be confused with *bodkin,* dagger).

HAMLET: We'll ha 't tomorrow night. You could, for
545   need, study a speech of some dozen or sixteen lines,
         which I would set down and insert in 't, could you
         not?
FIRST PLAYER: Ay, my lord.
HAMLET: Very well. Follow that lord, and look you
550   mock him not. — My good friends, I'll leave you till
         night. You are welcome to Elsinore.
                          (*Exeunt Polonius and Players.*)
ROSENCRANTZ: Good my lord!
                 (*Exeunt [Rosencrantz and Guildenstern].*)
HAMLET: Ay, so, God buy you. — Now I am alone.
         O, what a rogue and peasant slave am I!
555   Is it not monstrous that this player here,
         But in a fiction, in a dream of passion,
         Could force his soul so to his own conceit°
         That from her working all his visage wann'd,°
         Tears in his eyes, distraction in his aspect,
560   A broken voice, and his whole function suiting
         With forms to his conceit?° And all for nothing!
         For Hecuba!
         What's Hecuba to him, or he to Hecuba,
         That he should weep for her? What would he do,
565   Had he the motive and the cue for passion
         That I have? He would drown the stage with tears
         And cleave the general ear with horrid speech,
         Make mad the guilty and appall the free,°
         Confound the ignorant, and amaze indeed
570   The very faculties of eyes and ears. Yet I,
         A dull and muddy-mettled° rascal, peak,°
         Like John-a-dreams,° unpregnant of° my cause,
         And can say nothing — no, not for a king
         Upon whose property° and most dear life
575   A damn'd defeat was made. Am I a coward?
         Who calls me villain? Breaks my pate across?
         Plucks off my beard, and blows it in my face?
         Tweaks me by the nose? Gives me the lie° i' th'
            throat,
         As deep as to the lungs? Who does me this?
580   Ha, 'swounds, I should take it; for it cannot be
         But I am pigeon-liver'd,° and lack gall
         To make oppression bitter, or ere this
         I should have fatted all the region kites°
         With this slave's offal. Bloody, bawdy villain!
585   Remorseless, treacherous, lecherous, kindless° villain!
         [O, vengeance!]
         Why, what an ass am I! This is most brave,
         That I, the son of a dear father murder'd,

Prompted to my revenge by heaven and hell,
Must, like a whore, unpack my heart with words,   590
And fall a-cursing, like a very drab,°
A stallion!° Fie upon 't, foh! About,° my brains!
Hum, I have heard
That guilty creatures sitting at a play
Have by the very cunning of the scene   595
Been struck so to the soul that presently°
They have proclaim'd their malefactions;
For murder, though it have no tongue, will speak
With most miraculous organ. I'll have these players
Play something like the murder of my father   600
Before mine uncle. I'll observe his looks;
I'll tent° him to the quick. If 'a do blench,°
I know my course. The spirit that I have seen
May be the devil, and the devil hath power
T' assume a pleasing shape; yea, and perhaps   605
Out of my weakness and my melancholy,
As he is very potent with such spirits,°
Abuses° me to damn me. I'll have grounds
More relative° than this. The play's the thing
Wherein I'll catch the conscience of the King.   610
                                            (*Exit.*)

{*ACT III • Scene I*}°

(*Enter King, Queen, Polonius, Ophelia, Rosencrantz,
Guildenstern, Lords.*)

KING: And can you, by no drift of conference,°
      Get from him why he puts on this confusion,
      Grating so harshly all his days of quiet
      With turbulent and dangerous lunacy?
ROSENCRANTZ: He does confess he feels himself
            distracted,   5
      But from what cause 'a will by no means speak.
GUILDENSTERN: Nor do we find him forward° to be
            sounded,°
      But with a crafty madness keeps aloof
      When we would bring him on to some confession
      Of his true state.
QUEEN: Did he receive you well?   10
ROSENCRANTZ: Most like a gentleman.
GUILDENSTERN: But with much forcing of his
            disposition.°
ROSENCRANTZ: Niggard of question,° but of our
            demands
      Most free in his reply.

---

557. **conceit:** Conception. 558. **wann'd:** Grew pale.
560–61. **his whole . . . conceit:** His whole being responded with
actions to suit his thought. 568. **free:** Innocent. 571. **muddy-
mettled:** Dull-spirited. **peak:** Mope, pine. 572. **John-a-
dreams:** Sleepy dreaming idler. **unpregnant of:** Not quickened
by. 574. **property:** The crown; perhaps also character, quality.
578. **Gives me the lie:** Calls me a liar. 581. **pigeon-liver'd:** The
pigeon or dove was popularly supposed to be mild because it
secreted no gall. 583. **region kites:** Kites (birds of prey) of the
air, from the vicinity. 585. **kindless:** Unnatural.

591. **drab:** Prostitute. 592. **stallion:** Prostitute (male or female). (Many editors follow the Folio reading of *scullion.*)
About: About it, to work. 596. **presently:** At once.
602. **tent:** Probe. **blench:** Quail, flinch. 607. **spirits:**
Humors (of melancholy). 608. **Abuses:** Deludes. 609. **relative:** Closely related, pertinent. **III, i. Location:** The castle.
1. **drift of conference:** Direction of conversation. 7. **forward:**
Willing. **sounded:** Tested deeply. 12. **disposition:** Inclination. 13. **question:** Conversation.

QUEEN: Did you assay° him
15   To any pastime?
ROSENCRANTZ: Madam, it so fell out that certain players
     We o'er-raught° on the way. Of these we told him,
     And there did seem in him a kind of joy
     To hear of it. They are here about the court,
20   And, as I think, they have already order
     This night to play before him.
POLONIUS: 'Tis most true,
     And he beseech'd me to entreat your Majesties
     To hear and see the matter.
KING: With all my heart, and it doth much content me
25   To hear him so inclin'd.
     Good gentlemen, give him a further edge,°
     And drive his purpose into these delights.
ROSENCRANTZ: We shall, my lord.

           (Exeunt Rosencrantz and Guildenstern.)

KING: Sweet Gertrude, leave us too,
     For we have closely° sent for Hamlet hither,
30   That he, as 'twere by accident, may here
     Affront° Ophelia.
     Her father and myself, [lawful espials,°]
     Will so bestow ourselves that seeing, unseen,
     We may of their encounter frankly judge,
35   And gather by him, as he is behav'd,
     If 't be th' affliction of his love or no
     That thus he suffers for.
QUEEN: I shall obey you.
     And for your part, Ophelia, I do wish
     That your good beauties be the happy cause
40   Of Hamlet's wildness. So shall I hope your virtues
     Will bring him to his wonted way again,
     To both your honors.
OPHELIA: Madam, I wish it may.
                                        [Exit Queen.]
POLONIUS: Ophelia, walk you here. — Gracious,° so
          please you,
     We will bestow ourselves. [To Ophelia.] Read on
          this book,   [Gives her a book.]
45   That show of such an exercise° may color°
     Your loneliness. We are oft to blame in this —
     'Tis too much prov'd° — that with devotion's visage
     And pious action we do sugar o'er
     The devil himself.
50 KING [aside]: O, 'tis too true!
     How smart a lash that speech doth give my
          conscience!
     The harlot's cheek, beautied with plast'ring art,
     Is not more ugly to° the thing° that helps it

Than is my deed to my most painted word.
     O heavy burden!   55
POLONIUS: I hear him coming. Let's withdraw, my lord.
                              [King and Polonius withdraw.°]
(Enter Hamlet. [Ophelia pretends to read a book.])

HAMLET: To be, or not to be, that is the question:
     Whether 'tis nobler in the mind to suffer
     The slings and arrows of outrageous fortune,
     Or to take arms against a sea of troubles,   60
     And by opposing end them. To die, to sleep —
     No more — and by a sleep to say we end
     The heart-ache and the thousand natural shocks
     That flesh is heir to. 'Tis a consummation
     Devoutly to be wish'd. To die, to sleep;   65
     To sleep, perchance to dream. Ay, there's the rub,°
     For in that sleep of death what dreams may come
     When we have shuffled° off this mortal coil,°
     Must give us pause. There's the respect°
     That makes calamity of so long life.°   70
     For who would bear the whips and scorns of time,
     Th' oppressor's wrong, the proud man's contumely,°
     The pangs of despis'd° love, the law's delay,
     The insolence of office,° and the spurns°
     That patient merit of th' unworthy takes,   75
     When he himself might his quietus° make
     With a bare bodkin?° Who would fardels° bear,
     To grunt and sweat under a weary life,
     But that the dread of something after death,
     The undiscover'd country from whose bourn°   80
     No traveler returns, puzzles the will,
     And makes us rather bear those ills we have
     Than fly to others that we know not of?
     Thus conscience does make cowards of us all
     And thus the native hue° of resolution   85
     Is sicklied o'er with the pale cast° of thought,
     And enterprises of great pitch° and moment°
     With this regard° their currents° turn awry,
     And lose the name of action. — Soft you now,
     The fair Ophelia. Nymph, in thy orisons°   90
     Be all my sins remb'red.
OPHELIA: Good my lord,
     How does your honor for this many a day?
HAMLET: I humbly thank you; well, well, well.
OPHELIA: My lord, I have remembrances of yours,

---

14. assay: Try to win.   17. o'er-raught: Overtook and passed.
26. edge: Incitement.   29. closely: Privately.   31. Affront:
Confront, meet.   32. espials: Spies.   43. Gracious: Your
Grace (i.e., the King).   45. exercise: Act of devotion. (The
book she reads is one of devotion.)   color: Give a plausible
appearance to.   47. too much prov'd: Too often shown to be
true, too often practiced.   53. to: Compared to.   thing: I.e.,
the cosmetic.

56. [S.D.] withdraw: The King and Polonius may retire behind
an arras. The stage directions specify that they "enter" again
near the end of the scene.   66. rub: Literally, an obstacle
in the game of bowls.   68. shuffled: Sloughed, cast.   coil:
Turmoil.   69. respect: Consideration.   70. of . . . life: So
long-lived.   72. contumely: Insolent abuse.   73. despis'd: Rejected.   74. office: Officialdom.   spurns: Insults.   76. qui-
etus: Acquittance; here, death.   77. bodkin: Dagger.   fardels:
Burdens.   80. bourn: Boundary.   85. native hue: Natural
color, complexion.   86. cast: Shade of color.   87. pitch:
Height (as of a falcon's flight).   moment: Importance.   88. regard: Respect, consideration.   currents: Courses.   90. orisons:
Prayers.

95   That I have longed long to re-deliver.
        I pray you, now receive them.   [*Offers tokens.*]
HAMLET: No, not I, I never gave you aught.
OPHELIA: My honor'd lord, you know right well you
            did,
        And with them words of so sweet breath compos'd
100   As made these things more rich. Their perfume lost,
        Take these again, for to the noble mind
        Rich gifts wax poor when givers prove unkind.
        There, my lord.   [*Gives tokens.*]
HAMLET: Ha, ha! Are you honest?°
105 OPHELIA: My lord?
HAMLET: Are you fair?°
OPHELIA: What means your lordship?
HAMLET: That if you be honest and fair, your honesty°
        should admit no discourse° to your beauty.
110 OPHELIA: Could beauty, my lord, have better com-
        merce° than with honesty?
HAMLET: Ay, truly, for the power of beauty will sooner
        transform honesty from what it is to a bawd than the
        force of honesty can translate beauty into his like-
115   ness. This was sometime° a paradox,° but now the
        time° gives it proof. I did love you once.
OPHELIA: Indeed, my lord, you made me believe so.
HAMLET: You should not have believ'd me, for virtue
        cannot so inoculate° our old stock but we shall relish
120   of it.° I lov'd you not.
OPHELIA: I was the more deceiv'd.
HAMLET: Get thee to a nunn'ry.° Why wouldst thou be a
        breeder of sinners? I am myself indifferent honest;°
        but yet I could accuse me of such things that it were
125   better my mother had not borne me: I am very proud,
        revengeful, ambitious, with more offenses at my
        beck° than I have thoughts to put them in, imagina-
        tion to give them shape, or time to act them in. What
        should such fellows as I do crawling between earth
130   and heaven? We are arrant knaves, all; believe none
        of us. Go thy ways to a nunn'ry. Where's your father?
OPHELIA: At home, my lord.
HAMLET: Let the doors be shut upon him, that he may
        play the fool nowhere but in 's own house.
135   Farewell.
OPHELIA: O, help him, you sweet heavens!
HAMLET: If thou dost marry, I'll give thee this plague for
        thy dowry: be thou as chaste as ice, as pure as snow,
        thou shalt not escape calumny. Get thee to a nunn'ry,
140   farewell. Or, if thou wilt needs marry, marry a fool,

        for wise men know well enough what monsters° you°
        make of them. To a nunn'ry, go, and quickly too.
        Farewell.
OPHELIA: Heavenly powers, restore him!
HAMLET: I have heard of your paintings too, well   145
        enough. God hath given you one face, and you make
        yourselves another. You jig,° and amble, and you
        lisp, you nickname God's creatures, and make your
        wantonness your ignorance.° Go to, I'll no more on
        't; it hath made me mad. I say, we will have no moe   150
        marriage. Those that are married already — all but
        one — shall live. The rest shall keep as they are. To a
        nunn'ry, go.   (*Exit.*)
OPHELIA: O, what a noble mind is here o'erthrown!
        The courtier's, soldier's, scholar's, eye, tongue, sword,   155
        Th' expectancy and rose of the fair state,°
        The glass of fashion and the mold of form,°
        Th' observ'd of all observers,° quite, quite down!
        And I, of ladies most deject and wretched,
        That suck'd the honey of his music vows,   160
        Now see that noble and most sovereign reason,
        Like sweet bells jangled, out of time and harsh,
        That unmatch'd form and feature of blown° youth
        Blasted with ecstasy.° O, woe is me,
        T' have seen what I have seen, see what I see!   165

(*Enter King and Polonius.*)

KING: Love? His affections do not that way tend;
        Nor what he spake, though it lack'd form a little,
        Was not like madness. There's something in his soul,
        O'er which his melancholy sits on brood,
        And I do doubt° the hatch and the disclose°   170
        Will be some danger; which for to prevent,
        I have in quick determination
        Thus set it down: he shall with speed to England,
        For the demand of° our neglected tribute.
        Haply the seas and countries different   175
        With variable° objects shall expel
        This something-settled° matter in his heart,
        Whereon his brains still beating puts him thus
        From fashion of himself.° What think you on 't?
POLONIUS: It shall do well. But yet do I believe   180
        The origin and commencement of his grief
        Sprung from neglected love. — How now, Ophelia?
        You need not tell us what Lord Hamlet said;

---

104. honest: (1) Truthful; (2) chaste.   **106. fair:** (1) Beautiful; (2) just, honorable.   **108. your honesty:** Your chastity. **109. discourse:** Familiar dealings.   **110–11. commerce:** Dealings.   **115. sometime:** Formerly.   **paradox:** A view opposite to commonly held opinion.   **115–16. the time:** The present age.   **119. inoculate:** Graft, be engrafted to.   **119–20. but . . . it:** That we do not still have about us a taste of the old stock; i.e., retain our sinfulness.   **122. nunn'ry:** (1) Convent, (2) brothel.   **123. indifferent honest:** Reasonably virtuous. **127. beck:** Command.

141. monsters: An allusion to the horns of a cuckold.   **you:** You women.   **147. jig:** Dance and sing affectedly and wantonly.   **148–49. make . . . ignorance:** Excuse your affection on the grounds of your ignorance.   **156. Th' expectancy . . . state:** The hope and ornament of the kingdom made fair (by him).   **157. The glass . . . form:** The mirror of fashion and the pattern of courtly behavior.   **158. observ'd . . . observers:** The center of attention and honor in the court.   **163. blown:** Blooming.   **164. ecstasy:** Madness.   **170. doubt:** Fear.   **disclose:** Disclosure.   **174. For . . . of:** To demand.   **176. variable:** Various.   **177. something-settled:** Somewhat settled. **179. From . . . himself:** Out of his natural manner.

We heard it all. — My lord, do as you please,
185 But, if you hold it fit, after the play
Let his queen mother all alone entreat him
To show his grief. Let her be round° with him;
And I'll be plac'd, so please you, in the ear
Of all their conference. If she find him not,
190 To England send him, or confine him where
Your wisdom best shall think.
KING: It shall be so.
Madness in great ones must not unwatch'd go.

                                        (*Exeunt.*)

{*Scene II*}°

(*Enter Hamlet and three of the Players.*)

HAMLET: Speak the speech, I pray you, as I pronounc'd
it to you, trippingly on the tongue. But if you mouth
it, as many of our players° do, I had as lief the town-
crier spoke my lines. Nor do not saw the air too
5   much with your hand, thus, but use all gently; for in
the very torrent, tempest, and, as I may say, whirlwind of your passion, you must acquire and beget a
temperance that may give it smoothness. O, it
offends me to the soul to hear a robustious° periwig-
10   pated° fellow tear a passion to tatters, to very rags, to
split the ears of the groundlings,° who for the most
part are capable of° nothing but inexplicable dumb-
shows and noise. I would have such a fellow whipp'd
for o'er-doing Termagant.° It out-herods Herod.°
15   Pray you, avoid it.
FIRST PLAYER: I warrant your honor.
HAMLET: Be not too tame neither, but let your own discretion be your tutor. Suit the action to the word, the
word to the action, with this special observance, that
20   you o'erstep not the modesty of nature. For anything
so o'erdone is from° the purpose of playing, whose
end, both at the first and now, was and is, to hold, as
't were, the mirror up to nature, to show virtue her
feature, scorn her own image, and the very age and
25   body of the time his° form and pressure.° Now this
overdone, or come tardy off,° though it makes the
unskillful laugh, cannot but make the judicious

---

187. **round:** Blunt. III, II. **Location:** The castle. **3. our
players:** Indefinite use; i.e., *players nowadays.* **9. robus-
tious:** Violent, boisterous. **9–10. periwig-pated:** Wearing a
wig. **11. groundlings:** Spectators who paid least and stood in
the yard of the theater. **12. capable of:** Susceptible of being influenced by. **14. Termagant:** A god of the Saracens; a character in the St. Nicholas play, where one of his worshipers,
leaving him in charge of goods, returns to find them stolen;
whereupon he beats the god or idol, which howls vociferously.
Herod: Herod of Jewry. (A character in *The Slaughter of the
Innocents* and other cycle plays. The part was played with great
noise and fury.) **21. from:** Contrary to. **25. his:** Its. **pressure:** Stamp, impressed character. **26. come tardy off:** Inade-
quately done.

---

grieve, the censure of which one° must in your
allowance o'erweigh a whole theater of others. O,
there be players that I have seen play, and heard oth-   30
ers praise, and that highly, not to speak it profanely,
that, neither having th' accent of Christians nor the
gait of Christian, pagan, nor man, have so strutted
and bellow'd that I have thought some of nature's
journeymen° had made men and not made them   35
well, they imitated humanity so abominably.
FIRST PLAYER: I hope we have reform'd that indiffer-
ently° with us, sir.
HAMLET: O, reform it altogether. And let those that play
your clowns speak no more than is set down for   40
them; for there be of them° that will themselves
laugh, to set on some quantity of barren° spectators
to laugh too, though in the mean time some necessary question of the play be then to be consider'd.
That's villainous, and shows a most pitiful ambition   45
in the fool that uses it. Go, make you ready.

                                        [*Exeunt Players.*]

(*Enter Polonius, Guildenstern, and Rosencrantz.*)

How now, my lord? Will the King hear this piece of
work?
POLONIUS: And the Queen too, and that presently.°
HAMLET: Bid the players make haste.   50

                                        [*Exit Polonius.*]

Will you two help to hasten them?
ROSENCRANTZ: Ay, my lord.   (*Exeunt they two.*)
HAMLET: What ho, Horatio!

(*Enter Horatio.*)

HORATIO: Here, sweet lord, at your service.
HAMLET: Horatio, thou art e'en as just a man
As e'er my conversation cop'd withal.°   55
HORATIO: O, my dear lord —
HAMLET: Nay, do not think I flatter;
For what advancement may I hope from thee
That no revenue hast but thy good spirits,
To feed and clothe thee? Why should the poor be
    flatter'd?
No, let the candied° tongue lick absurd pomp,   60
And crook the pregnant° hinges of the knee
Where thrift° may follow fawning. Dost thou hear?
Since my dear soul was mistress of her choice
And could of men distinguish her election,
Sh' hath seal'd thee for herself, for thou hast been   65
As one, in suff'ring all, that suffers nothing,
A man that Fortune's buffets and rewards
Hast ta'en with equal thanks; and blest are those

---

28. **the censure . . . one:** The judgment of even one of whom.
35. **journeymen:** Laborers not yet masters in their trade.
37–38. **indifferently:** Tolerably. **41. of them:** Some among
them. **42. barren:** I.e., of wit. **49. presently:** At once.
55. **my . . . withal:** My contact with people provided opportunity for encounter with. **60. candied:** Sugared, flattering.
61. **pregnant:** Compliant. **62. thrift:** Profit.

Whose blood° and judgment are so well
   commeddled°
70 That they are not a pipe for Fortune's finger
    To sound what stop° she please. Give me that
       man
    That is not passion's slave, and I will wear him
    In my heart's core, ay, in my heart of heart,
    As I do thee. — Something too much of this. —
75 There is a play tonight before the King.
    One scene of it comes near the circumstance
    Which I have told thee of my father's death.
    I prithee, when thou seest that act afoot,
    Even with the very comment of thy soul°
80 Observe my uncle. If his occulted° guilt
    Do not itself unkennel in one speech,
    It is a damned° ghost that we have seen,
    And my imaginations are as foul
    As Vulcan's stithy.° Give him heedful note,
85 For I mine eyes will rivet to his face,
    And after we will both our judgments join
    In censure of his seeming.°
HORATIO: Well, my lord.
    If 'a steal aught the whilst this play is playing,
    And scape detecting, I will pay the theft.

([*Flourish.*] *Enter trumpets and kettledrums, King,
Queen, Polonius, Ophelia, [Rosencrantz, Guildenstern,
and other Lords, with Guards carrying torches].*)

90 HAMLET: They are coming to the play. I must be idle. Get
        you a place.   [*The King, Queen, and courtiers sit.*]
KING: How fares our cousin Hamlet?
HAMLET: Excellent, i' faith, of the chameleon's dish:°
        I eat the air, promise-cramm'd. You cannot feed ca-
95   pons so.
KING: I have nothing with° this answer, Hamlet. These
        words are not mine.°
HAMLET: No, nor mine now. [*To Polonius.*] My lord,
        you played once i' th' university, you say?
100 POLONIUS: That did I, my lord; and was accounted a
        good actor.
HAMLET: What did you enact?
POLONIUS: I did enact Julius Caesar. I was killed i' th'
        Capitol; Brutus kill'd me.
105 HAMLET: It was a brute part of him to kill so capital a
        calf there. Be the players ready?
ROSENCRANTZ: Ay, my lord; they stay upon your
        patience.

---

69. blood: Passion. **commeddled:** Commingled. **71. stop:**
Hole in a wind instrument for controlling the sound.
79. very . . . soul: Inward and sagacious criticism. **80. oc-
culted:** Hidden. **82. damned:** In league with Satan.
84. stithy: Smithy, place of stiths (anvils). **87. censure of
his seeming:** Judgment of his appearance or behavior.
93. chameleon's dish: Chameleons were supposed to feed on
air. Hamlet deliberately misinterprets the King's *fares* as *feeds.*
By his phrase *eat the air* he also plays on the idea of feeding
himself with the promise of succession, of being the *heir.*
96. have . . . with: Make nothing of. **97. are not mine:** Do
not respond to what I asked.

QUEEN: Come hither, my dear Hamlet, sit by me.
HAMLET: No, good mother, here's metal more attractive.   110
POLONIUS [*to the King*]: O, ho, do you mark that?
HAMLET: Lady, shall I lie in your lap?
                        [*Lying down at Ophelia's feet.*]
OPHELIA: No, my lord.
[HAMLET: I mean, my head upon your lap?
OPHELIA: Ay, my lord.]   115
HAMLET: Do you think I meant country° matters?
OPHELIA: I think nothing, my lord.
HAMLET: That's a fair thought to lie between maids' legs.
OPHELIA: What is, my lord?
HAMLET: Nothing.   120
OPHELIA: You are merry, my lord.
HAMLET: Who, I?
OPHELIA: Ay, my lord.
HAMLET: O God, your only jig-maker.° What should a
        man do but be merry? For look you how cheerfully   125
        my mother looks, and my father died within 's° two
        hours.
OPHELIA: Nay, 'tis twice two months, my lord.
HAMLET: So long? Nay then, let the devil wear black for
        I'll have a suit of sables.° O heavens! Die two months   130
        ago, and not forgotten yet? Then there's hope a great
        man's memory may outlive his life half a year. But,
        by 'r lady, 'a must build churches, then, or else shall
        'a suffer not thinking on,° with the hobby-horse,
        whose epitaph is "For, O, for, O, the hobby-horse is   135
        forgot."°

(*The trumpets sound. Dumb show follows.*)

(*Enter a King and a Queen [very lovingly]; the Queen
embracing him, and he her. [She kneels and makes show
of protestation unto him.] He takes her up, and declines
his head upon her neck. He lies him down upon a bank
of flowers. She, seeing him asleep, leaves him. Anon
comes in another man, takes off his crown, kisses it,
pours poison in the sleeper's ears, and leaves him. The
Queen returns; finds the King dead, makes passionate
action. The Poisoner, with some three or four, come in
again, seem to condole with her. The dead body is carried away. The Poisoner woos the Queen with gifts; she
seems harsh awhile but in the end accepts love.*)
                                        [*Exeunt.*]
OPHELIA: What means this, my lord?
HAMLET: Marry, this' miching mallecho;° it means
        mischief.

---

116. country: With a bawdy pun. **124. only jig-maker:** Very
best composer of jigs (song and dance). **126. within 's:** Within
this. **130. suit of sables:** Garments trimmed with the fur of
the sable and hence suited for a wealthy person, not a mourner
(with a pun on *sable* black). **134. suffer . . . on:** Undergo oblivion. **135–36. "For . . . forgot":** Verse of a song occurring
also in *Love's Labor's Lost,* III, i, 30. The hobby-horse was a
character made up to resemble a horse, appearing in the Morris
dance and such May-game sports. This song laments the disappearance of such customs under pressure from the Puritans.
138. this' miching mallecho: This is sneaking mischief.

140 OPHELIA: Belike° this show imports the argument° of
the play.

(*Enter Prologue.*)

HAMLET: We shall know by this fellow. The players cannot keep counsel;° they'll tell all.
OPHELIA: Will 'a tell us what this show meant?
145 HAMLET: Ay, or any show that you will show him. Be
not you° asham'd to show, he'll not shame to tell you
what it means.
OPHELIA: You are naught, you are naught.° I'll mark the
play.
150 PROLOGUE: For us, and for our tragedy,
Here stooping° to your clemency,
We beg your hearing patiently.   [*Exit.*]
HAMLET: Is this a prologue, or the posy of a ring?°
OPHELIA: 'Tis brief, my lord.
155 HAMLET: As woman's love.

(*Enter [two Players as] King and Queen.*)

PLAYER KING: Full thirty times hath Phoebus' cart°
gone round
Neptune's salt wash° and Tellus'° orbed ground,
And thirty dozen moons with borrowed° sheen
About the world have times twelve thirties been,
160 Since love our hearts and Hymen° did our hands
Unite commutual° in most sacred bands.
PLAYER QUEEN: So many journeys may the sun and
moon
Make us again count o'er ere love be done!
But, woe is me, you are so sick of late,
165 So far from cheer and from your former state,
That I distrust you. Yet, though I distrust,°
Discomfort you, my lord, it nothing° must.
For women's fear and love hold quantity;°
In neither aught, or in extremity.
170 Now, what my love is, proof° hath made you know,
And as my love is siz'd, my fear is so.
Where love is great, the littlest doubts are fear;
Where little fears grow great, great love grows
there.
PLAYER KING: Faith, I must leave thee, love, and
shortly too;
175 My operant° powers their functions leave to do.°
And thou shalt live in this fair world behind,
Honor'd, belov'd; and haply one as kind
For husband shalt thou —

PLAYER QUEEN: O, confound the rest!
Such love must needs be treason in my breast.
In second husband let me be accurst!   180
None wed the second but who kill'd the first.
HAMLET: Wormwood, wormwood.
PLAYER QUEEN: The instances° that second marriage
move°
Are base respects of thrift,° but none of love.
A second time I kill my husband dead,   185
When second husband kisses me in bed.
PLAYER KING: I do believe you think what now you
speak,
But what we do determine oft we break.
Purpose is but the slave to memory,°
Of violent birth, but poor validity,°   190
Which now, like fruit unripe, sticks on the tree,
But fall unshaken when they mellow be.
Most necessary 'tis that we forget
To pay ourselves what to ourselves is debt.°
What to ourselves in passion we propose,   195
The passion ending, doth the purpose lose.
The violence of either grief or joy
Their own enactures° with themselves destroy.
Where joy most revels, grief doth most lament;
Grief joys, joy grieves, on slender accident.   200
This world is not for aye,° nor 'tis not strange
That even our loves should with our fortunes
change;
For 'tis a question left us yet to prove,
Whether love lead fortune, or else fortune love.
The great man down, you mark his favorite flies;   205
The poor advanc'd makes friends of enemies.
And hitherto doth love on fortune tend;
For who not needs° shall never lack a friend,
And who in want° a hollow friend doth try,°
Directly seasons him° his enemy.   210
But, orderly to end where I begun,
Our wills and fates do so contrary run
That our devices still° are overthrown;
Our thoughts are ours, their ends° none of our own.
So think thou wilt no second husband wed,   215
But die thy thoughts when thy first lord is dead.
PLAYER QUEEN: Nor earth to me give food, nor heaven
light,
Sport and repose lock from me day and night,
To desperation turn my trust and hope,
An anchor's cheer° in prison be my scope!°   220

---

140. **Belike:** Probably.   **argument:** Plot.   143. **counsel:** Secret.
145–46. **Be not you:** If you are not.   148. **naught:** Indecent.
151. **stooping:** Bowing.   153. **posy . . . ring:** Brief motto in
verse inscribed in a ring.   156. **Phoebus' cart:** The sun god's
chariot.   157. **salt wash:** The sea.   **Tellus:** Goddess of the
earth, of the *orbed ground.*   158. **borrowed:** Reflected.
160. **Hymen:** God of matrimony.   161. **commutual:** Mutually.
166. **distrust:** Am anxious about.   167. **nothing:** Not at all.
168. **hold quantity:** Keep proportion with one another.
170. **proof:** Experience.   175. **operant:** Active.   **leave to do:**
Cease to perform.

183. **instances:** Motives.   **move:** Motivate.   184. **base . . .
thrift:** Ignoble considerations of material prosperity.   189. **Purpose . . . memory:** Our good intentions are subject to forgetfulness.   190. **validity:** Strength, durability.   193–94. **Most . . .
debt:** It's inevitable that in time we forget the obligations we have
imposed on ourselves.   198. **enactures:** Fulfillments.   201. **aye:**
Ever.   208. **who not needs:** He who is not in need (of wealth).
209. **who in want:** He who is in need.   **try:** Test (his generosity).
210. **seasons him:** Ripens him into.   213. **devices still:** Intentions
continually.   214. **ends:** Results.   220. **anchor's cheer:** Anchor-
ite's or hermit's fare.   **my scope:** The extent of my happiness.

Each opposite° that blanks° the face of joy
Meet what I would have well and it destroy!
Both here and hence° pursue me lasting strife,
If, once a widow, ever I be wife!

225 HAMLET: If she should break it now!
PLAYER KING: 'Tis deeply sworn. Sweet, leave me here
awhile;
My spirits grow dull, and fain I would beguile
The tedious day with sleep.   [Sleeps.]
PLAYER QUEEN: Sleep rock thy brain,
230 And never come mischance between us twain!
                                        [Exit.]
HAMLET: Madam, how like you this play?
QUEEN: The lady doth protest too much, methinks.
HAMLET: O, but she'll keep her word.
KING: Have you heard the argument?° Is there no of-
235 fense in 't?
HAMLET: No, no, they do but jest, poison in jest; no of-
fense i' th' world.
KING: What do you call the play?
HAMLET: "The Mouse-trap." Marry, how? Tropically.°
240 This play is the image of a murder done in Vienna.
Gonzago is the Duke's name; his wife, Baptista. You
shall see anon. 'Tis a knavish piece of work, but what
of that? Your Majesty, and we that have free° souls, it
touches us not. Let the gall'd jade° winch,° our with-
245 ers° are unwrung.°

(Enter Lucianus.)

This is one Lucianus, nephew to the King.
OPHELIA: You are as good as a chorus,° my lord.
HAMLET: I could interpret between you and your love, if
I could see the puppets dallying.°
250 OPHELIA: You are keen, my lord, you are keen.
HAMLET: It would cost you a groaning to take off mine
edge.
OPHELIA: Still better, and worse.°
HAMLET: So° you mistake° your husbands. Begin, mur-
255 derer, leave thy damnable faces, and begin. Come,
the croaking raven doth bellow for revenge.
LUCIANUS: Thoughts black, hands apt, drugs fit, and
time agreeing,

Confederate season,° else no creature seeing,
Thou mixture rank, of midnight weeds collected,   260
With Hecate's ban° thrice blasted, thrice infected,
Thy natural magic and dire property
On wholesome life usurp immediately.
          [Pours the poison into the sleeper's ears.]
HAMLET: 'A poisons him i' th' garden for his estate. His
name's Gonzago. The story is extant, and written in   265
very choice Italian. You shall see anon how the mur-
derer gets the love of Gonzago's wife.
                              [Claudius rises.]
OPHELIA: The King rises.
[HAMLET: What, frighted with false fire?°]
QUEEN: How fares my lord?   270
POLONIUS: Give o'er the play.
KING: Give me some light. Away!
POLONIUS: Lights, lights, lights!

          (Exeunt all but Hamlet and Horatio.)

HAMLET: "Why, let the strucken deer go weep,
The hart ungalled° play.   275
For some must watch,° while some must sleep;
Thus runs the world away."°
Would not this,° sir, and a forest of feathers° — if the
rest of my fortunes turn Turk with° me — with two
Provincial roses° on my raz'd° shoes, get me a fellow-   280
ship in a cry of players?°
HORATIO: Half a share.
HAMLET: A whole one, I.
"For thou dost know, O Damon dear,
This realm dismantled° was   285
Of Jove himself, and now reigns here
A very, very — pajock."°
HORATIO: You might have rhym'd.
HAMLET: O good Horatio, I'll take the ghost's word for
a thousand pound. Didst perceive?   290
HORATIO: Very well, my lord.
HAMLET: Upon the talk of pois'ning?
HORATIO: I did very well note him.
HAMLET: Ah, ha! Come, some music! Come, the re-
corders!°   295

222. opposite: Adverse thing. blanks: Causes to blanch or
grow pale. 223. hence: In the life hereafter. 234. argument:
Plot. 239. Tropically: Figuratively. (The first quarto reading,
trapically, suggests a pun on trap in Mouse-trap.) 243. free:
Guiltless. 244. gall'd jade: Horse whose hide is rubbed by
saddle or harness. winch: Wince. 244–45. withers: The
part between the horse's shoulder blades. 245. unwrung: Not
rubbed sore. 247. chorus: In many Elizabethan plays the
forthcoming action was explained by an actor known as the
"chorus"; at a puppet show the actor who spoke the dialogue
was known as an "interpreter," as indicated by the lines following. 249. dallying: With sexual suggestion, continued in keen,
i.e., sexually aroused, groaning, i.e., moaning in pregnancy,
and edge, i.e., sexual desire or impetuosity. 253. Still . . .
worse: More keen-witted and less decorous. 254. So: Even
thus (in marriage). mistake: Mistake, take erringly, false-
heartedly.

259. Confederate season: The time and occasion conspiring (to
assist the murderer). 261. Hecate's ban: The curse of Hecate,
the goddess of witchcraft. 269. false fire: The blank discharge
of a gun loaded with powder but not shot. 275. ungalled:
Unafflicted. 276. watch: Remain awake. 274–77. Why . . .
away: Probably from an old ballad, with allusion to the
popular belief that a wounded deer retires to weep and die;
cf. As You Like It, II, i, 66. 278. this: The play. feathers:
Allusion to the plumes that Elizabethan actors were fond of
wearing. 279. turn Turk with: Turn renegade against, go
back on. 280. Provincial roses: Rosettes of ribbon like the
roses of a part of France. raz'd: With ornamental slashing.
280–81. fellowship . . . players: Partnership in a theatrical
company. 285. dismantled: Stripped, divested. 287. pajock:
Peacock, a bird with a bad reputation (here substituted for the
obvious rhyme-word ass). 295. recorders: Wind instruments
like the flute.

"For if the King like not the comedy,
Why then, belike, he likes it not, perdy"°
Come, some music!

(Enter Rosencrantz and Guildenstern.)

GUILDENSTERN: Good my lord, vouchsafe me a word
300   with you.
HAMLET: Sir, a whole history.
GUILDENSTERN: The King, sir —
HAMLET: Ay, sir, what of him?
GUILDENSTERN: Is in his retirement marvelous dis-
305   temp'red.
HAMLET: With drink, sir?
GUILDENSTERN: No, my lord, with choler.°
HAMLET: Your wisdom should show itself more richer
    to signify this to the doctor, for for me to put him to
310   his purgation would perhaps plunge him into more
    choler.
GUILDENSTERN: Good my lord, put your discourse into
    some frame° and start not so wildly from my affair.
HAMLET: I am tame, sir. Pronounce.
315 GUILDENSTERN: The Queen, your mother, in most great
    affliction of spirit, hath sent me to you.
HAMLET: You are welcome.
GUILDENSTERN: Nay, good my lord, this courtesy is not
    of the right breed. If it shall please you to make me a
320   wholesome answer, I will do your mother's com-
    mandment; if not, your pardon° and my return shall
    be the end of my business.
HAMLET: Sir, I cannot.
ROSENCRANTZ: What, my lord?
325 HAMLET: Make you a wholesome answer; my wit's dis-
    eas'd. But, sir, such answer as I can make, you shall
    command, or rather, as you say, my mother. There-
    fore no more, but to the matter. My mother, you
    say —
330 ROSENCRANTZ: Then thus she says: your behavior hath
    struck her into amazement and admiration.°
HAMLET: O wonderful son, that can so stonish a
    mother! But is there no sequel at the heels of this
    mother's admiration? Impart.
335 ROSENCRANTZ: She desires to speak with you in her
    closet,° ere you go to bed.
HAMLET: We shall obey, were she ten times our mother.
    Have you any further trade with us?
ROSENCRANTZ: My lord, you once did love me.
340 HAMLET: And do still, by these pickers and stealers.°
ROSENCRANTZ: Good my lord, what is your cause of dis-
    temper? You do surely bar the door upon your own
    liberty, if you deny your griefs to your friend.

HAMLET: Sir, I lack advancement.
ROSENCRANTZ: How can that be, when you have the   345
    voice of the King himself for your succession in
    Denmark?
HAMLET: Ay, sir, but "While the grass grows"° — the
    proverb is something° musty.

(Enter the Players with recorders.)

O, the recorders! Let me see one. [*He takes a re-*   350
corder.] To withdraw° with you: why do you go about
to recover the wind° of me, as if you would drive me
into a toil?°
GUILDENSTERN: O, my lord, if my duty be too bold, my
    love is too unmannerly.°   355
HAMLET: I do not well understand that. Will you play
    upon this pipe?
GUILDENSTERN: My lord, I cannot.
HAMLET: I pray you.
GUILDENSTERN: Believe me, I cannot.   360
HAMLET: I do beseech you.
GUILDENSTERN: I know no touch of it, my lord.
HAMLET: It is as easy as lying. Govern these ventages°
    with your fingers and thumb, give it breath with your
    mouth, and it will discourse most eloquent music.   365
    Look you, these are the stops.
GUILDENSTERN: But these cannot I command to any
    utt'rance of harmony; I have not the skill.
HAMLET: Why, look you now, how unworthy a thing
    you make of me! You would play upon me, you   370
    would seem to know my stops, you would pluck out
    the heart of my mystery, you would sound me from
    my lowest note to the top of my compass,° and there
    is much music, excellent voice, in this little organ,°
    yet cannot you make it speak. 'Sblood, do you think I   375
    am easier to be play'd on than a pipe? Call me what
    instrument you will, though you can fret° me, you
    cannot play upon me.

(Enter Polonius.)

God bless you, sir!
POLONIUS: My lord, the Queen would speak with you,   380
    and presently.°
HAMLET: Do you see yonder cloud that's almost in
    shape of a camel?
POLONIUS: By th' mass, and 'tis like a camel, indeed.
HAMLET: Methinks it is like a weasel.   385
POLONIUS: It is back'd like a weasel.

---

297. perdy: A corruption of the French *par dieu,* by God.
307. choler: Anger. (But Hamlet takes the word in its more
basic humors sense of *bilious disorder.*) **313. frame:** Order.
321. pardon: Permission to depart. **331. admiration:** Wonder.
336. closet: Private chamber. **340. pickers and stealers:**
Hands (so called from the catechism, "to keep my hands from
picking and stealing").

348. While . . . grows: The rest of the proverb is "the silly
horse starves"; Hamlet may not live long enough to succeed to
the kingdom. **349. something:** Somewhat. **351. withdraw:**
Speak privately. **352. recover the wind:** Get the windward
side. **353. toil:** Snare. **354–55. if . . . unmannerly:** If I am
using an unmannerly boldness, it is my love that occasions it.
363. ventages: Stops of the recorder. **373. compass:** Range
(of voice). **374. organ:** Musical instrument. **377. fret:** Irritate (with a quibble on *fret* meaning the piece of wood, gut,
or metal that regulates the fingering on an instrument).
381. presently: At once.

HAMLET: Or like a whale?

POLONIUS: Very like a whale.

HAMLET: Then I will come to my mother by and by.°

390 [Aside.] They fool me° to the top of my bent.° — I
will come by and by.

POLONIUS: I will say so.   [Exit.]

HAMLET: "By and by" is easily said. Leave me, friends.

[Exeunt all but Hamlet.]

'Tis now the very witching time° of night,
395 When churchyards yawn and hell itself breathes out
Contagion to this world. Now could I drink hot
blood,
And do such bitter business as the day
Would quake to look on. Soft, now to my mother.
O heart, lose not thy nature! Let not ever
400 The soul of Nero° enter this firm bosom.
Let me be cruel, not unnatural;
I will speak daggers to her, but use none.
My tongue and soul in this be hypocrites:
How in my words somever° she be shent,°
405 To give them seals° never, my soul, consent!

(Exit.)

{Scene III}°

(Enter King, Rosencrantz, and Guildenstern.)

KING: I like him not, nor stands it safe with us
To let his madness range. Therefore prepare you.
I your commission will forthwith dispatch,°
And he to England shall along with you.
5 The terms° of our estate° may not endure
Hazard so near 's as doth hourly grow
Out of his brows.°

GUILDENSTERN: We will ourselves provide.
Most holy and religious fear it is
To keep those many many bodies safe
10 That live and feed upon your Majesty.

ROSENCRANTZ: The single and peculiar° life is bound
With all the strength and armor of the mind
To keep itself from noyance,° but much more
That spirit upon whose weal depends and rests
15 The lives of many. The cess° of majesty
Dies not alone, but like a gulf° doth draw
What's near it with it; or it is a messy wheel

Fix'd on the summit of the highest mount,
To whose huge spokes ten thousand lesser things
Are mortis'd and adjoin'd, which, when it falls,   20
Each small annexment, petty consequence,
Attends° the boist'rous ruin. Never alone
Did the King sigh, but with a general groan.

KING: Arm° you, I pray you, to this speedy voyage,
For we will fetters put about this fear,   25
Which now goes too free-footed.

ROSENCRANTZ: We will haste us.

(Exeunt Gentlemen [Rosencrantz
and Guildenstern].)

(Enter Polonius.)

POLONIUS: My lord, he's going to his mother's closet.
Behind the arras° I'll convey myself
To hear the process.° I'll warrant she'll tax him
home,°
And, as you said, and wisely was it said,   30
'Tis meet that some more audience than a mother,
Since nature makes them partial, should o'erhear
The speech, of vantage.° Fare you well, my liege.
I'll call upon you ere you go to bed,
And tell you what I know.

KING: Thanks, dear my lord.   35

(Exit [Polonius].)

O, my offense is rank, it smells to heaven;
It hath the primal eldest curse° upon 't,
A brother's murder. Pray can I not,
Though inclination be as sharp as will.°
My stronger guilt defeats my strong intent,   40
And, like a man to double business bound,
I stand in pause where I shall first begin,
And both neglect. What if this cursed hand
Were thicker than itself with brother's blood,
Is there not rain enough in the sweet heavens   45
To wash it white as snow? Whereto serves mercy
But to confront the visage of offense?°
And what's in prayer but this twofold force,
To be forestalled° ere we come to fall,
Or pardon'd being down? Then I'll look up;   50
My fault is past. But, O, what form of prayer
Can serve my turn? "Forgive me my foul
murder"?
That cannot be, since I am still possess'd
Of those effects for which I did the murder,
My crown, mine own ambition, and my queen.   55

---

389. by and by: Immediately.   **390. fool me:** Make me play the fool.   **top of my bent:** Limit of my ability or endurance (literally, the extent to which a bow may be bent).   **394. witching time:** Time when spells are cast and evil is abroad.   **400. Nero:** Murderer of his mother, Agrippina.   **404. How . . . somever:** However much by my words.   **shent:** Rebuked.   **405. give them seals:** Confirm them with deeds.   **III, III. Location:** The castle.   **3. dispatch:** Prepare, cause to be drawn up.   **5. terms:** Condition, circumstances.   **our estate:** My royal position.   **7. brows:** Effronteries, threatening frowns (?), brain (?).   **11. single and peculiar:** Individual and private.   **13. noyance:** Harm.   **15. cess:** Decease.   **16. gulf:** Whirlpool.

22. Attends: Participates in.   **24. Arm:** Prepare.   **28. arras:** Screen of tapestry placed around the walls of household apartments. (On the Elizabethan stage, the arras was presumably over a door or discovery space in the tiring-house façade.)   **29. process:** Proceedings.   **tax him home:** Reprove him severely.   **33. of vantage:** From an advantageous place.   **37. primal eldest curse:** The curse of Cain, the first murderer; he killed his brother Abel.   **39. Though . . . will:** Though my desire is as strong as my determination.   **46–47. Whereto . . . offense:** For what function does mercy serve other than to undo the effects of sin?   **49. forestalled:** Prevented (from sinning).

May one be pardon'd and retain th' offense?
In the corrupted currents° of this world
Offense's gilded hand° may shove by justice,
And oft 'tis seen the wicked prize° itself
60 Buys out the law. But 'tis not so above.
There is no shuffling,° there the action lies°
In his° true nature, and we ourselves compell'd,
Even to the teeth and forehead° of our faults,
To give in evidence. What then? What rests?°
65 Try what repentance can. What can it not?
Yet what can it, when one cannot repent?
O wretched state! O bosom black as death!
O limed° soul, that, struggling to be free,
Art more engag'd!° Help, angels! Make assay.°
70 Bow, stubborn knees, and heart with strings of steel,
Be soft as sinews of the new-born babe!
All may be well.

                                                    [*He kneels.*]

(*Enter Hamlet* [*with sword drawn*].)

HAMLET: Now might I do it pat,° now 'a is a-praying;
And now I'll do 't. And so 'a goes to heaven;
75 And so am I reveng'd. That would be scann'd:°
A villain kills my father, and for that,
I, his sole son, do this same villain send
To heaven.
Why, this is hire and salary, not revenge.
80 'A took my father grossly,° full of bread,°
With all his crimes broad blown,° as flush° as May;
And how his audit° stands who knows save
        heaven?
But in our circumstance and course° of thought,
'Tis heavy with him. And am I then reveng'd,
85 To take him in the purging of his soul,
When he is fit and season'd for his passage?
No!
Up, sword, and know thou a more horrid hent.°
                                    [*Puts up his sword.*]
When he is drunk asleep, or in his rage,
90 Or in th' incestuous pleasure of his bed,
At game a-swearing, or about some act
That has no relish of salvation in 't —
Then trip him, that his heels may kick at heaven,
And that his soul may be as damn'd and black

As hell, whereto it goes. My mother stays.   95
This physic° but prolongs thy sickly days.   (*Exit.*)
KING: My words fly up, my thoughts remain
        below.
Words without thoughts never to heaven go.
                                                    (*Exit.*)

{*Scene IV*}°

(*Enter* [*Queen*] *Gertrude and Polonius.*)

POLONIUS: 'A will come straight. Look you lay° home
        to him.
Tell him his pranks have been too broad° to bear
        with,
And that your Grace hath screen'd and stood
        between
Much heat° and him. I'll sconce° me even here.
Pray you, be round° [with him.   5
HAMLET (*within*): Mother, mother, mother!]
QUEEN: I'll warrant you, fear me not.
Withdraw, I hear him coming.
                        [*Polonius hides behind the arras.*]

(*Enter Hamlet.*)

HAMLET: Now, mother, what's the matter?
QUEEN: Hamlet, thou hast thy father° much offended. 10
HAMLET: Mother, you have my father much offended.
QUEEN: Come, come, you answer with an idle° tongue.
HAMLET: Go, go, you question with a wicked tongue.
QUEEN: Why, how now, Hamlet?
HAMLET: What's the matter now?
QUEEN: Have you forgot me?
HAMLET: No, by the rood,° not so: 15
You are the Queen, your husband's brother's wife
And — would it were not so! — you are my mother.
QUEEN: Nay, then, I'll set those to you that can speak.
HAMLET: Come, come, and sit you down; you shall not
        budge.
You go not till I set you up a glass   20
Where you may see the inmost part of you.
QUEEN: What wilt thou do? Thou wilt not murder me?
Help, ho!
POLONIUS [*behind*]: What, ho! Help!
HAMLET [*drawing*]: How now? A rat? Dead, for a
        ducat, dead!   25
                        [*Makes a pass through the arras.*]
POLONIUS [*behind*]: O, I am slain! [*Falls and dies.*]
QUEEN: O me, what hast thou done?
HAMLET: Nay, I know not. Is it the King?
QUEEN: O, what a rash and bloody deed is this!

---

57. **currents:** Courses.   58. **gilded hand:** Hand offering gold
as a bribe.   59. **wicked prize:** Prize won by wickedness.
61. **shuffling:** Escape by trickery.   **the action lies:** The accusation is made manifest, comes up for consideration (a legal
metaphor).   62. **his:** Its.   63. **teeth and forehead:** Face to face,
concealing nothing.   64. **rests:** Remains.   68. **limed:** Caught
as with birdlime, a sticky substance used to ensnare birds.
69. **engag'd:** Embedded.   **assay:** Trial.   73. **pat:** Opportunely.
75. **would be scann'd:** Needs to be looked into.   80. **grossly:**
Not spiritually prepared.   **full of bread:** Enjoying his worldly
pleasures. (See Ezek. 16:49.)   81. **crimes broad blown:** Sins
in full bloom.   **flush:** Lusty.   82. **audit:** Account.   83. **in . . .
course:** As we see it in our mortal situation.   88. **know . . .
hent:** Await to be grasped by me on a more horrid occasion.

96. **physic:** Purging (by prayer).   **III, IV. Location:** The queen's
private chamber.   1. **lay:** Thrust (i.e., reprove him soundly).
2. **broad:** Unrestrained.   4. **Much heat:** The king's anger.
sconce: Ensconce, hide.   5. **round:** Blunt.   10. **thy father:**
Your stepfather, Claudius.   12. **idle:** Foolish.   15. **rood:** Cross.

FAR LEFT: Michael Pennington as
Hamlet. NEAR LEFT: A scene from the
Royal Shakespeare Company's 1980
production. BELOW LEFT: Hamlet,
played by Kenneth Branagh, looks on
at the celebration of his mother's
marriage to his uncle Claudius.
Gertrude is played by Julie Christie
and Claudius by Sir Derek Jacobi.
Branagh directed this 1996 film.
RIGHT: The grave-digger holds up
Yorick's skull as Hamlet and Horatio
(Tom Wilkinson) look on. BELOW
RIGHT: Carol Royle as Ophelia with
Hamlet in the nunnery scene.

HAMLET: A bloody deed — almost as bad, good
    mother,
30   As kill a king, and marry with his brother.
QUEEN: As kill a king!
HAMLET: Ay, lady, it was my word.
    [Parts the arras and discovers Polonius.]
    Thou wretched, rash, intruding fool, farewell!
    I took thee for thy better. Take thy fortune.
    Thou find'st to be too busy is some danger. —
35   Leave wringing of your hands. Peace, sit you down,
    And let me wring your heart, for so I shall,
    If it be made of penetrable stuff,
    If damned custom° have not braz'd° it so
    That it be proof° and bulwark against sense.°
QUEEN: What have I done, that thou dar'st wag thy
40   tongue
    In noise so rude against me?
HAMLET: Such an art
    That blurs the grace and blush of modesty,
    Calls virtue hypocrite, takes off the rose
    From the fair forehead of an innocent love
45   And sets a blister° there, makes marriage-vows
    As false as dicers' oaths. O, such a deed
    As from the body of contraction° plucks
    The very soul, and sweet religion° makes
    A rhapsody° of words. Heaven's face does glow
50   O'er this solidity and compound mass
    With heated visage, as against the doom,
    Is thought-sick at the act.°
QUEEN   Ay me, what act,
    That roars so loud and thunders in the index?°
HAMLET: Look here, upon this picture, and on this,
55   The counterfeit presentment° of two brothers.
    [Shows her two likenesses.]
    See, what a grace was seated on this brow:
    Hyperion's° curls, the front° of Jove himself,
    An eye like Mars, to threaten and command,
    A station° like the herald Mercury
60   New-lighted on a heaven-kissing hill —
    A combination and a form indeed,
    Where every god did seem to set his seal,
    To give the world assurance of a man.
    This was your husband. Look you now, what
    follows:
65   Here is your husband, like a mildew'd ear,°
    Blasting his wholesome brother. Have you eyes?

Could you on this fair mountain leave to feed,
And batten° on this moor?° Ha, have you eyes?
You cannot call it love, for at your age
The heyday° in the blood is tame, it's humble,   70
And waits upon the judgment, and what judgment
Would step from this to this? Sense,° sure, you
    have,
Else could you not have motion, but sure that
    sense
Is apoplex'd,° for madness would not err,
Nor sense to ecstasy was ne'er so thrall'd   75
But it reserv'd some quantity of choice
To serve in such a difference. What devil was 't
That thus hath cozen'd° you at hoodman-blind?°
Eyes without feeling, feeling without sight,
Ears without hands or eyes, smelling sans° all,   80
Or but a sickly part of one true sense
Could not so mope.°
O shame, where is thy blush? Rebellious hell,
If thou canst mutine° in a matron's bones,
To flaming youth let virtue be as wax,   85
And melt in her own fire. Proclaim no shame
When the compulsive ardor gives the charge,
Since frost itself as actively doth burn,
And reason panders will.°
QUEEN: O Hamlet, speak no more!   90
Thou turn'st mine eyes into my very soul,
And there I see such black and grained° spots
As will not leave their tinct.°
HAMLET: Nay, but to live
In the rank sweat of an enseamed° bed,
Stew'd in corruption, honeying and making love   95
Over the nasty sty —
QUEEN: O, speak to me no more.
These words, like daggers, enter in my ears.
No more, sweet Hamlet!
HAMLET: A murderer and a villain,
A slave that is not twentieth part the tithe°   100
Of your precedent° lord, a vice° of kings,
A cutpurse of the empire and the rule,

---

38. damned custom: Habitual wickedness. **braz'd:** Brazened, hardened. **39. proof:** Armor. **sense:** Feeling. **45. sets a blister:** Brands as a harlot. **47. contraction:** The marriage contract. **48. religion:** Religious vows. **49. rhapsody:** Senseless string. **49–52. Heaven's . . . act:** Heaven's face flushes with anger to look down upon this solid world, this compound mass, with hot face as though the day of doom were near, and is thought-sick at the deed (i.e., Gertrude's marriage). **53. index:** Table of contents, prelude, or preface. **55. counterfeit presentment:** Portrayed representation. **57. Hyperion:** The sun god. **front:** Brow. **59. station:** Manner of standing. **65. ear:** I.e., of grain.

68. batten: Gorge. **moor:** Barren upland. **70. heyday:** State of excitement. **72. Sense:** Perception through the five senses (the functions of the middle or sensible soul). **74. apoplex'd:** Paralyzed. (Hamlet goes on to explain that without such a paralysis of will, mere madness would not so err, nor would the five senses so enthrall themselves to *ecstasy* or lunacy; even such deranged states of mind would be able to make the obvious choice between Hamlet Senior and Claudius.) **78. cozen'd:** Cheated. **hoodman-blind:** Blindman's bluff. **80. sans:** Without. **82. mope:** Be dazed, act aimlessly. **84. mutine:** Mutiny. **86–89. Proclaim . . . will:** Call it no shameful business when the compelling ardor of youth delivers the attack, i.e., commits lechery, since the frost of advanced age burns with as active a fire of lust and reason perverts itself by fomenting lust rather than restraining it. **92. grained:** Dyed in grain, indelible. **93. tinct:** Color. **94. enseamed:** Laden with grease. **100. tithe:** Tenth part. **101. precedent:** Former (i.e., the elder Hamlet). **vice:** Buffoon (a reference to the vice of the morality plays).

That from a shelf the precious diadem stole,
And put it in his pocket!
105 QUEEN: No more!

(*Enter Ghost [in his nightgown].*)

HAMLET: A king of shreds and patches° —
Save me, and hover o'er me with your wings,
You heavenly guards! What would your gracious
figure?
QUEEN: Alas, he's mad!
110 HAMLET: Do you not come your tardy son to chide,
That, laps'd in time and passion,° lets go by
Th' important° acting of your dread command?
O, say!
GHOST: Do not forget. This visitation
115 Is but to whet thy almost blunted purpose.
But, look, amazement° on thy mother sits.
O, step between her and her fighting soul!
Conceit° in weakest bodies strongest works.
Speak to her, Hamlet.
HAMLET: How is it with you, lady?
120 QUEEN: Alas, how is 't with you,
That you do bend your eye on vacancy,
And with th' incorporal° air do hold discourse?
Forth at your eyes your spirits wildly peep,
And, as the sleeping soldiers in th' alarm,
125 Your bedded° hair, like life in excrements,°
Start up and stand an° end. O gentle son,
Upon the heat and flame of thy distemper
Sprinkle cool patience. Whereon do you look?
HAMLET: On him, on him! Look you how pale he
glares!
130 His form and cause conjoin'd,° preaching to stones,
Would make them capable.° — Do not look upon
me,
Lest with this piteous action you convert
My stern effects.° Then what I have to do
Will want true color° — tears perchance for blood.
135 QUEEN: To whom do you speak this?
HAMLET: Do you see nothing there?
QUEEN: Nothing at all, yet all that is I see.
HAMLET: Nor did you nothing hear?
QUEEN: No, nothing but ourselves.
140 HAMLET: Why, look you there, look how it steals away!
My father, in his habit° as he lived!
Look, where he goes, even now, out at the portal!
(*Exit Ghost.*)

QUEEN: This is the very coinage of your brain.
This bodiless creation ecstasy°
Is very cunning in.   145
HAMLET: Ecstasy?
My pulse, as yours, doth temperately keep time,
And makes as healthful music. It is not madness
That I have utter'd. Bring me to the test,
And I the matter will reword, which madness   150
Would gambol° from. Mother, for love of grace,
Lay not that flattering unction° to your soul
That not your trespass but my madness speaks.
It will but skin and film the ulcerous place,
Whiles rank corruption, mining° all within,   155
Infects unseen. Confess yourself to heaven,
Repent what's past, avoid what is to come,
And do not spread the compost° on the weeds
To make them ranker. Forgive me this my virtue;°
For in the fatness° of these pursy° times   160
Virtue itself of vice must pardon beg,
Yea, curb° and woo for leave° to do him good.
QUEEN: O Hamlet, thou hast cleft my heart in twain.
HAMLET: O, throw away the worser part of it,
And live the purer with the other half.   165
Good night. But go not to my uncle's bed;
Assume a virtue, if you have it not.
That monster, custom, who all sense doth eat,°
Of habits devil,° is angel yet in this,
That to the use of actions fair and good   170
He likewise gives a frock or livery°
That aptly is put on. Refrain tonight,
And that shall lend a kind of easiness
To the next abstinence; the next more easy;
For use° almost can change the stamp of nature, 175
And either°. . . the devil, or throw him out
With wondrous potency. Once more, good night;
And when you are desirous to be bless'd,°
I'll blessing beg of you. For this same lord,
[*Pointing to Polonius.*]
I do repent; but heaven hath pleas'd it so   180
To punish me with this, and this with me,
That I must be their scourge and minister.°
I will bestow° him, and will answer well

---

106. **shreds and patches:** Motley, the traditional costume of the clown or fool.   111. **laps'd . . . passion:** Having allowed time to lapse and passion to cool.   112. **important:** Importunate, urgent.   116. **amazement:** Distraction.   118. **Conceit:** Imagination.   122. **incorporal:** Immaterial.   125. **bedded:** Laid in smooth layers. **excrements:** Outgrowths.   126. **an:** On.   130. **His . . . conjoin'd:** His appearance joined to his cause for speaking.   131. **capable:** Receptive.   132–33. **convert . . . effects:** Divert me from my stern duty.   134. **want true color:** Lack plausibility so that (with a play on the normal sense of *color*) I shall shed tears instead of blood.   141. **habit:** Dress.

144. **ecstasy:** Madness.   151. **gambol:** Skip away.   152. **unction:** Ointment.   155. **mining:** Working under the surface.   158. **compost:** Manure.   159. **this my virtue:** My virtuous talk in reproving you.   160. **fatness:** Grossness. **pursy:** Short-winded, corpulent.   162. **curb:** Bow, bend the knee. **leave:** Permission.   168. **who . . . eat:** Who consumes all proper or natural feeling.   169. **Of habits devil:** Devil-like in prompting evil habits.   171. **livery:** An outer appearance, a customary garb (and hence a predisposition easily assumed in time of stress).   175. **use:** Habit.   176. **And either:** A defective line usually emended by inserting the word *master* after *either*, following the fourth quarto and early editors.   178. **be bless'd:** Become blessed, i.e., repentant.   182. **their scourge and minister:** Agent of heavenly retribution. (By *scourge*, Hamlet also suggests that he himself will eventually suffer punishment in the process of fulfilling heaven's will.)   183. **bestow:** Stow, dispose of.

The death I gave him. So, again, good night.
185   I must be cruel only to be kind.
Thus bad begins and worse remains behind.°
One word more, good lady.
QUEEN: What shall I do?
HAMLET: Not this, by no means, that I bid you do:
Let the bloat° king tempt you again to bed,
190   Pinch wanton on your cheek, call you his mouse,
And let him, for a pair of reechy° kisses,
Or paddling in your neck with his damn'd fingers,
Make you to ravel all this matter out,
That I essentially am not in madness,
195   But mad in craft. 'Twere good° you let him know,
For who that's but a queen, fair, sober, wise,
Would from a paddock,° from a bat, a gib,°
Such dear concernings° hide? Who would do so?
No, in despite of sense and secrecy,
200   Unpeg the basket° on the house's top,
Let the birds fly, and, like the famous ape,°
To try conclusions,° in the basket creep
And break your own neck down.
QUEEN: Be thou assur'd, if words be made of breath,
205   And breath of life, I have no life to breathe
What thou hast said to me.
HAMLET: I must to England; you know that?
QUEEN: Alack,
I had forgot. 'Tis so concluded on.
HAMLET: There's letters seal'd, and my two school-
fellows,
210   Whom I will trust as I will adders fang'd,
They bear the mandate; they must sweep my way,°
And marshal me to knavery. Let it work.
For 'tis the sport to have the enginer°
Hoist with° his own petar,° and 't shall go hard
215   But I will delve one yard below their mines,°
And blow them at the moon. O, 'tis most sweet,
When in one line two crafts° directly meet.
This man shall set me packing.°
I'll lug the guts into the neighbor room.
220   Mother, good night indeed. This counselor
Is now most still, most secret, and most grave,
Who was in life a foolish prating knave.

186. behind: To come.   189. bloat: Bloated.   191. reechy:
Dirty, filthy.   195. good: Said ironically; also the following
eight lines.   197. paddock: Toad.   gib: Tomcat.   198. dear
concernings: Important affairs.   200. Unpeg the basket: Open
the cage, i.e., let out the secret.   201. famous ape: In a story
now lost.   202. conclusions: Experiments (in which the ape
apparently enters a cage from which birds have been released
and then tries to fly out of the cage as they have done, falling
to his death).   211. sweep my way: Go before me.   213. en-
giner: Constructor of military contrivances.   214. Hoist with:
Blown up by.   petar: Petard, an explosive used to blow in a
door or make a breach.   215. mines: Tunnels used in warfare
to undermine the enemy's emplacements; Hamlet will counter-
mine by going under their mines.   217. crafts: Acts of guile,
plots.   218. set me packing: Set me to making schemes, and set
me to lugging (him) and, also, send me off in a hurry.

Come, sir, to draw toward an end° with you.
Good night, mother.

(Exeunt [severally, Hamlet dragging in Polonius].)

{ACT IV • Scene 1}°

(Enter King and Queen, with Rosencrantz and Guildenstern.)

KING: There's matter in these sighs, these profound
heaves
You must translate; 'tis fit we understand them.
Where is your son?
QUEEN: Bestow this place on us a little while.

[Exeunt Rosencrantz and Guildenstern.]

Ah, mine own lord, what have I seen tonight!   5
KING: What, Gertrude? How does Hamlet?
QUEEN: Mad as the sea and wind when both contend
Which is the mightier. In his lawless fit,
Behind the arras hearing something stir,
Whips out his rapier, cries, "A rat, a rat!"   10
And, in this brainish apprehension,° kills
The unseen good old man.
KING: O heavy deed!
It had been so with us, had we been there.
His liberty is full of threats to all —
To you yourself, to us, to everyone.   15
Alas, how shall this bloody deed be answer'd?
It will be laid to us, whose providence°
Should have kept short,° restrain'd, and out of
haunt°
This mad young man. But so much was our love
We would not understand what was most fit,   20
But, like the owner of a foul disease,
To keep it from divulging,° let it feed
Even on the pith of life. Where is he gone?
QUEEN: To draw apart the body he hath kill'd,
O'er whom his very madness, like some ore°   25
Among a mineral° of metals base,
Shows itself pure: 'a weeps for what is done.
KING: O Gertrude, come away!
The sun no sooner shall the mountains touch
But we will ship him hence, and this vile deed   30
We must, with all our majesty and skill,
Both countenance and excuse. Ho, Guildenstern!

(Enter Rosencrantz and Guildenstern.)

Friends both, go join you with some further aid.
Hamlet in madness hath Polonius slain,
And from his mother's closet hath he dragg'd him.   35

223. draw . . . end: Finish up (with a pun on draw, pull).
IV, I. Location: The castle.   11. brainish apprehension: Head-
strong conception.   17. providence: Foresight.   18. short:
On a short tether.   out of haunt: Secluded.   22. divulging:
Becoming evident.   25. ore: Vein of gold.   26. mineral: Mine.

Go seek him out; speak fair, and bring the body
Into the chapel. I pray you, haste in this.

    [*Exeunt Rosencrantz and Guildenstern.*]

Come, Gertrude, we'll call up our wisest friends
And let them know both what we mean to do
40 And what's untimely done° . . . .
Whose whisper o'er the world's diameter,°
As level° as the cannon to his blank,°
Transports his pois'ned shot, may miss our
  name,
And hit the woundless° air. O, come away!
45 My soul is full of discord and dismay. (*Exeunt.*)

{*Scene II*}°

(*Enter Hamlet.*)

HAMLET: Safely stow'd.
[ROSENCRANTZ, GUILDENSTERN (*within*): Hamlet! Lord
 Hamlet!]
HAMLET: But soft, what noise? Who calls on Hamlet?
5 O, here they come.

(*Enter Rosencrantz and Guildenstern.*)

ROSENCRANTZ: What have you done, my lord, with the
 dead body?
HAMLET: Compounded it with dust, whereto 'tis kin.
ROSENCRANTZ: Tell us where 'tis, that we may take it
 thence
And bear it to the chapel.
10 HAMLET: Do not believe it.
ROSENCRANTZ: Believe what?
HAMLET: That I can keep your counsel and not mine
 own. Besides, to be demanded of° a sponge, what
 replication° should be made by the son of a king?
15 ROSENCRANTZ: Take you me for a sponge, my lord?
HAMLET: Ay, sir, that soaks up the King's countenance,°
 his rewards, his authorities. But such officers do the
 King best service in the end. He keeps them, like an
 ape an apple, in the corner of his jaw, first mouth'd,
20 to be last swallow'd. When he needs what you have
 glean'd, it is but squeezing you, and, sponge, you
 shall be dry again.
ROSENCRANTZ: I understand you not, my lord.
HAMLET: I am glad of it. A knavish speech sleeps in° a
25 foolish ear.
ROSENCRANTZ: My lord, you must tell us where the
 body is, and go with us to the King.

HAMLET: The body is with the King, but the King is not
 with the body.° The King is a thing —
GUILDENSTERN: A thing, my lord?   30
HAMLET: Of nothing.° Bring me to him. [Hide fox, and
 all after.°]   (*Exeunt.*)

{*Scene III*}°

(*Enter King, and two or three.*)

KING: I have sent to seek him, and to find the body.
How dangerous is it that this man goes loose!
Yet must not we put the strong law on him.
He's lov'd of the distracted° multitude,
Who like not in their judgment, but their eyes, 5
And where 'tis so, th' offender's scourge° is weigh'd,°
But never the offense. To bear° all smooth and even,
This sudden sending him away must seem
Deliberate pause.° Diseases desperate grown
By desperate appliance are reliev'd,   10
Or not at all.

(*Enter Rosencrantz, [Guildenstern,] and all the rest.*)

     How now? What hath befall'n?
ROSENCRANTZ: Where the dead body is bestow'd, my
 lord,
We cannot get from him.
KING: But where is he?
ROSENCRANTZ: Without, my lord; guarded, to know
 your pleasure.
KING: Bring him before us.
ROSENCRANTZ: Ho! Bring in the lord. 15

(*They enter [with Hamlet].*)

KING: Now, Hamlet, where's Polonius?
HAMLET: At supper.
KING: At supper? Where?
HAMLET: Not where he eats, but where 'a is eaten. A
 certain convocation of politic worms° are e'en at 20
 him. Your worm is your only emperor for diet.° We
 fat all creatures else to fat us, and we fat ourselves for
 maggots. Your fat king and your lean beggar is but
 variable service,° two dishes, but to one table —
 that's the end.   25

---

29. The . . . body: Perhaps alludes to the legal commonplace of
"the king's two bodies," which drew a distinction between the
sacred office of kingship and the particular mortal who possessed it at any given time. **31. Of nothing:** Of no account.
31–32. Hide . . . after: An old signal cry in the game of hide-
and-seek, suggesting that Hamlet now runs away from them.
IV, III. Location: The castle. **4. distracted:** Fickle, unstable.
6. scourge: Punishment. **weigh'd:** Taken into consideration.
7. bear: Manage. **9. Deliberate pause:** Carefully considered
action. **20. politic worms:** Crafty worms (suited to a master
spy like Polonius). **21. diet:** Food, eating (with perhaps a
punning reference to the Diet of Worms, a famous convocation held in 1521). **24. variable service:** Different courses of a
single meal.

---

40. And . . . done: A defective line; conjectures as to the missing words include *so, haply, slander* (Capell and others); *for,
haply, slander* (Theobald and others). **41. diameter:** Extent
from side to side. **42. As level:** With as direct aim. **blank:**
White spot in the center of a target. **44. woundless:** Invulnerable. **IV, II. Location:** The castle. **13. demanded of:** Questioned by. **14. replication:** Reply. **16. countenance:** Favor.
24. sleeps in: Has no meaning to.

KING: Alas, alas!

HAMLET: A man may fish with the worm that hath eat°
of a king, and eat of the fish that hath fed of that
worm.

30 KING: What dost thou mean by this?

HAMLET: Nothing but to show you how a king may go a
progress° through the guts of a beggar.

KING: Where is Polonius?

HAMLET: In heaven. Send thither to see. If your messen-
35 ger find him not there, seek him i' th' other place
yourself. But if indeed you find him not within this
month, you shall nose him as you go up the stairs
into the lobby.

KING [to some Attendants]: Go seek him there.

40 HAMLET: 'A will stay till you come.

                                    [Exit Attendants.]

KING: Hamlet, this deed, for thine especial safety. —
Which we do tender,° as we dearly° grieve
For that which thou hast done — must send thee
    hence
[With fiery quickness.] Therefore prepare thyself.
45 The bark° is ready, and the wind at help,
Th' associates tend,° and everything is bent°
For England.

HAMLET: For England!

KING: Ay, Hamlet.

50 HAMLET: Good.

KING: So is it, if thou knew'st our purposes.

HAMLET: I see a cherub° that sees them. But, come, for
England! Farewell, dear mother.

KING: Thy loving father, Hamlet.

55 HAMLET: My mother. Father and mother is man and
wife, man and wife is one flesh, and so, my mother.
Come, for England!   (Exit.)

KING: Follow him at foot;° tempt him with speed
    aboard.
Delay it not; I'll have him hence tonight.
60 Away! For everything is seal'd and done
That else leans on° th' affair. Pray you, make haste.

                        [Exeunt all but the King.]

And, England,° if my love thou hold'st at aught —
As my great power thereof may give thee sense,
Since yet thy cicatrice° looks raw and red
65 After the Danish sword, and thy free awe°
Pays homage to us — thou mayst not coldly set°
Our sovereign process,° which imports at full,
By letters congruing° to that effect,
The present° death of Hamlet. Do it, England,

For like the hectic° in my blood he rages,   70
And thou must cure me. Till I know 'tis done,
Howe'er my haps,° my joys were ne'er begun.

                                          (Exit.)

{Scene IV}°

(Enter Fortinbras with his Army over the stage.)

FORTINBRAS: Go, captain, from me greet the Danish
    king.
Tell him that, by his license,° Fortinbras
Craves the conveyance° of a promis'd march
Over his kingdom. You know the rendezvous.
If that his Majesty would aught with us,   5
We shall express our duty in his eye;°
And let him know so.

CAPTAIN: I will do 't, my lord.

FORTINBRAS: Go softly° on.   [Exeunt all but the
                                              Captain.]

(Enter Hamlet, Rosencrantz, [Guildenstern,] etc.)

HAMLET: Good sir, whose powers° are these?

CAPTAIN: They are of Norway, sir.   10

HAMLET: How purposed, sir, I pray you?

CAPTAIN: Against some part of Poland.

HAMLET: Who commands them, sir?

CAPTAIN: The nephew to old Norway, Fortinbras.

HAMLET: Goes it against the main° of Poland, sir,   15
Or for some frontier?

CAPTAIN: Truly to speak, and with no addition,°
We go to gain a little patch of ground
That hath in it no profit but the name.
To pay° five ducats, five, I would not farm it;°   20
Nor will it yield to Norway or the Pole
A ranker° rate, should it be sold in fee.°

HAMLET: Why, then the Polack never will defend it.

CAPTAIN: Yes, it is already garrison'd.

HAMLET: Two thousand souls and twenty thousand
    ducats   25
Will not debate the question of this straw.°
This is th' imposthume° of much wealth and
    peace,
That inward breaks, and shows no cause without
Why the man dies. I humbly thank you, sir.

CAPTAIN: God buy you, sir.   [Exit.]

ROSENCRANTZ: Will 't please you go, my lord?   30

HAMLET: I'll be with you straight. Go a little before.

                        [Exit all except Hamlet.]

---

27. eat: Eaten (pronounced "et"). 32. progress: Royal journey of state. 42. tender: Regard, hold dear. dearly: Intensely. 45. bark: Sailing vessel. 46. tend: Wait. bent: In
readiness. 52. cherub: Cherubim are angels of knowledge.
58. at foot: Close behind, at heel. 61. leans on: Bears upon,
is related to. 62. England: King of England. 64. cicatrice:
Scar. 65. free awe: Voluntary show of respect. 66. set:
Esteem. 67. process: Command. 68. congruing: Agreeing.
69. present: Immediate.

70. hectic: Persistent fever. 72. haps: Fortunes. IV. IV. Location: The coast of Denmark. 2. license: Permission. 3. conveyance: Escort, convoy. 6. eye: Presence. 8. softly: Slowly.
9. powers: Forces. 15. main: Main part. 17. addition: Exaggeration. 20. To pay: I.e., for a yearly rental of. farm it:
Take a lease of it. 22. ranker: Higher. in fee: Fee simple,
outright. 26. debate . . . straw: Settle this trifling matter.
27. imposthume: Abscess.

How all occasions do inform against° me,
And spur my dull revenge! What is a man,
If his chief good and market of° his time
35 Be but to sleep and feed? A beast, no more.
Sure he that made us with such large discourse,°
Looking before and after, gave us not
That capability and god-like reason
To fust° in us unus'd. Now, whether it be
40 Bestial oblivion,° or some craven scruple
Of thinking too precisely on th' event° —
A thought which, quarter'd, hath but one part
wisdom
And ever three parts coward — I do not know
Why yet I live to say "This thing's to do,"
45 Sith° I have cause and will and strength and means
To do 't. Examples gross° as earth exhort me:
Witness this army of such mass and charge°
Led by a delicate and tender prince,
Whose spirit, with divine ambition puff'd
50 Makes mouths° at the invisible event,
Exposing what is mortal and unsure
To all that fortune, death, and danger dare,
Even for an egg-shell. Rightly to be great
Is not to stir without great argument,
55 But greatly to find quarrel in a straw
When honor's at the stake. How stand I then,
That have a father kill'd, a mother stain'd,
Excitements of° my reason and my blood,
And let all sleep, while, to my shame, I see
60 The imminent death of twenty thousand men,
That, for a fantasy° and trick° of fame,
Go to their graves like beds, fight for a plot°
Whereon the numbers cannot try the cause,°
Which is not tomb enough and continent°
65 To hide the slain? O, from this time forth,
My thoughts be bloody, or be nothing worth!

                                             (*Exit.*)

{*Scene V*}°

(*Enter Horatio, [Queen] Gertrude, and a Gentleman.*)

QUEEN: I will not speak with her.
GENTLEMAN: She is importunate, indeed distract.
    Her mood will needs be pitied.
QUEEN: What would she have?
GENTLEMAN: She speaks much of her father, says she
    hears

There's tricks° i' th' world, and hems, and beats her
    heart,°   5
Spurns enviously at straws,° speaks things in doubt°
That carry but half sense. Her speech is nothing,
Yet the unshaped use° of it doth move
The hearers to collection;° they yawn° at it,
And botch° the words up fit to their own thoughts,   10
Which, as her winks and nods and gestures yield°
    them,
Indeed would make one think there might be
    thought,°
Though nothing sure, yet much unhappily.
HORATIO: 'twere good she were spoken with, for she
    may strew
Dangerous conjectures in ill-breeding° minds.   15
QUEEN: Let her come in.   [*Exit Gentlemen.*]
    [*Aside.*] To my sick soul, as sin's true nature is,
Each toy° seems prologue to some great amiss.°
So full of artless jealousy is guilt,
It spills itself in fearing to be spilt.°   20

(*Enter Ophelia [distracted].*)

OPHELIA: Where is the beauteous majesty of Denmark?
QUEEN: How now, Ophelia?
OPHELIA (*she sings*): "How should I your true love
    know
        From another one?
    By his cockle hat° and staff,   25
        And his sandal shoon."°
QUEEN: Alas, sweet lady, what imports this song?
OPHELIA: Say you? Nay, pray you, mark.
    "He is dead and gone, lady,   (*Song.*)
        He is dead and gone;   30
    At his head a grass-green turf,
        At his heels a stone."
    O, ho!
QUEEN: Nay, but Ophelia —
OPHELIA: Pray you mark.   35
    [*Sings.*] "White his shroud as the mountain
        snow"—

(*Enter King.*)

QUEEN: Alas, look here, my lord.
OPHELIA: "Larded° all with flowers   (*Song.*)
        Which bewept to the ground did not go
        With true-love showers."   40

---

32. **inform against:** Denounce, betray; take shape against.
34. **market of:** Profit of compensation for. 36. **discourse:** Power
of reasoning. 39. **fust:** Grow moldy. 40. **oblivion:** Forgetfulness. 41. **event:** Outcome. 45. **Sith:** Since. 46. **gross:**
Obvious. 47. **charge:** Expense. 50. **Makes mouths:** Makes
scornful faces. 58. **Excitements of:** Promptings by. 61. **fan-**
tasy: Fanciful caprice. **trick:** Trifle. 62. **plot:** I.e., of ground.
63. **Whereon . . . cause:** On which there is insufficient room for
the soldiers needed to engage in a military contest. 64. **conti-**
nent: Receptacle, container. **IV, v. Location:** The castle.

5. **tricks:** Deceptions. **heart:** Breast. 6. **Spurns . . . straws:**
Kicks spitefully, takes offense at trifles. **in doubt:** Obscurely.
8. **unshaped use:** Distracted manner. 9. **collection:** Inference,
a guess at some sort of meaning. **yawn:** Wonder, grasp.
10. **botch:** Patch. 11. **yield:** Delivery, bring forth (her words).
12. **thought:** Conjectured. 15. **ill-breeding:** Prone to suspect
the worst. 18. **toy:** Trifle. **amiss:** Calamity. 19–20. **So . . .**
spilt: Guilt is so full of suspicion that it unskillfully betrays
itself in fearing betrayal. 25. **cockle hat:** Hat with cockleshell
stuck in it as a sign that the wearer had been a pilgrim to the
shrine of St. James of Compostella in Spain. 26. **shoon:**
Shoes. 38. **Larded:** Decorated.

KING: How do you, pretty lady?

OPHELIA: Well, God 'ild° you! They say the owl° was a
baker's daughter. Lord, we know what we are, but
know not what we may be. God be at your table!

45 KING: Conceit° upon her father.

OPHELIA: Pray let's have no words of this; but when
they ask you what it means, say you this:

"Tomorrow is Saint Valentine's° day.   (Song.)
All in the morning betime,
50   And I a maid at your window,
     To be your Valentine.
Then up he rose, and donn'd his clo'es,
     And dupp'd° the chamber-door,
Let in the maid, that out a maid
55   Never departed more."

KING: Pretty Ophelia!

OPHELIA: Indeed, la, without an oath, I'll make an end
on 't:

[Sings.] "By Gis° and by Saint Charity,
60   Alack, and fie for shame!
Young men will do 't, if they come to 't;
     By Cock,° they are to blame.
Quoth she, 'Before you tumbled me,
     You promised me to wed.'"
65 He answers:
"'So would I ha' done, by yonder sun,
     An thou hadst not come to my bed.'"

KING: How long hath she been thus?

OPHELIA: I hope all will be well. We must be patient, but
70 I cannot choose but weep, to think they would lay
him i' th' cold ground. My brother shall know of it;
and so I thank you for your good counsel. Come, my
coach! Good night, ladies; good night, sweet ladies;
good night, good night.

                                        [Exit.]

KING: Follow her close; give her good watch, I pray
75   you.   [Exit Horatio.]
O, this is the poison of deep grief; it springs
All from her father's death — and now behold!
O Gertrude, Gertrude,
When sorrows come, they come not single spies,°
80 But in battalions. First, her father slain;
Next, your son gone, and he most violent
     author
Of his own just remove; the people muddied,°
Thick and unwholesome in their thoughts and
     whispers,
For good Polonius' death; and we have done but
     greenly,°

In hugger-mugger° to inter him; poor Ophelia   85
Divided from herself and her fair judgment,
Without the which we are pictures, or mere
     beasts;
Last, and as much containing as all these,
Her brother is in secret come from France,
Feeds on his wonder, keeps himself in clouds,°   90
And wants° not buzzers° to infect his ear
With pestilent speeches of his father's death,
Wherein necessity, of matter beggar'd,°
Will nothing stick our person to arraign
In ear and ear.° O my dear Gertrude, this,   95
Like to a murd'ring-piece,° in many places
Gives me superfluous death.   (A noise within.)

[QUEEN: Alack, what noise is this?]

KING: Attend!
Where are my Switzers?° Let them guard the door. 100

(Enter a Messenger.)

What is the matter?

MESSENGER: Save yourself, my lord!
The ocean, overpeering of his list,°
Eats not the flats° with more impiteous° haste
Than young Laertes, in a riotous head,°
O'erbears your officers. The rabble call him lord, 105
And, as° the world were now but to begin,
Antiquity forgot, custom not known,
The ratifiers and props° of every word,°
They cry, "Choose we! Laertes shall be king!"
Caps, hands, and tongues applaud it to the
     clouds,   110
"Laertes shall be king, Laertes king!"
                                     (A noise within.)

QUEEN: How cheerfully on the false trail they cry!
O, this is counter,° you false Danish dogs!

(Enter Laertes with others.)

KING: The doors are broke.

LAERTES: Where is this King? Sirs, stand you all
     without.   115

ALL: No, let's come in.

LAERTES: I pray you, give me leave.

ALL: We will, we will.

                     [They retire without the door.]

LAERTES: I thank you. Keep the door. O thou vile king,
Give me my father!

---

42. **God 'ild:** God yield or reward.   **owl:** Refers to a legend
about a baker's daughter who was turned into an owl for refusing Jesus bread.   45. **Conceit:** Brooding.   48. **Valentine's:**
This song alludes to the belief that the first girl seen by a man
on the morning of this day was his valentine or true love.
53. **dupp'd:** Opened.   59. **Gis:** Jesus.   62. **Cock:** A perversion
of *God* in oaths.   79. **spies:** Scouts sent in advance of the main
force.   82. **muddied:** Stirred up, confused.   84. **greenly:**
Imprudently, foolishly.

85. **hugger-mugger:** Secret haste.   90. **in clouds:** i.e., of suspicion and rumor.   91. **wants:** Lacks.   **buzzers:** Gossipers,
informers.   93. **of matter beggar'd:** Unprovided with facts.
95. **Will . . . and ear:** Will not hesitate to accuse my (royal) person in everybody's ears.   96. **murd'ring-piece:** Cannon loaded
so as to scatter its shot.   100. **Switzers:** Swiss guards, mer-
cenaries.   102. **overpeering of his list:** Overflowing its shore.
103. **flats:** Flatlands near shore.   **impiteous:** Pitiless.   104. **head:**
Armed force.   106. **as:** As if.   108. **ratifiers and props:** Refer
to *antiquity* and *custom*.   **word:** Promise.   113. **counter:** A
hunting term meaning to follow the trail in a direction opposite
to that which the game has taken.

QUEEN: Calmly, good Laertes.
                              [*She tries to hold him back.*]
LAERTES: That drop of blood that's calm proclaims me
120   bastard,
         Cries cuckold to my father, brands the harlot
         Even here, between the chaste unsmirched brow
         Of my true mother.
KING: What is the cause, Laertes,
         That thy rebellion looks so giant-like?
125   Let him go, Gertrude. Do not fear our° person.
         There's such divinity doth hedge a king
         That treason can but peep to what it would,°
         Acts little of his will.° Tell me, Laertes,
         Why thou art thus incens'd. Let him go, Gertrude.
         Speak, man.
LAERTES: Where is my father?
130 KING: Dead.
     QUEEN: But not by him.
     KING: Let him demand his fill.
     LAERTES: How came he dead? I'll not be juggled with.
         To hell, allegiance! Vows, to the blackest devil!
         Conscience and grace, to the profoundest pit!
135   I dare damnation. To this point I stand,
         That both the worlds I give to negligence,°
         Let come what comes, only I'll be reveng'd
         Most throughly° for my father.
     KING: Who shall stay you?
     LAERTES: My will, not all the world's.°
140   And for my means, I'll husband them so well,
         They shall go far with little.
     KING: Good Laertes,
         If you desire to know the certainty
         Of your dear father, is 't writ in your revenge
         That, swoopstake,° you will draw both friend and
              foe,
145   Winner and loser?
     LAERTES: None but his enemies.
     KING: Will you know them then?
     LAERTES: To his good friends thus wide I'll ope my
              arms,
         And, like the kind life-rend'ring pelican,°
         Repast° them with my blood.
     KING: Why, now you speak
150   Like a good child and a true gentleman.
         That I am guiltless of your father's death,
         And am most sensibly° in grief for it,

It shall as level° to your judgment 'pear
As day does to your eye.
              (*A noise within:*) "Let her come in."
LAERTES: How now? What noise is that?   155

(*Enter Ophelia.*)

O heat, dry up my brains! Tears seven times salt
Burn out the sense and virtue° of mine eye!
By heaven, thy madness shall be paid with
     weight°
Till our scale turn the beam.° O rose of May!
Dear maid, kind sister, sweet Ophelia!   160
O heavens, is 't possible a young maid's wits
Should be as mortal as an old man's life?
[Nature is fine in° love, and where 'tis fine,
It sends some precious instance° of itself
After the thing it loves.°]   165
OPHELIA: "They bore him barefac'd on the bier;
                                        (*Song.*)
     [Hey non nonny, nonny, hey nonny,]
     And in his grave rain'd many a tear"—
     Fare you well, my dove!
LAERTES: Hadst thou thy wits, and didst persuade°
     revenge,   170
     It could not move thus.
OPHELIA: You must sing "A-down a-down,
     And you call him a-down-a."
     O, how the wheel° becomes it! It is the false steward°
     that stole his master's daughter.   175
LAERTES: This nothing's more than matter.°
OPHELIA: There's rosemary,° that's for remembrance;
     pray you, love, remember. And there is pansies,° that's
     for thoughts.
LAERTES: A document° in madness, thoughts and remem-   180
     brance fitted.
OPHELIA: There's fennel° for you, and columbines.°
     There's rue° for you, and here's some for me; we may
     call it herb of grace o' Sundays. You may wear your
     rue with a difference.° There's a daisy.° I would give 185

---

125. **fear our:** Fear for my.   127. **can . . . would:** Can only glance; as from far off or through a barrier, at what it would intend.   128. **Acts . . . will:** (But) performs little of what it intends.   136. **both . . . negligence:** Both this world and the next are of no consequence to me.   138. **throughly:** Thoroughly. 139. **My will . . . world's:** I'll stop (*stay*) when my will is accomplished, not for anyone else's.   144. **swoopstake:** Literally, taking all stakes on the gambling table at once, i.e., indiscriminately; *draw* is also a gambling term.   148. **pelican:** Refers to the belief that the female pelican fed its young with its own blood.   149. **Repast:** Feed.   152. **sensibly:** Feelingly.

153. **level:** Plain.   157. **virtue:** Faculty, power.   158. **paid with weight:** Repaid, avenged equally or more.   159. **beam:** Crossbar of a balance.   163. **fine in:** Refined by.   164. **instance:** Token.   165. **After . . . loves:** Into the grave, along with Polonius.   170. **persuade:** Argue cogently for.   174. **wheel:** Spinning wheel as accompaniment to the song, or refrain.   **false steward:** The story is unknown.   176. **This . . . matter:** This seeming nonsense is more meaningful than sane utterance. 177. **rosemary:** Used as a symbol of remembrance both at weddings and at funerals.   178. **pansies:** Emblems of love and courtship; perhaps from French *pensées,* thoughts.   180. **document:** Instruction, lesson.   182. **fennel:** Emblem of flattery. **columbines:** Emblems of unchastity (?) or ingratitude (?). 183. **rue:** Emblem of repentance; when mingled with holy water, it was known as *herb of grace.*   185. **with a difference:** Suggests that Ophelia and the queen have different causes of sorrow and repentance; perhaps with a play on *rue* in the sense of ruth, pity.   **daisy:** Emblem of dissembling, faithlessness.

you some violets,° but they wither'd all when my
father died. They say 'e made a good end —
[*Sings.*] "For bonny sweet Robin is all my joy."
LAERTES: Thought° and affliction, passion, hell itself,
190   She turns to favor° and to prettiness.
OPHELIA: "And will 'a not come again? (*Song.*)
　　　And will 'a not come again?
　　　　　No, no, he is dead,
　　　　　Go to thy death-bed,
195   He never will come again.

　　　"His beard was as white as snow,
　　　All flaxen was his poll.°
　　　　　He is gone, he is gone,
　　　　　And we cast away moan.
200   God 'a' mercy on his soul!
And of all Christians' souls, I pray God. God buy you.
　　　　　　　　　　　　　　　[*Exit.*]
LAERTES: Do you see this, O God?
KING: Laertes, I must commune with your grief,
　　Or you deny me right. Go but apart,
205   Make choice of whom your wisest friends you will,
　　And they shall hear and judge 'twixt you and me.
　　If by direct or by collateral° hand
　　They find us touch'd,° we will our kingdom give,
　　Our crown, our life, and all that we call ours,
210   To you in satisfaction; but if not,
　　Be you content to lend your patience to us,
　　And we shall jointly labor with your soul
　　To give it due content.
LAERTES:　　　　　　　Let this be so.
　　His means of death, his obscure funeral —
215   No trophy,° sword, nor hatchment° o'er his bones,
　　No noble rite nor formal ostentation° —
　　Cry to be heard, as 'twere from heaven to earth,
　　That I must call 't in question.
KING:　　　　　　　　　So you shall;
　　And where th' offense is, let the great ax fall.
220   I pray you go with me.　　　　　(*Exeunt.*)

{Scene VI}°

(*Enter Horatio and others.*)

HORATIO: What are they that would speak with me?
GENTLEMAN: Seafaring men, sir. They say they have let-
　　ters for you.
HORATIO: Let them come in.　　　　[*Exit Gentleman.*]
5　　I do not know from what part of the world
　　I should be greeted, if not from lord Hamlet.

(*Enter Sailors.*)

FIRST SAILOR: God bless you sir.
HORATIO: Let him bless thee too.
FIRST SAILOR: 'A shall, sir, an 't please him. There's a let-
　　ter for you, sir — it came from th' ambassador that   10
　　was bound for England — if your name be Horatio,
　　as I am let to know it is.　　　　[*Gives letter.*]
HORATIO [*reads*]: "Horatio, when thou shalt have over-
　　look'd this, give these fellows some means° to the
　　King; they have letters for him. Ere we were two days   15
　　old at sea, a pirate of very warlike appointment° gave
　　us chase. Finding ourselves too slow of sail, we put
　　on a compell'd valor, and in the grapple I boarded
　　them. On the instant they got clear of our ship, so I
　　alone became their prisoner. They have dealt with me   20
　　like thieves of mercy,° but they knew what they did: I
　　am to do a good turn for them. Let the King have the
　　letters I have sent, and repair thou to me with as
　　much speed as thou wouldest fly death. I have words
　　to speak in thine ear will make thee dumb; yet are   25
　　they much too light for the bore° of the matter. These
　　good fellows will bring thee where I am. Rosencrantz
　　and Guildenstern hold their course for England. Of
　　them I have much to tell thee. Farewell.
　　　　　　He that thou knowest thine, Hamlet."   30
　　Come, I will give you way for these your letters,
　　And do 't the speedier that you may direct me
　　To him from whom you brought them.　　(*Exeunt.*)

{Scene VII}°

(*Enter King and Laertes.*)

KING: Now must your conscience my acquittance seal,°
　　And you must put me in your heart for friend,
　　Sith you have heard, and with a knowing ear,
　　That he which hath your noble father slain
　　Pursued my life.
LAERTES:　　　　It well appears. But tell me   5
　　Why you proceeded not against these feats°
　　So criminal and so capital° in nature,
　　As by your safety, greatness, wisdom, all things else,
　　You mainly° were stirr'd up.
KING:　　　　　　　O, for two special reasons,
　　Which may to you, perhaps, seem much unsinew'd,°   10
　　But yet to me th' are strong. The Queen his mother
　　Lives almost by his looks, and for myself —
　　My virtue or my plague, be it either which —
　　She's so conjunctive° to my life and soul
　　That, as the star moves not but in his sphere,°   15

---

186. **violets:** Emblems of faithfulness.　189. **Thought:** Melancholy.　190. **favor:** Grace.　197. **poll:** Head.　207. **collateral:**
Indirect.　208. **us touch'd:** Me implicated.　215. **trophy:** Memorial.　**hatchment:** Tablet displaying the armorial bearings of a
deceased person.　216. **ostentation:** Ceremony.　IV, VI. **Location:** The castle.

14. **means:** Means of access.　16. **appointment:** Equipage.
21. **thieves of mercy:** Merciful thieves.　26. **bore:** Caliber, i.e.,
importance.　IV, VII. **Location:** The castle.　1. **my acquittance
seal:** Confirm or acknowledge my innocence.　6. **feats:** Acts.
7. **capital:** Punishable by death.　9. **mainly:** Greatly.　10. **unsinew'd:** Weak.　14. **conjunctive:** Closely united.　15. **sphere:**
The hollow sphere in which, according to Ptolemaic astronomy, the planets moved.

I could not but by her. The other motive,
Why to a public count° I might not go,
Is the great love the general gender° bear him,
Who, dipping all his faults in their affection,
20 Would, like the spring° that turneth wood to stone,
Convert his gyves° to graces, so that my arrows,
Too slightly timber'd° for so loud° a wind,
Would have reverted to my bow again
And not where I had aim'd them.

25 LAERTES: And so have I a noble father lost,
A sister driven into desp'rate terms,°
Whose worth, if praises may go back° again,
Stood challenger on mount° of all the age
For her perfections. But my revenge will come.

KING: Break not your sleeps for that. You must not
30   think
That we are made of stuff so flat and dull
That we can let our beard be shook with danger
And think it pastime. You shortly shall hear more.
I lov'd your father, and we love ourself;
35 And that, I hope, will teach you to imagine —

(*Enter a Messenger with letters.*)

[How now? What news?]
MESSENGER: [Letters, my lord, from Hamlet:]
These to your Majesty, this to the Queen.
                                        [*Gives letters.*]
KING: From Hamlet? Who brought them?
MESSENGER: Sailors, my lord, they say; I saw them not.
40   They were given me by Claudio. He receiv'd them
Of him that brought them.
KING: Laertes, you shall hear them.
Leave us.   [*Exit Messenger.*]
[*Reads.*] "High and mighty, you shall know I am set
naked° on your kingdom. Tomorrow shall I beg leave
45 to see your kingly eyes, when I shall, first asking your
pardon° thereunto, recount the occasion of my sud-
den and more strange return.   Hamlet."
What should this mean? Are all the rest come back?
Or is it some abuse,° and no such thing?
LAERTES: Know you the hand?
50 KING: 'Tis Hamlet's character.° "Naked!"
And in a postscript here, he says "alone."
Can you devise° me?
LAERTES: I am lost in it, my lord. But let him come.
It warms the very sickness in my heart
55 That I shall live and tell him to his teeth,
"Thus didst thou."

KING: If it be so, Laertes —
As how should it be so? How otherwise?° —
Will you be ruled by me?
LAERTES: Ay, my lord,
So° you will not o'errule me to a peace.
KING: To thine own peace. If he be now returned,   60
As checking at° his voyage, and that he means
No more to undertake it, I will work him
To an exploit, now ripe in my device,
Under the which he shall not choose but fall;
And for his death no wind of blame shall breathe,   65
But even his mother shall uncharge the practice°
And call it accident.
LAERTES: My lord, I will be rul'd,
The rather if you could devise it so
That I might be the organ.°
KING: It falls right.
You have been talk'd of since your travel much,   70
And that in Hamlet's hearing, for a quality
Wherein, they say, you shine. Your sum of parts°
Did not together pluck such envy from him
As did that one, and that, in my regard,
Of the unworthiest siege.°   75
LAERTES: What part is that, my lord?
KING: A very riband in the cap of youth,
Yet needful too, for youth no less becomes
The light and careless livery that it wears
Than settled age his sables° and his weeds,°   80
Importing health° and graveness. Two months since
Here was a gentleman of Normandy.
I have seen myself, and serv'd against, the French,
And they can well° on horseback, but this gallant
Had witchcraft in 't; he grew unto his seat,   85
And to such wondrous doing brought his horse
As had he been incorps'd and demi-natured°
With the brave beast. So far he topp'd° my thought
That I, in forgery° of shapes and tricks,
Come short of what he did.
LAERTES: A Norman was 't?   90
KING: A Norman.
LAERTES: Upon my life, Lamord.
KING: The very same.
LAERTES: I know him well. He is the brooch° indeed
And gem of all the nation.
KING: He made confession° of you,   95

---

17. **count:** Account, reckoning. 18. **general gender:** Common people. 20. **spring:** A spring with such a concentration of lime that it coats a piece of wood with limestone, in effect gilding it. 21. **gyves:** Fetters (which, gilded by the people's praise, would look like badges of honor). 22. **slightly timber'd:** Light. **loud:** Strong. 26. **terms:** State, condition. 27. **go back:** Recall Ophelia's former virtues. 28. **on mount:** On high. 44. **naked:** Destitute, unarmed, without following. 46. **pardon:** Permission. 49. **abuse:** Deceit. 50. **character:** Handwriting. 52. **devise:** Explain to.

57. **As . . . otherwise:** How can this (Hamlet's return) be true? Yet how otherwise than true (since we have the evidence of his letter). 59. **So:** Provided that. 61. **checking at:** Turning aside from (like a falcon leaving the quarry to fly at a chance bird). 66. **uncharge the practice:** Acquit the stratagem of being a plot. 69. **organ:** Agent, instrument. 72. **Your . . . parts:** All your other virtues. 75. **unworthiest siege:** Least important rank. 80. **sables:** Rich robes furred with sable. **weeds:** Garments. 81. **Importing health:** Indicating prosperity. 84. **can well:** Are skilled. 87. **incorps'd and demi-natur'd:** Of one body and nearly of one nature (like the centaur). 88. **topp'd:** Surpassed. 89. **forgery:** Invention. 93. **brooch:** Ornament. 95. **confession:** Admission of superiority.

And gave you such a masterly report
For art and exercise in your defense,
And for your rapier most especial,
That he cried out, 'twould be a sight indeed,
If one could match you. The scrimers° of their
100   nation,
He swore, had neither motion, guard, nor eye,
If you oppos'd them. Sir, this report of his
Did Hamlet so envenom with his envy
That he could nothing do but wish and beg
105   Your sudden coming o'er to play° with you.
Now, out of this —
LAERTES: What out of this, my lord?
KING: Laertes, was your father dear to you?
Or are you like the painting of a sorrow,
A face without a heart?
LAERTES: Why ask you this?
110 KING: Not that I think you did not love your father,
But that I know love is begun by time,°
And that I see, in passages of proof,°
Time qualifies° the spark and fire of it.
There lives within the very flame of love
115   A kind of wick or snuff° that will abate it,
And nothing is at a like goodness still,°
For goodness, growing to a plurisy,°
Dies in his own too much.° That° we would do,
We should do when we would; for this "would"
          changes
120   And hath abatements° and delays as many
As there are tongues, are hands, are accidents,°
And then this "should" is like a spendthrift's sigh,°
That hurts by easing.° But, to the quick o' th' ulcer;
Hamlet comes back. What would you undertake
125   To show yourself your father's son in deed
More than in words?
LAERTES: To cut his throat i' th' church!
KING: No place, indeed, should murder sanctuarize;°
Revenge should have no bounds. But, good Laertes,
Will you do this,° keep close within your chamber.
130   Hamlet return'd shall know you are come home.
We'll put on those° shall praise your excellence
And set a double varnish on the fame
The Frenchman gave you, bring you in fine°
          together,

And wager on your heads. He, being remiss,°
Most generous,° and free from all contriving,   135
Will not peruse the foils, so that, with ease,
Or with a little shuffling, you may choose
A sword unbated,° and in a pass of practice°
Requite him for your father.
LAERTES: I will do 't.
And for that purpose I'll anoint my sword.   140
I bought an unction° of a mountebank°
So mortal that, but dip a knife in it,
Where it draws blood no cataplasm° so rare,
Collected from all simples° that have virtue
Under the moon, can save the thing from death   145
That is but scratch'd withal. I'll touch my point
With this contagion, that, if I gall° him slightly,
It may be death.
KING: Let's further think of this,
Weigh what convenience both of time and means
May fit us to our shape.° If this should fail,   150
And that our drift look through our bad
          performance,°
'Twere better not assay'd. Therefore this project
Should have a back or second, that might hold
If this did blast in proof.° Soft, let me see.
We'll make a solemn wager on your cunnings —   155
I ha 't!
When in your motion you are hot and dry —
As° make your bouts more violent to that end —
And that he calls for drink, I'll have prepar'd him
A chalice for the nonce,° whereon but sipping,   160
If he by chance escape your venom'd stuck,°
Our purpose may hold there. [A cry within.] But
          stay, what noise?

(Enter Queen.)

QUEEN: One woe doth tread upon another's heel,
So fast they follow. Your sister's drowned, Laertes.
LAERTES: Drown'd! O, where?   165
QUEEN: There is a willow grows askant° the brook
That shows his hoar° leaves in the glassy stream;
Therewith fantastic garlands did she make
Of crow-flowers, nettles, daisies, and long purples°
That liberal° shepherds give a grosser name,   170
But our cold° maids do dead men's fingers call them.
There on the pendent boughs her crownet° weeds

100. scrimers: Fencers.   **105. play:** Fence.   **111. begun by time:** Subject to change.   **112. passages of proof:** Actual instances.   **113. qualifies:** Weakens.   **115. snuff:** The charred part of a candlewick.   **116. nothing . . . still:** Nothing remains at a constant level of perfection.   **117. plurisy:** Excess, plethora.   **118. in . . . much:** Of its own excess.   **That:** That which.   **120. abatements:** Diminutions.   **121. accidents:** Occurrences, incidents.   **122. spendthrift's sigh:** An allusion to the belief that each sigh cost the heart a drop of blood.   **123. hurts by easing:** Costs the heart blood even while it affords emotional relief.   **127. sanctuarize:** Protect from punishment (alludes to the right of sanctuary with which certain religious places were invested).   **129. Will you do this:** If you wish to do this.   **131. put on those:** Instigate those who.   **133. in fine:** Finally.

134. remiss: Negligently unsuspicious.   **135. generous:** Noble-minded.   **138. unbated:** Not blunted, having no button.   **pass of practice:** Treacherous thrust.   **141. unction:** Ointment.   **mountebank:** Quack doctor.   **143. cataplasm:** Plaster or poultice.   **144. simples:** Herbs.   **147. gall:** Graze, wound.   **150. shape:** Part that we propose to act.   **151. drift . . . performance:** i.e., intention be disclosed by our bungling.   **154. blast in proof:** Burst in the test (like a cannon).   **158. As:** And you should.   **160. nonce:** Occasion.   **161. stuck:** Thrust (from *stoccado*, a fencing term).   **166. askant:** Aslant.   **167. hoar:** White or gray.   **169. long purples:** Early purple orchids.   **170. liberal:** Free-spoken.   **171. cold:** Chaste.   **172. crownet:** Made into a chaplet or coronet.

Clamb'ring to hang, an envious sliver° broke,
When down her weedy° trophies and herself
Fell in the weeping brook. Her clothes spread
175   wide,
And mermaid-like awhile they bore her up,
Which time she chanted snatches of old lauds,°
As one incapable° of her own distress,
Or like a creature native and indued°
180   Unto that element. But long it could not be
Till that her garments, heavy with their drink,
Pull'd the poor wretch from her melodious lay
To muddy death.
LAERTES: Alas, then she is drown'd?
QUEEN: Drown'd, drown'd.
LAERTES: Too much of water hast thou, poor
185   Ophelia,
And therefore I forbid my tears. But yet
It is our trick;° nature her custom holds,
Let shame say what it will. [*He weeps.*] When these
     are gone,
The woman will be out.° Adieu, my lord.
190   I have a speech of fire, that fain would blaze,
But that this folly drowns it.   (*Exit.*)
KING: Let's follow, Gertrude.
How much I had to do to calm his rage!
Now fear I this will give it start again;
Therefore let's follow.   (*Exeunt.*)

{*ACT V* • *Scene I*}°

(*Enter two Clowns*° [*with spades, etc.*])

FIRST CLOWN: Is she to be buried in Christian burial
     when she willfully seeks her own salvation?
SECOND CLOWN: I tell thee she is; therefore make her
     grave straight.° The crowner° hath sat on her, and
5   finds it Christian burial.
FIRST CLOWN: How can that be, unless she drown'd her-
     self in her own defense?
SECOND CLOWN: Why, 'tis found so.
FIRST CLOWN: It must be "se offendendo";° it cannot
10   be else. For here lies the point: if I drown myself
     wittingly, it argues an act, and an act hath three
     branches — it is to act, to do, and to perform.
     Argal,° she drown'd herself wittingly.
SECOND CLOWN: Nay, but hear you, goodman delver —

FIRST CLOWN: Give me leave. Here lies the water; good.   15
     Here stands the man; good. If the man go to this
     water, and drown himself, it is, will he,° nill he, he
     goes, mark you that. But if the water come to him
     and drown him, he drowns not himself. Argal, he
     that is not guilty of his own death shortens not his   20
     own life.
SECOND CLOWN: But is this law?
FIRST CLOWN: Ay, marry, is 't — crowner's quest° law.
SECOND CLOWN: Will you ha' the truth on 't? If this had
     not been a gentlewoman, she should have been   25
     buried out o' Christian burial.
FIRST CLOWN: Why, there thou say'st.° And the more
     pity that great folk should have count'nance° in this
     world to drown or hang themselves, more than their
     even-Christen.° Come, my spade. There is no ancient   30
     gentlemen but gard'ners, ditchers, and grave-makers.
     They hold up Adam's profession.
SECOND CLOWN: Was he a gentleman?
FIRST CLOWN: 'A was the first that ever bore arms.
[SECOND CLOWN: Why, he had none.   35
FIRST CLOWN: What, art a heathen? How dost thou
     understand the Scripture? The Scripture says "Adam
     digg'd." Could he dig without arms?] I'll put another
     question to thee. If thou answerest me not to the pur-
     pose, confess thyself° —   40
SECOND CLOWN: Go to.
FIRST CLOWN: What is he that builds stronger than
     either the mason, the shipwright, or the carpenter?
SECOND CLOWN: The gallows-maker, for that frame
     outlives a thousand tenants.   45
FIRST CLOWN: I like thy wit well, in good faith. The gal-
     lows does well, but how does it well? It does well to
     those that do ill. Now thou dost ill to say the gallows
     is built stronger than the church. Argal, the gallows
     may do well to thee. To 't again, come.   50
SECOND CLOWN: "Who builds stronger than a mason, a
     shipwright, or a carpenter?"
FIRST CLOWN: Ay, tell me that, and unyoke.°
SECOND CLOWN: Marry, now I can tell.
FIRST CLOWN: To 't.   55
SECOND CLOWN: Mass,° I cannot tell.

(*Enter Hamlet and Horatio* [*at a distance*].)

FIRST CLOWN: Cudgel thy brains no more about it, for
     your dull ass will not mend his pace with beating;
     and, when you are ask'd this question next, say "a
     grave-maker." The houses he makes lasts till dooms-   60
     day. Go, get thee in, and fetch me a stoup° of liquor.

[*Exit Second Clown. First Clown digs.*]

---

173. **envious sliver:** Malicious branch.   174. **weedy:** I.e., of plants.   177. **lauds:** Hymns.   178. **incapable:** Lacking capacity to apprehend.   179. **indued:** Adapted by nature.   187. **It is our trick:** Weeping is our natural way (when sad). 188–89. **When . . . out:** When my tears are all shed, the woman in me will be expended, satisfied.   **V, I. Location:** A churchyard.   [S.D.] *Clowns:* Rustics.   4. **straight:** Straightway, immediately.   **crowner:** Coroner.   9. **se offendendo:** A comic mistake for *se defendendo,* term used in verdicts of justifiable homicide.   13. **Argal:** Corruption of *ergo,* therefore.

17. **will he:** Will he not.   23. **quest:** Inquest.   27. **there thou say'st:** That's right.   28. **count'nance:** Privilege.   30. **even-Christen:** Fellow Christian.   40. **confess thyself:** The saying continues, "and be hanged."   53. **unyoke:** After this great effort you may unharness the team of your wits.   56. **Mass:** By the Mass.   61. **stoup:** Two-quart measure.

(Song.)

"In youth, when I did love, did love,°
    Methought it was very sweet,
To contract — O — the time for — a — my behove,°
    O, methought there — a — was nothing — a —
65   meet."°

HAMLET: Has this fellow no feeling of his business, that
'a sings at grave-making?

HORATIO: Custom hath made it in him a property of
easiness.°

70 HAMLET: 'Tis e'en so. The hand of little employment
hath the daintier sense.°

(Song.)

FIRST CLOWN: "But age, with his stealing steps,
    Hath claw'd me in his clutch,
And hath shipped me into the land,°
75   As if I had never been such."

[Throws up a skull.]

HAMLET: That skull had a tongue in it, and could sing
once. How the knave jowls° it to the ground, as if
'twere Cain's jaw-bone, that did the first murder!
This might be the pate of a politician,° which this ass
80 now o'erreaches,° one that would circumvent God,
might it not?

HORATIO: It might, my lord.

HAMLET: Or of a courtier, which could say "Good morrow, sweet lord! How dost thou, sweet lord?" This
85 might be my Lord Such-a-one, that prais'd my Lord
Such-a-one's horse when 'a meant to beg it, might it
not?

HORATIO: Ay, my lord.

HAMLET: Why, e'en so, and now my Lady Worm's, chap-
90 less,° and knock'd about the mazzard° with a sex-
ton's spade. Here's fine revolution,° an° we had the
trick to see 't. Did these bones cost no more the breeding,° but to play at loggats° with them? Mine ache to
think on 't.

(Song.)

95 FIRST CLOWN: "A pick-axe, and a spade, a spade,
    For and° a shrouding sheet;
O, a pit of clay for to be made
    For such a guest is meet."

[Throws up another skull.]

HAMLET: There's another. Why may not that be the skull
of a lawyer? Where be his quiddities° now, his quil- 100
lities,° his cases, his tenures,° and his tricks? Why
does he suffer this mad knave now to knock him
about the sconce° with a dirty shovel, and will not
tell him of his action of battery? Hum! This fellow
might be in 's time a great buyer of land, with his 105
statutes, his recognizances,° his fines, his double°
vouchers,° his recoveries.° [Is this the fine of his fines,
and the recovery of his recoveries,] to have his fine
pate full of fine dirt?° Will his vouchers vouch him
no more of his purchases, and double [ones too], 110
than the length and breadth of a pair of indentures?°
The very conveyances° of his lands will scarcely lie in
this box,° and must th' inheritor° himself have no
more, ha?

HORATIO: Not a jot more, my lord. 115

HAMLET: Is not parchment made of sheep-skins?

HORATIO: Ay, my lord, and of calf-skins too.

HAMLET: They are sheep and calves which seek out
assurance in that.° I will speak to this fellow. —
Whose grave's this, sirrah?° 120

FIRST CLOWN: Mine, sir.
  [Sings.] "O, a pit of clay for to be made
  [For such a guest is meet]."

HAMLET: I think it be thine, indeed, for thou liest in 't.

FIRST CLOWN: You lie out on 't, sir, and therefore 'tis not 125
yours. For my part, I do not lie in 't, yet it is mine.

HAMLET: Thou dost lie in 't, to be in 't and say it is thine.
'Tis for the dead, not for the quick;° therefore thou
liest.

FIRST CLOWN: 'Tis a quick lie, sir; 'twill away again 130
from me to you.

HAMLET: What man dost thou dig it for?

FIRST CLOWN: For no man, sir.

HAMLET: What woman, then?

FIRST CLOWN: For none, neither. 135

HAMLET: Who is to be buried in 't?

FIRST CLOWN: One that was a woman, sir, but, rest her
soul, she's dead.

---

62. In . . . love: This and the two following stanzas, with nonsensical variations, are from a poem attributed to Lord Vaux
and printed in *Tottel's Miscellany* (1557). The *O* and *a*
(for "ah") seemingly are the grunts of the digger. 64. To
contract . . . behove: To make a betrothal agreement for my benefit (?). 65. meet: Suitable, i.e., more suitable. 68–69. property of easiness: Something he can do easily and without
thinking. 71. daintier sense: More delicate sense of feeling.
74. into the land: Toward my grave (?) (but note the lack of
rhyme in *steps, land*). 77. jowls: Dashes. 79. politician:
Schemer, plotter. 80. o'erreaches: Circumvents, gets the better
of (with a quibble on the literal sense). 89–90. chapless: Having no lower jaw. 90. mazzard: Head (literally, a drinking
vessel). 91. revolution: Change. an: If. 92–93. the breeding: In the breeding, raising. 93. loggats: A game in which
pieces of hardwood are thrown to lie as near as possible to a
stake. 96. For and: And moreover.

100. quiddities: Subtleties, quibbles (from Latin *quid*, a thing).
100–01. quillities: Verbal niceties, subtle distinctions (variation
of *quiddities*). 101. tenures: The holding of a piece of property or office, or the conditions or period of such holding.
103. sconce: Head. 106. statutes, recognizances: Legal documents guaranteeing a debt by attaching land and property.
106–07. fines, recoveries: Ways of converting entailed estates
into "fee simple" or freehold. 106. double: Signed by two signatories. 107. vouchers: Guarantees of the legality of a title
to real estate. 107–09. fine of his fines . . . fine pate . . . fine
dirt: End of his legal maneuvers . . . elegant head . . . minutely
sifted dirt. 111. pair of indentures: Legal document drawn up
in duplicate on a single sheet and then cut apart on a zigzag line
so that each pair was uniquely matched. (Hamlet may refer to
two rows of teeth, or dentures.) 112. conveyances: Deeds.
113. this box: The skull. inheritor: Possessor, owner. 119. assurance in that: Safety in legal parchments. 120. sirrah: Term
of address to inferiors. 128. quick: Living.

HAMLET: How absolute° the knave is! We must speak by
140   the card,° or equivocation° will undo us. By the
Lord, Horatio, this three years I have taken note of it:
the age is grown so pick'd° that the toe of the peasant
comes so near the heel of the courtier, he galls his
kibe.° How long hast thou been a grave-maker?

145   FIRST CLOWN: Of all the days i' th' year, I came to 't that
day that our last king Hamlet overcame Fortinbras.

HAMLET: How long is that since?

FIRST CLOWN: Cannot you tell that? Every fool can tell
that. It was that very day that young Hamlet was
150   born — he that is mad, and sent into England.

HAMLET: Ay, marry, why was he sent into England?

FIRST CLOWN: Why, because 'a was mad. 'A shall recover
his wits there, or, if 'a do not, 'tis no great matter there.

HAMLET: Why?

155   FIRST CLOWN: 'Twill not be seen in him there. There the
men are as mad as he.

HAMLET: How came he mad?

FIRST CLOWN: Very strangely, they say.

HAMLET: How strangely?

160   FIRST CLOWN: Faith, e'en with losing his wits.

HAMLET: Upon what ground?

FIRST CLOWN: Why, here in Denmark. I have been sex-
ton here, man and boy, thirty years.

HAMLET: How long will a man lie i' th' earth ere he rot?

165   FIRST CLOWN: Faith, if 'a be not rotten before 'a die —
as we have many pocky° corses [now-a-days], that
will scarce hold the laying in —'a will last you some
eight year or nine year. A tanner will last you nine
year.

170   HAMLET: Why he more than another?

FIRST CLOWN: Why, sir, his hide is so tann'd with his
trade that 'a will keep out water a great while, and
your water is a sore decayer of your whoreson dead
body. [*Picks up a skull*] Here's a skull now hath lain
175   you° i' th' earth three and twenty years.

HAMLET: Whose was it?

FIRST CLOWN: A whoreson mad fellow's it was. Whose
do you think it was?

HAMLET: Nay, I know not.

180   FIRST CLOWN: A pestilence on him for a mad rogue! 'A
pour'd a flagon of Rhenish° on my head once. This
same skull, sir, was Yorick's skull, the King's jester.

HAMLET: This?

FIRST CLOWN: E'en that.

185   HAMLET: [Let me see.] [*Takes the skull.*] Alas, poor
Yorick! I knew him, Horatio, a fellow of infinite jest,
of most excellent fancy. He hath borne me on his
back a thousand times; and now, how abhorr'd in my

imagination it is! My gorge rises at it. Here hung
those lips that I have kiss'd I know not how oft.   190
Where be your gibes now? Your gambols, your
songs, your flashes of merriment that were wont to
set the table on a roar? Not one now, to mock your
own grinning? Quite chap-fall'n?° Now get you to
my lady's chamber, and tell her, let her paint an inch   195
thick, to this favor° she must come; make her laugh
at that. Prithee, Horatio, tell me one thing.

HORATIO: What's that, my lord?

HAMLET: Dost thou think Alexander look'd o' this fashion i' th' earth?   200

HORATIO: E'en so.

HAMLET: And smelt so? Pah! [*Puts down the skull.*]

HORATIO: E'en so, my lord.

HAMLET: To what base uses we may return, Horatio!
Why may not imagination trace the noble dust of   205
Alexander, till 'a find it stopping a bung-hole?

HORATIO: 'twere to consider too curiously,° to consider
so.

HAMLET: No, faith, not a jot, but to follow him thither
with modesty° enough, and likelihood to lead it. [As   210
thus]: Alexander died, Alexander was buried, Alexander returneth to dust; the dust is earth; of earth we
make loam;° and why of that loam, whereto he was
converted, might they not stop a beer-barrel?
Imperious° Caesar, dead and turn'd to clay,   215
Might stop a hole to keep the wind away.
O, that that earth which kept the world in awe
Should patch a wall t' expel the winter's flaw!°
But soft, but soft awhile! Here comes the King.

(*Enter King, Queen, Laertes, and the Corse [of Ophelia,
in procession, with Priest, Lords etc.].*)

The Queen, the courtiers. Who is this they follow?   220
And with such maimed rites? This doth betoken
The corse they follow did with desp'rate hand
Fordo it° own life. 'Twas of some estate.°
Couch° we awhile, and mark.

            [*He and Horatio conceal themselves.
            Ophelia's body is taken to the grave.*]

LAERTES: What ceremony else?   225

HAMLET [*to Horatio*]: That is Laertes, a very noble
youth. Mark.

LAERTES: What ceremony else?

PRIEST: Her obsequies have been as far enlarg'd
As we have warranty. Her death was doubtful,
And, but that great command o'ersways the order,   230
She should in ground unsanctified been lodg'd
Till the last trumpet. For° charitable prayers,
Shards,° flints, and pebbles should be thrown on her.

---

139. **absolute:** Positive, decided.   139–40. **by the card:** By
the mariner's card on which the points of the compass were
marked, i.e., with precision.   140. **equivocation:** Ambiguity
in the use of terms.   142. **pick'd:** Refined, fastidious.
143–44. **galls his kibe:** Chafes the courtier's chilblain (a swelling or sore caused by cold).   166. **pocky:** Rotten, diseased (literally, with the pox, or syphilis).   174–75. **lain you:** Lain.
181. **Rhenish:** Rhine wine.

194. **chap-fall'n:** (1) Lacking the lower jaw; (2) dejected.
196. **favor:** Aspect, appearance.   207. **curiously:** Minutely.
210. **modesty:** Moderation.   213. **loam:** Clay mixture for
brickmaking or other clay use.   215. **Imperious:** Imperial.
218. **flaw:** Gust of wind.   223. **Fordo it:** Destroy its.   **estate:**
Rank.   224. **Couch:** Hide, lurk.   232. **For:** In place of.
233. **Shards:** Broken bits of pottery.

Yet here she is allow'd her virgin crants,°
235   Her maiden strewments,° and the bringing home
Of bell and burial.°
LAERTES: Must there no more be done?
PRIEST: No more be done.
We should profane the service of the dead
To sing a requiem and such rest to her
As to peace-parted souls.
240   LAERTES: Lay her i' th' earth,
And from her fair and unpolluted flesh
May violets° spring! I tell thee, churlish priest,
A minist'ring angel shall my sister be
When thou liest howling!
HAMLET [to Horatio]:   What, the fair Ophelia!
QUEEN [scattering flowers]: Sweets to the sweet!
245   Farewell.
I hoped thou shouldst have been my Hamlet's wife.
I thought thy bride-bed to have deck'd, sweet maid,
And not have strew'd thy grave.
LAERTES: O, treble woe
Fall ten times treble on that cursed head
250   Whose wicked deed thy most ingenious sense°
Depriv'd thee of! Hold off the earth awhile,
Till I have caught her once more in mine arms.
          [Leaps into the grave and embraces Ophelia.]
Now pile your dust upon the quick and dead,
Till of this flat a mountain you have made
255   T 'o'ertop old Pelion,° or the skyish head
Of blue Olympus.°
HAMLET [coming forward]: What is he whose grief
Bears such an emphasis, whose phrase of sorrow
Conjures the wand'ring stars,° and makes them stand
260   Like wonder-wounded hearers? This is I,
Hamlet the Dane.°
LAERTES: The devil take thy soul!
                              [Grappling with him.]
HAMLET: Thou pray'st not well.
I prithee, take thy fingers from my throat;
For, though I am not splenitive° and rash,
265   Yet have I in me something dangerous,
Which let thy wisdom fear. Hold off thy hand.
KING: Pluck them asunder.
QUEEN: Hamlet, Hamlet!
ALL: Gentlemen!
HORATIO: Good my lord, be quiet.
                    [Hamlet and Horatio are parted.]
HAMLET: Why, I will fight with him upon this theme
270   Until my eyelids will no longer wag.
QUEEN: O my son, what theme?

HAMLET: I lov'd Ophelia. Forty thousand brothers
Could not with all their quantity of love
Make up my sum. What wilt thou do for her?
KING: O, he is mad, Laertes.   275
QUEEN: For love of God, forbear him.
HAMLET: 'Swounds,° show me what thou' do.
Woo 't° weep? Woo 't fight? Woo 't fast? Woo 't tear
          thyself?
Woo 't drink up eisel?° Eat a crocodile?
I'll do 't. Dost thou come here to whine?   280
To outface me with leaping in her grave?
Be buried quick° with her, and so will I.
And, if thou prate of mountains, let them throw
Millions of acres on us, till our ground,
Singeing his pate° against the burning zone,°   285
Make Ossa° like a wart! Nay, an thou 'lt mouth,°
I'll rant as well as thou.
QUEEN: This is mere° madness,
And thus a while the fit will work on him;
Anon, as patient as the female dove
When that her golden couplets° are disclos'd,° 290
His silence will sit drooping.
HAMLET: Hear you, sir.
What is the reason that you use me thus?
I lov'd you ever. But it is no matter.
Let Hercules himself do what he may,
The cat will mew, and dog will have his day.°   295
KING: I pray thee, good Horatio, wait upon him.

                    (Exit Hamlet and Horatio.)

[To Laertes.] Strengthen your patience in° our last
          night's speech;
We'll put the matter to the present push.° —
Good Gertrude, set some watch over your son. —
This grave shall have a living° monument.   300
An hour of quiet shortly shall we see;
Till then, in patience our proceeding be.   (Exeunt.)

{Scene II}°

(Enter Hamlet and Horatio.)

HAMLET: So much for this, sir; now shall you see the
          other.°
You do remember all the circumstance?

234. crants: Garland.   235. strewments: Traditional strewing of flowers.   235–36. bringing . . . burial: Laying to rest of the body in consecrated ground, to the sound of the bell.   242. violets: See IV, v, 186 and note.   250. ingenious sense: Mind endowed with finest qualities.   255, 256. Pelion, Olympus: Mountains in the north of Thessaly; see also Ossa at line 286.   259. wand'ring stars: Planets.   261. the Dane: This title normally signifies the king, see I, i, 15 and note.   264. splenitive: Quick-tempered.

277. 'Swounds: By His (Christ's) wounds.   278. Woo 't: Wilt thou.   279. eisel: Vinegar.   282. quick: Alive.   285. his pate: Its head, i.e., top.   burning zone: Sun's orbit.   286. Ossa: Another mountain in Thessaly. (In their war against the Olympian gods, the giants attempted to heap Ossa, Pelion, and Olympus on one another to scale heaven.)   mouth: Rant.   287. mere: Utter.   290. golden couplets: Two baby pigeons, covered with yellow down.   disclos'd: Hatched.   294–95. Let . . . day: Despite any blustering attempts at interference every person will sooner or later do what he must do.   297. in: By recalling.   298. present push: Immediate test.   300. living: Lasting; also refers (for Laertes' benefit) to the plot against Hamlet. V, II. Location: The castle.   1. see the other: Hear the other news.

HORATIO: Remember it, my lord!
HAMLET: Sir, in my heart there was a kind of
    fighting
5   That would not let me sleep. Methought I lay
    Worse than the mutines° in the bilboes.° Rashly,°
    And prais'd be rashness for it — let us know,°
    Our indiscretion sometime serves us well
    When our deep plots do pall,° and that should
    learn° us
10   There's a divinity that shapes our ends,
    Rough-hew° them how we will —
HORATIO: That is most certain.
HAMLET: Up from my cabin,
    My sea-gown scarf'd about me, in the dark
    Grop'd I to find out them, had my desire,
15   Finger'd° their packet, and in fine° withdrew
    To mine own room again, making so bold,
    My fears forgetting manners, to unseal
    Their grand commission; where I found, Horatio —
    Ah, royal knavery! — an exact command,
20   Larded° with many several sorts of reasons
    Importing° Denmark's health and England's too,
    With, ho, such bugs° and goblins in my life,°
    That, on the supervise,° no leisure bated,°
    No, not to stay the grinding of the axe,
    My head should be struck off.
25 HORATIO: Is 't possible?
HAMLET: Here's the commission; read it at more
    leisure.   [*Gives document.*]
    But wilt thou hear now how I did proceed?
HORATIO: I beseech you.
HAMLET: Being thus benetted round with villainies,
30   Or I could make a prologue to my brains,
    They had begun the play.° I sat me down,
    Devis'd a new commission, wrote it fair.°
    I once did hold it, as our statists° do,
    A baseness° to write fair, and labor'd much
35   How to forget that learning, but, sir, now
    It did me yeoman's° service. Wilt thou know
    Th' effect° of what I wrote?
HORATIO: Ay, good my lord.
HAMLET: An earnest conjuration from the King,
    As England was his faithful tributary,
40   As love between them like the palm might flourish,
    As peace should still her wheaten garland° wear

And stand a comma° 'tween their amities,
And many such-like as's° of great charge,°
That, on the view and knowing of these contents,
Without debasement further, more or less,   45
He should those bearers put to sudden death,
Not shriving time° allow'd.
HORATIO: How was this seal'd?
HAMLET: Why, even in that was heaven ordinant.°
    I had my father's signet° in my purse,
    Which was the model of that Danish seal;   50
    Folded the writ up in the form of th' other,
    Subscrib'd° it, gave 't th' impression,° plac'd it
    safely,
    The changeling° never known. Now, the next day
    Was our sea-fight, and what to this was sequent
    Thou knowest already.   55
HORATIO: So Guildenstern and Rosencrantz go to 't.
HAMLET: [Why, man, they did make love to this
    employment.]
    They are not near my conscience. Their defeat
    Does by their own insinuation° grow.
    'Tis dangerous when the baser nature comes   60
    Between the pass° and fell° incensed points
    Of mighty opposites.
HORATIO: Why, what a king is this!
HAMLET: Does it not, think thee, stand° me now
    upon —
    He that hath killed my king and whor'd my mother,
    Popp'd in between th' election° and my hopes, 65
    Thrown out his angle° for my proper° life,
    And with such coz'nage° — is 't not perfect
    conscience
    [To quit° him with this arm? And is 't not to be
    damn'd
    To let this canker° of our nature come
    In further evil?   70
HORATIO: It must be shortly known to him from
    England
    What is the issue of the business there.
HAMLET: It will be short. The interim is mine,
    And a man's life 's no more than to say "One."°
    But I am very sorry, good Horatio,   75
    That to Laertes I forgot myself,
    For by the image of my cause I see
    The portraiture of his. I'll court his favors.

---

6. mutines: Mutineers. **bilboes:** Shackles. **Rashly:** On impulse (this adverb goes with lines 12ff.). **7. know:** Acknowledge. **9. pall:** Fail. **learn:** Teach. **11. Rough-hew:** Shape roughly. **15. Finger'd:** Pilfered, pinched. **in fine:** Finally, in conclusion. **20. Larded:** Enriched. **21. Importing:** Relating to. **22. bugs:** Bugbears, hobgoblins. **in my life:** To be feared if I were allowed to live. **23. supervise:** Reading. **leisure bated:** Delay allowed. **30–31. Or . . . play:** Before I could consciously turn my brain to the matter, it had started working on a plan. (*Or* means *ere.*) **32. fair:** In a clear hand. **33. statists:** Statesmen. **34. baseness:** Lower-class trait. **36. yeoman's:** Substantial, workmanlike. **37. effect:** Purport. **41. wheaten garland:** Symbolic of fruitful agriculture, of peace.

42. comma: Indicating continuity, link. **43. as's:** (1) The "whereases" of formal document, (2) asses. **charge:** (1) Import, (2) burden. **47. shriving time:** Time for confession and absolution. **48. ordinant:** Directing. **49. signet:** Small seal. **52. Subscrib'd:** Signed. **impression:** With a wax seal. **53. changeling:** The substituted letter (literally, a fairy child substituted for a human one). **59. insinuation:** Interference. **61. pass:** Thrust. **fell:** Fierce. **63. stand:** Become incumbent. **65. election:** The Danish monarch was "elected" by a small number of high-ranking electors. **66. angle:** Fishing line. **proper:** Very. **67. coz'nage:** Trickery. **68. quit:** Repay. **69. canker:** Ulcer. **74. a man's . . . "One":** To take a man's life requires no more than to count to one as one duels.

But, sure, the bravery° of his grief did put me
Into a tow'ring passion.

80 HORATIO: Peace, who comes here?]

(*Enter a Courtier [Osric].*)

OSRIC: Your lordship is right welcome back to Denmark.
HAMLET: I humbly thank you, sir. [*To Horatio.*] Dost
know this water-fly?
HORATIO: No, my good lord.
85 HAMLET: Thy state is the more gracious, for 'tis a vice to
know him. He hath much land, and fertile. Let a
beast be lord of beasts, and his crib shall stand at the
King's mess.° 'Tis a chough,° but, as I say, spacious in
the possession of dirt.
90 OSRIC: Sweet lord, if your lordship were at leisure, I
should impart a thing to you from his Majesty.
HAMLET: I will receive it, sir, with all diligence of spirit.
Put your bonnet to his right use; 'tis for the head.
OSRIC: I thank your lordship, it is very hot.
95 HAMLET: No, believe me, 'tis very cold; the wind is
northerly.
OSRIC: It is indifferent° cold, my lord, indeed.
HAMLET: But yet methinks it is very sultry and hot for
my complexion.°
100 OSRIC: Exceedingly, my lord; it is very sultry, as
'twere — I cannot tell how. My lord, his Majesty
bade me signify to you that 'a has laid a great wager
on your head. Sir, this is the matter —
HAMLET: I beseech you, remember —
[*Hamlet moves him to put on his hat.*]
105 OSRIC: Nay, good my lord; for my ease,° in good faith.
Sir, here is newly come to court Laertes — believe
me, an absolute gentleman, full of most excellent
differences,° of very soft society° and great showing.° Indeed, to speak feelingly° of him, he is the
110 card° or calendar° of gentry,° for you shall find in him
the continent of what part° a gentleman would see.
HAMLET: Sir, his definement° suffers no perdition° in
you, though, I know, to divide him inventorially°
would dozy° th' arithmetic of memory, and yet
115 but yaw° neither° in respect of° his quick sail. But,
in the verity of extolment,° I take him to be a soul of

great article,° and his infusion° of such dearth and
rareness,° as, to make true diction° of him, his
semblable° is his mirror, and who else would trace°
him, his umbrage,° nothing more.   120
OSRIC: Your lordship speaks most infallibly of him.
HAMLET: The concernancy,° sir? Why do we wrap the
gentleman in our more rawer breath?°
OSRIC: Sir?
HORATIO: Is 't not possible to understand in another   125
tongue?° You will do 't,° sir, really.
HAMLET: What imports the nomination° of this gentle-
man?
OSRIC: Of Laertes?
HORATIO [*to Hamlet*]: His purse is empty already; all 's   130
golden words are spent.
HAMLET: Of him, sir.
OSRIC: I know you are not ignorant —
HAMLET: I would you did, sir; yet, in faith, if you did, it
would not much approve° me. Well, sir?   135
OSRIC: You are not ignorant of what excellence Laertes
is —
HAMLET: I dare not confess that, lest I should compare°
with him in excellence; but to know a man well were
to know himself.°   140
OSRIC: I mean, sir, for his weapon; but in the imputation
laid on him by them,° in his meed° he's unfellow'd.°
HAMLET: What's his weapon?
OSRIC: Rapier and dagger.
HAMLET: That's two of his weapons — but well.   145
OSRIC: The King, sir, hath wager'd with him six Barbary
horses, against the which he has impawn'd,° as I take
it, six French rapiers and poniards, with their
assigns,° as girdle, hangers,° and so. Three of the carriages,° in faith, are very dear to fancy,° very respon-   150
sive° to the hilts, most delicate° carriages, and of very
liberal conceit.°

---

79. bravery: Bravado. **86–88. Let . . . mess:** If a man, no
matter how beastlike, is as rich in possessions as Osric, he may
eat at the king's table. **88. chough:** Chattering jackdaw.
97. indifferent: Somewhat. **99. complexion:** Temperament.
105. for my ease: A conventional reply declining the invitation
to put his hat back on. **108. differences:** Special qualities.
soft society: Agreeable manners. **108–09. great showing:** Distinguished appearance. **109. feelingly:** With just perception.
110. card: Chart, map. **calendar:** Guide. **gentry:** Good
breeding. **111. the continent . . . part:** One who contains in
him all the qualities (a *continent* is that which contains).
112. definement: Definition. (Hamlet proceeds to mock Osric
by using his lofty diction back at him.) **perdition:** Loss,
diminution. **113. divide him inventorially:** Enumerate his
graces. **114. dozy:** Dizzy. **115. yaw:** To move unsteadily
(said of a ship). **neither:** For all that. **in respect of:** In comparison with. **116. in . . . extolment:** In true praise (of him).

117. article: Moment or importance. **infusion:** Essence, character imparted by nature. **117–18. dearth and rareness:**
Rarity. **118. make true diction:** Speak truly. **119. sem-
blable:** Only true likeness. **who . . . trace:** Any other person
who would wish to follow. **120. umbrage:** Shadow.
122. concernancy: Import, relevance. **123. breath:** Speech.
125–26. to understand . . . tongue: For Osric to understand
when someone else speaks in his manner. (Horatio twits Osric
for not being able to understand the kind of flowery speech he
himself uses when Hamlet speaks in such a vein.) **126. You
will do't:** You can if you try. **127. nomination:** Naming.
135. approve: Commend. **138. compare:** Seem to compete.
139–40. but . . . himself: For, to recognize excellence in another man, one must know oneself. **141–42. imputation . . .
them:** Reputation given him by others. **142. meed:** Merit.
unfellow'd: Unmatched. **147. impawn'd:** Staked, wagered.
149. assigns: Appurtenances. **hangers:** Straps on the sword
belt (*girdle*) from which the sword hung. **149–50. carriages:**
An affected way of saying *hangers;* literally, gun-carriages.
150. dear to fancy: Fancifully designed, tasteful. **150–51. responsive:** Corresponding closely, matching. **151. delicate:**
I.e., in workmanship. **152. liberal conceit:** Elaborate design.

HAMLET: What call you the carriages?

155 HORATIO [*to Hamlet*]: I knew you must be edified by the margent° ere you had done.

OSRIC: The carriages, sir, are the hangers.

HAMLET: The phrase would be more germane to the matter if we could carry a cannon by our sides; I would it might be hangers till then. But, on: six 160 Barb'ry horses against six French swords, their assigns, and three liberal-conceited carriages; that's the French bet against the Danish. Why is this impawn'd, as you call it?

OSRIC: The King, sir, hath laid,° sir, that in a dozen 165 passes° between yourself and him, he shall not exceed you three hits. He hath laid on twelve for nine, and it would come to immediate trial, if your lordship would vouchsafe the answer.

HAMLET: How if I answer no?

170 OSRIC: I mean, my lord, the opposition of your person in trial.

HAMLET: Sir, I will walk here in the hall. If it please his Majesty, it is the breathing time° of day with me. Let the foils be brought, the gentleman willing, and the 175 King hold his purpose, I will win for him an I can; if not, I will gain nothing but my shame and the odd hits.

OSRIC: Shall I deliver you so?

HAMLET: To this effect, sir — after what flourish your 180 nature will.

OSRIC: I commend my duty to your lordship.

HAMLET: Yours, yours. [*Exit Osric.*] He does well to commend it himself; there are no tongues else for 's turn.

185 HORATIO: This lapwing° runs away with the shell on his head.

HAMLET: 'A did comply, sir, with his dug,° before 'a suck'd it. Thus has he — and many more of the same breed that I know the drossy° age dotes on — only 190 got the tune° of the time and, out of an habit of encounter,° a kind of yesty° collection,° which carries them through and through the most fann'd and winnow'd° opinions; and do but blow them to their trial, the bubbles are out.°

(*Enter a Lord.*)

155. **margent:** Margin of a book, place for explanatory notes. 164. **laid:** Wagered.   165. **passes:** Bouts. (The odds of the betting are hard to explain. Possibly the king bets that Hamlet will win at least five out of twelve, at which point Laertes raises the odds against himself by betting he will win nine.) 173. **breathing time:** Exercise period.   185. **lapwing:** A bird that draws intruders away from its nest and was thought to run about when newly hatched with its head in the shell; a seeming reference to Osric's hat.   187. **comply . . . dug:** Observe ceremonious formality toward his mother's teat. 189. **drossy:** Frivolous.   190. **tune:** Temper, mood, manner of speech.   190–91. **habit of encounter:** Demeanor of social intercourse.   191. **yesty:** Yeasty, frothy.   **collection:** i.e., of current phrases.   192–93. **fann'd and winnow'd:** Select and refined.   193–94. **blow . . . out:** Put them to the test, and their ignorance is exposed.

195 LORD: My lord, his Majesty commended him to you by young Osric, who brings back to him that you attend him in the hall. He sends to know if your pleasure hold to play with Laertes, or that you will take longer time.

200 HAMLET: I am constant to my purposes; they follow the King's pleasure. If his fitness speaks,° mine is ready; now or whensoever, provided I be so able as now.

LORD: The King and Queen and all are coming down.

HAMLET: In happy time.°

205 LORD: The Queen desires you to use some gentle entertainment° to Laertes before you fall to play.

HAMLET: She well instructs me.   [*Exit Lord.*]

HORATIO: You will lose, my lord.

HAMLET: I do not think so. Since he went into France, I 210 have been in continual practice; I shall win at the odds. But thou wouldst not think how ill all's here about my heart; but it is no matter.

HORATIO: Nay, good my lord —

HAMLET: It is but foolery, but it is such a kind of gain- 215 giving,° as would perhaps trouble a woman.

HORATIO: If your mind dislike anything, obey it. I will forestall their repair hither, and say you are not fit.

HAMLET: Not a whit, we defy augury. There is special providence in the fall of a sparrow. If it be now, 'tis 220 not to come; if it be not to come, it will be now, if it be not now, yet it will come. The readiness is all. Since no man of aught he leaves knows what is 't to leave betimes,° let be.

(*A table prepar'd. [Enter] trumpets, drums, and Officers with cushions; King, Queen, [Osric,] and all the State; foils, daggers, [and wine borne in;] and Laertes.*)

KING: Come, Hamlet, come, and take this hand from me.

          [*The King puts Laertes' hand into Hamlet's.*]

HAMLET: Give me your pardon, sir. I have done you wrong, 225
But pardon 't, as you are a gentleman.
This presence° knows,
And you must needs have heard, how I am punish'd
With a sore distraction. What I have done
That might your nature, honor, and exception° 230
Roughly awake, I here proclaim was madness.
Was 't Hamlet wrong'd Laertes? Never Hamlet.
If Hamlet from himself be ta'en away,
And when he's not himself does wrong Laertes,
Then Hamlet does it not, Hamlet denies it. 235
Who does it, then? His madness. If 't be so,
Hamlet is of the faction that is wrong'd;
His madness is poor Hamlet's enemy.

201. **If . . . speaks:** If his readiness answers to the time. 204. **In happy time:** A phrase of courtesy indicating acceptance. 206. **entertainment:** Greeting.   214–15. **gain-giving:** Misgiving.   222–23. **what . . . betimes:** What is the best time to leave it.   227. **presence:** Royal assembly.   230. **exception:** Disapproval.

[Sir, in this audience,]
240 Let my disclaiming from a purpos'd evil
Free me so far in your most generous thoughts
That I have shot my arrow o'er the house
And hurt my brother.
LAERTES: I am satisfied in nature,°
Whose motive in this case should stir me most
245 To my revenge. But in my terms of honor
I stand aloof, and will no reconcilement
Till by some elder masters of known honor
I have a voice° and precedent of peace
To keep my name ungor'd. But till that time,
250 I do receive your offer'd love like love,
And will not wrong it.
HAMLET: I embrace it freely,
And will this brothers' wager frankly play.
Give us the foils. Come on.
LAERTES: Come, one for me.
HAMLET: I'll be your foil,° Laertes. In mine ignorance
255 Your skill shall, like a star i' th' darkest night,
Stick fiery off° indeed.
LAERTES: You mock me, sir.
HAMLET: No, by this hand.
KING: Give them the foils, young Osric. Cousin Hamlet,
You know the wager?
HAMLET: Very well, my lord.
260 Your Grace has laid the odds o' th' weaker side.
KING: I do not fear it; I have seen you both.
But since he is better'd,° we have therefore odds.
LAERTES: This is too heavy, let me see another.
              [Exchanges his foil for another.]
HAMLET: This likes me well. These foils have all a
length?
              [They prepare to play.]
265 OSRIC: Ay, my good lord.
KING: Set me the stoups of wine upon that table.
If Hamlet give the first or second hit,
Or quit° in answer of the third exchange,
Let all the battlements their ordnance fire.
270 The King shall drink to Hamlet's better breath,
And in the cup an union° shall he throw,
Richer than that which four successive kings
In Denmark's crown have worn. Give me the cups,
And let the kettle° to the trumpet speak,
275 The trumpet to the cannoneer without,
The cannons to the heavens, the heaven to earth,
"Now the King drinks to Hamlet." Come, begin.
              (Trumpets the while.)
And you, the judges, bear a wary eye.

HAMLET: Come on sir.
LAERTES: Come, my lord.   [They play. Hamlet scores 280
                                        a hit.]
HAMLET: One.
LAERTES: No.
HAMLET: Judgment.
OSRIC: A hit, a very palpable hit.
              (Drum, trumpets, and shot. Flourish.
                        A piece goes off.)
LAERTES: Well, again.
KING: Stay, give me drink. Hamlet, this pearl is thine. 285
      [He throws a pearl in Hamlet's cup and drinks.]
Here's to thy health. Give him the cup.
HAMLET: I'll play this bout first set it by awhile.
Come. [They play.] Another hit; what say you?
LAERTES: A touch, a touch. I do confess 't.
KING: Our son shall win.
QUEEN: He's fat,° and scant of breath. 290
Here, Hamlet, take my napkin,° rub thy brows.
The Queen carouses° to thy fortune, Hamlet.
HAMLET: Good madam!
KING: Gertrude, do not drink.
QUEEN: I will, my lord; I pray you pardon me. 295
              [Drinks.]
KING [aside]: It is the pois'ned cup. It is too late.
HAMLET: I dare not drink yet, madam; by and by.
QUEEN: Come, let me wipe thy face.
LAERTES [to King]: My lord, I'll hit him now.
KING: I do not think 't.
LAERTES [aside]: And yet it is almost against my
conscience. 300
HAMLET: Come, for the third Laertes. You do but dally.
I pray you, pass with your best violence;
I am afeard you make a wanton of me.°
LAERTES: Say you so? Come on.   [They play.]
OSRIC: Nothing, neither way. 305
LAERTES: Have at you now!
      [Laertes wounds Hamlet; then, in scuffling,
        they change rapiers,° and Hamlet wounds
                                        Laertes.]
KING: Part them! They are incens'd.
HAMLET: Nay, come, again.   [The Queen falls.]
OSRIC: Look to the Queen there, ho!
HORATIO: They bleed on both sides. How is it, my lord?
OSRIC: How is 't, Laertes?
LAERTES: Why, as a woodcock° to mine own springe,°
Osric; 310
I am justly kill'd with mine own treachery.

---

243. **in nature:** As to my personal feelings. **248. voice:** Authoritative pronouncement. **254. foil:** Thin metal background which sets a jewel off (with pun on the blunted rapier for fencing). **256. Stick fiery off:** Stand out brilliantly. **262. is better'd:** Has improved; is the odds-on favorite. **268. quit:** Repay (with a hit). **271. union:** Pearl (so called, according to Pliny's *Natural History,* IX, because pearls are *unique,* never identical). **274. kettle:** Kettledrum.

290. **fat:** Not physically fit, out of training. **291. napkin:** Handkerchief. **292. carouses:** Drinks a toast. **303. make . . . me:** Treat me like a spoiled child, holding back to give me an advantage. **306. [s.d.] in scuffling, they change rapiers:** This stage direction occurs in the Folio. According to a widespread stage tradition, Hamlet receives a scratch, realizes that Laertes' sword is unbated, and accordingly forces an exchange. **310. woodcock:** A bird, a type of stupidity or as a decoy. **springe:** Trap, snare.

HAMLET: How does the Queen?

KING: She swoons to see them bleed.

QUEEN: No, no, the drink, the drink — O my dear
      Hamlet —
   The drink, the drink! I am pois'ned.   [Dies.]

315 HAMLET: O villainy! Ho, let the door be lock'd!
   Treachery! Seek it out.   [Laertes falls.]

LAERTES: It is here, Hamlet. Hamlet, thou art
      slain.
   No med'cine in the world can do thee good;
   In thee there is not half an hour's life.

320   The treacherous instrument is in thy hand,
   Unbated° and envenom'd. The foul practice
   Hath turn'd itself on me. Lo, here I lie,
   Never to rise again. Thy mother's pois'ned.
   I can no more. The King, the King's to blame.

HAMLET: The point envenom'd too? Then, venom, to
325   thy work.   [Stabs the King.]

ALL: Treason! Treason!

KING: O, yet defend me, friends; I am but hurt.

HAMLET: Here, thou incestuous, murd'rous, damned
      Dane,

               [He forces the King to drink
                    the poisoned cup.]
   Drink off this potion. Is thy union° here?
   Follow my mother.   [King dies.]

330 LAERTES: He is justly serv'd.
   It is a poison temper'd° by himself.
   Exchange forgiveness with me, noble Hamlet.
   Mine and my father's death come not upon thee,
   Nor thine on me!   [Dies.]

335 HAMLET: Heaven make thee free of it! I follow thee.
   I am dead, Horatio. Wretched Queen, adieu!
   You that look pale and tremble at this chance,
   That are but mutes° or audience to this act,
   Had I but time — as this fell° sergeant,° Death,
340   Is strict in his arrest — O, I could tell you —
   But let it be. Horatio, I am dead;
   Thou livest. Report me and my cause aright
   To the unsatisfied.

HORATIO: Never believe it.
   I am more an antique Roman° than a Dane.
   Here's yet some liquor left.

         [He attempts to drink from the poisoned cup.
                    Hamlet prevents him.]

345 HAMLET: As th' art a man,
   Give me the cup! Let go! By heaven, I'll ha 't.
   O God, Horatio, what a wounded name,
   Things standing thus unknown, shall I leave behind
      me!
   If thou didst ever hold me in thy heart,

Absent thee from felicity awhile,   350
And in this harsh world draw thy breath in pain
To tell my story.
         (A march afar off [and a volley within].)
              What warlike noise is this?

OSRIC: Young Fortinbras, with conquest come from
      Poland,
   To the ambassadors of England gives
   This warlike volley.

HAMLET: O, I die, Horatio!   355
   The potent poison quite o'ercrows° my spirit.
   I cannot live to hear the news from England,
   But I do prophesy th' election lights
   On Fortinbras. He has my dying voice.°
   So tell him, with th' occurrents° more and less   360
   Which have solicited° — the rest is silence.   [Dies.]

HORATIO: Now cracks a noble heart. Good night,
      sweet prince;
   And flights of angels sing thee to thy rest!
                              [March within.]
   Why does the drum come hither?

(Enter Fortinbras, with the [English] Ambassadors [with
drum, colors, and attendants].)

FORTINBRAS: Where is this sight?

HORATIO: What is it you would see?   365
   If aught of woe or wonder, cease your search.

FORTINBRAS: This quarry° cries on havoc.° O proud
      Death.
   What feast is toward° in thine eternal cell,
   That thou so many princes at a shot
   So bloodily hast struck?

FIRST AMBASSADOR: The sight is dismal;   370
   And our affairs from England come too late.
   The ears are senseless that should give us hearing,
   To tell him his commandment is fulfill'd,
   That Rosencrantz and Guildenstern are dead.
   Where should we have our thanks?

HORATIO: Not from his° mouth,   375
   Had it th' ability of life to thank you.
   He never gave commandment for their death.
   But since, so jump° upon this bloody question,°
   You from the Polack wars, and you from
      England,
   Are here arriv'd, give order that these bodies   380
   High on a stage° be placed to the view,
   And let me speak to th' yet unknowing world
   How these things came about. So shall you hear
   Of carnal, bloody, and unnatural acts,
   Of accidental judgments,° casual° slaughters,   385

---

321. **Unbated:** Not blunted with a button.   329. **union:** Pearl (see line 271; with grim puns on the word's other meanings: marriage, shared death[?]).   331. **temper'd:** Mixed.
338. **mutes:** Silent observers.   339. **fell:** Cruel.   **sergeant:** Sheriff's officer.   344. **Roman:** It was the Roman custom to follow masters in death.

356. **o'ercrows:** Triumphs over.   359. **voice:** Vote.   360. **occurrents:** Events, incidents.   361. **solicited:** Moved, urged.
367. **quarry:** Heap of dead.   **cries on havoc:** Proclaims a general slaughter.   368. **toward:** In preparation.   375. **his:** Claudius's.   378. **jump:** Precisely.   **question:** Dispute.   381. **stage:** Platform.   385. **judgments:** Retributions.   **casual:** Occurring by chance.

Of deaths put on° by cunning and forc'd cause,
And, in this upshot, purposes mistook
Fall'n on th' inventors' heads. All this can I
Truly deliver.
FORTINBRAS: Let us haste to hear it,
390   And call the noblest to the audience.
For me, with sorrow I embrace my fortune.
I have some rights of memory° in this kingdom,
Which now to claim my vantage° doth invite me.
HORATIO: Of that I shall have also cause to speak,
And from his mouth whose voice will draw on
395   more.°
But let this same be presently° perform'd,

Even while men's minds are wild, lest more
    mischance
On° plots and errors happen.
FORTINBRAS: Let four captains
Bear Hamlet, like a soldier, to the stage,
For he was likely, had he been put on,°   400
To have prov'd most royal; and, for his passage,°
The soldiers' music and the rite of war
Speak loudly for him.
Take up the bodies. Such a sight as this
Becomes the field,° but here shows much amiss.   405
Go, bid the soldiers shoot.
        (*Exeunt* [*marching, bearing off the dead bodies;
                a peal of ordnance is shot off*].)

386. put on: Instigated.   **392. of memory:** Traditional, remembered.   **393. vantage:** Presence at this opportune moment.   **395. voice . . . more:** Vote will influence still others. **396. presently:** Immediately.

398. On: On the basis of.   **400. put on:** Invested in royal office and so put to the test.   **401. passage:** Death.   **405. field:** I.e., of battle.

COMMENTARIES

The modern era of Shakespeare criticism probably begins with Samuel Taylor Coleridge, whose lectures on Shakespeare were instrumental in helping a generation of early-nineteenth-century theatergoers take the playwright seriously. Coleridge, adapting the ideas of the German romantic critic Friedrich Schlegel, reached a wide and generally popular audience. His work centers on the character of Hamlet and his problems in the play, examining how Hamlet reveals himself both to us and to himself.

Sigmund Freud sees in *Hamlet* the seeds of the Oedipus complex that he had already identified in Sophocles' *Oedipus Rex*. The question of how one psychoanalyzes a literary character is perhaps best raised in Freud's essay. Later, a follower of Freud, Ernest Jones, wrote an entire book on Hamlet, analyzing him from the psychoanalytic perspective.

T. S. Eliot, speaking as a careful and noted student of Elizabethan and Jacobean drama, begins to point out some of the difficulties he sees with *Hamlet*. It is fascinating to see how great poets such as Coleridge and Eliot can approach the same play from such diverse points of view.

In a contemporary review of *Hamlet*, John Lahr focuses on the director's sense of pacing — commenting that Jonathan Kent cuts an hour off the length of *Hamlet*, thus making it, as he says, more of a "people's *Hamlet*."

Samuel Taylor Coleridge (1772–1834)
ON *HAMLET*   *1812*

Samuel Taylor Coleridge was the first modern English critic of Shakespeare to de-
velop influential readings of the great plays. He visited atheneums and lyceums (in-
stitutions promoting learning) on both sides of the Atlantic delivering his lectures
on Shakespeare, and his interpretations stimulated a new age of thoughtful criti-
cism. His lecture on Hamlet *includes a careful reading of difficult lines, but it also*
centers on questions of the relationship of Shakespeare to his creation. Further, the
mental state of Hamlet becomes of central interest to Coleridge and a basis of
much of his observation.

The seeming inconsistencies in the conduct and character of Hamlet have long
exercised the conjectural ingenuity of critics; and, as we are always loath to suppose that the cause of defective apprehension is in ourselves, the mystery has been
too commonly explained by the very easy process of setting it down as in fact inexplicable, and by resolving the phenomenon into a misgrowth or *lusus* of the capricious and irregular genius of Shakespeare. The shallow and stupid arrogance of
these vulgar and indolent decisions I would fain do my best to expose. I believe the
character of Hamlet may be traced to Shakespeare's deep and accurate science in
mental philosophy. Indeed, that this character must have some connection with the
common fundamental laws of our nature may be assumed from the fact that Hamlet has been the darling of every country in which the literature of England has been
fostered. In order to understand him, it is essential that we should reflect on the
constitution of our own minds. Man is distinguished from the brute animals in proportion as thought prevails over sense: but in the healthy processes of the mind, a
balance is constantly maintained between the impressions from outward objects
and the inward operations of the intellect: — for if there be an overbalance in the
contemplative faculty, man thereby becomes the creature of mere meditation, and
loses his natural power of action. Now one of Shakespeare's modes of creating
characters is to conceive any one intellectual or moral faculty in morbid excess, and
then to place himself, Shakespeare, thus mutilated or diseased, under given circumstances. In Hamlet he seems to have wished to exemplify the moral necessity of a
due balance between our attention to the objects of our senses, and our meditation
on the workings of our minds, — an *equilibrium* between the real and the imaginary worlds. In Hamlet this balance is disturbed: his thoughts, and the images of
his fancy, are far more vivid than his actual perceptions, and his very perceptions,
instantly passing through the *medium* of his contemplations, acquire, as they pass,
a form and a color not naturally their own. Hence we see a great, an almost enormous, intellectual activity, and a proportionate aversion to real action, consequent
upon it, with all its symptoms and accompanying qualities. This character Shakespeare places in circumstances, under which it is obliged to act on the spur of the
moment: — Hamlet is brave and careless of death; but he vacillates from sensibility, and procrastinates from thought, and loses the power of action in the energy of
resolve. Thus it is that this tragedy presents a direct contrast to that of Macbeth;
the one proceeds with the utmost slowness, the other with a crowded and breathless rapidity.

The effect of this overbalance of the imaginative power is beautifully illustrated in the everlasting broodings and superfluous activities of Hamlet's mind, which, unseated from its healthy relation, is constantly occupied with the world within, and abstracted from the world without, — giving substance to shadows, and throwing a mist over all commonplace actualities. It is the nature of thought to be indefinite; — definiteness belongs to external imagery alone. Hence it is that the sense of sublimity arises, not from the sight of an outward object, but from the beholder's reflection upon it; — not from the sensuous impression, but from the imaginative reflex. Few have seen a celebrated waterfall without feeling something akin to disappointment: it is only subsequently that the image comes back full into the mind, and brings with it a train of grand or beautiful associations. Hamlet feels this; his senses are in a state of trance, and he looks upon external things as hieroglyphics. His soliloquy —

Oh! that this too, too solid flesh would melt, &c.

springs from that craving after the indefinite — for that which is not — which most easily besets men of genius; and the self-delusion common to this temper of mind is finely exemplified in the character which Hamlet gives of himself: —

> — It can not be
> But I am pigeon-livered, and lack gall
> To make oppression bitter.

He mistakes the seeing his chains for the breaking of them, delays action till action is of no use, and dies the victim of mere circumstance and accident.[. . .]

Act I, scene IV. The unimportant conversation with which this scene opens is a proof of Shakespeare's minute knowledge of human nature. It is a well-established fact, that on the brink of any serious enterprise, or event of moment, men almost invariably endeavor to elude the pressure of their own thoughts by turning aside to trivial objects and familiar circumstances: thus this dialogue on the platform begins with remarks on the coldness of the air, and inquiries, obliquely connected, indeed, with the expected hour of the visitation, but thrown out in a seeming vacuity of topics, as to the striking of the clock and so forth. The same desire to escape from the impending thought is carried on in Hamlet's account of, and moralizing on, the Danish custom of wassailing: he runs off from the particular to the universal, and in his repugnance to personal and individual concerns, escapes, as it were, from himself in generalizations, and smothers the impatience and uneasy feelings of the moment in abstract reasoning. Besides this, another purpose is answered; — for by thus entangling the attention of the audience in the nice distinctions and parenthetical sentences of this speech of Hamlet's, Shakespeare takes them completely by surprise on the appearance of the Ghost, which comes upon them in all the suddenness of its visionary character. Indeed, no modern writer would have dared, like Shakespeare, to have preceded this last visitation by two distinct appearances, — or could have contrived that the third should rise upon the former two in impressiveness and solemnity of interest.

But in addition to all the other excellences of Hamlet's speech concerning the wassail-music — so finely revealing the predominant idealism, the ratiocinative° meditativeness, of his character — it has the advantage of giving nature and probability to the impassioned continuity of the speech instantly directed to the Ghost.

---

ratiocinative: Reasoned.

The *momentum* had been given to his mental activity; the full current of the thoughts and words had set in, and the very forgetfulness, in the fervor of his augmentation, of the purpose for which he was there, aided in preventing the appearance from benumbing the mind. Consequently, it acted as a new impulse, — a sudden stroke which increased the velocity of the body already in motion, whilst it altered the direction. The copresence of Horatio, Marcellus, and Bernardo is most judiciously contrived; for it renders the courage of Hamlet and his impetuous eloquence perfectly intelligible. The knowledge, — the unthought of consciousness, — the sensation, — of human auditors — of flesh and blood sympathists — acts as a support and a stimulation of *a tergo,* while the front of the mind, the whole consciousness of the speaker, is filled, yea, absorbed, by the apparition. Add too, that the apparition itself has by its previous appearances been brought nearer to a thing of this world. This accrescence° of objectivity in a Ghost that yet retains all its ghostly attributes and fearful subjectivity, is truly wonderful.

Act I, scene v. Hamlet's speech: —

O all you host of heaven! O earth! What else?
And shall I couple hell? —

I remember nothing equal to this burst unless it be the first speech of Prometheus in the Greek drama, after the exit of Vulcan and the two Afrites. But Shakespeare alone could have produced the vow of Hamlet to make his memory a blank of all maxims and generalized truths, that "observation had copied there,"— followed immediately by the speaker noting down the generalized fact,

That one may smile, and smile, and be a villain!

Marcellus: Hillo, ho, ho, my lord!
Hamlet: Hillo, ho, ho, boy! come bird, come, &c.

This part of the scene after Hamlet's interview with the Ghost has been charged with an improbable eccentricity. But the truth is that after the mind has been stretched beyond its usual pitch and tone, it must either sink into exhaustion and inanity, or seek relief by change. It is thus well known, that persons conversant in deeds of cruelty contrive to escape from conscience by connecting something of the ludicrous with them, and by inventing grotesque terms and a certain technical phraseology to disguise the horror of their practices. Indeed, paradoxical as it may appear, the terrible by a law of the human mind always touches on the verge of the ludicrous. Both arise from the perception of something out of the common order of things — something, in fact, out of its place; and if from this we can abstract danger, the uncommonness will alone remain, and the sense of the ridiculous be excited. The close alliance of these opposites — they are not contraries — appears from the circumstance, that laughter is equally the expression of extreme anguish and horror as of joy: as there are tears of sorrow and tears of joy, so is there a laugh of terror and a laugh of merriment. These complex causes will naturally have produced in Hamlet the disposition to escape from his own feelings of the overwhelming and supernatural by a wild transition to the ludicrous, — a sort of cunning bravado, bordering on the flights of delirium. For you may, perhaps, observe that Hamlet's wildness is but half false; he plays that subtle trick of pretending to act only when he is very near really being what he acts.

---

accrescence: Accumulation or concentration.

Sigmund Freud (1856–1939)

HAMLET'S SCRUPLES

1900–1930°

Sigmund Freud was the most celebrated psychiatrist of the twentieth century. He was especially interested in Greek myth, as his comments on Oedipus Rex *suggest.* Hamlet *was another play that took on mythic proportions for him, in part because Freud saw in Hamlet the operation of his famous theory of the Oedipus complex. In the following excerpt Freud examines the events of the play that bear on his theory.*

Another of the great creations of tragic poetry, Shakespeare's *Hamlet*, has its roots in the same soil as *Oedipus Rex*. But the changed treatment of the same material reveals the whole difference in the mental life of these two widely separated epochs of civilization: the secular advance of repression in the emotional life of mankind. In the *Oedipus* the child's wishful fantasy that underlies it is brought into the open and realized as it would be in a dream. In *Hamlet* it remains repressed; and — just as in the case of a neurosis — we only learn of its existence from its inhibiting consequences. Strangely enough, the overwhelming effect produced by the more modern tragedy has turned out to be compatible with the fact that people have remained completely in the dark as to the hero's character. The play is built up on Hamlet's hesitations over fulfilling the task of revenge that is assigned to him; but its text offers no reasons or motives for these hesitations and an immense variety of attempts at interpreting them have failed to produce a result. According to the view which was originated by Goethe and is still the prevailing one today, Hamlet represents the type of man whose power of direct action is paralyzed by an excessive development of his intellect. (He is "sicklied o'er with the pale cast of thought.") According to another view, the dramatist has tried to portray a pathologically irresolute character which might be classed as neurasthenic.° The plot of the drama shows us, however, that Hamlet is far from being represented as a person incapable of taking any action. We see him doing so on two occasions: first in a sudden outburst of temper, when he runs his sword through the eavesdropper behind the arras, and secondly in a premeditated and even crafty fashion, when, with all the callousness of a Renaissance prince, he sends the two courtiers to the death that had been planned for himself. What is it, then, that inhibits him in fulfilling the task set him by his father's ghost? The answer, once again, is that it is the peculiar nature of the task. Hamlet is able to do anything — except take vengeance on the man who did away with his father and took that father's place with his mother, the man who shows him the repressed wishes of his own childhood realized. Thus the loathing which should drive him on to revenge is replaced in him by self-reproaches, by scruples of conscience, which remind him that he himself is literally no better than the sinner whom he is to punish. Here I have translated into conscious terms what was bound to remain unconscious in Hamlet's mind; and if anyone is inclined to call him a hysteric, I can only accept the fact as one that is

---

1900–1930: Freud's *Interpretation of Dreams,* from which this excerpt is taken, was first published in 1900 and updated regularly by Freud through eight editions. This passage is taken from the eighth edition, published in 1930.
neurasthenic: One who suffers from fatigue, loss of energy, and feelings of inadequacy.

implied by my interpretation. The distaste for sexuality expressed by Hamlet in his conversation with Ophelia fits in very well with this: the same distaste which was destined to take possession of the poet's mind more and more during the years that followed, and which reached its extreme expression in *Timon of Athens*. For it can of course only be the poet's own mind which confronts us in Hamlet. I observe in a book on Shakespeare by Georg Brandes (1896) a statement that *Hamlet* was written immediately after the death of Shakespeare's father (in 1601), that is, under the immediate impact of his bereavement and, as we may well assume, while his childhood feelings about his father had been freshly revived. It is known, too, that Shakespeare's own son who died at an early age bore the name of "Hamnet," which is identical with "Hamlet." Just as *Hamlet* deals with the relation of a son to his parents, so *Macbeth* (written at approximately the same period) is concerned with the subject of childlessness. But just as all neurotic symptoms, and, for that matter, dreams, are capable of being "overinterpreted" and indeed need to be if they are to be fully understood, so all genuinely creative writings are the product of more than a single motive and more than a single impulse in the poet's mind, and are open to more than a single interpretation. In what I have written I have only attempted to interpret the deepest layer of impulses in the mind of the creative writer.

T. S. Eliot (1888–1965)
HAMLET AND HIS PROBLEMS   *1934*

Not only a leading poet of the twentieth-century modernist period, T. S. Eliot also produced extremely interesting criticism of Elizabethan literature. His several collections of essays have in some cases defined important critical terms that later readers have used to gain insight into great writers. One of those terms is developed here: the objective correlative, which Eliot feels is missing in Hamlet. *His argument is provocative and revealing.*

Few critics have ever admitted that *Hamlet* the play is the primary problem, and Hamlet the character only secondary. And Hamlet the character has had an especial temptation for that most dangerous type of critic: the critic with a mind which is naturally of the creative order, but which through some weakness in creative power exercises itself in criticism instead. These minds often find in Hamlet a vicarious existence for their own artistic realization. Such a mind had Goethe, who made of Hamlet a Werther; and such had Coleridge who made of Hamlet a Coleridge; and probably neither of these men in writing about Hamlet remembered that his first business was to study a work of art. The kind of criticism that Goethe and Coleridge produced, in writing of Hamlet, is the most misleading kind possible. For they both possessed unquestionable critical insight, and both make their critical aberrations the more plausible by the substitution — of their own Hamlet for Shakespeare's — which their creative gift effects. We should be thankful that Walter Pater° did not fix his attention on this play.

Walter Pater: English writer and critic (1839–1894). His writings were often overelaborate.

Two writers of our time, Mr. J. M. Robertson and Professor Stoll of the University of Minnesota, have issued small books which can be praised for moving in the other direction. Mr. Stoll performs a service in recalling to our attention the labors of the critics of the seventeenth and eighteenth centuries, observing that

> they knew less about psychology than more recent Hamlet critics, but they were nearer in spirit to Shakespeare's art; and as they insisted on the importance of the effect of the whole rather than on the importance of the leading character, they were nearer, in their old-fashioned way, to the secret of dramatic art in general.

Qua work of art, the work of art cannot be interpreted; there is nothing to interpret; we can only criticize it according to standards, in comparison to other works of art; and for "interpretation" the chief task is the presentation of relevant historical facts which the reader is not assumed to know. Mr. Robertson points out, very pertinently, how critics have failed in their "interpretation" of *Hamlet* by ignoring what ought to be very obvious: that *Hamlet* is a stratification, that it represents the efforts of a series of men, each making what he could out of the work of his predecessors. The *Hamlet* of Shakespeare will appear to us very differently if, instead of treating the whole action of the play as due to Shakespeare's design, we perceive his *Hamlet* to be superposed upon much cruder material which persists even in the final form.

We know that there was an older play by Thomas Kyd, that extraordinary dramatic (if not poetic) genius who was in all probability the author of two plays so dissimilar as the *Spanish Tragedy* and *Arden of Feversham;* and what this play was like we can guess from three clues: from the *Spanish Tragedy* itself, from the tale of Belleforest upon which Kyd's *Hamlet* must have been based, and from a version acted in Germany in Shakespeare's lifetime which bears strong evidence of having been adapted from the earlier, not from the later, play. From these three sources it is clear that in the earlier play the motive was a revenge motive simply; that the action or delay is caused, as in the *Spanish Tragedy,* solely by the difficulty of assassinating a monarch surrounded by guards; and that the "madness" of Hamlet was feigned in order to escape suspicion, and successfully. In the final play of Shakespeare, on the other hand, there is a motive which is more important than that of revenge, and which explicitly "blunts" the latter; the delay in revenge is unexplained on grounds of necessity or expediency; and the effect of the "madness" is not to lull but to arouse the king's suspicion. The alteration is not complete enough, however, to be convincing. Furthermore, there are verbal parallels so close to the *Spanish Tragedy* as to leave no doubt that in places Shakespeare was merely *revising* the text of Kyd. And finally there are unexplained scenes — the Polonius-Laertes and the Polonius-Reynaldo scenes — for which there is little excuse; these scenes are not in the verse style of Kyd, and not beyond doubt in the style of Shakespeare. These Mr. Robertson believes to be scenes in the original play of Kyd reworked by a third hand, perhaps Chapman,° before Shakespeare touched the play. And he concludes, with very strong show of reason, that the original play of Kyd was, like certain other revenge plays, in two parts of five acts. The upshot of Mr. Robertson's examination is, we believe, irrefragable: that Shakespeare's *Hamlet,* so far as it is Shakespeare's, is a play dealing with the effect of a mother's guilt upon her son, and that Shakespeare was unable to impose this motive successfully upon the "intractable" material of the old play.

Chapman: George Chapman (1559?–1634), Elizabethan poet and playwright.

Of the intractability there can be no doubt. So far from being Shakespeare's masterpiece, the play is most certainly an artistic failure. In several ways the play is puzzling, and disquieting as is none of the others. Of all the plays it is the longest and is possibly the one on which Shakespeare spent most pains; and yet he has left in it superfluous and inconsistent scenes which even hasty revision should have noticed. The versification is variable. Lines like

> Look, the morn, in russet mantle clad,
> Walks o'er the dew of yon high eastern hill,

are of the Shakespeare of *Romeo and Juliet*. The lines in act V, scene II,

> Sir, in my heart there was a kind of fighting
> That would not let me sleep . . .
> Up from my cabin,
> My sea-grown scarf'd about me, in the dark
> Grop'd I to find out them: had my desire;
> Finger'd their packet;

are of his quite mature. Both workmanship and thought are in an unstable position. We are surely justified in attributing the play, with that other profoundly interesting play of "intractable" material and astonishing versification, *Measure for Measure*, to a period of crisis, after which follow the tragic successes which culminate in *Coriolanus*. *Coriolanus* may be not as "interesting" as *Hamlet*, but it is, with *Antony and Cleopatra*, Shakespeare's most assured artistic success. And probably more people have thought *Hamlet* a work of art because they found it interesting, than have found it interesting because it is a work of art. It is the *Mona Lisa* of literature.

The grounds of *Hamlet*'s failure are not immediately obvious. Mr. Robertson is undoubtedly correct in concluding that the essential emotion of the play is the feeling of a son toward a guilty mother:

> [Hamlet's] tone is that of one who has suffered tortures on the score of his mother's degradation. . . . The guilt of a mother is an almost intolerable motive for drama, but it had to be maintained and emphasized to supply a psychological solution, or rather a hint of one.

This, however, is by no means the whole story. It is not merely the "guilt of a mother" that cannot be handled as Shakespeare handled the suspicion of Othello, the infatuation of Antony, or the pride of Coriolanus. The subject might conceivably have expanded into a tragedy like these, intelligible, self-complete, in the sunlight. *Hamlet*, like the sonnets, is full of some stuff that the writer could not drag to light, contemplate, or manipulate into art. And when we search for this feeling, we find it, as in the sonnets, very difficult to localize. You cannot point to it in the speeches; indeed, if you examine the two famous soliloquies you see the versification of Shakespeare, but a content which might be claimed by another, perhaps by the author of the *Revenge of Bussy d'Ambois*,° act V, scene I. We find Shakespeare's Hamlet not in the action, not in any quotations that we might select, so much as in an unmistakable tone which is unmistakably not in the earlier play.

Revenge of Bussy d'Ambois: Tragedy (1610–1611) by George Chapman, dealing with the reluctance of Clement d'Ambois to avenge his brother's death.

The only way of expressing emotion in the form of art is by finding an "objective correlative"; in other words, a set of objects, a situation, a chain of events which shall be the formula of that *particular* emotion; such that when the external facts, which must terminate in sensory experience, are given, the emotion is immediately evoked. If you examine any of Shakespeare's more successful tragedies, you will find this exact equivalence; you will find that the state of mind of Lady Macbeth walking in her sleep has been communicated to you by a skillful accumulation of imagined sensory impressions; the words of Macbeth on hearing of his wife's death strike us as if, given the sequence of events, these words were automatically released by the last event in the series. The artistic "inevitability" lies in this complete adequacy of the external to the emotion; and this is precisely what is deficient in *Hamlet*. Hamlet (the man) is dominated by an emotion which is inexpressible, because it is in *excess* of the facts as they appear. And the supposed identity of Hamlet with his author is genuine to this point: that Hamlet's bafflement at the absence of objective equivalent to his feelings is a prolongation of the bafflement of his creator in the face of his artistic problem. Hamlet is up against the difficulty that his disgust is occasioned by his mother, but that his mother is not an adequate equivalent for it; his disgust envelops and exceeds her. It is thus a feeling which he cannot understand; he cannot objectify it, and it therefore remains to poison life and obstruct action. None of the possible actions can satisfy it; and nothing that Shakespeare can do with the plot can express Hamlet for him. And it must be noticed that the very nature of the *données* of the problem precludes objective equivalence. To have heightened the criminality of Gertrude would have been to provide the formula for a totally different emotion in Hamlet; it is just *because* her character is so negative and insignificant that she arouses in Hamlet the feeling which she is incapable of representing.

The "madness" of Hamlet lay to Shakespeare's hand; in the earlier play a simple ruse, and to the end, we may presume, understood as a ruse by the audience. For Shakespeare it is less than madness and more than feigned. The levity of Hamlet, his repetition of phrase, his puns, are not part of a deliberate plan of dissimulation, but a form of emotional relief. In the character Hamlet it is the buffoonery of an emotion which can find no outlet in action; in the dramatist it is the buffoonery of an emotion which he cannot express in art. The intense feeling, ecstatic or terrible, without an object or exceeding its object, is something which every person of sensibility has known; it is doubtless a subject of study for pathologists. It often occurs in adolescence: the ordinary person puts these feelings to sleep, or trims down his feelings to fit the business world; the artist keeps them alive by his ability to intensify the world to his emotions. The Hamlet of Laforgue° is an adolescent; the Hamlet of Shakespeare is not, he has not that explanation and excuse. We must simply admit that here Shakespeare tackled a problem which proved too much for him. Why he attempted it at all is an insoluble puzzle; under compulsion of what experience he attempted to express the inexpressibly horrible, we cannot ever know. We need a great many facts in his biography; and we should like to know whether, and when, and after or at the same time as what personal experience, he read Montaigne's *Apologie de Raimond Sebond*. We should have, finally, to know something which is by hypothesis unknowable, for we assume it to be an experience which, in the manner indicated, exceeded the facts. We should have to understand things which Shakespeare did not understand himself.

Laforgue: Jules Laforgue (1860–1887), French poet who was an important influence on Eliot.

John Lahr (b. 1941)
REVIEW OF *HAMLET*   *1994*

As John Lahr reminds us, any review of Hamlet *always discusses the lead actor.*
All past productions are identified in terms of the actor who played the part. Lahr,
like most reviewers, centers first on Ralph Fiennes's performance in the title role.
He then goes on, focusing on elements such as costumes and stage settings as a way
of describing the overall production.

Hamlet is a play that tests the best actors of each generation, and also each generation's sense of itself. Over the last thirty years, in England, no fewer than three
*Hamlet*s have served as such cultural bellwethers. In 1965, during the Vietnam
War, David Warner gave us an untidy undergraduate Hamlet who was frustrated
by Denmark's military-industrial complex. In 1980, as Britain's economy went into
a weird free fall, Jonathan Pryce's *Hamlet* was possessed by the ghost of his father,
who spoke through him in a frightening supernatural flirtation with madness. And
now, in the neutral, post-Thatcher nineties, Ralph Fiennes has pitched his drop-
dead matinee-idol profile and the modesty of his sensitive soul into a postmodern
Hamlet whose refusal to risk interpretation reflects Britain's current bland and
winded times.

Fiennes, an intelligent, reticent player, seems almost as unwilling to enter the
vortex of Hamlet's torment as Hamlet himself is to take action. Fiennes radiates an
elegance of spirit that rivets the audience with its sense of unspoken mystery. His
performance is a stylish event, much more the "mould of form" than the "glass of
fashion." He has a mellow, reedy voice that filters Shakespeare's gorgeous complexity and gives the language an accessible colloquial ring. Fiennes is not one for
grand histrionic gestures. His personality doesn't take up a lot of space. He compels attention by his decency, not by his declaiming. Fiennes, who has limpid green
eyes and tousled chestnut hair, and who is a laid-back, brooding, romantic star, is
catnip to the public and oxygen at the box office. (The Almeida Theatre Company's
production, which began its much ballyhooed life at the Hackney Empire, the wonderful old music-hall venue in London's East End, has arrived at the Belasco for a
fourteen-week Broadway engagement.) This *Hamlet* has been designed to be a
people's *Hamlet,* which is to say a *Hamlet* in which the plot, not the psychology, is
complicated, and in which the cast works the room instead of working for meaning. Inevitably, therefore, Fiennes's Hamlet is not a navel-gazing scholar or an
alienated adolescent or a demented psychological case study. His Hamlet turns out
to be the guy Horatio always said he was: a "sweet prince," a sort of rogue and
pleasant slave.

The director, Jonathan Kent, who last year transferred the Almeida's *Medea,*
with Diana Rigg, to Broadway with great success, has set the play in Edwardian
England and has lopped an hour off the playing time. The speed favors breadth
over depth; the streamlining suits the cut of Fiennes's jib, and he wears James Ache-
son's period clothes well. What we have here is a ripping Shakespearean yarn that
shows off the thrills and chills of the story's melodramatic elements: the ghost of a
murdered king, a mother's hasty marriage to her husband's murderer, a prince
driven to near-madness and revenge, a lovelorn suicide, a lot of ghoulish high jinks
around graves, a terrific sword fight, and a quadruple poisoning. The result is lucid

without being moving: a kind of aerobic *Hamlet,* which works hard to keep up the pace while going nowhere.

The lights come up on a bare, raked stage, and the sound of crashing waves fills the auditorium. In the background, the environs of Elsinore are suggested by faint, blurred beams of light projected through a murky scrim on which the outlines of rocks are just visible. A sentinel climbs up through a trapdoor — more for effect than for sense, it seems, like many things in this production. "Who's there?" he calls. That's the play; the whole existential ball of wax. Hamlet's entire dramatic journey is foreshadowed in these first words. He, too, must penetrate the surrounding darkness and tease out the reality of his parents, of the corrupt court, and of himself. By finally taking action — which means accepting loss, including the loss of his own life, Hamlet sees clear into the heart of things and achieves his adulthood. In this sense, *Hamlet* is both a detective story and a metaphysical investigation. The practical and the philosophical aspects of the tale need time to build properly, as the saying goes, "No delay, no play." But here, with the proceedings speeded up, the text is not so much examined as *done.* It's significant that Fiennes attacks the "To be, or not to be" soliloquy, which sets out Hamlet's spiritual quandary, by coming toward us in manic stutter steps and turning the famous meditation into yapping thought. He skirts the issue of interpretation by turning talk into behavior. The image is novel but little nuance comes across the footlights. In this ranting mode, dissembling a madness that is really giddy grief, the barefoot Fiennes grabs Ophelia's crotch and insolently shoves Claudius's shoulder. But Fiennes can't really get up a convincingly antic head of steam. He is slow to kindle and never really burns. He's not so much tormented as pissed off.

Fiennes has his best moment with the grave-digger (the excellent grizzled Terence Rigby, who also plays Hamlet's father's ghost and the Player King). Listening to the Gravedigger expound matter-of-factly on how a body decomposes, and learning that a skull he has unearthed belonged to Yorick, the former King's jester, Hamlet gently takes this relic of his old acquaintance from the grave-digger. "This?" Fiennes says, uttering the word with a huge sense of recognition, wonder, and sadness. His sensitivity and the mournfulness of the moment coalesce. "Where be your gibes now? your gambols? your songs? your flashes of merriment, that were wont to set the table on a roar?" Fiennes says, with a delicacy that delivers Shakespeare's observations about mortality like a punch to the heart.

The production's obsession with surface has its most effective expression in Peter J. Davison's sets. He creates a dark, lugubrious officialdom of behemoth ceilings, heavy brown-stained doors, and large shuttered windows that turn the actors into scuttling Lilliputians. Hamlet is first seen framed by one of these gigantic windows, standing upstage with his back turned away from the bustle of power, whose aggrandizement is reflected in the monumentality that surrounds it. Still, Davison, too, succumbs to the production's impulse to startle rather than compel. The ghost is conjured up on a high platform behind the scrim. There, lit from above by the white glare of a halogen lamp and announced by a jolt of electronic sound, Hamlet's dead father appears twice, in his carapace of armor: a "Star Wars" effect that is a projection of commercial instincts more than of Hamlet's unconscious. Similarly, Jonathan Kent's eye for business is sometimes shrewder than his eye for detail. When Laertes and Hamlet take turns leaping into Ophelia's grave and embracing her body, each trying to outdo the remorse of the other, the poor dead girl bobs up and down like a hand puppet. And at the finale, when Fortinbras

(Rupert Penry-Jones, who is also Fiennes's understudy) arrives to take over the kingdom that Hamlet has died to save, his Aryan good looks and the gray capes of his lieutenants make it seem as if the Luftwaffe had invaded Denmark.

In American theatrical circles, the definition of a genius is anybody from England. But the prestige of this production can't hide the unevenness of its seasoned supporting cast, who prove the adage that British actors are either tours de force or forced to tour. Besides Terence Rigby, only the lanky, bearded Peter Eyre, as Polonius, breathes distinctive life into his role. Eyre plays the meddling bureaucrat as a long drink of cold water: cleaning his pince-nez as he counsels his hot-headed son to "neither a borrower, nor a lender be," and withholding his hand from Laertes when he goes, Eyre misses no opportunity to have fun with the old blowhard's pedantry. Polonius rushes to the Queen with a letter that Hamlet has sent his daughter, and reads it to her as a presenting symptom of Hamlet's lunacy. Reciting "To the celestial and my soul's idol, the most beautified Ophelia," Eyre's Polonius bristles with dopey patrician disdain. "That's an ill phrase, a vile phrase, 'beautified' is a vile phrase," he says, and gets one of the evening's best laughs.

Others are not so much at home in Shakespeare's climate of delirium. Tara FitzGerald, a talented young actress with a bright future, flounders as Ophelia. There is nothing fractured or vulnerable about her, and when Ophelia goes mad FitzGerald won't let her rip. FitzGerald's behavior — the compulsive walking back and forth, the sexual taunts directed at Claudius — feels tame and glib: a trick of the mind, not a journey of the heart. Often, when English actors are nowhere near the center of their parts they rely on the power of their articulate voices; James Laurenson's Claudius falls into the trap of such posturing. Claudius is John Gotti with a pedigree — carnal, vicious, powerhungry, ruthless — but Laurenson gives us chicanery on the half shell. He does a lot of Urgent Shakespeare Acting. A few wheeling turns upstage, some nips at the top of his hand, a little booming oratory, and — presto! — you have a villain. This stock rep stuff is also dished up by the beautiful Francesca Annis, as a Gertrude who can't manage much grief at the sight of Ophelia's dementia but does manage a long, lingering kiss with Hamlet. It's a bit of business that has become the theatrical baggage of the role in this century, but the incestuous overtone seems inappropriate, especially in such an unanalytic production.

A word about Hamlet's duel. Jonathan Kent and the fight director, William Hobbs, have built up this face-off between idealism and treachery into a scintillating contest that takes excellent advantage of the story's melodrama. A cream-colored tarp is rolled downstage for the match, and the court sits watching upstage right, in gray upholstered chairs. Hamlet fights with graceful, playful enthusiasm, unaware that he's up against the double whammy of Laertes' poisoned sword and Claudius's poisoned chalice. Hamlet gets the first couple of touches; then Laertes' temper flares, and he cuts Hamlet. They scuffle, and in the hurly-burly their swords get mixed up. Hamlet chases Laertes around the room, sending chairs flying and courtiers scurrying for safety. It's exciting and well-staged hokom, in which Laertes ends up hoist with his own petard. At that point, the Queen, who has drunk from the chalice, collapses; then the Grand Guignol of Shakespeare's ending quickly plays itself out. At the finale, Fortinbras's men lift Hamlet's corpse on their shoulders and, swaying, carry him slowly upstage and toward the light beyond. Fiennes's head falls back, giving the audience one last glimpse of the star. Even backward, upside down, and dead, Fiennes exits looking good.

OTHELLO

Othello was one of Shakespeare's most popular plays, produced frequently in his lifetime and throughout the seventeenth century. Although the date of composition is uncertain, we do know that the earliest recorded production was November 1, 1604, in the old Banqueting Hall at the court of King James I and his wife, Anne of Denmark. This detail is interesting because it coincides with the later production — during the same winter season and at the same theater — of Ben Jonson's *Masque of Blackness,* which was specifically commissioned by Queen Anne so that she could "paint herself black" along with the ladies in her retinue.

There seems to have been a vogue for blackness in England at the time. A great many Moors — the term, as Shakespeare and others of his time use it, means a dark-skinned person from Africa — were living in England at the end of Queen Elizabeth's reign and the beginning of King James's, the period of both performances. Though her government had given Moors "full diplomatic recognition" as a gesture of thanks for their conquest of England's enemy Spain, in 1601 Queen Elizabeth was so alarmed by the number of blacks in England that she appointed a foreign merchant to transport them from the kingdom. In 1604 a delegation of Arabs visited London, and their customs and style caused some stir, both of admiration and concern. While the color black was symbolically associated by white people with the devil and moral turpitude, and the practice of slavery was already advanced, a number of black African noblemen had traveled to England, and some had returned to Africa as translators and intermediaries in trading expeditions.

Aaron, a Moor in Shakespeare's *Titus Andronicus* (1594), was dark-skinned and a villain. Early on, however, Shakespeare represents black characters in other entertainments as noble. He establishes the noble birth and character of Othello, for instance, who tells us, "I am black" (III, iii, 263). The character of Othello, a general of the Venetian forces, derives from an early Italian story by Geraldi Cinthio published in 1566 in Italian and 1584 in French. Shakespeare might have read either one. He adapted the story, adding new characters, reinterpreting the action, and completely reimagining Othello, Desdemona, and Iago.

The setting, Venice, was exotic for Elizabethan audiences, but it was appropriate for establishing a character who was unusual and something of "the other," as, for example, Shylock was in the earlier *Merchant of Venice* (1596–1597). It was especially felicitous a choice of setting for Othello's generalship because the Venetian republic, by law, had to have a foreigner as general of the armies. No one in the play disputes Othello's leadership and soldiership — not even Iago.

While the play makes great use of the contrasts of black and white, light and dark, evening and day, both to establish mood and to imply moral values, the central action is not devoted to issues relative to Othello's race. The opening scenes reveal that Brabantio, Desdemona's father, and Iago, Othello's ensign, are capable of racial slurs. But each speaks out of anger and disappointment. The official governors of Venice never once imply racial inequity, nor do they condone any disrespect for Othello. Indeed, they support him in his marriage once they hear Desdemona indicate her willing choice of Othello as her mate.

The dramatic action centers on Iago's bitter disappointment at having been passed over for promotion in favor of Cassio, whom he regards as an inexperienced boy. Cassio is well enough regarded by Othello and others to end the play as governor of Mauritania, the country in northwest Africa that was settled by Berbers and from which the name Moors is derived. Even if Cassio was preferred because he was the intermediary between Othello and Desdemona, and even though he has the weakness of sometimes being an unsoldierly drunk, he proves more worthy than the villainous Iago, who virtually personifies the devil. At the end of the play, Othello, understanding how terribly he has been betrayed, wishes to look at Iago's foot to see if, like the devil's, it is cleft.

In some productions of the play, Iago almost steals the show. His soliloquies indicating how he will manipulate the characters to achieve his evil ends are so powerful as to chill an audience. He seems to be the force driving the action, while Othello struggles like a fly in the web of his deceit. Yet Othello is the great character in the drama. He rises majestically to deliver some of the greatest speeches Shakespeare ever wrote. Eventually, his initial innocence is replaced by rage and anger. Iago purposely infects Othello with jealousy, implying that his young, new wife Desdemona is dallying with Cassio. He offers "ocular proof" but proof that would not be convincing if Othello were not anxious to be convinced. Iago moves Othello from a contented man — a soldier at peace with himself — to a deracinated jealous husband.

Watching the progress of that action rivets the audience. Seeing how the villain Iago improvises at every turn to take advantage of each opportunity to present false "evidence" fascinates audience and reader alike. Ironically, the symbolism of blackness is reversed in Iago, whose inner soul is dark and hell bound, while Othello is led to commit a heinous crime whose horror he ultimately recognizes. He pays with his own death by his own hand. Our sympathy is with him at the end of the play, despite his moments of frightening anger and horror. He has been used by a lesser man, and what has permitted him to be deceived — as interpreted by some critics — is his essential innocence and goodness.

Among the patterns of imagery in the play, those connected with animals — such as the pig, the barbary horse, and the black ram — support Iago's efforts to emphasize Othello's bestiality. When he claims that Othello and Desdemona are "making the beast with two backs," he wishes to enlist Brabantio's aid in humiliating Othello and perhaps damaging his reputation with the Duke of Venice. The careful manipulation of this imagery helps Iago forward his plan even before he knows what it is.

Othello himself stands as one of the towering figures in Shakespeare's works, challenging actors in his own day and in ours. Desdemona may be faulted for her willfulness in marrying without her father's knowledge or permission — at the time a grave infraction. But the audience forgives her if only because it is obvious that nothing she could have said would have convinced her father to look kindly on Othello as a son-in-law. And while passion is at the core of the play, it may not have been passion alone that caused her to act as she did.

Othello in Performance

The first recorded production of *Othello* was November 1604 at the court of King James. But public performances probably were held at the Globe Theatre sometime that year or the following. Although no reliable performance records are available, we know that the play was produced by Shakespeare's company, The King's Men, both at the Globe in April 1610 and in Oxford in September of the same year. It was performed again in 1629, 1635, and 1636. It was popular in the eighteenth and nineteenth centuries as well as in the twentieth century and is among Shakespeare's most produced plays.

The first Othello was Richard Burbage, Shakespeare's finest actor in one of his finest roles. He wore Elizabethan clothes with no special effort to adopt a Moorish costume. We have no record of his makeup, and the only eyewitness account describes him as a "grieved Moor." However, judging from the tradition maintained up to 1709, when we have a portrait of Othello, we can assume he was played as a black man. The play enjoyed such popularity that it constantly attracted the most gifted actors of the day.

The nineteenth century produced several notable Othellos, but it also saw the beginning of a trend in which Othello became "tawny" rather than black. He became what was then known as a "white Moor." Edmund Kean, the greatest actor of his day, portrayed Othello in this fashion to extraordinary acclaim. The first black actor to play Othello was Ira Aldridge, an American on the London stage in the nineteenth century.

In modern times, two productions stand out as milestones: Paul Robeson's in New York in 1943–1944 and Laurence Olivier's in London in 1964. Robeson was known as a great singer but had performed onstage in Eugene O'Neill's *The Emperor Jones* prior to *Othello*. His physical presence on stage was striking in every way, especially when linked with his commanding voice. Martin Wine describes him as the "outstanding 'romantic' Othello of our time," by which he means a sympathetic and moving Othello. The Broadway production played for more performances than nearly any American production of Shakespeare up to that time. James Earl Jones, who played the role many years later, was in the audience and felt that Robeson's command of the concept of honor was singular and has never been approached since.

Laurence Olivier had himself made up not just as a black man but as a black African. Some critics were impressed by the achievement, but others felt it was still difficult to accept the idea of a white actor in the part. Yet Olivier's version was taut, powerful, and one of his greatest achievements. He took comfort in the fact that Shakespeare wrote the role for a white actor and did not worry over the shift in tradition. Martin Wine described his performance as "the most controversial" performance of our time. Olivier's interpretation was of an egotistical Othello, one who was tormented by neurotic tendencies and even a touch of paranoia. Olivier's Othello was less a man of the Renaissance than a man of modern times.

Most modern productions have made use of effective lighting, emphasizing the opening darkness of the drama. They also make use of simple staging, using archways effectively and suggestions of buildings, ships and sails, and sometimes Moorish architectural details.

William Shakespeare (1564–1616)
OTHELLO THE MOOR OF VENICE   *1604*

The Names of the Actors

OTHELLO, THE MOOR
BRABANTIO, [*a Venetian senator,*] *father to Desdemona*
CASSIO, *an honorable lieutenant* [*to Othello*]
IAGO, [*Othello's ancient,*] *a villain*
RODERIGO, *a gulled gentleman*
DUKE OF VENICE
SENATORS [*of Venice*]
MONTANO, *governor of Cyprus*
LODOVICO AND GRATIANO, [*kinsmen to Brabantio,*]
    two noble Venetians
SAILORS
CLOWNS
DESDEMONA, *wife to Othello*
EMILIA, *wife to Iago*
BIANCA, *a courtesan*
[MESSENGER, HERALD, OFFICERS, VENETIAN
    GENTLEMEN, MUSICIANS, ATTENDANTS]

Scene: *Venice and Cyprus*]

ACT I • *Scene 1*

A street in Venice.

Enter Roderigo and Iago.

RODERIGO: Tush, never tell me! I take it much
    unkindly
    That thou, Iago, who hast had my purse
    As if the strings were thine, shouldst know of this.°
IAGO: 'Sblood,° but you'll not hear me!
5   If ever I did dream of such a matter,
    Abhor me.
RODERIGO: Thou told'st me thou didst hold him in thy
    hate.
IAGO: Despise me if I do not. Three great ones of the
    city,
    In personal suit to make me his lieutenant,
10   Off-capped to him;° and, by the faith of man,
    I know my price; I am worth no worse a place.
    But he, as loving his own pride and purposes,
    Evades them with a bombast circumstance.°
    Horribly stuffed with epithets of war;
15   [And, in conclusion,]
    Nonsuits° my mediators; for, "Certes," says he,

I, I. 3. **this:** I.e., Desdemona's elopement.   5. **'Sblood:** By God's blood.   10. **him:** I.e., Othello.   13. **a bombast circumstance:** Pompous circumlocution.   16. **Nonsuits:** Rejects.

"I have already chose my officer."
And what was he?
Forsooth, a great arithmetician,°
One Michael Cassio, a Florentine   20
(A fellow almost damned in a fair wife°)
That never set a squadron in the field,
Nor the division of a battle knows
More than a spinster; unless the bookish theoric,
Wherein the togèd consuls can propose   25
As masterly as he. Mere prattle without practice
Is all his soldiership. But he, sir, had th' election;
And I (of whom his eyes had seen the proof
At Rhodes, at Cyprus, and on other grounds
Christian and heathen) must be belee'd and calmed°   30
By debitor and creditor; this counter-caster,°
He, in good time, must his lieutenant be,
And I — God bless the mark! — his Moorship's
    ancient.°
RODERIGO: By heaven, I rather would have been his
    hangman.
IAGO: Why, there's no remedy; 'tis the curse of service. 35
    Preferment goes by letter and affection,°
    And not by old gradation, where each second
    Stood heir to th' first. Now, sir, be judge yourself,
    Whether I in any just term am affined°
    To love the Moor.
RODERIGO: I would not follow him then.   40
IAGO: O, sir, content you;
    I follow him to serve my turn upon him.
    We cannot all be masters, nor all masters
    Cannot be truly followed. You shall mark
    Many a duteous and knee-crooking knave   45
    That, doting on his own obsequious bondage,
    Wears out his time, much like his master's ass,
    For naught but provender; and when he's old,
        cashiered.°
    Whip me such honest knaves! Others there are
    Who, trimmed° in forms and visages of duty,   50
    Keep yet their hearts attending on themselves;
    And, throwing but shows of service on their lords,
    Do well thrive by them, and when they have lined
        their coats,
    Do themselves homage. These fellows have some
        soul;

19. **arithmetician:** Theoretician.   21. **almost . . . wife:** (An obscure allusion; Cassio is unmarried, but see IV, I, 115–16).   30. **belee'd and calmed:** Left in the lurch.   31. **counter-caster:** Bookkeeper.   33. **ancient:** Ensign.   36. **affection:** Favoritism.   39. **affined:** Obliged.   48. **cashiered:** Turned off.   50. **trimmed:** Dressed up.

55   And such a one do I profess myself. For, sir,
      It is as sure as you are Roderigo,
      Were I the Moor, I would not be Iago.
      In following him, I follow but myself;
      Heaven is my judge, not I for love and duty,
60   But seeming so, for my peculiar end;
      For when my outward action doth demonstrate
      The native act and figure of my heart°
      In compliment extern,° 'tis not long after
      But I will wear my heart upon my sleeve
65   For daws to peck at; I am not what I am.
RODERIGO: What a full fortune does the thick-lips°
          owe°
      If he can carry't thus!
IAGO: Call up her father,
      Rouse him. Make after him, poison his delight,
      Proclaim him in the streets. Incense her kinsmen,
70   And though he in a fertile climate dwell,
      Plague him with flies; though that his joy be joy,
      Yet throw such changes of vexation on't
      As it may lose some color.
RODERIGO: Here is her father's house. I'll call aloud.
75 IAGO: Do, with like timorous° accent and dire yell
      As when, by night and negligence, the fire
      Is spied in populous cities.
RODERIGO: What, ho, Brabantio! Signior Brabantio,
          ho!
IAGO: Awake! What, ho, Brabantio! Thieves! thieves!
          thieves!
80   Look to your house, your daughter, and your bags!
      Thieves! thieves!

Brabantio at a window.°

BRABANTIO (*above*): What is the reason of this terrible
          summons?
      What is the matter there?
RODERIGO: Signior, is all your family within?
IAGO: Are your doors locked?
85 BRABANTIO: Why, wherefore ask you this?
IAGO: Zounds, sir, y' are robbed! For shame, put on
          your gown!
      Your heart is burst; you have lost half your soul.
      Even now, now, very now, an old black ram
      Is tupping your white ewe. Arise, arise!
90   Awake the snorting° citizens with the bell.
      Or else the devil will make a grandsire of you.
      Arise, I say!
BRABANTIO: What, have you lost your wits?
RODERIGO: Most reverend signior, do you know my
          voice?
95 BRABANTIO: Not I. What are you?
RODERIGO: My name is Roderigo.

BRABANTIO: The worser welcome!
      I have charged thee not to haunt about my doors.
      In honest plainness thou hast heard me say
      My daughter is not for thee; and now, in madness,
      Being full of supper and distemp'ring draughts,   100
      Upon malicious knavery dost thou come
      To start my quiet.
RODERIGO: Sir, sir, sir —
BRABANTIO: But thou must needs be sure
      My spirit and my place have in them power   105
      To make this bitter to thee.
RODERIGO: Patience, good sir.
BRABANTIO: What tell'st thou me of robbing? This is
          Venice;
      My house is not a grange.°
RODERIGO: Most grave Brabantio,
      In simple and pure soul I come to you.
IAGO: Zounds, sir, you are one of those that will not   110
      serve God if the devil bid you. Because we come to do
      you service, and you think we are ruffians, you'll
      have your daughter covered with a Barbary horse;
      you'll have your nephews° neigh to you; you'll have
      coursers for cousins, and gennets for germans.°   115
BRABANTIO: What profane wretch art thou?
IAGO: I am one, sir, that comes to tell you your daughter
      and the Moor are now making the beast with two
      backs.
BRABANTIO: Thou are a villain.
IAGO: You are — a senator.   120
BRABANTIO: This thou shalt answer. I know thee,
          Roderigo.
RODERIGO: Sir, I will answer anything. But I beseech
          you,
      If't be your pleasure and most wise consent,
      As partly I find it is, that your fair daughter,
      At this odd-even° and dull watch o' th' night,   125
      Transported, with no worse nor better guard
      But with a knave of common hire, a gondolier,
      To the gross clasps of a lascivious Moor —
      If this be known to you, and your allowance,°
      We then have done you bold and saucy wrongs;   130
      But if you know not this, my manners tell me
      We have your wrong rebuke. Do not believe
      That, from the sense° of all civility,
      I thus would play and trifle with your reverence.
      Your daughter, if you have not given her leave,   135
      I say again, hath made a gross revolt,
      Tying her duty, beauty, wit, and fortunes
      In an extravagant and wheeling° stranger
      Of here and everywhere. Straight satisfy yourself.
      If she be in her chamber, or your house,   140
      Let loose on me the justice of the state
      For thus deluding you.

---

62. The . . . heart: What I really believe and intend.   63. compliment extern: Outward appearance.   66. thick-lips: An Elizabethan epithet for blacks, including Moors.   owe: Own.
75. timorous: Terrifying.   [S.D.] *Brabantio at a window:* (Added
from quarto).   90. snorting: Snoring.

108. grange: Isolated farmhouse.   114. nephews: I.e., grandsons.
115. gennets for germans: Spanish horses for near kinsmen.
125. odd-even: Between night and morning.   129. allowance:
Approval.   133. from the sense: In violation.   138. extravagant and wheeling: Expatriate and roving.

BRABANTIO: Strike on the tinder, ho!
Give me a taper! Call up all my people!
This accident° is not unlike my dream.
145 Belief of it oppresses me already.
Light, I say! light!   *Exit [above].*
IAGO: Farewell, for I must leave you.
It seems not meet, nor wholesome to my place,
To be produced — as, if I stay, I shall —
Against the Moor. For I do know the state,
150 However this may gall him with some check,°
Cannot with safety cast° him; for he's embarked
With such loud reason to the Cyprus wars,
Which even now stand in act,° that for their souls
Another of his fathom° they have none
155 To lead their business; in which regard,
Though I do hate him as I do hell-pains,
Yet, for necessity of present life,
I must show out a flag and sign of love,
Which is indeed but sign. That you shall surely find
  him,
160 Lead to the Sagittary° the raisèd search;
And there will I be with him. So farewell.   *Exit.*

*Enter [below] Brabantio in his nightgown,° and Servants
with torches.*

BRABANTIO: It is too true an evil. Gone she is;
And what's to come of my despisèd time
Is naught but bitterness. Now, Roderigo,
165 Where didst thou see her? — O unhappy girl! —
With the Moor, say'st thou? — Who would be a
  father? —
How didst thou know 'twas she! — O, she deceives
  me
Past thought! — What said she to you? — Get moe°
  tapers!
Raise all my kindred! — Are they married, think
  you?
170 RODERIGO: Truly I think they are.
BRABANTIO: O heaven! How got she out? O treason of
  the blood!
Fathers, from hence trust not your daughters' minds
By what you see them act. Is there not charms
By which the property° of youth and maidhood
175 May be abused? Have you not read, Roderigo,
Of some such thing?
RODERIGO: Yes, sir, I have indeed.
BRABANTIO: Call up my brother. — O, would you had
  had her! —
Some one way, some another. — Do you know
Where we may apprehend her and the Moor?
180 RODERIGO: I think I can discover him, if you please
To get good guard and go along with me.
BRABANTIO: I pray you lead on. At every house I'll call;

I may command at most. — Get weapons, ho!
And raise some special officers of night. —
On, good Roderigo; I'll deserve° your pains.   185
                                        Exeunt.

Scene II

Before the lodgings of Othello.

Enter Othello, Iago, and Attendants with torches.

IAGO: Though in the trade of war I have slain men,
Yet do I hold it very stuff o' th' conscience
To do no contrived murther. I lack iniquity
Sometimes to do me service. Nine or ten times
I had thought t' have yerked° him here under the
  ribs.   5
OTHELLO: 'Tis better as it is.
IAGO: Nay, but he prated,
And spoke such scurvy and provoking terms
Against your honor
That with the little godliness I have
I did full hard forbear him. But I pray you, sir,   10
Are you fast° married? Be assured of this,
That the magnifico° is much beloved,
And hath in his effect a voice potential°
As double° as the Duke's. He will divorce you,
Or put upon you what restraint and grievance   15
The law, with all his might to enforce it on,
Will give him cable.
OTHELLO: Let him do his spite.
My services which I have done the signiory°
Shall out-tongue his complaints. 'Tis yet to
  know° —
Which, when I know that boasting is an honor,   20
I shall promulgate — I fetch my life and being
From men of royal siege;° and my demerits°
May speak unbonneted to as proud a fortune
As this that I have reached.° For know, Iago,
But that I love the gentle Desdemona,   25
I would not my unhousèd° free condition
Put into circumscription and confine
For the sea's worth. But look what lights come
  yond?
IAGO: Those are the raisèd father and his friends.
You were best go in.
OTHELLO: Not I; I must be found.   30
My parts, my title, and my perfect soul°
Shall manifest me rightly. Is it they?
IAGO: By Janus, I think no.

144. **accident:** Occurrence.   150. **check:** Reprimand.   151. **cast:**
Discharge.   153. **stand in act:** Are going on.   154. **fathom:**
Capacity.   160. **Sagittary:** An inn.   [s.d.] ***nightgown:*** Dress-
ing gown.   168. **moe:** More.   174. **property:** Nature.

185. **deserve:** Show gratitude for.   I, ɪɪ. 5. **yerked:** Stabbed.
11. **fast:** Securely.   12. **magnifico:** Grandee (Brabantio).
13. **potential:** Powerful.   14. **double:** Doubly influential.
18. **signiory:** Venetian government.   19. **yet to know:** Still
not generally known.   22. **siege:** Rank. **dermits:** Deserts.
24. **May speak . . . reached:** Are equal, I modestly assert, to
those of Desdemona's family.   26. **unhousèd:** Unrestrained.
31. **perfect soul:** Stainless conscience.

Enter Cassio, with torches, Officers.

OTHELLO: The servants of the Duke, and my
    lieutenant.
35   The goodness of the night upon you, friends!
    What is the news?
CASSIO: The Duke does greet you, general;
    And he requires your haste-post-haste appearance
    Even on the instant.
OTHELLO: What's the matter, think you?
CASSIO: Something from Cyprus, as I may divine.
40   It is a business of some heat. The galleys
    Have sent a dozen sequent° messengers
    This very night at one another's heels,
    And many of the consuls, raised and met,
    Are at the Duke's already. You have been hotly
      called for;
45   When, being not at your lodging to be found,
    The Senate hath sent about three several quests
    To search you out.
OTHELLO: 'Tis well I am found by you.
    I will but spend a word here in the house,
    And go with you.   [*Exit*]
CASSIO: Ancient, what makes he here?
50 IAGO: Faith, he to-night hath boarded a land carack.°
    If it prove lawful prize, he's made for ever.
CASSIO: I do not understand.
IAGO: He's married.
CASSIO: To who?

[*Enter Othello.*]

IAGO: Marry, to — Come, captain, will you go?
OTHELLO: Have
    with you.
CASSIO: Here comes another troop to seek for you.

*Enter Brabantio, Roderigo, and others with lights and
weapons.*

55 IAGO: It is Brabantio. General, be advised.
    He comes to bad intent.
OTHELLO: Holla! stand there!
RODERIGO: Signior, it is the Moor.
BRABANTIO: Down with him, thief!

[*They draw on both sides.*]

IAGO: You, Roderigo! Come, sir, I am for you.
OTHELLO: Keep up° your bright swords, for the dew
    will rust them.
60   Good signior, you shall more command with years
    Than with your weapons.
BRABANTIO: O thou foul thief, where hast thou stowed
    my daughter?
    Damned as thou art, thou hast enchanted her!
    For I'll refer me to all things of sense,
65   If she in chains of magic were not bound,
    Whether a maid so tender, fair, and happy,

So opposite to marriage that she shunned
The wealthy curlèd darlings of our nation,
Would ever have, t' incur a general mock,
Run from her guardage to the sooty bosom   70
Of such a thing as thou — to fear, not to delight.
Judge me the world if 'tis not gross in sense°
That thou hast practiced on her with foul charms,
Abused her delicate youth with drugs or minerals
That weaken motion.° I'll have't disputed on;   75
'Tis probable, and palpable to thinking.
I therefore apprehend and do attach° thee
For an abuser of the world, a practicer
Of arts inhibited and out of warrant.
Lay hold upon him. If he do resist,   80
Subdue him at his peril.
OTHELLO: Hold your hands,
Both you of my inclining and the rest.
Were it my cue to fight, I should have known it
Without a prompter. Where will you that I go
To answer this your charge?
BRABANTIO: To prison, till fit time   85
Of law and course of direct session°
Call thee to answer.
OTHELLO: What if I do obey?
How may the Duke be therewith satisfied,
Whose messengers are here about my side
Upon some present business of the state   90
To bring me to him?
OFFICER: 'Tis true, most worthy signior.
The Duke's in council, and your noble self
I am sure is sent for.
BRABANTIO: How? The Duke in council?
In this time of the night? Bring him away.
Mine's not an idle° cause. The Duke himself,   95
Or any of my brothers of the state,
Cannot but feel this wrong as 'twere their own;
For if such actions may have passage free,
Bondslaves and pagans shall our statesmen be.
                        Exeunt.

Scene III

The Venetian Senate Chamber.

*Enter Duke and Senators, set at a table, with lights and
Attendants.*

DUKE: There is no composition° in these news
    That gives them credit.
1. SENATOR: Indeed they are disproportioned.
    My letters say a hundred and seven galleys.
DUKE: And mine a hundred forty.
2. SENATOR: And mine two hundred.
    But though they jump° not on a just account —   5

---

41. **sequent:** Consecutive.   50. **carack:** Treasure ship.   59. **Keep
up:** I.e., sheath.   72. **gross in sense:** Obvious.   75. **motion:** Perception.   77. **attach:** Arrest.   86. **direct session:** Regular trial.   95. **idle:** Trifling.   I, III. 1. **composition:** Consistency.   5. **jump:** Agree.

As in these cases where the aim° reports
'Tis oft with difference — yet do they all confirm
A Turkish fleet, and bearing up to Cyprus.
DUKE: Nay, it is possible enough to judgment.
10   I do not so secure me° in the error
But the main article° I do approve°
In fearful sense.
SAILOR (*within*):   What, ho! what, ho! what, ho!
OFFICER: A messenger from the galleys.

Enter Sailor.

DUKE: Now, what's the business?
SAILOR: The Turkish preparation makes for Rhodes.
15   So was I bid report here to the state
By Signior Angelo.
DUKE: How say you by this change?
1. SENATOR: This cannot be
By no assay° of reason. 'Tis a pageant
To keep us in false gaze.° When we consider
20   Th' importancy of Cyprus to the Turk,
And let ourselves again but understand
That, as it more concerns the Turk than Rhodes,
So may he with more facile question bear° it,
For that it stands not in such warlike brace,°
25   But altogether lacks th' abilities
That Rhodes is dressed in — if we make thought of
this,
We must not think the Turk is so unskillful
To leave that latest which concerns him first,
Neglecting an attempt of ease and gain
30   To wake and wage° a danger profitless.
DUKE: Nay, in all confidence, he's not for Rhodes.
OFFICER: Here is more news.

Enter a Messenger.

MESSENGER: The Ottomites, reverend and gracious,
Steering with due course toward the isle of Rhodes,
35   Have there injointed them with an after fleet.
1. SENATOR: Ay, so I thought. How many, as you guess?
MESSENGER: Of thirty sail; and now they do restem°
Their backward course, bearing with frank
appearance
Their purposes toward Cyprus, Signior Montano,
40   Your trusty and most valiant servitor,
With his free duty recommends you thus,
And prays you to believe him.
DUKE: 'Tis certain then for Cyprus.
Marcus Luccicos,° is not he in town?
45   1. SENATOR: He's now in Florence.
DUKE: Write from us to him; post, post-haste dispatch.
1. SENATOR: Here comes Brabantio and the valiant
Moor.

---

6. **aim:** Conjecture.   10. **so secure me:** Take such comfort.
11. **article:** Substance.   **approve:** Accept.   18. **assay:** Test.
19. **in false gaze:** Looking the wrong way.   23. **with . . .
bear:** More easily capture.   24. **brace:** Posture of defense.
30. **wake and wage:** Rouse and risk.   37. **restem:** Steer again.
44. **Marcus Luccicos:** (Presumably a Venetian envoy).

---

*Enter Brabantio, Othello, Cassio, Iago, Roderigo, and
Officers.*

DUKE: Valiant Othello, we must straight employ you
Against the general enemy Ottoman.

[*To Brabantio.*]

I did not see you. Welcome, gentle signior.   50
We lacked your counsel and your help to-night.
BRABANTIO: So did I yours. Good your grace, pardon
me.
Neither my place, nor aught I heard of business,
Hath raised me from my bed; nor doth the general
care
Take hold on me; for my particular grief   55
Is of so floodgate° and o'erbearing nature
That it engluts° and swallows other sorrows,
And it is still itself.
DUKE: Why, what's the matter?
BRABANTIO: My daughter! O, my daughter!
ALL: Dead?
BRABANTIO: Ay, to me.
She is abused, stol'n from me, and corrupted   60
By spells and medicines bought of mountebanks;
For nature so prepost'rously to err,
Being not deficient,° blind, or lame of sense,
Sans witchcraft could not.
DUKE: Whoe'er he be that in this foul proceeding   65
Hath thus beguiled your daughter of herself,
And you of her, the bloody book of law
You shall yourself read in the bitter letter
After your own sense; yea, though our proper° son
Stood in your action.°
BRABANTIO: Humbly I thank your grace.   70
Here is the man — this Moor, whom now, it seems,
Your special mandate for the state affairs
Hath hither brought.
ALL: We are very sorry for't.
DUKE [*to Othello*]: What, in your own part, can you
say to this?
BRABANTIO: Nothing, but this is so.   75
OTHELLO: Most potent, grave, and reverend signiors,
My very noble, and approved° good masters,
That I have ta'en away this old man's daughter,
It is most true; true I have married her.
The very head and front of my offending   80
Hath this extent, no more. Rude° am I in my
speech,
And little blessed with the soft phrase of peace;
For since these arms of mine had seven years' pith°
Till now some nine moons wasted, they have used
Their dearest action in the tented field;   85
And little of this great world can I speak
More than pertains to feats of broil and battle;

---

56. **floodgate:** Torrential.   57. **engluts:** Devours.   63. **deficient:** Feeble-minded.   69. **our proper:** My own.   70. **Stood
in your action:** Were accused by you.   77. **approved:** Tested by
experience.   81. **Rude:** Unpolished.   83. **pith:** Strength.

And therefore little shall I grace my cause
In speaking for myself. Yet, by your gracious
    patience,
90   I will a round° unvarnished tale deliver
Of my whole course of love — what drugs, what
    charms,
What conjuration, and what mighty magic
(For such proceeding am I charged withal)
I won his daughter.
BRABANTIO: A maiden never bold;
95   Of spirit so still and quiet that her motion
Blushed° at herself; and she — in spite of nature,
Of years, of country, credit, everything —
To fall in love with what she feared to look on!
It is a judgment maimed and most imperfect
100   That will confess perfection so could err
Against all rules of nature, and must be driven
To find out practices° of cunning hell
Why this should be. I therefore vouch° again
That with some mixtures pow'rful o'er the blood,°
105   Or with some dram, conjured to this effect,
He wrought upon her.
DUKE: To vouch this is no proof,
Without more certain and more overt test
Than these thin habits° and poor likelihoods
Of modern seeming° do prefer against him.
110   1. SENATOR: But, Othello, speak.
Did you by indirect and forcèd° courses
Subdue and poison this young maid's affections?
Or came it by request, and such fair question°
As soul to soul affordeth?
OTHELLO: I do beseech you,
115   Send for the lady to the Sagittary
And let her speak of me before her father.
If you do find me foul in her report,
The trust, the office, I do hold of you
Not only take away, but let your sentence
Even fall upon my life.
120   DUKE: Fetch Desdemona hither.
OTHELLO: Ancient, conduct them; you best know the
    place.

Exit [*Iago, with*] *two or three* [*Attendants*].

And till she come, as truly as to heaven
I do confess the vices of my blood,
So justly to your grave ears I'll present
125   How I did thrive in this fair lady's love,
And she in mine.
DUKE: Say it, Othello.
OTHELLO: Her father loved me, oft invited me;
Still° questioned me the story of my life
130   From year to year — the battles, sieges, fortunes

That I have passed.
I ran it through, even from my boyish days
To th' very moment that he bade me tell it.
Wherein I spoke of most disastrous chances,
Of moving accidents by flood and field;   135
Of hairbreadth scapes i' th' imminent deadly
    breach;
Of being taken by the insolent foe
And sold to slavery; of my redemption thence
And portance° in my travels' history;
Wherein of anters° vast and deserts idle,   140
Rough quarries, rocks, and hills whose heads touch
    heaven,
It was my hint° to speak — such was the process;
And of the Cannibals that each other eat,
The Anthropophagi,° and men whose heads
Do grow beneath their shoulders. This to hear   145
Would Desdemona seriously incline;
But still the house affairs would draw her thence;
Which ever as she could with haste dispatch,
She'ld come again, and with a greedy ear
Devour up my discourse. Which I observing,   150
Took once a pliant° hour, and found good means
To draw from her a prayer of earnest heart
That I would all my pilgrimage dilate,°
Whereof by parcels° she had something heard,
But not intentively.° I did consent,   155
And often did beguile her of her tears
When I did speak of some distressful stroke
That my youth suffered. My story being done,
She gave me for my pains a world of sighs.
She swore, i' faith, 'twas strange, 'twas passing
    strange;   160
'Twas pitiful, 'twas wondrous pitiful.
She wished she had not heard it; yet she wished
That heaven had made her such a man. She thanked
    me;
And bade me, if I had a friend that loved her,
I should but teach him how to tell my story,   165
And that would woo her. Upon this hint° I spake.
She loved me for the dangers I had passed,
And I loved her that she did pity them.
This only is the witchcraft I have used.
Here comes the lady. Let her witness it.   170

Enter Desdemona, Iago, Attendants.

DUKE: I think this tale would win my daughter too.
    Good Brabantio,
Take up this mangled matter at the best.
Men do their broken weapons rather use
Than their bare hands.
BRABANTIO: I pray you hear her speak.   175

90. **round**: Plain.   95–96. **her motion Blushed**: Her own emotions caused her to blush.   102. **practices**: Plots.   103. **vouch**: Assert.   104. **blood**: Passions.   108. **thin habits**: Slight appearances.   109. **modern seeming**: Everyday supposition. 111. **forcèd**: Violent.   113. **question**: Conversation.   129. **Still**: Continually.

139. **portance**: Behavior.   140. **anters**: Caves.   142. **hint**: Occasion.   144. **Anthropophagi**: Man-eaters.   151. **pliant**: Propitious.   153. **dilate**: Recount in full.   154. **parcels**: Portions.   155. **intentively**: With full attention.   166. **hint**: Opportunity.

If she confess that she was half the wooer,
Destruction on my head if my bad blame
Light on the man! Come hither, gentle mistress.
Do you perceive in all this noble company
Where most you owe obedience?

180 DESDEMONA: My noble father,
I do perceive here a divided duty.
To you I am bound for life and education;°
My life and education both do learn me
How to respect you: you are the lord of duty;

185 I am hitherto your daughter. But here's my husband;
And so much duty as my mother showed
To you, preferring you before her father,
So much I challenge° that I may profess
Due to the Moor my lord.

BRABANTIO: God be with you! I have done.
190 Please it your grace, on to the state affairs.
I had rather to adopt a child than get° it.
Come hither, Moor.
I here do give thee that with all my heart
Which, but thou hast already, with all my heart

195 I would keep from thee. For your sake,° jewel,
I am glad at soul I have no other child;
For thy escape° would teach me tyranny,
To hang clogs on them. I have done, my lord.

DUKE: Let me speak like yourself° and lay a sentence°
200 Which, as a grise° or step, may help these lovers
[Into your favor.]
When remedies are past, the griefs are ended
By seeing the worst, which late on hopes depended.
To mourn a mischief that is past and gone

205 Is the next way to draw new mischief on.
What cannot be preserved when fortune takes,
Patience her injury a mock'ry makes.
The robbed that smiles steals something from the
    thief;
He robs himself that spends a bootless grief.

210 BRABANTIO: So let the Turk of Cyprus us beguile:
We lose it not so long as we can smile.
He bears the sentence well that nothing bears
But the free comfort which from thence he hears;
But he bears both the sentence and the sorrow

215 That to pay grief must of poor patience borrow.
These sentences, to sugar, or to gall,
Being strong on both sides, are equivocal.
But words are words. I never yet did hear
That the bruisèd heart was piercèd through the ear.

220 Beseech you, now to the affairs of state.

DUKE: The Turk with a most mighty preparation makes
for Cyprus. Othello, the fortitude° of the place is best
known to you; and though we have there a substitute of most allowed° sufficiency, yet opinion,° a more

sovereign mistress of effects, throws a more safer   225
voice on you. You must therefore be content to slub-
ber° the gloss of your new fortunes with this more
stubborn and boist'rous expedition.

OTHELLO: The tyrant custom, most grave senators,
Hath made the flinty and steel couch of war   230
My thrice-driven bed of down. I do agnize
A natural and prompt alacrity
I find in hardness;° and do undertake
These present wars against the Ottomites.
Most humbly, therefore, bending to your state,   235
I crave fit disposition for my wife,
Due reference of place, and exhibition,°
With such accommodation and besort°
As levels° with her breeding.

DUKE: If you please,
Be't at her father's.

BRABANTIO: I will not have it so.   240

OTHELLO: Nor I.

DESDEMONA: Nor I. I would not there reside,
To put my father in impatient thoughts
By being in his eye. Most gracious Duke,
To my unfolding lend your prosperous° ear,   245
And let me find a charter in your voice,
T' assist my simpleness.°

DUKE: What would you, Desdemona?

DESDEMONA: That I did love the Moor to live with
    him,
My downright violence, and storm of fortunes,   250
May trumpet to the world. My heart's subdued
Even to the very quality of my lord.
I saw Othello's visage in his mind,
And to his honors and his valiant parts
Did I my soul and fortunes consecrate.   255
So that, dear lords, if I be left behind,
A moth of peace, and he go to the war,
The rites for which I love him are bereft me,
And I a heavy interim shall support
By his dear absence. Let me go with him.   260

OTHELLO: Let her have your voice.
Vouch with me, heaven, I therefore beg it not
To please the palate of my appetite,
Not to comply with heat° — the young affects°
In me defunct — and proper satisfaction;   265
But to be free and bounteous to her mind;
And heaven defend your good souls that you think
I will your serious and great business scant
When she is with me. No, when light-winged toys
Of feathered Cupid seel° with wanton dullness   270
My speculative and officed instruments,°

---

182. **education:** Upbringing.   189. **challenge:** Claim the right.
191. **get:** Beget.   195. **For your sake:** Because of you.   197. **escape:** Escapade.   199. **like yourself:** As you should.   **sentence:**
Maxim.   200. **grise:** Step.   222. **fortitude:** Fortification.
224. **allowed:** Acknowledged.   **opinion:** Public opinion.

227. **slubber:** Sully.   231–33. **agnize . . . hardness:** Recognize
in myself a natural and easy response to hardship.   237. **exhibition:** Allowance of money.   238. **besort:** Suitable company.
239. **levels:** Corresponds.   245. **prosperous:** Favorable.
247. **simpleness:** Lack of skill.   264. **heat:** Passions.   **young
affects:** Tendencies of youth.   270. **seel:** Blind.   271. **My . . .
instruments:** My perceptive and responsible faculties.

That° my disports corrupt and taint my business,
Let housewives make a skillet of my helm,
And all indign° and base adversities
275   Make head against my estimation!°
DUKE: Be it as you shall privately determine,
Either for her stay or going. Th' affair cries haste,
And speed must answer it.
1. SENATOR: You must away to-night.
OTHELLO: With all my heart.
280   DUKE: At nine i' th' morning here we'll meet again.
Othello, leave some officer behind,
And he shall our commission bring to you,
With such things else of quality and respect
As doth import° you.
OTHELLO: So please your grace, my ancient;
285   A man he is of honesty and trust
To his conveyance I assign my wife,
With what else needful your good grace shall
        think
To be sent after me.
DUKE: Let it be so.
Good night to every one.
        [To Brabantio.]   And, noble signior,
290   If virtue no delighted° beauty lack,
Your son-in-law is far more fair than black.
1. SENATOR: Adieu, brave Moor. Use Desdemona well.
BRABANTIO: Look to her, Moor, if thou hast eyes to see:
She has deceived her father, and may thee.

                Exeunt [Duke, Senators, Officers, etc.].

295   OTHELLO: My life upon her faith! — Honest Iago,
My Desdemona must I leave to thee.
I prithee let thy wife attend on her,
And bring them after in the best advantage.°
Come, Desdemona. I have but an hour
300   Of love, of worldly matters and direction,
To spend with thee. We must obey the time.

                Exit Moor and Desdemona.

RODERIGO: Iago, —
IAGO: What say'st thou, noble heart?
RODERIGO: What will I do, think'st thou?
305   IAGO: Why, go to bed and sleep.
RODERIGO: I will incontinently° drown myself.
IAGO: If thou dost, I shall never love thee after. Why,
        thou silly gentleman!
RODERIGO: It is silliness to live when to live is torment;
310   and then have we a prescription to die when death is
        our physician.
IAGO: O villainous! I have looked upon the world for
        four times seven years; and since I could distinguish
        betwixt a benefit and an injury, I never found man
315   that knew how to love himself. Ere I would say I

would drown myself for the love of a guinea hen, I
would change my humanity with a baboon.
RODERIGO: What should I do? I confess it is my shame
        to be so fond, but it is not in my virtue to amend it.
IAGO: Virtue? a fig! 'Tis in ourselves that we are thus or   320
        thus. Our bodies are our gardens, to which our wills
        are gardeners; so that if we will plant nettles or sow
        lettuce, set hyssop and weed up thyme, supply it with
        one gender° of herbs or distract it with many —
        either to have it sterile with idleness or manured with   325
        industry — why, the power and corrigible authority°
        of this lies in our wills. If the balance of our lives had
        not one scale of reason to poise° another of sensual-
        ity, the blood and baseness° of our natures would
        conduct us to most preposterous conclusions. But we   330
        have reason to cool our raging motions,° our carnal
        strings, our unbitted° lusts; whereof I take this that
        you call love to be a sect or scion.°
RODERIGO: It cannot be.
IAGO: It is merely a lust of the blood and a permission of   335
        the will. Come, be a man! Drown thyself? Drown
        cats and blind puppies! I have professed me thy
        friend, and I confess me knit to thy deserving with
        cables of perdurable toughness. I could never better
        stead thee than now. Put money in thy purse. Follow   340
        thou the wars; defeat thy favor° with an usurped
        beard. I say, put money in thy purse. It cannot be that
        Desdemona should long continue her love to the
        Moor — put money in thy purse — nor he his to her.
        It was a violent commencement in her, and thou shalt   345
        see an answerable sequestration° — put but money
        in thy purse. These Moors are changeable in their
        wills — fill thy purse with money. The food that to
        him now is as luscious as locusts shall be to him
        shortly as bitter as coloquintida.° She must change   350
        for youth: when she is sated with his body, she will
        find the error of her choice. [She must have change,
        she must.] Therefore put money in thy purse. If thou
        wilt needs damn thyself, do it a more delicate way
        than drowning. Make° all the money thou canst. If   355
        sanctimony and a frail vow betwixt an erring° bar-
        barian and a supersubtle Venetian be not too hard
        for my wits and all the tribe of hell, thou shalt enjoy
        her. Therefore make money. A pox of drowning thy-
        self! 'Tis clean out of the way. Seek thou rather to   360
        be hanged in compassing thy joy than to be drowned
        and go without her.
RODERIGO: Wilt thou be fast to my hopes, if I depend on
        the issue?
IAGO: Thou art sure of me. Go, make money. I have told   365
        thee often, and I retell thee again and again, I hate the

---

272. **That:** So that.   274. **indign:** Unworthy.   275. **estimation:** Reputation.   284. **import:** Concern.   290. **delighted:**
Delightful.   298. **in the best advantage:** At the best opportunity.   306. **incontinently:** Forthwith.

324. **gender:** Species.   326. **corrigible authority:** Corrective
power.   328. **poise:** Counterbalance.   329. **blood and baseness:** Animal instincts.   331. **motions:** Appetites.   332. **unbit-
ted:** Uncontrolled.   333. **sect or scion:** Offshoot, cutting.
341. **defeat thy favor:** Spoil thy appearance.   346. **sequestra-
tion:** Estrangement.   350. **coloquintida:** A medicine.
355. **Make:** Raise.   356. **erring:** Wandering.

Moor. My cause is hearted;° thine hath no less rea-
son. Let us be conjunctive in our revenge against him.
If thou canst cuckold him, thou dost thyself a plea-
370 sure, me a sport. There are many events in the womb
of time, which will be delivered. Traverse,° go, pro-
vide thy money! We will have more of this tomorrow.
Adieu.
RODERIGO: Where shall we meet i' th' morning?
375 IAGO: At my lodging.
RODERIGO: I'll be with thee betimes.
IAGO: Go to, farewell — Do you hear, Roderigo?
[RODERIGO: What say you?
IAGO: No more of drowning, do you hear?
380 RODERIGO: I am changed.
IAGO: Go to, farewell. Put money enough in your
        purse.]
RODERIGO: I'll sell all my land.   *Exit.*
IAGO: Thus do I ever make my fool my purse;
        For I mine own gained knowledge should profane
385   If I would time expend with such a snipe°
        But for my sport and profit. I hate the Moor;
        And it is thought abroad that 'twixt my sheets
        H'as done my office. I know not if't be true;
        But I, for mere suspicion in that kind,
390   Will do as if for surety. He holds me well;°
        The better shall my purpose work on him.
        Cassio's a proper man. Let me see now:
        To get his place, and to plume up° my will
        In double knavery — How, how? — Let's see: —
395   After some time, to abuse Othello's ears
        That he is too familiar with his wife.
        He hath a person and a smooth dispose°
        To be suspected — framed to make women false.
        The Moor is of a free° and open nature
400   That thinks men honest that but seem to be so;
        And will as tenderly be led by th' nose
        As asses are.
        I have't! It is engend'red! Hell and night
        Must bring this monstrous birth to the world's light.
                                                      Exit.

ACT II • *Scene I*

An open place in Cyprus, near the harbor.

Enter Montano and two Gentlemen.

MONTANO: What from the cape can you discern at sea?
1. GENTLEMAN: Nothing at all: it is a high-wrought
        flood.
        I cannot 'twixt the heaven and the main
        Descry a sail.
5 MONTANO: Methinks the wind hath spoke aloud at land;

A fuller blast ne'er shook our battlements.
If it hath ruffianed so upon the sea,
What ribs of oak, when mountains melt on them,
Can hold the mortise?° What shall we hear of this?
2. GENTLEMAN: A segregation° of the Turkish fleet.   10
For do but stand upon the foaming shore,
The chidden billow seems to pelt the clouds;
The wind-shaked surge, with high and monstrous
        mane,
Seems to cast water on the burning Bear
And quench the Guards° of th' ever-fixèd pole.°   15
I never did like molestation° view
On the enchafèd flood.
MONTANO: If that the Turkish fleet
Be not ensheltered and embayed, they are drowned;
It is impossible to bear it out.

Enter a third Gentleman.

3. GENTLEMAN: News, lads! Our wars are done.   20
The desperate tempest hath so banged the Turks
That their designment halts.° A noble ship of Venice
Hath seen a grievous wrack and sufferance°
On most part of their fleet.
MONTANO: How? Is this true?
3. GENTLEMAN: The ship is here put in, 25
A Veronesa;° Michael Cassio,
Lieutenant to the warlike Moor Othello,
Is come on shore; the Moor himself at sea,
And is in full commission here for Cyprus.
MONTANO: I am glad on't. 'Tis a worthy governor.   30
3. GENTLEMAN: But his same Cassio, though he speak
        of comfort
Touching the Turkish loss, yet he looks sadly
And prays the Moor be safe, for they were parted
With foul and violent tempest.
MONTANO: Pray heaven he be;
For I have served him, and the man commands   35
Like a full soldier. Let's to the seaside, ho!
As well to see the vessel that's come in
As to throw out our eyes for brave Othello,
Even till we make the main and th' aerial blue
An indistinct regard.°
3. GENTLEMAN: Come, let's do so;   40
For every minute is expectancy
Of more arrivance.

Enter Cassio.

CASSIO: Thanks, you the valiant of this warlike isle,
That so approve the Moor! O, let the heavens
Give him defense against the elements,   45
For I have lost him on a dangerous sea!
MONTANO: Is he well shipped?

---

367. **My cause is hearted:** My heart is in it.   371. **Traverse:** Forward march.   385. **snipe:** Fool.   390. **well:** In high regard.
393. **plume up:** Gratify.   397. **dispose:** Manner.   399. **free:**
Frank.

II, I. 9. **hold the mortise:** Hold their joints together.   10. **segregation:** Scattering.   15. **Guards:** Stars near the North Star.
pole: Polestar.   16. **molestation:** Tumult.   22. **designment halts:**
Plan is crippled.   23. **sufferance:** Disaster.   26. **Veronesa:**
Ship furnished by Verona.   40. **An indistinct regard:** Indistinguishable.

CASSIO: His bark is stoutly timbered, and his pilot
  Of very expert and approved allowance;
50 Therefore my hopes, not surfeited to death,°
  Stand in bold cure.°
    (*Within.*)   A sail, a sail, a sail!

Enter a messenger.

CASSIO: What noise?
MESSENGER: The town is empty; on the brow o' th' sea
  Stand ranks of people, and they cry "A sail!"
55 CASSIO: My hopes do shape him for the governor.

A shot.

2. GENTLEMAN: They do discharge their shot of
    courtesy:
  Our friends at least.
CASSIO: I pray you, sir, go forth
  And give us truth who 'tis that is arrived.
2. GENTLEMAN: I shall.   *Exit.*
MONTANO: But, good lieutenant, is your general
60 wived?
CASSIO: Most fortunately. He hath achieved a maid
  That paragons° description and wild fame;
  One that excels the quirks° of blazoning° pens,
  And in th' essential vesture of creation
  Does tire the ingener.°

Enter Second Gentleman.

65   How now? Who has put in?
2. GENTLEMAN: 'Tis one Iago, ancient to the general.
CASSIO: H'as had most favorable and happy speed:
  Tempests themselves, high seas, and howling winds,
  The guttered° rocks and congregated sands,
70 Traitors ensteeped° to clog the guiltless keel,
  As having sense of beauty, do omit
  Their mortal° natures, letting go safely by
  The divine Desdemona.
MONTANO: What is she?
CASSIO: She that I spake of, our great captain's captain,
75 Left in the conduct of the bold Iago,
  Whose footing° here anticipates our thoughts
  A se'nnight's° speed. Great Jove, Othello guard,
  And swell his sail with thine own pow'rful breath,
  That he may bless this bay with his tall ship,
80 Make love's quick pants in Desdemona's arms,
  Give renewed fire to our extinced spirits,
  [And bring all Cyprus comfort!]

*Enter Desdemona, Iago, Roderigo, and Emilia [with
Attendants].*

                  O, behold!

---

50. **surfeited to death:** Overindulged. **51. in bold cure:** A good
chance of fulfillment. **62. paragons:** Surpasses. **63. quirks:**
Ingenuities. **blazoning:** Describing. **64–65. And . . . ingener:**
Merely to describe her as God made her exhausts her praiser.
69. guttered: Jagged. **70. ensteeped:** Submerged. **72. mortal:** Deadly. **76. footing:** Landing. **77. se'nnight's:** Week's.

The riches of the ship is come on shore!
You men of Cyprus, let her have your knees.°
Hail to thee, lady! and the grace of heaven,   85
Before, behind thee, and on every hand,
Enwheel thee round!
DESDEMONA: I thank you, valiant Cassio.
  What tidings can you tell me of my lord?
CASSIO: He is not yet arrived; nor know I aught
  But that he's well and will be shortly here.   90
DESDEMONA: O but I fear! How lost you company?
CASSIO: The great contention of the sea and skies
  Parted our fellowship.
    (*Within.*)   A sail, a sail! [*A shot.*]
                        But hark. A sail!
2. GENTLEMAN: They give their greeting to the citadel;
  This likewise is a friend.
CASSIO: See for the news.   95

           [*Exit Gentleman.*]

  Good ancient, you are welcome.
    [*To Emilia.*]   Welcome, mistress. —
  Let it not gall your patience, good Iago,
  That I extend my manners. 'Tis my breeding
  That gives me this bold show of courtesy.

[*Kisses Emilia.*°]

IAGO: Sir, would she give you so much of her lips   100
  As of her tongue she oft bestows on me,
  You would have enough.
DESDEMONA: Alas, she has no speech!
IAGO: In faith, too much.
  I find it still when I have list to sleep.
  Marry, before your ladyship, I grant,   105
  She puts her tongue a little in her heart
  And chides with thinking.
EMILIA: You have little cause to say so.
IAGO: Come on, come on! You are pictures out of
    doors,
  Bells in your parlors, wildcats in your kitchens,   110
  Saints in your injuries, devils being offended,
  Players in your housewifery,° and housewives° in
    your beds.
DESDEMONA: O, fie upon thee, slanderer!
IAGO: Nay, it is true, or else I am a Turk:
  You rise to play, and go to bed to work.   115
EMILIA: You shall not write my praise.
IAGO: No, let me out.
DESDEMONA: What wouldst thou write of me, if thou
    shouldst praise me?
IAGO: O gentle lady, do not put me to't,
  For I am nothing if not critical.
DESDEMONA: Come on, assay.° — There's one gone to
    the harbor?   120

---

84. **knees:** I.e., kneeling. [S.D.] *Kisses Emilia:* (Kissing was a
common Elizabethan form of social courtesy). **112. housewifery:** Housekeeping. **housewives:** Hussies. **120. assay:** Try.

IAGO: Ay, madam.

DESDEMONA: I am not merry; but I do beguile
  The thing I am by seeming otherwise. —
  Come, how wouldst thou praise me?

125 IAGO: I am about it; but indeed my invention
  Comes from my pate as birdlime° does from
    frieze° —
  It plucks out brains and all. But my Muse labors,
  And thus she is delivered:
  If she be fair and wise, fairness and wit —
130 The one's for use, the other useth it.

DESDEMONA: Well praised! How if she be black° and
  witty?

IAGO: If she be black, and thereto have a wit,
  She'll find a white that shall her blackness fit.

DESDEMONA: Worse and worse!

135 EMILIA: How if fair and foolish?

IAGO: She never yet was foolish that was fair,
  For even her folly° helped her to an heir.

DESDEMONA: These are old fond° paradoxes to make
  fools laugh i' th' alehouse. What miserable praise
140 hast thou for her that's foul° and foolish?

IAGO: There's none so foul, and foolish thereunto,
  But does foul pranks which fair and wise ones do.

DESDEMONA: O heavy ignorance! Thou praisest the
  worst best. But what praise couldst thou bestow on a
145 deserving woman indeed — one that in the authority
  of her merit did justly put on the vouch° of very malice itself?

IAGO: She that was ever fair, and never proud;
  Had tongue at will, and yet was never loud;
150 Never lacked gold, and yet went never gay;
  Fled from her wish, and yet said "Now I may";
  She that, being ang'red, her revenge being nigh,
  Bade her wrong stay, and her displeasure fly;
  She that in wisdom never was so frail
155 To change the cod's head for the salmon's tail;°
  She that could think, and ne'er disclose her mind;
  See suitors following, and not look behind:
  She was a wight (if ever such wight were) —

DESDEMONA: To do what?

160 IAGO: To suckle fools and chronicle small beer.°

DESDEMONA: O most lame and impotent conclusion!
  Do not learn of him, Emilia, though he be thy husband. How say you, Cassio? Is he not a most profane
  and liberal° counsellor?

165 CASSIO: He speaks home,° madam. You may relish him
  more in the soldier than in the scholar.

IAGO [aside]: He takes her by the palm. Ay, well said,
  whisper! With as little a web as this will I ensnare as

great a fly as Cassio. Ay, smile upon her, do! I will
gyve thee in thine own courtship.° — You say true; 170
'tis so, indeed! — If such tricks as these strip you out
of your lieutenantry, it had been better you had not
kissed your three fingers so oft — which now again
you are most apt to play the sir° in. Very good! well
kissed! an excellent courtesy! 'Tis so, indeed. Yet 175
again your fingers to your lips? Would they were
clyster pipes° for your sake! (*Trumpet within.*) The
Moor! I know his trumpet.

CASSIO: 'Tis truly so.

DESDEMONA: Let's meet him and receive him. 180

CASSIO: Lo, where he comes.

Enter Othello and Attendants.

OTHELLO: O my fair warrior!

DESDEMONA: My dear Othello!

OTHELLO: It gives me wonder great as my content
  To see you here before me. O my soul's joy!
  If after every tempest come such calms, 185
  May the winds blow till they have wakened death!
  And let the laboring bark climb hills of seas
  Olympus-high, and duck again as low
  As hell's from heaven! If it were now to die,
  'Twere now to be most happy;° for I fear 190
  My soul hath her content so absolute
  That not another comfort like to this
  Succeeds in unknown fate.

DESDEMONA: The heavens forbid
  But that our loves and comforts should increase
  Even as our days do grow.

OTHELLO: Amen to that, sweet powers! 195
  I cannot speak enough of this content;
  It stops me here; it is too much of joy.
  And this, and this, the greatest discords be

They kiss.

  That e'er our hearts shall make!

IAGO [aside]:   O, you are well
  tuned now!
  But I'll set down° the pegs that make this music, 200
  As honest as I am.

OTHELLO: Come, let us to the castle.
  News, friends! Our wars are done; the Turks are
    drowned.
  How does my old acquaintance of this isle? —
  Honey, you shall be well desired° in Cyprus;
  I have found great love amongst them. O my sweet, 205
  I prattle out of fashion, and I dote
  In mine own comforts. I prithee, good Iago,
  Go to the bay and disembark my coffers.
  Bring thou the master° to the citadel;

---

126. **birdlime:** A sticky paste. **freize:** Rough cloth.
131. **black:** Brunette. 137. **folly:** Wantonness. 138. **fond:**
Foolish. 140. **foul:** Ugly. 146. **put on the vouch:** Compel
the approval. 155. **To . . . tail:** I.e., to exchange the good for
the poor but expensive. 160. **chronicle small beer:** Keep petty
household accounts. 164. **profane and liberal:** Worldly and
licentious. 165. **home:** Bluntly.

---

170. **gyve . . . courtship:** Manacle you by means of your
courtly manners. 174. **sir:** Courtly gentleman. 177. **clyster
pipes:** Syringes. 190. **happy:** Fortunate. 200. **set down:**
Loosen. 204. **well desired:** Warmly welcomed. 209. **master:**
Ship captain.

Sir Laurence Olivier as Othello and
Maggie Smith as Desdemona in a tense
moment in his National Theatre
production of *Othello* in London, 1964.

John Douglas Thomas as Othello and
Jennifer Mudge Tucker as Desdemona in
the Trinity Repertory production of
Othello, Providence, Rhode Island, 1998.

210   He is a good one, and his worthiness
       Does challenge° much respect. — Come,
           Desdemona,
       Once more well met at Cyprus.

                    Exit Othello [with all but Iago and Roderigo].

IAGO: [*to an Attendant, who goes out*]: Do thou meet
       me presently at the harbor. [*To Roderigo*.] Come
215   hither. If thou be'st valiant (as they say base men
       being in love have then a nobility in their natures
       more than is native to them), list me. The lieutenant
       to-night watches on the court of guard.° First, I must
       tell thee this: Desdemona is directly in love with him.
220 RODERIGO: With him? Why, 'tis not possible.
       IAGO: Lay thy finger thus,° and let thy soul be instructed.
       Mark me with what violence she first loved the
       Moor, but for bragging and telling her fantastical
       lies; and will she love him still for prating? Let not
225   thy discreet heart think it. Her eye must be fed; and
       what delight shall she have to look on the devil?
       When the blood is made dull with the act of sport,
       there should be, again to inflame it, and to give sati-
       ety a fresh appetite, loveliness in favor, sympathy in
230   years, manners, and beauties; all which the Moor is
       defective in. Now for want of these required con-
       veniences,° her delicate tenderness will find itself
       abused, begin to heave the gorge,° disrelish and
       abhor the Moor. Very nature will instruct her in it
       and compel her to some second choice. Now, sir, this
235   granted — as it is a most pregnant° and unforced
       position — who stands so eminent in the degree of
       this fortune as Cassio does? A knave very voluble; no
       further conscionable° than in putting on the mere
       form of civil and humane° seeming for the better
240   compassing of his salt° and most hidden loose affec-
       tion? Why, none! why, none! A slipper° and subtle
       knave; a finder-out of occasions; that has an eye can
       stamp and counterfeit advantages, though true advan-
       tage never present itself; a devilish knave! Besides,
245   the knave is handsome, young, and hath all those
       requisites in him that folly and green minds look
       after. A pestilent complete knave! and the woman
       hath found him already.
250 RODERIGO: I cannot believe that in her; she's full of
       most blessed condition.°
       IAGO: Blessed fig's-end! The wine she drinks is made of
       grapes. If she had been blessed, she would never have
       loved the Moor. Blessed pudding! Didst thou not see
255   her paddle with the palm of his hand? Didst not
       mark that?
       RODERIGO: Yes, that I did; but that was but courtesy.

IAGO: Lechery, by this hand! an index and obscure
       prologue to the history of lust and foul thoughts.
       They met so near with their lips that their breaths   260
       embraced together. Villainous thoughts, Roderigo!
       When these mutualities° so marshal the way, hard at
       hand comes the master and main exercise, th' incor-
       porate° conclusion. Pish! But, sir, be you ruled by me:
       I have brought you from Venice. Watch you to-night;   265
       for the command, I'll lay't upon you. Cassio knows
       you not. I'll not be far from you: do you find some
       occasion to anger Cassio, either by speaking too
       loud, or tainting° his discipline, or from what other
       course you please which the time shall more favor-   270
       ably minister.
RODERIGO: Well.
IAGO: Sir, he's rash and very sudden in choler,° and haply
       with his truncheon may strike at you. Provoke him
       that he may; for even out of that will I cause these of 275
       Cyprus to mutiny; whose qualification° shall come
       into no true taste° again but by the displanting of
       Cassio. So shall you have a shorter journey to your
       desires by the means I shall then have to prefer°
       them; and the impediment most profitably removed   280
       without the which there were no expectation of our
       prosperity.
RODERIGO: I will do this if you can bring it to any
       opportunity.
IAGO: I warrant thee. Meet me by and by at the citadel; I 285
       must fetch his necessaries ashore. Farewell.
RODERIGO: Adieu.   *Exit.*
IAGO: That Cassio loves her, I do well believe't;
       That she loves him, 'tis apt° and of great credit.
       The Moor, howbeit that I endure him not,   290
       Is of a constant, loving, noble nature,
       And I dare think he'll prove to Desdemona
       A most dear husband. Now I do love her too;
       Not out of absolute lust, though peradventure
       I stand accountant° for as great a sin,   295
       But partly led to diet° my revenge,
       For that I do suspect the lusty Moor
       Hath leaped into my seat; the thought whereof
       Doth, like a poisonous mineral, gnaw my inwards;
       And nothing can or shall content my soul   300
       Till I am evened with him, wife for wife;
       Or failing so, yet that I put the Moor
       At least into a jealousy so strong
       That judgment cannot cure. Which thing to do,
       If this poor trash of Venice, whom I trash°   305
       For° his quick hunting, stand the putting on,°
       I'll have our Michael Cassio on the hip,°

---

262. mutualities: Exchanges.   **263–64. incorporate:** Carnal.
269. tainting: Discrediting.   **273. sudden in choler:** Violent in
anger.   **276. qualification:** Appeasement.   **277. true taste:**
Satisfactory state.   **279. prefer:** Advance.   **289. apt:** Probable.
295. accountant: Accountable.   **296. diet:** Feed.   **305. I trash:**
I weight down (in order to keep under control).   **306. For:** In
order to develop.   **stand the putting on:** Responds to my incit-
ing.   **307. on the hip:** At my mercy.

---

211. challenge: Deserve.   **218. court of guard:** Headquarters.
221. thus: I.e., on your lips.   **231–32. conveniences:** Compati-
bilities.   **233. heave the gorge:** Be nauseated.   **236. pregnant:**
Evident.   **239. conscionable:** Conscientious.   **240. humane:**
Polite.   **241. salt:** Lecherous.   **242. slipper:** Slippery.
251. condition: Character.

Abuse him to the Moor in the rank garb°
(For I fear Cassio with my nightcap too),
310   Make the Moor thank me, love me, and reward me
For making him egregiously an ass
And practicing upon° his peace and quiet
Even to madness. 'Tis here, but yet confused:
Knavery's plain face is never seen till used.   *Exit.*

Scene II

A street in Cyprus.

Enter Othello's Herald, with a proclamation.

HERALD: It is Othello's pleasure, our noble and valiant
general, that, upon certain tidings now arrived,
importing the mere perdition° of the Turkish fleet,
every man put himself into triumph; some to dance,
5   some to make bonfires, each man to what sport and
revels his addiction leads him. For, besides these beneficial news, it is the celebration of his nuptial. So
much was his pleasure should be proclaimed. All
offices° are open, and there is full liberty of feasting
10   from the present hour of five till the bell have told
eleven. Heaven bless the isle of Cyprus and our noble
general Othello!   *Exit.*

Scene III

The Cyprian Castle.

Enter Othello, Desdemona, Cassio, and Attendants.

OTHELLO: Good Michael, look you to the guard to-
night.
Let's teach ourselves that honorable stop,
Not to outsport discretion.
CASSIO: Iago hath direction what to do;
5   But not withstanding, with my personal eye
Will I look to't.
OTHELLO: Iago is most honest.
Michael, good night. To-morrow with your earliest
Let me have speech with you.
[*To Desdemona.*]   Come, my dear love.
The purchase made, the fruits are to ensue;
10   That profit's yet to come 'tween me and you. —
Good night.

          Exit [Othello with Desdemona and Attendants].

Enter Iago.

CASSIO: Welcome, Iago. We must to the watch.
IAGO: Not this hour, lieutenant; 'tis not yet ten o' th'
clock. Our general cast° us thus early for the love of

his Desdemona; who let us not therefore blame. He   15
hath not yet made wanton the night with her, and she
is sport for Jove.
CASSIO: She's a most exquisite lady.
IAGO: And, I'll warrant her, full of game.
CASSIO: Indeed, she's a most fresh and delicate creature.   20
IAGO: What an eye she has! Methinks it sounds a parley
to provocation.
CASSIO: An inviting eye; and yet methinks right modest.
IAGO: And when she speaks, is it not an alarum to love?
CASSIO: She is indeed perfection.   25
IAGO: Well, happiness to their sheets! Come, lieutenant,
I have a stoup° of wine, and here without are a brace
of Cyprus gallants that would fain have a measure to
the health of black Othello.
CASSIO: Not to-night, good Iago. I have very poor and   30
unhappy brains for drinking; I could well wish cour-
tesy would invent some other custom of entertain-
ment.
IAGO: O, they are our friends. But one cup! I'll drink for
you.   35
CASSIO: I have drunk but one cup to-night, and that was
craftily qualified° too; and behold what innovation°
it makes here. I am unfortunate in the infirmity and
dare not task my weakness with any more.
IAGO: What, man! 'Tis a night of revels: the gallants de-   40
sire it.
CASSIO: Where are they?
IAGO: Here at the door; I pray you call them in.
CASSIO: I'll do't, but it dislikes me.   *Exit.*
IAGO: If I can fasten but one cup upon him   45
With that which he hath drunk to-night already,
He'll be as full of quarrel and offense
As my young mistress' dog. Now my sick fool
Roderigo,
Whom love hath turned almost the wrong side out,
To Desdemona hath to-night caroused   50
Potations pottle-deep;° and he's to watch.
Three lads of Cyprus — noble swelling spirits,
That hold their honors in a wary distance,°
The very elements° of this warlike isle —
Have I to-night flustered with flowing cups,   55
And they watch too. Now, 'mongst this flock of
drunkards
Am I to put our Cassio in some action
That may offend the isle.

*Enter Cassio, Montano, and Gentlemen [; Servants fol-
lowing with wine].*

          But here they come.
If consequence do but approve my dream,
My boat sails freely, both with wind and stream.   60
CASSIO: 'Fore God, they have given me a rouse° already.

---

308. **rank garb:** Gross manner.   312. **practicing upon:** Plotting against.   II, ɪɪ. 3. **mere perdition:** Complete destruction.
9. **offices:** Kitchens and storerooms.   II, ɪɪɪ. 14. **cast:** Dismissed.

27. **stoup:** Two-quart tankard.   37. **qualified:** Diluted.   **innovation:** Disturbance.   51. **pottle-deep:** Bottoms up.   53. **That
. . . distance:** Very sensitive about their honor.   54. **very elements:** True representatives.   61. **rouse:** Bumper.

MONTANO: Good faith, a little one; not past a pint, as I
    am a soldier.
IAGO: Some wine, ho!
    [*Sings*.]
65 And let me the canakin clink, clink;
    And let me the canakin clink
        A soldier's a man;
        A life's but a span,
    Why then, let a soldier drink.
70 Some wine, boys!
CASSIO: 'Fore God, an excellent song!
IAGO: I learned it in England, where indeed they are most
    potent in potting. Your Dane, your German, and your
    swag-bellied Hollander — Drink, ho! — are nothing
75 to your English.
CASSIO: Is your Englishman so expert in his drinking?
IAGO: Why, he drinks you with facility your Dane dead
    drunk; he sweats not to overthrow your Almain; he
    gives your Hollander a vomit ere the next pottle can
80 be filled.
CASSIO: To the health of our general!
MONTANO: I am for it, lieutenant, and I'll do you
        justice.
IAGO: O sweet England!
    [*Sings*.]
85 King Stephen was a worthy peer;
        His breeches cost him but a crown;
    He held 'em sixpence all too dear,
        With that he called the tailor lown.°
    He was a wight of high renown,
90   And thou art but of low degree.
    'Tis pride that pulls the country down;
        Then take thine auld cloak about thee.
    Some wine, ho!
CASSIO: 'Fore God, this is a more exquisite song than
95 the other.
IAGO: Will you hear't again?
CASSIO: No, for I hold him to be unworthy of his place
    that does those things.° Well, God's above all; and
    there be souls must be saved, and there be souls must
100 not be saved.
IAGO: It's true, good lieutenant.
CASSIO: For mine own part — no offense to the general,
    nor any man of quality — I hope to be saved.
IAGO: And so do I too, lieutenant.
105 CASSIO: Ay but, by your leave, not before me. The lieu-
    tenant is to be saved before the ancient. Let's have no
    more of this; let's to our affairs. — God forgive us
    our sins! — Gentlemen, let's look to our business. Do
    not think, gentlemen, I am drunk. This is my ancient;
110 this is my right hand, and this is my left. I am not
    drunk now. I can stand well enough, and I speak well
    enough.
ALL: Excellent well!
CASSIO: Why, very well then. You must not think then
115 that I am drunk.   *Exit.*

88. **lown:** Rascal.   98. **does . . . things:** I.e., behaves in this
fashion.

MONTANO: To th' platform, masters. Come, let's set the
    watch.
IAGO: You see this fellow that is gone before.
    He's a soldier fit to stand by Caesar
    And give direction; and do but see his vice.
    'Tis to his virtue a just equinox,°   120
    The one as long as th' other. 'Tis pity of him.
    I fear the trust Othello puts him in,
    On some odd time of his infirmity,
    Will shake this island.
MONTANO: But is he often thus?
IAGO: 'Tis evermore his prologue to his sleep: 125
    He'll watch the horologe a double set°
    If drink rock not his cradle.
MONTANO: It were well
    The general were put in mind of it.
    Perhaps he sees it not, or his good nature
    Prizes the virtue that appears in Cassio   130
    And looks not on his evils. Is not this true?

Enter Roderigo.

IAGO [*aside to him*]: How now, Roderigo?
    I pray you after the lieutenant, go!   *Exit Roderigo.*
MONTANO: And 'tis great pity that the noble Moor
    Should hazard such a place as his own second   135
    With one of an ingraft° infirmity.
    It were an honest action to say
    So to the Moor.
IAGO: Not I, for this fair island!
    I do love Cassio well and would do much
    To cure him of this evil.
        (*Within:* Help! help!)
                        But hark! What noise?   140

Enter Cassio, driving in Roderigo.

CASSIO: Zounds, you rogue! you rascal!
MONTANO: What's the matter, lieutenant?
CASSIO: A knave to
    teach me my duty?
    I'll beat the knave into a twiggen° bottle.
RODERIGO: Beat me?
CASSIO: Dost thou prate, rogue?

[*Strikes him.*]

MONTANO: Nay, good lieutenant!

[*Stays him.*]

    I pray you, sir, hold your hand.
CASSIO: Let me go, sir,   145
    Or I'll knock you o'er the mazzard.°
MONTANO: Come, come,
    you're drunk!
CASSIO: Drunk?

They fight.

120. **just equinox:** Exact equivalent.   126. **watch . . . set:** Stay
awake twice around the clock.   136. **ingraft:** I.e., ingrained.
143. **twiggen:** Wicker-covered.   146. **mazzard:** Head.

IAGO [*aside to Roderigo*]: Away, I say! Go out and cry
    a mutiny!   *Exit Roderigo.*
    Nay, good lieutenant. God's will, gentlemen!
    Help, ho! — lieutenant — sir — Montano — sir —
150   Help, masters! — Here's a goodly watch indeed!

A bell rung.

    Who's that which rings the bell? Diablo, ho!
    The town will rise.° God's will, lieutenant, hold!
    You'll be shamed for ever.

Enter Othello and Gentlemen with weapons.

OTHELLO: What is the matter here?
MONTANO: Zounds, I bleed still. I am hurt to th' death.

He dies.

155 OTHELLO: Hold for your lives!
IAGO: Hold, hold! Lieutenant — sir — Montano —
    gentlemen!
    Have you forgot all sense of place and duty?
    Hold! The general speaks to you. Hold, for shame!
OTHELLO: Why, how now ho? From whence ariseth
    this?
160   Are we turned Turks, and to ourselves do that
    Which heaven hath forbid the Ottomites?
    For Christian shame put by this barbarous brawl!
    He that stirs next to carve for° his own rage
    Holds his soul light; he dies upon his motion.
165   Silence that dreadful bell! It frights the isle
    From her propriety.° What is the matter, masters?
    Honest Iago, that looks dead with grieving,
    Speak. Who began this? On thy love, I charge thee.
IAGO: I do not know. Friends all, but now, even now,
170   In quarter,° and in terms like bride and groom
    Devesting them for bed; and then, but now —
    As if some planet had unwitted men —
    Swords out, and tilting one at other's breast
    In opposition bloody. I cannot speak
175   Any beginning to this peevish odds,°
    And would in action glorious I had lost
    Those legs that brought me to a part of it!
OTHELLO: How comes it, Michael, you are thus
    forgot?
CASSIO: I pray you pardon me; I cannot speak.
OTHELLO: Worthy Montano, you were wont to be
180   civil;
    The gravity and stillness of your youth
    The world hath noted, and your name is great
    In months of wisest censure.° What's the matter
    That you unlace° your reputation thus
185   And spend your rich opinion° for the name
    Of a night-brawler? Give me answer to it.
MONTANO: Worthy Othello, I am hurt to danger.
    Your officer, Iago, can inform you,

While I spare speech, which something now
    offends° me,
Of all that I do know; nor know I aught   190
By me that's said or done amiss this night,
Unless self-charity be sometimes a vice,
And to defend ourselves it be a sin
When violence assails us.
OTHELLO: Now, by heaven,
    My blood° begins my safer guides to rule,   195
    And passion, having my best judgment collied,°
    Assays° to lead the way. If I once stir
    Or do but lift this arm, the best of you
    Shall sink in my rebuke. Give me to know
    How this foul rout began, who set it on;   200
    And he that is approved in° this offense,
    Though he had twinned with me, both at a birth,
    Shall lose me. What! in a town of war,
    Yet wild, the people's hearts brimful of fear,
    To manage° private and domestic quarrel?   205
    In night, and on the court and guard of safety?
    'Tis monstrous. Iago, who began't?
MONTANO: If partially affined, or leagued in office,°
    Thou dost deliver more or less than truth,
    Thou art no soldier.
IAGO: Touch me not so near.   210
    I had rather have this tongue cut from my mouth
    Than it should do offense to Michael Cassio;
    Yet I persuade myself, to speak the truth
    Shall nothing wrong him. This it is, general.
    Montano and myself being in speech,   215
    There comes a fellow crying out for help,
    And Cassio following him with determined sword
    To execute° upon him. Sir, this gentleman
    Steps in to Cassio and entreats his pause.
    Myself the crying fellow did pursue,   220
    Lest by his clamor — as it so fell out —
    The town might fall in fright. He, swift of foot,
    Outran my purpose; and I returned then rather
    For that I heard the clink and fall of swords,
    And Cassio high in oath;° which till to-night   225
    I ne'er might say before. When I came back —
    For this was brief — I found them close together
    At blow and thrust, even as again they were
    When you yourself did part them.
    More of this matter cannot I report;   230
    But men are men; the best sometimes forget.
    Though Cassio did some little wrong to him,
    As men in rage strike those that wish them best,
    Yet surely Cassio I believe received
    From him that fled some strange indignity,   235
    Which patience could not pass.°

---

152. **rise:** Grow riotous.   163. **carve for:** Indulge.   166. **pro-**
priety: Proper self.   170. **quarter:** Friendliness.   175. **peevish**
odds: Childish quarrel.   183. **censure:** Judgment.   184. **un-**
lace: Undo.   185. **rich opinion:** High reputation.

189. **offends:** Pains.   195. **blood:** Passion.   196. **collied:**
Darkened.   197. **Assays:** Tries.   201. **approved in:** Proved
guilty of.   205. **manage:** Carry on.   208. **partially . . . office:**
Prejudiced by comradeship or official relations.   218. **execute:**
Work his will.   225. **high in oath:** Cursing.   236. **pass:** Pass
over, ignore.

OTHELLO:　　　　　　　　　　　I know, Iago,
　　Thy honesty and love doth mince this matter,
　　Making it light to Cassio. Cassio, I love thee;
　　But never more be officer of mine.

Enter Desdemona, attended.

240　　Look if my gentle love be not raised up!
　　I'll make thee an example.
DESDEMONA:　　　　　　　　　What's the matter?
OTHELLO: All's well now, sweeting; come away to bed.

[*To Montano.*]

　　Sir, for your hurts, myself will be your surgeon.
　　Lead him off.

[*Montano is led off.*]

245　　Iago, look with care about the town
　　And silence those whom this vile brawl distracted.°
　　Come, Desdemona; 'tis the soldiers' life
　　To have their balmy slumbers waked with strife.

Exit [with all but Iago and Cassio].

IAGO: What, are you hurt, lieutenant?
250　CASSIO: Ay, past all surgery.
IAGO: Marry, God forbid!
CASSIO: Reputation, reputation, reputation! O, I have
　　lost my reputation! I have lost the immortal part of
　　myself, and what remains is bestial. My reputation,
255　Iago, my reputation!
IAGO: As I am an honest man, I thought you had re-
　　ceived some bodily wound. There is more sense in
　　that than in reputation. Reputation is an idle and
　　most false imposition; oft got without merit and lost
260　without deserving. You have lost no reputation at all
　　unless you repute yourself such a loser. What, man!
　　there are ways to recover° the general again. You are
　　but now cast in his mood° — a punishment more in
　　policy than in malice, even so as one would beat his
265　offenseless dog to affright an imperious lion. Sue to
　　him again, and he's yours.
CASSIO: I will rather sue to be despised than to deceive
　　so good a commander with so slight, so drunken,
　　and so indiscreet an officer. Drunk! and speak par-
270　rot!° and squabble! swagger! swear! and discourse
　　fustian° with one's own shadow! O thou invisible
　　spirit of wine, if thou hast no name to be known by,
　　let us call thee devil!
IAGO: What was he that you followed with your sword?
275　What had he done to you?
CASSIO: I know not.
IAGO: Is't possible?
CASSIO: I remember a mass of things, but nothing dis-
　　tinctly; a quarrel, but nothing wherefore. O God, that
280　men should put an enemy in their mouths to steal

away their brains! that we should with joy, pleas-
ance, revel, and applause° transform ourselves into
beasts!
IAGO: Why, but you are now well enough. How came
　　you thus recovered?　　　　　　　　　　　285
CASSIO: It hath pleased the devil drunkenness to give
　　place to the devil wrath. One unperfectness shows
　　me another, to make me frankly despise myself.
IAGO: Come, you are too severe a moraler. As the time,
　　the place, and the condition of this country stands, I　290
　　could heartily wish this had not so befall'n; but since
　　it is as it is, mend it for your own good.
CASSIO: I will ask him for my place again: he shall tell
　　me I am a drunkard! Had I as many mouths as
　　Hydra,° such an answer would stop them all. To be　295
　　now a sensible man, by and by a fool, and presently a
　　beast! O strange! Every inordinate cup is unblest,
　　and the ingredient° is a devil.
IAGO: Come, come, good wine is a good familiar crea-
　　ture if it be well used. Exclaim no more against it.　300
　　And, good lieutenant, I think you think I love you.
CASSIO: I have well approved° it, sir. I drunk!
IAGO: You or any man living may be drunk at some
　　time, man. I'll tell you what you shall do. Our gen-
　　eral's wife is now the general. I may say so in this　305
　　respect, for that he hath devoted and given up him-
　　self to the contemplation, mark, and denotement of
　　her parts and graces. Confess yourself freely to her;
　　importune her help to put you in your place again.
　　She is of so free,° so kind, so apt, so blessed a disposi-　310
　　tion she holds it a vice in her goodness not to do
　　more than she is requested. This broken joint be-
　　tween you and her husband entreat her to splinter;°
　　and my fortunes against any lay° worth naming, this
　　crack of your love shall grow stronger than it was　315
　　before.
CASSIO: You advise me well.
IAGO: I protest, in the sincerity of love and honest kind-
　　ness.
CASSIO: I think it freely; and betimes in the morning will　320
　　I beseech the virtuous Desdemona to undertake for
　　me. I am desperate of my fortunes if they check me
　　here.
IAGO: You are in the right. Good night, lieutenant; I must
　　to the watch.　　　　　　　　　　　　325
CASSIO: Good night, honest Iago.　　　　*Exit Cassio.*
IAGO: And what's he then that says I play the villain,
　　When this advice is free I give and honest,
　　Probal° to thinking, and indeed the course
　　To win the Moor again? For 'tis most easy　　330
　　Th' inclining Desdemona to subdue°
　　In an honest suit; she's framed as fruitful

---

246. **distracted:** Excited.　262. **recover:** Regain favor with.
263. **in his mood:** Dismissed because of his anger.　269–70. **parrot:** Meaningless phrases.　271. **fustian:** Bombastic nonsense.

282. **applause:** Desire to please.　295. **Hydra:** Monster with
many heads.　298. **ingredient:** Contents.　302. **approved:**
Proved.　310. **free:** Bounteous.　313. **splinter:** Bind up with
splints.　314. **lay:** Wager.　329. **Probal:** Probable.　331. **subdue:** Persuade.

As the free elements. And then for her
To win the Moor — were't to renounce his baptism,
335   All seals and symbols of redeemèd sin —
His soul is so enfettered to her love
That she may make, unmake, do what she list,
Even as her appetite shall play the god
With his weak function. How am I then a villain
340   To counsel Cassio to this parallel° course,
Directly to his good? Divinity° of hell!
When devils will the blackest sins put on,°
They do suggest at first with heavenly shows,
As I do now. For whiles this honest fool
345   Plies Desdemona to repair his fortunes,
And she for him pleads strongly to the Moor,
I'll pour this pestilence into his ear,
That she repeals him° for her body's lust;
And by how much she strives to do him good,
350   She shall undo her credit with the Moor.
So will I turn her virtue into pitch,
And out of her own goodness make the net
That shall enmesh them all.

Enter Roderigo.

                              How, now, Roderigo?
RODERIGO: I do follow here in the chase, not like a
355   hound that hunts, but one that fills up the cry.° My
money is almost spent; I have been to-night exceedingly well cudgelled; and I think the issue will be — I
shall have so much experience for my pains; and so,
with no money at all, and a little more wit, return
360   again to Venice.
IAGO: How poor are they that have not patience!
What wound did ever heal but by degrees?
Thou know'st we work by wit, and not by
    witchcraft;
And wit depends on dilatory time.
365   Does't not go well? Cassio hath beaten thee,
And thou by that small hurt hast cashiered Cassio.°
Though other things grow fair against the sun,
Yet fruits that blossom first will first be ripe.
Content thyself awhile. By the mass, 'tis morning!
370   Pleasure and action make the hours seem short.
Retire thee; go where thou art billeted.
Away, I say! Thou shalt know more hereafter.
Nay, get thee gone!   *Exit Roderigo.*
                        Two things are to be done:
My wife must move for Cassio to her mistress;
375   I'll set her on;
Myself the while to draw the Moor apart
And bring him jump° when he may Cassio find
Soliciting his wife. Ay, that's the way!
Dull no device by coldness and delay.   *Exit.*

---

340. **parallel:** Corresponding.   341. **Divinity:** Theology.
342. **put on:** Incite.   348. **repeals him:** Seeks his recall.
355. **cry:** Pack.   366. **cashiered Cassio:** Maneuvered Cassio's
discharge.   377. **jump:** At the exact moment.

ACT III • *Scene I*

Before the chamber of Othello and Desdemona.

Enter Cassio, with Musicians and the Clown.

CASSIO: Masters, play here, I will content° your pains:
Something that's brief; and bid "Good morrow,
    general."

[They play.]

CLOWN: Why, masters, ha' your instruments been in
Naples,° that they speak i' th' nose thus?
MUSICIAN: How, sir, how?   5
CLOWN: Are these, I pray you, called wind instruments?
MUSICIAN: Ay, marry, are they, sir.
CLOWN: O, thereby hangs a tail.
MUSICIAN: Whereby hangs a tail, sir?
CLOWN: Marry, sir, by many a wind instrument that I   10
know. But, masters, here's money for you; and the
general so likes your music that he desires you, for
love's sake, to make no more noise with it.
MUSICIAN: Well, sir, we will not.
CLOWN: If you have any music that may not be heard,   15
to't again: but, as they say, to hear music the general
does not greatly care.
MUSICIAN: We have none such, sir.
CLOWN: Then put up your pipes in your bag, for I'll
away. Go, vanish into air, away!   20

            Exit Musician [with his fellows].

CASSIO: Dost thou hear, my honest friend?
CLOWN: No, I hear not your honest friend. I hear you.
CASSIO: Prithee keep up thy quillets.° There's a poor
piece of gold for thee. If the gentlewoman that at-
tends the general's wife be stirring, tell her there's one   25
Cassio entreats her a little favor of speech. Wilt thou
do this?
CLOWN: She is stirring sir. If she will stir hither, I shall
seem to notify unto her.
CASSIO: [Do, good my friend.]   *Exit Clown.*

Enter Iago.

                        In happy time,° Iago.   30
IAGO: You have not been abed then?
CASSIO: Why, no; the day had broke
Before we parted. I have made bold, Iago,
To send in to your wife: my suit to her
Is that she will to virtuous Desdemona   35
Procure me some access.
IAGO: I'll send her to you presently;
And I'll devise a mean to draw the Moor
Out of the way, that your converse and
    business
May be more free.

III, I. 1. content: Reward.   **4. Naples:** (Notorious for its association with venereal disease).   **23. quillets:** Quips.   **30. In
happy time:** Well met.

CASSIO: I humbly thank you for't.　　　　　*Exit [Iago].*
40　　　　　　　　　　　　　　　I never knew
　　A Florentine° more kind and honest.

Enter Emilia.

EMILIA: Good morrow, good lieutenant. I am sorry
　　For your displeasure: but all will sure be well.
　　The general and his wife are talking of it,
45　　And she speaks for you stoutly. The Moor replied
　　That he you hurt is of great fame in Cyprus
　　And great affinity,° and that in wholesome wisdom
　　He might not but refuse you; but he protests he
　　　　loves you,
　　And needs no other suitor but his likings
50　　[To take the safest occasion° by the front°]
　　To bring you in again.
CASSIO:　　　　　　Yet I beseech you,
　　If you think fit, or that it may be done,
　　Give me advantage of some brief discourse
　　With Desdemona alone.
EMILIA:　　　　　　Pray you come in.
55　　I will bestow you where you shall have time
　　To speak your bosom° freely.
CASSIO:　　　　　　I am much bound to you.

　　　　　　　　　　　　　　　　　Exeunt.

Scene II

The castle.

Enter Othello, Iago, and Gentlemen.

OTHELLO: These letters give, Iago, to the pilot
　　And by him do my duties to the Senate.
　　That done, I will be walking on the works;°
　　Repair there to me.
IAGO:　　　　　　Well, my good lord, I'll do't.
5　OTHELLO: This fortification, gentlemen, shall we see't?
GENTLEMEN: We'll wait upon your lordship.　　*Exeunt.*

Scene III

The castle grounds.

Enter Desdemona, Cassio, and Emilia.

DESDEMONA: Be thou assured, good Cassio, I will do
　　All my abilities in thy behalf.
EMILIA: Good madam, do. I warrant it grieves my
　　　　husband
　　As if the cause were his.
DESDEMONA: O, that's an honest fellow. Do not doubt,
5　　Cassio,

---

41. **Florentine:** I.e., even a Florentine (like Cassio; Iago was
a Venetian). **47. affinity:** Family connections. **50. occasion:**
Opportunity. **front:** Forelock. **56. your bosom:** Your
inmost thoughts. **III, II. 3. works:** Fortifications.

　　But I will have my lord and you again
　　As friendly as you were.
CASSIO:　　　　　　Bounteous madam,
　　Whatever shall become of Michael Cassio,
　　He's never anything but your true servant.
DESDEMONA: I know't; I thank you. You do love my
　　　　lord;　　　　　　　　　　　　　　　10
　　You have known him long; and be you well assured
　　He shall in strangeness° stand no farther off
　　Than in a politic distance.°
CASSIO:　　　　　　Ay, but, lady,
　　That policy may either last so long,
　　Or feed upon such nice and waterish diet,°　　　15
　　Or breed itself so out of circumstance,
　　That, I being absent, and my place supplied,
　　My general will forget my love and service.
DESDEMONA: Do not doubt° that; before Emilia here
　　I give thee warrant of thy place. Assure thee,　　20
　　If I do vow a friendship, I'll perform it
　　To the last article. My lord shall never rest;
　　I'll watch him tame° and talk him out of patience;
　　His bed shall seem a school, his board a shrift;°
　　I'll intermingle everything he does　　　　　25
　　With Cassio's suit. Therefore be merry, Cassio,
　　For thy solicitor shall rather die
　　Than give thy cause away.

Enter Othello and Iago [at a distance].

EMILIA: Madam, here comes my lord.
CASSIO: Madam, I'll take my leave.　　　　　　30
DESDEMONA: Why, stay, and hear me speak.
CASSIO: Madam, not now: I am very ill at ease,
　　Unfit for mine own purposes.
DESDEMONA: Well, do your discretion.　　*Exit Cassio.*
IAGO: Ha! I like not that.
OTHELLO:　　　　　What dost thou say?　　　35
IAGO: Nothing, my lord; or if — I know not what.
OTHELLO: Was not that Cassio parted from my wife?
IAGO: Cassio, my lord? No, sure, I cannot think it,
　　That he would steal away so guilty-like,
　　Seeing your coming.
OTHELLO:　　　　　I do believe 'twas he.　　40
DESDEMONA: How now, my lord?
　　I have been talking with a suitor here,
　　A man that languishes in your displeasure.
OTHELLO: What is't you mean?
DESDEMONA: Why, your lieutenant, Cassio. Good my
　　　　lord,　　　　　　　　　　　　　　　45
　　If I have any grace or power to move you,
　　His present° reconciliation take;
　　For if he be not one that truly loves you,
　　That errs in ignorance, and not in cunning,

III, III. 12. strangeness: Aloofness. **13. Than . . . distance:**
Than wise policy requires. **15. Or . . . diet:** Or be continued for
such slight reasons. **19. doubt:** Fear. **23. watch him tame:**
Keep him awake until he gives in. **24. shrift:** Confessional.
47. present: Immediate.

50   I have no judgment in an honest face,
      I prithee call him back.
OTHELLO: Went he hence now?
DESDEMONA: Yes, faith; so humbled
      That he hath left part of his grief with me
      To suffer with him. Good love, call him back.
OTHELLO: Not now, sweet Desdemon; some other
55   time.
DESDEMONA: But shall't be shortly?
OTHELLO: The sooner, sweet, for you.
DESDEMONA: Shall't be to-night at supper?
OTHELLO: No, not to-night.
DESDEMONA: To-morrow dinner then?
OTHELLO: I shall not dine at home;
      I meet the captains at the citadel.
DESDEMONA: Why then, to-morrow night, or Tuesday
60   morn,
      On Tuesday noon or night, or Wednesday morn.
      I prithee name the time, but let it not
      Exceed three days. I' faith, he's penitent;
      And yet his trespass, in our common reason
65   (Save that, they say, the wars must make examples
      Out of their best), is not almost° a fault
      T' incur a private check.° When shall he come?
      Tell me, Othello. I wonder in my soul
      What you could ask me that I should deny
      Or stand so mamm'ring on.° What? Michael
70   Cassio,
      That came a-wooing with you, and so many a
        time,
      When I have spoke of you dispraisingly,
      Hath ta'en your part — to have so much to do
      To bring him in? By'r Lady, I could do much —
OTHELLO: Prithee no more. Let him come when he
75   will!
      I will deny thee nothing.
DESDEMONA: Why, this is not a boon;
      'Tis as I should entreat you wear your gloves,
      Or feed on nourishing dishes, or keep you warm,
      Or sue to you to do a peculiar profit
80   To your own person. Nay, when I have a suit
      Wherein I mean to touch your love indeed,
      It shall be full of poise and difficult weight,
      And fearful° to be granted.
OTHELLO: I will deny thee nothing!
      Whereon I do beseech thee grant me this,
85   To leave me but a little to myself.
DESDEMONA: Shall I deny you? No. Farewell, my lord.
OTHELLO: Farewell, my Desdemon: I'll come to thee
        straight.
DESDEMONA: Emilia, come. — Be as your fancies teach
        you;
      Whate'er you be, I am obedient.   Exit [with Emilia].
90   OTHELLO: Excellent wretch!° Perdition catch my soul

      But I do love thee! and when I love thee not,
      Chaos is come again.
IAGO: My noble lord —
OTHELLO: What dost thou say, Iago?
IAGO: Did Michael Cassio, when you wooed my lady,
      Know of your love?   95
OTHELLO: He did, from first to last. Why dost thou
        ask?
IAGO: But for a satisfaction of my thought;
      No further harm.
OTHELLO: Why of thy thought, Iago?
IAGO: I did not think he had been acquainted with her.
OTHELLO: O, yes, and went between us° very oft.   100
IAGO: Indeed?
OTHELLO: Indeed? Ay, indeed! Discern'st thou aught in
        that?
      Is he not honest?
IAGO: Honest, my lord?
OTHELLO: Honest. Ay, honest.
IAGO: My lord, for aught I know.
OTHELLO: What dost thou think?
IAGO: Think, my lord?
OTHELLO: Think, my lord?   105
      By heaven, he echoes me,
      As if there were some monster in his thought
      Too hideous to be shown. Thou dost mean
        something:
      I heard thee say even now, thou lik'st not that,
      When Cassio left my wife. What didst not like?   110
      And when I told thee he was of my counsel
      In my whole course of wooing, thou cried'st
        "Indeed?"
      And didst contract and purse thy brow together,
      As if thou then hadst shut up in thy brain
      Some horrible conceit.° If thou dost love me,   115
      Show me thy thought.
IAGO: My lord, you know I love you.
OTHELLO: I think thou dost;
      And, for I know thou'rt full of love and honesty
      And weigh'st thy words before thou giv'st them
        breath,
      Therefore these stops of thine fright me the more;   120
      For such things in a false disloyal knave
      Are tricks of custom; but in a man that's just
      They are close dilations, working from the heart
      That passion cannot rule.°
IAGO: For Michael Cassio,
      I dare be sworn I think that he is honest.   125
OTHELLO: I think so too.
IAGO: Men should be what they seem;
      Or those that be not, would they might seem none!°
OTHELLO: Certain, men should be what they seem.
IAGO: Why then, I think Cassio's an honest man.

---

66. **not almost:** Hardly.   67. **a private check:** Even a private
reprimand.   70. **mamm'ring on:** Hesitating about.   83. **fearful:** Dangerous.   90. **wretch:** (A term of endearment).

100. **went . . . us:** (I.e., as messenger).   115. **conceit:** Fancy.
123–24. **close dilations . . . rule:** Secret emotions which well up
in spite of restraint.   127. **seem none:** I.e., not pretend to be
men when they are really monsters.

130 OTHELLO: Nay, yet there's more in this.
        I prithee speak to me as to thy thinkings,
        As thou dost ruminate, and give thy worst of
            thoughts
        The worst of words.
     IAGO: Good my lord, pardon me:
        Though I am bound to every act of duty,
135   I am not bound to that all slaves are free to.°
        Utter my thoughts? Why, say they are vile and false,
        As where's that palace whereinto foul things
        Sometimes intrude not? Who has a breast so pure
        But some uncleanly apprehensions
140   Keep leets and law days,° and in Sessions sit
        With meditations lawful?
     OTHELLO: Thou dost conspire against thy friend, Iago,
        If thou but think'st him wronged, and mak'st his ear
        A stranger to thy thoughts.
     IAGO: I do beseech you —
145   Though I perchance am vicious in my guess
        (As I confess it is my nature's plague
        To spy into abuses, and oft my jealousy°
        Shapes faults that are not), that your wisdom yet
        From one that so imperfectly conjects°
150   Would take no notice, nor build yourself a trouble
        Out of his scattering and unsure observance.
        It were not for your quiet nor your good,
        Nor for my manhood, honesty, and wisdom,
        To let you know my thoughts.
     OTHELLO: What dost thou mean?
155 IAGO: Good name in man and woman, dear my lord,
        Is the immediate° jewel of their souls.
        Who steals my purse steals trash; 'tis something,
            nothing,
        'Twas mine, 'tis his, and has been slave to
            thousands;
        But he that filches from me my good name
160   Robs me of that which not enriches him
        And makes me poor indeed.
     OTHELLO: By heaven, I'll know thy thoughts!
     IAGO: You cannot, if my heart were in your hand;
        Nor shall not whilst 'tis in my custody.
     OTHELLO: Ha!
165 IAGO: O, beware, my lord, of jealousy!
        It is the green-eyed monster, which doth mock°
        The meat it feeds on. That cuckold lives in bliss
        Who, certain of his fate, loves not his wronger;
        But O, what damnèd minutes tells he o'er
170   Who dotes, yet doubts — suspects, yet strongly loves!
     OTHELLO: O misery!
     IAGO: Poor and content is rich, and rich enough;
        But riches fineless° is as poor as winter
        To him that ever fears he shall be poor.

        Good God, the souls of all my tribe defend   175
        From jealousy!
     OTHELLO: Why, why is this?
        Think'st thou I'd make a life of jealousy,
        To follow still the changes of the moon
        With fresh suspicions? No! To be once in doubt
        Is once to be resolved. Exchange me for a goat   180
        When I shall turn the business of my soul
        To such exsufflicate and blown° surmises,
        Matching this inference. 'Tis not to make me jealous
        To say my wife is fair, feeds well, loves company,
        Is free of speech, sings, plays, and dances;   185
        Where virtue is, these are more virtuous.
        Nor from mine own weak merits will I draw
        The smallest fear or doubt of her revolt,°
        For she had eyes, and chose me. No, Iago;
        I'll see before I doubt; when I doubt, prove;   190
        And on the proof there is no more but this —
        Away at once with love or jealousy!
     IAGO: I am glad of this; for now I shall have reason
        To show the love and duty that I bear you
        With franker spirit. Therefore, as I am bound,   195
        Receive it from me. I speak not yet of proof.
        Look at your wife; observe her well with Cassio;
        Wear your eyes thus, not jealous nor secure:°
        I would not have your free and noble nature,
        Out of self-bounty,° be abused. Look to't.   200
        I know our country disposition well:
        In Venice they do let God see the pranks
        They dare not show their husbands; their best
            conscience
        Is not to leave't undone, but keep't unknown.
     OTHELLO: Dost thou say so?   205
     IAGO: She did deceive her father, marrying you;
        And when she seemed to shake and fear your looks,
        She loved them most.
     OTHELLO: And so she did.
     IAGO: Why, go to then!
        She that, so young, could give out such a seeming
        To seel° her father's eyes up close as oak° —   210
        He thought 'twas witchcraft — but I am much to
            blame.
        I humbly do beseech you of your pardon
        For too much loving you.
     OTHELLO: I am bound to thee for ever.
     IAGO: I see this hath a little dashed your spirits.
     OTHELLO: Not a jot, not a jot.
     IAGO: I' faith, I fear it has.   215
        I hope you will consider what is spoke
        Comes from my love. But I do see y' are moved.
        I am to pray you not to strain my speech
        To grosser issues° nor to larger reach
        Than to suspicion.   220

135. **bound . . . free to:** Bound to tell that which even slaves are
allowed to keep to themselves.   140. **leets and law days:** Sit-
tings of the courts.   147. **jealousy:** Suspicion.   149. **conjects:**
Conjectures.   156. **immediate:** Nearest the heart.   166. **mock:**
Play with, like a cat with mouse.   173. **fineless:** Unlimited.

182. **exsufflicate and blown:** Spat out and flyblown.   188. **revolt:** Unfaithfulness.   198. **secure:** Overconfident.   200. **self-
bounty:** Natural goodness.   210. **seel:** Close.   **oak:** Oak grain.
219. **To grosser issues:** To mean something more monstrous.

Laurence Fishburne, Othello, and Kenneth Branagh, Iago, in Oliver Parker's 1995 film version of *Othello*.

OTHELLO: I will not.
IAGO: Should you do so, my lord,
  My speech should fall into such vile success°
  As my thoughts aim not at. Cassio's my worthy
        friend —
  My lord, I see y' are moved.
OTHELLO: No, not much moved:
225 I do not think but Desdemona's honest.°
IAGO: Long live she so! and long live you to think so!
OTHELLO: And yet, how nature erring from itself —
IAGO: Ay, there's the point! as (to be bold with you)
  Not to affect many proposèd matches
230 Of her own clime, complexion, and degree,
  Whereto we see in all things nature tends —
  Foh! one may smell in such a will most rank,
  Foul disproportions, thought unnatural —
  But pardon me — I do not in position°
235 Distinctly speak of her; though I may fear
  Her will, recoiling° to her better judgment,
  May fall to match° you with her country forms,
  And happily° repent.
OTHELLO: Farewell, farewell!
  If more thou dost perceive, let me know more.
240 Set on thy wife to observe. Leave me, Iago.
IAGO: My lord, I take my leave.   [*Going.*]
OTHELLO: Why did I marry? This honest creature
        doubtless
  Sees and knows more, much more, than he unfolds.

222. **vile success:** Evil outcome.   225. **honest:** Chaste.
234. **position:** Definite assertion.   236. **recoiling:** Reverting.
237. **fall to match:** Happen to compare.   238. **happily:** Haply,
perhaps.

IAGO [*returns*]: My lord, I would I might entreat your
        honor
  To scan this thing no further: leave it to time.   245
  Although 'tis fit that Cassio have his place,
  For sure he fills it up with great ability,
  Yet, if you please to hold off a while,
  You shall by that perceive him and his means.
  Note if your lady strain his entertainment°   250
  With any strong or vehement importunity;
  Much will be seen in that. In the mean time
  Let me be thought too busy° in my fears
  (As worthy cause I have to fear I am)
  And hold her free,° I do beseech your honor.   255
OTHELLO: Fear not my government.°
IAGO: I once more take my leave.   *Exit.*
OTHELLO: This fellow 's of exceeding honesty,
  And knows all qualities,° with a learned spirit
  Of° human dealings. If I do prove her haggard,°   260
  Though that her jesses° were my dear heartstrings,
  I'd whistle her off and let her down the wind
  To prey at fortune.° Haply, for I am black
  And have not those soft parts of conversation°
  That chamberers° have, or for I am declined   265
  Into the vale of years — yet that's not much —

250. **strain his entertainment:** Urge his recall.   253. **busy:**
Meddlesome.   255. **hold her free:** Consider her guiltless.
256. **government:** Self-control.   259. **qualities:** Natures.
259–60. **learned spirit Of:** Mind informed about.   260. **haggard:** A wild hawk.   261. **jesses:** Thongs for controlling a
hawk.   262–63. **whistle . . . fortune:** Turn her out and let her
take care of herself.   264. **soft . . . conversation:** Ingratiating
manners.   265. **chamberers:** Courtiers.

She's gone. I am abused, and my relief
Must be to loathe her. O curse of marriage,
That we can call these delicate creatures ours,
270 And not their appetites! I had rather be a toad
And live upon the vapor of a dungeon
Than keep a corner in the thing I love
For others' uses. Yet 'tis the plague of great ones;°
Prerogatived° are they less than the base.
275 'Tis destiny unshunnable, like death.
Even then this forkèd plague° is fated to us
When we do quicken.° Look where she comes.

Enter Desdemona and Emilia.

If she be false, O, then heaven mocks itself!
I'll not believe't.
DESDEMONA: How now, my dear Othello?
280 Your dinner, and the generous° islanders
By you invited, do attend your presence.
OTHELLO: I am to blame.
DESDEMONA: Why do you speak so faintly?
Are you not well?
OTHELLO: I have a pain upon my forehead, here.
DESDEMONA: Faith, that's with watching;° 'twill away
285 again.
Let me but bind it hard, within this hour
It will be well.
OTHELLO: Your napkin° is too little;

[*He pushes the handkerchief from him, and it falls unnoticed.*]

Let it° alone. Come, I'll go in with you.
DESDEMONA: I am very sorry that you are not well.

Exit [with Othello].

290 EMILIA: I am glad I have found this napkin;
This was her first remembrance from the Moor,
My wayward husband hath a hundred times
Wooed me to steal it; but she so loves the token
(For he conjured her she should ever keep it)
295 That she reserves it evermore about her
To kiss and talk to. I'll have the work ta'en out°
And give't Iago.
What he will do with it heaven knows, not I;
I nothing but to please his fantasy.°

Enter Iago.

300 IAGO: How now? What do you here alone?
EMILIA: Do not you chide; I have a thing for you.
IAGO: A thing for me? It is a common thing —
EMILIA: Ha?
IAGO: To have a foolish wife.

EMILIA: O, is that all? What will you give me now   305
For that same handkerchief?
IAGO: What handkerchief?
EMILIA: What handkerchief!
Why, that the Moor first gave to Desdemona;
That which so often you did bid me steal.
IAGO: Hast stol'n it from her?   310
EMILIA: No, faith; she let it drop by negligence,
And to th' advantage,° I, being here, took't up.
Look, here it is.
IAGO: A good wench! Give it me.
EMILIA: What will you do with't, that you have been so
earnest
To have me filch it?
IAGO: Why, what is that to you?   315

[*Snatches it.*]

EMILIA: If it be not for some purpose of import,°
Give't me again. Poor lady, she'll run mad
When she shall lack it.
IAGO: Be not acknown on't;° I have use for it.
Go, leave me.   *Exit Emilia.*   320
I will in Cassio's lodgings lose this napkin
And let him find it. Trifles light as air
Are to the jealous confirmations strong
As proofs of holy writ. This may do something.
The Moor already changes with my poison: 325
Dangerous conceits° are in their nature poisons,
Which at the first are scarce found to distaste,
But with a little act upon the blood
Burn like the mines of sulphur.

Enter Othello.

                                I did say so.
Look where he comes! Not poppy nor mandragora,°   330
Nor all the drowsy syrups of the world,
Shall ever med'cine thee to that sweet sleep
Which thou owedst yesterday.
OTHELLO: Ha! ha! false to me?
IAGO: Why, how now, general? No more of that!
OTHELLO: Avaunt! be gone! Thou hast set me on the
rack.   335
I swear 'tis better to be much abused
Than but to know't a little.
IAGO: How now, my lord?
OTHELLO: What sense had I of her stol'n hours of lust?
I saw't not, thought it not, it harmed not me;
I slept the next night well, fed well, was free° and
merry;   340
I found not Cassio's kisses on her lips
He that is robbed, not wanting° what is stol'n,
Let him not know't, and he's not robbed at all.
IAGO: I am sorry to hear this.

273. **great ones:** Prominent men.   274. **Prerogatived:** Privileged.   276. **forkèd plaque:** I.e., horns of a cuckold.   277. **do quicken:** Are born.   280. **generous:** Noble.   285. **watching:** Working late.   287. **napkin:** Handkerchief.   288. **it:** I.e., his forehead.   296. **work ta'en out:** Pattern copied.   299. **fantasy:** Whim.

312. **to th' advantage:** Opportunely.   316. **import:** Importance.   319. **Be . . . on't:** Do not acknowledge it.   326. **conceits:** Ideas.   330. **mandragora:** A narcotic.   340. **free:** Carefree.   342. **wanting:** Missing.

345 OTHELLO: I had been happy if the general camp,
    Pioneers° and all, had tasted her sweet body,
    So I had nothing known. O, now for ever
    Farewell the tranquil mind! farewell content!
    Farewell the plumèd troop, and the big° wars
350   That make ambition virtue! O, farewell!
    Farewell the neighing steed and the shrill trump,
    The spirit-stirring drum, th' ear-piercing fife,
    The royal banner, and all quality,
    Pride, pomp, and circumstance° of glorious war!
355   And O you mortal engines° whose rude throats
    Th' immortal Jove's dread clamors counterfeit,°
    Farewell! Othello's occupation's gone!
    IAGO: Is't possible, my lord?
    OTHELLO: Villain, be sure thou prove my love a
        whore!
360   Be sure of it; give me the ocular proof;
    Or, by the worth of mine eternal soul,
    Thou hadst been better have been born a dog
    Than answer my waked wrath!
    IAGO: Is't come to this?
    OTHELLO: Make me to see't; or at the least so prove it
365   That the probation° bear no hinge nor loop
    To hang a doubt on — or woe upon thy life!
    IAGO: My noble lord —
    OTHELLO: If thou dost slander her and torture me,
    Never pray more; abandon all remorse;
370   On horror's head horrors accumulate;
    Do deeds to make heaven weep, all earth amazed;
    For nothing canst thou to damnation add
    Greater than that.
    IAGO: O grace! O heaven forgive me!
    Are you a man? Have you a soul or sense? —
375   God b' wi' you! take mine office. O wretched fool,
    That liv'st to make thine honesty a vice!
    O monstrous world! Take note, take note, O world,
    To be direct and honest is not safe.
    I thank you for this profit;° and from hence
380   I'll love no friend, sith love breeds such offense.
    OTHELLO: Nay, stay. Thou shouldst be honest.
    IAGO: I should be wise; for honesty's a fool
    And loses that it works for.
    OTHELLO: By the world,
    I think my wife be honest, and think she is not;
385   I think that thou art just, and think thou art not.
    I'll have some proof. Her name, that was as fresh
    As Dian's visage, is now begrimed and black
    As mine own face. If there be cords, or knives,
    Poison, or fire, or suffocating streams,
390   I'll not endure it. Would I were satisfied!°
    IAGO: I see, sir, you are eaten up with passion:
    I do repent me that I put it to you.
    You would be satisfied?

OTHELLO: Would? Nay, I will.
IAGO: And may; but how? how satisfied, my lord?
    Would you, the supervisor,° grossly gape on? 395
    Behold her topped?
OTHELLO: Death and damnation! O!
IAGO: It were a tedious difficulty, I think,
    To bring them to that prospect. Damn them then,
    If ever mortal eyes do see them bolster°
    More than their own! What then? How then? 400
    What shall I say? Where's satisfaction?
    It is impossible you should see this,
    Were they as prime° as goats, as hot as monkeys,
    As salt° as wolves in pride,° and fools as gross
    As ignorance made drunk. But yet, I say, 405
    If imputation and strong circumstances
    Which lead directly to the door of truth
    Will give you satisfaction, you may have't.
OTHELLO: Give me a living reason she's disloyal.
IAGO: I do not like the office. 410
    But sith I am ent'red in this cause so far,
    Pricked to't by foolish honesty and love,
    I will go on. I lay with Cassio lately,
    And being troubled with a raging tooth,
    I could not sleep. 415
    There are a kind of men so loose of soul
    That in their sleeps will mutter their affairs.
    One of this kind is Cassio.
    In sleep I heard him say, "Sweet Desdemona,
    Let us be wary, let us hide our loves!" 420
    And then, sir, would he gripe and wring my
        hand,
    Cry "O sweet creature!" and then kiss me hard,
    As if he plucked up kisses by the roots
    That grew upon my lips; then laid his leg
    Over my thigh, and sighed, and kissed, and then 425
    Cried "Cursèd fate that gave thee to the Moor!"
OTHELLO: O monstrous! monstrous!
IAGO: Nay, this was but
    his dream.
OTHELLO: But this denoted a foregone conclusion;°
    'Tis a shrewd doubt,° though it be but a dream.
IAGO: And this may help to thicken other proofs 430
    That do demonstrate thinly.
OTHELLO: I'll tear her all to pieces!
IAGO: Nay, but be wise. Yet we see nothing done;
    She may be honest yet. Tell me but this —
    Have you not sometimes seen a handkerchief
    Spotted with strawberries in your wife's hand? 435
OTHELLO: I gave her such a one; 'twas my first gift.
IAGO: I know not that; but such a handkerchief —
    I am sure it was your wife's — did I to-day
    See Cassio wipe his beard with.
OTHELLO: If it be that —

---

346. Pioneers: Sappers, laborers. **349. big:** Stately. **354. circumstance:** Pageantry. **355. mortal engines:** Deadly artillery. **356. counterfeit:** Imitate. **365. probation:** Proof. **379. profit:** Profitable lesson. **390. satisfied:** Completely informed.

395. supervisor: Spectator. **399. bolster:** Lie together. **403. prime:** Lustful. **404. salt:** Lecherous. **pride:** Heat. **428. foregone conclusion:** Previous experience. **429. a shrewd doubt:** Cursedly suspicious.

440 IAGO: If it be that, or any that was hers,
        It speaks against her with the other proofs.
      OTHELLO: O, that the slave had forty thousand lives!
        One is too poor, too weak for my revenge.
        Now do I see 'tis true. Look here, Iago:
445   All my fond love thus do I blow to heaven.
        'Tis gone.
        Arise, black vengeance, from the hollow hell!
        Yield up, O love, thy crown and hearted throne
        To tyrannous hate! Swell, bosom, with thy
          fraught,°
        For 'tis of aspics'° tongues!
450 IAGO: Yet be content.
      OTHELLO: O, blood, blood, blood!
      IAGO: Patience, I say. Your mind perhaps may
          change.
      OTHELLO: Never, Iago. Like to the Pontic sea,°
        Whose icy current and compulsive course
455   Ne'er feels retiring ebb, but keeps due on
        To the Propontic and the Hellespont,
        Even so my bloody thoughts, with violent pace,
        Shall ne'er look back, ne'er ebb to humble love,
        Till that a capable° and wide revenge
        Swallow them up.
460   (*He kneels.*)   Now, by yond marble heaven,
        In the due reverence of a sacred vow
        I here engage my words.
      IAGO: Do not rise yet.

      (*Iago kneels.*)

        Witness, you ever-burning lights above,
        You elements that clip° us round about,
465   Witness that here Iago doth give up
        The execution° of his wit,° hands, heart
        To wronged Othello's service! Let him command,
        And to obey shall be in me remorse,°
        What bloody business ever.

      [*They rise.*]

      OTHELLO: I greet thy love,
        Not with vain thanks but with acceptance
470   bounteous,
        And will upon the instant put thee to't.
        Within these three days let me hear thee say
        That Cassio's not alive.
      IAGO: My friend is dead; 'tis done at your request.
475   But let her live.
      OTHELLO: Damn her, lewd minx! O, damn her! damn
          her!
        Come, go with me apart. I will withdraw
        To furnish me with some swift means of death
        For the fair devil. Now art thou my lieutenant.
480 IAGO: I am your own forever.   *Exeunt.*

---

449. **fraught:** Burden.   450. **aspics:** Deadly poisonous snakes.
453. **Pontic sea:** Black Sea.   459. **capable:** All-embracing.
464. **clip:** Encompass.   466. **execution:** Activities. **wit:**
Mind.   468. **remorse:** Pity.

Scene IV

The environs of the castle.

Enter Desdemona, Emilia, and Clown.

DESDEMONA: Do you know, sirrah, where Lieutenant
    Cassio lies?°
CLOWN: I dare not say he lies anywhere.
DESDEMONA: Why, man?
CLOWN: He's a soldier, and for me to say a soldier lies is   5
    stabbing.
DESDEMONA: Go to. Where lodges he?
CLOWN: To tell you where he lodges is to tell you where
    I lie.
DESDEMONA: Can anything be made of this?   10
CLOWN: I know not where he lodges; and for me to
    devise a lodging, and say he lies here or he lies there,
    were to lie in mine own throat.
DESDEMONA: Can you enquire him out, and be edified
    by report?   15
CLOWN: I will catechize the world for him; that is, make
    questions, and by them answer.
DESDEMONA: Seek him, bid him come hither. Tell him I
    have moved° my lord on his behalf and hope all will
    be well.   20
CLOWN: To do this is within the compass of man's wit,
    and therefore I'll attempt the doing of it.   *Exit.*
DESDEMONA: Where should I lose that handkerchief,
    Emilia?
EMILIA: I know not, madam.   25
DESDEMONA: Believe me, I had rather have lost my
      purse
    Full of crusadoes,° and but my noble Moor
    Is true of mind, and made of no such baseness
    As jealous creatures are, it were enough
    To put him to ill thinking.
EMILIA: Is he not jealous?   30
DESDEMONA: Who? he? I think the sun where he was
      born
    Drew all such humors° from him.

Enter Othello.

EMILIA: Look where he comes.
DESDEMONA: I will not leave him now till Cassio
    Be called to him — How is't with you, my lord?
OTHELLO: Well, my good lady. [*Aside.*] O, hardness to
      dissemble! —   35
    How do you, Desdemona?
DESDEMONA: Well, my good lord.
OTHELLO: Give me your hand. This hand is moist, my
      lady.
DESDEMONA: It yet hath felt no age nor known no
      sorrow.
OTHELLO: This argues fruitfulness and liberal heart.

III, IV. 2. lies: Lives, lodges.   **19. moved:** Made proposals to.
27. crusadoes: Portuguese gold coins.   **32. humors:** Inclinations.

40   Hot, hot, and moist. This hand of yours requires
     A sequester° from liberty, fasting and prayer,
     Much castigation, exercise devout;
     For here's a young and sweating devil here
     That commonly rebels. 'Tis a good hand,
     A frank one.
45 DESDEMONA: You may, indeed, say so;
     For 'twas that hand that gave away my heart.
     OTHELLO: A liberal hand! The hearts of old gave
     hands;
     But our new heraldry° is hands, not hearts.
     DESDEMONA: I cannot speak of this. Come now, your
     promise!
50 OTHELLO: What promise, chuck?
     DESDEMONA: I have sent to bid Cassio come speak
     with you.
     OTHELLO: I have a salt and sorry rheum° offends me.
     Lend me thy handkerchief.
     DESDEMONA: Here, my lord.
     OTHELLO: That which I gave you.
     DESDEMONA: I have it not about me.
     OTHELLO: Not?
     DESDEMONA: No, faith, my lord.
55 OTHELLO: That's a fault.
     That handkerchief
     Did an Egyptian° to my mother give.
     She was a charmer,° and could almost read
     The thoughts of people. She told her, while she kept
     it,
60   'Twould make her amiable° and subdue my father
     Entirely to her love; but if she lost it
     Or made a gift of it, my father's eye
     Should hold her loathèd, and his spirits should hunt
     After new fancies. She, dying, gave it me,
65   And bid me, when my fate would have me wive;
     To give it her. I did so; and take heed on't;
     Make it a darling like your precious eye.
     To lose't or give't away were such perdition°
     As nothing else could match.
     DESDEMONA: Is't possible?
70 OTHELLO: 'Tis true. There's magic in the web of it.
     A sibyl that had numb'red in the world
     The sun to course two hundred compasses,°
     In her prophetic fury sewed the work;
     The worms were hallowed that did breed the silk;
75   And it was dyed in mummy° which the skillful
     Conserved of maidens' hearts.
     DESDEMONA: I' faith? Is't true?
     OTHELLO: Most veritable. Therefore look to't well.
     DESDEMONA: Then would to God that I had never
     seen't!

OTHELLO: Ha! Wherefore?
DESDEMONA: Why do you speak so startingly and
     rash?   80
OTHELLO: Is't lost? Is't gone? Speak, is it out o' th'
     way?
DESDEMONA: Heaven bless us!
OTHELLO: Say you?
DESDEMONA: It is not lost. But what an if it were?
OTHELLO: How?   85
DESDEMONA: I say it is not lost.
OTHELLO: Fetch't, let me see't!
DESDEMONA: Why, so I can, sir; but I will not now.
     This is a trick to put° me from my suit:
     Pray you let Cassio be received again.
OTHELLO: Fetch me the handkerchief! My mind
     misgives.   90
DESDEMONA: Come, come!
     You'll never meet a more sufficient man.
OTHELLO: The handkerchief!
[DESDEMONA: I pray talk me of Cassio.
OTHELLO: The handkerchief!]
DESDEMONA: A man that all his time°
     Hath founded his good fortunes on your love,   95
     Shared dangers with you —
OTHELLO: The handkerchief!
DESDEMONA: I' faith, you are to blame.
OTHELLO: Zounds!   *Exit Othello.*
EMILIA: Is not this man jealous?   100
DESDEMONA: I ne'er saw this before.
     Sure there's some wonder in this
     handkerchief;
     I am most unhappy in the loss of it.
EMILIA: 'Tis not a year or two shows us a man.
     They are all but stomachs, and we all but food;   105
     They eat us hungerly, and when they are full,
     They belch us.

Enter Iago and Cassio.

              Look you — Cassio and my husband!
IAGO: There is no other way; 'tis she must do't.
     And lo the happiness!° Go and importune her.
DESDEMONA: How now, good Cassio? What's the news
     with you?   110
CASSIO: Madam, my former suit. I do beseech you
     That by your virtuous means I may again
     Exist, and be a member of his love
     Whom I with all the office of my heart
     Entirely honor. I would not be delayed.   115
     If my offense be of such mortal kind
     That neither service past, nor present sorrows,
     Nor purposed merit in futurity,
     Can ransom me into his love again,
     But to know so must be my benefit.   120
     So shall I clothe me in a forced content,

---

41. **sequester:** Removal.   48. **heraldry:** Heraldic symbolism.
52. **salt . . . rheum:** Distressing head cold.   57. **Egyptian:** Gypsy.
58. **charmer:** Sorceress.   60. **amiable:** Lovable.   68. **perdition:** Disaster.   72. **compasses:** Annual rounds.   75. **mummy:** A drug made from mummies.

88. **put:** Divert.   94. **all . . . time:** During his whole career.
109. **happiness:** Good luck.

And shut myself up in° some other course,
To fortune's alms.
DESDEMONA: Alas, thrice-gentle Cassio!
My advocation° is not now in tune.
125   My lord is not my lord; nor should I know him,
Were he in favor° as in humor altered.
So help me every spirit sanctified
As I have spoken for you all my best
And stood within the blank° of his displeasure
130   For my free speech! You must a while be patient.
What I can do I will; and more I will
Than for myself I dare. Let that suffice you.
IAGO: Is my lord angry?
EMILIA: He went hence but now,
And certainly in strange unquietness.
135   IAGO: Can he be angry? I have seen the cannon
When it hath blown his ranks into the air
And, like the devil, from his very arm
Puffed his own brother — and is he angry?
Something of moment then. I will go meet him.
140   There's matter in't indeed if he be angry.
DESDEMONA: I prithee do so.   *Exit [Iago].*
                      Something sure of state,°
Either from Venice or some unhatched practice°
Made demonstrable here in Cyprus to him,
Hath puddled° his clear spirit; and in such cases
145   Men's natures wrangle with inferior things,
Though great ones are their object. 'Tis even so;
For let our finger ache, and it endues°
Our other, healthful members even to a sense
Of pain. Nay, we must think men are not gods,
150   Nor of them look for such observancy
As fits the bridal. Beshrew me much, Emilia,
I was, unhandsome warrior° as I am,
Arraigning his unkindness with my soul;°
But now I find I had suborned the witness,
155   And he's indicted falsely.
EMILIA: Pray heaven it be state matters, as you
        think,
And no conception nor no jealous toy°
Concerning you.
DESDEMONA: Alas the day! I never gave him cause.
160   EMILIA: But jealous souls will not be answered so;
They are not ever jealous for the cause,
But jealous for they're jealous. 'Tis a monster
Begot upon itself,° born on itself.
DESDEMONA: Heaven keep that monster from Othello's
        mind!

EMILIA: Lady, amen.   165
DESDEMONA: I will go seek him. Cassio, walk here
    about:
If I do find him fit, I'll move your suit
And seek to effect it to my uttermost.
CASSIO: I humbly thank your ladyship.

                    Exeunt Desdemona and Emilia.
Enter Bianca.

BIANCA: Save you, friend Cassio!
CASSIO: What make you from home?   170
How is't with you, my most fair Bianca?
I' faith, sweet love, I was coming to your house.
BIANCA: And I was going to your lodging, Cassio.
What, keep a week away? seven days and nights?
Eightscore eight hours? and lovers' absent hours,   175
More tedious than the dial° eightscore times?
O weary reck'ning!
CASSIO: Pardon me, Bianca:
I have this while with leaden thoughts been pressed;
But I shall in a more continuate° time
Strike off this score of absence. Sweet Bianca,   180

[*Gives her Desdemona's handkerchief.*]

Take me this work out.°
BIANCA: O Cassio, whence came this?
This is some token from a newer friend.
To the felt absence now I feel a cause.
Is't come to this? Well, well.
CASSIO: Go to, woman!
Throw your vile guesses in the devil's teeth,   185
From whence you have them. You are jealous now
That this is from some mistress, some
        remembrance.
No, by my faith, Bianca.
BIANCA: Why, whose is it?
CASSIO: I know not, sweet; I found it in my chamber.
I like the work° well; ere it be demanded,   190
As like enough it will, I'd have it copied.
Take it and do't, and leave me for this time.
BIANCA: Leave you? Wherefore?
CASSIO: I do attend here on the general
And think it no addition, nor my wish,   195
To have him see me womaned.
BIANCA: Why, I pray you?
CASSIO: Not that I love you not.
BIANCA: But that you do not love me!
I pray you bring me on the way a little,
And say if I shall see you soon at night.
CASSIO: 'Tis but a little way that I can bring you,   200
For I attend here; but I'll see you soon.
BIANCA: 'Tis very good. I must be circumstanced.°
                              Exeunt.

---

122. **shut myself up in:** Confine myself to.   124. **advocation:**
Advocacy.   126. **favor:** Appearance.   129. **blank:** Bull's-eye
of the target.   141. **state:** Public affairs.   142. **unhatched
practice:** Budding plot.   144. **puddled:** Muddied.   147. **en-
dues:** Brings.   152. **unhandsome warrior:** Inadequate soldier.
153. **Arraigning . . . soul:** Indicting his unkindness before the
bar of my soul.   157. **toy:** Fancy.   163. **Begot . . . itself:** Self-
engendered.

---

176. **dial:** Clock.   179. **continuate:** Uninterrupted.   181. **Take
. . . out:** Copy this embroidery for me.   190. **work:** Needlework.   202. **circumstanced:** Governed by circumstances.

ACT IV • Scene I

The environs of the castle.

Enter Othello and Iago.

IAGO: Will you think so?
OTHELLO: Think so, Iago?
IAGO: What,
    To kiss in private?
OTHELLO: An unauthorized kiss.
IAGO: Or to be naked with her friend in bed
    An hour or more, not meaning any harm?
5 OTHELLO: Naked in bed, Iago, and not mean harm?
    It is hypocrisy against the devil.°
    They that mean virtuously, and yet do so,
    The devil their virtue tempts, and they tempt
        heaven.
IAGO: So they do nothing, 'tis a venial slip.
10   But if I give my wife a handkerchief —
OTHELLO: What then?
IAGO: Why, then 'tis hers, my lord; and being hers,
    She may, I think, bestow't on any man.
OTHELLO: She is protectress of her honor too;
15   May she give that?
IAGO: Her honor is an essence that's not seen;
    They have it very oft that have it not.
    But for the handkerchief —
OTHELLO: By heaven, I would most gladly have forgot
        it!
20   Thou said'st — O, it comes o'er my memory
    As doth the raven o'er the infected° house,
    Boding to all! — he had my handkerchief.
IAGO: Ay, what of that?
OTHELLO: That's not so good now.
IAGO: What
    If I had said I had seen him do you wrong?
25   Or heard him say — as knaves be such abroad
    Who having, by their own importunate suit,
    Or voluntary dotage of some mistress,
    Convincèd or supplied° them, cannot choose
    But they must blab —
OTHELLO: Hath he said anything?
30 IAGO: He hath, my lord; but be you well assured,
    No more than he'll unswear.
OTHELLO: What hath he said?
IAGO: Faith, that he did — I know not what he did.
OTHELLO: What? what?
IAGO: Lie —
OTHELLO: With her?
35 IAGO: With her, on her; what you will.
OTHELLO: Lie with her? lie on her? — We say lie on
    her when they belie her. — Lie with her! Zounds,
    that's   fulsome. — Handkerchief — confessions —
    handkerchief! — To confess, and be hanged for his

labor — first to be hanged, and then to confess! 40
    I tremble at it. Nature would not invest herself in
    such shadowing passion without some instruction.°
    It is not words that shakes me thus. — Pish! Noses,
    ears, and lips? Is't possible? — Confess? — Hand-
    kerchief? — O devil!   45

(Falls in a trance.)

IAGO: Work on,
    My med'cine, work! Thus credulous fools are
        caught,
    And many worthy and chaste dames even thus,
    All guiltless, meet reproach. — What, ho! my lord!
    My lord, I say! Othello!

Enter Cassio.

                              How now, Cassio?   50
CASSIO: What's the matter?
IAGO: My lord is fall'n into an epilepsy.
    This is his second fit; he had one yesterday.
CASSIO: Rub him about the temples.
IAGO: No, forbear.
    The lethargy° must have his quiet course.   55
    If not, he foams at mouth, and by and by
    Breaks out to savage madness. Look, he stirs.
    Do you withdraw yourself a little while.
    He will recover straight. When he is gone,
    I would on great occasion speak with you.   60
                              [*Exit Cassio.*]
    How is it, general? Have you not hurt your head?
OTHELLO: Dost thou mock me?
IAGO: I mock you? No, by heaven.
    Would you would bear your fortune like a man!
OTHELLO: A hornèd man's° a monster and a beast.
IAGO: There's many a beast then in a populous city, 65
    And many a civil monster.
OTHELLO: Did he confess it?
IAGO: Good sir, be a man.
    Think every bearded fellow that's but yoked
    May draw with you. There's millions now alive
    That nightly lie in those unproper° beds   70
    Which they dare swear peculiar:° your case is better.
    O, 'tis the spite of hell, the fiend's arch-mock,
    To lip a wanton in a secure° couch,
    And to suppose her chaste! No, let me know;
    And knowing what I am, I know what she shall be. 75
OTHELLO: O, thou art wise! 'Tis certain.
IAGO: Stand you
        awhile apart;
    Confine yourself but in a patient list.°
    Whilst you were here, o'erwhelmèd with your
        grief —

IV, I. 6. **hypocrisy . . . devil:** I.e., feigned sin instead of feigned
virtue.   21. **infected:** Plague-stricken.   28. **Convincèd or supplied:** Overcome or gratified.

41–42. **Nature . . . instruction:** My natural faculties would not
be so overcome by passion without reason.   55. **lethargy:**
Coma.   64. **hornèd man:** Cuckold.   70. **unproper:** Not exclusively their own.   71. **peculiar:** Exclusively their own.
73. **secure:** Free from fear of rivalry.   77. **in a patient list:**
Within the limits of self-control.

A passion most unsuiting such a man —
80　Cassio came hither. I shifted him away
And laid good 'scuse upon your ecstasy,°
Bade him anon return, and here speak with me;
The which he promised. Do but encave° yourself
And mark the fleers, the gibes, and notable scorns
85　That dwell in every region of his face;
For I will make him tell the tale anew —
Where, how, how oft, how long ago, and when
He hath, and is again to cope° your wife.
I say, but mark his gesture. Marry, patience!
90　Or I shall say y'are all in all in spleen,°
And nothing of a man.
OTHELLO:　　　　　　　Dost thou hear, Iago?
I will be found most cunning in my patience;
But — dost thou hear? — most bloody.
IAGO:　　　　　　　　　That's not amiss:
But yet keep time in all. Will you withdraw?

[Othello retires.]

95　Now will I question Cassio of Bianca,
A huswife° that by selling her desires
Buys herself bread and clothes. It is a creature
That dotes on Cassio, as 'tis the strumpet's plague
To beguile many and be beguiled by one.
100　He, when he hears of her, cannot refrain
From the excess of laughter. Here he comes.

Enter Cassio.

As he shall smile, Othello shall go mad;
And his unbookish° jealousy must conster°
Poor Cassio's smiles, gestures, and light behavior
105　Quite in the wrong. How do you now, lieutenant?
CASSIO: The worser that you give me the addition°
Whose want even kills me.
IAGO: Ply Desdemona well, and you are sure on't.
Now, if this suit lay in Bianca's power,
How quickly should you speed!
110　CASSIO:　　　　　　　　Alas, poor caitiff!°
OTHELLO: Look how he laughs already!
IAGO: I never knew a woman love man so.
CASSIO: Alas, poor rogue! I think, i' faith, she loves me.
OTHELLO: Now he denies it faintly, and laughs it out.
IAGO: Do you hear, Cassio?
115　OTHELLO:　　　　　　　Now he importunes him
To tell it o'er. Go to! Well said, well said!
IAGO: She gives out that you shall marry her.
Do you intend it?
CASSIO: Ha, ha, ha!
120　OTHELLO: Do you triumph, Roman? Do you triumph?
CASSIO: I marry her? What, a customer?° Prithee bear
some charity to my wit; do not think it so unwhole-
some. Ha, ha, ha!

---

81. **ecstasy:** Trance.　83. **encave:** Conceal.　88. **cope:** Meet.
90. **all in all in spleen:** Wholly overcome by your passion.
96. **huswife:** Hussy.　103. **unbookish:** Uninstructed.　**conster:**
Construe, interpret.　106. **addition:** Title.　110. **caitiff:** Wretch.
121. **customer:** Prostitute.

OTHELLO: So, so, so, so! They laugh that win!
IAGO: Faith, the cry goes that you shall marry her.　125
CASSIO: Prithee say true.
IAGO: I am a very villain else.
OTHELLO: Have you scored me?° Well.
CASSIO: This is the monkey's own giving out. She is per-
suaded I will marry her out of her own love and flat-　130
tery, not out of my promise.
OTHELLO: Iago beckons° me; now he begins the story.
CASSIO: She was here even now; she haunts me in every
place. I was t' other day talking on the sea bank with
certain Venetians, and thither comes the bauble,°　135
and, by this hand, she falls me thus about my neck —
OTHELLO: Crying "O dear Cassio!" as it were. His gesture imports it.
CASSIO: So hangs, and lolls, and weeps upon me; so
shakes and pulls me! Ha, ha, ha!　140
OTHELLO: Now he tells how she plucked him to my
chamber. O, I see that nose of yours, but not that dog
I shall throw it to.
CASSIO: Well, I must leave her company.

Enter Bianca.

IAGO: Before me! Look where she comes.　145
CASSIO: 'Tis such another fitchew!° marry, a perfumed
one. What do you mean by this haunting of me?
BIANCA: Let the devil and his dam haunt you! What did
you mean by that same handkerchief you gave me
even now? I was a fine fool to take it. I must take out　150
the whole work? A likely piece of work that you
should find it in your chamber and know not who
left it there! This is some minx's token, and I must
take out the work? There! Give it your hobby-horse.°
Wheresoever you had it, I'll take out no work on't.　155
CASSIO: How now, my sweet Bianca? How now? how
now?
OTHELLO: By heaven, that should be my handkerchief!
BIANCA: An you'll come to supper to-night, you may; an
you will not, come when you are next prepared for.　160
　　　　　　　　　　　　　　　　Exit.
IAGO: After her, after her!
CASSIO: Faith, I must; she'll rail in the street else.
IAGO: Will you sup there?
CASSIO: Yes, I intend so.
IAGO: Well, I may chance to see you; for I would very　165
fain speak with you.
CASSIO: Prithee come. Will you?
IAGO: Go to! say no more.　　　　　　　*Exit Cassio.*
OTHELLO [*comes forward*]: How shall I murder him,
Iago?　170
IAGO: Did you perceive how he laughed at his vice?°
OTHELLO: O Iago!
IAGO: And did you see the handkerchief?
OTHELLO: Was that mine?

---

128. **scored me:** Settled my account (?).　132. **beckons:** Signals.　135. **bauble:** Plaything.　146. **fitchew:** Polecat (slang for
whore).　154. **hobby-horse:** Harlot.　171. **vice:** I.e., vicious
conduct.

175   IAGO: Yours, by this hand! And to see how he prizes° the
      foolish woman your wife! She gave it him, and he
      hath giv'n it his whore.
      OTHELLO: I would have him nine years a-killing — A
      fine woman! a fair woman! a sweet woman!
180   IAGO: Nay, you must forget that.
      OTHELLO: Ay, let her rot, and perish, and be damned to-
      night; for she shall not live. No, my heart is turned to
      stone; I strike it, and it hurts my hand. O, the world
      hath not a sweeter creature! She might lie by an
185   emperor's side and command him tasks.
      IAGO: Nay, that's not your way.
      OTHELLO: Hang her! I do but say what she is. So deli-
      cate with her needle! an admirable musician! O, she
      will sing the savageness out of a bear! Of so high and
190   plenteous wit and invention° —
      IAGO: She's the worse for all this.
      OTHELLO: O, a thousand thousand times! And then, of
      so gentle a condition!°
      IAGO: Ay, too gentle.
195   OTHELLO: Nay, that's certain. But yet the pity of it, Iago!
      O Iago, the pity of it, Iago!
      IAGO: If you are so fond over her iniquity, give her
      patent° to offend; for if it touch not you, it comes
      near nobody.
200   OTHELLO: I will chop her into messes! Cuckold me!
      IAGO: O, 'tis foul in her.
      OTHELLO: With mine officer!
      IAGO: That's fouler.
      OTHELLO: Get me some poison, Iago, this night. I'll not
205   expostulate with her, lest her body and beauty unpro-
      vide° my mind again. This night, Iago!
      IAGO: Do it not with poison. Strangle her in her bed,
      even the bed she hath contaminated.
      OTHELLO: Good, good! The justice of it pleases. Very
210   good!
      IAGO: And for Cassio, let me be his undertaker,° you
      shall hear more by midnight.
      OTHELLO: Excellent good!

      A trumpet.

      What trumpet is that same?
      IAGO: I warrant something from Venice.

      Enter Lodovico, Desdemona, and Attendants.

215   'Tis Lodovico.
      This comes from the Duke; and see, your wife is
      with him.
      LODOVICO: God save you, worthy general!
      OTHELLO: With all my
      heart, sir.
      LODOVICO: The Duke and senators of Venice greet
      you.

      [*Gives him a letter.*]

      OTHELLO: I kiss the instrument of their pleasures.

      [*Opens the letter and reads.*]

      DESDEMONA: And what's the news, good cousin
      Lodovico?   220
      IAGO: I am very glad to see you, signior.
      Welcome to Cyprus.
      LODOVICO: I thank you. How does Lieutenant
      Cassio?
      IAGO: Lives, sir.
      DESDEMONA: Cousin, there's fall'n between him and
      my lord
      An unkind breach; but you shall make all well.   225
      OTHELLO: Are you sure of that?
      DESDEMONA: My lord?
      OTHELLO [*reads*]: "This fail you not to do, as you
      will — "
      LODOVICO: He did not call; he's busy in the paper.
      Is there division 'twixt thy lord and Cassio?   230
      DESDEMONA: A most unhappy one. I would do much
      T' atone° them, for the love I bear to Cassio.
      OTHELLO: Fire and brimstone!
      DESDEMONA: My lord?
      OTHELLO: Are you wise?
      DESDEMONA: What, is he angry?
      LODOVICO: May be the letter
      moved him;
      For, as I think, they do command him home,   235
      Deputing Cassio in his government.
      DESDEMONA: By my troth, I am glad on't.
      OTHELLO: Indeed?
      DESDEMONA: My lord?
      OTHELLO: I am glad to see you mad.°
      DESDEMONA: Why, sweet Othello —
      OTHELLO: Devil!

      [*Strikes her.*]

      DESDEMONA: I have not deserved this.   240
      LODOVICO: My lord, this would not be believed in
      Venice,
      Though I should swear I saw't. 'Tis very much.
      Make her amends; she weeps.
      OTHELLO: O devil, devil!
      If that the earth could teem° with woman's tears,
      Each drop she falls would prove a crocodile.°   245
      Out of my sight!
      DESDEMONA: I will not stay to offend you.
                                              [*Going.*]
      LODOVICO: Truly, an obedient lady.
      I do beseech your lordship call her back.
      OTHELLO: Mistress!
      DESDEMONA: My lord?
      OTHELLO: What would you with her, sir?   250
      LODOVICO: Who? I, my lord?

---

175. **prizes:** Values.   190. **invention:** Imagination.   193. **condition:** Disposition.   198. **patent:** License.   205. **unprovide:**
Disarm.   211. **be his undertaker:** Undertake to deal with him.

232. **atone:** Reconcile.   238. **mad:** I.e., waggish.   244. **teem:**
Breed.   245. **crocodile:** (Crocodiles were supposed to shed
hypocritical tears to lure men to destruction).

Paul Robeson in the 1930 London production of *Othello*.

Paul Robeson as Othello in the 1943 New York production, directed by Margaret Webster.

OTHELLO: Ay! You did wish that I would make her
    turn.
    Sir, she can turn, and turn, and yet go on
    And turn again; and she can weep, sir, weep;
255   And she's obedient; as you say, obedient,
    Very obedient. — Proceed you in your tears. —
    Concerning this, sir — O well-painted passion!° —
    I am commanded home. — Get you away;
    I'll send for you anon. — Sir, I obey the mandate
260   And will return to Venice. — Hence, avaunt!

                      [Exit Desdemona.]

    Cassio shall have my place. And, sir, to-night
    I do entreat that we may sup together.
    You are welcome, sir, to Cyprus — Goats and
      monkeys!

                          Exit.

LODOVICO: Is this the noble Moor whom our full
    Senate
265   Call all in all sufficient? Is this the nature
    Whom passion could not shake? whose solid virtue
    The shot of accident nor dart of chance
    Could neither graze nor pierce?
IAGO: He is much changed.
LODOVICO: Are his wits safe? Is he not light of brain?
270 IAGO: He's that he is; I may not breathe my censure.
    What he might be — if what he might he is not —
    I would to heaven he were!
LODOVICO: What, strike his wife?
IAGO: Faith, that was not so well; yet would I knew
    That stroke would prove the worst!
LODOVICO: Is it his use?°
275   Or did the letters work upon his blood
    And new-create this fault?
IAGO: Alas, alas!
    It is not honesty in me to speak
    What I have seen and known. You shall observe
      him,
    And his own courses will denote him so
280   That I may save my speech. Do but go after
    And mark how he continues.
LODOVICO: I am sorry that I am deceived in him.

                         Exeunt.

Scene II

Within the castle.

Enter Othello and Emilia.

OTHELLO: You have seen nothing then?
EMILIA: Nor ever heard, nor ever did suspect.
OTHELLO: Yes, you have seen Cassio and she together.
EMILIA: But then I saw no harm, and then I heard
5   Each syllable that breath made up between them.
OTHELLO: What, did they never whisper?

---

257. **passion:** Grief.   274. **use:** Custom.

EMILIA: Never, my lord.
OTHELLO: Nor send you out o' th' way?
EMILIA: Never.
OTHELLO: To fetch her fan, her gloves, her mask, nor
    nothing?
EMILIA: Never, my lord.   10
OTHELLO: That's strange.
EMILIA: I durst, my lord, to wager she is honest,
    Lay down my soul at stake. If you think other,
    Remove your thought; it doth abuse your bosom.°
    If any wretch have put this in your head,   15
    Let heaven requite it with the serpent's curse!°
    For if she be not honest, chaste, and true,
    There's no man happy; the purest of their wives
    Is foul as slander.
OTHELLO: Bid her come hither. Go.

                         Exit Emilia.

    She says enough; yet she's a simple bawd   20
    That cannot say as much. This is a subtle whore,
    A closet lock and key of villainous secrets;
    And yet she'll kneel and pray; I have seen her do't.

Enter Desdemona and Emilia.

DESDEMONA: My lord, what is your will?
OTHELLO: Pray, chuck,
    come hither.
DESDEMONA: What is your pleasure?
OTHELLO: Let me see your eyes. 25
    Look in my face.
DESDEMONA: What horrible fancy's this?
OTHELLO [*to Emilia*]: Some of your function, mistress.
    Leave procreants° alone and shut the door;
    Cough or cry hem if anybody come.
    Your mystery, your mystery!° Nay, dispatch! 30

                         Exit Emilia.

DESDEMONA: Upon my knees, what doth your speech
    import?
    I understand a fury in your words,
    [But not the words.]
OTHELLO: Why, what art thou?
DESDEMONA: Your wife, my lord;
    your true
    And loyal wife.
OTHELLO: Come, swear it, damn thyself; 35
    Lest, being like one of heaven,° the devils
      themselves
    Should fear to seize thee. Therefore be double-
      damned —
    Swear thou art honest.°
DESDEMONA: Heaven doth truly know it.
OTHELLO: Heaven truly knows that thou art false as
    hell.

IV, II. 14. **abuse . . . bosom:** Deceive your heart. 16. **serpent's curse:** (Cf. Genesis 3:14). 28. **procreants:** Mating couples.
30. **mystery:** Trade, occupation. 36. **being . . . heaven:** Looking like an angel. 38. **honest:** Chaste.

DESDEMONA: To whom, my lord? With whom? How
40   am I false?
OTHELLO: Ah, Desdemona! away! away! away!
DESDEMONA: Alas the heavy day! Why do you weep?
      Am I the motive of these tears, my lord?
      If haply you my father do suspect
45   An instrument° of this your calling back,
      Lay not your blame on me. If you have lost him,
      Why, I have lost him too.
OTHELLO: Had it pleased heaven
      To try me with affliction, had they rained
      All kinds of sores and shames on my bare head,
50   Steeped me in poverty to the very lips,
      Given to captivity me and my utmost hopes,
      I should have found in some place of my soul
      A drop of patience. But, alas, to make me
      A fixèd figure for the time of scorn°
55   To point his slow unmoving finger at!
      Yet could I bear that too; well, very well.
      But there where I have garnered up my heart,
      Where either I must live or bear no life,
      The fountain from the which my current runs
60   Or else dries up — to be discarded thence,
      Or keep it as a cistern for foul toads
      To knot and gender in — turn thy complexion
          there,°
      Patience, thou young and rose-lipped cherubin!
      Ay, there look grim as hell!
65 DESDEMONA: I hope my noble lord esteems me honest.
OTHELLO: O, ay; as summer flies are in the shambles,°
      That quicken° even with blowing. O thou weed,
      Who art so lovely fair, and smell'st so sweet,
      That the sense aches at thee, would thou hadst ne'er
          been born!
DESDEMONA: Alas, what ignorant sin have I
70   committed?
OTHELLO: Was this fair paper, this most goodly book,
      Made to write "whore" upon? What committed?
      Committed? O thou public commoner!°
      I should make very forges of my cheeks
75   That would to cinders burn up modesty,
      Did I but speak thy deeds. What committed?
      Heaven stops the nose at it, and the moon winks;°
      The bawdy wind, that kisses all it meets,
      Is hushed within the hollow mine of earth
80   And will not hear it. What committed?
      Impudent strumpet!
DESDEMONA: By heaven, you do me wrong!
OTHELLO: Are not you a strumpet?
DESDEMONA: No, as I am a Christian!
      If to preserve this vessel for my lord
      From any other foul unlawful touch
85   Be not to be a strumpet, I am none.

45. **An instrument:** To be the cause. 54. **time of scorn:** Scornful world. 62. **turn thy complexion there:** Change thy color at that point. 66. **shambles:** Slaughterhouse. 67. **quicken:** Come to life. 73. **commoner:** Harlot. 77. **winks:** Closes her eyes.

OTHELLO: What, not a whore?
DESDEMONA: No, as I shall be saved!
OTHELLO: Is't possible?
DESDEMONA: O, heaven forgive us!
OTHELLO: I cry you mercy° then.
      I took you for that cunning whore of Venice
      That married with Othello. — [Calling.] You,
          mistress,   90
      That have the office opposite to Saint Peter
      And keep the gate of hell!

Enter Emilia.

                          You, you, ay, you!
      We have done our course; there's money for your
          pains:
      I pray you turn the key, and keep our counsel. *Exit.*
EMILIA: Alas, what does this gentleman conceive?   95
      How do you, madam? How do you, my good lady?
DESDEMONA: Faith, half asleep.°
EMILIA: Good madam, what's the matter with my lord?
DESDEMONA: With who?
EMILIA: Why, with my lord, madam.   100
DESDEMONA: Who is thy lord?
EMILIA: He that is yours, sweet lady.
DESDEMONA: I have none. Do not talk to me, Emilia.
      I cannot weep; nor answer have I none
      But what should go by water. Prithee to-night
      Lay on my bed my wedding sheets, remember;   105
      And call thy husband hither.
EMILIA: Here's a change indeed!
                                                    Exit.
DESDEMONA: 'Tis meet I should be used so, very meet.
      How have I been behaved, that he might stick
      The small'st opinion° on my least misuse?°

Enter Iago and Emilia.

IAGO: What is your pleasure, madam? How is't with
      you?   110
DESDEMONA: I cannot tell. Those that do teach young
          babes
      Do it with gentle means and easy tasks:
      He might have chid me so; for, in good faith,
      I am a child to chiding.
IAGO: What is the matter, lady?
EMILIA: Alas, Iago, my lord hath so bewhored her,   115
      Thrown such despite and heavy terms upon her
      As true hearts cannot bear.
DESDEMONA: Am I that name, Iago?
IAGO: What name, fair lady?
DESDEMONA: Such as she said my lord did say I was.
EMILIA: He called her whore. A beggar in his drink   120
      Could not have laid such terms upon his callet.°
IAGO: Why did he so?
DESDEMONA: I do not know; I am sure I am none such.

88. **cry you mercy:** Beg your pardon. 97. **half asleep:** I.e., stunned. 109. **small'st opinion:** Least suspicion. **least misuse:** Slightest misconduct. 121. **callet:** Whore.

IAGO: Do not weep, do not weep. Alas the day!

125 EMILIA: Hath she forsook so many noble matches,
     Her father and her country, and her friends,
     To be called whore? Would it not make one weep?

DESDEMONA: It is my wretched fortune.

IAGO: Beshrew him for't!
     How comes this trick° upon him?

DESDEMONA: Nay, heaven doth know.

130 EMILIA: I will be hanged if some eternal villain,
     Some busy and insinuating rogue,
     Some cogging, cozening° slave, to get some office,
     Have not devised this slander. I'll be hanged else.

IAGO: Fie, there is no such man! It is impossible.

135 DESDEMONA: If any such there be, heaven pardon him!

EMILIA: A halter pardon him! and hell gnaw his bones!
     Why should he call her whore? Who keeps her
        company?
     What place? what time? what form? what likelihood?
     The Moor 's abused by some most villainous knave,

140 Some base notorious knave, some scurvy fellow.
     O heaven, that such companions° thou 'dst unfold,°
     And put in every honest hand a whip
     To lash the rascals naked through the world
     Even from the east to th' west!

IAGO: Speak within door.°

145 EMILIA: O, fie upon them! Some such squire he was
     That turned your wit the seamy side without
     And made you to suspect me with the Moor.

IAGO: You are a fool. Go to.

DESDEMONA: Alas, Iago,
     What shall I do to win my lord again?

150 Good friend, go to him; for, by this light of heaven,
     I know not how I lost him. Here I kneel:
     If e'er my will did trespass 'gainst his love
     Either in discourse° of thought or actual deed,
     Or that mine eyes, mine ears, or any sense

155 Delighted them in any other form,
     Or that I do not yet, and ever did,
     And ever will (though he do shake me off
     To beggarly divorcement) love him dearly,
     Comfort forswear° me! Unkindness may do much;

160 And his unkindness may defeat° my life,
     But never taint my love. I cannot say "whore."
     It does abhor me now I speak the word;
     To do the act that might the addition earn
     Not the world's mass of vanity could make me.

165 IAGO: I pray you be content. 'Tis but his humor.
     The business of the state does him offense,
     [And he does chide with you.]

DESDEMONA: If 'twere no other —

IAGO: 'Tis but so, I warrant.

[*Trumpets within.*]

Hark how these instruments summon you to supper.
The messengers of Venice stay the meat: 170
Go in, and weep not. All things shall be well.

        Exeunt Desdemona and Emilia.

Enter Roderigo.

     How now, Roderigo?

RODERIGO: I do not find that thou deal'st justly with me.

IAGO: What in the contrary?

RODERIGO: Every day thou daff'st me with some   175
     device,° Iago, and rather, as it seems to me now,
     keep'st from me all conveniency° than suppliest me
     with the least advantage of hope. I will indeed no
     longer endure it; nor am I yet persuaded to put up in
     peace what already I have foolishly suffered.   180

IAGO: Will you hear me, Roderigo?

RODERIGO: Faith, I have heard too much; for your
     words and performances are no kin together.

IAGO: You charge me most unjustly.

RODERIGO: With naught but truth. I have wasted myself   185
     out of my means. The jewels you have had from me
     to deliver to Desdemona would half have corrupted a
     votarist.° You have told me she hath received them,
     and returned me expectations and comforts of sud-
     den respect° and acquaintance; but I find none.   190

IAGO: Well, go to; very well.

RODERIGO: Very well! go to! I cannot go to, man; nor
     'tis not very well. By this hand, I say 'tis very scurvy,
     and begin to find myself fopped° in it.

IAGO: Very well.   195

RODERIGO: I tell you 'tis not very well. I will make my-
     self known to Desdemona. If she will return me my
     jewels, I will give over my suit and repent my unlaw-
     ful solicitation; if not, assure yourself I will seek satis-
     faction of you.   200

IAGO: You have said now.

RODERIGO: Ay, and said nothing but what I protest in-
     tendment of doing.

IAGO: Why, now I see there's mettle in thee; and even
     from this instant do build on thee a better opinion   205
     than ever before. Give me thy hand, Roderigo. Thou
     has taken against me a most just exception; but yet I
     protest I have dealt most directly° in thy affair.

RODERIGO: It hath not appeared.

IAGO: I grant indeed it hath not appeared, and your   210
     suspicion is not without wit and judgment. But,
     Roderigo, if thou hast that in thee indeed which I
     have greater reason to believe now than ever, I mean
     purpose, courage, and valor, this night show it. If
     thou the next night following enjoy not Desdemona,   215
     take me from this world with treachery and devise
     engines for° my life.

---

129. **trick:** Freakish behavior. 132. **cogging, cozening:** Cheating, defrauding. 141. **companions:** Rogues. **unfold:** Expose. 144. **within door:** With restraint. 153. **discourse:** Course. 159. **Comfort forswear:** Happiness forsake. 160. **defeat:** Destroy.

175–76. **thou . . . device:** You put me off with some trick. 177. **conveniency:** Favorable opportunities. 188. **votarist:** Nun. 190. **sudden respect:** Immediate notice. 194. **fopped:** Duped. 208. **directly:** Straightforwardly. 217. **engines for:** Plots against.

RODERIGO: Well, what is it? Is it within reason and compass?

220 IAGO: Sir, there is especial commission come from
Venice to depute Cassio in Othello's place.

RODERIGO: Is that true? Why, then Othello and Desdemona again to Venice.

IAGO: O, no; he goes into Mauritania and takes away
225 with him the fair Desdemona, unless his abode be lingered here° by some accident; wherein none can be
so determinate° as the removing of Cassio.

RODERIGO: How do you mean removing of him?

IAGO: Why, by making him uncapable of Othello's
230 place — knocking out his brains.

RODERIGO: And that you would have me to do?

IAGO: Ay, if you dare do yourself a profit and a right. He
sups to-night with a harlotry, and thither will I go to
him. He knows not yet of his honorable fortune. If
235 you will watch his going thence, which I will fashion
to fall out between twelve and one, you may take
him at your pleasure. I will be near to second your
attempt, and he shall fall between us. Come, stand
not amazed at it, but go along with me. I will show
240 you such a necessity in his death that you shall think
yourself bound to put it on him. It is now high supper time, and the night grows to waste. About it!

RODERIGO: I will hear further reason for this.

IAGO: And you shall be satisfied.   *Exeunt.*

Scene III

Within the castle.

*Enter Othello, Lodovico, Desdemona, Emilia, and
Attendants.*

LODOVICO: I do beseech you, sir, trouble yourself no
further.

OTHELLO: O, pardon me; 'twill do me good to walk.

LODOVICO: Madam, good night. I humbly thank your
ladyship.

DESDEMONA: Your honor is most welcome.

OTHELLO: Will you
walk, sir?
5   O, Desdemona —

DESDEMONA: My lord?

OTHELLO: Get you to bed on th' instant; I will be
returned forthwith. Dismiss your attendant there.
Look 't be done.

10 DESDEMONA: I will, my lord.

        Exit [Othello, with Lodovico and Attendants].

EMILIA: How goes it now? He looks gentler than he
did.

DESDEMONA: He says he will return incontinent.°

He hath commanded me to go to bed,
And bade me to dismiss you.

EMILIA: Dismiss me?

DESDEMONA: It was his bidding; therefore, good
Emilia,   15
Give me my nightly wearing, and adieu.
We must not now displease him.

EMILIA: I would you had never seen him!

DESDEMONA: So would not I. My love doth so approve
him
That even his stubbornness,° his checks,° his
frowns —   20
Prithee unpin me — have grace and favor in them.

EMILIA: I have laid those sheets you bade me on the bed.

DESDEMONA: All's one. Good faith, how foolish are
our minds!
If I do die before thee, prithee shroud me
In one of those same sheets.

EMILIA: Come, come! You talk.   25

DESDEMONA: My mother had a maid called Barbary.
She was in love; and he she loved proved mad°
And did forsake her. She had a song of "Willow";
An old thing 'twas; but it expressed her fortune,
And she died singing it. That song to-night   30
Will not go from my mind; I have much to do
But to go hang my head all at one side
And sing it like poor Barbary. Prithee dispatch.

EMILIA: Shall I go fetch your nightgown?°

DESDEMONA: No, unpin me here.   35
This Lodovico is a proper man.

EMILIA: A very handsome man.

DESDEMONA: He speaks well.

EMILIA: I know a lady in Venice would have walked
barefoot to Palestine for a touch of his nether lip.   40

DESDEMONA (*sings*):
    "The poor soul sat sighing by a sycamore tree
    Sing all a green willow;
    Her hand on her bosom, her head on her knee,
    Sing willow, willow, willow.
    The fresh streams ran by her and murmured her
        moans;   45
    Sing willow, willow, willow;
    Her salt tears fell from her, and soft'ned the
        stones" —
Lay by these.
    "Sing willow, willow, willow" —
Prithee hie thee;° he'll come anon.   50
    "Sing all a green willow must be my garland.
    Let nobody blame him; his scorn I approve" —
Nay, that's not next. Hark! who is 't that knocks?

EMILIA: It's the wind.

DESDEMONA (*sings*):
    "I call my love false love; but what said he then?   55
    Sing willow, willow, willow:

225–26. **abode . . . here:** Stay here be extended.   **226. deter-
minate:** Effective.   **IV, III. 12. incontinent:** At once.

20. **stubbornness:** Roughness.   **checks:** Rebukes.   **27. mad:**
Wild, faithless.   **34. nightgown:** Dressing gown.   **50. hie thee:**
Hurry.

If I court moe women, you'll couch with moe
   men."
So get thee gone; good night. Mine eyes do itch.
   Doth that bode weeping?
EMILIA: 'Tis neither here nor there.
DESDEMONA: I have heard it said so. O, these men,
60   these men!
   Dost thou in conscience think — tell me, Emilia —
   That there be women do abuse their husbands
   In such gross kind?
EMILIA: There be some such, no question.
DESDEMONA: Wouldst thou do such a deed for all the
   world?
EMILIA: Why, would not you?
65 DESDEMONA: No, by this heavenly light!
EMILIA: Nor I neither by this heavenly light.
   I might do't as well i' th' dark.
DESDEMONA: Wouldst thou do such a deed for all the
   world?
70 EMILIA: The world's a huge thing; it is a great price for a
   small vice.
DESDEMONA: In troth, I think thou wouldst not.
EMILIA: In troth, I think I should; and undo't when I had
   done it. Marry, I would not do such a thing for a
75   joint-ring,° nor for measures of lawn, nor for gowns,
   petticoats, nor caps, nor any petty exhibition;° but,
   for all the whole world — 'Ud's pity! who would not
   make her husband a cuckold to make him a monarch? I should venture purgatory for't.
80 DESDEMONA: Beshrew me if I would do such a wrong
   For the whole world.
EMILIA: Why, the wrong is but a wrong i' th' world; and
   having the world for your labor, 'tis a wrong in your
   own world, and you might quickly make it right.
85 DESDEMONA: I do not think there is any such woman.
EMILIA: Yes, a dozen; and as many to th' vantage° as
   Would store° the world they played for.
   But I do think it is their husbands' faults
   If wives do fall. Say that they slack their duties
90   And pour our treasures into foreign laps;
   Or else break out in peevish° jealousies,
   Throwing restraint upon us; or say they strike us,
   Or scant our former having° in despite —
   Why, we have galls;° and though we have some
      grace,
95   Yet have we some revenge. Let husbands know
   Their wives have sense like them. They see, and
      smell,
   And have their palates both for sweet and sour,
   As husbands have. What is it that they do
   When they change us for others? Is it sport?
100   I think it is. And doth affection breed it?
   I think it doth. Is't frailty that thus errs?

It is so too. And have not we affections,
   Desires for sport, and frailty, as men have?
   Then let them use us well; else let them know,
   The ills we do, their ills instruct us so.   105
DESDEMONA: Good night, good night. God me such
   usage° send,
   Not to pick bad from bad, but by bad mend!
                             Exeunt.

ACT V • *Scene 1*

A street in Cyprus.

Enter Iago and Roderigo.

IAGO: Here, stand behind this bulk;° straight will he
   come.
   Wear thy good rapier bare, and put it home.
   Quick, quick! Fear nothing; I'll be at thy elbow.
   It makes us, or it mars us — think on that,
   And fix most firm thy resolution.   5
RODERIGO: Be near at hand; I may miscarry in't.
IAGO: Here, at thy hand. Be bold, and take thy stand.

[Stands aside.]

RODERIGO: I have no great devotion to the deed,
   And yet he hath given me satisfying reasons.
   'Tis but a man gone. Forth my sword! He dies!   10
IAGO: I have rubbed this young quat° almost to the
   sense,°
   And he grows angry. Now whether he kill Cassio,
   Or Cassio him, or each do kill the other,
   Every way makes my gain. Live Roderigo,
   He calls me to a restitution large   15
   Of gold and jewels that I bobbed° from him
   As gifts to Desdemona.
   It must not be. If Cassio do remain,
   He hath a daily beauty in his life
   That makes me ugly; and besides, the Moor   20
   May unfold me to him; there stand I in much peril.
   No, he must die. Be't so! I hear him coming.

Enter Cassio.

RODERIGO: I know his gait. 'Tis he. Villain, thou diest!

[Makes a pass at Cassio.]

CASSIO: That thrust had been mine enemy indeed
   But that my coat° is better than thou know'st.   25
   I will make proof of thine.

[Draws, and wounds Roderigo.]

RODERIGO: O, I am slain!

      [Iago darts from concealment behind Cassio,
          wounds him in the leg, and exits.]

---

75. **joint-ring:** Ring made in separable halves. 76. **exhibition:** Gift. 86. **to th' vantage:** Besides. 87. **store:** Populate.
91. **peevish:** Senseless. 93. **having:** Allowance. 94. **galls:**
Spirits to resent.

106. **usage:** Habits. V, I. 1. **bulk:** Projecting shop-front.
11. **quat:** Pimple. **sense:** Quick. 16. **bobbed:** Swindled.
25. **coat:** Undershirt of mail.

CASSIO: I am maimed for ever. Help, ho! Murder! murder!

[*Falls.*]
Enter Othello.

OTHELLO: The voice of Cassio. Iago keeps his word.
RODERIGO: O, villain that I am!
OTHELLO: It is even so.
30 CASSIO: O, help, ho! light! a surgeon!
OTHELLO: 'Tis he. O brave Iago, honest and just,
    That hast such noble sense of thy friend's wrong!
    Thou teachest me. Minion,° your dear lies dead,
    And your unblest fate hies.° Strumpet, I come.
    Forth of my heart those charms, thine eyes, are
35   blotted.
    Thy bed, lust-stained, shall with lust's blood be
        spotted.   *Exit Othello.*

Enter Lodovico and Gratiano.

CASSIO: What, ho? No watch? No passage?° Murder!
    murder!
GRATIANO: 'Tis some mischance. The cry is very
    direful.
CASSIO: O, help!
40 LODOVICO: Hark!
RODERIGO: O wretched villain!
LODOVICO: Two or three groan. It is a heavy° night.
    These may be counterfeits. Let's think't unsafe
    To come in to the cry without more help.
45 RODERIGO: Nobody come? Then shall I bleed to death.
LODOVICO: Hark!

Enter Iago, with a light.

GRATIANO: Here's one comes in his shirt, with light
    and weapons.
IAGO: Who's there? Whose noise is this that cries on°
    murder?
LODOVICO: We do not know.
IAGO: Did not you hear a cry?
CASSIO: Here, here! For heaven's sake, help me!
IAGO: What's
50   the matter?
GRATIANO: This is Othello's ancient, as I take it.
LODOVICO: The same indeed, a very valiant fellow.
IAGO: What are you here that cry so grievously?
CASSIO: Iago? O, I am spoiled, undone by villains!
55   Give me some help.
IAGO: O me, lieutenant! What villains have done this?
CASSIO: I think that one of them is hereabout
    And cannot make° away.
IAGO: O treacherous villains!

[*To Lodovico and Gratiano.*]

    What are you there? Come in, and give some help.

RODERIGO: O, help me here!   60
CASSIO: That's one of them.
IAGO: O murd'rous slave! O villain!

[*Stabs Roderigo.*]

RODERIGO: O damned Iago! O inhuman dog!
IAGO: Kill men i' th' dark? — Where be these bloody
    thieves? —
    How silent is this town! — Ho! murder! murder! —
    What may you be? Are you of good or evil?   65
LODOVICO: As you shall prove us, praise us.
IAGO: Signior Lodovico?
LODOVICO: He, sir.
IAGO: I cry you mercy. Here's Cassio hurt by villains.
GRATIANO: Cassio?   70
IAGO: How is't, brother?
CASSIO: My leg is cut in two.
IAGO: Marry,° heaven forbid!
    Light, gentlemen. I'll bind it with my shirt.

Enter Bianca.

BIANCA: What is the matter, ho? Who is't that cried?
IAGO: Who is't that cried?   75
BIANCA: O my dear Cassio! my sweet Cassio!
    O Cassio, Cassio, Cassio!
IAGO: O notable strumpet! — Cassio, may you suspect
    Who they should be that have thus mangled you?
CASSIO: No.   80
GRATIANO: I am sorry to find you thus. I have been to
    seek you.
IAGO: Lend me a garter. So. O for a chair°
    To bear him easily hence!
BIANCA: Alas, he faints! O Cassio, Cassio, Cassio!
IAGO: Gentlemen all, I do suspect this trash   85
    To be a party in this injury. —
    Patience a while, good Cassio. — Come, come!
    Lend me a light. Know we this face or no?
    Alas, my friend and my dear countryman
    Roderigo? No — Yes, sure. — O heaven, Roderigo!   90
GRATIANO: What, of Venice?
IAGO: Even he, sir. Did you know him?
GRATIANO: Know him? Ay.
IAGO: Signior Gratiano? I cry your gentle pardon.
    These bloody accidents must excuse my manners
    That so neglected you.
GRATIANO: I am glad to see you.   95
IAGO: How do you, Cassio? — O, a chair, a chair!
GRATIANO: Roderigo?
IAGO: He, he, 'tis he!

[*A chair brought in.*]

    O, that's well said;° the chair.
    Some good man bear him carefully from hence.   100
    I'll fetch the general's surgeon. [*To Bianca.*] For you,
        mistress,

---

33. Minion: Mistress. **34. hies:** Hurries on. **37. passage:**
Passersby. **42. heavy:** Cloudy, dark. **48. cries on:** Raises the
cry of. **58. make:** Get.

72. Marry: (From "By Mary"). **82. chair:** Litter. **99. well
said:** Well done.

Save you your labor. — He that lies slain here,
Cassio,
Was my dear friend. What malice was between you?
CASSIO: None in the world; nor do I know the man.
IAGO [*to Bianca*]: What, look you pale? — O, bear him
105   out o' th' air.

                      [*Cassio and Roderigo are borne off.*]

Stay you, good gentlemen. — Look you pale,
    mistress! —
Do you perceive the gastness° of her eye? —
Nay, if you stare, we shall hear more anon.
Behold her well; I pray you look upon her.
110   Do you see, gentlemen? Nay, guiltiness will speak.
Though tongues were out of use.

Enter Emilia.

EMILIA: 'Las, what's the matter? What's the matter,
    husband?
IAGO: Cassio hath here been set on in the dark
By Roderigo, and fellows that are scaped.
115   He's almost slain, and Roderigo dead.
EMILIA: Alas, good gentlemen! alas, good Cassio!
IAGO: This is the fruits of whoring. Prithee, Emilia,
Go know of Cassio where he supped to-night.

[*To Bianca.*]

    What, do you shake at that?
BIANCA: He supped at my house; but I therefore shake
120   not.
IAGO: O, did he so? I charge you go with me.
EMILIA: Fie, fie upon thee, strumpet!
BIANCA: I am no strumpet, but of life as honest°
As you that thus abuse me.
EMILIA: As I? Foh! fie upon thee!
125 IAGO: Kind gentlemen, let's go see poor Cassio dressed.

[*To Bianca.*]

    Come, mistress, you must tell 's another tale.
Emilia, run you to the citadel
And tell my lord and lady what hath happed.

                                [*Exit Emilia.*]

Will you go on afore?   *Exeunt* [*all but Iago*].
                      This is the night
130   That either makes me or fordoes° me quite.   [*Exit.*]

Scene II

A bedchamber in the castle.

Desdemona [*asleep*] *in her bed. Enter Othello with a light.*

OTHELLO: It is the cause, it is the cause,° my soul.
Let me not name it to you, you chaste stars!

It is the cause. Yet I'll not shed her blood,
Nor scar that whiter skin of hers than snow,
And smooth as monumental alabaster.   5
Yet she must die, else she'll betray more men.
Put out the light, and then put out the light.
If I quench thee, thou flaming minister,°
I can again thy former light restore,
Should I repent me; but once put out thy light,   10
Thou cunning'st pattern of excelling nature,
I know not where is that Promethean heat°
That can thy light relume.° When I have plucked the
    rose,
I cannot give it vital growth again;
It needs must wither. I'll smell thee on the tree.   15

(*He kisses her.*)

O balmy breath, that dost almost persuade
Justice to break her sword! One more, one more!
Be thus when thou art dead, and I will kill thee,
And love thee after. One more, and that's the last!
So sweet was ne'er so fatal. I must weep,   20
But they are cruel tears. This sorrow's heavenly;
It strikes where it doth love. She wakes.
DESDEMONA: Who's there? Othello?
OTHELLO: Ay, Desdemona.
DESDEMONA: Will you come to bed, my lord?
OTHELLO: Have you prayed to-night, Desdemon?
DESDEMONA: Ay,
    my lord.   25
OTHELLO: If you bethink yourself of any crime°
Unreconciled as yet to heaven and grace,
Solicit for it straight.
DESDEMONA: Alack, my lord, what may you mean by
    that?
OTHELLO: Well, do it, and be brief; I will walk by.   30
I would not kill thy unprepared spirit.
No, heaven forfend!° I would not kill thy soul.
DESDEMONA: Talk you of killing?
OTHELLO: Ay, I do.
DESDEMONA: Then heaven
Have mercy on me!
OTHELLO: Amen, with all my heart!
DESDEMONA: If you say so, I hope you will not kill me. 35
OTHELLO: Hum!
DESDEMONA: And yet I fear you; for you're fatal then
When your eyes roll so. Why I should fear I know
    not,
Since guiltiness I know not; but yet I feel I fear.
OTHELLO: Think on thy sins.
DESDEMONA: They are loves I bear to you. 40
OTHELLO: Ay, and for that thou diest.
DESDEMONA: That death 's unnatural that kills for
    loving.
Alas, why gnaw you so your nether lip?
Some bloody passion shakes your very frame.

---

107. **gastness:** Terror. 123. **honest:** Chaste. 130. **fordoes:**
Destroys. **V, II. 1. cause:** Cause of justice.

8. **minister:** Servant. 12. **Promethean heat:** Divine fire. 13. **relume:** Relight. 26. **crime:** Sin. 32. **forfend:** Forbid.

45   These are portents,° but yet I hope, I hope,
         They do not point on me.
OTHELLO: Peace and be still!
DESDEMONA: I will so. What's the matter?
OTHELLO: That handkerchief which I so loved and
         gave thee
         Thou gav'st to Cassio.
DESDEMONA: No, by my life and soul!
         Send for the man and ask him.
50 OTHELLO: Sweet soul, take heed,
         Take heed of perjury; thou art on thy deathbed.
DESDEMONA: Ay, but not yet to die.
OTHELLO: Yes, presently.°
         Therefore confess thee freely of thy sin;
         For to deny each article with oath
55   Cannot remove nor choke the strong conception°
         That I do groan withal. Thou art to die.
DESDEMONA: Then Lord have mercy on me!
OTHELLO: I say amen.
DESDEMONA: And have you mercy too! I never did
         Offend° you in my life; never loved Cassio
60   But with such general warranty of heaven
         As I might love. I never gave him token.
OTHELLO: By heaven, I saw my handkerchief in's hand!
         O perjured woman! thou dost stone my heart,°
         And mak'st me call what I intend to do
65   A murder, which I thought a sacrifice.
         I saw the handkerchief.
DESDEMONA: He found it then.
         I never gave it him. Send for him hither.
         Let him confess a truth.
OTHELLO: He hath confessed.
DESDEMONA: What, my lord?
OTHELLO: That he hath used thee.
DESDEMONA: How? Unlawfully?
70 OTHELLO: Ay.
DESDEMONA: He will not say so.
OTHELLO: No, his mouth is stopped.
         Honest Iago hath ta'en order° for't.
DESDEMONA: O, my fear interprets. What, is he dead?
OTHELLO: Had all his hairs been lives, my great
         revenge
75   Had stomach for them all.
DESDEMONA: Alas, he is betrayed, and I undone!
OTHELLO: Out, strumpet! Weep'st thou for him to my
         face?
DESDEMONA: O, banish me, my lord, but kill me not!
OTHELLO: Down, strumpet!
80 DESDEMONA: Kill me to-morrow; let me live to-night!
OTHELLO: Nay, if you strive —
DESDEMONA: But half an hour!
OTHELLO: Being done, there is no pause.
DESDEMONA: But while I say one prayer!
OTHELLO: It is too late.

---

45. **portents:** Signs of impending violence.   52. **presently:** At
once.   55. **conception:** Belief.   59. **Offend:** Wrong.   63. **stone
my heart:** Turn my heart to stone.   72. **ta'en order:** Taken
measures.

(*Smothers her.*)

[DESDEMONA: O Lord, Lord, Lord!]

Emilia at the door.

EMILIA (*calls within*): My lord, my lord! What, ho! my
         lord, my lord!   85
OTHELLO: What noise is this? Not dead? not yet quite
         dead?
         I that am cruel am yet merciful;
         I would not have thee linger in thy pain.
         So, so.
EMILIA (*within*): What, ho! my lord, my lord!
OTHELLO: Who's there?   90
EMILIA (*within*): O, good my lord, I would speak a
         word with you!
OTHELLO: Yes, 'tis Emilia. — By and by.° — She's
         dead. —
         'Tis like she comes to speak of Cassio's death.
         The noise was here. Ha! no more moving?
         Still as the grave. — Shall she come in? Were't
         good! —   95
         I think she stirs again. No. — What's best to do?
         If she come in, she'll sure speak to my wife.
         My wife! my wife! what wife! I have no wife.
         O, insupportable! O heavy hour!
         Methinks it should be now a huge eclipse   100
         Of sun and moon, and that th' affrighted globe
         Should yawn° at alteration.
EMILIA (*within*):   I do beseech you
         That I may speak with you, O good my lord!
OTHELLO: I had forgot thee. O, come in, Emilia.
         Soft, by and by. — Let me the curtains draw. —   105

[*Closes the bed-curtains.*]

         Where art thou?

[*Opens the door.*]
Enter Emilia.
                                  What's the matter with thee now?
EMILIA: O my good lord, yonder's foul murder done!
OTHELLO: What? Now?
EMILIA: But now, my lord.
OTHELLO: It is the very error° of the moon.   110
         She comes more nearer earth than she was wont
         And makes men mad.
EMILIA: Cassio, my lord, hath killed a young Venetian
         Called Roderigo.
OTHELLO: Roderigo killed?
         And Cassio killed?
EMILIA: No, Cassio is not killed.   115
OTHELLO: Not Cassio killed? Then murder's out of
         tune,
         And sweet revenge grows harsh.
DESDEMONA: O, falsely, falsely murdered?

---

92. **By and by:** Just a moment (addressed to Emilia).
102. **yawn:** Open, as in an earthquake.   110. **error:** Straying
off course.

EMILIA: O, Lord!
    what cry is that?
OTHELLO: That? What?
120 EMILIA: Out and alas! that was my lady's voice.
    Help! help, ho! help! O lady, speak again!
    Sweet Desdemona! O sweet mistress, speak!
DESDEMONA: A guiltless death I die.
EMILIA: O, who hath done this deed?
125 DESDEMONA: Nobody — I myself. Farewell.
    Commend° me to my kind lord. O, farewell!

(*She dies.*)

OTHELLO: Why, how should she be murd'red?
EMILIA: Alas,
    who knows?
OTHELLO: You heard her say herself, it was not I.
EMILIA: She said so. I must needs report the truth.
130 OTHELLO: She's like a liar gone to burning hell!
    'Twas I that killed her.
EMILIA: O, the more angel she,
    And you the blacker devil!
OTHELLO: She turned to folly, and she was a whore.
EMILIA: Thou dost belie her, and thou art a devil.
OTHELLO: She was false as water.°
EMILIA: Thou art rash as fire
135   to say
    That she was false. O, she was heavenly true!
OTHELLO: Cassio did top her. Ask thy husband else.
    O, I were damned beneath all depth in hell
    But that I did proceed upon just grounds
140   To this extremity. Thy husband knew it all.
EMILIA: My husband?
OTHELLO: Thy husband.
EMILIA: That she was false to wedlock?
OTHELLO: Ay, with Cassio. Nay, had she been true,
145   If heaven would make me such another world
    Of one entire and perfect chrysolite,°
    I'ld not have sold her for it.
EMILIA: My husband?
OTHELLO: Ay 'twas he that told me first.
    An honest man he is, and hates the slime
    That sticks on filthy deeds.
150 EMILIA: My husband?
OTHELLO: What needs this iterance,° woman? I say thy
    husband.
EMILIA: O mistress, villainy hath made mocks with
    love!
    My husband say that she was false?
OTHELLO: He, woman.
    I say, thy husband. Dost understand the word?
155   My friend, thy husband; honest, honest Iago.
EMILIA: If he say so, may his pernicious soul
    Rot half a grain a day! he lies to th' heart.
    She was too fond of her most filthy bargain.
OTHELLO: Ha!

EMILIA: Do thy worst.   160
    This deed of thine is no more worthy heaven
    Than thou wast worthy her.
OTHELLO: Peace, you were best.
EMILIA: Thou hast not half the power to do me harm
    As I have to be hurt.° O gull! O dolt!
    As ignorant as dirt! thou hast done a deed —   165
    I care not for thy sword; I'll make thee known,
    Though I lost twenty lives. Help! help! Ho! help!
    The Moor hath killed my mistress! Murder!
    murder!

Enter Montano, Gratiano, Iago, and others.

MONTANO: What is the matter? How now, general?
EMILIA: O, are you come, Iago? You have done well,   170
    That men must lay their murders on your neck.
GRATIANO: What is the matter?
EMILIA: Disprove this villain, if thou be'st a man.
    He says thou told'st him that his wife was false.
    I know thou didst not; thou'rt not such a villain.   175
    Speak, for my heart is full.
IAGO: I told him what I thought, and told no more
    Than what he found himself was apt and true.
EMILIA: But did you ever tell him she was false?
IAGO: I did.   180
EMILIA: You told a lie, an odious damnèd lie!
    Upon my soul, a lie! a wicked lie!
    She false with Cassio? Did you say with Cassio?
IAGO: With Cassio, mistress. Go to, charm° your
    tongue.
EMILIA: I will not charm my tongue; I am bound to
    speak: 185
    My mistress here lies murdered in her bed —
ALL: O heavens forfend!
EMILIA: And your reports have set the murder on.
OTHELLO: Nay, stare not, masters. It is true indeed.
GRATIANO: 'Tis a strange truth.   190
MONTANO: O monstrous act!
EMILIA: Villainy, villainy, villainy!
    I think upon't — I think I smell't! — O villainy!
    I thought so then. — I'll kill myself for grief. —
    O villainy, villainy!
IAGO: What, are you mad? I charge you get you home.   195
EMILIA: Good gentlemen, let me have leave to speak.
    'Tis proper I obey him, but not now.
    Perchance, Iago, I will ne'er go home.
OTHELLO: O! O! O!   (*Falls on the bed.*)
EMILIA: Nay, lay thee down and roar!
    For thou hast killed the sweetest innocent   200
    That e'er did lift up eye.
OTHELLO: O, she was foul!

[*Rises.*]

    I scarce did know you, uncle. There lies your niece,
    Whose breath, indeed, these hands have newly
    stopped.

---

126. Commend: Remember.   **135. water:** (Which is yielding).
146. chrysolite: (Precious topaz).   **151. iterance:** Repetition.

164. to be hurt: To endure hurt.   **184. charm:** Cast a spell on.

I know this act shows° horrible and grim.

GRATIANO: Poor Desdemon! I am glad thy father's
205　　dead.
Thy match was mortal to him, and pure grief
Shore his old thread in twain. Did he live now,
This sight would make him do a desperate turn;°
Yea, curse his better angel from his side,
210　And fall to reprobation.°

OTHELLO: 'Tis pitiful; but yet Iago knows
That she with Cassio hath the act of shame
A thousand times committed. Cassio confessed it;
And she did gratify° his amorous works
215　With that recognizance° and pledge of love
Which I first gave her. I saw it in his hand.
It was a handkerchief, an antique token
My father gave my mother.

EMILIA: O God! O heavenly God!

IAGO: Zounds, hold your peace!

220　EMILIA:　　　　　　　'Twill out, 'twill out! I peace?
No, I will speak as liberal as the north,°
Let heaven and men and devils, let them all,
All, all, cry shame against me, yet I'll speak.

IAGO: Be wise, and get you home.

EMILIA:　　　　　　　　　　I will not.

[*Iago draws and threatens Emilia.*]

GRATIANO:　　　　　　　　　　Fie!
225　Your sword upon a woman?

EMILIA: O thou dull Moor, that handkerchief thou
　　speak'st of
I found by fortune, and did give my husband;
For often with a solemn earnestness —
More than indeed belonged to such a trifle —
He begged of me to steal 't.

230　IAGO:　　　　　　　　Villainous whore!

EMILIA: She give it Cassio? No, alas, I found it,
And I did give 't my husband.

IAGO:　　　　　　　　　Filth, thou liest!

EMILIA: By heaven, I do not, I do not, gentlemen.
O murd'rous coxcomb! what should such a fool
Do with so good a wife?

235　OTHELLO:　　　　　　Are there no stones° in heaven
But what serves for the thunder? Precious villain!

*The Moor runs at Iago [but is disarmed by Montano].
Iago kills his wife.*

GRATIANO: The woman falls. Sure he hath killed his
　　wife.

EMILIA: Ay, ay. O, lay me by my mistress' side.

　　　　　　　　　　　　　　　Exit Iago.

GRATIANO: He's gone, but his wife's killed.

MONTANO: 'Tis a notorious° villain. Take you this
240　　weapon,

Which I have here recovered from the Moor.
Come, guard the door without. Let him not pass,
But kill him rather. I'll after that same villain,
For 'tis a damnèd slave.

　　Exit [Montano, with all but Othello and Emilia].

OTHELLO:　　　　　　I am not valiant neither;
But every puny whisper° gets my sword.　　　　245
But why should honor outlive honesty?
Let it go all.

EMILIA:　　　　What did thy song bode, lady?
Hark, canst thou hear me? I will play the swan,
And die in music. [*Sings.*] "Willow, willow, willow."
Moor, she was chaste. She loved thee, cruel Moor:　250
So come my soul to bliss as I speak true.
So speaking as I think, alas, I die.

(*She dies.*)

OTHELLO: I have another weapon in this chamber;
It is a sword of Spain, the ice brook's° temper.
O, here it is. — Uncle, I must come forth.　　　255

GRATIANO (*within*): If thou attempt it, it will cost thee
　　dear.
Thou hast no weapon, and perforce must suffer.

OTHELLO: Look in upon me then and speak with me,
Or, naked° as I am, I will assault thee.

[*Enter Gratiano.*]

GRATIANO: What is the matter?

OTHELLO:　　　　　　Behold, I have a weapon;　260
A better never did itself sustain
Upon a soldier's thigh. I have seen the day
That with this little arm and this good sword
I have made my way through more impediments
Than twenty times your stop.° But O vain boast!　265
Who can control his fate? 'Tis not so now.
Be not afraid, though you do see me weaponed.
Here is my journey's end, here is my butt,°
And very seamark° of my utmost sail:
Do you go back dismayed? 'Tis a lost° fear.　　270
Man but a rush° against Othello's breast,
And he retires. Where should Othello go?
Now, how dost thou look now? O ill-starred
　　wench!
Pale as thy smock! When we shall meet at compt,°
This look of thine will hurl my soul from heaven,　275
And fiends will snatch at it. Cold, cold, my girl?
Even like thy chastity.
O cursèd, cursèd slave! Whip me, ye devils,
From the possession of this heavenly sight!
Blow me about in winds! roast me in sulphur!　　280

---

204. shows: Appears.　207. turn: Act.　209. reprobation: Rejection by God, damnation.　214. gratify: Reward.　215. recognizance: Token.　221. liberal as the north: Unchecked as the north wind blows.　235. stones: Bolts like those used for thunderbolts.　240. notorious: Notable.

245. puny whisper: Whippersnapper.　254. ice brook: I.e., a Spanish blade, tempered in cold running water.　259. naked: Disarmed.　265. stop: Power to stop.　268. butt: Limit. 269. seamark: Beacon, destination.　270. lost: Wasted. 271. Man but a rush: Wield only a reed.　274. compt: Final accounting, Last Judgment.

Wash me in steep-down gulfs of liquid fire!
Oh Desdemon! dead Desdemon! dead! Oh! Oh!

Enter Lodovico, Montano, Iago [as prisoner], and Officers; Cassio in a chair.

LODOVICO: Where is this rash and most unfortunate
    man?
OTHELLO: That's he that was Othello. Here I am.
285 LODOVICO: Where is that viper? Bring the villain forth.
OTHELLO: I look down towards his feet° — but that's a
    fable.
    If that thou be'st a devil, I cannot kill thee.

[Wounds Iago.]

LODOVICO: Wrench his sword from him.

[Othello is disarmed.]

IAGO: I bleed, sir, but not killed.
OTHELLO: I am not sorry neither. I'ld have thee live;
290   For in my sense, 'tis happiness to die.
LODOVICO: O thou Othello that wert once so good,
    Fall'n in the practice° of a damnèd slave,
    What shall be said to thee?
OTHELLO: Why, anything;
    An honorable murderer, if you will;
295   For naught did I in hate, but all in honor.
LODOVICO: This wretch hath part confessed his
    villainy.
    Did you and he consent in° Cassio's death?
OTHELLO: Ay.
CASSIO: Dear general, I never gave you cause.
300 OTHELLO: I do believe it, and I ask your pardon.
    Will you, I pray, demand that demi-devil
    Why he hath thus ensnared my soul and body?
IAGO: Demand me nothing. What you know, you
    know.
    From this time forth I never will speak word.
LODOVICO: What, not to pray?
305 GRATIANO: Torments will ope your lips.
OTHELLO: Well, thou dost best.
LODOVICO: Sir, you shall understand what hath
    befall'n,
    Which, as I think, you know not. Here is a letter
    Found in the pocket of the slain Roderigo;
310   And here another. The one of them imports
    The death of Cassio to be undertook
    By Roderigo.
OTHELLO: O villain!
CASSIO: Most heathenish and most gross!
LODOVICO: Now here's another discontented paper
315   Found in the pocket too; and this, it seems,
    Roderigo mean t' have sent this damnèd villain;
    But that, belike, Iago in the nick°
    Came in and satisfied him.

OTHELLO: O thou pernicious caitiff! —
    How came you, Cassio, by that handkerchief
    That was my wife's?
CASSIO: I found it in my chamber;   320
    And he himself confessed but even now
    That there he dropped it for a special purpose
    Which wrought to his desire.
OTHELLO: O fool! fool! fool!
CASSIO: There is besides in Roderigo's letter,
    How he upbraids Iago that he made him   325
    Brave me upon the watch; whereon it came
    That I was cast;° and even but now he spake,
    After long seeming dead — Iago hurt him,
    Iago set him on.
LODOVICO: You must forsake this room and go with
    us.   330
    Your power and your command is taken off,
    And Cassio rules in Cyprus. For this slave,
    If there be any cunning cruelty
    That can torment him much and hold him long,
    It shall be his. You shall close prisoner rest   335
    Till that the nature of your fault be known
    To the Venetian state. Come, bring away.
OTHELLO: Soft you! a word or two before you go.
    I have done the state some service, and they
      know't.
    No more of that. I pray you, in your letters,   340
    When you shall these unlucky° deeds relate,
    Speak of me as I am. Nothing extenuate,
    Nor set down aught in malice. Then must you
      speak
    Of one that loved not wisely, but too well;
    Of one not easily jealous, but, being wrought,   345
    Perplexed° in the extreme; of one whose hand,
    Like the base Judean,° threw a pearl away
    Richer than all his tribe; of one whose subdued°
      eyes,
    Albeit unusèd to the melting mood,
    Drop tears as fast as the Arabian trees   350
    Their med'cinable gum. Set you down this.
    And say besides that in Aleppo once,
    Where a malignant and a turbaned Turk
    Beat a Venetian and traduced the state,
    I took by th' throat the circumcisèd dog   355
    And smote him — thus.

(He stabs himself.)

LODOVICO: O bloody period!°
GRATIANO: All that's spoke is marred.
OTHELLO: I kissed thee ere I killed thee. No way but
    this,
    Killing myself, to die upon a kiss.

(He [falls upon the bed and] dies.)

---

286. **I . . . feet:** I.e., to see if they are cloven, like the Devil's.
292. **practice:** Plot.   297. **consent in:** Agree upon.   317. **nick:**
Nick of time.

327. **cast:** Dismissed.   341. **unlucky:** Fatal.   346. **Perplexed:**
Distracted.   347. **Judean:** Judas Iscariot (?) (quarto reads "Indian").   348. **subdued:** I.e., conquered by grief.   357. **period:**
Ending.

CASSIO: This did I fear, but thought he had no
360   weapon;
          For he was great of heart.
      LODOVICO [*to Iago*]:   O Spartan dog,
          More fell° than anguish, hunger, or the sea!
          Look on the tragic loading of this bed.
          This is thy work. The object poisons sight;
365   Let it be hid.° Gratiano, keep the house,

And seize upon° the fortunes of the Moor,
For they succeed on you. To you, lord governor,
Remains the censure° of this hellish villain,
The time, the place, the torture. O, enforce it!
Myself will straight aboard, and to the state   370
This heavy act with heavy heart relate.

Exeunt.

---

362. fell: Cruel.   **365. Let it be hid:** I.e., draw the bed curtains.

366. seize upon: Take legal possession of.   **368. censure:** Judicial sentence.

COMMENTARIES

The great Shakespeare critic A. C. Bradley examines Othello's character in a portion of his series of lectures on the play. His approach is to probe Othello's essential nature, beginning with the premise that Othello is not by nature jealous but that Iago makes him so. Virginia Mason Vaughan offers insights into the way in which one of the greatest nineteenth-century English actors prepared for the role and what he felt he had to trim from the text in order to satisfy midcentury audiences. John Holstrom's review of Laurence Olivier's singular performance in the newly founded Royal Shakespeare Company in 1964 is mixed. He praises Olivier but complains of the ensemble around him. This review touches on the ways in which even a memorable performance can be marred by a questionable production.

A. C. Bradley (*1851–1935*)
OTHELLO'S CHARACTER   *1904*

Among his distinguished lectures on Shakespearean tragedy, A. C. Bradley meditated on the essential nature of Othello. He sees him as a relatively simple man, especially in contrast to Iago, whom Bradley sees as more highly charged and luminous in the play. But what he sees in Othello is nobility, the same nobility that scores of theatergoers have seen on stages throughout the world.

The character of Othello is comparatively simple, but, as I have dwelt on the prominence of intrigue and accident in the play, it is desirable to show how essentially the success of Iago's plot is connected with this character. Othello's description of himself as

    one not easily jealous, but, being wrought,
Perplexed in the extreme,

is perfectly just. His tragedy lies in this — that his whole nature was indisposed to jealousy and yet was such that he was unusually open to deception and, if once wrought to passion, likely to act with little reflection, with no delay, and in the most decisive manner conceivable.

Let me first set aside a mistaken view. I do not mean the ridiculous notion that Othello was jealous by temperament, but the idea, which has some little plausibility, that the play is primarily a study of a noble barbarian, who has become a Christian and has imbibed some of the civilization of his employers, but who retains beneath the surface the savage passions of his Moorish blood and also the suspiciousness regarding female chastity common among Oriental peoples, and that the last three Acts depict the outburst of these original feelings through the thin crust of Venetian culture. It would take too long to discuss this idea,[1] and it would perhaps be useless to do so, for all arguments against it must end in an appeal to the reader's understanding of Shakespeare. If he thinks it is like Shakespeare to look at things in this manner; that he had a historical mind and occupied himself with problems of "Kulturgeschichte"; that he labored to make his Romans perfectly Roman, to give a correct view of the Britons in the days of Lear or Cymbeline, to portray in Hamlet a stage of the moral consciousness not yet reached by the people around him, the reader will also think this interpretation of *Othello* probable. To me it appears hopelessly un-Shakespearean. I could as easily believe that Chaucer meant the Wife of Bath for a study of the peculiarities of Somersetshire. I do not mean that Othello's race is a matter of no account. It has, as we shall presently see, its importance in the play. It makes a difference to our idea of him; it makes a difference to the action and catastrophe. But in regard to the essentials of his character it is not important; and if anyone had told Shakespeare that no Englishman would have acted like the Moor and had congratulated him on the accuracy of his racial psychology, I am sure he would have laughed.

Othello is, in one sense of the word, by far the most romantic figure among Shakespeare's heroes; and he is so partly from the strange life of war and adventure which he has lived from childhood. He does not belong to our world, and he seems to enter it we know not whence — almost as if from wonderland. There is something mysterious in his descent from men of royal siege; in his wanderings in vast deserts and among marvelous peoples; in his tales of magic handkerchiefs and prophetic Sibyls; in the sudden vague glimpses we get of numberless battles and sieges in which he has played the hero and has borne a charmed life; even in chance references to his baptism, his being sold to slavery, his sojourn in Aleppo.

And he is not merely a romantic figure; his own nature is romantic. He has not, indeed, the meditative or speculative imagination of Hamlet; but in the strictest sense of the word he is more poetic than Hamlet. Indeed, if one recalls Othello's most famous speeches — those that begin, "Her father loved me," "O now for ever," "Never, Iago," "Had it pleased Heaven," "It is the cause," "Behold, I have a weapon," "Soft you, a word or two before you go"— and if one places side by side with these speeches an equal number by any other hero, one will not doubt that Othello is the greatest poet of them all. There is the same poetry in his casual phrases — like "These nine moons wasted," "Keep up your bright swords, for the dew will rust them," "You chaste stars," "It is a sword of Spain, the ice-brook's

---

[1]The reader who is tempted by it should, however, first ask himself whether Othello does act like a barbarian or like a man who, though wrought almost to madness, does "all in honour."

temper," "It is the very error of the moon"— and in those brief expressions of intense feeling which ever since have been taken as the absolute expression, like

> If it were now to die,
> 'Twere now to be most happy; for, I fear,
> My soul hath her content so absolute
> That not another comfort like to this
> Succeeds in unknown fate,

or

> If she be false, O then heaven mocks itself,
> I'll not believe it;

or

> No, my heart is turned to stone; I strike it, and it hurts
>   my hand,

or

> But yet the pity of it, Iago! O Iago, the pity of it, Iago!

or

>   O thou weed,
> Who are so lovely fair and smell'st so sweet
> That the sense aches at thee, would thou hadst ne'er been
>   born.

And this imagination, we feel, has accompanied his whole life. He has watched with a poet's eye the Arabian trees dropping their med'cinable gum, and the Indian throwing away his chance-found pearl; and has gazed in a fascinated dream at the Pontic sea rushing, never to return, to the Propontic and the Hellespont; and has felt as no other man ever felt (for he speaks of it as none other ever did) the poetry of the pride, pomp, and circumstance of glorious war.

So he comes before us, dark and grand, with a light upon him from the sun where he was born; but no longer young, and now grave, self-controlled, steeled by the experience of countless perils, hardships, and vicissitudes, at once simple and stately in bearing and in speech, a great man naturally modest but fully conscious of his worth, proud of his services to the State, unawed by dignitaries and unelated by honors, secure, it would seem, against all dangers from without and all rebellion from within. And he comes to have his life crowned with the final glory of love, a love as strange, adventurous and romantic as any passage of his eventful history, filling his heart with tenderness and his imagination with ecstasy. For there is no love, not that of Romeo in his youth, more steeped in imagination than Othello's.

The sources of danger in this character are revealed but too clearly by the story. In the first place, Othello's mind, for all its poetry, is very simple. He is not observant. His nature tends outward. He is quite free from introspection and is not given to reflection. Emotion excites his imagination, but it confuses and dulls his intellect. On this side he is the very opposite of Hamlet, with whom, however, he shares a great openness and trustfulness of nature. In addition, he has little experience of the corrupt products of civilized life and is ignorant of European women.

In the second place, for all his dignity and massive calm (and he has greater dignity than any other of Shakespeare's men), he is by nature full of the most vehement passion. Shakespeare emphasizes his self-control, not only by the wonderful pictures of the First Act, but by references to the past. Lodovico, amazed at his violence, exclaims:

> Is this the noble Moor whom our full Senate
> Call all in all sufficient? Is this the nature
> Whom passion could not shake? whose solid virtue
> The shot of accident nor dart of chance
> Could neither graze nor pierce?

Iago, who has here no motive for lying, asks:

> Can he be angry? I have seen the cannon
> When it hath blown his ranks into the air,
> And, like the devil, from his very arm
> Puffed his own brother — and can he be angry?[2]

This, and other aspects of his character, are best exhibited by a single line — one of Shakespeare's miracles — the words by which Othello silences in a moment the night brawl between his attendants and those of Brabantio:

> Keep up your bright swords, for the dew will rust them.

And the same self-control is strikingly shown where Othello endeavors to elicit some explanation of the fight between Cassio and Montano. Here, however, there occur ominous words, which make us feel how necessary was this self-control, and make us admire it the more:

> Now, by heaven,
> My blood begins my safer guides to rule,
> And passion, having my best judgment collied,
> Assays to lead the way.

We remember these words later, when the sun of reason is "collied," blackened and blotted out in total eclipse.

Lastly, Othello's nature is all of one piece. His trust, where he trusts, is absolute. Hesitation is almost impossible to him. He is extremely self-reliant, and decides and acts instantaneously. If stirred to indignation, as "in Aleppo once," he answers with one lightning stroke. Love, if he loves, must be to him the heaven where either he must live or bear no life. If such a passion as jealousy seizes him, it will swell into a well-nigh uncontrollable flood. He will press for immediate conviction or immediate relief. Convinced, he will act with the authority of a judge and the swiftness of a man in mortal pain. Undeceived, he will do like execution on himself.

This character is so noble, Othello's feelings and actions follow so inevitably from it and from the forces brought to bear on it, and his sufferings are so heartrending that he stirs, I believe, in most readers a passion of mingled love and pity which they feel for no other hero in Shakespeare and to which not even Mr. Swinburne can do more than justice. Yet there are some critics and not a few readers who cherish a grudge against him. They do not merely think that in the later stages of his temptation he showed a certain obtuseness and that, to speak pedantically, he acted with unjustifiable precipitance and violence; no one, I sup-

---

[2]For the actor, then, to represent him as violently angry when he cashiers Cassio is an utter mistake.

pose, denies that. But even when they admit that he was not of a jealous temper, they consider that he *was* "easily jealous"; they seem to think that it was inexcusable in him to feel any suspicion of his wife at all; and they blame him for never suspecting Iago or asking him for evidence. I refer to this attitude of mind chiefly in order to draw attention to certain points in the story. It comes partly from mere inattention (for Othello did suspect Iago and did ask him for evidence); partly from a misconstruction of the text which makes Othello appear jealous long before he really is so; and partly from failure to realize certain essential facts. I will begin with these.

(1) Othello, we have seen, was trustful and thorough in his trust. He put entire confidence in the honesty of Iago, who had not only been his companion in arms but, as he believed, had just proved his faithfulness in the matter of the marriage. This confidence was misplaced, and we happen to know it; but it was no sign of stupidity in Othello. For his opinion of Iago was the opinion of practically everyone who knew him: and that opinion was that Iago was before all things "honest," his very faults being those of excess in honesty. This being so, even if Othello had not been trustful and simple, it would have been quite unnatural in him to be unmoved by the warnings of so honest a friend, warnings offered with extreme reluctance and manifestly from a sense of a friend's duty.[3] *Any* husband would have been troubled by them.

(2) Iago does not bring these warnings to a husband who had lived with a wife for months and years and knew her like his sister or his bosom friend. Nor is there any ground in Othello's character for supposing that, if he had been such a man, he would have felt and acted as he does in the play. But he was newly married; in the circumstances he cannot have known much of Desdemona before his marriage; and further he was conscious of being under the spell of a feeling which can give glory to the truth but can also give it to a dream.

(3) This consciousness in any imaginative man is enough, in such circumstances, to destroy his confidence in his powers of perception. In Othello's case, after a long and most artful preparation, there now comes, to reinforce its effect, the suggestions that he is not an Italian, nor even a European; that he is totally ignorant of the thoughts and the customary morality of Venetian women;[4] that he had himself seen in Desdemona's deception of her father how perfect an actress she could be. As he listens in horror, for a moment at least the past is revealed to him in a new and dreadful light, and the ground seems to sink under his feet. These suggestions are followed by a tentative but hideous and humiliating insinuation of what his honest and much-experienced friend fears may be the true explanation of Desdemona's rejection of acceptable suitors and of her strange, and naturally temporary, preference for a black man. Here Iago goes too far. He sees something in Othello's face that frightens him, and he breaks off. Nor does this idea take any hold of Othello's mind. But it is not surprising that his utter powerlessness to repel it on the ground of knowledge of his wife, or even of that instinctive interpretation

---

[3]It is important to observe that, in his attempt to arrive at the facts about Cassio's drunken misdemeanor, Othello had just had an example of Iago's unwillingness to tell the whole truth where it must injure a friend. No wonder he feels in the temptation scene that "this honest creature doubtless Sees and knows more, much more, than he unfolds."

[4]To represent that Venetian women do not regard adultery so seriously as Othello does, and again that Othello would be wise to accept the situation like an Italian husband, is one of Iago's most artful and most maddening devices.

of character which is possible between persons of the same race,[5] should complete his misery, so that he feels he can bear no more, and abruptly dismisses his friend (III, iii, 238).

Now I repeat that *any* man situated as Othello was would have been disturbed by Iago's communications, and I add that many men would have been made wildly jealous. But up to this point, where Iago is dismissed, Othello, I must maintain, does not show jealousy. His confidence is shaken, he is confused and deeply troubled, he feels even horror; but he is not yet jealous in the proper sense of that word. In his soliloquy (III, iii, 258 ff.) the beginning of this passion may be traced; but it is only after an interval of solitude, when he has had time to dwell on the idea presented to him, and especially after statements of fact, not mere general grounds of suspicion, are offered, that the passion lays hold of him. Even then, however, and indeed to the very end, he is quite unlike the essentially jealous man, quite unlike Leontes. No doubt the thought of another man's possessing the woman he loves is intolerable to him; no doubt the sense of insult and the impulse of revenge are at times most violent; and these are the feelings of jealousy proper. But these are not the chief or the deepest source of Othello's suffering. It is the wreck of his faith and his love. It is the feeling,

> If she be false, oh then Heaven mocks itself;

the feeling,

> O Iago, the pity of it, Iago!

the feeling,

> But there where I have garner'd up my heart,
> Where either I must live, or bear no life;
> The fountain from the which my current runs,
> Or else dries up — to be discarded thence. . . .

You will find nothing like this in Leontes.

Up to this point, it appears to me, there is not a syllable to be said against Othello. But the play is a tragedy, and from this point we may abandon the ungrateful and undramatic task of awarding praise and blame. When Othello, after a brief interval, reenters (III, iii, 330), we see at once that the poison has been at work, and "burns like the mines of sulphur."

> Look where he comes! Not poppy, nor mandragora,
> Nor all the drowsy syrups of the world,
> Shall ever medicine thee to that sweet sleep
> Which thou owedst yesterday.

He is "on the rack," in an agony so unbearable that he cannot endure the sight of Iago. Anticipating the probability that Iago has spared him the whole truth, he feels that in that case his life is over and his "occupation gone" with all its glories. But he has not abandoned hope. The bare possibility that his friend is deliberately deceiv-

---

[5]If the reader has ever chanced to see an African violently excited, he may have been startled to observe how completely at a loss he was to interpret those bodily expressions of passion which in a fellow countryman he understands at once, and in a European foreigner with somewhat less certainty. The effect of difference in blood in increasing Othello's bewilderment regarding his wife is not sufficiently realized. The same effect has to be remembered in regard to Desdemona's mistakes in dealing with Othello in his anger.

ing him — though such a deception would be a thing so monstrously wicked that he can hardly conceive it credible — is a kind of hope. He furiously demands proof, ocular proof. And when he is compelled to see that he is demanding an impossibility he still demands evidence. He forces it from the unwilling witness, and hears the maddening tale of Cassio's dream. It is enough. And if it were not enough, has he not sometimes seen a handkerchief spotted with strawberries in his wife's hand? Yes, it was his first gift to her.

> I know not that; but such a handkerchief —
> I am sure it was your wife's — did I to-day
> See Cassio wipe his beard with.

"If it be that," he answers — but what need to test the fact? The "madness of revenge" is in his blood, and hesitation is a thing he never knew. He passes judgment and controls himself only to make his sentence a solemn vow.

The Othello of the Fourth Act is Othello in his fall. His fall is never complete, but he is much changed. Toward the close of the temptation scene he becomes at times most terrible, but his grandeur remains almost undiminished. Even in the following scene (III, iv), where he goes to test Desdemona in the matter of the handkerchief and receives a fatal confirmation of her guilt, our sympathy with him is hardly touched by any feeling of humiliation. But in the Fourth Act "Chaos has come." A slight interval of time may be admitted here. It is but slight; for it was necessary for Iago to hurry on, and terribly dangerous to leave a chance for a meeting of Cassio with Othello; and his insight into Othello's nature taught him that his plan was to deliver blow on blow, and never to allow his victim to recover from the confusion of the first shock. Still there is a slight interval; and when Othello reappears we see at a glance that he is a changed man. He is physically exhausted, and his mind is dazed. He sees everything blurred through a mist of blood and tears. He has actually forgotten the incident of the handkerchief and has to be reminded of it. When Iago, perceiving that he can now risk almost any lie, tells him that Cassio has confessed his guilt, Othello, the hero who has seemed to us only second to Coriolanus in physical power, trembles all over; he mutters disjointed words; a blackness suddenly intervenes between his eyes and the world; he takes it for the shuddering testimony of nature to the horror he has just heard, and he falls senseless to the ground. When he recovers it is to watch Cassio, as he imagines, laughing over his shame. It is an imposition so gross, and should have been one so perilous, that Iago would never have ventured it before. But he is safe now. The sight only adds to the confusion of intellect the madness of rage; and a ravenous thirst for revenge, contending with emotions of infinite longing and regret, conquers them. The delay till nightfall is torture to him. His self-control has wholly deserted him, and he strikes his wife in the presence of the Venetian envoy. He is so lost to all sense of reality that he never asks himself what will follow the deaths of Cassio and his wife. An ineradicable instinct of justice, rather than any last quiver of hope, leads him to question Emilia; but nothing could convince him now, and there follows the dreadful scene of accusation; and then, to allow us the relief of burning hatred and burning tears, the interview of Desdemona with Iago, and that last talk of hers with Emilia, and her last song.

But before the end there is again a change. The supposed death of Cassio (v, i) satiates the thirst for vengeance. The Othello who enters the bedchamber with the words,

> It is the cause, it is the cause, my soul,

is not the man of the Fourth Act. The deed he is bound to do is no murder, but a sacrifice. He is to save Desdemona from herself, not in hate but in honor; in honor, and also in love. His anger has passed; a boundless sorrow has taken its place; and

> this sorrow's heavenly:
> It strikes where it doth love.

Even when, at the sight of her apparent obduracy, and at the hearing of words which by a crowning fatality can only reconvince him of her guilt, these feelings give way to others, it is to righteous indignation they give way, not to rage; and, terribly painful as this scene is, there is almost nothing here to diminish the admiration and love which heighten pity. And pity itself vanishes, and love and admiration alone remain, in the majestic dignity and sovereign ascendancy of the close. Chaos has come and gone; and the Othello of the Council Chamber and the quay of Cyprus has returned or a greater and nobler Othello still. As he speaks those final words in which all the glory and agony of his life — long ago in India and Arabia and Aleppo, and afterward in Venice, and now in Cyprus — seem to pass before us, like the pictures that flash before the eyes of a drowning man, a triumphant scorn for the fetters of the flesh and the littleness of all the lives that must survive him sweeps our grief away, and when he dies upon a kiss the most painful of all tragedies leaves us for the moment free from pain, and exulting in the power of "love and man's unconquerable mind."

Virginia Mason Vaughan (b. 1947)
MACREADY'S OTHELLO   1994

In her discussion of Othello's *performance history, Virginia Mason Vaughan describes one of the greatest Shakespearean actors of the mid-nineteenth century. William Charles Macready (1793–1873) was born in England and performed in London and throughout the United States. His care in producing* Othello, *including his willingness to edit out sensitive lines, gives us an interesting insight into the history of the play's production.*

Alan Downer, Macready's biographer, describes the tragedian's acting methods: "In the study and rehearsal of a part, Macready searched for character traits which an audience would recognize as natural, and by the skillful use of pause, transition, and colloquialism strove to convey the poet's meaning."[1] One technique was the "Macready pause," a slight hesitation within the speech in imitation of a natural speaking voice. Macready used these pauses to make Othello seem more realistic. On 1 November 1836, he recorded: "I think I acted Othello well with considerable spirit, and more *pause* than I generally allow myself, which is an undoubted

---

[1] Alan Downer, *The Eminent Tragedian: William Charles Macready* (Cambridge: Harvard University Press, 1966), p. 80. See also Bertram Joseph, *The Tragic Actor* (London: Routledge and Kegan Paul, 1959), pp. 284–320, for a discussion of Macready's acting style and the traits of his competitors, including Vandenhoff, Phelps, and Kean.

improvement."[2] Again, on 7 November: "Acted Othello, not exactly well, but again derived great benefit from *taking time* between my sentences."[3] Macready also used specific stage business to achieve what he thought would be a more natural effect. Downer observes, for example, that "To further contribute to the reality of the senate scene in *Othello* he played with his back to the audience."[4]

The productions Macready mounted at Covent Garden and Drury Lane demonstrate his meticulousness over scenic design and costume. George Ellis prepared watercolor drawings of costumes and scenery from the Covent Garden *Othello* for Charles Kean; seven scenic drawings, now in the Folger Shakespeare Library,[5] show careful attention to detail. The first is a wash of the Rialto that was also used for *The Merchant of Venice,* complete with bridge, canal, gondola, and Renaissance buildings in the background. The second scene is the citadel of Famagusta on the isle of Cyprus. It consists of three layers: the front panel shows the castle wall and cannons pointing out to sea; the middle panel portrays a castle turret, while the back panel opens to a prospect across the harbor. The third scene is a gateway leading from outside the castle to the inside. The drunken revels of *Othello,* act II, scene III, would be staged before these gates. The fourth watercolor is an ornate chamber in the castle, suitable for the temptation scene, the fifth an antechamber in the castle, ornamented with carved scrolled walls. The sixth set is a piazza outside an Italian Renaissance building, flanked by columns. Last, of course, is the bedchamber. The bed, hidden in the center back alcove, is ornately decked with labial curtains. At first the bed's upstage location seems to marginalize Desdemona, but three sets of brightly colored curtains draped above lure the eye inward toward the recess. The entire set, in contrast to the grim action of the murder, is brightly colored in shades of blue, pink, and yellow.

Macready's elaborate scenery was symptomatic of his efforts to produce Shakespeare in historically accurate settings. Shattuck demonstrates the tragedian's meticulous attention to historical detail when he produced *King John.*[6] This concern was not confined to the history plays, however. For *Othello* accuracy meant realistic scenes from Renaissance Venice (the Rialto, bridge, canal, gondolas, and Doge's Palace) and Cyprus (the citadel at Famagusta). Though they were painted after the fact, these watercolors demonstrate the extravagant beauty of Macready's 1837 Covent Garden *Othello,* a beauty that set a high standard for subsequent spectacular, historically based productions.

Macready's quest for scenic harmony included detailed attention to costumes. For London productions no expense was spared. Watercolor sketches of the Covent Garden costumes[7] are just as detailed and colorful as the scenic designs. They too may have been used, where appropriate, in *The Merchant of Venice.* Brabantio wears a red robe trimmed with ermine over a black doublet. Gratiano, in

[2]William Charles Macready, *The Diaries of William Charles Macready,* ed. William Toynbee (London: Chapman and Hall, Ltd., 1912), v. 1, p. 354.

[3]Ibid., p. 357.

[4]Downer, *Eminent Tragedian,* p. 75.

[5]The promptbooks described below are listed in Charles H. Shattuck's *The Shakespeare Promptbooks: A Descriptive Catalogue* (Urbana: University of Illinois Press, 1965). This particular promptbook, Folger 14, is listed in Shattuck as no. 26 (p. 359).

[6]See Charles H. Shattuck, *William Charles Macready's King John* (Urbana: University of Illinois Press, 1962).

[7]Folger Promptbook 15, Shattuck 27. (See note 5 above.)

contrast, appears in a black robe with red doublet. Othello's red tunic is fringed with gold to match his gold cape. Iago is dressed in a buff doublet with a green vest and gold trim. He wears red hose and black shoes. Later, he changes to buff leggings and a blue jacket. Cassio is foppish. He sports a plumed hat, green vest, and a gold doublet slashed to show red beneath. Lodovico is more decorous in silver and blue, with hat, cape, doublet, and hose. Montano wears a long white gown trimmed in red with a gold sash. The Venetian guard appears in sixteenth-century armor, while servants are appareled in rough brown jackets and doublets. White lace signifies Desdemona's purity, whereas black (with a red underskirt) suggests Emilia's earthiness. Tissue of gold or silver bespeaks an exalted station.

Red, black, gold, white, and blue — the colors create that harmonious effect Macready so cherished. Othello's red aligned him with the Venetian Senators, figures of law and authority. Emilia's red petticoat picks up the color scheme, but her scarlet indicates easy virtue. Each scene is chromatically planned, even the bed curtains' labial folds — the shapes and colors, like the acting, should suggest the emotions represented onstage.

The grandeur of Macready's Covent Garden *Othello* is best conveyed by the Senate Council scene (I, III). Macready's promptbook notes:

> The Senators are discov'd seated on an elevated platform, up the sides, and aX the back of the stage. Ten in Red Gowns- / including the Duke-Gratiano-and Brabantio / aX at back- Thirty- / including Lodovico / - in Black Gowns, with large open ermin'd sleeves, -at sides R & L. - The Duke's seat is slightly elevated above the others.- The Secretary is seated, - writing, and faces the duke.[8]

This scene was the culmination of Macready's search in *Othello* productions for historical accuracy; this was the Doge and his Council as he envisioned it from historical research and his own visits to Venice. Macready even covered the walls of the Doge's Hall with Titians and Tintorettos.[9] He was pleased with the result: his diary of 16 October 1837 exudes that "The Council of Forty was a scene of beautiful effect, one of the most real things I ever saw."[10]

Productions in the provinces and the United States could never be this elaborate, but traveling stars could carry their costumes with them; the Moor, at least, could be seen in appropriate splendor. Even through the swamps of Georgia, from Savannah to Mobile, Macready carted mammoth trunks of resplendent costumes so that he could represent his characters as he envisioned them.

Costumes aside, Macready's careful preparation was often wasted when he left London to play with provincial casts or journeyed to the backwoods of America. Although he was a difficult, egocentric man who often upstaged his fellow actors, as Kean had before him, one can sympathize with the meticulous actor faced with inadequate theatres and poorly prepared casts. In Liverpool, 31 January 1850, Macready found that "The Roderigo, Mr. Brown was *drunk!*"[11] Later that year in

[8]Folger Promptbook 13, Shattuck 25.

[9]Julie Hankey, Ed., *Othello* by William Shakespeare (Bristol: Bristol Classical Press, 1987), p. 153.

[10]William Charles Macready, *Macready's Reminiscences: and Selections from His Diaries and Letters,* ed. Sir Frederick Pollock (New York: Harper & Brothers, 1875), p. 416.

[11]Toynbee, *Diaries,* vol. II, p. 446.

Birmingham, Macready acted with an Othello who "actually *belaboured* [him] in the third act; it was so bad that at last [he] was obliged to resist the gentleman's 'corporal chastisement' and decline his shaking and pummelling!"[12] Perhaps such treatment was Macready's just punishment for rough handling of Desdemonas like Helena Faucit Martin. The wonder is that the perfectionist Macready could act at all with provincial and American casts too reluctant to rehearse and rather short on theatrical talent.

That Macready traveled from city to city, cast to cast, and performed Shakespeare's *Othello* night after night testifies to the uniformity of mid-nineteenth-century productions. As manager at Covent Garden and Drury Lane, Macready supervised his ideal *Othello,* a carefully designed performance in which scenery, costumes, blocking, and acting created a harmonious experience. In the provinces or outside New York and Philadelphia, the council scene might have two Senators instead of forty, but the blocking was substantially the same. So was the text.

A collation of the 1839 Macready acting edition with its predecessors — Mrs. Inchbald's (ca. 1808), Kemble's (1814), and Oxberry's (based on Edmund Kean's performances, 1819) — shows that Macready's Covent Garden *Othello* was somewhat more chaste and sensitive to the delicate feelings of his audiences than his predecessors'. Like Oxberry, but unlike Kemble and Inchbald, Macready's Iago makes no reference to "making the beast with two backs." Macready's Senate scene is by design much grander, requiring forty Senators rather than his predecessors' seven. Othello's cannibals and anthropophagi are quietly eliminated in keeping with the hero's dignity. On the Cyprus quay Macready drops Iago's reference to wives as "Players in your housewifery and housewives in your beds" (II, i, 111). Iago's observation that Othello "hath not yet made wanton the night with her . . ." (II, ii, 16) is also removed. Instead of "Happiness to their sheets!" Iago cries, "Happiness to them!" In the temptation scene, lines 463 to 467 are cut, whereas Inchbald and Kemble had retained them. Macready and Oxberry also root out the kisses from Cassio's dream. The major cuts from the eighteenth century — clown, Bianca, fit, willow song scene — persist. Macready's fastidiousness climaxes in act IV, scene ii, where he removes "Oh thou weed . . . That the sense aches at thee" (67–69) and "Was this fair paper . . . made to write whore upon" (71–72). He also substitutes the tame "one" for "strumpet" and "whore." In the next scene, Desdemona is not allowed to ask for her nightly apparel. Macready restores the original "Let me the curtains draw" (V, ii, 105), probably in reference to stage business. Hankey notes contemporary accounts of Macready's "thrilling effect" of thrusting his dark face through the curtains at Emilia's knock.[13] He closes the play — as Kean had done in performance — with Othello's last words.

Macready's purified text drops, in other words, all references to sheets, beds, going to bed, adultery, and sex. The bed behind half-closed curtains perhaps symbolizes the hidden sexuality underlying the play. While nothing remains in the revised language to offend a Victorian, the subject — adultery — was indeed salacious. Yet *Othello* was popular among all audiences, and no one apparently condemned the plot as immoral.

---

[12]Ibid., p. 463.
[13]Hankey, *Othello,* p. 317.

John Holstrom
GOING IT ALONE: A REVIEW OF OLIVIER'S OTHELLO   1964

Laurence Olivier has been considered one of the greatest Othellos of our time, but in this review John Holstrom finds fault with the production. He is careful to note that Olivier's portrayal of Othello is "a towering success," but he does so in the context of condemning most of the rest of the production. Holstrom makes us aware that for the play to work well, the cast must be balanced and equal to the measure of Othello himself.

There are differing opinions about foils. I don't mean those fencing things, or the wrappings of chocolate bars, but the setting of unobtrusive nonprecious metal into which a jewel is sunk, to shine the brighter against its dull background. This, in theatrical terms, was the view of those actor-managers (a dying if not dead race now) who surrounded themselves with a weak, untalented company so that they could shine out alone, without fear of distracting competition.

Others, however, believe that a precious stone is made more brilliant, not less, by being set in fine silver; others again have been made painfully aware that the effect of a great virtuoso performance on the stage is not heightened but cheapened by unworthy support from the rest of the cast. Acting isn't a finished form like plastic art. It has to be born again each time the curtain rises. The dynamism of a performance depends on intermeshing with a rhythm established by the lesser cogs; its character depends on relationships.

So I feel bitterly disappointed that when a theatrical jewel of great price — the long-awaited Olivier Othello, no less — finally comes our way, it should have been set in so feebly uninspired a production (by John Dexter, incredibly enough) and such a dreary, characterless cast that its power is lamed, its brilliance made to look suspect and its imaginative flights too often left to crash from their trapezes.

Sir Laurence has been quoted as saying, a few years back, that one of the reasons he hadn't attempted Othello was unwillingness to black up and sweat blood only to have the show stolen by some brilliant young fellow playing Iago. True enough, this can happen. Iago is infinitely the easier and more rewarding part, and it's rare (though it has been managed) for an actor not to be pretty striking in it. But Olivier is no fool. Having decided to do it, he wouldn't let vanity or insecurity betray him into doing an actor-manager on us, when *Othello* was at stake. This one knows. And yet the net result, at the National Theatre, has been as bad as if he had.

Essentially, make no mistake about it, his Othello is a towering success. Its lines are drawn as bravely and clearly as only a master can. This is a humorous, coolly intelligent Moor, quick to detect any false note, who could only be blinded to Iago's treachery by the deepest trust in him. He must lean on Iago with the absolute reliance many great officers have had in their serjeant-majors. Iago must therefore be a man with a different but entirely convincing mask for Othello, Cassio, Roderigo, Emilia, all the people he's intricately involved with. He must gaze into Othello's eyes with the passionate, worried devotion of a great hound. He must equally convince everyone else that he has their welfare at heart, come what may.

And at the National Theatre, what Iago do we get? We get a good little character actor called Frank Finlay, who has been puffed-up by the Royal Court claque into a thoroughly bad leading one. In Northern character parts, like Willie Mossop in *Hobson's Choice,* Finlay is admirable. As Stogumber in *Saint Joan* he was a pain. As Iago he is a national disaster, because he's giving no support at all to what would have been (but isn't) the greatest Othello of our day. Finlay's Iago is as nonexistent as Errol John's Othello was in the same building a year ago. Buff-jerkined, he lopes busily about the stage with a constant flow of neat, overelaborate gesture. He orates with flexed eyeballs and tirelessly bared teeth, spitting out each word with equal emphasis, like a punch-drunk Methodist preacher who's past caring what, if anything, it means. It's as crude, boring, and perfunctory an Iago as we'll see for a while: and the tragedy is that it gives Olivier nothing to play against and thus makes him seem sometimes unconvincing, sometimes artificial.

For this Othello, a highly wrought conception, desperately needs support. Olivier starts at a low pitch, with slightly thickened voice, working lightly and gracefully towards the sentiment and later the troubled guts of the part. In the marvelous temptation scene, he instantly registers a flicker of unease about the vanishing Cassio, but defers actual seriousness till audaciously late in the scene, holding the most delicate balance between joking and credence, keeping Iago's insinuations at bay in a kind of ironic game. He is also a Christian Othello, with a cross on his chest, and it's only when his control snaps that he tears the cross off and prays ("Now by yond marble heaven") as a Mohammedan. The epileptic fit remains a threat, nearly recurring more than once after the actual swoon. The great Propontic speeches are half-chanted, almost like Grand Opera, and it's here most of all that Olivier, supported by no sort of grandeur or passion in the rest, seems overcalculated in his isolation. The end is touchingly and beautifully done, with a return to the earlier poise and tenderness.

It could have been great. With even an averagely good Iago it probably would have been. And with a decent production and a fine Iago — the best in recent memory have been Richard Burton's rock-solid beast and Leo McKern's magnificent creation wasted on poor Errol John last year — it would have been something to tell our grandchildren about. But when all's said, this is a first attempt, not a last. Olivier is in his prime. Burton and McKern are still around, and so is Vladek Sheybal, that marvellous Pole who in spite of his accent would probably be the best Iago of all. As for the National Theatre Company, only six months old, it's already time for a ruthless shake-up.

One word of praise to Maggie Smith for a Desdemona of considerable dignity and delicacy. Her face, perhaps, is too ineradicably sly, and the mournful little voice, so perfect in comedy, is sometimes a problem in tragedy. But she was sweetly serious, besides sporting a most wringable neck.

A CULTURAL CASEBOOK

The Issue of Race and Othello

1600

ABDVLGVAHID.

LEGATVS REGIS BARBARIÆ
IN ANGLIAM.

ÆTATIS:42.

Abdul El-Ouahed Ben Messasud, Moorish Ambassador to Queen Elizabeth I (reigned 1558–1603). Oil on panel. Artist unknown.

By the sixteenth century, Elizabethan England had already inherited the seeds of racial prejudice. Explorers and adventurers of the fourteenth and fifteenth centuries had written of distant, culturally exotic nations whose inhabitants were dark-skinned. In Shakespeare's time, enough Africans lived in London and in other large coastal towns that theater audiences would have had some contact with black people. Late in her reign, the strong presence of Africans in England provoked Queen Elizabeth to order some of them sent back to Africa. Understanding his times, Shakespeare knew that his audience would be prejudiced against Othello — just as certain characters in the play itself are prejudiced. He crafted his play to stimulate conflicting emotional responses in his audience — creating the black Othello as a noble, grand, and imposing figure whose flaw, jealousy, and his willingness to trust his white officer, Iago, combine to seal his fate. Playing with his audience's notion of good and evil and black and white, Shakespeare confronts Renaissance racism with irony.

Some early critics disputed whether Shakespeare had in mind a "tawny" Moor or a "black" Moor for the title character. While the nineteenth-century stage preferred a light-skinned Othello, twentieth-century versions preferred a black Othello, usually with a black actor playing the role. Some great Othellos have been performed by white actors with the reasoning that Shakespeare wrote the part for Richard Burbage, who was white and one of the greatest actors of his day. Today the role is usually reserved for black actors, with a number of outstanding performances by Moses Gunn, James Earl Jones, and others.

The documents compiled here help us to consider *Othello* in the context of racial prejudice, both in Shakespeare's time and our own. Sir John Mandeville's *Travels,* dating 1357, demonstrates that early reports about the existence of black civilizations had reached Europe. Ethiopians were known to the English and referred to as Moors. Around the time of the first performance of *Othello,* an Arab delegation in London drew attention with its exotic fashions and styles. By the time *Othello* was performed, the English audience would have understood from general knowledge and experience what a "dark-visaged" man — either from north or central Africa — would have looked like.

Sir John Mandeville attempted to explain the nature of both Egypt and neighboring Ethiopia. He maintained that the inhabitants had been turned black by the heat of the sun. Much later, Richard Eden translated a travel book by Peter Martyr written in 1530. The single paragraph included in this casebook indicates that blacks were already present in Quarequa, a mountainous region of Haiti and the Dominican Republic. Eden theorizes that these black inhabitants were the descendants of seafaring Africans who were blown off course and landed in the Caribbean.

A Muslim convert to Christianity, Leo Africanus (as he became known to Europeans) wrote *A Geographical Historie of Africa* in 1550. It was expanded and revised for an English audience by John Pory in 1600. The book was a popular treatise that answered the needs of the curious to learn about Africa. In a sometimes fanciful fashion, it describes regions and nations as well as peoples, customs, and religious practices.

In "Othello and Color Prejudice," G. K. Hunter, a distinguished modern Shakespeare scholar, asserts that "Shakespeare intended his hero to be a black man." Hunter clarifies this statement with reference to other Renaissance works and writers. Margaret Webster, who directed the great performance of Paul Robeson in *Othello* in 1943, discusses the question of race in the play from the perspective of the mid-twentieth century. Her focus is on Desdemona as much as on Othello. Peter Marks reviewed Patrick Stewart (of *Star Trek* fame) in a production that had an all-black cast except for Stewart's portrayal of Othello. Marks felt that the result "tends to take the racial issue off the table." Whether that is the case or not, we should attempt to know as much as we can about the prejudices and understandings of Shakespeare's time as well as those of our own in regard to *Othello*.

In addition to the material in this Casebook, we should refer to Ben Jonson's *Masque of Blackness*, which follows. It was commissioned by Queen Anne for the court of King James I and was performed the same year and in the same theater as *Othello*. In some ways Jonson's *Masque* can be seen as a commentary on the age and perhaps on *Othello*.

Sir John Mandeville (c. 1300–1372)
FROM *MANDEVILLE'S TRAVELS*   1357

TRANSLATED FROM THE FRENCH BY COTTON TITUS

Mandeville's Travels, written in France in 1357, was one of the most popular travel books of the late Middle Ages and early Renaissance. Some of it is fantasy; some of it is gathered from the travels of many people. Othello's line concerning "men whose heads / Do grow beneath their shoulders" (I, III, 144–45) comes from this well-known book. The excerpts here point to contemporary views of Africans available to Shakespeare.

And between Egypt and Nubia it hath well a twelve journeys of desert. And men of Nubia be Christian, but they be black as the Moors for great heat of the sun.

In Egypt there be five provinces; one that hight° Sa'id, that other that hight Damanhur, another Rosetta that is an isle in Nile, another Alexandria, and another the land of Damietta. That city was wont to be right strong, but it was twice won of the Christian men. And therefore after that the Saracens beat down the walls, and with the walls and the towers thereof the Saracens made another city more far from the sea and cleped it the New Damietta, so that now no man dwelleth at the rather town of Damietta. At that city of Damietta is one of the havens of Egypt. And at Alexandria is that other, that is a full strong city, but there is no water to drink but if it come by conduit from Nile that entereth into their cisterns; and whoso stopped that water from them, they might not endure there. In Egypt there be but few fortlets or castles because that the country is so strong of himself.

Note of a Marvel   At the deserts of Egypt was a worthy man that was an holy hermit,[1] and there met with him a monster; that is to say, a monster is a thing deformed against kind both of man or of beast or of anything else, and that is cleped° a monster. And this

---

hight: Is called.
[1]St. Anthony or St. Paul the Hermit.
cleped: Named.

monster that met with this holy hermit was as it had been a man that had two horns trenchant on his forehead, and he had a body like a man to the navel, and beneath he had the body like a goat. And the hermit asked him what he was, and the monster answered him and said he was a deadly creature such as God had formed and dwelled in those deserts in purchasing his sustenance; and besought the hermit that he would pray God for him, the which that came from Heaven for to save all mankind, and was born of a maiden, and suffered passion and death, as we well know, by whom we live and be. And yet is the head with the two horns of that monster at Alexandria for a marvel.

In Egypt is the city of Heliopolis, that is to say the city of the sun. In that city there is a temple made round after the shape of the Temple of Jerusalem. The priests of that temple have all their writings under the date of the fowl that is cleped Phoenix, and there is none but one in all the world. And he cometh to burn himself upon the altar of that temple at the end of five hundred year, for so long he liveth. And at the five hundred years' end the priests array their altar honestly and put thereupon spices and sulphur vif and other things that will burn lightly, and the bird Phoenix cometh and burneth himself to ashes. And the first day next after men find in the ashes a worm; and the second day next after men find a bird quick and perfect; and the third day next after he flieth his way. And so there is no more birds of that kind in all the world but it alone, and truly that is a great miracle of God. And men may well liken that bird unto God because that there is no God but one, and also that Our Lord arose from death to life the third day.[. . .]

Beside the land of Chaldea is the land of Amazonia, that is the land of Feminia. And in that realm is all women and no man, not as some men say that men may not live there but for because that the women will not suffer no men amongst them to be their sovereigns. For sometime there was a king in that country, and men married as in other countries. And so befell that the king had war with them of Scythia, the which king hight Scolopitus, that was slain in battle and all the good blood of his realm. And when the queen and all the other noble ladies saw that they were all widows, and that all the royal blood was lost, they armed them and as creatures out of wit they slew all the men of the country that were left, for they would that all the women were widows as the queen and they were.

And from that time hitherwards they never would suffer man to dwell amongst them longer than seven days and seven nights, nor that no child that were male should dwell amongst them longer than he were nourished and then sent to his father. And when they will have any company of man, then they draw them towards the lands marching next to them. And then they have their loves that use them, and they dwell with them an eight days or ten, and then go home again. And if they have any knave child, they keep it a certain time and then send it to the father when he can go alone and eat by himself, or else they slay it. And if it be a female, they do away that one pap with an hot iron. And if it be a woman of great lineage, they do away the left pap that they may the better bear a shield. And if it be a woman on foot, they do away the right pap for to shoot with bow Turkish, for they shoot well with bows.

In that land they have a queen that governeth all that land, and all they be obedient to her. And always they make their queen by election that is most worthy in arms, for they be right good warriors and orped° and wise, noble, and worthy. And they go often time insold to help of other kings in their wars for gold and silver as

---

orped: Valiant.

other soldiers do, and they maintain themselves right vigorously. This land of Amazonia is an isle all environed with the sea save in two places where be two entries. And beyond that water dwell the men that be their paramours and their loves, where they go to solace them when they will.

Beside Amazonia is the land of *terra Margine,* that is a great country and a full delectable. And for the goodness of the country King Alexander let first make there the city of Alexandria (and yet he made twelve cities of the same name), but that city is now cleped Seleucia.

And from that other coast of Chaldea toward the south is Ethiopia, a great country that stretcheth to the end of Egypt. Ethiopia is departed into two principal parts, and that is in the east part and in the meridional part, the which part meridional is cleped Mauretania. And the folk of that country be black enough and more black than in the other part, and they be cleped Moors. In that part is a well that in the day it is so cold that no man may drink thereof, and in the night it is so hot that no man may suffer his hand therein. And beyond that part toward the south to pass by the Sea Ocean is a great land and a great country, but men may not dwell there for the fervent burning of the sun, so is it passing hot in that country. In Ethiopia all the rivers and all the waters be troubled, and they be some deal salt for the great heat that is there.

And the folk of that country be lightly drunk and have but little appetite to meat. And they have commonly the flux of the womb, and they live not long. In Ethiopia be many diverse folk. And Ethiopia is cleped Cusis. In that country be folk that have but one foot, and they go so blithe that it is marvel, and the foot is so large that it shadoweth all the body against the sun when they will lie and rest them. In Ethiopia, when the children be young and little, they be all yellow, and when that they wax of age that yellowness turneth to be all black. In Ethiopia is the city of Savah and the land of the which one of the three kings that presented Our Lord in Bethlehem was king of.

Richard Eden (1521?–1576)
FROM *DECADES OF THE NEW WORLD*   1555

Around 1555, Richard Eden translated the work of Peter Martyr, written originally in 1530. Eden added his own material to Martyr's book and produced a popular "introduction" to the New World. In this excerpt he comments on black inhabitants of a mountainous region of Hispaniola (now Haiti and the Dominican Republic), whom he assumes arrived in the New World by accident.

There is a region not past two days journey distant from *Quarequa,* in which they found only black Moors: and those exceeding fierce and cruel. They suppose that in time past certain black moors sailed thither out of *Aethiopia* to rob: and that by shipwreck or some other chance, they were driven to those mountains. Th[e] inhabitants of *Quarequa* live in continual war and debate with these black men.

Leo Africanus (c. 1485–c. 1554)
and John Pory (1572–1635)
From *A Geographical Historie of Africa*   1550, 1600

The travel accounts of Leo Africanus, born al-Hasan ibn Muhammad al-Wazzān Al-Zayyātī, were widely read in Elizabethan England. Most important in shaping the Elizabethans' impressions of Africans was his work, A Geographical Historie of Africa *(1550), which was revised and expanded by another traveler, John Pory, in 1600. The first two excerpts that follow are by Pory, who emphasizes certain negative features of north African outlaws. Africanus, born in Granada, explains later in his account that he owes his birth to Africa, and balances the picture by stressing the civility, liberality, and fidelity of the Moors inhabiting the desert of Libya.*

The People of Cafri, Part of the Lower Ethiopia

The people of this place called in the Arabian tongue Cafri, Cafres, or Cafates, that is to say, lawless or outlaws, are for the most part exceeding black of color, which very thing may be a sufficient argument, that the sun is not the sole or chief cause of their blackness; for in diverse other countries where the heat thereof is far more scorching and intolerable, there are tawny, brown, yellowish, ash-colored, and white people; so that the cause thereof seemeth rather to be of an hereditary quality transfused from the parents, than the intemperature of an hot climate, though it also may be some furtherance thereunto. The Hollanders in the year 1595, entering the harbor of Saint Bras, somewhat to the east of Cabo das Agulhas, had conversation and truck with some of these Cafres, whom they found to be a stout and valiant people, but very base and contemptible in their behavior and apparel, being clad in ox and sheeps skins, wrapped about their shoulders with the hairy sides inward, in form of a mantle. Their weapons are a kind of small slender darts or pikes, some whereof are headed with some kind of metal, the residue being unheaded, and hardened only at the points with fire. They cover their private parts with a sheeps tail, which is bound up before and behind with a girdle. Their home-beasts are, like those of Spaine, very well limbed and proportioned. Their sheep are great and fair, not having any wool on their backs, but a kind of harsh hair like goats. Other particulars by them observed, for brevitys sake, I omit.

The Kingdom of Damut

The kingdom of Damut (as *Sanutus* affirmeth) doth border upon the kingdom of Xoa, and is enclosed on either side with the lake of Barcena, and the land of Zanguebar. Howbeit others place Damut between the kingdoms of Vangue and Goiame toward the west, which opinion seemeth most probable. This country aboundeth with gold, ginger, grapes, corn, and beasts of all sorts. The slaves of this kingdom are much esteemed, and are commonly sold throughout all Arabia, Persia, and Egypt, where they prove most valiant soldiers. The greater part of the people of Damut are Gentiles, and the residue Christians, who have certain monasteries. In this kingdom is that exceeding high and dreadful mountain (having one narrow passage only to ascend by), whither the *Prete* sendeth his nobles which are convicted of any heinous crime, to suffer ignominious death with hunger and cold. About the fountains of Nilus some say, that there are Amazones or women-warriors, most valiant and redoubted, which use bows and arrows, and live under the government of a Queen: as likewise the people called Cafri or Cafates, being as black as pitch, and of a mighty stature, and (as some think) descended of the Jewes; but now they are idolators, and most deadly enemies to the Christians; for they make continual assaults upon the Abassins, despoiling them both of life and goods: but all the day-time they lie lurking in mountains, woods, and deep valleys.

The Manners and Customs of the African People, which Inhabit the Desert of Libya

The women of this nation be gross, corpulent, and of a swart complexion. They are fattest upon their breast and paps, but slender about the girdle-stead. Very civil they are, after their manner, both in speech and gestures: sometimes they will accept of a kiss; but whoso tempteth them farther, putteth his own life in hazard. For by reason of jealousy you may see them daily one to be the death and destruction of another, and that in such savage and brutish manner, that in this case they will show no compassion at all. And they seem to be more wise in this behalf than divers of our people for they will by no means match themselves unto an harlot. The liberality of this people hath at all times been exceeding great. And when any travelers may pass through their dry and desert territories, they will never repair to their tents, neither will they themselves travel upon the common highway. And if any caravan or multitude of merchants will pass those deserts, they are bound to pay certain custom unto the prince of the said people, namely, for every camels load a piece of cloth worth a ducat. Upon a time I remember that traveling in the company of certain merchants over the desert by them called Araoan, it was our chance there to meet with the prince of Zanaga; who, after he had received his due custom, invited the said company of merchants, for their recreation, to go and abide with him in his tents four or five days. Howbeit, because his tents were too far out of our way, and for that we should have wandered farther than we thought good, esteeming it more convenient for us to hold on our direct course, we refused his gentle offer, and for his courtesy gave him great thanks. But nor being satisfied therewith, he commanded that our camels should proceed on forward, but the merchants he carried along with him, and gave them very sumptuous entertainment of his place of abode. Where we were no sooner arrived, but this good prince caused camels of all kinds and ostriches, which he had hunted and taken by the way, to be killed for his household provision. Howbeit we requested him not to make such daily slaughters of his camels; affirming moreover, that we never used to eat the flesh of a geld camel, but when all other victuals failed us. Whereunto he answered, that he should deal uncivilly, if he welcomed so worthy and so seldom-seen guests with the killing of small cattle only. Wherefore he wished us to fall to such provision as was set before us. Here might you have seen great plenty of roasted and sodden flesh: their roasted ostriches were brought to the table in wicker platters, being seasoned with sundry kinds of herbs and spices. Their bread made of Mill and panicke was of a most savory and pleasant taste: and always at the end of dinner or supper we had plenty of dates and great store of milk served in. Yea, this bountiful and noble prince, that he might sufficiently show how welcome we were unto him, would together with his nobility always bear us company: howbeit we ever dined and supped apart by our selves. Moreover he caused certain religious and most learned men to come unto our banquet; who, all the time we remained with the said prince, used not to eat any bread at all, but fed only upon flesh and milk. Whereat we being somewhat amazed, the good prince gently told us, that they all were born in such places whereas no kind of grain would grow: howbeit that himself, for the entertainment of strangers, had great plenty of corn laid up in store. Wherefore he bad us to be of good cheer, saying that he would eat only of such things as his own native soil afforded: affirming moreover, that bread was yet in use among them at their feast of passover, and at other feasts also, whereupon they used to offer sacrifice. And thus we remained with him for the space of two days; all which time, what wonderful and magnificent cheer we had made us, would seem incredible to report. But the third day, being desirous to take our leave, the prince accompanied us to that place where we overtook our camels and company sent before. And this I dare most deeply take mine oath on, that we spent the said prince ten times more, than our custom which he received came to. We thought it not amiss here to set down this history, to declare in some sort the courtesy and liberality of the said nation. Neither could the prince aforesaid understand our language nor we his; but all our speech to and fro was made by an interpreter. And this which we have here recorded as touching this nation, is likewise to be understood of the other four nations above mentioned, which are dispersed over the residue of the Numidian deserts.

The Commendable Actions and Virtues of the Africans

Those Arabians which inhabit in Barbarie or upon the coast of the Mediterran sea, are greatly addicted unto the study of good arts and sciences: and those things which concern their law and religion are esteemed by them in the first place. Moreover they have been heretofore most studious of the Mathematics, of Philosophy, and of Astrology: but these arts (as it is aforesaid) were four hundred years ago, utterly destroyed and taken away by the chief professors of their law. The inhabitants of cities do most religiously observe and reverence those things which appertain unto their religion: yea they honor those doctors and priests, of whom they learn their law, as if they were petty-gods. Their Churches they frequent very diligently, to the end they may repeat certain prescript and formal prayers; most superstitiously persuading themselves that the same day wherein they make their prayers, it is not lawful for them to wash certain of their members, when as at other times they will wash their whole bodies. Whereof we will (by Gods help) discourse more at large in the second Book of this present treatise, when we shall fall into the mentioning of *Mahumet* and of his religion. Moreover those which inhabit Barbarie are of great cunning & dexterity for building & for mathematical inventions, which a man may easily conjecture by their artificial works. Most honest people they are, and destitute of all fraud and guile; not only embracing all simplicity and truth, but also practicing the same throughout the whole course of their lives: albeit certain Latin authors, which have written of the same regions, are far otherwise of opinion. Likewise they are most strong and valiant people, especially those which dwell upon the mountains. They keep their covenant most faithfully; insomuch that they had rather die than break promise. No nation in the world is so subject unto jealousy; for they will rather lease their lives, than put up any disgrace in the behalf of their women. So desirous they are of riches and honor, that therein no other people can go beyond them. They travel in a manner over the whole world to exercise traffic. For they are continually to be seen in Aegypt, in Aethiopia, in Arabia, Persia, India, and Turkie: and whithersoever they go, they are most honorably esteemed of: for none of them will possess any art, unless he hath attained unto great exactness and perfection therein. They have always been much delighted with all kind of civility and modest behavior: and it is accounted heinous among them for any man to utter in company, any bawdy or unseemly word. They have always in mind this sentence of a grave author; Give place to thy superior. If any youth in presence of his father, his uncle, or any other of his kindred, doth sing or talk aught of love matters, he is deemed to be worthy of grievous punishment. Whatsoever lad or youth there lighteth by chance into any company which discourseth of love, no sooner heareth nor understandeth what their talk tendeth unto, but immediately he withdraweth himself from among them. These are the things which we thought most worthy of relation as concerning the civility, humanity, and upright dealing of the Barbarians: let us now proceed unto the residue. Those Arabians which dwell in tents, that is to say, which bring up cattle, are of a more liberal and civil disposition: to wit, they are in their kind as devout, valiant, patient, courteous, hospitable, and as honest in life and conversation as any other people. They be most faithful observers of their word and promise; insomuch that the people, which before we said to dwell in the mountains, are greatly stirred up with emulation of their virtues. Howbeit the said mountainers, both for learning, for virtue, and for religion, are thought much inferior to the Numidians, albeit they have little or no knowledge at all in natural philosophy. They are reported likewise to be most skilful warriors, to be valiant, and exceeding lovers and practicers of all humanity. Also, the Moors and Arabians inhabiting Libya are somewhat civil of behavior, being plain dealers, void of dissimulation, favorable to strangers, and lovers of simplicity. Those which we before named white, or tawny Moors, are steadfast in friendship: as likewise, they indifferently and favorably esteem of other nations: and wholly endeavor themselves in this one thing, namely, that they may lead a most pleasant and jocund life. Moreover they maintain most learned professors of liberal arts, and such men are most devout in their religion. Neither is there any people in all Africa that lead a more happy and honorable life.

G. K. Hunter (b. 1920)
FROM *"OTHELLO AND COLOR PREJUDICE"*   1978

In attempting to determine Shakespeare's motives in portraying Othello as a black Moor, G. K. Hunter, a professor at Yale University, has examined the evidence suggesting the associations an Elizabethan audience would have made with the color black. In this excerpt he establishes the common color prejudice that would have been present in Shakespeare's audience and implies that Shakespeare consciously worked against it.

It is generally admitted today that Shakespeare was a practical man of the theater: however careless he may have been about maintaining consistency for the exact *reader* of his plays, he was not likely to introduce a theatrical novelty which would only puzzle his audience; it does not seem wise, therefore, to dismiss his theatrical innovations as if they were unintentional. The blackness of Othello is a case in point. Shakespeare largely modified the story he took over from Cinthio: he made a tragic hero out of Cinthio's passionate and bloody lover; he gave him a royal origin, a Christian baptism, a romantic *bravura* of manner, and, most impor-

[Read as the British Academy Shakespeare Lecture, 19 April 1967. First published in *The Proceedings of the British Academy*, liii (1967).]

tant of all, an orotund magnificence of diction. Yet, changing all this, he did not change his color and so produced a daring theatrical novelty — a black hero for a white community — a novelty which remains too daring for many recent theatrical audiences. Shakespeare cannot merely have carried over the color of Othello by being too lazy or too uninterested to meddle with it; for no actor, spending the time in "blacking-up," and hence no producer, could be indifferent to such an innovation, especially in that age, devoted to "imitation" and hostile to "originality." In fact, the repeated references to Othello's color in the play and the wider net of images of dark and light spread across the diction, show that Shakespeare was not only not unaware of the implication of his hero's color but was indeed intensely aware of it as one of the primary factors in his play.[1] I am therefore assuming in this lecture that the blackness of Othello has a theatrical purpose, and I intend to try to suggest what it was possible for that purpose to have been.

Shakespeare intended his hero to be a black man — that much I take for granted;[2] what is unknown is what the idea of a black man suggested to Shakespeare, and what reaction the appearance of a black man on the stage was calculated to produce. It is fairly certain, however, that some modern reactions are not likely to have been shared by the Elizabethans. The modern theater-going European intellectual, with a background of cultivated superiority to "color problems" in other continents, would often choose to regard Othello as a fellow man and to watch the story — which could so easily be reduced to its headline level: "sheltered white girl errs: said, 'Color does not matter' "— with a sense of freedom from such prejudices. But this lofty fair-mindedness may be too lofty for Shakespeare's play and not take the European any nearer the Othello of Shakespeare than the lady from Maryland quoted in the Furness New Variorum edition: "In studying the play of *Othello,* I have always *imagined* its hero a white man." Both views, that the color of Othello does not matter and that it matters too much to be tolerable, err, I suggest, by oversimplifying. Shakespeare was clearly deliberate in keeping Othello's color; and it is obvious that he counted on some positive audience reaction to this color; but it is equally obvious that he did not wish the audience to dismiss Othello as a stereotype.[. . .]

Modern rationalizations about "color" tend to be different from those of the Middle Ages and Renaissance. We are powerfully aware of the relativism of viewpoints; we distinguish easily between different racial cultures; and explicit arguments about the mingling of the races usually begin at the economic and social level and only move to questions of God's providence at the lunatic fringe.

The Elizabethans also had a powerful sense of the economic threat posed by the foreign groups they had daily contact with — Flemings or Frenchmen — but they had little or no continuous contact with "Moors" and no sense of economic threat from them. This did not mean, however, that they had no racial or color prejudice. They had, to start with, the basic common man's attitude that all foreigners are curious and inferior — the more foreign the more inferior, in the sense of the proverb quoted by Purchas: "Three Moors to a Portuguese; three Portuguese to an Englishman."[3] They had also the basic and ancient sense that black is the color of

[1]See R. B. Heilman, "More Fair Than Black: Light and Dark in *Othello,*" *Essays in Criticism,* i (1951), 313–35.

[2]I ignore the many treatises devoted to proving that he was of tawny or sunburnt color. These are, however, very worthy of study, as documents of prejudice.[. . .]

[3]See M. P. Tilley, *A Dictionary of Proverbs* (1950), M. 1132.

sin and death, "the badge of hell, the hue of dungeons, and the school of night" (as Shakespeare himself says).[4] This supposition is found all over the world (even in darkest Africa)[5] from the earliest to the latest times; which suggests a response to the basic antinomy of day and night. Certainly in the West there is a continuous and documented cultural tradition depending on it.[6][. . .]

An extreme example of this status of the Moor appears in the report of the pageant for the baptism of Prince Henry in 1594. It had been arranged that a lion should pull the triumphal car; but the lion could not be used, so a Moor was substituted.[7]

Renaissance scepticism and the voyages of discovery might seem, at first sight, to have destroyed the ignorance on which such thoughtless equations of black men and devils depended. But this does not prove to have been so. The voyagers brought back some accurate reports of black and heathen; but they often saw, or said they saw, what they expected to see — the marvels of the East.[8] In any case the vocabulary at their disposal frustrated any attempt at scientific discrimination. The world was still seen largely, in terms of vocabulary, as a network of religious names. The word "Moor" had no clear racial status. Elizabethan authors describe "Moors" as existing all over the globe. We hear of "Mores of Malabar" from Spenser,[9] of Moors in Malacca from James Lancaster,[10] of Moors in Guinea from Eden,[11] of Moors in Ethiopia from Lodge,[12] of Moors in Fukien from Willes,[13] of Moors in America from Marlowe[14] and sundry others. There seem to be Moors everywhere; but only everywhere, we should note, in that outer circuit of non-Christian lands where the saving grace of Jerusalem is weakest in its whitening power. Throughout the Elizabethan period there seems to remain considerable confusion whether the Moor is a human being or a monster. In the "plat" of the perished play of *Tamar Cam* (1592) we are told of an entry of "Tartars, Geates, Amozins, Nagars, ollive cullord moores, Caniballs, Hermophrodites, Pigmies," etc. — a characteristic medley.[15] In *Volpone* we are given a list of the undesirables

---

[4]*Love's Labour's Lost*, IV, III, 250 f.

[5]See V. W. Turner, "Colour Classification in Ndembu Ritual," *Anthropological Approaches to the Study of Religion*, ed. M. Banton (1966); Arthur Leib, "The Mystical Significance of Colours in . . . Madagascar," *Folk-lore*, lvii (1946), 128–33; Joan Westcott, "The Sculpture and Myths of Eshu-Elegba, the Yoruba Trickster," *Africa*, xxxii (1962).

[6]See E. Hoffman-Krayer and H. Bächtold-Stäubli, *Handwörterbuch des deutschen Aberglaubens* [1927], s.v. Schwartz.

[7]See *A True Reportary of the Baptisme of Frederik Henry, Prince of Scotland* (1594) (S.T.C. 13163).

[8]See R. Wittkower, "Marvels of the East," *Journal of the Warburg and Courtauld Institutes*, v (1942), 159–97.[. . .]

[9]*Faerie Queene*, VI, VII, 43.

[10]R. Hakluyt, *Principal Navigations* (Glasgow, 1903–1905 edition), vi. 399.

[11]Peter Martyr Anglerius, tr. R. Eden, *The History of Travel* (1577), fl. 348v.

[12]*Works* (Hunterian Society), ii. 52.

[13]Hakluyt, vi. 321 (where it is quite clear that "Moorish" means "Mahomedan."

[14]*Doctor Faustus* (*Works*, ed. C. F. Tucker Brooke, p. 150). Compare the "black Indians" in A. Brewer's *The Lovesick King* (Bang's Materialien [1907], 952 f.) and in B. Googe's *The Popish Kingdom* (translated from H. Kirchmeyer) (1570) — 1880 ed., p. 39 — and the "African Indians" in *Sir Thomas Stukeley* (1596) — Tudor Facsimile Texts, 2169.

[15]*Henslowe Papers*, ed. W. W. Greg (1907), p. 148. Compare the "Negro-Tartars" in *Gesta Grayorum* (M.S.R. 46) and the "Negarian Tartars" (ibid. 52).

that Volpone has coupled with to produce his Fool, Dwarf, and Hermaphrodite. The supposed parents are described as

> beggars,
> Gipsies and Jews and black-moors.[16]

The geographical vagueness of these authors does not mean, however, that they are vague in their sense of an antithetical relationship between "Moors" (wherever they live) and civilized white Christians. The first meaning given to the word "Moor" in *O.E.D.* is "Mahomedan" (with examples up to 1629); but in many of the examples this seems to mean no more than "infidel," non-Christian. The pressure that defines the word is more negative than positive. Like *Barbarian* and *Gentile* (or *Wog*) it was a word for "people not like us,"[17] so signaled by color. The word *Gentile* itself had still the religious sense of *Pagan,* and the combined phrase "Moors and Gentiles" is used regularly to represent the religious gamut of non-Christian possibilities (see *O.E.D.* for examples). Similarly, *Barbary* was not simply a place in Africa, but also the unclearly located home of Barbarism, as in Chaucer (Franklin's Tale, 1451, Man of Law's Tale, 183).

I have suggested above that the discoveries of the voyagers contributed little to Renaissance scientific or nontheological explanations of the world. And this was particularly true of the problems raised by the black-skinned races. No scientific explanation of black skins had ever been achieved, though doctors had long disputed it. Lodovicus Caelius Rhodiginus in his *Lectionum Antiquarum libri XXX* (1620) can cite column after column of authorities; but all without conclusive answers. We hear among the latest reports of Africa collected in T. Astley's *New General Collection of Voyages* (1745) that the blackness of the Negro is "a Topic that has given Rise to numberless Conjectures and great Disputes among the Learned in Europe" (ii, 269). Sir Thomas Browne in three essays in his *Pseudodoxia Epidemica* (VI, x–xii) not only declared that the subject was "amply and satisfactorily discussed as we know by no man" but proceeded to remedy this by way of amplitude rather than satisfactoriness. The theological explanation was left in possession of the field. Adam and Eve, it was assumed, were white; it follows that the creation of the black races can only be ascribed to some subsequent *fiat.* The two favorite possibilities were the cursing of Cain and the cursing of Ham or Cham and his posterity — and sometimes these two were assumed to be different expressions of the same event; at least one might allege, with Sir Walter Ralegh, that "the sonnes of Cham did possesse the vices of the sonnes of Cain."[18] The Cham explanation had the great advantage that "the threefold world" of tradition could be described in terms of the three sons of Noah — Japhet having produced the Europeans, Shem the Asiatics, while the posterity of Ham occupied Africa, or, in a more sophisticated version, "the Meridionall or southern partes of the world both in Asia and Africa"[19] — sophisticated, we should notice, without altering the basic theological assumption that Cham's posterity were banished to the most uncomfortable part of the globe, and a foretaste of the Hell to come. This geographical

[16]Ben Jonson, *Volpone,* I, v, 44 f.
[17]So that "Wogs begin at Calais," etc.
[18]*The History of the World,* I, VI, 2.
[19]A. Willet, *Hexapla in Genesin* (1605), p. 119.

assumption fitted in with the wisdom that the etymological doctors had in the Middle Ages been able to glean from the name *Ham* — defined as "*Cham: calidus, et ipse ex praesagio futuri cognominatus est. Posteritas enim eius eam terrae partem possedit quae vicino sole calentior est.*"[20] When this is linked to the other point made in relation to the Cham story — that his posterity were cursed to be slaves[21] — one can see how conveniently and plausibly such a view fitted the facts and desires found in the early navigators. Azurara, the chronicler of Prince Henry the Navigator's voyages, tells us that it was natural to find blackamoors as the slaves of lighter skinned men:

> these blacks were Moors (i.e. Mahomedans) like the others, though their slaves, in accordance with ancient custom which I believe to have been because of the curse which, after the Deluge, Noah laid upon his son Cain [*sic*], cursing him in this way: that his race should be subject to all the other races in the world. And from his race these blacks are descended.[22]

The qualities of the "Moors" who appear on the Elizabethan stage are hardly at all affected by Elizabethan knowledge of real Moors from real geographical locations, and, given the literary modes available, this is hardly surprising. It is true that the first important Moor-role — that of Muly Hamet in Peele's *The Battle of Alcazar* (c. 1589) — tells the story of a real man (with whom Queen Elizabeth had a treaty) in a real historical situation. But the dramatic focus that Peele manages to give to his Moorish character is largely dependent on the devil and underworld associations he can suggest for him — making him call up "Fiends, Fairies, hags that fight in beds of steel" and causing him to show more acquaintance with the geography of hell than with that of Africa. Aaron in *Titus Andronicus* is liberated from even such slender ties as associate Muly Hamet with geography. Aaron is in the play as the representative of a world of generalized barbarism, which is Gothic in Tamora and Moorish in Aaron, and unfocused in both. The purpose of the play is served by a general opposition between Roman order and Barbarian disorder. Shakespeare has the doubtful distinction of making explicit here (perhaps for the first time in English literature) the projection of black wickedness in terms of negro sexuality. The relationship between Tamora and Aaron is meant, clearly enough, to shock our normal sensibilities and their black baby is present as an emblem of disorder. In this respect, as in most others, Eleazer in *Lust's Dominion* (c. 1600) — the third pre-*Othello* stage-Moor — is copied from Aaron. The location of this play (Spain) gives a historically plausible excuse to present the devil in his favorite human form — "that of a Negro or Moor," but does not really use the locale to establish any racial points.

These characters provide the dominant images that must have been present in the minds of Shakespeare's original audience when they entered the Globe to see a play called *The Moor of Venice* — an expectation of pagan devilry set against white Christian civilization — excessive civilization perhaps in Venice, but civilization at least "like us." Even those who knew Cinthio's story of the Moor of Venice could not have had very different expectations, which may be summed up from the

---

[20] Isidore of Seville, *Etymologiae*, VII, VI, 17. (*Patrologia Latina*, lxxxii, col. 276.)
[21] See St Ambrose, *Comment. in epist. ad Philippenses* (*P.L.* xvii, col. 432). [. . .]
[22] *Discovery and Conquest of Guinea* (Hakluyt Society, XCV [1896], 54).

story told by Bandello (III, XXI) in which a master beats his Moorish servant, and the servant in revenge rapes and murders his wife and children.[23] Bandello draws an illuminating moral:

> By this I intend it to appear that a man should not be served by this sort of slave; for they are seldom found faithful, and at best they are full of filth, unclean, and stink all the time like goats. But all this is as nothing put beside the savage cruelty that reigns in them.

It is in such terms that the play opens. We hear from men like us of a man not like us, of "his Moorship," "the Moor," "the thick-lips," "an old black ram," "a Barbary horse," "the devil," of "the gross clasps of a lascivious Moor." The sexual fear and disgust that lie behind so much racial prejudice are exposed for our derisive expectations to fasten upon them. And we are at this point bound to agree with these valuations, for no alternative view is revealed. There is, of course, a certain comic *brio* which helps to distance the whole situation, and neither Brabantio, nor Iago nor Roderigo can wholly command our identification. None the less we are drawn on to await the entry of a traditional Moor figure, the kind of person we came to the theatre expecting to find.

When the second scene begins, however, it is clear that Shakespeare is bent to ends other than the fulfilment of these expectations. The Iago/Roderigo relationship of I, i, is repeated in the Iago/Othello relationship of the opening of I, II; but Othello's response to the real-seeming circumstance with which Iago lards his discourse is very different from the hungrily self-absorbed questionings of Roderigo. Othello draws on an inward certainty about himself, a radiant clarity about his own well-founded moral position. This is no "lascivious Moor," but a great Christian gentleman, against whom Iago's insinuations break like water against granite. Not only is Othello a Christian, moreover; he is the leader of Christendom in the last and highest sense in which Christendom existed as a viable entity, crusading against the "black pagans." He is to defend Cyprus against the Turk, "hellish horseleaches of Christian blood."[24] It was the fall of Cyprus which produced the alliance of Lepanto, and we should associate Othello with the emotion that Europe continued to feel — till well after the date of *Othello* — about that victory and about Don John of Austria.

Shakespeare has presented to us a traditional view of what Moors are like, i.e., gross, disgusting, inferior, carrying the symbol of their damnation on their skin; and has caught our overeasy assent to such assumptions in the grip of a guilt which associates us and our assent with the white man representative of such views in the play — Iago. Othello acquires the glamour of an innocent man that *we* have wronged, and an admiration stronger than he could have achieved by virtue plainly represented:

> . . . as these black masks
> Proclaim an enshield beauty ten times louder
> Than beauty could, displayed.

[23]M. Bandello, *Novelle,* Book III, novel xxi, derived from Pontanus (*Opera, i, 25, b*), and translated by F. Belleforest, *Histoires tragiques.* The story was apparently Englished in ballad form, in 1569, 1570, and again in 1624, 1675. See E. Hyder Rollins, "Analytical Index" (*Studies in Philology,* xxi [1924]), item 2542: "a strange petyful novell Dyscoursynge of a noble Lorde and his lady with thayre ij children executed by a blacke morryon."

[24]Hakluyt, *Principal Navigations* (1903–5 ed.), V. 122.

(Is it an accident that Shakespeare wrote these lines from *Measure for Measure* in approximately the same year as he wrote *Othello*?) Iago is a "civilized" man; but where, for the "inferior" Othello, appearance and reality, statement and truth are linked indissolubly, civilization for Iago consists largely of a capacity to manipulate appearances and probabilities:

> For when my outward action doth demonstrate
> The native act and figure of my heart
> In compliment extern, 'tis not long after
> But I will wear my heart upon my sleeve
> For daws to peck at: I am not what I am.

Othello may be "the devil" in appearance: but it is the "fair" Iago who gives birth to the dark realities of sin and death in the play:

> It is engender'd. Hell and night
> Must bring this monstrous birth to the world's light

The relationship between these two is developed in terms of appearance and reality. Othello controls the reality of action; Iago the "appearance" of talk about action; Iago the Italian is isolated (even from his wife), envious, enigmatic (even to himself), self-centered; Othello the "extravagant and wheeling stranger" is surrounded and protected by a network of duties, obligations, esteems, pious to his father-in-law, deferential to his superiors, kind to his subordinates, loving to his wife. To sum up, assuming that *soul* is reality and *body* is appearance, we may say that Iago is the white man with the black soul while Othello is the black man with the white soul. Long before Blake's little black boy had said

> I am black, but oh my soul is white.
> White as an angel is the English child,
> But I am black as if bereaved of light.

and before Kipling's Gunga Din:

> An' for all 'is dirty 'ide
> 'E was white, clear white inside . . .
> You're a better man than I am, Gunga Din!

Othello had represented the guilty awareness of Europe that the "foreigner type" is only the type we do not know, whose foreignness vanishes when we have better acquaintance; that the prejudicial foreign appearance may conceal a vision of truth, as Brabantio is told:

> If virtue no delighted beauty lack
> Your son-in-law is far more fair than black.

This reality of fairness in Othello provides a principal function for Desdemona in the play. Her love is of a spiritual intensity, of a strong simplicity equal to that of Othello himself, and pierces without effort beyond appearance, into reality:

> I saw Othello's visage in his mind.

Her love is a daring act of faith, beyond reason or social propriety. Like Beauty in the fairytale she denies the beastly (or devilish) appearance to proclaim her allegiance to the invisible reality. And she does so throughout the play, even when the case for the appearance seems most strong and when Iago's power over appearances rides highest. Even when on the point of death at Othello's hands, she gives testimony to her faith (martyr in the true sense of the word):

> Commend me to my *kind* lord.

Othello is then a play which manipulates our sympathies, supposing that we will have brought to the theater a set of careless assumptions about "Moors." It assumes also that we will find it easy to abandon these as the play brings them into focus and identifies them with Iago, draws its elaborate distinction between the external appearance of devilishness and the inner reality.

Margaret Webster (1905–1972)
SHAKESPEARE WITHOUT TEARS   *1942*

Margaret Webster directed the notable Broadway performance of Othello *with Paul Robeson in 1943–1944. In this excerpt from her memoirs, she comments on the question of race and its importance to the play. She focuses on Desdemona and her motives in marrying a black man whom her father could not accept. She connects this important detail to Othello's "acceptance of the possibility of Desdemona's infidelity."*

The question of Othello's race is of paramount importance to the play. There has been much controversy as to Shakespeare's intention. It is improbable that he troubled himself greatly with ethnological exactness. The Moor, to an Elizabethan, was a blackamoor, an African, an Ethiopian. Shakespeare's other Moor, Aaron, in *Titus Andronicus,* is specifically black; he has thick lips and a fleece of woolly hair. The Prince of Morocco in *The Merchant of Venice* bears "the shadowed livery of the burnished sun," and even Portia recoils from his "complexion" which he himself is at great pains to excuse.

Othello is repeatedly described, both by himself and others, as black; not pale beige, but black; and for a century and a half after the play's first presentation he was so represented on the stage. But after this the close consideration of nice minds began to discern something not quite ladylike about Desdemona's marrying a black man with thick lips. They cannot have been more horrified than Brabantio, her father, who thought that only witchcraft could have caused "nature so preposterously to err," or more convinced of the disastrous outcome of such a match than Iago, who looked upon it as nothing but a "frail vow between an erring Barbarian and a supersubtle Venetian," and declared, with his invincible cynicism, that "when she is sated with his body, she will find the error of her choice: She must have change; she must!"

It is very apparent, and vital to the play, that Othello himself was very conscious of these same considerations and quiveringly aware of what the judgment of the world would be upon his marriage. It is one of the most potent factors in his acceptance of the possibility of Desdemona's infidelity. And she herself loses much in the quality of her steadfastness and courage if it be supposed that she simply married against her father's wishes a man who chanced to be a little darker than his fellows, instead of daring a marriage which would cause universal condemnation among

Ron Canada as Iago and Patrick Stewart as Othello, in the Shakespeare Theater's 1997–1998 production of *Othello* in Washington, D.C., directed by Jude Kelly. In this version Stewart played Othello with an all-black cast.

the ladies of polite society. To scamp this consideration in the play is to deprive Othello of his greatest weakness, Desdemona of her highest strength, Iago of his skill and judgment, Emilia of a powerful factor in her behavior both to her master and her mistress, and Venice itself of an arrogance in toleration which was one of the principal hallmarks of its civilization — a civilization which frames, first and last, the soaring emotions of the play.

After these three tragedies, Shakespeare will never again take us into so passion-tossed a world, never set his actors to release themselves so fully from the normal restraints of polite behavior, never pound his audience into submission by the relentless power of words. He will give us a jealous man in Leontes, an ambitious one in Octavius, an embittered outcast in Timon, but it will not be the sacrificial jealousy of Othello, the haunted ambition of Macbeth, or the madness of Lear. Nothing that happens in the later plays will carry us beyond the sphere where reason is still a comfortable guide. Nor will man ever again cry with such anguish to the stars to shield him from the unbearable responsibility of the world he has fashioned. The theatre will revert to its normal self, its walls solid and comfortably bounding the two hours' traffic of make-believe. There will be plenty of technical problems to be faced. *Antony and Cleopatra* especially will call for a width and range of vision; many of the plays to come will need adroit and lavish handling. But never again will the hearts of players and audience be so swept with the mystery of life and the bitter release of death.

Peter Marks
REVIEW OF PATRICK STEWART AS OTHELLO   *1997*

Patrick Stewart is probably best known for his role as Jean-Luc Picard on Star Trek, *but before that he was with the Royal Shakespeare Company in England and has acted in many Shakespeare plays. This review finds him as a white Othello in an all-black production, so that the racial roles are reversed. Marks, surprisingly, finds that such an approach downplays the racial issues.*

In the past, white actors who played Othello inevitably became obsessed with makeup. "The whole thing will be in the lips and the color," Laurence Olivier observed in a 1964 *Life* magazine interview, in the midst of preparing his legendary portrayal. "I'll use just a little tiny touch of lake and a lot more brown and a little mauve."

The rules over the centuries for Caucasians contriving Othello's blackness were, by the standard of modern sensibilities, comically rigid: "A tawny tinge is now the color used for the gallant Moor," instructed an 1827 book on theater makeup. Today, of course, an Othello in blackface might justifiably be subject to catcalls. So is there any way a white performer can comfortably be cast in the part?

Patrick Stewart and the British director Jude Kelly have come upon one: eliminate the makeup altogether. In their kinetic, earth-toned, eye-filling production at the Shakespeare Theater here, Othello, played by Mr. Stewart, is white. The Venetians, from noble Cassio to twisted Iago to doomed Desdemona, are black. And in the race reversing, the company seeks to shatter stereotypes and remind playgoers of the endlessly adaptive nature of Shakespeare's exploration of otherness.

Thanks to some moving and polished performances by Teagle F. Bougere as Cassio, Franchelle Stewart Dorn as Emilia, Patrice Johnson as Desdemona, and, above all, to Mr. Stewart's captivating, devastatingly human portrayal, this *Othello* does not reveal itself as a curiosity but as a fascinating study of the fragile border between possessive love and obliterating paranoia.

Interestingly, the racial turning of the tables does not tilt the play toward ham-handed irony; rather, it tends to take the racial issue off the table. Though a few glaring casting problems, having more to do with technique than philosophy, deny the production the glowing mark of distinction it might have earned, the overall sensitivity and quality of the effort is ample justification for the risks its creators took.

The vigorous, sinewy Mr. Stewart, wearing a hoop earring and a serpentine tattoo on the back of his shaved head, is Ms. Kelly's chief insurance that her version never seems a mere trick. In this modern-dress production, she places him at the helm of a mercenary force that occupies Cyprus, rendered strikingly by Robert Innes Hopkins as a bomb-strafed fortress. (A romantic score by Michael Ward adds Italianate warmth.) The most controversial use of color in the play, however, may be in Mr. Hopkins's costumes: the Venetians' plum-colored fatigues (the Cypriots wear tangerine) make the actors look like members of a United Nations peacekeeping unit as outfitted by Banana Republic.

Othello himself is often played as a towering man of honor, a virtual stone figure on a pedestal. Untethered in other important ways from the role's history, Mr. Stewart finds in his Othello a charmed soldier of fortune more interested in making love than war. There is sigh-inducing passion in his poetic recall of how he wooed Desdemona with words. "She loved me for the dangers I had passed / And I loved her that she did pity them," he says, and it's abundantly clear in Mr. Stewart's rapturous gaze that this is the conquest he most highly treasures.

The speech is delivered during an early scene in which Othello is engaged by Venice's noblemen to rout the Turks from Cyprus; it's also one of the moments in which the play's racial tensions are most apparent. Brabantio, Desdemona's father (Darrell Carey), opposes his daughter's secret marriage, and he makes his objections plain.

In traditional productions, surrounded by a roomful of white faces, Othello seems a figure of strength and sympathy. But when Othello is a white military leader — what more recognizable authority figure exists in Western culture? — it's hard to feel particularly sorry for him. It's an instance in which race reversal does not jibe with an audience's sense of the way the world beyond the theater works.

More troublesome in this production, however, is the disappointingly wan battle of wills between Othello and his nemesis, Iago. The villainous underling who flatly announces, "I hate the Moor," is in some ways the play's most accessible character. He speaks to the audience constantly; we watch the drama unfold, in a sense, over his shoulder. Ms. Kelly's notion is an Iago who is a bitterly frustrated minor officer, passed over for promotions and even asked, humiliatingly, to carry Othello's luggage ashore.

But Ron Canada provides a dishearteningly wooden Iago, which robs his scenes with Mr. Stewart of their delicious cat-and-mouse aspect. The performance also unbalances Iago's encounters with Roderigo (Jimonn Cole), the jealous suitor he manipulates. Mr. Cole goes way over the top in his sniveling fool of a Roderigo, in what seems a vain attempt to energize his exchanges with Mr. Canada.

The tonic in this production comes in its portrayal of domestic disintegration. Ms. Johnson and Mr. Stewart have a winsome rapport that makes their marriage a true coupling, and until her fiery death scene, Ms. Dorn, as Iago's mate, conveys the dead-eyed complacency of a battered doormat. Mr. Stewart is never anything less than uncanny in his psychological portrait: it's like watching an autopsy on human feeling. The precise moment at which Iago first plants doubt about Desdemona's constancy registers on Mr. Stewart's intense features; you sense the tragic events to follow in the terrifying blink of his eye.

This fine actor, so magnetic a Prospero in George Wolfe's 1995 *Tempest*, seems to get better and better. Next time around, it might be even more rewarding to see his Iago.

Ben Jonson

Known primarily as a writer of comedies such as *Every Man in His Humor* (1598) and *Every Man out of His Humor* (1599) in the reign of Elizabeth I, Jonson's most interesting plays were performed during the reign (called the Jacobean period) of her successor, King James I. *Volpone* (1606) and *The Alchemist* (1610) stand today as Jonson's most often produced plays. Both are broad comedies: *Volpone* plays on the foxiness of a dying man who is anxious to see which of his heirs is worthy, and *The Alchemist* is a satire on the wiliness of con men who pretend to know how to transmute base metal into gold. All of these plays were highly regarded in Jacobean times. In addition to his comedies, Jonson's tragedies *Sejanus* (1603) and *Catiline* (1611) earned him the description of "best in tragedy" from a contemporary who maintained a diary devoted to his experiences in the theater.

Jonson led an exciting life. Born after his father died, he was placed in the Westminster School at the expense of its master, William Camden, author of the famous survey *Britannia*. There Jonson learned Latin and Greek but he himself said that instead of attending a university, he practiced his trade. Because Jonson's stepfather was a bricklayer, it has been assumed that Jonson learned that trade. He eventually grew tired of bricklaying and managed to get a job as an actor. In 1598, while a member of Philip Henslowe's theater, he killed a fellow actor in a brawl. He claimed self-defense and was granted "benefit of clergy," which was accorded those who could read and translate a Latin passage, but as punishment he carried a brand on his thumb from Tyburn, the place of execution and punishment, for the rest of his life.

For Jonson the stage was a way of making a living. He aspired to be a pure poet and was accorded great honor in his lifetime by other poets. But he could not, even with the patronage of important noblemen, eke out a sufficient living writing only poetry. Jonson was imprisoned in Elizabeth's reign for writing an offensive play, *The Isle of Dogs* (1597), and in the early years of King James's reign, which began on March 24, 1603, play writing continued to be dangerous. Toward the end of 1605, Jonson teamed with George Chapman and William Marston to write *Eastward Ho!,* a comedy that ridiculed the Scots (James I was a Scot). Jonson and Chapman were imprisoned, but Jonson eventually contacted enough important people to secure his release, probably in October, claiming that the few offensive lines had been written by Marston, who had fled London to avoid prison. Then in November the great Gunpowder Plot — remembered today with bonfires on November 5, Guy Fawkes Day — cast a dangerous shadow over him. Led by the Catholic conspirator Guy Fawkes, the Gunpowder Plot was a plan to kill the king, his advisors, and all members of the hierarchy of the Church and Parliament. Guy Fawkes's use of the pseudonym John Johnson, together with Jonson's conversion to Catholicism, may have resulted in the playwright's becoming a suspect. Luckily, he was well known in James's court and was able to demonstrate his loyalty and innocence.

For most of his life Jonson made his living by writing for the public stage, but he was by no means always successful. Although many of his plays are today regarded as among the most important of the late Renaissance, tastes changed during his lifetime, and by the end of his life he found himself no longer in vogue.

Jonson won considerable acclaim as a writer in the court of James I and Queen Anne. He composed entertainments and masques designed to be associated with important state occasions. The masque was a dramatic form that enjoyed great popularity for close to a century and a half. It was restricted to the entertainment and participation of royalty and courtiers. As its name implies, characters were sometimes masked to represent abstract ideas such as Blackness or Beauty or mythic characters such as Albion, an allegory for England itself.

Inigo Jones (1573–1652), brought to court by Queen Anne, collaborated with Jonson to make the Jacobean masque a dazzling spectacle. Jones was a painter and architect who had traveled abroad and returned to England with members of Anne's court when Anne ascended the British throne. He was responsible for designing costumes, scenery, special effects, and lighting. He introduced Italian theater machinery and techniques into his entertainments. The Jacobean masque was elaborate, sensational, and so enormously expensive that it is said to have contributed to the impoverishment of the crown inherited by James's successor, Charles I.

THE MASQUE OF BLACKNESS

Apparently dissatisfied with Samuel Daniel, the poet and writer who had produced the first masque for her court, Queen Anne turned to Ben Jonson and asked him to create a masque in which she and some of her court ladies could paint themselves black and pretend to be Moors. The source for her inspiration is unclear, but she may have encountered African emissaries in London or otherwise been aware of the presence of numerous Africans in London. During the later years of her reign, Queen Elizabeth felt there were too many black Africans in London and ordered them sent abroad. James does not seem to have followed her example.

The Masque of Blackness was the first of Ben Jonson's many masques. It was performed January 6, 1605, in the same theater and around the same time as Othello. Inigo Jones's machinery impressed the audience, which included foreign emissaries, such as the Venetian and Spanish ambassadors. Sir Dudley Carleton, present at the performance, was not pleased that the Queen and her attendants had painted themselves black. He feared that kissing the hands of the masquers might blacken his face. He may have been familiar with earlier royal entertainments in which black characters were represented with long black gloves and black cloth masks.

Jonson's opening description of the setting is extensive because in masques the costumes and imaginative figures took on great importance. But his text is also ingenious. Given the assignment to produce a masque for blackamoors, he invented the conceit that "the Ethiops were as fair / As other dames, now black with black despair." Hence, the narrative moves these figures toward recovering their original brightness by seeking a nation whose name ends in *"-tania"* and residing there for thirteen days. Their journey takes them to Mauretania, Lusitania, and Aquitania, but none of those nations can avail them. Finally, Britannia fulfills their desire, and the masque ends with the prospect of their remaining another twelve nights.

The daughters of Niger are described as beautiful women, all the more beautiful because of their black skin and hair, but in Jonson's masque they encounter a Eurocentric point of view expressed by "some few / Poor brainsick men" who convince them that they should be "fair." The word "fair" in Elizabethan English means primarily beautiful, but it also means light in color. The point of the masque is to emphasize the beauty of the daughters (who are played by the Queen and her attendants) and to restore them to their original fairness.

One important feature of the masque is the representation of figures in an allegorical fashion. In other words, Oceanus is not a psychologically real character but a figure who represents the ocean. Niger is the river, Aethiopia the nation. All the characters in the masque follow this pattern. When the Queen and her attendants dance (line 302), they assume allegorical identities. The Queen is Euphoris, or Happiness, and her symbol is a "golden tree laden with fruit." The dance that the Queen and her attendants perform is the highlight of the masque, and the courtiers who participated felt it to be a joyful and exciting occasion.

The Masque of Blackness, like all Jacobean masques, was a multimedia event, like a modern "happening." The lines of dialogue are carefully crafted, and the narrative suitably dramatic. But it is the music, the song, the dance, and the machinery of the setting — the rocking and moving seashell and the sudden appearances of characters — that make the masque successful and impressive. As far as we know, masques such as this were not performed more than once or twice, partly because of expense and partly because of the demand for novelty in a relatively small court.

The speaking characters were played by professional actors, but all the other roles were drawn from the court. That way the poetry could be heard and the drama maintained without stressing the courtiers, who would have had, with very few exceptions, no aspirations toward the stage.

The Masque of Blackness in Performance

Since the masque is preeminently a performance piece, we must credit the spectacle over the poetry and dialogue. Even Jonson, early in his collaboration, pays homage to Inigo Jones's innovations in the masque. Sir Dudley Carleton, who was present at the performance in the old banqueting house, had much to say about it. His comments help us imagine the scene:

> On Twelfth-Day . . . at night, we had the Queen's masque in the Banqueting House, or rather her pageant. There was a great engine at the lower end of the room, which had motion, and in it were the images of sea horses, with other terrible fishes, which were ridden by Moors; the indecorum was, that there was all fish and no water. At the further end was a great shell in the form of a scallop, wherein were four seats; on

Inigo Jones, Costume for a Nymph, Daughter of Niger. Jonson described the masquers: "The attire of [the] *Masquers* was alike, in all, without difference: the colors, *azure,* and *silver*; (their hair thick, and curled upright in tresses, like *Pyramids*), but returned on the top with a scroll and antique dressing of feathers, and jewels interlaced with ropes of pearl. And, for the front, ear, neck, and wrists, the ornament was of the most choice and orient pearl; best setting off from the black."

the lowest sat the Queen with my lady Bedford; on the rest were placed the ladies . . . their apparel was rich, but too courtesan-like for such great ones. Instead of vizards, their faces, and arms up to elbows, were painted black, which was disguise sufficient, for they were hard to be known; *but it became them nothing so well as their own red and white, and you cannot imagine a more ugly sight than a troop of lean-cheeked Moors.* The Spanish and Venetian Ambassadors were both present, and sat by the King in state; at which Monsieur Beaumont [the French ambassador] quarrels so extremely that he saith the whole court is Spanish . . . the night's work was concluded with a banquet in the great chamber, which was so seriously assaulted that down went tables and trestles before one bit was touched.

Masques are occasionally performed today but in nothing like their original form. The costs for the *Masque of Blackness* exceeded £3,000, a fortune of hundreds of thousands of dollars in today's money.

Ben Jonson *(1572–1637)*

THE MASQUE OF BLACKNESS

1605

List of Characters

OCEANUS
NIGER
AETHIOPIA
TRITONS, SEA-MAIDS, NYMPHS, THE DAUGHTERS OF
  NIGER, *and* OCEANIAE

The honor and splendor of these spectacles was such in the performance as, could those hours have lasted, this of mine now had been a most unprofitable work. But, when it is the fate even of the greatest and most
5 absolute° births to need and borrow a life of posterity, little had been done to the study of magnificence° in these° if presently with the rage of the people, who, as a part of greatness, are privileged by custom to deface their carcases,° the spirits had also perished. In duty,
10 therefore, to that majesty who gave them their authority and grace, and, no less than the most royal of predecessors, deserves eminent celebration for these solemnities, I add this later hand to redeem them° as well from ignorance as envy, two common evils, the one of censure, the
15 other of oblivion.

Pliny, Solinus, Ptolemy, and of late Leo the African, remember° unto us a river in Ethiopia famous by the name of Niger, of which the people were called *Nigritae*, now Negroes, and are the blackest nation of the world.
20 This river taketh spring out of a certain lake,° eastward, and after a long race falleth into the western ocean. Hence, because it was her majesty's will to have them° blackamores at first, the invention° was derived by me, and presented thus.

25 *First, for the scene, was drawn a Landtschap°* con-
sisting of small woods, and here and there a void place
filled with huntings;° which falling,° an artificial sea was
seen to shoot forth, as if it flowed to the land, raised
with waves which seemed to move, and in some places
30 *the billow to break, as imitating that orderly disorder*
which is common in nature. In front of this sea were
placed six tritons in moving and sprightly actions, their

upper parts human, save that their hairs were blue, as
partaking of the sea color, their desinent° parts fish,
mounted above their heads, and all varied in disposi-
35 *tion.° From their backs were borne out certain light*
pieces of taffeta as if carried by the wind, and their mu-
sic made out of wreathed shells. Behind these a pair of
sea-maids, for song, were as conspicuously seated; be-
tween which two great sea-horses, as big as the life, put
40 *forth themselves, the one mounting aloft and writhing*
his head from the other, which seemed to sink forwards
(so intended for variation, and that the figure behind
might come off better); upon their backs Oceanus and
Niger were advanced.

45 *Oceanus presented in a human form, the color of his*
flesh blue, and shadowed° with a robe of sea-green; his
head grey and horned, as he is described by the ancients;
his beard of the like mixed color. He was garlanded with
algae, or sea-grass, and in his hand a trident.
50 *Niger in form and color of an Ethiop, his hair and*
rare° beard curled, shadowed with a blue and bright
mantle; his front,° neck and wrists adorned with pearl;
and crowned with an artificial wreath of cane and
paper-rush.°
55 *These induced° the masquers, which were twelve*
nymphs, Negroes, and the daughters of Niger, attended
by so many of the Oceaniae,° which were their light-
bearers.

The masquers were placed in a great concave shell
60 *like mother of pearl, curiously° made to move on those*
waters and rise with the billow; the top thereof was
stuck with a chevron of lights which, indented to the
proportion of the shell, struck a glorious beam upon
them as they were seated one above another; so that
65 *they were all seen, but in an extravagant° order.*

On sides of the shell did swim six huge sea-monsters,
varied in their shape and dispositions,° bearing on their
backs the twelve torch-bearers, who were planted there
in several greces,° so as the backs of some were seen,
70 *some in purfle,° or side, others in face; and all having*
their lights burning out of whelks or murex shells.

The attire of the masquers was alike in all, without
difference: the colors, azure and silver; their hair thick
and curled upright in tresses, like pyramids, but returned
75

---

5. **absolute**: Perfect; here, noble.   6. **magnificence**: According to Aristotle, the virtue of monarchs.   7. **these**: I.e., masques. **7–9. people . . . carcases**: At the end of the masque, the audience was traditionally permitted to tear down the scenery and plunder the decorations.   13. **them**: The "spirits" of line 9. 17. **remember**: Mention.   20. **lake**: Lake Chad.   22. **them**: The masquers.   **invention**: Device of the masque.   25. **Landtschap**: Landscape.   27. **huntings**: Animals hunting their prey. **which falling**: The landscape-curtain was released from above, and fell to the floor in front of the stage to reveal the scene.

34. **desinent**: Terminal.   35–36. **disposition**: Arrangement. 47. **shadowed**: Covered.   52. **rare**: Thin.   53. **front**: Forehead. 55. **paper-rush**: Papyrus.   56. **induced**: Brought in.   58. **Oceaniae**: Sea nymphs, daughters of Oceanus.   61. **curiously**: Artfully.   66. **extravagant**: (1) Unusual; (2) moving about in an extraordinary way.   68. **dispositions**: Positions.   70. **greces**: Steps.   71. **purfle**: Profile.

*on the top with a scroll and antique dressing of feathers
and jewels interlaced with ropes of pearl. And for the
front,° ear, neck and wrists, the ornament was of the
most choice and orient pearl, best setting off from the*
80 *black.*

*For the light-bearers, sea-green, waved about the
skirts with gold and silver; their hair loose and flowing,
garlanded with sea-grass, and that stuck with branches
of coral.*

85 *These thus presented,° the scene behind seemed a
vast sea, and united with this that flowed forth, from
the termination or horizon of which (being the level of
the state,° which was placed in the upper end of the
hall) was drawn, by the lines of perspective, the whole*
90 *work shooting downwards from the eye; which decorum made it more conspicuous, and caught the eye afar
off with a wandering beauty. To which was added an
obscure and cloudy night-piece that made the whole set
off. So much for the bodily part, which was of Master*
95 *Inigo Jones° his design and act.*

*By this,° one of the tritons, with the two sea-maids,
began to sing to the others' loud music, their voices
being a tenor and two trebles.°*

SONG:
　　　Sound, sound aloud
100　The welcome of the orient flood
　　　Into the west;
　　　Fair Niger, son to great Oceanus,
　　　Now honored thus,
　　　With all his beauteous race,
105　Who, though but black in face,
　　　Yet are they bright,
　　　And full of life and light,
　　　To prove that beauty best
　　　Which not the color but the feature°
110　Assures unto the creature.

OCEANUS: Be silent now the ceremony's done,
　　　And Niger, say, how comes it, lovely son,
　　　That thou, the Ethiop's river, so far east,
　　　Art seen to fall into th'extremest west
115　Of me, the king of floods, Oceanus,
　　　And in mine empire's heart salute me thus?
　　　My ceaseless current now amazèd stands
　　　To see thy labor through so many lands
　　　Mix thy fresh billow with my brackish stream,
120　And in thy sweetness stretch thy diadem
　　　To these far distant and unequalled skies,
　　　This squarèd circle of celestial bodies.°

NIGER: Divine Oceanus, 'tis not strange at all
　　　That, since the immortal souls of creatures mortal

Mix with their bodies, yet reserve forever　　125
A power of separation, I should sever
My fresh streams from thy brackish, like things
　　　fixed,
Though with thy powerful saltness thus far mixed.
Virtue, though chained to earth, will still live free,
And hell itself must yield to industry.°　　130

OCEANUS: But what's the end of thy herculean labors
　　　Extended to these calm and blessèd shores?

NIGER: To do a kind and careful father's part,
　　　In satisfying every pensive heart
　　　Of these my daughters, my most lovèd birth:　135
　　　Who, though they were the first formed dames of
　　　　　earth,
　　　And in whose sparkling and refulgent eyes
　　　The glorious sun did still delight to rise;
　　　Though he — the best judge and most formal cause°
　　　Of all dames' beauties — in their firm hues draws　140
　　　Signs of his fervent'st love, and thereby shows
　　　That in their black° the perfect'st beauty grows,
　　　Since the fixed color of their curlèd hair,
　　　Which is the highest grace of dames most fair,
　　　No cares, no age can change, or there display　145
　　　The fearful tincture of abhorrèd grey,
　　　Since Death herself (herself being pale and blue)
　　　Can never alter their most faithful hue;
　　　All which are arguments to prove how far
　　　Their beauties conquer in great beauty's war,　150
　　　And more, how near divinity they be
　　　That stand from passion or decay so free.
　　　Yet since the fabulous voices of some few
　　　Poor brainsick men, styled poets here with you,
　　　Have with such envy of their graces sung　155
　　　The painted beauties other empires sprung,
　　　Letting their loose and wingèd fictions fly
　　　To infect all climates, yea, our purity;
　　　As of one Phaëton,° that fired the world,
　　　And that before his heedless flames were hurled　160
　　　About the globe, the Ethiops were as fair
　　　As other dames, now black with black despair;
　　　And in respect of their complexions changed,
　　　Are eachwhere since for luckless creatures ranged.
　　　Which when my daughters heard, as women are　165
　　　Most jealous of their beauties, fear and care
　　　Possessed them° whole; yea, and believing them,
　　　They wept such ceaseless tears into my stream
　　　That it hath thus far overflowed his shore
　　　To seek them patience, who have since e'ermore　170
　　　As the sun riseth charged his burning throne

---

78. **front:** Forehead.　85. **presented:** Having been presented.
87–88. **level . . . state:** Height of the royal throne.　95. **Inigo
Jones** (1573–1652): Architect and stage designer, Jonson's
collaborator throughout his career as court masque writer.
96. **this:** This time.　98. **trebles:** Sopranos.　109. **feature:**
Form.　122. **squarèd . . . bodies:** I.e., heavenly bodies perfectly transformed into an earthly realm.

130. **hell . . . industry:** From Horace, Odes I, iii, 36: "herculean effort overcame hell"; alluded to in the next line.
139. **formal cause:** Creator of the form or essence; Aristotelian
terminology.　142. **black:** Synonymous with ugly in Elizabethan English.　159. **Phaëton:** Son of Phoebus Apollo, the
sun god. He was allowed to drive the chariot of the sun, but
could not control the horses, and Zeus destroyed him lest he set
the world afire.　167. **them:** The poets. (Jonson)

With volleys of revilings, 'cause he shone
On their scorched cheeks with such intemperate
   fires,
And other dames made queens of all desires.
175 To frustrate which strange error oft I sought,
Though most in vain, against a settled thought
As women's are, till they confirmed at length
By miracle what I with so much strength
Of argument resisted; else they feigned:
180 For in the lake where their first spring they gained,
As they sat cooling their soft limbs one night,
Appeared a face all circumfused with light —
And sure they saw't, for Ethiops never dream —
Wherein they might decipher through the stream
185 These words:

  That they a land must forthwith seek
  Whose termination, of the Greek,
  Sounds -tania; where bright Sol,° that heat
  Their bloods, doth never rise or set,
190   But in his journey passeth by,
  And leaves that climate of the sky
  To comfort of a greater light,
  Who forms all beauty with his sight.

  In search of this have we three princedoms passed
195 That speak out -tania in their accents last;
Black Mauretania° first, and secondly
Swarth° Lusitania;° next we did descry
Rich Aquitania,° and yet cannot find
The place unto these longing nymphs designed.°
200 Instruct and aid me, great Oceanus:
What land is this that now appears to us?
OCEANUS: This land that lifts into the temperate air
His snowy cliff is Albion° the fair,
So called of Neptune's son, who ruleth here;
205 For whose dear guard, myself four thousand year,
Since old Deucalion's° days, have walked the round
About his empire, proud to see him crowned
Above my waves.

At this the moon was discovered in the upper part of
210 *the house, triumphant in a silver throne made in figure*
of a pyramis.° Her garments white and silver, the dress-
ing of her head antique, and crowned with a luminary,
or sphere of light, which striking on the clouds, and
heightened with silver, reflected as natural clouds do by
215 *the splendor of the moon. The heaven about her was*
vaulted with blue silk and set with stars of silver which
had in them their several lights burning. The sudden
sight of which made Niger to interrupt Oceanus with
this present° passion.

188. **Sol:** The sun.   196. **Mauretania:** The land of the Moors, including modern Morocco and part of Algeria.   197. **Swarth:** Swarthy. **Lusitania:** Portugal and western Spain.   198. **Aquitania:** Southwestern France.   199. **designed:** Indicated.   203. **Albion:** Traditional poetic name for England.   206. **Deucalion:** A Greek Noah, survivor of the universal flood.   211. **pyramis:** Pyramid.   219. *present:* Immediate.

NIGER: O see, our silver star!   220
Whose pure, auspicious light greets us thus far!
Great Aethiopia,° goddess of our shore,
Since with particular worship we adore
Thy general brightness, let particular grace
Shine on my zealous daughters: show the place   225
Which long their longings urged their eyes to see.
Beautify them, which long have deified thee.
AETHIOPIA: Niger, be glad; resume thy native cheer.
Thy daughters' labors have their period° here,
And so thy errors.° I was that bright face   230
Reflected by the lake, in which thy race
Read mystic lines; which skill Pythagoras
First taught to men by a reverberate° glass.°
This blessèd isle doth with that -tania end,
Which there they saw inscribed, and shall extend   235
Wished satisfaction to their best desires.
Britannia, which the triple world° admires,
This isle hath now recovered for her name,°
Where reign those beauties that with so much fame
The sacred muses' sons have honorèd,   240
And from bright Hesperus° to Eos° spread.
With that great name Britannia, this blessed isle
Hath won her ancient dignity and style,°
A world divided from the world, and tried
The abstract of it in his general pride.°   245
For were the world with all his wealth a ring,
Britannia, whose new name° makes all tongues sing,
Might be a diamond worthy to enchase° it,
Ruled by a sun that to this height doth grace it,
Whose beams shine day and night, and are of force   250
To blanch an Ethiop, and revive a corse.°
His light sciential° is, and, past mere nature,
Can salve the rude defects of every creature.
  Call forth thy honored daughters, then,
  And let them, 'fore the Britain men,   255
  Indent° the land with those pure traces°
  They flow with in their native graces.
  Invite them boldly to the shore;
  Their beauties shall be scorched no more;
  This sun is temperate, and refines   260
  All things on which his radiance shines.

222. **Aethiopia:** The moon goddess.   229. **period:** End.   230. **errors:** With a quibble on "wanderings."   233. **reverberate:** Reflecting.   232–33. **Pythagoras . . . glass:** Pythagoras was supposedly able to reflect messages onto the moon by writing in blood on a mirror.   237. **triple world:** Heaven, earth, and the underworld.   238. **recovered . . . name:** See line 247 and gloss.   241. **Hesperus:** Evening, the west. **Eos:** Dawn, the east.   243. **style:** Characterization.   244–45. **tried . . . pride:** Experienced the ideal of it through England's own pride in herself. "His" refers to England, despite "her" two lines earlier.   247. **new name:** The name Great Britain was coined when James VI of Scotland became king also of England and Wales in 1604. It was not officially adopted, however, until 1707.   248. **enchase:** Set in.   251. **corse:** Corpse.   252. **sciential:** Endowed with the powers of science.   256. **Indent:** Leave footprints on.   **traces:** Footsteps.

Here the tritons sounded, and they danced on shore, every couple as they advanced severally presenting their fans, in one of which were inscribed their mixed names,
265 *in the other a mute hieroglyphic expressing their mixed qualities. (Which manner of symbol I rather chose than imprese,° as well for strangeness as relishing of antiquity, and more applying to that original doctrine of sculpture which the Egyptians are said first to have*
270 *brought from the Ethiopians.)*

The names		The symbols
The queen	*Euphoris°*	A golden tree° laden with fruit.
1.		
Countess of Bedford	*Aglaia°*	
275 Lady Herbert	*Diaphane°*	The figure icosahedron° of crystal.
2.		
Countess of Derby	*Eucampse°*	
Lady Rich	*Ocyte°*	A pair of naked feet in a river.°
3.		
280 Countess of Suffolk	*Kathare°*	
Lady Bevill	*Notis°*	The salamander° simple.
4.		
Lady Effingham	*Psychrote°*	
Lady Elizabeth Howard	*Glycyte°*	A cloud full of rain,° dropping.
285		
5.		
Lady Susan de Vere	*Malacia°*	
Lady Wroth	*Baryte°*	An urn, sphered with wine.°
6.		
Lady Walsingham	*Periphere°*	

290   The names of the Oceaniae were: *Doris, Petraea, Ocyrhoe, Cydippe, Glauce, Tyche, Beroe, Acaste, Clytia, Ianthe, Lycoris, Plexaure.*

---

267. imprese: Emblems.   **272. *Euphoris:*** Abundance.   **golden tree:** Symbol of fertility.   **274. *Aglaia:*** Splendor.   **275. *Diaphane:*** Transparent.   **276. icosahedron:** A twenty-sided figure symbolizing water.   **277. *Eucampse:*** Flexibility.   **278. Ocyte:** Swiftness.   **279. naked . . . river:** Symbolizing purity.   **280. *Kathare:*** Spotless.   **281. *Notis:*** Moisture.   **salamander:** Which is not harmed by fire and can extinguish it.   **283. Psychrote:** Coldness.   **284. *Glycyte:*** Sweetness.   **284–85. cloud . . . rain:** Symbolizing education.   **286. *Malacia:*** Delicacy.   **287. *Baryte:*** Weight.   **287–88. urn . . . wine:** Obscure, but the whole symbolizes the globe of earth.   **289. *Periphere:*** Revolving, circular.

Their own single dance ended, as they were about to make choice of their men, one from the sea was heard to call 'em with this charm, sung by a tenor voice.   295

SONG:
Come away, come away,
We grow jealous of your stay;
If you do not stop your ear,
We shall have more cause to fear
Sirens of the land, than they   300
To doubt the sirens of the sea.

*Here they danced with their men several measures°
and corantos.° All which ended, they were again accited°
to sea with a song of two trebles,° whose cadences were
iterated by a double echo from several parts of the land.*   305

SONG:
                    Daughters of the subtle flood,
                         Do not let earth longer entertain you;
1ST ECHO: Let earth longer entertain you.
2ST ECHO: Longer entertain you.
                    'Tis to them enough of good   310
                    That you give this little hope to gain you.
1ST ECHO: Give this little hope to gain you.
2ND ECHO: Little hope to gain you.
                    If they love,
                         You shall quickly see;   315
                    For when to flight you move,
                    They'll follow you, the more you flee.
1ST ECHO: Follow you, the more you flee.
2ND ECHO: The more you flee.
                    If not, impute it each to other's matter;   320
                    They are but earth —
1ST ECHO: But earth,
2ND ECHO: Earth —
                         And what you vowed was water.
1ST ECHO: And what you vowed was water.   325
2ND ECHO: You vowed was water.
AETHIOPIA: Enough, bright nymphs, the night grows old,
And we are grieved we cannot hold
You longer light; but comfort take.
Your father only to the lake   330
Shall make return; yourselves, with feasts,
Must here remain the Ocean's guests.
Nor shall this veil the sun hath cast
Above your blood more summers last;
For which, you shall observe these rites: 335
Thirteen times thrice, on thirteen nights
(So often as I fill my sphere
With glorious light throughout the year),
You shall, when all things else do sleep
Save your chaste thoughts, with reverence steep   340

---

302. *measures:* Slow dances.   **303. *corantos:*** Dances with a running or gliding step.   **accited:** Summoned.   **304. *trebles:*** Sopranos.

Your bodies in that purer brine
And wholesome dew called rosmarine;°
Then with that soft and gentler° foam,
Of which the ocean yet yields some,
345 Whereof bright Venus, beauty's queen,
Is said to have begotten been,
You shall your gentler limbs o'er-lave,
And for your pains perfection have;
So that, this night, the year gone round,°
350 You do again salute this ground,
And in the beams of yond' bright sun
Your faces dry, and all is done.

*At which, in a dance they returned to the sea, where
they took their shell, and with this full song went out.*

342. rosmarine: Sea dew.   **343. gentler:** Very gentle.   **349. year
. . . round:** The sequel, however, was not produced until 1608.

Song:
Now Dian° with her burning face   355
   Declines apace,
  By which our waters know
  To ebb, that late did flow.
Back seas, back nymphs, but with a forward grace
  Keep, still, your reverence to the place;   360
And shout with joy of favor you have won
  In sight of Albion, Neptune's son.

*So ended the first masque, which, beside the singular
grace of music and dances, had that success in the nobility of performance as nothing needs to the illustration   365
but the memory by whom it was personated.*

355. Dian: The moon.

COMMENTARY

Eldred Jones (b. 1925)
AFRICA IN ENGLISH MASQUE AND PAGEANTRY   1965

In his book, Othello's Countrymen *(1965), Eldred Jones offers an extensive
review of the appearance of Africans in English entertainments. While the heyday
of the masque form is brief, it offered numerous opportunities to portray Africans
even before Ben Jonson's* Masque of Blackness. *What Jones demonstrates is that
the traditions and attitudes depicted in the masques were deeply ingrained in
English culture. Jonson relied on tradition as he developed his material.*

The English masque had only a short vogue. From its emergence as a distinct art
form with a name of its own, to its disappearance as a significant form, the period
stretches over less than a century and a half. Reckoning from the days when by the
combined efforts of Ben Jonson and Inigo Jones the masque rose to its final form,
the period shrinks to a little over three decades. But, from its earliest beginnings to
its disappearance, figures from Africa frequently contributed to the splendor and
strangeness of both the spectacle and the poetry of the masque. Like the form itself,
these African figures were at first vague and ill-defined, bearing little relevance to
any overall theme, and frequently having no connection with Africa except in
name. But later, as the masque took a settled form, they became more defined and
more deliberately related both to their supposed place of origin and to the themes
of the masques in which they appeared. For instance, figures which in the earliest

masques would have been described as "Moors" or "Blackamoors" appear in Jonson's *Masque of Blacknesse* as the "Daughters of Niger" against a background of both ancient and modern authorities: "Pliny, Solinus, Ptolemy, and of late Leo the African."

Whatever may have been the character or the strength of the stimulus which the English masque undoubtedly received from Renaissance Italy, certain of its features are to be found in activities which had been part of English life since medieval times. The dance was the nucleus around which the other features of the masque came to be established, and dancing, especially the dance called "Morisce" or "Morisco," had been an essential part of English medieval village festivals from earliest times. One of the customs associated with Morris dancing was the blackening of the faces of the participants. This tradition of blackening was also a feature of other popular activities in medieval England. The folk processions, the sword dance and the folk drama, all show an employment of the grotesque of which blackening was only one feature.

One of the most interesting characters in the medieval mummers play was the king of Egypt, who had a black face and who was accepted by tradition as the father of St. George. The devils in the mystery plays were also usually portrayed as black, and indeed some local traditions required all the participants in the mummers play to have black faces. The term "Moriscoe" (with its associations with "Moor" and "Morocco") and the king of Egypt also suggest a possible link between the English medieval dramatic tradition and Africa.

The practice of blackening was transferred to the more sophisticated court "disguisings" of the sixteenth century. In the earliest surviving description of a courtly festivity which involved blackening, the terms "Egipcians," "Moreskoes," and "blacke Moors" appear. In this masquelike performance in 1510, Henry VIII and the Earl of Essex had come in "appareled after Turkey fashion," while "the torchebearers were appareyled in Crymosyn satyne and grene, lyke Moreskoes, their faces blacke. . . ." Later in the same proceedings, six ladies also appeared "their heads rouled in plesauntes and typpers lyke the Egipcians, embroudered with gold. Their faces, neckes, armes and handes, covered with fyne plesaunce blacke . . . so that the same ladies seemed to be nigrost [sic] or blacke Mores." In this festivity, as in earlier entertainments of this kind, the black characters were merely decorative. The strangeness of their appearance had an exotic impact, and that was all that was required at that time. But it was this tradition which, continuing, made Queen Anne request Ben Jonson to make the characters in his masque of 1605 "Black-mores at first."

The Elizabethan outdoor pageant also frequently employed "Moors," and here again this use seems to have been linked with the use of grotesque characters in the medieval pageant. A king of Moors appeared in a pageant undertaken by the London drapers in 1522, and a surviving list of expenses in connection with it gives some indication of his function. The relevant entry records

> payment of 5s. to John Wakelyn, for playing the king of Moors, (the company finding him his apparell, his stage, and wyld fire).

Robert Withington, who notes this entry, draws the interesting conclusion that the "wyld fire" seems to connect the king of Moors here with the "wild man" or "green man" whose function in medieval pageantry was to clear a way through the crowd for the procession by using "wyld-fire" or fireworks. The king of Moors seems then to have crept into the later "procession" or "entertainment" as a grotesque character, to compel the crowds back by his strange appearance and his use of fireworks. (Individual items of the king's costume suggest that his appearance was spectacular: "the said king's girdle, his garland or turban of white feathers and black satin, sylver paper for his shoes, &c. .") In later outdoor pageants this crude function was refined so that the "Moor" or "king of Moors" appeared as a principal speaking character, often acting as the Presenter. In George Peele's pageant of 1585, for instance, the Presenter is described as "him that rid on a luzern before the Pageant, apparelled like a Moor." In Middleton's *Triumph of Truth* (1613) and Anthony Munday's *Chrysanaleia* (1616) similarly important functions were reserved for a Moor.

The popularity of Moors in masques can be judged by the number of references in surviving records either to masques specifically called masques of Moors, or to masques involving such characters, during the reigns of Edward VI, Elizabeth, and James I. The charges for a "Masque of Young Moors" given during Shrovetide 1547, in which King Edward took part, make very interesting reading, for they give illuminating information about the costuming of these characters. The blackening was effected through the use of black gloves, nether stockings, and face masks. These items are mentioned in the long list of charges: "To Rychard Lees of London mercer for viij yards d. of black vellett for gloves above thelbow for mores . . ."; "To hughe Eston the kynges hosyer for the makyng of xiiij peyres of nether stockes of lether black for mores"; a payment to "Nycholas modena straynger . . . for the trymyng Coloring and lyning of xvj vezars or maskes for moores." Some attempt was made to disguise the hair by giving the Moors "Cappes made with Cowrse budge." The elaborate costumes included "belles to hange at the skyrtes of the mores garments" and "dartes with brode heddes and ffethers of sylver. . . ." During the same reign, the accounts show that there was a masque involving Moors on 6 January 1551 and a masque of female Moors at Christmas 1551.

The accounts relating to the reign of Philip and Mary do not refer to any Moors in masques. In view of the apparent popularity of Moors in masques during Edward's reign, and the fact that a year after Elizabeth's accession they seem to have resumed their popularity and continued to hold it up to and during the reign of James I, this seems to indicate a significant temporary change of taste. One is led to speculate on whether portrayals of Moors were suspended out of deference to Philip, who, having had closer dealings with Moors, may have felt touchier on the subject than English monarchs.

Whatever the reasons were for the disappearance of Moors from masques during the reign of Philip and Mary, they reappeared in all their grandeur soon after Queen Elizabeth's accession. An inventory (dated 27 April 1560) of the wardrobe of the Office of the Revels refers to a masque of six Barbarians, and a masque of six Moors. The masque of Barbarians was performed on 1 January 1560, according to a note in the inventory, while the masque of Moors whose date is less certain is placed by E. K. Chambers on 29 January 1559.

There are no more references to masques involving African characters until 1579. (The records of the intervening years are either lost or are very incomplete.) But even this one masque referred to was not performed, although a Willyam Lyzard was paid "for patorns for the mores maske that should have served on Shrovetuesday." There are no other references to masques with Africans in Queen Elizabeth's reign.

Before we encounter our next Africans in masques, early in the reign of James I, a remarkable transformation had taken place. The masque had borrowed from the pageants and processions the use of poetry, and this new form had been employed by the gentlemen of the Inns of Court in their *Gesta Grayorum* (1595). Thus when the masque emerges under James I it emerges as a new form, a form worthy to engage the minds of serious poets. For a short while the English masque flourished as a serious art.

Queen Anne, who was to take a leading part in Ben Jonson's first court masque, expressed a wish "to have them [the masquers] Black-mores at first." This was not in itself a strange request. Now, however, more was involved than mere dressing-up. There had to be a poetic theme which would justify the introduction of black characters. It was therefore logical that Jonson should choose an African theme. His masquers thus emerged as "twelve Nymphs, Negro's, and the daughters of Niger . . ." since Negroes were "the blackest nation of the world." Niger himself was "in forme and colour of an Aethiope; his haire, and rare beard curled. . . ."

Around these characters Jonson weaves an ingenious story, using, whenever he so required, the fictions of the ancients to augment the fruits of his own imagination. The result is an engaging fable. The daughters of Niger had suddenly discovered, while reading Ovid, that they were not, after all, the most beautiful creatures in the world, and that their present color was the result of Phaeton's action:

> And, that, before his heedlesse flames were hurld
> About the Globe, the Aethiopes were as faire,
> As other Dames . . .

The now disillusioned and distracted girls cursed the sun for disfiguring them ("A custome of the Aethiopes, notable in Herod[otus] and Diod[orus] Sic[ulus]. See Plinie Nat. Hist. Lib. 5, cap. 8," adds a helpful Jonson) until they saw in a vision ("for Aethiopes never dreame") that they would recover their beauty if they traveled to a land with the termination "Tania." After passing through " 'blacke Mauritania, Swarth Lusitania and Rich Aquitania," they arrive in Britannia, the end of their quest. Here the beams of a "Sunne" (James),

> are of force
> To blanch an Aethiope, and revive a Cor's [sic].

All they had to do was to bathe thirteen nights in the ocean, and they would gain whiteness and beauty.

Jonson, once he had hit on the idea of black characters, wove both the poetry and, in so far as he controlled Inigo Jones, costume and scenery around them. The costumes and setting were carefully based on pale colors — silver and azure — with "jewells interlaced with ropes of pearle . . . best setting off from the black." The poetry is shot through with contrasts — light and darkness, black and white, death and life, the sun and the moon, and, by total implication, Africa and Europe. Niger's daughters for instance are thus described:

> Who, though but blacke in face,
> Yet, are they bright,
> And full of life and light.

In what must have been a *tour de force* in Elizabethan ears, Niger maintains that the black complexion is the most beautiful:

That, in their black, the prefectst beauty growes;
Since the fix't colour of their curled haire,
(Which is the highest grace of dames most faire)
No cares, no age can change; or there display
The fearefull tincture of abhorred *Gray*;
Since *Death* her selfe (her selfe being pale and blue)
Can never alter their most faithfull hiew.

Nothing as intricately harmonized as *The Masque of Blacknesse* had been attempted in the masque form before. It is a perfect blend of matter and manner; in it the extravagance which was germane to the masque is controlled by a disciplined imagination. This opinion was obviously not shared by Sir Dudley Carleton, whose comments on this presentation are preserved for us. Sir Dudley's criticisms of the scenery, that "there was all Fish and no Water," and of the apparel —"to light and Curtizan-light [sic] for such great ones"— show a literal rather than a literary mind. He, however, notes an interesting detail, namely that the masquers used paint (and not the usual velvet masks) to disguise their complexions:

> Instead of Vizzards, their Faces and Arms up to the Elbows, were painted black, which was Disguise sufficient, for they were hard to be known; but it became them nothing so well as their red and white, and you cannot imagine a more ugly Sight, then a Troop of lean-cheek'd Moors.

The thirteen days promised in *The Masque of Blacknesse* ran into three years before the daughters of Niger, by then washed white, were to return to the stage in *The Masque of Beauty*, which was presented in 1608.

Pedro Calderón
de la Barca

Calderón is one of Spain's greatest poets and dramatists of the Golden Age — the early and mid-seventeenth century. This was a time when Lope de Vega (1562–1635) dominated the stage and fashioned the form of the popular drama as a three-act structure, with the opening act establishing the issues and characters, the second act developing the conflict, and the third act resolving the problems raised by the drama. Lope established the form of the *comedia* (tragicomic social drama) in his *The New Art of Play Writing* (1609). Calderón followed Lope's structure.

The Golden Age also produced Spain's greatest painters — El Greco (1541–1614), Murillo (1617–1682), and Velásquez (1599–1660). The activity and significance of art in this period may be underscored by noting that during most of this period, King Philip IV brought artists to court and provided them with studios. Velásquez painted many portraits of King Philip, who visited his studio daily. Likewise, the theater was nurtured by the court throughout this period. Lope was the first court playwright, and when he died in 1635, Calderón took his place.

Calderón came from a well-to-do family ruled by a difficult and tyrannical father. He went first to the University of Alcalá and then to the university at Salamanca, where he studied law and probably theology. He changed his original plan to become a priest and began writing plays in 1623. Apparently the king or perhaps the powerful prime minister, Olivares, became aware of his work and brought him into the court circle, giving him the opportunity to produce a variety of plays. Despite the fact that Spain's power and wealth were eroding rapidly, Philip's court maintained a strenuous program of lavish entertainment. Some historians have seen this behavior as an escapist refusal to believe that most of the immense wealth in gold and silver brought back twice yearly from the Americas was already mortgaged on wars, insurrections, and entertainment. Not long after Calderón died, the nation was virtually bankrupt.

The opportunities afforded him at court made it possible for Calderón to produce elaborate entertainments, especially after Olivares built a new court suitable for more brilliant productions in 1634. The old court, the Alcázar, was dark, small, and depressing. The new court was large, elegant, and expressive. It demanded a steady stream of entertainments.

The popular stage was often an open-air theater similar to the Elizabethan theater of Shakespeare's time. Scenery was minimal, costumes rarely more than suggestions, and lighting natural. Plays were put on in the afternoon at 3 o'clock in the summer and at 2 o'clock in the winter. But at court lighting was provided by candles and oil lamps, scenic backgrounds were possible, and costuming was imaginative.

In Calderón's remarkable output as a playwright he may have produced as many as a hundred one-act religious plays for the feast of Corpus Christi. These *auto sacramentales* are allegorical plays, usually about saints' lives and similar to medieval miracle plays. Some of these plays were widely admired, such as *The Constant Prince* (1629), about the martyrdom of Portuguese prince Ferdinand; *The Wonder-Working Magician* (1637), about a Faust character; and *The Two Lovers of Heaven* (1640). Nearly eighty of these plays survive.

Calderón wrote many secular dramas as well as *zarzuelas,* a form that combined music, dance, and drama and that developed into his operas, in which the dialogue is set to music. Among his most important secular plays are *The Surgeon of His Honor* (1635), *Life Is a Dream* (1635), *The Mayor of Zalamea* (1640), and *Daughter of the Air* (1653). Each of these plays is powerful, but *Life Is a Dream* has become the longest-lived and the most often produced of his plays. He wrote it in his favorite baroque style — *Gongorism,* named for an earlier baroque poet, Luis de Góngora y Argote (1561–1627), whose style is marked by references to mythology, stylistic excesses, and complexity of language and thought. In translation many of such stylistic effects are lost, although *Life Is a Dream* is marked by complexity of thought even in English.

In 1651 Calderón took religious orders and retired from the popular stage, but he continued to write for the court. He eventually became an honorary chaplain to Philip and spent much of his time at court in Madrid even while officially assigned to Toledo.

LIFE IS A DREAM

The central action of *Life Is a Dream* is the conversion, or "rebirth," of Prince Segismund. The action of the subplot is the recovery of Rosaura's honor after her seduction by the foreign duke Astolfo. These two strands of action intertwine when Rosaura helps Segismund begin to understand the true nature of the world, and he helps her regain her honor once he is recognized by the people of Poland as the true heir of his father.

Life Is a Dream, often called Spain's *Hamlet,* is one of Calderón's philosophical plays. It centers on self-discovery and the untrustworthiness of illusion. Like Hamlet, Segismund spends part of the second act of the play trying to decide the truth of his experiences: Were they real, or were they a dream? Is life real or a dream? The concept of life as a dream comes from eastern thought and was commonly discussed in the seventeenth century. Skepticism — the reluctance to believe in the knowledge gathered by the senses — was widespread in this age. Both Shakespeare and Calderón were influenced by the revival of classical skepticism, and both examined experience in an effort to discover truth.

When the play opens, Segismund is imprisoned and baffled at his lack of freedom. He does not know that his horoscope predicted at his birth that he would grow up to be a tyrant who would conquer his father, King Basil. As a result Basil placed him in a prison with Clotaldo as his guard and tutor. But the aging Basil, concerned with the succession of his throne, has second thoughts and suspects that the horoscope might be wrong. He releases Segismund to observe his behavior: if he seems tyrannical, he will be reimprisoned and told that his moments of freedom were a dream; if he is prudent, he will inherit the crown.

Rosaura arrives searching for Astolfo, the man who wronged her. She is disguised as a man and is present when Basil experiments with freeing Segismund. Segismund behaves tyrannically, doing what he wants when he wants with no thought for anyone else. He is in a sense a "natural" man because he had not been socialized in a normal family or in normal surroundings. But before he is returned to prison, he falls in love with Rosaura, and his love for her begins the process of his conversion.

Once returned to prison, Segismund believes his experience of freedom was a dream until he reflects on Rosaura. His memory of her begins to convince him that he truly experienced freedom after all. Ultimately, the people resist the imposition of a foreign king, Astolfo, Duke of Muscovy, and storm the prison to free Segismund. He is a changed man who realizes that he must temper his desires and consider other people's feelings. At the head of an army, he defeats his father, Basil. When his father bows before him, he in turn bows before his father, thus demonstrating his allegiance and his conversion from a wrathful tyrant. Rosaura is a central part of Segismund's metamorphosis. She may be an allegorical representation of beauty, feminine (and therefore civilizing) beauty, or humanity. Segismund pledges to help her recover her honor. Prince Astolfo is revealed as a seducer, and Segismund is a wiser and more compassionate person.

Life Is a Dream in Performance

Like *Hamlet,* Calderón's *Life Is a Dream* has been produced often since its first appearance in 1635. Ironically, modern productions in Spain are infrequent because the Spanish are reluctant to tamper with the original verse, which is difficult and unusual. On the other hand, Federico García Lorca produced it in Spain in 1932 respecting the conventions of classic Spanish theater. The Teatro Español produced a full version in 1982. Productions in other parts of the world have, since the first English version in London in 1899, been frequent and interesting. Among the several modern New York versions was the 1981 production directed by María Irene Fornés. Ann Bogart did a highly praised "pictorially 'Spanish'" production in Cambridge, Massachusetts, in 1989 using Edwin Honig's translation. José Rivera's somewhat vaudevillean adaptation appeared in Hartford in 1998 and in New York in 2000, titled *Sueño.*

Another recent production was that by the Royal Lyceum Theatre Company of Scotland at the Brooklyn Academy of Music in 1999. This was a high-energy, powerful drama concentrating on the pain and bewilderment of Segismund, who appeared much of the time bearing a large chain, symbolic of his imprisonment. The stage was simple: a twenty-five-foot circle of broken stones over which hung a huge picture-frame mirror tilted to show only part of the action and to mirror the reality of the stage action in an unreal way throughout. The director, Calixto Bieito, from Barcelona, compressed the action into one two-hour act, relying for clarity on some long speeches of exposition and explanation. He also included two Spanish musicians singing Flamenco songs and beating Flamenco rhythms in the background — a haunting accompaniment. As in most modern productions, Clifford's translation attempted to make the language fresh for its own time rather than emulate the archaisms and poetic complexities of the original. John Clifford's translation was not literal but poetic and approximate.

Pedro Calderón de la Barca (1600–1681)

LIFE IS A DREAM   *1635*
TRANSLATED BY ROY CAMPBELL

Dramatis Personae

BASIL, *King of Poland*
SEGISMUND, *Prince*
ASTOLFO, *Duke of Muscovy*
CLOTALDO, *old man*
CLARION, *a comical servant*
ROSAURA, *a lady*
STELLA, *a princess*
Soldiers, guards, musicians, servants, retines, women

The scene is laid in the court of Poland, a nearby fortress, and the open country.

ACT I

(*On one side a craggy mountain: on the other a rude tower whose base serves as a prison for Segismund. The door facing the spectators is open. The action begins at nightfall.*)

(*Rosaura, dressed as a man, appears on the rocks climbing down to the plain: behind her comes Clarion.*)

ROSAURA: You headlong hippogriff who match the gale
   In rushing to and fro, you lightning-flicker
   Who give no light, you scaleless fish, you bird
   Who have no coloured plumes, you animal
5   Who have no natural instinct, tell me whither
   You lead me stumbling through this labyrinth
   Of naked crags! Stay here upon this peak
   And be a Phaëton to the brute-creation!
   For I, pathless save only for the track
10   The laws of destiny dictate for me,
   Shall, blind and desperate, descend this height

   Whose furrowed brows are frowning at the sun.
   How rudely, Poland, you receive a stranger
   (Hardly arrived, but to be treated hardly)
   And write her entry down in blood with thorns.   15
   My plight attests this well, but after all,
   Where did the wretchèd ever pity find?
CLARION: Say *two* so wretchèd. Don't you leave me out
   When you complain! If we two sallied out
   From our own country, questing high adventure,   20
   And after so much madness and misfortune
   Are still two here, and were two when we fell
   Down those rough crags — shall I not be offended
   To share the trouble yet forego the credit?
ROSAURA: I did not give you shares in my complaint   25
   So as not to rob you of the right to sorrow
   Upon your own account. There's such relief
   In venting grief that a philosopher
   Once said that sorrows should not be bemoaned
   But sought for pleasure.
CLARION: Philosopher?   30
   I call him a long-bearded, drunken sot
   And would they'd cudgelled him a thousand blows
   To give him something worth his while lamenting!
   But, madam, what should we do, by ourselves,
   On foot and lost at this late hour of day,   35
   Here on this desert mountain far away —
   The sun departing after fresh horizons?
ROSAURA: Clarion, how can I answer, being both
   The partner of your plight and your dilemma?
CLARION: Would anyone believe such strange events?   40
ROSAURA: If there my sight is not deceived by fancy,
   In the last timid light that yet remains
   I seem to see a building.
CLARION: Either my hopes
   Are lying or I see the signs myself.

ROSAURA: Between the towering crags, there stands so
45   small
        A royal palace that the lynx-eyed sun
        Could scarce perceive it at midday, so rude
        In architecture that it seems but one
        Rock more down-toppled from the sun-kissed crags
        That form the jaggèd crest.
50 CLARION: Let's go closer,
        For we have stared enough: it would be better
        To let the inmates make us welcome.
    ROSAURA: See:
        The door, or, rather, that funereal gap,
        Is yawning wide — whence night itself seems born,
55   Flowing out from its black, rugged centre.

    (*A sound of chains is heard.*)

    CLARION: Heavens! What's that I hear?
    ROSAURA: I have become
        A block immovable of ice and fire.
    CLARION: Was that a little chain? Why, I'll be
        hanged
        If that is not the clanking ghost of some
60   Past galley-slave — my terror proves it is!
    SEGISMUND: Oh, miserable me! Unhappy me!
    ROSAURA: How sad a cry that is! I fear new trials
        And torments.
    CLARION: It's a fearful sound.
    ROSAURA: Oh, come,
        My Clarion, let us fly from suffering!
65 CLARION: I'm in such sorry trim, I've not the spirit
        Even to run away.
    ROSAURA: And if you had,
        You'd not have seen that door, not known of it.
        When one's in doubt, the common saying goes
        One walks between two lights.
    CLARION: I'm the reverse.
        It's not that way with me.
70 ROSAURA: What then disturbs you?
    CLARION: I walk in doubt between two darknesses.
    ROSAURA: Is not that feeble exhalation there
        A light? That pallid star whose fainting tremors,
        Pulsing a doubtful warmth of glimmering rays,
75   Make even darker with its spectral glow
        That gloomy habitation? Yes! because
        By its reflection (though so far away)
        I recognise a prison, grim and sombre,
        The sepulchre of some poor living carcase.
80   And, more to wonder at, a man lies there
        Clothed in the hides of savage beasts, with limbs
        Loaded with fetters, and a single lamp
        For company. So, since we cannot flee,
        Let us stay here and listen to his plaint
        And what his sorrows are.
85 SEGISMUND: Unhappy me!
        Oh, miserable me! You heavens above,
        I try to think what crime I've done against you
        By being born. Although to have been born,
        I know, is an offence, and with just cause
90   I bear the rigours of your punishment:

Since to be born is man's worst crime. But yet
I long to know (to clarify my doubts)
What greater crime, apart from being born,
Can thus have earned my greater chastisement.
Aren't others born like me? And yet they seem   95
To boast a freedom that I've never known.
The bird is born, and in the hues of beauty
Clothed with its plumes, yet scarce has it become
A feathered posy — or a flower with wings —
When through ethereal halls it cuts its way,   100
Refusing the kind shelter of its nest.
And I, who have more soul than any bird,
Must have less liberty?
The beast is born, and with its hide bright-painted,
In lovely tints, has scarce become a spangled   105
And starry constellation (thanks to the skilful
Brush of the Painter) than its earthly needs
Teach it the cruelty to prowl and kill,
The monster of its labyrinth of flowers.
Yet I, with better instincts than a beast,   110
Must have less liberty?
The fish is born, the birth of spawn and slime,
That does not even live by breathing air.
No sooner does it feel itself a skiff
Of silver scales upon the wave than swiftly   115
It roves about in all directions taking
The measure of immensity as far
As its cold blood's capacity allows.
Yet I, with greater freedom of the will,
Must have less liberty?   120
The brook is born, and like a snake unwinds
Among the flowers. No sooner, silver serpent,
Does it break through the blooms than it regales
And thanks them with its music for their kindness,
Which opens to its course the majesty   125
Of the wide plain. Yet I, with far more life,
Must have less liberty?
This fills me with such passion, I become
Like the volcano Etna, and could tear
Pieces of my own heart out of my breast!   130
What law, justice, or reason can decree
That man alone should never know the joys
And be alone excepted from the rights
God grants a fish, a bird, a beast, a brook?
ROSAURA: His words have filled me full of fear and
        pity.   135
SEGISMUND: Who is it overheard my speech? Clotaldo?
CLARION: Say "yes!"
ROSAURA: It's only a poor wretch, alas,
    Who in these cold ravines has overheard
    Your sorrows.
SEGISMUND: Then I'll kill you.

(*Seizes her.*)

    So as to leave no witness of my frailty.   140
    I'll tear you into bits with these strong arms!
CLARION: I'm deaf. I wasn't able to hear that.
ROSAURA: If you were human born, it is enough
    That I should kneel to you for you to spare me.

SEGISMUND: Your voice has softened me, your presence
145   halted me,
And now, confusingly, I feel respect
For you. Who are you? Though here I have learned
So little of the world, since this grim tower
Has been my cradle and my sepulchre;
150 And though since I was born (if you can say
I really have been born) I've only seen
This rustic desert where in misery
I dwell alone, a living skeleton,
An animated corpse; and though till now,
155 I never spoke, save to one man who hears
My griefs and through whose converse I have heard
News of the earth and of the sky; and though,
To astound you more, and make you call me
A human monster, I dwell here, and am
160 A man of the wild animals, a beast
Among the race of men; and though in such
Misfortune, I have studied human laws,
Instructed by the birds, and learned to measure
The circles of the gentle stars, you only
165 Have curbed my furious rage, amazed my vision,
And filled with wonderment my sense of hearing.
Each time I look at you, I feel new wonder!
The more I see of you, the more I long
To go on seeing more of you. I think
170 My eyes are dropsical, to go on drinking
What it is death for them to drink, because
They go on drinking that which I am dying
To see and that which, seen, will deal me death.
Yet let me gaze on you and die, since I
175 Am so bewitched I can no longer think
What not seeing you would do to me — the sight
Itself being fatal! that would be more hard
Than dying, madness, rage, and fiercest grief:
It would be life — worst fate of all because
180 The gift of life to such a wretchèd man
Would be the gift of death to happiness!
ROSAURA: Astonished as I look, amazed to hear,
I know not what to say nor what to ask.
All I can say is that heaven guided me
185 Here to be comforted, if it is comfort
To see another sadder than oneself.
They say a sage philosopher of old,
Being so poor and miserable that he
Lived on the few plain herbs he could collect,
190 One day exclaimed: "Could any man be poorer
Or sadder than myself?"— when, turning round,
He saw the very answer to his words.
For there another sage philosopher
Was picking up the scraps he'd thrown away.
195 I lived cursing my fortune in this world
And asked within me: "Is there any other
Suffers so hard a fate?" Now out of pity
You've given me the answer. For within me
I find upon reflection that my griefs
200 Would be as joys to you and you'd receive them
To give you pleasure. So if they perchance
In any measure may afford relief,

Listen attentively to my misfortune
And take what is left over for yourself.
I am . . .   205
CLOTALDO (Within): Guards of the tower! You
    sluggards
Or cowards, you have let two people pass
Into the prison bounds . . .
ROSAURA: Here's more confusion!
SEGISMUND: That is Clotaldo, keeper of my prison.
Are my misfortunes still not at an end?   210
CLOTALDO: Come. Be alert, and either seize or slay
    them
Before they can resist!
VOICES (Within):   Treason! Betrayal!
CLARION: Guards of the tower who let us pass
    unhindered,
Since there's a choice, to seize us would be simpler.

(*Enter Clotaldo with soldiers. He holds a pistol and they all wear masks.*)

CLOTALDO (*Aside to the soldiers*):
    Cover your faces, all! It's a precaution   215
Imperative that nobody should know us
While we are here.
CLARION: What's this? A masquerade?
CLOTALDO: O you, who ignorantly passed the bounds
And limits of this region, banned to all —
Against the king's decree which has forbidden   220
That any should find out the prodigy
Hidden in these ravines — yield up your weapons
Or else this pistol, like a snake of metal,
Will spit the piercing venom of two shots
With scandalous assault upon the air.   225
SEGISMUND: Tyrannic master, ere you harm these people
Let my life be the spoil of these sad bonds
In which (I swear it by Almighty God)
I'll sooner rend myself with hands and teeth
Amid these rocks than see them harmed and mourn   230
Their suffering.
CLOTALDO: Since you know, Segismund,
That your misfortunes are so huge that, even
Before your birth, you died by heaven's decree,
And since you know these walls and binding chains
Are but the brakes and curbs to your proud frenzies,   235
What use is it to bluster?

(*To the guards.*)

                      Shut the door
Of this close prison! Hide him in its depths!
SEGISMUND: Ah, heavens, how justly you denied me
    freedom!
For like a Titan I would rise against you,
Pile jasper mountains high on stone foundations   240
And climb to burst the windows of the sun!
CLOTALDO: Perhaps you suffer so much pain today
Just to forestall that feat.
ROSAURA: Now that I see
How angry pride offends you, I'd be foolish
Not to plead humbly at your feet for life.   245

ABOVE: John Ortiz as Segismund hangs over Rosaura (Michi Barall) and Clarion (Jan Leslie Hardin), who contemplate the significance of his imprisonment. From José Rivera's Hartford Stage Company 1998 production of *Sueño*. The visual impact of this scene recollects Leonardo da Vinci's drawing of the "measure of man" as well as emblems of the crucifixion. RIGHT TOP: Segismund (John Ortiz) in prison holding his symbolic chains while Rosaura looks on in José Rivera's production of *Sueño* at the Hartford Stage. RIGHT BOTTOM: George Anton as Segismund in Calixto Bieito's Royal Lyceum Theatre production of *Life Is a Dream* at the Brooklyn Academy of Music, October 1999. The chains he carries symbolize his imprisonment and his torment.

Be moved by me to pity. It would be
Notoriously harsh that neither pride
Nor humbleness found favour in your eyes!
CLARION: And if neither Humility nor Pride
    Impress you (characters of note who act   250
    And motivate a thousand mystery plays)
    Let me, here, who am neither proud nor humble,
    But merely something halfway in between,
    Plead to you both for shelter and for aid.
CLOTALDO: Ho, there!
SOLDIER: Sir?
CLOTALDO: Take their weapons. Bind
    their eyes   255
    So that they cannot see the way they're led.
ROSAURA: This is my sword. To nobody but you
    I yield it, since you're, after all, the chief.
    I cannot yield to one of meaner rank.
CLARION: My sword is such that I will freely give it   260
    To the most mean and wretched.

(*To one soldier.*)

                        Take it, you!
ROSAURA: And if I have to die, I'll leave it to you
    In witness of your mercy. It's a pledge
    Of great worth and may justly be esteemed
    For someone's sake who wore it long ago.   265
CLOTALDO (*Apart*): Each moment seems to bring me
    new misfortune!
ROSAURA: Because of that, I ask you to preserve
    This sword with care. Since if inconstant Fate
    Consents to the remission of my sentence,
    It has to win me honour. Though I know not   270
    The secret that it carries, I do know
    It has got one — unless I trick myself —
    And prize it just as the sole legacy
    My father left me.
CLOTALDO: Who then was your father?
ROSAURA: I never knew.
CLOTALDO: And why have you come here?   275
ROSAURA: I came to Poland to avenge a wrong.
CLOTALDO (*Apart*):
    Sacred heavens!

(*On taking the sword he becomes very perturbed.*)

              What's this? Still worse and worse.
    I am perplexed and troubled with more fears.

(*Aloud.*)

    Tell me: who gave that sword to you?
ROSAURA: A woman.
CLOTALDO: Her name?
ROSAURA: A secret I am forced to keep.   280
CLOTALDO: What makes you think this sword contains
    a secret?
ROSAURA: That she who gave it to me said: "Depart
    To Poland. There with subtlety and art
    Display it so that all the leading people
    And noblemen can see you wearing it,   285
    And I know well that there's a lord among them

Who will both shelter you and grant you favour."
But, lest he should be dead, she did not name him.
CLOTALDO (*Aside*): Protect me, heavens! What is this I
    hear?
290 I cannot say if real or imagined
But here's the sword I gave fair Violante
In token that, whoever in the future
Should come from her to me wearing this sword,
Would find in me a tender father's love.
295 Alas, what can I do in such a pass,
When he who brings the sword to win my favour
Brings it to find his own red death instead
Arriving at my feet condemned already?
What strange perplexity! How hard a fate!
300 What an inconstant fortune to be plagued with!
This is my son not only by all signs
But also by the promptings of my heart,
Since, seeing him, my heart seems to cry out
To him, and beat its wings, and, though unable
305 To break the locks, behaves as one shut in,
Who, hearing noises in the street outside,
Cranes from the window-ledge. Just so, not knowing
What's really happening, but hearing sounds,
My heart runs to my eyes which are its windows
310 And out of them flows into bitter tears.
Protect me, heaven! What am I to do?
To take him to the king is certain death.
To hide him is to break my sacred oath
And the strong law of homage. From one side
315 Love of one's own, and from the other loyalty —
Call me to yield. Loyalty to my king
(Why do I doubt?) comes before life and honour.
Then live my loyalty, and let him die!
When I remember, furthermore, he came
320 To avenge an injury — a man insulted
And unavenged is in disgrace. My son
Therefore he is not, nor of noble blood.
But if some danger has mischanced, from which
No one escapes, since honour is so fragile
325 That any act can smash it, and it takes
A stain from any breath of air, what more
Could any nobleman have done than he,
Who, at the cost of so much risk and danger,
Comes to avenge his honour? Since he's so brave
330 He is my son, and my blood's in his veins.
And so betwixt the one doubt and the other,
The most important mean between extremes
Is to go to the king and tell the truth —
That he's my son, to kill, if so he wishes.
335 Perhaps my loyalty thus will move his mercy
And if I thus can merit a live son
I'll help him to avenge his injury.
But if the king prove constant in his rigour
And deal him death, he'll die in ignorance
That I'm his father.

(*Aloud to Rosaura and Clarion.*)

340   Come then, strangers, come!
And do not fear that you have no companions
In your misfortunes, since, in equal doubt,
Tossed between life and death, I cannot guess
Which is the greater evil or the less.

(*A hall at the royal palace, in court.*)

(*Enter Astolfo and soldiers at one side: from the other
side Princess Stella and ladies. Military music and salvos.*)

ASTOLFO: To greet your excellent bright beams
As brilliant as a comet's rays,   345
The drums and brasses mix their praise
With those of fountains, birds, and streams.
With sounds alike, in like amaze,
Your heavenly face each voice salutes,
Which puts them in such lively fettle,   350
The trumpets sound like birds of metal,
The songbirds play like feathered flutes.
And thus they greet you, fair señora —
The salvos, as their queen, the brasses,
As to Minerva when she passes,   355
The songbirds to the bright Aurora,
And all the flowers and leaves and grasses
As doing homage unto Flora,
Because you come to cheat the day
Which now the night has covered o'er —   360
Aurora in your spruce array,
Flora in peace, Pallas in war,
But in my heart the queen of May.
STELLA: If human voice could match with acts
You would have been unwise to say   365
Hyperboles that a few facts
May well refute some other day
Confounding all this martial fuss
With which I struggle daringly,
Since flatteries you proffer thus   370
Do not accord with what I see.
Take heed that it's an evil thing
And worthy of a brute accursed,
Loud praises with your mouth to sing
When in your heart you wish the worst.   375
ASTOLFO: Stella, you have been badly misinformed
If you doubt my good faith. Here let me beg you
To listen to my plea and hear me out.
The third Eugtorgius died, the King of Poland.
Basil, his heir, had two fair sisters who   380
Bore you, my cousin, and myself. I would not
Tire you with all that happened here. You know
Clorilene was our mother who enjoys,
Under a better reign, her starry throne.
She was the elder. Lovely Recisunda   385
(Whom may God cherish for a thousand years!)
The younger one, my mother and your aunt,
Was wed in Muscovy. Now to return:
Basil has yielded to the feebleness
Of age, loves learnèd study more than women,   390
Has lost his wife, is childless, will not marry.
And so it comes that you and I both claim
The heirdom of the realm. You claim that you
Were daughter to the elder daughter. I
                                                         395

Say that my being born a man, although
Son of the younger daughter, gives me title
To be preferred. We've told the king, our uncle,
Of both of our intentions. And he answered
400 That he would judge between our rival claims,
For which the time and place appointed was
Today and here. For that same reason I
Have left my native Muscovy. With that
Intent I come — not seeking to wage war
405 But so that you might thus wage war on me!
May Love, wise god, make true what people say
(Your "people" is a wise astrologer)
By settling this through your being chosen queen —
Queen and my consort, sovereign of my will;
410 My uncle crowning you, for greater honour;
Your courage conquering, as it deserves;
My love applauding you, its emperor!
STELLA: To such chivalrous gallantry, my breast
Cannot hold out. The imperial monarchy
415 I wish were mine only to make it yours —
Although my love is not quite satisfied
That you are to be trusted since your speech
Is somewhat contradicted by that portrait
You carry in the locket round your neck.
420 ASTOLFO: I'll give you satisfaction as to that.

(*Drums.*)

But these loud instruments will not permit it
That sound the arrival of the king and council.

(*Enter King Basil with his following.*)

STELLA: Wise Thales . . .
ASTOLFO: Learned Euclid . . .
STELLA: Among the signs . . .
ASTOLFO: Among the stars . . .
STELLA: Where you preside in power . . .
425 ASTOLFO: Where you reside . . .
STELLA: And plot their paths . . .
ASTOLFO: And trace their fiery trails . . .
STELLA: Describing . . .
ASTOLFO: . . . Measuring and judging them . . .
STELLA: Please read my stars that I, in humble
          bonds . . .
ASTOLFO: Please read them, so that I in soft
          embraces . . .
STELLA: May twine as ivy to this tree!
430 ASTOLFO: May find
Myself upon my knees before these feet!
BASIL: Come and embrace me, niece and nephew. Trust
me,
Since you're both loyal to my loving precepts,
And come here so affectionately both —
435 In nothing shall I leave you cause to cavil,
And both of you as equals will be treated.
The gravity of what I have to tell
Oppresses me, and all I ask of you
Is silence: the event itself will claim
440 Your wonderment. So be attentive now,
Belovèd niece and nephew, illustrious courtiers,

Relatives, friends, and subjects! You all know
That for my learning I have merited
The surname of The Learnèd, since the brush
Of great Timanthes, and Lisippus' marbles —   445
Stemming oblivion (consequence of time) —
Proclaimed me to mankind Basil the Great.
You know the science that I most affect
And most esteem is subtle mathematics
(By which I forestall time, cheat fame itself)   450
Whose office is to show things gradually.
For when I look my tables up and see,
Present before me, all the news and actions
Of centuries to come, I gain on Time —
Since Time recounts whatever I have said   455
After I say it. Those snowflaking haloes,
Those canopies of crystal spread on high,
Lit by the sun, cut by the circling moon,
Those diamond orbs, those globes of radiant crystal
Which the bright stars adorn, on which the signs   460
Parade in blazing excellence, have been
My chiefest study all through my long years.
They are the volumes on whose adamantine
Pages, bound up in sapphire, heaven writes,
In lines of burnished gold and vivid letters,   465
All that is due to happen, whether adverse
Or else benign. I read them in a flash,
So quickly that my spirit tracks their movements —
Whatever road they take, whatever goal
They aim at. Would to heaven that before   470
My genius had been the commentary
Writ in their margins, or the index to
Their pages, that my life had been the rubble,
The ruin, and destruction of their wrath,
And that my tragedy in them had ended,   475
Because, to the unlucky, even their merit
Is like a hostile knife, and he whom knowledge
Injures is but a murderer to himself.
And this I say myself, though my misfortunes
Say it far better, which, to marvel at,   480
I beg once more for silence from you all.
With my late wife, the queen, I had a son,
Unhappy son, to greet whose birth the heavens
Wore themselves out in prodigies and portents.
Ere the sun's light brought him live burial   485
Out of the womb (for birth resembles death)
His mother many times, in the delirium
And fancies of her sleep, saw a fierce monster
Bursting her entrails in a human form,
Born spattered with her lifeblood, dealing death,   490
The human viper of this century!
The day came for his birth, and every presage
Was then fulfilled, for tardily or never
Do the more cruel ones prove false. At birth
His horoscope was such that the bright sun,   495
Stained in its blood, entered ferociously
Into a duel with the moon above.
The whole earth seemed a rampart for the strife
Of heaven's two lights, who — though not hand-to-
          hand —

500 Fought light-to-light to gain the mastery!
The worst eclipse the sun has ever suffered
Since Christ's own death horrified earth and sky.
The whole earth overflowed with conflagrations
So that it seemed the final paroxysm
505 Of existence. The skies grew dark. Buildings shook.
The clouds rained stones. The rivers ran with
    blood.
In this delirious frenzy of the sun,
Thus, Segismund was born into the world,
Giving a foretaste of his character
510 By killing his own mother, seeming to speak thus
By his ferocity: "I am a man,
Because I have begun now to repay
All kindnesses with evil." To my studies
I went forthwith, and saw in all I studied
515 That Segismund would be the most outrageous
Of all men, the most cruel of all princes,
And impious of all monarchs, by whose acts
The kingdom would be torn up and divided
So as to be a school of treachery
520 And an academy of vices. He,
Risen in fury, amidst crimes and horrors,
Was born to trample me (with shame I say it)
And make of my grey hairs his very carpet.
Who is there but believes an evil Fate?
525 And more if he discovers it himself,
For self-love lends its credit to our studies.
So I, believing in the Fates, and in
The havoc that their prophecies predestined,
Determined to cage up this newborn tiger
530 To see if on the stars we sages have
Some power. I gave out that the prince had died
Stillborn, and, well-forewarned, I built a tower
Amidst the cliffs and boulders on yon mountains
Over whose tops the light scarce finds its way,
535 So stubbornly their obelisks and crags
Defend the entry to them. The strict laws
And edicts that I published then (declaring
That nobody might enter the forbidden
Part of the range) were passed on that account.
540 There Segismund lives to this day, a captive,
Poor and in misery, where, save Clotaldo,
His guardian, none have seen or talked to him.
The latter has instructed him in all
Branches of knowledge and in the Catholic faith,
545 Alone the witness of his misery.
There are three things to be considered now:
Firstly, Poland, that I love you greatly,
So much that I would free you from the oppression
And servitude of such a tyrant king.
550 He would not be a kindly ruler who
Would put his realm and homeland in such danger.
The second fact that I must bear in mind
Is this: that to deny my flesh and blood
The rights which law, both human and divine,
Concedes, would not accord with Christian
555   charity,
For no law says that, to prevent another

Being a tyrant, I may be one myself,
And if my son's a tyrant, to prevent him
From doing outrage, I myself should do it.
Now here's the third and last point I would speak
    of,   560
Namely, how great an error it has been
To give too much belief to things predicted,
Because, even if his inclination should
Dictate some headlong, rash precipitancies,
They may perhaps not conquer him entirely,   565
For the most accursèd destiny, the most
Violent inclination, the most impious
Planet — all can but influence, not force,
The free will which man holds direct from God.
And so, between one motive and another   570
Vacillating discursively, I hit
On a solution that will stun you all.
I shall tomorrow, but without his knowing
He is my son — your king — place Segismund
(For that's the name with which he was baptised)   575
Here on my throne, beneath my canopy,
Yes, in my very place, that he may govern you
And take command. And you must all be here
To swear him fealty as his loyal subjects.
Three things may follow from this test, and these   580
I'll set against the three which I proposed.
The first is that should the prince prove prudent,
Stable, and benign — thus giving the lie
To all that prophecy reports of him —
Then you'll enjoy in him your rightful ruler   585
Who was so long a courtier of the mountains
And neighbour to the beasts. Here is the second:
If he prove proud, rash, cruel, and outrageous,
And with a loosened rein gallop unheeding
Across the plains of vice, I shall have done   590
My duty, and fulfilled my obligation
Of mercy. If I then re-imprison him,
That's incontestably a kingly deed —
Not cruelty but merited chastisement.
The third thing's this: that if the prince should be 595
As I've described him, then — by the love I feel
For you, my vassals — I shall give you worthier
Rulers to wear the sceptre and the crown;
Because your king and queen will be my nephew
And niece, each with an equal right to rule,   600
Each gaining the inheritance he merits,
And joined in faith of holy matrimony.
This I command you as a king, I ask you
As a kind father, as a sage I pray you,
As an experienced old man I tell you,   605
And (if it's true, as Spanish Seneca
Says, that the king is slave unto his nation)
This, as a humble slave, I beg of you.
ASTOLFO: If it behoves me to reply (being
The person most involved in this affair)   610
Then, in the name of all, let Segismund
Appear! It is enough that he's your son!
ALL: Give us our prince: we want him for our king!
BASIL: Subjects, I thank you for your kindly favour.

615   Accompany these, my two Atlases,
            Back to their rooms. Tomorrow you shall see him.
ALL: Long live the great King Basil! Long live Basil!

(*Exeunt all, accompanying Stella and Astolfo. The King remains.*)

(*Enter Clotaldo with Rosaura and Clarion.*)

CLOTALDO: May I have leave to speak, sire?
BASIL: Oh, Clotaldo!
            You're very welcome.
CLOTALDO: Thus to kneel before you
620   Is always welcome, sire — yet not today
            When sad and evil Fate destroys the joy
            Your presence normally concedes.
BASIL: What's wrong?
CLOTALDO: A great misfortune, sire, has come upon me
            Just when I should have met it with rejoicing.
BASIL: Continue.
625 CLOTALDO: Sire, this beautiful young man
            Who inadvertently and daringly
            Came to the tower, wherein he saw the prince,
            Is my . . .
BASIL: Do not afflict yourself, Clotaldo.
            Had it not been just now, I should have minded,
630   I must confess. But I've revealed the secret,
            And now it does not matter if he knows it.
            Attend me afterwards. I've many things
            To tell you. You in turn have many things
            To do for me. You'll be my minister,
635   I warn you, in the most momentous action
            The world has ever seen. These prisoners, lest you
            Should think I blame your oversight, I'll pardon.
                                                   (*Exit.*)
CLOTALDO: Long may you live, great sire! A thousand
            years!

(*Aside.*)

            Heaven improves our fates. I shall not tell him
640   Now that he is my son, since it's not needed
            Till he's avenged.

(*Aloud.*)

            Strangers, you may go free.
ROSAURA: Humbly I kiss your feet.
CLARION: Whilst I'll just *miss* them —
            Old friends will hardly quibble at one letter.
645 ROSAURA: You've granted me my life, sir. I remain
            Your servant and eternally your debtor.
CLOTALDO: No! It was not your life I gave you. No!
            Since any wellborn man who, unavenged,
            Nurses an insult does not live at all.
650   And seeing you have told me that you came
            For that sole reason, it was not life I spared —
            Life in disgrace is not a life at all.

(*Aside.*)

            I see this spurs him.
ROSAURA: Freely I confess it —
            Although you spared my life, it was no life.

But I will wipe my honour's stain so spotless   655
            That after I have vanquished all my dangers
            Life well may seem a shining gift from you.
CLOTALDO: Take here your burnished steel: 'twill be
            enough,
            Bathed in your enemies' red blood, to right you.
            For steel that once was mine (I mean of course   660
            Just for the time I've had it in my keeping)
            Should know how to avenge you.
ROSAURA: Now, in your name I gird it on once more
            And on it I will swear to take revenge
            Although my foe were even mightier.   665
CLOTALDO: Is he so powerful?
ROSAURA: So much so that . . .
            Although I have no doubt in your discretion . . .
            I say no more because I'd not estrange
            Your clemency.
CLOTALDO: You would have won me had you told me,
            since   670
            That would prevent me helping him.

(*Aside.*)

            If only I could discover who he is!
ROSAURA: So that you'll not think that I value lightly
            Such confidence, know that my adversary
            Is no less than Astolfo, Duke of Muscovy.   675
CLOTALDO (*Aside*): (I hardly can withstand the grief it
            gives me
            For it is worse than aught I could imagine!
            Let us inquire of him some further facts.)

(*Aloud.*)

            If you were born a Muscovite, your ruler
            Could never have affronted you. Go back   680
            Home to your country. Leave this headstrong valour.
            It will destroy you.
ROSAURA: Though he's been my prince,
            I know that he has done me an affront.
CLOTALDO: Even though he slapped your face, that's
            no affront.

(*Aside.*)

            O heavens!
ROSAURA: My insult was far deeper!
CLOTALDO: Tell it: 685
            Since nothing I imagine could be deeper.
ROSAURA: Yes. I will tell it, yet, I know not why,
            With such respect I look upon your face,
            I venerate you with such true affection,
            With such high estimation do I weigh you,   690
            That I scarce dare to tell you — these men's clothes
            Are an enigma, not what they appear.
            So now you know. Judge if it's no affront
            That here Astolfo comes to wed with Stella
            Although betrothed to me. I've said enough.   695

                            (*Exeunt Rosaura and Clarion.*)

CLOTALDO: Here! Listen! Wait! What mazed
            confusion!

It is a labyrinth wherein the reason
Can find no clue. My family honour's injured.
The enemy's all powerful. I'm a vassal
700   And she's a woman. Heavens! Show a path
Although I don't believe there is a way!
There's nought but evil bodings in the sky.
The whole world is a prodigy, say I.

ACT II

(*A Hall in the Royal Palace.*)

(*Enter Basil and Clotaldo.*)

CLOTALDO: All has been done according to your
        orders.
BASIL: Tell me, Clotaldo, how it went?
CLOTALDO: Why, thus:
I took to Segismund a calming drug
Wherein are mixed herbs of especial virtue,
5   Tyrannous is their overpowering strength,
Which seize and steal and alienate man's gift
Of reasoning, thus making a live corpse
Of him. His violence evaporated
With all his faculties and senses too.
10   There is no need to prove it's possible
Because experience teaches us that medicine
Is full of natural secrets, that there is no
Animal, plant, or stone that has not got
Appointed properties. If human malice
15   Explores a thousand poisons which deal death,
Who then can doubt, that being so, that other
Poisons, less violent, cause only sleep?
But (leaving that doubt aside, as proven false
By every evidence) hear then the sequel:
20   I went down into Segismund's close prison
Bearing the drink wherein, with opium,
Henbane and poppies had been mixed. With him
I talked a little while of the humanities,
In which dumb Nature has instructed him,
25   The mountains and the heavens and the stars,
In whose divine academies he learned
Rhetoric from the birds and the wild creatures.
To lift his spirit to the enterprise
Which you require of him, I chose for subject
30   The swiftness of a stalwart eagle, who,
Deriding the base region of the wind,
Rises into the sphere reserved for fire,
A feathered lightning, an untethered comet.
Then I extolled such lofty flight and said:
35   "After all, he's the king of birds, and so
Takes precedence, by right, over the rest."
No more was needful for, in taking up
Majesty for his subject, he discoursed
With pride and high ambition, as his blood
40   Naturally moves, incites, and spurs him on
To grand and lofty things, and so he said
That in the restless kingdom of the birds
There should be those who swear obedience, too!

"In this, my miseries console me greatly,
Because if I'm a vassal here, it's only   45
By force, and not by choice. Of my own will
I would not yield in rank to any man."
Seeing that he grew furious — since this touched
The theme of his own griefs — I gave the potion
And scarcely had it passed from cup to breast   50
Before he yielded all his strength to slumber.
A chill sweat ran through all his limbs and veins.
Had I not known that this was mere feigned death
I would have thought him dead. Then came the men
To whom you've trusted this experiment,   55
Who placed him in a coach and brought him here
To your own rooms, where all things were
        prepared
In royalty and grandeur as befitting
His person. In your own bed they have laid him
Where, when the torpor wanes, they'll do him
        service   60
As if he were Your Majesty himself.
All has been done as you have ordered it,
And if I have obeyed you well, my lord,
I'd beg a favour (pardon me this freedom) —
To know what your intention is in thus   65
Transporting Segismund here to the palace.
BASIL: Your curiosity is just, Clotaldo,
And yours alone I'll satisfy. The star
Which governs Segismund, my son, in life,
Threatens a thousand tragedies and woes.   70
And now I wish to see whether the stars
(Which never lie — and having shown to us
So many cruel signs seem yet more certain)
May yet be brought to moderate their sentence,
Whether by prudence charmed or valour won,   75
For man does have the power to rule his stars.
I would examine this, bringing him here
Where he may know he is my son, and make
Trial of his talent. If magnanimously
He conquers and controls himself, he'll reign,   80
But if he proves a tyrant and is cruel,
Back to his chains he'll go. Now, you will ask,
Why did we bring him sleeping in this manner
For the experiment? I'll satisfy you,
Down to the smallest detail, with my answer.   85
If he knows that he is my son today,
And if tomorrow he should find himself
Once more reduced to prison, to misery,
He would despair entirely, knowing truly
Who, and whose son, he is. What consolation   90
Could he derive, then, from his lot? So I
Contrive to leave an exit for such grief,
By making him believe it was a dream.
By these means we may learn two things at once:
First, his character — for he will really be   95
Awake in all he thinks and all his actions;
Second, his consolation — which would be
(If he should wake in prison on the morrow,
Although he saw himself obeyed today)
That he might understand he had been dreaming,   100

And he will not be wrong, for in this world,
Clotaldo, all who live are only dreaming.
CLOTALDO: I've proofs enough to doubt of your
success,
But now it is too late to remedy it.
105 From what I can make out, I think he's wakened
And that he's coming this way, by the sound.
BASIL: I shall withdraw. You, as his tutor, go
And guide him through his new bewilderments
By answering his queries with the truth.
110 CLOTALDO: You give me leave to tell the truth of it?
BASIL: Yes, because knowing all things, he may find
Known perils are the easiest to conquer.

(*Exit Basil.*)

(*Enter Clarion.*)

CLARION: It cost me four whacks to get here so quickly.
I caught them from a red-haired halberdier
115 Sprouting a ginger beard over his livery,
And I've come to see what's going on.
No windows give a better view than those
A man brings with him in his head, not asking
For tickets of admission or paid seats,
120 Since at all functions, festivals, or feasts
He looks out with the same nice self-composure.
CLOTALDO (*Aside*): Here's Clarion who's the servant of
that person —
That trader in woes, importer from Poland
Of my disgrace.

(*Aloud.*)

Come, Clarion, what news?
125 CLARION: Item the first: encouraged by the fact
Your clemency's disposed to venge her insult,
Rosaura has resumed her proper clothing.
CLOTALDO: That's right: it's less indecorous and bold.
CLARION: Item: she's changed her name, and given out
That she's your niece. And now they've made so
130 much
Of her that she's been raised to maid of honour
To the unique and only princess, Stella.
CLOTALDO: That's right: her honour stands to my
account.
CLARION: Indeed she merely bides the time till you
135 Will settle all accounts about her honour.
CLOTALDO: Biding the time is wise, for in the end
It's Time that's going to settle all accounts!
CLARION: Item: that she's attended like a queen,
Because they take her for your niece. Item:
140 That I, who trudged along with her, am dying
Of hunger. Nobody remembers me,
Nor yet remembers that I'm like my name
And (should I sound my Clarion) could tell
All to the king and Stella and Astolfo.
145 For I am both a Clarion and a servant —
Two things which ill-accord with secrecy.
If silence should, by chance, let slip my hand,
Then there's a chorus which would fit me well:
"Dawn-breaking Clarion plays no better tune!"

CLOTALDO: You've reason for complaint. I'll satisfy it   150
If you'll but serve me . . .
CLARION: Hush, here's Segismund!

(*Enter musicians, singing, and servants arraying Segismund, who seems amazed.*)

SEGISMUND: Heavens above! What's this that I am
seeing?
I wonder at it all, with naught of fear!
But with a mighty doubt, I disbelieve it!
I? — in a sumptuous palace? I — encircled   155
With rich brocades and silks? I — overwhelmed
With servants in such brilliant liveries?
I — to awake in such a gorgeous bed?
I — in the middle of so many footmen
Who clothe me in rich garments? I'm awake: 160
It would be false to take this for a dream.
Am I not Segismund? Heavens! disabuse me
If I'm mistaken. Say, what could have happened
In my imagination while I slept —
That I should find myself in such a place?   165
But why should I worry, whatever it was?
I'll let myself be served and entertained —
Befall what may.
FIRST SERVANT (*Aside to Second Servant and Clarion*):
                         He's very melancholy!
SECOND SERVANT: Who would not be, considering all
that's happened
To him?
CLARION: I would not be!
SECOND SERVANT: You, speak to him.   170
FIRST SERVANT: Shall they begin to sing again?
SEGISMUND: Why, no,
I would not have them sing.
SECOND SERVANT: You're so distraught,
I wish you entertained.
SEGISMUND: My griefs are such
That no mere voices can amuse me now —
Only the martial music pleased my mind.   175
CLOTALDO: Your Highness, mighty prince, give me
your hand
To kiss. I'm glad to be the first to offer
Obedience at your feet.
SEGISMUND (*Aside*):   This is Clotaldo.
How is it he, that tyrannised my thralldom,
Should now be treating me with such respect?   180

(*Aloud.*)

Tell me what's happening all around me here.
CLOTALDO: With the perplexities of your new state,
Your reason will encounter many doubts,
But I shall try to free you from them all
(If that may be) because you now must know   185
You are hereditary Prince of Poland.
If you have been withdrawn from public sight
Under restraint, it was in strict obedience
To Fate's inclemency, which will permit
A thousand woes to fall upon this empire   190
The moment that you wear the sovereign's crown.

But trusting that you'll prudently defeat
Your own malignant stars (since they can be
Controlled by magnanimity) you've been
195 Brought to this palace from the tower you knew
Even while your soul was yielded up to sleep.
My lord the king, your father, will be coming
To see you, and from him you'll learn the rest.
SEGISMUND: Then, vile, infamous traitor, what have I
200 To know more than this fact of who I am,
To show my pride and power from this day onward?
How have you played your country such a treason
As to deny me, against law and right,
The rank which is my own?
CLOTALDO: Unhappy me!
SEGISMUND: You were a traitor to the law, a flattering
205   liar
To your own king, and cruel to myself.
And so the king, the law, and I condemn you,
After such fierce misfortunes as I've borne,
To die here by my hands.
SECOND SERVANT: My lord!
SEGISMUND: Let none
210 Get in the way. It is in vain. By God!
If you intrude, I'll throw you through the window.
SECOND SERVANT: Clotaldo, fly!
CLOTALDO: Alas, poor Segismund!
That you should show such pride, all unaware
That you are dreaming this.
                          (*Exit.*)
SECOND SERVANT: Take care! Take care!
SEGISMUND: Get out!
215 SECOND SERVANT: He was obeying the king's orders.
SEGISMUND: In an injustice, no one should obey
The king, and I'm his prince.
SECOND SERVANT: He had no right
To look into the rights and wrongs of it.
SEGISMUND: You must be mad to answer back at me.
CLARION: The prince is right. It's you who're in the
220   wrong!
SECOND SERVANT: Who gave you right to speak?
CLARION: I simply took it.
SEGISMUND: And who are you?
CLARION: I am the go-between,
And in this art I think I am a master —
Since I'm the greatest jackanapes alive.
SEGISMUND (*To Clarion*):
225 In all this new world, you're the only one
Of the whole crowd who pleases me.
CLARION: Why, my lord,
I am the best pleaser of Segismunds
That ever was: ask anybody here!

(*Enter Astolfo.*)

ASTOLFO: Blessèd the day, a thousand times, my prince,
230 On which you landed here on Polish soil
To fill with so much splendour and delight
Our wide horizons, like the break of day!
For you arise as does the rising sun

Out of the rugged mountains, far away.
Shine forth then! And although so tardily   235
You bind the glittering laurels on your brows,
The longer may they last you still unwithered.
SEGISMUND: God save you.
ASTOLFO: That you do not know me, sir,
Is some excuse for greeting me without
The honour due to me. I am Astolfo   240
The Duke of Muscovy. You are my cousin.
We are of equal rank.
SEGISMUND: Then if I say,
"God save you," do I not display good feeling?
But since you take such note of who you are,
The next time that I see you, I shall say   245
"God save you *not*," if you would like that better.
SECOND SERVANT (*To Astolfo*):
Your Highness, make allowance for his breeding
Amongst the mountains. So he deals with all.

(*To Segismund.*)

Astolfo does take precedence, Your Highness —
SEGISMUND: I have no patience with the way he came   250
To make his solemn speech, then put his hat on!
SECOND SERVANT: He's a grandee!
SEGISMUND: I'm grander than grandees!
SECOND SERVANT: For all that, there should be respect
    between you,
More than among the rest.
SEGISMUND: And who told you
To mix in my affairs?   255

(*Enter Stella.*)

STELLA: Many times welcome to Your Royal Highness,
Now come to grace the dais that receives him
With gratitude and love. Long may you live
August and eminent, despite all snares,
And count your life by centuries, not years!   260
SEGISMUND (*Aside to Clarion*):
Now tell me, who's this sovereign deity
At whose divinest feet Heaven lays down
The fleece of its aurora in the east?
CLARION: Sir, it's your cousin Stella.
SEGISMUND: She were better
Named "sun" than "star"!

(*To Stella.*)

                      Though your speech was fair, 265
Just to have seen you and been conquered by you
Suffices for a welcome in itself.
To find myself so blessed beyond my merit
What can I do but thank you, lovely Stella,
For you could add more brilliance and delight   270
To the most blazing star? When you get up
What work is left the sun to do? O give me
Your hand to kiss, from out whose cup of snow
The solar horses drink the fires of day!
STELLA: Be a more gentle courtier.
ASTOLFO: I am lost.   275

SECOND SERVANT: I know Astolfo's hurt. I must divert
    him.

(*To Segismund.*)

    Sir, you should know that thus to woo so boldly
    Is most improper. And, besides, Astolfo . . .
SEGISMUND: Did I not tell you not to meddle with me?
SECOND SERVANT: I only say what's just.
SEGISMUND: All this annoys me.
280   Nothing seems just to me but what I want.
SECOND SERVANT: Why, sir, I heard you say that no
    obedience
    Or service should be lent to what's unjust.
SEGISMUND: You also heard me say that I would throw
    Anyone who annoys me from that balcony.
SECOND SERVANT: With men like me you cannot do
285   such things.
SEGISMUND: No? Well, by God, I'll have to prove it
    then!

(*He takes him in his arms and rushes out, followed by
many, to return soon after.*)

ASTOLFO: What on earth have I seen? Can it be true?
STELLA: Go, all, and stop him!
SEGISMUND (*Returning*):   From the balcony
    He's fallen in the sea. How strange it seems!
290 ASTOLFO: Measure your acts of violence, my lord:
    From crags to palaces, the distance is
    As great as that between man and the beasts.
SEGISMUND: Well, since you are for speaking out so
    boldly,
    Perhaps one day you'll find that on your shoulders
295   You have no head to place your hat upon.
                      (*Exit Astolfo.*)

(*Enter Basil.*)

BASIL: What's happened here?
SEGISMUND: Nothing at all. A man
    Wearied me, so I threw him in the sea.
CLARION (*To Segismund*):
    Be warned. That is the king.
BASIL: On the first day,
    So soon, your coming here has cost a life?
300 SEGISMUND: He said I couldn't: so I won the bet.
BASIL: It grieves me, Prince, that, when I hoped to see
    you
    Forewarned, and overriding Fate, in triumph
    Over your stars, the first thing I should see
    Should be such rigour — that your first deed here
305   Should be a grievous homicide. Alas!
    With what love, now, can I offer my arms,
    Knowing your own have learned to kill already?
    Who sees a dirk, red from a mortal wound,
    But does not fear it? Who can see the place
310   Soaking in blood, where late a man was murdered,
    But even the strongest must respond to nature?
    So in your arms seeing the instrument
    Of death, and looking on a blood-soaked place,

    I must withdraw myself from your embrace,
    And though I thought in loving bonds to bind   315
    Your neck, yet fear withholds me from your arms.
SEGISMUND: Without your loving arms I can sustain
    Myself as usual. That such a loving father
    Could treat me with such cruelty, could thrust me
    From his side ungratefully, could rear me   320
    As a wild beast, could hold me for a monster,
    And pray that I were dead, that such a father
    Withholds his arms from winding round my neck,
    Seems unimportant, seeing that he deprives
    Me of my very being as a man.   325
BASIL: Would to heaven I had never granted it,
    For then I never would have heard your voice,
    Nor seen your outrages.
SEGISMUND: Had you denied
    Me being, then I would not have complained,
    But that you took it from me when you gave it —   330
    That is my quarrel with you. Though to give
    Is the most singular and noble action,
    It is the basest action if one gives
    Only to take away.
BASIL: How well you thank me
    For being raised from pauper to a prince!   335
SEGISMUND: In this what is there I should thank you
    for?
    You tyrant of my will! If you are old
    And feeble, and you die, what can you give me
    More than what is my own by right of birth?
    You are my father and my king, therefore   340
    This grandeur comes to me by natural law.
    Therefore, despite my present state, I'm not
    Indebted to you, rather can I claim
    Account of all those years in which you robbed me
    Of life and being, liberty, and honour.   345
    You ought to thank me that I press no claim
    Since you're my debtor, even to bankruptcy.
BASIL: Barbarous and outrageous brute! The
    heavens
    Have no fulfilled their prophecy: I call
    Them to bear witness to your pride. Although   350
    You know now, disillusioned, who you are,
    And see yourself where you take precedence,
    Take heed of this I say: be kind and humble
    Since it may be that you are only dreaming,
    Although it seems to you you're wide-awake.   355
                      (*Exit Basil.*)
SEGISMUND: Can I perhaps be dreaming, though I
    seem
    So wide-awake? No: I am not asleep,
    Since I can touch, and realise what I
    Have been before, and what I am today.
    And if you even now relented, Father,   360
    There'd be no cure since I know who I am
    And you cannot, for all your sighs and groans,
    Cheat me of my hereditary crown.
    And if I was submissive in my chains
    Before, then I was ignorant of what I am,   365

Which I now know (and likewise know that I
Am partly man but partly beast as well).

(*Enter Rosaura in woman's clothing.*)

ROSAURA (*Aside*): I came in Stella's train. I am afraid
    Of meeting with Astolfo, since Clotaldo
370   Says he must not know who I am, not see me,
    Because (he says) it touches on my honour.
    And well I trust Clotaldo since I owe him
    The safety of my life and honour both.
CLARION: What pleases you, and what do you admire
375   Most, of the things you've seen here in the world?
SEGISMUND: Why, nothing that I could not have
      foreseen —
    Except the loveliness of women! Once,
    I read among the books I had out there
    That who owes God most grateful contemplation
380   Is Man: who is himself a tiny world.
    But I think who owes God more grateful study
    Is Woman — since she is a tiny heaven,
    Having as much more beauty than a man
    As heaven than earth. And even more, I say,
385   If she's the one that I am looking at.
ROSAURA (*Aside*): That is the prince. I'll go.
SEGISMUND: Stop! Woman! Wait!
    Don't join the sunset with the breaking day
    By fading out so fast. If east and west
    Should clash like that, the day would surely suffer
390   A syncope. But what is this I see?
ROSAURA: What I am looking at I doubt, and yet
    Believe.
SEGISMUND (*Aside*): This beauty I have seen before.
ROSAURA (*Aside*): This pomp and grandeur I have seen
      before
    Cooped in a narrow dungeon.
395 SEGISMUND (*Aside*):   I have found
    My life at last.

(*Aloud.*)

                Woman (for that sole word
    Outsoars all wooing flattery of speech
    From one that is a man), woman, who are you?
    If even long before I ever saw you
400   You owed me adoration as your prince,
    How much the more should you be conquered by
      me
    Now I recall I've seen you once before!
    Who are you, beauteous woman?
ROSAURA (*Aside*):   I'll pretend.

(*Aloud.*)

    In Stella's train, I am a luckless lady.
SEGISMUND: Say no such thing. You are the sun from
405   which
    The minor star that's Stella draws its life,
    Since she receives the splendour of your rays.
    I've seen how in the kingdom of sweet odours,
    Commander of the squadrons of the flowers,
410   The rose's deity presides, and is

Their empress by divine right of her beauty.
Among the precious stones which can be listed
In the academy of mines, I've seen
The diamond much preferred above the rest,
And crowned their emperor, for shining brightest.   415
In the revolving empire of the stars
The morning star takes pride among the others.
In their perfected spheres, when the sun calls
The planets to his council, he presides
And is the very oracle of day.   420
Then if among stars, gems, planet, and flowers
The fairest are exalted, why do you
Wait on a lesser beauty than yourself
Who are, in greater excellence and beauty,
The sun, the morning star, the diamond, and the
    rose!   425

(*Enter Clotaldo, who remains by the stage-curtain.*)

CLOTALDO (*Aside*):
    I wish to curb him, since I brought him up.
    But, what is this?
ROSAURA: I reverence your favour,
    And yet reply, rhetorical, with silence,
    For when one's mind is clumsy and untaught,
    He answers best who does not speak at all.   430
SEGISMUND: Stay! Do not go! How can you wish to go
    And leave me darkened by my doubts?
ROSAURA: Your Highness,
    I beg your leave to go.
SEGISMUND: To go so rudely
    Is not to beg my leave but just to take it.
ROSAURA: But if you will not grant it, I must take it.   435
SEGISMUND: That were to change my courtesy to
      rudeness.
    Resistance is like venom to my patience.
ROSAURA: But even if this deadly, raging venom
    Should overcome your patience, yet you dare not
    And could not treat me with dishonour, sir.   440
SEGISMUND: Why, just to see then if I can, and dare
      to —
    You'll make me lose the fear I bear your beauty,
    Since the impossible is always tempting
    To me. Why, only now I threw a man
    Over this balcony who said I couldn't: 445
    And so to find out if I can or not
    I'll throw your honour through the window too.
CLOTALDO (*Aside*):
    He seems determined in this course. Oh, heavens!
    What's to be done that for a second time
    My honour's threatened by a mad desire?   450
ROSAURA: Then with good reason it was prophesied
    Your tyranny would wreak this kingdom
    Outrageous scandals, treasons, crimes, and deaths.
    But what can such a creature do as you
    Who are not even a man, save in the name —   455
    Inhuman, barbarous, cruel, and unbending
    As the wild beasts amongst whom you were nursed?
SEGISMUND: That you should not insult me in this way
    I spoke to you most courteously, and thought

460 I'd thereby get my way; but if you curse me thus
Even when I am speaking gently, why,
By the living God, I'll really give you cause.
Ho there! Clear out, the lot of you, at once!
Leave her to me! Close all the doors upon us.
Let no one enter!

(*Exeunt Clarion and other attendants.*)

465 ROSAURA: I am lost . . . I warn you . . .
SEGISMUND: I am a tyrant and you plead in vain.
CLOTALDO (*Aside*):
Oh, what a monstrous thing! I must restrain him
Even if I die for it.

(*Aloud.*)

                        Sir! Wait! Look here!
SEGISMUND: A second time you have provoked my
    anger,
470 You feeble, mad old man! Do you prize lightly
My wrath and rigour that you've gone so far?
CLOTALDO: Brought by the accents of her voice, I
    came
To tell you you must be more peaceful
If still you hope to reign, and warn you that
475 You should not be so cruel, though you rule —
Since this, perhaps, is nothing but a dream.
SEGISMUND: When you refer to disillusionment
You rouse me near to madness. Now you'll see,
Here as I kill you, if it's truth or dreaming!

(*As he tries to pull out his dagger, Clotaldo restrains him
and throws himself on his knees before him.*)

CLOTALDO: It's thus I'd save my life: and hope to do
480   so —
SEGISMUND: Take your presumptuous hand from off
    this steel.
CLOTALDO: Till people come to hold your rage and
    fury
I shall not let you go.
ROSAURA: O heavens!
SEGISMUND: Loose it,

(*They struggle.*)

I say, or else — you interfering fool —
485 I'll crush you to your death in my strong arms!
ROSAURA: Come quickly! Here's Clotaldo being killed!
                                    (*Exit.*)

(*Astolfo appears as Clotaldo falls on the floor, and the
former stands between Segismund and Clotaldo.*)

ASTOLFO: Why, what is this, most valiant prince?
        What? Staining
Your doughty steel in such old, frozen blood?
For shame! For shame! Sheathe your illustrious
    weapon!
490 SEGISMUND: When it is stained in his infamous blood!
ASTOLFO: At my feet here he has found sanctuary
And there he's safe, for it will serve him well.
SEGISMUND: Then serve me well by dying, for like this

I will avenge myself for your behaviour
In trying to annoy me first of all.   495
ASTOLFO: To draw in self-defense offends no king,
Though in his palace.

(*Astolfo draws his sword and they fight.*)

CLOTALDO (*To Astolfo*): Do not anger him!

(*Enter Basil, Stella, and attendants.*)

BASIL: Hold! Hold! What's this? Fighting with naked
    swords?
STELLA (*Aside*): It is Astolfo! How my heart misgives
    me!   500
BASIL: Why, what has happened here?
ASTOLFO: Nothing, my Lord,
Since you've arrived.

(*Both sheathe their swords.*)

SEGISMUND: Much, though you *have* arrived.
I tried to kill the old man.
BASIL: Had you no
Respect for those white hairs?
CLOTALDO: Sire, since they're only
Mine, as you well can see, it does not matter!   505
SEGISMUND: It is in vain you'd have me hold white hairs
In such respect, since one day you may find
Your own white locks prostrated at my feet
For still I have not taken vengeance on you
For the foul way in which you had me reared.   510
                                    (*Exit.*)
BASIL: Before that happens you will sleep once more
Where you were reared, and where what's happened
    may
Seem just a dream (being mere earthly glory).

(*All save Astolfo and Stella leave.*)

ASTOLFO: How seldom does prediction fail, when evil!
How oft, foretelling good! Exact in harm,   515
Doubtful in benefit! Oh, what a great
Astrologer would be one who foretold
Nothing but harms, since there's no doubt at all
That they are always due! In Segismund
And me the case is illustrated clearly.   520
In him, crimes, cruelties, deaths, and disasters
Were well predicted, since they all came true.
But in my own case, to predict for me
(As I foresaw beholding rays which cast
The sun into the shade and outface heaven)   525
Triumphs and trophies, happiness and praise,
Was false — and yet was true: it's only just
That when predictions start with promised favours
They should end in disdain.
STELLA: I do not doubt
Your protestations are most heartfelt; only   530
They're not for me, but for another lady
Whose portrait you were wearing round your neck
Slung in a locket when you first arrived.
Since it is so, she only can deserve
These wooing flatteries. Let her repay you   535

For in affairs of love, flatteries and vows
Made for another are mere forged credentials.

(*Rosaura enters but waits by the curtain.*)

ROSAURA (*Aside*): Thanks be to God, my troubles are
    near ended!
    To judge from what I see, I've naught to fear.
540 ASTOLFO: I will expel that portrait from my breast
    To make room for the image of your beauty
    And keep it there. For there where Stella is
    Can be no room for shade, and where the sun is
    No place for any star. I'll fetch the portrait.

(*Aside.*)

545   Forgive me, beautiful Rosaura, that,
    When absent, men and women seldom keep
    More faith than this.
                        (*Exit.*)

(*Rosaura comes forward.*)

ROSAURA (*Aside*): I could not hear a word. I was afraid
    That they would see me.
STELLA: Oh, Astrea!
ROSAURA: My lady!
550 STELLA: I am delighted that you came. Because
    To you alone would I confide a secret.
ROSAURA: Thereby you greatly honour me, your
    servant.
STELLA: Astrea, in the brief time I have known you
    I've given you the latchkey of my will.
555   For that, and being who you are, I'll tell you
    A secret which I've very often hidden
    Even from myself.
ROSAURA: I am your slave.
STELLA: Then, briefly:
    Astolfo, who's my cousin (the word cousin
    Suffices, since some things are plainly said
560   Even by thinking them), is to wed me
    If Fortune thus can wipe so many cares
    Away with one great joy. But I am troubled
    In that, the day he first came here, he carried
    A portrait of a lady round his neck.
565   I spoke to him about it courteously.
    He was most amiable, he loves me well,
    And now he's gone for it. I am embarrassed
    That he should give it me himself. Wait here,
    And tell him to deliver it to you.
570   Do not say more. Since you're discreet and fair:
    You'll surely know just what love is.
                        (*Exit.*)
ROSAURA: Great heavens!
    How I wish that I did not! For who could be
    So prudent or so skilful as would know
    What to advise herself in such a case?
575   Lives there a person on this earth today
    Who's more beset by the inclement stars,
    Who has more cares besieging him, or fights
    So many dire calamities at once?
    What can I do in such bewilderment

Wherein it seems impossible to find   580
Relief or comfort? Since my first misfortune
No other thing has chanced or happened to me
But was a new misfortune. In succession
Inheritors and heirs of their own selves
(Just like the Phoenix, his own son and father)   585
Misfortunes reproduce themselves, are born,
And live by dying. In their sepulchre
The ashes they consume are hot forever.
A sage once said misfortunes must be cowards
Because they never dare to walk alone   590
But come in crowds. I say they are most valiant
Because they always charge so bravely on
And never turn their backs. Who charges with them
May dare all things because there is no fear
That they'll ever desert him; and I say it   595
Because in all my life I never once
Knew them to leave me, nor will they grow tired
Of me till, wounded and shot through and through
By Fate, I fall into the arms of death.
Alas, what can I do in this dilemma?   600
If I reveal myself, then old Clotaldo,
To whom I owe my life, may take offence,
Because he told me to await the cure
And mending of my honour in concealment.
If I don't tell Astolfo who I am   605
And he detects me, how can I dissimulate?
Since even if I say I am not I,
The voice, the language, and the eyes will falter,
Because the soul will tell them that they lie.
What shall I do? It is in vain to study   610
What I should do, when I know very well
That, whatsoever way I choose to act,
When the time comes I'll do as sorrow bids,
For no one has control over his sorrows.
Then since my soul dares not decide its actions   615
Let sorrow fill my cup and let my grief
Reach its extremity and, out of doubts
And vain appearances, once and for all
Come out into the light — and Heaven shield me!

(*Enter Astolfo.*)

ASTOLFO: Here, lady, is the portrait . . . but . . . great
    God!   620
ROSAURA: Why does Your Highness halt, and stare
    astonished?
ASTOLFO: Rosaura! Why, to see you here!
ROSAURA: Rosaura?
    Sir, you mistake me for some other lady.
    I am Astrea, and my humble station
    Deserves no perturbation such as yours.   625
ASTOLFO: Enough of this pretence, Rosaura, since
    The soul can never lie. Though as Astrea
    I see you now, I love you as Rosaura.
ROSAURA: Not having understood Your Highness'
    meaning
    I can make no reply except to say   630
    That Stella (who might be the star of Venus)
    Told me to wait here and to tell you from her

635 To give to me the portrait you were fetching
(Which seems a very logical request)
And I myself will take it to my lady.
Thus Stella bids: even the slightest things
Which do me harm are governed by some star.

ASTOLFO: Even if you could make a greater effort
How poorly you dissimulate, Rosaura!

640 Tell your poor eyes they do not harmonise
With your own voice, because they needs must
            jangle
When the whole instrument is out of tune.
You cannot match the falsehood of your words
With the sincerity of what you're feeling.

645 ROSAURA: All I can say is — that I want the portrait.

ASTOLFO: As you require a fiction, with a fiction
I shall reply. Go and tell Stella this:
That I esteem her so, it seems unworthy
Only to send the counterfeit to her

650 And that I'm sending her the original.
And you, take the original along with you,
Taking yourself to her.

ROSAURA: When a man starts
Forth on a definite task, resolved and valiant,
Though he be offered a far greater prize

655 Than what he seeks, yet he returns with failure
If he returns without his task performed.
I came to get that portrait. Though I bear
The original with me, of greater value,
I would return in failure and contempt

660 Without the copy. Give it me, Your Highness,
Since I cannot return without it.

ASTOLFO: But
If I don't give it you, how can you do so?

ROSAURA: Like this, ungrateful man! I'll take it from
        you.

(*She tries to wrest it from him.*)

ASTOLFO: It is in vain.

ROSAURA: By God, it shall not come
Into another woman's hands!

665 ASTOLFO: You're terrifying!

ROSAURA: And you're perfidious!

ASTOLFO: Enough, my dear
        Rosaura!

ROSAURA: I, your dear? You lie, you villain!

(*They are both clutching the portrait.*)

(*Enter Stella.*)

STELLA: Astrea and Astolfo, what does this mean?

ASTOLFO (*Aside*): Here's Stella.

ROSAURA (*Aside*):   Love, grant me the
        strength to win
My portrait.

(*To Stella.*)

670   If you want to know, my lady,
What this is all about, I will explain.

ASTOLFO (*To Rosaura, aside*):
        What do you mean?

ROSAURA: You told me to await
Astolfo here and ask him for a portrait
On your behalf. I waited here alone

675 And as one thought suggests another thought,
Thinking of portraits, I recalled my own
Was here inside my sleeve. When one's alone,
One is diverted by a foolish trifle
And so I took it out to look at it.

680 It slipped and fell, just as Astolfo here,
Bringing the portrait of the other lady,
Came to deliver it to you as promised.
He picked my portrait up, and so unwilling
Is he to give away the one you asked for,

685 Instead of doing so, he seized upon
The other portrait which is mine alone
And will not give it back though I entreated
And begged him to return it. I was angry
And tried to snatch it back. That's it he's holding,

690 And you can see yourself if it's not mine.

STELLA: Let go the portrait.

(*She snatches it from him.*)

ASTOLFO: Madam!

STELLA: The draughtsman
Was not unkind to truth.

ROSAURA: Is it not mine?

STELLA: Why, who could doubt it?

ROSAURA: Ask him for the other.

STELLA: Here, take your own, Astrea. You may leave us.

ROSAURA (*Aside*): Now I have got my portrait, come
        what will.

695   (*Exit.*)

STELLA: Now give me up the portrait that I asked for
Although I'll see and speak to you no more.
I do not wish to leave it in your power
Having been once so foolish as to beg it.

ASTOLFO (*Aside*): Now how can I get out of this foul
        trap?   700

(*To Stella.*)

Beautiful Stella, though I would obey you,
And serve you in all ways, I cannot give you
The portrait, since . . .

STELLA: You are a crude, coarse villain
And ruffian of a wooer. For the portrait —
I do not want it now, since, if I had it,   705
It would remind me I had asked you for it.

                                              (*Exit.*)

ASTOLFO: Listen! Look! Wait! Let me explain!

(*Aside.*)

                                        Oh, damn
Rosaura! How the devil did she get
To Poland for my ruin and her own?

(*The prison of Segismund in the tower.*)

(*Segismund lying on the ground loaded with fetters and clothed in skins as before. Clotaldo, two attendants, and Clarion.*)

CLOTALDO: Here you must leave him — since his
710   reckless pride
      Ends here today where it began.
ATTENDANT: His chain
      I'll rivet as it used to be before.
CLARION: O Prince, you'd better not awake too soon
      To find how lost you are, how changed your fate,
715   And that your fancied glory of an hour
      Was but a shade of life, a flame of death!
CLOTALDO: For one who knows so well to wield his
      tongue
      It's fit a worthy place should be provided
      With lots of room and lots of time to argue.
720   This is the fellow that you have to seize

(*To the attendants.*)

      And that's the room in which you are to lock him.

(*Points to the nearest cell.*)

CLARION: Why me?
CLOTALDO: Because a Clarion who knows
      Too many secrets must be kept in gaol —
      A place where even clarions are silent.
725   CLARION: Have I, by chance, wanted to kill my father
      Or thrown an Icarus from a balcony?
      Am I asleep or dreaming? To what end
      Do you imprison me?
CLOTALDO: You're Clarion.
CLARION: Well, say I swear to be a cornet now,
730   A silent one, a wretched instrument . . . ?

(*They hustle him off.*)

(*Clotaldo remains.*)

(*Enter Basil, wearing a mask.*)

BASIL: Clotaldo.
CLOTALDO: Sire . . . and is it thus alone
      Your Majesty has come?
BASIL: Vain curiosity
      To see what happens here to Segismund.
CLOTALDO: See where he lies, reduced to misery!
735   BASIL: Unhappy prince! Born at a fatal moment!
      Come waken him, now he has lost his strength
      With all the opium he's drunk.
CLOTALDO: He's stirring
      And talking to himself.
BASIL: What is he dreaming?
      Let's listen now.
SEGISMUND: He who chastises tyrants
740   Is a most pious prince . . . Now let Clotaldo
      Die by my hand . . . my father kiss my feet . . .
CLOTALDO: He threatens me with death!
BASIL: And me with insult
      And cruelty.
CLOTALDO: He'd take my life away.
BASIL: And he'd humiliate me at his feet.
SEGISMUND (*Still in a dream*):
745   Throughout the expanse of this world's theatre
      I'll show my peerless valour, let my vengeance

Be wreaked, and the Prince Segismund be seen
To triumph — over his father . . . but, alas!

(*Awakening.*)

   Where am I?
BASIL (*To Clotaldo*): Since he must not see me here,   750
   I'll listen further off. You know your cue.

(*Retires to one side.*)

SEGISMUND: Can this be I? Am I the same who, chained
   And long imprisoned, rose to such a state?
   Are you not still my sepulchre and grave,
   You dismal tower? God! What things I have
      dreamed!   755
CLOTALDO (*Aside*): Now I must go to him to
   disenchant him.

(*Aloud.*)

   Awake already?
SEGISMUND: Yes: it was high time.
CLOTALDO: What? Do you have to spend all day
      asleep?
   Since I was following the eagle's flight
   With tardy discourse, have you still lain here   760
   Without awaking?
SEGISMUND: No. Nor even now
   Am I awake. It seems I've always slept,
   Since, if I've dreamed what I've just seen and heard
   Palpably and for certain, then I am dreaming
   What I see now — nor is it strange I'm tired,   765
   Since what I, sleeping, see, tells me that I
   Was dreaming when I thought I was awake.
CLOTALDO: Tell me your dream.
SEGISMUND: That's if it *was* a dream!
   No, I'll not tell you what I dreamed; but what
   I lived and saw, Clotaldo, I *will* tell you.   770
   I woke up in a bed that might have been
   The cradle of the flowers, woven by Spring.
   A thousand nobles, bowing, called me Prince,
   Attiring me in jewels, pomp, and splendour.
   My equanimity you turned to rapture   775
   Telling me that I was the Prince of Poland.
CLOTALDO: I must have got a fine reward!
SEGISMUND: Not so:
   For as a traitor, twice, with rage and fury,
   I tried to kill you.
CLOTALDO: Such cruelty to me?
SEGISMUND: I was the lord of all, on all I took revenge, 780
   Except I loved one woman . . . I believe
   That *that* was true, though all the rest has faded.
                                    (*Exit Basil.*)
CLOTALDO (*Aside*): I see the king was moved, to hear
   him speak.

(*Aloud.*)

   Talking of eagles made you dream of empires,
   But even in your dreams it's good to honour   785
   Those who have cared for you and brought you up.

For Segismund, even in dreams, I warn you
Nothing is lost by trying to do good.

(*Exit.*)

SEGISMUND: That's true, and therefore let us subjugate
790 The bestial side, this fury and ambition,
Against the time when we may dream once more,
As certainly we shall, for this strange world
Is such that but to live here is to dream.
And now experience shows me that each man
795 Dreams what he is until he is awakened.
The king dreams he's a king and in this fiction
Lives, rules, administers with royal pomp.
Yet all the borrowed praises that he earns
Are written in the wind, and he is changed
800 (How sad a fate!) by death to dust and ashes.
What man is there alive who'd seek to reign
Since he must wake into the dream that's death.
The rich man dreams his wealth which is his care
And woe. The poor man dreams his sufferings.
805 He dreams who thrives and prospers in this life.
He dreams who toils and strives. He dreams who
injures,
Offends, and insults. So that in this world
Everyone dreams the thing he is, though no one
Can understand it. I dream I am here,
810 Chained in these fetters. Yet I dreamed just now
I was in a more flattering, lofty station.
What is this life? A frenzy, an illusion,
A shadow, a delirium, a fiction.
The greatest good's but little, and this life
815 Is but a dream, and dreams are only dreams.

ACT III

(*The tower.*)

(*Enter Clarion.*)

CLARION: I'm held in an enchanted tower, because
Of all I know. What would they do to me
For all I don't know, since — for all I know —
They're killing me by starving me to death.
5 O that a man so hungry as myself
Should live to die of hunger while alive!
I am so sorry for myself that others
May well say "I can well believe it," since
This silence ill accords with my name "Clarion,"
10 And I just can't shut up. My fellows here?
Spiders and rats — fine feathered songsters those!
My head's still ringing with a dream of fifes
And trumpets and a lot of noisy humbug
And long processions as of penitents
15 With crosses, winding up and down, while some
Faint at the sight of blood besmirching others.
But now to tell the truth, I am in prison.
For knowing secrets, I am kept shut in,
Strictly observed as if I were a Sunday,
20 And feeling sadder than a Tuesday, where
I neither eat nor drink. They say a secret
Is sacred and should be as strictly kept
As any saint's day on the calendar.
Saint Secret's Day for me's a working day
Because I'm never idle then. The penance   25
I suffer here is merited, I say:
Because being a lackey, I was silent,
Which, in a servant, is a sacrilege.

(*A noise of drums and trumpets.*)

FIRST SOLDIER (*Within*):
Here is the tower in which he is imprisoned.
Smash in the door and enter, everybody!   30
CLARION: Great God! They've come to seek me. That
is certain
Because they say I'm here. What can they want?

(*Enter several soldiers.*)

FIRST SOLDIER: Go in.
SECOND SOLDIER: He's here!
CLARION: No, he's not here!
ALL THE SOLDIERS: Our lord!
CLARION: What, are they drunk?
FIRST SOLDIER: You are our rightful prince.
We do not want and never shall allow   35
A stranger to supplant our trueborn prince.
Give us your feet to kiss!
ALL THE SOLDIERS: Long live the prince!
CLARION: Bless me, if it's not real! In this strange
kingdom
It seems the custom, everyday, to take
Some fellow and to make him prince and then   40
Shut him back in this tower. That *must* be it!
So I must play my role.
ALL THE SOLDIERS: Give us your feet.
CLARION: I can't. They're necessary. After all
What sort of use would be a footless prince?
SECOND SOLDIER: All of us told your father, as one
man,   45
We want no prince of Muscovy but you!
CLARION: You weren't respectful to my father? Shame!
FIRST SOLDIER: It was our loyalty that made us tell him.
CLARION: If it was loyalty, you have my pardon.
SECOND SOLDIER: Restore your empire. Long live
Segismund!   50
CLARION (*Aside*): That is the name they seem to give to
all
These counterfeited princes.

(*Enter Segismund.*)

SEGISMUND: Who called Segismund?
CLARION (*Aside*): I seem to be a hollow sort of prince.
FIRST SOLDIER: Which of you's Segismund?
SEGISMUND: I am.
SECOND SOLDIER (*To Clarion*):   Then, why,
Rash fool, did you impersonate the prince   55
Segismund?
CLARION: What? I, Segismund? Yourselves
Be-Segismunded me without request.
All yours was both the rashness and the folly.

FIRST SOLDIER: Prince Segismund, whom we acclaim
    our lord,
60   Your father, great King Basil, in his fear
    That heaven would fulfil a prophecy
    That one day he would kneel before your feet
    Wishes now to deprive you of the throne
    And give it to the Duke of Muscovy.
65   For this he called a council, but the people
    Discovered his design and knowing, now,
    They have a native king, will have no stranger.
    So scorning the fierce threats of destiny,
    We've come to seek you in your very prison,
70   That aided by the arms of the whole people,
    We may restore you to the crown and sceptre,
    Taking them from the tyrant's grasp. Come, then:
    Assembling here, in this wide desert region,
    Hosts of plebeians, bandits, and freebooters,
75   Acclaim you king. Your liberty awaits you!
    Hark to its voice!

(*Shouts within.*)

               Long life to Segismund!
SEGISMUND: Once more, you heavens will that I should
    dream
    Of grandeur, once again, 'twixt doubts and shades,
    Behold the majesty of pomp and power
80   Vanish into the wind, once more you wish
    That I should taste the disillusion and
    The risk by which all human power is humbled,
    Of which all human power should live aware.
    It must not be. I'll not be once again
85   Put through my paces by my fortune's stars.
    And since I know this life is all a dream,
    Depart, vain shades, who feign, to my dead senses,
    That you have voice and body, having neither!
    I want no more feigned majesty, fantastic
90   Display, no void illusions, that one gust
    Can scatter like the almond tree in flower,
    Whose rosy buds, without advice or warning,
    Dawn in the air too soon and then, as one,
    Are all extinguished, fade, and fall, and wither
95   In the first gust of wind that comes along!
    I know you well. I know you well by now.
    I know that all that happens in yourselves
    Happens as in a sleeping man. For me
    There are no more delusions and deceptions
100   Since I well know this life is all a dream.
SECOND SOLDIER: If you think we are cheating, just
    sweep
    Your gaze along these towering peaks, and see
    The hosts that wait to welcome and obey you.
SEGISMUND: Already once before I've seen such crowds
105   Distinctly, quite as vividly as these:
    And yet it was a dream.
SECOND SOLDIER: No great event
    Can come without forerunners to announce it
    And this is the real meaning of your dream.
SEGISMUND: Yes, you say well. It was the fore-
    announcement

And just in case it was correct, my soul,   110
    (Since life's so short) let's dream the dream anew!
    But it must be attentively, aware
    That we'll awake from pleasure in the end.
    Forewarned of that, the shock's not so abrupt,
    The disillusion's less. Evils anticipated   115
    Lose half their sting. And armed with this
        precaution —
    That power, even when we're sure of it, is borrowed
    And must be given back to its true owner —
    We can risk anything and dare the worst.
    Subjects, I thank you for your loyalty.   120
    In me you have a leader who will free you,
    Bravely and skilfully, from foreign rule.
    Sound now to arms, you'll soon behold my valour.
    Against my father I must march and bring
    Truth from the stars. Yes: he must kneel to me.   125

(*Aside.*)

    But yet, since I may wake before he kneels,
    Perhaps I'd better not proclaim what may not
        happen.
ALL: Long live Segismund!

(*Enter Clotaldo.*)

CLOTALDO: Gracious heavens! What is
    This riot here?
SEGISMUND: Clotaldo!
CLOTALDO: Sir!

(*Aside.*)

                    He'll prove
    His cruelty on me.
CLARION: I bet he throws him   130
    Over the mountain.
CLOTALDO: At your royal feet
    I kneel, knowing my penalty is death.
SEGISMUND: Rise, rise, my foster father, from the
    ground,
    For you must be the compass and the guide
    In which I trust. You brought me up, and I   135
    Know what I owe your loyalty. Embrace me!
CLOTALDO: What's that you say?
SEGISMUND: I know I'm in a dream,
    But I would like to act well, since good actions,
    Even in a dream, are not entirely lost.
CLOTALDO: Since doing good is now to be your glory,   140
    You will not be offended that I too
    Should do what's right. You march against your
        father!
    I cannot give you help against my king.
    Here at your feet, my lord, I plead for death.
SEGISMUND (*Aloud*): Villain!

(*Aside.*)

                But let us suffer this annoyance.   145
    Though my rage would slay him, yet he's loyal.
    A man does not deserve to die for that.
    How many angry passions does this leash

Restrain in me, this curb of knowing well
150 That I must wake and find myself alone!
SECOND SOLDIER: All this fine talk, Clotaldo, is a cruel
Spurn of the public welfare. We are loyal
Who wish our own prince to reign over us.
CLOTALDO: Such loyalty, after the king were dead,
155 Would honour you. But while the king is living
He is our absolute, unquestioned lord.
There's no excuse for subjects who oppose
His sovereignty in arms.
FIRST SOLDIER: We'll soon see well
Enough, Clotaldo, what this loyalty
Is worth.
160 CLOTALDO: You would be better if you had some.
It is the greatest prize.
SEGISMUND: Peace, peace, I pray you.
CLOTALDO: My lord!
SEGISMUND: Clotaldo, if your feelings
Are truly thus, go you, and serve the king;
That's prudence, loyalty, and common sense.
165 But do not argue here with anyone
Whether it's right or wrong, for every man
Has his own honour.
CLOTALDO: Humbly I take my leave.
                                        (*Exit.*)
SEGISMUND: Now sound the drums and march in rank
and order
Straight to the palace.
ALL: Long live Segismund!
170 SEGISMUND: Fortune, we go to reign! Do not awake me
If I am dreaming! Do not let me fall
Asleep if it is true! To act with virtue
Is what matters, since if this proves true,
175 If not, we win us friends against the time
When we at last awake.

(*A room in the Royal Palace.*)

(*Enter Basil and Astolfo.*)

BASIL: Whose prudence can rein in a bolting horse?
Who can restrain a river's pride, in spate?
Whose valour can withstand a crag dislodged
180 And hurtling downwards from a mountain peak?
All these are easier by far than to hold back
A crowd's proud fury, once it has been roused.
It has two voices, both proclaiming war,
And you can hear them echoing through the
mountains,
185 Some shouting "Segismund," others "Astolfo."
The scene I set for swearing of allegiance
Lends but an added horror to this strife:
It has become the back cloth to a stage
Where Fortune plays out tragedies in blood.
190 ASTOLFO: My lord, forget the happiness and wealth
You promised me from your most blessèd hand.
If Poland, which I hope to rule, refuses
Obedience to my right, grudging me honour,
It is because I've got to earn it first.

Give me a horse, that I with angry pride   195
May match the thunder in my voice and ride
To strike, like lightning, terror far and wide.
                                        (*Exit Astolfo.*)
BASIL: No remedy for what's infallible!
What is foreseen is perilous indeed!
If something has to be, there's no way out;   200
In trying to evade it, you but court it.
This law is pitiless and horrible.
Thinking one can evade the risk, one meets it:
My own precautions have been my undoing,
And I myself have quite destroyed my kingdom. 205

(*Enter Stella.*)

STELLA: If you, my lord, in person do not try
To curb the vast commotion that has started
In all the streets between the rival factions,
You'll see your kingdom, swamped in waves of
crimson,
Swimming in its own blood, with nothing left   210
But havoc, dire calamity, and woe.
So frightful is the damage to your empire
That, seen, it strikes amazement; heard, despair.
The sun's obscured, the very winds are hindered.
Each stone is a memorial to the dead.   215
Each flower springs from a grave while every building
Appears a mausoleum, and each soldier
A premature and walking skeleton.

(*Enter Clotaldo.*)

CLOTALDO: Praise be to God, I reach your feet alive!
BASIL: Clotaldo! What's the news of Segismund?   220
CLOTALDO: The crowd, a headstrong monster blind
with rage,
Entered his dungeon tower and set him free.
He, now exalted for the second time,
Conducts himself with valour, boasting how
He will bring down the truth out of the stars. 225
BASIL: Give me a horse, that I myself, in person,
May vanquish such a base, ungrateful son!
For I, in the defence of my own crown,
Shall do by steel what science failed to do.
                                        (*Exit.*)
STELLA: I'll be Bellona to your Sun, and try   230
To write my name next yours in history.
I'll ride as though I flew on outstretched wings
That I may vie with Pallas.
                                        (*Exit.*)

(*Enter Rosaura, holding back Clotaldo.*)

ROSAURA: I know that all is war, Clotaldo, yet
Although your valour calls you to the front,   235
First hear me out. You know quite well that I
Arrived in Poland poor and miserable,
Where, shielded by your valour, I found mercy.
You told me to conceal myself, and stay
Here in the palace, hiding from Astolfo.   240
He saw me in the end, and so insulted
My honour that (although he saw me clearly)

He nightly speaks with Stella in the garden.
I have the key to it and I will show you
245   How you can enter there and end my cares.
Thus bold, resolved, and strong, you can recover
My honour, since you're ready to avenge me
By killing him.
CLOTALDO: It's true that I intended,
Since first I saw you (having heard your tale)
250   With my own life to rectify your wrongs.
The first step that I took was bid you dress
According to your sex, for fear Astolfo
Might see you as you were, and deem you
        wanton.
I was devising how we could recover
255   Your honour (so much did it weigh on me)
Even though we had to kill him. (A wild plan —
Though since he's not my king, I would not flinch
From killing him.) But then, when suddenly
Segismund tried to kill me, it was he
260   Who saved my life with his surpassing valour.
Consider: how can I requite Astolfo
With death for giving me my life so bravely,
And when my soul is full of gratitude?
So torn between the two of you I stand —
265   Rosaura, whose life I saved, and Astolfo,
Who saved my life. What's to be done? Which
        side
To take, and whom to help, I cannot judge.
What I owe you in that I gave you life
I owe to him in that he gave me life.
270   And so there is no course that I can take
To satisfy my love. I am a person
Who has to act, yet suffer either way.
ROSAURA: I should not have to tell so brave a man
That if it is nobility to give,
275   It's baseness to receive. That being so
You owe no gratitude to him, admitting
That it was he who gave you life, and you
Who gave me life, since he forced you to take
A meaner role, and through me you assumed
280   A generous role. So you should side with me:
My cause is so far worthier than his own
As giving is than taking.
CLOTALDO: Though nobility
Is with the giver, it is gratitude
That dwells with the receiver. As a giver
285   I have the name of being generous:
Then grant me that of being grateful too
And let me earn the title and be grateful,
As I am liberal, giving or receiving.
ROSAURA: You granted me my life, at the same time
290   Telling me it was worthless, since dishonoured,
And therefore was no life. Therefore from you
I have received no life at all. And since
You should be liberal first and grateful after
(Since so you said yourself) I now entreat you
295   Give me the life, the life you never gave me!
As giving magnifies the most, give first
And then be grateful after, if you will!

CLOTALDO: Won by your argument, I will be
        liberal.
Rosaura, I shall give you my estate
And you shall seek a convent, there to live.   300
This measure is a happy thought, for, see,
Fleeing a crime, you find a sanctuary.
For when the empire's threatened with disasters
And is divided thus, I, born a noble,
Am not the man who would augment its woes.   305
So with this remedy which I have chosen
I remain loyal to the kingdom, generous
To you, and also grateful to Astolfo.
And thus I choose the course that suits you best.
Were I your father, what could I do more?   310
ROSAURA: Were you my father, then I would accept
The insult. Since you are not, I refuse.
CLOTALDO: What do you hope to do then?
ROSAURA: Kill the duke!
CLOTALDO: A girl who never even knew her father
Armed with such courage?
ROSAURA: Yes.
CLOTALDO: What spurs you on?   315
ROSAURA: My good name.
CLOTALDO: In Astolfo you will find . . .
ROSAURA: My honour rides on him and strikes him
        down!
CLOTALDO: Your king, too, Stella's husband!
ROSAURA: Never, never
Shall that be, by almighty God, I swear!
CLOTALDO: Why, this is madness!
ROSAURA: Yes it is!
CLOTALDO: Restrain it.   320
ROSAURA: That I cannot.
CLOTALDO: Then you are lost forever!
ROSAURA: I know it!
CLOTALDO: Life and honour both together!
ROSAURA: I well believe it!
CLOTALDO: What do you intend?
ROSAURA: My death.
CLOTALDO: This is despair and desperation.
ROSAURA: It's honour.
CLOTALDO: It is nonsense.
ROSAURA: It is valour.   325
CLOTALDO: It's frenzy.
ROSAURA: Yes, it's anger! Yes, it's fury!
CLOTALDO: In short you cannot moderate your
        passion?
ROSAURA: No.
CLOTALDO: Who is there to help you?
ROSAURA: I, myself.
CLOTALDO: There is no cure?
ROSAURA: There is no cure!
CLOTALDO: Think well
If there's not some way out . . .
ROSAURA: Some other way   330
To do away with me . . .
                                            (Exit.)
CLOTALDO: If you are lost,
My daughter, let us both be lost together!

(*In the country.*)

(*Enter Segismund clothed in skins. Soldiers marching.
Clarion. Drums beating.*)

SEGISMUND: If Rome, today, could see me here, renewing
    Her olden triumphs, she might laugh to see
335 A wild beast in command of mighty armies,
    A wild beast, to whose fiery aspirations
    The firmament were all too slight a conquest!
    But stoop your flight, my spirit. Do not thus
    Be puffed to pride by these uncertain plaudits
340 Which, when I wake, will turn to bitterness
    In that I won them only to be lost.
    The less I value them, the less I'll miss them.

(*A trumpet sounds.*)

CLARION: Upon a rapid courser (pray excuse me,
    Since if it comes to mind I must describe it)
345 In which it seems an atlas was designed
    Since if its body is earth, its soul is fire
    Within its breast, its foam appears the sea,
    The wind its breath, and chaos its condition,
    Since in its soul, its foam, its breath and flesh,
350 It seems a monster of fire, earth, sea, and wind,
    Upon the horse, all of a patchwork colour,
    Dappled, and rushing forward at the will
    Of one who plies the spur, so that it flies
    Rather than runs — see how a woman rides
    Boldly into your presence.°
355 SEGISMUND: Her light blinds me.
CLARION: Good God! Why, here's Rosaura!
SEGISMUND: It is heaven
    That has restored her to my sight once more.

(*Enter Rosaura with sword and dagger in riding costume.*)

ROSAURA: Generous Segismund, whose majesty
    Heroically rises in the lustre
360 Of his great deeds out of his night of shadows,
    And as the greatest planet, in the arms
    Of his aurora, lustrously returns
    To plants and roses, over hills and seas,
    When, crowned with gold, he looks abroad, dispersing
365 Radiance, flashing his rays, bathing the summits,
    And broidering the fringes of the foam,
    So may you dawn upon the world, bright sun
    Of Poland, that a poor unhappy woman
    May fall before your feet and beg protection
370 Both as a woman and unfortunate —
    Two things that must oblige you, sire, as one
    Who prize yourself as valiant, each of them
    More than suffices for your chivalry.
    Three times you have beheld me now, three times
375 Been ignorant of who I am, because

351–55. Upon a . . . presence: Clarion's speech is a parody of
exaggerated style including Calderón's. [R.C.]

Three times you saw me in a different clothing.
The first time you mistook me for a man,
Within that rigorous prison, where your hardships
Made mine seem pleasure. Next time, as a woman,
You saw me, when your pomp and majesty   380
Were as a dream, a phantasm, a shade.
The third time is today when, as a monster
Of both the sexes, in a woman's costume
I bear a soldier's arms. But to dispose you
The better to compassion, hear my story.   385
My mother was a noble in the court
Of Moscow, who, since most unfortunate,
Must have been beautiful. Then came a traitor
And cast his eyes on her (I do not name him,
Not knowing who he is). Yet I deduce   390
That he was valiant too from my own valour,
Since he gave form to me — and I could wish
I had been born in pagan times, that I might
Persuade myself he was some god of those
Who rain in showers of gold, turn into swans   395
Or bulls, for Danaës, Ledas, or Europas.
That's strange: I thought I was just rambling on
By telling old perfidious myths, yet find
I've told you how my mother was cajoled.
Oh, she was beautiful as no one else   400
Has been, but was unfortunate like all.
He swore to wed her (that's an old excuse)
And this trick reached so nearly to her heart
That thought must weep, recalling it today.
The tyrant left her only with his sword   405
As Aeneas left Troy. I sheathed its blade here
Upon my thigh, and I will bare it too
Before the ending of this history.
Out of this union, this poor link which neither
Could bind the marriage nor handcuff the crime,   410
Myself was born, her image and her portrait,
Not in her beauty, but in her misfortune,
For mine's the same. That's all I need to say.
The most that I can tell you of myself
Is that the man who robbed me of the spoils   415
And trophies of my honour is Astolfo.
Alas! to name him my heart rages so
(As hearts will do when men name enemies).
Astolfo was my faithless and ungrateful
Lord, who (quite forgetful of our happiness,   420
Since of a past love even the memory fades)
Came here to claim the throne and marry Stella
For she's the star who rises as I set.
It's hard to credit that a star should sunder
Lovers the stars had made comfortable!   425
So hurt was I, so villainously cheated,
That I became mad, brokenhearted, sick,
Half wild with grief, and like to die, with all
Hell's own confusion ciphered on my mind
Like Babel's incoherence. Mutely I told   430
My griefs (since woes and griefs declare themselves
Better than can the mouth, by their effects),
When, with my mother (we were by ourselves),
She broke the prison of my pent-up sorrows

435 And from my breast they all rushed forth in troops.
I felt no shyness, for in knowing surely
That one to whom one's errors are recounted
Has also been an ally in her own,
One finds relief and rest, since bad example
440 Can sometimes serve for a good purpose too.
She heard my plaint with pity, and she tried
To palliate my sorrows with her own.
How easily do judges pardon error
When they've offended too! An example,
445 A warning, in herself, she did not trust
To idleness, or the slow cure of time,
Nor try to find a remedy for her honour
In my misfortunes, but, with better counsel,
She bade me follow him to Poland here
450 And with prodigious gallantry persuade him
To pay the debt to honour that he owes me.
So that it would be easier to travel,
She bade me don male clothing, and took down
This ancient sword which I am wearing now.
455 Now it is time that I unsheathe the blade
As I was bid, for, trusting in its sign,
She said: "Depart to Poland, show this sword
That all the nobles may behold it well,
And it may be that one of them will take
460 Pity on you, and counsel you, and shield you."
I came to Poland and, you will remember,
Entered your cave. You looked at me in wonder.
Clotaldo passionately took my part
To plead for mercy to the king, who spared me,
465 Then, when he heard my story, bade me change
Into my own clothes and attend on Stella,
There to disturb Astolfo's love and stop
Their marriage. Again you saw me in woman's dress
And were confused by the discrepancy.
470 But let's pass to what's new: Clotaldo, now
Persuaded that Astolfo must, with Stella,
Come to the throne, dissuades me from my purpose,
Against the interests of my name and honour.
But seeing you, O valiant Segismund,
475 Are claiming your revenge, now that the heavens
Have burst the prison of your rustic tower,
(Wherein you were the tiger of your sorrows,
The rock of sufferings and direful pains)
And sent you forth against your sire and country,
480 I come to aid you, mingling Dian's silks
With the hard steel of Pallas. Now, strong Captain,
It well behoves us both to stop this marriage —
Me, lest my promised husband should be wed,
You, lest, when their estates are joined, they weigh
485 More powerfully against your victory.
I come, as a mere woman, to persuade you
To right my shame; but, as a man, I come
To help you battle for your crown. As woman,
To melt your heart, here at your feet I fall;
490 But, as a man, I come to serve you bravely
Both with my person and my steel, and thus,
If you today should woo me as a woman,
Then I should have to kill you as a man would

In honourable service of my honour;
Since I must be three things today at once —   495
Passionate, to persuade you: womanly,
To ply you with my woes: manly, to gain
Honour in battle.
SEGISMUND: Heavens! If it is true I'm dreaming,
Suspend my memory, for in a dream
So many things could not occur. Great heavens!   500
If I could only come free of them all!
Or never think of any! Who ever felt
Such grievous doubts? If I but dreamed that triumph
In which I found myself, how can this woman
Refer me to such sure and certain facts?   505
Then all of it was true and not a dream.
But if it be the truth, why does my past life
Call it a dream? This breeds the same confusion.
Are dreams and glories so alike, that fictions
Are held for truths, realities for lies?   510
Is there so little difference in them both
That one should question whether what one sees
And tastes is true or false? What? Is the copy
So near to the original that doubt
Exists between them? Then if that is so,   515
And grandeur, power, majesty, and pomp,
Must all evaporate like shades at morning,
Let's profit by it, this time, to enjoy
That which we only can enjoy in dreams.
Rosaura's in my power: my soul adores her beauty.   520
Let's take the chance. Let love break every law
On which she has relied in coming here
And kneeling, trustful, prostrate at my feet.
This is a dream. If so, dream pleasures now
Since they must turn to sorrows in the end!   525
But with my own opinions, I begin
Once again to convince myself. Let's think.
If it is but vainglory and a dream,
Who for mere human vainglory would lose
True glory? What past blessing is not merely   530
A dream? Who has known heroic glories,
That deep within himself, as he recalls them,
Has never doubted that they might be dreams?
But if this all should end in disenchantment,
Seeing that pleasure is a lovely flame   535
That's soon converted into dust and ashes
By any wind that blows, then let us seek
That which endures in thrifty, lasting fame
In which no pleasures sleep, nor grandeurs dream.
Rosaura's without honour. In a prince   540
It's worthier to restore it than to steal it.
I shall restore it, by the living God,
Before I win my throne! Let's shun the danger
And fly from the temptation which is strong!
Then sound to arms!   545

(*To a soldier.*)

Today I must give battle before darkness
Buries the rays of gold in green-black waves!
ROSAURA: My lord! Alas, you stand apart, and offer
No word of pity for my plight. How is it

550 You neither hear nor see me nor even yet
Have turned your face on me?
SEGISMUND: Rosaura, for your
   honour's sake
I must be cruel to you, to be kind.
My voice must not reply to you because
My honour must reply to you. I am silent
555 Because my deeds must speak to you alone.
I do not look at you since, in such straits,
Having to see your honour is requited,
I must not see your beauty.
                              (*Exit with soldiers.*)
ROSAURA: What strange enigma's this? After such
   trouble
560 Still to be treated with more doubtful riddles!

(*Enter Clarion.*)

CLARION: Madam, may you be visited just now?
ROSAURA: Why, Clarion, where have you been all this
   time?
CLARION: Shut in the tower, consulting cards
About my death: "to be or not to be."
And it was a near thing.
ROSAURA: Why?
565 CLARION: Because I know
The secret who you are: in fact, Clotaldo . . .

(*Drums.*)

But hush what noise is that?
ROSAURA: What can it be?
CLARION: From the beleaguered palace a whole
   squadron
Is charging forth to harry and defeat
That of fierce Segismund.
570 ROSAURA: Why, what a coward
Am I, not to be at his side, the terror
And scandal of the world, while such fierce strife
Presses all round in lawless anarchy.
                                          (*Exit.*)
VOICES OF SOME: Long live our king!
VOICES OF OTHERS: Long live our liberty!
575 CLARION: Long live both king and liberty. Yes, live!
And welcome to them both! I do not worry.
In all this pother, I behave like Nero
Who never grieved at what was going on.
If I had anything to grieve about
580 It would be me, myself. Well hidden here,
Now, I can watch the sport that's going on.
This place is safe and hidden between crags,
And since death cannot find me here, two figs for
   death!

(*He hides. Drums and the clash of arms are heard.*)

(*Enter Basil, Clotaldo, and Astolfo, fleeing.*)

BASIL: Was ever king so hapless as myself
Or father more ill used?
585 CLOTALDO: Your beaten army
Rush down, in all directions, in disorder.
ASTOLFO: The traitors win!

BASIL: In battles such as these
Those on the winning side are ever "loyal,"
And traitors the defeated. Come, Clotaldo,
Let's flee from the inhuman cruelty   590
Of my fierce son!

(*Shots are fired within. Clarion falls wounded.*)

CLARION: Heavens, save me!
ASTOLFO: Who is this
Unhappy soldier bleeding at our feet?
CLARION: I am a most unlucky man who, wishing
To guard myself from death, have sought it out
By fleeing from it. Shunning it, I found it,   595
Because, to death, no hiding-place is secret.
So you can argue that whoever shuns it
Most carefully runs into it the quickest.
Turn, then, once more into the thick of battle:
There is more safety there amidst the fire   600
And clash of arms than here on this secluded
Mountain, because no hidden path is safe
From the inclemency of Fate; and so,
Although you flee from death, yet you may find it
Quicker than you expect, if God so wills.   605

(*He falls dead.*)

BASIL: "If God so wills". . . With what strange
   eloquence
This corpse persuades our ignorance and error
To better knowledge, speaking from the mouth
Of its fell wound, where the red liquid flowing
Seems like a bloody tongue which teaches us   610
That the activities of man are vain
When they are pitted against higher powers.
For I, who wished to liberate my country
From murder and sedition, gave it up
To the same ills from which I would have saved it.   615
CLOTALDO: Though Fate, my lord, knows every path,
   and finds
Him whom it seeks even in the midst of crags
And thickets, it is not a Christian judgment
To say there is no refuge from its fury.
A prudent man can conquer Fate itself.   620
Though you are not exempted from misfortune,
Take action to escape it while you can!
ASTOLFO: Clotaldo speaks as one mature in
   prudence,
And I as one in valour's youthful prime.
Among the thickets of this mount is hidden   625
A horse, the very birth of the swift wind.
Flee on him, and I'll guard you in the rear.
BASIL: If it is God's will I should die, or if
Death waits here for my coming, I will seek
Him out today, and meet him face to face.   630

(*Enter Segismund, Stella, Rosaura, soldiers, and their train.*)

A SOLDIER: Amongst the thickets of this mountain
The king is hiding.
SEGISMUND: Seek him out at once!

Leave no foot of the summit unexplored
But search from stem to stem and branch to branch!
CLOTALDO: Fly, sir!
BASIL: What for?
635   ASTOLFO: What do you mean to do?
BASIL: Astolfo, stand aside!
CLOTALDO: What is your wish?
BASIL: To take a cure I've needed for sometime.

(*To Segismund.*)

If you have come to seek me, here I am.

(*Kneeling.*)

Your father, prince, kneels humbly at your feet.
640   The white snow of my hair is now your carpet.
Tread on my neck and trample on my crown!
Lay low and drag my dignity in dust!
Take vengeance on my honour! Make a slave
Of me and, after all I've done to thwart them,
645   Let Fate fulfil its edict and claim homage
And Heaven fulfil its oracles at last!
SEGISMUND: Illustrious court of Poland, who have been
The witnesses of such unwonted wonders,
Attend to me, and hear your prince speak out.
What Heaven decrees and God writes with his
650   finger
(Whose prints and ciphers are the azure leaves
Adorned with golden lettering of the stars)
Never deceives nor lies. They only lie
Who seek to penetrate the mystery
655   And, having reached it, use it to ill purpose.
My father, who is here to evade the fury
Of my proud nature, made me a wild beast:
So, when I, by my birth of gallant stock,
My generous blood, and inbred grace and valour,
660   Might well have proved both gentle and forbearing,
The very mode of life to which he forced me,
The sort of bringing up I had to bear
Sufficed to make me savage in my passions.
What a strange method of restraining them!
665   If one were to tell any man: "One day
You will be killed by an inhuman monster,"
Would it be the best method he could choose
To wake that monster when it was asleep?
Or if they told him: "That sword which you're
      wearing
670   Will be your death," what sort of cure were it
To draw it forth and aim it at his breast?
Or if they told him: "Deep blue gulfs of water
Will one day be your sepulchre and grave
Beneath a silver monument of foam,"
675   He would be mad to hurl himself in headlong
When the sea highest heaved its snowy mountains
And crystalline sierras plumed with spray.
The same has happened to the king as to him
Who wakes a beast which threatens death, to him
680   Who draws a naked sword because he fears it,
To him who dives into the stormy breakers.

Though my ferocious nature (hear me now)
Was like a sleeping beast, my inborn rage
A sheathèd sword, my wrath a quiet ripple,
Fate should not be coerced by man's injustice —   685
This rouses more resentment. So it is
That he who seeks to tame his fortune must
Resort to moderation and to measure.
He who foresees an evil cannot conquer it.
Thus in advance, for though humility   690
Can overcome it, this it can do only
When the occasion's there, for there's no way
To dodge one's fate and thus evade the issue.
Let this strange spectacle serve as example —
This prodigy, this horror, and this wonder,   695
Because it is no less than one, to see,
After such measures and precautions taken
To thwart it, that a father thus should kneel
At his son's feet, a kingdom thus be shattered.
This was the sentence of the heavens above,   700
Which he could not evade, much though he tried.
Can I, younger in age, less brave, and less
In science than the king, conquer that fate?

(*To the King.*)

Sire, rise, give me your hand, now that the
      heavens
Have shown you that you erred as to the method   705
To vanquish them. Humbly I kneel before you
And offer you my neck to tread upon.
BASIL: Son, such a great and noble act restores you
Straight to my heart. Oh, true and worthy prince!
You have won both the laurel and the palm.   710
Crown yourself with your deeds! For you *have*
      conquered!
ALL: Long live Segismund! Long live Segismund!
SEGISMUND: Since I have other victories to win,
The greatest of them all awaits me now:
To conquer my own self. Astolfo, give   715
Your hand here to Rosaura, for you know
It is a debt of honour and must be paid.
ASTOLFO: Although, it's true, I owe some
      obligations —
She does not know her name or who she is,
It would be base to wed a woman who . . .   720
CLOTALDO: Hold! Wait! Rosaura's of as noble stock
As yours, Astolfo. In the open field
I'll prove it with my sword. She is my daughter
And that should be enough.
ASTOLFO: What do you say?
CLOTALDO: Until I saw her married, righted,
      honoured,   725
I did not wish for it to be discovered.
It's a long story but she is my daughter.
ASTOLFO: That being so, I'm glad to keep my word.
SEGISMUND: And now, so that the princess Stella
      here
Will not remain disconsolate to lose   730
A prince of so much valour, here I offer

My hand to her, no less in birth and rank.
Give me your hand.
STELLA: I gain by meriting
So great a happiness.
SEGISMUND: And now, Clotaldo,
735   So long so loyal to my father, come
To my arms. Ask me anything you wish.
FIRST SOLDIER: If thus you treat a man who never
        served you,
What about me who led the revolution
And brought you from your dungeon in the tower?
What will you give me?
740   SEGISMUND: That same tower and dungeon
From which you never shall emerge till death.
No traitor is of use after his treason.

BASIL: All wonder at your wisdom!
ASTOLFO: What a change
Of character!
ROSAURA: How wise and prudent!
SEGISMUND: Why
Do you wonder? Why do you marvel, since   745
It was a dream that taught me and I still
Fear to wake up once more in my close dungeon?
Though that may never happen, it's enough
To dream it might, for thus I came to learn
That all our human happiness must pass   750
Away like any dream, and I would here
Enjoy it fully ere it glide away,
Asking (for noble hearts are prone to pardon)
Pardon for faults in the actors or the play.

COMMENTARIES

Michael Billington (b. 1939)
REVIEW OF THE 1998 EDINBURGH FESTIVAL
PRODUCTION OF *LIFE IS A DREAM*   *1998*

> *Billington's review of the play emphasizes the energy and excitement created on stage. But it also emphasizes the optimism inherent in the play, the thought that even one as isolated and brutalized as Segismundo (Segismund) could discover in himself the qualities needed to change his life.*

The marriage of foreign and native talent doesn't always work. But the Edinburgh Festival, along with the Barbican Centre, has had the bright idea of inviting a Catalan director-designer team, Calixto Bieito and Carles Pujol, to stage Calderón's 1635 masterpiece, *Life Is a Dream,* in John Clifford's new translation with a British multiracial cast. The result is sensational.

For a start Calderón's play ushers us into a strange, labyrinthine world, one that deals both with the illusory nature of existence and the possibility of change. The story itself concerns a Polish prince, Segismundo, who has been kept imprisoned since birth in a dark tower. The reason? His father Basilio's fear of a prediction that his son would usurp his throne. And, when the savage Segismundo is briefly released, he fulfils Basilio's worst fears by committing rape and murder. But although he is quickly bunged back in the tower, Segismundo is once more set free by an uprising. This time, however, he behaves not like a bestial tyrant but with enlightened wisdom: defeating his father in battle, he forgives him and forges reconciliation.

Like all great plays, Calderón's work looks both backwards and forwards. *Oedipus Rex* comes to mind in the prophecy that ironically rebounds on those who seek to avoid it: the reduction of Segismundo, through social isolation, to animalistic savagery, also suggests Sophocles's Philoctetes. But the hero's belief, after his brief restoration to power, that "life's an illusion, a shadow, a fiction" prefigures Pirandello. And even his conclusion that our existence is no more than "empty air" has a touch of Borges and Beckett.

Yet what is extraordinary about the play is its optimism. Segismundo, not surprisingly, harps on the idea that life is a waking dream, that power, wealth, and pleasure are all illusory. Yet Calderón, far from drawing the conclusion that Camus later came to in *The Myth of Sisyphus* that all man's actions are therefore "senseless, absurd, useless," argues the exact opposite. He emerges as an apostle of change and a champion of free will. We may all be shadows, but, Calderón suggests, evil can still be defeated. As a message, it is a refreshing antidote to the arid determinism of the absurd.

The play emerges as a mix of magic realism and phantasmagoric ritual; and that shifting quality is perfectly caught by Bieito and his codesigner, Pujol. The stage itself is a circular cinder-track. Above it hovers a giant mirror which at first accurately reflects the characters. It is then tilted crazily to suggest the disordered world of Segismundo's prince-for-a-day tyranny. Finally, it is angled so the audience sees itself, a reminder that we are watching a theatrical spectacle and that we are as much role-players as anyone on the stage.

The Catalan team, including costume-designer Merce Paloma, also brings out the play's political implications. Dress is modern, so that Segismundo's paternalistic jailer sports a military uniform and his father a vivid, multicolored robe. On one level, the play becomes a parable about fascism and a world in which brutal solitary confinement is followed by equally arbitrary release.

The modernity of the message is also visible in the acting. George Anton plays the imprisoned prince with a ruthless lack of sentimentality. He is an angular, desperate, animalistic figure who, on release from prison, instantly hurls an old retainer out of the window, dives under the skirts of the king's niece for some inappropriate sex, and curls up on the throne to play cards with Sylvester McCoy's anarchic clown.

The production is least successful in handling the complex subplot: one in which the heroine, Rosaura, returns from Moscow in male attire to recover her lover and, in the process, rediscovers her long-lost father. This is no fault of the Irish actress, Olwen Fouere, who has a genuinely androgynous quality that enables her to shift shape ending "as a kind of monster carrying man's weapons but wearing women's clothes." The blame lies largely with Calderón, who gives Rosaura an outrageously long speech that cries out to be cut.

But this is still a notable occasion in which John Clifford's translation reclaims a Spanish masterpiece for the modern stage. There was once a bad Oxford production of the play that was rudely dubbed *Life's a Scream*. On this occasion, Calderón's vision of the illusion of existence is caught with painterly precision.

Ed Morales
REVIEW OF JOSÉ RIVERA'S PRODUCTION OF *SUEÑO*   *1998*

In this extensive discussion of José Rivera's adaptation of Life Is a Dream, *Morales examines the reasoning behind Rivera's reworking of Calderón's language and his emphasis on the philosophical issues that lie beneath the surface of the play. Morales also gives us some insight into the challenges faced by a modern producer of a seventeenth-century drama, especially in light of the ways in which both the theater and its audiences have changed.*

Sueño, José Rivera's adaptation of Calderón de la Barca's classic *La Vida es Sueño (Life Is a Dream),* starts out impressively enough. When John Ortiz's hirsute, muscular, and scantily clad body appears onstage suspended in midair by long red ropes, Hartford Stage Company audiences can't help but hold their collective breath and expect a wild theatrical ride. Ortiz plays Segismundo, the son of a Spanish monarch held in a dungeon because of his original sin — killing his mother in childbirth — but about to be freed from his misery to have a go at his birthright as a ruler. The sharp contrast between his captivity and deliverance causes Segismundo to blur the line between reality and dreams, and allows Calderón to explore the big philosophical questions (What is existence? *Is* life a dream, and if so, who is dreaming *us*? God?) that have made *La Vida es Sueño* so enduring. However, it's hard not to wonder what kind of resonance these issues can have for a twentieth-century audience, when a good chunk of reality is virtual or simulated.

At first glance, *Sueño*'s theatrical strategy seems to be a variation on what might be called the New York Shakespeare Festival style of reinventing the classics. The characters engage in a contemporary sassiness; they draw out some of the contemporaneous subtext from seventeenth-century situations; and traditionally cross-dressed roles are augmented by nontraditionally cross-dressed ones. But on closer inspection, Rivera's *Sueño* proves to be a true adaptation, not a recontextualization; there are no TV sets or gang paraphernalia in this production. The costumes are faithful to their origins in Spain. Indeed, it's not the surface aspects of the production that offer a contemporary spin on Calderón's metaphysical musings: it is the *language* that has been changed, shifting from the baroque Spanish verse of the 1600s to the contemporary rhythms of America at the end of the twentieth century.

From Segismundo's opening soliloquies, where he proclaims himself "a storm of chemical responses pretending to have a soul," Rivera has reclaimed Calderón's florid use of metaphor and made it his own, spiced with science, sarcasm, and sweetness. "I wanted to find the language Calderón would have used if he was a forty-two-year-old playwright living in California," the theater and television writer says on the phone from his home in Los Angeles. That blending of the contemporary and the antiquated can have some surprising results. For instance, when Segismundo says he is "God's wild virus," you can feel all the implications of imagined or real modern-day plagues while simultaneously acknowledging their roots in an empire engaged in conquering a New World.

Rivera was not only faced with the task of reinventing Calderón's language, but also the challenge of making the play, which is long on plot and short on characterization, "actable." By doing case studies of people who had experienced long-term isolation, Rivera was able to create a realistic psychological profile for Segismundo and enliven his character with appropriate behavior, particularly in the early scenes between him and Rosaura (Michi Barall), a young noblewoman bent on revenge. Long monologues were replaced with short, snappy, almost sit-com-esque interactions, a possible by-product of the time Rivera has done in Hollywood. (The writer professes to have given up television work, particularly since the demise of *Eerie, Indiana,* a series he created that some claim was too smart to remain on the air.)

In this way, the wordplay between Lord Astolfo (Damian Young) and Princess Estrella (Alene Dawson) — two scheming nobles who have their eyes on the throne — is one of the highlights of the production. "Flowers are dishrags compared to you," carps Astolfo in his parodic wooing of a noblewoman in line to succeed the reigning monarch. "Helen? A slutbox. . . . Aphrodite? Maggot poop." Young and Jan Leslie Harding, in her drag interpretation of Rosaura's clownish manservant Clarin (the character is traditionally played by a male), provide comic relief from the dark antics Segismundo engages in when he's given a chance to prove he might be worthy of nobility.

By showcasing these underlying comedic moments, *Sueño* moves away from the tragically cerebral aura that traditionally surrounds Calderón's work. Nevertheless, the play's dramatic impact is reinvigorated by Rivera's commitment to updating its contextual underpinnings. In the post-Freud era, there are echoes of the Oedipus complex in Segismundo's attacks on his father Basilio's kingship. Perhaps more important, their relationship strongly resembles the one between Prospero and Caliban in *The Tempest.* Segismundo is portrayed as a vulgar, uneducated beast, an id looking to inflict severe psychological, as well as physical, pain. Basilio, on the other hand, seems to be uncertain about his moral imperative: he is vaguely aware of his own complicity in the brutal conquest of the New World. Even as he obsesses over a lunar eclipse (the evil omen that marks the birth of his son), another spherical object, the Aztec calendar, lurks center stage for much of the play.

For Rivera, this zigzagging between the old and the new in some ways mirrors the ambivalence of the Hispanic phenomenon, and may explain Latino interest in the Hartford Stage production. (The fact that the theatre coordinated a major community relations drive didn't hurt either.) According to Rivera, while Hispanics may not feel directly connected to Spain, they still relate to intrinsic elements of the culture. "There's this code of honor that we all seem to be struggling with," muses Rivera. "Being Latino in the U.S. is like being caught in the middle between tradition and nontradition. But we have come to feel comfortable with contradiction."

While Rivera's rewrite may make Calderón's work more accessible and contemporary, *Sueño* has even more profound implications. Instead of saying, "If the Fates decree that now's your time to die / There's nothing you can do," Clarin declares, "If God wants your ass, he's going to get your ass." While the change works as humor, these lines are also helping Rivera establish the idea that the presence of mortal life is no longer just an extension of the proof of the existence of God. "In the original, Segismundo gets attached to the idea that if everything is a dream, the dreamer must be God," says Rivera. "What my version is trying to say is that the idea of God is unreliable."

In transferring Calderón's psyche into his own, Rivera is making a statement about American reality and the way it represents the difference between Old World and New World thinking. The romantic pairings that climax the original — Astolfo-Rosaura and Segismundo-Estrella — are reversed. Rosaura turns her back on nobility and urges Segismundo to join her in a quest for free will and the overturning of the rigid class structures of Europe. It's a moment that brings out an idea buried in Calderón's text, that a New World is about to begin. In José Rivera's own sly and spiritual way, *Sueño* carries the enormous implication that we're on the verge of that kind of history happening all over again.

Matt Wolf
THE *HAMLET* OF SPAIN, IN A FEVERED STAGING   *1999*

Matt Wolf reviews the 1999 London production of Life Is a Dream, *connecting the play to Calderón's near-contemporary, William Shakespeare. In certain ways Wolf sees Segismundo as a version of Hamlet. Like Hamlet, Segismundo quests for the truth and is never sure he has found it. And like Hamlet, Segismundo has been denied a portion of his birthright.*

Imagine a play that suggests Shakespeare — particularly *Hamlet* or *The Tempest* — filtered through a Pirandellian prism, with an enormous gilt-edged mirror suspended forbiddingly above the action and a gravel-strewn set providing its own aural soundscape.

That is one way of describing the production of *Life Is a Dream* that the Royal Lyceum Theater Company of Scotland will present on Tuesday at the Brooklyn Academy of Music. The Spanish director Calixto Bieito's fevered staging of the defining seventeenth-century play by Pedro Calderón de la Barca will have six performances at the Harvey Theater as part of the 1999 Next Wave Festival.

In Spain, Calderón's play enjoys something of the status of *Hamlet,* with which it shares an interest in man at his most self-avowedly anguished. Indeed, professing in John Clifford's contemporary translation that "humankind's greatest crime is to be born," Calderón's antiheroic prince, Segismundo (played by George Anton), recalls the racked metaphysician that is Shakespeare's Danish prince.

Segismundo has been sequestered from birth in a tower because of fears by his father, the king, Basilio (Jeffery Kissoon), that his son will rise up against him. The prince is then briefly released upon adulthood, only to be imprisoned once more, a caged animal capable, we discover later, of very real mercy.

And though he finds a vengeful ally of sorts in Rosaura (Olwen Fouere), the spurned lover whose separate fate provides the main subplot, Segismundo ends the play a free and potentially noble man — if, that is, freedom and nobility mean anything in the elision between wakefulness and sleep that is the true terrain of *Life Is a Dream.*

"What I love about it is it's a very questioning play," said Mr. Clifford, the translator, from his home in Edinburgh. "It's asking fundamental questions, starting with, 'What are we doing here?' " (His translation, he said, draws less from the accepted 1635 text than from an earlier published version dating to 1630.)

Mr. Bieito's production was first seen at the 1998 Edinburgh International Festival, where several critics found it a high point of the theater program ("The two hours pass like, well, a dream," wrote Charles Spencer in the *Daily Telegraph*). After a hiatus, the production toured last month to London as part of the Barbican International Theater Event (BITE '99) season.

His aim, Mr. Bieito said after the London opening, was to invigorate anew a play barely known in Britain or the United States, notwithstanding its affinities to the Elizabethans as well as to countless modernist writers, including Pirandello and Ionesco.

"For me, it was easier to work in Britain," said Mr. Bieito, thirty-five, of a rare directing assignment away from Barcelona, where he has lived since he was fifteen. Among his credits back home: a Catalan-language version in 1997 of the Broadway musical *Company,* whose songs include the very appropriately titled "Barcelona."

"In Spain," said the director, who doubles as his own designer (with Carles Pujol), "you have all the pressure all the time of tradition, of people thinking what *Life Is a Dream* must be." But in Scotland, he said, "I was freed to do the play and to renew it. Classical theater must not be classical, it must be fresh."

The result is a multicultural staging defiantly un-British in its impetuousness and vigor, especially coming from a writer who, Mr. Clifford said, "has an unfortunate reputation as a rigid Catholic theologian."

And Graham Sheffield, the Barbican's artistic director, said, "Calixto seems to have made the play modern without sacrificing its traditional roots; its physicality is frightening."

The play's animalistic passions more often than not fall to Mr. Anton, thirty-four, a Scot who spends much of the evening raising his voice and shedding his clothes as he charts Segismundo's journey from a Caliban figure to a Prospero of sorts.

The actor compared Mr. Bieito to a boxing coach. "When you were in the ring, as it were, he was hot," Mr. Anton said of his director. "He'd be at your side going, 'Quieter, quieter,' and then, 'Punch, punch, punch.'"

That may be because, said Mr. Kissoon, the performer, the director "wants to wake us up."

Late Seventeenth- and Eighteenth-Century Drama

The Restoration: Rebirth of Drama

Theater in England continued to thrive after Shakespeare's death, with a host of successful playwrights, including John Webster (1580?–1638?), Francis Beaumont (c. 1584–1616) and his collaborator John Fletcher (1579–1625), Philip Massinger (1583–1640), Thomas Middleton (1580–1627), John Ford (1586–c. 1655), and James Shirley (1596–1666). All these playwrights were busy working independently or in collaboration. Fletcher, chosen successor to Shakespeare at the Globe, furnished the theater with as many as four plays a year. But in 1642 long-standing religious and political conflicts between King Charles I and Parliament finally erupted into civil war, with the Parliament, under the influence of Puritanism, eventually winning.

The Puritans were religious extremists with narrow, specific values. They were essentially an emerging merchant class of well-to-do citizens who viewed the aristocracy as wastrels. Theater for them was associated with both the aristocracy and the low life. Theatergoing was synonymous with wasting time, the theaters were often a focus for immoral activity, and the neighborhoods around the theaters were as unsavory as any in England. Under the Puritan government, all theaters in England were closed for almost twenty years. When the new king, Charles II, was crowned in 1660, those that had not been converted to other uses had become completely outmoded.

As a young prince, Charles, with his mother and brother, had been sent to the Continent in the early stages of the civil war. When his father, Charles I, was beheaded, the future king and his family were in France, where they were in a position to see the remarkable achievements of French comedy and French classical tragedy. Charles II developed a taste for theater that accompanied him back to England. And when he returned in triumph to usher in the exciting and swashbuckling period known as the Restoration, he permitted favorites to build new theaters.

Theater on the Continent: Neoclassicism

Interaction among the leading European countries — England, Spain, and France — was sporadic at best in the seventeenth century because of intermittent wars among the nations, yet the development of theater in all three countries took similar turns throughout the early 1600s.

By the 1630s, the French were aware of Spanish achievements in the theater and Pierre Corneille (1606–1684), who emerged as France's leading playwright of the time, adapted a Spanish story by de Castro that became one of his most important plays, *Le Cid*.

By the time Charles II took up residence in France in the 1640s, the French had developed a suave, polished, and intellectually demanding approach to drama. Corneille and the neoclassicists were part of a large movement in European culture and the arts that tried to codify and emulate the achievement of the ancients. Qualities such as harmony, symmetry, balance in everything structural, and clear moral themes were most in evidence. Because NEOCLASSICISM valued thought over feeling, the thematic material in neoclassical drama was very important. That material was sometimes political, reflecting the values of Augustan Rome — 27 B.C. to A.D. 17 — when Caesar Augustus lived and when it was appropriate to think in terms of subordinating the self to the interests of the state. Neoclassical dramatists focused on honor, moral integrity, self-sacrifice, and heroic political subjects.

One school of critics held playwrights strictly to the Aristotelian concepts of the unities of time, place, character, and action. These "rules critics" demanded a perfect observance of the unities — that is, they wanted a play to have one plot, a single action that takes place in one day, and a single setting. In most cases the plays that satisfied them are now often thought of as static, cold, limited, and dull. Their perfection is seen today as rigid and emotionally icy.

Corneille's work did not please such critics, and they turned to a much younger competitor, Jean Racine (1639–1699), who brought the tradition of French tragedy to its fullest. Most of his plays are on classical subjects, beginning in 1667 with *Andromache*, continuing with *Britannicus* (1669), *Iphigenia* (1674), and *Mithridate* (1673), and ending in 1677 with his most famous and possibly best play, *Phaedra*.

Phaedra is a deeply passionate, moral play centering on the love of Phaedra for her stepson, Hippolytus. Venus is responsible for her incestuous love — which is the playwright's way of saying that Phaedra is impelled by the gods or by destiny, almost against her will.

The French stage, unlike the English, never substituted boys for female roles, and so plays such as *Phaedra* were opportunities for brilliant actresses. Phaedra, in particular, dominates the stage — she is a commanding and infinitely complex figure. It is no wonder that this play was a favorite of Sarah Bernhardt (1844–1923), one of France's greatest actresses.

French Comedy: Molière

At the same time that Racine commanded the tragic stage, Jean Baptiste Poquelin (1622–1673), known as Molière, began his dominance of the comic stage. He was aware of Racine's achievements and applauded them strongly. His career started with a small theater company that spent most of its time touring the countryside beyond Paris. When the company settled in Paris, its plays were influenced by some of the stock characters and situations of the commedia dell'arte, but they also began to reflect Molière's own genius for composition.

Seeing the company in 1658, King Louis XIV found it so much to his liking that he installed it in a theater and demanded to see more of its work. From that time on, Molière wrote, produced, and acted in one comedy after another, most of which have become part of the permanent repertoire of the French stage. Plays such as *The Misanthrope* (1666), *The Miser* (1669), *The Bourgeois Gentleman* (1670), *The Imaginary Invalid* (1673), and his satire on the theme of religious hypocrisy, *Tartuffe* (1669), are also staged all over the world.

Theater in England: Restoration Comedy of Manners

When the theaters reopened in England in the 1660s, they needed new plays. Times and tastes had changed, England had suffered enormous upheaval, and the Puritan-dominated, theater-darkened past was quickly undone. The new age wanted glitter, excitement, sensuality, and dramatic dazzle. Audiences wanted upbeat comedies that poked fun at the stuffed shirts of society and at old-fashioned institutions and fashions.

Several important physical changes took effect immediately. The new stages were in indoor theaters using artificial light. They could be operated year-round, and the price for seats varied according to location. The middle-priced seats were in the pit before the proscenium-arched stage (Figure 9). The first-level boxes against the walls were most expensive, while the lowest-priced seats were in the upper ranges of the balconies.

The new indoor theaters were generally adapted from spaces designed for courtly events. They were rectangular, often twice as long as they were wide, and usually lighted by candles in chandeliers. The proscenium frame around the stage appeared in the new theaters. Eventually, movable scenery and changeable painted backdrops helped the playwrights create their illusions, although some plays of the period could easily be performed on a bare stage.

Once English women were permitted to take part in theater, actresses appeared who commanded the stage immediately. The actresses of the period were bright, witty, and charming and were often the most important draw for seventeenth-century audiences. Nell Gwynne (1650–1687), one of the most famous actresses of her day and mistress to Charles II, became a legend of the English stage.

Among England's notable playwrights from 1660 through the eighteenth century were Aphra Behn (1640–1689), the first professional woman playwright on the English stage and author of *The Rover,* one of the most frequently performed plays of the period; William Wycherley (1640–1716), whose *The Plain Dealer,* indebted to Molière, and *The Country Wife* are regarded as his best work; William Congreve (1670–1729), whose *The Way of the World* is justly famous; and Richard Brinsley Sheridan (1751–1816), whose *School for Scandal* is still bright, lively, and engaging for modern audiences. Other important playwrights whose work is still performed are George Farquhar (1678–1707), especially known for *The Beaux Stratagem* (1707), John Gay (1685–1732), whose *Beggar's Opera* has been revived constantly since its first performance in 1728, and Oliver Goldsmith (1730–1774), author of *She Stoops to Conquer* (1773).

John Dryden (1631–1700), perhaps the most highly regarded English playwright from 1664 to 1677, collaborated in adaptations of Shakespeare's plays, but he became popular for his heroic dramas in rhymed verse: *The Indian Queen* (1664), its sequel *The Indian Emperor* (1665), *Tyrannick Love* (1669), and the two-part, ten-act *The Conquest of Granada* (1670). Montezuma is at the center of the first two plays; *Tyrannick Love* concerns the martyrdom

Figure 9. Conjectural reconstruction of an early Restoration theater. By Peter Kahn, Cornell University.

of St. Catherine by the Roman emperor, Maximin. *The Conquest of Granada* focuses on internal conflicts among the Moors fighting for survival in Spain. Almanzor, the main character, is considered one of Dryden's most accomplished creations. *Aureng-Zebe* (1675), his last effort in heroic rhymed drama, focuses on Aureng-Zebe, emperor of India and among the most rational and moral of his characters. Its plot and love complications are extremely dense and its mood somewhat melancholy. Today the heroic plays of the 1660s resemble high-style melodramas, but they were enormously popular in their time.

Dryden was also successful writing comedies such as *The Wild Gallant* (1663) and *The Rival Ladies* (1664). His tragicomedies were popular in his time and represent some of his most imaginative dramatic efforts. *Marriage à-la-Mode* (1672) is still highly regarded, especially for Dryden's songs. Among his experiments in opera is a version of Milton's *Paradise Lost* that he called *The State of Innocence and the Fall of Man* (1677) in which he rhymed some of Milton's blank verse. This work was never performed, although it remains a curiosity of the age. Dryden is also to be noted for his critical writing on drama, such as his famous *Of Dramatick Poesie* (1668) and *Of Heroick Plays* (1672), which laid down the theory behind his dramas and opened the questions of dramatic practice for examination.

Marriages of convenience are often the target of Restoration playwrights. The aristocratic attitude toward marriage usually centered on the union of "suitable" mates whose families were of the same social level and who were financially attractive to one another. Consequently, sometimes impoverished gentlemen of good name would seek out wealthy women and vice versa. The grounds for marriage were sometimes based on love but more often on financial or social convenience. As a result, the emotional expressions between marriage partners, as in Congreve's *The Way of the World,* are restricted and cautious. It is not until the end of the eighteenth century that the sentimental comedy appears, introducing recognizable emotional responses that appear to moderns as normal. Aristocratic attitudes toward marriage are evident in drama as late as the end of the nineteenth century, as in Oscar Wilde's *The Importance of Being Earnest.*

The English playwrights produced a wide range of comedy, drawing on their understanding of the audience's desire for bright, gay, and witty entertainment. The comedies of the period came to be known in the twentieth century as COMEDIES OF MANNERS because they reveal the foibles of the society that watched them. Society enjoyed laughing at itself. Although some of the English drama of the eighteenth century developed a moralistic tone and was often heavily classical, the earlier RESTORATION COMEDIES were less interested in reforming the society than in capitalizing on its faults.

Eighteenth-Century Drama

Eighteenth-century Europe absorbed much of the spirit of France and the French neoclassicists. England, like other European countries, began to see the effects of neoclassicism in the arts and literature. Emulation of classical art and classical values was common throughout Europe, and critics established standards of excellence in the arts to guarantee quality.

The most famous name in eighteenth-century English drama is David Garrick (1717–1779), the legendary actor and manager of the Drury Lane Theatre. The theaters, including his own, often reworked French drama and earlier English and Italian drama, but they began to develop a new SENTIMENTAL COMEDY to balance the neoclassical heroic tragedies of the period. It was a comedy in which the emotions of the audience were played on, manipulated, and exploited to arouse sympathy for the characters in the play.

Sentimental comedy flourished after 1720, but Colley Cibber (1671–1757) is sometimes credited with beginning the sentimental comedy with his *Love's Last Shift* (1696). The play centers on Loveless, who wanders from his marriage only to find that his wife has disguised herself as a prostitute to win him back. As in all sentimental comedies, what the audience most wants is what it gets: a certain amount of tears, a contrasting amount of laughter, and a happy ending. Cibber was especially well known as an actor for his portrayal of fops, his way of poking satiric fun at his own society and its pretensions.

Sir Richard Steele (1672–1729) wrote one of the best-known sentimental comedies, *The Conscious Lovers* (1722). Steele's coauthor of *The Spectator,* Joseph Addison (1672–1719), also distinguished himself with his contribution to the heroic tragedy of the age, the long neoclassical *Cato* (1713). It was considered to be the finest example of the moral heroic style. Today it is not a playable drama because the action is too slow, the speeches too long, and the theme too obscure, although it is a perfect model of what the age preferred in heroic tragedy. George Lillo (1693–1739) in *The London Merchant* (1731) produced a bourgeois tragedy in which the main character was from the middle class. It was one of the most frequently produced plays of its time.

The audiences at the time enjoyed bright, amusing comedies that often criticized wayward youth, overprotective parents, dishonest financial dealings, and social expectations. Their taste in tragedies veered toward a moralizing heroism that extolled the ideals of dedication to the values of the community and self-sacrifice on the part of the hero.

Late Seventeenth- and Eighteenth-Century Drama Timeline

DATE	THEATER	POLITICAL	SOCIAL/CULTURAL
1600–1700	**1606–1684:** French playwright Pierre Corneille, author of *Le Cid* (1636)	**1605:** Gun Powder Plot in London; execution of Guy Fawkes	**1608–1674:** John Milton, English author
	1622–1673: Molière (born John Baptiste Poquelin), French dramatist and actor, author of *The Misanthrope* (1666), *Tartuffe* (1667), and *The Learned Ladies* (1672)		**1610:** Galileo's first observations through a telescope
			1620: Voyage of the Mayflower
	c. 1634–1691: Sir George Etherege, author of *Love in a Tub* and *The Man of Mode* (1676)		**1631–1700:** John Dryden, English author and playwright
	1635–1710: Thomas Betterton, perhaps the Restoration's most important actor		
	1639–1699: Jean Baptiste Racine, French playwright, author of *Phaedre* (1677)		
	1640–1689: Aphra Behn, first professional woman playwright in the English theater, author of *The Rover* (1677–1680)	**1642:** Beginning of the English Civil War	
		1643: Louis XIV becomes king of France at age four.	
	1650–1687: Nell Gwynne, English actress and mistress of Charles II	**1649:** King Charles I of England is beheaded by Parliament.	
	1656: First use of Italianate scenery in England in a production of *The Siege of Rhodes*, designed by John Webb	**1655:** Oliver Cromwell prohibits Anglican church services and divides England into eleven districts governed by major-generals.	
	1658: Molière's troupe, the Illustre Théâtre, is invited to perform at the court of Louis XIV. The company is subsequently given permission to remain in Paris, as the Troupe de Monsieur, and allowed to use the Petit Bourbon for public performances.	**1658:** Cromwell dissolves Parliament.	
	1660: Theatrical activity resumes in London (after being halted in 1642) when Charles II issues patents to Thomas Killigrew and William Davenant. Women are permitted on the English stage for the first time.	**1660:** Restoration of the English monarchy and end of the Commonwealth. Charles II, son of the executed Charles I, is crowned.	**1660:** Dutch Boers settle on the Cape of Good Hope. **1661–1731:** Daniel Defoe, English author

Late Seventeenth- and Eighteenth-Century Drama Timeline (continued)

DATE	THEATER	POLITICAL	SOCIAL/CULTURAL
1600–1700 (continued)	**1664:** Japanese playwright Fukui Yagozaemon writes *The Outcast's Revenge*, the first full-length kabuki play.	**1664:** The British annex New Amsterdam and rename it New York.	**1664–1666:** Isaac Newton (1642–1727), English mathematician and physicist, discovers the law of universal gravitation and begins to develop calculus.
	1670–1729: William Congreve, author of *Love for Love* (1695) and *The Way of the World* (1700)	**1682:** Louis XIV moves the French court to Versailles.	**1665:** Plague devastates London.
	1680: The Comédie Française, the first national theater, opens in Paris.	**1682–1725:** Peter the Great reigns as czar of Russia and calls for political and cultural reforms.	**1666:** Great Fire of London
	1695–1715: Proliferation of female playwrights in England. Thirty-seven new plays by women are produced on the London stage during this period by playwrights such as Mary Pix (1666–1706), Susanna Centlivre (c. 1670–1723), Mary Delarivière Manley (c. 1672–1724), and Catharine Trotter (1679–1749).	**1685:** Louis XIV revokes the Edict of Nantes, and persecution of the Huguenots (French Protestants) ensues.	**1685–1750:** J. S. Bach, German composer
		1688: William of Orange invades England with the encouragement of prominent Protestants, who fear James II's Catholicism. James flees to France and then England. William III and Mary II (daughter of James II) are crowned in 1689.	**1687:** Isaac Newton, English scientist, publishes *Mathematical Principles*.
			1688–1704: Alexander Pope, English poet
	1698: Jeremy Collier's *A Short View of the Immorality and Profaneness of the English Stage*, the most effective of several attacks on the theater published at the turn of the century	**1690:** An Irish uprising in favor of James II is suppressed by William III at the Battle of the Boyne.	**1692:** Salem witchcraft trials
		1697: The last remains of Mayan civilization destroyed by the Spanish.	**1694–1778:** François Marie Arouet de Voltaire, French author often described as the embodiment of the Enlightenment
1700–1800		**1703:** Peter the Great lays the foundation for St. Petersburg.	**1703–1758:** Jonathan Edwards, American theologian
	1707–1793: Carlo Goldoni, Italian playwright, author of *The Servant of Two Masters* (1743)	**1707:** The Act of Union unites Scotland and England, which become Great Britain.	**1709–1784:** Samuel Johnson, English literary critic, scholar, poet, and lexicographer
	1717–1779: David Garrick, greatest English actor of the eighteenth century and owner and manager of the Drury Lane Theatre in London	**1714:** The House of Hanover begins its rule with the accession of George I.	
		1715: Louis XIV, France's Sun King, dies.	
	1720–1806: Carlo Gozzi, Italian playwright, author of *King Stag* (1762) and *Turandot* (1762)		**1720:** First serialization of novels in newspapers
			1724: Emmanuel Kant, German metaphysic philosopher

Late Seventeenth- and Eighteenth-Century Drama Timeline (continued)

DATE	THEATER	POLITICAL	SOCIAL/CULTURAL
1700–1800 (continued)	**1728:** John Gay (1685–1732) writes *The Beggar's Opera*, arguably the most popular English play of the eighteenth century.		**1726:** Jonathan Swift writes *Gulliver's Travels.*
	1729–1781: Gotthold Ephraim Lessing, Germany's first important playwright, author of *Minna von Barnhelm* (1767) and *Emilia Galotti* (1772)		**1732:** Covent Garden opera house opens in London. **1732:** Franz Josef Haydn, prolific Austrian composer
	1737: The Licensing Act in England prohibits the performance of any play not previously licensed by the Lord Chamberlain. A number of such laws regulating theatrical activity are enacted throughout the eighteenth century.	**1740:** Frederick the Great introduces freedom of press and worship in Prussia.	**1742:** Cotton factories are established in Birmingham and Northampton, England. **1746–1828:** Francisco de Goya, Spanish painter and political cartoonist
	1749–1832: Johann Wolfgang von Goethe, German writer. His early works include the play *Götz von Berlichingen* (1773) and the novel *The Sorrows of Young Werther* (1774).		**1751:** Dennis Diderot, French writer and philosopher, publishes the first volume of his *Encyclopédie.*
	1751–1816: Richard Brinsley Sheridan, playwright and statesman, author of *The School for Scandal* (1777)	**1756–1763:** Frederick begins the Seven Years War pitting Prussia and Great Britain against Russia, Austria, and France.	**1756–1791:** Wolfgang Amadeus Mozart, Austrian classical composer **1757–1827:** William Blake, Romantic poet and artist, author of *Songs of Innocence* and *Songs of Experience*
	1762: English actor-manager David Garrick prohibits audience members from sitting on the stage.	**1762:** Catherine the Great (b. 1729) becomes empress of Russia after overthrowing her husband, Peter III; she reigns until her death in 1796.	**1759–1797:** Mary Wollstonecraft, English writer and early feminist, author of *Vindication of the Rights of Woman* (1792) **1762:** The Sorbonne library opens in Paris.
		1763: The Treaty of Paris ends the Seven Years War. Prussia emerges as an important European power. France loses many colonial possessions.	
		1765: British Parliament passes the Stamp Act. Nine colonies draw up a declaration of rights and liberties.	
	c. 1769: Spectators are banned from sitting on the stage in Paris.	**1766:** Catherine the Great grants freedom of worship in Russia.	

Molière

Molière (1622–1673, born Jean Baptiste Poquelin) came from a family attached to the glittering court of King Louis XIV, the Sun King. His father had purchased an appointment to the king, and as a result the family was familiar with the exciting court life of Paris, although not on intimate terms with the courtiers who surrounded the king. Molière's father was a furnisher and upholsterer to the king; the family, while well-to-do and enjoying some power, was still apart from royalty and the privileged aristocracy.

Molière's education was exceptional. He went to Jesuit schools and spent more than five years at Collège de Clermont, which he left in 1641 having studied both the humanities and philosophy. His knowledge of philosophy was unusually deep, and his background in the classics was exceptionally strong. He also took a law degree in 1641 at Orléans, but never practiced. His father's dream was that his son should inherit his appointment as furnisher to the king, thereby guaranteeing himself a comfortable future.

That, however, was not to be. Instead of following the law, Molière decided at the last minute to abandon his secure future, change his name so as not to scandalize his family, and take up a career in the theater. He began by joining a company of actors run by the Béjart family. They established a theater based in Paris called the Illustre Théâtre. It was run by Madeleine Béjart, with whom Molière had a professional and personal relationship until she died in 1672. Eventually, Molière began writing plays but only after he had worked extensively as an actor.

The famed commedia dell'arte actor Tiberio Fiorillo, known as Scaramouche, was a close friend of Molière and perhaps responsible for Molière's choice of a career in theater. Scaramouche may have been part of the Illustre Théâtre, or he may have acted in it on occasion. Unfortunately, the Illustre Théâtre lasted only a year. It was one of several Parisian theatrical groups, and none of them prospered.

The company went bankrupt in 1644, and Molière, forced to leave Paris for about thirteen years, played in the provinces and remote towns. Before leaving Paris he had to be bailed out of debtors' prison. What was left of the Béjart group merged with another company on tour, and Molière became director of that company. During this time he suffered most of the indignities typical of the traveling life, including impoverishment.

In October 1658 Louis XIV saw Molière's troupe acting in one of his comedies at the Louvre. The royal court was so impressed with what it saw that the king gave him the use of a theater. Molière's work remained immensely popular and controversial. He acted in his own plays, produced his own plays, and wrote a succession of major works that are still favorites.

Because other companies envied his success and favor with the king, a number of "scandals" arose around some of his plays. The first play to invite controversy was *The School for Wives* (1662), in which Arnolphe reacts in horror to the infidelities he sees in the wives all around him. He decides that his wife-to-be must be raised far from the world, where she will be ignorant of the wayward lives of the Parisians. A man who intends to seduce her tells Arnolphe (not knowing who he is) how he will get her out of Arnolphe's grasp. The play is highly comic, but groups of theatergoers protested that it was immoral and scandalous. In response Molière wrote *Criticism of the School for Wives* (1663), in which the debate over the play is enacted.

One of Molière's most popular plays, *Tartuffe* (written in 1664), concerns a religious hypocrite who weasels his way into a noble household and then goes about trying to seduce its mistress. Molière envisioned the religious con man as his target in this play, and the name *Tartuffe* became shorthand for a religious hypocrite. The name still implies hypocrisy in France.

A French church group, the Society of the Holy Sacrament, thought it was being portrayed in the title role and protested that the play was immoral and offensive. The society's condemnation of the play effectively prevented it from being performed. Molière tried rewriting *Tartuffe,* but the society would not approve its production.

In 1669 the Society of the Holy Sacrament was dissolved in a restructuring of the French church, and *Tartuffe* was finally permitted to be played to large audiences. Theatergoers loved the play and found great amusement in the sly, lecherous rogue who completely beguiles Orgon, the man who thinks Tartuffe is a great saint and who introduces him into his household. In most modern productions Tartuffe is played broadly, almost as a caricature or a clown. Audiences find him amusing, scabrous, and irresistible. They usually find the play irresistible, as well, because it involves crafty maneuvering onstage and complicated deceptions.

Among Molière's other successes are *The Miser* (1668), *The Bourgeois Gentleman* (1670), and his final play, *The Imaginary Invalid* (1673). Molière had a bad cough for most of the last decade of his life, which onstage he often made to seem the cough of the character he was playing. But Molière was genuinely ill; he died on stage, playing the title role of *The Imaginary Invalid.*

THE MISANTHROPE

The Misanthrope (1666) in its own age was not the most successful of Molière's plays, but it has certainly been one of the most produced of all the plays in his canon. Typical of his work, it derives from a close and careful observation of French life and manners. Recently, English-language audiences have been able to savor this play in Richard Wilbur's superb translation, which catches the sharpness of the French wit and the elegance of the verse — both hallmarks of French seventeenth-century drama.

In one sense the play is based on the type of improbability that marks Greek New Comedy. It portrays the romance of two very different people, Alceste, the misanthrope who speaks his mind and brashly tells people what he thinks of them, and Célimène, the coquette who rarely says what she thinks but who enjoys the attention of many suitors. She enjoys society and her capacity to dominate it. Alceste cannot abide society and its superficialities. At the end of the play he resolves to leave it.

A revelation in the play is that while Alceste and Célimène are different on the surface, beneath the surface they are similar. They are both extreme types who behave extremely. Célimène carries coquetry to great lengths, leading on as many men as possible. Alceste is the epitome of a misanthrope, refusing to flatter people just to make them feel good. He says that he must tell the truth, and he does — even when it hurts, perhaps especially when it hurts. For him to fall in love with a coquette who must deceive those around her to keep herself at the center of attention is a wonderful comic irony. But beneath that irony lies the thought that Alceste himself may have flaws that are the opposite of Célimène's.

The ending of *The Misanthrope,* which avoids the marriage of the protagonists (a more typical ending of comedies), may have contributed to the disappointment of its initial audiences. Another comic playwright would have brought the two lovers together. But Molière chose a more complex and, for some, a less satisfying ending. While two secondary characters marry, the main characters — Alceste and Célimène — agree to disagree and decide to live separately after all. Molière leaves his audience simply hoping that the two will change their minds. But as the play ends, the audience has no real reason to expect that they will.

This is a very French drama. The society is elegant, formal, and mannered. Molière knows every character and reveals each one totally. The surface elegance of the verse is such that the manners of the society seem polished, artificial, and ritualistic without being especially deceptive. The deception in this play is not at the center of things nor does the play depend on mix-ups and misapprehensions for its success. This in itself gives us a rather intriguing hint about Molière's intentions. The theme of honesty is at the play's center, but it is no simple thing to decide, in a social situation such as these characters enjoy, exactly how honest honesty should be or when honesty is the best policy. Alceste has one view and Célimène has another.

Molière enjoys pitting the values of Célimène and Alceste against one another, but it is clear that he does not want to offer sweeping or simple solutions to their conflict. Instead, he is content to leave his audience thinking and wondering.

The Misanthrope in Performance

The first full production of *The Misanthrope* was on June 4, 1666, with Molière as Alceste and his wife as Célimène. Most of the players who joined them were aware that Alceste was modeled after Molière himself and that Molière was poking fun at himself and his marriage. Molière made the part more comical than serious. The French national theater, Comédie-Française, records some fifteen hundred performances of the play between 1680 and 1960, making it one of the most performed of all French comedies. Late in the eighteenth century, actors began playing Alceste as a serious character, as he is played today.

The first important American production in English was by Richard Mansfield, who acted the part of Alceste in New York in 1905. The reviews noted that "his embodiment of Alceste is vibrant with pain. . . . He smiles, but it is always the smile of bitterness." Richard Wilbur's verse translation played in the tiny Theatre East in New York in 1956 while the original rhymed French version with a French company played simultaneously at the Winter Garden on Broadway. Both productions were very successful. Wilbur's version has since played virtually all over America, with several productions in New York in the 1960s, 70s, and 80s. The West Side Repertory Theater performed it in modern black tie and tails in 1991, with James Jacobus as Alceste. *The Misanthrope* has also had innumerable college productions since Wilbur's translation, which has, at least in the United States, become the standard version.

Tony Harrison also translated the play for the British National Theatre in 1975 with Alec McCowan as Alceste and Diana Rigg as Célimène. Reviews were mixed, but the play was said to have "the brilliance of a tiara of diamonds."

Molière [*Jean Baptiste Poquelin*] *(1622–1673)*

THE MISANTHROPE   *1666*

TRANSLATED BY RICHARD WILBUR

Characters

ALCESTE, *in love with Célimène*
PHILINTE, *Alceste's friend*
ORONTE, *in love with Célimène*
CÉLIMÈNE, *Alceste's beloved*
ÉLIANTE, *Célimène's cousin*
ARSINOÉ, *a friend of Célimène's*
ACASTE }
CLITANDRE } *Marquesses*
BASQUE, *Célimène's servant*
A GUARD *of the Marshalsea*
DUBOIS, *Alceste's valet*

The scene throughout is in Célimène's house at Paris.

ACT I • *Scene I* [*Philinte, Alceste.*]

PHILINTE: Now, what's got into you?
ALCESTE (*seated*):   Kindly leave me alone.
PHILINTE: Come, come, what is it? This lugubrious
    tone . . .
ALCESTE: Leave me, I said; you spoil my solitude.
PHILINTE: Oh, listen to me, now, and don't be rude.
ALCESTE: I choose to be rude, Sir, and to be hard of
    hearing.   5
PHILINTE: These ugly moods of yours are not
    endearing;

Friends though we are, I really must insist . . .
ALCESTE (*abruptly rising*): Friends? Friends, you say?
    Well, cross me off your list.
I've been your friend till now, as you well know;
But after what I saw a moment ago   10
I tell you flatly that our ways must part.
I wish no place in a dishonest heart.
PHILINTE: Why, what have I done, Alceste? Is this quite
    just?
ALCESTE: My God, you ought to die of self-disgust.
I call your conduct inexcusable, Sir,   15
And every man of honor will concur.
I see you almost hug a man to death,
Exclaim for joy until you're out of breath,
And supplement these loving demonstrations
With endless offers, vows, and protestations;   20
Then when I ask you "Who was that?" I find
That you can barely bring his name to mind!
Once the man's back is turned, you cease to love
    him,
And speak with absolute indifference of him!
By God, I say it's base and scandalous   25
To falsify the heart's affections thus;
If I caught myself behaving in such a way,
I'd hang myself for shame, without delay.
PHILINTE: It hardly seems a hanging matter to me;
I hope that you will take it graciously   30
If I extend myself a slight reprieve,

And live a little longer, by your leave.
ALCESTE: How dare you joke about a crime so grave?
PHILINTE: What crime? How else are people to behave?
35   ALCESTE: I'd have them be sincere, and never part
       With any word that isn't from the heart.
     PHILINTE: When someone greets us with a show of
         pleasure,
       It's but polite to give him equal measure,
       Return his love the best that we know how,
40   And trade him offer for offer, vow for vow.
     ALCESTE: No, no, this formula you'd have me follow,
       However fashionable, is false and hollow,
       And I despise the frenzied operations
       Of all these barterers of protestations,
45   These lavishers of meaningless embraces
       These utterers of obliging commonplaces,
       Who court and flatter everyone on earth
       And praise the fool no less than the man of worth.
       Should you rejoice that someone fondles you,
50   Offers his love and service, swears to be true,
       And fills your ears with praises of your name,
       When to the first damned fop he'll say the same?
       No, no: no self-respecting heart would dream
       Of prizing so promiscuous an esteem;
55   However high the praise, there's nothing worse
       Than sharing honors with the universe.
       Esteem is founded on comparison:
       To honor all men is to honor none.
       Since you embrace this indiscriminate vice
60   Your friendship comes at far too cheap a price;
       I spurn the easy tribute of a heart
       Which will not set the worthy man apart:
       I choose, Sir, to be chosen; and in fine,
       The friend of mankind is no friend of mine.
65   PHILINTE: But in polite society, custom decrees
       That we show certain outward courtesies . . .
     ALCESTE: Ah, no! we should condemn with all our
         force
       Such false and artificial intercourse.
       Let men behave like men; let them display
70   Their inmost hearts in everything they say;
       Let the heart speak, and let our sentiments
       Not mask themselves in silly compliments.
     PHILINTE: In certain cases it would be uncouth
       And most absurd to speak the naked truth;
75   With all respect for your exalted notions,
       It's often best to veil one's true emotions.
       Wouldn't the social fabric come undone
       If we were wholly frank with everyone?
       Suppose you met with someone you couldn't bear;
80   Would you inform him of it then and there?
     ALCESTE: Yes.
     PHILINTE: Then you'd tell old Emilie it's pathetic
       The way she daubs her features with cosmetic
       And plays the gay coquette at sixty-four?
     ALCESTE: I would.
     PHILINTE: And you'd call Dorilas a bore,
85   And tell him every ear at court is lame
       From hearing him brag about his noble name?

ALCESTE: Precisely.
PHILINTE: Ah, you're joking.
ALCESTE: *Au contraire.*°
       In this regard there's none I'd choose to spare.
       All are corrupt; there's nothing to be seen
       In court or town but aggravates my spleen.°   90
       I fall into deep gloom and melancholy
       When I survey the scene of human folly,
       Finding on every hand base flattery,
       Injustice, fraud, self-interest, treachery. . . .
       Ah, it's too much; mankind has grown so base,   95
       I mean to break with the whole human race.
     PHILINTE: This philosophic rage is a bit extreme;
       You've no idea how comical you seem;
       Indeed, we're like those brothers in the play
       Called *School for Husbands,*° one of whom was
         prey . . .   100
     ALCESTE: Enough, now! None of your stupid similes.
     PHILINTE: Then let's have no more tirades, if you
         please.
       The world won't change, whatever you say or do;
       And since plain speaking means so much to you,
       I'll tell you plainly that by being frank   105
       You've earned the reputation of a crank,
       And that you're thought ridiculous when you rage
       And rant against the manners of the age.
     ALCESTE: So much the better; just what I wish to hear.
       No news could be more grateful to my ear.   110
       All men are so detestable in my eyes,
       I should be sorry if they thought me wise.
     PHILINTE: Your hatred's very sweeping, is it not?
     ALCESTE: Quite right: I hate the whole degraded lot.
     PHILINTE: Must all poor human creatures be embraced, 115
       Without distinction, by your vast distaste?
       Even in these bad times, there are surely a few . . .
     ALCESTE: No, I include all men in one dim view:
       Some men I hate for being rogues: the others
       I hate because they treat the rogues like brothers, 120
       And, lacking a virtuous scorn for what is vile,
       Receive the villain with a complaisant smile.
       Notice how tolerant people choose to be
       Toward that bold rascal who's at law with me.
       His social polish can't conceal his nature;   125
       One sees at once that he's a treacherous creature;
       No one could possibly be taken in
       By those soft speeches and that sugary grin.
       The whole world knows the shady means by
         which
       The low-brow's grown so powerful and rich,   130
       And risen to a rank so bright and high
       That virtue can but blush, and merit sigh.

87. *Au contraire:* On the contrary. 90. spleen: A body organ
thought to be the seat of melancholy, one of the four humors of
medieval physiology. **100. *School for Husbands:*** A play by
Molière (1661) in which two brothers, Sganarelle and Ariste,
are guardians of two orphan girls. Sganarelle hopes to marry
one of the girls, Isabelle, but she frees herself by trickery from
his domineering ways and marries someone else.

Whenever his name comes up in conversation,
None will defend his wretched reputation;
135 Call him knave, liar, scoundrel, and all the rest,
Each head will nod, and no one will protest.
And yet his smirk is seen in every house,
He's greeted everywhere with smiles and bows,
And when there's any honor that can be got
140 By pulling strings, he'll get it, like as not.
My God! It chills my heart to see the ways
Men come to terms with evil nowadays
Sometimes, I swear, I'm moved to flee and find
Some desert land unfouled by humankind.
145 PHILINTE: Come, let's forget the follies of the times
And pardon mankind for its petty crimes;
Let's have an end of rantings and of railings,
And show some leniency toward human failings.
This world requires a pliant rectitude;
150 Too stern a virtue makes one stiff and rude;
Good sense views all extremes with detestation,
And bids us to be noble in moderation.
The rigid virtues of the ancient days
Are not for us; they jar with all our ways
155 And ask of us too lofty a perfection.
Wise men accept their times without objection,
And there's no greater folly, if you ask me,
Than trying to reform society.
Like you, I see each day a hundred and one
160 Unhandsome deeds that might be better done,
But still, for all the faults that meet my view,
I'm never known to storm and rave like you.
I take men as they are, or let them be,
And teach my soul to bear their frailty;
165 And whether in court or town, whatever the scene,
My phlegm's° as philosophic as your spleen.
ALCESTE: This phlegm which you so eloquently
commend,
Does nothing ever rile it up, my friend?
Suppose some man you trust should treacherously
170 Conspire to rob you of your property,
And do his best to wreck your reputation?
Wouldn't you feel a certain indignation?
PHILINTE: Why, no. These faults of which you so
complain
Are part of human nature, I maintain,
175 And it's no more a matter for disgust
That men are knavish, selfish and unjust,
Than that the vulture dines upon the dead,
And wolves are furious, and apes ill-bred.
ALCESTE: Shall I see myself betrayed, robbed, torn to
bits,
180 And not . . . Oh, let's be still and rest our wits.
Enough of reasoning, now. I've had my fill.
PHILINTE: Indeed, you would do well, Sir, to be still.
Rage less at your opponent, and give some thought
To how you'll win this lawsuit that he's brought.
185 ALCESTE: I assure you I'll do nothing of the sort.

166. phlegm: In medieval physiology, the humor thought to be
cold and moist and to cause sluggishness.

PHILINTE: Then who will plead your case before the
court?
ALCESTE: Reason and right and justice will plead for
me.
PHILINTE: Oh, Lord. What judges do you plan to see?
ALCESTE: Why, none. The justice of my cause is clear.
PHILINTE: Of course, man; but there's politics to
fear . . .   190
ALCESTE: No, I refuse to lift a hand. That's flat.
I'm either right, or wrong.
PHILINTE: Don't count on that.
ALCESTE: No, I'll do nothing.
PHILINTE: Your enemy's influence
Is great, you know . . .
ALCESTE: That makes no difference.
PHILINTE: It will; you'll see.
ALCESTE: Must honor bow to guile?   195
If so, I shall be proud to lose the trial.
PHILINTE: Oh, really . . .
ALCESTE: I'll discover by this case
Whether or not men are sufficiently base
And impudent and villainous and perverse
To do me wrong before the universe.   200
PHILINTE: What a man!
ALCESTE: Oh, I could wish, whatever the cost,
Just for the beauty of it, that my trial were lost.
PHILINTE: If people heard you talking so, Alceste,
They'd split their sides. Your name would be a jest.
ALCESTE: So much the worse for jesters.
PHILINTE: May I enquire   205
Whether this rectitude you so admire,
And these hard virtues you're enamored of
Are qualities of the lady whom you love?
It much surprises me that you, who seem
To view mankind with furious disesteem,   210
Have yet found something to enchant your eyes
Amidst a species which you so despise.
And what is more amazing, I'm afraid,
Is the most curious choice your heart has made.
The honest Éliante is fond of you,   215
Arsinoé, the prude, admires you too;
And yet your spirit's been perversely led
To choose the flighty Célimène instead,
Whose brittle malice and coquettish ways
So typify the manners of our days.   220
How is it that the traits you most abhor
Are bearable in this lady you adore?
Are you so blind with love that you can't find them?
Or do you contrive, in her case, not to mind them?
ALCESTE: My love for that young widow's not the kind   225
That can't perceive defects; no, I'm not blind.
I see her faults, despite my ardent love,
And all I see I fervently reprove.
And yet I'm weak; for all her falsity,
That woman knows the art of pleasing me,   230
And though I never cease complaining of her,
I swear I cannot manage not to love her.
Her charm outweighs her faults; I can but aim
To cleanse her spirit in my love's pure flame.

235   PHILINTE: That's no small task; I wish you all success.
  You think then that she loves you?
  ALCESTE: Heavens, yes!
  I wouldn't love her did she not love me.
  PHILINTE: Well, if her taste for you is plain to see,
  Why do these rivals cause you such despair?
240   ALCESTE: True love, Sir, is possessive, and cannot bear
  To share with all the world. I'm here today
  To tell her she must send that mob away.
  PHILINTE: If I were you, and had your choice to make,
  Éliante, her cousin, would be the one I'd take;
245   That honest heart, which cares for you alone,
  Would harmonize far better with your own.
  ALCESTE: True, true: each day my reason tells me so;
  But reason doesn't rule in love, you know.
  PHILINTE: I fear some bitter sorrow is in store;
250   This love . . .

Scene II [*Oronte, Alceste, Philinte.*]

ORONTE (*to Alceste*): The servants told me at the door
  That Éliante and Célimène were out,
  But when I heard, dear Sir, that you were about,
  I came to say, without exaggeration,
5   That I hold you in the vastest admiration,
  And that it's always been my dearest desire
  To be the friend of one I so admire.
  I hope to see my love of merit requited,
  And you and I in friendship's bond united.
10   I'm sure you won't refuse — if I may be frank —
  A friend of my devotedness — and rank.

(*During this speech of Oronte's Alceste is abstracted
and seems unaware that he is being spoken to. He only
breaks off his reverie when Oronte says:*)

  It was for you, if you please, that my words were
    intended.
  ALCESTE: For me, Sir?
  ORONTE: Yes, for you. You're not offended?
  ALCESTE: By no means. But this much surprises me . . .
15   The honor comes most unexpectedly . . .
  ORONTE: My high regard should not astonish you;
  The whole world feels the same. It is your due.
  ALCESTE: Sir . . .
  ORONTE: Why, in all the State there isn't one
  Can match your merits; they shine, Sir, like the sun.
  ALCESTE: Sir . . .
20   ORONTE: You are higher in my estimation
  Than all that's most illustrious in the nation.
  ALCESTE: Sir . . .
  ORONTE: If I lie, may heaven strike me dead!
  To show you that I mean what I have said,
  Permit me, Sir, to embrace you most sincerely,
25   And swear that I will prize our friendship dearly.
  Give me your hand. And now, Sir, if you choose,
  We'll make our vows.
  ALCESTE: Sir . . .
  ORONTE: What! You refuse?

ALCESTE: Sir, it's a very great honor you extend:
  But friendship is a sacred thing, my friend;
  It would be profanation to bestow   30
  The name of friend on one you hardly know.
  All parts are better played when well-rehearsed
  Let's put off friendship, and get acquainted first.
  We may discover it would be unwise
  To try to make our natures harmonize.   35
  ORONTE: By heaven! You're sagacious to the core;
  This speech has made me admire you even more.
  Let time, then, bring us closer day by day;
  Meanwhile, I shall be yours in every way.
  If, for example, there should be anything   40
  You wish at court, I'll mention it to the King.
  I have his ear, of course; it's quite well known
  That I am much in favor with the throne.
  In short, I am your servant. And now, dear friend,
  Since you have such fine judgment, I intend   45
  To please you, if I can, with a small sonnet
  I wrote not long ago. Please comment on it,
  And tell me whether I ought to publish it.
  ALCESTE: You must excuse me, Sir; I'm hardly fit
  To judge such matters.
  ORONTE: Why not?
  ALCESTE: I am. I fear,   50
  Inclined to be unfashionably sincere.
  ORONTE: Just what I ask; I'd take no satisfaction
  In anything but your sincere reaction.
  I beg you not to dream of being kind.
  ALCESTE: Since you desire it, Sir, I'll speak my mind.   55
  ORONTE: *Sonnet.* It's a sonnet. . . . *Hope.* . . . The
    poem's addressed
  To a lady who wakened hopes within my breast.
  Hope . . . this is not the pompous sort of thing,
  Just modest little verses, with a tender ring.
  ALCESTE: Well, we shall see.
  ORONTE: *Hope* . . . I'm anxious to hear   60
  Whether the style seems properly smooth and clear,
  And whether the choice of words is good or bad.
  ALCESTE: We'll see, we'll see.
  ORONTE: Perhaps I ought to add
  That it took me only a quarter-hour to write it.
  ALCESTE: The time's irrelevant, Sir: kindly recite it.   65
  ORONTE (*reading*): Hope comforts us awhile, 'tis true,
  Lulling our cares with careless laughter,
  And yet such joy is full of rue,
  My Phyllis, if nothing follows after.
  PHILINTE: I'm charmed by this already; the style's
    delightful.   70
  ALCESTE (*sotto voce,° to Philinte*): How can you say
    that? Why, the thing is frightful.
  ORONTE: Your fair face smiled on me awhile,
  But was it kindness so to enchant me?
  'Twould have been fairer not to smile,
  If hope was all you meant to grant me.   75
  PHILINTE: What a clever thought! How handsomely
    you phrase it!

71. [S.D.] *sotto voce:* In a soft voice or stage whisper.

ALCESTE (*sotto voce, to Philinte*): You know the thing
    is trash. How dare you praise it?
ORONTE: If it's to be my passion's fate
    Thus everlastingly to wait,
80   Then death will come to set me free:
    For death is fairer than the fair;
    Phyllis, to hope is to despair
    When one must hope eternally.
PHILINTE: The close is exquisite — full of feeling and
    grace.
ALCESTE (*sotto voce, aside*): Oh, blast the close; you'd
85   better close your face
    Before you send your lying soul to hell.
PHILINTE: I can't remember a poem I've liked so well.
ALCESTE (*sotto voce, aside*): Good Lord!
ORONTE (*to Philinte*):   I fear you're
    flattering me a bit.
PHILINTE: Oh, no!
ALCESTE (*sotto voce, aside*): What else d'you call it, you
    hypocrite?
ORONTE (*to Alceste*): But you, Sir, keep your promise
90   now: don't shrink
    From telling me sincerely what you think.
ALCESTE: Sir, these are delicate matters; we all desire
    To be told that we've the true poetic fire.
    But once, to one whose name I shall not mention
95   I said, regarding some verse of his invention,
    That gentlemen should rigorously control
    That itch to write which often afflicts the soul;
    That one should curb the heady inclination
    To publicize one's little avocation
100   And that in showing off one's works of art
    One often plays a very clownish part.
ORONTE: Are you suggesting in a devious way
    That I ought not . . .
ALCESTE: Oh, that I do not say.
    Further, I told him that no fault is worse
105   Than that of writing frigid, lifeless verse,
    And that the merest whisper of such a shame
    Suffices to destroy a man's good name.
ORONTE: D'you mean to say my sonnet's dull and
    trite?
ALCESTE: I don't say that. But I went on to cite
110   Numerous cases of once-respected men
    Who came to grief by taking up the pen.
ORONTE: And am I like them? Do I write so poorly?
ALCESTE: I don't say that. But I told this person, "Surely
    You're under no necessity to compose;
115   Why you should wish to publish, heaven knows.
    There's no excuse for printing tedious rot
    Unless one writes for bread, as you do not.
    Resist temptation, then, I beg of you;
    Conceal your pastimes from the public view;
120   And don't give up, on any provocation,
    Your present high and courtly reputation,
    To purchase at a greedy printer's shop
    The name of silly author and scribbling fop."
    These were the points I tried to make him see.

ORONTE: I sense that they are also aimed at me,   125
    But now — about my sonnet — I'd like to be told . . .
ALCESTE: Frankly, that sonnet should be pigeonholed.
    You've chosen the worst models to imitate.
    The style's unnatural. Let me illustrate:
    For example, Your fair face smiled on me awhile,   130
    Followed by, 'Twould have been fairer not to smile!
    Or this: such joy is full of rue;
    Or this: For death is fairer than the fair;
    Or, Phyllis, to hope is to despair
    When one must hope eternally!   135
    This artificial style, that's all the fashion,
    Has neither taste, nor honesty, nor passion;
    It's nothing but a sort of wordy play,
    And nature never spoke in such a way.
    What, in this shallow age, is not debased?   140
    Our fathers, though less refined, had better taste;
    I'd barter all that men admire today
    For one old love song I shall try to say:
    If the King had given me for my own
    Paris, his citadel,   145
    And I for that must leave alone
    Her whom I love so well,
    I'd say then to the Crown,
    Take back your glittering town;
    My darling is more fair, I swear,   150
    My darling is more fair.
    The rhyme's not rich, the style is rough and old,
    But don't you see that it's the purest gold
    Beside the tinsel nonsense now preferred,
    And that there's passion in its every word?   155
    If the King had given me for my own
    Paris, his citadel,
    And I for that must leave alone
    Her whom I love so well,
    I'd say then to the Crown,   160
    Take back your glittering town;
    My darling is more fair, I swear,
    My darling is more fair.
    There speaks a loving heart. (*To Philinte.*) You're
    laughing, eh?
    Laugh on, my precious wit. Whatever you say,   165
    I hold that song's worth all the bibelots°
    That people hail today with ah's and oh's.
ORONTE: And I maintain my sonnet's very good.
ALCESTE: It's not at all surprising that you should.
    You have your reasons; permit me to have mine   170
    For thinking that you cannot write a line.
ORONTE: Others have praised my sonnet to the skies.
ALCESTE: I lack their art of telling pleasant lies.
ORONTE: You seem to think you've got no end of wit.
ALCESTE: To praise your verse, I'd need still more of it.   175
ORONTE: I'm not in need of your approval, Sir.
ALCESTE: That's good; you couldn't have it if you were.
ORONTE: Come now, I'll lend you the subject of my
    sonnet;
    I'd like to see you try to improve upon it.

166. bibelots: Trinkets.

ALCESTE: I might, by chance, write something just as
180   shoddy;
    But then I wouldn't show it to everybody.
ORONTE: You're most opinionated and conceited.
ALCESTE: Go find your flatterers, and be better treated.
ORONTE: Look here, my little fellow, pray watch your
    tone.
ALCESTE: My great big fellow, you'd better watch your
185   own.
PHILINTE (*stepping between them*): Oh, please, please,
    gentlemen! This will never do.
ORONTE: The fault is mine, and I leave the field to you.
    I am your servant, Sir, in every way.
ALCESTE: And I, Sir, am your most abject valet.

Scene III {*Philinte, Alceste.*}

PHILINTE: Well, as you see, sincerity in excess
    Can get you into a very pretty mess;
    Oronte was hungry for appreciation. . . .
ALCESTE: Don't speak to me.
PHILINTE: What?
ALCESTE: No more conversation.
PHILINTE: Really, now . . .
ALCESTE: Leave me alone.
PHILINTE: If I . . .
5   ALCESTE: Out of my sight!
PHILINTE: But what . . .
ALCESTE: I won't listen.
PHILINTE: But . . .
ALCESTE: Silence!
PHILINTE: Now, it is polite . . .
ALCESTE: By heaven, I've had enough. Don't follow
    me.
PHILINTE: Ah, you're just joking. I'll keep you
    company.

ACT II • Scene I {*Alceste, Célimène.*}

ALCESTE: Shall I speak plainly, Madam? I confess
    Your conduct gives me infinite distress,
    And my resentment's grown too hot to smother.
    Soon, I foresee, we'll break with one another.
5   If I said otherwise, I should deceive you;
    Sooner or later, I shall be forced to leave you,
    And if I swore that we shall never part
    I should misread the omens of my heart.
CÉLIMÈNE: You kindly saw me home, it would appear,
10   So as to pour invectives in my ear.
ALCESTE: I've no desire to quarrel. But I deplore
    Your inability to shut the door
    On all these suitors who beset you so.
    There's what annoys me, if you care to know.
15   CÉLIMÈNE: Is it my fault that all these men pursue me?
    Am I to blame if they're attracted to me?
    And when they gently beg an audience,
    Ought I to take a stick and drive them hence?

ALCESTE: Madam, there's no necessity for a stick;
    A less responsive heart would do the trick.   20
    Of your attractiveness I don't complain;
    But those your charms attract, you then detain
    By a most melting and receptive manner,
    And so enlist their hearts beneath your banner.
    It's the agreeable hopes which you excite   25
    That keep these lovers round you day and night;
    Were they less liberally smiled upon,
    That sighing troop would very soon be gone.
    But tell me, Madam, why it is that lately
    This man Clitandre interests you so greatly?   30
    Because of what high merits do you deem
    Him worthy of the honor of your esteem?
    Is it that your admiring glances linger
    On the splendidly long nail of his little finger?
    Or do you share the general deep respect   35
    For the blond wig he chooses to affect?
    Are you in love with his embroidered hose?
    Do you adore his ribbons and his bows?
    Or is it that this paragon bewitches
    Your tasteful eye with his vast German breeches?   40
    Perhaps his giggle, or his falsetto voice,
    Makes him the latest gallant of your choice?
CÉLIMÈNE: You're much mistaken to resent him so.
    Why I put up with him you surely know:
    My lawsuit's very shortly to be tried,   45
    And I must have his influence on my side.
ALCESTE: Then lose your lawsuit, Madam, or let it
    drop;
    Don't torture me by humoring such a fop.
CÉLIMÈNE: You're jealous of the whole world, Sir.
ALCESTE: That's true,
    Since the whole world is well-received by you.   50
CÉLIMÈNE: That my good nature is so unconfined
    Should serve to pacify your jealous mind;
    Were I to smile on one, and scorn the rest,
    Then you might have some cause to be distressed.
ALCESTE: Well, if I mustn't be jealous, tell me, then,   55
    Just how I'm better treated than other men.
CÉLIMÈNE: You know you have my love. Will that not
    do?
ALCESTE: What proof have I that what you say is true?
CÉLIMÈNE: I would expect, Sir, that my having said it
    Might give the statement a sufficient credit.   60
ALCESTE: But how can I be sure that you don't tell
    The selfsame thing to other men as well?
CÉLIMÈNE: What a gallant speech! How flattering to
    me!
    What a sweet creature you make me out to be!
    Well then, to save you from the pangs of doubt,   65
    All that I've said I hereby cancel out;
    Now, none but yourself shall make a monkey of
    you:
    Are you content?
ALCESTE: Why, why am I doomed to love you?
    I swear that I shall bless the blissful hour
    When this poor heart's no longer in your power!   70
    I make no secret of it: I've done my best

To exorcise this passion from my breast
But thus far all in vain; it will not go;
It's for my sins that I must love you so.
CÉLIMÈNE: Your love for me is matchless, Sir; that's
75   clear.
ALCESTE: Indeed, in all the world it has no peer;
        Words can't describe the nature of my passion,
        And no man ever loved in such a fashion.
CÉLIMÈNE: Yes, it's a brand-new fashion, I agree:
80   You show your love by castigating me,
        And all your speeches are enraged and rude.
        I've never been so furiously wooed.
ALCESTE: Yet you could calm that fury, if you chose.
        Come, shall we bring our quarrels to a close?
85   Let's speak with open hearts, then, and begin . . .

Scene II [*Célimène, Alceste, Basque.*]

CÉLIMÈNE: What is it?
BASQUE: Acaste is here.
CÉLIMÈNE: Well, send him in.

Scene III [*Célimène, Alceste.*]

ALCESTE: What! Shall we never be alone at all?
        You're always ready to receive a call,
        And you can't bear, for ten ticks of the clock,
        Not to keep open house for all who knock.
5   CÉLIMÈNE: I couldn't refuse him: he'd be most put out.
ALCESTE: Surely that's not worth worrying about.
CÉLIMÈNE: Acaste would never forgive me if he guessed
        That I consider him a dreadful pest.
ALCESTE: If he's a pest, why bother with him then?
10 CÉLIMÈNE: Heavens! One can't antagonize such men;
        Why, they're the chartered gossips of the court,
        And have a say in things of every sort.
        One must receive them, and be full of charm;
        They're no great help, but they can do you harm,
15   And though your influence be ever so great,
        They're hardly the best people to alienate.
ALCESTE: I see, dear lady, that you could make a case
        For putting up with the whole human race;
        These friendships that you calculate so nicely . . .

Scene IV [*Alceste, Célimène, Basque.*]

BASQUE: Madam, Clitandre is here as well.
ALCESTE: Precisely.
CÉLIMÈNE: Where are you going?
ALCESTE: Elsewhere.
CÉLIMÈNE: Stay.
ALCESTE: No, no.
CÉLIMÈNE: Stay, Sir.
ALCESTE: I can't.
CÉLIMÈNE: I wish it.
ALCESTE: No, I must go.

I beg you, Madam, not to press the matter;
You know I have no taste for idle chatter.   5
CÉLIMÈNE: Stay. I command you.
ALCESTE: No, I cannot stay.
CÉLIMÈNE: Very well; you have my leave to go away.

Scene V [*Éliante, Philinte, Acaste, Clitandre,
Alceste, Célimène, Basque.*]

ÉLIANTE (*to Célimène*): The Marquesses have kindly
        come to call.
        Were they announced?
CÉLIMÈNE: Yes. Basque, bring chairs for all.

(*Basque provides the chairs and exits.*)

        (*To Alceste.*) You haven't gone?
ALCESTE: No; and I shan't depart
        Till you decide who's foremost in your heart.
CÉLIMÈNE: Oh, hush.
ALCESTE: It's time to choose; take them, or me.   5
CÉLIMÈNE: You're mad.
ALCESTE: I'm not, as you shall shortly see.
CÉLIMÈNE: Oh?
ALCESTE: You'll decide.
CÉLIMÈNE: You're joking now, dear friend.
ALCESTE: No, no; you'll choose; my patience is at an
        end.
CLITANDRE: Madam, I come from court, where poor
        Cléonte
        Behaved like a perfect fool, as is his wont.
        Has he no friend to counsel him, I wonder,   10
        And teach him less unerringly to blunder?
CÉLIMÈNE: It's true, the man's a most accomplished
        dunce;
        His gauche behavior charms the eye at once;
        And every time one sees him, on my word,   15
        His manner's grown a trifle more absurd.
ACASTE: Speaking of dunces, I've just now conversed
        With old Damon, who's one of the very worst;
        I stood a lifetime in the broiling sun
        Before his dreary monologue was done.   20
CÉLIMÈNE: Oh, he's a wondrous talker, and has the
        power
        To tell you nothing hour after hour:
        If, by mistake, he ever came to the point,
        The shock would put his jawbone out of joint.
ÉLIANTE (*to Philinte*): The conversation takes its usual
        turn,   25
        And all our dear friends' ears will shortly burn.
CLITANDRE: Timante's a character, Madam.
CÉLIMÈNE: Isn't he, though?
        A man of mystery from top to toe,
        Who moves about in a romantic mist
        On secret missions which do not exist.   30
        His talk is full of eyebrows and grimaces;
        How tired one gets of his momentous faces;
        He's always whispering something confidential

Which turns out to be quite inconsequential;
35   Nothing's too slight for him to mystify;
He even whispers when he says "good-by."
ACASTE: Tell us about Géralde.
CÉLIMÈNE: That tiresome ass.
He mixes only with the titled class,
And fawns on dukes and princes, and is bored
40   With anyone who's not at least a lord.
The man's obsessed with rank, and his discourses
Are all of hounds and carriages and horses;
He uses Christian names with all the great,
And the word Milord, with him, is out of date.
45   CLITANDRE: He's very taken with Bélisc, I hear.
CÉLIMÈNE: She is the dreariest company, poor dear.
Whenever she comes to call, I grope about
To find some topic which will draw her out,
But, owing to her dry and faint replies,
50   The conversation wilts, and droops, and dies.
In vain one hopes to animate her face
By mentioning the ultimate commonplace;
But sun or shower, even hail or frost
Are matters she can instantly exhaust.
55   Meanwhile her visit, painful though it is,
Drags on and on through mute eternities,
And though you ask the time, and yawn, and
          yawn,
She sits there like a stone and won't be gone.
ACASTE: Now for Adraste.
CÉLIMÈNE: Oh, that conceited elf
60   Has a gigantic passion for himself;
He rails against the court, and cannot bear it
That none will recognize his hidden merit;
All honors given to others give offense
To his imaginary excellence.
CLITANDRE: What about young Cléon? His house,
65   they say,
Is full of the best society, night and day.
CÉLIMÈNE: His cook has made him popular, not he:
It's Cléon's table that people come to see.
ÉLIANTE: He gives a splendid dinner, you must admit.
70   CÉLIMÈNE: But must he serve himself along with it?
For my taste, he's a most insipid dish
Whose presence sours the wine and spoils the fish.
PHILINTE: Damis, his uncle is admired no end.
What's your opinion, Madam?
CÉLIMÈNE: Why, he's my friend.
75   PHILINTE: He seems a decent fellow, and rather clever.
CÉLIMÈNE: He works too hard at cleverness,
          however.
I hate to see him sweat and struggle so
To fill his conversation with *bons mots*.°
Since he's decided to become a wit
80   His taste's so pure that nothing pleases it;
He scolds at all the latest books and plays,
Thinking that wit must never stoop to praise,
That finding fault's a sign of intellect,

78. *bons mots:* Clever remarks, witticisms.

That all appreciation is abject,
And that by damning everything in sight   85
One shows oneself in a distinguished light.
He's scornful even of our conversations:
Their trivial nature sorely tries his patience;
He folds his arms, and stands above the battle,
And listens sadly to our childish prattle.   90
ACASTE: Wonderful, Madam! You've hit him off
          precisely.
CLITANDRE: No one can sketch a character so nicely.
ALCESTE: How bravely, Sirs, you cut and thrust
          at all
These absent fools, till one by one they fall:
But let one come in sight, and you'll at once   95
Embrace the man you lately called a dunce,
Telling him in a tone sincere and fervent
How proud you are to be his humble servant.
CLITANDRE: Why pick on us? *Madame's* been speaking,
          Sir.
And you should quarrel, if you must, with her.   100
ALCESTE: No, no, by God, the fault is yours, because
You lead her on with laughter and applause,
And make her think that she's the more delightful
The more her talk is scandalous and spiteful.
Oh, she would stoop to malice far, far less   105
If no such claque approved her cleverness.
It's flatterers like you whose foolish praise
Nourishes all the vices of these days.
PHILINTE: But why protest when someone ridicules
Those you'd condemn, yourself, as knaves or
          fools?   110
CÉLIMÈNE: Why, Sir? Because he loves to make a
          fuss.
You don't expect him to agree with us,
When there's an opportunity to express
His heaven-sent spirit of contrariness?
What other people think, he can't abide;   115
Whatever they say, he's on the other side;
He lives in deadly terror of agreeing;
'Twould make him seem an ordinary being.
Indeed, he's so in love with contradiction,
He'll turn against his most profound conviction   120
And with a furious eloquence deplore it,
If only someone else is speaking for it.
ALCESTE: Go on, dear lady, mock me as you please;
You have your audience in ecstasies.
PHILINTE: But what she says is true: you have a way   125
Of bridling at whatever people say;
Whether they praise or blame, your angry spirit
Is equally unsatisfied to hear it.
ALCESTE: Men, Sir, are always wrong, and that's the
          reason
That righteous anger's never out of season;   130
All that I hear in all their conversation
Is flattering praise or reckless condemnation.
CÉLIMÈNE: But . . .
ALCESTE: No, no, Madam, I am forced to state
That you have pleasures which I deprecate,

135   And that these others, here, are much to blame
       For nourishing the faults which are your shame.
  CLITANDRE: I shan't defend myself, Sir; but I vow
       I'd thought this lady faultless until now.
  ACASTE: I see her charms and graces, which are many;
140   But as for faults, I've never noticed any.
  ALCESTE: I see them, Sir; and rather than ignore them,
       I strenuously criticize her for them.
       The more one loves, the more one should object
       To every blemish, every least defect.
145   Were I this lady, I would soon get rid
       Of lovers who approved of all I did,
       And by their slack indulgence and applause
       Endorsed my follies and excused my flaws.
  CÉLIMÈNE: If all hearts beat according to your
       measure,
150   The dawn of love would be the end of pleasure;
       And love would find its perfect consummation
       In ecstasies of rage and reprobation.
  ÉLIANTE: Love, as a rule, affects men otherwise
       And lovers rarely love to criticize.
155   They see their lady as a charming blur,
       And find all things commendable in her.
       If she has any blemish, fault, or shame,
       They will redeem it by a pleasing name.
       The pale-faced lady's lily-white, perforce;
160   The swarthy one's a sweet brunette, of course;
       The spindly lady has a slender grace;
       The fat one has a most majestic pace;
       The plain one, with her dress in disarray
       They classify as *beauté négligée;*°
165   The hulking one's a goddess in their eyes,
       The dwarf, a concentrate of Paradise;
       The haughty lady has a noble mind;
       The mean one's witty, and the dull one's kind;
       The chatterbox has liveliness and verve,
170   The mute one has a virtuous reserve.
       So lovers manage, in their passion's cause,
       To love their ladies even for their flaws.
  ALCESTE: But I still say . . .
  CÉLIMÈNE   I think it would be nice
       To stroll around the gallery once or twice.
       What! You're not going, Sirs?
175 CLITANDRE AND ACASTE: No, Madam, no.
  ALCESTE: You seem to be in terror lest they go.
       Do what you will, Sirs; leave, or linger on,
       But I shan't go till after you are gone.
  ACASTE: I'm free to linger, unless I should perceive
180   *Madame* is tired, and wishes me to leave.
  CLITANDRE: And as for me, I needn't go today
       Until the hour of the King's *coucher.*°
  CÉLIMÈNE (*to Alceste*): You're joking, surely?
  ALCESTE: Not in the
       least; we'll see
       Whether you'd rather part with them, or me.

164. beauté négligée: Slovenly beauty.   **182. the King's *coucher*:**
The King's bedtime, a ceremonial occasion.

Scene VI [*Alceste, Célimène, Éliante, Acaste,
Philinte, Clitandre, Basque.*]

BASQUE (*to Alceste*): Sir, there's a fellow here who bids
      me state
      That he must see you, and that it can't wait.
ALCESTE: Tell him that I have no such pressing affairs.
BASQUE: It's a long tailcoat that this fellow wears,
     With gold all over.
CÉLIMÈNE (*to Alceste*):   You'd best go down and see.
     Or — have him enter.   5

Scene VII [*Alceste, Célimène, Éliante, Acaste,
Philinte, Clitandre, Guard.*]

ALCESTE (*confronting the Guard*):   Well, what do you
      want with me?
      Come in. Sir.
GUARD: I've a word, Sir, for your ear.
ALCESTE: Speak it aloud, Sir; I shall strive to hear.
GUARD: The Marshals have instructed me to say
     You must report to them without delay.   5
ALCESTE: Who? Me, Sir?
GUARD: Yes, Sir; you.
ALCESTE: But what do they want?
PHILINTE (*to Alceste*): To scotch your silly quarrel with
     Oronte.
CÉLIMÈNE (*to Philinte*): What quarrel?
PHILINTE: Oronte and he have
     fallen out
     Over some verse he spoke his mind about;
     The Marshals wish to arbitrate the matter.   10
ALCESTE: Never shall I equivocate or flatter!
PHILINTE: You'd best obey their summons; come, let's
     go.
ALCESTE: How can they mend our quarrel, I'd like to
     know?
     Am I to make a cowardly retraction,
     And praise those jingles to his satisfaction?   15
     I'll not recant; I've judged that sonnet rightly.
     It's bad.
PHILINTE: But you might say so more politely . . .
ALCESTE: I'll not back down; his verses make me sick.
PHILINTE: If only you could be more politic!
     But come, let's go.
ALCESTE: I'll go, but I won't unsay   20
     A single word.
PHILINTE: Well, let's be on our way.
ALCESTE: Till I am ordered by my lord the King
     To praise that poem, I shall say the thing
     Is scandalous, by God, and that the poet
     Ought to be hanged for having the nerve to show it. 25

(*To Clitandre and Acaste, who are laughing.*)

     By heaven, Sirs, I really didn't know
     That I was being humorous.

Scene from the Williamstown Theatre Festival's 1973 production of *The Misanthrope,* directed by Austin Pendleton.

CÉLIMÈNE: Go, Sir, go;
  Settle your business.
ALCESTE: I shall, and when I'm through,
  I shall return to settle things with you.

ACT III • *Scene 1 [Clitandre, Acaste.]*

CLITANDRE: Dear Marquess, how contented you
    appear;
  All things delight you, nothing mars your cheer.
  Can you, in perfect honesty, declare
  That you've a right to be so debonair?
5 ACASTE: By Jove, when I survey myself, I find
  No cause whatever for distress of mind.
  I'm young and rich; I can in modesty
  Lay claim to an exalted pedigree;
  And owing to my name and my condition
10 I shall not want for honors and position.
  Then as to courage, that most precious trait,
  I seem to have it, as was proved of late
  Upon the field of honor, where my bearing,
  They say, was very cool and rather daring.
15 I've wit, of course; and taste in such perfection
  That I can judge without the least reflection,

And at the theater, which is my delight,
Can make or break a play on opening night,
And lead the crowd in hisses or bravos,
And generally be known as one who knows.   20
I'm clever, handsome, gracefully polite;
My waist is small, my teeth are strong and white;
As for my dress, the world's astonished eyes
Assure me that I bear away the prize.
I find myself in favor everywhere,   25
Honored by men, and worshiped by the fair;
And since these things are so, it seems to me
I'm justified in my complacency.
CLITANDRE: Well, if so many ladies hold you dear,
  Why do you press a hopeless courtship here?   30
ACASTE: Hopeless, you say? I'm not the sort of fool
  That likes his ladies difficult and cool.
  Men who are awkward, shy, and peasantish
  May pine for heartless beauties, if they wish,
  Grovel before them, bear their cruelties,   35
  Woo them with tears and sighs and bended knees,
  And hope by dogged faithfulness to gain
  What their poor merits never could obtain.
  For men like me, however, it makes no sense
  To love on trust, and foot the whole expense.   40
  Whatever any lady's merits be,

I think, thank God, that I'm as choice as she;
That if my heart is kind enough to burn
For her, she owes me something in return;
45   And that in any proper love affair
The partners must invest an equal share.
CLITANDRE: You think, then, that our hostess favors
        you?
ACASTE: I've reason to believe that that is true.
CLITANDRE: How did you come to such a mad
        conclusion?
50   You're blind, dear fellow. This is sheer delusion.
ACASTE: All right, then: I'm deluded and I'm blind.
CLITANDRE: Whatever put the notion in your mind?
ACASTE: Delusion.
CLITANDRE: What persuades you that you're right?
ACASTE: I'm blind.
CLITANDRE: But have you any proofs to cite?
ACASTE: I tell you I'm deluded.
55   CLITANDRE: Have you, then,
        Received some secret pledge from Célimène?
ACASTE: Oh, no: she scorns me.
CLITANDRE: Tell me the truth, I beg.
ACASTE: She just can't bear me.
CLITANDRE: Ah, don't pull my leg.
        Tell me what hope she's given you, I pray.
60   ACASTE: I'm hopeless, and it's you who win the day.
        She hates me thoroughly, and I'm so vexed
        I mean to hang myself on Tuesday next.
CLITANDRE: Dear Marquess, let us have an armistice
        And make a treaty. What do you say to this?
65   If ever one of us can plainly prove
        That Célimène encourages his love,
        The other must abandon hope, and yield,
        And leave him in possession of the field.
ACASTE: Now, there's a bargain that appeals to me;
70   With all my heart, dear Marquess, I agree.
        But hush.

Scene II [*Célimène, Acaste, Clitandre.*]

CÉLIMÈNE: Still here?
CLITANDRE: 'Twas love that stayed our feet.
CÉLIMÈNE: I think I heard a carriage in the street.
        Whose is it? D'you know?

Scene III [*Célimène, Acaste, Clitandre, Basque.*]

BASQUE: Arsinoé is here, *Madame.*
CÉLIMÈNE: Arsinoé, you say? Oh, dear.
BASQUE: Éliante is entertaining her below.
CÉLIMÈNE: What brings the creature here, I'd like to
        know?
5   ACASTE: They say she's dreadfully prudish, but in fact
        I think her piety . . .
CÉLIMÈNE: It's all an act.
        At heart she's worldly, and her poor success
        In snaring men explains her prudishness.

It breaks her heart to see the beaux and gallants
Engrossed by other women's charms and talents,   10
And so she's always in a jealous rage
Against the faulty standards of the age.
She lets the world believe that she's a prude
To justify her loveless solitude,
And strives to put a brand of moral shame   15
On all the graces that she cannot claim.
But still she'd love a lover; and Alceste
Appears to be the one she'd love the best.
His visits here are poison to her pride;
She seems to think I've lured him from her side   20
And everywhere, at court or in the town,
The spiteful, envious woman runs me down.
In short, she's just as stupid as can be,
Vicious and arrogant in the last degree,
And . . .   25

Scene IV [*Arsinoé, Célimène, Clitandre, Acaste.*]

CÉLIMÈNE: Ah! What happy chance has brought you
        here?
        I've thought about you ever so much, my dear.
ARSINOÉ: I've come to tell you something you should
        know.
CÉLIMÈNE: How good of you to think of doing so!

(*Clitandre and Acaste go out, laughing.*)

Scene V [*Arsinoé, Célimène.*]

ARSINOÉ: It's just as well those gentlemen didn't tarry.
CÉLIMÈNE: Shall we sit down?
ARSINOÉ: That won't be necessary.
        Madam, the flame of friendship ought to burn
        Brightest in matters of the most concern,
        And as there's nothing which concerns us more   5
        Than honor, I have hastened to your door
        To bring you, as your friend, some information
        About the status of your reputation.
        I visited, last night, some virtuous folk,
        And, quite by chance, it was of you they spoke;   10
        There was, I fear, no tendency to praise
        Your light behavior and your dashing ways.
        The quantity of gentlemen you see
        And your by now notorious coquetry
        Were both so vehemently criticized   15
        By everyone, that I was much surprised.
        Of course, I needn't tell you where I stood;
        I came to your defense as best I could,
        Assured them you were harmless, and declared
        Your soul was absolutely unimpaired.   20
        But there are some things, you must realize,
        One can't excuse, however hard one tries,
        And I was forced at last into conceding
        That your behavior, Madam, is misleading,
        That it makes a bad impression, giving rise   25

To ugly gossip and obscene surmise,
And that if you were more *overtly* good,
You wouldn't be so much misunderstood.
Not that I think you've been unchaste — no! no!
30 The saints preserve me from a thought so low!
But mere good conscience never did suffice:
One must avoid the outward show of vice.
Madam, you're too intelligent, I'm sure,
To think my motives anything but pure
35 In offering you this counsel — which I do
Out of a zealous interest in you.
CÉLIMÈNE: Madam, I haven't taken you amiss;
I'm very much obliged to you for this;
And I'll at once discharge the obligation
40 By telling you about *your* reputation.
You've been so friendly as to let me know
What certain people say of me, and so
I mean to follow your benign example
By offering you a somewhat similar sample.
45 The other day, I went to an affair
And found some most distinguished people there
Discussing piety, both false and true.
The conversation soon came round to you.
Alas! Your prudery and bustling zeal
50 Appeared to have a very slight appeal.
Your affectation of a grave demeanor,
Your endless talk of virtue and of honor,
The aptitude of your suspicious mind
For finding sin where there is none to find,
55 Your towering self-esteem, that pitying face
With which you contemplate the human race,
Your sermonizings and your sharp aspersions
On people's pure and innocent diversions —
All these were mentioned, Madam, and, in fact,
60 Were roundly and concertedly attacked.
"What good," they said, "are all these outward
      shows,
When everything belies her pious pose?
She prays incessantly, but then, they say,
She beats her maids and cheats them of their pay;
65 She shows her zeal in every holy place,
But still she's vain enough to paint her face;
She holds that naked statues are immoral,
But with a naked *man* she'd have no quarrel."
Of course, I said to everybody there
70 That they were being viciously unfair;
But still they were disposed to criticize you,
And all agreed that someone should advise you
To leave the morals of the world alone,
And worry rather more about your own.
They felt that one's self-knowledge should be
75   great
Before one thinks of setting others straight;
That one should learn the art of living well
Before one threatens other men with hell,
And that the Church is best equipped, no doubt,
80 To guide our souls and root our vices out.
Madam, you're too intelligent, I'm sure,
To think my motives anything but pure

In offering you this counsel — which I do
Out of a zealous interest in you.
ARSINOÉ: I dared not hope for gratitude, but I   85
Did not expect so acid a reply;
I judge, since you've been so extremely tart,
That my good counsel pierced you to the heart.
CÉLIMÈNE: Far from it, Madam. Indeed, it seems to me
We ought to trade advice more frequently.   90
One's vision of oneself is so defective
That it would be an excellent corrective.
If you are willing, Madam, let's arrange
Shortly to have another frank exchange
In which we'll tell each other, *entre nous,*°   95
What you've heard tell of me, and I of you.
ARSINOÉ: Oh, people never censure you, my dear;
It's me they criticize. Or so I hear.
CÉLIMÈNE: Madam, I think we either blame or praise
According to our taste and length of days.   100
There is a time of life for coquetry,
And there's a season, too, for prudery.
When all one's charms are gone, it is, I'm sure,
Good strategy to be devout and pure:
It makes one seem a little less forsaken.   105
Some day, perhaps, I'll take the road you've taken:
Time brings all things. But I have time aplenty,
And see no cause to be a prude at twenty.
ARSINOÉ: You give your age in such a gloating tone
That one would think I was an ancient crone;   110
We're not so far apart, in sober truth,
That you can mock me with a boast of youth!
Madam, you baffle me. I wish I knew
What moves you to provoke me as you do.
CÉLIMÈNE: For my part, Madam, I should like to know   115
Why you abuse me everywhere you go.
Is it my fault, dear lady, that your hand
Is not, alas, in very great demand?
If men admire me, if they pay me court
And daily make me offers of the sort   120
You'd dearly love to have them make to you,
How can I help it? What would you have me do?
If what you want is lovers, please feel free
To take as many as you can from me.
ARSINOÉ: Oh, come. D'you think the world is losing
      sleep   125
Over the flock of lovers which you keep,
Or that we find it difficult to guess
What price you pay for their devotedness?
Surely you don't expect us to suppose
Mere merit could attract so many beaux?   130
It's not your virtue that they're dazzled by;
Nor is it virtuous love for which they sigh.
You're fooling no one, Madam; the world's not
      blind;
There's many a lady heaven has designed
To call men's noblest, tenderest feelings out,   135
Who has no lovers dogging her about;
From which it's plain that lovers nowadays

95. *entre nous:* Between ourselves.

Must be acquired in bold and shameless ways,
And only pay one court for such reward
140 As modesty and virtue can't afford.
Then don't be quite so puffed up, if you please,
About your tawdry little victories;
Try, if you can, to be a shade less vain,
And treat the world with somewhat less disdain.
145 If one were envious of your amours,
One soon could have a following like yours;
Lovers are no great trouble to collect
If one prefers them to one's self-respect.
CÉLIMÈNE: Collect them then, my dear; I'd love to see
150 You demonstrate that charming theory;
Who knows, you might . . .
ARSINOÉ: Now, Madam, that will do;
It's time to end this trying interview.
My coach is late in coming to your door,
Or I'd have taken leave of you before.
CÉLIMÈNE: Oh, please don't feel that you must rush
155   away;
I'd be delighted, Madam, if you'd stay.
However, lest my conversation bore you,
Let me provide some better company for you;
This gentleman, who comes most apropos,
160 Will please you more than I could do, I know.

Scene VI [*Alceste, Célimène, Arsinoé.*]

CÉLIMÈNE: Alceste, I have a little note to write
Which simply must go out before tonight;
Please entertain *Madame;* I'm sure that she
Will overlook my incivility.

Scene VII [*Alceste, Arsinoé.*]

ARSINOÉ: Well, Sir, our hostess graciously contrives
For us to chat until my coach arrives;
And I shall be forever in her debt
For granting me this little *tête-à-tête.*°
5   We women very rightly give our hearts
To men of noble character and parts,
And your especial merits, dear Alceste
Have roused the deepest sympathy in my breast.
Oh, how I wish they had sufficient sense
10   At court, to recognize your excellence!
They wrong you greatly, Sir. How it must hurt you
Never to be rewarded for your virtue!
ALCESTE: Why, Madam, what cause have I to feel
        aggrieved?
What great and brilliant thing have I achieved?
15   What service have I rendered to the King
That I should look to him for anything?
ARSINOÉ: Not everyone who's honored by the State
Has done great services. A man must wait

4. *tête-à-tête:* French for "head-to-head," in private conversation.

Till time and fortune offer him the chance.
Your merit, Sir, is obvious at a glance,   20
And . . .
ALCESTE: Ah, forget my merit; I am not neglected.
The court, I think, can hardly be expected
To mine men's souls for merit, and unearth
Our hidden virtues and our secret worth.
ARSINOÉ: *Some* virtues, though, are far too bright to
        hide;   25
Yours are acknowledged, Sir, on every side.
Indeed, I've heard you warmly praised of late
By persons of considerable weight.
ALCESTE: This fawning age has praise for everyone,
And all distinctions, Madam, are undone.   30
All things have equal honor nowadays,
And no one should be gratified by praise.
To be admired, one only need exist,
And every lackey's on the honors list.
ARSINOÉ: I only wish, Sir, that you had your eye   35
On some position at court, however high;
You'd only have to hint at such a notion
For me to set the proper wheels in motion
I've certain friendships I'd be glad to use
To get you any office you might choose.   40
ALCESTE: Madam, I fear that any such ambition
Is wholly foreign to my disposition.
The soul God gave me isn't of the sort
That prospers in the weather of a court.
It's all too obvious that I don't possess   45
The virtues necessary for success.
My one great talent is for speaking plain;
I've never learned to flatter or to feign;
And anyone so stupidly sincere
Had best not seek a courtier's career.   50
Outside the court, I know, one must dispense
With honors, privilege, and influence;
But still one gains the right, foregoing these,
Not to be tortured by the wish to please.
One needn't live in dread of snubs and slights,   55
Nor praise the verse that every idiot writes,
Nor humor silly Marquesses, nor bestow
Politic sighs on Madam So-and-So.
ARSINOÉ: Forget the court, then; let the matter rest.
But I've another cause to be distressed   60
About your present situation, Sir.
It's to your love affair that I refer.
She whom you love, and who pretends to love you,
Is, I regret to say, unworthy of you.
ALCESTE: Why, Madam? Can you seriously intend   65
To make so grave a charge against your friend?
ARSINOÉ: Alas, I must. I've stood aside too long
And let that lady do you grievous wrong;
But now my debt to conscience shall be paid:
I tell you that your love has been betrayed.   70
ALCESTE: I thank you, Madam; you're extremely kind.
Such words are soothing to a lover's mind.
ARSINOÉ: Yes, though she *is* my friend, I say again
You're very much too good for Célimène.
She's wantonly misled you from the start.   75

ALCESTE: You may be right; who knows another's heart?
     But ask yourself if it's the part of charity
     To shake my soul with doubts of her sincerity.
ARSINOÉ: Well, if you'd rather be a dupe than doubt
     her,
80   That's your affair. I'll say no more about her.
ALCESTE: Madam, you know that doubt and vague
     suspicion
     Are painful to a man in my position;
     It's most unkind to worry me this way
     Unless you've some real proof of what you say.
85   ARSINOÉ: Sir, say no more: all doubts shall be removed,
     And all that I've been saying shall be proved.
     You've only to escort me home, and there
     We'll look into the heart of this affair.
     I've ocular evidence which will persuade you
80   Beyond a doubt, that Célimène's betrayed you.
     Then, if you're saddened by that revelation,
     Perhaps I can provide some consolation.

ACT IV • *Scene I* [*Éliante, Philinte.*]

PHILINTE: Madam, he acted like a stubborn child
     I thought they never would be reconciled;
     In vain we reasoned, threatened, and appealed;
     He stood his ground and simply would not yield.
5   The Marshals, I feel sure have never heard
     An argument so splendidly absurd.
     "No, gentlemen," said he, "I'll not retract.
     His verse is bad: extremely bad, in fact.
     Surely it does the man no harm to know it.
10   Does it disgrace him, not to be a poet?
     A gentleman may be respected still,
     Whether he writes a sonnet well or ill.
     That I dislike his verse should not offend him;
     In all that touches honor, I commend him;
15   He's noble, brave, and virtuous — but I fear
     He can't in truth be called a sonneteer.
     I'll gladly praise his wardrobe; I'll endorse
     His dancing, or the way he sits a horse;
     But, gentlemen, I cannot praise his rhyme.
20   In fact, it ought to be a capital crime
     For anyone so sadly unendowed
     To write a sonnet, and read the thing aloud."
     At length he fell into a gentler mood
     And, striking a concessive attitude,
25   He paid Oronte the following courtesies:
     "Sir, I regret that I'm so hard to please,
     And I'm profoundly sorry that your lyric
     Failed to provoke me to a panegyric."°
     After these curious words, the two embraced
30   And then the hearing was adjourned — in haste.
ÉLIANTE: His conduct has been very singular lately;
     Still, I confess that I respect him greatly.
     The honesty in which he takes such pride
     Has — to my mind — its noble, heroic side.

---

28. **panegyric:** Elaborate praise.

In this false age, such candor seems outrageous;   35
     But I could wish that it were more contagious.
PHILINTE: What most intrigues me in our friend Alceste
     Is the grand passion that rages in his breast.
     The sullen humors he's compounded of
     Should not, I think, dispose his heart to love;   40
     But since they do, it puzzles me still more
     That he should choose your cousin to adore.
ÉLIANTE: It does, indeed, belie the theory
     That love is born of gentle sympathy,
     And that the tender passion must be based   45
     On sweet accords of temper and of taste.
PHILINTE: Does she return his love, do you suppose?
ÉLIANTE: Ah, that's a difficult question, Sir. Who
     knows?
     How can we judge the truth of her devotion?
     Her heart's a stranger to its own emotion.   50
     Sometimes it thinks it loves, when no love's there;
     At other times it loves quite unaware.
PHILINTE: I rather think Alceste is in for more
     Distress and sorrow than he's bargained for;
     Were he of my mind, Madam, his affection   55
     Would turn in quite a different direction,
     And we would see him more responsive to
     The kind regard which he receives from you.
ÉLIANTE: Sir, I believe in frankness, and I'm inclined
     In matters of the heart, to speak my mind.   60
     I don't oppose his love for her; indeed,
     I hope with all my heart that he'll succeed,
     And were it in my power, I'd rejoice
     In giving him the lady of his choice.
     But if, as happens frequently enough   65
     In love affairs, he meets with a rebuff —
     If Célimène should grant some rival's suit —
     I'd gladly play the role of substitute;
     Nor would his tender speeches please me less
     Because they'd once been made without success.   70
PHILINTE: Well, Madam, as for me, I don't oppose
     Your hopes in this affair; and heaven knows
     That in my conversations with the man
     I plead your cause as often as I can.
     But if those two should marry, and so remove   75
     All chance that he will offer you his love,
     Then I'll declare my own, and hope to see
     Your gracious favor pass from him to me.
     In short, should you be cheated of Alceste,
     I'd be most happy to be second best.   80
ÉLIANTE: Philinte, you're teasing.
PHILINTE: Ah, Madam, never fear;
     No words of mine were ever so sincere
     And I shall live in fretful expectation
     Till I can make a fuller declaration.

Scene II [*Alceste, Éliante, Philinte.*]

ALCESTE: Avenge me, Madam! I must have satisfaction,
     Or this great wrong will drive me to distraction!
ÉLIANTE: Why, what's the matter? What's upset you so?

ALCESTE: Madam, I've had a mortal, mortal blow.
5   If Chaos repossessed the universe,
   I swear I'd not be shaken any worse.
   I'm ruined. . . . I can say no more. . . . My soul . . .
ÉLIANTE: Do try, Sir, to regain your self-control.
ALCESTE: Just heaven! Why were so much beauty and
     grace
10   Bestowed on one so vicious and so base?
ÉLIANTE: Once more, Sir, tell us
ALCESTE: My world has gone to wrack:
   I'm — I'm betrayed; she's stabbed me in the back:
   Yes, Célimène (who would have thought it of her?)
   Is false to me, and has another lover.
ÉLIANTE: Are you quite certain? Can you prove these
15   things?
PHILINTE: Lovers are prey to wild imaginings
   And jealous fancies. No doubt there's some
     mistake. . . .
ALCESTE: Mind your own business, Sir, for heaven's
   sake.
   (*To Éliante.*) Madam, I have the proof that you
   demand
20   Here in my pocket, penned by her own hand.
   Yes, all the shameful evidence one could want
   Lies in this letter written to Oronte —
   Oronte! whom I felt sure she couldn't love,
   And hardly bothered to be jealous of.
25 PHILINTE: Still, in a letter, appearances may deceive;
   This may not be so bad as you believe.
ALCESTE: Once more I beg you, Sir, to let me be;
   Tend to your own affairs; leave mine to me.
ÉLIANTE: Compose yourself; this anguish that you
   feel . . .
30 ALCESTE: Is something, Madam, you alone can heal.
   My outraged heart, beside itself with grief,
   Appeals to you for comfort and relief.
   Avenge me on your cousin, whose unjust
   And faithless nature has deceived my trust;
35   Avenge a crime your pure soul must detest.
ÉLIANTE: But how, Sir?
ALCESTE: Madam, this heart within my breast
   Is yours; pray take it; redeem my heart from her,
   And so avenge me on my torturer.
   Let her be punished by the fond emotion,
40   The ardent love, the bottomless devotion,
   The faithful worship which this heart of mine
   Will offer up to yours as to a shrine.
ÉLIANTE: You have my sympathy, Sir, in all you suffer;
   Nor do I scorn the noble heart you offer;
45   But I suspect you'll soon be mollified
   And this desire for vengeance will subside.
   When some belovèd hand has done us wrong
   We thirst for retribution — but not for long;
   However dark the deed that she's committed,
50   A lovely culprit's very soon acquitted.
   Nothing's so stormy as an injured lover,
   And yet no storm so quickly passes over.
ALCESTE: No, Madam, no — this is no lovers' spat;
   I'll not forgive her, it's gone too far for that;

My mind's made up; I'll kill myself before   55
   I waste my hopes upon her any more.
   Ah, here she is. My wrath intensifies.
   I shall confront her with her tricks and lies,
   And crush her utterly, and bring you then
   A heart no longer slave to Célimène.   60

Scene III [*Célimène, Alceste.*]

ALCESTE (*aside*): Sweet heaven, help me to control my
   passion.
CÉLIMÈNE (*aside*): Oh, Lord. (*To Alceste.*) Why stand
   there staring in that fashion?
   And what d'you mean by those dramatic sighs,
   And that malignant glitter in your eyes?
ALCESTE: I mean that sins which cause the blood to
   freeze   5
   Look innocent beside your treacheries;
   That nothing Hell's or Heaven's wrath could do
   Ever produced so bad a thing as you.
CÉLIMÈNE: Your compliments were always sweet and
   pretty.
ALCESTE: Madam, it's not the moment to be witty.   10
   No, blush and hang your head; you've ample
   reason,
   Since I've the fullest evidence of your treason.
   Ah, this is what my sad heart prophesied;
   Now all my anxious fears are verified;
   My dark suspicion and my gloomy doubt   15
   Divined the truth, and now the truth is out.
   For all your trickery, I was not deceived;
   It was my bitter stars that I believed.
   But don't imagine that you'll go scot-free;
   You shan't misuse me with impunity.   20
   I know that love's irrational and blind;
   I know the heart's not subject to the mind,
   And can't be reasoned into beating faster;
   I know each soul is free to choose its master;
   Therefore had you but spoken from the heart,   25
   Rejecting my attention from the start,
   I'd have no grievance, or at any rate
   I could complain of nothing but my fate.
   Ah, but so falsely to encourage me —
   That was a treason and a treachery   30
   For which you cannot suffer too severely,
   And you shall pay for that behavior dearly.
   Yes, now I have no pity, not a shred;
   My temper's out of hand, I've lost my head
   Shocked by the knowledge of your double-
     dealings,   35
   My reason can't restrain my savage feelings;
   A righteous wrath deprives me of my senses,
   And I won't answer for the consequences.
CÉLIMÈNE: What does this outburst mean? Will you
   please explain?
   Have you, by any chance, gone quite insane?   40
ALCESTE: Yes, yes, I went insane the day I fell
   A victim to your black and fatal spell,

Thinking to meet with some sincerity
Among the treacherous charms that beckoned me.
CÉLIMÈNE: Pooh. Of what treachery can you
45   complain?
ALCESTE: How sly you are, how cleverly you feign!
But you'll not victimize me any more.
Look: here's a document you've seen before.
This evidence, which I acquired today,
50   Leaves you, I think, without a thing to say.
CÉLIMÈNE: Is this what sent you into such a fit?
ALCESTE: You should be blushing at the sight of it.
CÉLIMÈNE: Ought I to blush? I truly don't see why.
ALCESTE: Ah, now you're being bold as well as sly;
55   Since there's no signature, perhaps you'll claim . . .
CÉLIMÈNE: I wrote it, whether or not it bears my name.
ALCESTE: And you can view with equanimity
his proof of your disloyalty to me!
CÉLIMÈNE: Oh, don't be so outrageous and extreme.
60 ALCESTE: You take this matter lightly, it would seem.
Was it no wrong to me, no shame to you,
That you should send Oronte this *billet-doux*?°
CÉLIMÈNE: Oronte! Who said it was for him?
ALCESTE: Why, those
Who brought me this example of your prose.
65   But what's the difference? If you wrote the letter
To someone else, it pleases me no better.
My grievance and your guilt remain the same.
CÉLIMÈNE: But need you rage, and need I blush for
    shame,
If this was written to a *woman* friend?
70 ALCESTE: Ah! Most ingenious. I'm impressed no end;
And after that incredible evasion
Your guilt is clear. I need no more persuasion.
How dare you try so clumsy a deception?
D'you think I'm wholly wanting in perception?
75   Come, come, let's see how brazenly you'll try
To bolster up so palpable a lie:
Kindly construe this ardent closing section
As nothing more than sisterly affection!
Here, let me read it. Tell me, if you dare to,
That this is for a woman . . .
80 CÉLIMÈNE: I don't dare to.
What right have you to badger and berate me,
And so high-handedly interrogate me?
ALCESTE: Now, don't be angry; all I ask of you
Is that you justify a phrase or two . . .
85 CÉLIMÈNE: No, I shall not. I utterly refuse,
And you may take those phrases as you choose.
ALCESTE: Just show me how this letter could be meant
For a woman's eyes, and I shall be content.
CÉLIMÈNE: No, no, it's for Oronte; you're perfectly
    right.
90   I welcome his attentions with delight,
I prize his character and his intellect
And everything is just as you suspect.
Come, do your worst now; give your rage free rein;
But kindly cease to bicker and complain.

62. ***billet-doux:*** Love letter.

ALCESTE (*aside*): Good God! Could anything be more
    inhuman?   95
Was ever a heart so mangled by a woman?
When I complain of how she has betrayed me,
She bridles, and commences to upbraid me!
She tries my tortured patience to the limit;
She won't deny her guilt; she glories in it!   100
And yet my heart's too faint and cowardly
To break these chains of passion, and be free,
To scorn her as it should, and rise above
This unrewarded, mad, and bitter love.
(*To Célimène.*) Ah, traitress, in how confident a
    fashion   105
You take advantage of my helpless passion,
And use my weakness for your faithless charms
To make me once again throw down my arms!
But do at least deny this black transgression;
Take back that mocking and perverse confession;   110
Defend this letter and your innocence,
And I, poor fool, will aid in your defense.
Pretend, pretend, that you are just and true,
And I shall make myself believe in you.
CÉLIMÈNE: Oh, stop it. Don't be such a jealous dunce,   115
Or I shall leave off loving you at once.
Just why should I *pretend*? What could impel me
To stoop so low as that? And kindly tell me
Why, if I loved another, I shouldn't merely
Inform you of it, simply and sincerely!   120
I've told you where you stand, and that admission
Should altogether clear me of suspicion;
After so generous a guarantee
What right have you to harbor doubts of me?
Since women are (from natural reticence)   125
Reluctant to declare their sentiments,
And since the honor of our sex requires
That we conceal our amorous desires,
Ought any man for whom such laws are broken
To question what the oracle has spoken?   130
Should he not rather feel an obligation
To trust that most obliging declaration?
Enough, now. Your suspicions quite disgust me;
Why should I love a man who doesn't trust me?
I cannot understand why I continue,   135
Fool that I am, to take an interest in you.
I ought to choose a man less prone to doubt,
And give you something to be vexed about.
ALCESTE: Ah, what a poor enchanted fool I am;
These gentle words, no doubt, were all a sham,   140
But destiny requires me to entrust
My happiness to you, and so I must.
I'll love you to the bitter end, and see
How false and treacherous you dare to be.
CÉLIMÈNE: No, you don't really love me as you ought.   145
ALCESTE: I love you more than can be said or thought;
Indeed, I wish you were in such distress
That I might show my deep devotedness.
Yes, I could wish that you were wretchedly poor,
Unloved, uncherished, utterly obscure;   150
That fate had set you down upon the earth

Without possessions, rank, or gentle birth;
Then, by the offer of my heart, I might
Repair the great injustice of your plight;
155   I'd raise you from the dust, and proudly prove
The purity and vastness of my love.
CÉLIMÈNE: This is a strange benevolence indeed!
    God grant that I may never be in need. . . .
    Ah, here's Monsieur Dubois in quaint disguise.

Scene IV [*Célimène, Alceste, Dubois.*]

ALCESTE: Well, why this costume? Why those frightened
       eyes?
    What ails you?
DUBOIS: Well, Sir, things are most mysterious.
ALCESTE: What do you mean?
DUBOIS: I fear they're very serious.
ALCESTE: What?
DUBOIS: Shall I speak more loudly?
ALCESTE: Yes; speak out.
DUBOIS: Isn't there someone here, Sir?
5 ALCESTE: Speak, you lout!
    Stop wasting time.
DUBOIS: Sir, we must slip away.
ALCESTE: How's that?
DUBOIS: We must decamp without delay.
ALCESTE: Explain yourself.
DUBOIS: I tell you we must fly.
ALCESTE: What for?
DUBOIS: We mustn't pause to say good-by.
ALCESTE: Now what d'you mean by all of this, you
10   clown?
DUBOIS: I mean, Sir, that we've got to leave this town.
ALCESTE: I'll tear you limb from limb and joint from
       joint
    If you don't come more quickly to the point.
DUBOIS: Well, Sir, today a man in a black suit,
15   Who wore a black and ugly scowl to boot,
Left us a document scrawled in such a hand
As even Satan couldn't understand.
It bears upon your lawsuit, I don't doubt;
But all hell's devils couldn't make it out.
20 ALCESTE: Well, well, go on. What then? I fail to see
    How this event obliges us to flee.
DUBOIS: Well, Sir, an hour later, hardly more,
A gentleman who's often called before
Came looking for you in an anxious way.
25   Not finding you, he asked me to convey
(Knowing I could be trusted with the same)
The following message. . . . Now, what *was* his
       name?
ALCESTE: Forget his name, you idiot. What did he say?
DUBOIS: Well, it was one of your friends, Sir, anyway.
30   He warned you to begone, and he suggested
That if you stay, you may well be arrested.
ALCESTE: What? Nothing more specific? Think, man,
       think!
DUBOIS: No, Sir. He had me bring him pen and ink,

And dashed you off a letter which, I'm sure,
Will render things distinctly less obscure.   35
ALCESTE: Well — let me have it!
CÉLIMÈNE: What *is* this all about?
ALCESTE: God knows; but I have hopes of finding out.
    How long am I to wait, you blitherer?
DUBOIS: (*after a protracted search for the letter*):
    I must have left it on your table, Sir.
ALCESTE: I ought to . . .
CÉLIMÈNE: No, no, keep your self-control;   40
    Go find out what's behind his rigmarole.
ALCESTE: It seems that fate, no matter what I do,
Has sworn that I may not converse with you;
But, Madam, pray permit your faithful lover
To try once more before the day is over.   45

ACT V • *Scene I* [*Alceste, Philinte.*]

ALCESTE: No, it's too much. My mind's made up, I tell
       you.
PHILINTE: Why should this blow, however hard,
       compel you . . .
ALCESTE: No, no, don't waste your breath in argument;
Nothing you say will alter my intent;
This age is vile, and I've made up my mind   5
To have no further commerce with mankind.
Did not truth, honor, decency, and the laws
Oppose my enemy and approve my cause?
My claims were justified in all men's sight;
I put my trust in equity and right;   10
Yet, to my horror and the world's disgrace,
Justice is mocked, and I have lost my case!
A scoundrel whose dishonesty is notorious
Emerges from another lie victorious!
Honor and right condone his brazen fraud,   15
While rectitude and decency applaud!
Before his smirking face, the truth stands charmed,
And virtue conquered, and the law disarmed!
His crime is sanctioned by a court decree!
And not content with what he's done to me,   20
The dog now seeks to ruin me by stating
That I composed a book now circulating,
A book so wholly criminal and vicious
That even to speak its title is seditious!
Meanwhile Oronte, my rival, lends his credit   25
To the same libelous tale, and helps to spread it!
Oronte! a man of honor and of rank,
With whom I've been entirely fair and frank;
Who sought me out and forced me, willy-nilly,
To judge some verse I found extremely silly;   30
And who, because I properly refused
To flatter him, or see the truth abused,
Abets my enemy in a rotten slander!
There's the reward of honesty and candor!
The man will hate me to the end of time   35
For failing to commend his wretched rhyme!
And not this man alone, but all humanity
Do what they do from interest and vanity;

They prate of honor, truth, and righteousness,
40   But lie, betray, and swindle nonetheless.
Come then: man's villainy is too much to bear;
Let's leave this jungle and this jackal's lair.
Yes! treacherous and savage race of men,
You shall not look upon my face again.
45 PHILINTE: Oh, don't rush into exile prematurely;
Things aren't as dreadful as you make them, surely.
It's rather obvious, since you're still at large,
That people don't believe your enemy's charge.
Indeed, his tale's so patently untrue
50   It may do more harm to him than you.
    ALCESTE: Nothing could do that scoundrel any harm:
His frank corruption is his greatest charm,
And, far from hurting him, a further shame
Would only serve to magnify his name.
55 PHILINTE: In any case, his bald prevarication
Has done no injury to your reputation,
And you may feel secure in that regard.
As for your lawsuit, it should not be hard
To have the case reopened, and contest
This judgment . . .
60 ALCESTE: No, no, let the verdict rest.
Whatever cruel penalty it may bring,
I wouldn't have it changed for anything.
It shows the times' injustice with such clarity
That I shall pass it down to our posterity
65   As a great proof and signal demonstration
Of the black wickedness of this generation.
It may cost twenty thousand francs; but I
Shall pay their twenty thousand, and gain thereby
The right to storm and rage at human evil,
70   And send the race of mankind to the devil.
PHILINTE: Listen to me . . .
    ALCESTE: Why? What can you possibly say?
Don't argue, Sir; your labor's thrown away.
Do you propose to offer lame excuses
For men's behavior and the times' abuses?
75 PHILINTE: No, all you say I'll readily concede:
This is a low, conniving age, indeed;
Nothing but trickery prospers nowadays,
And people ought to mend their shabby ways.
Yes, man's a beastly creature; but must we then
80   Abandon the society of men?
Here in the world, each human frailty
Provides occasion for philosophy,
And that is virtue's noblest exercise;
If honesty shone forth from all men's eyes,
85   If every heart were frank and kind and just,
What could our virtues do but gather dust
(Since their employment is to help us bear
The villainies of men without despair)?
A heart well-armed with virtue can endure . . .
90 ALCESTE: Sir, you're a matchless reasoner, to be sure;
Your words are fine and full of cogency;
But don't waste time and eloquence on me.
My reason bids me go, for my own good.
My tongue won't lie and flatter as it should;
95   God knows what frankness it might next commit,

And what I'd suffer on account of it.
Pray let me wait for Célimène's return
In peace and quiet. I shall shortly learn,
By her response to what I have in view,
Whether her love for me is feigned or true.   100
PHILINTE: Till then, let's visit Éliante upstairs.
ALCESTE: No, I am too weighed down with somber
    cares.
Go to her, do; and leave me with my gloom
Here in the darkened corner of this room.
PHILINTE: Why, that's no sort of company, my friend;   105
I'll see if Éliante will not descend.

Scene II [*Célimène, Oronte, Alceste.*]

ORONTE: Yes, Madam, if you wish me to remain
Your true and ardent lover, you must deign
To give me some more positive assurance.
All this suspense is quite beyond endurance.
If your heart shares the sweet desires of mine,   5
Show me as much by some convincing sign;
And here's the sign I urgently suggest:
That you no longer tolerate Alceste,
But sacrifice him to my love, and sever
All your relations with the man forever.   10
CÉLIMÈNE: Why do you suddenly dislike him so?
You praised him to the skies not long ago.
ORONTE: Madam, that's not the point. I'm here to find
Which way your tender feelings are inclined.
Choose, if you please, between Alceste and me,   15
And I shall stay or go accordingly.
ALCESTE (*emerging from the corner*): Yes, Madam,
    choose; this gentleman's demand
Is wholly just, and I support his stand.
I too am true and ardent; I too am here
To ask that you make your feelings clear.   20
No more delays, now; no equivocation;
The time has come to make your declaration.
ORONTE: Sir, I've no wish in any way to be
An obstacle to your felicity.
ALCESTE: Sir, I've no wish to share her heart with you; 25
That may sound jealous, but at least it's true.
ORONTE: If, weighing us, she leans in your
    direction . . .
ALCESTE: If she regards you with the least affection . . .
ORONTE: I swear I'll yield her to you there and then.
ALCESTE: I swear I'll never see her face again.   30
ORONTE: Now, Madam, tell us what we've come to
    hear.
ALCESTE: Madam, speak openly and have no fear.
ORONTE: Just say which one is to remain your lover.
ALCESTE: Just name one name, and it will all be over.
ORONTE: What! Is it possible that you're undecided?   35
ALCESTE: What! Can your feelings possibly be divided?
CÉLIMÈNE: Enough: this inquisition's gone too far:
How utterly unreasonable you are!
Not that I couldn't make the choice with ease;
My heart has no conflicting sympathies   40

I know full well which one of you I favor,
And you'd not see me hesitate or waver.
But how can you expect me to reveal
So cruelly and bluntly what I feel?
45   I think it altogether too unpleasant
To choose between two men when both are present;
One's heart has means more subtle and more kind
Of letting its affections be divined,
Nor need one be uncharitably plain
50   To let a lover know he loves in vain.
ORONTE: No, no, speak plainly; I for one can stand it.
I beg you to be frank.
ALCESTE: And I demand it.
The simple truth is what I wish to know,
And there's no need for softening the blow.
55   You've made an art of pleasing everyone,
But now your days of coquetry are done:
You have no choice now, Madam, but to choose,
For I'll know what to think if you refuse;
I'll take your silence for a clear admission
60   That I'm entitled to my worst suspicion.
ORONTE: I thank you for this ultimatum, Sir.
And I may say I heartily concur.
CÉLIMÈNE: Really, this foolishness is very wearing:
Must you be so unjust and overbearing?
65   Haven't I told you why I must demur?
Ah, here's Éliante; I'll put the case to her.

Scene III [*Éliante, Philinte, Célimène, Oronte,
Alceste.*]

CÉLIMÈNE: Cousin, I'm being persecuted here
By these two persons, who, it would appear,
Will not be satisfied till I confess
Which one I love the more, and which the less,
5   And tell the latter to his face that he
Is henceforth banished from my company.
Tell me, has ever such a thing been done?
ÉLIANTE: You'd best not turn to me; I'm not the one
To back you in a matter of this kind:
10   I'm all for those who frankly speak their mind.
ORONTE: Madam, you'll search in vain for a defender.
ALCESTE: You're beaten, Madam, and may as well
surrender.
ORONTE: Speak, speak, you must; and end this awful
strain.
ALCESTE: Or don't, and your position will be plain.
15   ORONTE: A single word will close this painful scene.
ALCESTE: But if you're silent, I'll know what you mean.

Scene IV [*Arsinoé, Célimène, Éliante, Alceste,
Philinte, Acaste, Clitandre, Oronte.*]

ACASTE (*to Célimène*): Madam, with all due deference,
we two
Have come to pick a little bone with you.

CLITANDRE (*to Oronte and Alceste*): I'm glad you're
present, Sirs, as you'll soon learn,
Our business here is also your concern.
ARSINOÉ (*to Célimène*): Madam, I visit you so soon
again   5
Only because of these two gentlemen,
Who came to me indignant and aggrieved
About a crime too base to be believed.
Knowing your virtue, having such confidence in it,
I couldn't think you guilty for a minute,   10
In spite of all their telling evidence;
And, rising above our little difference
I've hastened here in friendship's name to see
You clear yourself of this great calumny.
ACASTE: Yes, Madam, let us see with what
composure   15
You'll manage to respond to this disclosure.
You lately sent Clitandre this tender note.
CLITANDRE: And this one, for Acaste, you also
wrote.
ACASTE (*to Oronte and Alceste*): You'll recognize this
writing, Sirs, I think;
The lady is so free with pen and ink   20
That you must know it all too well, I fear.
But listen: this is something you should hear.

"How absurd you are to condemn my lightheart-
edness in society, and to accuse me of being happiest
in the company of others. Nothing could be more   25
unjust; and if you do not come to me instantly and
beg pardon for saying such a thing, I shall never forgive you as long as I live. Our big bumbling friend the
Viscount . . ."

What a shame that he's not here.   30

"Our big bumbling friend the Viscount, whose
name stands first in your complaint, is hardly a man
to my taste; and ever since the day I watched him
spend three-quarters of an hour spitting into a well,
so as to make circles in the water, I have been unable 35
to think highly of him. As for the little Marquess . . ."

In all modesty, gentlemen, that is I.

"As for the little Marquess, who sat squeezing my
hand for such a long while yesterday, I find him in all   40
respects the most trifling creature alive; and the only
things of value about him are his cape and his sword.
As for the man with the green ribbons . . ."

(*To Alceste.*) It's your turn now, Sir.

"As for the man with the green ribbons, he   45
amuses me now and then with his bluntness and his
bearish ill-humor; but there are many times indeed
when I think him the greatest bore in the world. And
as for the sonneteer . . ."

50   (*To Oronte.*) Here's your helping.

        "And as for the sonneteer, who has taken it into
        his head to be witty, and insists on being an author in
        the teeth of opinion, I simply cannot be bothered to
        listen to him, and his prose wearies me quite as much
55   as his poetry. Be assured that I am not always so well-
        entertained as you suppose; that I long for your
        company, more than I dare to say, at all these enter-
        tainments to which people drag me; and that the
        presence of those one loves is the true and perfect
60   seasoning to all one's pleasures."

        CLITANDRE: And now for me.

        "Clitandre, whom you mention, and who so
        pesters me with his saccharine speeches, is the last
        man on earth for whom I could feel any affection. He
65   is quite mad to suppose that I love him, and so are
        you, to doubt that you are loved. Do come to your
        senses; exchange your suppositions for his; and visit
        me as often as possible, to help me bear the annoy-
        ance of his unwelcome attentions."

70   It's sweet character that these letters show,
        And what to call it, Madam, you well know.
        Enough. We're off to make the world acquainted
        With this sublime self-portrait that you've painted.
        ACASTE: Madam, I'll make you no farewell oration;
75   No, you're not worthy of my indignation.
        Far choicer hearts than yours, as you'll discover,
        Would like this little Marquess for a lover.

Scene V [*Célimène, Éliante, Arsinoé, Alceste,
Oronte, Philinte.*]

ORONTE: So! After all those loving letters you wrote,
        You turn on me like this, and cut my throat!
        And your dissembling, faithless heart, I find,
        Has pledged itself by turns to all mankind!
5   How blind I've been! But now I clearly see;
        I thank you, Madam, for enlightening me.
        My heart is mine once more, and I'm content;
        The loss of it shall be your punishment.
        (*To Alceste.*) Sir, she is yours; I'll seek no more to
            stand
10   Between your wishes and this lady's hand.

Scene VI [*Célimène, Éliante, Arsinoé, Alceste,
Philinte.*]

ARSINOÉ: (*to Célimène*): Madam, I'm forced to speak.
            I'm far too stirred
        To keep my counsel, after what I've heard.
        I'm shocked and staggered by your want of morals.

        It's not my way to mix in others' quarrels;
        But really, when this fine and noble spirit,   5
        This man of honor and surpassing merit,
        Laid down the offering of his heart before you,
        How *could* you . . .
ALCESTE: Madam, permit me, I implore you,
        To represent myself in this debate.
        Don't bother, please, to be my advocate.   10
        My heart, in any case, could not afford
        To give your services their due reward;
        And if I chose, for consolation's sake,
        Some other lady, 'twould not be you I'd take.
ARSINOÉ: What makes you think you could, Sir? And
            how dare you   15
        Imply that I've been trying to ensnare you?
        If you can for a moment entertain
        Such flattering fancies, you're extremely vain.
        I'm not so interested as you suppose
        In Célimène's discarded gigolos.   20
        Get rid of that absurd illusion, do.
        Women like me are not for such as you.
        Stay with this creature, to whom you're so
            attached;
        I've never seen two people better matched.

Scene VII [*Célimène, Éliante, Alceste, Philinte.*]

ALCESTE (*to Célimène*): Well, I've been still throughout
            this exposé,
        Till everyone but me has said his say.
        Come, have I shown sufficient self-restraint?
        And may I now . . .
CÉLIMÈNE: Yes, make your just complaint.
        Reproach me freely, call me what you will;   5
        You've every right to say I've used you ill.
        I've wronged you, I confess it; and in my shame
        I'll make no effort to escape the blame.
        The anger of those others I could despise;
        My guilt toward you I sadly recognize.   10
        Your wrath is wholly justified, I fear
        I know how culpable I must appear,
        I know all things bespeak my treachery,
        And that, in short, you've grounds for hating me.
        Do so; I give you leave.
ALCESTE: Ah, traitress — how,   15
        How should I cease to love you, even now?
        Though mind and will were passionately bent
        On hating you, my heart would not consent.
        (*To Éliante and Philinte.*) Be witness to my
            madness, both of you;
        See what infatuation drives one to;   20
        But wait; my folly's only just begun,
        And I shall prove to you before I'm done
        How strange the human heart is, and how far
        From rational we sorry creatures are.
        (*To Célimène.*) Woman, I'm willing to forget your
            shame,   25

And clothe your treacheries in a sweeter name;
I'll call them youthful errors, instead of crimes,
And lay the blame on these corrupting times.
My one condition is that you agree
30   To share my chosen fate, and fly with me
To that wild, trackless, solitary place
In which I shall forget the human race.
Only by such a course can you atone
For those atrocious letters; by that alone
35   Can you remove my present horror of you,
And make it possible for me to love you.
CÉLIMÈNE: What! *I* renounce the world at my young
        age,
And die of boredom in some hermitage?
ALCESTE: Ah, if you really loved me as you ought,
You wouldn't give the world a moment's
40   thought;
Must you have me, and all the world beside?
CÉLIMÈNE: Alas, at twenty one is terrified
Of solitude. I fear I lack the force
And depth of soul to take so stern a course.
45   But if my hand in marriage will content you,
Why, there's a plan which I might well consent to,
And . . .
ALCESTE: No, I detest you now. I could excuse
Everything else, but since you thus refuse
50   To love me wholly, as a wife should do,
And see the world in me, as I in you,
Go! I reject your hand, and disenthrall
My heart from your enchantments, once for all.

Scene VIII [Éliante, Alceste, Philinte.]

ALCESTE (*to Éliante*): Madam, your virtuous beauty
        has no peer;
Of all this world you only are sincere;
I've long esteemed you highly, as you know;
Permit me ever to esteem you so,
And if I do not now request your hand,   5
Forgive me, Madam, and try to understand.
I feel unworthy of it; I sense that fate
Does not intend me for the married state,
That I should do you wrong by offering you
My shattered heart's unhappy residue,   10
And that in short . . .
ÉLIANTE: Your argument's well taken:
Nor need you fear that I shall feel forsaken.
Were I to offer him this hand of mine,
Your friend Philinte, I think, would not decline.
PHILINTE: Ah, Madam, that's my heart's most
        cherished goal,   15
For which I'd gladly give my life and soul.
ALCESTE (*to Éliante and Philinte*): May you be true to
        all you now profess,
And so deserve unending happiness.
Meanwhile, betrayed and wronged in everything,
I'll flee this bitter world where vice is king,   20
And seek some spot unpeopled and apart
Where I'll be free to have an honest heart.
PHILINTE: Come, Madam, let's do everything we can
To change the mind of this unhappy man.

COMMENTARY

Lionel Gossman (b. 1929)
ALCESTE'S LOVE FOR CÉLIMÈNE   *1963*

What underlies Alceste's unlikely infatuation with Célimène? Gossman suggests that Alceste is playing to the very people of fashion whom he affects to look down on; consequently, he must conceal the real reasons for his love.

In reality, Alceste's love for Célimène is neither super-rational (above all reason and all explanation) nor irrational (below all reason and explanation). It is quite simply a peculiar and contradictory fascination which goes by the name of love in the vocabulary of the Alcestes of the world. It *can* be explained, and the explanation reveals that far from being the sincere and spontaneous being he says he is, Alceste is as calculating as anyone else.

It is precisely because Célimène is the most sought after and *worldly* of women (to all *appearances* the most unsuitable for Alceste) that he falls in love with her. It is not Célimène that Alceste loves or desires. She is irrelevant *as a person* to his "love." It is the world that he seeks to reach and possess through her. To have at his feet this woman whom all the world admires and courts would be to win the recognition of the world for himself. Alceste's love is entirely mediated by those very "gens à la mode"° for whom he so loudly protests his contempt. He "loves" Célimène because she has what he wants — the admiration of the world — and cannot admit he wants, without at the same time admitting that he is not the free, frank, and independent person he wants to be admired as. The object of his desire is thus also his unavowed rival, and this *for the very same reason* that she is the object of his desire. While he protests his love for Célimène, Alceste must therefore conceal the real reason for this love by affecting to deplore her participation in the "false" society of the *gens à la mode* and to despise her charms and her popularity. The final break with Célimène strikingly illustrates the ambiguity that characterizes Alceste's entire relationship with her from the beginning. Alceste calls on witnesses to observe how superior and disinterested his love is compared to the love of the elegant suitors who have abandoned Célimène, while at the same time he affirms before them his own contempt for it as unworthy of him:

Vous voyez ce que peut une indigne tendresse,
Et je vous fais tous deux *témoins* de ma foiblesse.
Mais, à vous dire vrai, ce n'est pas encor tout,
Et *vous allez me voir* la pousser jusqu'au bout,
Montrer que c'est à tort que sages on nous nomme,
Et que dans tous les coeurs il est toujours de l'homme.
[V, VII, 19–24][1]

Having once proved how different his love is from that of Célimène's frivolous and calculating suitors, however, Alceste is only too quick to use her unwillingness to follow him to his desert as an excuse to drop her. Célimène without her suitors can have no attraction for Alceste.

Those who fall for Alceste's argument about the irrationality of passion are his dupes. Alceste cannot accept in the front rank of his own consciousness, or admit to others, that his whole life is pure posturing before others, that he who claims to be sincere and spontaneous is as preoccupied with the public as anybody and as mediated by it as those whom he charges with acting parts for others. Is he not, after all, the only person in the world who does not posture, whose emotions spring directly from the heart and who speaks nothing but what he really thinks and feels? Alceste uses the myth of the irrationality of passion to hide from others and from himself a character that is every bit as cold and ungenerous as the characters of those he criticizes for their coldness and lack of generosity.[. . .]

Alceste's life is in an important sense a life not of participation but of demonstration. This is one way in which he differs from the tragic heroes of Racine. The scandalous contradiction between the ideal and the real, between being and appearance, between the world of absolute values and the world of contingent opportunities is at the heart of seventeenth-century tragedy. There is never any danger, however, that Alceste will share in the somber destinies of Racine's heroes. His

---

"gens à la mode": Fashionable people.
[1]V, IV, 1751–56 of original text; italics added by Gossman.

world is far removed from theirs. He does not stake his destiny, as Junie or Andromaque or Monime° does, on living an authentic life in a world of inauthenticity. The inauthenticity of the world is not a menace to him; on the contrary, it is the very source of all his satisfactions. It provides the basis for his own superiority and he spends his time not in a real struggle to reach authenticity, but in endless efforts to have his superiority recognized by the very world of inauthenticity which he affects to detest. The absence of value in the world becomes, with Alceste, a matter for personal self-congratulation. Far from threatening his existence, the world of lies and deceit founds it. He exhausts himself in theatrical gestures, because all his wrestling with the ideal and the real, all his disgust with the world's falseness, however painfully experienced subjectively, is, objectively viewed, nothing but vain, ineffectual, and deeply inauthentic posturing. He does not really suffer because life is full of pretense and selfishness, because men have made their lives so vain and stupid. He suffers because he cannot bear to be like others and because others refuse him the adulation which he wants from them.[. . .]

Alceste acts the part of an absolute, but no one accepts his absoluteness: He loses his lawsuit, he fails to make Célimène submit to him, and he is laughed at by the world at large. He is an absolute in the world of his own conceptualizing alone, and thither he withdraws to decide for himself the fate of all his battles. The desert to which Alceste has always thought of withdrawing and to which he makes as if to withdraw at the end of the comedy is the world of his own mind. In it there is nothing to contradict his absoluteness, but there is unfortunately nothing to confirm it either. Alceste's difficulty is that his absoluteness can be experienced as real only with reference to others. Withdrawal to the desert cannot therefore be a final solution. It can only be an *act*, just as his rejection of Philinte at the beginning of the play was an act. This withdrawal requires an audience to watch it; and this hermit seeks not to escape but to be pursued. Alceste's withdrawal is simply a pose. And this is the very marrow of Molière's play. Alceste literally *joue la comédie*.° He is perpetually play-acting, whether we think of his passion for Célimène or of his passion for justice, and in this respect he resembles Molière's other comic heroes.

Junie . . . Andromaque . . . Monime: Characters in plays by Racine.
joue la comédie: Plays a sham part; play-acts.

Aphra Behn

Although not technically the first English woman playwright or the first woman to earn a living by her pen, Aphra Behn (c. 1640–1689) was the first notably successful woman playwright. She wrote twenty plays, several novels, among them *Oroonoko* (c. 1688), and *Poems on Several Occasions* (1684). She also published translations and edited volumes of poetry.

Behn grew up in an England governed by the Puritan Commonwealth. Throughout the 1650s Cromwell was Protector, and the theaters were closed. The Puritans were, in her eyes, dull, hypocritical, and repressive. Her allegiance was with the Stuarts, whose King Charles I was beheaded by order of Parliament in 1649. His sons, Charles and James, were forced into exile on the Continent, along with many Stuart courtiers, such as the gallants who appear in *The Rover*. When Charles II was restored to the throne in 1660, the period known as the Restoration began. Behn was twenty years old.

Very little is known of her, and much of that is guesswork based on her writing. For example, *Oroonoko* is a novel set in Surinam, which was a British colony when she visited there with members of her family in 1663–1664. Her father, who had been appointed lieutenant-general of Surinam, died, and she returned to London. She married Mr. Behn, possibly a Dutch merchant in England, who died two years later. She seems to have been persuaded by the writer and theater manager Thomas Killigrew to become an English spy in Antwerp. She was residing there when the great fire of 1666 destroyed most of London. Her services were so little valued that she was not paid and ended up for a brief time in debtors' prison when she returned to England.

Once out of prison, she took advantage of her friendship with Thomas Betterton, who belonged to a theater company at Lincoln's Inn Fields. He played the lead in her first play, *The Forced Marriage* (1670), which ran successfully for six nights. The record for the first run of a play was thirteen nights. In 1670 Behn reached a mostly courtly audience, those politically aligned with Charles II or somehow involved in court politics.

Behn succeeded again with *The Amorous Prince* following *The Forced Marriage* in 1671. Those first two plays were wholly original, but she quickly resorted to the Shakespearean device of adapting the work of others. Like Shakespeare, she made considerable changes and constantly improved the material she borrowed. After the success of *The Rover* (1677), she was accused of plagiarism and answered the charge in the Postscript to the play. She did borrow some characters and details from Thomas Killigrew's *Thomaso; or, The Wanderer*, a closet drama, or play intended to be read, not staged (1654; published 1664); but, as she says in her Postscript, no one would have taken notice if her play were not so successful — and written by a woman. Playwrights commonly adapted earlier material because they had to produce many plays in a short time to earn a meager living.

The theme of her first play, loveless and unhappy marriages arranged by families, recurs throughout Behn's work. All we know about her own marriage is that it was brief; she did not remarry despite having long-term relationships. But she concerned herself with the fate of women in her society. A young woman could not hope to marry if she were not a virgin. Once she was married, a woman's property became her husband's, and her legal identity was melded with his. Consequently, she was at her husband's mercy since she had no recourse in law against any of his excesses.

However, the alternative to marriage was considered worse. If a woman was seduced, and people found out, she could expect to lose her status and forsake marriage. As a result, she would be forced to earn her own living, a harsh prospect since women were not given the same education as men and could not take part in any of the professions. One fate of many such women was to become prostitutes. In the meantime men pursued their goal of seduction, as they do in *The Rover* and other Behn plays, with no thought given to the welfare of the women they seduced. Furthermore, they frequently threatened women with rape if the women were uncompliant. The theme of rape echoes through Behn's plays. By necessity Behn had to appeal to a predominantly male audience, but even so she expresses some of her deeper concerns for the welfare of her sex. She exposes the unfairness and pain of arranged marriages and portrays women as complex and intelligent. Her work seems to bear the influence of Shakespeare's female characters, such as Helena and Hermia in *A Midsummer Night's Dream* and Beatrice in *Much Ado about Nothing*.

Behn's plays include *Abdelazer* (1676), *The Town Fop* (1676), *The Lucky Chance* (1686), and *The Emperor of the Moon* (1687). Her last play, *The Widow Ranter* (1689), produced posthumously, was a failure. But it is an interesting portrait of the settlement of the Virginias, based on her experience in the New World. The prefaces to Behn's plays treat important issues, such as the unequal education of women. She points out, however, that in playwriting the lack of education in Greek and Latin is no handicap. She reminds her readers that Shakespeare and Jonson did very well with limited education, and that "gownmen" (scholars) talked incessantly and to little account. What was needed for the stage was experience and a good ear, and Aphra Behn had both.

THE ROVER; OR, THE BANISHED CAVALIERS

The English rakes who swagger through this play are displaced Royalist cavaliers who lived perilously in exile during the Puritan interregnum of the 1650s as they awaited the restoration of Charles II to the throne. Their concerns in Naples are warlike and lusty. Their frequent dueling delighted the audiences of 1677 and caused *The Rover* to be one of Behn's best-received plays. Beneath the brawling, however, is a more serious struggle between the sexes.

It is pre-Lenten carnival time in Naples, when all the people dress in masquerade. The players in *The Rover* disguise themselves — Hellena as a gypsy or a page, Belvile as Antonio, the others in costumes that make them unrecognizable — from the first act to the last. Such masquerading permits the young men and women to meet and talk without supervision. Among the characters, the most stable are Florinda and Belvile, who love each other from the beginning and who end up married despite the objections of Florinda's brother Pedro and their father, who has promised Florinda to Don Vincentio, a wealthy old man.

Behn's favorite theme of arranged or forced marriage thus surfaces quickly in this play, and much of the action involves its circumvention. A related theme also develops quickly: forcible rape. The Cavaliers, or rakes, treat women of lower social class as if they were whores. In this play Florinda faces rape not once but twice. First Willmore, the Rover, treats her as "an errant harlot" and forces her to scream "rape" (III, v). When Frederick and Belvile intervene, he explains that he was drunk and not to blame. Florinda's second close call comes with Blunt. When she runs into his apartment to escape discovery on the street, Blunt decides to avenge his disgrace at the hands of Lucetta by raping Florinda — thus punishing the entire sex for his mishandling. This time Frederick, without knowing who Florinda is, decides both to help Blunt and to rape her as well. When she gives them a ring that reveals her to be an aristocrat, a woman of quality, Frederick says, "'twould anger us vilely to be trussed up for a rape upon a maid of quality, when we only believe we ruffle a harlot" (IV, v, 150–53).

These scenes are painful from our modern perspective and must have been even more so to women in Behn's audience. Part of her purpose, though, is to point out that men treated women differently according to class. Aristocrats such as these cavaliers were sometimes willfully brutal toward women in a lower class. Behn builds sympathy for Florinda and, by extension, for all women who are treated viciously by men. It is conceivable that some men in the audiences of Behn's day might not have been conscious of her purpose, since they may have approved of behavior such as Blunt's and Frederick's.

Like Florinda, the other female characters in *The Rover* face obstacles with wit and resourcefulness, but not all the women are successful. Behn's portrait of the courtesan Angellica is laced with irony. Against her will and better judgment, Angellica finds herself falling in love with Willmore. When she takes Willmore as a lover without demanding from him the usual thousand crowns, her handmaid Moretta watches in horror, realizing that her mistress is giving away something she would normally sell at a dear price. Angellica is smitten by Willmore — just as Hellena is smitten by the same rover — but once Willmore enjoys Angellica's pleasures, he dismisses her from his mind. Angellica the courtesan knows that this is the way men relate to women. But Angellica the woman, who gave Willmore her "virgin heart," is as deceived as any woman could be.

Hellena, promised to the church as a nun by her father, begins the play revealing her plans to avoid the convent at all costs. Her brother Pedro does not say so, but he seems to expect that when she is in the convent he will have access to the 300,000 crowns her uncle has bequeathed her. Pedro attempts to force Hellena to "marry" the church in the same way that he attempts to force Florinda to marry a man she does not love. Neither sister will have any of it.

The play centers more on the success of Florinda and Hellena than it does on Belvile or Willmore. Hellena, by virtue of her wit — which is equal to Willmore's — and her understanding of social realities, forces Willmore to submit to her will. He is all for making love, but she demands that Hymen, the god of marriage, be invoked before their lovemaking. When he tells her that she should be content with love and not demand marriage, she replies, "What shall I get? A cradle full of noise and mischief, with a pack of repentance at my back?" She is more than his match. The play ends with Florinda, Hellena, and Valeria all winning the husbands of their choice on their own terms.

The Rover; or, The Banished Cavaliers in Performance

King Charles II attended the March 24, 1677, production of *The Rover,* and successive royal performances were commanded before different monarchs in 1724 and 1729. Some seventy performances of the play took place between 1700 and 1725, and even more were recorded between 1726 and 1760. However, after 1790 the play was not produced for many decades.

Today's productions indicate a modern understanding of the play's feminist themes and its subtle wit-play between the sexes. The Folger Theater Group in Washington, D.C., produced the work in 1982, playing it broadly for its humor. Critics praised the play for its vitality but complained that the production overdid the "business"— stage gestures, movement, and action — and did not clearly deliver the lines. Christopher Reeve played Willmore in the Williamstown Theater production in 1987, with Kate Burton as Florinda. The director, John Rubinstein, moved the setting from Naples to the West Indies. One of the most interesting, although not wholly satisfying, productions was in 1986 by the Royal Shakespeare Company. Jeremy Irons played Willmore and Imogen Stubbs played Hellena. The director, John Barton, adapted the text using the earlier source play *Thomaso; or, The Wanderer* by Thomas Killigrew. Critics of the Royal Shakespeare production were struck by the modernity of Behn's play.

Aphra Behn (1640–1689)

THE ROVER; OR, THE BANISHED CAVALIERS   *1677*

PROLOGUE

Wits, like physicians, never can agree,
When of a different society.
And Rabel's drops° were never more cried down
By all the learned doctors of the town,
5 Than a new play whose author is unknown.
Nor can those doctors with more malice sue
(And powerful purses) the dissenting few,
Than those, with an insulting pride, do rail
At all who are not of their own cabal.°
10   If a young poet hit your humor right,
You judge him then out of revenge and spite.
So amongst men there are ridiculous elves,
Who monkeys hate for being too like themselves.
So that the reason of the grand debate
15 Why wit so oft is damned when good plays take,
Is that you censure as you love, or hate.
        Thus like a learned conclave poets sit,
Catholic° judges both of sense and wit,
And damn or save as they themselves think fit.
20 Yet those who to others' faults are so severe,
Are not so perfect but themselves may err.
Some write correct, indeed, but then the whole
(Bating° their own dull stuff i'th' play) is stole:
As bees do suck from flowers their honeydew,
25 So they rob others striving to please you.
        Some write their characters genteel and fine,
But then they do so toil for every line,
That what to you does easy seem, and plain,
Is the hard issue of their laboring brain.
30 And some th' effects of all their pains, we see,
Is but to mimic good extempore.°
Others, by long converse about the town,
Have wit enough to write a lewd lampoon,
But their chief skill lies in a bawdy song.
35 In short, the only wit that's now in fashion,
Is but the gleanings of good conversation.
As for the author of this coming play,
I asked him what he thought fit I should say
In thanks for your good company today:
40 He called me fool, and said it was well known
You came not here for our sakes, but your own.

New plays are stuffed with wits, and with deboches,°
That crowd and sweat like cits° in May-Day°
  coaches.°

WRITTEN BY A PERSON OF QUALITY

The Actors' Names

[Men]
DON ANTONIO, *the Viceroy's son*
DON PEDRO, *a noble Spaniard, his friend*
BELVILE, *an English colonel in love with Florinda*
WILLMORE, *the Rover*
FREDERICK, *an English gentleman, and friend to Belvile
  and Blunt*
BLUNT, *an English country gentleman*
STEPHANO, *servant to Don Pedro*
PHILIPPO, *Lucetta's gallant*
SANCHO, *pimp to Lucetta*
BISKEY *and* SEBASTIAN, *two bravos° to Angellica*
OFFICER *and* SOLDIERS
[DIEGO,] *Page to Don Antonio*

[Women]
FLORINDA, *sister to Don Pedro*
HELLENA, *a gay young woman designed for a nun, and
  sister to Florinda*
VALERIA, *a kinswoman to Florinda*
ANGELLICA BIANCA, *a famous courtesan*
MORETTA, *her woman*
CALLIS, *governess to Florinda and Hellena*
LUCETTA, *a jilting wench*
SERVANTS, *other* MASQUERADERS, MEN *and* WOMEN

The Scene: *Naples, in Carnival time.*

ACT I • *Scene 1*

(*A Chamber. Enter Florinda and Hellena.*)

FLORINDA: What an impertinent thing is a young girl
  bred in a nunnery! How full of questions! Prithee no
  more, Hellena; I have told thee more than thou
  understand'st already.

---

3. Rabel's drops: A patent medicine. **9. cabal:** A small, secret
political group. **18. Catholic:** Having broad tastes or interests.
23. Bating: Leaving out. **31. extempore:** A performance given
without a script or rehearsal.

42. deboches: Orgies, debauches. **43. cits:** Residents of cities.
May-Day: May 1, celebrated as a spring festival. **coaches:**
Carriages on parade during a May Day celebration. **[The
Actors' Names] bravos:** Villains, adventurers.

5   HELLENA: The more's my grief. I would fain know as
       much as you, which makes me so inquisitive; nor is't
       enough I know you're a lover, unless you tell me too
       who 'tis you sigh for.
    FLORINDA: When you're a lover I'll think you fit for a
10   secret of that nature.
    HELLENA: 'Tis true, I never was a lover yet, but I begin
       to have a shrewd guess what 'tis to be so, and fancy it
       very pretty to sigh, and sing, and blush, and wish,
       and dream and wish, and long and wish to see the
15   man, and when I do, look pale and tremble, just as
       you did when my brother brought home the fine
       English colonel to see you. What do you call him?
       Don Belvile?
    FLORINDA: Fie, Hellena.
20   HELLENA: That blush betrays you. I am sure 'tis so. Or is
       it Don Antonio the Viceroy's son? Or perhaps the
       rich old Don Vincentio, whom my father designs you
       for a husband? Why do you blush again?
    FLORINDA: With indignation; and how near soever my
25   father thinks I am to marrying that hated object, I
       shall let him see I understand better what's due to my
       beauty, birth, and fortune, and more to my soul, than
       to obey those unjust commands.
    HELLENA: Now hang me, if I don't love thee for that
30   dear disobedience. I love mischief strangely, as most
       of our sex do who are come to love nothing else.
       But tell me, dear Florinda, don't you love that fine
       Anglese?° For I vow, next to loving him myself, 'twill
       please me most that you do so, for he is so gay and so
35   handsome.
    FLORINDA: Hellena, a maid designed for a nun ought
       not to be so curious in a discourse of love.
    HELLENA: And dost thou think that ever I'll be a nun?
       Or at least till I'm so old I'm fit for nothing else?
40   Faith no, sister; and that which makes me long to
       know whether you love Belvile, is because I hope he
       has some mad companion or other that will spoil my
       devotion. Nay, I'm resolved to provide myself this
       Carnival, if there be e'er a handsome proper fellow of
45   my humor above ground,° though I ask first.
    FLORINDA: Prithee be not so wild.
    HELLENA: Now you have provided yourself of a man
       you take no care of poor me. Prithee tell me, what
       dost thou see about me that is unfit for love? Have I
50   not a world of youth? A humor gay? A beauty pass-
       able? A vigor desirable? Well shaped? Clean limbed?
       Sweet breathed? And sense enough to know how all
       these ought to be employed to the best advantage?
       Yes, I do and will; therefore lay aside your hopes of
55   my fortune by my being a devote,° and tell me how
       you came acquainted with this Belvile. For I perceive
       you knew him before he came to Naples.
    FLORINDA: Yes, I knew him at the siege of Pamplona; he

33. *Anglese*: The English colonel Belvile.   **45. above ground:**
In the real world (i.e., outside the convent).   **55. devote:** Nun.

was then a colonel of French horse,° who when the
town was ransacked, nobly treated my brother and   60
myself, preserving us from all insolences. And I must
own, besides great obligations, I have I know not
what that pleads kindly for him about my heart, and
will suffer no other to enter. But see, my brother.

(*Enter Don Pedro, Stephano with a masking habit,*° *and
Callis.*)

PEDRO: Good morrow, sister. Pray when saw you your   65
   lover Don Vincentio?
FLORINDA: I know not, sir. Callis, when was he here?
   For I consider it so little I know not when it was.
PEDRO: I have a command from my father here to tell
   you you ought not to despise him, a man of so vast a   70
   fortune, and such a passion for you. — Stephano, my
   things.

(*Puts on his masking habit.*)

FLORINDA: A passion for me? 'Tis more than e'er I saw,
   or he had a desire should be known. I hate Vincentio,
   sir, and I would not have a man so dear to me as my   75
   brother follow the ill customs of our country and
   make a slave of his sister. And, sir, my father's will
   I'm sure you may divert.
PEDRO: I know not how dear I am to you, but I wish only
   to be ranked in your esteem equal with the English   80
   colonel Belvile. Why do you frown and blush? Is
   there any guilt belongs to the name of that cavalier?
FLORINDA: I'll not deny I value Belvile. When I was
   exposed to such dangers as the licensed lust of common soldiers threatened when rage and conquest   85
   flew through the city, then Belvile, this criminal for
   my sake, threw himself into all dangers to save my
   honor. And will you not allow him my esteem?
PEDRO: Yes, pay him what you will in honor, but you
   must consider Don Vincentio's fortune, and the join-   90
   ture° he'll make you.
FLORINDA: Let him consider my youth, beauty, and fortune, which ought not to be thrown away on his age
   and jointure.
PEDRO: 'Tis true, he's not so young and fine a gentleman   95
   as that Belvile. But what jewels will that cavalier
   present you with? Those of his eyes and heart?
HELLENA: And are not those better than any Don Vincentio has brought from the Indies?
PEDRO: Why, how now! Has your nunnery breeding   100
   taught you to understand the value of hearts and eyes?
HELLENA: Better than to believe Vincentio's deserve
   value from any woman. He may perhaps increase her
   bags, but not her family.°

59. of French horse: In the French cavalry.   **64.** [S.D.] ***masking
habit:*** Costume for the Carnival masquerades.   **90–91. jointure:** An estate given by a husband to a wife in lieu of her
dowry.   **103–04. increase her bags . . . family:** Give her material goods but not enhance her family's standing.

105   PEDRO: This is fine! Go! Up to your devotion! You are not designed for the conversation of lovers.

HELLENA (*aside*): Nor saints yet a while, I hope. — Is't not enough you make a nun of me, but you must cast my sister away too, exposing her to a worse confine-
110   ment than a religious life?

PEDRO: The girl's mad! It is a confinement to be carried into the country to an ancient villa belonging to the family of the Vincentios these five hundred years, and have no other prospect than that pleasing one of see-
115   ing all her own that meets her eyes: a fine air, large fields, and gardens where she may walk and gather flowers?

HELLENA: When, by moonlight? For I am sure she dares not encounter with the heat of the sun; that were a
120   task only for Don Vincentio and his Indian breeding, who loves it in the dog days.° And if these be her daily divertissements,° what are those of the night? To lie in a wide moth-eaten bed-chamber with furni-ture in fashion in the reign of King Sancho the First;°
125   the bed, that which his forefathers lived and died in.

PEDRO: Very well.

HELLENA: This apartment, new furbrushed° and fitted out for the young wife, he out of freedom makes his dressing room; and being a frugal and a jealous cox-
130   comb,° instead of a valet to uncase° his feeble car-cass, he desires you to do that office. Signs of favor, I'll assure you, and such as you must not hope for unless your woman be out of the way.

PEDRO: Have you done yet?

135   HELLENA: That honor being past, the giant stretches itself, yawns and sighs a belch or two loud as a mus-ket, throws himself into bed, and expects you in his foul sheets; and ere you can get yourself undressed, calls you with a snore or two. And are not these fine
140   blessings to a young lady?

PEDRO: Have you done yet?

HELLENA: And this man you must kiss, nay you must kiss none but him too, and nuzzle through his beard to find his lips. And this you must submit to for
145   threescore years, and all for a jointure.

PEDRO: For all your character of Don Vincentio, she is as like to marry him as she was before.

HELLENA: Marry Don Vincentio! Hang me, such a wed-lock would be worse than adultery with another man.
150   I had rather see her in the *Hostel de Dieu,*° to waste her youth there in vows, and be a handmaid to lazars° and cripples, than to lose it in such a marriage.

PEDRO: You have considered, sister, that Belvile has no fortune to bring you to; banished his country, de-
155   spised at home, and pitied abroad.

HELLENA: What then? The Viceroy's son is better than

that old Sir Fifty. Don Vincentio! Don Indian! He thinks he's trading to Gambo° still, and would barter himself — that bell and bauble — for your youth and fortune.   160

PEDRO: Callis, take her hence and lock her up all this Carnival, and at Lent she shall begin her everlasting penance in a monastery.

HELLENA: I care not; I had rather be a nun than be obliged to marry as you would have me if I were de-   165
signed for't.

PEDRO: Do not fear the blessing of that choice. You shall be a nun.

HELLENA (*aside*): Shall I so? You may chance to be mis-taken in my way of devotion. A nun! Yes, I am like to   170
make a fine nun! I have an excellent humor for a grate!° No, I'll have a saint of my own to pray to shortly, if I like any that dares venture on me.

PEDRO: Callis, make it your business to watch this wild-cat. — As for you, Florinda, I've only tried you all   175
this while and urged my father's will; but mine is that you would love Antonio: He is brave and young, and all that can complete the happiness of a gallant maid. This absence of my father will give us opportunity to free you from Vincentio by marrying here, which you   180
must do tomorrow.

FLORINDA: Tomorrow!

PEDRO: Tomorrow, or 'twill be too late. 'Tis not my friendship to Antonio which makes me urge this, but love to thee and hatred to Vincentio; therefore resolve   185
upon tomorrow.

FLORINDA: Sir, I shall strive to do as shall become your sister.

PEDRO: I'll both believe and trust you. Adieu.

(*Exeunt*° *Pedro and Stephano.*)

HELLENA: As becomes his sister! That is to be as resolved   190
your way as he is his.

(*Hellena goes to Callis.*)

FLORINDA: I ne'er till now perceived my ruin near. I've no defense against Antonio's love, For he has all the advantages of nature, The moving arguments of youth and fortune.   195

HELLENA: But hark you, Callis, you will not be so cruel to lock me up indeed, will you?

CALLIS: I must obey the commands I have. Besides, do you consider what a life you are going to lead?

HELLENA: Yes, Callis, that of a nun; and till then I'll be in-   200
debted a world of prayers to you if you'll let me now see what I never did, the divertissements of a Carnival.

CALLIS: What, go in masquerade? 'Twill be a fine fare-well to the world, I take it. Pray what would you do there?   205

HELLENA: That which all the world does, as I am told:

---

121. **dog days:** The hot days of summer.   122. **divertissements:** Amusements.   124. **King Sancho the First:** King of Spain, probably Sancho I of Castile (970–1035).   127. **new fur-brushed:** Refurbished.   129–30. **coxcomb:** Conceited person, fop.   130. **uncase:** Disrobe.   150. *Hostel de Dieu:* Hospital operated by a group of nuns.   151. **lazars:** Lepers.

158. **Gambo:** British colony in West Africa.   172. **grate:** The grille covering the windows in a convent (i.e., the convent). 189. [s.d.] *Exeunt:* Latin for "they go out."

Be as mad as the rest and take all innocent freedoms.
Sister, you'll go too, will you not? Come, prithee be
not sad. We'll outwit twenty brothers if you'll be
210 ruled by me. Come, put off this dull humor with your
clothes, and assume one as gay and as fantastic as the
dress my cousin Valeria and I have provided, and let's
ramble.

FLORINDA: Callis, will you give us leave to go?

215 CALLIS (*aside*): I have a youthful itch of going myself. —
Madam, if I thought your brother might not know it,
and I might wait on you; for by my troth I'll not trust
young girls alone.

FLORINDA: Thou seest my brother's gone already, and
220 thou shalt attend and watch us.

(*Enter Stephano.*)

STEPHANO: Madam, the habits are come, and your
cousin Valeria is dressed and stays for you.

FLORINDA (*aside*): 'Tis well. I'll write a note, and if I
chance to see Belvile and want an opportunity to
225 speak to him, that shall let him know what I've
resolved in favor of him.

HELLENA: Come, let's in and dress us.   (*Exeunt.*)

Scene II

(*A long street. Enter Belvile, melancholy; Blunt and
Frederick.*)

FREDERICK: Why, what the devil ails the colonel, in a
time when all the world is gay to look like mere Lent
thus? Hadst thou been long enough in Naples to
have been in love, I should have sworn some such
5 judgment had befallen thee.

BELVILE: No, I have made no new amours since I came
to Naples.

FREDERICK: You have left none behind you in Paris?

BELVILE: Neither.

10 FREDERICK: I cannot divine the cause then, unless the
old cause, the want of money.

BLUNT: And another old cause, the want of a wench.
Would not that revive you?

BELVILE: You are mistaken, Ned.

15 BLUNT: Nay, 'adsheartlikins,° then thou'rt past cure.

FREDERICK: I have found it out: Thou hast renewed thy
acquaintance with the lady that cost thee so many
sighs at the siege of Pamplona — pox on't, what d'ye
call her — her brother's a noble Spaniard, nephew to
20 the dead general. Florinda. Ay, Florinda. And will
nothing serve thy turn but that damned virtuous
woman, whom on my conscience thou lov'st in spite
too, because thou seest little or no possibility of gaining her.

25 BELVILE: Thou art mistaken; I have int'rest enough in
that lovely virgin's heart to make me proud and vain,

were it not abated by the severity of a brother, who,
perceiving my happiness —

FREDERICK: Has civilly forbid thee the house?

BELVILE: 'Tis so, to make way for a powerful rival, the   30
Viceroy's son, who has the advantage of me in being
a man of fortune, a Spaniard, and her brother's
friend; which gives him liberty to make his court,
whilst I have recourse only to letters and distant
looks from her window, which are as soft and kind as   35
those which heaven sends down on penitents.

BLUNT: Heyday! 'Adsheartlikins, simile! By this light the
man is quite spoiled. Fred, what the devil are we made
of that we cannot be thus concerned for a wench?
'Adsheartlikins, our Cupids are like the cooks of the   40
camp: They can roast or boil a woman, but they have
none of the fine tricks to set 'em off; no hogoes° to
make the sauce pleasant and the stomach sharp.

FREDERICK: I dare swear I have had a hundred as young,
kind, and handsome as this Florinda; and dogs eat   45
me if they were not as troublesome to me i'th' morning as they were welcome o'er night.

BLUNT: And yet I warrant he would not touch another
woman if he might have her for nothing.

BELVILE: That's thy joy, a cheap whore.   50

BLUNT: Why, 'adsheartlikins, I love a frank soul. When
did you ever hear of an honest woman that took a
man's money? I warrant 'em good ones. But gentlemen, you may be free; you have been kept so poor
with parliaments and protectors that the little stock   55
you have is not worth preserving. But I thank my
stars I had more grace than to forfeit my estate by
cavaliering.

BELVILE: Methinks only following the court should be
sufficient to entitle 'em to that.   60

BLUNT: 'Adsheartlikins, they know I follow it to do it
no good, unless they pick a hole in my coat for lending you money now and then, which is a greater
crime to my conscience, gentlemen, than to the commonwealth.   65

(*Enter Willmore.*)

WILLMORE: Ha! Dear Belvile! Noble colonel!

BELVILE: Willmore! Welcome ashore, my dear rover!
What happy wind blew us this good fortune?

WILLMORE: Let me salute my dear Fred, and then command me. — How is't, honest lad?   70

FREDERICK: Fair, sir, the old compliment, infinitely the
better to see my dear mad Willmore again. Prithee,
why camest thou ashore? And where's the Prince?°

WILLMORE: He's well, and reigns still lord of the wat'ry
element. I must aboard again within a day or two,   75
and my business ashore was only to enjoy myself a
little this Carnival.

BELVILE: Pray know our new friend, sir; he's but bashful, a raw traveler, but honest, stout, and one of us.

---

15. 'adsheartlikins: Expostulation equivalent to "As God loves
us."

42. hogoes: Relishes.   **73. Prince:** Charles II, in exile on the
Continent during the reign of Cromwell.

(Embraces Blunt.)

80 WILLMORE: That you esteem him gives him an int'rest here.

BLUNT: Your servant, sir.

WILLMORE: But well, faith, I'm glad to meet you again in a warm climate, where the kind sun has its godlike
85 power still over the wine and women. Love and mirth are my business in Naples, and if I mistake not the place, here's an excellent market for chapmen° of my humor.

BELVILE: See, here be those kind merchants of love you
90 look for.

(Enter several men in masking habits, some playing on music, others dancing after; women dressed like courtesans, with papers pinned on their breasts, and baskets of flowers in their hands.)

BLUNT: 'Adsheartlikins, what have we here?

FREDERICK: Now the game begins.

WILLMORE: Fine pretty creatures! May a stranger have leave to look and love? What's here? "Roses for every
95 month"?   *(Reads the papers.)*

BLUNT: Roses for every month? What means that?

BELVILE: They are, or would have you think they're courtesans, who here in Naples are to be hired by the month.

100 WILLMORE: Kind and obliging to inform us, pray where do these roses grow? I would fain plant some of 'em in a bed of mine.

WOMAN: Beware such roses, sir.

WILLMORE: A pox of fear: I'll be baked with thee
105 between a pair of sheets, and that's thy proper still; so I might but strew such roses over me and under me. Fair one, would you would give me leave to gather at your bush this idle month; I would go near to make somebody smell of it all the year after.

110 BELVILE: And thou hast need of such a remedy, for thou stink'st of tar and ropes' ends like a dock or pesthouse.

(The Woman puts herself into the hands of a man and exeunt.)

WILLMORE: Nay, nay, you shall not leave me so.

BELVILE: By all means use no violence here.

WILLMORE: Death! Just as I was going to be damnably
115 in love, to have her led off! I could pluck that rose out of his hand, and even kiss the bed the bush grew in.

FREDERICK: No friend to love like a long voyage at sea.

BLUNT: Except a nunnery, Fred.

WILLMORE: Death! But will they not be kind? Quickly
120 be kind? Thou know'st I'm no tame sigher, but a rampant lion of the forest.

(Advances from the farther end of the scenes two men dressed all over with horns° of several sorts, making grimaces at one another, with papers pinned on their backs.)

87. **chapmen:** Merchants, in this case merchants of love.
121. [S.D.] *horns:* Emblem of the cuckold, a man whose wife is unfaithful.

BELVILE: Oh the fantastical rogues, how they're dressed! 'Tis a satire against the whole sex.

WILLMORE: Is this a fruit that grows in this warm country?   125

BELVILE: Yes, 'tis pretty to see these Italians start, swell, and stab at the word cuckold, and yet stumble at horns on every threshold.

WILLMORE: See what's on their back. *(Reads.)* "Flowers of every night." Ah, rogue! And more sweet than   130
roses of every month! This is a gardener of Adam's own breeding.

(They dance.)

BELVILE: What think you of these grave people? Is a wake in Essex half so mad or extravagant?

WILLMORE: I like their sober grave way; 'tis a kind of   135
legal authorized fornication, where the men are not chid° for't, nor the women despised, as amongst our dull English. Even the monsieurs° want that part of good manners.

BELVILE: But here in Italy, a monsieur is the humblest   140
best-bred gentleman: Duels are so baffled by bravos that an age shows not one but between a Frenchman and a hangman, who is as much too hard for him on the Piazza as they are for a Dutchman on the New Bridge. But see, another crew.   145

(Enter Florinda, Hellena, and Valeria, dressed like gypsies; Callis and Stephano, Lucetta, Philippo, and Sancho in masquerade.)

HELLENA: Sister, there's your Englishman, and with him a handsome proper fellow. I'll to him, and instead of telling him his fortune, try my own.

WILLMORE: Gypsies, on my life. Sure these will prattle if a man cross their hands.° *(Goes to Hellena.)* — Dear,   150
pretty, and, I hope, young devil, will you tell an amorous stranger what luck he's like to have?

HELLENA: Have a care how you venture with me, sir, lest I pick your pocket, which will more vex your English humor than an Italian fortune will please you.   155

WILLMORE: How the devil cam'st thou to know my country and humor?

HELLENA: The first I guess by a certain forward impudence, which does not displease me at this time; and the loss of your money will vex you because I hope   160
you have but very little to lose.

WILLMORE: Egad, child, thou'rt i'th' right; it is so little I dare not offer it thee for a kindness. But cannot you divine what other things of more value I have about me that I would more willingly part with?   165

HELLENA: Indeed no, that's the business of a witch, and I am but a gypsy yet. Yet without looking in your hand, I have a parlous° guess 'tis some foolish heart you mean, an inconstant English heart, as little worth stealing as your purse.   170

137. **chid:** Chided, reproached.   138. **monsieurs:** Frenchmen.
150. **cross their hands:** Cross their hands with silver: pay them to tell his fortune.   168. **parlous:** Dangerously cunning, clever (from *perilous*).

WILLMORE: Nay, then thou dost deal with the devil, that's certain. Thou hast guessed as right as if thou hadst been one of that number it has languished for. I find you'll be better acquainted with it, nor can you take it in a better time; for I am come from sea, child, and Venus not being propitious to me in her own element,° I have a world of love in store. Would you would be good-natured and take some on't° off my hands.

HELLENA: Why, I could be inclined that way, but for a foolish vow I am going to make to die a maid.

WILLMORE: Then thou art damned without redemption, and as I am a good Christian, I ought in charity to divert so wicked a design. Therefore prithee, dear creature, let me know quickly when and where I shall begin to set a helping hand to so good a work.

HELLENA: If you should prevail with my tender heart, as I begin to fear you will, for you have horrible loving eyes, there will be difficulty in't that you'll hardly undergo for my sake.

WILLMORE: Faith, child, I have been bred in dangers, and wear a sword that has been employed in a worse cause than for a handsome kind woman. Name the danger; let it be anything but a long siege, and I'll undertake it.

HELLENA: Can you storm?

WILLMORE: Oh, most furiously.

HELLENA: What think you of a nunnery wall? For he that wins me must gain that first.

WILLMORE: A nun! Oh, now I love thee for't! There's no sinner like a young saint. Nay, now there's no denying me; the old law had no curse to a woman like dying a maid: Witness Jeptha's daughter.°

HELLENA: A very good text this, if well handled; and I perceive, Father Captain, you would impose no severe penance on her who were inclined to console herself before she took orders.°

WILLMORE: If she be young and handsome.

HELLENA: Ay, there's it. But if she be not —

WILLMORE: By this hand, child, I have an implicit faith, and dare venture on thee with all faults. Besides, 'tis more meritorious to leave the world when thou hast tasted and proved the pleasure on't. Then 'twill be a virtue in thee, which now will be pure ignorance.

HELLENA: I perceive, good Father Captain, you design only to make me fit for heaven. But if, on the contrary, you should quite divert me from it, and bring me back to the world again, I should have a new man to seek, I find. And what a grief that will be; for when I begin, I fancy I shall love like anything; I never tried yet.

WILLMORE: Egad, and that's kind! Prithee, dear creature, give me credit for a heart, for faith, I'm a very honest fellow. Oh, I long to come first to the banquet of love! And such a swinging appetite I bring. Oh, I'm impatient. Thy lodging, sweetheart, thy lodging, or I'm a dead man!

HELLENA: Why must we be either guilty of fornication or murder if we converse with you men? And is there no difference between leave to love me, and leave to lie with me?

WILLMORE: Faith, child, they were made to go together.

LUCETTA (*pointing to Blunt*): Are you sure this is the man?

SANCHO: When did I mistake your game?

LUCETTA: This is a stranger, I know by his gazing; if he be brisk he'll venture to follow me, and then, if I understand my trade, he's mine. He's English, too, and they say that's a sort of good-natured loving people, and have generally so kind an opinion of themselves that a woman with any wit may flatter 'em into any sort of fool she pleases.

(*She often passes by Blunt and gazes on him; he struts and cocks, and walks and gazes on her.*)

BLUNT: 'Tis so, she is taken; I have beauties which my false glass° at home did not discover.

FLORINDA (*aside*): This woman watches me so, I shall get no opportunity to discover myself to him, and so miss the intent of my coming. — [*To Belvile.*] But as I was saying, sir, by this line you should be a lover. (*Looking in his hand.*)

BELVILE: I thought how right you guessed: All men are in love, or pretend to be so. Come, let me go; I'm weary of this fooling.   (*Walks away.*)

FLORINDA: I will not, sir, till you have confessed whether the passion that you have vowed Florinda be true or false.

(*She holds him; he strives to get from her.*)

BELVILE: Florinda!   (*Turns quick toward her.*)

FLORINDA: Softly.

BELVILE: Thou hast nam'd one will fix me here forever.

FLORINDA: She'll be disappointed then, who expects you this night at the garden gate. And if you fail not, as — (*Looks on Callis, who observes 'em.*) Let me see the other hand — you will go near to do, she vows to die or make you happy.

BELVILE: What canst thou mean?

FLORINDA: That which I say. Farewell.

(*Offers to go.*)

BELVILE: O charming sibyl,° stay; complete that joy which as it is will turn into distraction! Where must I be? At the garden gate? I know it. At night, you say? I'll sooner forfeit heaven than disobey.

(*Enter Don Pedro and other maskers, and pass over the stage.*)

---

176. **Venus . . . element:** Venus, the goddess of love, was supposedly born from the foam of the sea. 178. **on't:** Of it. 201. **Jeptha's daughter:** To fulfill a vow, Jeptha sacrificed his only child, a virgin daughter, whom he allowed to go off to the mountains for two months to "bewail" her virginity before he killed her. "And it became a custom in Israel that the daughters of Israel went year by year to lament the daughter of Jeptha . . . four days in the year" (Judges 11:39–40). 205. **took orders:** Entered the convent.

242. **false glass:** Lying mirror. 263. **sibyl:** A female prophet; fortune-teller.

CALLIS: Madam, your brother's here.

FLORINDA: Take this to instruct you farther.

(*Gives him a letter, and goes off.*)

FREDERICK: Have a care, sir, what you promise; this may
270   be a trap laid by her brother to ruin you.

BELVILE: Do not disturb my happiness with doubts.

(*Opens the letter.*)

WILLMORE: My dear pretty creature, a thousand blessings on thee! Still in this habit, you say? And after
dinner at this place?

275 HELLENA: Yes, if you will swear to keep your heart and
not bestow it between this and that.

WILLMORE: By all the little gods of love, I swear; I'll
leave it with you, and if you run away with it, those
deities of justice will revenge me.

(*Exeunt all the women [except Lucetta].*)

280 FREDERICK: Do you know the hand?

BELVILE: 'Tis Florinda's.
All blessings fall upon the virtuous maid.

FREDERICK: Nay, no idolatry; a sober sacrifice I'll allow
you.

285 BELVILE: Oh friends, the welcom'st news! The softest
letter! Nay, you shall all see it. And could you now be
serious, I might be made the happiest man the sun
shines on!

WILLMORE: The reason of this mighty joy?

290 BELVILE: See how kindly she invites me to deliver her
from the threatened violence of her brother. Will you
not assist me?

WILLMORE: I know not what thou mean'st, but I'll make
one at any mischief where a woman's concerned. But
295   she'll be grateful to us for the favor, will she not?

BELVILE: How mean you?

WILLMORE: How should I mean? Thou know'st there's
but one way for a woman to oblige me.

BELVILE: Do not profane; the maid is nicely virtuous.

300 WILLMORE: Who, pox, then she's fit for nothing but a
husband. Let her e'en go, colonel.

FREDERICK: Peace, she's the colonel's mistress, sir.

WILLMORE: Let her be the devil; if she be thy mistress,
I'll serve her. Name the way.

305 BELVILE: Read here this postscript. (*Gives him a letter.*)

WILLMORE (*reads*): "At ten at night, at the garden gate,
of which, if I cannot get the key, I will contrive a
way over the wall. Come attended with a friend or
two."— Kind heart, if we three cannot weave a string
310   to let her down a garden wall, 'twere pity but the
hangman wove one for us all.

FREDERICK: Let her alone for that; your woman's wit,
your fair kind woman, will outtrick a broker or a
Jew, and contrive like a Jesuit° in chains. But see,
315   Ned Blunt is stolen out after the lure of a damsel.

(*Exeunt Blunt and Lucetta.*)

BELVILE: So, he'll scarce find his way home again unless
we get him cried by the bellman in the market place.
And 'twould sound prettily: "A lost English boy of
thirty."

FREDERICK: I hope 'tis some common crafty sinner, one   320
that will fit him. It may be she'll sell him for Peru:°
The rogue's sturdy, and would work well in a mine.
At least I hope she'll dress him for our mirth, cheat
him of all, then have him well-favoredly banged, and
turned out at midnight.   325

WILLMORE: Prithee what humor is he of, that you wish
him so well?

BELVILE: Why, of an English elder brother's humor: educated in a nursery, with a maid to tend him till fifteen,
and lies with his grandmother till he's of age; one that   330
knows no pleasure beyond riding to the next fair, or
going up to London with his right worshipful father
in parliament time, wearing gay clothes, or making
honorable love to his lady mother's laundry maid;
gets drunk at a hunting match, and ten to one then   335
gives some proofs of his prowess. A pox upon him,
he's our banker, and has all our cash about him; and
if he fail, we are all broke.

FREDERICK: Oh, let him alone for that matter; he's of a
damned stingy quality that will secure our stock. I   340
know not in what danger it were indeed if the jilt
should pretend she's in love with him, for 'tis a kind
believing coxcomb; otherwise, if he part with more
than a piece of eight,° geld° him — for which offer he
may chance to be beaten if she be a whore of the first   345
rank.

BELVILE: Nay, the rogue will not be easily beaten; he's
stout enough. Perhaps if they talk beyond his capacity he may chance to exercise his courage upon some
of them, else I'm sure they'll find it as difficult to beat 350
as to please him.

WILLMORE: 'Tis a lucky devil to light upon so kind a
wench!

FREDERICK: Thou hadst a great deal of talk with thy
little gypsy; couldst thou do no good upon her? For   355
mine was hardhearted.

WILLMORE: Hang her, she was some damned honest
person of quality, I'm sure, she was so very free and
witty. If her face be but answerable to her wit and
humor, I would be bound to constancy this month to   360
gain her. In the meantime, have you made no kind
acquaintance since you came to town? You do not
use to be honest° so long, gentlemen.

FREDERICK: Faith, love has kept us honest: We have
been all fir'd with a beauty newly come to town, the   365
famous Paduana° Angellica Bianca.

WILLMORE: What, the mistress of the dead Spanish
general?

---

314. Jew . . . Jesuit: Anti-Semitic and anti-Catholic attitudes of the time portrayed Jews and Jesuits as cunning and not worthy of trust.

321. sell him for Peru: Sell him as a slave.   **344. piece of eight:** Spanish money.   **geld:** Castrate.   **363. honest:** Sexually inactive.   **366. Paduana:** Angellica was born in Padua, Italy.

BELVILE: Yes, she's now the only ador'd beauty of all
370   the youth in Naples, who put on all their charms to
       appear lovely in her sight: Their coaches, liveries, and
       themselves all gay as on a monarch's birthday to
       attract the eyes of this fair charmer, while she has
       the pleasure to behold all languish for her that see
375   her.
FREDERICK: 'Tis pretty to see with how much love the
       men regard her, and how much envy the women.
WILLMORE: What gallant has she?
BELVILE: None; she's exposed to sale, and four days in
380   the week she's yours, for so much a month.
WILLMORE: The very thought of it quenches all manner
       of fire in me. Yet prithee, let's see her.
BELVILE: Let's first to dinner, and after that we'll pass the
       day as you please. But at night ye must all be at my
385   devotion.
WILLMORE: I will not fail you.   [*Exeunt.*]

ACT II • *Scene I*

(*The long street. Enter Belvile and Frederick in masking
habits, and Willmore in his own clothes, with a vizard°
in his hand.*)

WILLMORE: But why thus disguised and muzzled?
BELVILE: Because whatever extravagances we commit in
       these faces, our own may not be obliged to answer
       'em.
5 WILLMORE: I should have changed my eternal buff,°
       too; but no matter, my little gypsy would not have
       found me out then. For if she should change hers, it is
       impossible I should know her unless I should hear her
       prattle. A pox on't, I cannot get her out of my head.
10   Pray heaven, if ever I do see her again, she prove
       damnably ugly, that I may fortify myself against her
       tongue.
BELVILE: Have a care of love, for o' my conscience she
       was not of a quality to give thee any hopes.
15 WILLMORE: Pox on 'em, why do they draw a man in
       then? She has played with my heart so, that 'twill
       never lie still till I have met with some kind wench
       that will play the game out with me. Oh, for my arms
       full of soft, white, kind woman — such as I fancy
20   Angellica.
BELVILE: This is her house, if you were but in stock to
       get admittance. They have not dined yet; I perceive
       the picture is not out.°

(*Enter Blunt.*)

WILLMORE: I long to see the shadow of the fair sub-
25   stance; a man may gaze on that for nothing.

II, I. [S.D.] *vizard*: Face mask.   **5. buff**: Military coat made of
buff (leather).   **23. picture is not out**: Hanging her picture outside the house is a sign that she is open for business. (See lines
111–12 later in the scene.)

BLUNT: Colonel, thy hand. And thine, Fred. I have been
       an ass, a deluded fool, a very coxcomb from my birth
       till this hour, and heartily repent my little faith.
BELVILE: What the devil's the matter with thee, Ned?
BLUNT: Oh, such a mistress, Fred! Such a girl!   30
WILLMORE: Ha! Where?
FREDERICK: Ay, where?
BLUNT: So fond, so amorous, so toying, and so fine! And
       all for sheer love, ye rogue! Oh, how she looked and
       kissed! And soothed my heart from my bosom! I can- 35
       not think I was awake, and yet methinks I see and
       feel her charms still. Fred, try if she have not left the
       taste of her balmy kisses upon my lips. (*Kisses him.*)
BELVILE: Ha! Ha! Ha!
WILLMORE: Death, man, where is she?   40
BLUNT: What a dog was I to stay in dull England so
       long! How have I laughed at the colonel when he
       sighed for love! But now the little archer° has re-
       venged him! And by this one dart I can guess at all his
       joys, which then I took for fancies, mere dreams and   45
       fables. Well, I'm resolved to sell all in Essex and plant
       here forever.
BELVILE: What a blessing 'tis, thou hast a mistress thou
       dar'st boast of; for I know thy humor is rather to
       have a proclaimed clap than a secret amour.   50
WILLMORE: Dost know her name?
BLUNT: Her name? No, 'adsheartlikins. What care I for
       names? She's fair, young, brisk and kind, even to rav-
       ishment! And what a pox care I for knowing her by
       any other title?   55
WILLMORE: Didst give her anything?
BLUNT: Give her? Ha! Ha! Ha! Why, she's a person of
       quality. That's a good one! Give her? 'Adsheartlikins,
       dost think such creatures are to be bought? Or are we
       provided for such a purchase? Give her, quoth ye?   60
       Why, she presented me with this bracelet for the toy
       of a diamond I used to wear. No, gentlemen, Ned
       Blunt is not everybody. She expects me again tonight.
WILLMORE: Egad, that's well; we'll all go.
BLUNT: Not a soul! No, gentlemen, you are wits; I am a   65
       dull country rogue, I.
FREDERICK: Well, sir, for all your person of quality, I
       shall be very glad to understand your purse be se-
       cure; 'tis our whole estate at present, which we are
       loath to hazard in one bottom.° Come sir, unlade.   70
BLUNT: Take the necessary trifle useless now to me, that
       am beloved by such a gentlewoman. 'Adsheartlikins,
       money! Here, take mine too.
FREDERICK: No, keep that to be cozened,° that we may
       laugh.   75
WILLMORE: Cozened? Death! Would I could meet with
       one that would cozen me of all the love I could spare
       tonight.
FREDERICK: Pox, 'tis some common whore, upon my life.
BLUNT: A whore? Yes, with such clothes, such jewels,   80

---

43. little archer: Cupid.   **70. hazard in one bottom**: Keep in
one place, as in the hold (bottom) of a ship.   **74. cozened**:
Cheated.

such a house, such furniture, and so attended! A whore!

BELVILE: Why yes, sir, they are whores, though they'll neither entertain you with drinking, swearing, or
85 bawdry; are whores in all those gay clothes and right° jewels; are whores with those great houses richly furnished with velvet beds, store of plate,° handsome attendance, and fine coaches; are whores, and errant° ones.

90 WILLMORE: Pox on't, where do these fine whores live?

BELVILE: Where no rogues in office, ycleped° constables, dare give 'em laws, nor the wine-inspired bullies of the town break their windows; yet they are whores though this Essex calf° believe 'em persons of quality.

95 BLUNT: 'Adsheartlikins, y'are all fools. There are things about this Essex calf that shall take with the ladies, beyond all your wit and parts. This shape and size, gentlemen, are not to be despised; my waist, too, tolerably long, with other inviting signs that shall be
100 nameless.

WILLMORE: Egad, I believe he may have met with some person of quality that may be kind to him.

BELVILE: Dost thou perceive any such tempting things about him that should make a fine woman, and of
105 quality, pick him out from all mankind to throw away her youth and beauty upon; nay, and her dear heart, too? No, no, Angellica has raised the price too high.

WILLMORE: May she languish for mankind till she die,
110 and be damned for that one sin alone.

(*Enter two Bravos and hang up a great picture of Angellica's against the balcony, and two little ones at each side of the door.*)

BELVILE: See there the fair sign to the inn where a man may lodge that's fool enough to give her price.

(*Willmore gazes on the picture.*)

BLUNT: 'Adsheartlikins, gentlemen, what's this?

BELVILE: A famous courtesan, that's to be sold.

115 BLUNT: How? To be sold? Nay, then I have nothing to say to her. Sold? What impudence is practiced in this country; with what order and decency whoring's established here by virtue of the Inquisition!° Come, let's be gone; I'm sure we're no chapmen for this
120 commodity.

FREDERICK: Thou art none, I'm sure, unless thou couldst have her in thy bed at a price of a coach in the street.

WILLMORE: How wondrous fair she is! A thousand crowns a month? By heaven, as many kingdoms were
125 too little! A plague of this poverty, of which I ne'er

complain but when it hinders my approach to beauty which virtue ne'er could purchase.

(*Turns from the picture.*)

BLUNT: What's this? (*Reads.*) "A thousand crowns a month"! 'Adsheartlikins, here's a sum! Sure 'tis a mistake. — [*To one of the Bravos.*] Hark you, friend, 130 does she take or give so much by the month?

FREDERICK: A thousand crowns! Why, 'tis a portion for the Infanta!°

BLUNT: Hark ye, friends, won't she trust?°

BRAVO: This is a trade, sir, that cannot live by credit. 135

(*Enter Don Pedro in masquerade, followed by Stephano.*)

BELVILE: See, here's more company; let's walk off a while.

(*Exeunt English,° Pedro reads.*)

PEDRO: Fetch me a thousand crowns; I never wished to buy this beauty at an easier rate. (*Passes off.*)

(*Enter Angellica and Moretta in the balcony, and draw a silk curtain.*)

ANGELLICA: Prithee, what said those fellows to thee?

BRAVO: Madam, the first were admirers of beauty only, 140 but no purchasers; they were merry with your price and picture, laughed at the sum, and so passed off.

ANGELLICA: No matter, I'm not displeased with their rallying; their wonder feeds my vanity, and he that wishes but to buy gives me more pride than he that 145 gives my price can make my pleasure.

BRAVO: Madam, the last I knew through all his disguises to be Don Pedro, nephew to the general, and who was with him in Pamplona.

ANGELLICA: Don Pedro? My old gallant's nephew? 150 When his uncle died he left him a vast sum of money; it is he who was so in love with me at Padua, and who used to make the general so jealous.

MORETTA: Is this he that used to prance before our window, and take such care to show himself an amorous 155 ass? If I am not mistaken, he is the likeliest man to give your price.

ANGELLICA: The man is brave and generous, but of a humor so uneasy and inconstant that the victory over his heart is as soon lost as won; a slave that can add 160 little to the triumph of the conqueror. But inconstancy's the sin of all mankind, therefore I'm resolved that nothing but gold shall charm my heart.

MORETTA: I'm glad on't; 'tis only interest that women of our profession ought to consider, though I wonder 165 what has kept you from that general disease of our sex so long; I mean, that of being in love.

ANGELLICA: A kind but sullen star under which I had the happiness to be born. Yet I have had no time for love; the bravest and noblest of mankind have purchased 170

---

86. right: Real. **87. plate:** Silverware. **89. errant:** Unmitigated. **91. ycleped:** Past participle of *clepe:* called. **94. Essex calf:** Derogatory term meaning "fool," referring to Essex, England, Blunt's home. **118. Inquisition:** The Spanish Inquisition (1478–1834) forced prostitutes out of Spain and into neighboring countries.

132–33. portion for the Infanta: Dowry for the Spanish princess. **134. trust:** Extend credit for payment. **136. [S.D.]** *English:* All the English characters.

Ann Reinking and Edward Hermann
in the Williamstown Theatre
Festival's 1987 production of *The
Rover,* directed by John Rubinstein.

my favors at so dear a rate, as if no coin but gold
were current with our trade. But here's Don Pedro
again; fetch me my lute, for 'tis for him or Don Antonio the Viceroy's son that I have spread my nets.

(*Enter at one door Don Pedro, Stephano; Don Antonio
and Diego* [*his page*] *at the other door, with people following him in masquerade, antically attired, some with
music. They both go up to the picture.*)

175 ANTONIO: A thousand crowns! Had not the painter flattered her, I should not think it dear.
PEDRO: Flattered her? By heaven, he cannot. I have seen
the original, nor is there one charm here more than
adorns her face and eyes; all this soft and sweet, with
180 a certain languishing air that no artist can represent.

ANTONIO: What I heard of her beauty before had fired
my soul, but this confirmation of it has blown it to a
flame.
PEDRO: Ha!
PAGE: Sir, I have known you throw away a thousand   185
crowns on a worse face, and though y'are near your
marriage, you may venture a little love here; Florinda
will not miss it.
PEDRO (*aside*): Ha! Florinda! Sure 'tis Antonio.
ANTONIO: Florinda! Name not those distant joys; there's   190
not one thought of her will check my passion here.
PEDRO [*aside*]: Florinda scorned! (*A noise of a lute
above.*) And all my hopes defeated of the possession
of Angellica! (*Antonio gazes up.*) Her injuries, by
heaven, he shall not boast of!   195

(*Song to a lute above.*)

SONG
　　[I]
　　When Damon first began to love
　　He languished in a soft desire,
　　And knew not how the gods to move,
　　　　To lessen or increase his fire.
200　*For Caelia in her charming eyes*
　　Wore all love's sweets, and all his cruelties.

　　II
　　But as beneath a shade he lay,
　　Weaving of flowers for Caelia's hair,
　　She chanced to lead her flock that way,
205　　*And saw the am'rous shepherd there.*
　　She gazed around upon the place,
　　And saw the grove, resembling night,
　　　　To all the joys of love invite,
　　Whilst guilty smiles and blushes dressed her face.
210　*At this the bashful youth all transport grew,*
　　And with kind force he taught the virgin how
　　　　To yield what all his sighs could never do.

(*Angellica throws open the curtains and bows to Antonio, who pulls off his vizard and bows and blows up kisses. Pedro, unseen, looks in's face. [The curtains close.]*)

ANTONIO: By heaven, she's charming fair!
PEDRO (*aside*): 'Tis he, the false Antonio!
ANTONIO (*to the Bravo*): Friend, where must I pay my
215　　off'ring of love?
　　My thousand crowns I mean.
PEDRO: That off'ring I have designed to make,
　　And yours will come too late.
ANTONIO: Prithee begone; I shall grow angry else,
220　　And then thou art not safe.
PEDRO: My anger may be fatal, sir, as yours,
　　And he that enters here may prove this truth.
ANTONIO: I know not who thou art, but I am sure
　　thou'rt worth my killing, for aiming at Angellica.
　　　　　　　　　　　　　(*They draw and fight.*)

(*Enter Willmore and Blunt, who draw and part 'em.*)

225　BLUNT: 'Adsheartlikins, here's fine doings.
　　WILLMORE: Tilting for the wench, I'm sure. Nay, gad, if
　　　　that would win her I have as good a sword as the best
　　　　of ye. Put up, put up, and take another time and
　　　　place, for this is designed for lovers only.
　　　　　　　　　　　　　　　(*They all put up.*)
PEDRO: We are prevented; dare you meet me tomorrow
230　　on the Molo?°
　　For I've a title to a better quarrel,
　　That of Florinda, in whose credulous heart
　　Thou'st made an int'rest, and destroyed my hopes.
ANTONIO: Dare!
235　　I'll meet thee there as early as the day.

230. **Molo:** Wharf.

PEDRO: We will come thus disguised, that whosoever
　　chance to get the better, he may escape unknown.
ANTONIO: It shall be so.

　　　　　　　(*Exeunt Pedro and Stephano.*)

— Who should this rival be? Unless the English
colonel, of whom I've often heard Don Pedro speak.　240
It must be he, and time he were removed who lays a
claim to all my happiness.

(*Willmore, having gazed all this while on the picture[s], pulls down a little one.*)

WILLMORE: This posture's loose and negligent;
　　The sight on't would beget a warm desire
　　In souls whom impotence and age had chilled.　　245
　　This must along with me.
BRAVO: What means this rudeness, sir? Restore the
　　picture.
ANTONIO: Ha! Rudeness committed to the fair Angel-
　　lica! — Restore the picture, sir.　　　　　　　250
WILLMORE: Indeed I will not, sir.
ANTONIO: By heaven, but you shall.
WILLMORE: Nay, do not show your sword; if you do, by
　　this dear beauty, I will show mine too.
ANTONIO: What right can you pretend to't?　　　　255
WILLMORE: That of possession, which I will maintain.
　　You, perhaps, have a thousand crowns to give for the
　　original.
ANTONIO: No matter, sir, you shall restore the picture.

(*[The curtains open.] Angellica and Moretta above.*)

ANGELLICA: Oh, Moretta, what's the matter?　　　260
ANTONIO: Or leave your life behind.
WILLMORE: Death! You lie; I will do neither.

(*They fight. The Spaniards join with Antonio, Blunt laying on like mad.*)

ANGELLICA: Hold, I command you, if for me you fight.

(*They leave off and bow.*)

WILLMORE [*aside*]: How heavenly fair she is! Ah, plague
　　of her price!　　　　　　　　　　　　　265
ANGELLICA: You sir, in buff, you that appear a soldier,
　　that first began this insolence —
WILLMORE: 'Tis true, I did so, if you call it insolence for
　　a man to preserve himself. I saw your charming pic-
　　ture and was wounded; quite through my soul each　270
　　pointed beauty ran; and wanting a thousand crowns
　　to procure my remedy, I laid this little picture to my
　　bosom, which, if you cannot allow me, I'll resign.
ANGELLICA: No, you may keep the trifle.
ANTONIO: You shall first ask me leave, and this.　　275

(*Fight again as before.*)

(*Enter Belvile and Frederick, who join with the English.*)

ANGELLICA: Hold! Will you ruin me? — Biskey! Sebast-
　　ian! Part 'em!

(*The Spaniards are beaten off.*)

MORETTA: Oh, madam, we're undone. A pox upon that rude fellow; he's set on to ruin us. We shall never see good days again till all these fighting poor rogues are sent to the galleys.

280

(*Enter Belvile, Blunt, Frederick, and Willmore with's shirt bloody.*)

BLUNT: 'Adsheartlikins, beat me at this sport and I'll ne'er wear sword more.

BELVILE (*to Willmore*): The devil's in thee for a mad fellow; thou art always one at an unlucky adventure. Come, let's be gone whilst we're safe, and remember these are Spaniards, a sort of people that know how to revenge an affront.

285

FREDERICK: You bleed! I hope you are not wounded.

WILLMORE: Not much. A plague on your dons; if they fight no better they'll ne'er recover Flanders.° What the devil was't to them that I took down the picture?

290

BLUNT: Took it! 'Adsheartlikins, we'll have the great one too; 'tis ours by conquest. Prithee help me up and I'll pull it down.

295

ANGELLICA [*to Willmore*]: Stay, sir, and ere you affront me farther let me know how you durst commit this outrage. To you I speak, sir, for you appear a gentleman.

WILLMORE: To me, madam? — Gentlemen, your servant.

300

(*Belvile stays him.*°)

BELVILE: Is the devil in thee? Dost know the danger of ent'ring the house of an incensed courtesan?

WILLMORE: I thank you for your care, but there are other matters in hand, there are, though we have no great temptation. Death! Let me go!

305

FREDERICK: Yes, to your lodging if you will, but not in here. Damn these gay harlots; by this hand I'll have as sound and handsome a whore for a patacoon.° Death, man, she'll murder thee!

WILLMORE: Oh, fear me not. Shall I not venture where a beauty calls? A lovely charming beauty! For fear of danger? When, by heaven, there's none so great as to long for her whilst I want money to purchase her.

310

FREDERICK: Therefore 'tis loss of time unless you had the thousand crowns to pay.

315

WILLMORE: It may be she may give a favor; at least I shall have the pleasure of saluting her when I enter and when I depart.

BELVILE: Pox, she'll as soon lie with thee as kiss thee, and sooner stab than do either. You shall not go.

320

ANGELLICA: Fear not, sir, all I have to wound with is my eyes.

BLUNT: Let him go. 'Adsheartlikins, I believe the gentlewoman means well.

---

291. **ne'er recover Flanders:** In 1659 the Spanish gave Flanders, which had been part of the Spanish Netherlands, to France as settlement to end a war.   300. [s.d.] *stays him:* Keeps him from leaving.   308. **patacoon:** Portuguese or Spanish coin of small denomination.

BELVILE: Well, take thy fortune; we'll expect you in the next street. Farewell, fool, farewell.

325

WILLMORE: Bye, colonel.   (*Goes in.*)

FREDERICK: The rogue's stark mad for a wench.

(*Exeunt.*)

Scene II

(*A fine chamber. Enter Willmore, Angellica, and Moretta.*)

ANGELLICA: Insolent sir, how durst you pull down my picture?

WILLMORE: Rather, how durst you set it up to tempt poor am'rous mortals with so much excellence, which I find you have but too well consulted by the unmerciful price you set upon't. Is all this heaven of beauty shown to move despair in those that cannot buy? And can you think th'effects of that despair should be less extravagant than I have shown?

5

ANGELLICA: I sent for you to ask my pardon, sir, not to aggravate your crime. I thought I should have seen you at my feet imploring it.

10

WILLMORE: You are deceived. I came to rail at you, and rail such truths too, as shall let you see the vanity of that pride which taught you how to set such price on sin.

15

For such it is whilst that which is love's due
Is meanly bartered for.

ANGELLICA: Ha! Ha! Ha! Alas, good captain, what pity 'tis your edifying doctrine will do no good upon me. Moretta, fetch the gentleman a glass,° and let him survey himself to see what charms he has. — (*Aside, in a soft tone.*) And guess my business.

20

MORETTA: He knows himself of old: I believe those breeches and he have been acquainted ever since he was beaten at Worcester.°

25

ANGELLICA: Nay, do not abuse the poor creature.

MORETTA: Good weather-beaten corporal, will you march off? We have no need of your doctrine, though you have of our charity. But at present we have no scraps; we can afford no kindness for God's sake. In fine, sirrah, the price is too high i'th' mouth° for you, therefore troop, I say.

30

WILLMORE: Here, good forewoman of the shop, serve me and I'll be gone.

35

MORETTA: Keep it to pay your laundress; your linen stinks of the gun room. For here's no selling by retail.

WILLMORE: Thou hast sold plenty of thy stale ware at a cheap rate.

MORETTA: Ay, the more silly kind heart I, but this is an age wherein beauty is at higher rates. In fine, you know the price of this.

40

WILLMORE: I grant you 'tis here set down, a thousand crowns a month. Pray, how much may come to my

---

21. **glass:** Mirror.   26. **Worcester:** Charles II was routed by Cromwell at Worcester in 1651 and was forced into exile on the Continent.   32. **high i'th' mouth:** High.

45   share for a pistole?° Bawd, take your black lead° and
      sum it up, that I may have a pistole's worth of this
      vain gay thing, and I'll trouble you no more.
    MORETTA: Pox on him, he'll fret me to death! Abom-
      inable fellow, I tell thee we only sell by the whole
50   piece.
    WILLMORE: 'Tis very hard, the whole cargo or nothing.
      Faith, madam, my stock will not reach it; I cannot be
      your chapman. Yet I have countrymen in town, mer-
      chants of love like me; I'll see if they'll put in for a
55   share. We cannot lose much by it, and what we have
      no use for, we'll sell upon the Friday's mart at "Who
      gives more?"— I am studying, madam, how to pur-
      chase you, though at present I am unprovided of
      money.
60 ANGELLICA (aside): Sure this from any other man would
      anger me; nor shall he know the conquest he has
      made. — Poor angry man, how I despise this railing.
    WILLMORE: Yes, I am poor. But I'm a gentleman,
      And one that scorns this baseness which you practice.
65   Poor as I am I would not sell myself,
      No, not to gain your charming high-prized person.
      Though I admire you strangely for your beauty,
      Yet I contemn your mind.
      And yet I would at any rate enjoy you;
70   At your own rate; but cannot. See here
      The only sum I can command on earth:
      I know not where to eat when this is gone.
      Yet such a slave I am to love and beauty
      This last reserve I'll sacrifice to enjoy you.
75   Nay, do not frown, I know you're to be bought,
      And would be bought by me. By me,
      For a meaning trifling sum, if I could pay it down.
      Which happy knowledge I will still repeat,
      And lay it to my heart: It has a virtue in't,
      And soon will cure those wounds your eyes have
80   made.
      And yet, there's something so divinely powerful
        there —
      Nay, I will gaze, to let you see my strength.

    (Holds her, looks on her, and pauses and sighs.)

      By heav'n, bright creature, I would not for the world
      Thy fame were half so fair as is thy face.

    (Turns her away from him.)

    ANGELLICA (aside): His words go through me to the
85   very soul. —
      If you have nothing else to say to me —
    WILLMORE: Yes, you shall hear how infamous you are —
      For which I do not hate thee —
      But that secures my heart, and all the flames it feels
90   Are but so many lusts:
      I know it by their sudden bold intrusion.
      The fire's impatient and betrays; 'tis false.

44–45. how much . . . pistole: How much will my pistole (a
Spanish coin) buy?   45. black lead: Pencil.

For had it been the purer flame of love,
I should have pined and languished at your feet,
Ere found the impudence to have discovered it.   95
I now dare stand your scorn and your denial.
MORETTA: Sure she's bewitched, that she can stand thus
  tamely and hear his saucy railing. — Sirrah, will you
  be gone?
ANGELLICA (to Moretta): How dare you take this lib-   100
  erty! Withdraw! — Pray tell me, sir, are not you
  guilty of the same mercenary crime? When a lady is
  proposed to you for a wife, you never ask how fair,
  discreet, or virtuous she is, but what's her fortune;
  which, if but small, you cry "She will not do my busi-   105
  ness," and basely leave her, though she languish for
  you. Say, is not this as poor?
WILLMORE: It is a barbarous custom, which I will scorn
  to defend in our sex, and do despise in yours.
ANGELLICA: Thou'rt a brave fellow! Put up thy gold,
  and know,   110
  That were thy fortune as large as is thy soul,
  Thou shouldst not buy my love
  Couldst thou forget those mean effects of vanity
  Which set me out to sale,
  And as a lover prize my yielding joys.   115
  Canst thou believe they'll be entirely thine,
  Without considering they were mercenary?
WILLMORE: I cannot tell, I must bethink me first.
  (Aside.) Ha! Death, I'm going to believe her.
ANGELLICA: Prithee confirm that faith, or if thou canst
  not,   120
  Flatter me a little: 'Twill please me from thy mouth.
WILLMORE (aside): Curse on thy charming tongue!
    Dost thou return
  My feigned contempt with so much subtlety? —
  Thou'st found the easiest way into my heart,
  Though I yet know that all thou say'st is false.   125

(Turning from her in rage.)

ANGELLICA: By all that's good, 'tis real;
  I never loved before, though oft a mistress.
  Shall my first vows be slighted?
WILLMORE (aside): What can she mean?
ANGELLICA (in an angry tone): I find you cannot credit
  me.   130
WILLMORE: I know you take me for an errant ass,
  An ass that may be soothed into belief,
  And then be used at pleasure;
  But, madam, I have been so often cheated
  By perjured, soft, deluding hypocrites,   135
  That I've no faith left for the cozening sex,
  Especially for women of your trade.
ANGELLICA: The low esteem you have of me perhaps
  May bring my heart again:
  For I have pride that yet surmounts my love.   140

(She turns with pride; he holds her.)

WILLMORE: Throw off this pride, this enemy to bliss,
  And show the power of love: 'Tis with those arms
  I can be only vanquished, made a slave.

ANGELLICA: Is all my mighty expectation vanished?
145   No, I will not hear thee talk; thou hast a charm
   In every word that draws my heart away,
   And all the thousand trophies I designed
   Thou hast undone. Why art thou soft?
   Thy looks are bravely rough, and meant for war.
150   Couldst thou not storm on still?
   I then perhaps had been as free as thou.
  WILLMORE (*aside*): Death, how she throws her fire
     about my soul! —
   Take heed, fair creature, how you raise my hopes,
   Which once assumed pretends to all dominion:
155   There's not a joy thou hast in store
   I shall not then command.
   For which I'll pay you back my soul, my life!
   Come, let's begin th'account this happy minute!
  ANGELLICA: And will you pay me then the price I ask?
  WILLMORE: Oh, why dost thou draw me from an
160   awful worship,
   By showing thou art no divinity.
   Conceal the fiend, and show me all the angel!
   Keep me but ignorant, and I'll be devout
   And pay my vows forever at this shrine.

(*Kneels and kisses her hand.*)

165 ANGELLICA: The pay I mean is but thy love for mine.
   Can you give that?
  WILLMORE: Entirely. Come, let's withdraw where I'll
   renew my vows, and breathe 'em with such ardor
   thou shalt not doubt my zeal.
170 ANGELLICA: Thou hast a power too strong to be resisted.

(*Exeunt Willmore and Angellica.*)

MORETTA: Now my curse go with you! Is all our project
   fallen to this? To love the only enemy to our trade?
   Nay, to love such a shameroon;° a very beggar; nay, a
   pirate beggar, whose business is to rifle and be gone;
175   a no-purchase, no-pay tatterdemalion,° and English
   picaroon;° a rogue that fights for daily drink, and
   takes a pride in being loyally lousy? Oh, I could curse
   now, if I durst. This is the fate of most whores.
   Trophies, which from believing fops we win,
180   *Are spoils to those who cozen us again.*   [*Exit.*]

ACT III • *Scene 1*

(*A street. Enter Florinda, Valeria, Hellena, in antic° different dresses from what they were in before; Callis attending.*)

FLORINDA: I wonder what should make my brother in so
   ill a humor? I hope he has not found out our ramble
   this morning.

HELLENA: No, if he had, we should have heard on't at
   both ears, and have been mewed up° this afternoon,   5
   which I would not for the world should have happened. Hey ho, I'm as sad as a lover's lute.
VALERIA: Well, methinks we have learnt this trade of
   gypsies as readily as if we had been bred upon the
   road to Loretto;° and yet I did so fumble when I told   10
   the stranger his fortune that I was afraid I should
   have told my own and yours by mistake. But methinks Hellena has been very serious ever since.
FLORINDA: I would give my garters she were in love, to be
   revenged upon her for abusing me. How is't, Hellena?   15
HELLENA: Ah, would I had never seen my mad monsieur. And yet, for all your laughing, I am not in love.
   And yet this small acquaintance, o' my conscience,
   will never out of my head.
VALERIA: Ha! Ha! Ha! I laugh to think how thou art fit-   20
   ted with a lover, a fellow that I warrant loves every
   new face he sees.
HELLENA: Hum, he has not kept his word with me here,
   and may be taken up. That thought is not very pleasant to me. What the deuce should this be now that I   25
   feel?
VALERIA: What is't like?
HELLENA: Nay, the Lord knows, but if I should be
   hanged I cannot choose but be angry and afraid
   when I think that mad fellow should be in love with   30
   anybody but me. What to think of myself I know not:
   Would I could meet with some true damned gypsy,
   that I might know my fortune.
VALERIA: Know it! Why there's nothing so easy: Thou
   wilt love this wand'ring inconstant till thou find'st   35
   thyself hanged about his neck, and then be as mad to
   get free again.
FLORINDA: Yes, Valeria, we shall see her bestride his
   baggage horse and follow him to the campaign.
HELLENA: So, so, now you are provided for there's no   40
   care taken of poor me. But since you have set my
   heart a-wishing, I am resolved to know for what, I
   will not die of the pip,° so I will not.
FLORINDA: Art thou mad to talk so? Who will like thee
   well enough to have thee, that hears what a mad   45
   wench thou art?
HELLENA: Like me? I don't intend every he that likes me
   shall have me, but he that I like. I should have stayed
   in the nunnery still if I had liked my lady abbess as
   well as she liked me. No, I came thence not, as my   50
   wise brother imagines, to take an eternal farewell of
   the world, but to love and to be beloved; and I will be
   beloved, or I'll get one of your men, so I will.
VALERIA: Am I put into° the number of lovers?

---

173. **shameroon:** Shameful person.   175. **tatterdemalion:** Ragamuffin.   176. **picaroon:** Wandering rogue.   III, I. [S.D.] *antic:* Absurd, ludicrous, strange.

5. **mewed up:** Shut in, imprisoned.   10. **Loretto:** Loreto is an Italian town on the Adriatic coast, a destination for pilgrims visiting the cottage of the Virgin Mary.   43. **pip:** A disease of poultry and birds, applied vaguely, usually humorously, to various ailments in humans.   54. **Am I put into:** Do you include me among?

55 HELLENA: You? Why, coz, I know thou'rt too good-
natured to leave us in any design; thou wouldst venture a cast° though thou comest off a loser, especially
with such a gamester. I observed your man, and your
willing ear incline that way; and if you are not a
60 lover, 'tis an art soon learnt — that I find.   (*Sighs.*)
FLORINDA: I wonder how you learnt to love so easily. I
had a thousand charms to meet my eyes and ears ere I
could yield, and 'twas the knowledge of Belvile's
merit, not the surprising person, took my soul. Thou
65 art too rash, to give a heart at first sight.
HELLENA: Hang your considering lover! I never thought
beyond the fancy that 'twas a very pretty, idle, silly
kind of pleasure to pass one's time with: to write little
soft nonsensical billets,° and with great difficulty and
70 danger receive answers in which I shall have my
beauty praised, my wit admired, though little or
none, and have the vanity and power to know I am
desirable. Then I have the more inclination that way
because I am to be a nun, and so shall not be sus-
75 pected to have any such earthly thoughts about me;
but when I walk thus — and sigh thus — they'll
think my mind's upon my monastery, and cry, "How
happy 'tis she's so resolved." But not a word of man.
FLORINDA: What a mad creature's this!
80 HELLENA: I'll warrant, if my brother hears either of you
sigh, he cries gravely, "I fear you have the indiscretion to be in love, but take heed of the honor of our
house, and your own unspotted fame"; and so he
conjures on till he has laid the soft winged god in
85 your hearts, or broke the bird's nest.° But see, here
comes your lover, but where's my inconstant? Let's
step aside, and we may learn something.

(*Go aside.*)

(*Enter Belvile, Frederick, and Blunt.*)

BELVILE: What means this! The picture's taken in.
BLUNT: It may be the wench is good-natured, and will be
90 kind gratis.° Your friend's a proper handsome fellow.
BELVILE: I rather think she has cut his throat and is fled;
I am mad he should throw himself into dangers. Pox
on't, I shall want him, too, at night. Let's knock and
ask for him.
95 HELLENA: My heart goes a-pit, a-pat, for fear 'tis my
man they talk of.

(*Knock; Moretta above.*)

MORETTA: What would you have?
BELVILE: Tell the stranger that entered here about two
hours ago that his friends stay here for him.
100 MORETTA: A curse upon him for Moretta: Would he
were at the devil! But he's coming to you.

(*Enter Willmore.*)

HELLENA: Ay, ay 'tis he. Oh, how this vexes me!

BELVILE: And how and how, dear lad, has fortune
smiled? Are we to break her windows, or raise up
altars to her, hah?   105
WILLMORE: Does not my fortune sit triumphant on my
brow? Dost not see the little wanton god there all gay
and smiling? Have I not an air about my face and
eyes that distinguish me from the crowd of common
lovers? By heaven, Cupid's quiver has not half so   110
many darts as her eyes! Oh, such a *bona roba*!° To
sleep in her arms is lying *in fresco*,° all perfumed air
about me.
HELLENA (*aside*): Here's fine encouragement for me to
fool on!   115
WILLMORE: Hark'ee, where didst thou purchase that
rich Canary° we drank today? Tell me, that I may
adore the spigot and sacrifice to the butt.° The juice
was divine; into which I must dip my rosary, and
then bless all things that I would have bold or fortu-   120
nate.
BELVILE: Well, sir, let's go take a bottle and hear the
story of your success.
FREDERICK: Would not French wine do better?
WILLMORE: Damn the hungry balderdash!° Cheerful   125
sack° has a generous virtue in't inspiring a successful
confidence, gives eloquence to the tongue and vigor
to the soul, and has in a few hours completed all my
hopes and wishes! There's nothing left to raise a new
desire in me. Come, let's be gay and wanton. And,   130
gentlemen, study; study what you want, for here are
friends that will supply gentlemen. [*Jingles gold.*]
Hark what a charming sound they make! 'Tis he and
she gold whilst here, and shall beget new pleasures
every moment.   135
BLUNT: But hark'ee, sir, you are not married, are you?
WILLMORE: All the honey of matrimony but none of the
sting, friend.
BLUNT: 'Adsheartlikins, thou'rt a fortunate rogue!
WILLMORE: I am so, sir: let these inform you! Ha, how   140
sweetly they chime! Pox of poverty: It makes a man a
slave, makes wit and honor sneak. My soul grew lean
and rusty for want of credit.
BLUNT: 'Adsheartlikins, this I like well; it looks like my
lucky bargain! Oh, how I long for the approach of   145
my squire, that is to conduct me to her house again.
Why, here's two provided for!
FREDERICK: By this light, y'are happy men.
BLUNT: Fortune is pleased to smile on us, gentlemen, to
smile on us.   150

(*Enter Sancho and pulls down Blunt by the sleeve; they go aside.*)

SANCHO: Sir, my lady expects you. She has removed all
that might oppose your will and pleasure, and is impatient till you come.

56–57. **venture a cast:** Throw the dice.   69. **billets:** Brief letters, notes.   84–85. **laid . . . bird's nest:** Ruined your chances.
90. **gratis:** Free of charge.

111. *bona roba:* A courtesan.   112. *in fresco:* In the fresh air out
of doors.   117. **Canary:** A light sweet wine from the Canary
Islands.   118. **butt:** Large wine cask.   125. **hungry balderdash:**
Cheap mixture of liquor.   126. **sack:** Dry white Spanish wine.

BLUNT: Sir, I'll attend you. — Oh the happiest rogue! I'll
155 take no leave, lest they either dog me or stay me.
                                    (*Exit with Sancho.*)
BELVILE: But then the little gypsy is forgot?
WILLMORE: A mischief on thee for putting her into my
   thoughts! I had quite forgot her else, and this night's
   debauch had drunk her quite down.
160 HELLENA: Had it so, good captain!

(*Claps him on the back.*)

WILLMORE (*aside*): Ha! I hope she did not hear me!
HELLENA: What, afraid of such a champion?
WILLMORE: Oh, you're a fine lady of your word, are you
   not? To make a man languish a whole day —
165 HELLENA: In tedious search of me.
WILLMORE: Egad, child, thou'rt in the right. Hadst thou
   seen what a melancholy dog I have been ever since I
   was a lover, how I have walked the streets like a
   Capuchin,° with my hands in my sleeves — faith,
170 sweetheart, thou wouldst pity me.
HELLENA [*aside*]: Now if I should be hanged I can't be
   angry with him, he dissembles so heartily. — Alas,
   good captain, what pains you have taken; now were I
   ungrateful not to reward so true a servant.
175 WILLMORE: Poor soul, that's kindly said; I see thou
   barest a conscience. Come then, for a beginning
   show me thy dear face.
HELLENA: I'm afraid, my small acquaintance, you have
   been staying that swinging stomach you boasted of
180 this morning. I then remember my little collation°
   would have gone down with you without the sauce
   of a handsome face. Is your stomach so queasy now?
WILLMORE: Faith, long fasting, child, spoils a man's
   appetite. Yet if you durst treat, I could so lay about
185 me still —
HELLENA: And would you fall to before a priest says
   grace?
WILLMORE: O fie, fie, what an old out-of-fashioned
   thing hast thou named? Thou couldst not dash me
190 more out of countenance shouldst thou show me an
   ugly face.

(*Whilst he is seemingly courting Hellena, enter Angellica, Moretta, Biskey, and Sebastian, all in masquerade.
Angellica sees Willmore and stares.*)

ANGELLICA: Heavens, 'tis he! And passionately fond to
   see another woman!
MORETTA: What could you less expect from such a
195 swaggerer?
ANGELLICA: Expect? As much as I paid him: a heart
      entire,
   Which I had pride enough to think when'er I gave,
   It would have raised the man above the vulgar,
   Made him all soul, and that all soft and constant.
200 HELLENA: You see, captain, how willing I am to be
   friends with you, till time and ill luck make us lovers;

---

169. **Capuchin:** Franciscan monk.   180. **collation:** Snack.

and ask you the question first rather than put your
modesty to the blush by asking me. For alas, I know
you captains are such strict men, and such severe
observers of your vows to chastity, that 'twill be hard 205
to prevail with your tender conscience to marry a
young willing maid.
WILLMORE: Do not abuse me, for fear I should take thee
   at thy word and marry thee indeed, which I'm sure
   will be revenge sufficient.   210
HELLENA: O' my conscience, that will be our destiny,
   because we are both of one humor: I am as inconstant as you, for I have considered, captain, that a
   handsome woman has a great deal to do whilst her
   face is good. For then is our harvest-time to gather 215
   friends, and should I in these days of my youth catch
   a fit of foolish constancy, I were undone: 'tis loitering
   by daylight in our great journey. Therefore, I declare
   I'll allow but one year for love, one year for indifference, and one year for hate; and then go hang your- 220
   self, for I profess myself the gay, the kind, and the
   inconstant. The devil's in't if this won't please you!
WILLMORE: Oh, most damnably. I have a heart with a
   hole quite through it too; no prison mine, to keep a
   mistress in.   225
ANGELLICA (*aside*): Perjured man! How I believe thee
   now!
HELLENA: Well, I see our business as well as humors are
   alike: yours to cozen as many maids as will trust you,
   and I as many men as have faith. See if I have not as 230
   desperate a lying look as you can have for the heart
   of you. (*Pulls off her vizard; he starts.*) How do you
   like it, captain?
WILLMORE: Like it! By heaven, I never saw so much
   beauty! Oh, the charms of those sprightly black eyes! 235
   That strangely fair face, full of smiles and dimples!
   Those soft round melting cherry lips and small even
   white teeth! Not to be expressed, but silently adored!
   [*She replaces her mask.*] Oh, one look more, and strike
   me dumb, or I shall repeat nothing else till I'm mad. 240

(*He seems to court her to pull off her vizard; she refuses.*)

ANGELLICA: I can endure no more. Nor is it fit to interrupt him, for if I do, my jealousy has so destroyed my
   reason I shall undo him. Therefore I'll retire, and you,
   Sebastian (*to one of her Bravos*), follow that woman
   and learn who 'tis; while you (*to the other Bravo*) tell 245
   the fugitive I would speak to him instantly.   (*Exit.*)

(*This while Florinda is talking to Belvile, who stands
sullenly; Frederick courting Valeria.*)

VALERIA [*to Belvile*]: Prithee, dear stranger, be not so
   sullen, for though you have lost your love you see my
   friend frankly offers you hers to play with in the
   meantime.   250
BELVILE: Faith, madam, I am sorry I can't play at her
   game.
FREDERICK [*to Valeria*]: Pray leave your intercession and
   mind your own affair. They'll better agree apart: He's

255   a modest sigher in company, but alone no woman
       'scapes him.
       FLORINDA [*aside*]: Sure he does but rally. Yet, if it should
       be true? I'll tempt him farther. — Believe me, noble
       stranger, I'm no common mistress. And for a little
260   proof on't, wear this jewel.° Nay, take it, sir, 'tis
       right, and bills of exchange may sometimes miscarry.
       BELVILE: Madam, why am I chose out of all mankind to
       be the object of your bounty?
       VALERIA: There's another civil question asked.
265   FREDERICK [*aside*]: Pox of's modesty; it spoils his own
       markets and hinders mine.
       FLORINDA: Sir, from my window I have often seen you,
       and women of my quality have so few opportunities
       for love that we ought to lose none.
270   FREDERICK [*to Valeria*]: Ay, this is something! Here's a
       woman! When shall I be blest with so much kindness
       from your fair mouth? — (*Aside to Belvile.*) Take the
       jewel, fool!
       BELVILE: You tempt me strangely, madam, every way —
275   FLORINDA (*aside*): So, if I find him false, my whole
       repose is gone.
       BELVILE: And but for a vow I've made to a very fair lady,
       this goodness had subdued me.
       FREDERICK [*aside to Belvile*]: Pox on't, be kind, in pity
280   to me be kind. For I am to thrive here but as you treat
       her friend.
       HELLENA: Tell me what you did in yonder house, and I'll
       unmask.
       WILLMORE: Yonder house? Oh, I went to a — to —
285   why, there's a friend of mine lives there.
       HELLENA: What, a she or a he friend?
       WILLMORE: A man, upon honor, a man. A she friend?
       No, no, madam, you have done my business, I thank
       you.
290   HELLENA: And was't your man friend that had more
       darts in's eyes than Cupid carries in's whole budget
       of arrows?
       WILLMORE: So —
       HELLENA: "Ah, such a *bona roba*! To be in her arms is
295   lying *in fresco*, all perfumed air about me." Was this
       your man friend too?
       WILLMORE: So —
       HELLENA: That gave you the he and the she gold, that
       begets young pleasures?
300   WILLMORE: Well, well, madam, then you can see there
       are ladies in the world that will not be cruel. There
       are, madam, there are.
       HELLENA: And there be men, too, as fine, wild, incon-
       stant fellows as yourself. There be, captain, there be,
305   if you go to that now. Therefore, I'm resolved —
       WILLMORE: Oh!
       HELLENA: To see your face no more —
       WILLMORE: Oh!
       HELLENA: Till tomorrow.
310   WILLMORE: Egad, you frighted me.
       HELLENA: Nor then neither, unless you'll swear never to
       see that lady more.

       260. jewel: A locket with her picture in it.

WILLMORE: See her! Why, never to think of womankind
       again.
HELLENA: Kneel and swear.   315

(*Kneels, she gives him her hand.*)

WILLMORE: I do, never to think, to see, to love, nor lie,
       with any but thyself.
HELLENA: Kiss the book.
WILLMORE: Oh, most religiously.   (*Kisses her hand.*)
HELLENA: Now what a wicked creature am I, to damn a   320
       proper fellow.
CALLIS (*to Florinda*): Madam, I'll stay no longer: 'tis
       e'en dark.
FLORINDA [*to Belvile*]: However, sir, I'll leave this with
       you, that when I'm gone you may repent the oppor-   325
       tunity you have lost by your modesty.

       (*Gives him the jewel, which is her picture, and exit.
       He gazes after her.*)

WILLMORE [*to Hellena*]: 'Twill be an age till tomorrow,
       and till then I will most impatiently expect you.
       Adieu, my dear pretty angel.

       (*Exeunt all the women.*)

BELVILE: Ha! Florinda's picture! 'Twas she herself. What   330
       a dull dog was I! I would have given the world for
       one minute's discourse with her.
FREDERICK: This comes of your modesty. Ah, pox o' your
       vow; 'twas ten to one but we had lost the jewel by't.
BELVILE: Willmore, the blessed'st opportunity lost!   335
       Florinda, friends, Florinda!
WILLMORE: Ah, rogue! Such black eyes! Such a face!
       Such a mouth! Such teeth! And so much wit!
BELVILE: All, all, and a thousand charms besides.
WILLMORE: Why, dost thou know her?   340
BELVILE: Know her! Ay, ay, and a pox take me with all
       my heart for being so modest.
WILLMORE: But hark'ee, friend of mine, are you my rival?
       And have I been only beating the bush all this while?
BELVILE: I understand thee not. I'm mad! See here —   345

(*Shows the picture.*)

WILLMORE: Ha! Whose picture's this? 'Tis a fine wench!
FREDERICK: The colonel's mistress, sir.
WILLMORE: Oh, oh, here. (*Gives the picture back.*) I
       thought't had been another prize. Come, come, a
       bottle will set thee right again.   350
BELVILE: I am content to try, and by that time 'twill be
       late enough for our design.
WILLMORE: Agreed.
       Love does all day the soul's great empire keep,
       But wine at night lulls the soft god asleep.   355
                                          (*Exeunt.*)

Scene II

(*Lucetta's house. Enter Blunt and Lucetta with a light.*)

LUCETTA: Now we are safe and free: no fears of the com-
       ing home of my old jealous husband, which made me

a little thoughtful when you came in first. But now
love is all the business of my soul.

5   BLUNT: I am transported! — (*Aside.*) Pox on't, that I
had but some fine things to say to her, such as lovers
use. I was a fool not to learn of Fred a little by heart
before I came. Something I must say. 'Adsheartlikins,
sweet soul, I am not used to compliment, but I'm an
10   honest gentleman, and thy humble servant.

  LUCETTA: I have nothing to pay for so great a favor, but
such a love as cannot but be great, since at first sight
of that sweet face and shape it made me your absolute captive.

15   BLUNT (*aside*): Kind heart, how prettily she talks! Egad,
I'll show her husband a Spanish trick: Send him out
of the world and marry her; she's damnably in love
with me, and will ne'er mind settlements,° and so
there's that saved.

20   LUCETTA: Well, sir, I'll go and undress me, and be with
you instantly.

  BLUNT: Make haste then, for 'adsheartlikins, dear soul,
thou canst not guess at the pain of a longing lover
when his joys are drawn within the compass of a few
25   minutes.

  LUCETTA: You speak my sense, and I'll make haste to
prove it.   (*Exit.*)

  BLUNT: 'Tis a rare girl, and this one night's enjoyment
with her will be worth all the days I ever passed in
30   Essex. Would she would go with me into England,
though to say truth, there's plenty of whores already.
Put a pox on 'em, they are such mercenary prodigal
whores that they want such a one as this, that's free
and generous, to give 'em good examples. Why, what
35   a house she has, how rich and fine!

(*Enter Sancho.*)

  SANCHO: Sir, my lady has sent me to conduct you to her
chamber.

  BLUNT: Sir, I shall be proud to follow. — (*Aside.*) Here's
one of her servants too; 'adsheartlikins, by this garb
40   and gravity he might be a justice of peace in Essex,
and is but a pimp here.

                                      (*Exeunt.*)

Scene III

(*The scene changes to a chamber with an alcove bed in't,
a table, etc.; Lucetta in bed. Enter Sancho and Blunt,
who takes the candle of Sancho at the door.*)

  SANCHO: Sir, my commission reaches no farther.

  BLUNT: Sir, I'll excuse your compliment.

                                  [*Exit Sancho.*]

  — What, in bed, my sweet mistress?

  LUCETTA: You see, I still outdo you in kindness.

5   BLUNT: And thou shalt see what haste I'll make to quit
scores. Oh, the luckiest rogue!

---

18. will ne'er mind settlements: Won't require the gifts of property usually settled on a wife after marriage.

(*He undresses himself.*)

  LUCETTA: Should you be false or cruel now —

  BLUNT: False! 'Adsheartlikins, what dost thou take me
for, a Jew? An insensible heathen? A pox of thy old
jealous husband: An° he were dead, egad, sweet soul,   10
it should be none of my fault if I did not marry thee.

  LUCETTA: It never should be mine.

  BLUNT: Good soul! I'm the fortunatest dog!

  LUCETTA: Are you not undressed yet?

  BLUNT: As much as my impatience will permit.   15

(*Goes toward the bed in his shirt, drawers, etc.*)

  LUCETTA: Hold, sir, put out the light; it may betray us
else.

  BLUNT: Anything; I need no other light but that of thine
eyes. — (*Aside.*) 'Adsheartlikins, there I think I had it.

(*Puts out the candle; the bed descends; he gropes about
to find it.*)

  Why, why, where am I got? What, not yet? Where are   20
you, sweetest? — Ah, the rogue's silent now. A pretty
love-trick this; how she'll laugh at me anon! — You
need not, my dear rogue, you need not! I'm all on fire
already; come, come, now call me, in pity. — Sure
I'm enchanted! I have been round the chamber, and   25
can find neither woman nor bed. I locked the door;
I'm sure she cannot go that way, or if she could, the
bed could not. — Enough, enough, my pretty wanton; do not carry the jest too far! (*Lights on a trap,
and is let down.*) — Ha! Betrayed! Dogs! Rogues!   30
Pimps! Help! Help!

(*Enter Lucetta, Philippo, and Sancho with a light.*)

  PHILIPPO: Ha! Ha! Ha! He's dispatched finely.

  LUCETTA: Now, sir, had I been coy, we had missed of this
booty.

  PHILIPPO: Nay, when I saw 'twas a substantial fool, I   35
was mollified. But when you dote upon a serenading
coxcomb, upon a face, fine clothes, and a lute, it
makes me rage.

  LUCETTA: You know I was never guilty of that folly, my
dear Philippo, but with yourself. But come, let's see   40
what we have got by this.

  PHILIPPO: A rich coat; sword and hat; these breeches,
too, are well lined! See here, a gold watch! A purse —
Ha! Gold! At least two hundred pistoles! A bunch of
diamond rings, and one with the family arms! A gold   45
box, with a medal of his king, and his lady mother's
picture! These were sacred relics, believe me. See, the
waistband of his breeches have a mine of gold — old
queen Bess's!° We have a quarrel to her ever since
eighty-eight,° and may therefore justify the theft: The   50
Inquisition might have committed it.

  LUCETTA: See, a bracelet of bowed gold! These his sisters
tied about his arm at parting. But well, for all this, I

---

10. **An:** If.   48–49. **old queen Bess's:** Queen Elizabeth I (reigned
1558–1603).   50. **eighty-eight:** The year the Spanish Armada
was defeated by the English (1588).

55   fear his being a stranger may make a noise and hinder our trade with them hereafter.

PHILIPPO: That's our security: He is not only a stranger
to us, but to the country too. The common shore°
into which he is descended, thou know'st, conducts
60   him into another street, which this light will hinder
him from ever finding again. He knows neither your
name, nor that of the street where your house is; nay,
nor the way to his own lodgings.

LUCETTA: And art thou not an unmerciful rogue, not to
afford him one night for all this? I should not have
65   been such a Jew.

PHILIPPO: Blame me not, Lucetta, to keep as much of
thee as I can to myself. Come, that thought makes me
wanton; let's to bed. — Sancho, lock up these.

This is the fleece which fools do bear,
70   *Designed for witty men to shear.*   (*Exeunt.*)

Scene IV

(*The scene changes, and discovers Blunt creeping out of
a common shore; his face, etc., all dirty.*)

BLUNT (*climbing up*): Oh, Lord, I am got out at last,
and, which is a miracle, without a clue. And now to
damning and cursing! But if that would ease me,
where shall I begin? With my fortune, myself, or the
5   quean° that cozened me? What a dog was I to believe
in woman! Oh, coxcomb! Ignorant conceited coxcomb! To fancy she could be enamored with my person! At first sight enamored! Oh, I'm a cursed puppy!
'Tis plain, fool was writ upon my forehead! She per-
10   ceived it; saw the Essex calf there. For what allure-
ments could there be in this countenance, which I can
endure because I'm acquainted with it. Oh dull, silly
dog, to be thus soothed into a cozening! Had I been
drunk, I might fondly have credited the young quean;
15   but as I was in my right wits to be thus cheated, confirms it: I am a dull believing English country fop. But
my comrades! Death and the devil, there's the worst
of all! Then a ballad will be sung tomorrow on the
Prado,° to a lousy tune of the enchanted squire and
20   the annihilated damsel. But Fred — that rogue —
and the colonel will abuse me beyond all Christian
patience. Had she left me my clothes, I have a bill of
exchange at home would have saved my credit. But
now all hope is taken from me. Well, I'll home, if I
25   can find the way, with this consolation: that I am not
the first kind believing coxcomb; but there are, gallants, many such good natures amongst ye.

*And though you've better arts to hide your follies,
'Adsheartlikins, y'are all as errant cullies.°*

(*Exit.*)

---

57. **common shore:** Sewer.   5. **quean:** Harlot, tramp.
18–19. **ballad . . . Prado:** A song satirizing him will be sung on the
Prado, a fashionable promenade in Madrid, for common amusement.   27. *cullies:* A cully is one easily fooled; a simpleton.

Scene V

(*Scene: the garden in the night. Enter Florinda in an undress,° with a key and a little box.*)

FLORINDA: Well, thus far I'm in my way to happiness. I
have got myself free from Callis; my brother too, I
find by yonder light, is got into his cabinet,° and
thinks not of me; I have by good fortune got the key
of the garden back door. I'll open it to prevent   5
Belvile's knocking: A little noise will now alarm my
brother. Now am I as fearful as a young thief.
(*Unlocks the door.*) Hark! What noise is that? Oh,
'twas the wind that played amongst the boughs.
Belvile stays long, methinks; it's time. Stay, for fear of   10
a surprise, I'll hide these jewels in yonder jasmine.

(*She goes to lay down the box.*)

(*Enter Willmore, drunk.*)

WILLMORE: What the devil is become of these fellows
Belvile and Frederick? They promised to stay at the
next corner for me, but who the devil knows the corner of a full moon? Now, whereabouts am I? Ha,   15
what have we here? A garden! A very convenient
place to sleep in. Ha! What has God sent us here? A
female! By this light, a woman! I'm a dog if it be not
a very wench!

FLORINDA: He's come! Ha! Who's there?   20
WILLMORE: Sweet soul, let me salute thy shoestring.
FLORINDA [*aside*]: 'Tis not my Belvile. Good heavens, I
know him not! — Who are you, and from whence
come you?
WILLMORE: Prithee, prithee, child, not so many hard   25
questions! Let it suffice I am here, child. Come, come
kiss me.
FLORINDA: Good gods! What luck is mine?
WILLMORE: Only good luck, child, parlous° good luck.
Come hither. —'Tis a delicate shining wench. By this   30
hand, she's perfumed, and smells like any nosegay. —
Prithee, dear soul, let's not play the fool and lose
time — precious time. For as Gad shall save me, I'm
as honest a fellow as breathes, though I'm a little dis-
guised° at present. Come, I say. Why, thou mayst be   35
free with me: I'll be very secret. I'll not boast who
'twas obliged me, not I; for hang me if I know thy
name.
FLORINDA: Heavens! What a filthy beast is this!
WILLMORE: I am so, and thou ought'st the sooner to lie 40
with me for that reason. For look you, child, there
will be no sin in't, because 'twas neither designed nor
premeditated: 'Tis pure accident on both sides. That's
a certain thing now. Indeed, should I make love to
you, and you vow fidelity, and swear and lie till you   45
believed and yielded — that were to make it willful
fornication, the crying sin of the nation. Thou art,

III, v. [S.D.] *undress:* Undergarment.   3. **cabinet:** Private room.
29. **parlous:** Excessively, with pun on *perilous.*   34–35. **disguised:** I.e., by liquor.

therefore, as thou art a good Christian, obliged in conscience to deny me nothing. Now, come be kind
50 without any more idle prating.
FLORINDA: Oh, I am ruined! Wicked man, unhand me!
WILLMORE: Wicked? Egad, child, a judge, were he young and vigorous, and saw those eyes of thine, would know 'twas they gave the first blow, the first
55 provocation. Come, prithee let's lose no time, I say. This is a fine convenient place.
FLORINDA: Sir, let me go, I conjure° you, or I'll call out.
WILLMORE: Ay, ay, you were best to call witness to see how finely you treat me. Do!
60 FLORINDA: I'll cry murder, rape, or anything, if you do not instantly let me go!
WILLMORE: A rape? Come, come, you lie, you baggage, you lie. What! I'll warrant you would fain have the world believe now that you are not so forward as
65 I. No, not you. Why at this time of night was your cobweb door set open, dear spider, but to catch flies? Ha! Come, or I shall be damnably angry. Why, what a coil° is here!
FLORINDA: Sir, can you think —
70 WILLMORE: That you would do't for nothing? Oh, oh, I find what you would be at. Look here, here's a pistole for you. Here's a work indeed! Here, take it, I say!
FLORINDA: For heaven's sake, sir, as you're a gentleman —
75 WILLMORE: So now, now, she would be wheedling me for more! What, you will not take it then? You are resolved you will not? Come, come, take it or I'll put it up again, for look ye, I never give more. Why, how now, mistress, are you so high i'th' mouth a pistole
80 won't down with you? Ha! Why, what a work's here! In good time! Come, no struggling to be gone. But an y'are good at a dumb wrestle, I'm for ye. Look ye, I'm for ye.   (*She struggles with him.*)

(*Enter Belvile and Frederick.*)

BELVILE: The door is open. A pox of this mad fellow!
85 I'm angry that we've lost him; I durst have sworn he had followed us.
FREDERICK: But you were so hasty, colonel, to be gone.
FLORINDA: Help! Help! Murder! Help! Oh, I am ruined!
BELVILE: Ha! Sure that's Florinda's voice! (*Comes up to
90 them.*) A man! — Villain, let go that lady!

(*A noise; Willmore turns and draws; Frederick interposes.*)

FLORINDA: Belvile! Heavens! My brother too is coming, and 'twill be impossible to escape. Belvile, I conjure you to walk under my chamber window, from whence I'll give you some instructions what to do.
95 This rude man has undone us.   (*Exit.*)
WILLMORE: Belvile!

(*Enter Pedro, Stephano, and other servants, with lights.*)

PEDRO: I'm betrayed! Run, Stephano, and see if Florinda be safe.

(*Exit Stephano.*)

(*They fight, and Pedro's party beats 'em out.*)

— So, whoe'er they be, all is not well. I'll to Florinda's chamber.   (*Going out, meets Stephano.*) 100
STEPHANO: You need not, sir: The poor lady's fast asleep, and thinks no harm. I would not awake her, sir, for fear of frighting her with your danger.
PEDRO: I'm glad she's there. — Rascals, how came the garden door open?   105
STEPHANO: That question comes too late, sir. Some of my fellow servants masquerading, I'll warrant.
PEDRO: Masquerading! A lewd custom to debauch our youth! There's something more in this than I imagine.

(*Exeunt.*)

Scene VI

(*Scene changes to the street. Enter Belvile in rage, Frederick holding him, Willmore melancholy.*)

WILLMORE: Why, how the devil should I know Florinda?
BELVILE: Ah, plague of your ignorance! If it had not been Florinda, must you be a beast? A brute? A senseless swine?
WILLMORE: Well, sir, you see I am endued° with patience: I can bear. Though egad, y'are very free with 5 me, methinks. I was in good hopes the quarrel would have been on my side, for so uncivilly interrupting me.
BELVILE: Peace, brute, whilst thou'rt safe. Oh, I'm distracted! 10
WILLMORE: Nay, nay, I'm an unlucky dog, that's certain.
BELVILE: Ah, curse upon the star that ruled my birth, or whatsoever other influence that makes me still so wretched. 15
WILLMORE: Thou break'st my heart with these complaints. There is no star in fault, no influence but sack, the cursed sack I drunk.
FREDERICK: Why, how the devil came you so drunk?
WILLMORE: Why, how the devil came you so sober? 20
BELVILE: A curse upon his thin skull, he was always beforehand that way.
FREDERICK: Prithee, dear colonel, forgive him; he's sorry for his fault.
BELVILE: He's always so after he has done a mischief. A 25 plague on all such brutes!
WILLMORE: By this light, I took her for an errant harlot.
BELVILE: Damn your debauched opinion! Tell me, sot, hadst thou so much sense and light about thee to distinguish her woman, and couldst not see something 30 about her face and person to strike an awful reverence into thy soul?

---

57. **conjure:** Entreat, implore.   68. **coil:** Noisy disturbance.

5. **endued:** Endowed.

WILLMORE: Faith no, I considered her as mere a woman
as I could wish.
35 BELVILE: 'Sdeath, I have no patience. Draw, or I'll kill
you!
WILLMORE: Let that alone till tomorrow, and if I set not
all right again, use your pleasure.
BELVILE: Tomorrow! Damn it,
40 The spiteful light will lead me to no happiness.
Tomorrow is Antonio's, and perhaps
Guides him to my undoing. Oh, that I could meet
This rival, this powerful fortunate!
WILLMORE: What then?
45 BELVILE: Let thy own reason, or my rage, instruct thee.
WILLMORE: I shall be finely informed then, no doubt.
Hear me, colonel, hear me; show me the man and I'll
do his business.
BELVILE: I know him no more than thou, or if I did I
50 should not need thy aid.
WILLMORE: This you say is Angellica's house; I prom-
ised the kind baggage to lie with her tonight.

(Offers to go in.)

(Enter Antonio and his Page. Antonio knocks on the hilt
of's sword.)

ANTONIO: You paid the thousand crowns I directed?
PAGE: To the lady's old woman, sir, I did.
55 WILLMORE: Who the devil have we here?
BELVILE: I'll now plant myself under Florinda's window,
and if I find no comfort there, I'll die.

(Exeunt Belvile and Frederick.)
(Enter Moretta.)

MORETTA: Page?
PAGE: Here's my lord.
60 WILLMORE: How is this? A picaroon going to board my
frigate? — Here's one chase gun for you!

(Drawing his sword, justles Antonio, who turns and
draws. They fight; Antonio falls.)

MORETTA: Oh, bless us! We're all undone!

(Runs in and shuts the door.)

PAGE: Help! Murder!

(Belvile returns at the noise of fighting.)

BELVILE: Ha! The mad rogue's engaged in some unlucky
65 adventure again.

(Enter two or three Masqueraders.)

MASQUERADER: Ha! A man killed!
WILLMORE: How, a man killed? Then I'll go home to
sleep.

(Puts up and reels out. Exeunt Masqueraders
another way.)

BELVILE: Who should it be? Pray heaven the rogue is
70 safe, for all my quarrel to him.

(As Belvile is groping about, enter an Officer and six
Soldiers.)

SOLDIER: Who's there?
OFFICER: So, here's one dispatched. Secure the mur-
derer.
BELVILE: Do not mistake my charity for murder! I came
to his assistance! (Soldiers sieze on Belvile.) 75
OFFICER: That shall be tried, sir. St. Jago! Swords drawn
in the Carnival time! (Goes to Antonio.)
ANTONIO: Thy hand, prithee.
OFFICER: Ha! Don Antonio! Look well to the villain
there. — How is it, sir? 80
ANTONIO: I'm hurt.
BELVILE: Has my humanity made me a criminal?
OFFICER: Away with him!
BELVILE: What a curst chance is this!

(Exeunt soldiers with Belvile.)

ANTONIO [aside]: This is the man that has set upon me 85
twice. — (To the officer.) Carry him to my apartment
till you have further orders from me.

(Exit Antonio, led.)

ACT IV • Scene I

(A fine room. Discovers Belvile as by dark alone.)

BELVILE: When shall I be weary of railing on fortune,
who is resolved never to turn with smiles upon me?
Two such defeats in one night none but the devil and
that mad rogue could have contrived to have plagued
me with. I am here a prisoner. But where, heaven 5
knows. And if there be murder done, I can soon
decide the fate of a stranger in a nation without
mercy. Yet this is nothing to the torture my soul bows
with when I think of losing my fair, my dear
Florinda. Hark, my door opens. A light! A man, and 10
seems of quality. Armed, too! Now shall I die like a
dog, without defense.

(Enter Antonio in a nightgown, with a light; his arm in a
scarf, and a sword under his arm. He sets the candle on
the table.)

ANTONIO: Sir, I come to know what injuries I have done
you, that could provoke you to so mean an action as
to attack me basely without allowing time for my 15
defense?
BELVILE: Sir, for a man in my circumstances to plead
innocence would look like fear. But view me well,
and you will find no marks of coward on me, nor
anything that betrays that brutality you accuse me 20
with.
ANTONIO: In vain, sir, you impose upon my sense. You
are not only he who drew on me last night, but yesterday before the same house, that of Angellica. Yet
there is something in your face and mien° that makes 25
me wish I were mistaken.

25. mien: Demeanor, appearance.

BELVILE: I own I fought today in the defense of a friend of mine with whom you, if you're the same, and your party were first engaged. Perhaps you think this
30 crime enough to kill me; but if you do, I cannot fear you'll do it basely.

ANTONIO: No sir, I'll make you fit for a defense with this.   (*Gives him the sword.*)

BELVILE: This gallantry surprises me, nor know I how to
35 use this present, sir, against a man so brave.

ANTONIO: You shall not need. For know, I come to snatch you from a danger that is decreed against you: perhaps your life, or long imprisonment. And 'twas with so much courage you offended, I cannot see you
40 punished.

BELVILE: How shall I pay this generosity?

ANTONIO: It had been safer to have killed another than have attempted me. To show your danger, sir, I'll let you know my quality: And 'tis the Viceroy's son
45 whom you have wounded.

BELVILE: The Viceroy's son! — (*Aside.*) Death and confusion! Was this plague reserved to complete all the rest? Obliged by° him, the man of all the world I would destroy!

50 ANTONIO: You seem disordered, sir.

BELVILE: Yes, trust me, I am, and 'tis with pain that man receives such bounties who wants the power to pay 'em back again.

ANTONIO: To gallant spirits 'tis indeed uneasy, but you
55 may quickly overpay me, sir.

BELVILE (*aside*): Then I am well. Kind heaven, but set us even, that I may fight with him and keep my honor safe. — Oh, I'm impatient, sir, to be discounting the mighty debt I owe you. Command me quickly.

60 ANTONIO: I have a quarrel with a rival, sir, about the maid we love.

BELVILE (*aside*): Death, 'tis Florinda he means! That thought destroys my reason, and I shall kill him.

ANTONIO: My rival, sir, is one has all the virtues man
65 can boast of —

BELVILE (*aside*): Death, who should this be?

ANTONIO: He challenged me to meet him on the Molo as soon as day appeared, but last night's quarrel has made my arm unfit to guide a sword.

70 BELVILE: I apprehend you, sir. You'd have me kill the man that lays a claim to the maid you speak of. I'll do't. I'll fly to do't!

ANTONIO: Sir, do you know her?

BELVILE: No, sir, but 'tis enough she is admired by you.

75 ANTONIO: Sir, I shall rob you of the glory on't, for you must fight under my name and dress.

BELVILE: That opinion must be strangely obliging that makes you think I can personate the brave Antonio, whom I can but strive to imitate.

80 ANTONIO: You say too much to my advantage. Come, sir, the day appears that calls you forth. Within, sir, is the habit.°   (*Exit Antonio.*)

---

48. Obliged by: Favored by.   **82. habit:** Antonio's clothing.

BELVILE: Fantastic fortune, thou deceitful light,
    That cheats the wearied traveler by night,
    Though on a precipice each step you tread,   85
    I am resolved to follow where you lead.   (*Exit.*)

Scene II

(*The Molo. Enter Florinda and Callis in masks, with Stephano.*)

FLORINDA (*aside*): I'm dying with my fears: Belvile's not coming as I expected under my window makes me believe that all those fears are true. — Canst thou not tell with whom my brother fights?

STEPHANO: No, madam, they were both in masquerade.   5
    I was by when they challenged one another, and they had decided the quarrel then, but were prevented by some cavaliers; which made 'em put it off till now. But I am sure 'tis about you they fight.

FLORINDA (*aside*): Nay, then, 'tis with Belvile, for what   10
    other lover have I that dares fight for me except Antonio, and he is too much in favor with my brother. If it be he, for whom shall I direct my prayers to heaven?

STEPHANO: Madam, I must leave you, for if my master see me, I shall be hanged for being your conductor. I   15
    escaped narrowly for the excuse I made for you last night i'th' garden.

FLORINDA: I'll reward thee for't. Prithee, no more.
                    (*Exit Stephano.*)

(*Enter Don Pedro in his masking habit.*)

PEDRO: Antonio's late today; the place will fill, and we may be prevented.   (*Walks about.*)   20

FLORINDA (*aside*): Antonio? Sure I heard amiss.

PEDRO: But who will not excuse a happy lover
    When soft fair arms confine the yielding neck,
    And the kind whisper languishingly breathes
    "Must you be gone so soon?"   25
    Sure I had dwelt forever on her bosom —
    But stay, he's here.

(*Enter Belvile dressed in Antonio's clothes.*)

FLORINDA [*aside*]: 'Tis not Belvile; half my fears are vanished.

PEDRO: Antonio!   30

BELVILE (*aside*): This must be he. — You're early, sir; I do not use to be outdone this way.

PEDRO: The wretched, sir, are watchful, and 'tis enough you've the advantage of me in Angellica.

BELVILE (*aside*): Angellica! Or° I've mistook my man, or   35
    else Antonio! Can he forget his interest in Florinda and fight for common prize?

PEDRO: Come, sir, you know our terms.

BELVILE (*aside*): By heaven, not I. — No talking; I am ready, sir.   40

(*Offers to fight; Florinda runs in.*)

---

35. Or: Either.

FLORINDA (*to Belvile*): Oh, hold! Whoever you be, I do
    conjure you hold! If you strike here, I die!
PEDRO: Florinda!
BELVILE: Florinda imploring for my rival!
45 PEDRO: Away; this kindness is unseasonable.

(*Puts her by; they fight; she runs in just as Belvile disarms Pedro.*)

FLORINDA: Who are you, sir, that dares deny my prayers?
BELVILE: Thy prayers destroy him; if thou wouldst preserve him, do that thou'rt unacquainted with, and
    curse him.
                         (*She holds him.*)
50 FLORINDA: By all you hold most dear, by her you love,
    I do conjure you, touch him not.
BELVILE: By her I love?
    See, I obey, and at your feet resign
    The useless trophy of my victory.

(*Lays his sword at her feet.*)

55 PEDRO: Antonio, you've done enough to prove you love
    Florinda.
BELVILE: Love Florinda! Does heaven love adoration,
    prayer, or penitence? Love her? Here, sir, your sword
    again.

(*Snatches up the sword and gives it to him.*)

60   Upon this truth I'll fight my life away.
PEDRO: No, you've redeemed my sister, and my friendship.

(*He gives him Florinda, and pulls off his vizard to show his face, and puts it on again.*)

BELVILE: Don Pedro!
PEDRO: Can you resign your claims to other women,
65   and give your heart entirely to Florinda?
BELVILE: Entire, as dying saints' confessions are!
    I can delay my happiness no longer:
    This minute let me make Florinda mine.
PEDRO: This minute let it be. No time so proper: This
70   night my father will arrive from Rome, and possibly
    may hinder what we purpose.
FLORINDA: O, heavens! This minute?

(*Enter Masqueraders and pass over.*)

BELVILE: Oh, do not ruin me!
PEDRO: The place begins to fill, and that we may not be
75   observed, do you walk off to St. Peter's church,
    where I will meet you and conclude your happiness.
BELVILE: I'll meet you there. — (*Aside.*) If there be no
    more saints' churches in Naples.
FLORINDA: Oh, stay, sir, and recall your hasty doom!
80   Alas, I have not yet prepared my heart
    To entertain so strange a guest.
PEDRO: Away; this silly modesty is assumed too late.
BELVILE: Heaven, madam, what do you do?
FLORINDA: Do? Despise the man that lays a tyrant's
    claim
85   To what he ought to conquer by submission.

BELVILE: You do not know me. Move a little this way.
                        (*Draws her aside.*)
FLORINDA: Yes, you may force me even to the altar,
    But not the holy man that offers there
    Shall force me to be thine.

(*Pedro talks to Callis this while.*)

BELVILE: Oh, do not lose so blest an opportunity!   90

(*Pulls off his vizard.*)

    See, 'tis your Belvile, not Antonio,
    Whom your mistaken scorn and anger ruins.
FLORINDA: Belvile!
    Where was my soul it could not meet thy voice,
    And take this knowledge in.   95

(*As they are talking, enter Willmore, finely dressed, and Frederick.*)

WILLMORE: No intelligence? No news of Belvile yet?
    Well, I am the most unlucky rascal in nature. Ha! Am
    I deceived, or is it he? Look, Fred! 'Tis he, my dear
    Belvile!

(*Runs and embraces him; Belvile's vizard falls out on's hand.*)

BELVILE: Hell and confusion seize thee!   100
PEDRO: Ha! Belvile! I beg your pardon, sir.

(*Takes Florinda from him.*)

BELVILE: Nay, touch her not. She's mine by conquest, sir;
    I won her by my sword.
WILLMORE: Didst thou so? And egad, child, we'll keep
    her by the sword.   105

(*Draws on Pedro; Belvile goes between.*)

BELVILE: Stand off!
    Thou'rt so profanely lewd, so curst by heaven,
    All quarrels thou espousest must be fatal.
WILLMORE: Nay, an you be so hot, my valor's coy,
    And shall be courted when you want it next.   110
                        (*Puts up his sword.*)
BELVILE (*to Pedro*): You know I ought to claim a
    victor's right,
    But you're the brother to divine Florinda,
    To whom I'm such a slave. To purchase her
    I durst not hurt the man she holds so dear.
PEDRO: 'Twas by Antonio's, not by Belvile's
    sword   115
    This question should have been decided, sir.
    I must confess much to your bravery's due,
    Both now and when I met you last in arms;
    But I am nicely punctual in my word,
    As men of honor ought, and beg your pardon: 120
    For this mistake another time shall clear.

(*Aside to Florinda as they are going out.*)

    — This was some plot between you and Belvile,
    But I'll prevent you.
                 [*Exeunt Pedro and Florinda.*]

(*Belvile looks after her and begins to walk up and down in rage.*)

WILLMORE: Do not be modest now and lose the woman.
125   But if we shall fetch her back so —
BELVILE: Do not speak to me!
WILLMORE: Not speak to you? Egad, I'll speak to you, and will be answered, too.
BELVILE: Will you, sir?
130   WILLMORE: I know I've done some mischief, but I'm so dull a puppy that I'm the son of a whore if I know how or where. Prithee inform my understanding.
BELVILE: Leave me, I say, and leave me instantly!
WILLMORE: I will not leave you in this humor, nor till I
135   know my crime.
BELVILE: Death, I'll tell you, sir —

(*Draws and runs at Willmore; he runs out, Belvile after him; Frederick interposes.*)

(*Enter Angellica, Moretta, and Sebastian.*)

ANGELLICA: Ha! Sebastian, is that not Willmore? Haste! haste and bring him back.

[*Exit Sebastian.*]

FREDERICK [*aside*]: The colonel's mad: I never saw him
140   thus before. I'll after 'em lest he do some mischief, for I am sure Willmore will not draw on him.   (*Exit.*)
ANGELLICA: I am all rage! My first desires defeated! For one for aught he knows that has no Other merit than her quality, Her being Don Pedro's sister. He loves her!
145   I know 'tis so. Dull, dull, insensible, He will not see me now, though oft invited, And broke his word last night. False perjured man! He that but yesterday fought for my favors, And would have made his life a sacrifice
150   To've gained one night with me, Must now be hired and courted to my arms.
MORETTA: I told you what would come on't, but Moretta's an old doting fool. Why did you give him five hundred crowns, but to set himself out for other
155   lovers? You should have kept him poor if you had meant to have had any good from him.
ANGELLICA: Oh, name not such mean trifles! Had I given Him all my youth has earned from sin, I had not lost a thought nor sigh upon't.
160   But I have given him my eternal rest, My whole repose, my future joys, my heart! My virgin heart, Moretta! Oh, 'tis gone!
MORETTA: Curse on him, here he comes. How fine she has made him, too.
165
(*Enter Willmore and Sebastian; Angellica turns and walks away.*)

WILLMORE: How now, turned shadow? Fly when I pursue, and follow when I fly? (*Sings.*)
Stay, gentle shadow of my dove,
    And tell me ere I go,

Whether the substance may not prove   170
    A fleeting thing like you.

(*As she turns she looks on him.*)

There's a soft kind look remaining yet.
ANGELLICA: Well, sir, you may be gay: All happiness, all joys pursue you still. Fortune's your slave, and gives you every hour choice of new hearts and beauties, till   175
you are cloyed° with the repeated bliss which others vainly languish for. But know, false man, that I shall be revenged.

(*Turns away in rage.*)

WILLMORE: So, gad, there are of those faint-hearted lovers, whom such a sharp lesson next their hearts   180
would make as impotent as fourscore.° Pox o' this whining; my business is to laugh and love. A pox on't, I hate your sullen lover: A man shall lose as much time to put you in humor now as would serve to gain a new woman.   185
ANGELLICA: I scorn to cool that fire I cannot raise, Or do the drudgery of your virtuous mistress.
WILLMORE: A virtuous mistress? Death, what a thing thou hast found out for me! Why, what the devil should I do with a virtuous woman, a sort of ill-   190
natured creatures that take a pride to torment a lover. Virtue is but an infirmity in woman, a disease that renders even the handsome ungrateful; whilst the ill-favored, for want of solicitations and address, only fancy themselves so. I have lain with a woman of   195
quality who has all the while been railing at whores.
ANGELLICA: I will not answer for your mistress's virtue, Though she be young enough to know no guilt; And I could wish you would persuade my heart 'Twas the two hundred thousand crowns you courted.   200
WILLMORE: Two hundred thousand crowns! What story's this? What trick? What woman, ha?
ANGELLICA: How strange you make it. Have you forgot the creature you entertained on the Piazzo last night?   205
WILLMORE (*aside*): Ha! My gypsy worth two hundred thousand crowns! Oh, how I long to be with her! Pox, I knew she was of quality.
ANGELLICA: False man! I see my ruin in thy face. How many vows you breathed upon my bosom   210
Never to be unjust. Have you forgot so soon?
WILLMORE: Faith, no; I was just coming to repeat 'em. But here's a humor indeed would make a man a saint. — (*Aside.*) Would she would be angry enough to leave me, and command me not to wait on her.   215

(*Enter Hellena dressed in man's clothes.*)

HELLENA: This must be Angellica: I know it by her mumping° matron here. Ay, ay, 'tis she. My mad captain's with her, too, for all his swearing. How this

---

176. **cloyed:** Full to bursting.   181. **as fourscore:** As an eighty-year-old.   217. **mumping:** Moping.

220 unconstant humor makes me love him! — Pray, good
grave gentlewoman, is not this Angellica?

MORETTA: My too young sir, it is. — [*Aside.*] I hope 'tis
one from Don Antonio.   (*Goes to Angellica.*)

HELLENA (*aside*): Well, something I'll do to vex him for
this.

225 ANGELLICA: I will not speak with him. Am I in humor to
receive a lover?

WILLMORE: Not speak with him? Why, I'll be gone, and
wait your idler minutes. Can I show less obedience to
the thing I love so fondly?

(*Offers to go.*)

230 ANGELLICA: A fine excuse this! Stay —

WILLMORE: And hinder your advantage? Should I repay
your bounties so ungratefully?

ANGELLICA [*to Hellena*]: Come hither, boy. —
[*To Willmore.*] That I may let you see

235 How much above the advantages you name
I prize one minute's joy with you.

WILLMORE (*impatient to be gone*): Oh, you destroy me
with this endearment. — [*Aside.*] Death, how shall
I get away? — Madam, 'twill not be fit I should be

240 seen with you. Besides, it will not be convenient. And
I've a friend — that's dangerously sick.

ANGELLICA: I see you're impatient. Yet you shall stay.

WILLMORE (*aside*): And miss my assignation with my
gypsy.

(*Walks about impatiently; Moretta brings Hellena, who
addresses herself to Angellica.*)

245 HELLENA: Madam,
You'll hardly pardon my intrusion
When you shall know my business,
And I'm too young to tell my tale with art;
But there must be a wondrous store of goodness

250 Where so much beauty dwells.

ANGELLICA: A pretty advocate, whoever sent thee.
Prithee proceed.

(*To Willmore, who is stealing off.*)

          — Nay, sir, you shall not go.

WILLMORE (*aside*): Then I shall lose my dear gypsy forever. Pox on't, she stays me out of spite.

255 HELLENA: I am related to a lady, madam,
Young, rich, and nobly born, but has the fate
To be in love with a young English gentleman.
Strangely she loves him, at first sight she loved him,
But did adore him when she heard him speak;

260 For he, she said, had charms in every word
That failed not to surprise, to wound and conquer.

WILLMORE (*aside*): Ha! Egad, I hope this concerns me.

ANGELLICA (*aside*): 'Tis my false man he means. Would
he were gone:
This praise will raise his pride, and ruin me.
(*To Willmore.*) — Well,

265 Since you are so impatient to be gone,
I will release you, sir.

WILLMORE (*aside*): Nay, then I'm sure 'twas me he
spoke of: This cannot be the effects of kindness in

her. — No, Madam, I've considered better on't, and
will not give you cause of jealousy.   270

ANGELLICA: But sir, I've business that —

WILLMORE: This shall not do; I know 'tis but to try me.

ANGELLICA: Well, to your story, boy. — (*Aside*). Though
'twill undo me.

HELLENA: With this addition to his other beauties,   275
He won her unresisting tender heart.
He vowed, and sighed, and swore he loved her
dearly;
And she believed the cunning flatterer,
And thought herself the happiest maid alive.
Today was the appointed time by both   280
To consummate their bliss:
The virgin, altar, and the priest were dressed;
And whilst she languished for th'expected
bridegroom,
She heard he paid his broken vows to you.

WILLMORE (*aside*): So, this is some dear rogue that's in   285
love with me, and this way lets me know it. Or, if
it be not me, he means someone whose place I may
supply.

ANGELLICA: Now I perceive
The cause of thy impatience to be gone,   290
And all the business of this glorious dress.

WILLMORE: Damn the young prater; I know not what
he means.

HELLENA: Madam,
In your fair eyes I read too much concern   295
To tell my further business.

ANGELLICA: Prithee, sweet youth, talk on: Thou mayst
perhaps
Raise here a storm that may undo my passion,
And then I'll grant thee anything.

HELLENA: Madam, 'tis to entreat you (oh
unreasonable)   300
You would not see this stranger.
For if you do, she vows you are undone;
Though nature never made a man so excellent,
And sure he 'ad been a god, but for inconstancy.

WILLMORE (*aside*): Ah, rogue, how finely he's instructed! 305
'Tis plain, some woman that has seen me *en passant*.°

ANGELLICA: Oh, I shall burst with jealousy! Do you
know the man you speak of?

HELLENA: Yes, madam, he used to be in buff and scarlet.

ANGELLICA (*to Willmore*): Thou false as hell, what canst   310
thou say to this?

WILLMORE: By heaven —

ANGELLICA: Hold, do not damn thyself —

HELLENA: Nor hope to be believed.

(*He walks about; they follow.*)

ANGELLICA: Oh perjured man!   315
Is't thus you pay my generous passion back?

HELLENA: Why would you, sir, abuse my lady's faith?

ANGELLICA: And use me so unhumanely.

HELLENA: A maid so young, so innocent —

---

306. en passant: In passing.

320 WILLMORE: Ah, young devil!

ANGELLICA: Dost thou not know thy life is in my power?

HELLENA: Or think my lady cannot be revenged?

WILLMORE (*aside*): So, so, the storm comes finely on.

ANGELLICA: Now thou art silent: Guilt has struck thee
325   dumb.

Oh, hadst thou still been so, I'd lived in safety.

(*She turns away and weeps.*)

WILLMORE (*aside to Hellena*): Sweetheart, the lady's name and house — quickly! I'm impatient to be with her.

(*Looks toward Angellica to watch her turning, and as she comes towards them he meets her.*)

330 HELLENA (*aside*): So, now is he for another woman.

WILLMORE: The impudent'st young thing in nature:
I cannot persuade him out of his error, madam.

ANGELLICA: I know he's in the right; yet thou'st a tongue
That would persuade him to deny his faith.

(*In rage walks away.*)

335 WILLMORE (*said softly to Hellena*): Her name, her name, dear boy!

HELLENA: Have you forgot it, sir?

WILLMORE (*aside*): Oh, I perceive he's not to know I am a stranger to his lady. — Yes, yes, I do know, but I
340   have forgot the — (*Angellica turns.*) — By heaven, such early confidence I never saw.

ANGELLICA: Did I not charge you with this mistress, sir?
Which you denied, though I beheld your perjury.
This little generosity of thine has rendered back my heart.   (*Walks away.*)

345 WILLMORE (*to Hellena*): So, you have made sweet work here, my little mischief. Look your lady be kind and good-natured now, or I shall have but a cursed bargain on't. (*Angellica turns toward them.*) — The rogue's bred up to mischief; art thou so great a fool
350   to credit him?

ANGELLICA: Yes, I do, and you in vain impose upon me. Come hither, boy. Is not this he you spake of?

HELLENA: I think it is. I cannot swear, but I vow he has just such another lying lover's look.

(*Hellena looks in his face; he gazes on her.*)

355 WILLMORE (*aside*): Ha! Do I not know that face? By heaven, my little gypsy! What a dull dog was I: Had I but looked that way I'd known her. Are all my hopes of a new woman banished? — Egad, if I do not fit thee for this, hang me. — [*To Angellica.*] Madam, I
360   have found out the plot.

HELLENA [*aside*]: Oh lord, what does he say? Am I discovered now?

WILLMORE: Do you see this young spark here?

HELLENA [*aside*]: He'll tell her who I am.

365 WILLMORE: Who do you think this is?

HELLENA [*aside*]: Ay, ay, he does know me. — Nay, dear captain, I am undone if you discover me.

WILLMORE: Nay, nay, no cogging;° she shall know what a precious mistress I have.

HELLENA: Will you be such a devil?   370

WILLMORE: Nay, nay, I'll teach you to spoil sport you will not make. — This small ambassador comes not from a person of quality, as you imagine and he says, but from a very errant gypsy: the talking'st, prating'st, canting'st little animal thou ever saw'st.   375

ANGELLICA: What news you tell me, that's the thing I mean.

HELLENA (*aside*): Would I were well off the place! If ever I go a-captain-hunting again —

WILLMORE: Mean that thing? That gypsy thing? Thou   380
mayst as well be jealous of thy monkey or parrot as of her. A German motion° were worth a dozen of her, and a dream were a better enjoyment — a creature of a constitution fitter for heaven than man.

HELLENA (*aside*): Though I'm sure he lies, yet this vexes   385
me.

ANGELLICA: You are mistaken: she's a Spanish woman made up of no such dull materials.

WILLMORE: Materials? Egad, an she be made of any that will either dispense or admit of love, I'll be   390
bound to continence.

HELLENA (*aside to him*): Unreasonable man, do you think so?

WILLMORE: You may return, my little brazen head, and tell your lady, that till she be handsome enough to be   395
beloved, or I dull enough to be religious, there will be small hopes of me.

ANGELLICA: Did you not promise, then, to marry her?

WILLMORE: Not I, by heaven.

ANGELLICA: You cannot undeceive my fears and tor-   400
ments, till you have vowed you will not marry her.

HELLENA (*aside*): If he swears that, he'll be revenged on me indeed for all my rogueries.

ANGELLICA: I know what arguments you'll bring against me: fortune and honor.   405

WILLMORE: Honor! I tell you, I hate it in your sex; and those that fancy themselves possessed of that foppery are the most impertinently troublesome of all womankind, and will transgress nine commandments to keep one. And to satisfy your jealousy, I   410
swear —

HELLENA (*aside to him*): Oh, no swearing, dear captain.

WILLMORE: If it were possible I should ever be inclined to marry, it should be some kind young sinner: one that has generosity enough to give a favor hand-   415
somely to one that can ask it discreetly, one that has wit enough to manage an intrigue of love. Oh, how civil such a wench is to a man that does her the honor to marry her.

ANGELLICA: By heaven, there's no faith in anything he   420
says.

(*Enter Sebastian.*)

368. cogging: Fawning, coaxing.   **382. motion:** Puppet show.

SEBASTIAN: Madam, Don Antonio —
ANGELLICA: Come hither.
HELLENA [aside]: Ha! Antonio! He may be coming
425   hither, and he'll certainly discover me. I'll therefore
retire without a ceremony.   (Exit Hellena.)
ANGELLICA: I'll see him. Get my coach ready.
SEBASTIAN: It waits you, madam.
WILLMORE [aside]: This is lucky. — What, madam, now
430   I may be gone and leave you to the enjoyment of my
rival?
ANGELLICA: Dull man, that canst not see how ill, how
poor,
That false dissimulation looks. Be gone,
And never let me see thy cozening face again,
435   Lest I relapse and kill thee.
WILLMORE: Yes, you can spare me now. Farewell, till
you're in better humor. — [Aside.] I'm glad of this
release. Now for my gypsy:
For though to worse we change, yet still we find
440   New joys, new charms, in a new miss that's kind.
                    (Exit Willmore.)
ANGELLICA: He's gone, and in this ague° of my soul
The shivering fit returns.
Oh, with what willing haste he took his leave,
As if the longed-for minute were arrived
445   Of some blest assignation.
In vain I have consulted all my charms,
In vain this beauty prized, in vain believed
My eyes could kindle any lasting fires;
I had forgot my name, my infamy,
450   And the reproach that honor lays on those
That dare pretend a sober passion here.
Nice reputation, though it leave behind
More virtues than inhabit where that dwells,
Yet that once gone, those virtues shine no more.
455   Then since I am not fit to be beloved,
I am resolved to think on a revenge
On him that soothed° me thus to my undoing.
                    (Exeunt.)

Scene III

(*A street. Enter Florinda and Valeria in habits different
from what they have been seen in.*)

FLORINDA: We're happily escaped, and yet I tremble
still.
VALERIA: A lover, and fear? Why, I am but half an one,
and yet I have courage for any attempt. Would Hel-
5   lena were here: I would fain have had her as deep in
this mischief as we; she'll fare but ill else, I doubt.
FLORINDA: She pretended a visit to the Augustine nuns;
but I believe some other design carried her out; pray
heaven we light on her. Prithee, what didst do with
10   Callis?

---
441. ague: Fever, accompanied by shivering.   **457. soothed:**
Advised.

VALERIA: When I saw no reason would do good on her, I
followed her into the wardrobe, and as she was looking for something in a great chest, I toppled her in by
the heels, snatched the key of the apartment where
you were confined, locked her in, and left her bawl-   15
ing for help.
FLORINDA: 'Tis well you resolve to follow my fortunes,
for thou darest never appear at home again after such
an action.
VALERIA: That's according as the young stranger and I   20
shall agree. But to our business. I delivered your note
to Belvile when I got out under pretense of going to
mass. I found him at his lodging, and believe me it
came seasonably, for never was man in so desperate a
condition. I told him of your resolution of making   25
your escape today if your brother would be absent
long enough to permit you; if not, to die rather than
be Antonio's.
FLORINDA: Thou should'st have told him I was confined
to my chamber upon my brother's suspicion that the   30
business on the Molo was a plot laid between him
and I.
VALERIA: I said all this, and told him your brother was
now gone to his devotion; and he resolves to visit
every church till he find him, and not only undeceive   35
him in that, but caress him so as shall delay his return
home.
FLORINDA: Oh heavens! He's here, and Belvile with him,
too.
(*They put on their vizards.*)

(*Enter Don Pedro, Belvile, Willmore; Belvile and Don
Pedro seeming in serious discourse.*)

VALERIA: Walk boldly by them, and I'll come at a dis-   40
tance, lest he suspect us.

(*She walks by them and looks back on them.*)

WILLMORE: Ha! A woman, and of excellent mien!
PEDRO: She throws a kind look back on you.
WILLMORE: Death, 'tis a likely wench and that kind
look shall not be cast away. I'll follow her.   45
BELVILE: Prithee do not.
WILLMORE: Do not? By heavens, to the antipodies,°
with such an invitation.

                    (*She goes out, and Willmore follows her.*)

BELVILE: 'Tis a mad fellow for a wench.

(*Enter Frederick.*)

FREDERICK: Oh, colonel, such news!   50
BELVILE: Prithee what?
FREDERICK: News that will make you laugh in spite of
fortune.
BELVILE: What, Blunt has had some damned trick put
upon him? Cheated, banged, or clapped?°   55

---
47. antipodies: Antipodes; parts of the earth diametrically opposite.   **55. clapped:** Given gonorrhea.

FREDERICK: Cheated, sir, rarely cheated of all but his shirt and drawers; the unconscionable whore too turned him out before consummation, so that, traversing the streets at midnight, the watch found him
60 in this *fresco* and conducted him home. By heaven, 'tis such a sight, and yet I durst as well been hanged as laughed at him or pity him: He beats all that do but ask him a question, and is in such an humor.

PEDRO: Who is't has met with this ill usage, sir?

65 BELVILE: A friend of ours whom you must see for mirth's sake. — (*Aside.*) I'll employ him to give Florinda time for an escape.

PEDRO: What is he?

BELVILE: A young countryman of ours, one that has
70 been educated at so plentiful a rate he yet ne'er knew the want of money; and 'twill be a great jest to see how simply he'll look without it. For my part, I'll lend him none: And the rogue know not how to put on a borrowing face and ask first, I'll let him see how
75 good 'tis to play our parts whilst I play his. Prithee, Fred, do you go home and keep him in that posture till we come.   (*Exeunt.*)

(*Enter Florinda from the farther end of the scene, looking behind her.*)

FLORINDA: I am followed still. Ha! My brother too advancing this way! Good heavens defend me from
80 being seen by him!   (*She goes off.*)

(*Enter Willmore, and after him Valeria, at a little distance.*)

WILLMORE: Ah, there she sails! She looks back as she were willing to be boarded; I'll warrant her prize.°

                      (*He goes out, Valeria following.*)

(*Enter Hellena, just as he goes out, with a page.*)

HELLENA: Ha, is not that my captain that has a woman in chase? 'Tis not Angellica. — Boy, follow those
85 people at a distance, and bring me an account where they go in.   (*Exit Page.*)
    — I'll find his haunts, and plague him everywhere. Ha! My brother!

                      (*Belvile, Willmore, Pedro cross the stage;*
                      Hellena runs off.)

Scene IV

(*Scene changes to another street. Enter Florinda.*)

FLORINDA: What shall I do? My brother now pursues me. Will no kind power protect me from his tyranny? Ha! Here's a door open; I'll venture in, since nothing can be worse than to fall into his hands. My life and
5 honor are at stake, and my necessity has no choice.
                      (*She goes in.*)

82. **warrant her prize:** Consider her worthy of pursuing.

(*Enter Valeria, Hellena's Page peeping after Florinda.*)

PAGE: Here she went in; I shall remember this house.
                      (*Exit Boy.*)

VALERIA: This is Belvile's lodging, she's gone in as readily as if she knew it. Ha! Here's that mad fellow again; I dare not venture in. I'll watch my opportunity.
                      (*Goes aside.*)

(*Enter Willmore, gazing about him.*)

WILLMORE: I have lost her hereabouts. Pox on't, she 10
must not 'scape me so.   (*Goes out.*)

Scene V

(*Scene changes to Blunt's chamber, discovers him sitting on a couch in his shirt and drawers, reading.*)

BLUNT: So, now my mind's a little at peace, since I have resolved revenge. A pox on this tailor, though, for not bringing home the clothes I bespoke. And a pox of all poor cavaliers: A man can never keep a spare suit for 'em, and I shall have these rogues come in and find me 5
naked, and then I'm undone. But I'm resolved to arm myself: The rascals shall not insult over me too much. (*Puts on an old rusty sword and buff belt.*) Now, how like a morris dancer° I am equipped! A fine ladylike whore to cheat me thus without affording me a kind- 10
ness for my money! A pox light on her, I shall never be reconciled to the sex more; she has made me as faithless as a physician, as uncharitable as a churchman, and as ill-natured as a poet. Oh, how I'll use all womankind hereafter! What would I give to have one of 15
'em within my reach now! Any mortal thing in petticoats, kind fortune, send me, and I'll forgive thy last night's malice. — Here's a cursed book, too — a warning to all young travelers — that can instruct me how to prevent such mischiefs now 'tis too late. Well, 20
'tis a rare convenient thing to read a little now and then, as well as hawk and hunt.

                      (*Sits down again and reads.*)

(*Enter to him Florinda.*)

FLORINDA: This house is haunted, sure: 'Tis well furnished, and no living thing inhabits it. Ha! A man! Heavens, how he's attired! Sure 'tis some rope 25
dancer, or fencing master. I tremble now for fear, and yet I must venture now to speak to him. — Sir, if I may not interrupt your meditations —

                      (*He starts up and gazes.*)

BLUNT: Ha, what's here? Are my wishes granted? And is not that a she creature? 'Adsheartlikins, 'tis. — What 30
wretched thing art thou, ha?

FLORINDA: Charitable sir, you've told yourself already

IV, v, 9. **morris dancer:** The morris dance is a lively dance performed by men wearing costumes and bells.

what I am: a very wretched maid, forced by a strange unlucky accident to seek a safety here, and must be ruined if you do not grant it.

BLUNT: Ruined! Is there any ruin so inevitable as that which now threatens thee? Dost thou know, miserable woman, into what den of mischiefs thou art fallen; what abyss of confusion, ha? Dost not see something in my looks that frights thy guilty soul, and makes thee wish to change that shape of woman for any humble animal, or devil? For those were safer for thee, and less mischievous.

FLORINDA: Alas, what mean you, sir? I must confess, your looks have something in 'em makes me fear, but I beseech you, as you seem a gentleman, pity a harmless virgin that takes your house for sanctuary.

BLUNT: Talk on, talk on; and weep, too, till my faith so return. Do, flatter me out of my senses again. A harmless virgin with a pox; as much one as t'other, 'adsheartlikins. Why, what the devil, can I not be safe in my house for you, not in my chamber? Nay, not even being naked too cannot secure me? This is an impudence greater than has invaded me yet. Come, no resistance.   (*Pulls her rudely.*)

FLORINDA: Dare you be so cruel?

BLUNT: Cruel? 'Adsheartlikins, as a galley slave, or a Spanish whore. Cruel? Yes, I will kiss and beat thee all over, kiss and see thee all over; thou shalt lie with me too, not that I care for the enjoyment, but to let thee see I have ta'en deliberated malice to thee, and will be revenged on one whore for the sins of another. I will smile and deceive thee; flatter thee, and beat thee; embrace thee and rob thee, as she did me; fawn on thee, and strip thee stark naked; then hang thee out at my window by the heels, with a paper of scurvy verses fastened to thy breast in praise of damnable women. Come, come, along.

FLORINDA: Alas, sir, must I be sacrificed for the crimes of the most infamous of my sex? I never understood the sins you name.

BLUNT: Do, persuade the fool you love him, or that, one of you can be just or honest; tell me I was not an easy coxcomb, or any strange impossible tale: It will be believed sooner than thy false showers or protestations. A generation of damned hypocrites! To flatter my very clothes from my back! Dissembling witches! Are these the returns you make an honest gentleman that trusts, believes, and loves you? But if I be not even with you — Come along, or I shall — (*Pulls her again.*)

(*Enter Frederick.*)

FREDERICK: Ha, what's here to do?

BLUNT: 'Adsheartlikins, Fred, I am glad thou art come, to be a witness of my dire revenge.

FREDERICK: What's this, a person of quality too, who is upon the ramble° to supply the defects of some grave impotent husband?

---

85. **upon the ramble:** Rambling, wandering.

BLUNT: No, this has another pretense: Some very unfortunate accident brought her hither, to save a life pursued by I know not who or why, and forced to take sanctuary here at fool's haven. 'Adsheartlikins, to me of all mankind for protection? Is the ass to be cajoled again, think ye? No, young one, no prayers or tears shall mitigate my rage; therefore prepare for both my pleasures of enjoyment and revenge. For I am resolved to make up my loss here on thy body: I'll take it out in kindness and in beating.

FREDERICK: Now, mistress of mine, what do you think of this?

FLORINDA: I think he will not, dares not be so barbarous.

FREDERICK: Have a care, Blunt, she fetched a deep sigh; she is enamored with thy shirt and drawers. She'll strip thee even of that; there are of her calling such unconscionable baggages and such dexterous thieves, they'll flea° a man and he shall ne'er miss his skin till he feels the cold. There was a countryman of ours robbed of a row of teeth whilst he was a-sleeping, which the jilt made him buy again when he waked. You see, lady, how little reason we have to trust you.

BLUNT: 'Adsheartlikins, why this is most abominable!

FLORINDA: Some such devils there may be, but by all that's holy, I am none such. I entered here to save a life in danger.

BLUNT: For no goodness, I'll warrant her.

FREDERICK: Faith, damsel, you had e'en confessed the plain truth, for we are fellows not to be caught twice in the same trap. Look on that wreck: a tight vessel when he set out of haven, well trimmed and laden. And see how a female picaroon of this island of rogues has shattered him, and canst thou hope for any mercy?

BLUNT: No, no, gentlewoman, come along; 'adsheartlikins, we must be better acquainted. — We'll both lie with her, and then let me alone to bang her.

FREDERICK: I'm ready to serve you in matters of revenge that has a double pleasure in't.

BLUNT: Well said. — You hear, little one, how you are condemned by public vote to the bed within; there's no resisting your destiny, sweetheart.

(*Pulls her.*)

FLORINDA: Stay, sir. I have seen you with Belvile, an English cavalier. For his sake, use me kindly. You know him, sir.

BLUNT: Belvile? Why yes, sweeting, we do know Belvile, and wish he were with us now. He's a cormorant at whore and bacon:° He'd have a limb or two of thee, my virgin pullet. But 'tis no matter; we'll leave him the bones to pick.

FLORINDA: Sir, if you have any esteem for that Belvile, I conjure you to treat me with more gentleness; he'll thank you for the justice.

FREDERICK: Hark'ee, Blunt, I doubt we are mistaken in this matter.

---

104. **flea:** Strip off the skin (flay).   **133–34. cormorant . . . bacon:** Glutton for sex.

FLORINDA: Sir, if you find me not worth Belvile's care, use me as you please. And that you may think I merit better treatment than you threaten, pray take this
145 present.

(*Gives him a ring; he looks on it.*)

BLUNT: Hum, a diamond! Why, 'tis a wonderful virtue now that lies in this ring, a mollifying virtue. 'Adsheartlikins, there's more persuasive rhetoric in't than all her sex can utter.
150 FREDERICK: I begin to suspect something, and 'twould anger us vilely to be trussed up for a rape upon a maid of quality, when we only believe we ruffle a harlot.
BLUNT: Thou art a credulous fellow, but 'adsheartlikins, I have no faith yet. Why, my saint prattled as par-
155 lously as this does; she gave me a bracelet, too, a devil on her! But I sent my man to sell it today for necessaries, and it proved as counterfeit as her vows of love.
FREDERICK: However, let it reprieve her till we see
160 Belvile.
BLUNT: That's hard, yet I will grant it.

(*Enter a Servant.*)

SERVANT: Oh, sir, the colonel is just come in with his new friend and a Spaniard of quality, and talks of having you to dinner with 'em.
165 BLUNT: 'Adsheartlikins, I'm undone! I would not see 'em for the world. Hark'ee, Fred, lock up the wench in your chamber.
FREDERICK: Fear nothing, madam: Whate'er he threatens, you are safe whilst in my hands.

(*Exeunt Frederick and Florinda.*)

170 BLUNT: And sirrah, upon your life, say I am not at home, or that I'm asleep, or — or — anything. Away; I'll prevent their coming this way.

(*Locks the door, and exeunt.*)

ACT V

(*Blunt's chamber. After a great knocking as at his chamber door, enter Blunt softly crossing the stage, in his shirt and drawers as before.*)

[VOICES] (*call within*): Ned! Ned Blunt! Ned Blunt!
BLUNT: The rogues are up in arms. 'Adsheartlikins, this villainous Frederick has betrayed me: They have heard of my blessed fortune.
5 [VOICES] (*and knocking within*): Ned Blunt! Ned! Ned!
BELVILE [*within*]: Why, he's dead, sir, without dispute dead, sir, without dispute dead; he has not been seen today. Let's break open the door. Here, boy —
BLUNT: Ha, break open the door? 'Adsheartlikins, that
10 mad fellow will be as good as his word.
BELVILE [*within*]: Boy, bring something to force the door.

(*A great noise within, at the door again.*)

BLUNT: So, now must I speak in my own defense, I'll try what rhetoric will do. — Hold, hold! What do you mean, gentlemen, what do you mean?
BELVILE (*within*): Oh, rogue, art alive? Prithee open the 15 door and convince us.
BLUNT: Yes, I am alive, gentlemen, but at present a little busy.
BELVILE (*within*): How, Blunt grown a man of business? Come, come, open and let's see this miracle. 20
BLUNT: No, no, no, no, gentlemen, 'tis no great business. But — I am — at — my devotion. 'Adsheartlikins, will you not allow a man time to pray?
BELVILE (*within*): Turned religious? A greater wonder than the first! Therefore open quickly, or we shall 25 unhinge, we shall.
BLUNT [*aside*]: This won't do. — Why hark'ee, colonel, to tell you the truth, I am about a necessary affair of life: I have a wench with me. You apprehend me? — The devil's in't if they be so uncivil as to disturb me 30 now.
WILLMORE [*within*]: How, a wench? Nay then, we must enter and partake. No resistance. Unless it be your lady of quality, and then we'll keep our distance.
BLUNT: So, the business is out. 35
WILLMORE [*within*]: Come, come, lend's more hands to the door. Now heave, all together. (*Breaks open the door.*) So, well done, my boys.

(*Enter Belvile [and his Page], Willmore, Frederick, and Pedro. Blunt looks simply, they all laugh at him; he lays his hand on his sword, and comes up to Willmore.*)

BLUNT: Hark'ee, sir, laugh out your laugh quickly, d'ye hear, and be gone. I shall spoil your sport else, 'ads- 40 heartlikins, sir. I shall. The jest has been carried on too long. — (*Aside.*) A plague upon my tailor!
WILLMORE: 'Sdeath, how the whore has dressed him! Faith, sir, I'm sorry.
BLUNT: Are you so, sir? Keep't to yourself then, sir, I 45 advise you, d'ye hear, for I can as little endure your pity as his mirth.

(*Lays his hand on's sword.*)

BELVILE: Indeed, Willmore, thou wert a little too rough with Ned Blunt's mistress. Call a person of quality whore, and one so young, so handsome, and so elo- 50 quent? Ha, ha, he.
BLUNT: Hark'ee, sir, you know me, and know I can be angry. Have a care, for 'adsheartlikins, I can fight, too, I can, sir. Do you mark me? No more.
BELVILE: Why so peevish, good Ned? Some disappoint- 55 ments, I'll warrant. What, did the jealous count, her husband, return just in the nick?
BLUNT: Or the devil, sir. (*They laugh.*) D'ye laugh? Look ye settle me a good sober countenance, and that quickly, too, or you shall know Ned Blunt is not — 60
BELVILE: Not everybody, we know that.
BLUNT: Not an ass to be laughed at, sir.
WILLMORE: Unconscionable sinner! To bring a lover so near his happiness — a vigorous passionate lover —

65 and then not only cheat him of his movables, but his very desires, too.

BELVILE: Ah, sir, a mistress is a trifle with Blunt; he'll have a dozen the next time he looks abroad. His eyes have charms not to be resisted; there needs no more
70 than to expose that taking person to the view of the fair, and he leads 'em all in triumph.

PEDRO: Sir, though I'm a stranger to you, I am ashamed at the rudeness of my nation; and could you learn who did it, would assist you to make an example of
75 'em.

BLUNT: Why ay, there's one speaks sense now, and handsomely. And let me tell you, gentlemen, I should not have showed myself like a jack pudding° thus to have made you mirth, but that I have revenge within my
80 power. For know, I have got into my possession a female, who had better have fallen under any curse than the ruin I design her. 'Adsheartlikins, she assaulted me here in my own lodgings, and had doubtless committed a rape upon me, had not this sword defended
85 me.

FREDERICK: I know not that, but o' my conscience thou had ravished her, had she not redeemed herself with a ring. Let's see't, Blunt.

(*Blunt shows the ring.*)

BELVILE [*aside*]: Ha! The ring I gave Florinda when we
90 exchanged our vows! — Hark'ee, Blunt —

(*Goes to whisper to him.*)

WILLMORE: No whispering, good colonel, there's a woman in the case. No whispering.

BELVILE [*aside to Blunt*]: Hark'ee, fool, be advised, and conceal both the ring and the story for your reputa-
95 tion's sake. Do not let people know what despised cullies we English are; to be cheated and abused by one whore, and another rather bribe thee than be kind to thee, is an infamy to our nation.

WILLMORE: Come, come, where's the wench? We'll see
100 her; let her be what she will, we'll see her.

PEDRO: Ay, ay, let us see her. I can soon discover whether she be of quality, or for your diversion.

BLUNT: She's in Fred's custody.

WILLMORE: Come, come, the key —

(*To Frederick, who gives him the key; they are going.*)

105 BELVILE [*aside*]: Death, what shall I do? — Stay, gentlemen. — [*Aside.*] Yet if I hinder 'em, I shall discover all. — Hold, let's go one at once.° Give me the key.

WILLMORE: Nay, hold there, colonel, I'll go first.

FREDERICK: Nay, no dispute, Ned and I have the propri-
110 ety of her.

WILLMORE: Damn propriety! Then we'll draw cuts. (*Belvile goes to whisper [to] Willmore.*) Nay, no corruption, good colonel. Come, the longest sword carries her.

---

78. jack pudding: Clown.   **107. one at once:** One after the other.

(*They all draw, forgetting Don Pedro, being a Spaniard, had the longest.*)

BLUNT: I yield up my interest to you, gentlemen, and 115 that will be revenge sufficient.

WILLMORE (*to Pedro*): The wench is yours. — [*Aside.*] Pox of his Toledo,° I had forgot that.

FREDERICK: Come, sir, I'll conduct you to the lady.

(*Exeunt Frederick and Pedro.*)

BELVILE (*aside*): To hinder him will certainly discover 120 her. — Dost know, dull beast, what mischief thou hast done?

(*Willmore walking up and down, out of humor.*)

WILLMORE: Ay, ay, to trust our fortune to lots! A devil on't, 'twas madness, that's the truth on't.

BELVILE: Oh, intolerable sot — 125

(*Enter Florinda running, masked, Pedro after her; Willmore gazing round her.*)

FLORINDA (*aside*): Good heaven defend me from discovery!

PEDRO: 'Tis but in vain to fly me; you're fallen to my lot.

BELVILE [*aside*]: Sure she's undiscovered yet, but now I 130 fear there is no way to bring her off.

WILLMORE [*aside*]: Why, what a pox, is not this my woman, the same I followed but now?

(*Pedro talking to Florinda, who walks up and down.*)

PEDRO: As if I did not know ye, and your business here.

FLORINDA (*aside*): Good heaven, I fear he does indeed!

PEDRO: Come, pray be kind; I know you meant to be so 135 when you entered here, for these are proper gentlemen.

WILLMORE: But sir, perhaps the lady will not be imposed upon: She'll choose her man.

PEDRO: I am better bred than not to leave her choice 140 free.

(*Enter Valeria, and is surprised at sight of Don Pedro.*)

VALERIA (*aside*): Don Pedro here! There's no avoiding him.

FLORINDA (*aside*): Valeria! Then I'm undone.

VALERIA (*to Pedro, running to him*): Oh, I have found 145 you, sir! The strangest accident — if I had breath — to tell it.

PEDRO: Speak! Is Florinda safe? Hellena well?

VALERIA: Ay, ay, sir. Florinda is safe. — [*Aside.*] From any fears of you. 150

PEDRO: Why, where's Florinda? Speak!

VALERIA: Ay, where indeed, sir; I wish I could inform you. But to hold you no longer in doubt —

FLORINDA (*aside*): Oh, what will she say?

VALERIA: She's fled away in the habit — of one of her 155 pages, sir. But Callis thinks you may retrieve her yet,

---

118. Toledo: His sword, which won the draw, was made in Toledo, Spain.

if you make haste away. She'll tell you, sir, the rest. — (*Aside.*) If you can find her out.

PEDRO: Dishonorable girl, she has undone my aim. —
160   [*To Belvile.*] Sir, you see my necessity of leaving you, and I hope you'll pardon it. My sister, I know, will make her flight to you, and if she do, I shall expect she should be rendered back.

BELVILE: I shall consult my love and honor, sir.
                                              (*Exit Pedro.*)
165 FLORINDA (*to Valeria*): My dear preserver, let me embrace thee.

WILLMORE: What the devil's all this?

BLUNT: Mystery, by this light.

VALERIA: Come, come, make haste and get yourselves
170   married quickly, for your brother will return again.

BELVILE: I'm so surprised with fears and joys, so amazed to find you here in safety, I can scarce persuade my heart into a faith of what I see.

WILLMORE: Hark'ee, colonel, is this that mistress who
175   has cost you so many sighs, and me so many quarrels with you?

BELVILE: It is. — [*To Florinda.*] Pray give him the honor of your hand.

WILLMORE: Thus it must be received, then. (*Kneels and*
180   *kisses her hand.*) And with it give your pardon, too.

FLORINDA: The friend to Belvile may command me anything.

WILLMORE (*aside*): Death, would I might; 'tis a surprising beauty.

185 BELVILE: Boy, run and fetch a father instantly.
                                              (*Exit Boy.*)
FREDERICK: So, now do I stand like a dog, and have not a syllable to plead my own cause with. By this hand, madam, I was never thoroughly confounded before, nor shall I ever more dare look up with confidence,
190   till you are pleased to pardon me.

FLORINDA: Sir, I'll be reconciled to you on one condition: that you'll follow the example of your friend in marrying a maid that does not hate you, and whose fortune, I believe, will not be unwelcome to you.

195 FREDERICK: Madam, had I no inclinations that way, I should obey your kind commands.

BELVILE: Who, Fred marry? He has so few inclinations for womankind that had he been possessed of paradise he might have continued there to this day, if no
200   crime but love could have disinherited him.

FREDERICK: Oh, I do not use to boast of my intrigues.

BELVILE: Boast! Why, thou cost nothing but boast. And I dare swear, wert thou as innocent from the sin of the grape as thou art from the apple, thou might'st yet
205   claim that right in Eden which our first parents lost by too much loving.

FREDERICK: I wish this lady would think me so modest a man.

VALERIA: She would be sorry then, and not like you half
210   so well. And I should be loath to break my word with you, which was, that if your friend and mine agreed, it should be a match between you and I.
                                              (*She gives him her hand.*)

FREDERICK: Bear witness, colonel, 'tis a bargain.
                                              (*Kisses her hand.*)
BLUNT (*to Florinda*): I have a pardon to beg, too; but 'adsheartlikins, I am so out of countenance that I'm a   215
dog if I can say anything to purpose.

FLORINDA: Sir, I heartily forgive you all.

BLUNT: That's nobly said, sweet lady. — Belvile, prithee present her her ring again, for I find I have not courage to approach her myself.   220

(*Gives him the ring; he gives it to Florinda.*)

(*Enter Boy.*)

BOY: Sir, I have brought the father that you sent for.
                                              [*Exit Boy.*]
BELVILE: 'Tis well. And now, my dear Florinda, let's fly to complete that mighty joy we have so long wished and sighed for. — Come, Fred, you'll follow?

FREDERICK: Your example, sir, 'twas ever my ambition   225
in war, and must be so in love.

WILLMORE: And must not I see this juggling° knot tied?

BELVILE: No, thou shalt do us better service and be our guard, lest Don Pedro's sudden return interrupt the ceremony.   230

WILLMORE: Content; I'll secure this pass.

        (*Exeunt Belvile, Florinda, Frederick, and Valeria.*)

(*Enter Boy.*)

BOY (*to Willmore*): Sir, there's a lady without would speak to you.

WILLMORE: Conduct her in; I dare not quit my post.

BOY [*to Blunt*]: And sir, your tailor waits you in your   235
chamber.

BLUNT: Some comfort yet: I shall not dance naked at the wedding.

                                              (*Exeunt Blunt and Boy.*)

(*Enter again the Boy, conducting in Angellica in a masking habit and a vizard. Willmore runs to her.*)

WILLMORE [*aside*]: This can be none but my pretty gypsy. — Oh, I see you can follow as well as fly.   240
Come, confess thyself the most malicious devil in nature; you think you have done my business with Angellica —

ANGELLICA: Stand off, base villain!

(*She draws a pistol and holds it to his breast.*)

WILLMORE: Ha, 'tis not she! Who art thou, and what's   245
thy business?

ANGELLICA: One thou hast injured, and who comes to kill thee for't.

WILLMORE: What the devil canst thou mean?

ANGELLICA: By all my hopes to kill thee —   250

(*Holds still the pistol to his breast; he going back, she following still.*)

WILLMORE: Prithee, on what acquaintance? For I know thee not.

227. juggling: Based on trickery or deception.

ANGELLICA: Behold this face so lost to thy
    remembrance,   (*Pulls off her vizard.*)
    And then call all thy sins about thy soul
255   And let 'em die with thee.
WILLMORE: Angellica!
ANGELLICA: Yes, traitor! Does not thy guilty blood run
    shivering through thy veins? Hast thou no horror at
    this sight, that tells thee thou hast not long to boast
260   thy shameful conquest?
WILLMORE: Faith, no, child. My blood keeps its old
    ebbs and flows still, and that usual heat too, that
    could oblige thee with a kindness, had I but opportu-
    nity.
265 ANGELLICA: Devil! Dost wanton with my pain? Have at
    thy heart!
WILLMORE: Hold, dear virago!° Hold thy hand a little; I
    am not now at leisure to be killed. Hold and hear
    me. — (*Aside.*) Death, I think she's in earnest.
270 ANGELLICA (*aside, turning from him*): Oh, if I take not
    heed, my coward heart will leave me to his mercy. —
    What have you, sir, to say? — But should I hear thee,
    thoud'st talk away all that is brave about me, and I
    have vowed thy death by all that's sacred.

(*Follows him with the pistol to his breast.*)

275 WILLMORE: Why then, there's an end of a proper hand-
    some fellow, that might 'a lived to have done good
    service yet. That's all I can say to't.
ANGELLICA (*pausingly*): Yet — I would give thee time
    for — penitence.
280 WILLMORE: Faith, child, I thank God I have ever took
    care to lead a good, sober, hopeful life, and am of a
    religion that teaches me to believe I shall depart in
    peace.
ANGELLICA: So will the devil! Tell me,
285   How many poor believing fools thou hast undone?
    How many hearts thou hast betrayed to ruin?
    Yet these are little mischiefs to the ills
    Thou'st taught mine to commit: Thou'st taught it
      love.
WILLMORE: Egad, 'twas shrewdly hurt the while.
290 ANGELLICA: Love, that has robbed it of its unconcern,
    Of all that pride that taught me how to value it.
    And in its room
    A mean submissive passion was conveyed,
    That made me humbly bow, which I ne'er did
295   To anything but heaven.
    Thou, perjured man, didst this; and with thy
      oaths,
    Which on thy knees thou didst devoutly make,
    Softened my yielding heart, and then I was a slave.
    Yet still had been content to've worn my chains,
300   Worn 'em with vanity and joy forever,
    Hadst thou not broke those vows that put them on.
    'Twas then I was undone.

(*All this while follows him with the pistol to his breast.*)

267. **virago:** A woman of great stature, strength, and courage.

WILLMORE: Broke my vows? Why, where hast thou
    lived? Amongst the gods? For I never heard of mortal
    man that has not broke a thousand vows.   305
ANGELLICA: Oh, impudence!
WILLMORE: Angellica, that beauty has been too long
    tempting, not to have made a thousand lovers lan-
    guish; who, in the amorous fever, no doubt have
    sworn like me. Did they all die in that faith, still   310
    adoring? I do not think they did.
ANGELLICA: No, faithless man; had I repaid their vows,
    as I did shine, I would have killed the ingrateful that
    had abandoned me.
WILLMORE: This old general has quite spoiled thee: 315
    Nothing makes a woman so vain as being flattered.
    Your old lover ever supplies the defects of age with
    intolerable dotage, vast charge, and that which you
    call constancy; and attributing all this to your own
    merits, you domineer, and throw your favors in's   320
    teeth, upbraiding him still with the defects of age,
    and cuckold him as often as he deceives your expec-
    tations. But the gay, young, brisk lover, that brings
    his equal fires, and can give you dart for dart, you'll
    find will be as nice as you sometimes.   325
ANGELLICA: All this thou'st made me know, for which I
    hate thee.
    Had I remained in innocent security,
    I should have thought all men were born my slaves,
    And worn my power like lightning in my eyes,
    To have destroyed at pleasure when offended.   330
    But when love held the mirror, the undeceiving
      glass
    Reflected all the weakness of my soul, and made me
      know
    My richest treasure being lost, my honor,
    All the remaining spoil could not be worth
    The conqueror's care or value.   335
    Oh, how I fell, like a long-worshiped idol,
    Discovering all the cheat.
    Would not the incense and rich sacrifice
    Which blind devotion offered at my altars
    Have fallen to thee?   340
    Why wouldst thou then destroy my fancied power?
WILLMORE: By heaven, thou'rt brave, and I admire
    thee strangely.
    I wish I were that dull, that constant thing
    Which thou wouldst have, and nature never meant
    me.
    I must, like cheerful birds, sing in all groves,   345
    And perch on every bough,
    Billing the next kind she that flies to meet me;
    Yet, after all, could build my nest with thee,
    Thither repairing when I'd loved my round,
    And still reserve a tributary flame.   350
    To gain your credit, I'll pay you back your charity,
    And be obliged for nothing but for love.

(*Offers her a purse of gold.*)

ANGELLICA: Oh, that thou wert in earnest!
    So mean a thought of me

355 Would turn my rage to scorn, and I should pity
        thee,
     And give thee leave to live;
     Which for the public safety of our sex,
     And my own private injuries, I dare not do.
     Prepare —   (*Follows still, as before.*)
360 I will no more be tempted with replies.
WILLMORE: Sure —
ANGELLICA: Another word will damn thee! I've heard
     thee talk too long.

(*She follows him with the pistol ready to shoot; he retires, still amazed. Enter Don Antonio, his arm in a
scarf, and lays hold on the pistol.*)

ANTONIO: Ha! Angellica!
365 ANGELLICA: Antonio! What devil brought thee hither?
     ANTONIO: Love and curiosity, seeing your coach at door.
        Let me disarm you of this unbecoming instrument of
        death. (*Takes away the pistol.*) Amongst the number
        of your slaves was there not one worthy the honor to
370   have fought your quarrel? — [*To Willmore.*] Who
        are you, sir, that are so very wretched to merit death
        from her?
     WILLMORE: One, sir, that could have made a better end
        of an amorous quarrel without you, than with you.
375 ANTONIO: Sure 'tis some rival. Ha! The very man took
        down her picture yesterday; the very same that set on
        me last night! Blessed opportunity —

(*Offers to shoot him.*)

ANGELLICA: Hold, you're mistaken, sir.
ANTONIO: By heaven, the very same! — Sir, what pre-
380   tensions have you to this lady?
     WILLMORE: Sir, I do not use to be examined, and am ill
        at all disputes but this —

(*Draws; Antonio offers to shoot.*)

ANGELLICA (*to Willmore*): Oh, hold! You see he's
        armed with certain death.
     — And you, Antonio, I command you hold,
385   By all the passion you've so lately vowed me.

(*Enter Don Pedro, sees Antonio, and stays.*)

PEDRO (*aside*): Ha! Antonio! And Angellica!
ANTONIO: When I refuse obedience to your will,
        May you destroy me with your mortal hate.
        By all that's holy, I adore you so,
390   That even my rival, who has charms enough
        To make him fall a victim to my jealousy,
        Shall live; nay, and have leave to love on still.
PEDRO (*aside*): What's this I hear?
ANGELLICA (*pointing to Willmore*): Ah thus, 'twas thus
        he talked, and I believed.
395   Antonio, yesterday
        I'd not have sold my interest in his heart
        For all the sword has won and lost in battle.
        — But now, to show my utmost of contempt,
        I give thee life; which, if thou wouldst preserve,
400   Live where my eyes may never see thee more.

Live to undo someone whose soul may prove
So bravely constant to revenge my love.

             (*Goes out. Antonio follows, but Pedro
                              pulls him back.*)

PEDRO: Antonio, stay.
ANTONIO: Don Pedro!
PEDRO: What coward fear was that prevented thee from   405
     meeting me this morning on the Molo?
ANTONIO: Meet thee?
PEDRO: Yes, me; I was the man that dared thee to't.
ANTONIO: Hast thou so often seen me fight in war, to
     find no better cause to excuse my absence? I sent my   410
     sword and one to do thee right, finding myself unca-
     pable to use a sword.
PEDRO: But 'twas Florinda's quarrel that we fought, and
     you, to show how little you esteemed her, sent me
     your rival, giving him your interest. But I have found   415
     the cause of this affront, and when I meet you fit for
     the dispute, I'll tell you my resentment.
ANTONIO: I shall be ready, sir, ere long, to do you rea-
     son.   (*Exit Antonio.*)
PEDRO: If I could find Florinda, now whilst my anger's   420
     high, I think I should be kind, and give her to Belvile
     in revenge.
WILLMORE: Faith, sir, I know not what you would do,
     but I believe the priest within has been so kind.
PEDRO: How? My sister married?   425
WILLMORE: I hope by this time he is, and bedded too, or
     he has not my longings about him.
PEDRO: Dares he do this? Does he not fear my power?
WILLMORE: Faith, not at all; if you will go in and thank
     him for the favor he has done your sister, so; if not,   430
     sir, my power's greater in this house than yours: I have
     a damned surly crew here that will keep you till the
     next tide, and then clap you on board for prize. My
     ship lies but a league off the Molo, and we shall show
     your donship a damned Tramontana° rover's trick.   435

(*Enter Belvile.*)

BELVILE: This rogue's in some new mischief. Ha! Pedro
     returned!
PEDRO: Colonel Belvile, I hear you have married my sis-
     ter.
BELVILE: You have heard truth then, sir.   440
PEDRO: Have I so? Then, sir, I wish you joy.
BELVILE: How?
PEDRO: By this embrace I do, and I am glad on't.
BELVILE: Are you in earnest?
PEDRO: By our long friendship and my obligations to   445
     thee, I am; the sudden change I'll give you reasons for
     anon. Come, lead me to my sister, that she may know
     I now approve her choice.

                         (*Exit Belvile with Pedro.*)

(*Willmore goes to follow them. Enter Hellena, as before
in boy's clothes, and pulls him back.*)

---

435. Tramontana: Region of Italy north of the Alps.

WILLMORE: Ha! My gypsy! Now a thousand blessings
450   on thee for this kindness. Egad, child, I was e'en in
despair of ever seeing thee again; my friends are all
provided for within, each man his kind woman.

HELLENA: Ha! I thought they had served me some such
trick!

455 WILLMORE: And I was e'en resolved to go aboard, and
condemn myself to my lone cabin, and the thoughts
of thee.

HELLENA: And could you have left me behind? Would
you have been so ill natured?

460 WILLMORE: Why, 'twould have broke my heart, child.
But since we are met again, I defy foul weather to
part us.

HELLENA: And would you be a faithful friend now, if a
maid should trust you?

465 WILLMORE: For a friend I cannot promise: Thou art of a
form so excellent, a face and humor too good for
cold dull friendship. I am parlously afraid of being in
love, child; and you have not forgotten how severely
you have used me?

470 HELLENA: That's all one; such usage you must still look
for: to find out all your haunts, to rail at you to all
that love you, till I have made you love only me in
your own defense, because nobody else will love you.

WILLMORE: But hast thou no better quality to recom-
475   mend thyself by?

HELLENA: Faith, none, captain. Why, twill be the greater
charity to take me for thy mistress. I am a lone child,
a kind of orphan lover, and why I should die a maid,
and in a captain's hands too, I do not understand.

480 WILLMORE: Egad, I was never clawed away with broad-
sides from any female before. Thou hast one virtue I
adore — good nature. I hate a coy demure mistress,
she's as troublesome as a colt, I'll break none. No,
give me a mad mistress when mewed, and in flying,
485   one I dare trust upon the wing, that whilst she's kind
will come to the lure.°

HELLENA: Nay, as kind as you will, good captain, whilst
it lasts. But let's lose no time.

WILLMORE: My time's as precious to me as thine can be.
490   Therefore, dear creature, since we are so well agreed,
let's retire to my chamber; and if ever thou wert
treated with such savory love! Come, my bed's prepared for such a guest all clean and sweet as thy fair
self. I love to steal a dish and a bottle with a friend,
495   and hate long graces. Come, let's retire and fall to.

HELLENA: 'Tis but getting my consent, and the business
is soon done. Let but old gaffer Hymen° and his
priest say amen to's, and I dare lay my mother's
daughter by as proper a fellow as your father's son,
500   without fear or blushing.

WILLMORE: Hold, hold, no bug words,° child. Priest
and Hymen? Prithee add a hangman to 'em to make

up the consort. No, no, we'll have no vows but love,
child, nor witness but the lover: The kind deity
enjoins naught but love and enjoy. Hymen and priest   505
wait still upon portion and jointure; love and beauty
have their own ceremonies. Marriage is as certain a
bane to love as lending money is to friendship. I'll
neither ask nor give a vow, though I could be content
to turn gypsy and become a left-handed bridegroom   510
to have the pleasure of working that great miracle of
making a maid a mother, if you durst venture. 'Tis
upse gypsy° that, and if I miss I'll lose my labor.

HELLENA: And if you do not lose, what shall I get? A
cradle full of noise and mischief, with a pack of   515
repentance at my back? Can you teach me to weave
incle° to pass my time with? 'Tis upse gypsy that, too.

WILLMORE: I can teach thee to weave a true love's knot
better.

HELLENA: So can my dog.   520

WILLMORE: Well, I see we are both upon our guards,
and I see there's no way to conquer good nature but
by yielding. Here, give me thy hand: One kiss, and I
am thine.

HELLENA: One kiss! How like my page he speaks! I am   525
resolved you shall have none, for asking such a
sneaking sum. He that will be satisfied with one kiss
will never die of that longing. Good friend single-
kiss, is all your talking come to this? A kiss, a
caudle!° Farewell, captain single-kiss.   530

(Going out; he stays her.)

WILLMORE: Nay, if we part so, let me die like a bird
upon a bough, at the sheriff's charge. By heaven,
both the Indies shall not buy thee from me. I adore
thy humor and will marry thee, and we are so of one
humor it must be a bargain. Give me thy hand.   535
(Kisses her hand.) And now let the blind ones, love
and fortune, do their worst.

HELLENA: Why, god-a-mercy, captain!

WILLMORE: But hark'ee: the bargain is now made, but is
it not fit we should know each other's names, that   540
when we have reason to curse one another hereafter,
and people ask me who 'tis I give to the devil, I may
at least be able to tell what family you came of?

HELLENA: Good reason, captain, and where I have
cause, as I doubt not but I shall have plentiful, that I   545
may know at whom to throw my — blessings, I
beseech ye your name.

WILLMORE: I am called Robert the Constant.

HELLENA: A very fine name! Pray was it your faulkner°
or butler that christened you? Do they not use to   550
whistle when they call you?

WILLMORE: I hope you have a better, that a man may
name without crossing himself — you are so merry
with mine.

484–86. flying . . . lure: I.e., one who will be faithful as long as
that doesn't interfere with her wishes.   **497. Hymen:** God of
marriage.   **501. bug words:** Words that inspire fear.

513. upse gypsy: Gypsy fashion.   **517. incle:** Linen yarn or
tape.   **530. caudle:** A warm drink made of gruel and wine or
ale, sweetened and spiced, given to the sick.   **549. faulkner:**
Falconer, trainer of hawks.

555   HELLENA: I am called Hellena the Inconstant.

(*Enter Pedro, Belvile, Florinda, Frederick, Valeria.*)

PEDRO: Ha! Hellena!

FLORINDA: Hellena!

HELLENA: The very same. Ha! My brother! Now, captain, show your love and courage; stand to your arms
560   and defend me bravely, or I am lost forever.

PEDRO: What's this I hear? False girl, how came you hither, and what's your business? Speak!

(*Goes roughly to her.*)

WILLMORE: Hold off, sir; you have leave to parley° only.

(*Puts himself between.*)

HELLENA: I had e'en as good tell it, as you guess it. Faith,
565   brother, my business is the same with all living creatures of my age: to love and be beloved — and here's the man.

PEDRO: Perfidious maid, hast thou deceived me too; deceived thyself and heaven?

570   HELLENA: 'Tis time enough to make my peace with that;
Be you but kind, let me alone with heaven.

PEDRO: Belvile, I did not expect this false play from you. Was't not enough you'd gain Florinda, which I pardoned, but your lewd friends too must be enriched
575   with the spoils of a noble family?

BELVILE: Faith, sir, I am as much surprised at this as you can be. Yet, sir, my friends are gentlemen, and ought to be esteemed for their misfortunes, since they have the glory to suffer with the best of men and kings.
580   'Tis true, he's a rover of fortune, yet a prince aboard his little wooden world.

PEDRO: What's this to the maintenance of a woman of her birth and quality?

WILLMORE: Faith, sir, I can boast of nothing but a
585   sword which does me right where'er I come, and has defended a worse cause than a woman's, and since I loved her before I either knew her birth or name, I must pursue my resolution and marry her.

PEDRO: And is all your holy intent of becoming a nun
590   debauched into a desire of man?

HELLENA: Why, I have considered the matter, brother, and find the three hundred thousand crowns my uncle left me, and you cannot keep from me, will be better laid out in love than in religion, and turn to as
595   good an account. Let most voices carry it: for heaven or the captain?

ALL CRY: A captain! A captain!

HELLENA: Look ye, sir, 'tis a clear case.

PEDRO: Oh, I am mad! — (*Aside.*) If I refuse, my life's in
600   danger. — Come, there's one motive induces me. Take her; I shall now be free from fears of her honor. Guard it you now, if you can; I have been a slave to't long enough.   (*Gives her to him.*)

WILLMORE: Faith, sir, I am of a nation that are of opinion a woman's honor is not worth guarding when she   605
has a mind to part with it.

HELLENA: Well said, captain.

PEDRO (*to Valeria*): This was your plot, mistress, but I hope you have married one that will revenge my quarrel to you.   610

VALERIA: There's no altering destiny, sir.

PEDRO: Sooner than a woman's will; therefore I forgive you all, and wish you may get my father's pardon as easily, which I fear.

(*Enter Blunt dressed in a Spanish habit, looking very ridiculous; his Man adjusting his band.*)

MAN: 'Tis very well, sir.   615

BLUNT: Well, sir! 'Adsheartlikins, I tell you 'tis damnable ill, sir. A Spanish habit! Good Lord! Could the devil and my tailor devise no other punishment for me but the mode of a nation I abominate?

BELVILE: What's the matter, Ned?   620

BLUNT: Pray view me round, and judge.

(*Turns round.*)

BELVILE: I must confess thou art a kind of an odd figure.

BLUNT: In a Spanish habit with a vengeance! I had rather be in the Inquisition for Judaism° than in this doublet and breeches; a pillory were an easy collar to this,   625
three handfuls high; and these shoes, too, are worse than the stocks, with the sole an inch shorter than my foot. In fine, gentlemen, methinks I look like a bag of bays° stuffed full of fool's flesh.

BELVILE: Methinks 'tis well, and makes thee look e'en   630
cavalier. Come, sir, settle your face and salute our friends. Lady —

BLUNT (*to Hellena*): Ha! Sayst thou so, my little rover? Lady, if you be one, give me leave to kiss your hand, and tell you, 'adsheartlikins, for all I look so, I am   635
your humble servant. A pox of my Spanish habit!
(*Music is heard to play.*)

WILLMORE: Hark! What's this?

(*Enter Boy.*)

BOY: Sir, as the custom is, the gay people in masquerade, who make every man's house their own, are coming up.   640

(*Enter several men and women in masking habits, with music; they put themselves in order and dance.*)

BLUNT: 'Adsheartlikins, would 'twere lawful to pull off their false faces, that I might see if my doxy° were not amongst 'em.

BELVILE (*to the maskers*): Ladies and gentlemen, since you are come so *a propos,*° you must take a small   645
collation with us.

---

563. **parley:** Speak or discuss.

624. **Inquisition for Judaism:** The Spanish Inquisition, which persecuted heretics, Jews, and Muslims.   628–29. **bag of bays:** Spices wrapped in cloth and used for flavoring in cooking.   642. **doxy:** Mistress, prostitute.   645. *a propos:* In a timely fashion; appropriately.

WILLMORE (*to Hellena*): Whilst we'll to the good man
    within, who stays to give us a cast of his office.°
    Have you no trembling at the near approach?
650 HELLENA: No more than you have in an engagement or
    a tempest.
    WILLMORE: Egad, thou'rt a brave girl, and I admire thy
    love and courage.
        Lead on; no other dangers they can dread,
655   *Who venture in the storms o'th' marriage bed.*
                                                            (*Exeunt.*)

EPILOGUE

The banished cavaliers! A roving blade!
A popish carnival! A masquerade!
The devil's in't if this will please the nation
In these our blessed times of reformation,
5   When conventickling° is so much in fashion.
    And yet —
    That mutinous tribe less factions do beget,
    Than your continual differing in wit.
    Your judgment's, as your passion's, a disease:
10   Nor muse nor miss your appetite can please;
    You're grown as nice as queasy consciences,
    Whose each convulsion, when the spirit moves,
    Damns everything that maggot° disapproves.
        With canting° rule you would the stage refine,
15   And to dull method all our sense confine.
    With th'insolence of commonwealths you rule,
    Where each gay fop and politic grave fool
    On monarch wit impose, without control.
    As for the last, who seldom sees a play,
20   Unless it be the old Blackfriars° way;
    Shaking his empty noddle o'er bamboo,°
    He cries, "Good faith, these plays will never do!
    Ah, sir, in my young days, what lofty wit,
    What high-strained scenes of fighting there were writ.
25   These are slight airy toys. But tell me, pray,
    What has the House of Commons done today?"
    Then shows his politics, to let you see
    Of state affairs he'll judge as notably
    As he can do of wit and poetry.
30   The younger sparks, who hither do resort,
    Cry,
    "Pox o' your genteel things! Give us more sport'!

Damn me, I'm sure 'twill never please the court."
    Such fops are never pleased, unless the play
Be stuffed with fools as brisk and dull as they.   35
Such might the half-crown spare, and in a glass
At home behold a more accomplished ass.
Where they may set their cravats, wigs, and faces,
And practice all their buffoonry grimaces:
See how this huff becomes, this damny,° stare,   40
Which they at home may act because they dare,
But must with prudent caution do elsewhere.
Oh that our Nokes, or Tony Lee,° could show
A fop but half so much to th' life as you.

POSTSCRIPT

This play had been sooner in print, but for a report
about the town (made by some either very malicious
or very ignorant) that 'twas *Thomaso*° altered; which
made the booksellers fear some trouble from the proprietor of that admirable play, which indeed has wit   5
enough to stock a poet, and is not to be pieced or
mended by any but the excellent author himself. That
I have stolen some hints from it, may be a proof that
I valued it more than to pretend to alter it, had I the
dexterity of some poets, who are not more expert in   10
stealing than in the art of concealing, and who even
that way outdo the Spartan boys.° I might have
appropriated all to myself; but I, vainly proud of my
judgment, hang out the sign of Angellica (the only
stolen object) to give notice where a great part of the   15
wit dwelt; though if the *Play of the Novella*° were as
well worth remembering as *Thomaso*, they might
(bating° the name) have as well said I took it from
thence. I will only say the plot and business (not to
boast on't) is my own; as for the words and charac-   20
ters, I leave the reader to judge and compare 'em with
Thomaso, to whom I recommend the great entertainment of reading it. Though had this succeeded ill, I
should have had no need of imploring that justice
from the critics, who are naturally so kind to any that   25
pretend to usurp their dominion, especially of our
sex: They would doubtless have given me the whole
honor on't. Therefore I will only say in English what
the famous Vergil does in Latin: I make verses, and
others have the fame.   30

---

648. stays . . . office: The priest waits to perform his office, i.e.,
to marry them.   **5. conventickling:** A pun. A conventicle was a
secret meeting of religious dissenters (those who were not members of the Church of England).   **13. maggot:** Conscience.
14. canting: Hypocritical.   **20. Blackfriars:** The Blackfriars
Theatre (1576–1655), considered old-fashioned in Behn's time.
21. o'er bamboo: Over a cane, implying old age.

40. damny: Damn me.   **43. Nokes . . . Lee:** The best low comedians of the day. James Nokes performed in Thomas Betterton's company.   **3. *Thomaso:*** Thomas Killigrew's *Thomaso;
or, The Wanderer* (1654; published 1664).   **12. Spartan boys:**
Those who hid in the Trojan horse.   **16. *Play of the Novella:***
The Novella (1632) by Richard Brome, from which Behn borrowed several ideas.   **18. bating:** Excepting.

COMMENTARIES

Virginia Woolf (1882–1941)
ON APHRA BEHN
1929

Virginia Woolf was a leading experimental writer of fiction in the first half of the twentieth century. She is known for the novels Mrs. Dalloway *(1925),* To the Lighthouse *(1927), and* Orlando *(1928) and for her essays, including* A Room of One's Own *(1929), from which this excerpt comes. Woolf was one of the first modern commentators to call attention to the extraordinary achievement of Aphra Behn.*

With Mrs. Behn we turn a very important corner on the road. We leave behind, shut up in their parks among their folios, those solitary great ladies who wrote without audience or criticism, for their own delight alone. We come to town and rub shoulders with ordinary people in the streets. Mrs. Behn was a middle-class woman with all the plebeian virtues of humor, vitality, and courage; a woman forced by the death of her husband and some unfortunate adventures of her own to make her living by her wits. She had to work on equal terms with men. She made, by working very hard, enough to live on. The importance of that fact outweighs anything that she actually wrote, even the splendid "A Thousand Martyrs I Have Made," or "Love in Fantastic Triumph Sat," for here begins the freedom of the mind, or rather the possibility that in the course of time the mind will be free to write what it likes. For now that Aphra Behn had done it, girls could go to their parents and say, You need not give me an allowance; I can make money by my pen. Of course the answer for many years to come was, Yes, by living the life of Aphra Behn! Death would be better! and the door was slammed faster than ever. That profoundly interesting subject, the value that men set upon women's chastity and its effect upon their education, here suggests itself for discussion, and might provide an interesting book if any student at Girton or Newnham cared to go into the matter. Lady Dudley, sitting in diamonds among the midges of a Scottish moor, might serve for frontispiece. Lord Dudley, the *Times* said when Lady Dudley died the other day, "a man of cultivated taste and many accomplishments, was benevolent and bountiful, but whimsically despotic. He insisted upon his wife's wearing full dress, even at the remotest shooting-lodge in the Highlands; he loaded her with gorgeous jewels," and so on, "he gave her everything — always excepting any measure of responsibility." Then Lord Dudley had a stroke and she nursed him and ruled his estates with supreme competence for ever after. That whimsical despotism was in the nineteenth century too.

But to return. Aphra Behn proved that money could be made by writing at the sacrifice, perhaps, of certain agreeable qualities; and so by degrees writing became not merely a sign of folly and a distracted mind, but was of practical importance. A husband might die, or some disaster overtake the family. Hundreds of women began as the eighteenth century drew on to add to their pin money, or to come to the rescue of their families by making translations or writing the innumerable bad novels which have ceased to be recorded even in textbooks, but are to be picked up in the fourpenny boxes in the Charing Cross Road. The extreme activity of mind which showed itself in the later eighteenth century among women — the talking, and the meeting, the writing of essays on Shakespeare, the translating of the classics — was founded on the solid fact that women could make money by writing. Money dignifies what is frivolous if unpaid for. It might still be well to sneer at "blue stockings with an itch for scribbling," but it could not be denied that they could put money in their purses. Thus, towards the end of the eighteenth century a change came about which, if I were rewriting history, I should describe more fully and think of greater importance than the Crusades or the Wars of the Roses. The middle-class woman began to write. For if *Pride and Prejudice* matters, and *Middlemarch* and *Vilette* and *Wuthering Heights* matter, then it matters far more than I can prove in an hour's discourse that women generally, and not merely the lonely aristocrat shut up in her country house among her folios and her flatterers, took to writing. Without those forerunners, Jane Austen and the Brontës and George Eliot could no more have written than Shakespeare could have written without Marlowe, or Marlowe without Chaucer, or Chaucer without those forgotten poets who paved the ways and tamed the natural savagery of the tongue. For masterpieces are not single and solitary births; they are the outcome of many years of thinking in common, of thinking by the body of the people, so that the experience of the mass is behind the single voice. Jane Austen should have laid a wreath upon the grave of Fanny Burney, and George Eliot done homage to the robust shade of Eliza Carter — the valiant old woman who tied a bell to her bedstead in order that she might wake early and learn Greek. All women together ought to let flowers fall upon the tomb of Aphra Behn, which is, most scandalously but rather appropriately, in Westminster Abbey,° for it was she who earned them the right to speak their minds. It is she — shady and amorous as she was — who makes it not quite fantastic for me to say to you tonight: Earn five hundred a year by your wits.

Westminster Abbey: The burial place in London of British royalty as well as distinguished citizens, including, in the Poets' Corner, famous writers.

Elaine Hobby (b. 1956)
COURTSHIP AND MARRIAGE IN *THE ROVER*   1989

Elaine Hobby closely examines The Rover *to help us understand the conventions of romantic love in Aphra Behn's work. Her essay is especially enlightening on the questions of marriage and rape and on the differences in the viewpoints of men and women characters in the play. Hobby notes the complexities implied in the characterization of Angellica, the courtesan.*

Commonly, Behn's plays feature at least two pairs of young lovers, whose attitudes to love and marriage serve as contrasting strategies in courtship. A common pattern is that of the "constant couple," who remain true to one another, and finally marry, despite parental opposition and, usually, confusions over one another's true identity and conduct. These lovers are not, however, idyllically well matched or perfectly happy. In *The Rover*, Florinda and Belvile are just such a constant couple. From the beginning they are in love with one another, and resolved to accept no other partner. Except for her stubbornness on this one issue, Florinda is all quiet obedience, failing to argue her case against an arranged marriage. Her passivity is no ideal. Twice in the course of the play she narrowly escapes being raped by the friends of her beloved, and on each occasion is only saved because her obvious high social class causes her attackers to hesitate, fearing retribution from her relatives. The second of these incidents is a nightmare scene where, seeking refuge in Blunt's house, she is regarded by him as the perfect target for his revenge against all women (and Lucetta in particular) for making fun of him. When Frederick, the play's great upholder of patriarchal morality, arrives, the two men agree to rape her.

> BLUNT: We'll both lie with her, and then let me alone to bang her.
> FREDERICK: I'm ready to serve you in matters of revenge that has a double pleasure in't.
> (IV, v, 123–26)

In a world where men can choose to rape a woman, any woman, for spite, there is no safety for the romantic heroine. In Behn's plays, as in her novels, rape or the threat of it is shown to be an almost routine masculine strategy to bully and manipulate women. In *The Amorous Prince*, Frederick threatens to rape Laura at knifepoint to humble her for scorning him, and in the same play Silvio threatens to rape his "sister" Cleonte. Sir Timothy Tawdrey in *The Town-Fopp*, when threatening to rape Phillis, tells her that old patriarchal lie: that all women want to be forcibly taken. Phillis's fate is the most terrible of all. Having no economic choices (like Philadelphia in Behn's novel *The Unfortunate Happy Lady*), she has no option but to marry her would-be rapist.

Setting out with a theme of courtship and marriage, Behn writes about rape and prostitution, constructing scenarios that show how closely connected these fates are for women. Where Florinda's reliance on "true love" for her salvation twice brings her to the brink of being raped, the courtesan Angellica Bianca in the same play is betrayed by her final inability to escape from the tempting lies of romance. Early in the play, she makes a cool assessment of women's position, explaining that she had opted to sell her body for the solid return of financial reward, rather than trusting to illusory male fidelity: "Nothing but gold shall charm my heart" (II, 1, 163). She knows, too, that marriage for money is a no less mercenary affair than prostitution. Disaster arrives, however, because she has seriously misjudged the power structure of her society. She arrives in town hoping to captivate either the viceroy's son Don Antonio, or Don Pedro, the nephew of her deceased "protector." Had she been married to her old lover, Don Pedro would have been her kin, and had some social duty to support her. As it is, she is left to live on her wits and her transitory physical charms. When Willmore, the "rover" of the title, finally rejects her in favor of the wealthy virgin Hellena, she is forced to recognize that her chosen independence was illusory. In a world where men make the rules, her only salable item is her virginity. Having sold that in the wrong market, she is damned.

When Angellica falls hopelessly for the feckless Willmore, she wants to believe that love and romance can be dissociated from social and economic structures, that "true love" in her world can be above financial considerations. She calls on him to see things her way and, blinded by this desire, does not recognize that he is using her for his pleasure.

> ANGELLICA: Thou'rt a brave fellow! Put up thy gold, and know,
> That were thy fortune large as is thy soul,
> Thou shouldst not buy my love
> Couldst thou forget these mean effects of vanity
> Which set me out to sale,
> And as a lover prize my yielding joys.
> Canst thou believe they'll be entirely thine,
> Without considering they were mercenary?   (II, II, 110–17)

In the course of the play, Willmore's repeated answer to this is a resounding "No." Having worshiped her beauty, tasted the pleasures of her body, and spent her money to attract a wealthier woman, he leaves her for a better catch.

Angellica is a troubling and uncomfortable figure in the play, disrupting the wit and airiness of scenes between Hellena and Willmore and undercutting the conventional "happy ending" of true lovers united. Realizing she has been betrayed by Willmore despite giving him "My virgin heart . . . Oh! 'tis gone!" (IV, II, 163) she plots her revenge "for the public safety of our sex" (V, 357). Trapping him at gunpoint she decides, however, to let him live: he is not worth the trouble of an execution: "But now, to show my utmost of contempt, / I give thee life" (V, 398–99). Through Willmore, she has learned that male protestations of devotion, and all their courtly love rhetoric, are for them just a game. There is no true power, no safety, for women.[. . .]

In many of Behn's plays, men's obsessions with their courtship conventions prevent them from understanding the women they address. Romance is a male invention, and women are jeopardized and often betrayed if they believe such declarations of undying passion. The task for the witty heroine who is at the center of many of Behn's plays, as Hellena is in *The Rover*, is to discover as much as possible about her man's true intentions, beneath his courtly facade. Willmore refers to both Angellica and to Hellena as his "angel" in high-flown rhetoric, but where Angellica is briefly fooled by this worship, Hellena is quite clear-sighted about the limit of his commitment. As far as possible, she takes control of her situation, disguising herself and playing parts, testing out and then capturing the man she has chosen. Disguised, she watches him court and promise fidelity to Angellica, and in a bitter but witty scene mocks him, throwing back at him the overblown promises she has heard him make (III, I). She has no interest in traditional courtship rituals, thinking them "a very pretty, idle, silly kind of pleasure to pass one's time with" (III, I, 67–68), but she is not deceived by Willmore's forthright arguments in favor of unfettered sensuality. She knows already what Angellica shows the audience: Marriage is a necessity for women, otherwise, as she challenges Willmore, "What shall I get? A cradle full of noise and mischief, with a pack of repentance at my back?" (V, 514–16).

She gets her man, but it is a tawdry victory and the audience knows it, with Angellica there to remind them. Willmore has shown himself to be insensitive, capricious, and dangerous to women, and there is no reason to imagine that he will be faithful to Hellena for longer than the month that he originally resolves to sacrifice to gain her. In *The Second Part of the Rover*, where Willmore again chooses between two women (and this time chooses the prostitute), it is revealed in passing that Hellena had died at sea within three months of the marriage.

The world of courtship and marriage depicted by Behn in these plays is a bleak one. Bright, witty women like Hellena use daring and imagination in a desperate attempt to evade the arranged marriages or confinements to nunneries destined them by their families. They race against time, trying their best to negotiate when all power lies in others' hands. None of the dashing young blades they choose and test out are admirable characters, but they seem preferable to a fool like Haunce van Ezel (in *The Dutch Lover*) or an odious tyrant like Octavio (in *The Feign'd Curtizans*). Woven in with the wit and humor, music and spectacle, are hard, sober women's truths about the debauchery of the Restoration court and its acolytes. Armed with wit and driven by necessity, like her heroines, Aphra Behn succeeded in dramatizing in marketable form the dilemmas that faced her and her sisters.

William Congreve

Although born in England, William Congreve (1670–1729) was educated in Ireland, first at Kilkenny School and then at Trinity College, Dublin. Jonathan Swift, whose poetry praised Congreve, was also at Kilkenny and Trinity during part of this time. They were lifelong friends and central figures in literary London. Later, Congreve read law at the Middle Temple in London and was able to make good use of his legal training in several of his plays.

Congreve's literary career began with a novel, *Incognita* (1691), which he wrote in his teens. John Dryden praised the novel and, later, his plays. After Congreve's first play was produced, the poet Thomas Southerne named Congreve the likely inheritor of Dryden's crown as poet laureate.

His first play, *The Old Bachelor* (1693) was an immediate success, establishing him as an important playwright. Later in 1693 he produced his second play, *The Double Dealer,* which had a mixed reception. Dryden, in a letter, said, "The women thinke he has exposed their Bitchery too much and the Gentlemen are offended with him; for the discovery of their follyes: & the way of their Intrigues, under the notion of Friendship to their Ladyes Husbands." Maskwell, the double dealer, is a classic manipulator who forwards his own interests while damaging those of other characters. Congreve defended the play as a moral fable, and it was not until Queen Mary requested a command performance that the play was restored in the eyes of the public. *Love for Love* (1695) was for many years Congreve's most popular and best-liked play. It is the story of the worthy Valentine, who is about to lose an inheritance to a younger brother. In the end Valentine's intelligence wins out, and by pretending madness he secures his beloved, the wealthy heiress Angelica, as well as his own estate. Thomas Betterton, the acclaimed Restoration actor, played Valentine in the first performances; his theater company at Lincoln's Inn Fields produced all of Congreve's work. John Gielgud played Valentine in London, opening on April 8, 1943, to considerable acclaim and continuing for 471 performances through World War II. Laurence Olivier and Lynn Redgrave played in the 1965 revival, also a success. Congreve's one tragedy, *The Mourning Bride* (1697), was very successful although it has not been revived in the twentieth century.

Congreve's career as a playwright lasted only seven years. He left the stage after the production of *The Way of the World* (1700), ostensibly because of its cool reception. Although not technically a failure, the play was not received with the enthusiasm Congreve thought it deserved. He was stung by the criticism of Jeremy Collier in *A Short View of the Immorality and Profaneness of the English Stage* (1698). Congreve was also annoyed by the rise of the new sentimental middle-class drama. He spent the rest of his life writing occasional poetry, such as *A Pindarique Ode on the Victorious Progress of Her Majesties Arms* (1706), and libretti for several operas: *The Judgment of Paris* (1701), *A Hymn to Harmony* (1703), and *The Tears of Amarylis* (1703). He spent much of his later years as a retiring gentleman in the company of the duchess of Marlborough, with whom he probably had a child, Lady Mary Godolphin, who inherited his estate.

Congreve was buried in the Poet's Corner of Westminster Abbey, near the grave of Aphra Behn, who is buried at the entrance to the cloisters. Critics in his time and in succeeding generations have regarded his plays as among the purest examples of the English comic style of the late seventeenth century. *The Way of the World* has been especially singled out for praise because while it is witty, brisk, and amusing, it is pungent and serious at the core, with characters whose intelligence and essential worth help animate a drama that vies with the achievement of Molière.

THE WAY OF THE WORLD

The Way of the World (1700), Congreve's fifth and last play, has been his most enduring and — taking the long view — his most successful. It is an intellectual romp, with plot twists, disguises, and numerous complications. The names of the characters — Fainall, Mirabell, Wilfull, Witwoud, Waitwell, and Petulant — indicate Congreve's use of stock or TYPE CHARACTERS, characters immediately recognizable for their stereotypical behavior and traits. However, he always moves beneath the surfaces of types and reveals a satisfying complexity. Type characters have been used to advantage in all ages of comic drama but especially so in the English Restoration.

Congreve's genius shows up in his witty use of REPARTEE, or quick replies. He is a master of the one-liner and the RIPOSTE, a sharp return in speech. Wit was a rapier in the late seventeenth century, to be used for the amusement of those intelligent enough to follow the exchanges. Early on, Witwoud says, "A wit should no more be sincere than a woman constant; one argues a decay of parts, as t'other of beauty." Mirabell tells Mrs. Fainall, "You should have just so much disgust for your husband as may be sufficient to make you relish your lover." Such witty comment on early eighteenth-century marriage, once we get to know Fainall and his essential viciousness, takes on a serious cast.

The plot of *The Way of the World* centers on marriage, adultery, and family fortunes. Man-about-town Mirabell wishes to marry Mrs. Millamant, who has inherited six thousand pounds and will receive another six thousand pounds if she marries in accord with the wishes of her aunt, Lady Wishfort (an older woman "full of the vigor of fifty-five"). Lady Wishfort, however, feels betrayed by Mirabell, who pretended to love her to get close to Millamant. Lady Wishfort wants Millamant to marry Sir Wilfull Witwoud, and Mirabell's efforts to make Lady Wishfort relent in this wish are carried forth on a wave of deception, disguise, and comic mixups. Mirabell and Millamant resemble traditional Shakespearean lovers such as Petruchio and Katharine in *The Taming of the Shrew* and Benedick and Beatrice in *Much Ado about Nothing*. They also resemble Aphra Behn's Willmore and Hellena and Molière's Alceste and Célimène. Millamant is every bit a match for Mirabell, and, as a result, their comic scenes are intense and engaging even as they reveal the limits of Congreve's society.

The "contract" scene in act IV, in which Millamant and Mirabell discuss their intentions to marry, is both funny and very serious. Their use of legal language in what is ostensibly a romantic situation is pointedly ironic. Millamant is no starry-eyed bride. She knows that once she is married all her possessions will belong to her husband; she will be like his chattel, to do with as he pleases. Having had the advantage of studying the marriages around her, she covenants in this scene for her independence.

The villain in the play is Fainall. While having an affair with Mrs. Marwood, he discovers that she is seriously attracted to Mirabell. No longer interested in Mrs. Marwood, he cannot turn away from her because she can expose him to his wife as an adulterer. Fainall's wife is Lady Wishfort's daughter, once married to a Mr. Languish, who has died. Before becoming involved with Fainall, Mrs. Fainall was Mirabell's mistress, but when she feared she was pregnant, Mirabell arranged the hasty marriage to Fainall, knowing that Fainall needed the widow's money and that Mrs. Fainall needed the respectability of marriage. It turned out that Mrs. Fainall was not pregnant and now regrets her marriage. In act II when she asks Mirabell why she married, he responds: "Why do we daily commit disagreeable and dangerous actions? To save that idol, reputation." Of her husband Fainall, he says, "When you are weary of him, you know your remedy." (The epigraph at the beginning of the play warns us that adultery is the subject of the drama.) These circumstances demonstrate that Fainall, for all his villainy, is also being used by the Wishfort family.

Mirabell, like Fainall, is a manipulator but is not a villain at heart. He respects Millamant and manages ultimately to find a way to undo Fainall's schemes to control Millamant's fortune. The play does not end with everyone happy, but with Mirabell and Millamant possessing the advantage and looking forward to marriage and children. Eventually, all deceptions are revealed, the proper lovers are joined, and the complications are smoothed out. Because of its careful examination of the relationship between the sexes and of the impediments a sophisticated society can throw between them, *The Way of the World* is virtually a timeless comedy.

The Way of the World in Performance

After the play's initial poor reception, Alexander Pope praised *The Way of the World* as having "so much bullion in it as would serve to lace fifty modern comedies." It was revived relatively soon after 1701 in London and, according to theater historian Emmet Avery, it played 285 times in the eighteenth century. It was one of the first plays at the new Covent Garden Theatre on December 7, 1732, and is said to be among the most produced English comedies ever since. It is manifestly a vehicle for female stars. The great actress Dame Peggy Ashcroft, along with Dame Edith Evans, starred in the London production of 1942. The play has been done steadily in the United States since the 1920s. The Tyrone Guthrie Theater in Minneapolis produced it in 1965 to rave notices; Jessica Tandy as Lady Wishfort essentially stole the show. Britain's Actor's

Company brought it to the Brooklyn Academy of Music in 1974, with the characters wearing cutaway formal clothes, top hats, and tails instead of eighteenth-century garb. The production used telephones and other modern conveniences to demonstrate that the play is not a museum piece. Robin Phillips's 1976 Stratford, Ontario, production was described as "nothing short of brilliant." Maggie Smith played Millamant several times in the 1980s, joining Jessica Tandy in her role as Lady Wishfort. Smith's performance in the January 1985 London production underscored the fact that the role is ideal for a great comic actress. She made the play her own.

William Congreve *(1670–1729)*

THE WAY OF THE WORLD   *1700*

Audire est operae pretium, procedere recte
Qui moechis non vultis.   — HORACE, *Satires*°

— Metuat doti deprensa.°

PROLOGUE

(Spoken by Mr. Fainall.)

Of those few fools who with ill stars are curst,
Sure scribbling fools, call'd poets, fare the worst;
For they're a sort of fools which Fortune makes,
And after she has made 'em fools, forsakes.
5   With Nature's oafs 'tis quite a different case,
For Fortune favors all her idiot-race;
In her° own nest the cuckoo-eggs we find,
O'er which she broods to hatch the
      changeling-kind.°
No portion for her own she has to spare,
10   So much she dotes on her adopted care.
   Poets are bubbles,° by the town drawn in,
Suffer'd at first some trifling stakes to win;
But what unequal hazards do they run!
Each time they write, they venture all they've won;

The squire that's buttered° still, is sure to be
      undone.   15
This author, heretofore, has found your favor,
But pleads no merit from his past behavior.
To build on that might prove a vain presumption,
Should grants to poets made admit resumption;
And in Parnassus° he must lose his seat,   20
If that be found a forfeited estate.
   He owns, with toil he wrought the following
      scenes,
But, if they're naught, ne'er spare him for his pains;
Damn him the more; have no commiseration
For dullness on mature deliberation.   25
He swears he'll not resent one hiss'd-off scene,
Nor, like those peevish wits, his play maintain,
Who, to assert their sense, your taste arraign.
Some plot we think he has, and some new thought;
Some humor too, no farce; but that's a fault.   30
Satire, he thinks, you ought not to expect;
For so reform'd a town who dares correct?
To please, this time, has been his sole pretense;
He'll not instruct, lest it should give offense.
Should he by chance a knave or fool expose,   35
That hurts none here, sure here are none of those.
In short, our play shall (with your leave to show it)
Give you one instance of a passive poet,
Who to your judgments yields all resignation;
So save or damn, after your own discretion.   40

[Epigraphs] *Audire . . . vultis:* Horace, *Satires* I.2.37–38. "Ye that do not wish well to the proceedings of adulterers, it is worth your while to hear how they are hampered on all sides" (trans. Christopher Smart).   *Metuat doti deprensa:* Ibid., line 131. The context of the lines in which the epigraph appears is "Nor am I apprehensive, while I am in her company, . . . lest the maid . . . should be in apprehension for her limbs, *the detected wife for her portion* [dowry], I for myself" (trans. Smart).   **7. her:** Fortune's.   **8. O'er which . . . changeling-kind:** The cuckoo lays its eggs in the nests of other birds to whom they are left to be hatched. The implication is that Fortune is favorable to fools.   **11. bubbles:** Dupes.

15. buttered: Abundantly flattered.   **20. Parnassus:** The Greek mountain sacred to Apollo and the Muses.

Dramatis Personae

Men

FAINALL, *in love with Mrs. Marwood*
MIRABELL, *in love with Mrs. Millamant*
WITWOUD, }
PETULANT, } *followers of Mrs. Millamant*
SIR WILFULL WITWOUD, *half brother to Witwoud, and nephew to Lady Wishfort*
WAITWELL, *servant to Mirabell*

Women

LADY WISHFORT, *enemy to Mirabell, for having falsely pretended love to her*
MRS. MILLAMANT, *a fine lady, niece to Lady Wishfort, and loves Mirabell*
MRS. MARWOOD, *friend to Mr. Fainall, and likes Mirabell*
MRS. FAINALL, *daughter to Lady Wishfort, and wife to Fainall, formerly friend to Mirabell*
FOIBLE, *woman to Lady Wishfort*
MINCING, *woman to Mrs. Millamant*
BETTY, *waiting-maid at a chocolate-house*
PEG, *maid to Lady Wishfort*
DANCERS, FOOTMEN, *and* ATTENDANTS

Scene: *London. The time equal to that of the presentation.*

ACT I

(*A Chocolate-House. Mirabell and Fainall, rising from cards; Betty waiting.*)

MIRABELL: You are a fortunate man, Mr. Fainall.
FAINALL: Have we done?
MIRABELL: What you please. I'll play on to entertain you.
5 FAINALL: No, I'll give you your revenge another time, when you are not so indifferent; you are thinking of something else now, and play too negligently. The coldness of a losing gamester lessens the pleasure of the winner. I'd no more play with a man that slighted
10 his ill fortune than I'd make love to a woman who undervalued the loss of her reputation.
MIRABELL: You have a taste extremely delicate and are for refining on your pleasures.
FAINALL: Prithee, why so reserved? Something has put
15 you out of humor.
MIRABELL: Not at all. I happen to be grave today, and you are gay; that's all.
FAINALL: Confess, Millamant and you quarreled last night, after I left you; my fair cousin has some
20 humors° that would tempt the patience of a Stoic.°

---

20. humors: Moods. **Stoic:** One who subscribes to the Stoic school of philosophy, which teaches freedom from passion and indifference to pleasure and pain.

What, some coxcomb° came in, and was well received by her, while you were by.
MIRABELL: Witwoud and Petulant, and what was worse, her aunt, your wife's mother, my evil genius; or to sum up all in her own name, my old Lady Wish-
25 fort came in.
FAINALL: Oh, there it is then! She has a lasting passion for you, and with reason. What, then my wife was there?
MIRABELL: Yes, and Mrs. Marwood, and three or four
30 more, whom I never saw before. Seeing me, they all put on their grave faces, whispered one another; then complained aloud of the vapors,° and after fell into a profound silence.
FAINALL: They had a mind to be rid of you.
35
MIRABELL: For which reason I resolved not to stir. At last the good old lady broke through her painful taciturnity with an invective against long visits. I would not have understood her, but Millamant joining in the argument, I rose, and, with a constrained smile,
40 told her, I thought nothing was so easy as to know when a visit began to be troublesome. She reddened, and I withdrew, without expecting° her reply.
FAINALL: You were to blame to resent what she spoke only in compliance with her aunt.
45
MIRABELL: She is more mistress of herself than to be under the necessity of such a resignation.
FAINALL: What? though half her fortune depends upon her marrying with my lady's approbation?
MIRABELL: I was then in such a humor that I should
50 have been better pleased if she had been less discreet.
FAINALL: Now I remember, I wonder not they were weary of you. Last night was one of their cabal nights; they have 'em three times a week, and meet by turns at one another's apartments, where they come
55 together like the coroner's inquest, to sit upon the murdered reputations of the week. You and I are excluded; and it was once proposed that all the male sex should be excepted. But somebody moved that, to avoid scandal, there might be one man of the com-
60 munity; upon which motion Witwoud and Petulant were enrolled members.°
MIRABELL: And who may have been the foundress of this sect? My Lady Wishfort, I warrant, who publishes her detestation of mankind, and full of the
65 vigor of fifty-five, declares for a friend° and ratafia,° and let posterity shift for itself, she'll breed no more.
FAINALL: The discovery of your sham addresses to her, to conceal your love to her niece, has provoked this separation; had you dissembled better, things might
70 have continued in the state of nature.
MIRABELL: I did as much as man could, with any rea-

---

21. coxcomb: Conceited person, fop. **33. vapors:** Boredom.
43. expecting: Awaiting. **61–62. Witwoud . . . members:** The implication is that Witwoud and Petulant are but half-men.
66. friend: Lover. When applied to a lady, the word carries the meaning of "mistress." **ratafia:** Fruit-flavored liqueur.

sonable conscience; I proceeded to the very last act of flattery with her, and was guilty of a song in her com-

75 mendation. Nay, I got a friend to put her into a lampoon, and compliment her with the imputation of an affair with a young fellow, which I carried so far that I told her the malicious town took notice that she was grown fat of a sudden; and when she lay in of a

80 dropsy,° persuaded her she was reported to be in labor. The devil's in't, if an old woman is to be flattered further, unless a man should endeavor downright personally to debauch° her; and that my virtue forbade me. But for the discovery of this amour I am

85 indebted to your friend, or your wife's friend, Mrs. Marwood.

FAINALL: What should provoke her to be your enemy, unless she has made you advances which you have slighted? Women do not easily forgive omissions of

90 that nature.

MIRABELL: She was always civil to me till of late. I confess I am not one of those coxcombs who are apt to interpret a woman's good manners to her prejudice, and think that she who does not refuse 'em every-

95 thing can refuse 'em nothing.

FAINALL: You are a gallant man, Mirabell; and though you may have cruelty enough not to satisfy a lady's longing, you have too much generosity not to be tender of her honor. Yet you speak with an indifference

100 which seems to be affected, and confesses you are conscious of a negligence.

MIRABELL: You pursue the argument with a distrust that seems to be unaffected, and confesses you are conscious of a concern for which the lady is more

105 indebted to you than is your wife.

FAINALL: Fie, fie, friend! If you grow censorious, I must leave you. I'll look upon the gamesters in the next room.

MIRABELL: Who are they?

110 FAINALL: Petulant and Witwoud. (*To Betty.*) Bring me some chocolate.   (*Exit.*)

MIRABELL: Betty, what says your clock?

BETTY: Turned of the last canonical hour,° sir.

(*Exit.*)

MIRABELL: How pertinently the jade° answers me!

115 (*Looking on his watch.*) Ha? almost one o'clock! O, y'are come!

(*Enter a Footman.*)

Well, is the grand affair over? You have been something tedious.

FOOTMAN: Sir, there's such coupling at Pancras° that they

stand behind one another, as 'twere in a country dance.   120
Ours was the last couple to lead up, and no hopes appearing of dispatch, besides the parson growing hoarse, we were afraid his lungs would have failed before it came to our turn, so we drove round to Duke's place,° and there they were riveted in a trice.°   125

MIRABELL: So, you are sure they are married.

FOOTMAN: Married and bedded, sir; I am witness.

MIRABELL: Have you the certificate?

FOOTMAN: Here it is, sir.

MIRABELL: Has the tailor brought Waitwell's clothes   130
home, and the new liveries?

FOOTMAN: Yes, sir.

MIRABELL: That's well. Do you go home again, d'ye hear, and adjourn the consummation till further order; bid Waitwell shake his ears, and Dame Partlet°   135
rustle up her feathers, and meet me at one o'clock by Rosamond's Pond,° that I may see her before she returns to her lady; and as you tender your ears, be secret.

(*Exit Footman.*)

(*Reenter Fainall and Betty.*)

FAINALL: Joy of your success, Mirabell; you look   140
pleased.

MIRABELL: Aye, I have been engaged in a matter of some sort of mirth, which is not yet ripe for discovery. I am glad this is not a cabal night. I wonder, Fainall, that you who are married, and of consequence should be   145
discreet, will suffer your wife to be of such a party.

FAINALL: Faith, I am not jealous. Besides, most who are engaged are women and relations; and for the men, they are of a kind too contemptible to give scandal.

MIRABELL: I am of another opinion. The greater the   150
coxcomb, always the more the scandal; for a woman who is not a fool can have but one reason for associating with a man who is one.

FAINALL: Are you jealous as often as you see Witwoud entertained by Millamant?   155

MIRABELL: Of her understanding I am, if not of her person.

FAINALL: You do her wrong; for, to give her her due, she has wit.

MIRABELL: She has beauty enough to make any man   160
think so, and complaisance enough not to contradict him who shall tell her so.

FAINALL: For a passionate lover, methinks you are a man somewhat too discerning in the failings of your mistress.   165

MIRABELL: And for a discerning man, somewhat too passionate a lover; for I like her with all her faults, nay, like her for her faults. Her follies are so natural,

---

80. dropsy: An excessive accumulation of fluid in the body. **83. debauch:** Seduce.   **113. canonical hour:** It was only during the canonical hours (eight in the morning to twelve noon) that marriages could be legally performed.   **114. jade:** Derogatory term for a woman.   **119. Pancras:** St. Pancras Church, where marriages were performed without license and outside the canonical hours.

125. Duke's place: St. James's Church, Aldgate.   **riveted in a trice:** Married quickly.   **135. Dame Partlet:** Refers to Foible, who has just been married to Waitwell. "Partlet" derives from Pertelote, the hen in Chaucer's "Nun's Priest's Tale."   **137. Rosamond's Pond:** A lake in St. James's Park.

170 or so artful, that they become her, and those affectations which in another woman would be odious,
serve but to make her more agreeable. I'll tell thee,
Fainall, she once used me with that insolence, that in
revenge I took her to pieces, sifted° her, and separated her failings, I studied 'em, and got 'em by rote.°
175 The catalogue was so large that I was not without
hopes one day or other to hate her heartily: To which
end I so used° myself to think of 'em that at length,
contrary to my design and expectation, they gave me
every hour less and less disturbance, till in a few days
180 it became habitual to me to remember 'em without
being displeased. They are now grown as familiar to
me as my own frailties; and in all probability, in a
little time longer I shall like 'em as well.

FAINALL: Marry her, marry her! Be half as well acquainted
185 with her charms as you are with her defects, and my
life on't, you are your own man again.

MIRABELL: Say you so?

FAINALL: Aye, aye, I have experience; I have a wife, and
so forth.

(Enter a Messenger.)

190 MESSENGER: Is one Squire Witwoud here?

BETTY: Yes; what's your business?

MESSENGER: I have a letter for him, from his brother Sir
Wilfull, which I am charged to deliver into his own
hands.

195 BETTY: He's in the next room, friend; that way.

(Exit Messenger.)

MIRABELL: What, is the chief of that noble family in
town, Sir Wilfull Witwoud?

FAINALL: He is expected today. Do you know him?

MIRABELL: I have seen him. He promises to be an extra-
200 ordinary° person; I think you have the honor to be
related to him.

FAINALL: Yes, he is half brother to this Witwoud by a
former wife, who was sister to my Lady Wishfort, my
wife's mother. If you marry Millamant, you must call
205 cousins too.

MIRABELL: I had rather be his relation than his acquaintance.

FAINALL: He comes to town in order to equip himself for
travel.

210 MIRABELL: For travel! Why the man that I mean is
above forty.°

FAINALL: No matter for that; 'tis for the honor of
England that all Europe should know we have block-
heads of all ages.

215 MIRABELL: I wonder there is not an act of parliament to
save the credit of the nation, and prohibit the expor-
tation of fools.

FAINALL: By no means; 'tis better as 'tis. 'Tis better to
trade with a little loss than to be quite eaten up with
being overstocked.   220

MIRABELL: Pray, are the follies of this knight-errant and
those of the squire his brother anything related?

FAINALL: Not at all; Witwoud grows by the knight, like
a medlar grafted on a crab.° One will melt in your
mouth, and t'other set your teeth on edge; one is all   225
pulp, and the other all core.

MIRABELL: So one will be rotten before he be ripe, and
the other will be rotten without ever being ripe at all.

FAINALL: Sir Wilfull is an odd mixture of bashfulness
and obstinacy. But when he's drunk, he's as loving as   230
the monster in *The Tempest,*° and much after the
same manner. To give t'other his due, he has something of good nature and does not always want wit.

MIRABELL: Not always; but as often as his memory fails
him, and his commonplace° of comparisons. He is a   235
fool with a good memory and some few scraps of
other folks' wit. He is one whose conversation can
never be approved, yet it is now and then to be
endured. He has indeed one good quality, he is not
exceptious;° for he so passionately affects the reputa- 240
tion of understanding raillery° that he will construe
an affront into a jest and call downright rudeness
and ill language, satire and fire.

FAINALL: If you have a mind to finish his picture, you
have an opportunity to do it at full length. Behold the 245
original!

(Enter Witwoud.)

WITWOUD: Afford me your compassion, my dears! Pity
me, Fainall! Mirabell, pity me!

MIRABELL: I do from my soul.

FAINALL: Why, what's the matter?   250

WITWOUD: No letters for me, Betty?

BETTY: Did not a messenger bring you one but now, sir?

WITWOUD: Aye, but no other?

BETTY: No, sir.

WITWOUD: That's hard, that's very hard. A messenger, a   255
mule, a beast of burden! He has brought me a letter
from the fool my brother, as heavy as a panegyric°
in a funeral sermon, or a copy of commendatory
verses from one poet to another. And what's worse,
'tis as sure a forerunner of the author as an epistle   260
dedicatory.

MIRABELL: A fool, and your brother, Witwoud!

WITWOUD: Aye, aye, my half brother. My half brother
he is, no nearer upon honor.

MIRABELL: Then 'tis possible he may be but half a fool.   265

---

173. **sifted:** Examined closely. 174. **by rote:** In a mechanical way. 177. **used:** Accustomed. 199–200. **extraordinary:**
Somewhat eccentric. 211. **above forty:** It was customary for a
gentleman of quality to make a "grand tour" of continental
capitals in his early twenties.

224. **medlar grafted on a crab:** The medlar is like a crab apple
and is edible only when it begins to decay. The crab apple is
always sour. 231. **the monster in *The Tempest*:** Caliban (or
Sycorax) in the adaptation of Shakespeare's play by John Dryden and Sir William Davenant (1667). 235. **commonplace:**
Commonplace book; scrapbook. 240. **exceptious:** Inclined
to take exceptions. 241. **raillery:** Good-humored ridicule;
banter. 257. **panegyric:** Eulogy, especially involving elaborate
praise.

WITWOUD: Good, good, Mirabell, *le drôle*!° Good, good; hang him, don't let's talk of him. Fainall, how does your lady? Gad, I say anything in the world to get this fellow out of my head. I beg pardon that I should ask a man of pleasure and the town a question at once so foreign and domestic.° But I talk like an old maid at a marriage, I don't know what I say; but she's the best woman in the world.°

FAINALL: 'Tis well you don't know what you say, or else your commendation would go near to make me either vain or jealous.

WITWOUD: No man in town lives well with a wife but Fainall. Your judgment, Mirabell?

MIRABELL: You had better step and ask his wife, if you would be credibly informed.

WITWOUD: Mirabell.

MIRABELL: Aye.

WITWOUD: My dear, I ask ten thousand pardons; gad, I have forgot what I was going to say to you!

MIRABELL: I thank you heartily, heartily.

WITWOUD: No, but prithee excuse me; my memory is such a memory.

MIRABELL: Have a care of such apologies, Witwoud; for I never knew a fool but he affected to complain, either of the spleen° or his memory.

FAINALL: What have you done with Petulant?

WITWOUD: He's reckoning his money — my money it was. I have no luck today.

FAINALL: You may allow him to win of you at play, for you are sure to be too hard for him at repartee;° since you monopolize the wit that is between you, the fortune must be his, of course.

MIRABELL: I don't find that Petulant confesses the superiority of wit to be your talent, Witwoud.

WITWOUD: Come, come, you are malicious now, and would breed debates. Petulant's my friend, and a very honest fellow, and a very pretty fellow, and has a smattering — faith and troth,° a pretty deal of an odd sort of a small wit; nay, I'll do him justice. I'm his friend, I won't wrong him. And if he had any judgment in the world, he would not be altogether contemptible. Come, come, don't detract from the merits of my friend.

FAINALL: You don't take your friend to be over-nicely bred?

WITWOUD: No, no, hang him, the rogue has no manners at all, that I must own. No more breeding than a bum-baily,° that I grant you. 'Tis pity, faith; the fellow has fire and life.

MIRABELL: What, courage?

WITWOUD: Hum, faith I don't know as to that; I can't say as to that. Yes, faith, in a controversy he'll contradict anybody.

MIRABELL: Though 'twere a man whom he feared, or a woman whom he loved.

WITWOUD: Well, well, he does not always think before he speaks; we have all our failings. You are too hard upon him, you are, faith. Let me excuse him. I can defend most of his faults, except one or two. One he has, that's the truth on't; if he were my brother, I could not acquit him. That indeed I could wish were otherwise.

MIRABELL: Aye, marry, what's that, Witwoud?

WITWOUD: Oh, pardon me! Expose the infirmities of my friend? No, my dear, excuse me there.

FAINALL: What, I warrant he's unsincere, or 'tis some such trifle.

WITWOUD: No, no, what if he be? 'Tis no matter for that; his wit will excuse that. A wit should no more be sincere than a woman constant; one argues a decay of parts,° as t'other of beauty.

MIRABELL: Maybe you think him too positive?

WITWOUD: No, no, his being positive is an incentive to argument, and keeps up conversation.

FAINALL: Too illiterate?

WITWOUD: That! that's his happiness; his want of learning gives him the more opportunities to show his natural parts.

MIRABELL: He wants words?

WITWOUD: Aye, but I like him for that now; for his want of words gives me the pleasure very often to explain his meaning.

FAINALL: He's impudent?

WITWOUD: No, that's not it.

MIRABELL: Vain?

WITWOUD: No.

MIRABELL: What! he speaks unseasonable truths sometimes, because he has not wit enough to invent an evasion?

WITWOUD: Truths! ha! ha! ha! No, no; since you will have it, I mean he never speaks truth at all, that's all. He will lie like a chambermaid, or a woman of quality's porter. Now that is a fault.

(*Enter a Coachman.*)

COACHMAN: Is Master Petulant here, mistress?

BETTY: Yes.

COACHMAN: Three gentlewomen in a coach would speak with him.

FAINALL: O brave Petulant! Three!

BETTY: I'll tell him.

COACHMAN: You must bring two dishes of chocolate and a glass of cinnamon-water.°

(*Exeunt*° *Betty and Coachman.*)

---

266. *le drôle:* The wag.   **271. foreign and domestic:** Since he knows (by gossip) that the Fainall marriage is not working out very well, Witwoud plays on the words "foreign and domestic."   **273. best woman in the world:** I.e., Mrs. Fainall. Witwoud realizes that he has blundered into a rather delicate situation.   **290. spleen:** Ill humor; peevishness.   **295. repartee:** Adroitness and cleverness in making replies in conversation.   **303. troth:** Loyalty, faithfulness.   **313. bum-baily:** An under-bailiff, a minor court officer.

335. parts: Personal endowments.   **365. cinnamon-water:** A cordial of spirits, cinnamon, and hot water, prescribed to aid digestion.   [s.d.] *Exeunt:* Latin for "they go out."

WITWOUD: That should be for two fasting strumpets,° and a bawd troubled with wind.° Now you may know what the three are.

MIRABELL: You are very free with your friend's acquaintance.

WITWOUD: Aye, aye, friendship without freedom is as dull as love without enjoyment, or wine without toasting. But to tell you a secret, these are trulls° whom he allows coach-hire, and something more, by the week, to call on him once a day at public places.

MIRABELL: How!

WITWOUD: You shall see how he won't go to 'em, because there's no more company here to take notice of him. Why, this is nothing to what he used to do; before he found out this way, I have known him call for himself.

FAINALL: Call for himself? What dost thou mean?

WITWOUD: Mean! Why, he would slip you out° of this chocolate-house, just when you had been talking to him; as soon as your back was turned, whip, he was gone! Then trip to his lodging, clap on a hood and scarf, and a mask, slap into a hackney-coach, and drive hither to the door again in a trice, where he would send in for himself; that I mean, call for himself, wait for himself. Nay, and what's more, not finding himself, sometimes leave a letter for himself.

MIRABELL: I confess this is something extraordinary. I believe he waits for himself now, he is so long a-coming. Oh! I ask his pardon.

(*Enter Petulant and Betty.*)

BETTY: Sir, the coach stays.

PETULANT: Well, well, I come. 'Sbud,° a man had as good be a professed midwife as a professed whoremaster, at this rate! To be knocked up and raised at all hours, and in all places! Pox on 'em, I won't come! D'ye hear, tell 'em I won't come. Let 'em snivel and cry their hearts out.

FAINALL: You are very cruel, Petulant.

PETULANT: All's one, let it pass. I have a humor to be cruel.

MIRABELL: I hope they are not persons of condition° that you use at this rate.

PETULANT: Condition! Condition's a dried fig, if I am not in humor! By this hand, if they were your — a — a — your what-d'ye-call-'ems themselves, they must wait or rub off,° if I want appetite.°

MIRABELL: What-d'ye-call-'ems! What are they, Witwoud?

WITWOUD: Empresses, my dear; by your what-d'ye-call-'ems he means sultana queens.

PETULANT: Aye, Roxolanas.°

MIRABELL: Cry you mercy!

FAINALL: Witwoud says they are —

PETULANT: What does he say th'are?

WITWOUD: I? Fine ladies, I say.

PETULANT: Pass on, Witwoud. Harkee, by this light his relations: two co-heiresses his cousins, and an old aunt, who loves caterwauling° better than a conventicle.°

WITWOUD: Ha! ha! ha! I had a mind to see how the rogue would come off. Ha! ha! ha! Gad, I can't be angry with him, if he had said they were my mother and my sisters.

MIRABELL: No!

WITWOUD: No; the rogue's wit and readiness of invention charm me. Dear Petulant!

BETTY: They are gone, sir, in great anger.

PETULANT: Enough, let 'em trundle. Anger helps complexion, saves paint.°

FAINALL: This continence is all dissembled; this is in order to have something to brag of the next time he makes court to Millamant, and swear he has abandoned the whole sex for her sake.

MIRABELL: Have you not left off your impudent pretensions there yet? I shall cut your throat some time or other, Petulant, about that business.

PETULANT: Aye, aye, let that pass. There are other throats to be cut.

MIRABELL: Meaning mine, sir?

PETULANT: Not I. I mean nobody; I know nothing. But there are uncles and nephews in the world, and they may be rivals. What then? All's one for that.

MIRABELL: How! harkee Petulant, come hither. Explain, or I shall call your interpreter.°

PETULANT: Explain! I know nothing. Why, you have an uncle, have you not, lately come to town, and lodges by my Lady Wishfort's?

MIRABELL: True.

PETULANT: Why, that's enough. You and he are not friends; and if he should marry and have a child, you may be disinherited, ha?

MIRABELL: Where hast thou stumbled upon all this truth?

PETULANT: All's one for that; why, then say I know something.

MIRABELL: Come, thou art an honest fellow, Petulant, and shalt make love to my mistress, thou sha't,° faith. What hast thou heard of my uncle?

PETULANT: I? Nothing I. If throats are to be cut, let swords clash! Snug's the word;° I shrug and am silent.

MIRABELL: Oh, raillery, raillery! Come, I know thou art in the women's secrets. What, you're a cabalist; I

---

366. strumpets: Prostitutes.   **367. wind:** Air in the stomach or bowels.   **373. trulls:** Women of easy virtue.   **382. slip you out:** Slip out.   **395. 'Sbud:** "God's blood," a mild oath. **404. condition:** Social distinction.   **409. rub off:** Go away. **want appetite:** Lack desire for them.   **414. Roxolanas:** Roxolana is the name of the Turkish sultana in Davenant's *The Siege of Rhodes* (1656), one of the first "heroic plays."

421. caterwauling: Noisy quarreling.   **421–22. conventicle:** A meetinghouse of nonconformist religious sects, especially Presbyterians.   **432. paint:** Makeup.   **447. interpreter:** Possibly a second, as in a duel.   **460. sha't:** Slangy contraction for "shalt." **463. Snug's the word:** In modern slang, "Mum's the word."

know you stayed at Millamant's last night, after I
went. Was there any mention made of my uncle or
me? Tell me. If thou hadst but good nature equal to
470 thy wit, Petulant, Tony Witwoud, who is now thy
competitor in fame, would show as dim by thee as a
dead whiting's° eye by a pearl of orient;° he would no
more be seen by thee than Mercury is by the sun.°
Come, I'm sure thou wo't° tell me.

475 PETULANT: If I do, will you grant me common sense then
for the future?

MIRABELL: Faith, I'll do what I can for thee, and I'll
pray that Heaven may grant it thee in the meantime.

PETULANT: Well, harkee.

(*Mirabell and Petulant talk apart.*)

480 FAINALL: Petulant and you both will find Mirabell as
warm a rival as a lover.

WITWOUD: Pshaw! pshaw! That she laughs at Petulant
is plain. And for my part, but that it is almost a fashion to admire her, I should — Harkee, to tell you a
485 secret, but let it go no further; between friends, I shall
never break my heart for her.

FAINALL: How!

WITWOUD: She's handsome; but she's a sort of an uncertain woman.

490 FAINALL: I thought you had died for her.

WITWOUD: Umh — no —

FAINALL: She has wit.

WITWOUD: 'Tis what she will hardly allow anybody
else. Now, demme,° I should hate that, if she were as
495 handsome as Cleopatra. Mirabell is not so sure of her
as he thinks for.

FAINALL: Why do you think so?

WITWOUD: We stayed pretty late there last night, and
heard something of an uncle to Mirabell, who is
500 lately come to town, and is between him and the best
part of his estate. Mirabell and he are at some distance, as my Lady Wishfort has been told; and you
know she hates Mirabell worse than a Quaker hates
a parrot,° or than a fishmonger hates a hard frost.°
505 Whether this uncle has seen Mrs. Millamant or not, I
cannot say; but there were items of such a treaty
being in embryo, and if it should come to life, poor
Mirabell would be in some sort unfortunately
fobbed,° i'faith.

510 FAINALL: 'Tis impossible Millamant should hearken to
it.

WITWOUD: Faith, my dear, I can't tell; she's a woman,
and a kind of a humorist.°

MIRABELL: And this° is the sum of what you could collect last night?   515

PETULANT: The quintessence. Maybe Witwoud knows
more; he stayed longer. Besides, they never mind him;
they say anything before him.

MIRABELL: I thought you had been the greatest favorite.

PETULANT: Aye, *tête à tête,*° but not in public, because I   520
make remarks.

MIRABELL: You do?

PETULANT: Aye, aye, pox, I'm malicious, man! Now he's
soft, you know; they are not in awe of him. The fellow's well bred; he's what you call a what-d'ye-call-   525
'em, a fine gentleman; but he's silly withal.

MIRABELL: I thank you. I know as much as my curiosity
requires. Fainall, are you for the Mall?°

FAINALL: Aye, I'll take a turn before dinner.

WITWOUD: Aye, we'll walk in the Park; the ladies talked   530
of being there.

MIRABELL: I thought you were obliged to watch for
your brother Sir Wilfull's arrival.

WITWOUD: No, no, he comes to his aunt's, my Lady
Wishfort. Pox on him! I shall be troubled with him   535
too; what shall I do with the fool?

PETULANT: Beg him for his estate, that I may beg you
afterwards; and so have but one trouble with you
both.

WITWOUD: O rare Petulant! Thou art as quick as fire in   540
a frosty morning; thou shalt to the Mall with us, and
we'll be very severe.

PETULANT: Enough, I'm in a humor to be severe.

MIRABELL: Are you? Pray then walk by yourselves: Let
us not be accessory to your putting the ladies out of   545
countenance with your senseless ribaldry,° which you
roar out aloud as often as they pass by you; and
when you have made a handsome woman blush, then
you think you have been severe.

PETULANT: What, what? Then let 'em either show their   550
innocence by not understanding what they hear, or
else show their discretion by not hearing what they
would not be thought to understand.

MIRABELL: But hast not thou then sense enough to
know that thou oughtest to be most ashamed thyself,   555
when thou hast put another out of countenance?

PETULANT: Not I, by this hand! I always take blushing
either for a sign of guilt or ill breeding.

MIRABELL: I confess you ought to think so. You are in
the right, that you may plead the error of your judg-   560
ment in defense of your practice.

    Where modesty's ill manners, 'tis but fit
    That impudence and malice pass for wit.

(*Exeunt.*)

---

472. **whiting:** A kind of codfish.   **pearl of orient:** Said to be
particularly brilliant.   473. **than Mercury is by the sun:**
The planet nearest the sun and of very low magnitude.
474. **wo't:** Wilt.   494. **demme:** Contraction of "damn me."
503–04. **Quaker . . . parrot:** Parrots are proverbially known to
swear.   504. **fishmonger . . . frost:** Fishmongers peddled fish
and consequently hated very cold weather.   509. **fobbed:**
Cheated.   513. **humorist:** A moody or capricious person,
hence unreliable.

514. **And this:** During the dialogue of Fainall and Witwoud,
Mirabell and Petulant have been talking "apart." They now
reenter the general dialogue.   520. *tête à tête:* Head to head.
528. **Mall:** A fashionable walk in St. James's Park.   546. **ribaldry:** Coarse behavior or language.

Scene from an updated version of *The Way of the World* directed by Sharon Ott in 1992 at the Huntington Theatre in Boston.

ACT II

(*St. James's Park. Enter Mrs. Fainall and Mrs. Marwood.*)

MRS. FAINALL: Aye, aye, dear Marwood, if we will be happy, we must find the means in ourselves, and among ourselves. Men are ever in extremes, either doting or averse. While they are lovers, if they have
5 fire and sense, their jealousies are insupportable. And when they cease to love (we ought to think at least) they loathe; they look upon us with horror and distaste; they meet us like the ghosts of what we were, and as from such, fly from us.
10 MRS. MARWOOD: True, 'tis an unhappy circumstance of life that love should ever die before us; and that the man so often should outlive the lover. But say what you will, 'tis better to be left than never to have been loved. To pass our youth in dull indifference, to
15 refuse the sweets of life because they once must leave us, is as preposterous as to wish to have been born old, because we one day must be old. For my part, my youth may wear and waste, but it shall never rust in my possession.

MRS. FAINALL: Then it seems you dissemble an aversion   20
to mankind, only in compliance to my mother's humor?

MRS. MARWOOD: Certainly. To be free,° I have no taste of those insipid dry discourses with which our sex of force must entertain themselves, apart from men. We   25
may affect endearments to each other, profess eternal friendships, and seem to dote like lovers; but 'tis not in our natures long to persevere. Love will resume his empire in our breasts; and every heart, or soon or late, receive and readmit him as its lawful tyrant.   30

MRS. FAINALL: Bless me, how have I been deceived! Why, you profess a libertine!°

MRS. MARWOOD: You see my friendship by my free-

23. **free:** Frank.   32. **profess a libertine:** Speak as one who leads a loose, unconventional life.

dom. Come, be as sincere, acknowledge that your
35   sentiments agree with mine.
MRS. FAINALL: Never!
MRS. MARWOOD: You hate mankind?
MRS. FAINALL: Heartily, inveterately.
MRS. MARWOOD: Your husband?
40 MRS. FAINALL: Most transcendently; aye, though I say
    it, meritoriously.
MRS. MARWOOD: Give me your hand upon it.
MRS. FAINALL: There.
MRS. MARWOOD: I join with you; what I have said has
45   been to try you.
MRS. FAINALL: Is it possible? Dost thou hate those
    vipers, men?
MRS. MARWOOD: I have done hating 'em; and am now
    come to despise 'em; the next thing I have to do, is
50   eternally to forget 'em.
MRS. FAINALL: There spoke the spirit of an Amazon, a
    Penthesilea!°
MRS. MARWOOD: And yet I am thinking sometimes to
    carry my aversion further.
55 MRS. FAINALL: How?
MRS. MARWOOD: Faith, by marrying; if I could but find
    one that loved me very well and would be thoroughly
    sensible of ill usage, I think I should do myself the
    violence of undergoing the ceremony.
60 MRS. FAINALL: You would not make him a cuckold?
MRS. MARWOOD: No, but I'd make him believe I did,
    and that's as bad.
MRS. FAINALL: Why had not you as good do it?
MRS. MARWOOD: Oh, if he should ever discover it, he
65   would then know the worst, and be out of his pain;
    but I would have him ever to continue upon the rack
    of fear and jealousy.
MRS. FAINALL: Ingenious mischief! Would thou wert
    married to Mirabell.
70 MRS. MARWOOD: Would I were!
MRS. FAINALL: You change color.
MRS. MARWOOD: Because I hate him.
MRS. FAINALL: So do I; but I can hear him named. But
    what reason have you to hate him in particular?
75 MRS. MARWOOD: I never loved him; he is, and always
    was, insufferably proud.
MRS. FAINALL: By the reason you give for your aversion,
    one would think it dissembled; for you have laid a
    fault to his charge of which his enemies must acquit
80   him.
MRS. MARWOOD: Oh, then it seems you are one of his
    favorable enemies. Methinks you look a little pale,
    and now you flush again.
MRS. FAINALL: Do I? I think I am a little sick o' the
85   sudden.
MRS. MARWOOD: What ails you?

52. Penthesilea: Queen of the Amazons, the mythical race of
women warriors. After befriending Priam following the death
of Hector, she was killed by Achilles, who fell in love with her
as she lay dying.

MRS. FAINALL: My husband. Don't you see him? He
    turned short upon me unawares, and has almost
    overcome me.

(*Enter Fainall and Mirabell.*)

MRS. MARWOOD: Ha! ha! ha! He comes opportunely   90
    for you.
MRS. FAINALL: For you, for he has brought Mirabell
    with him.
FAINALL: My dear!
MRS. FAINALL: My soul!   95
FAINALL: You don't look well today, child.
MRS. FAINALL: D'ye think so?
MIRABELL: He is the only man that does, madam.
MRS. FAINALL: The only man that would tell me so at
    least; and the only man from whom I could hear it   100
    without mortification.
FAINALL: O my dear, I am satisfied of your tenderness; I
    know you cannot resent anything from me, especially
    what is in effect of my concern.
MRS. FAINALL: Mr. Mirabell, my mother interrupted   105
    you in a pleasant relation last night; I would fain hear
    it out.
MIRABELL: The persons concerned in that affair have
    yet a tolerable reputation. I am afraid Mr. Fainall will
    be censorious.   110
MRS. FAINALL: He has a humor more prevailing than his
    curiosity and will willingly dispense with the hearing
    of one scandalous story, to avoid giving an occasion
    to make another by being seen to walk with his wife.
    This way, Mr. Mirabell, and I dare promise you will   115
    oblige us both.

(*Exeunt Mrs. Fainall and Mirabell.*)

FAINALL: Excellent creature! Well, sure if I should live to
    be rid of my wife, I should be a miserable man.
MRS. MARWOOD: Aye!
FAINALL: For having only that one hope, the accom-   120
    plishment of it, of consequence, must put an end to
    all my hopes; and what a wretch is he who must sur-
    vive his hopes! Nothing remains when that day
    comes, but to sit down and weep like Alexander,°
    when he wanted other worlds to conquer.   125
MRS. MARWOOD: Will you not follow 'em?
FAINALL: Faith, I think not.
MRS. MARWOOD: Pray let us; I have a reason.
FAINALL: You are not jealous?
MRS. MARWOOD: Of whom?   130
FAINALL: Of Mirabell.
MRS. MARWOOD: If I am, is it inconsistent with my love
    to you that I am tender of your honor?
FAINALL: You would intimate, then, as if there were a
    fellow-feeling between my wife and him.   135
MRS. MARWOOD: I think she does not hate him to that
    degree she would be thought.

124. Alexander: Alexander the Great (356–323 B.C.), the powerful ruler and conqueror.

FAINALL: But he, I fear, is too insensible.

MRS. MARWOOD: It may be you are deceived.

140 FAINALL: It may be so. I do now begin to apprehend it.

MRS. MARWOOD: What?

FAINALL: That I have been deceived, madam, and you are false.

MRS. MARWOOD: That I am false! What mean you?

145 FAINALL: To let you know I see through all your little arts. Come, you both love him; and both have equally dissembled your aversion. Your mutual jealousies of one another have made you clash till you have both struck fire. I have seen the warm confes-

150 sion reddening on your cheeks and sparkling from your eyes.

MRS. MARWOOD: You do me wrong.

FAINALL: I do not. 'Twas for my ease to oversee° and willfully neglect the gross advances made him by my

155 wife; that by permitting her to be engaged, I might continue unsuspected in my pleasures, and take you oftener to my arms in full security. But could you think, because the nodding husband would not awake, that e'er the watchful lover slept?

160 MRS. MARWOOD: And wherewithal can you reproach me?

FAINALL: With infidelity, with loving another, with love of Mirabell.

MRS. MARWOOD: 'Tis false! I challenge you to show an

165 instance that can confirm your groundless accusation. I hate him.

FAINALL: And wherefore do you hate him? He is insensible, and your resentment follows his neglect. An instance? The injuries you have done him are a proof,

170 your interposing in his love. What cause had you to make discoveries of his pretended passion? to undeceive the credulous aunt, and be the officious obstacle of his match with Millamant?

MRS. MARWOOD: My obligations to my lady urged me;

175 I had professed a friendship to her, and could not see her easy nature so abused by that dissembler.

FAINALL: What, was it conscience then? Professed a friendship! Oh, the pious friendships of the female sex!

180 MRS. MARWOOD: More tender, more sincere, and more enduring, than all the vain and empty vows of men, whether professing love to us, or mutual faith to one another.

FAINALL: Ha! ha! ha! You are my wife's friend too.

185 MRS. MARWOOD: Shame and ingratitude! Do you reproach me? You, you upbraid me? Have I been false to her, through strict fidelity to you, and sacrificed my friendship to keep my love inviolate? And have you the baseness to charge me with the guilt, un-

190 mindful of the merit? To you it should be meritorious, that I have been vicious, and do you reflect that guilt upon me, which should lie buried in your bosom?

FAINALL: You misinterpret my reproof. I meant but to remind you of the slight account you once could

153. oversee: Overlook.

make of strictest ties, when set in competition with 195 your love to me.

MRS. MARWOOD: 'Tis false; you urged it with deliberate malice! 'Twas spoke in scorn, and I never will forgive it.

FAINALL: Your guilt, not your resentment, begets your 200 rage. If yet you loved, you could forgive a jealousy; but you are stung to find that you are discovered.

MRS. MARWOOD: It shall be all discovered. You too shall be discovered, be sure you shall. I can but be exposed. If I do it myself, I shall prevent° your baseness. 205

FAINALL: Why, what will you do?

MRS. MARWOOD: Disclose it to your wife; own what has passed between us.

FAINALL: Frenzy!

MRS. MARWOOD: By all my wrongs I'll do't! I'll publish 210 to the world the injuries you have done me, both in my fame and fortune! With both I trusted you, you bankrupt in honor, as indigent of wealth.

FAINALL: Your fame I have preserved. Your fortune has been bestowed as the prodigality of your love would 215 have it, in pleasures which we both have shared. Yet, had not you been false, I had ere this repaid it. 'Tis true, had you permitted Mirabell with Millamant to have stolen their marriage, my lady had been incensed beyond all means of reconcilement, Milla- 220 mant had forfeited the moiety° of her fortune, which then would have descended to my wife. And wherefore did I marry, but to make lawful prize of a rich widow's wealth, and squander it on love and you?

MRS. MARWOOD: Deceit and frivolous pretense! 225

FAINALL: Death, am I not married! What's pretense? Am I not imprisoned, fettered? Have I not a wife? nay a wife that was a widow, a young widow, a handsome widow; and would be again a widow, but that I have a heart of proof,° and something of a constitution to 230 bustle through the ways of wedlock and this world! Will you yet be reconciled to truth and me?

MRS. MARWOOD: Impossible. Truth and you are inconsistent. I hate you, and shall for ever.

FAINALL: For loving you? 235

MRS. MARWOOD: I loathe the name of love after such usage; and next to the guilt with which you would asperse me, I scorn you most. Farewell!

FAINALL: Nay, we must not part thus.

MRS. MARWOOD: Let me go. 240

FAINALL: Come, I'm sorry.

MRS. MARWOOD: I care not, let me go, break my hands, do! I'd leave 'em to get loose.

FAINALL: I would not hurt you for the world. Have I no other hold to keep you here? 245

MRS. MARWOOD: Well, I have deserved it all.

FAINALL: You know I love you.

MRS. MARWOOD: Poor dissembling! Oh, that — well, It is not yet —

205. prevent: Anticipate.   221. moiety: Half.   230. heart of proof: A heart that is proof against such wishes.

250 FAINALL: What? what is it not? what is it not yet? It is not yet too late —

MRS. MARWOOD: No, it is not yet too late; I have that comfort.

FAINALL: It is, to love another.

255 MRS. MARWOOD: But not to loathe, detest, abhor mankind, myself, and the whole treacherous world.

FAINALL: Nay, this is extravagance. Come, I ask your pardon. No tears. I was to blame; I could not love you and be easy in my doubts. Pray, forbear. I believe

260 you. I'm convinced I've done you wrong; and any way, every way will make amends. I'll hate my wife yet more, damn her! I'll part with her, rob her of all she's worth, and we'll retire somewhere, anywhere, to another world. I'll marry thee; be pacified.

265 'Sdeath,° they come; hide your face, your tears. You have a mask;° wear it a moment. This way, this way. Be persuaded.

(*Exeunt.*)

(*Reenter Mirabell and Mrs. Fainall.*)

MRS. FAINALL: They are here yet.

MIRABELL: They are turning into the other walk.

270 MRS. FAINALL: While I only hated my husband, I could bear to see him; but since I have despised him, he's too offensive.

MIRABELL: Oh, you should hate with prudence.

MRS. FAINALL: Yes, for I have loved with indiscretion.

275 MIRABELL: You should have just so much disgust for your husband as may be sufficient to make you relish your lover.

MRS. FAINALL: You have been the cause that I have loved without bounds, and would you set limits to

280 that aversion of which you have been the occasion? Why did you make me marry this man?

MIRABELL: Why do we daily commit disagreeable and dangerous actions? To save that idol, reputation. If the familiarities of our loves had produced that con-

285 sequence of which you were apprehensive, where could you have fixed a father's name with credit, but on a husband?° I knew Fainall to be a man lavish of his morals, an interested and professing° friend, a false and a designing lover; yet one whose wit and

290 outward fair behavior have gained a reputation with the town enough to make that woman stand excused who has suffered herself to be won by his addresses. A better man ought not to have been sacrificed to the occasion; a worse had not answered to the purpose.

295 When you are weary of him, you know your remedy.

265. 'Sdeath: "God's death," an oath.   266. mask: Ladies' masks were fashionable and reputable except when worn at the theater, where they were construed as the mark of a loose woman.   283–87. If the familiarities . . . husband: Mirabell refers to his affair with Mrs. Fainall, after the death of her first husband, Mr. Languish, and prior to her marriage to Fainall. She feared that she was pregnant by Mirabell, and as a result Mirabell urged her marriage to Fainall.   288. professing: Self-interested and dissembling.

MRS. FAINALL: I ought to stand in some degree of credit with you, Mirabell.

MIRABELL: In justice to you, I have made you privy to my whole design, and put it in your power to ruin or advance my fortune. 300

MRS. FAINALL: Whom have you instructed to represent your pretended uncle?

MIRABELL: Waitwell, my servant.

MRS. FAINALL: He is an humble servant° to Foible, my mother's woman, and may win her to your interest. 305

MIRABELL: Care is taken for that. She is won and worn by this time. They were married this morning.

MRS. FAINALL: Who?

MIRABELL: Waitwell and Foible. I would not tempt my servant to betray me by trusting him too far. If your 310 mother, in hopes to ruin me, should consent to marry my pretended uncle, he might, like Mosca in *The Fox*,° stand upon terms;° so I made him sure beforehand.

MRS. FAINALL: So if my poor mother is caught in a con- 315 tract, you will discover the imposture betimes, and release her by producing a certificate of her gallant's former marriage?

MIRABELL: Yes, upon condition that she consent to my marriage with her niece, and surrender the moiety of 320 her fortune in her possession.°

MRS. FAINALL: She talked last night of endeavoring at a match between Millamant and your uncle.

MIRABELL: That was by Foible's direction, and my instruction, that she might seem to carry it more privately.° 325

MRS. FAINALL: Well, I have an opinion of your success for I believe my lady will do anything to get a husband; and when she has this, which you have provided for her, I suppose she will submit to anything to get rid of him. 330

MIRABELL: Yes, I think the good lady would marry anything that resembled a man, though 'twere no more than what a butler could pinch out of a napkin.°

MRS. FAINALL: Female frailty! We must all come to it, if we live to be old and feel the craving of a false 335 appetite when the true is decayed.

MIRABELL: An old woman's appetite is depraved like that of a girl. 'Tis the green sickness° of a second

304. servant: Suitor.   312–13. Mosca . . . *Fox*: Mosca, the crafty servant in Ben Jonson's play *Volpone; or, The Fox* (1606).   313. stand upon terms: Insist on the proper terms of a binding contract, as Mosca does in the denouement of the Jonson play.   319–21. condition that she . . . possession: Lady Wishfort has control of half of Mrs. Millamant's (her niece's) fortune, which Millamant will acquire on her marriage, provided Lady Wishfort approves of the match; should Millamant marry without her aunt's approval, she forfeits the half of her fortune in trust.   325. she might . . . privately: I.e., to allay any suspicions Lady Wishfort might have about the validity of Mirabell's "uncle."   333. pinch out of a napkin: It was fashionable to pinch table napkins into curious and fancy shapes.   338. green sickness: An anemia prevalent in adolescent girls, marked by a sallow yellow-green complexion.

340 childhood; and, like the faint offer of a latter spring, serves but to usher in the fall, and withers in an affected bloom.

MRS. FAINALL: Here's your mistress.

(*Enter Mrs. Millamant, Witwoud, and Mincing.*)

MIRABELL: Here she comes, i'faith, full sail, with her fan spread and streamers out, and a shoal of fools for
345 tenders.° Ha, no, I cry her mercy!

MRS. FAINALL: I see but one poor empty sculler,° and he tows her woman after him.

MIRABELL (*to Mrs. Millamant*): You seem to be unattended, madam. You used to have the *beau monde*°
350 throng after you, and a flock of gay, fine perukes° hovering round you.

WITWOUD: Like moths about a candle. I had like to have lost my comparison for want of breath.

MRS. MILLAMANT: Oh, I have denied myself airs today. I
355 have walked as fast through the crowd —

WITWOUD: As a favorite just disgraced, and with as few followers.

MRS. MILLAMANT: Dear Mr. Witwoud, truce with your similitudes;° for I'm as sick of 'em —
360 WITWOUD: As a physician of a good air. I cannot help it, madam, though 'tis against myself.

MRS. MILLAMANT: Yet again! Mincing, stand between me and his wit.

WITWOUD: Do, Mrs. Mincing, like a screen before a
365 great fire. I confess I do blaze today; I am too bright.

MRS. FAINALL: But, dear Millamant, why were you so long?

MRS. MILLAMANT: Long! Lord, have I not made violent haste? I have asked every living thing I met for you; I
370 have inquired after you, as after a new fashion.

WITWOUD: Madam, truce with your similitudes. No, you met her husband, and did not ask him for her.

MIRABELL: By your leave, Witwoud, that were like inquiring after an old fashion, to ask a husband for
375 his wife.

WITWOUD: Hum, a hit! a hit! a palpable hit!° I confess it.

MRS. FAINALL: You were dressed before I came abroad.

MRS. MILLAMANT: Aye, that's true. Oh, but then I had — Mincing, what had I? Why was I so long?

380 MINCING: O mem,° your laship° stayed to peruse a pecket° of letters.

MRS. MILLAMANT: Oh, aye, letters; I had letters. I am persecuted with letters. I hate letters. Nobody knows how to write letters, and yet one has 'em, one does
385 not know why. They serve one to pin up one's hair.

WITWOUD: Is that the way? Pray, madam, do you pin up your hair with all your letters? I find I must keep copies.

MRS. MILLAMANT: Only with those in verse, Mr. Witwoud. I never pin up my hair with prose, I think I
390 tried once, Mincing.

MINCING: O mem, I shall never forget it.

MRS. MILLAMANT: Aye, poor Mincing tiffed° and tiffed all the morning.

MINCING: Till I had the cremp in my fingers, I'll vow,
395 mem. And all to no purpose. But when your laship pins it up with poetry, it sits so pleasant the next day as anything, and is so pure and so crips.°

WITWOUD: Indeed, so crips?

MINCING: You're such a critic, Mr. Witwoud.
400 MRS. MILLAMANT: Mirabell, did you take exceptions last night? Oh, aye, and went away. Now I think on't, I'm angry. No, now I think on't, I'm pleased; for I believe I gave you some pain.

MIRABELL: Does that please you?
405 MRS. MILLAMANT: Infinitely; I love to give pain.

MIRABELL: You would affect a cruelty which is not in your nature; your true vanity is in the power of pleasing.

MRS. MILLAMANT: Oh, I ask your pardon for that. One's
410 cruelty is one's power; and when one parts with one's cruelty, one parts with one's power; and when one has parted with that, I fancy one's old and ugly.

MIRABELL: Aye, aye, suffer your cruelty to ruin the object of your power, to destroy your lover, and then
415 how vain, how lost a thing you'll be! Nay, 'tis true: You are no longer handsome when you've lost your lover; your beauty dies upon the instant. For beauty is the lover's gift; 'tis he bestows your charms, your glass is all a cheat. The ugly and the old, whom the
420 looking-glass mortifies, yet after commendation° can be flattered by it, and discover beauties in it; for that reflects our praises, rather than your face.

MRS. MILLAMANT: Oh, the vanity of these men! Fainall, d'ye hear him? If they did not commend us, we were
425 not handsome! Now, you must know they could not commend one, if one was not handsome. Beauty the lover's gift! Lord, what is a lover, that it can give? Why, one makes lovers as fast as one pleases, and they live as long as one pleases, and they die as soon
430 as one pleases; and then, if one pleases, one makes more.

WITWOUD: Very pretty. Why, you make no more of making of lovers, madam, than of making so many card matches.°
435 MRS. MILLAMANT: One no more owes one's beauty to a lover than one's wit to an echo. They can but reflect what we look and say; vain empty things if we are silent or unseen, and want a being.

---

345. **tenders:** Small boats that attend larger ships.   346. **sculler:** A man operating a rowboat; i.e., Witwoud.   349. *beau monde:* People of fashion.   350. **perukes:** Suitors, referring to the wigs worn by gentlemen of the period.   359. **similitudes:** Witwoud is a tireless (and tiresome) maker of comparisons, or similes. See "his commonplace [book] of comparisons" in act I.   376. **a palpable hit:** See Osric in *Hamlet*, V, II: "A hit, a very palpable hit."   380. **mem:** Madam. **laship:** Ladyship.   381. **pecket:** Packet.

393. **tiffed:** Arranged.   398. **crips:** Crisp.   421. **commendation:** Praise.   435. **card matches:** Matches made from pieces of heavy paper tipped with sulfur.

440 MIRABELL: Yet to those two vain empty things you owe
     two° the greatest pleasures of your life.
     MRS. MILLAMANT: How so?
     MIRABELL: To your lover you owe the pleasure of hear-
     ing yourselves praised; and to an echo the pleasure of
445 hearing yourselves talk.
     WITWOUD: But I know a lady that loves talking so inces-
     santly, she won't give an echo fair play; she has that
     everlasting rotation of tongue, that an echo must
     wait till she dies, before it can catch her last words.
450 MRS. MILLAMANT: Oh, fiction! Fainall, let us leave these
     men.
     MIRABELL (aside to Mrs. Fainall): Draw off Witwoud.
     MRS. FAINALL: Immediately. I have a word or two for
     Mr. Witwoud.

     (Exeunt Witwoud and Mrs. Fainall.)

455 MIRABELL: I would beg a little private audience too.
     You had the tyranny to deny me last night, though
     you knew I came to impart a secret to you that con-
     cerned my love.
     MRS. MILLAMANT: You saw I was engaged.
460 MIRABELL: Unkind! You had the leisure to entertain a
     herd of fools; things who visit you from their exces-
     sive idleness, bestowing on your easiness that time
     which is the encumbrance of their lives. How can you
     find delight in such society? It is impossible they
465 should admire you; they are not capable. Or if they
     were, it should be to you as a mortification, for sure
     to please a fool is some degree of folly.
     MRS. MILLAMANT: I please myself. Besides, sometimes
     to converse with fools is for my health.
470 MIRABELL: Your health! Is there a worse disease than
     the conversation of fools?
     MRS. MILLAMANT: Yes, the vapors; fools are physic° for
     it, next to assafetida.°
     MIRABELL: You are not in a course of fools?°
475 MRS. MILLAMANT: Mirabell, if you persist in this offen-
     sive freedom, you'll displease me. I think I must
     resolve, after all, not to have you; we shan't agree.
     MIRABELL: Not in our physic, it may be.
     MRS. MILLAMANT: And yet our distemper,° in all likeli-
480 hood, will be the same; for we shall be sick of one
     another. I shan't endure to be reprimanded nor
     instructed; 'tis so dull to act always by advice, and so
     tedious to be told of one's faults — I can't bear it.
     Well, I won't have you, Mirabell. I'm resolved — I
485 think — you may go. Ha! ha! ha! What would you
     give that you could help loving me?
     MIRABELL: I would give something that you did not
     know I could not help it.
     MRS. MILLAMANT: Come, don't look grave then. Well,
490 what do you say to me?

MIRABELL: I say that a man may as soon make a friend
by his wit, or a fortune by his honesty, as win a
woman with plain dealing° and sincerity.
MRS. MILLAMANT: Sententious Mirabell! Prithee, don't
look with that violent and inflexible wise face, like   495
Solomon at the dividing of the child° in an old tapestry hanging.
MIRABELL: You are merry, madam, but I would persuade you for a moment to be serious.
MRS. MILLAMANT: What, with that face? No, if you   500
keep your countenance, 'tis impossible I should hold
mine. Well, after all, there is something very moving
in a lovesick face. Ha! ha! ha! Well, I won't laugh;
don't be peevish. Heigho! now I'll be melancholy, as
melancholy as a watchlight.° Well, Mirabell, if ever   505
you will win me, woo me now. Nay, if you are so
tedious, fare you well; I see they are walking away.
MIRABELL: Can you not find in the variety of your disposition one moment —
MRS. MILLAMANT: To hear you tell me Foible's married,   510
and your plot like to speed? No.
MIRABELL: But how you came to know it —
MRS. MILLAMANT: Without the help of the devil, you
can't imagine; unless she should tell me herself.
Which of the two it may have been, I will leave you   515
to consider; and when you have done thinking of
that, think of me.

     (Exeunt Mrs. Millamant with Mincing.)

MIRABELL: I have something more — Gone! Think of
you! To think of a whirlwind, though 'twere in a
whirlwind, were a case of more steady contempla-   520
tion; a very tranquility of mind and mansion. A fellow that lives in a windmill has not a more whimsical
dwelling than the heart of a man that is lodged in a
woman. There is no point of the compass to which
they cannot turn, and by which they are not turned;   525
and by one as well as another; for motion, not
method, is their occupation. To know this, and yet
continue to be in love, is to be made wise from the
dictates of reason, and yet persevere to play the fool
by the force of instinct. Oh, here come my pair of   530
turtles!° What, billing so sweetly? Is not Valentine's
Day over with you yet?

(Enter Waitwell and Foible.)

Sirrah, Waitwell, why, sure you think you were married
for your own recreation, and not for my conveniency.

---

441. **two:** Two of.   472. **physic:** Medicine.   473. **assafetida:** A
gum resin prescribed by doctors as an antidote to "the vapors."
474. **course of fools:** Series of treatments.   479. **distemper:** Illness.

493. **plain dealing:** Honesty, frankness.   496. **Solomon . . .
child:** The Old Testament Solomon, king of Israel, was known
for his wisdom. When confronted with two women both claiming to be the mother of a newborn baby, Solomon said he
would divide the baby in two and give one half to each woman.
When one of the women told the king not to slay the baby but
to let it live and give it whole to the other woman, Solomon declared the first woman the baby's true mother (I Kings 3:16–28).
505. **watchlight:** A small night candle.   530–31. **pair of turtles:**
Turtle doves; lovers.

535 WAITWELL: Your pardon, sir. With submission, we have indeed been solacing° in lawful delights; but still with an eye to business, sir. I have instructed her as well as I could. If she can take your directions as readily as my instructions, sir, your affairs are in a prosperous way.

540 MIRABELL: Give you joy, Mrs. Foible.

FOIBLE: O las, sir, I'm so ashamed! I'm afraid my lady has been in a thousand inquietudes for me. But I protest, sir, I made as much haste as I could.

WAITWELL: That she did indeed, sir. It was my fault that 545 she did not make more.

MIRABELL: That I believe.

FOIBLE: But I told my lady as you instructed me, sir that I had a prospect of seeing Sir Rowland, your uncle; and that I would put her ladyship's picture in my 550 pocket to show him, which I'll be sure to say has made him so enamored of her beauty, that he burns with impatience to lie at her ladyship's feet and worship the original.

MIRABELL: Excellent Foible! Matrimony has made you 555 eloquent in love.

WAITWELL: I think she has profited, sir. I think so.

FOIBLE: You have seen Madam Millamant, sir?

MIRABELL: Yes.

FOIBLE: I told her, sir, because I did not know that you 560 might find an opportunity; she had so much company last night.

MIRABELL: Your diligence will merit more. In the mean- time — *(Gives money.)*

FOIBLE: O dear sir, your humble servant!

565 WAITWELL: Spouse.

MIRABELL: Stand off, sir, not a penny! Go on and pros- per, Foible; the lease shall be made good and the farm stocked, if we succeed.°

FOIBLE: I don't question your generosity, sir; and you 570 need not doubt of success. If you have no more com- mands, sir, I'll be gone, I'm sure my lady is at her toi- let and can't dress till I come. Oh, dear, I'm sure that *(looking out)* was Mrs. Marwood that went by in a mask; if she has seen me with you, I'm sure she'll tell 575 my lady. I'll make haste home and prevent her. Your servant, sir. B'w'y,° Waitwell. *(Exit.)*

WAITWELL: Sir Rowland, if you please. The jade's so pert upon her preferment° she forgets herself.

MIRABELL: Come, sir, will you endeavor to forget your- 580 self, and transform into Sir Rowland?

WAITWELL: Why, sir, it will be impossible I should re- member myself. Married, knighted, and attended° all in one day! 'Tis enough to make any forget himself. The difficulty will be how to recover my acquain- 585 tance and familiarity with my former self, and fall from my transformation to a reformation into Wait- well. Nay, I shan't be quite the same Waitwell nei-

---

ther; for, now I remember me, I'm married and can't be my own man again.

Aye, there's my grief; that's the sad change of life, 590 To lose my title, and yet keep my wife.

(Exeunt.)

ACT III

(A room in Lady Wishfort's house. Lady Wishfort at her toilet, Peg waiting.)

LADY WISHFORT: Merciful! no news of Foible yet?

PEG: No, madam.

LADY WISHFORT: I have no more patience. If I have not fretted myself till I am pale again, there's no veracity in me! Fetch me the red; the red, do you hear, sweet- 5 heart? An arrant ash-color, as I'm a person! Look you how this wench stirs! Why dost thou not fetch me a little red? Didst thou not hear me, mopus?°

PEG: The red ratafia° does your ladyship mean, or the cherry-brandy? 10

LADY WISHFORT: Ratafia, fool! No, fool! Not the ra- tafia, fool! Grant me patience! I mean the Spanish paper,° idiot; complexion, darling. Paint, paint, paint; dost thou understand that, changeling,° dangling thy hands like bobbins° before thee? Why dost thou not 15 stir, puppet? thou wooden thing upon wires!

PEG: Lord, madam, your ladyship is so impatient! I cannot come at the paint, madam; Mrs. Foible has locked it up and carried the key with her.

LADY WISHFORT: A pox take you both! Fetch me the 20 cherry-brandy then. *(Exit Peg.)* I'm as pale and as faint, I look like Mrs. Qualmsick, the curate's wife, that's always breeding. Wench, come, come, wench, what art thou doing? sipping? tasting? Save thee, dost thou not know the bottle? 25

(Reenter Peg with a bottle and china cup.)

PEG: Madam, I was looking for a cup.

LADY WISHFORT: A cup, save thee! and what a cup hast thou brought! Does thou take me for a fairy, to drink out of an acorn? Why didst thou not bring thy thimble? Hast thou ne'er a brass thimble clinking in 30 thy pocket with a bit of nutmeg? I warrant thee. Come, fill, fill! So; again. *(One knocks.)* See who that is. Set down the bottle first. Here, here under the table. What, wouldst thou go with the bottle in thy hand, like a tapster?° As I'm a person, this wench has 35 lived in an inn upon the road, before she came to me, like Maritornes the Asturian in *Don Quixote*!° No Foible yet?

---

536. solacing: Taking pleasure. 567–68. the lease . . . suc- ceed: I.e., "If our little plot succeeds, I'll be even more gener- ous." 576. B'w'y: A slurred form of "God be with you." 578. preferment: Her advancement in the world; her new status as a wife. 582. attended: Waited upon.

8. mopus: Idiot; dull-witted girl. 9. ratafia: Fruit-flavored brandy. 12–13. Spanish paper: Cosmetic rouge. 14. change- ling: Simpleton. 15. bobbins: Spools of yarn. 35. tapster: A person who taps beer in a tavern. 37. Maritornes . . . *Don Quixote*: In Cervantes's *Don Quixote* (part 1, chapter 16), Maritornes is an Austrian chambermaid with whom the Don fancies himself in love.

PEG: No, madam; Mrs. Marwood.

40　LADY WISHFORT: Oh, Marwood; let her come in. Come in, good Marwood.

(*Enter Mrs. Marwood.*)

MRS. MARWOOD: I'm surprised to find your ladyship in *déshabillé*° at this time of day.

LADY WISHFORT: Foible's a lost thing; has been abroad
45　since morning, and never heard of since.

MRS. MARWOOD: I saw her but now, as I came masked through the park, in conference with Mirabell.

LADY WISHFORT: With Mirabell! You call my blood into my face, with mentioning that traitor. She durst not
50　have the confidence! I sent her to negotiate an affair in which, if I'm detected, I'm undone. If that wheedling villain has wrought upon Foible to detect me, I'm ruined. O my dear friend, I'm a wretch of wretches if I'm detected.

55　MRS. MARWOOD: O madam, you cannot suspect Mrs. Foible's integrity.

LADY WISHFORT: Oh, he carries poison in his tongue that would corrupt integrity itself! If she has given him an opportunity, she has as good as put her
60　integrity into his hands. Ah, dear Marwood, what's integrity to an opportunity? Hark! I hear her! Go, you thing, and send her in. (*Exit Peg.*) Dear friend, retire into my closet,° that I may examine her with more freedom. You'll pardon me, dear friend; I can
65　make bold with you. There are books over the chimney, Quarles° and Prynne,° and the *Short View of the Stage,*° with Bunyan's works,° to entertain you.

(*Exit Mrs. Marwood.*)

(*Enter Foible.*)

O Foible, where hast thou been? What hast thou been doing?

70　FOIBLE: Madam, I have seen the party.

LADY WISHFORT: But what hast thou done?

FOIBLE: Nay, 'tis your ladyship has done, and are to do; I have only promised. But a man so enamored, so transported! Well, if worshiping of pictures be a sin,
75　poor Sir Rowland, I say.

LADY WISHFORT: The miniature has been counted like. But hast thou not betrayed me, Foible? Hast thou not detected me to that faithless Mirabell? What hadst

thou to do with him in the Park? Answer me, has he
got nothing out of thee?　80

FOIBLE (*aside*): So the devil has been beforehand with me. What shall I say? (*Aloud.*) Alas, madam, could I help it, if I met that confident thing? Was I in fault? If you had heard how he used me, and all upon your ladyship's account, I'm sure you would not suspect　85
my fidelity. Nay, if that had been the worst, I could have borne; but he had a fling at your ladyship too. And then I could not hold; but i'faith I gave him his own.

LADY WISHFORT: Me? what did the filthy fellow say?　90

FOIBLE: O madam! 'tis a shame to say what he said, with his taunts and his fleers, tossing up his nose. "Humh!" says he. "What, you are a-hatching some plot," says he, "you are so early abroad, or catering," says he, "Ferreting for some disbanded° officer,　95
I warrant. Half-pay is but thin subsistence," says he. "Well, what pension does your lady propose? Let me see," says he. "What, she must come down pretty deep now, she's superannuated,"° says he, "and —"

LADY WISHFORT: Ods° my life, I'll have him, I'll have　100
him murdered! I'll have him poisoned! Where does he eat? I'll marry a drawer° to have him poisoned in his wine! I'll send for Robin° from Locket's° immediately.

FOIBLE: Poison him? Poisoning's too good for him.　105
Starve him, madam, starve him; marry Sir Rowland, and get him disinherited. Oh, you would bless yourself to hear what he said!

LADY WISHFORT: A villain! "superannuated"!

FOIBLE: "Humh," says he. "I hear you are laying　110
designs against me too," says he, "and Mrs. Millamant is to marry my uncle" (he does not suspect a word of your ladyship); "but," says he, "I'll fit you for that." "I warrant you," says he. "I'll hamper you for that," says he. "You and your old frippery° too,"　115
says he. "I'll handle you —"

LADY WISHFORT: Audacious villain! "handle" me; would he durst! "Frippery! old frippery!" Was there ever such a foul-mouthed fellow? I'll be married to-morrow; I'll be contracted tonight.　120

FOIBLE: The sooner the better, madam.

LADY WISHFORT: Will Sir Rowland be here, sayest thou? When, Foible?

FOIBLE: Incontinently,° madam. No new sheriff's wife expects the return of her husband after knighthood　125
with that impatience in which Sir Rowland burns for the dear hour of kissing your ladyship's hands after dinner.

---

43. déshabillé: Casual attire.　**63. closet:** Private sitting room.　**66. Quarles:** Francis Quarles, devotional poet, author of *Emblems, Divine and Moral* (1635).　**Prynne:** William Prynne, Puritan author of *Histrio-Mastix* (1633), an attack on the immorality of the stage.　**66–67. Short View of the Stage:** By Jeremy Collier an attack on "the Immorality and Profaneness of the English Stage" (1698), directly aimed at the earlier plays of Congreve. Dryden answered the censures of Collier in his Preface to the *Fables* (1700).　**67. Bunyan's works:** John Bunyan, the great Puritan writer and preacher. A one-volume edition of the *Works of That Eminent Servant of Christ, Mr. John Bunyan* had appeared in 1692.

95. disbanded: Discharged.　**99. superannuated:** Old and infirm.　**100. Ods:** "God's."　**102. drawer:** One who draws wine or ale; a waiter.　**103. Robin:** Common name for a waiter.　**Locket's:** A fashionable restaurant at Charing Cross.　**115. old frippery:** Old clothes, as applied to Lady Wishfort, "old clotheshorse."　**124. Incontinently:** Immediately, and with the added suggestion of passionate impatience.

LADY WISHFORT: "Frippery! superannuated! frippery!"
130 I'll frippery the villain; I'll reduce him to frippery and
rags! A tatterdemalion!° I hope to see him hung with
tatters, like a Long Lane penthouse° or a gibbet thief.
A slander-mouthed railer! I warrant the spendthrift
prodigal's in debt as much as the million lottery,° or
135 the whole court upon a birthday.° I'll spoil his credit
with his tailor. Yes, he shall have my niece with her
fortune, he shall!
FOIBLE: He! I hope to see him lodge in Ludgate° first,
and angle into Blackfriars° for brass farthings with
140 an old mitten.°
LADY WISHFORT: Aye, dear Foible; thank thee for that,
dear Foible. He has put me out of all patience. I shall
never recompose my features to receive Sir Rowland
with any economy of face.° This wretch has fretted
145 me that I am absolutely decayed. Look, Foible.
FOIBLE: Your ladyship has frowned a little too rashly,
indeed, madam. There are some cracks discernible in
the white varnish.
LADY WISHFORT: Let me see the glass. "Cracks," sayest
150 thou? Why I am arrantly fleaed;° I look like an old
peeled wall. Thou must repair me, Foible, before Sir
Rowland comes, or I shall never keep up to my picture.°
FOIBLE: I warrant you, madam, a little art once made
155 your picture like you; and now a little of the same art
must make you like your picture. Your picture must
sit for you, madam.
LADY WISHFORT: But art thou sure Sir Rowland will not
fail to come? Or will 'a not fail when he does come?
160 Will he be importunate, Foible, and push? For if he
should not be importunate, I shall never break decorums. I shall die with confusion, if I am forced to
advance. Oh no, I can never advance! I shall swoon if
he should expect advances. No, I hope Sir Rowland
165 is better bred than to put a lady to the necessity of
breaking her forms. I won't be too coy neither. I
won't give him despair; but a little disdain is not
amiss, a little scorn is alluring.
FOIBLE: A little scorn becomes your ladyship.

131. **tatterdemalion:** Ragamuffin.   132. **Long Lane penthouse:**
A shed with a sloping roof in Long Lane, a district famous for
its shops of old and secondhand clothes.   134. **million lottery:**
A wild scheme to raise a million pounds by the sale of lottery
tickets.   135. **the whole . . . birthday:** Since custom demanded
gifts on such an occasion, a royal birthday was an expensive
event.   138. **Ludgate:** The debtors' prison.   139. **angle into
Blackfriars:** Ludgate Prison abutted on the precinct of Blackfriars, the area of London between Ludgate Hill and the river.
140. **old mitten:** It was the practice of Ludgate prisoners to beg
money from passersby, probably by lowering an old mitten on
a string from a high window.   144. **economy of face:** The
sense is that Lady Wishfort has been so distressed by Foible's
account of Mirabell's words that her makeup has been ruined,
and the cosmetics necessary to make her face presentable to
Sir Rowland will be very expensive.   150. **fleaed:** Flayed;
skinned.   152–53. **keep . . . picture:** I.e., "look as lovely as I
do in my picture."

LADY WISHFORT: Yes, but tenderness becomes me best, 170
a sort of dyingness. You see that picture has a sort of
a — ha, Foible? a swimmingness in the eyes. Yes, I'll
look so. My niece affects it; but she wants features. Is
Sir Rowland handsome? Let my toilet be removed.
I'll dress above. I'll receive Sir Rowland here. Is he 175
handsome? Don't answer me. I won't know; I'll be
surprised, I'll be taken by surprise.
FOIBLE: By storm, madam. Sir Rowland's a brisk man.
LADY WISHFORT: Is he! Oh, then he'll importune, if he's
a brisk man. I shall save decorums if Sir Rowland 180
importunes. I have a mortal terror at the apprehension of offending against decorums. Oh, I'm glad he's
a brisk man. Let my things be removed, good Foible.
(*Exit.*)

(*Enter Mrs. Fainall.*)

MRS. FAINALL: O Foible, I have been in a fright, lest I
should come too late! That devil Marwood saw you 185
in the Park with Mirabell, and I'm afraid will discover it to my lady.
FOIBLE: Discover what, madam?
MRS. FAINALL: Nay, nay, put not on that strange face. I
am privy to the whole design, and know that Wait- 190
well, to whom thou wert this morning married, is to
personate Mirabell's uncle, and as such, winning my
lady, to involve her in those difficulties from which
Mirabell only must release her, by his making his
conditions to have my cousin and her fortune left to 195
her own disposal.
FOIBLE: O dear madam, I beg your pardon. It was not
my confidence in your ladyship that was deficient;
but I thought the former good correspondence between your ladyship and Mr. Mirabell might have 200
hindered his communicating this secret.
MRS. FAINALL: Dear Foible, forget that.
FOIBLE: O dear madam, Mr. Mirabell is such a sweet,
winning gentleman, but your ladyship is the pattern
of generosity. Sweet lady, to be so good! Mr. Mirabell 205
cannot choose but be grateful. I find your ladyship
has his heart still. Now, madam, I can safely tell your
ladyship our success. Mrs. Marwood had told my
lady, but I warrant I managed myself. I turned it all
for the better. I told my lady that Mr. Mirabell railed 210
at her. I laid horrid things to his charge, I'll vow; and
my lady is so incensed that she'll be contracted to Sir
Rowland tonight, she says. I warrant I worked her
up, that he may have her for asking for, as they say of
a Welsh maidenhead. 215
MRS. FAINALL: O rare Foible!
FOIBLE: I beg your ladyship to acquaint Mr. Mirabell of
his success. I would be seen as little as possible to
speak to him; besides, I believe Madam Marwood
watches me. She has a month's mind;° but I know 220
Mr. Mirabell can't abide her. (*Calls.*) John! Remove
my lady's toilet. Madam, your servant. My lady is so
impatient, I fear she'll come for me if I stay.

220. **month's mind:** A longing, desire.

Chris Christman and Tag Tanalski in the 1986 production of *Way of the World* at the Spingold Theater, Brandeis University.

MRS. FAINALL: I'll go with you up the back stairs, lest I
225   should meet her.   (*Exeunt.*)

(*Reenter Mrs. Marwood alone.*)

MRS. MARWOOD: Indeed, Mrs. Engine,° is it thus with
you? Are you become a go-between of this importance? Yes, I shall watch you. Why, this wench is the
230   *passe-partout,* a very master-key to everybody's
strong-box. My friend Fainall,° have you carried it so
swimmingly? I thought there was something in it; but
it seems it's over with you.° Your loathing is not from
a want of appetite then, but from a surfeit. Else you
could never be so cool to fall from a principal to be
235   an assistant; to procure for him! "A pattern of generosity," that I confess. Well, Mr. Fainall, you have
met with your match. O man, man! woman, woman!
the devil's an ass; if I were a painter, I would draw
him like an idiot, a driveller with a bib and bells.
240   Man should have his head and horns,° and woman

the rest of him. Poor simple fiend! "Madam Marwood has a month's mind, but he can't abide her."
'Twere better for him you had not been his confessor
in that affair, without° you could have kept his counsel closer. I shall not prove another "pattern of gen-   245
erosity." He has not obliged me to that with those
excesses of himself; and now I'll have none of him.
Here comes the good lady, panting ripe; with a heart
full of hope, and a head full of care, like any chemist
upon the day of projection.°   250

(*Reenter Lady Wishfort.*)

LADY WISHFORT: O dear Marwood, what shall I say for
this rude forgetfulness? But my dear friend is all
goodness.
MRS. MARWOOD: No apologies, dear madam. I have
been very well entertained.   255
LADY WISHFORT: As I'm a person, I am in a very chaos
to think I should so forget myself, but I have such an
olio of affairs,° really I know not what to do. (*Calls.*)

226. Mrs. Engine: I.e., Foible, the agent of the plot, which Mrs.
Marwood has discovered by eavesdropping on the discourse
between Foible and Mrs. Fainall.   **230. Fainall:** Mrs. Fainall.
232. it seems . . . you: Among other things, Mrs. Marwood has
learned of Mrs. Fainall's affair with Mirabell before her marriage to Fainall.   **240. horns:** The traditional sign of the cuckold, a man whose wife is unfaithful.

244. without: Unless.   **249–50. like any chemist . . . projection:** The comparison refers to the attempts of the alchemists to
transmute base metals into gold. The "day of projection" is the
last day of the experiment, when success or failure will be
known.   **257–58. such an olio of affairs:** I.e., "such a number
of things on my mind."

Foible! I expect my nephew, Sir Wilfull, every mo-
260   ment too. (*Calls.*) Why, Foible! He means to travel
for improvement.
MRS. MARWOOD: Methinks Sir Wilfull should rather
think of marrying than travelling at his years. I hear
he is turned of forty.
265   LADY WISHFORT: Oh, he's in less danger of being spoiled
by his travels. I am against my nephew's marrying too
young. It will be time enough when he comes back
and has acquired discretion to choose for himself.
MRS. MARWOOD: Methinks Mrs. Millamant and he
270   would make a very fit match. He may travel afterwards. 'Tis a thing very usual with young gentlemen.
LADY WISHFORT: I promise you I have thought on't; and
since 'tis your judgment, I'll think on't again. I assure
you I will; I value your judgment extremely. On my
275   word, I'll propose it.

(*Reenter Foible.*)

Come, come, Foible, I had forgot my nephew will be
here before dinner. I must make haste.
FOIBLE: Mr. Witwoud and Mr. Petulant are come to
dine with your ladyship.
280   LADY WISHFORT: Oh, dear, I can't appear till I am
dressed. Dear Marwood, shall I be free with you
again, and beg you to entertain 'em? I'll make all
imaginable haste. Dear friend, excuse me.

(*Exeunt Lady Wishfort and Foible.*)

(*Enter Mrs. Millamant and Mincing.*)

MRS. MILLAMANT: Sure never anything was so unbred
285   as that odious man! Marwood, your servant.
MRS. MARWOOD: You have a color; what's the matter?
MRS. MILLAMANT: That horrid fellow, Petulant, has
provoked me into a flame. I have broke my fan.
Mincing, lend me yours; is not all the powder out of
290   my hair?
MRS. MARWOOD: No. What has he done?
MRS. MILLAMANT: Nay, he has done nothing; he has
only talked. Nay, he has said nothing neither; but he
has contradicted everything that has been said. For
295   my part, I thought Witwoud and he would have
quarreled.
MINCING: I vow, mem, I thought once they would have
fit.°
MRS. MILLAMANT: Well, 'tis a lamentable thing, I swear,
300   that one has not the liberty of choosing one's acquaintance as one does one's clothes.
MRS. MARWOOD: If we had that liberty, we should be as
weary of one set of acquaintance, though never so
good, as we are of one suit, though never so fine. A
305   fool and a doily stuff° would now and then find days
of grace, and be worn for variety.
MRS. MILLAMANT: I could consent to wear 'em, if they
would wear alike; but fools never wear out, they are

298. **fit:** Fought.   305. **doily stuff:** A coarse woolen material.

such *drap-de-Berry*° things! without one could give
'em to one's chambermaid after a day or two.   310
MRS. MARWOOD: 'Twere better so indeed. Or what
think you of the playhouse? A fine, gay, glossy fool
should be given there, like a new masking habit, after
the masquerade is over, and we have done with the
disguise. For a fool's visit is always a disguise, and   315
never admitted by a woman of wit, but to blind° her
affair with a lover of sense. If you would but appear
barefaced now, and own Mirabell, you might as easily put off Petulant and Witwoud as your hood and
scarf. And indeed 'tis time, for the town has found it;   320
the secret is grown too big for the pretense. 'Tis like
Mrs. Primly's great belly, she may lace it down
before, but it burnishes° on her hips. Indeed, Millamant, you can no more conceal it than my Lady
Strammel can her face, that goodly face, which, in   325
defiance of her Rhenish-wine tea,° will not be comprehended in a mask.°
MRS. MILLAMANT: I'll take my death, Marwood, you
are more censorious than a decayed beauty, or a discarded toast. Mincing, tell the men they may come   330
up. My aunt is not dressing here; their folly is less
provoking than your malice. (*Exit Mincing.*) "The
town has found it!" What has it found? That Mirabell loves me is no more a secret than it is a secret
that you discovered it to my aunt, or than the reason   335
why you discovered it is a secret.
MRS. MARWOOD: You are nettled.°
MRS. MILLAMANT: You're mistaken. Ridiculous!
MRS. MARWOOD: Indeed, my dear, you'll tear another
fan, if you don't mitigate those violent airs.   340
MRS. MILLAMANT: O silly! ha! ha! ha! I could laugh immoderately. Poor Mirabell! His constancy to me has
quite destroyed his complaisance for all the world
beside. I swear, I never enjoined it him to be so coy. If
I had the vanity to think he would obey me, I would   345
command him to show more gallantry. 'Tis hardly
well-bred to be so particular° on one hand, and so insensible on the other. But I despair to prevail, and so
let him follow his own way, ha! ha! ha! Pardon me,
dear creature, I must laugh, ha! ha! ha! though I   350
grant you 'tis a little barbarous, ha! ha! ha!
MRS. MARWOOD: What pity 'tis, so much fine raillery,
and delivered with so significant gesture, should be
so unhappily directed to miscarry!
MRS. MILLAMANT: Ha? Dear creature, I ask your par-   355
don. I swear I did not mind you.°
MRS. MARWOOD: Mr. Mirabell and you both may think

309. *drap-de-Berry:* Woolen cloth, probably coarse, from the
French province of Berry.   316. **blind:** Camouflage.   323. **bur-
nishes:** Is all the more evident.   326. **Rhenish-wine tea:** Rhenish
white wine was supposed to reduce corpulence.   326–27. **will
not . . . mask:** The sense is that the lady's face was so fat that no
mask would fit it.   337. **nettled:** Annoyed.   347. **particular:**
Attentive to one lady (i.e., Millamant).   356. **I did not mind
you:** "I did not have you in mind."

it a thing impossible, when I shall tell him by telling
you —

360 MRS. MILLAMANT: Oh, dear, what? For it is the same
thing if I hear it, ha! ha! ha!

MRS. MARWOOD: That I detest him, hate him, madam.

MRS. MILLAMANT: O madam, why so do I. And yet the
creature loves me, ha! ha! ha! How can one forbear
365 laughing to think of it! I am a sibyl° if I am not
amazed to think what he can see in me. I'll take my
death, I think you are handsomer and, within a year
or two as young; if you could but stay for me, I
should overtake you, but that cannot be. Well, that
370 thought makes me melancholic. Now, I'll be sad.

MRS. MARWOOD: Your merry note may be changed
sooner than you think.

MRS. MILLAMANT: D'ye say so? Then I'm resolved I'll
have a song to keep up my spirits.

(Reenter Mincing.)

375 MINCING: The gentlemen stay but to comb,° madam,
and will wait on you.

MRS. MILLAMANT: Desire Mrs. —, that is in the next
room, to sing the song I would have learnt yesterday.
You shall hear it, madam, not that there's any great
380 matter in it, but 'tis agreeable to my humor.

(Song.)

[*Set by Mr. John Eccles.*]

I

Love's but the frailty of the mind,
When 'tis not with ambition join'd;
A sickly flame, which, if not fed, expires,
And feeding, wastes in self-consuming fires.

II

385 'Tis not to wound a wanton boy
Or am'rous youth, that gives the joy;
But 'tis the glory to have pierc'd a swain,
For whom inferior beauties sigh'd in vain.

III

Then I alone the conquest prize,
390 When I insult a rival's eyes;
If there's delight in love, 'tis when I see
That heart, which others bleed for, bleed for me.

(Enter Petulant and Witwoud.)

MRS. MILLAMANT: Is your animosity composed, gentlemen?

395 WITWOUD: Raillery, raillery, madam; we have no animosity. We hit off a little wit now and then, but no
animosity. The falling-out of wits is like the falling-
out of lovers; we agree in the main, like treble and
bass. Ha, Petulant?

PETULANT: Aye, in the main, but when I have a humor to   400
contradict.

WITWOUD: Aye, when he has a humor to contradict,
then I contradict too. What, I know my cue. Then we
contradict one another like two battledores; for contradictions beget one another like Jews.   405

PETULANT: If he says black's black, if I have a humor to
say 'tis blue, let that pass; all's one for that. If I have a
humor to prove it, it must be granted.

WITWOUD: Not positively must, but it may, it may.

PETULANT: Yes, it positively must, upon proof positive.   410

WITWOUD: Aye, upon proof positive it must; but upon
proof presumptive it only may. That's a logical distinction now, madam.

MRS. MARWOOD: I perceive your debates are of importance and very learnedly handled.   415

PETULANT: Importance is one thing, and learning's
another; but a debate's a debate, that I assert.

WITWOUD: Petulant's an enemy to learning; he relies altogether on his parts.

PETULANT: No, I'm no enemy to learning; it hurts not me.   420

MRS. MARWOOD: That's a sign indeed it's no enemy to
you.

PETULANT: No, no, it's no enemy to anybody but them
that have it.

MRS. MILLAMANT: Well, an illiterate man's my aversion;   425
I wonder at the impudence of any illiterate man to
offer to make love.

WITWOUD: That I confess I wonder at too.

MRS. MILLAMANT: Ah! to marry an ignorant that can
hardly read or write!   430

PETULANT: Why should a man be any further from being
married, though he can't read, than he is from being
hanged? The ordinary's° paid for setting the psalm,
and the parish priest for reading the ceremony. And
for the rest which is to follow in both cases, a man   435
may do it without book; so all's one for that.

MRS. MILLAMANT: D'ye hear the creature? Lord, here's
company; I'll be gone.

(Exeunt Mrs. Millamant and Mincing.)

*(Enter Sir Wilfull Witwoud in a riding dress, and a Foot-
man to Lady Wishfort.)*

WITWOUD: In the name of Bartlemew and his fair,° what
have we here?   440

MRS. MARWOOD: 'Tis your brother, I fancy. Don't you
know him?

WITWOUD: Not I. Yes, I think it is he. I've almost forgot
him; I have not seen him since the Revolution.°

---

365. **sibyl:** A female prophet or seer.   375. **comb:** I.e., comb
their wigs.

433. **ordinary's:** The ordinary was the chaplain of a prison,
who prepared criminals for death.   439. **Bartlemew and his
fair:** Bartholomew Fair was held in August of each year at
Smithfield. Since it was specially renowned for its sale of country cloths, Witwoud may here be referring to the inappropriate-
ness of his brother's riding habit in a London drawing room.
444. **Revolution:** The bloodless Revolution of 1688, which
marked the defeat of James II and the accession to the throne of
William and Mary.

445 FOOTMAN (*to Sir Wilfull*): Sir, my lady's dressing. Here's company; if you please to walk in, in the meantime.

SIR WILFULL: Dressing! What, it's but morning here, I warrant, with you in London; we should count it towards afternoon in our parts, down in Shropshire.

450 Why then, belike my aunt han't dined yet, ha, friend?

FOOTMAN: Your aunt, sir?

SIR WILFULL: My aunt, sir! Yes, my aunt, sir, and your lady, sir; your lady is my aunt, sir. Why, what, dost thou not know me, friend? Why, then send some-

455 body hither that does. How long hast thou lived with thy lady, fellow, ha?

FOOTMAN: A week, sir; longer than anybody else in the house, except my lady's woman.

SIR WILFULL: Why then, belike thou dost not know thy

460 lady, if thou seest her, ha, friend?

FOOTMAN: Why truly, sir, I cannot safely swear to her face in a morning, before she is dressed. 'Tis like I may give a shrewd guess at her by this time.

SIR WILFULL: Well, prithee try what thou canst do; if

465 thou canst not guess, inquire her out, dost hear, fellow? And tell her, her nephew, Sir Wilfull Witwoud, is in the house.

FOOTMAN: I shall, sir.

SIR WILFULL: Hold ye, hear me, friend; a word with you

470 in your ear. Prithee who are these gallants?

FOOTMAN: Really, sir, I can't tell; here come so many here, 'tis hard to know 'em all. (*Exit.*)

SIR WILFULL: Oons,° this fellow knows less than a starling;° I don't think 'a knows his own name.

475 MRS. MARWOOD: Mr. Witwoud, your brother is not behind-hand in forgetfulness; I fancy he has forgot you too.

WITWOUD: I hope so. The devil take him that remembers first, I say.

480 SIR WILFULL: Save you, gentlemen and lady!

MRS. MARWOOD: For shame, Mr. Witwoud; why won't you speak to him? And you, sir.

WITWOUD: Petulant, speak.

PETULANT: And you, sir.

485 SIR WILFULL: No offense, I hope.

(*Salutes Mrs. Marwood.*)

MRS. MARWOOD: No sure, sir.

WITWOUD: This is a vile dog; I see that already. No offense! Ha! ha! ha! to him; to him, Petulant, smoke° him.

490 PETULANT: It seems as if you had come a journey, sir; hem, hem. (*Surveying him round.*)

SIR WILFULL: Very likely, sir, that it may seem so.

PETULANT: No offense, I hope, sir.

WITWOUD: Smoke the boots, the boots; Petulant, the

495 boots, ha! ha! ha!

SIR WILFULL: Maybe not, sir; thereafter as 'tis meant,° sir.

---

473. Oons: "God's wounds," an oath. **473–74. starling:** Proverbially a stupid bird. **488. smoke:** "To affront a stranger at his coming in" (Summers, *Dictionary of the Canting Crew*). **496. as 'tis meant:** "According to the way it is meant."

PETULANT: Sir, I presume upon the information of your boots.

SIR WILFULL: Why, 'tis like you may, sir. If you are not 500 satisfied with the information of my boots, sir, if you will step to the stable, you may inquire further of my horse, sir.

PETULANT: Your horse, sir! Your horse is an ass, sir!

SIR WILFULL: Do you speak by way of offense, sir? 505

MRS. MARWOOD: The gentleman's merry, that's all, sir. (*Aside.*) 'Slife,° we shall have a quarrel betwixt an horse and an ass, before they find one another out. (*Aloud.*) You must not take anything amiss from your friends, sir. You are among your friends here, 510 though it may be you don't know it. If I am not mistaken, you are Sir Wilfull Witwoud.

SIR WILFULL: Right, lady; I am Sir Wilfull Witwoud, so I write myself; no offense to anybody, I hope; and nephew to the Lady Wishfort of this mansion. 515

MRS. MARWOOD: Don't you know this gentleman, sir?

SIR WILFULL: Hum! What, sure 'tis not — yea by'r Lady, but 'tis. 'Sheart° I know not whether 'tis or no. Yea, but 'tis, by the Wrekin.° Brother Antony! What, Tony, i'faith! What, dost thou not know me? By'r Lady, nor 520 I thee, thou art so becravated° and so beperiwigged.° 'Sheart, why dost not speak? Art thou o'erjoyed?

WITWOUD: Odso, brother, is it you? Your servant, brother.

SIR WILFULL: Your servant! Why, yours, sir. Your ser- 525 vant again, 'sheart, and your friend and servant to that, and a — (*puff*) and a flapdragon for your service,° sir! and a hare's foot, and a hare's scut° for your service, sir, an you be so cold and so courtly!

WITWOUD: No offense, I hope, brother. 530

SIR WILFULL: 'Sheart, sir, but there is, and much offense! A pox, is this your Inns o' Court° breeding, not to know your friends and your relations, your elders and your betters?

WITWOUD: Why, brother Wilfull of Salop,° you may be 535 as short as a Shrewsbury° cake, if you please. But I tell you 'tis not modish to know relations in town. You think you're in the country, where great lubberly° brothers slabber° and kiss one another when they meet, like a call of serjeants.° 'Tis not the fash- 540 ion here, 'tis not indeed, dear brother.

SIR WILFULL: The fashion's a fool; and you're a fop, dear brother. 'Sheart, I've suspected this. By'r Lady, I

---

507. 'Slife: "God's life." **518. 'Sheart:** "God's heart." **519. Wrekin:** A hill in his native Shropshire. **521. becravated:** Wearing a cravat, or tie. **beperiwigged:** Wearing a wig. **527–28. flapdragon . . . service:** Derived from the game of catching raisins out of burning brandy; meaning "a fig for your service." **528. scut:** Tail. **532. Inns o' Court:** The center of the legal world of London, used for the city itself. Sir Wilfull, the country squire, simply asks if Witwoud's rudeness is a mark of city manners. **535. Salop:** Another name for Shropshire. **536. Shrewsbury:** The capital of Shropshire. **538–39. lubberly:** Loutish. **539. slabber:** Slobber. **540. serjeants:** When sergeants-at-law are admitted to the bar.

conjectured you were a fop, since you began to
change the style of your letters, and write in a scrap
of paper, gilt round the edges, no broader than a *subpoena.*° I might expect this when you left off, "Honored brother," and "hoping you are in good health,"
and so forth, to begin with a "Rat me,° knight, I'm so
sick of a last night's debauch," ods heart, and then
tell a familiar tale of a cock and a bull,° and a whore
and a bottle, and so conclude. You could write news
before you were out of your time,° when you lived
with honest Pumple Nose, the attorney of Furnival's
Inn,° you could entreat to be remembered then to
your friends round the Wrekin. We could have
gazettes, then, and *Dawks's Letter,*° and the *Weekly
Bill,*° till of late days.

PETULANT: 'Slife, Witwoud, were you ever an attorney's
clerk? of the family of the Furnivals? Ha! ha! ha!

WITWOUD: Aye, aye, but that was but for a while, not
long, not long. Pshaw! I was not in my own power
then; an orphan, and this fellow was my guardian.
Aye, aye, I was glad to consent to that man to come
to London. He had the disposal of me then. If I had
not agreed to that, I might have been bound prentice
to a felt maker in Shrewsbury; this fellow would have
bound me to a maker of felts.

SIR WILFULL: 'Sheart, and better than to be bound to a
maker of fops, where, I suppose, you have served
your time; and now you may set up for yourself.

MRS. MARWOOD: You intend to travel, sir, as I'm
informed.

SIR WILFULL: Belike I may, madam. I may chance to sail
upon the salt seas, if my mind hold.

PETULANT: And the wind serve.

SIR WILFULL: Serve or not serve, I shan't ask license of
you, sir; nor the weathercock your companion. I
direct my discourse to the lady, sir. 'Tis like my aunt
may have told you, madam. Yes, I have settled my
concerns, I may say now, and am minded to see foreign parts. If an how that the peace° holds, whereby,
that is, taxes abate.

MRS. MARWOOD: I thought you had designed for France
at all adventures.°

SIR WILFULL: I can't tell that; 'tis like I may, and 'tis like
I may not. I am somewhat dainty in making a resolution, because when I make it, I keep it. I don't stand
shill I, shall I,° then; if I say't, I'll do't. But I have

thoughts to tarry a small matter in town, to learn
somewhat of your lingo first, before I cross the seas.
I'd gladly have a spice of your French, as they say,
whereby to hold discourse in foreign countries.

MRS. MARWOOD: Here's an academy in town for that
use.

SIR WILFULL: There is? 'Tis like there may.

MRS. MARWOOD: No doubt you will return very much
improved.

WITWOUD: Yes, refined, like a Dutch skipper from a
whale-fishing.

(*Reenter Lady Wishfort with Fainall.*)

LADY WISHFORT: Nephew, you are welcome.

SIR WILFULL: Aunt, your servant.

FAINALL: Sir Wilfull, your most faithful servant.

SIR WILFULL: Cousin Fainall, give me your hand.

LADY WISHFORT: Cousin Witwoud, your servant; Mr.
Petulant, your servant. Nephew, you are welcome
again. Will you drink anything after your journey,
nephew, before you eat? Dinner's almost ready.

SIR WILFULL: I'm very well, I thank you, aunt; however,
I thank you for your courteous offer. 'Sheart I was
afraid you would have been in the fashion too, and
have remembered to have forgot your relations.
Here's your cousin Tony; belike I mayn't call him
brother for fear of offense.

LADY WISHFORT: O, he's a rallier,° nephew. My cousin's
a wit; and your great wits always rally their best
friends to choose.° When you have been abroad,
nephew, you'll understand raillery better.

(*Fainall and Mrs. Marwood talk apart.*)

SIR WILFULL: Why then, let him hold his tongue in the
meantime, and rail when that day comes.

(*Reenter Mincing.*)

MINCING: Mem, I come to acquaint your laship that
dinner is impatient?

SIR WILFULL: Impatient? Why then, belike it won't stay
till I pull off my boots. Sweetheart, can you help me
to a pair of slippers? My man's with the horses, I
warrant.

LADY WISHFORT: Fie, fie, nephew, you would not pull
off your boots here. Go down into the hall; dinner
shall stay for you. My nephew's a little unbred; you'll
pardon him, madam. Gentlemen, will you walk?
Marwood?

MRS. MARWOOD: I'll follow you, madam, before Sir
Wilfull is ready.

(*Exeunt all but Mrs. Marwood and Fainall.*)

FAINALL: Why then, Foible's a bawd, an arrant, rank,
match-making bawd. And I, it seems, am a husband,
a rank husband; and my wife a very arrant, rank

546–47. *subpoena:* A legal summons.   **549. "Rat me":** Contraction of the oath "May God rot me."   **551. tale . . . bull:** A
wildly exaggerated tale.   **553. out of your time:** I.e., before he
had finished his legal apprenticeship.   **554–55. Furnival's Inn:**
One of the Inns of Court (Chancery) attached to Lincoln's Inn.
557. *Dawks's Letter:* A newsletter with a wide circulation in the
provinces.   **557–58. *Weekly Bill:*** It reported all deaths in and
around London.   **582. peace:** The Treaty of Ryswick (1697),
which temporarily terminated the war between France on the
one hand and England and her Continental allies on the other.
585. at all adventures: In any case.   **589. shill I, shall I:** Shilly-
shally. Sir Wilfull is saying that he is not an indecisive man.

615. rallier: A railer; one who delights in raillery, gentle mockery.   **617. to choose:** As they like.

wife, all in the way of the world. 'Sdeath, to be a
cuckold by anticipation, a cuckold in embryo!° Sure I
was born with budding antlers, like a young satyr, or
640   a citizen's child.° 'Sdeath! to be outwitted, to be out-
jilted, outmatrimonied! If I had kept my speed like a
stag, 'twere somewhat; but to crawl after, with my
horns, like a snail, and be out-stripped by my wife,
'tis scurvy wedlock.

645   MRS. MARWOOD: Then shake it off. You have often
wished for an opportunity to part; and now you have
it. But first prevent their plot; the half of Millamant's
fortune is too considerable to be parted with, to a
foe, to Mirabell.

650   FAINALL: Damn him! that had been mine, had you not
made that fond° discovery. That had been forfeited,
had they been married. My wife had added luster to
my horns by that increase of fortune, I could have
worn 'em tipped with gold, though my forehead had
655   been furnished like a deputy lieutenant's hall.°

MRS. MARWOOD: They may prove a cap of mainte-
nance° to you still, if you can away with° your wife.
And she's no worse than when you had her. I dare
swear she had given up her game before she was
660   married.

FAINALL: Hum! that may be.

MRS. MARWOOD: You married her to keep you; and if
you can contrive to have her keep you better than
you expected, why should you not keep her longer
665   than you intended?

FAINALL: The means, the means.

MRS. MARWOOD: Discover to my lady your wife's conduct; threaten to part with her. My lady loves her,
and will come to any composition° to save her repu-
670   tation. Take the opportunity of breaking it, just upon
the discovery of this imposture. My lady will be
enraged beyond bounds, and sacrifice niece and fortune and all, at that conjuncture. And let me alone to
keep her warm; if she should flag in her part, I will
675   not fail to prompt her.

FAINALL: Faith, this has an appearance.°

MRS. MARWOOD: I'm sorry I hinted to my lady to

endeavor a match between Millamant and Sir Wilfull; that may be an obstacle.

FAINALL: Oh, for that matter leave me to manage him;   680
I'll disable him for that. He will drink like a Dane;°
after dinner, I'll set his hand in.°

MRS. MARWOOD: Well, how do you stand affected
towards your lady?

FAINALL: Why, faith, I'm thinking of it. Let me see. I am   685
married already, so that's over. My wife has played
the jade with me; well, that's over too. I never loved
her, or if I had, why, that would have been over too
by this time. Jealous of her I cannot be, for I am certain; so there's an end of jealousy. Weary of her I am,   690
and shall be. No, there's no end of that; no, no, that
were too much to hope. Thus far concerning my
repose; now for my reputation. As to my own, I married not for it, so that's out of the question. And as to
my part in my wife's, why, she had parted with hers   695
before; so bringing none to me, she can take none
from me. 'Tis against all rule of play that I should
lose to one who has not wherewithal to stake.

MRS. MARWOOD: Besides, you forget marriage is honor-
able.   700

FAINALL: Hum! Faith, and that's well thought on. Marriage is honorable, as you say; and if so, wherefore
should cuckoldom be a discredit, being derived from
so honorable a root?

MRS. MARWOOD: Nay, I know not; if the root be honor-   705
able, why not the branches?°

FAINALL: So, so; why, this point's clear. Well, how do we
proceed?

MRS. MARWOOD: I will contrive a letter which shall be
delivered to my lady at the time when that rascal who   710
is to act Sir Rowland is with her. It shall come as
from an unknown hand, for the less I appear to
know of the truth, the better I can play the incendiary. Besides, I would not have Foible provoked if I
could help it, because you know she knows some   715
passages.° Nay, I expect all will come out; but let the
mine be sprung first, and then I care not if I am discovered.

FAINALL: If the worst come to the worst, I'll turn my
wife to grass,° I have already a deed of settlement of   720
the best part of her estate, which I wheedled out of
her; and that you shall partake at least.

MRS. MARWOOD: I hope you are convinced that I hate
Mirabell now; you'll be no more jealous?

FAINALL: Jealous! No, by this kiss. Let husbands be jeal-   725
ous; but let the lover still believe. Or if he doubt, let it
be only to endear his pleasure, and prepare the joy
that follows, when he proves his mistress true. But let

637–38. **to be . . . embryo:** In their "talk apart," Mrs. Marwood has told Mr. Fainall what she has learned of his wife's
affair with Mirabell before her marriage to Fainall.   640. **citizen's child:** I.e., a cuckold's child. Many a child of an honest citizen was fathered by a gentleman of the town.   651. **fond:**
Foolish.   654–55. **forehead . . . hall:** I.e., though he had been
cuckolded as many times as there are antlers of stags and deer
decorating the country mansion of a deputy lieutenant.
656–57. **cap of maintenance:** A term in heraldry. The coat of
arms of a royal bastard sometimes included a cap with two
points behind, like the horns of a cuckold. Mrs. Marwood puns
on the word *maintenance* since she is insinuating that, armed
with this new information concerning his wife, Fainall may be
in a better position to blackmail Lady Wishfort to the amount
of Millamant's fortune that she controls.   657. **away with:**
Continue to tolerate.   669. **come to any composition:** Agree to
anything.   676. **an appearance:** Possibilities.

681. **drink like a Dane:** The Danes were known as heavy
drinkers.   682. **I'll set . . . in:** I.e., "I'll involve him in the
plot."   706. **branches:** I.e., the cuckold's horns.   715–16. **she
knows some passages:** I.e., Foible knows of Mrs. Marwood's
affair with Mr. Fainall and may divulge it. Indeed, she does,
in the denouement of act V.   719–20. **turn . . . grass:** Turn her
out, as he would an animal to graze.

730 husbands' doubts convert to endless jealousy; or if
they have belief, let it corrupt to superstition and
blind credulity. I am single, and will herd no more
with 'em. True, I wear the badge, but I'll disown the
order. And since I take my leave of 'em, I care not if I
leave 'em a common motto to their common crest.

735   All husbands must or pain or shame endure
        The wise too jealous are, fools too secure.

                                              (*Exeunt.*)

ACT IV

(*[Scene continues.] Enter Lady Wishfort and Foible.*)

LADY WISHFORT: Is Sir Rowland coming, sayest thou,
Foible? and are things in order?

FOIBLE: Yes, madam, I have put wax-lights in the
sconces, and placed the footmen in a row in the hall,
5 in their best liveries, with the coachman and postillion to fill up the equipage.

LADY WISHFORT: Have you pulvilled° the coachman
and postillion, that they may not stink of the stable
when Sir Rowland comes by?

10 FOIBLE: Yes, madam.

LADY WISHFORT: And are the dancers and the music
ready, that he may be entertained in all points with
correspondence to his passion?

FOIBLE: All is ready, madam.

15 LADY WISHFORT: And — well, and how do I look,
Foible?

FOIBLE: Most killing well, madam.

LADY WISHFORT: Well, and how shall I receive him? In
what figure shall I give his heart the first impression?
20 There is a great deal in the first impression. Shall I
sit? No, I won't sit, I'll walk; aye, I'll walk from the
door upon his entrance; and then turn full upon him.
No, that will be too sudden. I'll lie, aye, I'll lie down.
I'll receive him in my little dressing-room; there's a
25 couch. Yes, yes, I'll give the first impression on a
couch. I won't lie neither, but loll and lean upon one
elbow; with one foot a little dangling off, jogging in a
thoughtful way. Yes, and then as soon as he appears,
start, aye, start and be surprised, and rise to meet him
30 in a pretty disorder. Yes, oh, nothing is more alluring
than a levee° from a couch, in some confusion; it
shows the foot to advantage, and furnishes with
blushes and recomposing airs beyond comparison.
Hark! there's a coach.

35 FOIBLE: 'Tis he, madam.

LADY WISHFORT: Oh dear, has my nephew made his
addresses to Millamant? I ordered him.

FOIBLE: Sir Wilfull is set in to drinking, madam, in the
parlor.

40 LADY WISHFORT: Ods my life, I'll send him to her. Call
her down, Foible; bring her hither. I'll send him as I

go. When they are together, then come to me, Foible,
that I may not be too long alone with Sir Rowland.

                                              (*Exit.*)

(*Enter Mrs. Millamant and Mrs. Fainall.*)

FOIBLE: Madam, I stayed here to tell your ladyship that
Mr. Mirabell has waited this half hour for an oppor- 45
tunity to talk with you, though my lady's orders were
to leave you and Sir Wilfull together. Shall I tell Mr.
Mirabell that you are at leisure?

MRS. MILLAMANT: No, what would the dear man have?
I am thoughtful, and would amuse myself; bid him 50
come another time.
    "There never yet was woman made,
    Nor shall, but to be curs'd."°
                          (*Repeating and walking about.*)
That's hard!

MRS. FAINALL: You are very fond of Sir John Suckling 55
today, Millamant, and the poets.

MRS. MILLAMANT: He? Aye, and filthy verses; so I am.

FOIBLE: Sir Wilfull is coming, madam. Shall I send Mr.
Mirabell away?

MRS. MILLAMANT: Aye, if you please, Foible, send him 60
away, or send him hither; just as you will, dear
Foible. I think I'll see him; shall I? Aye, let the wretch
come.
                                       (*Exit Foible.*)
    "Thyrsis, a youth of the inspired train."°
                                       (*Repeating.*)
Dear Fainall, entertain Sir Wilfull. Thou hast philos- 65
ophy to undergo° a fool; thou art married and hast
patience. I would confer with my own thoughts.

MRS. FAINALL: I am obliged to you, that you would
make me your proxy in this affair; but I have business of my own.   70

(*Enter Sir Wilfull.*)

O Sir Wilfull, you are come at the critical instant.
There's your mistress up to the ears in love and contemplation; pursue your point, now or never.

SIR WILFULL: Yes; my aunt will have it so. I would
gladly have been encouraged with a bottle or two, 75
because I'm somewhat wary at first, before I am
acquainted. (*This while Millamant walks about
repeating to herself.*) But I hope, after a time, I shall
break my mind; that is, upon further acquaintance.
So for the present, cousin, I'll take my leave. If so be 80
you'll be so kind to make my excuse, I'll return to my
company.

MRS. FAINALL: Oh, fie, Sir Wilfull! What, you must not
be daunted.

---

7. **pulvilled:** Scented with a sweet-smelling powder.   31. **levee:**
Rising.

52–53. "**There never . . . curs'd**": The opening lines of a poem
by Sir John Suckling (1609–1642).   64. "**Thyrsis . . . train**":
The first line of *The Story of Phoebus and Daphne, Applied*, a
poem by Edmund Waller (1606–1687), a poet much admired
by Dryden and renowned for the "sweetness" of his verse.
66. **undergo:** Put up with.

SIR WILFULL: Daunted! No, that's not it. It is not so
much for that; for if so be that I set on't, I'll do't. But
only for the present; 'tis sufficient till further acquaintance, that's all. Your servant.

MRS. FAINALL: Nay, I'll swear you shall never lose so
favorable an opportunity, if I can help it. I'll leave
you together and lock the door.   (*Exit.*)

SIR WILFULL: Nay, nay, cousin. I have forgot my gloves.
What d'ye do? 'Sheart, 'a has locked the door indeed,
I think. Nay, Cousin Fainall, open the door! Pshaw,
what a vixen trick is this? Nay, now 'a has seen me
too. Cousin, I made bold to pass through as it were. I
think this door's enchanted!

MRS. MILLAMANT (*repeating*):
    "I prithee spare me, gentle boy,
    Press me no more for that slight toy —"°

SIR WILFULL: Anan?° Cousin, your servant.

MRS. MILLAMANT (*repeating*):
    "That foolish trifle of a heart —"
    Sir Wilfull!

SIR WILFULL: Yes. Your servant. No offense, I hope,
cousin.

MRS. MILLAMANT (*repeating*):
    "I swear it will not do its part,
    Though thou dost shine, employ'st thy pow'r and
        art."
    Natural, easy Suckling!

SIR WILFULL: Anan? Suckling? No such suckling neither, cousin, nor stripling! I thank Heaven, I'm no
minor.

MRS. MILLAMANT: Ah, rustic! ruder than Gothic.°

SIR WILFULL: Well, well, I shall understand your lingo
one of these days, cousin; in the meanwhile I must
answer in plain English.

MRS. MILLAMANT: Have you any business with me, Sir
Wilfull?

SIR WILFULL: Not at present, cousin. Yes, I made bold
to see, to come and know if that how you were disposed to fetch a walk this evening; if so be that I
might not be troublesome, I would have fought° a
walk with you.

MRS. MILLAMANT: A walk! What then?

SIR WILFULL: Nay, nothing. Only for the walk's sake,
that's all.

MRS. MILLAMANT: I nauseate walking; 'tis a country
diversion. I loathe the country and everything that
relates to it.

SIR WILFULL: Indeed! hah! Look ye, look ye, you do?
Nay, 'tis like you may. Here are choice of pastimes
here in town, as plays and the like; that must be confessed indeed.

MRS. MILLAMANT: *Ah, l'étourdi!*° I hate the town too.

SIR WILFULL: Dear heart, that's much. Hah! that you
should hate 'em both! Hah! 'tis like you may; there
are some can't relish the town, and others can't away
with the country. 'Tis like you may be one of those,
cousin.

MRS. MILLAMANT: Ha! ha! ha! Yes, 'tis like I may. You
have nothing further to say to me?

SIR WILFULL: Not at present, cousin. 'Tis like when I
have an opportunity to be more private, I may break
my mind in some measure. I conjecture you partly
guess — however, that's as time shall try; but spare to
speak and spare to speed,° as they say.

MRS. MILLAMANT: If it is of no great importance, Sir
Wilfull, you will oblige me to leave me; I have just
now a little business —

SIR WILFULL: Enough, enough, cousin, yes, yes, all a
case;° when you're disposed, when you're disposed.
Now's as well as another time; and another time as
well as now. All's one for that. Yes, yes, if your concerns call you, there's no haste; it will keep cold, as
they say. Cousin, your servant. I think this door's
locked.

MRS. MILLAMANT: You may go this way, sir.

SIR WILFULL: Your servant; then with your leave I'll
return to my company.

MRS. MILLAMANT: Aye, aye; ha! ha! ha!
    "Like Phoebus sung the no less am'rous boy."°

(*Enter Mirabell.*)

MIRABELL: "Like Daphne, she, as lovely and as coy."°
Do you lock yourself up from me, to make my search
more curious?° Or is this pretty artifice contrived, to
signify that here the chase must end and my pursuit
be crowned, for you can fly no further?

MRS. MILLAMANT: Vanity! No. I'll fly and be followed
to the last moment. Though I am upon the very verge
of matrimony, I expect you should solicit me as much
as if I were wavering at the grate of a monastery, with
one foot over the threshold. I'll be solicited to the
very last, nay, and afterwards.

MIRABELL: What, after the last?

MRS. MILLAMANT: Oh, I should think I was poor and
had nothing to bestow, if I were reduced to an inglo-
rious ease and freed from the agreeable fatigues of
solicitation.

MIRABELL: But do not you know that when favors are
conferred upon instant and tedious solicitation, that
they diminish in their value, and that both the giver
loses the grace, and the receiver lessens his pleasure?

99–100. "I prithee . . . toy": The first two lines of a "Song" by
Suckling. The three lines quoted by Millamant in her next two
speeches complete the first stanza of the poem.   **101. Anan:** "I
beg your pardon."   **111. Gothic:** The Restoration and early
eighteenth century considered the civilization of the Goths and
"Gothic" art rude and barbarous.   **120. fought:** A provincial
form of "fetched."

132. l'étourdi: The silly fellow.   **143–44. spare to speak . . .
speed:** Proverb meaning "If you hold your tongue, you won't
get along in the world."   **148–49. all a case:** Idiomatic for "It's
all the same."   **159. "Like Phoebus . . . boy":** The third line of
Waller's *Story of Phoebus and Daphne, Applied.*   **160. "Like
Daphne . . . coy":** The fourth line of Waller's poem. Mirabell
completes the couplet begun by Millamant.   **162. curious:**
Difficult.

180 MRS. MILLAMANT: It may be in things of common application; but never sure in love. Oh, I hate a lover that
can dare to think he draws a moment's air independent on the bounty of his mistress. There is not so
impudent a thing in nature as the saucy look of an
185 assured man, confident of success. The pedantic arrogance of a very husband has not so pragmatical° an
air. Ah! I'll never marry, unless I am first made sure of
my will and pleasure.

MIRABELL: Would you have 'em both before marriage?
190 Or will you be contented with the first now, and stay
for the other till after grace?

MRS. MILLAMANT: Ah! don't be impertinent. My dear
liberty, shall I leave thee? My faithful solitude, my
darling contemplation, must I bid you then adieu?
195 Ay-h adieu, my morning thoughts, agreeable wak-
ings, indolent slumbers, all ye *douceurs*,° ye *sommeils du matin*,° adieu. I can't do't, 'tis more than
impossible. Positively, Mirabell, I'll lie abed in a
morning as long as I please.

200 MIRABELL: Then I'll get up in a morning as early as I
please.

MRS. MILLAMANT: Ah! idle creature, get up when you
will. And d'ye hear, I won't be called names after I'm
married; positively I won't be called names.

205 MIRABELL: Names!

MRS. MILLAMANT: Aye, as wife, spouse, my dear, joy,
jewel, love, sweetheart, and the rest of that nauseous
cant, in which men and their wives are so fulsomely
familiar; I shall never bear that. Good Mirabell,
210 don't let us be familiar or fond, nor kiss before folks,
like my Lady Fadler and Sir Francis; nor go to Hyde
Park together the first Sunday in a new chariot, to
provoke eyes and whispers, and then never be seen
there together again, as if we were proud of one
215 another the first week, and ashamed of one another
ever after. Let us never visit together, nor go to a play
together. But let us be very strange and well-bred; let
us be as strange as if we had been married a great
while, and as well-bred as if we were not married at
220 all.

MIRABELL: Have you any more conditions to offer?
Hitherto your demands are pretty reasonable.

MRS. MILLAMANT: Trifles! As liberty to pay and receive
visits to and from whom I please; to write and receive
225 letters, without interrogatories° or wry faces on your
part; to wear what I please, and choose conversation
with regard only to my own taste; to have no obligation upon me to converse with wits that I don't like,
because they are your acquaintance, or to be intimate
230 with fools, because they may be your relations. Come
to dinner when I please; dine in my dressing-room
when I'm out of humor, without giving a reason. To
have my closet inviolate; to be sole empress of my

tea-table, which you must never presume to approach without first asking leave. And lastly, wher- 235
ever I am, you shall always knock at the door before
you come in. These articles subscribed, if I continue
to endure you a little longer, I may by degrees
dwindle into a wife.

MIRABELL: Your bill of fare is something advanced in 240
this latter account. Well, have I liberty to offer conditions, that when you are dwindled into a wife, I may
not be beyond measure enlarged into a husband?

MRS. MILLAMANT: You have free leave. Propose your
utmost; speak and spare not. 245

MIRABELL: I thank you. *Imprimis*° then, I covenant°
that your acquaintance be general; that you admit no
sworn confidante, or intimate of your own sex; no
she-friend to screen her affairs under your countenance, and tempt you to make trial of a mutual 250
secrecy. No decoy-duck to wheedle° you a fop,
scrambling° to the play in a mask; then bring you
home in a pretended fright, when you think you shall
be found out, and rail at me for missing the play, and
disappointing the frolic which you had to pick me up 255
and prove my constancy.

MRS. MILLAMANT: Detestable *imprimis*! I go to the play
in a mask!

MIRABELL: *Item,*° I article that you continue to like your
own face, as long as I shall; and while it passes cur- 260
rent with me, that you endeavor not to new-coin it.
To which end, together with all vizards for the day, I
prohibit all masks for the night, made of oiled skins
and I know not what: hog's bones, hare's gall, pig
water, and the marrow of a roasted cat.° In short, I 265
forbid all commerce with the gentle-woman in What-
d'ye-call-it Court. *Item,* I shut my doors against all
bawds with baskets, and pennyworths of muslin,
china, fans, atlases,° etc. *Item,* when you shall be
breeding — 270

MRS. MILLAMANT: Ah! name it not.

MIRABELL: Which may be presumed, with a blessing on
our endeavors —

MRS. MILLAMANT: Odious endeavors!

MIRABELL: I denounce against all strait-lacing, squeez- 275
ing for a shape, till you mold my boy's head like a
sugar-loaf, and instead of a man child, make me
father to a crooked billet.° Lastly, to the dominion of
the tea-table I submit, but with *proviso* that you
exceed not in your province, but restrain yourself to 280
native and simple tea-table drinks, as tea, chocolate,
and coffee, as likewise to genuine and authorized
tea-table talk, such as mending of fashions, spoiling
reputations, railing at absent friends, and so forth;
but that on no account you encroach upon the men's 285
prerogative, and presume to drink healths, or toast

---

186. **pragmatical:** Officious.   196. *douceurs:* Sweet pleasures.
196–97. *sommeils du matin:* Morning sleep.   225. **interrogatories:** Prying questions.

246. *Imprimis:* First.   **covenant:** Decree.   251. **wheedle:** Procure.   252. **scrambling:** Going without suitable dignity.
259. *Item:* In addition.   264–65. **hog's bones ... cat:** All
were ingredients in cosmetics.   269. **atlases:** A kind of satin.
278. **billet:** Stick.

fellows; for prevention of which, I banish all foreign forces, all auxiliaries to the tea-table, as orange brandy, all aniseed, cinnamon, citron, and Barbados waters, together with ratafia and the most noble spirit of clary.° But for cowslip wine, poppy water, and all dormitives,° those I allow. These *provisos* admitted, in other things I may prove a tractable and complying husband.

MRS. MILLAMANT: O horrid *provisos*! filthy strongwaters! I toast fellows, odious men! I hate your odious *provisos*.

MIRABELL: Then we're agreed. Shall I kiss your hand upon the contract? And here comes one to be a witness to the sealing of the deed.

(*Reenter Mrs. Fainall.*)

MRS. MILLAMANT: Fainall, what shall I do? Shall I have him? I think I must have him.

MRS. FAINALL: Aye, aye, take him, take him; what should you do?

MRS. MILLAMANT: Well then — I'll take my death I'm in a horrid fright. Fainall, I shall never say it. Well — I think — I'll endure you.

MRS. FAINALL: Fie! fie! have him, have him, and tell him so in plain terms; for I am sure you have a mind to him.

MRS. MILLAMANT: Are you? I think I have; and the horrid man looks as if he thought so too. Well, you ridiculous thing you, I'll have you; I won't be kissed, nor I won't be thanked. Here, kiss my hand though. So, hold your tongue now; don't say a word.

MRS. FAINALL: Mirabell, there's a necessity for your obedience; you have neither time to talk nor stay. My mother is coming; and in my conscience, if she should see you, would fall into fits and maybe not recover, time enough to return to Sir Rowland, who, as Foible tells me, is in a fair way to succeed. Therefore spare your ecstasies for another occasion, and slip down the back stairs, where Foible waits to consult you.

MRS. MILLAMANT: Aye, go, go. In the meantime I suppose you have said something to please me.

MIRABELL: I am all obedience.   (*Exit.*)

MRS. FAINALL: Yonder Sir Wilfull's drunk, and so noisy that my mother has been forced to leave Sir Rowland to appease him; but he answers her only with singing and drinking. What they may have done by this time I know not; but Petulant and he were upon quarreling as I came by.

MRS. MILLAMANT: Well, if Mirabell should not make a good husband, I am a lost thing; for I find I love him violently.

MRS. FAINALL: So it seems; for you mind not what's said to you. If you doubt him, you had best take up with Sir Wilfull.

MRS. MILLAMANT: How can you name that superannuated lubber? Foh!

(*Enter Witwoud, from drinking.*)

MRS. FAINALL: So, is the fray made up, that you have left 'em?

WITWOUD: Left 'em? I could stay no longer. I have laughed like ten christenings; I am tipsy with laughing. If I had stayed any longer I should have burst; I must have been let out and pieced in the sides like an unsized camlet.° Yes, yes, the fray is composed; my lady came in like a *noli prosequi*° and stopped the proceedings.

MRS. MILLAMANT: What was the dispute?

WITWOUD: That's the jest; there was no dispute. They could neither of 'em speak for rage, and so fell asputtering at one another like two roasting apples.

(*Enter Petulant, drunk.*)

Now, Petulant? All's over, all's well? Gad, my head begins to whim° it about. Why dost thou not speak? Thou art both as drunk and as mute as a fish.

PETULANT: Look you, Mrs. Millamant, if you can love me, dear nymph, say it, and that's the conclusion. Pass on, or pass off; that's all.

WITWOUD: Thou hast uttered volumes, folios, in less than *decimo sexto*,° my dear Lacedemonian.° Sirrah, Petulant, thou art an epitomizer of words.°

PETULANT: Witwoud, you are an annihilator of sense.

WITWOUD: Thou art a retailer of phrases and dost deal in remnants of remnants, like a maker of pincushions; thou art in truth (metaphorically speaking) a speaker of shorthand.

PETULANT: Thou art (without a figure) just one half of an ass, and Baldwin° yonder, thy half brother, is the rest. A Gemini° of asses split would make just four of you.

WITWOUD: Thou dost bite, my dear mustard seed; kiss me for that.

PETULANT: Stand off! I'll kiss no more males. I have kissed your twin yonder in a humor of reconciliation, till he (*hiccup*) rises upon my stomach like a radish.

MRS. MILLAMANT: Eh! filthy creature! What was the quarrel?

PETULANT: There was no quarrel; there might have been a quarrel.

WITWOUD: If there had been words enow between 'em to have expressed provocation, they had gone together by the ears like a pair of castanets.

288–91. **orange brandy . . . clary:** All these "auxiliaries" were cordials made of brandy and variously flavored. 292. **dormitives:** Sedatives.

347. **unsized camlet:** I.e., like a piece of unstiffened satin. 348. **noli prosequi:** A legal term meaning that the plaintiff does not wish to continue the prosecution. 355. **whim:** Spin. 361. **decimo sexto:** A very tiny book. **Lacedemonian:** Spartan. (The Spartans were known to be very laconic people, that is, terse in their speech.) 362. **thou art . . . words:** I.e., "You say much in few words." 369. **Baldwin:** The name of the ass in the medieval tale *Reynard the Fox*. 370. **Gemini:** Matched pair of twins. The constellation Gemini derives its name from the twin stars Castor and Pollux.

PETULANT: You were the quarrel.

MRS. MILLAMANT: Me!

385   PETULANT: If I have a humor to quarrel, I can make less
matters conclude premises. If you are not handsome,
what then, if I have a humor to prove it? If I shall
have my reward, say so; if not, fight for your face the
next time yourself. I'll go sleep.

390   WITWOUD: Do, wrap thyself up like a wood louse, and
dream revenge; and hear me, if thou canst learn to
write by tomorrow morning, pen me a challenge. I'll
carry it for thee.

PETULANT: Carry your mistress's monkey a spider! Go

395   flea dogs, and read romances! I'll go to bed to my
maid.   (*Exit.*)

MRS. FAINALL: He's horridly drunk. How came you all
in this pickle?

WITWOUD: A plot! a plot! to get rid of the knight. Your

400   husband's advice; but he sneaked off.

(*Reenter Sir Wilfull drunk, and Lady Wishfort.*)

LADY WISHFORT: Out upon't, out upon't! At years of discretion, and comport yourself at this rantipole° rate!

SIR WILFULL: No offense, aunt.

LADY WISHFORT: Offense? As I'm a person, I'm

405   ashamed of you. Fogh! how you stink of wine! D'ye
think my niece will ever endure such a borachio!°
you're an absolute borachio.

SIR WILFULL: Borachio!

LADY WISHFORT: At a time when you should commence

410   an amour, and put your best foot foremost —

SIR WILFULL: 'Sheart, an you grutch° me your liquor,
make a bill. Give me more drink, and take my purse.

(*Sings.*) "Prithee fill me the glass

415   Till it laugh in my face,
With ale that is potent and mellow;
        He that whines for a lass
        Is an ignorant ass,
For a bumper has not its fellow."

But if you would have me marry my cousin, say the

420   word, and I'll do't. Wilfull will do't; that's the word.
Wilfull will do't; that's my crest. My motto I have
forgot.

LADY WISHFORT: My nephew's a little overtaken,°
cousin, but 'tis with drinking your health. O' my

425   word you are obliged to him.

SIR WILFULL: *In vino veritas,*° aunt. If I drunk your
health today, cousin, I am a borachio. But if you have
a mind to be married, say the word, and send for the
piper; Wilfull will do't. If not, dust it away, and let's

430   have t'other round. Tony! Ods-heart, where's Tony?

---

402. rantipole: Wild.   **406. borachio:** Spanish for "wine bag,"
a drunkard. Shakespeare has a character named Borachio in
Much Ado about Nothing.   **411. grutch:** Grudge.   **423. overtaken:** Overcome by drink.   **426. *In vino veritas:*** "In wine
(there is) truth."

Tony's an honest fellow; but he spits after a bumper,
and that's a fault.

(*Sings.*) "We'll drink, and we'll never ha' done,
        boys,
    Put the glass then around with the sun, boys;
Let Apollo's example invite us;   435
    For he's drunk every night,
    And that makes him so bright,
That he's able next morning to light us."

The sun's a good pimple,° an honest soaker, he has a
cellar at your Antipodes.° If I travel, aunt, I touch at   440
your Antipodes; your Antipodes are a good, rascally
sort of topsy-turvy fellows. If I had a bumper, I'd
stand upon my head and drink a health to 'em. A
match or no match, cousin, with the hard name.
Aunt, Wilfull will do't. If she has her maidenhead, let 445
her look to't, if she has not, let her keep her own
counsel in the meantime, and cry out at the nine
months' end.

MRS. MILLAMANT: Your pardon, madam, I can stay no
longer. Sir Wilfull grows very powerful. Egh! how he   450
smells! I shall be overcome if I stay. Come, cousin.

(*Exeunt Mrs. Millamant and Mrs. Fainall.*)

LADY WISHFORT: Smells! he would poison a tallow-
chandler° and his family! Beastly creature, I know
not what to do with him. Travel, quotha! aye, travel,
travel, get thee gone, get thee but far enough, to the 455
Saracens, or the Tartars, or the Turks, for thou art
not fit to live in a Christian commonwealth, thou
beastly pagan!

SIR WILFULL: Turks, no; no Turks, aunt; your Turks are
infidels, and believe not in the grape. Your Maho-   460
metan, your Mussulman, is a dry stinkard.° No offense, aunt. My map says that your Turk is not so
honest a man as your Christian. I cannot find by the
map that your mufti° is orthodox; whereby it is a
plain case that orthodox is a hard word, aunt, and   465
(*hiccup*) Greek for claret.

(*Sings.*) "To drink is a Christian diversion,
Unknown to the Turk or the Persian
        Let Mahometan fools
        Live by heathenish rules,   470
And be damn'd over teacups and coffee!
        But let British lads sing,
        Crown a health to the king,
And a fig for your sultan and sophy!"°

Ah, Tony!   475

---

439. pimple: Drinking companion.   **440. Antipodes:** The opposite end of the world, or its inhabitants.   **452–53. tallow-
chandler:** Candle maker.   **461. dry stinkard:** A miserable
nondrinker. Mohammedans drink neither wine nor spirits.
464. mufti: An expert in Mohammedan religious law.
474. sophy: A former title of the Persian shah.

(*Enter Foible, and whispers [to] Lady Wishfort.*)

LADY WISHFORT (*aside to Foible*): Sir Rowland impatient? Good lack! what shall I do with this beastly
tumbril?° (*Aloud.*) Go lie down and sleep, you sot!
or, as I'm a person, I'll have you bastinadoed° with
480 broomsticks. Call up the wenches with broomsticks.

(*Exit Foible.*)

SIR WILFULL: Ahey! Wenches, where are the wenches?
LADY WISHFORT: Dear Cousin Witwoud, get him away,
and you will bind me to you inviolably. I have an
affair of moment that invades me with some precipi-
485 tation. You will oblige me to all futurity.
WITWOUD: Come, knight. Pox on him, I don't know
what to say to him. Will you go to a cock match?
SIR WILFULL: With a wench, Tony? Is she a shakebag,°
Sirrah? Let me bite your cheek° for that.
490 WITWOUD: Horrible! he has a breath like a bagpipe!
Aye, aye, come, will you march, my Salopian?°
SIR WILFULL: Lead on, little Tony, I'll follow thee, my
Anthony, my Tantony. Sirrah, thou shalt be my
Tantony, and I'll be thy pig.°
495   "And a fig for your sultan and sophy."

(*Exit singing with Witwoud.*)

LADY WISHFORT: This will never do. It will never make
a match; at least before he has been abroad.

(*Enter Waitwell, disguised as Sir Rowland.*)

Dear Sir Rowland, I am confounded with confusion
at the retrospection of my own rudeness! I have more
500 pardons to ask than the Pope distributes in the Year
of Jubilee.° But I hope, where there is likely to be so
near an alliance, we may unbend the severity of decorum, and dispense with a little ceremony.
WAITWELL: My impatience, madam, is the effect of my
505 transport; and till I have the possession of your
adorable person, I am tantalized on the rack, and do
but hang, madam, on the tenter° of expectation.
LADY WISHFORT: You have excess of gallantry, Sir Rowland, and press things to a conclusion with a most
510 prevailing vehemence. But a day or two for decency
of marriage —
WAITWELL: For decency of funeral, madam! The delay
will break my heart; or, if that should fail, I shall be
poisoned. My nephew will get an inkling of my
515 designs, and poison me — and I would willingly
starve him before I die; I would gladly go out of the
world with that satisfaction. That would be some

comfort to me, if I could but live so long as to be
revenged on that unnatural viper.
LADY WISHFORT: Is he so unnatural, say you? Truly I   520
would contribute much both to the saving of your
life, and the accomplishment of your revenge. Not
that I respect myself, though he has been a perfidious
wretch to me.
WAITWELL: Perfidious to you!   525
LADY WISHFORT: O Sir Rowland, the hours that he has
died away at my feet, the tears that he has shed, the
oaths that he has sworn, the palpitations that he has
felt, the trances and the tremblings, the ardors and
the ecstasies, the kneelings and the risings, the heart- 530
heavings and the hand-gripings, the pangs and the
pathetic regards of his protesting eyes! Oh, no memory can register!
WAITWELL: What, my rival! Is the rebel my rival? 'A
dies.   535
LADY WISHFORT: No, don't kill him at once, Sir Rowland; starve him gradually, inch by inch.
WAITWELL: I'll do't. In three weeks he shall be barefoot;
in a month out at knees with begging an alms. He
shall starve upward and upward, till he has nothing   540
living but his head, and then go out in a stink like a
candle's end upon a save-all.°
LADY WISHFORT: Well, Sir Rowland, you have the way.
You are no novice in the labyrinth of love; you have
the clue. But as I am a person, Sir Rowland, you must 545
not attribute my yielding to any sinister appetite, or
indigestion of widowhood; nor impute my complacency to any lethargy of continence. I hope you do
not think me prone to any iteration° of nuptials.
WAITWELL: Far be it from me —   550
LADY WISHFORT: If you do, I protest I must recede, or
think that I have made a prostitution of decorums;
but in the vehemence of compassion, and to save the
life of a person of so much importance —
WAITWELL: I esteem it so.   555
LADY WISHFORT: Or else you wrong my condescension.
WAITWELL: I do not, I do not!
LADY WISHFORT: Indeed you do.
WAITWELL: I do not, fair shrine of virtue!
LADY WISHFORT: If you think the least scruple of carnal- 560
ity° was an ingredient —
WAITWELL: Dear madam, no. You are all camphire° and
frankincense, all chastity and odor.
LADY WISHFORT: Or that —

(*Reenter Foible.*)

FOIBLE: Madam, the dancers are ready; and there's one   565
with a letter, who must deliver it into your own hands.

---

478. **tumbril:** Dump-cart. 479. **bastinadoed:** Beaten.
488. **shake-bag:** A term in cock fighting for a very game or
sporting cock. 489. **bite your cheek:** I.e., "give you a big
kiss." 491. **Salopian:** Shropshireman. 494. **pig:** In art and
legend, the pig is associated with St. Anthony the Great.
500–01. **Year of Jubilee:** The year (approximately every
twenty-fifth) in which the pope grants general remission from
the consequences of sin. 507. **tenter:** A tenterhook.

542. **save-all:** A device in a candlestick to ensure that the candle
will be completely burned. 549. **iteration:** Repetition. The
sense seems to be that Lady Wishfort hopes Sir Rowland will
not suspect her of a willingness to marry just any man.
560–61. **carnality:** Sensuality, lust. 562. **camphire:** Camphor
was believed to reduce sexual desire.

LADY WISHFORT: Sir Rowland, will you give me leave? Think favorably, judge candidly, and conclude you have found a person who would suffer racks in
570 honor's cause, dear Sir Rowland, and will wait on you incessantly.°   (*Exit.*)
WAITWELL: Fie, fie! What a slavery have I undergone! Spouse, hast thou any cordial? I want spirits.
FOIBLE: What a washy° rogue art thou, to pant thus for
575 a quarter of an hour's lying and swearing to a fine lady!
WAITWELL: Oh, she is the antidote to desire! Spouse, thou wilt fare the worse for't. I shall have no appetite to "iteration of nuptials" this eight-and-forty hours.
580 By this hand I'd rather be a chair-man° in the dog days° than act Sir Rowland till this time tomorrow!

(*Reenter Lady Wishfort, with a letter.*)

LADY WISHFORT: Call in the dancers. Sir Rowland, we'll sit, if you please, and see the entertainment. (*Dance.*) Now, with your permission, Sir Rowland, I will
585 peruse my letter. I would open it in your presence, because I would not make you uneasy. If it should make you uneasy, I would burn it — speak if it does — but you may see, the superscription is like a woman's hand.
590 FOIBLE (*aside to Waitwell*): By Heaven! Mrs. Marwood's; I know it. My heart aches. Get it from her.
WAITWELL: A woman's hand? No, madam, that's no woman's hand; I see that already. That's somebody whose throat must be cut.
595 LADY WISHFORT: Nay, Sir Rowland, since you give me a proof of your passion by your jealousy, I promise you I'll make a return, by a frank communication. You shall see it; we'll open it together. Look you here. (*Reads.*) "Madam, though unknown to you." Look
600 you there; 'tis from nobody that I know. "I have that honor for your character, that I think myself obliged to let you know you are abused. He who pretends to be Sir Rowland is a cheat and a rascal." Oh, heavens! what's this?
605 FOIBLE (*aside*): Unfortunate! all's ruined!
WAITWELL: How, how, let me see, let me see! (*Reading.*) "A rascal, and disguised and suborned° for that imposture." O villainy! O villainy! "by the contrivance of —"
610 LADY WISHFORT: I shall faint, I shall die, oh!
FOIBLE (*aside to Waitwell*): Say 'tis your nephew's hand. Quickly, his plot, swear, swear it!
WAITWELL: Here's a villain! Madam, don't you perceive it? don't you see it?
615 LADY WISHFORT: Too well, too well! I have seen too much.

WAITWELL: I told you at first I knew the hand. A woman's hand? The rascal writes a sort of a large hand, your Roman hand. I saw there was a throat to be cut presently. If he were my son, as he is my 620 nephew, I'd pistol him!
FOIBLE: Oh, treachery! But are you sure, Sir Rowland, it is his writing?
WAITWELL: Sure? Am I here? Do I live? Do I love this pearl of India? I have twenty letters in my pocket 625 from him in the same character.°
LADY WISHFORT: How!
FOIBLE: Oh, what luck it is, Sir Rowland, that you were present at this juncture! This was the business that brought Mr. Mirabell disguised to Madam Milla- 630 mant this afternoon. I thought something was contriving, when he stole by me and would have hid his face.
LADY WISHFORT: How, how! I heard the villain was in the house indeed; and now I remember, my niece 635 went away abruptly, when Sir Wilfull was to have made his addresses.
FOIBLE: Then, then, madam, Mr. Mirabell waited for her in her chamber, but I would not tell your ladyship to discompose° you when you were to receive Sir 640 Rowland.
WAITWELL: Enough, his date is short.
FOIBLE: No, good Sir Rowland, don't incur the law.
WAITWELL: Law? I care not for law. I can but die, and 'tis in a good cause. My lady shall be satisfied of my 645 truth and innocence, though it cost me my life.
LADY WISHFORT: No, dear Sir Rowland, don't fight; if you should be killed, I must never show my face; or hanged! Oh, consider my reputation, Sir Rowland! No, you shan't fight. I'll go in and examine my niece; 650 I'll make her confess. I conjure you, Sir Rowland, by all your love, not to fight.
WAITWELL: I am charmed, madam; I obey. But some proof you must let me give you; I'll go for a black box, which contains the writings of my whole estate, 655 and deliver that into your hands.
LADY WISHFORT: Aye, dear Sir Rowland, that will be some comfort; bring the black box.
WAITWELL: And may I presume to bring a contract to be signed this night? May I hope so far?   660
LADY WISHFORT: Bring what you will; but come alive, pray come alive. Oh, this is a happy discovery!
WAITWELL: Dead or alive I'll come, and married we will be in spite of treachery; aye, and get an heir that shall defeat the last remaining glimpse of hope in my aban- 665 doned nephew. Come, my buxom widow.
    Ere long you shall substantial proof receive,
    That I'm an arrant knight — °
FOIBLE (*aside*):   Or arrant° knave.
                                              (*Exeunt.*)

---

571. **incessantly:** Immediately.   574. **washy:** Weak.   580. **chair-man:** A sedan-chair carrier.   580–81. **dog days:** The sultriest days of the summer, a period of about six weeks beginning in early July.   607. **suborned:** Bribed.

626. **character:** Handwriting.   640. **discompose:** Distress, upset.   668. **arrant knight:** I.e., a true knight-errant.   **arrant:** Downright.

ACT V

([*Scene continues.*] *Enter Lady Wishfort and Foible.*)

LADY WISHFORT: Out of my house, out of my house, thou viper! thou serpent, that I have fostered! thou bosom traitress, that I raised from nothing! Begone! begone! begone! go! go! That I took from washing of old gauze and weaving of dead hair, with a bleak blue nose, over a chafing-dish of starved embers, and dining behind a traverse rag,° in a shop no bigger than a birdcage! Go, go! starve again, do, do!

FOIBLE: Dear madam, I'll beg your pardon on my knees.

LADY WISHFORT: Away! out! out! Go set up for yourself again! Do, drive a trade, do, with your three-penny-worth of small ware flaunting upon a pack-thread under a brandy-seller's bulk,° or against a dead wall by a ballad-monger! Go, hang out an old frisoneer-gorget,° with a yard of yellow colberteen° again. Do; an old gnawed mask, two rows of pins, and a child's fiddle; a glass necklace with the beads broken, and a quilted nightcap with one ear. Go, go, drive a trade! These were your commodities, you treacherous trull! this was the merchandise you dealt in, when I took you into my house, placed you next myself, and made you governante of my whole family! You have forgot this, have you, now you have feathered your nest?

FOIBLE: No, no, dear madam. Do but hear me; have but a moment's patience. I'll confess all. Mr. Mirabell seduced me; I am not the first that he has wheedled with his dissembling tongue. Your ladyship's own wisdom has been deluded by him, then how should I, a poor ignorant, defend myself? O madam, if you knew but what he promised me, and how he assured me your ladyship should come to no damage? Or else the wealth of the Indies should not have bribed me to conspire against so good, so sweet, so kind a lady as you have been to me.

LADY WISHFORT: No damage? What, to betray me, to marry me to a cast-servingman?° To make me a receptacle, a hospital for a decayed pimp? "No damage"? O thou frontless° impudence, more than a big-bellied actress!

FOIBLE: Pray do but hear me, madam; he could not marry your ladyship, madam. No indeed; his marriage was to have been void in law, for he was married to me first, to secure your ladyship. He could not have bedded your ladyship; for if he had consummated with your ladyship, he must have run the risk of the law and been put upon his clergy.° Yes indeed, I inquired of the law in that case before I would meddle or make.°

LADY WISHFORT: What, then I have been your property, have I? I have been convenient to you, it seems! While you were catering for Mirabell, I have been broker° for you? What, have you made a passive bawd of me? This exceeds all precedent; I am brought to fine uses, to become a botcher° of second-hand marriages between Abigails° and Andrews!° I'll couple you! Yes, I'll baste you together, you and your Philander!° I'll Duke's-Place you, as I'm a person! Your turtle is in custody already; you shall coo in the same cage, if there be constable or warrant in the parish. (*Exit.*)

FOIBLE: Oh, that ever I was born! Oh, that I was ever married! A bride! aye, I shall be a Bridewell-bride.° Oh!

(*Enter Mrs. Fainall.*)

MRS. FAINALL: Poor Foible, what's the matter?

FOIBLE: O madam, my lady's gone for a constable. I shall be had to a justice, and put to Bridewell to beat hemp. Poor Waitwell's gone to prison already.

MRS. FAINALL: Have a good heart, Foible; Mirabell's gone to give security for him. This is all Marwood's and my husband's doing.

FOIBLE: Yes, yes, I know it, madam; she was in my lady's closet, and overheard all that you said to me before dinner. She sent the letter to my lady; and that missing effect, Mr. Fainall laid this plot to arrest Waitwell, when he pretended to go for the papers; and in the meantime Mrs. Marwood declared all to my lady.

MRS. FAINALL: Was there no mention made of me in the letter? My mother does not suspect my being in the confederacy? I fancy Marwood has not told her, though she has told my husband.

FOIBLE: Yes, madam; but my lady did not see that part. We stifled the letter before she read so far. Has that mischievous devil told Mr. Fainall of your ladyship then?

MRS. FAINALL: Aye, all's out, my affair with Mirabell, everything discovered. This is the last day of our living together; that's my comfort.

FOIBLE: Indeed, madam, and so 'tis a comfort if you knew all. He has been even with your ladyship; which I could have told you long enough since, but I love to keep peace and quietness by my good will. I had rather bring friends together than set 'em at distance. But Mrs. Marwood and he are nearer related than ever their parents thought for.

---

7. traverse rag: A curtain or hanging that serves as a screen. **13. bulk:** A booth where brandy is sold. **14–15. frisoneer-gorget:** A kind of wimple, or head covering, made of coarse woolen cloth. **15. colberteen:** A French lace of inferior quality. **36. cast-servingman:** A discharged servant. **38. frontless:** Shameless. **46. put upon his clergy:** Forced to plead benefit of clergy. Clergy (and, later, people who could read or write) could claim exemption from punishment imposed by a secular court.

48. meddle or make: A colloquialism for "get mixed up in this business." **52. broker:** Marriage broker. **54. botcher:** A maker or mender. **55. Abigails:** A maidservant in Beaumont and Fletcher's play *The Scornful Lady.* **Andrews:** A manservant in Fletcher and Massinger's *The Elder Brother.* **57. Philander:** The lover in Beaumont and Fletcher's *The Laws of Candy.* **62. Bridewell-bride:** Bridewell was a house of correction.

95   MRS. FAINALL: Sayest thou so, Foible? Canst thou prove this?

FOIBLE: I can take my oath of it, madam; so can Mrs. Mincing. We have had many a fair word from Madam Marwood, to conceal something that passed
100   in our chamber one evening when you were at Hyde Park and we were thought to have gone awalking; but we went up unawares, though we were sworn to secrecy too. Madam Marwood took a book and swore us upon it, but it was but a book of poems. So
105   long as it was not a Bible oath, we may break it with a safe conscience.

MRS. FAINALL: This discovery is the most opportune thing I could wish. Now, Mincing?

(Enter Mincing.)

MINCING: My lady° would speak with Mrs. Foible,
110   mem. Mr. Mirabell is with her; he has set your spouse at liberty, Mrs. Foible, and would have you hide yourself in my lady's closet till my old lady's anger is abated. Oh, my old lady is in a perilous passion at something Mr. Fainall has said, he swears, and my
115   old lady cries. There's a fearful hurricane, I vow. He says, mem, how that he'll have my lady's fortune made over to him, or he'll be divorced.

MRS. FAINALL: Does your lady or Mirabell know that?

MINCING: Yes, mem, they have sent me to see if Sir Wil-
120   full be sober and to bring him to them. My lady is resolved to have him, I think, rather than lose such a vast sum as six thousand pound. Oh, come, Mrs. Foible, I hear my old lady.

MRS. FAINALL: Foible, you must tell Mincing that she
125   must prepare to vouch° when I call her.

FOIBLE: Yes, yes, madam.

MINCING: O yes, mem, I'll vouch anything for your ladyship's service, be what it will.

(Exeunt Mincing and Foible.)

(Reenter Lady Wishfort, with, Mrs. Marwood.)

LADY WISHFORT: O my dear friend, how can I enumer-
130   ate the benefits that I have received from your goodness? To you I owe the timely discovery of the false vows of Mirabell, to you I owe the detection of the impostor, Sir Rowland. And now you are become an intercessor with my son-in-law, to save the honor of
135   my house, and compound for the frailties of my daughter. Well, friend, you are enough to reconcile me to the bad world, or else I would retire to deserts and solitudes, and feed harmless sheep by groves and purling streams. Dear Marwood, let us leave the
140   world, and retire by ourselves and be shepherdesses.

MRS. MARWOOD: Let us first dispatch the affair in hand, madam. We shall have leisure to think of retirement afterwards. Here is one who is concerned in the treaty.

LADY WISHFORT: O daughter, daughter, is it possible

thou shouldst be my child, bone of my bone, and   145
flesh of my flesh, and, as I may say, another me, and yet transgress the most minute particle of severe virtue? Is it possible you should lean aside to iniquity, who have been cast in the direct mold of virtue? I have not only been a mold but a pattern for you, and   150
a model for you, after you were brought into the world.

MRS. FAINALL: I don't understand your ladyship.

LADY WISHFORT: Not understand? Why, have you not been naught?° Have you not been sophisticated?°   155
Not understand? Here I am ruined to compound° for your caprices and your cuckoldoms. I must pawn my plate and my jewels, and ruin my niece, and all little enough.

MRS. FAINALL: I am wronged and abused, and so are   160
you. 'Tis a false accusation, as false as hell, as false as your friend there, aye, or your friend's friend, my false husband.

MRS. MARWOOD: My friend, Mrs. Fainall? Your husband my friend? What do you mean?   165

MRS. FAINALL: I know what I mean, madam, and so do you; and so shall the world at a time convenient.

MRS. MARWOOD: I am sorry to see you so passionate, madam. More temper° would look more like innocence. But I have done. I am sorry my zeal to serve   170
your ladyship and family should admit of misconstruction, or make me liable to affronts. You will pardon me, madam, if I meddle no more with an affair in which I am not personally concerned.

LADY WISHFORT: O dear friend, I am so ashamed that   175
you should meet with such returns! *(To Mrs. Fainall.)* You ought to ask pardon on your knees, ungrateful creature; she deserves more from you than all your life can accomplish. *(To Mrs. Marwood.)* Oh, don't leave me destitute in this perplexity! No, stick to me,   180
my good genius.

MRS. FAINALL: I tell you, madam, you're abused. Stick to you? Aye, like a leech, to suck your best blood; she'll drop off when she's full. Madam, you shan't pawn a bodkin,° nor part with a brass counter,° in   185
composition for me. I defy 'em all. Let 'em prove their aspersions; I know my own innocence, and dare stand a trial.   *(Exit.)*

LADY WISHFORT: Why, if she should be innocent, if she should be wronged after all, ha? I don't know what   190
to think; and, I promise you, her education has been unexceptionable.° I may say it; for I chiefly made it my own care to initiate her very infancy in the rudiments of virtue, and to impress upon her tender years a young odium° and aversion to the very sight of   195

109. **My lady:** I.e., Millamant.   125. **vouch:** Testify.

155. **naught:** Naughty, wicked.   **sophisticated:** Corrupted, debauched.   156. **compound:** Compensate. Lady Wishfort refers to Mr. Fainall's blackmailing tactics.   169. **temper:** Temperateness.   185. **bodkin:** Needle or hairpin.   **brass counter:** A farthing (a quarter of a penny).   192. **unexceptionable:** Exemplary.   195. **odium:** Dislike.

men. Aye, friend, she would ha' shrieked if she had but seen a man, till she was in her teens. As I'm a person 'tis true. She was never suffered to play with a male child, though but in coats; nay, her very babies° were of the feminine gender. Oh, she never looked a man in the face but her own father, or the chaplain, and him we made a shift° to put upon her for a woman, by the help of his long garments and his sleek face, till she was going in her fifteen.°

MRS. MARWOOD: 'Twas much she should be deceived so long.

LADY WISHFORT: I warrant you, or she would never have borne to have been catechized by him; and have heard his long lectures against singing and dancing, and such debaucheries, and going to filthy plays and profane music meetings, where the lewd trebles squeak nothing but bawdy, and the basses roar blasphemy. Oh, she would have swooned at the sight or name of an obscene playbook! And can I think, after all this, that my daughter can be naught? What, a whore? and thought it excommunication to set her foot within the door of a playhouse! O dear friend, I can't believe it, no, no! As she says, let him prove it, let him prove it.

MRS. MARWOOD: Prove it, madam? What, and have your name prostituted in a public court? yours and your daughter's reputation worried at the bar by a pack of bawling lawyers? To be ushered in with an Oyez° of scandal, and have your case opened by an old fumbling lecher in a quoif° like a man-midwife; to bring your daughter's infamy to light; to be a theme for legal punsters and quibblers by the statute, and become a jest against a rule of court, where there is no precedent for a jest in any record, not even in Doomsday Book;° to discompose the gravity of the bench, and provoke naughty interrogatories in more naughty law Latin, while the good judge, tickled with the proceeding, simpers under a gray beard, and fidges° off and on his cushion as if he had swallowed cantharides,° or sat upon cow-itch!°

LADY WISHFORT: Oh, 'tis very hard!

MRS. MARWOOD: And then to have my young revelers of the Temple° take notes, like prentices at a conventicle;° and after, talk it over again in Commons,° or before drawers in an eating-house.

LADY WISHFORT: Worse and worse!

199. **babies:** Dolls.   202. **made a shift:** Devised a plan. 204. **in her fifteen:** Into her fifteenth year.   224. *Oyez*: The court crier's call for silence.   225. **quoif:** Coif, the lawyer's white cap.   230. **Doomsday Book:** A record of a survey of the lands of England made by order of William the Conqueror. 234. **fidges:** Fidgets.   235. **cantharides:** A powder made from dried beetles and used medicinally as a skin irritant.   **cow-itch:** Cowage, a plant that causes intense itching.   238. **Temple:** The courts of law.   238–39. **prentices at a conventicle:** It was customary for a Puritan master to require his apprentice to take notes on the Sunday sermon in the meetinghouse (conventicle). 239. **Commons:** The dining hall.

MRS. MARWOOD: Nay, this is nothing; if it would end here, 'twere well. But it must, after this, be consigned by the shorthand writers to the public press; and from thence be transferred to the hands, nay into the throats and lungs of hawkers,° with voices more licentious than the loud flounder-man's.° And this you must hear till you are stunned; nay, you must hear nothing else for some days.

LADY WISHFORT: Oh, 'tis insupportable! No, no, dear friend; make it up, make it up; aye, aye, I'll compound. I'll give up all, myself and my all, my niece and her all, anything, everything for composition.

MRS. MARWOOD: Nay, madam, I advise nothing; I only lay before you, as a friend, the inconveniencies which perhaps you have overseen. Here comes Mr. Fainall; if he will be satisfied to huddle up all in silence, I shall be glad. You must think I would rather congratulate than condole with you.

(Enter Fainall.)

LADY WISHFORT: Aye, aye, I do not doubt it, dear Marwood; no, no, I do not doubt it.

FAINALL: Well, madam, I have suffered myself to be overcome by the importunity of this lady, your friend, and am content you shall enjoy your own proper estate during life, on condition you oblige yourself never to marry, under such penalty as I think convenient.

LADY WISHFORT: Never to marry?

FAINALL: No more Sir Rowlands; the next imposture may not be so timely detected.

MRS. MARWOOD: That condition, I dare answer, my lady will consent to, without difficulty; she has already but too much experienced the perfidiousness of men. Besides, madam, when we retire to our pastoral solitude, we shall bid adieu to all other thoughts.

LADY WISHFORT: Aye, that's true; but in case of necessity, as of health, or some such emergency —

FAINALL: Oh, if you are prescribed marriage, you shall be considered; I will only reserve to myself the power to choose for you. If your physic be wholesome, it matters not who is your apothecary. Next, my wife shall settle on me the remainder of her fortune, not made over already; and for her maintenance depend entirely on my discretion.

LADY WISHFORT: This is most inhumanly savage, exceeding the barbarity of a Muscovite° husband.

FAINALL: I learned it from his Czarish majesty's retinue,° in a winter evening's conference over brandy and pepper, amongst other secrets of matrimony and policy, as they are at present practiced in the northern hemisphere. But this must be agreed unto, and that positively. Lastly, I will be endowed, in right of my

246. **hawkers:** Peddlers.   247. **flounder-man:** An actual flounder seller, well known to the Londoners of the day and noted for his "loud, but not unmusical" voice.   286. **Muscovite:** Russian.   287. **Czarish majesty's retinue:** Referring to Peter the Great's visit to England in 1697.

wife, with that six thousand pound, which is the moiety of Mrs. Millamant's fortune in your posses-
295 sion; and which she has forfeited (as will appear by the last will and testament of your deceased husband, Sir Jonathan Wishfort) by her disobedience in contracting herself against your consent or knowledge, and by refusing the offered match with Sir Wilfull
300 Witwoud, which you, like a careful aunt, had provided for her.

LADY WISHFORT: My nephew was *non compos*,° and could not make his addresses.

FAINALL: I come to make demands. I'll hear no objections.

305 LADY WISHFORT: You will grant me time to consider?

FAINALL: Yes, while the instrument° is drawing, to which you must set your hand till more sufficient deeds can be perfected; which I will take care shall be done with all possible speed. In the meanwhile I will
310 go for the said instrument, and till my return you may balance this matter in your own discretion. *(Exit.)*

LADY WISHFORT: This insolence is beyond all precedent, all parallel; must I be subject to this merciless villain?

MRS. MARWOOD: 'Tis severe indeed, madam, that you
315 should smart for your daughter's wantonness.

LADY WISHFORT: 'Twas against my consent that she married this barbarian, but she would have him, though her year° was not out. Ah! her first husband, my son Languish, would not have carried it thus.
320 Well, that was my choice, this is hers; she is matched now with a witness.° I shall be mad! Dear friend, is there no comfort for me? Must I live to be confiscated at this rebel-rate?° Here come two more of my Egyptian plagues° too.

(Enter Mrs. Millamant and Sir Wilfull Witwoud.)

325 SIR WILFULL: Aunt, your servant.

LADY WISHFORT: Out, caterpillar, call not me aunt! I know thee not!

SIR WILFULL: I confess I have been a little in disguise,° as they say. 'Sheart! and I'm sorry for't. What would
330 you have? I hope I committed no offense, aunt, and if I did, I am willing to make satisfaction; and what can a man say fairer? If I have broke anything, I'll pay for't, an it cost a pound. And so let that content for what's past, and make no more words. For what's to
335 come, to pleasure you I'm willing to marry my cousin. So pray let's all be friends; she and I are agreed upon the matter before a witness.

LADY WISHFORT: How's this, dear niece? Have I any comfort? Can this be true?

MRS. MILLAMANT: I am content to be a sacrifice to your 340 repose, madam; and to convince you that I had no hand in the plot, as you were misinformed, I have laid my commands on Mirabell to come in person, and be a witness that I give my hand to this flower of knighthood; and for the contract that passed be- 345 tween Mirabell and me, I have obliged him to make a resignation of it in your ladyship's presence. He is without, and waits your leave for admittance.

LADY WISHFORT: Well, I'll swear I am something revived at this testimony of your obedience; but I can- 350 not admit that traitor. I fear I cannot fortify myself to support his appearance. He is as terrible to me as a Gorgon;° if I see him, I fear I shall turn to stone, petrify incessantly.

MRS. MILLAMANT: If you disoblige him, he may resent 355 your refusal, and insist upon the contract still. Then 'tis the last time he will be offensive to you.

LADY WISHFORT: Are you sure it will be the last time? If I were sure of that! Shall I never see him again?

MRS. MILLAMANT: Sir Wilfull, you and he are to travel 360 together, are you not?

SIR WILFULL: 'Sheart, the gentleman's a civil gentleman, aunt; let him come in. Why, we are sworn brothers and fellow travelers. We are to be Pylades and Orestes,° he and I. He is to be my interpreter in foreign parts. 365 He has been overseas once already; and with *proviso* that I marry my cousin, will cross 'em once again, only to bear me company. 'Sheart, I'll call him in. An I set on't once, he shall come in; and see who'll hinder him. 370

(Goes to the door and hems.)

MRS. MARWOOD: This is precious fooling, if it would pass; but I'll know the bottom of it.

LADY WISHFORT: O dear Marwood, you are not going?

MRS. MARWOOD: Not far, madam; I'll return immediately.   *(Exit.)* 375

(Reenter Sir Wilfull with Mirabell.)

SIR WILFULL: Look up, man, I'll stand by you; 'sbud and she do frown, she can't kill you, besides, harkee, she dare not frown desperately, because her face is none of her own. 'Sheart, an she should, her forehead would wrinkle like the coat of a cream cheese; but 380 mum for that, fellow traveler.

MIRABELL: If a deep sense of the many injuries I have offered to so good a lady, with a sincere remorse and a hearty contrition, can but obtain the least glance of compassion, I am too happy. Ah, madam, there was 385 a time! But let it be forgotten. I confess I have deservedly forfeited the high place I once held, of sighing at your feet. Nay, kill me not, by turning from me

---

302. non compos: I.e., *non compos mentis,* not in his right mind. **306. instrument:** Formal agreement.   **318. her year:** Period of mourning for her first husband.   **321. with a witness:** Colloquialism meaning "with a vengeance."   **222–23. Must I live . . . rebel-rate:** The sense is "Must I live to see my property and fortune confiscated in this piratical fashion?"   **324. Egyptian plagues:** Referring to the plagues of Egypt recorded in Exodus 7ff.   **328. disguise:** Drunk.

353. Gorgon: Any one of the three sisters in Greek legend (Medusa was one) whose hair was wreathed with snakes and whose glance turned the beholder to stone.   **364. Pylades and Orestes:** In Greek legend Pylades was the loyal and trusted friend of Orestes, son of Agamemnon and brother of Elektra.

390 in disdain. I come not to plead for favor; nay, not for pardon. I am a suppliant only for pity. I am going where I shall never behold you more.

SIR WILFULL: How, fellow traveler! You shall go by yourself then.

395 MIRABELL: Let me be pitied first, and afterwards forgotten. I ask no more.

SIR WILFULL: By'r lady, a very reasonable request, and will cost you nothing, aunt. Come, come, forgive and forget, aunt; why, you must, an you are a Christian.

MIRABELL: Consider, madam, in reality you could not
400 receive much prejudice; it was an innocent device, though I confess it had a face of guiltiness. It was at most an artifice which love contrived, and errors which love produces have ever been accounted venial. At least think it is punishment enough that I
405 have lost what in my heart I hold most dear, that to your cruel indignation I have offered up this beauty, and with her my peace and quiet; nay, all my hopes of future comfort.

SIR WILFULL: An he does not move me, would I may
410 never be o' the quorum!° An it were not as good a deed as to drink, to give her to him again, I would I might never take shipping! Aunt, if you don't forgive quickly, I shall melt, I can tell you that. My contract went no farther than a little mouth-glue, and that's
415 hardly dry; one doleful sigh more from my fellow traveler, and 'tis dissolved.

LADY WISHFORT: Well, nephew, upon your account — ah, he has a false insinuating tongue! Well, sir, I will stifle my just resentment at my nephew's request. I will
420 endeavor what I can to forget, but on *proviso* that you resign the contract with my niece immediately.

MIRABELL: It is in writing, and with papers of concern; but I have sent my servant for it, and will deliver it to you, with all acknowledgments for your transcen-
425 dent goodness.

LADY WISHFORT (*aside*): Oh, he has witchcraft in his eyes and tongue! When I did not see him, I could have bribed a villain to his assassination; but his appearance rakes the embers which have so long lain
430 smothered in my breast.

(*Reenter Fainall and Mrs. Marwood.*)

FAINALL: Your date of deliberation, madam, is expired. Here is the instrument; are you prepared to sign?

LADY WISHFORT: If I were prepared, I am not empowered. My niece exerts a lawful claim, having matched
435 herself by my direction to Sir Wilfull.

FAINALL: That sham is too gross to pass on me, though 'tis imposed on you, madam.

MRS. MILLAMANT: Sir, I have given my consent.

MIRABELL: And, sir, I have resigned my pretensions.

440 SIR WILFULL: And, sir, I assert my right; and will maintain it in defiance of you, sir, and of your instrument. 'Sheart, an you talk of an instrument, sir, I have an old

410. **quorum:** An indispensable member of the legal bench.

fox° by my thigh shall hack your instrument of ram vellum° to shreds, sir! It shall not be sufficient for a *mittimus*° or a tailor's measure.° Therefore withdraw 445 your instrument, sir, or, by'r lady, I shall draw mine.

LADY WISHFORT: Hold, nephew, hold!

MRS. MILLAMANT: Good Sir Wilfull, respite° your valor.

FAINALL: Indeed? Are you provided of your guard, with your single beefeater° there? But I'm prepared for you, 450 and insist upon my first proposal. You shall submit your own estate to my management and absolutely make over my wife's to my sole use, as pursuant to the purpose and tenor of this other covenant. (*To Mrs. Millamant.*) I suppose, madam, your consent is 455 not requisite in this case; nor, Mr. Mirabell, your resignation; nor, Sir Wilfull, your right. You may draw your fox if you please, sir, and make a Bear Garden° flourish somewhere else; for here it will not avail. — This, my Lady Wishfort, must be subscribed, or your 460 darling daughter's turned adrift, like a leaky hulk, to sink or swim, as she and the current of this lewd town can agree.

LADY WISHFORT: Is there no means, no remedy to stop my ruin? Ungrateful wretch! dost thou not owe thy 465 being, thy subsistence, to my daughter's fortune?

FAINALL: I'll answer you when I have the rest of it in my possession.

MIRABELL (*to Lady Wishfort*): But that you would not accept of a remedy from my hands — I own I have 470 not deserved you should owe any obligation to me; or else perhaps I could advise —

LADY WISHFORT: Oh, what? what? to save me and my child from ruin, from want, I'll forgive all that's past; nay, I'll consent to anything to come, to be delivered 475 from this tyranny.

MIRABELL: Aye, madam, but that is too late; my reward is intercepted. You have disposed of her who only could have made me a compensation for all my services. But be it as it may, I am resolved I'll serve you; 480 you shall not be wronged in this savage manner.

LADY WISHFORT: How! Dear Mr. Mirabell, can you be so generous at last? But it is not possible. Harkee, I'll break my nephew's match; you shall have my niece yet, and all her fortune, if you can but save me from 485 this imminent danger.

MIRABELL: Will you? I take you at your word. I ask no more. I must have leave for two criminals to appear.

LADY WISHFORT: Aye, aye; anybody, anybody!

MIRABELL: Foible is one, and a penitent. 490

(*Reenter Mrs. Fainall, Foible, and Mincing.*)

---

443. **fox:** Sword.   443–44. **ram vellum:** Parchment (made from sheepskin).   445. *mittimus:* Legal term for a warrant of commitment to prison.   **tailor's measure:** Tailors' measurements were recorded on parchment.   448. **respite:** Control. 450. **beefeater:** A guard of the Tower of London.   458. **Bear Garden:** Bear baiting was a popular amusement in the London of the day, and the gardens in which it took place were notorious for brawls and rowdy behavior.

MRS. MARWOOD (*to Fainall*): O my shame! (*Mirabell and Lady Wishfort go to Mrs. Fainall and Foible.*) These corrupt things are brought hither to expose me.

FAINALL: If it must all come out, why let 'em know it; 'tis
495 but the way of the world. That shall not urge me to relinquish or abate one tittle of my terms; no, I will insist the more.

FOIBLE: Yes indeed, madam; I'll take my Bible oath of it.

MINCING: And so will I, mem.

500 LADY WISHFORT: O Marwood. Marwood, art thou false? my friend deceive me? Hast thou been a wicked accomplice with that profligate man?

MRS. MARWOOD: Have you so much ingratitude and injustice, to give credit against your friend to the
505 aspersions of two such mercenary trulls?

MINCING: "Mercenary," mem? I scorn your words. 'Tis true we found you and Mr. Fainall in the blue garret; by the same token, you swore us to secrecy upon Messalina's poems.° "Mercenary?" No, if we would
510 have been mercenary, we should have held our tongues; you would have bribed us sufficiently.

FAINALL: Go, you are an insignificant thing! Well, what are you the better for this? Is this Mr. Mirabell's expedient? I'll be put off no longer. You thing, that
515 was a wife, shall smart for this! I will not leave thee wherewithal to hide thy shame; your body shall be naked as your reputation.

MRS. FAINALL: I despise you, and defy your malice! You have aspersed me wrongfully. I have proved your
520 falsehood. Go, you and your treacherous — I will not name it, but starve together, perish!

FAINALL: Not while you are worth a groat,° indeed, my dear. Madam, I'll be fooled no longer.

LADY WISHFORT: Ah, Mr. Mirabell, this is small com-
525 fort, the detection of this affair.

MIRABELL: Oh, in good time. Your leave for the other offender and penitent to appear, madam.

(*Enter Waitwell, with a box of writings.*)

LADY WISHFORT: O Sir Rowland! Well, rascal?

WAITWELL: What your ladyship pleases. I have brought
530 the black box at last, madam.

MIRABELL: Give it me. Madam, you remember your promise.

LADY WISHFORT: Aye, dear sir.

MIRABELL: Where are the gentlemen?

535 WAITWELL: At hand, sir, rubbing their eyes; just risen from sleep.

FAINALL: 'Sdeath, what's this to me? I'll not wait your private concerns.

(*Enter Petulant and Witwoud.*)

509. **Messalina's poems:** Mincing means a volume of "miscellaneous" poems. Her mistake presents an amusing irony, since Messalina, the wife of the Roman Emperor Claudius, was notorious for her avarice, treachery, and dissoluteness.
522. **groat:** An old silver coin worth about fourpence.

PETULANT: How now? What's the matter? Whose hand's out?°   540

WITWOUD: Heyday! what, are you all got together, like players at the end of the last act?

MIRABELL: You may remember, gentlemen, I once requested your hands as witnesses to a certain parchment.   545

WITWOUD: Aye, I do; my hand I remember. Petulant set his mark.

MIRABELL: You wrong him, his name is fairly written, as shall appear. You do not remember, gentlemen, anything of what that parchment contained?   550

(*Undoing the box.*)

WITWOUD: No.

PETULANT: Not I. I writ. I read nothing.

MIRABELL: Very well; now you shall know. Madam, your promise.

LADY WISHFORT: Aye, aye, sir, upon my honor.   555

MIRABELL: Mr. Fainall, it is now time that you should know that your lady, while she was at her own disposal, and before you had by your insinuations wheedled her out of a pretended settlement of the greatest part of her fortune —   560

FAINALL: Sir! pretended!

MIRABELL: Yes, sir. I say that this lady, while a widow, having it seems received some cautions respecting your inconstancy and tyranny of temper, which from her own partial opinion and fondness of you she   565 could never have suspected — she did, I say, by the wholesome advice of friends and of sages learned in the laws of this land, deliver this same as her act and deed to me in trust, and to the uses within mentioned. You may read if you please (*holding out the   570 parchment*), though perhaps what is written on the back may serve your occasions.

FAINALL: Very likely, sir. What's here? Damnation! (*Reads.*) "A deed of conveyance of the whole estate real of Arabella Languish, widow, in trust to Edward   575 Mirabell." Confusion!

MIRABELL: Even so, sir; 'tis the way of the world, sir, of the widows of the world. I suppose this deed may bear an elder° date than what you have obtained from your lady?   580

FAINALL: Perfidious fiend! Then thus I'll be revenged.

(*Offers to run at Mrs. Fainall.*)

SIR WILFULL: Hold, sir! Now you may make your Bear Garden flourish somewhere else, sir.

FAINALL: Mirabell, you shall hear of this, sir; be sure you shall. (*To Sir Wilfull.*) Let me pass, oaf!   585

(*Exit.*)

MRS. FAINALL (*to Mrs. Marwood*): Madam, you seem to stifle your resentment; you had better give it vent.

MRS. MARWOOD: Yes, it shall have vent, and to your confusion; or I'll perish in the attempt.   (*Exit.*)

539–40. **Whose hand's out:** "What is the trouble?"   579. **elder:** Earlier.

590 LADY WISHFORT: O daughter, daughter, 'tis plain thou hast inherited thy mother's prudence.

MRS. FAINALL: Thank Mr. Mirabell, a cautious friend, to whose advice all is owing.

595 LADY WISHFORT: Well, Mr. Mirabell, you have kept your promise, and I must perform mine. First, I pardon, for your sake, Sir Rowland there, and Foible. The next thing is to break the matter to my nephew, and how to do that —

600 MIRABELL: For that, madam, give yourself no trouble; let me have your consent. Sir Wilfull is my friend; he has had compassion upon lovers, and generously engaged a volunteer° in this action, for our service, and now designs to prosecute his travels.

605 SIR WILFULL: 'Sheart, aunt, I have no mind to marry. My cousin's a fine lady, and the gentleman loves her, and she loves him, and they deserve one another; my resolution is to see foreign parts. I have set on't, and when I'm set on't, I must do't. And if these two gentlemen would travel too, I think they may be spared.

610 PETULANT: For my part, I say little; I think things are best off or on.°

WITWOUD: Egad, I understand nothing of the matter; I'm in a maze yet, like a dog in a dancing school.

615 LADY WISHFORT: Well, sir, take her, and with her all the joy I can give you.

MRS. MILLAMANT: Why does not the man take me? Would you have me give myself to you over again?

MIRABELL: Aye, and over and over again; (*kisses her hand*) for I would have you as often as possibly I can. 620 Well, Heaven grant I love you not too well; that's all my fear.

SIR WILFULL: 'Sheart, you'll have time enough to toy° after you're married; or if you will toy now, let us 625 have a dance in the meantime, that we who are not lovers may have some other employment besides looking on.

MIRABELL: With all my heart, dear Sir Wilfull. What shall we do for music?

630 FOIBLE: Oh, sir, some that were provided for Sir Rowland's entertainment are yet within call.

(*A dance.*)

LADY WISHFORT: As I am a person, I can hold out no longer. I have wasted my spirits so today already that I am ready to sink under the fatigue; and I cannot but 635 have some fears upon me yet that my son Fainall will pursue some desperate course.

MIRABELL: Madam, disquiet not yourself on that account; to my knowledge his circumstances are such, he must of force° comply. For my part, I will contribute all that in me lies to a reunion; in the 640 meantime, madam (*to Mrs. Fainall*), let me before these witnesses restore to you this deed of trust; it may be a means, well-managed, to make you live easily together.

From hence let those be warn'd, who mean to wed,
Lest mutual falsehood stain the bridal bed; 645
For each deceiver to his cost may find
That marriage frauds too oft are paid in kind.

(*Exeunt omnes.*)°

EPILOGUE

(*Spoken by Mrs. Millamant.*)

After our Epilogue this crowd dismisses,
I'm thinking how this play'll be pull'd to pieces.
But pray consider, ere you doom its fall,
How hard a thing 'twould be to please you all.
There are some critics so with spleen diseas'd, 5
They scarcely come inclining to be pleas'd;
And sure he must have more than mortal skill,
Who pleases any one against his will.
Then, all bad poets we are sure are foes,
And how their number's swell'd the town well knows; 10
In shoals I've mark'd 'em judging in the pit;
Though they're on no pretense for judgment fit,
But that they have been damn'd for want of wit.
Since when they, by their own offenses taught,
Set up for spies on plays, and finding fault. 15
Others there are whose malice we'd prevent;
Such who watch plays with scurrilous intent
To mark out who by characters are meant.
And though no perfect likeness they can trace,
Yet each pretends to know the copy'd face. 20
These with false glosses° feed their own ill nature,
And turn to libel what was meant a satire.°
May such malicious fops this fortune find,
To think themselves alone the fools design'd;
If any are so arrogantly vain, 25
To think they singly can support a scene,
And furnish fool enough to entertain.
For well the learn'd and the judicious know
That satire scorns to stoop so meanly low
As any one abstracted° fop to show. 30
For, as when painters form a matchless face
They from each fair one catch some diff'rent grace;
And shining features in one portrait blend,
To which no single beauty must pretend;
So poets oft do in one piece expose 35
Whole *belles assemblées*° of coquettes and beaux.

---

602. a volunteer: As a volunteer. **611. off or on:** One way or the other. **622. toy:** Play. **638. of force:** Of necessity.

647. [S.D.] *omnes:* Latin for "all." **21. glosses:** Marginal notes. **21–22. nature . . . satire:** According to seventeenth-century pronunciation, "nature" and "satire" were good rhymes. **30. abstracted:** Particular. **36.** *belles assemblées:* Fine gatherings.

COMMENTARIES

Howard Taubman (1907–1996)
REVIEW OF *THE WAY OF THE WORLD*   1965

Howard Taubman reviewed one of the notable modern productions of The Way
of the World, *starring Zoe Caldwell, a British actress who went on to win numerous awards. The question of accents, which Taubman discusses, is important for
any audience, since the lines are often rapid-fire and the wit razor-sharp. Caldwell's
authenticity and style charmed Taubman, who was pleased enough with the production to forgive its minor flaws.*

There are many good reasons to justify going out of one's way for the Minnesota Theater Company's *The Way of the World,* and hardly the least of them is
Congreve himself. But an excellent one is to enjoy the impeccable high-comedy
playing of Zoe Caldwell as Millamant.

Jessica Tandy brings a raffish gusto to Lady Wishfort, Nancy Wickwire is a cool,
suave intriguer as Marwood, Robert Pastene is all showy manners and hard bar-
gainer as Fainall, Robert Milli conveys the shrewd charm of Mirabell. But it is Miss
Caldwell who is unfaltering in every velvet thrust.

Not an inflection or a gesture is out of place in this handsomely composed portrait of a wise and witty young woman of the London world of 1700. In Tanya
Moiseiwitch's modish clothes, with their headdresses and trains, Miss Caldwell
moves with the poised self-knowledge of one who has stepped out of a Restoration
drawing room.

Her face with its pale make-up, obviously the careful concern of a young
woman of breeding who will not look vulgarly outdoorsy, rarely betrays an emotion. The eyes are detached but brighten occasionally with mischief. The voice is
silken, but what humor there is in the phrasing — not catchpenny humor but the
sense of fun that sparkles in a civilized mind.

When Miss Caldwell talks of being persecuted by letters, there is amusement in
the weariness of her tone. When she reads the poems of Sir John Suckling to confuse
addle-brained Sir Wilfull, it is as if only she and we were privy to the dry jesting.

When she sets forth the conditions on which she will agree to marry Mirabell,
she does so with a mingling of seriousness and laughter that suits perfectly Congreve's milieu and style. And Mr. Milli's response in kind gives the necessary fillip
to a scene that has not lost its edge in 265 years.

Douglas Campbell has directed *The Way of the World* with a relish of its manners and mannerisms. Miss Moiseiwitch's designs with their suggestion of colorful
elegancies turn the open stage of the Tyrone Guthrie Theater into a garden or
boudoir with equal felicity.

The over-all tone of the production, with its occasional background of Purcell music and with its ingratiating concluding dance, is admirable. But the Minnesota Theater Company would be deluding itself if it thought that it had met all the challenges implicit in a Congreve revival.

The balance of the performance is not always right. One or two players handle the Restoration extravagances self-consciously, making their points too obviously. Several others lack the flexibility of movement and diction needed for this kind of work.

And what is to be done about the mélange of accents with which Congreve's glittering English is spoken?

Consider Miss Tandy, Miss Wickwire and Miss Caldwell, all of whom know their business and speak well. Miss Wickwire's speech has the flatness of the American timbre. Miss Tandy's seems now to be an accommodation between her native English and the American approach. Miss Caldwell's enunciation and rhythm have the ring of authenticity. As for some of the company's younger members, they are struggling in deep, unfamiliar waters.

But if we are going to wait for perfection, we will never attempt revivals of the classics. It is better to do a Congreve with forces not equal in all parts than not to do him at all, provided, of course, you have such delightful exemplars as Miss Caldwell to show the irresistible way.

William Congreve (1670–1729)
AMENDMENTS OF MR. COLLIER'S FALSE
AND IMPERFECT CITATIONS, ETC.   *1698*

In 1698 an alarmed clergyman, Jeremy Collier, expressed horror at the licentiousness of the Restoration theater. In A Short View of the Immorality and Profaneness of the English Stage, *he attacked modern dramatists for deriving amusement from adulterous behavior. Collier detested what he felt was the lewdness of language and action on stage. He created a backlash of sentiment by catching the ear of the reigning king and queen, William and Mary. When Congreve responded, he attacked Collier on the grounds that he quoted passages out of context and therefore did not grasp the true moral meaning of satiric drama, which was meant to improve manners.*

I have no intention to examine all the absurdities and falsehoods in Mr. Collier's book.[1] To use the gentleman's own metaphor in his preface, an inventory of such a warehouse would be a large work. My detection of his malice and ignorance, of his sophistry and vast assurance, will lie within a narrow compass and only bear a proportion to so much of his book as concerns myself.

Least of all would I undertake to defend the corruptions of the stage. Indeed, if I were so inclined, Mr. Collier has given me no occasion, for the greater part of those examples which he has produced are only demonstrations of his own impurity. They only savor of his utterance and were sweet enough till tainted by his breath.

[1]*A Short View of the Immorality and Profaneness of the English Stage.*

I will not justify any of my own errors. I am sensible of many, and if Mr. Collier has by any accident stumbled on one or two, I will freely give them up to him. . . .

My intention, therefore, is to do little else but to restore those passages to their primitive station which have suffered so much in being transplanted by him. I will remove 'em from his dunghill and replant 'em in the field of nature; and when I have washed 'em of that filth which they have contracted in passing through his very dirty hands, let their own innocence protect them.

Mr. Collier, in the high vigor of his obscenity, first commits a rape upon my words and then arraigns 'em of immodesty; he has barbarity enough to accuse the very virgins that he has deflowered. . . . Where the expression is unblameable in its own clear and genuine signification, he enters into it himself like the evil spirit; he possesses the innocent phrase and makes it bellow forth his own blasphemies. . . .

To reprimand him a little in his own words, if these passages produced by Mr. Collier are obscene and profane, why were they raked in and disturbed unless it were to conjure up vice and revive impurities? Indeed, Mr. Collier has a very untoward way with him. His pen has such a libertine stroke that 'tis a question whether the practice or the reproof be the more licentious.

He teaches those vices he would correct and writes more like a pimp than a p———. Since the business must be undertaken, why was not the thought blanched, the expression made remote, and the ill features cast into shadows? . . . He has blackened the thoughts with his own smut. The expression that was remote, he has brought nearer. . . .

Before I proceed, for method's sake I must premise some few things to the reader, which if he thinks in his conscience are too much to be granted me I desire he would proceed no further in his perusal of these animadversions but return to Mr. Collier's *Short View, etc.*

First, I desire that I may lay down Aristotle's definition of comedy, which has been the compass by which all the comic poets since his time have steered their course. . . . Comedy, says Aristotle, is an imitation of the worse sort of people. . . . He does not mean the worse sort of people in respect to their quality but in respect to their manners. . . . There are crimes too daring and too horrid for comedy, but the vices most frequent and which are the common practice of the looser sort of livers are the subject matter of comedy. He tells us farther that they must be exposed after a ridiculous manner, for men are to be laughed out of their vices in comedy. The business of comedy is to delight as well as to instruct, and as vicious people are made ashamed of their follies or faults by seeing them exposed in a ridiculous manner, so are good people at once both warned and diverted at their expense.

Thus much I thought necessary to premise, that by showing the nature and end of comedy, we may be prepared to expect characters agreeable to it.

Secondly, since comic poets are obliged by the laws of comedy and to the intent that comedy may answer its true end and purpose, abovementioned, to represent vicious and foolish characters, in consideration of this, I desire that it may not be imputed to the persuasion or private sentiments of the author if at any time one of these vicious characters in any of his plays shall behave himself foolishly or immorally in word or deed. I hope I am not yet unreasonable; it were very hard that a painter should be believed to resemble all the ugly faces that he draws.

Thirdly, I must desire the impartial reader not to consider any expression or passage cited from any play as it appears in Mr. Collier's book, nor to pass any sentence or censure upon it out of its proper scene or alienated from the character by which it is spoken, for in that place alone and in his mouth alone can it have its proper and true signification. . . .

Fourthly, because Mr. Collier, in his chapter of the profaneness of the stage, has founded great part of his accusation upon the liberty which poets take of using some words in their plays which have been sometimes employed by the translators of the Holy Scriptures, I desire that the following distinction may be admitted, viz., that when words are applied to sacred things, and with a purpose to treat of sacred things, they ought to be understood accordingly, but when they are otherwise applied, the diversity of the subject gives a diversity of signification. And, in truth, he might as well except against the common use of the alphabet in poetry because the same letters are necessary to the spelling of words which are mentioned in sacred writ. . . .

It may not be impertinent in this place to remind the reader of a very common expedient which is made use of to recommend the instruction of our plays, which is this. After the action of the play is over and the delight of the representation at an end, there is generally care taken that the moral of the whole shall be summed up and delivered to the audience in the very last and concluding lines of the poem. The intention of this is that the delight of the representation may not so strongly possess the minds of the audience as to make them forget or oversee the instruction. It is the last thing said, that it may make the last impression, and it is always comprehended in a few lines and put into rhyme, that it may be easy and engaging to the memory.[. . .]

Mr. Collier, in his second chapter, charges the stage with profaneness. Almost all the quotations which he has made from my plays in this chapter are represented falsely or by halves, so that I have very little to do in their vindication but to represent 'em as they are in the original fairly and at length and to fill up the blanks which this worthy, honest gentleman has left.[. . .]

I come now to his chapter of the immorality of the stage. His objections here are rather objections against comedy in general than against mine or anybody's comedies in particular. He says the sparks that marry up the top ladies and are rewarded with wives and fortunes in the last acts are generally debauched characters. In answer to this, I refer to my first and second proposition. He is a little particular in his remarks upon Valentine in *Love for Love*. . . . Valentine is in debt and in love; he has honesty enough to close with a hard bargain rather than not pay his debts, in the first act; and he has generosity and sincerity enough in the last act to sacrifice everything to his love, and when he is in danger of losing his mistress thinks everything else of little worth. This, I hope, may be allowed a reason for the lady to say, "He has virtues." They are such in respect to her, and her once saying so in the last act is all the notice that is taken of his virtue quite through the play.

Mr. Collier says he is prodigal. He was prodigal and is shown in the first act under hard circumstances, which are the effects of his prodigality. That he is unnatural and undutiful, I don't understand: he has indeed a very unnatural father, and if he does not very passively submit to his tyranny and barbarous usage, I conceive there is a moral to be applied from thence to such fathers. That he is profane and obscene is a false accusation and without any evidence. In short, the character is a mixed character; his faults are fewer than his good qualities and as the world goes he may pass well enough for the best character in a comedy, where even the best must be shown to have faults, that the best spectators may be warned not to think too well of themselves. . . .

To give him his due, he seems everywhere to write more from prejudice than opinion; he rails when he should reason and for gentle reproofs uses scurrilous reproaches. . . . If there is any spirit in his arguments, it evaporates and flies off unseen through the heat of his passion. . . . That which shows the face of wit in his writing has indeed no more than the face, for the head is wanting.

Arnold Aronson (b. 1948)
COMEDY, MANNERS, AND BRICKBATS   *1991*

Arnold Aronson centers his comments on The Way of the World *on the 1991 production at the Public Theater in New York. He reviews Jeremy Collier's attack on the theaters of the time and then comments on the current production. His discussion is less a review than an effort to position the comedy in relation to historical events and early eighteenth-century attitudes toward sex and marriage.*

Currently at the Public Theater and opening Tuesday is an elitist play that has been attacked roundly by conservative moralists, led by a demagogic clergyman. But it will not be shut down by incensed watchdog groups, since the play is nearly 300 years old: William Congreve's classic *The Way of the World,* in a revival directed by David Greenspan.

First presented in 1700, the work is generally considered the artistic culmination of the Restoration comedy of manners. The exquisite language, rapier-sharp repartee, and labyrinthine plot make the play somewhat daunting for modern audiences and actors. Yet the antipathy faced by Congreve and his colleagues in the late seventeenth century was not unlike that of many theater artists today.

Jeremy Collier, a parson who campaigned against the stage with a vengeance, attacked Restoration playwrights in his famous 1698 diatribe, *A Short View of the Immorality and Profaneness of the English Stage.* He criticized them for "smuttiness of expression" and "swearing" and condemned a theater that "degrades human nature, sinks reason into appetite, and breaks down the distinction between man and beast." He was joined by the monarchs William and Mary and by members of Parliament who sought to restrict public behavior in the theater.

How could the situation have reached this state less than 100 years after Shakespeare? Whereas Elizabethan London had supported some half-dozen theaters catering to thousands of spectators, Restoration London never filled more than two theaters attended by an audience numbering in the hundreds, most of whom were associated with the court.

The transition began in 1642 when the Puritan rebellion led by Oliver Cromwell overthrew the monarchy. All the theaters were closed, and most of the courtiers escaped to Paris, where they remained until 1660, when Charles II took the throne. The returning nobility brought back a taste for French theater, especially its novel practice — for the English — of employing actresses. Under Charles II and James II the theater nearly became the private domain of the court. Thus the fops, pompous gallants, wits, and hypocrites who populate the plays (and bear the names of their characteristics — such as, in this play, Witwoud and Lady Wishfort, pronounced

"Wish-for-it") are typically seen as both vicious caricatures and realistic portraits of the audience.

The plots usually revolve around sexual intrigue, and infidelity seems taken for granted — it is *The Way of the World*. Easily lost in this play is the fact that the seemingly admirable Mirabell (André Braugher) had an affair with Lady Wishfort's (Ruth Maleczech) daughter (Mary Shultz), and when he thought she might be pregnant, foisted her on his friend Fainall (René Rivera), who marries her, though he is having an affair with Mrs. Marwood (Caris Corfman).

The accusations of immorality focused, not surprisingly, on sexual content and disregarded the fact that such plays were satirical. The playwrights tried to defend themselves, through pamphlets and jibes in their texts. But the attackers achieved their end. The theaters began to censor themselves, the small audiences declined further, and Congreve ceased writing. A decade later, plays were emphasizing moral virtues, and comedies, like those by George Farquhar, stressed sentiment and natural goodness, while the settings changed to the countryside, where city slickers received their comeuppance.

What critics at the time failed to realize was that Restoration comedies are not about sex. A kiss is rare and seems almost vulgar when it occurs. The plays are about human passions sublimated into a brilliant display of language. It is excess and lack of control that is evil in Congreve's world. Rationality, order, and command over passions and language are rewarded. This may not be the same as morality, but it *is* civility.

Nineteenth-Century Drama through the Turn of the Century

Technical Innovations

Technically, theaters changed more during the period between 1800 and 1900 than in any comparable earlier period. The introduction of gas jets early in the century had a major effect. Now, light could be dimmed or raised as needed; the house could be gradually and entirely darkened. With gaslight onstage, selective lighting contributed to the emotional effect of plays and allowed actors to move deeper into the stage instead of playing important scenes on the apron. With the advent of elaborate scenery, as in the Drottningholm Theater in Sweden, lighting devices were often placed behind the proscenium pillars and scenery so that actors were more visible when they stood within the proscenium. The changes did not take place overnight, but as new theaters were built in the early nineteenth century (and as older theaters were refurbished) the apron shrank and the front doors leading to it disappeared. That change reinforced the nineteenth-century practice of treating the proscenium opening as the imaginary "fourth wall" of a room. The elaborate framing of Chicago's Auditorium (1889, Figure 10) allowed for complex lighting systems as well as the framing of the proscenium, which acts as a "window" into the dramatic action.

Numerous other technical innovations were introduced into the new theaters, such as London's Drury Lane Theatre, which was rebuilt in 1812. Highly sophisticated machinery lifted actors from below the stage, and flies or fly galleries above the stage permitted scene changes and other dramatic alterations and effects. The technical resources of the modern theaters in Europe were extraordinary by midcentury.

Romantic Drama

The architectural and lighting changes were complex and uneven, but they accompanied changes in styles of acting, styles of plays, and the content of plays. Early nineteenth-century English Romantic poets produced a variety of plays espousing a new philosophy of the individual, a philosophy of democracy, and a cry for personal liberation, but unfortunately their plays failed to capture the popular stage. William Wordsworth's *The Borderers* (1796–1797), concerning political struggles on the border between England and Scotland,

Figure 10. Elaborately decorated proscenium arch. Auditorium, Chicago, 1889.

was a failure. A recent production (1989) at Yale University revealed its static, declamatory nature. Even a play with an inherently dramatic subject such as *The Fall of Robespierre* (1794) by Robert Southey and Samuel Taylor Coleridge — concerning the violent excesses of the French Revolution of 1789 — could not stir popular audiences. John Keats wrote *Otho the Great* (1819) about a tenth-century dispute between brothers and a father and son. He hoped that the great actor and producer Edmund Kean would want to produce the play, but Kean declined. Percy Bysshe Shelley wrote *The Cenci* (1819) when he was in Italy, hoping it would be produced on the English stage, but it was banned by the censors. The style of Shelley's play has been compared with John Webster's *The Dutchess of Malfi* (1613); its themes include violent death and insanity. George Gordon, Lord Byron, wrote several plays that had admirers but were not successful. *Manfred* (1817) is a CLOSET DRAMA — a play meant to be read, not produced. It presents a powerful portrait of a brooding intellect that could, in some ways, be compared with Hamlet. Allardyce Nicoll, the British drama historian and critic, has said of this and other Romantic plays that "audiences and readers familiar with *Lear* and *Macbeth* and *Othello* could not be expected to feel a thrill of wonder and delight in the contemplation of works so closely akin to these in general aim and yet so far removed from them in freshness of imaginative power."

French and German Romantic dramatists were more successful than their English counterparts. Johann Wolfgang von Goethe (1749–1832), one of Germany's most important playwrights, produced a number of successful plays in the late eighteenth century. Then came his masterpiece, *Faust* (1808, 1832), in two parts, with a scope and grandeur of concept that challenged the theaters of his day. The play opens in heaven, with Mephistopheles presenting his plan for tempting Faust; Faust signs over his soul to Mephistopheles in return for one moment of perfect joy. Faust was willing to risk all in his efforts to live life to its fullest, and despite his sins he was admired as a hero. Faust's self-analytic individualism, marked by a love of excess and a capacity for deep feeling and frightening intensity, has fascinated the German mind ever since Goethe rediscovered him. His development of Faust as a psychologically complex character contrasts with Marlowe's version in *Doctor Faustus*.

Another important force in German theater was Johann Cristoph Friedrich von Schiller (1759–1805), whose early play *The Robbers* (1781) was written when he was twenty-two. This still-popular (and still-produced) play reminds English audiences of the legend of Robin Hood since its hero, Karl von Moor, is a robber admirable for his generosity and seriousness. His adversary is his evil brother, who dominates the castle, the emblem of local repressive political power. Schiller was a highly successful playwright throughout the late eighteenth century. In the early nineteenth century he produced several popular historical plays such as *Maria Stuart* (1800) on Scotland's Queen Mary, the ill-fated cousin of Queen Elizabeth I. *The Maid of Orleans* (1801) told the story of Joan of Arc, the French heroine who led her army to victory only to be burned at the stake to satisfy political and religious exigencies. Both plays evoke deep sympathy for their heroines and both have been noted for their sentimentality. His last play, *William Tell* (1804), like *The Robbers*, tells the story of a heroic individual's fight against the oppressive forces of an evil baron. Schiller made the story of William Tell universal, and his theatrical successes were soon known throughout Europe and the Americas.

In France, the Romantic tragedy held sway for some time in the 1830s. Victor Hugo (1802–1885) had a great success in *Hernani* (1830), although critics and writers who insisted on classical rules were so disturbed by its innovation that they made disturbances in the theater. They attended only to jeer the pardon of Hernani, an outlaw, by Don Carlos, king of Spain. At the end Hernani and Donna Sol, his loved one, drink a poison so as to die together because they could not live together. Alexandre Dumas (1802–1879), soon to be famous as a novelist, produced a number of successful, influential plays, among them *Henry III and His Court* (1829) and *The Tower of Nesle* (1832).

Melodrama

MELODRAMA developed in Germany and France in the mid- and late eighteenth century. The *melo* in *melodrama* means "song"; incidental music was a hallmark of melodrama. In England certain regulations separated Covent Garden, Drury Lane, and the Haymarket — the three "major" theaters with exclusive licenses to produce spoken drama — from the "minor" theaters, which had to produce musical plays such as burlettas, which resembled our comic operettas. Eventually, the minor theaters began to produce plays with spoken dialogue and accompanying music, heralding a new, popular style. Melodrama proved to be one of the most durable innovations of the late eighteenth century.

In Germany, August Friedrich Ferdinand von Kotzebue (1761–1819) and in France Guilbert de Pixérécourt (1773–1844), who coined the term *melodrama,* began developing the melodramatic play. Many of these dramas used background music that altered according to the mood of the scene, a tradition that continues in films and on television. Nineteenth-century melodramas featured familiar crises: the virtuous maiden fallen into the hands of an unscrupulous landlord; the father who, lamenting over a portrait of his dead wife, discovers that he is speaking to his — until then — lost daughter. Nineteenth-century melodramas had well-defined heroes, heroines, and villains. The plots were filled with surprises and unlikely twists designed to amaze and delight the audience. Most of the plays were explicitly sentimental, depending on a strong emotional appeal with clear-cut and relatively decisive endings.

Though not popular later on, the plays of Kotzebue and Pixérécourt pleased their contemporary audiences and helped establish melodrama as a dominant style for the first six decades of the nineteenth century. Kotzebue published thirty-six plays (twenty-two were produced) and enjoyed an immense popularity in England and the United States. Translated into several languages, his works influenced later popular playwrights, who admired his ability to invent and resolve complex plot situations. An example of the ending of *La-Peyrouse* (1798) may provide a taste of the mode. The hero, cast ashore on a desert island, falls in love with the "savage" Malvina. When he rejoins his wife, Adelaide, he is presented with the problem of what to do with Malvina. Here is the women's solution:

> MALVINA (*turning affectionately, yet with trembling to Adelaide*): I have prayed for thee, and for myself — let us be sisters!
> ADELAIDE: Sisters! (*She remains some moments lost in thought.*) Sisters! Sweet girl, you have awakened a consoling idea in my bosom! Yes, we will be sisters, and this man shall be our brother! Share him we cannot, nor can either possess him singly. (*With enthusiasm.*) We, the sisters, will inhabit one hut, he shall dwell in another. We will educate our children, he shall assist us both — by day we will make but one family, at night we will separate — how say you? will you consent? . . . (*Extending her arms to La-Peyrouse.*) A sisterly embrace!

In France Pixérécourt produced a similar and highly successful drama that pleased his audiences. Not everyone was pleased, however. Goethe resigned his office from the Weimar Court Theatre when Pixérécourt's *The Dog of Montargis* was produced in 1816 because he did not want to be associated with any play that had a dog as its hero.

Not all these plays have been forgotten. Alexandre Dumas's *La Dame aux camélias* (Camille) was a theatrical hit in 1852 and has remained popular ever since, inspiring the Verdi opera *La Traviata* (1853) and revivals and adaptations up to the present, including the British playwright Pam Gems's feminist version (1987), starring Kathleen Turner. Based on a woman Dumas knew in

Paris, it is the story of a wealthy young man who falls in love with a courtesan, Marguerite Gauthier. Like Angellica in *The Rover,* she has manipulated men throughout her life, but now she is truly in love with Armand. The young man's father opposes the match, but even he is moved by the majesty of their love. Eventually, the father faces Marguerite and convinces her that if she really loves his son, she will let him go since their union can bring nothing but harm to Armand. She then fabricates a contempt for Armand and dismisses him, broken-hearted. Later, after they have been separated and she has fallen deathly ill, Armand learns the truth and rushes to her. On her deathbed Armand professes his love as she dies in his arms.

In the United States, George Aiken produced another long-lasting and influential drama, *Uncle Tom's Cabin* (1852), based on Harriet Beecher Stowe's novel. Stowe, a prominent northern abolitionist, poured all her anger at slavery into her novel. Aiken's stage version played for three hundred nights in its first production and across the nation more than a quarter of a million times. Some of its characters — Uncle Tom, Little Eva, Sambo, Topsy, and Simon Legree — live on in the popular imagination, but despite the contemporary interest in Stowe and in this play, the paternalistic subtitle, "Life among the Lowly," marks its era.

The Well-Made Play

Early in the nineteenth century, a Frenchman with an unusual theatrical gift for pleasing popular audiences began a career that spanned fifty successful years. Eugène Scribe (1791–1861) may have produced as many as four or five hundred plays. He employed collaborators and mined novels and stories for his plots, producing tragedies, comedies, opera libretti, and vaudeville one-act pieces. He quickly determined that the plot held the attention of the audience and that rambling character studies were of lesser interest. Consequently, he developed a formula for dramatic action and made sure that all his works fit into it. The result was the creation of a "factory" for making plays. Among the elements of Scribe's formula were the following:

1. A careful exposition telling the audience what the situation is, usually including one or more secrets to be revealed later.
2. Surprises, such as letters to be opened at a critical moment and identities to be revealed later.
3. Suspense that builds steadily throughout the play, usually sustained by cliff-hanging situations and characters who miss each other by way of carefully timed entrances and exits. At critical moments, characters lose important papers or misplace identifying jewelry, for instance.
4. A CLIMAX late in the play when the secrets are revealed and the hero confronts his antagonists and succeeds.
5. A DENOUEMENT, the resolution of the drama when all the loose ends are drawn together and explanations are made that render all the action plausible.

It should be evident from this description that the WELL-MADE PLAY still thrives, not only on the stage but also in films and on television. Scribe's emphasis on plot was sensational for his time, and his success was unrivaled; however, none of his plays has survived in contemporary performance. Only one, *Adrienne*

Lecouvreur (1849), the story of a famous actress poisoned by a rival, is mentioned by critics as interesting because of its depth of characterization. Scribe was superficial and brilliant — a winning combination in theater at the time. He had numerous imitators and prepared the way for later developments in theater.

The Rise of Realism

Technical changes in theaters during the latter part of the nineteenth century continued at a rapid pace. When limelight was added to gas, the result was bright, intense lighting onstage; in the last decades of the century electric light heralded a new era in lighting design. Good lighting generally demanded detailed and authentic scenery; the dreamy light produced by gas often hid imperfections that were now impossible to disguise. The new Madison Square Theater (1879) in New York was built with elevators that allowed its stage, complete with detailed and realistic scenery as well as actors, to be raised into position. European theaters had developed similar capacities.

In the 1840s accurate period costumes began to be the norm for historical plays. In the Elizabethan theater, contemporary clothing had been worn onstage, but by the mid-1800s costume designers were researching historical periods and producing costumes that aimed at historical accuracy.

In addition to offering lifelike scenery, lighting, and costumes, the theaters of the latter part of the century also featured plays whose circumstances and language were recognizable, contemporary, and believable. Even the sentimental melodramas seemed more realistic than productions of *King Lear* or *Macbeth*, plays that were still popular. The work of Scribe, including his historical plays, used a relatively prosaic everyday language. The situations may not seem absolutely lifelike to our eyes, but in their day they prepared the way for realism.

Changes in philosophy also contributed to the development of a realistic drama. Émile Zola (1840–1902) preached a doctrine of NATURALISM, demanding that drama avoid the artificiality of convoluted plot and urging a drama of natural, lifelike action. He intended his work to help change social conditions in France. His naturalistic novel *Nana* (1880) focused on a courtesan whose life came to a terrifying end. The play *Thérèse Raquin* (1873), based on Zola's novel of the same name, told the story of a woman and her lover who murder her husband and then commit suicide out of a sense of mutual guilt. There are no twists, surprises, or even much suspense in the play. Zola's subjects seem to have been uniformly grim, and naturalism became associated with the darker side of life.

REALISM, which avoided mechanical "clockwork" plots with their artificially contrived conclusions, began in the later years of the eighteenth century (some scholars claim to see evidence of it even earlier, in the work of Middleton) and progressed steadily to the end of the nineteenth century. In the realistic plays of Henrik Ibsen (1828–1906) and August Strindberg (1849–1912), the details of the setting, the costuming, and the circumstances of the action were so fully realized as to convince audiences that they were listening in on life itself. (See Figure 11 for an example of a realistic stage setting.)

In England, Oscar Wilde (1854–1900), poet, novelist, and playwright, offered an alternative to both melodrama and realistic drama near the end of

Figure 11. Realistic setting in a 1941 production of Anton Chekhov's *The Cherry Orchard*.

the century. Wilde had spent much of his literary life promoting the philosophy of art for art's sake. He asserted that the pleasure of poetry was in its sounds, images, and thoughts. Poetry and drama did not serve religious, political, social, or even personal goals. For Wilde, art served itself. He was such a brilliant conversationalist that the Irish poet-playwright W. B. Yeats declared him the only person he ever heard who spoke complete, rounded sentences that sounded as if he had written and polished them the night before. His witticisms were often barbed and vicious but always incisive and perceptive. He became famous for his bright, witty comedies. *The Importance of Being Earnest* (1895), sometimes wrongly accused of being about nothing, is the most performed. It is an unsentimental, witty, and sometimes brittle comedy that dissects English upper-class attitudes that most of his audience would have taken for granted.

Wilde competed with numerous comic playwrights in England and abroad, such as the enormously successful Arthur Wing Pinero (1855–1934) and W. S. Gilbert (1836–1911) in England and Georges Feydeau (1862–1921) in France. None, though, could manage the unusual combination of wit and seriousness that marks Wilde's achievement. Another important competitor was also an Irish playwright, Bernard Shaw (1856–1950), whose plays were also comic and serious, such as *Arms and the Man* (1894), *You Never Can Tell* (1898), and *Pygmalion* (1913). But Shaw is probably best known for his plays of ideas — plays in which an underlying idea or principle drives the action — such as *Mrs. Warren's Profession* (1898), *Man and Superman* (1903), and *Major Barbara* (1905).

After a disappointing beginning as a playwright, Anton Chekhov (1860–1904) worked with the Moscow Arts Theatre under the directorship of Konstantin Stanislavski (1865–1938), one of the most influential figures in modern western drama. Stanislavski emphasized "inner realism" by having the actor become the character even in situations off stage by developing improvisational experiences to let the actor explore the character in situations other than those within the play. The Stanislavski Method helped the actor become the part, rather than just play the part. Chekhov and Stanislavski worked together to produce Chekhov's plays at a time when Chekhov felt himself a failure as a dramatist.

The first production of Chekhov's *The Seagull* (1896), his sixth major staged play, was a failure. Stanislavski convinced Chekhov to give it to his company to produce, resulting in an important triumph. Chekhov then reworked an earlier play into *Uncle Vanya* (1899) for Stanislavski and it, too, was a hit. *Three Sisters* (1901) was not successful in its first performances, but it later became known as one of Chekhov's finest works. His last play, *The Cherry Orchard* (1904), was put on by Stanislavski's company and has become one of the most important works of twentieth-century drama. Chekhov died of a heart attack soon after the play's first production. Today Chekhov's legacy continues, with all his major plays staged throughout the world in the latter half of the twentieth century. Thus one of the most important nineteenth-century writers led the way to new developments in twentieth-century drama that are still evident today on the stage as well as in films and on television. Modern treatments of Chekhov's plays include Michael Picardie's adaptation of *The Cherry Orchard* to South Africa and Brian Friel's adaptation to Ireland. Mustapha Matura's *Trinidad Sisters* (1988) moves *Three Sisters* to Trinidad, demonstrating in part the universal appeal of Chekhov's plays.

Nineteenth-Century Drama Timeline

DATE	THEATER	POLITICAL	SOCIAL/CULTURAL
1700–1800	**1759–1805:** Friedrich von Schiller, German playwright, author of *The Robbers* (1781) and *Maria Stuart* (1800)		
	1761–1819: August Friedrich Ferdinand von Kotsebue, German playwright and one of the early developers of melodrama	**1775:** The American War of Independence begins at Concord, Massachusetts.	**1770–1827:** Ludwig van Beethoven, German composer
			1775–1817: Jane Austen, English novelist
	1767–1787: *Sturm und Drang* period in German drama featuring the work of Goethe, Schiller, and others who rebelled against eighteenth-century rationalism	**1776:** The Declaration of Independence is signed.	
		1783: Peace of Versailles: Britain recognizes the independence of the United States.	
	1773: The Swedish National Theater is established in Stockholm.	**1789:** French revolutionaries storm the Bastille as the French revolution sweeps over French society.	**1792–1822:** Percy Bysshe Shelley, English Romantic poet
	1773–1844: Guilbert de Pixérécourt, French playwright generally credited with originating the melodrama	**1793:** Louis XVI and his queen, Marie Antoinette, are guillotined. The reign of terror, a purge instituted by the revolutionary government of France, claims 35,000 lives in one year.	**1793:** Eli Whitney (1765–1825) invents the cotton gin.
			1795: British forces occupy the Cape of Good Hope.
			1795–1821: John Keats, English Romantic poet
	1791–1861: Eugène Scribe, French playwright, developer of the "well-made" play, author of *Adrienne Lecouvreur* (1849)	**1799:** Napoleon Bonaparte overthrows the Directory of France, the moderate government that replaced the government of terror.	**1798:** *Lyrical Ballads* is published by Wordsworth and Coleridge.
			1799–1837: Alexander Pushkin, Russian poet
1800–1900	**1806–1872:** Edwin Forrest, America's first great native-born actor	**1803:** The Louisiana Purchase doubles the area of the United States.	**1802–1885:** Victor Hugo, French novelist
		1804: Napoleon I (1769–1821) declares himself emperor of France.	**1803–1882:** Ralph Waldo Emerson, American Transcendental philosopher, clergyman, and author
	1808 and 1832: German writer Johann Wolfgang von Goethe (1749–1832) produces his masterpiece, *Faust* (in two parts).	**1805:** Admiral Horatio Nelson's victory over Napoleon at Trafalgar establishes the supremacy of British naval forces.	**1805:** Gas lighting is introduced in Great Britain.
	1809–1852: Nikolai Gogol, Russian playwright, author of *The Inspector General* (1836)	**1811–1820:** The Regency period: George, Prince of Wales, acts as regent for George III, who was declared insane.	**1809–1852:** Louis Braille, French inventor of reading system for the blind
	1813–1837: Georg Büchner, German playwright, author of *Danton's Death* (1835) and *Woyzeck* (1836)	**1812:** The U.S. declares war on Britain.	**1812–1870:** Charles Dickens, English novelist
		1814: Treaty of Ghent ends the War of 1812; Britain is defeated.	

Nineteenth-Century Drama Timeline (continued)

DATE	THEATER	POLITICAL	SOCIAL/CULTURAL
1800–1900 (continued)	**1816:** Chestnut Street Theater in Philadelphia is the first theater to illuminate its stage with gas lighting. **1822–1890:** Dion Boucicault, Irish American actor and writer of popular melodramas, among them *The Octoroon* (1859) and *The Colleen Bawn* (1860) **1828–1906:** Henrik Ibsen, Norwegian playwright. Among his best-known works are *A Doll House* (1879) and *Hedda Gabler* (1890). **1830:** *Hernani*, by the French novelist and playwright Victor Hugo (1802–1885), traditionally marks the beginning of French romanticism. **1837:** William Charles Macready (1793–1873), an English actor, is the first to use the limelight (or Drummond light), a prototype of the spotlight. **1840–1902:** Émile Zola, French writer and promoter of naturalism in literature. Among his works is the novel (also a play) *Thérèse Raquin* (1873).	**1815:** Napoleon is decisively defeated at the Battle of Waterloo. **1818:** Shaka ascends the Zulu throne in Southern Africa and initiates a period of military reform; he is assassinated in 1828. **1820:** Accession of George IV **1820:** The Missouri Compromise admits Maine as a free state and Missouri as a slave state. **1821:** Mexico declares its independence. **1823:** The Monroe Doctrine closes the American continent to European colonization. **1837:** Queen Victoria begins her sixty-four-year reign in England. **1839:** Beginning of the First opium War between England and China. The war ends in 1842 with the Treaty of Nanjing, which turns over Hong Kong to England and opens several Chinese ports to Western trade.	**1816–1855:** Charlotte Bronte, English novelist **1817–1862:** Henry David Thoreau, American Transcendental writer and naturalist **1820–1906:** Susan B. Anthony, American leader of the women's suffrage movement **1821–1881:** Fyodor Dostoevsky, Russian novelist **1828–1910:** Leo Tolstoy, Russian novelist and philosopher **1830–1886:** Emily Dickinson, American poet **1831:** William Lloyd Garrison (1805–1879), American abolitionist, founds the *Liberator*. **1833–1897:** Johannes Brahms, German composer **1839:** Louis Daguerre (1789–1851) invents the daguerreotype, an early type of photograph. **1840–1893:** Peter Ilyich Tchaikovsky, Russian composer **1843–1916:** Henry James, American realist novelist **1844:** The telegraph is used for the first time. **1845:** Frederick Douglass (c. 1817–1895), African American abolitionist, publishes *Narrative of the Life of Frederick Douglass*.
	1849: The Astor Place Riot in New York is a result of the rivalry between the actors William Charles Macready and Edwin Forrest; twenty-two people are killed. **1849–1923:** Sarah Bernhardt, French performer, perhaps the greatest actress of the nineteenth century **1849–1912:** August Strindberg, Swedish playwright. Among his works are *Miss Julie* (1888) and *The Dream Play* (1902).	**1846–1848:** Mexican War over the United States' annexation of Texas. The Treaty of Guadalupe Hildago (1848) cedes Texas to the United States. **1852:** Napoleon III declares himself emperor of France and rules until 1871.	**1845–1849:** The great potato famine in Ireland kills nearly a million Irish; 1,600,000 immigrate to the United States. **1848:** The First U.S. Women's Rights Convention is held in Seneca Falls, N.Y. **1848:** California gold rush **1848:** Karl Marx, German political philosopher, writes *The Communist Manifesto*, with Friedrich Engels. **1850:** Tennyson succeeds Wordsworth as poet laureate of Great Britain. **1851:** Herman Melville (1819–1891) publishes *Moby Dick*. **1852:** Harriet Beecher Stowe (1811–1896) publishes *Uncle Tom's Cabin*.

Nineteenth-Century Drama Timeline (continued)

DATE	THEATER	POLITICAL	SOCIAL/CULTURAL
1800–1900 (continued)	**1854–1900:** Oscar Wilde, English writer. His plays include *A Woman of No Importance* (1893) and *The Importance of Being Earnest* (1895).	**1857:** Czar Alexander II begins emancipation of serfs in Russia.	**1854–1856:** Scottish explorer David Livingstone crosses Africa.
	1856–1950: Bernard Shaw, Irish playwright. Among his works are *Mrs. Warren's Profession* (1898), *Major Barbara* (1905), and *Pygmalion* (1912).	**1860:** Abraham Lincoln is elected president. South Carolina secedes from the Union. **1861:** Italy is unified under Victor Emmanuel II.	
	1860–1904: Anton Chekhov, Russian writer, author of *The Seagull* (1896) and *The Cherry Orchard* (1903)	**1861–1865:** The Civil War is fought in the United States. **1862:** Otto von Bismarck is appointed prime minister of Prussia.	**1859:** Charles Darwin (1809–1882) publishes *On the Origin of Species by Natural Selection.* **1860s:** Louis Pasteur (1822–1895), French chemist, develops pasteurization. **1865–1939:** William Butler Yeats, Irish poet and playwright
	1870–1900: Golden Age of Peking (Beijing) Opera **1871–1896:** Gilbert and Sullivan write their comic operas, among them *H.M.S. Pinafore* (1878) and *The Pirates of Penzance* (1879).	**1865:** Abraham Lincoln is assassinated by the actor John Wilkes Booth at Ford's Theatre in Washington, D.C. **1869:** The Suez Canal opens. **1870–1871:** Franco-Prussian War	**1869:** The first transcontinental railroad in the United States is completed. **1869–1959:** Frank Lloyd Wright, preeminent American architect
	1876: Opening of Richard Wagner's Festival Theater in Bayreuth, Germany. Among his works is the four-part *Der Ring des Nibelungen* (1853–1874).	**1871:** The German Empire is founded under Kaiser Wilhelm I. **1876:** At the Battle of the Little Bighorn, the Sioux defeat General George Custer's troops.	**1876:** Alexander Graham Bell (1847–1922) invents the telephone. **1877:** Thomas Edison (1847–1931) invents the phonograph. **1879:** Thomas Edison invents the lightbulb.
	1881: The Savoy Theatre is the first theater in London to be completely illuminated by electric light. **1887:** Théâtre Libre is founded in Paris by André Antoine to pursue naturalism in subject matter and staging.	**1885:** The Congo becomes a personal possession of King Leopold II of Belgium. **1890:** The Battle of Wounded Knee ends the American Indians' wars of resistance; two hundred Indians are killed by the U.S. Army.	
	1890–1930: Vaudeville becomes one of the most popular forms of entertainment in the United States. **1896:** The first revolving stage is installed by Karl Lautenschlager at the Residenz Theater in Munich. **1898:** The Moscow Art Theatre is founded under the direction of Konstantin Stanislavsky and Vladimir Nemirovich-Danchenko.	**1898:** The Spanish-American War. Cuban patriots demand independence and receive the military support of the United States. The 1898 Treaty of Paris gives Puerto Rico, Guam, the Philippines, and Cuba to the United States. **1899–1902:** The Boer War (South African War) ends British supremacy in South Africa.	**1898–1976:** Paul Robeson, African American singer, actor, and civil rights activist

Henrik Ibsen

Using the new style of realism, Henrik Ibsen (1828–1906) slowly and painfully became the most influential modern dramatist. Subjects that had been ignored on the stage became the center of his work. But his rise to fame was anything but direct. His family was extremely poor, and as a youth he worked in a drugstore in Grimstad, a seaport town in Norway. At seventeen he had an illegitimate child with a servant girl. At twenty-one he wrote his first play, in verse. In 1850, at the age of twenty-two, he left Grimstad for Oslo (then called Christiana) to become a student, but within a year he joined the new National Theater and stayed for six years, writing and directing.

In the 1850s he wrote numerous plays that did not bring him recognition: *St. John's Eve* (1853), *Lady Inger of Østraat* (1855), *Olaf Liljekrans* (1857),

Henrik Ibsen at age sixty-eight, six years after the first production of *Hedda Gabler*. He was the most influential playwright in Europe when this photograph was taken in 1896.

and *The Vikings at Helgeland* (1857). In the early 1860s, with a wife and daughter to support, he went through a period of serious self-doubt and despair, and his first play in five years, *Love's Comedy* (1862), was turned down for performance. Eventually, he got a job with the Christiana Theater and had a rare success with *The Pretenders* (1864), a historical play about thirteenth-century warriors vying for the vacant throne of Norway.

His breakthrough came with the publication in 1866 of the verse play *Brand,* which was written to be read and not performed. (It was first produced in 1885.) It is the portrait of a clergyman who takes the strictures of religion so seriously that he rejects the New Testament doctrine of love and accepts the Old Testament doctrine of the will of God. He destroys himself in the process and ends the play on a mountaintop in the Ice Church, facing an avalanche about to kill him. Out of the clouds comes the answer to his questions of whether love or will achieves salvation: "He is the God of Love." *Brand* made Ibsen famous. He followed it with another successful closet drama, *Peer Gynt* (1867), about a character, quite unlike Brand, who avoids the rigors of morality and ends up unable to know if he has been saved or condemned.

Despite these successes, Ibsen still struggled for recognition. It was not until 1877 that he had his first success in a play that experimented with the new realistic style of drama: *The Pillars of Society,* which probed behind the hypocrisies of Karsten Bernick, a merchant who prospers by all manner of double-dealing and betrayal of his relatives. Eventually, he admits his crimes but, instead of being punished, is welcomed back into society and is more successful than ever. This play gave Ibsen a reputation in Germany, where it was frequently performed, and prepared him for his great successes. *A Doll House* (1879), which he wrote in Italy, came two years later. It was more fully realistic in style than *The Pillars of Society* and, while immensely successful in Scandinavia, did not become widely known elsewhere for another ten years.

His next play, *Ghosts* (1881), was denounced violently because it dared to treat a subject that had been taboo on the stage: syphilis. *Ghosts* introduced a respectable family, the Alvings, who harbor the secret that the late father contracted the disease and passed it on to Oswald, his son. In addition, the theme of incest is suggested in the presence of Alving's illegitimate daughter, Regina, who falls in love with Oswald. This kind of material was so foreign to the late nineteenth-century stage that Ibsen was vilified and isolated by the literary community in Norway. He chose exile for a time in Rome, Amalfi, and Munich.

Ibsen's last years were filled with activity. He wrote some of his best-known plays in rapid succession: *An Enemy of the People* (1882), *The Wild Duck* (1884), *Hedda Gabler* (1890), *The Master Builder* (1892), and *John Gabriel Borkman* (1896). In 1891 he returned to live in Norway, where he died fifteen years later.

The most influential European dramatist in the late nineteenth century, Ibsen inspired emerging writers in the United States, Ireland, and many other nations. But his full influence was not felt until the early decades of the twentieth century, when other writers were able to spread the revolutionary doctrine that was implied in realism as practiced by Ibsen and Strindberg. Being direct, honest, and unsparing in treating character and theme became the normal mode of serious drama after Ibsen.

A DOLL HOUSE

Once Henrik Ibsen found his voice as a realist playwright, he began to develop plays centering on social problems and the problems of the individual struggling against the demands of society. In *A Doll House* (1879) he focused on the repression of women. It was a subject that deeply offended conservatives and was very much on the minds of progressive and liberal Scandinavians. It was therefore a rather daring theme. The play opens with the dutiful, eager wife Nora Helmer twittering like a lark and pattering like a squirrel pleasing her husband, Torvald. Helmer is consumed with propriety. As far as he is concerned, Nora is only a woman, an empty-headed ornament in a house designed to keep his life functioning smoothly.

Nora is portrayed as a macaroon-eating, sweet-toothed creature looking for ways to please her husband. When she reveals that she borrowed the money that took them to Italy for a year to save her husband's life, she shows us that she is made of much stronger stuff than anyone has given her credit for. Yet the manner in which she borrowed the money is technically criminal because she had to forge her father's signature, and she now finds herself at the mercy of the lender, Nils Krogstad.

From a modern perspective, Nora's action seems daring and imaginative rather than merely illegal and surreptitious. Torvald Helmer's moralistic position is to us essentially stifling. He condemns Nora's father for a similar failure

LEFT: For this 1906 production of Ibsen's *The Wild Duck,* the director, André Antoine, had the set constructed of Norwegian pine to achieve a high degree of realism. ABOVE: Edvard Munch's 1906 stage design for Max Reinhardt's production of Ibsen's *Ghosts* at the Kammerspiele in Berlin. Although *Ghosts* (1881) was written in Ibsen's realistic style, Munch's expressionistic lines and shadows seem to reflect the tendencies in Ibsen's late plays to move beyond realism to a more dreamlike structure.

to secure proper signatures, just as he condemns Nils Krogstad for doing the same. He condemns people for their crimes without considering their circumstances or motives. He is moralistic rather than moral.

The atmosphere of the Helmer household is oppressive. Everything is set up to amuse Torvald, and he lacks any awareness that other people might be his equal. Early in the play Ibsen establishes Nora's longings: she explains that to pay back her loan she has had to take in copying work, and rather than resent her labor, she observes that it made her feel wonderful, the way a man must feel. Ibsen said that his intention in the play was not primarily to promote the emancipation of women; it was to establish, as Ibsen's biographer Michael Meyer says, "that the primary duty of anyone was to find out who he or she really was and to become that person."

However, the play from the first was seen as addressing the problems of women, especially married women who were treated as their husbands' property. When the play was first performed, the slam of the door at Nora's leaving was much louder than it is today. It was shocking to late nineteenth-century society, which took Torvald Helmer's attitudes for granted. The first audiences probably were split in their opinions about Nora's actions. As Meyer reminds us, "No play had ever before contributed so momentously to the social debate, or been so widely and furiously discussed among people who were not normally interested in theatrical or even artistic matters." Although the critics in Copenhagen and England were very negative, the audiences were filled with curiosity and flocked to the theaters to see the play.

What the audiences saw was that once Nora is awakened, the kind of life Torvald imagines for her is death to Nora. Torvald cannot see how his self-absorbed concern and fear for his own social standing reveal his limitations and selfishness. Nora sees immediately the limits of his concern, and her only choice is to leave him so that she can grow morally and spiritually.

What she does and where she goes have been a matter of speculation since the play was first performed. Ibsen refused to encourage any specific conjecture. It is enough that she has the courage to leave. But the ending of the play bothered audiences as well as critics, and it was performed in Germany in 1880 with a happy ending that Ibsen himself wrote to forestall anyone else from doing so. The first German actress to play the part insisted that she would personally never leave her children and therefore would not do the play as written. In the revised version, instead of leaving, Nora is led to the door of her children's room and falls weeping as the curtain goes down. The so-called happy-ending version was played for a while in England and elsewhere. No one was satisfied with this ending, and eventually the play reverted to its original form.

Through the proscenium arch of the theater in Ibsen's day audiences were permitted to eavesdrop on themselves, since Ibsen clearly was analyzing their own mores. In a way the audience was looking at a dollhouse; but instead of containing miniature furniture and miniature people, it contained replicas of those watching. That very sense of intimacy, made possible by the late nineteenth-century theater, heightened the intensity of the play.

A Doll House in Performance

A Doll House was first produced in the Royal Theatre, Copenhagen, in December 1879. Despite its immediate success in Scandinavia and Germany, two years passed before the play appeared elsewhere and ten years before it appeared in England and America in a complete and accurate text. Further, the early German version (February 1880), with Hedwig Niemann-Raabe as Nora, had to be revised with a happy ending because the actress refused to play the original ending. Fortunately, the "happy ending," in which Nora does not leave home, was not successful and Niemann-Raabe eventually played the part as written. An adaptation, also with the happy ending, titled *The Child Wife*, was produced in Milwaukee in 1882. While the first professional London production of the play in 1889 found favor with the public, it was attacked in the press for being "unnatural, immoral and, in its concluding scene, essentially undramatic." Among other things, Ibsen was being condemned for not providing a vibrant plot.

Among the play's memorable performances was Ethel Barrymore's version in New York in 1905. Barrymore was praised for a brilliant interpretation of "the child wife." Ruth Gordon played the part to acclaim in 1937, as did Claire Bloom in 1971 on the stage and in 1973 in film. Jane Fonda played in Joseph Losey's film version of 1973. The Norwegian actress Liv Ullmann performed the role in Lincoln Center in 1975 and was praised as "the most enchanting," the "most honest" Nora that the critic Walter Kerr had seen. Other critics were less kind, but it was a successful run. One of the most riveting of modern productions starred Janet McTeer in Anthony Page's revival of *A Doll House*. This production began in London in 1997 and transferred to New York for a Broadway run the same year. Ben Brantley of the *New York Times* said of it, "Nothing can prepare you for the initial shock of Ms.

McTeer's performance, which transforms the passive Nora Helmer, Ibsen's childlike plaything of a wife, into an electric, even aggressive presence" revealing "previously hidden nuances in Ibsen's landmark work." This production was faithful to the production values of Ibsen's original, using an essentially Victorian-era setting with period costumes. Janet McTeer's energy transformed the play and gave Nora a new dimension that made the audience feel that she would do better than merely survive when she left her home. The play is performed regularly in college and regional theaters in the United States and elsewhere.

Henrik Ibsen (1828–1906)

A Doll House

1879

TRANSLATED BY ROLF FJELDE

The Characters

Torvald Helmer, *a lawyer*
Nora, *his wife*
Dr. Rank
Mrs. Linde
Nils Krogstad, *a bank clerk*
The Helmers' Three Small Children
Anne-Marie, *their nurse*
Helene, *a maid*
A Delivery Boy

The action takes place in Helmer's residence.

ACT I

(*A comfortable room, tastefully but not expensively furnished. A door to the right in the back wall leads to the entryway; another to the left leads to Helmer's study. Between these doors, a piano. Midway in the left-hand wall a door, and further back a window. Near the window a round table with an armchair and a small sofa. In the right-hand wall, toward the rear, a door, and nearer the foreground a porcelain stove with two armchairs and a rocking chair beside it. Between the stove and the side door, a small table. Engravings on the walls. An*

As Fjelde explains in his foreword to the translation, he does not use the possessive "A Doll's House" because "the house is not Nora's, as the possessive implies." Fjelde believes that Ibsen includes Torvald with Nora in the original title, "for the two of them at the play's opening are still posing like the little marzipan bride and groom atop the wedding cake."

étagère° *with china figures and other small art objects; a small bookcase with richly bound books; the floor carpeted; a fire burning in the stove. It is a winter day.*)

(*A bell rings in the entryway; shortly after we hear the door being unlocked. Nora comes into the room, humming happily to herself; she is wearing street clothes and carries an armload of packages, which she puts down on the table to the right. She has left the hall door open, and through it a Delivery Boy is seen holding a Christmas tree and a basket, which he gives to the Maid who let them in.*)

Nora: Hide the tree well, Helene. The children mustn't get a glimpse of it till this evening, after it's trimmed. (*To the Delivery Boy, taking out her purse.*) How much?

Delivery Boy: Fifty, ma'am.

Nora: There's a crown. No, keep the change. (*The Boy thanks her and leaves. Nora shuts the door. She laughs softly to herself while taking off her street things. Drawing a bag of macaroons from her pocket, she eats a couple, then steals over and listens at her husband's study door.*) Yes, he's home. (*Hums again as she moves to the table right.*)

Helmer (*from the study*): Is that my little lark twittering out there?

Nora (*busy opening some packages*): Yes, it is.

Helmer: Is that my squirrel rummaging around?

Nora: Yes!

Helmer: When did my squirrel get in?

Nora: Just now. (*Putting the macaroon bag in her pocket and wiping her mouth.*) Do come in, Torvald, and see what I've bought.

[s.d.] **étagère:** Cabinet with shelves.

HELMER: Can't be disturbed. (*After a moment he opens the door and peers in, pen in hand.*) Bought, you say? All that there? Has the little spendthrift been out throwing money around again?

NORA: Oh, but Torvald, this year we really should let ourselves go a bit. It's the first Christmas we haven't had to economize.

HELMER: But you know we can't go squandering.

NORA: Oh yes, Torvald, we can squander a little now. Can't we? Just a tiny, wee bit. Now that you've got a big salary and are going to make piles and piles of money.

HELMER: Yes — starting New Year's. But then it's a full three months till the raise comes through.

NORA: Pooh! We can borrow that long.

HELMER: Nora! (*Goes over and playfully takes her by the ear.*) Are your scatterbrains off again? What if today I borrowed a thousand crowns, and you squandered them over Christmas week, and then on New Year's Eve a roof tile fell on my head, and I lay there —

NORA (*putting her hand on his mouth*): Oh! Don't say such things!

HELMER: Yes, but what if it happened — then what?

NORA: If anything so awful happened, then it just wouldn't matter if I had debts or not.

HELMER: Well, but the people I'd borrowed from?

NORA: Them? Who cares about them! They're strangers.

HELMER: Nora, Nora, how like a woman! No, but seriously, Nora, you know what I think about that. No debts! Never borrow! Something of freedom's lost — and something of beauty, too — from a home that's founded on borrowing and debt. We've made a brave stand up to now, the two of us; and we'll go right on like that the little while we have to.

NORA (*going toward the stove*): Yes, whatever you say, Torvald.

HELMER (*following her*): Now, now, the little lark's wings mustn't droop. Come on, don't be a sulky squirrel. (*Taking out his wallet.*) Nora, guess what I have here.

NORA (*turning quickly*): Money!

HELMER: There, see. (*Hands her some notes.*) Good grief, I know how costs go up in a house at Christmastime.

NORA: Ten — twenty — thirty — forty. Oh, thank you, Torvald; I can manage no end on this.

HELMER: You really will have to.

NORA: Oh yes, I promise I will! But come here so I can show you everything I bought. And so cheap! Look, new clothes for Ivar here — and a sword. Here a horse and a trumpet for Bob. And a doll and a doll's bed here for Emmy; they're nothing much, but she'll tear them to bits in no time anyway. And here I have dress material and handkerchiefs for the maids. Old Anne-Marie really deserves something more.

HELMER: And what's in that package there?

NORA (*with a cry*): Torvald, no! You can't see that till tonight!

HELMER: I see. But tell me now, you little prodigal, what have you thought of for yourself?

NORA: For myself? Oh, I don't want anything at all.

HELMER: Of course you do. Tell me just what — within reason — you'd most like to have.

NORA: I honestly don't know. Oh, listen, Torvald —

HELMER: Well?

NORA (*fumbling at his coat buttons, without looking at him*): If you want to give me something, then maybe you could — you could —

HELMER: Come on, out with it.

NORA (*hurriedly*): You could give me money, Torvald. No more than you think you can spare; then one of these days I'll buy something with it.

HELMER: But Nora —

NORA: Oh, please, Torvald darling, do that! I beg you, please. Then I could hang the bills in pretty gilt paper on the Christmas tree. Wouldn't that be fun?

HELMER: What are those little birds called that always fly through their fortunes?

NORA: Oh yes, spendthrifts; I know all that. But let's do as I say, Torvald; then I'll have time to decide what I really need most. That's very sensible, isn't it?

HELMER (*smiling*): Yes, very — that is, if you actually hung onto the money I give you, and you actually used it to buy yourself something. But it goes for the house and for all sorts of foolish things, and then I only have to lay out some more.

NORA: Oh, but Torvald —

HELMER: Don't deny it, my dear little Nora. (*Putting his arm around her waist.*) Spendthrifts are sweet, but they use up a frightful amount of money. It's incredible what it costs a man to feed such birds.

NORA: Oh, how can you say that! Really, I save everything I can.

HELMER (*laughing*): Yes, that's the truth. Everything you can. But that's nothing at all.

NORA (*humming, with a smile of quiet satisfaction*): Hm, if you only knew what expenses we larks and squirrels have, Torvald.

HELMER: You're an odd little one. Exactly the way your father was. You're never at a loss for scaring up money; but the moment you have it, it runs right out through your fingers; you never know what you've done with it. Well, one takes you as you are. It's deep in your blood. Yes, these things are hereditary, Nora.

NORA: Ah, I could wish I'd inherited many of Papa's qualities.

HELMER: And I couldn't wish you anything but just what you are, my sweet little lark. But wait; it seems to me you have a very — what should I call it? — a very suspicious look today —

NORA: I do?

HELMER: You certainly do. Look me straight in the eye.

NORA (*looking at him*): Well?

HELMER (*shaking an admonitory finger*): Surely my sweet tooth hasn't been running riot in town today, has she?

NORA: No. Why do you imagine that?

HELMER: My sweet tooth really didn't make a little detour through the confectioner's?

NORA: No, I assure you, Torvald —

HELMER: Hasn't nibbled some pastry?

NORA: No, not at all.

HELMER: Not even munched a macaroon or two?

NORA: No, Torvald, I assure you, really —

HELMER: There, there now. Of course I'm only joking.

NORA (*going to the table, right*): You know I could never think of going against you.

HELMER: No, I understand that; and you *have* given me your word. (*Going over to her.*) Well, you keep your little Christmas secrets to yourself, Nora darling. I expect they'll come to light this evening, when the tree is lit.

NORA: Did you remember to ask Dr. Rank?

HELMER: No. But there's no need for that, it's assumed he'll be dining with us. All the same, I'll ask him when he stops by here this morning. I've ordered some fine wine. Nora, you can't imagine how I'm looking forward to this evening.

NORA: So am I. And what fun for the children, Torvald!

HELMER: Ah, it's so gratifying to know that one's gotten a safe, secure job, and with a comfortable salary. It's a great satisfaction, isn't it?

NORA: Oh, it's wonderful!

HELMER: Remember last Christmas? Three whole weeks before, you shut yourself in every evening till long after midnight, making flowers for the Christmas tree, and all the other decorations to surprise us. Ugh, that was the dullest time I've ever lived through.

NORA: It wasn't at all dull for me.

HELMER (*smiling*): But the outcome *was* pretty sorry, Nora.

NORA: Oh, don't tease me with that again. How could I help it that the cat came in and tore everything to shreds.

HELMER: No, poor thing, you certainly couldn't. You wanted so much to please us all, and that's what counts. But it's just as well that the hard times are past.

NORA: Yes, it's really wonderful.

HELMER: Now I don't have to sit here alone, boring myself, and you don't have to tire your precious eyes and your fair little delicate hands —

NORA (*clapping her hands*): No, is it really true, Torvald, I don't have to? Oh, how wonderfully lovely to hear! (*Taking his arm.*) Now I'll tell you just how I've thought we should plan things. Right after Christmas — (*The doorbell rings.*) Oh, the bell. (*Straightening the room up a bit.*) Somebody would have to come. What a bore!

HELMER: I'm not at home to visitors, don't forget.

MAID (*from the hall doorway*): Ma'am, a lady to see you —

NORA: All right, let her come in.

MAID (*to Helmer*): And the doctor's just come too.

HELMER: Did he go right to my study?

MAID: Yes, he did.

(*Helmer goes into his room. The Maid shows in Mrs. Linde, dressed in traveling clothes, and shuts the door after her.*)

MRS. LINDE (*in a dispirited and somewhat hesitant voice*): Hello, Nora.

NORA (*uncertain*): Hello —

MRS. LINDE: You don't recognize me.

NORA: No, I don't know — but wait, I think — (*Exclaiming.*) What! Kristine! Is it really you?

MRS. LINDE: Yes, it's me.

NORA: Kristine! To think I didn't recognize you. But then, how could I? (*More quietly.*) How you've changed, Kristine!

MRS. LINDE: Yes, no doubt I have. In nine — ten long years.

NORA: Is it so long since we met! Yes, it's all of that. Oh, these last eight years have been a happy time, believe me. And so now you've come in to town, too. Made the long trip in the winter. That took courage.

MRS. LINDE: I just got here by ship this morning.

NORA: To enjoy yourself over Christmas, of course. Oh, how lovely! Yes, enjoy ourselves, we'll do that. But take your coat off. You're not still cold? (*Helping her.*) There now, let's get cozy here by the stove. No, the easy chair there! I'll take the rocker here. (*Seizing her hands.*) Yes, now you have your old look again; it was only in that first moment. You're a bit more pale, Kristine — and maybe a bit thinner.

MRS. LINDE: And much, much older, Nora.

NORA: Yes, perhaps a bit older; a tiny, tiny bit; not much at all. (*Stopping short; suddenly serious.*) Oh, but thoughtless me, to sit here, chattering away. Sweet, good Kristine, can you forgive me?

MRS. LINDE: What do you mean, Nora?

NORA (*softly*): Poor Kristine, you've become a widow.

MRS. LINDE: Yes, three years ago.

NORA: Oh, I knew it, of course; I read it in the papers. Oh, Kristine, you must believe me; I often thought of writing you then, but I kept postponing it, and something always interfered.

MRS. LINDE: Nora dear, I understand completely.

NORA: No, it was awful of me, Kristine. You poor thing, how much you must have gone through. And he left you nothing?

MRS. LINDE: No.

NORA: And no children?

MRS. LINDE: No.

NORA: Nothing at all, then?

MRS. LINDE: Not even a sense of loss to feed on.

NORA (*looking incredulously at her*): But Kristine, how could that be?

MRS. LINDE (*smiling wearily and smoothing her hair*): Oh, sometimes it happens, Nora.

NORA: So completely alone. How terribly hard that must be for you. I have three lovely children. You can't see them now; they're out with the maid. But now you must tell me everything —

MRS. LINDE: No, no, no, tell me about yourself.

NORA: No, you begin. Today I don't want to be selfish. I want to think only of you today. But there is something I must tell you. Did you hear of the wonderful luck we had recently?

MRS. LINDE: No, what's that?

NORA: My husband's been made manager in the bank, just think!

MRS. LINDE: Your husband? How marvelous!

NORA: Isn't it? Being a lawyer is such an uncertain living, you know, especially if one won't touch any cases that aren't clean and decent. And of course Torvald would never do that, and I'm with him completely there. Oh, we're simply delighted, believe me! He'll join the bank right after New Year's and start getting a huge salary and lots of commissions. From now on we can live quite differently — just as we want. Oh, Kristine, I feel so light and happy! Won't it be lovely to have stacks of money and not a care in the world?

MRS. LINDE: Well, anyway, it would be lovely to have enough for necessities.

NORA: No, not just for necessities, but stacks and stacks of money!

MRS. LINDE (*smiling*): Nora, Nora, aren't you sensible yet? Back in school you were such a free spender.

NORA (*with a quiet laugh*): Yes, that's what Torvald still says. (*Shaking her finger.*) But "Nora, Nora" isn't as silly as you all think. Really, we've been in no position for me to go squandering. We've had to work, both of us.

MRS. LINDE: You too?

NORA: Yes, at odd jobs — needlework, crocheting, embroidery, and such — (*casually*) and other things too. You remember that Torvald left the department when we were married? There was no chance of promotion in his office, and of course he needed to earn more money. But that first year he drove himself terribly. He took on all kinds of extra work that kept him going morning and night. It wore him down, and then he fell deathly ill. The doctors said it was essential for him to travel south.

MRS. LINDE: Yes, didn't you spend a whole year in Italy?

NORA: That's right. It wasn't easy to get away, you know. Ivar had just been born. But of course we had to go. Oh, that was a beautiful trip, and it saved Torvald's life. But it cost a frightful sum, Kristine.

MRS. LINDE: I can well imagine.

NORA: Four thousand, eight hundred crowns it cost. That's really a lot of money.

MRS. LINDE: But it's lucky you had it when you needed it.

NORA: Well, as it was, we got it from Papa.

MRS. LINDE: I see. It was just about the time your father died.

NORA: Yes, just about then. And, you know, I couldn't make that trip out to nurse him. I had to stay here, expecting Ivar any moment, and with my poor sick Torvald to care for. Dearest Papa, I never saw him again, Kristine. Oh, that was the worst time I've known in all my marriage.

MRS. LINDE: I know how you loved him. And then you went off to Italy?

NORA: Yes. We had the means now, and the doctors urged us. So we left a month after.

MRS. LINDE: And your husband came back completely cured?

NORA: Sound as a drum!

MRS. LINDE: But — the doctor?

NORA: Who?

MRS. LINDE: I thought the maid said he was a doctor, the man who came in with me.

NORA: Yes, that was Dr. Rank — but he's not making a sick call. He's our closest friend, and he stops by at least once a day. No, Torvald hasn't had a sick moment since, and the children are fit and strong, and I am, too. (*Jumping up and clapping her hands.*) Oh, dear God, Kristine, what a lovely thing to live and be happy! But how disgusting of me — I'm talking of nothing but my own affairs. (*Sits on a stool close by Kristine, arms resting across her knees.*) Oh, don't be angry with me! Tell me, is it really true that you weren't in love with your husband? Why did you marry him, then?

MRS. LINDE: My mother was still alive, but bedridden and helpless — and I had my two younger brothers to look after. In all conscience, I didn't think I could turn him down.

NORA: No, you were right there. But was he rich at the time?

MRS. LINDE: He was very well off, I'd say. But the business was shaky, Nora. When he died, it all fell apart, and nothing was left.

NORA: And then — ?

MRS. LINDE: Yes, so I had to scrape up a living with a little shop and a little teaching and whatever else I could find. The last three years have been like one endless workday without a rest for me. Now, it's over, Nora. My poor mother doesn't need me, for she's passed on. Nor the boys, either; they're working now and can take care of themselves.

NORA: How free you must feel —

MRS. LINDE: No — only unspeakably empty. Nothing to live for now. (*Standing up anxiously.*) That's why I couldn't take it any longer out in that desolate hole. Maybe here it'll be easier to find something to do and keep my mind occupied. If I could only be lucky enough to get a steady job, some office work —

NORA: Oh, but Kristine, that's so dreadfully tiring, and you already look so tired. It would be much better for you if you could go off to a bathing resort.

MRS. LINDE (*going toward the window*): I have no father to give me travel money, Nora.

NORA (*rising*): Oh, don't be angry with me.

MRS. LINDE (*going to her*): Nora dear, don't you be angry with me. The worst of my kind of situation is all the bitterness that's stored away. No one to work for, and yet you're always having to snap up your

opportunities. You have to live; and so you grow selfish. When you told me the happy change in your lot,
do you know I was delighted less for your sakes than
for mine?

NORA: How so? Oh, I see. You think maybe Torvald
could do something for you.

MRS. LINDE: Yes, that's what I thought.

NORA: And he will, Kristine! Just leave it to me; I'll
bring it up so delicately — find something attractive
to humor him with. Oh, I'm so eager to help you.

MRS. LINDE: How very kind of you, Nora, to be so concerned over me — doubly kind, considering you
really know so little of life's burdens yourself.

NORA: I — ? I know so little — ?

MRS. LINDE (*smiling*): Well, my heavens — a little needlework and such — Nora, you're just a child.

NORA (*tossing her head and pacing the floor*): You don't
have to act so superior.

MRS. LINDE: Oh?

NORA: You're just like the others. You all think I'm incapable of anything serious —

MRS. LINDE: Come now —

NORA: That I've never had to face the raw world.

MRS. LINDE: Nora dear, you've just been telling me all
your troubles.

NORA: Hm! Trivial! (*Quietly.*) I haven't told you the big
thing.

MRS. LINDE: Big thing? What do you mean?

NORA: You look down on me so, Kristine, but you
shouldn't. You're proud that you worked so long and
hard for your mother.

MRS. LINDE: I don't look down on a soul. But it is true:
I'm proud — and happy, too — to think it was given
to me to make my mother's last days almost free of
care.

NORA: And you're also proud thinking of what you've
done for your brothers.

MRS. LINDE: I feel I've a right to be.

NORA: I agree. But listen to this, Kristine — I've also got
something to be proud and happy for.

MRS. LINDE: I don't doubt it. But whatever do you mean?

NORA: Not so loud. What if Torvald heard! He mustn't,
not for anything in the world. Nobody must know,
Kristine. No one but you.

MRS. LINDE: But what is it, then?

NORA: Come here. (*Drawing her down beside her on
the sofa.*) It's true — I've also got something to be
proud and happy for. I'm the one who saved Torvald's life.

MRS. LINDE: Saved — ? Saved how?

NORA: I told you about the trip to Italy. Torvald never
would have lived if he hadn't gone south —

MRS. LINDE: Of course; your father gave you the
means —

NORA (*smiling*): That's what Torvald and all the rest
think, but —

MRS. LINDE: But — ?

NORA: Papa didn't give us a pin. I was the one who
raised the money.

MRS. LINDE: You? That whole amount?

NORA: Four thousand, eight hundred crowns. What do
you say to that?

MRS. LINDE: But Nora, how was it possible? Did you
win the lottery?

NORA (*disdainfully*): The lottery? Pooh! No art to that.

MRS. LINDE: But where did you get it from then?

NORA (*humming, with a mysterious smile*): Hmm, tra-
la-la-la.

MRS. LINDE: Because you couldn't have borrowed it.

NORA: No? Why not?

MRS. LINDE: A wife can't borrow without her husband's
consent.

NORA (*tossing her head*): Oh, but a wife with a little
business sense, a wife who knows how to manage —

MRS. LINDE: Nora, I simply don't understand —

NORA: You don't have to. Whoever said I *borrowed* the
money? I could have gotten it other ways. (*Throwing
herself back on the sofa.*) I could have gotten it from
some admirer or other. After all, a girl with my ravishing appeal —

MRS. LINDE: You lunatic.

NORA: I'll bet you're eaten up with curiosity, Kristine.

MRS. LINDE: Now listen here, Nora — you haven't
done something indiscreet?

NORA (*sitting up again*): Is it indiscreet to save your husband's life?

MRS. LINDE: I think it's indiscreet that without his
knowledge you —

NORA: But that's the point: He mustn't know! My Lord,
can't you understand? He mustn't ever know the
close call he had. It was to *me* the doctors came to
say his life was in danger — that nothing could save
him but a stay in the south. Didn't I try strategy then!
I began talking about how lovely it would be for me
to travel abroad like other young wives; I begged and
I cried; I told him please to remember my condition,
to be kind and indulge me; and then I dropped a hint
that he could easily take out a loan. But at that, Kristine, he nearly exploded. He said I was frivolous, and
it was his duty as man of the house not to indulge me
in whims and fancies — as I think he called them.
Aha, I thought, now you'll just have to be saved —
and that's when I saw my chance.

MRS. LINDE: And your father never told Torvald the
money wasn't from him?

NORA: No, never. Papa died right about then. I'd considered bringing him into my secret and begging him
never to tell. But he was too sick at the time — and
then, sadly, it didn't matter.

MRS. LINDE: And you've never confided in your husband since?

NORA: For heaven's sake, no! Are you serious? He's so
strict on that subject. Besides — Torvald, with all his
masculine pride — how painfully humiliating for
him if he ever found out he was in debt to me. That
would just ruin our relationship. Our beautiful,
happy home would never be the same.

MRS. LINDE: Won't you ever tell him?

NORA (*thoughtfully, half smiling*): Yes — maybe some-time years from now, when I'm no longer so attractive. Don't laugh! I only mean when Torvald loves me less than now, when he stops enjoying my dancing and dressing up and reciting for him. Then it might be wise to have something in reserve — (*Breaking off.*) How ridiculous! That'll never happen — Well, Kristine, what do you think of my big secret? I'm capable of something too, hm? You can imagine, of course, how this thing hangs over me. It really hasn't been easy meeting the payments on time. In the business world there's what they call quarterly interest and what they call amortization, and these are always so terribly hard to manage. I've had to skimp a little here and there, wherever I could, you know. I could hardly spare anything from my house allowance, because Torvald has to live well. I couldn't let the children go poorly dressed; whatever I got for them, I felt I had to use up completely — the darlings!

MRS. LINDE: Poor Nora, so it had to come out of your own budget, then?

NORA: Yes, of course. But I was the one most responsible, too. Every time Torvald gave me money for new clothes and such, I never used more than half; always bought the simplest, cheapest outfits. It was a godsend that everything looks so well on me that Torvald never noticed. But it did weigh me down at times, Kristine. It *is* such a joy to wear fine things. You understand.

MRS. LINDE: Oh, of course.

NORA: And then I found other ways of making money. Last winter I was lucky enough to get a lot of copying to do. I locked myself in and sat writing every evening till late in the night. Ah, I was tired so often, dead tired. But still it was wonderful fun, sitting and working like that, earning money. It was almost like being a man.

MRS. LINDE: But how much have you paid off this way so far?

NORA: That's hard to say, exactly. These accounts, you know, aren't easy to figure. I only know that I've paid out all I could scrape together. Time and again I haven't known where to turn. (*Smiling.*) Then I'd sit here dreaming of a rich old gentleman who had fallen in love with me —

MRS. LINDE: What! Who is he?

NORA: Oh, really! And that he'd died, and when his will was opened, there in big letters it said, "All my fortune shall be paid over in cash, immediately, to that enchanting Mrs. Nora Helmer."

MRS. LINDE: But Nora dear — who *was* this gentleman?

NORA: Good grief, can't you understand? The old man never existed; that was only something I'd dream up time and again whenever I was at my wits' end for money. But it makes no difference now; the old fossil can go where he pleases for all I care; I don't need him or his will — because now I'm free. (*Jumping up.*) Oh, how lovely to think of that, Kristine! Care-free! To know you're carefree, utterly carefree; to be able to romp and play with the children, and to keep up a beautiful, charming home — everything just the way Torvald likes it! And think, spring is coming, with big blue skies. Maybe we can travel a little then. Maybe I'll see the ocean again. Oh yes, it *is* so marvelous to live and be happy!

(*The front doorbell rings.*)

MRS. LINDE (*rising*): There's the bell. It's probably best that I go.

NORA: No, stay. No one's expected. It must be for Torvald.

MAID (*from the hall doorway*): Excuse me, ma'am — there's a gentleman here to see Mr. Helmer, but I didn't know — since the doctor's with him —

NORA: Who is the gentleman?

KROGSTAD (*from the doorway*): It's me, Mrs. Helmer.

(*Mrs. Linde starts and turns away toward the window.*)

NORA (*stepping toward him, tense, her voice a whisper*): You? What is it? Why do you want to speak to my husband?

KROGSTAD: Bank business — after a fashion. I have a small job in the investment bank, and I hear now your husband is going to be our chief —

NORA: In other words, it's —

KROGSTAD: Just dry business, Mrs. Helmer. Nothing but that.

NORA: Yes, then please be good enough to step into the study. (*She nods indifferently as she sees him out by the hall door, then returns and begins stirring up the stove.*)

MRS. LINDE: Nora — who was that man?

NORA: That was a Mr. Krogstad — a lawyer.

MRS. LINDE: Then it really was him.

NORA: Do you know that person?

MRS. LINDE: I did once — many years ago. For a time he was a law clerk in our town.

NORA: Yes, he's been that.

MRS. LINDE: How he's changed.

NORA: I understand he had a very unhappy marriage.

MRS. LINDE: He's a widower now.

NORA: With a number of children. There now, it's burning. (*She closes the stove door and moves the rocker a bit to one side.*)

MRS. LINDE: They say he has a hand in all kinds of business.

NORA: Oh? That may be true; I wouldn't know. But let's not think about business. It's so dull.

(*Dr. Rank enters from Helmer's study.*)

RANK (*still in the doorway*): No, no, really — I don't want to intrude, I'd just as soon talk a little while with your wife. (*Shuts the door, then notices Mrs. Linde.*) Oh, beg pardon. I'm intruding here too.

NORA: No, not at all. (*Introducing him.*) Dr. Rank, Mrs. Linde.

RANK: Well now, that's a name much heard in this

house. I believe I passed the lady on the stairs as I came.

MRS. LINDE: Yes, I take the stairs very slowly. They're rather hard on me.

RANK: Uh-hm, some touch of internal weakness?

MRS. LINDE: More overexertion, I'd say.

RANK: Nothing else? Then you're probably here in town to rest up in a round of parties?

MRS. LINDE: I'm here to look for work.

RANK: Is that the best cure for overexertion?

MRS. LINDE: One has to live, Doctor.

RANK: Yes, there's a common prejudice to that effect.

NORA: Oh, come on, Dr. Rank — you really do want to live yourself.

RANK: Yes, I really do. Wretched as I am, I'll gladly prolong my torment indefinitely. All my patients feel like that. And it's quite the same, too, with the morally sick. Right at this moment there's one of those moral invalids in there with Helmer —

MRS. LINDE (*softly*): Ah!

NORA: Who do you mean?

RANK: Oh, it's a lawyer, Krogstad, a type you wouldn't know. His character is rotten to the root — but even he began chattering all-importantly about how he had to *live.*

NORA: Oh? What did he want to talk to Torvald about?

RANK: I really don't know. I only heard something about the bank.

NORA: I didn't know that Krog — that this man Krogstad had anything to do with the bank.

RANK: Yes, he's gotten some kind of berth down there. (*To Mrs. Linde.*) I don't know if you also have, in your neck of the woods, a type of person who scuttles about breathlessly, sniffing out hints of moral corruption, and then maneuvers his victim into some sort of key position where he can keep an eye on him. It's the healthy these days that are out in the cold.

MRS. LINDE: All the same, it's the sick who most need to be taken in.

RANK (*with a shrug*): Yes, there we have it. That's the concept that's turning society into a sanatorium.

(*Nora, lost in her thoughts, breaks out into quiet laughter and claps her hands.*)

RANK: Why do you laugh at that? Do you have any real idea of what society is?

NORA: What do I care about dreary old society? I was laughing at something quite different — something terribly funny. Tell me, Doctor — is everyone who works in the bank dependent now on Torvald?

RANK: Is that what you find so terribly funny?

NORA (*smiling and humming*): Never mind, never mind! (*Pacing the floor.*) Yes, that's really immensely amusing: that we — that Torvald has so much power now over all those people. (*Taking the bag out of her pocket.*) Dr. Rank, a little macaroon on that?

RANK: See here, macaroons! I thought they were contraband here.

NORA: Yes, but these are some that Kristine gave me.

MRS. LINDE: What? I — ?

NORA: Now, now, don't be afraid. You couldn't possibly know that Torvald had forbidden them. You see, he's worried they'll ruin my teeth. But hmp! Just this once! Isn't that so, Dr. Rank? Help yourself! (*Puts a macaroon in his mouth.*) And you too, Kristine. And I'll also have one, only a little one — or two, at the most. (*Walking about again.*) Now I'm really tremendously happy. Now's there's just one last thing in the world that I have an enormous desire to do.

RANK: Well! And what's that?

NORA: It's something I have such a consuming desire to say so Torvald could hear.

RANK: And why can't you say it?

NORA: I don't dare. It's quite shocking.

MRS. LINDE: Shocking?

RANK: Well, then it isn't advisable. But in front of us you certainly can. What do you have such a desire to say so Torvald could hear?

NORA: I have such a huge desire to say — to hell and be damned!

RANK: Are you crazy?

MRS. LINDE: My goodness, Nora!

RANK: Go on, say it. Here he is.

NORA (*hiding the macaroon bag*): Shh, shh, shh!

(*Helmer comes in from his study, hat in hand, overcoat over his arm.*)

NORA (*going toward him*): Well, Torvald dear, are you through with him?

HELMER: Yes, he just left.

NORA: Let me introduce you — this is Kristine, who's arrived here in town.

HELMER: Kristine — ? I'm sorry, but I don't know —

NORA: Mrs. Linde, Torvald dear. Mrs. Kristine Linde.

HELMER: Of course. A childhood friend of my wife's, no doubt?

MRS. LINDE: Yes, we knew each other in those days.

NORA: And just think, she made the long trip down here in order to talk to you.

HELMER: What's this?

MRS. LINDE: Well, not exactly —

NORA: You see, Kristine is remarkably clever in office work, and so she's terribly eager to come under a capable man's supervision and add more to what she already knows —

HELMER: Very wise, Mrs. Linde.

NORA: And then when she heard that you'd become a bank manager — the story was wired out to the papers — then she came in as fast as she could and — Really, Torvald, for my sake you can do a little something for Kristine, can't you?

HELMER: Yes, it's not at all impossible. Mrs. Linde, I suppose you're a widow?

MRS. LINDE: Yes.

HELMER: Any experience in office work?

MRS. LINDE: Yes, a good deal.

HELMER: Well, it's quite likely that I can make an opening for you —

NORA (*clapping her hands*): You see, you see!

HELMER: You've come at a lucky moment, Mrs. Linde.

MRS. LINDE: Oh, how can I thank you?

HELMER: Not necessary. (*Putting his overcoat on.*) But today you'll have to excuse me —

RANK: Wait, I'll go with you. (*He fetches his coat from the hall and warms it at the stove.*)

NORA: Don't stay out long, dear.

HELMER: An hour; no more.

NORA: Are you going too, Kristine?

MRS. LINDE (*putting on her winter garments*): Yes, I have to see about a room now.

HELMER: Then perhaps we can all walk together.

NORA (*helping her*): What a shame we're so cramped here, but it's quite impossible for us to —

MRS. LINDE: Oh, don't even think of it! Good-bye, Nora dear, and thanks for everything.

NORA: Good-bye for now. Of course you'll be back this evening. And you too, Dr. Rank. What? If you're well enough? Oh, you've got to be! Wrap up tight now.

(*In a ripple of small talk the company moves out into the hall; children's voices are heard outside on the steps.*)

NORA: There they are! There they are! (*She runs to open the door. The children come in with their nurse, Anne-Marie.*) Come in, come in! (*Bends down and kisses them.*) Oh, you darlings — ! Look at them, Kristine. Aren't they lovely!

RANK: No loitering in the draft here.

HELMER: Come, Mrs. Linde — this place is unbearable now for anyone but mothers.

(*Dr. Rank, Helmer, and Mrs. Linde go down the stairs. Anne-Marie goes into the living room with the children. Nora follows, after closing the hall door.*)

NORA: How fresh and strong you look. Oh, such red cheeks you have! Like apples and roses. (*The children interrupt her throughout the following.*) And it was so much fun? That's wonderful. Really? You pulled both Emmy and Bob on the sled? Imagine, all together! Yes, you're a clever boy, Ivar. Oh, let me hold her a bit, Anne-Marie. My sweet little doll baby! (*Takes the smallest from the nurse and dances with her.*) Yes, yes, Mama will dance with Bob as well. What? Did you throw snowballs? Oh, if I'd only been there! No, don't bother, Anne-Marie — I'll undress them myself. Oh yes, let me. It's such fun. Go in and rest; you look half frozen. There's hot coffee waiting for you on the stove. (*The nurse goes into the room to the left. Nora takes the children's winter things off, throwing them about, while the children talk to her all at once.*) Is that so? A big dog chased you? But it didn't bite? No, dogs never bite little, lovely doll babies. Don't peek in the packages, Ivar! What is it? Yes, wouldn't you like to know. No, no, it's an ugly something. Well? Shall we play? What shall we play? Hide-and-seek? Yes, let's play hide-and-seek. Bob must hide first. I must? Yes, let me hide first. (*Laughing and shouting, she and the chil-*

dren play in and out of the living room and the adjoining room to the right. At last Nora hides under the table. The children come storming in, search, but cannot find her, then hear her muffled laughter, dash over to the table, lift the cloth up and find her. Wild shouting. She creeps forward as if to scare them. More shouts. Meanwhile, a knock at the hall door; no one has noticed it. Now the door half opens, and Krogstad appears. He waits a moment; the game goes on.*)

KROGSTAD: Beg pardon, Mrs. Helmer —

NORA (*with a strangled cry, turning and scrambling to her knees*): Oh! What do you want?

KROGSTAD: Excuse me. The outer door was ajar; it must be someone forgot to shut it —

NORA (*rising*): My husband isn't home, Mr. Krogstad.

KROGSTAD: I know that.

NORA: Yes — then what do you want here?

KROGSTAD: A word with you.

NORA: With — ? (*To the children, quietly.*) Go in to Anne-Marie. What? No, the strange man won't hurt Mama. When he's gone, we'll play some more. (*She leads the children into the room to the left and shuts the door after them. Then, tense and nervous:*) You want to speak to me?

KROGSTAD: Yes, I want to.

NORA: Today? But it's not yet the first of the month —

KROGSTAD: No, it's Christmas Eve. It's going to be up to you how merry a Christmas you have.

NORA: What is it you want? Today I absolutely can't —

KROGSTAD: We won't talk about that till later. This is something else. You do have a moment to spare, I suppose?

NORA: Oh yes, of course — I do, except —

KROGSTAD: Good. I was sitting over at Olsen's Restaurant when I saw your husband go down the street —

NORA: Yes?

KROGSTAD: With a lady.

NORA: Yes. So?

KROGSTAD: If you'll pardon my asking: Wasn't that lady a Mrs. Linde?

NORA: Yes.

KROGSTAD: Just now come into town?

NORA: Yes, today.

KROGSTAD: She's a good friend of yours?

NORA: Yes, she is. But I don't see —

KROGSTAD: I also knew her once.

NORA: I'm aware of that.

KROGSTAD: Oh? You know all about it. I thought so. Well, then let me ask you short and sweet: Is Mrs. Linde getting a job in the bank?

NORA: What makes you think you can cross-examine me, Mr. Krogstad — you, one of my husband's employees? But since you ask, you might as well know — yes, Mrs. Linde's going to be taken on at the bank. And I'm the one who spoke for her Mr. Krogstad. Now you know.

KROGSTAD: So I guessed right.

NORA (*pacing up and down*): Oh, one does have a tiny

bit of influence, I should hope. Just because I am a woman, don't think it means that — When one has a subordinate position, Mr. Krogstad, one really ought to be careful about pushing somebody who — hm —

KROGSTAD: Who has influence?

NORA: That's right.

KROGSTAD (*in a different tone*): Mrs. Helmer, would you be good enough to use your influence on my behalf?

NORA: What? What do you mean?

KROGSTAD: Would you please make sure that I keep my subordinate position in the bank?

NORA: What does that mean? Who's thinking of taking away your position?

KROGSTAD: Oh, don't play the innocent with me. I'm quite aware that your friend would hardly relish the chance of running into me again; and I'm also aware now whom I can thank for being turned out.

NORA: But I promise you —

KROGSTAD: Yes, yes, yes, to the point: There's still time, and I'm advising you to use your influence to prevent it.

NORA: But Mr. Krogstad, I have absolutely no influence.

KROGSTAD: You haven't? I thought you were just saying —

NORA: You shouldn't take me so literally. I! How can you believe that I have any such influence over my husband?

KROGSTAD: Oh, I've known your husband from our student days. I don't think the great bank manager's more steadfast than any other married man.

NORA: You speak insolently about my husband, and I'll show you the door.

KROGSTAD: The lady has spirit.

NORA: I'm not afraid of you any longer. After New Year's, I'll soon be done with the whole business.

KROGSTAD: (*restraining himself*): Now listen to me, Mrs. Helmer. If necessary, I'll fight for my little job in the bank as if it were life itself.

NORA: Yes, so it seems.

KROGSTAD: It's not just a matter of income; that's the least of it. It's something else — All right, out with it! Look, this is the thing. You know, just like all the others, of course, that once, a good many years ago, I did something rather rash.

NORA: I've heard rumors to that effect.

KROGSTAD: The case never got into court; but all the same, every door was closed in my face from then on. So I took up those various activities you know about. I had to grab hold somewhere; and I dare say I haven't been among the worst. But now I want to drop all that. My boys are growing up. For their sakes, I'll have to win back as much respect as possible here in town. That job in the bank was like the first rung in my ladder. And now your husband wants to kick me right back down in the mud again.

NORA: But for heaven's sake, Mr. Krogstad, it's simply not in my power to help you.

KROGSTAD: That's because you haven't the will to — but I have the means to make you.

NORA: You certainly won't tell my husband that I owe you money?

KROGSTAD: Hm — what if I told him that?

NORA: That would be shameful of you. (*Nearly in tears.*) This secret — my joy and my pride — that he should learn it in such a crude and disgusting way — learn it from you. You'd expose me to the most horrible unpleasantness —

KROGSTAD: Only unpleasantness?

NORA (*vehemently*): But go on and try. It'll turn out the worse for you, because then my husband will really see what a crook you are, and then you'll never be able to hold your job.

KROGSTAD: I asked if it was just domestic unpleasantness you were afraid of?

NORA: If my husband finds out, then of course he'll pay what I owe at once, and then we'd be through with you for good.

KROGSTAD (*a step closer*): Listen, Mrs. Helmer — you've either got a very bad memory, or else no head at all for business. I'd better put you a little more in touch with the facts.

NORA: What do you mean?

KROGSTAD: When your husband was sick, you came to me for a loan of four thousand, eight hundred crowns.

NORA: Where else could I go?

KROGSTAD: I promised to get you that sum —

NORA: And you got it.

KROGSTAD: I promised to get you that sum, on certain conditions. You were so involved in your husband's illness, and so eager to finance your trip, that I guess you didn't think out all the details. It might just be a good idea to remind you. I promised you the money on the strength of a note I drew up.

NORA: Yes, and that I signed.

KROGSTAD: Right. But at the bottom I added some lines for your father to guarantee the loan. He was supposed to sign down there.

NORA: Supposed to? He did sign.

KROGSTAD: I left the date blank. In other words, your father would have dated his signature himself. Do you remember that?

NORA: Yes, I think —

KROGSTAD: Then I gave you the note for you to mail to your father. Isn't that so?

NORA: Yes.

KROGSTAD: And naturally you sent it at once — because only some five, six days later you brought me the note, properly signed. And with that, the money was yours.

NORA: Well, then; I've made my payments regularly, haven't I?

KROGSTAD: More or less. But — getting back to the point — those were hard times for you then, Mrs. Helmer.

NORA: Yes, they were.

KROGSTAD: Your father was very ill, I believe.

NORA: He was near the end.

KROGSTAD: He died soon after?

NORA: Yes.

KROGSTAD: Tell me, Mrs. Helmer, do you happen to recall the date of your father's death? The day of the month, I mean.

NORA: Papa died the twenty-ninth of September.

KROGSTAD: That's quite correct; I've already looked into that. And now we come to a curious thing — (*taking out a paper*) which I simply cannot comprehend.

NORA: Curious thing? I don't know —

KROGSTAD: This is the curious thing: that your father co-signed the note for your loan three days after his death.

NORA: How — ? I don't understand.

KROGSTAD: Your father died the twenty-ninth of September. But look. Here your father dated his signature October second. Isn't that curious, Mrs. Helmer? (*Nora is silent.*) Can you explain it to me? (*Nora remains silent.*) It's also remarkable that the words "October second" and the year aren't written in your father's hand, but rather in one that I think I know. Well, it's easy to understand. Your father forgot perhaps to date his signature, and then someone or other added it, a bit sloppily, before anyone knew of his death. There's nothing wrong in that. It all comes down to the signature. And there's no question about *that*, Mrs. Helmer. It really *was* your father who signed his own name here, wasn't it?

NORA (*after a short silence, throwing her head back and looking squarely at him*): No, it wasn't. *I* signed Papa's name.

TOP: Nora (Claire Bloom) is troubled as Helmer (Donald Madden) kisses her in Patrick Garland's 1971 production. RIGHT: Helmer, Nora, and Mrs. Linde (Patricia Elliott) discuss the possibility of finding a suitable job for Mrs. Linde in the bank. FAR RIGHT: Krogstad (Robert Gerringer) explains the seriousness of her actions to Nora.

KROGSTAD: Wait, now — are you fully aware that this is a dangerous confession?

NORA: Why? You'll soon get your money.

KROGSTAD: Let me ask you a question — why didn't you send the paper to your father?

NORA: That was impossible. Papa was so sick. If I'd asked him for his signature, I also would have had to tell him what the money was for. But I couldn't tell him, sick as he was, that my husband's life was in danger. That was just impossible.

KROGSTAD: Then it would have been better if you'd given up the trip abroad.

NORA: I couldn't possibly. The trip was to save my husband's life. I couldn't give that up.

KROGSTAD: But didn't you ever consider that this was a fraud against me?

NORA: I couldn't let myself be bothered by that. You weren't any concern of mine. I couldn't stand you, with all those cold complications you made, even though you knew how badly off my husband was.

KROGSTAD: Mrs. Helmer, obviously you haven't the vaguest idea of what you've involved yourself in. But I can tell you this: It was nothing more and nothing worse that I once did — and it wrecked my whole reputation.

NORA: You? Do you expect me to believe that you ever acted bravely to save your wife's life?

KROGSTAD: Laws don't inquire into motives.

NORA: Then they must be very poor laws.

KROGSTAD: Poor or not — if I introduce this paper in court, you'll be judged according to law.

NORA: This I refuse to believe. A daughter hasn't a right to protect her dying father from anxiety and care? A wife hasn't a right to save her husband's life? I don't know much about laws, but I'm sure that somewhere in the books these things are allowed. And you don't know anything about it — you who practice the law? You must be an awful lawyer, Mr. Krogstad.

KROGSTAD: Could be. But business — the kind of business we two are mixed up in — don't you think I know about that? All right. Do what you want now. But I'm telling you *this:* If I get shoved down a second time, you're going to keep me company. (*He bows and goes out through the hall.*)

NORA (*pensive for a moment, then tossing her head*): Oh, really! Trying to frighten me! I'm not so silly as all that. (*Begins gathering up the children's clothes, but soon stops.*) But — ? No, but that's impossible! I did it out of love.

THE CHILDREN (*in the doorway, left*): Mama, that strange man's gone out the door.

NORA: Yes, yes, I know it. But don't tell anyone about the strange man. Do you hear? Not even Papa!

THE CHILDREN: No, Mama. But now will you play again?

NORA: No, not now.

THE CHILDREN: Oh, but Mama, you promised.

NORA: Yes, but I can't now. Go inside; I have too much to do. Go in, go in, my sweet darlings. (*She herds them gently back in the room and shuts the door after them. Settling on the sofa, she takes up a piece of embroidery and makes some stitches, but soon stops abruptly.*) No! (*Throws the work aside, rises, goes to the hall door and calls out.*) Helene! Let me have the tree in here. (*Goes to the table, left, opens the table drawer, and stops again.*) No, but that's utterly impossible!

MAID (*with the Christmas tree*): Where should I put it, ma'am?

NORA: There. The middle of the floor.

MAID: Should I bring anything else?

NORA: No, thanks. I have what I need.

(*The Maid, who has set the tree down, goes out.*)

NORA (*absorbed in trimming the tree*): Candles here — and flowers here. That terrible creature! Talk, talk, talk! There's nothing to it at all. The tree's going to be lovely. I'll do anything to please you Torvald. I'll sing for you, dance for you —

(*Helmer comes in from the hall, with a sheaf of papers under his arm.*)

NORA: Oh! You're back so soon?

HELMER: Yes. Has anyone been here?

NORA: Here? No.

HELMER: That's odd. I saw Krogstad leaving the front door.

NORA: So? Oh yes, that's true. Krogstad was here a moment.

HELMER: Nora, I can see by your face that he's been here, begging you to put in a good word for him.

NORA: Yes.

HELMER: And it was supposed to seem like your own idea? You were to hide it from me that he'd been here. He asked you that, too, didn't he?

NORA: Yes, Torvald, but —

HELMER: Nora, Nora, and you could fall for that? Talk with that sort of person and promise him anything? And then in the bargain, tell me an untruth.

NORA: An untruth — ?

HELMER: Didn't you say that no one had been here? (*Wagging his finger.*) My little songbird must never do that again. A songbird needs a clean beak to warble with. No false notes. (*Putting his arm about her waist.*) That's the way it should be, isn't it? Yes, I'm sure of it. (*Releasing her.*) And so, enough of that. (*Sitting by the stove.*) Ah, how snug and cozy it is here. (*Leafing among his papers.*)

NORA (*busy with the tree, after a short pause*): Torvald!

HELMER: Yes.

NORA: I'm so much looking forward to the Stenborgs' costume party, day after tomorrow.

HELMER: And I can't wait to see what you'll surprise me with.

NORA: Oh, that stupid business!

HELMER: What?

NORA: I can't find anything that's right. Everything seems so ridiculous, so inane.

HELMER: So my little Nora's come to *that* recognition?

NORA (*going behind his chair, her arms resting on its back*): Are you very busy, Torvald?

HELMER: Oh —

NORA: What papers are those?

HELMER: Bank matters.

NORA: Already?

HELMER: I've gotten full authority from the retiring management to make all necessary changes in personnel and procedure. I'll need Christmas week for that. I want to have everything in order by New Year's.

NORA: So that was the reason this poor Krogstad —

HELMER: Hm.

NORA (*still leaning on the chair and slowly stroking the nape of his neck*): If you weren't so very busy, I would have asked you an enormous favor, Torvald.

HELMER: Let's hear. What is it?

NORA: You know, there isn't anyone who has your good taste — and I want so much to look well at the cos-

tume party. Torvald, couldn't you take over and decide what I should be and plan my costume?

HELMER: Ah, is my stubborn little creature calling for a lifeguard?

NORA: Yes, Torvald, I can't get anywhere without your help.

HELMER: All right — I'll think it over. We'll hit on something.

NORA: Oh, how sweet of you. (*Goes to the tree again. Pause.*) Aren't the red flowers pretty — ? But tell me, was it really such a crime that this Krogstad committed?

HELMER: Forgery. Do you have any idea what that means?

NORA: Couldn't he have done it out of need?

HELMER: Yes, or thoughtlessness, like so many others. I'm not so heartless that I'd condemn a man categorically for just one mistake.

NORA: No, of course not, Torvald!

HELMER: Plenty of men have redeemed themselves by openly confessing their crimes and taking their punishment.

NORA: Punishment — ?

HELMER: But now Krogstad didn't go that way. He got himself out by sharp practices, and that's the real cause of his moral breakdown.

NORA: Do you really think that would — ?

HELMER: Just imagine how a man with that sort of guilt in him has to lie and cheat and deceive on all sides, has to wear a mask even with the nearest and dearest he has, even with his own wife and children. And with the children, Nora — that's where it's most horrible.

NORA: Why?

HELMER: Because that kind of atmosphere of lies infects the whole life of a home. Every breath the children take in is filled with the germs of something degenerate.

NORA (*coming closer behind him*): Are you sure of that?

HELMER: Oh, I've seen it often enough as a lawyer. Almost everyone who goes bad early in life has a mother who's a chronic liar.

NORA: Why just — the mother?

HELMER: It's usually the mother's influence that's dominant, but the father's works in the same way, of course. Every lawyer is quite familiar with it. And still this Krogstad's been going home year in, year out, poisoning his own children with lies and pretense; that's why I call him morally lost. (*Reaching his hands out toward her.*) So my sweet little Nora must promise me never to plead his cause. Your hand on it. Come, come, what's this? Give me your hand. There, now. All settled. I can tell you it'd be impossible for me to work alongside of him. I literally feel physically revolted when I'm anywhere near such a person.

NORA (*withdraws her hand and goes to the other side of the Christmas tree*): How hot it is here! And I've got so much to do.

HELMER (*getting up and gathering his papers*): Yes, and I have to think about getting some of these read through before dinner. I'll think about your costume, too. And something to hang on the tree in gilt paper, I may even see about that. (*Putting his hand on her head.*) Oh you, my darling little songbird. (*He goes into his study and closes the door after him.*)

NORA (*softly, after a silence*): Oh, really! It isn't so. It's impossible. It must be impossible.

ANNE-MARIE (*in the doorway left*): The children are begging so hard to come in to Mama.

NORA: No, no, no, don't let them in to me! You stay with them, Anne-Marie.

ANNE-MARIE: Of course, ma'am. (*Closes the door.*)

NORA (*pale with terror*): Hurt my children — ! Poison my home? (*A moment's pause; then she tosses her head.*) That's not true. Never. Never in all the world.

ACT II

(*Same room. Beside the piano the Christmas tree now stands stripped of ornament, burned-down candle stubs on its ragged branches. Nora's street clothes lie on the sofa. Nora, alone in the room, moves restlessly about; at last she stops at the sofa and picks up her coat.*)

NORA (*dropping the coat again*): Someone's coming! (*Goes toward the door, listens.*) No — there's no one. Of course — nobody's coming today, Christmas Day — or tomorrow, either. But maybe — (*Opens the door and looks out.*) No, nothing in the mailbox. Quite empty. (*Coming forward.*) What nonsense! He won't do anything serious. Nothing terrible could happen. It's impossible. Why, I have three small children.

(*Anne-Marie, with a large carton, comes in from the room to the left.*)

ANNE-MARIE: Well, at last I found the box with the masquerade clothes.

NORA: Thanks. Put it on the table.

ANNE-MARIE (*does so*): But they're all pretty much of a mess.

NORA: Ahh! I'd love to rip them in a million pieces!

ANNE-MARIE: Oh, mercy, they can be fixed right up. Just a little patience.

NORA: Yes, I'll go get Mrs. Linde to help me.

ANNE-MARIE: Out again now? In this nasty weather? Miss Nora will catch cold — get sick.

NORA: Oh, worse things could happen — How are the children?

ANNE-MARIE: The poor mites are playing with their Christmas presents, but —

NORA: Do they ask for me much?

ANNE-MARIE: They're so used to having Mama around, you know.

NORA: Yes, but Anne-Marie, I *can't* be together with them as much as I was.

ANNE-MARIE: Well, small children get used to anything.

NORA: You think so? Do you think they'd forget their mother if she was gone for good?

ANNE-MARIE: Oh, mercy — gone for good!

NORA: Wait, tell me. Anne-Marie — I've wondered so often — how could you ever have the heart to give your child over to strangers?

ANNE-MARIE: But I had to, you know, to become little Nora's nurse.

NORA: Yes, but how could you *do* it?

ANNE-MARIE: When I could get such a good place? A girl who's poor and who's gotten in trouble is glad enough for that. Because that slippery fish, he didn't do a thing for me, you know.

NORA: But your daughter's surely forgotten you.

ANNE-MARIE: Oh, she certainly has not. She's written to me, both when she was confirmed and when she was married.

NORA (*clasping her about the neck*): You old Anne-Marie, you were a good mother for me when I was little.

ANNE-MARIE: Poor little Nora, with no other mother but me.

NORA: And if the babies didn't have one, then I know that you'd — What silly talk! (*Opening the carton.*) Go in to them. Now I'll have to — Tomorrow you can see how lovely I'll look.

ANNE-MARIE: Oh, there won't be anyone at the party as lovely as Miss Nora. (*She goes off into the room, left.*)

NORA (*begins unpacking the box, but soon throws it aside*): Oh, if I dared to go out. If only nobody would come. If only nothing would happen here while I'm out. What craziness — nobody's coming. Just don't think. This muff — needs a brushing. Beautiful gloves, beautiful gloves. Let it go. Let it go! One, two, three, four, five, six — (*With a cry.*) Oh, there they are! (*Poises to move toward the door, but remains irresolutely standing. Mrs. Linde enters from the hall, where she has removed her street clothes.*)

NORA: Oh, it's you, Kristine. There's no one else out there? How good that you've come.

MRS. LINDE: I hear you were up asking for me.

NORA: Yes, I just stopped by. There's something you really can help me with. Let's get settled on the sofa. Look, there's going to be a costume party tomorrow evening at the Stenborgs' right above us, and now Torvald wants me to go as a Neapolitan peasant girl and dance the tarantella that I learned in Capri.

MRS. LINDE: Really, are you giving a whole performance?

NORA: Torvald says yes, I should. See, here's the dress. Torvald had it made for me down there; but now it's all so tattered that I just don't know —

MRS. LINDE: Oh, we'll fix that up in no time. It's nothing more than the trimmings — they're a bit loose here and there. Needle and thread? Good, now we have what we need.

NORA: Oh, how sweet of you!

MRS. LINDE (*sewing*): So you'll be in disguise tomorrow, Nora. You know what? I'll stop by then for a moment and have a look at you all dressed up. But listen, I've absolutely forgotten to thank you for that pleasant evening yesterday.

NORA (*getting up and walking about*): I don't think it was as pleasant as usual yesterday. You should have come to town a bit sooner, Kristine — Yes, Torvald really knows how to give a home elegance and charm.

MRS. LINDE: And you do, too, if you ask me. You're not your father's daughter for nothing. But tell me, is Dr. Rank always so down in the mouth as yesterday?

NORA: No, that was quite an exception. But he goes around critically ill all the time — tuberculosis of the spine, poor man. You know, his father was a disgusting thing who kept mistresses and so on — and that's why the son's been sickly from birth.

MRS. LINDE (*lets her sewing fall to her lap*): But my dearest Nora, how do you know about such things?

NORA (*walking more jauntily*): Hmp! When you've had three children, then you've had a few visits from — from women who know something of medicine, and they tell you this and that.

MRS. LINDE (*resumes sewing; a short pause*): Does Dr. Rank come here every day?

NORA: Every blessed day. He's Torvald's best friend from childhood, and *my* good friend, too. Dr. Rank almost belongs to this house.

MRS. LINDE: But tell me — is he quite sincere? I mean, doesn't he rather enjoy flattering people?

NORA: Just the opposite. Why do you think that?

MRS. LINDE: When you introduced us yesterday, he was proclaiming that he'd often heard my name in this house; but later I noticed that your husband hadn't the slightest idea who I really was. So how could Dr. Rank — ?

NORA: But it's all true, Kristine. You see, Torvald loves me beyond words, and, as he puts it, he'd like to keep me all to himself. For a long time he'd almost be jealous if I even mentioned any of my old friends back home. So of course I dropped that. But with Dr. Rank I talk a lot about such things because he likes hearing about them.

MRS. LINDE: Now listen, Nora; in many ways you're still like a child. I'm a good deal older than you, with a little more experience. I'll tell you something: You ought to put an end to all this with Dr. Rank.

NORA: What should I put an end to?

MRS. LINDE: Both parts of it, I think. Yesterday you said something about a rich admirer who'd provide you with money —

NORA: Yes, one who doesn't exist — worse luck. So?

MRS. LINDE: Is Dr. Rank well off?

NORA: Yes, he is.

MRS. LINDE: With no dependents?

NORA: No, no one. But —

MRS. LINDE: And he's over here every day?

NORA: Yes, I told you that.

MRS. LINDE: How can a man of such refinement be so grasping?

NORA: I don't follow you at all.

MRS. LINDE: Now don't try to hide it, Nora. You think I can't guess who loaned you the forty-eight hundred crowns?

NORA: Are you out of your mind? How could you think such a thing! A friend of ours, who comes here every single day. What an intolerable situation that would have been!

MRS. LINDE: Then it really wasn't him.

NORA: No, absolutely not. It never even crossed my mind for a moment — And he had nothing to lend in those days; his inheritance came later.

MRS. LINDE: Well, I think that was a stroke of luck for you, Nora dear.

NORA: No, it never would have occurred to me to ask Dr. Rank — Still, I'm quite sure that if I had asked him —

MRS. LINDE: Which you won't, of course.

NORA: No, of course not. I can't see that I'd ever need to. But I'm quite positive that if I talked to Dr. Rank —

MRS. LINDE: Behind your husband's back?

NORA: I've got to clear up this other thing; *that's* also behind his back. I've *got* to clear it all up.

MRS. LINDE: Yes, I was saying that yesterday, but —

NORA (*pacing up and down*): A man handles these problems so much better than a woman —

MRS. LINDE: One's husband does, yes.

NORA: Nonsense. (*Stopping.*) When you pay everything you owe, then you get your note back, right?

MRS. LINDE: Yes, naturally.

NORA: And can rip it into a million pieces and burn it up — that filthy scrap of paper!

MRS. LINDE (*looking hard at her, laying her sewing aside, and rising slowly*): Nora, you're hiding something from me.

NORA: You can see it in my face?

MRS. LINDE: Something's happened to you since yesterday morning. Nora, what is it?

NORA (*hurrying toward her*): Kristine! (*Listening.*) Shh! Torvald's home. Look, go in with the children a while. Torvald can't bear all this snipping and stitching. Let Anne-Marie help you.

MRS. LINDE (*gathering up some of the things*): All right, but I'm not leaving here until we've talked this out. (*She disappears into the room, left, as Torvald enters from the hall.*)

NORA: Oh, how I've been waiting for you, Torvald dear.

HELMER: Was that the dressmaker?

NORA: No, that was Kristine. She's helping me fix up my costume. You know, it's going to be quite attractive.

HELMER: Yes, wasn't that a bright idea I had?

NORA: Brilliant! But then wasn't I good as well to give in to you?

HELMER: Good — because you give in to your husband's judgment? All right, you little goose, I know you didn't mean it like that. But I won't disturb you. You'll want to have a fitting, I suppose.

NORA: And you'll be working?

HELMER: Yes. (*Indicating a bundle of papers.*) See. I've been down to the bank. (*Starts toward his study.*)

NORA: Torvald.

HELMER (*stops*): Yes.

NORA: If your little squirrel begged you, with all her heart and soul, for something — ?

HELMER: What's that?

NORA: Then would you do it?

HELMER: First, naturally, I'd have to know what it was.

NORA: Your squirrel would scamper about and do tricks, if you'd only be sweet and give in.

HELMER: Out with it.

NORA: Your lark would be singing high and low in every room —

HELMER: Come on, she does that anyway.

NORA: I'd be a wood nymph and dance for you in the moonlight.

HELMER: Nora — don't tell me it's that same business from this morning?

NORA (*coming closer*): Yes, Torvald, I beg you, please!

HELMER: And you actually have the nerve to drag that up again?

NORA: Yes, yes, you've got to give in to me; you *have* to let Krogstad keep his job in the bank.

HELMER: My dear Nora, I've slated his job for Mrs. Linde.

NORA: That's awfully kind of you. But you could just fire another clerk instead of Krogstad.

HELMER: This is the most incredible stubbornness! Because you go and give an impulsive promise to speak up for him, I'm expected to —

NORA: That's not the reason, Torvald. It's for your own sake. That man does writing for the worst papers; you said it yourself. He could do you any amount of harm. I'm scared to death of him —

HELMER: Ah, I understand. It's the old memories haunting you.

NORA: What do you mean by that?

HELMER: Of course, you re thinking about your father.

NORA: Yes, all right. Just remember how those nasty gossips wrote in the papers about Papa and slandered him so cruelly. I think they'd have had him dismissed if the department hadn't sent you up to investigate, and if you hadn't been so kind and open-minded toward him.

HELMER: My dear Nora, there's a notable difference between your father and me. Your father's official career was hardly above reproach. But mine is; and I hope it'll stay that way as long as I hold my position.

NORA: Oh, who can ever tell what vicious minds can invent? We could be so snug and happy now in our quiet, carefree home — you and I and the children, Torvald! That's why I'm pleading with you so —

HELMER: And just by pleading for him you make it impossible for me to keep him on. It's already known at the bank that I'm firing Krogstad. What if it's rumored around now that the new bank manager was vetoed by his wife —

NORA: Yes, what then — ?

HELMER: Oh yes — as long as our little bundle of stubbornness gets her way — ! I should go and make myself ridiculous in front of the whole office — give people the idea I can be swayed by all kinds of outside pressure. Oh, you can bet I'd feel the effects of that soon enough! Besides — there's something that rules Krogstad right out at the bank as long as I'm the manager.

NORA: What's that?

HELMER: His moral failings I could maybe overlook if I had to —

NORA: Yes, Torvald, why not?

HELMER: And I hear he's quite efficient on the job. But he was a crony of mine back in my teens — one of those rash friendships that crop up again and again to embarrass you later in life. Well, I might as well say it straight out: We're on a first-name basis. And that tactless fool makes no effort at all to hide it in front of others. Quite the contrary — he thinks that entitles him to take a familiar air around me, and so every other second he comes booming out with his, "Yes, Torvald!" and "Sure thing, Torvald!" I tell you, it's been excruciating for me. He's out to make my place in the bank unbearable.

NORA: Torvald, you can't be serious about all this.

HELMER: Oh no? Why not?

NORA: Because these are such petty considerations.

HELMER: What are you saying? Petty? You think I'm petty!

NORA: No, just the opposite, Torvald dear. That's exactly why —

HELMER: Never mind. You call my motives petty; then I might as well be just that. Petty! All right! We'll put a stop to this for good. (*Goes to the hall door and calls.*) Helene!

NORA: What do you want?

HELMER (*searching among his papers*): A decision. (*The Maid comes in.*) Look here; take this letter; go out with it at once. Get hold of a messenger and have him deliver it. Quick now. It's already addressed. Wait, here's some money.

MAID: Yes, sir. (*She leaves with the letter.*)

HELMER (*straightening his papers*): There, now, little Miss Willful.

NORA (*breathlessly*): Torvald, what was that letter?

HELMER: Krogstad's notice.

NORA: Call it back, Torvald! There's still time. Oh, Torvald, call it back! Do it for my sake — for your sake, for the children's sake! Do you hear, Torvald; do it! You don't know how this can harm us.

HELMER: Too late.

NORA: Yes, too late.

HELMER: Nora, dear, I can forgive you this panic, even though basically you're insulting me. Yes, you are! Or isn't it an insult to think that *I* should be afraid of a courtroom hack's revenge? But I forgive you anyway, because this shows so beautifully how much you love me. (*Takes her in his arms.*) This is the way it should be, my darling Nora. Whatever comes, you'll see: When it really counts, I have strength and courage enough as a man to take on the whole weight myself.

NORA (*terrified*): What do you mean by that?

HELMER: The whole weight, I said.

NORA (*resolutely*): No, never in all the world.

HELMER: Good. So we'll share it, Nora, as man and wife. That's as it should be. (*Fondling her.*) Are you happy now? There, there, there — not these frightened dove's eyes. It's nothing at all but empty fantasies — Now you should run through your tarantella and practice your tambourine. I'll go to the inner office, and shut both doors, so I won't hear a thing; you can make all the noise you like. (*Turning in the doorway.*) And when Rank comes, just tell him where he can find me. (*He nods to her and goes with his papers into the study, closing the door.*)

NORA (*standing as though rooted, dazed with fright, in a whisper*): He really could do it. He will do it. He'll do it in spite of everything. No, not that, never, never! Anything but that! Escape! A way out — (*The doorbell rings.*) Dr. Rank! Anything but that! *Any-thing*, whatever it is! (*Her hands pass over her face, smoothing it; she pulls herself together, goes over and opens the hall door. Dr. Rank stands outside, hang-ing his fur coat up. During the following scene, it begins getting dark.*)

NORA: Hello, Dr. Rank. I recognized your ring. But you mustn't go in to Torvald yet; I believe he's working.

RANK: And you?

NORA: For you, I always have an hour to spare — you know that. (*He has entered, and she shuts the door after him.*)

RANK: Many thanks. I'll make use of these hours while I can.

NORA: What do you mean by that? While you can?

RANK: Does that disturb you?

NORA: Well, it's such an odd phrase. Is anything going to happen?

RANK: What's going to happen is what I've been expect-ing so long — but I honestly didn't think it would come so soon.

NORA (*gripping his arm*): What is it you've found out? Dr. Rank, you have to tell me!

RANK (*sitting by the stove*): It's all over with me. There's nothing to be done about it.

NORA (*breathing easier*): Is it you — then — ?

RANK: Who else? There's no point in lying to one's self. I'm the most miserable of all my patients, Mrs. Helmer. These past few days I've been auditing my internal accounts. Bankrupt! Within a month I'll probably be laid out and rotting in the churchyard.

NORA: Oh, what a horrible thing to say.

RANK: The thing itself is horrible. But the worst of it is all the other horror before it's over. There's only one final examination left; when I'm finished with that, I'll know about when my disintegration will begin. There's something I want to say. Helmer with his sen-

sitivity has such a sharp distaste for anything ugly. I don't want him near my sickroom.

NORA: Oh, but Dr. Rank —

RANK: I won't have him in there. Under no condition. I'll lock my door to him — As soon as I'm completely sure of the worst, I'll send you my calling card marked with a black cross, and you'll know then the wreck has started to come apart.

NORA: No, today you're completely unreasonable. And I wanted you so much to be in a really good humor.

RANK: With death up my sleeve? And then to suffer this way for somebody else's sins. Is there any justice in that? And in every single family, in some way or another, this inevitable retribution of nature goes on —

NORA (*her hands pressed over her ears*): Oh, stuff! Cheer up! Please — be gay!

RANK: Yes, I'd just as soon laugh at it all. My poor, inno-cent spine, serving time for my father's gay army days.

NORA (*by the table, left*): He was so infatuated with asparagus tips and pâté de foie gras, wasn't that it?

RANK: Yes — and with truffles.

NORA: Truffles, yes. And then with oysters, I suppose?

RANK: Yes, tons of oysters, naturally.

NORA: And then the port and champagne to go with it. It's so sad that all these delectable things have to strike at our bones.

RANK: Especially when they strike at the unhappy bones that never shared in the fun.

NORA: Ah, that's the saddest of all.

RANK (*looks searchingly at her*): Hm.

NORA (*after a moment*): Why did you smile?

RANK: No, it was you who laughed.

NORA: No, it was you who smiled, Dr. Rank!

RANK (*getting up*): You're even a bigger tease than I'd thought.

NORA: I'm full of wild ideas today.

RANK: That's obvious.

NORA (*putting both hands on his shoulders*): Dear, dear Dr. Rank, you'll never die for Torvald and me.

RANK: Oh, that loss you'll easily get over. Those who go away are soon forgotten.

NORA (*looks fearfully at him*): You believe that?

RANK: One makes new connections, and then —

NORA: Who makes new connections?

RANK: Both you and Torvald will when I'm gone. I'd say you're well under way already. What was that Mrs. Linde doing here last evening?

NORA: Oh, come — you can't be jealous of poor Kris-tine?

RANK: Oh yes, I am. She'll be my successor here in the house. When I'm down under, that woman will prob-ably —

NORA: Shh! Not so loud. She's right in there.

RANK: Today as well. So you see.

NORA: Only to sew on my dress. Good gracious, how unreasonable you are. (*Sitting on the sofa.*) Be nice now, Dr. Rank. Tomorrow you'll see how beautifully

I'll dance; and you can imagine then that I'm dancing only for you — yes, and of course for Torvald, too — that's understood. (*Takes various items out of the carton.*) Dr. Rank, sit over here and I'll show you something.

RANK (*sitting*): What's that?

NORA: Look here. Look.

RANK: Silk stockings.

NORA: Flesh-colored. Aren't they lovely? Now it's so dark here, but tomorrow — No, no, no, just look at the feet. Oh well, you might as well look at the rest.

RANK: Hm —

NORA: Why do you look so critical? Don't you believe they'll fit?

RANK: I've never had any chance to form an opinion on that.

NORA (*glancing at him a moment*): Shame on you. (*Hits him lightly on the ear with the stockings.*) That's for you. (*Puts them away again.*)

RANK: And what other splendors am I going to see now?

NORA: Not the least bit more, because you've been naughty. (*She hunts a little and rummages among her things.*)

RANK (*after a short silence*): When I sit here together with you like this, completely easy and open, then I don't know — I simply can't imagine — whatever would have become of me if I'd never come into this house.

NORA (*smiling*): Yes, I really think you feel completely at ease with us.

RANK (*more quietly, staring straight ahead*): And then to have to go away from it all —

NORA: Nonsense, you're not going away.

RANK (*his voice unchanged*): — and not even be able to leave some poor show of gratitude behind, scarcely a fleeting regret — no more than a vacant place that anyone can fill.

NORA: And if I asked you now for — No —

RANK: For what?

NORA: For a great proof of your friendship —

RANK: Yes, yes?

NORA: No, I mean — for an exceptionally big favor —

RANK: Would you really, for once, make me so happy?

NORA: Oh, you haven't the vaguest idea what it is.

RANK: All right, then tell me.

NORA: No, but I can't, Dr. Rank — it's all out of reason. It's advice and help, too — and a favor —

RANK: So much the better. I can't fathom what you're hinting at. Just speak out. Don't you trust me?

NORA: Of course. More than anyone else. You're my best and truest friend, I'm sure. That's why I want to talk to you. All right, then, Dr. Rank: There's something you can help me prevent. You know how deeply, how inexpressibly dearly Torvald loves me; he'd never hesitate a second to give up his life for me.

RANK (*leaning close to her*): Nora — do you think he's the only one —

NORA (*with a slight start*): Who — ?

RANK: Who'd gladly give up his life for you.

NORA (*heavily*): I see.

RANK: I swore to myself you should know this before I'm gone. I'll never find a better chance. Yes, Nora, now you know. And also you know now that you can trust me beyond anyone else.

NORA (*rising, natural and calm*): Let me by.

RANK (*making room for her, but still sitting*): Nora —

NORA (*in the hall doorway*): Helene, bring the lamp in. (*Goes over to the stove.*) Ah, dear Dr. Rank, that was really mean of you.

RANK (*getting up*): That I've loved you just as deeply as somebody else? Was *that* mean?

NORA: No, but that you came out and told me. That was quite unnecessary —

RANK: What do you mean? Have you known — ?

(*The Maid comes in with the lamp, sets it on the table, and goes out again.*)

RANK: Nora — Mrs. Helmer — I'm asking you: Have you known about it?

NORA: Oh, how can I tell what I know or don't know? Really, I don't know what to say — Why did you have to be so clumsy, Dr. Rank! Everything was so good.

RANK: Well, in any case, you now have the knowledge that my body and soul are at your command. So won't you speak out?

NORA (*looking at him*): After that?

RANK: Please, just let me know what it is.

NORA: You can't know anything now.

RANK: I have to. You mustn't punish me like this. Give me the chance to do whatever is humanly possible for you.

NORA: Now there's nothing you can do for me. Besides, actually, I don't need any help. You'll see — it's only my fantasies. That's what it is. Of course! (*Sits in the rocker, looks at him, and smiles.*) What a nice one you are, Dr. Rank. Aren't you a little bit ashamed, now that the lamp is here?

RANK: No, not exactly. But perhaps I'd better go — for good?

NORA: No, you certainly can't do that. You must come here just as you always have. You know Torvald can't do without you.

RANK: Yes, but *you*?

NORA: You know how much I enjoy it when you're here.

RANK: That's precisely what threw me off. You're a mystery to me. So many times I've felt you'd almost rather be with me than with Helmer.

NORA: Yes — you see, there are some people that one loves most and other people that one would almost prefer being with.

RANK: Yes, there's something to that.

NORA: When I was back home, of course I loved Papa most. But I always thought it was so much fun when I could sneak down to the maids' quarters, because they never tried to improve me, and it was always so amusing, the way they talked to each other.

RANK: Aha, so it's their place that I've filled.

NORA (*jumping up and going to him*): Oh, dear, sweet Dr. Rank, that's not what I meant at all. But you can understand that with Torvald it's just the same as with Papa —

(*The Maid enters from the hall.*)

MAID: Ma'am — please! (*She whispers to Nora and hands her a calling card.*)

NORA (*glancing at the card*): Ah! (*Slips it into her pocket.*)

RANK: Anything wrong?

NORA: No, no, not at all. It's only some — it's my new dress —

RANK: Really? But — there's your dress.

NORA: Oh, that. But this is another one — I ordered it — Torvald mustn't know —

RANK: Ah, now we have the big secret.

NORA: That's right. Just go in with him — he's back in the inner study. Keep him there as long as —

RANK: Don't worry. He won't get away. (*Goes into the study.*)

NORA (*to the Maid*): And he's standing waiting in the kitchen?

MAID: Yes, he came up by the back stairs.

NORA: But didn't you tell him somebody was here?

MAID: Yes, but that didn't do any good.

NORA: He won't leave?

MAID: No, he won't go till he's talked with you, ma'am.

NORA: Let him come in, then — but quietly. Helene, don't breathe a word about this. It's a surprise for my husband.

MAID: Yes, yes, I understand — (*Goes out.*)

NORA: This horror — it's going to happen. No, no, no, it can't happen, it mustn't. (*She goes and bolts Helmer's door. The Maid opens the hall door for Krogstad and shuts it behind him. He is dressed for travel in a fur coat, boots, and a fur cap.*)

NORA (*going toward him*): Talk softly. My husband's home.

KROGSTAD: Well, good for him.

NORA: What do you want?

KROGSTAD: Some information.

NORA: Hurry up, then. What is it?

KROGSTAD: You know, of course, that I got my notice.

NORA: I couldn't prevent it, Mr. Krogstad. I fought for you to the bitter end, but nothing worked.

KROGSTAD: Does your husband's love for you run so thin? He knows everything I can expose you to, and all the same he dares to —

NORA: How can you imagine he knows anything about this?

KROGSTAD: Ah, no — I can't imagine it either, now. It's not at all like my fine Torvald Helmer to have so much guts —

NORA: Mr. Krogstad, I demand respect for my husband!

KROGSTAD: Why, of course — all due respect. But since the lady's keeping it so carefully hidden, may I presume to ask if you're also a bit better informed than yesterday about what you've actually done?

NORA: More than you ever could teach me.

KROGSTAD: Yes, I *am* such an awful lawyer.

NORA: What is it you want from me?

KROGSTAD: Just a glimpse of how you are, Mrs. Helmer. I've been thinking about you all day long. A cashier, a night-court scribbler, a — well, a type like me also has a little of what they call a heart, you know.

NORA: Then show it. Think of my children.

KROGSTAD: Did you or your husband ever think of mine? But never mind. I simply wanted to tell you that you don't need to take this thing too seriously. For the present, I'm not proceeding with any action.

NORA: Oh no, really! Well — I knew that.

KROGSTAD: Everything can be settled in a friendly spirit. It doesn't have to get around town at all; it can stay just among us three.

NORA: My husband must never know anything of this.

KROGSTAD: How can you manage that? Perhaps you can pay me the balance?

NORA: No, not right now.

KROGSTAD: Or you know some way of raising the money in a day or two?

NORA: No way that I'm willing to use.

KROGSTAD: Well, it wouldn't have done you any good, anyway. If you stood in front of me with a fistful of bills, you still couldn't buy your signature back.

NORA: Then tell me what you're going to do with it.

KROGSTAD: I'll just hold onto it — keep it on file. There's no outsider who'll even get wind of it. So if you've been thinking of taking some desperate step —

NORA: I have.

KROGSTAD: Been thinking of running away from home —

NORA: I have!

KROGSTAD: Or even of something worse —

NORA: How could you guess that?

KROGSTAD: You can drop those thoughts.

NORA: How could you guess I was thinking of *that*?

KROGSTAD: Most of us think about *that* at first. I thought about it too, but I discovered I hadn't the courage —

NORA (*lifelessly*): I don't either.

KROGSTAD (*relieved*): That's true, you haven't the courage? You too?

NORA: I don't have it — I don't have it.

KROGSTAD: It would be terribly stupid, anyway. After that first storm at home blows out, why, then — I have here in my pocket a letter for your husband —

NORA: Telling everything?

KROGSTAD: As charitably as possible.

NORA (*quickly*): He mustn't ever get that letter. Tear it up. I'll find some way to get money.

KROGSTAD: Beg pardon, Mrs. Helmer, but I think I just told you —

NORA: Oh, I don't mean the money I owe you. Let me know how much you want from my husband, and I'll manage it.

KROGSTAD: I don't want any money from your husband.

NORA: What do you want, then?

KROGSTAD: I'll tell you what. I want to recoup, Mrs. Helmer; I want to get on in the world — and there's where your husband can help me. For a year and a half I've kept myself clean of anything disreputable — all that time struggling with the worst conditions; but I was satisfied, working my way up step by step. Now I've been written right off, and I'm just not in the mood to come crawling back. I tell you, I want to move on. I want to get back in the bank — in a better position. Your husband can set up a job for me —

NORA: He'll never do that!

KROGSTAD: He'll do it. I know him. He won't dare breathe a word of protest. And once I'm in there together with him, you just wait and see! Inside of a year, I'll be the manager's right-hand man. It'll be Nils Krogstad, not Torvald Helmer, who runs the bank.

NORA: You'll never see the day!

KROGSTAD: Maybe you think you can —

NORA: I have the courage now — for *that*.

KROGSTAD: Oh, you don't scare me. A smart, spoiled lady like you —

NORA: You'll see; you'll see!

KROGSTAD: Under the ice, maybe? Down in the freezing, coal-black water? There, till you float up in the spring, ugly unrecognizable, with your hair falling out —

NORA: You don't frighten me.

KROGSTAD: Nor do you frighten me. One doesn't do these things, Mrs. Helmer. Besides what good would it be? I'd still have him safe in my pocket.

NORA: Afterwards? When I'm no longer — ?

KROGSTAD: Are you forgetting that *I'll* be in control then over your final reputation? (*Nora stands speechless, staring at him.*) Good; now I've warned you. Don't do anything stupid. When Helmer's read my letter, I'll be waiting for his reply. And bear in mind that it's your husband himself who's forced me back to my old ways. I'll never forgive him for that. Goodbye, Mrs. Helmer. (*He goes out through the hall.*)

NORA (*goes to the hall door, opens it a crack, and listens*): He's gone. Didn't leave the letter. Oh no, no, that's impossible too! (*Opening the door more and more.*) What's that? He's standing outside — not going downstairs. He's thinking it over? Maybe he'll — ? (*A letter falls in the mailbox; then Krogstad's footsteps are heard, dying away down a flight of stairs. Nora gives a muffled cry and runs over toward the sofa table. A short pause.*) In the mailbox. (*Slips warily over to the hall door.*) It's lying there. Torvald, Torvald — now we're lost!

MRS. LINDE (*entering with the costume from the room, left*): There now, I can't see anything else to mend. Perhaps you'd like to try —

NORA (*in a hoarse whisper*): Kristine, come here.

MRS. LINDE (*tossing the dress on the sofa*): What's wrong? You look upset.

NORA: Come here. See that letter? There! Look — through the glass in the mailbox.

MRS. LINDE: Yes, yes, I see it.

NORA: That letter's from Krogstad —

MRS. LINDE: Nora — it's Krogstad who loaned you the money!

NORA: Yes, and now Torvald will find out everything.

MRS. LINDE: Believe me, Nora, it's best for both of you.

NORA: There's more you don't know. I forged a name.

MRS. LINDE: But for heaven's sake — ?

NORA: I only want to tell you that, Kristine, so that you can be my witness.

MRS. LINDE: Witness? Why should I — ?

NORA: If I should go out of my mind — it could easily happen —

MRS. LINDE: Nora!

NORA: Or anything else occurred — so I couldn't be present here —

MRS. LINDE: Nora, Nora, you aren't yourself at all!

NORA: And someone should try to take on the whole weight, all of the guilt, you follow me —

MRS. LINDE: Yes, of course, but why do you think — ?

NORA: Then you're the witness that it isn't true, Kristine. I'm very much myself; my mind right now is perfectly clear; and I'm telling you: Nobody else has known about this; I alone did everything. Remember that.

MRS. LINDE: I will. But I don't understand all this.

NORA: Oh, how could you ever understand it? It's the miracle now that's going to take place.

MRS. LINDE: The miracle?

NORA: Yes, the miracle. But it's so awful, Kristine. It mustn't take place, not for anything in the world.

MRS. LINDE: I'm going right over and talk with Krogstad.

NORA: Don't go near him; he'll do you some terrible harm!

MRS. LINDE: There was a time once when he'd gladly have done anything for me.

NORA: He?

MRS. LINDE: Where does he live?

NORA: Oh, how do I know? Yes. (*Searches in her pocket.*) Here's his card. But the letter, the letter — !

HELMER (*from the study, knocking on the door*): Nora!

NORA (*with a cry of fear*): Oh! What is it? What do you want?

HELMER: Now, now, don't be so frightened. We're not coming in. You locked the door — are you trying on the dress?

NORA: Yes, I'm trying it. I'll look just beautiful, Torvald.

MRS. LINDE (*who has read the card*): He's living right around the corner.

NORA: Yes, but what's the use? We're lost. The letter's in the box.

MRS. LINDE: And your husband has the key?

NORA: Yes, always.

MRS. LINDE: Krogstad can ask for his letter back unread; he can find some excuse —

NORA: But it's just this time that Torvald usually —

MRS. LINDE: Stall him. Keep him in there. I'll be back as quick as I can. (*She hurries out through the hall entrance.*)

NORA (*goes to Helmer's door, opens it, and peers in*): Torvald!

HELMER (*from the inner study*): Well — does one dare set foot in one's own living room at last? Come on, Rank, now we'll get a look — (*In the doorway.*) But what's this?

NORA: What, Torvald dear?

HELMER: Rank had me expecting some grand masquerade.

RANK (*in the doorway*): That was my impression, but I must have been wrong.

NORA: No one can admire me in my splendor — not till tomorrow.

HELMER: But Nora dear, you look so exhausted. Have you practiced too hard?

NORA: No, I haven't practiced at all yet.

HELMER: You know, it's necessary —

NORA: Oh, it's absolutely necessary, Torvald. But I can't get anywhere without your help. I've forgotten the whole thing completely.

HELMER: Ah, we'll soon take care of that.

NORA: Yes, take care of me, Torvald, please! Promise me that? Oh, I'm so nervous. That big party — You must give up everything this evening for me. No business — don't even touch your pen. Yes? Dear Torvald, promise?

HELMER: It's a promise. Tonight I'm totally at your service — you little helpless thing. Hm — but first there's one thing I want to — (*Goes toward the hall door.*)

NORA: What are you looking for?

HELMER: Just to see if there's any mail.

NORA: No, no, don't do that, Torvald!

HELMER: Now what?

NORA: Torvald, please. There isn't any.

HELMER: Let me look, though. (*Starts out. Nora, at the piano, strikes the first notes of the tarantella. Helmer, at the door, stops.*) Aha!

NORA: I can't dance tomorrow if I don't practice with you.

HELMER (*going over to her*): Nora dear, are you really so frightened?

NORA: Yes, so terribly frightened. Let me practice right now; there's still time before dinner. Oh, sit down and play for me, Torvald. Direct me. Teach me, the way you always have.

HELMER: Gladly, if it's what you want. (*Sits at the piano.*)

NORA (*snatches the tambourine up from the box, then a long, varicolored shawl, which she throws around herself, whereupon she springs forward and cries out*): Play for me now! Now I'll dance!

(*Helmer plays and Nora dances. Rank stands behind Helmer at the piano and looks on.*)

HELMER (*as he plays*): Slower. Slow down.

NORA: Can't change it.

HELMER: Not so violent, Nora!

NORA: Has to be just like this.

HELMER (*stopping*): No, no, that won't do at all.

NORA (*laughing and swinging her tambourine*): Isn't that what I told you?

RANK: Let me play for her.

HELMER (*getting up*): Yes, go on. I can teach her more easily then.

(*Rank sits at the piano and plays, Nora dances more and more wildly. Helmer has stationed himself by the stove and repeatedly gives her directions; she seems not to hear them; her hair loosens and falls over her shoulders; she does not notice, but goes on dancing. Mrs. Linde enters.*)

MRS. LINDE (*standing dumbfounded at the door*): Ah — !

NORA (*still dancing*): See what fun, Kristine!

HELMER: But Nora darling, you dance as if your life were at stake.

NORA: And it is.

HELMER: Rank, stop! This is pure madness. Stop it, I say!

(*Rank breaks off playing, and Nora halts abruptly.*)

HELMER (*going over to her*): I never would have believed it. You've forgotten everything I taught you.

NORA (*throwing away the tambourine*): You see for yourself.

HELMER: Well, there's certainly room for instruction here.

NORA: Yes, you see how important it is. You've got to teach me to the very last minute. Promise me that, Torvald?

HELMER: You can bet on it.

NORA: You mustn't, either today or tomorrow, think about anything else but me; you mustn't open any letters — or the mailbox —

HELMER: Ah, it's still the fear of that man —

NORA: Oh yes, yes, that too.

HELMER: Nora, it's written all over you — there's already a letter from him out there.

NORA: I don't know. I guess so. But you mustn't read such things now; there mustn't be anything ugly between us before it's all over.

RANK (*quietly to Helmer*): You shouldn't deny her.

HELMER (*putting his arm around her*): The child can have her way. But tomorrow night, after you've danced —

NORA: Then you'll be free.

MAID (*in the doorway, right*): Ma'am, dinner is served.

NORA: We'll be wanting champagne, Helene.

MAID: Very good, ma'am. (*Goes out.*)

HELMER: So — a regular banquet, hm?

NORA: Yes, a banquet — champagne till daybreak! (*Calling out.*) And some macaroons, Helene. Heaps of them — just this once.

HELMER (*taking her hands*): Now, now, now — no hysterics. Be my own little lark again.

NORA: Oh, I will soon enough. But go on in — and you, Dr. Rank. Kristine, help me put up my hair.

RANK (*whispering, as they go*): There's nothing wrong — really wrong, is there?

HELMER: Oh, of course not. It's nothing more than this childish anxiety I was telling you about. (*They go out, right.*)

NORA: Well?

MRS. LINDE: Left town.

NORA: I could see by your face.

MRS. LINDE: He'll be home tomorrow evening. I wrote him a note.

NORA: You shouldn't have. Don't try to stop anything now. After all, it's a wonderful joy, this waiting here for the miracle.

MRS. LINDE: What is it you're waiting for?

NORA: Oh, you can't understand that. Go in to them; I'll be along in a moment.

(*Mrs. Linde goes into the dining room. Nora stands a short while as if composing herself; then she looks at her watch.*)

NORA: Five. Seven hours to midnight. Twenty-four hours to the midnight after, and then the tarantella's done. Seven and twenty-four? Thirty-one hours to live.

HELMER (*in the doorway, right*): What's become of the little lark?

NORA (*going toward him with open arms*): Here's your lark!

ACT III

(*Same scene. The table, with chairs around it, has been moved to the center of the room. A lamp on the table is lit. The hall door stands open. Dance music drifts down from the floor above. Mrs. Linde sits at the table, absently paging through a book, trying to read, but apparently unable to focus her thoughts. Once or twice she pauses, tensely listening for a sound at the outer entrance.*)

MRS. LINDE (*glancing at her watch*): Not yet — and there's hardly any time left. If only he's not — (*Listening again.*) Ah, there it is. (*She goes out in the hall and cautiously opens the outer door. Quiet footsteps are heard on the stairs. She whispers.*) Come in. Nobody's here.

KROGSTAD (*in the doorway*): I found a note from you at home. What's back of all this?

MRS. LINDE: I just *had* to talk to you.

KROGSTAD: Oh? And it just *had* to be here in this house?

MRS. LINDE: At my place it was impossible; my room hasn't a private entrance. Come in, we're all alone. The maid's asleep, and the Helmers are at the dance upstairs.

KROGSTAD (*entering the room*): Well, well, the Helmers are dancing tonight? Really?

MRS. LINDE: Yes, why not?

KROGSTAD: How true — why not?

MRS. LINDE: All right, Krogstad, let's talk.

KROGSTAD: Do we two have anything more to talk about?

MRS. LINDE: We have a great deal to talk about.

KROGSTAD: I wouldn't have thought so.

MRS. LINDE: No, because you've never understood me, really.

KROGSTAD: Was there anything more to understand — except what's all too common in life? A calculating woman throws over a man the moment a better catch comes by.

MRS. LINDE: You think I'm so thoroughly calculating? You think I broke it off lightly?

KROGSTAD: Didn't you?

MRS. LINDE: Nils — is that what you really thought?

KROGSTAD: If you cared, then why did you write me the way you did?

MRS. LINDE: What else could I do? If I had to break off with you, then it was my job as well to root out everything you felt for me.

KROGSTAD (*wringing his hands*): So that was it. And this — all this, simply for money!

MRS. LINDE: Don't forget I had a helpless mother and two small brothers. We couldn't wait for you, Nils; you had such a long road ahead of you then.

KROGSTAD: That may be; but you still hadn't the right to abandon me for somebody else's sake.

MRS. LINDE: Yes — I don't know. So many, many times I've asked myself if I did have that right.

KROGSTAD (*more softly*): When I lost you, it was as if all the solid ground dissolved from under my feet. Look at me; I'm a half-drowned man now, hanging onto a wreck.

MRS. LINDE: Help may be near.

KROGSTAD: It was near — but then you came and blocked it off.

MRS. LINDE: Without my knowing it, Nils. Today for the first time I learned that it's you I'm replacing at the bank.

KROGSTAD: All right — I believe you. But now that you know, will you step aside?

MRS. LINDE: No, because that wouldn't benefit you in the slightest.

KROGSTAD: Not "benefit" me, hm! I'd step aside anyway.

MRS. LINDE: I've learned to be realistic. Life and hard, bitter necessity have taught me that.

KROGSTAD: And life's taught me never to trust fine phrases.

MRS. LINDE: Then life's taught you a very sound thing. But you do have to trust in actions, don't you?

KROGSTAD: What does that mean?

MRS. LINDE: You said you were hanging on like a half-drowned man to a wreck.

KROGSTAD: I've good reason to say that.

MRS. LINDE: I'm also like a half-drowned woman on a wreck. No one to suffer with; no one to care for.

KROGSTAD: You made your choice.

MRS. LINDE: There wasn't any choice then.

KROGSTAD: So — what of it?

MRS. LINDE: Nils, if only we two shipwrecked people could reach across to each other.

KROGSTAD: What are you saying?

MRS. LINDE: Two on one wreck are at least better off than each on his own.

KROGSTAD: Kristine!

MRS. LINDE: Why do you think I came into town?

KROGSTAD: Did you really have some thought of me?

MRS. LINDE: I have to work to go on living. All my born days, as long as I can remember, I've worked, and it's been my best and my only joy. But now I'm completely alone in the world; it frightens me to be so empty and lost. To work for yourself — there's no joy in that. Nils, give me something — someone to work for.

KROGSTAD: I don't believe all this. It's just some hysterical feminine urge to go out and make a noble sacrifice.

MRS. LINDE: Have you ever found me to be hysterical?

KROGSTAD: Can you honestly mean this? Tell me — do you know everything about my past?

MRS. LINDE: Yes.

KROGSTAD: And you know what they think I'm worth around here.

MRS. LINDE: From what you were saying before, it would seem that with me you could have been another person.

KROGSTAD: I'm positive of that.

MRS. LINDE: Couldn't it happen still?

KROGSTAD: Kristine — you're saying this in all seriousness? Yes, you are! I can see it in you. And do you really have the courage, then — ?

MRS. LINDE: I need to have someone to care for, and your children need a mother. We both need each other. Nils, I have faith that you're good at heart — I'll risk everything together with you.

KROGSTAD (gripping her hands): Kristine, thank you, thank you — Now I know I can win back a place in their eyes. Yes — but I forgot —

MRS. LINDE (listening): Shh! The tarantella. Go now! Go on!

KROGSTAD: Why? What is it?

MRS. LINDE: Hear the dance up there? When that's over, they'll be coming down.

KROGSTAD: Oh, then I'll go. But — it's all pointless. Of course, you don't know the move I made against the Helmers.

MRS. LINDE: Yes, Nils, I know.

KROGSTAD: And all the same, you have the courage to — ?

MRS. LINDE: I know how far despair can drive a man like you.

KROGSTAD: Oh, if I only could take it all back.

MRS. LINDE: You easily could — your letter's still lying in the mailbox.

KROGSTAD: Are you sure of that?

MRS. LINDE: Positive. But —

KROGSTAD (looks at her searchingly): Is that the meaning of it, then? You'll save your friend at any price. Tell me straight out. Is that it?

MRS. LINDE: Nils — anyone who's sold herself for somebody else once isn't going to do it again.

KROGSTAD: I'll demand my letter back.

MRS. LINDE: No, no.

KROGSTAD: Yes, of course. I'll stay here till Helmer comes down; I'll tell him to give me my letter again — that it only involves my dismissal — that he shouldn't read it —

MRS. LINDE: No, Nils, don't call the letter back.

KROGSTAD: But wasn't that exactly why you wrote me to come here?

MRS. LINDE: Yes, in that first panic. But it's been a whole day and night since then, and in that time I've seen such incredible things in this house. Helmer's got to learn everything; this dreadful secret has to be aired; those two have to come to a full understanding; all these lies and evasions can't go on.

KROGSTAD: Well, then, if you want to chance it. But at least there's one thing I can do, and do right away —

MRS. LINDE (listening): Go now, go, quick! The dance is over. We're not safe another second.

KROGSTAD: I'll wait for you downstairs.

MRS. LINDE: Yes, please do; take me home.

KROGSTAD: I can't believe it; I've never been so happy. (He leaves by way of the outer door; the door between the room and the hall stays open.)

MRS. LINDE (straightening up a bit and getting together her street clothes): How different now! How different! Someone to work for, to live for — a home to build. Well, it is worth the try! Oh, if they'd only come! (Listening.) Ah, there they are. Bundle up. (She picks up her hat and coat. Nora's and Helmer's voices can be heard outside; a key turns in the lock, and Helmer brings Nora into the hall almost by force. She is wearing the Italian costume with a large black shawl about her; he has on evening dress, with a black domino open over it.)

NORA (struggling in the doorway): No, no, no, not inside! I'm going up again. I don't want to leave so soon.

HELMER: But Nora dear —

NORA: Oh, I beg you, please, Torvald. From the bottom of my heart, please — only an hour more!

HELMER: Not a single minute, Nora darling. You know our agreement. Come on, in we go; you'll catch cold out here. (In spite of her resistance, he gently draws her into the room.)

MRS. LINDE: Good evening.

NORA: Kristine!

HELMER: Why, Mrs. Linde — are you here so late?

MRS. LINDE: Yes, I'm sorry, but I did want to see Nora in costume.

NORA: Have you been sitting here, waiting for me?

MRS. LINDE: Yes. I didn't come early enough; you were all upstairs; and then I thought I really couldn't leave without seeing you.

HELMER (*removing Nora's shawl*): Yes, take a good look. She's worth looking at, I can tell you that, Mrs. Linde. Isn't she lovely?

MRS. LINDE: Yes, I should say —

HELMER: A dream of loveliness, isn't she? That's what everyone thought at the party, too. But she's horribly stubborn — this sweet little thing. What's to be done with her? Can you imagine, I almost had to use force to pry her away.

NORA: Oh, Torvald, you're going to regret you didn't indulge me, even for just a half hour more.

HELMER: There, you see. She danced her tarantella and got a tumultuous hand — which was well earned, although the performance may have been a bit too naturalistic — I mean it rather overstepped the proprieties of art. But never mind — what's important is, she made a success, an overwhelming success. You think I could let her stay on after that and spoil the effect? Oh no; I took my lovely little Capri girl — my capricious little Capri girl, I should say — took her under my arm; one quick tour of the ballroom, a curtsy to every side, and then — as they say in novels — the beautiful vision disappeared. An exit should always be effective, Mrs. Linde, but that's what I can't get Nora to grasp. Phew, It's hot in here. (*Flings the domino on a chair and opens the door to his room.*) Why's it dark in here? Oh yes, of course. Excuse me. (*He goes in and lights a couple of candles.*)

NORA (*in a sharp, breathless whisper*): So?

MRS. LINDE (*quietly*): I talked with him.

NORA: And — ?

MRS. LINDE: Nora — you must tell your husband everything.

NORA (*dully*): I knew it.

MRS. LINDE: You've got nothing to fear from Krogstad, but you have to speak out.

NORA: I won't tell.

MRS. LINDE: Then the letter will.

NORA: Thanks, Kristine. I know now what's to be done. Shh!

HELMER (*reentering*): Well, then, Mrs. Linde — have you admired her?

MRS. LINDE: Yes, and now I'll say good night.

HELMER: Oh, come, so soon? Is this yours, this knitting?

MRS. LINDE: Yes, thanks. I nearly forgot it.

HELMER: Do you knit, then?

MRS. LINDE: Oh yes.

HELMER: You know what? You should embroider instead.

MRS. LINDE: Really? Why?

HELMER: Yes, because it's a lot prettier. See here, one holds the embroidery so, in the left hand, and then one guides the needle with the right — so — in an easy, sweeping curve — right?

MRS. LINDE: Yes, I guess that's —

HELMER: But, on the other hand, knitting — it can never be anything but ugly. Look, see here, the arms tucked in, the knitting needles going up and down — there's something Chinese about it. Ah, that was really a glorious champagne they served.

MRS. LINDE: Yes, good night, Nora, and don't be stubborn anymore.

HELMER: Well put, Mrs. Linde!

MRS. LINDE: Good night, Mr. Helmer.

HELMER (*accompanying her to the door*): Good night, good night. I hope you get home all right. I'd be very happy to — but you don't have far to go. Good night, good night. (*She leaves. He shuts the door after her and returns.*) There, now, at last we got her out the door. She's a deadly bore, that creature.

NORA: Aren't you pretty tired, Torvald?

HELMER: No, not a bit.

NORA: You're not sleepy?

HELMER: Not at all. On the contrary, I'm feeling quite exhilarated. But you? Yes, you really look tired and sleepy.

NORA: Yes, I'm very tired. Soon now I'll sleep.

HELMER: See! You see! I was right all along that we shouldn't stay longer.

NORA: Whatever you do is always right.

HELMER (*kissing her brow*): Now my little lark talks sense. Say, did you notice what a time Rank was having tonight?

NORA: Oh, was he? I didn't get to speak with him.

HELMER: I scarcely did either, but it's a long time since I've seen him in such high spirits. (*Gazes at her a moment, then comes nearer her.*) Hm — it's marvelous, though, to be back home again — to be completely alone with you. Oh, you bewitchingly lovely young woman!

NORA: Torvald, don't look at me like that!

HELMER: Can't I look at my richest treasure? At all that beauty that's mine, mine alone — completely and utterly.

NORA (*moving around to the other side of the table*): You mustn't talk to me that way tonight.

HELMER (*following her*): The tarantella is still in your blood. I can see — and it makes you even more enticing. Listen. The guests are beginning to go. (*Dropping his voice.*) Nora — it'll soon be quiet through this whole house.

NORA: Yes, I hope so.

HELMER: You do, don't you, my love? Do you realize — when I'm out at a party like this with you — do you know why I talk to you so little, and keep such a distance away; just send you a stolen look now and then — you know why I do it? It's because I'm imagining then that you're my secret darling, my secret young bride-to-be, and that no one suspects there's anything between us.

NORA: Yes, yes; oh, yes, I know you're always thinking of me.

HELMER: And then when we leave and I place the shawl over those fine young rounded shoulders — over that wonderful curving neck — then I pretend that you're my young bride, that we're just coming from the wedding, that for the first time I'm bringing you into my house — that for the first time I'm alone with you — completely alone with you, your trembling young beauty! All this evening I've longed for nothing but you. When I saw you turn and sway in the tarantella — my blood was pounding till I couldn't stand it — that's why I brought you down here so early —

NORA: Go away, Torvald! Leave me alone. I don't want all this.

HELMER: What do you mean? Nora, you're teasing me. You will, won't you? Aren't I your husband — ?

(A knock at the outside door.)

NORA *(startled)*: What's that?

HELMER *(going toward the hall)*: Who is it?

RANK *(outside)*: It's me. May I come in a moment?

HELMER *(with quiet irritation)*: Oh, what does he want now? *(Aloud.)* Hold on. *(Goes and opens the door.)* Oh, how nice that you didn't just pass us by!

RANK: I thought I heard your voice, and then I wanted so badly to have a look in. *(Lightly glancing about.)* Ah, me, these old familiar haunts. You have it snug and cozy in here, you two.

HELMER: You seemed to be having it pretty cozy upstairs, too.

RANK: Absolutely. Why shouldn't I? Why not take in everything in life? As much as you can, anyway, and as long as you can. The wine was superb —

HELMER: The champagne especially.

RANK: You noticed that too? It's amazing how much I could guzzle down.

NORA: Torvald also drank a lot of champagne this evening.

RANK: Oh?

NORA: Yes, and that always makes him so entertaining.

RANK: Well, why shouldn't one have a pleasant evening after a well-spent day?

HELMER: Well spent? I'm afraid I can't claim that.

RANK *(slapping him on the back)*: But I can, you see!

NORA: Dr. Rank, you must have done some scientific research today.

RANK: Quite so.

HELMER: Come now — little Nora talking about scientific research!

NORA: And can I congratulate you on the results?

RANK: Indeed you may.

NORA: Then they were good?

RANK: The best possible for both doctor and patient — certainty.

NORA *(quickly and searchingly)*: Certainty?

RANK: Complete certainty. So don't I owe myself a gay evening afterwards?

NORA: Yes, you're right, Dr. Rank.

HELMER: I'm with you — just so long as you don't have to suffer for it in the morning.

RANK: Well, one never gets something for nothing in life.

NORA: Dr. Rank — are you very fond of masquerade parties?

RANK: Yes, if there's a good array of odd disguises —

NORA: Tell me, what should we two go as at the next masquerade?

HELMER: You little featherhead — already thinking of the next!

RANK: We two? I'll tell you what: You must go as Charmed Life —

HELMER: Yes, but find a costume for that!

RANK: Your wife can appear just as she looks every day.

HELMER: That was nicely put. But don't you know what you're going to be?

RANK: Yes, Helmer, I've made up my mind.

HELMER: Well?

RANK: At the next masquerade I'm going to be invisible.

HELMER: That's a funny idea.

RANK: They say there's a hat — black, huge — have you never heard of the hat that makes you invisible? You put it on, and then no one on earth can see you.

HELMER *(suppressing a smile)*: Ah, of course.

RANK: But I'm quite forgetting what I came for. Helmer, give me a cigar, one of the dark Havanas.

HELMER: With the greatest pleasure. *(Holds out his case.)*

RANK: Thanks. *(Takes one and cuts off the tip.)*

NORA *(striking a match)*: Let me give you a light.

RANK: Thank you. *(She holds the match for him; he lights the cigar.)* And now good-bye.

HELMER: Good-bye, good-bye, old friend.

NORA: Sleep well, Doctor.

RANK: Thanks for that wish.

NORA: Wish me the same.

RANK: You? All right, if you like — Sleep well. And thanks for the light. *(He nods to them both and leaves.)*

HELMER *(his voice subdued)*: He's been drinking heavily.

NORA *(absently)*: Could be. *(Helmer takes his keys from his pocket and goes out in the hall.)* Torvald — what are you after?

HELMER: Got to empty the mailbox; it's nearly full. There won't be room for the morning papers.

NORA: Are you working tonight?

HELMER: You know I'm not. Why — what's this? Someone's been at the lock.

NORA: At the lock — ?

HELMER: Yes, I'm positive. What do you suppose — ? I can't imagine one of the maids — ? Here's a broken hairpin. Nora, it's yours —

NORA *(quickly)*: Then it must be the children —

HELMER: You'd better break them of that. Hm, hm — well, opened it after all. *(Takes the contents out and calls into the kitchen.*) Helene! Helene, would you put out the lamp in the hall. (*He returns to the room, shutting the hall door, then displays the handful of mail.*) Look how it's piled up. (*Sorting through them.*) Now what's this?

NORA (*at the window*): The letter! Oh, Torvald, no!

HELMER: Two calling cards — from Rank.

NORA: From Dr. Rank?

HELMER (*examining them*): "Dr. Rank, Consulting Physician." They were on top. He must have dropped them in as he left.

NORA: Is there anything on them?

HELMER: There's a black cross over the name. See? That's a gruesome notion. He could almost be announcing his own death.

NORA: That's just what he's doing.

HELMER: What! You've heard something? Something he's told you?

NORA: Yes. That when those cards came, he'd be taking his leave of us. He'll shut himself in now and die.

HELMER: Ah, my poor friend! Of course I knew he wouldn't be here much longer. But so soon — And then to hide himself away like a wounded animal.

NORA: If it has to happen, then it's best it happens in silence — don't you think so, Torvald?

HELMER (*pacing up and down*): He's grown right into our lives. I simply can't imagine him gone. He with his suffering and loneliness — like a dark cloud setting off our sunlit happiness. Well, maybe it's best this way. For him, at least. (*Standing still.*) And maybe for us too, Nora. Now we're thrown back on each other, completely. (*Embracing her.*) Oh you, my darling wife, how can I hold you close enough? You know what, Nora — time and again I've wished you were in some terrible danger, just so I could stake my life and soul and everything, for your sake.

NORA (*tearing herself away, her voice firm and decisive*): Now you must read your mail, Torvald.

HELMER: No, no, not tonight. I want to stay with you, dearest.

NORA: With a dying friend on your mind?

HELMER: You're right. We've both had a shock. There's ugliness between us — these thoughts of death and corruption. We'll have to get free of them first. Until then — we'll stay apart.

NORA (*clinging about his neck*): Torvald — good night! Good night!

HELMER (*kissing her on the cheek*): Good night, little songbird. Sleep well, Nora. I'll be reading my mail now. (*He takes the letters into his room and shuts the door after him.*)

NORA (*with bewildered glances, groping about, seizing Helmer's domino, throwing it around her, and speaking in short, hoarse, broken whispers*): Never see him again. Never, never. (*Putting her shawl over her head.*) Never see the children either — them, too. Never, never. Oh, the freezing black water! The depths — down — Oh, I wish it were over — He has it now; he's reading it — now. Oh no, no, not yet.

Torvald, good-bye, you and the children — (*She starts for the hall; as she does, Helmer throws open his door and stands with an open letter in his hand.*)

HELMER: Nora!

NORA (*screams*): Oh — !

HELMER: What is this? You know what's in this letter?

NORA: Yes, I know. Let me go! Let me out!

HELMER (*holding her back*): Where are you going?

NORA (*struggling to break loose*): You can't save me, Torvald!

HELMER (*slumping back*): True! Then it's true what he writes? How horrible! No, no, it's impossible — it can't be true.

NORA: It *is* true. I've loved you more than all this world.

HELMER: Ah, none of your slippery tricks.

NORA (*taking one step toward him*): Torvald — !

HELMER: What *is* this you've blundered into!

NORA: Just let me loose. You're not going to suffer for my sake. You're not going to take on my guilt.

HELMER: No more playacting. (*Locks the hall door.*) You stay right here and give me a reckoning. You understand what you've done? Answer! You understand?

NORA (*looking squarely at him, her face hardening*): Yes. I'm beginning to understand everything now.

HELMER (*striding about*): Oh, what an awful awakening! In all these eight years — she who was my pride and joy — a hypocrite, a liar — worse, worse — a criminal! How infinitely disgusting it all is! The shame! (*Nora says nothing and goes on looking straight at him. He stops in front of her.*) I should have suspected something of the kind. I should have known. All your father's flimsy values — Be still! All your father's flimsy values have come out in you. No religion, no morals, no sense of duty — Oh, how I'm punished for letting him off! I did it for your sake, and you repay me like this.

NORA: Yes, like this.

HELMER: Now you've wrecked all my happiness — ruined my whole future. Oh, it's awful to think of. I'm in a cheap little grafter's hands; he can do anything he wants with me, ask for anything, play with me like a puppet — and I can't breathe a word. I'll be swept down miserably into the depths on account of a featherbrained woman.

NORA: When I'm gone from this world, you'll be free.

HELMER: Oh, quit posing. Your father had a mess of those speeches too. What good would that ever do me if you were gone from this world, as you say? Not the slightest. He can still make the whole thing known; and if he does, I could be falsely suspected as your accomplice. They might even think that I was behind it — that I put you up to it. And all that I can thank you for — you that I've coddled the whole of our marriage. Can you see now what you've done to me?

NORA (*icily calm*): Yes.

HELMER: It's so incredible, I just can't grasp it. But we'll have to patch up whatever we can. Take off the shawl. I said, take it off! I've got to appease him somehow or other. The thing has to be hushed up at any cost. And as for you and me, it's got to seem like everything between us is just as it was — to the outside world, that is. You'll go right on living in this house, of course. But you can't be allowed to bring up the children; I don't dare trust you with them — Oh, to have to say this to someone I've loved so much! Well, that's done with. From now on happiness doesn't matter; all that matters is saving the bits and pieces, the appearance — (*The doorbell rings. Helmer starts.*) What's that? And so late. Maybe the worst — ? You think he'd — ? Hide, Nora! Say you're sick. (*Nora remains standing motionless. Helmer goes and opens the door.*)

MAID (*half dressed, in the hall*): A letter for Mrs. Helmer.

HELMER: I'll take it. (*Snatches the letter and shuts the door.*) Yes, it's from him. You don't get it; I'm reading it myself.

NORA: Then read it.

HELMER (*by the lamp*): I hardly dare. We may be ruined, you and I. But — I've got to know. (*Rips open the letter, skims through a few lines, glances at an enclosure, then cries out joyfully.*) Nora! (*Nora looks inquiringly at him.*) Nora! Wait — better check it again — Yes, yes, it's true. I'm saved. Nora, I'm saved!

NORA: And I?

HELMER: You too, of course. We're both saved, both of us. Look. He's sent back your note. He says he's sorry and ashamed — that a happy development in his life — oh, who cares what he says! Nora, we're saved! No one can hurt you. Oh, Nora, Nora — but first, this ugliness all has to go. Let me see — (*Takes a look at the note.*) No, I don't want to see it; I want the whole thing to fade like a dream. (*Tears the note and both letters to pieces, throws them into the stove and watches them burn.*) There — now there's nothing left — He wrote that since Christmas Eve you — Oh, they must have been three terrible days for you, Nora.

NORA: I fought a hard fight.

HELMER: And suffered pain and saw no escape but — No, we're not going to dwell on anything unpleasant. We'll just be grateful and keep on repeating: It's over now, it's over! You hear me, Nora? You don't seem to realize — it's over. What's it mean — that frozen look? Oh, poor little Nora, I understand. You can't believe I've forgiven you. But I have, Nora; I swear I have. I know that what you did, you did out of love for me.

NORA: That's true.

HELMER: You loved me the way a wife ought to love her husband. It's simply the means that you couldn't judge. But you think I love you any the less for not knowing how to handle your affairs? No, no — just lean on me; I'll guide you and teach you. I wouldn't be a man if this feminine helplessness didn't make you twice as attractive to me. You mustn't mind

those sharp words I said — that was all in the first confusion of thinking my world had collapsed. I've forgiven you, Nora; I swear I've forgiven you.

NORA: My thanks for your forgiveness. (*She goes out through the door, right.*)

HELMER: No, wait — (*Peers in.*) What are you doing in there?

NORA (*inside*): Getting out of my costume.

HELMER (*by the open door*): Yes, do that. Try to calm yourself and collect your thoughts again, my frightened little songbird. You can rest easy now; I've got wide wings to shelter you with. (*Walking about close by the door.*) How snug and nice our home is, Nora. You're safe here; I'll keep you like a hunted dove I've rescued out of a hawk's claws. I'll bring peace to your poor, shuddering heart. Gradually it'll happen, Nora; you'll see. Tomorrow all this will look different to you; then everything will be as it was. I won't have to go on repeating I forgive you; you'll feel it for yourself. How can you imagine I'd ever conceivably want to disown you — or even blame you in any way? Ah, you don't know a man's heart, Nora. For a man there's something indescribably sweet and satisfying in knowing he's forgiven his wife — and forgiven her out of a full and open heart. It's as if she belongs to him in two ways now: In a sense he's given her fresh into the world again, and she's become his wife and his child as well. From now on that's what you'll be to me — you little, bewildered, helpless thing. Don't be afraid of anything, Nora; just open your heart to me, and I'll be conscience and will to you both — (*Nora enters in her regular clothes.*) What's this? Not in bed? You've changed your dress?

NORA: Yes, Torvald, I've changed my dress.

HELMER: But why now, so late?

NORA: Tonight I'm not sleeping.

HELMER: But Nora dear —

NORA (*looking at her watch*): It's still not so very late. Sit down, Torvald; we have a lot to talk over. (*She sits at one side of the table.*)

HELMER: Nora — what is this? That hard expression —

NORA: Sit down. This'll take some time. I have a lot to say.

HELMER (*sitting at the table directly opposite her*): You worry me, Nora. And I don't understand you.

NORA: No, that's exactly it. You don't understand me. And I've never understood you either — until tonight. No, don't interrupt. You can just listen to what I say. We're closing out accounts, Torvald.

HELMER: How do you mean that?

NORA (*after a short pause*): Doesn't anything strike you about our sitting here like this?

HELMER: What's that?

NORA: We've been married now eight years. Doesn't it occur to you that this is the first time we two, you and I, man and wife, have ever talked seriously together?

HELMER: What do you mean — seriously?

NORA: In eight whole years — longer even — right from

our first acquaintance, we've never exchanged a serious word on any serious thing.

HELMER: You mean I should constantly go and involve you in problems you couldn't possibly help me with?

NORA: I'm not talking of problems. I'm saying that we've never sat down seriously together and tried to get to the bottom of anything.

HELMER: But dearest, what good would that ever do you?

NORA: That's the point right there: You've never understood me. I've been wronged greatly, Torvald — first by Papa, and then by you.

HELMER: What! By us — the two people who've loved you more than anyone else?

NORA (*shaking her head*): You never loved me. You've thought it fun to be in love with me, that's all.

HELMER: Nora, what a thing to say!

NORA: Yes, it's true now, Torvald. When I lived at home with Papa, he told me all his opinions, so I had the same ones too; or if they were different I hid them, since he wouldn't have cared for that. He used to call me his doll-child, and he played with me the way I played with my dolls. Then I came into your house —

HELMER: How can you speak of our marriage like that?

NORA (*unperturbed*): I mean, then I went from Papa's hands into yours. You arranged everything to your own taste, and so I got the same taste as you — or I pretended to; I can't remember. I guess a little of both, first one, then the other. Now when I look back, it seems as if I'd lived here like a beggar — just from hand to mouth. I've lived by doing tricks for you, Torvald. But that's the way you wanted it. It's a great sin what you and Papa did to me. You're to blame that nothing's become of me.

HELMER: Nora, how unfair and ungrateful you are! Haven't you been happy here?

NORA: No, never. I thought so — but I never have.

HELMER: Not — not happy!

NORA: No, only lighthearted. And you've always been so kind to me. But our home's been nothing but a playpen. I've been your doll-wife here, just as at home I was Papa's doll-child. And in turn the children have been my dolls. I thought it was fun when you played with me, just as they thought it fun when I played with them. That's been our marriage, Torvald.

HELMER: There's some truth in what you're saying — under all the raving exaggeration. But it'll all be different after this. Playtime's over; now for the schooling.

NORA: Whose schooling — mine or the children's?

HELMER: Both yours and the children's, dearest.

NORA: Oh, Torvald, you're not the man to teach me to be a good wife to you.

HELMER: And you can say that?

NORA: And I — how am I equipped to bring up children?

HELMER: Nora!

NORA: Didn't you say a moment ago that that was no job to trust me with?

HELMER: In a flare of temper! Why fasten on that?

NORA: Yes, but you were so very right. I'm not up to the job. There's another job I have to do first. I have to try to educate myself. You can't help me with that. I've got to do it alone. And that's why I'm leaving you now.

HELMER (*jumping up*): What's that?

NORA: I have to stand completely alone, if I'm ever going to discover myself and the world out there. So I can't go on living with you.

HELMER: Nora, Nora!

NORA: I want to leave right away. Kristine should put me up for the night —

HELMER: You're insane! You've no right! I forbid you!

NORA: From here on, there's no use forbidding me anything. I'll take with me whatever is mine. I don't want a thing from you, either now or later.

HELMER: What kind of madness is this!

NORA: Tomorrow I'm going home — I mean, home where I came from. It'll be easier up there to find something to do.

HELMER: Oh, you blind, incompetent child!

NORA: I must learn to be competent, Torvald.

HELMER: Abandon your home, your husband, your children! And you're not even thinking what people will say.

NORA: I can't be concerned about that. I only know how essential this is.

HELMER: Oh, it's outrageous. So you'll run out like this on your most sacred vows.

NORA: What do you think are my most sacred vows?

HELMER: And I have to tell you that! Aren't they your duties to your husband and children?

NORA: I have other duties equally sacred.

HELMER: That isn't true. What duties are they?

NORA: Duties to myself.

HELMER: Before all else, you're a wife and a mother.

NORA: I don't believe in that anymore. I believe that before all else, I'm a human being, no less than you — or anyway, I ought to try to become one. I know the majority thinks you're right, Torvald, and plenty of books agree with you, too. But I can't go on believing what the majority says, or what's written in books. I have to think over these things myself and try to understand them.

HELMER: Why can't you understand your place in your own home? On a point like that, isn't there one everlasting guide you can turn to? Where's your religion?

NORA: Oh, Torvald, I'm really not sure what religion is.

HELMER: What — ?

NORA: I only know what the minister said when I was confirmed. He told me religion was this thing and that. When I get clear and away by myself, I'll go into that problem too. I'll see if what the minister said was right, or, in any case, if it's right for me.

HELMER: A young woman your age shouldn't talk like that. If religion can't move you, I can try to rouse your conscience. You do have some moral feeling? Or, tell me — has that gone too?

NORA: It's not easy to answer that, Torvald. I simply don't know. I'm all confused about these things. I just know I see them so differently from you. I find out for one thing, that the law's not at all what I'd thought — but I can't get it through my head that the law is fair. A woman hasn't a right to protect her dying father or save her husband's life! I can't believe that.

HELMER: You talk like a child. You don't know anything of the world you live in.

NORA: No, I don't. But now I'll begin to learn for myself. I'll try to discover who's right, the world or I.

HELMER: Nora, you're sick; you've got a fever. I almost think you're out of your head.

NORA: I've never felt more clearheaded and sure in my life.

HELMER: And — clearheaded and sure — you're leaving your husband and children?

NORA: Yes.

HELMER: Then there's only one possible reason.

NORA: What?

HELMER: You no longer love me.

NORA: No. That's exactly it.

HELMER: Nora! You can't be serious!

NORA: Oh, this is so hard, Torvald — you've been so kind to me always. But I can't help it. I don't love you anymore.

HELMER (*struggling for composure*): Are you also clearheaded and sure about that?

NORA: Yes, completely. That's why I can't go on staying here.

HELMER: Can you tell me what I did to lose your love?

NORA: Yes, I can tell you. It was this evening when the miraculous thing didn't come — then I knew you weren't the man I'd imagined.

HELMER: Be more explicit; I don't follow you.

NORA: I've waited now so patiently eight long years — for, my Lord, I know miracles don't come every day. Then this crisis broke over me, and such a certainty filled me: *Now* the miraculous event would occur. While Krogstad's letter was lying out there, I never for an instant dreamed that you could give in to his terms. I was so utterly sure you'd say to him: Go on, tell your tale to the whole wide world. And when he'd done that —

HELMER: Yes, what then? When I'd delivered my own wife into shame and disgrace — !

NORA: When he'd done that, I was so utterly sure that you'd step forward, take the blame on yourself and say: I am the guilty one.

HELMER: Nora — !

NORA: You're thinking I'd never accept such a sacrifice from you? No, of course not. But what good would my protests be against you? That was the miracle I was waiting for, in terror and hope. And to stave that off, I would have taken my life.

HELMER: I'd gladly work for you day and night, Nora — and take on pain and deprivation. But there's no one who gives up honor for love.

Janet McTeer as Nora Helmer in Anthony Page's production of *A Doll House* at the Belasco Theater on Broadway, 1997. McTeer's interpretation of the role electrified audiences who, according to Ben Brantley, found "previously hidden nuances in Ibsen's landmark work."

NORA: Millions of women have done just that.

HELMER: Oh, you think and talk like a silly child.

NORA: Perhaps. But you neither think nor talk like the man I could join myself to. When your big fright was over — and it wasn't from any threat against me, only for what might damage you — when all the danger was past, for you it was just as if nothing had happened. I was exactly the same, your little lark, your doll, that you'd have to handle with double care now that I'd turned out so brittle and frail. (*Gets up.*) Torvald — in that instant it dawned on me that for eight years I've been living here with a stranger, and that I'd even conceived three children — oh, I can't stand the thought of it! I could tear myself to bits.

HELMER (*heavily*): I see. There's a gulf that's opened between us — that's clear. Oh, but Nora, can't we bridge it somehow?

NORA: The way I am now, I'm no wife for you.

HELMER: I have the strength to make myself over.

NORA: Maybe — if your doll gets taken away.

HELMER: But to part! To part from you! No, Nora, no — I can't imagine it.

NORA (*going out, right*): All the more reason why it has to be. (*She reenters with her coat and a small overnight bag, which she puts on a chair by the table.*)

HELMER: Nora, Nora, not now! Wait till tomorrow.

NORA: I can't spend the night in a strange man's room.

HELMER: But couldn't we live here like brother and sister —

NORA: You know very well how long that would last. (*Throws her shawl about her.*) Good-bye, Torvald. I won't look in on the children. I know they're in better hands than mine. The way I am now, I'm no use to them.

HELMER: But someday, Nora — someday — ?

NORA: How can I tell? I haven't the least idea what'll become of me.

HELMER: But you're my wife, now and wherever you go.

NORA: Listen, Torvald — I've heard that when a wife deserts her husband's house just as I'm doing, then the law frees him from all responsibility. In any case, I'm freeing you from being responsible. Don't feel yourself bound, any more than I will. There has to be absolute freedom for us both. Here, take your ring back. Give me mine.

HELMER: That too?

NORA: That too.

HELMER: There it is.

NORA: Good. Well, now it's all over. I'm putting the keys here. The maids know all about keeping up the house — better than I do. Tomorrow, after I've left town, Kristine will stop by to pack up everything that's mine from home. I'd like those things shipped up to me.

HELMER: Over! All over! Nora, won't you ever think about me?

NORA: I'm sure I'll think of you often, and about the children and the house here.

HELMER: May I write you?

NORA: No — never. You're not to do that.

HELMER: Oh, but let me send you —

NORA: Nothing. Nothing.

HELMER: Or help you if you need it.

NORA: No. I accept nothing from strangers.

HELMER: Nora — can I never be more than a stranger to you?

NORA (*picking up the overnight bag*): Ah, Torvald — it would take the greatest miracle of all —

HELMER: Tell me the greatest miracle!

NORA: You and I both would have to transform ourselves to the point that — Oh, Torvald, I've stopped believing in miracles.

HELMER: But I'll believe. Tell me! Transform ourselves to the point that — ?

NORA: That our living together could be a true marriage. (*She goes out down the hall.*)

HELMER (*sinks down on a chair by the door, face buried in his hands*): Nora! Nora! (*Looking about and rising.*) Empty. She's gone. (*A sudden hope leaps in him.*) The greatest miracle — ?

(*From below, the sound of a door slamming shut.*)

COMMENTARIES

Ibsen wrote about his own work, both in his letters to producers and actors and in his notes describing the development of his plays. Such notes reveal his concern, his insights as he wrote the plays, and his motives. Sometimes what he says about the plays does not completely square with modern interpretations. On the other hand, he explains in his notes that the circumstances of women in modern society were much on his mind when he was working on *A Doll House*.

Ibsen's "Notes for the Modern Tragedy" is remarkable for suggesting a separate sensibility (spiritual law) for men and for women. His observations about the society in which women live — and in which Nora is confounded — sound as if they could have been written a century later than they were. When

Bernard Shaw wrote his comments on *A Doll House,* the play was a popular shocker; Shaw's observations were designed to help audiences interpret the play's actions more carefully. He is one of the earliest critics of the play, and one must remember while reading Shaw that some productions of the play changed the ending to make it happy. Muriel C. Bradbrook's discussion of *A Doll House* focuses on the moral bankruptcy of Nora's situation, which is to say the situation of all wives of the period.

Henrik Ibsen (1828–1906)
NOTES FOR THE MODERN TRAGEDY   *1878*
TRANSLATED BY A. G. CHATER

Ibsen's first notes for A Doll House *were jotted down on October 19, 1878. They show that his thinking on the relations between men and women was considerably sophisticated and that the material for the play had been gestating. His comments indicate that the essentially male society he knew was one of his central concerns in the play.*

There are two kinds of spiritual law, two kinds of conscience, one in man and another, altogether different, in woman. They do not understand each other; but in practical life the woman is judged by man's law, as though she were not a woman but a man.

The wife in the play ends by having no idea of what is right or wrong; natural feeling on the one hand and belief in authority on the other have altogether bewildered her.

A woman cannot be herself in the society of the present day, which is an exclusively masculine society, with laws framed by men and with a judicial system that judges feminine conduct from a masculine point of view.

She has committed forgery, and she is proud of it; for she did it out of love for her husband, to save his life. But this husband with his commonplace principles of honor is on the side of the law and looks at the question from the masculine point of view.

Spiritual conflicts. Oppressed and bewildered by the belief in authority, she loses faith in her moral right and ability to bring up her children. Bitterness. A mother in modern society, like certain insects who go away and die when she has done her duty in the propagation of the race. Love of life, of home, of husband and children and family. Now and then a womanly shaking off of her thoughts. Sudden return of anxiety and terror. She must bear it all alone. The catastrophe approaches, inexorably, inevitably. Despair, conflict, and destruction.

(Krogstad has acted dishonorably and thereby become well-to-do; now his prosperity does not help him, he cannot recover his honor.)

Bernard Shaw (1856–1950)
A DOLL'S HOUSE   *1891*

One of the first English men of letters to pay close attention to Ibsen's work was Bernard Shaw. While beginning to write his own plays, Shaw also spent time in the theater as a critic. His landmark book The Quintessence of Ibsenism *(1891; rev. ed. 1913), in which this comment on A Doll House appears, is a thorough discussion not only of the individual plays that Ibsen had produced but also of their implication for future literature. Shaw saw the significance of the new realism and its implications for the audiences of the late nineteenth century. He saw, too, that Ibsen's brand of realism would have an effect on the beliefs of his audiences, that Ibsen's drama was a drama of important ideas. In the following excerpt Shaw is especially sensitive to the feminist issues that are at the heart of the play, and he pays close attention to Nora's character development.*

Unfortunately, *Pillars of Society,* as a propagandist play, is disabled by the circumstance that the hero, being a fraudulent hypocrite in the ordinary police-court sense of the phrase, would hardly be accepted as a typical pillar of society by the class he represents. Accordingly, Ibsen took care next time to make his idealist irreproachable from the standpoint of the ordinary idealist morality. In the famous *Doll's House,* the pillar of society who owns the doll is a model husband, father, and citizen. In his little household, with the three darling children and the affectionate little wife, all on the most loving terms with one another, we have the sweet home, the womanly woman, the happy family life of the idealist's dream. Mrs. Nora Helmer is happy in the belief that she has attained a valid realization of all these illusions; that she is an ideal wife and mother; and that Helmer is an ideal husband who would, if the necessity arose, give his life to save her reputation. A few simply contrived incidents disabuse her effectually on all these points. One of her earliest acts of devotion to her husband has been the secret raising of a sum of money to enable him to make a tour which was necessary to restore his health. As he would have broken down sooner than go into debt, she has had to persuade him that the money was a gift from her father. It was really obtained from a moneylender, who refused to make her the loan unless she induced her father to endorse the promissory note. This being impossible, as her father was dying at the time, she took the shortest way out of the difficulty by writing the name herself, to the entire satisfaction of the moneylender, who, though not at all duped, knew that forged bills are often the surest to be paid. Since then she has slaved in secret at scrivener's work until she has nearly paid off the debt.

At this point Helmer is made manager of the bank in which he is employed; and the moneylender, wishing to obtain a post there, uses the forged bill to force Nora to exert her influence with Helmer on his behalf. But she, having a hearty contempt for the man, cannot be persuaded by him that there was any harm in putting her father's name on the bill, and ridicules the suggestion that the law would not recognize that she was right under the circumstances. It is her husband's own contemptuous denunciation of a forgery formerly committed by the moneylender himself that destroys her self-satisfaction and opens her eyes to her ignorance of the serious business of the world to which her husband belongs: the world outside the home he shares with her. When he goes on to tell her that commercial dishonesty is generally to be traced to the influence of bad mothers, she begins to perceive that the happy way in which she plays with the children, and the care she takes to dress them nicely, are not sufficient to constitute her a fit person to train them. To redeem the forged bill, she resolves to borrow the balance due upon it from an intimate friend of the family. She has learnt to coax her husband into giving her what she asks by appealing to his affection for her: that is, by playing all sorts of pretty tricks until he is wheedled into an amorous humor. This plan she has adopted without thinking about it, instinctively taking the line of least resistance with him. And now she naturally takes the same line with her husband's friend. An unexpected declaration of love from him is the result; and it at once explains to her the real nature of the domestic influence she has been so proud of.

All her illusions about herself are now shattered. She sees herself as an ignorant and silly woman, a dangerous mother, and a wife kept for her husband's pleasure merely; but she clings all the harder to her illusion about him: he is still the ideal husband who would make any sacrifice to rescue her from ruin. She resolves to kill herself rather than allow him to destroy his own career by taking the forgery on himself to save her reputation. The final disillusion comes when he, instead of at once proposing to pursue this ideal line of conduct when he hears of the forgery, naturally enough flies into a vulgar rage and heaps invective on her for disgracing him. Then she sees that their whole family life has been a fiction: their home a mere doll's house in which they have been playing at ideal husband and father, wife and mother. So she leaves him then and there and goes out into the real world to find out its reality for herself, and to gain some position not fundamentally false, refusing to see her children again until she is fit to be in charge of them, or to live with him until she and he become capable of a more honorable relation to one another. He at first cannot understand what has happened, and flourishes the shattered ideals over her as if they were as potent as ever. He presents the course most agreeable to him — that of her staying at home and avoiding a scandal — as her duty to her husband, to her children, and to her religion; but the magic of these disguises is gone; and at last even he understands what has really happened, and sits down alone to wonder whether that more honorable relation can ever come to pass between them.

Muriel C. Bradbrook (1909–1993)
A DOLL'S HOUSE: IBSEN THE MORALIST   *1948*

In her important study of Ibsen, Ibsen: The Norwegian, *Muriel Bradbrook discusses all the important plays, but she reserves a special place for* A Doll House. *In her analysis she suggests that Nora slowly discovers the fundamental bankruptcy of her marriage. Bradbrook calls it "eight years' prostitution." She also shows the true extent of Torvald's possessiveness and immaturity. As Bradbrook says, the true moment of recognition — in the Greek tragic sense — occurs when Nora sees both herself and Torvald in their true nature. Bradbrook also helps us see the full implication of Nora's leaving her home. She can never hope again for the comforts she has enjoyed as Torvald's wife.*

Poor Nora, living by playing her tricks like a little pet animal, sensing how to manage Torvald by those pettinesses in his character she does not know she knows of, is too vulnerably sympathetic to find her life-work in reading John Stuart Mill. At the end she still does not understand the strange world in which she has done wrong by forging a signature. She does understand that she has lived by what Virginia Woolf called "the slow waterlogged sinking of her will into his." And this picture is built up for her and for us by the power of structural implication, a form of writing particularly suited to drama, where the latent possibilities of a long stretch of past time can be thrown into relief by a crisis. In *A Doll's House*, the past is not only lighted up by the present, as a transparency might be lit up with a lamp; the past is changed by the present so that it becomes a different thing. Nora's marriage becomes eight years' prostitution, as she gradually learns the true nature of her relations with Torvald and the true nature of Torvald's feelings for her.

In Act I, no less than six different episodes bring out the war that is secretly waged between his masculine dictatorship and her feminine wiles:

Her wheedling him for money with a simple transference: "Let us do as *you* suggest. . . ."

Her promise to Christine: "Just leave it to me: I will broach the matter very cleverly." She is evidently habituated to and aware of her own technique.

Her description of how she tried to coax Torvald into taking the holiday and how she was saving up the story of the bond "for when I am no longer as good-looking as I am now." She knows the precarious nature of her hold.

Her method of asking work for Christine by putting Christine also into a (completely bogus) position of worshiping subservience to Torvald.

Her boast to Krogstad about her influence. Whilst this may be a justifiable triumph over her tormentor, it is an unconscious betrayal of Torvald (witness his fury in Act II at the idea of being thought uxorious).

After this faceted exposition, the treatment grows much broader. Nora admits Torvald's jealousy: Yet she flirts with Rank, aware but not acknowledging the grounds of her control. The pressure of implication remains constant throughout: It is comparable with the effect of a dialect, coloring all that is said. To take a few lines at random from the dialogue of Nora and Rank in Act II:

> NORA (*putting her hand on his shoulder*): Dear, dear Dr. Rank! Death mustn't take you away from Torvald and me. [Nora is getting demonstrative as she senses Rank's responsiveness, and her hopes of obtaining a loan from him rise. Hence her warmth of feeling, purely seductive.]
>
> RANK: It is a loss you will easily recover from. Those who are gone away are soon forgotten. [Poor Rank is reminded by that "Torvald and me" how little he really counts to Nora.]
>
> NORA (*anxiously*): Do you believe that? [Rank has awakened her thoughts of what may happen if *she* has to go away.]

Her methods grow more desperate — the open appeal to Torvald to keep Krogstad and the frantic expedient of the tarantella. In the last act her fate is upon her; yet in spite of all her terror and Torvald's tipsy amorousness, she still believes in his chivalry and devotion. This extraordinary self-deception is perhaps the subtlest and most telling implication of all. Practice had left her theory unshaken: So when the crash comes, she cries, "I have been living with a strange man," yet it was but the kind of man her actions had always implied him to be. Her vanity had completely prevented her from recognizing what she was doing, even though she had become such an expert at doing it.

Torvald is more gradually revealed. In the first act he appears indulgent, perhaps a trifle inclined to nag about the macaroons and to preach, but virtually a more efficient David Copperfield curbing a rather better-trained Dora. In the second act, his resentment and his pleasure alike uncover the deeper bases of his dominance. His anger at the prospect of being thought under his wife's influence and his fury at the imputation of narrow-mindedness show that it is really based on his own cowardice, the need for something weaker to bully: This is confirmed when he gloats over Nora's panic as evidence of her love for him, and over her agitation in the tarantella ("you little helpless thing!"). His love of order and his fastidiousness, when joined to such qualities, betray a set personality; and the last act shows that he has neither control nor sympathy on the physical level. But he is no fool, and his integrity is not all cowardice. Doubtless, debt or forgery really was abhorrent to him.

The climax of the play comes when Nora sees Torvald and sees herself: It is an *anagnorisis,* a recognition. Her life is cored like an apple. For she has had no life apart from this. Behind the irrelevant program for self-education there stands a woman, pitifully inexperienced, numbed by emotional shock, but with a newfound will to face what has happened, to accept her bankruptcy, as, in a very different way, Peer Gynt had at last accepted his.

"Yes, I am beginning to understand. . . ." she says. "What you did," observes the now magnanimous Torvald, "you did out of love for me." "That is true," says Nora: And she calls him to a "settling of accounts," not in any spirit of hostility but in an attempt to organize vacancy. "I have made nothing of my life. . . . I must stand quite alone . . . it is necessary to me . . ." That is really the program. *Ainsi tout leur a craqué dans les mains.*°

The spare and laminated speech gains its effect by inference and riddle. But these are the characteristic virtues of Norse. Irony is its natural weapon. Ibsen was working with the grain of the language. It was no accident that it fell to a Norwegian to take that most finely tooled art, the drama, and bring it to a point and precision so nice that literally not a phrase is without its direct contribution to the structure. The unrelenting cohesion of *A Doll's House* is perhaps, like that of the *Oedipus the King,* too hard on the playgoer; he is allowed no relief. Nora cannot coo to her baby without saying: "My sweet little *baby doll!*" or play with her children without choosing, significantly, *Hide and Seek.* Ibsen will not allow the smallest action to escape from the psychopathology of everyday life. However, a play cannot be acted so that every moment is tense with significance, and, in practice, an actor, for the sake of light and shade, will probably slur some of Ibsen's points, deliberately or unconsciously. The tension between the characters is such that the slightest movement of one sets all the others quivering. But this is partly because they are seen with such detachment, like a clear-cut intaglio. The play is, above all, articulated.

That is not to say that it is the mere dissection of a problem. Perhaps Rank and Mrs. Linde would have been more subtly wrought into the action at a later date; but the tight control kept over Nora and Torvald does not mean that they can be

---

Ainsi . . . mains: Thus everything has shattered in their hands.

exhausted by analysis or staled by custom. They are so far in advance of the characters of *Pillars of Society* that they are capable of the surprising yet inevitable development that marks the character conceived "in the round," the character that is, in Ibsen's phrase, fully "seen."

Consider, for example, Torvald's soliloquy whilst Nora is taking off her masquerade dress. It recalls at one moment Dickens's most unctuous hypocrites — "Here I will protect you like a hunted dove that I have saved from the claws of the hawk!"— at another Meredith's Willoughby Patterne° —"Only be frank and open with me and I will be both will and conscience to you"— yet from broadest caricature to sharpest analysis, it remains the self-glorified strut of the one character, the bank clerk in his pride, cousin to Peer Gynt, that typical Norwegian, and to Hjalmer Ekdal, the toiling breadwinner of the studio.

Whilst the Ibsenites might have conceded that Torvald is Art, they would probably have contended that Nora is Truth. Nora, however, is much more than a Revolting Wife. She is not a sour misanthropist or a fighting suffragette, but a lovely young woman who knows that she still holds her husband firmly infatuated after eight years of marriage. . . .

In leaving her husband Nora is seeking a fuller life as a human being. She is emancipating herself. Yet the seeking itself is also a renunciation, a kind of death — "I must stand alone." No less than Falk, or the hero of *On the Vidda,* she gives up something that has been her whole life. She is as broken as Torvald in the end: But she is a strong character and he is a weak one. In the "happy ending" which Ibsen reluctantly allowed to be used, it was the sight of the children that persuaded her to stay, and unless it is remembered that leaving Torvald means leaving the children, the full measure of Nora's decision cannot be taken. An actress gets her chance to make this point in the reply to Torvald's plea that Nora should stay for the children's sake.

It should be remembered, too, that the seriousness of the step she takes is lost on the present generation. She was putting herself outside society, inviting insult, destitution, and loneliness. She went out into a very dark night.

Willoughby Patterne: The protagonist in George Meredith's novel *The Egoist* (1879), an arrogant aristocrat who lacks awareness of the needs and desires of the women in his life.

HEDDA GABLER

Hedda Gabler (1890) is today Ibsen's most produced and perhaps his most respected play, but at first it provoked a more uniformly negative response than did any of his other plays. Critics were alarmed at the depressing environment that Ibsen created, and some Scandinavians were especially annoyed by the sense that Ibsen was condemning their entire society. The critics denounced the play "as a base escape of moral sewage gas" and Hedda herself as "acrawl with the foulest passions of humanity."

Hedda Gabler is an intense, powerful woman living in a world totally dominated by men. She is herself dominated by her memory of her father, General Gabler, a man of action whose pistols she now uses to amuse herself. What she enjoys is something of the general's prerogative: the shaping of the destiny of men, especially the manner of their death. Her rejection of anything she deems bourgeois, including sex, which seems to repulse her, drives her to reject the baby she is about to have and to lure Eilert Løvborg to her only to destroy him.

She wants to be an independent woman just as her father was independent and free. She chooses marriage not because she wants to give herself to George Tesman but because she anticipates, on the strength of his expectations of a professorship, a life of comfort and influence. The play opens on Hedda's return from her wedding trip abroad, with the question of whether or not she is pregnant, but Hedda is not interested in children or domesticity. We realize that Hedda and Tesman's marriage is bound for failure, and that Tesman cannot see the truth about her.

Eilert Løvborg, Hedda's friend before she married, is also Tesman's professional rival. Løvborg has the fire and genius needed to be truly distinguished — unlike Tesman, who is most comfortable gathering material for other people's books. But Løvborg is intemperate, doing everything to excess, including drinking. Hedda drives Løvborg to drink after he has been "renovated" by her friend Mrs. Elvsted. This is only one way in which Hedda's cruelty is revealed. She abuses the innocent Aunt Julia and actually burns Løvborg's book because it was created in part by Mrs. Elvsted and is therefore their "baby."

Hedda is a frustrated woman who cannot satisfy herself in the stifling society she hoped to dominate. To ensure that Løvborg commits suicide in an elegant, romantic way, she gives him one of General Gabler's pistols, but her dreams for a romantic shot in the temple are shattered when Judge Brack reveals that Løvborg actually died miserably in a brothel from a pistol that discharged into his "stomach — more or less."

Hedda watches on as Mrs. Elvsted and Tesman team up to rewrite Løvborg's lost book, and when she turns from them she discovers that she has lost all her independence. Judge Brack knows about the pistol, and it is clear that the price of silence is her becoming his mistress.

Hedda's fate has been variously interpreted. Is she a worthwhile character? Is her behavior excusable because she is a woman in a society that will value her not for what she can do but only for who she is? Is her fate determined by the fact that as a woman she cannot live the life she knows she should? Hedda does some frightful things in the play, but how are we to take her? She is clearly larger than anyone else in the play, and certainly more interesting. The men are all weak: Tesman is tied to his aunt's apron strings; Løvborg cannot control himself; and Brack is corrupt. Mrs. Elvsted is a sympathetic character, but her ambition is to be nothing more than a helpmate. None of these fates would satisfy Hedda; her action at the end of the play is almost inevitable.

The sense in which this is a realistic play is qualified by Ibsen's adherence to most of the standards of classical theater. The characters, plot, and setting are established according to the Scribean principles of the well-made play, and the effort to maintain a sense that the play is a "slice of life" seems minimal. The play is structured in four acts, and its rhythms resemble those of a tragedy. There is no attempt to raise issues that are especially shocking to the society or the audiences, as Ibsen had done, for instance, in dealing with syphilis in his play *Ghosts*.

The way we are to interpret Hedda is complicated by some facts that we know about the composition of the play. When Ibsen was writing it, he was himself an unfulfilled husband, with a profoundly repressed sex life. But he was also famous and as a result attracted a great many young women who were interested in him sexually. One of these, Emilie Bardach, age eighteen, fell in love with him, and he with her. They agreed to go off together, but soon Ibsen had second thoughts. He was afraid to take the chance of happiness when it was finally offered.

Ibsen's biographer, Michael Meyer, in a commentary on the play refers to Hedda Gabler as "a merciless self-portrait of Ibsen in skirts." The psychologist Arne Duve has argued that Hedda is a portrait of Ibsen's "repressed and crippled emotional life." Whether this biographical interpretation is fully warranted is difficult to say, but if it is true, then the character of Hedda and our interpretation of the play are intensely complicated.

Hedda Gabler in Performance

In January 1891 *Hedda Gabler* debuted in Munich and that year played elsewhere in Germany, as well as in Scandinavia and England. It was not well received. Feeling Hedda to be evil, the public and the press called the play incoherent and unpleasant. French audiences even jeered the first performances in Paris. The play withstood its unfavorable reception, though, and was eventually a worldwide success. In February 1899 the great theorist of acting, Konstantin Stanislavsky, played the part of Løvborg in the Moscow Arts Theatre's first production of an Ibsen play.

Blanche Bates first played Hedda Gabler in the United States in Philadelphia in 1904, and the reviews read as if they deplored a real woman when they spoke about Hedda's "degeneracy." Its performance in New York in 1918 met with critical attacks and the accusation that it was essentially meaningless. Critical taste changed, however, and by 1948 it was praised because it proved itself resistant to being dated or old-fashioned.

Ingmar Bergman's 1968 Stockholm production moved to England in 1970 with Maggie Smith as an "icily aware" Hedda. Bergman, an eminent filmmaker, divided the stage in two so that characters, especially Hedda, could exit from a scene but linger at a doorway to eavesdrop on the other characters' conversations. One critic said, "At times the drama seems to be taking place in different levels of the mind."

Trevor Nunn's production at the National Theater in Washington, D.C., in 1975 relied on Glenda Jackson as Hedda, but critics complained that she played the part as if it were comedic. No such complaints were raised, however, when Nunn's production was made into a film (1976), which won Jackson a nomination for an Academy Award. Martha Plimpton is the most recent Hedda in a production at the Long Wharf Theatre in New Haven in April 2000.

Henrik Ibsen (1828–1906)

HEDDA GABLER   *1890*
TRANSLATED BY ROLF FJELDE

The Characters

GEORGE TESMAN, *research fellow in cultural history*
HEDDA TESMAN, *his wife*
MISS JULIANA TESMAN, *his aunt*
MRS. ELVSTED
JUDGE BRACK
EILERT LØVBORG
BERTA, *the Tesmans' maid*

The action takes place in Tesman's residence in the fashionable part of town.

ACT I

(*A large, attractively furnished drawing room, decorated in dark colors. In the rear wall, a wide doorway with curtains drawn back. The doorway opens into a smaller room in the same style as the drawing room. In the right wall of the front room, a folding door that leads to the hall. In the left wall opposite, a glass door, with curtains similarly drawn back. Through the panes one can see part of an overhanging veranda and trees in autumn colors. In the foreground is an oval table, with tablecloth and chairs around it. By the right wall, a wide, dark porcelain stove, a high-backed armchair, a cushioned footstool, and two taborets.° In the right-hand corner, a settee with a small round table in front. Nearer, on the left and slightly out from the wall, a piano. On either side of the doorway in back, étagères° with terra cotta and majolica ornaments. Against the back wall of the inner room, a sofa, a table, and a couple of chairs can be seen. Above this sofa hangs a portrait of a handsome, elderly man in a general's uniform. Over the table, a hanging lamp with an opalescent glass shade. A number of bouquets of flowers are placed about the drawing room in vases and glasses. Others lie on the tables. The floors in both rooms are covered with thick carpets. Morning light. The sun shines in through the glass door.*)

(*Miss Juliana Tesman, wearing a hat and carrying a parasol, comes in from the hall, followed by Berta, who holds a bouquet wrapped in paper. Miss Tesman is a lady around sixty-five with a kind and good-natured look, nicely but simply dressed in a gray tailored suit. Berta is a maid somewhat past middle age, with a plain and rather provincial appearance.*)

[S.D.] *taborets:* Stools without back or arms.   [S.D.] étagères: Cabinets with shelves.

MISS TESMAN (*stops close by the door, listens, and says softly*): Goodness, I don't think they're even up yet!
BERTA (*also softly*): That's just what I said, Miss Juliana. Remember how late the steamer got in last night. Yes, and afterward! My gracious, how much the young bride had to unpack before she could get to bed.
MISS TESMAN: Well, then — let them enjoy a good rest. But they must have some of this fresh morning air when they do come down. (*She goes to the glass door and opens it wide.*)
BERTA (*by the table, perplexed, with the bouquet in her hand*): I swear there isn't a bit of space left. I think I'll have to put it here, miss. (*Places the bouquet on the piano.*)
MISS TESMAN: So now you have a new mistress, Berta dear. Lord knows it was misery for me to give you up.
BERTA (*on the verge of tears*): And for me, miss! What can I say? All those many blessed years I've been in your service, you and Miss Rina.
MISS TESMAN: We must take it calmly, Berta. There's really nothing else to do. George needs you here in this house, you know that. You've looked after him since he was a little boy.
BERTA: Yes, but miss, I'm all the time thinking of her lying at home. Poor thing — completely helpless. And with that new maid! She'll never take proper care of an invalid, that one.
MISS TESMAN: Oh, I'll manage to teach her. And most of it, you know, I'll do myself. So you mustn't be worrying over my poor sister.
BERTA: Well, but there's something else too, miss. I'm really so afraid I won't please the young mistress.
MISS TESMAN: Oh, well — there might be something or other at first —
BERTA: Because she's so very particular.
MISS TESMAN: Well of course. General Gabler's daughter. What a life she had in the general's day! Remember seeing her out with her father — how she'd go galloping past in that long black riding outfit, with a feather in her hat?
BERTA: Oh yes — I remember! But I never would have dreamed then that she and George Tesman would make a match of it.
MISS TESMAN: Nor I either. But now, Berta — before I forget: From now on, you mustn't say George Tesman. You must call him Doctor Tesman.
BERTA: Yes, the young mistress said the same thing — last night, right after they came in the door. Is that true then, miss?

MISS TESMAN: Yes, absolutely. Think of it, Berta — they gave him his doctor's degree. Abroad, that is — on this trip you know. I hadn't heard one word about it, till he told me down on the pier.

BERTA: Well, he's clever enough to be anything. But I never thought he'd go in for curing people.

MISS TESMAN: No, he wasn't made that kind of doctor. (*Nods significantly.*) But as a matter of fact, you may soon now have something still greater to call him.

BERTA: Oh, really! What's that, miss?

MISS TESMAN (*smiling*): Hm, wouldn't you like to know! (*Moved.*) Ah, dear God — if only my poor brother could look up from his grave and see what his little boy has become! (*Glancing about.*) But what's this, Berta? Why, you've taken all the slipcovers off the furniture — ?

BERTA: Madam told me to. She doesn't like covers on chairs, she said.

MISS TESMAN: Are they going to make this their regular living room, then?

BERTA: It seems so — with her. For his part — the doctor — he said nothing.

(*George Tesman enters the inner room from the right, singing to himself and carrying an empty, unstrapped suitcase. He is a youngish-looking man of thirty-three, medium sized, with an open, round, cheerful face, blond hair and beard. He is somewhat carelessly dressed in comfortable lounging clothes.*)

MISS TESMAN: Good morning, good morning, George!

TESMAN (*in the doorway*): Aunt Julie! Dear Aunt Julie! (*Goes over and warmly shakes her hand.*) Way out here — so early in the day — uh?

MISS TESMAN: Yes, you know I simply had to look in on you a moment.

TESMAN: And that without a decent night's sleep.

MISS TESMAN: Oh, that's nothing at all to me.

TESMAN: Well, then you did get home all right from the pier? Uh?

MISS TESMAN: Why, of course I did — thank goodness. Judge Brack was good enough to see me right to my door.

TESMAN: We were sorry we couldn't drive you up. But you saw for yourself — Hedda had all those boxes to bring along.

MISS TESMAN: Yes, that was quite something, the number of boxes she had.

BERTA (*to Tesman*): Should I go in and ask Mrs. Tesman if there's anything I can help her with?

TESMAN: No, thanks, Berta — don't bother. She said she'd ring if she needed anything.

BERTA (*going off toward the right*): All right.

TESMAN: But wait now — you can take this suitcase with you.

BERTA (*taking it*): I'll put it away in the attic. (*She goes out by the hall door.*)

TESMAN: Just think, Aunt Julie — I had that whole suitcase stuffed full of notes. You just can't imagine all I've managed to find, rummaging through archives. Marvelous old documents that nobody knew existed —

MISS TESMAN: Yes, you've really not wasted any time on your wedding trip, George.

TESMAN: I certainly haven't. But do take your hat off, Auntie. Here — let me help you — uh?

MISS TESMAN (*as he does so*): Goodness — this is exactly as if you were still back at home with us.

TESMAN (*turning the hat in his hand and studying it from all sides*): My — what elegant hats you go in for!

MISS TESMAN: I bought that for Hedda's sake.

TESMAN: For Hedda's sake? Uh?

MISS TESMAN: Yes, so Hedda wouldn't feel ashamed of me if we walked down the street together.

TESMAN (*patting her cheek*): You think of everything, Aunt Julie! (*Laying the hat on a chair by the table.*) So — look, suppose we sit down on the sofa and have a little chat till Hedda comes. (*They settle themselves. She puts her parasol on the corner of the sofa.*)

MISS TESMAN (*takes both of his hands and gazes at him*): How wonderful it is having you here, right before my eyes again, George! You — dear Jochum's own boy!

TESMAN: And for me too, to see you again, Aunt Julie! You, who've been father and mother to me both.

MISS TESMAN: Yes, I'm sure you'll always keep a place in your heart for your old aunts.

TESMAN: But Auntie Rina — hm? Isn't she any better?

MISS TESMAN: Oh no — we can hardly expect that she'll ever be better, poor thing. She lies there, just as she has all these years. May God let me keep her a little while longer! Because otherwise, George, I don't know what I'd do with my life. The more so now, when I don't have you to look after.

TESMAN (*patting her on the back*): There, there, there —

MISS TESMAN (*suddenly changing her tone*): No, but to think of it, that now you're a married man! And that it was *you* who carried off Hedda Gabler. The beautiful Hedda Gabler! Imagine! She, who always had so many admirers!

TESMAN (*hums a little and smiles complacently*): Yes, I rather suspect I have several friends who'd like to trade places with me.

MISS TESMAN: And then to have such a wedding trip! Five — almost six months —

TESMAN: Well, remember, I used it for research, too. All those libraries I had to check — and so many books to read!

MISS TESMAN: Yes, no doubt. (*More confidentially; lowering her voice.*) But now listen, George — isn't there something — something special you have to tell me?

TESMAN: From the trip?

MISS TESMAN: Yes.

TESMAN: No, I can't think of anything beyond what I wrote in my letters. I got my doctor's degree down there — but I told you that yesterday.

MISS TESMAN: Yes, of course. But I mean — whether you have any kind of — expectations — ?

TESMAN: Expectations?

MISS TESMAN: My goodness, George — I'm your old aunt!

TESMAN: Why, naturally I have expectations.

MISS TESMAN: Ah!

TESMAN: I have every expectation in the world of becoming a professor shortly.

MISS TESMAN: Oh, a professor, yes —

TESMAN: Or I might as well say, I'm sure of it. But, Aunt Julie — you know that perfectly well yourself.

MISS TESMAN (*with a little laugh*): That's right, so I do. (*Changing the subject.*) But we were talking about your trip. It must have cost a terrible amount of money.

TESMAN: Well, that big fellowship, you know — it took us a good part of the way.

MISS TESMAN: But I don't see how you could stretch it enough for two.

TESMAN: No, that's not so easy to see — uh?

MISS TESMAN: And especially traveling with a lady. For I hear tell that's much more expensive.

TESMAN: Yes, of course — it's a bit more expensive. But Hedda just had to have that trip. She *had* to. There was nothing else to be done.

MISS TESMAN: No, no, I guess not. A honeymoon abroad seems to be the thing nowadays. But tell me — have you had a good look around your house?

TESMAN: You can bet I have! I've been up since daybreak.

MISS TESMAN: And how does it strike you, all in all?

TESMAN: First-rate! Absolutely first-rate! Only I don't know what we'll do with the two empty rooms between the back parlor and Hedda's bedroom.

MISS TESMAN (*laughing again*): Oh, my dear George, I think you can use them — as time goes on.

TESMAN: Yes, you're quite right about that, Aunt Julie! In time, as I build up my library — uh?

MISS TESMAN: Of course, my dear boy. It was your library I meant.

TESMAN: I'm happiest now for Hedda's sake. Before we were engaged, she used to say so many times there was no place she'd rather live than here, in Secretary Falk's town house.

MISS TESMAN: Yes, and then to have it come on the market just after you'd sailed.

TESMAN: We really have had luck, haven't we?

MISS TESMAN: But expensive, George dear! You'll find it expensive, all this here.

TESMAN (*looks at her, somewhat crestfallen*): Yes, I suppose I will.

MISS TESMAN: Oh, Lord, yes!

TESMAN: How much do you think? Approximately? Hm?

MISS TESMAN: It's impossible to say till the bills are all in.

TESMAN: Well, fortunately Judge Brack has gotten me quite easy terms. That's what he wrote Hedda.

MISS TESMAN: Don't worry yourself about that, dear. I've also put up security to cover the carpets and furniture.

TESMAN: Security? Aunt Julie, dear — you? What kind of security could *you* give?

MISS TESMAN: I took out a mortgage on our pension.

TESMAN (*jumping up*): What! On your — and Auntie Rina's pension!

MISS TESMAN: I saw nothing else to do.

TESMAN (*standing in front of her*): But you're out of your mind, Aunt Julie! That pension — it's all Aunt Rina and you have to live on.

MISS TESMAN: Now, now — don't make so much of it. It's only a formality; Judge Brack said so. He was good enough to arrange the whole thing for me. Just a formality, he said.

TESMAN: That's all well enough. But still —

MISS TESMAN: You'll be drawing your own salary now. And good gracious, if we have to lay out a bit, just now at the start — why, it's no more than a pleasure for us.

TESMAN: Oh, Aunt Julie — you never get tired of making sacrifices for me!

MISS TESMAN (*rises and places her hands on his shoulders*): What other joy do I have in this world than smoothing the path for you, my dear boy? You, without father or mother to turn to. And now we've come to the goal, George! Things may have looked black at times; but now, thank heaven, you've made it.

TESMAN: Yes, it's remarkable, really, how everything's turned out for the best.

MISS TESMAN: Yes — and those who stood against you — who wanted to bar your way — they've gone down. They've fallen, George. The one most dangerous to you — he fell farthest. And he's lying there now, in the bed he made — poor, misguided creature.

TESMAN: Have you heard any news of Eilert? I mean, since I went away.

MISS TESMAN: Only that he's supposed to have brought out a new book.

TESMAN: What's that? Eilert Løvborg? Just recently, uh?

MISS TESMAN: So they say. But considering everything, it can hardly amount to much. Ah, but when *your* new book comes out — it'll be a different story, George! What will it be about?

TESMAN: It's going to treat the domestic handicrafts of Brabant in the Middle Ages.

MISS TESMAN: Just imagine — that you can write about things like that!

TESMAN: Actually, the book may take quite a while yet. I have this tremendous collection of material to put in order, you know.

MISS TESMAN: Yes, collecting and ordering — you do that so well. You're not my brother's son for nothing.

TESMAN: I look forward so much to getting started. Especially now, with a comfortable home of my own to work in.

MISS TESMAN: And most of all, dear, now that you've won her, the wife of your heart.

TESMAN (*embracing her*): Yes, yes, Aunt Julie! Hedda — that's the most beautiful part of it all! (*Glancing toward the doorway.*) But I think she's coming — uh?

(*Hedda enters from the left through the inner room. She is a woman of twenty-nine. Her face and figure show breeding and distinction; her complexion is pallid and opaque. Her steel gray eyes express a cool, unruffled calm. Her hair is an attractive medium brown, but not particularly abundant. She wears a tasteful, rather loose-fitting gown.)*

MISS TESMAN (*going to meet Hedda*): Good morning, Hedda dear — how good to see you!

HEDDA (*holding out her hand*): Good morning, my dear Miss Tesman! Calling so early? This *is* kind of you.

MISS TESMAN (*slightly embarrassed*): Well — did the bride sleep well in her new home?

HEDDA: Oh yes, thanks. Quite adequately.

TESMAN: Adequately! Oh, I like that, Hedda! You were sleeping like a stone when I got up.

HEDDA: Fortunately. But of course one has to grow accustomed to anything new, Miss Tesman — little by little. (*Looking toward the left.*) Oh! That maid has left the door open — and the sunlight's just flooding in.

MISS TESMAN (*going toward the door*): Well, we can close it.

HEDDA: No, no — don't! (*To Tesman.*) There, dear, draw the curtains. It gives a softer light.

TESMAN (*by the glass door*): All right — all right. Look, Hedda — now you have shade and fresh air both.

HEDDA: Yes, we really need some fresh air here, with all these piles of flowers — But — won't you sit down, Miss Tesman?

MISS TESMAN: Oh no, thank you. Now that I know that everything's fine — thank goodness — I will have to run along home. My sister's lying there waiting, poor thing.

TESMAN: Give her my very, very best, won't you? And say I'll be looking in on her later today.

MISS TESMAN: Oh, you can be sure I will. But what do you know, George — (*Searching in her bag.*) — I nearly forgot. I have something here for you.

TESMAN: What's that, Aunt Julie? Hm?

MISS TESMAN (*brings out a flat package wrapped in newspaper and hands it to him*): There, dear. Look.

TESMAN (*opening it*): Oh, my — you kept them for me, Aunt Julie! Hedda! That's really touching! Uh!

HEDDA (*by the* étagère *on the right*): Yes, dear, what is it?

TESMAN: My old bedroom slippers! My slippers!

HEDDA: Oh yes. I remember how often you spoke of them during the trip.

TESMAN: Yes, I missed them terribly. (*Going over to her.*) Now you can see them, Hedda!

HEDDA (*moves toward the stove*): Thanks, but I really don't care to.

TESMAN (*following her*): Imagine — Auntie Rina lay and embroidered them, sick as she was. Oh, you couldn't believe how many memories are bound up in them.

HEDDA (*at the table*): But not for me.

MISS TESMAN: I think Hedda is right, George.

TESMAN: Yes, but I only thought, now that she's part of the family —

HEDDA (*interrupting*): We're never going to manage with this maid, Tesman.

MISS TESMAN: Not manage with Berta?

TESMAN: But dear — why do you say that? Uh?

HEDDA (*pointing*): See there! She's left her old hat lying out on a chair.

TESMAN (*shocked; dropping the slippers*): But Hedda — !

HEDDA: Suppose someone came in and saw it.

TESMAN: Hedda — that's Aunt Julie's hat!

HEDDA: Really?

MISS TESMAN (*picking it up*): That's right, it's mine. And what's more, it certainly is not old — Mrs. Tesman.

HEDDA: I really hadn't looked closely at it, Miss Tesman.

MISS TESMAN (*putting on the hat*): It's actually the first time I've had it on. The very first time.

TESMAN: And it's lovely, too. Most attractive!

MISS TESMAN: Oh, it's hardly all that, George. (*Looks about.*) My parasol — ? Ah, here. (*Takes it.*) For that's mine too. (*Murmurs.*) Not Berta's.

TESMAN: New hat and new parasol! Just imagine, Hedda!

HEDDA: Quite charming, really.

TESMAN: Yes, aren't they, huh? But Auntie, take a good look at Hedda before you leave. See how charming *she* is!

MISS TESMAN: But George dear, there's nothing new in that. Hedda's been lovely all her life. (*She nods and starts out, right.*)

TESMAN (*following her*): But have you noticed how plump and buxom she's grown? How much she's filled out on the trip?

HEDDA (*crossing the room*): Oh, do be quiet — !

MISS TESMAN (*who has stopped and turned*): Filled out?

TESMAN: Of course, you can't see it so well when she has that dressing gown on. But I, who have the opportunity to —

HEDDA (*by the glass door, impatiently*): Oh, you have no opportunity for anything!

TESMAN: It must have been the mountain air, down in the Tyrol —

HEDDA (*brusquely interrupting*): I'm exactly as I was when I left.

TESMAN: Yes, that's your claim. But you certainly are not. Auntie, don't you agree?

MISS TESMAN (*gazing at her with folded hands*): Hedda is lovely — lovely — lovely. (*Goes up to her, takes her head in both hands, bends it down and kisses her hair.*) God bless and keep Hedda Tesman — for George's sake.

HEDDA (*gently freeing herself*): Oh — ! Let me go.

MISS TESMAN (*with quiet feeling*): I won't let a day go by without looking in on you two.

TESMAN: Yes, please do that, Aunt Julie! Uh?

MISS TESMAN: Good-bye — good-bye!

(She goes out by the hall door. Tesman accompanies her, leaving the door half open. He can be heard reiterating

his greetings to Aunt Rina and his thanks for the slippers. At the same time, Hedda moves about the room, raising her arms and clenching her fists as if in a frenzy. Then she flings back the curtains from the glass door and stands there, looking out. A moment later Tesman comes back, closing the door after him.)

TESMAN (*retrieving the slippers from the floor*): What are you standing and looking at, Hedda?

HEDDA (*again calm and controlled*): I'm just looking at the leaves — they're so yellow — and so withered.

TESMAN (*wraps up the slippers and puts them on the table*): Yes, well, we're into September now.

HEDDA (*once more restless*): Yes, to think — that already we're in — in September.

TESMAN: Didn't Aunt Julie seem a bit strange? A little — almost formal? What do you suppose was bothering her? Hm?

HEDDA: I hardly know her at all. Isn't that how she usually is?

TESMAN: No, not like this, today.

HEDDA (*leaving the glass door*): Do you think this thing with the hat upset her?

TESMAN: Oh, not very much. A little, just at the moment, perhaps —

HEDDA: But really, what kind of manners has she — to go throwing her hat about in a drawing room! It's just not proper.

TESMAN: Well, you can be sure Aunt Julie won't do it again.

HEDDA: Anyhow, I'll manage to smooth it over with her.

TESMAN: Yes, Hedda dear, I wish you would!

HEDDA: When you go in to see them later on, you might ask her out for the evening.

TESMAN: Yes, I'll do that. And there's something else you could do that would make her terribly happy.

HEDDA: Oh?

TESMAN: If only you could bring yourself to speak to her warmly, by her first name. For my sake, Hedda? Uh?

HEDDA: No, no — don't ask me to do that. I told you this once before. I'll try to call her "Aunt." That should be enough.

TESMAN: Oh, all right. I was only thinking, now that you belong to the family —

HEDDA: Hm — I really don't know — (*She crosses the room to the doorway.*)

TESMAN (*after a pause*): Is something the matter, Hedda? Uh?

HEDDA: I'm just looking at my old piano. It doesn't really fit in with all these other things.

TESMAN: With the first salary I draw, we can see about trading it in on a new one.

HEDDA: No, not traded in. I don't want to part with it. We can put it there, in the inner room, and get another here in its place. When there's a chance, I mean.

TESMAN (*slightly cast down*): Yes, we could do that, of course.

HEDDA (*picks up the bouquet from the piano*): These flowers weren't here when we got in last night.

TESMAN: Aunt Julie must have brought them for you.

HEDDA (*examining the bouquet*): A visiting card. (*Takes it out and reads it.*) "Will stop back later today." Can you guess who this is from?

TESMAN: No. Who? Hm?

HEDDA: It says, Mrs. Elvsted.

TESMAN: No, really? Sheriff Elvsted's wife. Miss Rysing, she used to be.

HEDDA: Exactly. The one with the irritating hair that she was always showing off. An old flame of yours, I've heard.

TESMAN (*laughing*): Oh, that wasn't for long. And it was before I knew you, Hedda. But imagine — that she's here in town.

HEDDA: It's odd that she calls on us. I've hardly seen her since we were in school.

TESMAN: Yes, I haven't seen her either — since God knows when. I wonder how she can stand living in such an out-of-the-way place. Hm?

HEDDA (*thinks a moment, then bursts out*): But wait — isn't it somewhere up in those parts that he — that Eilert Løvborg lives?

TESMAN: Yes, it's someplace right around there. (*Berta enters by the hall door.*)

BERTA: She's back again, ma'am — that lady who stopped by and left the flowers an hour ago. (*Pointing.*) The ones you have in your hand, ma'am.

HEDDA: Oh, is she? Good. Would you ask her to come in.

(*Berta opens the door for Mrs. Elvsted and goes out. Mrs. Elvsted is a slender woman with soft, pretty features. Her eyes are light blue, large, round, and somewhat prominent, with a startled, questioning look. Her hair is remarkably light, almost a white-gold, and unusually abundant and wavy. She is a couple of years younger than Hedda. She wears a dark visiting dress, tasteful, but not quite in the latest fashion.*)

HEDDA (*going to greet her warmly*): Good morning, my dear Mrs. Elvsted. How delightful to see you again!

MRS. ELVSTED (*nervously; struggling to control herself*): Yes, it's a very long time since we last met.

TESMAN (*gives her his hand*): Or since *we* met, uh?

HEDDA: Thank you for your beautiful flowers —

MRS. ELVSTED: Oh, that's nothing — I would have come straight out here yesterday afternoon, but then I heard you weren't at home —

TESMAN: Have you just now come to town? Uh?

MRS. ELVSTED: I got in yesterday toward noon. Oh, I was in desperation when I heard that you weren't at home.

HEDDA: Desperation! Why?

TESMAN: But my dear Mrs. Rysing — Mrs. Elvsted, I mean —

HEDDA: You're not in some kind of trouble?

MRS. ELVSTED: Yes, I am. And I don't know another living soul down here I can turn to.

HEDDA (*putting the bouquet down on the table*): Come, then — let's sit here on the sofa —

MRS. ELVSTED: Oh, I can't sit down. I'm really too much on edge!

HEDDA: Why, of course you can. Come here.

(*She draws Mrs. Elvsted down on the sofa and sits beside her.*)

TESMAN: Well? What is it, Mrs. Elvsted?

HEDDA: Has anything particular happened at home?

MRS. ELVSTED: Yes, that's both it — and not it. Oh, I do want so much that you don't misunderstand me —

HEDDA: But then the best thing, Mrs. Elvsted, is simply to speak your mind.

TESMAN: Because I suppose that's why you've come. Hm?

MRS. ELVSTED: Oh yes, that's why. Well, then, I have to tell you — if you don't already know — that Eilert Løvborg's also in town.

HEDDA: Løvborg — !

TESMAN: What! Is Eilert Løvborg back! Just think, Hedda!

HEDDA: Good Lord, I can hear.

MRS. ELVSTED: He's been back all of a week's time now. A whole week — in this dangerous town! Alone! With all the bad company that's around.

HEDDA: But my dear Mrs. Elvsted, what does *he* have to do with you?

MRS. ELVSTED (*glances anxiously at her and says quickly*): He was the children's tutor.

HEDDA: Your children's?

MRS. ELVSTED: My husband's. I have none.

HEDDA: Your stepchildren's, then.

MRS. ELVSTED: Yes.

TESMAN (*somewhat hesitantly*): But was he — I don't know quite how to put it — was he sufficiently — responsible in his habits for such a job? Uh?

MRS. ELVSTED: In these last two years, there wasn't a word to be said against him.

TESMAN: Not a word? Just think of that, Hedda!

HEDDA: I heard it.

MRS. ELVSTED: Not even a murmur, I can assure you! Nothing. But anyway — now that I know he's here — in this big city — and with so much money in his hands — then I'm just frightened to death for him.

TESMAN: But why didn't he stay up there where he was? With you and your husband? Uh?

MRS. ELVSTED: After the book came out, he just couldn't rest content with us.

TESMAN: Yes, that's right — Aunt Julie was saying he'd published a new book.

MRS. ELVSTED: Yes, a great new book, on the course of civilization — in all its stages. It's been out two weeks. And now it's been bought and read so much — and it's made a tremendous stir —

TESMAN: Has it really? It must be something he's had lying around from his better days.

MRS. ELVSTED: Years back, you mean?

TESMAN: I suppose.

MRS. ELVSTED: No, he's written it all up there with us. Now — in this last year.

TESMAN: That's marvelous to hear. Hedda! Just imagine!

MRS. ELVSTED: Yes, if only it can go on like this!

HEDDA: Have you seen him here in town?

MRS. ELVSTED: No, not yet. I had such trouble finding out his address. But this morning I got it at last.

HEDDA (*looks searchingly at her*): I must say it seems rather odd of your husband —

MRS. ELVSTED (*with a nervous start*): Of my husband —! What?

HEDDA: To send you to town on this sort of errand. Not to come and look after his friend himself.

MRS. ELVSTED: No, no, my husband hasn't the time for that. And then I had — some shopping to do.

HEDDA (*with a slight smile*): Oh, that's different.

MRS. ELVSTED (*getting up quickly and uneasily*): I beg you, please, Mr. Tesman — be good to Eilert Løvborg if he comes to you. And he will, I'm sure. You know — you were such good friends in the old days. And you're both doing the same kind of work. The same type of research — from what I can gather.

TESMAN: We were once, at any rate.

MRS. ELVSTED: Yes, and that's why I'm asking you, please — you too — to keep an eye on him. Oh, you will do that, Mr. Tesman — promise me that?

TESMAN: I'll be only too glad to, Mrs. Rysing —

HEDDA: Elvsted.

TESMAN: I'll certainly do everything in my power for Eilert. You can depend on that.

MRS. ELVSTED: Oh, how terribly kind of you! (*Pressing his hands.*) Many, many thanks! (*Frightened.*) He means so much to my husband, you know.

HEDDA (*rising*): You ought to write him, dear. He might not come by on his own.

TESMAN: Yes, that probably would be the best, Hedda? Hm?

HEDDA: And the sooner the better. Right now, I'd say.

MRS. ELVSTED (*imploringly*): Oh yes, if you could!

TESMAN: I'll write him this very moment. Have you got his address, Mrs. — Mrs. Elvsted?

MRS. ELVSTED: Yes. (*Takes a slip of paper from her pocket and hands it to him.*) Here it is.

TESMAN: Good, good. Then I'll go in — (*Looking about.*) But wait — my slippers? Ah! Here. (*Takes the package and starts to leave.*)

HEDDA: Write him a really warm, friendly letter. Nice and long, too.

TESMAN: Don't worry, I will.

MRS. ELVSTED: But please, not a word that I asked you to!

TESMAN: No, that goes without saying. Uh? (*Leaves by the inner room, to the right.*)

HEDDA (*goes over to Mrs. Elvsted, smiles, and speaks softly*): How's that! Now we've killed two birds with one stone.

MRS. ELVSTED: What do you mean?

HEDDA: Didn't you see that I wanted him out of the room?

MRS. ELVSTED: Yes, to write the letter —

HEDDA: But also to talk with you alone.

MRS. ELVSTED (*confused*): About this same thing?

HEDDA: Precisely.

MRS. ELVSTED (*upset*): But Mrs. Tesman, there's nothing more to say! Nothing!

HEDDA: Oh yes, but there is. There's a great deal more — I can see that. Come, sit here — and let's speak openly now, the two of us. (*She forces Mrs. Elvsted down into the armchair by the stove and sits on one of the taborets.*)

MRS. ELVSTED (*anxiously glancing at her watch*): But Mrs. Tesman, dear — I was just planning to leave.

HEDDA: Oh, you can't be in such a rush — Now! Tell me a little about how things are going at home.

MRS. ELVSTED: Oh, that's the last thing I'd ever want to discuss.

HEDDA: But with me, dear — ? After all, we were in school together.

MRS. ELVSTED: Yes, but you were a class ahead of me. Oh, I was terribly afraid of you then!

HEDDA: Afraid of me?

MRS. ELVSTED: Yes, terribly. Because whenever we met on the stairs, you'd always pull my hair.

HEDDA: Did I really?

MRS. ELVSTED: Yes, and once you said you would burn it off.

HEDDA: Oh, that was just foolish talk, you know.

MRS. ELVSTED: Yes, but I was so stupid then. And, anyway, since then — we've drifted so far — far apart from each other. We've moved in such different circles.

HEDDA: Well, let's try now to come closer again. Listen, at school we were quite good friends, and we called each other by our first names —

MRS. ELVSTED: No, I'm sure you're mistaken.

HEDDA: Oh, I couldn't be! I remember it clearly. And that's why we have to be perfectly open, just as we were. (*Moves the stool nearer Mrs. Elvsted.*) There now! (*Kissing her cheek.*) You have to call me Hedda.

MRS. ELVSTED (*pressing and patting her hands*): Oh, you're so good and kind — ! It's not at all what I'm used to.

HEDDA: There, there! And I'm going to call you my own dear Thora.

MRS. ELVSTED: My name is Thea.

HEDDA: Oh yes, of course. I meant Thea. (*Looks at her compassionately.*) So you're not much used to goodness or kindness, Thea? In your own home?

MRS. ELVSTED: If only I had a home! But I don't. I never have.

HEDDA (*glances quickly at her*): I thought it had to be something like that.

MRS. ELVSTED (*gazing helplessly into space*): Yes — yes — yes.

HEDDA: I can't quite remember now — but wasn't it as a housekeeper that you first came up to the Elvsteds?

MRS. ELVSTED: Actually as a governess. But his wife — his first wife — she was an invalid and mostly kept to her bed. So I had to take care of the house too.

HEDDA: But finally you became mistress of the house yourself.

MRS. ELVSTED (*heavily*): Yes, I did.

HEDDA: Let me see — about how long ago was that?

MRS. ELVSTED: That I was married?

HEDDA: Yes.

MRS. ELVSTED: It's five years now.

HEDDA: That's right. It must be.

MRS. ELVSTED: Oh, these five years — ! Or the last two or three, anyway. Oh, if you only knew, Mrs. Tesman —

HEDDA (*gives her hand a little slap*): Mrs. Tesman! Now, Thea!

MRS. ELVSTED: I'm sorry; I'll try — Yes, if you could only understand — Hedda —

HEDDA (*casually*): Eilert Løvborg has lived up there about three years too, hasn't he?

MRS. ELVSTED (*looks at her doubtfully*): Eilert Løvborg? Yes — he has.

HEDDA: Had you already known him here in town?

MRS. ELVSTED: Hardly at all. Well, I mean — by name, of course.

HEDDA: But up there — I suppose he'd visit you both?

MRS. ELVSTED: Yes, he came to see us every day. He was tutoring the children, you know. Because, in the long run, I couldn't do it all myself.

HEDDA: No, that's obvious. And your husband — ? I suppose he often has to be away?

MRS. ELVSTED: Yes, you can imagine, as sheriff, how much traveling he does around in the district.

HEDDA (*leaning against the chair arm*): Thea — my poor, sweet Thea — now you must tell me everything — just as it is.

MRS. ELVSTED: Well, then you have to ask the questions.

HEDDA: What sort of man is your husband, Thea? I mean — you know — to be with. Is he good to you?

MRS. ELVSTED (*evasively*): He believes he does everything for the best.

HEDDA: I only think he must be much too old for you. More than twenty years older, isn't he?

MRS. ELVSTED (*irritated*): That's true. Along with everything else. I just can't stand him! We haven't a single thought in common. Nothing at all — he and I.

HEDDA: But doesn't he care for you all the same — in his own way?

MRS. ELVSTED: Oh, I don't know what he feels. I'm no more than useful to him. And then it doesn't cost much to keep me. I'm inexpensive.

HEDDA: That's stupid of you.

MRS. ELVSTED (*shaking her head*): It can't be otherwise. Not with him. He really doesn't care for anyone but himself — and maybe a little for the children.

HEDDA: And for Eilert Løvborg, Thea.

MRS. ELVSTED (*looking at her*): Eilert Løvborg! Why do you think so?

HEDDA: But my dear — it seems to me, when he sends you all the way into town to look after him — (*Smiles almost imperceptibly.*) Besides, it's what you told my husband.

MRS. ELVSTED (*with a little nervous shudder*): Really? Yes, I suppose I did. (*In a quiet outburst.*) No — I might as well tell you here and now! It's bound to come out in time.

HEDDA: But my dear Thea — ?

MRS. ELVSTED: All right, then! My husband never knew I was coming here.

HEDDA: What! Your husband never knew —

MRS. ELVSTED: Of course not. Anyway, he wasn't at home. Off traveling somewhere. Oh, I couldn't bear it any longer, Hedda. It was impossible! I would have been so alone up there now.

HEDDA: Well? What then?

MRS. ELVSTED: So I packed a few of my things together — the barest necessities — without saying a word. And I slipped away from the house.

HEDDA: Right then and there?

MRS. ELVSTED: Yes, and took the train straight into town.

HEDDA: But my dearest girl — that you could dare to do such a thing!

MRS. ELVSTED (*rising and walking about the room*): What else could I possibly do!

HEDDA: But what do you think your husband will say when you go back home?

MRS. ELVSTED (*by the table, looking at her*): Back to him?

HEDDA: Yes, of course.

MRS. ELVSTED: I'll never go back to him.

HEDDA (*rising and approaching her*): You mean you've left, in dead earnest, for good?

MRS. ELVSTED: Yes. There didn't seem anything else to do.

HEDDA: But — to go away so openly.

MRS. ELVSTED: Oh, you can't keep a thing like that secret.

HEDDA: But what do you think people will say about you, Thea?

MRS. ELVSTED: God knows they'll say what they please. (*Sitting wearily and sadly on the sofa.*) I only did what I had to do.

HEDDA (*after a short silence*): What do you plan on now? What kind of work?

MRS. ELVSTED: I don't know yet. I only know I have to live here, where Eilert Løvborg is — if I'm going to live at all.

HEDDA (*moves a chair over from the table, sits beside her, and strokes her hands*): Thea dear — how did this — this friendship — between you and Eilert Løvborg come about?

MRS. ELVSTED: Oh, it happened little by little. I got some kind of power, almost, over him.

HEDDA: Really?

MRS. ELVSTED: He gave up his old habits. Not because I'd asked him to. I never dared do that. But he could tell they upset me, and so he dropped them.

HEDDA (*hiding an involuntary, scornful smile*): My dear little Thea — just as they say — you rehabilitated him.

MRS. ELVSTED: Well, he says so, at any rate. And he — on his part — he's made a real human being out of

me. Taught me to think — and understand so many things.

HEDDA: You mean he tutored you also?

MRS. ELVSTED: No, not exactly. But he'd talk to me — talk endlessly on about one thing after another. And then came the wonderful, happy time when I could share in his work! When I could help him!

HEDDA: Could you really?

MRS. ELVSTED: Yes! Whenever he wrote anything, we'd always work on it together.

HEDDA: Like two true companions.

MRS. ELVSTED (*eagerly*): Companions! You know, Hedda — that's what he said too! Oh, I ought to feel so happy — but I can't. I just don't know if it's going to last.

HEDDA: You're no more sure of him than that?

MRS. ELVSTED (*despondently*): There's a woman's shadow between Eilert Løvborg and me.

HEDDA (*looks at her intently*): Who could that be?

MRS. ELVSTED: I don't know. Someone out of his — his past. Someone he's really never forgotten.

HEDDA: What has he said — about this!

MRS. ELVSTED: It's only once — and just vaguely — that he touched on it.

HEDDA: Well! And what did he say!

MRS. ELVSTED: He said that when they broke off she was going to shoot him with a pistol.

HEDDA (*with cold constraint*): That's nonsense! Nobody behaves that way around here.

MRS. ELVSTED: No. And that's why I think it must have been that redheaded singer that at one time he —

HEDDA: Yes, quite likely.

MRS. ELVSTED: I remember they used to say about her that she carried loaded weapons.

HEDDA: Ah — then of course it must have been her.

MRS. ELVSTED (*wringing her hands*): But you know what, Hedda — I've heard that this singer — that she's in town again! Oh, it has me out of my mind —

HEDDA (*glancing toward the inner room*): Shh! Tesman's coming. (*Gets up and whispers.*) Thea — keep all this just between us.

MRS. ELVSTED (*jumping up*): Oh yes! In heaven's name — !

(*George Tesman, with a letter in his hand, enters from the right through the inner room.*)

TESMAN: There, now — the letter's signed and sealed.

HEDDA: That's fine. I think Mrs. Elvsted was just leaving. Wait a minute. I'll go with you to the garden gate.

TESMAN: Hedda, dear — could Berta maybe look after this?

HEDDA (*taking the letter*): I'll tell her to.

(*Berta enters from the hall.*)

BERTA: Judge Brack is here and says he'd like to greet you and the Doctor, ma'am.

HEDDA: Yes, ask Judge Brack to come in. And, here — put this letter in the mail.

BERTA (*takes the letter*): Yes, ma'am.

(*She opens the door for Judge Brack and goes out. Brack is a man of forty-five, thickset, yet well built, with supple movements. His face is roundish, with a distinguished profile. His hair is short, still mostly black, and carefully groomed. His eyes are bright and lively. Thick eyebrows; a mustache to match, with neatly clipped ends. He wears a trimly tailored walking suit, a bit too youthful for his age. Uses a monocle, which he now and then lets fall.*)

JUDGE BRACK (*hat in hand, bowing*): May one dare to call so early?

HEDDA: Of course one may.

TESMAN (*shakes his hand*): You're always welcome here. (*Introducing him.*) Judge Brack — Miss Rysing —

HEDDA: Ah — !

BRACK (*bowing*): I'm delighted.

HEDDA (*looks at him and laughs*): It's really a treat to see you by daylight, Judge!

BRACK: You find me — changed?

HEDDA: Yes. A bit younger, I think.

BRACK: Thank you, most kindly.

TESMAN: But what do you say for Hedda, uh? Doesn't she look flourishing? She's actually —

HEDDA: Oh, leave me out of it! You might thank Judge Brack for all the trouble he's gone to —

BRACK: Nonsense — it was a pleasure —

HEDDA: Yes, you're a true friend. But here's Thea, standing here, aching to get away. Excuse me, Judge; I'll be right back.

(*Mutual good-byes. Mrs. Elvsted and Hedda go out by the hall door.*)

BRACK: So — is your wife fairly well satisfied, then — ?

TESMAN: Yes, we can't thank you enough. Of course — I gather there's some rearrangement called for here and there. And one or two things are lacking. We still have to buy a few minor items.

BRACK: Really?

TESMAN: But that's nothing for you to worry about. Hedda said she'd pick up those things herself. Why don't we sit down, hm?

BRACK: Thanks. Just for a moment. (*Sits by the table.*) There's something I'd like to discuss with you, Tesman.

TESMAN: What? Oh, I understand! (*Sitting.*) It's the serious part of the banquet we're coming to, uh?

BRACK: Oh, as far as money matters go, there's no great rush — though I must say I wish we'd managed things a bit more economically.

TESMAN: But that was completely impossible! Think about Hedda, Judge! You, who know her so well — I simply couldn't have her live like a grocer's wife.

BRACK: No, no — that's the trouble, exactly.

TESMAN: And then — fortunately — it can't be long before I get my appointment.

BRACK: Well, you know — these things can often hang fire.

TESMAN: Have you heard something further? Hm?

BRACK: Nothing really definite — (*Changing the sub-*

ject.) But incidentally — I do have one piece of news for you.

TESMAN: Well?

BRACK: Your old friend Eilert Løvborg is back in town.

TESMAN: I already know.

BRACK: Oh? How did you hear?

TESMAN: She told me. The lady that left with Hedda.

BRACK: I see. What was her name again? I didn't quite catch it —

TESMAN: Mrs. Elvsted.

BRACK: Aha — Sheriff Elvsted's wife. Yes — it's up near them he's been staying.

TESMAN: And, just think — what a pleasure to hear that he's completely stable again!

BRACK: Yes, that's what they claim.

TESMAN: And that he's published a new book, uh?

BRACK: Oh yes!

TESMAN: And it's created quite a sensation.

BRACK: An extraordinary sensation.

TESMAN: Just imagine — isn't that marvelous? He, with his remarkable talents — I was so very afraid that he'd really gone down for good.

BRACK: That's what everyone thought.

TESMAN: But I've no idea what he'll find to do now. How on earth can he ever make a living? Hm?

(*During the last words, Hedda comes in by the hall door.*)

HEDDA (*to Brack, laughing, with a touch of scorn*): Tesman always goes around worrying about how people are going to make a living.

TESMAN: My Lord — it's poor Eilert Løvborg we're talking of, dear.

HEDDA (*glancing quickly at him*): Oh, really? (*Sits in the armchair by the stove and asks casually.*) What's the matter with him?

TESMAN: Well — he must have run through his inheritance long ago. And he can't write a new book every year. Uh? So I was asking, really, what's going to become of him.

BRACK: Perhaps I can shed some light on that.

TESMAN: Oh?

BRACK: You must remember that he does have relatives with a great deal of influence.

TESMAN: Yes, but they've washed their hands of him altogether.

BRACK: They used to call him the family's white hope.

TESMAN: They used to, yes! But he spoiled all that himself.

HEDDA: Who knows? (*With a slight smile.*) He's been rehabilitated up at the Elvsteds —

BRACK: And then this book that he's published —

TESMAN: Oh, well, let's hope they really help him some way or other. I just now wrote to him. Hedda dear, I asked him out here this evening.

BRACK: But my dear fellow, you're coming to my stag party this evening. You promised down on the pier last night.

HEDDA: Had you forgotten, Tesman?

TESMAN: Yes, I absolutely had.

BRACK: For that matter, you can rest assured that he'd never come.

TESMAN: What makes you say that, hm?

BRACK (*hesitating, rising and leaning on the back of the chair*): My dear Tesman — and you too, Mrs. Tesman — I can't, in all conscience, let you go on without knowing something that — that —

TESMAN: Something involving Eilert — ?

BRACK: Both you and him.

TESMAN: But my dear Judge, then tell us!

BRACK: You must be prepared that your appointment may not come through as quickly as you've wished or expected.

TESMAN (*jumping up nervously*): Has something gone wrong? Uh?

BRACK: It may turn out that there'll have to be a competition for the post —

TESMAN: A competition! Imagine, Hedda!

HEDDA (*leaning further back in the chair*): Ah, there — you see!

TESMAN: But with whom! You can't mean — ?

BRACK: Yes, exactly. With Eilert Løvborg.

TESMAN (*striking his hands together*): No, no — that's completely unthinkable! It's impossible! Uh?

BRACK: Hm — but it may come about, all the same.

TESMAN: No, but, Judge Brack — that would just be incredibly inconsiderate toward me! (*Waving his arms.*) Yes, because — you know — I'm a married man! We married on my prospects, Hedda and I. We went into debt. And even borrowed money from Aunt Julie. Because that job — my Lord, it was as good as promised to me, uh?

BRACK: Easy now — I'm sure you'll get the appointment. But you will have to compete for it.

HEDDA (*motionless in the armchair*): Just think, Tesman — it will be like a kind of championship match.

TESMAN: But Hedda dearest, how can you take it so calmly!

HEDDA (*as before*): I'm not the least bit calm. I can't wait to see how it turns out.

BRACK: In any case, Mrs. Tesman, it's well that you know now how things stand. I mean — with respect to those little purchases I hear you've been threatening to make.

HEDDA: This business can't change anything.

BRACK: I see! Well, that's another matter. Good-bye. (*To Tesman.*) When I take my afternoon walk, I'll stop by and fetch you.

TESMAN: Oh yes, please do — I don't know where I'm at.

HEDDA (*leaning back and reaching out her hand*): Good-bye, Judge. And come again soon.

BRACK: Many thanks. Good-bye now.

TESMAN (*accompanying him to the door*): Good-bye, Judge! You really must excuse me —

(*Brack goes out by the hall door.*)

TESMAN (*pacing about the room*): Oh, Hedda — one should never go off and lose oneself in dreams, uh?

HEDDA (*looks at him and smiles*): Do *you* do *that*?

TESMAN: No use denying it. It was living in dreams to go and get married and set up house on nothing but expectations.

HEDDA: Perhaps you're right about that.

TESMAN: Well, at least we have our comfortable home, Hedda! The home that we always wanted. That we both fell in love with, I could almost say. Hm?

HEDDA (*rising slowly and wearily*): It was part of our bargain that we'd live in society — that we'd keep a great house —

TESMAN: Yes, of course — how I'd looked forward to that! Imagine — seeing you as a hostess — in our own select circle of friends! Yes, yes — well for a while, we two will just have to get on by ourselves, Hedda. Perhaps have Aunt Julie here now and then. Oh, you — for you I wanted to have things so — so utterly different — !

HEDDA: Naturally this means I can't have a butler now.

TESMAN: Oh no — I'm sorry, a butler — we can't even talk about that, you know.

HEDDA: And the riding horse I was going to have —

TESMAN (*appalled*): Riding horse!

HEDDA: I suppose I can't think of that anymore.

TESMAN: Good Lord, no — that's obvious!

HEDDA (*crossing the room*): Well, at least I have one thing left to amuse myself with.

TESMAN (*beaming*): Ah, thank heaven for that! What is it, Hedda? Uh?

HEDDA (*in the center doorway, looking at him with veiled scorn*): My pistols, George.

TESMAN (*in fright*): Your pistols!

HEDDA (*her eyes cold*): General Gabler's pistols. (*She goes through the inner room and out to the left.*)

TESMAN (*runs to the center doorway and calls after her*): No, for heaven's sake, Hedda darling — don't touch those dangerous things! For my sake, Hedda! Uh?

ACT II

(*The rooms at the Tesmans', same as in the first act, except that the piano has been moved out and an elegant little writing table with a bookcase put in its place. A smaller table stands by the sofa to the left. Most of the flowers have been removed. Mrs. Elvsted's bouquet stands on the large table in the foreground. It is afternoon.*)

(*Hedda, dressed to receive callers, is alone in the room. She stands by the open glass door, loading a revolver. The match to it lies in an open pistol case on the writing table.*)

HEDDA (*looking down into the garden and calling*): Good to see you again, Judge!

BRACK (*heard from below, at a distance*): Likewise, Mrs. Tesman!

HEDDA (*raises the pistol and aims*): And now, Judge, I'm going to shoot you!

BRACK (*shouting from below*): No — no — no! Don't point that thing at me!

HEDDA: That's what comes of sneaking in the back way. (*She fires.*)

BRACK (*nearer*): Are you out of your mind — !

HEDDA: Oh dear — I didn't hit you, did I?

BRACK (*still outside*): Just stop this nonsense!

HEDDA: All right, you can come in, Judge.

(*Judge Brack, dressed for a stag party, enters through the glass door. He carries a light overcoat on his arm.*)

BRACK: Good God! Are you still playing such games? What are you shooting at?

HEDDA: Oh, I was just shooting into the sky.

BRACK (*gently taking the pistol out of her hand*): Permit me. (*Looks at it.*) Ah, this one — I know it well. (*Glancing around.*) Where's the case? Ah, here. (*Puts the pistol away and shuts the case.*) We'll have no more of that kind of fun today.

HEDDA: Well, what in heaven's name do you want me to do with myself?

BRACK: You haven't had any visitors?

HEDDA (*closing the glass door*): Not a single one. All of our set are still in the country, I guess.

BRACK: And Tesman isn't home either?

HEDDA (*at the writing table, putting the pistol case away in a drawer*): No. Right after lunch he ran over to his aunts. He didn't expect you so soon.

BRACK: Hm — I should have realized. That was stupid of me.

HEDDA (*turning her head and looking at him*): Why stupid?

BRACK: Because in that case I would have stopped by a little bit — earlier.

HEDDA (*crossing the room*): Well, you'd have found no one here then at all. I've been up in my room dressing since lunch.

BRACK: And there's not the least little crack in the door we could have conferred through.

HEDDA: You forgot to arrange it.

BRACK: Also stupid of me.

HEDDA: Well, we'll just have to settle down here — and wait. Tesman won't be back for a while.

BRACK: Don't worry, I can be patient.

(*Hedda sits in the corner of the sofa. Brack lays his coat over the back of the nearest chair and sits down, keeping his hat in his hand. A short pause. They look at each other.*)

HEDDA: Well?

BRACK (*in the same tone*): Well?

HEDDA: I spoke first.

BRACK (*leaning slightly forward*): Then let's have a nice little cozy chat, Mrs. Hedda.

HEDDA (*leaning further back on the sofa*): Doesn't it seem like a whole eternity since the last time we talked together? Oh, a few words last night and this morning — but they don't count.

BRACK: You mean, like this — between ourselves? Just the two of us?

HEDDA: Well, more or less.

BRACK: There wasn't a day that I didn't wish you were home again.

HEDDA: And I was wishing exactly the same.

BRACK: You? Really, Mrs. Hedda? And I thought you were having such a marvelous time on this trip.

HEDDA: Oh, you can imagine!

BRACK: But that's what Tesman always wrote.

HEDDA: Oh, him! There's nothing he likes better than grubbing around in libraries and copying out old parchments, or whatever you call them.

BRACK (*with a touch of malice*): But after all, it's his calling in life. In good part, anyway.

HEDDA: Yes, that's true. So there's nothing wrong with it — But what about *me*! Oh, Judge, you don't know — I've been so dreadfully bored.

BRACK (*sympathetically*): You really mean that? In all seriousness?

HEDDA: Well, you can understand — ! To go for a whole six months without meeting a soul who knew the least bit about our circle. No one that one could talk to about our kind of things.

BRACK: Ah, yes — I think that would bother me too.

HEDDA: But then the most unbearable thing of all —

BRACK: What?

HEDDA: To be everlastingly together with — with one and the same person —

BRACK (*nodding in agreement*): Morning, noon, and night — yes. At every conceivable hour.

HEDDA: I said "everlastingly."

BRACK: All right. But with our good friend Tesman I really should have thought —

HEDDA: My dear Judge, Tesman is — a specialist.

BRACK: Undeniably.

HEDDA: And specialists aren't at all amusing to travel with. Not in the long run, anyway.

BRACK: Not even — the specialist that one *loves*.

HEDDA: Ugh — don't use that syrupy word!

BRACK (*startled*): What's that, Mrs. Hedda!

HEDDA (*half laughing, half annoyed*): Well, just try it yourself! Try listening to the history of civilization morning, noon, and —

BRACK: Everlastingly.

HEDDA: Yes! Yes! And then all this business about domestic crafts in the Middle Ages — ! That really is just too revolting!

BRACK (*looks searchingly at her*): But tell me — I can't see how it ever came about that — ? Hm —

HEDDA: That George Tesman and I could make a match?

BRACK: All right, let's put it that way.

HEDDA: Good Lord, does it seem so remarkable?

BRACK: Well, yes — and no, Mrs. Hedda.

HEDDA: I really had danced myself out, Judge. My time was up. (*With a slight shudder.*) Ugh! No, I don't want to say that. Or think it, either.

BRACK: You certainly have no reason to.

HEDDA: Oh — reasons — (*Watching him carefully.*) And George Tesman — he is, after all, a thoroughly acceptable choice.

BRACK: Acceptable and dependable, beyond a doubt.

HEDDA: And I don't find anything especially ridiculous about him. Do you?

BRACK: Ridiculous? No-o-o, I wouldn't say that.

HEDDA: Hm. Anyway, he works incredibly hard on his research! There's every chance that, in time, he could still make a name for himself.

BRACK (*looking at her with some uncertainty*): I thought you believed, like everyone else, that he was going to be quite famous some day.

HEDDA (*wearily*): Yes, so I did. And then when he kept pressing and pleading to be allowed to take care of me — I didn't see why I ought to resist.

BRACK: No. From that point of view, of course not —

HEDDA: It was certainly more than my other admirers were willing to do for me, Judge.

BRACK (*laughing*): Well, I can't exactly answer for all the others. But as far as I'm concerned, you know that I've always cherished a — a certain respect for the marriage bond. Generally speaking, that is.

HEDDA (*bantering*): Oh, I never really held out any hopes for *you.*

BRACK: All I want is to have a warm circle of intimate friends, where I can be of use one way or another, with the freedom to come and go as — as a trusted friend —

HEDDA: Of the man of the house, you mean?

BRACK (*with a bow*): Frankly — I prefer the lady. But the man, too, of course, in his place. That kind of — let's say, triangular arrangement — you can't imagine how satisfying it can be all around.

HEDDA: Yes, I must say I longed for some third person so many times on that trip. Oh — those endless tête-à-têtes° in railway compartments — !

BRACK: Fortunately the wedding trip's over now.

HEDDA (*shaking her head*): The trip will go on — and on. I've only come to one stop on the line.

BRACK: Well, then what you do is jump out — and stretch yourself a little, Mrs. Hedda.

HEDDA: I'll never jump out.

BRACK: Never?

HEDDA: No. Because there's always someone on the platform who —

BRACK (*with a laugh*): Who looks at your legs, is that it?

HEDDA: Precisely.

BRACK: Yes, but after all —

HEDDA (*with a disdainful gesture*): I'm not interested. I'd rather keep my seat — right here, where I am. Tête-à-tête.

BRACK: Well, but suppose a third person came on board and joined the couple.

HEDDA: Ah! That's entirely different.

BRACK: A trusted friend, who understands —

HEDDA: And can talk about all kinds of lively things —

BRACK: Who's not in the least a specialist.

HEDDA (*with an audible sigh*): Yes, that would be a relief.

tête-à-têtes: Face-to-face conversations.

BRACK (*hearing the front door open and glancing toward it*): The triangle is complete.

HEDDA (*lowering her voice*): And the train goes on.

(*George Tesman, in a gray walking suit and a soft felt hat, enters from the hall. He has a good number of unbound books under his arm and in his pockets.*)

TESMAN (*going up to the table by the corner settee*): Phew! Let me tell you, that's hot work — carrying all these. (*Setting the books down.*) I'm actually sweating, Hedda. And what's this — you're already here, Judge? Hm? Berta didn't tell me.

BRACK (*rising*): I came in through the garden.

HEDDA: What are all these books you've gotten?

TESMAN (*stands leafing through them*): They're new publications in my special field. I absolutely need them.

HEDDA: Your special field?

BRACK: Of course. Books in his special field, Mrs. Tesman.

(*Brack and Hedda exchange a knowing smile.*)

HEDDA: You need still more books in your special field?

TESMAN: Hedda, my dear, it's impossible ever to have too many. You have to keep up with what's written and published.

HEDDA: Oh, I suppose so.

TESMAN (*searching among the books*): And look — I picked up Eilert Løvborg's new book too. (*Offering it to her.*) Maybe you'd like to have a look at it? Uh?

HEDDA: No, thank you. Or — well, perhaps later.

TESMAN: I skimmed through some of it on the way home.

HEDDA: Well, what do you think of it — as a specialist?

TESMAN: I think it's amazing how well it holds up. He's never written like this before. (*Gathers up the books.*) But I'll take these into the study now. I can't wait to cut the pages° — ! And then I better dress up a bit. (*To Brack.*) We don't have to rush right off, do we? Hm?

BRACK: No, not at all. There's ample time.

TESMAN: Ah, then I'll be at my leisure. (*Starts out with the books, but pauses and turns in the doorway.*) Oh, incidentally, Hedda — Aunt Julie won't be by to see you this evening.

HEDDA: She won't? I suppose it's that business with the hat?

TESMAN: Don't be silly. How can you think that of Aunt Julie? Imagine — ! No, it's Auntie Rina — she's very ill.

HEDDA: She always is.

TESMAN: Yes, but today she really took a turn for the worse.

HEDDA: Well, then it's only right for her sister to stay with her. I'll have to bear with it.

cut the pages: Book pages were printed on large sheets of paper that were folded and bound in groups of four. Readers had to trim the edges to separate the pages.

TESMAN: But you can't imagine how delighted Aunt Julie was all the same — because you'd filled out so nicely on the trip!

HEDDA (*under her breath; rising*): Oh, these eternal aunts!

TESMAN: What?

HEDDA (*going over to the glass door*): Nothing.

TESMAN: All right, then. (*He goes through the inner room and out, right.*)

BRACK: What were you saying about a hat?

HEDDA: Oh, it's something that happened with Miss Tesman this morning. She'd put her hat down over there on the chair. (*Looks at him and smiles.*) And I pretended I thought it was the maid's.

BRACK (*shaking his head*): But my dear Mrs. Hedda, how could you do that! Hurt that fine old lady!

HEDDA (*nervously, pacing the room*): Well, it's — these things come over me, just like that, suddenly. And I can't hold back. (*Throws herself down in the armchair by the stove.*) Oh, I don't know myself how to explain it.

BRACK (*behind the armchair*): You're not really happy — that's the heart of it.

HEDDA (*gazing straight ahead*): And I don't know why I ought to be — happy. Or maybe you can tell me why?

BRACK: Yes — among other things, because you've gotten just the home you've always wanted.

HEDDA (*looks up at him and laughs*): You believe that story too?

BRACK: You mean there's nothing to it?

HEDDA: Oh, yes — there's something to it.

BRACK: Well?

HEDDA: There's this much to it, that I used Tesman as my escort home from parties last summer —

BRACK: Unfortunately — I was going in another direction then.

HEDDA: How true. Yes, you had other directions to go last summer.

BRACK (*laughing*): For shame, Mrs. Hedda! Well — so you and Tesman — ?

HEDDA: Yes, so one evening we walked by this place. And Tesman, poor thing, was writhing in torment, because he couldn't find anything to say. And I felt sorry for a man of such learning —

BRACK (*smiling skeptically*): Did you? Hm —

HEDDA: No, I honestly did. And so — just to help him off the hook — I came out with some rash remark about this lovely house being where I'd always wanted to live.

BRACK: No more than that?

HEDDA: No more that evening.

BRACK: But afterward?

HEDDA: Yes, my rashness had its consequences, Judge.

BRACK: I'm afraid our rashness all too often does Mrs. Hedda.

HEDDA: Thanks! But don't you see, it was this passion for the old Falk mansion that drew George Tesman and me together! It was nothing more than that, that

brought on our engagement and the marriage and the wedding trip and everything else. Oh yes, Judge — I was going to say, you make your bed and then you lie in it.

BRACK: But that's priceless! So actually you couldn't care less about all this?

HEDDA: God knows, not in the least.

BRACK: But even now? Now that we've made it somewhat comfortable for you here?

HEDDA: Ugh — all the rooms seem to smell of lavender and dried roses. But maybe that scent was brought in by Aunt Julie.

BRACK (*laughing*): No, I think it's a bequest from the late Mrs. Falk.

HEDDA: Yes, there's something in it of the odor of death. It's like a corsage — the day after the dance. (*Folds her hands behind her neck, leans back in her chair, and looks at him.*) Oh, my dear Judge — you can't imagine how horribly I'm going to bore myself here.

BRACK: But couldn't you find some goal in life to work toward? Others do, Mrs. Hedda.

HEDDA: A goal — that would really absorb me?

BRACK: Yes, preferably.

HEDDA: God only knows what that could be. I often wonder if — (*Breaks off.*) But that's impossible too.

BRACK: Who knows? Tell me.

HEDDA: I was thinking — if I could get Tesman to go into politics.

BRACK (*laughing*): Tesman! No, I can promise you — politics is absolutely out of his line.

HEDDA: No, I can believe you. But even so, I wonder if I could get him into it?

BRACK: Well, what satisfaction would you have in that, if he can't succeed? Why push him in that direction?

HEDDA: Because, I've told you, I'm bored! (*After a pause.*) Then you think it's really out of the question that he could ever be a cabinet minister?

BRACK: Hm — you see, Mrs. Hedda — to be anything like that, he'd have to be fairly wealthy to start with.

HEDDA (*rising impatiently*): Yes, there it is! It's this tight little world I've stumbled into — (*Crossing the room.*) That's what makes life so miserable! So utterly ludicrous! Because that's what it *is*.

BRACK: I'd say the fault lies elsewhere.

HEDDA: Where?

BRACK: You've never experienced anything that's really stirred you.

HEDDA: Anything serious, you mean.

BRACK: Well, you can call it that, if you like. But now perhaps it's on the way.

HEDDA (*tossing her head*): Oh, you mean all the fuss over that wretched professorship! But that's Tesman's problem. I'm not going to give it a single thought.

BRACK: No, that isn't — ah, never mind. But suppose you were to be confronted now by what — in rather elegant language — is called your most solemn responsibility. (*Smiling.*) A new responsibility, Mrs. Hedda.

Marit Gronhaug as Hedda in
the 1986 Rogaland Teater
(Norway) production of
Hedda Gabler in London.

HEDDA (*angrily*): Be quiet! You'll never see me like that!

BRACK (*delicately*): We'll discuss it again in a year's time — at the latest.

HEDDA (*curtly*): I have no talent for such things, Judge. I won't have responsibilities!

BRACK: Don't you think you've a talent for what almost every woman finds the most meaningful —

HEDDA (*over by the glass door*): Oh, I told you, be quiet! I often think I have talent for only one thing in life.

BRACK (*moving closer*): And what, may I ask, is that?

HEDDA (*stands looking out*): Boring myself to death. And that's the truth. (*Turns, looks toward the inner room, and laughs.*) See what I mean! Here comes the professor.

BRACK (*in a low tone of warning*): Ah-ah-ah, Mrs. Hedda!

(*George Tesman, dressed for the party, with hat and gloves in hand, enters from the right through the inner room.*)

TESMAN: Hedda — there's been no word from Eilert Løvborg, has there? Hm?

HEDDA: No.

TESMAN: Well, he's bound to be here soon then. You'll see.

BRACK: You really believe he'll come?

TESMAN: Yes, I'm almost positive of it. Because I'm sure they're nothing but rumors, what you told us this morning.

BRACK: Oh?

TESMAN: Yes. At least Aunt Julie said she couldn't for the world believe that he'd stand in my way again. Can you imagine that!

BRACK: So, then everything's well and good.

TESMAN (*putting his hat with the gloves inside on a chair to the right*): Yes, but I really would like to wait for him as long as possible.

BRACK: We have plenty of time for that. There's no one due at my place till seven or half past.

TESMAN: Why, then we can keep Hedda company for a while. And see what turns up. Uh?

HEDDA (*taking Brack's hat and coat over to the settee*): And if worst comes to worst, Mr. Løvborg can sit and talk with me.

BRACK (*trying to take his things himself*): Ah, please, Mrs. Tesman — ! What do you mean by "worst," in this case?

HEDDA: If he won't go with you and Tesman.

TESMAN (*looks doubtfully at her*): But Hedda dear — is it quite right that he stays with you here? Uh? Remember that Aunt Julie isn't coming.

HEDDA: No, but Mrs. Elvsted is. The three of us can have tea together.

TESMAN: Oh, well, that's all right.

BRACK (*smiling*): And that might be the soundest plan for him too.

HEDDA: Why?

BRACK: Well, really, Mrs. Tesman, you've made enough pointed remarks about my little bachelor parties. You've always said they're only fit for men of the strictest principles.

HEDDA: But Mr. Løvborg is surely a man of principle now. After all, a reformed sinner —

(*Berta appears at the hall door.*)

BERTA: Ma'am, there's a gentleman here who'd like to see you —

HEDDA: Yes, show him in.

TESMAN (*softly*): I'm sure it's him! Just think!

(*Eilert Løvborg enters from the hall. He is lean and gaunt, the same age as Tesman, but looks older and rather exhausted. His hair and beard are dark brown, his face long and pale, but with reddish patches over the cheekbones. He is dressed in a trim black suit, quite new, and holds dark gloves and a top hat in his hand. He hesitates by the door and bows abruptly. He seems somewhat embarrassed.*)

TESMAN (*crosses over and shakes his hand*): Ah, my dear Eilert — so at last we meet again!

EILERT LØVBORG (*speaking in a hushed voice*): Thanks for your letter, George! (*Approaching Hedda.*) May I shake hands with you too, Mrs. Tesman?

HEDDA (*taking his hand*): So glad to see you, Mr. Løvborg. (*Gesturing with her hand.*) I don't know if you two gentlemen — ?

LØVBORG (*bowing slightly*): Judge Brack, I believe.

BRACK (*reciprocating*): Of course. It's been some years —

TESMAN (*to Løvborg, with his hands on his shoulders*): And now, Eilert, make yourself at home, completely! Right, Hedda? I hear you'll be settling down here in town again? Uh?

LØVBORG: I plan to.

TESMAN: Well, that makes sense. Listen — I just got hold of your new book. But I really haven't had time to read it yet.

LØVBORG: You can save yourself the bother.

TESMAN: Why? What do you mean?

LØVBORG: There's very little to it.

TESMAN: Imagine — you can say that!

BRACK: But it's won such high praise, I hear.

LØVBORG: That's exactly what I wanted. So I wrote a book that everyone could agree with.

BRACK: Very sound.

TESMAN: Yes, but my dear Eilert — !

LØVBORG: Because now I want to build up my position again — and try to make a fresh start.

TESMAN (*somewhat distressed*): Yes, that is what you want, I suppose. Uh?

LØVBORG (*smiling, puts down his hat and takes a thick manila envelope out of his pocket*): But when this comes out — George Tesman — you'll have to read it. Because this is the real book — the one that speaks for my true self.

TESMAN: Oh, really? What sort of book is that?

LØVBORG: It's the sequel.

TESMAN: Sequel? To what?

LØVBORG: To the book.

TESMAN: The one just out?

LØVBORG: Of course.

TESMAN: Yes, but my dear Eilert — that comes right down to our own time!

LØVBORG: Yes, it does. And this one deals with the future.

TESMAN: The future! But good Lord, there's nothing we know about that!

LØVBORG: True. But there are one or two things worth saying about it all the same. (*Opens the envelope.*) Here, take a look —

TESMAN: But that's not your handwriting.

LØVBORG: I dictated it. (*Paging through the manuscript.*) It's divided into two sections. The first is about the forces shaping the civilization of the future. And the second part, here — (*paging further on*) suggests what lines of development it's likely to take.

TESMAN: How extraordinary! It never would have occurred to me to write about anything like that.

HEDDA (*at the glass door, drumming on the pane*): Hm — no, of course not.

LØVBORG (*puts the manuscript back in the envelope and lays it on the table*): I brought it along because I thought I might read you a bit of it this evening.

TESMAN: Ah, that's very good of you, Eilert; but this evening — (*Glancing at Brack.*) I'm really not sure that it's possible —

LØVBORG: Well, some other time, then. There's no hurry.

BRACK: I should explain, Mr. Løvborg — there's a little party at my place tonight. Mostly for Tesman, you understand.

LØVBORG (*looking for his hat*): Ah — then I won't stay —

BRACK: No, listen — won't you give me the pleasure of having you join us?

LØVBORG (*sharply and decisively*): No, I can't. Thanks very much.

BRACK: Oh, nonsense! Do that. We'll be a small, select group. And you can bet we'll have it "lively," as Mrs. Hed — Mrs. Tesman says.

LØVBORG: I don't doubt it. But nevertheless —

BRACK: You could bring your manuscript with you and read it to Tesman there, at my place. I have a spare room you could use.

TESMAN: Why, of course, Eilert — you could do that, couldn't you? Uh?

HEDDA (*intervening*): But dear, if Mr. Løvborg simply doesn't want to! I'm sure Mr. Løvborg would much prefer to settle down here and have supper with me.

LØVBORG (*looking at her*): With you, Mrs. Tesman!

HEDDA: And with Mrs. Elvsted.

LØVBORG: Ah. (*Casually.*) I saw her a moment this afternoon.

HEDDA: Oh, did you? Well, she'll be here soon. So it's almost essential for you to stay, Mr. Løvborg. Otherwise, she'll have no one to see her home.

LØVBORG: That's true. Yes, thank you, Mrs. Tesman — I'll be staying, then.

HEDDA: Then let me just tell the maid —

(*She goes to the hall door and rings. Berta enters. Hedda talks to her quietly and points toward the inner room. Berta nods and goes out again.*)

TESMAN (*at the same time, to Løvborg*): Tell me, Eilert — is it this new material — about the future — that you're going to be lecturing on?

LØVBORG: Yes.

TESMAN: Because I heard at the bookstore that you'll be giving a lecture series here this autumn.

LØVBORG: I intend to. I hope you won't be offended, Tesman.

TESMAN: Why, of course not! But — ?

LØVBORG: I can easily understand that it makes things rather difficult for you.

TESMAN (*dispiritedly*): Oh, I could hardly expect that for my sake you'd —

LØVBORG: But I'm going to wait till you have your appointment.

TESMAN: You'll wait! Yes, but — but — you're not competing for it, then? Uh?

LØVBORG: No. I only want to win in the eyes of the world.

TESMAN: But, my Lord — then Aunt Julie was right after all! Oh yes — I knew it all along! Hedda! Can you imagine — Eilert Løvborg won't stand in our way!

HEDDA (*brusquely*): Our way? Leave me out of it.

(*She goes up toward the inner room where Berta is putting a tray with decanters and glasses on the table. Hedda nods her approval and comes back again. Berta goes out.*)

TESMAN (*at the same time*): But you, Judge — what do you say to all this? Uh?

BRACK: Well, I'd say that victory and honor — hm — after all, they're very sweet —

TESMAN: Yes, of course. But still —

HEDDA (*regarding Tesman with a cold smile*): You look as if you'd been struck by lightning.

TESMAN: Yes — something like it — I guess —

BRACK: That's because a thunderstorm just passed over us, Mrs. Tesman.

HEDDA (*pointing toward the inner room*): Won't you gentlemen please help yourselves to a glass of cold punch?

BRACK (*looking at his watch*): A parting cup? That's not such a bad idea.

TESMAN: Marvelous, Hedda! Simply marvelous! The way I feel now, with this weight off my mind —

HEDDA: Please, Mr. Løvborg, you too.

LØVBORG (*with a gesture of refusal*): No, thank you. Not for me.

BRACK: Good Lord, cold punch — it isn't poison, you know.

LØVBORG: Perhaps not for everyone.

HEDDA: I'll keep Mr. Løvborg company a while.

TESMAN: All right, Hedda dear, you do that.

(*He and Brack go into the inner room, sit down, drink punch, smoke cigarettes, and talk animatedly during the*

following. *Løvborg remains standing by the stove. Hedda goes to the writing table.*)

HEDDA (*slightly raising her voice*): I can show you some photographs, if you like. Tesman and I traveled through the Tyrol on our way home.

(*She brings over an album and lays it on the table by the sofa, seating herself in the farthest corner. Eilert Løvborg comes closer, stops and looks at her. Then he takes a chair and sits down on her left, his back toward the inner room.*)

HEDDA (*opening the album*): You see this view of the mountains, Mr. Løvborg. That's the Ortler group. Tesman's labeled them underneath. Here it is: "The Ortler group, near Meran."

LØVBORG (*whose eyes have never left her, speaking in a low, soft voice*): Hedda — Gabler!

HEDDA (*with a quick glance at him*): Ah! Shh!

LØVBORG (*repeating softly*): Hedda Gabler!

HEDDA (*looks at the album*): Yes, I used to be called that. In those days — when we two knew each other.

LØVBORG: And from now on — for the rest of my life — I have to teach myself not to say Hedda Gabler.

HEDDA (*turning the pages*): Yes, you have to. And I think you ought to start practicing it. The sooner the better, I'd say.

LØVBORG (*resentment in his voice*): Hedda Gabler married? And to George Tesman!

HEDDA: Yes — that's how it goes.

LØVBORG: Oh, Hedda, Hedda — how could you throw yourself away like that!

HEDDA (*looks at him sharply*): All right — no more of that!

LØVBORG: What do you mean?

(*Tesman comes in and over to the sofa.*)

HEDDA (*hears him coming and says casually*): And this one, Mr. Løvborg, was taken from the Val d'Ampezzo. Just look at the peaks of those mountains. (*Looks warmly up at Tesman.*) Now what were those marvelous mountains called, dear?

TESMAN: Let me see. Oh, those are the Dolomites.

HEDDA: Why, of course! Those are the Dolomites, Mr. Løvborg.

TESMAN: Hedda dear — I only wanted to ask if we shouldn't bring in some punch anyway. At least for you, hm?

HEDDA: Yes, thank you. And a couple of *petits fours*, please.

TESMAN: No cigarettes?

HEDDA: No.

TESMAN: Right.

(*He goes through the inner room and out to the right. Brack remains sitting inside, keeping his eye from time to time on Hedda and Løvborg.*)

LØVBORG (*softly, as before*): Answer me, Hedda — how could you go and do such a thing?

HEDDA (*apparently immersed in the album*): If you keep on saying Hedda like that to me, I won't talk to you.

LØVBORG: Can't I say Hedda even when we're alone?

HEDDA: No. You can think it, but you mustn't say it like that.

LØVBORG: Ah, I understand. It offends your — love for George Tesman.

HEDDA (*glances at him and smiles*): Love? You *are* absurd!

LØVBORG: Then you don't love him!

HEDDA: I don't expect to be unfaithful, either. I'm not having any of that!

LØVBORG: Hedda, just answer me one thing —

HEDDA: Shh!

(*Tesman, carrying a tray, enters from the inner room.*)

TESMAN: Look out! Here come the goodies. (*He sets the tray on the table.*)

HEDDA: Why do you do the serving?

TESMAN (*filling the glasses*): Because I think it's such fun to wait on you, Hedda.

HEDDA: But now you've poured out two glasses. And you know Mr. Løvborg doesn't want —

TESMAN: Well, but Mrs. Elvsted will be along soon.

HEDDA: Yes, that's right — Mrs. Elvsted —

TESMAN: Had you forgotten her? Uh?

HEDDA: We've been so caught up in these. (*Showing him a picture.*) Do you remember this little village?

TESMAN: Oh, that's the one just below the Brenner Pass! It was there that we stayed overnight —

HEDDA: And met all those lively summer people.

TESMAN: Yes, that's the place. Just think — if we could have had you with us, Eilert! My! (*He goes back and sits beside Brack.*)

LØVBORG: Answer me just one thing, Hedda —

HEDDA: Yes?

LØVBORG: Was there no love with respect to me, either? Not a spark — not one glimmer of love at all?

HEDDA: I wonder, really, was there? To me it was as if we were two true companions — two very close friends. (*Smiling.*) You, especially, were so open with me.

LØVBORG: You wanted it that way.

HEDDA: When I look back on it now, there was really something beautiful and fascinating — and daring, it seems to me, about — about our secret closeness — our companionship that no one, not a soul, suspected.

LØVBORG: Yes, Hedda, that's true! Wasn't there? When I'd come over to your father's in the afternoon — and the general sat by the window reading his papers — with his back to us —

HEDDA: And we'd sit on the corner sofa —

LØVBORG: Always with the same illustrated magazine in front of us —

HEDDA: Yes, for the lack of an album.

LØVBORG: Yes, Hedda — and the confessions I used to make — telling you things about myself that no one else knew of then. About the way I'd go out, the

drinking, the madness that went on day and night, for days at a time. Ah, what power was it in you, Hedda, that made me tell you such things?

HEDDA: You think it was some kind of power in me?

LØVBORG: How else can I explain it? And all those — those devious questions you asked me — and —

HEDDA: That you understood so remarkably well —

LØVBORG: To think you could sit there and ask such questions! So boldly.

HEDDA: Deviously, please.

LØVBORG: Yes, but boldly, all the same. Interrogating me about — all that kind of thing!

HEDDA: And to think you could answer, Mr. Løvborg.

LØVBORG: Yes, that's exactly what I don't understand — now, looking back. But tell me, Hedda — the root of that bond between us, wasn't it love? Didn't you feel, on your part, as if you wanted to cleanse and absolve me — when I brought those confessions to you? Wasn't that it?

HEDDA: No, not quite.

LØVBORG: What was your power, then?

HEDDA: Do you find it so very surprising that a young girl — if there's no chance of anyone knowing —

LØVBORG: Yes?

HEDDA: That she'd like some glimpse of a world that —

LØVBORG: That — ?

HEDDA: That she's forbidden to know anything about.

LØVBORG: So that was it?

HEDDA: Partly. Partly that, I guess.

LØVBORG: Companionship in a thirst for life. But why, then, couldn't it have gone on?

HEDDA: But that was your fault.

LØVBORG: You broke it off.

HEDDA: Yes, when that closeness of ours threatened to grow more serious. Shame on you, Eilert Løvborg! How could you violate my trust when I'd been so — so bold with my friendship?

LØVBORG (*clenching his fists*): Oh, why didn't you do what you said! Why didn't you shoot me down!

HEDDA: I'm — much too afraid of scandal.

LØVBORG: Yes, Hedda, you're a coward at heart.

HEDDA: A terrible coward. (*Changing her tone.*) But that was lucky for you. And now you're so nicely consoled at the Elvsteds'.

LØVBORG: I know what Thea's been telling you.

HEDDA: And perhaps you've been telling her all about us?

LØVBORG: Not a word. She's too stupid for that sort of thing.

HEDDA: Stupid?

LØVBORG: When it comes to those things, she's stupid.

HEDDA: And I'm a coward. (*Leans closer, without looking him in the eyes, and speaks softly.*) But there is something now that I can tell you.

LØVBORG (*intently*): What?

HEDDA: When I didn't dare shoot you —

LØVBORG: Yes?

HEDDA: That wasn't my worst cowardice — that night.

LØVBORG (*looks at her a moment, understands, and*

LEFT: Hedda (Glenda Jackson) and Mrs. Elvsted (Jennie Linden) in the 1975 Royal Shakespeare Company production of *Hedda Gabler* at the Aldwych. BELOW LEFT: Hedda and Eilert Løvborg (Patrick Stewart). RIGHT: Mrs. Elvsted and Hedda.

whispers passionately): Oh, Hedda! Hedda Gabler! Now I begin to see it, the hidden reason why we've been so close! You and I — ! . . . It was the hunger for *life* in you —

HEDDA (*quietly, with a sharp glance*): Careful! That's no way to think!

(*It has begun to grow dark. The hall door is opened from without by Berta.*)

HEDDA (*clapping the album shut and calling out with a smile*): Well, at last! Thea dear — please come in!

(*Mrs. Elvsted enters from the hall. She is in evening dress. The door is closed behind her.*)

HEDDA (*on the sofa, stretching her arms out toward her*): Thea, my sweet — I thought you were never coming!

(*In passing, Mrs. Elvsted exchanges light greetings with the gentlemen in the inner room, then comes over to the table and extends her hand to Hedda. Løvborg has gotten up. He and Mrs. Elvsted greet each other with a silent nod.*)

MRS. ELVSTED: Perhaps I ought to go in and talk a bit with your husband?

HEDDA: Oh, nonsense. Let them be. They're leaving soon.

MRS. ELVSTED: They're leaving?

HEDDA: Yes, for a drinking party.

MRS. ELVSTED (*quickly, to Løvborg*): But you're not?

LØVBORG: No.

HEDDA: Mr. Løvborg — is staying with us.

MRS. ELVSTED (*taking a chair, about to sit down beside him*): Oh, it's so good to be here!

HEDDA: No, no, Thea dear! Not there! You have to come over here by me. I want to be in the middle.

MRS. ELVSTED: Any way you please.

(*She goes around the table and sits on the sofa to Hedda's right. Løvborg resumes his seat.*)

LØVBORG (*after a brief pause, to Hedda*): Isn't she lovely to look at?

HEDDA (*lightly stroking her hair*): Only to look at?

LØVBORG: Yes. Because we two — she and I — we really *are* true companions. We trust each other completely. We can talk things out together without any reservations —

HEDDA: Never anything devious, Mr. Løvborg?

LØVBORG: Well —

MRS. ELVSTED (*quietly, leaning close to Hedda*): Oh, Hedda, you don't know how happy I am! Just think — he says that I've inspired him.

HEDDA (*regarding her with a smile*): Really, dear; did he say that?

LØVBORG: And then the courage she has, Mrs. Tesman, when it's put to the test.

MRS. ELVSTED: Good heavens, me! Courage!

LØVBORG: Enormous courage — where I'm concerned.

HEDDA: Yes, courage — yes! If one only had that.

LØVBORG: Then what?

HEDDA: Then life might still be bearable. (*Suddenly changing her tone.*) But now, Thea dearest — you really must have a nice cold glass of punch.

MRS. ELVSTED: No, thank you. I never drink that sort of thing.

HEDDA: Well, then you, Mr. Løvborg.

LØVBORG: Thanks, not for me either.

MRS. ELVSTED: No, not for him either!

HEDDA (*looking intently at him*): But if I insist?

LØVBORG: Makes no difference.

HEDDA (*with a laugh*): Poor me, then I have no power over you at all?

LØVBORG: Not in that area.

HEDDA: But seriously, I think you ought to, all the same. For your own sake.

MRS. ELVSTED: But Hedda — !

LØVBORG: Why do you think so?

HEDDA: Or, to be more exact, for others' sakes.

LØVBORG: Oh?

HEDDA: Otherwise, people might get the idea that you're not very bold at heart. That you're not really sure of yourself at all.

MRS. ELVSTED (*softly*): Oh, Hedda, don't — !

LØVBORG: People can think whatever they like, for all I care.

MRS. ELVSTED (*happily*): Yes, that's right!

HEDDA: I saw it so clearly in Judge Brack a moment ago.

LØVBORG: What did you see?

HEDDA: The contempt in his smile when you didn't dare join them for a drink.

LØVBORG: Didn't dare! Obviously I'd rather stay here and talk with you.

MRS. ELVSTED: That's only reasonable, Hedda.

HEDDA: But how could the judge know that? And besides, I noticed him smile and glance at Tesman when you couldn't bring yourself to go to their wretched little party.

LØVBORG: Couldn't! Are you saying I couldn't?

HEDDA: *I'm* not. But that's the way Judge Brack sees it.

LØVBORG: All right, let him.

HEDDA: Then you won't go along?

LØVBORG: I'm staying here with you and Thea.

MRS. ELVSTED: Yes, Hedda — you can be sure he is!

HEDDA (*smiles and nods approvingly at Løvborg*): I see. Firm as a rock. True to principle, to the end of time. There, that's what a man ought to be! (*Turning to Mrs. Elvsted and patting her.*) Well, now, didn't I tell you that, when you came here so distraught this morning —

LØVBORG (*surprised*): Distraught?

MRS. ELVSTED (*terrified*): Hedda — ! But Hedda — !

HEDDA: Can't you see for yourself? There's no need at all for your going around so deathly afraid that —

(*Changing her tone.*) There! Now we can all enjoy ourselves!

LØVBORG (*shaken*): What is all this, Mrs. Tesman?

MRS. ELVSTED: Oh, God, oh, God, Hedda! What are you saying! What are you doing!

HEDDA: Not so loud. That disgusting judge is watching you.

LØVBORG: So deathly afraid? For my sake?

MRS. ELVSTED (*in a low moan*): Oh, Hedda, you've made me so miserable!

LØVBORG (*looks intently at her a moment, his face drawn*): So that's how completely you trusted me.

MRS. ELVSTED (*imploringly*): Oh, my dearest — if you'll only listen — !

LØVBORG (*takes one of the glasses of punch, raises it, and says in a low, hoarse voice*): Your health, Thea! (*He empties the glass, puts it down, and takes the other.*)

MRS. ELVSTED (*softly*): Oh, Hedda, Hedda — how could you want such a thing!

HEDDA: Want it? I? Are you crazy?

LØVBORG: And your health too, Mrs. Tesman. Thanks for the truth. Long live truth! (*Drains the glass and starts to refill it.*)

HEDDA (*laying her hand on his arm*): All right — no more for now. Remember, you're going to a party.

MRS. ELVSTED: No, no, no!

HEDDA: Shh! They're watching you.

LØVBORG (*putting down his glass*): Now, Thea — tell me honestly —

MRS. ELVSTED: Yes!

LØVBORG: Did your husband know that you followed me?

MRS. ELVSTED (*wringing her hands*): Oh, Hedda — listen to him!

LØVBORG: Did you have it arranged, you and he, that you should come down into town and spy on me? Or maybe he got you to do it himself? Ah, yes — I'm sure he needed me back in the office! Or maybe he missed my hand at cards?

MRS. ELVSTED (*softly, in anguish*): Oh, Eilert, Eilert — !

LØVBORG (*seizing his glass to fill it*): Skoal to the old sheriff, too!

HEDDA (*stopping him*): That's enough. Don't forget, you're giving a reading for Tesman.

LØVBORG (*calmly, setting down his glass*): That was stupid of me, Thea. I mean, taking it like this. Don't be angry at me, my dearest. You'll see — you and all the others — that if I stumbled and fell — I'm back on my feet again now! With your help, Thea.

MRS. ELVSTED (*radiant with joy*): Oh, thank God — !

(*Brack, in the meantime, has looked at his watch. He and Tesman stand up and enter the drawing room.*)

BRACK (*takes his hat and overcoat*): Well, Mrs. Tesman, our time is up.

HEDDA: I suppose it is.

LØVBORG (*rising*): Mine too, Judge.

MRS. ELVSTED (*softly pleading*): Oh, Eilert — don't!

HEDDA (*pinching her arm*): They can hear you!

MRS. ELVSTED (*with a small cry*): Ow!

LØVBORG (*to Brack*): You were kind enough to ask me along.

BRACK: Oh, then you *are* coming, after all?

LØVBORG: Yes, thank you.

BRACK: I'm delighted —

LØVBORG (*putting the manila envelope in his pocket, to Tesman*): I'd like to show you one or two things before I turn this in.

TESMAN: Just think — how exciting! But Hedda dear. how will Mrs. Elvsted get home? Uh?

HEDDA: Oh, we'll hit on something.

LØVBORG (*glancing toward the ladies*): Mrs. Elvsted? Don't worry, I'll stop back and fetch her. (*Coming nearer.*) Say about ten o'clock, Mrs. Tesman? Will that do?

HEDDA: Yes. That will do very nicely.

TESMAN: Well, then everything's all set. But you mustn't expect *me* that early, Hedda.

HEDDA: Dear, you stay as long — just as long as you like.

MRS. ELVSTED (*with suppressed anxiety*): Mr. Løvborg — I'll be waiting here till you come.

LØVBORG (*his hat in his hand*): Yes, I understand.

BRACK: So, gentlemen — the excursion train is leaving! I hope it's going to be lively, as a certain fair lady puts it.

HEDDA: Ah, if only that fair lady could be there, invisible — !

BRACK: Why invisible?

HEDDA: To hear a little of your unadulterated liveliness, Judge.

BRACK (*laughs*): I wouldn't advise the fair lady to try.

TESMAN (*also laughing*): Hedda, you are the limit! What an idea!

BRACK: Well, good night. Good night, ladies.

LØVBORG (*bowing*): About ten o'clock, then.

(*Brack, Løvborg, and Tesman go out the hall door. At the same time, Berta enters from the inner room with a lighted lamp, which she sets on the drawing room table, then goes out the same way.*)

MRS. ELVSTED (*having risen, moving restlessly about the room*): Hedda — Hedda — what's going to come of all this?

HEDDA: At ten o'clock — he'll be here. I can see him now — with vine leaves in his hair — fiery and bold —

MRS. ELVSTED: Oh, how good that would be!

HEDDA: And then, you'll see — he'll be back in control of himself. He'll be a free man, then, for the rest of his days.

MRS. ELVSTED: Oh, God — if only he comes as you see him now!

HEDDA: He'll come back like that, and no other way! (*Gets up and goes closer.*) Go on and doubt him as much as you like. I believe in him. And now we'll find out —

MRS. ELVSTED: There's something behind what you're doing, Hedda.

HEDDA: Yes, there is. For once in my life, I want to have power over a human being.

MRS. ELVSTED: But don't you have that?

HEDDA: I don't have it. I've never had it.

MRS. ELVSTED: Not with your husband?

HEDDA: Yes, what a bargain *that* was! Oh, if you only could understand how poor I am. And you're allowed to be so rich! (*Passionately throws her arms about her.*) I think I'll burn your hair off, after all!

MRS. ELVSTED: Let go! Let me go! I'm afraid of you, Hedda!

BERTA (*in the doorway to the inner room*): Supper's waiting in the dining room, ma'am.

HEDDA: All right, we're coming.

MRS. ELVSTED: No, no, no! I'd rather go home alone! Right away — now!

HEDDA: Nonsense! First you're going to have tea, you little fool. And then — ten o'clock — Eilert Løvborg comes — with vine leaves in his hair.

(*She drags Mrs. Elvsted, almost by force, toward the doorway.*)

ACT III

(*The same rooms at the Tesmans'. The curtains are down across the doorway to the inner room, and also across the glass door. The lamp, shaded and turned down low, is burning on the table. The door to the stove stands open; the fire has nearly gone out.*)

(*Mrs. Elvsted, wrapped in a large shawl, with her feet up on a footstool, lies back in the armchair close by the stove. Hedda, fully dressed, is asleep on the sofa, with a blanket over her. After a pause, Mrs. Elvsted suddenly sits straight up in the chair, listening tensely. Then she sinks wearily back again.*)

MRS. ELVSTED (*in a low moan*): Not yet — oh, God — oh, God — not yet!

(*Berta slips in cautiously by the hall door. She holds a letter in her hand.*)

MRS. ELVSTED (*turns and whispers anxiously*): Yes? Has anyone come?

BERTA (*softly*): Yes, a girl just now stopped by with this letter.

MRS. ELVSTED (*quickly, reaching out her hand*): A letter! Give it to me!

BERTA: No, it's for the Doctor, ma'am.

MRS. ELVSTED: Oh.

BERTA: It was Miss Tesman's maid that brought it. I'll leave it here on the table.

MRS. ELVSTED: Yes, do.

BERTA (*putting the letter down*): I think I'd best put out the lamp. It's smoking.

MRS. ELVSTED: Yes, put it out. It'll be daylight soon.

BERTA (*does so*): It's broad daylight already, ma'am.

MRS. ELVSTED: It's daylight! And still no one's come — !

BERTA: Oh, mercy — I knew it would go like this.

MRS. ELVSTED: You knew?

BERTA: Yes, when I saw that a certain gentleman was back here in town — and that he went off with them. We've heard plenty about that gentleman over the years.

MRS. ELVSTED: Don't talk so loud. You'll wake Mrs. Tesman.

BERTA (*looks toward the sofa and sighs*): Goodness me — yes, let her sleep, poor thing. Should I put a bit more on the fire?

MRS. ELVSTED: Thanks, not for me.

BERTA: All right. (*She goes quietly out the hall door.*)

HEDDA (*wakes as the door shuts and looks up*): What's that?

MRS. ELVSTED: It was just the maid —

HEDDA (*glancing about*): In here — ? Oh yes, I remember now. (*Sits up on the sofa, stretches, and rubs her eyes.*) What time is it, Thea?

MRS. ELVSTED (*looking at her watch*): It's after seven.

HEDDA: When did Tesman get in?

MRS. ELVSTED: He isn't back.

HEDDA: Not back yet?

MRS. ELVSTED (*getting up*): No one's come in.

HEDDA: And we sat here and waited up for them till four o'clock —

MRS. ELVSTED (*wringing her hands*): And *how* I've waited for him!

HEDDA (*yawns, and speaks with her hand in front of her mouth*): Oh, dear — we could have saved ourselves the trouble.

MRS. ELVSTED: Did you get any sleep?

HEDDA: Oh yes. I slept quite well, I think. Didn't you?

MRS. ELVSTED: No, not at all. I couldn't, Hedda! It was just impossible.

HEDDA (*rising and going toward her*): There, there, now! There's nothing to worry about. It's not hard to guess what happened.

MRS. ELVSTED: Oh, what? Tell me!

HEDDA: Well, it's clear that the party must have gone on till all hours —

MRS. ELVSTED: Oh, Lord, yes — it must have. But even so —

HEDDA: And then, of course, Tesman didn't want to come home and make a commotion in the middle of the night. (*Laughs.*) Probably didn't care to show himself, either — so full of his party spirits.

MRS. ELVSTED: But where else could he have gone?

HEDDA: He must have gone up to his aunts' to sleep. They keep his old room ready.

MRS. ELVSTED: No, he can't be with them. Because he just now got a letter from Miss Tesman. It's over there.

HEDDA: Oh? (*Looking at the address.*) Yes, that's Aunt Julie's handwriting, all right. Well, then he must have stayed over at Judge Brack's. And Eilert Løvborg — he's sitting with vine leaves in his hair, reading away.

MRS. ELVSTED: Oh, Hedda, you say these things, and you really don't believe them at all.

HEDDA: You're such a little fool, Thea.

MRS. ELVSTED: That's true; I guess I am.

HEDDA: And you really look dead tired.

MRS. ELVSTED: Yes, I feel dead tired.

HEDDA: Well, you just do as I say, then. Go in my room and stretch out on the bed for a while.

MRS. ELVSTED: No, no — I still wouldn't get any sleep.

HEDDA: Why, of course you would.

MRS. ELVSTED: Well, but your husband's sure to be home now soon. And I've got to know right away —

HEDDA: I'll call you the moment he comes.

MRS. ELVSTED: Yes? Promise me, Hedda?

HEDDA: You can count on it. Just go and get some sleep.

MRS. ELVSTED: Thanks. I'll try. (*She goes out through the inner room.*)

(*Hedda goes over to the glass door and draws the curtains back. Bright daylight streams into the room. She goes over to the writing table, takes out a small hand mirror, regards herself and arranges her hair. She then goes to the hall door and presses the bell. After a moment, Berta enters.*)

BERTA: Did you want something, ma'am?

HEDDA: Yes, you can build up the fire. I'm freezing in here.

BERTA: Why, my goodness — we'll have it warm in no time. (*She rakes the embers together and puts some wood on, then stops and listens.*) There's the front doorbell, ma'am.

HEDDA: Go see who it is. I'll take care of the stove.

BERTA: It'll be burning soon. (*She goes out the hall door.*)

(*Hedda kneels on the footstool and lays more wood on the fire. After a moment, George Tesman comes in from the hall. He looks tired and rather serious. He tiptoes toward the doorway to the inner room and is about to slip through the curtains.*)

HEDDA (*at the stove, without looking up*): Good morning.

TESMAN (*turns*): Hedda! (*Approaching her.*) But what on earth — ! You're up so early? Uh?

HEDDA: Yes, I'm up quite early today.

TESMAN: And I was so sure you were still in bed sleeping. Isn't that something, Hedda!

HEDDA: Not so loud. Mrs. Elvsted's resting in my room.

TESMAN: Was Mrs. Elvsted here all night?

HEDDA: Well, no one returned to take her home.

TESMAN: No, I guess that's right.

HEDDA (*shuts the door to the stove and gets up*): So — did you enjoy your party?

TESMAN: Were you worried about me? Hm?

HEDDA: No, that never occurred to me. I just asked if you'd had a good time.

TESMAN: Oh yes, I really did, for once. But more at the beginning, I'd say — when Eilert read to me out of his book. We got there more than an hour too soon — imagine! And Brack had so much to get ready. But then Eilert read to me.

HEDDA (*sitting at the right-hand side of the table*): Well? Tell me about it —

TESMAN (*sitting on a footstool by the stove*): Really, Hedda — you can't imagine what a book that's going to be! I do believe it's one of the most remarkable things ever written. Just think!

HEDDA: Yes, I don't mean the book —

TESMAN: But I have to make a confession, Hedda. When he'd finished reading — I had such a nasty feeling —

HEDDA: Nasty?

TESMAN: I found myself envying Eilert, that he was able to write such a book. Can you imagine, Hedda!

HEDDA: Oh yes, I can imagine!

TESMAN: And then how sad to see — that with all his gifts — he's still quite irreclaimable.

HEDDA: Don't you mean that he has more courage to live than the others?

TESMAN: Good Lord, no — I mean, he simply can't take his pleasures in moderation.

HEDDA: Well, what happened then — at the end?

TESMAN: I suppose I'd have to say it turned into an orgy, Hedda.

HEDDA: Were there vine leaves in his hair?

TESMAN: Vine leaves? Not that I noticed. But he gave a long, muddled speech in honor of the woman who'd inspired his work. Yes, that was his phrase for it.

HEDDA: Did he give her name?

TESMAN: No, he didn't. But it seems to me it has to be Mrs. Elvsted. Wait and see!

HEDDA: Oh? Where did you leave him?

TESMAN: On the way here. We broke up — the last of us — all together. And Brack came along with us too, to get a little fresh air. And then we did want to make sure that Eilert got home safe. Because he really had a load on, you know.

HEDDA: He must have.

TESMAN: But here's the curious part of it, Hedda. Or perhaps I should say, the distressing part. Oh, I'm almost ashamed to speak of it — for Eilert's sake —

HEDDA: Yes, go on —

TESMAN: Well, as we were walking toward town, you see, I happened to drop back a little behind the others. Only for a minute or two — you follow me?

HEDDA: Yes, yes, so — ?

TESMAN: And then when I was catching up with the rest of them, what do you think I found on the sidewalk? Uh?

HEDDA: Oh, how should I know!

TESMAN: You mustn't breathe a word to anyone, Hedda — you hear me? Promise me that, for Eilert's sake. (*Takes a manila envelope out of his coat pocket.*) Just think — I found this.

HEDDA: Isn't that what he had with him yesterday?

TESMAN: That's right. It's the whole of his precious, irreplaceable manuscript. And he went and lost it — without even noticing. Can you imagine, Hedda! How distressing —

HEDDA: But why didn't you give it right back to him?

TESMAN: No, I didn't dare do that — in the state he was in —

HEDDA: And you didn't tell any of the others you'd found it?

TESMAN: Of course not. I'd never do that, you know — for Eilert's sake.

HEDDA: Then there's no one who knows you have Eilert Løvborg's manuscript?

TESMAN: No. And no one must ever know, either.

HEDDA: What did you say to him afterwards?

TESMAN: I had no chance at all to speak with him. As soon as we reached the edge of town, he and a couple of others got away from us and disappeared. Imagine!

HEDDA: Oh? I expect they saw him home.

TESMAN: Yes, they probably did, I suppose. And also Brack went home.

HEDDA: And where've you been carrying on since then?

TESMAN: Well, I and some of the others — we were invited up by one of the fellows and had morning coffee at his place. Or a post-midnight snack, maybe — uh? But as soon as I've had a little rest — and given poor Eilert time to sleep it off, then I've got to take this back to him.

HEDDA (*reaching out for the envelope*): No — don't give it back! Not yet, I mean. Let me read it first.

TESMAN: Hedda dearest, no. My Lord, I can't do that.

HEDDA: You can't?

TESMAN: No. Why, you can just imagine the anguish he'll feel when he wakes up and misses the manuscript. He hasn't any copy of it, you know. He told me that himself.

HEDDA (*looks searchingly at him*): Can't such a work be rewritten? I mean, over again?

TESMAN: Oh, I don't see how it could. Because the inspiration, you know —

HEDDA: Yes, yes — that's the thing, I suppose. (*Casually.*) Oh, by the way — there's a letter for you.

TESMAN: No, really — ?

HEDDA (*handing it to him*): It came early this morning.

TESMAN: Dear, from Aunt Julie! What could that be? (*Sets the envelope on the other taboret, opens the letter, skims through it, and springs to his feet.*) Oh, Hedda — she says poor Auntie Rina's dying!

HEDDA: It's no more than we've been expecting.

TESMAN: And if I want to see her one last time, I've got to hurry. I'll have to hop right over.

HEDDA (*suppressing a smile*): Hop?

TESMAN: Oh, Hedda dearest, if you could only bring yourself to come with me! Think of it!

HEDDA (*rises and dismisses the thought wearily*): No no, don't ask me to do such things. I don't want to look on sickness and death. I want to be free of everything ugly.

TESMAN: Yes, all right, then — (*Dashing about.*) My hat — ? My overcoat — ? Oh, in the hall — I do hope I'm not there too late, Hedda! Hm?

HEDDA: Oh, if you hurry —

(*Berta appears at the hall door.*)

BERTA: Judge Brack's outside, asking if he might stop in.
TESMAN: At a time like this! No, I can't possibly see him now.
HEDDA: But I can. (*To Berta.*) Ask the judge to come in.

(*Berta goes out.*)

HEDDA (*quickly, in a whisper*): Tesman, the manuscript! (*She snatches it from the taboret.*)
TESMAN: Yes, give it here!
HEDDA: No, no, I'll keep it till you're back.

(*She moves over to the writing table and slips it in the bookcase. Tesman stands flustered, unable to get his gloves on. Brack enters from the hall.*)

HEDDA: Well, aren't you the early bird.
BRACK: Yes, wouldn't you say so? (*To Tesman.*) Are you off and away too?
TESMAN: Yes, I absolutely have to get over to my aunts'. Just think — the invalid one, she's dying.
BRACK: Good Lord, she is? But then you mustn't let me detain you. Not at a moment like this —
TESMAN: Yes, I really must run — Good-bye! Good-bye! (*He goes hurriedly out the hall door.*)
HEDDA: It would seem you had quite a time of it last night, Judge.
BRACK: I've not been out of my clothes yet, Mrs. Hedda.
HEDDA: Not you, either?
BRACK: No, as you can see. But what's Tesman been telling you about our night's adventures?
HEDDA: Oh, some tedious tale. Something about stopping up somewhere for coffee.
BRACK: Yes, I know all about the coffee party. Eilert Løvborg wasn't with them, I expect?
HEDDA: No, they'd already taken him home.
BRACK: Tesman, as well.
HEDDA: No, but he said some others had.
BRACK (*smiles*): George Tesman is really a simple soul, Mrs. Hedda.
HEDDA: God knows he's that. But was there something else that went on?
BRACK: Oh, you might say so.
HEDDA: Well, now! Let's sit down, Judge; you'll talk more easily then.

(*She sits at the left-hand side of the table, with Brack at the long side, near her.*)

HEDDA: So?
BRACK: I had particular reasons for keeping track of my guests — or, I should say, certain of my guests, last night.
HEDDA: And among them Eilert Løvborg, perhaps?
BRACK: To be frank — yes.
HEDDA: Now you really have me curious —
BRACK: You know where he and a couple of the others spent the rest of the night, Mrs. Hedda?
HEDDA: Tell me — if it's fit to be told.

BRACK: Oh, it's very much fit to be told. Well, it seems they showed up at a quite animated soiree.
HEDDA: Of the lively sort.
BRACK: Of the liveliest.
HEDDA: Do go on, Judge —
BRACK: Løvborg, and the others also, had advance invitations. I knew all about it. But Løvborg had begged off, because now, of course, he was supposed to have become a new man, as you know.
HEDDA: Up at the Elvsteds', yes. But he went anyway?
BRACK: Well, you see, Mrs. Hedda — unfortunately the spirit moved him up at my place last evening —
HEDDA: Yes, I hear that he *was* inspired there.
BRACK: To a very powerful degree, I'd say. Well, so his mind turned to other things, that's clear. We males, sad to say — we're not always so true to principle as we ought to be.
HEDDA: Oh, I'm sure you're an exception, Judge. But what about Løvborg — ?
BRACK: Well, to cut it short — the result was that he wound up in Mademoiselle Diana's parlors.
HEDDA: Mademoiselle Diana's?
BRACK: It was Mademoiselle Diana who was holding the soiree. For a select circle of lady friends and admirers.
HEDDA: Is she a red-haired woman?
BRACK: Precisely.
HEDDA: Sort of a — singer?
BRACK: Oh yes — she's that too. And also a mighty huntress — of men, Mrs. Hedda. You've undoubtedly heard about her. Løvborg was one of her ruling favorites — back there in his palmy° days.
HEDDA: And how did all this end?
BRACK: Less amicably, it seems. She gave him a most tender welcoming, with open arms, but before long she'd taken to fists.
HEDDA: Against Løvborg?
BRACK: That's right. He accused her or her friends of having robbed him. He claimed that his wallet was missing — along with some other things. In short, he must have made a frightful scene.
HEDDA: And what did it come to?
BRACK: It came to a regular free-for-all, the men and the women both. Luckily the police finally got there.
HEDDA: The police too?
BRACK: Yes. But it's likely to prove an expensive little romp for Eilert Løvborg. That crazy fool.
HEDDA: So?
BRACK: He apparently made violent resistance. Struck one of the officers on the side of the head and ripped his coat. So they took him along to the station house.
HEDDA: Where did you hear all this?
BRACK: From the police themselves.
HEDDA (*gazing straight ahead*): So that's how it went. Then he had no vine leaves in his hair.
BRACK: Vine leaves, Mrs. Hedda?
HEDDA (*changing her tone*): But tell me, Judge — just why do you go around like this, spying on Eilert Løvborg?

palmy: Prosperous.

BRACK: In the first place, it's hardly a matter of no concern to me, if it's brought out during the investigation that he'd come direct from my house.

HEDDA: There'll be an investigation — ?

BRACK: Naturally. Anyway, that takes care of itself. But I felt that as a friend of the family I owed you and Tesman a full account of his nocturnal exploits.

HEDDA: Why, exactly?

BRACK: Well, because I have a strong suspicion that he'll try to use you as a kind of screen.

HEDDA: Oh, how could you ever think such a thing!

BRACK: Good Lord — we're really not blind, Mrs. Hedda. You'll see! This Mrs. Elvsted, she won't be going home now so quickly.

HEDDA: Well, even supposing there were something between them, there are plenty of other places where they could meet.

BRACK: Not one single home. From now on, every decent house will be closed to Eilert Løvborg.

HEDDA: So mine ought to be too, is that what you mean?

BRACK: Yes. I'll admit I'd find it more than annoying if that gentleman were to have free access here. If he came like an intruder, an irrelevancy, forcing his way into —

HEDDA: Into the triangle?

BRACK: Precisely. It would almost be like turning me out of my home.

HEDDA (*looks at him with a smile*): I see. The one cock of the walk — that's what you want to be.

BRACK (*nodding slowly and lowering his voice*): Yes, that's what I want to be. And that's what I'll fight for — with every means at my disposal.

HEDDA (*her smile vanishing*): You can be a dangerous person, can't you — in a tight corner.

BRACK: Do you think so?

HEDDA: Yes, now I'm beginning to think so. And I'm thoroughly grateful — that you have no kind of hold over me.

BRACK (*with an ambiguous laugh*): Ah, yes, Mrs. Hedda — perhaps you're right about that. If I had, then who knows just what I might do?

HEDDA: Now you listen here, Judge! That sounds too much like a threat.

BRACK (*rising*): Oh, nothing of the kind! A triangle, after all — is best fortified and defended by volunteers.

HEDDA: There we're agreed.

BRACK: Well, now that I've said all I have to say, I'd better get back to town. Good-bye, Mrs. Hedda. (*He goes toward the glass door.*)

HEDDA (*rising*): Are you going through the garden?

BRACK: Yes, I find it's shorter.

HEDDA: Yes, and then it's the back way, too.

BRACK: How true. I have nothing against back ways. At certain times they can be rather piquant.

HEDDA: You mean, when somebody's sharpshooting?

BRACK (*in the doorway, laughing*): Oh, people don't shoot their tame roosters!

HEDDA (*also laughing*): I guess not. Not when there's only one —

(*Still laughing, they nod good-bye to each other. He goes. She shuts the door after him, then stands for a moment, quite serious, looking out. She then goes over and glances through the curtains to the inner room. Moves to the writing table, takes Løvborg's envelope from the bookcase, and is about to page through it, when Berta's voice is heard loudly in the hall. Hedda turns and listens. She hurriedly locks the envelope in the drawer and lays the key on the inkstand. Eilert Løvborg, with his overcoat on and his hat in his hand, throws open the hall door. He looks confused and excited.*)

LØVBORG (*turned toward the hall*): And I'm telling you, I have to go in! I will, you hear me! (*He shuts the door, turns, sees Hedda, immediately gains control of himself and bows.*)

HEDDA (*at the writing table*): Well, Mr. Løvborg, it's late to call for Thea.

LØVBORG: Or rather early to call on you. You must forgive me.

HEDDA: How did you know she was still with me?

LØVBORG: They said at her lodgings that she'd been out all night.

HEDDA (*goes to the center table*): Did you notice anything in their faces when they said that?

LØVBORG (*looking at her inquiringly*): Notice anything?

HEDDA: I mean, did it look like they had their own thoughts on the matter?

LØVBORG (*suddenly understanding*): Oh yes, that's true? I'm dragging her down with me! Actually, I didn't notice anything. Tesman — I don't suppose he's up yet?

HEDDA: No, I don't think so.

LØVBORG: When did he get in?

HEDDA: Very late.

LØVBORG: Did he tell you anything?

HEDDA: Well, I heard you'd had a high time of it out at Judge Brack's.

LØVBORG: Anything else?

HEDDA: No, I don't think so. As a matter of fact, I was terribly sleepy —

(*Mrs. Elvsted comes in through the curtains to the inner room.*)

MRS. ELVSTED (*running toward him*): Oh, Eilert! At last — !

LØVBORG: Yes, at last. And too late.

MRS. ELVSTED (*looking anxiously at him*): What's too late?

LØVBORG: Everything's too late now. It's over with me.

MRS. ELVSTED: Oh no, no — don't say that!

LØVBORG: You'll say the same thing when you've heard —

MRS. ELVSTED: I won't hear anything!

HEDDA: Maybe you'd prefer to talk with her alone. I can leave.

LØVBORG: No, stay — you too. Please.

MRS. ELVSTED: But I tell you, I don't want to hear anything!

ABOVE LEFT: Hedda silhouetted near a portrait of her father, the General, in the Hartford Stage Company's 1988 production. ABOVE RIGHT: Tesman (Scott Wentworth), Løvborg (Richard Bekins), and Hedda (Mary Layne) discuss Løvborg's manuscript. LEFT: Tesman and Mrs. Elvsted (Elisabeth Berridge) plan to rewrite Løvborg's lost manuscript. ABOVE FAR RIGHT: Judge Brack (William Duff-Griffin) examines Hedda's father's pistol.

LØVBORG: It's nothing about last night.

MRS. ELVSTED: What is it, then —

LØVBORG: It's simply this, that from now on, we separate.

MRS. ELVSTED: Separate!

HEDDA (*involuntarily*): I knew it!

LØVBORG: Because I have no more use for you, Thea.

MRS. ELVSTED: And you can stand there and say that! No more use for me! Then I'm not going to help you now, as I have? We're not going to go on working together?

LØVBORG: I have no plans for any more work.

MRS. ELVSTED (*in desperation*): Then what will I do with my life?

LØVBORG: You must try to go on living as if you'd never known me.

MRS. ELVSTED: But I can't do that!

LØVBORG: You must try to, Thea. You'll have to go home again —

MRS. ELVSTED (*in a fury of protest*): Never! No! Where you are, that's where I want to be! I won't be driven away like this! I'm going to stay right here — and be together with you when the book comes out.

HEDDA (*in a tense whisper*): Ah, yes — the book!

LØVBORG (*looks at her*): My book and Thea's — for that's what it is.

MRS. ELVSTED: Yes, that's what I feel it is. And that's why I have the right, as well, to be with you when it comes out. I want to see you covered with honor and respect again. And the joy — I want to share the joy of it with you too.

LØVBORG: Thea — our book's never coming out.

HEDDA: Ah!

MRS. ELVSTED: Never coming out!

LØVBORG: *Can* never come out.

MRS. ELVSTED (*with anguished foreboding*): Eilert — what have you done with the manuscript?

HEDDA (*watching him intently*): Yes, the manuscript — ?

MRS. ELVSTED: Where is it!

LØVBORG: Oh, Thea — don't ask me that.

MRS. ELVSTED: Yes, yes, I have to know. I've got a right to know, this minute!

LØVBORG: The manuscript — well, you see — I tore the manuscript into a thousand pieces.

MRS. ELVSTED (*screams*): Oh no, no — !

HEDDA (*involuntarily*): But that just isn't — !

LØVBORG (*looks at her*): Isn't so, you think?

HEDDA (*composing herself*): All right. Of course; if you say it yourself. But it sounds so incredible —

LØVBORG: It's true, all the same.

MRS. ELVSTED (*wringing her hands*): Oh, God — oh, God, Hedda — to tear his own work to bits!

LØVBORG: I've torn my own life to bits. So why not tear up my life's work as well —

MRS. ELVSTED: And you did this thing last night!

LØVBORG: Yes, you heard me. In a thousand pieces. And scattered them into the fjord. Far out. At least there, there's clean salt water. Let them drift out to sea — drift with the tide and the wind. And after a while, they'll sink. Deeper and deeper. As I will, Thea.

MRS. ELVSTED: Do you know, Eilert, this thing you've done with the book — for the rest of my life it will seem to me as if you'd killed a little child.

LØVBORG: You're right. It was like murdering a child.

MRS. ELVSTED: But how could you do it — ! It was my child too.

HEDDA (*almost inaudible*): Ah, the child —

MRS. ELVSTED (*breathes heavily*): Then it *is* all over. Yes, yes, I'm going now, Hedda.

HEDDA: But you're not leaving town, are you?

MRS. ELVSTED: Oh, I don't know myself what I'll do. Everything's dark for me now. (*She goes out the hall door.*)

HEDDA (*stands waiting a moment*): You're not going to take her home, then, Mr. Løvborg?

LØVBORG: I? Through the streets? So people could see that she'd been with me?

HEDDA: I don't know what else may have happened last night. But is it so completely irredeemable?

LØVBORG: It won't just end with last night — I know that well enough. But the thing is, I've lost all desire for that kind of life. I don't want to start it again, not now. It's the courage and daring for life — that's what she's broken in me.

HEDDA (*staring straight ahead*): To think that pretty little fool could have a man's fate in her hands. (*Looks at him.*) But still, how could you treat her so heartlessly?

LØVBORG: Oh, don't say it was heartless!

HEDDA: To go ahead and destroy what's filled her whole being for months and years! That's not heartless?

LØVBORG: To you, Hedda — I can tell the truth.

HEDDA: The truth?

LØVBORG: Promise me first — give me your word that what I tell you now, you'll never let Thea know.

HEDDA: You have my word.

LØVBORG: Good. I can tell you, then, that what I said here just now isn't true.

HEDDA: About the manuscript?

LØVBORG: Yes. I didn't tear it up — or throw it in the fjord.

HEDDA: No, but — where is it, then?

LØVBORG: I've destroyed it all the same, Hedda. Utterly destroyed it.

HEDDA: I don't understand.

LØVBORG: Thea said that what I've done, for her was like killing a child.

HEDDA: Yes — that's what she said.

LØVBORG: But killing his child — that's not the worst thing a father can do.

HEDDA: *That's* not the worst?

LØVBORG: No. I wanted to spare Thea the worst.

HEDDA: And what's that — the worst?

LØVBORG: Suppose now, Hedda, that a man — in the early morning hours, say — after a wild, drunken night, comes home to his child's mother and says: "Listen — I've been out to this place and that — here and there. And I had our child with me. In this place and that. And I lost the child. Just lost it. God only

knows what hands it's come into. Or who's got hold of it."

HEDDA: Well — but when all's said and done — it was only a book —

LØVBORG: Thea's pure soul was in that book.

HEDDA: Yes, I understand.

LØVBORG: Well, then you can understand that for her and me there's no future possible any more.

HEDDA: What do you intend to do?

LØVBORG: Nothing. Just put an end to it all. The sooner the better.

HEDDA (*coming a step closer*): Eilert Løvborg — listen to me. Couldn't you arrange that — that it's done beautifully?

LØVBORG: Beautifully? (*Smiles.*) With vine leaves in my hair, as you used to dream in the old days —

HEDDA: No. I don't believe in vine leaves anymore. But beautifully, all the same. For this once — ! Good-bye! You must go now — and never come here again.

LØVBORG: Good-bye, then. And give my best to George Tesman. (*He turns to leave.*)

HEDDA: No, wait. I want you to have a souvenir from me.

(*She goes to the writing desk and opens the drawer and the pistol case, then comes back to Løvborg with one of the pistols.*)

LØVBORG (*looks at her*): That? Is that the souvenir?

HEDDA (*nods slowly*): Do you recognize it? It was aimed at you once.

LØVBORG: You should have used it then.

HEDDA: Here! Use it now.

LØVBORG (*puts the pistol in his breast pocket*): Thanks.

HEDDA: And beautifully, Eilert Løvborg. Promise me that!

LØVBORG: Good-bye, Hedda Gabler.

(*He goes out the hall door. Hedda listens a moment at the door. Then she goes over to the writing table, takes out the envelope with the manuscript, glances inside, pulls some of the sheets half out and looks at them. She then goes over to the armchair by the stove and sits, with the envelope in her lap. After a moment, she opens the stove door, then brings out the manuscript.*)

HEDDA (*throwing some of the sheets into the fire and whispering to herself*): Now I'm burning your child, Thea! You, with your curly hair! (*Throwing another sheaf in the stove.*) Your child and Eilert Løvborg's. (*Throwing in the rest.*) Now I'm burning — I'm burning the child.

ACT IV

(*The same rooms at the Tesmans'. It is evening. The drawing room is in darkness. The inner room is lit by the hanging lamp over the table. The curtains are drawn across the glass door. Hedda, dressed in black, is pacing back and forth in the dark room. She then enters the inner room, moving out of sight toward the left. Several chords are heard on the piano. She comes in view again, returning into the drawing room. Berta enters from the right through the inner room with a lighted lamp, which she puts on the table in front of the settee in the drawing room. Her eyes are red from crying, and she has black ribbons on her cap. She goes quietly and discreetly out to the right. Hedda moves to the glass door, lifts the curtains aside slightly, and gazes out into the darkness.)*

(Shortly after, Miss Tesman, in mourning, with a hat and veil, comes in from the hall. Hedda goes toward her, extending her hand.)

MISS TESMAN: Well, Hedda, here I am, all dressed in mourning. My poor sister's ordeal is finally over.

HEDDA: As you see, I've already heard. Tesman sent me a note.

MISS TESMAN: Yes, he promised he would. But all the same I thought that, to Hedda — here in the house of life — I ought to bear the news of death myself.

HEDDA: That was very kind of you.

MISS TESMAN: Ah, Rina ought not to have passed on just now. This is no time for grief in Hedda's house.

HEDDA (*changing the subject*): She had a peaceful death, then, Miss Tesman?

MISS TESMAN: Oh, she went so calmly, so beautifully. And so inexpressibly happy that she could see George once again. And say good-bye to him properly. Is it possible that he's still not home?

HEDDA: No, he wrote that I shouldn't expect him too early. But won't you sit down?

MISS TESMAN: No, thank you, my dear — blessed Hedda. I'd love to, but I have so little time. I want to see her dressed and made ready as best as I can. She should go to her grave looking her finest.

HEDDA: Can't I help you with something?

MISS TESMAN: Oh, you mustn't think of it. This is nothing for Hedda Tesman to put her hands to. Or let her thoughts dwell on, either. Not at a time like this, no.

HEDDA: Ah, thoughts — they're not so easy to control —

MISS TESMAN (*continuing*): Well, there's life for you. At my house now we'll be sewing a shroud for Rina. And here, too, there'll be sewing soon, I imagine. But a far different kind, praise God!

(George Tesman enters from the hall.)

HEDDA: Well, at last! It's about time.

TESMAN: Are you here, Aunt Julie? With Hedda? Think of that!

MISS TESMAN: I was just this minute leaving, dear boy. Well, did you get done all you promised you would?

TESMAN: No, I'm really afraid I've forgotten half. I'll have to run over and see you tomorrow. My brain's completely in a whirl today. I can't keep my thoughts together.

MISS TESMAN: But George dear, you mustn't take it that way.

TESMAN: Oh? Well, how should I, then?

MISS TESMAN: You should rejoice in your grief. Rejoice in everything that's happened, as I do.

TESMAN: Oh yes, of course. You're thinking of Auntie Rina.

HEDDA: It's going to be lonely for you, Miss Tesman.

MISS TESMAN: For the first few days, yes. But it won't be for long, I hope. I won't let dear Rina's little room stand empty.

TESMAN: No? Who would you want to have in it? Hm?

MISS TESMAN: Oh, there's always some poor invalid in need of care and attention.

HEDDA: Would you really take another burden like that on yourself?

MISS TESMAN: Burden! Mercy on you, child — it's been no burden for me.

HEDDA: But now, with a stranger —

MISS TESMAN: Oh, you soon make friends with an invalid. And I do so much need someone to live for — I, too. Well, thank God, in this house as well, there soon ought to be work that an old aunt can turn her hand to.

HEDDA: Oh, forget about us —

TESMAN: Yes, think how pleasant it could be for the three of us if —

HEDDA: If — ?

TESMAN (*uneasily*): Oh, nothing. It'll all take care of itself. Let's hope so. Uh?

MISS TESMAN: Ah, yes. Well, I expect you two have things to talk about. (*Smiles.*) And perhaps Hedda has something to tell you, George. Good-bye. I'll have to get home now to Rina. (*Turning at the door.*) Goodness me, how strange! Now Rina's both with me and with poor dear Jochum as well.

TESMAN: Yes, imagine that, Aunt Julie! Hm?

(Miss Tesman goes out the hall door.)

HEDDA (*follows Tesman with a cold, probing look*): I almost think you feel this death more than she.

TESMAN: Oh, it's not just Auntie Rina's death. It's Eilert who has me worried.

HEDDA (*quickly*): Any news about him?

TESMAN: I stopped up at his place this afternoon, thinking to tell him that the manuscript was safe.

HEDDA: Well? Didn't you see him then?

TESMAN: No, he wasn't home. But afterward I met Mrs. Elvsted, and she said he'd been here early this morning.

HEDDA: Yes, right after you left.

TESMAN: And apparently he said he'd torn his manuscript up. Uh?

HEDDA: Yes, he claimed that he had.

TESMAN: But good Lord, then he must have been completely demented! Well, then I guess you didn't dare give it back to him, Hedda, did you?

HEDDA: No, he didn't get it.

TESMAN: But you did tell him we had it, I suppose?

HEDDA: No. (*Quickly.*) Did you tell Mrs. Elvsted anything?

TESMAN: No, I thought I'd better not. But you should

have said something to him. Just think, if he goes off in desperation and does himself some harm! Give me the manuscript, Hedda! I'm taking it back to him right away. Where do you have it?

HEDDA (*cold and impassive, leaning against the armchair*): I don't have it anymore.

TESMAN: You don't have it! What on earth do you mean by that?

HEDDA: I burned it — the whole thing.

TESMAN (*with a start of terror*): Burned it! Burned Eilert Løvborg's manuscript!

HEDDA: Stop shouting. The maid could hear you.

TESMAN: Burned it! But my God in heaven — ! No, no, no — that's impossible!

HEDDA: Yes, but it's true, all the same.

TESMAN: But do you realize what you've done, Hedda! It's illegal disposition of lost property. Just think! Yes, you can ask Judge Brack; he'll tell you.

HEDDA: It would be wiser not mentioning this — either to the judge or to anyone else.

TESMAN: But how could you go and do such an incredible thing! Whatever put it into your head? What got into you, anyway? Answer me! Well?

HEDDA (*suppressing an almost imperceptible smile*): I did it for your sake, George.

TESMAN: For my sake!

HEDDA: When you came home this morning and told about how he'd read to you —

TESMAN: Yes, yes, then what?

HEDDA: Then you confessed that you envied him this book.

TESMAN: Good Lord, I didn't mean it literally.

HEDDA: Never mind. I still couldn't bear the thought that anyone should eclipse you.

TESMAN (*in an outburst of mingled doubt and joy*): Hedda — is this true, what you say! Yes, but — but — I never dreamed you could show your love like this. Imagine!

HEDDA: Well, then it's best you know that — that I'm going to — (*Impatiently, breaking off.*) No, no — you ask your Aunt Julie. She's the one who can tell you.

TESMAN: Oh, I'm beginning to understand you, Hedda! (*Claps his hands together.*) Good heavens, no! Is it actually *that*! Can it be? Uh?

HEDDA: Don't shout so. The maid can hear you.

TESMAN: The maid! Oh, Hedda, you're priceless, really! The maid — but that's Berta! Why, I'll go out and tell her myself.

HEDDA (*clenching her fists in despair*): Oh, I'll die — I'll die of all this!

TESMAN: Of what, Hedda? Uh?

HEDDA: Of all these — absurdities — George.

TESMAN: Absurdities? What's absurd about my being so happy? Well, all right — I guess there's no point in my saying anything to Berta.

HEDDA: Oh, go ahead — why not that, too?

TESMAN: No, no, not yet. But Aunt Julie will have to hear. And then, that you've started to call me George, too! Imagine! Oh, Aunt Julie will be so glad — so glad!

HEDDA: When she hears that I burned Eilert Løvborg's book — for your sake?

TESMAN: Well, as far as that goes — this thing with the book — of course, no one's to know about that. But that you have a love that burns for me Hedda — Aunt Julie can certainly share in that! You know, I wonder, really, if things such as this are common among young wives? Hm?

HEDDA: I think you should ask Aunt Julie about that, too.

TESMAN: Yes, I definitely will, when I have the chance.

(*Mrs. Elvsted, dressed as on her first visit, with hat and coat, comes in the hall door.*)

MRS. ELVSTED (*greets them hurriedly and speaks in agitation*): Oh, Hedda dear, don't be annoyed that I'm back again.

HEDDA: Has something happened, Thea?

TESMAN: Something with Eilert Løvborg? Uh?

MRS. ELVSTED: Yes, I'm so terribly afraid he's met with an accident.

HEDDA (*seizing her arm*): Ah — you think so!

TESMAN: But, Mrs. Elvsted, where did you get that idea?

MRS. ELVSTED: Well, because I heard them speaking of him at the boardinghouse, just as I came in. Oh, there are the most incredible rumors about him in town today.

TESMAN: Yes, you know, I heard them too! And yet I could swear that he went right home to bed last night. Imagine!

HEDDA: Well — what did they say at the boardinghouse?

MRS. ELVSTED: Oh, I couldn't get anything clearly. They either didn't know much themselves, or else — They stopped talking when they saw me. And I didn't dare to ask.

TESMAN (*restlessly moving about*): Let's hope — let's hope you misunderstood them, Mrs. Elvsted!

MRS. ELVSTED: No, no, I'm sure they were talking of him. And then I heard them say something or other about the hospital, or —

TESMAN: The hospital!

HEDDA: No — but that's impossible!

MRS. ELVSTED: Oh, I'm so deathly afraid for him now. And later I went up to his lodging to ask about him.

HEDDA: But was that very wise to do, Thea?

MRS. ELVSTED: What else could I do? I couldn't bear the uncertainty any longer.

TESMAN: But didn't you find him there either? Hm?

MRS. ELVSTED: No. And no one had any word of him. He hadn't been in since yesterday afternoon, they said.

TESMAN: Yesterday! Imagine them saying that!

MRS. ELVSTED: I think there can only be one reason — something terrible must have happened to him!

TESMAN: Hedda dear — suppose I went over and made a few inquiries — ?

HEDDA: No, no — don't you get mixed up in this business.

(*Judge Brack, with hat in hand, enters from the hall, Berta letting him in and shutting the door after him. He looks grave and bows silently.*)

TESMAN: Oh, is that you, Judge? Uh?

BRACK: Yes, it's imperative that I see you this evening.

TESMAN: I can see that you've heard the news from Aunt Julie.

BRACK: Among other things, yes.

TESMAN: It's sad, isn't it? Uh?

BRACK: Well, my dear Tesman, that depends on how you look at it.

TESMAN (*eyes him doubtfully*): Has anything else happened?

BRACK: Yes, as a matter of fact.

HEDDA (*intently*): Something distressing, Judge?

BRACK: Again, that depends on how you look at it, Mrs. Tesman.

MRS. ELVSTED (*in an uncontrollable outburst*): Oh, it's something about Eilert Løvborg!

BRACK (*glancing at her*): Now how did you hit upon that, Mrs. Elvsted? Have you, perhaps, heard something already — ?

MRS. ELVSTED (*in confusion*): No, no, nothing like that — but —

TESMAN: Oh, for heaven's sake, tell us!

BRACK (*with a shrug*): Well — I'm sorry, but — Eilert Løvborg's been taken to the hospital. He's dying.

MRS. ELVSTED (*crying out*): Oh, God, oh, God — !

TESMAN: To the hospital! And dying!

HEDDA (*involuntarily*): All so soon — !

MRS. ELVSTED (*wailing*): And we parted in anger, Hedda!

HEDDA (*in a whisper*): Thea — be careful, Thea!

MRS. ELVSTED (*ignoring her*): I have to see him! I have to see him alive!

BRACK: No use, Mrs. Elvsted. No one's allowed in to see him.

MRS. ELVSTED: Oh, but tell me, at least, what happened to him! What is it?

TESMAN: Don't tell me he tried to — ! Uh?

HEDDA: Yes, he did, I'm sure of it.

TESMAN: Hedda — how can you say — !

BRACK (*his eyes steadily on her*): Unhappily, you've guessed exactly right, Mrs. Tesman.

MRS. ELVSTED: Oh, how horrible!

TESMAN: Did it himself! Imagine!

HEDDA: Shot himself!

BRACK: Again, exactly right, Mrs. Tesman.

MRS. ELVSTED (*trying to control herself*): When did it happen, Mr. Brack?

BRACK: This afternoon. Between three and four.

TESMAN: But good Lord — where did he do it, then? Hm?

BRACK (*hesitating slightly*): Where? Why — in his room, I suppose.

MRS. ELVSTED: No, that can't be right. I was there between six and seven.

BRACK: Well, somewhere else, then. I don't know exactly. I only know he was found like that. Shot — in the chest.

MRS. ELVSTED: What a horrible thought! That he should end that way!

HEDDA (*to Brack*): In the chest, you say.

BRACK: Yes — I told you.

HEDDA: Not the temple?

BRACK: In the chest, Mrs. Tesman.

HEDDA: Well — well, the chest is just as good.

BRACK: Why, Mrs. Tesman?

HEDDA (*evasively*): Oh, nothing — never mind.

TESMAN: And the wound is critical, you say? Uh?

BRACK: The wound is absolutely fatal. Most likely, it's over already.

MRS. ELVSTED: Yes, yes, I can feel that it is! It's over! All over! Oh, Hedda — !

TESMAN: But tell me now — how did you learn about this?

BRACK (*brusquely*): One of the police. Someone I talked to.

HEDDA (*in a clear, bold voice*): At last, something truly done!

TESMAN (*shocked*): My God, what are you saying, Hedda!

HEDDA: I'm saying there's beauty in all this.

BRACK: Hm, Mrs. Tesman.

TESMAN: Beauty! What an idea!

MRS. ELVSTED: Oh, Hedda, how can you talk about beauty in such a thing?

HEDDA: Eilert Løvborg's settled accounts with himself. He's had the courage to do what — what had to be done.

MRS. ELVSTED: Don't you believe it! It never happened like that. When he did this, he was in a delirium!

TESMAN: In despair, you mean.

HEDDA: No, he wasn't. I'm certain of that.

MRS. ELVSTED: But he was! In delirium! The way he was when he tore up our book.

BRACK (*startled*): The book? His manuscript, you mean? He tore it up?

MRS. ELVSTED: Yes. Last night.

TESMAN (*in a low whisper*): Oh, Hedda, we'll never come clear of all this.

BRACK: Hm, that's very strange.

TESMAN (*walking about the room*): To think Eilert could be gone like that! And then not to have left behind the one thing that could have made his name live on.

MRS. ELVSTED: Oh, if it could only be put together again!

TESMAN: Yes, imagine if that were possible! I don't know what I wouldn't give —

MRS. ELVSTED: Perhaps it can, Mr. Tesman.

TESMAN: What do you mean?

MRS. ELVSTED (*searching in the pockets of her dress*): Look here. I've kept all these notes that he used to dictate from.

HEDDA (*coming a step closer*): Ah — !

TESMAN: You've kept them, Mrs. Elvsted! Uh?

MRS. ELVSTED: Yes, here they are. I took them along when I left home. And they've stayed right here in my pocket —

TESMAN: Oh, let me look!

MRS. ELVSTED (*hands him a sheaf of small papers*): But they're in such a mess. All mixed up.

TESMAN: But just think, if we could decipher them, even so! Maybe the two of us could help each other —

MRS. ELVSTED: Oh yes! At least, we could try —

TESMAN: We can do it! We *must*! I'll give my whole life to this!

HEDDA: You, George. Your life?

TESMAN: Yes. Or, let's say, all the time I can spare. My own research will have to wait. You can understand, Hedda. Hm! It's something I owe to Eilert's memory.

HEDDA: Perhaps.

TESMAN: And so, my dear Mrs. Elvsted, let's see if we can't join forces. Good Lord, there's no use brooding over what's gone by. Uh? We must try to compose our thoughts as much as we can, in order that —

MRS. ELVSTED: Yes, yes, Mr. Tesman, I'll do the best I can.

TESMAN: Come on, then. Let's look over these notes right away. Where shall we sit? Here? No, in there, in the back room. Excuse us, Judge. You come with me, Mrs. Elvsted.

MRS. ELVSTED: Dear God — if only we can do this!

(*Tesman and Mrs. Elvsted go into the inner room. She takes off her hat and coat. They both sit at the table under the hanging lamp and become totally immersed in examining the papers. Hedda goes toward the stove and sits in the armchair. After a moment Brack goes over by her.*)

HEDDA (*her voice lowered*): Ah, Judge — what a liberation it is, this act of Eilert Løvborg's.

BRACK: Liberation, Mrs. Hedda? Well, yes, for him; you could certainly say he's been liberated —

HEDDA: I mean for me. It's liberating to know that there can still actually be a free and courageous action in this world. Something that shimmers with spontaneous beauty.

BRACK (*smiling*): Hm — my dear Mrs. Hedda —

HEDDA: Oh, I already know what you're going to say. Because you're a kind of specialist too, you know, just like — Oh, well!

BRACK (*looking fixedly at her*): Eilert Løvborg meant more to you than you're willing to admit, perhaps even to yourself. Or am I wrong about that?

HEDDA: I won't answer that sort of question. I simply know that Eilert Løvborg's had the courage to live life after his own mind. And now — this last great act, filled with beauty! That he had the strength and the will to break away from the banquet of life — so young.

BRACK: It grieves me, Mrs. Hedda — but I'm afraid I have to disburden you of this beautiful illusion.

HEDDA: Illusion?

BRACK: One that, in any case, you'd soon be deprived of.

HEDDA: And what's that?

BRACK: He didn't shoot himself — of his own free will.

HEDDA: He didn't — !

BRACK: No. This whole affair didn't go off quite the way I described it.

HEDDA (*in suspense*): You've hidden something? What is it?

BRACK: For poor Mrs. Elvsted's sake, I did a little editing here and there.

HEDDA: Where?

BRACK: First, the fact that he's already dead.

HEDDA: In the hospital?

BRACK: Yes. Without regaining consciousness.

HEDDA: What else did you hide?

BRACK: That the incident didn't occur in his room.

HEDDA: Well, that's rather unimportant.

BRACK: Not entirely. Suppose I were to tell you that Eilert Løvborg was found shot in — in Mademoiselle Diana's boudoir.

HEDDA (*half rises, then sinks back again*): That's impossible, Judge! He wouldn't have gone there again today!

BRACK: He was there this afternoon. He went there, demanding something he said they'd stolen from him. Kept raving about a lost child —

HEDDA: Ah — so that was it —

BRACK: I thought perhaps that might be his manuscript. But, I hear now, he destroyed that himself. So it must have been his wallet.

HEDDA: I suppose so. Then, there — that's where they found him.

BRACK: Yes, there. With a discharged pistol in his breast pocket. The bullet had wounded him fatally.

HEDDA: In the chest — yes.

BRACK: No — in the stomach — more or less.

HEDDA (*stares up at him with a look of revulsion*): That too! What is it, this — this curse — that everything I touch turns ridiculous and vile?

BRACK: There's something else, Mrs. Hedda. Another ugly aspect to the case.

HEDDA: What's that?

BRACK: The pistol he was carrying —

HEDDA (*breathlessly*): Well! What about it?

BRACK: He must have stolen it.

HEDDA (*springs up*): Stolen! That's not true! He didn't!

BRACK: It seems impossible otherwise. He must have stolen it — shh!

(*Tesman and Mrs. Elvsted have gotten up from the table in the inner room and come into the drawing room.*)

TESMAN (*with both hands full of papers*): Hedda dear — it's nearly impossible to see in there under that overhead lamp. You know?

HEDDA: Yes, I know.

TESMAN: Do you think it would be all right if we used your table for a while? Hm?

HEDDA: Yes, I don't mind. (*Quickly.*) Wait! No, let me clear it off first.

TESMAN: Oh, don't bother, Hedda. There's plenty of room.

HEDDA: No, no, let me just clear it off, can't you? I'll put all this in by the piano. There!

(*She has pulled out an object covered with sheet music from under the bookcase, adds more music to it, and carries the whole thing into the inner room and off left. Tesman puts the scraps of paper on the writing table and moves the lamp over from the corner table. He and Mrs. Elvsted sit down and go on with their work. Hedda comes back.*)

HEDDA (*behind Mrs. Elvsted's chair, gently ruffling her hair*): Well, my sweet little Thea — how is it going with Eilert Løvborg's monument?

MRS. ELVSTED (*looking despondently up at her*): Oh, dear — it's going to be terribly hard to set these in order.

TESMAN: It's got to be done. There's just no alternative. Besides, setting other people's papers in order — it's exactly what I can do best.

(*Hedda goes over by the stove and sits on one of the taborets. Brack stands over her, leaning on the armchair.*)

HEDDA (*whispering*): What did you say about the pistol?

BRACK (*softly*): That he must have stolen it.

HEDDA: Why, necessarily, that?

BRACK: Because every other explanation would seem impossible, Mrs. Hedda.

HEDDA: I see.

BRACK (*glancing at her*): Of course, Eilert Løvborg was here this morning. Wasn't he?

HEDDA: Yes.

BRACK: Were you alone with him?

HEDDA: Yes, briefly.

BRACK: Did you leave the room while he was here?

HEDDA: No.

BRACK: Consider. You didn't leave, even for a moment.

HEDDA: Well, yes, perhaps, just for a moment — into the hall.

BRACK: And where did you have your pistol case?

HEDDA: I had it put away in —

BRACK: Yes, Mrs. Hedda?

HEDDA: It was lying over there, on the writing table.

BRACK: Have you looked since to see if both pistols are there?

HEDDA: No.

BRACK: No need to. I saw the pistol. Løvborg had it on him. I knew it immediately, from yesterday. And other days too.

HEDDA: Do you have it, maybe?

BRACK: No, the police have it.

HEDDA: What will they do with it?

BRACK: Try to trace it to the owner.

HEDDA: Do you think they'll succeed?

BRACK (*bending over her and whispering*): No, Hedda Gabler — as long as I keep quiet.

HEDDA (*looking at him anxiously*): And if you don't keep quiet — then what?

BRACK (*with a shrug*): Counsel could always claim that the pistol was stolen.

HEDDA (*decisively*): I'd rather die!

BRACK (*smiling*): People *say* such things. But they don't *do* them.

HEDDA (*without answering*): And what, then, if the pistol wasn't stolen. And they found the owner. What would happen?

BRACK: Well, Hedda — there'd be a scandal.

HEDDA: A scandal!

BRACK: A scandal, yes — the kind you're so deathly afraid of. Naturally, you'd appear in court — you and Mademoiselle Diana. She'd have to explain how the whole thing occurred. Whether it was an accident or homicide. Was he trying to pull the pistol out of his pocket to threaten her? Is that why it went off? Or had she torn the pistol out of his hand, shot him, and slipped it back in his pocket again? It's rather like her to do that, you know. She's a powerful woman, this Mademoiselle Diana.

HEDDA: But all that sordid business is no concern of mine.

BRACK: No. But you'll have to answer the question: Why did you give Eilert Løvborg the pistol? And what conclusions will people draw from the fact that you did give it to him?

HEDDA (*her head sinking*): That's true. I hadn't thought of that.

BRACK: Well, luckily there's no danger, as long as I keep quiet.

HEDDA: So I'm in your power, Judge. You have your hold over me from now on.

BRACK (*whispers more softly*): My dearest Hedda — believe me — I won't abuse my position.

HEDDA: All the same, I'm in your power. Tied to your will and desire. Not free. Not free, then! (*Rises impetuously.*) No — I can't bear the thought of it. Never!

BRACK (*looks at her half mockingly*): One usually manages to adjust to the inevitable.

HEDDA (*returning his look*): Yes, perhaps so. (*She goes over to the writing table. Suppressing an involuntary smile, she imitates Tesman's intonation.*) Well? Getting on with it, George? Uh?

TESMAN: Goodness knows, dear. It's going to mean months and months of work, in any case.

HEDDA (*as before*): Imagine that! (*Runs her hand lightly through Mrs. Elvsted's hair.*) Don't you find it strange, Thea? Here you are, sitting now beside Tesman — just as you used to sit with Eilert Løvborg.

MRS. ELVSTED: Oh, if I could only inspire your husband in the same way.

HEDDA: Oh, that will surely come — in time.

TESMAN: Yes, you know what, Hedda — I really think I'm beginning to feel something of the kind. But you go back and sit with Judge Brack.

HEDDA: Is there nothing the two of you need from me now?

TESMAN: No, nothing in the world. (*Turning his head.*)

From now on, Judge, you'll have to be good enough to keep Hedda company.

BRACK (*with a glance at Hedda*): I'll take the greatest pleasure in that.

HEDDA: Thanks. But I'm tired this evening. I want to rest a while in there on the sofa.

TESMAN: Yes, do that, dear. Uh?

(*Hedda goes into the inner room, pulling the curtains closed after her. Short pause. Suddenly she is heard playing a wild dance melody on the piano.*)

MRS. ELVSTED (*starting up from her chair*): Oh — what's that?

TESMAN (*running to the center doorway*): But Hedda dearest — don't go playing dance music tonight! Think of Auntie Rina! And Eilert, too!

HEDDA (*putting her head out between the curtains*): And Auntie Julie. And all the rest of them. From now on I'll be quiet. (*She closes the curtains again.*)

TESMAN (*at the writing table*): She can't feel very happy seeing us do this melancholy work. You know what, Mrs. Elvsted — you must move in with Aunt Julie. Then I can come over evenings. And then we can sit and work *there*. Uh?

MRS. ELVSTED: Yes, perhaps that would be best —

HEDDA: I can hear everything you say, Tesman. But what will I do evenings over here?

TESMAN (*leafing through the notes*): Oh, I'm sure Judge Brack will be good enough to stop by and see you.

BRACK (*in the armchair, calling out gaily*): I couldn't miss an evening, Mrs. Tesman! We'll have great times here together, the two of us!

HEDDA (*in a clear, ringing voice*): Yes, you can hope so, Judge, can't you? You, the one cock of the walk —

(*A shot is heard within. Tesman, Mrs. Elvsted, and Brack start from their chairs.*)

TESMAN: Oh, now she's fooling with those pistols again.

(*He throws the curtains back and runs in. Mrs. Elvsted follows. Hedda lies, lifeless, stretched out on the sofa. Confusion and cries. Berta comes in, bewildered, from the right.*)

TESMAN (*shrieking to Brack*): Shot herself! Shot herself in the temple! Can you imagine!

BRACK (*in the armchair, prostrated*): But good God! People don't *do* such things!

COMMENTARIES

   Henrik Ibsen's notes on *Hedda Gabler* show us what a complex process he went through to conceive the character and to put her in action. One sees his method of sketching out the action of the play and then commenting to himself on what the action implies. Caroline W. Mayerson's extensive commentary gives us insight into the symbolic levels of meaning in the play. Since the play has been considered a masterpiece of realism, some critics have assumed that it has no symbolic texture. Mayerson counters that view with a detailed analysis. Jan Kott's interpretation of Hedda's pistols, which he sees as explicit sexual symbols, helps to explain Mayerson's claim that the drama, while realistic, does not ignore the deeper significance of its own imagery. Clive Barnes reviews Glenda Jackson's 1975 portrayal of Hedda in the Royal Shakespeare Company's production, finding in her a powerful "mistress of her own fate."

Henrik Ibsen (1828–1906)
NOTES FOR *HEDDA GABLER*   *1890*

TRANSLATED BY EVERT SPRINCHORN

Like most playwrights, Ibsen kept a notebook into which he jotted ideas as he was writing his plays. The notes that follow are some of those he gathered as he was writing Hedda Gabler. *They show how his mind worked on the material, how he considered alternatives to what he was doing, and how he permitted his material to grow and develop.*

¶ One talks about building railways and highways for the cause of progress. But no, no, that is not what is needed. Space must be cleared so that the spirit of man can make its great turnabout. For it has gone astray. The spirit of man has gone astray. . . .

¶ *Notes:* One evening as Hedda and Tesman, together with some others, were on their way home from a party, Hedda remarked as they walked by a charming house that was where she would like to live. She meant it, but she said it only to keep the conversation with Tesman going. "He simply cannot carry on a conversation."

The house was actually for rent or sale. Tesman had been pointed out as the coming young man. And later when he proposed, and let slip that he too had dreamed of living there, she accepted.

He too had liked the house very much.

They get married. And they rent the house.[1]

But when Hedda returns as a young wife, with a vague sense of responsibility, the whole thing seems distasteful to her. She conceives a kind of hatred for the house just because it has become her home. She confides this to Brack. She evades the question with Tesman.

¶ The play shall deal with "the impossible," that is, to aspire to and strive for something which is against all the conventions, against that which is acceptable to conscious minds — Hedda's included.

¶ The episode of the hat makes Aunt Rising° lose her composure. She leaves — That it could be taken for the maid's hat — no, that's going too far!

That my hat, which I've had for over nine years, could be taken for the maid's — no, that's really too much! . . .

¶ Very few true parents are to be found in the world. Most people grow up under the influence of aunts or uncles — either neglected and misunderstood or else spoiled. . . .

¶ Hedda feels herself demoniacally attracted by the tendencies of the times. But she lacks courage. Her thoughts remain theories, ineffective dreams.

---

[1]Both of them, each in his and her own way, have seen in their common love for this house a sign of their mutual understanding. As if they sought and were drawn to a common home.

Then he rents the house. They get married and go abroad. He orders the house bought and his aunt furnishes it at his expense. Now it is their home. It is theirs and yet it is not, because it is not paid for. Everything depends on his getting the professorship. [Ibsen's note.]

Aunt Rising: Ibsen also spelled it *Rysing*. She became Aunt Juliana Tesman in the final version of the play.

¶ The feminine imagination is not active and independently creative like the masculine. It needs a bit of reality as a help.

¶ Løvborg has had inclinations toward "the bohemian life." Hedda is attracted in the same direction, but she does not dare to take the leap.

¶ Buried deep within Hedda there is a level of poetry. But the environment frightens her. Suppose she were to make herself ridiculous!

¶ Hedda realizes that she, much more than Thea, has abandoned her husband.

¶ The newly wedded couple return home in September — as the summer is dying. In the second act they sit in the garden — but with their coats on.

¶ Being frightened by one's own voice. Something strange, foreign.

¶ Newest Plan: The festivities in Tesman's garden — and Løvborg's defeat — already prepared for in the 1st act. Second act: the party —

¶ Hedda energetically refuses to serve as hostess. She will not celebrate their marriage because (in her opinion, it isn't a marriage). . . .

¶ Hedda is the type of woman in her position and with her character. She marries Tesman but she devotes her imagination to Eilert Løvborg. She leans back in her chair, closes her eyes, and dreams of his adventures. . . . This is the enormous difference: Mrs. Elvsted "works for his moral improvement." But for Hedda he is the object of cowardly, tempting daydreams. In reality she does not have the courage to be a part of anything like that. Then she realizes her condition. Caught! Can't comprehend it. Ridiculous! Ridiculous!

¶ The traditional delusion that one man and one woman are made for each other. Hedda has her roots in the conventional. She marries Tesman but she dreams of Eilert Løvborg. . . . She is disgusted by the latter's flight from life. He believes that this has raised him in her estimation. . . . Thea Elvsted is the conventional, sentimental, hysterical Philistine.

¶ Those Philistines, Mrs. E. and Tesman, explain my behavior by saying first I drink myself drunk and that the rest is done in insanity. It's a flight from reality which is an absolute necessity to me.

¶ *E. L.:* Give me something — a flower — at our parting. Hedda hands him the revolver.

Then Tesman arrives: Has he gone? "Yes." Do you think he will still compete against me? No, I don't think so. You can set your mind at rest.

¶ Tesman relates that when they were in Gratz she did not want to visit her relatives —

He misunderstands her real motives.

¶ In the last act as Tesman, Mrs. Elvsted, and Miss Rysing are consulting, Hedda plays in the small room at the back. She stops. The conversation continues. She appears in the doorway — Good night — I'm going now. Do you need me for anything? Tesman: No, nothing at all. Good night, my dear! . . . The shot is fired —

¶ Conclusion: All rush into the back room. Brack sinks as if paralyzed into a chair near the stove: But God have mercy — people don't *do* such things!

¶ When Hedda hints at her ideas to Brack, he says: Yes, yes, that's extraordinarily amusing — Ha ha ha! He does not understand that she is quite serious.

¶ Hedda is right in this: There is no love on Tesman's part. Nor on the aunt's part. However full of love she may be.

Eilert Løvborg has a double nature. It is a fiction that one loves only one person. He loves two — or many — alternately (to put it frivolously). But how can he explain his position? Mrs. Elvsted, who forces him to behave correctly, runs away from her husband. Hedda, who drives him beyond all limits, draws back at the thought of a scandal.

¶ Neither he nor Mrs. Elvsted understands the point. Tesman reads in the manuscript that was left behind about "the two ideals." Mrs. Elvsted can't explain to him what E. L. meant. Then comes the burlesque note: Both T. and Mrs. E. are going to devote their future lives to interpreting the mystery.

¶ Tesman thinks that Hedda hates E. L.

Mrs. Elvsted thinks so too.

Hedda sees their delusion but dares not disabuse them of it. There is something beautiful about having an aim in life. Even if it is a delusion —

She cannot do it. Take part in someone else's.

That is when she shoots herself.

The destroyed manuscript is entitled "The ~~Philosophy~~ Ethics of Future Society."

¶ Tesman is on the verge of losing his head. All this work meaningless. New thoughts! New visions! A whole new world! Then the two of them sit there, trying to find the meaning in it. Can't make any sense of it. . . .

¶ The greatest misery in this world is that so many have nothing to do but pursue happiness without being able to find it. . . .

¶ The simile: The journey of life = the journey on a train.

H.: One doesn't usually jump out of the compartment.

No, not when the train is moving.

Nor stand still when it is stationary. There's always someone on the platform, staring in.

¶ *Hedda:* Dream of a scandal — yes, I understand that well enough. But commit one — no, no, no.

¶ *Løvborg:* Now I understand. My ideal was an illusion. You aren't a bit better than I. Now I have nothing left to live for. Except pleasure — dissipation — as you call it . . . Wait, here's a present (The pistol)

¶ Tesman is nearsighted. Wears glasses. My, what a beautiful rose! Then he stuck his nose in the cactus. Ever since then — !

¶ NB: The mutual hatred of women. Women have no influence on external matters of government. Therefore they want to have an influence on souls. And then so many of them have no aim in life (the lack thereof is inherited) —

¶ Men and women don't belong to the same century. . . . What a great prejudice that one should love only *one*! . . .

¶ The demoniacal element in Hedda is this: She wants to exert her influence on someone — But once she has done so, she despises him. . . . The manuscript?

¶ In the third act Hedda questions Mrs. Elvsted. But if he's like that, why is he worth holding on to. . . . Yes, yes, I know — . . .

¶ NB!! The reversal in the play occurs during the big scene between Hedda and E. L. *He:* What a wretched business it is to conform to the existing morals. It would be ideal if a man of the present could live the life of the future. What a miserable business it is to fight over a professorship!

Hedda — that lovely girl! *H.:* No! *E. L.:* Yes, I'm going to say it. That lovely, cold girl — cold as marble.

I'm not dissipated fundamentally. But the life of reality isn't livable — . . .

¶ Life becomes for Hedda a ridiculous affair that isn't "worth seeing through to the end."

¶ The happiest mission in life is to place the people of today in the conditions of the future.

L.: Never put a child in this world, H.!

¶ When Brack speaks of a "triangular affair," Hedda thinks about what is going to happen and refers ambiguously to it. Brack doesn't understand.

¶ Brack cannot bear to be in a house where there are small children. "Children shouldn't be allowed to exist until they are fourteen or fifteen. That is, girls. What about boys? Shouldn't be allowed to exist at all — or else they should be raised outside the house."

¶ H. admits that children have always been a horror to her too.

¶ Hedda is strongly but imprecisely opposed to the idea that one should love "the family." The aunts mean nothing to her.

¶ It liberated Hedda's spirit to serve as a confessor to E. L. Her sympathy has secretly been on his side — But it became ugly when the public found out everything. Then she backed out.

¶ Main Points: (1) They are not all made to be mothers. (2) They are passionate but they are afraid of scandal. (3) They perceive that the times are full of missions worth devoting one's life to, but they cannot discover them.

¶ And besides Tesman is not exactly a professional, but he is a specialist. The Middle Ages are dead —

¶ T.: Now there you see also the great advantages to my studies. I can lose manuscripts and rewrite them — no inspiration needed —

¶ Hedda is completely taken up by the child that is to come, but when it is born she dreads what is to follow —

¶ Hedda must say somewhere in the play that she did not like to get out of her compartment while on the trip. Why not? I don't like to show my legs. . . . Ah, Mrs. H., but they do indeed show themselves. Nevertheless, I don't.

¶ Shot herself! Shot herself!

Brack (collapsing in the easy chair): But great God — people don't *do* such things!

¶ NB!! Eilert Løvborg believes that a comradeship must be formed between man and woman out of which the truly spiritual human being can arise. Whatever else the two of them do is of no concern. This is what the people around him do not understand. To them he is dissolute. Inwardly he is not.

¶ If a man can have several male friends, why can't he have several lady friends?

¶ It is precisely the sensual feelings that are aroused while in the company of his female "friends" or "comrades" that seek release in his excesses.

¶ Now I'm going. Don't you have some little remembrance to give me — ? You have flowers — and so many other things — (The story of the pistol from before) — But you won't use it anyhow —

¶ In the fourth act when Hedda finds out that he has shot himself, she is jubilant. . . . He had courage.

Here is the rest of the manuscript.

¶ Conclusion: Life isn't tragic. . . . Life is ridiculous. . . . And that's what I can't bear.

¶ Do you know what happens in novels? All those who kill themselves — through the head — not in the stomach. . . . How ridiculous — how baroque — . . .

Caroline W. Mayerson (b. 1907)
THEMATIC SYMBOLS IN *HEDDA GABLER*   1965

Sometimes the designation of realism has been applied to Ibsen in such a way as to suggest that all we get in his plays is a slice of life, with details that are meaningless except that they are there. The fact is that, like Gustave Flaubert, James Joyce, August Strindberg, and other realistic writers of his time, Ibsen was a craftsman who tried to make every detail in his plays add up to something. Caroline Mayerson shows us how loaded with significance certain otherwise innocent-looking objects are in Hedda Gabler. *She begins with Thea's hair, the manuscript that Løvborg loses, and General Gabler's pistols. In analyzing them, she shows us just how rich the surfaces of Ibsen's plays can be.*

During the course of the play, Ibsen places considerable emphasis upon Thea's hair, upon the manuscript as her "child," and upon General Gabler's pistols, and his treatment of these items suggests that he intended them to have symbolic significance. We shall be concerned in this essay with determining this significance and its effect upon the total meaning of the play. My analysis of the three symbols in their relationship to the theme, the characters, and the action will be based upon several broad assumptions which reflect views of Ibsen's concepts and methods implied or expressed by a number of previous commentators: (1) In *Hedda Gabler,* Ibsen examines the possibility of attaining freedom and fulfillment in modern society. (2) Hedda is a woman, not a monster; neurotic, but not psychotic. Thus, she may be held accountable for her behavior. But she is spiritually sterile. Her yearning for self-realization through exercise of her natural endowments is in conflict with her enslavement to a narrow standard of conduct. This conflict is complicated by her incomplete understanding of what freedom and fulfillment mean and how they may be achieved. She fails to realize that one must earn his inheritance in order to possess it, and she romanticizes the destructive and sensational aspects of Dionysiac ecstasy without perceiving that its true end is regeneration through sublimation of the ego in a larger unity. (3) Ibsen, as an experienced artist, was aware of the impact of minutiae and the need for integrating these with the general impression to be projected; therefore we may regard his descriptions, his stage directions, and his properties, no less than his dialogue, as means whereby intention and significance are conveyed.

While all the other characters in *Hedda Gabler* are implicitly compared to Hedda and serve, in one way or another, to throw light upon her personality, Thea Elvsted is the one with whom she is most obviously contrasted. Furthermore, their contest for the control of Loevborg is the most prominent external conflict in the play. The sterility-fertility antithesis from which central action proceeds is chiefly realized through the opposition of these two. Hedda is pregnant, and Thea is physically barren. But in emotionally repudiating her unborn child, Hedda rejects what Ibsen considered woman's opportunity to advance the march of progress.[1] The

---

[1]Cf. Ibsen's speech to the Norwegian Women's Rights League (1898): "It is women who are to solve the social problems. As mothers they are to do it. And only as such can they do it. Here lies a great task for woman" (*Speeches and New Letters of Henrik Ibsen,* trans. Arne Kildal [Boston, 1901], 66).

many other symptoms of her psychic sterility need little enlargement. Unwilling to give or even share herself, she maintains her independence at the price of complete frustration. Ibsen uses Thea, on the other hand, to indicate a way to freedom which Hedda never apprehends. Through her ability to extend herself in comradeship with Loevborg, Thea not only brings about the rebirth of his creative powers, but merges her own best self with his to produce a prophecy of the future, conceivably of the "Third Kingdom," in which Ibsen believed that the ideals of the past would coalesce in a new and more perfect unity. Having lost herself to find herself, she almost instinctively breaks with the mores of her culture in order to ensure continuance of function. Despite her palpitating femininity, she is the most truly emancipated person in the play. And it is she who wins at least a limited victory in the end. Although Loevborg has failed her, her fecundity is indefatigable; as Hedda kills herself, Thea is busily preparing to recreate her "child" with Tesman, thereby at once enabling him to realize his own little talents and weakening even further the tenuous bond which ties him to Hedda.

The contrast outlined above is reinforced by the procreative imagery of the play. The manuscript is Loevborg's and Thea's "child," the idea of progress born of a union between individuals who have freed themselves from the preconceptions of their environment.[2] This manuscript the sterile Hedda throws into the fire at the climax of her vindictive passion. Her impulse to annihilate by burning is directed both toward Thea's "child" and toward Thea's hair and calls attention to the relationship between them. Even without other indications that Ibsen was using hair as a symbol of fertility, such an inference might be made from the words which accompany the destruction of the manuscript:

> Now I am burning your child, Thea! Burning it, curly-locks! Your child and Eilert Loevborg's. I am burning — I am burning your child.

There is, however, considerable evidence, both before and after this scene, that Thea's hair is a sign of that potency which Hedda envies even while she ridicules and bullies its possessor. Ibsen, of course, had ample precedent for employing hair as a symbol of fertility. Perhaps the best support for the argument that he made a literary adaptation of this well-known, ancient idea in *Hedda Gabler* is a summary of the instances in which the hair is mentioned.

Although Ibsen's unobtrusive description of the hair of each of these women at her initial entrance may seem at the time only a casual stroke in the sketch, it assumes importance in retrospect. Hedda's hair is "not particularly abundant," whereas Thea's is "unusually abundant and wavy." Hedda's strongest impression of Thea is of that abundance: She recalls her as "the girl with the irritating hair, that she was always showing off." Moreover, Thea fearfully recollects Hedda's schoolgirl reaction to it: ". . . When we met on the stairs you used always to pull my hair. . . . Yes, and once you said you would burn it off my head." When Thea and Loevborg first meet in the play, Hedda seats herself, significantly, between them; the brief exchange of questions and answers which ensues is notable for its overtones: "Is not she [Thea] lovely to look at?" Loevborg asks. Hedda, lightly stroking Thea's hair, answers, "Only to look at?" Loevborg understands the innuendo, for he replies, "Yes. For we two — she and I — we two are real comrades."

[2]Cf. Ibsen's statement: "I firmly believe in the capacity for procreation and development of ideals" (*Speeches and New Letters*, 57).

Later, when the women are alone, Hedda, now fully informed of the extent to which Thea has realized her generative powers, laments her own meager endowment and renews her threat in its adolescent terms:

> Oh, if you could only understand how poor I am, and fate has made you so rich! (Clasps her passionately in her arms.) I think I must burn your hair off after all.

Hedda's violent gesture and Thea's almost hysterical reaction ("Let me go! Let me go! I am afraid of you, Hedda!") indicate the dangerous seriousness of words which otherwise might be mistaken for a joke; the threat prepares us for the burning of the manuscript, which follows in Act III. In the last tense scene of the play Hedda twice handles Thea's hair. The reader's imagination readily constructs the expressions and gestures whereby an actress could show Hedda's true attitude toward the hair which Ibsen directs her to ruffle "gently" and to pass her hands "softly through." The first gesture follows immediately upon an important action — Hedda has just removed the pistol to the inner room. The second accompanies dialogue which for the last time emphasizes Hedda's association of the hair with Thea's fertility and which brings home to Hedda her own predicament:

> HEDDA (*passes her hands softly through Mrs. Elvsted's hair*): Doesn't it seem strange to you, Thea? Here you are sitting with Tesman — just as you used to sit with Eilert Loevborg?
> MRS. ELVSTED: Ah, if I could only inspire your husband in the same way!
> HEDDA: Oh, that will come too — in time.
> TESMAN: Yes, do you know, Hedda — I really think I begin to feel something of the sort. But won't you go to sit with Brack again?
> HEDDA: Is there nothing I can do to help you two?
> TESMAN: No, nothing in the world.

These scenes in which the hair plays a part not only call attention to Hedda's limitations but show her reaction to her partial apprehension of them. In adapting a primitive symbol, Ibsen slightly altered its conventional meaning, substituting psychic for physical potency. Its primitivistic associations nevertheless pervade the fundamental relationships between the two women. The weapons Hedda uses against Thea are her hands and fire. The shock of the climactic scene results chiefly from seeing the savage emerge from behind her veneer of sophistication — the Hedda who feeds the manuscript to the flames is a naked woman engaged in a barbaric act. In contrast, the Hedda who handles her father's pistols is self-consciously cloaked in illusions of her hereditary participation in a chivalric tradition.

The pistols, like many other symbols used by Ibsen, quite obviously are not merely symbols, but have important plot function as well. Moreover, their symbolic significance cannot be reduced to a simple formula, but must be thought of in the light of the complex of associations which they carry as Hedda's legacy from General Gabler. Through Hedda's attitude toward and uses of the pistols, Ibsen constantly reminds us that Hedda "is to be regarded rather as her father's daughter than as her husband's wife."[3] Clearly the pistols are linked with certain values in her background which Hedda cherishes. Complete definition of these values is difficult without a more thorough knowledge of Ibsen's conception of a Norwegian general than the play or contemporary comment on it allows. Perhaps, as Brandes said, nineteenth-century audiences recognized that Hedda's pretensions to dignity

---

[3]*The Correspondence of Henrik Ibsen*, trans. & ed. Mary Morison (London, 1905), 435.

and grandeur as a general's daughter were falsely based, "that a Norwegian general is a cavalry officer, who as a rule, has never smelt powder, and whose pistols are innocent of bloodshed."[4] Such a realization, however, by no means nullifies the *theoretical* attributes and privileges of generalship to which Hedda aspires. Possibly Ibsen intended us to understand that Hedda is a member of a second generation of "ham actors" who betray their proud tradition by their melodramatic posturings. But it is this tradition, however ignoble its carrier, to which the pistols and Hedda (in her own mind) belong, and it is, after all, the general only as glimpsed through his daughter's ambitions and conceptions of worth that is of real importance in the play. These conceptions, as embodied in Hedda's romantic ideal of manhood, may be synthesized from the action and dialogue. The aristocrat possesses, above all, courage and self-control. He expresses himself through direct and independent action, living to capacity and scorning security and public opinion. Danger only piques big appetite, and death with honor is the victory to be plucked from defeat. But the recklessness of this Hotspur is tempered by a disciplined will, by means of which he "beautifully" orders both his own actions and those of others on whom his power is imposed. Such a one uses his pistols with deliberation, with calculated aim. He shoots straight — to defend his life or his honor, and to maintain his authority. Pistols, however, have no intrinsic glamor. Of the several possible accoutrements of a general, his pistols are those least likely to evoke thoughts of chivalric principles and most likely to recall the menace of the power vested in him. And such power, as *Hedda Gabler* shows us, delivered into the hands of a confused and irresponsible egotist, brings only meaningless destruction to all who come within its range.

The manipulation of the pistols throughout the play is a mockery of their traditional role. Except at target practice, Hedda does not even shoot straight until her suicide. Her potential danger is recognized by both men whom she threatens, but both understand (Brack, immediately; Loevborg, in Act II) that her threat is a theatrical gesture and that she has no real intention of acting directly, in defiance of the conventions which bid her "go roundabout." Her crass dishonesty in her sexual encounters is highlighted by this gun play. She uses the pistols, to be sure, to ward off or warn off encroachments upon her "honor." This honor, however, is rooted in social expedience rather than in a moral code. Having indirectly encouraged Loevborg by a succession of intimate *tête-à-têtes*, she poses as an outraged maiden when he makes amorous advances, thereby, as she later hints, thwarting her own emotional needs. Subsequently she sells her body to Tesman as cynically as (and far less honestly than) Madame Diana sells hers, then deliberately participates in the form, if not the substance, of marital infidelity with Brack in order to relieve her boredom. Both Hedda and Brack become aware of the cold ruthlessness of the other and the consequent danger to the loser if the delicate equilibrium of their relationship should be disturbed. But until the end Brack is so complacently convinced that Hedda is his female counterpart that he has no fear she will do more than shoot over his head; even as she lies dead, he can hardly believe that she has resorted to direct action —"People don't do such things."

The part the pistols play in Loevborg's death makes a central contribution to our understanding of the degree to which the ideals they represent are distorted by the clouded perspective from which Hedda views them. She has no real compre-

[4]Georg Brandes, *Henrik Ibsen. Björnstjerne Björnson: Critical Studies* (New York, 1899), 94.

hension of, nor interest in, the vital creative powers Thea helps Loevborg to realize. Instead, she glorifies his weaknesses, mistaking bravado for courage, the indulgence of physical appetites for godlike participation in "the banquet of life," a flight from reality for a heroic quest for totality of experience. Even more important is the fact that as she inhibits her own instinctive urge for fulfillment, she romanticizes its converse. Thus, having instigated his ruin, she incites Loevborg to commit suicide with her pistol. This radical denial of the will to live she arbitrarily invests with the heroism and beauty one associates with a sacrificial death; Hedda is incapable of making the distinction between an exhibitionistic gesture which inflates the ego and the tragic death, in which the ego is sublimated in order that the values of life may be extended and reborn.

Her inability to perceive the difference between melodrama and tragedy accounts for the disparity between Hedda's presumptive view of her own suicide and our evaluation of its significance. Ibsen with diabolical irony arranged a situation which bears close superficial resemblance to the traditional tragic end. Symbolically withdrawing herself from the bourgeois environment into the inner chamber which contains the relics of her earlier life, Hedda plays a "wild dance" upon her piano and, beneath her father's portrait, shoots herself "beautifully" through the temple with her father's pistol. She dies to vindicate her heritage of independence; with disciplined and direct aim she at last defeats the Bogy, which hitherto she has unsuccessfully attempted to circumvent. So Hedda would see her death, we are led to believe, could she be both principal and spectator; and no doubt she would find high-sounding phrases with which to memorialize it. But of course it is Brack and Tesman who have the curtain lines, and these lines show how little of her intent Hedda has conveyed to her world. And we, having the opportunity to judge the act with relation to its full context, may properly interpret it as the final self-dramatization of the consistently sterile protagonist. Hedda gains no insight; her death affirms nothing of importance. She never understands why, at her touch, everything becomes "ludicrous and mean." She dies to escape a sordid situation that is largely of her own making; she will not face reality nor assume responsibility for the consequences of her acts. The pistols, having descended to a coward and a cheat, bring only death without honor.

It would appear, then, that the symbols, while they do not carry the whole thematic burden of *Hedda Gabler,* illuminate the meaning of the characters and the action with which they are associated. As Eric Bentley has suggested, the characters, like those in the other plays of Ibsen's last period, are the living dead who dwell in a waste-land that resembles T. S. Eliot's. And, like Eliot later, Ibsen emphasized the aridity of the present by contrasting it with the heroic past. Indeed, *Hedda Gabler* may be thought of as a mock-tragedy, a sardonically contrived travesty of tragic action, which Ibsen shows us is no longer possible in the world of the play. This world is sick with a disease less curable than that of Oedipus's Thebes or Hamlet's Denmark. For its hereditary leaders are shrunken in stature, maimed and paralyzed by their enslavement to the ideals of the dominant middle class. With the other hollow men, they despise but nonetheless worship the false gods of respectability and security, paying only lip service to their ancestral principles. Such geniuses as this society produces are, when left to themselves, too weak to do more than batter their own heads against constricting barriers. They dissipate their talents and so fail in their mission as prophets and disseminators of Western culture; its interpretation is left to the unimaginative pedant, picking over the dry bones of the past. Women, the natural seminal vesicles of that culture, the mothers of the future, are those most cruelly inhibited by the sterilizing atmosphere of their environment. At one extreme is Aunt Julia, the genteel spinster, overcompensating for her starved emotions with obsessive self-dedication. At the other is Diana, the harlot. Even Thea, the progenitive spirit, the girl with the abundant hair, is a frail and colorless repository for the seeds of generation. Her break with convention when it threatens her maternity is shown to be the one mode of escape from the fate that overtakes the others. But Ibsen gives her triumph, too, a ludicrous twist. Hardly having begun the mourning song for her Adonis, she brings forth her embryonic offspring from her pocket and proceeds to mold it into shape with the aid of a Tesman — an echo of the classic death and rebirth, to be sure, but one not likely to produce the glorious Third Kingdom of which Ibsen dreamed. And appropriately holding the center of the stage throughout is Hedda, in whom the shadows of the past still struggle in a losing battle with the sterile specter of the present. Her pistols are engraved with insignia which the others understand not at all and which she only dimly comprehends. Her colossal egotism, her lack of self-knowledge, her cowardice, render her search for fulfillment but a succession of futile blunders which culminate in the supreme futility of death. Like Peer Gynt, she is fit only for the ladle of the button-molder;° she fails to realize a capacity either for great good or for great evil. Her mirror-image wears the mask of tragedy, but Ibsen makes certain that we see the horns and pointed ears of the satyr protruding from behind it.

button-molder: At the end of Ibsen's play *Peer Gynt,* the Button Molder tries to melt Peer in his ladle, an action that symbolizes loss of identity.

Jan Kott (b. 1914)
ON *HEDDA GABLER*   *1984*

> *Jan Kott's sexual analysis of Hedda's pistols introduces important levels of metaphor into a play that is already laden with sexual imagery.*

Chekhov wrote: "If in the first act a gun hangs on the wall, in the last act it must go off." In laying down this dramatic precept, he must surely have had *Hedda Gabler* in mind. Hedda inherits two pistols from her father. She fires the first one over Judge Brack's head when he approaches the house from the garden; and again at the end, when she shoots herself. The other pistol is fired offstage. It kills Eilert Loevborg. But the two pistols in *Hedda Gabler* are not only props exploited by Ibsen with iron-clad dramatic logic and preordained consequences; they also have sexual undertones. A Scandinavian Madame Bovary, well read in romantic novels, gives Loevborg a pistol: "use it now . . . and beautifully." But the fatal shot wounds him "in the stomach — more or less," and is fired in the parlor of the red-haired Mademoiselle Diana.

Ibsen's setting for *Hedda Gabler* is striking. The action takes place in a spacious salon with French windows which open out on a veranda and a garden in the "fashionable part of town," not a fjord. The windows are curtained; the theater had already learned the advantages of gaslight.

In the first scene, Hedda orders the curtains drawn. She can't stand sunlight. This is our first glimpse of her character. The salon is spacious and the furniture arrangement makes it possible for two separate conversations to be carried on at the same time. The old-fashioned *a parte*° is no longer necessary. Chekhov borrowed this "contrapuntal" dialogue from Ibsen and masterfully refined it.

The crucial part of the stage design is the room in the background, with a huge portrait of "a handsome, elderly man in a general's uniform" hanging on the wall behind the sofa. In the last scene Hedda will enter this room, draw the curtains, and shoot herself in front of her father's portrait. Hedda Tesman, two months pregnant, kills Hedda Gabler. The inner room, whose only exit leads to the salon in the foreground, is at once the concrete and the symbolic setting of the conflict between the Father/superego and the id. By shooting herself, Hedda kills the shadow of her Father and the child she never wanted. The "shadow" of the father kills the daughter. In contrast to the earlier dramas [by Ibsen], *Lady from the Sea* and *Rosmersholm,* where the prehistory of the conflicts, traumas, and sexual complexes festers beneath the surface, and though continuing to grow they are never seen, in *Hedda Gabler* nothing remains unspoken.

In this case study of a neurosis, the mother's place is left empty. Hedda was raised by her father, who would have preferred a son. She rode horses and learned to shoot guns. In school, like a tomboy, she pulled her girlfriends' hair. She can barely resist pulling Thea's blond locks in Act II. In the last *Hedda Gabler* I saw, in Bochum in 1977, Peter Zadek directed the scene of Hedda's and Thea's drinking bout with distinct lesbian undertones. It is an extreme though not arbitrary reading of the text. In this record of sexual neurosis, the inversion and displacement of libido are intended. Thirty-year-old Hedda Gabler is frigid.

General Gabler's daughter not only wants to rule in a man's world. Unable to assume her female sexual role, she escapes by playing out the male one in her imagination. She demands that Loevborg initiate her into masculine rites and describe his visits to the red-haired Diana. Imaginary sex is vicarious. Hedda, rejecting the traditional roles of wife and mother, is condemned to live vicariously, full of the frustration and sense of emptiness which she calls deadly boredom. Madame Bovary's love affairs with shallow men were substitutions for the romantic ecstasies she read about in contemporary novels. For General Gabler's daughter these flights and escapes are ruled out. She has only her inner room "with its heavy curtains and her father's portrait."

It is not only sexual fulfillment that Hedda strives for through imagination. Until the very last scene, all her passions and hatreds are realized only by acts of substitution. The manuscript of Loevborg's new book is twice called his and Thea's "child"; Hedda commits a substitute "infanticide" by burning it in the fireplace. The pistol shot above Judge Brack's head was a substitute murder and a substitute sexual act. Fear paralyzed her twice before: once when she was afraid to shoot Loevborg for his aggressive advances, and then a second time when she was afraid to sleep with him. Handing the pistol to Loevborg is murder by intent: The shot that kills him, in keeping with the logic of the dramaturgy, symbolically castrates him as well.

In coded messages, myths, dreams, and unconscious acts, opposite terms are interchangeable: They assume the guise of their antitheses. As in Racine and Chekhov

---

a parte: Keeping different conversations separate from one another as if in different spaces.

(although in Chekhov it is deeply hidden), the appeal of death in Ibsen disguises itself as the pulse of life, the instinct toward self-destruction is masked as libido. *Hedda Gabler* appears to return to the realistic technique of the earlier dramas, but along with *Rosmersholm,* it marks the beginning of Ibsen's last cycle of plays, from *Little Eyolf* to *When We Dead Awaken,* each of which repeats the theme of sexual frustration leading to self-destruction. With the exception of his final masterpiece, *John Gabriel Borkman,* in all these plays the balance between the realistic world and its symbolic projection is broken.

In his biography of Ibsen (1957), Michael Meyer entitled his chapter on *Hedda Gabler* "Portrait of the Dramatist as a Young Woman." "*Madame Bovary — c'est moi,*" Flaubert once wrote, and Hedda Gabler is in some sense Ibsen's alter ego. The psychoanalysis of Hedda would no doubt become the merciless psychoanalysis of her author. But in psychoanalytic interpretations of the author or of his work Ibsen's invention and artistic discoveries are usually neglected, and what is even more important, the historical context, the customs and atmospheric realism of the *fin de siècle,*° are altogether lost.

Ibsen never read a page of Freud. Neither did Strindberg. In the early 1890s Freud began his first methodical studies of hysteria; in 1895 he announced his first analysis of dreams; and he used the term "psychoanalysis" for the first time in 1896. The Scandinavian Miss Julies and Heddas were finding their dramatists in Strindberg and Ibsen while the Viennese Julies and Heddas were finding their analyst in Freud.

Clive Barnes (b. 1927)
REVIEW OF *HEDDA GABLER*   1975

> *Barnes appreciates the originality of interpretation in this Royal Shakespeare production of* Hedda Gabler. *He admires the way the production reveals Ibsen's "satirical malevolent humor" and his contempt for the "shabby way life was lived." In keeping with this focus, director Trevor Nunn and actress Glenda Jackson create a Hedda who is the "vicious mistress of her own fate"—a Hedda "to chill the mind."*

We all knew that Washington was rapidly becoming an important theater town, but the idea that a major imported production, from Britain's Royal Shakespeare Company, no less, and starring Glenda Jackson, should bypass New York and play Washington may seem outlandish. Yet that is precisely what is happening to Trevor Nunn's new staging of Ibsen's *Hedda Gabler,* which began life in Australia this season, appeared in Los Angeles and last night opened at the National Theater here, on its way home to its London premiere.

Washington's gain is very pointedly New York's loss, for this production — which I caught at today's matinee — is an adornment even to the Royal Shakespeare Company repertory. It is a beautiful and provoking rethinking of this modern classic and could be a landmark for English-speaking versions of Ibsen.

---

fin de siècle: Turn of the century.

Everyone is aware of the humor in Ibsen, and most productions try to steer clear of laughs. The freshness of this new staging is [that] it on the contrary tries to steer into them. Mr Nunn most persuasively takes literally Hedda's remark, twice-repeated, incidentally, that her life is a "grotesque farce," and he seizes every opportunity to point up Ibsen's satirical, malevolent humor, until the final stroke of tragic irony comes with Hedda's death.

The entire production is a dusty window on shallow, silly and selfish people caught frozen in a cold, monochromatic provincial landscape. This Hedda is no wilful child of circumstances but the vicious mistress of her own fate, an impartial force of evil leading an almost whimsical danse macabre.

In this view of Ibsen everyone is flayed. We see Ibsen's cynical view of bourgeois parochialism most clearly perhaps in plays such as *An Enemy of the People,* but this staging of *Hedda* helps to show that the playwright's contempt for the shabby way life was lived runs throughout all his work.

The production's bitter and emphatic insistence upon Ibsen's sardonic mockery of convention is not its only claim to originality. Mr. Nunn — and in this he treads a path not unlike that earlier taken by Ingmar Bergman in the same play — focuses on the smallness of Hedda's world. This is a petty story, full of small-scale lies, defections, vanities and betrayals. Here only Hedda is larger than the life of the play, and she is monstrous, a female Machiavel.

Part of the enclosed atmosphere of this complacent microcosm is provided by the repetitiveness of Ibsen's convoluted but commonplace use of language. We are accustomed to the repetition of Tesman's monotonous "What about that!" which he tags onto sentences like a catch phrase. Mr. Nunn, who has produced his own English adaptation of the original, stresses elsewhere the flatness of the language, with his constant repeating of simple words such as "beautiful." The verbal result is a kind of mad, comic oppressiveness.

At the storm center of any *Hedda* must stand Hedda herself, and in Mr. Nunn's conception and Miss Jackson's portrayal, she is an unforgettable, all but unforgivable, harpy. But if to understand is to forgive, then this Hedda must be forgiven, for few portrayals of the role can have been so dense, complex and yet, at last, comprehensible.

This Hedda has a wonderful snub-nosed arrogance, a remarkable way of flapping her hands in affectation. She is as cold as the submerged part of the iceberg, and she exhibits all the hugging charm of a boa constrictor. This is a merciless yet beautiful performance, reaching its terrible and great climax in its paroxysms of pure triumph when Hedda sends Eilert to his death, and then with calculated hatred burns his manuscript. This is a Hedda to chill the mind.

The rest of the cast offers Miss Jackson the perfect ensemble for her performance. Peter Eyre's Tesman, her husband, makes an interestingly irresolute spider figure, with thinning hair and hardening arteries, old out of his time. Timothy West, totally unctuous, sniffing superciliously and smiling pithily under raised eyebrows, is a splendidly menacing Judge Brack, while Patrick Stewart as a gruff, withdrawn Eilert Luvborg and Jennie Linden as a terrified victim of a Mrs. Elvsted are equally part of Mr. Nunn's picture.

And picture it is, for one of the abiding impressions of this fine *Hedda* is left by the lighting of Andy Phillips and the designs of John Napier, all in browns and grays (even the flowers are brown) and conceived all in nineteenth-century Scandinavian-modern, with stuffed sofas and art-nouveau stained glass. It is the ridiculous common-place world of sudden death.

August Strindberg

The Swedish playwright August Strindberg (1849–1912) wrote fifty-eight plays, more than a dozen novels, and more than a hundred short stories, all collected now in fifty-five volumes. Much of the time he was producing this astonishing body of work, he was the victim of persistent paranoia, suffered the destruction of three marriages, and lived through a major nervous breakdown.

He was a man of enormous complexity whose work has traditionally been broken into two parts. The first comprises the work he wrote up to 1894, which includes *The Father* (1877), *Miss Julie* (1888), *The Creditors* (1889), and other naturalistic plays; the second comprises work he wrote after 1897, including *To Damascus* (1898–1901), *There Are Crimes and Crimes* (1899), *Easter,* and *The Dance of Death* (both 1901), *A Dream Play* (1902), and *Ghost Sonata* (1907). These are largely expressionist plays. EXPRESSIONISM disregarded the strict demands of naturalism to present a "slice of life" without artistic shaping of plot and resolution. Instead, expressionist drama used materials that resembled dreams — or nightmares — and focused on symbolic actions and a subjective interpretation of the world. Strindberg's later drama is often symbolic, taut, and psychological. His novel *Inferno* (1897) not only marks the transition between his early and late work; it gives this period of his life its name. Strindberg's *Inferno* period was a time of madness and paranoic behavior that virtually redirected his life for more than three years. During this time he was convinced that the secrets of life were wrapped in the occult, and his energies went into alchemical experiments and studies of cabalistic lore.

The first period of his dramatic career began with *Master Olof* (1872), a historical drama that he chose to write in prose, which he felt was a more natural medium than verse, the convention for such plays at the time. The play was turned down, and he rewrote it in verse in 1876. It was rejected for a second time by the Royal Dramatic Theater but was finally produced the following year. At that time, Strindberg recorded: "In 1877 Antoine opened his Théâtre Libre in Paris, and *Thérèse Raquin,* although nothing but an adapted novel, became the dominant model. It was the powerful theme and the concentrated form that showed innovation, although the unity of time was not yet observed, and curtain falls were retained. It was then I wrote my dramas: *Lady Julie, The Father,* and *Creditors.*" *Thérèse Raquin,* Émile Zola's naturalistic play, inspired Strindberg to move further toward his own interpretation of naturalism, which is perhaps most evident in *Miss Julie.* Strindberg was more subjective in his approach to naturalism, less scientific and deterministic, than Zola. Whereas Zola's approach might be described as "photographic" realism, Strindberg's was more selective and impressionistic but no less honest and true. He saw his characters operating out of "a whole series of deeply buried motives." They were not necessarily the product of their biology or their social circumstances, as the naturalists of Zola's stripe sometimes implied. Yet Strindberg saw clearly that class distinctions helped determine the behavior of many people. He seemed to accept the view that people were not created by their class but rather belonged to their class because of the kind of people they were. Strindberg probed deeply into the psychology of his characters, whose emotional lives, rather than outward social qualities, determined their actions.

Strindberg is often described as a woman-hater, a misogynist. For periods of his life he seems to have been misogynistic, but he was nonetheless extremely contradictory in both behavior and belief. There is no simple way to talk about Strindberg's attitude toward women. On the one hand, he is conventional in his thinking that women belong in the home. On the other hand, he married a highly successful actress, Siri von Essen. As he said in a letter in 1895, "Woman is to me the earth and all its glory, the bond that binds, and of all the evil the worst evil I have seen is the female sex." A decade later in *A Blue Book,* he wrote, "When I approach a woman as a lover, I look up to her, I see something of the mother in her, and this I respect. I assume a subordinate position, become childish and puerile and actually am subordinate, like most men. . . . I put her on a pedestal." As in many things, including his attitude toward dramatic techniques and style, Strindberg is a mass of contradictions and complexities of the sort sometimes associated with genius.

MISS JULIE

Miss Julie, the daughter of a count, and Jean, the count's valet, come from strikingly different social backgrounds. In ordinary circumstances, they might not have been on friendly terms, much less have become lovers, as they do. But the count is away, and Miss Julie and Jean are drawn into a sexual liaison marked by a struggle for dominance and control. Miss Julie's fiancé has been disposed of before the play begins because he refused to debase himself slavishly to her will. She is a free spirit, but her breeding is suspect because her mother, like her, took a lover and defied the count. Miss Julie's mother rebelled against her husband and punished him by burning their house down after the insurance expired. As further punishment and abasement, she humiliated the count by arranging to have her lover loan him the money to rebuild the house. Thus, Miss Julie's heritage is one of independence, rebellion, and unorthodoxy.

Under her mother's tutelage, Miss Julie was raised to manipulate men, but she cannot accept them totally. She also seems to feel a mixture of contempt for herself as a woman along with her contempt for men. In his preface to the play, Strindberg says that Julie is a modern "half-woman" "man-hater" who sells herself for honors of various kinds. (See the commentary on p. 762.)

The play has a mysterious quality. It takes place on Midsummer Eve, when lovers reveal themselves to one another and when almost anything can happen. In primitive fertility rites it was a time associated with sexual awakening. Kristine mentions that it is the feast of St. John and alludes to his beheading for spurning Salome's advances. Jean (French for John) in one tense moment of the play beheads Julie's pet bird as a sign of the violence pent up in him. This incident also foreshadows Miss Julie's death.

The fairy-tale quality that creeps into the play — as in *A Midsummer Night's Dream*, set on the same day — may seem out of place in a realistic drama, but it is profoundly compelling. It is also typical of Strindberg, who often uses symbolism to suggest a dream quality and deepen the significance of the action. (Dreams are a part of reality that modern playwrights have taken great pains to explore.)

The count himself, Julie's father, never appears in the play, but his presence is always ominous and intense, again much as in a fairy tale. Jean tells Miss Julie that he would willingly kill himself if the count were to order it. The cook, Kristine, like a witch, demands retribution because she was spurned by Jean, who once was her lover. Near the end of the play she prevents Julie and Jean from running away from the count by impounding the horses in the stable, thus wreaking her revenge on both of them.

Although Julie may be seen as the princess, Jean has very little claim to being Prince Charming of the play, especially since he has little strength of character. He feels superior to his station as a valet, and Strindberg in his preface refers to him as a nobleman. However, like Kristine, he is coarse beneath his outwardly polished appearance. His highest ambition is to be the proprietor of a first-class hotel, a prospect he wants to share with Julie.

One of the most striking passages in the play is the story Jean tells Julie almost reluctantly. He tries to explain to her what it feels like to be "down below," where she has never been. When he was a boy, he thought of the apple trees in her father's garden as part of the "Garden of Eden, guarded by angry angels." He entered this enchanted place with his mother to weed onions and wandered into the outhouse — a building like a Turkish pavilion whose function he could not guess. While he was exploring it, he heard someone coming and had to exit beneath the outhouse and hide himself under a pile of weeds and "wet dirt that stank." From his hiding place he saw Julie in a pink dress and white stockings. He rushed to the millpond and jumped in to wash the filth off himself. Ironically, only a few moments after he tells her this story, he calls her a whore, and she, in response, says, "Oh, God in heaven, end my wretched life! Take me away from the filth I'm sinking into! Save me! Save me!"

Miss Julie falls under the power of her lover and cannot redirect her life; she sinks deeper and deeper into "filth." She has few choices at the end of the play, and the conclusion to *Miss Julie* is swift. The contrast between the willfulness of Julie and the caution of Jean makes their situation especially desperate. When Julie leaves at the end of the play to seal her fate, we sense the terrible weight of their society's values. Those values are symbolized by the return of the count and the expectations he had of Julie's behavior while he was gone.

Miss Julie in Performance

The first planned professional production of *Miss Julie* was canceled at the last minute by censors in Copenhagen on March 1, 1889. Although the play was performed privately on March 14, 1889, in Copenhagen University's Students' Union, it was not performed professionally in Stockholm until 1906. Some important early productions of the play were in Paris in Antoine's distinguished Théâtre Libre in 1893 and in Berlin in Max Reinhardt's Kleine Theater in 1904. Reinhardt produced seventeen of Strindberg's plays and was one of his great champions. In 1907 Strindberg produced the play in his own Intimate Theatre in Stockholm, where it ran intermittently for 134 showings. He even arranged a special performance for Bernard Shaw. The first London production was in 1912, but since the 1930s it has been revived many times, with many distinguished actors in all three major roles.

Among the notable modern productions is the Old Vic's 1966 version directed by Michael Elliott, with Maggie Smith and Albert Finney starring. The Baxter Theatre of Johannesburg, South Africa, produced the play in 1985 with the black actor John Kani as Jean and the white Afrikaner actress Sandra Prinsloo as Julie. Some white audiences considered that casting as outrageous. The sensational Ingmar Bergman production at the Brooklyn Academy of Music in 1991 stretched the play to two hours and made it more of a domestic tragedy — as John Simon said, "more like us, more believable, and, therefore, more terrifying."

Filmed at least five times, *Miss Julie* has been televised as well. It is one of the most produced of modern plays.

August Strindberg (1849–1912)

Miss Julie

1888

TRANSLATED BY HARRY G. CARLSON

Characters

MISS JULIE, *25 years old*
JEAN, *her father's valet, 30 years old*
KRISTINE, *her father's cook, 35 years old*

(*The action takes place in the Count's kitchen on midsummer eve.*)

Setting: (*A large kitchen, the ceiling and side walls of which are hidden by draperies. The rear wall runs diagonally from down left to up right. On the wall down left are two shelves with copper, iron, and pewter utensils; the shelves are lined with scalloped paper. Visible to the right is most of a set of large, arched glass doors, through which can be seen a fountain with a statue of Cupid, lilac bushes in bloom, and the tops of some Lombardy poplars. At down left is the corner of a large tiled stove; a portion of its hood is showing. At right, one end of the servants' white pine dining table juts out; several chairs stand around it. The stove is decorated with birch branches; juniper twigs are strewn on the floor. On the end of the table stands a large Japanese spice jar, filled with lilac blossoms. An ice box, a sink, and a washstand. Above the door is an old-fashioned bell on a spring; to the left of the door, the mouthpiece of a speaking tube is visible.*)

(*Kristine is frying something on the stove. She is wearing a light-colored cotton dress and an apron. Jean enters. He is wearing livery and carries a pair of high riding boots with spurs, which he puts down on the floor where they can be seen by the audience.*)

JEAN: Miss Julie's crazy again tonight; absolutely crazy!

KRISTINE: So you finally came back?

JEAN: I took the Count to the station and when I returned past the barn I stopped in for a dance. Who do I see but Miss Julie leading off the dance with the gamekeeper! But as soon as she saw me she rushed over to ask me for the next waltz. And she's been waltzing ever since — I've never seen anything like it. She's crazy!

KRISTINE: She always has been, but never as bad as the last two weeks since her engagement was broken off.

JEAN: Yes, I wonder what the real story was there. He was a gentleman, even if he wasn't rich. Ah! These people have such romantic ideas. (*Sits at the end of the table.*) Still, it's strange, isn't it? I mean that she'd rather stay home with the servants on midsummer eve instead of going with her father to visit relatives?

KRISTINE: She's probably embarrassed after that row with her fiancé.

JEAN: Probably! He gave a good account of himself, though. Do you know how it happened, Kristine? I saw it, you know, though I didn't let on I had.

KRISTINE: No! You saw it?

JEAN: Yes, I did. ——— That evening they were out near the stable, and she was "training" him — as she called it. Do you know what she did? She made him jump over her riding crop, the way you'd teach a dog to jump. He jumped twice and she hit him each time. But the third time he grabbed the crop out of her hand, hit her with it across the cheek, and broke it in pieces. Then he left.

KRISTINE: So, that's what happened! I can't believe it!

JEAN: Yes, that's the way it went! ——— What have you got for me that's tasty, Kristine?

KRISTINE (*serving him from the pan*): Oh, it's only a piece of kidney I cut from the veal roast.

JEAN (*smelling the food*): Beautiful! That's my favorite *délice.*° (*Feeling the plate.*) But you could have warmed the plate!

KRISTINE: You're fussier than the Count himself, once you start! (*She pulls his hair affectionately.*)

JEAN (*angry*): Stop it, leave my hair alone! You know I'm touchy about that.

KRISTINE: Now, now, it's only love, you know that. (*Jean eats. Kristine opens a bottle of beer.*)

JEAN: Beer? On midsummer eve? No thank you! I can do better than that. (*Opens a drawer in the table and takes out a bottle of red wine with yellow sealing wax.*) See that? Yellow seal! Give me a glass! A wine glass! I'm drinking this *pur.*°

KRISTINE (*returns to the stove and puts on a small saucepan*): God help the woman who gets you for a husband! What a fussbudget.

JEAN: Nonsense! You'd be damned lucky to get a man like me. It certainly hasn't done you any harm to have people call me your sweetheart. (*Tastes the wine.*) Good! Very good! Just needs a little warming. (*Warms the glass between his hands.*) We bought this in Dijon. Four francs a liter, not counting the cost of the bottle, or the customs duty. ——— What are you cooking now? It stinks like hell!

KRISTINE: Oh, some slop Miss Julie wants to give Diana.

JEAN: Watch your language, Kristine. But why should you have to cook for that damn mutt on midsummer eve? Is she sick?

KRISTINE: Yes, she's sick! She sneaked out with the gate-keeper's dog — and now there's hell to pay. Miss Julie won't have it!

JEAN: Miss Julie has too much pride about some things and not enough about others, just like her mother was. The Countess was most at home in the kitchen and the cowsheds, but a *one*-horse carriage wasn't elegant enough for her. The cuffs of her blouse were dirty, but she had to have her coat of arms on her cuff-links. ——— And Miss Julie won't take proper care of herself either. If you ask me, she just isn't refined. Just now, when she was dancing in the barn, she pulled the gamekeeper away from Anna and made him dance with her. *We* wouldn't behave like that, but that's what happens when aristocrats pretend they're common people — they get *common!* ——— But she is quite a woman! Magnificent! What shoulders, and what — et cetera!

KRISTINE: Oh, don't overdo it! I've heard what Clara says, and she dresses her.

JEAN: Ha, Clara! You're all jealous of each other! I've been out riding with her. . . . And the way she dances!

KRISTINE: Listen, Jean! You're going to dance with me, when I'm finished here, aren't you?

JEAN: Of course I will.

KRISTINE: Promise?

JEAN: Promise? When I say I'll do something, I do it! By the way, the kidney was very good. (*Corks the bottle.*)

JULIE (*in the doorway to someone outside*): I'll be right back! You go ahead for now! (*Jean sneaks the bottle back into the table drawer and gets up respectfully. Miss Julie enters and crosses to Kristine by the stove.*) Well? Is it ready? (*Kristine indicates that Jean is present.*)

JEAN (*gallantly*): Are you ladies up to something secret?

JULIE (*flicking her handkerchief in his face*): None of your business!

JEAN: Hmm! I like the smell of violets!

JULIE (*coquettishly*): Shame on you! So you know about perfumes, too? You certainly know how to dance. Ah, ah! No peeking! Go away.

JEAN (*boldly but respectfully*): Are you brewing up a magic potion for midsummer eve? Something to prophesy by under a lucky star, so you'll catch a glimpse of your future husband!

JULIE (*caustically*): You'd need sharp eyes to see him! (*To Kristine.*) Pour out half a bottle and cork it well. ——— Come and dance a schottische° with me, Jean . . .

JEAN (*hesitating*): I don't want to be impolite to anyone, and I've already promised this dance to Kristine . . .

JULIE: Oh, she can have another one — can't you, Kristine? Won't you lend me Jean?

KRISTINE: It's not up to me, ma'am. (*To Jean.*) If the mistress is so generous, it wouldn't do for you to say no. Go on, Jean, and thank her for the honor.

JEAN: To be honest, and no offense intended, I wonder whether it's wise for you to dance twice running with the same partner, especially since these people are quick to jump to conclusions . . .

JULIE (*flaring up*): What's that? What sort of conclusions? What do you mean?

JEAN (*submissively*): If you don't understand, ma'am, I must speak more plainly. It doesn't look good to play favorites with your servants. . . .

---

délice: Delight. *pur:* Pure; the first drink from the bottle.

schottische: A Scottish round dance resembling a polka.

JULIE: Play favorites! What an idea! I'm astonished! As mistress of the house, I honor your dance with my presence. And when I dance, I want to dance with someone who can lead, so I won't look ridiculous.

JEAN: As you order, ma'am! I'm at your service!

JULIE (*gently*): Don't take it as an order! On a night like this we're all just ordinary people having fun, so we'll forget about rank. Now, take my arm! ——— Don't worry, Kristine! I won't steal your sweetheart! (*Jean offers his arm and leads Miss Julie out.*)

Mime

(*The following should be played as if the actress playing Kristine were really alone. When she has to, she turns her back to the audience. She does not look toward them, nor does she hurry as if she were afraid they would grow impatient. Schottische music played on a fiddle sounds in the distance. Kristine hums along with the music. She clears the table, washes the dishes, dries them, and puts them away. She takes off her apron. From a table drawer she removes a small mirror and leans it against the bowl of lilacs on the table. She lights a candle, heats a hairpin over the flame, and uses it to set a curl on her forehead. She crosses to the door and listens, then returns to the table. She finds the handkerchief Miss Julie left behind, picks it up, and smells it. Then, preoccupied, she spreads it out, stretches it, smoothes out the wrinkles, and folds it into quarters, and so forth.*)

JEAN (*enters alone*): God, she really *is* crazy! What a way to dance! Everybody's laughing at her behind her back. What do you make of it, Kristine?

KRISTINE: Ah! It's that time of the month for her, and she always gets peculiar like that. Are you going to dance with me now?

JEAN: You're not mad at me, are you, for leaving . . . ?

KRISTINE: Of course not! ——— Why should I be, for a little thing like that? Besides, I know my place . . .

JEAN (*puts his arm around her waist*): You're a sensible girl, Kristine, and you'd make a good wife . . .

JULIE (*entering; uncomfortably surprised; with forced good humor*): What a charming escort — running away from his partner.

JEAN: On the contrary, Miss Julie. Don't you see how I rushed back to the partner I abandoned!

JULIE (*changing her tone*): You know, you're a superb dancer! ——— But why are you wearing livery on a holiday? Take it off at once!

JEAN: Then I must ask you to go outside for a moment. You see, my black coat is hanging over here . . . (*Gestures and crosses right.*)

JULIE: Are you embarrassed about changing your coat in front of me? Well, go in your room then. Either that or stay and I'll turn my back.

JEAN: With your permission, ma'am! (*He crosses right. His arm is visible as he changes his jacket.*)

JULIE (*to Kristine*): Tell me, Kristine — you two are so close — . Is Jean your fiancé?

KRISTINE: Fiancé? Yes, if you wish. We can call him that.

JULIE: What do you mean?

KRISTINE: You had a fiancé yourself, didn't you? So . . .

JULIE: Well, we were properly engaged . . .

KRISTINE: But nothing came of it, did it? (*Jean returns dressed in a frock coat and bowler hat.*)

JULIE: *Très gentil, monsieur Jean! Très gentil!*

JEAN: *Vous voulez plaisanter, madame!*

JULIE: *Et vous voulez parler français!°* Where did you learn that?

JEAN: In Switzerland, when I was wine steward in one of the biggest hotels in Lucerne!

JULIE: You look like a real gentleman in that coat! *Charmant!°* (*Sits at the table.*)

JEAN: Oh, you're flattering me!

JULIE (*offended*): Flattering you?

JEAN: My natural modesty forbids me to believe that you would really compliment someone like me, and so I took the liberty of assuming that you were exaggerating, which polite people call flattering.

JULIE: Where did you learn to talk like that? You must have been to the theater often.

JEAN: Of course. And I've done a lot of traveling.

JULIE: But you come from here, don't you?

JEAN: My father was a farmhand on the district attorney's estate nearby. I used to see you when you were little, but you never noticed me.

JULIE: No! Really?

JEAN: Sure. I remember one time especially . . . but I can't talk about that.

JULIE: Oh, come now! Why not? Just this once!

JEAN: No, I really couldn't, not now. Some other time, perhaps.

JULIE: Why some other time? What's so dangerous about now?

JEAN: It's not dangerous, but there are obstacles. ——— Her, for example. (*Indicating Kristine, who has fallen asleep in a chair by the stove.*)

JULIE: What a pleasant wife she'll make! She probably snores, too.

JEAN: No, she doesn't, but she talks in her sleep.

JULIE (*cynically*): How do *you* know?

JEAN (*audaciously*): I've heard her! (*Pause, during which they stare at each other.*)

JULIE: Why don't you sit down?

JEAN: I couldn't do that in your presence.

JULIE: But if I order you to?

JEAN: Then I'd obey.

JULIE: Sit down, then. ——— No, wait. Can you get me something to drink first?

JEAN: I don't know what we have in the ice box. I think there's only beer.

JULIE: Why do you say "only"? My tastes are so simple I

Très gentil . . . français!: Very pleasing, Mr. Jean! Very pleasing. You would trifle with me, madam! And you want to speak French!   *Charmant!*: Charming!

prefer beer to wine. (*Jean takes a bottle of beer from the ice box and opens it. He looks for a glass and a plate in the cupboard and serves her.*)

JEAN: Here you are, ma'am.

JULIE: Thank you. Won't you have something yourself?

JEAN: I'm not partial to beer, but if it's an order . . .

JULIE: An order? ——— Surely a gentleman can keep his lady company.

JEAN: You're right, of course. (*Opens a bottle and gets a glass.*)

JULIE: Now, drink to my health! (*He hesitates.*) What? A man of the world — and shy?

JEAN (*in mock romantic fashion, he kneels and raises his glass*): *Skål* to my mistress!

JULIE: Bravo! ——— Now kiss my shoe, to finish it properly. (*Jean hesitates, then boldly seizes her foot and kisses it lightly.*) Perfect! You should have been an actor.

JEAN (*rising*): That's enough now, Miss Julie! Someone might come in and see us.

JULIE: What of it?

JEAN: People talk, that's what! If you knew how their tongues were wagging just now at the dance, you'd . . .

JULIE: What were they saying? Tell me! ——— Sit down!

JEAN (*sits*): I don't want to hurt you, but they were saying things ——— suggestive things, that, that . . . well, you can figure it out for yourself! You're not a child. If a woman is seen drinking alone with a man — let alone a servant — at night — then . . .

JULIE: Then what? Besides, we're not alone. Kristine is here.

JEAN: Asleep!

JULIE: Then I'll wake her up. (*Rising.*) Kristine! Are you asleep? (*Kristine mumbles in her sleep.*)

JULIE: Kristine! ——— She certainly can sleep!

KRISTINE (*in her sleep*): The Count's boots are brushed — put the coffee on — right away, right away — uh, huh — oh!

JULIE (*grabbing Kristine's nose*): Will you wake up!

JEAN (*severely*): Leave her alone — let her sleep!

JULIE (*sharply*): What?

JEAN: Someone who's been standing over a stove all day has a right to be tired by now. Sleep should be respected . . .

JULIE (*changing her tone*): What a considerate thought — it does you credit — thank you! (*Offering her hand.*) Come outside and pick some lilacs for me! (*During the following, Kristine awakens and shambles sleepily off right to bed.*)

JEAN: Go with you?

JULIE: With me!

JEAN: We couldn't do that! Absolutely not!

JULIE: I don't understand. Surely you don't imagine . . .

JEAN: No, I don't, but the others might.

JULIE: What? That I've fallen in love with a servant?

JEAN: I'm not a conceited man, but such things happen — and for these people, nothing is sacred.

JULIE: I do believe you're an aristocrat!

JEAN: Yes, I am.

JULIE: And I'm stepping down . . .

JEAN: Don't step down, Miss Julie, take my advice. No one'll believe you stepped down voluntarily. People will always say you fell.

JULIE: I have a higher opinion of people than you. Come and see! ——— Come! (*She stares at him broodingly.*)

JEAN: You're very strange, do you know that?

JULIE: Perhaps! But so are you! ——— For that matter, everything is strange. Life, people, everything. Like floating scum, drifting on and on across the water, until it sinks down and down! That reminds me of a dream I have now and then. I've climbed up on top of a pillar. I sit there and see no way of getting down. I get dizzy when I look down, and I must get down, but I don't have the courage to jump. I can't hold on firmly, and I long to be able to fall, but I don't fall. And yet I'll have no peace until I get down, no rest unless I get down, down on the ground! And if I did get down to the ground, I'd want to be under the earth . . . Have you ever felt anything like that?

JEAN: No. I dream that I'm lying under a high tree in a dark forest. I want to get up, up on top, and look out over the bright landscape, where the sun is shining, and plunder the bird's nest up there, where the golden eggs lie. And I climb and climb, but the trunk's so thick and smooth, and it's so far to the first branch. But I know if I just reached that first branch, I'd go right to the top, like up a ladder. I haven't reached it yet, but I will, even if it's only in a dream!

JULIE: Here I am chattering with you about dreams. Come, let's go out! Just into the park! (*She offers him her arm, and they start to leave.*)

JEAN: We'll have to sleep on nine midsummer flowers, Miss Julie, to make our dreams come true! (*They turn at the door. Jean puts his hand to his eye.*)

JULIE: Did you get something in your eye?

JEAN: It's nothing — just a speck — it'll be gone in a minute.

JULIE: My sleeve must have brushed against you. Sit down and let me help you. (*She takes him by the arm and seats him. She tilts his head back and with the tip of a handkerchief tries to remove the speck.*) Sit still, absolutely still! (*She slaps his hand.*) Didn't you hear me? ——— Why, you're trembling; the big, strong man is trembling! (*Feels his biceps.*) What muscles you have!

JEAN (*warning*): Miss Julie!

JULIE: Yes, *monsieur* Jean.

JEAN: *Attention! Je ne suis qu'un homme!*°

JULIE Will you sit still! ——— There! Now it's gone! Kiss my hand and thank me.

JEAN (*rising*): Miss Julie, listen to me! ——— Kristine has gone to bed! ——— Will you listen to me!

JULIE: Kiss my hand first!

Attention! Je ne suis qu'un homme!: Watch out! I am only a man!

JEAN: Listen to me!

JULIE: Kiss my hand first!

JEAN: All right, but you've only yourself to blame!

JULIE: For what?

JEAN: For what? Are you still a child at twenty-five? Don't you know that it's dangerous to play with fire?

JULIE: Not for me. I'm insured.

JEAN (*boldly*): No, you're not! But even if you were, there's combustible material close by.

JULIE: Meaning you?

JEAN: Yes! Not because it's me, but because I'm young ———

JULIE: And handsome — what incredible conceit! A Don Juan perhaps! Or a Joseph!° Yes, that's it, I do believe you're a Joseph!

JEAN: Do you?

JULIE: I'm almost afraid so. (*Jean boldly tries to put his arm around her waist and kiss her. She slaps his face.*) How dare you?

JEAN: Are you serious or joking?

JULIE: Serious.

JEAN: Then so was what just happened. You play games too seriously, and that's dangerous. Well, I'm tired of games. You'll excuse me if I get back to work. I haven't done the Count's boots yet and it's long past midnight.

JULIE: Put the boots down!

JEAN: No! It's the work I have to do. I never agreed to be your playmate, and never will. It's beneath me.

JULIE: You're proud.

JEAN: In certain ways, but not in others.

JULIE: Have you ever been in love?

JEAN: We don't use that word, but I've been fond of many girls, and once I was sick because I couldn't have the one I wanted. That's right, sick, like those princes in the Arabian Nights — who couldn't eat or drink because of love.

JULIE: Who was she? (*Jean is silent.*) Who was she?

JEAN: You can't force me to tell you that.

JULIE: But if I ask you as an equal, as a — friend! Who was she?

JEAN: You!

JULIE (*sits*): How amusing . . .

JEAN: Yes, if you like! It was ridiculous! ——— You see, that was the story I didn't want to tell you earlier. Maybe I will now. Do you know how the world looks from down below? ——— Of course you don't. Neither do hawks and falcons, whose backs we can't see because they're usually soaring up there above us. I grew up in a shack with seven brothers and sisters and a pig, in the middle of a wasteland, where there wasn't a single tree. But from our window I could see the tops of apple trees above the wall of your father's garden. That was the Garden of Eden, guarded by angry angels with flaming swords.

Don Juan . . . Joseph: Don Juan in Spanish legend is a seducer of women; in Genesis, Joseph resists the advances of Potiphar's wife.

All the same, the other boys and I managed to find our way to the Tree of Life. ——— Now you think I'm contemptible, I suppose.

JULIE: Oh, all boys steal apples.

JEAN: You say that, but you think I'm contemptible anyway. Oh well! One day I went into the Garden of Eden with my mother, to weed the onion beds. Near the vegetable garden was a small Turkish pavilion in the shadow of jasmine bushes and over-grown with honeysuckle. I had no idea what it was used for, but I'd never seen such a beautiful building. People went in and came out again, and one day the door was left open. I sneaked close and saw walls covered with pictures of kings and emperors, and red curtains with fringes at the windows — now you know the place I mean. I ——— (*Breaks off a sprig of lilac and holds it in front of Miss Julie's nose.*) ——— I'd never been inside the manor house, never seen anything except the church — but this was more beautiful. From then on, no matter where my thoughts wandered, they returned — there. And gradually I got a longing to experience, just once, the full pleasure of — *enfin,*° I sneaked in, saw, and marveled! But then I heard someone coming! There was only one exit for ladies and gentlemen, but for me there was another, and I had no choice but to take it! (*Miss Julie, who has taken the lilac sprig, lets it fall on the table.*) Afterwards, I started running. I crashed through a raspberry bush, flew over a strawberry patch, and came up onto the rose terrace. There I caught sight of a pink dress and a pair of white stockings — it was you. I crawled under a pile of weeds, and I mean under — under thistles that pricked me and wet dirt that stank. And I looked at you as you walked among the roses, and I thought: If it's true that a thief can enter heaven and be with the angels, then why can't a farm-hand's son here on God's earth enter the manor house garden and play with the Count's daughter?

JULIE (*romantically*): Do you think all poor children would have thought the way you did?

JEAN (*at first hesitant, then with conviction*): If *all* poor — yes — of course. Of course!

JULIE: It must be terrible to be poor!

JEAN (*with exaggerated suffering*): Oh, Miss Julie! Oh! ——— A dog can lie on the Countess's sofa, a horse can have his nose patted by a young lady's hand, but a servant ——— (*Changing his tone.*) ——— oh, I know — now and then you find one with enough stuff in him to get ahead in the world, but how often? ——— Anyhow, do you know what I did then? ——— I jumped in the millstream with my clothes on, was pulled out, and got a beating. But the following Sunday, when my father and all the others went to my grandmother's, I arranged to stay home. I scrubbed myself with soap and water, put on my best clothes, and went to church so that I could see you! I saw you and returned home, determined to

enfin: Finally.

die. But I wanted to die beautifully and pleasantly, without pain. And then I remembered that it was dangerous to sleep under an elder bush. We had a big one, and it was in full flower. I plundered its treasures and bedded down under them in the oat bin. Have you ever noticed how smooth oats are? — and soft to the touch, like human skin . . . ! Well, I shut the lid and closed my eyes. I fell asleep and woke up feeling very sick. But I didn't die, as you can see. What was I after? ———— I don't know. There was no hope of winning you, of course. ———— You were a symbol of the hopelessness of ever rising out of the class in which I was born.

JULIE: You're a charming storyteller. Did you ever go to school?

JEAN: A bit, but I've read lots of novels and been to the theater often. And then I've listened to people like you talk — that's where I learned most.

JULIE: Do you listen to what we say?

JEAN: Naturally! And I've heard plenty, too, driving the carriage or rowing the boat. Once I heard you and a friend . . .

JULIE: Oh? ———— What did you hear?

JEAN: I'd better not say. But I was surprised a little. I couldn't imagine where you learned such words. Maybe at bottom there isn't such a great difference between people as we think.

JULIE: Shame on you! We don't act like you when we're engaged.

JEAN (*staring at her*): Is that true? ———— You don't have to play innocent with me, Miss . . .

JULIE: The man I gave my love to was a swine.

JEAN: That's what you all say — afterwards.

JULIE: All?

JEAN: I think so. I know I've heard that phrase before, on similar occasions.

JULIE: What occasions?

JEAN: Like the one I'm talking about. The last time . . .

JULIE (*rising*): Quiet! I don't want to hear any more!

JEAN: That's interesting — that's what *she* said, too. Well, if you'll excuse me, I'm going to bed.

JULIE (*gently*): To bed? On midsummer eve?

JEAN: Yes! Dancing with the rabble out there doesn't amuse me much.

JULIE: Get the key to the boat and row me out on the lake. I want to see the sun come up.

JEAN: Is that wise?

JULIE: Are you worried about your reputation?

JEAN: Why not? Why should I risk looking ridiculous and getting fired without a reference, just when I'm trying to establish myself. Besides, I think I owe something to Kristine.

JULIE: So, now it's Kristine . . .

JEAN: Yes, but you, too. ———— Take my advice, go up and go to bed!

JULIE: Am I to obey you?

JEAN: Just this once — for your own good! Please! It's very late. Drowsiness makes people giddy and liable to lose their heads! Go to bed! Besides — unless I'm mistaken — I hear the others coming to look for me. And if they find us together, you'll be lost!

(*The Chorus approaches, singing.*)

The swineherd found his true love
a pretty girl so fair,
The swineherd found his true love
but let the girl beware.

For then he saw the princess
the princess on the golden hill,
but then saw the princess,
so much fairer still.

So the swineherd and the princess
they danced the whole night through,
and he forgot his first love,
to her he was untrue.

And when the long night ended,
and in the light of day, of day,
the dancing too was ended,
and the princess could not stay.

Then the swineherd lost his true love,
and the princess grieves him still,
and never more she'll wander
from atop the golden hill.

JULIE: I know all these people and I love them, just as they love me. Let them come in and you'll see.

JEAN: No, Miss Julie, they don't love you. They take your food, but they spit on it! Believe me! Listen to them, listen to what they're singing! ———— No, don't listen to them!

JULIE (*listening*): What are they singing?

JEAN: It's a dirty song! About you and me!

JULIE: Disgusting! Oh! How deceitful! ————

JEAN: The rabble is always cowardly! And in a battle like this, you don't fight; you can only run away!

JULIE: Run away? But where? We can't go out — or into Kristine's room.

JEAN: True. But there's my room. Necessity knows no rules. Besides, you can trust me. I'm your friend and I respect you.

JULIE: But suppose — suppose they look for you in there?

JEAN: I'll bolt the door, and if anyone tries to break in, I'll shoot! ———— Come! (*On his knees.*) Come!

JULIE (*urgently*): Promise me. . . ?

JEAN: I swear! (*Miss Julie runs off right. Jean hastens after her.*)

Ballet

(*Led by a fiddler, the servants and farm people enter, dressed festively, with flowers in their hats. On the table they place a small barrel of beer and a keg of schnapps, both garlanded. Glasses are brought out, and the drink-*

STRINDBERG • MISS JULIE **753**

ing starts. A dance circle is formed and "The Swineherd and the Princess" is sung. When the dance is finished, everyone leaves, singing.)

(Miss Julie enters alone. She notices the mess in the kitchen, wrings her hands, then takes out her powder puff and powders her nose.)

JEAN (*enters, agitated*): There, you see? And you heard them. We can't possibly stay here now, you know that.

JULIE: Yes, I know. But what can we do?

JEAN: Leave, travel, far away from here.

JULIE: Travel? Yes, but where?

JEAN: To Switzerland, to the Italian lakes. Have you ever been there?

JULIE: No. Is it beautiful?

JEAN: Oh, an eternal summer — oranges growing everywhere, laurel trees, always green . . .

JULIE: But what'll we do there?

JEAN: I'll open a hotel — with first-class service for first-class people.

JULIE: Hotel?

JEAN: That's the life, you know. Always new faces, new languages. No time to worry or be nervous. No hunting for something to do — there's always work to be done: bells ringing night and day, train whistles blowing, carriages coming and going, and all the while gold rolling into the till! That's the life!

JULIE: Yes, it sounds wonderful. But what'll I do?

JEAN: You'll be mistress of the house: the jewel in our crown! With your looks . . . and your manner — oh — success is guaranteed! It'll be wonderful! You'll sit in your office like a queen and push an electric button to set your slaves in motion. The guests will file past your throne and timidly lay their treasures before you. —— You have no idea how people tremble when they get their bill. —— I'll salt the bills° and you'll sweeten them with your prettiest smile. —— Let's get away from here —— *(Takes a timetable out of his pocket.)* —— Right away, on the next train! —— We'll be in Malmö six-thirty tomorrow morning, Hamburg at eight-forty; from Frankfort to Basel will take a day, then on to Como by way of the St. Gotthard Tunnel, in, let's see, three days. Three days!

JULIE: That's all very well! But Jean — you must give me courage! —— Tell me you love me! Put your arms around me!

JEAN (*hesitating*): I want to — but I don't dare. Not in this house, not again. I love you — never doubt that — you don't doubt it, do you, Miss Julie?

JULIE (*shy; very feminine*): "Miss!" —— Call me Julie! There are no barriers between us anymore. Call me Julie!

JEAN (*tormented*): I can't! There'll always be barriers between us as long as we stay in this house. —— There's the past and there's the Count. I've never met anyone I had such respect for. —— When I see his gloves lying on a chair, I feel small. —— When I

salt the bills: Inflate or pad the bills.

hear that bell up there ring, I jump like a skittish horse. —— And when I look at his boots standing there so stiff and proud, I feel like bowing! (*Kicking the boots.*) Superstitions and prejudices we learned as children — but they can easily be forgotten. If I can just get to another country, a republic, people will bow and scrape when they see my livery — *they'll* bow and scrape, you hear, not me! I wasn't born to cringe. I've got stuff in me, I've got character, and if I can only grab onto that first branch, you watch me climb! I'm a servant today, but next year I'll own my own hotel. In ten years I'll have enough to retire. Then I'll go to Rumania and be decorated. I could — mind you I said *could* — end up a count!

JULIE: Wonderful, wonderful!

JEAN: Ah, in Rumania you just buy your title, and so you'll be a countess after all. My countess!

JULIE: But I don't care about that — that's what I'm putting behind me! Show me you love me, otherwise — otherwise, what am I?

JEAN: I'll show you a thousand times — afterwards! Not here! And whatever you do, no emotional outbursts, or we'll both be lost! We must think this through coolly, like sensible people. (*He takes out a cigar, snips the end, and lights it.*) You sit there, and I'll sit here. We'll talk as if nothing happened.

JULIE (*desperately*): Oh, my God! Have you no feelings?

JEAN: Me? No one has more feelings than I do, but I know how to control them.

JULIE: A little while ago you could kiss my shoe — and now!

JEAN (*harshly*): Yes, but that was before. Now we have other things to think about.

JULIE: Don't speak harshly to me!

JEAN: I'm not — just sensibly! We've already done one foolish thing, let's not have any more. The Count could return any minute, and by then we've got to decide what to do with our lives. What do you think of my plans for the future? Do you approve?

JULIE: They sound reasonable enough. I have only one question: For such a big undertaking you need capital — do you have it?

JEAN (*chewing on the cigar*): Me? Certainly! I have my professional expertise, my wide experience, and my knowledge of languages. That's capital enough, I should think!

JULIE: But all that won't even buy a train ticket.

JEAN: That's true. That's why I'm looking for a partner to advance me the money.

JULIE: Where will you find one quickly enough?

JEAN: That's up to you, if you want to come with me.

JULIE: But I can't; I have no money of my own. (*Pause.*)

JEAN: Then it's all off . . .

JULIE: And . . .

JEAN: Things stay as they are.

JULIE: Do you think I'm going to stay in this house as your lover? With all the servants pointing their fingers at me? Do you imagine I can face my father after this? No! Take me away from here, away from

Helen Mirren as Miss Julie in a 1971 production of
Strindberg's play.

special! (*He opens a drawer in the table, takes out a
wine bottle, and fills two glasses already used.*)

JULIE: Where did you get that wine?

JEAN: From the cellar.

JULIE: My father's burgundy!

JEAN: That'll do for his son-in-law, won't it?

JULIE: And I drink beer! Beer!

JEAN: That only shows I have better taste.

JULIE: Thief!

JEAN: Planning to tell?

JULIE: Oh, oh! Accomplice of a common thief! Was I
drunk? Have I been walking in a dream the whole
evening? Midsummer eve! A time of innocent fun!

JEAN: Innocent, eh?

JULIE (*pacing back and forth*): Is there anyone on earth
more miserable than I am at this moment?

JEAN: Why should you be? After such a conquest? Think
of Kristine in there. Don't you think she has feelings,
too?

JULIE: I thought so awhile ago, but not any more. No, a
servant is a servant . . .

JEAN: And a whore is a whore!

JULIE (*on her knees, her hands clasped*): Oh, God in
heaven, end my wretched life! Take me away from
the filth I'm sinking into! Save me! Save me!

JEAN: I can't deny I feel sorry for you. When I lay in that
onion bed and saw you in the rose garden, well . . . I'll
be frank . . . I had the same dirty thoughts all boys
have.

JULIE: And you wanted to die for me!

JEAN: In the oat bin? That was just talk.

JULIE: A lie, in other words!

JEAN (*beginning to feel sleepy*): More or less! I got the
idea from a newspaper story about a chimney sweep
who curled up in a firewood bin full of lilacs because
he got a summons for not supporting his illegitimate
child . . .

JULIE: So, that's what you're like . . .

JEAN: I had to think of something. And that's the kind of
story women always go for.

JULIE: Swine!

JEAN: *Merde!*

JULIE: And now you've seen the hawk's back . . .

JEAN: Not exactly its *back* . . .

JULIE: And I was to be the first branch . . .

JEAN: But the branch was rotten . . .

JULIE: I was to be the sign on the hotel . . .

JEAN: And I the hotel . . .

JULIE: Sit at your desk, entice your customers, pad their
bills . . .

JEAN: That I'd do myself . . .

JULIE: How can anyone be so thoroughly filthy?

JEAN: Better clean up then!

JULIE: You lackey, you menial, stand up, when I speak to
you!

JEAN: Menial's strumpet, lackey's whore, shut up and
get out of here! Who are you to lecture me on coarseness? None of my kind is ever as coarse as you were
tonight. Do you think one of your maids would

shame and dishonor ——— Oh, what have I done!
My God, my God! (*She cries.*)

JEAN: Now, don't start that old song! ——— What have
you done? The same as many others before you.

JULIE (*screaming convulsively*): And now you think I'm
contemptible! ——— I'm falling, I'm falling!

JEAN: Fall down to my level and I'll lift you up again.

JULIE: What terrible power drew me to you? The attraction of the weak to the strong? The falling to the rising? Or was it love? Was this love? Do you know
what love is?

JEAN: Me? What do you take me for? You don't think
this was my first time, do you?

JULIE: The things you say, the thoughts you think!

JEAN: That's the way I was taught, and that's the way I
am! Now don't get excited and don't play the grand
lady, because we're in the same boat now! ———
Come on, Julie, I'll pour you a glass of something

throw herself at a man the way you did? Have you ever seen any girl of my class offer herself like that? I've only seen it among animals and streetwalkers.

JULIE (*crushed*): You're right. Hit me, trample on me. I don't deserve any better. I'm worthless. But help me! If you see any way out of this, help me, Jean, please!

JEAN (*more gently*): I'd be lying if I didn't admit to a sense of triumph in all this, but do you think that a person like me would have dared even to look at someone like you if you hadn't invited it? I'm still amazed . . .

JULIE: And proud . . .

JEAN: Why not? Though I must say it was too easy to be really exciting.

JULIE: Go on, hit me, hit me harder!

JEAN (*rising*): No! Forgive me for what I've said! I don't hit a man when he's down, let alone a woman. I can't deny though, that I'm pleased to find out that what looked so dazzling to us from below was only tinsel, that the hawk's back was only gray, after all, that the lovely complexion was only powder, that those polished fingernails had black edges, and that a dirty handkerchief is still dirty, even if it smells of perfume . . . ! On the other hand, it hurts me to find out that what I was striving for wasn't finer, more substantial. It hurts me to see you sunk so low that you're inferior to your own cook. It hurts like watching flowers beaten down by autumn rains and turned into mud.

JULIE: You talk as if you were already above me.

JEAN: I am. You see, I could make you a countess, but you could never make me a count.

JULIE: But I'm the child of a count — something you could never be!

JEAN: That's true. But I could be the father of counts — if . . .

JULIE: But you're a thief. I'm not.

JEAN: There are worse things than being a thief! Besides, when I'm working in a house, I consider myself sort of a member of the family, like one of the children. And you don't call it stealing when a child snatches a berry off a full bush. (*His passion is aroused again.*) Miss Julie, you're a glorious woman, much too good for someone like me! You were drinking and you lost your head. Now you want to cover up your mistake by telling yourself that you love me! You don't. Maybe there was a physical attraction — but then your love is no better than mine. —— I could never be satisfied to be no more than an animal to you, and I could never arouse real love in you.

JULIE: Are you sure of that?

JEAN: You're suggesting it's possible —— Oh, I could fall in love with you, no doubt about it. You're beautiful, you're refined —— (*approaching and taking her hand*) —— cultured, lovable when you want to be, and once you start a fire in a man, it never goes out. (*Putting his arm around her waist.*) You're like hot, spicy wine, and one kiss from you . . . (*He tries to lead her out, but she slowly frees herself.*)

JULIE: Let me go!? —— You'll never win me like that.

JEAN: *How* then? —— Not like that? Not with caresses and pretty speeches. Not with plans about the future or rescue from disgrace! *How* then?

JULIE: How? How? I don't know! —— I have no idea! —— I detest you as I detest rats, but I can't escape from you.

JEAN: Escape with me!

JULIE (*pulling herself together*): Escape? Yes, we must escape! —— But I'm so tired. Give me a glass of wine? (*Jean pours the wine. She looks at her watch.*) But we must talk first. We still have a little time. (*She drains the glass, then holds it out for more.*)

JEAN: Don't drink so fast. It'll go to your head.

JULIE: What does it matter?

JEAN: What does it matter? It's vulgar to get drunk! What did you want to tell me?

JULIE: We must escape! But first we must talk, I mean I must talk. You've done all the talking up to now. You told about your life, now I want to tell about mine, so we'll know all about each other before we go off together.

JEAN: Just a minute! Forgive me! If you don't want to regret it afterwards, you'd better think twice before revealing any secrets about yourself.

JULIE: Aren't you my friend?

JEAN: Yes, sometimes! But don't rely on me.

JULIE: You're only saying that. —— Besides, everyone already knows my secrets. —— You see, my mother was a commoner — very humble background. She was brought up believing in social equality, women's rights, and all that. The idea of marriage repelled her. So, when my father proposed, she replied that she would never become his wife, but he could be her lover. He insisted that he didn't want the woman he loved to be less respected than he. But his passion ruled him, and when she explained that the world's respect meant nothing to her, he accepted her conditions.

But now his friends avoided him and his life was restricted to taking care of the estate, which couldn't satisfy him. I came into the world — against my mother's wishes, as far as I can understand. She wanted to bring me up as a child of nature, and, what's more, to learn everything a boy had to learn, so that I might be an example of how a woman can be as good as a man. I had to wear boy's clothes and learn to take care of horses, but I was never allowed in the cowshed. I had to groom and harness the horses and go hunting — and even had to watch them slaughter animals — that was disgusting! On the estate men were put on women's jobs and women on men's jobs — with the result that the property became run down and we became the laughingstock of the district. Finally, my father must have awakened from his trance because he rebelled and changed everything his way. My parents were then married quietly. Mother became ill — I don't know what illness it was — but she often had convulsions, hid in the attic and in the garden, and sometimes stayed out all night. Then came the great fire, which you've heard about. The house, the stables, and the cowshed all burned down, under very curious circumstances, suggesting arson, because the accident happened the day after the insurance had expired. The quarterly premium my father sent in was delayed because of a messenger's carelessness and didn't arrive in time. (*She fills her glass and drinks.*)

JEAN: Don't drink any more!

JULIE: Oh, what does it matter. —— We were left penniless and had to sleep in the carriages. My father had no idea where to find money to rebuild the house because he had so slighted his old friends that they had forgotten him. Then my mother suggested that he borrow from a childhood friend of hers, a brick manufacturer who lived nearby. Father got the loan without having to pay interest, which surprised him. And that's how the estate was rebuilt. —— (*Drinks again.*) Do you know who started the fire?

JEAN: The Countess, your mother.

JULIE: Do you know who the brick manufacturer was?

JEAN: Your mother's lover?

JULIE: Do you know whose money it was?

JEAN: Wait a moment — no, I don't.

JULIE: It was my mother's.

JEAN: You mean the Count's, unless they didn't sign an agreement when they were married.

JULIE: They didn't. —— My mother had a small inheritance which she didn't want under my father's control, so she entrusted it to her — friend.

JEAN: Who stole it!

JULIE: Exactly! He kept it. —— All this my father found out, but he couldn't bring it to court, couldn't repay his wife's lover, couldn't prove it was his wife's money! It was my mother's revenge for being forced into marriage against her will. It nearly drove him to suicide — there was a rumor that he tried with a pistol, but failed. So, he managed to live through it and my mother had to suffer for what she'd done. You can imagine that those were a terrible five years for me. I loved my father, but I sided with my mother because I didn't know the circumstances. I learned from her to hate men — you've heard how she hated the whole male sex — and I swore to her I'd never be a slave to any man.

JEAN: But you got engaged to that lawyer.

JULIE: In order to make him my slave.

JEAN: And he wasn't willing?

JULIE: He was willing, all right, but I wouldn't let him. I got tired of him.

JEAN: I saw it — out near the stable.

JULIE: What did you see?

JEAN: I saw — how he broke off the engagement.

JULIE: That's a lie! I was the one who broke it off. Has he said that he did? That swine . . .

JEAN: He was no swine, I'm sure. So, you hate men, Miss Julie?

JULIE: Yes! —— Most of the time! But sometimes — when the weakness comes, when passion burns! Oh, God, will the fire never die out?

JEAN: Do you hate me, too?

JULIE: Immeasurably! I'd like to have you put to death, like an animal . . .

JEAN: I see — the penalty for bestiality — the woman gets two years at hard labor and the animal is put to death. Right?

JULIE: Exactly!

JEAN: But there's no prosecutor here — and no animal. So, what'll we do?

JULIE: Go away!

JEAN: To torment each other to death?

JULIE: No! To be happy for — two days, a week, as long as we can be happy, and then — die . . .

JEAN: Die? That's stupid! It's better to open a hotel!

JULIE (*without listening*): —— on the shore of Lake Como, where the sun always shines, where the laurels are green at Christmas and the oranges glow.

JEAN: Lake Como is a rainy hole, and I never saw any oranges outside the stores. But tourists are attracted there because there are plenty of villas to be rented out to lovers, and that's a profitable business. —— Do you know why? Because they sign a lease for six months — and then leave after three weeks!

JULIE (*naively*): Why after three weeks?

JEAN: They quarrel, of course! But they still have to pay the rent in full! And so you rent the villas out again. And that's the way it goes, time after time. There's never a shortage of love — even if it doesn't last long!

JULIE: You don't want to die with me?

JEAN: I don't want to die at all! For one thing, I like living, and for another, I think suicide is a crime against the Providence which gave us life.

JULIE: You believe in God? *You?*

JEAN: Of course I do. And I go to church every other Sunday. —— To be honest, I'm tired of all this, and I'm going to bed.

JULIE: Are you? And do you think I can let it go at that? A man owes something to the woman he's shamed.

JEAN (*taking out his purse and throwing a silver coin on the table*): Here! I don't like owing anything to anybody.

JULIE (*pretending not to notice the insult*): Do you know what the law states . . .

JEAN: Unfortunately the law doesn't state any punishment for the woman who seduces a man!

JULIE (*as before*): Do you see any way out but to leave, get married, and then separate?

JEAN: Suppose I refuse such a *mésalliance?°*

JULIE: *Mésalliance* . . .

JEAN: Yes, for me! You see, I come from better stock than you. There's no arsonist in my family.

JULIE: How do you know?

JEAN: You can't prove otherwise. We don't keep charts

---

mésalliance: Misalliance or mismatch, especially regarding relative social status.

on our ancestors — there's just the police records! But I've read about your family. Do you know who the founder was? He was a miller who let the king sleep with his wife one night during the Danish War. I don't have any noble ancestors like that. I don't have any noble ancestors at all, but I could become one myself.

JULIE: This is what I get for opening my heart to someone unworthy, for giving my family's honor . . .

JEAN: Dishonor! ——— Well, I told you so: When people drink, they talk, and talk is dangerous!

JULIE: Oh, how I regret it! ——— How I regret it! ——— If you at least loved me.

JEAN: For the last time ——— what do you want? Shall I cry; shall I jump over your riding crop? Shall I kiss you and lure you off to Lake Como for three weeks, and then God knows what. . . ? What shall I do? What do you want? This is getting painfully embarrassing! But that's what happens when you stick your nose in women's business. Miss Julie! I see that you're unhappy. I know you're suffering, but I can't understand you. We don't have such romantic ideas; there's not this kind of hate between us. Love is a game we play when we get time off from work, but we don't have all day and night, like you. I think you're sick, really sick. Your mother was crazy, and her ideas have poisoned your life.

JULIE: Be kind to me. At least now you're talking like a human being.

JEAN: Be human yourself, then. You spit on me, and you won't let me wipe myself off ———

JULIE: Help me! Help me! Just tell me what to do, where to go!

JEAN: In God's name, if I only knew myself!

JULIE: I've been crazy, out of my mind, but isn't there any way out?

JEAN: Stay here and keep calm! No one knows anything!

JULIE: Impossible! The others know and Kristine knows.

JEAN: No they don't, and they'd never believe a thing like that!

JULIE (*hesitantly*): But — it could happen again!

JEAN: That's true!

JULIE: And then?

JEAN (*frightened*): Then? ——— Why didn't I think about that? Yes, there is only one thing to do — get away from here! Right away! I can't come with you, then we'd be finished, so you'll have to go alone — away — anywhere!

JULIE: Alone? ——— Where? ——— I can't do that!

JEAN: You must! And before the Count gets back! If you stay, you know what'll happen. Once you make a mistake like this, you want to continue because the damage has already been done. . . . Then you get bolder and bolder — until finally you're caught! So leave! Later you can write to the Count and confess everything — except that it was me! He'll never guess who it was, and he's not going to be eager to find out, anyway.

JULIE: I'll go if you come with me.

JEAN: Are you out of your head? Miss Julie runs away with her servant! In two days it would be in the newspapers, and that's something your father would never live through.

JULIE: I can't go and I can't stay! Help me! I'm so tired, so terribly tired. ——— Order me! Set me in motion — I can't think or act on my own . . .

JEAN: What miserable creatures you people are! You strut around with your noses in the air as if you were the lords of creation! All right, I'll order you. Go upstairs and get dressed! Get some money for the trip, and then come back down!

JULIE (*in a half-whisper*): Come up with me!

JEAN: To your room? ——— Now you're crazy again! (*Hesitates for a moment.*) No! Go, at once! (*Takes her hand to lead her out.*)

JULIE (*as she leaves*): Speak kindly to me, Jean!

JEAN: An order always sounds unkind — now you know how it feels. (*Jean, alone, sighs with relief. He sits at the table, takes out a notebook and pencil, and begins adding up figures, counting aloud as he works. He continues in dumb show until Kristine enters, dressed for church. She is carrying a white tie and shirt front.*)

KRISTINE: Lord Jesus, what a mess! What have you been up to?

JEAN: Oh, Miss Julie dragged everybody in here. You mean you didn't hear anything? You must have been sleeping soundly.

KRISTINE: Like a log.

JEAN: And dressed for church already?

KRISTINE: Of course! You remember you promised to come with me to communion today!

JEAN: Oh, yes, that's right. ——— And you brought my things. Come on, then! (*He sits down. Kristine starts to put on his shirt front and tie. Pause. Jean begins sleepily.*) What's the gospel text for today?

KRISTINE: On St. John's Day? — the beheading of John the Baptist, I should think!

JEAN: Ah, that'll be a long one, for sure. ——— Hey, you're choking me! ——— Oh, I'm sleepy, so sleepy!

KRISTINE: Yes, what have you been doing, up all night? Your face is absolutely green.

JEAN: I've been sitting here gabbing with Miss Julie.

KRISTINE: She has no idea what's proper, that one! (*Pause.*)

JEAN: You know, Kristine . . .

KRISTINE: What?

JEAN: It's really strange when you think about it. ——— Her!

KRISTINE: What's so strange?

JEAN: Everything! (*Pause.*)

KRISTINE (*looking at the half-empty glasses standing on the table*): Have you been drinking together, too?

JEAN: Yes.

KRISTINE: Shame on you! ——— Look me in the eye!

JEAN: Well?

KRISTINE: Is it possible? Is it possible?

JEAN (*thinking it over for a moment*): Yes, it is.

KRISTINE: Ugh! I never would have believed it! No, shame on you, shame!

JEAN: You're not jealous of her, are you?

KRISTINE: No, not of her! If it had been Clara or Sofie I'd have scratched your eyes out! ——— I don't know why, but that's the way I feel. ——— Oh, it's disgusting!

JEAN: Are you angry at her, then?

KRISTINE: No, at you! That was an awful thing to do, awful! Poor girl! ——— No, I don't care who knows it — I won't stay in a house where we can't respect the people we work for.

JEAN: Why should we respect them?

KRISTINE: You're so clever, you tell me! Do you want to wait on people who can't behave decently? Do you? You disgrace yourself that way, if you ask me.

JEAN: But it's a comfort to know they aren't any better than us.

KRISTINE: Not for me. If they're no better, what do we have to strive for to better ourselves. ——— And think of the Count! Think of him! As if he hasn't had enough misery in his life! Lord Jesus! No, I won't stay in this house any longer! ——— And it had to be with someone like you! If it had been that lawyer, if it had been a real gentleman . . .

JEAN: What do you mean?

KRISTINE: Oh, you're all right for what you are, but there are men and gentlemen, after all! ——— No, this business with Miss Julie I can never forget. She was so proud, so arrogant with men, you wouldn't have believed she could just go and give herself — and to someone like you! And she was going to have poor Diana shot for running after the gatekeepers' mutt! ——— Yes, I'm giving my notice, I mean it — I won't stay here any longer. On the twenty-fourth of October, I leave!

JEAN: And then?

KRISTINE: Well, since the subject has come up, it's about time you looked around for something since we're going to get married, in any case.

JEAN: Where am I going to look? I couldn't find a job like this if I was married.

KRISTINE: No, that's true. But you can find work as a porter or as a caretaker in some government office. The state doesn't pay much, I know, but it's secure, and there's a pension for the wife and children . . .

JEAN (grimacing): That's all very well, but it's a bit early for me to think about dying for a wife and children. My ambitions are a little higher than that.

KRISTINE: Your ambitions, yes! Well, you have obligations, too! Think about them!

JEAN: Don't start nagging me about obligations. I know what I have to do! (Listening for something outside.) Besides, this is something we have plenty of time to think over. Go and get ready for church.

KRISTINE: Who's that walking around up there?

JEAN: I don't know, unless it's Clara.

KRISTINE (going): You don't suppose it's the Count, who came home without us hearing him?

JEAN (frightened): The Count? No, I don't think so. He'd have rung.

KRISTINE (going): Well, God help us! I've never seen anything like this before. (The sun has risen and shines through the treetops in the park. The light shifts gradually until it slants in through the windows. Jean goes to the door and signals. Miss Julie enters, dressed in travel clothes and carrying a small bird cage, covered with a cloth, which she places on a chair.)

JULIE: I'm ready now.

JEAN: Shh! Kristine is awake.

JULIE (very nervous during the following): Does she suspect something?

JEAN: She doesn't know anything. But my God, you look awful!

JULIE: Why? How do I look?

JEAN: You're pale as a ghost and — excuse me, but your face is dirty.

JULIE: Let me wash up then. ——— (She goes to the basin and washes her hands and face.) Give me a towel! ——— Oh ——— the sun's coming up.

JEAN: Then the goblins will disappear.

JULIE: Yes, there must have been goblins out last night! ——— Jean, listen, come with me! I have some money now.

JEAN (hesitantly): Enough?

JULIE: Enough to start with. Come with me! I just can't travel alone on a day like this — midsummer day on a stuffy train — jammed in among crowds of people staring at me. Eternal delays at every station, while I'd wish I had wings. No, I can't, I can't! And then there'll be memories, memories of midsummer days when I was little. The church — decorated with birch leaves and lilacs; dinner at the big table with relatives and friends, the afternoons in the park, dancing, music, flowers, and games. Oh, no matter how far we travel, the memories will follow in the baggage car, with remorse and guilt!

JEAN: I'll go with you — but right away, before it's too late. Right this minute!

JULIE: Get dressed, then! (Picking up the bird cage.)

JEAN: But no baggage! It would give us away!

JULIE: No, nothing! Only what we can have in the compartment with us.

JEAN (has taken his hat): What've you got there? What is it?

JULIE: It's only my greenfinch. I couldn't leave her behind.

JEAN: What? Bring a bird cage with us? You're out of your head! Put it down!

JULIE: It's the only thing I'm taking from my home — the only living being that loves me, since Diana was unfaithful. Don't be cruel! Let me take her!

JEAN: Put the cage down, I said! ——— And don't talk so loudly — Kristine will hear us!

JULIE: No, I won't leave her in the hands of strangers! I'd rather you killed her.

JEAN: Bring the thing here, then, I'll cut its head off!

JULIE: Oh! But don't hurt her! Don't . . . no, I can't.

JEAN: Bring it here! I can!

JULIE (*taking the bird out of the cage and kissing it*): Oh, my little Serena, must you die and leave your mistress?

JEAN: Please don't make a scene! Your whole future is at stake! Hurry up! (*He snatches the bird from her, carries it over to the chopping block, and picks up a meat cleaver. Miss Julie turns away.*) You should have learned how to slaughter chickens instead of how to fire pistols. (*He chops off the bird's head.*) Then you wouldn't feel faint at the sight of blood.

JULIE (*screaming*): Kill me, too! Kill me! You, who can slaughter an innocent animal without blinking an eye! Oh, how I hate, how I detest you! There's blood between us now! I curse the moment I set eyes on you! I curse the moment I was conceived in my mother's womb!

JEAN: What good does cursing do? Let's go!

JULIE (*approaching the chopping block, as if drawn against her will*): No, I don't want to go yet. I can't . . . until I see . . . Shh! I hear a carriage ——— (*She listens, but her eyes never leave the cleaver and the chopping block.*) Do you think I can't stand the sight of blood? You think I'm so weak . . . Oh — I'd like to see your blood and your brains on a chopping block! ——— I'd like to see your whole sex swimming in a sea of blood, like my little bird . . . I think I could drink from your skull! I'd like to bathe my feet in your open chest and eat your heart roasted whole! ——— You think I'm weak. You think I love you because my womb craved your seed. You think I want to carry your spawn under my heart and nourish it with my blood — bear your child and take your name! By the way, what is your family name? I've never heard it. ——— Do you have one? I was to be Mrs. Bootblack — or Madame Pigsty. ——— You dog, who wears my collar, you lackey, who bears my coat of arms on your buttons — do I have to share you with my cook, compete with my own servant? Oh! Oh! Oh! ——— You think I'm a coward who wants to run away! No, now I'm staying — and let the storm break! My father will come home . . . to find his desk broken open . . . and his money gone! Then he'll ring — that bell . . . twice for his valet — and then he'll send for the police . . . and then I'll tell everything! Everything! Oh, what a relief it'll be to have it all end — if only it will end! ——— And then he'll have a stroke and die . . . That'll be the end of all of us — and there'll be peace . . . quiet . . . eternal rest! ——— And then our coat of arms will be broken against his coffin — the family title extinct — but the valet's line will go on in an orphanage . . . win laurels in the gutter, and end in jail!

JEAN: There's the blue blood talking! Very good, Miss Julie! Just don't let that miller out of the closet! (*Kristine enters, dressed for church, with a psalm-book in her hand.*)

JULIE (*rushing to Kristine and falling into her arms, as if seeking protection*): Help me, Kristine! Help me against this man!

KRISTINE (*unmoved and cold*): What a fine way to behave on a Sunday morning! (*Sees the chopping block.*) And look at this mess! ——— What does all this mean? Why all this screaming and carrying on?

JULIE: Kristine! You're a woman and my friend! Beware of this swine!

JEAN (*uncomfortable*): While you ladies discuss this, I'll go in and shave. (*Slips off right.*)

JULIE: You must listen to me so you'll understand!

KRISTINE: No, I could never understand such disgusting behavior! Where are you off to in your traveling clothes? ——— And he had his hat on. ——— Well? ——— Well?

JULIE: Listen to me, Kristine! Listen, and I'll tell you everything ———

KRISTINE: I don't want to hear it . . .

JULIE: But you must listen to me . . .

KRISTINE: What about? If it's about this silliness with Jean, I'm not interested, because it's none of my business. But if you're thinking of tricking him into running out, we'll soon put a stop to that!

JULIE (*extremely nervous*): Try to be calm now, Kristine, and listen to me! I can't stay here, and neither can Jean — so we must go away . . .

KRISTINE: Hm, hm!

JULIE (*brightening*): You see, I just had an idea ——— What if all three of us go — abroad — to Switzerland and start a hotel together? ——— I have money, you see — and Jean and I could run it — and I thought you, you could take care of the kitchen . . . Wouldn't that be wonderful? ——— Say yes! And come with us, and then everything will be settled! ——— Oh, do say yes! (*Embracing Kristine and patting her warmly.*)

KRISTINE (*coolly, thoughtfully*): Hm, hm!

JULIE (*presto tempo*):° You've never traveled, Kristine. ——— You must get out and see the world. You can't imagine how much fun it is to travel by train — always new faces — new countries. ——— And when we get to Hamburg, we'll stop off at the zoo — you'll like that. ——— and then we'll go to the theater and the opera — and when we get to Munich, dear, there we have museums, with Rubens and Raphael, the great painters, as you know. ——— You've heard of Munich, where King Ludwig lived — the king who went mad. ——— And then we'll see his castles — they're still there and they're like castles in fairy tales. ——— And from there it isn't far to Switzerland — and the Alps. ——— Imagine — the Alps have snow on them even in the middle of summer! ——— And oranges grow there and laurel trees that are green all year round ——— (*Jean can be seen in the wings right, sharpening his razor on a strop which he holds with his teeth and his left hand. He*

presto tempo: At a rapid pace.

listens to the conversation with satisfaction, nodding now and then in approval. Miss Julie continues tempo prestissimo.)° And then we'll start a hotel — and I'll be at the desk, while Jean greets the guests . . . does the shopping . . . writes letters. ——— You have no idea what a life it'll be — the train whistles blowing and the carriages arriving and the bells ringing in the rooms and down in the restaurant. ——— And I'll make out the bills — and I know how to salt them! . . . You'll never believe how timid travelers are when they have to pay their bills! ——— And you — you'll be in charge of the kitchen. ——— Naturally, you won't have to stand over the stove yourself. ——— And since you're going to be seen by people, you'll have to wear beautiful clothes. ——— And you, with your looks — no, I'm not flattering you — one fine day you'll grab yourself a husband! ——— You'll see! ——— A rich Englishman — they're so easy to ——— *(Slowing down.)* ——— catch — and then we'll get rich — and build ourselves a villa on Lake Como. ——— It's true it rains there a little now and then, but ——— *(Dully.)* ——— the sun has to shine sometimes — although it looks dark — and then . . . of course we could always come back home again ——— *(Pause.)* ——— here — or somewhere else ———

KRISTINE: Listen, Miss Julie, do you believe all this?

JULIE *(crushed)*: Do I believe it?

KRISTINE: Yes!

JULIE *(wearily)*: I don't know. I don't believe in anything anymore. *(She sinks down on the bench and cradles her head in her arms on the table.)* Nothing! Nothing at all!

KRISTINE *(turning right to where Jean is standing)*: So, you thought you'd run out!

JEAN *(embarrassed; puts the razor on the table)*: Run out? That's no way to put it. You hear Miss Julie's plan, and even if she is tired after being up all night, it's still a practical plan.

KRISTINE: Now you listen to me! Did you think I'd work as a cook for that . . .

JEAN *(sharply)*: You watch what you say in front of your mistress! Do you understand?

KRISTINE: Mistress!

JEAN: Yes!

KRISTINE: Listen to him! Listen to him!

JEAN: Yes, you listen! It'd do you good to listen more and talk less! Miss Julie is your mistress. If you despise her, you have to despise yourself for the same reason!

KRISTINE: I've always had enough self-respect ———

JEAN: ——— to be able to despise other people!

KRISTINE: ——— to stop me from doing anything that's beneath me. You can't say that the Count's cook has been up to something with the groom or the swineherd! Can you?

JEAN: No, you were lucky enough to get hold of a gentleman!

KRISTINE: Yes, a gentleman who sells the Count's oats from the stable.

JEAN: You should talk — taking a commission from the grocer and bribes from the butcher.

KRISTINE: What?

JEAN: And you say you can't respect your employers any longer. You, you, you!

KRISTINE: Are you coming to church with me, now? You could use a good sermon after your fine deed!

JEAN: No, I'm not going to church today. You'll have to go alone and confess what you've been up to.

KRISTINE: Yes, I'll do that, and I'll bring back enough forgiveness for you, too. The Savior suffered and died on the Cross for all our sins, and if we go to Him with faith and a penitent heart, He takes all our sins on Himself.

JEAN: Even grocery sins?

JULIE: And do you believe that, Kristine?

KRISTINE: It's my living faith, as sure as I stand here. It's the faith I learned as a child, Miss Julie, and kept ever since. "Where sin abounded, grace did much more abound!"

JULIE: Oh, if I only had your faith. If only . . .

KRISTINE: Well, you see, we can't have it without God's special grace, and that isn't given to everyone ———

JULIE: Who is it given to then?

KRISTINE: That's the great secret of the workings of grace, Miss Julie, and God is no respecter of persons, for the last shall be the first . . .

JULIE: Then He does respect the last.

KRISTINE *(continuing)*: . . . and it is easier for a camel to go through the eye of a needle, than for a rich man to enter the Kingdom of God. That's how it is, Miss Julie! Anyhow, I'm going now — alone, and on the way I'm going to tell the groom not to let any horses out, in case anyone wants to leave before the Count gets back! ——— Goodbye! *(Leaves.)*

JEAN: What a witch! ——— And all this because of a greenfinch! ———

JULIE *(dully)*: Never mind the greenfinch! ——— Can you see any way out of this? Any end to it?

JEAN *(thinking)*: No!

JULIE: What would you do in my place?

JEAN: In your place? Let's see — as a person of position, as a woman who had — fallen. I don't know — wait, now I know.

JULIE *(taking the razor and making a gesture)*: You mean like this?

JEAN: Yes! But — understand — *I* wouldn't do it! That's the difference between us!

JULIE: Because you're a man and I'm a woman? What sort of difference is that?

JEAN: The usual difference — between a man and a woman.

JULIE *(with the razor in her hand)*: I want to, but I can't! ——— My father couldn't either, the time he should have done it.

tempo prestissimo: At a very rapid pace.

JEAN: No, he shouldn't have! He had to revenge himself first.

JULIE: And now my mother is revenged again, through me.

JEAN: Didn't you ever love your father, Miss Julie?

JULIE: Oh yes, deeply, but I've hated him, too. I must have done so without realizing it! It was he who brought me up to despise my own sex, making me half woman, half man. Whose fault is what's happened? My father's, my mother's, my own? My own? I don't have anything that's my own. I don't have a single thought that I didn't get from my father, not an emotion that I didn't get from my mother, and this last idea — that all people are equal — I got that from my fiancé. ——— That's why I called him a swine! How can it be my fault? Shall I let Jesus take on the blame, the way Kristine does? ——— No, I'm too proud to do that and too sensible — thanks to my father's teachings. ——— And as for someone rich not going to heaven, that's a lie. But Kristine won't get in — how will she explain the money she has in the savings bank? Whose fault is it? ——— What does it matter whose fault it is? I'm still the one who has to bear the blame, face the consequences . . .

JEAN: Yes, but . . . (*The bell rings sharply twice. Miss Julie jumps up. Jean changes his coat.*) The Count is back! Do you suppose Kristine — (*He goes to the speaking tube, taps the lid, and listens.*)

JULIE: He's been to his desk!

JEAN: It's Jean, sir! (*Listening; the audience cannot hear the Count's voice.*) Yes, sir! (*Listening.*) Yes, sir! Right away! (*Listening.*) At once, sir! (*Listening.*) I see, in half an hour!

JULIE (*desperately frightened*): What did he say? Dear Lord, what did he say?

JEAN: He wants his boots and his coffee in half an hour.

JULIE: So, in half an hour! Oh, I'm so tired. I'm not able to do anything. I can't repent, can't run away, can't stay, can't live — can't die! Help me now! Order me, and I'll obey like a dog! Do me this last service, save my honor, save his name! You know what I *should* do, but don't have the will to . . . You will it, you order me to do it!

JEAN: I don't know why ——— but now I can't either ——— I don't understand. ——— It's as if this coat made it impossible for me to order you to do anything. ——— And now, since the Count spoke to me — I — I can't really explain it — but — ah, it's the damn lackey in me! ——— I think if the Count came down here now — and ordered me to cut my throat, I'd do it on the spot.

JULIE: Then pretend you're he, and I'm you! ——— You gave such a good performance before when you knelt at my feet. ——— You were a real nobleman. ——— Or — have you ever seen a hypnotist in the theater? (*Jean nods.*) He says to his subject: "Take the broom," and he takes it. He says: "Sweep," and he sweeps ———

JEAN: But the subject has to be asleep.

JULIE (*ecstatically*): I'm already asleep. ——— The whole room is like smoke around me . . . and you look like an iron stove . . . shaped like a man in black, with a tall hat — and your eyes glow like coals when the fire is dying — and your face is a white patch, like ashes ——— (*The sunlight has reached the floor and now shines on Jean.*) ——— it's so warm and good ——— (*She rubs her hands as if warming them before a fire.*) ——— and bright — and so peaceful!

JEAN (*taking the razor and putting it in her hand*): Here's the broom! Go now while it's bright — out to the barn — and . . . (*Whispers in her ear.*)

JULIE (*awake*): Thank you. I'm going now to rest! But just tell me — that those who are first can also receive the gift of grace. Say it, even if you don't believe it.

JEAN: The first? No, I can't ——— But wait — Miss Julie — now I know! You're no longer among the first — you're now among — the last!

JULIE: That's true. ——— I'm among the very last. I'm the last one of all! Oh! ——— But now I can't go! ——— Tell me once more to go!

JEAN: No, now I can't either! I can't!

JULIE: And the first shall be the last!

JEAN: Don't think, don't think! You're taking all my strength from me, making me a coward. ——— What was that? I thought the bell moved! ——— No! Shall we stuff paper in it? ——— To be so afraid of a bell! ——— But it isn't just a bell. ——— There's someone behind it — a hand sets it in motion — and something else sets the hand in motion. ——— Maybe if you cover your ears — cover your ears! But then it rings even louder! rings until someone answers. ——— And then it's too late! And then the police come — and — then ——— (*The bell rings twice loudly. Jean flinches, then straightens up.*) It's horrible! But there's no other way! ——— Go! (*Miss Julie walks firmly out through the door.*)

COMMENTARY

August Strindberg (1849–1912)
FROM THE PREFACE TO *MISS JULIE*   *1888*

TRANSLATED BY HARRY G. CARLSON

Strindberg's preface sets out his intentions in writing Miss Julie, *a play concerned with the problem of "social climbing or falling, of higher or lower, better or worse, man or woman." He discusses the struggle for dominance between Miss Julie and Jean, and characterizes Miss Julie as a woman forced to "wreak vengeance" on herself.*

Miss Julie is a modern character. Not that the man-hating half-woman has not existed in all ages but because now that she has been discovered, she has come out in the open to make herself heard. The half-woman is a type who pushes her way ahead, selling herself nowadays for power, decorations, honors, and diplomas, as formerly she used to do for money. The type implies a retrogressive step in evolution, an inferior species who cannot endure. Unfortunately, they are able to pass on their wretchedness; degenerate men seem unconsciously to choose their mates from among them. And so they breed, producing an indeterminate sex for whom life is a torture. Fortunately, the offspring go under either because they are out of harmony with reality or because their repressed instincts break out uncontrollably or because their hopes of achieving equality with men are crushed. The type is tragic, revealing the drama of a desperate struggle against Nature, tragic as the romantic heritage now being dissipated by naturalism, which has a contrary aim: happiness, and happiness belongs only to the strong and skillful species.

But Miss Julie is also: a relic of the old warrior nobility now giving way to a new nobility of nerve and intellect, a victim of her own flawed constitution, a victim of the discord caused in a family by a mother's "crime," a victim of the delusions and conditions of her age — and together these are the equivalent of the concept of Destiny, or Universal Law, of antiquity. Guilt has been abolished by the naturalist, along with God, but the consequences of an action — punishment, imprisonment or the fear of it — that he cannot erase, for the simple reason that they remain, whether he pronounces acquittal or not. Those who have been injured are not as kind and understanding as an unscathed outsider can afford to be. Even if her father felt constrained not to seek revenge, his daughter would wreak vengeance upon herself, as she does here, out of an innate or acquired sense of honor, which the upper classes inherit — from where? From barbarism, from the ancient Aryan home of the race, from medieval chivalry. It is a beautiful thing, but nowadays a hindrance to the survival of the race. It is the nobleman's harikari, which compels him to slit open his own stomach when someone insults him and which survives in a modified form in the duel, that privilege of the nobility. That is why Jean, the servant, lives, while Miss Julie cannot live without honor. The slave's advantage over the nobleman is that he lacks this fatal preoccupation with honor. But in all of us Aryans there is something of the nobleman, or a Don Quixote. And so we sympathize with the suicide, whose act means a loss of honor. We are noblemen enough to be pained when we see the mighty fallen and as superfluous as a corpse, yes, even if the fallen should rise again and make amends through an honorable act. The servant Jean is a race-founder, someone in whom the process of differentiation can be detected. Born the son of a tenant farmer, he has educated himself in the things a gentleman should know. He has been quick to learn, has finely developed senses (smell, taste, sight) and a feeling for what is beautiful. He is already moving up in the world and is not embarrassed about using other people's help. He is alienated from his fellow servants, despising them as parts of a past he has already put behind him. He fears and flees them because they know his secrets, pry into his intentions, envy his rise, and look forward eagerly to his fall. Hence his dual, indecisive nature, vacillating between sympathy for people in high social positions and hatred for those who currently occupy those positions. He is an aristocrat, as he himself says, has learned the secrets of good society, is polished on the surface but coarse beneath, wears a frock coat tastefully but without any guarantee that his body is clean.

He has respect for Miss Julie, but is afraid of Kristine because she knows his dangerous secrets. He is sufficiently callous not to let the night's events disturb his plans for the future. With both a slave's brutality and a master's lack of squeamishness, he can see blood without fainting and shake off misfortune easily. Consequently, he comes through the struggle unscathed and will probably end up an innkeeper. And even if *he* does not become a Rumanian count, his son will become a university student and possibly a county police commissioner. . . .

Apart from the fact that Jean is rising in the world, he is superior to Miss Julie because he is a man. Sexually, he is an aristocrat because of his masculine strength, his more keenly developed senses, and his capacity for taking the initiative. His sense of inferiority is mostly due to the social circumstances in which he happens to be living, and he can probably shed it along with his valet's jacket.

His slave mentality expresses itself in the fearful respect he has for the Count (the boots) and his religious superstition; but he respects the Count mainly as the occupant of the kind of high position to which he himself aspires; and the respect remains even after he has conquered the daughter of the house and seen how empty the lovely shell was.

I do not believe that love in any "higher" sense can exist between two people of such different natures, and so I have Miss Julie's love as something she fabricates in order to protect and excuse herself; and I have Jean suppose himself capable of loving her under other social circumstances. I think it is the same with love as with the hyacinth, which must take root in darkness *before* it can produce a sturdy flower. Here a flower shoots up, blooms, and goes to seed all at once, and that is why it dies so quickly.

Oscar Wilde

Oscar Fingal O'Flahertie Wills Wilde (1854–1900) was born to a famous eye surgeon who maintained a home in Dublin's most exclusive neighborhood. Wilde's mother, known by her literary name as Speranza, was noted for collecting Irish folk stories in the western hills in the late 1870s. Her work was important to later literature, but it was especially important for its timing, since most of the storytellers in Ireland were gone by the turn of the century.

Wilde was a brilliant classics scholar at Trinity College, Dublin, where his tutor was the legendary Mahaffy, who later traveled with him in France. After Trinity, he went to Magdalen College, Oxford, where he took a distinguished degree. Among his influences in Oxford was Slade Professor of Art John Ruskin, with whom Wilde had long walks and talks. Ruskin had published important books on northern Gothic art and on Italian art, especially the art of Venice. Art was one of Wilde's primary passions, especially decoration and the decorative arts. He agreed with Walter Pater, a contemporary art critic, that art must best serve the needs of art. He felt, for example, that poetry did not serve religious, political, social, or biographical goals. Its ends were aesthetic and its pleasures were in its sounds, images, and thoughts.

Partly because of his brilliance and partly because he was one of the age's greatest conversationalists, he was soon in the company of the famous and amusing people of his generation. Some of his conversational gift is apparent in his plays.

By his own admission, his life was marked by an overindulgence in sensuality: "What paradox was to me in the sphere of thought, perversity became to me in the sphere of passion." He married Constance Lloyd in 1884 and soon had two sons. But by 1891 he had already had several homosexual liaisons, one of which was to bring him to ruin. His relationship with the much younger Lord Alfred Douglas ended with Douglas's father, the marquis of Queensberry, publicly denouncing Wilde as a sodomite. Wilde sued for libel but lost. As a result, in 1895 he was tried for sodomy, convicted, and sentenced to two years' hard labor. Wilde's actions have been seen as self-destructive, but they are also consistent with his efforts to force society to examine its own hypocrisy. Unfortunately, his efforts in court and prison ruined him, and he died in exile in Paris three years after his release.

His best-known novel, *The Picture of Dorian Gray* (1890; expanded 1891), is the story of a young man whose sensual life eats away at him and eventually destroys him. The novel's failure led Wilde to try the stage, where he was a signal success. Remarkably, all his plays were written in the period between 1891 and his imprisonment in 1895. Most of his plays — *Salomé* (1891), *Lady Windermere's Fan* (1892), *A Woman of No Importance* (1893), *An Ideal Husband* (1895), and *The Importance of Being Earnest* (1895) — rank as witty, insightful, and sharp commentaries on the upper-class British society he knew best. They owe a great deal to eighteenth-century comedies, such as William Congreve's *The Way of the World*. But they also owe a great deal to English and European farces and comedies of his own time, many of which he seems to have studied closely. Unlike those plays — many have never been published and no longer exist — Wilde's are still funny and still seem pertinent even though the class he criticized has long vanished.

The Importance of Being Earnest was a remarkable success when it opened at St. James's Theatre on Valentine's Day 1895, but it closed in two months after fewer than one hundred performances when the scandal of Wilde's conviction became public. Wilde's reputation as playwright was made and broken in a matter of a few years, and it was not restored until after his death.

THE IMPORTANCE OF BEING EARNEST

The play was originally written in four acts, but because the producer requested it be cut, Wilde reworked it into three acts, agreeing that the excisions made the play stronger. Its subtitle, *A Trivial Comedy for Serious People*, has prompted commentators to think of the play as farcical fluff, a play about little or nothing that is nonetheless profoundly amusing. The *New York Times* commented after its first U.S. opening, "The thing is as slight in structure and as devoid of purpose as a paper balloon, but it is extraordinarily funny." Recent critics have challenged this view on the grounds that its subject matter centers on the questions of identity and reality. One current view is that its surfaces are slight but that beneath the surface is a commentary on a society that judges things only by appearance.

The primary characters are Algernon Moncrieff and Jack Worthing, young gentlemen of marriageable age. Among the women are Algernon's cousin Gwendolen Fairfax, who adores the name Ernest and is in love with Jack; Lady Bracknell, her mother; and Cecily Cardew, Jack's ward. Bunbury, referred to by Algernon, seems to be a character, but is instead an invention. He is a convenience for Algernon, a country friend whose illnesses Algernon uses to avoid social events he dislikes, such as Lady Bracknell's dinners. Jack, who lives in the country, has created a similar figure to help him escape to town — an imaginary brother Ernest. In town, Jack pretends to be Ernest; and all his town acquaintances, including Algernon and Gwendolen, know Jack by that name.

The similarities with Congreve's *The Way of the World* are striking. The question of marriage is central in both plays, and attitudes toward marriage in Wilde's social class are among the targets of his satire. When Lady Bracknell probes into Jack Worthing's background, she discovers the distressing news about his family "line": Jack is a foundling who had been left in a handbag in Victoria Station. His family "line" is the Brighton Line. Gwendolen could also have stepped from a Congreve comedy. She is determined to have Jack Worthing, and when he seems sluggish about proposing she prompts him, offering a critique of his proposal by telling him he seems inexperienced at it.

The play owes perhaps even more to the farces of the 1880s and 1890s and a great deal to the well-made play of Eugène Scribe and his successors. Critics often compare Wilde to Alexandre Dumas, the author of *La Dame aux camélias* (*Camille*), because both writers fashioned their plays with a considerable degree of artificiality, planting information in the first act that would prove the solution to problems in the last act. They also play with questions of identity, disguise, and revelation at the last minute in much the way Wilde does here when he reveals the identity of Ernest.

In melodramas and well-made plays, the revelation at the end was not that the potential husband had the right name so much as that he had the right background: he was an aristocrat and not the commoner he seemed to be. Wilde has fun with this convention and many others. In an instant, he ridicules the trick of revealing the hero to be "marriageable" because of his birth by emphasizing the triviality of a name. Yet names are of great importance (as Shakespeare tells us in *Romeo and Juliet*), and the earnestness implied in Ernest is one ingredient that helps Jack Worthing succeed.

Kerry Powell has demonstrated that almost every device in *The Importance of Being Earnest* was drawn from a contemporary farce or comedy. The device of the child lost in a piece of luggage was used in *The Lost Child* (1863), and *The Foundling* (1894) actually takes place in Brighton. The name Bunbury and the concept of "Bunburying" come from *The Godpapa* (1891). Even the device of baptism was used in *Crimes and Christening* (1891). Wilde was adept at taking the theater conventions his audience was most familiar with and using them to his own ends — to entertain his audience, but at the same time to help him put an extra edge on his satire.

The Importance of Being Earnest in Performance

After the first production closed down in 1895, the play was revived in London in 1898 and 1902, but an even more successful production in 1909 saw 324 performances. The benchmark for a truly successful play in those days seems to have been one hundred performances, and Wilde would have felt vindicated by the 1909 production, had he lived to see it. *The Importance of Being Earnest* has been produced so often in England and the United States that only a few productions can be taken into account here. The first New York production was in 1902. John Gielgud and Edith Evans played in the 1939 London production and then again in 1942. In 1947 Gielgud played in New York with Clifton Webb and Estelle Winwood. The reviews were especially strong, calling the play "as insolently monocled in manner and as killingly high-toned in language as mischievous tomfoolery can make it."

The play inspired at least five musicals between 1927 and 1984. The 1979 production at Stratford, Ontario, was called "a perfect play in a perfect production." An unsuccessful production by the Berlin Play Actors in 1987 used all men and relied on insights drawn from transvestite performers, but it was badly received. University productions of the play are fairly common, although, like the Yale Repertory production in 1986, they are not always able to pull off the comic demands of the play's exacting language. The original four-act version of the play, discovered in 1977 in the New York Public Library, was produced in Ohio in the John Carroll University's Marinello Theater in 1985. It was more a curiosity than a triumph. The 1993 production at the Aldwych in London received great praise for its dazzling sets that "matched Wilde's word pictures with bold stage pictures." Maggie Smith played Lady Bracknell.

The play is a witty tour de force of language. Its surfaces gleam, and the best productions play it straight.

Oscar Wilde (1854–1900)

THE IMPORTANCE OF BEING EARNEST
A TRIVIAL COMEDY FOR SERIOUS PEOPLE

1895

The Persons of the Play

JOHN WORTHING, J.P., *of the Manor House, Woolton, Hertfordshire*
ALGERNON MONCRIEFF, *his friend*
REV. CANON CHASUBLE, D.D., *rector of Woolton*
MERRIMAN, *butler to Mr. Worthing*
LANE, *Mr. Moncrieff's manservant*
LADY BRACKNELL
HON. GWENDOLEN FAIRFAX, *her daughter*
CECILY CARDEW, *John Worthing's ward*
MISS PRISM, *her governess*

The Scenes of the Play

Act I: *Algernon Moncrieff's Flat in Half Moon Street, W.*
Act II: *The Garden at the Manor House, Woolton*
Act III: *Morning Room at the Manor House, Woolton*

ACT I

(*Scene: Morning room in Algernon's flat in Half Moon Street. The room is luxuriously and artistically furnished. The sound of a piano is heard in the adjoining room. Lane is arranging afternoon tea on the table, and after the music has ceased, Algernon enters.*)

ALGERNON: Did you hear what I was playing, Lane?
LANE: I didn't think it polite to listen, sir.
ALGERNON: I'm sorry for that, for your sake. I don't play accurately — anyone can play accurately — but I play with wonderful expression. As far as the piano is concerned, sentiment is my forte. I keep science for Life.
LANE: Yes, sir.

ALGERNON: And, speaking of the science of Life, have you got the cucumber sandwiches cut for Lady Bracknell?
LANE: Yes, sir.   (*Hands them on a salver.*)
ALGERNON (*inspects them, takes two, and sits down on the sofa*): Oh! — by the way, Lane, I see from your book that on Thursday night, when Lord Shoreham and Mr. Worthing were dining with me, eight bottles of champagne are entered as having been consumed.
LANE: Yes, sir; eight bottles and a pint.
ALGERNON: Why is it that at a bachelor's establishment the servants invariably drink the champagne? I ask merely for information.
LANE: I attribute it to the superior quality of the wine, sir. I have often observed that in married households the champagne is rarely of a first-rate brand.
ALGERNON: Good heavens! Is marriage so demoralizing as that?
LANE: I believe it *is* a very pleasant state, sir. I have had very little experience of it myself up to the present. I have only been married once. That was in consequence of a misunderstanding between myself and a young person.
ALGERNON (*languidly*): I don't know that I am much interested in your family life, Lane.
LANE: No, sir; it is not a very interesting subject. I never think of it myself.
ALGERNON: Very natural, I am sure. That will do, Lane, thank you.
LANE: Thank you, sir.   (*Lane goes out.*)
ALGERNON: Lane's views on marriage seem somewhat lax. Really, if the lower orders don't set us a good example, what on earth is the use of them? They seem, as a class, to have absolutely no sense of moral responsibility.

(*Enter Lane.*)

LANE: Mr. Ernest Worthing.

(*Enter Jack. Lane goes out.*)

ALGERNON: How are you, my dear Ernest? What brings you up to town?

JACK: Oh, pleasure, pleasure! What else should bring one anywhere? Eating as usual, I see, Algy!

ALGERNON (*stiffly*): I believe it is customary in good society to take some slight refreshment at five o'clock. Where have you been since last Thursday?

JACK (*sitting down on the sofa*): In the country.

ALGERNON: What on earth do you do there?

JACK (*pulling off his gloves*): When one is in town one amuses oneself. When one is in the country one amuses other people. It is excessively boring.

ALGERNON: And who are the people you amuse?

JACK (*airily*): Oh, neighbors, neighbors.

ALGERNON: Got nice neighbors in your part of Shropshire?

JACK: Perfectly horrid! Never speak to one of them.

ALGERNON: How immensely you must amuse them! (*Goes over and takes sandwich.*) By the way, Shropshire is your county, is it not?

JACK: Eh? Shropshire? Yes, of course. Hallo! Why all these cups? Why cucumber sandwiches? Why such reckless extravagance in one so young? Who is coming to tea?

ALGERNON: Oh! merely Aunt Augusta and Gwendolen.

JACK: How perfectly delightful!

ALGERNON: Yes, that is all very well; but I am afraid Aunt Augusta won't quite approve of your being here.

JACK: May I ask why?

ALGERNON: My dear fellow, the way you flirt with Gwendolen is perfectly disgraceful. It is almost as bad as the way Gwendolen flirts with you.

JACK: I am in love with Gwendolen. I have come up to town expressly to propose to her.

ALGERNON: I thought you had come up for pleasure? — I call that business.

JACK: How utterly unromantic you are!

ALGERNON: I really don't see anything romantic in proposing. It is very romantic to be in love. But there is nothing romantic about a definite proposal. Why, one may be accepted. One usually is, I believe. Then the excitement is all over. The very essence of romance is uncertainty. If ever I get married, I'll certainly try to forget the fact.

JACK: I have no doubt about that, dear Algy. The Divorce Court was specially invented for people whose memories are so curiously constituted.

ALGERNON: Oh! there is no use speculating on that subject. Divorces are made in heaven — (*Jack puts out his hand to take a sandwich. Algernon at once interferes.*) Please don't touch the cucumber sandwiches. They are ordered specially for Aunt Augusta. (*Takes one and eats it.*)

JACK: Well, you have been eating them all the time.

ALGERNON: That is quite a different matter. She is my aunt. (*Takes plate from below.*) Have some bread and butter. The bread and butter is for Gwendolen. Gwendolen is devoted to bread and butter.

JACK (*advancing to table and helping himself*): And very good bread and butter it is too.

ALGERNON: Well, my dear fellow, you need not eat as if you were going to eat it all. You behave as if you were married to her already. You are not married to her already, and I don't think you ever will be.

JACK: Why on earth do you say that?

ALGERNON: Well, in the first place, girls never marry the men they flirt with. Girls don't think it right.

JACK: Oh, that is nonsense!

ALGERNON: It isn't. It is a great truth. It accounts for the extraordinary number of bachelors that one sees all over the place. In the second place, I don't give my consent.

JACK: Your consent!

ALGERNON: My dear fellow, Gwendolen is my first cousin. And before I allow you to marry her, you will have to clear up the whole question of Cecily.

(*Rings bell.*)

JACK: Cecily! What on earth do you mean? What do you mean, Algy, by Cecily? I don't know anyone of the name of Cecily.

(*Enter Lane.*)

ALGERNON: Bring me that cigarette case Mr. Worthing left in the smoking room the last time he dined here.

LANE: Yes, sir.   (*Lane goes out.*)

JACK: Do you mean to say you have had my cigarette case all this time? I wish to goodness you had let me know. I have been writing frantic letters to Scotland Yard about it. I was very nearly offering a large reward.

ALGERNON: Well, I wish you would offer one. I happen to be more than usually hard up.

JACK: There is no good offering a large reward now that the thing is found.

(*Enter Lane with the cigarette case on a salver. Algernon takes it at once. Lane goes out.*)

ALGERNON: I think that is rather mean of you, Ernest, I must say. (*Opens case and examines it.*) However, it makes no matter, for, now that I look at the inscription inside, I find that the thing isn't yours after all.

JACK: Of course it's mine. (*Moving to him.*) You have seen me with it a hundred times, and you have no right whatsoever to read what is written inside. It is a very ungentlemanly thing to read a private cigarette case.

ALGERNON: Oh! it is absurd to have a hard-and-fast rule about what one should read and what one shouldn't. More than half of modern culture depends on what one shouldn't read.

JACK: I am quite aware of the fact, and I don't propose to discuss modern culture. It isn't the sort of thing one should talk of in private. I simply want my cigarette case back.

ALGERNON: Yes; but this isn't your cigarette case. This cigarette case is a present from someone of the name of Cecily, and you said you didn't know anyone of that name.

JACK: Well, if you want to know, Cecily happens to be my aunt.

ALGERNON: Your aunt!

JACK: Yes. Charming old lady she is, too. Lives at Tunbridge Wells. Just give it back to me, Algy.

ALGERNON (*retreating to back of sofa*): But why does she call herself little Cecily if she is your aunt and lives at Tunbridge Wells? (*Reading.*) "From little Cecily with her fondest love."

JACK (*moving to sofa and kneeling upon it*): My dear fellow, what on earth is there in that? Some aunts are tall, some aunts are not tall. That is a matter that surely an aunt may be allowed to decide for herself. You seem to think that every aunt should be exactly like your aunt! That is absurd! For heaven's sake give me back my cigarette case.

(*Follows Algernon round the room.*)

ALGERNON: Yes. But why does your aunt call you her uncle? "From little Cecily, with her fondest love to her dear Uncle Jack." There is no objection, I admit, to an aunt being a small aunt, but why an aunt, no matter what her size may be, should call her own nephew her uncle, I can't quite make out. Besides, your name isn't Jack at all; it is Ernest.

JACK: It isn't Ernest; it's Jack.

ALGERNON: You have always told me it was Ernest. I have introduced you to everyone as Ernest. You answer to the name of Ernest. You look as if your name was Ernest. You are the most earnest looking person I ever saw in my life. It is perfectly absurd your saying that your name isn't Ernest. It's on your cards. Here is one of them (*taking it from case*) "Mr. Ernest Worthing, B.4, The Albany." I'll keep this as a proof that your name is Ernest if ever you attempt to deny it to me, or to Gwendolen, or to anyone else.

(*Puts the card in his pocket.*)

JACK: Well, my name is Ernest in town and Jack in the country, and the cigarette case was given to me in the country.

ALGERNON: Yes, but that does not account for the fact that your small Aunt Cecily, who lives at Tunbridge Wells, calls you her dear uncle. Come, old boy, you had much better have the thing out at once.

JACK: My dear Algy, you talk exactly as if you were a dentist. It is very vulgar to talk like a dentist when one isn't a dentist. It produces a false impression.

ALGERNON: Well, that is exactly what dentists always do. Now, go on! Tell me the whole thing. I may mention that I have always suspected you of being a confirmed and secret Bunburyist; and I am quite sure of it now.

JACK: Bunburyist? What on earth do you mean by a Bunburyist?

ALGERNON: I'll reveal to you the meaning of that incomparable expression as soon as you are kind enough to inform me why you are Ernest in town and Jack in the country.

JACK: Well, produce my cigarette case first.

ALGERNON: Here it is. (*Hands cigarette case.*) Now produce your explanation, and pray make it improbable.

(*Sits on sofa.*)

JACK: My dear fellow, there is nothing improbable about my explanation at all. In fact it's perfectly ordinary. Old Mr. Thomas Cardew, who adopted me when I was a little boy, made me in his will guardian to his granddaughter, Miss Cecily Cardew. Cecily, who addresses me as her uncle from motives of respect that you could not possibly appreciate, lives at my place in the country under the charge of her admirable governess, Miss Prism.

ALGERNON: Where is that place in the country, by the way?

JACK: That is nothing to you, dear boy. You are not going to be invited — I may tell you candidly that the place is not in Shropshire.

ALGERNON: I suspected that, my dear fellow! I have Bunburyed all over Shropshire on two separate occasions. Now, go on. Why are you Ernest in town and Jack in the country?

JACK: My dear Algy, I don't know whether you will be able to understand my real motives. You are hardly serious enough. When one is placed in the position of guardian, one has to adopt a very high moral tone on all subjects. It's one's duty to do so. And as a high moral tone can hardly be said to conduce very much to either one's health or one's happiness, in order to get up to town I have always pretended to have a younger brother of the name of Ernest, who lives in the Albany, and gets into the most dreadful scrapes. That, my dear Algy, is the whole truth pure and simple.

ALGERNON: The truth is rarely pure and never simple. Modern life would be very tedious if it were either and modern literature a complete impossibility!

JACK: That wouldn't be at all a bad thing.

ALGERNON: Literary criticism is not your forte, my dear fellow. Don't try it. You should leave that to people who haven't been at a university. They do it so well in the daily papers. What you really are is a Bunburyist. I was quite right in saying you were a Bunburyist. You are one of the most advanced Bunburyists I know.

JACK: What on earth do you mean?

ALGERNON: You have invented a very useful younger brother called Ernest, in order that you may be able to come up to town as often as you like. I have invented an invaluable permanent invalid called Bunbury, in order that I may be able to go down into the country whenever I choose. Bunbury is perfectly invaluable. If it wasn't for Bunbury's extraordinary bad health, for instance, I wouldn't be able to dine with you at Willis's tonight, for I have been really engaged to Aunt Augusta for more than a week.

JACK: I haven't asked you to dine with me anywhere tonight.

ALGERNON: I know. You are absurdly careless about sending out invitations. It is very foolish of you. Nothing annoys people so much as not receiving invitations.

JACK: You had much better dine with your Aunt Augusta.

ALGERNON: I haven't the smallest intention of doing anything of the kind. To begin with, I dined there on Monday, and once a week is quite enough to dine with one's own relations. In the second place, whenever I do dine there I am always treated as a member of the family, and sent down with° either no woman at all, or two. In the third place, I know perfectly well whom she will place me next to, tonight. She will place me next Mary Farquhar, who always flirts with her own husband across the dinner table. That is not very pleasant. Indeed, it is not even decent — and that sort of thing is enormously on the increase. The amount of women in London who flirt with their own husbands is perfectly scandalous. It looks so bad. It is simply washing one's clean linen in public. Besides, now that I know you to be a confirmed Bunburyist I naturally want to talk to you about Bunburying. I want to tell you the rules.

JACK: I'm not a Bunburyist at all. If Gwendolen accepts me, I am going to kill my brother, indeed I think I'll kill him in any case. Cecily is a little too much interested in him. It is rather a bore. So I am going to get rid of Ernest. And I strongly advise you to do the same with Mr. — with your invalid friend who has the absurd name.

ALGERNON: Nothing will induce me to part with Bunbury, and if you ever get married, which seems to me extremely problematic, you will be very glad to know Bunbury. A man who marries without knowing Bunbury has a very tedious time of it.

JACK: That is nonsense. If I marry a charming girl like Gwendolen, and she is the only girl I ever saw in my life that I would marry, I certainly won't want to know Bunbury.

ALGERNON: Then your wife will. You don't seem to realize, that in married life three is company and two is none.

JACK (sententiously): That, my dear young friend, is the theory that the corrupt French drama has been propounding for the last fifty years.

ALGERNON: Yes; and that the happy English home has proved in half the time.

JACK: For heaven's sake, don't try to be cynical. It's perfectly easy to be cynical.

ALGERNON: My dear fellow, it isn't easy to be anything nowadays. There's such a lot of beastly competition about. (The sound of an electric bell is heard.) Ah! that must be Aunt Augusta. Only relatives, or creditors, ever ring in that Wagnerian° manner. Now, if I

get her out of the way for ten minutes, so that you can have an opportunity for proposing to Gwendolen, may I dine with you tonight at Willis's?

JACK: I suppose so, if you want to.

ALGERNON: Yes, but you must be serious about it. I hate people who are not serious about meals. It is so shallow of them.

(Enter Lane.)

LANE: Lady Bracknell and Miss Fairfax.

(Algernon goes forward to meet them. Enter Lady Bracknell and Gwendolen.)

LADY BRACKNELL: Good afternoon, dear Algernon, I hope you are behaving very well.

ALGERNON: I'm feeling very well, Aunt Augusta.

LADY BRACKNELL: That's not quite the same thing. In fact the two things rarely go together.

(Sees Jack and bows to him with icy coldness.)

ALGERNON (to Gwendolen): Dear me, you are smart!

GWENDOLEN: I am always smart! Aren't I, Mr. Worthing?

JACK: You're quite perfect, Miss Fairfax.

GWENDOLEN: Oh! I hope I am not that. It would leave no room for developments, and I intend to develop in many directions.

(Gwendolen and Jack sit down together in the corner.)

LADY BRACKNELL: I'm sorry if we are a little late Algernon, but I was obliged to call on dear Lady Harbury. I hadn't been there since her poor husband's death. I never saw a woman so altered; she looks quite twenty years younger. And now I'll have a cup of tea, and one of those nice cucumber sandwiches you promised me.

ALGERNON: Certainly, Aunt Augusta.

(Goes over to tea table.)

LADY BRACKNELL: Won't you come and sit here, Gwendolen?

GWENDOLEN: Thanks, Mama, I'm quite comfortable where I am.

ALGERNON (picking up empty plate in horror): Good heavens! Lane! Why are there no cucumber sandwiches? I ordered them specially.

LANE (gravely): There were no cucumbers in the market this morning, sir. I went down twice.

ALGERNON: No cucumbers!

LANE: No, sir. Not even for ready money.

ALGERNON: That will do, Lane, thank you.

LANE: Thank you, sir. (Goes out.)

ALGERNON: I am greatly distressed, Aunt Augusta, about there being no cucumbers, not even for ready money.

LADY BRACKNELL: It really makes no matter, Algernon. I had some crumpets with Lady Harbury, who seems to me to be living entirely for pleasure now.

ALGERNON: I hear her hair has turned quite gold from grief.

---

sent down with: Assigned a woman to escort into the dining room for dinner. Wagnerian: Referring to the operas of Richard Wagner (1813–1883), whose music was popularly thought to be loud.

LADY BRACKNELL: It certainly has changed its color. From what cause I, of course, cannot say. (*Algernon crosses and hands tea.*) Thank you. I've quite a treat for you tonight, Algernon. I am going to send you down with Mary Farquhar. She is such a nice woman, and so attentive to her husband. It's delightful to watch them.

ALGERNON: I am afraid, Aunt Augusta, I shall have to give up the pleasure of dining with you tonight after all.

LADY BRACKNELL (*frowning*): I hope not, Algernon. It would put my table completely out. Your uncle would have to dine upstairs. Fortunately he is accustomed to that.

ALGERNON: It is a great bore, and, I need hardly say, a terrible disappointment to me, but the fact is I have just had a telegram to say that my poor friend Bunbury is very ill again. (*Exchanges glances with Jack.*) They seem to think I should be with him.

LADY BRACKNELL: It is very strange. This Mr. Bunbury seems to suffer from curiously bad health.

ALGERNON: Yes; poor Bunbury is a dreadful invalid.

LADY BRACKNELL: Well, I must say, Algernon, that I think it is high time that Mr. Bunbury made up his mind whether he was going to live or to die. This shilly-shallying with the question is absurd. Nor do I in any way approve of the modern sympathy with invalids. I consider it morbid. Illness of any kind is hardly a thing to be encouraged in others. Health is the primary duty of life. I am always telling that to your poor uncle, but he never seems to take much notice — as far as any improvement in his ailments goes. I should be much obliged if you would ask Mr. Bunbury, from me, to be kind enough not to have a relapse on Saturday, for I rely on you to arrange my music for me. It is my last reception, and one wants something that will encourage conversation, particularly at the end of the season when everyone has practically said whatever they had to say, which, in most cases, was probably not much.

ALGERNON: I'll speak to Bunbury, Aunt Augusta, if he is still conscious, and I think I can promise you he'll be all right by Saturday. Of course the music is a great difficulty. You see, if one plays good music, people don't listen, and if one plays bad music people don't talk. But I'll run over the program I've drawn out, if you will kindly come into the next room for a moment.

LADY BRACKNELL: Thank you, Algernon. It is very thoughtful of you. (*Rising, and following Algernon.*) I'm sure the program will be delightful, after a few expurgations. French songs I cannot possibly allow. People always seem to think that they are improper, and either look shocked, which is vulgar, or laugh, which is worse. But German sounds a thoroughly respectable language, and indeed, I believe is so. Gwendolen, you will accompany me.

GWENDOLEN: Certainly, Mama.

(*Lady Bracknell and Algernon go into the music room. Gwendolen remains behind.*)

JACK: Charming day it has been, Miss Fairfax.

GWENDOLEN: Pray don't talk to me about the weather Mr. Worthing. Whenever people talk to me about the weather, I always feel quite certain that they mean something else. And that makes me so nervous.

JACK: I do mean something else.

GWENDOLEN: I thought so. In fact, I am never wrong.

JACK: And I would like to be allowed to take advantage of Lady Bracknell's temporary absence —

GWENDOLEN: I would certainly advise you to do so. Mama has a way of coming back suddenly into a room that I have often had to speak to her about.

JACK (*nervously*): Miss Fairfax, ever since I met you I have admired you more than any girl — I have ever met since — I met you.

GWENDOLEN: Yes, I am quite aware of the fact. And I often wish that in public, at any rate, you had been more demonstrative. For me you have always had an irresistible fascination. Even before I met you I was far from indifferent to you. (*Jack looks at her in amazement.*) We live, as I hope you know Mr. Worthing, in an age of ideals. The fact is constantly mentioned in the more expensive monthly magazines, and has reached the provincial pulpits I am told: And my ideal has always been to love someone of the name of Ernest. There is something in that name that inspires absolute confidence. The moment Algernon first mentioned to me that he had a friend called Ernest, I knew I was destined to love you.

JACK: You really love me, Gwendolen?

GWENDOLEN: Passionately!

JACK: Darling! You don't know how happy you've made me.

GWENDOLEN: My own Ernest!

JACK: But you don't mean to say that you couldn't love me if my name wasn't Ernest?

GWENDOLEN: But your name is Ernest.

JACK: Yes, I know it is. But supposing it was something else? Do you mean to say you couldn't love me then?

GWENDOLEN (*glibly*): Ah! that is clearly a metaphysical speculation, and like most metaphysical speculations has very little reference at all to the actual facts of real life, as we know them.

JACK: Personally, darling, to speak quite candidly, I don't much care about the name of Ernest — I don't think the name suits me at all.

GWENDOLEN: It suits you perfectly. It is a divine name. It has a music of its own. It produces vibrations.

JACK: Well, really, Gwendolen, I must say that I think there are lots of other much nicer names. I think Jack, for instance, a charming name.

GWENDOLEN: Jack? — No, there is very little music in the name Jack, if any at all, indeed. It does not thrill. It produces absolutely no vibrations — I have known several Jacks, and they all, without exception, were more than usually plain. Besides, Jack is a notorious domesticity for John! And I pity any woman who is married to a man called John. She would probably never be allowed to know the entrancing pleasure of a single moment's solitude. The only really safe name is Ernest.

JACK: Gwendolen, I must get christened at once — I mean we must get married at once. There is no time to be lost.

GWENDOLEN: Married, Mr. Worthing?

JACK (*astounded*): Well — surely. You know that I love you, and you led me to believe, Miss Fairfax that you were not absolutely indifferent to me.

GWENDOLEN: I adore you. But you haven't proposed to me yet. Nothing has been said at all about marriage. The subject has not even been touched on.

JACK: Well — may I propose to you now?

GWENDOLEN: I think it would be an admirable opportunity. And to spare you any possible disappointment, Mr. Worthing, I think it only fair to tell you quite frankly beforehand that I am fully determined to accept you.

JACK: Gwendolen!

GWENDOLEN: Yes, Mr. Worthing, what have you got to say to me?

JACK: You know what I have got to say to you.

GWENDOLEN: Yes, but you don't say it.

JACK: Gwendolen, will you marry me?

(*Goes on his knees.*)

GWENDOLEN: Of course I will, darling. How long you have been about it! I am afraid you have had very little experience in how to propose.

JACK: My own one, I have never loved anyone in the world but you.

GWENDOLEN: Yes, but men often propose for practice. I know my brother Gerald does. All my girlfriends tell me so. What wonderfully blue eyes you have, Ernest! They are quite, quite blue. I hope you will always look at me just like that, especially when there are other people present.

(*Enter Lady Bracknell.*)

LADY BRACKNELL: Mr. Worthing! Rise, sir, from this semirecumbent posture. It is most indecorous.

GWENDOLEN: Mama! (*He tries to rise; she restrains him.*) I must beg you to retire. This is no place for you. Besides, Mr. Worthing has not quite finished yet.

LADY BRACKNELL: Finished what, may I ask?

GWENDOLEN: I am engaged to Mr. Worthing, Mama.

(*They rise together.*)

LADY BRACKNELL: Pardon me, you are not engaged to anyone. When you do become engaged to someone, I, or your father, should his health permit him, will inform you of the fact. An engagement should come on a young girl as a surprise, pleasant or unpleasant, as the case may be. It is hardly a matter that she could be allowed to arrange for herself — And now I have a few questions to put to you, Mr. Worthing. While I am making these inquiries, you, Gwendolen, will wait for me below in the carriage.

GWENDOLEN (*reproachfully*): Mama!

LADY BRACKNELL: In the carriage, Gwendolen! (*Gwendolen goes to the door. She and Jack blow kisses to each other behind Lady Bracknell's back. Lady Bracknell looks vaguely about as if she could not understand what the noise was. Finally turns round.*) Gwendolen, the carriage!

GWENDOLEN: Yes, Mama.

(*Goes out, looking back at Jack.*)

LADY BRACKNELL (*sitting down*): You can take a seat, Mr. Worthing.

(*Looks in her pocket for notebook and pencil.*)

JACK: Thank you, Lady Bracknell, I prefer standing.

LADY BRACKNELL (*pencil and notebook in hand*): I feel bound to tell you that you are not down on my list of eligible young men, although I have the same list as the dear Duchess of Bolton has. We work together, in fact. However, I am quite ready to enter your name, should your answers be what a really affectionate mother requires. Do you smoke?

JACK: Well, yes, I must admit I smoke.

LADY BRACKNELL: I am glad to hear it. A man should always have an occupation of some kind. There are far too many idle men in London as it is. How old are you?

JACK: Twenty-nine.

LADY BRACKNELL: A very good age to be married at. I have always been of opinion that a man who desires to get married should know either everything or nothing. Which do you know?

JACK (*after some hesitation*): I know nothing, Lady Bracknell.

LADY BRACKNELL: I am pleased to hear it. I do not approve of anything that tampers with natural ignorance. Ignorance is like a delicate exotic fruit; touch it and the bloom is gone. The whole theory of modern education is radically unsound. Fortunately in England, at any rate, education produces no effect whatsoever. If it did, it would prove a serious danger to the upper classes, and probably lead to acts of violence in Grosvenor Square. What is your income?

JACK: Between seven and eight thousand a year.

LADY BRACKNELL (*makes a note in her book*): In land, or in investments?

JACK: In investments, chiefly.

LADY BRACKNELL: That is satisfactory. What between the duties expected of one during one's lifetime, and the duties exacted from one after one's death, land has ceased to be either a profit or a pleasure. It gives one position, and prevents one from keeping it up. That's all that can be said about land.

JACK: I have a country house with some land, of course, attached to it, about fifteen hundred acres, I believe; but I don't depend on that for my real income. In fact, as far as I can make out, the poachers are the only people who make anything out of it.

LADY BRACKNELL: A country house! How many bedrooms? Well, that point can be cleared up afterwards. You have a town house, I hope? A girl with a simple, unspoiled nature, like Gwendolen, could hardly be expected to reside in the country.

JACK: Well, I own a house in Belgrave Square, but it is let by the year to Lady Bloxham. Of course, I can get it back whenever I like, at six months' notice.

LADY BRACKNELL: Lady Bloxham? I don't know her.

JACK: Oh, she goes about very little. She is a lady considerably advanced in years.

LADY BRACKNELL: Ah, nowadays that is no guarantee of respectability of character. What number in Belgrave Square?

JACK: 149.

LADY BRACKNELL (*shaking her head*): The unfashionable side. I thought there was something. However, that could easily be altered.

JACK: Do you mean the fashion, or the side?

LADY BRACKNELL (*sternly*): Both, if necessary, I presume. What are your politics?

JACK: Well, I am afraid I really have none. I am a Liberal Unionist.

LADY BRACKNELL: Oh, they count as Tories. They dine with us. Or come in the evening, at any rate. Now to minor matters. Are your parents living?

JACK: I have lost both my parents.

LADY BRACKNELL: Both? To lose one parent may be regarded as a misfortune — to lose *both* seems like carelessness. Who was your father? He was evidently a man of some wealth. Was he born in what the Radical papers call the purple of commerce, or did he rise from the ranks of the aristocracy?

JACK: I am afraid I really don't know. The fact is, Lady Bracknell, I said I had lost my parents. It would be nearer the truth to say that my parents seem to have lost me — I don't actually know who I am by birth. I was — well, I was found.

LADY BRACKNELL: Found!

JACK: The late Mr. Thomas Cardew, an old gentleman of a very charitable and kindly disposition, found me, and gave me the name of Worthing, because he happened to have a first-class ticket for Worthing in his pocket at the time. Worthing is a place in Sussex. It is a seaside resort.

LADY BRACKNELL: Where did the charitable gentleman who had a first-class ticket for this seaside resort find you?

JACK (*gravely*): In a handbag.

LADY BRACKNELL: A handbag?

JACK (*very seriously*): Yes, Lady Bracknell. I was in a handbag — a somewhat large, black leather handbag, with handles to it — an ordinary handbag in fact.

LADY BRACKNELL: In what locality did this Mr. James, or Thomas, Cardew come across this ordinary handbag?

JACK: In the cloakroom at Victoria Station. It was given to him in mistake for his own.

LADY BRACKNELL: The cloakroom at Victoria Station?

JACK: Yes. The Brighton line.

LADY BRACKNELL: The line is immaterial. Mr. Worthing, I confess I feel somewhat bewildered by what you have just told me. To be born, or at any rate bred, in a handbag, whether it had handles or not, seems to me to display a contempt for the ordinary decencies of family life that reminds one of the worst excesses of the French Revolution. And I presume you know what that unfortunate movement led to? As for the particular locality in which the handbag was found, a cloakroom at a railway station might serve to conceal a social indiscretion — has probably, indeed, been used for that purpose before now — but it could hardly be regarded as an assured basis for a recognized position in good society.

JACK: May I ask you then what you would advise me to do? I need hardly say I would do anything in the world to ensure Gwendolen's happiness.

LADY BRACKNELL: I would strongly advise you, Mr. Worthing, to try and acquire some relations as soon as possible, and to make a definite effort to produce at any rate one parent of either sex, before the season is quite over.

JACK: Well, I don't see how I could possibly manage to do that. I can produce the handbag at any moment. It is in my dressing room at home. I really think that should satisfy you, Lady Bracknell.

LADY BRACKNELL: Me, sir! What has it to do with me? You can hardly imagine that I and Lord Bracknell would dream of allowing our only daughter — a girl brought up with the utmost care — to marry into a cloakroom, and form an alliance with a parcel? Good morning, Mr. Worthing!

(*Lady Bracknell sweeps out in majestic indignation.*)

JACK: Good morning! (*Algernon, from the other room, strikes up the Wedding March. Jack looks perfectly furious, and goes to the door.*) For goodness' sake don't play that ghastly tune, Algy! How idiotic you are!

(*The music stops, and Algernon enters cheerily.*)

ALGERNON: Didn't it go off all right, old boy? You don't mean to say Gwendolen refused you? I know it is a way she has. She is always refusing people. I think it is most ill-natured of her.

JACK: Oh, Gwendolen is as right as a trivet. As far as she is concerned, we are engaged. Her mother is perfectly unbearable. Never met such a Gorgon° — I don't really know what a Gorgon is like, but I am quite sure that Lady Bracknell is one. In any case, she is a monster, without being a myth, which is rather unfair. I beg your pardon, Algy, I suppose I shouldn't talk about your own aunt in that way before you.

ALGERNON: My dear boy, I love hearing my relations abused. It is the only thing that makes me put up with them at all. Relations are simply a tedious pack of people, who haven't got the remotest knowledge

---

Gorgon: In Greek myth, one of three very ugly sisters who had, among other characteristics, serpents for hair.

of how to live, nor the smallest instinct about when to die.

JACK: Oh, that is nonsense!

ALGERNON: It isn't!

JACK: Well, I won't argue about the matter. You always want to argue about things.

ALGERNON: That is exactly what things were originally made for.

JACK: Upon my word, if I thought that, I'd shoot myself — (*A pause.*) You don't think there is any chance of Gwendolen becoming like her mother in about a hundred and fifty years, do you Algy?

ALGERNON: All women become like their mothers. That is their tragedy. No man does. That's his.

JACK: Is that clever?

ALGERNON: It is perfectly phrased! and quite as true as any observation in civilized life should be.

JACK: I am sick to death of cleverness. Everybody is clever nowadays. You can't go anywhere without meeting clever people. The thing has become an absolute public nuisance. I wish to goodness we had a few fools left.

ALGERNON: We have.

JACK: I should extremely like to meet them. What do they talk about?

ALGERNON: The fools? Oh! about the clever people, of course.

JACK: What fools!

ALGERNON: By the way, did you tell Gwendolen the truth about your being Ernest in town, and Jack in the country?

JACK (*in a very patronizing manner*): My dear fellow, the truth isn't quite the sort of thing one tells to a nice sweet refined girl. What extraordinary ideas you have about the way to behave to a woman!

ALGERNON: The only way to behave to a woman is to make love to her if she is pretty, and to someone else if she is plain.

JACK: Oh, that is nonsense.

ALGERNON: What about your brother? What about the profligate Ernest?

JACK: Oh, before the end of the week I shall have got rid of him. I'll say he died in Paris of apoplexy. Lots of people die of apoplexy, quite suddenly, don't they?

ALGERNON: Yes, but it's hereditary, my dear fellow. It's a sort of thing that runs in families. You had much better say a severe chill.

JACK: You are sure a severe chill isn't hereditary, or anything of that kind?

ALGERNON: Of course it isn't!

JACK: Very well, then. My poor brother Ernest is carried off suddenly in Paris, by a severe chill. That gets rid of him.

ALGERNON: But I thought you said that — Miss Cardew was a little too much interested in your poor brother Ernest? Won't she feel his loss a good deal?

JACK: Oh, that is all right. Cecily is not a silly romantic girl, I am glad to say. She has got a capital appetite,

goes long walks, and pays no attention at all to her lessons.

ALGERNON: I would rather like to see Cecily.

JACK: I will take very good care you never do. She is excessively pretty, and she is only just eighteen.

ALGERNON: Have you told Gwendolen yet that you have an excessively pretty ward who is only just eighteen?

JACK: Oh! one doesn't blurt these things out to people. Cecily and Gwendolen are perfectly certain to be extremely great friends. I'll bet you anything you like that half an hour after they have met, they will be calling each other sister.

ALGERNON: Women only do that when they have called each other a lot of other things first. Now, my dear boy, if we want to get a good table at Willis's, we really must go and dress. Do you know it is nearly seven?

JACK: (*irritably*): Oh! it always is nearly seven.

ALGERNON: Well, I'm hungry.

JACK: I never knew you when you weren't —

ALGERNON: What shall we do after dinner? Go to a theater?

JACK: Oh, no! I loathe listening.

ALGERNON: Well, let us go to the Club?

JACK: Oh, no! I hate talking.

ALGERNON: Well, we might trot round to the Empire° at ten?

JACK: Oh, no! I can't bear looking at things. It is so silly.

ALGERNON: Well, what shall we do?

JACK: Nothing!

ALGERNON: It is awfully hard work doing nothing. However, I don't mind hard work where there is no definite object of any kind.

(*Enter Lane.*)

LANE: Miss Fairfax.

(*Enter Gwendolen. Lane goes out.*)

ALGERNON: Gwendolen, upon my word!

GWENDOLEN: Algy, kindly turn your back. I have something very particular to say to Mr. Worthing.

ALGERNON: Really, Gwendolen, I don't think I can allow this at all.

GWENDOLEN: Algy, you always adopt a strictly immoral attitude towards life. You are not quite old enough to do that.

(*Algernon retires to the fireplace.*)

JACK: My own darling!

GWENDOLEN: Ernest, we may never be married. From the expression on Mama's face I fear we never shall. Few parents nowadays pay any regard to what their children say to them. The old-fashioned respect for the young is fast dying out. Whatever influence I ever had over Mama, I lost at the age of three. But although she may prevent us from becoming man and wife, and I may marry someone else, and marry often,

Empire: Empire Theatre, a London music hall that was also a rendezvous for prostitutes.

Scene from the Huntington Theatre Company's production of *The Importance of Being Earnest.*

nothing that she can possibly do can alter my eternal devotion to you.

JACK: Dear Gwendolen!

GWENDOLEN: The story of your romantic origin, as related to me by Mama, with unpleasing comments, has naturally stirred the deeper fibers of my nature. Your Christian name has an irresistible fascination. The simplicity of your character makes you exquisitely incomprehensible to me. Your town address at the Albany I have. What is your address in the country?

JACK: The Manor House, Woolton, Hertfordshire.

(*Algernon, who has been carefully listening, smiles to himself, and writes the address on his shirt cuff. Then picks up the Railway Guide.*)

GWENDOLEN: There is a good postal service, I suppose? It may be necessary to do something desperate. That of course will require serious consideration. I will communicate with you daily.

JACK: My own one!

GWENDOLEN: How long do you remain in town?

JACK: Till Monday.

GWENDOLEN: Good! Algy, you may turn round now.

ALGERNON: Thanks, I've turned round already.

GWENDOLEN: You may also ring the bell.

JACK: You will let me see you to your carriage, my own darling?

GWENDOLEN: Certainly.

JACK (*to Lane, who now enters*): I will see Miss Fairfax out.

LANE: Yes, sir.   (*Jack and Gwendolen go off.*)

(*Lane presents several letters on a salver to Algernon. It is to be surmised that they are bills, as Algernon, after looking at the envelopes, tears them up.*)

ALGERNON: A glass of sherry, Lane.

LANE: Yes, sir.

ALGERNON: Tomorrow, Lane, I'm going Bunburying.

LANE: Yes, sir.

ALGERNON: I shall probably not be back till Monday. You can put up my dress clothes, my smoking jacket, and all the Bunbury suits —

LANE: Yes, sir.   (*Handing sherry.*)

ALGERNON: I hope tomorrow will be a fine day, Lane.

LANE: It never is, sir.

ALGERNON: Lane, you're a perfect pessimist.

LANE: I do my best to give satisfaction, sir.

(*Enter Jack. Lane goes off.*)

JACK: There's a sensible, intellectual girl! the only girl I ever cared for in my life. (*Algernon is laughing immoderately.*) What on earth are you so amused at?

ALGERNON: Oh, I'm a little anxious about poor Bunbury, that is all.

JACK: If you don't take care, your friend Bunbury will get you into a serious scrape some day.

ALGERNON: I love scrapes. They are the only things that are never serious.

JACK: Oh, that's nonsense, Algy. You never talk anything but nonsense.

ALGERNON: Nobody ever does.

(*Jack looks indignantly at him, and leaves the room. Algernon lights a cigarette, reads his shirt cuff, and smiles.*)

ACT II

(*Scene: Garden at the Manor House. A flight of gray stone steps leads up to the house. The garden, an old-fashioned one, full of roses. Time of year, July. Basket chairs, and a table covered with books, are set under a large yew tree. Miss Prism discovered seated at the table. Cecily is at the back watering flowers.*)

MISS PRISM (*calling*): Cecily, Cecily! Surely such a utilitarian occupation as the watering of flowers is rather Moulton's duty than yours? Especially at a moment when intellectual pleasures await you. Your German grammar is on the table. Pray open it at page fifteen. We will repeat yesterday's lesson.

CECILY (*coming over very slowly*): But I don't like German. It isn't at all a becoming language. I know perfectly well that I look quite plain after my German lesson.

MISS PRISM: Child, you know how anxious your guardian is that you should improve yourself in every way. He laid particular stress on your German, as he was leaving for town yesterday. Indeed, he always lays stress on your German when he is leaving for town.

CECILY: Dear Uncle Jack is so very serious! Sometimes he is so serious that I think he cannot be quite well.

MISS PRISM (*drawing herself up*): Your guardian enjoys the best of health, and his gravity of demeanor is especially to be commended in one so comparatively young as he is. I know no one who has a higher sense of duty and responsibility.

CECILY: I suppose that is why he often looks a little bored when we three are together.

MISS PRISM: Cecily! I am surprised at you. Mr. Worthing has many troubles in his life. Idle merriment and triviality would be out of place in his conversation. You must remember his constant anxiety about that unfortunate young man his brother.

CECILY: I wish Uncle Jack would allow that unfortunate young man, his brother, to come down here some-times. We might have a good influence over him, Miss Prism. I am sure you certainly would. You know German, and geology, and things of that kind influence a man very much.

(*Cecily begins to write in her diary.*)

MISS PRISM (*shaking her head*): I do not think that even I could produce any effect on a character that according to his own brother's admission is irretrievably weak and vacillating. Indeed I am not sure that I would desire to reclaim him. I am not in favor of this modern mania for turning bad people into good people at a moment's notice. As a man sows so let him reap. You must put away your diary, Cecily. I really don't see why you should keep a diary at all.

CECILY: I keep a diary in order to enter the wonderful secrets of my life. If I didn't write them down I should probably forget all about them.

MISS PRISM: Memory, my dear Cecily, is the diary that we all carry about with us.

CECILY: Yes, but it usually chronicles the things that have never happened, and couldn't possibly have happened. I believe that Memory is responsible for nearly all the three-volume novels that Mudie sends us.

MISS PRISM: Do not speak slightingly of the three-volume novel, Cecily. I wrote one myself in earlier days.

CECILY: Did you really, Miss Prism? How wonderfully clever you are! I hope it did not end happily? I don't like novels that end happily. They depress me so much.

MISS PRISM: The good ended happily, and the bad unhappily. That is what Fiction means.

CECILY: I suppose so. But it seems very unfair. And was your novel ever published?

MISS PRISM: Alas! no. The manuscript unfortunately was abandoned. I use the word in the sense of lost or mislaid. To your work, child, these speculations are profitless.

CECILY (*smiling*): But I see dear Dr. Chasuble coming up through the garden.

MISS PRISM (*rising and advancing*): Dr. Chasuble! This is indeed a pleasure.

(*Enter Canon Chasuble.*)

CHASUBLE: And how are we this morning? Miss Prism, you are, I trust, well?

CECILY: Miss Prism has just been complaining of a slight headache. I think it would do her so much good to have a short stroll with you in the park, Dr. Chasuble.

MISS PRISM: Cecily, I have not mentioned anything about a headache.

CECILY: No, dear Miss Prism, I know that, but I felt instinctively that you had a headache. Indeed I was thinking about that, and not about my German lesson, when the Rector came in.

CHASUBLE: I hope, Cecily, you are not inattentive.

CECILY: Oh, I am afraid I am.

CHASUBLE: That is strange. Were I fortunate enough to be Miss Prism's pupil, I would hang upon her lips.

(*Miss Prism glares.*) I spoke metaphorically. — My metaphor was drawn from bees. Ahem! Mr. Worthing, I suppose, has not returned from town yet?

MISS PRISM: We do not expect him till Monday afternoon.

CHASUBLE: Ah yes, he usually likes to spend his Sunday in London. He is not one of those whose sole aim is enjoyment, as, by all accounts, that unfortunate young man his brother seems to be. But I must not disturb Egeria° and her pupil any longer.

MISS PRISM: Egeria? My name is Laetitia, Doctor.

CHASUBLE (*bowing*): A classical allusion merely, drawn from the Pagan authors. I shall see you both no doubt at Evensong?

MISS PRISM: I think, dear Doctor, I will have a stroll with you. I find I have a headache after all, and a walk might do it good.

CHASUBLE: With pleasure, Miss Prism, with pleasure. We might go as far as the schools and back.

MISS PRISM: That would be delightful. Cecily, you will read your Political Economy in my absence. The chapter on the Fall of the Rupee° you may omit. It is somewhat too sensational. Even these metallic problems have their melodramatic side.

(*Goes down the garden with Dr. Chasuble.*)

CECILY (*picks up books and throws them back on table*): Horrid Political Economy! Horrid Geography! Horrid, horrid German!

(*Enter Merriman with a card on a salver.*)

MERRIMAN: Mr. Ernest Worthing has just driven over from the station. He has brought his luggage with him.

CECILY (*takes the card and reads it*): "Mr. Ernest Worthing, B.4, The Albany, W." Uncle Jack's brother! Did you tell him Mr. Worthing was in town?

MERRIMAN: Yes, Miss. He seemed very much disappointed. I mentioned that you and Miss Prism were in the garden. He said he was anxious to speak to you privately for a moment.

CECILY: Ask Mr. Ernest Worthing to come here. I suppose you had better talk to the housekeeper about a room for him.

MERRIMAN: Yes, Miss. (*Merriman goes off.*)

CECILY: I have never met any really wicked person before. I feel rather frightened. I am so afraid he will look just like everyone else.

(*Enter Algernon, very gay and debonair.*)

He does!

ALGERNON (*raising his hat*): You are my little cousin Cecily, I'm sure.

CECILY: You are under some strange mistake. I am not little. In fact, I believe I am more than usually tall for my age (*Algernon is rather taken aback.*) But I am

your cousin Cecily. You, I see from your card, are Uncle Jack's brother, my cousin Ernest, my wicked cousin Ernest.

ALGERNON: Oh! I am not really wicked at all, Cousin Cecily. You mustn't think that I am wicked.

CECILY: If you are not, then you have certainly been deceiving us all in a very inexcusable manner. I hope you have not been leading a double life, pretending to be wicked and being really good all the time. That would be hypocrisy.

ALGERNON (*looks at her in amazement*): Oh! Of course I have been rather reckless.

CECILY: I am glad to hear it.

ALGERNON: In fact, now you mention the subject, I have been very bad in my own small way.

CECILY: I don't think you should be so proud of that, though I am sure it must have been very pleasant.

ALGERNON: It is much pleasanter being here with you.

CECILY: I can't understand how you are here at all. Uncle Jack won't be back till Monday afternoon.

ALGERNON: That is a great disappointment. I am obliged to go up by the first train on Monday morning. I have a business appointment that I am anxious — to miss.

CECILY: Couldn't you miss it anywhere but in London?

ALGERNON: No: the appointment is in London.

CECILY: Well, I know, of course, how important it is not to keep a business engagement, if one wants to retain any sense of the beauty of life, but still I think you had better wait till Uncle Jack arrives. I know he wants to speak to you about your emigrating.

ALGERNON: About my what?

CECILY: Your emigrating. He has gone up to buy your outfit.

ALGERNON: I certainly wouldn't let Jack buy my outfit. He has no taste in neckties at all.

CECILY: I don't think you will require neckties. Uncle Jack is sending you to Australia.

ALGERNON: Australia! I'd sooner die.

CECILY: Well, he said at dinner on Wednesday night, that you would have to choose between this world, the next world, and Australia.

ALGERNON: Oh, well! The accounts I have received of Australia and the next world are not particularly encouraging. This world is good enough for me, Cousin Cecily.

CECILY: Yes, but are you good enough for it?

ALGERNON: I'm afraid I'm not that. That is why I want you to reform me. You might make that your mission, if you don't mind, Cousin Cecily.

CECILY: I'm afraid I've no time, this afternoon.

ALGERNON: Well, would you mind my reforming myself this afternoon?

CECILY: It is rather quixotic° of you. But I think you should try.

ALGERNON: I will. I feel better already.

CECILY: You are looking a little worse.

Egeria: Roman goddess of water.   **Fall of the Rupee:** Reference to the Indian rupee, whose steady deflation between 1873 and 1893 caused the Indian governments finally to close the mints.

quixotic: Foolishly impractical, from the idealistic hero of Cervantes' *Don Quixote.*

ALGERNON: That is because I am hungry.

CECILY: How thoughtless of me. I should have remembered that when one is going to lead an entirely new life, one requires regular and wholesome meals. Won't you come in?

ALGERNON: Thank you. Might I have a buttonhole° first? I never have any appetite unless I have a buttonhole first.

CECILY: A Maréchal Niel?°

ALGERNON: No, I'd sooner have a pink rose.

CECILY: Why?   (*Cuts a flower.*)

ALGERNON: Because you are like a pink rose, Cousin Cecily.

CECILY: I don't think it can be right for you to talk to me like that. Miss Prism never says such things to me.

ALGERNON: Then Miss Prism is a shortsighted old lady. (*Cecily puts the rose in his buttonhole.*) You are the prettiest girl I ever saw.

CECILY: Miss Prism says that all good looks are a snare.

ALGERNON: They are a snare that every sensible man would like to be caught in.

CECILY: Oh! I don't think I would care to catch a sensible man. I shouldn't know what to talk to him about.

(*They pass into the house. Miss Prism and Dr. Chasuble return.*)

MISS PRISM: You are too much alone, dear Dr. Chasuble. You should get married. A misanthrope I can understand — a womanthrope, never!

CHASUBLE (*with a scholar's shudder*): Believe me, I do not deserve so neologistic a phrase. The precept as well as the practice of the Primitive Church was distinctly against matrimony.

MISS PRISM (*sententiously*): That is obviously the reason why the Primitive Church has not lasted up to the present day. And you do not seem to realize, dear Doctor, that by persistently remaining single, a man converts himself into a permanent public temptation. Men should be more careful; this very celibacy leads weaker vessels astray.

CHASUBLE: But is a man not equally attractive when married?

MISS PRISM: No married man is ever attractive except to his wife.

CHASUBLE: And often, I've been told, not even to her.

MISS PRISM: That depends on the intellectual sympathies of the woman. Maturity can always be depended on. Ripeness can be trusted. Young women are green. (*Dr. Chasuble starts.*) I spoke horticulturally. My metaphor was drawn from fruits. But where is Cecily?

CHASUBLE: Perhaps she followed us to the schools.

(*Enter Jack slowly from the back of the garden. He is dressed in the deepest mourning, with crepe hatband and black gloves.*)

MISS PRISM: Mr. Worthing!

CHASUBLE: Mr. Worthing?

MISS PRISM: This is indeed a surprise. We did not look for you till Monday afternoon.

JACK (*shakes Miss Prism's hand in a tragic manner*): I have returned sooner than I expected. Dr. Chasuble, I hope you are well?

CHASUBLE: Dear Mr. Worthing, I trust this garb of woe does not betoken some terrible calamity?

JACK: My brother.

MISS PRISM: More shameful debts and extravagance?

CHASUBLE: Still leading his life of pleasure?

JACK (*shaking his head*): Dead!

CHASUBLE: Your brother Ernest dead?

JACK: Quite dead.

MISS PRISM: What a lesson for him! I trust he will profit by it.

CHASUBLE: Mr. Worthing, I offer you my sincere condolence. You have at least the consolation of knowing that you were always the most generous and forgiving of brothers.

JACK: Poor Ernest! He had many faults, but it is a sad, sad blow.

CHASUBLE: Very sad indeed. Were you with him at the end?

JACK: No. He died abroad, in Paris, in fact. I had a telegram last night from the manager of the Grand Hotel.

CHASUBLE: Was the cause of death mentioned?

JACK: A severe chill, it seems.

MISS PRISM: As a man sows, so shall he reap.

CHASUBLE (*raising his hand*): Charity, dear Miss Prism, charity! None of us are perfect. I myself am peculiarly susceptible to drafts. Will the interment take place here?

JACK: No. He seemed to have expressed a desire to be buried in Paris.

CHASUBLE: In Paris! (*Shakes his head.*) I fear that hardly points to any very serious state of mind at the last. You would no doubt wish me to make some slight allusion to this tragic domestic affliction next Sunday. (*Jack presses his hand convulsively.*) My sermon on the meaning of the manna in the wilderness can be adapted to almost any occasion, joyful, or, as in the present case, distressing. (*All sigh.*) I have preached it at harvest celebrations, christenings, confirmations, on days of humiliation and festal days. The last time I delivered it was in the Cathedral, as a charity sermon on behalf of the Society for the Prevention of Discontent among the Upper Orders. The Bishop, who was present, was much struck by some of the analogies I drew.

JACK: Ah! that reminds me, you mentioned christenings I think, Dr. Chasuble? I suppose you know how to christen all right? (*Dr. Chasuble looks astounded.*) I mean, of course, you are continually christening, aren't you?

MISS PRISM: It is, I regret to say, one of the Rector's most constant duties in this parish. I have often spoken to the poorer classes on the subject. But they don't seem to know what thrift is.

---

buttonhole: Boutonniere.   **Maréchal Niel:** A yellow rose.

CHASUBLE: But is there any particular infant in whom you are interested, Mr. Worthing? Your brother was, I believe, unmarried, was he not?

JACK: Oh yes.

MISS PRISM (*bitterly*): People who live entirely for pleasure usually are.

JACK: But it is not for any child, dear Doctor. I am very fond of children. No! the fact is, I would like to be christened myself, this afternoon, if you have nothing better to do.

CHASUBLE: But surely, Mr. Worthing, you have been christened already?

JACK: I don't remember anything about it.

CHASUBLE: But have you any grave doubts on the subject?

JACK: I certainly intend to have. Of course I don't know if the thing would bother you in any way, or if you think I am a little too old now.

CHASUBLE: Not at all. The sprinkling, and, indeed, the immersion of adults is a perfectly canonical practice.

JACK: Immersion!

CHASUBLE: You need have no apprehensions. Sprinkling is all that is necessary, or indeed I think advisable. Our weather is so changeable. At what hour would you wish the ceremony performed?

JACK: Oh, I might trot round about five if that would suit you.

CHASUBLE: Perfectly, perfectly! In fact I have two similar ceremonies to perform at that time. A case of twins that occurred recently in one of the outlying cottages on your own estate. Poor Jenkins the carter, a most hardworking man.

JACK: Oh! I don't see much fun in being christened along with other babies. It would be childish. Would half-past five do?

CHASUBLE: Admirably! Admirably! (*Takes out watch.*) And now, dear Mr. Worthing, I will not intrude any longer into a house of sorrow. I would merely beg you not to be too much bowed down by grief. What seem to us bitter trials are often blessings in disguise.

MISS PRISM: This seems to me a blessing of an extremely obvious kind.

(*Enter Cecily from the house.*)

CECILY: Uncle Jack! Oh, I am pleased to see you back. But what horrid clothes you have got on! Do go and change them.

MISS PRISM: Cecily!

CHASUBLE: My child! my child!

(*Cecily goes towards Jack; he kisses her brow in a melancholy manner.*)

CECILY: What is the matter, Uncle Jack? Do look happy! You look as if you had toothache, and I have got such a surprise for you. Who do you think is in the dining room? Your brother!

JACK: Who?

CECILY: Your brother Ernest. He arrived about half an hour ago.

JACK: What nonsense! I haven't got a brother.

CECILY: Oh, don't say that. However badly he may have behaved to you in the past he is still your brother. You couldn't be so heartless as to disown him. I'll tell him to come out. And you will shake hands with him, won't you, Uncle Jack?

(*Runs back into the house.*)

CHASUBLE: These are very joyful tidings.

MISS PRISM: After we had all been resigned to his loss, his sudden return seems to me peculiarly distressing.

JACK: My brother is in the dining room? I don't know what it all means. I think it is perfectly absurd.

(*Enter Algernon and Cecily hand in hand. They come slowly up to Jack.*)

JACK: Good heavens!   (*Motions Algernon away.*)

ALGERNON: Brother John, I have come down from town to tell you that I am very sorry for all the trouble I have given you, and that I intend to lead a better life in the future.

(*Jack glares at him and does not take his hand.*)

CECILY: Uncle Jack, you are not going to refuse your own brother's hand?

JACK: Nothing will induce me to take his hand. I think his coming down here disgraceful. He knows perfectly well why.

CECILY: Uncle Jack, do be nice. There is some good in everyone. Ernest has just been telling me about his poor invalid friend Mr. Bunbury whom he goes to visit so often. And surely there must be much good in one who is kind to an invalid, and leaves the pleasures of London to sit by a bed of pain.

JACK Oh! he has been talking about Bunbury has he?

CECILY: Yes, he has told me all about poor Mr. Bunbury, and his terrible state of health.

JACK: Bunbury! Well, I won't have him talk to you about Bunbury or about anything else. It is enough to drive one perfectly frantic.

ALGERNON: Of course I admit that the faults were all on my side. But I must say that I think that Brother John's coldness to me is peculiarly painful. I expected a more enthusiastic welcome, especially considering it is the first time I have come here.

CECILY: Uncle Jack, if you don't shake hands with Ernest I will never forgive you.

JACK: Never forgive me?

CECILY: Never, never, never!

JACK: Well, this is the last time I shall ever do it.

(*Shakes hands with Algernon and glares.*)

CHASUBLE: It's pleasant, is it not, to see so perfect a reconciliation? I think we might leave the two brothers together.

MISS PRISM: Cecily, you will come with us.

CECILY: Certainly, Miss Prism. My little task of reconciliation is over.

CHASUBLE: You have done a beautiful action today, dear child.

MISS PRISM: We must not be premature in our judgments.

CECILY: I feel very happy.   (*They all go off.*)

JACK: You young scoundrel, Algy, you must get out of this place as soon as possible. I don't allow any Bunburying here.

(*Enter Merriman.*)

MERRIMAN: I have put Mr. Ernest's things in the room next to yours, sir. I suppose that is all right?

JACK: What?

MERRIMAN: Mr. Ernest's luggage, sir. I have unpacked it and put it in the room next to your own.

JACK: His luggage?

MERRIMAN: Yes, sir. Three portmanteaus, a dressing case, two hatboxes, and a large luncheon basket.

ALGERNON: I am afraid I can't stay more than a week this time.

JACK: Merriman, order the dog cart at once. Mr. Ernest has been suddenly called back to town.

MERRIMAN: Yes, sir.   (*Goes back into the house.*)

ALGERNON: What a fearful liar you are, Jack. I have not been called back to town at all.

JACK: Yes, you have.

ALGERNON: I haven't heard anyone call me.

JACK: Your duty as a gentleman calls you back.

ALGERNON: My duty as a gentleman has never interfered with my pleasures in the smallest degree.

JACK: I can quite understand that.

ALGERNON: Well, Cecily is a darling.

JACK: You are not to talk of Miss Cardew like that. I don't like it.

ALGERNON: Well, I don't like your clothes. You look perfectly ridiculous in them. Why on earth don't you go up and change? It is perfectly childish to be in deep mourning for a man who is actually staying for a whole week in your house as a guest. I call it grotesque.

JACK: You are certainly not staying with me for a whole week as a guest or anything else. You have got to leave — by the four-five train.

ALGERNON: I certainly won't leave you so long as you are in mourning. It would be most unfriendly. If I were in mourning you would stay with me, I suppose. I should think it very unkind if you didn't.

JACK: Well, will you go if I change my clothes?

ALGERNON: Yes, if you are not too long. I never saw anybody take so long to dress, and with such little result.

JACK: Well, at any rate, that is better than being always overdressed as you are.

ALGERNON: If I am occasionally a little overdressed, I make up for it by being always immensely overeducated.

JACK: Your vanity is ridiculous, your conduct an outrage, and your presence in my garden utterly absurd. However, you have got to catch the four-five, and I hope you will have a pleasant journey back to town. This Bunburying, as you call it, has not been a great success for you.

                                      (*Goes into the house.*)

ALGERNON: I think it has been a great success. I'm in love with Cecily, and that is everything.

(*Enter Cecily at the back of the garden. She picks up the can and begins to water the flowers.*)

But I must see her before I go, and make arrangements for another Bunbury. Ah, there she is.

CECILY: Oh, I merely came back to water the roses. I thought you were with Uncle Jack.

ALGERNON: He's gone to order the dog cart for me.

CECILY: Oh, is he going to take you for a nice drive?

ALGERNON: He's going to send me away.

CECILY: Then have we got to part?

ALGERNON: I am afraid so. It's a very painful parting.

CECILY: It is always painful to part from people whom one has known for a very brief space of time. The absence of old friends one can endure with equanimity. But even a momentary separation from anyone to whom one has just been introduced is almost unbearable.

ALGERNON: Thank you.

(*Enter Merriman.*)

MERRIMAN: The dog cart is at the door, sir.

(*Algernon looks appealingly at Cecily.*)

CECILY: It can wait, Merriman — for — five minutes.

MERRIMAN: Yes, miss.   (*Exit Merriman.*)

ALGERNON: I hope, Cecily, I shall not offend you if I state quite frankly and openly that you seem to me to be in every way the visible personification of absolute perfection.

CECILY: I think your frankness does you great credit, Ernest. If you will allow me I will copy your remarks into my diary.

                (*Goes over to table and begins writing in diary.*)

ALGERNON: Do you really keep a diary? I'd give anything to look at it. May I?

CECILY: Oh no. (*Puts her hand over it.*) You see, it is simply a very young girl's record of her own thoughts and impressions, and consequently meant for publication. When it appears in volume form I hope you will order a copy. But pray, Ernest, don't stop. I delight in taking down from dictation. I have reached "absolute perfection." You can go on. I am quite ready for more.

ALGERNON (*somewhat taken aback*): Ahem! Ahem!

CECILY: Oh, don't cough, Ernest. When one is dictating one should speak fluently and not cough. Besides, I don't know how to spell a cough.

(*Writes as Algernon speaks.*)

ALGERNON (*speaking very rapidly*): Cecily, ever since I first looked upon your wonderful and incomparable beauty, I have dared to love you wildly, passionately, devotedly, hopelessly.

CECILY: I don't think that you should tell me that you love me wildly, passionately, devotedly, hopelessly. Hopelessly doesn't seem to make much sense, does it?

ALGERNON: Cecily!

(*Enter Merriman.*)

MERRIMAN: The dog cart is waiting, sir.

ALGERNON: Tell it to come round next week, at the same hour.

MERRIMAN (*looks at Cecily, who makes no sign*): Yes, sir.   (*Merriman retires.*)

CECILY: Uncle Jack would be very much annoyed if he knew you were staying on till next week, at the same hour.

ALGERNON: Oh, I don't care about Jack. I don't care for anybody in the whole world but you. I love you, Cecily. You will marry me, won't you?

CECILY: You silly boy! Of course. Why, we have been engaged for the last three months.

ALGERNON: For the last three months?

CECILY: Yes, it will be exactly three months on Thursday.

ALGERNON: But how did we become engaged?

CECILY: Well, ever since dear Uncle Jack first confessed to us that he had a younger brother who was very wicked and bad, you of course have formed the chief topic of conversation between myself and Miss Prism. And of course a man who is much talked about is always very attractive. One feels there must be something in him after all. I daresay it was foolish of me, but I fell in love with you, Ernest.

ALGERNON: Darling! And when was the engagement actually settled?

CECILY: On the 14th of February last. Worn out by your entire ignorance of my existence, I determined to end the matter one way or the other, and after a long struggle with myself I accepted you under this dear old tree here. The next day I bought this little ring in your name, and this is the little bangle with the true lovers' knot I promised you always to wear.

ALGERNON: Did I give you this? It's very pretty, isn't it?

CECILY: Yes, you've wonderfully good taste, Ernest. It's the excuse I've always given for your leading such a bad life. And this is the box in which I keep all your dear letters.

(*Kneels at table, opens box, and produces letters tied up with blue ribbon.*)

ALGERNON: My letters! But my own sweet Cecily, I have never written you any letters.

CECILY: You need hardly remind me of that, Ernest. I remember only too well that I was forced to write your letters for you. I wrote always three times a week, and sometimes oftener.

ALGERNON: Oh, do let me read them, Cecily!

CECILY: Oh, I couldn't possibly. They would make you far too conceited. (*Replaces box.*) The three you wrote me after I had broken off the engagement are so beautiful, and so badly spelled, that even now I can hardly read them without crying a little.

ALGERNON: But was our engagement ever broken off?

CECILY: Of course it was. On the 22nd of last March. You can see the entry if you like. (*Shows diary.*)

"Today I broke off my engagement with Ernest. I feel it is better to do so. The weather still continues charming."

ALGERNON: But why on earth did you break it off? What had I done? I had done nothing at all. Cecily, I am very much hurt indeed to hear you broke it off. Particularly when the weather was so charming.

CECILY: It would hardly have been a really serious engagement if it hadn't been broken off at least once. But I forgave you before the week was out.

ALGERNON (*crossing to her, and kneeling*): What a perfect angel you are, Cecily.

CECILY: You dear romantic boy. (*He kisses her; she puts her fingers through his hair.*) I hope your hair curls naturally, does it?

ALGERNON: Yes, darling, with a little help from others.

CECILY: I am so glad.

ALGERNON: You'll never break off our engagement again, Cecily?

CECILY: I don't think I could break it off now that I have actually met you. Besides, of course, there is the question of your name.

ALGERNON (*nervously*): Yes, of course.

CECILY: You must not laugh at me, darling, but it had always been a girlish dream of mine to love someone whose name was Ernest. (*Algernon rises, Cecily also.*) There is something in that name that seems to inspire absolute confidence. I pity any poor married woman whose husband is not called Ernest.

ALGERNON: But, my dear child, do you mean to say you could not love me if I had some other name?

CECILY: But what name?

ALGERNON: Oh, any name you like — Algernon — for instance —

CECILY: But I don't like the name of Algernon.

ALGERNON: Well, my own dear, sweet, loving little darling, I really can't see why you should object to the name of Algernon. It is not at all a bad name. In fact, it is rather an aristocratic name. Half of the chaps who get into the Bankruptcy Court are called Algernon. But seriously, Cecily — (*moving to her*) — if my name was Algy, couldn't you love me?

CECILY (*rising*): I might respect you, Ernest, I might admire your character, but I fear that I should not be able to give you my undivided attention.

ALGERNON: Ahem! Cecily! (*Picking up hat.*) Your Rector here is, I suppose, thoroughly experienced in the practice of all the rites and ceremonials of the Church?

CECILY: Oh yes. Dr. Chasuble is a most learned man. He has never written a single book, so you can imagine how much he knows.

ALGERNON: I must see him at once on a most important christening — I mean on most important business.

CECILY: Oh!

ALGERNON: I shan't be away more than half an hour.

CECILY: Considering that we have been engaged since February the 14th, and that I only met you today for the first time, I think it is rather hard that you should leave me for so long a period as half an hour. Couldn't you make it twenty minutes?

ALGERNON: I'll be back in no time.

(*Kisses her and rushes down the garden.*)

CECILY: What an impetuous boy he is! I like his hair so much. I must enter his proposal in my diary.

(*Enter Merriman.*)

MERRIMAN: A Miss Fairfax has just called to see Mr. Worthing. On very important business Miss Fairfax states.

CECILY: Isn't Mr. Worthing in his library?

MERRIMAN: Mr. Worthing went over in the direction of the Rectory some time ago.

CECILY: Pray ask the lady to come out here; Mr. Worthing is sure to be back soon. And you can bring tea.

MERRIMAN: Yes, miss.   (*Goes out.*)

CECILY: Miss Fairfax! I suppose one of the many good elderly women who are associated with Uncle Jack in some of his philanthropic work in London. I don't quite like women who are interested in philanthropic work. I think it is so forward of them.

(*Enter Merriman.*)

MERRIMAN: Miss Fairfax.

(*Enter Gwendolen. Exit Merriman.*)

CECILY (*advancing to meet her*): Pray let me introduce myself to you. My name is Cecily Cardew.

GWENDOLEN: Cecily Cardew? (*Moving to her and shaking hands.*) What a very sweet name! Something tells me that we are going to be great friends. I like you already more than I can say. My first impressions of people are never wrong.

CECILY: How nice of you to like me so much after we have known each other such a comparatively short time. Pray sit down.

GWENDOLEN (*still standing up*): I may call you Cecily, may I not?

CECILY: With pleasure!

GWENDOLEN: And you will always call me Gwendolen, won't you?

CECILY: If you wish.

GWENDOLEN: Then that is all quite settled, is it not?

CECILY: I hope so.

(*A pause. They both sit down together.*)

GWENDOLEN: Perhaps this might be a favorable opportunity for my mentioning who I am. My father is Lord Bracknell. You have never heard of Papa, I suppose?

CECILY: I don't think so.

GWENDOLEN: Outside the family circle, Papa, I am glad to say, is entirely unknown. I think that is quite as it should be. The home seems to me to be the proper sphere for the man. And certainly once a man begins to neglect his domestic duties he becomes painfully effeminate, does he not? And I don't like that. It makes men so very attractive. Cecily, Mama, whose views on education are remarkably strict, has brought me up to be extremely shortsighted; it is part of her system, so do you mind my looking at you through my glasses?

CECILY: Oh! not at all, Gwendolen. I am very fond of being looked at.

GWENDOLEN (*after examining Cecily carefully through a lorgnette*): You are here on a short visit I suppose?

CECILY: Oh no! I live here.

GWENDOLEN (*severely*): Really? Your mother, no doubt, or some female relative of advanced years, resides here also?

CECILY: Oh no! I have no mother, nor, in fact, any relations.

GWENDOLEN: Indeed?

CECILY: My dear guardian, with the assistance of Miss Prism, has the arduous task of looking after me.

GWENDOLEN: Your guardian?

CECILY: Yes, I am Mr. Worthing's ward.

GWENDOLEN: Oh! It is strange he never mentioned to me that he had a ward. How secretive of him! He grows more interesting hourly. I am not sure, however, that the news inspires me with feelings of unmixed delight. (*Rising and going to her.*) I am very fond of you, Cecily; I have liked you ever since I met you! But I am bound to state that now that I know that you are Mr. Worthing's ward, I cannot help expressing a wish you were — well just a little older than you seem to be — and not quite so very alluring in appearance. In fact, if I may speak candidly —

CECILY: Pray do! I think that whenever one has anything unpleasant to say, one should always be quite candid.

GWENDOLEN: Well, to speak with perfect candor, Cecily, I wish that you were fully forty-two, and more than usually plain for your age. Ernest has a strong upright nature. He is the very soul of truth and honor. Disloyalty would be as impossible to him as deception. But even men of the noblest possible moral character are extremely susceptible to the influence of the physical charms of others. Modern, no less than Ancient History, supplies us with many most painful examples of what I refer to. If it were not so, indeed, History would be quite unreadable.

CECILY: I beg your pardon, Gwendolen, did you say Ernest?

GWENDOLEN: Yes.

CECILY: Oh, but it is not Mr. Ernest Worthing who is my guardian. It is his brother — his elder brother.

GWENDOLEN (*sitting down again*): Ernest never mentioned to me that he had a brother.

CECILY: I am sorry to say they have not been on good terms for a long time.

GWENDOLEN: Ah! that accounts for it. And now that I think of it I have never heard any man mention his brother. The subject seems distasteful to most men. Cecily, you have lifted a load from my mind. I was growing almost anxious. It would have been terrible if any cloud had come across a friendship like ours, would it not? Of course you are quite, quite sure that it is not Mr. Ernest Worthing who is your guardian?

CECILY: Quite sure. (*A pause.*) In fact, I am going to be his.

GWENDOLEN (*inquiringly*): I beg your pardon?

CECILY (*rather shy and confidingly*): Dearest Gwendolen, there is no reason why I should make a secret of it to you. Our little county newspaper is sure to chronicle the fact next week. Mr. Ernest Worthing and I are engaged to be married.

GWENDOLEN (*quite politely, rising*): My darling Cecily, I think there must be some slight error. Mr. Ernest Worthing is engaged to me. The announcement will appear in the *Morning Post* on Saturday at the latest.

CECILY (*very politely, rising*): I am afraid you must be under some misconception. Ernest proposed to me exactly ten minutes ago.   (*Shows diary.*)

GWENDOLEN (*examines diary through her lorgnette carefully*): It is certainly very curious, for he asked me to be his wife yesterday afternoon at 5:30. If you would care to verify the incident, pray do so. (*Produces diary of her own.*) I never travel without my diary. One should always have something sensational to read in the train. I am so sorry, dear Cecily, if it is any disappointment to you, but I am afraid *I* have the prior claim.

CECILY: It would distress me more than I can tell you, dear Gwendolen, if it caused you any mental or physical anguish, but I feel bound to point out that since Ernest proposed to you he clearly has changed his mind.

GWENDOLEN (*meditatively*): If the poor fellow has been entrapped into any foolish promise I shall consider it my duty to rescue him at once, and with a firm hand.

CECILY (*thoughtfully and sadly*): Whatever unfortunate entanglement my dear boy may have got into, I will never reproach him with it after we are married.

GWENDOLEN: Do you allude to me, Miss Cardew, as an entanglement? You are presumptuous. On an occasion of this kind it becomes more than a moral duty to speak one's mind. It becomes a pleasure.

CECILY: Do you suggest, Miss Fairfax, that I entrapped Ernest into an engagement? How dare you? This is no time for wearing the shallow mask of manners. When I see a spade I call it a spade.

GWENDOLEN (*satirically*): I am glad to say that I have never seen a spade. It is obvious that our social spheres have been widely different.

(*Enter Merriman, followed by the Footman. He carries a salver, tablecloth, and plate stand. Cecily is about to retort. The presence of the servants exercises a restraining influence, under which both girls chafe.*)

MERRIMAN: Shall I lay tea here as usual, miss?

CECILY (*sternly, in a calm voice*): Yes, as usual.

(*Merriman begins to clear table and lay cloth. A long pause. Cecily and Gwendolen glare at each other.*)

GWENDOLEN: Are there many interesting walks in the vicinity, Miss Cardew?

CECILY: Oh! Yes! a great many. From the top of one of the hills quite close one can see five counties.

GWENDOLEN: Five counties! I don't think I should like that. I hate crowds.

CECILY (*sweetly*): I suppose that is why you live in town?

(*Gwendolen bites her lip, and beats her foot nervously with her parasol.*)

GWENDOLEN (*looking round*): Quite a well-kept garden this is, Miss Cardew.

CECILY: So glad you like it, Miss Fairfax.

GWENDOLEN: I had no idea there were any flowers in the country.

CECILY: Oh, flowers are as common here, Miss Fairfax, as people are in London.

GWENDOLEN: Personally I cannot understand how anybody manages to exist in the country, if anybody who is anybody does. The country always bores me to death.

CECILY: Ah! This is what the newspapers call agricultural depression, is it not? I believe the aristocracy are suffering very much from it just at present. It is almost an epidemic amongst them, I have been told. May I offer you some tea, Miss Fairfax?

GWENDOLEN (*with elaborate politeness*): Thank you. (*Aside.*) Detestable girl! But I require tea!

CECILY (*sweetly*): Sugar?

GWENDOLEN (*superciliously*): No, thank you. Sugar is not fashionable anymore.

(*Cecily looks angrily at her, takes up the tongs, and puts four lumps of sugar into the cup.*)

CECILY (*severely*): Cake or bread and butter?

GWENDOLEN (*in a bored manner*): Bread and butter, please. Cake is rarely seen at the best houses nowadays.

CECILY (*cuts a very large slice of cake, and puts it on the tray*): Hand that to Miss Fairfax.

(*Merriman does so, and goes out with Footman. Gwendolen drinks the tea and makes a grimace. Puts down cup at once, reaches out her hand to the bread and butter, looks at it, and finds it is cake. Rises in indignation.*)

GWENDOLEN: You have filled my tea with lumps of sugar, and though I asked most distinctly for bread and butter, you have given me cake. I am known for the gentleness of my disposition, and the extraordinary sweetness of my nature, but I warn you, Miss Cardew, you may go too far.

CECILY (*rising*): To save my poor, innocent, trusting boy from the machinations of any other girl there are no lengths to which I would not go.

GWENDOLEN: From the moment I saw you I distrusted you. I felt that you were false and deceitful. I am never deceived in such matters. My first impressions of people are invariably right.

CECILY: It seems to me, Miss Fairfax, that I am trespassing on your valuable time. No doubt you have many other calls of a similar character to make in the neighborhood.

(*Enter Jack.*)

GWENDOLEN (*catching sight of him*): Ernest! My own Ernest!

JACK: Gwendolen! Darling!   (*Offers to kiss her.*)

GWENDOLEN (*drawing back*): A moment! May I ask if you are engaged to be married to this young lady? (*Points to Cecily.*)

JACK (*laughing*): To dear little Cecily! Of course not! What could have put such an idea into your pretty little head?

GWENDOLEN: Thank you. You may!
                                    (*Offers her cheek.*)

CECILY (*very sweetly*): I knew there must be some misunderstanding, Miss Fairfax. The gentleman whose arm is at present round your waist is my dear guardian, Mr. John Worthing.

GWENDOLEN: I beg your pardon?

CECILY: This is Uncle Jack.

GWENDOLEN (*receding*): Jack! Oh!

(*Enter Algernon.*)

CECILY: Here is Ernest.

ALGERNON (*goes straight over to Cecily without noticing anyone else*): My own love!
                                    (*Offers to kiss her.*)

CECILY (*drawing back*): A moment, Ernest! May I ask you — are you engaged to be married to this young lady?

ALGERNON (*looking round*): To what young lady? Good heavens! Gwendolen!

CECILY: Yes! to good heavens, Gwendolen, I mean to Gwendolen.

ALGERNON (*laughing*): Of course not! What could have put such an idea into your pretty little head?

CECILY: Thank you. (*Presenting her cheek to be kissed.*) You may. (*Algernon kisses her.*)

GWENDOLEN: I felt there was some slight error, Miss Cardew. The gentleman who is now embracing you is my cousin, Mr. Algernon Moncrieff.

CECILY (*breaking away from Algernon*): Algernon Moncrieff! Oh!

(*The two girls move towards each other and put their arms round each other's waists as if for protection.*)

CECILY: Are you called Algernon?

ALGERNON: I cannot deny it.

CECILY: Oh!

GWENDOLEN: Is your name really John?

JACK (*standing rather proudly*): I could deny it if I liked. I could deny anything if I liked. But my name certainly is John. It has been John for years.

CECILY (*to Gwendolen*): A gross deception has been practiced on both of us.

GWENDOLEN: My poor wounded Cecily!

CECILY: My sweet wronged Gwendolen!

GWENDOLEN (*slowly and seriously*): You will call me sister, will you not?

(*They embrace. Jack and Algernon groan and walk up and down.*)

CECILY (*rather brightly*): There is just one question I would like to be allowed to ask my guardian.

GWENDOLEN: An admirable idea! Mr. Worthing, there is just one question I would like to be permitted to put to you. Where is your brother Ernest? We are both engaged to be married to your brother Ernest, so it is a matter of some importance to us to know where your brother Ernest is at present.

JACK (*slowly and hesitatingly*): Gwendolen — Cecily — it is very painful for me to be forced to speak the truth. It is the first time in my life that I have ever been reduced to such a painful position, and I am really quite inexperienced in doing anything of the kind. However I will tell you quite frankly that I have no brother Ernest. I have no brother at all. I never had a brother in my life, and I certainly have not the smallest intention of ever having one in the future.

CECILY (*surprised*): No brother at all?

JACK (*cheerily*): None!

GWENDOLEN (*severely*): Had you never a brother of any kind?

JACK (*pleasantly*): Never. Not even of any kind.

GWENDOLEN: I am afraid it is quite clear, Cecily, that neither of us is engaged to be married to anyone.

CECILY: It is not a very pleasant position for a young girl suddenly to find herself in. Is it?

GWENDOLEN: Let us go into the house. They will hardly venture to come after us there.

CECILY: No, men are so cowardly, aren't they?

(*They retire into the house with scornful looks.*)

JACK: This ghastly state of things is what you call Bunburying, I suppose?

ALGERNON: Yes, and a perfectly wonderful Bunbury it is. The most wonderful Bunbury I have ever had in my life.

JACK: Well, you've no right whatsoever to Bunbury here.

ALGERNON: That is absurd. One has a right to Bunbury anywhere one chooses. Every serious Bunburyist knows that.

JACK: Serious Bunburyist! Good heavens!

ALGERNON: Well, one must be serious about something, if one wants to have any amusement in life. I happen to be serious about Bunburying. What on earth you are serious about I haven't got the remotest idea. About everything, I should fancy. You have such an absolutely trivial nature.

JACK: Well, the only small satisfaction I have in the whole of this wretched business is that your friend Bunbury is quite exploded. You won't be able to run down to the country quite so often as you used to do, dear Algy. And a very good thing too.

ALGERNON: Your brother is a little off color, isn't he, dear Jack? You won't be able to disappear to London quite so frequently as your wicked custom was. And not a bad thing either.

JACK: As for your conduct towards Miss Cardew, I must say that your taking in a sweet, simple, innocent girl like that is quite inexcusable. To say nothing of the fact that she is my ward.

ALGERNON: I can see no possible defense at all for your deceiving a brilliant, clever, thoroughly experienced young lady like Miss Fairfax. To say nothing of the fact that she is my cousin.

JACK: I wanted to be engaged to Gwendolen, that is all. I love her.

ALGERNON: Well, I simply wanted to be engaged to Cecily. I adore her.

JACK: There is certainly no chance of your marrying Miss Cardew.

ALGERNON: I don't think there is much likelihood, Jack, of you and Miss Fairfax being united.

JACK: Well, that is no business of yours.

ALGERNON: If it was my business, I wouldn't talk about it. (*Begins to eat muffins.*) It is very vulgar to talk about one's business. Only people like stockbrokers do that, and then merely at dinner parties.

JACK: How you can sit there, calmly eating muffins when we are in this horrible trouble. I can't make out. You seem to me to be perfectly heartless.

ALGERNON: Well, I can't eat muffins in an agitated manner. The butter would probably get on my cuffs. One should always eat muffins quite calmly. It is the only way to eat them.

JACK: I say it's perfectly heartless your eating muffins at all, under the circumstances.

ALGERNON: When I am in trouble, eating is the only thing that consoles me. Indeed, when I am in really great trouble, as anyone who knows me intimately will tell you, I refuse everything except food and drink. At the present moment I am eating muffins because I am unhappy. Besides, I am particularly fond of muffins.   (*Rising.*)

JACK (*rising*): Well, that is no reason why you should eat them all in that greedy way.

(*Takes muffins from Algernon.*)

ALGERNON (*offering tea cake*): I wish you would have tea cake instead. I don't like tea cake.

JACK: Good heavens! I suppose a man may eat his own muffins in his own garden.

ALGERNON: But you have just said it was perfectly heartless to eat muffins.

JACK: I said it was perfectly heartless of you, under the circumstances. That is a very different thing.

ALGERNON: That may be, but the muffins are the same. (*He seizes the muffin dish from Jack.*)

JACK: Algy, I wish to goodness you would go.

ALGERNON: You can't possibly ask me to go without having some dinner. It's absurd. I never go without my dinner. No one ever does, except vegetarians and people like that. Besides I have just made arrangements with Dr. Chasuble to be christened at a quarter to six under the name of Ernest.

JACK: My dear fellow, the sooner you give up that nonsense the better. I made arrangements this morning with Dr. Chasuble to be christened myself at 5:30, and I naturally will take the name of Ernest. Gwendolen would wish it. We can't both be christened Ernest. It's absurd. Besides, I have a perfect right to be christened if I like. There is no evidence at all that I ever have been christened by anybody. I should think it extremely probable I never was, and so does Dr. Chasuble. It is entirely different in your case. You have been christened already.

ALGERNON: Yes, but I have not been christened for years.

JACK: Yes, but you have been christened. That is the important thing.

ALGERNON: Quite so. So I know my constitution can stand it. If you are not quite sure about your ever having been christened, I must say I think it rather dangerous your venturing on it now. It might make you very unwell. You can hardly have forgotten that someone very closely connected with you was very nearly carried off this week in Paris by a severe chill.

JACK: Yes, but you said yourself that a severe chill was not hereditary.

ALGERNON: It usen't to be, I know — but I daresay it is now. Science is always making wonderful improvements in things.

JACK (*picking up the muffin dish*): Oh, that is nonsense; you are always talking nonsense.

ALGERNON: Jack, you are at the muffins again! I wish you wouldn't. There are only two left. (*Takes them.*) I told you I was particularly fond of muffins.

JACK: But I hate tea cake.

ALGERNON: Why on earth then do you allow tea cake to be served up for your guests? What ideas you have of hospitality!

JACK: Algernon! I have already told you to go. I don't want you here. Why don't you go!

ALGERNON: I haven't quite finished my tea yet! and there is still one muffin left.

(*Jack groans, and sinks into a chair. Algernon still continues eating.*)

ACT III

(*Scene: Morning room at the Manor House. Gwendolen and Cecily are at the window, looking out into the garden.*)

GWENDOLEN: The fact that they did not follow us at once into the house, as anyone else would have done, seems to me to show that they have some sense of shame left.

CECILY: They have been eating muffins. That looks like repentance.

GWENDOLEN (*after a pause*): They don't seem to notice us at all. Couldn't you cough?

CECILY: But I haven't got a cough.

GWENDOLEN: They're looking at us. What effrontery!

CECILY: They're approaching. That's very forward of them.

GWENDOLEN: Let us preserve a dignified silence.

CECILY: Certainly. It's the only thing to do now.

(*Enter Jack followed by Algernon. They whistle some dreadful popular air from a British opera.*)

GWENDOLEN: This dignified silence seems to produce an unpleasant effect.

CECILY: A most distasteful one.

GWENDOLEN: But we will not be the first to speak.

CECILY: Certainly not.

GWENDOLEN: Mr. Worthing, I have something very particular to ask you. Much depends on your reply.

CECILY: Gwendolen, your common sense is invaluable. Mr. Moncrieff, kindly answer me the following question. Why did you pretend to be my guardian's brother?

ALGERNON: In order that I might have an opportunity of meeting you.

CECILY (to Gwendolen): That certainly seems a satisfactory explanation, does it not?

GWENDOLEN: Yes, dear, if you can believe him.

CECILY: I don't. But that does not affect the wonderful beauty of his answer.

GWENDOLEN: True. In matters of grave importance, style, not sincerity is the vital thing. Mr. Worthing, what explanation can you offer to me for pretending to have a brother? Was it in order that you might have an opportunity of coming up to town to see me as often as possible?

JACK: Can you doubt it, Miss Fairfax?

GWENDOLEN: I have the gravest doubts upon the subject. But I intend to crush them. This is not the moment for German skepticism. (Moving to Cecily.) Their explanations appear to be quite satisfactory, especially Mr. Worthing's. That seems to me to have the stamp of truth upon it.

CECILY: I am more than content with what Mr. Moncrieff said. His voice alone inspires one with absolute credulity.

GWENDOLEN: Then you think we should forgive them?

CECILY: Yes. I mean no.

GWENDOLEN: True! I had forgotten. There are principles at stake that one cannot surrender. Which of us should tell them? The task is not a pleasant one.

CECILY: Could we not both speak at the same time?

GWENDOLEN: An excellent idea! I nearly always speak at the same time as other people. Will you take the time from me?

CECILY: Certainly.

(Gwendolyn beats time with uplifted finger.)

GWENDOLEN and CECILY (speaking together): Your Christian names are still an insuperable barrier. That is all!

JACK and ALGERNON (speaking together): Our Christian names! Is that all? But we are going to be christened this afternoon.

GWENDOLEN (to Jack): For my sake you are prepared to do this terrible thing?

JACK: I am!

CECILY (to Algernon): To please me you are ready to face this fearful ordeal?

ALGERNON: I am!

GWENDOLEN: How absurd to talk of the equality of the sexes! Where questions of self-sacrifice are concerned, men are infinitely beyond us.

JACK: We are! (Clasps hands with Algernon.)

CECILY: They have moments of physical courage of which we women know absolutely nothing.

GWENDOLEN (to Jack): Darling!

ALGERNON (to Cecily): Darling!

(They fall into each other's arms.)

(Enter Merriman. When he enters he coughs loudly, seeing the situation.)

MERRIMAN: Ahem! Ahem! Lady Bracknell!

JACK: Good heavens!

(Enter Lady Bracknell. The couples separate, in alarm. Exit Merriman.)

LADY BRACKNELL: Gwendolen! What does this mean?

GWENDOLEN: Merely that I am engaged to be married to Mr. Worthing, Mama.

LADY BRACKNELL: Come here. Sit down. Sit down immediately. Hesitation of any kind is a sign of mental decay in the young, of physical weakness in the old. (Turns to Jack.) Apprised, sir, of my daughter's sudden flight by her trusty maid, whose confidence I purchased by means of a small coin, I followed her at once by a luggage train. Her unhappy father is, I am glad to say, under the impression that she is attending a more than usually lengthy lecture by the University Extension Scheme on the influence of a permanent income on thought. I do not propose to undeceive him. Indeed I have never undeceived him on any question. I would consider it wrong. But of course, you will clearly understand that all communication between yourself and my daughter must cease immediately from this moment. On this point, as indeed on all points, I am firm.

JACK: I am engaged to be married to Gwendolen, Lady Bracknell!

LADY BRACKNELL: You are nothing of the kind, sir. And now, as regards Algernon! — Algernon!

ALGERNON: Yes, Aunt Augusta.

LADY BRACKNELL: May I ask if it is in this house that your invalid friend Mr. Bunbury resides?

ALGERNON (stammering): Oh! No! Bunbury doesn't live here. Bunbury is somewhere else at present. In fact, Bunbury is dead.

LADY BRACKNELL: Dead! When did Mr. Bunbury die? His death must have been extremely sudden.

ALGERNON (airily): Oh! I killed Bunbury this afternoon. I mean poor Bunbury died this afternoon.

LADY BRACKNELL: What did he die of?

ALGERNON: Bunbury? Oh, he was quite exploded.

LADY BRACKNELL: Exploded! Was he the victim of a revolutionary outrage? I was not aware that Mr. Bunbury was interested in social legislation. If so, he is well punished for his morbidity.

ALGERNON: My dear Aunt Augusta, I mean he was found out! The doctors found out that Bunbury could not live, that is what I mean — so Bunbury died.

Eric Stoltz and Schuyler Grant propose a toast in the Irish Repertory Theatre's 1996 production of *The Importance of Being Earnest.*

LADY BRACKNELL: He seems to have had great confidence in the opinion of his physicians. I am glad, however, that he made up his mind at the last to some definite course of action, and acted under proper medical advice. And now that we have finally got rid of this Mr. Bunbury, may I ask, Mr. Worthing, who is that young person whose hand my nephew Algernon is now holding in what seems to me a peculiarly unnecessary manner?

JACK: That lady is Miss Cecily Cardew, my ward.

(*Lady Bracknell bows coldly to Cecily.*)

ALGERNON: I am engaged to be married to Cecily, Aunt Augusta.

LADY BRACKNELL: I beg your pardon?

CECILY: Mr. Moncrieff and I are engaged to be married, Lady Bracknell.

LADY BRACKNELL (*with a shiver, crossing to the sofa and sitting down*): I do not know whether there is anything peculiarly exciting in the air of this particular part of Hertfordshire, but the number of engagements that go on seems to me considerably above the proper average that statistics have laid down for our guidance. I think some preliminary inquiry on my part would not be out of place. Mr. Worthing, is Miss Cardew at all connected with any of the larger railway stations in London? I merely desire information. Until yesterday I had no idea that there were any families or persons whose origin was a Terminus.

(*Jack looks perfectly furious, but restrains himself.*)

JACK (*in a clear, cold voice*): Miss Cardew is the granddaughter of the late Mr. Thomas Cardew of 149, Belgrave Square, S.W.; Gervase Park, Dorking, Surrey; and the Sporran, Fifeshire, N.B.

LADY BRACKNELL: That sounds not unsatisfactory. Three addresses always inspire confidence, even in tradesmen. But what proof have I of their authenticity?

JACK: I have carefully preserved the Court Guides of the period. They are open to your inspection, Lady Bracknell.

LADY BRACKNELL (*grimly*): I have known strange errors in that publication.

JACK: Miss Cardew's family solicitors are Messrs. Markby, Markby, and Markby.

LADY BRACKNELL: Markby, Markby, and Markby? A firm of the very highest position in their profession. Indeed I am told that one of the Mr. Markbys is occasionally to be seen at dinner parties. So far I am satisfied.

JACK (*very irritably*): How extremely kind of you, Lady Bracknell! I have also in my possession, you will be pleased to hear, certificates of Miss Cardew's birth, baptism, whooping cough, registration, vaccination, confirmation, and the measles; both the German and the English variety.

LADY BRACKNELL: Ah! A life crowded with incident I see; though perhaps somewhat too exciting for a young girl. I am not myself in favor of premature experiences. (*Rises, looks at her watch.*) Gwendolen! the time approaches for our departure. We have not a moment to lose. As a matter of form, Mr. Worthing, I had better ask you if Miss Cardew has any little fortune?

JACK: Oh! about a hundred and thirty thousand pounds in the Funds. That is all. Good-bye, Lady Bracknell. So pleased to have seen you.

LADY BRACKNELL (*sitting down again*): A moment, Mr. Worthing. A hundred and thirty thousand pounds! And in the Funds! Miss Cardew seems to me a most attractive young lady, now that I look at her. Few girls of the present day have any really solid qualities, any of the qualities that last, and improve with time. We live, I regret to say, in an age of surfaces. (*To Cecily.*) Come over here, dear. (*Cecily goes across.*) Pretty child! your dress is sadly simple, and your hair seems almost as Nature might have left it. But we can soon alter all that. A thoroughly experienced French maid produces a really marvelous result in a very brief space of time. I remember recommending one to young Lady Lancing, and after three months her own husband did not know her.

JACK (*aside*): And after six months nobody knew her.

LADY BRACKNELL (*glares at Jack for a few moments. Then bends, with a practiced smile, to Cecily*): Kindly turn round, sweet child. (*Cecily turns completely round.*) No, the side view is what I want. (*Cecily presents her profile.*) Yes, quite as I expected. There are distinct social possibilities in your profile. The two weak points in our age are its want of principle and its want of profile. The chin a little higher, dear. Style largely depends on the way the chin is worn. They are worn very high, just at present. Algernon!

ALGERNON: Yes, Aunt Augusta!

LADY BRACKNELL: There are distinct social possibilities in Miss Cardew's profile.

ALGERNON: Cecily is the sweetest, dearest, prettiest girl in the whole world. And I don't care twopence about social possibilities.

LADY BRACKNELL: Never speak disrespectfully of Society, Algernon. Only people who can't get into it do that. (*To Cecily.*) Dear child, of course you know that Algernon has nothing but his debts to depend upon. But I do not approve of mercenary marriages. When I married Lord Bracknell I had no fortune of any kind. But I never dreamed for a moment of allowing that to stand in my way. Well, I suppose I must give my consent.

ALGERNON: Thank you, Aunt Augusta.

LADY BRACKNELL: Cecily, you may kiss me!

CECILY (*kisses her*): Thank you, Lady Bracknell.

LADY BRACKNELL: You may also address me as Aunt Augusta for the future.

CECILY: Thank you, Aunt Augusta.

LADY BRACKNELL: The marriage, I think, had better take place quite soon.

ALGERNON: Thank you, Aunt Augusta.

CECILY: Thank you, Aunt Augusta.

LADY BRACKNELL: To speak frankly, I am not in favor of long engagements. They give people the opportunity of finding out each other's character before marriage, which I think is never advisable.

JACK: I beg your pardon for interrupting you, Lady Bracknell, but this engagement is quite out of the question. I am Miss Cardew's guardian, and she cannot marry without my consent until she comes of age. That consent I absolutely decline to give.

LADY BRACKNELL: Upon what grounds may I ask? Algernon is an extremely, I may almost say an ostentatiously, eligible young man. He has nothing, but he looks everything. What more can one desire?

JACK: It pains me very much to have to speak frankly to you, Lady Bracknell, about your nephew, but the fact is that I do not approve at all of his moral character. I suspect him of being untruthful.

(*Algernon and Cecily look at him in indignant amazement.*)

LADY BRACKNELL: Untruthful! My nephew Algernon? Impossible! He is an Oxonian.°

JACK: I fear there can be no possible doubt about the matter. This afternoon, during my temporary absence in London on an important question of romance, he obtained admission to my house by means of the false pretense of being my brother. Under an assumed name he drank, I've just been informed by my butler, an entire pint bottle of my Perrier-Jouêt, Brut, '89; a wine I was specially reserving for myself. Continuing his disgraceful deception, he succeeded in the course of the afternoon in alienating the affections of my only ward. He subsequently stayed to tea, and devoured every single muffin. And what makes his conduct all the more heartless is, that he was perfectly well aware from the first that I have no brother, that I never had a brother, and that I don't intend to have a brother, not even of any kind. I distinctly told him so myself yesterday afternoon.

LADY BRACKNELL: Ahem! Mr. Worthing, after careful consideration I have decided entirely to overlook my nephew's conduct to you.

JACK: That is very generous of you, Lady Bracknell. My own decision, however, is unalterable. I decline to give my consent.

LADY BRACKNELL (*to Cecily*): Come here, sweet child. (*Cecily goes over.*) How old are you, dear?

CECILY: Well, I am really only eighteen, but I always admit to twenty when I go to evening parties.

Oxonian: Educated at Oxford University.

LADY BRACKNELL: You are perfectly right in making some slight alteration. Indeed, no woman should ever be quite accurate about her age. It looks so calculating — (*In a meditative manner.*) Eighteen but admitting to twenty at evening parties. Well, it will not be very long before you are of age and free from the restraints of tutelage. So I don't think your guardian's consent is, after all, a matter of any importance.

JACK: Pray excuse me, Lady Bracknell, for interrupting you again, but it is only fair to tell you that according to the terms of her grandfather's will Miss Cardew does not come legally of age till she is thirty-five.

LADY BRACKNELL: That does not seem to me to be a grave objection. Thirty-five is a very attractive age. London society is full of women of the very highest birth who have, of their own free choice, remained thirty-five for years. Lady Dumbleton is an instance in point. To my own knowledge she has been thirty-five ever since she arrived at the age of forty, which was many years ago now. I see no reason why our dear Cecily should not be even still more attractive at the age you mention than she is at present. There will be a large accumulation of property.

CECILY: Algy, could you wait for me till I was thirty-five?

ALGERNON: Of course I could, Cecily. You know I could.

CECILY: Yes, I felt it instinctively, but I couldn't wait all that time. I hate waiting even five minutes for anybody. It always makes me rather cross. I am not punctual myself, I know, but I do like punctuality in others, and waiting, even to be married, is quite out of the question.

ALGERNON: Then what is to be done, Cecily?

CECILY: I don't know, Mr. Moncrieff.

LADY BRACKNELL: My dear Mr. Worthing, as Miss Cardew states positively that she cannot wait till she is thirty-five — a remark which I am bound to say seems to me to show a somewhat impatient nature — I would beg of you to reconsider your decision.

JACK: But my dear Lady Bracknell, the matter is entirely in your own hands. The moment you consent to my marriage with Gwendolen, I will most gladly allow your nephew to form an alliance with my ward.

LADY BRACKNELL (*rising and drawing herself up*): You must be quite aware that what you propose is out of the question.

JACK: Then a passionate celibacy is all that any of us can look forward to.

LADY BRACKNELL: That is not the destiny I propose for Gwendolen. Algernon, of course, can choose for himself. (*Pulls out her watch.*) Come, dear; (*Gwendolen rises*) we have already missed five, if not six, trains. To miss any more might expose us to comment on the platform.

(*Enter Dr. Chasuble.*)

CHASUBLE: Everything is quite ready for the christenings.

LADY BRACKNELL: The christenings, sir! Is not that somewhat premature?

CHASUBLE (*looking rather puzzled, and pointing to Jack and Algernon*): Both these gentlemen have expressed a desire for immediate baptism.

LADY BRACKNELL: At their age? The idea is grotesque and irreligious! Algernon, I forbid you to be baptized. I will not hear of such excesses. Lord Bracknell would be highly displeased if he learned that that was the way in which you wasted your time and money.

CHASUBLE: Am I to understand then that there are to be no christenings at all this afternoon?

JACK: I don't think that, as things are now, it would be of much practical value to either of us, Dr. Chasuble.

CHASUBLE: I am grieved to hear such sentiments from you, Mr. Worthing. They savor of the heretical views of the Anabaptists,° views that I have completely refuted in four of my unpublished sermons. However, as your present mood seems to be one peculiarly secular, I will return to the church at once. Indeed, I have just been informed by the pew opener that for the last hour and a half Miss Prism has been waiting for me in the vestry.

LADY BRACKNELL (*starting*): Miss Prism! Did I hear you mention a Miss Prism?

CHASUBLE: Yes, Lady Bracknell. I am on my way to join her.

LADY BRACKNELL: Pray allow me to detain you for a moment. This matter may prove to be one of vital importance to Lord Bracknell and myself. Is this Miss Prism a female of repellent aspect, remotely connected with education?

CHASUBLE (*somewhat indignantly*): She is the most cultivated of ladies, and the very picture of respectability.

LADY BRACKNELL: It is obviously the same person. May I ask what position she holds in your household?

CHASUBLE (*severely*): I am a celibate, madam.

JACK (*interposing*): Miss Prism, Lady Bracknell, has been for the last three years Miss Cardew's esteemed governess and valued companion.

LADY BRACKNELL: In spite of what I hear of her, I must see her at once. Let her be sent for.

CHASUBLE (*looking off*): She approaches; she is nigh.

(*Enter Miss Prism hurriedly.*)

MISS PRISM: I was told you expected me in the vestry, dear Canon. I have been waiting for you there for an hour and three-quarters.

(*Catches sight of Lady Bracknell who has fixed her with a stony glare. Miss Prism grows pale and quails. She looks anxiously round as if desirous to escape.*)

LADY BRACKNELL (*in a severe, judicial voice*): Prism! (*Miss Prism bows her head in shame.*) Come here, Prism! (*Miss Prism approaches in a humble manner.*) Prism! Where is that baby? (*General consternation. The Canon starts back in horror. Algernon and Jack pretend to be anxious to shield Cecily and*

Anabaptists: A religious sect beginning in the sixteenth century and advocating adult baptism and church membership by adults only.

Gwendolen from hearing the details of a terrible public scandal.) Twenty-eight years ago, Prism, you left Lord Bracknell's house, Number 104, Upper Grosvenor Street, in charge of a perambulator that contained a baby, of the male sex. You never returned. A few weeks later, through the elaborate investigations of the Metropolitan police, the perambulator was discovered at midnight, standing by itself in a remote corner of Bayswater. It contained the manuscript of a three-volume novel of more than usually revolting sentimentality. (*Miss Prism starts in involuntary indignation.*) But the baby was not there! (*Everyone looks at Miss Prism.*) Prism! Where is that baby? (*A pause.*)

MISS PRISM: Lady Bracknell, I admit with shame that I do not know. I only wish I did. The plain facts of the case are these. On the morning of the day you mention, a day that is forever branded on my memory, I prepared as usual to take the baby out in its perambulator. I had also with me a somewhat old, but capacious handbag in which I had intended to place the manuscript of a work of fiction that I had written during my few unoccupied hours. In a moment of mental abstraction, for which I never can forgive myself, I deposited the manuscript in the bassinette, and placed the baby in the handbag.

JACK (*who has been listening attentively*): But where did you deposit the handbag?

MISS PRISM: Do not ask me, Mr. Worthing.

JACK: Miss Prism, this is a matter of no small importance to me. I insist on knowing where you deposited the handbag that contained that infant.

MISS PRISM: I left it in the cloakroom of one of the larger railway stations in London.

JACK: What railway station?

MISS PRISM (*quite crushed*): Victoria. The Brighton line. (*Sinks into a chair.*)

JACK: I must retire to my room for a moment. Gwendolen, wait here for me.

GWENDOLEN: If you are not too long, I will wait here for you all my life.

(*Exit Jack in great excitement.*)

CHASUBLE: What do you think this means, Lady Bracknell?

LADY BRACKNELL: I dare not even suspect, Dr. Chasuble. I need hardly tell you that in families of high position strange coincidences are not supposed to occur. They are hardly considered the thing.

(*Noises heard overhead as if someone was throwing trunks about. Everyone looks up.*)

CECILY: Uncle Jack seems strangely agitated.

CHASUBLE: Your guardian has a very emotional nature.

LADY BRACKNELL: This noise is extremely unpleasant. It sounds as if he was having an argument. I dislike arguments of any kind. They are always vulgar, and often convincing.

CHASUBLE (*looking up*): It has stopped now.

(*The noise is redoubled.*)

LADY BRACKNELL: I wish he would arrive at some conclusion.

GWENDOLEN: This suspense is terrible. I hope it will last.

(*Enter Jack with a handbag of black leather in his hand.*)

JACK (*rushing over to Miss Prism*): Is this the handbag, Miss Prism? Examine it carefully before you speak. The happiness of more than one life depends on your answer.

MISS PRISM (*calmly*): It seems to be mine. Yes, here is the injury it received through the upsetting of a Gower Street omnibus in younger and happier days. Here is the stain on the lining caused by the explosion of a temperance beverage, an incident that occurred at Leamington. And here, on the lock, are my initials. I had forgotten that in an extravagant mood I had had them placed there. The bag is undoubtedly mine. I am delighted to have it so unexpectedly restored to me. It has been a great inconvenience being without it all these years.

JACK (*in a pathetic voice*): Miss Prism, more is restored to you than this handbag. I was the baby you placed in it.

MISS PRISM (*amazed*): You?

JACK (*embracing her*): Yes — mother!

MISS PRISM (*recoiling in indignant astonishment*): Mr. Worthing! I am unmarried!

JACK: Unmarried! I do not deny that is a serious blow. But after all, who has the right to cast a stone against one who has suffered? Cannot repentance wipe out an act of folly? Why should there be one law for men, and another for women? Mother, I forgive you. (*Tries to embrace her again.*)

MISS PRISM (*still more indignant*): Mr. Worthing, there is some error. (*Pointing to Lady Bracknell.*) There is the lady who can tell you who you really are.

JACK (*after a pause*): Lady Bracknell, I hate to seem inquisitive, but would you kindly inform me who I am?

LADY BRACKNELL: I am afraid that the news I have to give you will not altogether please you. You are the son of my poor sister, Mrs. Moncrieff, and consequently Algernon's elder brother.

JACK: Algy's elder brother! Then I have a brother after all. I knew I had a brother! I always said I had a brother! Cecily, — how could you have ever doubted that I had a brother. (*Seizes hold of Algernon.*) Dr. Chasuble, my unfortunate brother. Miss Prism, my unfortunate brother. Gwendolen, my unfortunate brother. Algy, you young scoundrel, you will have to treat me with more respect in the future. You have never behaved to me like a brother in all your life.

ALGERNON: Well, not till today, old boy, I admit. I did my best, however, though I was out of practice.

(*Shakes hands.*)

GWENDOLEN (*to Jack*): My own! But what own are you? What is your Christian name, now that you have become someone else?

JACK: Good heavens! — I had quite forgotten that point. Your decision on the subject of my name is irrevocable, I suppose?

GWENDOLEN: I never change, except in my affections.

CECILY: What a noble nature you have, Gwendolen!

JACK: Then the question had better be cleared up at once. Aunt Augusta, a moment. At the time when Miss Prism left me in the handbag, had I been christened already?

LADY BRACKNELL: Every luxury that money could buy, including christening, had been lavished upon you by your fond and doting parents.

JACK: Then I was christened! That is settled. Now, what name was I given? Let me know the worst.

LADY BRACKNELL: Being the eldest son you were naturally christened after your father.

JACK (*irritably*): Yes, but what was my father's Christian name?

LADY BRACKNELL (*meditatively*): I cannot at the present moment recall what the General's Christian name was. But I have no doubt he had one. He was eccentric, I admit. But only in later years. And that was the result of the Indian climate, and marriage, and indigestion, and other things of that kind.

JACK: Algy! Can't you recollect what our father's Christian name was?

ALGERNON: My dear boy, we were never even on speaking terms. He died before I was a year old.

JACK: His name would appear in the Army Lists of the period, I suppose, Aunt Augusta?

LADY BRACKNELL: The General was essentially a man of peace, except in his domestic life. But I have no doubt his name would appear in any military directory.

JACK: The Army Lists of the last forty years are here. These delightful records should have been my constant study. (*Rushes to bookcase and tears the books out.*) M. Generals — Mallam, Maxbohm, Magley, what ghastly names they have — Markby, Migsby, Mobbs, Moncrieff! Lieutenant 1840, Captain, Lieutenant-Colonel, Colonel, General 1869, Christian names, Ernest John. (*Puts book very quietly down and speaks quite calmly.*) I always told you, Gwendolen, my name was Ernest, didn't I? Well, it is Ernest after all. I mean it naturally is Ernest.

LADY BRACKNELL: Yes, I remember now that the General was called Ernest. I knew I had some particular reason for disliking the name.

GWENDOLEN: Ernest! My own Ernest! I felt from the first that you could have no other name!

JACK: Gwendolen, it is a terrible thing for a man to find out suddenly that all his life he has been speaking nothing but the truth. Can you forgive me?

GWENDOLEN: I can. For I feel that you are sure to change.

JACK: My own one!

CHASUBLE (*to Miss Prism*): Laetitia! (*Embraces her.*)

MISS PRISM (*enthusiastically*): Frederick! At last!

ALGERNON: Cecily! (*Embraces her.*) At last!

JACK: Gwendolen! (*Embraces her.*) At last!

LADY BRACKNELL: My nephew, you seem to be displaying signs of triviality.

JACK: On the contrary, Aunt Augusta, I've now realized for the first time in my life the vital Importance of Being Earnest.

COMMENTARIES

Peter Raby (b. 1939)
AN UNPUBLISHED LETTER FROM OSCAR WILDE
ON *THE IMPORTANCE OF BEING EARNEST* 1991

Peter Raby introduces an 1894 letter from Oscar Wilde describing the plot of the play to his friend George Alexander. Wilde was under enormous financial pressure at the time and was eager to have his play produced. What we see in this letter is the human, vulnerable side of a witty, ironic comic playwright.

The full text of Oscar Wilde's first version of *The Importance of Being Earnest* has been lost for many years. Wilde sent it to George Alexander in July 1894, before leaving for a two-month holiday with his family in Worthing. He was desperate for money. Every encounter with Lord Alfred Douglas cost him more: he was overdrawn at the bank, and, so he claims in the letter, he had to bear the expenses of his mother's household as well as his own

Wilde's output during 1894 was astonishing: he completed *An Ideal Husband*, wrote the contrasting *A Florentine Tragedy* and most of *La Sainte Courtisane,* and embarked on an entirely new genre in *Earnest.* The more tumultuous and complex his private life, the more productive he became. He was in frequent correspondence with a number of producers and managers during the course of the year: with John Hare and Lewis Waller over *An Ideal Husband,* with Charles Frohman and Albert Palmer in New York in connection with a number of properties, both existing and unwritten, and with Dion Boucicault, who was producing *Lady Windermere's Fan* in Australia. Frohman, who controlled the American rights to *Lady Windermere's Fan,* was negotiating for *An Ideal Husband.* The year before, he had invited Wilde to write him a new play, perhaps a "modern *School for Scandal* style of play"; Wilde's American agent, the "brilliant delightful" Elizabeth Marbury, wrote to Wilde in July from Paris with details of Frohman's latest offer, which included an option on his next modern comedy. Albert Palmer was also angling for a comedy "with no real serious interest."

Completed plays and royalties were no longer enough to keep Wilde's finances buoyant. He turned his gift for story-telling to advantage in the form of the scenario. Alexander, generous and approachable, and the producer of Wilde's first great theatrical success, *Lady Windermere's Fan,* had expressed an interest in the new comedy. Wilde seems to have dashed off the *Earnest* scenario more to secure a £150 advance than because he thought the play right for a romantic actor of modern and costume pieces. (In fact, having received the advance, he rapidly backpedalled, suggesting the piece was too farcical, and sending Alexander a more suitable scenario from Worthing, something "strong" and serious, which Frank Harris eventually turned into *Mr and Mrs Daventry.*)

There are many stages between the outline of *Earnest* and the script which was played at the St James's Theatre on February 14, 1895, while the Marquess of Queensberry prowled around the building, unable to gain admission, and when Wilde's world was on the point of disintegration. There are some manuscript pages in a notebook in the Clark Library, at the University of California in Los Angeles, containing notes and scraps of dialogue, for example:

> Beautiful name — Ernest, I couldn't love anybody who wasn't called Ernest —
> Oh! don't say that Gwendolen. It sounds perfectly heartless of you — why should love be dependent on the action of an irresponsible godfather. Is a man's whole fortune to depend on the font. I am told that there was a moment when my father contemplated calling me John —

Another fragment seems to encapsulate a sharply visualized image:

> Gwen: Leave the room, Mamma. This is no place for you.
> Duchess: Mr Worthing rise from this semi-recumbent posture — it is most unbefitting.

The future Lady Bracknell springs fully armed from that one phrase. Indeed, the women characters — Prism, Gwendolen, Duchess — are throughout more vividly delineated in these early phases.

From these fragments, the play grew into a four-act version, with a brace of butlers named after Wilde's publishers, a gardener, and an ominous solicitor. There followed a collection of names with geographical or personal associations: Lancing, Shoreham, Bracknell, Blaxam, Bunbury, Maxbohm, Cardew. (Cicely Cardew, daughter of friends of Wilde, was born in 1893; her uncle was a director of the London and South East Railway, and the Cardew engine hauled the evening boat-train to Newhaven.) By Christmas, the new play had been promised to Charles Wyndham. When Alexander found he had a failure on his hands in Henry James's *Guy Domville,* Wyndham agreed to concede his rights in *Earnest,* provided Wilde wrote him an original play before completing yet another for Alexander. Alexander persuaded Wilde to compress *Earnest* into three acts (which was the form of the original scenario he had been shown). Wilde resisted for a little, but trusted Alexander's judgment; the play, he told Ada Leverson, "must go like a pistol shot." Wilde wanted to attend rehearsals, as he had for his previous London openings, but Douglas, "so beautiful is his nature," declined. Instead, Wilde accompanied Douglas on a final Bunbury to Algeria, returning alone for the final rehearsals of this play.

The following letter was described in Sotheby's Sale Catalogue for July 1933, under item 608, one of a number of Wilde's letters to her husband sold by Lady Alexander. The catalogue provided a synopsis, and reproduced one section. The text is taken from papers at the Clark Library. These are typewritten copies of letters from Wilde to Alexander, marked for inclusion in A.E.W. Mason's study, *Sir George Alexander and the St James's Theatre,* which was published in 1935. Mason wrote to Vyvyan Holland's solicitors, asking for permission to print excerpts, and bracketing those passages he wished to include: these papers are, most probably, Mason's originals. Mason printed only brief extracts from the opening and the last two paragraphs, and his book is the source for the extract printed in Sir Rupen Hart-Davis's edition of Wilde's *Letters.* So far as I am aware, the full letter has not been published before. It is reproduced here by permission of Mr Merlin Holland and the Clark Library (the letter is © Merlin Holland):

16, Tite Street,
S.W.

My dear Aleck,

Thanks for your letter. There really is nothing more to tell you about the comedy beyond what I said already. I mean that the real charm of the play, if it is to have charm, must be in the dialogue. The plot is slight, but, I think, adequate.

Act I. Evening party. 10 p.m.

Lord Alfred Rufford's rooms in Mayfair. Arrives from country Bertram Ashton his friend: a man of 25 or 30 years of age: his great friend.

Rufford asks him about his life. He tells him that he has a ward, etc. very young and pretty. That in the country he has to be serious, etc. that he comes to town to enjoy himself, and has invented a fictitious younger brother of the name of George — to whom all his misdeeds are put down. Rufford is deeply interested about the ward.

Guests arrive: the Duchess of Selby and her daughter, Lady Maud Rufford, with whom the guardian is in love — fin-de-siècle talk, a lot of guests — the guardian proposes to Lady Maud on his knees — enter Duchess —

Lady Maud. "Mamma, this is no place for you."

Scene: Duchess enquires for *her son Lord Alfred Rufford:* servant comes in with note to say that Lord Alfred has been suddenly called away to the country. Lady Maud vows eternal fidelity to the guardian whom she only knows under the name of *George* Ashton.

(P.S. The disclosure of the guardian of his double life is occasioned by Lord Alfred saying to him "You left your handkerchief here the last time you were up" (or cigarette case). The guardian takes it — the Lord A. says but "why, dear George, is it marked Bertram — who is Bertram Ashton?" Guardian discloses plot.)

Act II

The guardian's home — pretty cottage. Mabel Harbord, his ward, and her governess, Miss Prism, Governess of course dragon of propriety. Talk about the profligate George: maid comes in to say "Mr. George Ashton." — governess protests against his admission. Mabel insists. Enter Lord Alfred. Falls in love with ward at once. He is reproached with his bad life, etc. Expressed great repentance. They go to garden.

Enter guardian: Mabel comes in: "I have a great surprise for you — your brother is here"— Guardian, of course, denies having a brother. Mabel says "You cannot disown your own brother, whatever he has done."— and brings in Lord Alfred. Scene: also scene between two men alone. Finally Lord Alfred arrested for debt contracted by guardian: guardian delighted. Mabel, however, makes him forgive his brother and pay up. Guardian looks over bills and scolds Lord Alfred for profligacy.

Miss Prism backs the guardian up. Guardian then orders his brother out of the house. Mabel intercedes, and brother remains. Miss Prism has designs on the guardian — matrimonial — she is 40 at least — she believes he is proposing to her and accepts him — his consternation.

Act III. Mabel and the false brother. He proposes, and is accepted.

When Mabel is alone, Lady Maud, who only knows the guardian under the name of George, arrives alone. She tells Mabel she is engaged to George — scene naturally. Mabel retires: enter George, he kisses his sister naturally. Enter Mabel and sees them. Explanations, of course. Mabel breaks off the match on the ground that there is nothing to reform in George: she only consented to marry him because she thought he was bad and wanted guidance — He promises to be a bad husband — so as to give her an opportunity of making him a better man; she is a little mollified.

Enter guardian: he is reproached also by Lady Maud for his respectable life in the country: a J.P.: a county-councillor: a churchwarden: a philanthropist: a good example. He appeals to his life in London: she is mollified, on condition that he never lives in the country: the country is demoralising: it makes you respectable. "The simple fare at the Savoy: the quiet life in Piccadilly: the solitude of Mayfair is what you need, etc."

Enter Duchess in pursuit of her daughter — objects to both matches. Miss Prism, who had in early days been governess to the Duchess, sets it all right, without intending to do so — everything ends happily.

Result   Curtain

Author called.

Cigarette called.

Manager called.

Royalties for a year for author.

Manager credited with writing the play. He consoles himself for the slander with bag of red gold.

Fireworks

Of course this scenario is open to alterations: the third act, after entrance of Duchess, will have to be elaborated: also, the local doctor, or clergyman, must be brought in, in the play, for Prism.

Well, I think an amusing thing with lots of fun and wit might be made. If you think so, too, and care to have the refusal of it — do let me know — and send me £150. If, when the play is finished, you think it too slight — not serious enough — of course you have the £150 back — I want to go away and write it — and it could be ready in October — as I have nothing else to do — and Palmer is anxious to have a play from me for the States "with no real serious interest"— just a comedy.

In the meanwhile, my dear Aleck, I am so pressed for money, that I don't know what to do. Of course I am extravagant, but a great deal of my worries comes from the fact that I have had for three years to keep up two establishments — my dear Mother's as well as my own — like many Irish ladies she never gets her jointure° paid — small though it is — and naturally it falls on me — this is of course *quite private* but for these years I have had two houses on my shoulders — and of course, am extravagant besides — you have always been a good wise friend to me — so think what you can do.

Kind regards to Mrs. Aleck.

Ever,

OSCAR

jointure: A widow's portion of her husband's estate.

Peter Raby (b. 1939)
THE ORIGINS OF *THE IMPORTANCE OF BEING EARNEST*   1994

In this article, Peter Raby provides some insight into the origins of the play. Wilde wrote quickly, using material that was about him — including names of towns such as Worthing for his characters — so that one has the impression he reflected his environment in his work. However, it is also plain that Wilde lived at such a level that he had considerable need for the money his new farcical comedy was to provide.

Wilde, as the negotiations with Alexander[1] reveal, was acutely conscious of embarking on a new field with this play, referring to it as "farcical comedy" and, to another correspondent, as "quite nonsensical." Its first working title was "The Guardian," and the manuscript notebook in the Clark Library, which also contains speeches for *A Woman of No Importance*, seems to be an attempt at expanding aspects of the first scenario. Even at this early stage, some of the key names had shifted — indeed, only Miss Prism, of all the named characters, retains the same name from scenario to first performance, which gives her an unexpectedly high profile within the play's development. Lady Maud Rufford has become Lady Gwendolen; her mother retains the rank of Duchess; more significantly, Bertram/George Ashton, repeatedly referred to as "Guardian" in the scenario, has been transformed into Mr. Worthing. The importance of his Christian name is now central:

> LADY G: Beautiful name — Ernest. I couldn't love anybody who wasn't called Ernest —
> Oh! don't say that Gwendolen. it sounds perfectly heartless of you — why shd. love be dependent on the action of an irresponsible godfather. Is a man's whole fortune to depend on the font. I am told there was a moment when my father contemplated calling me John —
> How very cruel of him!
> I could love you under any other name —
> Could you love me if my name was Jane? or Maria?
> Devotedly —
> Then you have no sense of romance. Those are not names meant for moonlight.
> cd. you not love me if my name was Geoffrey —
> I might respect you, but love wd. be out of the question — Geoffrey! too straightforward. I cd forgive anything in my husband except passion for telling the truth. That wd. make married life unbearable.

The obsession with the name, and so with form, lies at the play's core, alongside the art of lying, which alone can make married life bearable. Two other quotations from these notes reinforce the theme. On the third page, detached from the dialogue, at an angle and underscored, is the phrase: "Mr. Bunbury — always ill —"; and on the fourth, the following resonant exchange, expanded from the scenario:

> GWEN: Leave the room, Mamma. This is no place for you.
> DUCHESS: Mr. Worthing rise from this semirecumbent posture — it is most unbefitting[2]

---

[1]**George Alexander (1858–1918):** English actor and manager of the St. James Theatre. He commissioned *Lady Windermere's Fan* from Wilde.
[2]AMS Notebook, William Andrews Clark Library, Los Angeles.

All the evidence points to Wilde constructing *The Importance of Being Earnest* with great rapidity and zest, incorporating material which lay conveniently at hand — names, incidents, circumstances — into an outline, and more crucially a tone and manner, which had already taken shape in his mind. The choice of the Sussex seaside resort of Worthing for the guardian's borrowed name follows his habit of incorporating place-names into the comedy he was composing (Hunstanton, Goring). Worthing was particularly apposite for a "serious," propertied Justice of the Peace, following the convention of English comedy of manners. Other neighboring seaside villages to surface in the final text are Lancing and Shoreham. The train journey which John Worthing's benefactor, Thomas Cardew, was about to embark on when he was mistakenly handed the black leather handbag was the very journey from Victoria Station on the Brighton line which Wilde would have taken with his family, who on this occasion included a "horrid ugly Swiss governess."[3]

Other names make links with contrasting aspects of Wilde's life. The guardian's great friend of the scenario was "Lord Alfred Rufford," a name Wilde had already used in the final version of *A Woman of No Importance*. This may have struck Wilde as too blatant a glance at Lord Alfred Douglas; Algernon Moncrieff, Scottish and aristocratic in sound, was more circumspect. (There are several Moncrieffs in the Army List of 1894, including one serving General, stationed in Dublin, of whom Wilde may have heard.) The Douglas connection remains through the character who moved from the Duchess of Selby via Lady Brancaster to Lady Bracknell, Bracknell being the Berkshire home of Douglas's mother, the Marchioness of Queensberry. Wilde's circle of homosexual friends is glanced at obliquely through a number of references. The name Ernest itself has been fully discussed in this context, most recently by Joseph Bristow.[4] "Lady Bloxham" commemorates Jack Bloxam, the editor of the *Chameleon,* in which Wilde's "Phrases and Philosophies for the Use of the Young" was published. B4 the Albany, Jack's London address, echoes the residence of Wilde's friend George Ives. There may, too, be another submerged reference, this time to Robbie Ross, in the name of Miss Cardew's family solicitors, "Markby, Markby, and Markby." There was, in fact, an old-established firm of London solicitors which incorporated the name of Markby. The firm had no dealings with Wilde, but Ross was friendly with one of the managing clerks and would call in to the office to see him. Wilde was not primarily creating a private reference but selecting brilliantly from a set of possibilities to create a particular resonance. Markby, Markby, and Markby conveys an air of respectability, indeed gentility, far removed from the less salubrious solicitors of the four-act version, Gribsby and Parker, in which "Gribsby" has the ring of a particularly ruthless, Dickensian kind of lawyer.

In one version, "Gribsby" had been "Hubbard." Wilde's meticulous care to achieve precisely the right name is recorded in an anecdote of Coulson Kernahan. Kernahan was correcting the proofs of *The Picture of Dorian Gray* and recalls Wilde cross-questioning him: "There's a picture framer — a mere tradesman — in my story, isn't there?" On hearing that he had called him Ashton, Wilde replied: "Ashton is a gentleman's name. And I've given it — God forgive me — to a tradesman!

---

[3]*Letters of Oscar Wilde,* ed. Rupert Hart-Davis (London, 1962), 360.
[4]*The Importance of Being Earnest and Related Writings,* ed. Joseph Bristow (London, 1992), 18–20.

It must be changed to Hubbard. Hubbard positively smells of the tradesman!"[5] Having hit on names which seemed especially apt, Wilde would use them repeatedly, at least, as with these two, in drafts. He would occasionally use a name as a private act of revenge. Max Beerbohm recorded that the names of Wilde's publishers, Lane and Matthews, with whom he was in dispute during the autumn of 1894, were both brought into service as manservant and butler, before Wilde relented at least in the case of Matthews, who became Merriman. There may, too, be a personal dimension to the Bunbury joke. Kerry Powell has drawn attention to the farce *Godpapa,* which included a character called Bunbury with an imaginary ailment.[6] Charles Brookfield was the coauthor of the farce and played Bunbury. Wilde disliked Brookfield, who had mocked him in the travesty *The Poet and the Puppets*: it would have given Wilde a particular pleasure to have infiltrated Brookfield surreptitiously into his own travesty and to have disposed of him so finally and satisfactorily.

Wilde's social ear was acute. The names of the two singleminded girls in his play are finely differentiated. Gwendolen Fairfax carries a certain weight and crisp urbanity, appropriate for Lady Bracknell's daughter, while Jack's ward, Cicely Cardew, has a musical lightness about it. Wilde was an undergraduate at Magdalen with two of the Cardew family. Miss Cecily Cardew was born in 1893, and Wilde reportedly promised, when staying with the Cardews at their country house, that he would name the heroine of his next play after her. (The Victorians would have pronounced "Cecily" as "Cicely," as was done in Nicholas Hytner's 1993 production at the Aldwych Theatre, London.) The Cardew connection may even have prompted Wilde's inventive use of the cloakroom at Victoria Station, for Christopher Baldock Cardew was a director of the London and South East Railway. On the other hand, it may simply have been a dimension of Wilde's genius to create artful fictions that uncannily but surreally echoed life.

Wilde's work is relentlessly self-referential. It also contrives to reflect, shadow, and finally subvert a wide range of contemporary plays. The parallels and motifs which Powell has set out in *Oscar Wilde and the Theatre of the 1890s* draw attention both to Wilde's affinities with an astonishing range of near-contemporary farce and to the specific example of Lestocq and Robson's *The Foundling,* which shared not only a number of common features with *The Importance of Being Earnest* but also a New York producer, Charles Frohman. *The Foundling* opened at Terry's on August 30, 1894. The time-scale is tight, and it cannot be established that Wilde saw a performance: he claimed he did not have the rail-fare to London before his luncheon at the Garrick with Alexander. The date on the typescript draft of Acts III and IV, September 19th, suggests completion some days before. The *Morning Post* of August 31, 1894, reported in its review that Dick Pennell, the hopeful bridegroom and Jack Worthing counterpart, is informed "that he is really a foundling, having been discovered, as a baby, in a bedroom of a hotel at Margate," whereupon Mrs Cotton, the girl's mother, declares that "he shall not be allowed to marry her daughter until he can satisfy her that his parentage is at least respectable." By the time Wilde had composed his first complete draft, he had an excellent opportu-

---

[5]Coulson Kernahan, *In Good Company: Some Personal Recollections of Swinburne, Lord Roberts, Watts-Dunton, Oscar Wilde, Edward Whymper, S. J. Stone and Stephen Philips* (London, 1917), 213.

[6]Kerry Powell, *Oscar Wilde and the Theatre of the 1890s* (Cambridge, 1990), 127.

nity to see *The Foundling* without traveling to London. One of the few communications from this period which can be dated precisely, a telegram to Ada Leverson, puts Wilde and Douglas in Worthing on September 22. On September 20, *The Foundling* was acted at the Brighton Theatre, Brighton being the actual setting of this seaside farce. A fortnight later, the more serious but near-farcical episode of Douglas's illness would be enacted at Brighton's Grand Hotel.

Wilde offered a brilliant and versatile synthesis of the genre of farcical comedy, as though he had been steeped in it all his life rather than coming to it as a new experiment. It is not an imitation but a subversion which at the same time develops it into a distinct and continuously surprising new form. The mood of hard-edged gaiety which infuses it is one which he was struggling to recapture in his own life. Telling Douglas about his luncheon with Gladys de Grey, with Reggie Lister and Aleck Yorke, he commented wistfully: "They want me to go to Paris with them on Thursday: they say one wears flannels and straw hats and dines in the Bois, but, of course, I have no money, as usual, and can't go."[7] This is the yearning of Ernest-in-town. But Wilde's earlier life was full of such impromptu outings, and a glance through some of the letters of his Oxford years reveals experiences which he seems to have drawn upon for the Bunbury-in-the-country scenes. Traveling to his uncle's Lincolnshire rectory, he accepted a lift from the station in a neighbor's dog-cart, and examined schools in geography and played lawn tennis, and argued with his uncle, who revenged himself "by preaching on Rome in the morning, and on humility in the evening";[8] and then, after the triumph of his First, he went to stay with Frank Miles at Bingham Rectory, where he played more lawn tennis, and ate strawberries, and where he found the four Miles daughters: "all very pretty indeed, one of them who is writing at the other side of the table quite lovely." The idyll, though, is not sufficiently like art or literature to be entirely perfect: "A wonderful garden with such white lilies and rose walks; only there are no serpents or apples it would be quite Paradise."[9] With *The Importance of Being Earnest*, Wilde constructed the glittering, uncompromising idyll of his last great fiction, with a full complement of apples and serpents.

In this artificially constructed world, at once like and unlike both farcical comedy and society, everyone invents what they desire, and everyone finally acquires it. Each character is resourcefully creative: diaries, three-volume novels, sermons, visiting cards, lists of eligible young men form the fabricated evidence which gives credibility to their fictions. Jack invents Ernest, Algernon impersonates him: Cecily and Gwendolen respond to the challenge, and the double fiction becomes reality, within the artificial world of the play. The emphasis on names, that apparently trivial pun which so irritated Sidney Grundy, turns out to be important after all. Form and style, not sincerity, are dominant, and, as Wilde predicted in his initial scenario, "everything ends happily." But the charm of the dialogue has all the practiced artifice of experience, and the serpent's irony makes itself felt in every phrase and cadence.

---

[7]*Letters of Oscar Wilde*, 358.
[8]*Letters of Oscar Wilde*, 14.
[9]*Letters of Oscar Wilde*, 16–17.

Anton Chekhov

Anton Chekhov (1860–1904) spent most of his childhood in relative poverty. His family managed to set up its household in Moscow after years spent in remote Taganrog, six hundred miles to the south. He studied medicine in Moscow and eventually took his degree. Though he practiced medicine most of his life, he said that if medicine was his wife, literature was his mistress. His earliest literary efforts were for the purpose of relieving his family's poverty, but it was not long before he earned more from writing than from medicine. By 1896 he had written more than three hundred short stories, most of them published in newspapers. Many of them are classics.

His first theatrical works, apart from his short farces, were not successful. *Ivanov* (1887–1889), rushed to production, was a failure, but its revised 1889 version, reflecting much of his personal life, was successful. *The Wood Demon* (1889), also a failure, helped Chekhov eventually produce his great plays: *The Seagull* (1896); *Uncle Vanya* (1897); *Three Sisters* (1901); and his last, *The Cherry Orchard* (1903). These plays essentially reshaped modern drama, creating a style that critic Richard Peace describes as a "subtle blend of naturalism and symbolism."

The Seagull attracted the attention of the Moscow Art Theatre. The play was not a success in its first production in 1896, but two years later it became one of the theater's triumphs. Konstantin Stanislavsky, the great Russian director and actor, played Trigorin, the lead character, but Chekhov felt that he was overacting. They often had disagreements about the playwright's work, but the Moscow Art Theatre supported Chekhov fully.

The surfaces of Chekhov's plays are so lifelike that at times one feels his dramatic purposes are submerged, and to an extent that is true. Chekhov is the master of the SUBTEXT, a technique in which the surface of the dialogue seems innocuous or meandering, but deeper meanings are implied. Madame Ranevskaya's musings about her childhood in act I of *The Cherry Orchard* contrast with the purposeful dialogue of Lopakhin. Her long speeches in act III talking about the "millstone" she loves in Paris are also meanderings, but they reveal an idealistic character doomed to suffer at the hands of a new generation of realists who have no time for her ramblings and sentimentalism.

Because Chekhov's subtexts are always present, to read his work requires close attention. One must constantly probe, analyze, ask what is implied by what is being said. Chekhov resists "explaining" his plays by having key characters give key thematic speeches. Instead, the meaning builds slowly. Our understanding of what a situation or circumstance finally means will change as we read and as we gather more understanding of the subtleties veiled by surfaces.

Chekhov's style is remarkable for its clarity; its surface is direct, simple, and effective. Even his short stories have a clear dramatic center, and the characters he chose to observe are exceptionally modern in that they are not heroes, not villains. The dramatic concept of a larger-than-life Oedipus or of *Hamlet*'s devilish Claudius is nowhere to be seen in his work. Chekhov's characters are limited, recognizable, and in many ways completely ordinary.

Chekhov's genius was in showing such characters' ambitions, pain, and successes. He was quite aware of important social changes taking place in Russia; the old aristocratic classes, who once owned serfs, were being reduced to a genteel impoverishment, while the children of former slaves were beginning to succeed in business and real estate ventures. Since Chekhov's grandfather had been a serf who bought his freedom in 1841, it is likely that Chekhov was especially supportive of such social change; we see evidence of that in his best plays.

THE CHERRY ORCHARD

The Cherry Orchard (1903), premiered on Chekhov's birthday, January 17, in 1904. The Moscow Art Theatre performance was directed by Konstantin Stanislavsky, an actor-director who pioneered a new method of realistic acting. (Stanislavsky is still read and admired the world over. His techniques were modified in the United States and form the basis of METHOD ACTING.) For the subtle effects that Chekhov wanted, however, he found Stanislavsky too stagey, flamboyant, and melodramatic. They argued hotly over what should happen in his plays, and often Stanislavsky prevailed.

One argument was over whether *The Cherry Orchard* was a tragedy. Chekhov steadfastly called it a comedy, but Stanislavsky saw the ruin of Madame Ranevskaya and the destruction of the cherry orchard as tragic. Chekhov perhaps saw it the same way, but he also considered its potential as the beginning of a new, more realistic life for Madame Ranevskaya and her brother Gayev. Their impracticality was an important cause of their having lost their wealth and estate.

How audiences interpret Lopakhin depends on how they view the ambition of the new class of businessmen whose zeal, work, and cleverness earn them the estates that previously they could have hoped only to work on. Social change is fueled by money, which replaces an inherited aristocracy with ambitious moneymakers who earn the power to force changes on the old, less flexible aristocrats. In Russia massive social change was eventually effected by revolution and the institution of communism. But *The Cherry Orchard* shows that change would have come to Russia in any event.

Perhaps Chekhov's peasant blood helped him see the play as more of a comedy than a tragedy, even though he portrays the characters with greater complexity than we might expect in comedy. Lopakhin is not a simple, unsympathetic character; Trofimov is not a simple dreamer. We need to look closely at what they do and why they do it. For example, when thinking about preserving the beauties of the cherry orchard, Trofimov reminds people that all of Russia is an orchard, that the world is filled with beautiful places. Such a view makes it difficult for him to feel nostalgia for aristocratic privilege.

Trofimov sounds a striking note about the practice of slavery in Russia. He tells Madame Ranevskaya and Gayev that they are living on credit, that they must repay debts to the Russian people. The cherry orchard is beautiful because each tree represents the soul of a serf. The beautiful class of people to which the impractical Madame Ranevskaya belongs owes its beauty and grace to the institution of slavery, and soon the note will be presented for payment. The sound of the breaking string in act I, repeated at the end of the play, is Chekhov's way of symbolizing the losses and changes represented in the play.

Madame Ranevskaya, however, cannot change. Her habits of mind are fully formed before the play begins; nothing that Lopakhin can say will help change her. Even though she knows she is dangerously in debt, she gives a gold coin to a beggar. *Noblesse oblige* — the duty of the upper class to help the poor — is still part of her ethos, even if it also involves her own ruin.

A sense of tragedy is apparent in Madame Ranevskaya's feelings and her helplessness. She seems incapable of transforming herself, no matter how much she may wish to change. We see her as a victim of fate, a fate that is formed by her expectations and training. But the play also contains comic and nonsensical moments, as, for example, in the byplay of Varya, Yasha, and Yepikhodov over a game of billiards in act III. In his letters Chekhov mentions that the play is happy and frivolous, "in places even a farce."

The Cherry Orchard in Performance

Since its first production in 1904, *The Cherry Orchard* has played to responsive audiences in Europe and abroad. It was produced in London in 1911, Berlin in 1919, and New York in 1923 (in Russian). Eva Le Gallienne produced it in New York in her English version in 1928. In 1968 she directed the play with Uta Hagen as Madame Ranevskaya. Tyrone Guthrie directed it at the Old Vic in 1933 and again in 1941. John Gielgud, Peggy Ashcroft, Judy Dench, and Dorothy Tutin performed in a powerful and well-reviewed version in London in 1961. When an all-black *Cherry Orchard* was produced by Joseph Papp in 1973, James Earl Jones was praised as a powerful Lopakhin.

Andrei Serban's 1977 production for Joseph Papp at Lincoln Center in New York was praised for its extraordinary stage effects. According to the reviewer at *Time* magazine,

> Serban's best images effectively magnify the play's conflict between the old order and the bright new world that is its doom: a frieze of peasants laboring beneath modern telegraph wires, a group of aristocrats watching the setting sun silhouette a factory on the horizon.

The American playwright Jean Claude van Italie has revised the text for contemporary audiences. His version, produced at the John Drew Theater of Guild Hall in East Hampton in July 1985, was directed by Elinor Renfield. Amanda Plummer played Anya and Joanna Merlin played Madame Ranevskaya. Peter Brook's 1987 New York production, with Brian Dennehy as a notable Lopakhin, had little scenery beyond a great number of Oriental rugs. It was played without intermissions at breakneck speed. *New York Times* critic Frank Rich said of it, "On this director's magic carpets, *The Cherry Orchard* flies." In 1997 Galina Volchek staged a Russian-language version in the Martin Beck Theater on Broadway. Critic Peter Marks said the play was "communicated vividly."

Anton Chekhov (1860–1904)

THE CHERRY ORCHARD   *1903*

TRANSLATED BY ANN DUNNIGAN

Characters

RANEVSKAYA, LYUBOV ANDREYEVNA, *a landowner*
ANYA, *her daughter, seventeen years old*
VARYA, *her adopted daughter, twenty-four years old*
GAYEV, LEONID ANDREYEVICH, *Madame Ranevskaya's brother*
LOPAKHIN, YERMOLAI ALEKSEYEVICH, *a merchant*
TROFIMOV, PYOTR SERGEYEVICH, *a student*
SEMYONOV-PISHCHIK, BORIS BORISOVICH, *a landowner*
CHARLOTTA IVANOVNA, *a governess*
YEPIKHODOV, SEMYON PANTELEYEVICH, *a clerk*
DUNYASHA, *a maid*
FIRS, *an old valet, eighty-seven years old*
YASHA, *a young footman*
A STRANGER
THE STATIONMASTER
A POST OFFICE CLERK
GUESTS, SERVANTS

The action takes place on Madame Ranevskaya's estate.

ACT I

(*A room that is still called the nursery. One of the doors leads into Anya's room. Dawn; the sun will soon rise. It is May, the cherry trees are in bloom, but it is cold in the orchard; there is a morning frost. The windows in the room are closed. Enter Dunyasha with a candle, and Lopakhin with a book in his hand.*)

LOPAKHIN: The train is in, thank God. What time is it?

DUNYASHA: Nearly two. (*Blows out the candle.*) It's already light.

LOPAKHIN: How late is the train, anyway? A couple of hours at least. (*Yawns and stretches.*) I'm a fine one! What a fool I've made of myself! Came here on purpose to meet them at the station, and then overslept. . . . Fell asleep in the chair. It's annoying. . . . You might have waked me.

DUNYASHA: I thought you had gone. (*Listens.*) They're coming now, I think!

LOPAKHIN (*listens*): No . . . they've got to get the luggage and one thing and another. (*Pause.*) Lyubov Andreyevna has lived abroad for five years, I don't know what she's like now. . . . She's a fine person. Sweet-tempered, simple. I remember when I was a boy of fifteen, my late father — he had a shop in the village then — gave me a punch in the face and made

my nose bleed. . . . We had come into the yard here for some reason or other, and he'd had a drop too much. Lyubov Andreyevna — I remember as if it were yesterday — still young, and so slender, led me to the washstand in this very room, the nursery. "Don't cry, little peasant," she said, "it will heal in time for your wedding. . . ." (*Pause.*) Little peasant . . . my father was a peasant, it's true, and here I am in a white waistcoat and tan shoes. Like a pig in a pastry shop. . . . I may be rich, I've made a lot of money, but if you think about it, analyze it, I'm a peasant through and through. (*Turning pages of the book.*) Here I've been reading this book, and I didn't understand a thing. Fell asleep over it. (*Pause.*)

DUNYASHA: The dogs didn't sleep all night: They can tell that their masters are coming.

LOPAKHIN: What's the matter with you, Dunyasha, you're so . . .

DUNYASHA: My hands are trembling. I'm going to faint.

LOPAKHIN: You're much too delicate, Dunyasha. You dress like a lady, and do your hair like one, too. It's not right. You should know your place.

(*Enter Yepikhodov with a bouquet, he wears a jacket and highly polished boots that squeak loudly. He drops the flowers as he comes in.*)

YEPIKHODOV (*picking up the flowers*): Here, the gardener sent these. He says you're to put them in the dining room. (*Hands the bouquet to Dunyasha.*)

LOPAKHIN: And bring me some kvas.°

DUNYASHA: Yes, sir. (*Goes out.*)

YEPIKHODOV: There's a frost this morning — three degrees — and the cherry trees are in bloom. I cannot approve of our climate. (*Sighs.*) I cannot. Our climate is not exactly conducive. And now, Yermolai Alekseyevich, permit me to append: The day before yesterday I bought myself a pair of boots, which, I venture to assure you, squeak so that it's quite infeasible. What should I grease them with?

LOPAKHIN: Leave me alone. You make me tired.

YEPIKHODOV: Every day some misfortune happens to me. But I don't complain, I'm used to it, I even smile.

(*Dunyasha enters, serves Lopakhin the kvas.*)

YEPIKHODOV: I'm going. (*Stumbles over a chair and upsets it.*) There! (*As if in triumph.*) Now you see, excuse the expression . . . the sort of circumstance,

---

kvas: A Russian beer.

incidentally. . . . It's really quite remarkable! (*Goes out.*)

DUNYASHA: You know, Yermolai Alekseyich, I have to confess that Yepikhodov has proposed to me.

LOPAKHIN: Ah!

DUNYASHA: And I simply don't know. . . . He's a quiet man, but sometimes, when he starts talking, you can't understand a thing he says. It's nice, and full of feeling, only it doesn't make sense. I sort of like him. He's madly in love with me. But he's an unlucky fellow: Every day something happens to him. They tease him about it around here; they call him Two-and-twenty Troubles.

LOPAKHIN (*listening*): I think I hear them coming . . .

DUNYASHA: They're coming! What's the matter with me? I'm cold all over.

LOPAKHIN: They're really coming. Let's go and meet them. Will she recognize me? It's five years since we've seen each other.

DUNYASHA (*agitated*): I'll faint this very minute . . . oh, I'm going to faint!

(*Two carriages are heard driving up to the house. Lopakhin and Dunyasha go out quickly. The stage is empty. There is a hubbub in the adjoining rooms. Firs hurriedly crosses the stage leaning on a stick. He has been to meet Lyubov Andreyevna and wears old fashioned livery and a high hat. He mutters something to himself, not a word of which can be understood. The noise offstage grows louder and louder. A voice: "Let's go through here. . . ." Enter Lyubov Andreyevna, Anya, Charlotta Ivanovna with a little dog on a chain, all in traveling dress; Varya wearing a coat and kerchief; Gayev, Semyonov-Pishchik, Lopakhin, Dunyasha with a bundle and parasol; servants with luggage — all walk through the room.*)

ANYA: Let's go this way. Do you remember, Mama, what room this is?

LYUBOV ANDREYEVNA: (*joyfully, through tears*): The nursery!

VARYA: How cold it is! My hands are numb. (*To Lyubov Andreyevna.*) Your rooms, both the white one and the violet one, are just as you left them, Mama.

LYUBOV ANDREYEVNA: The nursery . . . my dear, lovely nursery. . . . I used to sleep here when I was little. . . . (*Weeps.*) And now, like a child, I . . . (*Kisses her brother, Varya, then her brother again.*) Varya hasn't changed; she still looks like a nun. And I recognized Dunyasha. . . . (*Kisses Dunyasha.*)

GAYEV: The train was two hours late. How's that? What kind of management is that?

CHARLOTTA (*to Pishchik*): My dog even eats nuts.

PISHCHIK (*amazed*): Think of that now!

(*They all go out except Anya and Dunyasha.*)

DUNYASHA: We've been waiting and waiting for you. . . . (*Takes off Anya's coat and hat.*)

ANYA: I didn't sleep for four nights on the road . . . now I feel cold.

DUNYASHA: It was Lent when you went away, there was snow and frost then, but now? My darling! (*Laughs and kisses her.*) I've waited so long for you, my joy, my precious . . . I must tell you at once, I can't wait another minute. . . .

ANYA (*listlessly*): What now?

DUNYASHA: The clerk, Yepikhodov, proposed to me just after Easter.

ANYA: You always talk about the same thing. . . . (*Straightening her hair.*) I've lost all my hairpins. . . . (*She is so exhausted she can hardly stand.*)

DUNYASHA: I really don't know what to think. He loves me — he loves me so!

ANYA (*looking through the door into her room, tenderly*): My room, my windows . . . it's just as though I'd never been away. I am home! Tomorrow morning I'll get up and run into the orchard. . . . Oh, if I could only sleep! I didn't sleep during the entire journey, I was so tormented by anxiety.

DUNYASHA: Pyotr Sergeich arrived the day before yesterday.

ANYA (*joyfully*): Petya!

DUNYASHA: He's asleep in the bathhouse, he's staying there. "I'm afraid of being in the way," he said. (*Looks at her pocket watch.*) I ought to wake him up, but Varvara Mikhailovna told me not to. "Don't you wake him," she said.

(*Enter Varya with a bunch of keys at her waist.*)

VARYA: Dunyasha, coffee, quickly . . . Mama's asking for coffee.

DUNYASHA: This very minute. (*Goes out.*)

VARYA: Thank God, you've come! You're home again. (*Caressing her.*) My little darling has come back! My pretty one is here!

ANYA: I've been through so much.

VARYA: I can imagine!

ANYA: I left in Holy Week, it was cold then. Charlotta never stopped talking and doing her conjuring tricks the entire journey. Why did you saddle me with Charlotta?

VARYA: You couldn't have traveled alone, darling. At seventeen!

ANYA: When we arrived in Paris, it was cold, snowing. My French is awful. . . . Mama was living on the fifth floor, and when I got there, she had all sorts of Frenchmen and ladies with her, and an old priest with a little book, and it was full of smoke, dismal. Suddenly I felt sorry for Mama, so sorry. I took her head in my arms and held her close and couldn't let her go. Afterward she kept hugging me and crying. . . .

VARYA (*through her tears*): Don't talk about it, don't talk about it . . .

ANYA: She had already sold her villa near Mentone, and she had nothing left, nothing. And I hadn't so much as a kopeck left, we barely managed to get there. But Mama doesn't understand! When we had dinner in a station restaurant, she always ordered the most expensive dishes and tipped each of the waiters a ruble. Charlotta is the same. And Yasha also ordered a dinner, it was simply awful. You know, Yasha is Mama's footman; we brought him with us.

VARYA: I saw the rogue.

ANYA: Well, how are things? Have you paid the interest?

VARYA: How could we?

ANYA: Oh, my God, my God!

VARYA: In August the estate will be put up for sale.

ANYA: My God!

(*Lopakhin peeps in at the door and moos like a cow.*)

LOPAKHIN: Moo-o-o! (*Disappears.*)

VARYA (*through her tears*): What I couldn't do to him! (*Shakes her fist.*)

ANYA (*embracing Varya, softly*): Varya, has he proposed to you? (*Varya shakes her head.*) But he loves you. . . . Why don't you come to an understanding, what are you waiting for?

VARYA: I don't think anything will ever come of it. He's too busy, he has no time for me . . . he doesn't even notice me. I've washed my hands of him, it makes me miserable to see him. . . . Everyone talks of our wedding, they all congratulate me, and actually there's nothing to it — it's all like a dream. . . . (*In a different tone.*) You have a brooch like a bee.

ANYA (*sadly*): Mama bought it. (*Goes into her own room; speaks gaily, like a child.*) In Paris I went up in a balloon!

VARYA: My darling is home! My pretty one has come back!

(*Dunyasha has come in with the coffeepot and prepares coffee.*)

VARYA (*stands at the door of Anya's room*): You know, darling, all day long I'm busy looking after the house, but I keep dreaming. If we could marry you to a rich man I'd be at peace. I could go into a hermitage, then to Kiev, to Moscow, and from one holy place to another. . . . I'd go on and on. What a blessing!

ANYA: The birds are singing in the orchard. What time is it?

VARYA: It must be after two. Time you were asleep, darling. (*Goes into Anya's room.*) What a blessing!

(*Yasha enters with a lap robe and a traveling bag.*)

YASHA (*crosses the stage mincingly*): May one go through here?

DUNYASHA: A person would hardly recognize you, Yasha. Your stay abroad has done wonders for you.

YASHA: Hm. . . . And who are you?

DUNYASHA: When you left here I was only that high — (*indicating with her hand*). I'm Dunyasha, Fyodor Kozoyedov's daughter. You don't remember?

YASHA: Hm. . . . A little cucumber! (*Looks around, then embraces her; she cries out and drops a saucer. He quickly goes out.*)

VARYA (*in a tone of annoyance, from the doorway*): What's going on here?

DUNYASHA (*tearfully*): I broke a saucer.

VARYA: That's good luck.

ANYA: We ought to prepare Mama: Petya is here. . . .

VARYA: I gave orders not to wake him.

ANYA (*pensively*): Six years ago Father died, and a month later brother Grisha drowned in the river . . . a pretty little seven-year-old boy. Mama couldn't bear it and went away . . . went without looking back. . . . (*Shudders.*) How I understand her, if she only knew! (*Pause.*) And Petya Trofimov was Grisha's tutor, he may remind her. . . .

(*Enter Firs wearing a jacket and a white waistcoat.*)

FIRS (*goes to the coffeepot, anxiously*): The mistress will have her coffee here. (*Puts on white gloves.*) Is the coffee ready? (*To Dunyasha, sternly.*) You! Where's the cream?

DUNYASHA: Oh, my goodness! (*Quickly goes out.*)

FIRS (*fussing over the coffeepot*): Ah, what an addlepate! (*Mutters to himself.*) They've come back from Paris. . . . The master used to go to Paris . . . by carriage. . . . (*Laughs.*)

VARYA: What is it, Firs?

FIRS: If you please? (*Joyfully.*) My mistress has come home! At last! Now I can die. . . . (*Weeps with joy.*)

(*Enter Lyubov Andreyevna, Gayev, and Semyonov-Pishchik, the last wearing a sleeveless peasant coat of fine cloth and full trousers. Gayev, as he comes in, goes through the motions of playing billiards.*)

LYUBOV ANDREYEVNA: How does it go? Let's see if I can remember . . . cue ball into the corner! Double the rail to center table.

GAYEV: Cut shot into the corner! There was a time, sister, when you and I used to sleep here in this very room, and now I'm fifty-one, strange as it may seem. . . .

LOPAKHIN: Yes, time passes.

GAYEV: How's that?

LOPAKHIN: Time, I say, passes.

GAYEV: It smells of patchouli here.

ANYA: I'm going to bed. Good night, Mama. (*Kisses her mother.*)

LYUBOV ANDREYEVNA: My precious child. (*Kisses her hands.*) Are you glad to be home? I still feel dazed.

ANYA: Good night, Uncle.

GAYEV (*kisses her face and hands*): God bless you. How like your mother you are! (*To his sister.*) At her age you were exactly like her, Lyuba.

(*Anya shakes hands with Lopakhin and Pishchik and goes out, closing the door after her.*)

LYUBOV ANDREYEVNA: She's exhausted.

PISHCHIK: Must have been a long journey.

VARYA: Well, gentlemen? It's after two, high time you were going.

LYUBOV ANDREYEVNA (*laughs*): You haven't changed, Varya. (*Draws Varya to her and kisses her.*) I'll just drink my coffee and then we'll all go. (*Firs places a cushion under her feet.*) Thank you, my dear. I've got used to coffee. I drink it day and night. Thanks, dear old man. (*Kisses him.*)

VARYA: I'd better see if all the luggage has been brought in.

LYUBOV ANDREYEVNA: Is this really me sitting here? (*Laughs.*) I feel like jumping about and waving my arms. (*Buries her face in her hands.*) What if it's only a dream! God knows I love my country, love it dearly. I couldn't look out the train window, I was crying so! (*Through tears.*) But I must drink my coffee. Thank you, Firs, thank you, my dear old friend. I'm so glad you're still alive.

FIRS: The day before yesterday.

GAYEV: He's hard of hearing.

LOPAKHIN: I must go now, I'm leaving for Kharkov about five o'clock. It's so annoying! I wanted to have a good look at you, and have a talk. You're as splendid as ever.

PISHCHIK (*breathing heavily*): Even more beautiful. . . . Dressed like a Parisienne. . . . There goes my wagon, all four wheels!

LOPAKHIN: Your brother here, Leonid Andreich, says I'm a boor, a moneygrubber, but I don't mind. Let him talk. All I want is that you should trust me as you used to, and that your wonderful, touching eyes should look at me as they did then. Merciful God! My father was one of your father's serfs, and your grandfather's, but you yourself did so much for me once, that I've forgotten all that and love you as if you were my own kin — more than my kin.

LYUBOV ANDREYEVNA: I can't sit still, I simply cannot. (*Jumps up and walks about the room in great excitement.*) I cannot bear this joy. . . . Laugh at me, I'm silly. . . . My dear little bookcase . . . (*kisses bookcase*) my little table . . .

GAYEV: Nurse died while you were away.

LYUBOV ANDREYEVNA (*sits down and drinks coffee*): Yes, God rest her soul. They wrote me.

GAYEV: And Anastasy is dead. Petrushka Kosoi left me and is now with the police inspector in town. (*Takes a box of hard candies from his pocket and begins to suck one.*)

PISHCHIK: My daughter, Dashenka . . . sends her regards . . .

LOPAKHIN: I wish I could tell you something very pleasant and cheering. (*Glances at his watch.*) I must go directly, there's no time to talk, but . . . well, I'll say it in a couple of words. As you know, the cherry orchard is to be sold to pay your debts. The auction is set for August twenty-second, but you need not worry, my dear, you can sleep in peace, there is a way out. This is my plan. Now, please listen! Your estate is only twenty versts° from town, the railway runs close by, and if the cherry orchard and the land along the river were cut up into lots and leased for summer cottages, you'd have, at the very least, an income of twenty-five thousand a year.

GAYEV: Excuse me, what nonsense!

LYUBOV ANDREYEVNA: I don't quite understand you, Yermolai Alekseich.

LOPAKHIN: You will get, at the very least, twenty-five rubles a year for a two-and-a-half-acre lot, and if you advertise now, I guarantee you won't have a single plot of ground left by autumn, everything will be snapped up. In short, I congratulate you, you are saved. The site is splendid, the river is deep. Only, of course, the ground must be cleared . . . you must tear down all the old outbuildings, for instance, and this house, which is worthless, cut down the old cherry orchard —

LYUBOV ANDREYEVNA: Cut it down? Forgive me, my dear, but you don't know what you are talking about. If there is one thing in the whole province that is interesting, not to say remarkable, it's our cherry orchard.

LOPAKHIN: The only remarkable thing about this orchard is that it is very big. There's a crop of cherries every other year, and then you can't get rid of them, nobody buys them.

GAYEV: This orchard is even mentioned in the *Encyclopedia.*

LOPAKHIN (*glancing at his watch*): If we don't think of something and come to a decision, on the twenty-second of August the cherry orchard, and the entire estate, will be sold at auction. Make up your minds! There is no other way out, I swear to you. None whatsoever.

FIRS: In the old days, forty or fifty years ago, the cherries were dried, soaked, marinated, and made into jam, and they used to —

GAYEV: Be quiet, Firs.

FIRS: And they used to send cartloads of dried cherries to Moscow and Kharkov. And that brought in money! The dried cherries were soft and juicy in those days, sweet, fragrant. . . . They had a method then . . .

LYUBOV ANDREYEVNA: And what has become of that method now?

FIRS: Forgotten. Nobody remembers. . . .

PISHCHIK: How was it in Paris? What's it like there? Did you eat frogs?

LYUBOV ANDREYEVNA: I ate crocodiles.

PISHCHIK: Think of that now!

LOPAKHIN: There used to be only the gentry and the peasants living in the country, but now these summer people have appeared. All the towns, even the smallest ones, are surrounded by summer cottages. And it is safe to say that in another twenty years these people will multiply enormously. Now the summer resident only drinks tea on his porch, but it may well be that he'll take to cultivating his acre and then your cherry orchard will be a happy, rich, luxuriant —

GAYEV (*indignantly*): What nonsense!

(*Enter Varya and Yasha.*)

VARYA: There are two telegrams for you, Mama. (*Picks out a key and with a jingling sound opens an old-fashioned bookcase.*) Here they are.

versts: A verst is approximately equal to a kilometer, a little more than half a mile.

LYUBOV ANDREYEVNA: From Paris. (*Tears up the telegrams without reading them.*) That's all over. . . .

GAYEV: Do you know, Lyuba, how old this bookcase is? A week ago I pulled out the bottom drawer, and what do I see? Some figures burnt into it. The bookcase was made exactly a hundred years ago. What do you think of that? Eh? We could have celebrated its jubilee. It's an inanimate object, but nevertheless, for all that, it's a bookcase.

PISHCHIK: A hundred years . . . think of that now!

GAYEV: Yes . . . that is something. . . . (*Feeling the bookcase.*) Dear, honored bookcase. I salute thy existence, which for over one hundred years has served the glorious ideals of goodness and justice; thy silent appeal to fruitful endeavor, unflagging in the course of a hundred years, tearfully sustaining through generations of our family, courage and faith in a better future, and fostering in us ideals of goodness and social consciousness. . . .

(*A pause.*)

LOPAKHIN: Yes . . .

LYUBOV ANDREYEVNA: You are the same as ever, Lyonya.

GAYEV (*somewhat embarrassed*): Carom into the corner, cut shot to center table.

LOPAKHIN (*looks at his watch*): Well, time for me to go.

YASHA (*hands medicine to Lyubov Andreyevna*): Perhaps you will take your pills now.

PISHCHIK: Don't take medicaments, dearest lady, they do neither harm nor good. Let me have them, honored lady. (*Takes the pillbox, shakes the pills into his hand, blows on them, puts them into his mouth and washes them down with kvas.*) There!

LYUBOV ANDREYEVNA (*alarmed*): Why, you must be mad!

PISHCHIK: I've taken all the pills.

LOPAKHIN: What a glutton!

(*Everyone laughs.*)

FIRS: The gentleman stayed with us during Holy Week . . . ate half a bucket of pickles. . . . (*Mumbles.*)

LYUBOV ANDREYEVNA: What is he saying?

VARYA: He's been muttering like that for three years now. We've grown used to it.

YASHA: He's in his dotage.

(*Charlotta Ivanovna, very thin, tightly laced, in a white dress with a lorgnette at her belt, crosses the stage.*)

LOPAKHIN: Forgive me, Charlotta Ivanovna, I haven't had a chance to say how do you do to you. (*Tries to kiss her hand.*)

CHARLOTTA (*pulls her hand away*): If I permit you to kiss my hand you'll be wanting to kiss my elbow next, then my shoulder.

LOPAKHIN: I have no luck today. (*Everyone laughs.*) Charlotta Ivanovna, show us a trick!

LYUBOV ANDREYEVNA: Charlotta, show us a trick!

CHARLOTTA: No. I want to sleep. (*Goes out.*)

LOPAKHIN: In three weeks we'll meet again. (*Kisses Lyubov Andreyevna's hand.*) Good-bye till then. Time to go. (*To Gayev.*) Good-bye. (*Kisses Pishchik.*) Good-bye. (*Shakes hands with Varya, then with Firs and Yasha.*) I don't feel like going. (*To Lyubov Andreyevna.*) If you make up your mind about the summer cottages and come to a decision, let me know; I'll get you a loan of fifty thousand or so. Think it over seriously.

VARYA (*angrily*): Oh, why don't you go!

LOPAKHIN: I'm going, I'm going. (*Goes out.*)

GAYEV: Boor. Oh, pardon. Varya's going to marry him, he's Varya's young man.

VARYA: Uncle dear, you talk too much.

LYUBOV ANDREYEVNA: Well, Varya, I shall be very glad. He's a good man.

PISHCHIK: A man, I must truly say . . . most worthy. . . . And my Dashenka . . . says, too, that . . . says all sorts of things. (*Snores but wakes up at once.*) In any case, honored lady, oblige me . . . a loan of two hundred and forty rubles . . . tomorrow the interest on my mortgage is due. . . .

VARYA (*in alarm*): We have nothing, nothing at all!

LYUBOV ANDREYEVNA: I really haven't any money.

PISHCHIK: It'll turn up. (*Laughs.*) I never lose hope. Just when I thought everything was lost, that I was done for, lo and behold — the railway line ran through my land . . . and they paid me for it. And before you know it, something else will turn up, if not today — tomorrow. . . . Dashenka will win two hundred thousand . . . she's got a lottery ticket.

LYUBOV ANDREYEVNA: The coffee is finished, we can go to bed.

FIRS (*brushing Gayev's clothes, admonishingly*): You've put on the wrong trousers again. What am I to do with you?

VARYA (*softly*): Anya's asleep. (*Quietly opens the window.*) The sun has risen, it's no longer cold. Look, Mama dear, what wonderful trees! Oh, Lord, the air! The starlings are singing!

GAYEV (*opens another window*): The orchard is all white. You haven't forgotten, Lyuba? That long avenue there that runs straight — straight as a stretched-out strap; it gleams on moonlight nights. Remember? You've not forgotten?

LYUBOV ANDREYEVNA (*looking out the window at the orchard*): Oh, my childhood, my innocence! I used to sleep in this nursery, I looked out from here into the orchard, happiness awoke with me each morning, it was just as it is now, nothing has changed. (*Laughing with joy.*) All, all white! Oh, my orchard! After the dark, rainy autumn and the cold winter, you are young again, full of happiness, the heavenly angels have not forsaken you. . . . If I could cast off this heavy stone weighing on my breast and shoulders, if I could forget my past!

GAYEV: Yes, and the orchard will be sold for our debts, strange as it may seem. . . .

LYUBOV ANDREYEVNA: Look, our dead mother walks in the orchard . . . in a white dress! (*Laughs with joy.*) It is she!

GAYEV: Where?

VARYA: God be with you, Mama dear.

LYUBOV ANDREYEVNA: There's no one there, I just imagined it. To the right, as you turn to the summerhouse, a slender white sapling is bent over . . . it looks like a woman.

(*Enter Trofimov wearing a shabby student's uniform and spectacles.*)

LYUBOV ANDREYEVNA: What a wonderful orchard! The white masses of blossoms, the blue sky —

TROFIMOV: Lyubov Andreyevna! (*She looks around at him.*) I only want to pay my respects, then I'll go at once. (*Kisses her hand ardently.*) I was told to wait until morning, but I hadn't the patience.

(*Lyubov Andreyevna looks at him, puzzled.*)

VARYA (*through tears*): This is Petya Trofimov.

TROFIMOV: Petya Trofimov, I was Grisha's tutor. . . . Can I have changed so much?

(*Lyubov Andreyevna embraces him, quietly weeping.*)

GAYEV (*embarrassed*): There, there, Lyuba.

VARYA (*crying*): Didn't I tell you, Petya, to wait till tomorrow?

LYUBOV ANDREYEVNA: My Grisha . . . my little boy . . . Grisha . . . my son. . . .

VARYA: What can we do, Mama dear? It's God's will.

TROFIMOV (*gently, through tears*): Don't, don't. . . .

LYUBOV ANDREYEVNA (*quietly weeping*): My little boy dead, drowned. . . . Why? Why, my friend? (*In a lower voice.*) Anya is sleeping in there, and I'm talking loudly . . . making all this noise. . . . But Petya, why do you look so bad? Why have you grown so old?

TROFIMOV: A peasant woman in the train called me a mangy gentleman.

LYUBOV ANDREYEVNA: You were just a boy then, a charming little student, and now your hair is thin — and spectacles! Is it possible you are still a student? (*Goes toward the door.*)

TROFIMOV: I shall probably be an eternal student.

LYUBOV ANDREYEVNA (*kisses her brother, then Varya*): Now, go to bed. . . . You've grown older too, Leonid.

PISHCHIK (*follows her*): Well, seems to be time to sleep. . . . Oh, my gout! I'm staying the night. Lyubov Andreyevna, my soul, tomorrow morning . . . two hundred and forty rubles. . . .

GAYEV: He keeps at it.

PISHCHIK: Two hundred and forty rubles . . . to pay the interest on my mortgage.

LYUBOV ANDREYEVNA: I have no money, my friend.

PISHCHIK: My dear, I'll pay it back. . . . It's a trifling sum.

LYUBOV ANDREYEVNA: Well, all right, Leonid will give it to you. . . . Give it to him, Leonid.

GAYEV: Me give it to him! . . . Hold out your pocket!

LYUBOV ANDREYEVNA: It can't be helped, give it to him. . . . He needs it. . . . He'll pay it back.

(*Lyubov Andreyevna, Trofimov, Pishchik, and Firs go out. Gayev, Varya, and Yasha remain.*)

GAYEV: My sister hasn't yet lost her habit of squandering money. (*To Yasha.*) Go away, my good fellow, you smell of the henhouse.

YASHA (*with a smirk*): And you, Leonid Andreyevich, are just the same as ever.

GAYEV: How's that? (*To Varya.*) What did he say?

VARYA: Your mother has come from the village; she's been sitting in the servants' room since yesterday, waiting to see you. . . .

YASHA: Let her wait, for God's sake!

VARYA: Aren't you ashamed?

YASHA: A lot I need her! She could have come tomorrow. (*Goes out.*)

VARYA: Mama's the same as ever, she hasn't changed a bit. She'd give away everything, if she could.

GAYEV: Yes. . . . (*A pause.*) If a great many remedies are suggested for a disease, it means that the disease is incurable. I keep thinking, racking my brains, I have many remedies, a great many, and that means in effect, that I have none. It would be good to receive a legacy from someone, good to marry our Anya to a very rich man, good to go to Yaroslav and try our luck with our aunt, the Countess. She is very, very rich, you know.

VARYA (*crying*): If only God would help us!

GAYEV: Stop bawling. Auntie's very rich, but she doesn't like us. In the first place, sister married a lawyer, not a nobleman . . . (*Anya appears in the doorway.*) She married beneath her, and it cannot be said that she has conducted herself very virtuously. She is good, kind, charming, and I love her dearly, but no matter how much you allow for extenuating circumstances, you must admit she leads a sinful life. You feel it in her slightest movement.

VARYA (*in a whisper*): Anya is standing in the doorway.

GAYEV: What? (*Pause.*) Funny, something got into my right eye . . . I can't see very well. And Thursday, when I was in the district court . . .

(*Anya enters.*)

VARYA: Why aren't you asleep, Anya?

ANYA: I can't get to sleep. I just can't.

GAYEV: My little one! (*Kisses Anya's face and hands.*) My child. . . . (*Through tears.*) You are not my niece, you are my angel, you are everything to me. Believe me, believe . . .

ANYA: I believe you, Uncle. Everyone loves you and respects you, but, Uncle dear, you must keep quiet, just keep quiet. What were you saying just now about my mother, about your own sister? What made you say that?

GAYEV: Yes, yes. . . . (*Covers his face with her hand.*) Really, it's awful! My God! God help me! And today I made a speech to the bookcase . . . so stupid! And it was only when I had finished that I realized it was stupid.

VARYA: It's true, Uncle dear, you ought to keep quiet. Just don't talk, that's all.

ANYA: If you could keep from talking, it would make things easier for you, too.

GAYEV: I'll be quiet. (*Kisses Anya's and Varya's hands.*) I'll be quiet. Only this is about business. On Thursday I was in the district court, well, a group of us gathered together and began talking about one thing and another, this and that, and it seems it might be possible to arrange a loan on a promissory note to pay the interest at the bank.

VARYA: If only God would help us!

GAYEV: On Tuesday I'll go and talk it over again. (*To Varya.*) Stop bawling. (*To Anya.*) Your mama will talk to Lopakhin; he, of course, will not refuse her. . . . And as soon as you've rested, you will go to Yaroslav to the Countess, your great-aunt. In that way we shall be working from three directions — and our business is in the hat. We'll pay the interest, I'm certain of it. . . . (*Puts a candy in his mouth.*) On my honor, I'll swear by anything you like, the estate shall not be sold. (*Excitedly.*) By my happiness, I swear it! Here's my hand on it, call me a worthless, dishonorable man if I let it come to auction! I swear by my whole being!

ANYA (*a calm mood returns to her, she is happy*): How good you are, Uncle, how clever! (*Embraces him.*) Now I am at peace! I'm at peace! I'm happy!

(*Enter Firs.*)

FIRS (*reproachfully*): Leonid Andreich, have you no fear of God? When are you going to bed?

GAYEV: Presently, presently. Go away, Firs. I'll . . . all right, I'll undress myself. Well, children, bye-bye. . . . Details tomorrow, and now go to sleep. (*Kisses Anya and Varya.*) I am a man of the eighties. . . . They don't think much of that period today, nevertheless, I can say that in the course of my life I have suffered not a little for my convictions. It is not for nothing that the peasant loves me. You have to know the peasant! You have to know from what —

ANYA: There you go again, Uncle!

VARYA: Uncle dear, do be quiet.

FIRS (*angrily*): Leonid Andreich!

GAYEV: I'm coming, I'm coming. . . . Go to bed. A clean double rail shot to center table. . . . (*Goes out; Firs hobbles after him.*)

ANYA: I'm at peace now. I would rather not go to Yaroslav, I don't like my great-aunt, but still, I'm at peace, thanks to Uncle. (*She sits down.*)

VARYA: We must get some sleep. I'm going now. Oh, something unpleasant happened while you were away. In the old servants' quarters, as you know, there are only the old people: Yefimushka, Polya, Yevstignei, and, of course, Karp. They began letting in all sorts of rogues to spend the night — I didn't say anything. But then I heard they'd been spreading a rumor that I'd given an order for them to be fed nothing but dried peas. Out of stinginess, you

see. . . . It was all Yevstignei's doing. . . . Very well, I think, if that's how it is, you just wait. I send for Yevstignei . . . (*yawning*) he comes. . . . "How is it, Yevstignei," I say, "that you could be such a fool. . . ." (*Looks at Anya.*) She's fallen asleep. (*Takes her by the arm.*) Come to your little bed. . . . Come along. (*Leading her.*) My little darling fell asleep. Come. . . . (*They go.*)

(*In the distance, beyond the orchard, a shepherd is playing on a reed pipe. Trofimov crosses the stage and, seeing Varya and Anya, stops.*)

VARYA: Sh! She's asleep . . . asleep. . . . Come along, darling.

ANYA (*softly, half-asleep*): I'm so tired. . . . Those bells . . . Uncle . . . dear . . . Mama and Uncle . . .

VARYA: Come, darling, come along. (*They go into Anya's room.*)

TROFIMOV (*deeply moved*): My sunshine! My spring!

ACT II

(*A meadow. An old, lopsided, long-abandoned little chapel; near it a well, large stones that apparently were once tombstones, and an old bench. A road to the Gayev manor house can be seen. On one side, where the cherry orchard begins, tall poplars loom. In the distance a row of telegraph poles, and far, far away, on the horizon, the faint outline of a large town, which is visible only in very fine, clear weather. The sun will soon set. Charlotta, Yasha, and Dunyasha are sitting on the bench; Yepikhodov stands near playing something sad on the guitar. They are all lost in thought. Charlotta wears an old forage cap; she has taken a gun from her shoulder and is adjusting the buckle on the sling.*)

CHARLOTTA (*reflectively*): I haven't got a real passport, I don't know how old I am, but it always seems to me that I'm quite young. When I was a little girl, my father and mother used to travel from one fair to another giving performances — very good ones. And I did the *salto mortale*° and all sorts of tricks. Then when Papa and Mama died, a German lady took me to live with her and began teaching me. Good. I grew up and became a governess. But where I come from and who I am — I do not know. . . . Who my parents were — perhaps they weren't even married — I don't know. (*Takes a cucumber out of her pocket and eats it.*) I don't know anything. (*Pause.*) One wants so much to talk, but there isn't anyone to talk to . . . I have no one.

YEPIKHODOV (*plays the guitar and sings*): "What care I for the clamorous world, what's friend or foe to me?". . . How pleasant it is to play a mandolin!

DUNYASHA: That's a guitar, not a mandolin. (*Looks at herself in a hand mirror and powders her face.*)

salto mortale: Somersault.

YEPIKHODOV: To a madman, in love, it is a mandolin. . . . (*Sings.*) "Would that the heart were warmed by the flame of requited love . . ."

(*Yasha joins in.*)

CHARLOTTA: How horribly these people sing! . . . Pfui! Like jackals!

DUNYASHA (*to Yasha*): Really, how fortunate to have been abroad!

YASHA: Yes, to be sure. I cannot but agree with you there. (*Yawns, then lights a cigar.*)

YEPIKHODOV: It stands to reason. Abroad everything has long since been fully constituted.

YASHA: Obviously.

YEPIKHODOV: I am a cultivated man, I read all sorts of remarkable books, but I am in no way able to make out my own inclinations, what it is I really want, whether, strictly speaking, to live or to shoot myself; nevertheless, I always carry a revolver on me. Here it is. (*Shows revolver.*)

CHARLOTTA: Finished. Now I'm going. (*Slings the gun over her shoulder.*) You're a very clever man, Yepikhodov, and quite terrifying; women must be mad about you. Brrr! (*Starts to go.*) These clever people are all so stupid, there's no one for me to talk to. . . . Alone, always alone, I have no one . . . and who I am, and why I am, nobody knows. . . . (*Goes out unhurriedly.*)

YEPIKHODOV: Strictly speaking, all else aside, I must state regarding myself, that fate treats me unmercifully, as a storm does a small ship. If, let us assume, I am mistaken, then why, to mention a single instance, do I wake up this morning, and there on my chest see a spider of terrifying magnitude? . . . Like that. (*Indicates with both hands.*) And likewise, I take up some kvas to quench my thirst, and there see something in the highest degree unseemly, like a cockroach. (*Pause.*) Have you read Buckle?° (*Pause.*) If I may trouble you, Avdotya Fedorovna, I should like to have a word or two with you.

DUNYASHA: Go ahead.

YEPIKHODOV: I prefer to speak with you alone. . . . (*Sighs.*)

DUNYASHA (*embarrassed*): Very well . . . only first bring me my little cape . . . you'll find it by the cupboard. . . . It's rather damp here. . . .

YEPIKHODOV: Certainly, ma'am . . . I'll fetch it, ma'am. . . . Now I know what to do with my revolver. . . . (*Takes the guitar and goes off playing it.*)

YASHA: Two-and-twenty Troubles! Between ourselves, a stupid fellow. (*Yawns.*)

DUNYASHA: God forbid that he should shoot himself. (*Pause.*) I've grown so anxious, I'm always worried. I was only a little girl when I was taken into the master's house, and now I'm quite unused to the simple life, and my hands are white as can be, just like a lady's. I've become so delicate, so tender and ladylike, I'm afraid of everything. . . . Frightfully so. And, Yasha, if you deceive me, I just don't know what will become of my nerves.

YASHA (*kisses her*): You little cucumber! Of course, a girl should never forget herself. What I dislike above everything is when a girl doesn't conduct herself properly.

DUNYASHA: I'm passionately in love with you, you're educated, you can discuss anything. (*Pause.*)

YASHA (*yawns*): Yes. . . . As I see it, it's like this: If a girl loves somebody, that means she's immoral. (*Pause.*) Very pleasant smoking a cigar in the open air. . . . (*Listens.*) Someone's coming this way. . . . It's the masters. (*Dunyasha impulsively embraces him.*) You go home, as if you'd been to the river to bathe; take that path, otherwise they'll see you and suspect me of having a rendezvous with you. I can't endure that sort of thing.

DUNYASHA (*with a little cough*): My head is beginning to ache from your cigar. . . . (*Goes out.*)

(*Yasha remains, sitting near the chapel. Lyubov Andreyevna, Gayev, and Lopakhin enter.*)

LOPAKHIN: You must make up your mind once and for all — time won't stand still. The question, after all, is quite simple. Do you agree to lease the land for summer cottages or not? Answer in one word: Yes or no? Only one word!

LYUBOV ANDREYEVNA: Who is it that smokes those disgusting cigars out here? (*Sits down.*)

GAYEV: Now that the railway line is so near, it's made things convenient. (*Sits down.*) We went to town and had lunch . . . cue ball to the center! I feel like going to the house first and playing a game.

LYUBOV ANDREYEVNA: Later.

LOPAKHIN: Just one word! (*Imploringly.*) Do give me an answer!

GAYEV (*yawning*): How's that?

LYUBOV ANDREYEVNA (*looks into her purse*): Yesterday I had a lot of money, and today there's hardly any left. My poor Varya tries to economize by feeding everyone milk soup, and in the kitchen the old people get nothing but dried peas, while I squander money foolishly. . . . (*Drops the purse, scattering gold coins.*) There they go. . . . (*Vexed.*)

YASHA: Allow me, I'll pick them up in an instant. (*Picks up the money.*)

LYUBOV ANDREYEVNA: Please do, Yasha. And why did I go to town for lunch? . . . That miserable restaurant of yours with its music, and tablecloths smelling of soap. . . . Why drink so much, Lyonya? Why eat so much? Why talk so much? Today in the restaurant again you talked too much, and it was all so pointless. About the seventies, about the decadents. And to whom? Talking to waiters about the decadents!

LOPAKHIN: Yes.

GAYEV (*waving his hand*): I'm incorrigible, that's evi-

Buckle: Thomas Henry Buckle (1821–1862) was a radical historian who formulated a scientific basis for history emphasizing the interrelationship of climate, food production, population, and wealth.

dent. . . . (*Irritably to Yasha.*) Why do you keep twirling about in front of me?

YASHA (*laughs*): I can't help laughing when I hear your voice.

GAYEV (*to his sister*): Either he or I —

LYUBOV ANDREYEVNA: Go away, Yasha, run along.

YASHA (*hands Lyubov Andreyevna her purse*): I'm going, right away. (*Hardly able to contain his laughter.*) This very instant. . . . (*Goes out.*)

LOPAKHIN: That rich man, Deriganov, is prepared to buy the estate. They say he's coming to the auction himself.

LYUBOV ANDREYEVNA: Where did you hear that?

LOPAKHIN: That's what they're saying in town.

LYUBOV ANDREYEVNA: Our aunt in Yaroslav promised to send us something, but when and how much, no one knows.

LOPAKHIN: How much do you think she'll send? A hundred thousand? Two hundred?

LYUBOV ANDREYEVNA: Oh . . . ten or fifteen thousand, and we'll be thankful for that.

LOPAKHIN: Forgive me, but I have never seen such frivolous, such queer, unbusinesslike people as you, my friends. You are told in plain language that your estate is to be sold, and it's as though you don't understand it.

ABOVE: The spare set in Ron Daniel's 1993 production of *The Cherry Orchard* at the American Repertory Theatre highlights the characters' emotional isolation. RIGHT: Claire Bloom as Madame Ranevskaya.

LYUBOV ANDREYEVNA: But what are we to do? Tell us what to do.

LOPAKHIN: I tell you every day. Every day I say the same thing. Both the cherry orchard and the land must be leased for summer cottages, and it must be done now, as quickly as possible — the auction is close at hand. Try to understand! Once you definitely decide on the cottages, you can raise as much money as you like, and then you are saved.

LYUBOV ANDREYEVNA: Cottages, summer people — forgive me, but it's so vulgar.

GAYEV: I agree with you, absolutely.

LOPAKHIN: I'll either burst into tears, start shouting, or fall into a faint! I can't stand it! You've worn me out! (*To Gayev.*) You're an old woman!

GAYEV: How's that?

LOPAKHIN: An old woman! (*Starts to go.*)

LYUBOV ANDREYEVNA (*alarmed*): No, don't go, stay, my dear. I beg you. Perhaps we'll think of something!

LOPAKHIN: What is there to think of?

LYUBOV ANDREYEVNA: Don't go away, please. With you here it's more cheerful somehow. . . . (*Pause.*) I keep expecting something to happen, like the house caving in on us.

GAYEV (*in deep thought*): Double rail shot into the corner. . . . Cross table to the center. . . .

LYUBOV ANDREYEVNA: We have sinned so much. . . .

LOPAKHIN: What sins could you have —

GAYEV (*puts a candy into his mouth*): They say I've eaten up my entire fortune in candies. . . . (*Laughs.*)

LYUBOV ANDREYEVNA: Oh, my sins. . . . I've always squandered money recklessly, like a madwoman, and I married a man who did nothing but amass debts. My husband died from champagne — he drank terribly — then, to my sorrow, I fell in love with another man, lived with him, and just at that time — that was my first punishment, a blow on the head — my little boy was drowned . . . here in the river. And I went abroad, went away for good, never to return, never to see this river. . . . I closed my eyes and ran, beside myself, and *he* after me . . . callously, without pity. I bought a villa near Mentone, because he fell ill there, and for three years I had no rest, day or night. The sick man wore me out, my soul dried up. Then last year, when the villa was sold to pay my debts, I went to Paris, and there he stripped me of everything, and left me for another woman; I tried to poison myself. . . . So stupid, so shameful. . . . And suddenly I felt a longing for Russia, for my own country, for my little girl. . . . (*Wipes away her tears.*) Lord, Lord, be merciful, forgive my sins! Don't punish me anymore! (*Takes a telegram out of her pocket.*) This came today from Paris. . . . He asks my forgiveness, begs me to return. . . . (*Tears up telegram.*) Do I hear music? (*Listens.*)

GAYEV: That's our famous Jewish band. You remember, four violins, a flute, and double bass.

LYUBOV ANDREYEVNA: It's still in existence? We ought to send for them sometime and give a party.

LOPAKHIN (*listens*): I don't hear anything. . . . (*Sings softly.*) "The Germans, for pay, will turn Russians into Frenchmen, they say." (*Laughs.*) What a play I saw yesterday at the theater — very funny!

LYUBOV ANDREYEVNA: There was probably nothing funny about it. Instead of going to see plays you ought to look at yourselves a little more often. How drab your lives are, how full of futile talk!

LOPAKHIN: That's true. I must say, this life of ours is stupid. . . . (*Pause.*) My father was a peasant, an idiot; he understood nothing, taught me nothing; all he did was beat me when he was drunk, and always with a stick. As a matter of fact, I'm as big a blockhead and idiot as he was. I never learned anything, my handwriting's disgusting, I write like a pig — I'm ashamed to have people see it.

LYUBOV ANDREYEVNA: You ought to get married, my friend.

LOPAKHIN: Yes . . . that's true.

LYUBOV ANDREYEVNA: To our Varya. She's a nice girl.

LOPAKHIN: Yes.

LYUBOV ANDREYEVNA: She's a girl who comes from simple people, works all day long, but the main thing is she loves you. Besides, you've liked her for a long time now.

LOPAKHIN: Well? I've nothing against it. . . . She's a good girl. (*Pause.*)

GAYEV: I've been offered a place in the bank. Six thousand a year. . . . Have you heard?

LYUBOV ANDREYEVNA: How could you! You stay where you are. . . .

(*Firs enters carrying an overcoat.*)

FIRS (*to Gayev*): If you please, sir, put this on, it's damp.

GAYEV (*puts on the overcoat*): You're a pest, old man.

FIRS: Never mind. . . . You went off this morning without telling me. (*Looks him over.*)

LYUBOV ANDREYEVNA: How you have aged, Firs!

FIRS: What do you wish, madam?

LOPAKHIN: She says you've grown very old!

FIRS: I've lived a long time. They were arranging a marriage for me before your papa was born. . . . (*Laughs.*) I was already head footman when the emancipation came. At that time I wouldn't consent to my freedom, I stayed with the masters. . . . (*Pause.*) I remember, everyone was happy, but what they were happy about, they themselves didn't know.

LOPAKHIN: It was better in the old days. At least they flogged them.

FIRS (*not hearing*): Of course. The peasants kept to the masters, the masters kept to the peasants; but now they have all gone their own ways, you can't tell about anything.

GAYEV: Be quiet, Firs. Tomorrow I must go to town. I've been promised an introduction to a certain general who might let us have a loan.

LOPAKHIN: Nothing will come of it. And you can rest assured, you won't even pay the interest.

LYUBOV ANDREYEVNA: He's raving. There is no such general.

(*Enter Trofimov, Anya, and Varya.*)

GAYEV: Here come our young people.

ANYA: There's Mama.

LYUBOV ANDREYEVNA (*tenderly*): Come, come along, my darlings. (*Embraces Anya and Varya.*) If you only knew how I love you both! Sit here beside me — there, like that.

(*They all sit down.*)

LOPAKHIN: Our eternal student is always with the young ladies.

TROFIMOV: That's none of your business.

LOPAKHIN: He'll soon be fifty, but he's still a student.

TROFIMOV: Drop your stupid jokes.

LOPAKHIN: What are you so angry about, you queer fellow?

TROFIMOV: Just leave me alone.

LOPAKHIN (*laughs*): Let me ask you something: What do you make of me?

TROFIMOV: My idea of you, Yermolai Alekseich, is this: You're a rich man, you will soon be a millionaire. Just as the beast of prey, which devours everything that crosses its path, is necessary in the metabolic process, so are you necessary.

(*Everyone laughs.*)

VARYA: Petya, you'd better tell us something about the planets.

LYUBOV ANDREYEVNA: No, let's go on with yesterday's conversation.

TROFIMOV: What was it about?

GAYEV: About the proud man.

TROFIMOV: We talked a long time yesterday, but we didn't get anywhere. In the proud man, in your sense of the word, there's something mystical. And you may be right from your point of view, but if you look at it simply, without being abstruse, why even talk about pride? Is there any sense in it if, physiologically, man is poorly constructed, if, in the vast majority of cases, he is coarse, ignorant, and profoundly unhappy? We should stop admiring ourselves. We should just work, and that's all.

GAYEV: You die, anyway.

TROFIMOV: Who knows? And what does it mean — to die? It may be that man has a hundred senses, and at his death only the five that are known to us perish, and the other ninety-five go on living.

LYUBOV ANDREYEVNA: How clever you are, Petya!

LOPAKHIN (*ironically*): Terribly clever!

TROFIMOV: Mankind goes forward, perfecting its powers. Everything that is now unattainable will some day be comprehensible and within our grasp, only we must work, and help with all our might those who are seeking the truth. So far, among us here in Russia, only a very few work. The great majority of the intelligentsia that I know seek nothing, do nothing, and as yet are incapable of work. They call themselves the intelligentsia, yet they belittle their servants, treat the peasants like animals, are wretched students, never read anything serious, and do absolutely nothing; they only talk about science and know very little about art. They all look serious, have grim expressions, speak of weighty matters, and philosophize; and meanwhile anyone can see that the workers eat abominably, sleep without pillows, thirty or forty to a room, and everywhere there are bedbugs, stench, dampness, and immorality. . . . It's obvious that all our fine talk is merely to delude ourselves and others. Show me the day nurseries they are always talking about — and where are the reading rooms? They only write about them in novels, but in reality they don't exist. There is nothing but filth, vulgarity, asiaticism.° . . . I'm afraid of those very serious countenances, I don't like them, I'm afraid of serious conversations. We'd do better to remain silent.

LOPAKHIN: You know, I get up before five in the morning, and I work from morning to night; now, I'm always handling money, my own and other people's, and I see what people around me are like. You have only to start doing something to find out how few honest, decent people there are. Sometimes, when I can't sleep, I think: "Lord, Thou gavest us vast forests, boundless fields, broad horizons, and living in their midst we ourselves ought truly to be giants. . . ."

LYUBOV ANDREYEVNA: Now you want giants! They're good only in fairy tales, otherwise they're frightening.

(*Yepikhodov crosses at the rear of the stage, playing the guitar.*)

LYUBOV ANDREYEVNA (*pensively*): There goes Yepikhodov . . .

ANYA (*pensively*): There goes Yepikhodov . . .

GAYEV: The sun has set, ladies and gentlemen.

TROFIMOV: Yes.

GAYEV (*in a low voice, as though reciting*): Oh, Nature, wondrous Nature, you shine with eternal radiance, beautiful and indifferent; you, whom we call mother, unite within yourself both life and death, giving life and taking it away. . . .

VARYA (*beseechingly*): Uncle dear!

ANYA: Uncle, you're doing it again!

TROFIMOV: You'd better cue ball into the center.

GAYEV: I'll be silent, silent.

(*All sit lost in thought. The silence is broken only by the subdued muttering of Firs. Suddenly a distant sound is heard, as if from the sky, like the sound of a snapped string mournfully dying away.*)

LYUBOV ANDREYEVNA: What was that?

LOPAKHIN: I don't know. Somewhere far off in a mine shaft a bucket's broken loose. But somewhere very far away.

GAYEV: It might be a bird of some sort . . . like a heron.

---

asiaticism: Trofimov, expressing a common prejudice of the time, refers to Asian apathy.

TROFIMOV: Or an owl . . .

LYUBOV ANDREYEVNA (*shudders*): It's unpleasant somehow. . . . (*Pause.*)

FIRS: The same thing happened before the troubles: An owl hooted and the samovar hissed continually.

GAYEV: Before what troubles?

FIRS: Before the emancipation.

LYUBOV ANDREYEVNA: Come along, my friends, let us go, evening is falling. (*To Anya.*) There are tears in your eyes — what is it, my little one?

(*Embraces her.*)

ANYA: It's all right, Mama. It's nothing.

TROFIMOV: Someone is coming.

(*A Stranger appears wearing a shabby white forage cap and an overcoat. He is slightly drunk.*)

STRANGER: Permit me to inquire, can I go straight through here to the station?

GAYEV: You can. Follow the road.

STRANGER: I am deeply grateful to you. (*Coughs.*) Splendid weather. . . . (*Reciting.*) "My brother, my suffering brother . . . come to the Volga, whose groans". . . (*To Varya.*) Mademoiselle, will you oblige a hungry Russian with thirty kopecks?

(*Varya, frightened, cries out.*)

LOPAKHIN (*angrily*): There's a limit to everything.

LYUBOV ANDREYEVNA (*panic-stricken*): Here you are — take this. . . . (*Fumbles in her purse.*) I have no silver. . . . Never mind, here's a gold piece for you. . . .

STRANGER: I am deeply grateful to you. (*Goes off.*)

(*Laughter.*)

VARYA (*frightened*): I'm leaving . . . I'm leaving. . . . Oh, Mama, dear, there's nothing in the house for the servants to eat, and you give him a gold piece!

LYUBOV ANDREYEVNA: What's to be done with such a silly creature? When we get home I'll give you all I've got. Yermolai Alekseyevich, you'll lend me some more!

LOPAKHIN: At your service.

LYUBOV ANDREYEVNA: Come, my friends, it's time to go. Oh, Varya, we have definitely made a match for you. Congratulations!

VARYA (*through tears*): Mama, that's not something to joke about.

LOPAKHIN: "Aurelia, get thee to a nunnery . . ."°

GAYEV: Look, my hands are trembling: It's a long time since I've played a game of billiards.

LOPAKHIN: "Aurelia, O Nymph, in thy orisons, be all my sins remember'd!"

LYUBOV ANDREYEVNA: Let us go, my friends, it will soon be suppertime.

"**Aurelia . . . nunnery**": From Hamlet's famous line rejecting Ophelia (Lopakhin's next line is also from Shakespeare's *Hamlet*).

VARYA: He frightened me. My heart is simply pounding.

LOPAKHIN: Let me remind you, ladies and gentlemen: On the twenty-second of August the cherry orchard is to be sold. Think about that! — Think!

(*All go out except Trofimov and Anya.*)

ANYA (*laughs*): My thanks to the stranger for frightening Varya, now we are alone.

TROFIMOV: Varya is so afraid we might suddenly fall in love with each other that she hasn't left us alone for days. With her narrow mind she can't understand that we are above love. To avoid the petty and the illusory, which prevent our being free and happy — that is the aim and meaning of life. Forward! We are moving irresistibly toward the bright star that burns in the distance! Forward! Do not fall behind, friends!

ANYA (*clasping her hands*): How well you talk! (*Pause.*) It's marvelous here today!

TROFIMOV: Yes, the weather is wonderful.

ANYA: What have you done to me, Petya, that I no longer love the cherry orchard as I used to? I loved it so tenderly, it seemed to me there was no better place on earth than our orchard.

TROFIMOV: All Russia is our orchard. It is a great and beautiful land, and there are many wonderful places in it. (*Pause.*) Just think, Anya: Your grandfather, your great-grandfather, and all your ancestors were serf-owners, possessors of living souls. Don't you see that from every cherry tree, from every leaf and trunk, human beings are peering out at you? Don't you hear their voices? To possess living souls — that has corrupted all of you, those who lived before and you who are living now, so that your mother, you, your uncle, no longer perceive that you are living in debt, at someone else's expense, at the expense of those whom you wouldn't allow to cross your threshold. . . . We are at least two hundred years behind the times, we have as yet absolutely nothing, we have no definite attitude toward the past, we only philosophize, complain of boredom, or drink vodka. Yet it's quite clear that to begin to live we must first atone for the past, be done with it, and we can atone for it only by suffering, only by extraordinary, unceasing labor. Understand this, Anya.

ANYA: The house we live in hasn't really been ours for a long time, and I shall leave it, I give you my word.

TROFIMOV: If you have the keys of the household, throw them into the well and go. Be as free as the wind.

ANYA (*in ecstasy*): How well you put that!

TROFIMOV: Believe me, Anya, believe me! I am not yet thirty, I am young, still a student, but I have already been through so much! As soon as winter comes, I am hungry, sick, worried, poor as a beggar, and — where has not fate driven me! Where have I not been? And yet always, every minute of the day and night, my soul was filled with inexplicable premonitions. I have a premonition of happiness, Anya, I can see it . . .

ANYA: The moon is rising.

(*Yepikhodov is heard playing the same melancholy song on the guitar. The moon rises. Somewhere near the poplars Varya is looking for Anya and calling: "Anya, where are you?"*)

TROFIMOV: Yes, the moon is rising. (*Pause.*) There it is — happiness . . . it's coming, nearer and nearer, I can hear its footsteps. And if we do not see it, if we do not recognize it, what does it matter? Others will see it.

VARYA'S VOICE: Anya! Where are you?

TROFIMOV: That Varya again! (*Angrily.*) It's revolting!

ANYA: Well? Let's go down to the river. It's lovely there.

TROFIMOV: Come on. (*They go.*)

VARYA'S VOICE: Anya! Anya!

ACT III

(*The drawing room, separated by an arch from the ballroom. The chandelier is lighted. The Jewish band that was mentioned in act II is heard playing in the hall. It is evening. In the ballroom they are dancing a grand rond. The voice of Semyonov-Pishchik: "Promenade à une paire!"° They all enter the drawing room: Pishchik and Charlotta Ivanovna are the first couple, Trofimov and Lyubov Andreyevna the second, Anya and the Post-Office Clerk the third, Varya and the Stationmaster the fourth, etc. Varya, quietly weeping, dries her tears as she dances. Dunyasha is in the last couple. As they cross the drawing room Pishchik calls: "Grand rond, balancez!" and "Les cavaliers à genoux et remercier vos dames!"° Firs, wearing a dress coat, brings in a tray with seltzer water. Pishchik and Trofimov come into the drawing room.*)

PISHCHIK: I'm a full-blooded man, I've already had two strokes, and dancing's hard work for me, but as they say, "If you run with the pack, you can bark or not, but at least wag your tail." At that, I'm as strong as a horse. My late father — quite a joker he was, God rest his soul — used to say, talking about our origins, that the ancient line of Semyonov-Pishchik was descended from the very horse that Caligula had seated in the Senate.° . . . (*Sits down.*) But the trouble is — no money! A hungry dog believes in nothing but meat. . . . (*Snores but wakes up at once.*) It's the same with me — I can think of nothing but money. . . .

TROFIMOV: You know, there really is something equine about your figure.

PISHCHIK: Well, a horse is a fine animal. . . . You can sell a horse.

(*There is the sound of a billiard game in the next room. Varya appears in the archway.*)

"*Promenade à une paire!*": French for "Walk in pairs!" "*Grand rond . . . dames!*": Instructions in the dance: "Large circle!" and "Gentlemen, kneel down and thank your ladies!" **Caligula . . . Senate:** Caligula (A.D. 12–41), a cavalry soldier, was Roman emperor (A.D. 37–41).

TROFIMOV (*teasing her*): Madame Lopakhina! Madame Lopakhina!

VARYA (*angrily*): Mangy gentleman!

TROFIMOV: Yes, I am a mangy gentleman, and proud of it!

VARYA (*reflecting bitterly*): Here we've hired musicians, and what are we going to pay them with? (*Goes out.*)

TROFIMOV (*to Pishchik*): If the energy you have expended in the course of your life trying to find money to pay interest had gone into something else, ultimately, you might very well have turned the world upside down.

PISHCHIK: Nietzsche . . . the philosopher . . . the greatest, most renowned . . . a man of tremendous intellect . . . says in his works that it is possible to forge banknotes.

TROFIMOV: And have you read Nietzsche?

PISHCHIK: Well . . . Dashenka told me. I'm in such a state now that I'm just about ready for forging. . . . The day after tomorrow I have to pay three hundred and ten rubles . . . I've got a hundred and thirty. . . . (*Feels in his pocket, grows alarmed.*) The money is gone! I've lost the money! (*Tearfully.*) Where is my money? (*Joyfully.*) Here it is, inside the lining. . . . I'm all in a sweat. . . .

(*Lyubov Andreyevna and Charlotta Ivanovna come in.*)

LYUBOV ANDREYEVNA (*humming a* Lezginka):° Why does Leonid take so long? What is he doing in town? (*To Dunyasha.*) Dunyasha, offer the musicians some tea.

TROFIMOV: In all probability, the auction didn't take place.

LYUBOV ANDREYEVNA: It was the wrong time to have the musicians, the wrong time to give a dance. . . . Well, never mind. . . . (*Sits down and hums softly.*)

CHARLOTTA (*gives Pishchik a deck of cards*): Here's a deck of cards for you. Think of a card.

PISHCHIK: I've thought of one.

CHARLOTTA: Now shuffle the pack. Very good. And now, my dear Mr. Pishchik, hand it to me. *Ein, zwei, drei!*° Now look for it — it's in your side pocket.

PISHCHIK (*takes the card out of his side pocket*): The eight of spades — absolutely right! (*Amazed.*) Think of that, now!

CHARLOTTA (*holding the deck of cards in the palm of her hand, to Trofimov*): Quickly, tell me, which card is on top?

TROFIMOV: What? Well, the queen of spades.

CHARLOTTA: Right! (*To Pishchik.*) Now which card is on top?

PISHCHIK: The ace of hearts.

CHARLOTTA: Right! (*Claps her hands and the deck of cards disappears.*) What lovely weather we're having today! (*A mysterious feminine voice, which seems to come from under the floor, answers her: "Oh, yes,*

Lezginka: A lively Russian tune for a dance.   ***Ein, zwei, drei!*:** "One, two, three" (German).

splendid weather, madam.") You are so nice, you're my ideal. . . . (*The voice: "And I'm very fond of you, too, madam.*")

STATIONMASTER (*applauding*): Bravo, Madame Ventriloquist!

PISHCHIK (*amazed*): Think of that, now! Most enchanting Charlotta Ivanovna . . . I am simply in love with you. . . .

CHARLOTTA: In love? (*Shrugs her shoulders.*) Is it possible that you can love? *Guter Mensch, aber schlechter Musikant.*°

TROFIMOV (*claps Pishchik on the shoulder*): You old horse, you!

CHARLOTTA: Attention, please! One more trick. (*Takes a lap robe from a chair.*) Here's a very fine lap robe; I should like to sell it. (*Shakes it out.*) Doesn't anyone want to buy it?

PISHCHIK (*amazed*): Think of that, now!

CHARLOTTA: *Ein, zwei, drei!* (*Quickly raises the lap robe, behind it stands Anya, who curtsies, runs to her mother, embraces her, and runs back into the ballroom amid the general enthusiasm.*)

LYUBOV ANDREYEVNA (*applauding*): Bravo, bravo!

CHARLOTTA: Once again! *Ein, zwei, drei.* (*Raises the lap robe; behind it stands Varya, who bows.*)

PISHCHIK (*amazed*): Think of that, now!

CHARLOTTA: The end! (*Throws the robe at Pishchik, makes a curtsy, and runs out of the room.*)

PISHCHIK (*hurries after her*): The minx! . . . What a woman! What a woman! (*Goes out.*)

LYUBOV ANDREYEVNA: And Leonid still not here. What he is doing in town so long, I do not understand! It must be all over by now. Either the estate is sold, or the auction didn't take place — but why keep us in suspense so long!

VARYA (*trying to comfort her*): Uncle has bought it, I am certain of that.

TROFIMOV (*mockingly*): Yes.

VARYA: Great-aunt sent him power of attorney to buy it in her name and transfer the debt. She's doing it for Anya's sake. And I am sure, with God's help, Uncle will buy it.

LYUBOV ANDREYEVNA: Our great-aunt in Yaroslav sent fifteen thousand to buy the estate in her name — she doesn't trust us — but that's not even enough to pay the interest. (*Covers her face with her hands.*) Today my fate will be decided, my fate . . .

TROFIMOV (*teasing Varya*): Madame Lopakhina!

VARYA (*angrily*): Eternal student! Twice already you've been expelled from the university.

LYUBOV ANDREYEVNA: Why are you so cross, Varya? If he teases you about Lopakhin, what of it? Go ahead and marry Lopakhin if you want to. He's a nice man, he's interesting. And if you don't want to, don't. Nobody's forcing you, my pet.

Guter Mensch, aber schlechter Musikant: "Good man, but poor musician" (German).

VARYA: To be frank, Mama dear, I regard this matter seriously. He is a good man, I like him.

LYUBOV ANDREYEVNA: Then marry him. I don't know what you're waiting for!

VARYA: Mama, I can't propose to him myself. For the last two years everyone's been talking to me about him; everyone talks, but he is either silent or he jokes. I understand. He's getting rich, he's absorbed in business, he has no time for me. If I had some money, no matter how little, if it were only a hundred rubles, I'd drop everything and go far away. I'd go into a nunnery.

TROFIMOV: A blessing!

VARYA (*to Trofimov*): A student ought to be intelligent! (*In a gentle tone, tearfully.*) How homely you have grown, Petya, how old! (*To Lyubov Andreyevna, no longer crying.*) It's just that I cannot live without work, Mama. I must be doing something every minute.

(*Yasha enters.*)

YASHA (*barely able to suppress his laughter*): Yepikhodov has broken a billiard cue! (*Goes out.*)

VARYA: But why is Yepikhodov here? Who gave him permission to play billiards? I don't understand these people. . . . (*Goes out.*)

LYUBOV ANDREYEVNA: Don't tease her, Petya. You can see she's unhappy enough without that.

TROFIMOV: She's much too zealous, always meddling in other people's affairs. All summer long she's given Anya and me no peace — afraid a romance might develop. What business is it of hers? Besides, I've given no occasion for it, I am far removed from such banality. We are above love!

LYUBOV ANDREYEVNA: And I suppose I am beneath love. (*In great agitation.*) Why isn't Leonid here? If only I knew whether the estate had been sold or not! The disaster seems to me so incredible that I don't even know what to think, I'm lost. . . . I could scream this very instant . . . I could do something foolish. Save me, Petya. Talk to me, say something. . . .

TROFIMOV: Whether or not the estate is sold today — does it really matter? That's all done with long ago; there's no turning back, the path is overgrown. Be calm, my dear. One must not deceive oneself; at least once in one's life one ought to look the truth straight in the eye.

LYUBOV ANDREYEVNA: What truth? You can see where there is truth and where there isn't, but I seem to have lost my sight, I see nothing. You boldly settle all the important problems, but tell me, my dear boy, isn't it because you are young and have not yet had to suffer for a single one of your problems? You boldly look ahead, but isn't it because you neither see nor expect anything dreadful, since life is still hidden from your young eyes? You're bolder, more honest, deeper than we are, but think about it, be just a little bit magnanimous, and spare me. You see, I was born here, my mother and father lived here, and my grandfather. I love this house, without the cherry orchard my life has no meaning for me, and if it must be sold, then sell me with the orchard. . . . (*Embraces Trofimov and kisses him on the forehead.*) And my son was drowned here. . . . (*Weeps.*) Have pity on me, you good, kind man.

TROFIMOV: You know I feel for you with all my heart.

LYUBOV ANDREYEVNA: But that should have been said differently, quite differently. . . . (*Takes out her handkerchief and a telegram falls to the floor.*) My heart is heavy today, you can't imagine. It's so noisy here, my soul quivers at every sound, I tremble all over, and yet I can't go to my room. When I am alone the silence frightens me. Don't condemn me, Petya . . . I love you as if you were my own. I would gladly let you marry Anya, I swear it, only you must study, my dear, you must get your degree. You do nothing, fate simply tosses you from place to place — it's so strange. . . . Isn't that true? Isn't it? And you must do something about your beard, to make it grow somehow. . . . (*Laughs.*) You're so funny!

TROFIMOV (*picks up the telegram*): I have no desire to be an Adonis.°

LYUBOV ANDREYEVNA: That's a telegram from Paris. I get them every day. One yesterday, one today. That wild man has fallen ill again, he's in trouble again. . . . He begs my forgiveness, implores me to come, and really, I ought to go to Paris to be near him. Your face is stern, Petya, but what can one do, my dear? What am I to do? He is ill, he's alone and unhappy, and who will look after him there, who will keep him from making mistakes, who will give him his medicine on time? And why hide it or keep silent, I love him, that's clear. I love him, love him. . . . It's a millstone round my neck, I'm sinking to the bottom with it, but I love that stone, I cannot live without it. (*Presses Trofimov's hand.*) Don't think badly of me, Petya, and don't say anything to me, don't say anything. . . .

TROFIMOV (*through tears*): For God's sake, forgive my frankness: You know that he robbed you!

LYUBOV ANDREYEVNA: No, no, no, you mustn't say such things! (*Covers her ears.*)

TROFIMOV: But he's a scoundrel! You're the only one who doesn't know it! He's a petty scoundrel, a nonentity —

LYUBOV ANDREYEVNA (*angry, but controlling herself*): You are twenty-six or twenty-seven years old, but you're still a schoolboy!

TROFIMOV: That may be!

LYUBOV ANDREYEVNA: You should be a man, at your age you ought to understand those who love. And you ought to be in love yourself. (*Angrily.*) Yes, yes! It's not purity with you, it's simply prudery, you're a ridiculous crank, a freak —

TROFIMOV (*horrified*): What is she saying!

LYUBOV ANDREYEVNA: I am above love! You're not above love, you're just an addlepate, as Firs would say. Not to have a mistress at your age!

TROFIMOV (*in horror*): This is awful! What is she saying! . . . (*Goes quickly toward the ballroom.*) This is awful . . . I can't . . . I won't stay here. . . . (*Goes out, but immediately returns.*) All is over between us! (*Goes out to the hall.*)

LYUBOV ANDREYEVNA (*calls after him*): Petya, wait! You absurd creature, I was joking! Petya!

(*In the hall there is the sound of someone running quickly downstairs and suddenly falling with a crash. Anya and Varya scream, but a moment later laughter is heard.*)

LYUBOV ANDREYEVNA: What was that?

(*Anya runs in.*)

ANYA (*laughing*): Petya fell down the stairs! (*Runs out.*)

LYUBOV ANDREYEVNA: What a funny boy that Petya is!

(*The Stationmaster stands in the middle of the ballroom and recites A. Tolstoy's° "The Sinner." Everyone listens to him, but he has no sooner spoken a few lines than the sound of a waltz is heard from the hall and the recitation is broken off. They all dance. Trofimov, Anya, Varya, and Lyubov Andreyevna come in from the hall.*)

LYUBOV ANDREYEVNA: Come, Petya . . . come, you pure soul . . . please, forgive me. . . . Let's dance. . . . (*They dance.*)

(*Anya and Varya dance. Firs comes in, puts his stick by the side door. Yasha also comes into the drawing room and watches the dancers.*)

YASHA: What is it, grandpa?

FIRS: I don't feel well. In the old days, we used to have generals, barons, admirals, dancing at our balls, but now we send for the post office clerk and the stationmaster, and even they are none too eager to come. Somehow I've grown weak. The late master, their grandfather, dosed everyone with sealing wax, no matter what ailed them. I've been taking sealing wax every day for twenty years or more, maybe that's what's kept me alive.

YASHA: You bore me, grandpa. (*Yawns.*) High time you croaked.

FIRS: Ah, you . . . addlepate! (*Mumbles.*)

(*Trofimov and Lyubov Andreyevna dance from the ballroom into the drawing room.*)

LYUBOV ANDREYEVNA: *Merci.* I'll sit down a while. (*Sits.*) I'm tired.

(*Anya comes in.*)

ANYA (*excitedly*): There was a man in the kitchen just now saying that the cherry orchard was sold today.

Adonis: From Greek myth, a beautiful young man.

A. Tolstoy: Aleksey Konstantinovich Tolstoy (1817–1875), Russian novelist, dramatist, and poet.

LYUBOV ANDREYEVNA: Sold to whom?

ANYA: He didn't say. He's gone. (*Dances with Trofimov; they go into the ballroom.*)

YASHA: That was just some old man babbling. A stranger.

FIRS: Leonid Andreich is not back yet, still hasn't come. And he's wearing the light, between-seasons overcoat; like enough he'll catch cold. Ah, when they're young they're green.

LYUBOV ANDREYEVNA: This is killing me. Yasha, go and find out who it was sold to.

YASHA: But that old man left long ago. (*Laughs.*)

LYUBOV ANDREYEVNA (*slightly annoyed*): Well, what are you laughing at? What are you so happy about?

YASHA: That Yepikhodov is very funny! Hopeless! Two-and-twenty Troubles.

LYUBOV ANDREYEVNA: Firs, if the estate is sold, where will you go?

FIRS: Wherever you tell me to go, I'll go.

LYUBOV ANDREYEVNA: Why do you look like that? Aren't you well? You ought to go to bed.

FIRS: Yes. . . . (*With a smirk.*) Go to bed, and without me who will serve, who will see to things? I'm the only one in the whole house.

YASHA (*to Lyubov Andreyevna*): Lyubov Andreyevna! Permit me to make a request, be so kind! If you go back to Paris again, do me the favor of taking me with you. It is positively impossible for me to stay here. (*Looking around, then in a low voice.*) There's no need to say it, you can see for yourself, it's an uncivilized country, the people have no morals, and the boredom! The food they give us in the kitchen is unmentionable, and besides, there's this Firs who keeps walking about mumbling all sorts of inappropriate things. Take me with you, be so kind!

(*Enter Pishchik.*)

PISHCHIK: May I have the pleasure of a waltz with you, fairest lady? (*Lyubov Andreyevna goes with him.*) I really must borrow a hundred and eighty rubles from you, my charmer . . . I really must. . . . (*Dancing.*) Just a hundred and eighty rubles. . . . (*They pass into the ballroom.*)

YASHA (*softly sings*): "Wilt thou know my soul's unrest . . ."

(*In the ballroom a figure in a gray top hat and checked trousers is jumping about, waving its arms; there are shouts of "Bravo, Charlotta Ivanovna!"*)

DUNYASHA (*stopping to powder her face*): The young mistress told me to dance — there are lots of gentlemen and not enough ladies — but dancing makes me dizzy, and my heart begins to thump. Firs Nikolayevich, the post office clerk just said something to me that took my breath away.

(*The music grows more subdued.*)

FIRS: What did he say to you?

DUNYASHA: "You," he said, "are like a flower."

YASHA (*yawns*): What ignorance. . . . (*Goes out.*)

DUNYASHA: Like a flower. . . . I'm such a delicate girl, I just adore tender words.

FIRS: You'll get your head turned.

(*Enter Yepikhodov.*)

YEPIKHODOV: Avdotya Fyodorovna, you are not desirous of seeing me. . . . I might almost be some sort of insect. (*Sighs.*) Ah, life!

DUNYASHA: What is it you want?

YEPIKHODOV: Indubitably, you may be right. (*Sighs.*) But, of course, if one looks at it from a point of view, then, if I may so express myself, and you will forgive my frankness, you have completely reduced me to a state of mind. I know my fate, every day some misfortune befalls me, but I have long since grown accustomed to that; I look upon my fate with a smile. But you gave me your word, and although I —

DUNYASHA: Please, we'll talk about it later, but leave me in peace now. Just now I'm dreaming. . . . (*Plays with her fan.*)

YEPIKHODOV: Every day a misfortune, and yet, if I may so express myself, I merely smile, I even laugh.

(*Varya enters from the ballroom.*)

VARYA: Are you still here, Semyon? What a disrespectful man you are, really! (*To Dunyasha.*) Run along, Dunyasha. (*To Yepikhodov.*) First you play billiards and break a cue, then you wander about the drawing room as though you were a guest.

YEPIKHODOV: You cannot, if I may so express myself, penalize me.

VARYA: I am not penalizing you, I'm telling you. You do nothing but wander from one place to another, and you don't do your work. We keep a clerk, but for what, I don't know.

YEPIKHODOV (*offended*): Whether I work, or wander about, or eat, or play billiards, these are matters to be discussed only by persons of discernment, and my elders.

VARYA: You dare say that to me! (*Flaring up.*) You dare? You mean to say I have no discernment? Get out of here! This instant!

YEPIKHODOV (*intimidated*): I beg you to express yourself in a more delicate manner.

VARYA (*beside herself*): Get out, this very instant! Get out! (*He goes to the door, she follows him.*) Two-and-twenty Troubles! Don't let me set eyes on you again!

YEPIKHODOV (*goes out, his voice is heard behind the door*): I shall lodge a complaint against you!

VARYA: Oh, you're coming back? (*Seizes the stick left near the door by Firs.*) Come, come on. . . . Come, I'll show you. . . . Ah, so you're coming, are you? Then take that — (*Swings the stick just as Lopakhin enters.*)

LOPAKHIN: Thank you kindly.

VARYA (*angrily and mockingly*): I beg your pardon.

LOPAKHIN: Not at all. I humbly thank you for your charming reception.

VARYA: Don't mention it. (*Walks away, then looks back and gently asks.*) I didn't hurt you, did I?

LOPAKHIN: No, it's nothing. A huge bump coming up, that's all.

(*Voices in the ballroom: "Lopakhin has come! Yermolai Alekseich!" Pishchik enters.*)

PISHCHIK: As I live and breathe! (*Kisses Lopakhin.*) There is a whiff of cognac about you, dear soul. And we've been making merry here, too.

(*Enter Lyubov Andreyevna.*)

LYUBOV ANDREYEVNA: Is that you, Yermolai Alekseich? What kept you so long? Where's Leonid?

LOPAKHIN: Leonid Andreich arrived with me, he's coming . . .

LYUBOV ANDREYEVNA (*agitated*): Well, what happened? Did the sale take place? Tell me!

LOPAKHIN (*embarrassed, fearing to reveal his joy*): The auction was over by four o'clock. . . . We missed the train, had to wait till half past nine. (*Sighing heavily.*) Ugh! My head is swimming. . . .

(*Enter Gayev; he carries his purchases in one hand and wipes away his tears with the other.*)

LYUBOV ANDREYEVNA: Lyonya, what happened? Well, Lyonya? (*Impatiently, through tears.*) Be quick, for God's sake!

GAYEV (*not answering her, simply waves his hand. To Firs, weeping*): Here, take these. . . . There's anchovies, Kerch herrings. . . . I haven't eaten anything all day. . . . What I have been through! (*The click of billiard balls is heard through the open door to the billiard room, and Yasha's voice: "Seven and eighteen!" Gayev's expression changes, he is no longer weeping.*) I'm terribly tired. Firs, help me change. (*Goes through the ballroom to his own room, followed by Firs.*)

PISHCHIK: What happened at the auction? Come on, tell us!

LYUBOV ANDREYEVNA: Is the cherry orchard sold?

LOPAKHIN: It's sold.

LYUBOV ANDREYEVNA: Who bought it?

LOPAKHIN: I bought it. (*Pause.*)

(*Lyubov Andreyevna is overcome; she would fall to the floor if it were not for the chair and table near which she stands. Varya takes the keys from her belt and throws them on the floor in the middle of the drawing room and goes out.*)

LOPAKHIN: I bought it! Kindly wait a moment, ladies and gentlemen, my head is swimming. I can't talk. . . . (*Laughs.*) We arrived at the auction, Deriganov was already there. Leonid Andreich had only fifteen thousand, and straight off Deriganov bid thirty thousand over and above the mortgage. I saw how the land lay, so I got into the fight and bid forty. He bid forty-five. I bid fifty-five. In other words, he kept raising it by five thousand, and I by ten. Well, it

finally came to an end. I bid ninety thousand above the mortgage, and it was knocked down to me. The cherry orchard is now mine! Mine! (*Laughs uproariously.*) Lord! God in heaven! The cherry orchard is mine! Tell me I'm drunk, out of my mind, that I imagine it. . . . (*Stamps his feet.*) Don't laugh at me! If my father and my grandfather could only rise from their graves and see all that has happened, how their Yermolai, their beaten, half-literate Yermolai, who used to run about barefoot in winter, how that same Yermolai has bought an estate, the most beautiful estate in the whole world! I bought the estate where my father and grandfather were slaves, where they weren't even allowed in the kitchen. I'm asleep, this is just some dream of mine, it only seems to be. . . . It's the fruit of your imagination, hidden in the darkness of uncertainty. . . . (*Picks up the keys, smiling tenderly.*) She threw down the keys, wants to show that she's not mistress here anymore. . . . (*Jingles the keys.*) Well, no matter. (*The orchestra is heard tuning up.*) Hey, musicians, play, I want to hear you! Come on, everybody, and see how Yermolai Lopakhin will lay the ax to the cherry orchard, how the trees will fall to the ground! We're going to build summer cottages and our grandsons and great-grandsons will see a new life here. . . . Music! Strike up!

(*The orchestra plays. Lyubov Andreyevna sinks into a chair and weeps bitterly.*)

LOPAKHIN (*reproachfully*): Why didn't you listen to me, why? My poor friend, there's no turning back now. (*With tears.*) Oh, if only all this could be over quickly, if somehow our discordant, unhappy life could be changed!

PISHCHIK (*takes him by the arm; speaks in an undertone*): She's crying. Let's go into the ballroom, let her be alone. . . . Come on. . . . (*Leads him into the ballroom.*)

LOPAKHIN: What's happened? Musicians, play so I can hear you! Let everything be as I want it! (*Ironically.*) Here comes the new master, owner of the cherry orchard! (*Accidentally bumps into a little table, almost upsetting the candelabrum.*) I can pay for everything! (*Goes out with Pishchik.*)

(*There is no one left in either the drawing room or the ballroom except Lyubov Andreyevna, who sits huddled up and weeping bitterly. The music plays softly. Anya and Trofimov enter hurriedly. Anya goes to her mother and kneels before her. Trofimov remains in the doorway of the ballroom.*)

ANYA: Mama! . . . Mama, you're crying! Dear, kind, good Mama, my beautiful one, I love you . . . I bless you. The cherry orchard is sold, it's gone, that's true, true, but don't cry, Mama, life is still before you, you still have your good, pure soul. . . . Come with me, come, darling, we'll go away from here! . . . We'll plant a new orchard, more luxuriant than this one. You will see it and understand; and joy, quiet, deep joy, will sink into your soul, like the evening sun, and you will smile, Mama! Come, darling, let us go. . . .

ACT IV

(*The scene is the same as act I. There are neither curtains on the windows nor pictures on the walls, and only a little furniture piled up in one corner, as if for sale. There is a sense of emptiness. Near the outer door, at the rear of the stage, suitcases, traveling bags, etc., are piled up. Through the open door on the left the voices of Varya and Anya can be heard. Lopakhin stands waiting. Yasha is holding a tray with little glasses of champagne. In the hall, Yepikhodov is tying up a box. Offstage, at the rear, there is a hum of voices. It is the peasants who have come to say good-bye. Gayev's voice: "Thanks, brothers, thank you."*)*

YASHA: The peasants have come to say good-bye. In my opinion, Yermolai Alekseich, peasants are good-natured, but they don't know much.

(*The hum subsides. Lyubov Andreyevna enters from the hall with Gayev. She is not crying, but she is pale, her face twitches, and she cannot speak.*)

GAYEV: You gave them your purse, Lyuba. That won't do! That won't do!

LYUBOV ANDREYEVNA: I couldn't help it! I couldn't help it! (*They both go out.*)

LOPAKHIN (*in the doorway, calls after them*): Please, do me the honor of having a little glass at parting. I didn't think of bringing champagne from town, and at the station I found only one bottle. Please! What's the matter, friends, don't you want any? (*Walks away from the door.*) If I'd known that, I wouldn't have bought it. Well, then I won't drink any either. (*Yasha carefully sets the tray down on a chair.*) At least you have a glass, Yasha.

YASHA: To those who are departing! Good luck! (*Drinks.*) This champagne is not the real stuff, I can assure you.

LOPAKHIN: Eight rubles a bottle. (*Pause.*) It's devilish cold in here.

YASHA: They didn't light the stoves today; it doesn't matter, since we're leaving. (*Laughs.*)

LOPAKHIN: Why are you laughing?

YASHA: Because I'm pleased.

LOPAKHIN: It's October, yet it's sunny and still outside, like summer. Good for building. (*Looks at his watch, then calls through the door.*) Bear in mind, ladies and gentlemen, only forty-six minutes till train time! That means leaving for the station in twenty minutes. Better hurry up!

(*Trofimov enters from outside wearing an overcoat.*)

TROFIMOV: Seems to me it's time to start. The carriages are at the door. What the devil has become of my rubbers? They're lost. (*Calls through the door.*) Anya, my rubbers are not here. I can't find them.

LOPAKHIN: I've got to go to Kharkov. I'm taking the same train you are. I'm going to spend the winter in Kharkov. I've been hanging around here with you, and I'm sick and tired of loafing. I can't live without work, I don't know what to do with my hands; they dangle in some strange way, as if they didn't belong to me.

TROFIMOV: We'll soon be gone, then you can take up your useful labors again.

LOPAKHIN: Here, have a little drink.

TROFIMOV: No, I don't want any.

LOPAKHIN: So you're off for Moscow?

TROFIMOV: Yes, I'll see them into town, and tomorrow I'll go to Moscow.

LOPAKHIN: Yes. . . . Well, I expect the professors haven't been giving any lectures: They're waiting for you to come!

TROFIMOV: That's none of your business.

LOPAKHIN: How many years is it you've been studying at the university?

TROFIMOV: Can't you think of something new? That's stale and flat. (*Looks for his rubbers.*) You know we'll probably never see each other again, so allow me to give you one piece of advice at parting: Don't wave your arms about! Get out of that habit — of arm-waving. And another thing, building cottages and counting on the summer residents in time becoming independent farmers — that's just another form of arm-waving. Well, when all's said and done, I'm fond of you anyway. You have fine, delicate fingers, like an artist; you have a fine delicate soul.

LOPAKHIN (*embraces him*): Good-bye, my dear fellow. Thank you for everything. Let me give you some money for the journey, if you need it.

TROFIMOV: What for? I don't need it.

LOPAKHIN: But you haven't any!

TROFIMOV: I have. Thank you. I got some money for a translation. Here it is in my pocket. (*Anxiously.*) But where are my rubbers?

VARYA (*from the next room*): Here, take the nasty things! (*Flings a pair of rubbers onto the stage.*)

TROFIMOV: What are you so cross about, Varya? Hm. . . . But these are not my rubbers.

LOPAKHIN: In the spring I sowed three thousand acres of poppies, and now I've made forty thousand rubles clear. And when my poppies were in bloom, what a picture it was! So, I'm telling you, I've made forty thousand, which means I'm offering you a loan because I can afford to. Why turn up your nose? I'm a peasant — I speak bluntly.

TROFIMOV: Your father was a peasant, mine was a pharmacist — which proves absolutely nothing. (*Lopakhin takes out his wallet.*) No, don't — even if you gave me two hundred thousand I wouldn't take it. I'm a free man. And everything that is valued so highly and held so dear by all of you, rich and poor alike, has not the slightest power over me — it's like a feather floating in the air. I can get along without you, I can pass you by, I'm strong and proud.

Mankind is advancing toward the highest truth, the highest happiness attainable on earth, and I am in the front ranks!

LOPAKHIN: Will you get there?

TROFIMOV: I'll get there. (*Pause.*) I'll either get there or I'll show others the way to get there.

(*The sound of axes chopping down trees is heard in the distance.*)

LOPAKHIN: Well, good-bye, my dear fellow. It's time to go. We turn up our noses at one another, but life goes on just the same. When I work for a long time without stopping, my mind is easier, and it seems to me that I, too, know why I exist. But how many there are in Russia, brother, who exist nobody knows why. Well, it doesn't matter, that's not what makes the wheels go round. They say Leonid Andreich has taken a position in the bank, six thousand a year. . . . Only, of course, he won't stick it out, he's too lazy. . . .

ANYA (*in the doorway*): Mama asks you not to start cutting down the cherry orchard until she's gone.

TROFIMOV: Yes, really, not to have had the tact . . . (*Goes out through the hall.*)

LOPAKHIN: Right away, right away. . . . Ach, what people. . . . (*Follows Trofimov out.*)

ANYA: Has Firs been taken to the hospital?

YASHA: I told them this morning. They must have taken him.

ANYA (*to Yepikhodov, who is crossing the room*): Semyon Panteleich, please find out if Firs has been taken to the hospital.

YASHA (*offended*): I told Yegor this morning. Why ask a dozen times?

YEPIKHODOV: It is my conclusive opinion that the venerable Firs is beyond repair; it's time he was gathered to his fathers. And I can only envy him. (*Puts a suitcase down on a hatbox and crushes it.*) There you are! Of course! I knew it! (*Goes out.*)

YASHA (*mockingly*): Two-and-twenty Troubles!

VARYA (*through the door*): Has Firs been taken to the hospital?

ANYA: Yes, he has.

VARYA: Then why didn't they take the letter to the doctor?

ANYA: We must send it on after them. . . . (*Goes out.*)

VARYA (*from the adjoining room*): Where is Yasha? Tell him his mother has come to say good-bye to him.

YASHA (*waves his hand*): They really try my patience.

(*Dunyasha has been fussing with the luggage; now that Yasha is alone she goes up to him.*)

DUNYASHA: You might give me one little look, Yasha. You're going away . . . leaving me. . . . (*Cries and throws herself on his neck.*)

YASHA: What's there to cry about? (*Drinks champagne.*) In six days I'll be in Paris again. Tomorrow we'll take the express, off we go, and that's the last you'll see of us. I can hardly believe it. *Vive la France!* This place is not for me, I can't live here. . . . It can't be helped.

I've had enough of this ignorance — I'm fed up with it. (*Drinks champagne.*) What are you crying for? Behave yourself properly, then you won't cry.

DUNYASHA (*looks into a small mirror and powders her face*): Send me a letter from Paris. You know, I loved you, Yasha, how I loved you! I'm such a tender creature, Yasha!

YASHA: Here they come. (*Busies himself with the luggage, humming softly.*)

(*Enter Lyubov Andreyevna, Gayev, Charlotta Ivanovna.*)

GAYEV: We ought to be leaving. There's not much time now. (*Looks at Yasha.*) Who smells of herring?

LYUBOV ANDREYEVNA: In about ten minutes we should be getting into the carriages. (*Glances around the room.*) Good-bye, dear house, old grandfather. Winter will pass, spring will come, and you will no longer be here, they will tear you down. How much these walls have seen! (*Kisses her daughter warmly.*) My treasure, you are radiant, your eyes are sparkling like two diamonds. Are you glad? Very?

ANYA: Very! A new life is beginning, Mama!

GAYEV (*cheerfully*): Yes, indeed, everything is all right now. Before the cherry orchard was sold we were all worried and miserable, but afterward, when the question was finally settled once and for all, everybody calmed down and felt quite cheerful. . . . I'm in a bank now, a financier . . . cue ball into the center . . . and you, Lyuba, say what you like, you look better, no doubt about it.

LYUBOV ANDREYEVNA: Yes. My nerves are better, that's true. (*Her hat and coat are handed to her.*) I sleep well. Carry out my things, Yasha, it's time. (*To Anya.*) My little girl, we shall see each other soon. . . . I shall go to Paris and live there on the money your great-aunt sent to buy the estate — long live Auntie! — but that money won't last long.

ANYA: You'll come back soon, Mama, soon . . . won't you? I'll study hard and pass my high school examinations, and then I can work and help you. We'll read all sorts of books together, Mama. . . . Won't we? (*Kisses her mother's hand.*) We'll read in the autumn evenings, we'll read lots of books, and a new and wonderful world will open up before us. . . . (*Dreaming.*) Mama, come back. . . .

LYUBOV ANDREYEVNA: I'll come, my precious. (*Embraces her.*)

(*Enter Lopakhin, Charlotta Ivanovna is softly humming a song.*)

GAYEV: Happy Charlotta: She's singing!

CHARLOTTA (*picks up a bundle and holds it like a baby in swaddling clothes*): Bye, baby, bye. . . . (*A baby's crying is heard, "Wah! Wah!"*) Be quiet, my darling, my dear little boy. (*"Wah! Wah!"*) I'm so sorry for you! (*Throws the bundle down.*) You will find me a position, won't you? I can't go on like this.

LOPAKHIN: We'll find something, Charlotta Ivanovna, don't worry.

GAYEV: Everyone is leaving us, Varya's going away . . . all of a sudden nobody needs us.

CHARLOTTA: I have nowhere to go in town. I must go away. (*Hums.*) It doesn't matter . . .

(*Enter Pishchik.*)

LOPAKHIN: Nature's wonder!

PISHCHIK (*panting*): Ugh! Let me catch my breath. . . . I'm exhausted. . . . My esteemed friends. . . . Give me some water. . . .

GAYEV: After money, I suppose? Excuse me, I'm fleeing from temptation. . . . (*Goes out.*)

PISHCHIK: It's a long time since I've been to see you . . . fairest lady. . . . (*To Lopakhin*) So you're here. . . . Glad to see you, you intellectual giant. . . . Here . . . take it . . . four hundred rubles . . . I still owe you eight hundred and forty . . .

LOPAKHIN (*shrugs his shoulders in bewilderment*): I must be dreaming. . . . Where did you get it?

PISHCHIK: Wait . . . I'm hot. . . . A most extraordinary event. Some Englishmen came to my place and discovered some kind of white clay on my land. (*To Lyubov Andreyevna*) And four hundred for you . . . fairest, most wonderful lady. . . . (*Hands her the money.*) The rest later. (*Takes a drink of water.*) Just now a young man in the train was saying that a certain . . . great philosopher recommends jumping off roofs. . . . "Jump!" he says, and therein lies the whole problem. (*In amazement.*) Think of that, now! . . . Water!

LOPAKHIN: Who were those Englishmen?

PISHCHIK: I leased them the tract of land with the clay on it for twenty-four years. . . . And now, excuse me, I have no time . . . I must be trotting along . . . I'm going to Znoikov's . . . to Kardamanov's . . . I owe everybody. (*Drinks.*) Keep well . . . I'll drop in on Thursday . . .

LYUBOV ANDREYEVNA: We're just moving into town, and tomorrow I go abroad . . .

PISHCHIK: What? (*Alarmed.*) Why into town? That's why I see the furniture . . . suitcases. . . . Well, never mind. . . . (*Through tears.*) Never mind. . . . Men of the greatest intellect, those Englishmen. . . . Never mind. . . . Be happy . . . God will help you. . . . Never mind. . . . Everything in this world comes to an end. . . . (*Kisses Lyubov Andreyevna's hand.*) And should the news reach you that my end has come, just remember this old horse, and say: "There once lived a certain Semyonov-Pishchik, God rest his soul.". . . Splendid weather. . . . Yes. . . . (*Goes out greatly disconcerted, but immediately returns and speaks from the doorway.*) Dashenka sends her regards. (*Goes out.*)

LYUBOV ANDREYEVNA: Now we can go. I am leaving with two things on my mind. First — that Firs is sick. (*Looks at her watch.*) We still have about five minutes. . . .

ANYA: Mama, Firs has already been taken to the hospital. Yasha sent him there this morning.

LYUBOV ANDREYEVNA: My second concern is Varya. She's used to getting up early and working, and now, with no work to do, she's like a fish out of water. She's grown pale and thin, and cries all the time, poor girl. . . . (*Pauses.*) You know very well, Yermolai Alekseich, that I dreamed of marrying her to you, and everything pointed to your getting married. (*Whispers to Anya, who nods to Charlotta, and they both go out.*) She loves you, you are fond of her, and I don't know — I don't know why it is you seem to avoid each other. I can't understand it!

LOPAKHIN: To tell you the truth, I don't understand it myself. The whole thing is strange, somehow. . . . If there's still time, I'm ready right now. . . . Let's finish it up — and *basta*,° but without you I feel I'll never be able to propose to her.

LYUBOV ANDREYEVNA: Splendid! After all, it only takes a minute. I'll call her in at once. . . .

LOPAKHIN: And we even have the champagne. (*Looks at the glasses.*) Empty! Somebody's already drunk it. (*Yasha coughs.*) That's what you call lapping it up.

LYUBOV ANDREYEVNA (*animatedly*): Splendid! We'll leave you. . . . Yasha, *allez*!° I'll call her. . . . (*At the door.*) Varya, leave everything and come here. Come! (*Goes out with Yasha.*)

LOPAKHIN (*looking at his watch*): Yes. . . . (*Pause.*)

(*Behind the door there is smothered laughter and whispering; finally Varya enters.*)

VARYA (*looking over the luggage for a long time*): Strange, I can't seem to find it . . .

LOPAKHIN: What are you looking for?

VARYA: I packed it myself, and I can't remember . . . (*Pause.*)

LOPAKHIN: Where are you going now, Varya Mikhailovna?

VARYA: I? To the Ragulins'. . . . I've agreed to go there to look after the house . . . as a sort of housekeeper.

LOPAKHIN: At Yashnevo? That would be about seventy versts from here. (*Pause.*) Well, life in this house has come to an end. . . .

VARYA (*examining the luggage*): Where can it be? . . . Perhaps I put it in the trunk. . . . Yes, life in this house has come to an end . . . there'll be no more . . .

LOPAKHIN: And I'm off for Kharkov . . . by the next train. I have a lot to do. I'm leaving Yepikhodov here . . . I've taken him on.

VARYA: Really!

LOPAKHIN: Last year at this time it was already snowing, if you remember, but now it's still and sunny. It's cold though. . . . About three degrees of frost.

VARYA: I haven't looked. (*Pause.*) And besides, our thermometer's broken. (*Pause.*)

(*A voice from the yard calls: "Yermolai Alekseich!"*)

LOPAKHIN (*as if he had been waiting for a long time for the call*): Coming! (*Goes out quickly.*)

basta: Italian for "enough."   *allez!*: French for "go!"

(*Varya sits on the floor, lays her head on a bundle of clothes, and quietly sobs. The door opens and Lyubov Andreyevna enters cautiously.*)

LYUBOV ANDREYEVNA: Well? (*Pause.*) We must be going.

VARYA (*no longer crying, dries her eyes*): Yes, it's time, Mama dear. I can get to the Ragulins' today, if only we don't miss the train.

LYUBOV ANDREYEVNA (*in the doorway*): Anya, put your things on!

(*Enter Anya, then Gayev and Charlotta Ivanovna. Gayev wears a warm overcoat with a hood. The servants and coachmen come in. Yepikhodov bustles about the luggage.*)

LYUBOV ANDREYEVNA: Now we can be on our way.

ANYA (*joyfully*): On our way!

GAYEV: My friends, my dear, cherished friends! Leaving this house forever, can I pass over in silence, can I refrain from giving utterance, as we say farewell, to those feelings that now fill my whole being —

ANYA (*imploringly*): Uncle!

VARYA: Uncle dear, don't!

GAYEV (*forlornly*): Double the rail off the white to center table . . . yellow into the side pocket. . . . I'll be quiet. . . .

(*Enter Trofimov, then Lopakhin.*)

TROFIMOV: Well, ladies and gentlemen, it's time to go!

LOPAKHIN: Yepikhodov, my coat!

LYUBOV ANDREYEVNA: I'll sit here just one more minute. It's as though I had never before seen what the walls of this house were like, what the ceilings were like, and now I look at them hungrily, with such tender love . . .

GAYEV: I remember when I was six years old, sitting on this windowsill on Whitsunday, watching my father going to church . . .

LYUBOV ANDREYEVNA: Have they taken all the things?

LOPAKHIN: Everything, I think. (*Puts on his overcoat.*) Yepikhodov, see that everything is in order.

YEPIKHODOV (*in a hoarse voice*): Rest assured, Yermolai Alekseich!

LOPAKHIN: What's the matter with your voice?

YEPIKHODOV: Just drank some water . . . must have swallowed something.

YASHA (*contemptuously*): What ignorance!

LYUBOV ANDREYEVNA: When we go — there won't be a soul left here. . . .

LOPAKHIN: Till spring.

VARYA (*pulls an umbrella out of a bundle as though she were going to hit someone; Lopakhin pretends to be frightened*): Why are you — I never thought of such a thing!

TROFIMOV: Ladies and gentlemen, let's get into the carriages — it's time now! The train will soon be in!

VARYA: Petya, there they are — your rubbers, by the suitcase. (*Tearfully.*) And what dirty old things they are!

TROFIMOV (*putting on his rubbers*): Let's go, ladies and gentlemen!

GAYEV (*extremely upset, afraid of bursting into tears*): The train . . . the station. . . . Cross table to the center, double the rail . . . on the white into the corner.

LYUBOV ANDREYEVNA: Let us go!

GAYEV: Are we all here? No one in there? (*Locks the side door on the left.*) There are some things stored in there, we must lock up. Let's go!

ANYA: Good-bye, house! Good-bye, old life!

TROFIMOV: Hail to the new life! (*Goes out with Anya.*)

(*Varya looks around the room and slowly goes out. Yasha and Charlotta with her dog go out.*)

LOPAKHIN: And so, till spring. Come along, my friends. . . . Till we meet! (*Goes out.*)

(*Lyubov Andreyevna and Gayev are left alone. As though they had been waiting for this, they fall onto each other's necks and break into quiet, restrained sobs, afraid of being heard.*)

GAYEV (*in despair*): My sister, my sister. . . .

LYUBOV ANDREYEVNA: Oh, my dear, sweet, lovely orchard! . . . My life, my youth, my happiness, good-bye! . . . Good-bye!

ANYA'S VOICE (*gaily calling*): Mama!

TROFIMOV'S VOICE (*gay and excited*): Aa-oo!

LYUBOV ANDREYEVNA: One last look at these walls, these windows. . . . Mother loved to walk about in this room. . . .

GAYEV: My sister, my sister!

ANYA'S VOICE: Mama!

TROFIMOV'S VOICE: Aa-oo!

LYUBOV ANDREYEVNA: We're coming! (*They go out.*)

(*The stage is empty. There is the sound of doors being locked, then of the carriages driving away. It grows quiet. In the stillness there is the dull thud of an ax on a tree, a forlorn, melancholy sound. Footsteps are heard. From the door on the right Firs appears. He is dressed as always in a jacket and white waistcoat, and wears slippers. He is ill.*)

FIRS (*goes to the door and tries the handle*): Locked. They have gone. . . . (*Sits down on the sofa.*) They've forgotten me. . . . Never mind. . . . I'll sit here awhile. . . . I expect Leonid Andreich hasn't put on his fur coat and has gone off in his overcoat. (*Sighs anxiously.*) And I didn't see to it. . . . When they're young, they're green! (*Mumbles something which cannot be understood.*) I'll lie down awhile. . . . There's no strength left in you, nothing's left, nothing. . . . Ach, you . . . addlepate! (*Lies motionless.*)

(*A distant sound is heard that seems to come from the sky, the sound of a snapped string mournfully dying away. A stillness falls, and nothing is heard but the thud of the ax on a tree far away in the orchard.*)

COMMENTARIES

Anton Chekhov (1860–1904)

FROM *LETTERS OF ANTON CHEKOV*   *1888–1903*

TRANSLATED BY MICHAEL HENRY HEIM WITH SIMON KARLINSKY

Chekhov, like Ibsen, was an inveterate letter writer. In letters to family members and colleagues, he spoke quite frankly about his hopes, expectations, and difficulties regarding his work. Chekhov's letters concerning his purpose as an artist and his play The Cherry Orchard *give us some insight into the anxieties and hopes that Chekhov had for his work. His awareness of the difficulties he faced in his writing helps us understand how his plays developed into complex and demanding works.*

October 4, 1888

The people I fear are those who look for tendentiousness between the lines and are determined to see me as either liberal or conservative. I am neither liberal, nor conservative, nor gradualist, nor monk, nor indifferentist. I should like to be a free artist and nothing else. That is why I cultivate no particular predilection for policemen, butchers, scientists, writers, or the younger generation. I look upon tags and labels as prejudices. My holy of holies is the human body, health, intelligence, talent, inspiration, love and the most absolute freedom imaginable, freedom from violence and lies.

November 25, 1892

Keep in mind that the writers we call eternal or simply good, the writers who intoxicate us, have one highly important trait in common: They are moving towards something definite and beckon you to follow, and you feel with your entire being, not only with your mind, that they have a certain goal, like the ghost of Hamlet's father, which had a motive for coming and stirring Hamlet's imagination. Depending on their caliber, some have immediate goals — the abolition of serfdom, the liberation of one's country, politics, beauty, or simply vodka . . . — while the goals of others are more remote — God, life after death, the happiness of mankind, etc. The best of them are realistic and describe life as it is, but because each line is saturated with the consciousness of its goal, you feel life as it should be in addition to life as it is, and you are captivated by it. But what about us? Us! We describe life as it is and stop dead right there. We wouldn't lift a hoof if you lit into us with a whip. We have neither immediate nor remote goals, and there is an emptiness in our souls. We have no politics, we don't believe in revolution, there is no God, we're not afraid of ghosts, and I personally am not even afraid of death or blindness. If you want nothing, hope for nothing, and fear nothing, you cannot be an artist.

To K. S. Stanislavsky°
Yalta. Oct. 30, 1903

When I was writing Lopakhin, I thought of it as a part for you. If for any reason you don't care for it, take the part of Gayev. Lopakhin is a merchant, of course, but he is a very decent person in every sense. He must behave with perfect decorum, like an educated man, with no petty ways or tricks of any sort, and it seemed to me this part, the central one of the play, would come out brilliantly in your hands. . . . In choosing an actor for the part you must remember that Varya, a serious and religious girl, is in love with Lopakhin; she wouldn't be in love with a mere money-grubber. . . .

To Vl. I. Nemirovich-Danchenko°
Yalta. Nov. 2, 1903

. . . Pishchik is a Russian, an old man, worn out by the gout, age, and satiety; stout, dressed in a sleeveless undercoat (à la Simov [an actor in the Moscow Art Theatre]), boots without heels. Lopakhin — a white waistcoat, yellow shoes; when walking, swings his arms, a broad stride, thinks deeply while walking, walks as if on a straight line. Hair not short, and therefore often throws back his head; while in thought he passes his hand through his beard, combing it from the back forward, i.e., from the neck toward the mouth. Trofimov, I think, is clear. Varya — black dress, wide belt.

Three years I spent writing "The Cherry Orchard," and for three years I have been telling you that it is necessary to invite an actress for the role of Lyubov Andreyevna. And now you see you are trying to solve a puzzle that won't work out.

To K. S. Alekseyev (Stanislavsky)
Yalta. Nov. 5, 1903

The house in the play is two-storied, a large one. But in the third act does it not speak of a stairway leading down? Nevertheless, this third act worries me. . . . N. has it that the third act takes place in "some kind of hotel"; . . . evidently I made an error in the play. The action does not pass in "some kind of hotel," but in a *drawing-room*. If I mention a hotel in the play, which I cannot now doubt, after Vl. Iv.'s [Nemirovich-Danchenko] letter, please telegraph me. We must correct it; we cannot issue it thus, with grave errors distorting its meaning.

The house must be large, solid; wooden (like Aksakov's, which, I think, S. T. Morozov has seen) or stone, it is all the same. It is very old and imposing; country residents do not take such houses; such houses are usually wrecked and the material employed for the construction of a country house. The furniture is ancient, stylish, solid; ruin and debt have not affected the surroundings.

When they buy such a house, they reason thus: it is cheaper and easier to build a new and smaller one than to repair this old one.

Your shepherd played well. That was most essential.

K. S. Stanislavsky: Konstantin Stanislavsky (1863–1938), director with the Moscow Art Theatre, which produced most of Chekhov's plays.
Vl. I. Nemirovich-Danchenko: Vladimir Ivanovich Nemirovich-Danchenko (1858–1943), novelist and codirector of the Moscow Art Theatre.

Maxim Gorky (1868–1936)
FROM *RECOLLECTIONS*   *1921*

TRANSLATED BY KATHERINE MANSFIELD

Alexei Maximovitch Pyeshkov changed his name to Maxim Gorky, which in Russian means "Maxim the Bitter." His childhood and early years gave him great reason for bitterness because he was raised by a brutal grandfather who regularly beat Maxim and his mother. Once, when Maxim was eight, he attacked his grandfather with a bread knife for beating his frail and sick mother. Gorky spent many years tramping through Russia and became a writer of the common people. He was introduced to the Moscow Art Theatre by Chekhov, and his first play, The Lower Depths *(1902), starred Chekhov's wife, Olga Knipper. It was a mercilessly realistic portrait of the homeless, impoverished castaways of Russian life. It established Gorky as a major dramatist, and after the Russian revolution he became the most revered of Soviet writers.*

Reading Anton Chekhov's stories, one feels oneself in a melancholy day of late autumn, when the air is transparent and the outline of naked trees, narrow houses, grayish people, is sharp. Everything is strange, lonely, motionless, helpless. The horizon, blue and empty, melts into the pale sky, and its breath is terribly cold upon the earth, which is covered with frozen mud. The author's mind, like the autumn sun, shows up in hard outline the monotonous roads, the crooked streets, the little squalid houses in which tiny, miserable people are stifled by boredom and laziness and fill the houses with an unintelligible, drowsy bustle. . . .

Here is the lachrymose Ranevskaya and the other owners of *The Cherry Orchard,* egotistical like children, with the flabbiness of senility. They missed the right moment for dying; they whine, seeing nothing of what is going on around them, understanding nothing, parasites without the power of again taking root in life. The wretched little student, Trofimov, speaks eloquently of the necessity of working — and does nothing but amuse himself, out of sheer boredom, with stupid mockery of Varya, who works ceaselessly for the good of idlers. . . .

There passes before one a long file of men and women, slaves of their love, of their stupidity and idleness, of their greed for the good things of life; there walk the slaves of the dark fear of life; they straggle anxiously along, filling life with incoherent words about the future, feeling that in the present there is no place for them.

At moments out of the gray mass of them one hears the sound of a shot: Ivanov [*Ivanov*] or Treplev [in *The Seagull*] has guessed what he ought to do and has died.

Many of them have nice dreams of how pleasant life will be in three hundred years, but it occurs to none of them to ask themselves who will make life pleasant if we only dream.

In front of that dreary, gray crowd of helpless people there passed a great, wise, and observant man; he looked at all these dreary inhabitants of his country, and, with a sad smile, with a tone of gentle but deep reproach, with anguish in his face and in his heart, in a beautiful and sincere voice, he said to them:

"You live badly, my friends. It is shameful to live like that."

Virginia Woolf (1882–1941)
ON *THE CHERRY ORCHARD*   *1920*

Virginia Woolf was one of the most important experimental writers of fiction in the first half of the twentieth century. Her best-known works include Mrs. Dalloway *(1925),* To the Lighthouse *(1927),* Orlando *(1928),* A Room of One's Own *(1930), and* The Waves *(1931). But in addition to these landmark works, she wrote a huge number of essays and commentaries, not to mention letters that have now been gathered into five large volumes. Her insight into literature is always keen and original. Her approach, for instance, to a 1920 production of* The Cherry Orchard *is through language. She is naturally sensitive to careful use of language, and it is therefore important for her to observe that out of the apparently disjointed use of sentences comes extraordinary drama. She ends her commentary with an interesting comparison that delves into the realm of music — or, more properly, into an imaginative realm in which the theatergoers themselves are musical instruments.*

It is, as a rule, when a critic does not wish to commit himself or to trouble himself, that he refers to atmosphere. And, given time, something might be said in greater detail of the causes which produced this atmosphere — the strange dislocated sentences, each so erratic and yet cutting out the shape so firmly, of the realism, of the humor, of the artistic unity. But let the word atmosphere be taken literally to mean that Chekhov has contrived to shed over us a luminous vapor in which life appears as it is, without veils, transparent and visible to the depths. Long before the play was over, we seemed to have sunk below the surface of things and to be feeling our way among submerged but recognizable emotions. "I have no proper passport. I don't know how old I am; I always feel I am still young"— how the words go sounding on in one's mind — how the whole play resounds with such sentences, which reverberate, melt into each other, and pass far away out beyond everything! In short, if it is permissible to use such vague language, I do not know how better to describe the sensation at the end of *The Cherry Orchard*, than by saying that it sends one into the street feeling like a piano played upon at last, not in the middle only but all over the keyboard and with the lid left open so that the sound goes on.

John Corbin (1870–1959)
REVIEW OF *THE CHERRY ORCHARD*   *1923*

After brief praise for the Russian-language production of the Moscow Players, John Corbin's review centers itself entirely on an analysis of the play. Clearly, he sees the main characters as feckless and wasteful and has little sympathy for them. On the other hand, he sees in Lopakhin a man of industry and progress. His interpretation may well depend on the emphasis of the postrevolutionary Russian players, whose sympathies would certainly not have aligned with aristocrats.

The Moscow players proceeded last night from the lower depths of Gorky to the high comedy of Tchekhoff, revealing new artistic resources. Stanislavsky, Olga Knipper-Tchekhova, Moskvin, Leonidoff and half a dozen others entered with consummate ease into a rich variety of new characterizations. The stage management was less signal in its effects, but no less perfect. Yet for some reason *The Cherry Orchard* failed to stir the audience, even the Russian portion of it, as did *The Lower Depths* and even *Tsar Fyodor*.

This is a play of comedy values both high and light. The milleu is that of the ancient landed aristocracy, beautifully symbolized by an orchard of cherry trees in full bloom which surrounds the crumbling manor house. Quite obviously, these amiable folks have fallen away from the pristine vigor of their race.

The middle-aged brother and sister who live together are unconscious, ir-reclaimable spendthrifts, both of their shrinking purses and of their waning lives. With a little effort, one is made to feel, even with a modicum of mental concentration, calamity could be averted. But that is utterly beyond their vacuous and futile amiability; so their estate is sold over their heads and the leagues of gay cherry trees are felled to make way for suburban villas.

Beneath the graceful, easy-going surface of the play one feels rather than perceives a criticism on the Russia of two decades ago. Here is a woman of truly Slavic instability, passing with a single gesture from heartbreak to the gayety of a moment, from acutely maternal grief for an only child long dead to weak doting on a Parisian lover who is faithless to her and yet has power to hold her and batten on her bounty. Here is a man whose sentiment for the home of his ancestors breaks forth in fluent declaiming, quasi-poetic and quasi-philosophic, yet who cannot lift a finger to avert financial disaster.

In the entire cast only one person has normal human sense. Lopakhin is the son of a serf who has prospered in freedom. He is loyal enough to the old masters, dogging their footsteps with good advice. But in the end it is he who buys the estate and fells the cherry trees for the villas of an industrial population. It is as if Tchekhoff saw in the new middle class the hope of a disenchanted yet sounder and more progressive Russia. The war has halted that movement, but indications are not lacking that it is already resuming.

With such a theme developed by the subtly masterful act of Tchekhoff there is scope for comedy acting of the highest quality. It is more than likely that the company seized every opportunity and improved upon it. But to any one who does not understand Russian, judgment in such a matter is quite impossible. Where effects are to be achieved only by the subtlest intonation, the most delicate phrasing, it fares ill with those whose entire vocabulary is da, da.

As an example of the art of the most distinguished company that has visited our shores in modern memory, this production of *The Cherry Orchard* is abundantly worth seeing. The play in itself is of interest as the masterpiece of the man who, with Gorky, has touched the pinnacle of modern Russian comedy. But if some Moscovite should rise up and tell us that in any season our own stage produces casts as perfect and ensembles as finely studied in detail, it would be quite possible to believe him.

Peter Brook *(b. 1925)*
ON CHEKHOV   *1987*

Peter Brook has established himself as one of the most distinguished directors of recent years. He was educated at Oxford University and has been a director of the Royal Shakespeare Company in England. In 1987 he directed The Cherry Orchard *at the Brooklyn Academy of Music. Some of his thoughts as he prepared to direct the play are presented here, showing his awareness of Chekhov's "film sense" in a play that was written just as film was emerging as a popular form. He is also aware of Chekhov's personal vision of death and sees it expressed in the circumstances of the play.*

Chekhov always looked for what's natural; he wanted performances and productions to be as limpid as life itself. Chekhov's writing is extremely concentrated, employing a minimum of words; in a way, it is similar to Pinter or Beckett. As with them, it is construction that counts, rhythm, the purely theatrical poetry that comes not from beautiful words but from the right word at the right moment. In the theater, someone can say "yes" in such a way that the "yes" is no longer ordinary — it can become a beautiful word, because it is the perfect expression of what cannot be expressed in any other way. With Chekhov, periods, commas, points of suspension are all of a fundamental importance, as fundamental as the "pauses" precisely indicated by Beckett. If one fails to observe them, one loses the rhythm and tensions of the play. In Chekhov's work, the punctuation represents a series of coded messages which record characters' relationships and emotions, the moments at which ideas come together or follow their own course. The punctuation enables us to grasp what the words conceal.

Chekhov is like a perfect filmmaker. Instead of cutting from one image to another — perhaps from one place to another — he switches from one emotion to another just before it gets too heavy. At the precise moment when the spectator risks becoming too involved in a character, an unexpected situation cuts across: Nothing is stable. Chekhov portrays individuals and a society in a state of perpetual change, he is the dramatist of life's movement, simultaneously smiling and serious, amusing and bitter — completely free from the "music," the Slav "nostalgia" that Paris nightclubs still preserve. He often stated that his plays were comedies — this was the central issue of his conflict with Stanislavsky.

But it's wrong to conclude that *The Cherry Orchard* should be performed as a vaudeville. Chekhov is an infinitely detailed observer of the human comedy. As a doctor, he knew the meaning of certain kinds of behavior, how to discern what was essential, to expose what he diagnosed. Although he shows tenderness and an attentive sympathy, he never sentimentalizes. One doesn't imagine a doctor shedding tears over the illnesses of his patients. He learns how to balance compassion with distance.

In Chekhov's work, death is omnipresent — he knew it well — but there is nothing negative or unsavory in its presence. The awareness of death is balanced with a desire to live. His characters possess a sense of the present moment, and the need to taste it fully. As in great tragedies, one finds a harmony between life and death.

Chekhov died young, having traveled, written, and loved enormously, having taken part in the events of his day, in great schemes of social reform. He died shortly after asking for some champagne, and his coffin was transported in a wagon bearing the inscription "Fresh Oysters." His awareness of death, and of the precious moments that could be lived, endow his work with a sense of the relative: in other words, a viewpoint from which the tragic is always a bit absurd.

In Chekhov's work, each character has its own existence: not one of them resembles another, particularly in *The Cherry Orchard,* which presents a micro-cosm of the political tendencies of the time. There are those who believe in social transformations, others attached to a disappearing past. None of them can achieve satisfaction or plenitude, and seen from outside, their existences might well appear empty, senseless. But they all burn with intense desires. They are not disillusioned, quite the contrary: In their own ways, they are all searching for a better quality of life, emotionally and socially. Their drama is that society — the outside world — blocks their energy. The complexity of their behavior is not indicated in the words, it emerges from the mosaic construction of an infinite number of details. What is essential is to see that these are not plays about lethargic people. They are hyper-vital people in a lethargic world, forced to dramatize the minutest happening out of a passionate desire to live. They have not given up.

Bernard Shaw

The Irish playwright Bernard Shaw[1] (1856–1950) was astonishing not only for the range of his writing but also for the length and vigor of his life. He was a public figure for most of his days, with an especially keen ability to catch public attention and to make his presence felt. His early work was devoted to criticism in newspapers and then to a series of fairly successful novels. He began writing plays in his late thirties; once he began, he realized that he had discovered his vocation, and he went on to write more than fifty. Some of them, such as *Arms and the Man* (1894), *Candida* (1897), *Mrs. Warren's Profession* (1898), *Man and Superman* (1901–1903), *Major Barbara* (1905), *Pygmalion* (1913), *Heartbreak House* (1919), and *St. Joan* (1923), are among the most performed plays by any English-language writer of his time.

Shaw's gift of analysis and philosophical reflection created in his works a new kind of drama that has sometimes been named for him — Shavian. The term implies a deep interest in ideas rather than in character and a propensity for elaborate discourse between characters who represent different points of view. Shaw assumed that drama should amuse and entertain, but of much greater importance was his didactic motive. Drama should teach a lesson about something of great moral importance.

This is not to say that Shaw was unable to be entertaining. Some of his comedies, still played today, are bright and witty. *You Never Can Tell* (1898), a comedy about male-female relationships whose main character is a dentist, and *Pygmalion,* a comedy in which a man teaches a cockney girl how to speak with an upper-class accent with unexpected results, are both funny plays. *Pygmalion* was redone as a musical, *My Fair Lady,* and has been Shaw's most financially successful play.

Still, Shaw was basically a philosophical writer. His plays can usually be seen as having a specific theme on which the characters constantly discourse. Whether it is on the relation of England to Ireland, on the state of the medical profession, on genetics and propagation, or on poverty, Shaw always focused on an issue and even commented that Shakespeare's shortcoming was that his plays have no message.

Shaw frequently wrote elaborate and lengthy prefaces to his published plays. In his prefaces, Shaw takes time to explain — and fully explore — the messages of his plays. He discusses the questions of genetic planning and the improvement of the race in his preface to *Man and Superman*; in the preface to *Candida* he discusses the relationship of pity to love.

Shaw's lifelong socialism affected his work and his thinking, and he himself was a socialist politician for a short period. Consequently, it is not uncommon to see political concerns expressed and debated in his plays.

---

[1]Shaw was born George Bernard Shaw and is sometimes referred to as GBS. He disliked the name George and preferred to be addressed as Bernard Shaw.

Shaw's political ideas were shaped by his concern for economics as a discipline, beginning in 1882. In 1884 he joined the Fabian Society, established a year earlier as a group to study and promote socialism, and remained active until 1911. Fabianism, unlike Marxism or communism, believed that society need not be destroyed by revolution but could become an instrument of socialist reform. For this reason Fabianism was known as evolutionary socialism. *Fabian Essays* (1889), which Shaw edited, was used by study groups that sprouted up throughout England to spread Fabian socialist ideas through politics, religion, and society. The result of the movement was the organization of a new political party, the Labor Party (1893), which still exists. The socialist government of England in the 1960s and 1970s was a direct outgrowth of Fabian theories.

While Shaw studied economics, he grew to believe that all social values were built on an economic base. He developed this idea in his Fabian essays and maintained it throughout his plays. He also maintained a presence as a critic of theater and accepted Ibsen as a major playwright when most London critics found his work unacceptable. Shaw's *Quintessence of Ibsenism* (1891; revised after Ibsen's death in 1913) is still a useful commentary on that playwright's work. (See an excerpt from *Quintessence of Ibsenism* on pp. 690–91.)

MRS. WARREN'S PROFESSION

Shaw once described this play as being in "my most odious vein." It was written in 1894 and inspired by Janet Achurch, the actress who played Nora in Ibsen's *A Doll House*. Achurch told Shaw the story of a play she was writing based on Maupassant's short story "Yvette." Shaw adopted the idea and hoped that when he finished his play, Achurch would play Vivie, the heroine. Shaw owed a great deal to other playwrights who had touched on similar themes — although none as directly as Shaw — but his story of a mother-daughter relationship in which the mother was a prostitute was original in that it proposed a "new woman" for the heroine, Vivie, and refused to permit Mrs. Warren to express shame for her professional decisions. This was a highly daring play for its time.

Indeed, the play had only two private performances in London in 1902 before it premiered in the United States in 1905. The play was banned or protested in several cities, especially after its first performances. By the time it was given its first public performances in London in 1926, Shaw had lost interest in the play and simply felt it was too late in production. The Comédie Français considered it too amoral to produce as late as 1955, which demonstrates that Shaw hit a nerve that was not limited to the reactions of his own day.

The form of the play is essentially conventional for its time, although Shaw consciously employed techniques of Henrik Ibsen, whom he admired enough to have written the seminal study *The Quintessence of Ibsenism* (1891). He had learned from Ibsen how to address social issues directly and how to produce a female character whose ambiguities intrigue an audience. Ibsen's emphasis on the "new woman" — the independent woman who could make her own decisions and her own way — is evident in *Mrs. Warren's Profession.*

The men in the play are generally dependent on the women. Mrs. Warren has a good business sense and has used the capital provided her by Sir George Crofts so well that Crofts need no longer worry about his own welfare. In one sense he is a kept man, living on the earnings of a woman. The Reverend Samuel Gardner has converted from a roué and former client of Mrs. Warren to an overly pious churchman worried about his reputation. His son, Frank, may or may not be a brother to Vivie, and while the play ends with Vivie declaring that she doesn't care if he is her brother or not, the theme of incest seems underdeveloped. Yet Shaw felt it was an essential ingredient of the play. Frank plans not to work, is shiftless and indolent, and would be content to be supported by Vivie and her mother's money just as Crofts is content to bask in the security provided by Mrs. Warren.

The underlying theme of economic opportunities for women drives this play. The Victorians felt that prostitution, widespread in England, was one of the most serious social diseases of the time. But Shaw is keen enough in his analysis of English social life to realize that prostitutes were often forced into the profession because the alternatives were even worse. Mrs. Warren explains to Vivie in act 2 that she watched her two half-sisters follow the path of respectability: "One of them worked in a whitelead factory twelve hours a day for nine shillings a week until she died of lead poisoning. She only expected to get her hands a little paralyzed; but she died. The other was always held up to us as a model because she married a Government laborer in the Deptford victualling yard, and kept his room and the three children neat and tidy on eighteen shillings a week — until he took to drink."

The unrespectable sisters, Liz and Mrs. Warren, followed "the life" and ended up in control of their own situation. Liz, retired in a cathedral town, is emblematic of the height of respectability. Vivie is in a position to reject her mother's life as well as Croft's offer of marriage and wealth and Frank's offer of marriage and love. But she is in this position because her mother provided her with a man's education at Cambridge. She describes herself as a "wrangler" — a term meaning an honors student in mathematics but also implying achievement in debate. This position was formerly available only to men (as Praed implies when he says nothing like that happened "in my day").

Vivie ends the play in the secure knowledge that she will succeed in the law profession and that the limited options available to her mother will never be her only options. Vivie, then, is heroic, and the play comic in form.

Mrs. Warren's Profession in Performance

Mrs. Warren's Profession was produced privately in London on January 5, 1902, at the New Lyric Theater. On October 27, 1902, it was produced at the Hyperion Theater in New Haven, Connecticut, its first American production. H. Granville Barker, a distinguished actor and writer, played the part of Frank, and Fanny Brough was Mrs. Warren. It was performed again in New York in 1905 with the well-known actor, Richard Mansfield, but the police commissioner closed the play for "offending public decency." A special court hearing in 1906 proclaimed the play "not pleasant" but did not declare it indecent.

After performances in Berlin (1907) and Glasgow (1913), the play's first public performance in England took place in Birmingham in 1925, when the British censors finally cleared the play of charges of indecency. It ran in London at the Strand Theatre in 1926 for eighty-six performances.

John Loder and Estelle Winwood played Crofts and Mrs. Warren off-Broadway in 1950 for twenty-eight performances. Ruth Gordon and Lynn Redgrave played Mrs. Warren and Vivie in a 1976 New York Shakespeare Festival production in Lincoln Center that lasted for sixty-nine performances. Edward Herrmann played Frank, and Milo O'Shea played Reverend Gardner. Annual productions of the play have been staged since that time in Niagara-on-the-Lake, New Haven, Boston, Hartford, San Francisco, and London.

Bernard Shaw (1856–1950)

MRS. WARREN'S PROFESSION   *1898*

Characters

VIVIE WARREN
PRAED
MRS WARREN
SIR GEORGE CROFTS
FRANK GARDNER
REVEREND SAMUEL GARDNER

ACT I

Summer afternoon in a cottage garden on the eastern slope of a hill a little south of Haslemere in Surrey. Looking up the hill, the cottage is seen in the left hand corner of the garden, with its thatched roof and porch, and a large latticed window to the left of the porch. Farther back a little wing is built out, making an angle with the right side wall. From the end of this wing a paling curves across and forward, completely shutting in the garden, except for a gate on the right. The common rises uphill beyond the paling to the sky line. Some folded canvas garden chairs are leaning against the side bench in the porch. A lady's bicycle is propped against the wall, under the window. A little to the right of the porch a hammock is slung from two posts. A big canvas umbrella, stuck in the ground, keeps the sun off the hammock, in which a young lady lies reading and making notes, her head towards the cottage and her feet towards the gate. In front of the hammock, and within reach of her hand, is a common kitchen chair, with a pile of serious-looking books and a supply of writing paper upon it.

A gentleman walking on the common comes into sight from behind the cottage. He is hardly past middle age, with something of the artist about him, unconventionally but carefully dressed, and clean-shaven except for a moustache, with an eager, susceptible face and very amiable and considerate manners. He has silky black hair, with waves of grey and white in it. His eyebrows are white, his moustache black. He seems not certain of his way. He looks over the paling; takes stock of the place; and sees the young lady.

THE GENTLEMAN (*taking off his hat*): I beg your pardon. Can you direct me to Hindhead View — Mrs Alison's?

THE YOUNG LADY (*glancing up from her book*): This is Mrs Alison's. (*She resumes her work.*)

THE GENTLEMAN: Indeed! Perhaps — may I ask are you Miss Vivie Warren?

THE YOUNG LADY (*sharply, as she turns on her elbow to get a good look at him*): Yes.

THE GENTLEMAN (*daunted and conciliatory*): I'm afraid I appear intrusive. My name is Praed. (*Vivie at once throws her books upon the chair, and gets out of the hammock.*) Oh, pray dont let me disturb you.

VIVIE (*striding to the gate and opening it for him*): Come in, Mr Praed. (*He comes in.*) Glad to see you. (*She proffers her hand and takes his with a resolute and hearty grip. She is an attractive specimen of the sensible, able, highly educated young middle-class Englishwoman. Age 22. Prompt, strong, confident, self-possessed. Plain, business-like dress, but not dowdy. She wears a chatelaine at her belt, with a fountain pen and a paper knife among its pendants.*)

PRAED: Very kind of you indeed, Miss Warren. (*She shuts the gate with a vigorous slam: he passes in to the middle of the garden, exercising his fingers, which are slightly numbed by her greeting.*) Has your mother arrived?

VIVIE (*quickly, evidently scenting aggression*): Is she coming?

PRAED (*surprised*): Didnt you expect us?

VIVIE: No.

PRAED: Now, goodness me, I hope Ive not mistaken the day. That would be just like me, you know. Your mother arranged that she was to come down from London and that I was to come over from Horsham to be introduced to you.

VIVIE (*not at all pleased*): Did she? Hm! My mother has rather a trick of taking me by surprise — to see how I behave myself when she's away, I suppose. I fancy I shall take my mother very much by surprise one of these days, if she makes arrangements that concern me without consulting me beforehand. She hasnt come.

PRAED (*embarrassed*): I'm really very sorry.

VIVIE (*throwing off her displeasure*): It's not your fault, Mr Praed, is it? And I'm very glad youve come, believe me. You are the only one of my mother's friends I have asked her to bring to see me.

PRAED (*relieved and delighted*): Oh, now this is really very good of you, Miss Warren!

VIVIE: Will you come indoors; or would you rather sit out here whilst we talk?

PRAED: It will be nicer out here, dont you think?

VIVIE: Then I'll go and get you a chair. (*She goes to the porch for a garden chair.*)

PRAED (*following her*): Oh, pray, pray! Allow me. (*He lays hands on the chair.*)

VIVIE (*letting him take it*): Take care of your fingers: theyre rather dodgy things, those chairs. (*She goes across to the chair with the books on it; pitches them into the hammock; and brings the chair forward with one swing.*)

PRAED (*who has just unfolded his chair*): Oh, now do let me take that hard chair! I like hard chairs.

VIVIE: So do I. (*She sits down.*) Sit down, Mr Praed. (*This invitation she gives with genial peremptoriness, his anxiety to please her clearly striking her as a sign of weakness of character on his part.*)

PRAED: By the way, though, hadnt we better go to the station to meet your mother?

VIVIE (*coolly*): Why? She knows the way. (*Praed hesitates, and then sits down in the garden chair, rather disconcerted.*) Do you know, you are just like what I expected. I hope you are disposed to be friends with me.

PRAED (*again beaming*): Thank you, my dear Miss Warren: thank you. Dear me! I'm so glad your mother hasnt spoilt you!

VIVIE: How?

PRAED: Well, in making you too conventional. You know, my dear Miss Warren, I am a born anarchist. I hate authority. It spoils the relations between parent and child — even between mother and daughter. Now I was always afraid that your mother would strain her authority to make you very conventional. It's such a relief to find that she hasnt.

VIVIE: Oh! have I been behaving unconventionally?

PRAED: Oh no: oh dear no. At least not conventionally inconventionally, you understand. (*She nods. He goes on, with a cordial outburst.*) But it was so charming of you to say that you were disposed to be friends with me! You modern young ladies are splendid — perfectly splendid!

VIVIE (*dubiously*): Eh? (*Watching him with dawning disappointment as to the quality of his brains and character.*)

PRAED: When I was your age, young men and women were afraid of each other: there was no good fellowship — nothing real — only gallantry copied out of novels, and as vulgar and affected as it could be. Maidenly reserve! — gentlemanly chivalry! — always saying no when you meant yes! — simple purgatory for shy and sincere souls!

VIVIE: Yes, I imagine there must have been a frightful waste of time — especially women's time.

PRAED: Oh, waste of life, waste of everything. But things are improving. Do you know, I have been in a positive state of excitement about meeting you ever since your magnificent achievements at Cambridge — a thing unheard of in my day. It was perfectly splendid, your tieing with the third wrangler.° Just the right place, you know. The first wrangler is always a dreamy, morbid fellow, in whom the thing is pushed to the length of a disease.

VIVIE: It doesnt pay. I wouldnt do it again for the same money.

PRAED (*aghast*): The same money!

VIVIE: I did it for £50. Perhaps you dont know how it was. Mrs Latham, my tutor at Newnham, told my mother that I could distinguish myself in the mathematical tripos° if I went in for it in earnest. The papers were full just then of Phillipa Summers beating the senior wrangler — you remember about it; and nothing would please my mother but that I should do the same thing. I said flatly that it was not worth my while to face the grind since I was not going in for teaching; but I offered to try for fourth wrangler or thereabouts for £50. She closed with me at that, after a little grumbling; and I was better than my bargain. But I wouldnt do it again for that. £200 would have been nearer the mark.

PRAED (*much damped*): Lord bless me! Thats a very practical way of looking at it.

VIVIE: Did you expect to find me an unpractical person?

PRAED: No, no. But surely it's practical to consider not only the work these honors cost, but also the culture they bring.

---

wrangler: An honors student in mathematics. The term also implies achievement in debate.   **tripos:** An examination for the B.A. degree with honors at Cambridge University.

VIVIE: Culture! My dear Mr Praed: do you know what the mathematical tripos means? It means grind, grind, grind for six to eight hours a day at mathematics, and nothing but mathematics. I'm supposed to know something about science; but I know nothing except the mathematics it involves. I can make calculations for engineers, electricians, insurance companies, and so on; but I know next to nothing about engineering or electricity or insurance. I dont even know arithmetic well. Outside mathematics, lawn-tennis, eating, sleeping, cycling, and walking, I'm a more ignorant barbarian than any woman could possibly be who hadnt gone in for the tripos.

PRAED (*revolted*): What a monstrous, wicked, rascally system! I knew it! I felt at once that it meant destroying all that makes womanhood beautiful.

VIVIE: I dont object to it on that score in the least. I shall turn it to very good account, I assure you.

PRAED: Pooh! In what way?

VIVIE: I shall set up in chambers in the City and work at actuarial calculations and conveyancing. Under cover of that I shall do some law, with one eye on the Stock Exchange all the time. Ive come down here by myself to read law — not for a holiday, as my mother imagines. I hate holidays.

PRAED: You make my blood run cold. Are you to have no romance, no beauty in your life?

VIVIE: I dont care for either, I assure you.

PRAED: You cant mean that.

VIVIE: Oh yes I do. I like working and getting paid for it. When I'm tired of working, I like a comfortable chair, a cigar, a little whisky, and a novel with a good detective story in it.

PRAED (*in a frenzy of repudiation*): I dont believe it. I am an artist; and I cant believe it: I refuse to believe it. (*Enthusiastically.*) Ah, my dear Miss Warren, you havn't discovered yet, I see, what a wonderful world art can open up to you.

VIVIE: Yes I have. Last May I spent six weeks in London with Honoria Fraser. Mamma thought we were doing a round of sightseeing together; but I was really at Honoria's chambers in Chancery Lane every day, working away at actuarial calculations for her, and helping her as well as a greenhorn could. In the evenings we smoked and talked, and never dreamt of going out except for exercise. And I never enjoyed myself more in my life. I cleared all my expenses, and got initiated into the business without a fee into the bargain.

PRAED: But bless my heart and soul, Miss Warren, do you call that trying art?

VIVIE: Wait a bit. That wasnt the beginning. I went up to town on an invitation from some artistic people in Fitzjohn's Avenue: one of the girls was a Newnham chum. They took me to the National Gallery, to the Opera, and to a concert where the band played all the evening — Beethoven and Wagner and so on. I wouldnt go through that experience again for any-thing you could offer me. I held out for civility's sake until the third day; and then I said, plump out, that I couldnt stand any more of it, and went off to Chancery Lane. Now you know the sort of perfectly splendid modern young lady I am. How do you think I shall get on with my mother?

PRAED (*startled*): Well, I hope — er —

VIVIE: It's not so much what you hope as what you believe, that I want to know.

PRAED: Well, frankly, I am afraid your mother will be a little disappointed. Not from any shortcoming on your part — I dont mean that. But you are so different from her ideal.

VIVIE: What is her ideal like?

PRAED: Well, you must have observed, Miss Warren, that people who are dissatisfied with their own bringing up generally think that the world would be all right if everybody were to be brought up quite differently. Now your mother's life has been — er — I suppose you know —

VIVIE: I know nothing. (*Praed is appalled. His consternation grows as she continues.*) Thats exactly my difficulty. You forget, Mr. Praed, that I hardly know my mother. Since I was a child I have lived in England, at school or college, or with people paid to take charge of me. I have been boarded out all my life; and my mother has lived in Brussels or Vienna and never let me go to her. I only see her when she visits England for a few days. I dont complain: it's been very pleasant; for people have been very good to me; and there has always been plenty of money to make things smooth. But dont imagine I know anything about my mother. I know far less than you do.

PRAED (*very ill at ease*): In that case — (*He stops, quite at a loss. Then, with a forced attempt at gaiety*) But what nonsense we are talking! Of course you and your mother will get on capitally. (*He rises, and looks abroad at the view.*) What a charming little place you have here!

VIVIE (*unmoved*): If you think you are doing anything but confirming my worst suspicions by changing the subject like that, you must take me for a much greater fool than I hope I am.

PRAED: Your worst suspicions! Oh, pray dont say that. Now dont.

VIVIE: Why wont my mother's life bear being talked about?

PRAED: Pray think, Miss Vivie. It is natural that I should have a certain delicacy in talking to my old friend's daughter about her behind her back. You will have plenty of opportunity of talking to her about it when she comes. (*Anxiously*) I wonder what is keeping her.

VIVIE: No: she wont talk about it either. (*Rising*) However, I wont press you. Only, mind this, Mr Praed. I strongly suspect there will be a battle royal when my mother hears of my Chancery Lane project.

PRAED (*ruefully*): I'm afraid there will.

VIVIE: I shall win the battle, because I want nothing but

my fare to London to start there to-morrow earning my own living by devilling° for Honoria. Besides, I have no mysteries to keep up; and it seems she has. I shall use that advantage over her if necessary.

PRAED (*greatly shocked*): Oh no! No, pray. Youd not do such a thing.

VIVIE: Then tell me why not.

PRAED: I really cannot. I appeal to your good feeling. (*She smiles at his sentimentality.*) Besides, you may be too bold. Your mother is not to be trifled with when she's angry.

VIVIE: You cant frighten me, Mr Praed. In that month at Chancery Lane I had opportunities of taking the measure of one or two women very like my mother, who came to consult Honoria. You may back me to win. But if I hit harder in my ignorance than I need, remember that it is you who refuse to enlighten me. Now, let us drop the subject. (*She takes her chair and replaces it near the hammock with the same vigorous swing as before.*)

PRAED (*taking a desperate resolution*): One word, Miss Warren. I had better tell you. It's very difficult; but —

(*Mrs Warren and Sir George Crofts arrive at the gate. Mrs Warren is a woman between 40 and 50, good-looking, showily dressed in a brilliant hat and a gay blouse fitting tightly over her bust and flanked by fashionable sleeves. Rather spoiled and domineering, but, on the whole, a genial and fairly presentable old blackguard of a woman.*

Crofts is a tall, powerfully-built man of about 50, fashionably dressed in the style of a young man. Nasal voice, reedier than might be expected from his strong frame. Clean-shaven, bulldog jaws, large flat ears, and thick neck, gentlemanly combination of the most brutal types of city man, sporting man, and man about town.)

VIVIE: Here they are. (*Coming to them as they enter the garden.*) How do, mater. Mr Praed's been here this half hour, waiting for you.

MRS WARREN: Well, if youve been waiting, Praddy, it's your own fault: I thought youd have had the gumption to know I was coming by the 3:10 train. Vivie: put your hat on, dear: youll get sunburnt. Oh, I forgot to introduce you. Sir George Crofts: my little Vivie.

(*Crofts advances to Vivie with his most courtly manner. She nods, but makes no motion to shake hands.*)

CROFTS: May I shake hands with a young lady whom I have known by reputation very long as the daughter of one of my oldest friends?

VIVIE (*who has been looking him up and down sharply*): If you like. (*She takes his tenderly proffered hand and gives it a squeeze that makes him open his eyes; then turns away, and says to her mother.*) Will you come

---

devilling: To aid a professional (such as a lawyer or literary person) without fee or monetary recognition. This would constitute an apprenticeship.

---

in, or shall I get a couple more chairs? (*She goes into the porch for the chairs.*)

MRS WARREN: Well, George, what do you think of her?

CROFTS (*ruefully*): She has a powerful fist. Did you shake hands with her, Praed?

PRAED: Yes: it will pass off presently.

CROFTS: I hope so. (*Vivie reappears with two more chairs. He hurries to her assistance.*) Allow me.

MRS WARREN (*patronizingly*): Let Sir George help you with the chairs, dear.

VIVIE (*almost pitching the two into his arms*): Here you are. (*She dusts her hands and turns to Mrs Warren.*) Youd like some tea, wouldnt you?

MRS WARREN (*sitting in Praed's chair and fanning herself*): I'm dying for a drop to drink.

VIVIE: I'll see about it. (*She goes into the cottage. Sir George has by this time managed to unfold a chair and plant it beside Mrs Warren, on her left. He throws the other on the grass and sits down, looking dejected and rather foolish, with the handle of his stick in his mouth. Praed, still very uneasy, fidgets about the garden on their right.*)

MRS WARREN (*to Praed, looking at Crofts*): Just look at him, Praddy: he looks cheerful, dont he? He's been worrying my life out these three years to have that little girl of mine shewn to him; and now that Ive done it, he's quite out of countenance. (*Briskly.*) Come! sit up, George; and take your stick out of your mouth. (*Crofts sulkily obeys.*)

PRAED: I think, you know — if you dont mind my saying so — that we had better get out of the habit of thinking of her as a little girl. You see she has really distinguished herself; and I'm not sure, from what I have seen of her, that she is not older than any of us.

MRS WARREN (*greatly amused*): Only listen to him, George! Older than any of us! Well, she has been stuffing you nicely with her importance.

PRAED: But young people are particularly sensitive about being treated in that way.

MRS WARREN: Yes; and young people have to get all that nonsense taken out of them, and a good deal more besides. Dont you interfere, Praddy. I know how to treat my own child as well as you do. (*Praed, with a grave shake of his head, walks up the garden with his hands behind his back. Mrs Warren pretends to laugh, but looks after him with perceptible concern. Then she whispers to Crofts*) Whats the matter with him? What does he take it like that for?

CROFTS (*morosely*): Youre afraid of Praed.

MRS WARREN: What! Me! Afraid of dear old Praddy! Why, a fly wouldnt be afraid of him.

CROFTS: Youre afraid of him.

MRS WARREN (*angry*): I'll trouble you to mind your own business, and not try any of your sulks on me. I'm not afraid of you, anyhow. If you cant make yourself agreeable, youd better go home. (*She gets up, and, turning her back on him, finds herself face to face with Praed.*) Come, Praddy, I know it was only your tender-heartedness. Youre afraid I'll bully her.

PRAED: My dear Kitty: you think I'm offended. Dont imagine that: pray dont. But you know I often notice things that escape you; and though you never take my advice, you sometimes admit afterwards that you ought to have taken it.

MRS WARREN: Well, what do you notice now?

PRAED: Only that Vivie is a grown woman. Pray, Kitty, treat her with every respect.

MRS WARREN (*with genuine amazement*): Respect! Treat my own daughter with respect! What next, pray!

VIVIE (*appearing at the cottage door and calling to Mrs Warren*): Mother: will you come up to my room and take your bonnet off before tea?

MRS WARREN: Yes, dearie. (*She laughs indulgently at Praed and pats him on the cheek as she passes him on her way to the porch. She follows Vivie into the cottage.*)

CROFTS (*furtively*): I say, Praed.

PRAED: Yes.

CROFTS: I want to ask you a rather particular question.

PRAED: Certainly. (*He takes Mrs Warren's chair and sits close to Crofts.*)

CROFTS: Thats right: they might hear us from the window. Look here: did Kitty ever tell you who that girl's father is?

PRAED: Never.

CROFTS: Have you any suspicion of who it might be?

PRAED: None.

CROFTS (*not believing him*): I know, of course, that you perhaps might feel bound not to tell if she had said anything to you. But it's very awkward to be uncertain about it now that we shall be meeting the girl every day. We dont exactly know how we ought to feel towards her.

PRAED: What difference can that make? We take her on her own merits. What does it matter who her father was?

CROFTS (*suspiciously*): Then you know who he was?

PRAED (*with a touch of temper*): I said no just now. Did you not hear me?

CROFTS: Look here, Praed. I ask you as a particular favor. If you do know (*movement of protest from Praed*) — I only say, if you know, you might at least set my mind at rest about her. The fact is, I feel attracted towards her. Oh, dont be alarmed: it's quite an innocent feeling. Thats what puzzles me about it. Why, for all I know, *I* might be her father.

PRAED: You! Impossible! Oh no, nonsense!

CROFTS (*catching him up cunningly*): You know for certain that I'm not?

PRAED: I know nothing about it, I tell you, any more than you. But really, Crofts — oh no, it's out of the question. Theres not the least resemblance.

CROFTS: As to that, theres no resemblance between her and her mother that I can see. I suppose she's not your daughter, is she?

PRAED (*He meets the question with an indignant stare; then recovers himself with an effort and answers gently and gravely*): Now listen to me, my dear Crofts. I have nothing to do with that side of Mrs Warren's life, and never had. She has never spoken to me about it; and of course I have never spoken to her about it. Your delicacy will tell you that a handsome woman needs some friends who are not — well, not on that footing with her. The effect of her own beauty would become a torment to her if she could not escape from it occasionally. You are probably on much more confidential terms with Kitty than I am. Surely you can ask her the question yourself.

CROFTS (*rising impatiently*): I have asked her, often enough. But she's so determined to keep the child all to herself that she would deny that it ever had a father if she could. No: theres nothing to be got out of her — nothing that one can believe, anyhow. I'm thoroughly uncomfortable about it, Praed.

PRAED (*rising also*): Well, as you are, at all events, old enough to be her father, I dont mind agreeing that we both regard Miss Vivie in a parental way, as a young girl whom we are bound to protect and help. All the more, as the real father, whoever he was, was probably a black-guard. What do you say?

CROFTS (*aggressively*): I'm no older than you, if you come to that.

PRAED: Yes you are, my dear fellow: you were born old. I was born a boy: Ive never been able to feel the assurance of a grown-up man in my life.

MRS WARREN (*calling from within the cottage*): Praddee! George! Tea-ea-ea-ea!

CROFTS (*hastily*): She's calling us. (*He hurries in. Praed shakes his head bodingly, and is following slowly when he is hailed by a young gentleman who has just appeared on the common, and is making for the gate. He is a pleasant, pretty, smartly dressed, and entirely good-for-nothing young fellow, not long turned 20, with a charming voice and agreeably disrespectful manners. He carries a very light sporting magazine rifle.*)

THE YOUNG GENTLEMAN: Hallo! Praed!

PRAED: Why, Frank Gardner! (*Frank comes in and shakes hands cordially.*) What on earth are you doing here?

FRANK: Staying with my father.

PRAED: The Roman father?

FRANK: He's rector here. I'm living with my people this autumn for the sake of economy. Things came to a crisis in July: the Roman father had to pay my debts. He's stony broke in consequence; and so am I. What are you up to in these parts? Do you know the people here?

PRAED: Yes: I'm spending the day with a Miss Warren.

FRANK (*enthusiastically*): What! Do you know Vivie? Isnt she a jolly girl! I'm teaching her to shoot — you see (*shewing the rifle*)! I'm so glad she knows you: youre just the sort of fellow she ought to know. (*He smiles, and raises the charming voice almost to a singing tone as he exclaims.*) It's ever so jolly to find you here, Praed. Aint it now?

PRAED: I'm an old friend of her mother's. Mrs Warren brought me over to make her daughter's acquaintance.

FRANK: The mother! Is she here?

PRAED: Yes — inside, at tea.

MRS WARREN (*calling from within*): Prad-dee-ee-ee-eee! The tea-cake'll be cold.

PRAED (*calling*): Yes, Mrs Warren. In a moment. Ive just met a friend here.

MRS WARREN: A what?

PRAED (*louder*): A friend.

MRS WARREN: Bring him up.

PRAED: All right. (*To Frank.*) Will you accept the invitation?

FRANK (*incredulous, but immensely amused*): Is that Vivie's mother?

PRAED: Yes.

FRANK: By Jove! What a lark! Do you think she'll like me?

PRAED: Ive no doubt youll make yourself popular, as usual. Come in and try (*moving towards the house*).

FRANK: Stop a bit. (*Seriously.*) I want to take you into my confidence.

PRAED: Pray dont. It's only some fresh folly, like the barmaid at Redhill.

FRANK: It's ever so much more serious than that. You say youve only just met Vivie for the first time?

PRAED: Yes.

FRANK (*rhapsodically*): Then you can have no idea what a girl she is. Such character! Such sense! And her cleverness! Oh, my eye, Praed, but I can tell you she is clever! And the most loving little heart that —

CROFTS (*putting his head out of the window*): I say, Praed: what are you about? Do come along. (*He disappears.*)

FRANK: Hallo! Sort of chap that would take a prize at a dog show, aint he? Who's he?

PRAED: Sir George Crofts, an old friend of Mrs Warren's. I think we had better come in.

(*On their way to the porch they are interrupted by a call from the gate. Turning, they see an elderly clergyman looking over it.*)

THE CLERGYMAN (*calling*): Frank!

FRANK: Hello! (*To Praed.*) The Roman father. (*To the clergyman.*) Yes, gov'nor: all right: presently. (*To Praed.*) Look here, Praed: youd better go in to tea. I'll join you directly.

PRAED: Very good. (*He raises his hat to the clergyman, who acknowledges the salute distantly. Praed goes into the cottage. The clergyman remains stiffly outside the gate, with his hands on the top of it. The Rev. Samuel Gardner, a beneficed clergyman of the Established Church, is over 50. He is a pretentious, booming, noisy person, hopelessly asserting himself as a father and a clergyman without being able to command respect in either capacity.*)

REV. SAMUEL: Well, sir. Who are your friends here, if I may ask?

FRANK: Oh, it's all right, gov'nor! Come in.

REV. SAMUEL: No, sir; not until I know whose garden I am entering.

FRANK: It's all right. It's Miss Warren's.

REV. SAMUEL: I have not seen her at church since she came.

FRANK: Of course not: she's a third wrangler — ever so intellectual! — took a higher degree than you did; so why should she go to hear you preach?

REV. SAMUEL: Dont be disrespectful, sir.

FRANK: Oh, it dont matter: nobody hears us. Come in. (*He opens the gate, unceremoniously pulling his father with it into the garden.*) I want to introduce you to her. She and I get on rattling well together: she's charming. Do you remember the advice you gave me last July, gov'nor?

REV. SAMUEL (*severely*): Yes. I advised you to conquer your idleness and flippancy, and to work your way into an honorable profession and live on it and not upon me.

FRANK: No: thats what you thought of afterwards. What you actually said was that since I had neither brains nor money, I'd better turn my good looks to account my marrying somebody with both. Well, look here. Miss Warren has brains: you cant deny that.

REV. SAMUEL: Brains are not everything.

FRANK: No, of course not: theres the money —

REV. SAMUEL (*interrupting him austerely*): I was not thinking of money, sir. I was speaking of higher things — social position, for instance.

FRANK: I dont care a rap about that.

REV. SAMUEL: But I do, sir.

FRANK: Well, nobody wants you to marry her. Anyhow, she has what amounts to a high Cambridge degree; and she seems to have as much money as she wants.

REV. SAMUEL (*sinking into a feeble vein of humor*): I greatly doubt whether she has as much money as you will want.

FRANK: Oh, come: I havnt been so very extravagant. I live ever so quietly; I dont drink; I dont bet much; and I never go regularly on the razzle-dazzle as you did when you were my age.

REV. SAMUEL (*booming hollowly*): Silence, sir.

FRANK: Well, you told me yourself, when I was making ever such an ass of myself about the barmaid at Redhill, that you once offered a woman £50 for the letters you wrote to her when —

REV. SAMUEL (*terrified*): Sh-sh-sh, Frank, for Heaven's sake! (*He looks round apprehensively. Seeing no one within earshot he plucks up courage to boom again, but more subduedly.*) You are taking an ungentlemanly advantage of what I confided to you for your own good, to save you from an error you would have repented all your life long. Take warning by your father's follies, sir; and dont make them an excuse for your own.

FRANK: Did you ever hear the story of the Duke of Wellington and his letters?

REV. SAMUEL: No, sir; and I dont want to hear it.

FRANK: The old Iron Duke didnt throw away £50 — not he. He just wrote: "My dear Jenny: Publish and be damned! Yours affectionately, Wellington." Thats what you should have done.

REV. SAMUEL (*piteously*): Frank, my boy: when I wrote those letters I put myself into that woman's power. When I told you about her I put myself, to some extent, I am sorry to say, in your power. She refused my money with these words, which I shall never forget: "Knowledge is power," she said; "and I never sell power." Thats more than twenty years ago; and she has never made use of her power or caused me a moment's uneasiness. You are behaving worse to me than she did, Frank.

FRANK: Oh yes I dare say! Did you ever preach at her the way you preach at me every day?

REV. SAMUEL (*wounded almost to tears*): I leave you, sir. You are incorrigible. (*He turns towards the gate.*)

FRANK (*utterly unmoved*): Tell them I shant be home to tea, will you, gov'nor, like a good fellow? (*He goes towards the cottage door and is met by Vivie coming out, followed by Praed, Crofts, and Mrs Warren.*)

VIVIE (*to Frank*): Is that your father, Frank? I do so want to meet him.

FRANK: Certainly. (*Calling after his father*) Gov'nor. (*The Rev Samuel turns at the gate, fumbling nervously at his hat. Praed comes down the garden on the opposite side, beaming in anticipation of civilities. Crofts prowls about near the hammock, poking it with his stick to make it swing. Mrs Warren halts on the threshold, staring hard at the clergyman.*) Let me introduce — my father: Miss Warren.

VIVIE (*going to the clergyman and shaking his hand*): Very glad to see you here, Mr Gardner. Let me introduce everybody. Mr Gardner — Mr Frank Gardner — Mr Praed — Sir George Crofts, and — (*As the men are raising their hats to one another, Vivie is interrupted by an exclamation from her mother, who swoops down on the Reverend Samuel.*)

MRS WARREN: Why, it's Sam Gardner, gone into the church! Dont you know us, Sam? This is George Crofts, as large as life and twice as natural. Dont you remember me?

REV. SAMUEL (*very red*): I really — er —

MRS WARREN: Of course you do. Why, I have a whole album of your letters still: I came across them only the other day.

REV. SAMUEL (*miserably confused*): Miss Vavasour, I believe.

MRS WARREN (*correcting him quickly in a loud whisper*): Tch! Nonsense — Mrs. Warren: dont you see my daughter there?

ACT II

(*Inside the cottage after nightfall. Looking eastward from within instead of westward from without, the latticed window, with its curtains drawn, is now seen in the middle of the front wall of the cottage, with the porch door to the left of it. In the left-hand side wall is the door leading to the wing. Farther back against the same wall is a dresser with a candle and matches on it, and Frank's rifle standing beside them, with the barrel resting in the plate-rack. In the centre a table stands with a lighted lamp on it. Vivie's books and writing materials are on a table to the right of the window, against the wall. The fireplace is on the right, with a settle: there is no fire. Two of the chairs are set right and left of the table.*

The cottage door opens, showing a fine starlit night without; and Mrs. Warren, her shoulders wrapped in a shawl borrowed from Vivie, enters, followed by Frank. She has had enough of walking, and gives a gasp of relief as she unpins her hat; takes it off; sticks the pin through the crown; and puts it on the table.)

MRS WARREN: O Lord! I dont know which is the worst of the country, the walking or the sitting at home with nothing to do. I could do a whisky and soda now very well, if only they had such a thing in this place.

FRANK (*helping her to take off her shawl, and giving her shoulders the most delicate possible little caress with his fingers as he does so*): Perhaps Vivie's got some.

MRS WARREN (*glancing back at him for an instant from the corner of her eye as she detects the pressure*): Nonsense! What would a young girl like her be doing with such things! Never mind: it dont matter. (*She throws herself wearily into a chair at the table.*) I wonder how she passes her time here! I'd a good deal rather be in Vienna.

FRANK: Let me take you there. (*He folds the shawl neatly; hangs it on the back of the other chair; and sits down opposite Mrs Warren.*)

MRS WARREN: Get out! I'm beginning to think youre a chip of the old block.

FRANK: Like the gov'nor, eh?

MRS WARREN: Never you mind. What do you know about such things? Youre only a boy.

FRANK: Do come to Vienna with me? It'd be ever such larks.

MRS WARREN: No, thank you. Vienna is no place for you — at least not until youre a little older. (*She nods at him to emphasize this piece of advice. He makes a mock-piteous face, belied by his laughing eyes. She looks at him; then rises and goes to him.*) Now, look here, little boy (*taking his face in her hands and turning it up to her*): I know you through and through by your likeness to your father, better than you know yourself. Dont you go taking any silly ideas into your head about me. Do you hear?

FRANK (*gallantly wooing her with his voice*): Cant help it, my dear Mrs Warren: it runs in the family. (*She pretends to box his ears; then looks at the pretty, laughing, upturned face for a moment, tempted. At last she kisses him, and immediately turns away, out of patience with herself.*)

MRS WARREN: There! I shouldnt have done that. I am wicked. Never you mind, my dear: it's only a motherly kiss. Go and make love to Vivie.

FRANK: So I have.

MRS WARREN (*turning on him with a sharp note of alarm in her voice*): What!

FRANK: Vivie and I are ever such chums.

MRS WARREN: What do you mean? Now see here: I wont have any young scamp tampering with my little girl. Do you hear? I wont have it.

FRANK (*quite unabashed*): My dear Mrs Warren: dont you be alarmed. My intentions are honorable — ever so honorable; and your little girl is jolly well able to take care of herself. She dont need looking after half so much as her mother. She aint so handsome, you know.

MRS WARREN (*taken aback by his assurance*): Well, you have got a nice, healthy two inches thick of cheek all over you. I dont know where you got it — not from your father, anyhow. (*Voices and footsteps in the porch.*) Sh! I hear the others coming in. (*She sits down hastily.*) Remember: youve got your warning. (*The Rev. Samuel comes in, followed by Crofts.*) Well, what became of you two? And wheres Praddy and Vivie?

CROFTS (*putting his hat on the settle and his stick in the chimney corner*): They went up the hill. We went to the village. I wanted a drink. (*He sits down on the settle, putting his legs up along the seat.*)

MRS WARREN: Well, she oughtnt to go off like that without telling me. (*To Frank*) Get your father a chair, Frank: where are your manners? (*Frank springs up and gracefully offers his father his chair; then takes another from the wall and sits down at the table, in the middle, with his father on his right and Mrs Warren on his left.*) George: where are you going to stay to-night? You cant stay here. And whats Praddy going to do?

CROFTS: Gardner'll put me up.

MRS WARREN: Oh, no doubt youve taken care of yourself! But what about Praddy?

CROFTS: Dont know. I suppose he can sleep at the inn.

MRS WARREN: Havnt you room for him, Sam?

REV. SAMUEL: Well, er — you see, as rector here, I am not free to do as I like exactly. Er — what is Mr Praed's social position?

MRS WARREN: Oh, he's all right: he's an architect. What an old stick-in-the-mud you are, Sam!

FRANK: Yes, it's all right, gov'nor. He built that place down in Monmouthshire for the Duke of Beaufort — Tintern Abbey they call it. You must have heard of it. (*He winks with lightning smartness at Mrs Warren, and regards his father blandly.*)

REV. SAMUEL: Oh, in that case, of course we shall only be too happy. I suppose he knows the Duke of Beaufort personally.

FRANK: Oh, ever so intimately! We can stick him in Georgina's old room.

MRS WARREN: Well, thats settled. Now if those two would only come in and let us have supper. Theyve no right to stay out after dark like this.

CROFTS (*aggressively*): What harm are they doing you?

MRS WARREN: Well, harm or not, I dont like it.

FRANK: Better not wait for them, Mrs Warren. Praed will stay out as long as possible. He has never known before what it is to stray over the heath on a summer night with my Vivie.

CROFTS (*sitting up in some consternation*): I say, you know. Come!

REV. SAMUEL (*startled out of his professional manner into real force and sincerity*): Frank, once for all, it's out of the question. Mrs Warren will tell you that it's not to be thought of.

CROFTS: Of course not.

FRANK (*with enchanting placidity*): Is that so, Mrs Warren?

MRS WARREN (*reflectively*): Well, Sam, I dont know. If the girl wants to get married, no good can come of keeping her unmarried.

REV. SAMUEL (*astounded*): But married to him! — your daughter to my son! Only think: it's impossible.

CROFTS: Of course it's impossible. Dont be a fool, Kitty.

MRS WARREN (*nettled*): Why not? Isn't my daughter good enough for your son?

REV. SAMUEL: But surely, my dear Mrs Warren, you know the reason —

MRS WARREN (*defiantly*): I know no reasons. If you know any, you can tell them to the lad, or to the girl, or to your congregation, if you like.

REV. SAMUEL (*helplessly*): You know very well that I couldnt tell anyone the reasons. But my boy will believe me when I tell him there are reasons.

FRANK: Quite right, Dad: he will. But has your boy's conduct ever been influenced by your reasons?

CROFTS: You cant marry her; and thats all about it. (*He gets up and stands on the hearth, with his back to the fireplace, frowning determinedly.*)

MRS WARREN (*turning on him sharply*): What have you got to do with it, pray?

FRANK (*with his prettiest lyrical cadence*): Precisely what I was going to ask, myself, in my own graceful fashion.

CROFTS (*to Mrs Warren*): I suppose you dont want to marry the girl to a man younger than herself and without either a profession or twopence to keep her on. Ask Sam, if you dont believe me. (*To the Rev. Samuel.*) How much more money are you going to give him?

REV. SAMUEL: Not another penny. He has had his patrimony; and he spent the last of it in July. (*Mrs Warren's face falls.*)

CROFTS (*watching her*): There! I told you. (*He resumes his place on the settle and puts up his legs on the seat again, as if the matter were finally disposed of.*)

FRANK (*plaintively*): This is ever so mercenary. Do you suppose Miss Warren's going to marry for money? If we love one another —

MRS WARREN: Thank you. Your love's a pretty cheap commodity, my lad. If you have no means of keeping a wife, that settles it: you cant have Vivie.

FRANK (*much amused*): What do you say, gov'nor, eh?

REV. SAMUEL: I agree with Mrs Warren.

FRANK: And good old Crofts has already expressed his opinion.

CROFTS (*turning angrily on his elbow*): Look here: I want none of your cheek.

FRANK (*pointedly*): I'm ever so sorry to surprise you, Crofts; but you allowed yourself the liberty of speaking to me like a father a moment ago. One father is enough, thank you.

CROFTS (*contemptuously*): Yah! (*He turns away again.*)

FRANK (*rising*): Mrs Warren: I cannot give my Vivie up, even for your sake.

MRS WARREN (*muttering*): Young scamp!

FRANK (*continuing*): And as you no doubt intend to hold out other prospects to her, I shall lose no time in placing my case before her. (*They stare at him; and he begins to declaim gracefully*)

> He either fears his fate too much,
> Or his deserts are small,
> That dares not put it to the touch
> To gain or lose it all.

(*The cottage door opens whilst he is reciting; and Vivie and Praed come in. He breaks off. Praed puts his hat on the dresser. There is an immediate improvement in the company's behaviour. Crofts takes down his legs from the settle and pulls himself together as Praed joins him at the fireplace. Mrs Warren loses her ease of manner and takes refuge in querulousness.*)

MRS WARREN: Wherever you have been, Vivie?

VIVIE (*taking off her hat and throwing it carelessly on the table*): On the hill.

MRS WARREN: Well, you shouldnt go off like that without letting me know. How could I tell what had become of you — and night coming on too!

VIVIE (*going to the door of the inner room and opening it, ignoring her mother*): Now, about supper? We shall be rather crowded in here, I'm afraid.

MRS WARREN: Did you hear what I said, Vivie?

VIVIE (*quietly*): Yes, mother. (*Reverting to the supper difficulty.*) How many are we? (*Counting.*) One, two, three, four, five, six. Well, two will have to wait until the rest are done: Mrs Allison has only plates and knives for four.

PRAED: Oh, it doesnt matter about me. I —

VIVIE: You have had a long walk and are hungry, Mr Praed: you shall have your supper at once. I can wait myself. I want one person to wait with me. Frank: are you hungry?

FRANK: Not the least in the world — completely off my peck, in fact.

MRS WARREN (*to Crofts*): Neither are you, George. You can wait.

CROFTS: Oh, hang it, Ive eaten nothing since tea-time. Cant Sam do it?

FRANK: Would you starve my poor father?

REV. SAMUEL (*testily*): Allow me to speak for myself, sir. I am perfectly willing to wait.

VIVIE (*decisively*): Theres no need. Only two are wanted. (*She opens the door of the inner room.*) Will you take my mother in, Mr Gardner. (*The Rev. Samuel takes Mrs Warren; and they pass into the next room. Praed and Crofts follow. All except Praed clearly disapprove of the arrangement, but do not know how to resist it. Vivie stands at the door looking in at them.*) Can you squeeze past to that corner, Mr Praed: it's rather a tight fit. Take care of your coat against the white-wash — thats right. Now, are you all comfortable?

PRAED (*within*): Quite, thank you.

MRS WARREN (*within*): Leave the door open, dearie. (*Frank looks at Vivie; then steals to the cottage door and softly sets it wide open.*) Oh Lor, what a draught! Youd better shut it, dear. (*Vivie shuts it promptly. Frank noiselessly shuts the cottage door.*)

FRANK (*exulting*): Aha! Got rid of em. Well, Vivvums: what do you think of my governor?

VIVIE (*preoccupied and serious*): Ive hardly spoken to him. He doesnt strike me as being a particularly able person.

FRANK: Well, you know, the old man is not altogether such a fool as he looks. You see, he's rector here; and in trying to live up to it he makes a much bigger ass of himself than he really is. No, the gov'nor aint so bad, poor old chap; and I dont dislike him as much as you might expect. He means well. How do you think youll get on with him?

VIVIE (*rather grimly*): I dont think my future life will be much concerned with him, or with any of that old circle of my mother's, except perhaps Praed. What do you think of my mother?

FRANK: Really and truly?

VIVIE: Yes, really and truly.

FRANK: Well, she's ever so jolly. But she's rather a caution, isnt she? And Crofts! Oh, my eye, Crofts!

VIVIE: What a lot, Frank!

FRANK: What a crew!

VIVIE (*with intense contempt for them*): If I thought that I was like that — that I was going to be a waster, shifting along from one meal to another with no purpose, and no character, and no grit in me, I'd open an artery and bleed to death without one moment's hesitation.

FRANK: Oh no, you wouldnt. Why should they take any grind when they can afford not to? I wish I had their luck. No: what I object to is their form. It isnt the thing: it's slovenly, ever so slovenly.

VIVIE: Do you think your form will be any better when youre as old as Crofts, if you dont work?

FRANK: Of course I do — ever so much better. Vivvums mustnt lecture: her little boy's incorrigible. (*He attempts to take her face caressingly in his hands.*)

VIVIE (*striking his hands down sharply*): Off with you: Vivvums is not in a humor for petting her little boy this evening.

FRANK: How unkind!

VIVIE (*stamping at him*): Be serious. I'm serious.

FRANK: Good. Let us talk learnedly. Miss Warren: do you know that all the most advanced thinkers are agreed that half the diseases of modern civilization are due to starvation of the affections in the young. Now, I —

VIVIE (*cutting him short*): You are getting tiresome. (*She opens the inner door*) Have you room for Frank there? He's complaining of starvation.

MRS WARREN (*within*): Of course there is (*clatter of knives and glasses as she moves the things on the table.*) Here: theres room now beside me. Come along, Mr Frank.

FRANK (*aside to Vivie, as he goes*): Her little boy will be ever so even with his Vivvums for this. (*He goes into the other room.*)

MRS WARREN (*within*): Here, Vivie: come on you too, child. You must be famished. (*She enters, followed by Crofts, who holds the door open for Vivie with marked deference. She goes out without looking at him; and he shuts the door after her.*) Why, George, you cant be done: youve eaten nothing.

CROFTS: Oh, all I wanted was a drink. (*He thrusts his hands in his pockets, and begins prowling about the room, restless and sulky.*)

MRS WARREN: Well, I like enough to eat. But a little of that cold beef and cheese and lettuce goes a long way. (*With a sigh of only half repletion she sits down lazily at the table.*)

CROFTS: What do you go encouraging that young pup for?

MRS WARREN (*on the alert at once*): Now see here, George: what are you up to about that girl? Ive been watching your way of looking at her. Remember: I know you and what your looks mean.

CROFTS: Theres no harm in looking at her, is there?

MRS WARREN: I'd put you out and pack you back to London pretty soon if I saw any of your nonsense. My girl's little finger is more to me than your whole body and soul. (*Crofts receives this with a sneering grin. Mrs Warren, flushing a little at her failure to impose on him in the character of a theatrically devoted mother, adds in a lower key*) Make your mind easy: the young pup has no more chance than you have.

CROFTS: Maynt a man take an interest in a girl?

MRS WARREN: Not a man like you.

CROFTS: How old is she?

MRS WARREN: Never you mind how old she is.

CROFTS: Why do you make such a secret of it?

MRS WARREN: Because I choose.

CROFTS: Well, I'm not fifty yet; and my property is as good as ever it was —

MRS WARREN (*interrupting him*): Yes; because youre as stingy as youre vicious.

CROFTS (*continuing*): And a baronet isnt to be picked up every day. No other man in my position would put up with you for a mother-in-law. Why shouldnt she marry me?

MRS WARREN: You!

CROFTS: We three could live together quite comfortably.

I'd die before her and leave her a bouncing widow with plenty of money. Why not? It's been growing in my mind all the time Ive been walking with that fool inside there.

MRS WARREN (*revolted*): Yes: it's the sort of thing that would grow in your mind. (*He halts in his prowling; and the two look at one another, she steadfastly, with a sort of awe behind her contemptuous disgust: he stealthily, with a carnal gleam in his eye and a loose grin, tempting her.*)

CROFTS (*suddenly becoming anxious and urgent as he sees no sign of sympathy in her*): Look here, Kitty: youre a sensible woman: you neednt put on any moral airs. I'll ask no more questions; and you need answer none. I'll settle the whole property on her; and if you want a cheque for yourself on the wedding day, you can name any figure you like — in reason.

MRS WARREN: So it's come to that with you, George, like all the other worn out old creatures!

CROFTS (*savagely*): Damn you! (*She rises and turns fiercely on him; but the door of the inner room is opened just then; and the voices of the others are heard returning. Crofts, unable to recover his presence of mind, hurries out of the cottage. The clergyman comes back.*)

REV. SAMUEL (*looking round*): Where is Sir George.

MRS WARREN: Gone out to have a pipe. (*She goes to the fireplace, turning her back on him to compose herself. The clergyman goes to the table for his hat. Meanwhile Vivie comes in, followed by Frank, who collapses into the nearest chair with an air of extreme exhaustion. Mrs Warren looks round at Vivie and says, with her affectation of maternal patronage even more forced than usual.*) Well, dearie: have you had a good supper?

VIVIE: You know what Mrs Alison's suppers are. (*She turns to Frank and pets him.*) Poor Frank! was all the beef gone? did it get nothing but bread and cheese and ginger beer? (*Seriously, as if she had done quite enough trifling for one evening.*) Her butter is really awful. I must get some down from the stores.

FRANK: Do, in Heaven's name!

(*Vivie goes to the writing-table and makes a memorandum to order the butter. Praed comes in from the inner room, putting up his handkerchief, which he has been using as a napkin.*)

REV. SAMUEL: Frank, my boy: it is time for us to be thinking of home. Your mother does not know yet that we have visitors.

PRAED: I'm afraid we're giving trouble.

FRANK: Not the least in the world, Praed: my mother will be delighted to see you. She's a genuinely intellectual, artistic woman; and she sees nobody here from one year's end to another except the gov'nor; so you can imagine how jolly dull it pans out for her. (*To the Rev. Samuel.*) Youre not intellectual or artistic, are you, pater? So take Praed home at once; and I'll stay here and entertain Mrs Warren. Youll pick up

Crofts in the garden. He'll be excellent company for the bull-pup.

PRAED (*taking his hat from the dresser, and coming close to Frank*): Come with us, Frank. Mrs Warren has not seen Miss Vivie for a long time; and we have prevented them from having a moment together yet.

FRANK (*quite softened, and looking at Praed with romantic admiration*): Of course: I forgot. Ever so thanks for reminding me. Perfect gentleman, Praddy. Always were — my ideal through life. (*He rises to go, but pauses a moment between the two older men, and puts his hand on Praed's shoulder.*) Ah, if you had only been my father instead of this unworthy old man! (*He puts his other hand on his father's shoulder.*)

REV. SAMUEL (*blustering*): Silence, sir, silence: you are profane.

MRS WARREN (*laughing heartily*): You should keep him in better order, Sam. Good-night. Here: take George his hat and stick with my compliments.

REV. SAMUEL (*taking them*): Good-night. (*They shake hands. As he passes Vivie he shakes hands with her also and bids her good-night. Then, in booming command, to Frank*) Come along, sir, at once. (*He goes out. Meanwhile Frank has taken his cap from the dresser and his rifle from the rack. Praed shakes hands with Mrs Warren and Vivie and goes out, Mrs Warren accompanying him idly to the door and looking out after him as he goes across the garden. Frank silently begs a kiss from Vivie; but she, dismissing him with a stern glance, takes a couple of books and some paper from the writing-table, and sits down with them at the middle table, so as to have the benefit of the lamp.*)

FRANK (*at the door, taking Mrs Warren's hand*): Good-night, dear Mrs Warren. (*He squeezes her hand. She snatches it away, her lips tightening, and looks more than half disposed to box his ears. He laughs mischievously and runs off, clapping-to° the door behind him.*)

MRS WARREN (*coming back to her place at the table, opposite Vivie, resigning herself to an evening of boredom now that the men are gone*): Did you ever in your life hear anyone rattle on so? Isnt he a tease? (*She sits down.*) Now that I think of it, dearie, dont you go encouraging him. I'm sure he's a regular good-for-nothing.

VIVIE: Yes: I'm afraid poor Frank is a thorough good-for-nothing. I shall have to get rid of him; but I shall feel sorry for him, though he's not worth it, poor lad. That man Crofts does not seem to me to be good for much either, is he?

MRS WARREN (*galled by Vivie's cool tone*): What do you know of men, child, to talk that way about them? Youll have to make up your mind to see a good deal of Sir George Crofts, as he's a friend of mine.

VIVIE (*quite unmoved*): Why? Do you expect that we shall be much together — you and I, I mean?

MRS WARREN (*staring at her*): Of course — until youre married. Youre not going back to college again.

VIVIE: Do you think my way of life would suit you? I doubt it.

MRS WARREN: Your way of life! What do you mean?

VIVIE (*cutting a page of her book with the paper knife on her chatelaine*): Has it really never occurred to you, mother, that I have a way of life like other people?

MRS WARREN: What nonsense is this youre trying to talk? Do you want to shew your independence, now that youre a great little person at school? Dont be a fool, child.

VIVIE (*indulgently*): Thats all you have to say on the subject, is it, mother?

MRS WARREN (*puzzled, then angry*): Dont you keep on asking me questions like that. (*Violently*) Hold your tongue. (*Vivie works on, losing no time, and saying nothing.*) You and your way of life, indeed! What next? (*She looks at Vivie again. No reply.*) Your way of life will be what I please, so it will. (*Another pause.*) Ive been noticing these airs in you ever since you got that tripos or whatever you call it. If you think I'm going to put up with them youre mistaken; and the sooner you find it out, the better. (*Muttering.*) All I have to say on the subject, indeed! (*Again raising her voice angrily.*) Do you know who youre speaking to, Miss?

VIVIE (*looking across at her without raising her head from her book*): No. Who are you? What are you?

MRS WARREN (*rising breathless*): You young imp!

VIVIE: Everybody knows my reputation, my social standing, and the profession I intend to pursue. I know nothing about you. What is that way of life which you invite me to share with you and Sir George Crofts, pray?

MRS WARREN: Take care. I shall do something I'll be sorry for after, and you too.

VIVIE (*putting aside her books with cool decision*): Well, let us drop the subject until you are better able to face it. (*Looking critically at her mother*) You want some good walks and a little lawn tennis to set you up. You are shockingly out of condition: you were not able to manage twenty yards uphill to-day without stopping to pant; and your wrists are mere rolls of fat. Look at mine. (*She holds out her wrists.*)

MRS WARREN (*after looking at her helplessly, begins to whimper*): Vivie —

VIVIE (*springing up sharply*): Now pray dont begin to cry. Anything but that. I really cannot stand whimpering. I will go out of the room if you do.

MRS WARREN (*piteously*): Oh, my darling, how can you be so hard on me? Have I no rights over you as your mother?

VIVIE: Are you my mother?

MRS WARREN (*appalled*): Am I your mother! Oh, Vivie!

VIVIE: Then where are our relatives — my father — our family friends? You claim the rights of a mother: the

---

clapping-to: Slamming.

right to call me fool and child; to speak to me as no woman in authority over me at college dare speak to me; to dictate my way of life; and to force on me the acquaintance of a brute whom anyone can see to be the most vicious sort of London man about town. Before I give myself the trouble to resist such claims, I may as well find out whether they have any real existence.

MRS WARREN (*distracted, throwing herself on her knees*): Oh no, no. Stop, stop. I am your mother: I swear it. Oh, you cant mean to turn on me — my own child: it's not natural. You believe me, dont you? Say you believe me.

VIVIE: Who was my father?

MRS WARREN: You dont know what youre asking. I cant tell you.

VIVIE (*determinedly*): Oh yes you can, if you like. I have a right to know; and you know very well that I have that right. You can refuse to tell me, if you please; but if you do, you will see the last of me to-morrow morning.

MRS WARREN: Oh, it's too horrible to hear you talk like that. You wouldnt — you couldnt leave me.

VIVIE (*ruthlessly*): Yes, without a moment's hesitation, if you trifle with me about this. (*Shivering with disgust.*) How can I feel sure that I may not have the contaminated blood of that brutal waster in my veins?

MRS WARREN: No, no. On my oath it's not he, nor any of the rest that you have ever met. I'm certain of that, at least. (*Vivie's eyes fasten sternly on her mother as the significance of this flashes on her.*)

VIVIE (*slowly*): You are certain of that, at least. Ah! You mean that that is all you are certain of. (*Thoughtfully.*) I see. (*Mrs Warren buries her face in her hands.*) Dont do that, mother: you know you dont feel it a bit. (*Mrs Warren takes down her hands and looks up deplorably at Vivie, who takes out her watch and says*) Well, that is enough for to-night. At what hour would you like breakfast? Is half-past eight too early for you?

MRS WARREN (*wildly*): My God, what sort of woman are you?

VIVIE (*coolly*): The sort the world is mostly made of, I should hope. Otherwise I dont understand how it gets its business done. Come (*taking her mother by the wrist, and pulling her up pretty resolutely*): pull yourself together. Thats right.

MRS WARREN (*querulously*): Youre very rough with me, Vivie.

VIVIE: Nonsense. What about bed? It's past ten.

MRS WARREN (*passionately*): Whats the use of my going to bed? Do you think I could sleep?

VIVIE: Why not? I shall.

MRS WARREN: You! youve no heart. (*She suddenly breaks out vehemently in her natural tongue — the dialect of a woman of the people — with all her affectations of maternal authority and conventional manners gone, and an overwhelming inspiration of true conviction and scorn in her.*) Oh, I wont bear it: I

wont put up with the injustice of it. What might have you to set yourself up above me like this? You boast of what you are to me — to me, who gave you the chance of being what you are. What chance had I? Shame on you for a bad daughter and a stuck-up prude!

VIVIE (*cool and determined, but no longer confident; for her replies, which have sounded convincingly sensible and strong to her so far, now begin to ring rather woodenly and even priggishly against the new tone of her mother*): Dont think for a moment I set myself above you in any way. You attacked me with the conventional authority of a mother: I defended myself with the conventional superiority of a respectable woman. Frankly, I am not going to stand any of your nonsense; and when you drop it I shall not expect you to stand any of mine. I shall always respect your right to your own opinions and your own way of life.

MRS WARREN: My own opinions and my own way of life! Listen to her talking! Do you think I was brought up like you — able to pick and choose my own way of life? Do you think I did what I did because I liked it, or thought it right, or wouldnt rather have gone to college and been a lady if I'd had the chance?

VIVIE: Everybody has some choice, mother. The poorest girl alive may not be able to choose between being Queen of England or Principal of Newnham; but she can choose between ragpicking and flowerselling, according to her taste. People are always blaming their circumstances for what they are. I dont believe in circumstances. The people who get on in this world are the people who get up and look for the circumstances they want, and, if they cant find them, make them.

MRS WARREN: Oh, it's easy to talk, very easy, isnt it? Here! — would you like to know what my circumstances were?

VIVIE: Yes: you had better tell me. Wont you sit down?

MRS WARREN: Oh, I'll sit down: dont you be afraid. (*She plants her chair farther forward with brazen energy, and sits down. Vivie is impressed in spite of herself.*) D'you know what your gran'mother was?

VIVIE: No.

MRS WARREN: No, you dont. I do. She called herself a widow and had a fried-fish shop down by the Mint, and kept herself and four daughters out of it. Two of us were sisters: that was me and Liz; and we were both good-looking and well made. I suppose our father was a well-fed man: mother pretended he was a gentleman; but I dont know. The other two were only half sisters — undersized, ugly, starved looking, hard working, honest poor creatures: Liz and I would have half-murdered them if mother hadn't half-murdered us to keep our hands off them. They were the respectable ones. Well, what did they get by their respectability? I'll tell you. One of them worked in a white-lead factory twelve hours a day for nine shillings a week until she died of lead poisoning. She only expected to get her hands a little paralyzed; but she died. The other was always held up to us as a model because she married a Government laborer in the Deptford victualling yard, and kept his room and the three children neat and tidy on eighteen shillings a week — until he took to drink. That was worth being respectable for, wasnt it?

VIVIE (*now thoughtfully attentive*): Did you and your sister think so?

MRS WARREN: Liz didnt, I can tell you: she had more spirit. We both went to a church school — that was part of the ladylike airs we gave ourselves to be superior to the children that knew nothing and went nowhere — and we stayed there until Liz went out one night and never came back. I know the schoolmistress thought I'd soon follow her example; for the clergyman was always warning me that Lizzie'd end by jumping off Waterloo Bridge. Poor fool: that was all he knew about it! But I was more afraid of the whitelead factory than I was of the river; and so would you have been in my place. That clergyman got me a situation as scullery maid in a temperance restaurant where they sent out for anything you liked. Then I was waitress; and then I went to the bar at Waterloo station — fourteen hours a day serving drinks and washing glasses for four shillings a week and my board. That was considered a great promotion for me. Well, one cold, wretched night, when I was so tired I could hardly keep myself awake, who should come up for a half of Scotch but Lizzie, in a long fur cloak, elegant and comfortable, with a lot of sovereigns in her purse.

VIVIE (*grimly*): My aunt Lizzie!

MRS WARREN: Yes; and a very good aunt to have, too. She's living down at Winchester now, close to the cathedral, one of the most respectable ladies there — chaperones girls at the county ball, if you please. No river for Liz, thank you! You remind me of Liz a little: she was a first-rate business woman — saved money from the beginning — never let herself look too like what she was — never lost her head or threw away a chance. When she saw I'd grown up good-looking she said to me across the bar "What are you doing there, you little fool? wearing out your health and your appearance for other people's profit!" Liz was saving money then to take a house for herself in Brussels; and she thought we two could save faster than one. So she lent me some money and gave me a start; and I saved steadily and first paid her back, and then went into business with her as her partner. Why shouldnt I have done it? The house in Brussels was real high class — a much better place for a woman to be in than the factory where Anne Jane got poisoned. None of our girls were ever treated as I was treated in the scullery of that temperance place, or at the Waterloo bar, or at home. Would you have had me stay in them and become a worn out old drudge before I was forty?

VIVIE (*intensely interested by this time*): No; but why did you choose that business? Saving money and good management will succeed in any business.

MRS WARREN: Yes, saving money. But where can a woman get the money to save in any other business? Could you save out of four shillings a week and keep yourself dressed as well? Not you. Of course, if youre a plain woman and cant earn anything more; or if you have a turn for music, or the stage, or newspaper-writing: thats different. But neither Liz nor I had any turn for such things: all we had was our appearance and our turn for pleasing men. Do you think we were such fools as to let other people trade in our good looks by employing us as shopgirls, or barmaids, or waitresses, when we could trade in them ourselves and get all the profits instead of starvation wages? Not likely.

VIVIE: You were certainly quite justified — from the business point of view.

MRS WARREN: Yes; or any other point of view. What is any respectable girl brought up to do but to catch some rich man's fancy and get the benefit of his money by marrying him? — as if a marriage ceremony could make any difference in the right or wrong of the thing! Oh, the hypocrisy of the world makes me sick! Liz and I had to work and save and calculate just like other people; elseways we should be as poor as any good-for-nothing, drunken waster of a woman that thinks her luck will last for ever. (*With great energy.*) I despise such people: theyve no character; and if theres a thing I hate in a woman, it's want of character.

VIVIE: Come now, mother: frankly! Isnt it part of what you call character in a woman that she should greatly dislike such a way of making money?

MRS WARREN: Why, of course. Everybody dislikes having to work and make money; but they have to do it all the same. I'm sure Ive often pitied a poor girl, tired out and in low spirits, having to try to please some man that she doesnt care two straws for — some half-drunken fool that thinks he's making himself agreeable when he's teasing and worrying and disgusting a woman so that hardly any money could pay her for putting up with it. But she has to bear with disagreeables and take the rough with the smooth, just like a nurse in a hospital or anyone else. It's not work that any woman would do for pleasure, goodness knows; though to hear the pious people talk you would suppose it was a bed of roses.

VIVIE: Still you consider it worth while. It pays.

MRS WARREN: Of course it's worth while to a poor girl, if she can resist temptation and is good-looking and well conducted and sensible. It's far better than any other employment open to her. I always thought that oughtnt to be. It cant be right, Vivie, that there shouldnt be better opportunities for women. I stick to that: it's wrong. But it's so, right or wrong; and a girl must make the best of it. But of course it's not worth while for a lady. If you took to it youd be a fool; but I should have been a fool if I'd taken to anything else.

VIVIE (*more and more deeply moved*): Mother: suppose we were both as poor as you were in those wretched old days, are you quite sure that you wouldnt advise me to try the Waterloo bar, or marry a laborer, or even go into the factory?

MRS WARREN (*indignantly*): Of course not. What sort of mother do you take me for! How could you keep your self-respect in such starvation and slavery? And whats a woman worth? whats life worth? without self-respect! Why am I independent and able to give my daughter a first-rate education, when other women that had just as good opportunities are in the gutter?

BELOW: Vivie, played by Kate Goehring, listens to her mother, Mariette Hartley, reveal her secret in Bernard Shaw's *Mrs. Warren's Profession* at the Huntington Theatre, Boston, 1999.
RIGHT: Vivie and her mother console each other in *Mrs. Warren's Profession*, Huntington Theatre, Boston, 1999.

Because I always knew how to respect myself and control myself. Why is Liz looked up to in a cathedral town? The same reason. Where would we be now if we'd minded the clergyman's foolishness? Scrubbing floors for one and sixpence a day and nothing to look forward to but the workhouse infirmary. Dont you be led astray by people who dont know the world, my girl. The only way for a woman to provide for herself decently is for her to be good to some man that can afford to be good to her. If she's in his own station of life, let her make him marry her; but if she's far beneath him she cant expect it — why should she? It wouldnt be for her own happiness. Ask any lady in London society that has daughters; and she'll tell you the same, except that I tell you straight and she'll tell you crooked. Thats all the difference.

VIVIE (*fascinated, gazing at her*): My dear mother: you are a wonderful woman — you are stronger than all England. And are you really and truly not one wee bit doubtful — or — or — ashamed?

MRS WARREN: Well, of course, dearie, it's only good manners to be ashamed of it: it's expected from a woman. Women have to pretend to feel a great deal that they dont feel. Liz used to be angry with me for plumping out the truth about it. She used to say that when every woman could learn enough from what was going on in the world before her eyes, there was no need to talk about it to her. But then Liz was such a perfect lady! She had the true instinct of it; while I was always a bit of a vulgarian. I used to be so pleased when you sent me your photographs to see that you were growing up like Liz: youve just her ladylike, determined way. But I cant stand saying one thing when everyone knows I mean another. Whats the use in such hypocrisy? If people arrange the world that way for women, theres no good pretending that it's arranged the other way. I never was a bit ashamed really. I consider that I had a right to be proud that we managed everything so respectably, and never had a word against us, and that the girls were so well taken care of. Some of them did very well: one of them married an ambassador. But of course now I darent talk about such things: whatever would they think of us! (*She yawns.*) Oh dear! I do believe I'm getting sleepy after all. (*She stretches herself lazily, thoroughly relieved by her explosion, and placidly ready for her night's rest.*)

VIVIE: I believe it is I who will not be able to sleep now. (*She goes to the dresser and lights the candle. Then she extinguishes the lamp, darkening the room a good deal.*) Better let in some fresh air before locking up. (*She opens the cottage door, and finds that it is broad moonlight.*) What a beautiful night! Look! (*She draws aside the curtains of the window. The landscape is seen bathed in the radiance of the harvest moon rising over Blackdown.*)

MRS WARREN (*with a perfunctory glance at the scene*): Yes, dear; but take care you dont catch your death of cold from the night air.

VIVIE (*contemptuously*): Nonsense.

MRS WARREN (*querulously*): Oh yes: everything I say is nonsense, according to you.

VIVIE (*turning to her quickly*): No: really that is not so, mother. You have got completely the better of me tonight, though I intended it to be the other way. Let us be good friends now.

MRS WARREN (*shaking her head a little ruefully*): So it has been the other way. But I suppose I must give in to it. I always got the worst of it from Liz; and now I suppose it'll be the same with you.

VIVIE: Well, never mind. Come: good-night, dear old mother. (*She takes her mother in her arms.*)

MRS WARREN (*fondly*): I brought you up well, didnt I, dearie?

VIVIE: You did.

MRS WARREN: And youll be good to your poor old mother for it, wont you?

VIVIE: I will, dear. (*Kissing her*) Good-night.

MRS WARREN (*with unction*): Blessings on my own dearie darling — a mother's blessing! (*She embraces her daughter protectingly, instinctively looking upward as if to call down a blessing.*)

ACT III

(*In the Rectory garden next morning, with the sun shining and the birds in full song. The garden wall has a five-barred wooden gate, wide enough to admit a carriage, in the middle. Beside the gate hangs a bell on a coiled spring, communicating with a pull outside. The carriage drive comes down the middle of the garden and then swerves to its left, where it ends in a little gravelled circus opposite the Rectory porch. Beyond the gate is seen the dusty high road, parallel with the wall, bounded on the farther side by a strip of turf and an unfenced pine wood. On the lawn, between the house and the drive, is a clipped yew tree, with a garden bench in its shade. On the opposite side the garden is shut in by a box hedge; and there is a sundial on the turf, with an iron chair near it. A little path leads off through the box hedge, behind the sundial.*

Frank, seated on the chair near the sundial, on which he has placed the morning papers, is reading the Standard. *His father comes from the house, red-eyed and shivery, and meets Frank's eye with misgiving.*)

FRANK (*looking at his watch*): Half past eleven. Nice hour for a rector to come down to breakfast!

REV. SAMUEL: Dont mock, Frank: dont mock. I am a little — er — (*Shivering*) —

FRANK: Off colour?

REV. SAMUEL (*repudiating the expression*): No, sir: unwell this morning. Wheres your mother?

FRANK: Dont be alarmed: she's not here. Gone to town by the 11.13 with Bessie. She left several messages for you. Do you feel equal to receiving them now, or shall I wait till youve breakfasted?

REV. SAMUEL: I have breakfasted, sir. I am surprised at your mother going to town when we have people staying with us. Theyll think it very strange.

FRANK: Possibly she has considered that. At all events, if Crofts is going to stay here, and you are going to sit up every night with him until four, recalling the incidents of your fiery youth, it is clearly my mother's duty, as a prudent housekeeper, to go up to the stores and order a barrel of whisky and a few hundred siphons.

REV. SAMUEL: I did not observe that Sir George drank excessively.

FRANK: You were not in a condition to, gov'nor.

REV. SAMUEL: Do you mean to say that *I* —

FRANK (*calmly*): I never saw a beneficed clergyman less sober. The anecdotes you told about your past career were so awful that I really dont think Praed would have passed the night under your roof if it hadnt been for the way my mother and he took to one another.

REV. SAMUEL: Nonsense, sir. I am Sir George Crofts' host. I must talk to him about something; and he has only one subject. Where is Mr Praed now?

FRANK: He is driving my mother and Bessie to the station.

REV. SAMUEL: Is Crofts up yet?

FRANK: Oh, long ago. He hasnt turned a hair: he's in much better practice than you — has kept it up ever since, probably. He's taken himself off somewhere to smoke. (*Frank resumes his paper. The Rev. Samuel turns disconsolately towards the gate; then comes back irresolutely.*)

REV. SAMUEL: Er — Frank.

FRANK: Yes.

REV. SAMUEL: Do you think the Warrens will expect to be asked here after yesterday afternoon?

FRANK: Theyve been asked already. Crofts informed us at breakfast that you told him to bring Mrs Warren and Vivie over here to-day, and to invite them to make this house their home. It was after that communication that my mother found she must go to town by the 11.13 train.

REV. SAMUEL (*with despairing vehemence*): I never gave any such invitation. I never thought of such a thing.

FRANK (*compassionately*): How do you know, gov'nor, what you said and thought last night? Hallo! heres Praed back again.

PRAED (*coming in through the gate*): Good morning.

REV. SAMUEL: Good morning. I must apologize for not having met you at breakfast. I have a touch of — of —

FRANK: Clergyman's sore throat, Praed. Fortunately not chronic.

PRAED (*changing the subject*): Well, I must say your house is in a charming spot here. Really most charming.

REV. SAMUEL: Yes: it is indeed. Frank will take you for a walk, Mr Praed, if you like. I'll ask you to excuse me: I must take the opportunity to write my sermon while Mrs Gardner is away and you are all amusing yourselves. You wont mind, will you?

PRAED: Certainly not. Dont stand on the slightest ceremony with me.

REV. SAMUEL: Thank you. I'll — er — er — (*He stammers his way to the porch and vanishes into the house.*)

PRAED (*sitting down on the turf near Frank, and hugging his ankles*): Curious thing it must be writing a sermon every week.

FRANK: Ever so curious, if he did it. He buys em. He's gone for some soda water.

PRAED: My dear boy: I wish you would be more respectful to your father. You know you can be so nice when you like.

FRANK: My dear Praddy: you forget that I have to live with the governor. When two people live together — it dont matter whether theyre father and son, husband and wife, brother and sister — they cant keep up the polite humbug which comes so easy for ten minutes on an afternoon call. Now the governor, who unites to many admirable domestic qualities the irresoluteness of a sheep and the pompousness and aggressiveness of a jackass —

PRAED: No, pray, pray, my dear Frank, remember! He is your father.

FRANK: I give him due credit for that. But just imagine his telling Crofts to bring the Warrens over here! He must have been ever so drunk. You know, my dear Praddy, my mother wouldnt stand Mrs Warren for a moment. Vivie mustnt come here until she's gone back to town.

PRAED: But your mother doesnt know anything about Mrs Warren, does she?

FRANK: I dont know. Her journey to town looks as if she did. Not that my mother would mind in the ordinary way: she has stuck like a brick to lots of women who had got into trouble. But they were all nice women. Thats what makes the real difference. Mrs Warren, no doubt, has her merits; but she's ever so rowdy; and my mother simply wouldnt put up with her. So — hallo! (*This exclamation is provoked by the reappearance of the clergyman, who comes out of the house in haste and dismay.*)

REV. SAMUEL: Frank: Mrs Warren and her daughter are coming across the heath with Crofts: I saw them from the study windows. What am I to say about your mother?

FRANK (*jumping up energetically*): Stick on your hat and go out and say how delighted you are to see them; and that Frank's in the garden; and that mother and Bessie have been called to the bedside of a sick relative, and were ever so sorry they couldnt stop; and that you hope Mrs Warren slept well; and — and — say any blessed thing except the truth, and leave the rest to Providence.

REV. SAMUEL: But how are we to get rid of them afterwards?

FRANK: Theres no time to think of that now. Here! (*He*

bounds into the porch and returns immediately with a clerical felt hat, which he claps on his father's head.) Now: off with you. Praed and I'll wait here, to give the thing an unpremeditated air. (*The clergyman, dazed but obedient, hurries off through the gate. Praed gets up from the turf, and dusts himself.*)

FRANK: We must get that old lady back to town somehow, Praed. Come! honestly, dear Praddy, do you like seeing them together — Vivie and the old lady?

PRAED: Oh, why not?

FRANK (*his teeth on edge*): Dont it make your flesh creep ever so little? — that wicked old devil, up to every villainy under the sun, I'll swear, and Vivie — ugh!

PRAED: Hush, pray. Theyre coming. (*The clergyman and Crofts are seen coming along the road, followed by Mrs Warren and Vivie walking affectionately together.*)

FRANK: Look: she actually has her arm round the old woman's waist. It's her right arm: she began it. She's gone sentimental, by God! Ugh! ugh! Now do you feel the creeps? (*The clergyman opens the gate; and Mrs Warren and Vivie pass him and stand in the middle of the garden looking at the house. Frank, in an ecstasy of dissimulation, turns gaily to Mrs Warren, exclaiming*) Ever so delighted to see you, Mrs Warren. This quiet old rectory garden becomes you perfectly.

MRS WARREN: Well, I never! Did you hear that, George? He says I look well in a quiet old rectory garden.

REV. SAMUEL (*still holding the gate for Crofts, who loafs through it, heavily bored*): You look well everywhere, Mrs Warren.

FRANK: Bravo, gov'nor! Now look here: lets have an awful jolly time of it before lunch. First lets see the church. Everyone has to do that. It's a regular old thirteenth century church, you know: the gov'nor's ever so fond of it, because he got up a restoration fund and had it completely rebuilt six years ago. Praed will be able to show its points.

REV. SAMUEL (*mooning hospitably at them*): I shall be pleased, I'm sure, if Sir George and Mrs Warren really care about it.

MRS WARREN: Oh, come along and get it over. Itll do George good: I'll lay he doesnt trouble church much.

CROFTS (*turning back towards the gate*): Ive no objection.

REV. SAMUEL: Not that way. We go through the fields, if you dont mind. Round here. (*He leads the way by the little path through the box hedge.*)

CROFTS: Oh, all right. (*He goes with the parson. Praed follows with Mrs Warren. Vivie does not stir, but watches them until they have gone, with all the lines of purpose in her face marking it strongly.*)

FRANK: Aint you coming?

VIVIE: No. I want to give you a warning, Frank. You were making fun of my mother just now when you said that about the rectory garden. That is barred in future. Please treat my mother with as much respect as you treat your own.

FRANK: My dear Viv: she wouldnt appreciate it. She's not like my mother: the same treatment wouldnt do for both cases. But what on earth has happened to you? Last night we were perfectly agreed as to your mother and her set. This morning I find you attitudinizing sentimentally with your arm round your parent's waist.

VIVIE (*flushing*): Attitudinizing!

FRANK: That was how it struck me. First time I ever saw you do a second-rate thing.

VIVIE (*controlling herself*): Yes, Frank: there has been a change; but I dont think it a change for the worse. Yesterday I was a little prig.

FRANK: And to-day?

VIVIE (*wincing; then looking at him steadily*): To-day I know my mother better than you do.

FRANK: Heaven forbid!

VIVIE: What do you mean?

FRANK: Viv: theres a freemasonry among thoroughly immoral people that you know nothing of. Youve too much character. Thats the bond between your mother and me: thats why I know her better than youll ever know her.

VIVIE: You are wrong: you know nothing about her. If you knew the circumstances against which my mother had to struggle —

FRANK (*adroitly finishing the sentence for her*): I should know why she is what she is, shouldnt I? What difference would that make? Circumstances or no circumstances, Viv, you wont be able to stand your mother.

VIVIE (*very angry*): Why not?

FRANK: Because she's an old wretch, Viv. If you ever put your arm round her waist in my presence again, I'll shoot myself there and then as a protest against an exhibition which revolts me.

VIVIE: Must I choose between dropping your acquaintance and dropping my mother's?

FRANK (*gracefully*): That would put the old lady at ever such a disadvantage. No, Viv: your infatuated little boy will have to stick to you in any case. But he's all the more anxious that you shouldnt make mistakes. It's no use, Viv: your mother's impossible. She may be a good sort; but she's a bad lot, a very bad lot.

VIVIE (*hotly*): Frank — ! (*He stands his ground. She turns away and sits down on the bench under the yew tree, struggling to recover her self-command. Then she says*) Is she to be deserted by all the world because she's what you call a bad lot? Has she no right to live?

FRANK: No fear of that, Viv: she wont ever be deserted. (*He sits on the bench beside her.*)

VIVIE: But I am to desert her, I suppose.

FRANK (*babyishly, lulling her and making love to her with his voice*): Mustnt go live with her. Little family group of mother and daughter wouldnt be a success. Spoil our little group.

VIVIE (*falling under the spell*): What little group?

FRANK: The babes in the wood: Vivie and little Frank. (*He slips his arm round her waist and nestles against her like a weary child.*) Lets go and get covered up with leaves.

VIVIE (*rythmically, rocking him like a nurse*): Fast asleep, hand in hand, under the trees.

FRANK: The wise little girl with her silly little boy.

VIVIE: The dear little boy with his dowdy little girl.

FRANK: Ever so peaceful, and relieved from the imbecility of the little boy's father and the questionableness of the little girl's —

VIVIE (*smothering the word against her breast*): Sh-sh-sh-sh! little girl wants to forget all about her mother. (*They are silent for some moments, rocking one another. Then Vivie wakes up with a shock, exclaiming*) What a pair of fools we are! Come: sit up. Gracious! your hair. (*She smooths it.*) I wonder do all grown up people play in that childish way when nobody is looking. I never did it when I was a child.

FRANK: Neither did I. You are my first playmate. (*He catches her hand to kiss it, but checks himself to look round first. Very unexpectedly, he sees Crofts emerging from the box hedge.*) Oh damn!

VIVIE: Why damn, dear?

FRANK (*whispering*): Sh! Here's this brute Crofts. (*He sits farther away from her with an unconcerned air.*)

VIVIE: Dont be rude to him, Frank. I particularly wish to be polite to him. It will please my mother. (*Frank makes a wry face.*)

CROFTS: Could I have a few words with you, Miss Vivie?

VIVIE: Certainly.

CROFTS (*to Frank*): Youll excuse me, Gardner. Theyre waiting for you in the church, if you dont mind.

FRANK (*rising*): Anything to oblige you, Crofts — except church. If you want anything, Vivie, ring the gate bell, and a domestic will appear. (*He goes into the house with unruffled suavity.*)

CROFTS (*watching him with a crafty air as he disappears, and speaking to Vivie with an assumption of being on privileged terms with her*): Pleasant young fellow that, Miss Vivie. Pity he has no money, isnt it?

VIVIE: Do you think so?

CROFTS: Well, whats he to do? No profession, no property. Whats he good for?

VIVIE: I realize his disadvantages, Sir George.

CROFTS (*a little taken aback at being so precisely interpreted*): Oh, it's not that. But while we're in this world we're in it; and money's money. (*Vivie does not answer.*) Nice day, isnt it?

VIVIE (*with scarcely veiled contempt for this effort at conversation*): Very.

CROFTS (*with brutal good humor, as if he liked her pluck*): Well, thats not what I came to say. (*Affecting frankness*) Now listen, Miss Vivie. I'm quite aware that I'm not a young lady's man.

VIVIE: Indeed, Sir George?

CROFTS: No; and to tell you the honest truth I dont want to be either. But when I say a thing I mean it; when I feel sentiment I feel it in earnest; and what I value I pay hard money for. Thats the sort of man I am.

VIVIE: It does you great credit, I'm sure.

CROFTS: Oh, I dont mean to praise myself. I have my faults, Heaven knows: no man is more sensible of that than I am. I know I'm not perfect: thats one of the advantages of being a middle-aged man; for I'm not a young man, and I know it. But my code is a simple one, and, I think, a good one. Honor between man and man; fidelity between man and woman; and no cant about this religion or that religion, but an honest belief that things are making for good on the whole.

VIVIE (*with biting irony*): "A power, not ourselves, that makes for righteousness," eh?

CROFTS (*taking her seriously*): Oh, certainly, not ourselves, of course. You understand what I mean. (*He sits down beside her, as one who has found a kindred spirit.*) Well, now as to practical matters. You may have an idea that Ive flung my money about; but I havnt: I'm richer to-day than when I first came into the property. Ive used my knowledge of the world to invest my money in ways that other men have overlooked; and whatever else I may be, I'm a safe man from the money point of view.

VIVIE: It's very kind of you to tell me all this.

CROFTS: Oh well, come, Miss Vivie: you neednt pretend you dont see what I'm driving at. I want to settle down with a Lady Crofts. I suppose you think me very blunt, eh?

VIVIE: Not at all: I am much obliged to you for being so definite and business-like. I quite appreciate the offer: the money, the position, Lady Crofts, and so on. But I think I will say no, if you dont mind. I'd rather not. (*She rises, and strolls across to the sundial to get out of his immediate neighborhood.*)

CROFTS (*not at all discouraged, and taking advantage of the additional room left him on the seat to spread himself comfortably, as if a few preliminary refusals were part of the inevitable routine of courtship*): I'm in no hurry. It was only just to let you know in case young Gardner should try to trap you. Leave the question open.

VIVIE (*sharply*): My no is final. I wont go back from it. (*She looks authoritatively at him. He grins; leans forward with his elbows on his knees to prod with his stick at some unfortunate insect in the grass; and looks cunningly at her. She turns away impatiently.*)

CROFTS: I'm a good deal older than you — twenty-five years — quarter of a century. I shant live for ever; and I'll take care that you shall be well off when I'm gone.

VIVIE: I am proof against even that inducement, Sir George. Dont you think youd better take your answer? There is not the slightest chance of my altering it.

CROFTS (*rising, after a final slash at a daisy, and beginning to walk to and fro*): Well, no matter. I could tell you some things that would change your mind fast enough; but I wont, because I'd rather win you by honest affection. I was a good friend to your mother:

ask her whether I wasnt. She'd never have made the money that paid for your education if it hadnt been for my advice and help, not to mention the money I advanced her. There are not many men would have stood by her as I have. I put not less than £40,000 into it, from first to last.

VIVIE (*staring at him*): Do you mean to say you were my mother's business partner?

CROFTS: Yes. Now just think of all the trouble and the explanations it would save if we were to keep the whole thing in the family, so to speak. Ask your mother whether she'd like to have to explain all her affairs to a perfect stranger.

VIVIE: I see no difficulty, since I understand that the business is wound up, and the money invested.

CROFTS (*stopping short, amazed*): Wound up! Wind up a business thats paying 35 per cent in the worst years! Not likely. Who told you that?

VIVIE (*her color quite gone*): Do you mean that it is still —? (*She stops abruptly, and puts her hand on the sundial to support herself. Then she gets quickly to the iron chair and sits down.*) What business are you talking about?

CROFTS: Well, the fact is it's not what would be considered exactly a high-class business in my set — the county set, you know — our set it will be if you think better of my offer. Not that theres any mystery about it: dont think that. Of course you know by your mother's being in it that it's perfectly straight and honest. Ive known her for many years; and I can say of her that she'd cut off her hands sooner than touch anything that was not what it ought to be. I'll tell you all about it if you like. I dont know whether youve found in travelling how hard it is to find a really comfortable private hotel.

VIVIE (*sickened, averting her fate*): Yes: go on.

CROFTS: Well, thats all it is. Your mother has a genius for managing such things. We've got two in Brussels, one in Berlin, one in Vienna, and two in Buda-Pesth. Of course there are others besides ourselves in it; but we hold most of the capital; and your mother's indispensable as managing director. Youve noticed, I daresay, that she travels a good deal. But you see you cant mention such things in society. Once let out the word hotel and everybody says you keep a public-house. You wouldnt like people to say that of your mother, would you? Thats why we're so reserved about it. By the bye, youll keep it to yourself, wont you? Since it's been a secret so long, it had better remain so.

VIVIE: And this is the business you invite me to join you in?

CROFTS: Oh no. My wife shant be troubled with business. Youll not be in it more than youve always been.

VIVIE: I always been! What do you mean?

CROFTS: Only that youve always lived on it. It paid for your education and the dress you have on your back. Dont turn up your nose at business, Miss Vivie; where would your Newnhams and Girtons be without it?

VIVIE (*rising, almost beside herself*): Take care. I know what this business is.

CROFTS (*starting, with a suppressed oath*): Who told you?

VIVIE: Your partner — my mother.

CROFTS (*black with rage*): The old — (*Vivie looks quickly at him. He swallows the epithet and stands swearing and raging foully to himself. But he knows that his cue is to be sympathetic. He takes refuge in generous indignation.*) She ought to have had more consideration for you. I'd never have told you.

VIVIE: I think you would probably have told me when we were married: it would have been a convenient weapon to break me in with.

CROFTS (*quite sincerely*): I never intended that. On my word as a gentleman I didnt.

(*Vivie wonders at him. Her sense of the irony of his protest cools and braces her. She replies with contemptuous self-possession.*)

VIVIE: It does not matter. I suppose you understand that when we leave here to-day our acquaintance ceases.

CROFTS: Why? Is it for helping your mother?

VIVIE: My mother was a very poor woman who had no reasonable choice but to do as she did. You were a rich gentleman; and you did the same for the sake of 35 per cent. You are a pretty common sort of scoundrel, I think. That is my opinion of you.

CROFTS (*after a stare — not at all displeased, and much more at his ease on these frank terms than on their former ceremonious ones*): Ha, ha, ha, ha! Go it, little missie, go it: it doesnt hurt me and it amuses you. Why the devil shouldnt I invest my money that way? I take the interest on my capital like other people: I hope you dont think I dirty my own hands with the work. Come: you wouldnt refuse the acquaintance of my mother's cousin the Duke of Belgravia because some of the rents he gets are earned in queer ways. You wouldnt cut the Archbishop of Canterbury, I suppose, because the Ecclesiastical Commissioners have a few publicans and sinners among their tenants. Do you remember your Crofts scholarship at Newnham? Well, that was founded by my brother the M.P. He gets his 22 per cent out of a factory with 600 girls in it, and not one of them getting wages enough to live on. How d'ye suppose most of them manage? Ask your mother. And do you expect me to turn my back on 35 per cent when all the rest are pocketing what they can, like sensible men? No such fool! If youre going to pick and choose your acquaintances on moral principles, youd better clear out of this country, unless you want to cut yourself out of all decent society.

VIVIE (*conscience stricken*): You might go on to point out that I myself never asked where the money I spent came from. I believe I am just as bad as you.

CROFTS (*greatly reassured*): Of course you are; and a very good thing too! What harm does it do after all? (*Rallying her jocularly*) So you dont think me such a scoundrel now you come to think it over. Eh?

VIVIE: I have shared profits with you; and I admitted you just now to the familiarity of knowing what I think of you.

CROFTS (*with serious friendliness*): To be sure you did. You wont find me a bad sort; I dont go in for being superfine intellectually; but Ive plenty of honest human feeling; and the old Crofts breed comes out in a sort of instinctive hatred of anything low, in which I'm sure youll sympathize with me. Believe me, Miss Vivie, the world isnt such a bad place as the croakers make out. So long as you dont fly openly in the face of society, society doesnt ask any inconvenient questions; and it makes precious short work of the cads who do. There are no secrets better kept than the secrets that everybody guesses. In the society I can introduce you to, no lady or gentleman would so far forget themselves as to discuss my business affairs or your mother's. No man can offer you a safer position.

VIVIE (*studying him curiously*): I suppose you really think youre getting on famously with me.

CROFTS: Well, I hope I may flatter myself that you think better of me than you did at first.

VIVIE (*quietly*): I hardly find you worth thinking about at all now. (*She rises and turns towards the gate, pausing on her way to contemplate him and say almost gently, but with intense conviction*) When I think of the society that tolerates you, and the laws that protect you — when I think of how helpless nine out of ten young girls would be in the hands of you and my mother — the unmentionable woman and her capitalist bully —

CROFTS (*livid*): Damn you!

VIVIE: You need not. I am among the damned already.

(*She raises the latch of the gate to open it and go out. He follows her and puts his hand heavily on the top bar to prevent its opening.*)

CROFTS (*panting with fury*): Do you think I'll put up with this from you, you young devil, you?

VIVIE (*unmoved*): Be quiet. Some one will answer the bell. (*Without flinching a step she strikes the bell with the back of her hand. It clangs harshly; and he starts back involuntarily. Almost immediately Frank appears at the porch with his rifle.*)

FRANK (*with cheerful politeness*): Will you have the rifle, Viv; or shall I operate?

VIVIE: Frank: have you been listening?

FRANK: Only for the bell, I assure you; so that you shouldnt have to wait. I think I showed great insight into your character, Crofts.

CROFTS: For two pins I'd take that gun from you and break it across your head.

FRANK (*stalking him cautiously*): Pray dont. I'm ever so careless in handling firearms. Sure to be a fatal accident, with a reprimand from the coroner's jury for my negligence.

VIVIE: Put the rifle away, Frank: it's quite unnecessary.

FRANK: Quite right, Viv. Much more sportsmanlike to catch him in a trap. (*Crofts, understanding the insult, makes a threatening movement.*) Crofts: there are fifteen cartridges in the magazine here; and I am a dead shot at the present distance and at an object of your size.

CROFTS: Oh, you neednt be afraid. I'm not going to touch you.

FRANK: Ever so magnanimous of you under the circumstances! Thank you.

CROFTS: I'll just tell you this before I go. It may interest you, since youre so fond of one another. Allow me, Mister Frank, to introduce you to your half-sister, the eldest daughter of the Reverend Samuel Gardner. Miss Vivie: Your half-brother. Good morning. (*He goes out through the gate and along the road.*)

FRANK (*after a pause of stupefaction, raising the rifle*): Youll testify before the coroner that it's an accident, Viv. (*He takes aim at the retreating figure of Crofts. Vivie seizes the muzzle and pulls it round against her breast.*)

VIVIE: Fire now. You may.

FRANK (*dropping his end of the rifle hastily*): Stop! take care. (*She lets it go. It falls on the turf.*) Oh, youve given your little boy such a turn. Suppose it had gone off — ugh! (*He sinks on the garden seat, overcome.*)

VIVIE: Suppose it had: do you think it would not have been a relief to have some sharp physical pain tearing through me?

FRANK (*coaxingly*): Take it ever so easy, dear Viv. Remember: even if the rifle scared that fellow into telling the truth for the first time in his life, that only makes us the babes in the wood in earnest. (*He holds out his arms to her.*) Come and be covered up with leaves again.

VIVIE (*with a cry of disgust*): Ah, not that, not that. You make all my flesh creep.

FRANK: Why, whats the matter?

VIVIE: Good-bye. (*She makes for the gate.*)

FRANK (*jumping up*): Hallo! Stop! Viv! Viv! (*She turns in the gateway*) Where are you going to? Where shall we find you?

VIVIE: At Honoria Fraser's chambers, 67 Chancery Lane, for the rest of my life. (*She goes off quickly in the opposite direction to that taken by Crofts.*)

FRANK: But I say — wait — dash it! (*He runs after her.*)

ACT IV

(*Honoria Fraser's chambers in Chancery Lane. An office at the top of New Stone Buildings, with a plate-glass window, distempered walls, electric light, and a patent stove. Saturday afternoon. The chimneys of Lincoln's Inn and the western sky beyond are seen through the window. There is a double writing-table in the middle of the room, with a cigar box, ash pans, and a portable electric reading lamp almost snowed up in heaps of papers and books. This table has knee holes and chairs right and left and is very untidy. The clerk's desk, closed and tidy, with its high stool, is against the wall, near a door communicating with the inner rooms. In the opposite wall is the door leading to the public corridor. Its upper panel is of opaque glass, lettered in black on the outside, "Fraser and Warren." A baize screen hides the corner between this door and the window.*

Frank, in a fashionable light-colored coaching suit, with his stick, gloves, and white hat in his hands, is pacing up and down the office. Somebody tries the door with a key.)

FRANK (*calling*): Come in. It's not locked.

(*Vivie comes in, in her hat and jacket. She stops and stares at him.*)

VIVIE (*sternly*): What are you doing here?

FRANK: Waiting to see you. Ive been here for hours. Is this the way you attend to your business? (*He puts his hat and stick on the table, and perches himself with a vault on the clerk's stool, looking at her with every appearance of being in a specially restless, teasing, flippant mood.*)

VIVIE: Ive been away exactly twenty minutes for a cup of tea. (*She takes off her hat and jacket and hangs them up behind the screen.*) How did you get in?

FRANK: The staff had not left when I arrived. He's gone to play cricket on Primrose Hill. Why dont you employ a woman, and give your sex a chance?

VIVIE: What have you come for?

FRANK (*springing off the stool and coming close to her*): Viv: lets go and enjoy the Saturday half-holiday somewhere, like the staff. What do you say to Richmond, and then a music hall, and a jolly supper?

VIVIE: Cant afford it. I shall put in another six hours work before I go to bed.

FRANK: Cant afford it, cant we? Aha! Look here. (*He takes out a handful of sovereigns and makes them chink.*) Gold, Viv, gold!

VIVIE: Where did you get it?

FRANK: Gambling, Viv, gambling. Poker.

VIVIE: Pah! It's meaner than stealing it. No: I'm not coming. (*She sits down to work at the table, with her back to the glass door, and begins turning over the papers.*)

FRANK (*remonstrating piteously*): But, my dear Viv, I want to talk to you ever so seriously.

VIVIE: Very well: sit down in Honoria's chair and talk here. I like ten minutes chat after tea. (*He murmurs.*) No use groaning: I'm inexorable. (*He takes the opposite seat disconsolately.*) Pass that cigar box, will you?

FRANK (*pushing the cigar box across*): Nasty womanly habit. Nice men dont do it any longer.

VIVIE: Yes: they object to the smell in the office; and weve had to take to cigarets. See! (*She opens the box and takes out a cigaret, which she lights. She offers him one; but he shakes his head with a wry face. She settles herself comfortably in her chair, smoking.*) Go ahead.

FRANK: Well, I want to know what youve done — what arrangements youve made.

VIVIE: Everything was settled twenty minutes after I arrived here. Honoria has found the business too much for her this year; and she was on the point of sending for me and proposing a partnership when I walked in and told her I hadnt a farthing in the world. So I installed myself and packed her off for a fortnight's holiday. What happened at Haslemere when I left?

FRANK: Nothing at all. I said youd gone to town on particular business.

VIVIE: Well?

FRANK: Well, either they were too flabbergasted to say anything, or else Crofts had prepared your mother. Anyhow, she didnt say anything; and Crofts didnt say anything; and Praddy only stared. After tea they got up and went; and Ive not seen them since.

VIVIE (*nodding placidly with one eye on a wreath of smoke*): Thats all right.

FRANK (*looking round disparagingly*): Do you intend to stick in this confounded place?

VIVIE (*blowing the wreath decisively away, and sitting straight up*): Yes. These two days have given me back all my strength and self-possession. I will never take a holiday again as long as I live.

FRANK (*with a very wry face*): Mps! You look quite happy — and as hard as nails.

VIVIE (*grimly*): Well for me that I am!

FRANK (*rising*): Look here, Viv: we must have an explanation. We parted the other day under a complete misunderstanding.

VIVIE (*putting away the cigaret*): Well: clear it up.

FRANK: You remember what Crofts said?

VIVIE: Yes.

FRANK: That revelation was supposed to bring about a complete change in the nature of our feeling for one another. It placed us on the footing of brother and sister.

VIVIE: Yes.

FRANK: Have you ever had a brother?

VIVIE: No.

FRANK: Then you dont know what being brother and sister feels like? Now I have lots of sisters: Jessie and Georgina and the rest. The fraternal feeling is quite familiar to me; and I assure you my feeling for you is not the least in the world like it. The girls will go their way; I will go mine; and we shant care if we never see one another again. Thats brother and sister. But as to you, I cant be easy if I have to pass a week without seeing you. Thats not brother and sister. It's exactly what I felt an hour before Crofts made his revelation. In short, dear Viv, it's love's young dream.

VIVIE (*bitingly*): The same feeling, Frank, that brought your father to my mother's feet. Is that it?

FRANK (*revolted*): I very strongly object, Viv, to have my feelings compared to any which the Reverend Samuel is capable of harboring; and I object still more to a comparison of you to your mother. Besides, I dont believe the story. I have taxed my father with it, and obtained from him what I consider tantamount to a denial.

VIVIE: What did he say?

FRANK: He said he was sure there must be some mistake.

VIVIE: Do you believe him?

FRANK: I am prepared to take his word as against Crofts'.

VIVIE: Does it make any difference? I mean in your imagination or conscience; for of course it makes no real difference.

FRANK (*shaking his head*): None whatever to me.

VIVIE: Nor to me.

FRANK (*staring*): But this is ever so surprising! I thought our whole relations were altered in your imagination and conscience, as you put it, the moment those words were out of that brute's muzzle.

VIVIE: No: it was not that. I didnt believe him. I only wish I could.

FRANK: Eh?

VIVIE: I think brother and sister would be a very suitable relation for us.

FRANK: You really mean that?

VIVIE: Yes. It's the only relation I care for, even if we could afford any other. I mean that.

FRANK (*raising his eyebrows like one on whom a new light has dawned, and speaking with quite an effusion of chivalrous sentiment*): My dear Viv: why didnt you say so before? I am ever so sorry for persecuting you. I understand, of course.

VIVIE (*puzzled*): Understand what?

FRANK: Oh, I'm not a fool in the ordinary sense — only in the Scriptural sense of doing all the things the wise man declared to be folly, after trying them himself on the most extensive scale. I see I am no longer Vivvum's little boy. Dont be alarmed: I shall never call you Vivvums again — at least unless you get tired of your new little boy, whoever he may be.

VIVIE: My new little boy!

FRANK (*with conviction*): Must be a new little boy. Always happens that way. No other way, in fact.

VIVIE: None that you know of, fortunately for you.

(*Someone knocks at the door.*)

FRANK: My curse upon yon caller, whoe'er he be!

VIVIE: It's Praed. He's going to Italy and wants to say good-bye. I asked him to call this afternoon. Go and let him in.

FRANK: We can continue our conversation after his departure for Italy. I'll stay him out. (*He goes to the door and opens it.*) How are you, Praddy. Delighted to see you. Come in. (*Praed, dressed for travelling, comes in, in high spirits, excited by the beginning of his journey.*)

PRAED: How do you do, Miss Warren. (*She presses his hand cordially, though a certain sentimentality in his high spirits jars on her.*) I start in an hour from Holborn Viaduct. I wish I could persuade you to try Italy.

VIVIE: What for?

PRAED: Why, to saturate yourself with beauty and romance, of course. (*Vivie, with a shudder, turns her chair to the table, as if the work waiting for her there*

were a consolation and support to her. Praed sits opposite to her. Frank places a chair just behind Vivie, and drops lazily and carelessly into it, talking at her over his shoulder.*)

FRANK: No use, Praddy. Viv is a little Philistine. She is indifferent to my romance, and insensible to my beauty.

VIVIE: Mr Praed: once for all, there is no beauty and no romance in life for me. Life is what it is; and I am prepared to take it as it is.

PRAED (*enthusiastically*): You will not say that if you come to Verona and on to Venice. You will cry with delight at living in such a beautiful world.

FRANK: This is most eloquent, Praddy. Keep it up.

PRAED: Oh, I assure you *I* have cried — I shall cry again, I hope — at fifty! At your age, Miss Warren, you would not need to go so far as Verona. Your spirits would absolutely fly up at the mere sight of Ostend. You would be charmed with the gaiety, the vivacity, the happy air of Brussels. (*Vivie recoils*) Whats the matter?

FRANK: Hallo, Viv!

VIVIE (*to Praed, with deep reproach*): Can you find no better example of your beauty and romance than Brussels to talk to me about?

PRAED (*puzzled*): Of course it's very different from Verona. I dont suggest for a moment that —

VIVIE (*bitterly*): Probably the beauty and romance come to much the same in both places.

PRAED (*completely sobered and much concerned*): My dear Miss Warren: I — (*looking enquiringly at Frank*) Is anything the matter?

FRANK: She thinks your enthusiasm frivolous, Praddy. She's had ever such a serious call.

VIVIE (*sharply*): Hold your tongue, Frank. Dont be silly.

FRANK (*calmly*): Do you call this good manners, Praed?

PRAED (*anxious and considerate*): Shall I take him away, Miss Warren? I feel sure we have disturbed you at your work. (*He is about to rise.*)

VIVIE: Sit down: I'm not ready to go back to work yet. You both think I have an attack of nerves. Not a bit of it. But there are two subjects I want dropped, if you dont mind. One of them (*to Frank*) is love's young dream in any shape or form: the other (*to Praed*) is the romance and beauty of life, especially as exemplified by the gaiety of Brussels. You are welcome to any illusions you may have left on these subjects: I have none. If we three are to remain friends, I must be treated as a woman of business, permanently single (*to Frank*) and permanently unromantic (*to Praed*).

FRANK: I also shall remain permanently single until you change your mind. Praddy: change the subject. Be eloquent about something else.

PRAED (*diffidently*): I'm afraid theres nothing else in the world that I can talk about. The Gospel of Art is the only one I can preach. I know Miss Warren is a great devotee of the Gospel of Getting On; but we cant discuss that without hurting your feelings, Frank, since you are determined not to get on.

FRANK: Oh, dont mind my feelings. Give me some improving advice by all means: it does me ever so much good. Have another try to make a successful man of me, Viv. Come: lets have it all: energy, thrift, foresight, self-respect, character. Dont you hate people who have no character, Viv?

VIVIE (*wincing*): Oh, stop, stop: let us have no more of that horrible cant. Mr Praed: if there are really only those two gospels in the world, we had better all kill ourselves; for the same taint is in both, through and through.

FRANK (*looking critically at her*): There is a touch of poetry about you to-day, Viv, which has hitherto been lacking.

PRAED (*remonstrating*): My dear Frank: arnt you a little unsympathetic?

VIVIE (*merciless to herself*): No: it's good for me. It keeps me from being sentimental.

FRANK (*bantering her*): Checks your strong natural propensity that way, dont it?

VIVIE (*almost hysterically*): Oh yes: go on: dont spare me. I was sentimental for one moment in my life — beautifully sentimental — by moonlight; and now —

FRANK (*quickly*): I say, Viv: take care. Dont give yourself away.

VIVIE: Oh, do you think Mr Praed does not know all about my mother? (*Turning on Praed*) You had better have told me that morning, Mr Praed. You are very old fashioned in your delicacies, after all.

PRAED: Surely it is you who are a little old fashioned in your prejudices, Miss Warren. I feel bound to tell you, speaking as an artist, and believing that the most intimate human relationships are far beyond and above the scope of the law, that though I know that your mother is an unmarried woman, I do not respect her the less on that account. I respect her more.

FRANK (*airily*): Hear, hear!

VIVIE (*staring at him*): Is that all you know?

PRAED: Certainly that is all.

VIVIE: Then you neither of you know anything. Your guesses are innocence itself compared to the truth.

PRAED (*startled and indignant, preserving his politeness with an effort*): I hope not. (*More emphatically*) I hope not, Miss Warren. (*Frank's face shows that he does not share Praed's incredulity. Vivie utters an exclamation of impatience. Praed's chivalry droops before their conviction. He adds, slowly*) If there is anything worse — that is, anything else — are you sure you are right to tell us, Miss Warren?

VIVIE: I am sure that if I had the courage I should spend the rest of my life in telling it to everybody — in stamping and branding it into them until they felt their share in its shame and horror as I feel mine. There is nothing I despise more than the wicked convention that protects these things by forbidding a woman to mention them. And yet I cant tell you. The two infamous words that describe what my mother is are ringing in my ears and struggling on my tongue; but I cant utter them: my instinct is too strong for me.

(*She buries her face in her hands. The two men, astonished, stare at one another and then at her. She raises her head again desperately and takes a sheet of paper and a pen.*) Here: let me draft you a prospectus.

FRANK: Oh, she's mad. Do you hear, Viv, mad. Come: pull yourself together.

VIVIE: You shall see. (*She writes.*) "Paid up capital: not less than £40,000 standing in the name of Sir George Crofts, Baronet, the chief shareholder." What comes next? — I forget. Oh yes: "Premises at Brussels, Berlin, Vienna and Buda-Pesth. Managing director: Mrs Warren"; and now dont let us forget her qualifications: the two words. There! (*She pushes the paper to them.*) Oh, no: dont read it: dont! (*She snatches it back and tears it to pieces; then seizes her head in her hands and hides her face on the table. Frank, who has watched the writing carefully over her shoulder, and opened his eyes very widely at it, takes a card from his pocket; scribbles a couple of words; and silently hands it to Praed, who looks at it with amazement. Frank then remorsefully stoops over Vivie.*)

FRANK (*whispering tenderly*): Viv, dear: thats all right. I read what you wrote: so did Praddy. We understand. And we remain, as this leaves us at present, yours ever so devotedly. (*Vivie slowly raises her head.*)

PRAED: We do indeed, Miss Warren. I declare you are the most splendidly courageous woman I ever met. (*This sentimental compliment braces Vivie. She throws it away from her with an impatient shake, and forces herself to stand up, though not without some support from the table.*)

FRANK: Dont stir, Viv, if you dont want to. Take it easy.

VIVIE: Thank you. You can always depend on me for two things, not to cry and not to faint. (*She moves a few steps towards the door of the inner rooms, and stops close to Praed to say*) I shall need much more courage than that when I tell my mother that we have come to the parting of the ways. Now I must go into the next room for a moment to make myself neat again, if you dont mind.

PRAED: Shall we go away?

VIVIE: No: I'll be back presently. Only for a moment.

(*She goes into the other room, Praed opening the door for her.*)

PRAED: What an amazing revelation! I'm extremely disappointed in Crofts: I am indeed.

FRANK: I'm not in the least. I feel he's perfectly accounted for at last. But what a facer for me, Praddy! I cant marry her now.

PRAED (*sternly*): Frank! (*The two look at one another, Frank unruffled, Praed deeply indignant.*) Let me tell you, Gardner, that if you desert her now you will behave very despicably.

FRANK: Good old Praddy! Ever chivalrous! But you mistake: it's not the moral aspect of the case: it's the money aspect. I really cant bring myself to touch the old woman's money now?

PRAED: And was that what you were going to marry on?

FRANK: What else? *I* havnt any money, nor the smallest turn for making it. If I married Viv now she would have to support me; and I should cost her more than I am worth.

PRAED: But surely a clever, bright fellow like you can make something by your own brains.

FRANK: Oh yes, a little. (*He takes out his money again.*) I made all that yesterday — in an hour and a half. But I made it in a highly speculative business. No, dear Praddy: even if Jessie and Georgina marry millionaires and the governor dies after cutting them off with a shilling, I shall have only four hundred a year. And he wont die until he's three score and ten: he hasnt originality enough. I shall be on short allowance for the next twenty years. No short allowance for Viv, if I can help it. I withdraw gracefully and leave the field to the gilded youth of England. So thats settled. I shant worry her about it: I'll just send her a little note after we're gone. She'll understand.

PRAED (*grasping his hand*): Good fellow, Frank! I heartily beg your pardon. But must you never see her again?

FRANK: Never see her again! Hang it all, be reasonable. I shall come along as often as possible, and be her brother. I can not understand the absurd consequences you romantic people expect from the most ordinary transactions. (*A knock at the door.*) I wonder who this is. Would you mind opening the door? If it's a client it will look more respectable than if I appeared.

PRAED: Certainly. (*He goes to the door and opens it. Frank sits down in Vivie's chair to scribble a note.*) My dear Kitty: come in, come in.

(*Mrs Warren comes in, looking apprehensively round for Vivie. She has done her best to make herself matronly and dignified. The brilliant hat is replaced by a sober bonnet, and the gay blouse covered by a costly black silk mantle. She is pitiably anxious and ill at ease — evidently panic-stricken.*)

MRS WARREN (*to Frank*): What! Youre here, are you?

FRANK (*turning in his chair from his writing, but not rising*): Here, and charmed to see you. You come like a breath of spring.

MRS WARREN: Oh, get out with your nonsense. (*In a low voice*) Wheres Vivie?

(*Frank points expressively to the door of the inner room, but says nothing.*)

MRS WARREN (*sitting down suddenly and almost beginning to cry*): Praddy: wont she see me, dont you think?

PRAED: My dear Kitty: dont distress yourself. Why should she not?

MRS WARREN: Oh, you never can see why not: youre too amiable. Mr Frank: did she say anything to you?

FRANK (*folding his note*): She must see you, if (*very expressively*) you wait until she comes in.

MRS WARREN (*frightened*): Why shouldnt I wait?

(*Frank looks quizzically at her; puts his note carefully on the ink-bottle, so that Vivie cannot fail to find it when next she dips her pen; then rises and devotes his attention entirely to her.*)

FRANK: My dear Mrs Warren: suppose you were a sparrow — ever so tiny and pretty a sparrow hopping in the roadway — and you saw a steam roller coming in your direction, would you wait for it?

MRS WARREN: Oh, dont bother me with your sparrows. What did she run away from Haslemere like that for?

FRANK: I'm afraid she'll tell you if you wait until she comes back.

MRS WARREN: Do you want me to go away?

FRANK: No. I always want you to stay. But I advise you to go away.

MRS WARREN: What! And never see her again!

FRANK: Precisely.

MRS WARREN (*crying again*): Praddy: dont let him be cruel to me. (*She hastily checks her tears and wipes her eyes.*) She'll be so angry if she sees Ive been crying.

FRANK (*with a touch of real compassion in his airy tenderness*): You know that Praddy is the soul of kindness, Mrs Warren. Praddy: what do you say? Go or stay?

PRAED (*to Mrs Warren*): I really should be very sorry to cause you unnecessary pain; but I think perhaps you had better not wait. The fact is — (*Vivie is heard at the inner door.*)

FRANK: Sh! Too late. She's coming.

MRS WARREN: Dont tell her I was crying. (*Vivie comes in. She stops gravely on seeing Mrs Warren, who greets her with hysterical cheerfulness.*) Well, dearie. So here you are at last.

VIVIE: I am glad you have come: I want to speak to you. You said you were going, Frank, I think.

FRANK: Yes. Will you come with me, Mrs Warren? What do you say to a trip to Richmond, and the theatre in the evening? There is safety in Richmond. No steam roller there.

VIVIE: Nonsense, Frank. My mother will stay here.

MRS WARREN (*scared*): I dont know: perhaps I'd better go. We're disturbing you at your work.

VIVIE (*with quiet decision*): Mr Praed: please take Frank away. Sit down, mother. (*Mrs Warren obeys helplessly.*)

PRAED: Come, Frank. Good-bye, Miss Vivie.

VIVIE (*shaking hands*): Good-bye. A pleasant trip.

PRAED: Thank you: thank you. I hope so.

FRANK (*to Mrs Warren*): Good-bye: youd ever so much better have taken my advice. (*He shakes hands with her. Then airily to Vivie*) Bye-bye, Viv.

VIVIE: Good-bye. (*He goes out gaily without shaking hands with her. Praed follows. Vivie, composed and extremely grave, sits down in Honoria's chair, and waits for her mother to speak. Mrs Warren, dreading a pause, loses no time in beginning.*)

MRS WARREN: Well, Vivie, what did you go away like

that for without saying a word to me? How could you do such a thing! And what have you done to poor George? I wanted him to come with me; but he shuffled out of it. I could see that he was quite afraid of you. Only fancy: he wanted me not to come. As if (*trembling*) I should be afraid of you, dearie. (*Vivie's gravity deepens.*) But of course I told him it was all settled and comfortable between us, and that we were on the best of terms. (*She breaks down.*) Vivie: whats the meaning of this? (*She produces a paper from an envelope; comes to the table; and hands it across.*) I got it from the bank this morning.

VIVIE: It is my month's allowance. They sent it to me as usual the other day. I simply sent it back to be placed to your credit, and asked them to send you the lodgment receipt. In future I shall support myself.

MRS WARREN (*not daring to understand*): Wasnt it enough? Why didnt you tell me? (*With a cunning gleam in her eye*) I'll double it: I was intending to double it. Only let me know how much you want.

VIVIE: You know very well that that has nothing to do with it. From this time I go my own way in my own business and among my own friends. And you will go yours. (*She rises*) Good-bye.

MRS WARREN (*appalled*): Good-bye?

VIVIE: Yes: good-bye. Come: dont let us make a useless scene: you understand perfectly well. Sir George Crofts has told me the whole business.

MRS WARREN (*angrily*): Silly old — (*She swallows an epithet, and turns white at the narrowness of her escape from uttering it.*) He ought to have his tongue cut out. But I explained it all to you; and you said you didnt mind.

VIVIE (*steadfastly*): Excuse me: I do mind. You explained how it came about. That does not alter it.

(*Mrs Warren, silenced for a moment, looks forlornly at Vivie, who waits like a statue, secretly hoping that the combat is over. But the cunning expression comes back into Mrs Warren's face; and she bends across the table, sly and urgent, half whispering*)

MRS WARREN: Vivie: do you know how rich I am?

VIVIE: I have no doubt you are very rich.

MRS WARREN: But you dont know all that that means: youre too young. It means a new dress every day; it means theatres and balls every night; it means having the pick of all the gentlemen in Europe at your feet; it means a lovely house and plenty of servants; it means the choicest of eating and drinking; it means everything you like, everything you want, everything you can think of. And what are you here? A mere drudge, toiling and moiling early and late for your bare living and two cheap dresses a year. Think over it. (*Soothingly*) Youre shocked, I know. I can enter into your feelings; and I think they do you credit; but trust me, nobody will blame you: you may take my word for that. I know what young girls are; and I know youll think better of it when youve turned it over in your mind.

VIVIE: So thats how it's done, is it? You must have said all that to many a woman, mother, to have it so pat.

MRS WARREN (*passionately*): What harm am I asking you to do? (*Vivie turns away contemptuously. Mrs Warren follows her desperately*) Vivie: listen to me: you dont understand: youve been taught wrong on purpose: you dont know what the world is really like.

VIVIE (*arrested*): Taught wrong on purpose! What do you mean?

MRS WARREN: I mean that youre throwing away all your chances for nothing. You think that people are what they pretend to be — that the way you were taught at school and college to think right and proper is the way things really are. But it's not: it's all only a pretence, to keep the cowardly slavish common run of people quiet. Do you want to find that out, like other women, at forty, when youve thrown yourself away and lost your chances; or wont you take it in good time now from your own mother, that loves you and swears to you that it's truth — gospel truth? (*Urgently*) Vivie: the big people, the clever people, the managing people, all know it. They do as I do, and think what I think. I know plenty of them. I know them to speak to, to introduce you to, to make friends of for you. I dont mean anything wrong: thats what you dont understand: your head is full of ignorant ideas about me. What do the people that taught you know about life or about people like me? When did they ever meet me, or speak to me, or let anyone tell them about me? — the fools! Would they ever have done anything for you if I hadnt paid them? Havnt I told you that I want you to be respectable? Havnt I brought you up to be respectable? And how can you keep it up without my money and my influence and Lizzie's friends? Cant you see that youre cutting your own throat as well as breaking my heart in turning your back on me?

VIVIE: I recognise the Crofts philosophy of life, mother. I heard it all from him that day at the Gardners'.

MRS WARREN: You think I want to force that played-out old sot on you! I dont, Vivie: on my oath I dont.

VIVIE: It would not matter if you did: you would not succeed. (*Mrs Warren winces, deeply hurt by the implied indifference towards her affectionate intention. Vivie, neither understanding this nor concerning herself about it, goes on calmly*) Mother: you dont at all know the sort of person I am. I dont object to Crofts more than to any other coarsely built man of his class. To tell you the truth, I rather admire him for being strong-minded enough to enjoy himself in his own way and make plenty of money instead of living the usual shooting, hunting, dining-out, tailoring, loafing life of his set merely because all the rest do it. And I'm perfectly aware that if I'd been in the same circumstances as my aunt Liz, I'd have done exactly what she did. I dont think I'm more prejudiced or straitlaced than you: I think I'm less. I'm certain I'm less sentimental. I know very well that fashionable morality is all a pretence, and that if I took your money and devoted the rest of my life to spending it fashionably, I might be as worthless and vicious as the silliest woman could possibly want to be without having a word said to me about it. But I dont want to be worthless. I shouldnt enjoy trotting about the park to advertize my dressmaker and carriage builder, or being bored at the opera to show off a shop windowful of diamonds.

MRS WARREN (*bewildered*): But —

VIVIE: Wait a moment: Ive not done. Tell me why you continue your business now that you are independent of it. Your sister, you told me, has left all that behind her. Why dont you do the same?

MRS WARREN: Oh, it's all very easy for Liz: she likes good society, and has the air of being a lady. Imagine me in a cathedral town! Why, the very rooks in the trees would find me out even if I could stand the dulness of it. I must have work and excitement, or I should go melancholy mad. And what else is there for me to do? The life suits me: I'm fit for it and not for anything else. If I didnt do it somebody else would; so I dont do any real harm by it. And then it brings in money; and I like making money. No: it's no use: I cant give it up — not for anybody. But what need you know about it? I'll never mention it. I'll keep Crofts away. I'll not trouble you much: you see I have to be constantly running about from one place to another. Youll be quit of me altogether when I die.

VIVIE: No. I am my mother's daughter. I am like you: I must have work, and must make more money than I spend. But my work is not your work, and my way not your way. We must part. It will not make much difference to us: instead of meeting one another for perhaps a few months in twenty years, we shall never meet: thats all.

MRS WARREN (*her voice stifled in tears*): Vivie: I meant to have been more with you: I did indeed.

VIVIE: It's no use, mother: I am not to be changed by a few cheap tears and entreaties any more than you are, I dare say.

MRS WARREN (*wildly*): Oh, you call a mother's tears cheap.

VIVIE: They cost you nothing; and you ask me to give you the peace and quietness of my whole life in exchange for them. What use would my company be to you if you could get it? What have we two in common that could make either of us happy together?

MRS WARREN (*lapsing recklessly into her dialect*): We're mother and daughter. I want my daughter. Ive a right to you. Who is to care for me when I'm old? Plenty of girls have taken to me like daughters and cried at leaving me; but I let them all go because I had you to look forward to. I kept myself lonely for you. Youve no right to turn on me now and refuse to do your duty as a daughter.

VIVIE (*jarred and antagonized by the echo of the slums in her mother's voice*): My duty as a daughter! I thought we should come to that presently. Now once

for all, mother, you want a daughter and Frank wants a wife. I dont want a mother; and I dont want a husband. I have spared neither Frank nor myself in sending him about his business. Do you think I will spare you?

MRS WARREN (*violently*): Oh, I know the sort you are — no mercy for yourself or anyone else. *I* know. My experience has done that for me anyhow: I can tell the pious, canting, hard, selfish woman when I meet her. Well, keep yourself to yourself: *I* dont want you. But listen to this. Do you know what I would do with you if you were a baby again — aye, as sure as there's a Heaven above us?

VIVIE: Strangle me, perhaps.

MRS WARREN: No: I'd bring you up to be a real daughter to me, and not what you are now, with your pride and your prejudices and the college education you stole from me — yes, stole: deny it if you can: what was it but stealing? I'd bring you up in my own house, so I would.

VIVIE (*quietly*): In one of your own houses.

MRS WARREN (*screaming*): Listen to her! listen to how she spits on her mother's grey hairs! Oh, may you live to have your own daughter tear and trample on you as you have trampled on me. And you will: you will. No woman ever had luck with a mother's curse on her.

VIVIE: I wish you wouldnt rant, mother. It only hardens me. Come: I suppose I am the only young woman you ever had in your power that you did good to. Dont spoil it all now.

MRS WARREN: Yes, Heaven forgive me, it's true; and you are the only one that ever turned on me. Oh, the injustice of it, the injustice, the injustice! I always wanted to be a good woman. I tried honest work; and I was slave-driven until I cursed the day I ever heard of honest work. I was a good mother; and because I made my daughter a good woman she turns me out as if I was a leper. Oh, if I only had my life to live over again! I'd talk to that lying clergyman in the school. From this time forth, so help me Heaven in my last hour, I'll do wrong and nothing but wrong. And I'll prosper on it.

VIVIE: Yes: it's better to choose your line and go through with it. If I had been you, mother, I might have done as you did; but I should not have lived one life and believed in another. You are a conventional woman at heart. That is why I am bidding you good-bye now. I am right, am I not?

MRS WARREN (*taken aback*): Right to throw away all my money!

VIVIE: No: right to get rid of you? I should be a fool not to? Isnt that so?

MRS WARREN (*sulkily*): Oh well, yes, if you come to that, I suppose you are. But Lord help the world if everybody took to doing the right thing! And now I'd better go than stay where I'm not wanted. (*She turns to the door.*)

VIVIE (*kindly*): Wont you shake hands?

MRS WARREN (*after looking at her fiercely for a moment with a savage impulse to strike her*): No, thank you. Good-bye.

VIVIE (*matter-of-factly*): Good-bye. (*Mrs Warren goes out, slamming the door behind her. The strain on Vivie's face relaxes; her grave expression breaks up into one of joyous content; her breath goes out in a half sob, half laugh of intense relief. She goes buoyantly to her place at the writing-table; pushes the electric lamp out of the way; pulls over a great sheaf of papers; and is in the act of dipping her pen in the ink when she finds Frank's note. She opens it unconcernedly and reads it quickly, giving a little laugh at some quaint turn of expression in it.*) And good-bye, Frank. (*She tears the note up and tosses the pieces into the wastepaper basket without a second thought. Then she goes at her work with a plunge, and soon becomes absorbed in her figures.*)

COMMENTARIES

Theatre Magazine
A CONTEMPORARY REACTION TO
MRS. WARREN'S PROFESSION   1906

> *This attack on the play, along with Shaw's response to the Court of Special Sessions in New York, which cleared the play of indecency, gives us a good idea how many "proper" New Yorkers reacted to the subject matter Shaw felt important to present to audiences. It was printed in* Theatre Magazine *in 1906.*

Two judges, with a third one dissenting, in the Court of Special Sessions in New York City, have acquitted Arnold Daly of violating Section 385 of the Penal Code in having produced George Bernard Shaw's play, *Mrs. Warren's Profession*. This section provides against any indecent and suggestive act on the part of any performer. The decision is on a technical point. Mr. Shaw may get such comfort from it as he can, but he will find that no technique, either of Law or Art, can cure defects of material and substance. If he retains the right to produce, the public will retain the right to reject, and may exercise it. It may be that no court can take into consideration, in passing upon a given play, the entire philosophy and all the blatant flauntings of it in his various plays, publications, and utterances. But the public can. It can take care of itself. Statutes and codes are not needed for every offense. Here is a pseudo-anarchist who believes in no family tie (except for himself, perhaps), who proclaims free love, who preaches the seduction of our daughters by wholesale, not by means of wine suppers and "delicate" attentions, but by a false philosophy of specious half-truths; and, if anybody is swept into the dustbin, it will not be the American public. If Mr. Shaw is under a delusion to the contrary, his delusion of grandeur may not be technically amenable to the law of the courts, but it will be to the law of public opinion.

Mr. Shaw lost no time in rushing into print directly he learned of the decision. Few authors understand the value of sensational newspaper advertising so well as he. This is what was cabled in his name to the New York *Sun*:

> The main thing is that the decision states that the exposure of the social evil may lead to social reform. Whatever other comments the Court passed does not matter to me so long as that principle is admitted. According to one paper the Court deems the play disgusting. I shall continue to write similar disgusting things until some definite good is achieved.
>
> The entire blame for the agitation against *Mrs. Warren's Profession* lies in the hands of the New York critics. Their stupidity, inhumanity and scurrilous and obscene language in dealing with the play drove the poor, wretched little Police Commissioner to steps he was reluctant to take. No words of mine are adequate to describe my feelings toward these critics. They should all be gathered in a dustpan and thrown into a dust heap. Had they any sense of decency, they would make a barefooted pilgrimage somewhere or shoot themselves, but I don't suppose they will.
>
> I do not consider the decision of the Court complete unless it contains a recommendation for the imprisonment of all the editors and critics of the New York press who were responsible for bringing about this agitation. The remainder of my life will be devoted to forcing home their disgraceful attitude in the matter. With thousands of women in New York under the adverse influences with which I deal, they had a splendid opportunity of aiding the work, but their stupidity was too great to permit them to see other than sensational phases. In their ostrichlike dullness they imagine they know more about the subject than I do, but when I say a thing is so no sane person will accept their word against mine.
>
> The most scandalous lie they told was that *Mrs. Warren's Profession* was written for the purpose of making money. Any intelligent manager will tell you that a play which is dependent on pornographic situations is doomed to failure. For a week, perhaps, weak, degenerate debauchees may pay extravagant prices to see such a piece and then it is finished. The impression was spread in America that *Mrs. Warren's Profession* was a piece of that character. Its production cost me $5,000 out of my own pocket, besides injuring the receipts of other plays of mine on tour. Yet those who spent money to see *Mrs. Warren's Profession* in the hope of satisfying their mental lasciviousness have my most profound pity in their disappointment. They must hold me guilty of taking their money under false pretenses.

The only statement of any real interest in the foregoing effusion is that the production of *Mrs. Warren's Profession* cost Mr. Shaw $5,000 out of his own pocket. That may explain the willingness of managers and actors to experiment with these queer plays.

New York Times
EFFORTS AT CENSORSHIP OF
MRS. WARREN'S PROFESSION   *1905–1906*

The names in the series of articles written about the play in the New York Times
*in 1905 and 1906 became famous. McAdoo was a police commissioner, and
Anthony Comstock was a campaigner for decency who sought every opportunity
to uphold "public morality." Justice Olmsted was later associated with prohibition. These articles give us a clear view of the controversy surrounding the play and
the difficulties that Shaw felt in trying to protect Arnold Daly, who truly risked
being charged with wrongdoing. This is a typical effort at censorship of significant
literature.*

Comstock At It Again

Warns Arnold Daly against Playing Mrs. Warren's Profession

October 25, 1905

Copies of this interesting correspondence between Anthony Comstock of the
Society for the Suppression of Vice, who has strong views as to the value of the
works of George Bernard Shaw, and Arnold Daly, the actor, who is about to produce a new play by Mr. Shaw, entitled *Mrs. Warren's Profession,* came to the *New
York Times* last night. Here they are:

Society for the Suppression of Vice
New York, Oct. 20, 1905

Mr. Arnold Daly:

Dear Sir: I am informed that it is your intention to put upon the stage one of
Bernard Shaw's filthy products, entitled *Mrs. Warren's Profession.* I also understand that this play has been suppressed in London.

In order that you may not plead ignorance as to the laws and in the interpretation of the laws of this State, I beg to call your attention to the following decision
made by the Appellate Division in the case of *People vs. Dorris.* [Here Mr. Comstock quotes the decision.]

There are many other decisions besides this, but the language is so explicit in
this case, and as it is the utterance of the Appellate Division of the Supreme Court
of this State, in this district, it seems to me sufficient.

Yours very truly,

ANTHONY COMSTOCK,
Secretary

New York, Oct. 21, 1905

Mr. Anthony Comstock, Secretary Society for Suppression of Vice,
142 Nassau St., New York City:

Dear Sir:

You call *Mrs. Warren's Profession* a "filthy" play. I cannot believe that you have
read it; but, if so, your use of adjective is decorative, but not descriptive.

It is a strong sermon and a great moral lesson, and I cordially invite you to come to the Garrick Theatre on Wednesday or Thursday of next week, when I will be pleased to have you see a rehearsal of it.

Yours truly,

ARNOLD DALY

Shaw to Comstock: You Can't Scare Me

As to Daly, Believes a Rest in Prison Would Do Him Good

October 27, 1905

Special Cable to the New York Times [*Copyright, 1905*] LONDON, Oct. 26 — "Well, what is it now?" demanded George Bernard Shaw as, backed up to his grate fire, he received me this morning in his charming home, Adelphi Terrace.

I showed him a telegram to the effect that Anthony Comstock had warned Arnold Daly under threat of criminal prosecution not to produce Shaw's play, *Mrs. Warren's Profession.*

Shaw at once assumed that Comstock's warning was tantamount to a threat to imprison Daly, and commented on it in that sense. He said:

> You tell me Anthony Comstock threatens to put Arnold Daly in prison if he produces *Mrs. Warren's Profession,* and ask me what I have to say.
>
> Do you remember the classic telegram sent by Lord Clanricarde to his tenants in Ireland? "If you think you can intimidate me by shooting my agent you are very much mistaken."
>
> Well, all I can say is if Comstock thinks he can intimidate me by imprisoning Daly he does not quite know his man. Let him imprison Daly, by all means. A few months' rest and quiet would do Daly a great deal of good, and the scandal of his imprisonment would completely defeat Comstock's attempt to hide the fact that Mrs. Warren's "profession" exists because libertines pay women well to be evil, and often show them affection and respect, whilst pious people pay them infamously and drudge their bodies and souls to death at honest labor. [. . .]

Shaw's Play Stopped; The Manager Arrested

McAdoo Calls the Piece Revolting and Indecent — Warrants for the Players — Tickets Still on Sale Late in the Day, Notwithstanding Condemnation by the Press

November 1, 1905

Police Commissioner McAdoo took steps yesterday which stopped the further presentation at the Garrick Theatre of *Mrs. Warren's Profession,* George Bernard Shaw's play. Mr. McAdoo saw the performance on Monday night, and the first thing he did when he reached his office yesterday morning was to report to Mayor McClellan that the production was "revolting, indecent, and nauseating where it was not boring."

After talking with the Mayor, Mr. McAdoo wrote to Arnold Daly, ex-Senator Reynolds, who is said to be the owner of the theatre, and Samuel W. Gumpertz, its manager, telling them that he would prevent a second performance and arrest those participating therein. Later a warrant was issued by Magistrate Whitman calling for the arrest of Mr. Reynolds, Mr. Gumpertz, Mr. Daly, and the other actors and actresses in the cast, which was served by Inspector Brooks in person.

Mr. Gumpertz was arraigned in Jefferson Market Court. He was paroled upon his own recognizance until this morning at 11 o'clock.

The warrant charged a violation of that section of the Penal Code which relates to "offending public decency." Before his parole Mr. Gumpertz promised to be present this morning and to have the others named in the warrant, or such of them as were able to appear, in readiness for the hearing. He also said there would be no further performances for the present.

Shortly before the arrest of Mr. Gumpertz, but long after the receipt of Commissioner McAdoo's letter, the sale of tickets at the box office was stopped and the following notice was posted on the door of the theatre:

> Further performance of *Mrs. Warren's Profession* will be abandoned, owing to the universal condemnation of the press.
>
> ARNOLD DALY.

> Theatre closed to-night. Will reopen to-morrow night with *Candida*, original cast.

The Court Approves Bernard Shaw's Play

Mrs. Warren's Profession, *Legally Not Indecent, Justices Say — "Repellent Things" in it — But They May Do Good — Justice Olmsted Says That without Advertising It Wouldn't Last*

July 7, 1906

Bernard Shaw's play, *Mrs. Warren's Profession,* has successfully passed the censorship of Special Sessions. The Justices call the play "not pleasant," and declare it fraught with "shock producers" and "repellent things," but say that it is not indecent in the eyes of the law. They add, indeed, that it may become a medium of much needed social reforms.

These characterizations are made in a decision handed down yesterday by the court in the case of the people against Arnold Daly, the actor, and Samuel Gompertz, his manager, whose acquittal is ordered. Messrs. Daly and Gompertz were arrested on the evening of Oct. 20 last at the close of the opening performance of the play at the Garrick Theatre. They were tried in the Court of Special Sessions on April 19. Information was also lodged against Chrystal Herne and Mary Shaw, two of the actresses who appeared in the play.

The prevailing opinion in the case is written by Justice Olmsted, with Justice Wyatt concurring. Justice McAvoy dissented, but wrote no opinion. Justice Olmsted enters into an elaborate analysis of the theme of *Mrs. Warren's Profession,* and in some instances handles the author very much as a theatrical critic would on a first night. Here is the opinion in part:

> The complaining police officer, who was the sole witness, testified to no indecent or suggestive act on the part of the performer. The court is called upon on this state of fact to decide whether the language of the prompt book as spoken on the stage was a public nuisance per se because offensive to public decency. There is nothing in the words them-

selves, nor in any particular phrase or expression, which can be said to be indecent and the court is compelled to resort to the theme and motive of the play to find the indecency complained of. The theme is not a pleasant one.

Justice Olmsted then analyses the theme. This part is rather hard on Bernard Shaw. The Justice says:

> The dramatist has in this play used old and hackneyed materials, the common tool of scores of other playwrights, but he has used them more boldly — so boldly in fact that their tendency is to surprise and shock the audience. It must be said for him that he has in this play made vice less attractive than many other dramatists whose plays have never received the censorious attention of the police.
>
> The suggestion that the clergyman in the play is the father of Mrs. Warren's daughter, with the situation which makes the clergyman's acknowledged son a suitor for the daughter's hand, is another of the dramatist's shock producers, and there are other repellent things both in the play and in its characters: in fact, there is so little that is attractive in the drama that it is safe to predict that without the preliminary sensational advertisement of this proposed production its life on the boards would be short.

Justice Olmsted cites precedents to show that the test of criminality under the opinions of the higher courts is "whether a production is naturally calculated to excite in the spectator impure imagination and whether the other incidents and qualities, however attractive, are merely accessory to this as the primary or main purpose of the representation."

To the question whether Bernard Shaw's play in its essence is moral or immoral Justice Olmsted replies:

> If virtue does not receive its usual reward in this play, vice at least is presented in an odious light and its votaries are punished. The attack on social conditions is one which might result in effecting some needed social reforms. The court cannot refrain from suggesting, however, that the reforming influence of the play in this regard is minimized by the method of the attack.

In conclusion Justice Olmsted says:

> While the court may hold decided opinion regarding the fitness of this play as a stage production, when it comes to consider the question of criminality of the acts of these defendants in publicly producing it, it must make application of the principle of law laid down by the Court of Appeals as the test of criminality.
>
> Making such application in the case at bar, it appears that instead of exciting impure imagination in the mind of the spectator, that which is really excited is disgust; that the unlovely, the repellent, the disgusting in the play are merely accessories to the main purpose of the drama, which is an attack on certain social conditions relating to the employment of women which the dramatist believes, as do many others with him, should be reformed.
>
> Tried by this rule, the play does not come within the inhibition of the statute, and the defendants are acquitted.

Bernard Shaw (1856–1950)
PLAYS UNPLEASANT: *MRS. WARREN'S PROFESSION*   *1898*

Shaw included Mrs. Warren's Profession *in a group of three plays he titled "unpleasant." He explains in this excerpt from one of his prefaces (1898) that the subjects of these plays are not to be taken lightly by an audience out for an evening of fun but are serious and meant to be considered carefully.*

In *Mrs Warren's Profession* I have gone straight at the fact that, as Mrs Warren puts it, "the only way for a woman to provide for herself decently is for her to be good to some man that can afford to be good to her." There are some questions on which I am, like most Socialists, an extreme Individualist. I believe that any society which desires to found itself on a high standard of integrity of character in its units should organize itself in such a fashion as to make it possible too for all men and all women to maintain themselves in reasonable comfort by their industry without selling their affections and their convictions. At present we not only condemn women as a sex to attach themselves to "breadwinners," licitly or illicitly, on pain of heavy privation and disadvantage; but we have great prostitute classes of men: for instance, dramatists and journalists, to whom I myself belong, not to mention the legions of lawyers, doctors, clergymen, and platform politicians who are daily using their highest faculties to belie their real sentiments: a sin compared to which that of a woman who sells the use of her person for a few hours is too venial to be worth mentioning; for rich men without conviction are more dangerous in modern society than poor women without chastity. Hardly a pleasant subject this!

I must, however, warn my readers that my attacks are directed against themselves, not against my stage figures. They cannot too thoroughly understand that the guilt of defective social organization does not lie alone on the people who actually work the commercial makeshifts which the defects make inevitable, and who often, like Sartorius and Mrs Warren, display valuable executive capacities and even high moral virtues in their administration, but with the whole body of citizens whose public opinion, public action, and public contribution as ratepayers alone can replace Sartorius's slums with decent dwellings, Charteris's intrigues with reasonable marriage contracts, and Mrs Warren's profession with honorable industries guarded by a humane industrial code and a "moral minimum" wage.

Bernard Shaw (1856–1950)
FROM THE PREFACE TO *MRS. WARREN'S PROFESSION*   *1902*

Most of Shaw's prefaces to his plays address the issues of the plays themselves. This preface concentrates on the efforts of authorities to censor the play and prevent its production. Shaw gives us his views on censorship and on the public attitudes that viewed the play as threatening to public morality. However, he also goes on to comment on the issues of prostitution in the late nineteenth century and its relationship to the society that sustained it. As he puts it, even his supportive critics would not see themselves as responsible for the existence of the Mrs. Warrens among them.

The Author's Apology   *Mrs Warren's Profession* has been performed at last, after a delay of only eight years; and I have once more shared with Ibsen the triumphant amusement of startling all but the strongest-headed of the London theater critics clean out of the practice of their profession. No author who has ever known the exultation of sending the Press into an hysterical tumult of protest, of moral panic, of involuntary and frantic confession of sin, of a horror of conscience in which the power of distinguishing between the work of art on the stage and the real life of the spectator is confused and overwhelmed, will ever care for the stereotyped compliments which every successful farce or melodrama elicits from the newspapers. Give me that critic who rushed from my play to declare furiously that Sir George Crofts ought to be kicked. What a triumph for the actor, thus to reduce a jaded London journalist to the condition of the simple sailor in the Wapping gallery, who shouts execrations at Iago and warnings to Othello not to believe him! But dearer still than such simplicity is that sense of the sudden earthquake shock to the foundations of morality which sends a pallid crowd of critics into the street shrieking that the pillars of society are cracking and the ruin of the State at hand. Even the Ibsen champions of ten years ago remonstrate with me just as the veterans of those brave days remonstrated with them. Mr Grein, the hardy iconoclast who first launched my plays on the stage alongside *Ghosts* and *The Wild Ducks,* exclaims that I have shattered his ideals. Actually his ideals! What would Dr. Relling say? And Mr William Archer himself disowns me because I "cannot touch pitch without wallowing in it." Truly my play must be more needed than I knew; and yet I thought I knew how little the others know.

Do not suppose, however, that the consternation of the Press reflects any consternation among the general public. Anybody can upset the theater critics, in a turn of the wrist, by substituting for the romantic commonplaces of the stage the moral commonplaces of the pulpit, the platform, or the library. Play *Mrs Warren's Profession* to an audience of clerical members of the Christian Social Union and of women well experienced in Rescue, Temperance, and Girls' Club work, and no moral panic will arise: every man and woman present will know that as long as poverty makes virtue hideous and the spare pocket-money of rich bachelordom makes vice dazzling, their daily hand-to-hand fight against prostitution with prayer and persuasion, shelters and scanty alms, will be a losing one. There was a time when they were able to urge that though "the white-lead factory where Anne Jane was poisoned" may be a far more terrible place than Mrs Warren's house, yet hell is still more dreadful. Nowadays they no longer believe in hell; and the girls among whom they are working know that they did not believe in it, and would laugh at them if they did. So well have the rescuers learnt that Mrs Warren's defense of herself and indictment of society is the thing that most needs saying, that those who know me personally reproach me, not for writing this play, but for wasting my energies on "pleasant plays" for the amusement of frivolous people, when I can build up such excellent stage sermons on their own work. *Mrs Warren's Profession* is the one play of mine which I could submit to a censorship without doubt of the result; only, it must not be the censorship of the minor theater critic, nor of an innocent court official like the King's Reader of Plays, much less of people who consciously profit by Mrs Warren's profession, or who personally make use of it, or who hold the widely whispered view that it is an indispensable safety-valve for the protection of domestic virtue, or, above all, who are smitten with a sentimental affection for our fallen sister, and would "take her up tenderly, lift her with care, fashioned so slenderly, young, and *so* fair." Nor am I prepared to accept the verdict of the medical gentlemen who would compulsorily examine and register Mrs Warren, whilst leaving Mrs Warren's patrons, especially her military patrons, free to destroy her health and anybody else's without fear of reprisals. But I should be quite content to have my play judged by, say, a joint committee of the Central Vigilance Society and the Salvation Army. And the sterner moralists the members of the committee were, the better.[. . .]

I now come to those critics who, intellectually baffled by the problem in *Mrs Warren's Profession,* have made a virtue of running away from it. I will illustrate their method by a quotation from Dickens, taken from the fifth chapter of *Our Mutual Friend.*

> "Hem!" began Wegg. "This, Mr Boffin and Lady, is the first chapter of the first wollume of the *Decline and Fall of* ———" here he looked hard at the book, and stopped.
> "What's the matter, Wegg?"
> "Why, it comes into my mind, do you know, sir," said Wegg with an air of insinuating frankness (having first again looked hard at the book), "that you made a little mistake this morning, which I had meant to set you right in; only something put it out of my head. I think you said Rooshan Empire, sir?"
> "It is Rooshan; ain't it, Wegg?"
> "No, sir. Roman. Roman."
> "What's the difference, Wegg?"
> "The difference, sir?" Mr Wegg was faltering and in danger of breaking down, when a bright thought flashed upon him. "The difference, sir? There you place me in a difficulty, Mr Boffin. Suffice it to observe, that the difference is best postponed to some other occasion when Mrs Boffin does not honour us with her company. In Mrs Boffin's presence, sir, we had better drop it."
> Mr Wegg thus came out of his disadvantage with quite a chivalrous air, and not only that, but by dint of repeating with a manly delicacy, "In Mrs Boffin's presence, sir, we had better drop it!" turned the disadvantage on Boffin, who felt that he had committed himself in a very painful manner.

I am willing to let Mr Wegg drop it on these terms, provided I am allowed to mention here that *Mrs Warren's Profession* is a play for women; that it was written for women; that it has been performed and produced mainly through the determination of women that it should be performed and produced; that the enthusiasm of women made its first performance excitingly successful; and that not one of these women had any inducement to support it except their belief in the timeliness and the power of the lesson the play teaches. Those who were "surprised to see ladies present" were men; and when they proceeded to explain that the journals they represented could not possibly demoralize the public by describing such a play, their editors cruelly devoted the space saved by their delicacy to an elaborate and respectful account of the progress of a young lord's attempt to break the bank at Monte Carlo. A few days sooner Mrs Warren would have been crowded out of their papers by an exceptionally abominable police case. [. . .]

My old Independent Theater manager, Mr Grein, besides that reproach to me for shattering his ideals, complains that Mrs Warren is not wicked enough, and names several romancers who would have clothed her black soul with all the terrors of tragedy. I have no doubt they would; but if you please, my dear Mr. Grein, that is just what I did not want to do. Nothing would please our sanctimonious British public more than to throw the whole guilt of Mrs Warren's profession on Mrs Warren herself. Now the whole aim of my play is to throw that guilt on the

British public itself. You may remember that when he produced my first play, *Widowers' Houses,* exactly the same misunderstanding arose. When the virtuous young gentleman rose up in wrath against the slum landlord, the slum landlord very effectually shewed him that slums are the product, not of individual Harpagons, but of the indifference of virtuous young gentlemen to the condition of the city they live in, provided they live at the west end of it on money earned by somebody else's labor. The notion that prostitution is created by the wickedness of Mrs Warren is as silly as the notion — prevalent, nevertheless, to some extent in Temperance circles — that drunkenness is created by the wickedness of the publican. Mrs Warren is not a whit a worse woman than the reputable daughter who cannot endure her. Her indifference to the ultimate social consequences of her means of making money, and her discovery of that means by the ordinary method of taking the line of least resistance to getting it, are too common in English society to call for any special remark. Her vitality, her thrift, her energy, her outspokenness, her wise care of her daughter, and the managing capacity which has enabled her and her sister to climb from the fried fish shop down by the Mint to the establishments of which she boasts, are all high English social virtues. Her defense of herself is so overwhelming that it provokes the *St. James's Gazette* to declare that "the tendency of the play is wholly evil" because "it contains one of the boldest and most specious defenses of an immoral life for poor women that has ever been penned." Happily the *St James's Gazette* here speaks in its haste. Mrs Warren's defense of herself is not only bold and specious, but valid and unanswerable. But it is no defense at all of the vice which she organizes. It is no defense of an immoral life to say that the alternative offered by society collectively to poor women is a miserable life, starved, overworked, fetid, ailing, ugly. Though it is quite natural and *right* for Mrs Warren to choose what is, according to her lights, the least immoral alternative, it is none the less infamous of society to offer such alternatives. For the alternatives offered are not morality and immorality, but two sorts of immorality. The man who cannot see that starvation, overwork, dirt, and disease are as immoral as prostitution — that they are the vices and crimes of a nation, and not merely its misfortunes — is (to put it as politely as possible) a hopelessly Private Person.

The notion that Mrs Warren must be a fiend is only an example of the violence and passion which the slightest reference to sex rouses in undisciplined minds, and which makes it seem natural to our lawgivers to punish silly and negligible indecencies with a ferocity unknown in dealing with, for example, ruinous financial swindling. Had my play been entitled *Mr Warren's Profession,* and Mr Warren been a bookmaker, nobody would have expected me to make him a villain as well. Yet gambling is a vice, and bookmaking an institution, for which there is absolutely nothing to be said. The moral and economic evil done by trying to get other people's money without working for it (and this is the essence of gambling) is not only enormous but uncompensated. There are no two sides to the question of gambling, no circumstances which force us to tolerate it lest its suppression lead to worse things, no consensus of opinion among responsible classes, such as magistrates and military commanders, that it is a necessity, no Athenian records of gambling made splendid by the talents of its professors, no contention that instead of violating morals it only violates a legal institution which is in many respects oppressive and unnatural, no possible plea that the instinct on which it is founded is a vital one. Prostitution can confuse the issue with all these excuses: gambling has none of them. Consequently, if Mrs Warren must needs be a demon, a bookmaker must be a cacodemon. Well, does anybody who knows the sporting world really believe that bookmakers are worse than their neighbors? On the contrary, they have to be a good deal better; for in that world nearly everybody whose social rank does not exclude such an occupation would be a bookmaker if he could; but the strength of character required for handling large sums of money and for strict settlements and unflinching payment of losses is so rare that successful bookmakers are rare too. It may seem that at least public spirit cannot be one of a bookmaker's virtues; but I can testify from personal experience that excellent public work is done with money subscribed by bookmakers. It is true that there are abysses in bookmaking: for example, welshing. Mr Grein hints that there are abysses in Mrs Warren's profession also. So there are in every profession: the error lies in supposing that every member of them sounds these depths. I sit on a public body which prosecutes Mrs Warren zealously; and I can assure Mr Grein that she is often leniently dealt with because she has conducted her business "respectably" and held herself above its vilest branches. The degrees in infamy are as numerous and as scrupulously observed as the degrees in the peerage: the moralist's notion that there are depths at which the moral atmosphere ceases is as delusive as the rich man's notion that there are no social jealousies or snobberies among the very poor. No: had I drawn Mrs Warren as a fiend in human form, the very people who now rebuke me for flattering her would probably be the first to deride me for deducing character logically from occupation instead of observing it accurately in society.

One critic is so enslaved by this sort of logic that he calls my portraiture of the Reverend Samuel Gardner an attack on religion. According to this view Subaltern Iago is an attack on the army, Sir John Falstaff an attack on knighthood, and King Claudius an attack on royalty. Here again the clamor for naturalness and human feeling, raised by so many critics when they are confronted by the real thing on the stage, is really a clamor for the most mechanical and superficial sort of logic. The dramatic reason for making the clergyman what Mrs Warren calls "an old stick-in-the-mud," whose son, in spite of much capacity and charm, is a cynically worthless member of society, is to set up a mordant contrast between him and the woman of infamous profession, with her well brought-up, straightforward, hardworking daughter. The critics who have missed the contrast have doubtless observed often enough that many clergymen are in the Church through no genuine calling, but simply because, in circles which can command preferment, it is the refuge of "the fool of the family"; and that clergymen's sons are often conspicuous reactionists against the restraints imposed on them in childhood by their father's profession. These critics must know, too, from history if not from experience, that women as unscrupulous as Mrs Warren have distinguished themselves as administrators and rulers, both commercially and politically. But both observation and knowledge are left behind when journalists go to the theater. Once in their stalls, they assume that it is "natural" for clergymen to be saintly, for soldiers to be heroic, for lawyers to be hard-hearted, for sailors to be simple and generous, for doctors to perform miracles with little bottles, and for Mrs Warren to be a beast and a demon. All this is not only not natural, but not dramatic. A man's profession only enters into the drama of his life when it comes into conflict with his nature. The result of this conflict is tragic in Mrs Warren's case, and comic in the clergyman's case (at least we are savage enough to laugh at it); but in both cases it is illogical, and in both cases natural. I repeat, the critics who accuse me of sacrificing nature to logic are so sophisticated by their profession that to them logic is nature, and nature absurdity.

A Cultural Casebook

The "Woman Question" in the Late Nineteenth Century

The "woman question" was central to great controversy that swept throughout Europe and the United States during the nineteenth century and brought the circumstances of women to the attention of society. Prior to the industrial revolution, women worked side by side with men in the fields or in home-based industries. With the creation of a moneyed class made possible by the fruits of factory labor, however, women similar to Ibsen's Nora Helmer sought economic independence. Although wealthy and newly middle-class women were considered "angels of the house"—responsible for managing the household, supervising the children, and supporting their husband's efforts—eventually these women began to see the limitations of their role. As the philosopher John Stuart Mill put it, women were expected to be willing slaves, but some of them, like Nora in Ibsen's *A Doll House*, rebelled.

Ibsen's Nora Helmer and Hedda Gabler and Strindberg's Miss Julie offer views into the opportunities for women in the age. Marriage is the key to Nora's sense of self and satisfaction until she realizes how little her efforts to save her husband are appreciated. Marriage, Hedda's only hope of possessing power in her community, turns out to be less romantic and less empowering than she had hoped, so she becomes desperate. For Miss Julie, romance is not synonymous with marriage, but she realizes, too, that her virtue, once spent, can no longer give her power over men such as Jean. These plays demonstrate the limits of women's power in the second half of the nineteenth century.

The limited legal status of married women was increasingly unsatisfactory to wives during the latter part of the nineteenth century, and laws were passed to help them retain control over some of their own property as distinct from their husbands' property. Because divorce was difficult or impossible, separation usually ended in the ostracism of the woman. Many women in this era worked for reform, and several of the dramas of Ibsen and other Scandinavian writers argued for better treatment of women in society.

The economic limitations imposed on women were severe. Women of the upper-middle classes were expected not to work at all, whereas women of the lower classes living in cities had few choices. Women who did factory work risked injury and disease. As Mrs. Warren eloquently explains in Shaw's *Mrs. Warren's Profession*, even late in the nineteenth century, factory women aged quickly, had no job security, were dispensable, and often ended badly. One alternative was the choice made by Mrs. Warren, who avoided the early death of her sister Jane, victim of lead poisoning in a factory, by becoming a prostitute and then a madam.

In the Victorian era prostitution remained an almost universal fact of life. It enjoyed licensing in some places and toleration and graft in others. In England, the Contagious Diseases Acts, instituted between 1860 and 1870, supposedly protected sailors and other military personnel from venereal disease. The laws required all prostitutes in military regions to be examined by appointed officials. Prostitutes adjudged "sick" were confined in hospitals with little or no hope of being released. Politically active women who had been at the forefront of the equal rights movement and the quest for the vote were outraged at this unequal treatment of the participants in the act of prostitution. Eventually, their protests forced the government to repeal the Contagious Diseases Acts.

Some of the following documents point out the economic and social issues involved in prostitution in the period. Descriptions from brothel directories reveal the widely accepted "business" of running a brothel. Madams, "landladies" of the brothels, were managers who had risen from the ranks, and their number was not large, as Barbara Meil Hobson explains in "Successful Madams." The small number of madams who actually achieved financial independence is a point to remember when considering the achievement of Mrs. Warren in Shaw's play.

As this collection of documents attests, the debate over the "woman question" was conducted in the houses of Parliament, in the daily papers of many nations, and in the essays, dramas, and writings of authors such as August Strindberg. The plays of Ibsen, Strindberg, Shaw, and other writers of the period must be seen against the backdrop of the struggle for women's rights.

John Stuart Mill (1806–1873)
ON THE SUBJECTION OF WOMEN   *1869*

John Stuart Mill was an important philosopher in the mid-nineteenth century. He held to a philosophy of utilitarianism, which stressed the usefulness of actions and principles. His views on the subjection of women note that the superior strength of men had been turned into principles of law and behavior as if women were meant to be subjugated. According to Mill, women have been forced into wrongful submission.

From the very earliest twilight of human society, every woman (owing to the value attached to her by men, combined with her inferiority in muscular strength) was found in a state of bondage to some man. Laws and systems of polity always begin by recognizing the relations they find already existing between individuals. They convert what was a mere physical fact into a legal right, give it the sanction of society, and principally aim at the substitution of public and organized means of asserting and protecting these rights, instead of the irregular and lawless conflict of physical strength. Those who had already been compelled to obedience became in this manner legally bound to it.

All causes, social and natural, combine to make it unlikely that women should be collectively rebellious to the power of men. They are so far in a position different from all other subject classes, that their masters require something more from them than actual service. Men do not want solely the obedience of women, they want their sentiments. All men, except the most brutish, desire to have, in the woman most nearly connected with them, not a forced slave but a willing one, not a slave merely, but a favorite. They have therefore put everything in practice to enslave their minds. The masters of all other slaves rely, for maintaining obedience, on fear; either fear of themselves, or religious fears. The masters of women wanted more than simple obedience, and they turned the whole force of education to effect their purpose. All women are brought up from the very earliest years in the belief that their ideal of character is the very opposite to that of men; not self-will, and government by self-control, but submission, and yielding to the control of others. All the moralities tell them that it is the duty of women, and all the current sentimentalities that it is their nature, to live for others; to make complete abnegation of themselves, and to have no life but in their affections. And by their affections are meant the only ones they are allowed to have — those to the men with whom they are connected, or to the children who constitute an additional and indefeasible tie between them and a man. When we put together three things — first, the natural attraction between opposite sexes; secondly, the wife's entire dependence on the husband, every privilege or pleasure she has being either his gift, or depending entirely on his will; and lastly, that the principal object of human pursuit, consideration, and all objects of social ambition, can in general be sought or obtained by her only through him, it would be a miracle if the object of being attractive to men had not become the polar star of feminine education and formation of character. And, this great means of influence over the minds of women having been acquired, an instinct of selfishness made men avail themselves of it to the utmost as a means of holding women in subjection, by representing to them meekness, submissiveness, and resignation of all individual will into the hands of a man, as an essential part of sexual attractiveness. What is now called the nature of women is an eminently artificial thing — the result of forced repression in some directions, unnatural stimulation in others.

August Strindberg (1849–1912)
THE WOMAN QUESTION: WOMEN'S RIGHTS   *1884*
TRANSLATED FROM THE SWEDISH BY MARY SANDBACH

Though he eventually developed a reputation as a misogynist, the playwright August Strindberg published a forward-looking book on marriage early in his career. He was married to the actress Siri von Essen and living in Switzerland when he wrote The Last Word on the Woman Question *(1883). But it was hardly his last word on the subject. The very next year he wrote the novel* Getting Married. *The following excerpt is from the preface to part 1 of that work. Feminism had been a growing movement in Scandinavia and elsewhere, and while Strindberg's views may seem compatible with feminist ideals, he wrote the following declaration of women's rights in a state of irritation. He was apparently sick and tired of the woman question by 1884.*

Meanwhile, under present conditions, it is both impossible and harmful to detach the Woman Question from its context. Woman's desire for emancipation is identical with man's restless longing for freedom. Let us therefore liberate man from his prejudices, and we shall see that the emancipation of women will follow. But we must work together for our objective as friends, not as enemies. The woman of the future, be it a nearer or a more distant future, shall have an indisputable right to demand certain things and, in order to dispel the suspicion that I entertain reactionary ideas, I will now set these out under the following heading:

Woman's Rights

Which the laws of nature would grant her, but of which, thanks to our perverse social system (and not as a result of male tyranny), she has been deprived.

1. The right to the same education as men. I cannot too often repeat that by this I do not mean to imagine that she will be raised to man's level by learning all the unnecessary things with which he now has to stuff himself. Posterity, which will put an end to the difference between elementary and secondary schools, which will put an end to matriculation, and all other examinations, will one day feel obliged to establish a single civic examination which everyone will take, and which will replace confirmation. This examination will be the same for men and women, and will only require those examined to have a thorough knowledge of the arts of reading, writing, and arithmetic, a knowledge of the laws of their country, a knowledge of their civic rights and duties, and also of one living language. He who wants after that to learn what Cicero thought of Lucius Sulla, and what Moses intended to do with the children of Israel may do so, that is if he has time for such luxuries, for posterity will demand that every citizen shall support himself by bodily toil as nature intended.

2. Boys and girls shall attend the same schools, so that both sexes learn to know each other early in life. Things will not then be as they are today, when boys imagine that girls are angels, and girls that boys are knights. In this way we shall avoid all the silent sins of fantasy and precocity, for they are a result of the way in which the sexes are isolated.

3. The girl shall have the same freedom to "run wild" and choose what company she pleases.

4. There shall be complete equality between the sexes, which will do away with that revolting form of hypocrisy called gallantry, or politeness to ladies. A girl will not expect a boy to get up and give her his seat, for that is the hallmark of the subservient slave; and a brother will not get into the habit of expecting his sister to make his bed, or sew on his shirt buttons, for these are things he must do for himself.

5. Woman shall have the vote. In the future, when her confirmation consists of an examination in the laws that govern the community in which she lives, and when this community is obliged to present an annual report to its members, as companies do today, a woman will be just as well able to decide for whom or for what she will vote as a man.

6. Woman shall be eligible for all occupations, which should not be any more difficult to arrange under self-government than it is today when, inconsequently enough, she can become the monarch. Self-government will not be the same as government by professionals, but will be more like local government, that is a commission which can be performed in leisure moments. Is anyone wiser and better suited to govern than an old mother, who has learned through motherhood and running a household both how to rule and how to administrate? (Our forefathers had such a veneration for the wisdom of older women that they believed them to possess supernatural knowledge.)

7. This measure will mean that the moral code will become less rigid, and the law less strict, for a mother has learned to be more tolerant than anyone, and no one knows better than she how patient and how unexacting you must be with the erring children of man.

8. Woman shall be exempt from military service. Anyone who regards this as unjust should take into consideration the fact that nature exacts compensation from her in the form of heavy maternal duties. For that matter military service will not in future be regarded as particularly glorious. It will simply be a duty.

9. By a just distribution of the combined riches of nature the community of the future will ensure that all who are born receive sustenance and instruction. Marriage as a guarantee for these advantages will therefore become unnecessary. Man and wife will conclude a contract, verbal or written, for a union of any length they may decide, which they will have the right to dissolve when they please, without reference to law or gospel. It is true that this will not prevent a situation in which two males want to possess the same female, but the struggle will be less cruel, and the female will be the one to choose, — which is not the case at present — for no one in future will be obliged to marry for money or position, as neither of these things will exist. Selection will therefore be natural, and consequently the race will improve.

So much for the woman of the future and marriage. But there are things we can do to make reasonable improvements in the married state under present conditions. These are:

1. That boys and girls shall be allowed to mix more freely.

2. That the education of boys shall be simplified, so that it will not be unjust if the education of girls is simplified too.

3. The girl (like the boy) shall no longer be forced to learn so much about the past, but she shall be obliged to acquaint herself with the way in which society is governed today.

4. She may be given the vote at the earliest possible moment.

5. False gallantry will cease of itself, and men and women will associate together as men do now. But things shall not be as at present, when men have all male banquets, which end with a toast to the ladies, while the latter sit at home eating porridge and milk.

6. Civil marriage shall be introduced, and this will make divorce easier. Not that it is likely to become more frequent, but easier divorce will make the bonds feel less irksome, and will disabuse the man of the idea that he owns the woman. Children will still hold married couples together, unless the circumstances are very difficult.

Civil marriage would do away with the horrible legal ruling that necessitates warnings by the clergy, or obligatory "desertion."

7. The paragraphs in our laws about a husband's rights as a guardian shall be rescinded.

8. A woman shall come of age at eighteen without any reservations.

9. Deeds of settlement and the judicial division of property shall be obligatory on all married couples.

10. A woman (when her education is the same as that given to men) shall have the right to fill any post and practice any profession she pleases. (But if two million women were let loose on the labor market at the moment the result would be ruthless competition. Here — under present conditions — we must perhaps condescend to an inconsistency, unless by any chance, a surplus of labor accelerated the adoption of the new social system.)

11. When he marries a man shall be obliged to take out a life insurance policy, so that in the event of his death, his wife and children will not be left destitute. This is more especially his duty if he takes a woman away from a gainful occupation.

12. A woman shall keep her own name. She shall not have the right to take her husband's title in its feminine form, for a title under present conditions is a possession, often expensively acquired, and worth money. This proviso is necessary if there is to be equality, and it will prevent many women from being tempted to buy a title with their wealth. Boys shall take their father's name, and girls their mother's.

13. Separate bedrooms shall be the rule from the beginning. For a practice so offensive to "decency" as a common bedchamber brings its own punishment, and gives rise to confusion, distaste, satiety, and even worse things in a relationship. This rule will make a woman's position freer, and will give her the right to possess her own body.

14. If a woman is solely her husband's wife, and the mother of his children and has no independent occupation, she shall receive an allowance for clothes and recreation. She shall not have a salary, or receive clothes as presents, for which she has to say thank you. Moreover, she shall have the *right* to pay for her amusements herself, even when she is out with her husband, and thus be spared from always being *treated*.

15. If a married woman is gainfully occupied and does not run her own home, she shall be obliged to contribute from her earnings as much to the household as her husband does. If she also works in her home she shall be allowed to keep what she earns, for her work at home will thus come to be regarded as an extra contribution, and not as now, as the services rendered by a slave.

Johan Thorsten Sellin (1897–1994)
MARRIAGE AND DIVORCE IN SWEDEN   *1922*

Sellin discusses the rights of Swedish women in marriage before the sweeping changes invoked by the law of 1920. Prior to that time the wife was essentially at the mercy of her husband's decisions. She was bound to obey her husband's wishes on virtually all important issues, and her children were her husband's to educate or train as he liked. A wife's limitations were established under law.

Before the law of 1920 went into effect, the status of the wife, as far as the law was concerned, was, in spite of improvements, rather unfavorable in many respects, giving unmistakable evidence of the double standard, which the present law has succeeded in abolishing. She, first of all, followed her husband's estate in life; if he for some reason or other became poor, she was obliged to accept this fact with resignation, even though he might have been the cause of the poverty. Her husband's nationality was hers, and the choice of domicile was in his hands. Her only right to refuse to live where he determined to live depended on whether or not his decision would cause her life to be placed in jeopardy, expose her to injustice, or force her to move abroad. In the last mentioned case, she could refuse to comply with his wishes only if his business at the time of the marriage was not likely to take him abroad or if he was not appointed to some official position which necessitated foreign residence.

A wife was in duty bound to expend her energies and efforts for her family and her home, in accordance with her husband's wishes. This meant that she could not accept outside work without his permission, unless the needs of the family made it imperative. Although the law gave him no power to compel her to follow his wishes, he could refuse to support her or could ask the clergy to "warn" her, the first step toward separation from bed and board. With her husband's permission[1] she could conduct a business or engage in other profitable employment, but if he were legally disqualified to engage in business (due to official position as custom officer, public prosecutor, or tax collector) she shared his disability, even though she may have had his permission. If she failed to heed her husband's refusal, she could be fined like any other individual who conducted a business without license. When she worked lawfully, i.e., with her husband's permission, her earnings belonged to her, although it is not certain that what she purchased with these earnings became hers to do with as she chose.

A married mother had nothing to say in the bringing up of her own children, i.e., the law gave her no such right. Her husband was their guardian until they reached majority, chose their life's work, and gave away his daughters in marriage. If he abused his guardianship, the court could appoint someone else guardian, but in no instance could the mother be so appointed while the family remained undisrupted. She was thereby classified with "feeble-minded persons, heavy debtors, spendthrifts, enemies of the child, persons not yet twenty-five years of age, or so old and crippled that he cannot discharge his duties as guardian, etc." Only in case the husband went insane, deserted his wife, or for other reasons was unable to exercise his guardianship could she be substituted, and if he died, she took his place as guardian of her children — until she remarried. In case husband and wife belonged to different religious faiths, the former decided in which faith the children should be brought up.

As a rule, all the property of the spouses was joint, since in the majority of marriages no private property or income existed. Of this joint property the husband was the sole manager. His administrative powers extended even to his wife's private property, with the exception of her private real property. He decided upon the amount to be spent for the household expenses, for the education of the children, and even for his wife's personal needs. The latter had no right to

---

[1]The industrial and commercial acts of 1846 prohibited a woman to engage in business without her husband's permission and security.

demand anything from her husband, except necessities, even though she may have been the source of the entire family fortune. Most important of all, perhaps, was the fact that no matter how he managed the joint property, he owed his wife no accounting.

Richard Panofsky (b. 1943)
A NINETEENTH-CENTURY HUSBAND'S LETTER
TO HIS WIFE   *1844*

Richard Panofsky, a professor at the University of Massachusetts at Dartmouth, has provided a translated letter from a man named Marcus (1807–1865) to his wife Ulrike (1816–1888). The couple and their six children lived in nineteenth-century Hamburg, Germany. The letter establishes the conditions under which Marcus would take his wife back into his house after she had left him and the children. It also establishes exactly what he expects of his wife. According to Panofsky, Ulrike returned.

June 23, 1844

Dear Wife,

You have sinned greatly — and maybe I too; but this much is certain: Adam sinned after Eve had already sinned. So it is with us; you, alone, carry the guilt of all the misfortune which, however, I helped to enlarge later by my behavior. Listen now, since I still believe certain things to be necessary in order that we may have a peaceful life. If we want not only to be content for a day but forever, you will have to follow my wishes. So examine yourself and determine if you are strong enough to conquer your false ambitions and your stubbornness to submit to all the conditions, the fulfillment of which I cannot ignore. Every sensible person will tell you that all I ask of you is what is easily understood. If you insist on remaining stubborn, then do not return to my house, for you will never be happy with me; your husband, children, and the entire city threaten indifference or even contempt.

But if you decide to act *sensibly* and *correctly,* that is *justly* and *kindly,* then be certain that many in the world will envy you.

I am including here the paper which I read to you in front of the rabbi; ask anyone in your residence if the wishes expressed by me are not quite reasonable, and are of a kind to which every wife can agree for the welfare of domestic happiness. In any case, act in a way you think best.

When you decide to return, write to tell me on which day and hour you depart from Berlin and give me your itinerary whether by way of Kuestrin and Pinne or by way of Wollstein. I will then meet you at Wollstein or Pinne. I expect you will bring Solomon with you.

Don't travel unprepared. If you need money, ask your father.

May God enlighten your heart and mind.

I remain your so far unhappy,

[MARCUS]

Greetings to my parents, brothers, and sisters; also your brother. Show them what you wish, this letter, the enclosure, whatever you want. The children are fortunately healthy.

If you want to return with joy and peace, write me by return mail. In that case, I would rather send you a carriage. Maybe Madam Fraenkel will come along. . . .

[*Enclosure*]

My wife promises — for which every wife is obligated to her husband — to follow my wishes in everything and to strictly obey my orders. It is already self-evident that our marital relations have often been disturbed by the fact that my wife does not follow my wishes but believes herself to be entitled to act on her own, even if this is totally against my orders. In order not to have to remind my wife every second what my wishes are regarding homemaking and public conduct — wishes which I have often expressed — I want to make here a few rules which shall serve as a code of conduct. A home is best run if the work for each hour is planned ahead of time, if possible.

Servants get up no later than 5:00 A.M. in summer and 6:00 A.M. in winter, the children an hour later. The cook prepares breakfast. The nursemaid puts out clothes for every child, prepares water and sponge, cleans the combs, etc. The cook should stay in the kitchen unless there is time to clean the rooms. At least once a week the rooms should be cleaned whenever possible, but not all on the same day.

Every Wednesday, the people in the house should do a laundry. Every last Wednesday in the month, there shall be a large laundry with an outside washerwoman. At least every Monday, the seamstress shall come into the house to fix what is necessary.

Every Thursday or Friday, bread is baked for the week; I think it is best to buy grain and have it ground, but to knead it at home.

Every Friday special bread (Barches) should be bought for the evening meal.

The kitchen list will be prepared and discussed every Thursday evening, jointly, by me and my wife; but my wish is to be decisive.

After this, provisions are to be bought every Friday at the market. For this purpose, my wife, herself, will go to the market on Fridays, accompanied by a servant; she can substitute a special woman who does errands (*Faktorfrau*) if she wishes, but not a servant.

All expenditures have to be written down daily and punctually.

The children receive a bath every Thursday evening. The children's clothes must be kept in a specially appointed chest, with a separate compartment for each child with the child's name upon it. The boys' suits and girls' dresses are to be kept separately. To keep used laundry, there must be a hamper easily accessible. Equally important is the food storage box in which provisions are kept in order, locked and safe from vermin.

The kitchen should be kept in order. Once a week all woodwork and copper must be scoured. The lights and lamps have to be cleaned daily. Toward servants, one has to be strict and just. Therefore, one should not call them names which aren't suitable for a decent wife. One should give them enough nourishing food. Disobedience and obstinacy are to be referred to me.

My wife will never make visits in my absence. However, she should visit the synagogue every Saturday — at least once a month; also she should go for a walk with the children at least once a week.

Helen Watterson Moody (1859–1928)
WHAT IT MEANS TO BE A WIFE   *1899*

The Ladies Home Journal, *by no means a radical magazine in 1899, attempted to show wives how to best serve their husbands and themselves. Helen Watterson Moody, a frequent contributor to the* Journal, *emphasizes methods by which a wife can "Keep Love Secure."*

When a woman marries she assumes two new sets of relations — those of sentiment, through which she becomes the loving, faithful companion of one man and the mother of his children, and the economic relation, through which she becomes one of the great conserving and distributing agents of the world. Since I shall speak of these last two conditions later, I will now only consider that one sentimental relation whose beauty and holiness, if rightly assumed, give foundation to all the rest — that of wifehood.

Marriage is, or should be, primarily a relation of sentiment, yet the happiness of married life is decided by quite other things than sentiment — sturdy and steady moral qualities, good sense, and fair executive ability. I think the recognition of the fact that, though love is the supreme thing in married life, love alone is not enough, always comes to a newly married couple with a sense of surprise.

The Only Way to Keep Love Secure

In the first months of married life, love is so sufficient, and loving so simple, that there seems no other need in life. But by-and-by, when care begins to shadow them, when duties present themselves, and, strangely enough, conflict with each other, when convictions clash and tastes differ, then both husband and wife begin to realize that back of love must stand what I have called "steady and sturdy moral qualities" — justice, patience, honesty, and sincerity, and magnanimity. Indeed, on these depends the very continuance of love in marriage, for it is not possible to go on loving unless that is found which is worthy of love. I say this advisedly. I know the world is full of men and women who think, either because they like to think so, or sadly, because they must, that one can love where one does not respect. It seems to me that this does not ennoble one's ideal of love. One may pity, may have an infinite yearning tenderness over what one cannot respect, but love is of royal birth and recognizes only what is as royal as itself. The way, then, to keep love secure in married life is not so much to be anxiously watching and guarding lest it should escape, or crying that love has spread its wings because the first holiday romance is replaced by graver feeling, but by living along simply and honestly and frankly together, on a high plane, looking most and always toward "whatsoever things are true, whatsoever things are honest, whatsoever things are just, whatsoever things are pure, whatsoever things are lovely, whatsoever things are of good report." Then Love will be not a captive, but a most willing guest.

Marriage Is a Serious and Steady Occupation

That is why I say that the real happiness of married life depends largely upon the personal character that is put into it. Next in importance I place sound, good sense; and I mean by this that underlying sense of proportion by which one is able to discriminate the insignificant, the passing, the unimportant, from the grave, the permanent, the important — that capacity for steady, balancing thought which keeps one from impulsive words and rash deeds. A woman who is blessed with good sense does not consider at the start that marriage is a role to be skillfully and successfully enacted, or a grand frolic of which she is to be the admired and indulged center, or a mere incident in a life crowded with other activities. She knows that marriage is a serious and steady vocation, and that the true wife is one who enters marriage not thinking how much she can get out of it, but how much she can put into it. It is this larger conception of marriage which makes women dwell by their own firesides in sweet content with what is commonly called the "narrow limits of home," knowing well that no true home is narrow since it must give cover to "the whole primal mysteries of life — food, raiment, and work to earn them withal: love and marriage, birth and death, right-doing and wrong-doing — all these commonplaces of humanity which are most divine because they are most commonplace."

The way to make home a wide place to dwell in, is to bring a wide personality to dwell in it. Any home is just as wide as the maker, and can be no wider. When a woman understands this she is able to keep her head steady and her heart undisturbed over newspaper sketches about other women, in which each one of them is made to do the most remarkable and entirely unnecessary combination of things. [. . .]

Married Women Can Find Time If They Will

When I hear a married woman lament the lack of wide opportunities in her life I find myself wondering, in a kind of daze, what she means. If I inquire particularly, I usually discover that by lack of opportunities she means either the time for study and self-cultivation which she deeply desires, or else an opportunity for public activity and recognition. Well, both of these are good in their proper places, and there are few wives who will not be able to find some hours in the week to give to either one or the other. I suspect that in the case of those women who say they actually do not get time for study or music, or for an occasional club meeting, the trouble lies in the fact that they do not want to enough. For be sure of this, that in the long run a man or a woman usually finds time in life to do the thing that he or she wants to do most. A woman may desire the opportunity for self-culture and growth, but if she in her heart really prefers an hour of neighborhood gossip, or a piece of drawn linen for her luncheon table, or a vulgar profusion in the menu she offers her guests, she will have these and not the study. If, on the other hand, the intellectual quickening that comes from communion with big and earnest minds be the one thing in life that she feels she must have, be sure that in some degree she will have it — not enough of it, possibly, to satisfy her, but enough to make her life richer, because she will make her living less complex in order that she may have it.

RIGHT: Scene in a brothel, from the *National Police Gazette,* July 26, 1879. (© Collection of The New-York Historical Society)
BELOW: A scene from Hogarth's *Harlot's Progress:* A madam welcomes a newly arrived woman who will soon become part of the establishment. One of her customers looks eagerly on.

Flora Tristan (1803–1844)

London Journal: Prostitutes in London . . . All the Streets Are Full of Them   *1842*

TRANSLATED FROM THE FRENCH BY JEAN HAWKES

Flora Tristan, a French feminist, visited London often. Her journal was published in France in 1840 and translated into English in 1842. Among her many observations, her comments on the prostitutes of London establish the fact of their presence in remarkable numbers. Waterloo Bridge remained a notorious site for plying the trade of prostitution both in the late nineteenth century and afterward. Tristan's detailed account implies a deep sympathy for the women involved.

There are so many prostitutes in London that one sees them everywhere at any time of day; all the streets are full of them, but at certain times they flock in from outlying districts in which most of them live, and mingle with the crowds in theaters and public places. It is rare for them to take men home; their landlords would object, and besides their lodgings are unfit. They take their "captures" to the houses reserved for their trade. . . .

Between seven and eight o'clock one evening, accompanied by two friends armed with canes, I went to take a look at the new suburb which lies on either side of the long broad thoroughfare called Waterloo Road at the end of Waterloo Bridge. This neighborhood is almost entirely inhabited by prostitutes and people who live off prostitution; it is courting danger to go there alone at night. It was a hot summer evening; in every window and doorway women were laughing and joking with their protectors. Half dressed, some of them *naked to the waist,* they were a revolting sight, and the criminal, cynical expressions of their companions filled me with apprehension. These men are for the most part very good looking — young, vigorous, and well made — but their coarse and common air marks them as animals whose sole instinct is to satisfy their appetites. . . .

We went on our way and explored all the streets in the vicinity of Waterloo Road, then we sat upon the bridge to watch the women of the neighborhood flock past, as they do every night between the hours of eight and nine, on their way to the West End, where they ply their trade all through the night and return home between eight and nine in the morning. They infest the promenades and any other place where people gather, such as the approaches to the Stock Exchange, the various public buildings and the theaters, which they invade as soon as entry is reduced to half price. . . . After the play they move on to the "finishes"; these are squalid taverns or vast resplendent gin-palaces where people go to spend what remains of the night. . . .

I had heard descriptions of the debauchery to be seen at finishes, but could never bring myself to believe them. Now I was in London for the fourth time with the firm resolve to discover everything for myself. I determined to overcome my repugnance and go in person to one of these finishes. . . . The same friends who had accompanied me to the Waterloo Road again offered to be my guides. . . .

From the outside these "gin-palaces" with their carefully fastened shutters seem to be quietly slumbering; but no sooner has the doorkeeper admitted you by the little door reserved for the initiates than you are dazzled by the light of a thousand gas lamps. Upstairs there is a spacious salon divided down the middle; in one half there is a row of tables separated one from the other by wooden screens, as in all English restaurants. . . . In the other half there is a dais where the prostitutes parade in all their finery; seeking to arouse the men with their glances and remarks. . . .

Towards midnight the regular clients begin to arrive; several finishes are frequented by men in high society, and this is where the cream of the aristocracy gather. At first the young noblemen recline on the sofas, smoking and exchanging pleasantries with the women; then, when they have drunk enough for the fumes of champagne and Madeira to go to their heads, the illustrious scions of the English nobility, the very honorable members of Parliament remove their coats, untie their cravats, take off their waistcoats and braces, and proceed to set up their private boudoir in a public place. Why not make themselves at home, since they are paying out so much money for the right to display their contempt. . . . The orgy rises to a crescendo; between four and five o'clock in the morning it reaches its height.

At this point it takes a good deal of courage to remain in one's seat, a mute spectator of all that takes place. What a worthy use these English lords make of their immense fortunes! How fine and generous they are when they have lost the use of their reason and offer fifty, even a hundred guineas to a prostitute if she will lend herself to all the obscenities that drunkenness engenders. . . .

For in a finish there is no lack of entertainment. One of the favorite sports is to *ply a woman with drink* until she falls dead drunk upon the floor, then to make her swallow a draught compounded of *vinegar, mustard, and pepper;* this invariably throws the poor creature into horrible convulsions, and her spasms and contortions provoke the *honorable company* to gales of laughter and infinite amusement. Another diversion much appreciated at these fashionable gatherings is to empty the contents of the nearest glass upon the women as they lie insensible on the ground. I have seen satin dresses of no recognizable color, only a confused mass of stains; wine, brandy, beer, tea, coffee, cream, etc. . . . daubed all over them in a thousand fantastic shapes. . . . The air is heavy with the noxious odors of food, drink, tobacco, and others more fetid still which seize you by the throat, grip your temples in a vice, and make your senses reel: it is indescribably horrible! . . . However, this life, which continues relentlessly night after night, is the prostitute's sole hope of a fortune, for she has no hold on the Englishman when he is sober. *The sober Englishman is chaste to the point of prudery.*

It is usually between seven and eight o'clock in the morning when people leave the finish. The servants go out to look for cabs, and anyone still on his feet gathers up his clothes and returns home; as for the rest, the pot-boys dress them in the first garments that come to hand, bundle them into a cab, and tell the cabman where to deliver them. Often nobody knows their address; then they are deposited in the cellar and left to sleep in the straw. This place is known as the drunkards hole, and there they stay until they have recovered their wits sufficiently to say where they wish to be taken.

A LETTER TO THE *TIMES* (LONDON) FROM A PROSTITUTE

1858

After a concerted effort on the part of prominent London citizens to reduce prostitution in London, a prostitute who referred to herself as "one of that abandoned sisterhood" came forth with the following letter filled with suggestions about how to improve the circumstances of the prostitute and her customers. She hopes to avoid the "persecution" of individuals while London attempts to deal with a vice it considers a nuisance.

Sir:

Certain Persons have, as you know, commenced a crusade against London Prostitutes, and, if one of that abandoned sisterhood may presume to address you, grant me your attention.

The precept and example set me by parents, now, thank God, in their graves; the education likewise "thrown away" upon me, and my subsequent experience as a governess in a highly respectable family, were not necessary to the conviction that the class among which I may be numbered consists of outcasts whose undisguised pursuit is an offense to the laws of God and man.

I know that we are cut off from the moral, social, and religious worlds. . . . We need not be told of our ruin and degradation, because we never "fall" without being alive to the fact. A woman seduced may forgive her wrongs . . . it is impossible for her to forget what she is; society will not permit her to do so. . . . Do not suppose, then, that I would attempt to defend what transpires nightly in the Haymarket, in Coventry Street, or wherever women of my caste congregate. I do not ask you to countenance anything of the kind. No, Sir, give "Vice its own image" and do your duty.

But, while you yourself refrain from going a step too far, pray give a warning to others. It is one thing to put down a nuisance. It is another to persecute individuals. I will anticipate much that may fairly be said, and admit that if I live avowedly in defiance of those regulations which the community has established as essential to its well being. . . . I must expect to be checked in such openly vicious courses, for I believe the liberty of the subject should end where injustice to others begins. But pray tell those good gentlemen who are bent on "putting us down," that theirs is not only a delicate, but a difficult undertaking, and they should be careful lest they have more to answer for than they dream of in their philosophy.

The vice of London, Sir, is seen to float upon its surface; let it pass as the weed on its way to the ocean. If it accumulates so as to become offensive, disperse it. If it is otherwise annoying and cannot conveniently be avoided, deal with it accordingly.

Appoint commissioners who are fitted for the office, intelligent, respectable, and responsible gentlemen, and make it worth their while to devote themselves entirely to the reduction of the scandal complained of. Empower these officials to have us taken up and punished for riot or impropriety of any kind. But let not the "pelting petty officer," the ignorant constable of a few shillings a week, and it may be an unfeeling and unthinking brute, interfere with us as he will. Recollect it was man who made us what we are. It is man who pays for the finery, the rouge, and the gin . . . it is man who, when we apply ourselves to industry and honesty, employs us upon starvation wages; and if man had his way, and women's nature were not superior to his, there would be no virtue extant. Say, then, is it for man to persecute even the most profligate among us?

Pray, Sir, think of this, and tell those gentlemen whose speeches I read to act upon it. They may be husbands and fathers . . . and I allow for their parental solicitude. But if they be Christians they will imitate one who said, "Go, and sin no more," and not "move on," "anywhere, anywhere, out of the world."

Your humble servant,

ONE MORE UNFORTUNATE

Barbara Meil Hobson
SUCCESSFUL MADAMS

1987

In this brief excerpt Hobson describes prostitutes who became "successful entrepreneurs" and achieved positions similar to that of Mrs. Warren in Bernard Shaw's play. However, very few prostitutes ever became financially independent. Mrs. Warren is remarkable for her success, not for her profession.

On the other hand, the image of the prostitute as someone who accumulates savings from her trade, wisely invests her capital, and obtains a small fortune was not very realistic either. We know of some famous successful madams at the turn of

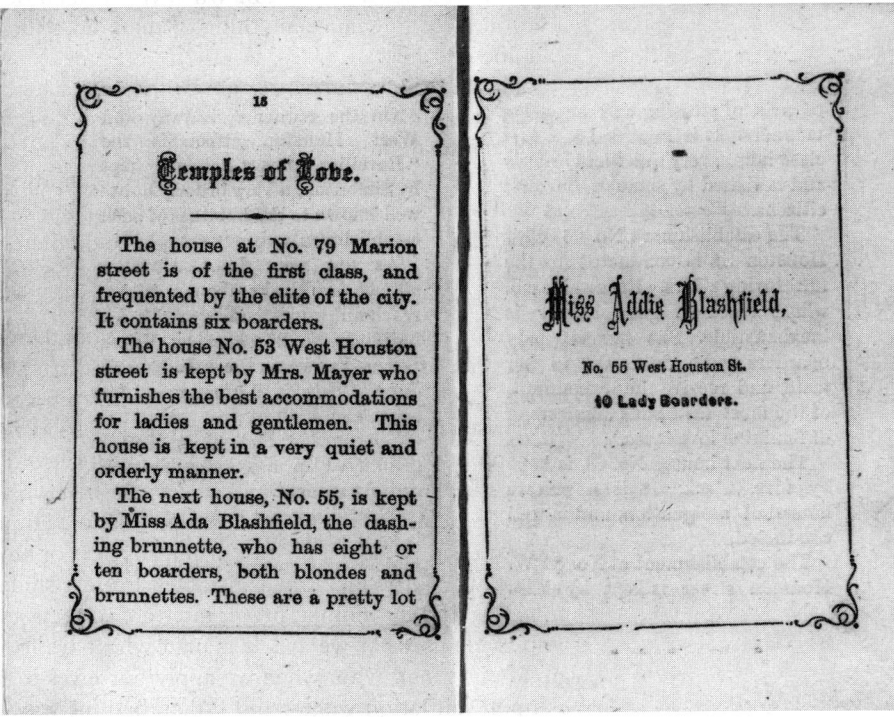

The Gentleman's Directory, Temples of Love, address listings, 1870. Published directories such as this one informed men where to find the best brothels. Even newspapers carried discreet advertisements when prostitutes changed houses so they would not lose their regular clientele. (© Collection of The New-York Historical Society)

the century, including the Everleigh sisters, who operated gilded palaces of vice in Chicago, and Nell Kimball, the famous "queen" of Storeyville. They were the successful entrepreneurs of the demimonde, and they even published their memoirs.

What little we know of typical prostitutes' futures suggests that few women achieved upward economic mobility through prostitution. The nineteenth-century police registers tell us that women in regulated prostitution were most likely to reenter traditional working class occupations. [. . .] The fees Swedish prostitutes had to pay for medical examinations, the percentages madams took for room and board, and the expenses for dress and cosmetics did not leave very much money for savings. Prostitutes in the high-class brothels in nineteenth-century American cities were paid high prices for their sexual services. But madams usually took 50 percent of a prostitute's receipts, and expenses were high. In addition, prostitutes in many of these cities had to take a cut from their earnings for police protection. Research on nineteenth-century St. Paul documents that career paths within prostitution were limited. Only four out of sixty-one brothel prostitutes listed in official records became madams, a revealing statistic in a city where prostitution was aboveboard — unofficially licensed.

Drama in the Early and Mid-Twentieth Century

The realist tradition in drama had certain EXPRESSIONIST qualities evident in the symbolic actions in Strindberg's *Miss Julie* and the romantic fantasies of Hedda in *Hedda Gabler*. But the surfaces of the plays appear realistic, consisting of a sequence of events that we might imagine happening in real life. The subject matter is also in the tradition of naturalism because it is drawn from life and not beautified or toned down for the middle-class audience.

But in the early to mid-twentieth century realistic drama took a new turn, incorporating distortions of reality that border on the unreal or *surreal*. From the time of Anton Chekhov in 1903 to Samuel Beckett in the 1950s, drama exploited the possibilities of realism, antirealism, and the poetic expansion of expressionism.

The Heritage of Realism

In the late nineteenth century realism was often perceived as too severe for an audience that had loved melodrama. Realistic plays forced comfortable audiences to observe psychological and physical problems that their status as members of the middle class usually allowed them to avoid. Audiences often protested loudly at this painful experience.

The technique of realism could, however, be adapted for many different purposes, and eventually realism was reshaped to satisfy middle-class sensibilities by commercial playwrights, who produced popular, pleasant plays. By the 1920s in Europe and the 1930s in America, theatergoing audiences expected plays to be realistic. Even the light comedies dominating the commercial stage were in a more or less realistic mode. Anything that disturbed the illusion of realism was thought to be a flaw.

Reactions to the comfortable use of realistic techniques were numerous, especially after the First World War. One extreme reaction was that of DADAISM. Through the Dadaists' chief propagandist, Tristan Tzara (1896–1963), the group promoted an art that was essentially enigmatic and incoherent to the average person. That was its point. The Dadaists blamed World War I on sensible, middle-class people who were logical and well intentioned but never questioned convention. The brief plays that were performed in many Dadaist clubs in Europe often featured actors speaking simultaneously so that nothing they said could be understood. The purpose was to confound the normal expectations of theatergoers.

Other developments were also making it possible for playwrights to experiment and move away from a strict reliance on "comfortable" realism. By World War I motion pictures began to make melodramatic entertainment available to most people in the world. Even when films were silent, they relied on techniques that had been common on the nineteenth-century stage. Their growing domination of popular dramatic entertainment provided an outlet for the expectations of middle-class audiences and freed more imaginative playwrights to experiment and develop in different directions.

Realism and Myth

The incorporation of myth in drama offered new opportunities to expand the limits of realism. Sigmund Freud's theories of psychoanalysis at the turn of the century stimulated a new interest in myth and dreams as a psychological link between people. Freud studied Greek myths for clues to the psychic state of his patients, and he published a number of commentaries on Greek plays and on *Hamlet.* (See excerpts on pp. 100–03 and pp. 384–85.) The psychologist Carl Jung, a follower of Freud who eventually split with him, helped give a powerful impetus to the interest in dreams and the symbolism of myth by suggesting that all members of a culture share an inborn knowledge of the basic myths of the culture. Jung postulated a collective unconscious, a repository of mythic material in the mind that all humans inherit as part of their birthright. This theory gave credence to the power of myth in everyday life; along with Freud's theories, it is one of the most important ideas empowering drama and other art forms in this century. Playwrights who used elements of myth in their plays produced a poetic form of realism that deals with a level of truth common to all humans.

Myth and Culture

Some non-European drama depends on interpretation of local myth in relation to the culture or cultures that produce it. Wole Soyinka's background as a Nigerian familiar with Yoruba culture and myth, along with his formal education in England, prepared him for a career that expanded the horizons of drama for both Nigerian and European audiences.

Soyinka's experimentation has spanned two traditions — modern European theater and modern ritual theater of the Yoruba people of Nigeria. Traditional Yoruba drama develops from religious celebrations and annual festivals and includes music and dance. Soyinka's plays, including *The Strong Breed,* concern themselves with African traditions and issues, but they often also explore mythic forces that link European and African cultures. His plays have been produced throughout the world and have demonstrated the universality of the community and the anxiety of the individual it sometimes breeds. Soyinka has also written critical studies on Yoruba tragedy and has interpreted, translated, and produced Greek tragedy.

Poetic Realism

The Abbey Theatre in Dublin, which functioned with distinction from the turn of the century, produced major works by John Millington Synge, W. B. Yeats, Sean O'Casey, and Lady Gregory. Lady Gregory's peasant plays concentrated on the charming, the amusing, and occasionally the grotesque. She tried to represent the dialect she heard in the west of Ireland, a dialect that was distinctive, poetic, and colorful. She also took advantage of local Irish myths and used some of them for her most powerful plays, such as *Dervorgilla* and *Grania*, both portraits of passionate women from Irish legend and myth.

John Millington Synge, like Lady Gregory, was interested in the twin forces of myth and peasant dialects. His plays are difficult to fit into a realist mold, although their surfaces are sometimes naturalistic. Some audiences reacted violently to his realistic portrayals of peasant life because they were unflattering. Synge's plays were sometimes directly connected with ancient Irish myth, as in *Deirdre of the Sorrows* (1910), which concerns a willful Irish princess who runs off with a young warrior and his brothers on the eve of her wedding to an old king. The story ends sadly for Deirdre, and she is regarded as a fated heroine, almost a Greek figure. Synge's most popular play, *The Playboy of the Western World,* a comedy with a few dark overtones, reveals his gift for emulating the Irish way of speaking English in Ireland's western county of Mayo. His creation of peasant dialogue remains one of his most important contributions to modern drama.

In the United States, Eugene O'Neill, influenced by Strindberg, experimented with realism, first by presenting stark, powerful plays that disturbed his audiences. *The Hairy Ape* (1922) portrayed a primitive coal stoker on a passenger liner who awakened base emotions in the more refined passengers. In *The Emperor Jones* (1921) O'Neill produced the first important American expressionist play. The shifting scenery, created by lighting, was dreamlike and at times frightening. The experience of the play reflected the frightening psychic experiences of the main character, Brutus Jones.

O'Neill also experimented with more poetic forms of realism. In *Desire under the Elms* (1924), he explores the myth of Phaedra — centering on her incestuous love for her husband's son — but sets it in rural New England on a rock-hard farm. In the tradition of realism, the play treats unpleasant themes: sons' distrust of their father and their dishonoring him, lust between a son and his stepmother, and the murder of a baby to "prove" love. But it is not simply realistic. Without its underpinning of myth, the play would be sordid, but the myth helps us see that fate operates even today, not in terms of messages from the gods but rather in terms of messages from our hearts and bodies. Lust is a force in nature that drives and destroys.

Meanwhile, in Fascist Spain, Federico García Lorca, also a poetic realist, was uncovering dark emotional centers of the psyche in his *House of Bernarda Alba* (1936), which explores erotic forces repressed and then set loose. Lorca was opposed to Fascism and was murdered by a Fascist agent. His plays reveal a bleakness of spirit that helps us imagine the darkness — moral and psychological — that enveloped Europe in the 1940s.

Social Realism

Ten years after *Desire under the Elms* enjoyed popularity, a taste for plays based on SOCIAL REALISM developed. This was realism with a political conscience. Because the world was in the throes of a depression that reduced many people to destitution and homelessness, drama began to aim at awakening governments to the consequences of unbridled capitalism and the depressions that freewheeling economies produced.

Plays like Jack Kirkland's *Tobacco Road* (1933), adapted from Erskine Caldwell's novel, presented a grim portrait of rural poverty in America. Sidney Kingsley's *Dead End* (1935) portrayed the life of virtually homeless boys on the Lower East Side of Manhattan. In the same year Maxwell Anderson produced a verse tragedy, *Winterset,* with gangsters and gangsterism at its core. Also in 1935 Clifford Odets produced *Waiting for Lefty,* an openly leftist labor drama. These plays' realist credentials lay primarily in their effort to show audiences portraits of life that might shock their middle-class sensibilities.

Realism and Expressionism

After Eugene O'Neill's experiments in combining myth and realism, later American dramatists looked for new ways to expand the resources of realism while retaining its power. The use of EXPRESSIONISM — often poetic in language and effect — was one solution that appealed to both Tennessee Williams and Arthur Miller. Expressionism developed in the first and second decades of the twentieth century. The movement began in Germany, and was influenced by some of Strindberg's work. Because expressionism takes many forms, there is no simple way to define the term except to see it as an alternative to realistic drama. Instead of having realistic sets, the stage may sometimes be barren or flooded with light or draped. Characters sometimes become symbolic; dialogue is often sharp, abrupt, enigmatic. The German theater saw its earliest developments in Frank Wedekind, whose first play, *Spring Awakening,* which explored sexual repression, abandoned a naturalistic style. His work influenced later German playwrights such as George Kaiser, Ernst Toller, Erwin Piscator, and Bertolt Brecht, whose *Three-Penny Opera* (1928) incorporated some of the hallmarks of expressionism, such as a music-hall atmosphere and broadly drawn characters.

Later American playwrights modified the characteristics of expressionism; they melded expressionist elements, such as fantastic sets and highly poetic diction, with a relatively realistic style. Tennessee Williams's *The Glass Menagerie* (1944) and Arthur Miller's *Death of a Salesman* (1949) both use expressionist techniques. Williams's poetic stage directions make clear that he is drawing on nonrealistic dramatic devices. He describes the scene as "memory and . . . therefore nonrealistic." He calls for an interior "rather dim and poetic," and he uses a character who also steps outside the staged action to serve as a narrator — one who "takes whatever license with dramatic convention as is convenient to his purposes." As the narrator tells his story, the walls of the building seem to melt away, revealing the inside of a house and the lives and fantasies of his mother and sister, both caught in their own distorted visions of life.

Arthur Miller's original image for *Death of a Salesman* was the inside of Willy Loman's mind; Jo Mielziner's expressionist set represented his idea as a cross-section of Loman's house. As the action in one room concluded, lights went up to begin action in another (Figure 12). This evocative staging influenced the production of numerous plays by later writers. In the original set, a scrim, or gauze screen, was painted with branches and leaves. When this scrim was lit from the front for memory scenes, the set was transformed to evoke an earlier time when the sons were boys.

Miller used expressionist techniques to create the hallucinatory sequences when Willy talks with Ben, the man who walked into the jungle poor and

Figure 12. Expressionistic setting in Arthur Miller's *Death of a Salesman.*

walked out a millionaire, and when Biff recalls seeing Willy with the woman in Boston.

While expressionism made some inroads in American theater, the techniques of realism persisted and developed. Lorraine Hansberry's *A Raisin in the Sun* (1959) uses basically realistic staging and dialogue to portray the difficulties of the members of one family in reaching for opportunity to overcome poverty. For Williams and Miller, expressionism offered a way to bring other worlds to bear on the staged action — the worlds of dream and fantasy. Hansberry does not use the expressionist techniques of Miller. Her only exotic touch is the visit of the African young man, Asagai, who offers a moment of cultural counterpoint. Hansberry's realism is essentially conservative.

Antirealism

SURREALISM (literally, "beyond realism") in the early twentieth century was based originally on an interpretation of experience not through the lucid mind of the waking person but through the mind of the dreamer, the unconscious mind that Freud described. Surrealism augmented or, for some playwrights, supplanted realism and became a means of distorting reality for emotional purposes.

When Pirandello's six characters come onstage looking for their author in *Six Characters in Search of an Author* (1921), no one believes that they are characters rather than actors. Pirandello's play is an examination of the realities we take for granted in drama. He turns the world of expectation in drama upside down. He reminds us that what we assume to be real is always questionable: we cannot be sure of anything; we must presume that things are true, and in some cases we must take them on faith.

Pirandello's philosophy dominated his stories, plays, and novels. His questioning of the certainty of human knowledge was designed to undermine his audience's faith in an absolute reality. Modern physicists have concurred with philosophers, ancient and modern, who question everyday reality. Pirandello was influenced by the modern theories of relativity that physicists were developing, and he found in them validation of his own attack on certainty.

Epic Theater

Bertolt Brecht (1898–1956) began writing plays just after World War I. He was a political dramatist who rejected the theater of his day, which valued the realistic "well-made play," in which all the parts fit perfectly together and function like a machine. His feeling was that such plays were too mechanical, like a "clockwork mouse."

Exploring the style of his predecessor Irwin Piscator, Brecht developed EPIC THEATER. The term implies a sequence of actions or episodes of the kind found in Homer's *Iliad*. In epic theater the sense of dramatic illusion is constantly voided by reminders from the stage that one is watching a play. Stark, harsh lighting, blank stages, placards announcing changes of scenes, bands playing music onstage, and long, discomfiting pauses make it impossible for an audience to become totally immersed in a realistic illusion. Brecht, offering a genuine alternative to realistic drama, wanted the audience to analyze the play's thematic content rather than to sit back and be entertained. He believed that realistic drama convinced audiences that the play's vision of reality described not just things as they are but things as they must be. Such drama, Brecht asserted, helped maintain the social problems that they portrayed by reinforcing, rather than challenging, their realities.

Brecht's *Mother Courage* (written in 1939 and produced in 1941) is an antiwar drama staged early in World War II. The use of song, an unreal setting, and an unusual historical perspective (the Thirty Years' War in the seventeenth century) help to achieve the "defamiliarization" that Brecht thought drama ought to produce in its audiences. The techniques of epic theater in *Galileo* and *The Good Woman of Setzuan* (1943) — a study of the immoralities that prosper under capitalism — were imitated by playwrights in the 1950s. Hardly a major play in that period is free of Brecht's influence.

Eugène Ionesco (1909–1994) is said to have been the first of the postwar absurdist dramatists, with his production of *The Bald Soprano* and *The Lesson* (both in 1951). Ionesco called them "anti-plays" because they avoided the normal causal relationship of actions and realistic expectations of conventional drama.

Absurdist Drama

The critic Martin Esslin coined the term THEATER OF THE ABSURD when describing the work of Samuel Beckett (1906–1989), the Irish playwright whose dramas often dispense with almost everything that makes the well-made play well made. Some of his plays have no actors onstage — amplified breathing is the only hint of human presence in one case. Some have little or no plot; others have no words. His theater is minimalist, offering a stage reality that seems cut to the bone, without the usual realistic devices of plot, character development, and intricate setting.

The theater of the absurd assumes that the world is meaningless, that meaning is a human concept, and that individuals must create significance and not rely on institutions or traditions to provide it. The absurdist movement grew out of EXISTENTIALISM, a postwar French philosophy demanding that the individual face the emptiness of the universe and create meaning in a life that has no essential meaning within itself. *Waiting for Godot* (1952) captured the modern imagination and established a landmark in absurdist drama.

In *Waiting for Godot* two tramps, Vladimir and Estragon, meet near a tree where they expect Godot to arrive to talk with them. The play has two acts that both end with a small boy explaining that Godot cannot come today but will come tomorrow. Godot is not coming, and the tramps who wait for Godot will wait forever. While they wait they entertain themselves with vaudeville routines and eventually are met by a rich man, Pozzo, and his slave, Lucky. Lucky, on the command "Think, pig," speaks in a stream of garbled phrases that evoke Western philosophy and religion but that remain meaningless. Pozzo and Lucky have no interest in joining Vladimir and Estragon in waiting for Godot. They leave the two alone, waiting — afraid to leave for fear of missing Godot, but uncertain that Godot will ever arrive.

Beckett seems to be saying that in an absurd world such gestures are necessary to create the sense of significance that people need to live. His characters' awareness of an audience and his refusal to create a drama in which an audience can "lose" itself in a comfortable surface of realistic illusion are all, in their own way, indebted to Brecht.

Beckett's *Krapp's Last Tape* (1958) places some extraordinary limitations on performance. Krapp is the only person onstage throughout the play, and his dialogues are with tapes of himself made many years before. The situation is absurd, but as Beckett reveals to us, the absurd has its own complexities, and situations such as Krapp's can sustain complex interpretations. Beckett expects his audience to analyze the drama, not merely be entertained.

The illusion of reality is shed almost entirely in *Endgame*. Hamm cannot move. His parents, both legless, are in trashcans onstage. Clov performs all the play's movement on a barren, cellarlike stage.

The great plays of this period reflect the values of the cultures from which they spring. They make comments on life in the modern world and question the values that the culture takes for granted. The drama of this part of the twentieth century is a drama of examination.

Early and Mid-Twentieth-Century Drama Timeline

DATE	THEATER	POLITICAL	SOCIAL/CULTURAL
1850–1900	**1854–1931:** David Belasco, American producer. Belasco uses pictorial realism in staging and creates "stars" on the New York stage.		
	1862–1928: Adolphe Appia, influential Swiss designer		
	1871–1909: John Millington Synge, Irish playwright, author of *Riders to the Sea* (1904) and *The Playboy of the Western World* (1907)		
	1872–1966: Edward Gordon Craig, influential English theatrical designer		
	1873–1943: Max Reinhardt, Austrian director, producer, and theorist		
	1880–1964: Sean O'Casey, Irish playwright, author of *Juno and the Paycock* (1924) and *The Plough and the Stars* (1926)		
	1887–1954: Robert Edmond Jones, revolutionary American scenic designer		
	1888–1953: Eugene O'Neill, American playwright. Among his works are *Desire under the Elms* (1924), *Mourning Becomes Electra* (1931), and *Long Day's Journey into Night* (1939–1941).		
	1898–1956: Bertolt Brecht, German playwright, author of *The Threepenny Opera* (1928), *Mother Courage* (1941), and *The Good Woman of Setzuan* (1943)		
	1898: The Irish Literary Society is founded by William Butler Yeats (1865–1939) and Lady Augusta Gregory (1863–1935). The group leads the way in creating an indigenous Irish theater.		

Early and Mid-Twentieth-Century Drama Timeline (continued)

DATE	THEATER	POLITICAL	SOCIAL/CULTURAL
1900–1950	**1904:** The Abbey Theatre, evolved from the Irish Literary Society founded by Yeats and Lady Gregory, opens in Dublin. **1905–1984:** Lillian Hellman, American playwright, author of *The Children's Hour* (1934) and *The Little Foxes* (1939). Other important American female playwrights of the period include Rachel Crothers (1876–1958), Zona Gale (1874–1938), and Susan Glaspell (1876–1948). **1906–1989:** Samuel Beckett, Irish playwright who wrote some of his plays in French. Among his works are *Waiting for Godot* (1952) and *Endgame* (1957). **1911–1983:** Tennessee Williams, American playwright, author of *The Glass Menagerie* (1945), *A Streetcar Named Desire* (1947), and *Cat on a Hot Tin Roof* (1955) **1915:** Arthur Miller, American playwright, born. Among his works are *Death of a Salesman* (1949) and *The Crucible* (1953). **1915:** George Cram Cook, Eugene O'Neill, and Susan Glaspell found the Province-town Players in Province-town, Massachusetts. **1917:** J. L. Williams's *Why Marry?* receives the first Pulitzer Prize for drama. **1918:** Formation of the Theater Guild in New York City **1919:** Actors Equity Association is officially recognized as a union in the United States. **1920:** Théâtre National Populaire is founded in Paris.	**1900:** The Boxer Rebellion attempts to curtail Western commercial interests in China. **1901:** Queen Victoria of England dies and is succeeded by her son Edward VII. **1904–1905:** Russo-Japanese War. Russia is defeated, and Japan emerges as a world power. **1905:** The Sinn Fein party is founded in Dublin. **1912:** Sun Yat Sen is elected president of the Republic of China and founds the Kuomintang. **1914:** World War I begins with the assassination of Austrian Archduke Franz Ferdinand in Sarajevo. **1916:** The Easter Rising in Ireland is suppressed by the British. **1917:** The Russian Revolution overthrows the czar and establishes Bolshevik control under V. I. Lenin. **1919:** The Treaty of Versailles formally ends World War I. **1920:** The Nineteenth Amendment grants women the right to vote. **1921:** Southern Ireland becomes the independent Republic of Ireland.	**1900–1971:** Louis Armstrong, African American jazz trumpet player **1900:** Sigmund Freud (1856–1939) writes *The Interpretation of Dreams.* **1901:** Ragtime music becomes popular in the United States. **1903:** Wilbur and Orville Wright's first flight **1905:** The first movie theater in the United States opens in New York City. **1905–1914:** Over 10 million immigrants arrive in the United States. **1906:** An earthquake and subsequent fire ravage San Francisco. **1907:** Picasso's (1881–1973) *Les Demoiselles d'Avignon* is significant to cubism movement in art. **1908:** Henry Ford (1863–1947) designs the Model T. **1910:** W. E. B. DuBois (1868–1963), African American civil rights leader and author, establishes the NAACP. **1912:** The ocean liner *Titanic* sinks, killing 1,513 passengers. **1913:** Niels Bohr (1885–1962) formulates his theory of atomic structure. **1914:** The Panama Canal is completed. **1915:** D. W. Griffith's film *The Birth of a Nation* is released. **c. 1916:** Albert Einstein (1879–1955) formulates his theory of relativity. **1916:** Jazz music evolves in New Orleans, Chicago, and New York City. **1918:** Influenza epidemic kills 22 million people worldwide by 1922. **1919:** The Bauhaus, an influential school of art and architecture, is established by Walter Gropius in Germany. **1920:** Prohibition begins in the United States.

Early and Mid-Twentieth-Century Drama Timeline (continued)

DATE	THEATER	POLITICAL	SOCIAL/CULTURAL
1900–1950 (continued)	**1921:** Italian playwright Luigi Pirandello (1867–1936) writes *Six Characters in Search of an Author.*	**1921:** Ku Klux Klan activities become violent throughout southern United States.	
	1923–1924: Moscow Art Theater visits the United States for the first time.	**1921:** Sacco and Vanzetti, Italian anarchists, are sentenced to death in the United States.	**1922:** T. S. Eliot (1888–1965) publishes *The Waste Land.*
		1922: Fascist dictator Benito Mussolini gains power in Italy.	**1922:** James Joyce (1882–1941) publishes *Ulysses.*
			1923: George Gershwin (1898–1937) performs *Rhapsody in Blue.*
		1924–1972: J. Edgar Hoover, director of the Federal Bureau of Investigation	**1925:** F. Scott Fitzgerald (1896–1940) publishes *The Great Gatsby.*
		1925: Adolf Hitler reorganizes the Nazi Party and publishes volume 1 of *Mein Kampf.*	**1925:** Margaret Sanger (1883–1966) organizes the first international birth control conference.
	1927: Neil Simon born. His plays include *The Odd Couple* (1965), *Chapter Two* (1979), and *Biloxi Blues* (1984).	**1928:** The Kellogg-Briand Pact, outlawing war, is signed in Paris by 65 states.	**1920s:** Harlem Renaissance: African American literature, music, and art flourish in New York City. Langston Hughes (1902–1967), Zora Neale Hurston (1901–1960), Jean Toomer (1894–1967), and many others publish.
	1930–1965: Lorraine Hansberry, African American playwright, author of *A Raisin in the Sun* (1959)	**c. 1928:** Joseph Stalin comes to power in the Soviet Union.	**1925:** John T. Scopes, schoolteacher, is tried for violating a Tennessee law that prohibits the teaching of the theory of evolution.
	1930: María Irene Fornés, Cuban playwright, born. Among her works are *Fefu and Her Friends* (1977) and *The Conduct of Life* (1985).	**1929:** The U.S. stock market crash begins the Great Depression.	**1926:** Ernest Hemingway (1899–1961) publishes *The Sun Also Rises.*
	1931: The Group Theatre is founded by Harold Clurman, Cheryl Crawford, and Lee Strasberg and operates for ten years.	**1933:** New Deal economic reforms attempt to provide recovery from the Depression.	**1926:** Duke Ellington's (1899–1974) first records appear.
		1933: Adolf Hitler comes to power in Germany. German labor unions and political parties other than the Nazi are suppressed. Nazis erect their first concentration camp; persecution of Jews begins in Germany.	**1927:** *The Jazz Singer* is the first "talkie" movie.
	1934: Wole Soyinka, Nigerian playwright, born. His works include *The Strong Breed* (1962) and *A Play of Giants* (1985).		**1927:** Charles Lindbergh (1902–1974) makes the first solo nonstop transatlantic flight.
			1927: Virginia Woolf (1882–1941), English novelist, publishes *To the Lighthouse.*
	1934: Socialist realism is declared the official artistic policy in Soviet theater.	**1933:** Prohibition is repealed.	**1929:** William Faulkner (1897–1962) publishes *The Sound and the Fury.*
		1935: Roosevelt signs the U.S. Social Security Act.	**1931:** Robert Frost (1874–1963) wins the Pulitzer Prize for *Collected Poems.*
	1935: The American plays *Dead End* by Sidney Kingsley, *Winterset* by Maxwell Anderson, and *Waiting for Lefty* by Clifford Odets are produced.	**1935:** The Nuremberg laws in Nazi Germany deprive German Jews of their citizenship and civil rights.	**1931:** The Empire State Building in New York City is completed.
		1935–1936: Italy's conquest of Ethiopia	**1932:** Aldous Huxley (1894–1963) publishes *Brave New World.*
		1936: Chiang Kai-shek declares war on Japan.	

Early and Mid-Twentieth-Century Drama Timeline (continued)

DATE	THEATER	POLITICAL	SOCIAL/CULTURAL
1900–1950 (continued)	**1935–1939:** The Federal Theatre Project operates in the United States under the auspices of the Works Progress Administration. **1936:** Federico García Lorca, Spanish playwright, writes *The House of Bernarda Alba.* **1937:** Peter Stein, influential German director, born. Among his important productions are *Peer Gynt* (1971) and the *Oresteia* (1980). **1938:** Antonín Artaud, French playwright and theorist, writes *The Theater and Its Double.*	**1936–1939:** Civil War in Spain results in Generalissimo Franco's consolidation of power. **1939:** England and France declare war on Germany and its allies. **1939:** Germany invades Poland. **1940:** Germany invades France. **1941:** Japan attacks Pearl Harbor, and the United States enters World War II. **1942:** Germany begins killing Jews and others in gas chambers. **1942:** The U.S. Army interns Japanese Americans in prison camps.	**1937:** Amelia Earhart (1897–1937), the first woman to fly across the Atlantic, vanishes over the Pacific Ocean. **1938:** Joe Louis (1914–1981), African American heavyweight boxer, defeats German Max Schmeling.
	1946: The Living Theatre is founded by Judith Malina and Julian Beck.	**1944:** Allies liberate France. **1945:** The United States drops atomic bombs on Hiroshima and Nagazaki, Japan. **1945:** Hitler commits suicide in Berlin, and Germany signs an unconditional surrender. **1946:** Juan Perón is elected president of Argentina.	**1943:** Penicillin is first used in the treatment of chronic diseases. **1940s:** The era of great musical theater begins in the United States, featuring the songs of Cole Porter (1891–1964), Richard Rodgers (1902–1979), and Oscar Hammerstein (1895–1960), among many others.
	1947: The Actors Studio is founded in New York City by Robert Lewis, Elia Kazan, and Cheryl Crawford. Lee Strasberg assumes control by 1948. **1947:** Beginning of the regional theater movement in the United States. Margo Jones opens an arena theater in Dallas, Nina Vance founds the Alley Theatre in Houston, and the Arena Stage opens in 1949 in Washington, D.C. **1949:** The Berliner Ensemble is founded in East Berlin.	**1947:** India proclaims independence and is divided into Pakistan and India. **1948:** The Republic of Israel is proclaimed by Jewish leaders in Palestine. **1948:** Indian leader Mahatma Gandhi is assassinated. **1949:** Mao Zedong announces the establishment of the People's Republic of China. **1949:** The North Atlantic Treaty Organization allies Canada, Western Europe, and the United States. **1949:** The apartheid system is established in South Africa.	**1947:** Jackie Robinson (1919–1972) becomes the first African American to sign a contract with a major baseball club.

John Millington Synge

John Millington Synge (1871–1909) was one of the brilliant discoveries of the Irish Literary Renaissance, which was largely the product of Lady Gregory and William Butler Yeats, the codirectors of the Abbey Theatre in Dublin. The Abbey ranks as one of the most influential and successful national theaters in European history. From 1904 to the present, it has been devoted to producing plays by Irish writers, some of whom have gone on to be ranked among the greatest of their age. Besides Synge, Bernard Shaw, Lady Gregory, Yeats, Sean O'Casey, and Brian Friel are among the many whose names still loom impressively as having contributed to the reputation of the Abbey.

Synge was gifted in languages, with a degree in German from Trinity College, Dublin. Also a violinist, he went to Paris to study music and live the bohemian life of the artist. It was there in 1896 that Yeats and Lady Gregory met him, persuading him to return to Ireland and write plays for what was to become the Abbey. They convinced him to spend time in the Aran Islands, the wildest part of Ireland. Yeats felt the Arans were an important source of the literary energy of the nation because the Islanders' colorful language sounded like English filtered through Irish Gaelic.

Synge wrote a number of important plays within less than ten years. Most of them remain in the repertory of modern drama: *In the Shadow of the Glen* (1903), *Riders to the Sea* (1904), *The Well of the Saints* (1905), *The Tinker's Wedding* (1907), *The Playboy of the Western World* (1907), and *Deirdre of the Sorrows* (1910). With the exception of *The Tinker's Wedding*, which is so anticlerical that it has never been given a production at the Abbey, they are all still regularly produced there.

Synge was not always a popular playwright in Ireland. He felt that he faithfully represented peasant ways, but his Dublin audiences often protested that he insulted the Irish. Synge's kind of realism, while not especially harsh or critical, was an unvarnished view of the west of Ireland. The Abbey audiences wanted an idealized portrait of their countrymen and countrywomen, not straightforward and sometimes embarrassing portraits such as the one Synge offered them in *The Playboy of the Western World.* That play caused riots in the Abbey Theatre when first performed.

Synge was shocked at the uproar; he had never expected his play to stimulate such a response. The question of realism was probably not on Synge's mind at all. *Playboy* is less a realistic play than is *Riders to the Sea,* and both are rooted not in any effort to force the audience to look at life as it is really lived but rather in the mythic and symbolic forces that underlie everyone's experiences of heroism, life, and death. The deep roots of both plays are in Irish myth and the Christian religion. Synge was amazed to think that audiences ignored those important aspects and that they focused on other, less significant issues.

Synge's early death robbed world drama of a figure who certainly would have been among the greatest writers of the century. As it is, his work is remarkable; but in his last play, *Deirdre of the Sorrows,* which he never finished, we can see the promise of a body of work that would have taken its place with the best plays of our time.

THE PLAYBOY OF THE WESTERN WORLD

The Playboy of the Western World (1907) is set in County Mayo in the west of Ireland. Synge once said it was the county with the most fairies in it, implying that its people lived close to the land in the old ways. The play was written for William Butler Yeats and Lady Gregory, directors of the famed Abbey Theatre in Dublin. Today it stands as one of the greatest achievements of the Irish Literary Renaissance.

The plot involves Pegeen Mike's harboring of Christy Mahon, a supposed murderer of his own father, and is derived from a similar story told to Yeats and Arthur Symons about a murderer whose flight west to the Aran Islands resulted in his escape to America. The people of the Arans felt that any man who murdered his father must have had a good reason and should be sheltered from the law.

The power of the Roman Catholic Church in Ireland is evident in the ways in which the characters, such as Pegeen's suitor, Shawn Keogh, acquiesce to the authority of the parish priest. However, a vein of adventure and perhaps lawlessness stimulates the female characters, especially Pegeen Mike and the Widow Quin. The Widow Quin is suspected of having murdered her husband by a pinprick that resulted in blood poisoning and sees a likely mate in Christy, who smashed his father over the head with a loy (a long, narrow spade used to dig potatoes).

When Christy Mahon enters the shebeen (a small drinking establishment) owned by Pegeen's father, he brings with him the novelty of one who, unlike the timid Shawn Keogh, has the courage to defy the law and set out on his own. Although his father bullied him throughout life and tried to force him to marry an older woman to acquire her farm, Christy has the better of him in an argument. The story Christy tells, somewhat exaggerated for effect, wins him the admiration of the women in the shebeen, who see him as a daring folk hero.

Later, encouraged to take part in local sporting games, he proves himself to be as courageous and heroic as his story led people to assume. Although the experienced Widow Quin presents herself as the likely wife for such a man, Pegeen sees in Christy the opportunity for an exciting life — and Christy prefers her for her youth and high spirit.

On one level, the conflict in the drama is between patterns that are familiar and possibilities that are unfamiliar, dangerous, and exciting. Pegeen Mike is conventional in her way, as we learn at the end of the play, but she is more receptive to adventure than most of the other village characters. On another level the conflict is between youth and age: Christy as son and Old Mahon as father. In the natural order of things, the father must eventually give way to the son, and this play dramatizes that process. But Christy also represents breaking away from the norm and taking risks, even at the expense of breaking the law. Yet Christy is innocent throughout the play. He is developing and maturing — beginning to see himself as others see him. By the end of the play, he has become a very different person from the one he was at the beginning.

Another important aspect of the play is suggested by the obvious significance of "Christy Mahon": Christy Man. The language and imagery of the play focus on the thrones of heaven, the angels, the stars, and even the devil, implying a spiritual connection between Christy and Christ. This connection is more obvious to a reader of the drama than to a viewer, in part because the intense action of the play in act III partially obscures the images and parallels.

The language of the play is one of Synge's great achievements. A trained musician with a fine ear, he spent time in rural Ireland listening to people talk while they did not know he was listening. He transcribed some of their speech as an aid to writing his own dialogue. That the contemporary Irish playwright Martin MacDonagh has learned from Synge is evident in the locutions of more modern characters. As Synge says in the preface to the play, he felt that in 1907 the people of the west were still speaking a poetic language that gave him an advantage as a playwright.

The Playboy of the Western World in Performance

The first production of *The Playboy of the Western World* in 1907 resulted in one of the most notorious reactions in the history of the Abbey Theatre. The audience seemed to have come with an antagonism toward Synge based on some of his earlier works. Things were quiet for a while, but the crowd broke out in savage anger when Christy in act III said, "It's Pegeen I'm seeking only, and what'd I care if you brought me a drift of chosen females, standing in their shifts itself, maybe, from this place to the Eastern World?" At the mention of "shifts," a term for a woman's slip, the audience began one of the worst riots the Abbey would ever see. It shut down the performance. At the root of the incident was the prevailing view that Synge had been disrespectful of the Irish peasant. In the United States in 1911, the Abbey presented the play to audiences who also rioted, but not until later in act III when Christy raises the loy to hit his father.

Eventually the anger over the play died down, and performances continued without serious incident. Today *The Playboy of the Western World* is one of the most popular Irish plays of the twentieth century. Eithne Dunne played Pegeen Mike and Burgess Meredith was Christy Mahon in the 1946 production in New York. Siobhan McKenna, praised as the greatest Irish actress of mid-century, took the role of Pegeen Mike in several productions in Ireland and abroad in the 1950s. She also starred in the film version of the play. The play has been produced frequently in London, New York, and Dublin since 1957. It was adapted and performed in the 1990s as *The Playboy of the West Indies,* demonstrating its appropriateness as a postcolonial drama.

The setting in most modern performances replicates the interior of an Irish shebeen, and the action of the sporting games takes place offstage, somewhat in the manner of the Greek drama. The dialogue brings with it the feel of the speech of people in the west of Ireland, whether the actors are Irish or not. Performances in 1998 by director Douglas Hughes at both the Steppenwolf Theatre Company of Chicago and the Long Wharf Theatre in New Haven — with Martha Plimpton as Pegeen Mike, Jim True as Christy, and Lanny Flaherty as Old Mahon — emphasized the father-and-son relationship in a manner that opened new avenues for interpretation. The performances demonstrated that almost a hundred years after its initial performance *The Playboy of the Western World* is timely, dynamic, and powerful.

John Millington Synge (1871–1909)
THE PLAYBOY OF THE WESTERN WORLD   *1907*

Persons in the Play

CHRISTOPHER MAHON, *called* CHRISTY
OLD MAHON, *his father, a squatter*
MICHAEL JAMES FLAHERTY, called MICHAEL JAMES, *a publican*
MARGARET FLAHERTY, called PEGEEN MIKE, *his daughter*
WIDOW QUIN, *a woman of about thirty*
SHAWN KEOGH, *her cousin, a young farmer*
PHILLY CULLEN and JIMMY FARRELL, *small farmers*
SARA TANSEY, SUSAN BRADY, and HONOR BLAKE, *village girls*
A BELLMAN°
SOME PEASANTS

(**Scene:** *The action takes place near a village, on a wild coast of Mayo. The first act passes on an evening of autumn, the other two acts on the following day.*)

ACT I

(**Scene:** *Country public-house or shebeen, very rough and untidy. There is a sort of counter on the right with shelves, holding many bottles and jugs, just seen above it. Empty barrels stand near the counter. At back, a little to left of counter, there is a door into the open air, then, more to the left, there is a settle with shelves above it, with more jugs, and a table beneath a window. At the left there is a large open fire-place, with turf fire, and a small door into inner room. Pegeen, a wild-looking*

Bellman: A town crier who rings a bell.

but fine girl, of about twenty, is writing at table. She is dressed in the usual peasant dress.)

PEGEEN (*slowly as she writes*): Six yards of stuff for to make a yellow gown. A pair of lace boots with lengthy heels on them and brassy eyes. A hat is suited for a wedding-day. A fine tooth comb. To be sent with three barrels of porter in Jimmy Farrell's creel cart on the evening of the coming Fair to Mister Michael James Flaherty. With the best compliments of this season. Margaret Flaherty.

SHAWN KEOGH (*a fat and fair young man comes in as she signs, looks round awkwardly, when he sees she is alone*): Where's himself?

PEGEEN (*without looking at him*): He's coming. (*She directs the letter.*) To Mister Sheamus Mulroy, Wine and Spirit Dealer, Castlebar.

SHAWN (*uneasily*): I didn't see him on the road.

PEGEEN: How would you see him (*licks stamp and puts it on letter*) and it dark night this half hour gone by?

SHAWN (*turning towards the door again*): I stood a while outside wondering would I have a right to pass on or to walk in and see you, Pegeen Mike (*comes to fire*), and I could hear the cows breathing, and sighing in the stillness of the air, and not a step moving any place from this gate to the bridge.

PEGEEN (*putting letter in envelope*): It's above at the cross-roads he is, meeting Philly Cullen; and a couple more are going along with him to Kate Cassidy's wake.

SHAWN (*looking at her blankly*): And he's going that length in the dark night?

PEGEEN (*impatiently*): He is surely, and leaving me lonesome on the scruff of the hill. (*She gets up and puts envelope on dresser, then winds clock.*) Isn't it long the nights are now, Shawn Keogh, to be leaving a poor girl with her own self counting the hours to the dawn of day?

SHAWN (*with awkward humor*): If it is, when we're wedded in a short while you'll have no call to complain, for I've little will to be walking off to wakes or weddings in the darkness of the night.

PEGEEN (*with rather scornful good humor*): You're making mighty certain, Shaneen, that I'll wed you now.

SHAWN: Aren't we after making a good bargain, the way we're only waiting these days on Father Reilly's dispensation from the bishops, or the Court of Rome.

PEGEEN (*looking at him teasingly, washing up at dresser*): It's a wonder, Shaneen, the Holy Father'd be taking notice of the likes of you; for if I was him I wouldn't bother with this place where you'll meet none but Red Linahan, has a squint in his eye, and Patcheen is lame in his heel, or the mad Mulrannies were driven from California and they lost in their wits. We're a queer lot these times to go troubling the Holy Father on his sacred seat.

SHAWN (*scandalized*): If we are, we're as good this place as another, maybe, and as good these times as we were for ever.

PEGEEN (*with scorn*): As good, is it? Where now will you meet the like of Daneen Sullivan knocked the eye from a peeler,° or Marcus Quin, God rest him, got six months for maiming ewes, and he a great warrant to tell stories of holy Ireland till he'd have the old women shedding down tears about their feet. Where will you find the like of them, I'm saying?

SHAWN (*timidly*): If you don't, it's a good job, maybe; for (*with peculiar emphasis on the words*) Father Reilly has small conceit to have that kind walking around and talking to the girls.

PEGEEN (*impatiently, throwing water from basin out of the door*): Stop tormenting me with Father Reilly (*imitating his voice*) when I'm asking only what way I'll pass these twelve hours of dark, and not take my death with the fear.

(*Looking out of door.*)

SHAWN (*timidly*): Would I fetch you the Widow Quin, maybe?

PEGEEN: Is it the like of that murderer? You'll not, surely.

SHAWN (*going to her, soothingly*): Then I'm thinking himself will stop along with you when he sees you taking on, for it'll be a long night-time with great darkness, and I'm after feeling a kind of fellow above in the furzy ditch, groaning wicked like a maddening dog, the way it's good cause you have, maybe, to be fearing now.

PEGEEN (*turning on him sharply*): What's that? Is it a man you seen?

SHAWN (*retreating*): I couldn't see him at all; but I heard

---

peeler: A police officer.

---

him groaning out, and breaking his heart. It should have been a young man from his words speaking.

PEGEEN (*going after him*): And you never went near to see was he hurted or what ailed him at all?

SHAWN: I did not, Pegeen Mike. It was a dark, lonesome place to be hearing the like of him.

PEGEEN: Well, you're a daring fellow, and if they find his corpse stretched above in the dews of dawn, what'll you say then to the peelers, or the Justice of the Peace?

SHAWN (*thunderstruck*): I wasn't thinking of that. For the love of God, Pegeen Mike, don't let on I was speaking of him. Don't tell your father and the men is coming above; for if they heard that story, they'd have great blabbing this night at the wake.

PEGEEN: I'll maybe tell them, and I'll maybe not.

SHAWN: They are coming at the door. Will you whisht, I'm saying?

PEGEEN: Whisht yourself.

(*She goes behind counter. Michael James, fat jovial publican, comes in followed by Philly Cullen, who is thin and mistrusting, and Jimmy Farrell, who is fat and amorous, about forty-five.*)

MEN (*together*): God bless you. The blessing of God on this place.

PEGEEN: God bless you kindly.

MICHAEL (*to men who go to the counter*): Sit down now, and take your rest. (*Crosses to Shawn at the fire.*) And how is it you are, Shawn Keogh? Are you coming over the sands to Kate Cassidy's wake?

SHAWN: I am not, Michael James. I'm going home the short cut to my bed.

PEGEEN (*speaking across the counter*): He's right too, and have you no shame, Michael James, to be quitting off for the whole night, and leaving myself lonesome in the shop?

MICHAEL (*good-humoredly*): Isn't it the same whether I go for the whole night or a part only? and I'm thinking it's a queer daughter you are if you'd have me crossing backward through the Stooks of the Dead Women,° with a drop taken.

PEGEEN: If I am a queer daughter, it's a queer father'd be leaving me lonesome these twelve hours of dark, and I piling the turf with the dogs barking, and the calves mooing, and my own teeth rattling with the fear.

JIMMY (*flatteringly*): What is there to hurt you, and you a fine, hardy girl would knock the head of any two men in the place?

PEGEEN (*working herself up*): Isn't there the harvest boys with their tongues red for drink, and the ten tinkers° is camped in the east glen, and the thousand militia — bad cess° to them! — walking idle through

---

Stooks of the Dead Women: A geological formation of standing rocks on the shore of County Kerry.
tinkers: Gypsies.
bad cess: Bad luck.

the land. There's lots surely to hurt me, and I won't stop alone in it, let himself do what he will.

MICHAEL: If you're that afeard, let Shawn Keogh stop along with you. It's the will of God, I'm thinking, himself should be seeing to you now.

(*They all turn on Shawn.*)

SHAWN (*in horrified confusion*): I would and welcome, Michael James, but I'm afeard of Father Reilly; and what at all would the Holy Father and the Cardinals of Rome be saying if they heard I did the like of that?

MICHAEL (*with contempt*): God help you! Can't you sit in by the hearth with the light lit and herself beyond in the room? You'll do that surely, for I've heard tell there's a queer fellow above, going mad or getting his death, maybe, in the gripe of the ditch, so she'd be safer this night with a person here.

SHAWN (*with plaintive despair*): I'm afeard of Father Reilly, I'm saying. Let you not be tempting me, and we near married itself.

PHILLY (*with cold contempt*): Lock him in the west room. He'll stay then and have no sin to be telling to the priest.

MICHAEL (*to Shawn, getting between him and the door*): Go up now.

SHAWN (*at the top of his voice*): Don't stop me, Michael James. Let me out of the door, I'm saying, for the love of the Almighty God. Let me out (*trying to dodge past him*). Let me out of it, and may God grant you His indulgence in the hour of need.

MICHAEL (*loudly*): Stop your noising, and sit down by the hearth.

(*Gives him a push and goes to counter laughing.*)

SHAWN (*turning back, wringing his hands*): Oh, Father Reilly and the saints of God, where will I hide myself to-day? Oh, St. Joseph and St. Patrick and St. Brigid, and St. James,° have mercy on me now!

(*Shawn turns round, sees door clear, and makes a rush for it.*)

MICHAEL (*catching him by the coat-tail*): You'd be going, is it?

SHAWN (*screaming*): Leave me go, Michael James, leave me go, you old Pagan, leave me go, or I'll get the curse of the priests on you, and of the scarlet-coated bishops of the courts of Rome.

(*With a sudden movement he pulls himself out of his coat, and disappears out of the door, leaving his coat in Michael's hands.*)

MICHAEL (*turning round, and holding up coat*): Well, there's the coat of a Christian man. Oh, there's sainted glory this day in the lonesome west; and by the will of God I've got you a decent man, Pegeen,

St. Joseph . . . St. James: An excess of saintly protection hints at Shawn's timidity.

you'll have no call to be spying after if you've a score of young girls, maybe, weeding in your fields.

PEGEEN (*taking up the defense of her property*): What right have you to be making game of a poor fellow for minding the priest, when it's your own fault is, not paying a penny pot-boy° to stand along with me and give me courage in the doing of my work?

(*She snaps the coat away from him, and goes behind counter with it.*)

MICHAEL (*taken aback*): Where would I get a pot-boy? Would you have me send the bellman screaming in the streets of Castlebar?

SHAWN (*opening the door a chink and putting in his head, in a small voice*): Michael James!

MICHAEL (*imitating him*): What ails you?

SHAWN: The queer dying fellow's beyond looking over the ditch. He's come up, I'm thinking, stealing your hens. (*Looks over his shoulder.*) God help me, he's following me now (*he runs into room*), and if he's heard what I said, he'll be having my life, and I going home lonesome in the darkness of the night.

(*For a perceptible moment they watch the door with curiosity. Some one coughs outside. Then Christy Mahon, a slight young man, comes in very tired and frightened and dirty.*)

CHRISTY (*in a small voice*): God save all here!

MEN: God save you kindly.

CHRISTY (*going to the counter*): I'd trouble you for a glass of porter, woman of the house.

(*He puts down coin.*)

PEGEEN (*serving him*): You're one of the tinkers, young fellow, is beyond camped in the glen?

CHRISTY: I am not; but I'm destroyed walking.

MICHAEL (*patronizingly*): Let you come up then to the fire. You're looking famished with the cold.

CHRISTY: God reward you. (*He takes up his glass and goes a little way across to the left, then stops and looks about him.*) Is it often the police do be coming into this place, master of the house?

MICHAEL: If you'd come in better hours, you'd have seen "Licensed for the sale of Beer and Spirits, to be consumed on the premises," written in white letters above the door, and what would the polis want spying on me, and not a decent house within four miles, the way every living Christian is a bona fide, saving one widow alone?

CHRISTY (*with relief*): It's a safe house, so.

(*He goes over to the fire, sighing and moaning. Then he sits down, putting his glass beside him and begins gnawing a turnip, too miserable to feel the others staring at him with curiosity.*)

MICHAEL (*going after him*): Is it yourself is fearing the polis? You're wanting, maybe?

pot-boy: A boy who serves drinks in a pub or tavern.

CHRISTY: There's many wanting.

MICHAEL: Many surely, with the broken harvest and the ended wars.° (*He picks up some stockings, etc., that are near the fire, and carries them away furtively.*) It should be larceny, I'm thinking?

CHRISTY (*dolefully*): I had it in my mind it was a different word and a bigger.

PEGEEN: There's a queer lad. Were you never slapped in school, young fellow, that you don't know the name of your deed?

CHRISTY (*bashfully*): I'm slow at learning, a middling scholar only.

MICHAEL: If you're a dunce itself, you'd have a right to know that larceny's robbing and stealing. Is it for the like of that you're wanting?

CHRISTY (*with a flash of family pride*): And I the son of a strong farmer (*with a sudden qualm*), God rest his soul, could have bought up the whole of your old house a while since, from the butt of his tailpocket, and not have missed the weight of it gone.

MICHAEL (*impressed*): If it's not stealing, it's maybe something big.

CHRISTY (*flattered*): Aye; it's maybe something big.

JIMMY: He's a wicked-looking young fellow. Maybe he followed after a young woman on a lonesome night.

CHRISTY (*shocked*): Oh, the saints forbid, mister; I was all times a decent lad.

PHILLY (*turning on Jimmy*): You're a silly man, Jimmy Farrell. He said his father was a farmer a while since, and there's himself now in a poor state. Maybe the land was grabbed from him, and he did what any decent man would do.

MICHAEL (*to Christy, mysteriously*): Was it bailiffs?

CHRISTY: The divil a one.

MICHAEL: Agents?

CHRISTY: The divil a one.

MICHAEL: Landlords?

CHRISTY (*peevishly*): Ah, not at all, I'm saying. You'd see the like of them stories on any little paper of a Munster town. But I'm not calling to mind any person, gentle, simple, judge or jury, did the like of me.

(*They all draw nearer with delighted curiosity.*)

PHILLY: Well, that lad's a puzzle-the-world.

JIMMY: He'd beat Dan Davies' circus, or the holy missioners making sermons on the villainy of man. Try him again, Philly.

PHILLY: Did you strike golden guineas out of solder, young fellow, or shilling coins itself?

CHRISTY: I did not, mister, not sixpence nor a farthing coin.

JIMMY: Did you marry three wives maybe? I'm told there's a sprinkling have done that among the holy Luthers° of the preaching north.

ended wars: The Boer War (1899–1902) in which many Irish fought in South Africa, had recently ended.
Luthers: Protestants.

CHRISTY (*shyly*): I never married with one, let alone with a couple or three.

PHILLY: Maybe he went fighting for the Boers,° the like of the man beyond, was judged to be hanged, quartered, and drawn. Were you off east, young fellow, fighting bloody wars for Kruger° and the freedom of the Boers?

CHRISTY: I never left my own parish till Tuesday was a week.

PEGEEN (*coming from counter*): He's done nothing, so. (*To Christy.*) If you didn't commit murder or a bad, nasty thing, or false coining, or robbery, or butchery, or the like of them, there isn't anything that would be worth your troubling for to run from now. You did nothing at all.

CHRISTY (*his feelings hurt*): That's an unkindly thing to be saying to a poor orphaned traveler, has a prison behind him, and hanging before, and hell's gap gaping below.

PEGEEN (*with a sign to the men to be quiet*): You're only saying it. You did nothing at all. A soft lad the like of you wouldn't slit the windpipe of a screeching sow.

CHRISTY (*offended*): You're not speaking the truth.

PEGEEN (*in mock rage*): Not speaking the truth, is it? Would you have me knock the head of you with the butt of the broom?

CHRISTY (*twisting round on her with a sharp cry of horror*): Don't strike me. I killed my poor father, Tuesday was a week, for doing the like of that.

PEGEEN (*with blank amazement*): Is it killed your father?

CHRISTY (*subsiding*): With the help of God I did surely, and that the Holy Immaculate Mother° may intercede for his soul.

PHILLY (*retreating with Jimmy*): There's a daring fellow.

JIMMY: Oh, glory be to God!

MICHAEL (*with great respect*): That was a hanging crime, mister honey. You should have had good reason for doing the like of that.

CHRISTY (*in a very reasonable tone*): He was a dirty man, God forgive him, and he getting old and crusty, the way I couldn't put up with him at all.

PEGEEN: And you shot him dead?

CHRISTY (*shaking his head*): I never used weapons. I've no license, and I'm a law-fearing man.

MICHAEL: It was with a hilted knife maybe? I'm told, in the big world it's bloody knives they use.

CHRISTY (*loudly, scandalized*): Do you take me for a slaughter-boy?

PEGEEN: You never hanged him, the way Jimmy Farrell hanged his dog from the license, and had it screeching

Boers: South Africans of Dutch or Huguenot (Protestant) ancestry.
Kruger: Paul Kruger (1825–1904) was a South African statesman.
Holy Immaculate Mother: Refers to the Virgin Mary, the mother of Jesus.

The 1946 Broadway production of *The Playboy of the Western World* with Eithne Dunn as Pegeen Mike and Burgess Meredith (seated with cane) as Christy Mahon. Barry Macollum, J. M. Kerrigan, and J. C. Nugent look on.

and wriggling three hours at the butt of a string, and himself swearing it was a dead dog, and the peelers swearing it had life?

CHRISTY: I did not then. I just riz the loy° and let fall the edge of it on the ridge of his skull, and he went down at my feet like an empty sack, and never let a grunt or groan from him at all.

MICHAEL (*making a sign to Pegeen to fill Christy's glass*): And what way weren't you hanged, mister? Did you bury him then?

CHRISTY (*considering*): Aye. I buried him then. Wasn't I digging spuds in the field?

MICHAEL: And the peelers never followed after you the eleven days that you're out?

CHRISTY (*shaking his head*): Never a one of them, and I walking forward facing hog, dog, or divil on the highway of the road.

PHILLY (*nodding wisely*): It's only with a common week-day kind of a murderer them lads would be trusting their carcase,° and that man should be a great terror when his temper's roused.

MICHAEL: He should then. (*To Christy.*) And where was it, mister honey, that you did the deed?

CHRISTY (*looking at him with suspicion*): Oh, a distant place, master of the house, a windy corner of high, distant hills.

PHILLY (*nodding with approval*): He's a close man, and he's right, surely.

loy: A long narrow spade used to dig potatoes.

carcase: Carcass.

PEGEEN: That'd be a lad with the sense of Solomon° to have for a pot-boy, Michael James, if it's the truth you're seeking one at all.

PHILLY: The peelers is fearing him, and if you'd that lad in the house there isn't one of them would come smelling around if the dogs itself were lapping poteen° from the dung-pit of the yard.

JIMMY: Bravery's a treasure in a lonesome place, and a lad would kill his father, I'm thinking, would face a foxy divil with a pitchpike on the flags of hell.

PEGEEN: It's the truth they're saying, and if I'd that lad in the house, I wouldn't be fearing the looséd kharki° cut-throats, or the walking dead.

CHRISTY (*swelling with surprise and triumph*): Well, glory be to God!

MICHAEL (*with deference*): Would you think well to stop here and be pot-boy, mister honey, if we gave you good wages, and didn't destroy you with the weight of work?

SHAWN (*coming forward uneasily*): That'd be a queer kind to bring into a decent quiet household with the like of Pegeen Mike.

PEGEEN (*very sharply*): Will you whisht? Who's speaking to you?

SHAWN (*retreating*): A bloody-handed murderer the like of . . .

PEGEEN (*snapping at him*): Whisht I am saying; we'll take no fooling from your like at all. (*To Christy with a honeyed voice.*) And you, young fellow, you'd have a right to stop, I'm thinking, for we'd do our all and utmost to content your needs.

CHRISTY (*overcome with wonder*): And I'd be safe in this place from the searching law?

CHRISTY: You would, surely. If they're not fearing you, itself, the peelers in this place is decent droughty° poor fellows, wouldn't touch a cur dog and not give warning in the dead of night.

PEGEEN (*very kindly and persuasively*): Let you stop a short while anyhow. Aren't you destroyed walking with your feet in bleeding blisters, and your whole skin needing washing like a Wicklow sheep.

CHRISTY (*looking round with satisfaction*): It's a nice room, and if it's not humbugging me you are, I'm thinking that I'll surely stay.

JIMMY (*jumps up*): Now, by the grace of God, herself will be safe this night, with a man killed his father holding danger from the door, and let you come on, Michael James, or they'll have the best stuff drunk at the wake.

MICHAEL (*going to the door with men*): And begging your pardon, mister, what name will we call you, for we'd like to know?

CHRISTY: Christopher Mahon.

MICHAEL: Well, God bless you, Christy, and a good rest till we meet again when the sun'll be rising to the noon of day.

CHRISTY: God bless you all.

MEN: God bless you.

(*They go out except Shawn, who lingers at door.*)

SHAWN (*to Pegeen*): Are you wanting me to stop along with you and keep you from harm?

PEGEEN (*gruffly*): Didn't you say you were fearing Father Reilly?

SHAWN: There'd be no harm staying now, I'm thinking, and himself in it too.

PEGEEN: You wouldn't stay when there was need for you, and let you step off nimble this time when there's none.

SHAWN: Didn't I say it was Father Reilly . . .

PEGEEN: Go on, then, to Father Reilly (*in a jeering tone*), and let him put you in the holy brotherhoods, and leave that lad to me.

SHAWN: If I meet the Widow Quin . . .

PEGEEN: Go on, I'm saying, and don't be waking this place with your noise. (*She hustles him out and bolts the door.*) That lad would wear the spirits from the saints of peace. (*Bustles about, then takes off her apron and pins it up in the window as a blind. Christy watching her timidly. Then she comes to him and speaks with bland good-humor.*) Let you stretch out now by the fire, young fellow. You should be destroyed traveling.

CHRISTY (*shyly again, drawing off his boots*): I'm tired, surely, walking wild eleven days, and waking fearful in the night.

(*He holds up one of his feet, feeling his blisters, and looking at them with compassion.*)

PEGEEN (*standing beside him, watching him with delight*): You should have had great people in your family, I'm thinking, with the little, small feet you have, and you with a kind of a quality name, the like of what you'd find on the great powers and potentates of France and Spain.

CHRISTY (*with pride*): We were great surely, with wide and windy acres of rich Munster° land.

PEGEEN: Wasn't I telling you, and you a fine, handsome young fellow with a noble brow?

CHRISTY (*with a flash of delighted surprise*): Is it me?

PEGEEN: Aye. Did you never hear that from the young girls where you come from in the west or south?

CHRISTY (*with venom*): I did not then. Oh, they're bloody liars in the naked parish where I grew a man.

PEGEEN: If they are itself, you've heard it these days, I'm thinking, and you walking the world telling out your story to young girls or old.

CHRISTY: I've told my story no place till this night, Pegeen Mike, and it's foolish I was here, maybe, to be

---

Solomon: A tenth-century B.C. king of Israel known for his words of wisdom recorded in the Book of Proverbs of the Old Testament.
poteen: Illegally distilled Irish whiskey.
kharki: Ex-British soldiers from the Boer War who wore khaki uniforms.
droughty: Interested in having a drink, thus sociable.

Munster: A province located in the south of Ireland.

Jim True (Christy Mahon) and Martha Plimpton (Pegeen Mike) in the Long Wharf Theatre's 1998 production directed by Doug Hughes.

talking free, but you're decent people, I'm thinking, and yourself a kindly woman, the way I wasn't fearing you at all.

PEGEEN (*filling a sack with straw*): You've said the like of that, maybe, in every cot and cabin where you've met a young girl on your way.

CHRISTY (*going over to her, gradually raising his voice*): I've said it nowhere till this night, I'm telling you, for I've seen none the like of you the eleven long days I am walking the world, looking over a low ditch or a high ditch on my north or my south, into stony scattered fields, or scribes of bog,° where you'd see young, limber girls, and fine prancing women making laughter with the men.

PEGEEN: If you weren't destroyed traveling, you'd have as much talk and streeleen,° I'm thinking, as Owen Roe O'Sullivan or the poets of the Dingle Bay, and I've heard all times it's the poets are your like, fine fiery fellows with great rages when their temper's roused.

CHRISTY (*drawing a little nearer to her*): You've a power of rings, God bless you, and would there be any offense if I was asking are you single now?

PEGEEN: What would I want wedding so young?

CHRISTY (*with relief*): We're alike, so.

PEGEEN (*she puts sack on settle° and beats it up*): I never killed my father. I'd be afeard to do that, except I was the like of yourself with blind rages tearing me within, for I'm thinking you should have had great tussling when the end was come.

CHRISTY (*expanding with delight at the first confidential talk he has ever had with a woman*): We had not then. It was a hard woman was come over the hill, and if he was always a crusty kind when he'd a hard

---

scribes of bog: Refers to peat bogs cut into bricks and ready for harvesting; the peat is burned as fuel.
streeleen: strolling or wandering aimlessly.

settle: A bench with a high, solid back and a closed foundation used for storage.

woman setting him on, not the divil himself or his four fathers could put up with him at all.

PEGEEN (*with curiosity*): And isn't it a great wonder that one wasn't fearing you?

CHRISTY (*very confidentially*): Up to the day I killed my father, there wasn't a person in Ireland knew the kind I was, and I there drinking, waking, eating, sleeping, a quiet, simple poor fellow with no man giving me heed.

PEGEEN (*getting a quilt out of the cupboard and putting it on the sack*): It was the girls were giving you heed maybe, and I'm thinking it's most conceit you'd have to be gaming with their like.

CHRISTY (*shaking his head, with simplicity*): Not the girls itself, and I won't tell you a lie. There wasn't anyone heeding me in that place saving only the dumb beasts of the field.

(*He sits down at fire.*)

PEGEEN (*with disappointment*): And I thinking you should have been living the like of a king of Norway or the Eastern world.

(*She comes and sits beside him after placing bread and mug of milk on the table.*)

CHRISTY (*laughing piteously*): The like of a king, is it? And I after toiling, moiling, digging, dodging from the dawn till dusk with never a sight of joy or sport saving only when I'd be abroad in the dark night poaching rabbits on hills, for I was a devil to poach, God forgive me, (*very naïvely*) and I near got six months for going with a dung fork and stabbing a fish.

PEGEEN: And it's that you'd call sport, is it, to be abroad in the darkness with yourself alone?

CHRISTY: I did, God help me, and there I'd be as happy as the sunshine of St. Martin's Day,° watching the light passing the north or the patches of fog, till I'd hear a rabbit starting to screech and I'd go running in the furze.° Then when I'd my full share I'd come walking down where you'd see the ducks and geese stretched sleeping on the highway of the road, and before I'd pass the dunghill, I'd hear himself snoring out, a loud lonesome snore he'd he making all times, the while he was sleeping, and he a man 'd be raging all times, the while he was waking, like a gaudy officer you'd hear cursing and damning and swearing oaths.

PEGEEN: Providence and Mercy, spare us all!

CHRISTY: It's that you'd say surely if you seen him and he after drinking for weeks, rising up in the red dawn, or before it maybe, and going out into the yard as naked as an ash tree in the moon of May, and shying clods against the visage of the stars till he'd put the fear of death into the banbhs° and the screeching sows.

St. Martin's Day: November 11th, the Feast of St. Martin.
furze: A spiny shrub with yellow flowers; also known as gorse.
banbhs: Piglets.

PEGEEN: I'd be well-nigh afeard of that lad myself, I'm thinking. And there was no one in it but the two of you alone?

CHRISTY: The divil a one, though he'd sons and daughters walking all great states and territories of the world, and not a one of them, to this day, but would say their seven curses on him, and they rousing up to let a cough or sneeze, maybe, in the deadness of the night.

PEGEEN (*nodding her head*): Well, you should have been a queer lot. I never cursed my father the like of that, though I'm twenty and more years of age.

CHRISTY: Then you'd have cursed mine, I'm telling you, and he a man never gave peace to any, saving when he'd get two months or three, or be locked in the asylums for battering peelers or assaulting men (*with depression*) the way it was a bitter life he led me till I did up a Tuesday and halve his skull.

PEGEEN (*putting her hand on his shoulder*): Well, you'll have peace in this place, Christy Mahon, and none to trouble you, and it's near time a fine lad like you should have your good share of the earth.

CHRISTY: It's time surely, and I a seemly fellow with great strength in me and bravery of . . .

(*Someone knocks.*)

CHRISTY (*clinging to Pegeen*): Oh, glory! it's late for knocking, and this last while I'm in terror of the peelers, and the walking dead.

(*Knocking again.*)

PEGEEN: Who's there?

VOICE (*outside*): Me.

PEGEEN: Who's me?

VOICE: The Widow Quin.

PEGEEN (*jumping up and giving him the bread and milk*): Go on now with your supper, and let on to be sleepy, for if she found you were such a warrant to talk, she'd be stringing gabble till the dawn of day. (*He takes bread and sits shyly with his back to the door.*)

PEGEEN (*opening door, with temper*): What ails you, or what is it you're wanting at this hour of the night?

WIDOW QUIN (*coming in a step and peering at Christy*): I'm after meeting Shawn Keogh and Father Reilly below, who told me of your curiosity man, and they fearing by this time he was maybe roaring, romping on your hands with drink.

PEGEEN (*pointing to Christy*): Look now is he roaring, and he stretched away drowsy with his supper and his mug of milk. Walk down and tell that to Father Reilly and to Shaneen Keogh.

WIDOW QUIN (*coming forward*): I'll not see them again, for I've their word to lead that lad forward for to lodge with me.

PEGEEN (*in blank amazement*): This night, is it?

WIDOW QUIN (*going over*): This night. "It isn't fitting," says the priesteen, "to have his likeness lodging with an orphaned girl." (*To Christy.*) God save you, mister!

CHRISTY (*shyly*): God save you kindly.

WIDOW QUIN (*looking at him with half-amazed curiosity*): Well, aren't you a little smiling fellow? It should have been great and bitter torments did rouse your spirits to a deed of blood.

CHRISTY (*doubtfully*): It should, maybe.

WIDOW QUIN: It's more than "maybe" I'm saying, and it'd soften my heart to see you sitting so simple with your cup and cake, and you fitter to be saying your catechism° than slaying your da.

PEGEEN (*at counter, washing glasses*): There's talking when any'd see he's fit to be holding his head high with the wonders of the world. Walk on from this, for I'll not have him tormented and he destroyed traveling since Tuesday was a week.

WIDOW QUIN (*peaceably*): We'll be walking surely when his supper's done, and you'll find we're great company, young fellow, when it's of the like of you and me you'd hear the penny poets singing in an August Fair.

CHRISTY (*innocently*): Did you kill your father?

PEGEEN (*contemptuously*): She did not. She hit himself with a worn pick, and the rusted poison did corrode his blood the way he never overed it, and died after. That was a sneaky kind of murder did win small glory with the boys itself.

(*She crosses to Christy's left.*)

WIDOW QUIN (*with good-humor*): If it didn't, maybe all knows a widow woman has buried her children and destroyed her man is a wiser comrade for a young lad than a girl, the like of you, who'd go helter-skeltering after any man would let you a wink upon the road.

PEGEEN (*breaking out into wild rage*): And you'll say that, Widow Quin, and you gasping with the rage you had racing the hill beyond to look on his face.

WIDOW QUIN (*laughing derisively*): Me, is it? Well, Father Reilly has cuteness° to divide you now. (*She pulls Christy up.*) There's great temptation in a man did slay his da, and we'd best be going, young fellow; so rise up and come with me.

PEGEEN (*seizing his arm*): He'll not stir. He's pot-boy in this place, and I'll not have him stolen off and kidnabbed while himself's abroad.

WIDOW QUIN: It'd be a crazy pot-boy'd lodge him in the shebeen where he works by day, so you'd have a right to come on, young fellow, till you see my little houseen, a perch off on the rising hill.

PEGEEN: Wait till morning, Christy Mahon. Wait till you lay eyes on her leaky thatch is growing more pasture for her buck goat than her square of fields, and she without a tramp itself to keep in order her place at all.

WIDOW QUIN: When you see me contriving in my little gardens, Christy Mahon, you'll swear the Lord God formed me to be living lone, and that there isn't my match in Mayo for thatching, or mowing, or shearing a sheep.

---

catechism: A summary of religious doctrine.
cuteness: Shrewdness.

PEGEEN (*with noisy scorn*): It's true the Lord God formed you to contrive indeed. Doesn't the world know you reared a black lamb at your own breast, so that the Lord Bishop of Connaught felt the elements of a Christian, and he eating it after in a kidney stew? Doesn't the world know you've been seen shaving the foxy skipper from France for a threepenny bit and a sop of grass tobacco would wring the liver from a mountain goat you'd meet leaping the hills?

WIDOW QUIN (*with amusement*): Do you hear her now, young fellow? Do you hear the way she'll be rating at your own self when a week is by?

PEGEEN (*to Christy*): Don't heed her. Tell her to go into her pigsty and not plague us here.

WIDOW QUIN: I'm going; but he'll come with me.

PEGEEN (*shaking him*): Are you dumb, young fellow?

CHRISTY (*timidly, to Widow Quin*): God increase you; but I'm pot-boy in this place, and it's here I'd liefer stay.

PEGEEN (*triumphantly*): Now you have heard him, and go on from this.

WIDOW QUIN (*looking round the room*): It's lonesome this hour crossing the hill, and if he won't come along with me, I'd have a right maybe to stop this night with yourselves. Let me stretch out on the settle, Pegeen Mike; and himself can lie by the hearth.

PEGEEN (*short and fiercely*): Faith, I won't. Quit off or I will send you now.

WIDOW QUIN (*gathering her shawl up*): Well, it's a terror to be aged a score. (*To Christy.*) God bless you now, young fellow, and let you be wary, or there's right torment will await you here if you go romancing with her like, and she waiting only, as they bade me say, on a sheepskin parchment to be wed with Shawn Keogh of Killakeen.

CHRISTY (*going to Pegeen as she bolts the door*): What's that she's after saying?

PEGEEN: Lies and blather, you've no call to mind. Well, isn't Shawn Keogh an impudent fellow to send up spying on me? Wait till I lay hands on him. Let him wait, I'm saying.

CHRISTY: And you're not wedding him at all?

PEGEEN: I wouldn't wed him if a bishop came walking for to join us here.

CHRISTY: That God in glory may be thanked for that.

PEGEEN: There's your bed now. I've put a quilt upon you I'm after quilting a while since with my own two hands, and you'd best stretch out now for your sleep, and may God give you a good rest till I call you in the morning when the cocks will crow.

CHRISTY (*as she goes to inner room*): May God and Mary and St. Patrick bless you and reward you, for your kindly talk. (*She shuts the door behind her. He settles his bed slowly, feeling the quilt with immense satisfaction.*) Well, it's a clean bed and soft with it, and it's great luck and company I've won me in the end of time — two fine women fighting for the likes of me — till I'm thinking this night wasn't I a foolish fellow not to kill my father in the years gone by.

ACT II

(**Scene:** *As before. Brilliant morning light. Christy, looking bright and cheerful, is cleaning a girl's boots.*)

CHRISTY (*to himself, counting jugs on dresser*): Half a hundred beyond. Ten there. A score that's above. Eighty jugs. Six cups and a broken one. Two plates. A power of glasses. Bottles, a school-master'd be hard set to count, and enough in them, I'm thinking, to drunken all the wealth and wisdom of the County Clare. (*He puts down the boot carefully.*) There's her boots now, nice and decent for her evening use, and isn't it grand brushes she has? (*He puts them down and goes by degrees to the looking-glass.*) Well, this'd be a fine place to be my whole life talking out with swearing Christians, in place of my old dogs and cat, and I stalking around, smoking my pipe and drinking my fill, and never a day's work but drawing a cork an odd time, or wiping a glass, or rinsing out a shiny tumbler for a decent man. (*He takes the looking-glass from the wall and puts it on the back of a chair; then sits down in front of it and begins washing his face.*) Didn't I know rightly I was handsome, though it was the divil's own mirror we had beyond, would twist a squint across an angel's brow; and I'll be growing fine from this day, the way I'll have a soft lovely skin on me and won't be the like of the clumsy young fellows do be ploughing all times in the earth and dung. (*He starts.*) Is she coming again? (*He looks out.*) Stranger girls. God help me, where'll I hide myself away and my long neck naked to the world? (*He looks out.*) I'd best go to the room maybe till I'm dressed again.

(*He gathers up his coat and the looking-glass, and runs into the inner room. The door is pushed open, and Susan Brady looks in, and knocks on door.*)

SUSAN: There's nobody in it.

(*Knocks again.*)

NELLY (*pushing her in and following her, with Honor Blake and Sara Tansey*): It'd be early for them both to be out walking the hill.

SUSAN: I'm thinking Shawn Keogh was making game of us and there's no such man in it at all.

HONOR (*pointing to straw and quilt*): Look at that. He's been sleeping there in the night. Well, it'll be a hard case if he's gone off now, the way we'll never set our eyes on a man killed his father, and we after rising early and destroying ourselves running fast on the hill.

NELLY: Are you thinking them's his boots?

SARA (*taking them up*): If they are, there should be his father's track on them. Did you never read in the papers the way murdered men do bleed and drip?

SUSAN: Is that blood there, Sara Tansey?

SARA (*smelling it*): That's bog water, I'm thinking, but it's his own they are surely, for I never seen the like of

them for whity mud, and red mud, and turf on them, and the fine sands of the sea. That man's been walking, I'm telling you.

(*She goes down right, putting on one of his boots.*)

SUSAN (*going to window*): Maybe he's stolen off to Bel-mullet with the boots of Michael James, and you'd have a right so to follow after him, Sara Tansey, and you the one yoked the ass cart and drove ten miles to set your eyes on the man bit the yellow lady's nostril on the northern shore.

(*She looks out.*)

SARA (*running to window with one boot on*): Don't be talking, and we fooled to-day. (*Putting on other boot.*) There's a pair do fit me well, and I'll be keeping them for walking to the priest, when you'd be ashamed this place, going up winter and summer with nothing worth while to confess at all.

HONOR (*who has been listening at the door*): Whisht! there's someone inside the room. (*She pushes door a chink open.*) It's a man.

(*Sara kicks off boots and puts them where they were. They all stand in a line looking through chink.*)

SARA: I'll call him. Mister! Mister! (*He puts in his head.*) Is Pegeen within?

CHRISTY (*coming in as meek as a mouse, with the looking-glass held behind his back*): She's above on the cnuceen,° seeking the nanny goats, the way she'd have a sup of goat's milk for to color my tea.

SARA: And asking your pardon, is it you's the man killed his father?

CHRISTY (*sidling toward the nail where the glass was hanging*): I am, God help me!

SARA (*taking eggs she has brought*): Then my thousand welcomes to you, and I've run up with a brace of duck's eggs for your food to-day. Pegeen's ducks is no use, but these are the real rich sort. Hold out your hand and you'll see it's no lie I'm telling you.

CHRISTY (*coming forward shyly, and holding out his left hand*): They're a great and weighty size.

SUSAN: And I run up with a pat of butter, for it'd be a poor thing to have you eating your spuds dry, and you after running a great way since you did destroy your da.

CHRISTY: Thank you kindly.

HONOR: And I brought you a little cut of cake, for you should have a thin stomach on you, and you that length walking the world.

NELLY: And I brought you a little laying pullet — boiled and all she is — was crushed at the fall of night by the curate's car. Feel the fat of that breast, mister.

CHRISTY: It's bursting, surely.

(*He feels it with the back of his hand, in which he holds the presents.*)

---

cnuceen: A little hill.

SARA: Will you pinch it? Is your right hand too sacred for to use at all? (*She slips round behind him.*) It's a glass he has. Well, I never seen to this day a man with a looking-glass held to his back. Them that kills their fathers is a vain lot surely.

(*Girls giggle.*)

CHRISTY (*smiling innocently and piling presents on glass*): I'm very thankful to you all to-day . . .

WIDOW QUIN (*coming in quickly, at door*): Sara Tansey, Susan Brady, Honor Blake! What in glory has you here at this hour of day?

GIRLS (*giggling*): That's the man killed his father.

WIDOW QUIN (*coming to them*): I know well it's the man; and I'm after putting him down in the sports below for racing, leaping, pitching, and the Lord knows what.

SARA (*exuberantly*): That's right, Widow Quin. I'll bet my dowry that he'll lick the world.

WIDOW QUIN: If you will, you'd have a right to have him fresh and nourished in place of nursing a feast. (*Taking presents.*) Are you fasting or fed, young fellow?

CHRISTY: Fasting, if you please.

WIDOW QUIN (*loudly*): Well, you're the lot. Stir up now and give him his breakfast. (*To Christy.*) Come here to me (*she puts him on bench beside her while the girls make tea and get his breakfast*) and let you tell us your story before Pegeen will come, in place of grinning your ears off like the moon of May.

CHRISTY (*beginning to be pleased*): It's a long story; you'd be destroyed listening.

WIDOW QUIN: Don't be letting on to be shy, a fine, gamey, treacherous lad the like of you. Was it in your house beyond you cracked his skull?

CHRISTY (*shy but flattered*): It was not. We were digging spuds in his cold, sloping, stony, divil's patch of a field.

WIDOW QUIN: And you went asking money of him, or making talk of getting a wife would drive him from his farm?

CHRISTY: I did not, then; but there I was, digging and digging, and "You squinting idiot," says he, "let you walk down now and tell the priest you'll wed the Widow Casey in a score of days."

WIDOW QUIN: And what kind was she?

CHRISTY (*with horror*): A walking terror from beyond the hills, and she two score and five years, and two hundredweights and five pounds in the weighing scales, with a limping leg on her, and a blinded eye, and she a woman of noted misbehavior with the old and young.

GIRLS (*clustering round him, serving him*): Glory be.

WIDOW QUIN: And what did he want driving you to wed with her?

(*She takes a bit of the chicken.*)

CHRISTY (*eating with growing satisfaction*): He was letting on I was wanting a protector from the harshness of the world, and he without a thought the whole while but how he'd have her hut to live in and her gold to drink.

WIDOW QUIN: There's maybe worse than a dry hearth and a widow woman and your glass at night. So you hit him then?

CHRISTY (*getting almost excited*): I did not. "I won't wed her," says I, "when all know she did suckle me for six weeks when I came into the world, and she a hag this day with a tongue on her has the crows and seabirds scattered, the way they wouldn't cast a shadow on her garden with the dread of her curse."

WIDOW QUIN (*teasingly*): That one should be right company.

SARA (*eagerly*): Don't mind her. Did you kill him then?

CHRISTY: "She's too good for the like of you," says he, "and go on now or I'll flatten you out like a crawling beast has passed under a dray."° "You will not if I can help it," says I. "Go on," says he, "or I'll have the divil making garters of your limbs to-night." "You will not if I can help it," says I.

(*He sits up, brandishing his mug.*)

SARA: You were right surely.

CHRISTY (*impressively*): With that the sun came out between the cloud and the hill, and it shining green in my face. "God have mercy on your soul," says he, lifting a scythe;° "or on your own," says I, raising the loy.

SUSAN: That's a grand story.

HONOR: He tells it lovely.

CHRISTY (*flattered and confident, waving bone*): He gave a drive with the scythe, and I gave a lep to the east. Then I turned around with my back to the north, and I hit a blow on the ridge of his skull, laid him stretched out, and he split to the knob of his gullet.

(*He raises the chicken bone to his Adam's apple.*)

GIRLS (*together*): Well, you're a marvel! Oh, God bless you! You're the lad surely!

SUSAN: "I'm thinking the Lord God sent him this road to make a second husband to the Widow Quin, and she with a great yearning to be wedded, though all dread her here. Lift him on her knee, Sara Tansey.

WIDOW QUIN: Don't tease him.

SARA (*going over to dresser and counter very quickly, and getting two glasses and porter*): You're heroes surely, and let you drink a supeen° with your arms linked like the outlandish lovers in the sailor's song. (*She links their arms and gives them the glasses.*) There now. Drink a health to the wonders of the western world, the pirates, preachers, poteen-makers, with the jobbing jockies;° parching peelers, and the juries fill their stomachs selling judgments of the English law.°

---

dray: A strong low cart without sides.
scythe: A tool with a long curved blade used for cutting grass.
supeen: A small drink.
jobbing jockies: Itinerant horse-breakers.
juries . . . English law: Juries accept bribes.

(*Brandishing the bottle.*)

WIDOW QUIN: That's a right toast, Sara Tansey. Now Christy.

(*They drink with their arms linked, he drinking with his left hand, she with her right. As they are drinking, Pegeen Mike comes in with a milk can and stands aghast. They all spring away from Christy. He goes down left. Widow Quin remains seated.*)

PEGEEN (*angrily, to Sara*): What is it you're wanting?

SARA (*twisting her apron*): An ounce of tobacco.

PEGEEN: Have you tuppence?

SARA: I've forgotten my purse.

PEGEEN: Then you'd best be getting it and not fooling us here. (*To the Widow Quin, with more elaborate scorn.*) And what is it you're wanting, Widow Quin?

WIDOW QUIN (*insolently*): A penn'orth of starch.

PEGEEN (*breaking out*): And you without a white shift or a shirt in your whole family since the drying of the flood. I've no starch for the like of you, and let you walk on now to Killamuck.

WIDOW QUIN (*turning to Christy, as she goes out with the girls*): Well, you're mighty huffy this day, Pegeen Mike, and, you young fellow, let you not forget the sports and racing when the noon is by.

(*They go out.*)

PEGEEN (*imperiously*): Fling out that rubbish and put them cups away. (*Christy tidies away in great haste.*) Shove in the bench by the wall. (*He does so.*) And hang that glass on the nail. What disturbed it at all?

CHRISTY (*very meekly*): I was making myself decent only, and this a fine country for young lovely girls.

PEGEEN (*sharply*): Whisht your talking of girls.

(*Goes to counter — right.*)

CHRISTY: Wouldn't any wish to be decent in a place . . .

PEGEEN: Whisht I'm saying.

CHRISTY (*looks at her face for a moment with great misgivings, then as a last effort, takes up a loy, and goes towards her, with feigned assurance*): It was with a loy the like of that I killed my father.

PEGEEN (*still sharply*): You've told me that story six times since the dawn of day.

CHRISTY (*reproachfully*): It's a queer thing you wouldn't care to be hearing it and them girls after walking four miles to be listening to me now.

PEGEEN (*turning round astonished*): Four miles.

CHRISTY (*apologetically*): Didn't himself say there were only four bona fides living in the place?

PEGEEN: It's bona fides° by the road they are, but that lot came over the river lepping the stones. It's not three perches when you go like that, and I was down this morning looking on the papers the post-boy does

have in his bag. (*With meaning and emphasis.*) For there was great news this day, Christopher Mahon.

(*She goes into room left.*)

CHRISTY (*suspiciously*): Is it news of my murder?

PEGEEN (*inside*): Murder, indeed.

CHRISTY (*loudly*): A murdered da?

PEGEEN (*coming in again and crossing right*): There was not, but a story filled half a page of the hanging of a man. Ah, that should be a fearful end, young fellow, and it worst of all for a man who destroyed his da, for the like of him would get small mercies, and when it's dead he is, they'd put him in a narrow grave, with cheap sacking wrapping him round, and pour down quicklime on his head, the way you'd see a woman pouring any frish-frash° from a cup.

CHRISTY (*very miserably*): Oh, God help me. Are you thinking I'm safe? You were saying at the fall of night, I was shut of jeopardy and I here with yourselves.

PEGEEN (*severely*): You'll be shut of jeopardy no place if you go talking with a pack of wild girls the like of them do be walking abroad with the peelers, talking whispers at the fall of night.

CHRISTY (*with terror*): And you're thinking they'd tell?

PEGEEN (*with mock sympathy*): Who knows, God help you.

CHRISTY (*loudly*): What joy would they have to bring hanging to the likes of me?

PEGEEN: It's queer joys they have, and who knows the thing they'd do, if it'd make the green stones cry itself to think of you swaying and swiggling at the butt of a rope, and you with a fine, stout neck, God bless you! the way you'd be a half an hour, in great anguish, getting your death.

CHRISTY (*getting his boots and putting them on*): If there's that terror of them, it'd be best, maybe, I went on wandering like Esau or Cain and Abel° on the sides of Neifin° or the Erris plain.°

PEGEEN (*beginning to play with him*): It would, maybe, for I've heard the Circuit judges this place is a heartless crew.

CHRISTY (*bitterly*): It's more than Judges this place is a heartless crew. (*Looking up at her.*) And isn't it a poor thing to be starting again and I a lonesome fellow will be looking out on women and girls the way the needy fallen spirits do be looking on the Lord?

PEGEEN: What call have you to be that lonesome when there's poor girls walking Mayo in their thousands now?

---

bona fides: Travelers living at least four miles from a pub could legally drink after hours. Thus they could drink in "good faith."

frish-frash: A thin cabbage soup.
Esau . . . Abel: Esau was deceived by his twin brother Jacob and forced for a time to live as a roving warrior without his father's blessing. According to Genesis, Cain murdered his brother Abel and was sentenced by God to restlessly wander the earth.
Neifin: Irish mountain range.
Erris plain: An area in the Irish countryside.

CHRISTY (*grimly*): It's well you know what call I have. It's well you know it's a lonesome thing to be passing small towns with the lights shining sideways when the night is down, or going in strange places with a dog noising before you and a dog noising behind, or drawn to the cities where you'd hear a voice kissing and talking deep love in every shadow of the ditch, and you passing on with an empty, hungry stomach failing from your heart.

PEGEEN: I'm thinking you're an odd man, Christy Mahon. The oddest walking fellow I ever set my eyes on to this hour to-day.

CHRISTY: What would any be but odd men and they living lonesome in the world?

PEGEEN: I'm not odd, and I'm my whole life with my father only.

CHRISTY (*with infinite admiration*): How would a lovely handsome woman the like of you be lonesome when all men should be thronging around to hear the sweetness of your voice, and the little infant children should be pestering your steps I'm thinking, and you walking the roads.

PEGEEN: I'm hard set to know what way a coaxing fellow the like of yourself should be lonesome either.

CHRISTY: Coaxing?

PEGEEN: Would you have me think a man never talked with the girls would have the words you've spoken to-day? It's only letting on you are to be lonesome, the way you'd get around me now.

CHRISTY: I wish to God I was letting on; but I was lonesome all times, and born lonesome, I'm thinking, as the moon of dawn.

(*Going to door.*)

PEGEEN (*puzzled by his talk*): Well, it's a story I'm not understanding at all why you'd be worse than another, Christy Mahon, and you a fine lad with the great savagery to destroy your da.

CHRISTY: It's little I'm understanding myself, saving only that my heart's scalded this day, and I going off stretching out the earth between us, the way I'll not be waking near you another dawn of the year till the two of us do arise to hope or judgment with the saints of God, and now I'd best be going with my wattle in my hand, for hanging is a poor thing (*turning to go*), and it's little welcome only is left me in this house to-day.

PEGEEN (*sharply*): Christy! (*He turns round.*) Come here to me. (*He goes towards her.*) Lay down that switch and throw some sods on the fire. You're pot-boy in this place, and I'll not have you mitch off° from us now.

CHRISTY: You were saying I'd be hanged if I stay.

PEGEEN (*quite kindly at last*): I'm after going down and reading the fearful crimes of Ireland for two weeks or three, and there wasn't a word of your murder. (*Get-*

ting up and going over to the counter.*) They've likely not found the body. You're safe so with ourselves.

CHRISTY (*astonished, slowly*): It's making game of me you were (*following her with fearful joy*), and I can stay so, working at your side, and I not lonesome from this mortal day.

PEGEEN: What's to hinder you from staying, except the widow woman or the young girls would inveigle you off?

CHRISTY (*with rapture*): And I'll have your words from this day filling my ears, and that look is come upon you meeting my two eyes, and I watching you loafing around in the warm sun, or rinsing your ankles when the night is come.

PEGEEN (*kindly, but a little embarrassed*): I'm thinking you'll be a loyal young lad to have working around, and if you vexed me a while since with your leaguing with the girls, I wouldn't give a thraneen° for a lad hadn't a mighty spirit in him and a gamey heart.

(*Shawn Keogh runs in carrying a cleeve° on his back, followed by the Widow Quin.*)

SHAWN (*to Pegeen*): I was passing below, and I seen your mountainy sheep eating cabbages in Jimmy's field. Run up or they'll be bursting surely.

PEGEEN: Oh, God mend them!

(*She puts a shawl over her head and runs out.*)

CHRISTY (*looking from one to the other. Still in high spirits*): I'd best go to her aid maybe. I'm handy with ewes.

WIDOW QUIN (*closing the door*): She can do that much, and there is Shaneen has long speeches for to tell you now.

(*She sits down with an amused smile.*)

SHAWN (*taking something from his pocket and offering it to Christy*): Do you see that, mister?

CHRISTY (*looking at it*): The half of a ticket to the Western States!°

SHAWN (*trembling with anxiety*): I'll give it to you and my new hat (*pulling it out of hamper*); and my breeches with the double seat (*pulling it off*); and my new coat is woven from the blackest shearings for three miles around (*giving him the coat*); I'll give you the whole of them, and my blessing, and the blessing of Father Reilly itself, maybe, if you'll quit from this and leave us in the peace we had till last night at the fall of dark.

CHRISTY (*with a new arrogance*): And for what is it you're wanting to get shut of me?

SHAWN (*looking to the Widow for help*): I'm a poor scholar with middling faculties to coin a lie, so I'll tell you the truth, Christy Mahon. I'm wedding with Peg-

---

mitch off: Disappear without leave.

thraneen: An object of little value.
cleeve: Meat cleaver.
Western States: The United States.

een beyond, and I don't think well of having a clever fearless man the like of you dwelling in her house.

CHRISTY (*almost pugnaciously*): And you'd be using bribery for to banish me?

SHAWN (*in an imploring voice*): Let you not take it badly, mister honey, isn't beyond the best place for you where you'll have golden chains and shiny coats and you riding upon hunters with the ladies of the land.

(*He makes an eager sign to the Widow Quin to come to help him.*)

WIDOW QUIN (*coming over*): It's true for him, and you'd best quit off and not have that poor girl setting her mind on you, for there's Shaneen thinks she wouldn't suit you though all is saying that she'll wed you now.

(*Christy beams with delight.*)

SHAWN (*in terrified earnest*): She wouldn't suit you, and she with the divil's own temper the way you'd be strangling one another in a score of days. (*He makes the movement of strangling with his hands.*) It's the like of me only that she's fit for, a quiet simple fellow wouldn't raise a hand upon her if she scratched itself.

WIDOW QUIN (*putting Shawn's hat on Christy*): Fit them clothes on you anyhow, young fellow, and he'd maybe loan them to you for the sports. (*Pushing him towards inner door.*) Fit them on and you can give your answer when you have them tried.

CHRISTY (*beaming, delighted with the clothes*): I will then. I'd like herself to see me in them tweeds and hat.

(*He goes into room and shuts the door.*)

SHAWN (*in great anxiety*): He'd like herself to see them. He'll not leave us, Widow Quin. He's a score of divils in him the way it's well nigh certain he will wed Pegeen.

WIDOW QUIN (*jeeringly*): It's true all girls are fond of courage and do hate the like of you.

SHAWN (*walking about in desperation*): Oh, Widow Quin, what'll I be doing now? I'd inform again him, but he'd burst from Kilmainham° and he'd be sure and certain to destroy me. If I wasn't so God-fearing, I'd near have courage to come behind him and run a pike into his side. Oh, it's a hard case to be an orphan and not to have your father that you're used to, and you'd easy kill and make yourself a hero in the sight of all. (*Coming up to her.*) Oh, Widow Quin, will you find me some contrivance when I've promised you a ewe?

WIDOW QUIN: A ewe's a small thing, but what would you give me if I did wed him and did save you so?

SHAWN (*with astonishment*): You?

WIDOW QUIN: Aye. Would you give me the red cow you

Kilmainham: A prison in Dublin.

have and the mountainy ram, and the right of way across your rye path, and a load of dung at Michaelmas,° and turbary° upon the western hill?

SHAWN (*radiant with hope*): I would surely, and I'd give you the wedding-ring I have, and the loan of a new suit, the way you'd have him decent on the wedding-day. I'd give you two kids for your dinner, and a gallon of poteen, and I'd call the piper on the long car to your wedding from Crossmolina or from Ballina. I'd give you . . .

WIDOW QUIN: That'll do so, and let you whisht, for he's coming now again.

(*Christy comes in very natty in the new clothes. Widow Quin goes to him admiringly.*)

WIDOW QUIN: If you seen yourself now, I'm thinking you'd be too proud to speak to us at all, and it'd be a pity surely to have your like sailing from Mayo to the Western World.

CHRISTY (*as proud as a peacock*): I'm not going. If this is a poor place itself, I'll make myself contented to be lodging here.

(*Widow Quin makes a sign to Shawn to leave them.*)

SHAWN: Well, I'm going measuring the race-course while the tide is low, so I'll leave you the garments and my blessing for the sports to-day. God bless you!

(*He wriggles out.*)

WIDOW QUIN (*admiring Christy*): Well, you're mighty spruce, young fellow. Sit down now while you're quiet till you talk with me.

CHRISTY (*swaggering*): I'm going abroad on the hillside for to seek Pegeen.

WIDOW QUIN: You'll have time and plenty for to seek Pegeen, and you heard me saying at the fall of night the two of us should be great company.

CHRISTY: From this out I'll have no want of company when all sorts is bringing me their food and clothing (*he swaggers to the door, tightening his belt*), the way they'd set their eyes upon a gallant orphan cleft his father with one blow to the breeches belt. (*He opens door, then staggers back.*) Saints of glory! Holy angels from the throne of light!

WIDOW QUIN (*going over*): What ails you?

CHRISTY: It's the walking spirit of my murdered da?

WIDOW QUIN (*looking out*): Is it that tramper?

CHRISTY (*wildly*): Where'll I hide my poor body from that ghost of hell?

(*The door is pushed open, and old Mahon appears on threshold. Christy darts in behind door.*)

WIDOW QUIN (*in great amusement*): God save you, my poor man.

Michaelmas: September 29th, the feast of St. Michael the Archangel.
turbary: The right to cut turf on someone else's property.

MAHON (*gruffly*): Did you see a young lad passing this way in the early morning or the fall of night?

WIDOW QUIN: You're a queer kind to walk in not saluting at all.

MAHON: Did you see the young lad?

WIDOW QUIN (*stiffly*): What kind was he?

MAHON: An ugly young streeler° with a murderous gob° on him, and a little switch in his hand. I met a tramper seen him coming this way at the fall of night.

WIDOW QUIN: There's harvest hundreds do be passing these days for the Sligo° boat. For what is it you're wanting him, my poor man?

MAHON: I want to destroy him for breaking the head on me with the clout of a loy. (*He takes off a big hat, and shows his head in a mass of bandages and plaster, with some pride.*) It was he did that, and amn't I a great wonder to think I've traced him ten days with that rent in my crown?

WIDOW QUIN (*taking his head in both hands and examining it with extreme delight*): That was a great blow. And who hit you? A robber maybe?

MAHON: It was my own son hit me, and he the divil a robber, or anything else, but a dirty, stuttering lout.

WIDOW QUIN (*letting go his skull and wiping her hands in her apron*): You'd best be wary of a mortified scalp, I think they call it, lepping around with that wound in the splendor of the sun. It was a bad blow surely, and you should have vexed him fearful to make him strike that gash in his da.

MAHON: Is it me?

WIDOW QUIN (*amusing herself*): Aye. And isn't it a great shame when the old and hardened do torment the young?

MAHON (*raging*): Torment him is it? And I after holding out with the patience of a martyred saint till there's nothing but destruction on, and I'm driven out in my old age with none to aid me.

WIDOW QUIN (*greatly amused*): It's a sacred wonder the way that wickedness will spoil a man.

MAHON: My wickedness, is it? Amn't I after saying it is himself has me destroyed, and he a liar on walls, a talker of folly, a man you'd see stretched the half of the day in the brown ferns with his belly to the sun.

WIDOW QUIN: Not working at all?

MAHON: The divil a work, or if he did itself, you'd see him raising up a haystack like the stalk of a rush, or driving our last cow till he broke her leg at the hip, and when he wasn't at that he'd be fooling over little birds he had — finches and felts — or making mugs at his own self in the bit of a glass we had hung on the wall.

WIDOW QUIN (*looking at Christy*): What way was he so foolish? It was running wild after the girls may be?

MAHON (*with a shout of derision*): Running wild, is it? If he seen a red petticoat coming swinging over the hill, he'd be off to hide in the sticks, and you'd see

him shooting out his sheep's eyes between the little twigs and the leaves, and his two ears rising like a hare looking out through a gap. Girls, indeed!

WIDOW QUIN: It was drink maybe?

MAHON: And he a poor fellow would get drunk on the smell of a pint. He'd a queer rotten stomach, I'm telling you, and when I gave him three pulls from my pipe a while since, he was taken with contortions till I had to send him in the ass cart to the females' nurse.

WIDOW QUIN (*clasping her hands*): Well, I never till this day heard tell of a man the like of that!

MAHON: I'd take a mighty oath you didn't surely, and wasn't he the laughing joke of every female woman where four baronies° meet, the way the girls would stop their weeding if they seen him coming the road to let a roar at him, and call him the looney of Mahon's.

WIDOW QUIN: I'd give the world and all to see the like of him. What kind was he?

MAHON: A small low fellow.

WIDOW QUIN: And dark?

MAHON: Dark and dirty.

WIDOW QUIN (*considering*): I'm thinking I seen him.

MAHON (*eagerly*): An ugly young blackguard.

WIDOW QUIN: A hideous, fearful villain, and the spit of you.

MAHON: What way is he fled?

WIDOW QUIN: Gone over the hills to catch a coasting steamer to the north or south.

MAHON: Could I pull up on him now?

WIDOW QUIN: If you'll cross the sands below where the tide is out, you'll be in it as soon as himself, for he had to go round ten miles by the top of the bay. (*She points to the door.*) Strike down by the head beyond and then follow on the roadway to the north and east.

(*Mahon goes abruptly.*)

WIDOW QUIN (*shouting after him*): Let you give him a good vengeance when you come up with him, but don't put yourself in the power of the law, for it'd be a poor thing to see a judge in his black cap reading out his sentence on a civil warrior the like of you.

(*She swings the door to and looks at Christy, who is cowering in terror, for a moment, then she bursts into a laugh.*)

WIDOW QUIN: Well, you're the walking Playboy° of the Western World, and that's the poor man you had divided to his breeches belt.

CHRISTY (*looking out: then, to her*): What'll Pegeen say when she hears that story? What'll she be saying to me now?

WIDOW QUIN: She'll knock the head of you, I'm thinking, and drive you from the door. God help her to be taking you for a wonder, and you a little schemer making up the story you destroyed your da.

---

streeler: A street tough.
gob: Mouth.
Sligo: A county on the northwest coast of Ireland.

baronies: Large tracts of privately owned land; equivalent to modern counties.
Playboy: A man who lives for the pursuit of pleasure.

CHRISTY (*turning to the door, nearly speechless with rage, half to himself*): To be letting on he was dead, and coming back to his life, and following after me like an old weazel tracing a rat, and coming in here laying desolation between my own self and the fine women of Ireland, and he a kind of carcase that you'd fling upon the sea . . .

WIDOW QUIN (*more soberly*): There's talking for a man's one only son.

CHRISTY (*breaking out*): His one son, is it? May I meet him with one tooth and it aching, and one eye to be seeing seven and seventy divils in the twists of the road, and one old timber leg on him to limp into the scalding grave. (*Looking out.*) There he is now crossing the strands, and that the Lord God would send a high wave to wash him from the world.

WIDOW QUIN (*scandalized*): Have you no shame? (*Putting her hand on his shoulder and turning him round.*) What ails you? Near crying, is it?

CHRISTY (*in despair and grief*): Amn't I after seeing the love-light of the star of knowledge shining from her brow, and hearing words would put you thinking on the holy Brigid speaking to the infant saints, and now she'll be turning again, and speaking hard words to me, like an old woman with a spavindy° ass she'd have, urging on a hill.

WIDOW QUIN: There's poetry talk for a girl you'd see itching and scratching, and she with a stale stink of poteen on her from selling in the shop.

CHRISTY (*impatiently*): It's her like is fitted to be handling merchandise in the heavens above, and what'll I be doing now, I ask you, and I a kind of wonder was jilted by the heavens when a day was by.

(*There is a distant noise of girls' voices. Widow Quin looks from window and comes to him, hurriedly.*)

WIDOW QUIN: You'll be doing like myself, I'm thinking, when I did destroy my man, for I'm above many's the day, odd times in great spirits, abroad in the sunshine, darning a stocking or stitching a shift; and odd times again looking out on the schooners, hookers, trawlers is sailing the sea, and I thinking on the gallant hairy fellows are drifting beyond, and myself long years living alone.

CHRISTY (*interested*): You're like me, so.

WIDOW QUIN: I am your like, and it's for that I'm taking a fancy to you, and I with my little houseen above where there'd be myself to tend you, and none to ask were you a murderer or what at all.

CHRISTY: And what would I be doing if I left Pegeen?

WIDOW QUIN: I've nice jobs you could be doing, gathering shells to make a whitewash for our hut within, building up a little goose-house, or stretching a new skin on an old curragh° I have, and if my hut is far

from all sides, it's there you'll meet the wisest old men, I tell you, at the corner of my wheel, and it's there yourself and me will have great times whispering and hugging. . . .

VOICES (*outside, calling far away*): Christy! Christy Mahon! Christy!

CHRISTY: Is it Pegeen Mike?

WIDOW QUIN: It's the young girls, I'm thinking, coming to bring you to the sports below, and what is it you'll have me to tell them now?

CHRISTY: Aid me for to win Pegeen. It's herself only that I'm seeking now. (*Widow Quin gets up and goes to window.*) Aid me for to win her, and I'll be asking God to stretch a hand to you in the hour of death, and lead you short cuts through the Meadows of Ease, and up the floor of Heaven to the Footstool of the Virgin's Son.°

WIDOW QUIN: There's praying.

VOICES (*nearer*): Christy! Christy Mahon!

CHRISTY (*with agitation*): They're coming. Will you swear to aid and save me for the love of Christ?

WIDOW QUIN (*looks at him for a moment*): If I aid you, will you swear to give me a right of way I want, and a mountainy ram, and a load of dung at Michaelmas, the time that you'll be master here?

CHRISTY: I will, by the elements and stars of night.

WIDOW QUIN: Then we'll not say a word of the old fellow, the way Pegeen won't know your story till the end of time.

CHRISTY: And if he chances to return again?

WIDOW QUIN: We'll swear he's a maniac and not your da. I could take an oath I seen him raving on the sands to-day.

(*Girls run in.*)

SUSAN: Come on to the sports below. Pegeen says you're to come.

SARA TANSEY: The lepping's° beginning, and we've a jockey's suit to fit upon you for the mule race on the sands below.

HONOR: Come on, will you?

CHRISTY: I will then if Pegeen's beyond.

SARA TANSEY: She's in the boreen° making game of Shaneen Keogh.

CHRISTY: Then I'll be going to her now.

(*He runs out followed by the girls.*)

WIDOW QUIN: Well, if the worst comes in the end of all, it'll be great game to see there's none to pity him but a widow woman, the like of me, has buried her children and destroyed her man.

(*She goes out.*)

---

spavindy: A variation of *spavin*, or a swelling on the hock of a donkey or horse associated with strain.
curragh: A traditional Irish boat with a keel made by stretching hide over a wicker frame.

Virgin's Son: Jesus Christ, son of the Virgin Mary, according to Roman Catholic doctrine.
lepping: Long-jumping.
boreen: A narrow country road.

ACT III

(**Scene:** *As before. Later in the day. Jimmy comes in, slightly drunk.*)

JIMMY (*calls*): Pegeen! (*Crosses to inner door.*) Pegeen Mike! (*Comes back again into the room.*) Pegeen! (*Philly comes in in the same state.*) (*To Philly.*) Did you see herself?

PHILLY: I did not; but I sent Shawn Keogh with the ass cart for to bear him home. (*Trying cupboards which are locked.*) Well, isn't he a nasty man to get into such staggers at a morning wake? and isn't herself the divil's daughter for locking, and she so fussy after that young gaffer, you might take your death with drought and none to heed you?

JIMMY: It's little wonder she'd be fussy, and he after bringing bankrupt ruin on the roulette man, and the trick-o'-the-loop man, and breaking the nose of the cockshot-man, and winning all in the sports below, racing, lepping, dancing, and the Lord knows what! He's right luck, I'm telling you.

PHILLY: If he has, he'll be rightly hobbled yet, and he not able to say ten words without making a brag of the way he killed his father, and the great blow he hit with the loy.

JIMMY: A man can't hang by his own informing, and his father should be rotten by now.

(*Old Mahon passes window slowly.*)

PHILLY: Supposing a man's digging spuds in that field with a long spade, and supposing he flings up the two halves of that skull, what'll be said then in the papers and the courts of law?

JIMMY: They'd say it was an old Dane, maybe, was drowned in the flood.° (*Old Mahon comes in and sits down near door listening.*) Did you never hear tell of the skulls they have in the city of Dublin, ranged out like blue jugs in a cabin of Connaught?

PHILLY: And you believe that?

JIMMY (*pugnaciously*): Didn't a lad see them and he after coming from harvesting in the Liverpool boat? "They have them there," says he, "making a show of the great people there was one time walking the world. White skulls and black skulls and yellow skulls, and some with full teeth, and some haven't only but one."

PHILLY: It was no lie, maybe, for when I was a young lad there was a graveyard beyond the house with the remnants of a man who had thighs as long as your arm. He was a horrid man, I'm telling you, and there was many a fine Sunday I'd put him together for fun, and he with shiny bones, you wouldn't meet the like of these days in the cities of the world.

MAHON (*getting up*): You wouldn't, is it? Lay your eyes on that skull, and tell me where and when there was another the like of it, is splintered only from the blow of a loy.

PHILLY: Glory be to God! And who hit you at all?

flood: Noah's flood, meaning a long time ago.

MAHON (*triumphantly*): It was my own son hit me. Would you believe that?

JIMMY: Well, there's wonders hidden in the heart of man!

PHILLY (*suspiciously*): And what way was it done?

MAHON (*wandering about the room*): I'm after walking hundreds and long scores of miles, winning clean beds and the fill of my belly four times in the day, and I doing nothing but telling stories of that naked truth. (*He comes to them a little aggressively.*) Give me a supeen and I'll tell you now.

(*Widow Quin comes in and stands aghast behind him. He is facing Jimmy and Philly, who are on the left.*)

JIMMY: Ask herself beyond. She's the stuff hidden in her shawl.

WIDOW QUIN (*coming to Mahon quickly*): You here, is it? You didn't go far at all?

MAHON: I seen the coasting steamer passing, and I got a drought upon me and a cramping leg, so I said, "The divil go along with him," and turned again. (*Looking under her shawl.*) And let you give me a supeen, for I'm destroyed traveling since Tuesday was a week.

WIDOW QUIN (*getting a glass, in a cajoling tone*): Sit down then by the fire and take your ease for a space. You've a right to be destroyed indeed, with your walking, and fighting, and facing the sun (*giving him poteen from a stone jar she has brought in*). There now is a drink for you, and may it be to your happiness and length of life.

MAHON (*taking glass greedily and sitting down by fire*): God increase you!

WIDOW QUIN (*taking men to the right stealthily*): Do you know what? That man's raving from his wound to-day, for I met him a while since telling a rambling tale of a tinker had him destroyed. Then he heard of Christy's deed, and he up and says it was his son had cracked his skull. O isn't madness a fright, for he'll go killing someone yet, and he thinking it's the man has struck him so?

JIMMY (*entirely convinced*): It's a fright, surely. I knew a party was kicked in the head by a red mare, and he went killing horses a great while, till he eat the insides of a clock and died after.

PHILLY (*with suspicion*): Did he see Christy?

WIDOW QUIN: He didn't. (*With a warning gesture.*) Let you not be putting him in mind of him, or you'll be likely summoned if there's murder done. (*Looking round at Mahon.*) Whisht! He's listening. Wait now till you hear me taking him easy and unraveling all. (*She goes to Mahon.*) And what way are you feeling, mister? Are you in contentment now?

MAHON (*slightly emotional from his drink*): I'm poorly only, for it's a hard story the way I'm left to-day, when it was I did tend him from his hour of birth, and he a dunce never reached his second book, the way he'd come from school, many's the day, with his legs lamed under him, and he blackened with his beatings like a tinker's ass. It's a hard story, I'm saying, the way some do have their next and nighest raising up a hand of murder on them, and some is lonesome getting their death with lamentation in the dead of night.

WIDOW QUIN (*not knowing what to say*): To hear you talking so quiet, who'd know you were the same fellow we seen pass to-day?

MAHON: I'm the same surely. The wrack and ruin of three score years; and it's a terror to live that length, I tell you, and to have your sons going to the dogs against you, and you wore out scolding them, and skelping° them, and God knows what.

PHILLY (*to Jimmy*): He's not raving. (*To Widow Quin.*) Will you ask him what kind was his son?

WIDOW QUIN (*to Mahon, with a peculiar look*): Was your son that hit you a lad of one year and a score maybe, a great hand at racing and lepping and licking the world?

MAHON (*turning on her with a roar of rage*): Didn't you hear me say he was the fool of men, the way from this out he'll know the orphan's lot with old and young making game of him and they swearing, raging, kicking at him like a mangy cur.

(*A great burst of cheering outside, some way off.*)

MAHON (*putting his hands to his ears*): What in the name of God do they want roaring below?

WIDOW QUIN (*with the shade of a smile*): They're cheering a young lad, the champion Playboy of the Western World.

(*More cheering.*)

MAHON (*going to window*): It'd split my heart to hear them, and I with pulses in my brain-pan for a week gone by. Is it racing they are?

JIMMY (*looking from door*): It is then. They are mounting him for the mule race will be run upon the sands. That's the playboy on the winkered mule.

MAHON (*puzzled*): That lad, is it? If you said it was a fool he was, I'd have laid a mighty oath he was the likeness of my wandering son (*uneasily, putting his hand to his head*). Faith, I'm thinking I'll go walking for to view the race.

WIDOW QUIN (*stopping him, sharply*): You will not. You'd best take the road to Belmullet, and not be dilly-dallying in this place where there isn't a spot you could sleep.

PHILLY (*coming forward*): Don't mind her. Mount there on the bench and you'll have a view of the whole. They're hurrying before the tide will rise, and it'd be near over if you went down the pathway through the crags below.

MAHON (*mounts on bench, Widow Quin beside him*): That's a right view again the edge of the sea. They're coming now from the point. He's leading. Who is he at all?

WIDOW QUIN: He's the champion of the world, I tell

you, and there isn't a hop'orth° isn't falling lucky to his hands to-day.

PHILLY (*looking out, interested in the race*): Look at that. They're pressing him now.

JIMMY: He'll win it yet.

PHILLY: Take your time, Jimmy Farrell. It's too soon to say.

WIDOW QUIN (*shouting*): Watch him taking the gate. There's riding.

JIMMY (*cheering*): More power to the young lad!

MAHON: He's passing the third.

JIMMY: He'll lick them yet!

WIDOW QUIN: He'd lick them if he was running races with a score itself.

MAHON: Look at the mule he has, kicking the stars.

WIDOW QUIN: There was a lep! (*Catching hold of Mahon in her excitement.*) He's fallen! He's mounted again! Faith, he's passing them all!

JIMMY: Look at him skelping her!

PHILLY: And the mountain girls hooshing° him on!

JIMMY: It's the last turn! The post's cleared for them now!

MAHON: Look at the narrow place. He'll be into the bogs! (*With a yell.*) Good rider! He's through it again!

JIMMY: He neck and neck!

MAHON: Good boy to him! Flames, but he's in!

(*Great cheering, in which all join.*)

MAHON (*with hesitation*): What's that? They're raising him up. They're coming this way. (*With a roar of rage and astonishment.*) It's Christy! by the stars of God! I'd know his way of spitting and he astride the moon.

(*He jumps down and makes for the door. but Widow Quin catches him and pulls him back.*)

WIDOW QUIN: Stay quiet, will you. That's not your son. (*To Jimmy.*) Stop him, or you'll get a month for the abetting of manslaughter and be fined as well.

JIMMY: I'll hold him.

MAHON (*struggling*): Let me out! Let me out, the lot of you! till I have my vengeance on his head to-day.

WIDOW QUIN (*shaking him, vehemently*): That's not your son. That's a man is going to make a marriage with the daughter of this house, a place with fine trade, with a license, and with poteen too.

MAHON (*amazed*): That man marrying a decent and a moneyed girl! Is it mad yous are? Is it in a crazy-house for females that I'm landed now?

WIDOW QUIN: It's mad yourself is with the blow upon your head. That lad is the wonder of the Western World.

MAHON: I seen it's my son.

WIDOW QUIN: You seen that you're mad. (*Cheering outside.*) Do you hear them cheering him in the zig-zags of the road? Aren't you after saying that your son's a

---

skelping: Striking or slapping.

hop'orth: Half-penny worth.
hooshing: Cheering.

fool, and how would they be cheering a true idiot born?

MAHON (*getting distressed*): It's maybe out of reason that that man's himself. (*Cheering again.*) There's none surely will go cheering him. Oh, I'm raving with a madness that would fright the world! (*He sits down with his hand to his head.*) There was one time I seen ten scarlet divils letting on they'd cork my spirit in a gallon can; and one time I seen rats as big as badgers sucking the life blood from the butt of my lug;° but I never till this day confused that dribbling idiot with a likely man. I'm destroyed surely.

WIDOW QUIN: And who'd wonder when it's your brain-pan that is gaping now?

MAHON: Then the blight of the sacred drought upon myself and him, for I never went mad to this day, and I not three weeks with the Limerick girls drinking myself silly, and parlatic° from the dusk to dawn. (*To Widow Quin, suddenly.*) Is my visage astray?

WIDOW QUIN: It is then. You're a sniggering maniac, a child could see.

MAHON (*getting up more cheerfully*): Then I'd best be going to the union beyond, and there'll be a welcome before me, I tell you (*with great pride*), and I a terrible and fearful case, the way that there I was one time, screeching in a straitened waistcoat, with seven doctors writing out my sayings in a printed book. Would you believe that?

WIDOW QUIN: If you're a wonder itself, you'd best be hasty, for them lads caught a maniac one time and pelted the poor creature till he ran out, raving and foaming, and was drowned in the sea.

MAHON (*with philosophy*): It's true mankind is the divil when your head's astray. Let me out now and I'll slip down the boreen, and not see them so.

WIDOW QUIN (*showing him out*): That's it. Run to the right, and not a one will see.

(*He runs off.*)

PHILLY (*wisely*): You're at some gaming, Widow Quin; but I'll walk after him and give him his dinner and a time to rest, and I'll see then if he's raving or as sane as you.

WIDOW QUIN (*annoyed*): If you go near that lad, let you be wary of your head, I'm saying. Didn't you hear him telling he was crazed at times?

PHILLY: I heard him telling a power; and I'm thinking we'll have right sport, before night will fall.

(*He goes out.*)

JIMMY: Well, Philly's a conceited and foolish man. How could that madman have his senses and his brain-pan slit? I'll go after them and see him turn on Philly now.

(*He goes; Widow Quin hides poteen behind counter. Then hubbub outside.*)

VOICES: There you are! Good jumper! Grand lepper! Darlint boy! He's the racer! Bear him on, will you!

(*Christy comes in, in Jockey's dress, with Pegeen Mike, Sara, and other girls, and men.*)

PEGEEN (*to crowd*): Go on now and don't destroy him and he drenching with sweat. Go along, I'm saying, and have your tug-of-warring till he's dried his skin.

CROWD: Here's his prizes! A bagpipes! A fiddle was played by a poet in the years gone by! A flat and three-thorned blackthorn would lick the scholars out of Dublin town!

CHRISTY (*taking prizes from the men*): Thank you kindly, the lot of you. But you'd say it was little only I did this day if you'd seen me a while since striking my one single blow.

TOWN CRIER (*outside, ringing a bell*): Take notice, last event of this day! Tug-of-warring on the green below! Come on, the lot of you! Great achievements for all Mayo men!

PEGEEN: Go on, and leave him for to rest and dry. Go on, I tell you, for he'll do no more. (*She bustles crowd out; Widow Quin following them.*)

MEN (*going*): Come on then. Good luck for the while!

PEGEEN (*radiantly, wiping his face with her shawl*): Well, you're the lad, and you'll have great times from this out when you could win that wealth of prizes, and you sweating in the heat of noon!

CHRISTY (*looking at her with delight*): I'll have great times if I win the crowning prize I'm seeking now, and that's your promise that you'll wed me in a fort-night, when our banns° is called.

PEGEEN (*backing away from him*): You've right daring to go ask me that, when all knows you'll be starting to some girl in your own townland, when your father's rotten in four months, or five.

CHRISTY (*indignantly*): Starting from you, is it? (*He follows her.*) I will not, then, and when the airs is warming in four months, or five, it's then yourself and me should be pacing Neifin in the dews of night, the times sweet smells do be rising, and you'd see a little shiny new moon, maybe, sinking on the hills.

PEGEEN (*looking at him playfully*): And it's that kind of a poacher's love you'd make, Christy Mahon, on the sides of Neifin, when the night is down?

CHRISTY: It's little you'll think if my love's a poacher's, or an earl's itself, when you'll feel my two hands stretched around you, and I squeezing kisses on your puckered lips, till I'd feel a kind of pity for the Lord God is all ages sitting lonesome in his golden chair.

PEGEEN: That'll be right fun, Christy Mahon, and any girl would walk her heart out before she'd meet a young man was your like for eloquence, or talk, at all.

CHRISTY (*encouraged*): Let you wait, to hear me talking, till we're astray in Erris, when Good Friday's by, drinking a sup from a well, and making mighty kisses

---

lug: Ear; reference to his former alcoholic hallucinations.
parlatic: Talkative.

banns: A public announcement (usually in the church) of an intended marriage.

with our wetted mouths, or gaming in a gap or sun-shine, with yourself stretched back unto your neck-lace, in the flowers of the earth.

PEGEEN (*in a lower voice, moved by his tone*): I'd be nice so, is it?

CHRISTY (*with rapture*): If the mitred bishops seen you that time, they'd be the like of the holy prophets, I'm thinking, do be straining the bars of Paradise to lay eyes on the Lady Helen of Troy, and she abroad, pac-ing back and forward, with a nosegay in her golden shawl.

PEGEEN (*with real tenderness*): And what is it I have, Christy Mahon, to make me fitting entertainment for the like of you, that has such poet's talking, and such bravery of heart?

CHRISTY (*in a low voice*): Isn't there the light of seven heavens in your heart alone, the way you'll be an angel's lamp to me from this out, and I abroad in the darkness, spearing salmons in the Owen, or the Car-rowmore?°

PEGEEN: If I was your wife, I'd be along with you those nights, Christy Mahon, the way you'd see I was a great hand at coaxing bailiffs, or coining funny nick-names for the stars of night.

CHRISTY: You, is it? Taking your death in the hailstones, or in the fogs of dawn.

PEGEEN: Yourself and me would shelter easy in a narrow bush, (*with a qualm of dread*) but we're only talking, maybe, for this would be a poor, thatched place to hold a fine lad is the like of you.

CHRISTY (*putting his arm round her*): If I wasn't a good Christian, it's on my naked knees I'd be saying my prayers and paters to every jackstraw you have roof-ing your head, and every stony pebble is paving the laneway to your door.

PEGEEN (*radiantly*): If that's the truth, I'll be burning candles from this out to the miracles of God that have brought you from the south to-day, and I, with my gowns bought ready, the way that I can wed you, and not wait at all.

CHRISTY: It's miracles, and that's the truth. Me there toiling a long while, and walking a long while, not knowing at all I was drawing all times nearer to this holy day.

PEGEEN: And myself, a girl, was tempted often to go sail-ing the seas till I'd marry a Jew-man, with ten kegs of gold, and I not knowing at all there was the like of you drawing nearer, like the stars of God.

CHRISTY: And to think I'm long years hearing women talking that talk, to all bloody fools, and this the first time I've heard the like of your voice talking sweetly for my own delight.

PEGEEN: And to think it's me is talking sweetly, Christy Mahon, and I the fright of seven townlands for my biting tongue. Well, the heart's a wonder; and, I'm

thinking, there won't be our like in Mayo, for gallant lovers, from this hour, to-day. (*Drunken singing is heard outside.*) There's my father coming from the wake, and when he's had his sleep we'll tell him, for he's peaceful then.

(*They separate.*)

MICHAEL (*singing outside*): The jailor and the turnkey
    They quickly ran us down,
And brought us back as prisoners
    Once more to Cavan town.

(*He comes in supported by Shawn.*)

There we lay bewailing
    All in a prison bound. . . .

(*He sees Christy. Goes and shakes him drunkenly by the hand, while Pegeen and Shawn talk on the left.*)

MICHAEL (*to Christy*): The blessing of God and the holy angels on your head, young fellow. I hear tell you're after winning all in the sports below; and wasn't it a shame I didn't bear you along with me to Kate Cas-sidy's wake, a fine, stout lad, the like of you, for you'd never see the match of it for flows of drink, the way when we sunk her bones at noonday in her nar-row grave, there were five men, aye, and six men, stretched out retching speechless on the holy stones.

CHRISTY (*uneasily, watching Pegeen*): Is that the truth?

MICHAEL: It is then, and aren't you a louty schemer to go burying your poor father unbeknownst when you'd a right to throw him on the crupper of a Kerry mule and drive him westwards, like holy Joseph in the days gone by, the way we could have given him a decent burial, and not have him rotting beyond, and not a Christian drinking a smart drop to the glory of his soul?

CHRISTY (*gruffly*): It's well enough he's lying, for the likes of him.

MICHAEL (*slapping him on the back*): Well, aren't you a hardened slayer? It'll be a poor thing for the house-hold man where you go sniffing for a female wife; and (*pointing to Shawn*) look beyond at that shy and decent Christian I have chosen for my daughter's hand, and I after getting the gilded dispensation° this day for to wed them now.

CHRISTY: And you'll be wedding them this day, is it?

MICHAEL (*drawing himself up*): Aye. Are you thinking, if I'm drunk itself, I'd leave my daughter living single with a little frisky rascal is the like of you?

PEGEEN (*breaking away from Shawn*): Is it the truth the dispensation's come?

MICHAEL (*triumphantly*): Father Reilly's after reading it in gallous Latin, and "It's come in the nick of time," says he; "so I'll wed them in a hurry, dreading that young gaffer who'd capsize the stars."

Owen . . . Carrowmore: The Owen, or Oweniny, is a river in County Mayo, Ireland. The Carrowmore is a large lake in the same region.

gilded dispensation: Because they are very distant cousins, Shawn felt the need of a dispensation that permitted them to marry under church law.

PEGEEN (*fiercely*): He's missed his nick of time, for it's that lad, Christy Mahon, that I'm wedding now.

MICHAEL (*loudly with horror*): You'd be making him a son to me, and he wet and crusted with his father's blood?

PEGEEN: Aye. Wouldn't it be a bitter thing for a girl to go marrying the like of Shaneen, and he a middling kind of a scarecrow, with no savagery or fine words in him at all?

MICHAEL (*gasping and sinking on a chair*): Oh, aren't you a heathen daughter to go shaking the fat of my heart, and I swamped and drownded with the weight of drink? Would you have them turning on me the way that I'd be roaring to the dawn of day with the wind upon my heart? Have you not a word to aid me, Shaneen? Are you not jealous at all?

SHANEEN (*in great misery*): I'd be afeard to be jealous of a man did slay his da.

PEGEEN: Well, it'd be a poor thing to go marrying your like. I'm seeing there's a world of peril for an orphan girl, and isn't it a great blessing I didn't wed you, before himself came walking from the west or south?

SHAWN: It's a queer story you'd go picking a dirty tramp up from the highways of the world.

PEGEEN (*playfully*): And you think you're a likely beau to go straying along with, the shiny Sundays of the opening year, when it's sooner on a bullock's liver you'd put a poor girl thinking than on the lily or the rose?

SHAWN: And have you no mind of my weight of passion, and the holy dispensation, and the drift of heifers I am giving, and the golden ring?

PEGEEN: I'm thinking you're too fine for the like of me, Shawn Keogh of Killakeen, and let you go off till you'd find a radiant lady with droves of bullocks on the plains of Meath,° and herself bedizened in the diamond jewelleries of Pharaoh's ma. That'd be your match, Shaneen. So God save you now!

(*She retreats behind Christy.*)

SHAWN: Won't you hear me telling you . . . ?

CHRISTY (*with ferocity*): Take yourself from this, young fellow, or I'll maybe add a murder to my deeds to-day.

MICHAEL (*springing up with a shriek*): Murder is it? Is it mad yous are? Would you go making murder in this place, and it piled with poteen for our drink tonight? Go on to the foreshore if it's fighting you want, where the rising tide will wash all traces from the memory of man.

(*Pushing Shawn towards Christy.*)

SHAWN (*shaking himself free, and getting behind Michael*): I'll not fight him, Michael James. I'd liefer live a bachelor, simmering in passions to the end of time, than face a lepping savage the like of him has descended from the Lord knows where. Strike him

Meath: A county in the east of Ireland.

yourself, Michael James, or you'll lose my drift of heifers and my blue bull from Sneem.

MICHAEL: Is it me fight him, when it's father-slaying he's bred to now? (*Pushing Shawn.*) Go on you fool and fight him now.

SHAWN (*coming forward a little*): Will I strike him with my hand?

MICHAEL: Take the loy is on your western side.

SHAWN: I'd be afeard of the gallows if I struck him with that.

CHRISTY (*taking up the loy*): Then I'll make you face the gallows or quit off from this.

(*Shawn flies out of the door.*)

CHRISTY: Well, fine weather be after him (*going to Michael, coaxingly*), and I'm thinking you wouldn't wish to have that quaking blackguard in your house at all. Let you give us your blessing and hear her swear her faith to me, for I'm mounted on the spring-tide° of the stars of luck, the way it'll be good for any to have me in the house.

PEGEEN (*at the other side of Michael*): Bless us now, for I swear to God I'll wed him, and I'll not renege.

MICHAEL (*standing up in the center, holding on to both of them*): It's the will of God, I'm thinking, that all should win an easy or a cruel end, and it's the will of God that all should rear up lengthy families for the nurture of the earth. What's a single man, I ask you, eating a bit in one house and drinking a sup in another, and he with no place of his own, like an old braying jackass strayed upon the rocks? (*To Christy.*) It's many would be in dread to bring your like into their house for to end them, maybe, with a sudden end; but I'm a decent man of Ireland, and I liefer face the grave untimely and I seeing a score of grandsons growing up little gallant swearers by the name of God, than go peopling my bedside with puny weeds the like of what you'd breed, I'm think-ing, out of Shaneen Keogh. (*He joins their hands.*) A daring fellow is the jewel of the world, and a man did split his father's middle with a single clout, should have the bravery of ten, so may God and Mary and St. Patrick bless you, and increase you from this mor-tal day.

CHRISTY AND PEGEEN: Amen, O Lord!

(*Hubbub outside.*)
(*Old Mahon rushes in, followed by all the crowd, and Widow Quin. He makes a rush at Christy, knocks him down, and begins to beat him.*)

PEGEEN (*dragging back his arm*): Stop that, will you. Who are you at all?

MAHON: His father, God forgive me!

PEGEEN (*drawing back*): Is it rose from the dead?

MAHON: Do you think I look so easy quenched with the tap of a loy?

springtide: A tide of greater than average range that occurs dur-ing a new and full moon.

(Beats Christy again.)

PEGEEN (*glaring at Christy*): And it's lies you told, letting on you had him slitted, and you nothing at all.

CHRISTY (*catching Mahon's stick*): He's not my father. He's a raving maniac would scare the world. (*Pointing to Widow Quin.*) Herself knows it is true.

CROWD: You're fooling Pegeen! The Widow Quin seen him this day, and you likely knew! You're a liar!

CHRISTY (*dumbfounded*): It's himself was a liar, lying stretched out with an open head on him, letting on he was dead.

MAHON: Weren't you off racing the hills before I got my breath with the start I had seeing you turn on me at all?

PEGEEN: And to think of the coaxing glory we had given him, and he after doing nothing but hitting a soft blow and chasing northward in a sweat of fear. Quit off from this.

CHRISTY (*piteously*): You've seen my doings this day, and let you save me from the old man; for why would you be in such a scorch of haste to spur me to destruction now?

PEGEEN: It's there your treachery is spurring me, till I'm hard set to think you're the one I'm after lacing in my heart-strings half-an-hour gone by. (*To Mahon.*) Take him on from this, for I think bad the world should see me raging for a Munster liar, and the fool of men.

MAHON: Rise up now to retribution, and come on with me.

CROWD (*jeeringly*): There's the playboy! There's the lad thought he'd rule the roost in Mayo. Slate° him now, mister.

CHRISTY (*getting up in shy terror*): What is it drives you to torment me here, when I'd asked the thunders of the might of God to blast me if I ever did hurt to any saving only that one single blow.

MAHON (*loudly*): If you didn't, you're a poor good-for-nothing, and isn't it by the like of you the sins of the whole world are committed?

CHRISTY (*raising his hands*): In the name of the Almighty God. . . .

MAHON: Leave troubling the Lord God. Would you have him sending down droughts, and fevers, and the old hen and the cholera morbus?

CHRISTY (*to Widow Quin*): Will you come between us and protect me now?

WIDOW QUIN: I've tried a lot, God help me, and my share is done.

CHRISTY (*looking round in desperation*): And I must go back into my torment is it, or run off like a vagabond straying through the Unions with the dusts of August making mudstains in the gullet of my throat, or the winds of March blowing on me till I'd take an oath I felt them making whistles of my ribs within?

SARA: Ask Pegeen to aid you. Her like does often change.

Slate: Thrash.

CHRISTY: I will not then, for there's torment in the splendor of her like, and she a girl any moon of midnight would take pride to meet, facing southwards on the heaths of Keel. But what did I want crawling forward to scorch my understanding at her flaming brow?

PEGEEN (*to Mahon, vehemently, fearing she will break into tears*): Take him on from this or I'll set the young lads to destroy him here.

MAHON (*going to him, shaking his stick*): Come on now if you wouldn't have the company to see you skelped.

PEGEEN (*half laughing, through her tears*): That's it, now the world will see him pandied,° and he an ugly liar was playing off the hero, and the fright of men.

CHRISTY (*to Mahon, very sharply*): Leave me go!

CROWD: That's it. Now Christy. If them two set fighting, it will lick the world.

MAHON (*making a grab at Christy*): Come here to me.

CHRISTY (*more threateningly*): Leave me go, I'm saying.

MAHON: I will maybe, when your legs is limping, and your back is blue.

CROWD: Keep it up, the two of you. I'll back the old one. Now the playboy.

CHRISTY (*in low and intense voice*): Shut your yelling, for if you're after making a mighty man of me this day by the power of a lie, you're setting me now to think if it's a poor thing to be lonesome, it's worse maybe to go mixing with the fools of earth.

(Mahon makes a movement towards him.)

CHRISTY (*almost shouting*): Keep off . . . lest I do show a blow unto the lot of you would set the guardian angels winking in the clouds above.

(He swings round with a sudden rapid movement and picks up a loy.)

CROWD (*half frightened, half amused*): He's going mad! Mind yourselves! Run from the idiot!

CHRISTY: If I am an idiot, I'm after hearing my voice this day saying words would raise the topknot on a poet in a merchant's town. I've won your racing, and your lepping, and . . .

MAHON: Shut your gullet and come on with me.

CHRISTY: I'm going, but I'll stretch you first.

(He runs at old Mahon with the loy, chases him out of the door, followed by crowd and Widow Quin. There is a great noise outside, then a yell, and dead silence for a moment. Christy comes in, half dazed, and goes to fire.)

WIDOW QUIN (*coming in, hurriedly, and going to him*): They're turning again you. Come on, or you'll be hanged, indeed.

CHRISTY: I'm thinking, from this out, Pegeen'll be giving me praises the same as in the hours gone by.

WIDOW QUIN (*impatiently*): Come by the back-door. I'd think bad to have you stifled on the gallows tree.

CHRISTY (*indignantly*): I will not, then. What good'd be my life-time, if I left Pegeen?

pandied: Punished.

WIDOW QUIN: Come on, and you'll be no worse than you were last night; and you with a double murder this time to be telling to the girls.

CHRISTY: I'll not leave Pegeen Mike.

WIDOW QUIN (*impatiently*): Isn't there the match of her in every parish public, from Binghamstown unto the plain of Meath? Come on, I tell you, and I'll find you finer sweethearts at each waning moon.

CHRISTY: It's Pegeen I'm seeking only, and what'd I care if you brought me a drift of chosen females, standing in their shifts itself, maybe, from this place to the Eastern World?

SARA (*runs in, pulling off one of her petticoats*): They're going to hang him. (*Holding out Petticoat and shawl.*) Fit these upon him, and let him run off to the east.

WIDOW QUIN: He's raving now; but we'll fit them on him, and I'll take him, in the ferry, to the Achill boat.

CHRISTY (*struggling feebly*): Leave me go, will you? when I'm thinking of my luck to-day, for she will wed me surely, and I a proven hero in the end of all.

(*They try to fasten petticoat round him.*)

WIDOW QUIN: Take his left hand, and we'll pull him now. Come on, young fellow.

CHRISTY (*suddenly starting up*): You'll be taking me from her? You're jealous, is it, of her wedding me? Go on from this.

(*He snatches up a stool, and threatens them with it.*)

WIDOW QUIN (*going*): It's in the mad-house they should put him, not in jail, at all. We'll go by the back-door, to call the doctor, and we'll save him so.

(*She goes out, with Sara, through inner room. Men crowd in the doorway. Christy sits down again by the fire.*)

MICHAEL (*in a terrified whisper*): Is the old lad killed surely?

PHILLY: I'm after feeling the last gasps quitting his heart.

(*They peer in at Christy.*)

MICHAEL (*with a rope*): Look at the way he is. Twist a hangman's knot on it, and slip it over his head, while he's not minding at all.

PHILLY: Let you take it, Shaneen. You're the soberest of all that's here.

SHAWN: Is it me to go near him, and he the wickedest and worst with me? Let you take it, Pegeen Mike.

PEGEEN: Come on, so.

(*She goes forward with the others, and they drop the double hitch over his head.*)

CHRISTY: What ails you?

SHAWN (*triumphantly, as they pull the rope tight on his arm*): Come on to the peelers, till they stretch you now.

CHRISTY: Me!

MICHAEL: If we took pity on you, the Lord God would, maybe, bring us ruin from the law to-day, so you'd best come easy, for hanging is an easy and a speedy end.

CHRISTY: I'll not stir. (*To Pegeen.*) And what is it you'll say to me, and I after doing it this time in the face of all?

PEGEEN: I'll say, a strange man is a marvel, with his mighty talk; but what's a squabble in your back-yard, and the blow of a loy, have taught me that there's a great gap between a gallous story and a dirty deed. (*To Men.*) Take him on from this, or the lot of us will be likely put on trial for his deed to-day.

CHRISTY (*with horror in his voice*): And it's yourself, will send me off, to have a horny-fingered hangman hitching his bloody slip-knots at the butt of my ear.

MEN (*pulling rope*): Come on, will you?

(*He is pulled down on the floor.*)

CHRISTY (*twisting his legs round the table*): Cut the rope, Pegeen, and I'll quit the lot of you, and live from this out, like the madmen of Keel, eating muck and green weeds, on the faces of the cliffs.

PEGEEN: And leave us to hang, is it, for a saucy liar, the like of you? (*To Men.*) Take him on, out from this.

SHAWN: Pull a twist on his neck, and squeeze him so.

PHILLY: Twist yourself. Sure he cannot hurt you, if you keep your distance from his teeth alone.

SHAWN: I'm afeard of him. (*To Pegeen.*) Lift a lighted sod, will you, and scorch his leg.

PEGEEN (*blowing the fire, with a bellows*): Leave go now, young fellow, or I'll scorch your shins.

CHRISTY: You're blowing for to torture me. (*His voice rising and growing stronger.*) That's your kind, is it? Then let the lot of you be wary, for, if I've to face the gallows, I'll have a gay march down, I tell you, and shed the blood of you before I die.

SHAWN (*in terror*): Keep a good hold, Philly. Be wary, for the love of God. For I'm thinking he would liefest wreak his pains on me.

CHRISTY (*almost gaily*): If I do lay my hands on you, it's the way you'll be at the fall of night, hanging as a scarecrow for the fowls of hell. Ah, you'll have a gallous jaunt I'm saying, coaching out through Limbo° with my father's ghost.

SHAWN (*to Pegeen*): Make haste, will you? Oh, isn't he a holy terror, and isn't it true for Father Reilly, that all drink's a curse that has the lot of you so shaky and uncertain now?

CHRISTY: If I can wring a neck among you, I'll have a royal judgment looking on the trembling jury in the courts of law. And won't there be crying out in Mayo the day I'm stretched upon the rope with ladies in their silks and satins sniveling in their lacy kerchiefs, and they rhyming songs and ballads on the terror of my fate?

Limbo: According to Roman Catholic doctrine, the dwelling of souls who are banned from heaven because they have not been baptized as Christians.

(*He squirms round on the floor and bites Shawn's leg.*)

SHAWN (*shrieking*): My leg's bit on me. He's the like of a mad dog, I'm thinking, the way that I will surely die.

CHRISTY (*delighted with himself*): You will then, the way you can shake out hell's flags of welcome for my coming in two weeks or three, for I'm thinking Satan hasn't many have killed their da in Kerry, and in Mayo too.

(*Old Mahon comes in behind on all fours and looks on unnoticed.*)

MEN (*to Pegeen*): Bring the sod, will you?

PEGEEN (*coming over*): God help him so. (*Burns his leg.*)

CHRISTY (*kicking and screaming*): O, glory be to God!

(*He kicks loose from the table, and they all drag him towards the door.*)

JIMMY (*seeing old Mahon*): Will you look what's come in?

(*They all drop Christy and run left.*)

CHRISTY (*scrambling on his knees face to face with old Mahon*): Are you coming to be killed a third time, or what ails you now?

MAHON: For what is it they have you tied?

CHRISTY: They're taking me to the peelers to have me hanged for slaying you.

MICHAEL (*apologetically*): It is the will of God that all should guard their little cabins from the treachery of law, and what would my daughter be doing if I was ruined or was hanged itself?

MAHON (*grimly, loosening Christy*): It's little I care if you put a bag on her back, and went picking cockles° till the hour of death; but my son and myself will be going our own way, and we'll have great times from this out telling stories of the villainy of Mayo, and the fools is here. (*To Christy, who is freed.*) Come on now.

CHRISTY: Go with you, is it? I will then, like a gallant captain with his heathen slave. Go on now and I'll see you from this day stewing my oatmeal and washing my spuds, for I'm master of all fights from now. (*Pushing Mahon.*) Go on, I'm saying.

MAHON: Is it me?

CHRISTY: Not a word out of you. Go on from this.

MAHON (*walking out and looking back at Christy over his shoulder*): Glory be to God! (*With a broad smile.*) I am crazy again!

(*Goes.*)

CHRISTY: Ten thousand blessings upon all that's here, for you've turned me a likely gaffer in the end of all, the way I'll go romancing through a romping lifetime from this hour to the dawning of the judgment day.

(*He goes out.*)

MICHAEL: By the will of God, we'll have peace now for our drinks. Will you draw the porter, Pegeen?

SHAWN (*going up to her*): It's a miracle Father Reilly can wed us in the end of all, and we'll have none to trouble us when his vicious bite is healed.

PEGEEN (*hitting him a box on the ear*): Quit my sight. (*Putting her shawl over her head and breaking out into wild lamentations.*) Oh my grief, I've lost him surely. I've lost the only Playboy of the Western World.

cockles: Edible mollusks that live in the sea.

COMMENTARY

W. G. Fay (1872–1947) *and*
Catherine Carswell (1879–1946)
PRODUCING THE *PLAYBOY*

1935

W. G. Fay and his brother Frank were responsible for training actors for the famed Abbey Theatre, where Synge's Playboy of the Western World *was first produced in 1907. He explains his misgivings about the original rehearsals and goes on to discuss the nature of the riots that all but darkened the theater. Fay implies that he would have been happy to have Synge make a few "sensible" changes. Synge, however, refused.*

I gave the *Playboy* long and careful rehearsal, doing my best to tone down the bitterness of it, and all the time with a sinking heart. I knew we were in for trouble, but it was my business to get Synge's play produced as nearly to his notions as possible in the circumstances and with the material at my disposal. All through the first act the play went splendidly, and I was beginning to feel hopeful, even cheerful. The second act, too, opened to plenty of laughter. We had not got to the beginning of the "rough stuff." But with the entrance of the Widow Quin the audience began to show signs of restlessness. Obviously they couldn't abide her; and when we came to my line about "all bloody fools," the trouble began in earnest, with hisses and cat-calls and all the other indications that the audience are not in love with you. Now that word "bloody" in the script had given me qualms, but Synge had insisted — and who was I to contradict him? — that in the West it was the casual mild expletive, like "bally," or "beastly," or "bloomin'." Yet how was Dublin to know that? In Dublin, as for that matter all over England and Scotland in those days, it was a "low" word, a pothouse° word. Quite a lot of years later, even, it provided the theatrical sensation of the London season when Bernard Shaw's Eliza Doolittle rapped it out in *Pygmalion*. Nowadays, I understand, it is so much a young lady's expression that no he-man ever dreams of using it. Synge was in advance of his time. There was therefore some excuse for the audience's protest, though it was needlessly violent. Yet the queer thing was that what turned the audience into a veritable mob of howling devils was not this vulgar expletive, but as irreproachable a word as there is in the English dictionary — the decent old-fashioned "shift" for the traditional undergarment of a woman. There is a point in the play where Christy (which in this case was poor me) says, "It's Pegeen I'm seeking only, and what'd I care if you brought me a drift of chosen females, standing in their shifts itself, maybe, from this place to the Eastern World." You may say that the image — a magnificent one, mark you — must have been shocking to so unsophisticated an audience as ours, but it was not the image that shocked them. It was the word, for the row was just as bad when Pegeen Mike herself said to the Widow Quin, "Is it you asking for a penn'orth of starch, with ne'er a shift or a shirt as long as you can remember?"

The last act opened with the house in an uproar, and by the time the curtain fell, the uproar had become a riot. Two or three times I tried to get them to let us finish for the sake of those who wanted to hear the play, but it was no use. They wanted a row and they were going to have one. There were free fights in the stalls. Mr. Hillis, our conductor, got his face damaged, and at one time it seemed as if the stage would be stormed. It was lucky for themselves that the patriots did not venture as far as that, for our call-boy,° who was also boiler attendant and general factotum, had armed himself with a big axe from the boiler room, and swore by all the saints in the calendar that he would chop the head off the first lad who came over the footlights. And knowing him, I haven't a shadow of doubt that he would have chopped.

This was on a Saturday night. Over Sunday the directors had to consider whether they would bow to the storm and withdraw the play, or face it out. Very properly they took the courageous course, and the company, though it was no joke for them, loyally supported their decision to go on playing at all costs. And so on

---

pothouse: A tavern.
call-boy: A boy who tells actors when it is time to go onstage.

the Monday night the curtain was rung up to a well-organized pandemonium, for the patriots had been busy over the weekend also. As it was impossible for any of us to be heard, I arranged with the cast that we should simply walk through the play, not speaking a word aloud, but changing positions and going through all the motions, so to speak. The noise was terrific, but we finished the play. It was not until the Thursday night that, in order to give a fair deal to those who had paid their money to hear, the directors had the police in the theater. We also had taken the precaution to pad the floor with felt, which frustrated the rhythmic stamping that had been the opposition's most effective device. Thus we were able once more to speak the lines, but our reputation as an Irish national institution was ruined. Not content with libeling the saintly Irish people, we had actually called in the tyrant Saxon's myrmidons to silence their righteous indignation! Of course the root of the trouble was that Synge had written a brilliant play about the Irish peasantry without any of the traditional sentiment or illusions that were then so dear to the Irish playgoer. He was accused of making a deliberate attack on the national character, whatever that may be. Even William Boyle was among the angriest of angry, though he had to confess that he had not seen the play but had only read the reports of the hubbub in the newspapers. To mark his loathing of us he withdrew all his plays, which I think was ungrateful, considering all we had done for him. [. . .]

We played *The Playboy* for the full number of advertised performances, matinee included. There was a debate conducted by Mr. Yeats in the theater on the following Monday, when both sides were given an opportunity of stating their views, but it was a rather futile meeting, I think. The incident was a lamentable business from every point of view, as the future proved. If it taught the public that they could not dictate the policy of the theater, that was all. However, you cannot beat the public in the end, as I had warned Synge and the other directors, because they can always boycott you. And that was what happened after *The Playboy*. For weeks on end we had to play to five or ten shillings a night — a full program to half a dozen people scattered all over the house. I used to invite them all into the stalls to sit together. You can play serious plays to a scattered audience, but you cannot play comedy unless somebody laughs, and people do not laugh unless they are sitting together. I lost friends who never forgave me for producing the play and myself taking the leading part, and who could not, or would not understand that it was my job to produce any play that my directors wanted, quite apart from my personal likes or dislikes. All our hard work from the November of the previous year was forgotten — all the previous plays that we had produced to the general delight. Where actors are concerned the public has a very short memory.

One thing that made Synge's plays difficult for a Dublin audience was that he actually knew the people he was writing about, whereas they only thought they did. One could get a fairly accurate and just criticism of a Gaelic play from anyone who spoke the language, for such a person had firsthand knowledge of the peasant. But I don't suppose half a dozen people in Dublin could have told you the difference in idiom and brogue between a man from the glens of Antrim and a man from Waterford, or between a Galway man and a Wicklow one. I myself knew these distinctions in a rough-and-ready way owing to my experience as a stroller and I knew how right Synge was. Time has justified him, for his dialect is now the standard one and is even used by Eugene O'Neill in America. And not only did the Dubliners fail to appreciate Synge's profound knowledge of rural Ireland, but they completely misunderstood the character of the man. He was popularly imagined as an outlandish ogre, actuated by hatred of the human race in general and of the Irish race in particular, and both willing to wound and unafraid to strike. Nothing could have been farther from the truth. Synge would never willingly have hurt anybody. He was one of the gentlest souls that ever breathed, and beloved by everybody who knew him. I never knew him lose his temper even in the most trying circumstances, and he was always full of jokes and good-humor that made even a long night journey on tour — and that is a severe test for anyone — a pleasure instead of the penance that it usually is.

A CULTURAL CASEBOOK

The Abbey Theatre and the Irish Literary Renaissance

The Abbey Theatre in 1946. Walter Macken's best-known play, *Mungo's Mansion,* and Lady Gregory's highly successful *The Workhouse Ward* were playing.

The Irish Literary Renaissance began in the last decade of the nineteenth century in a climate of Irish nationalism. At that time, the conditions that had led to general impoverishment and the great potato famine of the 1840s, when a million Irish died and more emigrated, were essentially intact. Ireland continued to be treated as a colonial outpost by the English, who exploited its agricultural resources and seized most of its desirable estates. The population shrank from eight million to four million between 1845 and 1895, and English rule remained indifferent to the growing demand for significant change. The result was a sense of inferiority experienced by many Irish and reinforced by the creation of the "stage Irishman," a comic buffoon who shuffled, bowed, and scraped subserviently in many English comedies.

The concept of a native Irish theater was conceived close to the turn of the twentieth century as the result of discussions among W. B. Yeats (1865–1939), Lady Isabella Augusta Gregory (1852–1932), George Moore (1852–1933), and Edward Martyn (1859–1923). The Fay brothers, William (1872–1947) and Frank (1871–1931) in *The Fays of the Abbey Theatre,* describe the theater's growth and development from the point of view of actors.

The theater went by several names as it evolved: the Irish Literary Theatre (1899), the Irish National Dramatic Company (1900), the Irish National Theatre Society (1902), and eventually, when Annie Horniman (1860–1937) provided the funds to lease a permanent space, it became the Irish National Theatre Society, Ltd. (Abbey Company) (1905) on Abbey Street. *The Countess Cathleen* by W. B. Yeats and *The Heather Field* by Edward Martyn, the project's first plays, were produced in the Antient Concert Rooms on May 8, 1899. Soon George Moore and other playwrights in Ireland began to contribute plays, and the theater became an important cultural center in Dublin. Joseph Holloway, the architect who helped remodel the original Abbey, and other regulars kept journals recording their playgoing experiences.

Before the Abbey Theatre, plays in Ireland were usually imported from England. Most were popular comedies or standard dramas by Molière or Shakespeare. Many were standard melodramas, such as the works of Dion Boucicault (1820–1890), a Dublin-born playwright who emigrated to America in 1853 and wrote *The Colleen Bawn* (1860), *Arrah-na-Pogue* (1864), and *The Shaughran* (1874) — all plays with an Irish setting popular in England and the United States. These plays, however, were broad entertainments without nationalistic purpose.

The political purpose of the Abbey was certainly sympathetic to nationalist goals. However, neither Yeats nor Lady Gregory was interested in promoting reform through violence. Both thought that the English would eventually grant home rule to Ireland without the need for an armed rebellion. Radical political organizations, such as Sinn Fein (We Ourselves), disagreed and tried to pressure the Abbey to accept their views. It never did, despite the fact that Yeats's one revolutionary play, *Cathleen ni Houlihan,* played at the Abbey Theatre during Easter week in 1916, when the armed uprising that eventually led to the founding of the Irish Free State in 1922 began.

Without question, the first genius of the theater was John Millington Synge, whose works caused disturbances and offended nationalist sensibilities. Instead of portraying the Irish peasant as innocent and glorious, Synge portrayed the peasant as prey to grandiosity, cowardice, and misperception — much like people anywhere. His *Playboy of the Western World* presented Dublin with a countryside full of people ready to make a hero out of a man who claimed to kill his "da." Such a portrait proved unacceptable to those who maintained a romantic image of the Irish peasant in his "lyrical green fields."

When it premiered in 1907, *The Playboy of the Western World* caused riots that ceased only when the police were called to maintain order. But even before that, in 1899, Yeats's *Countess Cathleen* was condemned by the Roman Catholic Church on moral grounds. In the play, set during the potato famine, two devils roam the countryside buying the souls of the poor. The Countess Cathleen redeems their souls by selling hers at a great price, using the funds to feed the people of the west. The controversy arose when clerics declared that no Irish woman would sell her soul. Students at the Jesuit University in Dublin signed a petition condemning the play. Eventually Yeats submitted the play for careful review by two priests who determined that the play should be produced.

The second genius of the Abbey was Sean O'Casey, whose first plays revived the theater in the 1920s after the civil war. His play *The Plough and the Stars* (1926) concerned the Easter uprising of 1916, which O'Casey did not participate in because he had quit the Irish Republican Brotherhood over a personal slight. The uprising did not achieve labor reform, which was one of his major interests. Some ten years later, in a mood of spite, he wrote the play. He presented the incendiary speeches of Patrick Pearse (1879–1916), one of Ireland's martyrs of 1916, in such an uncomplimentary fashion that patriots in the audience halted the performance by rioting. Eventually O'Casey went into exile to the London stage, where he became a world figure in drama like Bernard Shaw, whose *The Shewing-up of Blanco Posnet* appeared in 1909. Shaw (like Oscar Wilde) was Irish but was connected to the English stage and took little part in the workings of the Abbey.

Despite their resistance to specific political pressures, Yeats, Lady Gregory, and others were steadfast in their view that the Abbey Theatre was designed to elevate the status of Irish literature. Early actors who commuted from England by boat were revealed by their accents and mannerisms to be foreigners. The Irish audience detected any false notes whether by playwright or actor. The Fay brothers, who managed the actors early in the theater's development, saw that the new plays would achieve more immediate success with Irish actors. These Irish plays, often about Irish country people, needed an Irish presentation. That goal was achieved relatively early in the theater's development.

Many theaters now thrive in Northern Ireland and the Republic of Ireland, but the Abbey Theatre still functions as an important venue for Irish playwrights. The works of Brian Friel, Thomas Murphy, Conor McPherson, and other current Irish playwrights often are premiered at the Abbey. Martin McDonagh's plays were first produced in Galway, but the Abbey will most likely produce him too. The early work of Lady Gregory and W. B. Yeats created a solid foundation for a theater that is still vigorous and still contributing to world drama.

The texts compiled here reveal the early stages of the Abbey's development, including its stated purpose and criteria for selecting plays for production, as told by Lady Gregory. W. B. Yeats's 1902 one-act *Cathleen ni Houlihan* was one of the most successful plays of the early Abbey. It offers a portrait of Ireland as an old woman with the "walk of a queen" urging young men to leave their families and join the rebellion. Lady Gregory discusses how she collaborated with Yeats on writing *Cathleen,* and two pieces from the *United Irishman* review *Cathleen* and the other play on the night's double-bill — *Deirdre. Deirdre*'s author, George Russell (1867–1935), was a schoolmate of Yeats. Typesetters of his first short story had misprinted his pseudonym, Aeon, as A.E., and he retained the initials as a pen name. *Deirdre* is based on a romantic ancient Irish mythic tale of a woman fated to cause the death of her lover and destruction of the high king of Ireland. It is one of the most often told Irish tales.

In his memoir, W. G. Fay establishes the importance of "the art of acting" in the development of the theater. In an excerpt from his book, Peter Kavanagh describes the early history of the theater. W. B. Yeats relates the struggles of the theater in one of the issues of *Samhain* (an Irish word, pronounced "Sow-in," for the seasonal feast from October 31st to November 1st that marked the beginning of winter and of the Celtic new year — our modern-day celebration of Halloween is derived from it). *Samhain* was an irregularly published journal devoted to clarifying the philosophy and aims of the Abbey Theatre. Finally, the entry from the journal of Joseph Holloway, a faithful theatergoer and the architect who helped remodel the Abbey, records the *Playboy* riots of 1907. It also records Holloway's distaste for the play.

Lady Isabella Augusta Gregory (1852–1932)
OUR STATEMENT *and*   1898
ADVICE TO PLAYWRIGHTS   1913

In a single paragraph, Lady Gregory gives us the statement of purpose of the founders of the Abbey Theatre. Their ambition to show that Ireland "is not the home of buffoonery and of easy sentiment" countered the images presented on stages in England and sometimes in the United States of the "stage Irishman" who was cunning, shuffling, and subordinate. In "Advice to Playwrights," Lady Gregory explains what the Abbey was looking for in a good play. In the process, she also implies what the Abbey was not interested in: propaganda and moralistic dramas.

Our Statement

Our statement — it seems now a little pompous — began: "We propose to have performed in Dublin in the spring of every year certain Celtic and Irish plays, which whatever be their degree of excellence will be written with a high ambition, and so to build up a Celtic and Irish school of dramatic literature. We hope to find in Ireland an uncorrupted and imaginative audience trained to listen by its passion for oratory, and believe that our desire to bring upon the stage the deeper thoughts and emotions of Ireland will ensure for us a tolerant welcome, and that freedom to experiment which is not found in theatres of England, and without which no new movement in art or literature can succeed. We will show that Ireland is not the home of buffoonery and of easy sentiment, as it has been represented, but the home of an ancient idealism. We are confident of the support of all Irish people, who are weary of misrepresentation, in carrying out a work that is outside all the political questions that divide us."

Lady Gregory late in her career as playwright and director of the Abbey Theatre.

Advice to Playwrights   One of our heaviest tasks had been reading the plays sent in. For some years Mr. Yeats and I read every one of these; but now a committee reports on them first and sends back those that are quite impossible with a short printed notice:

> The Reading Committee of the National Theatre Society regret to say that the enclosed play, which you kindly submitted to them, is, for various reasons, not suitable for production by the Abbey Company.

If a play is not good enough to produce, but yet shows some skill in construction or dialogue, we send another printed form written by Mr. Yeats:

ADVICE TO PLAYWRIGHTS WHO ARE SENDING

PLAYS TO THE ABBEY, DUBLIN

The Abbey Theatre is a subsidised theatre with an educational object. It will, therefore, be useless as a rule to send it plays intended as popular entertainments and that alone, or originally written for performance by some popular actor at the popular theatres. A play to be suitable for performance at the Abbey should contain some criticism of life, founded on the experience or personal observation of the writer, or some vision of life, of Irish life by preference, important from its beauty or from some excellence of style; and this intellectual quality is not more necessary to tragedy than to the gayest comedy.

We do not desire propagandist plays, nor plays written mainly to serve some obvious moral purpose; for art seldom concerns itself with those interests or opinions that can be defended by argument, but with realities of emotion and character that become self-evident when made vivid to the imagination.

The dramatist should also banish from his mind the thought that there are some ingredients, the love-making of the popular stage for instance, especially fitted to give dramatic pleasure; for any knot of events, where there is passionate emotion and clash of will, can be made the subject matter of a play, and the less like a play it is at the first sight the better play may come of it in the end. Young writers should remember that they must get all their effects from the logical expression of their subject, and not by the addition of extraneous incidents; and that a work of art can have but one subject. A work of art, though it must have the effect of nature, is art because it is not nature, as Goethe said: and it must possess a unity unlike the accidental profusion of nature.

The Abbey Theatre is continually sent plays which show that their writers have not understood that the attainment of this unity by what is usually a long shaping and re-shaping of the plot, is the principal labour of the dramatist, and not the writing of the dialogue.

Before sending plays of any length, writers would often save themselves some trouble by sending a "Scenario," or scheme of the plot, together with one completely written act and getting the opinion of the Reading Committee as to its suitability before writing the whole play.

I find a note from Mr. Yeats:

> Some writer offers us a play which "unlike those at the Abbey," he says, is so constructed as to admit any topic or a scene laid in any country. It will under the circumstances, he says, "do good to all." I am sending him "Advice to Playwrights."

The advice was not always gratefully received. I wrote to Mr. Yeats:

> Such an absurd letter in the *Cork Sportsman,* suggesting that you make all other dramatists rewrite their plays to hide your own idiosyncrasy!

If a play shows real promise and a mind behind it, we write personally to the author, making criticisms and suggestions. We were accused for a while of smothering the work of young writers in order that we might produce our own, but time has done away with that libel, and we are very proud of the school of drama that has come into being through the creation of our Theatre. We were advised also to put on more popular work, work that would draw an audience for the moment from being topical, or because the author had friends in some league. But we went on giving what we thought good until it became popular. I wrote once, thinking we had yielded over much:

> I am sorry ——'s play has been so coldly received (a play that has since become a favourite one), but I think it is partly our own fault. It would have got a better welcome a year ago. We have been humouring our audience instead of educating it, which is the work we ought to do. It is not only giving so much —— and —— , it is the want of good work pressed on, and I believe the want of verse, which they respect anyhow. . . . I think the pressing on of Synge's two plays the best thing we can do for this season. We have a great backing now in his reputation. In the last battle, when we cried up his genius, we were supposed to do it for our own interest. . . . I only read Gerothwohl's speech after you left, and thought that sentence most excellent about the theatre he was connected with being intended "for art and a thinking Democracy." It is just what we set out to do, and now we are giving in to stupidity in a Democracy. I think the sentence should be used when we can.

One at least of the many gloomy prophecies written to Mr. Yeats at some time of trouble has not come true:

I am giving you the situation as it appears to me. Remember there is —— and —— and —— . An amalgamation of all the dissentients with a Gaelic dramatic society would leave Synge, Lady Gregory, and Boyle with yourself, and none of these have drawing power in Dublin. . . . You who initiated the theatre movement in Ireland, will be out of it.

William Butler Yeats (1865–1939)
CATHLEEN NI HOULIHAN   *1902*

W. B. Yeats, widely known as one of the greatest poets of the twentieth century, spent many years between 1899 and 1939 writing plays. Most of them appeared at the Abbey Theatre, of which he was the director. He sometimes complained in his poetry that he spent too much time and energy in the theater, but the fact is that he produced an extraordinary series of plays, some of which influenced the later work of fellow Irishman, Samuel Beckett.

Yeats's early dramatic work resulted from his sense that an Irish Literary Theatre needed Irish plays. His first play, also the first play produced by the group that would found the Abbey, *The Countess Cathleen* (1899), told the story of an Irish countess who, during the years of the Irish famine (in the 1840s), sold her soul to two devils in order to save the peasants from starvation. At the end of the play, God and the angels intervene, thwarting the devils and saving her soul. This play, the first offering of the Irish Literary Theatre, caused controversy but remained on the

Maud Gonne around the time she starred in *Cathleen ni Houlihan.*

stage despite petitions denouncing it on the grounds that no Irish woman would sell her soul to the devil.

Cathleen ni Houlihan (1902), Yeats's third play, was first performed by the predecessor to the Abbey Theatre, W. G. Fay's Irish National Theatre Society, in St. Teresa's Hall in Dublin. The company that would become known as the Abbey Theatre finally found a home in the fall of 1904. Lady Gregory's collaboration on *Cathleen ni Houlihan* helped Yeats achieve a pleasant and folk-sounding language, unusual in his work.

Yeats wrote the play for a woman with whom he had fallen in love: Maud Gonne (1866–1953), a member of a radical women's group fighting for women's rights as well as for a free and independent Ireland. In many ways Maud Gonne, who played the title role in the first production, embodied the ideals that the fictional Cathleen ni Houlihan represented. William Fay said of her, "Never again will there be such a splendid Kathleen as she; a beautiful tall woman with her great masses of golden hair and her voice that would charm the birds off the bough."

As Lady Gregory tells us, Yeats's play came to him in a dream in which an old woman arrives at the door of a young man about to be married. She appears on the eve of the uprising of 1798, when the French landed in Killala to support the Irish in their struggle against the English. The image of Ireland as an old woman transformed into a beautiful young woman had been part of Irish folklore for centuries, but Yeats's application of the story to this historical uprising was novel.

Cathleen ni Houlihan was extremely popular and generally well received. It played at the Abbey in a revival during Easter week in 1916, when Irish patriots, many of whom were known to Yeats, declared an Irish Republic and fought vainly against the British army for the nation's freedom. Many in the audience viewed it as a revolutionary drama, more revolutionary than Yeats had originally intended, and Yeats feared that his play had sent men to their death. Nonetheless, it remained one of his most popular plays.

CATHLEEN NI HOULIHAN

Persons in the Play

PETER GILLANE
MICHAEL GILLANE, *his son, going to be married*
PATRICK GILLANE, *a lad of twelve, Michael's brother*
BRIDGET GILLANE, *Peter's wife*
DELIA CAHEL, *engaged to Michael*
THE POOR OLD WOMAN
NEIGHBORS

(**Scene:** *Interior of a cottage close to Killala, in 1798. Bridget is standing at a table undoing a parcel. Peter is sitting at one side of the fire, Patrick at the other.*)

PETER: What is that sound I hear?
PATRICK: I don't hear anything. (*He listens.*) I hear it now. It's like cheering. (*He goes to the window and looks out.*) I wonder what they are cheering about. I don't see anybody.
PETER: It might be a hurling.°
PATRICK: There's no hurling today. It must be down in the town the cheering is.

---

hurling: An Irish sport.

BRIDGET: I suppose the boys must be having some sport of their own. Come over here, Peter, and look at Michael's wedding clothes.

PETER (*shifts his chair to table*): Those are grand clothes, indeed.

BRIDGET: You hadn't clothes like that when you married me, and no coat to put on of a Sunday more than any other day.

PETER: That is true, indeed. We never thought a son of our own would be wearing a suit of that sort for his wedding, or have so good a place to bring a wife to.

PATRICK (*who is still at the window*): There's an old woman coming down the road. I don't know is it here she is coming?

BRIDGET: It will be a neighbor coming to hear about Michael's wedding. Can you see who it is?

PATRICK: I think it is a stranger, but she's not coming to the house. She's turned into the gap that goes down where Maurteen and his sons are shearing sheep. (*He turns toward Bridget.*) Do you remember what Winny of the Cross-Roads was saying the other night about the strange woman that goes through the country whatever time there's war or trouble coming?

BRIDGET: Don't be bothering us about Winny's talk, but go and open the door for your brother. I hear him coming up the path.

PETER: I hope he has brought Delia's fortune with him safe, for fear her people might go back on the bargain and I after making it. Trouble enough I had making it.

(*Patrick opens the door and Michael comes in.*)

BRIDGET: What kept you, Michael? We were looking out for you this long time.

MICHAEL: I went round by the priest's house to bid him be ready to marry us tomorrow.

BRIDGET: Did he say anything?

MICHAEL: He said it was a very nice match, and that he was never better pleased to marry any two in his parish than myself and Delia Cahel.

PETER: Have you got the fortune, Michael?

MICHAEL: Here it is.

(*Michael puts bag on table and goes over and leans against chimney-jamb. Bridget, who has been all this time examining the clothes, pulling the seams and trying the lining of the pockets, etc., puts the clothes on the dresser.*)

PETER (*getting up and taking the bag in his hand and turning out the money*): Yes, I made the bargain well for you, Michael. Old John Cahel would sooner have kept a share of this a while longer. "Let me keep the half of it until the first boy is born," says he. "You will not," says I. "Whether there is or is not a boy, the whole hundred pounds must be in Michael's hands before he brings your daughter to the house." The wife spoke to him then, and he gave in at the end.

BRIDGET: You seem well pleased to be handling the money, Peter.

PETER: Indeed, I wish I had had the luck to get a hundred pounds, or twenty pounds itself, with the wife I married.

BRIDGET: Well, if I didn't bring much I didn't get much. What had you the day I married you but a flock of hens and you feeding them, and a few lambs and you driving them to the market at Ballina. (*She is vexed and bangs a jug on the dresser.*) If I brought no fortune I worked it out in my bones, laying down the baby, Michael that is standing there now, on a stook of straw, while I dug the potatoes, and never asking big dresses or anything but to be working.

PETER: That is true, indeed. (*He pats her arm.*)

BRIDGET: Leave me alone now till I ready the house for the woman that is to come into it.

PETER: You are the best woman in Ireland, but money is good, too. (*He begins handling the money again and sits down.*) I never thought to see so much money within my four walls. We can do great things now we have it. We can take the ten acres of land we have the chance of since Jamsie Dempsey died, and stock it. We will go to the fair of Ballina to buy the stock. Did Delia ask any of the money for her own use, Michael?

MICHAEL: She did not, indeed. She did not seem to take much notice of it, or to look at it at all.

BRIDGET: That's no wonder. Why would she look at it when she had yourself to look at, a fine, strong young man? It is proud she must be to get you; a good steady boy that will make use of the money, and not be running through it or spending it on drink like another.

PETER: It's likely Michael himself was not thinking much of the fortune either, but of what sort the girl was to look at.

MICHAEL (*coming over towards the table*): Well, you would like a nice comely girl to be beside you, and to go walking with you. The fortune only lasts for a while, but the woman will be there always.

PATRICK (*turning round from the window*): They are cheering again down in the town. Maybe they are landing horses from Enniscrone. They do be cheering when the horses take the water well.

MICHAEL: There are no horses in it. Where would they be going and no fair at hand? Go down to the town, Patrick, and see what is going on.

PATRICK (*opens the door to go out, but stops for a moment on the threshold*): Will Delia remember, do you think, to bring the greyhound pup she promised me when she would be coming to the house?

MICHAEL: She will surely.

(*Patrick goes out, leaving the door open.*)

PETER: It will be Patrick's turn next to be looking for a fortune, but he won't find it so easy to get it and he with no place of his own.

BRIDGET: I do be thinking sometimes, now things are going so well with us, and the Cahels such a good back to us in the district, and Delia's own uncle a priest, we might be put in the way of making Patrick a priest some day, and he so good at his books.

PETER: Time enough, time enough. You have always your head full of plans, Bridget.

BRIDGET: We will be well able to give him learning, and not to send him tramping the country like a poor scholar that lives on charity.

MICHAEL: They're not done cheering yet. (*He goes over to the door and stands there for a moment, putting up his hand to shade his eyes.*)

BRIDGET: Do you see anything?

MICHAEL: I see an old woman coming up the path.

BRIDGET: Who is it, I wonder? It must be the strange woman Patrick saw a while ago.

MICHAEL: I don't think it's one of the neighbors anyway, but she has her cloak over her face.

BRIDGET: It might be some poor woman heard we were making ready for the wedding and came to look for her share.

PETER: I may as well put the money out of sight. There is no use leaving it out for every stranger to look at.

(*He goes over to a large box in the corner, opens it and puts the bag in and fumbles at the lock.*)

MICHAEL: There she is father!

(*An Old Woman passes the window slowly. She looks at Michael as she passes.*)

I'd sooner a stranger not to come to the house the night before my wedding.

BRIDGET: Open the door, Michael; don't keep the poor woman waiting.

(*The Old Woman comes in. Michael stands aside to make way for her.*)

OLD WOMAN: God save all here!

PETER: God save you kindly!

OLD WOMAN: You have good shelter here.

PETER: You are welcome to whatever shelter we have.

BRIDGET: Sit down there by the fire and welcome.

OLD WOMAN (*warming her hands*): There is a hard wind outside.

(*Michael watches her curiously from the door. Peter comes over to the table.*)

PETER: Have you traveled far to-day?

OLD WOMAN: I have traveled far, very far; there are few have traveled so far as myself, and there's many a one that doesn't make me welcome. There was one that had strong sons I thought were friends of mine, but they were shearing their sheep, and they wouldn't listen to me.

PETER: It's a pity indeed for any person to have no place of their own.

OLD WOMAN: That's true for you indeed, and it's long I'm on the roads since I first went wandering.

BRIDGET: It is a wonder you are not worn out with so much wandering.

OLD WOMAN: Sometimes my feet are tired and my hands are quiet, but there is no quiet in my heart. When the people see me quiet, they think old age has come on me and that all the stir has gone out of me. But when the trouble is on me I must be talking to my friends.

BRIDGET: What was it put you wandering?

OLD WOMAN: Too many strangers in the house.

BRIDGET: Indeed you look as if you'd had your share of trouble.

OLD WOMAN: I have had trouble indeed.

BRIDGET: What was it put the trouble on you?

OLD WOMAN: My land that was taken from me.

PETER: Was it much land they took from you?

OLD WOMAN: My four beautiful green fields.°

PETER (*aside to Bridget*): Do you think could she be the widow Casey that was put out of her holding at Kilglass a while ago?

BRIDGET: She is not. I saw the widow Casey one time at the market in Ballina, a stout fresh woman.

PETER (*to Old Woman*): Did you hear a noise of cheering, and you coming up the hill?

OLD WOMAN: I thought I heard the noise I used to hear when my friends came to visit me. (*She begins singing half to herself.*)

> I will go cry with the woman,
> For yellow-haired Donough is dead,
> With a hempen rope for a neckcloth,
> And a white cloth on his head, —

MICHAEL (*coming from the door*): What is it that you are singing, ma'am?

OLD WOMAN: Singing I am about a man I knew one time, yellow-haired Donough that was hanged in Galway. (*She goes on singing, much louder.*)

> I am come to cry with you, woman,
> My hair is unwound and unbound;
> I remember him ploughing his field,
> Turning up the red side of the ground,
> And building his barn on the hill
> With the good mortared stone;
> O! we'd have pulled down the gallows
> Had it happened in Enniscrone!

MICHAEL: What was it brought him to his death?

OLD WOMAN: He died for love of me: many a man has died for love of me.

PETER (*aside to Bridget*): Her trouble has put her wits astray.

MICHAEL: Is it long since that song was made? Is it long since he got his death?

OLD WOMAN: Not long, not long. But there were others that died for love of me a long time ago.

MICHAEL: Were they neighbors of your own, ma'am?

OLD WOMAN: Come here beside me and I'll tell you about them.

(*Michael sits down beside her at the hearth.*)

There was a red man of the O'Donnells from the north, and a man of the O'Sullivans from the south, and there was one Brian that lost his life at Clontarf by the sea, and there were a great many in the west, some that died hundreds of years ago, and there are some that will die tomorrow.

---

fields: The four provinces of Ireland: Ulster, Munster, Leinster, and Connacht.

MICHAEL: Is it in the west that men will die tomorrow?

OLD WOMAN: Come nearer, nearer to me.

BRIDGET: Is she right, do you think? Or is she a woman from beyond the world?

PETER: She doesn't know well what she's talking about, with the want and the trouble she has gone through.

BRIDGET: The poor thing, we should treat her well.

PETER: Give her a drink of milk and a bit of the oaten cake.

BRIDGET: Maybe we should give her something along with that, to bring her on her way. A few pence or a shilling itself, and we with so much money in the house.

PETER: Indeed I'd not begrudge it to her if we had it to spare, but if we go running through what we have, we'll soon have to break the hundred pounds, and that would be a pity.

BRIDGET: Shame on you, Peter. Give her the shilling and your blessing with it, or our own luck will go from us.

(*Peter goes to the box and takes out a shilling.*)

BRIDGET (*to the Old Woman*): Will you have a drink of milk, ma'am?

OLD WOMAN: It is not food or drink that I want.

PETER (*offering the shilling*): Here is something for you.

OLD WOMAN: This is not what I want. It is not silver I want.

PETER: What is it you would be asking for?

OLD WOMAN: If anyone would give me help he must give me himself, he must give me all.

(*Peter goes over to the table staring at the shilling in his hand in a bewildered way, and stands whispering to Bridget.*)

MICHAEL: Have you no one to care you in your age, ma'am?

OLD WOMAN: I have not. With all the lovers that brought me their love, I never set out the bed for any.

MICHAEL: Are you lonely going the roads, ma'am?

OLD WOMAN: I have my thoughts and I have my hopes.

MICHAEL: What hopes have you to hold to?

OLD WOMAN: The hope of getting my beautiful fields back again; the hope of putting the strangers out of my house.

MICHAEL: What way will you do that, ma'am?

OLD WOMAN: I have good friends that will help me. They are gathering to help me now. I am not afraid. If they are put down to-day they will get the upper hand to-morrow. (*She gets up.*) I must be going to meet my friends. They are coming to help me and I must be there to welcome them. I must call the neighbours together to welcome them.

MICHAEL: I will go with you.

BRIDGET: It is not her friends you have to go and welcome, Michael; it is the girl coming into the house you have to welcome. You have plenty to do, it is food and drink you have to bring to the house. The woman that is coming home is not coming with empty hands; you would not have an empty house before her. (*To the Old Woman.*) Maybe you don't know, ma'am, that my son is going to be married to-morrow.

OLD WOMAN: It is not a man going to his marriage that I look to for help.

PETER (*to Bridget*): Who is she, do you think, at all?

BRIDGET: You did not tell us your name yet, ma'am.

OLD WOMAN: Some call me the Poor Old Woman, and there are some that call me Cathleen, the daughter of Houlihan.

PETER: I think I knew some one of that name, once. Who was it, I wonder? It must have been some one I knew when I was a boy. No, no; I remember, I heard it in a song.

OLD WOMAN (*who is standing in the doorway*): They are wondering that there were songs made for me; there have been many songs made for me. I heard one on the wind this morning. (*Sings.*)

> Do not make a great keening
> When the graves have been dug to-morrow.
> Do not call the white-scarfed riders

Maud Gonne (far right) in the
title role of Yeats's *Cathleen ni
Houlihan*, 1902.

> To the burying that shall be to-morrow.
> Do not spread food to call strangers
> To the wakes that shall be to-morrow;
> Do not give money for prayers
> For the dead that shall die to-morrow . . .
> They will have no need of prayers, they will have no need of prayers.

MICHAEL: I do not know what that song means, but tell me something I can do for you.

PETER: Come over to me, Michael.

MICHAEL: Hush, father, listen to her.

OLD WOMAN: It is a hard service they take that help me. Many that are red-cheeked now will be pale-cheeked; many that have been free to walk the hills and the bogs and the rushes, will be sent to walk hard streets in far countries; many a good plan will be broken; many that have gathered money will not stay to spend it; many a child will be born and there will be no father at its christening to give it a name. They that have red cheeks will have pale cheeks for my sake, and for all that, they will think they are well paid. (*She goes out; her voice is heard outside singing.*)

> They shall be remembered for ever,
> They shall be alive for ever,
> They shall be speaking for ever,
> The people shall hear them for ever.

BRIDGET (*to Peter*): Look at him, Peter; he has the look of a man that has got the touch. (*Raising her voice.*) Look here, Michael, at the wedding clothes. Such grand clothes as these are! You have a right to fit them on now, it would be a pity tomorrow if they did not fit. The boys would be laughing at you. Take them, Michael, and go into the room and fit them on. (*She puts them on his arm.*)

MICHAEL: What wedding are you talking of? What clothes will I be wearing to-morrow?

BRIDGET: These are the clothes you are going to wear when you marry Delia Cahel to-morrow.

MICHAEL: I had forgotten that. (*He looks at the clothes and turns towards the inner room, but stops at the sound of cheering outside.*)

PETER: There is the shouting come to our own door. What is it has happened?

(*Neighbors come crowding in, Patrick and Delia with them.*)

PATRICK: There are ships in the Bay; the French are landing at Killala!

(*Peter takes his pipe from his mouth and his hat off, and stands up. The clothes slip from Michael's arm.*)

DELIA: Michael!

(*He takes no notice.*)

　Michael!

(*He turns towards her.*)

　Why do you look at me like a stranger?

(*She drops his arm. Bridget goes over towards her.*)

PATRICK: The boys are all hurrying down the hillsides to join the French.
DELIA: Michael won't be going to join the French.
BRIDGET (*to Peter*): Tell him not to go, Peter.
PETER: It's no use. He doesn't hear a word we're saying.
BRIDGET: Try and coax him over to the fire.
DELIA: Michael, Michael! You won't leave me! You won't join the French, and we going to be married!

(*She puts her arms about him, he turns towards her as if about to yield.*)

(*Old Woman's voice outside.*)

　　They shall be speaking for ever,
　　The people shall hear them for ever.

(*Michael breaks away from Delia, stands for a second at the door, then rushes out, following the Old Woman's voice. Bridget takes Delia, who is crying silently, into her arms.*)

PETER (*to Patrick, laying a hand on his arm*): Did you see an old woman going down the path?
PATRICK: I did not, but I saw a young girl, and she had the walk of a queen.

Lady Isabella Augusta Gregory (1852–1932)
A COMMENT ON *CATHLEEN NI HOULIHAN*   1913

> *Lady Gregory provides some of the background for Yeats's play,* Cathleen ni Houlihan. *Her role in the construction of the play involved helping Yeats make the "country quality" of the dialogue as natural as possible. He admitted himself that the dialogue challenged him. In this passage, Lady Gregory relates the dream that inspired the play, as Yeats told it to her.*

Later in the year we wrote together *Kathleen ni Houlihan* and to that he wrote an introductory letter addressed to me: "One night I had a dream almost as distinct as a vision, of a cottage where there was well-being and firelight and talk of a marriage, and into the midst of that cottage there came an old woman in a long cloak. She was Ireland herself, that Kathleen ni Houlihan for whom so many songs have been sung and for whose sake so many have gone to their death. I thought if I could write this out as a little play, I could make others see my dream as I had seen it, but

I could not get down from that high window of dramatic verse, and in spite of all you had done for me, I had not the country speech. One has to live among the people, like you, of whom an old man said in my hearing, "She has been a serving maid among us," before one can think the thoughts of the people and speak with their tongue. We turned my dream into the little play, *Kathleen ni Houlihan,* and when we gave it to the little theatre in Dublin and found that working people liked it, you helped me to put my other dramatic fables into speech."

The United Irishman
REVIEWS OF YEATS'S *CATHLEEN NI HOULIHAN* AND A.E.'S *DEIRDRE*
1902

The United Irishman *was a weekly newspaper founded in 1899 by Arthur Griffith (1872–1922), who took a strong interest in the gestation of the Abbey Theatre. His paper was openly separatist and called for an independent Irish nation. He saw* Cathleen ni Houlihan, Deirdre, *and the founders of the Abbey as important elements in his plans for an Irish nation. The first of the following pieces was only one of several designed to stimulate public interest in the plays. The second is a highly complimentary review of the two plays, which were presented together at St. Teresa's Hall.*

Mr. Yeats's New Play

March 29, 1902

Mr. Yeats, who returned to Dublin a few days ago to attend the final rehearsals of his new play, in answer to some questions we submitted to him has kindly sent us the following reply:

"My subject is Ireland and its struggle for independence. The scene is laid in the West of Ireland at the time of the French landing. I have described a household preparing for the wedding of the son of the house. Everyone expects some good thing from the wedding. The bridegroom is thinking of his bride, the father of the fortune which will make them all more prosperous, and the mother of a plan of turning this prosperity to account by making her youngest son a priest, and the youngest son of a greyhound pup the bride promised to give him when she marries. Into this household comes Kathleen Ni Houlihan herself, and the bridegroom leaves his bride, and all the hopes come to nothing. It is the perpetual struggle of the cause of Ireland and every other ideal cause against private hopes and dreams, against all that we mean when we say the world. I have put into the mouth of Kathleen Ni Houlihan verses about those who have died or are about to die for her, and these verses are the key of the rest. She sings of one yellow-haired Donough in stanzas that were suggested to me by some old Gaelic folksong:

I will go cry with the woman,
   For yellow-haired Donough is dead,
With a hempen-rope for a neck-cloth,
   And a white cloth on his head.

> I am come to cry with you woman,
>   My hair is unbound and unwound:
> I remember him ploughing his field,
>   Turning up the red side of the ground.
>
> And building his barn on the hill,
>   With the good-mortared stone;
> Oh, we'd have pulled down the gallows,
>   Had it happened at Enniscrone.

And just before she goes out she sings:

> Do not make a great keening
>   When the graves have been dug to-morrow;
> Do not call the white-scarfed riders
>   To the buryings that shall be to-morrow;
> Do not spread food to call strangers,
>   To the wakes that shall be to-morrow.

And after a few words of dialogue she goes out crying:

> They shall be remembered for ever;
> They shall be alive for ever;
> They shall be speaking for ever,
> The people shall hear them for ever.

I have written the whole play in the English of the West of Ireland, the English of people who think in Irish. My play, *The Land of Heart's Desire,* was, in a sense, the call of the heart, the heart seeking its own dream; this play is the call of country, and I have a plan of following it up with a little play about the call of religion, and printing the three plays together some day."

From the *United Irishman*

April 12, 1902

The Irish National Theatre is a reality — the performances in St. Teresa's Hall last week made it so. Ten years hence people may wonder if there did exist a time when they regarded the production of Irish drama with the same perplexed astonishment as the Pink journalists regard the speaking of plain English. The greatest of our literary men have written us plays: Mr. W. G. Fay has trained Irishmen and Irishwomen to act them, and Inghinidhe na hEireann° has carried the work of successful production out. The critics who live by criticizing what nature denied them the faculty of appreciating, have never attempted constructive work, wisely enough, for the sake of their reputations. Those who saw that the real defect in the Irish Literary Theatre lay in its absolute dependence on the unsympathetic and even impossible British actor, set to work to provide the remedy. Without the aid of Mr. W. G. Fay and his brother the remedy could not have been provided. To these gentlemen's ability, patriotism, and enthusiasm is due the fact that within a little more than a year a company of Irishmen and Irishwomen capable of presenting two great plays like *Deirdre* and *Kathleen Ni Houlihan* has been formed, and the enthusiastic crowds that thronged St. Teresa's Hall on Wednesday, Thursday, and Friday nights last week recognized the great part Inghinidhe na hEireann and

---

Inghinidhe na hEireann: The Daughters of Erin, a nationalist group led by Maud Gonne.

Messrs. Fay have performed in making the Irish National Theatre independent and completely Irish. We have now great Irish plays, written for the Irish people by Irish *litterateurs,* acted by Irish actors, and produced in the Irish capital. So great was the enthusiasm excited that had the hall of St. Teresa's been available for three weeks instead of only the three nights advertised, we believe it would have been crowded with an appreciative audience each evening. Those who were unfortunate enough to be unable to attend on any of the nights or to procure admittance, if they essayed to attend, will be consoled to learn that later on in the year these plays and probably others will be given in Dublin in a larger and more convenient hall than St. Teresa's — for the free use of which the committee of the Total Abstinence Club deserves our thanks.

Something has been attempted and something has been done. We agree with Mr. Yeats that nothing save a victory on the battlefield could so strengthen the National spirit as the creation of an Irish Theatre, and though the battle victory is not yet within our power to achieve, it is within our power to create an Irish Theatre, and we are creating it — a Theatre where the heroic past of Ireland can be made to live again for us and give us inspiration and aspiration, as "A.E." has done in *Deirdre* — a Theatre where the spirit of our country can speak straight to our souls, rouse every noble emotion and rekindle the fires of patriotism, as Mr. Yeats has done in *Kathleen Ni Houlihan,* a Theatre in which, as Mr. Yeats said, all Ireland will walk the stage — the Ireland of the historic period as well as the Ireland of the sagas, where every dream that has stirred the heart of her people will inspire the playwright, where the story of Ireland will be told with sweetness, with dignity, and with simplicity — such a Theatre is worth a great sacrifice to upbuild. But there is little sacrifice needed. We have launched the Irish National Theatre successfully, and through it we shall be able to refresh ourselves, as Mr. Russell put it, at the enchanted spring of our race. Where there is a National Theatre there is always national spirit and movement; where there is none, there is usually subserviency and stagnation.

W. G. Fay *(1872–1947) and*
Catherine Carswell *(1879–1946)*
COMMUNITY DRAMA   *1935*

Willie Fay, one of the best actors in the first years of the Abbey Theatre, attempts to set the record straight in his book The Fays of the Abbey Theatre. *He contends that the theater's beginnings were much less literary than dramatic. From his perspective, acting came first, and the plays came later.*

Before starting upon the history of the Abbey Theatre, from which the whole of the great movement now known as the "little theater" and "community drama" took its origin, there is one point I want to make perfectly clear. I find that most people think of the Abbey Theatre as part and parcel of a national, or rather nationalist movement, that found literary expression in the work of men like W. B. Yeats and "A.E." and was represented in politics by Sinn Fein. They are apt to confuse it with the Irish Literary Theatre, which was dead and buried before the Abbey Theatre had been conceived, much less born. The only connection between the two was the purely personal one that Mr. Yeats was actively associated with both. The

Abbey Theatre's contacts with Sinn Fein were equally slight. We had, it is true, the nominal support of Arthur Griffith, but he was a most uncomfortable ally, and was readier with disparagement (or worse) than praise. He could never forgive us for refusing to subordinate our art to his politics. Another popular error identifies the name of Lady Gregory with the Abbey Theatre in a manner which she, I am sure, would have been the first to disclaim. As an author and director Lady Gregory rendered services of the greatest value, and for technical reasons, as will appear, she was made the nominal patentee; but the real *sage-femme°* of the Abbey Theatre, without whose aid it would have been still-born, was Miss Horniman, an Englishwoman who had no concern with Irish literature or politics but only an intense love of the art of the drama. And here now is my great point that can never be sufficiently emphasized. *The Abbey Theatre was first and foremost a theatrical, not a literary movement.* It was the creation not of men of letters but of actors. It is true that it discovered many dramatists of ability and at least one, J. M. Synge, of genius, who, being men of letters, appeal to other men of letters and so have received their full meed of praise, which nobody grudges them. But the playwrights were, so to speak, a supervening phenomenon. It was the zeal of the players that provided the conditions in which they were able to emerge. From time to time I shall have occasion to indicate some analogies between our work and Ibsen's, but these are only incidental and superficial. Fundamentally there is no analogy. On the contrary, the Irish experiment was the exact opposite of the Norwegian. Ibsen made a theater to suit his plays. We of the Abbey made our theater first and then got plays to suit it, which, I venture to submit, is the natural order — at any rate it is what the Elizabethans did. We were not literary men. Most of us were humble folk who had to live by hard and humdrum toil — almost, I might say

> rude mechanicals
> That work for bread upon Athenian stalls.

What bound us together was enthusiasm for the art of acting. If we had been limited by literary or political considerations we might have done some interesting work but we should have remained parochial. We should never have created, as we did, the "community drama."

sage-femme: Wise woman.

Peter Kavanagh (b. 1916)
THE ABBEY THEATRE   1950

Peter Kavanagh tells the story of the development of the Abbey Theatre by revealing the energies of the people involved. He describes them in terms that make them seem living, breathing characters rather than historical entities. He pays special attention to the contributions of Annie Horniman, who paid the way in the first years and made it possible for Yeats and Lady Gregory to have a theater in which to produce their works.

The Abbey Theatre opened for the first time on Saturday night, December 27, 1904. All seats — five hundred and sixty-two — were filled. Notabilities from the literary and political worlds were present: John Dillon, John Redmond, Stephen Gwynn, W. B. Yeats, A.E., Edward Martyn, Hugh Lane, John Masefield (representing the *Manchester Guardian*), and many others. Neither Lady Gregory nor Miss Horniman was present; Lady Gregory claims to have been ill and Miss Horniman had "urgent" business in England. Immediately before the curtain went up, Yeats consulted the stars; he found them quiet and fairly favorable, he told Lady Gregory. Had he consulted any ordinary Irishman, he might have received a more accurate prognostication.

The Dublin daily newspapers, impressed by the distinguished patrons of the Abbey, reported favorably. Even the *Irish Independent,* which had so violently attacked Synge's *In the Shadow of the Glen* a year before, now praised Yeats. It was otherwise with the weekly newspapers, which were mostly nationalistic. Arthur Griffith's *United Irishman* returned to the attack, pointing out that Synge was as decadent as Petronious and that "the theatre which started so well, can now only alternate a decadent wail with a Calvinistic groan."

One could not expect D. P. Moran, editor of the *Leader,* to be less antagonistic. All along, his dislike of Yeats and his associates had been so violent it blinded his judgment even to the merit of Synge's *Riders to the Sea;* he had described it as "a ghastly production" which "reminded me of a visit to a dissecting room." However, his slightly cynical account of the Abbey Theatre opening is significant, because it represented the attitude of the masses at this time.

As he entered the Abbey, Moran tells us, his first impression, after viewing the aristocratic, Anglo-Irish audience, was that he "had strayed by mistake into a prayer meeting of the foreign element in Ireland." He could not expect anything else, for the theater had been built by an Englishwoman and was owned by her. She did not trust her Anglo-Irish friends enough to hand the theater over to them, and the fact she retained full control made Moran suspicious that it might be one further attempt by the British Foreign Office to poison the Irish mind.

> We fear that Mr. Yeats, shrewd man though he is, will never touch the Irish heart. If the movement as it has been developed by Mr. Yeats, rang true even to the hearts of the consciously "superior" class who are so evident these times on the edges of real Ireland surely some one or more of them would have backed this illustrated chanting movement with their money, and not have left it to a woman of the English to supply the Society with a theatre. . . . We note that the ha'penny *Independent* was "got at" by the melancholy twilight advertising ring on Saturday and a nicely posed head of W. B. was the centrepiece in an illustrated puff of the poor What-is-it to be boomed. . . . We fear that the National Theatre Society is not worth criticism in a widely-read paper. . . . These "National" people who flutter and twitter *outside* the land of the Irish people do not interest the people. On Saturday night, the first night, when the male and female social butterflies who like chatter and feigned excitement, flock to these places, the house was only very partially filled [this was not true]. . . . Some of the audience amused us. When our eyes glanced over the stalls, it warmed our Irish hearts to think that we have given so many of those present at one time or another, a well-deserved correction. The Celtic Christmas was incarnate between the acts. Melancholy Greys chattered to Rhythmic Twilights. For us the play was principally at the other side of the footlights. . . . An amusing feature of this grey and twilight race is that they are so grey that they are quite unconscious that people "have the weight" of them and are laughing at their posings and posturings. They are expert advertisers, however, and are entitled to credit for their excellence in that useful art. . . .

In fairness to Moran, it must be noted that on more than one occasion he suspended his attack, when asked to do so by Yeats, so that the theater might be able to bring in an audience for a certain play.

When Yeats opened the Abbey Theatre, his bottomless contempt for public opinion was again apparent: he included Synge's *In the Shadow of the Glen* in the first program. Synge had written a new play, *The Well of the Saints,* and it had been in rehearsal since the previous June. It was a more controversial play than *In the Shadow of the Glen,* but Yeats played the latter because it was certain to displease, reserving *The Well of the Saints* for the second series of productions. Thanks to the novelty of having a new theater, many people attended during the first week, and a profit of fifty pounds was made.

The Well of the Saints, performed on February 4, lost sixty pounds and emptied the theater. This did not disturb Yeats; he was sure of the genius of Synge. "Irishmen," he told George Moore, "had written well before Synge, but they had written well by casting off Ireland; but Synge was the first man that Ireland had inspired." Moore continued:

> I asked if he were going to find his fortune in Ireland, his literary fortune, for *The Well of the Saints* had very nearly emptied the Abbey Theatre. We were twenty in the stalls: The Yeats family, Sarah Purser, William Bailey, John Eglinton, AE, Longworth, and dear Edward [Martyn], who supported the Abbey Theatre though he was averse from peasant plays. All this sneering at Catholic practices is utterly distasteful to me, he said to me. I can hear the whining voice of the proselytiser through it all. I never will go against my opinions, and when I hear the Sacred Name, I assure you — .

Having expressed his contempt for critics and public, Yeats was content to produce some noncontroversial plays, mostly comedies. *Kincora,* an historical play about Brian Boru written by Lady Gregory, appeared on March 25. It was well liked by the audience, and even the *United Irishman* praised it. On April 25 a first play by William Boyle, *The Building Fund,* also pleased, being partly of the commercial variety. *Land,* a peasant play by Padraic Colum, was performed in June. It was such a simple and innocent kind of play that critics of the Abbey agreed that Yeats and his associates had begun to see the light at last. But they were soon to be disillusioned.

These popular pieces were shown mainly because Yeats had not complete control of the selection of plays. A.E.'s democratic method was still the rule. But Yeats was moving to have this changed. He accomplished this through the cooperation of Miss Horniman.

First he reorganized the company, turning it into a professional group. He argued that to do good work, actors would need to devote their full time to the job. Miss Horniman guaranteed £600 for salaries. Willie Fay was made manager of the theater at a salary of 27 shillings per week, and to other members were given salaries of from 15 shillings to a pound. Only those who were really interested in the theater would accept such negligible wages, and many of the original actors left. In return for her guarantee Miss Horniman asked that the Society assure her of its good faith by becoming a limited liability society, thereby protecting her against any serious financial loss. There was some opposition to this, because it meant appointing three directors who might develop into dictators on policy and play selection. Yeats had foreseen this objection and was prepared for it. He had submitted one of his own plays anonymously to the Society, and the selection committee rejected it. Consequently, when the charge of dictatorship was made, he was able to argue that the dictatorship of the few who are of the highest intelligence is better than the democracy of the many. This rather shocking statement was difficult to reply to: it was answered by the secession of two thirds of the Society. This left only eight members: Yeats, Synge, Lady Gregory, Sara Allgood, Miss Esposito, Udolpho Wright, Frank Fay, and Willie Fay.

William Butler Yeats (1865–1939)
THE DRAMATIC MOVEMENT   *1904*

In Samhain *(1904), the official publication of the theater company, Yeats talks about the company's early struggles and provides insight into some of the daily issues that the founders had to confront. The economy of the theater is naturally impressive, but also notable is the concern Yeats voices over censorship, a problem that the Abbey skirted in part because of a technicality. The English stage was regularly censored, while the Abbey enjoyed relative freedom, which sometimes caused popular eruptions.*

William Butler Yeats in the early years of the Abbey Theatre.

The National Theatre Society has had great difficulties because of the lack of any suitable playhouse. It has been forced to perform in halls without proper lighting for the stage, and almost without dressing-rooms, and with level floors in the auditorium that prevented all but the people in the front row from seeing properly. These halls are expensive too, and the players of poetical drama in an age of musical comedy have light pockets. But now a generous English friend, Miss Horniman, has rearranged and in part rebuilt, at very considerable expense, the old Mechanics' Institute Theatre, now the Abbey Theatre, and given us the use of it without any charge, and I need not say that she has gained our gratitude, as she will gain the gratitude of our audience. The work of decoration and alteration has been done by Irishmen, and everything, with the exception of some few things that are not made here, or not of a good enough quality, has been manufactured in Ireland. The stained glass in the entrance hall is the work of Miss Sarah Purser and her apprentices, the large copper mirror-frames are from the new metal works at Youghal, and the pictures of some of our players are by an Irish artist. These details and some details of form and colour in the building, as a whole, have been arranged by Miss Horniman herself. [. . .]

At a time when drama was more vital than at present, unpaid actors, and actors with very little training, have influenced it deeply. The Mystery Plays and the Miracle Plays got their players at no great distance from the church door, and the classic drama of France had for a forerunner performances of Greek and Latin classics, given by students and people of quality, and even at its height Racine wrote two of his most famous tragedies to be played by young girls at school. This was before acting had got so far away from our natural instincts of expression. When the play is in verse, or in rhythmical prose, it does not gain by the change, and a company of amateurs, if they love literature, and are not self-conscious, and really do desire to do well, can often make a better hand of it than the ordinary professional company.

The greater number of their plays will, in all likelihood, be comedies of Irish country life, and here they need not fear competition, for they will know an Irish countryman as no professional can know him; but whatever they play, they will have one advantage the English amateur has not: there is in their blood a natural capacity for acting, and they have never, like him, become the mimics of well-known actors. The arts have always lost something of their sap when they have been cut off from the people as a whole; and when the theatre is perfectly alive, the audience, as at the Gaelic drama to-day in Gaelic-speaking districts, feels itself to be almost a part of the play. I have never felt that the dignity of art was imperilled when the audience at Dr. Hyde's *An Posadh*° cheered the bag of flour or the ham lent by some local shopkeepers to increase the bridal gifts. It was not merely because of its position in the play that the Greek chorus represented the people, and the old ballad-singers waited at the end of every verse till their audience had taken up the chorus; while Ritual, the most powerful form of drama, differs from the ordinary form, because everyone who hears it is also a player. Our modern theatre, with the seats always growing more expensive, and its dramatic art drifting always from the living impulse of life, and becoming more and more what Rossetti would have called "soulless self-reflections of man's skill," no longer gives pleasure to any imaginative mind. It is easy for us to hate England in this country, and we give that hatred something of nobility if we turn it now and again into hatred of the

An Posadh: The Wedding.

vulgarity of commercial syndicates, of all that commercial finish and pseudo-art she has done so much to cherish. Mr. Standish O'Grady has quoted somebody as saying, "The passions must be held in reverence, they must not, they cannot be excited at will," and the noble using of that old hatred will win for us sympathy and attention from all artists and people of good taste, and from those of England more than anywhere, for there is the need greatest.

Before this part of our work can be begun, it will be necessary to create a household of living art in Dublin, with principles that have become habits, and a public that has learnt to care for a play because it is a play, and not because it is serviceable to some cause. Our patent is not so wide[1] as we had hoped for, for we had hoped to have a patent as little restricted as that of the Gaiety or the Theatre Royal. We were, however, vigorously opposed by these theatres and by the Queen's Theatre, and the Solicitor-General, to meet them half-way, has restricted our patent to plays written by Irishmen or on Irish subjects or to foreign masterpieces, provided these masterpieces are not English. This has been done to make our competition against the existing theatres as unimportant as possible. It does not directly interfere with the work of our society to any serious extent, but it would have indirectly helped our work had such bodies as the Elizabethan Stage Society, which brought *Everyman* to Dublin some years ago, been able to hire the theatre from Miss Horniman, when it is not wanted by us, and to perform there without the limitations imposed by a special licence.

Everything that creates a theatrical audience is an advantage to us, and the small number of seats in our theatre would have kept away that kind of drama, in whatever language, which spoils an audience for good work.

The enquiry itself was not a little surprising, for the legal representatives of the theatres, being the representatives of Musical Comedy, were very anxious for the morals of the town. I had spoken of the Independent Theatre, and a lawyer wanted to know if a play of mine which attacked the institution of marriage had not been performed by it recently. I had spoken of M. Maeterlinck and of his indebtedness to a theatre somewhat similar to our own, and one of our witnesses, who knew no more about it than the questioner, was asked if a play by M. Maeterlinck called *L'Intruse*° had not been so immoral that it was received with a cry of horror in London. I have written no play about marriage, and the Independent Theatre died some twelve years ago, and *L'Intruse* might be played in a nursery with no worse effects than a little depression of spirits. Our opponents, having thus protested against our morals, went home with the fees of Musical Comedy in their pockets.

For all this, we are better off so far as the law is concerned than we would be in England. The theatrical law of Ireland was made by the Irish Parliament, and though the patent system, the usual method of the time, has outlived its use and come to an end everywhere but in Ireland, we must be grateful to that ruling caste of free spirits, that being free themselves they left the theatre in freedom. In England there is a Censor, who forbids you to take a subject from the Bible or from politics, or to picture public characters, or certain moral situations which are the foundation of some of the greatest plays of the world. When I was at the great American Catholic University of Notre-Dame I heard that the students had given a performance of *Oedipus the King*, and *Oedipus the King* is forbidden in London. A

---

[1]Our patent has been widened since. — 1923.
L'Intruse: The Intruder (1890).

censorship created in the eighteenth century by Walpole, because somebody had written against election bribery, has been distorted by a puritanism which is not the less an English invention for being a pretended hatred of vice and a real hatred of intellect. Nothing has ever suffered so many persecutions as the intellect, though it is never persecuted under its own name. It is but according to old usage when a law that cherishes Musical Comedy and permits to every second melodrama the central situation of *The Sign of the Cross*, attempted rape, becomes one of the secondary causes of the separation of the English theatre from life. It does not interfere with anything that makes money, and Musical Comedy, with its hints and innuendoes, and its consistently low view of life, makes a great deal, for money is always respectable; but would a group of artists and students see once again the master-pieces of the world, they would have to hide from the law as if they had been a school of thieves; or were we to take with us to London that beautiful Nativity Play of Dr. Hyde's, which was performed in Sligo Convent a few months ago, that holy vision of the central story of the world, as it is seen through the minds and the traditions of the poor, the constables might upset the cradle. And yet it is precisely these stories of the Bible that have all to themselves — in the imagination of English people, especially of the English poor — the place they share in this country with the stories of Finn and of Oisin and of Patrick.

Joseph Holloway (1861–1944)
JOURNAL ENTRIES ON THE *PLAYBOY* RIOTS   1907

Joseph Holloway, a Dublin architect and lifelong theatergoer, claimed to have seen virtually every interesting play produced in Dublin in his adult lifetime. He was familiar with many actors and producers as well, and Annie Horniman hired him to remodel the Mechanics' Theatre on Abbey Street for use by Yeats and Lady Gregory. His opinions on plays reflect attitudes common among those who loved theater in Dublin. Along with them, he condemned Synge's Playboy of the Western World, *the play that caused the police to arrive "in large numbers."*

Saturday, January 26.   The Abbey was thronged in the evening to witness the first performance of Synge's three-act comedy *The Playboy of the Western World*, which ended in fiasco owing to the coarseness of the dialogue. The audience bore with it for two and a half acts and even laughed with the dramatist at times, but an unusually brutally coarse remark put into the mouth of "Christopher Mahon," the playboy of the title, set the house off into hooting and hissing amid counter applause, and the din was kept up till the curtain closed in.

On coming out, Lady Gregory asked me, "What was the cause of the disturbance?"

And my monosyllabic answer was, "Blackguardism!"

To which she queried, "On which side?"

"The stage!" came from me pat, and then I passed on, and the incident was closed. . . .

"This is not Irish life!" said one of the voices from the pit, and despite the fact that Synge in a note on the program says, "I have used one or two words only that

I have not heard among the country people of Ireland, or spoken in my own nursery before I could read the newspapers," I maintain that his play of *The Playboy* is not a truthful or just picture of the Irish peasants, but simply the outpouring of a morbid, unhealthy mind ever seeking on the dunghill of life for the nastiness that lies concealed there. . . . Synge is the evil genius of the Abbey and Yeats his able lieutenant. Both dabble in the unhealthy. Lady Gregory, though she backs them up when they transgress good taste and cast decency to the winds, keeps clean in her plays, and William Boyle is ever and always wholesome. . . .

W. G. Fay as "Christopher Mahon," the hero, was inimitable in a very disagreeable role. Miss Maire O'Neill as "Margaret Flaherty," the publican's daughter who sets her cap at "Mahon" and gives the cold shoulder to "Shawn Keogh" (F. J. Fay), a sheepish admirer of her (played after the fashion of "Hyacinth Halvey" by Fay) was excellent, and Sara Allgood as "Widow Quin" who had designs on "Mahon" was also good. Two more undesirable specimens of Irish womankind could not be found in this isle I be thinking. A. Power, repulsively got-up, played "Old Mahon" with some effect. Arthur Sinclair as the drunken bar-keeper, and J. M. Kerrigan as "Jimmy Farrell," a small farmer, interpreted the characters . . . carefully. I only pitied the actors and actresses for having to give utterance to such gross sentiments and only wonder they did not refuse to speak some of the lines.

Sunday, January 27.   Met W. G. Fay and Mrs. Fay together with Frank on Pembroke Road while out for a walk, and we chatted about last night's fiasco, and the feeling of the actors during and leading up to the scene. The players had expected the piece's downfall sooner, and W. G. Fay expressed it that "Had I not cut out a lot of the matter, the audience would not have stood an act of it." I praised the acting and said it was a fine audience to play to. It frankly did not like the play and frankly expressed itself on the matter, having patiently listened to it until the fatal phrase came and proved the last straw. Frank excused Synge on the score that he has had no joy in his life, and until he has had some you may expect drab plays from him. . . . The influence of the Elizabethan dramatists was on Synge, and he loved vigorous speech. Frank partly defended him on this score. He told me Lawrence came round after the comedy and was in a terrible state about the piece. Both brothers wondered what would be the result of last night's scene, and I said, "Bad houses next week, but a return when the right stuff would be forthcoming again."

Susan Glaspell

Susan Glaspell (1876–1948) is an important figure in early twentieth-century American drama. Through her influence, serious theater began to thrive in an environment used to musicals, sentimental comedies, and fashionable revivals. She was born in Davenport, Iowa, to Irish immigrant parents and grew up writing. After graduating from Drake University, she took a job as a reporter and by 1901 had become a full-time writer. Her first novel, *The Glory of the Conquered: The Story of a Great Love,* published in 1909, earned her enough to spend a year in Paris. *The Visioning,* which followed in 1911, was set on an army base and presented a less sentimentalized world than did her first book. She published her first collection of stories, *Lifted Masks,* in 1912. Her best novel, *Fidelity,* was published in 1915, after she had returned to the United States.

In 1908 Glaspell first met her future husband, George Cram (Jig) Cook, a traveled intellectual and Harvard graduate who was teaching at Iowa University. After the initial meeting, Cook eventually married someone else, but five years later was divorced. Following Glaspell's return from Europe in 1913, they were reintroduced by mutual friends; they now felt that they had been fated for each other. They settled on Cape Cod and, with Mary Heaton Vorse, founded the Provincetown Players. The theater company became a highly influential platform for a number of important American writers, such as Djuna Barnes, Edna Ferber, and Edna St. Vincent Millay. Eugene O'Neill, a prominent member of the Provincetown Players, played roles in Glaspell's works, including *Trifles* (1916). Her earliest play — first produced in her living room then moved to the Provincetown Playhouse — was *Suppressed Desires* (1915), a spoof on the rage for using Freudian theories to explain everyday life. In a letter to the New York *Times* (February 13, 1920) she said that the play "is having fun with the people who went off their heads about psychoanalysis — went 'bugs'— when this subject reached the first circle in New York to know of it."

Glaspell's one-act plays, including *Close the Book* (1917), *A Woman's Honor* (1918), and *Tickless Time* (1919), were collected in 1920. Her first full-length play, *Bernice* (1919), centered on interpreting the character of a dead woman. Its success led to another full-length play, *The Verge* (1921), about a woman who tries to make a new reality around herself and begins with creating new kinds of plants. Some critics saw the protagonist as an admirable new woman; others saw her as neurotic. *The Inheritors* (1921), also a full-length drama, focuses on the third-generation inheritors of a Midwestern college who clash because one family has liberal views and one has conservative views. Her last play, winner of the Pulitzer Prize, was *Alison's House* (1930), based on the life of Emily Dickinson. The latter part of Glaspell's life was spent writing fiction, concentrating on four novels set in the Midwest about the struggles of women to maintain their ideals and values.

Jig Cook, a writer himself, and a partner in many of Glaspell's ventures, spent the last two years of his life living in Delphi, Greece, in the manner of the peasants living on Mount Parnassus near the temple of Apollo. He died in 1924, and when Glaspell returned to the United States she wrote a memoir of their life together called *The Road to the Temple*. In 1925 she broke with the Provincetown Players, who had moved in directions she did not approve of under the directorship of Eugene O'Neill. O'Neill tried to mollify Glaspell, but she never accepted his use of the theater company she and her husband had cofounded. When she died in 1948, she and O'Neill were essentially unreconciled.

TRIFLES

Trifles (1916) was apparently written as a companion piece for Eugene O'Neill's first produced play, the one-act *Bound East for Cardiff*. The two were put together to make a complete evening presentation. In one sense *Trifles* is a murder mystery, but in another it is a critique of the gender-rigid attitudes of the officials whose responsibility it is to investigate the death of John Wright. Its main character, Minnie Foster Wright, is never presented, only described as a sweet woman who loved to sing when she was young but who married a man who slowly stifled her joy in living.

The setting of the play is a kitchen where the women, Mrs. Peters and Mrs. Hale, remain throughout the action. They examine the condition of the room and by extension, the condition of Minnie Foster Wright. The men, examining the crime scene, the upstairs bedroom, spend much of the time offstage. They feel that they are examining the important evidence; yet when they return with their findings, they are unable to understand what led to the death of John Wright, who to them seems quite a normal farmer.

The women, however, by examining the messy condition of the kitchen, the state of Minnie's preserves, and the quilt she was working on, begin to understand the motive behind Wright's murder. When they get to the dead body of the songbird Minnie had valued, they understand things in a way that the men cannot. The men observe that women are concerned with trifles, things of no importance. But the truth is that the women understand the fate of Minnie Foster Wright and John Wright in a way that would be almost impossible for the men, given their sense of what is significant and what is a trifle.

In many ways the play is a study of gender differences and the way men's expectations and their sense of reality can distort the truth and deform a woman's life. In 1917 Glaspell wrote a short story, using all the same material, called "A Jury of Her Peers," implying that the only peers of Minnie Foster Wright would be women like Mrs. Hale and Mrs. Peters. In 1917, however, women could not vote and in most states could not serve on juries.

Trifles in Performance

The original production included Eugene O'Neill among its cast members and received a positive response, but after Glaspell's death most of her work fell out of fashion. *Trifles* was neglected until the early 1960s, when feminist interest helped revive her plays. Teacher and writer Sylvan Barnet included the play in his drama anthology, helping to bring it to the attention of contemporary viewers. Now produced most often by school and college groups, the play enjoys considerable popularity.

Susan Glaspell (1882–1948)

TRIFLES

1916

Characters

GEORGE HENDERSON, *county attorney*
HENRY PETERS, *sheriff*
LEWIS HALE, *a neighboring farmer*
MRS. PETERS
MRS. HALE

Scene: *The kitchen in the now abandoned farmhouse of John Wright, a gloomy kitchen, and left without having been put in order — the walls covered with a faded wall paper. Down right is a door leading to the parlor. On the right wall above this door is a built-in kitchen cupboard with shelves in the upper portion and drawers below. In the rear wall at right, up two steps is a door opening onto stairs leading to the second floor. In the rear wall at left is a door to the shed and from there to the outside. Between these two doors is an old-fashioned black iron stove. Running along the left wall from the shed door is an old iron sink and sink shelf, in which is set a hand pump. Downstage of the sink is an uncurtained window. Near the window is an old wooden rocker. Center stage is an unpainted wooden kitchen table with straight chairs on either side. There is a small chair down right. Unwashed pans under the sink, a loaf of bread outside the breadbox, a dish towel on the table — other signs of incompleted work. At the rear the shed door opens and the Sheriff comes in followed by the County Attorney and Hale. The Sheriff and Hale are men in middle life, the County Attorney is a young man; all are much bundled up and go at once to the stove. They are followed by the two women — the Sheriff's wife, Mrs. Peters, first: she is a slight wiry woman, a thin nervous face. Mrs. Hale is larger and would ordinarily be called more comfortable looking, but she is disturbed now and looks fearfully about as she enters. The women have come in slowly, and stand close together near the door.*

COUNTY ATTORNEY (*at stove rubbing his hands*): This feels good. Come up to the fire, ladies.

MRS. PETERS (*after taking a step forward*): I'm not — cold.

SHERIFF (*unbuttoning his overcoat and stepping away from the stove to right of table as if to mark the beginning of official business*): Now, Mr. Hale, before we move things about, you explain to Mr. Henderson just what you saw when you came here yesterday morning.

COUNTY ATTORNEY (*crossing down to left of the table*): By the way, has anything been moved? Are things just as you left them yesterday?

SHERIFF (*looking about*): It's just about the same. When it dropped below zero last night I thought I'd better send Frank out this morning to make a fire for us — (*sits right of center table*) no use getting pneumonia with a big case on, but I told him not to touch anything except the stove — and you know Frank.

COUNTY ATTORNEY: Somebody should have been left here yesterday.

SHERIFF: Oh — yesterday. When I had to send Frank to Morris Center for that man who went crazy — I want you to know I had my hands full yesterday. I knew you could get back from Omaha by today and as long as I went over everything here myself ———

COUNTY ATTORNEY: Well, Mr. Hale, tell just what happened when you came here yesterday morning.

HALE (*crossing down to above table*): Harry and I had started to town with a load of potatoes. We came along the road from my place and as I got here I said, "I'm going to see if I can't get John Wright to go in with me on a party telephone." I spoke to Wright about it once before and he put me off, saying folks talked too much anyway, and all he asked was peace and quiet — I guess you know about how much he talked himself; but I thought maybe if I went to the house and talked about it before his wife, though I said to Harry that I didn't know as what his wife wanted made much difference to John ——

COUNTY ATTORNEY: Let's talk about that later, Mr. Hale. I do want to talk about that, but tell now just what happened when you got to the house.

HALE: I didn't hear or see anything; I knocked at the door, and still it was all quiet inside. I knew they must be up, it was past eight o'clock. So I knocked again, and I thought I heard someone say, "Come in." I wasn't sure, I'm not sure yet, but I opened the door — this door (*indicating the door by which the two women are still standing*) and there in that rocker — (*pointing to it*) sat Mrs. Wright. (*They all look at the rocker down left.*)

COUNTY ATTORNEY: What — was she doing?

HALE: She was rockin' back and forth. She had her apron in her hand and was kind of — pleating it.

COUNTY ATTORNEY: And how did she — look?

HALE: Well, she looked queer.

COUNTY ATTORNEY: How do you mean — queer?

HALE: Well, as if she didn't know what she was going to do next. And kind of done up.

COUNTY ATTORNEY (*takes out notebook and pencil and sits left of center table*): How did she seem to feel about your coming?

HALE: Why, I don't think she minded — one way or other. She didn't pay much attention. I said, "How do, Mrs. Wright, it's cold, ain't it?" And she said, "Is it?"— and went on kind of pleating at her apron. Well, I was surprised: she didn't ask me to come up to the stove, or to set down, but just sat there, not even looking at me, so I said, "I want to see John." And then she — laughed. I guess you would call it a laugh. I thought of Harry and the team outside, so I said a little sharp: "Can't I see John?" "No," she says, kind o' dull like. "Ain't he home?" says I. "Yes," says she, "he's home." "Then why can't I see him?" I asked her, out of patience. "'Cause he's dead," says she. "*Dead?*" says I. She just nodded her head, not getting a bit excited, but rockin' back and forth. "Why — where is he?" says I, not knowing what to say. She just pointed upstairs — like that. (*Himself pointing to the room above.*) I started for the stairs, with the idea of going up there. I walked from there to here — then I says, "Why, what did he die of?" "He died of a rope round his neck," says she, and just went on pleatin' at her apron. Well, I went out and called Harry. I thought I might — need help. We went upstairs and there he was lyin'——

COUNTY ATTORNEY: I think I'd rather have you go into that upstairs, where you can point it all out. Just go on now with the rest of the story.

HALE: Well, my first thought was to get that rope off. It looked . . . (*stops: his face twitches*) . . . but Harry, he went up to him, and he said, "No, he's dead all right, and we'd better not touch anything." So we went right back downstairs. She was still sitting that same way. "Has anybody been notified?" I asked. "No," says she, unconcerned. "Who did this, Mrs. Wright?" said Harry. He said it businesslike — and she stopped pleatin' of her apron. "I don't know," she says. "You don't *know?*" says Harry. "No," says she. "Weren't you sleepin' in the bed with him?" says Harry. "Yes," says she, "but I was on the inside." "Somebody slipped a rope round his head and strangled him and you didn't wake up?" says Harry. "I didn't wake up," she said after him. We must 'a' looked as if we didn't see how that could be, for after a minute she said, "I sleep sound." Harry was going to ask her more questions but I said maybe we ought to let her tell her story first to the coroner, or the sheriff, so Harry went fast as he could to Rivers' place, where there's a telephone.

COUNTY ATTORNEY: And what did Mrs. Wright do when she knew that you had gone for the coroner?

HALE: She moved from the rocker to that chair over there (*pointing to a small chair in the down right corner*) and just sat there with her hands held together and looking down. I got a feeling that I ought to make some conversation, so I said I had come in to see if John wanted to put in a telephone, and at that she started to laugh, and then she stopped and looked at me — scared. (*The County Attorney, who has had his notebook out, makes a note.*) I dunno, maybe it wasn't scared. I wouldn't like to say it was. Soon Harry got back, and then Dr. Lloyd came and you, Mr. Peters, and so I guess that's all I know that you don't.

COUNTY ATTORNEY (*rising and looking around*): I guess we'll go upstairs first — and then out to the barn and around there. (*To the Sheriff.*) You're convinced that there was nothing important here — nothing that would point to any motive?

SHERIFF: Nothing here but kitchen things. (*The County Attorney, after again looking around the kitchen, opens the door of a cupboard closet in right wall. He brings a small chair from right — gets on it and looks on a shelf. Pulls his hand away, sticky.*)

COUNTY ATTORNEY: Here's a nice mess. (*The women draw nearer up to center.*)

MRS. PETERS (*to the other woman*): Oh, her fruit; it did freeze. (*To the Lawyer.*) She worried about that when it turned so cold. She said the fire'd go out and her jars would break.

SHERIFF (*rises*): Well, can you beat the woman! Held for murder and worryin' about her preserves.

COUNTY ATTORNEY (*getting down from chair*): I guess before we're through she may have something more serious than preserves to worry about. (*Crosses down right center.*)

HALE: Well, women are used to worrying over trifles. (*The two women move a little closer together.*)

COUNTY ATTORNEY (*with the gallantry of a young politician*): And yet, for all their worries, what would we do without the ladies? (*The women do not unbend. He goes below the center table to the sink, takes a dipperful of water from the pail, and pouring it into a basin, washes his hands. While he is doing this the Sheriff and Hale cross to cupboard, which they inspect. The County Attorney starts to wipe his hands on the roller towel, turns it for a cleaner place.*) Dirty towels! (*Kicks his foot against the pans under the sink.*) Not much of a housekeeper, would you say, ladies?

MRS. HALE (*stiffly*): There's a great deal of work to be done on a farm.

COUNTY ATTORNEY: To be sure. And yet (*with a little bow to her*) I know there are some Dickson County farmhouses which do not have such roller towels. (*He gives it a pull to expose its full-length again.*)

MRS. HALE: Those towels get dirty awful quick. Men's hands aren't always clean as they might be.

COUNTY ATTORNEY: Ah, loyal to your sex, I see. But you and Mrs. Wright were neighbors. I suppose you were friends, too.

MRS. HALE (*shaking her head*): I've not seen much of her of late years. I've not been in this house — it's more than a year.

COUNTY ATTORNEY (*crossing to women up center*): And why was that? You didn't like her?

MRS. HALE: I liked her all well enough. Farmer's wives have their hands full, Mr. Henderson. And then ——

COUNTY ATTORNEY: Yes —— ?

MRS. HALE (*looking about*): It never seemed a very cheerful place.

COUNTY ATTORNEY: No — it's not cheerful. I shouldn't say she had the homemaking instinct.

MRS. HALE: Well, I don't know as Wright had, either.

COUNTY ATTORNEY: You mean that they didn't get on very well?

MRS. HALE: No, I don't mean anything. But I don't think a place'd be any cheerfuller for John Wright's being in it.

COUNTY ATTORNEY: I'd like to talk more of that a little later. I want to get the lay of things upstairs now. (*He goes past the women to up right where the steps lead to a stair door.*)

SHERIFF: I suppose anything Mrs. Peters does'll be all right. She was to take in some clothes for her, you know, and a few little things. We left in such a hurry yesterday.

COUNTY ATTORNEY: Yes, but I would like to see what you take, Mrs. Peters, and keep an eye out for anything that might be of use to us.

MRS. PETERS: Yes, Mr. Henderson. (*The men leave by up right door to stairs. The women listen to the men's steps on the stairs, then look about the kitchen.*)

MRS. HALE (*crossing left to sink*): I'd hate to have men coming into my kitchen, snooping around and criticizing. (*She arranges the pans under sink which the lawyer had shoved out of place.*)

MRS. PETERS: Of course it's no more than their duty. (*Crosses to cupboard up right.*)

MRS. HALE: Duty's all right, but I guess that deputy sheriff that came out to make the fire might have got

a little of this on. (*Gives the roller towel a pull.*) Wish I'd though of that sooner. Seems mean to talk about her for not having things slicked up when she had to come away in such a hurry. (*Crosses right to Mrs. Peters at cupboard.*)

MRS. PETERS (*who has been looking through cupboard, lifts one end of towel that covers a pan*): She had bread set. (*Stands still.*)

MRS. HALE (*eyes fixed on a loaf of bread beside the breadbox, which is on a low shelf of the cupboard*): She was going to put this in there. (*Picks up loaf, abruptly drops it. In a manner of returning to familiar things.*) It's a shame about her fruit. I wonder if it's all gone. (*Gets up on chair and looks.*) I think there's some here that's all right, Mrs. Peters. Yes — here; (*holding it toward the window*) this is cherries, too. (*Looking again.*) I declare I believe that's the only one. (*Gets down, jar in hand. Goes to the sink and wipes it off on the outside.*) She'll feel awful bad after all her hard work in the hot weather. I remember the afternoon I put up my cherries last summer. (*She puts the jar on the big kitchen table, center of the room. With a sigh, is about to sit down in the rocking chair. Before she is seated realizes what chair it is; with a slow look at it, steps back. The chair which she has touched rocks back and forth. Mrs. Peters moves to center table and they both watch the chair rock for a moment or two.*)

MRS. PETERS (*shaking off the mood which the empty rocking chair has evoked. Now in a businesslike manner she speaks*): Well I must get those things from the front room closet. (*She goes to the door at the right but, after looking into the other room, steps back.*) You coming with me, Mrs. Hale? You could help me carry them. (*They go in the other room; reappear, Mrs. Peters carrying a dress, petticoat, and skirt, Mrs. Hale following with a pair of shoes.*) My, it's cold in there. (*She puts the clothes on the big table and hurries to the stove.*)

MRS. HALE (*right of center table examining the skirt*): Wright was close. I think maybe that's why she kept so much to herself. She didn't even belong to the Ladies' Aid. I suppose she felt she couldn't do her part, and then you don't enjoy things when you feel shabby. I heard she used to wear pretty clothes and be lively, when she was Minnie Foster, one of the town girls singing in the choir. But that — oh, that was thirty years ago. This all you want to take in?

MRS. PETERS: She said she wanted an apron. Funny thing to want, for there isn't much to get you dirty in jail, goodness knows. But I suppose just to make her feel more natural. (*Crosses to cupboard.*) She said they was in the top drawer in this cupboard. Yes, here. And then her little shawl that always hung behind the door. (*Opens stair door and looks.*) Yes, here it is. (*Quickly shuts door leading upstairs.*)

MRS. HALE (*abruptly moving toward her*): Mrs. Peters?

MRS. PETERS: Yes, Mrs. Hale? (*At up right door.*)

MRS. HALE: Do you think she did it?

Mrs. Peters (*in a frightened voice*): Oh, I don't know.

Mrs. Hale: Well, I don't think she did. Asking for an apron and her little shawl. Worrying about her fruit.

Mrs. Peters (*starts to speak, glances up, where footsteps are heard in the room above. In a low voice*): Mr. Peters says it looks bad for her. Mr. Henderson is awful sarcastic in a speech and he'll make fun of her sayin' she didn't wake up.

Mrs. Hale: Well, I guess John Wright didn't wake when they was slipping that rope under his neck.

Mrs. Peters (*crossing slowly to table and placing shawl and apron on table with other clothing*): No, it's strange. It must have been done awful crafty and still. They say it was such a — funny way to kill a man, rigging it all up like that.

Mrs. Hale (*crossing to left of Mrs. Peters at table*): That's just what Mr. Hale said. There was a gun in the house. He says that's what he can't understand.

Mrs. Peters: Mr. Henderson said coming out that what was needed for the case was a motive: something to show anger, or — sudden feeling.

Mrs. Hale (*who is standing by the table*): Well, I don't see any signs of anger around here. (*She puts her hand on the dish towel, which lies on the table, stands looking down at table, one-half of which is clean, the other half messy.*) It's wiped to here. (*Makes a move as if to finish work, then turns and looks at loaf of bread outside the breadbox. Drops towel. In that voice of coming back to familiar things.*) Wonder how they are finding things upstairs. (*Crossing below table to down right.*) I hope she had it a little more red-up° up there. You know, it seems kind of *sneaking*. Locking her up in town and then coming out here and trying to get her own house to turn against her!

Mrs. Peters: But, Mrs. Hale, the law is the law.

Mrs. Hale: I s'pose 'tis. (*Unbuttoning her coat.*) Better loosen up your things, Mrs. Peters. You won't feel them when you go out. (*Mrs. Peters takes off her fur tippet, goes to hang it on chair back left of table, stands looking at the work basket on floor near down left window.*)

Mrs. Peters: She was piecing a quilt. (*She brings the large sewing basket to the center table and they look at the bright pieces, Mrs. Hale above the table and Mrs. Peters left of it.*)

Mrs. Hale: It's a log cabin pattern. Pretty, isn't it? I wonder if she was goin' to quilt it or just knot it? (*Footsteps have been heard coming down the stairs. The Sheriff enters followed by Hale and the County Attorney.*)

Sheriff: They wonder if she was going to quilt it or just knot it! (*The men laugh, the women look abashed.*)

County Attorney (*rubbing his hands over the stove*): Frank's fire didn't do much up here, did it? Well, let's go out to the barn and get that cleared up. (*The men go outside by up left door.*)

red-up: (slang) Ready for company.

Mrs. Hale (*resentfully*): I don't know as there's anything so strange, our takin' up our time with little things while we're waiting for them to get the evidence. (*She sits in chair right of table smoothing out a block with decision.*) I don't see as it's anything to laugh about.

Mrs. Peters (*apologetically*): Of course they've got awful important things on their minds. (*Pulls up a chair and joins Mrs. Hale at the left of the table.*)

Mrs. Hale (*examining another block*): Mrs. Peters, look at this one. Here, this is the one she was working on, and look at the sewing! All the rest of it has been so nice and even. And look at this! It's all over the place! Why, it looks as if she didn't know what she was about! (*After she has said this they look at each other, then start to glance back at the door. After an instant Mrs. Hale has pulled at a knot and ripped the sewing.*)

Mrs. Peters: Oh, what are you doing, Mrs. Hale?

Mrs. Hale (*mildly*): Just pulling out a stitch or two that's not sewed very good. (*Threading a needle.*) Bad sewing always made me fidgety.

Mrs. Peters (*with a glance at the door, nervously*): I don't think we ought to touch things.

Mrs. Hale: I'll just finish up this end. (*Suddenly stopping and leaning forward.*) Mrs. Peters?

Mrs. Peters: Yes, Mrs. Hale?

Mrs. Hale: What do you suppose she was so nervous about?

Mrs. Peters: Oh — I don't know. I don't know as she was nervous. I sometimes sew awful queer when I'm just tired. (*Mrs. Hale starts to say something, looks at Mrs. Peters, then goes on sewing.*) Well, I must get these things wrapped up. They may be through sooner than we think. (*Putting apron and other things together.*) I wonder where I can find a piece of paper, and string. (*Rises.*)

Mrs. Hale: In that cupboard, maybe.

Mrs. Peters (*crosses right looking in cupboard*): Why, here's a bird-cage. (*Holds it up.*) Did she have a bird, Mrs. Hale?

Mrs. Hale: Why, I don't know whether she did or not — I've not been here for so long. There was a man around last year selling canaries cheap, but I don't know as she took one; maybe she did. She used to sing real pretty herself.

Mrs. Peters (*glancing around*): Seems funny to think of a bird here. But she must have had one, or why would she have a cage? I wonder what happened to it?

Mrs. Hale: I s'pose maybe the cat got it.

Mrs. Peters: No, she didn't have a cat. She's got that feeling some people have about cats — being afraid of them. My cat got in her room and she was real upset and asked me to take it out.

Mrs. Hale: My sister Bessie was like that. Queer, ain't it?

Mrs. Peters (*examining the cage*): Why, look at this door. It's broke. One hinge is pulled apart. (*Takes a step down to Mrs. Hale's right.*)

MRS. HALE (*looking too*): Looks as if someone must have been rough with it.

MRS. PETERS: Why, yes. (*She brings the cage forward and puts it on the table.*)

MRS. HALE (*glancing toward up left door*): I wish if they're going to find any evidence they'd be about it. I don't like this place.

MRS. PETERS: But I'm awful glad you came with me, Mrs. Hale. It would be lonesome for me sitting here alone.

MRS. HALE: It would, wouldn't it? (*Dropping her sewing.*) But I tell you what I do wish, Mrs. Peters. I wish I had come over sometimes when *she* was here. I — (*looking around the room*) — wish I had.

MRS. PETERS: But of course you were awful busy, Mrs. Hale — your house and your children.

MRS. HALE (*rises and crosses left*): I could've come. I stayed away because it weren't cheerful — and that's why I ought to have come. I — (*looking out left window*) — I've never liked this place. Maybe it's because it's down in a hollow and you don't see the road. I dunno what it is, but it's a lonesome place and always was. I wish I had come over to see Minnie Foster sometimes. I can see now — (*Shakes her head.*)

MRS. PETERS (*left of table and above it*): Well, you mustn't reproach yourself, Mrs. Hale. Somehow we just don't see how it is with other folks until — something turns up.

MRS. HALE: Not having children makes less work — but it makes a quiet house, and Wright out to work all day, and no company when he did come in. (*Turning from window.*) Did you know John Wright, Mrs. Peters?

MRS. PETERS: Not to know him; I've seen him in town. They say he was a good man.

MRS. HALE: Yes — good; he didn't drink, and kept his word as well as most, I guess, and paid his debts. But he was a hard man, Mrs. Peters. Just to pass the time of day with him — (*Shivers.*) Like a raw wind that gets to the bone. (*Pauses, her eye falling on the cage.*) I should think she would 'a' wanted a bird. But what do you suppose went with it?

MRS. PETERS: I don't know, unless it got sick and died. (*She reaches over and swings the broken door, swings it again, both women watch it.*)

MRS. HALE: You weren't raised round here, were you? (*Mrs. Peters shakes her head.*) You didn't know — her?

MRS. PETERS: Not till they brought her yesterday.

MRS. HALE: She — come to think of it, she was kind of like a bird herself — real sweet and pretty, but kind of timid and — fluttery. How — she — did — change. (*Silence: then as if struck by a happy thought and relieved to get back to everyday things. Crosses right above Mrs. Peters to cupboard, replaces small chair used to stand on to its original place down right.*) Tell you what, Mrs. Peters, why don't you take the quilt in with you? It might take up her mind.

MRS. PETERS: Why, I think that's a real nice idea, Mrs.

Hale. There couldn't possibly be any objection to it could there? Now, just what would I take? I wonder if her patches are in here — and her things. (*They look in the sewing basket.*)

MRS. HALE (*crosses to right of table*): Here's some red. I expect this has got sewing things in it. (*Brings out a fancy box.*) What a pretty box. Looks like something somebody would give you. Maybe her scissors are in here. (*Opens box. Suddenly puts her hand to her nose.*) Why —— (*Mrs. Peters bends nearer, then turns her face away.*) There's something wrapped up in this piece of silk.

MRS. PETERS: Why, this isn't her scissors.

MRS. HALE (*lifting the silk*): Oh, Mrs. Peters — it's —— — (*Mrs. Peters bends closer.*)

MRS. PETERS: It's the bird.

MRS. HALE: But, Mrs. Peters — look at it! Its neck! Look at its neck! It's all — other side *to*.

MRS. PETERS: Somebody — wrung — its — neck. (*Their eyes meet. A look of growing comprehension, of horror. Steps are heard outside. Mrs. Hale slips box under quilt pieces, and sinks into her chair. Enter Sheriff and County Attorney. Mrs. Peters steps down left and stands looking out of window.*)

COUNTY ATTORNEY (*as one turning from serious things to little pleasantries*): Well, ladies, have you decided whether she was going to quilt it or knot it? (*Crosses to center above table.*)

MRS. PETERS: We think she was going to — knot it. (*Sheriff crosses to right of stove, lifts stove lid, and glances at fire, then stands warming hands at stove.*)

COUNTY ATTORNEY: Well, that's interesting, I'm sure. (*Seeing the bird-cage.*) Has the bird flown?

MRS. HALE (*putting more quilt pieces over the box*): We think the — cat got it.

COUNTY ATTORNEY (*preoccupied*): Is there a cat? (*Mrs. Hale glances in a quick covert way at Mrs. Peters.*)

MRS. PETERS (*turning from window takes a step in*): Well, not *now*. They're superstitious, you know. They leave.

COUNTY ATTORNEY (*to Sheriff Peters, continuing an interrupted conversation*): No sign at all of anyone having come from the outside. Their own rope. Now let's go up again and go over it piece by piece. (*They start upstairs.*) It would have to have been someone who knew just the —— (*Mrs. Peters sits down left of table. The two women sit there not looking at one another, but as if peering into something and at the same time holding back. When they talk now it is in the manner of feeling their way over strange ground, as if afraid of what they are saying, but as if they cannot help saying it.*)

MRS. HALE (*hesistatively and in hushed voice*): She liked the bird. She was going to bury it in that pretty box.

MRS. PETERS (*in a whisper*): When I was a girl — my kitten — there was a boy took a hatchet, and before my eyes — and before I could get there —— (*Covers her face an instant.*) If they hadn't held me back I would have — (*catches herself, looks upstairs where steps are heard, falters weakly*) — hurt him.

MRS. HALE (*with a slow look around her*): I wonder how it would seem never to have had any children around. (*Pause.*) No, Wright wouldn't like the bird — a thing that sang. She used to sing. He killed that, too.

MRS. PETERS (*moving uneasily*): We don't know who killed the bird.

MRS. HALE: I knew John Wright.

MRS. PETERS: It was an awful thing was done in this house that night, Mrs. Hale. Killing a man while he slept, slipping a rope around his neck that choked the life out of him.

MRS. HALE: His neck. Choked the life out of him. (*Her hand goes out and rests on the bird-cage.*)

MRS. PETERS (*with rising voice*): We don't know who killed him. We don't *know*.

MRS. HALE (*her own feelings not interrupted*): If there'd been years and years of nothing, then a bird to sing to you, it would be awful — still, after the bird was still.

MRS. PETERS (*something within her speaking*): I know what stillness is. When we homesteaded in Dakota, and my first baby died — after he was two years old, and me with no other then ——

MRS. HALE (*moving*): How soon do you suppose they'll be through looking for the evidence?

MRS. PETERS: I know what stillness is. (*Pulling herself back.*) The law has got to punish crimes, Mrs. Hale.

MRS. HALE (*not as if answering that*): I wish you'd seen Minnie Foster when she wore a white dress with blue ribbons and stood up there in the choir and sang. (*A look around the room.*) Oh, I *wish* I'd come over here once in a while! That was a crime! That was a crime! Who's going to punish that?

MRS. PETERS (*looking upstairs*): We mustn't — take on.

MRS. HALE: I might have known she needed help! I know how things can be — for women. I tell you, it's queer, Mrs. Peters. We live close together and we live far apart. We all go through the same things — it's all just a different kind of the same thing. (*Brushes her eyes, noticing the jar of fruit, reaches out for it.*) If I was you I wouldn't tell her her fruit was gone. Tell her it *ain't*. Tell her it's all right. Take this in to prove it to her. She — she may never know whether it was broke or not.

MRS. PETERS (*takes the jar, looks about for something to wrap it in; takes petticoat from the clothes brought from the other room, very nervously begins winding this around the jar. In a false voice*): My, it's a good thing the men couldn't hear us. Wouldn't they just laugh! Getting all stirred up over a little thing like a — dead canary. As if they could have anything to do with — with — wouldn't they *laugh!* (*The men are heard coming downstairs.*)

MRS. HALE (*under her breath*): Maybe they would — maybe they wouldn't.

COUNTY ATTORNEY: No, Peters, it's all perfectly clear except a reason for doing it. But you know juries when it comes to women. If there was some definite thing. (*Crosses slowly to above table. Sheriff crosses down right. Mrs. Hale and Mrs. Peters remain seated at either side of table.*) Something to show — something to make a story about — a thing that would connect up with this strange way of doing it —— (*The women's eyes meet for an instant. Enter Hale from outer door.*)

HALE (*remaining by door*): Well, I've got the team around. Pretty cold out there.

COUNTY ATTORNEY: I'm going to stay awhile by myself. (*To the Sheriff.*) You can send Frank out for me, can't you? I want to go over everything. I'm not satisfied that we can't do better.

SHERIFF: Do you want to see what Mrs. Peters is going to take in? (*The Lawyer picks up the apron, laughs.*)

COUNTY ATTORNEY: Oh, I guess they're not very dangerous things the ladies have picked out. (*Moves a few things about, disturbing the quilt pieces which cover the box. Steps back.*) No, Mrs. Peters doesn't need supervising. For that matter a sheriff's wife is married to the law. Ever think of it that way, Mrs. Peters?

MRS. PETERS: Not — just that way.

SHERIFF (*chuckling*): Married to the law. (*Moves to down right door to the other room.*) I just want you to come in here a minute, George. We ought to take a look at these windows.

COUNTY ATTORNEY (*scoffingly*): Oh, windows!

SHERIFF: We'll be right out, Mr. Hale. (*Hale goes outside. The Sheriff follows the County Attorney into the room. Then Mrs. Hale rises, hands tight together, looking intensely at Mrs. Peters, whose eyes make a slow turn, finally meeting Mrs. Hale's. A moment Mrs. Hale holds her, then her own eyes point the way to where the box is concealed. Suddenly Mrs. Peters throws back quilt pieces and tries to put the box in the bag she is carrying. It is too big. She opens box, starts to take bird out, cannot touch it, goes to pieces, stands there helpless. Sound of a knob turning in the other room. Mrs. Hale snatches the box and puts it in the pocket of her big coat. Enter County Attorney and Sheriff, who remains down right.*)

COUNTY ATTORNEY (*crosses to up left door facetiously*): Well, Henry, at least we found out that she was not going to quilt it. She was going to — what is it you call it, ladies?

MRS. HALE (*standing center below table facing front, her hand against her pocket*): We call it — knot it, Mr. Henderson.

COMMENTARY

Christine Dymkowski (b. 1950)
ON THE EDGE: THE PLAYS OF SUSAN GLASPELL   *1988*

Christine Dymkowski sees Trifles *as a play that occupies the edge — the marginalized space reserved for women. The male figures in the play assume that their interests are central to the murder investigation, whereas Glaspell demonstrates that the most significant issues in the investigation are on the edge of men's attention, where they can never see them.*

The paradoxically central nature of the edge informs Glaspell's theatrical methods and themes. Her first play, *Trifles* (1916), illustrates its use in several ways, the irony of the title already having been noted. The plot revolves around the visit to a farmhouse by County Attorney Henderson and Sheriff Peters to investigate the murder of John Wright; they are accompanied by the farmer who discovered the murder and, almost incidentally, by the farmer's and sheriff's wives. The men's assumption is that Minnie Wright, already in custody for the crime, has killed her husband, and they are there to search the house for clues to a motive. The audience undoubtedly sees them as protagonists at the start of the play.

The stage directions immediately call attention to the women's marginality: the men, "much bundled up" against the freezing cold, "go at once to the stove" in the Wrights' kitchen, while the women who follow them in do so "slowly, and stand close together near the door." The separateness of the female and male worlds is thus immediately established visually and then reinforced by the dialogue:

> MRS. PETERS (*to the other woman*): Oh, her fruit; it did freeze. (*To the Lawyer.*) She worried about that when it turned so cold. . . .
>
> SHERIFF: Well, can you beat the women [*sic*]! Held for murder and worryin' about her preserves.
>
> COUNTY ATTORNEY: I guess before we're through she may have something more serious than preserves to worry about.
>
> HALE: Well, women are used to worrying over trifles.
>
> (*The two women move a little closer together.*)

Not surprisingly, the women are relegated to the kitchen, while the men's attention turns to the rest of the house, particularly the bedroom where the crime was committed: "You're convinced that there was nothing important here — nothing that would point to any motive," Henderson asks Peters, and is assured that there is "Nothing here but kitchen things." However, while the men view the kitchen as marginal to their purpose, the drama stays centered there where the women are: contrary to expectation, it becomes the central focus of the play.

Ironically, it is the kitchen that holds the clues to the desperation and loneliness of Minnie's life and yields the women the answers for which the men search in vain; moreover, the understanding that they do reach goes beyond the mere solving of the crime to a redefinition of what the crime was. Mrs. Hale blames herself for a failure of imagination: "Oh, I *wish* I'd come over here once in a while! That was a crime! That was a crime! Who's going to punish that? . . . I might have known she needed help! I know how things can be — for women. I tell you, it's queer, Mrs. Peters. We live close together and we live far apart. We all go through the same things — it's all just a different kind of the same thing." The empathy both women feel for Minnie leads them to suppress the evidence they have found, patiently enduring the men's condescension instead of competing with them on their own ground. Conventional moral values are overturned, just as the expected form of the murder mystery is ignored: the play differentiates between justice and law and shows that the traditional "solution" is no such thing.

Just as Glaspell sets the play in the seemingly marginal kitchen, she makes the absent Minnie Wright its focus, a tactic she was to use again in *Bernice* and *Alison's House;* although noted by critics, this use of an absent central character has not received much comment. It is yet another way in which Glaspell makes central the apparently marginal — indeed, in stage terms, the nonexistent.

Luigi Pirandello

Luigi Pirandello (1867–1936) was an Italian short-story writer and novelist, a secondary school teacher, and finally a playwright. His life was complicated by business failures that wiped out his personal income and threw his wife into a psychological depression that Pirandello quite bluntly described as madness. Out of his acquaintance with madness — he remained with his wife for fourteen years after she lost touch with reality — Pirandello claimed to have developed much of his attitude toward the shifting surfaces of appearances.

Pirandello's short stories and novels show the consistent pattern of his plays: a deep examination of what we know to be real and a questioning of our confidence in our beliefs. His novel *Shoot* (1915) questions the surfaces of cinema reality, which contemporary Italy had embraced with great enthusiasm. His relentless examination of the paradoxes of experience has given him a reputation for pessimism. He himself said, "I think of life as a very sad piece of buffoonery," and he insisted that people bear within them a deep need to deceive themselves "by creating a reality . . . which . . . is discovered to be vain and illusory."

As Pirandello was not a popular writer in Italy, much of his dramatic work was first performed abroad. But he did win the Nobel Prize for literature in 1934, an indication that his particular brand of modernism was indeed influential. At that time Pirandello was a member of the Fascist Party in Italy, although his participation was limited primarily to his work in the state-supported Art Theater of Rome, which he founded.

Pirandello's influence in modern theater resulted from his experimentation with the concept of realism that dominated drama from the time of Strindberg and Ibsen. The concept of the imaginary "fourth wall" of the stage through which the audience observed the action of characters in their living rooms had become the norm in theater. Pirandello, however, questioned all thought of norms by bringing the very idea of reality under philosophical scrutiny. His questioning helped playwrights around the world expand their approaches to theater in the early part of the twentieth century. Pirandello was one of the first, and one of the best, experimentalists.

Six Characters in Search of an Author

Pirandello's play is part of a trilogy: *Six Characters in Search of an Author* (1921), *Each in His Own Way* (1924), and *Tonight We Improvise* (1930). These plays all examine the impossibility of knowing reality. There is no objective truth to know, Pirandello tells us, and what we think of as reality is totally subjective, something that each of us maintains independently of other people and that none of us can communicate. We are, in other words, apart, sealed into our own limited world.

These ideas were hardly novel. Playwrights had dealt with them before, even during the Elizabethan age, at a time when — because of the Protestant Reformation — the absolute systems of reality promoted by the Roman Catholic Church had crumbled. Pirandello's plays were also produced during a period — the 1920s — when his culture was uncertain, frightened, and still reeling in shock from the destruction of World War I. In this depressed time, Pirandello's audience saw in his work a reflection of their own dispirited, fearful selves.

In a sense, *Six Characters in Search of an Author* is about the relationship between art and life, and especially about the relationship between drama and life. The premise of the play is absurd. In the middle of a rehearsal of a Pirandello play, several characters appear and request that an author be present to cobble them into a play. The stage manager assumes that they are presenting themselves as actors to be in a play, but they explain that they are not actors. They are real characters. This implies a paradox that characters are independent of the actors who play them (we are used to the characters being only on paper). When they demand actors to represent them, we know that one limit of impossibility has been reached.

The characters who appear are, in a sense, types: a father, a mother, a stepdaughter, a son, two silent figures — the boy and the child — and, finally, a milliner, Madame Pace. They share the stage with the actors of the company who are rehearsing the Pirandello play *Mixing It Up*. The six characters have been abandoned by their creator, the author who has absconded, leaving them in search of a substitute. The stepdaughter, late in the play, surmises that their author abandoned them "in a fit of depression, of disgust for the ordinary theater as the public knows it and likes it."

Pirandello uses his characters and their situation to comment on the life of the theater in the 1920s, and he also uses them to begin a series of speculations on the relationship of a public to the actors they see in plays, the characters the actors play, and the authors who create them. To an extent, the relationship between an author and his or her characters always implies a metaphor for the relationship between a creator and all creation. It is tempting to think of Samuel Beckett years later in his *Waiting for Godot* imagining an "author" having abandoned his creations because they failed to satisfy him. The six characters — or creations — who invade the stage in Pirandello's play have a firm sense of themselves and their actions. They bring with them a story — as all characters in plays do — and they invite the manager to participate in their stories, just as characters invite audiences to become one with their narratives.

One of the more amusing scenes depicts the characters' reactions to seeing actors play their parts. Since they are "real" characters, they have the utmost authority in knowing how their parts should be played, and they end up laughing at the inept efforts of the actors in act II. When the manager disputes with them, wondering why they protest so vigorously, they explain that they want to make sure the truth is told. The truth: the concept seems so simple on the surface, but in the situation that Pirandello has conceived, it is loaded with complexities that the stage manager cannot fathom.

By the time the question of truth has been raised, the manager has begun to get a sense of the poignancy of the story that these characters have to tell. He has also begun to see that he must let them continue to tell their story — except that they are not telling it, they are living it. When the climax of their story is reached in the last moments of the play, the line between what is acted and what is lived onstage has become almost completely blurred. When the play ends, it is difficult to know what has truly occurred and what has truly been acted out.

Six Characters in Search of an Author has endured because it still rings true in its examination of the relationship between art and life, illusion and reality. The very word *illusion* is rejected by the characters — as characters they are part of the illusion of reality. They reject the thought that they are literature, asserting, "This is Life, this is passion!"

Six Characters in Search of an Author in Performance

The 1916 Italian production of *Six Characters in Search of an Author* established Pirandello as a dramatist of major importance. The first London production was in the Kingsway Theatre in March 1922. The reviews were positive, and the audiences, although at times puzzled, were responsive to what the *Christian Science Monitor* called "one of the freshest and most original productions seen for a long time." The first production in New York was directed by Brock Pemberton at the Princess Theater in October 1922 with the distinguished American actress Florence Eldridge as the stepdaughter. One newspaper critic said, "Pirandello turns a powerful microscope on the dramatist's mental workshop — the modus operandi of play production — and after having destroyed our illusion, like a prestidigitator who shows us how a trick is done, expects us to believe in him."

Pirandello directed the play in Italian in London in 1925, and despite the audience's general inability to understand the language, the New Oxford Theatre was filled for every night of its run. He brought the company to the United States after the British censor determined that the play was "unsuitable for English audiences" and closed the play in London. It was not officially licensed for performance in England again until 1928.

Revivals of the play have been numerous. Three productions in New York in the 1930s preceded revivals in 1948 and 1955. London saw productions in February 1932 and November 1950. By the 1930s audience confusion had simmered down, and in 1932 one London critic declared, "Repetition cannot dull the brilliance of the play's attack on theatrical shams." Sir Ralph Richardson performed in London's West End in 1963. In 1955, Tyrone Guthrie's Phoenix Theater used a translation and adaptation by Guthrie and Michael Wager. The production was not successful, although critics liked the translation. Robert Brustein received extraordinary praise for his American Repertory Theatre (ART) production in 1985. Instead of having the six characters interrupt a Pirandello play, they interrupt the rehearsal of a Molière play, *Sganarelle,* which has roots in Italian commedia dell'arte, and which had been a highly successful ART production. This self-reference — in Pirandellian fashion — helped to blur the line between the realities on and off the stage. Boston critic Kevin Kelly said of the performance, "Brustein immediately links the paradox in Pirandello's theme about reality in illusion / illusion in reality to . . . the pragmatic fantasy of theater itself."

Luigi Pirandello (1867–1936)

SIX CHARACTERS IN SEARCH OF AN AUTHOR   *1921*
A COMEDY IN THE MAKING

TRANSLATED BY EDWARD STORER

Characters of the Comedy in the Making

THE FATHER
THE MOTHER
THE STEPDAUGHTER
THE SON
THE BOY ⎫
THE CHILD ⎬ *do not speak*
MADAME PACE

Actors of the Company

THE MANAGER
LEADING LADY
LEADING MAN
SECOND LADY LEAD
L'INGÉNUE
JUVENILE LEAD
OTHER ACTORS AND ACTRESSES
PROPERTY MAN
PROMPTER
MACHINIST
MANAGER'S SECRETARY
DOOR-KEEPER
SCENE SHIFTERS

Scene: *Daytime. The stage of a theater.*

(N.B.: *The Comedy is without acts or scenes. The performance is interrupted once, without the curtain being lowered, when the Manager and the chief characters withdraw to arrange a scenario. A second interruption of the action takes place when, by mistake, the stage hands let the curtain down.*)

ACT I

(*The spectators will find the curtain raised and the stage as it usually is during the daytime. It will be half dark, and empty, so that from the beginning the public may have the impression of an impromptu performance.*)

(*Prompter's box and a small table and chair for the Manager.*)

(*Two other small tables and several chairs scattered about as during rehearsals.*)

(*The Actors and Actresses of the company enter from the back of the stage: first one, then another, then two together; nine or ten in all. They are about to rehearse a Pirandello play: Mixing It Up. Some of the company move off toward their dressing rooms. The Prompter, who has the "book" under his arm, is waiting for the Manager in order to begin the rehearsal.*)

(*The Actors and Actresses, some standing, some sitting, chat and smoke. One perhaps reads a paper; another cons his part.*)

(*Finally, the Manager enters and goes to the table prepared for him. His Secretary brings him his mail, through which he glances. The Prompter takes his seat, turns on a light, and opens the "book."*)

THE MANAGER (*throwing a letter down on the table*): I can't see. (*To Property Man.*) Let's have a little light, please!

PROPERTY MAN: Yes, sir, yes, at once. (*A light comes down on to the stage.*)

THE MANAGER (*clapping his hands*): Come along! Come along! Second act of "Mixing It Up." (*Sits down.*)

(*The Actors and Actresses go from the front of the stage to the wings, all except the three who are to begin the rehearsal.*)

THE PROMPTER (*reading the "book"*): "Leo Gala's house. A curious room serving as dining-room and study."

THE MANAGER (*to Property Man*): Fix up the old red room.

PROPERTY MAN (*noting it down*): Red set. All right!

THE PROMPTER (*continuing to read from the "book"*): "Table already laid and writing desk with books and papers. Bookshelves. Exit rear to Leo's bedroom. Exit left to kitchen. Principal exit to right."

THE MANAGER (*energetically*): Well, you understand: The principal exit over there; here, the kitchen. (*Turning to actor who is to play the part of Socrates.*) You make your entrances and exits here. (*To Property Man.*) The baize doors at the rear, and curtains.

PROPERTY MAN (*noting it down*): Right!

PROMPTER (*reading as before*): "When the curtain rises, Leo Gala, dressed in cook's cap and apron, is busy beating an egg in a cup. Philip, also dressed as a cook, is beating another egg. Guidi Venanzi is seated and listening."

LEADING MAN (*to Manager*): Excuse me, but must I absolutely wear a cook's cap?

THE MANAGER (*annoyed*): I imagine so. It says so there anyway. (*Pointing to the "book."*)

LEADING MAN: But it's ridiculous!

THE MANAGER (*jumping up in a rage*): Ridiculous? Ridiculous? Is it my fault if France won't send us any more good comedies, and we are reduced to putting on Pirandello's works, where nobody understands anything, and where the author plays the fool with us all? (*The Actors grin. The Manager goes to Leading Man and shouts.*) Yes sir, you put on the cook's cap and beat eggs. Do you suppose that with all this egg-beating business you are on an ordinary stage? Get that out of your head. You represent the shell of the eggs you are beating! (*Laughter and comments among the Actors.*) Silence! and listen to my explanations, please! (*To Leading Man.*) "The empty form of reason without the fullness of instinct, which is blind."— You stand for reason, your wife is instinct. It's a mixing up of the parts, according to which you

who act your own part become the puppet of yourself. Do you understand?

LEADING MAN: I'm hanged if I do.

THE MANAGER: Neither do I. But let's get on with it. It's sure to be a glorious failure anyway. (*Confidentially.*) But I say, please face three-quarters. Otherwise, what with the abstruseness of the dialogue, and the public that won't be able to hear you, the whole thing will go to hell. Come on! come on!

PROMPTER: Pardon sir, may I get into my box? There's a bit of a draft.

THE MANAGER: Yes, yes, of course!

(*At this point, the Door-Keeper has entered from the stage door and advances toward the Manager's table, taking off his braided cap. During this maneuver, the Six Characters enter, and stop by the door at back of stage, so that when the Door-Keeper is about to announce their coming to the Manager, they are already on the stage. A tenuous light surrounds them, almost as if irradiated by them — the faint breath of their fantastic reality.*)

(*This light will disappear when they come forward toward the actors. They preserve, however, something of the dream lightness in which they seem almost suspended; but this does not detract from the essential reality of their forms and expressions.*)

(*He who is known as the Father is a man of about 50: hair, reddish in color, thin at the temples; he is not bald, however, thick mustaches, falling over his still fresh mouth, which often opens in an empty and uncertain smile. He is fattish, pale; with an especially wide forehead. He has blue, oval-shaped eyes, very clear and piercing. Wears light trousers and a dark jacket. He is alternatively mellifluous and violent in his manner.*)

(*The Mother seems crushed and terrified as if by an intolerable weight of shame and abasement. She is dressed in modest black and wears a thick widow's veil of crepe. When she lifts this, she reveals a waxlike face. She always keeps her eyes downcast.*)

(*The Stepdaughter is dashing, almost impudent, beautiful. She wears mourning too, but with great elegance. She shows contempt for the timid half-frightened manner of the wretched Boy (14 years old, and also dressed in black); on the other hand, she displays a lively tenderness for her little sister, the Child (about four), who is dressed in white, with a black silk sash at the waist.*)

(*The Son (22) is tall, severe in his attitude of contempt for the Father, supercilious and indifferent to the Mother. He looks as if he had come on the stage against his will.*)

DOOR-KEEPER (*cap in hand*): Excuse me, sir . . .

THE MANAGER (*rudely*): Eh? What is it?

DOOR-KEEPER (*timidly*): These people are asking for you, sir.

THE MANAGER (*furious*): I am rehearsing, and you know perfectly well no one's allowed to come in during rehearsals! (*Turning to the Characters.*) Who are you, please? What do you want?

THE FATHER (*coming forward a little, followed by the*

others who seem embarrassed): As a matter of fact . . . we have come here in search of an author . . .

THE MANAGER (*half angry, half amazed*): An author? What author?

THE FATHER: Any author, sir.

THE MANAGER: But there's no author here. We are not rehearsing a new piece.

THE STEPDAUGHTER (*vivaciously*): So much the better, so much the better! We can be your new piece.

AN ACTOR (*coming forward from the others*): Oh, do you hear that?

THE FATHER (*to Stepdaughter*): Yes, but if the author isn't here . . . (*To Manager.*) unless you would be willing . . .

THE MANAGER: You are trying to be funny.

THE FATHER: No, for Heaven's sake, what are you saying? We bring you a drama, sir.

THE STEPDAUGHTER: We may be your fortune.

THE MANAGER: Will you oblige me by going away? We haven't time to waste with mad people.

THE FATHER (*mellifluously*): Oh sir, you know well that life is full of infinite absurdities, which, strangely enough, do not even need to appear plausible, since they are true.

THE MANAGER: What the devil is he talking about?

THE FATHER: I say that to reverse the ordinary process may well be considered a madness: that is, to create credible situations, in order that they may appear true. But permit me to observe that if this be madness, it is the sole *raison d'être*° of your profession, gentlemen. (*The Actors look hurt and perplexed.*)

THE MANAGER (*getting up and looking at him*): So our profession seems to you one worthy of madmen then?

THE FATHER: Well, to make seem true that which isn't true . . . without any need . . . for a joke as it were . . . Isn't that your mission, gentlemen: to give life to fantastic characters on the stage?

THE MANAGER (*interpreting the rising anger of the Company*): But I would beg you to believe, my dear sir, that the profession of the comedian is a noble one. If today, as things go, the playwrights give us stupid comedies to play and puppets to represent instead of men, remember we are proud to have given life to immortal works here on these very boards! (*The Actors, satisfied, applaud their Manager.*)

THE FATHER (*interrupting furiously*): Exactly, perfectly, to living beings more alive than those who breathe and wear clothes: beings less real perhaps, but truer! I agree with you entirely. (*The Actors look at one another in amazement.*)

THE MANAGER: But what do you mean? Before, you said . . .

THE FATHER: No, excuse me, I meant it for you, sir, who were crying out that you had no time to lose with madmen, while no one better than yourself knows that nature uses the instrument of human fantasy in order to pursue her high creative purpose.

raison d'être: French for "reason to exist."

THE MANAGER: Very well, — but where does all this take us?

THE FATHER: Nowhere! It is merely to show you that one is born to life in many forms, in many shapes, as tree, or as stone, as water, as butterfly, or as woman. So one may also be born a character in a play.

THE MANAGER (*with feigned comic dismay*): So you and these other friends of yours have been born characters?

THE FATHER: Exactly, and alive as you see! (*Manager and Actors burst out laughing.*)

THE FATHER (*hurt*): I am sorry you laugh, because we carry in us a drama, as you can guess from this woman here veiled in black.

THE MANAGER (*losing patience at last and almost indignant*): Oh, chuck it! Get away please! Clear out of here! (*To Property Man.*) For Heaven's sake, turn them out!

THE FATHER (*resisting*): No, no, look here, we . . .

THE MANAGER (*roaring*): We come here to work, you know.

LEADING ACTOR: One cannot let oneself be made such a fool of.

THE FATHER (*determined, coming forward*): I marvel at your incredulity, gentlemen. Are you not accustomed to see the characters created by an author spring to life in yourselves and face each other? Just because there is no "book" (*pointing to the Prompter's box*) which contains us, you refuse to believe . . .

THE STEPDAUGHTER (*advances toward Manager, smiling and coquettish*): Believe me, we are really six most interesting characters, sir; sidetracked however.

THE FATHER: Yes, that is the word! (*To Manager all at once.*) In the sense, that is, that the author who created us alive no longer wished, or was no longer able, materially to put us into a work of art. And this was a real crime, sir, because he who has had the luck to be born a character can laugh even at death. He cannot die. The man, the writer, the instrument of the creation will die, but his creation does not die. And to live for ever, it does not need to have extraordinary gifts or to be able to work wonders. Who was Sancho Panza? Who was Don Abbondio?° Yet they live eternally because — live germs as they were — they had the fortune to find a fecundating matrix, a fantasy which could raise and nourish them: make them live for ever!

THE MANAGER: That is quite all right. But what do you want here, all of you?

THE FATHER: We want to live.

THE MANAGER (*ironically*): For Eternity?

THE FATHER: No, sir, only for a moment . . . in you.

AN ACTOR: Just listen to him!

LEADING LADY: They want to live, in us . . . !

JUVENILE LEAD (*pointing to the Stepdaughter*): I've no objection, as far as that one is concerned!

Sancho Panza . . . Don Abbondio: Memorable characters in novels: the squire in Cervantes's *Don Quixote* and the priest in Manzoni's *I Promessi Sposi* (*The Betrothed*), respectively.

THE FATHER: Look here! look here! The comedy has to be made. (*To the Manager.*) But if you and your actors are willing, we can soon concert it among ourselves.

THE MANAGER (*annoyed*): But what do you want to concert? We don't go in for concerts here. Here we play dramas and comedies!

THE FATHER: Exactly! That is just why we have come to you.

THE MANAGER: And where is the "book"?

THE FATHER: It is in us! (*The Actors laugh.*) The drama is in us, and we are the drama. We are impatient to play it. Our inner passion drives us on to this.

THE STEPDAUGHTER (*disdainful, alluring, treacherous full of impudence*): My passion, sir! Ah, if you only knew! My passion for him! (*Points to the Father and makes a pretense of embracing him. Then she breaks out into a loud laugh.*)

THE FATHER (*angrily*): Behave yourself! And please don't laugh in that fashion.

THE STEPDAUGHTER: With your permission, gentlemen, I, who am a two months orphan, will show you how I can dance and sing. (*Sings and then dances Prenez garde à Tchou-Tchin-Tchou.*)

Les chinois sont un peuple malin,
De Shangaî à Pékin,
Ils ont mis des écriteaux partout:
Prenez garde à Tchou-Tchin-Tchou.°

ACTORS AND ACTRESSES: Bravo! Well done! Tip-top!

THE MANAGER: Silence! This isn't a café concert, you know! (*Turning to the Father in consternation.*) Is she mad?

THE FATHER: Mad? No, she's worse than mad.

THE STEPDAUGHTER (*to Manager*): Worse? Worse? Listen! Stage this drama for us at once! Then you will see that at a certain moment I . . . when this little darling here. . . . (*Takes the Child by the hand and leads her to the Manager.*) Isn't she a dear? (*Takes her up and kisses her.*) Darling! Darling! (*Puts her down again and adds feelingly.*) Well, when God suddenly takes this dear little child away from that poor mother there; and this imbecile here (*seizing hold of the Boy roughly and pushing him forward*) does the stupidest things, like the fool he is, you will see me run away. Yes, gentlemen, I shall be off. But the moment hasn't arrived yet. After what has taken place between him and me (*indicates the Father with a horrible wink*) I can't remain any longer in this society, to have to witness the anguish of this mother here for that fool. . . . (*Indicates the Son.*) Look at him! Look at him! See how indifferent, how frigid he is, because he is the legitimate son. He despises me, despises him (*pointing to the Boy*), despises this baby

Prenez . . . Tchou: This French popular song is an adaptation of "Chu-Chin-Chow," an old Broadway show tune. "The Chinese are a sly people; / From Shanghai to Peking, / They've stuck up warning signs: / Beware of Tchou-Tchin-Tchou." (The words are funnier in French because *chou* means "cabbage.")

here; because . . . we are bastards. (*Goes to the Mother and embraces her.*) And he doesn't want to recognize her as his mother — she who is the common mother of us all. He looks down upon her as if she were only the mother of us three bastards. Wretch! (*She says all this very rapidly, excitedly. At the word "bastards" she raises her voice, and almost spits out the final "Wretch!"*)

THE MOTHER (*to the Manager, in anguish*): In the name of these two little children, I beg you. . . . (*She grows faint and is about to fall.*) Oh God!

THE FATHER (*coming forward to support her as do some of the Actors*): Quick, a chair, a chair for this poor widow!

THE ACTORS: Is it true? Has she really fainted?

THE MANAGER: Quick, a chair! Here!

(*One of the Actors brings a chair, the others proffer assistance. The Mother tries to prevent the Father from lifting the veil which covers her face.*)

THE FATHER: Look at her! Look at her!

THE MOTHER: No, no; stop it please!

THE FATHER (*raising her veil*): Let them see you!

THE MOTHER (*rising and covering her face with her hands, in desperation*): I beg you, sir, to prevent this man from carrying out his plan which is loathsome to me.

THE MANAGER (*dumbfounded*): I don't understand at all. What is the situation? (*To the Father.*) Is this lady your wife?

THE FATHER: Yes, gentlemen: my wife!

THE MANAGER: But how can she be a widow if you are alive? (*The Actors find relief for their astonishment in a loud laugh.*)

THE FATHER: Don't laugh! Don't laugh like that, for Heaven's sake. Her drama lies just here in this: she has had a lover, a man who ought to be here.

THE MOTHER (*with a cry*): No! No!

THE STEPDAUGHTER: Fortunately for her, he is dead. Two months ago as I said. We are in mourning, as you see.

THE FATHER: He isn't here, you see, not because he is dead. He isn't here — look at her a moment and you will understand — because her drama isn't a drama of the love of two men for whom she was incapable of feeling anything except possibly a little gratitude — gratitude not for me but for the other. She isn't a woman, she is a mother, and her drama — powerful, sir, I assure you — lies, as a matter of fact, all in these four children she has had by two men.

THE MOTHER: I had them? Have you got the courage to say that I wanted them? (*To the Company.*) It was his doing. It was he who gave me that other man, who forced me to go away with him.

THE STEPDAUGHTER: It isn't true.

THE MOTHER (*startled*): Not true, isn't it?

THE STEPDAUGHTER: No, it isn't true, it just isn't true.

THE MOTHER: And what can you know about it?

THE STEPDAUGHTER: It isn't true. Don't believe it. (*To Manager.*) Do you know why she says so? For that fellow there. (*Indicates the Son.*) She tortures herself, destroys herself on account of the neglect of that son there, and she wants him to believe that if she abandoned him when he was only two years old, it was because he (*indicates the Father*) made her do so.

THE MOTHER (*vigorously*): He forced me to it, and I call God to witness it. (*To the Manager.*) Ask him (*indicates Husband*) if it isn't true. Let him speak. You (*to Daughter*) are not in a position to know anything about it.

THE STEPDAUGHTER: I know you lived in peace and happiness with my father while he lived. Can you deny it?

THE MOTHER: No, I don't deny it. . . .

THE STEPDAUGHTER: He was always full of affection and kindness for you. (*To the Boy, angrily.*) It's true, isn't it? Tell them! Why don't you speak, you little fool?

THE MOTHER: Leave the poor boy alone. Why do you want to make me appear ungrateful, daughter? I don't want to offend your father. I have answered him that I didn't abandon my house and my son through any fault of mine, nor from any wilful passion.

THE FATHER: It is true. It was my doing.

LEADING MAN (*to the Company*): What a spectacle!

LEADING LADY: We are the audience this time.

JUVENILE LEAD: For once, in a way.

THE MANAGER (*beginning to get really interested*): Let's hear them out. Listen!

THE SON: Oh yes, you're going to hear a fine bit now. He will talk to you of the Demon of Experiment.

THE FATHER: You are a cynical imbecile. I've told you so already a hundred times. (*To the Manager.*) He tries to make fun of me on account of this expression which I have found to excuse myself with.

THE SON (*with disgust*): Yes, phrases! phrases!

THE FATHER: Phrases! Isn't everyone consoled when faced with a trouble or fact he doesn't understand, by a word, some simple word, which tells us nothing and yet calms us?

THE STEPDAUGHTER: Even in the case of remorse. In fact, especially then.

THE FATHER: Remorse? No, that isn't true. I've done more than use words to quiet the remorse in me.

THE STEPDAUGHTER: Yes, there was a bit of money too. Yes, yes, a bit of money. There were the hundred lire he was about to offer me in payment, gentlemen. . . . (*Sensation of horror among the Actors.*)

THE SON (*to the Stepdaughter*): This is vile.

THE STEPDAUGHTER: Vile? There they were in a pale blue envelope on a little mahogany table in the back of Madame Pace's shop. You know Madame Pace — one of those ladies who attract poor girls of good family into their ateliers, under the pretext of their selling *robes et manteaux.*°

THE SON: And he thinks he has bought the right to tyrannize over us all with those hundred lire he was going to pay; but which, fortunately — note this, gentlemen — he had no chance of paying.

---

robes et manteaux: French for "dresses and capes."

THE STEPDAUGHTER: It was a near thing, though, you know! (*Laughs ironically.*)

THE MOTHER (*protesting*): Shame, my daughter, shame!

THE STEPDAUGHTER: Shame indeed! This is my revenge! I am dying to live that scene . . . The room . . . I see it . . . Here is the window with the mantles exposed, there the divan, the looking-glass, a screen, there in front of the window the little mahogany table with the blue envelope containing one hundred lire. I see it. I see it. I could take hold of it. . . . But you, gentlemen, you ought to turn your backs now: I am almost nude, you know. But I don't blush: I leave that to him. (*Indicating Father.*)

THE MANAGER: I don't understand this at all.

THE FATHER: Naturally enough. I would ask you, sir, to exercise your authority a little here, and let me speak before you believe all she is trying to blame me with. Let me explain.

THE STEPDAUGHTER: Ah yes, explain it in your own way.

THE FATHER: But don't you see that the whole trouble lies here? In words, words. Each one of us has within him a whole world of things, each man of us his own special world. And how can we ever come to an understanding if I put in the words I utter the sense and value of things as I see them; while you who listen to me must inevitably translate them according to the conception of things each one of you has within himself. We think we understand each other, but we never really do. Look here! This woman (*indicating the Mother*) takes all my pity for her as a specially ferocious form of cruelty.

THE MOTHER: But you drove me away.

THE FATHER: Do you hear her? I drove her away! She believes I really sent her away.

THE MOTHER: You know how to talk, and I don't but, believe me, sir (*to Manager*), after he had married me . . . who knows why? . . . I was a poor insignificant woman. . . .

THE FATHER: But, good Heavens! it was just for your humility that I married you. I loved this simplicity in you. (*He stops when he sees she makes signs to contradict him, opens his arms wide in sign of desperation, seeing how hopeless it is to make himself understood.*) You see she denies it. Her mental deafness, believe me, is phenomenal, the limit: (*touches his forehead*) deaf, deaf, mentally deaf! She has plenty of feeling. Oh yes, a good heart for the children; but the brain — deaf, to the point of desperation — !

THE STEPDAUGHTER: Yes, but ask him how his intelligence has helped us.

THE FATHER: If we could see all the evil that may spring from good, what should we do? (*At this point the Leading Lady, who is biting her lips with rage at seeing the Leading Man flirting with the Stepdaughter, comes forward and speaks to the Manager.*)

LEADING LADY: Excuse me, but are we going to rehearse today?

MANAGER: Of course, of course; but let's hear them out.

JUVENILE LEAD: This is something quite new.

L'INGÉNUE: Most interesting!

LEADING LADY: Yes, for the people who like that kind of thing. (*Casts a glance at Leading Man.*)

THE MANAGER (*to Father*): You must please explain yourself quite clearly. (*Sits down.*)

THE FATHER: Very well then: listen! I had in my service a poor man, a clerk, a secretary of mine, full of devotion, who became friends with her. (*Indicating the Mother.*) They understood one another, were kindred souls in fact, without, however, the least suspicion of any evil existing. They were incapable even of thinking of it.

THE STEPDAUGHTER: So he thought of it — for them!

THE FATHER: That's not true. I meant to do good to them — and to myself, I confess, at the same time. Things had come to the point that I could not say a word to either of them without their making a mute appeal, one to the other, with their eyes. I could see them silently asking each other how I was to be kept in countenance, how I was to be kept quiet. And this, believe me, was just about enough of itself to keep me in a constant rage, to exasperate me beyond measure.

THE MANAGER: And why didn't you send him away then — this secretary of yours?

THE FATHER: Precisely what I did, sir. And then I had to watch this poor woman drifting forlornly about the house like an animal without a master, like an animal one has taken in out of pity.

THE MOTHER: Ah yes. . . !

THE FATHER (*suddenly turning to the Mother*): It's true about the son anyway, isn't it?

THE MOTHER: He took my son away from me first of all.

THE FATHER: But not from cruelty. I did it so that he should grow up healthy and strong by living in the country.

THE STEPDAUGHTER (*pointing to him ironically*): As one can see.

THE FATHER (*quickly*): Is it my fault if he has grown up like this? I sent him to a wet nurse in the country, a peasant, as *she* did not seem to me strong enough, though she is of humble origin. That was, anyway, the reason I married her. Unpleasant all this may be, but how can it be helped? My mistake possibly, but there we are! All my life I have had these confounded aspirations towards a certain moral sanity. (*At this point the Stepdaughter bursts into a noisy laugh.*) Oh, stop it! Stop it! I can't stand it.

THE MANAGER: Yes, please stop it, for Heaven's sake.

THE STEPDAUGHTER: But imagine moral sanity from him, if you please — the client of certain ateliers like that of Madame Pace!

THE FATHER: Fool! That is the proof that I am a man! This seeming contradiction, gentlemen, is the strongest proof that I stand here a live man before you. Why, it is just for this very incongruity in my nature that I have had to suffer what I have. I could not live by the side of that woman (*indicating the Mother*) any longer; but not so much for the boredom she inspired me with as for the pity I felt for her.

THE MOTHER: And so he turned me out — .

THE FATHER: — well provided for! Yes, I sent her to that man, gentlemen . . . to let her go free of me.

THE MOTHER: And to free himself.

THE FATHER: Yes, I admit it. It was also a liberation for me. But great evil has come of it. I meant well when I did it, and I did it more for her sake than mine. I swear it. (*Crosses his arms on his chest; then turns suddenly to the Mother.*) Did I ever lose sight of you until that other man carried you off to another town, like the angry fool he was? And on account of my pure interest in you . . . my pure interest, I repeat, that had no base motive in it . . . I watched with the tenderest concern the new family that grew up around her. She can bear witness to this. (*Points to the Stepdaughter.*)

THE STEPDAUGHTER: Oh yes, that's true enough. When I was a kiddie so so high, you know, with plaits over my shoulders and knickers longer than my skirts, I used to see him waiting outside the school for me to come out. He came to see how I was growing up.

THE FATHER: This is infamous, shameful!

THE STEPDAUGHTER: No. Why?

THE FATHER: Infamous! infamous! (*Then excitedly to Manager, explaining.*) After she (*indicating the Mother*) went away, my house seemed suddenly empty. She was my incubus, but she filled my house. I was like a dazed fly alone in the empty rooms. This boy here (*indicating the Son*) was educated away from home, and when he came back, he seemed to me to be no more mine. With no mother to stand between him and me, he grew up entirely for himself, on his own, apart, with no tie of intellect or affection binding him to me. And then — strange but true — I was driven, by curiosity at first and then by some tender sentiment, towards her family, which had come into being through my will. The thought of her began gradually to fill up the emptiness I felt all around me. I wanted to know if she were happy in living out the simple daily duties of life. I wanted to think of her as fortunate and happy because far away from the complicated torments of my spirit. And so, to have proof of this, I used to watch that child coming out of school.

THE STEPDAUGHTER: Yes, yes. True. He used to follow me in the street and smiled at me, waved his hand, like this. I would look at him with interest, wondering who he might be. I told my mother, who guessed at once. (*The Mother agrees with a nod.*) Then she didn't want to send me to school for some days; and when I finally went back, there he was again — looking so ridiculous — with a paper parcel in his hands. He came close to me, caressed me, and drew out a fine straw hat from the parcel, with a bouquet of flowers — all for me!

THE MANAGER: A bit discursive this, you know!

THE SON (*contemptuously*): Literature! Literature!

Scene from the 1984 American Repertory Theatre production of *Six Characters in Search of an Author,* directed by Robert Brustein.

THE FATHER: Literature indeed! This is life, this is passion!

THE MANAGER: It may be, but it won't act.

THE FATHER: I agree. This is only the part leading up. I don't suggest this should be staged. She (*pointing to the Stepdaughter*), as you see, is no longer the flapper with plaits down her back —

THE STEPDAUGHTER: — and knickers showing below the skirt!

THE FATHER: The drama is coming now, sir; something new, complex, most interesting.

THE STEPDAUGHTER: As soon as my father died . . .

THE FATHER: — there was absolute misery for them. They came back here, unknown to me. Through her stupidity! (*Pointing to the Mother.*) It is true she can barely write her own name; but she could anyhow have got her daughter to write to me that they were in need . . .

THE MOTHER: And how was I to divine all this sentiment in him?

THE FATHER: That is exactly your mistake, never to have guessed any of my sentiments.

THE MOTHER: After so many years apart, and all that had happened . . .

THE FATHER: Was it my fault if that fellow carried you away? It happened quite suddenly, for after he had obtained some job or other, I could find no trace of them; and so, not unnaturally, my interest in them dwindled. But the drama culminated unforeseen and violent on their return, when I was impelled by my miserable flesh that still lives. . . . Ah! what misery, what wretchedness is that of the man who is alone and disdains debasing *liaisons!* Not old enough to do without women, and not young enough to go and look for one without shame. Misery? It's worse than misery; it's a horror; for no woman can any longer give him love; and when a man feels this. . . . One ought to do without, you say? Yes, yes, I know. Each of us when he appears before his fellows is clothed in a certain dignity. But every man knows what unconfessable things pass within the secrecy of his own heart. One gives way to the temptation, only to rise from it again, afterwards, with a great eagerness to reestablish one's dignity, as if it were a tombstone to place on the grave of one's shame, and a monument to hide and sign the memory of our weaknesses. Everybody's in the same case. Some folks haven't the courage to say certain things, that's all!

THE STEPDAUGHTER: All appear to have the courage to do them though.

THE FATHER: Yes, but in secret. Therefore, you want more courage to say these things. Let a man but speak these things out, and folks at once label him a cynic. But it isn't true. He is like all the others, better indeed, because he isn't afraid to reveal with the light of the intelligence the red shame of human bestiality on which most men close their eyes so as not to see it.

Woman — for example, look at her case! She turns tantalizing inviting glances on you. You seize her. No sooner does she feel herself in your grasp than she closes her eyes. It is the sign of her mission, the sign by which she says to man: "Blind yourself, for I am blind."

THE STEPDAUGHTER: Sometimes she can close them no

more: when she no longer feels the need of hiding her shame to herself, but dry-eyed and dispassionately, sees only that of the man who has blinded himself without love. Oh, all these intellectual complications make me sick, disgust me — all this philosophy that uncovers the beast in man, and then seeks to save him, excuse him . . . I can't stand it, sir. When a man seeks to "simplify" life bestially, throwing aside every relic of humanity, every chaste aspiration, every pure feeling, all sense of ideality, duty, modesty, shame . . . then nothing is more revolting and nauseous than a certain kind of remorse — crocodiles' tears, that's what it is.

THE MANAGER: Let's come to the point. This is only discussion.

THE FATHER: Very good, sir! But a fact is like a sack which won't stand up when it's empty. In order that it may stand up, one has to put into it the reason and sentiment which have caused it to exist. I couldn't possibly know that after the death of that man, they had decided to return here, that they were in misery, and that she (*pointing to the Mother*) had gone to work as a modiste,° and at a shop of the type of that of Madame Pace.

THE STEPDAUGHTER: A real high-class modiste, you must know, gentlemen. In appearance, she works for the leaders of the best society; but she arranges matters so that these elegant ladies serve her purpose . . . without prejudice to other ladies who are . . . well . . . only so so.

THE MOTHER: You will believe me, gentlemen, that it never entered my mind that the old hag offered me work because she had her eye on my daughter.

THE STEPDAUGHTER: Poor mamma! Do you know, sir, what that woman did when I brought her back the work my mother had finished? She would point out to me that I had torn one of my frocks, and she would give it back to my mother to mend. It was I who paid for it, always I; while this poor creature here believed she was sacrificing herself for me and these two children here, sitting up at night sewing Madame Pace's robes.

THE MANAGER: And one day you met there . . .

THE STEPDAUGHTER: Him, him. Yes sir, an old client. There's a scene for you to play! Superb!

THE FATHER: She, the Mother arrived just then . . .

THE STEPDAUGHTER (*treacherously*): Almost in time!

THE FATHER (*crying out*): No, in time! in time! Fortunately I recognized her . . . in time. And I took them back home with me to my house. You can imagine now her position and mine; she, as you see her; and I who cannot look her in the face.

THE STEPDAUGHTER: Absurd! How can I possibly be expected — after that — to be a modest young miss, a fit person to go with his confounded aspirations for "a solid moral sanity"?

THE FATHER: For the drama lies all in this — in the con-

modiste: A person who makes fashionable clothing for women.

science that I have, that each one of us has. We believe this conscience to be a single thing, but it is many-sided. There is one for this person, and another for that. Diverse consciences. So we have this illusion of being one person for all, of having a personality that is unique in all our acts. But it isn't true. We perceive this when, tragically perhaps, in something we do, we are as it were, suspended, caught up in the air on a kind of hook. Then we perceive that all of us was not in that act, and that it would be an atrocious injustice to judge us by that action alone, as if all our existence were summed up in that one deed. Now do you understand the perfidy of this girl? She surprised me in a place, where she ought not to have known me, just as I could not exist for her; and she now seeks to attach to me a reality such as I could never suppose I should have to assume for her in a shameful and fleeting moment of my life. I feel this above all else. And the drama, you will see, acquires a tremendous value from this point. Then there is the position of the others . . . his. . . . (*Indicating the Son.*)

THE SON (*shrugging his shoulders scornfully*): Leave me alone! I don't come into this.

THE FATHER: What? You don't come into this?

THE SON: I've got nothing to do with it, and don't want to have; because you know well enough I wasn't made to be mixed up in all this with the rest of you.

THE STEPDAUGHTER: We are only vulgar folk! He is the fine gentleman. You may have noticed, Mr. Manager, that I fix him now and again with a look of scorn while he lowers his eyes — for he knows the evil he has done me.

THE SON (*scarcely looking at her*): I?

THE STEPDAUGHTER: You! you! I owe my life on the streets to you. Did you or did you not deny us, with your behavior, I won't say the intimacy of home, but even that mere hospitality which makes guests feel at their ease? We were intruders who had come to disturb the kingdom of your legitimacy. I should like to have you witness, Mr. Manager, certain scenes between him and me. He says I have tyrannized over everyone. But it was just his behavior which made me insist on the reason for which I had come into the house, — this reason he calls "vile"— into his house, with my mother who is his mother too. And I came as mistress of the house.

THE SON: It's easy for them to put me always in the wrong. But imagine, gentlemen, the position of a son, whose fate it is to see arrive one day at his home a young woman of impudent bearing, a young woman who inquires for his father, with whom who knows what business she has. This young man has then to witness her return bolder than ever, accompanied by that child there. He is obliged to watch her treat his father in an equivocal and confidential manner. She asks for money of him in a way that lets one suppose he must give it to her, *must,* do you understand, because he has every obligation to do so.

THE FATHER: But I have, as a matter of fact, this obligation. I owe it to your mother.

THE SON: How should I know? When had I ever seen or heard of her? One day there arrive with her (*indicating Stepdaughter*) that lad and this baby here. I am told: "This is *your* mother too, you know." I divine from her manner (*indicating Stepdaughter again*) why it is they have come home. I had rather not say what I feel and think about it. I shouldn't even care to confess to myself. No action can therefore be hoped for from me in this affair. Believe me, Mr. Manager, I am an "unrealized" character, dramatically speaking; and I find myself not at all at ease in their company. Leave me out of it, I beg you.

THE FATHER: What? It is just because you are so that . . .

THE SON: How do you know what I am like? When did you ever bother your head about me?

THE FATHER: I admit it. I admit it. But isn't that a situation in itself? This aloofness of yours which is so cruel to me and to your mother, who returns home and sees you almost for the first time grown up, who doesn't recognize you but knows you are her son. . . . (*Pointing out the Mother to the Manager.*) See, she's crying!

THE STEPDAUGHTER (*angrily, stamping her foot*): Like a fool!

THE FATHER (*indicating Stepdaughter*): She can't stand him, you know. (*Then referring again to the Son.*) He says he doesn't come into the affair, whereas he is really the hinge of the whole action. Look at that lad who is always clinging to his mother, frightened and humiliated. It is on account of this fellow here. Possibly his situation is the most painful of all. He feels himself a stranger more than the others. The poor little chap feels mortified, humiliated at being brought into a home out of charity as it were. (*In confidence.*) He is the image of his father. Hardly talks at all. Humble and quiet.

THE MANAGER: Oh, we'll cut him out. You've no notion what a nuisance boys are on the stage. . . .

THE FATHER: He disappears soon, you know. And the baby too. She is the first to vanish from the scene. The drama consists finally in this: when that mother reenters my house, her family born outside of it, and shall we say superimposed on the original, ends with the death of the little girl, the tragedy of the boy and the flight of the elder daughter. It cannot go on, because it is foreign to its surroundings. So after much torment, we three remain: I, the mother, that son. Then, owing to the disappearance of that extraneous family, we too find ourselves strange to one another. We find we are living in an atmosphere of mortal desolation which is the revenge, as he (*indicating Son*) scornfully said of the Demon of Experiment, that unfortunately hides in me. Thus, sir, you see when faith is lacking, it becomes impossible to create certain states of happiness, for we lack the necessary humility. Vaingloriously, we try to substitute ourselves for this faith, creating thus for the rest of the world a reality which we believe after their fashion, while, actually, it doesn't exist. For each one of us has his own reality to be respected before God, even when it is harmful to one's very self.

THE MANAGER: There is something in what you say. I assure you all this interests me very much. I begin to think there's the stuff for a drama in all this, and not a bad drama either.

THE STEPDAUGHTER (*coming forward*): When you've got a character like me . . .

THE FATHER (*shutting her up, all excited to learn the decision of the Manager*): You be quiet!

THE MANAGER (*reflecting, heedless of interruption*): It's new . . . hem . . . yes. . . .

THE FATHER: Absolutely new!

THE MANAGER: You've got a nerve though, I must say, to come here and fling it at me like this . . .

THE FATHER: You will understand, sir, born as we are for the stage . . .

THE MANAGER: Are you amateur actors then?

THE FATHER: No, I say born for the stage, because . . .

THE MANAGER: Oh, nonsense. You're an old hand, you know.

THE FATHER: No sir, no. We act that role for which we have been cast, that role which we are given in life. And in my own case, passion itself, as usually happens, becomes a trifle theatrical when it is exalted.

THE MANAGER: Well, well, that will do. But you see, without an author. . . . I could give you the address of an author if you like . . .

THE FATHER: No, no. Look here! You must be the author.

THE MANAGER: I? What are you talking about?

THE FATHER: Yes, you, you! Why not?

THE MANAGER: Because I have never been an author: that's why.

THE FATHER: Then why not turn author now? Everybody does it. You don't want any special qualities. Your task is made much easier by the fact that we are all here alive before you. . . .

THE MANAGER: It won't do.

THE FATHER: What? When you see us live our drama. . . .

THE MANAGER: Yes, that's all right. But you want someone to write it.

THE FATHER: No, no. Someone to take it down, possibly, while we play it, scene by scene! It will be enough to sketch it out at first, and then try it over.

THE MANAGER: Well . . . I am almost tempted. It's a bit of an idea. One might have a shot at it.

THE FATHER: Of course. You'll see what scenes will come out of it. I can give you one, at once . . .

THE MANAGER: By Jove, it tempts me. I'd like to have a go at it. Let's try it out. Come with me to my office. (*Turning to the Actors.*) You are at liberty for a bit, but don't step out of the theater for long. In a quarter of an hour, twenty minutes, all back here again! (*To the Father.*) We'll see what can be done. Who knows if we don't get something really extraordinary out of it?

THE FATHER: There's no doubt about it. They (*indicating the Characters*) had better come with us too, hadn't they ?

THE MANAGER: Yes, yes. Come on! come on! (*Moves away and then turning to the Actors.*) Be punctual, please! (*Manager and the Six Characters cross the stage and go off. The other Actors remain, looking at one another in astonishment.*)

LEADING MAN: Is he serious? What the devil does he want to do?

JUVENILE LEAD: This is rank madness.

THIRD ACTOR: Does he expect to knock up a drama in five minutes?

JUVENILE LEAD: Like the improvisers!

LEADING LADY: If he thinks I'm going to take part in a joke like this. . . .

JUVENILE LEAD: I'm out of it anyway.

FOURTH ACTOR: I should like to know who they are. (*Alludes to Characters.*)

THIRD ACTOR: What do you suppose? Madmen or rascals!

JUVENILE LEAD: And he takes them seriously!

L'INGÉNUE: Vanity! He fancies himself as an author now.

LEADING MAN: It's absolutely unheard of. If the stage has come to this . . . well I'm . . .

FIFTH ACTOR: It's rather a joke.

THIRD ACTOR: Well, we'll see what's going to happen next.

(*Thus talking, the Actors leave the stage, some going out by the little door at the back, others retiring to their dressing rooms.*)

(*The curtain remains up.*)

(*The action of the play is suspended for twenty minutes.*)

ACT II

(*The stage call-bells ring to warn the company that the play is about to begin again.*)

(*The Stepdaughter comes out of the Manager's office along with the Child and the Boy. As she comes out of the office, she cries: —*)

Nonsense! nonsense! Do it yourselves! I'm not going to mix myself up in this mess. (*Turning to the Child and coming quickly with her on to the stage.*) Come on, Rosetta, let's run!

(*The Boy follows them slowly, remaining a little behind and seeming perplexed.*)

THE STEPDAUGHTER (*stops, bends over the Child and takes the latter's face between her hands*): My little darling! You're frightened, aren't you? You don't know where we are, do you? (*Pretending to reply to a question of the Child.*) What is the stage? It's a place, baby, you know, where people play at being serious, a place where they act comedies. We've got to act a comedy now, dead serious, you know; and

you're in it also, little one. (*Embraces her, pressing the little head to her breast, and rocking the Child for a moment.*) Oh darling, darling, what a horrid comedy you've got to play! What a wretched part they've found for you! A garden . . . a fountain . . . look . . . just suppose, kiddie, it's here. Where, you say? Why, right here in the middle. It's all pretense you know. That's the trouble, my pet: it's all make-believe here. It's better to imagine it though, because if they fix it up for you, it'll only be painted cardboard, painted cardboard for the rockery, the water, the plants. . . . Ah, but I think a baby like this one would sooner have a make-believe fountain than a real one, so she could play with it. What a joke it'll be for the others! But for you, alas! not quite such a joke: you who are real, baby dear, and really play by a real fountain that is big and green and beautiful, with ever so many bamboos around it that are reflected in the water, and a whole lot of little ducks swimming about. . . . No, Rosetta, no, your mother doesn't bother about you on account of that wretch of a son there. I'm in the devil of a temper, and as for that lad. . . . (*Seizes Boy by the arm to force him to take one of his hands out of his pockets.*) What have you got there? What are you hiding? (*Pulls his hand out of his pocket, looks into it, and catches the glint of a revolver.*) Ah! where did you get this? (*The Boy, very pale in the face, looks at her, but does not answer.*) Idiot! If I'd been in your place, instead of killing myself, I'd have shot one of those two, or both of them: father and son.

(*The Father enters from the office, all excited from his work. The Manager follows him.*)

THE FATHER: Come on, come on dear! Come here for a minute! We've arranged everything. It's all fixed up.

THE MANAGER (*also excited*): If you please, young lady, there are one or two points to settle still. Will you come along?

THE STEPDAUGHTER (*following him toward the office*): Ouff! what's the good, if you've arranged everything.

(*The Father, Manager, and Stepdaughter go back into the office again [off] for a moment. At the same time, the Son, followed by the Mother, comes out.*)

THE SON (*looking at the three entering office*): Oh this is fine, fine! And to think I can't even get away!

(*The Mother attempts to look at him, but lowers her eyes immediately when he turns away from her. She then sits down. The Boy and the Child approach her. She casts a glance again at the Son, and speaks with humble tones, trying to draw him into conversation.*)

THE MOTHER: And isn't my punishment the worst of all? (*Then seeing from the Son's manner that he will not bother himself about her.*) My God! Why are you so cruel? Isn't it enough for one person to support all this torment? Must you then insist on others seeing it also?

THE SON (*half to himself, meaning the Mother to hear, however*): And they want to put it on the stage! If there was at least a reason for it! He thinks he has got at the meaning of it all. Just as if each one of us in every circumstance of life couldn't find his own explanation of it! (*Pauses.*) He complains he was discovered in a place where he ought not to have been seen, in a moment of his life which ought to have remained hidden and kept out of the reach of that convention which he has to maintain for other people. And what about my case? Haven't I had to reveal what no son ought ever to reveal: how father and mother live and are man and wife for themselves quite apart from that idea of father and mother which we give them? When this idea is revealed, our life is then linked at one point only to that man and that woman; and as such it should shame them, shouldn't it?

(*The Mother hides her face in her hands. From the dressing rooms and the little door at the back of the stage the Actors and Stage Manager return, followed by the Property Man and the Prompter. At the same moment, the Manager comes out of his office, accompanied by the Father and the Stepdaughter.*)

THE MANAGER: Come on, come on, ladies and gentlemen! Heh! you there, machinist!

MACHINIST: Yes sir?

THE MANAGER: Fix up the parlor with the floral decorations. Two wings and a drop with a door will do. Hurry up!

(*The Machinist runs off at once to prepare the scene and arranges it while the Manager talks with the Stage Manager, the Property Man, and the Prompter on matters of detail.*)

THE MANAGER (*to Property Man*): Just have a look, and see if there isn't a sofa or a divan in the wardrobe . . .

PROPERTY MAN: There's the green one.

THE STEPDAUGHTER: No no! Green won't do. It was yellow, ornamented with flowers — very large! and most comfortable!

PROPERTY MAN: There isn't one like that.

THE MANAGER: It doesn't matter. Use the one we've got.

THE STEPDAUGHTER: Doesn't matter? It's most important!

THE MANAGER: We're only trying it now. Please don't interfere. (*To Property Man.*) See if we've got a shop window — long and narrowish.

THE STEPDAUGHTER: And the little table! The little mahogany table for the pale blue envelope!

PROPERTY MAN (*to Manager*): There's that little gilt one.

THE MANAGER: That'll do fine.

THE FATHER: A mirror.

THE STEPDAUGHTER: And the screen! We must have a screen. Otherwise how can I manage?

PROPERTY MAN: That's all right, Miss. We've got any amount of them.

THE MANAGER (*to the Stepdaughter*): We want some clothes pegs too, don't we?

THE STEPDAUGHTER: Yes, several, several!

THE MANAGER: See how many we've got and bring them all.

PROPERTY MAN: All right!

(*The Property Man hurries off to obey his orders. While he is putting the things in their places, the Manager talks to the Prompter and then with the Characters and the Actors.*)

THE MANAGER (*to Prompter*): Take your seat. Look here: this is the outline of the scenes, act by act. (*Hands him some sheets of paper.*) And now I'm going to ask you to do something out of the ordinary.

PROMPTER: Take it down in shorthand?

THE MANAGER (*pleasantly surprised*): Exactly! Can you do shorthand?

PROMPTER: Yes, a little.

THE MANAGER: Good! (*Turning to a Stage Hand.*) Go and get some paper from my office, plenty, as much as you can find.

(*The Stage Hand goes off and soon returns with a handful of paper which he gives to the Prompter.*)

THE MANAGER (*to Prompter*): You follow the scenes as we play them, and try and get the points down, at any rate the most important ones. (*Then addressing the Actors.*) Clear the stage, ladies and gentlemen! Come over here (*pointing to the left*) and listen attentively.

LEADING LADY: But, excuse me, we . . .

THE MANAGER (*guessing her thought*): Don't worry! You won't have to improvise.

LEADING MAN: What have we to do then?

THE MANAGER: Nothing. For the moment you just watch and listen. Everybody will get his part written out afterwards. At present we're going to try the thing as best we can. They're going to act now.

THE FATHER (*as if fallen from the clouds into the confusion of the stage*): We? What do you mean, if you please, by a rehearsal?

THE MANAGER: A rehearsal for them. (*Points to the Actors.*)

THE FATHER: But since we are the characters . . .

THE MANAGER: All right: "characters" then, if you insist on calling yourselves such. But here, my dear sir, the characters don't act. Here the actors do the acting. The characters are there, in the "book" (*pointing toward Prompter's box*) — when there is a "book"!

THE FATHER: I won't contradict you; but excuse me, the actors aren't the characters. They want to be, they pretend to be, don't they? Now if these gentlemen here are fortunate enough to have us alive before them . . .

THE MANAGER: Oh, this is grand! You want to come before the public yourselves then?

THE FATHER: As we are. . . .

THE MANAGER: I can assure you it would be a magnificent spectacle!

LEADING MAN: What's the use of us here anyway then?

THE MANAGER: You're not going to pretend that you can

act? It makes me laugh! (*The Actors laugh.*) There, you see, they are laughing at the notion. But, by the way, I must cast the parts. That won't be difficult. They cast themselves. (*To the Second Lady Lead.*) You play the Mother. (*To the Father.*) We must find her a name.

THE FATHER: Amalia, sir.

THE MANAGER: But that is the real name of your wife. We don't want to call her by her real name.

THE FATHER: Why ever not, if it is her name? . . . Still, perhaps, if that lady must . . . (*Makes a slight motion of the hand to indicate the Second Lady Lead.*) I see this woman here (*means the Mother*) as Amalia. But do as you like. (*Gets more and more confused.*) I don't know what to say to you. Already, I begin to hear my own words ring false, as if they had another sound . . .

THE MANAGER: Don't you worry about it. It'll be our job to find the right tones. And as for her name, if you want her Amalia, Amalia it shall be; and if you don't like it, we'll find another! For the moment though, we'll call the characters in this way: (*To Juvenile Lead.*) You are the Son. (*To the Leading Lady.*) You naturally are the Stepdaughter. . . .

THE STEPDAUGHTER (*excitedly*): What? what? I, that woman there? (*Bursts out laughing.*)

THE MANAGER (*angry*): What is there to laugh at?

LEADING LADY (*indignant*): Nobody has ever dared to laugh at me. I insist on being treated with respect; otherwise I go away.

THE STEPDAUGHTER: No, no, excuse me . . . I am not laughing at you. . . .

THE MANAGER (*to Stepdaughter*): You ought to feel honored to be played by . . .

LEADING LADY (*at once, contemptuously*): "That woman there" . . .

THE STEPDAUGHTER: But I wasn't speaking of you, you know. I was speaking of myself — whom I can't see at all in you! That is all. I don't know . . . but . . . you . . . aren't in the least like me. . . .

THE FATHER: True. Here's the point. Look here, sir, our temperaments, our souls. . . .

THE MANAGER: Temperament, soul, be hanged! Do you suppose the spirit of the piece is in you? Nothing of the kind!

THE FATHER: What, haven't we our own temperaments, our own souls?

THE MANAGER: Not at all. Your soul or whatever you like to call it takes shape here. The actors give body and form to it, voice and gesture. And my actors — I may tell you — have given expression to much more lofty material than this little drama of yours, which may or may not hold up on the stage. But if it does, the merit of it, believe me, will be due to my actors.

THE FATHER: I don't dare contradict you, sir, but, believe me, it is a terrible suffering for us who are as we are, with these bodies of ours, these features to see. . . .

THE MANAGER (*cutting him short and out of patience*): Good heavens! The make-up will remedy all that, man, the make-up. . . .

THE FATHER: Maybe. But the voice, the gestures . . .

THE MANAGER: Now, look here! On the stage, you as yourself, cannot exist. The actor here acts you, and that's an end to it!

THE FATHER: I understand. And now I think I see why our author who conceived us as we are, all alive, didn't want to put us on the stage after all. I haven't the least desire to offend your actors. Far from it! But when I think that I am to be acted by . . . I don't know by whom. . . .

LEADING MAN (*on his dignity*): By me, if you've no objection!

THE FATHER (*humbly, mellifluously*): Honored, I assure you, sir. (*Bows.*) Still, I must say that try as this gentleman may, with all his good will and wonderful art, to absorb me into himself. . . .

LEADING MAN: Oh chuck it! "Wonderful art!" Withdraw that, please!

THE FATHER: The performance he will give, even doing his best with make-up to look like me. . . .

LEADING MAN: It will certainly be a bit difficult! (*The Actors laugh.*)

THE FATHER: Exactly! It will be difficult to act me as I really am. The effect will be rather — apart from the make-up — according as to how he supposes I am, as he senses me — if he does sense me — and not as I inside of myself feel myself to be. It seems to me then that account should be taken of this by everyone whose duty it may become to criticize us. . . .

THE MANAGER: Heavens! The man's starting to think about the critics now! Let them say what they like. It's up to us to put on the play if we can. (*Looking around.*) Come on! come on! Is the stage set? (*To the Actors and Characters.*) Stand back — stand back! Let me see, and don't let's lose any more time! (*To the Stepdaughter.*) Is it all right as it is now?

THE STEPDAUGHTER: Well, to tell the truth, I don't recognize the scene.

THE MANAGER: My dear lady, you can't possibly suppose that we can construct that shop of Madame Pace piece by piece here? (*To the Father.*) You said a white room with flowered wallpaper, didn't you?

THE FATHER: Yes.

THE MANAGER: Well then. We've got the furniture right more or less. Bring that little table a bit further forward. (*The Stage Hands obey the order. To Property Man.*) You go and find an envelope, if possible, a pale blue one; and give it to that gentleman. (*Indicates Father.*)

PROPERTY MAN: An ordinary envelope?

MANAGER AND FATHER: Yes, yes, an ordinary envelope.

PROPERTY MAN: At once, sir. (*Exit.*)

THE MANAGER: Ready, everyone! First scene — the Young Lady. (*The Leading Lady comes forward.*) No, no, you must wait. I meant her. (*Indicating the Stepdaughter.*) You just watch —

THE STEPDAUGHTER (*adding at once*): How I shall play it, how I shall live it! . . .

LEADING LADY (*offended*): I shall live it also, you may be sure, as soon as I begin!

THE MANAGER (*with his hands to his head*): Ladies and gentlemen, if you please! No more useless discussions! Scene I: the Young Lady with Madame Pace: Oh! (*Looks around as if lost.*) And this Madame Pace, where is she?

THE FATHER: She isn't with us, sir.

THE MANAGER: Then what the devil's to be done?

THE FATHER: But she is alive too.

THE MANAGER: Yes, but where is she?

THE FATHER: One minute. Let me speak! (*Turning to the Actresses.*) If these ladies would be so good as to give me their hats for a moment. . . .

THE ACTRESSES (*half surprised, half laughing, in chorus*): What? Why? Our hats? What does he say?

THE MANAGER: What are you going to do with the ladies' hats? (*The Actors laugh.*)

THE FATHER: Oh nothing. I just want to put them on these pegs for a moment. And one of the ladies will be so kind as to take off her mantle. . . .

THE ACTORS: Oh, what d'you think of that? Only the mantle? He must be mad.

SOME ACTRESSES: But why? Mantles as well?

THE FATHER: To hang them up here for a moment. Please be so kind, will you?

THE ACTRESSES (*taking off their hats, one or two also their cloaks, and going to hang them on the racks*): After all, why not? There you are! This is really funny. We've got to put them on show.

THE FATHER: Exactly; just like that, on show.

THE MANAGER: May we know why?

THE FATHER: I'll tell you. Who knows if, by arranging the stage for her, she does not come here herself, attracted by the very articles of her trade? (*Inviting the Actors to look toward the exit at back of stage.*) Look! Look!

(*The door at the back of stage opens and Madame Pace enters and takes a few steps forward. She is a fat, oldish woman with puffy oxygenated hair. She is rouged and powdered, dressed with a comical elegance in black silk. Round her waist is a long silver chain from which hangs a pair of scissors. The Stepdaughter runs over to her at once amid the stupor of the Actors.*)

THE STEPDAUGHTER (*turning toward her*): There she is! There she is!

THE FATHER (*radiant*): It's she! I said so, didn't I! There she is!

THE MANAGER (*conquering his surprise, and then becoming indignant*): What sort of a trick is this?

LEADING MAN (*almost at the same time*): What's going to happen next?

JUVENILE LEAD: Where does she come from?

L'INGÉNUE: They've been holding her in reserve, I guess.

LEADING LADY: A vulgar trick!

THE FATHER (*dominating the protests*): Excuse me, all of you! Why are you so anxious to destroy in the name of a vulgar, commonplace sense of truth, this reality which comes to birth attracted and formed by the magic of the stage itself, which has indeed more right to live here than you, since it is much truer than you — if you don't mind my saying so? Which is the actress among you who is to play Madame Pace? Well, here is Madame Pace herself. And you will allow, I fancy, that the actress who acts her will be less true than this woman here, who is herself in person. You see my daughter recognized her and went over to her at once. Now you're going to witness the scene!

(*But the scene between the Stepdaughter and Madame Pace has already begun despite the protest of the Actors and the reply of the Father. It has begun quietly, naturally, in a manner impossible for the stage. So when the Actors, called to attention by the Father, turn round and see Madame Pace, who has placed one hand under the Stepdaughter's chin to raise her head, they observe her at first with great attention, but hearing her speak in an unintelligible manner their interest begins to wane.*)

THE MANAGER: Well? well?

LEADING MAN: What does she say?

LEADING LADY: One can't hear a word.

JUVENILE LEAD: Louder! Louder please!

THE STEPDAUGHTER (*leaving Madame Pace, who smiles a Sphinx-like smile, and advancing toward the Actors*): Louder? Louder? What are you talking about? These aren't matters which can be shouted at the top of one's voice. If I have spoken them out loud, it was to shame him and have my revenge. (*Indicates Father.*) But for Madame it's quite a different matter.

THE MANAGER: Indeed? indeed? But here, you know people have got to make themselves heard, my dear. Even we who are on the stage can't hear you. What will it be when the public's in the theater? And anyway, you can very well speak up now among yourselves, since we shan't be present to listen to you as we are now. You've got to pretend to be alone in a room at the back of a shop where no one can hear you.

(*The Stepdaughter coquettishly and with a touch of malice makes a sign of disagreement two or three times with her finger.*)

THE MANAGER: What do you mean by no?

THE STEPDAUGHTER (*sotto voce,° mysteriously*): There's someone who will hear us if she (*indicating Madame Pace*) speaks out loud.

THE MANAGER (*in consternation*): What? Have you got someone else to spring on us now? (*The Actors burst out laughing.*)

THE FATHER: No, no sir. She is alluding to me. I've got to

---

sotto voce: In a soft voice or stage whisper.

be here — there behind that door, in waiting; and Madame Pace knows it. In fact, if you will allow me, I'll go there at once, so I can be quite ready. (*Moves away.*)

THE MANAGER (*stopping him*): No! wait! wait! We must observe the conventions of the theater. Before you are ready . . .

THE STEPDAUGHTER (*interrupting him*): No, get on with it at once! I'm just dying, I tell you, to act this scene. If he's ready, I'm more than ready.

THE MANAGER (*shouting*): But, my dear young lady, first of all, we must have the scene between you and this lady. . . . (*Indicates Madame Pace.*) Do you understand?

THE STEPDAUGHTER: Good Heavens! She's been telling me what you know already: that mama's work is badly done again, that the material's ruined; and that if I want her to continue to help us in our misery I must be patient. . . .

MADAME PACE (*coming forward with an air of great importance*): Yes indeed, sir, I no wanta take advantage of her, I no wanta be hard. . . .

(*Note: Madame Pace is supposed to talk in a jargon half Italian, half English.*)

THE MANAGER (*alarmed*): What? What? She talks like that? (*The Actors burst out laughing again.*)

THE STEPDAUGHTER (*also laughing*): Yes yes, that's the way she talks, half English, half Italian! Most comical it is!

MADAME PACE: Itta seem not verra polite gentlemen laugha atta me eeff I trya best speaka English.

THE MANAGER: *Diamine!°* Of course! Of course! Let her talk like that! Just what we want. Talk just like that, Madame, if you please! The effect will be certain. Exactly what was wanted to put a little comic relief into the crudity of the situation. Of course she talks like that! Magnificent!

THE STEPDAUGHTER: Magnificent? Certainly! When certain suggestions are made to one in language of that kind, the effect is certain, since it seems almost a joke. One feels inclined to laugh when one hears her talk about an "old signore" "who wanta talka nicely with you." Nice old signore, eh, Madame?

MADAME PACE: Not so old my dear, not so old! And even if you no like him, he won't make any scandal!

THE MOTHER (*jumping up amid the amazement and consternation of the Actors, who had not been noticing her. They move to restrain her*): You old devil! You murderess!

THE STEPDAUGHTER (*running over to calm her Mother*): Calm yourself, Mother, calm yourself! Please don't. . . .

THE FATHER (*going to her also at the same time*): Calm yourself! Don't get excited! Sit down now!

THE MOTHER: Well then, take that woman away out of my sight!

Diamine!: Italian for "Well, I'll be damned!"

THE STEPDAUGHTER (*to Manager*): It is impossible for my mother to remain here.

THE FATHER (*to Manager*): They can't be here together. And for this reason, you see: that woman there was not with us when we came. . . . If they are on together, the whole thing is given away inevitably, as you see.

THE MANAGER: It doesn't matter. This is only a first rough sketch — just to get an idea of the various points of the scene, even confusedly. . . . (*Turning to the Mother and leading her to her chair.*) Come along, my dear lady, sit down now, and let's get on with the scene. . . .

(*Meanwhile, the Stepdaughter, coming forward again, turns to Madame Pace.*)

THE STEPDAUGHTER: Come on, Madame, come on!

MADAME PACE (*offended*): No, no, *grazie*. I do not do anything witha your mother present.

THE STEPDAUGHTER: Nonsense! Introduce this "old signore" who wants to talk nicely to me. (*Addressing the Company imperiously.*) We've got to do this scene one way or another, haven't we? Come on! (*To Madame Pace.*) You can go!

MADAME PACE: Ah yes! I go'way! I go'way! Certainly! (*Exits furious.*)

THE STEPDAUGHTER (*to the Father*): Now you make your entry. No, you needn't go over there. Come here. Let's suppose you've already come in. Like that, yes! I'm here with bowed head, modest like. Come on! Out with your voice! Say "Good morning, Miss" in that peculiar tone, that special tone. . . .

THE MANAGER: Excuse me, but are you the Manager, or am I? (*To the Father, who looks undecided and perplexed.*) Get on with it, man! Go down there to the back of the stage. You needn't go off. Then come right forward here.

(*The Father does as he is told, looking troubled and perplexed at first. But as soon as he begins to move, the reality of the action affects him, and he begins to smile and to be more natural. The Actors watch intently.*)

THE MANAGER (*sotto voce, quickly to the Prompter in his box*): Ready! ready! Get ready to write now.

THE FATHER (*coming forward and speaking in a different tone*): Good afternoon, Miss!

THE STEPDAUGHTER (*head bowed down slightly, with restrained disgust*): Good afternoon!

THE FATHER (*looks under her hat which partly covers her face. Perceiving she is very young, he makes an exclamation, partly of surprise, partly of fear lest he compromise himself in a risky adventure*): Ah . . . but . . . ah . . . I say . . . this is not the first time that you have come here, is it?

THE STEPDAUGHTER (*modestly*): No sir.

THE FATHER: You've been here before, eh? (*Then seeing her nod agreement.*) More than once? (*Waits for her to answer, looks under her hat, smiles, and then says:*) Well then, there's no need to be so shy, is there? May I take off your hat?

THE STEPDAUGHTER (*anticipating him and with veiled disgust*): No sir . . . I'll do it myself. (*Takes it off quickly.*)

(*The Mother, who watches the progress of the scene with the Son and the other two children who cling to her, is on thorns; and follows with varying expressions of sorrow, indignation, anxiety, and horror the words and actions of the other two. From time to time she hides her face in her hands and sobs.*)

THE MOTHER: Oh, my God, my God!

THE FATHER (*playing his part with a touch of gallantry*): Give it to me! I'll put it down. (*Takes hat from her hands.*) But a dear little head like yours ought to have a smarter hat. Come and help me choose one from the stock, won't you?

L'INGÉNUE (*interrupting*): I say . . . those are our hats you know.

THE MANAGER (*furious*): Silence! silence! Don't try and be funny, if you please. . . . We're playing the scene now, I'd have you notice. (*To the Stepdaughter.*) Begin again, please!

THE STEPDAUGHTER (*continuing*): No thank you, sir.

THE FATHER: Oh, come now. Don't talk like that. You must take it. I shall be upset if you don't. There are some lovely little hats here; and then — Madame will be pleased. She expects it, anyway, you know.

THE STEPDAUGHTER: No, no! I couldn't wear it!

THE FATHER: Oh, you're thinking about what they'd say at home if they saw you come in with a new hat? My dear girl, there's always a way round these little matters, you know.

THE STEPDAUGHTER (*all keyed up*): No, it's not that. I couldn't wear it because I am . . . as you see . . . you might have noticed . . .

(*Showing her black dress.*)

THE FATHER: . . . in mourning! Of course: I beg your pardon: I'm frightfully sorry. . . .

THE STEPDAUGHTER (*forcing herself to conquer her indignation and nausea*): Stop! Stop! It's I who must thank you. There's no need for you to feel mortified or specially sorry. Don't think any more of what I've said. (*Tries to smile.*) I must forget that I am dressed so. . . .

THE MANAGER (*interrupting and turning to the Prompter*): Stop a minute! Stop! Don't write that down. Cut out that last bit. (*Then to the Father and Stepdaughter.*) Fine! it's going fine! (*To the Father only.*) And now you can go on as we arranged. (*To the Actors.*) Pretty good that scene, where he offers her the hat, eh?

THE STEPDAUGHTER: The best's coming now. Why can't we go on?

THE MANAGER: Have a little patience! (*To the Actors.*) Of course, it must be treated rather lightly.

LEADING MAN: Still, with a bit of go in it!

LEADING LADY: Of course! It's easy enough! (*To Leading Man.*) Shall you and I try it now?

LEADING MAN: Why, yes! I'll prepare my entrance. (*Exit in order to make his entrance.*)

THE MANAGER (*to Leading Lady*): See here! The scene between you and Madame Pace is finished. I'll have it written out properly after. You remain here . . . oh, where are you going?

LEADING LADY: One minute. I want to put my hat on again. (*Goes over to hatrack and puts her hat on her head.*)

THE MANAGER: Good! You stay here with your head bowed down a bit.

THE STEPDAUGHTER: But she isn't dressed in black.

LEADING LADY: But I shall be, and much more effectively than you.

THE MANAGER (*to Stepdaughter*): Be quiet please, and watch! You'll be able to learn something. (*Clapping his hands.*) Come on! come on! Entrance, please!

(*The door at rear of stage opens, and the Leading Man enters with the lively manner of an old gallant. The rendering of the scene by the Actors from the very first words is seen to be quite a different thing, though it has not in any way the air of a parody. Naturally, the Stepdaughter and the Father, not being able to recognize themselves in the Leading Lady and the Leading Man, who deliver their words in different tones and with a different psychology, express, sometimes with smiles, sometimes with gestures, the impression they receive.*)

LEADING MAN: Good afternoon, Miss . . .

THE FATHER (*at once unable to contain himself*): No! no!

(*The Stepdaughter, noticing the way the Leading Man enters, bursts out laughing.*)

THE MANAGER (*furious*): Silence! And you, please, just stop that laughing. If we go on like this, we shall never finish.

THE STEPDAUGHTER: Forgive me, sir but it's natural enough. This lady (*indicating Leading Lady*) stands there still; but if she is supposed to be me, I can assure you that if I heard anyone say "Good afternoon" in that manner and in that tone, I should burst out laughing as I did.

THE FATHER: Yes, yes, the manner, the tone . . .

THE MANAGER: Nonsense! Rubbish! Stand aside and let me see the action.

LEADING MAN: If I've got to represent an old fellow who's coming into a house of an equivocal character . . .

THE MANAGER: Don't listen to them, for Heaven's sake! Do it again! It goes fine. (*Waiting for the Actors to begin again.*) Well?

LEADING MAN: Good afternoon, Miss.

LEADING LADY: Good afternoon.

LEADING MAN (*imitating the gesture of the Father when he looked under the hat, and then expressing quite clearly first satisfaction and then fear*): Ah, but . . . I say . . . this is not the first time that you have come here, is it?

THE MANAGER: Good, but not quite so heavily. Like

this. (*Acts himself.*) "This isn't the first time that you have come here". . . (*To Leading Lady.*) And you say: "No, sir."

LEADING LADY: No, sir.

LEADING MAN: You've been here before, more than once.

THE MANAGER: No, no, stop! Let her nod "yes" first. "You've been here before, eh?" (*The Leading Lady lifts up her head slightly and closes her eyes as though in disgust. Then she inclines her head twice.*)

THE STEPDAUGHTER (*unable to contain herself*): Oh my God! (*Puts a hand to her mouth to prevent herself from laughing.*)

THE MANAGER (*turning round*): What's the matter?

THE STEPDAUGHTER: Nothing, nothing!

THE MANAGER (*to Leading Man*): Go on!

LEADING MAN: You've been here before, eh? Well then, there's no need to be so shy, is there? May I take off your hat?

(*The Leading Man says this last speech in such a tone and with such gestures that the Stepdaughter, though she has her hand to her mouth, cannot keep from laughing.*)

LEADING LADY (*indignant*): I'm not going to stop here to be made a fool of by that woman there.

LEADING MAN: Neither am I! I'm through with it!

THE MANAGER (*shouting to Stepdaughter*): Silence! for once and all, I tell you!

THE STEPDAUGHTER: Forgive me! forgive me!

THE MANAGER: You haven't any manners: that's what it is! You go too far.

THE FATHER (*endeavoring to intervene*): Yes, it's true, but excuse her . . .

THE MANAGER: Excuse what? It's absolutely disgusting.

THE FATHER: Yes, sir, but believe me, it has such a strange effect when . . .

THE MANAGER: Strange? Why strange? Where is it strange?

THE FATHER: No, sir; I admire your actors — this gentleman here, this lady; but they are certainly not us!

THE MANAGER: I should hope not. Evidently they cannot be you, if they are actors.

THE FATHER: Just so: actors! Both of them act our parts exceedingly well. But, believe me, it produces quite a different effect on us. They want to be us, but they aren't, all the same.

THE MANAGER: What is it then anyway?

THE FATHER: Something that is . . . that is theirs — and no longer ours . . .

THE MANAGER: But naturally, inevitably, I've told you so already.

THE FATHER: Yes, I understand . . . I understand . . .

THE MANAGER: Well then, let's have no more of it! (*Turning to the Actors.*) We'll have the rehearsals by ourselves, afterwards, in the ordinary way. I never could stand rehearsing with the author present. He's never satisfied! (*Turning to Father and Stepdaughter.*) Come on! Let's get on with it again; and try and see if you can't keep from laughing.

THE STEPDAUGHTER: Oh, I shan't laugh any more. There's a nice little bit coming from me now: you'll see.

THE MANAGER: Well then: when she says "Don't think any more of what I've said, I must forget, etc.," you (*addressing the Father*) come in sharp with "I understand"; and then you ask her . . .

THE STEPDAUGHTER (*interrupting*): What?

THE MANAGER: Why she is in mourning.

THE STEPDAUGHTER: Not at all! See here: when I told him that it was useless for me to be thinking about my wearing mourning, do you know how he answered me? "Ah well," he said, "then let's take off this little frock."

THE MANAGER: Great! Just what we want, to make a riot in the theater!

THE STEPDAUGHTER: But it's the truth!

THE MANAGER: What does that matter? Acting is our business here. Truth up to a certain point, but no further.

THE STEPDAUGHTER: What do you want to do then?

THE MANAGER: You'll see, you'll see! Leave it to me.

THE STEPDAUGHTER: No sir! What you want to do is to piece together a little romantic sentimental scene out of my disgust, out of all the reasons, each more cruel and viler than the other, why I am what I am. He is to ask me why I'm in mourning; and I'm to answer with tears in my eyes, that it is just two months since papa died. No sir, no! He's got to say to me, as he did say, "Well, let's take off this little dress at once." And I, with my two months' mourning in my heart, went there behind that screen, and with these fingers tingling with shame . . .

THE MANAGER (*running his hands through his hair*): For Heaven's sake! What are you saying?

THE STEPDAUGHTER (*crying out excitedly*): The truth! The truth!

THE MANAGER: It may be. I don't deny it, and I can understand all your horror; but you must surely see that you can't have this kind of thing on the stage. It won't go.

THE STEPDAUGHTER: Not possible, eh? Very well! I'm much obliged to you — but I'm off.

THE MANAGER: Now be reasonable! Don't lose your temper!

THE STEPDAUGHTER: I won't stop here! I won't! I can see you fixed it all up with him in your office. All this talk about what is possible for the stage . . . I understand! He wants to get at his complicated "cerebral drama," to have his famous remorses and torments acted; but I want to act my part, *my part!*

THE MANAGER: (*annoyed, shaking his shoulders*): Ah! Just *your* part! But, if you will pardon me, there are other parts than yours: His (*indicating the Father*) and hers (*indicating the Mother*)! On the stage you can't have a character becoming too prominent and overshadowing all the others. The thing is to pack them all into a neat little framework and then act what is actable. I am aware of the fact that everyone has his own interior life which he wants very much to put forward. But the difficulty lies in this fact: to set out just so much as is necessary for the stage, taking the other characters into consideration, and at the same time hint at the unrevealed interior life of each. I am willing to admit, my dear young lady, that from your point of view it would be a fine idea if each character could tell the public all his troubles in a nice monologue or a regular one hour lecture. (*Good humoredly.*) You must restrain yourself, my dear, and in your own interest, too; because this fury of yours, this exaggerated disgust you show, may make a bad impression, you know. After you have confessed to me that there were others before him at Madame Pace's and more than once . . .

THE STEPDAUGHTER (*bowing her head, impressed*): It's true. But remember those others mean him for me all the same.

THE MANAGER (*not understanding*): What? The others? What do you mean?

THE STEPDAUGHTER: For one who has gone wrong, sir, he who was responsible for the first fault is responsible for all that follow. He is responsible for my faults, was, even before I was born. Look at him, and see if it isn't true!

THE MANAGER: Well, well! And does the weight of so much responsibility seem nothing to you? Give him a chance to act it, to get it over!

THE STEPDAUGHTER: How? How can he act all his "noble remorses," all his "moral torments," if you want to spare him the horror of being discovered one day — after he had asked her what he did ask her — in the arms of her, that already fallen woman, that child, sir, that child he used to watch come out of school? (*She is moved.*)

(*The Mother at this point is overcome with emotion and breaks out into a fit of crying. All are touched. A long pause.*)

THE STEPDAUGHTER (*as soon as the Mother becomes a little quieter, adds resolutely and gravely*): At present, we are unknown to the public. Tomorrow, you will act us as you wish, treating us in your own manner. But do you really want to see drama, do you want to see it flash out as it really did?

THE MANAGER: Of course! That's just what I do want, so I can use as much of it as is possible.

THE STEPDAUGHTER: Well then, ask that Mother there to leave us.

THE MOTHER (*changing her low plaint into a sharp cry*): No! No! Don't permit, it, sir, don't permit it!

THE MANAGER: But it's only to try . . .

THE MOTHER: I can't bear it. I can't.

THE MANAGER: But since it has happened already . . . I don't understand!

THE MOTHER: It's taking place now. It happens all the time. My torment isn't a pretended one. I live and feel every minute of my torture. Those two children there — have you heard them speak? They can't speak anymore. They cling to me to keep my torment

actual and vivid for me. But for themselves, they do not exist, they aren't anymore. And she (*indicating the Stepdaughter*) has run away, she has left me, and is lost. If I now see her here before me, it is only to renew for me the tortures I have suffered for her too.

THE FATHER: The eternal moment! She (*indicating the Stepdaughter*) is here to catch me, fix me, and hold me eternally in the stocks for that one fleeting and shameful moment of my life. She can't give it up! And you, sir, cannot either fairly spare me . . .

THE MANAGER: I never said I didn't want to act it. It will form, as a matter of fact, the nucleus of the whole first act right up to her surprise. (*Indicates the Mother.*)

THE FATHER: Just so! This is my punishment: the passion in all of us that must culminate in her final cry.

THE STEPDAUGHTER: I can hear it still in my ears. It's driven me mad, that cry! — You can put me on as you like; it doesn't matter. Fully dressed, if you like — provided I have at least the arm bare; because, standing like this (*she goes close to the Father and leans her head on his breast*) with my head so, and my arms round his neck, I saw a vein pulsing in my arm here; and then, as if that live vein had awakened disgust in me, I closed my eyes like this, and let my head sink on his breast. (*Turning to the Mother.*) Cry out, mother! Cry out! (*Buries head in Father's breast, and with her shoulders raised as if to prevent her hearing the cry, adds in tones of intense emotion.*) Cry out as you did then!

THE MOTHER (*coming forward to separate them*): No! My daughter, my daughter! (*And after having pulled her away from him.*) You brute! you brute! She is my daughter! Don't you see she's my daughter?

THE MANAGER (*walking backward toward footlights*): Fine! fine! Damned good! And then, of course — curtain!

THE FATHER (*going toward him excitedly*): Yes, of course, because that's the way it really happened.

THE MANAGER (*convinced and pleased*): Oh, yes, no doubt about it. Curtain here, curtain!

(*At the reiterated cry of the Manager, the Machinist lets the curtain down, leaving the Manager and the Father in front of it before the footlights.*)

THE MANAGER: The darned idiot! I said "curtain" to show the act should end there, and he goes and lets it down in earnest. (*To the Father, while he pulls the curtain back to go on to the stage again.*) Yes, yes, it's all right. Effect certain! That's the right ending. I'll guarantee the first act at any rate.

ACT III

(*When the curtain goes up again, it is seen that the stage hands have shifted the bit of scenery used in the last part and have rigged up instead at the back of the stage a drop, with some trees, and one or two wings. A portion of a fountain basin is visible. The Mother is sitting on the right with the two children by her side. The Son is on the same side, but away from the others. He seems bored, angry, and full of shame. The Father and the Stepdaughter are also seated toward the right front. On the other side (left) are the Actors, much in the positions they occupied before the curtain was lowered. Only the Manager is standing up in the middle of the stage, with his hand closed over his mouth, in the act of meditating.)*

THE MANAGER (*shaking his shoulders after a brief pause*): Ah yes: the second act! Leave it to me, leave it all to me as we arranged, and you'll see! It'll go fine!

THE STEPDAUGHTER: Our entry into his house (*indicates Father*) in spite of him . . . (*Indicates the Son.*)

THE MANAGER (*out of patience*): Leave it to me, I tell you!

THE STEPDAUGHTER: Do let it be clear, at any rate, that it is in spite of my wishes.

THE MOTHER (*from her corner, shaking her head*): For all the good that's come of it . . .

THE STEPDAUGHTER (*turning toward her quickly*): It doesn't matter. The more harm done us, the more remorse for him.

THE MANAGER (*impatiently*): I understand! Good Heavens! I understand! I'm taking it into account.

THE MOTHER (*supplicatingly*): I beg you, sir, to let it appear quite plain that for conscience' sake I did try in every way . . .

THE STEPDAUGHTER (*interrupting indignantly and continuing for the Mother*): . . . to pacify me, to dissuade me from spiting him. (*To Manager.*) Do as she wants: satisfy her, because it is true! I enjoy it immensely. Anyhow, as you can see, the meeker she is, the more she tries to get at his heart, the more distant and aloof does he become.

THE MANAGER: Are we going to begin this second act or not?

THE STEPDAUGHTER: I'm not going to talk any more now. But I must tell you this: you can't have the whole action take place in the garden, as you suggest. It isn't possible!

THE MANAGER: Why not?

THE STEPDAUGHTER: Because he (*indicates the Son again*) is always shut up alone in his room. And then there's all the part of that poor dazed-looking boy there which takes place indoors.

THE MANAGER: Maybe! On the other hand, you will understand — we can't change scenes three or four times in one act.

LEADING MAN: They used to once.

THE MANAGER: Yes, when the public was up to the level of that child there.

LEADING LADY: It makes the illusion easier.

THE FATHER (*irritated*): The illusion! For Heaven's sake, don't say illusion. Please don't use that word, which is particularly painful for . . .

THE MANAGER (*astounded*): And why, if you please?

THE FATHER: It's painful, cruel, really cruel; and you ought to understand that.

THE MANAGER: But why? What ought we to say then? The illusion, I tell you, sir, which we've got to create for the audience. . . .

THE LEADING MAN: With our acting.

THE MANAGER: The illusion of a reality.

THE FATHER: I understand; but you, perhaps, do not understand us. Forgive me! You see . . . here for you and your actors, the thing is only — and rightly so . . . a kind of game. . . .

THE LEADING LADY (*interrupting indignantly*): A game! We're not children here, if you please! We are serious actors.

THE FATHER: I don't deny it. What I mean is the game, or play, of your art, which has to give, as the gentleman says, a perfect illusion of reality.

THE MANAGER: Precisely — !

THE FATHER: Now, if you consider the fact that we (*indicates himself and the other five Characters*), as we are, have no other reality outside of this illusion. . . .

THE MANAGER (*astonished, looking at his Actors, who are also amazed*): And what does that mean?

THE FATHER (*after watching them for a moment with a wan smile*): As I say, sir, that which is a game of art for you is our sole reality. (*Brief pause. He goes a step or two nearer the Manager and adds.*) But not only for us, you know, by the way. Just you think it over well. (*Looks him in the eyes.*) Can you tell me who you are?

THE MANAGER (*perplexed, half-smiling*): What? Who am I? I am myself.

THE FATHER: And if I were to tell you that that isn't true, because you and I . . . ?

THE MANAGER: I should say you were mad — ! (*The Actors laugh.*)

THE FATHER: You're quite right to laugh: because we are all making believe here. (*To Manager.*) And you can therefore object that it's only for a joke that that gentleman there (*indicates the Leading Man*), who naturally is himself, has to be me, who am on the contrary myself — this thing you see here. You see I've caught you in a trap! (*The Actors laugh.*)

THE MANAGER (*annoyed*): But we've had all this over once before. Do you want to begin again?

THE FATHER: No, no! That wasn't my meaning! In fact, I should like to request you to abandon this game of art (*looking at the Leading Lady as if anticipating her*) which you are accustomed to play here with your actors, and to ask you seriously once again: who are you?

THE MANAGER (*astonished and irritated, turning to his Actors*): If this fellow here hasn't got a nerve! A man who calls himself a character comes and asks me who I am!

THE FATHER (*with dignity, but not offended*): A character, sir, may always ask a man who he is. Because a character has really a life of his own, marked with his especial characteristics; for which reason he is always "somebody." But a man — I'm not speaking of you now — may very well be "nobody."

THE MANAGER: Yes, but you are asking these questions of me, the boss, the manager! Do you understand?

THE FATHER: But only in order to know if you, as you really are now, see yourself as you once were with all the illusions that were yours then, with all the things both inside and outside of you as they seemed to you — as they were then indeed for you. Well, sir, if you think of all those illusions that mean nothing to you now, of all those things which don't even *seem* to you to exist anymore, while once they *were* for you, don't you feel that — I won't say these boards — but the very earth under your feet is sinking away from you when you reflect that in the same way this *you* as you feel it today — all this present reality of yours — is fated to seem a mere illusion to you tomorrow?

THE MANAGER (*without having understood much, but astonished by the specious argument*): Well, well! And where does all this take us anyway?

THE FATHER: Oh, nowhere! It's only to show you that if we (*indicating the Characters*) have no other reality beyond the illusion, you too must not count overmuch on your reality as you feel it today, since, like that of yesterday, it may prove an illusion for you tomorrow.

THE MANAGER (*determining to make fun of him*): Ah, excellent! Then you'll be saying next that you, with this comedy of yours that you brought here to act, are truer and more real than I am.

THE FATHER (*with the greatest seriousness*): But of course, without doubt!

THE MANAGER: Ah, really?

THE FATHER: Why, I thought you'd understand that from the beginning.

THE MANAGER: More real than I?

THE FATHER: If your reality can change from one day to another. . . .

THE MANAGER: But everyone knows it can change. It is always changing, the same as anyone else's.

THE FATHER (*with a cry*): No, sir, not ours! Look here! That is the very difference! Our reality doesn't change: it can't change! It can't be other than what it is, because it is already fixed for ever. It's terrible. Ours is an immutable reality which should make you shudder when you approach us if you are really conscious of the fact that your reality is a mere transitory and fleeting illusion, taking this form today and that tomorrow, according to the conditions, according to your will, your sentiments, which in turn are controlled by an intellect that shows them to you today in one manner and tomorrow . . . who knows how? . . . Illusions of reality represented in this fatuous comedy of life that never ends, nor can ever end! Because if tomorrow it were to end . . . then why, all would be finished.

THE MANAGER: Oh for God's sake, will you *at least* finish with this philosophizing and let us try and shape this comedy which you yourself have brought me here? You argue and philosophize a bit too much, my dear sir. You know you seem to me almost, al-

most . . . (*Stops and looks him over from head to foot.*) Ah, by the way, I think you introduced yourself to me as a — what shall . . . we say — a "character," created by an author who did not afterward care to make a drama of his own creations.

THE FATHER: It is the simple truth, sir.

THE MANAGER: Nonsense! Cut that out, please! None of us believes it, because it isn't a thing, as you must recognize yourself, which one can believe seriously. If you want to know, it seems to me you are trying to imitate the manner of a certain author whom I heartily detest — I warn you — although I have unfortunately bound myself to put on one of his works. As a matter of fact, I was just starting to rehearse it, when you arrived. (*Turning to the Actors.*) And this is what we've gained — out of the frying-pan into the fire!

THE FATHER: I don't know to what author you may be alluding, but believe me I feel what I think; and I seem to be philosophizing only for those who do not think what they feel, because they blind themselves with their own sentiment. I know that for many people this self-blinding seems much more "human"; but the contrary is really true. For man never reasons so much and becomes so introspective as when he suffers, since he is anxious to get at the cause of his sufferings, to learn who has produced them, and whether it is just or unjust that he should have to bear them. On the other hand, when he is happy, he takes his happiness as it comes and doesn't analyze it, just as if happiness were his right. The animals suffer without reasoning about their sufferings. But take the case of a man who suffers and begins to reason about it. Oh no! it can't be allowed! Let him suffer like an animal, and then — ah yes, he is "human"!

THE MANAGER: Look here! Look here! You're off again, philosophizing worse than ever.

THE FATHER: Because I suffer, sir! I'm not philosophizing: I'm crying aloud the reason of my sufferings.

THE MANAGER (*makes brusque movement as he is taken with a new idea*): I should like to know if anyone has ever heard of a character who gets right out of his part and perorates and speechifies as you do. Have you ever heard of a case? I haven't.

THE FATHER: You have never met such a case, sir, because authors, as a rule, hide the labor of their creations. When the characters are really alive before their author, the latter does nothing but follow them in their action, in other words, in the situations which they suggest to him; and he has to will them the way they will themselves — for there's trouble if he doesn't. When a character is born, he acquires at once such an independence, even of his own author, that he can be imagined by everybody even in many other situations where the author never dreamed of placing him; and so he acquires for himself a meaning which the author never thought of giving him.

THE MANAGER: Yes, yes, I know this.

THE FATHER: What is there then to marvel at in us?

Imagine such a misfortune for characters as I have described to you: to be born of an author's fantasy, and be denied life by him; and then answer me if these characters left alive, and yet without life, weren't right in doing what they did do and are doing now, after they have attempted everything in their power to persuade him to give them their stage life. We've all tried him in turn, I, she (*indicating the Stepdaughter*) and she (*indicating the Mother*).

THE STEPDAUGHTER: It's true. I too have sought to tempt him, many, many times, when he has been sitting at his writing table, feeling a bit melancholy, at the twilight hour. He would sit in his armchair too lazy to switch on the light, and all the shadows that crept into his room were full of our presence coming to tempt him. (*As if she saw herself still there by the writing table, and was annoyed by the presence of the Actors.*) Oh, if you would only go away, go away and leave us alone — mother here with that son of hers — I with that child — that boy there always alone — and then I with him (*just hints at the Father*) — and then I alone, alone . . . in those shadows! (*Makes a sudden movement as if in the vision she has of herself illuminating those shadows she wanted to seize hold of herself.*) Ah! my life! my life! Oh, what scenes we proposed to him — and I tempted him more than any of the others!

THE FATHER: Maybe. But perhaps it was your fault that he refused to give us life: because you were too insistent, too troublesome.

THE STEPDAUGHTER: Nonsense! Didn't he make me so himself? (*Goes close to the Manager to tell him as if in confidence.*) In my opinion he abandoned us in a fit of depression, of disgust for the ordinary theater as the public knows it and likes it.

THE SON: Exactly what it was, sir; exactly that!

THE FATHER: Not at all! Don't believe it for a minute. Listen to me! You'll be doing quite right to modify, as you suggest, the excesses both of this girl here, who wants to do too much, and of this young man, who won't do anything at all.

THE SON: No, nothing!

THE MANAGER: You too get over the mark occasionally, my dear sir, if I may say so.

THE FATHER: I? When? Where?

THE MANAGER: Always! Continuously! Then there's this insistence of yours in trying to make us believe you are a character. And then too, you must really argue and philosophize less, you know, much less.

THE FATHER: Well, if you want to take away from me the possibility of representing the torment of my spirit which never gives me peace, you will be suppressing me: that's all. Every true man, sir, who is a little above the level of the beasts and plants does not live for the sake of living, without knowing how to live; but he lives so as to give a meaning and a value of his own to life. For me this is *everything*. I cannot give up this, just to represent a mere fact as she (*indicating the Stepdaughter*) wants. It's all very well for

her, since her "vendetta" lies in the "fact." I'm not going to do it. It destroys my *raison d'être*.

THE MANAGER: Your *raison d'être*! Oh, we're going ahead fine! First she starts off, and then you jump in. At this rate, we'll never finish.

THE FATHER: Now, don't be offended! Have it your own way — provided, however, that within the limits of the parts you assign us each one's sacrifice isn't too great.

THE MANAGER: You've got to understand that you can't go on arguing at your own pleasure. Drama is action, sir, action and not confounded philosophy.

THE FATHER: All right. I'll do just as much arguing and philosophizing as everybody does when he is considering his own torments.

THE MANAGER: If the drama permits! But for Heaven's sake, man, let's get along and come to the scene.

THE STEPDAUGHTER: It seems to me we've got too much action with our coming into his house. (*Indicating Father.*) You said, before, you couldn't change the scene every five minutes.

THE MANAGER: Of course not. What we've got to do is to combine and group up all the facts in one simultaneous, close-knit action. We can't have it as you want, with your little brother wandering like a ghost from room to room, hiding behind doors and meditating a project which — what did you say it did to him?

THE STEPDAUGHTER: Consumes him, sir, wastes him away!

THE MANAGER: Well, it may be. And then at the same time, you want the little girl there to be playing in the garden . . . one in the house, and the other in the garden; isn't that it?

THE STEPDAUGHTER: Yes, in the sun, in the sun! That is my only pleasure: to see her happy and careless in the garden after the misery and squalor of the horrible room where we all four slept together. And I had to sleep with her — I, do you understand? — with my vile contaminated body next to hers; with her holding me fast in her loving little arms. In the garden, whenever she spied me, she would run to take me by the hand. She didn't care for the big flowers, only the little ones; and she loved to show me them and pet me.

THE MANAGER: Well then, we'll have it in the garden. Everything shall happen in the garden; and we'll group the other scenes there. (*Calls a Stage Hand.*) Here, a backcloth with trees and something to do as a fountain basin. (*Turning round to look at the back of the stage.*) Ah, you've fixed it up. Good! (*To Stepdaughter.*) This is just to give an idea, of course. The Boy, instead of hiding behind the doors, will wander about here in the garden, hiding behind the trees. But it's going to be rather difficult to find a child to do that scene with you where she shows you the flowers. (*Turning to the Boy.*) Come forward a little, will you please? Let's try it now! Come along! come along! (*Then seeing him come shyly forward, full of fear and looking lost.*) It's a nice business, this lad here.

What's the matter with him? We'll have to give him a word or two to say. (*Goes close to him, puts a hand on his shoulders, and leads him behind one of the trees.*) Come on! come on! Let me see you a little! Hide here . . . yes, like that. Try and show your head just a little as if you were looking for someone. . . . (*Goes back to observe the effect, when the Boy at once goes through the action.*) Excellent! fine! (*Turning to Stepdaughter.*) Suppose the little girl there were to surprise him as he looks round, and run over to him, so we could give him a word or two to say?

THE STEPDAUGHTER: It's useless to hope he will speak, as long as that fellow there is here. . . . (*Indicates the Son.*) You must send him away first.

THE SON (*jumping up*): Delighted! Delighted! I don't ask for anything better. (*Begins to move away.*)

THE MANAGER (*at once stopping him*): No! No! Where are you going? Wait a bit!

(*The Mother gets up alarmed and terrified at the thought that he is really about to go away. Instinctively she lifts her arms to prevent him, without, however, leaving her seat.*)

THE SON (*to Manager, who stops him*): I've got nothing to do with this affair. Let me go, please! Let me go!

THE MANAGER: What do you mean by saying you've got nothing to do with this?

THE STEPDAUGHTER (*calmly, with irony*): Don't bother to stop him: he won't go away.

THE FATHER: He has to act the terrible scene in the garden with his mother.

THE SON (*suddenly resolute and with dignity*): I shall act nothing at all. I've said so from the very beginning. (*To the Manager.*) Let me go!

THE STEPDAUGHTER (*going over to the Manager*): Allow me? (*Puts down the Manager's arm which is restraining the Son.*) Well, go away then, if you want to! (*The Son looks at her with contempt and hatred. She laughs and says.*) You see, he can't, he can't go away! He is obliged to stay here, indissolubly bound to the chain. If I, who fly off when that happens which has to happen because I can't bear him — if I am still here and support that face and expression of his, you can well imagine that he is unable to move. He has to remain here, has to stop with that nice father of his, and that mother whose only son he is. (*Turning to the Mother.*) Come on, mother, come along! (*Turning to Manager to indicate her.*) You see, she was getting up to keep him back. (*To the Mother, beckoning her with her hand.*) Come on, come on! (*Then to Manager.*) You can imagine how little she wants to show these actors of yours what she really feels; but so eager is she to get near him that. . . . There, you see? She is willing to act her part. (*And in fact, the Mother approaches him; and as soon as the Stepdaughter has finished speaking, opens her arms to signify that she consents.*)

THE SON (*suddenly*): No! no! If I can't go away, then I'll stop here; but I repeat: I act nothing!

THE FATHER (*to Manager excitedly*): You can force him, sir.

THE SON: Nobody can force me.

THE FATHER: I can.

THE STEPDAUGHTER: Wait a minute, wait . . . First of all, the baby has to go to the fountain. . . . (*Runs to take the Child and leads her to the fountain.*)

THE MANAGER: Yes, yes of course; that's it. Both at the same time.

(*The Second Lady Lead and the Juvenile Lead at this point separate themselves from the group of Actors. One watches the Mother attentively; the other moves about studying the movements and manner of the Son whom he will have to act.*)

THE SON (*to Manager*): What do you mean by both at the same time? It isn't right. There was no scene between me and her. (*Indicates the Mother.*) Ask her how it was!

THE MOTHER: Yes, it's true. I had come into his room. . . .

THE SON: Into my room, do you understand? Nothing to do with the garden.

THE MANAGER: It doesn't matter. Haven't I told you we've got to group the action?

THE SON (*observing the Juvenile Lead studying him*): What do you want?

THE JUVENILE LEAD: Nothing! I was just looking at you.

THE SON (*turning toward the Second Lady Lead*): Ah! she's at it too: to re-act her part! (*Indicating the Mother.*)

THE MANAGER: Exactly! And it seems to me that you ought to be grateful to them for their interest.

THE SON: Yes, but haven't you yet perceived that it isn't possible to live in front of a mirror which not only freezes us with the image of ourselves, but throws our likeness back at us with a horrible grimace?

THE FATHER: That is true, absolutely true. You must see that.

THE MANAGER (*to Second Lady Lead and Juvenile Lead*): He's right! Move away from them!

THE SON: Do as you like. I'm out of this!

THE MANAGER: Be quiet, you, will you? And let me hear your mother! (*To Mother.*) You were saying you had entered. . . .

THE MOTHER: Yes, into his room, because I couldn't stand it any longer. I went to empty my heart to him of all the anguish that tortures me. . . . But as soon as he saw me come in. . . .

THE SON: Nothing happened! There was no scene. I went away, that's all! I don't care for scenes!

THE MOTHER: It's true, true. That's how it was.

THE MANAGER: Well now, we've got to do this bit between you and him. It's indispensable.

THE MOTHER: I'm ready . . . when you are ready. If you could only find a chance for me to tell him what I feel here in my heart.

THE FATHER (*going to Son in a great rage*): You'll do this for your mother, for your mother, do you understand?

THE SON (*quite determined*): I do nothing!

THE FATHER (*taking hold of him and shaking him*): For God's sake, do as I tell you! Don't you hear your mother asking you for a favor? Haven't you even got the guts to be a son?

THE SON (*taking hold of the Father*): No! No! And for God's sake stop it, or else.... (*General agitation. The Mother, frightened, tries to separate them.*)

THE MOTHER (*pleading*): Please! please!

THE FATHER (*not leaving hold of the Son*): You've got to obey, do you hear?

THE SON (*almost crying from rage*): What does it mean, this madness you've got? (*They separate.*) Have you no decency, that you insist on showing everyone our shame? I won't do it! I won't! And I stand for the will of our author in this. He didn't want to put us on the stage, after all!

THE MANAGER: Man alive! You came here . . .

THE SON (*indicating Father*): He did! I didn't!

THE MANAGER: Aren't you here now?

THE SON: It was his wish, and he dragged us along with him. He's told you not only the things that did happen, but also things that have never happened at all.

THE MANAGER: Well, tell me then what did happen. You went out of your room without saying a word?

THE SON: Without a word, so as to avoid a scene!

THE MANAGER: And then what did you do?

THE SON: Nothing . . . walking in the garden. . . . (*Hesitates for a moment with expression of gloom.*)

THE MANAGER (*coming closer to him, interested by his extraordinary reserve*): Well, well . . . walking in the garden. . . .

THE SON (*exasperated*): Why on earth do you insist? It's horrible!

(*The Mother trembles, sobs, and looks toward the fountain.*)

THE MANAGER (*slowly observing the glance and turning toward the Son with increasing apprehension*): The baby?

THE SON: There in the fountain. . . .

THE FATHER (*pointing with tender pity to the Mother*): She was following him at the moment. . . .

THE MANAGER (*to the Son anxiously*): And then you. . . .

THE SON: I ran over to her; I was jumping in to drag her out when I saw something that froze my blood . . . the boy standing stock still, with eyes like a madman's, watching his little drowned sister, in the fountain! (*The Stepdaughter bends over the fountain to hide the Child. She sobs.*) Then. . . . (*A revolver shot rings out behind the trees where the Boy is hidden.*)

THE MOTHER (*with a cry of terror runs over in that direction together with several of the Actors amid general confusion*): My son! My son! (*Then amid the cries and exclamations one hears her voice.*) Help! Help!

THE MANAGER (*pushing the Actors aside while they lift up the Boy and carry him off*): Is he really wounded?

SOME ACTORS: He's dead! dead!

OTHER ACTORS: No, no, it's only make-believe, it's only pretense!

THE FATHER (*with a terrible cry*): Pretense? Reality, sir, reality!

THE MANAGER: Pretense? Reality? To hell with it all! Never in my life has such a thing happened to me. I've lost a whole day over these people, a whole day!

COMMENTARY

John Corbin (1870–1959)
REVIEW OF *SIX CHARACTERS IN SEARCH OF AN AUTHOR*   1922

Corbin's review of the distinguished 1922 production of Six Characters in Search of an Author *reminds us how much the audiences loved the play. They stood clapping long after the last curtain. Florence Eldridge, who became famous for her role, is given relatively little attention here. Corbin instead focused his comments on the complexity of the play's comic premise.*

Philosophical fooling and shrewd criticism on the art of the theatre mingle in the Italian play which Brock Pemberton is presenting in translation at the Princess.

Imagine a playwright whose creative mind is haunted by six characters, the persons of a harrowing family drama, all urging insistently that they be given full and subtly shaded representation in the theatre. That is the normal condition of authentic creation; but as art consists in rigid elimination as well as in delicate emphasis, many of the aspirations of the six for self-expression have to be denied. Imagine next that the subject of their suffering is not sympathetic to the public, and that the only true and significant outcome is undramatic — not moving and inspiring, but static. That very often happens when a dramatist takes his real inspiration from life as it is actually lived, and in the supreme court of the manager's office he is nonsuited. There is no play.

But there are characters more live and vital than most of those that see the footlights. Imagine, finally, that these characters, still longing to live out their lives on the scene, go out in search of a more obliging author — and find a stage manager who has a company but no new play, only the stock stuff of a world somewhat deficient in new inspiration. Recognizing raw materials of interest and power, the enterprising business man undertakes to supply the place of the author. It seems to him a positive windfall to be relieved of that insistent and obnoxious incident of production. He will allow the six characters to live out their own lives while a secretary takes down the dialogue and his company stands by preparing to assume the parts. Magnificent!

Those who look upon ordinary rehearsals as a madhouse will receive illumination. Instead of a single author, long subdued in misery, the manager has his six orphans to contend with. The actors of his company, accustomed to have parts ruthlessly adapted to their personalities, are confronted each with a fury of unreason, demanding the absolute. For these characters, though the shadows of a dream, are "real" in the sense of being raw vitality unshaped to the necessities of art and the practical ends of the theatre. In the turmoil that ensues there is much satire on the foibles of player folk and managers and no little philosophy of dramatic art and dramatic criticism.

Margaret Wycherly is Mother in the roving dramatis personae and lends to the character genuine imagination and emotional power. Moffat Johnston is the garrulous father, eagerly philosophic and disquisitional. Florence Eldridge is the stepdaughter, overflowing with eager youth and charm. Throughout the production is able and highly competent. The audience last night, largely composed of folk of the theatre, rose to the novelty and humor of the idea and lingered long in applause after the brief three acts were over.

What the public will say to this rather slender and technical satire remains to be seen, but already it may be said that the season is indebted to Mr. Pemberton for one more exploration of strange fields and pastures new.

Eugene O'Neill

Eugene O'Neill (1888–1953) is a major figure in American drama. His enormous output is in the tradition of realism established by Strindberg and Ibsen, and his early plays, such as *Anna Christie* (1921), introduced Americans to the techniques of the great European realists. Realism for Americans was a move away from the sentimental comedies, the pathetic dramas, and the melodrama that dominated the American stage from before the Civil War to World War I. Some of O'Neill's plays, such as *Strange Interlude* (1928) and *Dynamo* (1929), were expressionist in style, demonstrating a considerable range. O'Neill rejected the kind of theater in which his father had thrived. James O'Neill had long been a stage star, traveling across the country in his production of *The Count of Monte Cristo,* which had made him rich but had also made him a prisoner of a single role.

Eugene O'Neill won the Pulitzer Prize for drama three times in the 1920s and the Nobel Prize for literature in 1936. Although not popular successes in his own day, his plays — including those published posthumously — are now mainstays of the American theater. Some of America's finest actors have taken a strong interest in his work, both producing his plays and acting in them on the stage and on television. From the 1950s to the 1990s, the late Colleen Dewhurst and Jason Robards, Jr., in particular, gave some magnificent performances and interpretations of O'Neill's work.

The young O'Neill was a romantic in the popular sense of the word. After a year at Princeton University, he began to travel on the sea. His jaunts took him to South America, and he once wound up virtually broke and without resources in Buenos Aires. When he returned to America, he studied for a year with George Pierce Baker, the most famous drama teacher of his day. Eventually, he took up residence in Provincetown, Massachusetts, where a group of people dedicated to theater — including the playwright Susan Glaspell — began to put on plays in their living rooms. When their audiences spilled over, the group created the Provincetown Playhouse, the theater in which many of O'Neill's earliest pieces were first performed.

The subjects of many of O'Neill's plays were not especially appealing to general theater audiences. Those who hoped for light comedy and a good laugh or light melodrama and a good cry found the intensity of his dark vision of the world to be overwhelming. They came for mere entertainment, and he was providing them with frightening visions of the soul's interior. The glum and painful surroundings of *Anna Christie* (1921) and the brutality of the lower-class coal stoker in *The Hairy Ape* (1922) were foreign to the comfortable middle-class audiences who supported commercial theater in America. They found O'Neill's characters to be haunted by family agonies, affections never given, ambitions never realized, pains never assuaged. Despite his remarkable abilities and the power of his drama, audiences often did not know what to make of him. To a large extent, his acceptance came on waves of shock, as had the acceptance of the Scandinavian realists.

O'Neill's early work is marked by a variety of experiments with theatrical effects and moods. He tried to use the primary influences of Greek drama in such plays as *Desire under the Elms* (1924), which has been described by critics as Greek tragedy, and *Mourning Becomes Electra* (1931), based on the *Oresteia,* which took three days to perform. But many of his early plays now seem dated and strange. His most impressive plays are his later work, such as *Ah, Wilderness!* (1933), *The Iceman Cometh* (1939), *Long Day's Journey into Night* (1939–1941), *A Moon for the Misbegotten* (1943), and *A Touch of the Poet* (1935–1942), which was performed posthumously in 1957.

DESIRE UNDER THE ELMS

Desire under the Elms (1924) is Eugene O'Neill's first effort at writing in the style of Greek tragedy. He did not follow the Greek tradition and choose a great figure of noble birth about whom the fates would unravel their mystery. Rather, he was deliberately democratic, choosing a New England farmer and his family as the protagonists of his drama. Just as fate animates a Greek tragedy, the emotional forces of jealousy, resentment, lust, and incestuous love animate *Desire under the Elms.*

O'Neill set his play on a typically rocky New England soil, which in many ways bears a striking resemblance to the rocky soil of Athens and the Greek coastline. The unyielding toughness of life on that land contrasts with the easy life to be made from gold mining in California. Ephraim Cabot, the seventy-five-year-old father, has been made hard and physically powerful by his work. He has just taken a third wife, the young and scheming Abbie. His youngest son, Eben, has decided to stay on the farm while his two other sons plan to go to California and put New England behind them.

The sense of having been dispossessed of his farm by his new stepmother drives Eben to hate Abbie, who has married the elder Cabot merely to inherit his farm. At first the sparring between Abbie and Eben is based on calculating self-interest, but eventually their feelings overpower them. Lust turns to love, and the son they produce is passed off as old Cabot's, although the townspeople have no illusion about whose child it is.

The farm itself is a powerful presence in the play. Whenever old Cabot thinks he should give up and follow the promise of easy money in California, he feels God's presence urging him to stay. God operates for Ephraim as the oracle in *Oedipus Rex* does, giving him a message that is painful but must be obeyed. The rocks on the farm are unforgiving, and so is the fate that Abbie and Eben face. Theirs is an impossible love; everything they do to prove their love condemns them even more. The forces of fate center on the farm. When the play opens, Eben says of it, "God! Purty!" When the play ends, the sheriff praises the farm and says he surely would like to own it, striking a clear note of irony: the agony of the play is rooted in lust — lust for the farm that parallels the lust between Abbie and Eben.

The play is haunted by the ghost of Eben's mother, whom Ephraim married primarily for her farm. Her ghost is exorcised only after the cycle of retribution has begun. Old Cabot has committed a crime against her, and now he must become the victim.

The language of the dialogue is that of New England in the mid-nineteenth century. Living in New England, O'Neill understood the ways and the language of its people. He seems to have imagined the "down-east" flavor of Maine in the language, and he has been careful to build the proper pronunciation into the dialogue. This folksy way of speaking helps emphasize the peasantlike qualities in these New England farmers. O'Neill's careful use of language is reminiscent of Synge's masterful representation of the Irish-English speech in *Playboy of the Western World*.

The language of O'Neill's characters has a rocky toughness at times. Characters are laconic — they often answer in a single word: "Ay-eh." Faithful to his vision of the simple speech of country folk, O'Neill avoids giving them elaborate poetic soliloquies. Instead, he shows how, despite their limited language, rural people feel profound emotions and act on them.

O'Neill carefully links Abbie with Queen Phaedra, who in Euripides' play *Hippolytus* and in Racine's seventeenth-century play *Phaedra* finds herself uncontrollably desiring her husband's son as a lover. Racine and Racine's audience could easily imagine such intense emotions overwhelming a noblewoman because they thought that nobility felt more intensely and lived more intensely than ordinary people. But O'Neill is trying to make his audience see that even unlettered farm people can feel as deeply as tragic heroes of any age do. The Cabots are victims of passion. They share their fate with the great families of the Greek tragedies.

Desire under the Elms in Performance

Desire under the Elms was first performed in Greenwich Village in 1924 under the auspices of the Provincetown Players. A year later it appeared on Broadway for thirty-six weeks, a long run for a tragedy. Its first reviewers were courteous but puzzled. They compared the play with earlier O'Neill works, remarking on its "tragic gloom and irony" and praising its language. At the Los Angeles production in 1926, the cast was arrested for "giving an obscene play." The sexual themes offended theatergoers in California, and even those who defended the play admitted that the text would be offensive to some members of the audience.

Because the English censor banned the play until 1938, its first European production was in Prague's National Theatre in 1925. Its Czech title translated as "The Farm under the Elms." The director used a highly stylized set influenced by the Moscow Art Theatre and later described as "a sort of two-storied wooded edifice . . . rather like a log cabin multiplied by four."

Other earlier European productions followed in Moscow in 1932, in Stockholm in 1933, and finally in London in 1940. The 1952 New York revival was not successful. The 1963 revival at the Circle in the Square in New York starred George C. Scott and his wife, Colleen Dewhurst. Jose Quintero, a notable interpreter of O'Neill, directed. Critics complained about "awkward" echoes of Greek tragedy while admitting that the play had an uncanny power despite its flaws. It ran for 380 performances.

The play has often been revived: in Boston in 1967; at the Berkshire Theater Festival in 1974; at the Roundabout Theater in New York, directed by Terry Schrieber, in 1984; and by numerous local theater groups. In 1978 Edward Thomas staged it at Connecticut College in New London as an opera. A creditable production, it emphasized the play's American folk qualities.

Eugene O'Neill (1888–1953)

DESIRE UNDER THE ELMS

1924

Characters

EPHRAIM CABOT
SIMEON }
PETER   } *his sons*
EBEN   }
ABBIE PUTNAM
YOUNG GIRL, TWO FARMERS, *the* FIDDLER, *a* SHERIFF, *and other folk from the neighboring farms.*

(Scene: *The action of the entire play takes place in, and immediately outside of, the Cabot farmhouse in New England, in the year 1850. The south end of the house faces front to a stone wall with a wooden gate at center opening on a country road. The house is in good condition but in need of paint. Its walls are a sickly grayish, the green of the shutters faded. Two enormous elms are on each side of the house. They bend their trailing branches down over the roof. They appear to protect and at the same time subdue. There is a sinister maternity in their aspect, a crushing, jealous absorption. They have developed from their intimate contact with the life of man in the house an appalling humaneness. They brood oppressively over the house. They are like exhausted women resting their sagging breasts and hands and hair on its roof, and when it rains their tears trickle down monotonously and rot on the shingles.*

There is a path running from the gate around the right corner of the house to the front door. A narrow porch is on this side. The end wall facing us has two windows in its upper story, two larger ones on the floor below. The two upper are those of the father's bedroom and that of the brothers. On the left, ground floor, is the kitchen — on the right, the parlor, the shades of which are always drawn down.)

PART I • *Scene 1*

(*Exterior of the farmhouse. It is sunset of a day at the beginning of summer in the year 1850. There is no wind and everything is still. The sky above the roof is suffused with deep colors, the green of the elms glows, but the house is in shadow, seeming pale and washed out by contrast.*)

(*A door opens and Eben Cabot comes to the end of the porch and stands looking down the road to the right. He has a large bell in his hand and this he swings mechanically, awakening a deafening clangor. Then he puts his hands on his hips and stares up at the sky. He sighs with a puzzled awe and blurts out with halting appreciation.*)

EBEN: God! Purty! (*His eyes fall and he stares about him frowningly. He is twenty-five, tall and sinewy. His face is well formed, good-looking, but its expression is resentful and defensive. His defiant, dark eyes remind one of a wild animal's in captivity. Each day is a cage in which he finds himself trapped but inwardly unsubdued. There is a fierce repressed vitality about him. He has black hair, mustache, a thin curly trace of beard. He is dressed in rough farm clothes.*)

(*He spits on the ground with intense disgust, turns, and goes back into the house.*)

(*Simeon and Peter come in from their work in the fields. They are tall men, much older than their half-brother [Simeon is thirty-nine and Peter thirty-seven], built on a squarer, simpler model, fleshier in body, more bovine and homelier in face, shrewder and more practical. Their shoulders stoop a bit from years of farm work. They clump heavily along in their clumsy thick-soled boots caked with earth. Their clothes, their faces, hands, bare arms, and throats are earth-stained. They smell of earth. They stand together for a moment in front of the house and, as if with the one impulse, stare dumbly up at the sky, leaning on their hoes. Their faces have a compressed, unresigned expression. As they look upward, this softens.*)

SIMEON (*grudgingly*): Purty.

PETER: Ay-eh.

SIMEON (*suddenly*): Eighteen year ago.

PETER: What?

SIMEON: Jenn. My woman. She died.

PETER: I'd fergot.

SIMEON: I rec'lect — now an' agin. Makes it lonesome. She'd hair long's a hoss' tail — an' yeller like gold!

PETER: Waal — she's gone. (*This with indifferent finality — then after a pause.*) They's gold in the West, Sim.

SIMEON (*still under the influence of sunset — vaguely*): In the sky?

PETER: Waal — in a manner o' speakin' — that's the promise. (*Growing excited.*) Gold in the sky — in the West — Golden Gate — Californi-a! — Goldest West! — fields o' gold!

SIMEON (*excited in his turn*): Fortunes layin' just atop o' the ground waitin' t' be picked! Solomon's mines, they says! (*For a moment they continue looking up at the sky — then their eyes drop.*)

PETER (*with sardonic bitterness*): Here — it's stones atop o' the ground — stones atop o' stones — makin' stone walls — year atop o' year — him 'n' yew 'n' me 'n' then Eben — makin' stone walls fur him to fence us in!

SIMEON: We've wuked. Give our strength. Give our years. Plowed 'em under in the ground — (*He stamps rebelliously.*) — rottin' — makin' soil for his crops! (*A pause.*) Waal — the farm pays good for hereabouts.

PETER: If we plowed in Californi-a, they'd be lumps o' gold in the furrow!

SIMEON: Californi-a's t'other side o' earth, a'most. We got t' calc'late —

PETER (*after a pause*): 'Twould be hard fur me, too, to give up what we've 'arned here by our sweat. (*A pause. Eben sticks his head out of the dining room window, listening.*)

SIMEON: Ay-eh. (*A pause.*) Mebbe — he'll die soon.

PETER (*doubtfully*): Mebbe.

SIMEON: Mebbe — fur all we knows — he's dead now.

PETER: Ye'd need proof.

SIMEON: He's been gone two months — with no word.

PETER: Left us in the fields an evenin' like this. Hitched up an' druv off into the West. That's plum onnateral. He hadn't never been off this farm 'ceptin' t' the village in thirty year or more, not since he married Eben's maw. (*A pause. Shrewdly.*) I calc'late we might git him declared crazy by the court.

SIMEON: He skinned 'em too slick. He got the best o' all on 'em. They'd never b'lieve him crazy. (*A pause.*) We got t' wait — till he's underground.

EBEN (*with a sardonic chuckle*): Honor thy father! (*They turn startled, and stare at him. He grins, then scowls.*) I pray he's died. (*They stare at him. He continues matter-of-factly.*) Supper's ready.

SIMEON AND PETER (*together*): Ay-eh.

EBEN (*gazing up at the sky*): Sun's downin' purty.

SIMEON AND PETER (*together*): Ay-eh. They's gold in the West.

EBEN: Ay-eh. (*Pointing.*) Yonder atop o' the hill pasture, ye mean?

SIMEON AND PETER (*together*): In Californi-a!

EBEN: Hunh? (*Stares at them indifferently for a second, then drawls.*) Waal — supper's gittin' cold. (*He turns back into kitchen.*)

SIMEON (*startled — smacks his lips*): I air hungry!

PETER (*sniffing*): I smells bacon!

SIMEON (*with hungry appreciation*): Bacon's good!

PETER (*in same tone*): Bacon's bacon! (*They turn, shouldering each other, their bodies bumping and rubbing together as they hurry clumsily to their food, like two friendly oxen toward their evening meal. They disappear around the right corner of house and can be heard entering the door.*)

Scene II

(*The color fades from the sky. Twilight begins. The interior of the kitchen is now visible. A pine table is at center, a cook-stove in the right rear corner, four rough wooden chairs, a tallow candle on the table. In the middle of the rear wall is fastened a big advertising poster with a ship in full sail and the word "California" in big letters. Kitchen utensils hang from nails. Everything is neat and in order but the atmosphere is of a men's camp kitchen rather than that of a home.*)

(*Places for three are laid. Eben takes boiled potatoes and bacon from the stove and puts them on the table, also a loaf of bread and a crock of water. Simeon and Peter shoulder in, slump down in their chairs without a word. Eben joins them. The three eat in silence for a moment, the two elder as naturally unrestrained as beasts of the field, Eben picking at his food without appetite, glancing at them with a tolerant dislike.*)

SIMEON (*suddenly turns to Eben*): Looky here! Ye'd oughtn't t' said that, Eben.

PETER: 'Twa'n't righteous.

EBEN: What?

SIMEON: Ye prayed he'd died.

EBEN: Waal — don't yew pray it? (*A pause.*)

PETER: He's our Paw.

EBEN (*violently*): Not mine!

SIMEON (*dryly*): Ye'd not let no one else say that about yer Maw! Ha! (*He gives one abrupt sardonic guffaw. Peter grins.*)

EBEN (*very pale*): I meant — I hain't his'n — I hain't like him — he hain't me!

PETER (*dryly*): Wait till ye've growed his age!

EBEN (*intensely*): I'm Maw — every drop o' blood! (*A pause. They stare at him with indifferent curiosity.*)

PETER (*reminiscently*): She was good t' Sim 'n' me. A good Stepmaw's scurse.

SIMEON: She was good t' everyone.

EBEN (*greatly moved, gets to his feet and makes an awkward bow to each of them — stammering*): I be thankful t' ye. I'm her — her heir. (*He sits down in confusion.*)

PETER (*after a pause — judicially*): She was good even t' him.

EBEN (*fiercely*): An' fur thanks he killed her!

SIMEON (*after a pause*): No one never kills nobody. It's allus somethin'. That's the murderer.

EBEN: Didn't he slave Maw t' death?

PETER: He's slaved himself t' death. He's slaved Sim 'n' me 'n' yew t' death — on'y none o' us hain't died — yit.

SIMEON: It's somethin' — drivin' him — t' drive us!

EBEN (*vengefully*): Waal — I hold him t' jedgment! (*Then scornfully.*) Somethin'! What's somethin'?

SIMEON: Dunno.

EBEN (*sardonically*): What's drivin' yew to Californi-a, mebbe? (*They look at him in surprise.*) Oh, I've heerd ye! (*Then, after a pause.*) But ye'll never go t' the gold fields!

PETER (*assertively*): Mebbe!

EBEN: Whar'll ye git the money?

PETER: We kin walk. It's an a'mighty ways — Californi-a — but if yew was t' put all the steps we've walked on this farm end t' end we'd be in the moon!

EBEN: The Injuns'll skulp ye on the plains.

SIMEON (*with grim humor*): We'll mebbe make 'em pay a hair fur a hair!

EBEN (*decisively*): But t'aint that. Ye won't never go because ye'll wait here fur yer share o' the farm, thinkin' allus he'll die soon.

SIMEON (*after a pause*): We've a right.

PETER: Two-thirds belongs t'us.

EBEN (*jumping to his feet*): Ye've no right! She wa'n't yewr Maw! It was her farm! Didn't he steal it from her? She's dead. It's my farm.

SIMEON (*sardonically*): Tell that t' Paw — when he comes! I'll bet ye a dollar he'll laugh — fur once in his life. Ha! (*He laughs himself in one single mirthless bark.*)

PETER (*amused in turn, echoes his brother*): Ha!

SIMEON (*after a pause*): What've ye got held agin us, Eben? Year arter year it's skulked in yer eye — somethin'.

PETER: Ay-eh.

EBEN: Ay-eh. They's somethin'. (*Suddenly exploding.*) Why didn't ye never stand between him 'n' my Maw when he was slavin' her to her grave — t' pay her back fur the kindness she done t' yew? (*There is a long pause. They stare at him in surprise.*)

SIMEON: Waal — the stock'd got t' be watered.

PETER: 'R they was woodin' t' do.

SIMEON: 'R plowin'.

PETER: 'R hayin'.

SIMEON: 'R spreadin' manure.

PETER: 'R weedin'.

SIMEON: 'R prunin'.

PETER: 'R milkin'.

EBEN (*breaking in harshly*): An' makin' walls — stone atop o' stone — makin' walls till yer heart's a stone ye heft up out o' the way o' growth onto a stone wall t' wall in yer heart!

SIMEON (*matter-of-factly*): We never had no time t' meddle.

PETER (*to Eben*): Yew was fifteen afore yer Maw died — an' big fur yer age. Why didn't ye never do nothin'?

EBEN (*harshly*): They was chores t' do, wasn't they? (*A pause — then slowly.*) It was on'y arter she died I come to think o' it. Me cookin' — doin' her work — that made me know her, suffer her sufferin' — she'd come back t' help — come back t' bile potatoes — come back t' fry bacon — come back t' bake biscuits — come back all cramped up t' shake the fire, an' carry ashes, her eyes weepin' an' bloody with smoke an' cinders same's they used t' be. She still comes back — stands by the stove thar in the evenin' — she can't find it nateral sleepin' an' restin' in peace. She can't git used t' bein' free — even in her grave.

SIMEON: She never complained none.

EBEN: She'd got too tired. She'd got too used t' bein' too tired. That was what he done. (*With vengeful passion.*) An' sooner'r later, I'll meddle. I'll say the thin's I didn't say then t' him! I'll yell 'em at the top o' my lungs. I'll see t' it my Maw gits some rest an' sleep in her grave! (*He sits down again, relapsing into a brooding silence. They look at him with a queer indifferent curiosity.*)

PETER (*after a pause*): Whar in tarnation d'ye s'pose he went, Sim?

SIMEON: Dunno. He druv off in the buggy, all spick an' span, with the mare all breshed an' shiny, druv off clackin' his tongue an' wavin' his whip. I remember it right well. I was finishin' plowin', it was spring an' May an' sunset, an' gold in the West, an' he druv off into it. I yells "Whar ye goin', Paw?" an' he hauls up by the stone wall a jiffy. His old snake's eyes was glitterin' in the sun like he'd been drinkin' a jugful an' he says with a mule's grin: "Don't ye run away till I come back!"

PETER: Wonder if he knowed we was wantin' fur Californi-a?

SIMEON: Mebbe. I didn't say nothin' and he says, lookin' kinder queer an' sick: "I been hearin' the hens cluckin' an' the roosters crowin' all the durn day. I been listenin't' the cows lowin' an' everythin' else kickin' up till I can't stand it no more. It's spring an' I'm feelin' damned," he says. "Damned like an old bare hickory tree fit on'y fur burnin'," he says. An' then I calc'late I must've looked a mite hopeful, fur he adds real spry and vicious: "But don't git no fool idee I'm dead. I've sworn t' live a hundred an' I'll do it, if on'y t' spite yer sinful greed! An' now I'm ridin' out t' learn God's message t' me in the spring, like the prophets done. An' yew git back t' yer plowin'," he says. An' he druv off singin' a hymn. I thought he was drunk — 'r I'd stopped him goin'.

EBEN (*scornfully*): No, ye wouldn't! Ye're scared o' him. He's stronger — inside — than both o' ye put together!

PETER (*sardonically*): An' yew — be yew Samson?°

EBEN: I'm gittin' stronger. I kin feel it growin' in me — growin' an' growin' — till it'll bust out — ! (*He gets up and puts on his coat and a hat. They watch him, gradually breaking into grins. Eben avoids their eyes sheepishly.*) I'm goin' out fur a spell — up the road.

PETER: T' the village.

SIMEON: T' see Minnie?

EBEN (*defiantly*): Ay-eh!

PETER (*jeeringly*): The Scarlet Woman!

SIMEON: Lust — that's what's growin' in ye!

EBEN: Waal — she's purty!

PETER: She's been purty fur twenty year.

SIMEON: A new coat o' paint'll make a heifer out of forty.

EBEN: She hain't forty!

PETER: If she hain't, she's teeterin' on the edge.

EBEN (*desperately*): What d'yew know —

PETER: All they is . . . Sim knew her — an' then me arter —

SIMEON: An' Paw kin tell yew somethin' too! He was fust!

EBEN: D'ye mean t' say he . . . ?

SIMEON (*with a grin*): Ay-eh! We air his heirs in every-thin'!

EBEN (*intensely*): That's more to it! That grows on it! It'll bust soon! (*Then violently.*) I'll go smash my fist in her face! (*He pulls open the door in rear violently.*)

SIMEON (*with a wink at Peter — drawlingly*): Mebbe — but the night's wa'm — purty — by the time ye git thar mebbe ye'll kiss her instead!

PETER: Sart'n he will! (*They both roar with coarse laughter. Eben rushes out and slams the door — then the outside front door — comes around the corner of the house and stands still by the gate, staring up at the sky.*)

SIMEON (*looking after him*): Like his Paw.

PETER: Dead spit an' image!

SIMEON: Dog'll eat dog!

PETER: Ay-eh. (*Pause. With yearning.*) Mebbe a year from now we'll be in Californi-a.

SIMEON: Ay-eh. (*A pause. Both yawn.*) Let's git t'bed. (*He blows out the candle. They go out door in rear. Eben stretches his arms up to the sky — rebelliously.*)

EBEN: Waal — thar's a star, an' somewhar's they's him, an' here's me, an' thar's Min up the road — in the same night. What if I does kiss her? She's like t'night, she's soft 'n' wa'm, her eyes kin wink like a star, her

Samson: A biblical hero known for his great physical strength.

mouth's wa'm, her arms're wa'm, she smells like a wa'm plowed field, she's purty . . . Ay-eh! By God A'mighty she's purty, an' I don't give a damn how many sins she's sinned afore mine or who she's sinned 'em with, my sin's as purty as any one on 'em! (*He strides off down the road to the left.*)

Scene III

(*It is the pitch darkness just before dawn. Eben comes in from the left and goes around to the porch, feeling his way, chuckling bitterly and cursing half-aloud to himself.*)

EBEN: The cussed old miser! (*He can be heard going in the front door. There is a pause as he goes upstairs, then a loud knock on the bedroom door of the brothers.*) Wake up!

SIMEON (*startledly*): Who's thar?

EBEN (*Pushing open the door and coming in, a lighted candle in his hand. The bedroom of the brothers is revealed. Its ceiling is the sloping roof. They can stand upright only close to the center dividing wall of the upstairs. Simeon and Peter are in a double bed, front. Eben's cot is to the rear. Eben has a mixture of silly grin and vicious scowl on his face.*): I be!

PETER (*angrily*): What in hell's-fire. . . ?

EBEN: I got news fur ye! Ha! (*He gives one abrupt sardonic guffaw.*)

SIMEON (*angrily*): Couldn't ye hold it 'til we'd got our sleep?

EBEN: It's nigh sunup. (*Then explosively.*) He's gone an' married agen!

SIMEON AND PETER (*explosively*): Paw?

EBEN: Got himself hitched to a female 'bout thirty-five — an' purty, they says . . .

SIMEON (*aghast*): It's a durn lie!

PETER: Who says?

SIMEON: They been stringin' ye!

EBEN: Think I'm a dunce, do ye? The hull village says. The preacher from New Dover, he brung the news — told it t'our preacher — New Dover, that's whar the old loon got himself hitched — that's whar the woman lived —

PETER (*no longer doubting — stunned*): Waal . . . !

SIMEON (*the same*): Waal . . . !

EBEN (*sitting down on a bed — with vicious hatred*): Ain't he a devil out o' hell? It's jest t' spite us — the damned old mule!

PETER (*after a pause*): Everythin'll go t'her now.

SIMEON: Ay-eh. (*A pause — dully.*) Waal — if it's done —

PETER: It's done us. (*Pause — then persuasively.*) They's gold in the fields o' Californi-a, Sim. No good a-stayin' here now.

SIMEON: Jest what I was a-thinkin'. (*Then with decision.*) S'well fust's last! Let's light out and git this mornin'.

PETER: Suits me.

EBEN: Ye must like walkin'.

SIMEON (*sardonically*): If ye'd grow wings on us we'd fly thar!

EBEN: Ye'd like ridin' better — on a boat, wouldn't ye? (*Fumbles in his pocket and takes out a crumpled sheet of foolscap.*) Waal, if ye sign this ye kin ride on a boat. I've had it writ out an' ready in case ye'd ever go. It says fur three hundred dollars t' each ye agree yewr shares o' the farm is sold t' me. (*They look suspiciously at the paper. A pause.*)

SIMEON (*wonderingly*): But if he's hitched agen —

PETER: An' whar'd yew git that sum o' money, anyways?

EBEN (*cunningly*): I know whar it's hid. I been waitin' — Maw told me. She knew whar it lay fur years, but she was waitin' . . . It's her'n — the money he hoarded from her farm an' hid from Maw. It's my money by rights now.

PETER: Whar's it hid?

EBEN (*cunningly*): Whar yew won't never find it without me. Maw spied on him —'r she'd never knowed. (*A pause. They look at him suspiciously, and he at them.*) Waal, is it fa'r trade?

SIMEON: Dunno.

PETER: Dunno.

SIMEON (*looking at window*): Sky's grayin'.

PETER: Ye better start the fire, Eben.

SIMEON: An' fix some vittles.

EBEN: Ay-eh. (*Then with a forced jocular heartiness.*) I'll git ye a good one. If ye're startin' t' hoof it t' Californi-a ye'll need somethin' that'll stick t' yer ribs. (*He turns to the door, adding meaningly.*) But ye kin ride on a boat if ye'll swap. (*He stops at the door and pauses. They stare at him.*)

SIMEON (*suspiciously*): Whar was ye all night?

EBEN (*defiantly*): Up t' Min's. (*Then slowly.*) Walkin' thar, fust I felt 's if I'd kiss her; then I got a-thinkin' o' what ye'd said o' him an' her an' I says, I'll bust her nose fur that! Then I got t' the village an' heerd the news an' I got madder'n hell an' run all the way t' Min's not knowin' what I'd do — (*He pauses — then sheepishly but more defiantly.*) Waal — when I seen her, I didn't hit her — nor I didn't kiss her nuther — I begun t' beller like a calf an' cuss at the same time, I was so durn mad — an' she got scared — an' I jest grabbed holt an' tuk her! (*Proudly.*) Yes, sirree! I tuk her. She may've been his'n — an' your'n, too — but she's mine now!

SIMEON (*dryly*): In love, air yew?

EBEN (*with lofty scorn*): Love! I don't take no stock in sech slop!

PETER (*winking at Simeon*): Mebbe Eben's aimin' t' marry, too.

SIMEON: Min'd make a true faithful he'pmeet! (*They snicker.*)

EBEN: What do I care fur her —'ceptin' she's round an' wa'm? The p'int is she was his'n — an' now she b'longs t' me! (*He goes to the door — then turns — rebelliously.*) An' Min hain't sech a bad un. They's worse'n Min in the world, I'll bet ye! Wait'll we see

this cow the Old Man's hitched t'! She'll beat Min, I got a notion! (*He starts to go out.*)

SIMEON (*suddenly*): Mebbe ye'll try t' make her your'n, too?

PETER: Ha! (*He gives a sardonic laugh of relish at this idea.*)

EBEN (*spitting with disgust*): Her — here — sleepin' with him — stealin' my Maw's farm! I'd as soon pet a skunk 'r kiss a snake! (*He goes out. The two stare after him suspiciously. A pause. They listen to his steps receding.*)

PETER: He's startin' the fire.

SIMEON: I'd like t' ride t' Californi-a — but —

PETER: Min might o' put some scheme in his head.

SIMEON: Mebbe it's all a lie 'bout Paw marryin'. We'd best wait an' see the bride.

PETER: An' don't sign nothin' till we does!

SIMEON: Nor till we've tested it's good money! (*Then with a grin.*) But if Paw's hitched we'd be sellin' Eben somethin' we'd never git nohow!

PETER: We'll wait an' see. (*Then with sudden vindictive anger.*) An' till he comes, let's yew 'n' me not wuk a lick, let Eben tend to thin's if he's a mind to, let's us jest sleep an' eat an' drink likker, an' let the hull damned farm go t' blazes!

SIMEON (*excitedly*): By God, we've 'arned a rest! We'll play rich fur a change. I hain't a-going to stir outa bed till breakfast's ready.

PETER: An' on the table!

SIMEON (*after a pause — thoughtfully*): What d'ye cal'c'late she'll be like — our new Maw? Like Eben thinks?

PETER: More'n' likely.

SIMEON (*vindictively*): Waal — I hope she's a she-devil that'll make him wish he was dead an' livin' in the pit o' hell fur comfort!

PETER (*fervently*): Amen!

SIMEON (*imitating his father's voice*): "I'm ridin' out t' learn God's message t' me in the spring like the prophets done," he says. I'll bet right then an' thar he knew plumb well he was goin' whorin', the stinkin' old hypocrite!

Scene IV

(*Same as scene II — shows the interior of the kitchen with a lighted candle on table. It is gray dawn outside. Simeon and Peter are just finishing their breakfast. Eben sits before his plate of untouched food, brooding frowningly.*)

PETER (*glancing at him rather irritably*): Lookin' glum don't help none.

SIMEON (*sarcastically*): Sorrowin' over his lust o' the flesh!

PETER (*with a grin*): Was she yer fust?

EBEN (*angrily*): None o'yer business. (*A pause.*) I was thinkin' o' him. I got a notion he's gittin' near — I kin feel him comin' on like yew kin feel malaria chill afore it takes ye.

PETER: It's too early yet.

SIMEON: Dunno. He'd like t' catch us nappin' — jest t' have somethin' t' hoss us 'round over.

PETER (*Mechanically gets to his feet. Simeon does the same.*): Waal — let's git t'wuk. (*They both plod mechanically toward the door before they realize. Then they stop short.*)

SIMEON (*grinning*): Ye're a cussed fool, Pete — and I be wuss! Let him see we hain't wukin'! We don't give a durn!

PETER (*as they go back to the table*): Not a damned durn! It'll serve t' show him we're done with him. (*They sit down again. Eben stares from one to the other with surprise.*)

SIMEON (*grins at him*): We're aimin' t' start bein' lilies o' the field.

PETER: Nary a toil 'r spin 'r lick o' wuk do we put in!

SIMEON: Ye're sole owner — till he comes — that's what ye wanted. Waal, ye got t' be sole hand, too.

PETER: The cows air bellerin'. Ye better hustle at the milkin'.

EBEN (*with excited joy*): Ye mean ye'll sign the paper?

SIMEON (*dryly*): Mebbe.

PETER: Mebbe.

SIMEON: We're considerin'. (*Peremptorily.*) Ye better git t' wuk.

EBEN (*with queer excitement*): It's Maw's farm agen! It's my farm! Them's my cows! I'll milk my durn fingers off fur cows o' mine! (*He goes out door in rear, they stare after him indifferently.*)

SIMEON: Like his Paw.

PETER: Dead spit 'n' image!

SIMEON: Waal — let dog eat dog! (*Eben comes out of front door and around the corner of the house. The sky is beginning to grow flushed with sunrise. Eben stops by the gate and stares around him with glowing, possessive eyes. He takes in the whole farm with his embracing glance of desire.*)

EBEN: It's purty! It's damned purty! It's mine! (*He suddenly throws his head back boldly and glares with hard, defiant eyes at the sky.*) Mine, d'ye hear? Mine! (*He turns and walks quickly off left, rear, toward the barn. The two brothers light their pipes.*)

SIMEON (*putting his muddy boots up on the table, tilting back his chair, and puffing defiantly*): Waal — this air solid comfort — fur once.

PETER: Ay-eh. (*He follows suit. A pause. Unconsciously they both sigh.*)

SIMEON (*suddenly*): He never was much o' a hand at milkin', Eben wa'n't.

PETER (*with a snort*): His hands air like hoofs! (*A pause.*)

SIMEON: Reach down the jug thar! Let's take a swaller. I'm feelin' kind o' low.

PETER: Good idee! (*He does so — gets two glasses — they pour out drinks of whisky.*) Here's t' the gold in Californi-a!

SIMEON: An' luck t' find it! (*They drink — puff resolutely — sigh — take their feet down from the table.*)

PETER: Likker don't pear t' sot right.

SIMEON: We hain't used t' it this early. (*A pause. They become very restless.*)

PETER: Gittin' close in this kitchen.

SIMEON (*with immense relief*): Let's git a breath o' air. (*They arise briskly and go out rear — appear around house and stop by the gate. They stare up at the sky with a numbed appreciation.*)

PETER: Purty!

SIMEON: Ay-eh. Gold's t' the East now.

PETER: Sun's startin' with us fur the Golden West.

SIMEON (*staring around the farm, his compressed face tightened, unable to conceal his emotion*): Waal — it's our last mornin' — mebbe.

PETER (*the same*): Ay-eh.

SIMEON (*stamps his foot on the earth and addresses it desperately*): Waal — ye've thirty year o' me buried in ye — spread out over ye — blood an' bone an' sweat — rotted away — fertilizin' ye — richin' yer soul — prime manure, by God, that's what I been t' ye!

PETER: Ay-eh! An' me.

SIMEON: An' yew, Peter. (*He sighs — then spits.*) Waal — no use'n cryin' over spilt milk.

PETER: They's gold in the West — an' freedom, mebbe. We been slaves t' stone walls here.

SIMEON (*defiantly*): We hain't nobody's slaves from this out — nor nothin's slaves nuther. (*A pause — restlessly.*) Speaking o' milk, wonder how Eben's managin'?

PETER: I s'pose he's managin'.

SIMEON: Mebbe we'd ought t' help — this once.

PETER: Mebbe. The cows knows us.

SIMEON: An' likes us. They don't know him much.

PETER: An' the hosses, an' pigs, an' chickens. They don't know him much.

SIMEON: They knows us like brothers — an' likes us! (*Proudly.*) Hain't we raised 'em t' be fust-rate, number one prize stock?

PETER: We hain't — not no more.

SIMEON (*dully*): I was fergittin'. (*Then resignedly.*) Waal, let's go help Eben a spell an' git waked up.

PETER: Suits me. (*They are starting off down left, rear, for the barn when Eben appears from there hurrying toward them, his face excited.*)

EBEN (*breathlessly*): Waal — har they be! The old mule an' the bride! I seen 'em from the barn down below at the turnin'.

PETER: How could ye tell that far?

EBEN: Hain't I as far-sight as he's near-sight? Don't I know the mare 'n' buggy, an' two people settin' in it? Who else . . . ? An' I tell ye I kin feel 'em a'comin', too! (*He squirms as if he had the itch.*)

PETER (*beginning to be angry*): Waal — let him do his own unhitchin'!

SIMEON (*angry in his turn*): Let's hustle in an' git our

bundles an' be a-goin' as he's a-comin'. I don't want never t' step inside the door agen arter he's back. (*They both start back around the corner of the house. Eben follows them.*)

EBEN (*anxiously*): Will ye sign it afore ye go?

PETER: Let's see the color o' the old skinflint's money an' we'll sign. (*They disappear left. The two brothers clump upstairs to get their bundles. Eben appears in the kitchen, runs to window, peers out, comes back and pulls up a strip of flooring in under stove, takes out a canvas bag and puts it on table, then sets the floorboard back in place. The two brothers appear a moment after. They carry old carpetbags.*)

EBEN (*puts his hand on bag guardingly*): Have ye signed?

SIMEON (*shows paper in his hand*): Ay-eh. (*Greedily.*) Be that the money?

EBEN (*opens bag and pours out pile of twenty-dollar gold pieces*): Twenty-dollar pieces — thirty of 'em. Count 'em. (*Peter does so, arranging them in stacks of five, biting one or two to test them.*)

PETER: Six hundred. (*He puts them in bag and puts it inside his shirt carefully.*)

SIMEON (*handing paper to Eben*): Har ye be.

EBEN (*after a glance, folds it carefully and hides it under his shirt — gratefully*): Thank yew.

PETER: Thank yew fur the ride.

SIMEON: We'll send ye a lump o' gold fur Christmas. (*A pause. Eben stares at them and they at him.*)

PETER (*awkwardly*): Waal — we're a-goin'.

SIMEON: Comin' out t' the yard?

EBEN: No. I'm waitin' in here a spell. (*Another silence. The brothers edge awkwardly to door in rear — then turn and stand.*)

SIMEON: Waal — good-by.

PETER: Good-by.

EBEN: Good-by. (*They go out. He sits down at the table, faces the stove and pulls out the paper. He looks from it to the stove. His face, lighted up by the shaft of sunlight from the window, has an expression of trance. His lips move. The two brothers come out to the gate.*)

PETER (*looking off toward barn*): Thar he be — un-hitchin'.

SIMEON (*with a chuckle*): I'll bet ye he's riled!

PETER: An thar she be.

SIMEON: Let's wait 'n' see what our new Maw looks like.

PETER (*with a grin*): An' give him our partin' cuss!

SIMEON (*grinning*): I feel like raisin' fun. I feel light in my head an' feet.

PETER: Me, too. I feel like laffin' till I'd split up the middle.

SIMEON: Reckon it's the likker?

PETER: No. My feet feel itchin' t' walk an' walk — an' jump high over thin's — an'. . . .

SIMEON: Dance? (*A pause.*)

PETER (*puzzled*): It's plumb onnateral.

SIMEON (*a light coming over his face*): I calc'late it's 'cause school's out. It's holiday. Fur once we're free!

PETER (*dazedly*): Free?

SIMEON: The halter's broke — the harness is busted — the fence bars is down — the stone walls air crumblin' an' tumblin'! We'll be kickin' up an' tearin' away down the road!

PETER (*drawing a deep breath — oratorically*): Anybody that wants this stinkin' old rock-pile of a farm kin hev it. T'ain't our'n, no sirree!

SIMEON (*takes the gate off its hinges and puts it under his arm*): We harby 'bolishes shet gates, an' open gates, an' all gates, by thunder!

PETER: We'll take it with us fur luck an' let 'er sail free down some river.

SIMEON (*as a sound of voices comes from left, rear*): Har they comes! (*The two brothers congeal into two stiff, grim-visaged statues. Ephraim Cabot and Abbie Putnam come in. Cabot is seventy-five, tall and gaunt, with great, wiry, concentrated power, but stoop-shouldered from toil. His face is as hard as if it were hewn out of a boulder, yet there is a weakness in it, a petty pride in its own narrow strength. His eyes are small, close together, and extremely near-sighted, blinking continually in the effort to focus on objects, their stare having a straining, ingrowing quality. He is dressed in his dismal black Sunday suit. Abbie is thirty-five, buxom, full of vitality. Her round face is pretty but marred by its rather gross sensuality. There is strength and obstinacy in her jaw, a hard determination in her eyes, and about her whole personality the same unsettled, untamed, desperate quality which is so apparent in Eben.*)

CABOT (*as they enter — a queer strangled emotion in his dry cracking voice*): Har we be t' hum, Abbie.

ABBIE (*with lust for the word*): Hum! (*Her eyes gloating on the house without seeming to see the two stiff figures at the gate.*) It's purty — purty! I can't b'lieve it's r'ally mine.

CABOT (*sharply*): Yewr'n? Mine! (*He stares at her penetratingly. She stares back. He adds relentingly.*) Our'n — mebbe! It was lonesome too long. I was growin' old in the spring. A hum's got t' hev a woman.

ABBIE (*her voice taking possession*): A woman's got t' hev a hum!

CABOT (*nodding uncertainly*): Ay-eh. (*Then irritably.*) Whar be they? Ain't thar nobody about —'r wukin' —'r nothin'?

ABBIE (*Sees the brothers. She returns their stare of cold appraising contempt with interest — slowly.*): Thar's two men loafin' at the gate an' starin' at me like a couple o' strayed hogs.

CABOT (*straining his eyes*): I kin see 'em — but I can't make out. . . .

SIMEON: It's Simeon.

PETER: It's Peter.

CABOT (*exploding*): Why hain't ye wukin'?

SIMEON (*dryly*): We're waitin' t' welcome ye hum — yew an' the bride!

CABOT (*confusedly*): Huh? Waal — this be yer new Maw, boys. (*She stares at them and they at her.*)

SIMEON (*turns away and spits contemptuously*): I see her!

PETER (*spits also*): An I see her!

ABBIE (*with the conqueror's conscious superiority*): I'll go in an' look at *my* house. (*She goes slowly around to porch.*)

SIMEON (*with a snort*): *Her* house!

PETER (*calls after her*): Ye'll find Eben inside. Ye better not tell him it's *yewr* house.

ABBIE (*mouthing the name*): Eben. (*Then quietly.*) I'll tell Eben.

CABOT (*with a contemptuous sneer*): Ye needn't heed Eben. Eben's a dumb fool — like his Maw — soft an' simple!

SIMEON (*with his sardonic burst of laughter*): Ha! Eben's a chip o' yew — spit 'n' image — hard 'n' bitter's a hickory tree! Dog'll eat dog. He'll eat ye yet, old man!

CABOT (*commandingly*): Ye git t' wuk.

SIMEON (*as Abbie disappears in house — winks at Peter and says tauntingly*): So that thar's our new Maw, be it? Whar in hell did ye dig her up? (*He and Peter laugh.*)

PETER: Ha! Ye'd better turn her in the pen with the other sows. (*They laugh uproariously, slapping their thighs.*)

CABOT (*so amazed at their effrontery that he stutters in confusion*): Simeon! Peter! What's come over ye? Air ye drunk?

SIMEON: We're free, old man — free o' yew an' the hull damned farm! (*They grow more and more hilarious and excited.*)

PETER: An' we're startin' out fur the gold fields o' Californi-a!

SIMEON: Ye kin take this place an' burn it!

PETER: An' bury it — fur all we cares!

SIMEON: We're free, old man! (*He cuts a caper.*)

PETER: Free! (*He gives a kick in the air.*)

SIMEON (*in a frenzy*): Whoop!

PETER: Whoop! (*They do an absurd Indian war dance about the old man who is petrified between rage and the fear that they are insane.*)

SIMEON: We're free as Injuns! Lucky we don't skulp ye!

PETER: An' burn yer barn an' kill the stock!

SIMEON: An' rape yer new woman! Whoop! (*He and Peter stop their dance, holding their sides, rocking with wild laughter.*)

CABOT (*edging away*): Lust fur gold — fur the sinful, easy gold o' Californi-a! It's made ye mad!

SIMEON (*tauntingly*): Wouldn't ye like us to send ye back some sinful gold, ye old sinner?

PETER: They's gold besides what's in Californi-a! (*He retreats back beyond the vision of the old man and takes the bag of money and flaunts it in the air above his head, laughing.*)

SIMEON: And sinfuller, too!

PETER: We'll be voyagin' on the sea! Whoop! (*He leaps up and down.*)

SIMEON: Livin' free! Whoop! (*He leaps in turn.*)

CABOT (*suddenly roaring with rage*): My cuss on ye!

SIMEON: Take our'n in trade fur it! Whoop!

CABOT: I'll hev ye both chained up in the asylum!

PETER: Ye old skinflint! Good-by!

SIMEON: Ye old blood sucker! Good-by!

CABOT: Go afore I . . . !

PETER: Whoop! (*He picks a stone from the road. Simeon does the same.*)

SIMEON: Maw'll be in the parlor.

PETER: Ay-eh! One! Two!

CABOT (*frightened*): What air ye . . . ?

PETER: Three! (*They both throw, the stones hitting the parlor window with a crash of glass, tearing the shade.*)

SIMEON: Whoop!

PETER: Whoop!

CABOT (*in a fury now, rushing toward them*): If I kin lay hands on ye — I'll break yer bones fur ye! (*But they beat a capering retreat before him, Simeon with the gate still under his arm. Cabot comes back, panting with impotent rage. Their voices as they go off take up the song of the gold-seekers to the old tune of "Oh, Susannah!"*)

"I jumped aboard the Liza ship,
And traveled on the sea,
And every time I thought of home
I wished it wasn't me!
Oh! Californi-a,
That's the land fur me!
I'm off to Californi-a!
With my wash bowl on my knee."

(*In the meantime, the window of the upper bedroom on right is raised and Abbie sticks her head out. She looks down at Cabot — with a sigh of relief.*)

ABBIE: Waal — that's the last o' them two, hain't it? (*He doesn't answer. Then in possessive tones.*) This here's a nice bedroom, Ephraim. It's a r'al nice bed. Is it my room, Ephraim?

CABOT (*grimly — without looking up*): Our'n! (*She cannot control a grimace of aversion and pulls back her head slowly and shuts the window. A sudden horrible thought seems to enter Cabot's head.*) They been up to somethin'! Mebbe — mebbe they've pizened the stock —'r somethin'! (*He almost runs off down toward the barn. A moment later the kitchen door is slowly pushed open and Abbie enters. For a moment she stands looking at Eben. He does not notice her at first. Her eyes take him in penetratingly with a calculating appraisal of his strength as against hers. But under this her desire is dimly awakened by his youth and good looks. Suddenly he becomes conscious of her presence and looks up. Their eyes meet. He leaps to his feet, glowering at her speechlessly.*)

ABBIE (*in her most seductive tones which she uses all*)

through this scene): Be you — Eben? I'm Abbie — (*She laughs.*) I mean, I'm yer new Maw.

EBEN (*viciously*): No, damn ye!

ABBIE (*as if she hadn't heard — with a queer smile*): Yer Paw's spoke a lot o' yew. . . .

EBEN: Ha!

ABBIE: Ye mustn't mind him. He's an old man. (*A long pause. They stare at each other.*) I don't want t' pretend playin' Maw t' ye, Eben. (*Admiringly.*) Ye're too big an' too strong fur that. I want t' be frens with ye. Mebbe with me fur a fren ye'd find ye'd like livin' here better. I kin make it easy fur ye with him, mebbe. (*With a scornful sense of power.*) I calc'late I kin git him t' do most anythin' fur me.

EBEN (*with bitter scorn*): Ha! (*They stare again, Eben obscurely moved, physically attracted to her — in forced stilted tones.*) Yew kin go t' the devil!

ABBIE (*calmly*): If cussin' me does ye good, cuss all ye've a mind t'. I'm all prepared t' have ye agin me — at fust. I don't blame ye nuther. I'd feel the same at any stranger comin' t' take my Maw's place. (*He shudders. She is watching him carefully.*) Yew must've cared a lot fur yewr Maw, didn't ye? My Maw died afore I'd growed. I don't remember her none. (*A pause.*) But yew won't hate me long, Eben. I'm not the wust in the world — an' yew an' me've got a lot in common. I kin tell that by lookin' at ye. Waal — I've had a hard life, too — oceans o' trouble an' nuthin' but wuk fur reward. I was a orphan early an' had t' wuk fur others in other folks' hums. Then I married an' he turned out a drunken spreer an' so he had to wuk fur others an' me too agen in other folks' hums, an' the baby died, an' my husband got sick an' died too, an' I was glad sayin' now I'm free fur once, on'y I diskivered right away all I was free fur was t'wuk agen in other folks' hums, doin' other folks' wuk till I'd most give up hope o' ever doin' my own wuk in my own hum, an' then your Paw come . . . (*Cabot appears returning from the barn. He comes to the gate and looks down the road the brothers have gone. A faint strain of their retreating voices is heard: "Oh, Californi-a! That's the place for me." He stands glowering, his fist clenched, his face grim with rage.*)

EBEN (*fighting against his growing attraction and sympathy — harshly*): An' bought yew — like a harlot! (*She is stung and flushes angrily. She has been sincerely moved by the recital of her troubles. He adds furiously.*) An' the price he's payin' ye — this farm — was my Maw's, damn ye! — an' mine now!

ABBIE (*with a cool laugh of confidence*): Yewr'n? We'll see 'bout that! (*Then strongly.*) Waal — what if I did need a hum? What else'd I marry an old man like him fur?

EBEN (*maliciously*): I'll tell him ye said that!

ABBIE (*smiling*): I'll say ye're lyin' a-purpose — an' he'll drive ye off the place!

EBEN: Ye devil!

ABBIE (*defying him*): This be my farm — this be my hum — this be my kitchen — !

EBEN (*furiously, as if he were going to attack her*): Shut up, damn ye!

ABBIE (*walks up to him — a queer coarse expression of desire in her face and body — slowly*): An' upstairs — that be my bedroom — an' my bed! (*He stares into her eyes, terribly confused and torn. She adds softly.*) I hain't bad nor mean —'ceptin' fur an enemy — but I got t' fight fur what's due me out o' life, if I ever 'spect t' git it. (*Then putting her hand on his arm — seductively.*) Let's yew 'n' me be frens, Eben.

EBEN (*stupidly — as if hypnotized*): Ay-eh. (*Then furiously flinging off her arm.*) No, ye durned old witch! I hate ye! (*He rushes out the door.*)

ABBIE (*looks after him smiling satisfiedly — then half to herself, mouthing the word*): Eben's nice. (*She looks at the table, proudly.*) I'll wash up *my* dishes now. (*Eben appears outside, slamming the door behind him. He comes around corner, stops on seeing his father, and stands staring at him with hate.*)

CABOT (*raising his arms to heaven in the fury he can no longer control*): Lord God o' Hosts, smite the undutiful sons with Thy wust cuss!

EBEN (*breaking in violently*): Yew 'n' yewr God! Allus cussin' folks — allus naggin' 'em!

CABOT (*oblivious to him — summoningly*): God o' the old! God o' the lonesome!

EBEN (*mockingly*): Naggin' His sheep t' sin! T' hell with yewr God! (*Cabot turns. He and Eben glower at each other.*)

CABOT (*harshly*): So it's yew. I might've knowed it. (*Shaking his finger threateningly at him.*) Blasphemin' fool! (*Then quickly.*) Why hain't ye t' wuk?

EBEN: Why hain't yew? They've went. I can't wuk it all alone.

CABOT (*contemptuously*): Nor noways! I'm wuth ten o' ye yit, old's I be! Ye'll never be more'n half a man! (*Then, matter-of-factly.*) Waal — let's git t' the barn. (*They go. A last faint note of the "Californi-a" song is heard from the distance. Abbie is washing her dishes.*)

PART II • *Scene I*

(*The exterior of the farmhouse, as in part I — a hot Sunday afternoon two months later. Abbie, dressed in her best, is discovered sitting in a rocker at the end of the porch. She rocks listlessly, enervated by the heat, staring in front of her with bored, half-closed eyes.*)

(*Eben sticks his head out of his bedroom window. He looks around furtively and tries to see — or hear — if anyone is on the porch, but although he has been careful to make no noise, Abbie has sensed his movement. She stops rocking, her face grows animated and eager, she waits attentively. Eben seems to feel her presence, he scowls back his thoughts of her and spits with exaggerated disdain — then withdraws back into the room. Abbie waits, holding her breath as she listens with passionate eagerness for every sound within the house.*)

(*Eben comes out. Their eyes meet; his falter. He is confused, he turns away and slams the door resentfully. At this gesture, Abbie laughs tantalizingly, amused but at the same time piqued and irritated. He scowls, strides off the porch to the path and starts to walk past her to the road with a grand swagger of ignoring her existence. He is dressed in his store suit, spruced up, his face shines from soap and water. Abbie leans forward on her chair, her eyes hard and angry now, and, as he passes her, gives a sneering, taunting chuckle.*)

EBEN (*stung — turns on her furiously*): What air yew cacklin' 'bout?

ABBIE (*triumphant*): Yew!

EBEN: What about me?

ABBIE: Ye look all slicked up like a prize bull.

EBEN (*with a sneer*): Waal — ye hain't so durned purty yerself, be ye? (*They stare into each other's eyes, his held by hers in spite of himself, hers glowingly possessive. Their physical attraction becomes a palpable force quivering in the hot air.*)

ABBIE (*softly*): Ye don't mean that, Eben. Ye may think ye mean it, mebbe, but ye don't. Ye can't. It's agin nature, Eben. Ye been fightin' yer nature ever since the day I come — tryin' t' tell yerself I hain't purty t'ye. (*She laughs a low humid laugh without taking her eyes from his. A pause — her body squirms desirously — she murmurs languorously.*) Hain't the sun strong an' hot? Ye kin feel it burnin' into the earth — Nature — makin' thin's grow — bigger 'n' bigger — burnin' inside ye — makin' ye want t' grow — into somethin' else — till ye're jined with it — an' it's your'n — but it owns ye, too — ant makes ye grow bigger — like a tree — like them elums — (*She laughs again softly, holding his eyes. He takes a step toward her, compelled against his will.*) Nature'll beat ye, Eben. Ye might's well own up t' it fust 's last.

EBEN (*trying to break from her spell — confusedly*): If Paw'd hear ye goin' on. . . . (*Resentfully.*) But ye've made such a damned idjit out o' the old devil . . . ! (*Abbie laughs.*)

ABBIE: Waal — hain't it easier fur yew with him changed softer?

EBEN (*defiantly*): No. I'm fightin' him — fightin' yew — fightin' fur Maw's rights t' her hum! (*This breaks her spell for him. He glowers at her.*) An' I'm onto ye. Ye hain't foolin' me a mite. Ye're aimin' t' swaller up everythin' an' make it your'n. Waal, you'll find I'm a heap sight bigger hunk nor yew kin chew! (*He turns from her with a sneer.*)

ABBIE (*trying to regain her ascendancy — seductively*): Eben!

EBEN: Leave me be! (*He starts to walk away.*)

ABBIE (*more commandingly*): Eben!

EBEN (*stops — resentfully*): What d'ye want?

ABBIE (*trying to conceal a growing excitement*): Whar air ye goin'?

EBEN (*with malicious nonchalance*): Oh — up the road a spell.

ABBIE: T' the village?

EBEN (*airily*): Mebbe.

ABBIE (*excitedly*): T' see that Min, I s'pose?

EBEN: Mebbe.

ABBIE (*weakly*): What d'ye want t' waste time on her fur?

EBEN (*revenging himself now — grinning at her*): Ye can't beat Nature, didn't ye say? (*He laughs and again starts to walk away.*)

ABBIE (*bursting out*): An ugly old hake!

EBEN (*with a tantalizing sneer*): She's purtier'n yew be!

ABBIE: That every wuthless drunk in the country has. . . .

EBEN (*tauntingly*): Mebbe — but she's better'n yew. She owns up fa'r 'n' squar' t' her doin's.

ABBIE (*furiously*): Don't ye dare compare. . . .

EBEN: She don't go sneakin' an' stealin' — what's mine.

ABBIE (*savagely seizing on his weak point*): Your'n? Yew mean — my farm?

EBEN: I mean the farm yew sold yerself fur like any other old whore — my farm!

ABBIE (*stung — fiercely*): Ye'll never live t' see the day when even a stinkin' weed on it'll belong t' ye! (*Then in a scream.*) Git out o' my sight! Go on t' yer slut — disgracin' yer Paw 'n' me! I'll git yer Paw t' horse-whip ye off the place if I want t'! Ye're only livin' here 'cause I tolerate ye! Git along! I hate the sight o' ye! (*She stops, panting and glaring at him.*)

EBEN (*returning her glance in kind*): An' I hate the sight o' yew! (*He turns and strides off up the road. She follows his retreating figure with concentrated hate. Old Cabot appears coming up from the barn. The hard, grim expression of his face has changed. He seems in some queer way softened, mellowed. His eyes have taken on a strange, incongruous dreamy quality. Yet there is no hint of physical weakness about him — rather he looks more robust and younger. Abbie sees him and turns away quickly with unconcealed aversion. He comes slowly up to her.*)

CABOT (*mildly*): War yew an' Eben quarrelin' agen?

ABBIE (*shortly*): No.

CABOT: Ye was talkie' a'mighty loud. (*He sits down on the edge of porch.*)

ABBIE (*snappishly*): If ye heerd us they hain't no need askin' questions.

CABOT: I didn't hear what ye said.

ABBIE (*relieved*): Waal — it wa'n't nothin' t' speak on.

CABOT (*after a pause*): Eben's queer.

ABBIE (*bitterly*): He's the dead spit 'n' image o' yew!

CABOT (*queerly interested*): D'ye think so, Abbie? (*After a pause, ruminatingly.*) Me 'n' Eben's allus fit 'n' fit. I never could b'ar him noways. He's so thunderin' soft — like his Maw.

ABBIE (*scornfully*): Ay-eh! 'Bout as soft as yew be!

CABOT (*as if he hadn't heard*): Mebbe I been too hard on him.

ABBIE (*jeeringly*): Waal — ye're gittin' soft now — soft as slop! That's what Eben was sayin'.

CABOT (*his face instantly grim and ominous*): Eben was sayin'? Waal, he'd best not do nothin' t' try me 'r he'll soon diskiver. . . . (*A pause. She keeps her face turned away. His gradually softens. He stares up at the sky.*) Purty, hain't it?

ABBIE (*crossly*): I don't see nothin' purty.

CABOT: The sky. Feels like a wa'm field up thar.

ABBIE (*sarcastically*): Air yew aimin' t' buy up over the farm too? (*She snickers contemptuously.*)

CABOT (*strangely*): I'd like t' own my place up thar. (*A pause.*) I'm gittin' old, Abbie. I'm gittin' ripe on the bough. (*A pause. She stares at him mystified. He goes on.*) It's allus lonesome cold in the house — even when it's bilin' hot outside. Hain't yew noticed?

ABBIE: No.

CABOT: It's wa'm down t' the barn — nice smellin' an' warm — with the cows. (*A pause.*) Cows is queer.

ABBIE: Like yew?

CABOT: Like Eben. (*A pause.*) I'm gittin' t' feel resigned t' Eben — jest as I got t' feel 'bout his Maw. I'm gittin' t' learn to b'ar his softness — jest like her'n. I cal'c'late I c'd a'most take t' him — if he wa'n't sech a dumb fool! (*A pause.*) I s'pose it's old age a-creepin' in my bones.

ABBIE (*indifferently*): Waal — ye hain't dead yet.

CABOT (*roused*): No, I hain't, yew bet — not by a hell of a sight — I'm sound 'n' tough as hickory! (*Then moodily.*) But arter three score and ten the Lord warns ye t' prepare. (*A pause.*) That's why Eben's come in my head. Now that his cussed sinful brothers is gone their path t' hell, they's no one left but Eben.

ABBIE (*resentfully*): They's me, hain't they? (*Agitatedly.*) What's all this sudden likin' ye've tuk to Eben? Why don't ye say nothin' 'bout me? Hain't I yer lawful wife?

CABOT (*simply*): Ay-eh. Ye be. (*A pause — he stares at her desirously — his eyes grow avid — then with a sudden movement he seizes her hands and squeezes them, declaiming in a queer camp meeting preacher's tempo.*) Yew air my Rose o' Sharon! Behold, yew air fair; yer eyes air doves; yer lips air like scarlet; yer two breasts air like two fawns; yer navel be like a round goblet; yer belly be like a heap o' wheat. . . . (*He covers her hand with kisses. She does not seem to notice. She stares before her with hard angry eyes.*)

ABBIE (*jerking her hands away — harshly*): So ye're plannin' t' leave the farm t' Eben, air ye?

CABOT (*dazedly*): Leave . . . ? (*Then with resentful obstinacy.*) I hain't a-givin' it t' no one!

ABBIE (*remorselessly*): Ye can't take it with ye.

CABOT (*thinks a moment — then reluctantly*): No, I cal'c'late not. (*After a pause — with a strange passion.*) But if I could, I would, by the Eternal! 'R if I could, in my dyin' hour, I'd set it afire an' watch it burn — this house an' every ear o' corn an' every tree down t' the last blade o' hay! I'd sit an' know it was all a-dying with me an' no one else'd ever own what was mine, what I'd made out o' nothin' with my own sweat 'n' blood! (*A pause — then he adds with a queer affection.*) 'Ceptin' the cows. Them I'd turn free.

ABBIE (*harshly*): An' me?

CABOT (*with a queer smile*): Ye'd be turned free, too.

ABBIE (*furiously*): So that's the thanks I git fur marryin' ye — t' have ye change kind to Eben who hates ye, an' talk o' turnin' me out in the road.

CABOT (*hastily*): Abbie! Ye know I wa'n't. . . .

ABBIE (*vengefully*): Just let me tell ye a thing or two 'bout Eben! Whar's he gone? T' see that harlot, Min! I tried fur t' stop him. Disgracin' yew an' me — on the Sabbath, too!

CABOT (*rather guiltily*): He's a sinner — nateral-born. It's lust eatin' his heart.

ABBIE (*enraged beyond endurance — wildly vindictive*): An' his lust fur me! Kin ye find excuses fur that?

CABOT (*stares at her — after a dead pause*): Lust — fur yew?

ABBIE (*defiantly*): He was tryin' t' make love t' me — when ye heerd us quarrelin'.

CABOT (*stares at her — then a terrible expression of rage comes over his face — he springs to his feet shaking all over*): By the A'mighty God — I'll end him!

ABBIE (*frightened now for Eben*): No! Don't ye!

CABOT (*violently*): I'll git the shotgun an' blow his soft brains t' the top o' them elums!

ABBIE (*throwing her arms around him*): No, Ephraim!

CABOT (*pushing her away violently*): I will, by God!

ABBIE (*in a quieting tone*): Listen, Ephraim. 'Twa'n't nothin' bad — on'y a boy's foolin' —'twa'n't meant serious — jest jokin' an' teasin'. . . .

CABOT: Then why did ye say — lust?

ABBIE: It must hev sounded wusser'n I meant. An' I was mad at thinkin' — ye'd leave him the farm.

CABOT (*quieter but still grim and cruel*): Waal then, I'll horsewhip him off the place if that much'll content ye.

ABBIE (*reaching out and taking his hand*): No. Don't think o' me! Ye mustn't drive him off. 'Tain't sensible. Who'll ye get to help ye on the farm? They's no one hereabouts.

CABOT (*considers this — then nodding his appreciation*): Ye got a head on ye. (*Then irritably.*) Waal, let him stay. (*He sits down on the edge of the porch. She sits beside him. He murmurs contemptuously.*) I oughtn't t' git riled so — at that 'ere fool calf. (*A pause.*) But har's the p'int. What son o' mine'll keep on here t' the farm — when the Lord does call me? Simeon an' Peter air gone t' hell — an' Eben's follerin' 'em.

ABBIE: They's me.

CABOT: Ye're on'y a woman.

ABBIE: I'm yewr wife.

CABOT: That hain't me. A son is me — my blood — mine. Mine ought t' git mine. An' then it's still mine — even though I be six foot under. D'ye see?

ABBIE (*giving him a look of hatred*): Ay-eh. I see. (*She becomes very thoughtful, her face growing shrewd, her eyes studying Cabot craftily.*)

CABOT: I'm gittin' old — ripe on the bough. (*Then with a sudden forced reassurance.*) Not but what I hain't a hard nut t' crack even yet — an' fur many a year t' come! By the Etarnal, I kin break most o' the young fellers' backs at any kind o' work any day o' the year!

ABBIE (*suddenly*): Mebbe the Lord'll give *us* a son.

CABOT (*turns and stares at her eagerly*): Ye mean — a son — t' me 'n' yew?

ABBIE (*with a cajoling smile*): Ye're a strong man yet, hain't ye? 'Tain't noways impossible, be it? We know that. Why d'ye stare so? Hain't ye never thought o' that afore? I been thinkin' o' it all along. Ay-eh — an' I been prayin' it'd happen, too.

CABOT (*his face growing full of joyous pride and a sort of religious ecstasy*): Ye been prayin', Abbie? — fur a son? — t' us?

ABBIE: Ay-eh. (*With a grim resolution.*) I want a son now.

CABOT (*excitedly clutching both of her hands in his*): It'd be the blessin' o' God, Abbie — the blessin' o' God A'mighty on me — in my old age — in my lone-someness! They hain't nothin' I wouldn't do fur ye then, Abbie. Ye'd hev on'y t' ask it — anythin' ye'd a mind t'!

ABBIE (*interrupting*): Would ye will the farm t' me then — t' me an' it . . . ?

CABOT (*vehemently*): I'd do anythin' ye axed, I tell ye! I swar it! May I be everlastin' damned t' hell if I wouldn't! (*He sinks to his knees pulling her down with him. He trembles all over with the fervor of his hopes.*) Pray t' the Lord agen, Abbie. It's the Sabbath! I'll jine ye! Two prayers air better nor one. "An' God hearkened unto Rachel"! An' God hearkened unto Abbie! Pray, Abbie! Pray fur him to hearken! (*He bows his head, mumbling. She pretends to do likewise but gives him a side glance of scorn and triumph.*)

Scene II

(*About eight in the evening. The interior of the two bed-rooms on the top floor is shown. Eben is sitting on the side of his bed in the room on the left. On account of the heat he has taken off everything but his undershirt and pants. His feet are bare. He faces front, brooding mood-ily, his chin propped on his hands, a desperate expression on his face.*)

   (*In the other room Cabot and Abbie are sitting side by side on the edge of their bed, an old four-poster with feather mattress. He is in his nightshirt, she in her night-dress. He is still in the queer, excited mood into which the notion of a son has thrown him. Both rooms are lighted dimly and flickeringly by tallow candles.*)

CABOT: The farm needs a son.

ABBIE: I need a son.

CABOT: Ay-eh. Sometimes ye air the farm an' sometimes the farm be yew. That's why I clove t'ye in my lone-someness. (*A pause. He pounds his knee with his fist.*) Me an' the farm has got t' beget a son!

ABBIE: Ye'd best go t' sleep. Ye're gittin' thin's all mixed.

CABOT (*with an impatient gesture*): No, I hain't. My mind's clear's a well. Ye don't know me, that's it. (*He stares hopelessly at the floor.*)

ABBIE (*indifferently*): Mebbe. (*In the next room Eben gets up and paces up and down distractedly. Abbie hears him. Her eyes fasten on the intervening wall with concentrated attention. Eben stops and stares. Their hot glances seem to meet through the wall. Unconsciously he stretches out his arms for her and she half rises. Then aware, he mutters a curse at him-self and flings himself face downward on the bed, his clenched fists above his head, his face buried in the pillow. Abbie relaxes with a faint sigh but her eyes remain fixed on the wall; she listens with all her attention for some movement from Eben.*)

CABOT (*suddenly raises his head and looks at her — scornfully*): Will ye ever know me — 'r will any man 'r woman? (*Shaking his head.*) No. I calc'late wa'n't t' be. (*He turns away. Abbie looks at the wall. Then, evidently unable to keep silent about his thoughts, without looking at his wife, he puts out his hand and clutches her knee. She starts violently, looks at him, sees he is not watching her, concentrates again on the wall, and pays no attention to what he says.*) Listen, Abbie. When I come here fifty odd year ago — I was jest twenty an' the strongest an' hardest ye ever seen — ten times as strong an' fifty times as hard as Eben. Waal — this place was nothin' but fields o' stones. Folks laughed when I tuk it. They couldn't know what I knowed. When ye kin make corn sprout out o' stones, God's livin' in yew! They wa'n't strong enuf fur that! They reckoned God was easy. They laughed. They don't laugh no more. Some died here-abouts. Some went West an' died. They're all under-ground — fur follerin' arter an easy God. God hain't easy. (*He shakes his head slowly.*) An' I growed hard. Folks kept allus sayin' he's a hard man like 'twas sin-ful t' be hard, so's at last I said back at 'em: Waal then, by thunder, ye'll git me hard an' see how ye like it! (*Then suddenly.*) But I give in t' weakness once. 'Twas arter I'd been here two year. I got weak — despairful — they was so many stones. They was a party leavin', givin' up, goin' West. I jined 'em. We tracked on 'n' on. We come t' broad medders, plains, whar the soil was black an' rich as gold. Nary a stone. Easy. Ye'd on'y to plow an' sow an' then set an' smoke yer pipe an' watch thin's grow. I could o' been a rich man — but somethin' in me fit me an' fit me — the voice o' God sayin': "This hain't wuth nothin' t' Me. Git ye back t' hum!" I got afeerd o' that voice an' I lit out back t' hum here, leavin' my claim an' crops t' whoever'd a mind t' take 'em. Ay-eh. I actolly give up what was rightful mine! God's hard, not easy! God's in the stones! Build my church on a rock — out o' stones an' I'll be in them! That's what He meant t' Peter! (*He sighs heavily — a pause.*) Stones. I picked 'em up an' piled 'em into walls. Ye kin read the years of my life in them walls, every day a hefted stone, climbin' over the hills up and down, fencin' in the fields that was mine, whar I'd made thin's grow out o' nothin' — like the will o' God, like the servant o' His hand. It wa'n't easy. It was hard an' He made me hard fur it. (*He pauses.*) All the time I kept gittin' lonesomer. I tuk a wife. She bore Simeon an' Peter. She was a good woman. She wuked hard. We was married twenty year. She never knowed me. She helped but she never knowed what she was helpin'. I was allus lonesome. She died. After that it wa'n't so lonesome fur a spell. (*A pause.*) I lost count o' the years. I had no time t' fool away countin' 'em. Sim an' Peter helped. The farm growed. It was all mine! When I thought o' that I didn't feel lonesome. (*A pause.*) But ye can't hitch yer mind t' one thin' day an' night. I tuk another wife — Eben's Maw. Her folks was contestin' me at law over my deeds t' the farm — my farm! That's why Eben keeps a-talkin' his fool talk o' this bein' his Maw's farm. She bore Eben. She was purty — but soft. She tried t' be hard. She couldn't. She never knowed me nor nothin'. It was lonesomer 'n hell with her. After a matter o' sixteen odd years, she died. (*A pause.*) I lived with the boys. They hated me 'cause I was hard. I hated them 'cause they was soft. They coveted the farm without knowin' what it meant. It made me bitter 'n wormwood. It aged me — them coveting what I'd made fur mine. Then this spring the call come — the voice o' God cryin' in my wilderness, in my lonesomeness — t' go out an' seek an' find! (*Turning to her with strange passion.*) I sought ye an' I found ye! Yew air my Rose o' Sharon! Yer eyes air like.... (*She has turned a blank face, resentful eyes to his. He stares at her for a moment — then harshly.*) Air ye any the wiser fur all I've told ye?

ABBIE (*confusedly*): Mebbe.

CABOT (*pushing her away from him — angrily*): Ye don't know nothin' — nor never will. If ye don't hev a son t' redeem ye.... (*This in a tone of cold threat.*)

ABBIE (*resentfully*): I've prayed, hain't I?

CABOT (*bitterly*): Pray agen — fur understandin'!

ABBIE (*a veiled threat in her tone*): Ye'll have a son out o' me, I promise ye.

CABOT: How kin ye promise?

ABBIE: I got second-sight mebbe. I kin foretell. (*She gives a queer smile.*)

CABOT: I believe ye have. Ye give me the chills sometimes. (*He shivers.*) It's cold in this house. It's oneasy. They's thin's pokin' about in the dark — in the corners. (*He pulls on his trousers, tucking in his nightshirt, and pulls on his boots.*)

ABBIE (*surprised*): Whar air ye goin'?

CABOT (*queerly*): Down whar it's restful — whar it's warm — down t' the barn. (*Bitterly.*) I kin talk t' the cows. They know. They know the farm an' me. They'll give me peace. (*He turns to go out the door.*)

ABBIE (*a bit frightenedly*): Air ye ailin' tonight, Ephraim?

CABOT: Growin'. Growin' ripe on the bough. (*He turns and goes, his boots clumping down the stairs. Eben sits up with a start, listening. Abbie is conscious of his movement and stares at the wall. Cabot comes out of the house around the corner and stands by the gate, blinking at the sky. He stretches up his hands in a tortured gesture.*) God A'mighty, call from the dark! (*He listens as if expecting an answer. Then his arms drop, he shakes his head and plods off toward the barn. Eben and Abbie stare at each other through the wall. Eben sighs heavily and Abbie echoes it. Both become terribly nervous, uneasy. Finally Abbie gets up and listens, her ear to the wall. He acts as if he saw every move she was making, he becomes resolutely still. She seems driven into a decision — goes out the door in rear determinedly. His eyes follow her. Then as the door of his room is opened softly, he turns away, waits in an attitude of strained fixity. Abbie stands for a second staring at him, her eyes burning with desire. Then with a little cry she runs over and throws her arms about his neck, she pulls his head back and covers his mouth with kisses. At first, he submits dumbly; then he puts his arms about her neck and returns her kisses, but finally, suddenly aware of his hatred, he hurls her away from him, springing to his feet. They stand speechless and breathless, panting like two animals.*)

ABBIE (*at last — painfully*): Ye shouldn't, Eben — ye shouldn't — I'd make ye happy!

EBEN (*harshly*): I don't want t' be happy — from yew!

ABBIE (*helplessly*): Ye do, Eben! Ye do! Why d'ye lie?

EBEN (*viciously*): I don't take t'ye, I tell ye! I hate the sight o' ye!

ABBIE (*with an uncertain troubled laugh*): Waal, I kissed ye anyways — an' ye kissed back — yer lips was burnin' — ye can't lie 'bout that! (*Intensely.*) If ye don't care, why did ye kiss me back — why was yer lips burnin'?

EBEN (*wiping his mouth*): It was like pizen on 'em. (*Then tauntingly.*) When I kissed ye back, mebbe I thought 'twas someone else.

ABBIE (*wildly*): Min?

EBEN: Mebbe.

ABBIE (*torturedly*): Did ye go t' see her? Did ye r'ally go? I thought ye mightn't. Is that why ye throwed me off jest now?

EBEN (*sneeringly*): What if it be?

ABBIE (*raging*): Then ye're a dog, Eben Cabot!

EBEN (*threateningly*): Ye can't talk that way t' me!

ABBIE (*with a shrill laugh*): Can't I? Did ye think I was in love with ye — a weak thin' like yew? Not much! I on'y wanted ye fur a purpose o' my own — an' I'll hev ye fur it yet 'cause I'm stronger'n yew be!

EBEN (*resentfully*): I knowed well it was on'y part o' yer plan t' swaller everythin'!

ABBIE (*tauntingly*): Mebbe!

EBEN (*furious*): Git out o' my room!

ABBIE: This air my room an' ye're on'y hired help!

EBEN (*threateningly*): Git out afore I murder ye!

ABBIE (*quite confident now*): I hain't a mite afeerd. Ye want me, don't ye? Yes, ye do! An' yer Paw's son'll never kill what he wants! Look at yer eyes! They's

Abbie in the 1988 Pushkin Theatre (Moscow) production of *Desire under the Elms*, directed by Mark Lamos of the Hartford Stage Company.

lust fur me in 'em, burnin' 'em up! Look at yer lips now! They're tremblin' an' longin' t' kiss me, an' yer teeth t' bite! (*He is watching her now with a horrible fascination. She laughs a crazy triumphant laugh.*) I'm a-goin' t' make all o' this hum my hum! They's one room hain't mine yet, but it's a-goin' t' be tonight. I'm a-goin' down now an' light up! (*She makes him a mocking bow.*) Won't ye come courtin' me in the best parlor, Mister Cabot?

EBEN (*staring at her — horribly confused — dully*): Don't ye dare! It hain't been opened since Maw died an' was laid out thar! Don't ye . . . ! (*But her eyes are fixed on his so burningly that his will seems to wither before hers. He stands swaying toward her helplessly.*)

ABBIE (*holding his eyes and putting all her will into her words as she backs out the door*): I'll expect ye afore long, Eben.

EBEN (*Stares after her for a while, walking toward the door. A light appears in the parlor window. He murmurs.*): In the parlor? (*This seems to arouse connotations, for he comes back and puts on his white shirt, collar, half ties the tie mechanically, puts on coat, takes his hat, stands barefooted looking about*

him in bewilderment, mutters wonderingly.) Maw! Whar air yew? (*Then goes slowly toward the door in rear.*)

Scene III

(*A few minutes later. The interior of the parlor is shown. A grim, repressed room like a tomb in which the family has been interred alive. Abbie sits on the edge of the horsehair sofa. She has lighted all the candles and the room is revealed in all its preserved ugliness. A change has come over the woman. She looks awed and frightened now, ready to run away.*)

(*The door is opened and Eben appears. His face wears an expression of obsessed confusion. He stands staring at her, his arms hanging disjointedly from his shoulders, his feet bare, his hat in his hand.*)

ABBIE (*after a pause — with a nervous, formal politeness*): Won't ye set?

EBEN (*dully*): Ay-eh. (*Mechanically he places his hat carefully on the floor near the door and sits stiffly beside her on the edge of the sofa. A pause. They both remain rigid, looking straight ahead with eyes full of fear.*)

ABBIE: When I fust come in — in the dark — they seemed somethin' here.

EBEN (*simply*): Maw.

ABBIE: I kin still feel — somethin'. . . .

EBEN: It's Maw.

ABBIE: At fust I was feered o' it. I wanted t' yell an' run. Now — since yew come — seems like it's growin' soft an' kind t' me. (*Addressing the air — queerly.*) Thank yew.

EBEN: Maw allus loved me.

ABBIE: Mebbe it knows I love yew, too. Mebbe that makes it kind t' me.

EBEN (*dully*): I dunno. I should think she'd hate ye.

ABBIE (*with certainty*): No. I kin feel it don't — not no more.

EBEN: Hate ye fur stealin' her place — here in her hum — settin' in her parlor whar she was laid — (*He suddenly stops, staring stupidly before him.*)

ABBIE: What is it, Eben?

EBEN (*in a whisper*): Seems like Maw didn't want me t' remind ye.

ABBIE (*excitedly*): I knowed, Eben! It's kind t' me! It don't b'ar me no grudges fur what I never knowed an' couldn't help!

EBEN: Maw b'ars him a grudge.

ABBIE: Waal, so does all o' us.

EBEN: Ay-eh. (*With passion.*) I does, by God!

ABBIE (*taking one of his hands in hers and patting it*): Thar! Don't git riled thinkin' o' him. Think o' yer Maw who's kind t' us. Tell me about yer Maw, Eben.

EBEN: They hain't nothin' much. She was kind. She was good.

ABBIE (*Putting one arm over his shoulder. He does not seem to notice — passionately.*): I'll be kind an' good t' ye!

EBEN: Sometimes she used t' sing fur me.

ABBIE: I'll sing fur ye!

EBEN: This was her hum. This was her farm.

ABBIE: This is my hum! This is my farm!

EBEN: He married her t' steal 'em. She was soft an' easy. He couldn't 'preciate her.

ABBIE: He can't 'preciate me!

EBEN: He murdered her with his hardness.

ABBIE: He's murderin' me!

EBEN: She died. (*A pause.*) Sometimes she used to sing fur me. (*He bursts into a fit of sobbing.*)

ABBIE (*both her arms around him — with wild passion*): I'll sing fur ye! I'll die fur ye! (*In spite of her overwhelming desire for him, there is a sincere maternal love in her manner and voice — a horribly frank mixture of lust and mother love.*) Don't cry, Eben! I'll take yer Maw's place! I'll be everythin' she was t' ye! Let me kiss ye, Eben! (*She pulls his head around. He makes a bewildered pretense of resistance. She is tender.*) Don't be afeered! I'll kiss ye pure, Eben — same 's if I was a Maw t' ye — an' ye

kin kiss me back 's if yew was my son — my boy — sayin' good-night t' me! Kiss me, Eben. (*They kiss in restrained fashion. Then suddenly wild passion overcomes her. She kisses him lustfully again and again and he flings his arms about her and returns her kisses. Suddenly, as in the bedroom, he frees himself from her violently and springs to his feet. He is trembling all over, in a strange state of terror. Abbie strains her arms toward him with fierce pleading.*) Don't ye leave me, Eben! Can't ye see it hain't enuf — lovin' ye like a Maw — can't ye see it's got t' be that an' more — much more — a hundred times more — fur me t' be happy — fur yew t' be happy?

EBEN (*to the presence he feels in the room*): Maw! Maw! What d'ye want? What air ye tellin' me?

ABBIE: She's tellin' ye t' love me. She knows I love ye an' I'll be good t' ye. Can't ye feel it? Don't ye know? She's tellin' ye t' love me, Eben!

EBEN: Ay-eh. I feel — mebbe she — but — I can't figger out — why — when ye've stole her place — here in her hum — in the parlor whar she was —

ABBIE (*fiercely*): She knows I love ye!

EBEN (*his face suddenly lighting up with a fierce, triumphant grin*): I see it! I sees why. It's her vengeance on him — so's she kin rest quiet in her grave!

ABBIE (*wildly*): Vengeance o' God on the hull o' us! What d'we give a durn? I love ye, Eben! God knows I love ye! (*She stretches out her arms for him.*)

EBEN (*throws himself on his knees beside the sofa and grabs her in his arms — releasing all his pent-up passion*): An' I love ye, Abbie! — now I kin say it! I been dyin' fur want o' ye — every hour since ye come! I love ye! (*Their lips meet in a fierce, bruising kiss.*)

Scene IV

(*Exterior of the farmhouse. It is just dawn. The front door at right is opened and Eben comes out and walks around to the gate. He is dressed in his working clothes. He seems changed. His face wears a bold and confident expression, he is grinning to himself with evident satisfaction. As he gets near the gate, the window of the parlor is heard opening and the shutters are flung back and Abbie sticks her head out. Her hair tumbles over her shoulders in disarray, her face is flushed, she looks at Eben with tender, languorous eyes and calls softly.*)

ABBIE: Eben. (*As he turns — playfully.*) Jest one more kiss afore ye go. I'm goin' to miss ye fearful all day.

EBEN: An' me yew, ye kin bet! (*He goes to her. They kiss several times. He draws away, laughingly.*) Thar. That's enuf, hain't it? Ye won't hev none left fur next time.

ABBIE: I got a million o' 'em left fur yew! (*Then a bit anxiously.*) D'ye r'ally love me, Eben?

EBEN (*emphatically*): I like ye better'n any gal I ever knowed! That's gospel!

ABBIE: Likin' hain't lovin'.

EBEN: Waal then — I love ye. Now air yew satisfied?

ABBIE: Ay-eh, I be. (*She smiles at him adoringly.*)

EBEN: I better git t' the barn. The old critter's liable t' suspicion an' come sneakin' up.

ABBIE (*with a confident laugh*): Let him! I kin allus pull the wool over his eyes. I'm goin' t' leave the shutters open and let in the sun 'n' air. This room's been dead long enuf. Now it's goin' t' be my room!

EBEN (*frowning*): Ay-eh.

ABBIE (*hastily*): I meant — our room.

EBEN: Ay-eh.

ABBIE: We made it our'n last night, didn't we? We give it life — our lovin' did. (*A pause.*)

EBEN (*with a strange look*): Maw's gone back t' her grave. She kin sleep now.

ABBIE: May she rest in peace! (*Then tenderly rebuking.*) Ye oughtn't t' talk o' sad thin's — this mornin'.

EBEN: It jest come up in my mind o' itself.

ABBIE: Don't let it. (*He doesn't answer. She yawns.*) Waal, I'm a-goin' t' steal a wink o' sleep. I'll tell the Old Man I hain't feelin' pert. Let him git his own vittles.

EBEN: I see him comin' from the barn. Ye better look smart an' git upstairs.

ABBIE: Ay-eh. Good-by. Don't ferget me. (*She throws him a kiss. He grins — then squares his shoulders and awaits his father confidently. Cabot walks slowly up from the left, staring up at the sky with a vague face.*)

EBEN (*jovially*): Mornin', Paw. Star-gazin' in daylight?

CABOT: Purty, hain't it?

EBEN (*looking around him possessively*): It's a durned purty farm.

CABOT: I mean the sky.

EBEN (*grinning*): How d'ye know? Them eyes o' your'n can't see that fur. (*This tickles his humor and he slaps his thigh and laughs.*) Ho-ho! That's a good un!

CABOT (*grimly sarcastic*): Ye're feelin' right chipper, hain't ye? Whar'd ye steal the likker?

EBEN (*good-naturedly*): 'Tain't likker. Jest life. (*Suddenly holding out his hand — soberly.*) Yew 'n' me is quits. Let's shake hands.

CABOT (*suspiciously*): What's come over ye?

EBEN: Then don't. Mebbe it's jest as well. (*A moment's pause.*) What's come over me? (*Queerly.*) Didn't ye feel her passin' — goin' back t' her grave?

CABOT (*dully*): Who?

EBEN: Maw. She kin rest now an' sleep content. She's quit with ye.

CABOT (*confusedly*): I rested. I slept good — down with the cows. They know how t' sleep. They're teachin' me.

EBEN (*suddenly jovial again*): Good fur the cows! Waal — ye better git t' work.

CABOT (*grimly amused*): Air yew bossin' me, ye calf?

EBEN (*beginning to laugh*): Ay-eh! I'm bossin' yew! Ha-ha-ha! See how ye like it! Ha-ha-ha! I'm the prize rooster o' this roost. Ha-ha-ha! (*He goes off toward the barn laughing.*)

CABOT (*looks after him with scornful pity*): Soft-headed. Like his Maw. Dead spit 'n' image. No hope in him! (*He spits with contemptuous disgust.*) A born fool! (*Then matter-of-factly.*) Waal — I'm gittin' peckish. (*He goes toward door.*)

PART III • *Scene* I

(*A night in late spring the following year. The kitchen and the two bedrooms upstairs are shown. The two bedrooms are dimly lighted by a tallow candle in each. Eben is sitting on the side of the bed in his room, his chin propped on his fists, his face a study of the struggle he is making to understand his conflicting emotions. The noisy laughter and music from below where a kitchen dance is in progress annoy and distract him. He scowls at the floor.*)

(*In the next room a cradle stands beside the double bed.*)

(*In the kitchen all is festivity. The stove has been taken down to give more room to the dancers. The chairs, with wooden benches added, have been pushed back against the walls. On these are seated, squeezed in tight against one another, farmers and their wives and their young folks of both sexes from the neighboring farms. They are all chattering and laughing loudly. They evidently have some secret joke in common. There is no end of winking, of nudging, of meaning nods of the head toward Cabot who, in a state of extreme hilarious excitement increased by the amount he has drunk, is standing near the rear door where there is a small keg of whisky and serving drinks to all the men. In the left corner, front, dividing the attention with her husband, Abbie is sitting in a rocking chair, a shawl wrapped about her shoulders. She is very pale, her face is thin and drawn, her eyes are fixed anxiously on the open door in rear as if waiting for someone.*)

(*The musician is tuning up his fiddle, seated in the far right corner. He is a lanky young fellow with a long, weak face. His pale eyes blink incessantly and he grins about him slyly with a greedy malice.*)

ABBIE (*suddenly turning to a young girl on her right*): Whar's Eben?

YOUNG GIRL (*eyeing her scornfully*): I dunno, Mrs. Cabot. I hain't seen Eben in ages. (*Meaningly.*) Seems like he's spent most o' his time t' hum since yew come.

ABBIE (*vaguely*): I tuk his Maw's place.

YOUNG GIRL: Ay-eh. So I've heerd. (*She turns away to retail this bit of gossip to her mother sitting next to her. Abbie turns to her left to a big stoutish middle-aged man whose flushed face and starting eyes show the amount of "likker" he has consumed.*)

ABBIE: Ye hain't seen Eben, hev ye?

MAN: No, I hain't. (*Then he adds with a wink.*) If yew hain't, who would?

ABBIE: He's the best dancer in the county. He'd ought t' come an' dance.

MAN (*with a wink*): Mebbe he's doin' the dutiful an' walkin' the kid t' sleep. It's a boy, hain't it?

ABBIE (*nodding vaguely*): Ay-eh — born two weeks back — purty's a picter.

MAN: They all is — t' their Maws. (*Then in a whisper, with a nudge and a leer.*) Listen, Abbie — if ye ever git tired o' Eben, remember me! Don't fergit now! (*He looks at her uncomprehending face for a second — then grunts disgustedly.*) Waal — guess I'll likker agin. (*He goes over and joins Cabot who is arguing noisily with an old farmer over cows. They all drink.*)

ABBIE (*this time appealing to nobody in particular*): Wonder what Eben's a-doin'? (*Her remark is repeated down the line with many a guffaw and titter until it reaches the fiddler. He fastens his blinking eyes on Abbie.*)

FIDDLER (*raising his voice*): Bet I kin tell ye, Abbie, what Eben's doin'! He's down t' the church offerin' up prayers o' thanksgivin'. (*They all titter expectantly.*)

A MAN: What fur? (*Another titter.*)

FIDDLER: 'Cause unto him a — (*He hesitates just long enough.*) brother is born! (*A roar of laughter. They all look from Abbie to Cabot. She is oblivious, staring at the door. Cabot, although he hasn't heard the words, is irritated by the laughter and steps forward, glaring about him. There is an immediate silence.*)

CABOT: What're ye all bleatin' about — like a flock o' goats? Why don't ye dance, damn ye? I axed ye here t' dance — t' eat, drink an' be merry — an' thar ye set cacklin' like a lot o' wet hens with the pip! Ye've swilled my likker an' guzzled my vittles like hogs, hain't ye? Then dance fur me, can't ye? That's fa'r an' squar', hain't it? (*A grumble of resentment goes around but they are all evidently in too much awe of him to express it openly.*)

FIDDLER (*slyly*): We're waitin' fur Eben. (*A suppressed laugh.*)

CABOT (*with a fierce exultation*): T'hell with Eben! Eben's done fur now! I got a new son! (*His mood switching with drunken suddenness.*) But ye needn't t' laugh at Eben, none o' ye! He's my blood, if he be a dumb fool. He's better nor any o' yew! He kin do a day's work a'most up t' what I kin — an' that'd put any o' yew pore critters t' shame!

FIDDLER: An' he kin do a good night's work, too! (*A roar of laughter.*)

CABOT: Laugh, ye damn fools! Ye're right jist the same, Fiddler. He kin work day an' night too, like I kin, if need be!

OLD FARMER (*from behind the keg where he is weaving drunkenly back and forth — with great simplicity*): They hain't many t' touch ye, Ephraim — a son at seventy-six. That's a hard man fur ye! I be on'y sixty-eight an' I couldn't do it. (*A roar of laughter in which Cabot joins uproariously.*)

CABOT (*slapping him on the back*): I'm sorry fur ye, Hi. I'd never suspicion sech weakness from a boy like yew!

OLD FARMER: An' I never reckoned yew had it in ye nuther, Ephraim. (*There is another laugh.*)

CABOT (*suddenly grim*): I got a lot in me — a hell of a lot — folks don't know on. (*Turning to the fiddler.*) Fiddle 'er up, durn ye! Give 'em somethin' t' dance t'! What air ye, an ornament? Hain't this a celebration? Then grease yer elbow an' go it!

FIDDLER (*seizes a drink which the Old Farmer holds out to him and downs it*): Here goes! (*He starts to fiddle "Lady of the Lake." Four young fellows and four girls form in two lines and dance a square dance. The Fiddler shouts directions for the different movements, keeping his words in the rhythm of the music and interspersing them with jocular personal remarks to the dancers themselves. The people seated along the walls stamp their feet and clap their hands in unison. Cabot is especially active in this respect. Only Abbie remains apathetic, staring at the door as if she were alone in a silent room.*)

FIDDLER: Swing your partner t' the right! That's it, Jim! Give her a b'ar hug. Her Maw hain't lookin'. (*Laughter.*) Change partners! That suits ye, don't it, Essie, now ye got Reub afore ye? Look at her redden up, will ye! Waal, life is short an' so's love, as the feller says. (*Laughter.*)

CABOT (*excitedly, stamping his foot*): Go it, boys! Go it, gals!

FIDDLER (*with a wink at the others*): Ye're the spryest seventy-six ever I sees, Ephraim! Now if ye'd on'y good eyesight . . . ! (*Suppressed laughter. He gives Cabot no chance to retort but roars.*) Promenade! Ye're walkin' like a bride down the aisle, Sarah! Waal, while they's life they's allus hope, I've heerd tell. Swing your partner to the left! Gosh A'mighty, look at Johnny Cook high-steppin'! They hain't goin' t' be much strength left fur howin' in the corn lot t'morrow. (*Laughter.*)

CABOT: Go it! Go it! (*Then suddenly, unable to restrain himself any longer, he prances into the midst of the dancers, scattering them, waving his arms about wildly.*) Ye're all hoofs! Git out o' my road! Give me room! I'll show ye dancin'. Ye're all too soft! (*He pushes them roughly away. They crowd back toward the walls, muttering, looking at him resentfully.*)

FIDDLER (*jeeringly*): Go it, Ephraim! Go it! (*He starts "Pop, Goes the Weasel," increasing the tempo with every verse until at the end he is fiddling crazily as fast as he can go.*)

CABOT (*Starts to dance, which he does very well and with tremendous vigor. Then he begins to improvise, cuts incredibly grotesque capers, leaping up and cracking his heels together, prancing around in a circle with body bent in an Indian war dance, then suddenly straightening up and kicking as high as he can with both legs. He is like a monkey on a string. And all the while he intersperses his antics with shouts and derisive comments.*): Whoop! Here's dancin' fur ye! Whoop! See that! Seventy-six, if I'm a day! Hard as iron yet! Beatin' the young 'uns like I allus done! Look at me! I'd invite ye t' dance on my hundredth birthday on'y ye'll all be dead by then. Ye're a sickly generation! Yer hearts air pink, not red! Yer veins is full o' mud an' water! I be the on'y man in the county! Whoop! See that! I'm a Injun! I've killed Injuns in the West afore ye was born — an' skulped 'em too! They's a arrer wound on my backside I c'd show ye! The hull tribe chased me. I outrun 'em all — with the arrer stuck in me! An' I tuk vengeance on 'em. Ten eyes fur an eye, that was my motter! Whoop! Look at me! I kin kick the ceilin' off the room! Whoop!

FIDDLER (*stops playing — exhaustedly*): God A'mighty, I got enuf. Ye got the devil's strength in ye.

CABOT (*delightedly*): Did I beat yew, too? Waal, ye played smart. Hev a swig. (*He pours whisky for himself and Fiddler. They drink. The others watch Cabot silently with cold, hostile eyes. There is a dead pause. The Fiddler rests. Cabot leans against the keg, panting, glaring around him confusedly. In the room above, Eben gets to his feet and tiptoes out the door in rear, appearing a moment later in the other bedroom. He moves silently, even frightenedly, toward the cradle and stands there looking down at the baby. His face is as vague as his reactions are confused, but there is a trace of tenderness, of interested discovery. At the same moment that he reaches the cradle, Abbie seems to sense something. She gets up weakly and goes to Cabot.*)

ABBIE: I'm goin' up t' the baby.

CABOT (*with real solicitation*): Air ye able fur the stairs? D'ye want me t' help ye, Abbie?

ABBIE: No. I'm able. I'll be down agen soon.

CABOT: Don't ye git wore out! He needs ye, remember — our son does! (*He grins affectionately, patting her on the back. She shrinks from his touch.*)

ABBIE (*dully*): Don't — tech me. I'm goin' — up. (*She goes. Cabot looks after her. A whisper goes around the room. Cabot turns. It ceases. He wipes his forehead streaming with sweat. He is breathing pantingly.*)

CABOT: I'm a-goin' out t' git fresh air. I'm feelin' a mite dizzy. Fiddle up thar! Dance, all o' ye! Here's likker fur them as wants it. Enjoy yerselves. I'll be back. (*He goes, closing the door behind him.*)

FIDDLER (*sarcastically*): Don't hurry none on our account! (*A suppressed laugh. He imitates Abbie.*) Whar's Eben? (*More laughter.*)

A WOMAN (*loudly*): What's happened in this house is plain as the nose on yer face! (*Abbie appears in the doorway upstairs and stands looking in surprise and adoration at Eben who does not see her.*)

A MAN: Ssshh! He's li'ble t' be listenin' at the door. That'd be like him. (*Their voices die to an intensive whispering. Their faces are concentrated on this gossip. A noise as of dead leaves in the wind comes from the room. Cabot has come out from the porch and stands by the gate, leaning on it, staring at the sky blinkingly. Abbie comes across the room silently. Eben does not notice her until quite near.*)

EBEN (*starting*): Abbie!

ABBIE: Ssshh! (*She throws her arms around him. They kiss — then bend over the cradle together.*) Ain't he purty? — dead spit 'n' image o' yew!

EBEN (*pleased*): Air he? I can't tell none.

ABBIE: E-zactly like!

EBEN (*frowningly*): I don't like this. I don't like lettin' on what's mine's his'n. I been doin' that all my life. I'm gittin' t' the end o' b'arin' it!

ABBIE (*putting her finger on his lips*): We're doin' the best we kin. We got t' wait. Somethin's bound t' happen. (*She puts her arms around him.*) I got t' go back.

EBEN: I'm goin' out. I can't b'ar it with the fiddle playin' an' the laughin'.

ABBIE: Don't git feelin' low. I love ye, Eben. Kiss me. (*He kisses her. They remain in each other's arms.*)

CABOT (*at the gate, confusedly*): Even the music can't drive it out — somethin'. Ye kin feel it droppin' off the elums, climbin' up the roof, sneakin' down the chimney, pokin' in the corners! They's no peace in houses, they's no rest livin' with folks. Somethin's always livin' with ye. (*With a deep sigh.*) I'll go t' the barn an' rest a spell. (*He goes wearily toward the barn.*)

FIDDLER (*tuning up*): Let's celebrate the old skunk gittin' fooled! We kin have some fun now he's went. (*He starts to fiddle "Turkey in the Straw." There is real merriment now. The young folks get up to dance.*)

Scene II

(*A half hour later — exterior — Eben is standing by the gate looking up at the sky, an expression of dumb pain bewildered by itself on his face. Cabot appears, returning from the barn, walking wearily, his eyes on the ground. He sees Eben and his whole mood immediately changes. He becomes excited, a cruel, triumphant grin comes to his lips, he strides up and slaps Eben on the back. From within comes the whining of the fiddle and the noise of stamping feet and laughing voices.*)

CABOT: So har ye be!

EBEN (*startled, stares at him with hatred for a moment — then dully*): Ay-eh.

CABOT (*surveying him jeeringly*): Why hain't ye been in t' dance? They was all axin' fur ye.

EBEN: Let 'em ax!

CABOT: They's a hull passel o' purty gals.

EBEN: T' hell with 'em!

CABOT: Ye'd ought t' be marryin' one o' 'em soon.

EBEN: I hain't marryin' no one.

CABOT: Ye might 'arn a share o' a farm that way.

EBEN (*with a sneer*): Like yew did, ye mean? I hain't that kind.

CABOT (*stung*): Ye lie! 'Twas yer Maw's folks aimed t' steal my farm from me.

EBEN: Other folks don't say so. (*After a pause — defiantly.*) An' I got a farm, anyways!

CABOT (*derisively*): Whar?

EBEN (*stamps a foot on the ground*): Har!

CABOT (*throws his head back and laughs coarsely*): Ho-ho! Ye hev, hev ye? Waal, that's a good un!

EBEN (*controlling himself — grimly*): Ye'll see!

CABOT (*stares at him suspiciously, trying to make him out — a pause — then with scornful confidence*): Ay-eh. I'll see. So'll ye. It's ye that's blind — blind as a mole underground. (*Eben suddenly laughs, one short sardonic bark: "Ha." A pause. Cabot peers at him with renewed suspicion.*) What air ye hawin' 'bout? (*Eben turns away without answering. Cabot grows angry.*) God A'mighty, yew air a dumb dunce! They's nothin' in that thick skull o' your'n but noise — like a empty keg it be! (*Eben doesn't seem to hear. Cabot's rage grows.*) Yewr farm! God A'mighty! If ye wa'n't a born donkey ye'd know ye'll never own stick nor stone on it, specially now arter him bein' born. It's his'n, I tell ye — his'n arter I die — but I'll live a hundred jest t' fool ye all — an' he'll be growed then — yewr age a'most! (*Eben laughs again his sardonic "Ha." This drives Cabot into a fury.*) Ha? Ye think ye kin git 'round that someways, do ye? Waal, it'll be her'n, too — Abbie's — ye won't git 'round her — she knows yer tricks — she'll be too much fur ye — she wants the farm her'n — she was afeerd o' ye — she told me ye was sneakin' 'round tryin' t' make love t' her t' git her on yer side ... ye ... ye mad fool, ye! (*He raises his clenched fists threateningly.*)

EBEN (*is confronting him, choking with rage*): Ye lie, ye old skunk! Abbie never said no sech thing!

CABOT (*suddenly triumphant when he sees how shaken Eben is*): She did. An' I says, I'll blow his brains t' the top o' them elums — an' she says no that hain't sense, who'll ye git t'help ye on the farm in his place — an' then she says yew'n me ought t' have a son — I know we kin, she says — an' I says, if we do, ye kin have anythin' I've got ye've a mind t'. An' she says, I wants Eben cut off so's this farm'll be mine when ye die! (*With terrible gloating.*) An' that's what's happened, hain't it? An' the farm's her'n! An' the dust o' the road — that's you'rn! Ha! Now who's hawin'?

EBEN (*has been listening, petrified with grief and rage — suddenly laughs wildly and brokenly*): Ha-ha-ha! So that's her sneakin' game — all along! — like I suspicioned at fust — t' swaller it all — an' me, too ...! (*Madly.*) I'll murder her! (*He springs toward the porch but Cabot is quicker and gets in between.*)

CABOT: No, ye don't!

EBEN: Git out o' my road! (*He tries to throw Cabot aside. They grapple in what becomes immediately a murderous struggle. The old man's concentrated strength is too much for Eben. Cabot gets one hand on his throat and presses him back across the stone wall. At the same moment, Abbie comes out on the porch. With a stifled cry she runs toward them.*)

ABBIE: Eben! Ephraim! (*She tugs at the hand on Eben's throat.*) Let go, Ephraim! Ye're chokin' him!

CABOT (*Removes his hand and flings Eben sideways full length on the grass, gasping and choking. With a cry, Abbie kneels beside him, trying to take his head on her lap, but he pushes her away. Cabot stands looking down with fierce triumph.*): Ye needn't t've fret, Abbie, I wa'n't aimin' t' kill him. He hain't wuth hangin' fur — not by a hell of a sight! (*More and more triumphantly.*) Seventy-six an' him not thirty yit — an' look whar he be fur thinkin' his Paw was easy! No, by God, I hain't easy! An' him upstairs, I'll raise him t' be like me! (*He turns to leave them.*) I'm goin' in an' dance! — sing an' celebrate! (*He walks to the porch — then turns with a great grin.*) I don't calc'late it's left in him, but if he gits pesky, Abbie, ye jest sing out. I'll come a-runnin' an' by the Etarnal, I'll put him across my knee an' birch him! Ha-ha-ha! (*He goes into the house laughing. A moment later his loud "whoop" is heard.*)

ABBIE (*tenderly*): Eben. Air ye hurt? (*She tries to kiss him but he pushes her violently away and struggles to a sitting position.*)

EBEN (*gaspingly*): T'hell — with ye!

ABBIE (*not believing her ears*): It's me, Eben — Abbie — don't ye know me?

EBEN (*glowering at her with hatred*): Ay-eh — I know ye — now! (*He suddenly breaks down, sobbing weakly.*)

ABBIE (*fearfully*): Eben — what's happened t' ye — why did ye look at me 's if ye hated me?

EBEN (*violently, between sobs and gasps*): I do hate ye! Ye're a whore — a damn trickin' whore!

ABBIE (*shrinking back horrified*): Eben! Ye don't know what ye're sayin'!

EBEN (*scrambling to his feet and following her — accusingly*): Ye're nothin' but a stinkin' passel o' lies! Ye've been lyin' t' me every word ye spoke, day an' night, since we fust — done it. Ye've kept sayin' ye loved me. ...

ABBIE (*frantically*): I do love ye! (*She takes his hand but he flings hers away.*)

EBEN (*unheeding*): Ye've made a fool o' me — a sick, dumb fool — a-purpose! Ye've been on'y playin' yer sneakin', stealin' game all along — gittin' me t' lie with ye so's ye'd hev a son he'd think was his'n, an' makin' him promise he'd give ye the farm and let me eat dust, if ye did git him a son! (*Staring at her with anguished, bewildered eyes.*) They must be a devil livin' in ye! T'ain't human t' be as bad as that be!

ABBIE (*stunned — dully*): He told yew ...?

EBEN: Hain't it true? It hain't no good in yew lyin'.

ABBIE (*pleadingly*): Eben, listen — ye must listen — it was long ago — afore we done nothin' — yew was scornin' me — goin' t' see Min — when I was lovin' ye — an' I said it t' him t' git vengeance on ye!

EBEN (*Unheedingly. With tortured passion.*): I wish ye was dead! I wish I was dead along with ye afore this come! (*Ragingly.*) But I'll git my vengeance too! I'll pray Maw t' come back t' help me — t' put her cuss on yew an' him!

ABBIE (*brokenly*): Don't ye, Eben! Don't ye! (*She throws herself on her knees before him, weeping.*) I didn't mean t' do bad t'ye! Fergive me, won't ye?

EBEN (*not seeming to hear her — fiercely*): I'll git squar' with the old skunk — an' yew! I'll tell him the truth 'bout the son he's so proud o'! Then I'll leave ye here t' pizen each other — with Maw comin' out o' her grave at nights — an' I'll go t' the gold fields o' Cali-forni-a whar Sim an' Peter be!

ABBIE (*terrified*): Ye won't — leave me? Ye can't!

EBEN (*with fierce determination*): I'm a-goin', I tell ye! I'll git rich thar an' come back an' fight him fur the farm he stole — an' I'll kick ye both out in the road — t' beg an' sleep in the woods — an' yer son along with ye — t' starve an' die! (*He is hysterical at the end.*)

ABBIE (*with a shudder — humbly*): He's yewr son, too, Eben.

EBEN (*torturedly*): I wish he never was born! I wish he'd die this minit! I wish I'd never sot eyes on him! It's him — yew havin' him — a-purpose t' steal — that's changed everythin'!

ABBIE (*gently*): Did ye believe I loved ye — afore he come?

EBEN: Aye-eh — like a dumb ox!

ABBIE: An' ye don't believe no more?

EBEN: B'lieve a lyin' thief! Ha!

ABBIE (*shudders — then humbly*): An' did ye r'ally love me afore?

EBEN (*brokenly*): Ay-eh — an' ye was trickin' me!

ABBIE: An' ye don't love me now!

EBEN (*violently*): I hate ye, I tell ye!

ABBIE: An' ye're truly goin' West — goin' t' leave me — all account o' him being born?

EBEN: I'm a-goin' in the mornin' — or may God strike me t' hell!

ABBIE (*after a pause — with a dreadful cold intensity — slowly*): If that's what his comin's done t' me — killin' yewr love — takin' yew away — my on'y joy — the on'y joy I ever knowed — like heaven t' me — purtier'n heaven — then I hate him, too, even if I be his Maw!

EBEN (*bitterly*): Lies! Ye love him! He'll steal the farm fur ye! (*Brokenly.*) But t'ain't the farm so much — not no more — it's yew foolin' me — gittin' me t' love ye — lyin' yew loved me — jest t' git a son t' steal!

ABBIE (*distractedly*): He won't steal! I'd kill him fust! I do love ye! I'll prove t' ye . . . !

EBEN (*harshly*): T'ain't no use lyin' no more. I'm deaf t' ye! (*He turns away.*) I hain't seein' ye agen. Good-by!

ABBIE (*pale with anguish*): Hain't ye even goin' t' kiss me — not once — arter all we loved?

EBEN (*in a hard voice*): I hain't wantin' t' kiss ye never agen! I'm wantin' t' forgit I ever sot eyes on ye!

ABBIE: Eben! — ye mustn't — wait a spell — I want t' tell ye. . . .

EBEN: I'm a-goin' in t' git drunk. I'm a-goin' t' dance.

ABBIE (*clinging to his arm — with passionate earnest-ness*): If I could make it —'s if he'd never come up between us — if I could prove t' ye I wa'n't schemin' t' steal from ye — so's everythin' could be jest the same with us, lovin' each other jest the same, kissin' an' happy the same's we've been happy afore he come — if I could do it — ye'd love me agen, wouldn't ye? Ye'd kiss me agen? Ye wouldn't never leave me, would ye?

EBEN (*moved*): I calc'late not. (*Then shaking her hand off his arm — with a bitter smile.*) But ye hain't God, be ye?

ABBIE (*exultantly*): Remember ye've promised! (*Then with strange intensity.*) Mebbe I kin take back one thin' God does!

EBEN (*peering at her*): Ye're gittin' cracked, hain't ye? (*Then going toward door.*) I'm a-goin' t' dance.

ABBIE (*calls after him intensely*): I'll prove t' ye! I'll prove I love ye better'n. . . . (*He goes in the door, not seeming to hear. She remains standing where she is, looking after him — then she finishes desperately.*) Better'n everythin' else in the world!

Scene III

(*Just before dawn in the morning — shows the kitchen and Cabot's bedroom. In the kitchen, by the light of a tallow candle on the table, Eben is sitting, his chin propped on his hands, his drawn face blank and expres-sionless. His carpetbag is on the floor beside him. In the bedroom, dimly lighted by a small whale-oil lamp, Cabot lies asleep. Abbie is bending over the cradle, lis-tening, her face full of terror yet with an undercurrent of desperate triumph. Suddenly, she breaks down and sobs, appears about to throw herself on her knees beside the cradle, but the old man turns restlessly, groaning in his sleep, and she controls herself, and, shrinking away from the cradle with a gesture of horror, backs swiftly toward the door in rear and goes out. A moment later she comes into the kitchen and, running to Eben, flings her arms about his neck and kisses him wildly. He hard-ens himself, he remains unmoved and cold, he keeps his eyes straight ahead.*)

ABBIE (*hysterically*): I done it, Eben! I told ye I'd do it! I've proved I love ye — better'n everythin' — so's ye can't never doubt me no more!

EBEN (*dully*): Whatever ye done, it hain't no good now.

ABBIE (*wildly*): Don't ye say that! Kiss me, Eben, won't ye? I need ye t' kiss me arter what I done! I need ye t' say ye love me!

EBEN (*kisses her without emotion — dully*): That's fur good-by. I'm a-goin' soon.

ABBIE: No! No! Ye won't go — not now!

EBEN (*going on with his own thoughts*): I been a-thinkin' — an' I hain't goin' t' tell Paw nothin'. I'll leave Maw t' take vengeance on ye. If I told him, the old skunk'd jest be stinkin' mean enuf to take it out on that baby. (*His voice showing emotion in spite of him.*) An' I don't want nothin' bad t' happen t' him.

He hain't t' blame fur yew. (*He adds with a certain queer pride.*) An' he looks like me! An' by God, he's mine! An' some day I'll be a-comin' back an' . . . !

ABBIE (*too absorbed in her own thoughts to listen to him — pleadingly*): They's no cause fur ye t' go now — they's no sense — it's all the same's it was — they's nothin' come b'tween us now — arter what I done!

EBEN (*Something in her voice arouses him. He stares at her a bit frightenedly.*): Ye look mad, Abbie. What did ye do?

ABBIE: I — I killed him, Eben.

EBEN (*amazed*): Ye killed him?

ABBIE (*dully*): Ay-eh.

EBEN (*recovering from his astonishment — savagely*): An' serves him right! But we got t' do somethin' quick t' make it look s'if the old skunk'd killed himself when he was drunk. We kin prove by 'em all how drunk he got.

ABBIE (*wildly*): No! No! Not him! (*Laughing distractedly.*) But that's what I ought t' done, hain't it? I oughter killed him instead! Why didn't ye tell me?

EBEN (*appalled*): Instead? What d'ye mean?

ABBIE: Not him.

EBEN (*his face grown ghastly*): Not — not that baby!

ABBIE (*dully*): Ay-eh!

EBEN (*falls to his knees as if he'd been struck — his voice trembling with horror*): Oh, God A'mighty! A'mighty God! Maw, whar was ye, why didn't ye stop her?

ABBIE (*simply*): She went back t' her grave that night we fust done it, remember? I hain't felt her about since. (*A pause. Eben hides his head in his hands, trembling all over as if he had the ague. She goes on dully.*) I left the piller over his little face. Then he killed himself. He stopped breathin'. (*She begins to weep softly.*)

EBEN (*rage beginning to mingle with grief*): He looked like me. He was mine, damn ye!

ABBIE (*slowly and brokenly*): I didn't want t' do it. I hated myself fur doin' it. I loved him. He was so purty — dead spit 'n' image o' yew. But I loved yew more — an' yew was goin' away — far off whar I'd never see ye agen, never kiss ye, never feel ye pressed agin me agen — an' ye said ye hated him fur havin' him — ye said ye hated him an' wished he was dead — ye said if it hain't been fur him comin' it'd be the same's afore between us.

EBEN (*unable to endure this, springs to his feet in a fury, threatening her, his twitching fingers seeming to reach out for her throat*): Ye lie! I never said — I never dreamed ye'd — I'd cut off my head afore I'd hurt his finger!

ABBIE (*piteously, sinking on her knees*): Eben, don't ye look at me like that — hatin' me — not after what I done fur ye — fur us — so's we could be happy agen —

EBEN (*furiously now*): Shut up, or I'll kill ye! I see yer game now — the same old sneakin' trick — ye're aimin' t' blame me fur the murder ye done!

ABBIE (*moaning — putting her hands over her ears*): Don't ye, Eben! Don't ye! (*She grasps his legs.*)

EBEN (*his mood suddenly changing to horror, shrinks away from her*): Don't ye tech me! Ye're pizen! How could ye — t' murder a pore little critter — Ye must've swapped yer soul t' hell! (*Suddenly raging.*) Ha! I kin see why ye done it! Not the lies ye jest told — but 'cause ye wanted t' steal agen — steal the last thin' ye'd left me — my part o' him — no, the hull o' him — ye saw he looked like me — ye knowed he was all mine — an' ye couldn't b'ar it — I know ye! Ye killed him fur bein' mine! (*All this has driven him almost insane. He makes a rush past her for the door — then turns — shaking both fists at her, violently.*) But I'll take vengeance now! I'll git the Sheriff! I'll tell him everythin'! Then I'll sing "I'm off to Californi-a!" an' go — gold — Golden Gate — gold sun — fields o' gold in the West! (*This last he half shouts, half croons incoherently, suddenly breaking off passionately.*) I'm a-goin' fur the Sheriff t' come an' git ye! I want ye tuk away, locked up from me! I can't stand t' luk at ye! Murderer an' thief 'r not, ye still tempt me! I'll give ye up t' the Sheriff! (*He turns and runs out, around the corner of house, panting and sobbing, and breaks into a swerving sprint down the road.*)

ABBIE (*struggling to her feet, runs to the door, calling after him*): I love ye, Eben! I love ye! (*She stops at the door weakly, swaying, about to fall.*) I don't care what ye do — if ye'll on'y love me agen — (*She falls limply to the floor in a faint.*)

Scene IV

(*About an hour later. Same as scene III. Shows the kitchen and Cabot's bedroom. It is after dawn. The sky is brilliant with the sunrise. In the kitchen, Abbie sits at the table, her body limp and exhausted, her head bowed down over her arms, her face hidden. Upstairs, Cabot is still asleep but awakens with a start. He looks toward the window and gives a snort of surprise and irritation — throws back the covers and begins hurriedly pulling on his clothes. Without looking behind him, he begins talking to Abbie whom he supposes beside him.*)

CABOT: Thunder 'n' lightin', Abbie! I hain't slept this late in fifty year! Looks 's if the sun was full riz a'most. Must've been the dancin' an' likker. Must be gittin' old. I hope Eben's t' wuk. Ye might've tuk the trouble t' rouse me, Abbie. (*He turns — sees no one there — surprised.*) Waal — whar air she? Gittin' vittles, I calc'late. (*He tiptoes to the cradle and peers down — proudly.*) Mornin', sonny. Purty's a picter! Sleepin' sound. He don't beller all night like most o' 'em. (*He goes quietly out the door in rear — a few moments later enters kitchen — sees Abbie — with satisfaction.*) So thar ye be. Ye got any vittles cooked?

ABBIE (*without moving*): No.

CABOT (*coming to her, almost sympathetically*): Ye feelin' sick?

ABBIE: No.

CABOT (*Pats her on shoulder. She shudders.*): Ye'd best lie down a spell. (*Half jocularly.*) Yer son'll be needin' ye soon. He'd ought t' wake up with a gnashin' appetite, the sound way he's sleepin'.

ABBIE (*shudders — then in a dead voice*): He hain't never goin' t' wake up.

CABOT (*jokingly*): Takes after me this mornin'. I hain't slept so late in . . .

ABBIE: He's dead.

CABOT (*stares at her — bewilderedly*): What. . . .

ABBIE: I killed him.

CABOT (*stepping back from her — aghast*): Air ye drunk —'r crazy —'r . . . ?

ABBIE (*suddenly lifts her head and turns on him — wildly*): I killed him, I tell ye! I smothered him. Go up an' see if ye don't b'lieve me!

(*Cabot stares at her a second, then bolts out the rear door, can be heard bounding up the stairs, and rushes into the bedroom and over to the cradle. Abbie has sunk back lifelessly into her former position. Cabot puts his hand down on the body in the crib. An expression of fear and horror comes over his face.*)

CABOT (*shrinking away — tremblingly*): God A'mighty! God A'mighty. (*He stumbles out the door — in a short while returns to the kitchen — comes to Abbie, the stunned expression still on his face — hoarsely.*) Why did ye do it? Why? (*As she doesn't answer, he grabs her violently by the shoulder and shakes her.*) I ax ye why ye done it! Ye'd better tell me 'r . . . !

ABBIE (*gives him a furious push which sends him staggering back and springs to her feet — with wild rage and hatred*): Don't ye dare tech me! What right hev ye t' question me 'bout him? He wa'n't yewr son! Think I'd have a son by yew? I'd die fust! I hate the sight o' ye an' allus did! It's yew I should've murdered, if I'd had good sense! I hate ye! I love Eben. I did from the fust. An' he was Eben's son — mine an' Eben's — not your'n!

CABOT (*stands looking at her dazedly — a pause — finding his words with an effort — dully*): That was it — what I felt — pokin' round the corners — while ye lied — holdin' yerself from me — sayin' ye'd already conceived — (*He lapses into crushed silence — then with a strange emotion.*) He's dead, sart'n. I felt his heart. Pore little critter! (*He blinks back one tear, wiping his sleeve across his nose.*)

ABBIE (*hysterically*): Don't ye! Don't ye! (*She sobs unrestrainedly.*)

CABOT (*with a concentrated effort that stiffens his body into a rigid line and hardens his face into a stony mask — through his teeth to himself*): I got t' be — like a stone — a rock o' jedgment! (*A pause. He gets complete control over himself — harshly.*) If he was Eben's, I be glad he air gone! An' mebbe I suspi-

cioned it all along. I felt they was somethin' onnateral — somewhars — the house got so lonesome — an' cold — drivin' me down t' the barn — t' the beasts o' the field. . . . Ay-eh. I must've suspicioned — somethin'. Ye didn't fool me — not altogether, leastways — I'm too old a bird — growin' ripe on the bough. . . . (*He becomes aware he is wandering, straightens again, looks at Abbie with a cruel grin.*) So ye'd liked t' hev murdered me 'steed o' him, would ye? Waal, I'll live to a hundred! I'll live t' see ye hung! I'll deliver ye up t' the jedgment o' God an' the law! I'll git the Sheriff now. (*Starts for the door.*)

ABBIE (*dully*): Ye needn't. Eben's gone fur him.

CABOT (*amazed*): Eben — gone fur the Sheriff?

ABBIE: Ay-eh.

CABOT: T' inform agen ye?

ABBIE: Ay-eh.

CABOT (*considers this — a pause — then in a hard voice*): Waal, I'm thankful fur him savin' me the trouble. I'll git t' wuk. (*He goes to the door — then turns — in a voice full of strange emotion.*) He'd ought t' been my son, Abbie. Ye'd ought t' loved me. I'm a man. If ye'd loved me, I'd never told no Sheriff on ye no matter what ye did, if they was t' brile me alive!

ABBIE (*defensively*): They's more to it nor yew know, makes him tell.

CABOT (*dryly*): Fur yewr sake, I hope they be. (*He goes out — comes around to the gate — stares up at the sky. His control relaxes. For a moment he is old and weary. He murmurs despairingly.*) God A'mighty, I be lonesomer'n ever! (*He hears running footsteps from the left, immediately is himself again. Eben runs in, panting exhaustedly, wild-eyed and mad looking. He lurches through the gate. Cabot grabs him by the shoulder. Eben stares at him dumbly.*) Did ye tell the Sheriff?

EBEN (*nodding stupidly*): Ay-eh.

CABOT (*gives him a push away that sends him sprawling — laughing with withering contempt*): Good fur ye! A prime chip o' yer Maw ye be! (*He goes toward the barn, laughing harshly. Eben scrambles to his feet. Suddenly Cabot turns — grimly threatening.*) Git off this farm when the Sheriff takes her — or, by God, he'll have t' come back an' git me fur murder, too! (*He stalks off. Eben does not appear to have heard him. He runs to the door and comes into the kitchen. Abbie looks up with a cry of anguished joy. Eben stumbles over and throws himself on his knees beside her sobbing brokenly.*)

EBEN: Fergive me!

ABBIE (*happily*): Eben! (*She kisses him and pulls his head over against her breast.*)

EBEN: I love ye! Fergive me!

ABBIE (*ecstatically*): I'd fergive ye all the sins in hell fur sayin' that! (*She kisses his head, pressing it to her with a fierce passion of possession.*)

EBEN (*brokenly*): But I told the Sheriff. He's comin' fur ye!

ABBIE: I kin b'ar what happens t' me — now!

EBEN: I woke him up. I told him. He says, wait 'til I git dressed. I was waiting. I got to thinkin' o' yew. I got to thinkin' how I'd loved ye. It hurt like somethin' was bustin' in my chest an' head. I got t' cryin'. I knowed sudden I loved ye yet, an' allus would love ye!

ABBIE (*caressing his hair — tenderly*): My boy, hain't ye?

EBEN: I begun t' run back. I cut across the fields an' through the woods. I thought ye might have time t' run away — with me — an' . . .

ABBIE (*shaking her head*): I got t' take my punishment — t' pay fur my sin.

EBEN: Then I want t' share it with ye.

ABBIE: Ye didn't do nothin'.

EBEN: I put it in yer head. I wisht he was dead! I as much as urged ye t' do it!

ABBIE: No. It was me alone!

EBEN: I'm as guilty as yew be! He was the child o' our sin.

ABBIE (*lifting her head as if defying God*): I don't repent that sin! I hain't askin' God t' fergive that!

EBEN: Nor me — but it led up t' the other — an' the murder ye did, ye did 'count o' me — an' it's my murder, too, I'll tell the Sheriff — an' if ye deny it, I'll say we planned it t'gether — an' they'll all b'lieve me, fur they suspicion everythin' we've done, an' it'll seem likely an' true to 'em. An' it is true — way down. I did help ye — somehow.

ABBIE (*laying her head on his — sobbing*): No! I don't want yew t' suffer!

EBEN: I got t' pay fur my part o' the sin! An' I'd suffer wuss leavin' ye, goin' West, thinkin' o' ye day an' night, bein' out when yew was in — (*lowering his voice*) 'r bein' alive when yew was dead. (*A pause.*) I want t' share with ye, Abbie — prison 'r death 'r hell 'r anythin'! (*He looks into her eyes and forces a trembling smile.*) If I'm sharin' with ye, I won't feel lonesome, leastways.

ABBIE (*weakly*): Eben! I won't let ye! I can't let ye!

EBEN (*kissing her — tenderly*): Ye can't he'p yerself. I got ye beat fur once!

ABBIE (*forcing a smile — adoringly*): I hain't beat — s'long's I got ye!

EBEN (*hears the sound of feet outside*): Ssshh! Listen! They've come t' take us!

ABBIE: No, it's him. Don't give him no chance to fight ye, Eben. Don't say nothin' — no matter what he says. An' I won't neither. (*It is Cabot. He comes up from the barn in a great state of excitement and strides into the house and then into the kitchen. Eben is kneeling beside Abbie, his arm around her, hers around him. They stare straight ahead.*)

CABOT (*Stares at them, his face hard. A long pause — vindictively.*): Ye make a slick pair o' murderin' turtle doves! Ye'd ought t' be both hung on the same limb an' left thar t' swing in the breeze an' rot — a warnin' t' old fools like me t' b'ar their lonesomeness alone — an' fur young fools like ye t' hobble their

lust. (*A pause. The excitement returns to his face, his eyes snap, he looks a bit crazy.*) I couldn't work today. I couldn't take no interest. T' hell with the farm! I'm leavin' it! I've turned the cows an' other stock loose! I've druv 'em into the woods whar they kin be free! By freein' 'em, I'm freein' myself! I'm quittin' here today! I'll set fire t' house an' barn an' watch 'em burn, an' I'll leave yer Maw t' haunt the ashes, an' I'll will the fields back t' God, so that nothin' human kin never touch 'em! I'll be a-goin' to Californi-a — t' jine Simeon an' Peter — true sons o' mine if they be dumb fools — an' the Cabots'll find Solomon's Mines t'gether! (*He suddenly cuts a mad caper.*) Whoop! What was the song they sung? "Oh, Californi-a! That's the land fur me." (*He sings this — then gets on his knees by the floorboard under which the money was hid.*) An' I'll sail thar on one o' the finest clippers I kin find! I've got the money! Pity ye didn't know whar this was hidden so's ye could steal. . . . (*He has pulled up the board. He stares — feels — stares again. A pause of dead silence. He slowly turns, slumping into a sitting position on the floor, his eyes like those of a dead fish, his face the sickly green of an attack of nausea. He swallows painfully several times — forces a weak smile at last.*) So — ye did steal it!

EBEN (*emotionlessly*): I swapped it t' Sim an' Peter fur their share o' the farm — t' pay their passage t' Californi-a.

CABOT (*with one sardonic*): Ha! (*He begins to recover. Gets slowly to his feet — strangely.*) I calc'late God give it to 'em — not yew! God's hard, not easy! Mebbe they's easy gold in the West but it hain't God's gold. It hain't fur me. I kin hear His voice warnin' me agen t' be hard an' stay on my farm. I kin see his hand usin' Eben t' steal t' keep me from weakness. I kin feel I be in the palm o' His hand, His fingers guidin' me. (*A pause — then he mutters sadly.*) It's a-goin' t' be lonesomer now than ever it war afore — an' I'm gittin' old, Lord — ripe on the bough. . . . (*Then stiffening.*) Waal — what d'ye want? God's lonesome, hain't He? God's hard an' lonesome! (*A pause. The Sheriff with two men comes up the road from the left. They move cautiously to the door. The Sheriff knocks on it with the butt of his pistol.*)

SHERIFF: Open in the name o' the law! (*They start.*)

CABOT: They've come fur ye. (*He goes to the rear door.*) Come in, Jim! (*The three men enter. Cabot meets them in doorway.*) Jest a minit, Jim. I got 'em safe here. (*The Sheriff nods. He and his companions remain in the doorway.*)

EBEN (*suddenly calls*): I lied this mornin', Jim. I helped her to do it. Ye kin take me, too.

ABBIE (*brokenly*): No!

CABOT: Take 'em both. (*He comes forward — stares at Eben with a trace of grudging admiration.*) Purty good — fur yew! Waal, I got t' round up the stock. Good-by.

EBEN: Good-by.

ABBIE: Good-by. (*Cabot turns and strides past the men — comes out and around the corner of the house, his shoulders squared, his face stony, and stalks grimly toward the barn. In the meantime the Sheriff and men have come into the room.*)

SHERIFF (*embarrassedly*): Waal — we'd best start.

ABBIE: Wait. (*Turns to Eben.*) I love ye, Eben.

EBEN: I love ye, Abbie. (*They kiss. The three men grin and shuffle embarrassedly. Eben takes Abbie's hand.*)

They go out the door in rear, the men following, and come from the house, walking hand in hand to the gate. Eben stops there and points to the sunrise sky.) Sun's a-rizin'. Purty, hain't it?

ABBIE: Ay-eh. (*They both stand for a moment looking up raptly in attitudes strangely aloof and devout.*)

SHERIFF (*looking around at the farm enviously — to his companions*): It's a jim-dandy farm, no denyin'. Wished I owned it!

COMMENTARY

Stark Young (*1881–1963*)
REVIEW OF *DESIRE UNDER THE ELMS*   *1924*

> *Stark Young's sensitive review of this play contrasted with other reviewers. He saw the work as a significant advance for O'Neill and extensively discusses the drama in terms that reveal its importance. Young also gives particular praise to Walter Huston's performance and to the work's farmhouse setting. His final comments praise the writing in a specific scene "written with such poetry and terrible beauty as we rarely see in theatre."*

Desire under the Elms, the first play by Eugene O'Neill to be produced since *Welded,* was presented last night at the Greenwich Village Theatre and proved to be as unlike that drama as it was unlike *The Hairy Ape* or *The Emperor Jones. Desire under the Elms* reverts in character to the earlier *Beyond the Horizon,* though it exhibits by comparison a fine progress in solidity and finish. It has less sentiment that this older piece and more passion; it is better written throughout; it has much tragic gloom and irony but a more mature conception and a more imaginative austerity.

Desire under the Elms is essentially a story of solitude, physical solitude, the solitude of the land, of men's dreams, of love, of life. The God behind the existence created on this New England farm is a harsh God, who is alone and is not understood. The minds of the people in this story are shaken and tinged with loneliness, with thwarted passion, with the trivial, the intense, the drab exaltation and denial of life. Underneath this solitude desire works, the redemption through love.

The children of old Cabot hate him. The youngest, the son of the second wife, remembers his dead mother, worked to death, and sees her about the place, risen from her grave. The father brings home a third wife. The two older sons go away to California; the younger stays and thinks to avenge his mother. In time he and the young wife come to love each other.

A son is born, which old Cabot thinks is to be heir to the farm, leaving the second wife's son adrift in the world. While a dance in honor of the newborn child goes on in the kitchen, the father and son quarrel outside; the son believes his father when he hears that the woman wanted a son only to cheat him out of the farm. He reviles her. To prove to him that it was the love of him and not the desire for the farm that had driven her to him, she kills the child. He runs off for the sheriff. The father turns the live stock loose in the woods and plans to go away, but when he finds the money gone from its hiding place, he believes that God another time has willed that he stand by the farm. The son returns from the sheriff's, he falls at the knees of the woman, takes part of the blame on himself, and they go away together to prison.

Robert Edmond Jones's setting for *Desire under the Elms* was profoundly dramatic. The end of a New England farmhouse with its overhanging elms was for all practical purposes built there on stage, with a wall of actual stone coming down to the footlights; a scene that was realistic but at the same time strangely and powerfully heightened in effect.

The general performance of the play was unusually adequate though not often on a level with the writing. Mary Morris, however, whose career as the fair Gertrude in *Fashion* last year was one of the flowers of the season's acting, played the wife in *Desire under the Elms* with a new and suppressed method that deepened at times into an admirable poignancy and a kind of grim, thin poetry that seemed the exact truth of her lines. Charles Ellis, though his work in earlier scenes was less successful or convincing, played with real poetry the passage where the boy is possessed with love for the woman and for his child. Walter Huston as the old man was everywhere trenchant, gaunt, fervid, harsh, as he should be in the part. In his ability to cover his gradations, to express the natural and convincing emotion, and to convey the harsh, inarticulate life embodied in this extraordinary portrait that Eugene O'Neill has drawn. Mr. Huston showed his talent and proved to be the best choice possible for the role.

The scene of *Desire under the Elms* that best illustrates the highest quality of the play is that in which we see the dance going on, the father outside the house, the young wife and her lover in the upstairs room in each other's arms beside the child's cradle, a scene written with such poetry and terrible beauty as we rarely see in the theatre, a scene that for these qualities of poetry, terror and at the same time unflinching realism rises above anything that Mr. O'Neill has written.

Federico García Lorca

Federico García Lorca (1898–1936) lived through some of the most troubling times of modern Spain. He was born in the countryside near Granada, Spain, and maintained a lifelong love of the Spanish village and country people. His father was a wealthy farmer, and his mother was a teacher who encouraged his early love of literature, art, and music. Lorca's talents were extraordinary. A fine pianist, he counted among his friends some of Spain's greatest musicians, including Manuel de Falla. Lorca painted throughout his life and maintained a close friendship with Salvador Dalí. His career in the university was not especially distinguished, but as a student he became famous for readings of his own poetry. He produced an early play, *The Butterfly's Evil Spell*, in 1920, the year before he published his first book of poems. His political leanings throughout his life were liberal and reformist, but his early years were spent living under a Spanish dictatorship. General elections ended Spain's monarchy and established the Second Spanish Republic in 1931, but Fascist leaders, notably Francisco Franco, began agitating for control. Standing for a free republic and prominent as a leftist, Lorca was killed suddenly and without explanation by Franco's forces in 1936, just two days before the start of the Spanish Civil War.

Lorca's dramatic work had developed steadily. His second play, *The Girl Who Waters the Sweet Basil Flower and the Inquisitive Prince* (1923), was a puppet show. Lorca, who especially enjoyed this form of drama, had bought his own puppet theater when he was fifteen. He designed the sets, and Manuel de Falla provided the music. Unfortunately, the manuscript for this play has been lost. Text for another puppet play of the same period, *The Billy-Club Puppets*, does exist, as do copies of some later dramatic sketches: *Buster Keaton's Promenade* (1926), which takes off on Buster Keaton's film character, and *The Public* (1933), one of several experimental surrealist plays. His first real success was *Mariana Pineda* (1927), produced in Granada. After suffering a personal crisis, perhaps connected to his growing awareness of his homosexuality, Lorca spent a year in New York, from which experience he wrote *The Poet in New York*, published — much later — in 1940.

Lorca returned to Spain and produced a number of plays in the early 1930s, such as *The Shoemaker's Prodigious Wife* (1930), *The Love of Don Perlimplín with Belisa in the Garden* (1933), and *Doña Rosita, the Spinster* (1935), the last of his plays to be produced during his lifetime. His three most important plays are generally referred to as folk tragedies: *Blood Wedding* (1933) and *Yerma* (1934) were produced in Madrid, and *The House of Bernarda Alba* was produced in Buenos Aires in 1945. These three plays were influenced by a great Spanish actress and producer, Margarita Xirgu, for whom the title role of Yerma was created.

Lorca's reputation flourished after the end of World War II, but because Spain's Fascist government continued until Franco's death in 1975, Lorca's work could not be produced in his native country until the 1980s. His gift was in combining poetry, music, original set designs, and a sense of the language of the country people who inspired his work. He had a feel for the pagan forces that informed the country people and aimed to show their creative power in everyday life. He celebrated instinctive, primitive religious feeling, the joy of living, the sexual energy of the universe, and the fullness of life.

THE HOUSE OF BERNARDA ALBA

Lorca diverged from his earlier poetic style when he created this play, sub-titled "a drama about women in the villages of Spain." He is on record as having said, "Not a drop of poetry! Reality! Realism!" Supposed to be as realistic and detailed as a "photographic document," the play pointed to some of the harsher realities of life for women in rural Spain. Indeed, only women appear in the play. Pepe el Romano, a young handsome man, betrothed to Angustias, Bernarda's eldest daughter (apparently for her money), is mentioned often but never appears. In the beginning of the third act, a stallion making loud sounds in his stall represents the symbolic force of sex in nature. Bernarda Alba demands that the stallion be freed before it brings the walls down, but at the same time she determines to keep her daughters hidden away in her house and under her thumb. The focus of the play is on Bernarda Alba's determination to preserve her dignity in her village. She wants to make sure that no one talks about her family disparagingly; she must keep up appearances even at the risk of smothering the sexual energies of her five daughters.

When the play opens, Bernarda's second husband has just died, and she declares that the household shall mourn for eight years. Her daughters would be shut in and not see a man for any of that time. However, since Angustias has her own money from her father, Bernarda's first husband, she is courted by Pepe el Romano. At the same time Pepe secretly expresses his true affection to Angustias's sister Adela, who is much closer to him in age and who would be a more suitable wife. Bernarda, however, is adamant about the period of mourning and eventually chases Pepe away with a shotgun after discovering that he has given in to his desires.

This is a play about the tyranny of Bernarda over her daughters. It portrays her desire to be respected in the community at all costs, even the cost of living a lie. It is also a play about "Women without men." Some critics have seen in the prisonlike atmosphere (note the constant reference to bars) a suggestion of the religious convent and the sexual repression it implies. The Cistercians, known as Bernardas, were an order of nuns familiar to Lorca. But Lorca is exploring a number of powerful forces in life: the power of the family and tradition, the power of religion and its structures of moral behavior, the power of economic necessity and the way it distorts lives, and the power of a political force that maintains itself through absolute authority. Most of these forces were evident in the Spain Lorca knew throughout his life. From 1932 much of his time was spent traveling with, and writing for, a government-sponsored touring company, La Barraca, that put on classic Spanish plays in remote towns around the nation. He had plenty of opportunity to observe everyday life in rural Spain. This play reveals some of its nature.

The House of Bernarda Alba in Performance

The first production of the play was in Buenos Aires in 1945, which Lorca visited shortly before he died, impressing those he met with his genius. South America has long found his work important; Lorca's play was produced in various South American countries long before it appeared in Spain. Eric Bentley staged a minimalist production of the play at the Abbey Theatre in Dublin in 1950, with Peggy Hayes as Bernarda and Angela Newmann as Adela. He describes this production in his *In Search of Theater* (1953) saying, "Ireland and Spain are two of the remaining vestiges of Catholic-peasant civilization. Lorca's play springs from this civilization, gives it amazingly full expression, and is a bitter rejection of it."

The play was given a limited production in Paris in the Studio des Champs-Élysées in 1946, employing a fine set with stark white walls and black wrought-iron bars across the windows. A New York production at the ANTA Playhouse lasted for seventeen performances in January 1951. Bentley had earlier speculated that the play would be very difficult to communicate to 1950s London or New York audiences, and he seems to have been correct. It was produced in New York again by Teatro Hispano, directed by Max Ferra, in early 1972. Bernarda was played by the Cuban actress Ofelia Gonzalez. Numerous productions in Europe followed; one of the most powerful was in 1986 at the Lyric Theatre in Hammersmith, London, directed by Nuria Espert. The sets and the lighting served to intensify the sense of overwhelming heat from the Andalusian sun. Paul Preston, in his review in the *Times Literary Supplement,* said, "Glenda Jackson's Bernarda is as stiff-backed as the most humourless prison governor or mother superior, dominating her brood with snarling sarcasm and fulminating looks." Joan Plowright played a powerful Poncia, but Patricia Hayes, as Bernarda's mother, was singled out for a stunning performance: "wearing muslin rags over white flesh like a feverish and ecstatic moth" (Michael Ratcliffe in the *Observer*). The play moved into the West End (London's Broadway) to the Globe Theatre in 1987 with the same cast. Among the most recent productions is the 1993 production in Northern Ireland at the adventurous women's company, the Charabanc Theatre Company. Lynne Parker adapted and directed the play to exceptional reviews, and the production toured twenty towns throughout Ireland and Northern Ireland before settling in at the Project Arts Centre in Dublin. The reviews of the production celebrated its excellence and explored the women's issues in the drama.

Federico García Lorca (1898–1936)

THE HOUSE OF BERNARDA ALBA　　　　*1936*

A DRAMA ABOUT WOMEN IN THE VILLAGES OF SPAIN

TRANSLATED BY JAMES GRAHAM-LUJÁN AND RICHARD L. O'CONNELL

Characters

BERNARDA (*age 60*)
MARÍA JOSEFA, *Bernarda's Mother* (*age 80*)
ANGUSTIAS, *Bernarda's Daughter* (*age 39*)
MAGDALENA, *Bernarda's Daughter* (*age 30*)
AMELIA, *Bernarda's Daughter* (*age 27*)
MARTIRIO, *Bernarda's Daughter* (*age 24*)
ADELA, *Bernarda's Daughter* (*age 20*)
A MAID (*age 50*)
LA PONCIA, *A Maid* (*age 60*)
PRUDENCIA (*age 50*)
WOMEN IN MOURNING

The writer states that these Three Acts are intended as a photographic document.

ACT 1

(*A very white room in Bernarda Alba's house. The walls are white. There are arched doorways with jute curtains tied back with tassels and ruffles. Wicker chairs. On the walls, pictures of unlikely landscapes full of nymphs or legendary kings.*

　It is summer. A great brooding silence fills the stage. It is empty when the curtain rises. Bells can be heard tolling outside.)

FIRST SERVANT (*entering*): The tolling of those bells hits me right between the eyes.

PONCIA (*she enters, eating bread and sausage*): More than two hours of mumbo jumbo. Priests are here from all the towns. The church looks beautiful. At the first responsory for the dead, Magdalena fainted.

FIRST SERVANT: She's the one who's left most alone.

PONCIA: She's the only one who loved her father. Ay! Thank God we're alone for a little. I came over to eat.

FIRST SERVANT: If Bernarda sees you . . . !

PONCIA: She's not eating today so she'd just as soon we'd all die of hunger! Domineering old tyrant! But she'll be fooled! I opened the sausage crock.

FIRST SERVANT (*with an anxious sadness*): Couldn't you give me some for my little girl, Poncia?

PONCIA: Go ahead! And take a fistful of peas too. She won't know the difference today.

VOICE (*within*): Bernarda!

PONCIA: There's the grandmother! Isn't she locked up tight?

FIRST SERVANT: Two turns of the key.

PONCIA: You'd better put the cross-bar up too. She's got the fingers of a lock-picker!

VOICE (*within*): Bernarda!

PONCIA (*shouting*): She's coming! (*to the servant*) Clean everything up good. If Bernarda doesn't find things shining, she'll pull out the few hairs I have left.

SERVANT: What a woman!

PONCIA: Tyrant over everyone around her. She's perfectly capable of sitting on your heart and watching you die for a whole year without turning off that cold little smile she wears on her wicked face. Scrub, scrub those dishes!

SERVANT: I've got blood on my hands from so much polishing of everything.

PONCIA: She's the cleanest, she's the decentest, she's the highest everything! A good rest her poor husband's earned!

(*The bells stop.*)

SERVANT: Did all the relatives come?

PONCIA: Just hers. His people hate her. They came to see him dead and make the sign of the cross over him; that's all.

SERVANT: Are there enough chairs?

PONCIA: More than enough. Let them sit on the floor. When Bernarda's father died people stopped coming under this roof. She doesn't want them to see her in her "domain." Curse her!

SERVANT: She's been good to you.

PONCIA: Thirty years washing her sheets. Thirty years eating her leftovers. Nights of watching when she had a cough. Whole days peeking through a crack in the shutters to spy on the neighbors and carry her the tale. Life without secrets one from the other. But in spite of that — curse her! May the "pain of the piercing nail" strike her in the eyes.

SERVANT: Poncia!

PONCIA: But I'm a good watchdog! I bark when I'm told and bite beggars' heels when she sics me on 'em. My sons work in her fields — both of them already married, but one of these days I'll have enough.

SERVANT: And then. . . ?

PONCIA: Then I'll lock myself up in a room with her and spit in her face — a whole year. "Bernarda, here's for this, that and the other!" Till I leave her — just like a lizard the boys have squashed. For that's what she is — she and her whole family! Not that I envy her her life. Five girls are left her, five ugly daughters — not counting Angustias the eldest, by her first husband, who has money — the rest of them, plenty of eyelets to embroider, plenty of linen petticoats, but bread and grapes when it comes to inheritance.

SERVANT: Well, *I'd* like to have what they've got!

PONCIA: All we have is our hands and a hole in God's earth.

SERVANT: And that's the only earth they'll ever leave to us — to us who have nothing!

PONCIA (*at the cupboard*): This glass has some specks.

SERVANT: Neither soap nor rag will take them off.

(*The bells toll.*)

PONCIA: The last prayer! I'm going over and listen. I certainly like the way our priest sings. In the Pater Noster his voice went up, and up — like a pitcher filling with water little by little. Of course, at the end his voice cracked, but it's glorious to hear it. No, there never was anybody like the old Sacristan — Tronchapinos. At my mother's Mass, may she rest in peace, he sang. The walls shook — and when he said "Amen," it was as if a wolf had come into the church.

(*Imitating him.*)

A-a-a-a-men!

(*She starts coughing.*)

SERVANT: Watch out — you'll strain your windpipe!

PONCIA: I'd rather strain something else!

(*Goes out laughing.*)
(*The servant scrubs. The bells toll.*)

SERVANT (*imitating the bells*): Dong, dong, dong. Dong, dong, dong. May God forgive him!

BEGGAR WOMAN (*at the door, with a little girl*): Blesséd be God!

SERVANT: Dong, dong, dong. I hope he waits many years for us! Dong, dong, dong.

BEGGAR (*loudly, a little annoyed*): Blesséd be God!

SERVANT (*annoyed*): Forever and ever!

BEGGAR: I came for the scraps.

(*The bells stop tolling.*)

SERVANT: You can go right out the way you came in. Today's scraps are for me.

BEGGAR: But you have somebody to take care of you — and my little girl and I are all alone!

SERVANT: Dogs are alone too, and they live.

BEGGAR: They always give them to me.

SERVANT: Get out of here! Who let you in anyway? You've already tracked up the place.

(*The beggar woman and little girl leave. The servant goes on scrubbing.*)

Floors finished with oil, cupboards, pedestals, iron beds — but us servants, we can suffer in silence —

and live in mud huts with a plate and a spoon. I hope someday not a one will be left to tell it.

(*The bells sound again.*)

Yes, yes — ring away. Let them pelt you in a coffin with gold inlay and brocade to carry it on — you're no less dead than I'll be, so take what's coming to you, Antonio María Benavides — stiff in your broadcloth suit and your high boots — take what's coming to you! You'll never again lift my skirts behind the corral door!

(*From the rear door, two by two, women in mourning with large shawls and black skirts and fans, begin to enter. They come in slowly until the stage is full.*)

SERVANT (*breaking into a wail*): Oh, Antonio María Benavides, now you'll never see these walls, nor break bread in this house again! I'm the one who loved you most of all your servants.

(*Pulling her hair.*)

Must I love on after you've gone? Must I go on living?

(*The two hundred women finish coming in, and Bernarda and her five daughters enter. Bernarda leans on a cane.*)

BERNARDA (*to the servant*): Silence!

SERVANT (*weeping*): Bernarda!

BERNARDA: Less shrieking and more work. You should have had all this cleaner for the wake. Get out. This isn't your place.

(*The servant goes off crying.*)

The poor are like animals — they seem to be made of different stuff.

FIRST WOMAN: The poor feel their sorrows too.

BERNARDA: But they forget them in front of a plateful of peas.

FIRST GIRL (*timidly*): Eating is necessary for living.

BERNARDA: At your age one doesn't talk in front of older people.

WOMAN: Be quiet, child.

BERNARDA: I've never taken lessons from anyone. Sit down.

(*They sit down. Pause. Loudly.*)

Magdalena, don't cry. If you want to cry, get under your bed. Do you hear me?

SECOND WOMAN (*to Bernarda*): Have you started to work the fields?

BERNARDA: Yesterday.

THIRD WOMAN: The sun comes down like lead.

FIRST WOMAN: I haven't known heat like this for years.

(*Pause. They all fan themselves.*)

BERNARDA: Is the lemonade ready?

PONCIA: Yes, Bernarda.

(*She brings in a large tray full of little white jars which she distributes.*)

BERNARDA: Give the men some.

PONCIA: They're already drinking in the patio.

BERNARDA: Let them get out the way they came in. I don't want them walking through here.

A GIRL (*to Angustias*): Pepe el Romano was with the men during the service.

ANGUSTIAS: There he was.

BERNARDA: His mother was there. She saw his mother. Neither she nor I saw Pepe . . .

GIRL: I thought . . .

BERNARDA: The one who *was* there was Darajalí, the widower. Very close to your Aunt. We all of us saw him.

SECOND WOMAN (*aside, in a low voice*): Wicked, worse than wicked woman!

THIRD WOMAN: A tongue like a knife!

BERNARDA: Women in church shouldn't look at any man but the priest — and him only because he wears skirts. To turn your head is to be looking for the warmth of corduroy.

FIRST WOMAN: Sanctimonious old snake!

PONCIA (*between her teeth*): Itching for a man's warmth.

BERNARDA (*beating with her cane on the floor*): Bléssed be God!

ALL (*crossing themselves*): Forever bléssed and praised.

BERNARDA: Rest in peace with holy company at your head.

ALL: Rest in peace!

BERNARDA: With the Angel Saint Michael, and his sword of justice.

ALL: Rest in peace!

BERNARDA: With the key that opens, and the hand that locks.

ALL: Rest in peace!

BERNARDA: With the most bléssed, and the little lights of the field.

ALL: Rest in peace!

BERNARDA: With our holy charity, and all souls on land and sea.

ALL: Rest in peace!

BERNARDA: Grant rest to your servant, Antonio María Benavides, and give him the crown of your bléssed glory.

ALL: Amen.

BERNARDA (*she rises and chants*): *Requiem aeternam donat eis domine.*

ALL (*standing and chanting in the Gregorian fashion*): *Et lux perpetua luce ab eis.°*

(*They cross themselves.*)

FIRST WOMAN: May you have health to pray for his soul. (*They start filing out.*)

THIRD WOMAN: You won't lack loaves of hot bread.

SECOND WOMAN: Nor a roof for your daughters.

(*They are all filing in front of Bernarda and going out. Angustias leaves by the door to the patio.*)

Requiem aeternam . . . ab eis: Eternal rest grant to him, O Lord. And let perpetual light shine on him.

FOURTH WOMAN: May you go on enjoying your wedding wheat.

PONCIA (*she enters, carrying a money bag*): From the men — this bag of money for Masses.

BERNARDA: Thank them — and let them have a glass of brandy.

GIRL (*to Magdalena*): Magdalena . . .

BERNARDA (*to Magdalena, who is starting to cry*): Sh-h-h-h!

(*She beats with her cane on the floor.*)

(*All the women have gone out.*)

BERNARDA (*to the women who have just left*): Go back to your houses and criticize everything you've seen! I hope it'll be many years before you pass under the archway of my door again.

PONCIA: You've nothing to complain about. The whole town came.

BERNARDA: Yes, to fill my house with the sweat from their wraps and the poison of their tongues.

AMELIA: Mother, don't talk like that.

BERNARDA: What other way is there to talk about this cursed village with no river — this village full of wells where you drink water always fearful it's been poisoned?

PONCIA: Look what they've done to the floor!

BERNARDA: As though a herd of goats had passed through.

(*Poncia cleans the floor.*)

Adela, give me a fan.

ADELA: Take this one.

(*She gives her a round fan with green and red flowers.*)

BERNARDA (*throwing the fan on the floor*): Is that the fan to give to a widow? Give me a black one and learn to respect your father's memory.

MARTIRIO: Take mine.

BERNARDA: And you?

MARTIRIO: I'm not hot.

BERNARDA: Well, look for another, because you'll need it. For the eight years of mourning, not a breath of air will get in this house from the street. We'll act as if we'd sealed up doors and windows with bricks. That's what happened in my father's house — and in my grandfather's house. Meantime, you can all start embroidering your hope-chest linens. I have twenty bolts of linen in the chest from which to cut sheets and coverlets. Magdalena can embroider them.

MAGDALENA: It's all the same to me.

ADELA (*sourly*): If you don't want to embroider them — they can go without. That way yours will look better.

MAGDALENA: Neither mine nor yours. I know I'm not going to marry. I'd rather carry sacks to the mill. Anything except sit here day after day in this dark room.

BERNARDA: That's what a woman is for.

MAGDALENA: Cursed be all women.

BERNARDA: In this house you'll do what I order. You

can't run with the story to your father any more. Needle and thread for women. Whiplash and mules for men. That's the way it has to be for people who have certain obligations.

(*Adela goes out.*)

VOICE: Bernarda! Let me out!

BERNARDA (*calling*): Let her out now!

(*The first servant enters.*)

FIRST SERVANT: I had a hard time holding her. In spite of her eighty years, your mother's strong as an oak.

BERNARDA: It runs in the family. My grandfather was the same way.

SERVANT: Several times during the wake I had to cover her mouth with an empty sack because she wanted to shout out to you to give her dishwater to drink at least, and some dogmeat, which is what she says you feed her.

MARTIRIO: She's mean!

BERNARDA (*to servant*): Let her get some fresh air in the patio.

SERVANT: She took her rings and the amethyst earrings out of the box, put them on, and told me she wants to get married.

(*The daughters laugh.*)

BERNARDA: Go with her and be careful she doesn't get near the well.

SERVANT: You don't need to be afraid she'll jump in.

BERNARDA: It's not that — but the neighbors can see her there from their windows.

(*The servant leaves.*)

MARTIRIO: We'll go change our clothes.

BERNARDA: Yes, but don't take the kerchiefs from your heads.

(*Adela enters.*)

And Angustias?

ADELA (*meaningfully*): I saw her looking out through the cracks of the back door. The men had just gone.

BERNARDA: And you, what were *you* doing at the door?

ADELA: I went there to see if the hens had laid.

BERNARDA: But the men had already gone!

ADELA (*meaningfully*): A group of them were still standing outside.

BERNARDA (*furiously*): Angustias! Angustias!

ANGUSTIAS (*entering*): Did you want something?

BERNARDA: For what — and at whom — were you looking?

ANGUSTIAS: Nobody.

BERNARDA: Is it decent for a woman of your class to be running after a man the day of her father's funeral? Answer me! Whom were you looking at?

(*Pause.*)

ANGUSTIAS: I . . .

BERNARDA: Yes, you!

ANGUSTIAS: Nobody.

BERNARDA: Soft! Honeytongue!

(*She strikes her.*)

PONCIA (*running to her*): Bernarda, calm down!

(*She holds her. Angustias weeps.*)

BERNARDA: Get out of here, all of you!

(*They all go out.*)

PONCIA: She did it not realizing what she was doing — although it's bad, of course. It really disgusted me to see her sneak along to the patio. Then she stood at the window listening to the men's talk, which, as usual, was not the sort one should listen to.

BERNARDA: That's what they come to funerals for. (*With curiosity.*) What were they talking about?

PONCIA: They were talking about Paca la Roseta. Last night they tied her husband up in a stall, stuck her on a horse behind the saddle, and carried her away to the depths of the olive grove.

BERNARDA: And what did she do?

PONCIA: She? She was just as happy — they say her breasts were exposed and Maximiliano held on to her as if he were playing a guitar. Terrible!

BERNARDA: And what happened?

PONCIA: What had to happen. They came back almost at daybreak. Paca la Roseta with her hair loose and a wreath of flowers on her head.

BERNARDA: She's the only bad woman we have in the village.

PONCIA: Because she's not from here. She's from far away. And those who went with her are the sons of outsiders too. The men from here aren't up to a thing like that.

BERNARDA: No, but they like to see it, and talk about it, and suck their fingers over it.

PONCIA: They were saying a lot more things.

BERNARDA (*looking from side to side with a certain fear*): What things?

PONCIA: I'm ashamed to talk about them.

BERNARDA: And my daughter heard them?

PONCIA: Of course!

BERNARDA: That one takes after her Aunts: white and mealy-mouthed and casting sheep's eyes at any little barber's compliment. Oh, what one has to go through and put up with so people will be decent and not too wild!

PONCIA: It's just that your daughters are of an age when they ought to have husbands. Mighty little trouble they give you. Angustias must be much more than thirty now.

BERNARDA: Exactly thirty-nine.

PONCIA: Imagine. And she's never had a beau . . .

BERNARDA (*furiously*): None of them has ever had a beau and they've never needed one! They get along very well.

PONCIA: I didn't mean to offend you.

BERNARDA: For a hundred miles around there's no one

good enough to come near them. The men in this town are not of their class. Do you want me to turn them over to the first shepherd?

PONCIA: You should have moved to another town.

BERNARDA: That's it. To sell them!

PONCIA: No, Bernarda, to change. . . . Of course, any place else, they'd be the poor ones.

BERNARDA: Hold your tormenting tongue!

PONCIA: One can't even talk to you. Do we, or do we not share secrets?

BERNARDA: We do not. You're a servant and I pay you. Nothing more.

PONCIA: But . . .

FIRST SERVANT (*entering*): Don Arturo's here. He's come to see about dividing the inheritance.

BERNARDA: Let's go. (*to the servant*) You start white-washing the patio. (*to La Poncia*) And you start putting all the dead man's clothes away in the chest.

PONCIA: We could give away some of the things.

BERNARDA: Nothing — not a button even! Not even the cloth we covered his face with.

(*She goes out slowly, leaning on her cane. At the door she turns to look at the two servants. They go out. She leaves.*)

(*Amelia and Martirio enter.*)

AMELIA: Did you take the medicine?

MARTIRIO: For all the good it'll do me.

AMELIA: But you took it?

MARTIRIO: I do things without any faith, but like clock-work.

AMELIA: Since the new doctor came you look livelier.

MARTIRIO: I feel the same.

AMELIA: Did you notice? Adelaida wasn't at the funeral.

MARTIRIO: I know. Her sweetheart doesn't let her go out even to the front doorstep. Before, she was gay. Now, not even powder on her face.

AMELIA: These days a girl doesn't know whether to have a beau or not.

MARTIRIO: It's all the same.

AMELIA: The whole trouble is all these wagging tongues that won't let us live. Adelaida has probably had a bad time.

MARTIRIO: She's afraid of our mother. Mother is the only one who knows the story of Adelaida's father and where he got his lands. Everytime she comes here, Mother twists the knife in the wound. Her father killed his first wife's husband in Cuba so he could marry her himself. Then he left her there and went off with another woman who already had one daughter, and then he took up with this other girl, Adelaida's mother, and married her after his second wife died insane.

AMELIA: But why isn't a man like that put in jail?

MARTIRIO: Because men help each other cover up things like that and no one's able to tell on them.

AMELIA: But Adelaida's not to blame for any of that.

MARTIRIO: No. But history repeats itself. I can see that everything is a terrible repetition. And she'll have the same fate as her mother and grandmother — both of them wife to the man who fathered her.

AMELIA: What an awful thing!

MARTIRIO: It's better never to look at a man. I've been afraid of them since I was a little girl. I'd see them in the yard, yoking the oxen and lifting grain sacks, shouting and stamping, and I was always afraid to grow up for fear one of them would suddenly take me in his arms. God has made me weak and ugly and has definitely put such things away from me.

AMELIA: Don't say that! Enrique Humanas was after you and he liked you.

MARTIRIO: That was just people's ideas! One time I stood in my nightgown at the window until daybreak because he let me know through his shepherd's little girl that he was going to come, and he didn't. It was all just talk. Then he married someone else who had more money than I.

AMELIA: And ugly as the devil.

MARTIRIO: What do men care about ugliness? All they care about is lands, yokes of oxen, and a submissive bitch who'll feed them.

AMELIA: Ay!

(*Magdalena enters.*)

MAGDALENA: What are you doing?

MARTIRIO: Just here.

AMELIA: And you?

MAGDALENA: I've been going through all the rooms. Just to walk a little, and look at Grandmother's needle-point pictures — the little woolen dog, and the black man wrestling with the lion — which we liked so much when we were children. Those were happier times. A wedding lasted ten days and evil tongues weren't in style. Today people are more refined. Brides wear white veils, just as in the cities, and we drink bottled wine, but we rot inside because of what people might say.

MARTIRIO: Lord knows what went on then!

AMELIA (*to Magdalena*): One of your shoelaces has come untied.

MAGDALENA: What of it?

AMELIA: You'll step on it and fall.

MAGDALENA: One less!

MARTIRIO: And Adela?

MAGDALENA: Ah! She put on the green dress she made to wear for her birthday, went out to the yard, and began shouting: "Chickens! Chickens, look at me!" I had to laugh.

AMELIA: If Mother had only seen her!

MAGDALENA: Poor little thing! She's the youngest one of us and still has her illusions. I'd give something to see her happy.

(*Pause. Angustias crosses the stage, carrying some towels.*)

ANGUSTIAS: What time is it?

MAGDALENA: It must be twelve.

ANGUSTIAS: So late?

AMELIA: It's about to strike.

(*Angustias goes out.*)

MAGDALENA (*meaningfully*): Do you know what?

(*Pointing after Angustias.*)

AMELIA: No.
MAGDALENA: Come on!
MARTIRIO: I don't know what you're talking about!
MAGDALENA: Both of you know it better than I do, always with your heads together, like two little sheep, but not letting anybody else in on it. I mean about Pepe el Romano!
MARTIRIO: Ah!
MAGDALENA (*mocking her*): Ah! The whole town's talking about it. Pepe el Romano is coming to marry Angustias. Last night he was walking around the house and I think he's going to send a declaration soon.
MARTIRIO: I'm glad. He's a good man.
AMELIA: Me too. Angustias is well off.
MAGDALENA: Neither one of you is glad.
MARTIRIO: Magdalena! What do you mean?
MAGDALENA: If he were coming because of Angustias' looks, for Angustias as a woman, I'd be glad too, but he's coming for her money. Even though Angustias is our sister, we're her family here and we know she's old and sickly, and always has been the least attractive one of us! Because if she looked like a dressed-up stick at twenty, what can she look like now, now that she's forty?
MARTIRIO: Don't talk like that. Luck comes to the one who least expects it.
AMELIA: But Magdalena's right after all! Angustias has all her father's money; she's the only rich one in the house and that's why, now that Father's dead and the money will be divided, they're coming for her.
MAGDALENA: Pepe el Romano is twenty-five years old and the best looking man around here. The natural thing would be for him to be after you, Amelia, or our Adela, who's twenty — not looking for the least likely one in this house, a woman who, like her father, talks through her nose.
MARTIRIO: Maybe he likes that!
MAGDALENA: I've never been able to bear your hypocrisy.
MARTIRIO: Heavens!

(*Adela enters.*)

MAGDALENA: Did the chickens see you?
ADELA: What did you want me to do?
AMELIA: If Mother sees you, she'll drag you by your hair!
ADELA: I had a lot of illusions about this dress. I'd planned to put it on the day we were going to eat watermelons at the well. There wouldn't have been another like it.
MARTIRIO: It's a lovely dress.
ADELA: And one that looks very good on me. It's the best thing Magdalena's ever cut.

MAGDALENA: And the chickens, what did they say to you?
ADELA: They presented me with a few fleas that riddled my legs.

(*They laugh.*)

MARTIRIO: What you can do is dye it black.
MAGDALENA: The best thing you can do is give it to Angustias for her wedding with Pepe el Romano.
ADELA (*with hidden emotion*): But Pepe el Romano . . .
AMELIA: Haven't you heard about it?
ADELA: No.
MAGDALENA: Well, now you know!
ADELA: But it can't be!
MAGDALENA: Money can do anything.
ADELA: Is that why she went out after the funeral and stood looking through the door?

(*Pause.*)

And that man would . . .
MAGDALENA: Would do anything.

(*Pause.*)

MARTIRIO: What are you thinking, Adela?
ADELA: I'm thinking that this mourning has caught me at the worst moment of my life for me to bear it.
MAGDALENA: You'll get used to it.
ADELA (*bursting out, crying with rage*): I will not get used to it! I can't be locked up. I don't want my skin to look like yours. I don't want my skin's whiteness lost in these rooms. Tomorrow I'm going to put on my green dress and go walking in the streets. I want to go out!

(*The first servant enters.*)

MAGDALENA (*in a tone of authority*): Adela!
SERVANT: The poor thing! How she misses her father. . . .

(*She goes out.*)

MARTIRIO: Hush!
AMELIA: What happens to one will happen to all of us.

(*Adela grows calm.*)

MAGDALENA: The servant almost heard you.
SERVANT (*entering*): Pepe el Romano is coming along at the end of the street.

(*Amelia, Martirio and Magdalena run hurriedly.*)

MAGDALENA: Let's go see him!

(*They leave rapidly.*)

SERVANT (*to Adela*): Aren't you going?
ADELA: It's nothing to me.
SERVANT: Since he has to turn the corner, you'll see him better from the window of your room.

(*The servant goes out. Adela is left on the stage, standing doubtfully; after a moment, she also leaves rapidly, going toward her room. Bernarda and La Poncia come in.*)

BERNARDA: Damned portions and shares.

PONCIA: What a lot of money is left to Angustias!

BERNARDA: Yes.

PONCIA: And for the others, considerably less.

BERNARDA: You've told me that three times now, when you know I don't want it mentioned! Considerably less; a lot less! Don't remind me any more.

(*Angustias comes in, her face heavily made up.*)

Angustias!

ANGUSTIAS: Mother.

BERNARDA: Have you dared to powder your face? Have you dared to wash your face on the day of your father's death?

ANGUSTIAS: He wasn't my father. Mine died a long time ago. Have you forgotten that already?

BERNARDA: You owe more to this man, father of your sisters, than to your own. Thanks to him, your fortune is intact.

ANGUSTIAS: We'll have to see about that first!

BERNARDA: Even out of decency! Out of respect!

ANGUSTIAS: Let me go out, mother!

BERNARDA: Let you go out? After I've taken that powder off your face, I will. Spineless! Painted hussy! Just like your aunts!

(*She removes the powder violently with her handkerchief.*)

Now get out!

PONCIA: Bernarda, don't be so hateful!

BERNARDA: Even though my mother is crazy, I still have my five senses and I know what I'm doing.

(*They all enter.*)

MAGDALENA: What's going on here?

BERNARDA: Nothing's "going on here"!

MAGDALENA (*to Angustias*): If you're fighting over the inheritance, you're the richest one and can hang on to it all.

ANGUSTIAS: Keep your tongue in your pocketbook!

BERNARDA (*beating on the floor*): Don't fool yourselves into thinking you'll sway me. Until I go out of this house feet first I'll give the orders for myself and for you!

(*Voices are heard and María Josefa, Bernarda's mother, enters. She is very old and has decked out her head and breast with flowers.*)

MARÍA JOSEFA: Bernarda, where is my mantilla? Nothing, nothing of what I own will be for any of you. Not my rings nor my black moiré dress. Because not a one of you is going to marry — not a one. Bernarda, give me my necklace of pearls.

BERNARDA (*to the servant*): Why did you let her get in here?

SERVANT (*trembling*): She got away from me!

MARÍA JOSEFA: I ran away because I want to marry — I want to get married to a beautiful manly man from the shore of the sea. Because here the men run from women.

BERNARDA: Hush, hush, Mother!

MARÍA JOSEFA: No, no — I won't hush. I don't want to see these single women, longing for marriage, turning their hearts to dust; and I want to go to my home town. Bernarda, I want a man to get married to and be happy with!

BERNARDA: Lock her up!

MARÍA JOSEFA: Let me go out, Bernarda!

(*The servant seizes María Josefa.*)

BERNARDA: Help her, all of you!

(*They all grab the old woman.*)

MARÍA JOSEFA: I want to get away from here! Bernarda! To get married by the shore of the sea — by the shore of the sea!

(*Quick curtain.*)

ACT 2

(*A white room in Bernarda's house. The doors on the left lead to the bedrooms. Bernarda's daughters are seated on low chairs, sewing. Magdalena is embroidering. La Poncia is with them.*)

ANGUSTIAS: I've cut the third sheet.

MARTIRIO: That one goes to Amelia.

MAGDALENA: Angustias, shall I put Pepe's initials here too?

ANGUSTIAS (*dryly*): No.

MAGDALENA (*calling, from off stage to Adela*): Adela, aren't you coming?

AMELIA: She's probably stretched out on the bed.

PONCIA: Something's wrong with that one. I find her restless, trembling, frightened — as if a lizard were between her breasts.

MARTIRIO: There's nothing, more or less, wrong with her than there is with all of us.

MAGDALENA: All of us except Angustias.

ANGUSTIAS: I feel fine, and anybody who doesn't like it can pop.

MAGDALENA: We all have to admit the nicest things about you are your figure and your tact.

ANGUSTIAS: Fortunately, I'll soon be out of this hell.

MAGDALENA: Maybe you won't get out!

MARTIRIO: Stop this talk!

ANGUSTIAS: Besides, a good dowry is better than dark eyes in one's face!

MAGDALENA: All you say just goes in one ear and out the other.

AMELIA (*to La Poncia*): Open the patio door and see if we can get a bit of a breeze.

(*La Poncia opens the door.*)

MARTIRIO: Last night I couldn't sleep because of the heat.

The women stand as witnesses in a scene from *The House of Bernarda Alba* directed by Julia Robinson at the Alba Tomi Theatre in New York in 1987.

AMELIA: Neither could I.

MAGDALENA: I got up for a bit of air. There was a black storm cloud and a few drops even fell.

PONCIA: It was one in the morning and the earth seemed to give off fire. I got up too. Angustias was still at the window with Pepe.

MAGDALENA (*with irony*): That late? What time did he leave?

ANGUSTIAS: Why do you ask, if you saw him?

AMELIA: He must have left about one-thirty.

ANGUSTIAS: Yes. How did you know?

AMELIA: I heard him cough and heard his mare's hoof-beats.

PONCIA: But I heard him leave around four.

ANGUSTIAS: It must have been someone else!

PONCIA: No, I'm sure of it!

AMELIA: That's what it seemed to me, too.

MAGDALENA: That's very strange!

(*Pause.*)

PONCIA: Listen, Angustias, what did he say to you the first time he came by your window?

ANGUSTIAS: Nothing. What should he say? Just talked.

MARTIRIO: It's certainly strange that two people who never knew each other should suddenly meet at a window and be engaged.

ANGUSTIAS: Well, I didn't mind.

AMELIA: I'd have felt very strange about it.

ANGUSTIAS: No, because when a man comes to a window he knows, from all the busybodies who come and go and fetch and carry, that he's going to be told "yes."

MARTIRIO: All right, but he'd have to ask you.

ANGUSTIAS: Of course!

AMELIA (*inquisitively*): And how did he ask you?

ANGUSTIAS: Why, no way: —"You know I'm after you. I need a good, well brought up woman, and that's you — if it's agreeable."

AMELIA: These things embarrass me!

ANGUSTIAS: They embarrass me too, but one has to go through it!

PONCIA: And did he say anything more?

ANGUSTIAS: Yes, he did all the talking.

MARTIRIO: And you?

ANGUSTIAS: I couldn't have said a word. My heart was almost coming out of my mouth. It was the first time I'd ever been alone at night with a man.

MAGDALENA: And such a handsome man.

ANGUSTIAS: He's not bad looking!

PONCIA: Those things happen among people who have an idea how to do things, who talk and say and move their hand. The first time my husband, Evaristo the Short-tailed, came to my window . . . Ha! Ha! Ha!

AMELIA: What happened?

PONCIA: It was very dark. I saw him coming along and as he went by he said, "Good evening." "Good evening," I said. Then we were both silent for more than half an hour. The sweat poured down my body. Then Evaristo got nearer and nearer as if he wanted to squeeze in through the bars and said in a very low voice —"Come here and let me feel you!"

(*They all laugh. Amelia gets up, runs, and looks through the door.*)

AMELIA: Ay, I thought mother was coming!

MAGDALENA: What she'd have done to us!

(*They go on laughing.*)

AMELIA: Sh-h-h! She'll hear us.

PONCIA: Then he acted very decently. Instead of getting some other idea, he went to raising birds, until he died. You aren't married but it's good for you to know, anyway, that two weeks after the wedding a man gives up the bed for the table, then the table for the tavern, and the woman who doesn't like it can just rot, weeping in a corner.

AMELIA: You liked it.

PONCIA: I learned how to handle him!

MARTIRIO: Is it true that you sometimes hit him?

PONCIA: Yes, and once I almost poked out one of his eyes!

MAGDALENA: All women ought to be like that!

PONCIA: I'm one of your mother's school. One time I don't know what he said to me, and then I killed all his birds — with the pestle!

(*They laugh.*)

MAGDALENA: Adela, child! Don't miss this.

AMELIA: Adela!

(*Pause.*)

MAGDALENA: I'll go see!

(*She goes out.*)

PONCIA: That child is sick!

MARTIRIO: Of course. She hardly sleeps!

PONCIA: What *does* she do, then?

MARTIRIO: How do I know what she does?

PONCIA: You probably know better than we do, since you sleep with just a wall between you.

ANGUSTIAS: Envy gnaws on people.

AMELIA: Don't exaggerate.

ANGUSTIAS: I can tell it in her eyes. She's getting the look of a crazy woman.

MARTIRIO: Don't talk about crazy women. This is one place you're not allowed to say that word.

(*Magdalena and Adela enter.*)

MAGDALENA: Didn't you say she was asleep?

ADELA: My body aches.

MARTIRIO (*with a hidden meaning*): Didn't you sleep well last night?

ADELA: Yes.

MARTIRIO: Then?

ADELA (*loudly*): Leave me alone. Awake or asleep, it's no affair of yours. I'll do whatever I want to with my body.

MARTIRIO: I was just concerned about you!

ADELA: Concerned? — curious! Weren't you sewing? Well, continue! I wish I were invisible so I could pass through a room without being asked where I was going!

SERVANT (*entering*): Bernarda is calling you. The man with the laces is here.

(*All but Adela and La Poncia go out, and as Martirio leaves, she looks fixedly at Adela.*)

ADELA: Don't look at me like that! If you want, I'll give you my eyes, for they're younger, and my back to improve that hump you have, but look the other way when I go by.

PONCIA: Adela, she's your sister, and the one who most loves you besides!

ADELA: She follows me everywhere. Sometimes she looks in my room to see if I'm sleeping. She won't let me breathe, and always, "Too bad about that face!" "Too bad about that body! It's going to waste!" But I won't let that happen. My body will be for whomever I choose.

PONCIA (*insinuatingly, in a low voice*): For Pepe el Romano, no?

ADELA (*frightened*): What do you mean?

PONCIA: What I said, Adela!

ADELA: Shut up!

PONCIA (*loudly*): Don't you think I've noticed?

ADELA: Lower your voice!

PONCIA: Then forget what you're thinking about!

ADELA: What do you know?

PONCIA: We old ones can see through walls. Where do you go when you get up at night?

ADELA: I wish you were blind!

PONCIA: But my head and hands are full of eyes, where something like this is concerned. I couldn't possibly guess your intentions. Why did you sit almost naked at your window, and with the light on and the window open, when Pepe passed by the second night he came to talk with your sister?

ADELA: That's not true!

PONCIA: Don't be a child! Leave your sister alone. And if you like Pepe el Romano, keep it to yourself.

(*Adela weeps.*)

Besides, who says you can't marry him? Your sister Angustias is sickly. She'll die with her first child. Narrow waisted, old — and out of my experience I can tell you she'll die. Then Pepe will do what al widowers do in these parts: he'll marry the youngest and most beautiful, and that's you. Live on that hope, forget him, anything; but don't go against God's law.

ADELA: Hush!

PONCIA: I won't hush!

ADELA: Mind your own business. Snooper, traitor!

PONCIA: I'm going to stick to you like a shadow!

ADELA: Instead of cleaning the house and then going to bed and praying for the dead, you root around like an old sow about goings on between men and women — so you can drool over them.

PONCIA: I keep watch; so people won't spit when they pass our door.

ADELA: What a tremendous affection you've suddenly conceived for my sister.

PONCIA: I don't have any affection for any of you. I

want to live in a decent house. I don't want to be dirtied in my old age!

ADELA: Save your advice. It's already too late. For I'd leap not over you, just a servant, but over my mother to put out this fire I feel in my legs and my mouth. What can you possibly say about me? That I lock myself in my room and will not open the door? That I don't sleep? I'm smarter than you! See if you can catch the hare with your hands.

PONCIA: Don't defy me, Adela, don't defy me! Because I can shout, light lamps, and make bells ring.

ADELA: Bring four thousand yellow flares and set them about the walls of the yard. No one can stop what has to happen.

PONCIA: You like him that much?

ADELA: That much! Looking in his eyes I seem to drink his blood in slowly.

PONCIA: I won't listen to you.

ADELA: Well, you'll have to. I've been afraid of you. But now I'm stronger than you!

(Angustias enters.)

ANGUSTIAS: Always arguing!

PONCIA: Certainly. She insists that in all this heat I have to go bring her I don't know what from the store.

ANGUSTIAS: Did you buy me the bottle of perfume?

PONCIA: The most expensive one. And the face powder. I put them on the table in your room.

(Angustias goes out.)

ADELA: And be quiet!

PONCIA: We'll see!

(Martirio and Amelia enter.)

MARTIRIO (*to Adela*): Did you see the laces?

AMELIA: Angustias', for her wedding sheets, are beautiful.

ADELA (*to Martirio, who is carrying some lace*): And these?

MARTIRIO: They're for me. For a nightgown.

ADELA (*with sarcasm*): One needs a sense of humor around here!

MARTIRIO (*meaningfully*): But only for me to look at. I don't have to exhibit myself before anybody.

PONCIA: No one ever sees us in our nightgowns.

MARTIRIO (*meaningfully, looking at Adela*): Sometimes they don't! But I love nice underwear. If I were rich, I'd have it made of Holland Cloth. It's one of the few tastes I've left.

PONCIA: These laces are beautiful for babies caps and christening gowns. I could never afford them for my own. Now let's see if Angustias will use them for hers. Once she starts having children, they'll keep her running night and day.

MAGDALENA: I don't intend to sew a stitch on them.

AMELIA: And much less bring up some stranger's children. Look how our neighbors across the road are — making sacrifices for four brats.

PONCIA: They're better off than you. There at least they laugh and you can hear them fight.

MARTIRIO: Well, you go work for them, then.

PONCIA: No, fate has sent me to this nunnery!

(Tiny bells are heard distantly as though through several thicknesses of wall.)

MAGDALENA: It's the men going back to work.

PONCIA: It was three o'clock a minute ago.

MARTIRIO: With this sun!

ADELA (*sitting down*): Ay! If only we could go out in the fields too!

MAGDALENA (*sitting down*): Each class does what it has to!

MARTIRIO (*sitting down*): That's it!

AMELIA (*sitting down*): Ay!

PONCIA: There's no happiness like that in the fields right at this time of year. Yesterday morning the reapers arrived. Forty or fifty handsome young men.

MAGDALENA: Where are they from this year?

PONCIA: From far, far away. They came from the mountains! Happy! Like weathered trees! Shouting and throwing stones! Last night a woman who dresses in sequins and dances, with an accordion, arrived, and fifteen of them made a deal with her to take her to the olive grove. I saw them from far away. The one who talked with her was a boy with green eyes — tight knit as a sheaf of wheat.

AMELIA: Really?

ADELA: Are you sure?

PONCIA: Years ago another one of those women came here, and I myself gave my eldest son some money so he could go. Men need things like that.

ADELA: Everything's forgiven *them*.

AMELIA: To be born a woman's the worst possible punishment.

MAGDALENA: Even our eyes aren't our own.

(A distant song is heard, coming nearer.)

PONCIA: There they are. They have a beautiful song.

AMELIA: They're going out to reap now.

CHORUS:
> The reapers have set out
> Looking for ripe wheat;
> They'll carry off the hearts
> Of any girls they meet.

(Tambourines and carrañacas are heard. Pause. They all listen in the silence cut by the sun.)

AMELIA: And they don't mind the sun!

MARTIRIO: They reap through flames.

ADELA: How I'd like to be a reaper so I could come and go as I pleased. Then we could forget what's eating us all.

MARTIRIO: What do you have to forget?

ADELA: Each one of us has something.

MARTIRIO (*intensely*): Each one!

PONCIA: Quiet! Quiet!

CHORUS (*very distantly*):
> Throw wide your doors and windows,

You girls who live in the town
The reaper asks you for roses
With which to deck his crown.

PONCIA: What a song!

MARTIRIO (*with nostalgia*):
Throw wide your doors and windows,
You girls who live in the town.

ADELA (*passionately*):
The reaper asks you for roses
With which to deck his crown.

(*The song grows more distant.*)

PONCIA: Now they're turning the corner.

ADELA: Let's watch them from the window of my room.

PONCIA: Be careful not to open the shutters too much because they're likely to give them a push to see who's looking.

(*The three leave. Martirio is left sitting on the low chair with her head between her hands.*)

AMELIA (*drawing near her*): What's wrong with you?

MARTIRIO: The heat makes me feel ill.

AMELIA: And it's no more than that?

MARTIRIO: I was wishing it were November, the rainy days, the frost — anything except this unending summertime.

AMELIA: It'll pass and come again.

MARTIRIO: Naturally.

(*Pause.*)

What time did you go to sleep last night?

AMELIA: I don't know. I sleep like a log. Why?

MARTIRIO: Nothing. Only I thought I heard someone in the yard.

AMELIA: Yes?

MARTIRIO: Very late.

AMELIA: And weren't you afraid?

MARTIRIO: No. I've heard it other nights.

AMELIA: We'd better watch out! Couldn't it have been the shepherds?

MARTIRIO: The shepherds come at six.

AMELIA: Maybe a young, unbroken mule?

MARTIRIO (*to herself, with double meaning*): That's it! That's it. An unbroken little mule.

AMELIA: We'll have to set a watch.

MARTIRIO: No. No. Don't say anything. It may be I've just imagined it.

AMELIA: Maybe.

(*Pause. Amelia starts to go.*)

MARTIRIO: Amelia!

AMELIA (*at the door*): What?

(*Pause.*)

MARTIRIO: Nothing.

(*Pause.*)

AMELIA: Why did you call me?

(*Pause.*)

MARTIRIO: It just came out. I didn't mean to.

(*Pause.*)

AMELIA: Lie down for a little.

ANGUSTIAS (*she bursts in furiously, in a manner that makes a great contrast with previous silence*): Where's that picture of Pepe I had under my pillow? Which one of you has it?

MARTIRIO: No one.

AMELIA: You'd think he was a silver St. Bartholomew.°

ANGUSTIAS: Where's the picture?

(*Poncia, Magdalena and Adela enter.*)

ADELA: What picture?

ANGUSTIAS: One of you has hidden it from me.

MAGDALENA: Do you have the effrontery to say that?

ANGUSTIAS: I had it in my room, and now it isn't there.

MARTIRIO: But couldn't it have jumped out into the yard at midnight? Pepe likes to walk around in the moonlight.

ANGUSTIAS: Don't joke with me! When he comes I'll tell him.

PONCIA: Don't do that! Because it'll turn up.

(*Looking at Adela.*)

ANGUSTIAS: I'd like to know which one of you has it.

ADELA (*looking at Martirio*): Somebody has it! But not me!

MARTIRIO (*with meaning*): Of course not you!

BERNARDA (*entering with her cane*): What scandal is this in my house in the heat's heavy silence? The neighbors must have their ears glued to the walls.

ANGUSTIAS: They've stolen my sweetheart's picture!

BERNARDA (*fiercely*): Who? Who?

ANGUSTIAS: They have!

BERNARDA: Which one of you?

(*Silence.*)

Answer me!

(*Silence.*) (*To La Poncia.*)

Search their rooms! Look in their beds. This comes of not tying you up with shorter leashes. But I'll teach you now! (*to Angustias*) Are you sure?

ANGUSTIAS: Yes.

BERNARDA: Did you look everywhere?

ANGUSTIAS: Yes, Mother.

(*They all stand in an embarrassed silence.*)

BERNARDA: At the end of my life — to make me drink the bitterest poison a mother knows. (*to Poncia*) Did you find it?

PONCIA: Here it is.

BERNARDA: Where did you find it?

PONCIA: It was . . .

BERNARDA: Say it! Don't be afraid.

PONCIA (*wonderingly*): Between the sheets in Martirio's bed.

silver St. Bartholomew: A medallion used for good fortune.

BERNARDA (*to Martirio*): Is that true?

MARTIRIO: It's true.

BERNARDA (*advancing on her, beating her with her cane*): You'll come to a bad end yet, you hypocrite! Trouble maker!

MARTIRIO (*fiercely*): Don't hit me, Mother!

BERNARDA: All I want to!

MARTIRIO: If I let you! You hear me? Get back!

PONCIA: Don't be disrespectful to your mother!

ANGUSTIAS (*holding Bernarda*): Let her go, please!

BERNARDA: Not even tears in your eyes.

MARTIRIO: I'm not going to cry just to please you.

BERNARDA: Why did you take the picture?

MARTIRIO: Can't I play a joke on my sister? What else would I want it for?

ADELA (*leaping forward, full of jealousy*): It wasn't a joke! You never liked to play jokes. It was something else bursting in her breast — trying to come out. Admit it openly now.

MARTIRIO: Hush, and don't make me speak; for if I should speak the walls would close together one against the other with shame.

ADELA: An evil tongue never stops inventing lies.

BERNARDA: Adela!

MAGDALENA: You're crazy.

AMELIA: And you stone us all with your evil suspicions.

MARTIRIO: But some others do things more wicked!

ADELA: Until all at once they stand forth stark naked and the river carries them along.

BERNARDA: Spiteful!

ANGUSTIAS: It's not my fault Pepe el Romano chose me!

ADELA: For your money.

ANGUSTIAS: Mother!

BERNARDA: Silence!

MARTIRIO: For your fields and your orchards.

MAGDALENA: That's only fair.

BERNARDA: Silence, I say! I saw the storm coming but I didn't think it'd burst so soon. Oh, what an avalanche of hate you've thrown on my heart! But I'm not old yet — I have five chains for you, and this house my father built, so not even the weeds will know of my desolation. Out of here!

(*They go out. Bernarda sits down desolately. La Poncia is standing close to the wall. Bernarda recovers herself, and beats on the floor.*)

I'll have to let them feel the weight of my hand! Bernarda, remember your duty!

PONCIA: May I speak?

BERNARDA: Speak. I'm sorry you heard. A stranger is always out of place in a family.

PONCIA: What I've seen, I've seen.

BERNARDA: Angustias must get married right away.

PONCIA: Certainly. We'll have to get her away from here.

BERNARDA: Not her, him!

PONCIA: Of course. He's the one to get away from here. You've thought it all out.

BERNARDA: I'm not thinking. These are things that shouldn't and can't be thought out. I give orders.

PONCIA: And you think he'll be satisfied to go away?

BERNARDA (*rising*): What are you imagining now?

PONCIA: He will, of course, marry Angustias.

BERNARDA: Speak up! I know you well enough to see that your knife's out for me.

PONCIA: I never knew a warning could be called murder.

BERNARDA: Have you some "warning" for me?

PONCIA: I'm not making any accusations, Bernarda. I'm only telling you to open your eyes and you'll see.

BERNARDA: See what?

PONCIA: You've always been smart, Bernarda. You've seen other people's sins a hundred miles away. Many times I've thought you could read minds. But, your children are your children, and now you're blind.

BERNARDA: Are you talking about Martirio?

PONCIA: Well, yes — about Martirio . . .

(*With curiosity.*)

I wonder why she hid the picture?

BERNARDA (*shielding her daughter*): After all, she says it was a joke. What else could it be?

PONCIA (*scornfully*): Do you believe that?

BERNARDA (*sternly*): I don't merely believe it. It's so!

PONCIA: Enough of this. We're talking about your family. But if we were talking about your neighbor across the way, what would it be?

BERNARDA: Now you're beginning to pull the point of the knife out.

PONCIA (*always cruelly*): No, Bernarda. Something very grave is happening here. I don't want to put the blame on your shoulders, but you've never given your daughters any freedom. Martirio is lovesick. I don't care what you say. Why didn't you let her marry Enrique Humanas? Why, on the very day he was coming to her window did you send him a message not to come?

BERNARDA (*loudly*): I'd do it a thousand times over! My blood won't mingle with the Humanas' while I live! His father was a shepherd.

PONCIA: And you see now what's happening to you with these airs!

BERNARDA: I have them because I can afford to. And you don't have them because you know where you came from!

PONCIA (*with hate*): Don't remind me! I'm old now. I've always been grateful for your protection.

BERNARDA (*emboldened*): You don't seem so!

PONCIA (*with hate, behind softness*): Martirio will forget this.

BERNARDA: And if she doesn't — the worse for her. I don't believe this is that "very grave thing" that's happening here. Nothing's happening here. It's just that you wish it would! And if it should happen one day, you can be sure it won't go beyond these walls.

PONCIA: I'm not so sure of that! There are people in town who can also read hidden thoughts, from afar.

BERNARDA: How you'd like to see me and my daughters on our way to a whorehouse!

PONCIA: No one knows her own destiny!

BERNARDA: I know my destiny! And my daughters! The whorehouse was for a certain woman, already dead. . . .

PONCIA (*fiercely*): Bernarda, respect the memory of my mother!

BERNARDA: Then don't plague me with your evil thoughts!

(*Pause.*)

PONCIA: I'd better stay out of everything.

BERNARDA: That's what you ought to do. Work and keep your mouth shut. The duty of all who work for a living.

PONCIA: But we can't do that. Don't you think it'd be better for Pepe to marry Martirio or . . . yes! . . . Adela?

BERNARDA: No, I *don't* think so.

PONCIA (*with meaning*): Adela! She's Romano's real sweetheart!

BERNARDA: Things are never the way we want them!

PONCIA: But it's hard work to turn them from their destined course. For Pepe to be with Angustias seems wrong to me — and to other people — and even to the wind. Who knows if they'll get what they want?

BERNARDA: There you go again! Sneaking up on me — giving me bad dreams. But I won't listen to you, because if all you say should come to pass — I'd scratch your face.

PONCIA: Frighten someone else with that.

BERNARDA: Fortunately, my daughters respect me and have never gone against my will!

PONCIA: That's right! But, as soon as they break loose they'll fly to the rooftops!

BERNARDA: And I'll bring them down with stones!

PONCIA: Oh, yes! You were always the bravest one!

BERNARDA: I've always enjoyed a good fight!

PONCIA: But aren't people strange. You should see Angustias' enthusiasm for her lover, at her age! And he seems very smitten too. Yesterday my oldest son told me that when he passed by with the oxen at four-thirty in the morning they were still talking.

BERNARDA: At four-thirty?

ANGUSTIAS (*entering*): That's a lie!

PONCIA: That's what he told me.

BERNARDA (*to Angustias*): Speak up!

ANGUSTIAS: For more than a week Pepe has been leaving at one. May God strike me dead if I'm lying.

MARTIRIO (*entering*): I heard him leave at four too.

BERNARDA: But did you see him with your eyes?

MARTIRIO: I didn't want to look out. Don't you talk now through the side window?

ANGUSTIAS: We talk through my bedroom window.

(*Adela appears at the door.*)

MARTIRIO: Then . . .

BERNARDA: What's going on here?

PONCIA: If you're not careful, you'll find out! At least Pepe was at *one* of your windows — and at four in the morning too!

BERNARDA: Are you sure of that?

PONCIA: You can't be sure of anything in this life!

ADELA: Mother, don't listen to someone who wants us to lose everything we have.

BERNARDA: I know how to take care of myself! If the townspeople want to come bearing false witness against me, they'll run into a stone wall! Don't any of you talk about this! Sometimes other people try to stir up a wave of filth to drown us.

MARTIRIO: I don't like to lie.

PONCIA: So there must be something.

BERNARDA: There won't be anything. I was born to have my eyes always open. Now I'll watch without closing them 'til I die.

ANGUSTIAS: I have the right to know.

BERNARDA: You don't have any right except to obey. No one's going to fetch and carry for me. (*to La Poncia*) And don't meddle in our affairs. No one will take a step without my knowing it.

SERVANT (*entering*): There's a big crowd at the top of the street, and all the neighbors are at their doors!

BERNARDA (*to Poncia*): Run see what's happening!

(*The girls are about to run out.*)

Where are you going? I always knew you for window-watching women and breakers of your mourning. All of you, to the patio!

(*They go out. Bernarda leaves. Distant shouts are heard.*)

(*Martirio and Adela enter and listen, not daring to step farther than the front door.*)

MARTIRIO: You can be thankful I didn't happen to open my mouth.

ADELA: I would have spoken too.

MARTIRIO: And what were you going to say? Wanting isn't doing!

ADELA: I do what I can and what happens to suit me. You've wanted to, but haven't been able.

MARTIRIO: You won't go on very long.

ADELA: I'll have everything!

MARTIRIO: I'll tear you out of his arms!

ADELA (*pleadingly*): Martirio, let me be!

MARTIRIO: None of us will have him!

ADELA: He wants me for his house!

MARTIRIO: I saw how he embraced you!

ADELA: I didn't want him to. It's as if I were dragged by a rope.

MARTIRIO: I'll see you dead first!

(*Magdalena and Angustias look in. The tumult is increasing. A servant enters with Bernarda. Poncia also enters from another door.*)

PONCIA: Bernarda!

BERNARDA: What's happening?

PONCIA: Librada's daughter, the unmarried one, had a child and no one knows whose it is!

ADELA: A child?

PONCIA: And to hide her shame she killed it and hid it

under the rocks, but the dogs, with more heart than most Christians, dug it out and, as though directed by the hand of God, left it at her door. Now they want to kill her. They're dragging her through the streets — and down the paths and across the olive groves the men are coming, shouting so the fields shake.

BERNARDA: Yes, let them all come with olive whips and hoe handles — let them all come and kill her!

ADELA: No, not to kill her!

MARTIRIO: Yes — and let us go out too!

BERNARDA: And let whoever loses her decency pay for it!

(*Outside a woman's shriek and a great clamor is heard.*)

ADELA: Let her escape! Don't you go out!

MARTIRIO (*looking at Adela*): Let her pay what she owes!

BERNARDA (*at the archway*): Finish her before the guards come! Hot coals in the place where she sinned!

ADELA (*holding her belly*): No! No!

BERNARDA: Kill her! Kill her!

(*Curtain.*)

ACT 3

(*Four white walls, lightly washed in blue, of the interior patio of Bernarda Alba's house. The doorways, illumined by the lights inside the rooms, give a tenuous glow to the stage. At the center there is a table with a shaded oil lamp about which Bernarda and her daughters are eating. La Poncia serves them. Prudencia sits apart. When the curtain rises, there is a great silence interrupted only by the noise of plates and silverware.*)

PRUDENCIA: I'm going. I've made you a long visit.

(*She rises.*)

BERNARDA: But wait, Prudencia. We never see one another.

PRUDENCIA: Have they sounded the last call to rosary?

PONCIA: Not yet.

(*Prudencia sits down again.*)

BERNARDA: And your husband, how's he getting on?

PRUDENCIA: The same.

BERNARDA: We never see him either.

PRUDENCIA: You know how he is. Since he quarrelled with his brothers over the inheritance, he hasn't used the front door. He takes a ladder and climbs over the back wall.

BERNARDA: He's a real man! And your daughter?

PRUDENCIA: He's never forgiven her.

BERNARDA: He's right.

PRUDENCIA: I don't know what he told you. I suffer because of it.

BERNARDA: A daughter who's disobedient stops being a daughter and becomes an enemy.

PRUDENCIA: I let water run. The only consolation I've

left is to take refuge in the church, but, since I'm losing my sight, I'll have to stop coming so the children won't make fun of me.

(*A heavy blow is heard against the walls.*)

What's that?

BERNARDA: The stallion. He's locked in the stall and he kicks against the wall of the house.

(*Shouting.*)

Tether him and take him out in the yard!

(*In a lower voice.*)

He must be too hot.

PRUDENCIA: Are you going to put the new mares to him?

BERNARDA: At daybreak.

PRUDENCIA: You've known how to increase your stock.

BERNARDA: By dint of money and struggling.

PONCIA (*interrupting*): And she has the best herd in these parts. It's a shame that prices are low.

BERNARDA: Do you want a little cheese and honey?

PRUDENCIA: I have no appetite.

(*The blow is heard again.*)

PONCIA: My God!

PRUDENCIA: It quivered in my chest.

BERNARDA (*rising, furiously*): Do I have to say things twice? Let him out to roll on the straw.

(*Pause. Then, as though speaking to the stableman.*)

Well then, lock the mares in the corral, but let him run free or he may kick down the walls.

(*She returns to the table and sits again.*)

Ay, what a life!

PRUDENCIA: You have to fight like a man.

BERNARDA: That's it.

(*Adela gets up from the table.*)

Where are you going?

ADELA: For a drink of water.

BERNARDA (*raising her voice*): Bring a pitcher of cool water. (*to Adela*) You can sit down. (*Adela sits down.*)

PRUDENCIA: And Angustias, when will she get married?

BERNARDA: They're coming to ask for her within three days.

PRUDENCIA: You must be happy.

ANGUSTIAS: Naturally!

AMELIA (*to Magdalena*): You've spilled the salt!

MAGDALENA: You can't possibly have worse luck than you're having.

AMELIA: It always brings bad luck.

BERNARDA: That's enough!

PRUDENCIA (*to Angustias*): Has he given you the ring yet?

ANGUSTIAS: Look at it.

(*She holds it out.*)

PRUDENCIA: It's beautiful. Three pearls. In my day, pearls signified tears.

ANGUSTIAS: But things have changed now.

ADELA: I don't think so. Things go on meaning the same. Engagement rings should be diamonds.

PONCIA: The most appropriate.

BERNARDA: With pearls or without them, things are as one proposes.

MARTIRIO: Or as God disposes.

PRUDENCIA: I've been told your furniture is beautiful.

BERNARDA: It cost sixteen thousand *reales*.°

PONCIA (*interrupting*): The best is the wardrobe with the mirror.

PRUDENCIA: I never saw a piece like that.

BERNARDA: We had chests.

PRUDENCIA: The important thing is that everything be for the best.

ADELA: And that you never know.

BERNARDA: There's no reason why it shouldn't be.

(*Bells are heard very distantly.*)

PRUDENCIA: The last call. (*to Angustias*) I'll be coming back to have you show me your clothes.

ANGUSTIAS: Whenever you like.

PRUDENCIA: Good evening — God bless you!

BERNARDA: Good-bye, Prudencia.

ALL FIVE DAUGHTERS (*at the same time*): God go with you!

(*Pause. Prudencia goes out.*)

BERNARDA: Well, we've eaten.

(*They rise.*)

ADELA: I'm going to walk as far as the gate to stretch my legs and get a bit of fresh air.

(*Magdalena sits down in a low chair and leans against the wall.*)

AMELIA: I'll go with you.

MARTIRIO: I too.

ADELA (*with contained hate*): I'm not going to get lost!

AMELIA: One needs company at night.

(*They go out. Bernarda sits down. Angustias is clearing the table.*)

BERNARDA: I've told you once already! I want you to talk to your sister Martirio. What happened about the picture was a joke and you must forget it.

ANGUSTIAS: You know she doesn't like me.

BERNARDA: Each one knows what she thinks inside. I don't pry into anyone's heart, but I want to put up a good front and have family harmony. You understand?

ANGUSTIAS: Yes.

BERNARDA: Then that's settled.

MAGDALENA (*she is almost asleep*): Besides, you'll be gone in no time.

(*She falls asleep.*)

reales: Spanish silver coin. Sixteen thousand would have been a great sum.

ANGUSTIAS: Not soon enough for me.

BERNARDA: What time did you stop talking last night?

ANGUSTIAS: Twelve-thirty.

BERNARDA: What does Pepe talk about?

ANGUSTIAS: I find him absent-minded. He always talks to me as though he were thinking of something else. If I ask him what's the matter, he answers — "We men have our worries."

BERNARDA: You shouldn't ask him. And when you're married, even less. Speak if he speaks, and look at him when he looks at you. That way you'll get along.

ANGUSTIAS: But, Mother, I think he's hiding things from me.

BERNARDA: Don't try to find out. Don't ask him, and above all, never let him see you cry.

ANGUSTIAS: I should be happy, but I'm not.

BERNARDA: It's all the same.

ANGUSTIAS: Many nights I watch Pepe very closely through the window bars and he seems to fade away — as though he were hidden in a cloud of dust like those raised by the flocks.

BERNARDA: That's just because you're not strong.

ANGUSTIAS: I hope so!

BERNARDA: Is he coming tonight?

ANGUSTIAS: No, he went into town with his mother.

BERNARDA: Good, we'll get to bed early. Magdalena!

ANGUSTIAS: She's asleep.

(*Adela, Martirio and Amelia enter.*)

AMELIA: What a dark night!

ADELA: You can't see two steps in front of you.

MARTIRIO: A good night for robbers, for anyone who needs to hide.

ADELA: The stallion was in the middle of the corral. White. Twice as large. Filling all the darkness.

AMELIA: It's true. It was frightening. Like a ghost.

ADELA: The sky has stars as big as fists.

MARTIRIO: This one stared at them till she almost cracked her neck.

ADELA: Don't you like them up there?

MARTIRIO: What goes on over the roof doesn't mean a thing to me. I have my hands full with what happens under it.

ADELA: Well, that's the way it goes with you!

BERNARDA: And it goes the same for you as for her.

ANGUSTIAS: Good night.

ADELA: Are you going to bed now?

ANGUSTIAS: Yes, Pepe isn't coming tonight.

(*She goes out.*)

ADELA: Mother, why, when a stars falls or lightning flashes, does one say:
Holy Barbara, blessed on high
May your name be in the sky
With holy water written high?

BERNARDA: The old people know many things we've forgotten.

AMELIA: I close my eyes so I won't see them.

ADELA: Not I. I like to see what's quiet and been quiet for years on end, running with fire.

MARTIRIO: But all that has nothing to do with us.

BERNARDA: And it's better not to think about it.

ADELA: What a beautiful night! I'd like to stay up till very late and enjoy the breeze from the fields.

BERNARDA: But we have to go to bed. Magdalena!

AMELIA: She's just dropped off.

BERNARDA: Magdalena!

MAGDALENA (annoyed): Leave me alone!

BERNARDA: To bed!

MAGDALENA (rising, in a bad humor): You don't give anyone a moment's peace!

(She goes off grumbling.)

AMELIA: Good night!

(She goes out.)

BERNARDA: You two get along, too.

MARTIRIO: How is it Angustias' sweetheart isn't coming tonight?

BERNARDA: He went on a trip.

MARTIRIO (looking at Adela): Ah!

ADELA: I'll see you in the morning!

(She goes out. Martirio drinks some water and goes out slowly, looking at the door to the yard. La Poncia enters.)

PONCIA: Are you still here?

BERNARDA: Enjoying this quiet and not seeing anywhere the "very grave thing" that's happening here — according to you.

PONCIA: Bernarda, let's not go any further with this.

BERNARDA: In this house there's no question of a yes or a no. My watchfulness can take care of anything.

PONCIA: Nothing's happening outside. That's true, all right. Your daughters act and are as though stuck in a cupboard. But neither you nor anyone else can keep watch inside a person's heart.

BERNARDA: My daughters breathe calmly enough.

PONCIA: That's your business, since you're their mother. I have enough to do just with serving you.

BERNARDA: Yes, you've turned quiet now.

PONCIA: I keep my place — that's all.

BERNARDA: The trouble is you've nothing to talk about. If there were grass in this house, you'd make it your business to put the neighbors' sheep to pasture here.

PONCIA: I hide more than you think.

BERNARDA: Do your sons still see Pepe at four in the morning? Are they still repeating this house's evil litany?

PONCIA: They say nothing.

BERNARDA: Because they can't. Because there's nothing for them to sink their teeth in. And all because my eyes keep constant watch!

PONCIA: Bernarda, I don't want to talk about this because I'm afraid of what you'll do. But don't you feel so safe.

BERNARDA: Very safe!

PONCIA: Who knows, lightning might strike suddenly. Who knows but what all of a sudden, in a rush of blood, your heart might stop.

BERNARDA: Nothing will happen here. I'm on guard now against all your suspicions.

PONCIA: All the better for you.

BERNARDA: Certainly, all the better!

SERVANT (entering): I've just finished with the dishes. Is there anything else, Bernarda?

BERNARDA (rising): Nothing. I'm going to get some rest.

PONCIA: What time do you want me to call you?

BERNARDA: No time. Tonight I intend to sleep well.

(She goes out.)

PONCIA: When you're powerless against the sea, it's easier to turn your back on it and not look at it.

SERVANT: She's so proud! She herself pulls the blindfold over her eyes.

PONCIA: I can do nothing. I tried to head things off, but now they frighten me too much. You feel this silence? — in each room there's a thunderstorm and the day it breaks, it'll sweep all of us along with it. But I've said what I had to say.

SERVANT: Bernarda thinks nothing can stand against her, yet she doesn't know the strength a man has among women alone.

PONCIA: It's not all the fault of Pepe el Romano. It's true last year he was running after Adela; and she was crazy about him — but she ought to keep her place and not lead him on. A man's a man.

SERVANT: And some there are who believe he didn't have to talk many times with Adela.

PONCIA: That's true.

(In a low voice.)

And some other things.

SERVANT: I don't know what's going to happen here.

PONCIA: How I'd like to sail across the sea and leave this house, this battleground, behind!

SERVANT: Bernarda's hurrying the wedding and it's possible nothing will happen.

PONCIA: Things have gone much too far already. Adela is set no matter what comes, and the rest of them watch without rest.

SERVANT: Martirio too. . . ?

PONCIA: That one's the worst. She's a pool of poison. She sees El Romano is not for her, and she'd sink the world if it were in her hand to do so.

SERVANT: How bad they all are!

PONCIA: They're women without men, that's all. And in such matters even blood is forgotten. Sh-h-h-h!

(She listens.)

SERVANT: What's the matter?

PONCIA (she rises): The dogs are barking.

SERVANT: Someone must have passed by the back door.

(Adela enters wearing a white petticoat and corselet.)

PONCIA: Aren't you in bed yet?

ADELA: I want a drink of water.

(*She drinks from a glass on the table.*)

PONCIA: I imagined you were asleep.

ADELA: I got thirsty and woke up. Aren't you two going to get some rest?

SERVANT: Soon now.

(*Adela goes out.*)

PONCIA: Let's go.

SERVANT: We've certainly earned some sleep. Bernarda doesn't let me rest the whole day.

PONCIA: Take the light.

SERVANT: The dogs are going mad.

PONCIA: They're not going to let us sleep.

(*They go out. The stage is left almost dark. María Josefa enters with a lamb in her arms.*)

MARÍA JOSEFA (*singing*):
> Little lamb, child of mine,
> Let's go to the shore of the sea,
> The tiny ant will be at his doorway,
> I'll nurse you and give you your bread.
> Bernarda, old leopard-face,
> And Magdalena, hyena-face,
> Little lamb . . .
> Rock, rock-a-bye,
> Let's go to the palms at Bethlehem's gate.

(*She laughs.*)

> Neither you nor I would want to sleep
> The door will open by itself
> And on the beach we'll go and hide
> In a little coral cabin.
> Bernarda, old leopard face,
> And Magdalena, hyena-face,
> Little lamb . . .
> Rock, rock-a-bye,
> Let's go to the palms at Bethlehem's gate.

(*She goes off singing.*)

(*Adela enters. She looks about cautiously and disappears out the door leading to the corral. Martirio enters by another door and stands in anguished watchfulness near the center of the stage. She also is in petticoats. She covers herself with a small black scarf. María Josefa crosses before her.*)

MARTIRIO: Grandmother, where are you going?

MARÍA JOSEFA: You are going to open the door for me? Who are you?

MARTIRIO: How did you get out here?

MARÍA JOSEFA: I escaped. You, who are you?

MARTIRIO: Go back to bed.

MARÍA JOSEFA: You're Martirio. Now I see you. Martirio, face of a martyr. And when are you going to have a baby? I've had this one.

MARTIRIO: Where did you get that lamb?

MARÍA JOSEFA: I know it's a lamb. But can't a lamb be a baby? It's better to have a lamb than not to have any-

thing. Old Bernarda, leopard-face, and Magdalena, hyena-face!

MARTIRIO: Don't shout.

MARÍA JOSEFA: It's true. Everything's very dark. Just because I have white hair you think I can't have babies, but I can — babies and babies and babies. This baby will have white hair, and I'd have *this* baby, and another, and this *one* other; and with all of us with snow white hair we'll be like the waves — one, then another, and another. Then we'll all sit down and all of us will have white heads, and we'll be seafoam. Why isn't there any seafoam here? Nothing but mourning shrouds here.

MARTIRIO: Hush, hush.

MARÍA JOSEFA: When my neighbor had a baby, I'd carry her some chocolate and later she'd bring me some, and so on — always and always and always. You'll have white hair, but your neighbors won't come. Now I have to go away, but I'm afraid the dogs will bite me. Won't you come with me as far as the fields? I don't like fields. I like houses, but open houses, and the neighbor women asleep in their beds with their little tiny tots, and the men outside sitting in their chairs. Pepe el Romano is a giant. All of you love him. But he's going to devour you because you're grains of wheat. No, not grains of wheat. Frogs with no tongues!

MARTIRIO (*angrily*): Come, off to bed with you.

(*She pushes her.*)

MARÍA JOSEFA: Yes, but then you'll open the door for me, won't you?

MARTIRIO: Of course.

MARÍA JOSEFA (*weeping*):
> Little lamb, child of mine,
> Let's go to the shore of the sea,
> The tiny ant will be at his doorway,
> I'll nurse you and give you your bread.

(*Martirio locks the door through which María Josefa came out and goes to the yard door. There she hesitates, but goes two steps farther.*)

MARTIRIO (*in a low voice*): Adela! (*Pause. She advances to the door. Then, calling.*) Adela!

(*Adela enters. Her hair is disarranged.*)

ADELA: And what are you looking for me for?

MARTIRIO: Keep away from him.

ADELA: Who are you to tell me that?

MARTIRIO: That's no place for a decent woman.

ADELA: How you wish *you'd* been there!

MARTIRIO (*shouting*): This is the moment for me to speak. This can't go on.

ADELA: This is just the beginning. I've had strength enough to push myself forward — the spirit and looks you lack. I've seen death under this roof, and gone out to look for what was mine, what belonged to me.

MARTIRIO: That soulless man came for another woman. You pushed yourself in front of him.

ADELA: He came for the money, but his eyes were always on me.

MARTIRIO: I won't allow you to snatch him away. He'll marry Angustias.

ADELA: You know better than I he doesn't love her.

MARTIRIO: I know.

ADELA: You know because you've seen — he loves me, me!

MARTIRIO (*desperately*): Yes.

ADELA (*close before her*): He loves me, *me!* He loves me, *me!*

MARTIRIO: Stick me with a knife if you like, but don't tell me that again.

ADELA: That's why you're trying to fix it so I won't go away with him. It makes no difference to you if he puts his arms around a woman he doesn't love. Nor does it to me. He could be a hundred years with Angustias, but for him to have his arms around me seems terrible to you — because you too love him! You love him!

MARTIRIO (*dramatically*): Yes! Let me say it without hiding my head. Yes! my breast's bitter, bursting like a pomegranate. I love him!

ADELA (*impulsively, hugging her*): Martirio, Martirio, I'm not to blame!

MARTIRIO: Don't put your arms around me! Don't try to smooth it over. My blood's no longer yours, and even though I try to think of you as a sister, I see you as just another woman.

(*She pushes her away.*)

ADELA: There's no way out here. Whoever has to drown — let her drown. Pepe is mine. He'll carry me to the rushes along the river bank. . . .

MARTIRIO: He won't!

ADELA: I can't stand this horrible house after the taste of his mouth. I'll be what he wants me to be. Everybody in the village against me, burning me with their fiery fingers; pursued by those who claim they're decent, and I'll wear, before them all, the crown of thorns that belongs to the mistress of a married man.

MARTIRIO: Hush!

ADELA: Yes, yes. (*In a low voice.*) Let's go to bed. Let's let him marry Angustias. I don't care any more, but I'll go off alone to a little house where he'll come to see me whenever he wants, whenever he feels like it.

MARTIRIO: That'll never happen! Not while I have a drop of blood left in my body.

ADELA: Not just weak you, but a wild horse I could force to his knees with just the strength of my little finger.

MARTIRIO: Don't raise that voice of yours to me. It irritates me. I have a heart full of a force so evil that, without my wanting to be, I'm drowned by it.

ADELA: You show us the way to love our sisters. God must have meant to leave me alone in the midst of darkness because I can see you as I've never seen you before.

(*A whistle is heard and Adela runs toward the door, but Martirio gets in front of her.*)

MARTIRIO: Where are you going?

ADELA: Get away from that door!

MARTIRIO: Get by me if you can!

ADELA: Get away!

(*They struggle.*)

MARTIRIO (*shouts*): Mother! Mother!

ADELA: Let me go!

(*Bernarda enters. She wears petticoats and a black shawl.*)

BERNARDA: Quiet! Quiet! How poor I am without even a man to help me!

MARTIRIO (*pointing to Adela*): She was with him. Look at those skirts covered with straw!

BERNARDA (*going furiously toward Adela*): That's the bed of a bad woman!

ADELA (*facing her*): There'll be an end to prison voices here! (*Adela snatches away her mother's cane and breaks it in two.*) This is what I do with the tyrant's cane. Not another step. No one but Pepe commands me!

(*Magdalena enters.*)

MAGDALENA: Adela!

(*La Poncia and Angustias enter.*)

ADELA: I'm his. (*to Angustias*) Know that — and go out in the yard and tell him. He'll be master in this house.

ANGUSTIAS: My God!

BERNARDA: The gun! Where's the gun?

(*She rushes out. La Poncia runs ahead of her. Amelia enters and looks on frightened, leaning her head against the wall. Behind her comes Martirio.*)

ADELA: No one can hold me back!

(*She tries to go out.*)

ANGUSTIAS (*holding her*): You're not getting out of here with your body's triumph! Thief! Disgrace of this house!

MAGDALENA: Let her go where we'll never see her again!

(*A shot is heard.*)

BERNARDA (*entering*): Just try looking for him now!

MARTIRIO (*entering*): That does away with Pepe el Romano.

ADELA: Pepe! My God! Pepe!

(*She runs out.*)

PONCIA: Did you kill him?

MARTIRIO: No. He raced away on his mare!

BERNARDA: It was my fault. A woman can't aim.

MAGDALENA: Then, why did you say . . . ?

MARTIRIO: For her! I'd like to pour a river of blood over her head!

PONCIA: Curse you!
MAGDALENA: Devil!
BERNARDA: Although it's better this way!

(*A thud is heard.*)

Adela! Adela!

PONCIA (*at her door*): Open this door!

BERNARDA: Open! Don't think the walls will hide your shame!

SERVANT (*entering*): All the neighbors are up!

BERNARDA (*in a low voice, but like a roar*): Open! Or I'll knock the door down!

(*Pause. Everything is silent.*)

Adela!

(*She walks away from the door.*)

A hammer!

(*La Poncia throws herself against the door. It opens and she goes in. As she enters, she screams and backs out.*)

What is it?

PONCIA (*she puts her hands to her throat*): May we never die like that!

(*The sisters fall back. The servant crosses herself. Bernarda screams and goes forward.*)

Don't go in!

BERNARDA: No, not I! Pepe, you're running now, alive in the darkness, under the trees, but another day you'll fall. Cut her down! My daughter died a virgin. Take her to another room and dress her as though she were a virgin. No one will say anything about this! She died a virgin. Tell them, so that at dawn, the bells will ring twice.

MARTIRIO: A thousand times happy she, who had him.

BERNARDA: And I want no weeping. Death must be looked at face to face. Silence!

(*To one daughter.*)

Be still, I said!

(*To another daughter.*)

Tears when you're alone! We'll drown ourselves in a sea of mourning. She, the youngest daughter of Bernarda Alba, died a virgin. Did you hear me? Silence, silence, I said. Silence!

COMMENTARY

John Gilmour (*b. 1939*)
RELIGION IN *THE HOUSE OF BERNARDA ALBA*   1992

> *In this commentary Gilmour examines the function of Christian faith in the play. He contrasts Christian charity with the repressive and ritualistic Christian regime that Bernarda imposes on her daughters. Gilmour also sees that the hypocrisy portrayed in the play is connected to Spain's intolerant social conditions at the time of Lorca's writing.*

Bernarda may be very scrupulous about the way in which her family should show respect for the dead, and very familiar with Catholic ritual, but that is as far as her Christianity extends. Religion for her seems to mean blind, unquestioning adherence to an established set of rules which are there to be observed solely for the purpose of keeping up appearances. Her daughter Magdalena's sad comment, "nos pudrimos por el qué dirán" [we rot inside because of what people might say], is an indication of the destructive effect which this code of behavior has on her family's well-being. Nowhere is there room in this scheme of things for the more positive and fundamental aspects of the Christian faith, notably love and charity towards others. Ronaldo Cueto, in a recent article in which he investigates the religious significance of the character Bernarda Alba, makes the interesting point that Bernardas are the name commonly given in Spain to nuns of the Cistercian order whose main tenet of faith is "God is love." Yet it is surely hard to find a character as far removed from the true Bernardine spirit of love as Lorca's protagonist. A life of rigid conformity has corrupted her entire being, destroyed her soul and poisoned her home and social environment. Angustia describes the atmosphere inside their home as "un infierno" [a hell] — a damning indictment indeed of Bernarda's supposedly Christian regime. Bernarda shows no sign of being a loving mother. She is not prepared to trust her daughters with any kind of freedom (La Poncia tells her, "Tú no has dejado a tus hijas libres" [you never gave your daughters any freedom]). She keeps them prisoner in their own house (Magdelena complains of being "sentada días y días dentro de esta sala oscura" [sitting day after day in this dark room]). Like Yerma's sisters-in-law, she considers it her duty to stand guard over the family's honour; she blindly assures La Poncia, "Mi vigilancia lo puede todo . . . aquí no pasa nada" [My eyes kept constant watch . . . nothing gets by me]. She happily ruins the few chances which her daughters have to fall in love, either through snobbery ("Su padre fue gañán" [His father was a shepherd] is her explanation of why Martirio could not marry Enrique Humanas) or through social convention (Angustias's rich inheritance puts paid to Adela's relationship with Pepe el Romano). She thinks nothing of resorting to physical violence against her children. Angustias and Martirio are beaten to the ground amid a barrage of expletives which show the intensity of her fury. Not even the loss of Adela can release any emotion from her. Her "no quiero llantos" (I want no weeping) is the cold reaction of a mother whose only care appears to be that her daughter must be laid out "como una doncella" (like a virgin). Her stoicism in the face of tragedy is so remarkable as to be unnatural.[. . .]

In their painful search for individual fulfillment, Lorca's tragic heroines in the rural plays reflect this bitter struggle to throw off the shackles of an ideologically dominant social institution which, in the eyes of the reformist Republicans of the 1930s, had for so long been synonymous with intolerance, immobilism, obscurantism and repression. Lorca may not have claimed allegiance to any particular left-wing political movement or party, but his depiction of a rural society, pious and ritualistic yet lacking the most basic Christian virtues, casts him as an outspoken opponent of conservative, bourgeois values. In short it is possibly his social conscience that makes him present religion in this negative manner.

Eugène Ionesco

Eugène Ionesco was born in 1909 in Slatina, a small town in Romania not far from Bucharest, to a Romanian father and a French mother. In 1911 the family moved to Paris, where his father studied law, and from 1917 to 1919 he and his sister attended boarding school in the country village of La Chapelle-Anthenaise. In a complex turn of events, his father divorced his mother secretly in Romania and took Eugène and his sister to live with him and his new wife. The move left Eugène very unhappy because he was more attached to his mother than to his father, and his father was a domineering and sometimes violent man. Eugène eventually left home when he was seventeen, while his sister, unable to tolerate their stepmother, rejoined their mother.

Ionesco studied French at the University of Bucharest. There he began his writing career and was noticed by a number of Romanian writers. Ionesco's first volume of poetry, *Elegies for Minuscule Creatures,* was published in 1931, but he later disowned it as the musings of an immature writer. He married in 1936, three months before his mother died, and taught high school French in Romania until 1939, when he returned to France. Although he and his wife were forced to return to Romania when World War II began Ionesco was permitted to teach in Bucharest until he made his way to Marseille in 1942 and weathered the rest of the war virtually in hiding and in relative poverty.

After the war Ionesco and his family (a daughter was born in 1944) moved back to Paris. While working as a proofreader he also used textbooks to teach himself English. His amusement at the essential nonsense of the phrases and expressions he encountered in the books led him to write his first play, *The Bald Soprano* (1950). In the play, he employs the kinds of clichéd expressions that appear in such books. Ultimately, as the critics have said, the play is about the certainty of a failure of communication.

Failure of communication is present in many of Ionesco's plays, and some commentators have pointed to the problems of his childhood as the source of his anxiety. Early in his life his parents were separated and his father presumed dead. Then his father reappeared only to later divorce Ionesco's mother and gain custody of their children in 1922 on the specious grounds that his wife deserted the family. Ionesco's journals of his early years record a tumultuous family life in which his mother appears as a virtual household slave. Some recurrent issues in his plays — including females as victims or as robotic extensions of their husband's will, and masculine figures as dark, tyrannical, and threatening — have led critics to credit his childhood experiences with having colored the main lines of his drama.

From the first performance of *The Bald Soprano,* soon linked with *The Lesson* (1951), Ionesco was considered a leader in a new wave of postwar drama. The first performance of *The Bald Soprano* entertained an audience of three, but all three were influential literary people in Paris, and the resultant word-of-mouth praise soon brought more people into the theater. In a short time

Ionesco was associated with the absurdist writers, and his plays were thought to be the beginning of absurdist drama. He was linked repeatedly with Samuel Beckett.

Ionesco was more comfortable with the term "anti-play," which is what he applied to *The Bald Soprano*. His theory was that realistic theater was dead, or certainly backward-looking. As an experimenter in avant-garde drama, Ionesco created fantasies that avoided realistic imitation and instead used symbol and language to penetrate a deeper level of meaning. He was not interested in the contemporary realistic drama or in the light entertainment of his day. He was also uninterested in the experiments of directors who tried to shock audiences. Instead, he intended the language in his plays to produce insight.

The ultimate success of *The Bald Soprano* and *The Lesson* has been remarkable. They established Ionesco as a powerful force in absurdist drama, along with Samuel Beckett. In his next play, *The Chairs* (1952), Old Woman and Old Man hire an Orator to deliver their message to the world. Instead of an audience, they draw only a collection of empty chairs. After they throw themselves out a window, calling, "Long live the Emperor!" the Orator steps forward to reveal that he can only speak gibberish. As an absurdist play, *The Chairs* remains a classic.

Among his other important plays are *Rhinoceros* (1959), *Exit the King* (1962), *Killing Game* (1970), and *Macbett* (1972). His later plays seem to move away from the stark experimentation of the early drama, a disappointment to some of his fans. However, audiences have disagreed. *Rhinoceros*, about people who mutate into animals, is one of his best-received plays among general theatergoers. In the last twenty years of his life, Ionesco wrote several prose works and concentrated on painting and lithography.

THE LESSON

Problems of communication lie at the heart of *The Lesson*. The professor is an old man who at first seems almost too timid to be a successful teacher. The pupil is a young woman who comes to him to study toward "the total doctorate." She seems at first to be bright, alert, and lively. The maid, wary and concerned, tries to warn the professor to be careful — especially to avoid instruction in philology, the study of words. He ignores her and proceeds to create havoc with unintelligible lessons on the origins of words.

Some commentators have seen an autobiographical quality in this play. The professor bears a resemblance to Ionesco's father, especially in his totalitarian zeal to control the pupil entirely. The maid resembles his mother, who was browbeaten by his father but remained sensible and controlled. The entire situation in the drama has also been compared to the political circumstances through which Ionesco lived in Europe, when fascism dominated Romania and conquered France. The pupil is essentially powerless in the play, partly because of her lack of knowledge. For example, she has minor problems naming the seasons and deciding if Paris is the capital of France. She is very good in addition and multiplication. But the professor complains that she cannot subtract: "It's not enough to integrate, you must also disintegrate," he tells her, implying that destruction and construction are equally necessary. But she is also powerless in part because she is very passive.

The professor soon moves into the realm of words: "The elements of linguistics and of comparative philology." The maid warns him, "Philology leads to calamity!" But he persists. His lectures become incomprehensible. The pupil attempts to respond to the lecture, but the professor stops her and embarks on long passages of dialogue that are all but incomprehensible. Eventually the pupil complains of a toothache, but nothing stops the professor in his tirade about "the neo-Spanish languages."

The once timid professor begins to dominate his pupil, while his pupil retreats and becomes more passive. The knife that the professor eventually wields — either real or imaginary, depending on the performance — delivers a sexualized assault that has been foreshadowed by the "lewd gleam" that the opening stage directions tell us occasionally comes into his eyes. The complicity of the maid, who prepares the entrance of the next pupil, may have been inspired by Ionesco's mother and stepmother's tolerance of his father's many infidelities.

The Lesson in Performance

Originally, *The Lesson* was written at the request of Maurice Cuvelier, who directed a tiny "pocket" theater in the district of Montparnasse. He wanted a play that could be done with a minimal set and few actors. The first performances were not especially successful. The audience was small. Some came because they had enjoyed the humor of *The Bald Soprano*, but *The Lesson* was dark and serious. Yet it was unmistakable in its direct attack on power. Totalitarianism was still alive in the world, and audiences certainly understood the connection between the play and contemporary life.

Quickly, the two plays were placed on the same bill and have been staged together for more than twelve thousand performances. In fact, they have played for forty years in Paris at the Théâtre de la Huchette, a small theater in which the audience feels that it is participating in an intimate part of theater history.

The early short plays lend themselves to being paired. *The Lesson* is also sometimes paired with *The Chairs,* as it was at the Royal Court Theatre in London in 1958. It took Ionesco a while before he could master the form of the full-length drama, as in *Rhinoceros.* Today some of his full-length plays and all three of his early one-act plays are produced in theaters around the world. Ionesco is not quite as shocking as he was in the 1950s, yet his work is still regarded as innovative and powerful.

Eugène Ionesco (1909–1994)

THE LESSON

1951

A COMIC DRAMA

TRANSLATED BY DONALD ALLEN

Characters

THE PROFESSOR, *aged fifty to sixty*
THE YOUNG PUPIL, *aged eighteen*
THE MAID, *aged forty-five to fifty*

Scene: *The office of the old professor, which also serves as a dining room. To the left, a door opens onto the apartment stairs; upstage, to the right, another door opens onto a corridor of the apartment. Upstage, a little left of center, a window, not very large, with plain curtains; on the outside sill of the window are ordinary potted plants. The low buildings with red roofs of a small town can be seen in the distance. The sky is grayish-blue. On the right stands a provincial buffet. The table doubles as a desk, it stands at stage center. There are three chairs around the table, and two more stand on each side of the window. Light-colored wallpaper, some shelves with books.*

(When the curtain rises the stage is empty, and it remains so for a few moments. Then we hear the doorbell ring.)

VOICE OF THE MAID (*from the corridor*): Yes. I'm coming.

(The Maid comes in, after having run down the stairs. She is stout, aged forty-five to fifty, red-faced, and wears a peasant woman's cap. She rushes in, slamming the door to the right behind her, and dries her hands on her apron as she runs towards the door on the left. Meanwhile we hear the doorbell ring again.)

MAID: Just a moment, I'm coming.

(She opens the door. A young Pupil, aged eighteen, enters. She is wearing a gray student's smock, a small white collar and carries a student's satchel under her arm.)

MAID: Good morning, miss.
PUPIL: Good morning, madam. Is the Professor at home?
MAID: Have you come for the lesson?
PUPIL: Yes, I have.
MAID: He's expecting you. Sit down for a moment. I'll tell him you're here.
PUPIL: Thank you.

(She seats herself near the table, facing the audience; the hall door is to her left; her back is to the other door, through which the Maid hurriedly exits, calling):

MAID: Professor, come down please, your pupil is here.

VOICE OF THE PROFESSOR (*rather reedy*): Thank you. I'm coming . . . in just a moment . . .

(The Maid exits; the Pupil draws in her legs, holds her satchel on her lap, and waits demurely. She casts a glance or two around the room, at the furniture, at the ceiling too. Then she takes a notebook out of her satchel, leafs through it, and stops to look at a page for a moment as though reviewing a lesson, as though taking a last look at her homework. She seems to be a well-brought-up girl, polite, but lively, gay, dynamic; a fresh smile is on her lips. During the course of the play she progressively loses the lively rhythm of her movement and her carriage, she becomes withdrawn. From gay and smiling she becomes progressively sad and morose; from very lively at the beginning, she becomes more and more fatigued and somnolent. Towards the end of the play her face must clearly express a nervous depression; her way of speaking shows the effects of this, her tongue becomes thick, words come to her memory with difficulty and emerge from her mouth with as much difficulty; she comes to a manner vaguely paralyzed, the beginning of aphasia.° Firm and determined at the beginning, so much so as to appear to be almost aggressive, she becomes more and more passive, until she is almost a mute and inert object, seemingly inanimate in the Professor's hands, to such an extent that when he makes his final gesture, she no longer reacts. Insensible, her reflexes deadened, only her eyes in an expressionless face will show inexpressible astonishment and fear. The transition from one manner to the other must of course be made imperceptibly.)

(The Professor enters. He is a little old man with a little white beard. He wears pince-nez,° a black skull cap, a long black schoolmaster's coat, trousers and shoes of black, detachable white collar, a black tie. Excessively polite, very timid, his voice deadened by his timidity, very proper, very much the teacher. He rubs his hands together constantly; occasionally a lewd gleam comes into his eyes and is quickly repressed.)

(During the course of the play his timidity will disappear progressively, imperceptibly; and the lewd gleams in his eyes will become a steady devouring flame in the

---

aphasia: Loss or impairment of the power to use or understand words.
pince-nez: Eyeglasses clipped to the nose by a spring.

end. From a manner that is inoffensive at the start, the Professor becomes more and more sure of himself, more and more nervous, aggressive, dominating, until he is able to do as he pleases with the Pupil, who has become, in his hands, a pitiful creature. Of course, the voice of the Professor must change too, from thin and reedy, to stronger and stronger, until at the end it is extremely powerful, ringing, sonorous, while the Pupil's voice changes from the very clear and ringing tones that she has at the beginning of the play until it is almost inaudible. In these first scenes the Professor might stammer very slightly.)

PROFESSOR: Good morning, young lady. You . . . I expect that you . . . that you are the new pupil?

PUPIL (*turns quickly with a lively and self-assured manner; she gets up, goes toward the Professor, and gives him her hand*): Yes, Professor. Good morning, Professor. As you see, I'm on time. I didn't want to be late.

PROFESSOR: That's fine, miss. Thank you, you didn't really need to hurry. I am very sorry to have kept you waiting . . . I was just finishing up . . . well . . . I'm sorry . . . You will excuse me, won't you?

PUPIL: Oh, certainly, Professor. It doesn't matter at all, Professor.

PROFESSOR: Please excuse me . . . Did you have any trouble finding the house?

PUPIL: No . . . Not at all. I just asked the way. Everybody knows you around here.

PROFESSOR: For thirty years I've lived in this town. You've not been here for long? How do you find it?

PUPIL: It's all right. The town is attractive and even agreeable, there's a nice park, a boarding school, a bishop, nice shops and streets . . .

PROFESSOR: That's very true, young lady. And yet, I'd just as soon live somewhere else. In Paris, or at least Bordeaux.

PUPIL: Do you like Bordeaux?

PROFESSOR: I don't know. I've never seen it.

PUPIL: But you know Paris?

PROFESSOR: No, I don't know it either, young lady, but if you'll permit me, can you tell me, Paris is the capital city of . . . miss?

PUPIL (*searching her memory for a moment, then, happily guessing*): Paris is the capital city of . . . France?

PROFESSOR: Yes, young lady, bravo, that's very good, that's perfect. My congratulations. You have your French geography at your fingertips. You know your chief cities.

PUPIL: Oh! I don't know them all yet, Professor, it's not quite that easy, I have trouble learning them.

PROFESSOR: Oh! it will come . . . you mustn't give up . . . young lady . . . I beg your pardon . . . have patience . . . little by little . . . You will see, it will come in time . . . What a nice day it is today . . . or rather, not so nice . . . Oh! but then yes it is nice. In short, it's not too bad a day, that's the main thing . . . ahem . . . ahem . . . it's not raining and it's not snowing either.

PUPIL: That would be most unusual, for it's summer now.

PROFESSOR: Excuse me, miss, I was just going to say so . . . but as you will learn, one must be ready for anything.

PUPIL: I guess so, Professor.

PROFESSOR: We can't be sure of anything, young lady, in this world.

PUPIL: The snow falls in the winter. Winter is one of the four seasons. The other three are . . . uh . . . spr . . .

PROFESSOR: Yes?

PUPIL: . . . ing, and then summer . . . and . . . uh . . .

PROFESSOR: It begins like "automobile," miss.

PUPIL: Ah, yes, autumn . . .

PROFESSOR: That's right, miss. That's a good answer, that's perfect. I am convinced that you will be a good pupil. You will make real progress. You are intelligent, you seem to me to be well informed, and you've a good memory.

PUPIL: I know my seasons, don't I, Professor?

PROFESSOR: Yes, indeed, miss . . . or almost. But it will come in time. In any case, you're coming along. Soon you'll know all the seasons, even with your eyes closed. Just as I do.

PUPIL: It's hard.

PROFESSOR: Oh, no. All it takes is a little effort, a little good will, miss. You will see. It will come, you may be sure of that.

PUPIL: Oh, I do hope so, Professor. I have a great thirst for knowledge. My parents also want me to get an education. They want me to specialize. They consider a little general culture, even if it is solid, is no longer enough, in these times.

PROFESSOR: Your parents, miss, are perfectly right. You must go on with your studies. Forgive me for saying so, but it is very necessary. Our contemporary life has become most complex.

PUPIL: And so very complicated too . . . My parents are fairly rich, I'm lucky. They can help me in my work, help me in my very advanced studies.

PROFESSOR: And you wish to qualify for . . . ?

PUPIL: Just as soon as possible, for the first doctor's orals. They're in three weeks' time.

PROFESSOR: You already have your high school diploma, if you'll pardon the question?

PUPIL: Yes, Professor, I have my science diploma and my arts diploma, too.

PROFESSOR: Ah, you're very far advanced, even perhaps too advanced for your age. And which doctorate do you wish to qualify for? In the physical sciences or in moral philosophy?

PUPIL: My parents are very much hoping — if you think it will be possible in such a short time — they very much hope that I can qualify for the total doctorate.

PROFESSOR: The total doctorate? . . . You have great courage, young lady, I congratulate you sincerely. We will try, miss, to do our best. In any case, you already know quite a bit, and at so young an age too.

PUPIL: Oh, Professor.

PROFESSOR: Then, if you'll permit me, pardon me, please, I do think that we ought to get to work. We have scarcely any time to lose.

PUPIL: Oh, but certainly, Professor, I want to. I beg you to.

PROFESSOR: Then, may I ask you to sit down . . . there . . . Will you permit me, miss, that is if you have no objections, to sit down opposite me?

PUPIL: Oh, of course, Professor, please do.

PROFESSOR: Thank you very much, miss. (*They sit down facing each other at the table, their profiles to the audience.*) There we are. Now have you brought your books and notebooks?

PUPIL (*taking notebooks and books out of her satchel*): Yes, Professor. Certainly, I have brought all that we'll need.

PROFESSOR: Perfect, miss. This is perfect. Now, if this doesn't bore you . . . shall we begin?

PUPIL: Yes, indeed, Professor, I am at your disposal.

PROFESSOR: At my disposal? (*A gleam comes into his eyes and is quickly extinguished; he begins to make a gesture that he suppresses at once.*) Oh, miss, it is I who am at your disposal. I am only your humble servant.

PUPIL: Oh, Professor . . .

PROFESSOR: If you will . . . now . . . we . . . we . . . I . . . I will begin by making a brief examination of your knowledge, past and present, so that we may chart our future course . . . Good. How is your perception of plurality?

PUPIL: It's rather vague . . . confused.

Professor: Good. We shall see.

(*He rubs his hands together. The Maid enters, and this appears to irritate the Professor. She goes to the buffet and looks for something, lingering.*)

PROFESSOR: Now, miss, would you like to do a little arithmetic, that is if you want to . . .

PUPIL: Oh, yes, Professor. Certainly, I ask nothing better.

PROFESSOR: It is rather a new science, a modern science, properly speaking, it is more a method than a science . . . And it is also a therapy. (*To the Maid:*) Have you finished, Marie?

MAID: Yes, Professor, I've found the plate. I'm just going . . .

PROFESSOR: Hurry up then. Please go along to the kitchen, if you will.

MAID: Yes, Professor, I'm going. (*She starts to go out.*) Excuse me, Professor, but take care, I urge you to remain calm.

PROFESSOR: You're being ridiculous, Marie. Now, don't worry.

MAID: That's what you always say.

PROFESSOR: I will not stand for your insinuations. I know perfectly well how to comport myself. I am old enough for that.

MAID: Precisely, Professor. You will do better not to start the young lady on arithmetic. Arithmetic is tiring, exhausting.

PROFESSOR: Not at my age. And anyhow, what business is it of yours? This is my concern. And I know what I'm doing. This is not your department.

MAID: Very well, Professor. But you can't say that I didn't warn you.

PROFESSOR: Marie, I can get along without your advice.

MAID: As you wish, Professor. (*She exits.*)

PROFESSOR: Miss, I hope you'll pardon this absurd interruption . . . Excuse this woman . . . She is always afraid that I'll tire myself. She fusses over my health.

PUPIL: Oh, that's quite all right, Professor. It shows that she's very devoted. She loves you very much. Good servants are rare.

PROFESSOR: She exaggerates. Her fears are stupid. But let's return to our arithmetical knitting.

PUPIL: I'm following you, Professor.

PROFESSOR (*wittily*): Without leaving your seat!

PUPIL (*appreciating his joke*): Like you, Professor.

PROFESSOR: Good. Let us arithmetize a little now.

PUPIL: Yes, gladly, Professor.

PROFESSOR: It wouldn't be too tiresome for you to tell me . . .

PUPIL: Not at all, Professor, go on.

PROFESSOR: How much are one and one?

PUPIL: One and one make two.

PROFESSOR (*marveling at the Pupil's knowledge*): Oh but that's very good. You appear to me to be well along in your studies. You should easily achieve the total doctorate, miss.

PUPIL: I'm so glad. Especially to have someone like you tell me this.

PROFESSOR: Let's push on: how much are two and one?

PUPIL: Three.

PROFESSOR: Three and one?

PUPIL: Four.

PROFESSOR: Four and one?

PUPIL: Five.

PROFESSOR: Five and one?

PUPIL: Six.

PROFESSOR: Six and one?

PUPIL: Seven.

PROFESSOR: Seven and one?

PUPIL: Eight.

PROFESSOR: Seven and one?

PUPIL: Eight again.

PROFESSOR: Very well answered. Seven and one?

PUPIL: Eight once more.

PROFESSOR: Perfect. Excellent. Seven and one?

PUPIL: Eight again. And sometimes nine.

PROFESSOR: Magnificent. You are magnificent. You are exquisite. I congratulate you warmly, miss. There's scarcely any point in going on. At addition you are a past master. Now, let's look at subtraction. Tell me, if you are not exhausted, how many are four minus three?

PUPIL: Four minus three? . . . Four minus three?

PROFESSOR: Yes. I mean to say: subtract three from four.

PUPIL: That makes . . . seven?

PROFESSOR: I am sorry but I'm obliged to contradict

you. Four minus three does not make seven. You are confused: four plus three makes seven, four minus three does not make seven . . . This is not addition anymore. We must subtract now.

PUPIL (*trying to understand*): Yes . . . yes . . .

PROFESSOR: Four minus three makes . . . How many? . . . How many?

PUPIL: Four?

PROFESSOR: No, miss, that's not it.

PUPIL: Three then.

PROFESSOR: Not that either, miss . . . Pardon, I'm sorry . . . I ought to say, that's not it . . . excuse me.

PUPIL: Four minus three . . . Four minus three . . . Four minus three? . . . But now doesn't that make ten?

PROFESSOR: Oh, certainly not, miss. It's not a matter of guessing, you've got to think it out. Let's try to deduce it together. Would you like to count?

PUPIL: Yes, Professor. One . . . two . . . uh . . .

PROFESSOR: You know how to count? How far can you count up to?

PUPIL: I can count to . . . infinity.

PROFESSOR: That's not possible, miss.

PUPIL: Well then, let's say to sixteen.

PROFESSOR: That is enough. One must know one's limits. Count then, if you will, please.

PUPIL: One . . . two . . . and after two, comes three . . . then four . . .

PROFESSOR: Stop there, miss. Which number is larger? Three or four?

PUPIL: Uh . . . three or four? Which is the larger? The larger of three or four? In what sense larger?

PROFESSOR: Some numbers are smaller and others are larger. In the large numbers there are more units than in the small . . .

PUPIL: Than in the small numbers?

PROFESSOR: Unless the small ones have smaller units. If they are very small, then there might be more units in the small numbers than in the large . . . if it is a question of other units . . .

PUPIL: In that case, the small numbers can be larger than the large numbers?

PROFESSOR: Let's not go into that. That would take us much too far. You must realize simply that more than numbers are involved here . . . there are also magnitudes, totals, there are groups, there are heaps, heaps of such things as plums, trucks, geese, prune pits, etc. To facilitate our work, let's merely suppose that we have only equal numbers, then the bigger numbers will be those that have the most units.

PUPIL: The one that has the most is the biggest? Ah, I understand, Professor, you are identifying quality with quantity.

PROFESSOR: That is too theoretical, miss, too theoretical. You needn't concern yourself with that. Let us take an example and reason from a definite case. Let's leave the general conclusions for later. We have the number four and the number three, and each has always the same number of units. Which number will be larger, the smaller or the larger?

PUPIL: Excuse me, Professor . . . What do you mean by the larger number? Is it the one that is not so small as the other?

PROFESSOR: That's it, miss, perfect. You have understood me very well.

PUPIL: Then, it is four.

PROFESSOR: What is four — larger or smaller than three?

PUPIL: Smaller . . . no, larger.

PROFESSOR: Excellent answer. How many units are there between three and four? . . . Or between four and three, if you prefer?

PUPIL: There aren't any units, Professor, between three and four. Four comes immediately after three; there is nothing at all between three and four!

PROFESSOR: I haven't made myself very well understood. No doubt, it is my fault. I've not been sufficiently clear.

PUPIL: No, Professor, it's my fault.

PROFESSOR: Look here. Here are three matches. And here is another one, that makes four. Now watch carefully — we have four matches. I take one away, now how many are left?

(*We don't see the matches, nor any of the objects that are mentioned. The Professor gets up from the table, writes on the imaginary blackboard with an imaginary piece of chalk, etc.*)

PUPIL: Five. If three and one make four, four and one make five.

PROFESSOR: That's not it. That's not it at all. You always have a tendency to add. But one must be able to subtract too. It's not enough to integrate, you must also disintegrate. That's the way life is. That's philosophy. That's science. That's progress, civilization.

PUPIL: Yes, Professor.

PROFESSOR: Let's return to our matches. I have four of them. You see, there are really four. I take one away, and there remain only . . .

PUPIL: I don't know, Professor.

PROFESSOR: Come now, think. It's not easy, I admit. Nevertheless, you've had enough training to make the intellectual effort required to arrive at an understanding. So?

PUPIL: I can't get it, Professor. I don't know, Professor.

PROFESSOR: Let us take a simpler example. If you had two noses, and I pulled one of them off . . . how many would you have left?

PUPIL: None.

PROFESSOR: What do you mean, none?

PUPIL: Yes, it's because you haven't pulled off any, that's why I have one now. If you had pulled it off, I wouldn't have it anymore.

PROFESSOR: You've not understood my example. Suppose that you have only one ear.

PUPIL: Yes, and then?

PROFESSOR: If I gave you another one, how many would you have then?

PUPIL: Two.

PROFESSOR: Good. And if I gave you still another ear. How many would you have then?

PUPIL: Three ears.

PROFESSOR: Now, I take one away . . . and there remain . . . how many ears?

PUPIL: Two.

PROFESSOR: Good. I take away still another one, how many do you have left?

PUPIL: Two.

PROFESSOR: No. You have two, I take one away, I eat one up, then how many do you have left?

PUPIL: Two.

PROFESSOR: I eat one of them . . . one.

PUPIL: Two.

PROFESSOR: One.

PUPIL: Two.

PROFESSOR: One!

PUPIL: Two!

PROFESSOR: One!!!

PUPIL: Two!!!

PROFESSOR: One!!!

PUPIL: Two!!!

PROFESSOR: One!!!

PUPIL: Two!!!

PROFESSOR: No. No. That's not right. The example is not . . . it's not convincing. Listen to me.

PUPIL: Yes, Professor.

PROFESSOR: You've got . . . you've got . . . you've got . . .

PUPIL: Ten fingers!

PROFESSOR: If you wish. Perfect. Good. You have then ten fingers.

PUPIL: Yes, Professor.

PROFESSOR: How many would you have if you had only five of them?

PUPIL: Ten, Professor.

PROFESSOR: That's not right!

PUPIL: But it is, Professor.

PROFESSOR: I tell you it's not!

PUPIL: You just told me that I had ten . . .

PROFESSOR: I also said, immediately afterwards, that you had five!

PUPIL: I don't have five, I've got ten!

PROFESSOR: Let's try another approach . . . for purposes of subtraction let's limit ourselves to the numbers from one to five . . . Wait now, miss, you'll soon see. I'm going to make you understand.

(*The Professor begins to write on the imaginary blackboard. He moves it closer to the Pupil, who turns around in order to see it.*)

PROFESSOR: Look here, miss . . . (*He pretends to draw a stick on the blackboard and the number 1 below the stick; then two sticks and the number 2 below, then three sticks and the number 3 below, then four sticks with the number 4 below.*) You see . . .

PUPIL: Yes, Professor.

PROFESSOR: These are sticks, miss, sticks. This is one stick, these are two sticks, and three sticks, then four sticks, then five sticks. One stick, two sticks, three

sticks, four and five sticks, these are numbers. When we count the sticks, each stick is a unit, miss . . . What have I just said?

PUPIL: "A unit, miss! What have I just said?"

PROFESSOR: Or a figure! Or a number! One, two, three, four, five, these are the elements of numeration, miss.

PUPIL (*hesitant*): Yes, Professor. The elements, figures, which are sticks, units and numbers . . .

PROFESSOR: At the same time . . . that's to say, in short — the whole of arithmetic is there.

PUPIL: Yes, Professor. Good, Professor. Thanks, Professor.

PROFESSOR: Now, count, if you will please, using these elements . . . add and subtract . . .

PUPIL (*as though trying to impress them on her memory*): Sticks are really fingers and numbers are units?

PROFESSOR: Hmm . . . so to speak. And then?

PUPIL: One could subtract two units from three units, but can one subtract two twos from three threes? And two figures from four numbers? And three numbers from one unit?

PROFESSOR: No, miss.

PUPIL: Why, Professor?

PROFESSOR: Because, miss.

PUPIL: Because why, Professor? Since one is the same as the other?

PROFESSOR: That's the way it is, miss. It can't be explained. This is only comprehensible through internal mathematical reasoning. Either you have it or you don't.

PUPIL: So much the worse for me.

PROFESSOR: Listen to me, miss, if you don't achieve a profound understanding of these principles, these arithmetical archetypes, you will never be able to perform correctly the functions of a polytechnician. Still less will you be able to teach a course in a polytechnical school . . . or the primary grades. I realize that this is not easy, it is very, very abstract . . . obviously . . . but unless you can comprehend the primary elements, how do you expect to be able to calculate mentally — and this is the least of the things that even an ordinary engineer must be able to do — how much, for example, are three billion seven hundred fifty-five million nine hundred ninety-eight thousand two hundred fifty-one, multiplied by five billion one hundred sixty-two million three hundred and three thousand five hundred and eight?

PUPIL (*very quickly*): That makes nineteen quintillion three hundred ninety quadrillion two trillion eight hundred forty-four billion two hundred nineteen million one hundred sixty-four thousand five hundred and eight . . .

PROFESSOR (*astonished*): No. I don't think so. That must make nineteen quintillion three hundred ninety quadrillion two trillion eight hundred forty-four billion two hundred nineteen million one hundred sixty-four thousand five hundred and nine . . .

PUPIL: . . . No . . . five hundred and eight . . .

PROFESSOR (*more and more astonished, calculating mentally*): Yes . . . you are right . . . the result is indeed . . . (*He mumbles unintelligibly*:) . . . quintillion, quadrillion, trillion, billion, million . . . (*Clearly*:) one hundred sixty-four thousand five hundred and eighty . . . (*Stupefied*:) But how did you know that, if you don't know the principles of arithmetical reasoning?

PUPIL: It's easy. Not being able to rely on my reasoning, I've memorized all the products of all possible multiplications.

PROFESSOR: That's pretty good . . . However, permit me to confess to you that that doesn't satisfy me, miss, and I do not congratulate you: in mathematics and in arithmetic especially, the thing that counts — for in arithmetic it is always necessary to count — the thing that counts is, above all, understanding . . . It is by mathematical reasoning, simultaneously inductive and deductive, that you ought to arrive at this result — as well as at any other result. Mathematics is the sworn enemy of memory, which is excellent otherwise, but disastrous, arithmetically speaking! . . . That's why I'm not happy with this . . . this won't do, not at all . . .

PUPIL (*desolated*): No, Professor.

PROFESSOR: Let's leave it for the moment. Let's go on to another exercise . . .

PUPIL: Yes, Professor.

MAID (*entering*): Hmm, hmm, Professor . . .

PROFESSOR (*who doesn't hear her*): It is unfortunate, miss, that you aren't further along in specialized mathematics . . .

MAID (*taking him by the sleeve*): Professor! Professor!

PROFESSOR: I fear that you will not be able to qualify for the total doctor's orals . . .

PUPIL: Yes, Professor, it's too bad!

PROFESSOR: Unless you . . . (*To the Maid*:) Let me be, Marie . . . Look here, why are you bothering me? Go back to the kitchen! To your pots and pans! Go away! Go away! (*To the Pupil*:) We will try to prepare you at least for the partial doctorate . . .

MAID: Professor! . . . Professor! . . . (*She pulls his sleeve.*)

PROFESSOR (*to the Maid*): Now leave me alone! Let me be! What's the meaning of this? . . . (*To the Pupil*:) I must therefore teach you, if you really do insist on attempting the partial doctorate . . .

PUPIL: Yes, Professor.

PROFESSOR: . . . The elements of linguistics and of comparative philology° . . .

MAID: No, Professor, no! . . . You mustn't do that! . . .

PROFESSOR: Marie, you're going too far!

MAID: Professor, especially not philology, philology leads to calamity . . .

PUPIL (*astonished*): To calamity? (*Smiling, a little stupidly*:) That's hard to believe.

PROFESSOR (*to the Maid*): That's enough now! Get out of here!

MAID: All right, Professor, all right. But you can't say that I didn't warn you! Philology leads to calamity!

PROFESSOR: I'm an adult, Marie!

PUPIL: Yes, Professor.

MAID: As you wish.

(*She exits.*)

PROFESSOR: Let's continue, miss.

PUPIL: Yes, Professor.

PROFESSOR: I want you to listen now with the greatest possible attention to a lecture I have prepared . . .

PUPIL: Yes, Professor!

PROFESSOR: . . . Thanks to which, in fifteen minutes' time, you will be able to acquire the fundamental principles of the linguistic and comparative philology of the neo-Spanish languages.

PUPIL: Yes, Professor, oh good!

(*She claps her hands.*)

PROFESSOR (*with authority*): Quiet! What do you mean by that?

PUPIL: I'm sorry, Professor.

(*Slowly, she replaces her hands on the table.*)

PROFESSOR: Quiet! (*He gets up, walks up and down the room, his hands behind his back; from time to time he stops at stage center or near the Pupil, and underlines his words with a gesture of his hand; he orates, but without being too emotional. The Pupil follows him with her eyes, occasionally with some difficulty, for she has to turn her head far around; once or twice, not more, she turns around completely.*) And now, miss, Spanish is truly the mother tongue which gave birth to all the neo-Spanish languages, of which Spanish, Latin, Italian, our own French, Portuguese, Romanian, Sardinian or Sardanapalian, Spanish and neo-Spanish — and also, in certain of its aspects, Turkish which is otherwise very close to Greek, which is only logical, since it is a fact that Turkey is a neighbor of Greece and Greece is even closer to Turkey than you are to me — this is only one more illustration of the very important linguistic law which states that geography and philology are twin sisters . . . You may take notes, miss.

PUPIL (*in a dull voice*): Yes, Professor!

PROFESSOR: That which distinguishes the neo-Spanish languages from each other and their idioms from the other linguistic groups, such as the group of languages called Austrian and neo-Austrian or Hapsburgian, as well as the Esperanto, Helvetian, Monacan, Swiss, Andorran, Basque, and jai alai° groups, and also the groups of diplomatic and technical languages — that which distinguishes them, I repeat, is their striking resemblance which makes it so hard to distinguish them from each other — I'm

---

philology: Study of language, linguistics.

jai alai: Game similar to handball.

speaking of the neo-Spanish languages which one is able to distinguish from each other, however, only thanks to their distinctive characteristics, absolutely indisputable proofs of their extraordinary resemblance, which renders indisputable their common origin, and which, at the same time, differentiates them profoundly — through the continuation of the distinctive traits which I've just cited.

PUPIL: Oooh! Ye-e-e-s-s-s, Professor!

PROFESSOR: But let's not linger over generalities . . .

PUPIL (*regretfully, but won over*): Oh, Professor . . .

PROFESSOR: This appears to interest you. All the better, all the better.

PUPIL: Oh, yes, Professor . . .

PROFESSOR: Don't worry, miss. We will come back to it later . . . That is if we come back to it at all. Who can say?

PUPIL (*enchanted in spite of everything*): Oh, yes, Professor.

PROFESSOR: Every tongue — you must know this, miss, and remember it *until the hour of your death* . . .

PUPIL: Oh! yes, Professor, until the hour of my death . . . Yes, Professor . . .

PROFESSOR: . . . And this, too, is a fundamental principle, every tongue is at bottom nothing but language, which necessarily implies that it is composed of sounds, or . . .

PUPIL: Phonemes . . .

PROFESSOR: Just what I was going to say. Don't parade your knowledge. You'd do better to listen.

PUPIL: All right, Professor. Yes, Professor.

PROFESSOR: The sounds, miss, must be seized on the wing as they fly so that they'll not fall on deaf ears. As a result, when you set out to articulate, it is recommended, insofar as possible, that you lift up your neck and chin very high, and rise up on the tips of your toes, you see, this way . . .

PUPIL: Yes, Professor.

PROFESSOR: Keep quiet. Remain seated, don't interrupt me . . . And project the sounds very loudly with all the force of your lungs in conjunction with that of your vocal cords. Like this, look: "Butterfly," "Eureka," "Trafalgar," "Papaya." This way, the sounds become filled with a warm air that is lighter than the surrounding air so that they can fly without danger of falling on deaf ears, which are veritable voids, tombs of sonorities. If you utter several sounds at an accelerated speed, they will automatically cling to each other, constituting thus syllables, words, even sentences, that is to say groupings of various importance, purely irrational assemblages of sounds, denuded of all sense, but for that very reason the more capable of maintaining themselves without danger at a high altitude in the air. By themselves, words charged with significance will fall, weighted down by their meaning, and in the end they always collapse, fall . . .

PUPIL: . . . On deaf ears.

PROFESSOR: That's it, but don't interrupt . . . and into

the worst confusion . . . Or else burst like balloons. Therefore, miss . . . (*The Pupil suddenly appears to be unwell.*) What's the matter?

PUPIL: I've got a toothache, Professor.

PROFESSOR: That's not important. We're not going to stop for anything so trivial. Let us go on . . .

PUPIL (*appearing to be in more and more pain*): Yes, Professor.

PROFESSOR: I draw your attention in passing to the consonants that change their nature in combinations. In this case *f* becomes *v*, *d* becomes *t*, *g* becomes *k*, and vice versa, as in these examples that I will cite for you: "That's all right," "hens and chickens," "Welsh rabbit," "lots of nothing," "not at all."[1]

PUPIL: I've got a toothache.

PROFESSOR: Let's continue.

PUPIL: Yes.

PROFESSOR: To resume: it takes years and years to learn to pronounce. Thanks to science, we can achieve this in a few minutes. In order to project words, sounds and all the rest, you must realize that it is necessary to pitilessly expel air from the lungs, and make it pass delicately, caressingly, over the vocal cords, which, like harps or leaves in the wind, will suddenly shake, agitate, vibrate, vibrate, vibrate or uvulate, or fricate or jostle against each other, or sibilate, sibilate, placing everything in movement, the uvula, the tongue, the palate, the teeth . . .

PUPIL: I have a toothache.

PROFESSOR: . . . And the lips . . . Finally the words come out through the nose, the mouth, the ears, the pores, drawing along with them all the organs that we have named, torn up by the roots, in a powerful, majestic flight, which is none other than what is called, improperly, the voice, whether modulated in singing or transformed into a terrible symphonic storm with a whole procession . . . of garlands of all kinds of flowers, of sonorous artifices: labials, dentals, occlusives, palatals, and others, some caressing, some bitter or violent.

PUPIL: Yes, Professor, I've got a toothache.

PROFESSOR: Let's go on, go on. As for the neo-Spanish languages, they are closely related, so closely to each other, that they can be considered as true second cousins. Moreover, they have the same mother: Spanishe, with a mute *e*. That is why it is so difficult to distinguish them from one another. That is why it is so useful to pronounce carefully, and to avoid errors in pronunciation. Pronunciation itself is worth a whole language. A bad pronunciation can get you into trouble. In this connection, permit me, parenthetically, to share a personal experience with you. (*Slight pause. The Professor goes over his memories for a moment; his features mellow, but he recovers at once.*) I was very young, little more than a child. It was during my military service. I had a friend in the regiment, a vicomte, who suffered from a rather

---

[1]All to be heavily elided. [Translator's note.]

serious defect in his pronunciation: he could not pronounce the letter *f*. Instead of *f*, he said *f*. Thus, instead of "Birds of a feather flock together," he said: "Birds of a feather flock together." He pronounced filly instead of filly, Firmin instead of Firmin, French bean instead of French bean, go frig yourself instead of go frig yourself, farrago instead of farrago, fee fi fo fum instead of fee fi fo fum, Philip instead of Philip, fictory instead of fictory, February instead of February, March–April instead of March–April, Gerard de Nerval and not as is correct — Gerard de Nerval, Mirabeau instead of Mirabeau, etc., instead of etc., and thus instead of etc., instead of etc., and thus and so forth. However, he managed to conceal his fault so effectively that, thanks to the hats he wore, no one ever noticed it.

PUPIL: Yes, I've got a toothache.

PROFESSOR (*abruptly changing his tone, his voice hardening*): Let's go on. We'll first consider the points of similarity in order the better to apprehend, later on, that which distinguishes all these languages from each other. The differences can scarcely be recognized by people who are not aware of them. Thus, all the words of all the languages . . .

PUPIL: Uh, yes? . . . I've got a toothache.

PROFESSOR: Let's continue . . . are always the same, just as all the suffixes, all the prefixes, all the terminations, all the roots . . .

PUPIL: Are the roots of words square?

PROFESSOR: Square or cube. That depends.

PUPIL: I've got a toothache.

PROFESSOR: Let's go on. Thus, to give you an example which is little more than an illustration, take the word "front" . . .

PUPIL: How do you want me to take it?

PROFESSOR: However you wish, so long as you take it, but above all do not interrupt.

PUPIL: I've got a toothache.

PROFESSOR: Let's continue . . . I said: Let's continue. Take now the word "front." Have you taken it?

PUPIL: Yes, yes, I've got it. My teeth, my teeth . . .

PROFESSOR: The word "front" is the root of "frontispiece." It is also to be found in "affronted." "Ispiece" is the suffix, and "af" the prefix. They are so called because they do not change. They don't want to.

PUPIL: I've got a toothache.

PROFESSOR: Let's go on. (*Rapidly:*) These prefixes are of Spanish origin. I hope you noticed that, did you?

PUPIL: Oh, how my tooth aches.

PROFESSOR: Let's continue. You've surely also noticed that they've not changed in French. And now, young lady, nothing has succeeded in changing them in Latin either, nor in Italian, nor in Portuguese, nor in Sardanapalian, nor in Sardanapali, nor in Romanian, nor in neo-Spanish, nor in Spanish, nor even in the Oriental: front, frontispiece, affronted, always the same word, invariably with the same root, the same suffix, the same prefix, in all the languages I have named. And it is always the same for all words.

PUPIL: In all languages, these words mean the same thing? I've got a toothache.

PROFESSOR: Absolutely. Moreover, it's more a notion than a word. In any case, you have always the same signification, the same composition, the same sound structure, not only for this word, but for all conceivable words, in all languages. For one single notion is expressed by one and the same word, and its synonyms, in all countries. Forget about your teeth.

PUPIL: I've got a toothache. Yes, yes, yes.

PROFESSOR: Good, let's go on. I tell you, let's go on . . . How would you say, for example, in French: roses of my grandmother are as yellow as my grandfather who was Asiatic?

PUPIL: My teeth ache, ache, ache.

PROFESSOR: Let's go on, let's go on, go ahead and answer, anyway.

PUPIL: In French?

PROFESSOR: In French.

PUPIL: Uhh . . . I should say in French: the roses of my grandmother are . . . ?

PROFESSOR: As yellow as my grandfather who was Asiatic . . .

PUPIL: Oh well, one would say, in French, I believe, the roses . . . of my . . . how do you say "grandmother" in French?

PROFESSOR: In French? Grandmother.

PUPIL: The roses of my grandmother are as yellow — in French, is it "yellow"?

PROFESSOR: Yes, of course!

PUPIL: Are as yellow as my grandfather when he got angry.

PROFESSOR: No . . . who was A . . .

PUPIL: . . . siatic . . . I've got a toothache.

PROFESSOR: That's it.

PUPIL: I've got a tooth . . .

PROFESSOR: Ache . . . so what . . . let's continue! And now translate the same sentence into Spanish, then into neo-Spanish . . .

PUPIL: In Spanish . . . this would be: the roses of my grandmother are as yellow as my grandfather who was Asiatic.

PROFESSOR: No. That's wrong.

PUPIL: And in neo-Spanish: the roses of my grandmother are as yellow as my grandfather who was Asiatic.

PROFESSOR: That's wrong. That's wrong. That's wrong. You have inverted it, you've confused Spanish with neo-Spanish, and neo-Spanish with Spanish . . . Oh . . . no . . . it's the other way around . . .

PUPIL: I've got a toothache. You're getting mixed up.

PROFESSOR: You're the one who is mixing me up. Pay attention and take notes. I will say the sentence to you in Spanish, then in neo-Spanish, and finally, in Latin. You will repeat after me. Pay attention, for the resemblances are great. In fact, they are identical resemblances. Listen, follow carefully . . .

PUPIL: I've got a tooth . . .

PROFESSOR: . . . Ache.

PUPIL: Let's go on . . . Ah! . . .

PROFESSOR: . . . In Spanish: the roses of my grandmother are as yellow as my grandfather who was Asiatic; in Latin; the roses of my grandmother are as yellow as my grandfather who was Asiatic. Do you detect the difference? Translate this into . . . Romanian.

PUPIL: The . . . how do you say "roses" in Romanian?

PROFESSOR: But "roses," what else?

PUPIL: It's not "roses"? Oh, how my tooth aches!

PROFESSOR: Certainly not, certainly not, since "roses" is a translation in Oriental of the French word "roses," in Spanish "roses," do you get it? In Sardinapali, "roses" . . .

PUPIL: Excuse me, Professor, but . . . Oh, my toothache! . . . I don't get the difference.

PROFESSOR: But it's so simple! So simple! It's a matter of having a certain experience, a technical experience and practice in these diverse languages, which are so diverse in spite of the fact that they present wholly identical characteristics. I'm going to try to give you a key . . .

PUPIL: Toothache . . .

PROFESSOR: That which differentiates these languages, is neither the words, which are absolutely the same, nor the structure of the sentence which is everywhere the same, nor the intonation, which does not offer any differences, nor the rhythm of the language . . . that which differentiates them . . . are you listening?

PUPIL: I've got a toothache.

PROFESSOR: Are you listening to me, young lady? Aah! We're going to lose our temper.

PUPIL: You're bothering me, Professor. I've got toothache.

PROFESSOR: Son of a cocker spaniel! Listen to me!

PUPIL: Oh well . . . yes . . . yes . . . go on . . .

PROFESSOR: That which distinguishes them from each other, on the one hand, and from their mother, Spanishe with its mute *e*, on the other hand . . . is . . .

PUPIL (*grimacing*): Is what?

PROFESSOR: Is an intangible thing. Something intangible that one is able to perceive only after very long study, with a great deal of trouble and the broadest experience . . .

PUPIL: Ah?

PROFESSOR: Yes, young lady. I cannot give any rule. One must have a feeling for it, and well, that's it. But in order to have it, one one must study, and then study some more.

PUPIL: Toothache.

PROFESSOR: All the same, there are some specific cases where words differ from one language to another . . . but we cannot base our knowledge on these cases, which are, so to speak, exceptional.

PUPIL: Oh, yes? . . . Oh, Professor, I've got a toothache.

PROFESSOR: Don't interrupt! Don't make me lose my temper! I can't answer for what I'll do. I was saying, then . . . Ah, yes, the exceptional cases, the so-called easily distinguished . . . or facilely distinguished . . . or conveniently . . . if you prefer . . . I repeat, if you prefer, for I see that you're not listening to me . . .

PUPIL: I've got a toothache.

PROFESSOR: I say then: in certain expressions in current usage, certain words differ totally from one language to another, so much so that the language employed is, in this case, considerably easier to identify. I'll give you an example: the neo-Spanish expression, famous in Madrid: "My country is the new Spain," becomes in Italian: "My country is . . ."

PUPIL: The new Spain.

PROFESSOR: No! "My country is Italy." Tell me now, by simple deduction, how do you say "Italy" in French?

PUPIL: I've got a toothache.

PROFESSOR: But it's so easy: for the word "Italy," in French we have the word "France," which is an exact translation of it. My country is France. And "France" in Oriental: "Orient!" My country is the Orient. And "Orient" in Portuguese: "Portugal!" The Oriental expression: My country is the Orient is translated then in the same fashion into Portuguese: My country is Portugal! And so on . . .

PUPIL: Oh, no more, no more. My teeth . . .

PROFESSOR: Ache! ache! ache! . . . I'm going to pull them out, I will! One more example. The word "capital" — it takes on, according to the language one speaks, a different meaning. That is to say that when a Spaniard says: "I reside in the capital," the word "capital" does not mean at all the same thing that a Portuguese means when he says: "I reside in the capital." All the more so in the case of a Frenchman, a neo-Spaniard, a Romanian, a Latin, a Sardanapali . . . Whenever you hear it, young lady — young lady, I'm saying this for you! Pooh! Whenever you hear the expression: "I reside in the capital," you will immediately and easily know whether this is Spanish or Spanish, or neo-Spanish, French, Oriental, Romanian, or Latin, for it is enough to know which metropolis is referred to by the person who pronounces the sentence . . . at the very moment he pronounces it . . . But these are almost the only precise examples that I can give you . . .

PUPIL: Oh dear! My teeth . . .

PROFESSOR: Silence! Or I'll bash in your skull!

PUPIL: Just try to! Skulldugger!°

(*The Professor seizes her wrist and twists it.*)

PUPIL: Oww!

PROFESSOR: Keep quiet now! Not a word!

PUPIL (*whimpering*): Toothache . . .

PROFESSOR: One thing that is the most . . . how shall I say it? . . . the most paradoxical . . . yes . . . that's the word . . . the most paradoxical thing, is that a lot of people who are completely illiterate speak these different languages . . . do you understand? What did I just say?

Skulldugger: A devious person.

PUPIL: . . . "Speak these different languages! What did I just say?"

PROFESSOR: You were lucky that time! . . . The common people speak a Spanish full or neo-Spanish words that they are entirely unaware of, all the while believing that they are speaking Latin . . . or they speak Latin, full of Oriental words, all the while believing that they're speaking Romanian . . . or Spanish, full of neo-Spanish, all the while believing that they're speaking Sardanapali, or Spanish . . . Do you understand?

PUPIL: Yes! yes! yes! yes! What more do want . . . ?

PROFESSOR: No insolence, my pet, or you'll be sorry . . . (*In a rage*:) But the worst of all, young lady, is that certain people, for example, in a Latin that they suppose is Spanish, say: "Both my kidneys are of the same kidney," in addressing themselves to a Frenchman who does not know a word of Spanish, but the latter understands it as if it were his own language. For that matter he thinks it is his own language. And the Frenchman will reply, in French: "Me too, sir, mine are too," and this will be perfectly comprehensible to a Spaniard, who will feel certain that the reply is in pure Spanish and that Spanish is being spoken . . . when, in reality, it was neither Spanish nor French, but Latin in the neo-Spanish dialect . . . Sit still, young lady, don't fidget, stop tapping your feet . . .

PUPIL: I've got a toothache.

PROFESSOR: How do you account for the fact that, in speaking without knowing which language they speak, or even while each of them believes that he is speaking another, the common people understand each other at all?

PUPIL: I wonder.

PROFESSOR: It is simply one of the inexplicable curiosities of the vulgar empiricism of the common people — not to be confused with experience! — a paradox, a non-sense, one of the aberrations of human nature, it is purely and simply instinct — to put it in a nutshell . . . That's what is involved here.

PUPIL: Hah! hah!

PROFESSOR: Instead of staring at the flies while I'm going to all this trouble . . . you would do much better to try to be more attentive . . . it is not I who is going to qualify for the partial doctor's orals . . . I passed mine a long time ago . . . and I've won my total doctorate, too . . . and my super-total diploma . . . Don't you realize that what I'm saying is for your own good?

PUPIL: Toothache!

PROFESSOR: Ill-mannered . . . It can't go on like this, it won't do, it won't do, it won't do . . .

PUPIL: I'm . . . listening . . . to you . . .

PROFESSOR: Ahah! In order to learn to distinguish all the different languages, as I've told you, there is nothing better than practice . . . Let's take them up in order. I am going to try to teach you all the translations of the word "knife."

PUPIL: Well, all right . . . if you want . . .

PROFESSOR (*calling the Maid*): Marie! Marie! She's not there . . . Marie! Marie . . . Marie, where are you? (*He opens the door on the right.*) Marie! . . .

(*He exits. The Pupil remains alone several minutes, staring into space, wearing a stupefied expression.*)

PROFESSOR (*offstage, in a shrill voice*): Marie! What are you up to? Why don't you come! When I call you, you must come! (*He re-enters, followed by Marie.*) It is I who gives the orders, do you hear? (*He points at the Pupil*): She doesn't understand anything, that girl. She doesn't understand!

MAID: Don't get into such a state, sir, you know where it'll end! You're going to go too far, you're going to go too far.

PROFESSOR: I'll be able to stop in time.

MAID: That's what you always say. I only wish I could see it.

PUPIL: I've got a toothache.

MAID: You see, it's starting, that's the symptom.

PROFESSOR: What symptom? Explain yourself? What do you mean?

PUPIL (*in a spiritless voice*): Yes, what do you mean? I've got a toothache.

MAID: The final symptom! The chief symptom!

PROFESSOR: Stupid! stupid! stupid! (*The Maid starts to exit.*) Don't go away like that! I called you to help me find the Spanish, neo-Spanish, Portuguese, French, Oriental, Romanian, Sardanapali, Latin and Spanish knives.

MAID (*severely*): Don't ask me. (*She exits.*)

PROFESSOR (*makes a gesture as though to protest, then refrains, a little helpless. Suddenly, he remembers*): Ah! (*He goes quickly to the drawer where he finds a big knife, invisible or real according to the preference of the director. He seizes it and brandishes it happily.*) Here is one, young lady, here is a knife. It's too bad that we only have this one, but we're going to try to make it serve for all the languages, anyway! It will be enough if you will pronounce the word "knife" in all the languages, while looking at the object, very closely, fixedly, and imagining that it is in the language that you are speaking.

PUPIL: I've got a toothache.

PROFESSOR (*almost singing, chanting*): Now, say "kni," like "kni," "fe," like "fe" . . . And look, look, look at it, watch it . . .

PUPIL: What is this one in? French, Italian or Spanish?

PROFESSOR: That doesn't matter now . . . That's not your concern. Say: "kni."

PUPIL: "Kni."

PROFESSOR: . . . "fe" . . . Look.

(*He brandishes the knife under the Pupil's eyes.*)

PUPIL: "fe" . . .

PROFESSOR: Again . . . Look at it.

PUPIL: Oh, no! My God! I've had enough. And besides, I've got a toothache, my feet hurt me, I've got a headache.

PROFESSOR (*abruptly*): Knife . . . look . . . knife . . . look . . . knife . . . look . . .

PUPIL: You're giving me an earache, too. Oh, your voice! It's so piercing!

PROFESSOR: Say: knife . . . kni . . . fe . . .

PUPIL: No! My ears hurt, I hurt all over . . .

PROFESSOR: I'm going to tear them off, your ears, that's what I'm going to do to you, and then they won't hurt you anymore, my pet.

PUPIL: Oh . . . you're hurting me, oh, you're hurting me . . .

PROFESSOR: Look, come on, quickly, repeat after me: "kni" . . .

PUPIL: Oh, since you insist . . . knife . . . knife . . . (*In a lucid moment, ironically*): Is that neo-Spanish . . . ?

PROFESSOR: If you like, yes, it's neo-Spanish, but hurry up . . . we haven't got time . . . And then, what do you mean by that insidious question? What are you up to?

PUPIL (*becoming more and more exhausted, weeping, desperate, at the same time both exasperated and in a trance*): Ah!

PROFESSOR: Repeat, watch. (*He imitates a cuckoo:*) Knife, knife . . . knife, knife . . . knife, knife . . . knife, knife . . .

PUPIL: Oh, my head . . . aches . . . (*With her hand she caressingly touches the parts of her body as she names them*): . . . My eyes . . .

PROFESSOR (*like a cuckoo*): Knife, knife . . . knife, knife . . . (*They are both standing. The Professor still brandishes his invisible knife, nearly beside himself, as he circles around her in a sort of scalp dance, but it is important that this not be exaggerated and that his dance steps be only suggested. The Pupil stands facing the audience, then recoils in the direction of the window, sickly, languid, victimized.*)

PROFESSOR: Repeat, repeat: knife . . . knife . . . knife . . .

PUPIL: I've got a pain . . . my throat, neck . . . oh, my shoulders . . . my breast . . . knife . . .

PROFESSOR: Knife . . . knife . . . knife . . .

PUPIL: My hips . . . knife . . . my thighs . . . kni . . .

PROFESSOR: Pronounce it carefully . . . knife . . . knife . . .

PUPIL: Knife . . . my throat . . .

PROFESSOR: Knife . . . knife . . .

PUPIL: Knife . . . my shoulders . . . my arms, my breast, my hips . . . knife . . . knife . . .

PROFESSOR: That's right . . . Now, you're pronouncing it well . . .

PUPIL: Knife . . . my breast . . . my stomach . . .

PROFESSOR (*changing his voice*): Pay attention . . . don't break my window . . . the knife kills . . .

PUPIL (*in a weak voice*): Yes, yes . . . the knife kills?

PROFESSOR (*striking the Pupil with a very spectacular blow of the knife*): Aaah! That'll teach you!

(*Pupil also cries "Aah!" then falls, flopping in an immodest position onto a chair which, as though by chance, is near the window. The murderer and his victim shout "Aaah!" at the same moment. After the first*

The Maid (Laura Napoli) warning the Professor (Christopher Sorenson) in the Cornell University Center for Theater Arts production of *The Lesson* during its 1997–1998 season.

blow of the knife, the Pupil flops onto the chair, her legs spread wide and hanging over both sides of the chair. The Professor remains standing in front of her, his back to the audience. After the first blow, he strikes her dead with a second slash of the knife, from bottom to top. After that blow a noticeable convulsion shakes his whole body.)

PROFESSOR (*winded, mumbling*): Bitch . . . Oh, that's good, that does me good . . . Ah! Ah! I'm exhausted . . . I can scarcely breathe . . . Aah! (*He breathes with difficulty; he falls — fortunately a chair is there; he mops his brow, mumbles some incomprehensible words; his breathing becomes normal. He gets up, looks at the knife in his hand, looks at the young girl, then as though he were waking up, in a panic:*) What have I done! What's going to happen to me now! What's going to happen! Oh! dear! Oh dear, I'm in trouble! Young lady, young lady, get up! (*He is agitated, still holding onto the invisible knife, which he doesn't know what to do with.*) Come now, young lady, the lesson is over . . . you may go . . . you can pay another time . . . Oh! she is dead . . . dea-ead . . . And by my knife . . . She is dea-ead . . . It's terrible. (*He calls the Maid:*) Marie! Marie! My good Marie, come here! Ah! Ah! (*The door on the right opens a little and Marie appears.)* No . . . don't come in . . . I made a mistake . . . I don't need you, Marie . . . I don't need you any-more . . . do you understand? . . .

(Maid enters wearing a stern expression, without saying a word. She sees the corpse.)

PROFESSOR *(in a voice less and less assured)*: I don't need you, Marie . . .

MAID *(sarcastic)*: Then, you're satisfied with your pupil, she's profited by your lesson?

PROFESSOR *(holding the knife behind his back)*: Yes, the lesson is finished . . . but . . . she . . . she's still there . . . she doesn't want to leave . . .

MAID *(very harshly)*: Is that a fact? . . .

PROFESSOR *(trembling)*: It wasn't I . . . it wasn't I . . . Marie . . . No . . . I assure you . . . it wasn't I, my little Marie . . .

MAID: And who was it? Who was it then? Me?

PROFESSOR: I don't know . . . maybe . . .

MAID: Or the cat?

PROFESSOR: That's possible . . . I don't know . . .

MAID: And today makes it the fortieth time! . . . And every day it's the same thing! Every day! You should be ashamed, at your age . . . and you're going to make yourself sick! You won't have any pupils left. That will serve you right.

PROFESSOR *(irritated)*: It wasn't my fault! She didn't want to learn! She was disobedient! She was a bad pupil! She didn't want to learn!

MAID: Liar! . . .

PROFESSOR *(craftily approaching the Maid, holding the knife behind his back)*: It's none of your business! *(He tries to strike her with a great blow of the knife; the Maid seizes his wrist in mid-gesture and twists it; the Professor lets the knife fall to the floor.)* . . . I'm sorry!

MAID *(gives him two loud, strong slaps; the Professor falls onto the floor, on his prat; he sobs)*: Little mur-derer! bastard! You're disgusting! You wanted to do that to me? I'm not one of your pupils, not me! *(She pulls him up by the collar, picks up his skullcap and puts it on his head; he's afraid she'll slap him again and holds his arm up to protect his face, like a child.)* Put the knife back where it belongs, go on! *(The Pro-fessor goes and puts it back in the drawer of the buf-fet, then comes back to her.)* Now didn't I warn you, just a little while ago: arithmetic leads to philology, and philology leads to crime . . .

PROFESSOR: You said "to calamity"!

MAID: It's the same thing.

PROFESSOR: I didn't understand you. I thought that "calamity" was a city and that you meant that philol-ogy leads to the city of Calamity . . .

MAID: Liar! Old fox! An intellectual like you is not going to make a mistake in the meanings of words. Don't try to pull the wool over my eyes.

PROFESSOR *(sobbing)*: I didn't kill her on purpose!

MAID: Are you sorry at least?

PROFESSOR: Oh, yes, Marie, I swear it to you!

MAID: I can't help feeling sorry for you! Ah! you're a good boy in spite of everything! I'll try to fix this. But don't start it again . . . it could give you a heart attack . . .

PROFESSOR: Yes, Marie! What are we going to do, now?

MAID: We're going to bury her . . . along with the thirty-nine others . . . that will make forty coffins . . . I'll call the undertakers and my lover, Father Au-guste . . . I'll order the wreaths . . .

PROFESSOR: Yes, Marie, thank you very much.

MAID: Well, that's that. And perhaps it won't be neces-sary to call Auguste, since you yourself are something of a priest at times, if one can believe the gossip.

PROFESSOR: In any case, don't spend too much on the wreaths. She didn't pay for her lesson.

MAID: Don't worry . . . The least you can do is cover her up with her smock, she's not decent that way. And then we'll carry her out . . .

PROFESSOR: Yes, Marie, yes. *(He covers up the body.)* There's a chance that we'll get pinched° . . . with forty coffins . . . Don't you think . . . people will be surprised . . . Suppose they ask us what's inside them?

MAID: Don't worry so much. We'll say that they're empty. And besides, people won't ask questions, they're used to it.

PROFESSOR: Even so . . .

MAID *(she takes out an armband with an insignia, per-haps the Nazi swastika)*: Wait, if you're afraid, wear this, then you won't have anything more to be afraid of. *(She puts the armband around his arm.)* . . . That's good politics.

PROFESSOR: Thanks, my little Marie. With this, I won't need to worry . . . You're a good girl, Marie . . . Very loyal . . .

MAID: That's enough. Come on, sir. Are you all right?

PROFESSOR: Yes, my little Marie. *(The Maid and the Professor take the body of the young girl, one by the shoulders, the other by the legs, and move towards the door on the right.)* Be careful. We don't want to hurt her.

(They exit. The stage remains empty for several mo-ments. We hear the doorbell ring at the left.)

VOICE OF THE MAID: Just a moment, I'm coming!

(She appears as she was at the beginning of the play, and goes towards the door. The doorbell rings again.)

MAID *(aside)*: She's certainly in a hurry, this one! *(Aloud:)* Just a moment! *(She goes to the door on the left, and opens it.)* Good morning, miss! You are the new pupil? You have come for the lesson? The Pro-fessor is expecting you. I'll go tell him that you've come. He'll be right down. Come in, miss, come in!

---

pinched: Caught.

Bertolt Brecht

Among the most inventive and influential of modern playwrights, Bertolt Brecht (1898–1956) has left a legacy of important plays and theories about how those plays should be produced. Throughout most of his career he felt that drama should inform and awaken sensibilities, not just entertain or anesthetize an audience. Most of his plays concern philosophical and political issues, and some of them so threatened the Nazi regime that his works were burned publicly in Germany during the Third Reich.

At nineteen, Brecht worked as an orderly in a hospital during the last months of World War I. Seeing so much carnage and misery in the medical wards made him a lifelong pacifist. After the war he began writing plays while a student in Munich. His first successes in the Munich theater took the form of commentary on returned war veterans and on the questions of duty and heroism — which he treated negatively. His rejection of spiritual concepts was influenced by his readings of Hegel and the doctrines of Marx's dialectical materialism. Marx's theories predicted class struggles and based most social values in economic realities. Brecht eventually moved to Berlin, the theatrical center of Germany, and by 1926 was on his way to becoming a Communist.

Finding the political pressures in early Nazi Germany too frightening and dangerous for his writing, Brecht went into exile in 1933. He lived for a time in Scandinavia and later in the United States. After World War II Brecht and his wife returned to Berlin where, in 1949, he founded the Berliner Ensemble, which produced most of his later work. Brecht chose East Berlin as his home, in part because he felt his work could best be understood in a Communist setting. One irony is that his work has been even more widely appreciated and accepted in the West than in the former Communist eastern bloc.

Brecht wrote his most popular play in 1928, a musical in collaboration with the German composer Kurt Weill: *The Threepenny Opera*. The model for this play, the English writer John Gay's 1728 ballad opera *The Beggar's Opera*, provided Brecht with a perfect platform on which to comment satirically on the political and economic circumstances in Germany two hundred years after Gay wrote. The success of the Brecht-Weill collaboration — the work is still performed regularly — is due in part to Brecht's capacity to create appealing underworld characters such as Polly Peachum and Macheath, known as Mack the Knife. Brecht's wife, Helene Weigel, played Mrs. Peachum, the madam of the brothel in which the action takes place. Kurt Weill's second wife, Lotte Lenya, was an overnight sensation in the part of Jenny. She had a highly acclaimed reprise in New York almost twenty-five years later.

Brecht's most successful plays are *Galileo* (1938–1939), *Mother Courage* (1939), *The Good Woman of Setzuan* (1943), *The Private Lives of the Master Race* (1945), and *The Caucasian Chalk Circle* (1948). But these represent only a tiny fraction of a mass of work, including plays, poetry, criticism, and fiction.

His output is extraordinary in volume and quality. It includes plays borrowed not only from Gay but also from Sophocles, Molière, Gorky, Shakespeare, and John Webster, among others.

Brecht developed a number of theories regarding drama. He used the term *epic theater* to distinguish his own theater from traditional Aristotelian drama. Brecht expected his audience to observe critically, to draw conclusions, and to participate in an intellectual argument with the work at hand. The confrontational relationship he intended was designed to engage the audience in analyzing what they saw rather than in identifying with the main characters or in enjoying a wash of sentimentality or emotion.

One of the ways Brecht achieved his ends was by making the theatricality of the production's props, lights, sets, and equipment visible, thereby reminding the members of the audience that they were seeing a play. He used the term ALIENATION to define the effect he wanted his theater to have on an audience. He hoped that by alienating his audience from the drama he would keep them emotionally detached and intellectually alert. Brecht's theater was political. He saw a connection between an audience that could analyze theater critically and an audience that could analyze reality critically — and see that social, political, and economic conditions were not "natural" or fixed immutably but could (and should) be changed.

Brecht's theories produced interesting results and helped stimulate audiences that expected to be entertained by realistic or sentimental plays. His style spread rapidly throughout the world of theater, and it is still being used and developed by contemporary playwrights such as Heiner Müller and performers such as Pina Bausch.

MOTHER COURAGE

Since *Mother Courage* was first produced in 1941 in Zurich, it has become a classic of modern theater, performed successfully in the United States and most other Western countries. Brecht conceived of the drama as a powerful antiwar play. He set it in Germany during the Thirty Years' War, in which the German Protestants, supported by countries such as France, Denmark, and England, fought against the Hapsburg empire, which was allied with the Holy Roman Empire and the German Catholic princes. The war was actually a combination of many wars fought during the period of thirty years. It was bloody and seemingly interminable, devastating Germany's towns and citizenry as well as its agriculture and commerce. The armies fought to control territory, economic markets, and the religious differences between German Lutherans and Roman Catholics.

Brecht was not interested in the immediate causes underlying the Thirty Years' War. He was making a case against war entirely, regardless of its cause. To do this, he deliberately avoided making his play realistic. The stage setting is essentially barren; and the play is structured in scenes that are very intense but that avoid any sense of continuity of action. Audiences cannot become involved in unfolding action; they must always remain conscious of themselves as audience. Moreover, the lighting is high intensity, almost cruel at times, spotlighting the action in a way that is completely unnatural. In the early productions, Brecht included slide projections of the headings that accompany each of the twelve scenes so that the audience was always reminded of the presence of the playwright and the fact that they were seeing a play. These headings provided yet another break in the continuity of the action.

Although the printed text does not convey it, the play as Brecht produced it employed long silences, some of which were unsettling to the audience. When Swiss Cheese, Mother Courage's "honest" son, has a moment of rest in scene 3, he is in an intense ring of stage light as he comments on sitting in the sun in his shirtsleeves. He is relaxing for the last time, and the intensity of the light becomes an ironic device: it exposes him as a thief, and he is dragged off to his death as a result of having stolen the cash box from the regiment. Swiss Cheese has been corrupted by the war, just as virtually everyone is corrupted.

Mother Courage herself lives off the war by selling goods to the soldiers. She and her children haul their wagon across the battlefields with no concern for who is winning, who is losing, or even where they are. Her only ambition is to stock her wagon, sell her goods, and make sure she does not get stuck with any useless inventory. When the chaplain tells her that peace has broken out, she laments their condition because without war the family has no livelihood.

As Mother Courage continues to pull her wagon across field after field, she learns how to survive. But she also loses her children, one by one, to the war. Eilif, seduced into joining the army by a recruitment officer, is led into battle thinking that war is a heroic adventure. Swiss Cheese thinks he found a good deal in a paymaster's uniform. Both are wrong: there is no security in war, and they eventually perish.

Kattrin, the daughter, is likewise a victim of the violence of war. Having been violated by a Swedish soldier, she becomes mute. Near the end of the play she is treated violently again, and the terrible scar on her face leaves her unmarriageable. At the end Kattrin dies while sounding an alarm to give the sleeping town warning of an imminent attack.

Finally, Mother Courage is left alone. She picks up her wagon and finds that she can maneuver it herself. The play ends as she circles the stage, with everything around her consumed by war.

Brecht's stated intentions were somewhat thwarted by the reactions of the play's first audiences. They were struck by the power of Brecht's characterization of Mother Courage and treated her with immense sympathy. They saw her as an indomitable woman whose strength in the face of adversity was so great that she could not be overwhelmed. But Brecht intended the audience to analyze Mother Courage further and to see in her a reflection of society's wrong values. She conducts business on the field of battle, paying no attention to the moral question of war itself. She makes her living from the war but cannot see that it is the war that causes her anguish.

In response to the audiences' sympathetic reactions, Brecht revised the play, adding new lines to help audiences see the venality of Mother Courage's motives. But subsequent audiences have continued to treat her as a survivor —

almost a biblical figure. Brecht's German critics saw her as a model for one who endures all the terrors of war and yet remains a testament for the resilience of humankind. No matter how one decides to interpret her, Mother Courage remains one of the most unusual and haunting characters in modern drama.

Mother Courage in Performance

Brecht wrote *Mother Courage* in three months, beginning in September 1939, while he and Helene Weigel were in Sweden in exile from Nazi Germany. Its first production was on April 19, 1941, in Zurich, Switzerland, while Brecht waited in Sweden for entry papers to the United States. Brecht and Weigel returned to Europe after the war. In 1948 they went to East Berlin to work with a new theater group explicitly to produce *Mother Courage* with Helene Weigel in the title role in January 1949. In October 1950 Brecht directed Thérèsa Giehse as Courage in Munich. Other productions were staged in provincial German towns and in other European cities, such as Rotterdam and Paris, both in 1951.

Brecht's productions are sometimes regarded as "canonical," although contemporary directors often modify his original plans. He usually began the performance with a half-curtain and a four-person orchestra playing an overture. Next, an unseen record player played a song associated with Courage; as Courage came on stage, she sang the second verse of her song herself. The stage had only a CYCLORAMA, a large curved curtain used as a backdrop, and a circle marked on the floor. This defined the space that was Mother Courage's world, and various sets were placed on the circle to accommodate successive scenes. The circle itself was a revolving turntable on which the wagon moved, going essentially nowhere. Brecht used placards to indicate changes in time and place as well as to indicate events in the life of Mother Courage and her children. The lighting was generally bright, and the effect was lively and colorful.

Brecht was not widely produced in the West during the cold war, but Leon Epp directed *Mother Courage* at the Volkstheater in Vienna in 1963. In the same year Jerome Robbins produced the play at the Martin Beck Theatre on Broadway, with sets by Ming Cho Lee. Anne Bancroft played Mother Courage, and Zohra Lampert was Kattrin. The reviews praised Bancroft for achieving a "lonely magnificence" at the end of the play and maintained that Brecht produced a considerable emotional intensity despite his theoretical distaste for such effects.

The next year Joseph Slowik produced the play in the Goodman Theater in Chicago with a partial student cast and the distinguished Eugenie Leontovich as Mother Courage. In England *Mother Courage* was produced twice in the 1950s in London. In 1961 and 1965 it was produced by the Old Vic. Numerous local theaters put on the play in the late 1960s and 1970s. In 1980 Ntozake Shange adapted it for its second New York production and reset it in the period after the American Civil War; Gloria Foster and Morgan Freeman had the major roles. Frank Rich praised the acting and the energy of the play but feared that Brecht's original vision was altered almost beyond recognition: Mother Courage becomes "an innocent victim of an entire system," which is exactly what Brecht argued against.

The Royal Shakespeare Company produced the play in London in 1984 with Judi Dench as Courage and Zoë Wanamaker as Kattrin. Both received fine reviews, as did the production itself. Diana Rigg was Mother Courage in the production at the Olivier Theatre in London (November 1995–January 1996), which featured a new colloquial translation by the playwright David Hare and which reset the play in the period of World War I. Like all these productions, it maintained the circular set that Brecht had originally used and experimented with Brecht's theories of alienation and distancing. The success of these productions indicates the play's appeal for our time.

Bertolt Brecht (1898–1956)

MOTHER COURAGE AND HER CHILDREN   *1939*
A CHRONICLE OF THE THIRTY YEARS' WAR

TRANSLATED BY JOHN WILLETT

Characters

MOTHER COURAGE
KATTRIN, *her dumb daughter*
EILIF, *the elder son*
SWISS CHEESE, *the younger son*
THE RECRUITER
THE SERGEANT
THE COOK
THE GENERAL
THE CHAPLAIN
THE ARMOURER
YVETTE POTTER
THE MAN WITH THE PATCH
ANOTHER SERGEANT
THE ANCIENT COLONEL
A CLERK
A YOUNG SOLDIER
AN OLDER SOLDIER
A PEASANT
THE PEASAN'TS WIFE
THE YOUNG MAN
THE OLD WOMAN
ANOTHER PEASANT
HIS WIFE
THE YOUNG PEASANT
THE ENSIGN
SOLDIERS
A VOICE

SCENE 1

(*Spring 1624. The Swedish Commander-in-Chief Count Oxenstierna is raising troops in Dalecarlia for the Polish campaign. The canteen woman Anna Fierling, known under the name of Mother Courage, loses one son.*)
(*Country road near a town.*)
(*A sergeant and a recruiter stand shivering.*)

RECRUITER: How can you muster a unit in a place like this? I've been thinking about suicide, sergeant. Here am I, got to find our commander four companies before the twelfth of the month, and people round here are so nasty I can't sleep nights. S'pose I get hold of some bloke and shut my eye to his pigeon chest and varicose veins, I get him proper drunk, he signs on the line, I'm just settling up, he goes for a piss, I follow him to the door because I smell a rat; bob's your uncle, he's off like a flea with the itch. No notion of word of honour, loyalty, faith, sense of duty. This place has shattered my confidence in the human race, sergeant.

SERGEANT: It's too long since they had a war here; stands to reason. Where's their sense of morality to come from? Peace — that's just a mess; takes a war to restore order. Peacetime, the human race runs wild. People and cattle get buggered about, who cares? Everyone eats just as he feels inclined, a hunk of cheese on top of his nice white bread, and a slice of fat on top of the cheese. How many young blokes and good horses in that town there, nobody knows; they never thought of counting. I been in places ain't seen a war for nigh seventy years: folks hadn't got names to them, couldn't tell one another apart. Takes a war to get proper nominal rolls and inventories — shoes in bundles and corn in bags, and man and beast properly numbered and carted off, cause it stands to reason: no order, no war.

RECRUITER: Too true.

SERGEANT: Same with all good things, it's a job to get a war going. But once it's blossomed out there's no holding it; folk start fighting shy of peace like punters what can't stop for fear of having to tot up what they lost. Before that it's war they're fighting shy of. It's something new to them.

RECRUITER: Hey, here's a cart coming. Two tarts with two young fellows. Stop her, sergeant. If this one's a flop I'm not standing around in your spring winds any longer, I can tell you.

(*Sound of a jew's-harp. Drawn by two young fellows, a covered cart rolls in. On it sit Mother Courage and her dumb daughter Kattrin.*)

MOTHER COURAGE: Morning, sergeant.

SERGEANT (*blocking the way*): Morning, all. And who are you?

MOTHER COURAGE: Business folk. (*Sings.*)

> You captains, tell the drums to slacken
> And give your infanteers a break:
> It's Mother Courage with her waggon
> Full of the finest boots they make.
> With crawling lice and looted cattle
> With lumbering guns and straggling kit —
> How can you flog them into battle
> Unless you get them boots that fit?
>> The new year's come. The watchmen shout.
>> The thaw sets in. The dead remain.
>> Whatever life has not died out
>> It staggers to its feet again.
>
> Captains, how can you make them face it —
> Marching to death without a brew?
> Courage has rum with which to lace it
> And boil their souls and bodies through.
> Their musket primed, their stomach hollow —
> Captains, your men don't look so well.
> So feed them up and let them follow
> While you command them into hell.
>> The new year's come. The watchmen shout.
>> The thaw sets in. The dead remain.
>> Wherever life has not died out
>> It staggers to its feet again.

SERGEANT: Halt! Who are you with, you trash?

THE ELDER SON: Second Finnish Regiment.

SERGEANT: Where's your papers?

MOTHER COURAGE: Papers?

THE YOUNGER SON: What, mean to say you don't know Mother Courage?

SERGEANT: Never heard of her. What's she called Courage for?

MOTHER COURAGE: Courage is the name they gave me because I was scared of going broke, sergeant, so I drove me cart right through the bombardment of Riga with fifty loaves of bread aboard. They were going mouldy, it was high time, hadn't any choice really.

SERGEANT: Don't be funny with me. Your papers.

MOTHER COURAGE (*pulling a bundle of papers from a tin box and climbing down off the cart*): That's all my papers, sergeant. You'll find a whole big missal from Altötting in Bavaria for wrapping gherkins in, and a road map of Moravia, the Lord knows when I'll ever get there, might as well chuck it away, and here's a stamped certificate that my horse hasn't got foot-and-mouth, only he's dead worse luck, cost fifteen florins he did — not me luckily. That enough paper for you?

SERGEANT: You pulling my leg? I'll knock that sauce out of you. S'pose you know you got to have a licence.

MOTHER COURAGE: Talk proper to me, do you mind, and don't you dare say I'm pulling your leg in front of my unsullied children, 'tain't decent, I got no time for you. My honest face, that's me licence with the Second Regiment, and if it's too difficult for you to read there's nowt I can do about it. Nobody's putting a stamp on that.

RECRUITER: Sergeant, methinks I smell insubordination in this individual. What's needed in our camp is obedience.

MOTHER COURAGE: Sausage, if you ask me.

SERGEANT: Name.

MOTHER COURAGE: Anna Fierling.

SERGEANT: You all called Fierling then?

MOTHER COURAGE: What'd you mean? It's me's called Fierling, not them.

SERGEANT: Aren't all this lot your children?

MOTHER COURAGE: You bet they are, but why should they all have to be called the same, eh? (*Pointing to her elder son.*) For instance, that one's called Eilif Nojocki — Why? his father always claimed he was called Kojocki or Mojocki or something. The boy remembers him clearly, except that the one he remembers was someone else, a Frenchie with a little beard. Aside from that he's got his father's wits; that man knew how to snitch a peasant's pants off his bum without him noticing. This way each of us has his own name, see.

SERGEANT: What, each one different?

MOTHER COURAGE: Don't tell me you ain't never come across that.

SERGEANT: So I s'pose he's a Chinaman? (*Pointing to the younger son.*)

MOTHER COURAGE: Wrong. Swiss.

SERGEANT: After the Frenchman?

MOTHER COURAGE: What Frenchman? I never heard tell of no Frenchman. You keep muddling things up, we'll be hanging around here till dark. A Swiss, but called Fejos, and the name has nowt to do with his father. He was called something quite different and was a fortifications engineer, only drunk all the time.

(*Swiss Cheese beams and nods; dumb Kattrin too is amused.*)

SERGEANT: How in hell can he be called Fejos?

MOTHER COURAGE: I don't like to be rude, sergeant, but

you ain't got much imagination, have you? Course he's called Fejos, because when he arrived I was with a Hungarian, very decent fellow, had terrible kidney trouble though he never touched a drop. The boy takes after him.

SERGEANT: But he wasn't his father . . .

MOTHER COURAGE: Took after him just the same. I call him Swiss Cheese. (*Pointing to her daughter.*) And that's Kattrin Haupt, she's half German.

SERGEANT: Nice family, I must say.

MOTHER COURAGE: Aye, me cart and me have seen the world.

SERGEANT: I'm writing all this down. (*He writes.*) And you're from Bamberg in Bavaria; how d'you come to be here?

MOTHER COURAGE: Can't wait till war chooses to visit Bamberg, can I?

RECRUITER (*to Eilif*): You two should be called Jacob Ox and Esau Ox, pulling the cart like that. I s'pose you never get out of harness?

EILIF: Ma, can I clobber him one? I wouldn't half like to.

MOTHER COURAGE: And I says you can't; just you stop where you are. And now two fine officers like you, I bet you could use a good pistol, or a belt buckle, yours is on its last legs, sergeant.

SERGEANT: I could use something else. Those boys are healthy as young birch trees, I observe: chests like barrels, solid leg muscles. So why are they dodging their military service, may I ask?

MOTHER COURAGE (*quickly*): Nowt doing, sergeant. Yours is no trade for my kids.

RECRUITER: But why not? There's good money in it, glory too. Flogging boots is women's work. (*To Eilif.*) Come here, let's see if you've muscles in you or if you're a chicken.

MOTHER COURAGE: He's a chicken. Give him a fierce look, he'll fall over.

RECRUITER: Killing a young bull that happens to be in his way. (*Wants to lead him off.*)

MOTHER COURAGE: Let him alone, will you? He's nowt for you folk.

RECRUITER: He was crudely offensive and talked about clobbering me. The two of us are going to step into that field and settle it man to man.

EILIF: Don't you worry, mum, I'll fix him.

MOTHER COURAGE: Stop there! You varmint! I know you, nowt but fights. There's a knife down his boot. A slasher, that's what he is.

RECRUITER: I'll draw it out of him like a milk-tooth. Come along, sonny.

MOTHER COURAGE: Sergeant, I'll tell the colonel. He'll have you both in irons. The lieutenant's going out with my daughter.

SERGEANT: No rough stuff, chum. (*To Mother Courage.*) What you got against military service? Wasn't his own father a soldier? Died a soldier's death, too? Said it yourself.

MOTHER COURAGE: He's nowt but a child. You want to

take him off to slaughterhouse, I know you lot. They'll give you five florins for him.

RECRUITER: First he's going to get a smart cap and boots, eh?

EILIF: Not from you.

MOTHER COURAGE: Let's both go fishing, said angler to worm. (*To Swiss Cheese.*) Run off, call out they're trying to kidnap your brother. (*She pulls a knife.*) Go on, you kidnap him, just try. I'll slit you open, trash. I'll teach you to make war with him. We're doing an honest trade in ham and linen, and we're peaceable folk.

SERGEANT: Peaceable I don't think; look at your knife. You should be ashamed of yourself; put that knife away, you old harridan. A minute back you were admitting you live off the war, how else should you live, what from? But how's anyone to have war without soldiers?

MOTHER COURAGE: No need for it to be my kids.

SERGEANT: Oh, you'd like war to eat the pips but spit out the apple? It's to fatten up your kids, but you won't invest in it. Got to look after itself, eh? And you called Courage, fancy that. Scared of the war that keeps you going? Your sons aren't scared of it, I can see that.

EILIF: Take more than a war to scare me.

SERGEANT: And why? Look at me: has army life done all that badly by me? Joined up at seventeen.

MOTHER COURAGE: Still got to reach seventy.

SERGEANT: I don't mind waiting.

MOTHER COURAGE: Under the sod, eh?

SERGEANT: You trying to insult me, saying I'll die?

MOTHER COURAGE: S'pose it's true? S'pose I can see the mark's on you? S'pose you look like a corpse on leave to me? Eh?

SWISS CHEESE: She's got second sight, Mother has.

RECRUITER: Go ahead, tell the sergeant's fortune, might amuse him.

MOTHER COURAGE: Gimme helmet. (*He gives it to her.*)

SERGEANT: It don't mean a bloody sausage. Anything for a laugh though.

MOTHER COURAGE (*taking out a sheet of parchment and tearing it up*): Eilif, Swiss Cheese and Kattrin, may all of us be torn apart like this if we lets ourselves get too mixed up in the war. (*To the sergeant.*) Just for you I'm doing it for free. Black's for death. I'm putting a big black cross on this slip of paper.

SWISS CHEESE: Leaving the other one blank, see?

MOTHER COURAGE: Then I fold them across and shake them. All of us is jumbled together like this from our mother's womb, and now draw a slip and you'll know. (*The sergeant hesitates.*)

RECRUITER (*to Eilif*): I don't take just anybody, they all know I'm choosey, but you got the kind of fire I like to see.

SERGEANT (*fishing in the helmet*): Too silly. Load of eyewash.

SWISS CHEESE: Drawn a black cross, he has. Write him off.

RECRUITER: They're having you on; not everybody's name's on a bullet.

SERGEANT (*hoarsely*): You've put me in the shit.

MOTHER COURAGE: Did that yourself the day you became a soldier. Come along, let's move on now. 'Tain't every day we have a war, I got to get stirring.

SERGEANT: God damn it, you can't kid me. We're taking that bastard of yours for a soldier.

EILIF: Swiss Cheese'd like to be a soldier too.

MOTHER COURAGE: First I've heard of that. You'll have to draw too, all three of you. (*She goes to the rear to mark crosses on further slips.*)

RECRUITER (*to Eilif*): One of the things they say against us is that it's all holy-holy in the Swedish camp; but that's a malicious rumour to do us down. There's no hymn-singing but Sundays, just a single verse, and then only for those got voices.

MOTHER COURAGE (*coming back with the slips, which she drops into the sergeant's helmet*): Trying to get away from their ma, the devils, off to war like calves to salt-lick. But I'm making you draw lots, and that'll show you the world is no vale of joys with "Come along, son, we need a few more generals." Sergeant, I'm so scared they won't get through the war. Such dreadful characters, all three of them. (*She hands the helmet to Eilif.*) Hey, come on, fish out your slip. (*He fishes one out, unfolds it. She snatches it from him.*) There you are, it's a cross. Oh, wretched mother that I am, o pain-racked giver of birth! Shall he die? Aye, in the springtime of life he is doomed. If he becomes a soldier he shall bite the dust, it's plain to see. He is too foolhardy, like his dad was. And if he ain't sensible he'll go the way of all flesh, his slip proves it. (*Shouts at him.*) You going to be sensible?

EILIF: Why not?

MOTHER COURAGE: Sensible thing is stay with your mother, never mind if they poke fun at you and call you chicken, just you laugh.

RECRUITER: If you're pissing in your pants I'll make do with your brother.

MOTHER COURAGE: I told you laugh. Go on, laugh. Now you draw, Swiss Cheese. I'm not so scared on account you're honest. (*He fishes in the helmet.*) Oh, why look at your slip in that strange way? It's got to be a blank. There can't be any cross on it. Surely I'm not going to lose *you*. (*She takes the slip.*) A cross? What, you too? Is that because you're so simple, perhaps? O Swiss Cheese, you too will be sunk if you don't stay utterly honest all the while, like I taught you from childhood when you brought the change back from the baker's. Else you can't save yourself. Look, sergeant, that's a black cross, ain't it?

SERGEANT: A cross, that's right. Can't think how I come to get one. I always stay in the rear. (*To the recruiter.*) There's no catch. Her own family get it too.

SWISS CHEESE: I get it too. But I listen to what I'm told.

MOTHER COURAGE (*to Kattrin*): And now you're the only one I know's all right, you're a cross yourself; got a kind heart you have. (*Holds the helmet up to*

her on the cart, but takes the slip out herself.) No, that's too much. That can't be right; must have made a mistake shuffling. Don't be too kind-hearted, Kattrin, you'll have to give it up, there's a cross above your path too. Lie doggo, girl, it can't be that hard once you're born dumb. Right, all of you know now. Look out for yourselves, you'll need to. And now up we get and on we go. (*She climbs on to the cart.*)

RECRUITER (*to the sergeant*): Do something.

SERGEANT: I don't feel very well.

RECRUITER: Must of caught a chill taking your helmet off in that wind. Involve her in a deal. (*Aloud.*) Might as well have a look at that belt-buckle, sergeant. After all, our friends here have to live by their business. Hey, you people, the sergeant wants to buy that belt-buckle.

MOTHER COURAGE: Half a florin. Two florins is what a belt like that's worth. (*Climbs down again.*)

SERGEANT: 'Tain't new. Let me get out of this damned wind and have a proper look at it. (*Goes behind the cart with the buckle.*)

MOTHER COURAGE: Ain't what I call windy.

SERGEANT: I s'pose it might be worth half a florin, it's silver.

MOTHER COURAGE (*joining him behind the cart*): It's six solid ounces.

RECRUITER (*to Eilif*): And then we men'll have one together. Got your bounty money here, come along. (*Eilif stands undecided.*)

MOTHER COURAGE: Half a florin it is.

SERGEANT: It beats me. I'm always at the rear. Sergeant's the safest job there is. You can send the others up front, cover themselves with glory. Me dinner hour's properly spoiled. Shan't be able to hold nowt down, I know.

MOTHER COURAGE: Mustn't let it prey on you so's you can't eat. Just stay at the rear. Here, take a swig of brandy, man. (*Gives him a drink.*)

RECRUITER (*has taken Eilif by the arm and is leading him away up stage*): Ten florins bounty money, then you're a gallant fellow fighting for the king and women'll be after you like flies. And you can clobber me for free for insulting you.

(*Exeunt both.°*)

(*Dumb Kattrin leans down from the cart and makes hoarse noises.*)

MOTHER COURAGE: All right, Kattrin, all right. Sergeant's just paying. (*Bites the half-florin.*) I got no faith in any kind of money. Burnt child, that's me, sergeant. This coin's good, though. And now let's get moving. Where's Eilif?

SWISS CHEESE: Went off with the recruiter.

MOTHER COURAGE (*stands quite still, then*): You simpleton. (*To Kattrin.*) 'Tain't your fault, you can't speak, I know.

SERGEANT: Could do with a swig yourself, ma. That's

Exeunt both: They both leave.

life. Plenty worse thing's than being a soldier. Want to live off war, but keep yourself and family out of it, eh?

MOTHER COURAGE: You'll have to help your brother pull now, Kattrin.

(*Brother and sister hitch themselves to the cart and start pulling. Mother Courage walks alongside. The cart rolls on.*)

SERGEANT (*looking after them*):
    Like the war to nourish you?
    Have to feed it something too.

SCENE 2

(*In the years 1625 and 1626 Mother Courage crosses Poland in the train of the Swedish armies. Before the fortress of Wallhof she meets her son again. Successful sale of a capon and heyday of her dashing son.*)
(*The general's tent.*)
(*Beside it, his kitchen. Thunder of cannon. The cook is arguing with Mother Courage, who wants to sell him a capon.*)

THE COOK: Sixty hellers for a miserable bird like that?

MOTHER COURAGE: Miserable bird? This fat brute? Mean to say some greedy old general — and watch your step if you got nowt for his dinner — can't afford sixty hellers for him?

THE COOK: I can get a dozen like that for ten hellers just down the road.

MOTHER COURAGE: What, a capon like this you can get just down the road? In time of siege, which means hunger that tears your guts. A rat you might get: "might" I say because they're all being gobbled up, five men spending best part of day chasing one hungry rat. Fifty hellers for a giant capon in time of siege!

THE COOK: But it ain't us having the siege, it's t'other side. We're conducting the siege, can't you get that in your head?

MOTHER COURAGE: But we got nowt to eat too, even worse than them in the town. Took it with them, didn't they? They're having a high old time, everyone says. And look at us! I been to the peasants, there's nowt there.

THE COOK: There's plenty. They're sitting on it.

MOTHER COURAGE (*triumphantly*): They ain't. They're bust, that's what they are. Just about starving. I saw some, were grubbing up roots from sheer hunger, licking their fingers after they boiled some old leather strap. That's way it is. And me got a capon here and supposed to take forty hellers for it.

THE COOK: Thirty, not forty. I said thirty.

MOTHER COURAGE: Here, this ain't just any old capon. It was such a gifted beast, I been told, it could only eat to music, had a military march of its own. It could count, it was that intelligent. And you say forty hellers is too much? General will make mincemeat of you if there's nowt on his table.

THE COOK: See what I'm doing? (*He takes a piece of beef and puts his knife to it.*) Here I got a bit of beef, I'm going to roast it. Make up your mind quick.

MOTHER COURAGE: Go on, roast it. It's last year's.

THE COOK: Last night's. That animal was still alive and kicking, I saw him myself.

MOTHER COURAGE: Alive and stinking, you mean.

THE COOK: I'll cook him five hours if need be. I'll just see if he's still tough. (*He cuts into it.*)

MOTHER COURAGE: Put plenty of pepper on it so his lordship the general don't smell the pong.

(*The general, a chaplain and Eilif enter the tent.*)

THE GENERAL (*slapping Eilif on the shoulder*): Now then, Eilif my son, into your general's tent with you and sit thou at my right hand. For you accomplished a deed of heroism, like a pious cavalier; and doing what you did for God, and in a war of religion at that, is something I commend in you most highly, you shall have a gold bracelet as soon as we've taken this town. Here we are, come to save their souls for them, and what do those insolent dung-encrusted yokels go and do? Drive their beef away from us. They stuff it into those priests of theirs all right, back and front, but you taught 'em manners, ha! So here's a pot of red wine for you, the two of us'll knock it back at one gulp. (*They do so.*) Piss all for the chaplain, the old bigot. And now, what would you like for dinner, my darling?

EILIF: A bit of meat, why not?

THE GENERAL: Cook! Meat!

THE COOK: And then he goes and brings guests when there's nowt there.

(*Mother Courage silences him so she can listen.*)

EILIF: Hungry job cutting down peasants.

MOTHER COURAGE: Jesus Christ, it's my Eilif.

THE COOK: Your what?

MOTHER COURAGE: My eldest boy. It's two years since I lost sight of him, they pinched him from me on the road, must think well of him if the general's asking him to dinner, and what kind of a dinner can you offer? Nowt. You heard what the visitor wishes to eat: meat. Take my tip, you settle for the capon, it'll be a florin.

THE GENERAL (*has sat down with Eilif, and bellows*): Food, Lamb, you foul cook, or I'll have your hide.

THE COOK: Give it over, dammit, this is blackmail.

MOTHER COURAGE: Didn't someone say it was a miserable bird?

THE COOK: Miserable; give it over, and a criminal price, fifty hellers.

MOTHER COURAGE: A florin, I said. For my eldest boy, the general's guest, no expense is too great for me.

THE COOK (*gives her the money*): You might at least pluck it while I see to the fire.

MOTHER COURAGE (*sits down to pluck the fowl*): He won't half be surprised to see me. He's my dashing clever son. Then I got a stupid one too, he's honest

Lotte Lenya as Mother Courage pulling her wagon in Brecht's 1979 Berliner Ensemble production of his play.

though. The girl's nowt. One good thing, she don't talk.

THE GENERAL: Drink up, my son, this is my best Falernian; only got a barrel or two left, but that's nothing to pay for a sign that there's still true faith to be found in my army. As for that shepherd of souls he can just look on, because all he does is preach, without the least idea how it's to be carried out. And now, my son Eilif, tell us more about the neat way you smashed those yokels and captured the twenty oxen. Let's hope they get here soon.

EILIF: A day or two at most.

MOTHER COURAGE: Thoughtful of our Eilif not to bring the oxen in till tomorrow, else you lot wouldn't have looked twice at my capon.

EILIF: Well, it was like this, see. I'd heard peasants had been driving the oxen they'd hidden, out of the forest into one particular wood, on the sly and mostly by night. That's where people from the town were

s'posed to come and pick them up. So I holds off and lets them drive their oxen together, reckoning they'd be better than me at finding 'em. I had my blokes slavering after the meat, cut their emergency rations even further for a couple of days till their mouths was watering at the least sound of any word beginning with "me-," like "measles" say.

THE GENERAL: Very clever of you.

EILIF: Possibly. The rest was a piece of cake. Except that the peasants had cudgels and outnumbered us three to one and made a murderous attack on us. Four of 'em shoved me into a thicket, knocked my sword from my hand and bawled out "Surrender!" What's the answer, I wondered; they're going to make mincemeat of me.

THE GENERAL: What did you do?

EILIF: I laughed.

THE GENERAL: You did what?

EILIF: Laughed. So we got talking. I put it on a business footing from the start, told them "Twenty florins a head's too much. I'll give you fifteen." As if I was meaning to pay. That threw them, and they began scratching their heads. In a flash I'd picked up my sword and was hacking 'em to pieces. Necessity's the mother of invention, eh, sir?

THE GENERAL: What is your view, pastor of souls?

THE CHAPLAIN: That phrase is not strictly speaking in the Bible, but when Our Lord turned the five loaves into five hundred there was no war on and he could tell people to love their neighbours as they'd had enough to eat. Today it's another story.

THE GENERAL (*laughs*): Quite another story. You can have a swig after all for that, you old Pharisee.° (*To Eilif.*) Hacked 'em to pieces, did you, so my gallant lads can get a proper bite to eat? What do the Scriptures say? "Whatsoever thou doest for the least of my brethren, thou doest for me." And what did you do for them? Got them a good square meal of beef, because they're not accustomed to mouldy bread, the old way was to fix a cold meal of rolls and wine in your helmet before you went out to fight for God.

EILIF: Aye, in a flash I'd picked up my sword and was hacking them to pieces.

THE GENERAL: You've the makings of a young Caesar. You ought to see the King.

EILIF: I have from a distance. He kind of glows. I'd like to model myself on him.

THE GENERAL: You've got something in common already. I appreciate soldiers like you, Eilif, men of courage. Somebody like that I treat as I would my own sort. (*He leads him over to the map.*) Have a look at the situation, Eilif; it's a long haul still.

MOTHER COURAGE (*who has been listening and now angrily plucks the fowl*): That must be a rotten general.

Pharisee: A member of a Jewish sect current in biblical days; the term is now commonly used to refer to a hypocritical, self-righteous person.

THE COOK: He's ravenous all right, but why rotten?

MOTHER COURAGE: Because he's got to have men of courage, that's why. If he knew how to plan a proper campaign what would he be needing men of courage for? Ordinary ones would do. It's always the same; whenever there's a load of special virtues around it means something stinks.

THE COOK: I thought it meant things is all right.

MOTHER COURAGE: No, that they stink. Look, s'pose some general or king is bone stupid and leads his men up shit creek, then those men've got to be fearless, there's another virtue for you. S'pose he's stingy and hires too few soldiers, then they got to be a crowd of Hercules's. And s'pose he's slapdash and don't give a bugger, then they got to be clever as monkeys else their number's up. Same way they got to show exceptional loyalty each time he gives them impossible jobs. Nowt but virtues no proper country and no decent king or general would ever need. In decent countries folk don't have to have virtues, the whole lot can be perfectly ordinary, average intelligence, and for all I know cowards.

THE GENERAL: I'll wager your father was a soldier.

EILIF: A great soldier, I been told. My mother warned me about it. There's a song I know.

THE GENERAL: Sing it to us. (*Roars.*) When's that dinner coming?

EILIF: It's called The Song of the Girl and the Soldier. (*He sings it, dancing a war dance with his sabre.*)

> The guns blaze away, and the bay'nit'll slay
> And the water can't hardly be colder.
> What's the answer to ice? Keep off's my advice!
> That's what the girl told the soldier.
> Next thing the soldier, wiv' a round up the spout
> Hears the band playing and gives a great shout:
> Why, it's marching what makes you a soldier!
> So it's down to the south and then northwards once
>   more:
> See him catching that bay'nit in his naked paw!
> That's what his comrades done told her.
>
> Oh, do not despise the advice of the wise
> Learn wisdom from those that are older
> And don't try for things that are out of your
>   reach —
> That's what the girl told the soldier.
> Next thing the soldier, his bay'nit in place
> Wades into the river and laughs in her face
> Though the water comes up to his shoulder.
> When the shingle roof glints in the light o' the
>   moon
> We'll be wiv' you again, not a moment too soon!
> That's what his comrades done told her.

MOTHER COURAGE (*takes up the song in the kitchen, beating on a pot with her spoon*):

> You'll go out like a light! And the sun'll take flight
> For your courage just makes us feel colder.

> Oh, that vanishing light! May God see that it's
>   right! —
> That's what the girl told the soldier.

EILIF: What's that?

MOTHER COURAGE (*continues singing*):

> Next thing the soldier, his bay'nit in place
> Was caught by the current and went down without
>   trace
> And the water couldn't hardly be colder.
> Then the shingle roof froze in the light o' the
>   moon
> As both soldier and ice drifted down to their
>   doom —
> And d'you know what his comrades done told her?
>
> He went out like a light. And the sunshine took
>   flight
> For his courage just made 'em feel colder.
> Oh, do not despise the advice of the wise!
> That's what the girl told the soldier.

THE GENERAL: The things they get up to in my kitchen these days.

EILIF (*Has gone into the kitchen. He flings his arms round his mother.*): Fancy seeing you again, ma! Where's the others?

MOTHER COURAGE (*in his arms*): Snug as a bug in a rug. They made Swiss Cheese paymaster of the Second Finnish; any road he'll stay out of fighting that way, I couldn't keep him out altogether.

EILIF: How's the old feet?

MOTHER COURAGE: Bit tricky getting me shoes on of a morning.

THE GENERAL (*has joined them*): So you're his mother, I hope you've got plenty more sons for me like this one.

EILIF: Ain't it my lucky day? You sitting out there in the kitchen, ma, hearing your son commended . . .

MOTHER COURAGE: You bet I heard. (*Slaps his face.*)

EILIF (*holding his cheek*): What's that for? Taking the oxen?

MOTHER COURAGE: No. Not surrendering when those four went for you and wanted to make mincemeat of you. Didn't I say you should look after yourself? You Finnish devil!

(*The general and the chaplain stand in the doorway laughing.*)

SCENE 3

(*Three years later Mother Courage is taken prisoner along with elements of a Finnish regiment. She manages to save her daughter, likewise her covered cart, but her honest son is killed.*)
(*Military camp.*)

(*Afternoon. A flagpole with the regimental pay. From her cart, festooned now with all kinds of goods, Mother Courage has stretched a washing line to a large cannon, across which she and Kattrin are folding the washing. She is bargaining at the same time with an armourer over a sack of shot. Swiss Cheese, now wearing a paymaster's uniform, is looking on. A comely person, Yvette Pottier, is sewing a gaily coloured hat, a glass of brandy before her. She is in her stockinged feet, having laid aside her red high-heeled boots.*)

THE ARMOURER: I'll let you have that shot for a couple of florins. It's cheap at the price, I got to have the money because the colonel's been boozing with his officers since two days back, and the drink's run out.

MOTHER COURAGE: That's troops' munitions. They catch me with that, I'm for court-martial. You crooks flog the shot, and troops got nowt to fire at enemy.

THE ARMOURER: Have a heart, can't you; you scratch my back and I'll scratch yours.

MOTHER COURAGE: I'm not taking army property. Not at that price.

THE ARMOURER: You can sell it on the q.t. tonight to the Fourth Regiment's armourer for five florins, eight even, if you let him have a receipt for twelve. He's right out of ammunition.

MOTHER COURAGE: Why not you do it?

THE ARMOURER: I don't trust him, he's a pal of mine.

MOTHER COURAGE (*takes the sack*): Gimme. (*To Kattrin.*) Take it away and pay him a florin and a half. (*The armourer protests.*) I said a florin and a half. (*Kattrin drags the sack upstage, the armourer following her. Mother Courage addresses Swiss Cheese.*) Here's your woollies, now look after them, it's October and autumn may set in any time. I ain't saying it's got to, cause I've learned nowt's got to come when you think it will, not even seasons of the year. But your regimental accounts got to add up right, come what may. Do they add up right?

SWISS CHEESE: Yes, mother.

MOTHER COURAGE: Don't you forget they made you paymaster cause you was honest, not dashing like your brother, and above all so stupid I bet you ain't even thought of clearing off with it, no not you. That's a big consolation to me. And don't lose those woollies.

SWISS CHEESE: No, mother, I'll put them under my mattress. (*Begins to go.*)

THE ARMOURER: I'll go along with you, paymaster.

MOTHER COURAGE: And don't you start learning him none of your tricks.

(*The armourer leaves with Swiss Cheese without any farewell gesture.*)

YVETTE (*waving to him*): No reason not to say goodbye, armourer.

MOTHER COURAGE (*to Yvette*): I don't like to see them together. He's wrong company for our Swiss Cheese. Oh well, war's off to a good start. Easily take four, five years before all countries are in. A bit of fore-sight, don't do nothing silly, and business'll flourish. Don't you know you ain't s'posed to drink before midday with your complaint?

YVETTE: Complaint, who says so, it's a libel.

MOTHER COURAGE: They all say so.

YVETTE: Because they're all telling lies, Mother Courage, and me at my wits' end cause they're all avoiding me like something the cat brought in thanks to those lies, what the hell am I remodelling my hat for? (*She throws it away.*) That's why I drink before midday. Never used to, gives you crows' feet, but now what the hell? All the Second Finnish know me. Ought to have stayed at home when my first fellow did me wrong. No good our sort being proud. Eat shit, that's what you got to do, or down you go.

MOTHER COURAGE: Now don't you start up again about that Pieter of yours and how it all happened, in front of my innocent daughter too.

YVETTE: She's the one should hear it, put her off love.

MOTHER COURAGE: Nobody can put 'em off that.

YVETTE: Then I'll go on, get it off my chest. It all starts with yours truly growing up in lovely Flanders, else I'd never of seen him and wouldn't be stuck here now in Poland, cause he was an army cook, fair-haired, a Dutchman but thin for once. Kattrin, watch out for the thin ones, only in those days I didn't know that, or that he'd got a girl already, or that they all called him Puffing Piet cause he never took his pipe out of his mouth when he was on the job, it meant that little to him. (*She sings the Song of Fraternisation.*)

When I was only sixteen
The foe came into our land.
He laid aside his sabre
And with a smile he took my hand.
After the May parade
The May light starts to fade.
The regiment dressed by the right
The drums were beaten, that's the drill.
The foe took us behind the hill
And fraternised all night.

There were so many foes then
But mine worked in the mess.
I loathed him in the daytime.
At night I loved him none the less.
After the May parade
The May light starts to fade.
The regiment dressed by the right
The drums were beaten, that's the drill.
The foe took us behind the hill
And fraternised all night.

The love which came upon me
Was wished on me by fate.
My friends could never grasp why
I found it hard to share their hate.
The fields were wet with dew
When sorrow first I knew.

The regiment dressed by the right
The drums were beaten, that's the drill.
And then the foe, my lover still
Went marching out of sight.

I followed him, fool that I was, but I never found him, and that was five years back. (*She walks unsteadily behind the cart.*)

MOTHER COURAGE: You left your hat here.

YVETTE: Anyone wants it can have it.

MOTHER COURAGE: Let that be a lesson, Kattrin. Don't you start anything with them soldiers. Love makes the world go round, I'm warning you. Even with fellows not in the army it's no bed of roses. He says he'd like to kiss the ground your feet walk on — reminds me, did you wash them yesterday? — and after that you're his skivvy. Be thankful you're dumb, then you can't contradict yourself and won't be wanting to bite your tongue off for speaking the truth; it's a godsend, being dumb is. And here comes the general's cook, now what's he after?

(*Enter the cook and the chaplain.*)

THE CHAPLAIN: I have a message for you from your son Eilif, and the cook has come along because you made such a profound impression on him.

THE COOK: I just came along to get a bit of air.

MOTHER COURAGE: That you can always do here if you behave yourself, and if you don't I can deal with you. What does he want? I got no spare cash.

THE CHAPLAIN: Actually I had a message for his brother the paymaster.

MOTHER COURAGE: He ain't here now nor anywhere else neither. He ain't his brother's paymaster. He's not to lead him into temptation nor be clever at his expense. (*Giving him money from the purse slung round her.*) Give him this, it's a sin, he's banking on mother's love and ought to be ashamed of himself.

THE COOK: Not for long, he'll have to be moving off with the regiment, might be to his death. Give him a bit extra, you'll be sorry later. You women are tough, then later on you're sorry. A little glass of brandy wouldn't have been a problem, but it wasn't offered and, who knows, a bloke may lie beneath the green sod and none of you people will ever be able to dig him up again.

THE CHAPLAIN: Don't give way to your feelings, cook. To fall in battle is a blessing, not an inconvenience, and why? It is a war of faith. None of your common wars but a special one, fought for the faith and therefore pleasing to God.

THE COOK: Very true. It's a war all right in one sense, what with requisitioning, murder and looting and the odd bit of rape thrown in, but different from all the other wars because it's a war of faith; stands to reason. But it's thirsty work at that, you must admit.

THE CHAPLAIN (*to Mother Courage, indicating the cook*): I tried to stop him, but he says he's taken a shine to you, you figure in his dreams.

THE COOK (*lighting a stumpy pipe*): Just want a glass of brandy from a fair hand, what harm in that? Only I'm groggy already cause the chaplain here's been telling such jokes all the way along you bet I'm still blushing.

MOTHER COURAGE: Him a clergyman too. I'd best give the pair of you a drink or you'll start making me immoral suggestions cause you've nowt else to do.

THE CHAPLAIN: Behold a temptation, said the court preacher, and fell. (*Turning back to look at Kattrin as he leaves.*) And who is this entrancing young person?

MOTHER COURAGE: That ain't an entrancing but a decent young person. (*The chaplain and the cook go behind the cart with Mother Courage. Kattrin looks after them, then walks away from her washing towards the hat. She picks it up and sits down, pulling the red boots towards her. Mother Courage can be heard in the background talking politics with the chaplain and the cook.*)

MOTHER COURAGE: Those Poles here in Poland had no business sticking their noses in. Right, our king moved in on them, horse and foot, but did they keep the peace? no, went and stuck their noses into their own affairs, they did, and fell on king just as he was quietly clearing off. They committed a breach of peace, that's what, so blood's on their own head.

THE CHAPLAIN: All our king minded about was freedom. The emperor had made slaves of them all, Poles and Germans alike, and the king had to liberate them.

THE COOK: Just what I say, your brandy's first rate, I weren't mistaken in your face, but talk of the king, it cost the king dear trying to give freedom to Germany, what with giving Sweden the salt tax, what cost the poor folk a bit, so I've heard, on top of which he had to have the Germans locked up and drawn and quartered cause they wanted to carry on slaving for the emperor. Course the king took a serious view when anybody didn't want to be free. He set out by just trying to protect Poland against bad people, particularly the emperor, then it started to become a habit till he ended up protecting the whole of Germany. They didn't half kick. So the poor old king's had nowt but trouble for all his kindness and expenses, and that's something he had to make up for by taxes of course, which caused bad blood, not that he'd let a little matter like that depress him. One thing he had on his side, God's word, that was a help. Because otherwise folk would of been saying he done it all for himself and to make a bit on the side. So he's always had a good conscience, which was the main point.

MOTHER COURAGE: Anyone can see you're no Swede or you wouldn't be talking that way about the Hero King.

THE CHAPLAIN: After all he provides the bread you eat.

THE COOK: I don't eat it, I bake it.

MOTHER COURAGE: They'll never beat him, and why, his men got faith in him. (*Seriously.*) To go by what the big shots say, they're waging war for almighty God and in the name of everything that's good and lovely. But look closer, they ain't so silly, they're wag-ing it for what they can get. Else little folk like me wouldn't be in it at all.

THE COOK: That's the way it is.

THE CHAPLAIN: As a Dutchman you'd do better to glance at the flag above your head before venting your opinions here in Poland.

MOTHER COURAGE: All good Lutherans here. Prosit!°

(*Kattrin has put on Yvette's hat and begun strutting around in imitation of her way of walking.*)

(*Suddenly there is a noise of cannon fire and shooting. Drums. Mother Courage, the cook and the chaplain rush out from behind the cart, the two last-named still carrying their glasses. The armourer and another soldier run up to the cannon and try to push it away.*)

MOTHER COURAGE: What's happening? Wait till I've taken my washing down, you louts! (*She tries to res-cue her washing.*)

THE ARMOURER: The Catholics! Broken through. Don't know if we'll get out of here. (*To the soldier.*) Get that gun shifted! (*Runs on.*)

THE COOK: God, I must find the general. Courage, I'll drop by in a day or two for another talk.

MOTHER COURAGE: Wait, you forgot your pipe.

THE COOK (*in the distance*): Keep it for me. I'll be need-ing it.

MOTHER COURAGE: Would happen just as we're making a bit of money.

THE CHAPLAIN: Ah well, I'll be going too. Indeed, if the enemy is so close as that it might be dangerous. Blesséd are the peacemakers is the motto in wartime. If only I had a cloak to cover me.

MOTHER COURAGE: I ain't lending no cloaks, not on your life. I been had too often.

THE CHAPLAIN: But my faith makes it particularly dan-gerous for me.

MOTHER COURAGE (*gets him a cloak*): Goes against my conscience, this does. Now you run along.

THE CHAPLAIN: Thank you, dear lady, that's very gener-ous of you, but I think it might be wiser for me to remain seated here; it could arouse suspicion and bring the enemy down on me if I were seen to run.

MOTHER COURAGE (*to the soldier*): Leave it, you fool, who's going to pay you for that? I'll look after it for you, you're risking your neck.

THE SOLDIER (*running away*): You can tell 'em I tried.

MOTHER COURAGE: Cross my heart. (*Sees her daughter with the hat.*) What you doing with that strumpet's hat? Take that lid off, you gone crazy? And the enemy arriving any minute! (*Pulls the hat off Kat-trin's head.*) Want 'em to pick you up and make a prostitute of you? And she's gone and put those boots on, whore of Babylon! Off with those boots! (*Tries to tug them off her.*) Jesus Christ, chaplain, gimme a hand, get those boots off her, I'll be right back. (*Runs to the cart.*)

Prosit!: Cheers!

YVETTE (*arrives, powdering her face*): Fancy that, the Catholics are coming. Where's my hat? Who's been kicking it around? I can't go about looking like this if the Catholics are coming. What'll they think of me? No mirror either. (*To the chaplain.*) How do I look? Too much powder?

THE CHAPLAIN: Exactly right.

YVETTE: And where are them red boots? (*Fails to find them as Kattrin hides her feet under her skirt.*) I left them here all right. Now I'll have to get to me tent barefoot. It's an outrage.

(*Exit.*)

(*Swiss Cheese runs in carrying in a small box.*)

MOTHER COURAGE (*Arrives with her hands full of ashes. To Kattrin.*): Here some ashes. (*To Swiss Cheese.*) What's that you're carrying?

SWISS CHEESE: Regimental cash box.

MOTHER COURAGE: Chuck it away. No more paymas-tering for you.

SWISS CHEESE: I'm responsible. (*He goes to the rear.*)

MOTHER COURAGE (*to the chaplain*): Take your clerical togs off, padre, or they'll spot you under that cloak. (*She rubs Kattrin's face with ash.*) Keep still, will you? There you are, a bit of muck and you'll be safe. What a disaster. Sentries were drunk. Hide your light under a bushel, it says. Take a soldier, specially a Catholic one, add a clean face, and there's your instant whore. For weeks they get nowt to eat, then soon as they manage to get it by looting they're falling on anything in skirts. That ought to do. Let's have a look. Not bad. Looks like you been grubbing in muckheap. Stop trembling. Nothing'll happen to you like that. (*To Swiss Cheese.*) Where d'you leave cash box?

SWISS CHEESE: Thought I'd put it in cart.

MOTHER COURAGE (*horrified*): What, my cart? Sheer criminal idiocy. Only take me eyes off you one in-stant. Hang us all three, they will.

SWISS CHEESE: I'll put it somewhere else then, or clear out with it.

MOTHER COURAGE: You sit on it, it's too late now.

THE CHAPLAIN (*who is changing his clothes downstage*): For heaven's sake, the flag!

MOTHER COURAGE (*hauls down the regimental flag*): Bozhe moi! I'd given up noticing it were there. Twenty-five years I've had it.

(*The thunder of cannon intensifies.*)

(*A morning three days later. The cannon has gone. Mother Courage, Kattrin, the chaplain and Swiss Cheese are sitting gloomily over a meal.*)

SWISS CHEESE: That's three days I been sitting around with nowt to do, and sergeant's always been kind to me but any moment now he'll start asking where's Swiss Cheese with the pay box?

MOTHER COURAGE: You thank your stars they ain't after you.

THE CHAPLAIN: What can I say? I can't even hold a ser-vice here, it might make trouble for me. Whosoever hath a full heart, his tongue runneth over, it says, but heaven help me if mine starts running over.

MOTHER COURAGE: That's how it goes. Here they sit, one with his faith and the other with his cash box. Dunno which is more dangerous.

THE CHAPLAIN: We are all of us in God's hands.

MOTHER COURAGE: Oh, I don't think it's as bad as that yet, though I must say I can't sleep nights. If it weren't for you, Swiss Cheese, things'd be easier. I think I got meself cleared. I told 'em I didn't hold with Antichrist, the Swedish one with horns on, and I'd observed left horn was a bit unserviceable. Half way through their interrogation I asked where I could get church candles not too dear. I knows the lingo cause Swiss Cheese's dad were Catholic, often used to make jokes about it, he did. They didn't believe me all that much, but they ain't got no regimental canteen lady. So they're winking an eye. Could turn out for the best, you know. We're prisoners, but same like fleas on dog.

THE CHAPLAIN: That's good milk. But we'll need to cut down our Swedish appetites a bit. After all, we've been defeated.

MOTHER COURAGE: Who's been defeated? Look, victory and defeat ain't bound to be same for the big shots up top as for them below, not by no means. Can be times the bottom lot find a defeat really pays them. Honour's lost, nowt else. I remember once up in Livonia our general took such a beating from enemy I got a horse off our baggage train in the confusion, pulled me cart seven months, he did, before we won and they checked up. As a rule you can say victory and defeat both come expensive to us ordinary folk. Best thing for us is when politics get bogged down solid. (To Swiss Cheese.) Eat up.

SWISS CHEESE: Got no appetite for it. What's sergeant to do when pay day comes round?

MOTHER COURAGE: They don't have pay days on a retreat.

SWISS CHEESE: It's their right, though. They needn't retreat if they don't get paid. Needn't stir a foot.

MOTHER COURAGE: Swiss Cheese, you're that conscientious it makes me quite nervous. I brought you up to be honest, you not being clever, but you got to know where to stop. Chaplain and me, we're off now to buy Catholic flag and some meat. Dunno anyone so good at sniffing meat, like sleepwalking it is, straight to target. I'd say he can pick out a good piece by the way his mouth starts watering. Well, thank goodness they're letting me go on trading. You don't ask tradespeople their faith but their prices. And Lutheran trousers keep cold out too.

THE CHAPLAIN: What did the mendicant say when he heard the Lutherans were going to turn everything in town and country topsy-turvy? "They'll always need beggars." (Mother Courage disappears into the cart.) So she's still worried about the cash box. So far they've taken us all for granted as part of the cart, but how long for?

SWISS CHEESE: I can get rid of it.

THE CHAPLAIN: That's almost more dangerous. Suppose you're seen. They have spies. Yesterday a fellow popped up out of the ditch in front of me just as I was relieving myself first thing. I was so scared I only just suppressed an ejaculatory prayer. That would have given me away all right. I think what they'd like best is to go sniffing people's excrement to see if they're Protestants. The spy was a little runt with a patch over one eye.

MOTHER COURAGE (clambering out of the cart with a basket): What have I found, you shameless creature? (She holds up the red boots in triumph.) Yvette's red high-heeled boots! Coolly went and pinched them, she did. Cause you put it in her head she was an enchanting young person. (She lays them in the basket.) I'm giving them back. Stealing Yvette's boots! She's wrecking herself for money. That's understandable. But you'd do it for nothing, for pleasure. What did I tell you: you're to wait till it's peace. No soldiers for you. You're not to start exhibiting yourself till it's peacetime.

THE CHAPLAIN: I don't find she exhibits herself.

MOTHER COURAGE: Too much for my liking. Let her be like a stone in Dalecarlia, where there's nowt else, so folk say "Can't see that cripple," that's how I'd lief have her. Then nowt'll happen to her. (To Swiss Cheese.) You leave that box where it is, d'you hear? And keep an eye on your sister, she needs it. The pair of you'll have me in grave yet. Sooner be minding a bagful of fleas.

(She leaves with the chaplain. Kattrin clears away the dishes.)

SWISS CHEESE: Won't be able to sit out in the sun in shirtsleeves much longer. (Kattrin points at a tree.) Aye, leaves turning yellow. (Kattrin asks by gestures if he wants a drink.) Don't want no drink. I'm thinking. (Pause.) Said she can't sleep. Best if I got rid of that box, found a good place for it. All right, let's have a glass. (Kattrin goes behind the cart.) I'll stuff it down the rat-hole by the river for the time being. Probably pick it up tonight before first light and take it to Regiment. How far can they have retreated in three days? Bet sergeant's surprised. I'm agreeably disappointed in you, Swiss Cheese, he'll say. I make you responsible for the cash, and you go and bring it back.

(As Kattrin emerges from behind the cart with a full glass in her hand, two men confront her. One is a sergeant, the other doffs his hat to her. He has a patch over one eye.)

THE MAN WITH THE PATCH: God be with you, mistress. Have you seen anyone round here from Second Finnish Regimental Headquarters?

(Kattrin, badly frightened, runs downstage, spilling the brandy. The two men look at one another, then withdraw on seeing Swiss Cheese sitting there.)

SWISS CHEESE (*interrupted in his thoughts*): You spilt half of it. What are those faces for? Jabbed yourself in eye? I don't get it. And I'll have to be off, I've thought it over, it's the only way. (*He gets up. She does everything possible to make him realise the danger. He only shrugs her off.*) Wish I knew what you're trying to say. Sure you mean well, poor creature, just can't get words out. What's it matter your spilling my brandy, I'll drink plenty more glasses yet, what's one more or less? (*He gets the box from the cart and takes it under his tunic.*) Be back in a moment. Don't hold me up now, or I'll be angry. I know you mean well. Too bad you can't speak.

(*As she tries to hold him back he kisses her and tears himself away. Exit. She is desperate, running hither and thither uttering little noises. The chaplain and Mother Courage return. Kattrin rushes to her mother.*)

MOTHER COURAGE: What's all this? Pull yourself together, love. They done something to you? Where's Swiss Cheese? Tell it me step by step, Kattrin. Mother understands you. What, so that bastard did take the box? I'll wrap it round his ears, the little hypocrite. Take your time and don't gabble, use your hands, I don't like it when you howl like a dog, what'll his reverence say? Makes him uncomfortable. What, a one-eyed man came along?

THE CHAPLAIN: That one-eyed man is a spy. Have they arrested Swiss Cheese? (*Kattrin shakes her head, shrugs her shoulders.*) We're done for.

MOTHER COURAGE (*fishes in her basket and brings out a Catholic flag, which the chaplain fixes to the mast*): Better hoist new flag.

THE CHAPLAIN (*bitterly*): All good Catholics here.

(*Voices are heard from the rear. The two men bring in Swiss Cheese.*)

SWISS CHEESE: Let me go, I got nowt. Don't twist my shoulder, I'm innocent.

SERGEANT: Here's where he came from. You know each other.

MOTHER COURAGE: Us? How?

SWISS CHEESE: I don't know her. Got no idea who she is, had nowt to do with them. I bought me dinner here, ten hellers it cost. You might have seen me sitting here, it was too salty.

SERGEANT: Who are you people, eh?

MOTHER COURAGE: We're law-abiding folk. That's right, he bought a dinner. Said it was too salty.

SERGEANT: Trying to pretend you don't know each other, that it?

MOTHER COURAGE: Why should I know him? Can't know everyone. I don't go asking 'em what they're called and are they a heretic; if he pays he ain't a heretic. You a heretic?

SWISS CHEESE: Go on.

THE CHAPLAIN: He sat there very properly, never opening his mouth except when eating. Then he had to.

SERGEANT: And who are you?

MOTHER COURAGE: He's just my potboy. Now I expect you gentlemen are thirsty, I'll get you a glass of brandy, you must be hot and tired with running.

SERGEANT: No brandy on duty. (*To Swiss Cheese.*) You were carrying something. Must have hidden it by the river. Was a bulge in your tunic when you left here.

MOTHER COURAGE: You sure it was him?

SWISS CHEESE: You must be thinking of someone else. I saw someone bounding off with a bulge in his tunic. I'm the wrong man.

MOTHER COURAGE: I'd say it was a misunderstanding too, such things happen. I'm a good judge of people, I'm Courage, you heard of me, everyone knows me, and I tell you that's an honest face he has.

SERGEANT: We're on the track of the Second Finnish Regiment's cash box. We got the description of the fellow responsible for it. Been trailing him two days. It's you.

SWISS CHEESE: It's not me.

SERGEANT: And you better cough it up, or you're a goner, you know. Where is it?

MOTHER COURAGE (*urgently*): Of course he'd give it over rather than be a goner. Right out he'd say: I got it, here it is, you're too strong. He ain't all that stupid. Speak up, stupid idiot, here's the sergeant giving you a chance.

SWISS CHEESE: S'pose I ain't got it.

SERGEANT: Then come along. We'll get it out of you. (*They lead him off.*)

MOTHER COURAGE (*calls after them*): He'd tell you. He's not that stupid. And don't you twist his shoulder! (*Runs after them.*)

(*Evening of the same day. The chaplain and dumb Kattrin are cleaning glasses and polishing knives.*)

THE CHAPLAIN: Cases like that, where somebody gets caught, are not unknown in religious history. It reminds me of the Passion of Our Lord and Saviour. There's an old song about that. (*He sings the Song of the Hours.°*)

In the first hour Jesus mild
Who had prayed since even
Was betrayed and led before
Pontius the heathen.

Pilate found him innocent
Free from fault and error
Therefore, having washed his hands
Sent him to King Herod.

In the third hour he was scourged
Stripped and clad in scarlet
And a plaited crown of thorns
Set upon his forehead.

Song of the Hours: Translated by Ralph Manheim.

On the Son of Man they spat
Mocked him and made merry.
Then the cross of death was brought
Given him to carry.

At the sixth hour with two thieves
To the cross they nailed him
And the people and the thieves
Mocked him and reviled him.

This is Jesus King of Jews
Cried they in derision
Till the sun withdrew its light
From that awful vision.

At the ninth hour Jesus wailed
Why hast thou me forsaken?
Soldiers brought him vinegar
Which he left untaken.

Then he yielded up the ghost
And the earth was shaken.
Rended was the temple's veil
And the saints were wakened.

Soldiers broke the two thieves' legs
As the night descended.
Thrust a spear in Jesus' side
When his life had ended.

Still they mocked, as from his wound
Flowed the blood and water
And blasphemed the Son of Man
With their cruel laughter.

MOTHER COURAGE (*entering excitedly*): It's touch and
go. They say sergeant's open to reason though. Only
we mustn't let on it's Swiss Cheese else they'll say we
helped him. It's a matter of money, that's all. But
where's money to come from? Hasn't Yvette been
round? I ran into her, she's got her hooks on some
colonel, maybe he'd buy her a canteen business.

THE CHAPLAIN: Do you really wish to sell?

MOTHER COURAGE: Where's money for sergeant to
come from?

THE CHAPLAIN: What'll you live on, then?

MOTHER COURAGE: That's just it.

(*Yvette Pottier arrives with an extremely ancient colonel.*)

YVETTE (*embracing Mother Courage*): My dear Courage, fancy seeing you so soon. (*Whispers.*) He's not
unwilling. (*Aloud.*) This is my good friend who
advises me in business matters. I happened to hear
you wanted to sell your cart on account of circumstances. I'll think it over.

MOTHER COURAGE: Pledge it, not sell, just not too much
hurry, 'tain't every day you find a cart like this in
wartime.

YVETTE (*disappointed*): Oh, pledge. I thought it was for
sale. I'm not so sure I'm interested. (*To the colonel.*)
How do you feel about it?

THE COLONEL: Just as you feel, pet.

MOTHER COURAGE: I'm only pledging it.

YVETTE: I thought you'd got to have the money.

MOTHER COURAGE (*firmly*): I got to have it, but sooner
run myself ragged looking for a bidder than sell outright. And why? The cart's our livelihood. It's a
chance for you, Yvette; who knows when you'll get
another like it and have a special friend to advise
you, am I right?

YVETTE: Yes, my friend thinks I should clinch it, but I'm
not sure. If it's only a pledge . . . so you agree we
ought to buy outright?

THE COLONEL: I agree, pet.

MOTHER COURAGE: Best look and see if you can find
anything for sale then; maybe you will if you don't
rush it, take your friend along with you, say a week
or fortnight, might find something suits you.

YVETTE: Then let's go looking. I adore going around
looking for things, I adore going around with you,
Poldi, it's such fun, isn't it? No matter if it takes a
fortnight. How soon would you pay the money back
if you got it?

MOTHER COURAGE: I'd pay back in two weeks, maybe
one.

YVETTE: I can't make up my mind, Poldi chéri, you
advise me. (*Takes the colonel aside.*) She's got to sell,
I know, no problem there. And there's that ensign,
you know, the fair-haired one, he'd be glad to lend
me the money. He's crazy about me, says there's
someone I remind him of. What do you advise?

THE COLONEL: You steer clear of him. He's no good.
He's only making use of you. I said I'd buy you something, didn't I, pussykins?

YVETTE: I oughtn't to let you. Of course if you think the
ensign might try to take advantage . . . Poldi, I'll
accept it from you.

THE COLONEL: That's how I feel too.

YVETTE: Is that your advice?

THE COLONEL: That is my advice.

YVETTE (*to Courage once more*): My friend's advice
would be to accept. Make me out a receipt saying the
cart's mine once two weeks are up, with all its contents, we'll check it now, I'll bring the two hundred
florins later. (*To the colonel.*) You go back to the
camp, I'll follow, I got to check it all and see there's
nothing missing from my cart. (*She kisses him. He
leaves. She climbs up on the cart.*) Not all that many
boots, are there?

MOTHER COURAGE: Yvette, it's no time for checking
your cart, s'posing it is yours. You promised you'd
talk to sergeant about Swiss Cheese, there ain't a
minute to lose, they say in an hour he'll be court-
martialled.

YVETTE: Just let me count the shirts.

MOTHER COURAGE (*pulling her down by the skirt*): You
bloody vampire. Swiss Cheese's life's at stake. And

not a word about who's making the offer, for God's sake, pretend it's your friend, else we're all done for cause we looked after him.

YVETTE: I fixed to meet that one-eyed fellow in the copse, he should be there by now.

THE CHAPLAIN: It doesn't have to be the whole two hundred either, I'd go up to a hundred and fifty, that may be enough.

MOTHER COURAGE: Since when has it been your money? You kindly keep out of this. You'll get your hotpot all right, don't worry. Hurry up and don't haggle, it's life or death. (*Pushes Yvette off.*)

THE CHAPLAIN: Far be it from me to interfere, but what are we going to live on? You're saddled with a daughter who can't earn her keep.

MOTHER COURAGE: I'm counting on regimental cash box, Mr. Clever. They'll allow it as his expenses.

THE CHAPLAIN: But will she get the message right?

MOTHER COURAGE: It's her interest I should spend her two hundred so she gets the cart. She's set on that, God knows how long that colonel of hers'll last. Kattrin, polish the knives, there's the pumice. And you, stop hanging round like Jesus on Mount of Olives,° get moving, wash them glasses, we'll have fifty or more of cavalry in tonight and I don't want to hear a lot of "I'm not accustomed to having to run about, oh my poor feet, we never ran in church." Thank the Lord they're corruptible. After all, they ain't wolves, just humans out for money. Corruption in humans is same as compassion in God. Corruption's our only hope. Long as we have it there'll be lenient sentences and even an innocent man'll have a chance of being let off.

YVETTE (*comes in panting*): They'll do it for two hundred. But it's got to be quick. Soon be out of their hands. Best thing is I go right away to my colonel with the one-eyed man. He's admitted he had the box, they put the thumbscrews on him. But he chucked it in the river soon as he saw they were on his track. The box is a write-off. I'll go and get the money from my colonel, shall I?

MOTHER COURAGE: Box is a write-off? How'm I to pay back two hundred then?

YVETTE: Oh, you thought you'd get it from the box, did you? And I was to be Joe Soap I suppose? Better not count on that. You'll have to pay up if you want Swiss Cheese back, or would you sooner I dropped the whole thing so's you could keep your cart?

MOTHER COURAGE: That's something I didn't allow for. Don't worry, you'll get your cart, I've said goodbye to it, had it seventeen years, I have. I just need a moment to think, it's bit sudden, what'm I to do, two hundred's too much for me, pity you didn't beat 'em down. Must keep a bit back, else any Tom, Dick and Harry'll be able to shove me in ditch. Go and tell

---

Jesus on Mount of Olives: The Bible shows Jesus on the Mount of Olives when he preaches the Sermon on the Mount and when he prays in anguish before his betrayal by Peter.

---

them I'll pay hundred and twenty florins, else it's all off, either way I'm losing me cart.

YVETTE: They won't do it. That one-eyed man's impatient already, keeps looking over his shoulder, he's so worked up. Hadn't I best pay them the whole two hundred?

MOTHER COURAGE (*in despair*): I can't pay that. Thirty years I been working. She's twenty-five already, and no husband. I got her to think of too. Don't push me, I know what I'm doing. Say a hundred and twenty, or it's off.

YVETTE: It's up to you. (*Rushes off.*)

(*Without looking at either the chaplain or her daughter, Mother Courage sits down to help Kattrin polish knives.*)

MOTHER COURAGE: Don't smash them glasses, they ain't ours now. Watch what you're doing, you'll cut yourself. Swiss Cheese'll be back, I'll pay two hundred if it comes to the pinch. You'll get your brother, love. For eighty florins we could fill a pack with goods and start again. Plenty of folk has to make do.

THE CHAPLAIN: The Lord will provide, it says.

MOTHER COURAGE: See they're properly dry. (*She cleans knives in silence. Kattrin suddenly runs behind the cart, sobbing.*)

YVETTE (*comes running in*): They won't do it. I told you so. The one-eyed man wanted to leave right away, said there was no point. He says he's just waiting for the drum-roll; that means sentence has been pronounced. I offered a hundred and fifty. He didn't even blink. I had to convince him to stay there so's I could have another word with you.

MOTHER COURAGE: Tell him I'll pay the two hundred. Hurry! (*Yvette runs off. They sit in silence. The chaplain has stopped polishing the glasses.*) I reckon I bargained too long.

(*In the distance drumming is heard. The chaplain gets up and goes to the rear. Mother Courage remains seated. It grows dark. The drumming stops. It grows light once more. Mother Courage is sitting exactly as before.*)

YVETTE (*arrives, very pale*): Well, you got what you asked for, with your haggling and trying to keep your cart. Eleven bullets they gave him, that's all. You don't deserve I should bother any more about you. But I did hear they don't believe the box really is in the river. They've an idea it's here and anyhow that you're connected with him. They're going to bring him here, see if you gives yourself away when you sees him. Thought I'd better warn you so's you don't recognise him, else you'll all be for it. They're right on my heels, best tell you quick. Shall I keep Kattrin away? (*Mother Courage shakes her head.*) Does she know? She mayn't have heard the drumming or know what it meant.

MOTHER COURAGE: She knows. Get her.

(*Yvette fetches Kattrin, who goes to her mother and stands beside her. Mother Courage takes her hand. Two lansequenets come carrying a stretcher with something lying on it covered by a sheet. The sergeant marches beside them. They set down the stretcher.*)

SERGEANT: Here's somebody we dunno the name of. It's got to be listed, though, so everything's shipshape. He had a meal here. Have a look, see if you know him. (*He removes the sheet.*) Know him? (*Mother Courage shakes her head.*) What, never see him before he had that meal here? (*Mother Courage shakes her head.*) Pick him up. Chuck him in the pit. He's got nobody knows him. (*They carry him away.*)

SCENE 4

(*Mother Courage sings the Song of the Grand Capitulation.*)
(*Outside an officer's tent.*)
(*Mother Courage is waiting. A clerk looks out of the tent.*)

THE CLERK: I know you. You had a paymaster from the Lutherans with you, what was in hiding. I'd not complain if I were you.

MOTHER COURAGE: But I got a complaint to make. I'm innocent, would look as how I'd a bad conscience if I let this pass. Slashed everything in me cart to pieces with their sabres, they did, then wanted I should pay five taler fine for nowt, I tell you, nowt.

CLERK: Take my tip, better shut up. We're short of canteens, so we let you go on trading, specially if you got a bad conscience and pay a fine now and then.

MOTHER COURAGE: I got a complaint.

CLERK: Have it your own way. Then you must wait till the captain's free. (*Withdraws inside the tent.*)

YOUNG SOLDIER (*enters aggressively*): Bouque la Madonne! Where's that bleeding pig of a captain what's took my reward money to swig with his tarts? I'll do him.

OLDER SOLDIER (*running after him*): Shut up. They'll put you in irons.

YOUNG SOLDIER: Out of there, you thief! I'll slice you into pork chops, I will. Pocketing my prize money after I'd swum the river, only one in the whole squadron, and now I can't even buy meself a beer. I'm not standing for that. Come on out there so I can cut you up!

OLDER SOLDIER: Blessed Mother of God, he's asking for trouble.

MOTHER COURAGE: Is it some reward he weren't paid?

YOUNG SOLDIER: Lemme go, I'll slash you too while I'm at it.

OLDER SOLDIER: He rescued the colonel's horse and got no reward for it. He's young yet, still wet behind the ears.

MOTHER COURAGE: Let him go, he ain't a dog you got to chain up. Wanting your reward is good sound sense. Why be a hero otherwise?

YOUNG SOLDIER: So's he can sit in there and booze. You're shit-scared, the lot of you. I done something special and I want my reward.

MOTHER COURAGE: Don't you shout at me, young fellow. Got me own worries, I have; any road you should spare your voice, be needing it when captain comes, else there'll be and you too hoarse to make a sound, which'll make it hard for him to clap you in irons till you turn blue. People what shouts like that can't keep it up ever; half an hour, and they have to be rocked to sleep, they're so tired.

YOUNG SOLDIER: I ain't tired and to hell with sleep. I'm hungry. They make our bread from acorns and hemp-seed, and they even skimp on that. He's whoring away my reward and I'm hungry. I'll do him.

MOTHER COURAGE: Oh I see, you're hungry. Last year that general of yours ordered you all off roads and across fields so corn should be trampled flat; I could've got ten florins for a pair of boots s'pose I'd had boots and s'pose anyone'd been able to pay ten florins. Thought he'd be well away from that area this year, he did, but here he is, still there, and hunger is great. I see what you're angry about.

YOUNG SOLDIER: I won't have it, don't talk to me, it ain't fair and I'm not standing for that.

MOTHER COURAGE: And you're right; but how long? How long you not standing for unfairness? One hour, two hours? Didn't ask yourself that, did you, but it's the whole point, and why, once you're in irons it's too bad if you suddenly finds you can put up with unfairness after all.

YOUNG SOLDIER: What am I listening to you for, I'd like to know? Bouque la Madonne, where's that captain?

MOTHER COURAGE: You been listening to me because you knows it's like what I say, your anger has gone up in smoke already, it was just a short one and you needed a long one, but where you going to get it from?

YOUNG SOLDIER: Are you trying to tell me asking for my reward is wrong?

MOTHER COURAGE: Not a bit. I'm just telling you your anger ain't long enough, it's good for nowt, pity. If you'd a long one I'd be trying to prod you on. Cut him up, the swine, would be my advice to you in that case; but how about if you don't cut him up cause you feels your tail going between your legs? Then I'd look silly and captain'd take it out on me.

OLDER SOLDIER: You're perfectly right, he's just a bit crazy.

YOUNG SOLDIER: Very well, let's see if I don't cut him up. (*Draws his sword.*) When he arrives I'm going to cut him up.

CLERK (*looks out*): The captain'll be here in one minute. Sit down.

(*The young soldier sits down.*)

MOTHER COURAGE: He's sitting now. See, what did I say? You're sitting now. Ah, how well they know us, no one need tell 'em how to go about it. Sit down! and, bingo, we're sitting. And sitting and sedition don't mix. Don't try to stand up, you won't stand the way you was standing before. I shouldn't worry about what I think; I'm no better, not one moment. Bought up all our fighting spirit, they have. Eh? S'pose I kick back, might be bad for business. Let me tell you a thing or two about the Grand Capitulation. (*She sings the Song of the Grand Capitulation.*)

Back when I was young, I was brought to realise
What a very special person I must be
(Not just any old cottager's daughter, what with my
    looks and my talents and my urge towards
    Higher Things)
And insisted that my soup should have no hairs in it.
No one makes a sucker out of me!
(All or nothing, only the best is good enough, each
    man for himself, nobody's telling *me* what to do.)
Then I heard a tit
Chirp: Wait a bit!
    And you'll be marching with the band
    In step, responding to command
    And striking up your little dance:
    Now we advance.
    And now: parade, form square!
    Then men swear God's there —
    Not the faintest chance!

In no time at all anyone who looked could see
That I'd learned to take my medicine with good
    grace.
(Two kids on my hands and look at the price of
    bread, and things they expect of you!)
When they finally came to feel that they were
    through with me
They'd got me grovelling on my face.
(Takes all sorts to make a world, you scratch my
    back and I'll scratch yours, no good banging
    your head against a brick wall.)
Then I heard that tit
Chirp: Wait a bit!
    And you'll be marching with the band
    In step, responding to command
    And striking up your little dance:
    Now they advance.
    And now: parade, form square!
    Then men swear God's there —
    Not the faintest chance!

I've known people tried to storm the summits:
There's no star too bright or seems too far away.
(Dogged does it, where there's a will there's a way,
    by hook or by crook.)
As each peak disclosed fresh peaks to come, it's
Strange how much a plain straw hat could weigh.
(You have to cut your coat according to your cloth.)
Then I hear the tit
Chirp: Wait a bit!
    And they'll be marching with the band
    In step, responding to command

And striking up their little dance:
Now they advance.
And now: parade, form square!
Then men swear God's there —
Not the faintest chance!

MOTHER COURAGE (*to the young soldier*): That's why I reckon you should stay there with your sword drawn if you're truly set on it and your anger's big enough, because you got grounds, I agree, but if your anger's a short one best leave right away.
YOUNG SOLDIER: Oh stuff it. (*He staggers off with the older soldier following.*)
CLERK (*sticks his head out*): Captain's here now. You can make your complaint.
MOTHER COURAGE: I changed me mind. I ain't complaining.

(*Exit.*)

SCENE 5

(*Two years have gone by. The war is spreading to new areas. Ceaselessly on the move, Courage's little cart crosses Poland, Moravia, Bavaria, Italy then Bavaria again. 1631. Tilly's victory at Magdeburg costs Mother Courage four officers' shirts.*)
(*Mother Courage's cart has stopped in a badly shot-up village. Thin military music in the distance. Two soldiers at the bar being served by Kattrin and Mother Courage. One of them has a lady's fur coat over his shoulders.*)

MOTHER COURAGE: Can't pay, that it? No money, no schnapps. They give us victory parades, but catch them giving men their pay.
SOLDIER: I want my schnapps. I missed the looting. That double-crossing general only allowed an hour's looting in the town. He ain't an inhuman monster, he said. Town must of paid him.
THE CHAPLAIN (*stumbles in*): There are people still lying in that yard. The peasant's family. Somebody give me a hand. I need linen.

(*The second soldier goes off with him. Kattrin becomes very excited and tries to make her mother produce linen.*)

MOTHER COURAGE: I got none. All my bandages was sold to regiment. I ain't tearing up my officer's shirts for that lot.
CHAPLAIN (*calling back*): I need linen, I tell you.
MOTHER COURAGE (*blocking Kattrin's way into the cart by sitting on the step*): I'm giving nowt. They'll never pay, and why, nowt to pay with.
CHAPLAIN (*bending over a woman he has carried in*): Why d'you stay around during the gunfire?
PEASANT WOMAN (*feebly*): Farm.
MOTHER COURAGE: Catch them abandoning anything. But now I'm s'posed to foot the bill. I won't do it.
FIRST SOLDIER: Those are Protestants. What they have to be Protestants for?

MOTHER COURAGE: They ain't bothering about faith. They lost their farm.

SECOND SOLDIER: They're no Protestants. They're Catholics like us.

FIRST SOLDIER: No way of sorting 'em out in a bombardment.

A PEASANT (*brought in by the chaplain*): My arm's gone.

THE CHAPLAIN: Where's that linen?

MOTHER COURAGE: I can't give nowt. What with expenses, taxes, loan interest and bribes. (*Making guttural noises, Kattrin raises a plank and threatens her mother with it.*) You gone plain crazy? Put that plank away or I'll paste you one, you cow. I'm giving nowt, don't want to, got to think of meself. (*The chaplain lifts her off the steps and sets her on the ground, then starts pulling out shirts and tearing them into strips.*) My officers' shirts! Half a florin apiece! I'm ruined. (*From the house comes the cry of a child in pain.*)

THE PEASANT: The baby's in there still. (*Kattrin dashes in.*)

THE CHAPLAIN (*to the woman*): Don't move. They'll get it out.

MOTHER COURAGE: Stop her, roof may fall in.

THE CHAPLAIN: I'm not going back in there.

MOTHER COURAGE (*torn both ways*): Don't waste my precious linen.

(*Kattrin brings a baby out of the ruins.*)

MOTHER COURAGE: How nice, found another baby to cart around? Give it to its ma this instant, unless you'd have me fighting for hours to get it off you, like last time, d'you hear? (*To the second soldier.*) Don't stand there gawping, you go back and tell them cut out that music, we can see it's a victory with our own eyes. All your victories mean to me is losses.

THE CHAPLAIN (*tying a bandage*): Blood's coming through.

(*Kattrin is rocking the baby and making lullaby noises.*)

MOTHER COURAGE: Look at her, happy as a queen in all this misery; give it back at once, its mother's coming round. (*She catches the first soldier, who has been attacking the drinks and is trying to make off with one of the bottles.*) Psia krew! Thought you'd score another victory, you animal? Now pay.

FIRST SOLDIER: I got nowt.

MOTHER COURAGE (*pulling the fur coat off his back*): Then leave that coat, it's stolen any road.

THE CHAPLAIN: There's still someone under there.

SCENE 6

(*Outside the Bavarian town of Ingolstadt Courage participates in the funeral of the late Imperial commander Tilly. Discussions are held about war heroes and the war's duration. The chaplain complains that his talents are lying fallow, and dumb Kattrin gets the red boots. The year is 1632.*)

(*Inside a canteen tent.*)

(*It has a bar towards the rear. Rain. Sound of drums and Funeral music. The chaplain and the regimental clerk are playing a board game. Mother Courage and her daughter are stocktaking.*)

THE CHAPLAIN: Now the funeral procession will be moving off.

MOTHER COURAGE: Too bad about commander in chief — twenty-two pairs those socks — he fell by accident, they say. Mist over fields, that was the trouble. General had just been haranguing a regiment saying they must fight to last man and last round, he was riding back when mist made him lose direction so he was up front and a bullet got him in midst of battle — only four hurricane lamps left. (*A whistle from the rear. She goes to the bar.*) You scrimshankers, dodging your commander in chief's funeral, scandal I call it. (*Pours drinks.*)

THE CLERK: They should never of paid troops out before the funeral. Instead of going now they're all getting pissed.

THE CHAPLAIN (*to the clerk*): Aren't you supposed to go to the funeral?

THE CLERK: Dodged it cause of the rain.

MOTHER COURAGE: It's different with you, your uniform might get wet. I heard they wanted to toll bells for funeral as usual, except it turned out all churches had been blown to smithereens by his orders, so poor old commander in chief won't be hearing no bells as they let the coffin down. They're going to let off three salvoes instead to cheer things up — seventeen belts.

SHOUTS (*from the bar*): Hey, Missis, a brandy!

MOTHER COURAGE: Let's see your money. No, I ain't having you in my tent with your disgusting boots. You can drink outside, rain or no rain. (*To the clerk.*) I'm only letting in sergeants and up. Commander in chief had been having his worries, they say. S'posed to have been trouble with Second Regiment cause he stopped their pay, said it was a war of faith and they should do it for free. (*Funeral march. All look to the rear.*)

THE CHAPLAIN: Now they'll be filing past the noble corpse.

MOTHER COURAGE: Can't help feeling sorry for those generals and emperors, there they are maybe thinking they're doing something extra special what folk'll talk about in years to come, and earning a public monument, like conquering the world for instance, that's a fine ambition for a general, how's he to know any better? I mean, he plagues hisself to death, then it all breaks down on account of ordinary folk what just wants their beer and bit of a chat, nowt higher. Finest plans get bolloxed up by the pettiness of them as should be carrying them out, because emperors can't do nowt themselves, they just counts on soldiers and people to back 'em up whatever happens, am I right?

THE CHAPLAIN (*laughs*): Courage, you're right, aside

from the soldiers. They do their best. Give me that lot outside there, for instance, drinking their brandy in the rain, and I'd guarantee to make you one war after another for a hundred years if need be, and I'm no trained general.

MOTHER COURAGE: You don't think war might end, then?

THE CHAPLAIN: What, because the commander in chief's gone? Don't be childish. They're two a penny, no shortage of heroes.

MOTHER COURAGE: Ee, I'm not asking for fun of it, but because I'm thinking whether to stock up, prices are low now, but if war's going to end it's money down the drain.

THE CHAPLAIN: I realise it's a serious question. There've always been people going round saying "the war can't go on for ever." I tell you there's nothing to stop it going on for ever. Of course there can be a bit of a breathing space. The war may need to get its second wind, it may even have an accident so to speak. There's no guarantee against that; nothing's perfect on this earth of ours. A perfect war, the sort you might say couldn't be improved on, that's something we shall probably never see. It can suddenly come to a standstill for some quite unforeseen reason, you can't allow for everything. A slight case of negligence, and it's bogged down up to the axles. And then it's a matter of hauling the war out of the mud again. But emperor and kings and popes will come to its rescue. So on the whole it has nothing serious to worry about, and will live to a ripe old age.

A SOLDIER (sings at the bar):

> A schnapps, landlord, you're late!
> A soldier cannot wait
> To do his emperor's orders.

> Make it a double, this is a holiday.

MOTHER COURAGE: S'pose I went by what you say . . .

THE CHAPLAIN: Think it out for yourself. What's to compete with the war?

THE SOLDIER (at the rear):

> Your breast, my girl, you're late!
> A soldier cannot wait
> To ride across the borders.

THE CLERK (unexpectedly): And what about peace? I'm from Bohemia and I'd like to go home some day.

THE CHAPLAIN: Would you indeed? Ah, peace. Where is the hole once the cheese has been eaten?

THE SOLDIER (at the rear):

> Lead trumps, my friend, you're late!
> A soldier cannot wait.
> His emperor needs him badly.

> Your blessing, priest, you're late!
> A soldier cannot wait.
> Must lay his life down gladly.

THE CLERK: In the long run lifes impossible if there's no peace.

THE CHAPLAIN: I'd say there's peace in war too; it has its peaceful moments. Because war satisfies all requirements, peaceable ones included, they're catered for, and it would simply fizzle out if they weren't. In war you can do a crap like in the depths of peacetime, then between one battle and the next you can have a beer, then even when you're moving up you can lay your head on your arms and have a bit of shuteye in the ditch, it's entirely possible. During a charge you can't play cards maybe, but nor can you in the depths of peacetime when you're ploughing, and after a victory there are various openings. You may get a leg blown off, then you start by making a lot of fuss as though it were serious, but afterwards you calm down or get given a schnapps, and you end up hopping around and the war's no worse off than before. And what's to stop you being fruitful and multiplying in the middle of all the butchery, behind a barn or something, in the long run you can't be held back from it, and then the war will have your progeny and can use them to carry on with. No, the war will always find an outlet, mark my words. Why should it ever stop?

(Kattrin has ceased working and is staring at the chaplain.)

MOTHER COURAGE: I'll buy fresh stock then. If you say so. (Kattrin suddenly flings a basket full of bottles to the ground and runs off.) Kattrin! (Laughs.) Damn me if she weren't waiting for peace. I promised her she'd get a husband soon as peace came. (Hurries after her.)

THE CLERK (standing up): I won. You been talking too much. Pay up.

MOTHER COURAGE (returning with Kattrin): Don't be silly, war'll go on a bit longer, and we'll make a bit more money, and peacetime'll be all the nicer for it. Now you go into town, that's ten minutes' walk at most, fetch things from Golden Lion, the expensive ones, we can fetch rest in cart later, it's all arranged, regimental clerk here will go with you. Nearly everybody's attending commander in chief's funeral, nowt can happen to you. Careful now, don't let them steal nowt, think of your dowry.

(Kattrin puts a cloth over her head and leaves with the clerk.)

THE CHAPLAIN: Is that all right to let her go with the clerk?

MOTHER COURAGE: She's not that pretty they'd want to ruin her.

THE CHAPLAIN: I admire the way you run your business and always win through. I see why they called you Courage.

MOTHER COURAGE: Poor folk got to have courage. Why, they're lost. Simply getting up in morning takes some doing in their situation. Or ploughing a field, and in a war at that. Mere fact they bring kids into world shows they got courage, cause there's no hope for them. They have to hang one another and slaughter one another, so just looking each other in face must call for courage. Being able to put up with emperor and pope shows supernatural courage, cause those two cost 'em their lives. (*She sits down, takes a little pipe from her purse and smokes.*) You might chop us a bit of kindling.

THE CHAPLAIN (*reluctantly removing his coat and preparing to chop up sticks*): I happen to be a pastor of souls, not a woodcutter.

MOTHER COURAGE: I got no soul, you see. Need firewood, though.

THE CHAPLAIN: Where's that stumpy pipe from?

MOTHER COURAGE: Just a pipe.

THE CHAPLAIN: What d'you mean, "just," it's a quite particular pipe, that.

MOTHER COURAGE: Aha?

THE CHAPLAIN: That stumpy pipe belongs to the Oxenstierna Regiment's cook.

MOTHER COURAGE: If you know that already why ask, Mr. Clever?

THE CHAPLAIN: Because I didn't know if you were aware what you're smoking. You might just have been rummaging around in your things, come across some old pipe or other, and used it out of sheer absence of mind.

MOTHER COURAGE: And why not?

THE CHAPLAIN: Because you didn't. You're smoking that deliberately.

MOTHER COURAGE: And why shouldn't I?

THE CHAPLAIN: Courage, I'm warning you. It's my duty. Probably you'll never clap eyes on the gentleman again, and that's no loss but your good fortune. He didn't make at all a reliable impression on me. Quite the opposite.

MOTHER COURAGE: Really? Nice fellow that.

THE CHAPLAIN: So he's what you would call a nice fellow? I wouldn't. Far be it from me to bear him the least ill-will, but nice is not what I would call him. More like one of those Don Juans, a slippery one. Have a look at that pipe if you don't believe me. You must admit it tells you a good deal about his character.

MOTHER COURAGE: Nowt that I can see. Worn out, I'd call it.

THE CHAPLAIN: Practically bitten through, you mean. A man of wrath. That is the pipe of an unscrupulous man of wrath; you must see that if you have any discrimination left.

MOTHER COURAGE: Don't chop my chopping block in two.

THE CHAPLAIN: I told you I'm not a woodcutter by trade. I studied to be a pastor of souls. My talent and abilities are being abused in this place, by manual labour. My God-given endowments are denied expression. It's a sin. You have never heard me preach. One sermon of mine can put a regiment in such a frame of mind it'll treat the enemy like a flock of sheep. Life to them is a smelly old foot cloth which they fling away in a vision of final victory. God has given me the gift of speech. I can preach so you'll lose all sense of sight and hearing.

MOTHER COURAGE: I don't wish to lose my sense of sight and hearing. Where'd that leave me?

THE CHAPLAIN: Courage, I have often thought that your dry way of talking conceals more than just a warm heart. You too are human and need warmth.

MOTHER COURAGE: Best way for us to get this tent warm is have plenty of firewood.

THE CHAPLAIN: Don't change the subject. Seriously, Courage, I sometimes ask myself what it would be like if our relationship were to become somewhat closer. I mean, given that the whirlwind of war has so strangely whirled us together.

MOTHER COURAGE: I'd say it was close enough. I cook meals for you and you run around and chop firewood for instance.

THE CHAPLAIN (*coming closer*): You know what I mean by closer; it's not a relationship founded on meals and wood-chopping and other such base necessities. Let your head speak, harden thyself not.

MOTHER COURAGE: Don't you come at me with that axe. That'd be too close a relationship.

THE CHAPLAIN: You shouldn't make a joke of it. I'm a serious person and I've thought about what I'm saying.

MOTHER COURAGE: Be sensible, padre. I like you. I don't want to row you. All I'm after is get myself and children through all this with my cart. I don't see it as mine, and I ain't in the mood for private affairs. Right now I'm taking a gamble, buying stores just when commander in chief's fallen and all the talk's of peace. Where d'you reckon you'd turn if I'm ruined? Don't know, do you? You chop us some kindling wood, then we can keep warm at night, that's quite something these times. What's this? (*She gets up. Enter Kattrin, out of breath, with a wound above her eye. She is carrying a variety of stuff: parcels, leather goods, a drum and so on.*)

MOTHER COURAGE: What happened, someone assault you? On way back? She was assaulted on her way back. Bet it was that trooper was getting drunk here. I shouldn't have let you go, love. Drop that stuff. Not too bad, just a flesh wound you got. I'll bandage it and in a week it'll be all right. Worse than wild beasts, they are. (*She ties up the wound.*)

THE CHAPLAIN: It's not them I blame. They never went raping back home. The fault lies with those that start wars, it brings humanity's lowest instincts to the surface.

MOTHER COURAGE: Calm down. Didn't clerk come back with you? That's because you're respectable, they don't bother. Wound ain't a deep one, won't leave no mark. There you are, all bandaged up. You'll get something, love, keep calm. Something I put aside for you, wait till you see. (*She delves into a*

sack and brings out Yvette's red high-heeled boots.)
Made you open your eyes, eh? Something you always
wanted. They're yours. Put 'em on quick, before I
change me mind. Won't leave no mark, and what if it
does? Ones I'm really sorry for's the ones they fancy.
Drag them around till they're worn out, they do.
Those they don't care for they leaves alive. I seen girls
before now had pretty faces, then in no time looking
fit to frighten a hyaena. Can't even go behind a bush
without risking trouble, horrible life they lead. Same
like with trees, straight well-shaped ones get chopped
down to make beams for houses and crooked ones
live happily ever after. So it's a stroke of luck for you
really. Them boots'll be all right, I greased them
before putting them away.

(*Kattrin leaves the boots where they are and crawls into
the cart.*)

THE CHAPLAIN: Let's hope she's not disfigured.
MOTHER COURAGE: She'll have a scar. No use her waiting for peacetime now.
THE CHAPLAIN: She didn't let them steal the things.
MOTHER COURAGE: Maybe I shouldn't have dinned that
into her so. Wish I knew what went on in that head
of hers. Just once she stayed out all night, once in all
those years. Afterwards she went around like before,
except she worked harder. Couldn't get her to tell
what had happened. Worried me quite a while, that
did. (*She collects the articles brought by Kattrin, and
sorts them angrily.*) That's war for you. Nice way to
get a living!

(*Sound of cannon fire.*)

THE CHAPLAIN: Now they'll be burying the commander
in chief. This is a historic moment.
MOTHER COURAGE: What I call a historic moment is
them bashing my daughter over the eye. She's half
wrecked already, won't get no husband now, and her
so crazy about kids; anyway, she's only dumb from
war, soldier stuffed something in her mouth when she
was little. As for Swiss Cheese I'll never see him again,
and where Eilif is God alone knows. War be damned.

SCENE 7

(*Mother Courage at the peak of her business career.*)
(*High road.*)
(*The chaplain, Mother Courage, and Kattrin are pulling
the cart, which is hung with new wares. Mother
Courage is wearing a necklace of silver coins.*)

MOTHER COURAGE: I won't have you folk spoiling my
war for me. I'm told it kills off the weak, but they're
write-off in peacetime too. And war gives its people a
better deal. (*She sings.*)

  And if you feel your forces fading
  You won't be there to share the fruits.

  But what is war but private trading
  That deals in blood instead of boots?

And what's the use of settling down? Them as does
are first to go. (*Sings.*)

  Some people think to live by looting
  The goods some others haven't got.
  You think it's just a line they're shooting
  Until you hear they have been shot.

  And some I saw dig six feet under
  In haste to lie down and pass out.
  Now they're at rest perhaps they wonder
  Just what was all their haste about.

(*They pull it further.*)

SCENE 8

(*The same year sees the death of the Swedish king Gus-
tavus Adolphus at the battle of Lützen. Peace threatens
to ruin Mother Courage's business. Courage's dashing
son performs one heroic deed too many and comes to a
sticky end.*)
(*Camp.*)
(*A summer morning. In front of the cart stand an old
woman and her son. The son carries a large sack of bedding.*)

MOTHER COURAGE'S VOICE (*from inside the cart*): Does
it need to be this ungodly hour?
THE YOUNG MAN: We walked twenty miles in the night
and got to be back today.
MOTHER COURAGE'S VOICE: What am I to do with bedding? Folk've got no houses.
THE YOUNG MAN: Best have a look first.
THE OLD WOMAN: This place is no good either. Come on.
THE YOUNG MAN: What, and have them sell the roof
over our head for taxes? She might pay three florins if
you throw in the bracelet. (*Bells start ringing.*) Listen,
mother.
VOICES (*from the rear*): Peace! Swedish king's been killed.
MOTHER COURAGE (*Sticks her head out of the cart. She
has not yet done her hair.*): What's that bell-ringing
about in mid-week?
THE CHAPLAIN (*crawling out from under the cart*):
What are they shouting? Peace?
MOTHER COURAGE: Don't tell me peace has broken out
just after I laid in new stock.
THE CHAPLAIN (*calling to the rear*): That true? Peace?
VOICES: Three weeks ago, they say, only no one told us.
THE CHAPLAIN (*to Courage*): What else would they be
ringing the bells for?
VOICES: A whole lot of Lutherans have driven into
town, they brought the news.
THE YOUNG MAN: Mother, it's peace. What's the matter?

(*The old woman has collapsed.*)

MOTHER COURAGE (*speaking into the cart*): Holy cow! Kattrin, peace! Put your black dress on, we're going to church. Least we can do for Swiss Cheese. Is it true, though?

THE YOUNG MAN: The people here say so. They've made peace. Can you get up? (*The old woman stands up dumbfounded.*) I'll get the saddlery going again. I promise. It'll all work out. Father will get his bedding back. Can you walk? (*To the chaplain.*) She came over queer. It's the news. She never thought there'd be peace again. Father always said so. We're going straight home. (*They go off.*)

MOTHER COURAGE'S VOICE: Give her a schnapps.

THE CHAPLAIN: They've already gone.

MOTHER COURAGE'S VOICE: What's up in camp?

THE CHAPLAIN: They're assembling. I'll go on over. Shouldn't I put on my clerical garb?

MOTHER COURAGE'S VOICE: Best check up before parading yourself as heretic. I'm glad about peace, never mind if I'm ruined. Any road I'll have got two of me children through the war. Be seeing Eilif again now.

THE CHAPLAIN: And who's that walking down the lines? Bless me, the army commander's cook.

THE COOK (*somewhat bedraggled and carrying a bundle*): What do I behold? The padre!

THE CHAPLAIN: Courage, we've got company.

(*Mother Courage clambers out.*)

THE COOK: I promised I'd drop over for a little talk soon as I had the time. I've not forgotten your brandy, Mrs. Fierling.

MOTHER COURAGE: Good grief, the general's cook! After all these years! Where's my eldest boy Eilif?

THE COOK: Hasn't he got here? He left before me, he was on his way to see you too.

THE CHAPLAIN: I shall don my clerical garb, just a moment.

(*Goes off behind the cart.*)

MOTHER COURAGE: Then he may be here any minute. (*Calls into the cart.*) Kattrin, Eilif's on his way. Get cook a glass of brandy, Kattrin! (*Kattrin does not appear.*) Drag your hair down over it, that's all right. Mr. Lamb's no stranger. (*Fetches the brandy herself.*) She don't like to come out, peace means nowt to her. Took too long coming, it did. They gave her a crack over one eye, you barely notice it now but she thinks folks are staring at her.

THE COOK: Ah yes. War. (*He and Mother Courage sit down.*)

MOTHER COURAGE: Cooky, you caught me at bad moment. I'm ruined.

THE COOK: What? That's hard.

MOTHER COURAGE: Peace'll wring my neck. I went and took chaplain's advice, laid in fresh stocks only t'other day. And now they're going to demobilise and I'll be left sitting on me wares.

THE COOK: What'd you want to go and listen to padre for? If I hadn't been in such a hurry that time, the Catholics arriving so quickly and all, I'd warned you against that man. All piss and wind, he is. So he's the authority around here, eh?

MOTHER COURAGE: He's been doing washing-up for me and helping pull.

THE COOK: Him pull! I bet he told you some of those jokes of his too, I know him, got a very unhealthy view of women, he has, all my good influence on him went for nowt. He ain't steady.

MOTHER COURAGE: You steady then?

THE COOK: Whatever else I ain't, I'm steady. Mud in your eye!

MOTHER COURAGE: Steady, that's nowt. I only had one steady fellow, thank God. Hardest I ever had to work in me life; he flogged the kids' blankets soon as autumn came, and he called me mouth-organ an unchristian instrument. Ask me, you ain't saying much for yourself admitting you're steady.

THE COOK: Still tough as nails, I see; but that's what I like about you.

MOTHER COURAGE: Now don't tell me you been dreaming of me nails.

THE COOK: Well, well, here we are, along with armistice bells and your brandy like what nobody else ever serves, it's famous, that is.

MOTHER COURAGE: I don't give two pins for your armistice bells just now. Can't see 'em handing out all the back pay what's owing, so where does that leave me with my famous brandy? Had your pay yet?

THE COOK (*hesitantly*): Not exactly. That's why we all shoved off. If that's how it is, I thought, I'll go and visit friends. So here I am sitting with you.

MOTHER COURAGE: Other words you got nowt.

THE COOK: High time they stopped that bloody clanging. Wouldn't mind getting into some sort of trade. I'm fed up being cook to that lot. I'm s'posed to rustle them up meals out of tree roots and old bootsoles, then they fling the hot soup in my face. Cook these days is a dog's life. Sooner do war service, only of course it's peacetime now. (*He sees the chaplain reappearing in his old garments.*) More about that later.

THE CHAPLAIN: It's still all right, only had a few moths in it.

THE COOK: Can't see why you bother. You won't get your old job back, who are you to inspire now to earn his pay honourably and lay down his life? What's more I got a bone to pick with you, cause you advised this lady to buy a lot of unnecessary goods saying war would go on for ever.

THE CHAPLAIN (*heatedly*): I'd like to know what concern that is of yours.

THE COOK: Because it's unscrupulous, that sort of thing is. How dare you meddle in other folks' business arrangements with your unwanted advice?

THE CHAPLAIN: Who's meddling? (*To Courage.*) I never knew this gentleman was such an intimate you had to account to him for everything.

MOTHER COURAGE: Keep your hair on, cook's only giving his personal opinion and you can't deny your war was a flop.

THE CHAPLAIN: You should not blaspheme against peace, Courage. You are a hyaena of the battlefield.

MOTHER COURAGE: I'm what?

THE COOK: If you're going to insult this lady you'll have to settle with me.

THE CHAPLAIN: It's not you I'm talking to. Your intentions are only too transparent. (*To Courage.*) But when I see you picking up peace betwixt your finger and your thumb like some dirty old snot-rag, then my humanity feels outraged; for then I see that you don't want peace but war, because you profit from it; in which case you shouldn't forget the ancient saying that whosoever sups with the devil needs a long spoon.

MOTHER COURAGE: I got no use for war, and war ain't got much use for me. But I'm not being called no hyaena, you and me's through.

THE CHAPLAIN: Then why grumble about peace when everybody's breathing sighs of relief? Because of some old junk in your cart?

MOTHER COURAGE: My goods ain't old junk but what I lives by, and you too up to now.

THE CHAPLAIN: Off war, in other words. Aha.

THE COOK (*to the chaplain*): You're old enough to know it's always a mistake offering advice. (*To Courage.*) Way things are, your best bet's to get rid of certain goods quick as you can before prices hit rock-bottom. Dress yourself and get moving, not a moment to lose.

MOTHER COURAGE: That ain't bad advice. I'll do that, I guess.

THE CHAPLAIN: Because cooky says it.

MOTHER COURAGE: Why couldn't you say it? He's right, I'd best go off to market. (*Goes inside the cart.*)

THE COOK: That's one to me, padre. You got no presence of mind. What you should of said was: what, me offer advice, all I done was discuss politics. Better not take me on. Cockfighting don't suit that get-up.

THE CHAPLAIN: If you don't stop your gob I'll murder you, get-up or no get-up.

THE COOK (*pulling off his boots and unwrapping his footcloths*): Pity the war made such a godless shit of you, else you'd easily get another parsonage now it's peacetime. Cooks won't be needed, there's nowt to cook, but faith goes on just the same, nowt changed in that direction.

THE CHAPLAIN: Mr. Lamb, I'm asking you not to elbow me out. Since I came down in the world I've become a better person. I couldn't preach to anyone now.

(*Enter Yvette Pottier in black, dressed up to the nines, carrying a cane. She is much older and fatter, and heavily powdered. She is followed by a manservant.*)

YVETTE: Hullo there, everybody. Is this Mother Courage's establishment?

THE CHAPLAIN: It is. And with whom have we the honour . . . ?

YVETTE: With the Countess Starhemberg, my good man. Where's Courage?

THE CHAPLAIN (*calls into the cart*): The Countess Starhemberg wishes to speak to you.

MOTHER COURAGE'S VOICE: Just coming.

YVETTE: It's Yvette.

MOTHER COURAGE'S VOICE: Oh, Yvette!

YVETTE: Come to see how you are. (*Sees the cook turn round aghast.*) Pieter!

THE COOK: Yvette!

YVETTE: Well I never! How d'you come to be here?

THE COOK: Got a lift.

THE CHAPLAIN: You know each other then? Intimately?

YVETTE: I should think so. (*She looks the cook over.*) Fat.

THE COOK: Not all that skinny yourself.

YVETTE: All the same I'm glad to see you, you shit. Gives me a chance to say what I think of you.

THE CHAPLAIN: You say it, in full; but don't start till Courage is out here.

MOTHER COURAGE (*coming out with all kinds of goods*): Yvette! (*They embrace.*) But what are you in mourning for?

YVETTE: Suits me, don't it? My husband the colonel died a few years back.

MOTHER COURAGE: That old fellow what nearly bought the cart?

YVETTE: His elder brother.

MOTHER COURAGE: Then you're sitting pretty. Nice to find somebody what's made it in this war.

YVETTE: Up and down and up again, that's the way it went.

MOTHER COURAGE: I'm not hearing a word against colonels, they make a mint of money.

THE CHAPLAIN: I would put my boots back on if I were you. (*To Yvette.*) You promised you would say what you think of the gentleman.

THE COOK: Don't kick up a stink here, Yvette.

MOTHER COURAGE: Yvette, this is a friend of mine.

YVETTE: That's old Puffing Piet.

THE COOK: Let's drop the nicknames. I'm called Lamb.

MOTHER COURAGE (*laughs*): Puffing Piet! Him as made all the women crazy! Here, I been looking after your pipe for you.

THE CHAPLAIN: Smoking it, too.

YVETTE: What luck I can warn you against him. Worst of the lot, he was, rampaging along the whole Flanders coastline. Got more girls in trouble than he has fingers.

THE COOK: That's all a long while ago. Tain't true anyhow.

YVETTE: Stand up when a lady brings you into the conversation! How I loved this man! All the time he had a little dark girl with bandy legs, got her in trouble too of course.

THE COOK: Got you into high society more like, far as I can see.

YVETTE: Shut your trap, you pathetic remnant! Better watch out for him, though; fellows like that are still dangerous even when on their last legs.

MOTHER COURAGE (*to Yvette*): Come along, got to get

rid of my stuff afore prices start dropping. You might be able to put a word in for me at regiment, with your connections. (*Calls into the cart.*) Kattrin, church is off, I'm going to market instead. When Eilif turns up, one of you give him a drink. (*Exit with Yvette.*)

YVETTE (*as she leaves*): Fancy a creature like that ever making me leave the straight and narrow path. Thank my lucky stars I managed to reach the top all the same. But I've cooked your goose, Puffing Piet, and that's something that'll be credited to me one day in the world to come.

THE CHAPLAIN: I would like to take as a text for our little talk "The mills of God grind slowly." Weren't you complaining about my jokes?

THE COOK: Dead out of luck, I am. It's like this, you see: I thought I might get a hot meal. Here am I starving, and now they'll be talking about me and she'll get quite a wrong picture. I think I'll clear out before she's back.

THE CHAPLAIN: I think so too.

THE COOK: Padre, I'm fed up already with this bloody peace. Human race has to go through fire and sword cause it's sinful from the cradle up. I wish I could be roasting a fat capon once again for the general, wherever he's got to, in mustard sauce with a carrot or two.

THE CHAPLAIN: Red cabbage. Red cabbage for a capon.

THE COOK: You're right, but carrots was what he had to have.

THE CHAPLAIN: No sense of what's fitting.

THE COOK: Not that it stopped you guzzling your share.

THE CHAPLAIN: With misgivings.

THE COOK: Anyway you must admit those were the days.

THE CHAPLAIN: I might admit it if pressed.

THE COOK: Now you've called her a hyaena your days here are finished. What you staring at?

THE CHAPLAIN: Eilif! (*Eilif arrives, followed by soldiers with pikes. His hands are fettered. His face is chalky-white.*) What's wrong?

EILIF: Where's mother?

THE CHAPLAIN: Gone into town.

EILIF: I heard she was around. They've allowed me to come and see her.

THE COOK (*to the soldiers*): What you doing with him?

A SOLDIER: Something not nice.

THE CHAPLAIN: What's he been up to?

THE SOLDIER: Broke into a peasant's place. The wife's dead.

THE CHAPLAIN: How could you do a thing like that?

EILIF: It's what I did last time, ain't it?

THE COOK: Aye, but it's peace now.

EILIF: Shut up. All right if I sit down till she comes?

THE SOLDIER: We've no time.

THE CHAPLAIN: In wartime they recommended him for that, sat him at the general's right hand. Dashing, it was, in those days. Any chance of a word with the provost-marshal?

THE SOLDIER: Wouldn't do no good. Taking some peasant's cattle, what's dashing about that?

THE COOK: Dumb, I call it.

EILIF: If I'd been dumb you'd of starved, clever bugger.

THE COOK: But as you were clever you're going to be shot.

THE CHAPLAIN: We'd better fetch Kattrin out anyhow.

EILIF: Sooner have a glass of schnapps, could do with that.

THE SOLDIER: No time, come along.

THE CHAPLAIN: And what shall we tell your mother?

EILIF: Tell her it wasn't any different, tell her it was the same thing. Or tell her nowt. (*The soldiers propel him away.*)

THE CHAPLAIN: I'll accompany you on your grievous journey.

EILIF: Don't need any bloody parsons.

THE CHAPLAIN: Wait and see. (*Follows him.*)

THE COOK (*calls after them*): I'll have to tell her, she'll want to see him.

THE CHAPLAIN: I wouldn't tell her anything. At most that he was here and will come again, maybe tomorrow. By then I'll be back and can break it to her. (*Hurries off.*)

(*The cook looks after him, shaking his head, then walks restlessly around. Finally he comes up to the cart.*)

THE COOK: Hoy! Don't you want to come out? I can understand you hiding away from peace. Like to do the same myself. Remember me, I'm general's cook? I was wondering if you'd a bit of something to eat while I wait for your mum. I don't half feel like a bit of pork, or bread even, just to fill the time. (*Peers inside.*) Head under blanket. (*Sound of gunfire off.*)

MOTHER COURAGE (*runs in, out of breath and with all her goods still*): Cooky, peacetime's over. War's been on again three days now. Heard news before selling me stuff, thank God. They're having a shooting match with Lutherans in town. We must get cart away at once. Kattrin, pack up! What you in the dumps for? What's wrong?

THE COOK: Nowt.

MOTHER COURAGE: Something is. I see it way you look.

THE COOK: Cause war's starting up again, I s'pose. Looks as if it'll be tomorrow night before I get next hot food inside me.

MOTHER COURAGE: You're lying, cooky.

THE COOK: Eilif was here. Had to leave almost at once, though.

MOTHER COURAGE: Was he now? Then we'll be seeing him on the march. I'm joining our side this time. How's he look?

THE COOK: Same as usual.

MOTHER COURAGE: Oh, he'll never change. Take more than war to steal him from me. Clever, he is. You going to help me get packed? (*Begins to pack up.*) What's his news? Still in general's good books? Say anything about his deeds of valour?

THE COOK (*glumly*): Repeated one of them, I'm told.

MOTHER COURAGE: Tell it me later, we got to move off. (*Kattrin appears.*) Kattrin, peacetime's finished now. We're moving on. (*To the cook.*) How about you?

THE COOK: Have to join up again.

MOTHER COURAGE: Why don't you . . . Where's padre?

THE COOK: Went into town with Eilif.

MOTHER COURAGE: Then you come along with us a way. Need somebody to help me.

THE COOK: That business with Yvette, you know . . .

MOTHER COURAGE: Done you no harm in my eyes. Opposite. Where there's smoke there's fire, they say. You coming along?

THE COOK: I won't say no.

MOTHER COURAGE: The Twelfth moved off already. Take the shaft. Here's a bit of bread. We must get round behind to Lutherans. Might even be seeing Eilif tonight. He's my favourite one. Short peace, wasn't it? Now we're off again. (*She sings as the cook and Kattrin harness themselves up.*)

> From Ulm to Metz, from Metz to Munich
> Courage will see the war gets fed.
> The war will show a well-filled tunic
> Given its daily shot of lead.
> But lead alone can hardly nourish
> It must have soldiers to subsist.
> It's you it needs to make it flourish.
> The war's still hungry. So enlist!

SCENE 9

(*It is the seventeenth year of the great war of faith. Germany has lost more than half her inhabitants. Those who survive the bloodbath are killed off by terrible epidemics. Once fertile areas are ravaged by famine, wolves roam the burnt-out towns. In autumn 1634 we find Courage in the Fichtelgebirge, off the main axis of the Swedish armies. The winter this year is early and harsh. Business is bad, so that there is nothing to do but beg. The cook gets a letter from Utrecht and is sent packing.*)
(*Outside a semi-dilapidated parsonage.*)
(*Grey morning in early winter. Gusts of wind. Mother Courage and the cook in shabby sheepskins, drawing the cart.*)

THE COOK: It's all dark, nobody up yet.

MOTHER COURAGE: Except it's parson's house. Have to crawl out of bed to ring bells. Then he'll have hot soup.

THE COOK: What from, when the whole village is burnt? We seen it.

MOTHER COURAGE: It's lived in, though, dog was barking.

THE COOK: S'pose parson's got, he'll give nowt.

MOTHER COURAGE: Maybe if we sing. . . .

THE COOK: I've had enough. (*Abruptly.*) Got a letter from Utrecht saying mother died of cholera and inn's mine. Here's letter if you don't believe me. No business of yours the way aunty goes on about my mode of existence, but have a look.

MOTHER COURAGE: (*Reads the letter.*) Lamb, I'm tired too of always being on the go. I feel like butcher's dog, dragging meat round customers and getting nowt off it. I got nowt left to sell, and folk got nowt left to buy nowt with. Saxony a fellow in rags tried landing me a stack of old books for two eggs, Württemberg they wanted to swap their plough for a titchy bag of salt. What's to plough for? Nowt growing no more, just brambles. In Pomerania villages are s'posed to have started in eating the younger kids, and nuns have been caught sticking folk up.

THE COOK: World's dying out.

MOTHER COURAGE: Sometimes I sees meself driving through hell with me cart selling brimstone, or across heaven with packed lunches for hungry souls. Give me my kids what's left, let's find some place they ain't shooting, and I'd like a few more years undisturbed.

THE COOK: You and me could get that inn going, Courage, think it over. Made up me mind in the night, I did: back to Utrecht with or without you, and starting today.

MOTHER COURAGE: Have to talk to Kattrin. That's a bit quick for me; I'm against making decisions all freezing cold and nowt inside you. Kattrin! (*Kattrin climbs out of the cart.*) Kattrin, got something to tell you. Cook and I want to go to Utrecht. He's been left an inn there. That'd be a settled place for you, let you meet a few people. Lots of 'em respect somebody mature, looks ain't everything. I'd like it too. I get on with cook. Say one thing for him, got a head for business. We'd have our meals for sure, not bad, eh? And your own bed too; like that, wouldn't you? Road's no life really. God knows how you might finish up. Lousy already, you are. Have to make up our minds, see, we could move with the Swedes, up north, they're somewhere up that way. (*She points to the left.*) Reckon that's fixed, Kattrin.

THE COOK: Anna, I got something private to say to you.

MOTHER COURAGE: Get back in cart, Kattrin.

(*Kattrin climbs back.*)

THE COOK: I had to interrupt, cause you don't understand, far as I can see. I didn't think there was need to say it, sticks out a mile. But if it don't, then let me tell you straight, no question of taking her along, not on your life. You get me, eh.

(*Kattrin sticks her head out of the cart behind them and listens.*)

MOTHER COURAGE: You mean I'm to leave Kattrin back here?

THE COOK: Use your imagination. Inn's got no room. It ain't one of the sort got three bar parlours. Put our backs in it we two'll get a living, but not three, no chance of that. She can keep cart.

MOTHER COURAGE: Thought she might find husband in Utrecht.

THE COOK: Go on, make me laugh. Find a husband, how? Dumb and that scar on top of it. And at her age?

MOTHER COURAGE: Don't talk so loud.

THE COOK: Loud or soft, no getting over facts. And that's another reason why I can't have her in the inn. Customers don't want to be looking at that all the time. Can't blame them.

MOTHER COURAGE: Shut your big mouth. I said not so loud.

THE COOK: Light's on in parson's house. We can try singing.

MOTHER COURAGE: Cooky, how's she to pull the cart on her own? War scares her. She'll never stand it. The dreams she must have . . . I hear her nights groaning. Mostly after a battle. What's she seeing in those dreams, I'd like to know. She's got a soft heart. Lately I found she'd got another hedgehog tucked away what we'd run over.

THE COOK: Inn's too small. (*Calls out.*) Ladies and gentlemen, domestic staff and other residents! We are now going to give you a song concerning Solomon, Julius Caesar and other famous personages what had bad luck. So's you can see we're respectable folk, which makes it difficult to carry on, particularly in winter. (*They sing.*)

> You saw sagacious Solomon
> You know what came of him.
> To him complexities seemed plain.
> He cursed the hour that gave birth to him
> And saw that everything was vain.
> How great and wise was Solomon!
> The world however didn't wait
> But soon observed what followed on.
> It's wisdom that had brought him to this state —
> How fortunate the man with none!

Yes, the virtues are dangerous stuff in this world, as this fine song proves, better not to have them and have a pleasant life and breakfast instead, hot soup for instance. Look at me: I haven't any but I'd like some. I'm a serving soldier but what good did my courage do me in all them battles, nowt, here I am starving and better have been shit-scared and stayed at home. For why?

> You saw courageous Caesar next
> You know what he became.
> They deified him in his life
> Then had him murdered just the same.
> And as they raised the fatal knife
> How loud he cried: You too, my son!
> The world however didn't wait
> But soon observed what followed on.
> It's courage that had brought him to that state.
> How fortunate the man with none!

(*Sotto voce.*) Don't even look out. (*Aloud.*) Ladies and gentlemen, domestic staff and other inmates! All right, you may say, gallantry never cooked a man's dinner, what about trying honesty? You can eat all you want then, or anyhow not stay sober. How about it?

> You heard of honest Socrates
> The man who never lied:
> They weren't so grateful as you'd think
> Instead the rulers fixed to have him tried
> And handed him the poisoned drink.
> How honest was the people's noble son!
> The world however didn't wait
> But soon observed what followed on.
> It's honesty that brought him to that state.
> How fortunate the man with none!

Ah yes, they say, be unselfish and share what you've got, but how about if you got nowt? It's all very well to say the do-gooders have a hard time, but you still got to have something. Aye, unselfishness is a rare virtue, cause it just don't pay.

> Saint Martin couldn't bear to see
> His fellows in distress.
> He met a poor man in the snow
> And shared his cloak with him, we know.
> Both of them therefore froze to death.
> His place in Heaven was surely won!
> The world however didn't wait
> But soon observed what followed on.
> Unselfishness had brought him to that state.
> How fortunate the man with none!

That's how it is with us. We're respectable folk, stick together, don't steal, don't murder, don't burn places down And all the time you might say we're sinking lower and lower, and it's true what the song says, and soup is few and far between, and if we weren't like this but thieves and murderers I dare say we'd be eating our fill. For virtues aren't their own reward, only wickednesses are, that's how the world goes and it didn't ought to.

> Here you can see respectable folk
> Keeping to God's own laws.
> So far he hasn't taken heed.
> You who sit safe and warm indoors
> Help to relieve our bitter need!
> How virtuously we had begun!
> The world however didn't wait
> But soon observed what followed on.
> It's fear of God that brought us to that state.
> How fortunate the man with none!

VOICE (*from above*): Hey, you there! Come on up! There's hot soup if you want.

MOTHER COURAGE: Lamb, me stomach won't stand nowt. 'Tain't that it ain't sensible, what you say, but is that your last word? We got on all right.

THE COOK: Last word. Think it over.

MOTHER COURAGE: I've nowt to think. I'm not leaving her here.

THE COOK: That's proper senseless, nothing I can do about it though. I'm not a brute, just the inn's a small one. So now we better get on up, or there'll be nowt here either and wasted time singing in the cold.

MOTHER COURAGE: I'll get Kattrin.

THE COOK: Better bring a bit back for her. Scare them if they sees three of us coming. (*Exeunt both.*)

(*Kattrin climbs out of the cart with a bundle. She looks around to see if the other two have gone. Then she takes an old pair of trousers of the cook's and a skirt of her mother's, and lays them side by side on one of the wheels, so that they are easily seen. She has finished and is picking up her bundle to go, when Mother Courage comes back from the house.*)

MOTHER COURAGE (*with a plate of soup*): Kattrin! Will you stop there? Kattrin! Where you off to with that bundle? Has devil himself taken you over? (*She examines the bundle.*) She's packed her things. You been listening? I told him nowt doing, Utrecht, his rotten inn, what'd we be up to there? You and me, inn's no place for us. Still plenty to be got out of war. (*She sees the trousers and the skirt.*) You're plain stupid. S'pose I'd seen that, and you gone away? (*She holds Kattrin back as she tries to break away.*) Don't you start thinking it's on your account I given him the push. It was cart, that's it. Catch me leaving my cart I'm used to, it ain't you, it's for cart. We'll go off in t'other direction, and we'll throw cook's stuff out so he finds it, silly man. (*She climbs in and throws out a few other articles in the direction of the trousers.*) There, he's out of our business now, and I ain't having nobody else in, ever. You and me'll carry on now. This winter will pass, same as all the others. Get hitched up, it looks like snow.

(*They both harness themselves to the cart, then wheel it round and drag it off. When the cook arrives he looks blankly at his kit.*)

SCENE 10

(*During the whole of 1635 Mother Courage and her daughter Kattrin travel over the highroads of central Germany, in the wake of the increasingly bedraggled armies.*)
(*High road.*)
(*Mother Courage and Kattrin are pulling the cart. They pass a peasant's house inside which there is a voice singing.*)

THE VOICE:

The roses in our arbour
Delight us with their show:
They have such lovely flowers
Repaying all our labour
After the summer showers.
Happy are those with gardens now:
They have such lovely flowers.

When winter winds are freezing
As through the woods they blow
Our home is warm and pleasing.
We fixed the thatch above it
With straw and moss we wove it.
Happy are those with shelter now
When winter winds are freezing.

(*Mother Courage and Kattrin pause to listen, then continue pulling.*)

SCENE 11

(*January 1636. The emperor's troops are threatening the Protestant town of Halle. The stone begins to speak. Mother Courage loses her daughter and trudges on alone. The war is a long way from being over.*)
(*The cart is standing, much the worse for wear, alongside a peasant's house with a huge thatched roof, backing on a wall of rock. It is night.*)
(*An ensign and three soldiers in heavy armour step out of the wood.*)

THE ENSIGN: I want no noise now. Anyone shouts, shove your pike into him.

FIRST SOLDIER: Have to knock them up, though, if we're to find a guide.

THE ENSIGN: Knocking sounds natural. Could be a cow bumping the stable wall.

(*The soldiers knock on the door of the house. The peasant's wife opens it. They stop her mouth. Two soldiers go in.*)

MAN'S VOICE (*within*): What is it?

(*The soldiers bring out the peasant and his son.*)

THE ENSIGN (*pointing at the cart, where Kattrin's head has appeared*): There's another one. (*A Soldier drags her out.*) Anyone else live here beside you lot?

THE PEASANTS: This is our son. And she's dumb. Her mother's gone into town to buy stuff. For their business, cause so many people's getting out and selling things cheap. They're just passing through. Canteen folk.

THE ENSIGN: I'm warning you, keep quiet, or if there's the least noise you get a pike across your nut. Now I want someone to come with us and show us the path to the town. (*Points to the young peasant.*) Here, you.

THE YOUNG PEASANT: I don't know no path.

SECOND SOLDIER (*grinning*): He don't know no path.

THE YOUNG PEASANT: I ain't helping Catholics.

THE ENSIGN (*to the second soldier*): Stick your pike in his ribs.

THE YOUNG PEASANT (*forced to his knees, with the pike threatening him*): I won't do it, not to save my life.

FIRST SOLDIER: I know what'll change his mind. (*Goes towards the stable.*) Two cows and an ox. Listen, you: if you're not reasonable I'll chop up your cattle.

THE YOUNG PEASANT: No, not that!

THE PEASANT'S WIFE (*weeps*): Please spare our cattle, captain, it'd be starving us to death.

THE ENSIGN: They're dead if he goes on being obstinate.

FIRST SOLDIER: I'm taking the ox first.

THE YOUNG PEASANT (*to his father*): Have I got to? (*The wife nods.*) Right.

THE PEASANT'S WIFE: And thank you kindly, captain, for sparing us, for ever and ever, Amen.

(*The peasant stops his wife from further expressions of gratitude.*)

FIRST SOLDIER: I knew the ox was what they minded about most, was I right?

(*Guided by the young peasant, the ensign and his men continue on their way.*)

THE PEASANT: What are they up to, I'd like to know. Nowt good.

THE PEASANT'S WIFE: Perhaps they're just scouting. What you doing?

THE PEASANT (*putting a ladder against the roof and climbing up it*): Seeing if they're on their own. (*From the top.*) Something moving in the wood. Can see something down by the quarry. And there are men in armour in the clearing. And a gun. That's at least a regiment. God's mercy on the town and everyone in it!

THE PEASANT'S WIFE: Any lights in the town?

THE PEASANT: No. They'll all be asleep. (*Climbs down.*) If those people get in they'll butcher the lot.

THE PEASANT'S WIFE: Sentries're bound to spot them first.

THE PEASANT: Sentry in the tower up the hill must have been killed, or he'd have blown his bugle.

THE PEASANT'S WIFE: If only there were more of us.

THE PEASANT: Just you and me and that cripple.

THE PEASANT'S WIFE: Nowt we can do, you'd say. . . .

THE PEASANT: Nowt.

THE PEASANT'S WIFE: Can't possibly run down there in the blackness.

THE PEASANT: Whole hillside's crawling with 'em. We could give a signal.

THE PEASANT'S WIFE: What, and have them butcher us too?

THE PEASANT: You're right, nowt we can do.

THE PEASANT'S WIFE (*to Kattrin*): Pray, poor creature, pray! Nowt we can do to stop bloodshed. You can't talk, maybe, but at least you can pray. He'll hear you if no one else can. I'll help you. (*All kneel, Kattrin behind the two peasants.*) Our Father, which art in Heaven, hear Thou our prayer, let not the town be destroyed with all what's in it sound asleep and suspecting nowt. Arouse Thou them that they may get up and go to the walls and see how the enemy approacheth with picks and guns in the blackness across fields below the slope. (*Turning to Kattrin.*) Guard Thou our mother and ensure that the watch-

man sleepeth not but wakes up, or it will be too late. Succour our brother-in-law also, he is inside there with his four children, spare Thou them, they are innocent and know nowt. (*To Kattrin, who gives a groan.*) One of them's not two yet, the eldest's seven. (*Kattrin stands up distractedly.*) Our Father, hear us, for only Thou canst help; we look to be doomed, for why, we are weak and have no pike and nowt and can risk nowt and are in Thy hand along with our cattle and all the farm, and same with the town, it too is in Thy hand and the enemy is before the walls in great strength.

(*Unobserved, Kattrin has slipped away to the cart and taken from it something which she hides beneath her apron; then she climbs up the ladder on to the stable roof.*)

THE PEASANT'S WIFE: Forget not the children, what are in danger, the littlest ones especially, the old folk what can't move, and every living creature.

THE PEASANT: And forgive us our trespasses as we forgive them that trespass against us. Amen.

(*Sitting on the roof, Kattrin begins to beat the drum which she has pulled out from under her apron.*)

THE PEASANT'S WIFE: Jesus Christ, what's she doing?

THE PEASANT: She's out of her mind.

THE PEASANT'S WIFE: Quick, get her down.

(*The peasant hurries to the ladder, but Kattrin pulls it up on to the roof.*)

THE PEASANT'S WIFE: She'll do us in.

THE PEASANT: Stop drumming at once, you cripple!

THE PEASANT'S WIFE: Bringing the Catholics down on us!

THE PEASANT (*looking for stones to throw*): I'll stone you.

THE PEASANT'S WIFE: Where's your feelings? Where's your heart? We're done for if they come down on us. Slit our throats, they will.

(*Kattrin stares into the distance towards the town and carries on drumming.*)

THE PEASANT'S WIFE (*to her husband*): I told you we shouldn't have allowed those vagabonds on to farm. What do they care if our last cows are taken?

THE ENSIGN (*runs in with his soldiers and the young peasant*): I'll cut you to ribbons, all of you!

THE PEASANT'S WIFE: Please, sir, it's not our fault, we couldn't help it. It was her sneaked up there. A foreigner.

THE ENSIGN: Where's the ladder?

THE PEASANT: There.

THE ENSIGN (*calls up*): I order you, throw that drum down.

(*Kattrin goes on drumming.*)

THE ENSIGN: You're all in this together. It'll be the end of you.

THE PEASANT: They been cutting pine trees in that wood. How about if we got one of the trunks and poked her off. . . .

FIRST SOLDIER (*to the ensign*): Permission to make a suggestion, sir! (*He whispers something in the ensign's ear.*) Listen, we got a suggestion could help you. Get down off there and come into town with us right away. Show us which your mother is and we'll see she ain't harmed.

(*Kattrin goes on drumming.*)

THE ENSIGN (*pushes him roughly aside*): She doesn't trust you; with a mug like yours it's not surprising. (*Calls up.*) Suppose I gave you my word? I can give my word of honour as an officer.

(*Kattrin drums harder.*)

THE ENSIGN: Is nothing sacred to her?

THE YOUNG PEASANT: There's more than her mother involved, sir.

FIRST SOLDIER: This can't go on much longer. They're bound to hear in the town.

THE ENSIGN: We'll have somehow to make a noise that's louder than her drumming. What can we make a noise with?

FIRST SOLDIER: Thought we weren't s'posed to make no noise.

THE ENSIGN: A harmless one, you fool. A peaceful one.

THE PEASANT: I could chop wood with my axe.

THE ENSIGN: Good: you chop. (*The peasant fetches his axe and attacks a tree-trunk.*) Chop harder! Harder! You're chopping for your life.

(*Kattrin has been listening, drumming less loudly the while. She now looks wildly round, and goes on drumming.*)

THE ENSIGN: Not loud enough. (*To the first soldier.*) You chop too.

THE PEASANT: Only got the one axe. (*Stops chopping.*)

THE ENSIGN: We'll have to set the farm on fire. Smoke her out, that's it.

THE PEASANT: It wouldn't help, captain. If the towns-people see a fire here they'll know what's up.

(*Kattrin has again been listening as she drums. At this point she laughs.*)

THE ENSIGN: Look at her laughing at us. I'm not having that. I'll shoot her down, and damn the conse-quences. Fetch the harquebus.

(*Three soldiers hurry off. Kattrin goes on drumming.*)

THE PEASANT'S WIFE: I got it, captain. That's their cart. If we smash it up she'll stop. Cart's all they got.

THE ENSIGN (*to the young peasant*): Smash it up. (*Calls up.*) We're going to smash up your cart if you don't stop drumming. (*The young peasant gives the cart a few feeble blows.*)

THE PEASANT'S WIFE: Stop it, you animal!

(*Desperately looking towards the cart, Kattrin emits pitiful noises. But she goes on drumming.*)

THE ENSIGN: Where are those clodhoppers with the harquebus?

FIRST SOLDIER: Can't have heard nowt in town yet, else we'd be hearing their guns.

THE ENSIGN (*calls up*): They can't hear you at all. And now we're going to shoot you down. For the last time: throw down that drum!

THE YOUNG PEASANT (*suddenly flings away his plank*): Go on drumming! Or they'll all be killed! Go on, go on. . . .

(*The soldier knocks him down and beats him with his pike. Kattrin starts to cry, but she goes on drumming.*)

THE PEASANT'S WIFE: Don't strike his back! For God's sake, you're beating him to death!

(*The soldiers hurry in with the harquebus.*)

SECOND SOLDIER: Colonel's frothing at the mouth, sir. We're all for court-martial.

THE ENSIGN: Set it up! Set it up! (*Calls up while the gun is being erected.*) For the very last time: stop drum-ming! (*Kattrin, in tears, drums as loud as she can.*) Fire! (*The soldiers fire. Kattrin is hit, gives a few more drumbeats and then slowly crumples.*)

THE ENSIGN: That's the end of that.

(*But Kattrin's last drumbeats are taken up by the town's cannon. In the distance can be heard a confused noise of tocsins and gunfire.*)

FIRST SOLDIER: She's made it.

SCENE 12

(*Before first light. Sound of the fifes and drums of troops marching off into the distance.*)
(*In front of the cart Mother Courage is squatting by her daughter. The peasant family are standing near her.*)

THE PEASANTS (*with hostility*): You must go, missis. There's only one more regiment behind that one. You can't go on your own.

MOTHER COURAGE: I think she's going to sleep. (*She sings.*)

> Lullaby baby
> What's that in the hay?
> Neighbours' kids grizzle
> But my kids are gay.
> Neighbours' are in tatters
> And you're dressed in lawn
> Cut down from the raiment an
> Angel has worn.
> Neighbours' kids go hungry
> And you shall eat cake
> Suppose it's too crumbly

You've only to speak.
Lullaby baby
What's that in the hay?
The one lies in Poland
The other — who can say?

Better if you'd not told her nowt about your brother-in-law's kids.

THE PEASANT: If you'd not gone into town to get your cut it might never of happened.

MOTHER COURAGE: Now she's asleep.

THE PEASANT'S WIFE: She ain't asleep. Can't you see she's passed over?

THE PEASANT: And it's high time you got away yourself. There are wolves around and, what's worse, marauders.

MOTHER COURAGE: Aye.

(*She goes and gets a tarpaulin to cover the dead girl with.*)

THE PEASANT'S WIFE: Ain't you got nobody else? What you could go to?

MOTHER COURAGE: Aye, one left. Eilif.

THE PEASANT (*as Mother Courage covers the dead girl*): Best look for him, then. We'll mind·her, see she gets proper burial. Don't you worry about that.

MOTHER COURAGE: Here's money for expenses.

(*She counts out coins into the peasant's hands. The peasant and his son shake hands with her and carry Kattrin away.*)

THE PEASANT'S WIFE (*as she leaves*): I'd hurry.

MOTHER COURAGE (*harnessing herself to the cart*): Hope I can pull cart all right by meself. Be all right, nowt much inside it. Got to get back in business again.

(*Another regiment with its fifes and drums marches past in the background.*)

MOTHER COURAGE (*tugging the cart*): Take me along!
(*Singing is heard from offstage.*)

With all its luck and all its danger
The war is dragging on a bit
Another hundred years or longer
The common man won't benefit.
Filthy his food, no soap to shave him
The regiment steals half his pay.
But still a miracle may save him:
Tomorrow is another day!
    The new year's come. The watchmen shout.
    The thaw sets in. The dead remain.
    Wherever life has not died out
    It staggers to its feet again.

COMMENTARIES

Bertolt Brecht (1898–1956)
THE ALIENATION EFFECT   *1964*

TRANSLATED BY JOHN WILLETT

> *In this short description, Brecht explains some of his theories of staging and acting. His alienation effect reminds the audience that the characters on stage are dramatic constructs, not real people suffering real emotions. As he explains, the A-effect is the opposite of traditional acting, which is designed to produce an empathy between actor and audience. The A-effect rejects that empathy.*

What follows represents an attempt to describe a technique of acting which was applied in certain theaters with a view to taking the incidents portrayed and alienating them from the spectator. The aim of this technique, known as the alienation effect, was to make the spectator adopt an attitude of inquiry and criticism in his approach to the incident. The means were artistic.

The first condition for the A-effect's application to this end is that stage and auditorium must be purged of everything "magical" and that no "hypnotic tensions" should be set up. This ruled out any attempt to make the stage convey the flavor of a particular place (a room at evening, a road in the autumn), or to create atmosphere by relaxing the tempo of the conversation. The audience was not "worked up" by a display of temperament or "swept away" by acting with tautened muscles; in short, no attempt was made to put it in a trance and give it the illusion of watching an ordinary unrehearsed event. As will be seen presently, the audience's tendency to plunge into such illusions has to be checked by specific artistic means.

The first condition for the achievement of the A-effect is that the actor must invest what he has to show with a definite gest of showing. It is of course necessary to drop the assumption that there is a fourth wall cutting the audience off from the stage and the consequent illusion that the stage action is taking place in reality and without an audience. That being so, it is possible for the actor in principle to address the audience directly.

It is well known that contact between audience and stage is normally made on the basis of empathy. Conventional actors devote their efforts so exclusively to bringing about this psychological operation that they may be said to see it as the principal aim of their art. Our introductory remarks will already have made it clear that the technique which produces an A-effect is the exact opposite of that which aims at empathy. The actor applying it is bound not to try to bring about the empathy operation.

Yet in his efforts to reproduce particular characters and show their behavior he need not renounce the means of empathy entirely. He uses these means just as any normal person with no particular acting talent would use them if he wanted to portray someone else, i.e., show how he behaves. This showing of other people's behavior happens time and again in ordinary life (witnesses of an accident demonstrating to newcomers how the victim behaved, a facetious person imitating a friend's walk, etc.), without those involved making the least effort to subject their spectators to an illusion. At the same time they do feel their way into their characters' skins with a view to acquiring their characteristics.

As has already been said, the actor too will make use of this psychological operation. But whereas the usual practice in acting is to execute it during the actual performance, in the hope of stimulating the spectator into a similar operation, he will achieve it only at an earlier stage, at some time during rehearsals.

To safeguard against an unduly "impulsive," frictionless and uncritical creation of characters and incidents, more reading rehearsals can be held than usual. The actor should refrain from living himself into the part prematurely in any way, and should go on functioning as long as possible as a reader (which does not mean a reader-aloud). An important step is memorizing one's first impressions.

When reading his part the actor's attitude should be one of a man who is astounded and contradicts. Not only the occurrence of the incidents, as he reads about them, but the conduct of the man he is playing, as he experiences it, must be weighed up by him and their peculiarities understood; none can be taken as given, as something that "was bound to turn out that way," that was "only to be expected from a character like that." Before memorizing the words he must memorize what he felt astounded at and where he felt impelled to contradict. For these are dynamic forces that he must preserve in creating his performance.

When he appears on the stage, besides what he actually is doing he will at all essential points discover, specify, imply what he is not doing; that is to say he will act in such a way that the alternative emerges as clearly as possible, that his acting allows the other possibilities to be inferred and only represents one out of the possible variants. He will say for instance "You'll pay for that," and not say "I forgive you." He detests his children; it is not the case that he loves them. He moves down stage left and not up stage right. Whatever he doesn't do must be contained and conserved in what he does. In this way every sentence and every gesture signifies a decision; the character remains under observation and is tested. The technical term for this procedure is "fixing the 'not . . . but.'"

The actor does not allow himself to become completely transformed on the stage into the character he is portraying. He is not Lear, Harpagon, Schweik; he shows them. He reproduces their remarks as authentically as he can; he puts forward their way of behaving to the best of his abilities and knowledge of men; but he never tries to persuade himself (and thereby others) that this amounts to a complete transformation. Actors will know what it means if I say that a typical kind of acting without this complete transformation takes place when a producer or colleague shows one how to play a particular passage. It is not his own part, so he is not completely transformed; he underlines the technical aspect and retains the attitude of someone just making suggestions.

Once the idea of total transformation is abandoned the actor speaks his part not as if he were improvising it himself but like a quotation. At the same time he obviously has to render all the quotation's overtones, the remark's full human and concrete shape; similarly the gesture he makes must have the full substance of a human gesture even though it now represents a copy.

Given this absence of total transformation in the acting there are three aids which may help to alienate the actions and remarks of the characters being portrayed:

1. Transposition into the third person.
2. Transposition into the past.
3. Speaking the stage directions out loud.

Using the third person and the past tense allows the actor to adopt the right attitude of detachment. In addition he will look for stage directions and remarks that comment on his lines, and speak them aloud at rehearsal ("He stood up and exclaimed angrily, not having eaten: . . . ," or "He had never been told so before, and didn't know if it was true or not," or "He smiled, and said with forced nonchalance: . . ."). Speaking the stage directions out loud in the third person results in a clash between two tones of voice, alienating the second of them, the text proper. This style of acting is further alienated by taking place on the stage after having already been outlined and announced in words. Transposing it into the past gives the speaker a standpoint from which he can look back at his sentence. The sentence too is thereby alienated without the speaker adopting an unreal point of view; unlike the spectator, he has read the play right through and is better placed to judge the sentence in accordance with the ending, with its consequences, than the former, who knows less and is more of a stranger to the sentence.

This composite process leads to an alienation of the text in the rehearsals which generally persists in the performance too. The directness of the relationship with the audience allows and indeed forces the actual speech delivery to be varied in accordance with the greater or smaller significance attaching to the sentences. Take the case of witnesses addressing a court. The underlinings, the characters' insistence on their remarks, must be developed as a piece of effective virtuosity. If the actor turns to the audience it must be a whole-hearted turn rather than the asides and soliloquizing technique of the old-fashioned theater. To get the full A-effect from the poetic medium the actor should start at rehearsal by paraphrasing the verse's content in vulgar prose, possibly accompanying this by the gestures designed for the verse. A daring and beautiful handling of verbal media will alienate the text. (Prose can be alienated by translation into the actor's native dialect.)

Gesture will be dealt with below, but it can at once be said that everything to do with the emotions has to be externalized; that is to say, it must be developed into a gesture. The actor has to find a sensibly perceptible outward expression for his character's emotions, preferably some action that gives away what is going on inside him. The emotion in question must be brought out, must lose all its restrictions so that it can be treated on a big scale. Special elegance, power and grace of gesture bring about the A-effect.

A masterly use of gesture can be seen in Chinese acting. The Chinese actor achieves the A-effect by being seen to observe his own movements.

Whatever the actor offers in the way of gesture, verse structure, etc., must be finished and bear the hallmarks of something rehearsed and rounded-off. The impression to be given is one of ease, which is at the same time one of difficulties overcome. The actor must make it possible for the audience to take his own art, his mastery of technique, lightly too. He puts an incident before the spectator with perfection and as he thinks it really happened or might have happened. He does not conceal the fact that he has rehearsed it, any more than an acrobat conceals his training, and he emphasizes that it is his own (actor's) account, view, version of the incident.

Because he doesn't identify himself with him he can pick a definite attitude to adopt towards the character whom he portrays, can show what he thinks of him and invite the spectator, who is likewise not asked to identify himself, to criticize the character portrayed.

The attitude which he adopts is a socially critical one. In his exposition of the incidents and in his characterization of the person he tries to bring out those features which come within society's sphere. In this way his performance becomes a discussion (about social conditions) with the audience he is addressing. He prompts the spectator to justify or abolish these conditions according to what class he belongs to.

The object of the A-effect is to alienate the social gest underlying every incident. By social gest is meant the mimetic and gestural expression of the social relationships prevailing between people of a given period.

It helps to formulate the incident for society, and to put it across in such a way that society is given the key, if titles are thought up for the scenes. These titles must have a historical quality.

This brings us to a crucial technical device: historicization.

The actor must play the incidents as historical ones. Historical incidents are unique, transitory incidents associated with particular periods. The conduct of the persons involved in them is not fixed and "universally human"; it includes elements that have been or may be overtaken by the course of history, and is subject to criticism from the immediately following period's point of view. The conduct of those born before us is alienated[1] from us by an incessant evolution.

It is up to the actor to treat present-day events and modes of behavior with the same detachment as the historian adopts with regard to those of the past. He must alienate these characters and incidents from us.

Characters and incidents from ordinary life, from our immediate surroundings, being familiar, strike us as more or less natural. Alienating them helps to make them seem remarkable to us. Science has carefully developed a technique of getting irritated with the everyday, "self-evident," universally accepted occurrence, and there is no reason why this infinitely useful attitude should not be taken over by art. It is an attitude which arose in science as a result of the growth in human productive powers. In art the same motive applies.

As for the emotions, the experimental use of the A-effect in the epic theater's German productions indicated that this way of acting too can stimulate them, though possibly a different class of emotion is involved from those of the orthodox theater. A critical attitude on the audience's part is a thoroughly artistic one. Nor does the actual practice of the A-effect seem anything like so unnatural as its description. Of course it is a way of acting that his nothing to do with stylization as commonly practiced. The main advantage of the epic theater with its A-effect, intended purely to show the world in such a way that it becomes manageable, is precisely its quality of being natural and earthly, its humor and its renunciation of all the mystical elements that have stuck to the orthodox theater from the old days.

[1]*Entfremdet.*

Bertolt Brecht (1898–1956)

Notes for *Mother Courage*, Scene 12   *1949*

TRANSLATED BY ERIC BENTLEY AND HUGO SCHMIDT

> *Brecht produced booklets for some of his work that supply a great deal of background information that does not appear in the text of the plays. Brecht's manner of producing his plays were important to him. While he did not expect every successive production to adhere strictly to the standards he established in commentaries such as this, he hoped his intentions would be substantially respected.*

Twelfth Scene
Courage Moves On

> *The peasants have to convince Courage that Kattrin is dead. Kattrin's lullaby. Mother Courage pays for Kattrin's funeral and receives the expressions of sympathy of the peasants. Mother Courage harnesses herself to her empty covered wagon. Still hoping to get back into business, she follows the tattered army.*

Basic Arrangement

The wagon stands on the empty stage. Mother Courage holds dead Kattrin's head in her lap. The peasants stand at the foot of the dead girl, huddled together and hostile. Courage talks as if her daughter were only sleeping, and deliberately overhears the reproach of the peasants that she was to blame for Kattrin's death.

Kattrin's lullaby. The mother's face is bent low over the face of the daughter. The song does not conciliate those who listen.

Mother Courage pays for Kattrin's funeral and receives expressions of sympathy from the peasants. After she has realized that her last child is dead, Courage gets up laboriously and hobbles around the corpse (right), along the footlights, behind the wagon. She returns with a tent cloth, and answers over her shoulder the peasant's question whether she had no one to turn to: "Oh yes, one. Eilif." And places the cloth over the body, with her back toward the footlights. At the head of the corpse, she pulls the cloth all the way over the face, then again takes her place behind the corpse. The peasant and his son shake hands with her and bow ceremoniously before carrying the body out (to the right). The peasant woman, too, shakes hands with Courage, walks to the right and stops once more, undecided. The two women exchange a few words, then the peasant woman exits.

Mother Courage harnesses herself to her empty covered wagon. Still hoping to get back into business, she follows the tattered army. Slowly, the old woman walks to the wagon, rolls up the rope which Dumb Kattrin had been pulling to this point, takes a stick, looks at it, slips it through the sling of the second rope, tucks the stick under her arm, and starts pulling. The turntable begins to move, and Courage circles the stage once. The curtain closes when she is upstage right for the second time.

The Peasants

The attitude of the peasants toward Courage is hostile. She got them into difficulties, and they will be saddled with her if she does not catch up with the regiments. Besides, she is to blame for the accident herself, in their opinion. And moreover the canteen woman is not part of the resident population, and now, in time of war, she belongs to the fleecers, cutthroats, and marauders in the wake of the armies. When they condole with her by shaking her hand, they merely follow custom.

The Bow

During this entire scene, Weigel, as Courage, showed an almost animal indifference. All the more beautiful was the deep bow that she made when the body was carried away.

The Lullaby

The lullaby must be sung without sentimentality and without the desire to arouse sentimentality. Otherwise, its significance does not get across. The thought that is the basis of this song is a murderous one: the child of this mother was supposed to be better off than other children of other mothers. Through a slight stress on the "you," Weigel revealed the treacherous hope of Courage to get her child, and perhaps only hers, through the war alive. The child to whom the most common things were denied was promised the uncommon.

Paying for the Funeral

Even when paying for the funeral, Weigel gave another hint at the character of Courage. She fished a few coins from her leather purse, put one back, and gave the rest to the peasant. The overpowering impression she gave of having been destroyed was not in the least diminished by this.

The Last Verse

While Courage slowly harnessed herself to her wagon, the last verse of her song was sung from the box in which the band had been placed. It expresses one more time her undestroyed hope to get something out of war anyway. It becomes more impressive in that it does not aim at the illusion that the song is actually sung by army units moving past in the distance.

Giehse in the Role of Courage

When covering up the body, Giehse put her head under the cloth, looking at her daughter one more time, before finally dropping it over her face.

Before she began pulling away her covered wagon — another beautiful variant — she looked into the distance, to figure out where to go, and before she started pulling, she blew her nose with her index finger.

Take Your Time

At the end of the play it is necessary that one see the wagon roll away. Naturally, the audience gets the idea when the wagon starts. If the movement is extended, a moment of irritation arises ("that's long enough, now"). If it is prolonged even further, deeper understanding sets in.

Pulling the Wagon in the Last Scene

For the 12th scene, farm house and stable with roof (of the 11th scene) were cleared away, and only the wagon and Dumb Kattrin's body were left. The act of dragging the wagon off — the large letters "Saxony" were pulled up (out of sight) when the music begins — took place on a completely empty stage: whereby one remembered the setting of the first scene. Courage and her wagon moved in a complete circle on the revolving stage. She passed the footlights once more. As usual, the stage was bathed in light.

Discoveries of the Realists

Wherein lies the effectiveness of Weigel's gesture when she mechanically puts one coin back into her purse, after having fished her money out, as she hands the peasant the funeral money for dead Kattrin? She shows that this tradeswoman, in all her grief, does not completely forget to count, since money is so hard to come by. And she shows this as a discovery about human nature that is shaped by certain conditions. This little feature has the power and the suddenness of a discovery. The art of the realists consists of digging out the truth from under the rubble of the evident, of connecting the particular with the general, of pinning down the unique within the larger process.

A Change of Text

After "I'll manage, there isn't much in it now," Courage added, in the Munich and then also in the Berlin production: "I must start up again in business."

Mother Courage Learns Nothing

In the last scene, Weigel's Courage appeared like an eighty-year-old woman. And she comprehends nothing. She reacts only to the statements that are connected with war, such as that one must not remain behind. She overhears the crude reproach of the peasants that Kattrin's death was her fault.

Courage's inability to learn from the unproductiveness of war was a prophecy in the year 1938 when the play was written. At the Berlin production in 1948 the desire was voiced that Courage should at least come to a realization in the play. To make it possible for the spectator to get something out of this realistic play, i.e., to make the spectator learn a lesson, theaters have to arrive at an acting style that does not seek an identification of the spectator with the protagonist.

Judging on the basis of reports of spectators and newspaper reviews, the Zurich world premiere — although artistically on a high level — presented only the image of war as a natural catastrophe and an inevitable fate, and thereby it underscored to the middle-class spectator in the orchestra his own indestructibility, his ability to survive. But even to the likewise middle-class Courage, the decision "Join in or don't join in" was always left open in the play. The production, it seems, must also have presented Courage's business dealings, profiteering, willingness to take risks, as quite natural, "eternally human" behavior, so that she had no other choice. Today, it is true, the man of the middle class can no longer stay out of war, as Courage could have. To him, a production of the play can probably teach nothing but a real hatred of war, and a certain insight into the fact that the big deals of which war consists are not made by the little people. In that sense, the play is more of a lesson than reality is, because here in the play the situation of war is more of an experimental situation, made for the sake of insights. I.e., the spectator attains the attitude of a student — as long as the acting style is correct. The part of the audience that belongs to the proletariat, i.e., the class that actually can struggle against and overcome war, should be given insight into the connection between business and war (again provided the acting style is correct): the proletariat as a class can do away with war by doing away with capitalism. Of course, as far as the proletarian part of the audience is concerned, one must also take into consideration the fact that this class is busy drawing its own conclusions — inside as well as outside the theater.

The Epic Element

The Epic element was certainly visible in the production at the Deutsches Theater — in the arrangement, in the presentation of the characters, in the minute execution of details, and in the pacing of the entire play. Also, contradictory elements were not eliminated but stressed, and the parts, visible as such, made a convincing whole. However, the goal of Epic Theater was not reached. Much became clear, but clarification was in the end absent. Only in a few recasting-rehearsals did it clearly emerge, for then the actors were only "pretending," i.e., they only showed to the newly added colleague the positions and intonations, and then the whole thing received that preciously loose, unlabored, non-urgent element that incites the spectator to have his own independent thoughts and feelings.

That the production did not have an Epic foundation was never remarked, however: which was probably the reason the actors did not dare provide one.

Concerning the Notes Themselves

We hope that the present notes, offering various explanations and inventions essential to the production of a play, will not have an air of spurious seriousness. It is admittedly hard to establish the lightness and casualness that are of the essence of theater. The arts, even when they are instructive, are forms of amusement.

Tennessee Williams

Tennessee Williams
pausing on the set of
Night of the Iguana at
London's Savoy Theatre
in 1965.

Tennessee Williams (1911–1983) was one of a handful of post–World War II American playwrights to achieve an international reputation. He was born Thomas Lanier Williams in Columbus, Mississippi, the son of a traveling shoe salesman who eventually moved the family to a dark and dreary tenement in St. Louis. A precocious child, Williams was given a typewriter by his mother when he was eleven years old. The instrument helped him create fantasy worlds that seemed more real, more important to him than the dark and sometimes threatening world in which he lived. His parents, expecting a third child, bought a house whose gloominess depressed virtually everyone in it. His mother and father found themselves arguing, and his sister, Rose, took refuge from the real world by closeting herself with a collection of glass animals.

Both Rose and Tennessee responded badly to their environment, and both had breakdowns. Tennessee was so ill that he suffered a partial paralysis of his legs, a disorder that made him a victim of bullies at school and a disappointment to his father at home. He could never participate in sports and was always somewhat frail; however, he was very advanced intellectually and published his first story when he was sixteen.

His education was sporadic. He attended the University of Missouri but, failing ROTC because of his physical limitations, soon dropped out to work in a shoe company. He then went to Washington University in St. Louis but dropped out again. Finally, he earned a bachelor's degree in playwriting at the State University of Iowa when he was twenty-four. During this time he was writing plays, some of which were produced at Washington University. Two years after he graduated, the Theatre Guild produced his first commercial play, *Battle of Angels* (1940), in Boston. It was such a distinct failure that he feared his fledgling career was stunted, but he kept writing and managed to live for a few years on foundation grants. It was not until the production of *The Glass Menagerie* (1944 in Chicago, 1945 in New York) that he achieved the kind of notice he knew he deserved. His first real success, the play was given the New York Drama Critics' Circle Award, the sign of his having achieved a measure of professional recognition and financial independence.

After trying several jobs, including an unsuccessful attempt at screenwriting, he had no more worries about work after *The Glass Menagerie* ran on Broadway for 561 performances. In 1947 his second success, *A Streetcar Named Desire*, starring the then unknown Marlon Brando, was an even bigger box-office smash. It ran for 855 performances and won the Pulitzer Prize. By the time Tennessee Williams was thirty-six, he was regarded as one of the most important playwrights in America.

Williams followed these successes with a number of plays that were not all as well received as his first works. *Summer and Smoke* (1948), *The Rose Tattoo* (1951), and *Camino Real* (1953) were met with measured enthusiasm from the public, although the critics thought highly of Williams's work. These plays were followed by the saga of a southern family, *Cat on a Hot Tin Roof*, which won all the major drama prizes in 1955, including the Pulitzer.

Williams's energy was unfailing in the next several years. He authored a screenplay, *Baby Doll*, with the legendary director Elia Kazan, in 1956. In 1958 he wrote a one-act play, *Suddenly Last Summer*, and in 1959 *Sweet Bird of Youth*. Some of his later plays are *The Night of the Iguana* (1961), *The Milk Train Doesn't Stop Here Anymore* (1963), and *Small Craft Warnings* (1972). He also wrote a novel and several volumes of short stories, establishing himself as an important writer in many genres. His sudden death in 1983 was a blow to the theater world.

THE GLASS MENAGERIE

Tennessee Williams has often been accused of exorcising his family demons in his plays and of therefore sometimes cloaking events in a personal symbolism that is impossible for an audience to penetrate totally. *The Glass Menagerie* (1944) certainly derives from his personal experience growing up in St. Louis in a tenement, the setting for the play. The characters are drawn from his own family, particularly the character Laura, who is based on his sister. But the symbolism in the play is not so obscure as to give an audience special difficulty.

In a way Williams thought of the play as a tribute to his sister, Rose. Rose's depressions were so severe that eventually she received a lobotomy, which rendered her more passive and more hopeless than before. The operation did not achieve anything positive, and Williams felt somewhat responsible because he had not urged the family to refuse the treatment.

In the play Amanda Wingfield is obsessed with finding gentlemen callers and a suitable career for her daughter, Laura, who walks with a slight limp and is exceedingly shy. Amanda lives in a world of imagination, endlessly retelling stories about a glorious past filled with suitors she could have had before she married. Amanda bullies Laura, whose only defense is to bury herself in her own fantasy world of spun-glass animals. Tom, the son and narrator of the play, is also a victim of Amanda's bullying, but he is more independent and better able to withstand her assaults.

Both children are great disappointments to Amanda. Tom is aloof, indolent, something like his father who is present only in his picture on the wall. Laura calls herself a cripple and has no self-esteem or hope for a future such as the one her mother conceives for her. Laura's shyness is almost uncontrollable. It has ruined any hope of a business career, to Amanda's intense distress. When Tom brings home Jim, and his sister recognizes him as a boy she admired from afar in high school, Laura is nearly too shy to come to the dinner table. And when it becomes clear that Jim is not the gentleman caller of Amanda's dreams, Amanda and Laura are left to face reality or to continue living in their fantasy worlds.

Amanda confronts Tom at the end of the play and asserts that he "live[s] in a dream" and "manufacture[s] illusions." She could be speaking about any character in the play, including Jim, who lives according to popular illusions about self-fulfillment. But the Wingfields in particular pay dearly for their illusions, perhaps Laura more than anyone because of her mother's inability to relinquish intense but unrealistic hopes for her daughter.

Williams's written presentation of the play provides more insights than usual for a reading audience. His stage directions are elaborate, poetic, and exceptionally evocative. Through Tom, as narrator, he says that the play is not realistic but rather is a memory play, an enactment of moments in Tom's memory.

Williams specifies a setting that is almost dreamlike, using Brechtian devices such as the visual images and screen legends flashed at appropriate moments. He uses music to establish a mood or stimulate an association. Because modern productions rarely follow Williams's directions, the dreamlike quality is sometimes lost. In fact, ironically, modern productions of this play are often realistic rather than symbolic, although they usually maintain the mood that Williams hoped to achieve.

The Glass Menagerie in Performance

The first production of *The Glass Menagerie* opened in Chicago on December 26, 1944, during World War II. Audiences were not drawn to it at first, but the critics' positive reviews began to attract people to the theater. In March 1945, when it was playing to full houses, the play transferred to New York and began a run of 561 performances. It won the Drama Critics' Circle Award as the best American play of the 1944–1945 season. Two road companies then toured the play around the country. The first London performance, in the large and distinguished Theatre Royal in Haymarket in July 1948, was directed by John Gielgud and starred Helen Hayes as Amanda Wingfield. A film version followed in 1950.

Revivals of the play have been both numerous and successful. Laurette Taylor, who played Amanda in the original New York production, set a standard with her interpretation of Williams's poetic language. Maureen Stapleton, whose more vigorous approach contrasted sharply with Taylor's, took the role in the 1965 production in the Brooks Atkinson Theater in New York. The critic Howard Taubman said, "Maureen Stapleton does not cause one to forget Miss Taylor. . . . Through the magic of her own sensitivity, she gives Amanda a strong, binding thread of sadness and tenderness." Katharine Hepburn's first television performance was as Amanda in 1973. "She gives a brilliant, multi-faceted performance that is surely the acting tour de force of the year," said Percy Shain. Jessica Tandy performed the role in 1983 at the Eugene O'Neill Theater in New York, with Amanda Plummer as Laura. *New York Times* critic Frank Rich declared, "This Amanda is tough, and even her most comic badgerings leave a bitter aftertaste." The British director of that production, John Dexter, used some of the flash cards that Williams specified in the original published version but that had been omitted from previous productions. They flashed important speeches on the scrim during the performance.

Joanne Woodward played Amanda in the 1986 revival at the Long Wharf Theater in New Haven in a version that had been performed at the Williamstown Theatre Festival in 1982. Treat Williams was the son, James Naughton was the suitor, and the Long Wharf production was impressively dreamlike and powerful. Woodward's husband, Paul Newman, directed this version in the 1987 film of the play.

Tennessee Williams (1911–1983)
THE GLASS MENAGERIE   *1944*

nobody, not even the rain, has such small hands — E. E. CUMMINGS

Production Notes by Tennessee Williams

Being a "memory play," *The Glass Menagerie* can be presented with unusual freedom of convention. Because of its considerably delicate or tenuous material, atmospheric touches and subtleties of direction play a particularly important part. Expressionism and all other unconventional techniques in drama have only one valid aim, and this is a closer approach to truth. When a play employs unconventional techniques, it is not, or certainly shouldn't be, trying to escape its responsibility of dealing with reality, or interpreting experience, but is actually or should be attempting to find a closer approach, or more penetrating and vivid expression of things as they are. The straight realistic play with its genuine frigidaire and authentic ice cubes, its characters that speak exactly as its audience speaks, corresponds to the academic landscape and has the same virtue of a photographic likeness. Everyone should know nowadays the unimportance of the photographic in art: that truth, life, or reality is an organic thing which the poetic imagination can represent or suggest, in essence, only through transformation, through changing into other forms than those which were merely present in appearance.

These remarks are not meant as a preface only to this particular play. They have to do with a conception of a new, plastic theatre which must take the place of the exhausted theatre of realistic conventions if the theatre is to resume vitality as a part of our culture.

The Screen Device. There is *only one important difference between the original and acting version of the play* and that is the *omission* in the latter of the device which I tentatively included in my *original* script. This device was the use of a screen on which were projected magic-lantern slides bearing images or titles. I do not regret the omission of this device from the present Broadway production. The extraordinary power of Miss Taylor's performance made it suitable to have the utmost simplicity in the physical production. But I think it may be interesting to some readers to see how this device was conceived. So I am putting it into the published manuscript. These images and legends, projected from behind, were cast on a section of wall between the front-room and dining-room areas, which should be indistinguishable from the rest when not in use.

The purpose of this will probably be apparent. It is to give accent to certain values in each scene. Each scene contains a particular point (or several) which is structurally the most important. In an episodic play, such as this, the basic structure or narrative line may be obscured from the audience; the effect may seem fragmentary rather than architectural. This may not be the fault of the play so much as a lack of attention in the audience. The legend or image upon the screen will strengthen the effect of what is merely allusion in the writing and allow the primary point to be made more simply and lightly than if the entire responsibility were on the spoken lines. Aside from this structural value, I think the screen will have a definite emotional appeal, less definable but just as important. An imaginative producer or director may invent many other uses for this device than those

indicated in the present script. In fact the possibilities of the device seem much larger to me than the instance of this play can possibly utilize.

The Music. Another extra-literary accent in this play is provided by the use of music. A single recurring tune, "The Glass Menagerie," is used to give emotional emphasis to suitable passages. This tune is like circus music, not when you are on the grounds or in the immediate vicinity of the parade, but when you are at some distance and very likely thinking of something else. It seems under those circumstances to continue almost interminably and it weaves in and out of your preoccupied consciousness; then it is the lightest, most delicate music in the world and perhaps the saddest. It expresses the surface vivacity of life with the underlying strain of immutable and inexpressible sorrow. When you look at a piece of delicately spun glass you think of two things: how beautiful it is and how easily it can be broken. Both of those ideas should be woven into the recurring tune, which dips in and out of the play as if it were carried on a wind that changes. It serves as a thread of connection and allusion between the narrator with his separate point in time and space and the subject of his story. Between each episode it returns as reference to the emotion, nostalgia, which is the first condition of the play. It is primarily Laura's music and therefore comes out most clearly when the play focuses upon her and the lovely fragility of glass which is her image.

The Lighting. The lighting in the play is not realistic. In keeping with the atmosphere of memory, the stage is dim. Shafts of light are focused on selected areas or actors, sometimes in contradistinction to what is the apparent center. For instance, in the quarrel scene between Tom and Amanda, in which Laura has no active part, the clearest pool of light is on her figure. This is also true of the supper scene, when her silent figure on the sofa should remain the visual center. The light upon Laura should be distinct from the others, having a peculiar pristine clarity such as light used in early religious portraits of female saints or madonnas. A certain correspondence to light in religious paintings, such as El Greco's, where the figures are radiant in atmosphere that is relatively dusky, could be effectively used throughout the play. (It will also permit a more effective use of the screen.) A free, imaginative use of light can be of enormous value in giving a mobile, plastic quality to plays of a more or less static nature.

Characters

AMANDA WINGFIELD, *the mother. A little woman of great but confused vitality clinging frantically to another time and place. Her characterization must be carefully created, not copied from type. She is not paranoiac, but her life is paranoia. There is much to admire in Amanda, and as much to love and pity as there is to laugh at. Certainly she has endurance and a kind of heroism, and though her foolishness makes her unwittingly cruel at times, there is tenderness in her slight person.*

LAURA WINGFIELD, *her daughter. Amanda, having failed to establish contact with reality, continues to live vitally in her illusions, but Laura's situation is even graver. A childhood illness has left her crippled, one leg slightly shorter than the other, and held in a brace. This defect need not be more than suggested on the stage. Stemming from this, Laura's separation increases till she is like a piece of her own glass collection, too exquisitely fragile to move from the shelf.*

TOM WINGFIELD, *her son. And the narrator of the play. A poet with a job in a warehouse. His nature is not remorseless, but to escape from a trap he has to act without pity.*

JIM O'CONNOR, *the gentleman caller. A nice, ordinary, young man.*

Scene: *An alley in St. Louis.*
Part I: *Preparation for a Gentleman Caller.*
Part II: *The Gentleman Calls.*
Time: *Now and the Past.*

SCENE 1

(*The Wingfield apartment is in the rear of the building, one of those vast hive-like conglomerations of cellular living-units that flower as warty growths in overcrowded urban centers of lower middle-class population and are symptomatic of the impulse of this largest and fundamentally enslaved section of American society to avoid fluidity and differentiation and to exist and function as one interfused mass of automatism.*)

(*The apartment faces an alley and is entered by a fire escape, a structure whose name is a touch of accidental poetic truth, for all of these huge buildings are always burning with the slow and implacable fires of human desperation. The fire escape is included in the set — that is, the landing of it and steps descending from it.*)

(*The scene is memory and is therefore nonrealistic. Memory takes a lot of poetic license. It omits some details; others are exaggerated, according to the emotional value of the articles it touches, for memory is*

seated predominantly in the heart. The interior is therefore rather dim and poetic.)

(*At the rise of the curtain, the audience is faced with the dark, grim rear wall of the Wingfield tenement. This building, which runs parallel to the footlights, is flanked on both sides by dark, narrow alleys which run into murky canyons of tangled clotheslines, garbage cans, and the sinister latticework of neighboring fire escapes. It is up and down these side alleys that exterior entrances and exits are made, during the play. At the end of Tom's opening commentary, the dark tenement wall slowly reveals (by means of a transparency) the interior of the ground floor Wingfield apartment.*)

(*Downstage is the living room, which also serves as a sleeping room for Laura, the sofa unfolding to make her bed. Upstage, center, and divided by a wide arch or second proscenium with transparent faded portieres (or second curtain), is the dining room. In an old-fashioned what-not in the living room are seen scores of transparent glass animals. A blown-up photograph of the father hangs on the wall of the living room, facing the audience, to the left of the archway. It is the face of a very handsome young man in a doughboy's First World War cap. He is gallantly smiling, ineluctably smiling, as if to say, "I will be smiling forever."*)

(*The audience hears and sees the opening scene in the dining room through both the transparent fourth wall of the building and the transparent gauze portieres of the dining-room arch. It is during this revealing scene that the fourth wall slowly ascends, out of sight. This transparent exterior wall is not brought down again until the very end of the play, during Tom's final speech.*)

(*The narrator is an undisguised convention of the play. He takes whatever license with dramatic convention is convenient to his purposes.*)

(*Tom enters dressed as a merchant sailor from alley, stage left, and strolls across the front of the stage to the fire escape. There he stops and lights a cigarette. He addresses the audience.*)

TOM: Yes, I have tricks in my pocket, I have things up my sleeve. But I am the opposite of a stage magician. He gives you illusion that has the appearance of truth. I give you truth in the pleasant disguise of illusion. To begin with, I turn back time. I reverse it to that quaint period, the thirties, when the huge middle class of America was matriculating in a school for the blind. Their eyes had failed them, or they had failed their eyes, and so they were having their fingers pressed forcibly down on the fiery Braille alphabet of a dissolving economy. In Spain there was revolution. Here there was only shouting and confusion. In Spain there was Guernica. Here there were disturbances of labor, sometimes pretty violent, in otherwise peaceful cities such as Chicago, Cleveland, Saint Louis. . . . This is the social background of the play.

(*Music.*)

The play is memory. Being a memory play, it is dimly lighted, it is sentimental, it is not realistic. In memory everything seems to happen to music. That explains the fiddle in the wings. I am the narrator of the play, and also a character in it. The other characters are my mother, Amanda, my sister, Laura, and a gentleman caller who appears in the final scenes. He is the most realistic character in the play, being an emissary from a world of reality that we were somehow set apart from. But since I have a poet's weakness for symbols, I am using this character also as a symbol; he is the long delayed but always expected something that we live for. There is a fifth character in the play who doesn't appear except in this larger-than-life photograph over the mantel. This is our father who left us a long time ago. He was a telephone man who fell in love with long distances; he gave up his job with the telephone company and skipped the light fantastic out of town . . . The last we heard of him was a picture postcard from Mazatlan, on the Pacific coast of Mexico, containing a message of two words —"Hello — Good-bye!" and no address. I think the rest of the play will explain itself. . . .

(*Amanda's voice becomes audible through the portieres.*)
(*Legend on Screen: "Où Sont les Neiges."*)°
(*He divides the portieres and enters the upstage area.*)
(*Amanda and Laura are seated at a drop-leaf table. Eating is indicated by gestures without food or utensils. Amanda faces the audience. Tom and Laura are seated in profile.*)
(*The interior has lit up softly and through the scrim we see Amanda and Laura seated at the table in the upstage area.*)

AMANDA (*calling*): Tom?
TOM: Yes, Mother.
AMANDA: We can't say grace until you come to the table!
TOM: Coming, Mother. (*He bows slightly and withdraws, reappearing a few moments later in his place at the table.*)
AMANDA (*to her son*): Honey, don't *push* with your *fingers*. If you have to push with something, the thing to push with is a crust of bread. And chew — chew! Animals have sections in their stomachs which enable them to digest food without mastication, but human beings are supposed to chew their food before they swallow it down. Eat food leisurely, son, and really enjoy it. A well-cooked meal has lots of delicate flavors that have to be held in the mouth for appreciation. So chew your food and give your salivary glands a chance to function!

(*Tom deliberately lays his imaginary fork down and pushes his chair back from the table.*)

TOM: I haven't enjoyed one bite of this dinner because of your constant directions on how to eat it. It's you

Où Sont les Neiges: Where are the snows [of yesteryear].

that makes me rush through meals with your hawk-like attention to every bite I take. Sickening — spoils my appetite — all this discussion of animals' secretion — salivary glands — mastication!
AMANDA (*lightly*): Temperament like a Metropolitan° star! (*He rises and crosses downstage.*) You're not excused from the table.
TOM: I'm getting a cigarette.
AMANDA: You smoke too much.

(*Laura rises.*)

LAURA: I'll bring in the blancmange.

(*He remains standing with his cigarette by the portieres during the following.*)

AMANDA (*rising*): No, sister, no, sister — you be the lady this time and I'll be the darky.
LAURA: I'm already up.
AMANDA: Resume your seat, little sister — I want you to stay fresh and pretty — for gentlemen callers!
LAURA: I'm not expecting any gentlemen callers.
AMANDA (*crossing out to kitchenette. Airily*): Sometimes they come when they are least expected! Why, I remember one Sunday afternoon in Blue Mountain — (*Enters kitchenette.*)
TOM: I know what's coming!
LAURA: Yes. But let her tell it.
TOM: Again?
LAURA: She loves to tell it.

(*Amanda returns with bowl of dessert.*)

AMANDA: One Sunday afternoon in Blue Mountain — your mother received — *seventeen!* — gentlemen callers! Why, sometimes there weren't chairs enough to accommodate them all. We had to send the nigger over to bring in folding chairs from the parish house.
TOM (*remaining at portieres*): How did you entertain those gentlemen callers?
AMANDA: I understood the art of conversation!
TOM: I bet you could talk.
AMANDA: Girls in those days *knew* how to talk, I can tell you.
TOM: Yes?

(*Image: Amanda as a girl on a porch greeting callers.*)

AMANDA: They knew how to entertain their gentlemen callers. It wasn't enough for a girl to be possessed of a pretty face and a graceful figure — although I wasn't slighted in either respect. She also needed to have a nimble wit and a tongue to meet all occasions.
TOM: What did you talk about?
AMANDA: Things of importance going on in the world! Never anything coarse or common or vulgar. (*She addresses Tom as though he were seated in the vacant chair at the table though he remains by portieres. He plays this scene as though he held the book.*) My callers were gentlemen — all! Among my

Metropolitan: The Metropolitan Opera in New York City.

callers were some of the most prominent young planters of the Mississippi Delta — planters and sons of planters!

(*Tom motions for music and a spot of light on Amanda.*)
  (*Her eyes lift, her face glows, her voice becomes rich and elegiac.*)
  (*Screen legend: "Où Sont les Neiges."*)

There was young Champ Laughlin who later became vice-president of the Delta Planters Bank. Hadley Stevenson who was drowned in Moon Lake and left his widow one hundred and fifty thousand in Government bonds. There were the Cutrere brothers, Wesley and Bates. Bates was one of my bright particular beaux! He got in a quarrel with that wild Wainright boy. They shot it out on the floor of Moon Lake Casino. Bates was shot through the stomach. Died in the ambulance on his way to Memphis. His widow was also well-provided for, came into eight or ten thousand acres, that's all. She married him on the rebound — never loved her — carried my picture on him the night he died! And there was that boy that every girl in the Delta had set her cap for! That beautiful, brilliant young Fitzhugh boy from Greene County!

TOM: What did he leave his widow?

AMANDA: He never married! Gracious, you talk as though all of my old admirers had turned up their toes to the daisies!

TOM: Isn't this the first you mentioned that still survives?

AMANDA: That Fitzhugh boy went North and made a fortune — came to be known as the Wolf of Wall Street! He had the Midas touch, whatever he touched turned to gold! And I could have been Mrs. Duncan J. Fitzhugh, mind you! But — I picked your *father!*

LAURA (*rising*): Mother, let me clear the table.

AMANDA: No, dear, you go in front and study your typewriter chart. Or practice your shorthand a little. Stay fresh and pretty! — It's almost time for our gentlemen callers to start arriving. (*She flounces girlishly toward the kitchenette.*) How many do you suppose we're going to entertain this afternoon?

(*Tom throws down the paper and jumps up with a groan.*)

LAURA (*alone in the dining room*): I don't believe we're going to receive any, Mother.

AMANDA (*reappearing, airily*): What? No one — not one? You must be joking! (*Laura nervously echoes her laugh. She slips in a fugitive manner through the half-open portieres and draws them gently behind her. A shaft of very clear light is thrown on her face against the faded tapestry of the curtains. Music: "The Glass Menagerie" under faintly. Lightly.*) Not one gentleman caller? It can't be true! There must be a flood, there must have been a tornado!

LAURA: It isn't a flood, it's not a tornado, Mother. I'm just not popular like you were in Blue Mountain. . . .
  (*Tom utters another groan. Laura glances at him

with a faint, apologetic smile. Her voice catching a little.*) Mother's afraid I'm going to be an old maid.

(*The scene dims out with "Glass Menagerie" music.*)

SCENE 2

("*Laura, Haven't You Ever Liked Some Boy?*")
  (*On the dark stage the screen is lighted with the image of blue roses.*)
  (*Gradually Laura's figure becomes apparent and the screen goes out.*)
  (*The music subsides.*)
  (*Laura is seated in the delicate ivory chair at the small clawfoot table.*)
  (*She wears a dress of soft violet material for a kimono — her hair tied back from her forehead with a ribbon.*)
  (*She is washing and polishing her collection of glass.*)
  (*Amanda appears on the fire escape steps. At the sound of her ascent, Laura catches her breath, thrusts the bowl of ornaments away and seats herself stiffly before the diagram of the typewriter keyboard as though it held her spellbound. Something has happened to Amanda. It is written in her face as she climbs to the landing: a look that is grim and hopeless and a little absurd.*)
  (*She has on one of those cheap or imitation velvety-looking cloth coats with imitation fur collar. Her hat is five or six years old, one of those dreadful cloche hats that were worn in the late twenties, and she is clasping an enormous black patent-leather pocketbook with nickel clasp and initials. This is her full-dress outfit, the one she usually wears to the D.A.R.°*)
  (*Before entering she looks through the door.*)
  (*She purses her lips, opens her eyes wide, rolls them upward and shakes her head.*)
  (*Then she slowly lets herself in the door. Seeing her mother's expression Laura touches her lips with a nervous gesture.*)

LAURA: Hello, Mother, I was — (*She makes a nervous gesture toward the chart on the wall. Amanda leans against the shut door and stares at Laura with a martyred look.*)

AMANDA: Deception? Deception? (*She slowly removes her hat and gloves, continuing the swift suffering stare. She lets the hat and gloves fall on the floor — a bit of acting.*)

LAURA (*shakily*): How was the D.A.R. meeting? (*Amanda slowly opens her purse and removes a dainty white handkerchief which she shakes out delicately and delicately touches to her lips and nostrils.*) Didn't you go to the D.A.R. meeting, Mother?

D.A.R.: Daughters of the American Revolution, a patriotic organization for women whose ancestors were involved in the American Revolutionary War.

AMANDA (*faintly, almost inaudibly*): — No. — No. (*Then more forcibly*). I did not have the strength — to go to the D.A.R. In fact, I did not have the courage! I wanted to find a hole in the ground and hide myself in it forever! (*She crosses slowly to the wall and removes the diagram of the typewriter keyboard. She holds it in front of her for a second, staring at it sweetly and sorrowfully — then bites her lips and tears it in two pieces.*)

LAURA (*faintly*): Why did you do that, Mother? (*Amanda repeats the same procedure with the chart of the Gregg Alphabet.*) Why are you —

AMANDA: Why? Why? How old are you, Laura?

LAURA: Mother, you know my age.

AMANDA: I thought that you were an adult; it seems that I was mistaken. (*She crosses slowly to the sofa and sinks down and stares at Laura.*)

LAURA: Please don't stare at me, Mother.

(*Amanda closes her eyes and lowers her head. Count ten.*)

AMANDA: What are we going to do, what is going to become of us, what is the future?

(*Count ten.*)

LAURA: Has something happened, Mother? (*Amanda draws a long breath and takes out the handkerchief again. Dabbing process.*) Mother, has — something happened?

AMANDA: I'll be all right in a minute. I'm just bewildered — (*Count five.*) — by life. . . .

LAURA: Mother, I wish that you would tell me what's happened.

AMANDA: As you know, I was supposed to be inducted into my office at the D.A.R. this afternoon. (*Image: a swarm of typewriters.*) But I stopped off at Rubicam's Business College to speak to your teachers about your having a cold and ask them what progress they thought you were making down there.

LAURA: Oh. . . .

AMANDA: I went to the typing instructor and introduced myself as your mother. She didn't know who you were. Wingfield, she said. We don't have any such student enrolled at the school! I assured her she did, that you had been going to classes since early in January. "I wonder," she said, "if you could be talking about that terribly shy little girl who dropped out of school after only a few days' attendance?" "No," I said, "Laura, my daughter, has been going to school every day for the past six weeks!" "Excuse me," she said. She took the attendance book out and there was your name, unmistakably printed, and all the dates you were absent until they decided that you had dropped out of school. I still said, "No, there must have been some mistake! There must have been some mix-up in the records!" And she said, "No — I remember her perfectly now. Her hands shook so that she couldn't hit the right keys! The first time I gave a speed test, she broke down completely — was sick at the stomach and almost had to be carried into the wash-room! After that morning she never showed up any more. We phoned the house but never got any answer" — while I was working at Famous and Barr, I suppose, demonstrating those — Oh! I felt so weak I could barely keep on my feet. I had to sit down while they got me a glass of water! Fifty dollars' tuition, all of our plans — my hopes and ambitions for you — just gone up the spout, just gone up the spout like that. (*Laura draws a long breath and gets awkwardly to her feet. She crosses to the victrola and winds it up.*) What are you doing?

LAURA: Oh! (*She releases the handle and returns to her seat.*)

AMANDA: Laura, where have you been going when you've gone out pretending that you were going to business college?

LAURA: I've just been going out walking.

AMANDA: That's not true.

LAURA: It is. I just went walking.

AMANDA: Walking? Walking? In winter? Deliberately courting pneumonia in that light coat? Where did you walk to, Laura?

LAURA: All sorts of places — mostly in the park.

AMANDA: Even after you'd started catching that cold?

LAURA: It was the lesser of two evils, Mother. (*Image: winter scene in park.*) I couldn't go back up. I — threw up — on the floor!

AMANDA: From half past seven till after five every day you mean to tell me you walked around in the park, because you wanted to make me think that you were still going to Rubicam's Business College?

LAURA: It wasn't as bad as it sounds. I went inside places to get warmed up.

AMANDA: Inside where?

LAURA: I went in the art museum and the bird houses at the Zoo. I visited the penguins every day! Sometimes I did without lunch and went to the movies. Lately I've been spending most of my afternoons in the Jewel-box, that big glass house where they raise the tropical flowers.

AMANDA: You did all this to deceive me, just for the deception? (*Laura looks down.*) Why?

LAURA: Mother, when you're disappointed, you get that awful suffering look on your face, like the picture of Jesus' mother in the museum!

AMANDA: Hush!

LAURA: I couldn't face it.

(*Pause. A whisper of strings.*)
(*Legend: "The Crust of Humility."*)

AMANDA (*hopelessly fingering the huge pocketbook*): So what are we going to do the rest of our lives? Stay home and watch the parades go by? Amuse ourselves with the glass menagerie, darling? Eternally play those worn-out phonograph records your father left as a painful reminder of him? We won't have a business career — we've given that up because it gave us nervous indigestion! (*Laughs wearily.*) What is there left but dependency all our lives? I know so well what becomes of unmarried women who aren't prepared to occupy a position. I've seen such pitiful cases in the South — barely tolerated spinsters living upon the grudging patronage of sister's husband or brother's wife! — stuck away in some little mousetrap of a room — encouraged by one in-law to visit another — little birdlike women without any nest — eating the crust of humility all their life! Is that the future that we've mapped out for ourselves? I swear it's the only alternative I can think of! It isn't a very pleasant alternative, is it? Of course — some girls do *marry*. (*Laura twists her hands nervously.*) Haven't you ever liked some boy?

LAURA: Yes. I liked one once. (*Rises.*) I came across his picture a while ago.

AMANDA (*with some interest*): He gave you his picture?

LAURA: No, it's in the yearbook.

AMANDA (*disappointed*): Oh — a high-school boy.

(*Screen image: Jim as high school hero bearing a silver cup.*)

LAURA: Yes. His name was Jim. (*Laura lifts the heavy annual from the clawfoot table.*) Here he is in *The Pirates of Penzance*.

AMANDA (*absently*): The what?

LAURA: The operetta the senior class put on. He had a wonderful voice and we sat across the aisle from each other Mondays, Wednesdays, and Fridays in the Aud. Here he is with the silver cup for debating! See his grin?

AMANDA (*absently*): He must have had a jolly disposition.

LAURA: He used to call me — Blue Roses.

(*Image: blue roses.*)

AMANDA: Why did he call you such a name as that?

LAURA: When I had that attack of pleurosis — he asked me what was the matter when I came back. I said pleurosis — he thought that I said Blue Roses! So that's what he always called me after that. Whenever he saw me, he'd holler, "Hello, Blue Roses!" I didn't care for the girl that he went out with. Emily Meisenbach. Emily was the best-dressed girl at Soldan. She never struck me, though, as being sincere . . . It says in the Personal Section — they're engaged. That's — six years ago! They must be married by now.

AMANDA: Girls that aren't cut out for business careers usually wind up married to some nice man. (*Gets up with a spark of revival.*) Sister, that's what you'll do!

(*Laura utters a startled, doubtful laugh. She reaches quickly for a piece of glass.*)

LAURA: But, Mother —

AMANDA: Yes? (*Crossing to photograph.*)

LAURA (*in a tone of frightened apology*): I'm — crippled!

(*Image: screen.*)

AMANDA: Nonsense! Laura, I've told you never, never to use that word. Why, you're not crippled, you just

have a little defect — hardly noticeable, even! When people have some slight disadvantage like that, they cultivate other things to make up for it — develop charm — and vivacity — and — *charm!* That's all you have to do! (*She turns again to the photograph.*) One thing your father had *plenty of* — was *charm!*

(*Tom motions to the fiddle in the wings.*)
(*The scene fades out with music.*)

SCENE 3

(*Legend on screen: "After the Fiasco —"*)
(*Tom speaks from the fire escape landing.*)

TOM: After the fiasco at Rubicam's Business College, the idea of getting a gentleman caller for Laura began to play a more important part in Mother's calculations. It became an obsession. Like some archetype of the universal unconscious, the image of the gentleman caller haunted our small apartment. . . . (*Image: young man at door with flowers.*) An evening at home rarely passed without some allusion to this image, this specter, this hope. . . . Even when he wasn't mentioned, his presence hung in Mother's preoccupied look and in my sister's frightened, apologetic manner — hung like a sentence passed upon the Wingfields! Mother was a woman of action as well as words. She began to take logical steps in the planned direction. Late that winter and in the early spring — realizing that extra money would be needed to properly feather the nest and plume the bird — she conducted a vigorous campaign on the telephone, roping in subscribers to one of those magazines for matrons called *The Home-maker's Companion*, the type of journal that features the serialized sublimations of ladies of letters who think in terms of delicate cuplike breasts, slim, tapering waists, rich, creamy thighs, eyes like wood smoke in autumn, fingers that soothe and caress like strains of music, bodies as powerful as Etruscan sculpture.

(*Screen image: glamor magazine cover.*)
(*Amanda enters with phone on long extension cord. She is spotted in the dim stage.*)

AMANDA: Ida Scott? This is Amanda Wingfield! We *missed* you at the D.A.R. last Monday! I said to myself: She's probably suffering with that sinus condition! How is that sinus condition? Horrors! Heaven have mercy! — You're a Christian martyr, yes, that's what you are, a Christian martyr! Well I just now happened to notice that your subscription to the *Companion*'s about to expire! Yes, it expires with the next issue, honey! — just when that wonderful new serial by Bessie Mae Hopper is getting off to such an exciting start. Oh, honey, it's something that you can't miss! You remember how *Gone with the Wind* took everybody by storm? You simply couldn't go out if you hadn't read it. All everybody *talked* was Scarlett O'Hara. Well, this is a book that critics already compare to *Gone with the Wind*. It's the *Gone with the Wind* of the post–World War generation! — What? — Burning? — Oh, honey, don't let them burn, go take a look in the oven and I'll hold the wire! Heavens — I think she's hung up!

(*Dim out.*)

(*Legend on screen: "You Think I'm in Love with Continental Shoemakers?"*)

(*Before the stage is lighted, the violent voices of Tom and Amanda are heard.*)

(*They are quarreling behind the portieres. In front of them stands Laura with clenched hands and panicky expression.*)

(*A clear pool of light on her figure throughout this scene.*)

TOM: What in Christ's name am I —

AMANDA (*shrilly*): Don't you use that —

TOM: Supposed to do!

AMANDA: Expression! Not in my —

TOM: Ohhh!

AMANDA: Presence! Have you gone out of your senses?

TOM: I have, that's true, *driven* out!

AMANDA: What is the matter with you, you — big — big — IDIOT!

TOM: Look — I've got *no thing,* no single thing —

AMANDA: Lower your voice!

TOM: In my life here that I can call my OWN! Everything is —

AMANDA: Stop that shouting!

TOM: Yesterday you confiscated my books! You had the nerve to —

AMANDA: I took that horrible novel back to the library — yes! That hideous book by that insane Mr. Lawrence. (*Tom laughs wildly.*) I cannot control the output of diseased minds or people who cater to them — (*Tom laughs still more wildly.*) BUT I WON'T ALLOW SUCH FILTH BROUGHT INTO MY HOUSE! No, no, no, no, no!

TOM: House, house! Who pays rent on it, who makes a slave of himself to —

AMANDA (*fairly screeching*): Don't you DARE to —

TOM: No, no, I mustn't say things! *I've* got to just —

AMANDA: Let me tell you —

TOM: I don't want to hear any more! (*He tears the portieres open. The upstage area is lit with a turgid smoky red glow.*)

(*Amanda's hair is in metal curlers and she wears a very old bathrobe, much too large for her slight figure, a relic of the faithless Mr. Wingfield.*)

(*An upright typewriter and a wild disarray of manuscripts are on the dropleaf table. The quarrel was probably precipitated by Amanda's interruption of his creative labor. A chair lying overthrown on the floor.*)

(*Their gesticulating shadows are cast on the ceiling by the fiery glow.*)

AMANDA: You *will* hear more, you —

TOM: No, I won't hear more, I'm going out!

AMANDA: You come right back in —

TOM: Out, out out! Because I'm —

AMANDA: Come back here, Tom Wingfield! I'm not through talking to you!

TOM: Oh, go —

LAURA (*desperately*): Tom!

AMANDA: You're going to listen, and no more insolence from you! I'm at the end of my patience! (*He comes back toward her.*)

TOM: What do you think I'm at? Aren't I supposed to have any patience to reach the end of, Mother? I know, I know. It seems unimportant to you, what I'm *doing* — what I *want* to do — having a little *difference* between them! You don't think that —

AMANDA: I think you've been doing things that you're ashamed of. That's why you act like this. I don't believe that you go every night to the movies. Nobody goes to the movies night after night. Nobody in their right minds goes to the movies as often as you pretend to. People don't go to the movies at nearly midnight, and movies don't let out at two A.M. Come in stumbling. Muttering to yourself like a maniac! You get three hours' sleep and then go to work. Oh, I can picture the way you're doing down there. Moping, doping, because you're in no condition.

TOM (*wildly*): No, I'm in no condition!

AMANDA: What right have you got to jeopardize your job? Jeopardize the security of us all? How do you think we'd manage if you were —

TOM: Listen! You think I'm crazy *about* the *warehouse?* (*He bends fiercely toward her slight figure.*) You think I'm in love with the Continental Shoemakers? You think I want to spend fifty-five *years* down there in that — *celotex interior!* with — *fluorescent* — *tubes!* Look! I'd rather somebody picked up a crowbar and battered out my brains — than go back mornings! I *go!* Every time you come in yelling that God damn "*Rise and Shine!*" "*Rise and Shine!*" I say to myself, "*How lucky dead* people are!" But I get up. I *go!* For sixty-five dollars a month I give up all that I dream of doing and being *ever!* And you say self — *self's* all I ever think of. Why, listen, if self is what I thought of, Mother, I'd be where he is — GONE! (*Pointing to father's picture.*) As far as the system of transportation reaches! (*He starts past her. She grabs his arm.*) Don't grab at me, Mother!

AMANDA: Where are you going?

TOM: I'm going to the *movies!*

AMANDA: I don't believe that lie!

TOM (*Crouching toward her, overtowering her tiny figure. She backs away, gasping.*): I'm going to opium dens! Yes, opium dens, dens of vice and criminals' hangouts, Mother. I've joined the Hogan gang, I'm a hired assassin, I carry a tommy-gun in a violin case! I run a string of cathouses in the Valley! They call me Killer, Killer Wingfield, I'm leading a double life, a simple, honest warehouse worker by day, by night, a dynamic *czar* of the *underworld, Mother.* I go to gambling casinos, I spin away fortunes on the roulette table! I wear a patch over one eye and a false mustache, sometimes I put on green whiskers. On those occasions they call me — *El Diablo!* Oh, I could tell you things to make you sleepless! My enemies plan to dynamite this place. They're going to blow us all skyhigh some night! I'll be glad, very happy, and so will you! You'll go up, up on a broomstick, over Blue Mountain with seventeen gentlemen callers! You ugly — babbling old — *witch.* . . . (*He goes through a series of violent, clumsy movements, seizing his overcoat, lunging to the door, pulling it fiercely open. The women watch him, aghast. His arm catches in the sleeve of the coat as he struggles to pull it on. For a moment he is pinioned by the bulky garment. With an outraged groan he tears the coat off again, splitting the shoulders of it, and hurls it across the room. It strikes against the shelf of Laura's glass collection, there is a tinkle of shattering glass. Laura cries out as if wounded.*)

(*Music legend: "The Glass Menagerie."*)

LAURA (*shrilly*): My glass! — menagerie. . . . (*She covers her face and turns away.*)

(*But Amanda is still stunned and stupefied by the "ugly witch" so that she barely notices this occurrence. Now she recovers her speech.*)

AMANDA (*in an awful voice*): I won't speak to you — until you apologize! (*She crosses through portieres and draws them together behind her. Tom is left with Laura. Laura clings weakly to the mantel with her face averted. Tom stares at her stupidly for a moment. Then he crosses to shelf. Drops awkwardly to his knees to collect the fallen glass, glancing at Laura as if he would speak but couldn't.*)

(*"The Glass Menagerie" steals in as the scene dims out.*)

SCENE 4

(*The interior is dark. Faint light in the alley.*)

(*A deep-voiced bell in a church is tolling the hour of five as the scene commences.*)

(*Tom appears at the top of the alley. After each solemn boom of the bell in the tower, he shakes a little noisemaker or rattle as if to express the tiny spasm of man in contrast to the sustained power and dignity of the Almighty. This and the unsteadiness of his advance make it evident that he has been drinking.*)

(*As he climbs the few steps to the fire escape landing light steals up inside. Laura appears in nightdress, observing Tom's empty bed in the front room.*)

(*Tom fishes in his pockets for the door key, removing a motley assortment of articles in the search, including a perfect shower of movie ticket stubs and an empty bottle. At last he finds the key, but just as he is about to*

insert it, it slips from his fingers. He strikes a match and crouches below the door.)

TOM (*bitterly*): One crack — and it falls through!

(*Laura opens the door.*)

LAURA: Tom! Tom, what are you doing?

TOM: Looking for a door key.

LAURA: Where have you been all this time?

TOM: I have been to the movies.

LAURA: All this time at the movies?

TOM: There was a very long program. There was a Garbo picture and a Mickey Mouse and a travelogue and a newsreel and a preview of coming attractions. And there was an organ solo and a collection for the milk fund — simultaneously — which ended up in a terrible fight between a fat lady and an usher!

LAURA (*innocently*): Did you have to stay through everything?

TOM: Of course! And, oh, I forgot! There was a big stage show! The headliner on this stage show was Malvolio the Magician. He performed wonderful tricks, many of them, such as pouring water back and forth between pitchers. First it turned to wine and then it turned to beer and then it turned to whiskey. I know it was whiskey it finally turned into because he needed somebody to come up out of the audience to help him, and I came up — both shows! It was Kentucky Straight Bourbon. A very generous fellow, he gave souvenirs. (*He pulls from his back pocket a shimmering rainbow-colored scarf.*) He gave me this. This is his magic scarf. You can have it, Laura. You wave it over a canary cage and you get a bowl of goldfish. You wave it over the goldfish bowl and they fly away canaries. . . . But the wonderfullest trick of all was the coffin trick. We nailed him into a coffin and he got out of the coffin without removing one nail. (*He has come inside.*) There is a trick that would come in handy for me — get me out of this 2 by 4 situation! (*Flops onto bed and starts removing shoes.*)

LAURA: Tom — Shhh!

TOM: What you shushing me for?

LAURA: You'll wake up Mother.

TOM: Goody, goody! Pay 'er back for all those "Rise an' Shines." (*Lies down, groaning.*) You know it don't take much intelligence to get yourself into a nailed-up coffin, Laura. But who in hell ever got himself out of one without removing one nail?

(*As if in answer, the father's grinning photograph lights up.*)

(*Scene dims out.*)

(*Immediately following: The church bell is heard striking six. At the sixth stroke the alarm clock goes off in Amanda's room, and after a few moments we hear her calling: "Rise and Shine! Rise and Shine! Laura, go tell your brother to rise and shine!"*)

TOM (*sitting up slowly*): I'll rise — but I won't shine.

(*The light increases.*)

AMANDA: Laura, tell your brother his coffee is ready.

(*Laura slips into front room.*)

LAURA: Tom! it's nearly seven. Don't make Mother nervous. (*He stares at her stupidly. Beseechingly.*) Tom, speak to Mother this morning. Make up with her, apologize, speak to her!

TOM: She won't to me. It's her that started not speaking.

LAURA: If you just say you're sorry she'll start speaking.

TOM: Her not speaking — is that such a tragedy?

LAURA: Please — please!

AMANDA (*calling from kitchenette*): Laura, are you going to do what I asked you to do, or do I have to get dressed and go out myself?

LAURA: Going, going — soon as I get on my coat! (*She pulls on a shapeless felt hat with nervous, jerky movement, pleadingly glancing at Tom. Rushes awkwardly for coat. The coat is one of Amanda's, inaccurately made over, the sleeves too short for Laura.*) Butter and what else?

AMANDA (*entering upstage*): Just butter. Tell them to charge it.

LAURA: Mother, they make such faces when I do that.

AMANDA: Sticks and stones may break my bones, but the expression on Mr. Garfinkel's face won't harm us! Tell your brother his coffee is getting cold.

LAURA (*at door*): Do what I asked you, will you, will you, Tom?

(*He looks sullenly away.*)

AMANDA: Laura, go now or just don't go at all!

LAURA (*rushing out*): Going — going! (*A second later she cries out. Tom springs up and crosses to the door. Amanda rushes anxiously in. Tom opens the door.*)

TOM: Laura?

LAURA: I'm all right. I slipped, but I'm all right.

AMANDA (*peering anxiously after her*): If anyone breaks a leg on those fire escape steps, the landlord ought to be sued for every cent he possesses! (*She shuts door. Remembers she isn't speaking and returns to other room.*)

(*As Tom enters listlessly for his coffee, she turns her back to him and stands rigidly facing the window on the gloomy gray vault of the areaway. Its light on her face with its aged but childish features is cruelly sharp, satirical as a Daumier print.*)

(*Music under: "Ave Maria."*)

(*Tom glances sheepishly but sullenly at her averted figure and slumps at the table. The coffee is scalding hot; he sips it and gasps and spits it back in the cup. At his gasp, Amanda catches her breath and half turns. Then catches herself and turns back to window.*)

(*Tom blows on his coffee, glancing sidewise at his mother. She clears her throat. Tom clears his. He starts to rise. Sinks back down again, scratches his head, clears his throat again. Amanda coughs. Tom raises his cup in both hands to blow on it, his eyes staring over the rim of it at his mother for several moments. Then he slowly sets the cup down and awkwardly and hesitantly rises from the chair.*)

TOM (*hoarsely*): Mother. I — I apologize. Mother. (*Amanda draws a quick, shuddering breath. Her face works grotesquely. She breaks into childlike tears.*) I'm sorry for what I said, for everything that I said, I didn't mean it.

AMANDA (*sobbingly*): My devotion has made me a witch and so I make myself hateful to my children!

TOM: *No*, you *don't*.

AMANDA: I worry so much, don't sleep, it makes me nervous!

TOM (*gently*): I understand that.

AMANDA: I've had to put up a solitary battle all these years. But you're my right-hand bower! Don't fall down, don't fail!

TOM (*gently*): I try, Mother.

AMANDA (*with great enthusiasm*): Try and you will SUCCEED! (*The notion makes her breathless.*) Why, you — you're just *full* of natural endowments! Both of my children — they're *unusual* children! Don't you think I know it? I'm so — *proud!* Happy and — feel I've — so much to be thankful for but — Promise me one thing, son!

TOM: What, Mother?

AMANDA: Promise, son, you'll — never be a drunkard!

LEFT: Laurette Taylor as Amanda in the original 1944 production of *The Glass Menagerie*. RIGHT: Julie Haydon as Laura. ABOVE: Jo Mielziner's drawing of the set for the original production of *The Glass Menagerie*.

TOM (*turns to her grinning*): I will never be a drunkard, Mother.

AMANDA: That's what frightened me so, that you'd be drinking! Eat a bowl of Purina!

TOM: Just coffee, Mother.

AMANDA: Shredded wheat biscuit?

TOM: No, no, Mother, just coffee.

AMANDA: You can't put in a day's work on an empty stomach. You've got ten minutes — don't gulp! Drinking too-hot liquids makes cancer of the stomach. . . . Put cream in.

TOM: No, thank you.

AMANDA: To cool it.

TOM: No! No, thank you, I want it black.

AMANDA: I know, but it's not good for you. We have to do all that we can to build ourselves up. In these trying times we live in, all that we have to cling to is — each other. . . . That's why it's so important to — Tom, I — I sent out your sister so I could discuss something with you. If you hadn't spoken I would have spoken to you. (*Sits down.*)

TOM (*gently*): What is it, Mother, that you want to discuss?

AMANDA: *Laura!*

(*Tom puts his cup down slowly.*)
(*Legend on screen: "Laura."*)
(*Music: "The Glass Menagerie."*)

TOM: — Oh. — Laura . . .

AMANDA (*touching his sleeve*): You know how Laura is. So quiet but — still water runs deep! She notices things and I think she — broods about them. (*Tom looks up.*) A few days ago I came in and she was crying.

TOM: What about?

AMANDA: You.

TOM: Me?

AMANDA: She has an idea that you're not happy here.

TOM: What gave her that idea?

AMANDA: What gives her any idea? However, you do act strangely. I — I'm not criticizing, understand *that!* I know your ambitions do not lie in the warehouse, that like everybody in the whole wide world — you've had to — make sacrifices, but — Tom — Tom — life's not easy, it calls for — Spartan endurance! There's so many things in my heart that I cannot describe to you! I've never told you but I — *loved your father. . . .*

TOM (*gently*): I know that, Mother.

AMANDA: And you — when I see you taking after his ways! Staying out late — and — well, you *had* been drinking the night you were in that — terrifying condition! Laura says that you hate the apartment and that you go out nights to get away from it! Is that true, Tom?

TOM: No. You say there's so much in your heart that you can't describe to me. That's true of me, too. There's so much in my heart that I can't describe to *you!* So let's respect each other's —

AMANDA: But, why — *why,* Tom — are you always so *restless?* Where do you go to, nights?

TOM: I — go to the movies.

AMANDA: Why do you go to the movies so much, Tom?

TOM: I go to the movies because — I like adventure. Adventure is something I don't have much of at work, so I go to the movies.

AMANDA: But, Tom, you go to the movies *entirely* too *much!*

TOM: I like a lot of adventure.

(*Amanda looks baffled, then hurt. As the familiar inquisition resumes he becomes hard and impatient again. Amanda slips back into her querulous attitude toward him.*)
(*Image on screen: sailing vessel with Jolly Roger.°*)

AMANDA: Most young men find adventure in their careers.

TOM: Then most young men are not employed in a warehouse.

AMANDA: The world is full of young men employed in warehouses and offices and factories.

TOM: Do all of them find adventure in their careers?

AMANDA: They do or they do without it! Not everybody has a craze for adventure.

TOM: Man is by instinct a lover, a hunter, a fighter, and none of those instincts are given much play at the warehouse!

AMANDA: Man is by instinct! Don't quote instinct to me! Instinct is something that people have got away from! It belongs to animals! Christian adults don't want it!

TOM: What do Christian adults want, then, Mother?

AMANDA: Superior things! Things of the mind and the spirit! Only animals have to satisfy instincts! Surely your aims are somewhat higher than theirs! Than monkeys — pigs —

TOM: I reckon they're not.

AMANDA: You're joking. However, that isn't what I wanted to discuss.

TOM (*rising*): I haven't much time.

AMANDA (*pushing his shoulders*): Sit down.

TOM: You want me to punch in red at the warehouse, Mother?

AMANDA: You have five minutes. I want to talk about Laura.

(*Legend: "Plans and Provisions."*)

TOM: All right! What about Laura?

AMANDA: We have to be making plans and provisions for her. She's older than you, two years, and nothing has happened. She just drifts along doing nothing. It frightens me terribly how she just drifts along.

TOM: I guess she's the type that people call home girls.

AMANDA: There's no such type, and if there is, it's a pity! That is unless the home is hers, with a husband!

Jolly Roger: The black flag with white skull and crossbones used by pirates.

Tom: What?

AMANDA: Oh, I can see the handwriting on the wall as plain as I see the nose in front of my face! It's terrifying! More and more you remind me of your father! He was out all hours without explanation — Then *left! Good-bye!* And me with a bag to hold. I saw that letter you got from the Merchant Marine. I know what you're dreaming of. I'm not standing here blindfolded. Very well, then. Then *do* it! But not till there's somebody to take your place.

Tom: What do you mean?

AMANDA: I mean that as soon as Laura has got somebody to take care of her, married, a home of her own, independent — why, then you'll be free to go wherever you please, on land, on sea, whichever way the wind blows you! But until that time you've got to look out for your sister. I don't say me because I'm old and don't matter! I say for your sister because she's young and dependent. I put her in business college — a dismal failure! Frightened her so it made her sick to her stomach. I took her over to the Young People's League at the church. Another fiasco. She spoke to nobody, nobody spoke to her. Now all she does is fool with those pieces of glass and play those worn-out records. What kind of a life is that for a girl to lead!

Tom: What can I do about it?

AMANDA: Overcome selfishness! Self, self, self is all that you ever think of! (*Tom springs up and crosses to get his coat. It is ugly and bulky. He pulls on a cap with earmuffs.*) Where is your muffler? Put your wool muffler on! (*He snatches it angrily from the closet and tosses it around his neck and pulls both ends tight.*) Tom! I haven't said what I had in mind to ask you.

Tom: I'm too late to —

AMANDA (*Catching his arms — very importunately. Then shyly*): Down at the warehouse, aren't there some — nice young men?

Tom: No!

AMANDA: There *must* be — *some* . . .

Tom: Mother —

(*Gesture.*)

AMANDA: Find out one that's clean-living — doesn't drink and — ask him out for sister!

Tom: What?

AMANDA: For *sister!* To *meet!* Get *acquainted!*

Tom (*stamping to door*): Oh, my go-osh!

AMANDA: Will you? (*He opens door. Imploringly.*) Will you? (*He starts down.*) Will you? *Will* you, dear?

Tom (*calling back*): YES!

(*Amanda closes the door hesitantly and with a troubled but faintly hopeful expression.*)
  (*Screen image: glamor magazine cover.*)
  (*Spot° Amanda at phone.*)

AMANDA: Ella Cartwright? This is Amanda Wingfield! How are you, honey? How is that kidney condition?

Spot: Spotlight.

(*Count five.*) Horrors! (*Count five.*) You're a Christian martyr, yes, honey, that's what you are, a Christian martyr! Well, I just happened to notice in my little red book that your subscription to the *Companion* has just run out! I knew that you wouldn't want to miss out on the wonderful serial starting in this new issue. It's by Bessie Mae Hopper, the first thing she's written since *Honeymoon for Three.* Wasn't that a strange and interesting story? Well, this one is even lovelier, I believe. It has a sophisticated society background. It's all about the horsey set on Long Island!

(*Fade out.*)

SCENE 5

(*Legend on screen "Annunciation." Fade with music.*)
  (*It is early dusk of a spring evening. Supper has just been finished in the Wingfield apartment. Amanda and Laura in light colored dresses are removing dishes from the table, in the upstage area, which is shadowy, their movements formalized almost as a dance or ritual, their moving forms as pale and silent as moths.*)
  (*Tom, in white shirt and trousers, rises from the table and crosses toward the fire escape.*)

AMANDA (*as he passes her*): Son, will you do me a favor?

Tom: What?

AMANDA: Comb your hair! You look so pretty when your hair is combed! (*Tom slouches on sofa with evening paper. Enormous caption "Franco Triumphs."*) There is only one respect in which I would like you to emulate your father.

Tom: What respect is that?

AMANDA: The care he always took of his appearance. He never allowed himself to look untidy. (*He throws down the paper and crosses to fire escape.*) Where are you going?

Tom: I'm going out to smoke.

AMANDA: You smoke too much. A pack a day at fifteen cents a pack. How much would that amount to in a month? Thirty times fifteen is how much, Tom? Figure it out and you will be astounded at what you could save. Enough to give you a night school course in accounting at Washington U! Just think what a wonderful thing that would be for you, son!

(*Tom is unmoved by the thought.*)

Tom: I'd rather smoke. (*He steps out on landing, letting the screen door slam.*)

AMANDA (*sharply*): I know! That's the tragedy of it. . . . (*Alone, she turns to look at her husband's picture.*)

(*Dance music: "All the World is Waiting for the Sunrise!"*)

Tom (*to the audience*): Across the alley from us was the Paradise Dance Hall. On evenings in spring the windows and doors were open and the music came outdoors. Sometimes the lights were turned out except for a large glass sphere that hung from the ceiling. It would turn slowly about and filter the dusk with delicate rainbow colors. Then the orchestra played a waltz or a tango, something that had a slow and sensuous rhythm. Couples would come outside, to the relative privacy of the alley. You could see them kissing behind ash-pits and telephone poles. This was the compensation for lives that passed like mine, without any change or adventure. Adventure and change were imminent in this year. They were waiting around the corner for all these kids. Suspended in the mist over Berchtesgaden, caught in the folds of Chamberlain's umbrella — In Spain there was Guernica!° But here there was only hot swing music and liquor, dance halls, bars, and movies, and sex that hung in the gloom like a chandelier and flooded the world with brief, deceptive rainbows. . . . All the world was waiting for bombardments!

(*Amanda turns from the picture and comes outside.*)

AMANDA (*sighing*): A fire escape landing's a poor excuse for a porch. (*She spreads a newspaper on a step and sits down, gracefully and demurely as if she were settling into a swing on a Mississippi veranda.*) What are you looking at?

TOM: The moon.

AMANDA: Is there a moon this evening?

TOM: It's rising over Garfinkel's Delicatessen.

AMANDA: So it is! A little silver slipper of a moon. Have you made a wish on it yet?

TOM: Um-hum.

AMANDA: What did you wish for?

TOM: That's a secret.

AMANDA: A secret, huh? Well, I won't tell mine either. I will be just as mysterious as you.

TOM: I bet I can guess what yours is.

AMANDA: Is my head so transparent?

TOM: You're not a sphinx.

AMANDA: No, I don't have secrets. I'll tell you what I wished for on the moon. Success and happiness for my precious children! I wish for that whenever there's a moon, and when there isn't a moon, I wish for it, too.

TOM: I thought perhaps you wished for a gentleman caller.

AMANDA: Why do you say that?

TOM: Don't you remember asking me to fetch one?

AMANDA: I remember suggesting that it would be nice for your sister if you brought home some nice young man from the warehouse. I think I've made that suggestion more than once.

Berchtesgaden . . . Chamberlain . . . Guernica: All references to the approaches of World War II in Europe. Berchtesgaden was Hitler's summer home; Neville Chamberlain was the prime minister of England who signed the Munich Pact, which was regarded as a capitulation to Hitler; and the Spanish town Guernica was destroyed by German bombs during the Spanish Civil War in the late 1930s.

TOM: Yes, you have made it repeatedly.

AMANDA: Well?

TOM: We are going to have one.

AMANDA: *What?*

TOM: A gentleman caller!

(*The annunciation is celebrated with music.*)
    (*Amanda rises.*)
    (*Image on screen: caller with bouquet.*)

AMANDA: You mean you have asked some nice young man to come over?

TOM: Yep. I've asked him to dinner.

AMANDA: You really did?

TOM: I did!

AMANDA: You did, and did he — *accept?*

TOM: He did!

AMANDA: Well, well — well, well! That's — lovely!

TOM: I thought that you would be pleased.

AMANDA: It's definite, then?

TOM: Very definite.

AMANDA: Soon?

TOM: Very soon.

AMANDA: For heaven's sake, stop putting on and tell me some things, will you?

TOM: What things do you want me to tell you?

AMANDA: *Naturally* I would like to know when he's *coming!*

TOM: He's coming tomorrow.

AMANDA: *Tomorrow?*

TOM: Yep. Tomorrow.

AMANDA: But, Tom!

TOM: Yes, Mother?

AMANDA: Tomorrow gives me no time!

TOM: Time for what?

AMANDA: Preparations! Why didn't you phone me at once, as soon as you asked him, the minute that he accepted? Then, don't you see, I could have been getting ready!

TOM: You don't have to make any fuss.

AMANDA: Oh, Tom, Tom, Tom, of course I have to make a fuss! I want things nice, not sloppy! Not thrown together. I'll certainly have to do some fast thinking, won't I?

TOM: I don't see why you have to think at all.

AMANDA: You just don't know. We can't have a gentleman caller in a pigsty! All my wedding silver has to be polished, the monogrammed table linen ought to be laundered! The windows have to be washed and fresh curtains put up. And how about clothes? We have to *wear* something, don't we?

TOM: Mother, this boy is no one to make a fuss over!

AMANDA: Do you realize he's the first young man we've introduced to your sister? It's terrible, dreadful, disgraceful that poor little sister has never received a single gentleman caller! Tom, come inside! (*She opens the screen door.*)

TOM: What for?

AMANDA: I want to ask you some things.

TOM: If you're going to make such a fuss, I'll call it off, I'll tell him not to come.

AMANDA: You certainly won't do anything of the kind. Nothing offends people worse than broken engagements. It simply means I'll have to work like a Turk! We won't be brilliant, but we'll pass inspection. Come on inside. (*Tom follows, groaning.*) Sit down.

TOM: Any particular place you would like me to sit?

AMANDA: Thank heavens I've got that new sofa! I'm also making payments on a floor lamp I'll have sent out! And put the chintz covers on, they'll brighten things up! Of course I'd hoped to have these walls repapered. . . . What is the young man's name?

TOM: His name is O'Connor.

AMANDA: That, of course, means fish — tomorrow is Friday!° I'll have that salmon loaf — with Durkee's dressing! What does he do? He works at the warehouse?

TOM: Of course! How else would I —

AMANDA: Tom, he — doesn't drink?

TOM: Why do you ask me that?

AMANDA: Your father *did!*

TOM: Don't get started on that!

AMANDA: He *does* drink, then?

TOM: Not that I know of!

AMANDA: Make sure, be certain! The last thing I want for my daughter's a boy who drinks!

TOM: Aren't you being a little premature? Mr. O'Connor has not yet appeared on the scene!

AMANDA: But will tomorrow. To meet your sister, and what do I know about his character? Nothing! Old maids are better off than wives of drunkards!

TOM: Oh, my God!

AMANDA: Be still!

TOM (*leaning forward to whisper*): Lots of fellows meet girls whom they don't marry!

AMANDA: Oh, talk sensibly, Tom — and don't be sarcastic! (*She has gotten a hairbrush.*)

TOM: What are you doing?

AMANDA: I'm brushing that cowlick down! What is this young man's position at the warehouse?

TOM (*submitting grimly to the brush and the interrogation*): This young man's position is that of a shipping clerk, Mother.

AMANDA: Sounds to me like a fairly responsible job, the sort of a job *you* would be in if you just had more *get-up.* What is his salary? Have you got any idea.

TOM: I would judge it to be approximately eighty-five dollars a month.

AMANDA: Well — not princely, but —

TOM: Twenty more than I make.

AMANDA: Yes, how well I know! But for a family man, eighty-five dollars a month is not much more than you can just get by on. . . .

TOM: Yes, but Mr. O'Connor is not a family man.

---

fish . . . Friday: Until the 1960s Catholics were prohibited from eating meat on Fridays.

AMANDA: He might be, mightn't he? Some time in the future?

TOM: I see. Plans and provisions.

AMANDA: You are the only young man that I know of who ignores the fact that the future becomes the present, the present the past, and the past turns into everlasting regret if you don't plan for it!

TOM: I will think that over and see what I can make of it.

AMANDA: Don't be supercilious with your mother! Tell me some more about this — what do you call him?

TOM: James D. O'Connor. The D. is for Delaney.

AMANDA: Irish on *both* sides! *Gracious!* And doesn't drink?

TOM: Shall I call him up and ask him right this minute?

AMANDA: The only way to find out about those things is to make discreet inquiries at the proper moment. When I was a girl in Blue Mountain and it was suspected that a young man drank, the girl whose attentions he had been receiving, if any girl *was,* would sometimes speak to the minister of his church, or rather her father would if her father was living, and sort of feel him out on the young man's character. That is the way such things are discreetly handled to keep a young woman from making a tragic mistake!

TOM: Then how did you happen to make a tragic mistake?

AMANDA: That innocent look of your father's had everyone fooled! He *smiled* — the world was *enchanted!* No girl can do worse than put herself at the mercy of a handsome appearance! I hope that Mr. O'Connor is not too good-looking.

TOM: No, he's not too good-looking. He's covered with freckles and hasn't too much of a nose.

AMANDA: He's not right-down homely, though?

TOM: Not right-down homely. Just medium homely, I'd say.

AMANDA: Character's what to look for in a man.

TOM: That's what I've always said, Mother.

AMANDA: You've never said anything of the kind and I suspect you would never give it a thought.

TOM: Don't be suspicious of me.

AMANDA: At least I hope he's the type that's up and coming.

TOM: I think he really goes in for self-improvement.

AMANDA: What reason have you to think so?

TOM: He goes to night school.

AMANDA (*beaming*): Splendid! What does he do, I mean study?

TOM: Radio engineering and public speaking!

AMANDA: Then he has visions of being advanced in the world! Any young man who studies public speaking is aiming to have an executive job some day! And radio engineering? A thing for the future! Both of these facts are very illuminating. Those are the sort of things that a mother should know concerning any young man who comes to call on her daughter. Seriously or — not.

TOM: One little warning. He doesn't know about Laura.

I didn't let on that we had dark ulterior motives. I just said, why don't you come have dinner with us? He said okay and that was the whole conversation.

AMANDA: I bet it was! You're eloquent as an oyster. However, he'll know about Laura when he gets here. When he sees how lovely and sweet and pretty she is, he'll thank his lucky stars he was asked to dinner.

TOM: Mother, you mustn't expect too much of Laura.

AMANDA: What do you mean?

TOM: Laura seems all those things to you and me because she's ours and we love her. We don't even notice she's crippled anymore.

AMANDA: Don't say crippled! You know that I never allow that word to be used!

TOM: But face facts, Mother. She is and — that's not all —

AMANDA: What do you mean not all?

TOM: Laura is very different from other girls.

AMANDA: I think the difference is all to her advantage.

TOM: Not quite all — in the eyes of others — strangers — she's terribly shy and lives in a world of her own and those things make her seem a little peculiar to people outside the house.

AMANDA: Don't say peculiar.

TOM: Face the facts. She is.

(*The dance-hall music changes to a tango that has a minor and somewhat ominous tone.*)

AMANDA: In what way is she peculiar — may I ask?

TOM (*gently*): She lives in a world of her own — a world of — little glass ornaments, Mother. . . . (*Gets up. Amanda remains holding brush, looking at him, troubled.*) She plays old phonograph records and — that's about all — (*He glances at himself in the mirror and crosses to door.*)

AMANDA (*sharply*): Where are you going?

TOM: I'm going to the movies. (*Out screen door.*)

AMANDA: Not to the movies, every night to the movies! (*Follows quickly to screen door.*) I don't believe you always go to the movies! (*He is gone. Amanda looks worriedly after him for a moment. Then vitality and optimism return and she turns from the door. Crossing to portieres.*) Laura! Laura! (*Laura answers from kitchenette.*)

LAURA: Yes, Mother.

AMANDA: Let those dishes go and come in front! (*Laura appears with dish towel. Gaily.*) Laura, come here and make a wish on the moon!

LAURA (*entering*): Moon — moon?

AMANDA: A little silver slipper of a moon. Look over your left shoulder, Laura, and make a wish! (*Laura looks faintly puzzled as if called out of sleep. Amanda seizes her shoulders and turns her at an angle by the door.*) Now! Now, darling, *wish!*

LAURA: What shall I wish for, Mother?

AMANDA (*her voice trembling and her eyes suddenly filling with tears*): Happiness! Good Fortune!

(*The violin rises and the stage dims out.*)

SCENE 6

(*Image: high school hero.*)

TOM: And so the following evening I brought Jim home to dinner. I had known Jim slightly in high school. In high school Jim was a hero. He had tremendous Irish good nature and vitality with the scrubbed and polished look of white chinaware. He seemed to move in a continual spotlight. He was a star in basketball, captain of the debating club, president of the senior class and the glee club and he sang the male lead in the annual light operas. He was always running or bounding, never just walking. He seemed always at the point of defeating the law of gravity. He was shooting with such velocity through his adolescence that you would logically expect him to arrive at nothing short of the White House by the time he was thirty. But Jim apparently ran into more interference after his graduation from Soldan. His speed had definitely slowed. Six years after he left high school he was holding a job that wasn't much better than mine.

(*Image: clerk.*)

He was the only one at the warehouse with whom I was on friendly terms. I was valuable to him as someone who could remember his former glory, who had seen him win basketball games and the silver cup in debating. He knew my secret practice of retiring to a cabinet of the washroom to work on poems when business was slack in the warehouse. He called me Shakespeare. And while the other boys in the warehouse regarded me with suspicious hostility, Jim took a humorous attitude toward me. Gradually his attitude affected the others, their hostility wore off and they also began to smile at me as people smile at an oddly fashioned dog who trots across their path at some distance.

I knew that Jim and Laura had known each other at Soldan, and I had heard Laura speak admiringly of his voice. I didn't know if Jim remembered her or not. In high school Laura had been as unobtrusive as Jim had been astonishing. If he did remember Laura, it was not as my sister, for when I asked him to dinner, he grinned and said, "You know, Shakespeare, I never thought of you as having folks!"

He was about to discover that I did. . . .

(*Light up stage.*)

(*Legend on screen: "The Accent of a Coming Foot."*)

(*Friday evening. It is about five o'clock of a late spring evening which comes "scattering poems in the sky."*)

(*A delicate lemony light is in the Wingfield apartment.*)

(*Amanda has worked like a Turk in preparation for the gentleman caller. The results are astonishing. The new floor lamp with its rose-silk shade is in place, a colored paper lantern conceals the broken light fixture in the ceiling, new billowing white curtains are at the windows, chintz covers are on chairs and sofa, a pair of new sofa pillows make their initial appearance.*)

(*Open boxes and tissue paper are scattered on the floor.*)

(*Laura stands in the middle with lifted arms while Amanda crouches before her, adjusting the hem of the new dress, devout and ritualistic. The dress is colored and designed by memory. The arrangement of Laura's hair is changed; it is softer and more becoming. A fragile, unearthly prettiness has come out in Laura: she is like a piece of translucent glass touched by light, given a momentary radiance, not actual, not lasting.*)

AMANDA (*impatiently*): Why are you trembling?
LAURA: Mother, you've made me so nervous!
AMANDA: How have I made you nervous?
LAURA: By all this fuss! You make it seem so important!
AMANDA: I don't understand you, Laura. You couldn't be satisfied with just sitting home, and yet whenever I try to arrange something for you, you seem to resist it. (*She gets up.*) Now take a look at yourself. No, wait! Wait just a moment — I have an idea!
LAURA: What is it now?

(*Amanda produces two powder puffs which she wraps in handkerchiefs and stuffs in Laura's bosom.*)

LAURA: Mother, what are you doing?
AMANDA: They call them "Gay Deceivers"!
LAURA: I won't wear them!
AMANDA: You will!
LAURA: Why should I?
AMANDA: Because, to be painfully honest, your chest is flat.
LAURA: You make it seem like we were setting a trap.
AMANDA: All pretty girls are a trap, a pretty trap, and men expect them to be. (*Legend: "A Pretty Trap."*) Now look at yourself, young lady. This is the prettiest you will ever be! I've got to fix myself now! You're going to be surprised by your mother's appearance! (*She crosses through portieres, humming gaily.*)

(*Laura moves slowly to the long mirror and stares solemnly at herself.*)

(*A wind blows the white curtains inward in a slow, graceful motion and with a faint, sorrowful sighing.*)

AMANDA (*offstage*): It isn't dark enough yet. (*She turns slowly before the mirror with a troubled look.*)

(*Legend on screen: "This Is My Sister: Celebrate Her with Strings!" Music.*)

AMANDA (*laughing, off*): I'm going to show you something. I'm going to make a spectacular appearance!
LAURA: What is it, Mother?
AMANDA: Possess your soul in patience — you will see! Something I've resurrected from that old trunk! Styles haven't changed so terribly much after all.... (*She parts the portieres.*) Now just look at your mother! (*She wears a girlish frock of yellowed voile with a blue silk sash. She carries a bunch of jonquils — the legend of her youth is nearly revived.*

Feverishly.) This is the dress in which I led the cotillion. Won the cakewalk twice at Sunset Hill, wore one spring to the Governor's ball in Jackson! See how I sashayed around the ballroom, Laura? (*She raises her skirt and does a mincing step around the room.*) I wore it on Sundays for my gentlemen callers! I had it on the day I met your father — I had malaria fever all that spring. The change of climate from East Tennessee to the Delta — weakened resistance — I had a little temperature all the time — not enough to be serious — just enough to make me restless and giddy! Invitations poured in — parties all over the Delta! — "Stay in bed," said Mother, "you have fever!"— but I just wouldn't. — I took quinine but kept on going, going! — Evenings, dances! — Afternoons, long, long rides! Picnics — lovely! — So lovely, that country in May. — All lacy with dogwood, literally flooded with jonquils! — That was the spring I had the craze for jonquils. Jonquils became an absolute obsession. Mother said, "Honey, there's no more room for jonquils." And still I kept on bringing in more jonquils. Whenever, wherever I saw them, I'd say, "Stop! Stop! I see jonquils!" I made the young men help me gather the jonquils! It was a joke, Amanda and her jonquils! Finally there were no more vases to hold them, every available space was filled with jonquils. No vases to hold them? All right, I'll hold them myself! And then I — (*She stops in front of the picture. Music.*) met your father! Malaria fever and jonquils and then — this — boy.... (*She switches on the rose-colored lamp.*) I hope they get here before it starts to rain. (*She crosses upstage and places the jonquils in bowl on table.*) I gave your brother a little extra change so he and Mr. O'Connor could take the service car home.
LAURA (*with altered look*): What did you say his name was?
AMANDA: O'Connor.
LAURA: What is his first name?
AMANDA: I don't remember. Oh, yes, I do. It was — Jim!

(*Laura sways slightly and catches hold of a chair.*)
(*Legend on screen: "Not Jim!"*)

LAURA (*faintly*): Not — Jim!
AMANDA: Yes, that was it, it was Jim! I've never known a Jim that wasn't nice!

(*Music: ominous.*)

LAURA: Are you sure his name is Jim O'Connor?
AMANDA: Yes. Why?
LAURA: Is he the one that Tom used to know in high school?
AMANDA: He didn't say so. I think he just got to know him at the warehouse.
LAURA: There was a Jim O'Connor we both knew in high school — (*Then, with effort.*) If that is the one that Tom is bringing to dinner — you'll have to excuse me, I won't come to the table.

AMANDA: What sort of nonsense is this?

LAURA: You asked me once if I'd ever liked a boy. Don't you remember I showed you this boy's picture?

AMANDA: You mean the boy you showed me in the year-book?

LAURA: Yes, that boy.

AMANDA: Laura, Laura, were you in love with that boy?

LAURA: I don't know, Mother. All I know is I couldn't sit at the table if it was him!

AMANDA: It won't be him! It isn't the least bit likely. But whether it is or not, you will come to the table. You will not be excused.

LAURA: I'll have to be, Mother.

AMANDA: I don't intend to humor your silliness, Laura. I've had too much from you and your brother, both! So just sit down and compose yourself till they come. Tom has forgotten his key so you'll have to let them in, when they arrive.

LAURA (*panicky*): Oh, Mother — *you* answer the door!

AMANDA (*lightly*): I'll be in the kitchen — busy!

LAURA: Oh, Mother, please answer the door, don't make me do it!

AMANDA (*crossing into kitchenette*): I've got to fix the dressing for the salmon. Fuss, fuss — silliness! — over a gentleman caller!

(*Door swings shut. Laura is left alone.*)

 (*Legend: "Terror!"*)

 (*She utters a low moan and turns off the lamp — sits stiffly on the edge of the sofa, knotting her fingers together.*)

 (*Legend on screen: "The Opening of a Door!"*)

 (*Tom and Jim appear on the fire escape steps and climb to landing. Hearing their approach, Laura rises with a panicky gesture. She retreats to the portieres.*)

 (*The doorbell. Laura catches her breath and touches her throat. Low drums.*)

AMANDA (*calling*): Laura, sweetheart! The door!

(*Laura stares at it without moving.*)

JIM: I think we just beat the rain.

TOM: Uh-huh. (*He rings again, nervously. Jim whistles and fishes for a cigarette.*)

AMANDA (*very, very gaily*): Laura, that is your brother and Mr. O'Connor! Will you let them in, darling?

(*Laura crosses toward kitchenette door.*)

LAURA (*breathlessly*): Mother — you go to the door!

(*Amanda steps out of kitchenette and stares furiously at Laura. She points imperiously at the door.*)

FAR LEFT: Amanda (Ruby Dee) and
Laura (Tonia Rowe) in the 1989 Arena
Stage production of *The Glass
Menagerie,* directed by Tazewell
Thompson. LEFT: Laura, Amanda, and
Tom (Jonathan Earl Peck). RIGHT:
Scene from *The Glass Menagerie.*

LAURA: Please, please!

AMANDA (*in a fierce whisper*): What is the matter with you, you silly thing?

LAURA (*desperately*): Please, you answer it, *please!*

AMANDA: I told you I wasn't going to humor you, Laura. Why have you chosen this moment to lose your mind?

LAURA: Please, please, please, you go!

AMANDA: You'll have to go to the door because I can't!

LAURA (*despairingly*): I can't either!

AMANDA: *Why?*

LAURA: I'm *sick!*

AMANDA: I'm sick, too — of your nonsense! Why can't you and your brother be normal people? Fantastic whims and behavior! (*Tom gives a long ring.*) Preposterous goings on! Can you give me one reason — (*Calls out lyrically.*) COMING! JUST ONE SECOND! —

why should you be afraid to open a door? Now you answer it, Laura!

LAURA: Oh, oh, oh . . . (*She returns through the portieres. Darts to the victrola and winds it frantically and turns it on.*)

AMANDA: Laura Wingfield, you march right to that door!

LAURA: Yes — yes, Mother!

(*A faraway, scratchy rendition of "Dardanella" softens the air and gives her strength to move through it. She slips to the door and draws it cautiously open.*)

(*Tom enters with the caller, Jim O'Connor.*)

TOM: Laura, this is Jim. Jim, this is my sister, Laura.

JIM (*stepping inside*): I didn't know that Shakespeare had a sister!

LAURA (*retreating stiff and trembling from the door*): How — how do you do?

JIM (*heartily extending his hand*): Okay!

(*Laura touches it hesitantly with hers.*)

JIM: Your hand's *cold*, Laura!

LAURA: Yes, well — I've been playing the victrola. . . .

JIM: Must have been playing classical music on it! You ought to play a little hot swing music to warm you up!

LAURA: Excuse me — I haven't finished playing the victrola. . . .

(*She turns awkwardly and hurries into the front room. She pauses a second by the victrola. Then catches her breath and darts through the portieres like a frightened deer.*)

JIM (*grinning*): What was the matter?

TOM: Oh — with Laura? Laura is — terribly shy.

JIM: Shy, huh? It's unusual to meet a shy girl nowadays. I don't believe you ever mentioned you had a sister.

TOM: Well, now you know. I have one. Here is the *Post Dispatch*. You want a piece of it?

JIM: Uh-huh.

TOM: What piece? The comics?

JIM: Sports! (*Glances at it.*) Ole Dizzy Dean is on his bad behavior.

TOM (*disinterest*): Yeah? (*Lights cigarette and crosses back to fire escape door.*)

JIM: Where are *you* going?

TOM: I'm going out on the terrace.

JIM (*goes after him*): You know, Shakespeare — I'm going to sell you a bill of goods!

TOM: What goods?

JIM: A course I'm taking.

TOM: Huh?

JIM: In public speaking! You and me, we're not the warehouse type.

TOM: Thanks — that's good news. But what has public speaking got to do with it?

JIM: It fits you for — executive positions!

TOM: Awww.

JIM: I tell you it's done a helluva lot for me.

(*Image: executive at desk.*)

TOM: In what respect?

JIM: In every! Ask yourself what is the difference between you an' me and men in the office down front? Brains? — No! — Ability? — No! Then what? Just one little thing —

TOM: What is that one little thing?

JIM: Primarily it amounts to — social poise! Being able to square up to people and hold your own on any social level!

AMANDA (*offstage*): Tom?

TOM: Yes, Mother?

AMANDA: Is that you and Mr. O'Connor?

TOM: Yes, Mother.

AMANDA: Well, you just make yourselves comfortable in there.

TOM: Yes, Mother.

AMANDA: Ask Mr. O'Connor if he would like to wash his hands.

JIM: Aw, — no — no — thank you — I took care of that at the warehouse. Tom —

TOM: Yes?

JIM: Mr. Mendoza was speaking to me about you.

TOM: Favorably?

JIM: What do you think?

TOM: Well —

JIM: You're going to be out of a job if you don't wake up.

TOM: I am waking up —

JIM: You show no signs.

TOM: The signs are interior.

(*Image on screen: the sailing vessel with Jolly Roger again.*)

TOM: I'm planning to change. (*He leans over the rail speaking with quiet exhilaration. The incandescent marquees and signs of the first-run movie houses light his face from across the alley. He looks like a voyager.*) I'm right at the point of committing myself to a future that doesn't include the warehouse and Mr. Mendoza or even a night school course in public speaking.

JIM: What are you gassing about?

TOM: I'm tired of the movies.

JIM: Movies!

TOM: Yes, movies! Look at them — (*A wave toward the marvels of Grand Avenue.*) All of those glamorous people — having adventures — hogging it all, gobbling the whole thing up! You know what happens? People go to the *movies* instead of *moving!* Hollywood characters are supposed to have all the adventures for everybody in America, while everybody in America sits in a dark room and watches them have them! Yes, until there's a war. That's when adventure becomes available to the masses! *Everyone's* dish, not only Gable's! Then the people in the dark room come out of the dark room to have some adventures themselves — Goody, goody! — It's our turn now, to go to the South Sea Island — to make a safari — to be exotic, far-off! — But I'm not patient. I don't want to wait till then. I'm tired of the *movies* and I am *about* to move!

JIM (*incredulously*): Move?

TOM: Yes.

JIM: When?

TOM: Soon!

JIM: Where? Where?

(*Theme three music seems to answer the question, while Tom thinks it over. He searches among his pockets.*)

TOM: I'm starting to boil inside. I know I seem dreamy, but inside — well, I'm boiling! Whenever I pick up a shoe, I shudder a little thinking how short life is and what I am doing! — Whatever that means. I know it doesn't mean shoes — except as something to wear on a traveler's feet! (*Finds paper.*) Look —

JIM: What?

TOM: I'm a member.

JIM (*reading*): The Union of Merchant Seamen.

TOM: I paid my dues this month, instead of the light bill.

JIM: You will regret it when they turn the lights off.

TOM: I won't be here.

JIM: How about your mother?

TOM: I'm like my father. The bastard son of a bastard! See how he grins? And he's been absent going on sixteen years!

JIM: You're just talking, you drip. How does your mother feel about it?

TOM: Shhh! — Here comes Mother! Mother is not acquainted with my plans!

AMANDA (*enters portieres*): Where are you all?

TOM: On the terrace, Mother.

(*They start inside. She advances to them. Tom is distinctly shocked at her appearance. Even Jim blinks a little. He is making his first contact with girlish Southern vivacity and in spite of the night school course in public speaking is somewhat thrown off the beam by the unexpected outlay of social charm.*)

(*Certain responses are attempted by Jim but are swept aside by Amanda's gay laughter and chatter. Tom is embarrassed but after the first shock Jim reacts very warmly. Grins and chuckles, is altogether won over.*)

(*Image: Amanda as a girl.*)

AMANDA (*coyly smiling, shaking her girlish ringlets*): Well, well, well, so this is Mr. O'Connor. Introductions entirely unnecessary. I've heard so much about you from my boy. I finally said to him, Tom — good gracious! — why don't you bring this paragon to supper? I'd like to meet this nice young man at the warehouse! — Instead of just hearing him sing your praises so much! I don't know why my son is so standoffish — that's not Southern behavior! Let's sit down and — I think we could stand a little more air in here! Tom, leave the door open. I felt a nice fresh breeze a moment ago. Where has it gone to? Mmm, so warm already! And not quite summer, even. We're going to burn up when summer really gets started. However, we're having — we're having a very light supper. I think light things are better fo' this time of year. The same as light clothes are. Light clothes an' light food are what warm weather calls fo'. You know our blood gets so thick during th' winter — it takes a while fo' us to *adjust* ou'selves! — when the season changes . . . It's come so quick this year. I wasn't prepared. All of a sudden — heavens! Already summer! — I ran to the trunk an' pulled out this light dress — Terribly old! Historical almost! But feels so good — so good an' co-ol, y'know. . . .

TOM: Mother —

AMANDA: Yes, honey?

TOM: How about — supper?

AMANDA: Honey, you go ask Sister if supper is ready! You know that Sister is in full charge of supper! Tell her you hungry boys are waiting for it. (*To Jim.*) Have you met Laura?

JIM: She —

AMANDA: Let you in? Oh, good, you've met already! It's rare for a girl as sweet an' pretty as Laura to be domestic! But Laura is, thank heavens, not only pretty but also very domestic. I'm not at all. I never was a bit. I never could make a thing but angel food cake. Well, in the South we had so many servants. Gone, gone, gone. All vestiges of gracious living! Gone completely! I wasn't prepared for what the future brought me. All of my gentlemen callers were sons of planters and so of course I assumed that I would be married to one and raise my family on a large piece of land with plenty of servants. But man proposes — and woman accepts the proposal! — To vary that old, old saying a little bit — I married no planter! I married a man who worked for the telephone company! — That gallantly smiling gentleman over there! (*Points to the picture.*) A telephone man who — fell in love with long distance! — Now he travels and I don't even know where! — But what am I going on for about my — tribulations! Tell me yours — I hope you don't have any! Tom?

TOM (*returning*): Yes, Mother?

AMANDA: Is supper nearly ready?

TOM: It looks to me like supper is on the table.

AMANDA: Let me look — (*She rises prettily and looks through portieres.*) Oh, lovely! — But where is Sister?

TOM: Laura is not feeling well and she says that she thinks she'd better not come to the table.

AMANDA: What? — Nonsense! — Laura? Oh, Laura!

LAURA (*offstage, faintly*): Yes, Mother.

AMANDA: You really must come to the table! We won't be seated until you come to the table! Come in, Mr. O'Connor. You sit over there, and I'll — Laura? Laura Wingfield! You're keeping us waiting, honey! We can't say grace until you come to the table!

(*The back door is pushed weakly open and Laura comes in. She is obviously quite faint, her lips trembling, her eyes wide and staring. She moves unsteadily toward the table.*)

(*Legend: "Terror!"*)

(*Outside a summer storm is coming abruptly. The white curtains billow inward at the windows and there is a sorrowful murmur and deep blue dusk.*)

(*Laura suddenly stumbles — she catches at a chair with a faint moan.*)

TOM: Laura!

AMANDA: Laura! (*There is a clap of thunder.*) (*Legend: "Ah!"*) (*Despairingly.*) Why, Laura, you *are* sick, darling! Tom, help your sister into the living room, dear! Sit in the living room, Laura — rest on the sofa. Well! (*To the gentleman caller.*) Standing over the hot stove made her ill! — I told her that it was just too warm this evening, but — (*Tom comes back in. Laura is on the sofa.*) Is Laura all right now?

TOM: Yes.

AMANDA: What *is* that? Rain? A nice cool rain has come up! (*She gives the gentleman caller a frightened look.*) I think we may — have grace — now . . . (*Tom looks at her stupidly.*) Tom, honey — you say grace!

TOM: Oh . . . "For these and all thy mercies —" (*They bow their heads, Amanda stealing a nervous glance at Jim. In the living room Laura, stretched on the sofa, clenches her hand to her lips, to hold back a shuddering sob.*) God's Holy Name be praised —

(*The scene dims out.*)

SCENE 7

(*A Souvenir*)

(*Half an hour later. Dinner is just being finished in the upstage area which is concealed by the drawn portieres.*)

(*As the curtain rises Laura is still huddled upon the sofa, her feet drawn under her, her head resting on a pale blue pillow, her eyes wide and mysteriously watchful. The new floor lamp with its shade of rose-colored silk gives a soft, becoming light to her face, bringing out the fragile, unearthly prettiness which usually escapes attention. There is a steady murmur of rain, but it is slackening and stops soon after the scene begins; the air outside becomes pale and luminous as the moon breaks out.*)

(*A moment after the curtain rises, the lights in both rooms flicker and go out.*)

JIM: Hey, there, Mr. Light Bulb!

(*Amanda laughs nervously.*)
(*Legend: "Suspension of a Public Service."*)

AMANDA: Where was Moses when the lights went out? Ha-ha. Do you know the answer to that one, Mr. O'Connor?

JIM: No, Ma'am, what's the answer?

AMANDA: In the dark! (*Jim laughs appreciably.*) Everybody sit still. I'll light the candles. Isn't it lucky we have them on the table? Where's a match? Which of you gentlemen can provide a match?

JIM: Here.

AMANDA: Thank you, sir.

JIM: Not at all, Ma'am!

AMANDA: I guess the fuse has burnt out. Mr. O'Connor, can you tell a burnt-out fuse? I know I can't and Tom is a total loss when it comes to mechanics. (*Sound: getting up: voices recede a little to kitchenette.*) Oh, be careful you don't bump into something. We don't want our gentleman caller to break his neck. Now wouldn't that be a fine howdy-do?

JIM: Ha-ha! Where is the fuse box?

AMANDA: Right here next to the stove. Can you see anything?

JIM: Just a minute.

AMANDA: Isn't electricity a mysterious thing? Wasn't it Benjamin Franklin who tied a key to a kite? We live in such a mysterious universe, don't we? Some people say that science clears up all the mysteries for us. In my opinion it only creates more! Have you found it yet?

JIM: No, Ma'am. All these fuses look okay to me.

AMANDA: Tom!

TOM: Yes, Mother?

AMANDA: That light bill I gave you several days ago. The one I told you we got the notices about?

TOM: Oh. — Yeah.

(*Legend: "Ha!"*)

AMANDA: You didn't neglect to pay it by any chance?

TOM: Why, I —

AMANDA: Didn't! I might have known it!

JIM: Shakespeare probably wrote a poem on that light bill, Mrs. Wingfield.

AMANDA: I might have known better than to trust him with it! There's such a high price for negligence in this world!

JIM: Maybe the poem will win a ten-dollar prize.

AMANDA: We'll just have to spend the remainder of the evening in the nineteenth century, before Mr. Edison made the Mazda lamp!

JIM: Candlelight is my favorite kind of light.

AMANDA: That shows you're romantic! But that's no excuse for Tom. Well, we got through dinner. Very considerate of them to let us get through dinner before they plunged us into everlasting darkness, wasn't it, Mr. O'Connor?

JIM: Ha-ha!

AMANDA: Tom, as a penalty for your carelessness you can help me with the dishes.

JIM: Let me give you a hand.

AMANDA: Indeed you will not!

JIM: I ought to be good for something.

AMANDA: Good for something? (*Her tone is rhapsodic.*) You? Why, Mr. O'Connor, nobody, *nobody's* given me this much entertainment in years — as you have!

JIM: Aw, now, Mrs. Wingfield!

AMANDA: I'm not exaggerating, not one bit! But Sister is all by her lonesome. You go keep her company in the parlor! I'll give you this lovely old candelabrum that used to be on the altar at the church of the Heavenly Rest. It was melted a little out of shape when the church burnt down. Lightning struck it one spring. Gypsy Jones was holding a revival at the time and he intimated that the church was destroyed because the Episcopalians gave card parties.

JIM: Ha-ha.

AMANDA: And how about coaxing Sister to drink a little wine? I think it would be good for her! Can you carry both at once?

JIM: Sure. I'm Superman!

AMANDA: Now, Thomas, get into this apron!

(*The door of kitchenette swings closed on Amanda's gay laughter; the flickering light approaches the portieres.*)

(*Laura sits up nervously as he enters. Her speech at first is low and breathless from the almost intolerable strain of being alone with a stranger.*)

(*The legend: "I Don't Suppose You Remember Me at All!"*)

(*In her first speeches in this scene, before Jim's warmth overcomes her paralyzing shyness, Laura's voice is thin and breathless as though she has just run up a steep flight of stairs.*)

(*Jim's attitude is gently humorous. In playing this scene it should be stressed that while the incident is apparently unimportant, it is to Laura the climax of her secret life.*)

JIM: Hello, there, Laura.

LAURA (*faintly*): Hello. (*She clears her throat.*)

JIM: How are you feeling now? Better?

LAURA: Yes. Yes, thank you.

JIM: This is for you. A little dandelion wine. (*He extends it toward her with extravagant gallantry.*)

LAURA: Thank you.

JIM: Drink it — but don't get drunk! (*He laughs heartily. Laura takes the glass uncertainly; laughs shyly.*) Where shall I set the candles?

LAURA: Oh — oh, anywhere . . .

JIM: How about here on the floor? Any objections?

LAURA: No.

JIM: I'll spread a newspaper under to catch the drippings. I like to sit on the floor. Mind if I do?

LAURA: Oh, no.

JIM: Give me a pillow?

LAURA: What?

JIM: A pillow!

LAURA: Oh . . . (*Hands him one quickly.*)

JIM: How about you? Don't you like to sit on the floor?

LAURA: Oh — yes.

JIM: Why don't you, then?

LAURA: I — will.

JIM: Take a pillow! (*Laura does. Sits on the other side of the candelabrum. Jim crosses his legs and smiles engagingly at her.*) I can't hardly see you sitting way over there.

LAURA: I can — see you.

JIM: I know, but that's not fair, I'm in the limelight. (*Laura moves her pillow closer.*) Good! Now I can see you! Comfortable?

LAURA: Yes.

JIM: So am I. Comfortable as a cow. Will you have some gum?

LAURA: No, thank you.

JIM: I think that I will indulge, with your permission. (*Musingly unwraps it and holds it up.*) Think of the fortune made by the guy that invented the first piece of chewing gum. Amazing, huh? The Wrigley Building is one of the sights of Chicago. — I saw it summer before last when I went up to the Century of Progress. Did you take in the Century of Progress?

LAURA: No, I didn't.

JIM: Well, it was quite a wonderful exposition. What impressed me most was the Hall of Science. Gives you an idea of what the future will be in America, even more wonderful than the present time is!

(*Pause. Smiling at her.*) Your brother tells me you're shy. Is that right, Laura?

LAURA: I — don't know.

JIM: I judge you to be an old-fashioned type of girl. Well, I think that's a pretty good type to be. Hope you don't think I'm being too personal — do you?

LAURA (*hastily, out of embarrassment*): I believe I *will* take a piece of gum, if you — don't mind. (*Clearing her throat.*) Mr. O'Connor, have you — kept up with your singing?

JIM: Singing? Me?

LAURA: Yes. I remember what a beautiful voice you had.

JIM: When did you hear me sing?

(*Voice offstage in the pause.*)

VOICE: (*offstage*): O blow, ye winds, heigh-ho,
　　A-roving I will go!
　　　I'm off to my love
　　　With a boxing glove —
　　Ten thousand miles away!

JIM: You say you've heard me sing?

LAURA: Oh, yes! Yes, very often . . . I — don't suppose you remember me — at all?

JIM (*smiling doubtfully*): You know I have an idea I've seen you before. I had that idea soon as you opened the door. It seemed almost like I was about to remember your name. But the name that I started to call you — wasn't a name! And so I stopped myself before I said it.

LAURA: Wasn't it — Blue Roses?

JIM (*Springs up. Grinning.*): Blue Roses! My gosh, yes — Blue Roses! That's what I had on my tongue when you opened the door! Isn't it funny what tricks your memory plays? I didn't connect you with the high school somehow or other. But that's where it was; it was high school. I didn't even know you were Shakespeare's sister! Gosh, I'm sorry.

LAURA: I didn't expect you to. You — barely knew me!

JIM: But we did have a speaking acquaintance, huh?

LAURA: Yes, we — spoke to each other.

JIM: When did you recognize me?

LAURA: Oh, right away!

JIM: Soon as I came in the door?

LAURA: When I heard your name I thought it was probably you. I knew that Tom used to know you a little in high school. So when you came in the door — Well, then I was — sure.

JIM: Why didn't you *say* something, then?

LAURA (*breathlessly*): I didn't know what to say, I was — too surprised!

JIM: For goodness' sakes! You know, this sure is funny!

LAURA: Yes! Yes, isn't it, though . . .

JIM: Didn't we have a class in something together?

LAURA: Yes, we did.

JIM: What class was that?

LAURA: It was — singing — Chorus!

JIM: Aw!

LAURA: I sat across the aisle from you in the Aud.

JIM: Aw.

LAURA: Mondays, Wednesdays, and Fridays.

JIM: Now I remember — you always came in late.

LAURA: Yes, it was so hard for me, getting upstairs. I had that brace on my leg — it clumped so loud!

JIM: I never heard any clumping.

LAURA (*wincing at the recollection*): To me it sounded like — thunder!

JIM: Well, well, well, I never even noticed.

LAURA: And everybody was seated before I came in. I had to walk in front of all those people. My seat was in the back row. I had to go clumping all the way up the aisle with everyone watching!

JIM: You shouldn't have been self-conscious.

LAURA: I know, but I was. It was always such a relief when the singing started.

JIM: Aw, yes, I've placed you now! I used to call you Blue Roses. How was it that I got started calling you that?

LAURA: I was out of school a little while with pleurosis. When I came back you asked me what was the matter. I said I had pleurosis — you thought I said Blue Roses. That's what you always called me after that!

JIM: I hope you didn't mind.

LAURA: Oh, no — I liked it. You see, I wasn't acquainted with many — people. . . .

JIM: As I remember you sort of stuck by yourself.

LAURA: I — I — never had much luck at — making friends.

JIM: I don't see why you wouldn't.

LAURA: Well, I — started out badly.

JIM: You mean being —

LAURA: Yes, it sort of — stood between me —

JIM: You shouldn't have let it!

LAURA: I know, but it did, and —

JIM: You were shy with people!

LAURA: I tried not to be but never could —

JIM: Overcome it?

LAURA: No, I — I never could!

JIM: I guess being shy is something you have to work out of kind of gradually.

LAURA (*sorrowfully*): Yes — I guess it —

JIM: Takes time!

LAURA: Yes —

JIM: People are not so dreadful when you know them. That's what you have to remember! And everybody has problems, not just you, but practically everybody has got some problems. You think of yourself as having the only problems, as being the only one who is disappointed. But just look around you and you will see lots of people as disappointed as you are. For instance, I hoped when I was going to high school that I would be further along at this time, six years later, than I am now — You remember that wonderful write-up I had in *The Torch*?

LAURA: Yes! (*She rises and crosses to table.*)

JIM: It said I was bound to succeed in anything I went into! (*Laura returns with the annual.*) Holy Jeez! *The Torch!* (*He accepts it reverently. They smile across it with mutual wonder. Laura crouches beside him and they begin to turn through it. Laura's shyness is dissolving in his warmth.*)

LAURA: Here you are in *Pirates of Penzance!*

JIM (*wistfully*): I sang the baritone lead in that operetta.

LAURA (*rapidly*): So — *beautifully!*

JIM (*protesting*): Aw —

LAURA: Yes, yes — beautifully — beautifully!

JIM: You heard me?

LAURA: All three times!

JIM: No!

LAURA: Yes!

JIM: All three performances?

LAURA (*looking down*): Yes.

JIM: Why?

LAURA: I — wanted to ask you to — autograph my program.

JIM: Why didn't you ask me to?

LAURA: You were always surrounded by your own friends so much that I never had a chance to.

JIM: You should have just —

LAURA: Well, I — thought you might think I was —

JIM: Thought I might think you was — what?

LAURA: Oh —

JIM (*with reflective relish*): I was beleaguered by females in those days.

LAURA: You were terribly popular!

JIM: Yeah —

LAURA: You had such a — friendly way —

JIM: I was spoiled in high school.

LAURA: Everybody — liked you!

JIM: Including you?

LAURA: I — yes, I — I did, too — (*She gently closes the book in her lap.*)

JIM: Well, well, well! — Give me that program, Laura. (*She hands it to him. He signs it with a flourish.*) There you are — better late than never!

LAURA: Oh, I — what a — surprise!

JIM: My signature isn't worth very much right now. But some day — maybe — it will increase in value! Being disappointed is one thing and being discouraged is something else. I am disappointed but I am not discouraged. I'm twenty-three years old. How old are you?

LAURA: I'll be twenty-four in June.

JIM: That's not old age!

LAURA: No, but —

JIM: You finished high school?

LAURA (*with difficulty*): I didn't go back.

JIM: You mean you dropped out?

LAURA: I made bad grades in my final examinations. (*She rises and replaces the book and the program. Her voice strained.*) How is — Emily Meisenbach getting along?

JIM: Oh, that kraut-head!

LAURA: Why do you call her that?

JIM: That's what she was.

LAURA: You're not still — going with her?

JIM: I never see her.

LAURA: It said in the Personal Section that you were — engaged!

JIM: I know, but I wasn't impressed by that — propaganda!

LAURA: It wasn't — the truth?

JIM: Only in Emily's optimistic opinion!

LAURA: Oh —

(*Legend: "What Have You Done since High School?"*)

(*Jim lights a cigarette and leans indolently back on his elbows smiling at Laura with a warmth and charm which lights her inwardly with altar candles. She remains by the table and turns in her hands a piece of glass to cover her tumult.*)

JIM (*after several reflective puffs on a cigarette*): What have you done since high school? (*She seems not to hear him.*) Huh? (*Laura looks up.*) I said what have you done since high school, Laura?

LAURA: Nothing much.

JIM: You must have been doing something these six long years.

LAURA: Yes.

JIM: Well, then, such as what?

LAURA: I took a business course at business college —

JIM: How did that work out?

LAURA: Well, not very — well — I had to drop out, it gave me — indigestion —

(*Jim laughs gently.*)

JIM: What are you doing now?

LAURA: I don't do anything — much. Oh, please don't think I sit around doing nothing! My glass collection takes up a good deal of my time. Glass is something you have to take good care of.

JIM: What did you say — about glass?

LAURA: Collection I said — I have one — (*She clears her throat and turns away again, acutely shy.*)

JIM (*abruptly*): You know what I judge to be the trouble with you? Inferiority complex! Know what that is? That's what they call it when someone low-rates himself! I understand it because I had it, too. Although my case was not so aggravated as yours seems to be. I had it until I took up public speaking, developed my voice, and learned that I had an aptitude for science. Before that time I never thought of myself as being outstanding in any way whatsoever! Now I've never made a regular study of it, but I have a friend who says I can analyze people better than doctors that make a profession of it. I don't claim that to be necessarily true, but I can sure guess a person's psychology, Laura! (*Takes out his gum.*) Excuse me, Laura. I always take it out when the flavor is gone. I'll use this scrap of paper to wrap it in. I know how it is to get it stuck on a shoe. Yep — that's what I judge to be your principal trouble. A lack of confidence in yourself as a person. You don't have the proper amount of faith in yourself. I'm basing that fact on a number of your remarks and also on certain observations I've made.

For instance that clumping you thought was so awful in high school. You say that you even dreaded to walk into class. You see what you did? You dropped out of school, you gave up an education because of a clump, which as far as I know was practically nonexistent! A little physical defect is what you have. Hardly noticeable even! Magnified thousands of times by imagination! You know what my strong advice to you is? Think of yourself as *superior* in some way!

LAURA: In what way would I think?

JIM: Why, man alive, Laura! Just look about you a little. What do you see? A world full of common people! All of 'em born and all of 'em going to die! Which of them has one-tenth of your good points! Or mine! Or anyone else's, as far as that goes — Gosh! Everybody excels in some one thing. Some in many! (*Unconsciously glances at himself in the mirror.*) All you've got to do is discover in what! Take me, for instance. (*He adjusts his tie at the mirror.*) My interest happens to lie in electro-dynamics. I'm taking a course in radio engineering at night school, Laura, on top of a fairly responsible job at the warehouse. I'm taking that course and studying public speaking.

LAURA: Ohhhh.

JIM: Because I believe in the future of television! (*Turning back to her.*) I wish to be ready to go up right along with it. Therefore I'm planning to get in on the ground floor. In fact, I've already made the right connections and all that remains is for the industry itself to get under way! Full steam — (*His eyes are starry.*) *Knowledge* — Zzzzzp! *Money* — Zzzzzzp! — *Power!* That's the cycle democracy is built on! (*His attitude is convincingly dynamic. Laura stares at him, even her shyness eclipsed in her absolute wonder. He suddenly grins.*) I guess you think I think a lot of myself!

LAURA: No — o-o-o, I —

JIM: Now how about you? Isn't there something you take more interest in than anything else?

LAURA: Well, I do — as I said — have my — glass collection —

(*A peal of girlish laughter from the kitchen.*)

JIM: I'm not right sure I know what you're talking about. What kind of glass is it?

LAURA: Little articles of it, they're ornaments mostly! Most of them are little animals made out of glass, the tiniest little animals in the world. Mother calls them a glass menagerie! Here's an example of one, if you'd like to see it! This one is one of the oldest. It's nearly thirteen. (*He stretches out his hand.*) (*Music: "The Glass Menagerie."*) Oh, be careful — if you breathe, it breaks!

JIM: I'd better not take it. I'm pretty clumsy with things.

LAURA: Go on, I trust you with him! (*Places it in his palm.*) There now — you're holding him gently! Hold him over the light, he loves the light! You see how the light shines through him?

JIM: It sure does shine!

LAURA: I shouldn't be partial, but he is my favorite one.

JIM: What kind of a thing is this one supposed to be?

LAURA: Haven't you noticed the single horn on his forehead?

JIM: A unicorn, huh?

LAURA: Mmm-hmmm!

JIM: Unicorns, aren't they extinct in the modern world?

LAURA: I know!

JIM: Poor little fellow, he must feel sort of lonesome.

LAURA (*smiling*): Well, if he does he doesn't complain about it. He stays on a shelf with some horses that don't have horns and all of them seem to get along nicely together.

JIM: How do you know?

LAURA (*lightly*): I haven't heard any arguments among them!

JIM (*grinning*): No arguments, huh? Well, that's a pretty good sign! Where shall I set him?

LAURA: Put him on the table. They all like a change of scenery once in a while!

JIM (*stretching*): Well, well, well, well — Look how big my shadow is when I stretch!

LAURA: Oh, oh, yes — it stretches across the ceiling!

JIM (*crossing to door*): I think it's stopped raining. (*Opens fire escape door.*) Where does the music come from?

LAURA: From the Paradise Dance Hall across the alley.

JIM: How about cutting the rug a little, Miss Wingfield?

LAURA: Oh, I —

JIM: Or is your program filled up? Let me have a look at it. (*Grasps imaginary card.*) Why, every dance is taken! I'll just have to scratch some out. (*Waltz music: "La Golondrina."*) Ahhh, a waltz! (*He executes some sweeping turns by himself then holds his arms toward Laura.*)

LAURA (*breathlessly*): I — can't dance!

JIM: There you go, that inferiority stuff!

LAURA: I've never danced in my life!

JIM: Come on, try!

LAURA: Oh, but I'd step on you!

JIM: I'm not made out of glass.

LAURA: How — how — how do we start?

JIM: Just leave it to me. You hold your arms out a little.

LAURA: Like this?

JIM: A little bit higher. Right. Now don't tighten up, that's the main thing about it — relax.

LAURA (*laughing breathlessly*): It's hard not to.

JIM: Okay.

LAURA: I'm afraid you can't budge me.

JIM: What do you bet I can't? (*He swings her into motion.*)

LAURA: Goodness, yes, you can!

JIM: Let yourself go, now, Laura, just let yourself go.

LAURA: I'm —

JIM: Come on!

LAURA: Trying!

JIM: Not so stiff — Easy does it!

LAURA: I know but I'm —

JIM: Loosen th' backbone! There now, that's a lot better.

LAURA: Am I?

JIM: Lots, lots better! (*He moves her about the room in a clumsy waltz.*)

LAURA: Oh, my!

JIM: Ha-ha!

LAURA: Oh, my goodness!

JIM: Ha-ha-ha! (*They suddenly bump into the table. Jim stops.*) What did we hit on?

LAURA: Table.

JIM: Did something fall off it? I think —

LAURA: Yes.

JIM: I hope that it wasn't the little glass horse with the horn!

LAURA: Yes.

JIM: Aw, aw, aw. Is it broken?

LAURA: Now it is just like all the other horses.

JIM: It's lost its —

LAURA: Horn! It doesn't matter. Maybe it's a blessing in disguise.

JIM: You'll never forgive me. I bet that that was your favorite piece of glass.

LAURA: I don't have favorites much. It's no tragedy, Freckles. Glass breaks so easily. No matter how careful you are. The traffic jars the shelves and things fall off them.

JIM: Still I'm awfully sorry that I was the cause.

LAURA (*smiling*): I'll just imagine he had an operation. The horn was removed to make him feel less — freakish! (*They both laugh.*) Now he will feel more at home with the other horses, the ones that don't have horns . . .

JIM: Ha-ha, that's very funny! (*Suddenly serious.*) I'm glad to see that you have a sense of humor. You know — you're — well — very different! Surprisingly different from anyone else I know! (*His voice becomes soft and hesitant with a genuine feeling.*) Do you mind me telling you that? (*Laura is abashed beyond speech.*) I mean it in a nice way . . . (*Laura nods shyly, looking away.*) You make me feel sort of — I don't know how to put it! I'm usually pretty good at expressing things, but — This is something that I don't know how to say! (*Laura touches her throat and clears it — turns the broken unicorn in her hands.*) (*Even softer.*) Has anyone ever told you that you were pretty? (*Pause: Music.*) (*Laura looks up slowly, with wonder, and shakes her head.*) Well, you are! In a very different way from anyone else. And all the nicer because of the difference, too. (*His voice becomes low and husky. Laura turns away, nearly faint with the novelty of her emotions.*) I wish that you were my sister. I'd teach you to have some confidence in yourself. The different people are not like other people, but being different is nothing to be ashamed of. Because other people are not such wonderful people. They're one hundred times one thousand. You're one times one! They walk all over the earth. You just stay here. They're common as — weeds, but — you — well, you're — *Blue Roses!*

(*Image on screen: blue roses.*)
  (*Music changes.*)

LAURA: But blue is wrong for — roses . . .

JIM: It's right for you — You're — pretty!

LAURA: In what respect am I pretty?

JIM: In all respects — believe me! Your eyes — your hair — are pretty! Your hands are pretty! (*He catches hold of her hand.*) You think I'm making this up because I'm invited to dinner and have to be nice. Oh, I could do that! I could put on an act for you, Laura, and say lots of things without being very sincere. But this time I am. I'm talking to you sincerely. I happened to notice you had this inferiority complex that keeps you from feeling comfortable with people. Somebody needs to build your confidence up and make you proud instead of shy and turning away and — blushing — Somebody ought to — Ought to — *kiss* you, Laura! (*His hand slips slowly up her arm to her shoulder.*) (*Music swells tumultuously.*) (*He suddenly turns her about and kisses her on the lips. When he releases her Laura sinks on the sofa with a bright, dazed look. Jim backs away and fishes in his pocket for a cigarette.*) (*Legend on screen: "Souvenir."*) Stumble-john! (*He lights the cigarette, avoiding her look. There is a peal of girlish laughter from Amanda in the kitchen. Laura slowly raises and opens her hand. It still contains the little broken glass animal. She looks at it with a tender, bewildered expression.*) Stumble-john! I shouldn't have done that — That was way off the beam. You don't smoke, do you? (*She looks up, smiling, not hearing the question. He sits beside her a little gingerly. She looks at him speechlessly — waiting. He coughs decorously and moves a little farther aside as he considers the situation and senses her feelings, dimly, with perturbation. Gently.*) Would you — care for a — mint? (*She doesn't seem to hear him but her look grows brighter even.*) Peppermint — Life Saver? My pocket's a regular drugstore — wherever I go . . . (*He pops a mint in his mouth. Then gulps and decides to make a clean breast of it. He speaks slowly and gingerly.*) Laura, you know, if I had a sister like you, I'd do the same thing as Tom. I'd bring out fellows and — introduce her to them. The right type of boys of a type to — appreciate her. Only — well — he made a mistake about me. Maybe I've got no call to be saying this. That may not have been the idea in having me over. But what if it was? There's nothing wrong about that. The only trouble is that in my case — I'm not in a situation to — do the right thing. I can't take down your number and say I'll phone. I can't call up next week and — ask for a date. I thought I had better explain the situation in case you misunderstood it and — hurt your feelings. . . . (*Pause. Slowly, very slowly, Laura's look changes, her eyes returning slowly from his to the ornament in her palm.*)

(*Amanda utters another gay laugh in the kitchen.*)

LAURA (*faintly*): You — won't — call again?

JIM: No, Laura, I can't. (*He rises from the sofa.*) As I was just explaining, I've — got strings on me, Laura, I've — been going steady! I go out all the time with a girl named Betty. She's a home-girl like you, and Catholic, and Irish, and in a great many ways we — get along fine. I met her last summer on a moonlight boat trip up the river to Alton, on the *Majestic.* Well — right away from the start it was — love! (*Legend: Love!*) (*Laura sways slightly forward and grips the arm of the sofa. He fails to notice, now enrapt in his own comfortable being.*) Being in love has made a new man of me! (*Leaning stiffly forward, clutching the arm of the sofa, Laura struggles visibly with her storm. But Jim is oblivious, she is a long way off.*) The power of love is really pretty tremendous! Love is something that — changes the whole world, Laura! (*The storm abates a little and Laura leans back. He notices her again.*) It happened that Betty's aunt took sick, she got a wire and had to go to Centralia. So Tom — when he asked me to dinner — I naturally just accepted the invitation, not knowing that you — that he — that I — (*He stops awkwardly.*) Huh — I'm a stumble-john! (*He flops back on the sofa. The holy candles in the altar of Laura's face have been snuffed out! There is a look of almost infinite desolation. Jim glances at her uneasily.*) I wish that you would — say something. (*She bites her lip which was trembling and then bravely smiles. She opens her hand again on the broken glass ornament. Then she gently takes his hand and raises it level with her own. She carefully places the unicorn in the palm of his hand, then pushes his fingers closed upon it.*) What are you — doing that for? You want me to have him? — Laura? (*She nods.*) What for?

LAURA: A — souvenir . . .

(*She rises unsteadily and crouches beside the victrola to wind it up.*)
  (*Legend on screen: "Things Have a Way of Turning out so Badly."*)
  (*Or Image: "Gentleman Caller Waving Goodbye! — Gaily."*)
  (*At this moment Amanda rushes brightly back in the front room. She bears a pitcher of fruit punch in an old-fashioned cut-glass pitcher and a plate of macaroons. The plate has a gold border and poppies painted on it.*)

AMANDA: Well, well, well! Isn't the air delightful after the shower? I've made you children a little liquid refreshment. (*Turns gaily to the gentleman caller.*) Jim, do you know that song about lemonade?
  "Lemonade, lemonade
    Made in the shade and stirred with a spade —
  Good enough for any old maid!"

JIM (*uneasily*): Ha-ha! No — I never heard it.

AMANDA: Why, Laura! You look so serious!

JIM: We were having a serious conversation.

AMANDA: Good! Now you're better acquainted!

JIM (*uncertainly*): Ha-ha! Yes.

AMANDA: You modern young people are much more serious-minded than my generation. I was so gay as a girl!

JIM: You haven't changed, Mrs. Wingfield.

AMANDA: Tonight I'm rejuvenated! The gaiety of the occasion, Mr. O'Connor! (*She tosses her head with a peal of laughter. Spills lemonade.*) Oooo! I'm baptizing myself!

JIM: Here — let me —

AMANDA (*setting the pitcher down*): There now. I discovered we had some maraschino cherries. I dumped them in, juice and all!

JIM: You shouldn't have gone to that trouble, Mrs. Wingfield.

AMANDA: Trouble, trouble? Why it was loads of fun! Didn't you hear me cutting up in the kitchen? I bet your ears were burning! I told Tom how out-done with him I was for keeping you to himself so long a time! He should have brought you over much, much sooner! Well, now that you've found your way, I want you to be a very frequent caller! Not just occasional but all the time. Oh, we're going to have a lot of gay times together! I see them coming! Mmm, just breathe that air! So fresh, and the moon's so pretty! I'll skip back out — I know where my place is when young folks are having a — serious conversation!

JIM: Oh, don't go out, Mrs. Wingfield. The fact of the matter is I've got to be going.

AMANDA: Going, now? You're joking! Why, it's only the shank of the evening, Mr. O'Connor!

JIM: Well, you know how it is.

AMANDA: You mean you're a young workingman and have to keep workingmen's hours. We'll let you off early tonight. But only on the condition that next time you stay later. What's the best night for you? Isn't Saturday night the best night for you workingmen?

JIM: I have a couple of time clocks to punch, Mrs. Wingfield. One at morning, another one at night!

AMANDA: My, but you *are* ambitious! You work at night, too?

JIM: No, Ma'am, not work but — Betty! (*He crosses deliberately to pick up his hat. The band at the Paradise Dance Hall goes into a tender waltz.*)

AMANDA: Betty? Betty? Who's — Betty! (*There is an ominous cracking sound in the sky.*)

JIM: Oh, just a girl. The girl I go steady with! (*He smiles charmingly. The sky falls.*)

(*Legend: "The Sky Falls."*)

AMANDA (*a long-drawn exhalation*): Ohhhh . . . Is it a serious romance, Mr. O'Connor?

JIM: We're going to be married the second Sunday in June.

AMANDA: Ohhhh — how nice! Tom didn't mention that you were engaged to be married.

JIM: The cat's not out of the bag at the warehouse yet. You know how they are. They call you Romeo and stuff like that. (*He stops at the oval mirror to put on his hat. He carefully shapes the brim and the crown*

to give a discreetly dashing effect.*) It's been a wonderful evening, Mrs. Wingfield. I guess this is what they mean by Southern hospitality.

AMANDA: It really wasn't anything at all.

JIM: I hope it don't seem like I'm rushing off. But I promised Betty I'd pick her up at the Wabash depot, an' by the time I get my jalopy down there her train'll be in. Some women are pretty upset if you keep 'em waiting.

AMANDA: Yes, I know — The tyranny of women! (*Extends her hand.*) Good-bye, Mr. O'Connor. I wish you luck — and happiness — and success! All three of them, and so does Laura! — Don't you, Laura?

LAURA: Yes!

JIM (*taking her hand*): Good-bye, Laura. I'm certainly going to treasure that souvenir. And don't you forget the good advice I gave you. (*Raises his voice to a cheery shout.*) So long, Shakespeare! Thanks again, ladies — Good night!

(*He grins and ducks jauntily out.*)

(*Still bravely grimacing, Amanda closes the door on the gentleman caller. Then she turns back to the room with a puzzled expression. She and Laura don't dare to face each other. Laura crouches beside the victrola to wind it.*)

AMANDA (*faintly*): Things have a way of turning out so badly. I don't believe that I would play the victrola. Well, well — well — Our gentleman caller was engaged to be married! Tom!

TOM (*from back*): Yes, Mother?

AMANDA: Come in here a minute. I want to tell you something awfully funny.

TOM (*enters with macaroon and a glass of the lemonade*): Has the gentleman caller gotten away already?

AMANDA: The gentleman caller has made an early departure. What a wonderful joke you played on us!

TOM: How do you mean?

AMANDA: You didn't mention that he was engaged to be married.

TOM: Jim? Engaged?

AMANDA: That's what he just informed us.

TOM: I'll be jiggered! I didn't know about that.

AMANDA: That seems very peculiar.

TOM: What's peculiar about it?

AMANDA: Didn't you call him your best friend down at the warehouse?

TOM: He is, but how did I know?

AMANDA: It seems extremely peculiar that you wouldn't know your best friend was going to be married!

TOM: The warehouse is where I work, not where I know things about people!

AMANDA: You don't know things anywhere! You live in a dream; you manufacture illusions! (*He crosses to door.*) Where are you going?

TOM: I'm going to the movies.

AMANDA: That's right, now that you've had us make such fools of ourselves. The effort, the preparations, all the expense! The new floor lamp, the rug, the clothes for Laura! All for what? To entertain some other girl's fiancé! Go to the movies, go! Don't think about us, a mother deserted, an unmarried sister who's crippled and has no job! Don't let anything interfere with your selfish pleasure! Just go, go, go — to the movies!

TOM: All right, I will! The more you shout about my selfishness to me the quicker I'll go, and I won't go to the movies!

AMANDA: Go, then! Then go to the moon — you selfish dreamer!

(*Tom smashes his glass on the floor. He plunges out on the fire escape, slamming the door. Laura screams — cut by door.*)

(*Dance hall music up. Tom goes to the rail and grips it desperately, lifting his face in the chill white moonlight penetrating the narrow abyss of the alley.*)

(*Legend on screen: "And so Good-bye . . ."*)

(*Tom's closing speech is timed with the interior pantomime. The interior scene is played as though viewed through soundproof glass. Amanda appears to be making a comforting speech to Laura who is huddled upon the sofa. Now that we cannot hear the mother's speech, her silliness is gone and she has dignity and tragic beauty. Laura's dark hair hides her face until at the end of the speech she lifts it to smile at her mother. Amanda's gestures are slow and graceful, almost dancelike, as she comforts the daughter. At the end of her speech she glances a moment at the father's picture — then withdraws through the portieres. At close of Tom's speech, Laura blows out the candles, ending the play.*)

TOM: I didn't go to the moon, I went much further — for time is the longest distance between two places — Not long after that I was fired for writing a poem on the lid of a shoebox. I left Saint Louis. I descended the steps of this fire escape for a last time and followed, from then on, in my father's footsteps, attempting to find in motion what was lost in space — I traveled around a great deal. The cities swept about me like dead leaves, leaves that were brightly colored but torn away from the branches. I would have stopped, but I was pursued by something. It always came upon me unawares, taking me altogether by surprise. Perhaps it was a familiar bit of music. Perhaps it was only a piece of transparent glass — Perhaps I am walking along a street at night, in some strange city, before I have found companions. I pass the lighted window of a shop where perfume is sold. The window is filled with pieces of colored glass, tiny transparent bottles in delicate colors, like bits of a shattered rainbow. Then all at once my sister touches my shoulder. I turn around and look into her eyes . . . Oh, Laura, Laura, I tried to leave you behind me, but I am more faithful than I intended to be! I reach for a cigarette, I cross the street, I run into the movies or a bar, I buy a drink, I speak to the nearest stranger — anything that can blow your candles out! (*Laura bends over the candles.*) — for nowadays the world is lit by lightning! Blow out your candles, Laura — and so good-bye. . . .

(*She blows the candles out.*)
(*The scene dissolves.*)

COMMENTARIES

Tennessee Williams is a fascinating figure in American drama. He was a forceful personality who charmed his friends and the public alike, although his life was often filled with uncertainties and unresolved problems. Some of his best work derived from his private agonies. His work was taken seriously almost from the first, and a body of criticism has developed around it, including biographies, personal reminiscences of collaborators, critical commentaries, and scholarship.

In the *New York Times* review of *The Glass Menagerie* (included here as a commentary), Lewis Nichols describes Laurette Taylor's performance as Amanda as "completely perfect." Donald Spoto, who wrote *The Kindness of Strangers: The Life of Tennessee Williams* (1985), says that Taylor, a powerful actress whose career had seemed finished when the part was offered to her, almost refused the role at first. But her interpretation established a point of reference to which later actresses had to pay homage. Spoto helps us understand the power of collaboration between actor and playwright that sometimes helps both expand their understanding of the work.

Benjamin Nelson explains that "*The Glass Menagerie* exhibits several of Williams's weaknesses as well as his strengths as a playwright." He discusses Williams's characterizations, especially of Laura and Amanda. He also points to "poetic passages" in the play that he feels are weaknesses. Ultimately, Nelson poses an interesting dramatic question: Is the play a tragedy? The search for an answer to this question involves a full consideration of the play's strengths and weaknesses, its success or failure.

Lewis Nichols (1903–1982)
REVIEW OF *THE GLASS MENAGERIE* 1945

Lewis Nichols's review of the New York premiere of The Glass Menagerie *focused on the stellar performance of Laurette Taylor, who played the Mother. Nichols also points out the quality of Williams's writing and his ear for "faintly sardonic dialogue." He saw the play as a superb vehicle for sublime acting.*

The theatre opened its Easter basket the night before and found it a particularly rich one. Preceded by warm and tender reports from Chicago, *The Glass Menagerie* opened at the Playhouse on Saturday, and immediately it was clear that for once the advance notes were not in error. Tennessee Williams's simple play forms the framework for some of the finest acting to be seen in many a day. "Memorable" is an overworked word, but that is the only one to describe Laurette Taylor's performance. March left the theatre like a lioness.

Miss Taylor's picture of a blowsy, impoverished woman who is living on memories of a flower-scented Southern past is completely perfect. It combines qualities of humor and human understanding. The Mother of the play is an amusing figure and a pathetic one. Aged, with two children, living in an apartment off an alley in St. Louis, she recalls her past glories, her seventeen suitors, the old and better life. She is a bit of a scold, a bit of a snob; her finery has worn threadbare, but she has kept it for occasions of state. Miss Taylor makes her a person known by any other name to everyone in her audience. That is art.

In the story the Mother is trying to do the best she can for her children. The son works in a warehouse, although he wants to go to far places. The daughter, a cripple, never has been able to finish school. She is shy, she spends her time collecting glass animals — the title comes from this — and playing old phonograph records. The Mother thinks it is time she is getting married, but there has never been a Gentleman Caller at the house. Finally the son brings home another man from the warehouse and out comes the finery and the heavy if bent candlestick. Even the Gentleman Caller fails. He is engaged to another girl.

Mr. Williams's play is not all of the same caliber. A strict perfectionist could easily find a good many flaws. There are some unconnected odds and ends which have little to do with the story: Snatches of talk about the war, bits of psychology, occasional moments of rather flowery writing. But Mr. Williams has a real ear for faintly sardonic dialogue, unexpected phrases and an affection for his characters.

Miss Taylor takes these many good passages and makes them sing. She plays softly and part of the time seems to be mumbling — a mumble that can be heard at the top of the gallery. Her accents, like the author's phrases, are unexpected, her gestures are vague and fluttery. There is no doubt she was a Southern belle; there is no doubt she is a great actress.

Eddie Dowling, who is coproducer, and, with Margo Jones, codirector, has the double job of narrator and the player of The Son. The narration is like that of *Our Town* and *I Remember Mama* and it probably is not essential to *The Glass Menagerie*. In the play itself Mr. Dowling gives his quiet, easy performance. Julie Haydon, very ethereal and slight, is good as the daughter, as is Anthony Ross as the Gentleman Caller. The Caller had been the hero in high school, but he, too, had been unsuccessful. Jo Mielziner's setting fits the play, as does Paul Bowles's music. In fact, everything fits. *The Glass Menagerie*, like spring, is a pleasure to have in the neighborhood.

Donald Spoto (b. 1941)
LAURETTE TAYLOR IN *THE GLASS MENAGERIE*   *1985*

Before the part of Amanda Wingfield was offered to her, Laurette Taylor had thought her career as an actress was over. Donald Spoto, the biographer of Tennessee Williams, gives us a vision of how persistence and devotion to someone of genuine talent produced a legend in American acting.

That month [December 1944], the details moved together swiftly. [Actor-producer-director Eddie] Dowling, who had directed actress Julie Haydon in *The Time of Your Life,*° convinced her that (although she was thirty-four) she would be credible as the lame, fragile Laura, a character at least a decade younger. She, in turn, took the play to her friend and mentor (later her husband), the formidable critic George Jean Nathan, whose approval she felt obligatory. At the same time, the forty-nine-year-old Dowling announced — without a smile — that he would play young (twentyish) Tom, the shoe-warehouse clerk and aspiring poet; for the role of the gentleman caller, Anthony Ross was hired. The remaining role to be cast was Amanda Wingfield — the "little woman of great but confused vitality," as Williams described her in the play, "clinging frantically to another time and place." The role demanded not mere competence, but the nuances of dramatic greatness. Nathan suggested Laurette Taylor. Dowling and [Audrey] Wood [Williams's agent] and Williams saw his wisdom; they also panicked.

Laurette Taylor, then sixty, had been up to the 1930s one of the great ladies of the American stage. Those who had seen her in *Peg O'My Heart* (in 1912) or *The Furies* (in 1928) or *Outward Bound* (in 1938) knew her gifts. But for almost ten years she had herself become a woman of great but confused vitality, and a confirmed alcoholic.

At that time, Taylor was living in sad withdrawal from the theater, at a hotel on East 60th Street, where she was daily attended by a drama student named Eloise

---

The Time of Your Life: A play (1939) by William Saroyan.

Sheldon. In return for acting lessons, the young woman cared for the practical details of Taylor's life and offered devoted companionship. The play reached Taylor by the circuitous route of Wood to Dowling to Haydon to Nathan to Sheldon to Taylor. It also bore a new title — *The Glass Menagerie.*

"Of course her first reaction was to turn it down," Eloise Sheldon Armen recalled years later; "she thought her career was over. But we prevailed on her to see that no one could bring this character to life the way she could." At last, with the loving encouragement of Eloise —"a small flame," as Laurette Taylor's daughter appreciatively wrote of the young student, "guiding [Taylor] back to the paths of everyday life"— she accepted the part. She did not, however, stop drinking, nor did she seem to give much attention to memorizing lines before or during rehearsals.

In November, Dowling (with, Williams insisted, Margo Jones as codirector) began rehearsals in New York prior to a scheduled Chicago tryout at the end of December. Terrified that something like the history of *Battle of Angels* would be repeated — not because of the new play's content (which could not have been more different) but because he no longer believed the play was anything but "rather dull, too nice"— Williams fled New York for St. Louis. There he was interviewed on his life and work and hopes by the drama critic of the *Star-Times,* a man named William Inge. The resulting article was full of inaccuracies, half-truths, and Williams's typical alterations of personal history; the resulting friendship was much more intense and dramatic.

But Audrey and Dowling would not allow Williams to be an absentee author, and in December he was summoned to Chicago. The situation, he quickly realized, was as bleak as the fierce winter that had already descended.

First of all, Laurette Taylor — with only a week remaining before the December 26 premiere — attended the final rehearsals in what can only be called an alcoholic stupor, barely summarizing the dialogue and so broadly defining the woman's Southern accent and character that, as Williams wrote . . . , she made the play sound like the Aunt Jemima Pancake Hour. In addition, Jo Mielziner's stage designs were being followed with great difficulty, and the music Williams had commissioned from his old acquaintance Paul Bowles sounded harsh through the theater's crude sound system. Luggage had not arrived; a winter storm raged; the Civic Theatre was inconvenient to Chicago's main theater district; there was no budget for advertising or publicity; and everyone in the company (except Eddie Dowling and Julie Haydon) — cast, crew, author — submerged the fear of failure in strong drink. Margo Jones, Williams wrote . . . , was like a scoutmaster leading a wayward and desperate troop to their doom.

As late as Christmas Eve, the lines of the play had been neither "frozen" (fixed by the producer and playwright to be performed as written) nor completely memorized. Laurette Taylor managed only a martini mumble, Dowling was demanding rewrites, and the cast was stumbling into props and one another. "Mr. Dowling," Williams said quietly that night, "art is experience remembered in tranquillity. And I find no tranquillity in Chicago."

The night after Christmas, *The Glass Menagerie* was somehow performed for a small, diffident audience. By the afternoon of the twenty-seventh, the box office had taken in only four hundred dollars, and the producers prepared a closing notice. But then Audrey telephoned them to read two brief reviews: Critic Claudia Cassidy, writing in the *Chicago Daily Tribune,* said the play had "the stamina of success . . . [it] knows people and how they tick. . . . If it is your play, as it is mine, it reaches out . . . and you are caught in its spell." And Ashton Stevens, in the *Herald American,* said *The Glass Menagerie* "has the courage of true poetry couched in colloquial prose."

Before the end of that day, the mayor of Chicago, at the urging of the Civic Theatre's management, authorized a fifty-percent ticket subsidy for municipal employees. On the third night, Laurette Taylor was not simply discharging a half-formed role, she was creating a legend, she had begun to draw a more wonderful portrait than anyone could have imagined — not Eddie Dowling (who resented the critics' subsequent raves about her), not Tennessee Williams nor Audrey Wood, not anyone connected with the play.

"Actually," according to the playwright, "she directed many of the scenes, particularly the ones between mother and daughter, and she did a top-notch job. She was continually working on her part, putting in little things and taking them out — almost every night in Chicago there was something new, but she never disturbed the central characterization. Everything she did was absolutely in character."

The closing notice was removed — not, however, because box-office business dramatically improved, but because Claudia Cassidy and Ashton Stevens had been championing the play, returning almost nightly and telling and writing about it almost daily. "It gripped players and audiences alike," Cassidy wrote on January 7, 1945, "and created one of those rare evenings in the theater that make 'stagestruck' an honorable word." By the middle of the month, no tickets were available. In an unusual example of journalistic salvation, a play was for once not lost but kept alive because of critical support.

Benjamin Nelson
PROBLEMS IN *THE GLASS MENAGERIE*   *1961*

Benjamin Nelson's analysis of Williams's play recognizes the power of the circumstances portrayed in the play. Nelson is concerned, however, that the characters, especially Laura, are not as fully and carefully drawn as they need to be to make the play truly powerful. He also criticizes Williams for creating a universe that "does not allow tragedy."

The Glass Menagerie exhibits several of Williams's weaknesses as well as his strengths as a playwright. The great strength of the play is of course the delicate, sympathetic, yet objective creation of meaningful people in a meaningful situation. Williams has caught a decisive and desperate moment in the lives of four individuals and given it illumination and a sense of deep meaning — no small feat for any writer.

His characterizations are not equally realized. He has been unable to create Laura on more than a single dimension, while Amanda is overwhelming in her multifaceted delineation. On a more technical level the play manifests a doubt on the part of its author toward the power of the written word. As a backdrop for *The Glass Menagerie,* Williams originally wished to use a screen to register emotions and present images from the past, present, and future. For example, when Jim

O'Connor confesses to the family that he is going steady with another girl, the legend on the screen is to read, "The Sky Falls." Fortunately, [actor-director] Eddie Dowling deleted these touches of the poet from his production, but the play still abounds with a number of pretentious statements on the part of Tom as Narrator.

I assume that the final scene between Amanda and Laura is played in pantomime because Williams wished to portray Amanda's dignity through her gestures and her daughter's reaction rather than through the mother's speech, which during the course of the drama has been either shrill, simpering, or saucy. But in relegating this scene to background silence while Tom makes a self-conscious statement about drifting like a dead leaf "attempting to find in motion what was lost in space," he has substituted a painfully pretentious narration for what could have been an intense and luminous moment between the two women.

Again, on the credit side of the author, his play presents genuine situation, motivation, and, as Joseph Wood Krutch has noted, "a hard substantial core of shrewd observation and deft, economical characterization." But Mr. Krutch also noted that "this hard core is enveloped in a fuzzy haze of pretentious, sentimental, pseudopoetic verbiage."[1] In *The Glass Menagerie,* the strained lyricism runs parallel with dialogue that is fresh, alive, and highly characteristic, particularly in the speech of Amanda. This dialogue fortunately dominates the proceedings, but the excess of self-conscious "poetical" passages is quite apparent and is a fault of which Williams is to be guilty in much of his later work.

But the great weakness of *The Glass Menagerie* does not lie in its author's artistic or technical deficiencies. The weakness lies at the core of the play and evolves out of what is to become the playwright's hardening philosophical commitment. We can begin to comprehend this when we ask ourselves whether or not *The Glass Menagerie* is a tragedy. It presents a tragic situation and characters who, despite their moodiness and foolishness and self-deception, possess a sense of the tragic. With the possible exception of Laura, they are intensely genuine and the destruction of their dreams and aspirations bears the illusion of great importance. But the play is not a tragedy. The universe of *The Glass Menagerie* does not allow tragedy.

Everyone in the play is a failure and in the course of their drama they all perish a little. Amanda, the most heroic of the quartet, is pitiful but not tragic because from the outset she is doomed to failure despite her desperate struggle to right things. None of these people are given the opportunity to triumph against a fate which is as malignant as it is implacable. Their struggle is a rear-guard action against life, a continuous retreat. This retreat may be moving, pathetic, melodramatic, or boisterous, but it is always a withdrawal. After all, what is the world outside the glass menagerie?

> There was only hot swing music and liquor, dance halls, bars, and movies, and sex that hung in the gloom like a chandelier and flooded the world with brief, deceptive rainbows. . . . All the world was waiting for bombardments! (p. 1112)

The world outside the Wingfield apartment is a world of illusions, also, even more deceptive and destructive than those held by Amanda and Laura. It is the world of *Stairs to the Roof* and this time the escape is not to a new star but into the individual and personal illusions fostered by each of the characters as his private defense against destruction. Jim waits for the day when his "zzzzzp!" will at last

[1]Joseph Wood Krutch, *The Nation* 14 April 1945:24.

disperse his fear and uncertainty; Laura creates her own sparkling, cold world which gives the illusion of warmth but is as eternal in its unreality as the glass from which it is composed; Amanda strikes out with all her power against her fate by clinging to the past as to a shield; and Tom, recognizing the plight of his family, can do no more than drift away from them, rudderless, frightened, and never really as far from Amanda and Laura as he knows he should be.

Not one of these individuals can cope with his situation. They struggle and their hopes and the destruction of these hopes possess a sense of great importance because Williams has created genuine people in an intensely genuine situation, but they lack the completeness to truly cope with their dilemma. They are not responsible for what has happened to them and they are much too helpless to do more than delay the inevitable. And destruction is inevitable because it is implicit in the universe of Tennessee Williams.

> For the sins of the world are really only its partialities, and these are what sufferings must atone for. . . . The nature of man is full of such makeshift arrangements, devised by himself to cover his incompletion. He feels a part of himself to be like a missing wall or a room left unfurnished and he tries as well as he can to make up for it. The use of imagination, resorting to dreams or the loftier purpose of art, is a mask he devises to cover his incompletion. Or violence such as a war, between two men or among a number of nations, is also a blind and senseless compensation for that which is not yet formed in human nature. Then there is still another compensation. This one is found in the principle of atonement, the surrender of self to violent treatment by others with the idea of thereby cleansing one's self of his guilt.[2]

This statement emanates from the core of Williams's thought and is perhaps his most illuminating commentary about himself and his work. It represents a philosophy, or let us say an attitude toward man in his universe, which is to manifest itself in all his work. It is taken from his short story, "Desire and the Black Masseur," which deals with the final compensation cited in the above quotation: purification through violence. In this tale, a man atones for what the author feels is a cosmic fragmentation and guilt by allowing — and actually furthering — his destruction by a cannibal. In *Battle of Angels* and *The Purification,* we find this same kind of violent cleansing.

The Glass Menagerie is a far cry from any of these works; it is the most nonviolent drama written by Williams. Nevertheless it adheres to the belief set forth in the short story. The underlying belief in *The Glass Menagerie* is that there is very little, if any, reason for living. Man is by nature incomplete because his universe is fragmented. There is nothing to be done about this condition because nothing *can* be done about it. Human guilt becomes a corollary of universal guilt and man's life is an atonement for the human condition. In each character in *The Glass Menagerie* there is a part "like a missing wall or a room left unfurnished and he tries as well as he can to make up for it." The mask devised by Laura and Amanda and Tom and Jim is "the use of imagination, resorting to dreams." The Wingfields are broken, fragmented people because "the sins of the world are really only its partialities." They are really not at all responsible for their condition, and thus are in no way able to cope with it. They are trapped in a determined universe. Without some kind of responsibility on the part of the protagonist there is opportunity neither for tragic elevation nor tragic fall. The Wingfields were doomed the moment they were

---

[2]Williams, "Desire and the Black Masseur," *One Arm and Other Stories* (New York, 1948), 85.

born. At best their struggles will allow them to survive . . . for a time. They will never be allowed to triumph. Thus their struggles, their hopes, and even their eventual destruction can never move far beyond pathos. The beauty and magic of *The Glass Menagerie* is that this pathos is genuine, objective, and deeply moving.

CAT ON A HOT TIN ROOF

The title of the play comes from an offhand remark made by Tennessee Williams's father, Cornelius Williams, who told his wife that she sometimes made him "as nervous as a cat on a hot tin roof." In the play's first production Williams said that he saw his father in the character of Big Daddy. Reminiscence and family memory are as apparent in this play as in most of his work. The secret ingredient in the play, the secret that haunts Brick and torments Maggie, is homosexuality and Brick's relationship with his now-dead friend Skipper. Maggie seduced Skipper to find out what his relation with Brick was, and when he was unable to perform sexually with her, she felt she knew the truth. The theme of homosexuality extends to the previous inhabitants of Maggie and Brick's bedroom, the bachelors Jack Straw and Peter Ochello, the original owners of the plantation. Williams's note that the two "shared this room all their lives together" implies that their relationship was that of lovers. Williams had already become fully aware of his own homosexuality, although he revealed that personal element only obliquely in works such as *Cat on a Hot Tin Roof* until he "came out" during a television interview with David Frost in 1970.

Williams said in his *Memoirs* that this play was his favorite: "I believe that in *Cat* I reached beyond myself, in the second act, to a kind of crude eloquence of expression in Big Daddy that I have managed to give no other character of my creation." Critics have said that one reason Williams liked the play is that he was able to observe the unities of time, place, and action. Brick is confined to his room because he has broken his ankle in a drunken competition at the high school track. The central action of the play, the celebration of Big Daddy's sixty-fifth birthday, is thus brought to the bedroom, which is also at the center of one of the principal tensions in the play.

Big Daddy owns a cotton plantation and both his sons are a disappointment to him. Gooper, with his ambitious wife and his five "no-neck monsters," is weak and unappealing. Even though Gooper has become a lawyer and produced children in an effort to please his father, Big Daddy sees him as possessing none of the masculine qualities he expects in his heir. Brick, a former football player and Big Daddy's favorite, slipped into debilitating alcoholism after Skipper's death. At the time of the play he has no career and few prospects. Maggie sees that the only way she can secure Big Daddy's blessing in the form of Brick's inheritance is by having a child. And with Brick keeping a sexual distance from her, she has to find a way to help him over his grief.

Because Williams made Brick's homosexuality more or less ambiguous, some critics felt that the play's structure was inconclusive. For example, they reasoned that one sexual failure on the part of Skipper did not prove anything about his sexual preference. They also felt that Maggie and Brick's sexual efforts after the curtain falls on the last act may not be successful at all.

Williams's original version of the play — before it was performed — differed from his final version. Originally, Big Daddy did not appear after act 2, and Maggie and Brick did not vow to have a child or to get together at all. The play was changed because its first director, Elia Kazan, felt that Big Daddy was too brilliant a character to leave out of act 3. He argued with Williams until, against his will, Williams revised act 3 to imply a more positive ending, to bring back Big Daddy — who tells an elephant joke that caused the censor to complain in 1955 — and to make Maggie a softer, less acerbic, and much more appealing character. Williams later said that he agreed that the revision made the play stronger, although he preferred his original ending. He later published the play with two act 3s so that regional and other theaters could choose the ending they preferred.

Cat on a Hot Tin Roof in Performance

The play premiered at the Morosco Theater in New York in March 1955 with Burl Ives, then known best as a folk singer, as Big Daddy, Barbara Bel Geddes as Maggie, Ben Gazzara as Brick, and Mildred Dunnock as Big Mama. This powerful cast made the play a huge success. After 694 performances in New York, it toured for another 268 performances. It won Williams his second Pulitzer Prize and his third Drama Critics' Circle Award for best play of the season. Elia Kazan not only directed the play but worked hard to help Williams alter his conception. Williams felt that the play should have a realistic production, since in his mind it was a realistic play. Kazan saw it otherwise and introduced soft lighting and a dreamy setting that established the play as moderately expressionistic.

London theaters were banned from performing the play as written, but a theater club produced it to mixed reviews in 1956. The film version originally was to have Grace Kelly as Maggie, but Elizabeth Taylor got the role, and Paul Newman played Brick. The film version removed all suggestions of homosexuality, focusing instead on Brick's immaturity and his need to grow up to the responsibilities of marriage. It was a highly successful film for its time.

Numerous revivals of the play have appeared in many countries, including a production in Tokyo in 1970. Williams revised the ending once more — putting back the elephant joke — for a restaging of the play in 1974 in Stratford, Connecticut, and then took it to New York for twenty weeks with Elizabeth Ashley as Maggie and Keir Dullea as Brick. That version (which we use in this book) was made into a television production in 1984 with Rip Torn as Big Daddy, Kim Stanley as Big Mama, Tommy Lee Jones as Brick, and Jessica Lange as Maggie. TV critic Richard Zoglin said, "The net effect is to retain the beefed-up dimensions of Maggie and Big Daddy from Broadway, but to leave Brick, at the end, a little more stuck in what Williams describes as a 'state of spiritual despair.'" *Newsweek* described the 1990 New York production, with Howard Davies directing Kathleen Turner as Maggie, as "one of the strongest Tennessee Williams revivals ever on Broadway." Charles Durning's Big Daddy was called "a powerhouse performance."

Tennessee Williams (1911–1983)

CAT ON A HOT TIN ROOF
1955

Characters

MARGARET
BRICK
MAE, *sometimes called Sister Woman*
BIG MAMA
DIXIE, *a little girl*
BIG DADDY
REVEREND TOOKER
GOOPER, *sometimes called Brother Man*
DOCTOR BAUGH, *pronounced "Baw"*
LACEY, *a Negro servant*
SOOKEY, *another*
CHILDREN

Notes for the Designer

The set is the bed-sitting-room of a plantation home in the Mississippi Delta. It is along an upstairs gallery which probably runs around the entire house; it has two pairs of very wide doors opening onto the gallery, showing white balustrades against a fair summer sky that fades into dusk and night during the course of the play, which occupies precisely the time of its performance, excepting, of course, the fifteen minutes of intermission.

Perhaps the style of the room is not what you would expect in the home of the Delta's biggest cotton planter. It is Victorian with a touch of the Far East. It hasn't changed much since it was occupied by the original owners of the place, Jack Straw and Peter Ochello, a pair of old bachelors who shared this room all their lives together. In other words, the room must evoke some ghosts; it is gently and poetically haunted by a relationship that must have involved a tenderness which was uncommon. This may be irrelevant or unnecessary, but I once saw a reproduction of a faded photograph of the verandah of Robert Louis Stevenson's home on that Samoan Island where he spent his last years, and there was a quality of tender light on weathered wood, such as porch furniture made of bamboo and wicker, exposed to tropical suns and tropical rains, which came to mind when I thought about the set for this play, bringing also to mind the grace and comfort of light, the reassurance it gives, on a late and fair afternoon in summer, the way that no matter what, even dread of death, is gently touched and soothed by it. For the set is the background for a play that deals with human extremities of emotion, and it needs that softness behind it.

The bathroom door, showing only pale-blue tile and silver towel racks, is in one side wall; the hall door in the opposite wall. Two articles of furniture need mention: a big double bed which staging should make a functional part of the set as often as suitable, the surface of which should be slightly raked to make figures on it seen more easily; and against the wall space between the two huge double doors upstage: a monumental monstrosity peculiar to our times, a *huge* console combination of radio-phonograph (hi-fi with three speakers), TV set, *and* liquor cabinet, bearing and containing many glasses and bottles, all in one piece, which is a composition of muted silver tones, and the opalescent tones of reflecting glass, a chromatic link, this thing, between the sepia (tawny gold) tones of the interior and the cool (white and blue) tones of the gallery and sky. This piece of furniture (?!), this monument, is a very complete and compact little shrine to virtually all the comforts and illusions behind which we hide from such things as the characters in the play are faced with. . . .

The set should be far less realistic than I have so far implied in this description of it. I think the walls below the ceiling should dissolve mysteriously into air; the set should be roofed by the sky; stars and moon suggested by traces of milky pallor, as if they were observed through a telescope lens out of focus.

Anything else I can think of? Oh, yes, fanlights (transoms shaped like an open glass fan) above all the doors in the set, with panes of blue and amber, and above all, the designer should take as many pains to give the actors room to move about freely (to show their restlessness, their passion for breaking out) as if it were a set for a ballet.

An evening in summer. The action is continuous with two intermissions.

ACT 1

(*At the rise of the curtain someone is taking a shower in the bathroom, the door of which is half open. A pretty young woman, with anxious lines in her face, enters the bedroom and crosses to the bathroom door.*)

MARGARET (*shouting above roar of water*): One of those no-neck monsters hit me with a hot buttered biscuit so I have t' change!

(*Margaret's voice is both rapid and drawling. In her long speeches she has the vocal tricks of a priest delivering a liturgical chant, the lines are almost sung, always continuing a little beyond her breath so she has to gasp for another. Sometimes she intersperses the lines with a little wordless singing, such as "Da-da-daaaa!"*)

(*Water turns off and Brick calls out to her, but is still unseen. A tone of politely feigned interest, masking indifference, or worse, is characteristic of his speech with Margaret.*)

BRICK: Wha'd you say, Maggie? Water was on s' loud I couldn't hearya. . . .

MARGARET: Well, I! — just remarked that! — one of th' no-neck monsters messed up m' lovely lace dress so I got t' — cha-a-ange. . . .

(*She opens and kicks shut drawers of the dresser.*)

BRICK: Why d'ya call Gooper's kiddies no-neck monsters?

MARGARET: Because they've got no necks! Isn't that a good enough reason?

BRICK: Don't they have any necks?

MARGARET: None visible. Their fat little heads are set on their fat little bodies without a bit of connection.

BRICK: That's too bad.

MARGARET: Yes, it's too bad because you can't wring their necks if they've got no necks to wring! Isn't that right, honey?

(*She steps out of her dress, stands in a slip of ivory satin and lace.*)

Yep, they're no-neck monsters, all no-neck people are monsters . . .

(*Children shriek downstairs.*)

Hear them? Hear them screaming? I don't know where their voice boxes are located since they don't have necks. I tell you I got so nervous at that table tonight I thought I would throw back my head and utter a scream you could hear across the Arkansas border an' parts of Louisiana an' Tennessee. I said to

your charming sister-in-law, Mae, honey, couldn't you feed those precious little things at a separate table with an oilcloth cover? They make such a mess an' the lace cloth looks *so* pretty! She made enormous eyes at me and said, "Ohhh, noooooo! On Big Daddy's birthday? Why, he would never forgive me!" Well, I want you to know, Big Daddy hadn't been at the table two minutes with those five no-neck monsters slobbering and drooling over their food before he threw down his fork an' shouted, "Fo' God's sake, Gooper, why don't you put them pigs at a trough in th' kitchen?" — Well, I swear, I simply could have di-ieed!

Think of it, Brick, they've got five of them and number six is coming. They've brought the whole bunch down here like animals to display at a county fair. Why, they have those children doin' tricks all the time! "Junior, show Big Daddy how you do this, show Big Daddy how you do that, say your little piece fo' Big Daddy, Sister. Show your dimples, Sugar. Brother, show Big Daddy how you stand on your head!" — It goes on all the time, along with constant little remarks and innuendos about the fact that you and I have not produced any children, are totally childless and therefore totally useless! — Of course it's comical but it's also disgusting since it's so obvious what they're up to!

BRICK (*without interest*): What are they up to, Maggie?

MARGARET: Why you know what they're up to!

BRICK (*appearing*): No, I don't know what they're up to.

(*He stands there in the bathroom doorway drying his hair with a towel and hanging onto the towel rack because one ankle is broken, plastered and bound. He is still slim and firm as a boy. His liquor hasn't started tearing him down outside. He has the additional charm of that cool air of detachment that people have who have given up the struggle. But now and then, when disturbed, something flashes behind it, like lightning in a fair sky, which shows that at some deeper level he is far from peaceful. Perhaps in a stronger light he would show some signs of deliquescence, but the fading, still warm light from the gallery treats him gently.*)

MARGARET: I'll tell you what they're up to, boy of mine! — They're up to cutting you out of your father's estate, and —

(*She freezes momentarily before her next remark. Her voice drops as if it were somehow a personally embarrassing admission.*)

— Now we know that Big Daddy's dyin' of — cancer. . . .

(*There are voices on the lawn below: long-drawn calls across distance. Margaret raises her lovely bare arms and powders her armpits with a light sigh.*)

(*She adjusts the angle of a magnifying mirror to straighten an eyelash, then rises fretfully saying:*)

There's so much light in the room it —

BRICK (*softly but sharply*): Do we?

MARGARET: Do we what?

BRICK: Know Big Daddy's dyin' of cancer?

MARGARET: Got the report today.

BRICK: Oh . . .

MARGARET (*letting down bamboo blinds which cast long, gold-fretted shadows over the room*): Yep, got th' report just now . . . it didn't surprise me, Baby. . . .

(*Her voice has range, and music; sometimes it drops low as a boy's and you have a sudden image of her playing boy's games as a child.*)

I recognized the symptoms soon's we got here last spring and I'm willin' to bet you that Brother Man and his wife were pretty sure of it, too. That more than likely explains why their usual summer migration to the coolness of the Great Smokies was passed up this summer in favor of — hustlin' down here ev'ry whipstitch with their whole screamin' tribe! And why so many allusions have been made to Rainbow Hill lately. You know what Rainbow Hill is? Place that's famous for treatin' alcoholics an' dope fiends in the movies!

BRICK: I'm not in the movies.

MARGARET: No, and you don't take dope. Otherwise you're a perfect candidate for Rainbow Hill, Baby, and that's where they aim to ship you — over my dead body! Yep, over my dead body they'll ship you there, but nothing would please them better. Then Brother Man could get a-hold of the purse strings and dole out remittances to us, maybe get power of attorney and sign checks for us and cut off our credit wherever, whenever he wanted! Son-of-a-bitch! — How'd you like that, Baby? — Well, you've been doin' just about ev'rything in your power to bring it about, you've just been doin' ev'rything you can think of to aid and abet them in this scheme of theirs! Quittin' work, devoting yourself to the occupation of drinkin'! — Breakin' your ankle last night on the high school athletic field: doin' what? Jumpin' hurdles? At two or three in the morning? Just fantastic! Got in the paper. *Clarksdale Register* carried a nice little item about it, human interest story about a well-known former athlete stagin' a one-man track meet on the Glorious Hill High School athletic field last night, but was slightly out of condition and didn't clear the first hurdle! Brother Man Gooper claims he exercised his influence t' keep it from goin' out over AP or UP or every goddamn "P."

But, Brick? You still have one big advantage!

(*During the above swift flood of words, Brick has reclined with contrapuntal leisure on the snowy surface of the bed and has rolled over carefully on his side or belly.*)

BRICK (*wryly*): Did you *say* something, Maggie?

MARGARET: Big Daddy dotes on you, honey. And he can't stand Brother Man and Brother Man's wife, that monster of fertility, Mae. Know how I know? By little expressions that flicker over his face when that woman is holding fo'th on one of her choice topics such as — how she refused twilight sleep!° — when the twins were delivered! Because she feels motherhood's an experience that a woman ought to experience fully! — in order to fully appreciate the wonder and beauty of it! HAH! — and how she made Brother Man come in an' stand beside her in the delivery room so he would not miss out on the "wonder and beauty" of it either! — producin' those noneck monsters. . . .

(*A speech of this kind would be antipathetic from almost anybody but Margaret; she makes it oddly funny, because her eyes constantly twinkle and her voice shakes with laughter which is basically indulgent.*)

— Big Daddy shares my attitude toward those two! As for me, well — I give him a laugh now and then and he tolerates me. In fact! — I sometimes suspect that Big Daddy harbors a little unconscious "lech" fo' me. . . .

BRICK: What makes you think that Big Daddy has a lech for you, Maggie?

MARGARET: Way he always drops his eyes down my body when I'm talkin' to him, drops his eyes to my boobs an' licks his old chops! Ha ha!

BRICK: That kind of talk is disgusting.

MARGARET: Did anyone ever tell you that you're an ass-aching Puritan, Brick?

I think it's mighty fine that that ole fellow, on the doorstep of death, still takes in my shape with what I think is deserved appreciation!

And you wanta know something else? Big Daddy didn't know how many little Maes and Goopers had been produced! "How many kids have you got?" he asked at the table, just like Brother Man and his wife were new acquaintances to him! Big Mama said he was jokin', but that ole boy wasn't jokin', Lord, no!

And when they infawmed him that they had five already and were turning out number six! — the news seemed to come as a sort of unpleasant surprise . . .

(*Children yell below.*)

Scream, monsters!

(*Turns to Brick with a sudden, gay, charming smile which fades as she notices that he is not looking at her but into fading gold space with a troubled expression.*)

(*It is constant rejection that makes her humor "bitchy."*)

Yes, you should of been at that supper-table, Baby.

(*Whenever she calls him "baby" the word is a soft caress.*)

Y'know, Big Daddy, bless his ole sweet soul, he's the dearest ole thing in the world, but he does hunch over his food as if he preferred not to notice anything

twilight sleep: Anesthesia.

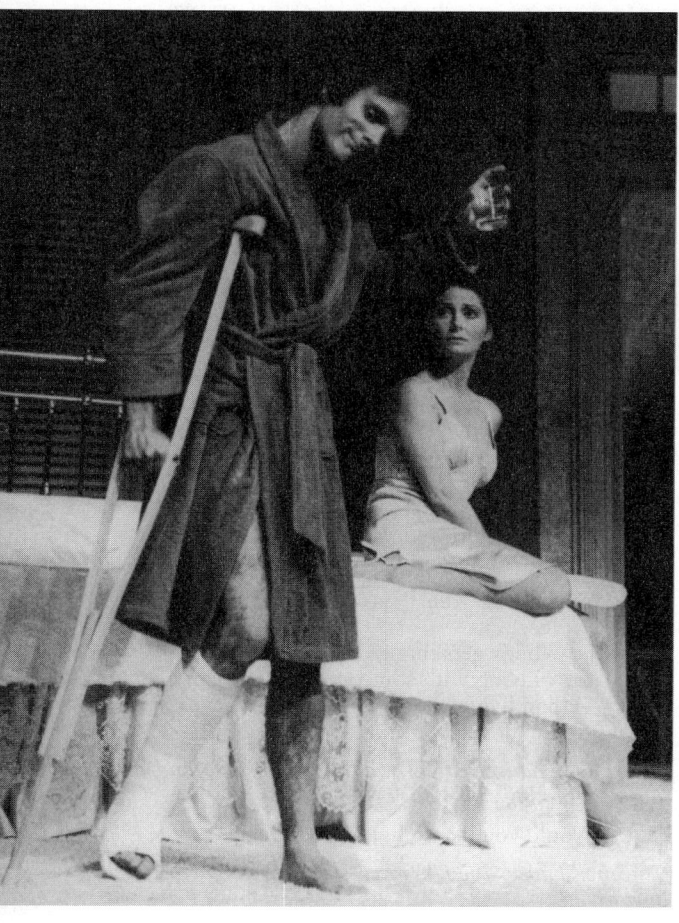

ABOVE LEFT: Maggie (Elizabeth
Ashley) in the 1974 American
Shakespeare Theater production
of *Cat on a Hot Tin Roof*. LEFT:
Brick (Keir Dullea) and Maggie.
ABOVE: Maggie and Big Daddy
(Fred Gwynne).

else. Well, Mae an' Gooper were side by side at the table, direckly across from Big Daddy, watchin' his face like hawks while they jawed an' jabbered about the cuteness an' brillance of th' no-neck monsters!

(*She giggles with a hand fluttering at her throat and her breast and her long throat arched.*)

(*She comes downstage and recreates the scene with voice and gesture.*)

And the no-neck monsters were ranged around the table, some in high chairs and some on th' *Books of Knowledge,* all in fancy little paper caps in honor of Big Daddy's birthday, and all through dinner, well, I want you to know that Brother Man an' his partner never once, for one moment, stopped exchanging pokes an' pinches an' kicks an' signs an' signals! — Why, they were like a couple of cardsharps fleecing a sucker. — Even Big Mama, bless her ole sweet soul, she isn't th' quickest an' brightest thing in the world, she finally noticed, at last, an' said to Gooper, "Gooper, what are you an' Mae makin' all these signs at each other about?" — I swear t' goodness, I nearly choked on my chicken!

(*Margaret, back at the dressing table, still doesn't see Brick. He is watching her with a look that is not quite definable — Amused? shocked? contemptuous? — part of those and part of something else.*)

Y'know — your brother Gooper still cherishes the illusion he took a giant step up on the social ladder when he married Miss Mae Flynn of the Memphis Flynns.

But I have a piece of Spanish news for Gooper. The Flynns never had a thing in this world but money and they lost that, they were nothing at all but fairly successful climbers. Of course, Mae Flynn came out in Memphis eight years before I made my debut in Nashville, but I had friends at Ward-Belmont who came from Memphis and they used to come to see me and I used to go to see them for Christmas and spring vacations, and so I know who rates an' who doesn't rate in Memphis society. Why, y'know ole Papa Flynn, he barely escaped doing time in the Federal pen for shady manipulations on th' stock market when his chain stores crashed, and as for Mae having been a cotton carnival queen, as they remind us so often, lest we forget, well, that's one honor that I don't envy her for! — Sit on a brass throne on a tacky float an' ride down Main Street, smilin', bowin', and blowin' kisses to all the trash on the street —

(*She picks out a pair of jeweled sandals and rushes to the dressing table.*)

Why, year before last, when Susan McPheeters was singled out fo' that honor, y'know what happened to her? Y'know what happened to poor little Susie McPheeters?

BRICK (*absently*): No. What happened to little Susie McPheeters?

MARGARET: Somebody spit tobacco juice in her face.

BRICK (*dreamily*): Somebody spit tobacco juice in her face?

MARGARET: That's right, some old drunk leaned out of a window in the Hotel Gayoso and yelled, "Hey, Queen, hey, hey, there, Queenie!" Poor Susie looked up and flashed him a radiant smile and he shot out a squirt of tobacco juice right in poor Susie's face.

BRICK: Well, what d'you know about that.

MARGARET (*gaily*): What do I know about it? I was there, I saw it!

BRICK (*absently*): Must have been kind of funny.

MARGARET: Susie didn't think so. Had hysterics. Screamed like a banshee. They had to stop th' parade an' remove her from her throne an' go on with —

(*She catches sight of him in the mirror, gasps slightly, wheels about to face him. Count ten.*)

— Why are you looking at me like that?

BRICK (*whistling softly, now*): Like what, Maggie?

MARGARET (*intensely, fearfully*): The way y' were lookin' at me just now, befo' I caught your eye in the mirror and you started t' whistle! I don't know how t' describe it but it froze my blood! — I've caught you lookin' at me like that so often lately. What are you thinkin' of when you look at me like that?

BRICK: I wasn't conscious of lookin' at you, Maggie.

MARGARET: Well, I was conscious of it! What were you thinkin'?

BRICK: I don't remember thinking of anything, Maggie.

MARGARET: Don't you think I know that — ? Don't you — ? — Think I know that — ?

BRICK (*cooly*): Know *what,* Maggie?

MARGARET (*struggling for expression*): That I've gone through this — *hideous!* — transformation, become — *hard! Frantic!*

(*Then she adds, almost tenderly:*)

— *cruel!!*
    That's what you've been observing in me lately. How could y' help but observe it? That's all right. I'm not — thin-skinned any more, can't afford t' be thin-skinned any more.

(*She is now recovering her power.*)

— But Brick? Brick?

BRICK: Did you say something?

MARGARET: I was *goin* t' say something: that I get — lonely. Very!

BRICK: Ev'rybody gets that . . .

MARGARET: Living with someone you love can be lonelier — than living entirely *alone!* — if the one that y' love doesn't love you. . . .

(*There is a pause. Brick hobbles downstage and asks, without looking at her:*)

BRICK: Would you like to live alone, Maggie?

(*Another pause: then — after she has caught a quick, hurt breath:*)

MARGARET: *No! — God! — I wouldn't!*

(*Another gasping breath. She forcibly controls what must have been an impulse to cry out. We see her deliberately, very forcibly, going all the way back to the world in which you can talk about ordinary matters.*)

Did you have a nice shower?
BRICK: Uh-huh.
MARGARET: Was the water cool?
BRICK: No.
MARGARET: But it made y' feel fresh, huh?
BRICK: Fresher. . . .
MARGARET: I know something would make y' feel *much* fresher!
BRICK: What?
MARGARET: An alcohol rub. Or cologne, a rub with cologne!
BRICK: That's good after a workout but I haven't been workin' out, Maggie.
MARGARET: You've kept in good shape, though.
BRICK (*indifferently*): You think so, Maggie?
MARGARET: I always thought drinkin' men lost their looks, but I was plainly mistaken.
BRICK (*wryly*): Why, thanks, Maggie.
MARGARET: You're the only drinkin' man I know that it never seems t' put fat on.
BRICK: I'm gettin' softer, Maggie.
MARGARET: Well, sooner or later it's bound to soften you up. It was just beginning to soften up Skipper when —

(*She stops short.*)

I'm sorry. I never could keep my fingers off a sore — I wish you *would* lose your looks. If you did it would make the martyrdom of Saint Maggie a little more bearable. But no such goddamn luck. I actually believe you've gotten better looking since you've gone on the bottle. Yeah, a person who didn't know you would think you'd never had a tense nerve in your body or a strained muscle.

(*There are sounds of croquet on the lawn below: the click of mallets, light voices, near and distant.*)

Of course, you always had that detached quality as if you were playing a game without much concern over whether you won or lost, and now that you've lost the game, not lost but just quit playing, you have that rare sort of charm that usually only happens in very old or hopelessly sick people, the charm of the defeated. — You look so cool, so cool, so enviably cool.
REVEREND TOOKER (*offstage right*): Now looka here, boy, lemme show you how to get outa that!
MARGARET: They're playing croquet. The moon has appeared and it's white, just beginning to turn a little bit yellow. . . .
    You were a wonderful lover. . . .
    Such a wonderful person to go to bed with, and I think mostly because you were really indifferent to it.

Isn't that right? Never had any anxiety about it, did it naturally, easily, slowly, with absolute confidence and perfect calm, more like opening a door for a lady or seating her at a table than giving expression to any longing for her. Your indifference made you wonderful at lovemaking — *strange?* — but true. . . .
REVEREND TOOKER: Oh! That's a beauty.
DOCTOR BAUGH: Yeah. I got you boxed.
MARGARET: You know, if I thought you would never, never, *never* make love to me again — I would go downstairs to the kitchen and pick out the longest and sharpest knife I could find and stick it straight into my heart, I swear that I would!
REVEREND TOOKER: Watch out, you're gonna miss it.
DOCTOR BAUGH: You just don't know me, boy!
MARGARET: But one thing I don't have is the charm of the defeated, my hat is still in the ring, and I am determined to win!

(*There is the sound of croquet mallets hitting croquet balls.*)

REVEREND TOOKER: Mmm — You're too slippery for me.
MARGARET: — What is the victory of a cat on a hot tin roof? — I wish I knew. . . .
    Just staying on it, I guess, as long as she can. . . .
DOCTOR BAUGH: Jus' like an eel, boy, jus' like an eel!

(*More croquet sounds.*)

MARGARET: Later tonight I'm going to tell you I love you an' maybe by that time you'll be drunk enough to believe me. Yes, they're playing croquet. . . .
    Big Daddy is dying of cancer. . . .
    What were you thinking of when I caught you looking at me like that? Were you thinking of Skipper?

(*Brick takes up his crutch, rises.*)

Oh, excuse me, forgive me, but laws of silence don't work! No, laws of silence don't work. . . .

(*Brick crosses to the bar, takes a quick drink, and rubs his head with a towel.*)

Laws of silence don't work. . . .
    When something is festering in your memory or your imagination, laws of silence don't work, it's just like shutting a door and locking it on a house on fire in hope of forgetting that the house is burning. But not facing a fire doesn't put it out. Silence about a thing just magnifies it. It grows and festers in silence, becomes malignant. . . .

(*He drops his crutch.*)

BRICK: Give me my crutch.

(*He has stopped rubbing his hair dry but still stands hanging onto the towel rack in a white towel-cloth robe.*)

MARGARET: Lean on me.
BRICK: No, just give me my crutch.

MARGARET: Lean on my shoulder.
BRICK: *I don't want to lean on your shoulder, I want my crutch!*

(*This is spoken like sudden lightning.*)

Are you going to give me my crutch or do I have to get down on my knees on the floor and —
MARGARET: *Here, here, take it, take it!*

(*She has thrust the crutch at him.*)

BRICK (*hobbling out*): Thanks . . .
MARGARET: We mustn't scream at each other, the walls in this house have ears. . . .

(*He hobbles directly to liquor cabinet to get a new drink.*)

— but that's the first time I've heard you raise your voice in a long time, Brick. A crack in the wall? — Of composure?
— I think that's a good sign. . . .
A sign of nerves in a player on the defensive!

(*Brick turns and smiles at her coolly over his fresh drink.*)

BRICK: It just hasn't happened yet, Maggie.
MARGARET: What?
BRICK: The click I get in my head when I've had enough of this stuff to make me peaceful. . . .
Will you do me a favor?
MARGARET: Maybe I will. What favor?
BRICK: Just, just keep your voice down!
MARGARET (*in a hoarse whisper*): I'll do you that favor, I'll speak in a whisper, if not shut up completely, if *you* will do *me* a favor and make that drink your last one till after the party.
BRICK: What party?
MARGARET: Big Daddy's birthday party.
BRICK: Is this Big Daddy's birthday?
MARGARET: You know this is Big Daddy's birthday!
BRICK: No, I don't, I forgot it.
MARGARET: Well, I remembered it for you . . .

(*They are both speaking as breathlessly as a pair of kids after a fight, drawing deep exhausted breaths and looking at each other with faraway eyes, shaking and panting together as if they had broken apart from a violent struggle.*)

BRICK: Good for you, Maggie.
MARGARET: You just have to scribble a few lines on this card.
BRICK: You scribble something, Maggie.
MARGARET: It's got to be your handwriting; it's your present, I've given him my present; it's got to be your handwriting!

(*The tension between them is building again, the voices becoming shrill once more.*)

BRICK: I didn't get him a present.
MARGARET: I got one for you.

BRICK: All right. You write the card, then.
MARGARET: And have him know you didn't remember his birthday?
BRICK: I didn't remember his birthday.
MARGARET: You don't have to prove you didn't!
BRICK: I don't want to fool him about it.
MARGARET: Just write "Love, Brick!" for God's —
BRICK: No.
MARGARET: You've *got* to!
BRICK: I don't have to do anything I don't want to do. You keep forgetting the conditions on which I agreed to stay on living with you.
MARGARET (*out before she knows it*): I'm not living with you. We occupy the same cage.
BRICK: You've got to remember the conditions agreed on.
SONNY (*offstage*): Mommy, give it to me. I had it first.
MAE: Hush.
MARGARET: They're impossible conditions!
BRICK: Then why don't you — ?
SONNY: I want it, I want it!
MAE: Get away!
MARGARET: HUSH! Who is out there? Is somebody at the door?

(*There are footsteps in hall.*)

MAE (*outside*): May I enter a moment?
MARGARET: Oh, *you*! Sure. Come in, Mae.

(*Mae enters bearing aloft the bow of a young lady's archery set.*)

MAE: Brick, is this thing yours?
MARGARET: Why, Sister Woman — that's my Diana Trophy. Won it at the intercollegiate archery contest on the Ole Miss campus.
MAE: It's a mighty dangerous thing to leave exposed round a house full of nawmal rid-blooded children attracted t'weapons.
MARGARET: "Nawmal rid-blooded children attracted t'weapons" ought t'be taught to keep their hands off things that don't belong to them.
MAE: Maggie, honey, if you had children of your own you'd know how funny that is. Will you please lock this up and put the key out of reach?
MARGARET: Sister Woman, nobody is plotting the destruction of your kiddies. — Brick and I still have our special archers' license. We're goin' deer-huntin' on Moon Lake as soon as the season starts. I love to run with dogs through chilly woods, run, run leap over obstructions —

(*She goes into the closet carrying the bow.*)

MAE: How's the injured ankle, Brick?
BRICK: Doesn't hurt. Just itches.
MAE: Oh, my! Brick — Brick, you should've been downstairs after supper! Kiddies put on a show. Polly played the piano, Buster an' Sonny drums, an' then they turned out the lights an' Dixie an' Trixie puh-fawmed a toe dance in fairy costume with *spahkluhs*! Big Daddy just beamed! He just beamed!

MARGARET (*from the closet with a sharp laugh*): Oh, I bet. It breaks my heart that we missed it!

(*She reenters.*)

But Mae? Why did y'give dawgs' names to all your kiddies?

MAE: *Dogs'* names?

MARGARET (*sweetly*): Dixie, Trixie, Buster, Sonny, Polly! — Sounds like four dogs and a parrot . . .

MAE: Maggie?

(*Margaret turns with a smile.*)

Why are you so catty?

MARGARET: Cause I'm a cat! But why can't *you* take a joke, Sister Woman?

MAE: Nothin' pleases me more than a joke that's funny. You know the real names of our kiddies. Buster's real name is Robert. Sonny's real name is Saunders. Trixie's real name is Marlene and Dixie's —

(*Gooper downstairs calls for her. "Hey, Mae! Sister Woman, intermission is over!" — She rushes to door, saying:*)

Intermission is over! See ya later!

MARGARET: I wonder what Dixie's real name is?

BRICK: Maggie, being catty doesn't help things any . . .

MARGARET: I know! *WHY!* — Am I so catty? — Cause I'm consumed with envy an' eaten up with longing? — Brick, I'm going to lay out your beautiful Shantung silk suit from Rome and one of your monogrammed silk shirts. I'll put your cuff links in it, those lovely star sapphires I get you to wear so rarely. . . .

BRICK: I can't get trousers on over this plaster cast.

MARGARET: Yes, you can, I'll help you.

BRICK: I'm not going to get dressed, Maggie.

MARGARET: Will you just put on a pair of white silk pajamas?

BRICK: Yes, I'll do that, Maggie.

MARGARET: *Thank* you, thank you so *much!*

BRICK: Don't mention it.

MARGARET: *Oh, Brick!* How long does it have t' go on? This punishment? Haven't I done time enough, haven't I served my term, can't I apply for a — pardon?

BRICK: Maggie, you're spoiling my liquor. Lately your voice always sounds like you'd been running upstairs to warn somebody that the house was on fire!

MARGARET: Well, no wonder, no wonder. Y'know what I feel like, Brick?
        I feel all the time like a cat on a hot tin roof!

BRICK: Then jump off the roof, jump off it, cats can jump off roofs and land on their four feet uninjured!

MARGARET: Oh, yes!

BRICK: Do it! — fo' God's sake, do it . . .

MARGARET: Do what?

BRICK: Take a lover!

MARGARET: I can't see a man but you! Even with my eyes closed, I just see you! Why don't you get ugly, Brick, why don't you please get fat or ugly or something so I could stand it?

(*She rushes to hall door, opens it, listens.*)

The concert is still going on! Bravo, no-necks, bravo!

(*She slams and locks door fiercely.*)

BRICK: What did you lock the door for?

MARGARET: To give us a little privacy for a while.

BRICK: You know better, Maggie.

MARGARET: No, I don't know better. . . .

(*She rushes to gallery doors, draws the rose-silk drapes across them.*)

BRICK: Don't make a fool of yourself.

MARGARET: I don't mind makin' a fool of myself over you!

BRICK: I mind, Maggie. I feel embarrassed for you.

MARGARET: Feel embarrassed! But don't continue my torture. I can't live on and on under these circumstances.

BRICK: You agreed to —

MARGARET: I know but —

BRICK: — Accept that condition!

MARGARET: *I CAN'T! CAN'T! CAN'T!*

(*She seizes his shoulder.*)

BRICK: Let go!

(*He breaks away from her and seizes the small boudoir chair and raises it like a lion-tamer facing a big circus cat.*)

(*Count five. She stares at him with her fist pressed to her mouth, then bursts into shrill, almost hysterical laughter. He remains grave for a moment, then grins and puts the chair down.*)

(*Big Mama calls through closed door.*)

BIG MAMA: Son? Son? Son?

BRICK: What is it, Big Mama?

BIG MAMA (*outside*): Oh, son! We got the most wonderful news about Big Daddy. I just had t' run up an' tell you right this —

(*She rattles the knob.*)

— What's this door doin', locked, faw? You all think there's robbers in the house?

MARGARET: Big Mama, Brick is dressin, he's not dressed yet.

BIG MAMA: That's all right, it won't be the first time I've seen Brick not dressed. Come on, open this door!

(*Margaret, with a grimace, goes to unlock and open the hall door, as Brick hobbles rapidly to the bathroom and kicks the door shut. Big Mama has disappeared from the hall.*)

MARGARET: Big Mama?

(*Big Mama appears through the opposite gallery doors behind Margaret, huffing and puffing like an old bulldog. She is a short, stout woman; her sixty years and 170 pounds have left her somewhat breathless most of the time; she's always tensed like a boxer, or rather, a*

Japanese wrestler. Her "family" was maybe a little superior to Big Daddy's, but not much. She wears a black or silver lace dress and at least half a million in flashy gems. She is very sincere.)

BIG MAMA (*loudly, startling Margaret*): Here — I come through Gooper's and Mae's gall'ry door. Where's Brick? *Brick* — Hurry on out of there son, I just have a second and want to give you the news about Big Daddy. — I hate locked doors in a house . . .

MARGARET (*with affected lightness*): I've noticed you do, Big Mama, but people have got to have *some* moments of privacy, don't they?

BIG MAMA: No, ma'am, not in *my* house. (*Without pause.*) Whacha took off you' dress faw? I thought that little lace dress was so sweet on yuh, honey.

MARGARET: I thought it looked sweet on me, too, but one of m' cute little table-partners used it for a napkin so — !

BIG MAMA (*picking up stockings on floor*): What?

MARGARET: You know, Big Mama, Mae and Gooper's so touchy about those children — thanks, Big Mama . . .

(*Big Mama has thrust the picked-up stockings in Margaret's hand with a grunt.*)

— that you just don't dare to suggest there's any room for improvement in their —

BIG MAMA: Brick, hurry out! — Shoot, Maggie, you just don't like children.

MARGARET: I do SO like children! Adore them! — well brought up!

BIG MAMA (*gentle — loving*): Well, why don't you have some and bring them up well, then, instead of all the time pickin' on Gooper's an' Mae's?

GOOPER (*shouting up the stairs*): Hey, hey, Big Mama, Betsy an' Hugh got to go, waitin' t' tell yuh g'by!

BIG MAMA: Tell 'em to hold their hawses, I'll be right down in a jiffy!

GOOPER: Yes ma'am!

(*She turns to the bathroom door and calls out.*)

BIG MAMA: Son? Can you hear me in there?

(*There is a muffled answer.*)

We just got the full report from the laboratory at the Ochsner Clinic, completely negative, son, ev'rything negative, right on down the line! Nothin' a-tall's wrong with him but some little functional thing called a spastic colon. Can you hear me, son?

MARGARET: He can hear you, Big Mama.

BIG MAMA: Then why don't he say something? God Almighty, a piece of news like that should make him shout. It made *me* shout, I can tell you. I shouted and sobbed and fell right down on my knees! — Look!

(*She pulls up her skirt.*)

See the bruises where I hit my kneecaps? Took both doctors to haul me back on my feet!

(*She laughs — she always laughs like hell at herself.*)

Big Daddy was furious with me! But ain't that wonderful news?

(*Facing bathroom again, she continues:*)

After all the anxiety we been through to git a report like that on Big Daddy's birthday? Big Daddy tried to hide how much of a load that news took off his mind, but didn't fool *me*. He was mighty close to crying about it *himself*!

(*Good-byes are shouted downstairs, and she rushes to door.*)

GOOPER: Big Mama!

BIG MAMA: *Hold those people down there, don't let them go!* — Now, git dressed we're all comin' up to this room fo' Big Daddy's birthday party because of your ankle. — How's his ankle, Maggie?

MARGARET: Well, he broke it, Big Mama.

BIG MAMA: I know he broke it.

(*A phone is ringing in hall. A Negro voice answers: "Mistuh Polly's res'dence."*)

I mean does it hurt him much still.

MARGARET: I'm afraid I can't give you that information, Big Mama. You'll have to ask Brick if it hurts much still or not.

SOOKEY (*in the hall*): It's Memphis, Mizz Polly, it's Miss Sally in Memphis.

BIG MAMA: Awright, Sookey.

(*Big Mama rushes into the hall and is heard shouting on the phone:*)

Hello, Miss Sally. How are you, Miss Sally? — Yes, well, I was just gonna call you about it. *Shoot!* —

MARGARET: Brick, don't!

(*Big Mama raises her voice to a bellow.*)

BIG MAMA: *Miss Sally? Don't ever call me from the Gayoso Lobby, too much talk goes on in that hotel lobby, no wonder you can't hear me!* Now listen, Miss Sally. They's nothin' serious wrong with Big Daddy. We got the report just now, they's nothin' wrong but a thing called a — spastic! SPASTIC! — colon . . .

(*She appears at the hall door and calls to Margaret.*)

— Maggie, come out here and talk to that fool on the phone. I'm shouted breathless!

MARGARET (*goes out and is heard sweetly at phone*): Miss Sally? This is Brick's wife, Maggie. So nice to hear your voice. Can you hear *mine*? Well, *good*! — Big Mama just wanted you to know that they've got the report from the Ochsner Clinic and what Big Daddy has is a spastic colon. Yes. Spastic colon, Miss Sally. That's right, spastic colon. *G'bye, Miss Sally, hope I'll see you real soon!*

(*Hangs up a little before Miss Sally was probably ready to terminate the talk. She returns through the hall door.*)

She heard me perfectly. I've discovered with deaf

people the thing to do is not shout at them but just enunciate clearly. My rich old Aunt Cornelia was deaf as the dead but I could make her hear me just by sayin' each word slowly, distinctly, close to her ear. I read her the *Commercial Appeal* ev'ry night, read her the classified ads in it, even, she never missed a word of it. But was she a mean ole thing! Know what I got when she died? Her unexpired subscriptions to five magazines and the Book-of-the-Month Club and a LIBRARY full of ev'ry dull book ever written! All else went to her hellcat of a sister . . . meaner than she was, even!

(*Big Mama has been straightening things up in the room during this speech.*)

BIG MAMA (*closing closet door on discarded clothes*): *Miss Sally sure is a case!* Big Daddy says she's always got her hand out fo' something. He's not mistaken. That poor ole thing always has her hand out fo' somethin'. I don't think Big Daddy gives her as much as he should.

GOOPER: Big Mama! Come on now! Betsy and Hugh can't wait no longer!

BIG MAMA (*shouting*): I'm comin'!

(*She starts out. At the hall door, turns and jerks a forefinger, first toward the bathroom door, then toward the liquor cabinet, meaning: "Has Brick been drinking?" Margaret pretends not to understand, cocks her head and raises her brows as if the pantomimic performance was completely mystifying to her.*)

(*Big Mama rushes back to Margaret:*)

Shoot! Stop playin' so dumb! — I mean has he been drinkin' that stuff much yet?

MARGARET (*with a little laugh*): Oh! I think he had a highball after supper.

BIG MAMA: Don't laugh about it! — Some single men stop drinkin' when they git married and others start! Brick never touched liquor before he — !

MARGARET (*crying out*): THAT'S NOT FAIR!

BIG MAMA: Fair or not fair I want to ask you a question, one question: D'you make Brick happy in bed?

MARGARET: Why don't you ask if he makes *me* happy in bed?

BIG MAMA: Because I know that —

MARGARET: *It works both ways!*

BIG MAMA: Something's not right! You're childless and my son drinks!

GOOPER: Come on, Big Mama!

(*Gooper has called her downstairs and she has rushed to the door on the line above. She turns at the door and points at the bed.*)

— When a marriage goes on the rocks, the rocks are *there*, right *there!*

MARGARET: *That's* —

(*Big Mama has swept out of the room and slammed the door.*)

— not — *fair* . . .

(*Margaret is alone, completely alone, and she feels it. She draws in, hunches her shoulders, raises her arms with fists clenched, shuts her eyes tight as a child about to be stabbed with a vaccination needle. When she opens her eyes again, what she sees is the long oval mirror and she rushes straight to it, stares into it with a grimace and says: "Who are you?" — Then she crouches a little and answers herself in a different voice which is high, thin, mocking: "I am Maggie the Cat!" — Straightens quickly as bathroom door opens a little and Brick calls out to her.*)

BRICK: Has Big Mama gone?

MARGARET: She's gone.

(*He opens the bathroom door and hobbles out, with his liquor glass now empty, straight to the liquor cabinet. He is whistling softly. Margaret's head pivots on her long, slender throat to watch him.*)

(*She raises a hand uncertainly to the base of her throat, as if it was difficult for her to swallow, before she speaks:*)

You know, our sex life didn't just peter out in the usual way, it was cut off short, long before the natural time for it to, and it's going to revive again, just as sudden as that. I'm confident of it. That's what I'm keeping myself attractive for. For the time when you'll see me again like other men see me. Yes, like other men see me. They still see me, Brick, and they like what they see. Uh-huh. Some of them would give their —

Look, Brick!

(*She stands before the long oval mirror, touches her breast and then her hips with her two hands.*)

How high my body stays on me! — Nothing has fallen on me — not a fraction. . . .

(*Her voice is soft and trembling: a pleading child's. At this moment as he turns to glance at her — a look which is like a player passing a ball to another player, third down and goal to go — she has to capture the audience in a grip so tight that she can hold it till the first intermission without any lapse of attention.*)

Other men still want me. My face looks strained, sometimes, but I've kept my figure as well as you've kept yours, and men admire it. I still turn heads on the street. Why, last week in Memphis everywhere that I went men's eyes burned holes in my clothes, at the country club and in restaurants and department stores, there wasn't a man I met or walked by that didn't just eat me up with his eyes and turn around when I passed him and look back at me. Why, at Alice's party for her New York cousins, the best-lookin' man in the crowd — followed me upstairs and tried to force his way in the powder room with me, followed me to the door and tried to force his way in!

BRICK: Why didn't you let him, Maggie?

MARGARET: Because I'm not that common, for one

thing. Not that I wasn't almost tempted to. You like to know who it was? It was Sonny Boy Maxwell, that's who!

BRICK: Oh, yeah, Sonny Boy Maxwell, he was a good end-runner but had a little injury to his back and had to quit.

MARGARET: He has no injury now and has no wife and still has a lech for me!

BRICK: I see no reason to lock him out of a powder room in that case.

MARGARET: And have someone catch me at it? I'm not that stupid. Oh, I might sometime cheat on you with someone, since you're so insultingly eager to have me do it! — But if I do, you can be damned sure it will be in a place and a time where no one but me and the man could possibly know. Because I'm not going to give you any excuse to divorce me for being unfaithful or anything else. . . .

BRICK: Maggie, I wouldn't divorce you for being unfaithful or anything else. Don't you know that? Hell. I'd be relieved to know that you'd found yourself a lover.

MARGARET: Well, I'm taking no chances. No, I'd rather stay on this hot tin roof.

BRICK: A hot tin roof's 'n uncomfo'table place t' stay on. . . .

(*He starts to whistle softly.*)

MARGARET (*through his whistle*): Yeah, but I can stay on it just as long as I have to.

BRICK: You could leave me, Maggie.

(*He resumes whistle. She wheels about to glare at him.*)

MARGARET: *Don't want to and will not!* Besides if I did, you don't have a cent to pay for it but what you get from Big Daddy and he's dying of cancer!

(*For the first time a realization of Big Daddy's doom seems to penetrate to Brick's consciousness, visibly, and he looks at Margaret.*)

BRICK: Big Mama just said he *wasn't*, that the report was okay.

MARGARET: That's what she thinks because she got the same story that they gave Big Daddy. And was just as taken in by it as he was, poor ole things. . . .

But tonight they're going to tell her the truth about it. When Big Daddy goes to bed, they're going to tell her that he is dying of cancer.

(*She slams the dresser drawer.*)

— It's malignant and it's terminal.

BRICK: Does Big Daddy know it?

MARGARET: Hell, do they *ever* know it? Nobody says, "You're dying." You have to fool them. They have to fool *themselves*.

BRICK: Why?

MARGARET: *Why?* Because human beings dream of life everlasting, that's the reason! But most of them want it on earth and not in heaven.

(*He gives a short, hard laugh at her touch of humor.*)

Well. . . . (*She touches up her mascara.*) That's how it is, anyhow. . . . (*She looks about.*) Where did I put down my cigarette? Don't want to burn up the homeplace, at least not with Mae and Gooper and their five monsters in it!

(*She has found it and sucks at it greedily. Blows out smoke and continues:*)

So this is Big Daddy's last birthday. And Mae and Gooper, they know it, oh, *they* know it, all right. They got the first information from the Ochsner Clinic. That's why they rushed down here with their no-neck monsters. Because. Do you know something? Big Daddy's made no will? Big Daddy's never made out any will in his life, and so this campaign's afoot to impress him, forcibly as possible, with the fact that you drink and I've borne no children!

(*He continues to stare at her a moment, then mutters something sharp but not audible and hobbles rather rapidly out onto the long gallery in the fading, much faded, gold light.*)

MARGARET (*continuing her liturgical chant*): Y'know, I'm *fond* of Big Daddy, I am genuinely fond of that old man, I really *am*, you know. . . .

BRICK (*faintly, vaguely*): Yes, I know you are. . . .

MARGARET: I've always sort of admired him in spite of his coarseness, his four-letter words and so forth. Because Big Daddy *is* what he *is*, and he makes no bones about it. He hasn't turned gentleman farmer, he's still a Mississippi redneck, as much of a redneck as he must have been when he was just overseer here on the old Jack Straw and Peter Ochello place. But he got hold of it an' built it into th' biggest an' finest plantation in the Delta. — I've always *liked* Big Daddy. . . .

(*She crosses to the proscenium.*)

Well, this is Big Daddy's last birthday. I'm sorry about it. But I'm facing the facts. It takes money to take care of a drinker and that's the office that I've been elected to lately.

BRICK: You don't have to take care of me.

MARGARET: Yes, I do. Two people in the same boat have got to take care of each other. At least you want money to buy more Echo Spring when this supply is exhausted, or will you be satisfied with a ten-cent beer?

Mae an' Gooper are plannin' to freeze us out of Big Daddy's estate because you drink and I'm childless. But we can defeat that plan. We're *going* to defeat that plan!

Brick, y'know, I've been so God damn disgustingly poor all my life! — That's the *truth*, Brick!

BRICK: I'm not sayin' it isn't.

MARGARET: Always had to suck up to people I couldn't

stand because they had money and I was poor as Job's turkey. You don't know what that's like. Well, I'll tell you, it's like you would feel a thousand miles away from Echo Spring! — And had to get back to it on that broken ankle . . . without a crutch!

That's how it feels to be as poor as Job's turkey and have to suck up to relatives that you hated because they had money and all you had was a bunch of hand-me-down clothes and a few old moldly three-percent government bonds. My daddy loved his liquor, he fell in love with his liquor the way you've fallen in love with Echo Spring! — And my poor Mama, having to maintain some semblance of social position, to keep appearances up, on an income of one hundred and fifty dollars a month on those old government bonds!

When I came out, the year that I made my debut, I had just two evening dresses! One Mother made me from a pattern in *Vogue*, the other a hand-me-down from a snotty rich cousin I hated!

— The dress that I married you in was my grandmother's weddin' gown. . . .

So that's why I'm like a cat on a hot tin roof!

(*Brick is still on the gallery. Someone below calls up to him in a warm Negro voice, "Hiya, Mistuh Brick, how yuh feelin'?" Brick raises his liquor glass as if that answered the question.*)

MARGARET: You can be young without money, but you can't be old without it. You've got to be old *with* money because to be old without it is just too awful, you've got to be one or the other, either *young* or *with money*, you can't be old and *without* it. — That's the *truth*, Brick. . . .

(*Brick whistles softly, vaguely.*)

Well, now I'm dressed, I'm all dressed, there's nothing else for me to do.

(*Forlornly, almost fearfully.*)

I'm dressed, all dressed, nothing else for me to do . . .

(*She moves about restlessly, aimlessly, and speaks, as if to herself.*)

What am I — ? Oh! — my bracelets. . . .

(*She starts working a collection of bracelets over her hands onto her wrists, about six on each, as she talks.*)

I've thought a whole lot about it and now I know when I made my mistake. Yes, I made my mistake when I told you the truth about that thing with Skipper. Never should have confessed it, a fatal error, tellin' you about that thing with Skipper.

BRICK: Maggie, shut up about Skipper. I mean it, Maggie; you got to shut up about Skipper.

MARGARET: You ought to understand that Skipper and I —

BRICK: You don't think I'm serious, Maggie? You're fooled by the fact that I am saying this quiet? Look,

Maggie. What you're doing is a dangerous thing to do. You're — you're — you're — foolin' with something that — nobody ought to fool with.

MARGARET: This time I'm going to finish what I have to say to you. Skipper and I made love, if love you could call it, because it made both of us feel a little bit closer to you. You see, you son of a bitch, you asked too much of people, of me, of him, of all the unlucky poor damned sons of bitches that happen to love you, and there was a whole pack of them, yes, there was a pack of them besides me and Skipper, you asked too goddamn much of people that loved you, you — superior creature! — you godlike being! — And so we made love to each other to dream it was you, both of us! Yes, yes, yes! Truth, truth! What's so awful about it? I like it, I think the truth is — yeah! I shouldn't have told you. . . .

BRICK (*holding his head unnaturally still and uptilted a bit*): It was Skipper that told me about it. Not you, Maggie.

MARGARET: I told you!

BRICK: After he told me!

MARGARET: What does it matter who — ?

DIXIE: I got your mallet, I got your mallet.

TRIXIE: Give it to me, give it to me. IT's mine.

(*Brick turns suddenly out upon the gallery and calls:*)

BRICK: Little girl! Hey, little girl!

LITTLE GIRL (*at a distance*): What, Uncle Brick?

BRICK: Tell the folks to come up! — Bring everybody upstairs!

TRIXIE: It's mine, it's mine.

MARGARET: I can't stop myself! I'd go on telling you this in front of them all, if I had to!

BRICK: Little girl! Go on, go on, will you? Do what I told you, call them!

DIXIE: Okay.

MARGARET: Because it's got to be told and you, you! — you never let me!

(*She sobs, then controls herself, and continues almost calmly.*)

It was one of those beautiful, ideal things they tell about in the Greek legends, it couldn't be anything else, you being you, and that's what made it so sad, that's what made it so awful, because it was love that never could be carried through to anything satisfying or even talked about plainly.

BRICK: Maggie, you gotta stop this.

MARGARET: Brick, I tell you, you got to believe me, Brick, I *do* understand all about it! I — I think it was — *noble!* Can't you tell I'm sincere when I say I respect it? My only point, the only point that I'm making, is life has got to be allowed to continue even after the *dream* of life is — all — over. . . .

(*Brick is without his crutch. Leaning on furniture, he crosses to pick it up as she continues as if possessed by a will outside herself:*)

ABOVE: Kathleen Turner as Maggie in the 1990 Eugene O'Neill Theatre production of *Cat on a Hot Tin Roof*, directed by Howard Davies. BELOW: Brick (Daniel Hugh Kelly) and Maggie. (Photos by Michael Tighe.)

Why I remember when we double-dated at college, Gladys Fitzgerald and I and you and Skipper, it was more like a date between you and Skipper. Gladys and I were just sort of tagging along as if it was necessary to chaperone you! — to make a good public impression —

BRICK (*turns to face her, half lifting his crutch*): Maggie, you want me to hit you with this crutch? Don't you know I could kill you with this crutch?

MARGARET: Good Lord, man, d' you think I'd care if you did?

BRICK: One man has one great good true thing in his life. One great good thing which is true! — I had friendship with Skipper. — You are naming it dirty!

MARGARET: I'm not naming it dirty! I am naming it clean.

BRICK: Not love with you, Maggie, but friendship with Skipper was that one great true thing, and you are naming it dirty!

MARGARET: Then you haven't been listenin', not understood what I'm saying! I'm naming it so damn clean that it killed poor Skipper! — You two had something that had to be kept on ice, yes, incorruptible, yes! — and death was the only icebox where you could keep it. . . .

BRICK: I married you, Maggie. Why would I marry you, Maggie, if I was — ?

MARGARET: Brick, let me finish! — I know, believe me I know, that it was only Skipper that harbored even any *unconscious* desire for anything not perfectly pure between you two! — Now let me skip a little. You married me early that summer we graduated out of Ole Miss, and we were happy, weren't we, we were blissful, yes, hit heaven together ev'ry time that we loved! But that fall you an' Skipper turned down wonderful offers of jobs in order to keep on bein' football heroes — pro-football heroes. You organized the Dixie Stars that fall, so you could keep on bein' teammates forever! But somethin' was not right with it! — Me included! — between you. Skipper began hittin' the bottle . . . you got a spinal injury — couldn't play the Thanksgivin' game in Chicago, watched it on TV from a traction bed in Toledo. I joined Skipper. The Dixie Stars lost because poor Skipper was drunk. We drank together that night all night in the bar of the Blackstone and when cold day was comin' up over the Lake an' we were comin' out drunk to take a dizzy look at it, I said, "SKIPPER! STOP LOVIN' MY HUSBAND OR TELL HIM HE'S GOT TO LET YOU ADMIT IT TO HIM!" — one way or another!

HE SLAPPED ME HARD ON THE MOUTH! — then turned and ran without stopping once, I am sure, all the way back into his room at the Blackstone. . . .

— When I came to his room that night, with a little scratch like a shy little mouse at his door, he made that pitiful, ineffectual little attempt to prove that what I had said wasn't true. . . .

(*Brick strikes at her with crutch, a blow that shatters the gemlike lamp on the table.*)

— In this way, I destroyed him, by telling him truth that he and his world which he was born and raised in, yours and his world, had told him could not be told?

— From then on Skipper was nothing at all but a receptacle for liquor and drugs. . . .

— *Who shot cock robin? I with my* —

(*She throws back her head with tight shut eyes.*)

— *merciful arrow!*

(*Brick strikes at her; misses.*)

Missed me! — Sorry, — I'm not tryin' to whitewash my behavior, Christ, no! Brick, I'm not good. I don't know why people have to pretend to be good, nobody's good. The rich or the well-to-do can afford to respect moral patterns, conventional moral patterns, but I could never afford to, yeah, but — I'm honest! Give me credit for just that, will you *please?* — Born poor, raised poor, expect to die poor unless I manage to get us something out of what Big Daddy leaves when he dies of cancer! But Brick?! — *Skipper is dead! I'm alive!* Maggie the cat is —

(*Brick hops awkwardly forward and strikes at her again with his crutch.*)

— *alive! I am alive, alive! I am . . .*

(*He hurls the crutch at her, across the bed she took refuge behind, and pitches forward on the floor as she completes her speech.*)

— *alive!*

(*A little girl, Dixie, bursts into the room, wearing an Indian war bonnet and firing a cap pistol at Margaret and shouting: "Bang, bang, bang!"*)

(*Laughter downstairs floats through the open hall door. Margaret had crouched gasping to bed at child's entrance. She now rises and says with cool fury:*)

Little girl, your mother or someone should teach you — (*gasping*) — to knock at a door before you come into a room. Otherwise people might think that you — lack — good breeding. . . .

DIXIE: Yanh, yanh, yanh, what is Uncle Brick doin' on th' floor?

BRICK: I tried to kill your Aunt Maggie, but I failed — and I fell. Little girl, give me my crutch so I can get up off th' floor.

MARGARET: Yes, give your uncle his crutch, he's a cripple, honey, he broke his ankle last night jumping hurdles on the high school athletic field!

DIXIE: What were you jumping hurdles for, Uncle Brick?

BRICK: Because I used to jump them, and people like to do what they used to do, even after they've stopped being able to do it. . . .

MARGARET: That's right, that's your answer, now go away, little girl.

(*Dixie fires cap pistol at Margaret three times.*)

> Stop, you stop that, monster! You little no-neck monster!

(*She seizes the cap pistol and hurls it through gallery doors.*)

DIXIE (*with a precocious instinct for the cruelest thing*): You're *jealous!* — You're just jealous because you can't have babies!

(*She sticks out her tongue at Margaret as she sashays past her with her stomach stuck out, to the gallery. Margaret slams the gallery doors and leans panting against them. There is a pause. Brick has replaced his spilt drink and sits, faraway, on the great four-poster bed.*)

MARGARET: You see? — they gloat over us being childless, even in front of their five little no-neck monsters!

(*Pauses. Voices approach on the stairs.*)

> Brick? — I've been to a doctor in Memphis, a — a gynecologist. . . .
>   I've been completely examined, and there is no reason why we can't have a child whenever we want one. And this is my time by the calendar to conceive. Are you listening to me? Are you? Are you LISTENING TO ME!

BRICK: Yes. I hear you, Maggie.

(*His attention returns to her inflamed face.*)

> — But how in hell on earth do you imagine — that you're going to have a child by a man that can't stand you?

MARGARET: That's a problem that I will have to work out.

(*She wheels about to face the hall door.*)

MAE (*offstage left*): Come on, Big Daddy. We're all goin' up to Brick's room.

(*From offstage left, voices: Reverend Tooker, Doctor Baugh, Mae.*)

MARGARET: *Here they come!*

(*The lights dim.*)

ACT 2

(*There is no lapse of time. Margaret and Brick are in the same positions they held at the end of act 1.*)

MARGARET (*at door*): *Here they come!*

(*Big Daddy appears first, a tall man with a fierce, anxious look, moving carefully not to betray his weakness even, or especially, to himself.*)

GOOPER: I read in the *Register* that you're getting a new memorial window.

(*Some of the people are approaching through the hall, others along the gallery: voices from both directions. Gooper and Reverend Tooker become visible outside gallery doors, and their voices come in clearly.*)
  (*They pause outside as Gooper lights a cigar.*)

REVEREND TOOKER (*vivaciously*): Oh, but St. Paul's in Grenada has three memorial windows, and the latest one is a Tiffany stained-glass window that cost twenty-five hundred dollars, a picture of Christ the Good Shepherd with a Lamb in His arms.

MARGARET: Big Daddy.

BIG DADDY: Well, Brick.

BRICK: Hello Big Daddy. — Congratulations!

BIG DADDY: — Crap. . . .

GOOPER: Who give that window, Preach?

REVEREND TOOKER: Clyde Fletcher's widow. Also presented St. Paul's with a baptismal font.

GOOPER: Y'know what somebody ought t' give your church is a *coolin'* system, Preach.

MAE (*almost religiously*): — Let's see now, they've had their *tyyy*-phoid shots, and their tetanus shots, their diphtheria shots and their hepatitis shots and their polio shots, they got *those* shots every month from May through September, and — Gooper? Hey! Gooper! — What all have the kiddies been shot faw?

REVEREND TOOKER: Yes, siree, Bob! And y'know what Gus Hamma's family gave in his memory to the church at Two Rivers? A complete new stone parish-house with a basketball court in the basement and a —

BIG DADDY (*uttering a loud barking laugh which is far from truly mirthful*): Hey, Preach! What's all this talk about memorials, Preach? Y' think somebody's about t' kick off around here? 'S that it?

(*Startled by this interjection, Reverend Tooker decides to laugh at the question almost as loud as he can.*)
  (*How he would answer the question we'll never know, as he's spared that embarrassment by the voice of Gooper's wife, Mae, rising high and clear as she appears with "Doc" Baugh, the family doctor, through the hall door.*)

MARGARET (*overlapping a bit*): Turn on the hi-fi, Brick! Let's have some music t' start off th' party with!

BRICK: You turn it on, Maggie.

(*The talk becomes so general that the room sounds like a great aviary of chattering birds. Only Brick remains unengaged, leaning upon the liquor cabinet with his faraway smile, an ice cube in a paper napkin with which he now and then rubs his forehead. He doesn't respond to Margaret's command. She bounds forward and stoops over the instrument panel of the console.*)

GOOPER: We gave 'em that thing for a third anniversary present, got three speakers in it.

(*The room is suddenly blasted by the climax of a Wagnerian opera or a Beethoven symphony.*)

BIG DADDY: *Turn that damn thing off!*

(*Almost instant silence, almost instantly broken by the shouting charge of Big Mama, entering through hall door like a charging rhino.*)

BIG MAMA: *Wha's my Brick, wha's mah precious baby!!*
BIG DADDY: *Sorry! Turn it back on!*

(*Everyone laughs very loud. Big Daddy is famous for his jokes at Big Mama's expense, and nobody laughs louder at these jokes than Big Mama herself, though sometimes they're pretty cruel and Big Mama has to pick up or fuss with something to cover the hurt that the loud laugh doesn't quite cover.*)

(*On this occasion, a happy occasion because the dread in her heart has also been lifted by the false report on Big Daddy's condition, she giggles, grotesquely, coyly, in Big Daddy's direction and bears down upon Brick, all very quick and alive.*)

BIG MAMA: Here he is, here's my precious baby! What's that you've got in your hand? You put that liquor down, son, your hand was made fo' holdin' somethin' better than that!
GOOPER: Look at Brick put it down!

(*Brick has obeyed Big Mama by draining the glass and handing it to her. Again everyone laughs, some high, some low.*)

BIG MAMA: Oh, you bad boy, you, you're my bad little boy. Give Big Mama a kiss, you bad boy, you! — Look at him shy away, will you? Brick never liked bein' kissed or made a fuss over, I guess because he's always had too much of it!
Son, you turn that thing off!

(*Brick has switched on the TV set.*)

I can't stand TV, radio was bad enough but TV has gone it one better, I mean — (*plops wheezing in chair*) — one worse, ha ha! Now what'm I sittin' down here faw? I want t' sit next to my sweetheart on the sofa, hold hands with him and love him up a little!

(*Big Mama has on a black and white figured chiffon. The large irregular patterns, like the markings of some massive animal, the luster of her great diamonds and many pearls, the brilliants set in the silver frames of her glasses, her riotous voice, booming laugh, have dominated the room since she entered. Big Daddy has been regarding her with a steady grimace of chronic annoyance.*)

BIG MAMA (*still louder*): Preacher, Preacher, hey, Preach! Give me you' hand an' help me up from this chair!
REVEREND TOOKER: None of your tricks, Big Mama!
BIG MAMA: What tricks? You give me you' hand so I can get up an' —

(*Reverend Tooker extends her his hand. She grabs it and pulls him into her lap with a shrill laugh that spans an octave in two notes.*)

Ever seen a preacher in a fat lady's lap? Hey, hey, folks! Ever seen a preacher in a fat lady's lap?

(*Big Mama is notorious throughout the Delta for this sort of inelegant horseplay. Margaret looks on with indulgent humor, sipping Dubonnet "on the rocks" and watching Brick, but Mae and Gooper exchange signs of humorless anxiety over these antics, the sort of behavior which Mae thinks may account for their failure to quite get in with the smartest young married set in Memphis, despite all. One of the Negroes, Lacey or Sookey, peeks in, cackling. They are waiting for a sign to bring in the cake and champagne. But Big Daddy's not amused. He doesn't understand why, in spite of the infinite mental relief he's received from the doctor's report, he still has these same old fox teeth in his guts. "This spastic condition is something else," he says to himself, but aloud he roars at Big Mama:*)

BIG DADDY: *BIG MAMA, WILL YOU QUIT HORSIN'?* — You're too old an' too fat fo' that sort of crazy kid stuff an' besides a woman with your blood pressure — she had two hundred last spring! — is riskin' a stroke when you mess around like that. . . .

(*Mae blows on a pitch pipe.*)

BIG MAMA: *Here comes Big Daddy's birthday!*

(*Negroes in white jackets enter with an enormous birthday cake ablaze with candles and carrying buckets of champagne with satin ribbons about the bottle necks.*)

(*Mae and Gooper strike up song, and everybody, including the Negroes and Children, joins in. Only Brick remains aloof.*)

EVERYONE: Happy birthday to you.
Happy birthday to you.
Happy birthday, Big Daddy —

(*Some sing: "Dear, Big Daddy!"*)

Happy birthday to you.

(*Some sing: "How old are you?"*)

(*Mae has come down center and is organizing her children like a chorus. She gives them a barely audible: "One, two, three!" and they are off in the new tune.*)

CHILDREN: Skinamarinka — dinka — dink
Skinamarinka — do
We love you.
Skinamarinka — dinka — dink
Skinamarinka — do.

(*All together, they turn to Big Daddy.*)

Big Daddy, you!

(*They turn back front, like a musical comedy chorus.*)

We love you in the morning;
We love you in the night.
We love you when we're with you,
And we love you out of sight.

Skinamarinka — dinka — dink
Skinamarinka — do.

(*Mae turns to Big Mama.*)

Big Mama, too!

(*Big Mama bursts into tears. The Negroes leave.*)

BIG DADDY: Now Ida, what the hell is the matter with
you?
MAE: She's just so happy.
BIG MAMA: I'm just so happy, Big Daddy, I have to cry
or something.

(*Sudden and loud in the hush:*)

Brick, do you know the wonderful news that Doc
Baugh got from the clinic about Big Daddy? Big
Daddy's one hundred percent!
MARGARET: Isn't that wonderful?
BIG MAMA: He's just one hundred percent. Passed the
examination with flying colors. Now that we know
there's nothing wrong with Big Daddy but a spastic
colon, I can tell you something. I was worried sick
half out of my mind, for fear that Big Daddy might
have a thing like —

(*Margaret cuts through this speech, jumping up and
exclaiming shrilly:*)

MARGARET: Brick, honey, aren't you going to give Big
Daddy his birthday present?

(*Passing by him, she snatches his liquor glass from him.*)
(*She picks up a fancily wrapped package.*)

Here it is, Big Daddy, this is from Brick!
BIG MAMA: This is the biggest birthday Big Daddy's ever
had, a hundred presents and bushels of telegrams
from —
MAE (*at same time*): What is it, Brick?
GOOPER: I bet 500 to 50 that Brick don't *know* what it
is.
BIG MAMA: The fun of presents is not knowing what
they are till you open the package. Open your
present, Big Daddy.
BIG DADDY: Open it you'self. I want to ask Brick somethin! Come here, Brick.
MARGARET: Big Daddy's callin' you, Brick.

(*She is opening the package.*)

BRICK: Tell Big Daddy I'm crippled.
BIG DADDY: I see you're crippled. I want to know how
you got crippled.
MARGARET (*making diversionary tactics*): Oh, look, oh,
look, why, it's a cashmere robe!

(*She holds the robe up for all to see.*)

MAE: You sound surprised, Maggie.
MARGARET: I never saw one before.
MAE: That's funny. — *Hah!*
MARGARET (*turning on her fiercely, with a brilliant
smile*): Why is it funny? All my family ever had was

family — and luxuries such as cashmere robes still
surprise me!
BIG DADDY (*ominously*): Quiet!
MAE (*heedless in her fury*): I don't see how you could be
so surprised when you bought it yourself at Loewen-
stein's in Memphis last Saturday. You know how I
know?
BIG DADDY: I said, Quiet!
MAE: — I know because the salesgirl that sold it to you
waited on me and said, Oh, Mrs. Pollitt, your sister-
in-law just bought a cashmere robe for your husband's father!
MARGARET: Sister Woman! Your talents are wasted as a
housewife and mother, you really ought to be with
the FBI or —
BIG DADDY: QUIET!

(*Reverend Tooker's reflexes are slower than the others'.
He finishes a sentence after the bellow.*)

REVEREND TOOKER (*to Doc Baugh*): — the Stork and
the Reaper are running neck and neck!

(*He starts to laugh gaily when he notices the silence and
Big Daddy's glare. His laugh dies falsely.*)

BIG DADDY: Preacher, I hope I'm not butting in on more
talk about memorial stained-glass windows, am I,
Preacher?

(*Reverend Tooker laughs feebly, then coughs dryly in
the embarrassed silence.*)

Preacher?
BIG MAMA: Now, Big Daddy, don't you pick on Preacher!
BIG DADDY (*raising his voice*): You ever hear that expression all hawk and no spit? You bring that expression to mind with that little dry cough of yours, all
hawk an' no spit. . . .

(*The pause is broken only by a short startled laugh from
Margaret, the only one there who is conscious of and
amused by the grotesque.*)

MAE (*raising her arms and jangling her bracelets*): I
wonder if the mosquitoes are active tonight?
BIG DADDY: What's that, Little Mama? Did you make
some remark?
MAE: Yes, I said I wondered if the mosquitoes would eat
us alive if we went out on the gallery for a while.
BIG DADDY: Well, if they do, I'll have your bones pulver-
ized for fertilizer!
BIG MAMA (*quickly*): Last week we had an airplane
spraying the place and I think it done some good, at
least I haven't had a —
BIG DADDY (*cutting her speech*): Brick, they tell me, if
what they tell me is true, that you done some jump-
ing last night on the high school athletic field?
BIG MAMA: Brick, Big Daddy is talking to you, son.
BRICK (*smiling vaguely over his drink*): What was that,
Big Daddy?
BIG DADDY: They said you done some jumping on the
high school track field last night.

BRICK: That's what they told me, too.

BIG DADDY: Was it jumping or humping that you were doing out there? What were you doing out there at three A.M., layin' a woman on that cinder track?

BIG MAMA: Big Daddy, you are off the sick-list, now, and I'm not going to excuse you for talkin' so —

BIG DADDY: Quiet!

BIG MAMA: — *nasty* in front of Preacher and —

BIG DADDY: *QUIET!* — I ast you, Brick, if you was cuttin' you'self a piece o' poon-tang last night on that cinder track? I thought maybe you were chasin' poon-tang on that track an' tripped over something in the heat of the chase — 'sthat it?

(*Gooper laughs, loud and false, others nervously following suit. Big Mama stamps her foot, and purses her lips, crossing to Mae and whispering something to her as Brick meets his father's hard, intent, grinning stare with a slow, vague smile that he offers all situations from behind the screen of his liquor.*)

BRICK: No, sir, I don't think so. . . .

MAE (*at the same time, sweetly*): Reverend Tooker, let's you and I take a stroll on the widow's walk.

(*She and the preacher go out on the gallery as Big Daddy says:*)

BIG DADDY: Then what the hell were you doing out there at three o'clock in the morning?

BRICK: Jumping the hurdles, Big Daddy, runnin' and jumpin' the hurdles, but those high hurdles have gotten too high for me, now.

BIG DADDY: Cause you was drunk?

BRICK (*his vague smile fading a little*): Sober I wouldn't have tried to jump the *low* ones. . . .

BIG MAMA (*quickly*): Big Daddy, blow out the candles on your birthday cake!

MARGARET (*at the same time*): I want to propose a toast to Big Daddy Pollitt on his sixty-fifth birthday, the biggest cotton planter in —

BIG DADDY (*bellowing with fury and disgust*): *I told you to stop it, now stop it, quit this — !*

BIG MAMA (*coming in front of Big Daddy with the cake*): Big Daddy, I will not allow you to talk that way, not even on your birthday, I —

BIG DADDY: I'll talk like I want to on my birthday, Ida, or any other goddamn day of the year and anybody here that don't like it knows what they can do!

BIG MAMA: You don't mean that!

BIG DADDY What makes you think I don't mean it?

(*Meanwhile various discreet signals have been exchanged and Gooper has also gone out on the gallery.*)

BIG MAMA: I just know you don't mean it.

BIG DADDY: You don't know a goddamn thing and you never did!

BIG MAMA: Big Daddy, you don't mean that.

BIG DADDY: Oh, yes, I do, oh, yes, I do, I mean it! I put up with a whole lot of crap around here because I thought I was dying. And you thought I was dying

and you started taking over, well, you can stop taking over now, Ida, because I'm not gonna die, you can just stop now this business of taking over because you're not taking over because I'm not dying, I went through the laboratory and the goddamn exploratory operation and there's nothing wrong with me but a spastic colon. And I'm not dying of cancer which you thought I was dying of. Ain't that so? Didn't you think that I was dying of cancer, Ida?

(*Almost everybody is out on the gallery but the two old people glaring at each other across the blazing cake.*)

(*Big Mama's chest heaves and she presses a fat fist to her mouth.*)

(*Big Daddy continues, hoarsely:*)

Ain't that so, Ida? Didn't you have an idea I was dying of cancer and now you could take control of this place and everything on it? I got that impression, I seemed to get that impression. Your loud voice everywhere, your fat old body butting in here and there!

BIG MAMA: Hush! The Preacher!

BIG DADDY: Fuck the goddamn preacher!

(*Big Mama gasps loudly and sits down on the sofa which is almost too small for her.*)

Did you hear what I said? I said fuck the goddamn preacher!

(*Somebody closes the gallery doors from outside just as there is a burst of fireworks and excited cries from the children.*)

BIG MAMA: I never seen you act like this before and I can't think what's got in you!

BIG DADDY: I went through all that laboratory and operation and all just so I would know if you or me was boss here! Well, now it turns out that I am and you ain't — and that's my birthday present — and my cake and champagne! — because for three years now you been gradually taking over. Bossing. Talking. Sashaying your fat old body around the place I made! I made this place! I was overseer on it! I was the overseer on the old Straw and Ochello plantation. I quit school at ten! I quit school at ten years old and went to work like a nigger in the fields. And I rose to be overseer of the Straw and Ochello plantation. And old Straw died and I was Ochello's partner and the place got bigger and bigger and bigger and bigger and bigger! I did all that myself with no goddamn help from you, and now you think you're just about to take over. Well, I am just about to tell you that you are not just about to take over, you are not just about to take over a God damn thing. Is that clear to you, Ida? Is that very plain to you, now? Is that understood completely? I been through the laboratory from A to Z. I've had the goddamn exploratory operation, and nothing is wrong with me but a spastic colon — made spastic, I guess, by *disgust!* By all the goddamn lies and liars that I have had to put up with and all the goddamn hypocrisy that I lived with all these forty years that we been livin' together!

    Hey! Ida!! Blow out the candles on the birthday cake! Purse up your lips and draw a deep breath and blow out the goddam candles on the cake!

BIG MAMA: Oh, Big Daddy, oh, oh, oh, Big Daddy!

BIG DADDY: What's the matter with you?

BIG MAMA: *In all these years you never believed that I loved you??*

BIG DADDY: Huh?

BIG MAMA: *And I did, I did so much, I did love you!* — I even loved your hate and your hardness, Big Daddy!

(*She sobs and rushes awkwardly out onto the gallery.*)

BIG DADDY (*to himself*): Wouldn't it be funny if that was true. . . .

(*A pause is followed by a burst of light in the sky from the fireworks.*)

    BRICK! HEY, BRICK!

(*He stands over his blazing birthday cake.*)

(*After some moments, Brick hobbles in on his crutch, holding his glass.*)

(*Margaret follows him with a bright, anxious smile.*)

    I didn't call you, Maggie. I called Brick.

MARGARET: I'm just delivering him to you.

(*She kisses Brick on the mouth which he immediately wipes with the back of his hand. She flies girlishly back out. Brick and his father are alone.*)

BIG DADDY: Why did you do that?

BRICK: Do what, Big Daddy?

BIG DADDY: Wipe her kiss off your mouth like she'd spit on you.

BRICK: I don't know. I wasn't conscious of it.

BIG DADDY: That woman of yours has a better shape on her than Gooper's but somehow or other they got the same look about them.

BRICK: What sort of look is that, Big Daddy?

BIG DADDY: I don't know how to describe it but it's the same look.

BRICK: They don't look peaceful, do they?

BIG DADDY: No, they sure in hell don't.

BRICK: They look nervous as cats?

BIG DADDY: That's right, they look nervous as cats.

BRICK: Nervous as a couple of cats on a hot tin roof?

BIG DADDY: That's right, boy, they look like a couple of cats on a hot tin roof. It's funny that you and Gooper being so different would pick out the same type of woman.

BRICK: Both of us married into society, Big Daddy.

BIG DADDY: Crap . . . I wonder what gives them both that look?

BRICK: Well. They're sittin' in the middle of a big piece of land, Big Daddy, twenty-eight thousand acres is a pretty big piece of land and so they're squaring off on it, each determined to knock off a bigger piece of it than the other whenever you let it go.

BIG DADDY: I got a surprise for those women. I'm not gonna let it go for a long time yet if that's what they're waiting for.

BRICK: That's right, Big Daddy. You just sit tight and let them scratch each other's eyes out. . . .

BIG DADDY: You bet your life I'm going to sit tight on it and let those sons of bitches scratch their eyes out, ha ha ha. . . .

    But Gooper's wife's a good breeder, you got to admit she's fertile. Hell, at supper tonight she had them all at the table and they had to put a couple of extra leafs in the table to make room for them, she's got five head of them, now, and another one's comin'.

BRICK: Yep, number six is comin' . . .

BIG DADDY: Six hell, she'll probably drop a litter next time. Brick, you know, I swear to God, I don't know the way it happens.

BRICK: The way what happens, Big Daddy?

BIG DADDY: You git you a piece of land, by hook or crook, an' things start growin' on it, things accumulate on it, and the first thing you know it's completely out of hand, completely out of hand!

BRICK: Well, they say nature hates a vacuum, Big Daddy.

BIG DADDY: That's what they say, but sometimes I think that a vacuum is a hell of a lot better than some of the stuff that nature replaces it with.

    Is someone out there by that door?

GOOPER: Hey Mae.

BRICK: Yep.

BIG DADDY: Who?

(*He has lowered his voice.*)

BRICK: Someone int'rested in what we say to each other.

BIG DADDY: Gooper? — *GOOPER!*

(*After a discreet pause, Mae appears in the gallery door.*)

MAE: Did you call Gooper, Big Daddy?

BIG DADDY: Aw, it was you.

MAE: Do you want Gooper, Big Daddy?

BIG DADDY: No, and I don't want you. I want some privacy here, while I'm having a confidential talk with my son Brick. Now it's too hot in here to close them doors, but if I have to close those fuckin' doors in order to have a private talk with my son Brick, just let me know and I'll close 'em. Because I hate eavesdroppers, I don't like any kind of sneakin' an' spyin'.

MAE: Why, Big Daddy —

BIG DADDY: You stood on the wrong side of the moon, it threw your shadow!

MAE: I was just —

BIG DADDY: You was just nothing but *spyin'* an you *know* it!

MAE (*begins to sniff and sob*): Oh, Big Daddy, you're so unkind for some reason to those that really love you!

BIG DADDY: Shut up, shut up, shut up! I'm going to move you and Gooper out of that room next to this! It's none of your goddamn business what goes on in here at night between Brick an' Maggie. You listen at night like a couple of rutten peekhole spies and go and give a report on what you hear to Big Mama an' she comes to me and says they say such and such and so and so about what they heard goin' on between Brick an' Maggie, and Jesus, it makes me sick. I'm goin' to move you an' Gooper out of that room, I can't stand sneakin' an' spyin', it makes me puke. . . .

(*Mae throws back her head and rolls her eyes heavenward and extends her arms as if invoking God's pity for this unjust martyrdom; then she presses a handkerchief to her nose and flies from the room with a loud swish of skirts.*)

BRICK (*now at the liquor cabinet*): They listen, do they?

BIG DADDY: Yeah. They listen and give reports to Big Mama on what goes on in here between you and Maggie. They say that —

(*He stops as if embarrassed.*)

— You won't sleep with her, that you sleep on the sofa. Is that true or not true? If you don't like Maggie, get rid of Maggie! — What are you doin' there now?

BRICK: Fresh'nin' up my drink.

BIG DADDY: Son, you know you got a real liquor problem?

BRICK: Yes, sir, yes, I know.

BIG DADDY: Is that why you quit sports-announcing, because of this liquor problem?

BRICK: Yes, sir, yes, sir, I guess so.

(*He smiles vaguely and amiably at his father across his replenished drink.*)

BIG DADDY: Son, don't guess about it, it's too important.

BRICK (*vaguely*): Yes, sir.

BIG DADDY: And listen to me, don't look at the damn chandelier. . . .

(*Pause. Big Daddy's voice is husky.*)

— Somethin' else we picked up at th' big fire-sale in Europe.

(*Another pause.*)

Life is important. There's nothing else to hold onto. A man that drinks is throwing his life away. Don't do it, hold onto your life. There's nothing else to hold onto. . . .

Sit down over here so we don't have to raise our voices, the walls have ears in this place.

BRICK (*hobbling over to sit on the sofa beside him*): All right, Big Daddy.

BIG DADDY: Quit! — how'd that come about? Some disappointment?

BRICK: I don't know. Do you?

BIG DADDY: I'm askin' you, God damn it! How in hell would I know if you don't?

BRICK: I just got out there and found that I had a mouth full of cotton. I was always two or three beats behind what was goin' on on the field and so I —

BIG DADDY: Quit!

BRICK (*amiably*): Yes, quit.

BIG DADDY: Son?

BRICK: Huh?

BIG DADDY (*inhales loudly and deeply from his cigar; then bends suddenly a little forward, exhaling loudly and raising a hand to his forehead*): — Whew! — ha ha! — I took in too much smoke, it made me a little lightheaded. . . .

(*The mantel clock chimes.*)

Why is it so damn hard for people to talk?

BRICK: Yeah. . . .

(*The clock goes on sweetly chiming till it has completed the stroke of ten.*)

— Nice peaceful-soundin' clock, I like to hear it all night. . . .

(*He slides low and comfortable on the sofa; Big Daddy sits up straight and rigid with some unspoken anxiety. All his gestures are tense and jerky as he talks. He wheezes and pants and sniffs through his nervous speech, glancing quickly, shyly, from time to time, at his son.*)

BIG DADDY: We got that clock the summer we wint to Europe, me an' Big Mama on that damn Cook's Tour, never had such an awful time in my life, I'm tellin' you, son, those gooks over there, they gouge your eyeballs out in their grand hotels. And Big Mama bought more stuff than you could haul in a couple of boxcars, that's no crap. Everywhere she wint on this whirlwind tour, she bought, bought, bought. Why, half that stuff she bought is still crated up in the cellar, under water last spring!

(*He laughs.*)

That Europe is nothin' on earth but a great big auction, that's all it is, that bunch of old worn-out places, it's just a big fire-sale, the whole fuckin' thing, an' Big Mama wint wild in it, why, you couldn't hold that woman with a mule's harness! Bought, bought, bought! — lucky I'm a rich man, yes siree, Bob, an' half that stuff is mildewin' in th' basement. It's lucky I'm a rich man, it sure is lucky, well, I'm a rich man, Brick, yep, I'm a mighty rich man.

(*His eyes light up for a moment.*)

Y'know how much I'm worth? Guess, Brick! Guess how much I'm worth!

(*Brick smiles vaguely over his drink.*)

Close on ten million in cash an' blue-chip stocks, outside, mind you, of twenty-eight thousand acres of the richest land this side of the valley Nile!

But a man can't buy his life with it, he can't buy back his life with it when his life has been spent, that's one thing not offered in the Europe fire-sale or in the American markets or any markets on earth, a man can't buy his life with it, he can't buy back his life when his life is finished. . . .

That's a sobering thought, a very sobering thought, and that's a thought that I was turning over in my head, over and over and over — until today. . . .

I'm wiser and sadder, Brick, for this experience which I just gone through. They's one thing else that I remember in Europe.

BRICK: What is that, Big Daddy?

BIG DADDY: The hills around Barcelona in the country of Spain and the children running over those bare hills in their bare skins beggin' like starvin' dogs with howls and screeches, and how fat the priests are on the streets of Barcelona, so many of them and so fat and so pleasant, ha ha! — Y'know I could feed that country? I got money enough to feed that goddamn country, but the human animal is a selfish beast and I don't reckon the money I passed out there to those howling children in the hills around Barcelona would more than upholster the chairs in this room, I mean pay to put a new cover on this chair!

Hell, I threw them money like you'd scatter feed corn for chickens, I threw money at them just to get rid of them long enough to climb back into th' car and — drive away. . . .

And then in Morocco, them Arabs, why, I remember one day in Marrakech, that old walled Arab city, I set on a broken-down wall to have a cigar, it was fearful hot there and this Arab woman stood in the road and looked at me till I was embarrassed, she stood stock still in the dusty hot road and looked at me till I was embarrassed. But listen to this. She had a naked child with her, a little naked girl with her, barely able to toddle, and after a while she set this child on the ground and give her a push and whispered something to her.

This child come toward me, barely able t' walk, come toddling up to me and —

Jesus, it makes you sick t' remember a thing like this! It stuck out its hand and tried to unbutton my trousers!

That child was not yet five! Can you believe me? Or do you think that I am making this up? I wint back to the hotel and said to Big Mama, Git packed! We're clearing out of this country. . . .

BRICK: Big Daddy, you're on a talkin' jag tonight.

BIG DADDY (*ignoring this remark*): Yes, sir, that's how it is, the human animal is a beast that dies but the fact that he's dying don't give him pity for others, no, sir, it —

— Did you say something?

BRICK: Yes.

BIG DADDY: What?

BRICK: Hand me over that crutch so I can get up.

BIG DADDY: Where you goin?

BRICK: I'm takin' a little short trip to Echo Spring.

BIG DADDY: To where?

BRICK: Liquor cabinet. . . .

BIG DADDY: Yes, sir, boy —

(*He hands Brick the crutch.*)

— the human animal is a beast that dies and if he's got money he buys and buys and buys and I think the reason he buys everything he can buy is that in the back of his mind he has the crazy hope that one of his purchases will be life everlasting! — Which it never can be. . . . The human animal is a beast that —

BRICK (*at the liquor cabinet*): Big Daddy, you sure are shootin' th' breeze here tonight.

(*There is a pause and voices are heard outside.*)

BIG DADDY: I been quiet here lately, spoke not a word, just sat and stared into space. I had something heavy weighing on my mind but tonight that load was took off me. That's why I'm talking. — The sky looks diff'rent to me. . . .

BRICK: You know what I like to hear most?

BIG DADDY: What?

BRICK: Solid quiet. Perfect unbroken quiet.

BIG DADDY: Why?

BRICK: Because it's more peaceful.

BIG DADDY: Man, you'll hear a lot of that in the grave.

(*He chuckles agreeably.*)

BRICK: Are you through talkin' to me?

BIG DADDY: Why are you so anxious to shut me up?

BRICK: Well, sir, ever so often you say to me, Brick, I want to have a talk with you, but when we talk, it never materializes. Nothing is said. You sit in a chair and gas about this and that and I look like I listen. I try to look like I listen, but I don't listen, not much. Communication is — awful hard between people an' — somehow between you and me, it just don't — happen.

BIG DADDY: Have you ever been scared? I mean have you ever felt downright terror of something?

(*He gets up.*)

Just one moment.

(*He looks off as if he were going to tell an important secret.*)

Brick?

BRICK: What?

BIG DADDY: Son, I thought I had it!

BRICK: Had what? Had what, Big Daddy?

BIG DADDY: Cancer!

BRICK: Oh . . .

BIG DADDY: I thought the old man made out of bones had laid his cold and heavy hand on my shoulder!

BRICK: Well, Big Daddy, you kept a tight mouth about it.

BIG DADDY: A pig squeals. A man keeps a tight mouth about it, in spite of a man not having a pig's advantage.

BRICK: What advantage is that?

BIG DADDY: Ignorance — of mortality — is a comfort. A man don't have that comfort, he's the only living thing that conceives of death, that knows what it is. The others go without knowing which is the way that anything living should go, go without knowing, without any knowledge of it, and yet a pig squeals, but a man sometimes, he can keep a tight mouth about it. Sometimes he —

(*There is a deep, smoldering ferocity in the old man.*)

— can keep a tight mouth about it. I wonder if —

BRICK: What, Big Daddy?

BIG DADDY: A whiskey highball would injure this spastic condition?

BRICK: No, sir, it might do it good.

BIG DADDY (*grins suddenly, wolfishly*): Jesus, I can't tell you! The sky is open! Christ, it's open again! It's open, boy, it's open!

(*Brick looks down at his drink.*)

BRICK: You feel better, Big Daddy?

BIG DADDY: Better? Hell! I can breathe! — All of my life I been like a doubled up fist. . . .

(*He pours a drink.*)

— Poundin', smashin', drivin'! — now I'm going to loosen these doubled-up hands and touch things *easy* with them. . . .

(*He spreads his hands as if caressing the air.*)

You know what I'm contemplating?

BRICK (*vaguely*): No, sir. What are you contemplating?

BIG DADDY: Ha ha! — *Pleasure!* — pleasure with *women!*

(*Brick's smile fades a little but lingers.*)

— Yes, boy. I'll tell you something that you might not guess. I still have desire for women and this is my sixty-fifth birthday.

BRICK: I think that's mighty remarkable, Big Daddy.

BIG DADDY: Remarkable?

BRICK: *Admirable*, Big Daddy.

BIG DADDY: You're damn right it is, remarkable and admirable both. I realize now that I never had me enough. I let many chances slip by because of scruples about it, scruples, convention — crap. . . . All that stuff is bull, bull, bull! — It took the shadow of death to make me see it. Now that shadow's lifted, I'm going to cut loose and have, what is it they call it, have me a — ball!

BRICK: A ball, huh?

BIG DADDY: That's right, a ball, a ball! Hell! — I slept with Big Mama till, let's see, five years ago, till I was sixty and she was fifty-eight, and never even liked her, never did!

(*The phone has been ringing down the hall. Big Mama enters, exclaiming:*)

BIG MAMA: Don't you men hear that phone ring? I heard it way out on the gall'ry.

BIG DADDY: There's five rooms off this front gall'ry that you could go through. Why do you go through this one?

(*Big Mama makes a playful face as she bustles out the hall door.*)

Hunh! — Why, when Big Mama goes out of a room, I can't remember what that woman looks like —

BIG MAMA: Hello.

BIG DADDY: — But when Big Mama comes back into the room, boy, then I see what she looks like, and I wish I didn't!

(*Bends over laughing at this joke till it hurts his guts and he straightens with a grimace. The laugh subsides to a chuckle as he puts the liquor glass a little distrustfully down the table.*)

BIG MAMA: Hello, Miss Sally.

(*Brick has risen and hobbled to the gallery doors.*)

BIG DADDY: Hey! Where you goin'?

BRICK: Out for a breather.

BIG DADDY: Not yet you ain't. Stay here till this talk is finished, young fellow.

BRICK: I thought it was finished, Big Daddy.

BIG DADDY: It ain't even begun.

BRICK: My mistake. Excuse me. I just wanted to feel that river breeze.

BIG DADDY: Set back down in that chair.

(*Big Mama's voice rises, carrying down the hall.*)

BIG MAMA: Miss Sally, you're a case! You're a caution, Miss Sally.

BIG DADDY: Jesus, she's talking to my old maid sister again.

BIG MAMA: Why didn't you give me a chance to explain it to you?

BIG DADDY: Brick, this stuff burns me.

BIG MAMA: Well, good-bye, now, Miss Sally. You come down real soon. Big Daddy's dying to see you.

BIG DADDY: Crap!

BIG MAMA: Yaiss, good-bye, Miss Sally. . . .

(*She hangs up and bellows with mirth. Big Daddy groans and covers his ears as she approaches.*)

(*Bursting in:*)

Big Daddy, that was Miss Sally callin' from Memphis again! You know what she done, Big Daddy? She called her doctor in Memphis to git him to tell her what that spastic thing is! Ha-*HAAAA!* — And called back to tell me how relieved she was that — Hey! Let me in!

(*Big Daddy has been holding the door half closed against her.*)

BIG DADDY: Naw I ain't. I told you not to come and go through this room. You just back out and go through those five other rooms.

BIG MAMA: Big Daddy? Big Daddy? Oh, Big Daddy! — You didn't mean those things you said to me, did you?

(*He shuts door firmly against her but she still calls.*)

Brick (Ben Gazzara) and Big Daddy (Burl Ives) in the original 1955 production of *Cat on a Hot Tin Roof,* directed by Elia Kazan.

Sweetheart? Sweetheart? Big Daddy? You didn't mean those awful things you said to me? — I know you didn't. I know you didn't mean those things in your heart. . . .

(*The childlike voice fades with a sob and her heavy foot-steps retreat down the hall. Brick has risen once more on his crutches and starts for the gallery again.*)

BIG DADDY: All I ask of that woman is that she leave me alone. But she can't admit to herself that she makes me sick. That comes of having slept with her too many years. Should of quit much sooner but that old woman she never got enough of it — and I was good in bed . . . I never should of wasted so much of it on her. . . . They say you got just so many and each one is numbered. Well, I got a few left in me, a few, and I'm going to pick me a good one to spend 'em on! I'm going to pick me a choice one, I don't care how much she costs, I'll smother her in — minks! Ha ha! I'll strip her naked and smother her in minks and choke her

with diamonds! Ha ha! I'll strip her naked and choke her with diamonds and smother her with minks and hump her from hell to breakfast. *Ha aha ha ha ha!*

MAE (*gaily at door*): Who's that laughin' in there?
GOOPER: Is Big Daddy laughin' in there?
BIG DADDY: Crap! — them two — *drips.* . . .

(*He goes over and touches Brick's shoulder.*)

Yes, son. Brick, boy. — I'm — *happy!* I'm happy, son, I'm happy!

(*He chokes a little and bites his under lip, pressing his head quickly, shyly against his son's head and then, coughing with embarrassment, goes uncertainly back to the table where he set down the glass. He drinks and makes a grimace as it burns his guts. Brick sighs and rises with effort.*)

What makes you so restless? Have you got ants in your britches?

BRICK: Yes, sir . . .

BIG DADDY: Why?

BRICK: — Something — hasn't — happened. . . .

BIG DADDY: Yeah? What is that!

BRICK (*sadly*): — the click. . . .

BIG DADDY: Did you say click?

BRICK: Yes, click.

BIG DADDY: What click?

BRICK: A click that I get in my head that makes me peaceful.

BIG DADDY: I sure in hell don't know what you're talking about, but it disturbs me.

BRICK: It's just a mechanical thing.

BIG DADDY: What is a mechanical thing?

BRICK: This click that I get in my head that makes me peaceful. I got to drink till I get it. It's just a mechanical thing, something like a — like a — like a —

BIG DADDY: Like a —

BRICK: Switch clicking off in my head, turning the hot light off and the cool night on and —

(*He looks up, smiling sadly.*)

— all of a sudden there's — peace!

BIG DADDY (*whistles long and soft with astonishment; he goes back to Brick and clasps his son's two shoulders*): Jesus! I didn't know it had gotten that bad with you. Why, boy, you're — *alcoholic!*

BRICK: That's the truth, Big Daddy. I'm alcoholic.

BIG DADDY: This shows how I — let things go!

BRICK: I have to hear that little click in my head that makes me peaceful. Usually I hear it sooner than this, sometimes as early as — noon, but —

— Today it's — dilatory. . . .

I just haven't got the right level of alcohol in my bloodstream yet!

(*This last statement is made with energy as he freshens his drink.*)

BIG DADDY: Uh — huh. Expecting death made me blind. I didn't have no idea that a son of mine was turning into a drunkard under my nose.

BRICK (*gently*): Well, now you do, Big Daddy, the news has penetrated.

BIG DADDY: UH-huh, yes, now I do, the news has — penetrated. . . .

BRICK: And so if you'll excuse me —

BIG DADDY: No, I won't excuse you.

BRICK: — I'd better sit by myself till I hear that click in my head, it's just a mechanical thing but it don't happen except when I'm alone or talking to no one. . . .

BIG DADDY: You got a long, long time to sit still, boy, and talk to no one, but now you're talkin' to me. At least I'm talking to you. And you set there and listen until I tell you the conversation is over!

BRICK: But this talk is like all the others we've ever had together in our lives! It's nowhere, nowhere! — it's — it's *painful*, Big Daddy. . . .

BIG DADDY: All right, then let it be painful, but don't you move from that chair! — I'm going to remove that crutch. . . .

(*He seizes the crutch and tosses it across room.*)

BRICK: I can hop on one foot, and if I fall, I can crawl!

BIG DADDY: If you ain't careful you're gonna crawl off this plantation and then, by Jesus, you'll have to hustle your drinks along Skid Row!

BRICK: That'll come, Big Daddy.

BIG DADDY: Naw, it won't. You're my son and I'm going to straighten you out; now that *I'm* straightened out, I'm going to straighten out you!

BRICK: Yeah?

BIG DADDY: Today the report come in from Ochsner Clinic. Y'know what they told me?

(*His face glows with triumph.*)

The only thing that they could detect with all the instruments of science in that great hospital is a little spastic condition of the colon! And nerves torn to pieces by all that worry about it.

(*A little girl bursts into room with a sparkler clutched in each fist, hops and shrieks like a monkey gone mad and rushes back out again as Big Daddy strikes at her.*)

(*Silence. The two men stare at each other. A woman laughs gaily outside.*)

I want you to know I breathed a sigh of relief almost as powerful as the Vicksburg tornado!

(*There is laughter outside, running footsteps, the soft, plushy sound and light of exploding rockets.*)

(*Brick stares at him soberly for a long moment; then makes a sort of startled sound in his nostrils and springs up on one foot and hops across the room to grab his crutch, swinging on the furniture for support. He gets the crutch and flees as if in horror for the gallery. His father seizes him by the sleeve of his white silk pajamas.*)

Stay here, you son of a bitch! — till I say go!

BRICK: I can't.

BIG DADDY: You sure in hell will, God damn it.

BRICK: No, I can't. We talk, you talk, in — circles! We get no where, no where! It's always the same, you say you want to talk to me and don't have a fuckin' thing to say to me!

BIG DADDY: Nothin' to say when I'm tellin' you I'm going to live when I thought I was dying?!

BRICK: Oh — *that!* — Is that what you have to say to me?

BIG DADDY: Why, you son of a bitch! Ain't that, ain't that — *important?!*

BRICK: Well, you said that, that's said, and now I —

BIG DADDY: Now you set back down.

BRICK: You're all balled up, you —

BIG DADDY: I ain't balled up!

BRICK: You are, you're all balled up!

BIG DADDY: Don't tell me what I am, you drunken whelp! I'm going to tear this coat sleeve off if you don't set down!

BRICK: Big Daddy —

BIG DADDY: Do what I tell you! I'm the boss here, now! I want you to know I'm back in the driver's seat now!

(*Big Mama rushes in, clutching her great heaving bosom.*)

BIG MAMA: Big Daddy!

BIG DADDY: What in hell do you want in here, Big Mama?

BIG MAMA: Oh, Big Daddy! Why are you shouting like that? I just cain't *stainnnnnnnd* — it. . . .

BIG DADDY (*raising the back of his hand above his head*): GIT! — outa here.

(*She rushes back out, sobbing.*)

BRICK (*softly, sadly*): Christ. . . .

BIG DADDY (*fiercely*): Yeah! Christ! — is right. . . .

(*Brick breaks loose and hobbles toward the gallery.*)
(*Big Daddy jerks his crutch from under Brick so he steps with the injured ankle. He utters a hissing cry of anguish, clutches a chair and pulls it over on top of him on the floor.*)

Son of a — tub of — hog fat. . . .

BRICK: Big Daddy! Give me my crutch.

(*Big Daddy throws the crutch out of reach.*)

Give me that crutch, Big Daddy.

BIG DADDY: Why do you drink?

BRICK: Don't know, give me my crutch!

BIG DADDY: You better think why you drink or give up drinking!

BRICK: Will you please give me my crutch so I can get up off this floor?

BIG DADDY: First you answer my question. Why do you drink? Why are you throwing your life away, boy, like somethin' disgusting you picked up on the street?

BRICK (*getting onto his knees*): Big Daddy, I'm in pain, I stepped on that foot.

BIG DADDY: Good! I'm glad you're not too numb with the liquor in you to feel some pain!

BRICK: You — spilled my — drink . . .

BIG DADDY: I'll make a bargain with you. You tell me why you drink and I'll hand you one. I'll pour you the liquor myself and hand it to you.

BRICK: Why do I drink?

BIG DADDY: Yea! Why?

BRICK: Give me a drink and I'll tell you.

BIG DADDY: Tell me first!

BRICK: I'll tell you in one word.

BIG DADDY: What word?

BRICK: DISGUST!

(*The clock chimes softly, sweetly. Big Daddy gives it a short, outraged glance.*)

Now how about that drink?

BIG DADDY: What are you disgusted with? You got to tell me that, first. Otherwise being disgusted don't make no sense!

BRICK: Give me my crutch.

BIG DADDY: You heard me, you got to tell me what I asked you first.

BRICK: I told you, I said to kill my disgust!

BIG DADDY: DISGUST WITH WHAT!

BRICK: You strike a hard bargain.

BIG DADDY: What are you disgusted with? — an' I'll pass you the liquor.

BRICK: I can hop on one foot, and if I fall, I can crawl.

BIG DADDY: You want liquor that bad?

BRICK (*dragging himself up, clinging to bedstead*): Yeah, I want it that bad.

BIG DADDY: If I give you a drink, will you tell me what it is you're disgusted with, Brick?

BRICK: Yes, sir, I will try to.

(*The old man pours him a drink and solemnly passes it to him.*)
(*There is silence as Brick drinks.*)

Have you ever heard the word "mendacity"?

BIG DADDY: Sure. Mendacity is one of them five dollar words that cheap politicians throw back and forth at each other.

BRICK: You know what it means?

BIG DADDY: Don't it mean lying and liars?

BRICK: Yes, sir, lying and liars.

BIG DADDY: Has someone been lying to you?

CHILDREN (*chanting in chorus offstage*):
We want Big Dad-dee!
We want Big Dad-dee!

(*Gooper appears in the gallery door.*)

GOOPER: Big Daddy, the kiddies are shouting for you out there.

BIG DADDY (*fiercely*): Keep out, Gooper!

GOOPER: 'Scuse *me*!

(*Big Daddy slams the doors after Gooper.*)

BIG DADDY: Who's been lying to you, has Margaret been lying to you, has your wife been lying to you about something, Brick?

BRICK: Not her. That wouldn't matter.

BIG DADDY: Then who's been lying to you, and what about?

BRICK: No one single person and no one lie. . . .

BIG DADDY: Then what, what then, for Christ's sake?

BRICK: — The whole, the whole — thing. . . .

BIG DADDY: Why are you rubbing your head? You got a headache?

BRICK: No, I'm tryin' to —

BIG DADDY: — Concentrate, but you can't because your brain's all soaked with liquor, is that the trouble? Wet brain!

(*He snatches the glass from Brick's hand.*)

What do you know about this mendacity thing? Hell! I could write a book on it! Don't you know that? I could write a book on it and still not cover the subject? Well, I could, I could write a goddamn book on it and still not cover the subject anywhere near enough!! — Think of all the lies I got to put up with! — Pretenses! Ain't that mendacity? Having to pretend stuff you don't think or feel or have any idea of? Having for instance to act like I care for Big Mama! — I haven't been able to stand the sight, sound, or smell of that woman for forty years now! — even when I *laid* her! — regular as a piston. . . .

Pretend to love that son of a bitch of a Gooper and his wife Mae and those five same screechers out there like parrots in a jungle? Jesus! Can't stand to look at 'em!

Church! — it bores the bejesus out of me but I go! — I go an' sit there and listen to the fool preacher!

Clubs! — Elks! Masons! Rotary! — *crap!*

(*A spasm of pain makes him clutch his belly. He sinks into a chair and his voice is softer and hoarser.*)

You I *do* like for some reason, did always have some kind of real feeling for — affection — respect — yes, always. . . .

You and being a success as a planter is all I ever had any devotion to in my whole life! — and that's the truth. . . .

I don't know why, but it is!

I've lived with mendacity! — Why can't *you* live with it? Hell, you *got* to live with it, there's nothing *else* to *live* with except mendacity, is there?

BRICK: Yes, sir. Yes, sir there is something else that you can live with!

BIG DADDY: What?

BRICK (*lifting his glass*): This! — Liquor. . . .

BIG DADDY: That's not living, that's dodging away from life.

BRICK: I want to dodge away from it.

BIG DADDY: Then why don't you kill yourself, man?

BRICK: I like to drink. . . .

BIG DADDY: Oh, God, I can't talk to you. . . .

BRICK: I'm sorry, Big Daddy.

BIG DADDY: Not as sorry as I am. I'll tell you something. A little while back when I thought my number was up —

(*This speech should have torrential pace and fury.*)

— before I found out it was just this — spastic — colon. I thought about you. Should I or should I not, if the jig was up, give you this place when I go — since I hate Gooper an' Mae an' know that they hate me, and since all five same monkeys are little Maes an' Goopers. — And I thought, No! — Then I thought, Yes! — I couldn't make up my mind. I hate Gooper and his five same monkeys and that bitch Mae! Why should I turn over twenty-eight thousand acres of the richest land this side of the valley Nile to not my kind? — But why in hell, on the other hand, Brick — should I subsidize a goddamn fool on the bottle? — Liked or not liked, well, maybe even — *loved!* — Why should I do that? — Subsidize worthless behavior? Rot? Corruption?

BRICK (*smiling*): I understand.

BIG DADDY: Well, if you do, you're smarter than I am, God damn it, because I don't understand. And this I will tell you frankly. I didn't make up my mind at all on that question and still to this day I ain't made out no will! — Well, now I don't *have* to. The pressure is gone. I can just wait and see if you pull yourself together or if you don't.

BRICK: That's right, Big Daddy.

BIG DADDY: You sound like you thought I was kidding.

BRICK (*rising*): No, sir, I know you're not kidding.

BIG DADDY: But you don't care — ?

BRICK (*hobbling toward the gallery door*): No, sir, I don't care. . . .

(*He stands in the gallery doorway as the night sky turns pink and green and gold with successive flashes of light.*)

BIG DADDY: WAIT! — Brick. . . .

(*His voice drops. Suddenly there is something shy, almost tender, in his restraining gesture.*)

Don't let's — leave it like this, like them other talks we've had, we've always — talked around things, we've — just talked around things for some fuckin' reason, I don't know what, it's always like something was left not spoken, something avoided because neither of us was honest enough with the — other. . . .

BRICK: I never lied to you, Big Daddy.

BIG DADDY: Did I ever to *you?*

BRICK: No, sir. . . .

BIG DADDY: Then there is at least two people that never lied to each other.

BRICK: But we've never *talked* to each other.

BIG DADDY: We can *now.*

BRICK: Big Daddy, there don't seem to be anything much to say.

BIG DADDY: You say that you drink to kill your disgust with lying.

BRICK: You said to give you a reason.

BIG DADDY: Is liquor the only thing that'll kill this disgust?

BRICK: Now. Yes.

BIG DADDY: But not once, huh?

BRICK: Not when I was still young an' believing. A drinking man's someone who wants to forget he isn't still young an' believing.

BIG DADDY: Believing what?

BRICK: Believing. . . .

BIG DADDY: Believing *what?*

BRICK (*stubbornly evasive*): Believing. . . .

BIG DADDY: I don't know what the hell you mean by believing and I don't think you know what you mean by believing, but if you still got sports in your blood, go back to sports announcing and —

BRICK: Sit in a glass box watching games I can't play? Describing what I can't do while players do it? Sweating out their disgust and confusion in contests I'm not fit for? Drinkin' a coke, half bourbon, so I can stand it? That's no goddamn good any more, no help — time just outran me, Big Daddy — got there first . . .

BIG DADDY: I think you're passing the buck.

BRICK: You know many drinkin' men?

BIG DADDY (*with a slight, charming smile*): I have known a fair number of that species.

BRICK: Could any of them tell you why he drank?

BIG DADDY: Yep, you're passin' the buck to things like time and disgust with "mendacity" and — crap! — if you got to use that kind of language about a thing, it's ninety-proof bull, and I'm not buying any.

BRICK: I had to give you a reason to get a drink!

BIG DADDY: You started drinkin' when your friend Skipper died.

(*Silence for five beats. Then Brick makes a startled movement, reaching for his crutch.*)

BRICK: What are you suggesting?

BIG DADDY: I'm suggesting nothing.

(*The shuffle and clop of Brick's rapid hobble away from his father's steady, grave attention.*)

— But Gooper an' Mae suggested that there was something not right exactly in your —

BRICK (*stopping short downstage as if backed to a wall*): "Not right"?

BIG DADDY: Not, well, exactly *normal* in your friend-ship with —

BRICK: They suggested that, too? I thought that was Maggie's suggestion.

(*Brick's detachment is at last broken through. His heart is accelerated; his forehead sweat-beaded; his breath becomes more rapid and his voice hoarse. The thing they're discussing, timidly and painfully on the side of Big Daddy, fiercely, violently on Brick's side, is the inadmissible thing that Skipper died to disavow between them. The fact that if it existed it had to be disavowed to "keep face" in the world they lived in, may be at the heart of the "mendacity" that Brick drinks to kill his disgust with. It may be the root of his collapse. Or maybe it is only a single manifestation of it, not even the most important. The bird that I hope to catch in the net of this play is not the solution of one man's psychological problem. I'm trying to catch the true quality of experience in a group of people, that cloudy, flickering, evanescent — fiercely charged! — interplay of live human beings in the thundercloud of a common crisis. Some mystery should be left in the revelation of character in a play, just as a great deal of mystery is always left in the revelation of character in life, even in one's own character to himself. This does not absolve the playwright of his duty to observe and probe as clearly and deeply as he legitimately can: But it should steer him away from "pat" conclusions, facile definitions which make a play just a play, not a snare for the truth of human experience.*)

(*The following scene should be played with great concentration, with most of the power leashed but palpable in what is left unspoken.*)

Who else's suggestion is it, is it *yours*? How many others thought that Skipper and I were —

BIG DADDY (*gently*): Now, hold on, hold on a minute, son. — I knocked around in my time.

BRICK: What's that got to do with —

BIG DADDY: I said "Hold on!" — I bummed, I bummed this country till I was —

BRICK: Whose suggestion, who else's suggestion is it?

BIG DADDY: Slept in hobo jungles and railroad Y's and flophouses in all cities before I —

BRICK: Oh, *you* think so, too, you call me your son and a queer. Oh! Maybe that's why you put Maggie and me in this room that was Jack Straw's and Peter Ochello's, in which that pair of old sisters slept in a double bed where both of 'em died!

BIG DADDY: *Now just don't go throwing rocks at —*

(*Suddenly Reverend Tooker appears in the gallery doors, his head slightly, playfully, fatuously cocked, with a practiced clergyman's smile, sincere as a birdcall blown on a hunter's whistle, the living embodiment of the pious, conventional lie.*)

(*Big Daddy gasps a little at this perfectly timed, but incongruous, apparition.*)

— What're you lookin' for, preacher?

REVEREND TOOKER: The gentleman's lavatory, ha ha! — heh, heh . . .

BIG DADDY (*with strained courtesy*): — Go back out and walk down to the other end of the gallery, Reverend Tooker, and use the bathroom connected with my bedroom, and if you can't find it, ask them where it is!

REVEREND TOOKER: Ah, thanks.

(*He goes out with a deprecatory chuckle.*)

BIG DADDY: It's hard to talk in this place . . .

BRICK: Son of a — !

BIG DADDY (*leaving a lot unspoken*): — I seen all things and understood a lot of them, till 1910. Christ, the year that — I had worn my shoes through, hocked my — I hopped off a yellow dog freight car half a mile down the road, slept in a wagon of cotton outside the gin — Jack Straw an' Peter Ochello took me in. Hired me to manage this place which grew into this one. — When Jack Straw died — why, old Peter Ochello quit eatin' like a dog does when its master's dead, and died, too!

BRICK: Christ!

BIG DADDY: I'm just saying I understand such —

BRICK (*violently*): Skipper is dead. I have not quit eating!

BIG DADDY: No, but you started drinking.

(*Brick wheels on his crutch and hurls his glass across the room shouting.*)

BRICK: YOU THINK SO, TOO?

(*Footsteps run on the gallery. There are women's calls.*)

(*Big Daddy goes toward the door.*)

(*Brick is transformed, as if a quiet mountain blew suddenly up in volcanic flame.*)

BRICK: You think so, too? You think so, too? You think me an' Skipper did, did, did! — *sodomy!* — together?

BIG DADDY: Hold — !
BRICK: That what you —
BIG DADDY: — *ON* — a minute!
BRICK: You think we did dirty things between us, Skipper an' —
BIG DADDY: Why are you shouting like that? Why are you —
BRICK: — Me, is that what you think of Skipper, is that —
BIG DADDY: — so excited? I don't think nothing. I don't know nothing. I'm simply telling you what —
BRICK: You think that Skipper and me were a pair of dirty old men?
BIG DADDY: Now that's —
BRICK: Straw? Ochello? A couple of —
BIG DADDY: Now just —
BRICK: — fucking sissies? Queers? Is that what you —
BIG DADDY: Shhh.
BRICK: — think?

(*He loses his balance and pitches to his knees without noticing the pain. He grabs the bed and drags himself up.*)

BIG DADDY: Jesus! — Whew. . . . Grab my hand!
BRICK: Naw, I don't want your hand. . . .
BIG DADDY: Well, I want yours. Git up!

(*He draws him up, keeps an arm about him with concern and affection.*)

You broken out in a sweat! You're panting like you'd run a race with —
BRICK (*freeing himself from his father's hold*): Big Daddy, you shock me, Big Daddy, you, you — *shock* me! Talkin' so —

(*He turns away from his father.*)

— casually! — about a — thing like that . . .
　　— Don't you know how people *feel* about things like that? How, how *disgusted* they are by things like that? Why, at Ole Miss when it was discovered a pledge to our fraternity, Skipper's and mine, did a, *attempted* to do a, unnatural thing with —
　　We not only dropped him like a hot rock! — We told him to git off the campus, and he did, he got! — All the way to —

(*He halts, breathless.*)

BIG DADDY: — Where?
BRICK: — North Africa, last I heard!
BIG DADDY: Well, I have come back from further away than that, I have just now returned from the other side of the moon, death's country, son, and I'm not easy to shock by anything here.

(*He comes downstage and faces out.*)

Always, anyhow, lived with too much space around me to be infected by ideas of other people. One thing you can grow on a big place more important than cotton! — is *tolerance!* — I grown it.

(*He returns toward Brick.*)

BRICK: Why can't exceptional friendship, *real, real, deep, deep friendship!* between two men be respected as something clean and decent without being thought of as —
BIG DADDY: It can, it is, for God's sake.
BRICK: — *Fairies.* . . .

(*In his utterance of this word, we gauge the wide and profound reach of the conventional mores he got from the world that crowned him with early laurel.*)

BIG DADDY: I told Mae an' Gooper —
BRICK: Frig Mae and Gooper, frig all dirty lies and liars! — Skipper and me had a clean, true thing between us! — had a clean friendship, practically all our lives, till Maggie got the idea you're talking about. Normal? No! — It was too rare to be normal, any true thing between two people is too rare to be normal. Oh, once in a while he put his hand on my shoulder or I'd put mine on his, oh, maybe even, when we were touring the country in profootball an' shared hotel rooms we'd reach across the space between the two beds and shake hands to say goodnight, yeah, one or two times we —
BIG DADDY: Brick, nobody thinks that that's not normal!
BRICK: Well, they're mistaken, it was! It was a pure an' true thing an' that's not normal.
MAE (*offstage*): Big Daddy, they're startin' the fireworks.

(*They both stare straight at each other for a long moment. The tension breaks and both turn away as if tired.*)

BIG DADDY: Yeah, it's — hard t' — talk. . . .
BRICK: All right, then, let's — let it go. . . .
BIG DADDY: Why did Skipper crack up? Why have you?

(*Brick looks back at his father again. He has already decided, without knowing that he has made this decision, that he is going to tell his father that he is dying of cancer. Only this could even the score between them: one inadmissible thing in return for another.*)

BRICK (*ominously*): All right. You're asking for it, Big Daddy. We're finally going to have that real true talk you wanted. It's too late to stop it, now, we got to carry it through and cover every subject.

(*He hobbles back to the liquor cabinet.*)

Uh-huh.

(*He opens the ice bucket and picks up the silver tongs with slow admiration of their frosty brightness.*)

Maggie declares that Skipper and I went into profootball after we left Ole Miss because we were scared to grow up . . .

(*He moves downstage with the shuffle and clop of a cripple on a crutch. As Margaret did when her speech became "recitative," he looks out into the house, commanding its attention by his direct, concentrated gaze — a broken, "tragically elegant" figure telling simply as much as he knows of "the Truth":*)

— Wanted to — keep on tossing — those long, long! — high, high! — passes that — couldn't be intercepted except by time, the aerial attack that made us famous! And so we did, we did, we kept it up for one season, that aerial attack, we held it high! — Yeah, but —

— that summer, Maggie, she laid the law down to me, said, Now or never, and so I married Maggie. . . .

BIG DADDY: How was Maggie in bed?

BRICK (*wryly*): Great! the greatest!

(*Big Daddy nods as if he thought so.*)

She went on the road that fall with the Dixie Stars. Oh, she made a great show of being the world's best sport. She wore a — wore a — tall bearskin cap! A shako, they call it, a dyed moleskin coat, a moleskin coat dyed red! — Cut up crazy! Rented hotel ballrooms for victory celebrations, wouldn't cancel them when it — turned out — defeat. . . .

   MAGGIE THE CAT! Ha ha!

(*Big Daddy nods.*)

— But Skipper, he had some fever which came back on him which doctors couldn't explain and I got that injury — turned out to be just a shadow on the X-ray plate — and a touch of bursitis. . . .

   I lay in a hospital bed, watched our games on TV, saw Maggie on the bench next to Skipper when he was hauled out of a game for stumbles, fumbles! — Burned me up the way she hung on his arm! — Y'know, I think that Maggie had always felt sort of left out because she and me never got any closer together than two people just get in bed, which is not much closer than two cats on a — fence humping. . . .

   So! She took this time to work on poor dumb Skipper. He was a less than average student at Ole Miss, you know that, don't you?! — Poured in his mind the dirty, false idea that what we were, him and me, was a frustrated case of that ole pair of sisters that lived in this room, Jack Straw and Peter Ochello! — He, poor Skipper, went to bed with Maggie to prove it wasn't true, and when it didn't work out, he thought it *was* true! — Skipper broke in two like a rotten stick — nobody ever turned so fast to a lush — or died of it so quick. . . .

   — Now are you satisfied?

(*Big Daddy has listened to this story, dividing the grain from the chaff. Now he looks at his son.*)

BIG DADDY: Are *you* satisfied?

BRICK: With what?

BIG DADDY: That half-ass story!

BRICK: What's half-ass about it?

BIG DADDY: Something's left out of that story. What did you leave out?

(*The phone has started ringing in the hall.*)

GOOPER (*offstage*): Hello.

(*As if it reminded him of something, Brick glances suddenly toward the sound and says:*)

BRICK: Yes! — I left out a long-distance call which I had from Skipper —

GOOPER: Speaking, go ahead.

BRICK: — In which he made a drunken confession to me and on which I hung up!

GOOPER: No.

BRICK: — Last time we spoke to each other in our lives . . .

GOOPER: No, sir.

BIG DADDY: You musta said something to him before you hung up.

BRICK: What could I say to him?

BIG DADDY: Anything. Something.

BRICK: Nothing.

BIG DADDY: Just hung up?

BRICK: Just hung up.

BIG DADDY: Uh-huh. Anyhow now! — we have tracked down the lie with which you're disgusted and which you are drinking to kill your disgust with, Brick. You been passing the buck. This disgust with mendacity is disgust with yourself.

   You! — dug the grave of your friend and kicked him in it! — before you'd face truth with him!

BRICK: *His* truth, not *mine*!

BIG DADDY: His truth, okay! But you wouldn't face it with him!

BRICK: Who *can* face truth? Can *you*?

BIG DADDY: Now don't start passin' the rotten buck again, boy!

BRICK: How about these birthday congratulations, these many, many happy returns of the day, when ev'rybody knows there won't be any except you!

(*Gooper, who has answered the hall phone, lets out a high, shrill laugh; the voice becomes audible saying: "No, no, you got it all wrong! Upside down! Are you crazy?"*)

(*Brick suddenly catches his breath as he realizes that he has made a shocking disclosure. He hobbles a few paces, then freezes, and without looking at his father's shocked face says:*)

Let's, let's — go out, now, and — watch the fireworks. Come on, Big Daddy.

(*Big Daddy moves suddenly forward and grabs hold of the boy's crutch like it was a weapon for which they were fighting for possession.*)

BIG DADDY: Oh, no, no! No one's going out! What did you start to say?

BRICK: I don't remember.

BIG DADDY: "Many happy returns when they know there won't be any"?

BRICK: Aw, hell, Big Daddy, forget it. Come on out on the gallery and look at the fireworks they're shooting off for your birthday. . . .

BIG DADDY: First you finish that remark you were makin' before you cut off. "Many happy returns when they know there won't be any"? — Ain't that what you just said?

BRICK: Look, now. I can get around without that crutch if I have to but it would be a lot easier on the furniture an' glassware if I didn't have to go swinging along like Tarzan of th' —

BIG DADDY: FINISH! WHAT YOU WAS SAYIN'!

(*An eerie green glow shows in sky behind him.*)

BRICK (*sucking the ice in his glass, speech becoming thick*): Leave th' place to Gooper and Mae an' their five little same little monkeys. All I want is —

BIG DADDY: "LEAVE TH' PLACE," did you say?

BRICK (*vaguely*): All twenty-eight thousand acres of the richest land this side of the valley Nile.

BIG DADDY: Who said I was "leaving the place" to Gooper or anybody? This is my sixty-fifth birthday! I got fifteen years or twenty years left in me! I'll outlive *you!* I'll bury you an' have to pay for your coffin!

BRICK: Sure. Many happy returns. Now let's go watch the fireworks, come on, let's —

BIG DADDY: Lying, have they been lying? About the report from th' — clinic? Did they, did they — find something? — *Cancer.* Maybe?

BRICK: Mendacity is a system that we live in. Liquor is one way out an' death's the other. . . .

(*He takes the crutch from Big Daddy's loose grip and swings out on the gallery leaving the doors open.*)
(*A song, "Pick a Bale of Cotton," is heard.*)

MAE (*appearing in door*): Oh, Big Daddy, the field hands are singin' fo' you!

BRICK: I'm sorry, Big Daddy. My head don't work any more and it's hard for me to understand how anybody could care if he lived or died or was dying or cared about anything but whether or not there was liquor left in the bottle and so I said what I said without thinking. In some ways I'm no better than the others, in some ways worse because I'm less alive. Maybe it's being alive that makes them lie, and being almost *not* alive makes me sort of accidentally truthful — I don't know but — anyway — we've been friends . . .

— And being friends is telling each other the truth. . . .

(*There is a pause.*)

You told *me!* I told *you!*

BIG DADDY (*slowly and passionately*): CHRIST — DAMN —

GOOPER (*offstage*): Let her go!

(*Fireworks offstage right.*)

BIG DADDY: — ALL — LYING SONS OF — LYING BITCHES!

(*He straightens at last and crosses to the inside door. At the door he turns and looks back as if he had some des-*

perate question he couldn't put into words. Then he nods reflectively and says in a hoarse voice:*)

Yes, all liars, all liars, all lying dying liars!

(*This is said slowly, slowly, with a fierce revulsion. He goes on out.*)

— Lying! Dying! Liars!

(*Brick remains motionless as the lights dim out and the curtain falls.*)

ACT 3

(*There is no lapse of time. Big Daddy is seen leaving as at the end of act 2.*)

BIG DADDY: ALL LYIN' — DYIN'! — LIARS! LIARS! — LIARS!

(*Margaret enters.*)

MARGARET: Brick, what in the name of God was goin' on in this room?

(*Dixie and Trixie enter through the doors and circle around Margaret shouting. Mae enters from the lower gallery window.*)

MAE: Dixie, Trixie, you quit that!

(*Gooper enters through the doors.*)

Gooper, will y' please get these kiddies to bed right now!

GOOPER: Mae, you seen Big Mama?

MAE: Not yet.

(*Gooper and kids exit through the doors. Reverend Tooker enters through the windows.*)

REVEREND TOOKER: Those kiddies are so full of vitality. I think I'll have to be starting back to town.

MAE: Not yet, Preacher. You know we regard you as a member of this family, one of our closest an' dearest, so you just got t' be with us when Doc Baugh gives Big Mama th' actual truth about th' report from the clinic.

MARGARET: Where do you think you're going?

BRICK: Out for some air.

MARGARET: Why'd Big Daddy shout "Liars"?

MAE: Has Big Daddy gone to bed, Brick?

GOOPER (*entering*): Now where is that old lady?

REVEREND TOOKER: I'll look for her.

(*He exits to the gallery.*)

MAE: Cain'tcha find her, Gooper?

GOOPER: She's avoidin' this talk.

MAE: I think she senses somethin'.

MARGARET (*going out on the gallery to Brick*): Brick, they're goin' to tell Big Mama the truth about Big Daddy and she's goin' to need you.

DOCTOR BAUGH: This is going to be painful.

MAE: Painful things caint always be avoided.

REVEREND TOOKER: I see Big Mama.

GOOPER: Hey, Big Mama, come here.

MAE: Hush, Gooper, don't holler.

BIG MAMA (*entering*): Too much smell of burnt fireworks makes me feel a little bit sick at my stomach. — Where is Big Daddy?

MAE: That's what I want to know, where has Big Daddy gone?

BIG MAMA: He must have turned in, I reckon he went to baid . . .

GOOPER: Well, then, now we can talk.

BIG MAMA: What *is* this talk, *what* talk?

(*Margaret appears on the gallery, talking to Doctor Baugh.*)

MARGARET (*musically*): My family freed their slaves ten years before abolition. My great-great-grandfather gave his slaves their freedom five years before the War between the States started!

MAE: Oh, for God's sake! Maggie's climbed back up in her family tree!

MARGARET (*sweetly*): What, Mae?

(*The pace must be very quick: great Southern animation.*)

BIG MAMA (*addressing them all*): I think Big Daddy was just worn out. He loves his family, he loves to have them around him, but it's a strain on his nerves. He wasn't himself tonight, Big Daddy wasn't himself, I could tell he was all worked up.

REVEREND TOOKER: I think he's remarkable.

BIG MAMA: Yaisss! Just remarkable. Did you all notice the food he ate at that table? Did you all notice the supper he put away? Why he ate like a hawss!

GOOPER: I hope he doesn't regret it.

BIG MAMA: What? Why that man — ate a huge piece of cawn bread with molasses on it! Helped himself twice to hoppin' John.

MARGARET: Big Daddy loves hoppin' John. — We had a real country dinner.

BIG MAMA (*overlapping Margaret*): Yaiss, he simply adores it! an' candied yams? Son? That man put away enough food at that table to stuff a *field* hand!

GOOPER (*with grim relish*): I hope he don't have to pay for it later on . . .

BIG MAMA (*fiercely*): What's *that*, Gooper?

MAE: Gooper says he hopes Big Daddy doesn't suffer tonight.

BIG MAMA: Oh, shoot, Gooper says, Gooper says! Why should Big Daddy suffer for satisfying a normal appetite? There's nothin' wrong with that man but nerves, he's sound as a dollar! And now he knows he is an' that's why he ate such a supper. He had a big load off his mind, knowin' he wasn't doomed t' — what he thought he was doomed to . . .

MARGARET (*sadly and sweetly*): Bless his old sweet soul . . .

BIG MAMA (*vaguely*): Yais, bless his heart, where's Brick?

MAE: Outside.

GOOPER: — Drinkin' . . .

BIG MAMA: I know he's drinkin'. Cain't I see he's drinkin' without you continually tellin' me that boy's drinkin'?

MARGARET: Good for you, Big Mama!

(*She applauds.*)

BIG MAMA: Other people *drink* and *have* drunk an' will *drink*, as long as they make that stuff an' put it in bottles.

MARGARET: That's the truth. I never trusted a man that didn't drink.

BIG MAMA: *Brick? Brick!*

MARGARET: He's still on the gall'ry. I'll go bring him in so we can talk.

BIG MAMA (*worriedly*): I don't know what this mysterious family conference is about.

(*Awkward silence. Big Mama looks from face to face, then belches slightly and mutters, "Excuse me . . . " She opens an ornamental fan suspended about her throat. A black lace fan to go with her black lace gown, and fans her wilting corsage, sniffing nervously and looking from face to face in the uncomfortable silence as Margaret calls "Brick?" and Brick sings to the moon on the gallery.*)

MARGARET: Brick, they're gonna tell Big Mama the truth an' she's gonna need you.

BIG MAMA: I don't know what's wrong here, you all have such long faces! Open that door on the hall and let some air circulate through here, will you please, Gooper?

MAE: I think we'd better leave that door closed, Big Mama, till after the talk.

MARGARET: Brick!

BIG MAMA: Reveren' Tooker, will *you* please open that door?

REVEREND TOOKER: I sure will, Big Mama.

MAE: I just didn't think we ought t' take any chance of Big Daddy hearin' a word of this discussion.

BIG MAMA: *I swan!* Nothing's going to be said in Big Daddy's house that he caint hear if he want to!

GOOPER: Well, Big Mama, it's —

(*Mae gives him a quick, hard poke to shut him up. He glares at her fiercely as she circles before him like a burlesque ballerina, raising her skinny bare arms over her head, jangling her bracelets, exclaiming:*)

MAE: *A breeze! A breeze!*

REVEREND TOOKER: I think this house is the coolest house in the Delta. — Did you all know that Halsey Banks's widow put air-conditioning units in the church and rectory at Friar's Point in memory of Halsey?

(*General conversation has resumed; everybody is chatting so that the stage sounds like a bird cage.*)

GOOPER: Too bad nobody cools your church off for you. I bet you sweat in that pulpit these hot Sundays, Reverend Tooker.

REVEREND TOOKER: Yes, my vestments are drenched. Last Sunday the gold in my chasuble faded into the purple.

GOOPER: Reveren', you musta been preachin' hell's fire last Sunday.

MAE (*at the same time to Doctor Baugh*): You reckon those vitamin B12 injections are what they're cracked up t' be, Doc Baugh?

DOCTOR BAUGH: Well, if you want to be stuck with something I guess they're as good to be stuck with as anything else.

BIG MAMA (*at the gallery door*): Maggie, Maggie, aren't you comin' with Brick?

MAE (*suddenly and loudly, creating a silence*): I have a strange feeling, I have a peculiar feeling!

BIG MAMA (*turning from the gallery*): What feeling?

MAE: That Brick said somethin' he shouldn't of said t' Big Daddy.

BIG MAMA: Now what on earth could Brick of said t' Big Daddy that he shouldn't say?

GOOPER: Big Mama, there's somethin' —

MAE: NOW, WAIT!

(*She rushes up to Big Mama and gives her a quick hug and kiss. Big Mama pushes her impatiently off.*)

DOCTOR BAUGH: In my day they had what they call the Keeley cure for heavy drinkers.

BIG MAMA: Shoot!

DOCTOR BAUGH: But now I understand they just take some kind of tablets.

GOOPER: They call them "Annie Bust" tablets.

BIG MAMA: Brick don't need to take *nothin'*.

(*Brick and Margaret appear in gallery doors, Big Mama unaware of his presence behind her.*)

That boy is just broken up over Skipper's death. You know how poor Skipper died. They gave him a big, big dose of that sodium amytal stuff at his home and then they called the ambulance and give him another big, big dose of it at the hospital and that and all of the alcohol in his system fo' months an' months just proved too much for his heart . . . I'm scared of needles! I'm more scared of a needle than the knife . . . I think more people have been needled out of this world than —

(*She stops short and wheels about.*)

Oh — here's Brick! My precious baby —

(*She turns upon Brick with short, fat arms extended, at the same time uttering a loud, short sob, which is both comic and touching. Brick smiles and bows slightly, making a burlesque gesture of gallantry for Margaret to pass before him into the room. Then he hobbles on his crutch directly to the liquor cabinet and there is absolute silence, with everybody looking at Brick as everybody*

has always looked at Brick when he spoke or moved or appeared. One by one he drops ice cubes in his glass, then suddenly, but not quickly, looks back over his shoulder with a wry, charming smile, and says:)

BRICK: I'm sorry! Anyone else?

BIG MAMA (*sadly*): No, son. I *wish* you wouldn't!

BRICK: I wish I didn't have to, Big Mama, but I'm still waiting for that click in my head which makes it all smooth out!

BIG MAMA: Ow, Brick, you — BREAK MY HEART!

MARGARET (*at same time*): Brick, go sit with Big Mama!

BIG MAMA: I just cain't staiiiiii-nnnnnnnd-it . . .

(*She sobs.*)

MAE: Now that we're all assembled —

GOOPER: We kin talk . . .

BIG MAMA: Breaks my heart . . .

MARGARET: Sit with Big Mama, Brick, and hold her hand.

(*Big Mama sniffs very loudly three times, almost like three drumbeats in the pocket of silence.*)

BRICK: You do that, Maggie. I'm a restless cripple. I got to stay on my crutch.

(*Brick hobbles to the gallery door; leans there as if waiting.*)

(*Mae sits beside Big Mama, while Gooper moves in front and sits on the end of the couch, facing her. Reverend Tooker moves nervously into the space between them; on the other side, Doctor Baugh stands looking at nothing in particular and lights a cigar. Margaret turns away.*)

BIG MAMA: Why're you all *surroundin'* me — like this? Why're you all starin' at me like this an' makin' signs at each other?

(*Reverend Tooker steps back startled.*)

MAE: Calm yourself, Big Mama.

BIG MAMA: Calm you'self, *you'self*, Sister Woman. How could I calm myself with everyone starin' at me as if big drops of blood had broken out on m'face? What's this all about, annh! What?

(*Gooper coughs and takes a center position.*)

GOOPER: Now, Doc Baugh.

MAE: Doc Baugh?

GOOPER: Big Mama wants to know the complete truth about the report we got from the Ochsner Clinic.

MAE (*eagerly*): — on Big Daddy's condition!

GOOPER: Yais, on Big Daddy's condition, we got to face it.

DOCTOR BAUGH: Well . . .

BIG MAMA (*terrified, rising*): Is there? Something? Something that I? Don't — know?

(*In these few words, this startled, very soft, question, Big Mama reviews the history of her forty-five years with Big Daddy, her great, almost embarrassingly true-hearted and simple-minded devotion to Big Daddy, who must have had something Brick has, who made himself loved so much by the "simple expedient" of not loving enough to disturb his charming detachment, also once coupled, like Brick, with virile beauty.)*

(Big Mama has a dignity at this moment; she almost stops being fat.)

DOCTOR BAUGH (*after a pause, uncomfortably*): Yes? — Well —

BIG MAMA: I!!! — want to — *knowwwwwww . . .*

(Immediately she thrusts her fist to her mouth as if to deny that statement. Then for some curious reason, she snatches the withered corsage from her breast and hurls it on the floor and steps on it with her short, fat feet.)

Somebody must be lyin'! — I want to know!

MAE: Sit down, Big Mama, sit down on this sofa.

MARGARET: Brick, go sit with Big Mama.

BIG MAMA: *What is it, what is it?*

DOCTOR BAUGH: I never have seen a more thorough examination than Big Daddy Pollitt was given in all my experience with the Ochsner Clinic.

GOOPER: It's one of the best in the country.

MAE: It's THE best in the country — bar *none!*

(For some reason she gives Gooper a violent poke as she goes past him. He slaps at her hand without removing his eyes from his mother's face.)

DOCTOR BAUGH: Of course they were ninety-nine and nine-tenths percent sure before they even started.

BIG MAMA: Sure of what, sure of what, sure of — what? — what?

(She catches her breath in a startled sob. Mae kisses her quickly. She thrusts Mae fiercely away from her, staring at the Doctor.)

MAE: Mommy, be a brave girl!

BRICK (*in the doorway, softly*): "By the light, by the light, Of the sil-ve-ry moo-oo-n . . . "

GOOPER: Shut up! — Brick.

BRICK: Sorry . . .

(He wanders out on the gallery.)

DOCTOR BAUGH: But now, you see, Big Mama, they cut a piece of this growth, a specimen of the tissue and —

BIG MAMA: Growth? You told Big Daddy —

DOCTOR BAUGH: Now wait.

BIG MAMA (*fiercely*): You told me and Big Daddy there wasn't a thing wrong with him but —

MAE: Big Mama, they always —

GOOPER: Let Doc Baugh talk, will yuh?

BIG MAMA: — little spastic condition of —

(Her breath gives out in a sob.)

DOCTOR BAUGH: Yes, that's what we told Big Daddy. But we had this bit of tissue run through the laboratory and I'm sorry to say the test was positive on it. It's — well — malignant . . .

(Pause.)

BIG MAMA: — Cancer?! Cancer?!

(Doctor Baugh nods gravely. Big Mama gives a long gasping cry.)

MAE AND GOOPER: Now, now, now, Big Mama, you had to know . . .

BIG MAMA: WHY DIDN'T THEY CUT IT OUT OF HIM? HANH? HANH?

DOCTOR BAUGH: Involved too much, Big Mama, too many organs affected.

MAE: Big Mama, the liver's affected and so's the kidneys, both! It's gone way past what they call a —

GOOPER: A surgical risk.

MAE: — Uh-huh . . .

(Big Mama draws a breath like a dying gasp.)

REVEREND TOOKER: Tch, tch, tch, tch, tch!

DOCTOR BAUGH: Yes it's gone past the knife.

MAE: *That's why he's turned yellow, Mommy!*

BIG MAMA: *Git away from me, git away from me, Mae!*

(She rises abruptly.)

I want Brick! Where's Brick? Where is my only son?

MAE: Mama! Did she say *"only* son"?

GOOPER: What does that make *me?*

MAE: A sober responsible man with five precious children! — *Six!*

BIG MAMA: I want Brick to tell me! Brick! Brick!

MARGARET (*rising from her reflections in a corner*): Brick was so upset he went back out.

BIG MAMA: *Brick!*

MARGARET: Mama, let *me* tell you!

BIG MAMA: No, no, leave me alone, you're not my blood!

GOOPER: *Mama, I'm your son!* Listen to *me!*

MAE: Gooper's your son, he's your first-born!

BIG MAMA: Gooper never liked Daddy.

MAE (*as if terribly shocked*): That's not TRUE!

(There is a pause. The minister coughs and rises.)

REVEREND TOOKER (*to Mae*): I think I'd better slip away at this point.

(Discreetly.)

Good night, good night, everybody, and God bless you all . . . on this place . . .

(He slips out.)

(Mae coughs and points at Big Mama.)

GOOPER: Well, Big Mama . . .

(He sighs.)

BIG MAMA: It's all a mistake, I know it's just a bad dream.

DOCTOR BAUGH: We're gonna keep Big Daddy as comfortable as we can.

BIG MAMA: Yes, it's just a bad dream, that's all it is, it's just an awful dream.

GOOPER: In my opinion Big Daddy is having some pain but won't admit that he has it.

BIG MAMA: Just a dream, a bad dream.

DOCTOR BAUGH: That's what lots of them do, they think if they don't admit they're having the pain they can sort of escape the fact of it.

GOOPER (*with relish*): Yes, they get sly about it, they get real sly about it.

MAE: Gooper and I think —

GOOPER: Shut up, Mae! Big Mama, I think — Big Daddy ought to be started on morphine.

BIG MAMA: Nobody's going to give Big Daddy morphine.

DOCTOR BAUGH: Now, Big Mama, when that pain strikes it's going to strike mighty hard and Big Daddy's going to need the needle to bear it.

BIG MAMA: I tell you, nobody's going to give him morphine.

MAE: Big Mama, you don't want to see Big Daddy suffer, you know you —

(*Gooper, standing beside her, gives her a savage poke.*)

DOCTOR BAUGH (*placing a package on the table*): I'm leaving this stuff here, so if there's a sudden attack you all won't have to send out for it.

MAE: I know how to give a hypo.

BIG MAMA: Nobody's gonna give Big Daddy morphine.

GOOPER: Mae took a course in nursing during the war.

MARGARET: Somehow I don't think Big Daddy would want Mae to give him a hypo.

MAE: You think he'd want *you* to do it?

DOCTOR BAUGH: Well . . .

(*Doctor Baugh rises.*)

GOOPER: Doctor Baugh is goin'.

DOCTOR BAUGH: Yes, I got to be goin'. Well, keep your chin up, Big Mama.

GOOPER (*with jocularity*): She's gonna keep *both* chins up, aren't you, Big Mama?

(*Big Mama sobs.*)

Now stop that, Big Mama.

GOOPER (*at the door with Doctor Baugh*): Well, Doc, we sure do appreciate all you done. I'm telling you, we're surely obligated to you for —

(*Doctor Baugh has gone out without a glance at him.*)

— I guess that doctor has got a lot on his mind but it wouldn't hurt him to act a little more human . . .

(*Big Mama sobs.*)

Now be a brave girl, Mommy.

BIG MAMA: It's not true, I know that it's just not true!

GOOPER: Mama, those tests are infallible!

BIG MAMA: Why are you so determined to see your father daid?

MAE: Big Mama!

MARGARET (*gently*): I know what Big Mama means.

MAE (*fiercely*): Oh, do you?

MARGARET (*quietly and very sadly*): Yes, I think I do.

MAE: For a newcomer in the family you sure do show a lot of understanding.

MARGARET: Understanding is needed on this place.

MAE: I guess you must have needed a lot of it in your family, Maggie, with your father's liquor problem and now you've got Brick with his!

MARGARET: Brick does not have a liquor problem at all. Brick is devoted to Big Daddy. This thing is a terrible strain on him.

BIG MAMA: Brick is Big Daddy's boy, but he drinks too much and it worries me and Big Daddy, and, Margaret, you've got to cooperate with us, you've got to cooperate with Big Daddy and me in getting Brick straightened out. Because it will break Big Daddy's heart if Brick don't pull himself together and take hold of things.

MAE: Take hold of *what* things, Big Mama?

BIG MAMA: The place.

(*There is a quick violent look between Mae and Gooper.*)

GOOPER: Big Mama, you've had a shock.

MAE: Yais, we've all had a shock, but . . .

GOOPER: Let's be realistic —

MAE: — Big Daddy would never, would *never*, be foolish enough to —

GOOPER: — put this place in irresponsible hands!

BIG MAMA: Big Daddy ain't going to leave the place in anybody's hands; Big Daddy is *not* going to die. I want you to get that in your heads, all of you!

MAE: Mommy, Mommy, Big Mama, we're just as hopeful an' optimistic as you are about Big Daddy's prospects, we have faith in *prayer* — but nevertheless there are certain matters that have to be discussed an' dealt with, because otherwise —

GOOPER: Eventualities have to be considered and now's the time . . . Mae, will you please get my brief case out of our room?

MAE: Yes, honey.

(*She rises and goes out through the hall door.*)

GOOPER (*standing over Big Mama*): Now, Big Mom. What you said just now was not at all true and you know it. I've always loved Big Daddy in my own quiet way. I never made a show of it, and I know that Big Daddy has always been fond of me in a quiet way, too, and he never made a show of it neither.

(*Mae returns with Gooper's brief case.*)

MAE: Here's your brief case, Gooper, honey.

GOOPER (*handing the brief case back to her*): Thank you . . . Of cou'se, my relationship with Big Daddy is different from Brick's.

MAE: You're eight years older'n Brick an' always had t' carry a bigger load of th' responsibilities than Brick ever had t' carry. He never carried a thing in his life but a football or a highball.

GOOPER: Mae, will y' let me talk, please?

MAE: Yes, honey.

GOOPER: Now, a twenty-eight-thousand-acre plantation's a mighty big thing t' run.

MAE: Almost singlehanded.

(*Margaret has gone out onto the gallery and can be heard calling softly to Brick.*)

BIG MAMA: You never had to run this place! What are you talking about? As if Big Daddy was dead and in his grave, you just helped him out with a few business details and had your law practice at the same time in Memphis!

MAE: Oh, Mommy, Mommy, Big Mommy! Let's be fair!

MARGARET: Brick!

MAE: Why, Gooper has given himself body and soul to keeping this place up for the past five years since Big Daddy's health started failing.

MARGARET: Brick!

MAE: Gooper won't say it, Gooper never thought of it as a duty, he just did it. And what did Brick do? Brick kept living in his past glory at college! Still a football player at twenty-seven!

MARGARET (*returning alone*): Who are you talking about now? Brick? A football player? He isn't a football player and you know it. Brick is a sports announcer on TV and one of the best-known ones in the country!

MAE: I'm talking about what he was.

MARGARET: Well, I wish you would just stop talking about my husband.

GOOPER: I've got a right to discuss my brother with other members of MY OWN family, which don't include *you*. Why don't you go out there and drink with Brick?

MARGARET: I've never seen such malice toward a brother.

GOOPER: How about his for me? Why, he can't stand to be in the same room with me!

MARGARET: This is a deliberate campaign of vilification for the most disgusting and sordid reason on earth, and I know what it is! It's *avarice, avarice, greed, greed!*

BIG MAMA: *Oh, I'll scream! I will scream in a moment unless this stops!*

(*Gooper has stalked up to Margaret with clenched fists at his sides as if he would strike her. Mae distorts her face again into a hideous grimace behind Margaret's back.*)

BIG MAMA (*sobs*): Margaret. Child. Come here. Sit next to Big Mama.

MARGARET: Precious Mommy. I'm sorry, I'm sorry, I — !

(*She bends her long graceful neck to press her forehead to Big Mama's bulging shoulder under its black chiffon.*)

MAE: How beautiful, how touching, this display of devotion! Do you know why she's childless? She's childless because that big beautiful athlete husband of hers won't go to bed with her!

GOOPER: You jest won't let me do this in a nice way, will yah? Aw right — I don't give a goddamn if Big Daddy likes me or don't like me or did or never did or will or will never! I'm just appealing to a sense of common decency and fair play. I'll tell you the truth. I've resented Big Daddy's partiality to Brick ever since Brick was born, and the way I've been treated like I was just barely good enough to spit on

and sometimes not even good enough for that. Big Daddy is dying of cancer, and it's spread all through him and it's attacked all his vital organs including the kidneys and right now he is sinking into uremia, and you all know what uremia is, it's poisoning of the whole system due to the failure of the body to eliminate its poisons.

MARGARET (*to herself, downstage, hissingly*): *Poisons, poisons! Venomous thoughts and words! In hearts and minds! — That's poisons!*

GOOPER (*overlapping her*): I am asking for a square deal, and, by God, I expect to get one. But if I don't get one, if there's any peculiar shenanigans going on around here behind my back, well, I'm not a corporation lawyer for nothing, I know how to protect my own interests.

(*Brick enters from the gallery with a tranquil, blurred smile, carrying an empty glass with him.*)

BRICK: Storm coming up.

GOOPER: Oh! A late arrival!

MAE: Behold the conquering hero comes!

GOOPER: The fabulous Brick Pollitt! Remember him? — Who could forget him!

MAE: He looks like he's been injured in a game!

GOOPER: Yep, I'm afraid you'll have to warm the bench at the Sugar Bowl this year, Brick!

(*Mae laughs shrilly.*)

Or was it the Rose Bowl that he made that famous run in? —

(*Thunder.*)

MAE: The punch bowl, honey. It was in the punch bowl, the cut-glass punch bowl!

GOOPER: Oh, that's right, I'm getting the bowls mixed up!

MARGARET: Why don't you stop venting your malice and envy on a sick boy?

BIG MAMA: *Now you two hush, I mean it, hush, all of you, hush!*

DAISY, SOOKEY: Storm! Storm comin'! Storm! Storm!

LACEY: Brightie, close them shutters.

GOOPER: Lacey, put the top up on my Cadillac, will yuh?

LACEY: Yes, suh, Mistah Pollitt!

GOOPER (*at the same time*): Big Mama, you know it's necessary for me t' go back to Memphis in th' mornin' t' represent the Parker estate in a lawsuit.

(*Mae sits on the bed and arranges papers she has taken from the brief case.*)

BIG MAMA: Is it, Gooper?

MAE: Yaiss.

GOOPER: That's why I'm forced to — to bring up a problem that —

MAE: Somethin' that's too important t' be put off!

GOOPER: If Brick was sober, he ought to be in on this.

MARGARET: Brick is present; we're present.

GOOPER: Well, good. I will now give you this outline my

partner, Tom Bullitt, an' me have drawn up — a sort of dummy — trusteeship.

MARGARET: Oh, that's it! You'll be in charge an dole out remittances, will you?

GOOPER: This we did as soon as we got the report on Big Daddy from th' Ochsner Laboratories. We did this thing, I mean we drew up this dummy outline with the advice and assistance of the Chairman of the Boa'd of Directors of th' Southern Plantahs Bank and Trust Company in Memphis, C. C. Bellowes, a man who handles estates for all th' prominent fam'lies in West Tennessee and th' Delta.

BIG MAMA: Gooper?

GOOPER (*crouching in front of Big Mama*): Now this is not — not final, or anything like it. This is just a preliminary outline. But it does provide a basis — a design — a — possible, feasible — *plan!*

MARGARET: Yes, I'll bet it's a plan.

(*Thunder.*)

MAE: It's a plan to protect the biggest estate in the Delta from irresponsibility an' —

BIG MAMA: Now you listen to me, all of you, you listen here! They's not goin' to be any more catty talk in my house! And Gooper, you put that away before I grab it out of your hand and tear it right up! I don't know what the hell's in it, and I don't want to know what the hell's in it. I'm talkin' in Big Daddy's language now; I'm his *wife*, not his *widow*, I'm still his *wife*! And I'm talkin' to you in his language an' —

GOOPER: Big Mama, what I have here is —

MAE (*at the same time*): Gooper explained that it's just a plan . . .

BIG MAMA: I don't care what you got there. Just put it back where it came from, an' don't let me see it again, not even the outside of the envelope of it! Is that understood? Basis! Plan! Preliminary! Design! I say — what is it Big Daddy always says when he's disgusted?

BRICK (*from the bar*): Big Daddy says "crap" when he's disgusted.

BIG MAMA (*rising*): That's right — CRAP! I say CRAP too, like Big Daddy!

(*Thunder.*)

MAE: Coarse language doesn't seem called for in this —

GOOPER: Somethin' in me is *deeply outraged* by hearin' you talk like this.

BIG MAMA: *Nobody's goin' to take nothin'!* — till Big Daddy lets go of it — maybe, just possibly, not — not even then! No, not even then!

(*Thunder.*)

MAE: Sookey, hurry up an' git that po'ch furniture cova-hed; want th' paint to come off?

GOOPER: Lacey, put mah car away!

LACEY: Caint, Mistah Pollitt, you got the keys!

GOOPER: Naw, you got 'em, man. Where th' keys to th' car, honey?

MAE: You got 'em in your pocket!

BRICK: "You can always hear me singin' this song, Show me the way to go home."

(*Thunder distantly.*)

BIG MAMA: Brick! Come here, Brick, I need you. Tonight Brick looks like he used to look when he was a little boy, just like he did when he played wild games and used to come home when I hollered myself hoarse for him, all sweaty and pink cheeked and sleepy, with his — red curls shining . . .

(*Brick draws aside as he does from all physical contact and continues the song in a whisper, opening the ice bucket and dropping in the ice cubes one by one as if he were mixing some important chemical formula.*)

(*Distant thunder.*)

Time goes by so fast. Nothin' can outrun it. Death commences too early — almost before you're half acquainted with life — you meet the other . . . Oh, you know we just got to love each other an' stay together, all of us, just as close as we can, especially now that such a *black* thing has come and moved into this place without invitation.

(*Awkwardly embracing Brick, she presses her head to his shoulder.*)

(*A dog howls offstage.*)

Oh, Brick, son of Big Daddy, Big Daddy does so love you. Y'know what would be his fondest dream come true? If before he passed on, if Big Daddy has to pass on . . .

(*A dog howls.*)

. . . you give him a child of yours, a grandson as much like his son as his son is like Big Daddy . . .

MARGARET: I know that's Big Daddy's dream.

BIG MAMA: That's his dream.

MAE: Such a pity that Maggie and Brick can't oblige.

BIG DADDY (*off downstage right on the gallery*): Looks like the wind was takin' liberties with this place.

SERVANT (*offstage*): Yes, sir, Mr. Pollitt.

MARGARET (*crossing to the right door*): Big Daddy's on the gall'ry.

(*Big Mama has turned toward the hall door at the sound of Big Daddy's voice on the gallery.*)

BIG MAMA: I can't stay here. He'll see somethin' in my eyes.

(*Big Daddy enters the room from upstage right.*)

BIG DADDY: Can I come in?

(*He puts his cigar in an ash tray.*)

MARGARET: Did the storm wake you up, Big Daddy?

BIG DADDY: Which stawm are you talkin' about — th' one outside or th' hullballoo in here?

(*Gooper squeezes past Big Daddy.*)

GOOPER: 'Scuse me.

(*Mae tries to squeeze past Big Daddy to join Gooper, but Big Daddy puts his arm firmly around her.*)

BIG DADDY: I heard some mighty loud talk. Sounded like somethin' important was bein' discussed. What was the powwow about?

MAE (*flustered*): Why — nothin', Big Daddy . . .

BIG DADDY (*crossing to extreme left center, taking Mae with him*): What is that pregnant-lookin' envelope you're puttin' back in your brief case, Gooper?

GOOPER (*at the foot of the bed, caught, as he stuffs papers into envelope*): That? Nothin', suh — nothin' much of anythin' at all . . .

BIG DADDY: Nothin'? It looks like a whole lot of nothin'!

(*He turns upstage to the group.*)

You all know th' story about th' young married couple —

GOOPER: Yes, sir!

BIG DADDY: Hello, Brick —

BRICK: Hello, Big Daddy.

(*The group is arranged in a semicircle above Big Daddy, Margaret at the extreme right, then Mae and Gooper, then Big Mama, with Brick at the left.*)

BIG DADDY: Young married couple took Junior out to th' zoo one Sunday, inspected all of God's creatures in their cages, with satisfaction.

GOOPER: Satisfaction.

BIG DADDY (*crossing to upstage center, facing front*): This afternoon was a warm afternoon in spring an' that ole elephant had somethin' else on his mind which was bigger'n peanuts. You know this story, Brick?

(*Gooper nods.*)

BRICK: No, sir, I don't know it.

BIG DADDY: Y'see, in th' cage adjoinin' they was a young female elephant in heat!

BIG MAMA (*at Big Daddy's shoulder*): Oh, Big Daddy!

BIG DADDY: What's the matter, preacher's gone, ain't he? All right. That female elephant in the next cage was permeatin' the atmosphere about her with a powerful and excitin' odor of female fertility! Huh! Ain't that a nice way to put it, Brick?

BRICK: Yes, sir, nothin' wrong with it.

BIG DADDY: Brick says th's nothin' wrong with it!

BIG MAMA: Oh, Big Daddy!

BIG DADDY (*crossing to downstage center*): So this ole bull elephant still had a couple of fornications left in him. He reared back his trunk an' got a whiff of that elephant lady next door! — began to paw at the dirt in his cage an' butt his head against the separatin' partition and, first thing y'know, there was a conspicuous change in his *profile* — very *conspicuous*! Ain't I tellin' this story in decent language, Brick?

BRICK: Yes, sir, too fuckin' decent!

BIG DADDY: So, the little boy pointed at it and said, "What's that?" His mama said, "Oh, that's — nothin'!" — His papa said, "She's spoiled!"

(*Big Daddy crosses to Brick at left.*)

You didn't laugh at that story, Brick.

(*Big Mama crosses to downstage right crying. Margaret goes to her. Mae and Gooper hold upstage right center.*)

BRICK: No, sir, I didn't laugh at that story.

BIG DADDY: What is the smell in this room? Don't you notice it, Brick? Don't you notice a powerful and obnoxious odor of mendacity in this room?

BRICK: Yes, sir, I think I do, sir.

GOOPER: Mae, Mae . . .

BIG DADDY: There is nothing more powerful. Is there, Brick?

BRICK: No, sir. No, sir, there isn't, an' nothin' more obnoxious.

BIG DADDY: Brick agrees with me. The odor of mendacity is a powerful and obnoxious odor an' the stawm hasn't blown it away from this room yet. You notice it, Gooper?

GOOPER: What, sir?

BIG DADDY: How about you, Sister Woman? You notice the unpleasant odor of mendacity in this room?

MAE: Why, Big Daddy, I don't even know what that is.

BIG DADDY: You can smell it. Hell it smells like death!

(*Big Mama sobs. Big Daddy looks toward her.*)

What's wrong with that fat woman over there, loaded with diamonds? Hey, what's-you-name, what's the matter with you?

MARGARET (*crossing toward Big Daddy*): She had a slight dizzy spell, Big Daddy.

BIG DADDY: You better watch that, Big Mama. A stroke is a bad way to go.

MARGARET (*crossing to Big Daddy at center*): Oh, Brick, Big Daddy has on your birthday present to him, Brick, he has on your cashmere robe, the softest material I have ever felt.

BIG DADDY: Yeah, this is my soft birthday, Maggie . . . Not my gold or my silver birthday, but my soft birthday, everything's got to be soft for Big Daddy on this soft birthday.

(*Maggie kneels before Big Daddy at center.*)

MARGARET: Big Daddy's got on his Chinese slippers that I gave him, Brick. Big Daddy, I haven't given you my big present yet, but now I will, now's the time for me to present it to you! I have an announcement to make!

MAE: What? What kind of announcement?

GOOPER: A sports announcement, Maggie?

MARGARET: Announcement of life beginning! A child is coming, sired by Brick, and out of Maggie the Cat! I have Brick's child in my body, an' that's my birthday present to Big Daddy on this birthday!

(*Big Daddy looks at Brick who crosses behind Big Daddy to downstage portal, left.*)

BIG DADDY: Get up, girl, get up off your knees, girl.

(*Big Daddy helps Margaret to rise. He crosses above her, to her right, bites off the end of a fresh cigar, taken from his bathrobe pocket, as he studies Margaret.*)

    Uh-huh, this girl has life in her body, that's no lie!
BIG MAMA: BIG DADDY'S DREAM COME TRUE!
BRICK: JESUS!
BIG DADDY (*crossing right below wicker stand*): Gooper, I want my lawyer in the mornin'.
BRICK: Where are you goin', Big Daddy?
BIG DADDY: Son, I'm goin' up on the roof, to the belvedere on th' roof to look over my kingdom before I give up my kingdom — twenty-eight thousand acres of th' richest land this side of the valley Nile!

(*He exits through right doors, and down right on the gallery.*)

BIG MAMA (*following*): Sweetheart, sweetheart, sweetheart — can I come with you?

(*She exits downstage right.*)
    (*Margaret is downstage center in the mirror area. Mae has joined Gooper and she gives him a fierce poke, making a low hissing sound and a grimace of fury.*)

GOOPER (*pushing her aside*): Brick, could you possibly spare me one small shot of that liquor?
BRICK: Why, help yourself, Gooper boy.
GOOPER: I will.
MAE (*shrilly*): Of course we know that this is — a lie.
GOOPER: *Be still, Mae.*
MAE: I won't be still! I know she's made this up!
GOOPER: Goddamn it, I said shut up!
MARGARET: Gracious! I didn't know that my little announcement was going to provoke such a storm!
MAE: *That* woman isn't *pregnant!*
GOOPER: Who said she was?
MAE: *She* did.
GOOPER: The doctor didn't. Doc Baugh didn't.
MARGARET: I haven't gone to Doc Baugh.
GOOPER: Then who'd you go to, Maggie?
MARGARET: One of the best gynecologists in the South.
GOOPER: Uh huh, uh huh! — I see . . .

(*He takes out a pencil and notebook.*)

    — May we have his name, please?
MARGARET: No, you may not, Mister Prosecuting Attorney!
MAE: He doesn't have any name, he doesn't exist!
MARGARET: Oh, he exists all right, and so does my child, Brick's baby!
MAE: You can't conceive a child by a man that won't sleep with you unless you think you're —

(*Brick has turned on the phonograph. A scat song cuts Mae's speech.*)

GOOPER: *Turn that off!*
MAE: We know it's a lie because we hear you in here; he won't sleep with you, we hear you! So don't imagine

you're going to put a trick over on us, to fool a dying man with a —

(*A long drawn cry of agony and rage fills the house. Margaret turns the phonograph down to a whisper. The cry is repeated.*)

MAE: Did you hear that, Gooper, did you hear that?
GOOPER: Sounds like the pain has struck.
MAE: Go see, Gooper!
GOOPER: Come along and leave these lovebirds together in their nest!

(*He goes out first. Mae follows but turns at the door, contorting her face and hissing at Margaret.*)

MAE: *Liar!*

(*She slams the door.*)
    (*Margaret exhales with relief and moves a little unsteadily to catch hold of Brick's arm.*)

MARGARET: Thank you for — keeping still . . .
BRICK: O.K., Maggie.
MARGARET: It was gallant of you to save my face!

(*He now pours down three shots in quick succession and stands waiting, silent. All at once he turns with a smile and says:*)

BRICK: *There!*
MARGARET: What?
BRICK: The *click* . . .

(*His gratitude seems almost infinite as he hobbles out on the gallery with a drink. We hear his crutch as he swings out of sight. Then, at some distance, he begins singing to himself a peaceful song. Margaret holds the big pillow forlornly as if it were her only companion, for a few moments, then throws it on the bed. She rushes to the liquor cabinet, gathers all the bottles in her arms, turns about undecidedly, then runs out of the room with them, leaving the door ajar on the dim yellow hall. Brick is heard hobbling back along the gallery, singing his peaceful song. He comes back in, sees the pillow on the bed, laughs lightly, sadly, picks it up. He has it under his arm as Margaret returns to the room. Margaret softly shuts the door and leans against it, smiling softly at Brick.*)

MARGARET: Brick, I used to think that you were stronger than me and I didn't want to be overpowered by you. But now, since you've taken to liquor — you know what? — I guess it's bad, but now I'm stronger than you and I can love you more truly! Don't move that pillow. I'll move it right back if you do! — Brick?

(*She turns out all the lamps but a single rose-silk-shaded one by the bed.*)

    I really have been to a doctor and I know what to do and — Brick? — this is my time by the calendar to conceive?
BRICK: Yes, I understand, Maggie. But how are you going to conceive a child by a man in love with his liquor?

MARGARET: By locking his liquor up and making him satisfy my desire before I unlock it!
BRICK: Is that what you've done, Maggie?
MARGARET: Look and see. That cabinet's mighty empty compared to before!
BRICK: Well, I'll be a son of a —

(*He reaches for his crutch but she beats him to it and rushes out on the gallery, hurls the crutch over the rail, and comes back in, panting.*)

MARGARET: And so tonight we're going to make the lie true, and when that's done, I'll bring the liquor back here and we'll get drunk together, here, tonight, in this place that death has come into . . . — What do you say?
BRICK: I don't say anything. I guess there's nothing to say.
MARGARET: Oh, you weak people, you weak, beautiful people! — who give up with such grace. What you want is someone to —

(*She turns out the rose-silk lamp.*)

— take hold of you. — Gently, gently with love hand your life back to you, like somethin' gold you let go of. I *do* love you, Brick, I *do*!
BRICK (*smiling with charming sadness*): Wouldn't it be funny if that was true?

COMMENTARIES

Tennessee Williams (1911–1983)
MEMOIRS
1972

Tennessee Williams published Memoirs *in 1972, after establishing himself as one of the most successful American playwrights. The two excerpts included here concern his feelings about* Cat on a Hot Tin Roof *and his feelings about being a writer.*

Well, now, about plays, what about them? Plays are written and then, if they are lucky, they are performed, and if their luck still holds, which is not too frequently the case, their performance is so successful that both audience and critics at the first night are aware that they are being offered a dramatic work which is both honest and entertaining and also somehow capable of engaging their aesthetic appreciation.

I have never liked to talk about the professional side of my life. Am I afraid that it is a bird that will be startled away by discussion, as by a hawk's shadow? Something like that, I suppose.

People are always asking me, at those symposia to which I've been subjected in recent years, which is my favorite among the plays I have written, the number of which eludes my recollection, and I either say to them, "Always the latest" or I succumb to my instinct for the truth and say, "I suppose it must be the published version of *Cat on a Hot Tin Roof.*"

That play comes closest to being both a work of art and a work of craft. It is really very well put together, in my opinion, and all its characters are amusing and credible and touching. Also it adheres to the valuable edict of Aristotle that a tragedy must have unity of time and place and magnitude of theme.

The set in *Cat* never changes and its running time is exactly the time of its action, meaning that one act, timewise, follows directly upon the other, and I know of no other modern American play in which this is accomplished.

However my reasons for liking *Cat* best are deeper than that. I believe that in *Cat* I reached beyond myself, in the second act, to a kind of crude eloquence of expression in Big Daddy that I have managed to give no other character of my creation.

The story of *Cat*'s production in 1954 and the disaster that followed upon its enormous success must be told now.

[Director Elia] Kazan immediately shared Audrey's [Wood, Williams's agent] enthusiasm for *Cat* but he said that it was faulty in one act. I assumed that he meant the first act, but no, it was the third act. He wanted a more admirable heroine than the Maggie offered in the original script.

Inwardly I disagreed. I thought that in Maggie I had presented a very true and moving portrait of a young woman whose frustration in love and whose practicality drove her to the literal seduction of an unwilling young man. Seduction is too soft a word. Brick was literally forced back to bed by Maggie, when she confiscated his booze . . .

Then I also had to violate my own intuition by having Big Daddy re-enter the stage in Act Three. I saw nothing for him to do in that act when he re-entered and I did not think that it was dramatically proper that he should re-enter. Consequently I had him tell "the elephant story." This was assaulted by censors. I was told it must be removed. The material which I then had to put in its place was always offensive to me.

I would not tell you this except for the consequences to me as a writer after *Cat* had received its Critics' Award and its Pulitzer.

Even though I always go crazy on opening nights, the New York opening of *Cat* was particularly dreadful. I thought it was a failure, a distortion of what I had intended. After the show was over I thought I had heard coughs all during the performance. I suppose there weren't that many, probably the usual number. And it did become my biggest, my longest-running play. But after the show was over on opening night, Kazan said, "Let's go to my apartment until the reviews are out." He was totally confident that it would be a hit. I met Audrey Wood outside, and at the time I was totally dependent on her for any creative confidence; and so I said, "Audrey, we're all going up to the Kazans' to wait for the notices." She said, "Oh no, I have other plans." I was hurt, and said something mean. . . .

What is it like being a writer? I would say it is like being free.

I know that some writers aren't free, they are professionally employed, which is quite a different thing.

Professionally, they are probably better writers in the conventional sense of "better." They have an ear to the ground of best-seller demands: They please their publishers and presumably their public as well.

But they are not free and so they are not what I regard a true writer as being.

To be free is to have achieved your life.

It means any number of freedoms.

It means the freedom to stop when you please, to go where and when you please, it means to be voyager here and there, one who flees many hotels, sad or happy, without obstruction and without much regret.

It means the freedom of being. And someone has wisely observed, if you can't be yourself, what's the point of being anything at all?

I am not a frequent reader nor quoter of Scriptures and yet I love a piece of advice which occurs among them:

"Let thy light so shine among men that they see thy good works and glorify thy Father which is in heaven."

There is a New Journalism, there is a New Criticism, there is a new look and style of cinema and theater, of practically everything that we live with, but what I think we most need is a New Morality.

And I think we've arrived at a point where that is a necessity of continued and bearable existence.

Brenda Murphy (b. 1950)
TENNESSEE WILLIAMS AND ELIA KAZAN
COLLABORATE ON *CAT*   *1991*

Theater is a collaborative art, and numerous plays have been altered because of suggestions of director or actor. The collaboration of Tennessee Williams and director Elia Kazan was special because both were powerful personalities and each respected the other. The Cat on a Hot Tin Roof *that we know is much different from the one that Williams first wrote. He was willing to make many of the creative changes suggested by Kazan.*

[Director Elia Kazan's] imagination stimulated by Big Daddy's rhetorical power, Kazan developed the production around the impetus of direct communication between the characters and the audience. At the beginning of Act 2, for example, he made a note to himself to have Big Daddy come downstage facing the audience and talk straight out to them while the others remained way upstage, even out on the gallery. Williams agreed with Kazan about the power of Big Daddy's character and the centrality of words in the play. In *Memoirs* he wrote, "In *Cat* I reached beyond myself, in the second act, to a kind of crude eloquence of expression in Big Daddy that I have managed to give no other character of my creation."[1]

Although Williams had incorporated the idea of addressing the audience in the "recitative" speeches of Maggie and Brick in the early scripts, he had not counted on what was in 1955 the radical concept that Kazan devised for the production. As Kazan noted in a later interview, the conventions of representational realism were so entrenched in the Broadway theater of the fifties that foregrounding the production's theatricality to the extent of having the characters address the audience directly had been considered anathema for many years. The last time he could remember it being done was in the production of *Our Town*° in 1938.[2]

---

[1]Tennessee Williams, *Memoirs* (Garden City: Doubleday, 1975).
   Our Town: In this play by Thornton Wilder, a character called the Stage Manager speaks to the audience throughout the play.
   [2]Michel Ciment, *Kazan on Kazan* (New York: Viking, 1974) 47.

Kazan's pride in this rejection of realistic convention and his continuing interest in subjectifying theatrical experience were evident in an interview he gave in the early sixties:

> I was busting out of the goddamned proscenium theater uptown. In *Cat on a Hot Tin Roof* I had everybody address the audience continually. Every time they had one of those long speeches they'd turn and say it to the audience. Nobody thought anything of it once we opened. But there was a hell of a lot of bitching about it before. . . . The whole second act of *Cat* was a long address by Burl Ives to the audience. I had him address various members of the audience . . . "what would *you* do?" is implicit in this kind of staging. It sucks the audience into the experience and emotion of that moment.[3]

Kazan wrote in his autobiography that he had to convince Williams to accept his notion of how Burl Ives would play the part of Big Daddy. When Kazan said he was going to bring Ives right down to the edge of the forestage, have him "look the audience right in the eye, and speak it directly to them," Williams protested that *Cat* was a realistic play, and should be kept within the representational conventions. When pressed by Kazan to say whether old cotton planters actually talked that eloquently and that long without interruption, Williams replied that they did. After all, who would dare interrupt them?[4] Nonetheless Kazan pursued his concept for the production in the face of Williams's skepticism, if not his opposition.

The Design

When the central dynamic of the production had been established as direct communication between the characters and the audience, it had to imbue all the elements of the stage language. Here Kazan reports that he did run into opposition from Williams, who had a clear idea of what he thought the set should be like, an image that had evolved as he had revised the play. In the notes for the designer he prepared for the script preceding the November pre-rehearsal version, Williams described the basic plan of the set that was eventually used for the production: a bed–sitting room in a Mississippi Delta plantation, opening onto an upstairs gallery and showing white balustrades against a fair summer sky that fades into dusk and night during the course of the play. This is what is needed to support the action of the play which, as Williams was fond of pointing out, observed the unities of time and place, the action of the play being confined to the single set and occupying exactly the amount of time it took to enact on stage. The lighting was obviously crucial for this play, to show the passage of time that is a central thematic concern as well as a structural one.

Beyond this, however, Williams's original image of the set was strikingly different from the set Kazan and Jo Mielziner eventually devised between them. Williams described the room as Victorian, with a touch of the Far East, and poetically haunted by the tender relationship of Jack Straw and Peter Ochello. He noted that the room should not have changed much since Straw and Ochello's time. To suggest the style for the design, Williams referred the designer to the reproduction he had seen of a faded photograph of the verandah of Robert Louis Stevenson's home in Samoa: "There was a quality of tender light on weathered wood, such as porch-furniture made of bamboo and wicker, exposed to tropical suns and tropical rains,

[3]Quoted in Richard Schechner and Theodore Hoffman, "'Look, There's the American Theatre': An Interview with Elia Kazan," *Tulane Drama Review,* 9 (Winter 1964): 71.
[4]Elia Kazan, *Elia Kazan: A Life* (New York: Knopf, 1988) 541–42.

which came to mind when I thought about the set for this play" (RV xiii).° The photograph, he wrote, also brought to mind "the grace and comfort of light, the reassurance it gives, on a late and fair afternoon in summer, the way that no matter what, even dread of death, is gently touched and soothed by it. For the set is the background for a play that deals with human extremities of emotion and needs that softness behind it" (RV xiii).

Williams described in detail the big, slightly raked, double bed and the "entertainment center" that were the most significant objects in the set, and then he cautioned the designer, lest he feel that the previous description confined him to literal realism. As in the published "Note for the Designer," Williams envisioned that "the set should be far less realistic than I have so far implied in this description of it": The walls should dissolve mysteriously into the air below the ceiling; the set should be roofed by the sky; stars and moon suggested by traces of milky pallor, as if they were observed through a telescope lens out of focus (RV xiv). The original note, however, added the idea that a spiral nebula might be faintly suggested in order to suggest the "mystery of the cosmos," which Williams thought should be a visible presence in the play, almost as present as an actor in it. He also thought that the cloud effects and the sound effects for the windstorm in Act 3 should be as unrealistic as the set. As he revised the script, however, Williams began to reconceptualize the set as well. In November he sent off a rewrite of the scene description suggesting that the room should appear to have been remodeled since Straw and Ochello's time, and now had an open, Japanese effect. The canopied bed, he suggested, could appear to have been removed from an Italian renaissance palazzo when Big Daddy and Big Mama raided Europe a few years previously.

When Kazan and Mielziner began talking about the design, their concept of a production that foregrounded the characters' rhetorical appeals to the audience became the central element in their discussion. Kazan has written:

> Jo Mielziner and I had read the play in the same way; we saw its great merit was its brilliant rhetoric and its theatricality. Jo didn't see the play as realistic any more than I did. If it was to be done realistically, I would have to contrive stage business to keep the old man talking those great second-act speeches turned out front and pretend that it was just another day in the life of the Pollitt family. This would, it seemed to me, amount to an apology to the audience for the glory of the author's language. It didn't seem like just another day in the life of a cotton planter's family to Jo or to me; it seemed like the best kind of theater, the kind we were interested in encouraging, the theater theatrical, not pretending any longer that an audience wasn't out there to be addressed but having a performer as great as Burl Ives acknowledge their presence at all times and even make eye contact with individuals.[5]

Accordingly, Kazan wrote, "I caused Jo to design our setting as I wished, a large, triangular platform, tipped toward the audience and holding only one piece of furniture, an ornate bed. This brought the play down to its essentials and made it impossible for it to be played any way except as I preferred."[6]

The set was not quite so spare as Kazan remembered it, but the central point of his statement, that the presentational impulse was the dominant aesthetic factor in

---

RV: The reading version of the play (New York: New American Library, 1958), which has both versions of the third act.

[5]Kazan 542–43.

[6]Kazan 543.

creating the design, has been fully corroborated by Mielziner. In his memoir, Mielziner described their discussion about the design much as Kazan did. Asked how he thought the "elephant story" should be handled proxemically, Mielziner told Kazan that he thought it should receive as much emphasis as possible: "I suggested that we have an area of the stage on which Big Daddy could come down close to the audience and deliver the lines with dramatic force." Mielziner wrote that Kazan was delighted with his answer, and "from this discussion grew the idea of creating a stage within the stage. It would be steeply raked toward the audience with one corner actually jutting out over the footlights. In its final form it turned out to be a sort of thrust stage."[7]

Mielziner's design was a departure from the subjective realism he had employed in *Menagerie, Streetcar,* and *Summer and Smoke,* in that he did not try to suggest through the material elements of the stage language that the events unfolding on stage were filtered through the mind of one of the characters. Instead, the design of the set projected the action out toward the audience, forcing it to become involved as though it were one of the characters. Extremely spare, the set was composed of two platforms, a large diamond-shaped one, a corner of which projected beyond the proscenium, and a smaller rectangle a foot lower at stage right. There were no doors, such actions as opening doors and looking into the mirror being mimed in this production. The only items of furniture Mielziner drew in his sketches were the primary material signifiers: the large bed, which signified both Maggie and Brick's failing marriage and the lingering memory of Straw and Ochello; the entertainment center, which signified both Brick's immediate goal of escape from reality and the vacuous materialism that Williams saw in the fifties; and the daybed, which signified Brick's withdrawal from Maggie, their marriage, and life in general. The actual set, however, also held a wicker night table and a large wicker armchair which could accommodate either Burl Ives or two of the other actors. The overall effect was of a large playing space down front where the actors could address the audience as if from a bare platform.

The lines of the design contributed to this effect. The perspective was such that the corner of the ceiling came down to a point slightly to the left of upstage center, helping to focus the audience's attention on the point of the diamond where the characters addressed the audience. Mielziner took Williams's hints to give lighting a central function in the play, running a scrim from floor to ceiling along two sides of the set with strips of black velour indicating the lines of the columns outside the windows of the room when the light of the moon was projected through them. To signify sunlight, slide projections of blinds were thrown on the scrims, while the gallery and the lawn beyond the windows were blocked out. When characters on the gallery or the lawn were to be seen, the lights behind the scrim were brought up, making the actors visible to the audience, as had been done with *Streetcar.*

Two follow-spots were used in the production. One, on the audience's left, highlighted Maggie throughout Act 1 and picked up Big Mama, Maggie, and Brick in Act 2, as they were in turn nominally being addressed by Big Daddy, who was downstage talking to the audience. In Act 3 the light again shone on Maggie almost without interruption. The follow-spot on the audience's right highlighted the characters Maggie was addressing in Act 1, chiefly Brick, as she had her turn at "recitative." It shone on Big Daddy throughout Act 2 and picked up Brick, Big Mama,

[7]*Designing for Theatre: A Memoir and a Portfolio* (New York: Bram Hall House, 1965) 183.

Gooper, Mae, and Maggie at various times during Act 3, emphasizing a significant entrance or a significant reaction indexically as it occurred. Contributing to the generally "golden" look of the production's lighting, the follow-spots were amber except when a character went out onto the gallery, when they were changed to blue. The follow-spots not only helped to avoid confusion by focusing the audience's attention where Kazan wanted it to be, they also contributed to the foregrounding of the theatricality in the production by "framing" specific characters and pieces of action. Kazan stylized the composition of his stage picture in *Cat*, and encoded a great deal of meaning through gesture, movement, and pose in the production. Using the follow-spots to highlight these formal compositions emphasized that what was happening onstage was not real life but theater.

In designing the furniture, both Kazan and Mielziner took their cue from Williams's earlier description of the set, emphasizing the qualities he had seen in the Robert Louis Stevenson photograph. Kazan had underlined elements of this description in his copy of the script. Listed together, they indicate quite well the direction Mielziner took with the design after their conferences:

> Delta's biggest cotton planter
> Far East
> The room must evoke some ghosts
> Gently . . . poetically haunted by a relationship . . . a tenderness which was uncommon
> Samoan Island
> tender light on weathered wood
> Bamboo . . . wicker
> [the entertainment center] monument . . . very complete . . . compact little shrine . . .
> all the comforts . . . illusions . . . hide [written in the margin, "Brick hides"] such
> things as the characters in the play are faced with (RV xii–xiv)

From these suggestions came the old wicker headboard with its huge and fantastically shaped design of two cornucopias, the matching wicker furniture, the carpet with its lushly fertile design of oversized flowers and vines, and the one object in the room that competed with the fertility symbol of the bed for the audience's attention, the oversized bar, hi-fi, radio, and television with its sleekly modern fifties lines. This object realized Williams's description of a compact modern shrine to all the comforts and illusions of contemporary life and signified Brick's retreat from human contact.

Kazan has said more than once that Williams did not like the set that Mielziner finally developed for *Cat* because he thought his play should be performed realistically. Kazan has also indicated that the set was a material signifier of his aesthetic vision in opposition to Williams's:

> I had the setting I'd asked for; Jo had given me what I wanted. Tennessee had approved of it earlier, when he was ready to approve of damn near anything I asked for, because I was the director he wanted. Now the setting was up onstage, too late to change, and on that setting there was only one way for any human to conduct himself: "out front" it's called. Dear Tennessee was stuck with my vision, like it or not.[8]

---

[8]Kazan 543.

Arthur Miller

Arthur Miller (b. 1915) has been the dean of American playwrights since the opening of *Death of a Salesman* in 1949. His steady output as a writer and a playwright began with his first publications after college in 1939, when he worked in the New York Federal Theatre Project, a branch of the Works Progress Administration (WPA), Franklin D. Roosevelt's huge Depression-era effort to put Americans back to work.

Miller, the son of a Jewish immigrant, was born and raised during his early years in the Harlem section of Manhattan and later in Brooklyn after his father's business failed. In high school Miller thought of himself more as an athlete than as a student, and he had trouble getting teachers' recommendations for college. After considerable struggle and waiting, he entered the University of Michigan, where his talent as a playwright emerged under the tutelage of Kenneth Rowe, his playwriting professor. His undergraduate plays won important university awards, and he became noticed by the Theatre Guild, a highly respected theater founded to present excellent plays (not necessarily commercial successes). His career was under way.

From 1939 to 1947 Miller wrote radio plays, screenplays, articles, stories, and a novel. His work covered a wide range of material, much of it growing out of his childhood memories of a tightly knit and somewhat eccentric family that provided him with a large gallery of characters. But he also dealt with political issues and problems of anti-Semitism, which was widespread in the 1930s and 1940s. Miller's political concerns have been a constant presence in his work since his earliest writings.

All My Sons (1947) was his first successful play. It ran on Broadway for three hundred performances, a remarkable record for a serious drama. The story centers on a man who knowingly produces defective parts for airplanes and then blames the subsequent crashes on his business partner, who is ruined and imprisoned. When the guilty man's son finds out the truth, he confronts his father and rebukes him. Ultimately, the man realizes not only that he has lost his son because of his deceit but that the dead pilots were also "all my sons." The play won the New York Drama Critics' Circle Award.

Miller's next play, *Death of a Salesman* (1949), was written in six weeks. Focusing on the American ideal of business success, its conclusions were a challenge to standard American business values. Willy Loman, first performed by Lee J. Cobb, was intended to be a warning for Americans in the postwar period of the cost of growing wealth and affluence.

Miller's next play, *The Crucible* (1953), portrayed witch-hunts of seventeenth-century New England, but most people recognized the subtext: it was about contemporary anti-Communist witch-hunts. In the late 1940s and early 1950s the House Un-American Activities Committee (HUAC) held hearings to uncover suspected Communists in all areas of American life, particularly the arts. Many writers, artists, and performers came under close, often unfair, scrutiny by HUAC for their own political views and allegiances and were often asked to testify against their friends. Many were blacklisted (prevented from working in commercial theaters and movie companies), some were imprisoned for not testifying at others' trials, and some had their reputations and careers destroyed.

Arthur Miller was fearless in facing down HUAC, and he was convicted of contempt of court for not testifying against his friends. For a time he too was blacklisted, but his contempt citation was reversed, and he was not imprisoned. Given his personal political stance during this dangerous time, it is not a surprise to find that he usually chooses to write about matters of social concern.

In the 1990s Miller became the darling of the London stage while at the same time being somewhat neglected in the United States. One full-scale play, *Broken Glass* (1994), played in regional theater before going to a brief run on Broadway and then a longer run in London's West End. The play concerns a woman who becomes paralyzed in response to *Kristallnacht* (night of crystal), a night of violent rampages against Jews and Jewish property that resulted in 91 Jewish dead, hundreds injured, and 7,500 businesses and 177 synagogues gutted. After November 9, 1938, it was clear that Jews were no longer safe in Hitler's Germany. The subject of the play is intense, significant, and still timely.

The Ride Down Mount Morgan had its premiere in London in 1991; it then took seven years to open in New York in 1998. Its protagonist, Lyman Felt, played by Patrick Stewart in New York, was conceived as a Reaganite go-getter of the late 1980s: economically rapacious, sexually voracious, and amoral. When Felt's Porsche crashes on a ride down Mount Morgan, his two wives discover one another at the hospital. The play proceeds, examining the ethical values that permit Felt to live as he does. George Wolfe produced the play at the Joseph Papp Public Theatre. The Broadway production opened at the Ambassador Theater in April 2000, again with Patrick Stewart. The play was nominated for a Tony Award.

DEATH OF A SALESMAN

Death of a Salesman (1949) was a hit from its first performances and has remained at the center of modern American drama ever since. It has been successful in China, where there were no salesmen, and in Europe, where many salesmen dominate certain industries. Everywhere this play has touched the hearts and minds of its audiences. Its success is a phenomenon of American drama.

The play was first performed in an experimental environment. Miller had originally conceived of a model of a man's head as the stage setting. He has said: "The first image that occurred to me which was to result in *Death of a*

Salesman was of an enormous face the height of the proscenium arch which would appear and then open up, and we would see the inside of a man's head. In fact, *The Inside of His Head* was the first title." This technique was not used, but when Miller worked with the director and producer of the first production, he helped develop a setting that became a model for the "American style" in drama. The multilevel set permitted the play to shift from Willy Loman and his wife, Linda, having a conversation in their kitchen to their son's bedroom on the second level of the house. The set permitted portions of the stage to be reserved for Willy's visions of his brother, Ben, and for scenes outside the house such as Willy's interlude with the woman in Boston.

In a way, the setup of the stage respected Miller's original plan, but instead of portraying a cross-section of Willy's head, it presented a metaphor for a cross-section of his life. The audience was not looking in on just a living room, as in the nineteenth-century Ibsenist approach, but on an entire house and an entire life.

Using a cross-section of a house as a metaphor was an especially important device in this play because of the play's allusions to Greek tragedy. The great Greek tragedies usually portray the destruction of a house — such as the house of Atreus — in which "house" stands for a whole family, not a building. When Shakespeare's Hamlet dies, for example, his entire line dies with him. The death in *Death of a Salesman* implies the destruction of a family holding certain beliefs that have been wrong from the start.

The life of the salesman has given Willy a sense of dignity and worth, and he imagines that the modern world has corrupted that sense by robbing salesmen of the value of their personality. He thinks that the modern world has failed him, but he is wrong. His original belief — that what counts is not *what* you know but *whom* you know and how well you are liked — lies at the heart of his failure. When the play opens, he already has failed at the traveling salesman's job because he can no longer drive to his assigned territory. He cannot sell what he needs to sell.

Willy has inculcated his beliefs in his sons, Happy and Biff, and both are as ineffectual as their father. Willy doted on Biff and encouraged him to become a high school football star at the expense of his studies. But when Biff cannot pass an important course, and his plans to make up the work are subverted by his disillusionment in his father, his dreams of a college football career vanish. He cannot change and recover from this defeat. Happy, like his father, builds castles in the air and assumes somehow that he will be successful, though he has nothing to back himself up with. He wants the glory — and he spends time in fanciful imaginings, as Willy does — but he cannot do the basic work that makes it possible to achieve glory. Ironically, it is the "anemic" Bernard — who studies hard, stresses personal honesty and diligence, and never brags — who is successful.

Linda supports Willy's illusions, allowing him to be a fraud by sharing — or pretending to believe — in his dream. Willy has permitted himself to feel that integrity, honesty, and fidelity are not as important as being well liked.

The play ends with Willy still unable to face the deceptions he has perpetuated. He commits suicide, believing that his sons will be able to follow in his footsteps and succeed where he did not; he thinks that his insurance money will save the house and the family. What he does not realize is that his sons are no more capable than he is. They have been corrupted by his thinking, his values, his beliefs. And they cannot solve the problems that overwhelmed him.

Death of a Salesman has been given a privileged position in American drama because it is a modern tragedy. Aristotle felt that only characters of noble birth could be tragic heroes, but Miller confounds this theory, as Eugene O'Neill did, by showing the human integrity in even the most humble characters. Miller's Willy Loman is not a peasant, nor is he noble. In fact, Miller took a frightening risk in producing a figure that we find hard to like. Willy wants to be well liked, but as an audience we find it difficult to like a person who whines, complains, and accepts petty immorality as a normal way of life. Despite his character, we are awed by his fate.

One Chinese commentator said, after the Chinese production, that China is filled with such dreamers as Willy. Certainly America has been filled with them. Willy stands as an aspect of our culture, commercial and otherwise, that is at the center of our reflection of ourselves. Perhaps we react so strongly to Willy because we are afraid that we might easily become a Willy Loman if we are not vigilant about our moral views, our psychological well-being, and the limits of our commitment to success. Willy Loman has mesmerized audiences in America in many different economic circumstances: prosperity, recession, rapid growth, and cautious development. No matter what those circumstances, we have looked at the play as if looking in a mirror. What we have seen has always involved us, although it has not always made us pleased with ourselves.

Death of a Salesman in Performance

Death of a Salesman opened on Broadway on February 10, 1949, and won virtually every prize available for drama, including the Pulitzer Prize and the New York Drama Critics' Circle Award for best play. It ran on Broadway for an incredible 742 performances. Elia Kazan, director, was instrumental in establishing the play's innovative staging. Lee J. Cobb was cast as Willy, Mildred Dunnock as Linda, Arthur Kennedy as Biff, and Cameron Mitchell as Happy. The London production in July 1949, with Paul Muni as Willy and Kevin McCarthy as Biff, lasted 204 performances. Robert Coleman said of the New York production: "An explosion of emotional dynamite was set off last evening in the Morosco [Theater]. . . . In fashioning *Death of a Salesman* for them, author Arthur Miller and director Elia Kazan have collaborated on as exciting and devastating a theatrical blast as the nerves of modern playgoers can stand." Of Cobb, Howard Barnes said, "Cobb contributes a mammoth and magnificent portrayal of the central character. In his hands the salesman's frustration and final suicide are a matter of tremendous import."

An all-black production was directed by Lee Sankowich in Baltimore in 1972. Miller, in the audience on that production's opening night, commented that the play had been well received in "many countries and cultures" and that the Baltimore production further underscored the universality of the play. George C. Scott was praised for the power of his performance as Willy in New York's Circle in the Square production in 1975. A Chinese production directed by Arthur Miller was enormously successful in the 1980s. In the most celebrated revival of the play Dustin Hoffman portrayed Willy, John Malkovich played Biff, and Michael Rudman directed at the Broadhurst Theatre in New York in 1984. The critic Benedict Nightingale said of that production: "Somewhere at the core of him [Willy] an elaborate battle is being fought between dishonesty and honesty, glitter and substance, appearance and reality, between the promises or supposed promises of society and the claims of the self, between what Willy professes to value and what, perhaps without knowing it, he actually does value." In 1985 Dustin Hoffman brought his production of Miller's play to television, where it was viewed by an estimated twenty-five million people.

On February 10, 1999, exactly fifty years to the day from its original opening, the play's most recent production opened with Brian Dennehy as Willy Loman. The production was conceived in Chicago by the Goodman Theater Company, and in its revival Dennehy was praised by critics and theater-goers alike for presenting a powerful portrayal of Willy Loman for a new generation. Critics praised the timelessness of the drama — ultimately crowning it as an American classic.

Arthur Miller (b. 1915)

DEATH OF A SALESMAN   *1949*

CERTAIN PRIVATE CONVERSATIONS IN TWO ACTS AND A REQUIEM

Characters

WILLY LOMAN	UNCLE BEN
LINDA	HOWARD WAGNER
BIFF	JENNY
HAPPY	STANLEY
BERNARD	MISS FORSYTHE
THE WOMAN	LETTA
CHARLEY	

The action takes place in Willy Loman's house and yard and in various places he visits in the New York and Boston of today.

(Throughout the play, in the stage directions, left and right mean stage left and stage right.)

ACT I

(A melody is heard, played upon a flute. It is small and fine, telling of grass and trees and the horizon. The curtain rises.)

*(Before us is the Salesman's house. We are aware of towering, angular shapes behind it, surrounding it on all sides. Only the blue light of the sky falls upon the house and forestage; the surrounding area shows an angry glow of orange. As more light appears, we see a solid vault of apartment houses around the small, fragile-*seeming home. An air of the dream clings to the place, a dream rising out of reality. The kitchen at center seems actual enough, for there is a kitchen table with three chairs, and a refrigerator. But no other fixtures are seen. At the back of the kitchen there is a draped entrance, which leads to the living room. To the right of the kitchen, on a level raised two feet, is a bedroom furnished only with a brass bedstead and a straight chair. On a shelf over the bed a silver athletic trophy stands. A window opens onto the apartment house at the side.)*

(Behind the kitchen, on a level raised six and a half feet, is the boys' bedroom, at present barely visible. Two beds are dimly seen, and at the back of the room a dormer window. [This bedroom is above the unseen living room.] At the left a stairway curves up to it from the kitchen.)

(The entire setting is wholly or, in some places, partially transparent. The roofline of the house is one-dimensional; under and over it we see the apartment buildings. Before the house lies an apron, curving beyond the forestage into the orchestra. This forward area serves as the back yard as well as the locale of all Willy's imaginings and of his city scenes. Whenever the action is in the present the actors observe the imaginary wall-lines, entering the house only through its door at the left. But in the scenes of the past these boundaries are broken, and characters enter or leave a room by stepping "through" a wall onto the forestage.)

(*From the right, Willy Loman, the Salesman, enters, carrying two large sample cases. The flute plays on. He hears but is not aware of it. He is past sixty years of age, dressed quietly. Even as he crosses the stage to the doorway of the house, his exhaustion is apparent. He unlocks the door, comes into the kitchen, and thankfully lets his burden down, feeling the soreness of his palms. A word-sigh escapes his lips — it might be "Oh, boy, oh, boy." He closes the door then carries his cases out into the living room, through the draped kitchen doorway.*)

(*Linda, his wife, has stirred in her bed at the right. She gets out and puts on a robe, listening. Most often jovial, she has developed an iron repression of her exceptions to Willy's behavior — she more than loves him, she admires him, as though his mercurial nature, his temper, his massive dreams and little cruelties, served her only as sharp reminders of the turbulent longings within him, longings which she shares but lacks the temperament to utter and follow to their end.*)

LINDA (*hearing Willy outside the bedroom, calls with some trepidation*): Willy!

WILLY: It's all right. I came back.

LINDA: Why? What happened? (*Slight pause.*) Did something happen, Willy?

WILLY: No, nothing happened.

LINDA: You didn't smash the car, did you?

WILLY (*with casual irritation*): I said nothing happened. Didn't you hear me?

LINDA: Don't you feel well?

WILLY: I'm tired to the death. (*The flute has faded away. He sits on the bed beside her, a little numb.*) I couldn't make it. I just couldn't make it, Linda.

LINDA (*very carefully, delicately*): Where were you all day? You look terrible.

WILLY: I got as far as a little above Yonkers. I stopped for a cup of coffee. Maybe it was the coffee.

LINDA: What?

WILLY (*after a pause*): I suddenly couldn't drive anymore. The car kept going off onto the shoulder, y'know?

LINDA (*helpfully*): Oh. Maybe it was the steering again. I don't think Angelo knows the Studebaker.

WILLY: No, it's me, it's me. Suddenly I realize I'm goin' sixty miles an hour and I don't remember the last five minutes. I'm — I can't seem to — keep my mind to it.

LINDA: Maybe it's your glasses. You never went for your new glasses.

WILLY: No, I see everything. I came back ten miles an hour. It took me nearly four hours from Yonkers.

LINDA (*resigned*): Well, you'll just have to take a rest, Willy, you can't continue this way.

WILLY: I just got back from Florida.

LINDA: But you didn't rest your mind. Your mind is overactive, and the mind is what counts, dear.

WILLY: I'll start out in the morning. Maybe I'll feel better in the morning. (*She is taking off his shoes.*) These goddam arch supports are killing me.

LINDA: Take an aspirin. Should I get you an aspirin? It'll soothe you.

WILLY (*with wonder*): I was driving along, you understand? And I was fine. I was even observing the scenery. You can imagine, me looking at scenery, on the road every week of my life. But it's so beautiful up there, Linda, the trees are so thick, and the sun is warm. I opened the windshield and just let the warm air bathe over me. And then all of a sudden I'm goin' off the road! I'm tellin' ya, I absolutely forgot I was driving. If I'd've gone the other way over the white line I might've killed somebody. So I went on again — and five minutes later I'm dreamin' again, and I nearly — (*He presses two fingers against his eyes.*) I have such thoughts, I have such strange thoughts.

LINDA: Willy, dear. Talk to them again. There's no reason why you can't work in New York.

WILLY: They don't need me in New York. I'm the New England man. I'm vital in New England.

LINDA: But you're sixty years old. They can't expect you to keep traveling every week.

WILLY: I'll have to send a wire to Portland. I'm supposed to see Brown and Morrison tomorrow morning at ten o'clock to show the line. Goddammit, I could sell them! (*He starts putting on his jacket.*)

LINDA (*taking the jacket from him*): Why don't you go down to the place tomorrow and tell Howard you've simply got to work in New York? You're too accommodating, dear.

WILLY: If old man Wagner was alive I'd a been in charge of New York now! That man was a prince, he was a masterful man. But that boy of his, that Howard, he don't appreciate. When I went north the first time, the Wagner Company didn't know where New England was!

LINDA: Why don't you tell those things to Howard, dear?

WILLY (*encouraged*): I will, I definitely will. Is there any cheese?

LINDA: I'll make you a sandwich.

WILLY: No, go to sleep. I'll take some milk. I'll be up right away. The boys in?

LINDA: They're sleeping. Happy took Biff on a date tonight.

WILLY (*interested*): That so?

LINDA: It was so nice to see them shaving together, one behind the other, in the bathroom. And going out together. You notice? The whole house smells of shaving lotion.

WILLY: Figure it out. Work a lifetime to pay off a house. You finally own it, and there's nobody to live in it.

LINDA: Well, dear, life is a casting off. It's always that way.

WILLY: No, no, some people — some people accomplish something. Did Biff say anything after I went this morning?

LINDA: You shouldn't have criticized him, Willy, especially after he just got off the train. You mustn't lose your temper with him.

WILLY: When the hell did I lose my temper? I simply asked him if he was making any money. Is that a criticism?

LINDA: But, dear, how could he make any money?

WILLY (*worried and angered*): There's such an undercurrent in him. He became a moody man. Did he apologize when I left this morning?

LINDA: He was crestfallen, Willy. You know how he admires you. I think if he finds himself, then you'll both be happier and not fight any more.

WILLY: How can he find himself on a farm? Is that a life? A farmhand? In the beginning, when he was young, I thought, well, a young man, it's good for him to tramp around, take a lot of different jobs. But it's more than ten years now and he has yet to make thirty-five dollars a week!

LINDA: He's finding himself, Willy.

WILLY: Not finding yourself at the age of thirty-four is a disgrace!

LINDA: Shh!

WILLY: The trouble is he's lazy, goddammit!

LINDA: Willy, please!

WILLY: Biff is a lazy bum!

LINDA: They're sleeping. Get something to eat. Go on down.

WILLY: Why did he come home? I would like to know what brought him home.

LINDA: I don't know. I think he's still lost, Willy. I think he's very lost.

WILLY: Biff Loman is lost. In the greatest country in the world a young man with such — personal attractiveness, gets lost. And such a hard worker. There's one thing about Biff — he's not lazy.

LINDA: Never.

WILLY (*with pity and resolve*): I'll see him in the morning; I'll have a nice talk with him. I'll get him a job selling. He could be big in no time. My God! Remember how they used to follow him around in high school? When he smiled at one of them their faces lit up. When he walked down the street . . . (*He loses himself in reminiscences.*)

LINDA (*trying to bring him out of it*): Willy, dear, I got a new kind of American-type cheese today. It's whipped.

WILLY: Why do you get American when I like Swiss?

LINDA: I just thought you'd like a change —

WILLY: I don't want a change! I want Swiss cheese. Why am I always being contradicted?

LINDA (*with a covering laugh*): I thought it would be a surprise.

WILLY: Why don't you open a window in here, for God's sake?

LINDA (*with infinite patience*): They're all open, dear.

WILLY: The way they boxed us in here. Bricks and windows, windows and bricks.

LINDA: We should've bought the land next door.

WILLY: The street is lined with cars. There's not a breath of fresh air in the neighborhood. The grass don't grow anymore, you can't raise a carrot in the back yard. They should've had a law against apartment houses. Remember those two beautiful elm trees out there? When I and Biff hung the swing between them?

LINDA: Yeah, like being a million miles from the city.

WILLY: They should've arrested the builder for cutting those down. They massacred the neighborhood. (*Lost.*) More and more I think of those days, Linda. This time of year it was lilac and wisteria. And then the peonies would come out, and the daffodils. What fragrance in this room!

LINDA: Well, after all, people had to move somewhere.

WILLY: No, there's more people now.

LINDA: I don't think there's more people. I think —

WILLY: There's more people! That's what's ruining this country! Population is getting out of control. The competition is maddening! Smell the stink from that apartment house! And another one on the other side . . . How can they whip cheese?

(*On Willy's last line, Biff and Happy raise themselves up in their beds, listening.*)

LINDA: Go down, try it. And be quiet.

WILLY (*turning to Linda, guiltily*): You're not worried about me, are you, sweetheart?

BIFF: What's the matter?

HAPPY: Listen!

LINDA: You've got too much on the ball to worry about.

WILLY: You're my foundation and my support, Linda.

LINDA: Just try to relax, dear. You make mountains out of molehills.

WILLY: I won't fight with him any more. If he wants to go back to Texas, let him go.

LINDA: He'll find his way.

WILLY: Sure. Certain men just don't get started till later in life. Like Thomas Edison, I think. Or B. F. Goodrich. One of them was deaf. (*He starts for the bedroom doorway.*) I'll put my money on Biff.

LINDA: And Willy — if it's warm Sunday we'll drive in the country. And we'll open the windshield, and take lunch.

WILLY: No, the windshields don't open on the new cars.

LINDA: But you opened it today.

WILLY: Me? I didn't. (*He stops.*) Now isn't that peculiar! Isn't that a remarkable — (*He breaks off in amazement and fright as the flute is heard distantly.*)

LINDA: What, darling?

WILLY: That is the most remarkable thing.

LINDA: What, dear?

WILLY: I was thinking of the Chevvy. (*Slight pause.*) Nineteen twenty-eight . . . when I had that red Chevvy — (*Breaks off.*) That funny? I coulda sworn I was driving that Chevvy today.

LINDA: Well, that's nothing. Something must've reminded you.

WILLY: Remarkable. Ts. Remember those days? The way Biff used to simonize that car? The dealer refused to believe there was eighty thousand miles on it. (*He shakes his head.*) Heh! (*To Linda.*) Close your eyes, I'll be right up. (*He walks out of the bedroom.*)

HAPPY (*to Biff*): Jesus, maybe he smashed up the car again!

LINDA (*calling after Willy*): Be careful on the stairs, dear! The cheese is on the middle shelf! (*She turns, goes over to the bed, takes his jacket, and goes out of the bedroom.*)

(*Light has risen on the boys' room. Unseen, Willy is heard talking to himself, "Eighty thousand miles," and a little laugh. Biff gets out of bed, comes downstage a bit, and stands attentively. Biff is two years older than his brother Happy, well built, but in these days bears a worn air and seems less self-assured. He has succeeded less, and his dreams are stronger and less acceptable than Happy's. Happy is tall, powerfully made. Sexuality is like a visible color on him, or a scent that many women have discovered. He, like his brother, is lost, but in a different way, for he has never allowed himself to turn his face toward defeat and is thus more confused and hard-skinned, although seemingly more content.*)

HAPPY (*getting out of bed*): He's going to get his license taken away if he keeps that up. I'm getting nervous about him, y'know, Biff?

BIFF: His eyes are going.

HAPPY: No, I've driven with him. He sees all right. He just doesn't keep his mind on it. I drove into the city with him last week. He stops at a green light and then it turns red and he goes. (*He laughs.*)

BIFF: Maybe he's color-blind.

HAPPY: Pop? Why he's got the finest eye for color in the business. You know that.

BIFF (*sitting down on his bed*): I'm going to sleep.

HAPPY: You're not still sour on Dad, are you, Biff?

BIFF: He's all right, I guess.

WILLY (*underneath them, in the living room*): Yes, sir, eighty thousand miles — eighty-two thousand!

BIFF: You smoking?

HAPPY (*holding out a pack of cigarettes*): Want one?

BIFF (*taking a cigarette*): I can never sleep when I smell it.

WILLY: What a simonizing job, heh!

HAPPY (*with deep sentiment*): Funny, Biff, y'know? Us sleeping in here again? The old beds. (*He pats his bed affectionately.*) All the talk that went across those two beds, huh? Our whole lives.

BIFF: Yeah. Lotta dreams and plans.

HAPPY (*with a deep and masculine laugh*): About five hundred women would like to know what was said in this room.

(*They share a soft laugh.*)

BIFF: Remember that big Betsy something — what the hell was her name — over on Bushwick Avenue?

HAPPY (*combing his hair*): With the collie dog!

BIFF: That's the one. I got you in there, remember?

HAPPY: Yeah, that was my first time — I think. Boy, there was a pig. (*They laugh, almost crudely.*) You taught me everything I know about women. Don't forget that.

BIFF: I bet you forgot how bashful you used to be. Especially with girls.

HAPPY: Oh, I still am, Biff.

BIFF: Oh, go on.

HAPPY: I just control it, that's all. I think I got less bashful and you got more so. What happened, Biff? Where's the old humor, the old confidence? (*He shakes Biff's knee. Biff gets up and moves restlessly about the room.*) What's the matter?

BIFF: Why does Dad mock me all the time?

HAPPY: He's not mocking you, he —

BIFF: Everything I say there's a twist of mockery on his face. I can't get near him.

HAPPY: He just wants you to make good, that's all. I wanted to talk to you about Dad for a long time, Biff. Something's — happening to him. He — talks to himself.

BIFF: I noticed that this morning. But he always mumbled.

HAPPY: But not so noticeable. It got so embarrassing I sent him to Florida. And you know something? Most of the time he's talking to you.

BIFF: What's he say about me?

HAPPY: I can't make it out.

BIFF: What's he say about me?

HAPPY: I think the fact that you're not settled, that you're still kind of up in the air . . .

BIFF: There's one or two other things depressing him, Happy.

HAPPY: What do you mean?

BIFF: Never mind. Just don't lay it all to me.

HAPPY: But I think if you just got started — I mean — is there any future for you out there?

BIFF: I tell ya, Hap, I don't know what the future is. I don't know — what I'm supposed to want.

HAPPY: What do you mean?

BIFF: Well, I spent six or seven years after high school trying to work myself up. Shipping clerk, salesman, business of one kind or another. And it's a measly manner of existence. To get on that subway on the hot mornings in summer. To devote your whole life to keeping stock, or making phone calls, or selling or buying. To suffer fifty weeks of the year for the sake of a two-week vacation, when all you really desire is to be outdoors, with your shirt off. And always to have to get ahead of the next fella. And still — that's how you build a future.

HAPPY: Well, you really enjoy it on a farm? Are you content out there?

BIFF (*with rising agitation*): Hap, I've had twenty or thirty different kinds of jobs since I left home before the war, and it always turns out the same. I just realized it lately. In Nebraska when I herded cattle, and the Dakotas, and Arizona, and now in Texas. It's why I came home now, I guess, because I realized it. This farm I work on, it's spring there now, see? And they've got about fifteen new colts. There's nothing more inspiring or — beautiful than the sight of a mare and a new colt. And it's cool there now, see?

Texas is cool now, and it's spring. And whenever spring comes to where I am, I suddenly get the feeling, my God, I'm not gettin' anywhere! What the hell am I doing, playing around with horses, twenty-eight dollars a week! I'm thirty-four years old, I oughta be makin' my future. That's when I come running home. And now, I get here, and I don't know what to do with myself. (*After a pause.*) I've always made a point of not wasting my life, and every time I come back here I know that all I've done is to waste my life.

HAPPY: You're a poet, you know that, Biff? You're a — you're an idealist!

BIFF: No, I'm mixed up very bad. Maybe I oughta get married. Maybe I oughta get stuck into something. Maybe that's my trouble. I'm like a boy. I'm not married, I'm not in business, I just — I'm like a boy. Are you content, Hap? You're a success, aren't you? Are you content?

HAPPY: Hell, no!

BIFF: Why? You're making money, aren't you?

HAPPY (*moving about with energy, expressiveness*): All I can do now is wait for the merchandise manager to die. And suppose I get to be merchandise manager? He's a good friend of mine, and he just built a terrific estate on Long Island. And he lived there about two months and sold it, and now he's building another one. He can't enjoy it once it's finished. And I know that's just what I would do. I don't know what the hell I'm workin' for. Sometimes I sit in my apartment — all alone. And I think of the rent I'm paying. And it's crazy. But then, it's what I always wanted. My own apartment, a car, and plenty of women. And still, goddammit, I'm lonely.

BIFF (*with enthusiasm*): Listen, why don't you come out West with me?

HAPPY: You and I, heh?

BIFF: Sure, maybe we could buy a ranch. Raise cattle, use our muscles. Men built like we are should be working out in the open.

HAPPY (*avidly*): The Loman Brothers, heh?

BIFF (*with vast affection*): Sure, we'd be known all over the counties!

HAPPY (*enthralled*): That's what I dream about, Biff. Sometimes I want to just rip my clothes off in the middle of the store and outbox that goddam merchandise manager. I mean I can outbox, outrun and outlift anybody in that store, and I have to take orders from those common, petty sons-of-bitches till I can't stand it anymore.

BIFF: I'm tellin' you, kid, if you were with me I'd be happy out there.

HAPPY (*enthused*): See, Biff, everybody around me is so false that I'm constantly lowering my ideals . . .

BIFF: Baby, together we'd stand up for one another, we'd have someone to trust.

HAPPY: If I were around you —

BIFF: Hap, the trouble is we weren't brought up to grub for money. I don't know how to do it.

HAPPY: Neither can I!

BIFF: Then let's go!

HAPPY: The only thing is — what can you make out there?

BIFF: But look at your friend. Builds an estate and then hasn't the peace of mind to live in it.

HAPPY: Yeah, but when he walks into the store the waves part in front of him. That's fifty-two thousand dollars a year coming through the revolving door, and I got more in my pinky finger than he's got in his head.

BIFF: Yeah, but you just said —

HAPPY: I gotta show some of those pompous, self-important executives over there that Hap Loman can make the grade. I want to walk into the store the way he walks in. Then I'll go with you, Biff. We'll be together yet, I swear. But take those two we had tonight. Now weren't they gorgeous creatures?

BIFF: Yeah, yeah, most gorgeous I've had in years.

HAPPY: I get that any time I want, Biff. Whenever I feel disgusted. The only trouble is, it gets like bowling or something. I just keep knockin' them over and it doesn't mean anything. You still run around a lot?

BIFF: Naa. I'd like to find a girl — steady, somebody with substance.

HAPPY: That's what I long for.

BIFF: Go on! You'd never come home.

HAPPY: I would! Somebody with character, with resistance! Like Mom, y'know? You're gonna call me a bastard when I tell you this. That girl Charlotte I was with tonight is engaged to be married in five weeks. (*He tries on his new hat.*)

BIFF: No kiddin'!

HAPPY: Sure, the guy's in line for the vice-presidency of the store. I don't know what gets into me, maybe I just have an overdeveloped sense of competition or something, but I went and ruined her, and furthermore I can't get rid of her. And he's the third executive I've done that to. Isn't that a crummy characteristic? And to top it all, I go to their weddings! (*Indignantly, but laughing.*) Like I'm not supposed to take bribes. Manufacturers offer me a hundred-dollar bill now and then to throw an order their way. You know how honest I am, but it's like this girl, see. I hate myself for it. Because I don't want the girl, and, still, I take it and — I love it!

BIFF: Let's go to sleep.

HAPPY: I guess we didn't settle anything, heh?

BIFF: I just got one idea that I think I'm going to try.

HAPPY: What's that?

BIFF: Remember Bill Oliver?

HAPPY: Sure, Oliver is very big now. You want to work for him again?

BIFF: No, but when I quit he said something to me. He put his arm on my shoulder, and he said, "Biff, if you ever need anything, come to me."

HAPPY: I remember that. That sounds good.

BIFF: I think I'll go to see him. If I could get ten thousand or even seven or eight thousand dollars I could buy a beautiful ranch.

HAPPY: I bet he'd back you. 'Cause he thought highly of you, Biff. I mean, they all do. You're well liked, Biff. That's why I say to come back here, and we both have the apartment. And I'm tellin' you, Biff, any babe you want . . .

BIFF: No, with a ranch I could do the work I like and still be something. I just wonder though. I wonder if Oliver still thinks I stole that carton of basketballs.

HAPPY: Oh, he probably forgot that long ago. It's almost ten years. You're too sensitive. Anyway, he didn't really fire you.

BIFF: Well, I think he was going to. I think that's why I quit. I was never sure whether he knew or not. I know he thought the world of me, though. I was the only one he'd let lock up the place.

WILLY (*below*): You gonna wash the engine, Biff?

HAPPY: Shh!

(*Biff looks at Happy, who is gazing down, listening. Willy is mumbling in the parlor.*)

HAPPY: You hear that?

(*They listen. Willy laughs warmly.*)

BIFF (*growing angry*): Doesn't he know Mom can hear that?

WILLY: Don't get your sweater dirty, Biff!

(*A look of pain crosses Biff's face.*)

HAPPY: Isn't that terrible? Don't leave again, will you? You'll find a job here. You gotta stick around. I don't know what to do about him, it's getting embarrassing.

WILLY: What a simonizing job!

BIFF: Mom's hearing that!

WILLY: No kiddin', Biff, you got a date? Wonderful!

HAPPY: Go on to sleep. But talk to him in the morning, will you?

BIFF (*reluctantly getting into bed*): With her in the house. Brother!

HAPPY (*getting into bed*): I wish you'd have a good talk with him.

(*The light on their room begins to fade.*)

BIFF (*to himself in bed*): That selfish, stupid . . .

HAPPY: Sh . . . Sleep, Biff.

(*Their light is out. Well before they have finished speaking, Willy's form is dimly seen below in the darkened kitchen. He opens the refrigerator, searches in there, and takes out a bottle of milk. The apartment houses are fading out, and the entire house and surroundings become covered with leaves. Music insinuates itself as the leaves appear.*)

WILLY: Just wanna be careful with those girls, Biff, that's all. Don't make any promises. No promises of any kind. Because a girl, y'know, they always believe what you tell 'em, and you're very young, Biff, you're too young to be talking seriously to girls.

(*Light rises on the kitchen. Willy, talking, shuts the refrigerator door and comes downstage to the kitchen table. He pours milk into a glass. He is totally immersed in himself, smiling faintly.*)

WILLY: Too young entirely, Biff. You want to watch your schooling first. Then when you're all set, there'll be plenty of girls for a boy like you. (*He smiles broadly at a kitchen chair.*) That so? The girls pay for you? (*He laughs.*) Boy, you must really be makin' a hit.

(*Willy is gradually addressing — physically — a point offstage, speaking through the wall of the kitchen, and his voice has been rising in volume to that of a normal conversation.*)

WILLY: I been wondering why you polish the car so careful. Ha! Don't leave the hubcaps, boys. Get the chamois to the hubcaps. Happy, use newspaper on the windows, it's the easiest thing. Show him how to do it, Biff! You see, Happy? Pad it up, use it like a pad. That's it, that's it, good work. You're doin' all right, Hap. (*He pauses, then nods in approbation for a few seconds, then looks upward.*) Biff, first thing we gotta do when we get time is clip that big branch over the house. Afraid it's gonna fall in a storm and hit the roof. Tell you what. We get a rope and sling her around, and then we climb up there with a couple of saws and take her down. Soon as you finish the car, boys, I wanna see ye. I got a surprise for you, boys.

BIFF (*offstage*): Whatta ya got, Dad?

WILLY: No, you finish first. Never leave a job till you're finished — remember that. (*Looking toward the "big trees."*) Biff, up in Albany I saw a beautiful hammock. I think I'll buy it next trip, and we'll hang it right between those two elms. Wouldn't that be something? Just swingin' there under those branches. Boy, that would be . . .

(*Young Biff and Young Happy appear from the direction Willy was addressing. Happy carries rags and a pail of water. Biff, wearing a sweater with a block "S," carries a football.*)

BIFF (*pointing in the direction of the car offstage*): How's that, Pop, professional?

WILLY: Terrific. Terrific job, boys. Good work, Biff.

HAPPY: Where's the surprise, Pop?

WILLY: In the back seat of the car.

HAPPY: Boy! (*He runs off.*)

BIFF: What is it, Dad? Tell me, what'd you buy?

WILLY (*laughing, cuffs him*): Never mind, something I want you to have.

BIFF (*turns and starts off*): What is it, Hap?

HAPPY (*offstage*): It's a punching bag!

BIFF: Oh, Pop!

WILLY: It's got Gene Tunney's signature on it!

(*Happy runs onstage with a punching bag.*)

BIFF: Gee, how'd you know we wanted a punching bag?

Biff (Kevin Anderson), Willy (Brian Dennehy), and Happy (Ted Koch) in a bright moment in
Robert Falls's 1999 Broadway revival of *Death of a Salesman*.

WILLY: Well, it's the finest thing for the timing.

HAPPY (*lies down on his back and pedals with his feet*):
I'm losing weight, you notice, Pop?

WILLY (*to Happy*): Jumping rope is good too.

BIFF: Did you see the new football I got?

WILLY (*examining the ball*): Where'd you get a new
ball?

BIFF: The coach told me to practice my passing.

WILLY: That so? And he gave you the ball, heh?

BIFF: Well, I borrowed it from the locker room. (*He
laughs confidentially.*)

WILLY (*laughing with him at the theft*): I want you to
return that.

HAPPY: I told you he wouldn't like it!

BIFF (*angrily*): Well, I'm bringing it back!

WILLY (*stopping the incipient argument, to Happy*):
Sure, he's gotta practice with a regulation ball,
doesn't he? (*To Biff.*) Coach'll probably congratulate
you on your initiative!

BIFF: Oh, he keeps congratulating my initiative all the
time, Pop.

WILLY: That's because he likes you. If somebody else

took that ball there'd be an uproar. So what's the
report, boys, what's the report?

BIFF: Where'd you go this time, Dad? Gee we were lonesome for you.

WILLY (*pleased, puts an arm around each boy and they
come down to the apron*): Lonesome, heh?

BIFF: Missed you every minute.

WILLY: Don't say? Tell you a secret, boys. Don't breathe
it to a soul. Someday I'll have my own business, and
I'll never have to leave home anymore.

HAPPY: Like Uncle Charley, heh?

WILLY: Bigger than Uncle Charley! Because Charley is
not — liked. He's liked, but he's not — well liked.

BIFF: Where'd you go this time, Dad?

WILLY: Well, I got on the road, and I went north to
Providence. Met the Mayor.

BIFF: The Mayor of Providence!

WILLY: He was sitting in the hotel lobby.

BIFF: What'd he say?

WILLY: He said, "Morning!" And I said, "You got a fine
city here, Mayor." And then he had coffee with me.
And then I went to Waterbury. Waterbury is a fine

city. Big clock city, the famous Waterbury clock. Sold a nice bill there. And then Boston — Boston is the cradle of the Revolution. A fine city. And a couple of other towns in Mass., and on to Portland and Bangor and straight home!

BIFF: Gee, I'd love to go with you sometime, Dad.

WILLY: Soon as summer comes.

HAPPY: Promise?

WILLY: You and Hap and I, and I'll show you all the towns. America is full of beautiful towns and fine, upstanding people. And they know me, boys, they know me up and down New England. The finest people. And when I bring you fellas up, there'll be open sesame for all of us, 'cause one thing, boys: I have friends. I can park my car in any street in New England, and the cops protect it like their own. This summer, heh?

BIFF AND HAPPY (*together*): Yeah! You bet!

WILLY: We'll take our bathing suits.

HAPPY: We'll carry your bags, Pop!

WILLY: Oh, won't that be something! Me comin' into the Boston stores with you boys carryin' my bags. What a sensation!

(*Biff is prancing around, practicing passing the ball.*)

WILLY: You nervous, Biff, about the game?

BIFF: Not if you're gonna be there.

WILLY: What do they say about you in school, now that they made you captain?

HAPPY: There's a crowd of girls behind him every time the classes change.

BIFF (*taking Willy's hand*): This Saturday, Pop, this Saturday — just for you, I'm going to break through for a touchdown.

HAPPY: You're supposed to pass.

BIFF: I'm takin' one play for Pop. You watch me, Pop, and when I take off my helmet, that means I'm breakin' out. Then you watch me crash through that line!

WILLY (*kisses Biff*): Oh, wait'll I tell this in Boston!

(*Bernard enters in knickers. He is younger than Biff, earnest and loyal, a worried boy.*)

BERNARD: Biff, where are you? You're supposed to study with me today.

WILLY: Hey, looka Bernard. What're you lookin' so anemic about, Bernard?

BERNARD: He's gotta study, Uncle Willy. He's got Regents next week.

HAPPY (*tauntingly, spinning Bernard around*): Let's box, Bernard!

BERNARD: Biff! (*He gets away from Happy.*) Listen, Biff, I heard Mr. Birnbaum say that if you don't start studyin' math he's gonna flunk you, and you won't graduate. I heard him!

WILLY: You better study with him, Biff. Go ahead now.

BERNARD: I heard him!

BIFF: Oh, Pop, you didn't see my sneakers! (*He holds up a foot for Willy to look at.*)

WILLY: Hey, that's a beautiful job of printing!

BERNARD (*wiping his glasses*): Just because he printed University of Virginia on his sneakers doesn't mean they've got to graduate him, Uncle Willy!

WILLY (*angrily*): What're you talking about? With scholarships to three universities they're gonna flunk him?

BERNARD: But I heard Mr. Birnbaum say —

WILLY: Don't be a pest, Bernard! (*To his boys.*) What an anemic!

BERNARD: Okay, I'm waiting for you in my house, Biff.

(*Bernard goes off. The Lomans laugh.*)

WILLY: Bernard is not well liked, is he?

BIFF: He's liked, but he's not well liked.

HAPPY: That's right, Pop.

WILLY: That's just what I mean. Bernard can get the best marks in school, y'understand, but when he gets out in the business world, y'understand, you are going to be five times ahead of him. That's why I thank Almighty God you're both built like Adonises. Because the man who makes an appearance in the business world, the man who creates personal interest, is the man who gets ahead. Be liked and you will never want. You take me, for instance. I never have to wait in line to see a buyer. "Willy Loman is here!" That's all they have to know, and I go right through.

BIFF: Did you knock them dead, Pop?

WILLY: Knocked 'em cold in Providence, slaughtered 'em in Boston.

HAPPY (*on his back, pedaling again*): I'm losing weight, you notice, Pop?

(*Linda enters as of old, a ribbon in her hair, carrying a basket of washing.*)

LINDA (*with youthful energy*): Hello, dear!

WILLY: Sweetheart!

LINDA: How'd the Chevvy run?

WILLY: Chevrolet, Linda, is the greatest car ever built. (*To the boys.*) Since when do you let your mother carry wash up the stairs?

BIFF: Grab hold there, boy!

HAPPY: Where to, Mom?

LINDA: Hang them up on the line. And you better go down to your friends, Biff. The cellar is full of boys. They don't know what to do with themselves.

BIFF: Ah, when Pop comes home they can wait!

WILLY (*laughs appreciatively*): You better go down and tell them what to do, Biff.

BIFF: I think I'll have them sweep out the furnace room.

WILLY: Good work, Biff.

BIFF (*goes through wall-line of kitchen to doorway at back and calls down*): Fellas! Everybody sweep out the furnace room! I'll be right down!

VOICES: All right! Okay, Biff.

BIFF: George and Sam and Frank, come out back! We're hangin' up the wash! Come on, Hap, on the double! (*He and Happy carry out the basket.*)

LINDA: The way they obey him!

WILLY: Well, that's training, the training. I'm tellin' you,

I was sellin' thousands and thousands, but I had to come home.

LINDA: Oh, the whole block'll be at that game. Did you sell anything?

WILLY: I did five hundred gross in Providence and seven hundred gross in Boston.

LINDA: No! Wait a minute, I've got a pencil. (*She pulls pencil and paper out of her apron pocket.*) That makes your commission . . . Two hundred — my God! Two hundred and twelve dollars!

WILLY: Well, I didn't figure it yet, but . . .

LINDA: How much did you do?

WILLY: Well, I — I did — about a hundred and eighty gross in Providence. Well, no — it came to — roughly two hundred gross on the whole trip.

LINDA (*without hesitation*): Two hundred gross. That's . . . (*She figures.*)

WILLY: The trouble was that three of the stores were half-closed for inventory in Boston. Otherwise I woulda broke records.

LINDA: Well, it makes seventy dollars and some pennies. That's very good.

WILLY: What do we owe?

LINDA: Well, on the first there's sixteen dollars on the refrigerator —

WILLY: Why sixteen?

LINDA: Well, the fan belt broke, so it was a dollar eighty.

WILLY: But it's brand new.

LINDA: Well, the man said that's the way it is. Till they work themselves in, y'know.

(*They move through the wall-line into the kitchen.*)

WILLY: I hope we didn't get stuck on that machine.

LINDA: They got the biggest ads of any of them!

WILLY: I know, it's a fine machine. What else?

LINDA: Well, there's nine-sixty for the washing machine. And for the vacuum cleaner there's three and a half due on the fifteenth. Then the roof, you got twenty-one dollars remaining.

WILLY: It don't leak, does it?

LINDA: No, they did a wonderful job. Then you owe Frank for the carburetor.

WILLY: I'm not going to pay that man! That goddam Chevrolet, they ought to prohibit the manufacture of that car!

LINDA: Well, you owe him three and a half. And odds and ends, comes to around a hundred and twenty dollars by the fifteenth.

WILLY: A hundred and twenty dollars! My God, if business don't pick up I don't know what I'm gonna do!

LINDA: Well, next week you'll do better.

WILLY: Oh, I'll knock 'em dead next week. I'll go to Hartford. I'm very well liked in Hartford. You know, the trouble is, Linda, people don't seem to take to me.

(*They move onto the forestage.*)

LINDA: Oh, don't be foolish.

WILLY: I know it when I walk in. They seem to laugh at me.

LINDA: Why? Why would they laugh at you? Don't talk that way, Willy.

(*Willy moves to the edge of the stage. Linda goes into the kitchen and starts to darn stockings.*)

WILLY: I don't know the reason for it, but they just pass me by. I'm not noticed.

LINDA: But you're doing wonderful, dear. You're making seventy to a hundred dollars a week.

WILLY: But I gotta be at it ten, twelve hours a day. Other men — I don't know — they do it easier. I don't know why — I can't stop myself — I talk too much. A man oughta come in with a few words. One thing about Charley. He's a man of few words, and they respect him.

LINDA: You don't talk too much, you're just lively.

WILLY (*smiling*): Well, I figure, what the hell, life is short, a couple of jokes. (*To himself.*) I joke too much! (*The smile goes.*)

LINDA: Why? You're —

WILLY: I'm fat. I'm very — foolish to look at, Linda. I didn't tell you, but Christmas time I happened to be calling on F. H. Stewarts, and a salesman I know, as I was going in to see the buyer I heard him say something about — walrus. And I — I cracked him right across the face. I won't take that. I simply will not take that. But they do laugh at me. I know that.

LINDA: Darling . . .

WILLY: I gotta overcome it. I know I gotta overcome it. I'm not dressing to advantage, maybe.

LINDA: Willy, darling, you're the handsomest man in the world —

WILLY: Oh, no, Linda.

LINDA: To me you are. (*Slight pause.*) The handsomest.

(*From the darkness is heard the laughter of a woman. Willy doesn't turn to it, but it continues through Linda's lines.*)

LINDA: And the boys, Willy. Few men are idolized by their children the way you are.

(*Music is heard as behind a scrim, to the left of the house, The Woman, dimly seen, is dressing.*)

WILLY (*with great feeling*): You're the best there is, Linda, you're a pal, you know that? On the road — on the road I want to grab you sometimes and just kiss the life outa you.

(*The laughter is loud now, and he moves into a brightening area at the left, where The Woman has come from behind the scrim and is standing, putting on her hat, looking into a "mirror" and laughing.*)

WILLY: 'Cause I get so lonely — especially when business is bad and there's nobody to talk to. I get the feeling that I'll never sell anything again, that I won't make a living for you, or a business, a business for the boys. (*He talks through The Woman's subsiding laughter; The Woman primps at the "mirror."*) There's so much I want to make for —

THE WOMAN: Me? You didn't make me, Willy. I picked you.

WILLY (*pleased*): You picked me?

THE WOMAN (*who is quite proper-looking, Willy's age*): I did. I've been sitting at that desk watching all the salesmen go by, day in, day out. But you've got such a sense of humor, and we do have such a good time together, don't we?

WILLY: Sure, sure. (*He takes her in his arms.*) Why do you have to go now?

THE WOMAN: It's two o'clock . . .

WILLY: No, come on in! (*He pulls her.*)

THE WOMAN: . . . my sisters'll be scandalized. When'll you be back?

WILLY: Oh, two weeks about. Will you come up again?

THE WOMAN: Sure thing. You do make me laugh. It's good for me. (*She squeezes his arm, kisses him.*) And I think you're a wonderful man.

WILLY: You picked me, heh?

THE WOMAN: Sure. Because you're so sweet. And such a kidder.

WILLY: Well, I'll see you next time I'm in Boston.

THE WOMAN: I'll put you right through to the buyers.

WILLY (*slapping her bottom*): Right. Well, bottoms up!

THE WOMAN (*slaps him gently and laughs*): You just kill me, Willy. (*He suddenly grabs her and kisses her roughly.*) You kill me. And thanks for the stockings. I love a lot of stockings. Well, good night.

WILLY: Good night. And keep your pores open!

THE WOMAN: Oh, Willy!

(*The Woman bursts out laughing, and Linda's laughter blends in. The Woman disappears into the dark. Now the area at the kitchen table brightens. Linda is sitting where she was at the kitchen table, but now is mending a pair of her silk stockings.*)

LINDA: You are, Willy. The handsomest man. You've got no reason to feel that —

WILLY (*coming out of The Woman's dimming area and going over to Linda*): I'll make it all up to you, Linda, I'll —

LINDA: There's nothing to make up, dear. You're doing fine, better than —

WILLY (*noticing her mending*): What's that?

LINDA: Just mending my stockings. They're so expensive —

WILLY (*angrily, taking them from her*): I won't have you mending stockings in this house! Now throw them out!

(*Linda puts the stockings in her pocket.*)

BERNARD (*entering on the run*): Where is he? If he doesn't study!

WILLY (*moving to the forestage, with great agitation*): You'll give him the answers!

BERNARD: I do, but I can't on a Regents! That's a state exam! They're liable to arrest me!

WILLY: Where is he? I'll whip him, I'll whip him!

LINDA: And he'd better give back that football, Willy, it's not nice.

WILLY: Biff! Where is he? Why is he taking everything?

LINDA: He's too rough with the girls, Willy. All the mothers are afraid of him!

WILLY: I'll whip him!

BERNARD: He's driving the car without a license!

(*The Woman's laugh is heard.*)

WILLY: Shut up!

LINDA: All the mothers —

WILLY: Shut up!

BERNARD (*backing quietly away and out*): Mr. Birnbaum says he's stuck up.

WILLY: Get outa here!

BERNARD: If he doesn't buckle down he'll flunk math! (*He goes off.*)

LINDA: He's right, Willy, you've gotta —

WILLY (*exploding at her*): There's nothing the matter with him! You want him to be a worm like Bernard? He's got spirit, personality . . .

(*As he speaks, Linda, almost in tears, exits into the living room. Willy is alone in the kitchen, wilting and staring. The leaves are gone. It is night again, and the apartment houses look down from behind.*)

WILLY: Loaded with it. Loaded! What is he stealing? He's giving it back, isn't he? Why is he stealing? What did I tell him? I never in my life told him anything but decent things.

(*Happy in pajamas has come down the stairs; Willy suddenly becomes aware of Happy's presence.*)

HAPPY: Let's go now, come on.

WILLY (*sitting down at the kitchen table*): Huh! Why did she have to wax the floors herself? Everytime she waxes the floors she keels over. She knows that!

HAPPY: Shh! Take it easy. What brought you back tonight?

WILLY: I got an awful scare. Nearly hit a kid in Yonkers. God! Why didn't I go to Alaska with my brother Ben that time! Ben! That man was a genius, that man was success incarnate! What a mistake! He begged me to go.

HAPPY: Well, there's no use in —

WILLY: You guys! There was a man started with the clothes on his back and ended up with diamond mines!

HAPPY: Boy, someday I'd like to know how he did it.

WILLY: What's the mystery? The man knew what he wanted and went out and got it! Walked into a jungle, and comes out, the age of twenty-one, and he's rich! The world is an oyster, but you don't crack it open on a mattress!

HAPPY: Pop, I told you I'm gonna retire you for life.

WILLY: You'll retire me for life on seventy goddam dollars a week? And your women and your car and your apartment, and you'll retire me for life! Christ's sake,

I couldn't get past Yonkers today! Where are you guys, where are you? The woods are burning! I can't drive a car!

(*Charley has appeared in the doorway. He is a large man, slow of speech, laconic, immovable. In all he says, despite what he says, there is pity, and, now, trepidation. He has a robe over pajamas, slippers on his feet. He enters the kitchen.*)

CHARLEY: Everything all right?
HAPPY: Yeah, Charley, everything's . . .
WILLY: What's the matter?
CHARLEY: I heard some noise. I thought something happened. Can't we do something about the walls? You sneeze in here, and in my house hats blow off.
HAPPY: Let's go to bed, Dad. Come on.

(*Charley signals to Happy to go.*)

WILLY: You go ahead, I'm not tired at the moment.
HAPPY (*to Willy*): Take it easy, huh? (*He exits.*)
WILLY: What're you doin' up?
CHARLEY (*sitting down at the kitchen table opposite Willy*): Couldn't sleep good. I had a heartburn.
WILLY: Well, you don't know how to eat.
CHARLEY: I eat with my mouth.
WILLY: No, you're ignorant. You gotta know about vitamins and things like that.
CHARLEY: Come on, let's shoot. Tire you out a little.
WILLY (*hesitantly*): All right. You got cards?
CHARLEY (*taking a deck from his pocket*): Yeah, I got them. Someplace. What is it with those vitamins?
WILLY (*dealing*): They build up your bones. Chemistry.
CHARLEY: Yeah, but there's no bones in a heartburn.
WILLY: What are you talkin' about? Do you know the first thing about it?
CHARLEY: Don't get insulted.
WILLY: Don't talk about something you don't know anything about.

(*They are playing. Pause.*)

CHARLEY: What're you doin' home?
WILLY: A little trouble with the car.
CHARLEY: Oh. (*Pause.*) I'd like to take a trip to California.
WILLY: Don't say.
CHARLEY: You want a job?
WILLY: I got a job, I told you that. (*After a slight pause.*) What the hell are you offering me a job for?
CHARLEY: Don't get insulted.
WILLY: Don't insult me.
CHARLEY: I don't see no sense in it. You don't have to go on this way.
WILLY: I got a good job. (*Slight pause.*) What do you keep comin' in here for?
CHARLEY: You want me to go?
WILLY (*after a pause, withering*): I can't understand it. He's going back to Texas again. What the hell is that?
CHARLEY: Let him go.

WILLY: I got nothin' to give him, Charley, I'm clean, I'm clean.
CHARLEY: He won't starve. None a them starve. Forget about him.
WILLY: Then what have I got to remember?
CHARLEY: You take it too hard. To hell with it. When a deposit bottle is broken you don't get your nickel back.
WILLY: That's easy enough for you to say.
CHARLEY: That ain't easy for me to say.
WILLY: Did you see the ceiling I put up in the living room?
CHARLEY: Yeah, that's a piece of work. To put up a ceiling is a mystery to me. How do you do it?
WILLY: What's the difference?
CHARLEY: Well, talk about it.
WILLY: You gonna put up a ceiling?
CHARLEY: How could I put up a ceiling?
WILLY: Then what the hell are you bothering me for?
CHARLEY: You're insulted again.
WILLY: A man who can't handle tools is not a man. You're disgusting.
CHARLEY: Don't call me disgusting, Willy.

(*Uncle Ben, carrying a valise and an umbrella, enters the forestage from around the right corner of the house. He is a stolid man, in his sixties, with a mustache and an authoritative air. He is utterly certain of his destiny, and there is an aura of far places about him. He enters exactly as Willy speaks.*)

WILLY: I'm getting awfully tired, Ben.

(*Ben's music is heard. Ben looks around at everything.*)

CHARLEY: Good, keep playing; you'll sleep better. Did you call me Ben?

(*Ben looks at his watch.*)

WILLY: That's funny. For a second there you reminded me of my brother Ben.
BEN: I only have a few minutes. (*He strolls, inspecting the place. Willy and Charley continue playing.*)
CHARLEY: You never heard from him again, heh? Since that time?
WILLY: Didn't Linda tell you? Couple of weeks ago we got a letter from his wife in Africa. He died.
CHARLEY: That so.
BEN (*chuckling*): So this is Brooklyn, eh?
CHARLEY: Maybe you're in for some of his money.
WILLY: Naa, he had seven sons. There's just one opportunity I had with that man . . .
BEN: I must make a train, William. There are several properties I'm looking at in Alaska.
WILLY: Sure, sure! If I'd gone with him to Alaska that time, everything would've been totally different.
CHARLIE: Go on, you'd froze to death up there.
WILLY: What're you talking about?
BEN: Opportunity is tremendous in Alaska, William. Surprised you're not up there.

WILLY: Sure, tremendous.

CHARLEY: Heh?

WILLY: There was the only man I ever met who knew the answers.

CHARLEY: Who?

BEN: How are you all?

WILLY (*taking a pot, smiling*): Fine, fine.

CHARLEY: Pretty sharp tonight.

BEN: Is Mother living with you?

WILLY: No, she died a long time ago.

CHARLEY: Who?

BEN: That's too bad. Fine specimen of a lady, Mother.

WILLY (*to Charley*): Heh?

BEN: I'd hoped to see the old girl.

CHARLEY: Who died?

BEN: Heard anything from Father, have you?

WILLY (*unnerved*): What do you mean, who died?

CHARLEY (*taking a pot*): What're you talkin' about?

BEN (*looking at his watch*): William, it's half-past eight!

WILLY (*as though to dispel his confusion he angrily stops Charley's hand*): That's my build!

CHARLEY: I put the ace —

WILLY: If you don't know how to play the game I'm not gonna throw my money away on you!

CHARLEY (*rising*): It was my ace, for God's sake!

WILLY: I'm through, I'm through!

BEN: When did Mother die?

WILLY: Long ago. Since the beginning you never knew how to play cards.

CHARLEY (*picks up the cards and goes to the door*): All right! Next time I'll bring a deck with five aces.

WILLY: I don't play that kind of game!

CHARLEY (*turning to him*): You ought to be ashamed of yourself!

WILLY: Yeah?

CHARLEY: Yeah! (*He goes out.*)

WILLY (*slamming the door after him*): Ignoramus!

BEN (*as Willy comes toward him through the wall-line of the kitchen*): So you're William.

WILLY (*shaking Ben's hand*): Ben! I've been waiting for you so long! What's the answer? How did you do it?

BEN: Oh, there's a story in that.

(*Linda enters the forestage, as of old, carrying the wash basket.*)

LINDA: Is this Ben?

BEN (*gallantly*): How do you do, my dear.

LINDA: Where've you been all these years? Willy's always wondered why you —

WILLY (*pulling Ben away from her impatiently*): Where is Dad? Didn't you follow him? How did you get started?

BEN: Well, I don't know how much you remember.

WILLY: Well, I was just a baby, of course, only three or four years old —

BEN: Three years and eleven months.

WILLY: What a memory, Ben!

BEN: I have many enterprises, William, and I have never kept books.

WILLY: I remember I was sitting under the wagon in — was it Nebraska?

BEN: It was South Dakota, and I gave you a bunch of wild flowers.

WILLY: I remember you walking away down some open road.

BEN (*laughing*): I was going to find Father in Alaska.

WILLY: Where is he?

BEN: At that age I had a very faulty view of geography, William. I discovered after a few days that I was heading due south, so instead of Alaska, I ended up in Africa.

LINDA: Africa!

WILLY: The Gold Coast!

BEN: Principally diamond mines.

LINDA: Diamond mines!

BEN: Yes, my dear. But I've only a few minutes —

WILLY: No! Boys! Boys! (*Young Biff and Happy appear.*) Listen to this. This is your Uncle Ben, a great man! Tell my boys, Ben!

BEN: Why, boys, when I was seventeen I walked into the jungle, and when I was twenty-one I walked out. (*He laughs.*) And by God I was rich.

WILLY (*to the boys*): You see what I been talking about? The greatest things can happen!

BEN (*glancing at his watch*): I have an appointment in Ketchikan Tuesday week.

WILLY: No, Ben! Please tell about Dad. I want my boys to hear. I want them to know the kind of stock they spring from. All I remember is a man with a big beard, and I was in Mamma's lap, sitting around a fire, and some kind of high music.

BEN: His flute. He played the flute.

WILLY: Sure, the flute, that's right!

(*New music is heard, a high, rollicking tune.*)

BEN: Father was a very great and a very wild-hearted man. We would start in Boston, and he'd toss the whole family into the wagon, and then he'd drive the team right across the country; through Ohio, and Indiana, Michigan, Illinois, and all the Western states. And we'd stop in the towns and sell the flutes that he'd made on the way. Great inventor Father. With one gadget he made more in a week than a man like you could make in a lifetime.

WILLY: That's just the way I'm bringing them up, Ben — rugged, well liked, all-around.

BEN: Yeah? (*To Biff.*) Hit that, boy — hard as you can. (*He pounds his stomach.*)

BIFF: Oh, no, sir!

BEN (*taking boxing stance*): Come on, get to me! (*He laughs.*)

WILLY: Go to it, Biff! Go ahead, show him!

BIFF: Okay! (*He cocks his fists and starts in.*)

LINDA (*to Willy*): Why must he fight, dear?

BEN (*sparring with Biff*): Good boy! Good boy!

WILLY: How's that, Ben, heh?

HAPPY: Give him the left, Biff!

LINDA: Why are you fighting?

BEN: Good boy! (*Suddenly comes in, trips Biff, and stands over him, the point of his umbrella poised over Biff's eye.*)

LINDA: Look out, Biff!

BIFF: Gee!

BEN (*patting Biff's knee*): Never fight fair with a stranger, boy. You'll never get out of the jungle that way. (*Taking Linda's hand and bowing.*) It was an honor and a pleasure to meet you, Linda.

LINDA (*withdrawing her hand coldly, frightened*): Have a nice — trip.

BEN (*to Willy*): And good luck with your — what do you do?

WILLY: Selling.

BEN: Yes. Well . . . (*He raises his hand in farewell to all.*)

WILLY: No, Ben, I don't want you to think . . . (*He takes Ben's arm to show him.*) It's Brooklyn, I know, but we hunt too.

BEN: Really, now.

WILLY: Oh, sure, there's snakes and rabbits and — that's why I moved out here. Why, Biff can fell any one of these trees in no time! Boys! Go right over to where they're building the apartment house and get some sand. We're gonna rebuild the entire front stoop right now! Watch this, Ben!

BIFF: Yes, sir! On the double, Hap!

HAPPY (*as he and Biff run off*): I lost weight, Pop, you notice?

(*Charley enters in knickers, even before the boys are gone.*)

CHARLEY: Listen, if they steal any more from that building the watchman'll put the cops on them!

LINDA (*to Willy*): Don't let Biff . . .

(*Ben laughs lustily.*)

WILLY: You shoulda seen the lumber they brought home last week. At least a dozen six-by-tens worth all kinds a money.

CHARLEY: Listen, if that watchman —

WILLY: I gave them hell, understand. But I got a couple of fearless characters there.

CHARLEY: Willy, the jails are full of fearless characters.

BEN (*clapping Willy on the back, with a laugh at Charley*): And the stock exchange, friend!

WILLY (*joining in Ben's laughter*): Where are the rest of your pants?

CHARLEY: My wife bought them.

WILLY: Now all you need is a golf club and you can go upstairs and go to sleep. (*To Ben.*) Great athlete! Between him and his son Bernard they can't hammer a nail!

BERNARD (*rushing in*): The watchman's chasing Biff!

WILLY (*angrily*): Shut up! He's not stealing anything!

LINDA (*alarmed, hurrying off left*): Where is he? Biff, dear! (*She exits.*)

WILLY (*moving toward the left, away from Ben*): There's nothing wrong. What's the matter with you?

BEN: Nervy boy. Good!

WILLY (*laughing*): Oh, nerves of iron, that Biff!

CHARLEY: Don't know what it is. My New England man comes back and he's bleedin', they murdered him up there.

WILLY: It's contacts, Charley, I got important contacts!

CHARLEY (*sarcastically*): Glad to hear it, Willy. Come in later, we'll shoot a little casino. I'll take some of your Portland money. (*He laughs at Willy and exits.*)

WILLY (*turning to Ben*): Business is bad, it's murderous. But not for me, of course.

BEN: I'll stop by on my way back to Africa.

WILLY (*longingly*): Can't you stay a few days? You're just what I need, Ben, because I — I have a fine position here, but I — well, Dad left when I was such a baby and I never had a chance to talk to him and I still feel — kind of temporary about myself.

BEN: I'll be late for my train.

(*They are at opposite ends of the stage.*)

WILLY: Ben, my boys — can't we talk? They'd go into the jaws of hell for me, see, but I —

BEN: William, you're being first-rate with your boys. Outstanding, manly chaps!

WILLY (*hanging on to his words*): Oh, Ben, that's good to hear! Because sometimes I'm afraid that I'm not teaching them the right kind of — Ben, how should I teach them?

BEN (*giving great weight to each word, and with a certain vicious audacity*): William, when I walked into the jungle, I was seventeen. When I walked out I was twenty-one. And, by God, I was rich! (*He goes off into darkness around the right corner of the house.*)

WILLY: . . . was rich! That's just the spirit I want to imbue them with! To walk into a jungle! I was right! I was right! I was right!

(*Ben is gone, but Willy is still speaking to him as Linda, in nightgown and robe, enters the kitchen, glances around for Willy, then goes to the door of the house, looks out and sees him. Comes down to his left. He looks at her.*)

LINDA: Willy, dear? Willy?

WILLY: I was right!

LINDA: Did you have some cheese? (*He can't answer.*) It's very late, darling. Come to bed, heh?

WILLY (*looking straight up*): Gotta break your neck to see a star in this yard.

LINDA: You coming in?

WILLY: Whatever happened to that diamond watch fob? Remember? When Ben came from Africa that time? Didn't he give me a watch fob with a diamond in it?

LINDA: You pawned it, dear. Twelve, thirteen years ago. For Biff's radio correspondence course.

WILLY: Gee, that was a beautiful thing. I'll take a walk.

LINDA: But you're in your slippers.

WILLY (*starting to go around the house at the left*): I was right! I was! (*Half to Linda, as he goes, shaking his head.*) What a man! There was a man worth talking to. I was right!

LINDA (*calling after* Willy): But in your slippers, Willy!

(*Willy is almost gone when Biff, in his pajamas, comes down the stairs and enters the kitchen.*)

BIFF: What is he doing out there?

LINDA: Sh!

BIFF: God Almighty, Mom, how long has he been doing this?

LINDA: Don't, he'll hear you.

BIFF: What the hell is the matter with him?

LINDA: It'll pass by morning.

BIFF: Shouldn't we do anything?

LINDA: Oh, my dear, you should do a lot of things, but there's nothing to do, so go to sleep.

(*Happy comes down the stair and sits on the steps.*)

HAPPY: I never heard him so loud, Mom.

LINDA: Well, come around more often, you'll hear him. (*She sits down at the table and mends the lining of Willy's jacket.*)

BIFF: Why didn't you ever write me about this, Mom?

LINDA: How would I write to you? For over three months you had no address.

BIFF: I was on the move. But you know I thought of you all the time. You know that, don't you, pal?

LINDA: I know, dear, I know. But he likes to have a letter. Just to know that there's still a possibility for better things.

BIFF: He's not like this all the time, is he?

LINDA: It's when you come home he's always the worst.

BIFF: When I come home?

LINDA: When you write you're coming, he's all smiles and talks about the future, and — he's just wonderful. And then the closer you seem to come, the more shaky he gets, and then, by the time you get here, he's arguing, and he seems angry at you. I think it's just that maybe he can't bring himself to — to open up to you. Why are you so hateful to each other? Why is that?

BIFF (*evasively*): I'm not hateful, Mom.

LINDA: But you no sooner come in the door than you're fighting!

BIFF: I don't know why. I mean to change. I'm tryin', Mom, you understand?

LINDA: Are you home to stay now?

BIFF: I don't know. I want to look around, see what's goin'.

LINDA: Biff, you can't look around all your life, can you?

BIFF: I just can't take hold, Mom. I can't take hold of some kind of a life.

LINDA: Biff, a man is not a bird, to come and go with the springtime.

BIFF: Your hair . . . (*He touches her hair.*) Your hair got so gray.

LINDA: Oh, it's been gray since you were in high school. I just stopped dyeing it, that's all.

BIFF: Dye it again, will ye? I don't want my pal looking old. (*He smiles.*)

LINDA: You're such a boy! You think you can go away for a year and . . . You've got to get it into your head now that one day you'll knock on this door and there'll be strange people here —

BIFF: What are you talking about? You're not even sixty, Mom.

LINDA: But what about your father?

BIFF (*lamely*): Well, I meant him too.

HAPPY: He admires Pop.

LINDA: Biff, dear, if you don't have any feeling for him, then you can't have any feeling for me.

BIFF: Sure I can, Mom.

LINDA: No. You can't just come to see me, because I love him. (*With a threat, but only a threat, of tears.*) He's the dearest man in the world to me, and I won't have anyone making him feel unwanted and low and blue. You've got to make up your mind now, darling, there's no leeway any more. Either he's your father and you pay him that respect, or else you're not to come here. I know he's not easy to get along with — nobody knows that better than me — but . . .

WILLY (*from the left, with a laugh*): Hey, hey, Biffo!

BIFF (*starting to go out after Willy*): What the hell is the matter with him? (*Happy stops him.*)

LINDA: Don't — don't go near him!

BIFF: Stop making excuses for him! He always, always wiped the floor with you. Never had an ounce of respect for you.

HAPPY: He's always had respect for —

BIFF: What the hell do you know about it?

HAPPY (*surlily*): Just don't call him crazy!

BIFF: He's got no character — Charley wouldn't do this. Not in his own house — spewing out that vomit from his mind.

HAPPY: Charley never had to cope with what he's got to.

BIFF: People are worse off than Willy Loman. Believe me, I've seen them!

LINDA: Then make Charley your father, Biff. You can't do that, can you? I don't say he's a great man. Willy Loman never made a lot of money. His name was never in the paper. He's not the finest character that ever lived. But he's a human being, and a terrible thing is happening to him. So attention must be paid. He's not to be allowed to fall into his grave like an old dog. Attention, attention must be finally paid to such a person. You called him crazy —

BIFF: I didn't mean —

LINDA: No, a lot of people think he's lost his — balance. But you don't have to be very smart to know what his trouble is. The man is exhausted.

HAPPY: Sure!

LINDA: A small man can be just as exhausted as a great man. He works for a company thirty-six years this March, opens up unheard-of territories to their trademark, and now in his old age they take his salary away.

HAPPY (*indignantly*): I didn't know that, Mom.

LINDA: You never asked, my dear! Now that you get your spending money someplace else you don't trouble your mind with him.

HAPPY: But I gave you money last —

LINDA: Christmas time, fifty dollars! To fix the hot water it cost ninety-seven fifty! For five weeks he's been on straight commission, like a beginner, an unknown!

BIFF: Those ungrateful bastards!

LINDA: Are they any worse than his sons? When he brought them business, when he was young, they were glad to see him. But now his old friends, the old buyers that loved him so and always found some order to hand him in a pinch — they're all dead, retired. He used to be able to make six, seven calls a day in Boston. Now he takes his valises out of the car and puts them back and takes them out again and he's exhausted. Instead of walking he talks now. He drives seven hundred miles, and when he gets there no one knows him anymore, no one welcomes him. And what goes through a man's mind, driving seven hundred miles home without having earned a cent? Why shouldn't he talk to himself? Why? When he has to go to Charley and borrow fifty dollars a week and pretend to me that it's his pay? How long can that go on? How long? You see what I'm sitting here and waiting for? And you tell me he has no character? The man who never worked a day but for your benefit? When does he get the medal for that? Is this his reward — to turn around at the age of sixty-three and find his sons, who he loved better than his life, one a philandering bum —

HAPPY: Mom!

LINDA: That's all you are, my baby! (*To Biff.*) And you! What happened to the love you had for him? You were such pals! How you used to talk to him on the phone every night! How lonely he was till he could come home to you!

BIFF: All right, Mom. I'll live here in my room, and I'll get a job. I'll keep away from him, that's all.

LINDA: No, Biff. You can't stay here and fight all the time.

BIFF: He threw me out of this house, remember that.

LINDA: Why did he do that? I never knew why.

BIFF: Because I know he's a fake and he doesn't like anybody around who knows!

LINDA: Why a fake? In what way? What do you mean?

BIFF: Just don't lay it all at my feet. It's between me and him — that's all I have to say. I'll chip in from now on. He'll settle for half my pay check. He'll be all right. I'm going to bed. (*He starts for the stairs.*)

LINDA: He won't be all right.

BIFF (*turning on the stairs, furiously*): I hate this city and I'll stay here. Now what do you want?

LINDA: He's dying, Biff.

(*Happy turns quickly to her, shocked.*)

BIFF (*after a pause*): Why is he dying?

LINDA: He's been trying to kill himself.

BIFF (*with great horror*): How?

LINDA: I live from day to day.

BIFF: What're you talking about?

LINDA: Remember I wrote you that he smashed up the car again? In February?

BIFF: Well?

LINDA: The insurance inspector came. He said that they have evidence. That all these accidents in the last year — weren't — weren't — accidents.

HAPPY: How can they tell that? That's a lie.

LINDA: It seems there's a woman . . . (*She takes a breath as*)

BIFF (*sharply but contained*): What woman?

LINDA (*simultaneously*): . . . and this woman . . .

LINDA: What?

BIFF: Nothing. Go ahead.

LINDA: What did you say?

BIFF: Nothing. I just said what woman?

HAPPY: What about her?

LINDA: Well, it seems she was walking down the road and saw his car. She says that he wasn't driving fast at all, and that he didn't skid. She says he came to that little bridge, and then deliberately smashed into the railing, and it was only the shallowness of the water that saved him.

BIFF: Oh, no, he probably just fell asleep again.

LINDA: I don't think he fell asleep.

BIFF: Why not?

LINDA: Last month . . . (*With great difficulty.*) Oh, boys, it's so hard to say a thing like this! He's just a big stupid man to you, but I tell you there's more good in him than in many other people. (*She chokes, wipes her eyes.*) I was looking for a fuse. The lights blew out, and I went down the cellar. And behind the fuse box — it happened to fall out — was a length of rubber pipe — just short.

HAPPY: No kidding!

LINDA: There's a little attachment on the end of it. I knew right away. And sure enough, on the bottom of the water heater there's a new little nipple on the gas pipe.

HAPPY (*angrily*): That — jerk.

BIFF: Did you have it taken off?

LINDA: I'm — I'm ashamed to. How can I mention it to him? Every day I go down and take away that little rubber pipe. But, when he comes home, I put it back where it was. How can I insult him that way? I don't know what to do. I live from day to day, boys. I tell you, I know every thought in his mind. It sounds so old-fashioned and silly, but I tell you he put his whole life into you and you've turned your backs on him. (*She is bent over in the chair, weeping, her face in her hands.*) Biff, I swear to God! Biff, his life is in your hands!

HAPPY (*to Biff*): How do you like that damned fool!

BIFF (*kissing her*): All right, pal, all right. It's all settled now. I've been remiss. I know that, Mom. But now I'll stay, and I swear to you, I'll apply myself. (*Kneeling in front of her, in a fever of self-reproach.*) It's just — you see, Mom, I don't fit in business. Not that I won't try. I'll try, and I'll make good.

HAPPY: Sure you will. The trouble with you in business was you never tried to please people.

BIFF: I know, I —

HAPPY: Like when you worked for Harrison's. Bob Harrison said you were tops, and then you go and do some damn fool thing like whistling whole songs in the elevator like a comedian.

BIFF (*against Happy*): So what? I like to whistle sometimes.

HAPPY: You don't raise a guy to a responsible job who whistles in the elevator!

LINDA: Well, don't argue about it now.

HAPPY: Like when you'd go off and swim in the middle of the day instead of taking the line around.

BIFF (*his resentment rising*): Well, don't you run off? You take off sometimes, don't you? On a nice summer day?

HAPPY: Yeah, but I cover myself!

LINDA: Boys!

HAPPY: If I'm going to take a fade the boss can call any number where I'm supposed to be and they'll swear to him that I just left. I'll tell you something that I hate to say, Biff, but in the business world some of them think you're crazy.

BIFF (*angered*): Screw the business world!

HAPPY: All right, screw it! Great, but cover yourself!

LINDA: Hap, Hap!

BIFF: I don't care what they think! They've laughed at Dad for years, and you know why? Because we don't belong in this nuthouse of a city! We should be mixing cement on some open plain, or — or carpenters. A carpenter is allowed to whistle!

(*Willy walks in from the entrance of the house, at left.*)

WILLY: Even your grandfather was better than a carpenter. (*Pause. They watch him.*) You never grew up. Bernard does not whistle in the elevator, I assure you.

BIFF (*as though to laugh Willy out of it*): Yeah, but you do, Pop.

WILLY: I never in my life whistled in an elevator! And who in the business world thinks I'm crazy?

BIFF: I didn't mean it like that, Pop. Now don't make a whole thing out of it, will ye?

WILLY: Go back to the West! Be a carpenter, a cowboy, enjoy yourself!

LINDA: Willy, he was just saying —

WILLY: I heard what he said!

HAPPY (*trying to quiet Willy*): Hey, Pop, come on now . . .

WILLY (*continuing over Happy's line*): They laugh at me, heh? Go to Filene's, go to the Hub, go to Slattery's, Boston. Call out the name Willy Loman and see what happens! Big shot!

BIFF: All right, Pop.

WILLY: Big!

BIFF: All right!

WILLY: Why do you always insult me?

BIFF: I didn't say a word. (*To Linda.*) Did I say a word?

LINDA: He didn't say anything, Willy.

WILLY (*going to the doorway of the living room*): All right, good night, good night.

LINDA: Willy, dear, he just decided . . .

WILLY (*to Biff*): If you get tired hanging around tomorrow, paint the ceiling I put up in the living room.

BIFF: I'm leaving early tomorrow.

HAPPY: He's going to see Bill Oliver, Pop.

WILLY (*interestedly*): Oliver? For what?

BIFF (*with reserve, but trying, trying*): He always said he'd stake me. I'd like to go into business, so maybe I can take him up on it.

LINDA: Isn't that wonderful?

WILLY: Don't interrupt. What's wonderful about it? There's fifty men in the City of New York who'd stake him. (*To Biff.*) Sporting goods?

BIFF: I guess so. I know something about it and —

WILLY: He knows something about it! You know sporting goods better than Spalding, for God's sake! How much is he giving you?

BIFF: I don't know, I didn't even see him yet, but —

WILLY: Then what're you talkin' about?

BIFF (*getting angry*): Well, all I said was I'm gonna see him, that's all!

WILLY (*turning away*): Ah, you're counting your chickens again.

BIFF (*starting left for the stairs*): Oh, Jesus, I'm going to sleep!

WILLY (*calling after him*): Don't curse in this house!

BIFF (*turning*): Since when did you get so clean?

HAPPY (*trying to stop them*): Wait a . . .

WILLY: Don't use that language to me! I won't have it!

HAPPY (*grabbing Biff, shouts*): Wait a minute! I got an idea. I got a feasible idea. Come here, Biff, let's talk this over now, let's talk some sense here. When I was down in Florida last time, I thought of a great idea to sell sporting goods. It just came back to me. You and I, Biff — we have a line, the Loman Line. We train a couple of weeks, and put on a couple of exhibitions, see?

WILLY: That's an idea!

HAPPY: Wait! We form two basketball teams, see? Two water polo teams. We play each other. It's a million dollars' worth of publicity. Two brothers, see? The Loman Brothers. Displays in the Royal Palms — all the hotels. And banners over the ring and the basketball court: "Loman Brothers." Baby, we could sell sporting goods!

WILLY: That is a one-million-dollar idea!

LINDA: Marvelous!

BIFF: I'm in great shape as far as that's concerned.

HAPPY: And the beauty of it is, Biff, it wouldn't be like a business. We'd be out playin' ball again . . .

BIFF (*enthused*): Yeah, that's . . .

WILLY: Million-dollar . . .

HAPPY: And you wouldn't get fed up with it, Biff. It'd be the family again. There'd be the old honor, and comradeship, and if you wanted to go off for a swim or somethin' — well, you'd do it! Without some smart cooky gettin' up ahead of you!

WILLY: Lick the world! You guys together could absolutely lick the civilized world.

BIFF: I'll see Oliver tomorrow. Hap, if we could work that out . . .

LINDA: Maybe things are beginning to —

WILLY (*wildly enthused, to Linda*): Stop interrupting! (*To Biff.*) But don't wear sport jacket and slacks when you see Oliver.

BIFF: No, I'll —

WILLY: A business suit, and talk as little as possible, and don't crack any jokes.

BIFF: He did like me. Always liked me.

LINDA: He loved you!

WILLY (*to Linda*): Will you stop! (*To Biff.*) Walk in very serious. You are not applying for a boy's job. Money is to pass. Be quiet, fine, and serious. Everybody likes a kidder, but nobody lends him money.

HAPPY: I'll try to get some myself, Biff. I'm sure I can.

WILLY: I see great things for you kids, I think your troubles are over. But remember, start big and you'll end big. Ask for fifteen. How much you gonna ask for?

BIFF: Gee, I don't know —

WILLY: And don't say "Gee." "Gee" is a boy's word. A man walking in for fifteen thousand dollars does not say "Gee!"

BIFF: Ten, I think, would be top though.

WILLY: Don't be so modest. You always started too low. Walk in with a big laugh. Don't look worried. Start off with a couple of your good stories to lighten things up. It's not what you say, it's how you say it — because personality always wins the day.

LINDA: Oliver always thought the highest of him —

WILLY: Will you let me talk?

BIFF: Don't yell at her, Pop, will ye?

WILLY (*angrily*): I was talking, wasn't I?

BIFF: I don't like you yelling at her all the time, and I'm tellin' you, that's all.

WILLY: What're you, takin' over this house?

LINDA: Willy —

WILLY (*turning to her*): Don't take his side all the time, goddammit!

BIFF (*furiously*): Stop yelling at her!

WILLY (*suddenly pulling on his cheek, beaten down, guilt ridden*): Give my best to Bill Oliver — he may remember me. (*He exits through the living room doorway.*)

LINDA (*her voice subdued*): What'd you have to start that for? (*Biff turns away.*) You see how sweet he was as soon as you talked hopefully? (*She goes over to Biff.*) Come up and say good night to him. Don't let him go to bed that way.

HAPPY: Come on, Biff, let's buck him up.

LINDA: Please, dear. Just say good night. It takes so little to make him happy. Come. (*She goes through the living room doorway, calling upstairs from within the living room.*) Your pajamas are hanging in the bathroom, Willy!

HAPPY (*looking toward where Linda went out*): What a woman! They broke the mold when they made her. You know that, Biff?

BIFF: He's off salary. My God, working on commission!

HAPPY: Well, let's face it: he's no hot-shot selling man. Except that sometimes, you have to admit, he's a sweet personality.

BIFF (*deciding*): Lend me ten bucks, will ye? I want to buy some new ties.

HAPPY: I'll take you to a place I know. Beautiful stuff. Wear one of my striped shirts tomorrow.

BIFF: She got gray. Mom got awful old. Gee, I'm gonna go in to Oliver tomorrow and knock him for a —

HAPPY: Come on up. Tell that to Dad. Let's give him a whirl. Come on.

BIFF (*steamed up*): You know, with ten thousand bucks, boy!

HAPPY (*as they go into the living room*): That's the talk, Biff, that's the first time I've heard the old confidence out of you! (*From within the living room, fading off.*) You're gonna live with me, kid, and any babe you want just say the word . . . (*The last lines are hardly heard. They are mounting the stairs to their parents' bedroom.*)

LINDA (*entering her bedroom and addressing Willy, who is in the bathroom. She is straightening the bed for him.*): Can you do anything about the shower? It drips.

WILLY (*from the bathroom*): All of a sudden everything falls to pieces. Goddam plumbing, oughta be sued, those people. I hardly finished putting it in and the thing . . . (*His words rumble off.*)

LINDA: I'm just wondering if Oliver will remember him. You think he might?

WILLY (*coming out of the bathroom in his pajamas*): Remember him? What's the matter with you, you crazy? If he'd've stayed with Oliver he'd be on top by now! Wait'll Oliver gets a look at him. You don't know the average caliber any more. The average young man today — (*he is getting into bed*) — is got a caliber of zero. Greatest thing in the world for him was to bum around.

(*Biff and Happy enter the bedroom. Slight pause.*)

WILLY (*stops short, looking at Biff*): Glad to hear it, boy.

HAPPY: He wanted to say good night to you, sport.

WILLY (*to Biff*): Yeah. Knock him dead, boy. What'd you want to tell me?

BIFF: Just take it easy, Pop. Good night. (*He turns to go.*)

WILLY (*unable to resist*): And if anything falls off the desk while you're talking to him — like a package or something — don't you pick it up. They have office boys for that.

LINDA: I'll make a big breakfast —

WILLY: Will you let me finish? (*To Biff.*) Tell him you were in the business in the West. Not farm work.

BIFF: All right, Dad.

LINDA: I think everything —

WILLY (*going right through her speech*): And don't undersell yourself. No less than fifteen thousand dollars.

BIFF (*unable to bear him*): Okay. Good night, Mom. (*He starts moving.*)

WILLY: Because you got a greatness in you, Biff, remember that. You got all kinds of greatness . . . (*He lies back, exhausted. Biff walks out.*)

LINDA (*calling after Biff*): Sleep well, darling!

HAPPY: I'm gonna get married, Mom. I wanted to tell you.

LINDA: Go to sleep, dear.

HAPPY (*going*): I just wanted to tell you.

WILLY: Keep up the good work. (*Happy exits.*) God . . . remember that Ebbets Field game? The championship of the city?

LINDA: Just rest. Should I sing to you?

WILLY: Yeah. Sing to me. (*Linda hums a soft lullaby.*) When that team came out — he was the tallest, remember?

LINDA: Oh, yes. And in gold.

(*Biff enters the darkened kitchen, takes a cigarette, and leaves the house. He comes downstage into a golden pool of light. He smokes, staring at the night.*)

WILLY: Like a young god. Hercules — something like that. And the sun, the sun all around him. Remember how he waved to me? Right up from the field, with the representatives of three colleges standing by? And the buyers I brought, and the cheers when he came out — Loman, Loman, Loman! God Almighty, he'll be great yet. A star like that, magnificent, can never really fade away!

(*The light on Willy is fading. The gas heater begins to glow through the kitchen wall, near the stairs, a blue flame beneath red coils.*)

LINDA (*timidly*): Willy dear, what has he got against you?

WILLY: I'm so tired. Don't talk anymore.

(*Biff slowly returns to the kitchen. He stops, stares toward the heater.*)

LINDA: Will you ask Howard to let you work in New York?

WILLY: First thing in the morning. Everything'll be all right.

(*Biff reaches behind the heater and draws out a length of rubber tubing. He is horrified and turns his head toward Willy's room, still dimly lit, from which the strains of Linda's desperate but monotonous humming rise.*)

WILLY (*staring through the window into the moonlight*): Gee, look at the moon moving between the buildings!

(*Biff wraps the tubing around his hand and quickly goes up the stairs.*)

ACT II

(*Music is heard, gay and bright. The curtain rises as the music fades away. Willy, in shirt sleeves is sitting at the kitchen table, sipping coffee, his hat in his lap. Linda is piling his cup when she can.*)

WILLY: Wonderful coffee. Meal in itself.

LINDA: Can I make you some eggs?

WILLY: No. Take a breath.

LINDA: You look so rested, dear.

WILLY: I slept like a dead one. First time in months. Imagine, sleeping till ten on a Tuesday morning. Boys left nice and early, heh?

LINDA: They were out of here by eight o'clock.

WILLY: Good work!

LINDA: It was so thrilling to see them leaving together. I can't get over the shaving lotion in this house!

WILLY (*smiling*): Mmm —

LINDA: Biff was very changed this morning. His whole attitude seemed to be hopeful. He couldn't wait to get downtown to see Oliver.

WILLY: He's heading for a change. There's no question, there simply are certain men that take longer to get — solidified. How did he dress?

LINDA: His blue suit. He's so handsome in that suit. He could be a — anything in that suit!

(*Willy gets up from the table. Linda holds his jacket for him.*)

WILLY: There's no question, no question at all. Gee, on the way home tonight I'd like to buy some seeds.

LINDA (*laughing*): That'd be wonderful. But not enough sun gets back there. Nothing'll grow any more.

WILLY: You wait, kid, before it's all over we're gonna get a little place out in the country, and I'll raise some vegetables, a couple of chickens . . .

LINDA: You'll do it yet, dear.

(*Willy walks out of his jacket. Linda follows him.*)

WILLY: And they'll get married, and come for a weekend. I'd build a little guest house. 'Cause I got so many fine tools, all I'd need would be a little lumber and some peace of mind.

LINDA (*joyfully*): I sewed the lining . . .

WILLY: I could build two guest houses, so they'd both come. Did he decide how much he's going to ask Oliver for?

LINDA (*getting him into the jacket*): He didn't mention it, but I imagine ten or fifteen thousand. You going to talk to Howard today?

WILLY: Yeah. I'll put it to him straight and simple. He'll just have to take me off the road.

LINDA: And Willy, don't forget to ask for a little advance, because we've got the insurance premium. It's the grace period now.

WILLY: That's a hundred . . . ?

LINDA: A hundred and eight, sixty-eight. Because we're a little short again.

WILLY: Why are we short?

LINDA: Well, you had the motor job on the car . . .

WILLY: That goddam Studebaker!

LINDA: And you got one more payment on the refrigerator . . .

WILLY: But it just broke again!

LINDA: Well, it's old, dear.

WILLY: I told you we should've bought a well-advertised machine. Charley bought a General Electric and it's twenty years old and it's still good, that son-of-a-bitch.

LINDA: But, Willy —

WILLY: Whoever heard of a Hastings refrigerator? Once in my life I would like to own something outright before it's broken! I'm always in a race with the junkyard! I just finished paying for the car and it's on its last legs. The refrigerator consumes belts like a goddamn maniac. They time those things. They time them so when you finally paid for them, they're used up.

LINDA (*buttoning up his jacket as he unbuttons it*): All told, about two hundred dollars would carry us, dear. But that includes the last payment on the mortgage. After this payment, Willy, the house belongs to us.

WILLY: It's twenty-five years!

LINDA: Biff was nine years old when we bought it.

WILLY: Well, that's a great thing. To weather a twenty-five year mortgage is —

LINDA: It's an accomplishment.

WILLY: All the cement, the lumber, the reconstruction I put in this house! There ain't a crack to be found in it anymore.

LINDA: Well, it served its purpose.

WILLY: What purpose? Some stranger'll come along, move in, and that's that. If only Biff would take this house, and raise a family . . . (*He starts to go.*) Good-by, I'm late.

LINDA (*suddenly remembering*): Oh, I forgot! You're supposed to meet them for dinner.

WILLY: Me?

LINDA: At Frank's Chop House on Forty-eighth near Sixth Avenue.

WILLY: Is that so! How about you?

LINDA: No, just the three of you. They're gonna blow you to a big meal!

WILLY: Don't say! Who thought of that?

LINDA: Biff came to me this morning, Willy, and he said, "Tell Dad, we want to blow him to a big meal." Be there six o'clock. You and your two boys are going to have dinner.

WILLY: Gee whiz! That's really somethin'. I'm gonna knock Howard for a loop, kid. I'll get an advance, and I'll come home with a New York job. Goddammit, now I'm gonna do it!

LINDA: Oh, that's the spirit, Willy!

WILLY: I will never get behind a wheel the rest of my life!

LINDA: It's changing, Willy, I can feel it changing!

WILLY: Beyond a question. G'by, I'm late. (*He starts to go again.*)

LINDA (*calling after him as she runs to the kitchen table for a handkerchief*): You got your glasses?

WILLY (*feels for them, then comes back in*): Yeah, yeah, got my glasses.

LINDA (*giving him the handkerchief*): And a handkerchief.

WILLY: Yeah, handkerchief.

LINDA: And your saccharine?

WILLY: Yeah, my saccharine.

LINDA: Be careful on the subway stairs.

(*She kisses him, and a silk stocking is seen hanging from her hand. Willy notices it.*)

WILLY: Will you stop mending stockings? At least while I'm in the house. It gets me nervous. I can't tell you. Please.

(*Linda hides the stocking in her hand as she follows Willy across the forestage in front of the house.*)

LINDA: Remember, Frank's Chop House.

WILLY (*passing the apron*): Maybe beets would grow out there.

LINDA (*laughing*): But you tried so many times.

WILLY: Yeah. Well, don't work hard today. (*He disappears around the right corner of the house.*)

LINDA: Be careful!

(*As Willy vanishes, Linda waves to him. Suddenly the phone rings. She runs across the stage and into the kitchen and lifts it.*)

LINDA: Hello? Oh, Biff! I'm so glad you called, I just . . . Yes, sure, I just told him. Yes, he'll be there for dinner at six o'clock, I didn't forget. Listen, I was just dying to tell you. You know that little rubber pipe I told you about? That he connected to the gas heater? I finally decided to go down the cellar this morning and take it away and destroy it. But it's gone! Imagine? He took it away himself, it isn't there! (*She listens.*) When? Oh, then you took it. Oh — nothing, it's just that I'd hoped he'd taken it away himself. Oh, I'm not worried, darling, because this morning he left in such high spirits, it was like the old days! I'm not afraid any more. Did Mr. Oliver see you? . . . Well, you wait there then. And make a nice impression on him, darling. Just don't perspire too much before you see him. And have a nice time with Dad. He may have big news too! . . . That's right, a New York job. And be sweet to him tonight, dear. Be loving to him. Because he's only a little boat looking for a harbor. (*She is trembling with sorrow and joy.*) Oh, that's wonderful, Biff, you'll save his life. Thanks, darling. Just put your arm around him when he comes into the restaurant. Give him a smile. That's the boy . . . Good-by, dear. . . . You got your comb? . . . That's fine. Good-by, Biff dear.

(*In the middle of her speech, Howard Wagner, thirty-six, wheels in a small typewriter table on which is a wire-recording machine and proceeds to plug it in. This is on the left forestage. Light slowly fades on Linda as it rises on Howard. Howard is intent on threading the machine and only glances over his shoulder as Willy appears.*)

WILLY: Pst! Pst!

HOWARD: Hello, Willy, come in.

WILLY: Like to have a little talk with you, Howard.

HOWARD: Sorry to keep you waiting. I'll be with you in a minute.

WILLY: What's that, Howard?

HOWARD: Didn't you ever see one of these? Wire recorder.

WILLY: Oh. Can we talk a minute?

HOWARD: Records things. Just got delivery yesterday. Been driving me crazy, the most terrific machine I ever saw in my life. I was up all night with it.

WILLY: What do you do with it?

HOWARD: I bought it for dictation, but you can do anything with it. Listen to this. I had it home last night. Listen to what I picked up. The first one is my daughter. Get this. (*He flicks the switch and "Roll out the Barrel" is heard being whistled.*) Listen to that kid whistle.

WILLY: That is lifelike, isn't it?

HOWARD: Seven years old. Get that tone.

WILLY: Ts, ts. Like to ask a little favor if you . . .

(*The whistling breaks off, and the voice of Howard's daughter is heard.*)

HIS DAUGHTER: Now you, Daddy.

HOWARD: She's crazy for me! (*Again the same song is whistled.*) That's me! Ha! (*He winks.*)

WILLY: You're very good!

(*The whistling breaks off again. The machine runs silent for a moment.*)

HOWARD: Sh! Get this now, this is my son.

HIS SON: "The capital of Alabama is Montgomery; the capital of Arizona is Phoenix; the capital of Arkansas is Little Rock; the capital of California is Sacramento . . ." (*and on, and on.*)

HOWARD (*holding up five fingers*): Five years old, Willy!

WILLY: He'll make an announcer some day!

HIS SON (*continuing*): "The capital . . ."

HOWARD: Get that — alphabetical order! (*The machine breaks off suddenly.*) Wait a minute. The maid kicked the plug out.

WILLY: It certainly is a —

HOWARD: Sh, for God's sake!

HIS SON: "It's nine o'clock, Bulova watch time. So I have to go to sleep."

WILLY: That really is —

HOWARD: Wait a minute! The next is my wife.

(*They wait.*)

HOWARD'S VOICE: "Go on, say something." (*Pause.*) "Well, you gonna talk?"

HIS WIFE: "I can't think of anything."

HOWARD'S VOICE: "Well, talk — it's turning."

HIS WIFE (*shyly, beaten*): "Hello." (*Silence.*) "Oh, Howard, I can't talk into this . . ."

HOWARD (*snapping the machine off*): That was my wife.

WILLY: That is a wonderful machine. Can we —

HOWARD: I tell you, Willy, I'm gonna take my camera, and my bandsaw, and all my hobbies, and out they go. This is the most fascinating relaxation I ever found.

WILLY: I think I'll get one myself.

HOWARD: Sure, they're only a hundred and a half. You can't do without it. Supposing you wanna hear Jack Benny, see? But you can't be at home at that hour. So you tell the maid to turn the radio on when Jack Benny comes on, and this automatically goes on with the radio . . .

WILLY: And when you come home you . . .

HOWARD: You can come home twelve o'clock, one o'clock, any time you like, and you get yourself a Coke and sit yourself down, throw the switch, and there's Jack Benny's program in the middle of the night!

WILLY: I'm definitely going to get one. Because lots of times I'm on the road, and I think to myself, what I must be missing on the radio!

HOWARD: Don't you have a radio in the car?

WILLY: Well, yeah, but who ever thinks of turning it on?

HOWARD: Say, aren't you supposed to be in Boston?

WILLY: That's what I want to talk to you about, Howard. You got a minute? (*He draws a chair in from the wing.*)

HOWARD: What happened? What're you doing here?

WILLY: Well . . .

HOWARD: You didn't crack up again, did you?

WILLY: Oh, no. No . . .

HOWARD: Geez, you had me worried there for a minute. What's the trouble?

WILLY: Well, tell you the truth, Howard. I've come to the decision that I'd rather not travel anymore.

HOWARD: Not travel! Well, what'll you do?

WILLY: Remember, Christmas time, when you had the party here? You said you'd try to think of some spot for me here in town.

HOWARD: With us?

WILLY: Well, sure.

HOWARD: Oh, yeah, yeah. I remember. Well, I couldn't think of anything for you, Willy.

WILLY: I tell ya, Howard. The kids are all grown up, y'know. I don't need much anymore. If I could take home — well, sixty-five dollars a week, I could swing it.

HOWARD: Yeah, but Willy, see I —

WILLY: I tell ya why, Howard. Speaking frankly and between the two of us, y'know — I'm just a little tired.

HOWARD: Oh, I could understand that, Willy. But you're a road man, Willy, and we do a road business. We've only got a half-dozen salesmen on the floor here.

WILLY: God knows, Howard, I never asked a favor of any man. But I was with the firm when your father used to carry you in here in his arms.

HOWARD: I know that, Willy, but —

WILLY: Your father came to me the day you were born and asked me what I thought of the name Howard, may he rest in peace.

HOWARD: I appreciate that, Willy, but there just is no

spot here for you. If I had a spot I'd slam you right in, but I just don't have a single solitary spot.

(*He looks for his lighter. Willy has picked it up and gives it to him. Pause.*)

WILLY (*with increasing anger*): Howard, all I need to set my table is fifty dollars a week.

HOWARD: But where am I going to put you, kid?

WILLY: Look, it isn't a question of whether I can sell merchandise, is it?

HOWARD: No, but it's business, kid, and everybody's gotta pull his own weight.

WILLY (*desperately*): Just let me tell you a story, Howard —

HOWARD: 'Cause you gotta admit, business is business.

WILLY (*angrily*): Business is definitely business, but just listen for a minute. You don't understand this. When I was a boy — eighteen, nineteen — I was already on the road. And there was a question in my mind as to whether selling had a future for me. Because in those days I had a yearning to go to Alaska. See, there were three gold strikes in one month in Alaska, and I felt like going out. Just for the ride, you might say.

HOWARD (*barely interested*): Don't say.

WILLY: Oh, yeah, my father lived many years in Alaska. He was an adventurous man. We've got quite a little streak of self-reliance in our family. I thought I'd go out with my older brother and try to locate him, and maybe settle in the North with the old man. And I was almost decided to go, when I met a salesman in the Parker House. His name was Dave Singleman. And he was eighty-four years old, and he'd drummed merchandise in thirty-one states. And old Dave, he'd go up to his room, y'understand, put on his green velvet slippers — I'll never forget — and pick up his phone and call the buyers, and without ever leaving his room, at the age of eighty-four, he made his living. And when I saw that, I realized that selling was the greatest career a man could want. 'Cause what could be more satisfying than to be able to go, at the age of eighty-four, into twenty or thirty different cities, and pick up a phone, and be remembered and loved and helped by so many different people? Do you know? When he died — and by the way he died the death of a salesman, in his green velvet slippers in the smoker of the New York, New Haven and Hartford, going into Boston — when he died, hundreds of salesmen and buyers were at his funeral. Things were sad on a lotta trains for months after that. (*He stands up. Howard has not looked at him.*) In those days there was personality in it, Howard. There was respect and comradeship, and gratitude in it. Today, it's all cut and dried, and there's no chance for bringing friendship to bear — or personality. You see what I mean? They don't know me any more.

HOWARD (*moving away, to the right*): That's just the thing, Willy.

WILLY: If I had forty dollars a week — that's all I'd need. Forty dollars, Howard.

HOWARD: Kid, I can't take blood from a stone, I —

WILLY (*desperation is on him now*): Howard, the year Al Smith was nominated, your father came to me and —

HOWARD (*starting to go off*): I've got to see some people, kid.

WILLY (*stopping him*): I'm talking about your father! There were promises made across this desk! You mustn't tell me you've got people to see — I put thirty-four years into this firm, Howard, and now I can't pay my insurance! You can't eat the orange and throw the peel away — a man is not a piece of fruit! (*After a pause.*) Now pay attention. Your father — in 1928 I had a big year. I averaged a hundred and seventy dollars a week in commissions.

HOWARD (*impatiently*): Now, Willy, you never averaged —

WILLY (*banging his hand on the desk*): I averaged a hundred and seventy dollars a week in the year of 1928! And your father came to me — or rather I was in the office here — it was right over this desk — and he put his hand on my shoulder —

HOWARD (*getting up*): You'll have to excuse me, Willy, I gotta see some people. Pull yourself together. (*Going out.*) I'll be back in a little while.

(*On Howard's exit, the light on his chair grows very bright and strange.*)

WILLY: Pull myself together! What the hell did I say to him? My God, I was yelling at him! How could I? (*Willy breaks off, staring at the light, which occupies the chair, animating it. He approaches this chair, standing across the desk from it.*) Frank, Frank, don't you remember what you told me that time? How you put your hand on my shoulder, and Frank . . . (*He leans on the desk and as he speaks the dead man's name he accidentally switches on the recorder, and instantly*)

HOWARD'S SON: ". . . of New York is Albany. The capital of Ohio is Cincinnati, the capital of Rhode Island is . . ." (*The recitation continues.*)

WILLY (*leaping away with fright, shouting*): Ha! Howard! Howard! Howard!

HOWARD (*rushing in*): What happened?

WILLY (*pointing at the machine, which continues nasally, childishly, with the capital cities*): Shut it off! Shut it off!

HOWARD (*pulling the plug out*): Look, Willy . . .

WILLY (*pressing his hands to his eyes*): I gotta get myself some coffee. I'll get some coffee . . .

(*Willy starts to walk out. Howard stops him.*)

HOWARD (*rolling up the cord*): Willy, look . . .

WILLY: I'll go to Boston.

HOWARD: Willy, you can't go to Boston for us.

WILLY: Why can't I go?

HOWARD: I don't want you to represent us. I've been meaning to tell you for a long time now.

WILLY: Howard, are you firing me?

HOWARD: I think you need a good long rest, Willy.

WILLY: Howard —

HOWARD: And when you feel better, come back, and we'll see if we can work something out.

WILLY: But I gotta earn money, Howard. I'm in no position to —

HOWARD: Where are your sons? Why don't your sons give you a hand?

WILLY: They're working on a very big deal.

HOWARD: This is no time for false pride, Willy. You go to your sons and you tell them that you're tired. You've got two great boys, haven't you?

WILLY: Oh, no question, no question, but in the meantime . . .

HOWARD: Then that's that, heh?

WILLY: All right, I'll go to Boston tomorrow.

HOWARD: No, no.

WILLY: I can't throw myself on my sons. I'm not a cripple!

HOWARD: Look, kid, I'm busy this morning.

WILLY (*grasping Howard's arm*): Howard, you've got to let me go to Boston!

HOWARD (*hard, keeping himself under control*): I've got a line of people to see this morning. Sit down, take five minutes, and pull yourself together, and then go home, will ya? I need the office, Willy. (*He starts to go, turns, remembering the recorder, starts to push off the table holding the recorder.*) Oh, yeah. Whenever you can this week, stop by and drop off the samples. You'll feel better, Willy, and then come back and we'll talk. Pull yourself together, kid, there's people outside.

(*Howard exits, pushing the table off left. Willy stares into space, exhausted. Now the music is heard — Ben's music — first distantly, then closer, closer. As Willy speaks, Ben enters from the right. He carries valise and umbrella.*)

WILLY: Oh, Ben, how did you do it? What is the answer? Did you wind up the Alaska deal already?

BEN: Doesn't take much time if you know what you're doing. Just a short business trip. Boarding ship in an hour. Wanted to say good-by.

WILLY: Ben, I've got to talk to you.

BEN (*glancing at his watch*): Haven't the time, William.

WILLY (*crossing the apron to Ben*): Ben, nothing's working out. I don't know what to do.

BEN: Now, look here, William. I've bought timberland in Alaska and I need a man to look after things for me.

WILLY: God, timberland! Me and my boys in those grand outdoors!

BEN: You've a new continent at your doorstep, William. Get out of these cities, they're full of talk and time payments and courts of law. Screw on your fists and you can fight for a fortune up there.

WILLY: Yes, yes! Linda, Linda!

(*Linda enters as of old, with the wash.*)

LINDA: Oh, you're back?

BEN: I haven't much time.

WILLY: No, wait! Linda, he's got a proposition for me in Alaska.

LINDA: But you've got — (*To Ben.*) He's got a beautiful job here.

WILLY: But in Alaska, kid, I could —

LINDA: You're doing well enough, Willy!

BEN (*to Linda*): Enough for what, my dear?

LINDA (*frightened of Ben and angry at him*): Don't say those things to him! Enough to be happy right here, right now. (*To Willy, while Ben laughs.*) Why must everybody conquer the world? You're well liked, and the boys love you, and someday — (*To Ben*) — why, old man Wagner told him just the other day that if he keeps it up he'll be a member of the firm, didn't he, Willy?

WILLY: Sure, sure. I am building something with this firm, Ben, and if a man is building something he must be on the right track, mustn't he?

BEN: What are you building? Lay your hand on it. Where is it?

WILLY (*hesitantly*): That's true, Linda, there's nothing.

LINDA: Why? (*To Ben.*) There's a man eighty-four years old —

WILLY: That's right, Ben, that's right. When I look at that man I say, what is there to worry about?

BEN: Bah!

WILLY: It's true, Ben. All he has to do is go into any city, pick up the phone, and he's making his living and you know why?

BEN (*picking up his valise*): I've got to go.

WILLY (*holding Ben back*): Look at this boy!

(*Biff, in his high school sweater, enters carrying suitcase. Happy carries Biff's shoulder guards, gold helmet, and football pants.*)

WILLY: Without a penny to his name, three great universities are begging for him, and from there the sky's the limit, because it's not what you do, Ben. It's who you know and the smile on your face! It's contacts, Ben, contacts! The whole wealth of Alaska passes over the lunch table at the Commodore Hotel, and that's the wonder, the wonder of this country, that a man can end with diamonds here on the basis of being liked! (*He turns to Biff.*) And that's why when you get out on that field today it's important. Because thousands of people will be rooting for you and loving you. (*To Ben, who has again begun to leave.*) And Ben! when he walks into a business office his name will sound out like a bell and all the doors will open to him! I've seen it, Ben, I've seen it a thousand times! You can't feel it with your hand like timber, but it's there!

BEN: Good-by, William.

WILLY: Ben, am I right? Don't you think I'm right? I value your advice.

BEN: There's a new continent at your doorstep, William. You could walk out rich. Rich! (*He is gone.*)

WILLY: We'll do it here, Ben! You hear me? We're gonna do it here!

(*Young Bernard rushes in. The gay music of the Boys is heard.*)

BERNARD: Oh, gee, I was afraid you left already!

WILLY: Why? What time is it?

BERNARD: It's half-past one!

WILLY: Well, come on, everybody! Ebbets Field next stop! Where's the pennants? (*He rushes through the wall-line of the kitchen and out into the living room.*)

LINDA (*to Biff*): Did you pack fresh underwear?

BIFF (*who has been limbering up*): I want to go!

BERNARD: Biff, I'm carrying your helmet, ain't I?

HAPPY: No, I'm carrying the helmet.

BERNARD: Oh, Biff, you promised me.

HAPPY: I'm carrying the helmet.

BERNARD: How am I going to get in the locker room?

LINDA: Let him carry the shoulder guards. (*She puts her coat and hat on in the kitchen.*)

BERNARD: Can I, Biff? 'Cause I told everybody I'm going to be in the locker room.

HAPPY: In Ebbets Field it's the clubhouse.

BERNARD: I meant the clubhouse. Biff!

HAPPY: Biff!

BIFF (*grandly, after a slight pause*): Let him carry the shoulder guards.

HAPPY (*as he gives Bernard the shoulder guards*): Stay close to us now.

(*Willy rushes in with the pennants.*)

WILLY (*handing them out*): Everybody wave when Biff comes out on the field. (*Happy and Bernard run off.*) You set now, boy?

(*The music has died away.*)

BIFF: Ready to go, Pop. Every muscle is ready.

WILLY (*at the edge of the apron*): You realize what this means?

BIFF: That's right, Pop.

WILLY (*feeling Biff's muscles*): You're comin' home this afternoon captain of the All-Scholastic Championship Team of the City of New York.

BIFF: I got it, Pop. And remember, pal, when I take off my helmet, that touchdown is for you.

WILLY: Let's go! (*He is starting out, with his arm around Biff, when Charley enters, as of old, in knickers.*) I got no room for you, Charley.

CHARLEY: Room? For what?

WILLY: In the car.

CHARLEY: You goin' for a ride? I wanted to shoot some casino.

WILLY (*furiously*): Casino! (*Incredulously.*) Don't you realize what today is?

LINDA: Oh, he knows, Willy. He's just kidding you.

WILLY: That's nothing to kid about!

CHARLEY: No, Linda, what's goin' on?

LINDA: He's playing in Ebbets Field.

CHARLEY: Baseball in this weather?

WILLY: Don't talk to him. Come on, come on! (*He is pushing them out.*)

CHARLEY: Wait a minute, didn't you hear the news?

WILLY: What?

CHARLEY: Don't you listen to the radio? Ebbets Field just blew up.

WILLY: You go to hell! (*Charley laughs. Pushing them out.*) Come on, come on! We're late.

CHARLEY (*as they go*): Knock a homer, Biff, knock a homer!

WILLY (*the last to leave, turning to Charley*): I don't think that was funny, Charley. This is the greatest day of his life.

CHARLEY: Willy, when are you going to grow up?

WILLY: Yeah, heh? When this game is over, Charley, you'll be laughing out of the other side of your face. They'll be calling him another Red Grange. Twenty-five thousand a year.

CHARLEY (*kidding*): Is that so?

WILLY: Yeah, that's so.

CHARLEY: Well, then, I'm sorry, Willy. But tell me something.

WILLY: What?

CHARLEY: Who is Red Grange?

WILLY: Put up your hands. Goddam you, put up your hands!

(*Charley, chuckling, shakes his head and walks away, around the left corner of the stage. Willy follows him. The music rises to a mocking frenzy.*)

WILLY: Who the hell do you think you are, better than everybody else? You don't know everything, you big, ignorant, stupid . . . Put up your hands!

(*Light rises, on the right side of the forestage, on a small table in the reception room of Charley's office. Traffic sounds are heard. Bernard, now mature, sits whistling to himself. A pair of tennis rackets and an overnight bag are on the floor beside him.*)

WILLY (*offstage*): What are you walking away for? Don't walk away! If you're going to say something say it to my face! I know you laugh at me behind my back. You'll laugh out of the other side of your goddam face after this game. Touchdown! Touchdown! Eighty thousand people! Touchdown! Right between the goal posts.

(*Bernard is a quiet, earnest, but self-assured young man. Willy's voice is coming from right upstage now. Bernard lowers his feet off the table and listens. Jenny, his father's secretary, enters.*)

JENNY (*distressed*): Say, Bernard, will you go out in the hall?

BERNARD: What is that noise? Who is it?

JENNY: Mr. Loman. He just got off the elevator.

BERNARD (*getting up*): Who's he arguing with?

JENNY: Nobody. There's nobody with him. I can't deal with him anymore, and your father gets all upset everytime he comes. I've got a lot of typing to do, and your father's waiting to sign it. Will you see him?

WILLY (*entering*): Touchdown! Touch — (*He sees*

Jenny.) Jenny, Jenny, good to see you. How're ya? Workin'? Or still honest?

JENNY: Fine. How've you been feeling?

WILLY: Not much any more, Jenny. Ha, ha! (*He is surprised to see the rackets.*)

BERNARD: Hello, Uncle Willy.

WILLY (*almost shocked*): Bernard! Well, look who's here! (*He comes quickly, guiltily, to Bernard and warmly shakes his hand.*)

BERNARD: How are you? Good to see you.

WILLY: What are you doing here?

BERNARD: Oh, just stopped by to see Pop. Get off my feet till my train leaves. I'm going to Washington in a few minutes.

WILLY: Is he in?

BERNARD: Yes, he's in his office with the accountant. Sit down.

WILLY (*sitting down*): What're you going to do in Washington?

BERNARD: Oh, just a case I've got there, Willy.

WILLY: That so? (*Indicating the rackets.*) You going to play tennis there?

BERNARD: I'm staying with a friend who's got a court.

WILLY: Don't say. His own tennis court. Must be fine people, I bet.

BERNARD: They are, very nice. Dad tells me Biff's in town.

WILLY (*with a big smile*): Yeah, Biff's in. Working on a very big deal, Bernard.

BERNARD: What's Biff doing?

WILLY: Well, he's been doing very big things in the West. But he decided to establish himself here. Very big. We're having dinner. Did I hear your wife had a boy?

BERNARD: That's right. Our second.

WILLY: Two boys! What do you know!

BERNARD: What kind of a deal has Biff got?

WILLY: Well, Bill Oliver — very big sporting-goods man — he wants Biff very badly. Called him in from the West. Long distance, carte blanche, special deliveries. Your friends have their own private tennis court?

BERNARD: You still with the old firm, Willy?

WILLY (*after a pause*): I'm — I'm overjoyed to see how you made the grade, Bernard, overjoyed. It's an encouraging thing to see a young man really — really — Looks very good for Biff — very — (*He breaks off, then.*) Bernard — (*He is so full of emotion, he breaks off again.*)

BERNARD: What is it, Willy?

WILLY (*small and alone*): What — what's the secret?

BERNARD: What secret?

WILLY: How — how did you? Why didn't he ever catch on?

BERNARD: I wouldn't know that, Willy.

WILLY (*confidentially, desperately*): You were his friend, his boyhood friend. There's something I don't understand about it. His life ended after that Ebbets Field game. From the age of seventeen nothing good ever happened to him.

BERNARD: He never trained himself for anything.

WILLY: But he did, he did. After high school he took so many correspondence courses. Radio mechanics; television; God knows what, and never made the slightest mark.

BERNARD (*taking off his glasses*): Willy, do you want to talk candidly?

WILLY (*rising, faces Bernard*): I regard you as a very brilliant man, Bernard. I value your advice.

BERNARD: Oh, the hell with the advice, Willy. I couldn't advise you. There's just one thing I've always wanted to ask you. When he was supposed to graduate, and the math teacher flunked him —

WILLY: Oh, that son-of-a-bitch ruined his life.

BERNARD: Yeah, but, Willy, all he had to do was go to summer school and make up that subject.

WILLY: That's right, that's right.

BERNARD: Did you tell him not to go to summer school?

WILLY: Me? I begged him to go. I ordered him to go!

BERNARD: Then why wouldn't he go?

WILLY: Why? Why! Bernard, that question has been trailing me like a ghost for the last fifteen years. He flunked the subject, and laid down and died like a hammer hit him!

BERNARD: Take it easy, kid.

WILLY: Let me talk to you — I got nobody to talk to. Bernard, Bernard, was it my fault? Y'see? It keeps going around in my mind, maybe I did something to him. I got nothing to give him.

BERNARD: Don't take it so hard.

WILLY: Why did he lay down? What is the story there? You were his friend!

BERNARD: Willy, I remember, it was June, and our grades came out. And he'd flunked math.

WILLY: That son-of-a-bitch!

BERNARD: No, it wasn't right then. Biff just got very angry, I remember, and he was ready to enroll in summer school.

WILLY (*surprised*): He was?

BERNARD: He wasn't beaten by it at all. But then, Willy, he disappeared from the block for almost a month. And I got the idea that he'd gone up to New England to see you. Did he have a talk with you then?

(*Willy stares in silence.*)

BERNARD: Willy?

WILLY (*with a strong edge of resentment in his voice*): Yeah, he came to Boston. What about it?

BERNARD: Well, just that when he came back — I'll never forget this, it always mystifies me. Because I'd thought so well of Biff, even though he'd always taken advantage of me. I loved him, Willy, y'know? And he came back after that month and took his sneakers — remember those sneakers with "University of Virginia" printed on them? He was so proud of those, wore them every day. And he took them down in the cellar, and burned them up in the furnace. We had a fist fight. It lasted at least half an hour. Just the two of us, punching each other down the cellar, and crying right through it. I've often thought of how strange it was that I knew he'd given up his life. What happened in Boston, Willy?

(*Willy looks at him as at an intruder.*)

BERNARD: I just bring it up because you asked me.

WILLY (*angrily*): Nothing. What do you mean, "What happened?" What's that got to do with anything?

BERNARD: Well, don't get sore.

WILLY: What are you trying to do, blame it on me? If a boy lays down is that my fault?

BERNARD: Now, Willy, don't get —

WILLY: Well, don't — don't talk to me that way! What does that mean, "What happened?"

(*Charley enters. He is in his vest, and he carries a bottle of bourbon.*)

CHARLEY: Hey, you're going to miss that train. (*He waves the bottle.*)

BERNARD: Yeah, I'm going. (*He takes the bottle.*) Thanks, Pop. (*He picks up his rackets and bag.*) Good-by, Willy, and don't worry about it. You know, "If at first you don't succeed . . ."

WILLY: Yes, I believe in that.

BERNARD: But sometimes, Willy, it's better for a man just to walk away.

WILLY: Walk away?

BERNARD: That's right.

WILLY: But if you can't walk away?

BERNARD (*after a slight pause*): I guess that's when it's tough. (*Extending his hand.*) Good-by, Willy.

WILLY (*shaking Bernard's hand*): Good-by, boy.

CHARLEY (*an arm on Bernard's shoulder*): How do you like this kid? Gonna argue a case in front of the Supreme Court.

BERNARD (*protesting*): Pop!

WILLY (*genuinely shocked, pained, and happy*): No! The Supreme Court!

BERNARD: I gotta run. 'By, Dad!

CHARLEY: Knock 'em dead, Bernard!

(*Bernard goes off.*)

WILLY (*as Charley takes out his wallet*): The Supreme Court! And he didn't even mention it!

CHARLEY (*counting out money on the desk*): He don't have to — he's gonna do it.

WILLY: And you never told him what to do, did you? You never took any interest in him.

CHARLEY: My salvation is that I never took any interest in anything. There's some money — fifty dollars. I got an accountant inside.

WILLY: Charley, look . . . (*With difficulty.*) I got my insurance to pay. If you can manage it — I need a hundred and ten dollars.

(*Charley doesn't reply for a moment; merely stops moving.*)

WILLY: I'd draw it from my bank but Linda would know, and I . . .

CHARLEY: Sit down, Willy.

WILLY (*moving toward the chair*): I'm keeping an account of everything, remember. I'll pay every penny back. (*He sits.*)

CHARLEY: Now listen to me, Willy.

WILLY: I want you to know I appreciate . . .

CHARLEY (*sitting down on the table*): Willy, what're you doin'? What the hell is goin' on in your head?

WILLY: Why? I'm simply . . .

CHARLEY: I offered you a job. You make fifty dollars a week. And I won't send you on the road.

WILLY: I've got a job.

CHARLEY: Without pay? What kind of a job is a job without pay? (*He rises.*) Now, look, kid, enough is enough. I'm no genius but I know when I'm being insulted.

WILLY: Insulted!

CHARLEY: Why don't you want to work for me?

WILLY: What's the matter with you? I've got a job.

CHARLEY: Then what're you walkin' in here every week for?

WILLY (*getting up*): Well, if you don't want me to walk in here —

CHARLEY: I'm offering you a job.

WILLY: I don't want your goddam job!

CHARLEY: When the hell are you going to grow up?

WILLY (*furiously*): You big ignoramus, if you say that to me again I'll rap you one! I don't care how big you are! (*He's ready to fight.*)

(*Pause.*)

CHARLEY (*kindly, going to him*): How much do you need, Willy?

WILLY: Charley, I'm strapped. I'm strapped. I don't know what to do. I was just fired.

CHARLEY: Howard fired you?

WILLY: That snotnose. Imagine that? I named him. I named him Howard.

CHARLEY: Willy, when're you gonna realize that them things don't mean anything? You named him Howard, but you can't sell that. The only thing you got in this world is what you can sell. And the funny thing is that you're a salesman, and you don't know that.

WILLY: I've always tried to think otherwise, I guess. I always felt that if a man was impressive, and well liked, that nothing —

CHARLEY: Why must everybody like you? Who liked J. P. Morgan?° Was he impressive? In a Turkish bath he'd look like a butcher. But with his pockets on he was very well liked. Now listen, Willy, I know you don't like me, and nobody can say I'm in love with you, but I'll give you a job because — just for the hell of it, put it that way. Now what do you say?

WILLY: I — I just can't work for you, Charley.

CHARLEY: What're you, jealous of me?

WILLY: I can't work for you, that's all, don't ask me why.

J. P. Morgan: (1837–1913), wealthy financier and art collector whose money was made chiefly in banking, railroads, and steel.

CHARLEY (*angered, takes out more bills*): You been jealous of me all your life, you dammed fool! Here, pay your insurance. (*He puts the money in Willy's hand.*)

WILLY: I'm keeping strict accounts.

CHARLEY: I've got some work to do. Take care of yourself. And pay your insurance.

WILLY (*moving to the right*): Funny, y'know? After all the highways, and the trains, and the appointments, and the years, you end up worth more dead than alive.

CHARLEY: Willy, nobody's worth nothin' dead. (*After a slight pause.*) Did you hear what I said?

(*Willy stands still, dreaming.*)

CHARLEY: Willy!

WILLY: Apologize to Bernard for me when you see him. I didn't mean to argue with him. He's a fine boy. They're all fine boys, and they'll end up big — all of them. Someday they'll all play tennis together. Wish me luck, Charley. He saw Bill Oliver today.

CHARLEY: Good luck.

WILLY (*on the verge of tears*): Charley, you're the only friend I got. Isn't that a remarkable thing? (*He goes out.*)

CHARLEY: Jesus!

(*Charley stares after him a moment and follows. All light blacks out. Suddenly raucous music is heard, and a red glow rises behind the screen at right. Stanley, a young waiter, appears, carrying a table, followed by Happy, who is carrying two chairs.*)

STANLEY (*putting the table down*): That's all right, Mr. Loman, I can handle it myself. (*He turns and takes the chairs from Happy and places them at the table.*)

HAPPY (*glancing around*): Oh, this is better.

STANLEY: Sure, in the front there you're in the middle of all kinds of noise. Whenever you got a party, Mr. Loman, you just tell me and I'll put you back here. Y'know, there's a lotta people they don't like it private, because when they go out they like to see a lotta action around them because they're sick and tired to stay in the house by theirself. But I know you, you ain't from Hackensack. You know what I mean?

HAPPY (*sitting down*): So how's it coming, Stanley?

STANLEY: Ah, it's a dog life. I only wish during the war they'd a took me in the Army. I coulda been dead by now.

HAPPY: My brother's back, Stanley.

STANLEY: Oh, he come back, heh? From the Far West.

HAPPY: Yeah, big cattle man, my brother, so treat him right. And my father's coming too.

STANLEY: Oh, your father too!

HAPPY: You got a couple of nice lobsters?

STANLEY: Hundred percent, big.

HAPPY: I want them with the claws.

STANLEY: Don't worry, I don't give you no mice. (*Happy laughs.*) How about some wine? It'll put a head on the meal.

HAPPY: No. You remember, Stanley, that recipe I brought you from overseas? With the champagne in it?

STANLEY: Oh, yeah, sure. I still got it tacked up yet in the kitchen. But that'll have to cost a buck apiece anyways.

HAPPY: That's all right.

STANLEY: What'd you, hit a number or somethin'?

HAPPY: No, it's a little celebration. My brother is — I think he pulled off a big deal today. I think we're going into business together.

STANLEY: Great! That's the best for you. Because a family business, you know what I mean? — that's the best.

HAPPY: That's what I think.

STANLEY: 'Cause what's the difference? Somebody steals? It's in the family. Know what I mean? (*Sotto voce.°*) Like this bartender here. The boss is goin' crazy what kinda leak he's got in the cash register. You put it in but it don't come out.

HAPPY (*raising his head*): Sh!

STANLEY: What?

HAPPY: You notice I wasn't lookin' right or left, was I?

STANLEY: No.

HAPPY: And my eyes are closed.

STANLEY: So what's the — ?

HAPPY: Strudel's comin'.

STANLEY (*catching on, looks around*): Ah, no, there's no —

(*He breaks off as a furred, lavishly dressed girl enters and sits at the next table. Both follow her with their eyes.*)

STANLEY: Geez, how'd ya know?

HAPPY: I got radar or something. (*Staring directly at her profile.*) Oooooooo . . . Stanley.

STANLEY: I think that's for you, Mr. Loman.

HAPPY: Look at that mouth. Oh, God. And the binoculars.

STANLEY: Geez, you got a life, Mr. Loman.

HAPPY: Wait on her.

STANLEY (*going to the girl's table*): Would you like a menu, ma'am?

GIRL: I'm expecting someone, but I'd like a —

HAPPY: Why don't you bring her — excuse me, miss, do you mind? I sell champagne, and I'd like you to try my brand. Bring her a champagne, Stanley.

GIRL: That's awfully nice of you.

HAPPY: Don't mention it. It's all company money. (*He laughs.*)

GIRL: That's a charming product to be selling, isn't it?

HAPPY: Oh, gets to be like everything else. Selling is selling, y'know.

GIRL: I suppose.

HAPPY: You don't happen to sell, do you?

GIRL: No, I don't sell.

HAPPY: Would you object to a compliment from a stranger? You ought to be on a magazine cover.

GIRL (*looking at him a little archly*): I have been.

(*Stanley comes in with a glass of champagne.*)

Sotto voce: In a soft voice or stage whisper.

HAPPY: What'd I say before, Stanley? You see? She's a cover girl.

STANLEY: Oh, I could see, I could see.

HAPPY (*to the Girl*): What magazine?

GIRL: Oh, a lot of them. (*She takes the drink.*) Thank you.

HAPPY: You know what they say in France, don't you? "Champagne is the drink of the complexion" — Hya, Biff!

(*Biff has entered and sits with Happy.*)

BIFF: Hello, kid. Sorry I'm late.

HAPPY: I just got here. Uh, Miss — ?

GIRL: Forsythe.

HAPPY: Miss Forsythe, this is my brother.

BIFF: Is Dad here?

HAPPY: His name is Biff. You might've heard of him. Great football player.

GIRL: Really? What team?

HAPPY: Are you familiar with football?

GIRL: No, I'm afraid I'm not.

HAPPY: Biff is quarterback with the New York Giants.

GIRL: Well, that is nice, isn't it? (*She drinks.*)

HAPPY: Good health.

GIRL: I'm happy to meet you.

HAPPY: That's my name. Hap. It's really Harold, but at West Point they called me Happy.

GIRL (*now really impressed*): Oh, I see. How do you do? (*She turns her profile.*)

BIFF: Isn't Dad coming?

HAPPY: You want her?

BIFF: Oh, I could never make that.

HAPPY: I remember the time that idea would never come into your head. Where's the old confidence Biff?

BIFF: I just saw Oliver —

HAPPY: Wait a minute. I've got to see that old confidence again. Do you want her? She's on call.

BIFF: Oh, no. (*He turns to look at the Girl.*)

HAPPY: I'm telling you. Watch this. (*Turning to the Girl*): Honey? (*She turns to him.*) Are you busy?

GIRL: Well, I am . . . but I could make a phone call.

HAPPY: Do that, will you, honey? And see if you can get a friend. We'll be here for a while. Biff is one of the greatest football players in the country.

GIRL (*standing up*): Well, I'm certainly happy to meet you.

HAPPY: Come back soon.

GIRL: I'll try.

HAPPY: Don't try, honey, try hard.

(*The Girl exits. Stanley follows, shaking his head in bewildered admiration.*)

HAPPY: Isn't that a shame now? A beautiful girl like that? That's why I can't get married. There's not a good woman in a thousand. New York is loaded with them, kid!

BIFF: Hap, look —

HAPPY: I told you she was on call!

BIFF (*strangely unnerved*): Cut it out, will ya? I want to say something to you.

HAPPY: Did you see Oliver?

BIFF: I saw him all right. Now look, I want to tell Dad a couple of things and I want you to help me.

HAPPY: What? Is he going to back you?

BIFF: Are you crazy? You're out of your goddam head, you know that?

HAPPY: Why? What happened?

BIFF (*breathlessly*): I did a terrible thing today, Hap. It's been the strangest day I ever went through. I'm all numb, I swear.

HAPPY: You mean he wouldn't see you?

BIFF: Well, I waited six hours for him, see? All day. Kept sending my name in. Even tried to date his secretary so she'd get me to him, but no soap.

HAPPY: Because you're not showin' the old confidence Biff. He remembered you, didn't he?

BIFF (*stopping Happy with a gesture*): Finally, about five o'clock, he comes out. Didn't remember who I was or anything. I felt like such an idiot, Hap.

HAPPY: Did you tell him my Florida idea?

BIFF: He walked away. I saw him for one minute. I got so mad I could've torn the walls down! How the hell did I ever get the idea I was a salesman there? I even believed myself that I'd been a salesman for him! And then he gave me one look and — I realized what a ridiculous lie my whole life has been! We've been talking in a dream for fifteen years. I was a shipping clerk.

HAPPY: What'd you do?

BIFF (*with great tension and wonder*): Well, he left, see. And the secretary went out. I was all alone in the waiting room. I don't know what came over me, Hap. The next thing I know I'm in his office — paneled walls, everything. I can't explain it. I — Hap, I took his fountain pen.

HAPPY: Geez, did he catch you?

BIFF: I ran out. I ran down all eleven flights. I ran and ran and ran.

HAPPY: That was an awful dumb — what'd you do that for?

BIFF (*agonized*): I don't know, I just — wanted to take something, I don't know. You gotta help me, Hap. I'm gonna tell Pop.

HAPPY: You crazy? What for?

BIFF: Hap, he's got to understand that I'm not the man somebody lends that kind of money to. He thinks I've been spiting him all these years and it's eating him up.

HAPPY: That's just it. You tell him something nice.

BIFF: I can't.

HAPPY: Say you got a lunch date with Oliver tomorrow.

BIFF: So what do I do tomorrow?

HAPPY: You leave the house tomorrow and come back at night and say Oliver is thinking it over. And he thinks it over for a couple of weeks, and gradually it fades away and nobody's the worse.

BIFF: But it'll go on forever!

HAPPY: Dad is never so happy as when he's looking forward to something!

(*Willy enters.*)

HAPPY: Hello, scout!

WILLY: Gee, I haven't been here in years!

(*Stanley has followed Willy in and sets a chair for him. Stanley starts off but Happy stops him.*)

HAPPY: Stanley!

(*Stanley stands by, waiting for an order.*)

BIFF (*going to Willy with guilt, as to an invalid*): Sit down, Pop. You want a drink?

WILLY: Sure, I don't mind.

BIFF: Let's get a load on.

WILLY: You look worried.

BIFF: N-no. (*To Stanley.*) Scotch all around. Make it doubles.

STANLEY: Doubles, right. (*He goes.*)

WILLY: You had a couple already, didn't you?

BIFF: Just a couple, yeah.

WILLY: Well, what happened, boy? (*Nodding affirmatively, with a smile.*) Everything go all right?

BIFF (*takes a breath, then reaches out and grasps Willy's hand*): Pal . . . (*He is smiling bravely, and Willy is smiling too.*) I had an experience today.

HAPPY: Terrific, Pop.

WILLY: That so? What happened?

BIFF (*high, slightly alcoholic, above the earth*): I'm going to tell you everything from first to last. It's been a strange day. (*Silence. He looks around, composes himself as best he can, but his breath keeps breaking the rhythm of his voice.*) I had to wait quite a while for him, and —

WILLY: Oliver?

BIFF: Yeah, Oliver. All day, as a matter of cold fact. And a lot of — instances — facts, Pop, facts about my life came back to me. Who was it, Pop? Who ever said I was a salesman with Oliver?

WILLY: Well, you were.

BIFF: No, Dad, I was a shipping clerk.

WILLY: But you were practically —

BIFF (*with determination*): Dad, I don't know who said it first, but I was never a salesman for Bill Oliver.

WILLY: What're you talking about?

BIFF: Let's hold on to the facts tonight, Pop. We're not going to get anywhere bullin' around. I was a shipping clerk.

WILLY (*angrily*): All right, now listen to me —

BIFF: Why don't you let me finish?

WILLY: I'm not interested in stories about the past or any crap of that kind because the woods are burning, boys, you understand? There's a big blaze going on all around. I was fired today.

BIFF (*shocked*): How could you be?

WILLY: I was fired, and I'm looking for a little good news to tell your mother, because the woman has waited and the woman has suffered. The gist of it is that I haven't got a story left in my head, Biff. So

don't give me a lecture about facts and aspects. I am not interested. Now what've you got to say to me?

(*Stanley enters with three drinks. They wait until he leaves.*)

WILLY: Did you see Oliver?

BIFF: Jesus, Dad!

WILLY: You mean you didn't go up there?

HAPPY: Sure he went up there.

BIFF: I did. I — saw him. How could they fire you?

WILLY (*on the edge of his chair*): What kind of a welcome did he give you?

BIFF: He won't even let you work on commission?

WILLY: I'm out! (*Driving.*) So tell me, he gave you a warm welcome?

HAPPY: Sure, Pop, sure!

BIFF (*driven*): Well, it was kind of —

WILLY: I was wondering if he'd remember you. (*To Happy.*) Imagine, man doesn't see him for ten, twelve years and gives him that kind of a welcome!

HAPPY: Damn right!

BIFF (*trying to return to the offensive*): Pop, look —

WILLY: You know why he remembered you, don't you? Because you impressed him in those days.

BIFF: Let's talk quietly and get this down to the facts, huh?

WILLY (*as though Biff had been interrupting*): Well, what happened? It's great news, Biff. Did he take you into his office or'd you talk in the waiting room?

BIFF: Well, he came in, see, and —

WILLY (*with a big smile*): What'd he say? Betcha he threw his arm around you.

BIFF: Well, he kinda —

WILLY: He's a fine man. (*To Happy.*) Very hard man to see, y'know.

HAPPY (*agreeing*): Oh, I know.

WILLY (*to Biff*): Is that where you had the drinks?

BIFF: Yeah, he gave me a couple of — no, no!

HAPPY (*cutting in*): He told him my Florida idea.

WILLY: Don't interrupt. (*To Biff.*) How'd he react to the Florida idea?

BIFF: Dad, will you give me a minute to explain?

WILLY: I've been waiting for you to explain since I sat down here! What happened? He took you into his office and what?

BIFF: Well — I talked. And — and he listened, see.

WILLY: Famous for the way he listens, y'know. What was his answer?

BIFF: His answer was — (*He breaks off, suddenly angry.*) Dad, you're not letting me tell you what I want to tell you!

WILLY (*accusing, angered*): You didn't see him, did you?

BIFF: I did see him!

WILLY: What'd you insult him or something? You insulted him, didn't you?

BIFF: Listen, will you let me out of it, will you just let me out of it!

HAPPY: What the hell!

WILLY: Tell me what happened!

BIFF (*to Happy*): I can't talk to him!

(*A single trumpet note jars the ear. The light of green leaves stains the house, which holds the air of night and a dream. Young Bernard enters and knocks on the door of the house.*)

YOUNG BERNARD (*frantically*): Mrs. Loman, Mrs. Loman!

HAPPY: Tell him what happened!

BIFF (*to Happy*): Shut up and leave me alone!

WILLY: No, no! You had to go and flunk math!

BIFF: What math? What're you talking about?

YOUNG BERNARD: Mrs. Loman, Mrs. Loman!

(*Linda appears in the house, as of old.*)

WILLY (*wildly*): Math, math, math!

BIFF: Take it easy, Pop!

YOUNG BERNARD: Mrs. Loman!

WILLY (*furiously*): If you hadn't flunked you'd've been set by now!

BIFF: Now, look, I'm gonna tell you what happened, and you're going to listen to me.

YOUNG BERNARD: Mrs. Loman!

BIFF: I waited six hours —

HAPPY: What the hell are you saying?

BIFF: I kept sending in my name but he wouldn't see me. So finally he . . . (*He continues unheard as light fades low on the restaurant.*)

YOUNG BERNARD: Biff flunked math!

LINDA: No!

YOUNG BERNARD: Birnbaum flunked him! They won't graduate him!

LINDA: But they have to. He's gotta go to the university. Where is he? Biff! Biff!

YOUNG BERNARD: No, he left. He went to Grand Central.

LINDA: Grand — You mean he went to Boston!

YOUNG BERNARD: Is Uncle Willy in Boston?

LINDA: Oh, maybe Willy can talk to the teacher. Oh, the poor, poor boy!

(*Light on house area snaps out.*)

BIFF (*at the table, now audible, holding up a gold fountain pen*): . . . so I'm washed up with Oliver, you understand? Are you listening to me?

WILLY (*at a loss*): Yeah, sure. If you hadn't flunked —

BIFF: Flunked what? What're you talking about?

WILLY: Don't blame everything on me! I didn't flunk math — you did! What pen?

HAPPY: That was awful dumb, Biff, a pen like that is worth —

WILLY (*seeing the pen for the first time*): You took Oliver's pen?

BIFF (*weakening*): Dad, I just explained it to you.

WILLY: You stole Bill Oliver's fountain pen!

BIFF: I didn't exactly steal it! That's just what I've been explaining to you!

HAPPY: He had it in his hand and just then Oliver walked in, so he got nervous and stuck it in his pocket!

WILLY: My God, Biff!

BIFF: I never intended to do it, Dad!

OPERATOR'S VOICE: Standish Arms, good evening!

WILLY (*shouting*): I'm not in my room!

BIFF (*frightened*): Dad, what's the matter? (*He and Happy stand up.*)

OPERATOR: Ringing Mr. Loman for you!

WILLY: I'm not there, stop it!

BIFF (*horrified, gets down on one knee before Willy*): Dad, I'll make good, I'll make good. (*Willy tries to get to his feet. Biff holds him down.*) Sit down now.

WILLY: No, you're no good, you're no good for anything.

BIFF: I am, Dad, I'll find something else, you understand? Now don't worry about anything. (*He holds up Willy's face.*) Talk to me, Dad.

OPERATOR: Mr. Loman does not answer. Shall I page him?

WILLY (*attempting to stand, as though to rush and silence the Operator*): No, no, no!

HAPPY: He'll strike something, Pop.

WILLY: No, no . . .

BIFF (*desperately, standing over Willy*): Pop, listen! Listen to me! I'm telling you something good. Oliver talked to his partner about the Florida idea. You listening? He — he talked to his partner, and he came to me . . . I'm going to be all right, you hear? Dad, listen to me, he said it was just a question of the amount!

WILLY: Then you . . . got it?

HAPPY: He's gonna be terrific, Pop!

WILLY (*trying to stand*): Then you got it, haven't you? You got it! You got it!

BIFF (*agonized, holds Willy down*): No, no. Look, Pop. I'm supposed to have lunch with them tomorrow. I'm just telling you this so you'll know that I can still make an impression, Pop. And I'll make good somewhere, but I can't go tomorrow, see?

WILLY: Why not? You simply —

BIFF: But the pen, Pop!

WILLY: You give it to him and tell him it was an oversight!

HAPPY: Sure, have lunch tomorrow!

BIFF: I can't say that —

WILLY: You were doing a crossword puzzle and accidentally used his pen!

BIFF: Listen, kid, I took those balls years ago, now I walk in with his fountain pen? That clinches it, don't you see? I can't face him like that! I'll try elsewhere.

PAGE'S VOICE: Paging Mr. Loman!

WILLY: Don't you want to be anything?

BIFF: Pop, how can I go back?

WILLY: You don't want to be anything, is that what's behind it?

BIFF (*now angry at Willy for not crediting his sympathy*): Don't take it that way! You think it was easy walking into that office after what I'd done to him? A team of horses couldn't have dragged me back to Bill Oliver!

WILLY: Then why'd you go?

BIFF: Why did I go? Why did I go! Look at you! Look at what's become of you!

(*Off left, The Woman laughs.*)

WILLY: Biff, you're going to go to that lunch tomorrow, or —

BIFF: I can't go. I've got no appointment!

HAPPY: Biff, for . . . !

WILLY: Are you spiting me?

BIFF: Don't take it that way! Goddammit!

WILLY (*strikes Biff and falters away from the table*): You rotten little louse! Are you spiting me?

THE WOMAN: Someone's at the door, Willy!

BIFF: I'm no good, can't you see what I am?

HAPPY (*separating them*): Hey, you're in a restaurant! Now cut it out, both of you! (*The girls enter.*) Hello, girls, sit down.

(*The Woman laughs, off left.*)

MISS FORSYTHE: I guess we might as well. This is Letta.

THE WOMAN: Willy, are you going to wake up?

BIFF (*ignoring Willy*): How're ya, miss, sit down. What do you drink?

MISS FORSYTHE: Letta might not be able to stay long.

LETTA: I gotta get up very early tomorrow. I got jury duty. I'm so excited! Were you fellows ever on a jury?

BIFF: No, but I been in front of them! (*The girls laugh.*) This is my father.

LETTA: Isn't he cute? Sit down with us, Pop.

HAPPY: Sit him down, Biff!

BIFF (*going to him*): Come on, slugger, drink us under the table. To hell with it! Come on, sit down, pal.

(*On Biff's last insistence, Willy is about to sit.*)

THE WOMAN (*now urgently*): Willy, are you going to answer the door!

(*The Woman's call pulls Willy back. He starts right, befuddled.*)

BIFF: Hey, where are you going?

WILLY: Open the door.

BIFF: The door?

WILLY: The washroom . . . the door . . . where's the door?

BIFF (*leading Willy to the left*): Just go straight down.

(*Willy moves left.*)

THE WOMAN: Willy, Willy, are you going to get up, get up, get up, get up?

(*Willy exits left.*)

LETTA: I think it's sweet you bring your daddy along.

MISS FORSYTHE: Oh, he isn't really your father!

BIFF (*at left, turning to her resentfully*): Miss Forsythe, you've just seen a prince walk by. A fine, troubled prince. A hard-working, unappreciated prince. A pal, you understand? A good companion. Always for his boys.

LETTA: That's so sweet.

HAPPY: Well, girls, what's the program? We're wasting time. Come on, Biff. Gather round. Where would you like to go?

BIFF: Why don't you do something for him?

HAPPY: Me!

BIFF: Don't you give a damn for him, Hap?

HAPPY: What're you talking about? I'm the one who —

BIFF: I sense it, you don't give a good goddam about him. (*He takes the rolled-up hose from his pocket and puts it on the table in front of Happy.*) Look what I found in the cellar, for Christ's sake. How can you bear to let it go on?

HAPPY: Me? Who goes away? Who runs off and —

BIFF: Yeah, but he doesn't mean anything to you. You could help him — I can't! Don't you understand what I'm talking about? He's going to kill himself, don't you know that?

HAPPY: Don't I know it! Me!

BIFF: Hap, help him! Jesus . . . help him . . . Help me, help me, I can't bear to look at his face! (*Ready to weep, he hurries out, up right.*)

HAPPY (*starting after him*): Where are you going?

MISS FORSYTHE: What's he so mad about?

HAPPY: Come on, girls, we'll catch up with him.

MISS FORSYTHE (*as Happy pushes her out*): Say, I don't like that temper of his!

HAPPY: He's just a little overstrung, he'll be all right!

WILLY (*off left, as The Woman laughs*): Don't answer! Don't answer!

LETTA: Don't you want to tell your father —

HAPPY: No, that's not my father. He's just a guy. Come on, we'll catch Biff, and, honey, we're going to paint this town! Stanley, where's the check! Hey, Stanley!

(*They exit. Stanley looks toward left.*)

STANLEY (*calling to Happy indignantly*): Mr. Loman! Mr. Loman!

(*Stanley picks up a chair and follows them off. Knocking is heard off left. The Woman enters, laughing. Willy follows her. She is in a black slip; he is buttoning his shirt. Raw, sensuous music accompanies their speech.*)

WILLY: Will you stop laughing? Will you stop?

THE WOMAN: Aren't you going to answer the door? He'll wake the whole hotel.

WILLY: I'm not expecting anybody.

THE WOMAN: Whyn't you have another drink, honey, and stop being so damn self-centered?

WILLY: I'm so lonely.

THE WOMAN: You know you ruined me, Willy? From now on, whenever you come to the office, I'll see that you go right through to the buyers. No waiting at my desk anymore, Willy. You ruined me.

WILLY: That's nice of you to say that.

THE WOMAN: Gee, you are self-centered! Why so sad?

You are the saddest, self-centeredest soul I ever did see-saw. (*She laughs. He kisses her.*) Come on inside, drummer boy. It's silly to be dressing in the middle of the night. (*As knocking is heard.*) Aren't you going to answer the door?

WILLY: They're knocking on the wrong door.

THE WOMAN: But I felt the knocking. And he heard us talking in here. Maybe the hotel's on fire!

WILLY (*his terror rising*): It's a mistake.

THE WOMAN: Then tell him to go away!

WILLY: There's nobody there.

THE WOMAN: It's getting on my nerves, Willy. There's somebody standing out there and it's getting on my nerves!

WILLY (*pushing her away from him*): All right, stay in the bathroom here, and don't come out. I think there's a law in Massachusetts about it, so don't come out. It may be that new room clerk. He looked very mean. So don't come out. It's a mistake, there's no fire.

(*The knocking is heard again. He takes a few steps away from her, and she vanishes into the wing. The light follows him, and now he is facing Young Biff, who carries a suitcase. Biff steps toward him. The music is gone.*)

BIFF: Why didn't you answer?

WILLY: Biff! What are you doing in Boston?

BIFF: Why didn't you answer? I've been knocking for five minutes, I called you on the phone —

WILLY: I just heard you. I was in the bathroom and had the door shut. Did anything happen home?

BIFF: Dad — I let you down.

WILLY: What do you mean?

BIFF: Dad . . .

WILLY: Biffo, what's this about? (*Putting his arm around Biff.*) Come on, let's go downstairs and get you a malted.

BIFF: Dad, I flunked math.

WILLY: Not for the term?

BIFF: The term. I haven't got enough credits to graduate.

WILLY: You mean to say Bernard wouldn't give you the answers?

BIFF: He did, he tried, but I only got a sixty-one.

WILLY: And they wouldn't give you four points?

BIFF: Birnbaum refused absolutely. I begged him, Pop, but he won't give me those points. You gotta talk to him before they close the school. Because if he saw the kind of man you are, and you just talked to him in your way, I'm sure he'd come through for me. The class came right before practice, see, and I didn't go enough. Would you talk to him? He'd like you, Pop. You know the way you could talk.

WILLY: You're on. We'll drive right back.

BIFF: Oh, Dad, good work! I'm sure he'll change it for you!

WILLY: Go downstairs and tell the clerk I'm checkin' out. Go right down.

BIFF: Yes, sir! See, the reason he hates me, Pop — one day he was late for class so I got up at the blackboard and imitated him. I crossed my eyes and talked with a lithp.

WILLY (*laughing*): You did? The kids like it?

BIFF: They nearly died laughing!

WILLY: Yeah? What'd you do?

BIFF: The thquare root of thixthy twee is . . . (*Willy bursts out laughing; Biff joins.*) And in the middle of it he walked in!

(*Willy laughs and The Woman joins in offstage.*)

WILLY (*without hesitation*): Hurry downstairs and —

BIFF: Somebody in there?

WILLY: No, that was next door.

(*The Woman laughs offstage.*)

BIFF: Somebody got in your bathroom!

WILLY: No, it's the next room, there's a party —

THE WOMAN (*enters, laughing. She lisps this.*): Can I come in? There's something in the bathtub, Willy, and it's moving!

(*Willy looks at Biff, who is staring open-mouthed and horrified at The Woman.*)

WILLY: Ah — you better go back to your room. They must be finished painting by now. They're painting her room so I let her take a shower here. Go back, go back . . . (*He pushes her.*)

THE WOMAN (*resisting*): But I've got to get dressed, Willy, I can't —

WILLY: Get out of here! Go back, go back . . . (*Suddenly striving for the ordinary.*) This is Miss Francis, Biff, she's a buyer. They're painting her room. Go back, Miss Francis, go back . . .

THE WOMAN: But my clothes, I can't go out naked in the hall!

WILLY (*pushing her offstage*): Get outa here! Go back, go back!

(*Biff slowly sits down on his suitcase as the argument continues offstage.*)

THE WOMAN: Where's my stockings? You promised me stockings, Willy!

WILLY: I have no stockings here!

THE WOMAN: You had two boxes of size nine sheers for me, and I want them!

WILLY: Here, for God's sake, will you get outa here!

THE WOMAN (*enters holding a box of stockings*): I just hope there's nobody in the hall. That's all I hope. (*To Biff.*) Are you football or baseball?

BIFF: Football.

THE WOMAN (*angry, humiliated*): That's me too. G'night. (*She snatches her clothes from Willy, and walks out.*)

WILLY (*after a pause*): Well, better get going. I want to get to the school first thing in the morning. Get my suits out of the closet. I'll get my valise. (*Biff doesn't move.*) What's the matter! (*Biff remains motionless, tears falling.*) She's a buyer. Buys for J. H. Simmons. She lives down the hall — they're painting. You don't imagine — (*He breaks off. After a pause.*) Now listen, pal, she's just a buyer. She sees merchandise in her room and they have to keep it looking just so . . . (*Pause. Assuming command.*) All right, get my suits. (*Biff doesn't move.*) Now stop crying and do as I say. I gave you an order. Biff, I gave you an order! Is that what you do when I give you an order? How dare you cry! (*Putting his arm around Biff.*) Now look, Biff, when you grow up you'll understand about these things. You mustn't — you mustn't overemphasize a thing like this. I'll see Birnbaum first thing in the morning.

BIFF: Never mind.

WILLY (*getting down beside Biff*): Never mind! He's going to give you those points. I'll see to it.

BIFF: He wouldn't listen to you.

WILLY: He certainly will listen to me. You need those points for the U. of Virginia.

BIFF: I'm not going there.

WILLY: Heh? If I can't get him to change that mark you'll make it up in summer school. You've got all summer to —

BIFF (*his weeping breaking from him*): Dad . . .

WILLY (*infected by it*): Oh, my boy . . .

BIFF: Dad . . .

WILLY: She's nothing to me, Biff. I was lonely, I was terribly lonely.

BIFF: You — you gave her Mama's stockings! (*His tears break through and he rises to go.*)

WILLY (*grabbing for Biff*): I gave you an order!

BIFF: Don't touch me, you — liar!

WILLY: Apologize for that!

BIFF: You fake! You phony little fake! You fake! (*Overcome, he turns quickly and weeping fully goes out with his suitcase. Willy is left on the floor on his knees.*)

WILLY: I gave you an order! Biff, come back here or I'll beat you! Come back here! I'll whip you!

(*Stanley comes quickly in from the right and stands in front of Willy.*)

WILLY (*shouts at Stanley*): I gave you an order . . .

STANLEY: Hey, let's pick it up, pick it up, Mr. Loman. (*He helps Willy to his feet.*) Your boys left with the chippies. They said they'll see you home.

(*A second waiter watches some distance away.*)

WILLY: But we were supposed to have dinner together.

(*Music is heard, Willy's theme.*)

STANLEY: Can you make it?

WILLY: I'll — sure, I can make it. (*Suddenly concerned about his clothes.*) Do I — I look all right?

STANLEY: Sure, you look all right. (*He flicks a speck off Willy's lapel.*)

WILLY: Here — here's a dollar.

STANLEY: Oh, your son paid me. It's all right.

WILLY (*putting it in Stanley's hand*): No, take it. You're a good boy.

STANLEY: Oh, no, you don't have to . . .

WILLY: Here — here's some more, I don't need it any-more. (*After a slight pause.*) Tell me — is there a seed store in the neighborhood?

STANLEY: Seeds? You mean like to plant?

(*As Willy turns, Stanley slips the money back into his jacket pocket.*)

WILLY: Yes. Carrots, peas . . .

STANLEY: Well, there's hardware stores on Sixth Avenue, but it may be too late now.

WILLY (*anxiously*): Oh, I'd better hurry. I've got to get some seeds. (*He starts off to the right.*) I've got to get some seeds, right away. Nothing's planted. I don't have a thing in the ground.

(*Willy hurries out as the light goes down. Stanley moves over to the right after him, watches him off. The other waiter has been staring at Willy.*)

STANLEY (*to the waiter*): Well, whatta you looking at?

(*The waiter picks up the chairs and moves off right. Stanley takes the table and follows him. The light fades on this area. There is a long pause, the sound of the flute coming over. The light gradually rises on the kitchen, which is empty. Happy appears at the door of the house, followed by Biff. Happy is carrying a large bunch of long-stemmed roses. He enters the kitchen, looks around for Linda. Not seeing her, he turns to Biff, who is just outside the house door, and makes a gesture with his hands, indicating "Not here, I guess." He looks into the living room and freezes. Inside, Linda, unseen, is seated, Willy's coat on her lap. She rises ominously and quietly and moves toward Happy, who backs up into the kitchen, afraid.*)

HAPPY: Hey, what're you doing up? (*Linda says nothing but moves toward him implacably.*) Where's Pop? (*He keeps backing to the right, and now Linda is in full view in the doorway to the living room.*) Is he sleeping?

LINDA: Where were you?

HAPPY (*trying to laugh it off*): We met two girls, Mom, very fine types. Here, we brought you some flowers. (*Offering them to her.*) Put them in your room, Ma.

(*She knocks them to the floor at Biff's feet. He has now come inside and closed the door behind him. She stares at Biff, silent.*)

HAPPY: Now what'd you do that for? Mom, I want you to have some flowers —

LINDA (*cutting Happy off, violently to Biff*): Don't you care whether he lives or dies?

HAPPY (*going to the stairs*): Come upstairs, Biff.

BIFF (*with a flare of disgust, to Happy*): Go away from me! (*To Linda.*) What do you mean, lives or dies? Nobody's dying around here, pal.

LINDA: Get out of my sight! Get out of here!

BIFF: I wanna see the boss.

LINDA: You're not going near him!

BIFF: Where is he? (*He moves into the living room and Linda follows.*)

LINDA (*shouting after Biff*): You invite him for dinner. He looks forward to it all day — (*Biff appears in his parents' bedroom, looks around, and exits*) — and then you desert him there. There's no stranger you'd do that to!

HAPPY: Why? He had a swell time with us. Listen, when I — (*Linda comes back into the kitchen*) — desert him I hope I don't outlive the day!

LINDA: Get out of here!

HAPPY: Now look, Mom . . .

LINDA: Did you have to go to women tonight? You and your lousy rotten whores!

(*Biff reenters the kitchen.*)

HAPPY: Mom, all we did was follow Biff around trying to cheer him up! (*To Biff.*) Boy, what a night you gave me!

LINDA: Get out of here, both of you, and don't come back! I don't want you tormenting him any more. Go on now, get your things together! (*To Biff.*) You can sleep in his apartment. (*She starts to pick up the flowers and stops herself.*) Pick up this stuff, I'm not your maid anymore. Pick it up, you bum, you!

(*Happy turns his back to her in refusal. Biff slowly moves over and gets down on his knees, picking up the flowers.*)

LINDA: You're a pair of animals! Not one, not another living soul would have had the cruelty to walk out on that man in a restaurant!

BIFF (*not looking at her*): Is that what he said?

LINDA: He didn't have to say anything. He was so humiliated he nearly limped when he came in.

HAPPY: But, Mom, he had a great time with us —

BIFF (*cutting him off violently*): Shut up!

(*Without another word, Happy goes upstairs.*)

LINDA: You! You didn't even go in to see if he was all right!

BIFF (*still on the floor in front of Linda, the flowers in his hand; with self-loathing*): No. Didn't. Didn't do a damned thing. How do you like that, heh? Left him babbling in a toilet.

LINDA: You louse. You . . .

BIFF: Now you hit it on the nose! (*He gets up, throws the flowers in the wastebasket.*) The scum of the earth, and you're looking at him!

LINDA: Get out of here!

BIFF: I gotta talk to the boss, Mom. Where is he?

LINDA: You're not going near him. Get out of this house!

BIFF (*with absolute assurance, determination*): No. We're gonna have an abrupt conversation, him and me.

LINDA: You're not talking to him.

(*Hammering is heard from outside the house, off right. Biff turns toward the noise.*)

LINDA (*suddenly pleading*): Will you please leave him alone?

BIFF: What's he doing out there?

LINDA: He's planting the garden!

BIFF (*quietly*): Now? Oh, my God!

(*Biff moves outside, Linda following. The light dies down on them and comes up on the center of the apron as Willy walks into it. He is carrying a flashlight, a hoe, and a handful of seed packets. He raps the top of the hoe sharply to fix it firmly, and then moves to the left, measuring off the distance with his foot. He holds the flashlight to look at the seed packets, reading off the instructions. He is in the blue of night.*)

WILLY: Carrots . . . quarter-inch apart. Rows . . . one-foot rows. (*He measures it off.*) One foot. (*He puts down a package and measures off.*) Beets. (*He puts down another package and measures again.*) Lettuce. (*He reads the package, puts it down.*) One foot — (*He breaks off as Ben appears at the right and moves slowly down to him.*) What a proposition, ts, ts. Terrific, terrific. 'Cause she's suffered, Ben, the woman has suffered. You understand me? A man can't go out the way he came in, Ben, a man has got to add up to something. You can't, you can't — (*Ben moves toward him as though to interrupt.*) You gotta consider, now. Don't answer so quick. Remember, it's a guaranteed twenty-thousand-dollar proposition. Now look, Ben, I want you to go through the ins and outs of this thing with me. I've got nobody to talk to, Ben, and the woman has suffered, you hear me?

BEN (*standing still, considering*): What's the proposition?

WILLY: It's twenty thousand dollars on the barrelhead. Guaranteed, gilt-edged, you understand?

BEN: You don't want to make a fool of yourself. They might not honor the policy.

WILLY: How can they dare refuse? Didn't I work like a coolie to meet every premium on the nose? And now they don't pay off? Impossible!

BEN: It's called a cowardly thing, William.

WILLY: Why? Does it take more guts to stand here the rest of my life ringing up a zero?

BEN (*yielding*): That's a point, William. (*He moves, thinking, turns.*) And twenty thousand — that is something one can feel with the hand, it is there.

WILLY (*now assured, with rising power*): Oh, Ben, that's the whole beauty of it! I see it like a diamond, shining in the dark, hard and rough, that I can pick up and touch in my hand. Not like — like an appointment! This would not be another damned-fool appointment, Ben, and it changes all the aspects. Because he thinks I'm nothing, see, and so he spites me. But the funeral — (*Straightening up.*) Ben, that funeral will be massive! They'll come from Maine, Massachusetts, Vermont, New Hampshire! All the old-timers with the strange license plates — that boy will be thunderstruck, Ben, because he never realized — I am known! Rhode Island, New York, New Jersey — I am known, Ben, and he'll see it with his eyes once and for all. He'll see what I am, Ben! He's in for a shock, that boy!

BEN (*coming down to the edge of the garden*): He'll call you a coward.

WILLY (*suddenly fearful*): No, that would be terrible.

BEN: Yes. And a damned fool.

WILLY: No, no, he mustn't, I won't have that! (*He is broken and desperate.*)

BEN: He'll hate you, William.

(*The gay music of the Boys is heard.*)

WILLY: Oh, Ben, how do we get back to all the great times? Used to be so full of light, and comradeship, the sleigh-riding in winter, and the ruddiness on his cheeks. And always some kind of good news coming up, always something nice coming up ahead. And never even let me carry the valises in the house, and simonizing, simonizing that little red car! Why, why can't I give him something and not have him hate me?

BEN: Let me think about it. (*He glances at his watch.*) I still have a little time. Remarkable proposition, but you've got to be sure you're not making a fool of yourself.

(*Ben drifts off upstage and goes out of sight. Biff comes down from the left.*)

WILLY (*suddenly conscious of Biff, turns and looks up at him, then begins picking up the packages of seeds in confusion*): Where the hell is that seed? (*Indignantly.*) You can't see nothing out here! They boxed in the whole goddam neighborhood!

BIFF: There are people all around here. Don't you realize that?

WILLY: I'm busy. Don't bother me.

BIFF (*taking the hoe from Willy*): I'm saying good-by to you, Pop. (*Willy looks at him, silent, unable to move.*) I'm not coming back any more.

WILLY: You're not going to see Oliver tomorrow?

BIFF: I've got no appointment, Dad.

WILLY: He put his arm around you, and you've got no appointment?

BIFF: Pop, get this now, will you? Everytime I've left it's been a fight that sent me out of here. Today I realized something about myself and I tried to explain it to you and I — I think I'm just not smart enough to make any sense out of it for you. To hell with whose fault it is or anything like that. (*He takes Willy's arm.*) Let's just wrap it up, heh? Come on in, we'll tell Mom. (*He gently tries to pull Willy to left.*)

WILLY (*frozen, immobile, with guilt in his voice*): No, I don't want to see her.

BIFF: Come on! (*He pulls again, and Willy tries to pull away.*)

WILLY (*highly nervous*): No, no, I don't want to see her.

BIFF (*tries to look into Willy's face, as if to find the answer there*): Why don't you want to see her?

WILLY (*more harshly now*): Don't bother me, will you?

BIFF: What do you mean, you don't want to see her? You don't want them calling you yellow, do you? This isn't your fault; it's me, I'm a bum. Now come

inside! (*Willy strains to get away.*) Did you hear what I said to you?

(*Willy pulls away and quickly goes by himself into the house. Biff follows.*)

LINDA (*to Willy*): Did you plant, dear?

BIFF (*at the door, to Linda*): All right, we had it out. I'm going and I'm not writing any more.

LINDA (*going to Willy in the kitchen*): I think that's the best way, dear. 'Cause there's no use drawing it out, you'll just never get along.

(*Willy doesn't respond.*)

BIFF: People ask where I am and what I'm doing, you don't know, and you don't care. That way it'll be off your mind and you can start brightening up again. All right? That clears it, doesn't it? (*Willy is silent, and Biff goes to him.*) You gonna wish me luck, scout? (*He extends his hand.*) What do you say?

LINDA: Shake his hand, Willy.

WILLY (*turning to her, seething with hurt*): There's no necessity to mention the pen at all, y'know.

BIFF (*gently*): I've got no appointment, Dad.

WILLY (*erupting fiercely*): He put his arm around . . . ?

BIFF: Dad, you're never going to see what I am, so what's the use of arguing? If I strike oil I'll send you a check. Meantime forget I'm alive.

WILLY (*to Linda*): Spite, see?

BIFF: Shake hands, Dad.

WILLY: Not my hand.

BIFF: I was hoping not to go this way.

WILLY: Well, this is the way you're going. Good-by.

(*Biff looks at him a moment, then turns sharply and goes to the stairs.*)

WILLY (*stops him with*): May you rot in hell if you leave this house!

BIFF (*turning*): Exactly what is it that you want from me?

WILLY: I want you to know, on the train, in the mountains, in the valleys, wherever you go, that you cut down your life for spite!

BIFF: No, no.

WILLY: Spite, spite, is the word of your undoing! And when you're down and out, remember what did it. When you're rotting somewhere beside the railroad tracks, remember, and don't you dare blame it on me!

BIFF: I'm not blaming it on you!

WILLY: I won't take the rap for this, you hear?

(*Happy comes down the stairs and stands on the bottom step, watching.*)

BIFF: That's just what I'm telling you!

WILLY (*sinking into a chair at a table, with full accusation*): You're trying to put a knife in me — don't think I don't know what you're doing!

BIFF: All right, phony! Then let's lay it on the line. (*He whips the rubber tube out of his pocket and puts it on the table.*)

Dustin Hoffman as Willy Loman in the 1985 film version of *Death of a Salesman*.

HAPPY: You crazy . . .

LINDA: Biff! (*She moves to grab the hose, but Biff holds it down with his hand.*)

BIFF: Leave it there! Don't move it!

WILLY (*not looking at it*): What is that?

BIFF: You know goddam well what that is.

WILLY (*caged, wanting to escape*): I never saw that.

BIFF: You saw it. The mice didn't bring it into the cellar! What is this supposed to do, make a hero out of you? This supposed to make me sorry for you?

WILLY: Never heard of it.

BIFF: There'll be no pity for you, you hear it? No pity!

WILLY (*to Linda*): You hear the spite!

BIFF: No, you're going to hear the truth — what you are and what I am!

LINDA: Stop it!

WILLY: Spite!

HAPPY (*coming down toward Biff*): You cut it now!

BIFF (*to Happy*): The man don't know who we are! The man is gonna know! (*To Willy.*) We never told the truth for ten minutes in this house!

HAPPY: We always told the truth!

BIFF (*turning on him*): You big blow, are you the assistant buyer? You're one of the two assistants to the assistant, aren't you?

HAPPY: Well, I'm practically . . .

BIFF: You're practically full of it! We all are! and I'm through with it. (*To Willy.*) Now hear this, Willy, this is me.

WILLY: I know you!

BIFF: You know why I had no address for three months? I stole a suit in Kansas City and I was in jail. (*To Linda, who is sobbing.*) Stop crying. I'm through with it.

(*Linda turns away from them, her hands covering her face.*)

WILLY: I suppose that's my fault!

BIFF: I stole myself out of every good job since high school!

WILLY: And whose fault is that?

BIFF: And I never got anywhere because you blew me so full of hot air I could never stand taking orders from anybody! That's whose fault it is!

WILLY: I hear that!

LINDA: Don't, Biff!

BIFF: It's goddam time you heard that! I had to be boss big shot in two weeks, and I'm through with it!

WILLY: Then hang yourself! For spite, hang yourself!

BIFF: No! Nobody's hanging himself, Willy! I ran down eleven flights with a pen in my hand today. And suddenly I stopped, you hear me? And in the middle of that office building, do you hear this? I stopped in the middle of that building and I saw — the sky. I saw the things that I love in this world. The work and the food and time to sit and smoke. And I looked at the pen and said to myself, what the hell am I grabbing this for? Why am I trying to become what I don't want to be? What am I doing in an office, making a contemptuous begging fool of myself, when all I want is out there, waiting for me the minute I say I know who I am! Why can't I say that, Willy? (*He tries to make Willy face him, but Willy pulls away and moves to the left.*)

WILLY (*with hatred, threateningly*): The door of your life is wide open!

BIFF: Pop! I'm a dime a dozen, and so are you!

WILLY (*turning on him now in an uncontrolled outburst*): I am not a dime a dozen! I am Willy Loman, and you are Biff Loman!

(*Biff starts for Willy, but is blocked by Happy. In his fury, Biff seems on the verge of attacking his father.*)

BIFF: I am not a leader of men, Willy, and neither are you. You were never anything but a hard-working drummer who landed in the ash can like all the rest of them! I'm one dollar an hour, Willy! I tried seven states and couldn't raise it. A buck an hour! Do you gather my meaning? I'm not bringing home any prizes any more, and you're going to stop waiting for me to bring them home!

WILLY (*directly to Biff*): You vengeful, spiteful mutt!

(*Biff breaks from Happy. Willy, in fright, starts up the stairs. Biff grabs him.*)

BIFF (*at the peak of his fury*): Pop, I'm nothing! I'm nothing, Pop. Can't you understand that? There's no spite in it any more. I'm just what I am, that's all.

(*Biff's fury has spent itself and he breaks down, sobbing, holding on to Willy, who dumbly fumbles for Biff's face.*)

WILLY (*astonished*): What're you doing? What're you doing? (*To Linda.*) Why is he crying?

BIFF (*crying, broken*): Will you let me go, for Christ's sake? Will you take that phony dream and burn it before something happens? (*Struggling to contain himself he pulls away and moves to the stairs.*) I'll go in the morning. Put him — put him to bed. (*Exhausted, Biff moves up the stairs to his room.*)

WILLY (*after a long pause, astonished, elevated*): Isn't that — isn't that remarkable? Biff — he likes me!

LINDA: He loves you, Willy!

HAPPY (*deeply moved*): Always did, Pop.

WILLY: Oh, Biff! (*Staring wildly.*) He cried! Cried to me. (*He is choking with his love, and now cries out his promise.*) That boy — that boy is going to be magnificent!

(*Ben appears in the light just outside the kitchen.*)

BEN: Yes, outstanding, with twenty thousand behind him.

LINDA (*sensing the racing of his mind, fearfully, carefully*): Now come to bed, Willy. It's all settled now.

WILLY (*finding it difficult not to rush out of the house*): Yes, we'll sleep. Come on. Go to sleep, Hap.

BEN: And it does take a great kind of a man to crack the jungle.

(*In accents of dread, Ben's idyllic music starts up.*)

HAPPY (*his arm around Linda*): I'm getting married, Pop, don't forget it. I'm changing everything. I'm gonna run that department before the year is up. You'll see, Mom. (*He kisses her.*)

BEN: The jungle is dark but full of diamonds, Willy.

(*Willy turns, moves, listening to Ben.*)

LINDA: Be good. You're both good boys, just act that way, that's all.

HAPPY: 'Night, Pop. (*He goes upstairs.*)

LINDA (*to Willy*): Come, dear.

BEN (*with greater force*): One must go in to fetch a diamond out.

WILLY (*to Linda, as he moves slowly along the edge of kitchen, toward the door*): I just want to get settled down, Linda. Let me sit alone for a little.

LINDA (*almost uttering her fear*): I want you upstairs.

WILLY (*taking her in his arms*): In a few minutes, Linda. I couldn't sleep right now. Go on, you look awful tired. (*He kisses her.*)

BEN: Not like an appointment at all. A diamond is rough and hard to the touch.

WILLY: Go on now. I'll be right up.

LINDA: I think this is the only way, Willy.

WILLY: Sure, it's the best thing.

BEN: Best thing!

WILLY: The only way. Everything is gonna be — go on, kid, get to bed. You look so tired.

LINDA: Come right up.

WILLY: Two minutes.

(*Linda goes into the living room, then reappears in her bedroom. Willy moves just outside the kitchen door.*)

Biff (Kevin Anderson) and Willy (Brian Dennehy) try to console one another in Robert Falls's 1999 production of *Death of a Salesman.*

WILLY: Loves me. (*Wonderingly.*) Always loved me. Isn't that a remarkable thing? Ben, he'll worship me for it!

BEN (*with promise*): It's dark there, but full of diamonds.

WILLY: Can you imagine that magnificence with twenty thousand dollars in his pocket?

LINDA (*calling from her room*): Willy! Come up!

WILLY (*calling into the kitchen*): Yes! yes. Coming! It's very smart, you realize that, don't you, sweetheart? Even Ben sees it. I gotta go, baby. 'By! 'By! (*Going over to Ben, almost dancing.*) Imagine? When the mail comes he'll be ahead of Bernard again!

BEN: A perfect proposition all around.

WILLY: Did you see how he cried to me? Oh, if I could kiss him, Ben!

BEN: Time, William, time!

WILLY: Oh, Ben, I always knew one way or another we were gonna make it, Biff and I!

BEN (*looking at his watch*): The boat. We'll be late. (*He moves slowly off into the darkness.*)

WILLY (*elegiacally, turning to the house*): Now when you kick off, boy, I want a seventy-yard boot, and get right down the field under the ball, and when you hit, hit low and hit hard, because it's important, boy. (*He swings around and faces the audience.*) There's all kinds of important people in the stands, and the first thing you know . . . (*Suddenly realizing he is alone.*) Ben! Ben, where do I . . . ? (*He makes a sudden movement of search.*) Ben, how do I . . . ?

LINDA (*calling*): Willy, you coming up?

WILLY (*uttering a gasp of fear, whirling about as if to quiet her*): Sh! (*He turns around as if to find his way; sounds, faces, voices, seem to be swarming in upon him and he flicks at them, crying, Sh! Sh! Suddenly music, faint and high, stops him. It rises in intensity, almost to an unbearable scream. He goes up and down on his toes, and rushes off around the house.*) Shhh!

LINDA: Willy?

(*There is no answer. Linda waits. Biff gets up off his bed. He is still in his clothes. Happy sits up. Biff stands listening.*)

LINDA (*with real fear*): Willy, answer me! Willy!

(*There is the sound of a car starting and moving away at full speed.*)

LINDA: No!

BIFF (*rushing down the stairs*): Pop!

(*As the car speeds off, the music crashes down in a frenzy of sound, which becomes the soft pulsation of a single cello string. Biff slowly returns to his bedroom. He and Happy gravely don their jackets. Linda slowly walks out of her room. The music has developed into a dead march. The leaves of day are appearing over everything. Charley and Bernard, somberly dressed, appear and knock on the kitchen door. Biff and Happy slowly descend the stairs to the kitchen as Charley and Bernard enter. All stop a moment when Linda, in clothes of mourning, bearing a little bunch of roses, comes through the draped doorway into the kitchen. She goes to Charley and takes his arm. Now all move toward the audience, through the wall-line of the kitchen. At the limit of the apron, Linda lays down the flowers, kneels, and sits back on her heels. All stare down at the grave.*)

REQUIEM

CHARLEY: It's getting dark, Linda.

(*Linda doesn't react. She stares at the grave.*)

BIFF: How about it, Mom? Better get some rest, heh? They'll be closing the gate soon.

(*Linda makes no move. Pause.*)

HAPPY (*deeply angered*): He had no right to do that. There was no necessity for it. We would've helped him.

CHARLEY (*grunting*): Hmmm.

BIFF: Come along, Mom.

LINDA: Why didn't anybody come?

CHARLEY: It was a very nice funeral.

LINDA: But where are all the people he knew? Maybe they blame him.

CHARLEY: Naa. It's a rough world, Linda. They wouldn't blame him.

LINDA: I can't understand it. At this time especially. First time in thirty-five years we were just about free and clear. He only needed a little salary. He was even finished with the dentist.

CHARLEY: No man only needs a little salary.

LINDA: I can't understand it.

BIFF: There were a lot of nice days. When he'd come home from a trip; or on Sundays, making the stoop; finishing the cellar; putting on the new porch; when he built the extra bathroom; and put up the garage. You know something, Charley, there's more of him in that front stoop than in all the sales he ever made.

CHARLEY: Yeah. He was a happy man with a batch of cement.

LINDA: He was so wonderful with his hands.

BIFF: He had the wrong dreams. All, all, wrong.

HAPPY (*almost ready to fight Biff*): Don't say that!

BIFF: He never knew who he was.

CHARLEY (*stopping Happy's movement and reply. To Biff*): Nobody dast blame this man. You don't understand: Willy was a salesman. And for a salesman, there is no rock bottom to the life. He don't put a bolt to a nut, he don't tell you the law or give you medicine. He's a man way out there in the blue, riding on a smile and a shoeshine. And when they start

not smiling back — that's an earthquake. And then you get yourself a couple of spots on your hat, and you're finished. Nobody dast blame this man. A salesman is got to dream, boy. It comes with the territory.

BIFF: Charley, the man didn't know who he was.

HAPPY (*infuriated*): Don't say that!

BIFF: Why don't you come with me, Happy?

HAPPY: I'm not licked that easily. I'm staying right in this city, and I'm gonna beat this racket! (*He looks at Biff, his chin set.*) The Loman Brothers!

BIFF: I know who I am, kid.

HAPPY: All right, boy. I'm gonna show you and everybody else that Willy Loman did not die in vain. He had a good dream. It's the only dream you can have — to come out number-one man. He fought it out here, and this is where I'm gonna win it for him.

BIFF (*with a hopeless glance at Happy, bends toward his mother*): Let's go, Mom.

LINDA: I'll be with you in a minute. Go on, Charley. (*He hesitates.*) I want to, just for a minute. I never had a chance to say good-by.

(*Charley moves away, followed by Happy. Biff remains a slight distance up and left of Linda. She sits there, summoning herself. The flute begins, not far away, playing behind her speech.*)

LINDA: Forgive me, dear. I can't cry. I don't know what it is, but I can't cry. I don't understand it. Why did you ever do that? Help me, Willy, I can't cry. It seems to me that you're just on another trip. I keep expecting you. Willy, dear, I can't cry. Why did you do it? I search and search and I search, and I can't understand it, Willy. I made the last payment on the house today. Today, dear. And there'll be nobody home. (*A sob rises in her throat.*) We're free and clear. (*Sobbing more fully, released.*) We're free. (*Biff comes slowly toward her.*) We're free . . . We're free . . .

(*Biff lifts her to her feet and moves out up right with her in his arms. Linda sobs quietly. Bernard and Charley come together and follow them, followed by Happy. Only the music of the flute is left on the darkening stage as over the house the hard towers of the apartment buildings rise into sharp focus, and the curtain falls.*)

COMMENTARIES

Arthur Miller (b. 1915)

IN MEMORIAM

"In Memoriam," a short story about a salesman written in 1932 when Arthur Miller was seventeen, was published in 1995 after it was discovered in the Arthur Miller Archive at the University of Texas's Harry Ransom library. A note on the manuscript indicates that the real Schoenzeit threw himself in front of an elevated railway train the day after the incident the story records. While not providing the model for Death of a Salesman, *the story reminds us that Miller had experience with men like Willy Loman.*

Sitting here now, thinking of him, he seems to be a romantic figure, but really he wasn't. Yet I couldn't venture to call him "commonplace." I never knew him intimately, yet I feel as though I knew him more closely, more thoroughly, than I know myself. His was a salesman's profession, if one may describe such dignified slavery as a profession, and though he tried to interest himself in his work he never became entirely molded into the pot of that business. His emotions were displayed at the wrong times always, and he never quite knew when to laugh. Perhaps, if I may say so, he never was complete. He had lost something vital. There was an air of quiet solitude, of cryptic wondering about both him and his name.

Although he was ever simply and immaculately dressed, I always imagined he had been dressed by someone else.

When I first heard his name, I wondered if he hadn't forgotten some other and had merely been called this by men. His last name was Schoenzeit; the first I never learned, but it had to be Alfred. He always seemed to need that name. Especially when he sat at the small glass-topped table in my father's showroom, slowly perusing the columns of the *Times,* with tears of perspiration dotting the reddened ridge that his gray felt hat had made around his head. The shined, bulgy-toed shoes placed flatly and it seemed carefully on the carpet, his overcoat folded neatly on a chair, the bow of his tie stuck so perfectly into the crevice of a starched, rounded collar completed a setting where I am sure he never belonged.

Schoenzeit, as everyone called him, often was gay. I might add "happy," but of the last I shall never be sure. He laughed as superciliously as any of the others when someone was the object of a quip. But these occasions were rare and never lasted, as far as he was concerned. Always he returned to his fogged manner, and after the joke had faded from his mind the light which seemed to brighten his countenance, too, disappeared, and he was once more enigmatic and incomprehensible.

I had, on several occasions, been alone with him, and may truthfully say I deeply pitied such a dejected soul. At one time it was necessary for him to go to the Bronx to interview a large retail drygoods store, and I was instructed to carry his samples. It was late spring, the sky was cloudless and blue, a yellow sun was slowly warming the cool morning air, and the usual city hurriers were plying their trade.

I had six coats in my arms, holding them against my chest, while he walked, leaning very slightly forward, by my side. His feet must have hurt him, for he pointed them outward, laying them flat on the ground at every step. When walking, he seemed to be striving against a stiff wind, his eyebrows peaked together, forming tiny creases at the bridge of his nose. His hat, placed straight on his head, shaded his eyes, which gazed seekingly ahead.

It was necessary to walk from Eighth to Third Avenue in order to reach the Elevated, and he offered many times to rest. I must have looked tired, because he turned to me once and laughed, saying in his cracked yet resonant baritone, "Hard work, eh, kid? Some business . . ." Of course, I didn't admit my weariness, and pitching my head to one side, raising my eyebrows and smiling, assured him that I was enjoying it as much as he was.

In due time, we approached the El, and about a block away he slowly and lightly touched my arm and, still looking ahead, he asked, "Arthur, do you get paid from the firm for carfare?" He said this in a low tone, as though he were trying to hide his point until it was absolutely necessary to take the plunge.

I thought for a moment and answered, "Well, whenever I have to go anywhere out of walking distance I am given money to ride, but I have no standing allowance for such purposes." He seemed to falter, and flushed a trifle before answering, and for a second I felt both rage and pity for this decrepit soul, who, it seemed, aged many years as he turned to me. I knew then that he felt as though his life were ended, that he was merely being pushed by outside forces. And though his body went on as before, the soul inside had crumpled and broken beyond repair.

He was asking me now for carfare. I knew he would rather have been pulled apart by a tiger, but he was asking me for carfare, a nickel to hold out to a corpulent, uninterested machine for his fare. My heart bled for him at that moment, and as we mounted the long stairway to the trains I realized that as low and shakingly embarrassed as I felt, his senses were that much more tormented and destroyed. And I marvelled at his poise under the circumstances. The coats were warm now against me, and I was thankful to God himself for this refuge for my gawky body which, with the expression of my eyes, must reveal to him my sensations.

I tried as best I could to make this situation seem as if it were common-place — I who had carried samples for so many salesmen. And when we reached the turnstile, I balanced my burden on one knee while I dipped my free hand into my pocket. Behind my throat, I cursed myself for not having the change. I turned from him in order to get the nickels required, and when I lifted my eyes to his figure I prayed, until my temples seemed to burst, for his salvation. At that moment, he looked so broken, so dejected and lost that I hastily lowered my gaze. He appeared to me then, as he stood there at the turnstile, like a small dog who has messed in the house, standing now, after his beating, waiting for his master to open the door to the back yard.

During the entire ride uptown, we two spoke but sparingly. The bright streets below changed constantly as we racketed past, and the windows of the houses facing the trains offered a haven for my confused and weary imagination.

He sold nothing that day and was profusely maltreated by the attending force at the buying office who, by virtue of their superior intelligence and ties to match, were vindicated even when they were consciously adding to the vicissitudes of a seller's life.

On the return trip, Alfred, as I subconsciously called him, became more voluble and questioned me as to my ambitions and my occupations in my leisure time.

Upon hearing that I owned an old car, he immediately became interested and spoke a little less haltingly than was his wont. From constant rebuff, he was loath to venture an opinion, and often embarrassed us both by ending a bountiful conversation unexpectedly.

He accompanied me to my father's place and, placing his hand on the small of my back, patted me lightly, and said with a faint smile, "Thanks, Arthur — and I'll . . . see you tomorrow."

With that farewell, he was off into the crowd, and his restless body faded slowly into the dark overcoats of unknowns as it willingly shrank from my sight.

I never saw him again and had forgotten him entirely when I heard of his death.

"Schoenzeit is dead," and my only recollection of that second when I heard those words is a slow exhaling of my breath and a cool, soft, glowing smile within my soul.

Arthur Miller *(b. 1915)*
TRAGEDY AND THE COMMON MAN   *1949*

One of the curious debates that arose around Death of a Salesman *was the question of whether it was a genuine tragedy. One of the requirements for traditional tragedy is that the hero be of noble birth. Miller countered that notion with a clear statement of modern purpose regarding tragedy.*

In this age few tragedies are written. It has often been held that the lack is due to a paucity of heroes among us, or else that modern man has had the blood drawn out of his organs of belief by the skepticism of science, and the heroic attack on life cannot feed on an attitude of reserve and circumspection. For one reason or another, we are often held to be below tragedy — or tragedy above us. The inevitable conclusion is, of course, that the tragic mode is archaic, fit only for the very highly placed, the kings or the kingly, and where this admission is not made in so many words it is most often implied.

I believe that the common man is as apt a subject for tragedy in its highest sense as kings were. On the face of it this ought to be obvious in the light of modern psychiatry, which bases its analysis upon classic formulations, such as the Oedipus and Orestes complexes, for instance, which were enacted by royal beings, but which apply to everyone in similar emotional situations.

More simply, when the question of tragedy in art is not at issue, we never hesitate to attribute to the well-placed and the exalted the very same mental processes as the lowly. And finally, if the exaltation of tragic action were truly a property of the high-bred character alone, it is inconceivable that the mass of mankind should cherish tragedy above all other forms, let alone be capable of understanding it.

As a general rule, to which there may be exceptions unknown to me, I think the tragic feeling is evoked in us when we are in the presence of a character who is ready to lay down his life, if need be, to secure one thing — his sense of personal dignity. From Orestes to Hamlet, Medea to Macbeth, the underlying struggle is that of the individual attempting to gain his "rightful" position in his society.

Sometimes he is one who has been displaced from it, sometimes one who seeks to attain it for the first time, but the fateful wound from which the inevitable events spiral is the wound of indignity, and its dominant force is indignation. Tragedy, then, is the consequence of a man's total compulsion to evaluate himself justly.

In the sense of having been initiated by the hero himself, the tale always reveals what has been called his "tragic flaw," a failing that is not peculiar to grand or elevated characters. Nor is it necessarily a weakness. The flaw, or crack in the character, is really nothing — and need be nothing — but his inherent unwillingness to remain passive in the face of what he conceives to be a challenge to his dignity, his image of his rightful status. Only the passive, only those who accept their lot without active retaliation, are "flawless." Most of us are in that category.

But there are among us today, as there always have been, those who act against the scheme of things that degrades them, and in the process of action everything we have accepted out of fear or insensitivity or ignorance is shaken before us and examined, and from this total onslaught by an individual against the seemingly stable cosmos surrounding us — from this total examination of the "unchangeable" environment — comes the terror and the fear that is classically associated with tragedy.

More important, from this total questioning of what has previously been unquestioned, we learn. And such a process is not beyond the common man. In revolutions around the world, these past thirty years, he has demonstrated again and again this inner dynamic of all tragedy.

Insistence upon the rank of the tragic hero, or the so-called nobility of his character, is really but a clinging to the outward forms of tragedy. If rank or nobility of character was indispensable, then it would follow that the problems of those with rank were the particular problems of tragedy. But surely the right of one monarch to capture the domain from another no longer raises our passions, nor are our concepts of justice what they were to the mind of an Elizabethan king.

The quality in such plays that does shake us, however, derives from the underlying fear of being displaced, the disaster inherent in being torn away from our chosen image of what and who we are in this world. Among us today this fear is as strong, and perhaps stronger, than it ever was. In fact, it is the common man who knows this fear best.

Now, if it is true that tragedy is the consequence of a man's total compulsion to evaluate himself justly, his destruction in the attempt posits a wrong or an evil in his environment. And this is precisely the morality of tragedy and its lesson. The discovery of the moral law, which is what the enlightenment of tragedy consists of, is not the discovery of some abstract or metaphysical quantity.

The tragic right is a condition of life, a condition in which the human personality is able to flower and realize itself. The wrong is the condition which suppresses man, perverts the flowing out of his love and creative instinct. Tragedy enlightens — and it must, in that it points the heroic finger at the enemy of man's freedom. The thrust for freedom is the quality in tragedy which exalts. The revolutionary questioning of the stable environment is what terrifies. In no way is the common man debarred from such thoughts or such actions.

Seen in this light, our lack of tragedy may be partially accounted for by the turn which modern literature has taken toward the purely psychiatric view of life, or the purely sociological. If all our miseries, our indignities, are born and bred within our minds, then all action, let alone the heroic action, is obviously impossible.

And if society alone is responsible for the cramping of our lives, then the protagonist must needs be so pure and faultless as to force us to deny his validity as a character. From neither of these views can tragedy derive, simply because neither represents a balanced concept of life. Above all else, tragedy requires the finest appreciation by the writer of cause and effect.

No tragedy can therefore come about when its author fears to question absolutely everything, when he regards any institution, habit, or custom as being either everlasting, immutable, or inevitable. In the tragic view the need of man to wholly realize himself is the only fixed star, and whatever it is that hedges his nature and lowers it is ripe for attack and examination. Which is not to say that tragedy must preach revolution.

The Greeks could probe the very heavenly origin of their ways and return to confirm the rightness of laws. And Job could face God in anger, demanding his right, and end in submission. But for a moment everything is in suspension, nothing is accepted, and in this stretching and tearing apart of the cosmos, in the very action of so doing, the character gains "size," the tragic stature which is spuriously attached to the royal or the highborn in our minds. The commonest of men may take on that stature to the extent of his willingness to throw all he has into the contest, the battle to secure his rightful place in his world.

There is a misconception of tragedy with which I have been struck in review after review, and in many conversations with writers and readers alike. It is the idea that tragedy is of necessity allied to pessimism. Even the dictionary says nothing more about the word than that it means a story with a sad or unhappy ending. This impression is so firmly fixed that I almost hesitate to claim that in truth tragedy implies more optimism in its author than does comedy, and that its final result ought to be the reinforcement of the onlooker's brightest opinions of the human animal.

For, if it is true to say that in essence the tragic hero is intent upon claiming his whole due as a personality, and if this struggle must be total and without reservation, then it automatically demonstrates the indestructible will of man to achieve his humanity.

The possibility of victory must be there in tragedy. Where pathos rules, where pathos is finally derived, a character has fought a battle he could not possibly have won. The pathetic is achieved when the protagonist is, by virtue of his witlessness, his insensitivity, or the very air he gives off, incapable of grappling with a much superior force.

Pathos truly is the mode for the pessimist. But tragedy requires a nicer balance between what is possible and what is impossible. And it is curious, although edifying, that the plays we revere, century after century, are the tragedies. In them, and in them alone, lies the belief — optimistic, if you will — in the perfectibility of man.

It is time, I think, that we who are without kings, took up this bright thread of our history and followed it to the only place it can possibly lead in our time — the heart and spirit of the average man.

Michiko Kakutani (b. 1955)

A SALESMAN WHO TRANSCENDS TIME 1999

Brian Dennehy revived Death of a Salesman *fifty years after its premiere and discovered that the audiences were as deeply moved in 1999 as they were in 1949. Michiko Kakutani perceives the center of interest in the play shifting in this new production to emphasize the relationship of a father with his sons. Kakutani notes that despite the play's flaws, its larger issues of love between father and son and longings for immortality have taken on even more significance.*

A half century after its premiere, *Death of a Salesman* has become an American classic — a perennial produced around the world, from Baltimore to Beijing, and routinely taught in high school English classes and mounted in community theaters. The play has become an institution, part of the accepted theater canon, and today even boasts its own Web site (www.deathofasalesman.com), where, in an ironic twist on its central theme, you will be able to purchase souvenirs.

With the opening on Wednesday of the Goodman Theater's new production of *Salesman* at the Eugene O'Neill Theatre on Broadway — fifty years to the day from the play's 1949 world premiere — it is clear that many of the debates that attended the original opening have long since become obsolete. We no longer question whether a play about a little man (a "low-man," as opposed to a king or powerful ruler) can be called a tragedy, just as we no longer question the ethnicity of the play's hero, the Jewishness or non-Jewishness of his locution.

At the same time, however, other debates persist. While *Salesman* opened to — and has continued to enjoy — enormous popular success, both the play and its author have maintained a less than stellar reputation among many highbrow critics. *Salesman* has been debunked as a didactic commentary on the bankruptcy of the American dream of success, while Mr. Miller has been dismissed as an epigone of Ibsenism, a preachy, pompous, and, yes, portentous writer who belongs, like Clifford Odets and Lillian Hellman, to a middlebrow, premodernist past. In retrospect, it is an overly simplistic judgment — especially when it comes to *Salesman,* Mr. Miller's most famous, most enduring, and in many ways most anomalous play.

Oddly enough, Mr. Miller's own ponderous pronouncements have tended to reinforce the perception of his work as an outmoded form of social realism. In one 1950 essay, he argued that *Death of a Salesman* — which chronicles the last day in the life of a salesman named Willy Loman, who has lost his job and, he fears, the love of his son Biff — is "the tragedy of a man who did believe that he alone was not meeting the qualifications laid down for mankind by those clean-shaven frontiersmen who inhabit the peaks of broadcasting and advertising offices."

Willy the failed salesman and willful suicide, Mr. Miller suggested in his own autobiography, represents the fate of a true believer in America's false dream of success: "This pseudo life that thought to touch the clouds by standing on top of a refrigerator, waving a paid-up mortgage at the moon, victorious at last." His singleminded pursuit of success has blinded him to the love of his own family, robbed him of his sense of self, and left him to subsist on a diet of illusions.

In contrast to Eugene O'Neill, who declared that he was "interested only in the relation of man and God," Mr. Miller has implied that the tragedy in his own work springs from the relation between man and the conditions that suppress him and pervert "the flowing out of his love and creative instinct." The playwright's own unhappy experiences during the Depression and the 1950s, when he was convicted of contempt of Congress for refusing to name names before the House Un-American Activities Committee, persuaded him, he has said, that politics "determines the exteriors of your personality," and he remained convinced, he once stated, that all serious plays ultimately address a single question: "How may a man make of the outside world a home?"

Truly great work, he declared in a 1958 interview, is "that work which will show at one and the same time the power and force of the human will working with and against the force of society upon it."

Yet in Robert Falls's darkly hued new staging from Chicago, *Death of a Salesman* seems less a social drama about what Harold Clurman called "the breakdown of the whole concept of salesmanship inherent in our society" than a fierce portrait of a father and son, caught in a fatal embrace of love and resentment and guilt. And Brian Dennehy's Willy Loman seems less a man, in Mr. Miller's words, who "embodies in himself some of the most terrible conflicts running through the streets of America today" than a perpetual adolescent caught in the dizzying gap between reality and his own expectations. This Willy Loman, like Dustin Hoffman's in 1984 on Broadway, may not be a tragic figure — to the last moment, self-awareness continues to elude him — but like Kierkegaard's "unhappiest man," he is a touching one, subsisting on past memory and future hope. His dilemmas are more psychological than sociological, more existential than environmental.

The play's structure, too, seems a far cry from the rough-hewn carpentry often associated with Mr. Miller's work. There is a dreamlike quality to *Salesman*, an expressionistic invocation of shifting moods and time frames that helps conceal the creaky stage machinery apparent in so many other Miller plays from *All My Sons* (1947) to *Broken Glass* (1994).

Certainly *Salesman*, too, has its problems: a paint-by-numbers Freudianism, a conveniently withheld secret that overshadows the second act, and supporting characters who are little more than cardboard cutouts. As written, Willy's long-suffering wife, Linda, is basically a doormat — a passive accomplice in her husband's denial, what we would today call an enabler. And Willy's successful brother, Ben — who walked into the jungle at seventeen, and walked out at twenty-one a rich man with diamonds in his pockets — remains a transparent symbol of rough and ready capitalism, a Horatio Alger joke.

These flaws, however, are subsumed by the play's visceral and deeply affecting portrait of father and son: Willy, intent for years on passing on to his son his own tarnished dreams; and Biff, finally shorn of those illusions, intent on making his father face the hard facts of his existence. The play limns Willy's fears of losing Biff's love and his own longings for immortality — his desire not just to be liked, but to be well liked — and it immerses the audience in Willy's conflicted, contradictory state of mind. In fact, Mr. Miller once noted that his original title for *Salesman* was "The Inside of His Head."

The play was constructed on the premise that Willy, in his growing panic and confusion, sees time not as a continuum but as a simultaneity of moments past and present. In the play's confessional structure, current anxieties fade into remembered guilts, and dreams and regrets blur and overlap — a structure not dissimilar to the narrative strategy adopted by Mr. Miller in his own 1987 autobiography, *Timebends*. The play, Mr. Miller wrote in that book, was meant to "cut through time like a knife through a layer cake or a road through a mountain revealing its geologic layers."

In later works like *After the Fall* (1964) and *The Price* (1968), Mr. Miller would again try to focus on his characters' inner lives, but never again with such urgency and skill as in *Salesman*. His other better-known plays would remain rooted in more topical concerns and feature characters who are more clearly symbols than flesh-and-blood human beings. *All My Sons* (1947) depicts a businessman — read greedy capitalist — covering up his role in the manufacture of defective parts that doomed twenty-one Air Force planes during World War II. *The Crucible* (1953) uses the Salem witch hunts of the late 1600s as a metaphor for the Communist witch hunts of the 1950s. *A View from the Bridge* (1955) examines the costs of McCarthy-era betrayal through its portrait of a longshoreman who rats on two illegal immigrants. *The American Clock* (1980), inspired by Studs Terkel's *Hard Times*, attempts to provide a panoramic portrait of the Depression. And *The Ride Down Mount Morgan* (1991) casts a cold eye on the rampant selfishness of the Reagan era. All too often in these works, Mr. Miller's efforts to "prove the theme" result in sanctimonious speechifying, message-driven melodramatics and two-dimensional characters who come across as illustrations of one or more social ills.

In recent years, the most successful productions of these works have played down the political, polemic aspects of the texts, to reveal their psychological subtext, the bedrock emotions of sexual passion and familial love, betrayal and guilt that lurk beneath the sociology. Last year, the Roundabout Theater Company's highly acclaimed production of *A View from the Bridge* shrugged off the play's McCarthy-era echoes to focus on the hero's secret obsession with his wife's teenage niece and the psychosexual drives that lead him to commit a shocking act of betrayal. Nicholas Hytner's dazzling 1996 movie version of *The Crucible* similarly stripped away that play's McCarthy-era moorings: by firmly grounding the story in the particulars of seventeenth-century Salem, the film uncovered the story's primal drama, its fascination with the consequences of lying and deception and sexual repression.

The success of such productions underscores the current renaissance that Mr. Miller has been enjoying — not just in England, where his work has found a ready audience among theatergoers reared, since the heyday of anti-Thatcherism, on politically committed playwriting, but also here in the States, where the Signature Theater Company recently completed a yearlong retrospective of his plays in New York.

What accounts for Mr. Miller's continuing appeal? Perhaps some of the very aspects of his work that seem so old-fashioned — his moral seriousness and fondness for mythic intonations (inspired by his favorite works, the Bible and Greek tragedies) — are refreshing anomalies in this age of relentless irony and cynicism.

In a day when the avant-garde has insistently purveyed a vision of a fractured, fragmented world, Mr. Miller's assumption that "life has meaning" appeals to our vestigial belief (or hope) that the dots *can* be connected, that a pattern *can* be found in the carpet. And in a day when the arts are increasingly becoming a form of entertainment, when the commercial theater has increasingly given us slice-of-life dramas, brittle satires, and glitzy theme-park musicals, his efforts, however ham-handed, to address the large questions of right and wrong suggest that the theater still matters, that it can still provide a venue for intellectual debate.

Indeed, his plays attest to his own belief that works of art can "change the consciousness of people and their estimate of who they are and what they stand for."

Brenda Murphy (b. 1950)
DEATH OF A SALESMAN: THE DESIGN PROCESS   *1995*

Brenda Murphy examines the process by which the design for the set began to take shape. The distinguished set designer Jo Mielziner was presented with a highly novel concept in the action of the play, and his solution has spawned many imitations. His solution was to concentrate on the salesman's house, presenting it in a dramatic cross-section.

While the casting proceeded, the biggest unanswered question about the script, the design concept, was being addressed. On September 24, Jo Mielziner received a call from Kermit Bloomgarden asking whether he could come straight over and talk to him about "something very interesting." After learning that Kazan hoped to begin rehearsal of the play in two weeks, Mielziner left the meeting with the *Salesman* script to read. During that afternoon and evening, Mielziner began to understand the difficulty of the job he was faced with: "It was not only that there were so many different scenic locations but that the action demanded instantaneous time changes from the present to the past and back again. Actors playing a contemporaneous scene suddenly went back fifteen years in exactly the same setting — the Salesman's house."

As he looked for a design solution to the many changes in scene and time demanded by the script, Mielziner hit on the concept that was to become the key to the production:

> The most important visual symbol in the play — the real background of the story — was the Salesman's house. Therefore, why should that house not be the main set, with all the other scenes — the corner of a graveyard, a hotel room in Boston, the corner of a business office, a lawyer's consultation room, and so on — played on a forestage? If I designed these little scenes in segments and fragments, with easily moved props and fluid lighting effects, I might be able, without ever lowering the curtain, to achieve the easy flow that the author dearly wanted.

The problem was that developing this design scheme would require more than the two weeks that remained before rehearsals were scheduled to begin. Miller would have to make substantial revisions in the script to change blackouts at the end of each scene to instantaneous scene changes, and Kazan would have to reconceive the whole production. What's more, if the play's opening was delayed, the pre-Broadway theatre bookings and the New York opening would have to be canceled and rescheduled. Mielziner asked for a meeting with Bloomgarden, Miller, and Kazan for that afternoon.

A long discussion followed Mielziner's presentation of his ideas on September 25. In the end, the aesthetic advantages of the single-set design scheme built around the material symbol of the house were determined to far outweigh the difficulties:

> To Arthur Miller, a design scheme allowing him as author to blend scenes at will without even the shortest break for physical changes was a significant decision. To Kazan, with his strong sense of movement, stimulated by his already proven genius as a film director, the scheme would permit use of some of the best cinematic techniques.

In the end, it was decided to postpone the start of rehearsals until the end of December and the New York opening until 10 February, allowing enough time for

Miller's revisions and Kazan's rethinking of the direction as well as for the development of the design. Kazan was to consider Mielziner's "concept of a house standing like a specter behind all the scenes of the play, always present as it might be always present in Willy's mind, wherever his travels take him, even behind the office he visits, even behind the Boston hotel room and above his grave plot," the "single most critically important contribution and the key to the way [he] directed the play." Eloquently described by Miller on the opening pages of the published play, it has served the same purpose for millions of readers who have never seen a production of *Death of a Salesman.*

Mielziner set to work immediately to realize his ideas scenically. He made a number of rough sketches over the next few days, along with a ground plan of the stage, and worked on a breakdown of the script, which gave a page reference for each key scene and a notation of the needed lighting, scenery, props, and elevations. On September 28, he flew to Boston, where Kazan was rehearsing the pre-Broadway previews for *Love Life,* and went over his ideas at a breakfast meeting, leaving his director "after a brief hour with about ninety-percent approval." During the next week, Mielziner made about twenty black-and-white sketches representing the scenic design of the whole production and set his assistants to work on translating his sketches into an accurate floor plan and building a scale model of the set. When he met on October 4 with Bloomgarden, Kazan, and Miller, the designer had "a group of ground plans and sketches that . . . solved the major puzzles and were at least indications of the right style" for the production.

Mielziner's set was the culmination of a style of design he had been developing in his productions of Tennessee Williams's plays. In *The Glass Menagerie, A Streetcar Named Desire,* and *Summer and Smoke,* he had combined translucent scenery, expert lighting effects, and sets that went, as the eye traveled upward, from drab realistic interiors to light, delicate frameworks that were mere suggestions of buildings. The result was a style that was beginning to be recognized as his signature and that signaled to audiences a subjective realism in the play that juxtaposed ostensibly objective reality with a character's fantasy as easily as the scenery juxtaposed realism with symbolic abstraction.

Mielziner's *Salesman* set developed from his careful reading of the dialogue and the brief descriptive note that Miller had given him. Miller's note read: "[The house] had once been surrounded by open country, but it was now hemmed in with apartment houses. Trees that used to shade the house against the open sky and hot summer sun now were for the most part dead or dying." In the dialogue, Mielziner had underlined the lines "Boxed us in here"; "Bricks and windows, windows and bricks"; and "beautiful elm trees out there." From these visual suggestions, he conceived a tri-level set for the house, with Willy and Linda's bedroom on the lower floor, at stage right, one step up from the kitchen, which, at center stage, formed the largest playing space. On the far left of the kitchen were steps leading up to the boys' bedroom, above and behind the kitchen. All three rooms could be seen simultaneously. Although there was no wall between the parents' bedroom and the kitchen, the rear wall of each room was hung with translucent backdrops stenciled with "wallpaper" patterns. The lower floor also contained a bed, several chairs, a table, a telephone stand, and a refrigerator. Mielziner's original sketches also showed the hot water heater in the kitchen, but it was eventually hidden behind a curtain because it had become intrusive.

Rising above the lower floor there were only the skeletal rafters representing the gabled roof line and a platform holding the boys' beds and a chest. Behind the house was a translucent backdrop with two trees, the outline of the roof, and the boys' dormer window painted on the facing side. On the back were painted the outlines of bare, rectangular buildings with rectangular windows. When lit from the front with a soft golden light, the backdrop showed the Lomans' house as it used to be, a small but brave structure rising with hope and light to the sky. When lit from the back with a threatening reddish glow, it showed the house in the play's present, its fragile skeleton threatened by the huge, glowering apartment buildings.

On October 4, the main design problems that remained were lack of room for movement on the stage and transitions in time. The lack of room was solved only on December 8, when Kazan convinced Bloomgarden to take eleven seats out of the first row (at a cost of $323.40 per week in receipts) in order to extend the forestage. One of the biggest transition problems was getting Biff and Hap from the scene in their bedroom dressed in pajamas to the immediately following scene in which they appear to Willy in the kitchen as they were in the past, dressed in football uniforms. To manage this without closing the curtain or blacking the stage out, Mielziner had elevators built into the boys' beds so the actors could be moved unnoticed from one scene to the other. In order to give them time for a costume change, Miller expanded Willy's monologue about polishing the car by several minutes.

As the autumn progressed, Mielziner confronted the questions of lighting and props. Arthur Miller remembers that Mielziner and lighting expert Eddie Kook together "once worked an entire afternoon lighting a chair." The chair was the one that Willy addresses as if it were his old boss Frank Wagner in Howard's office, reminding him of the promises he had made. As Willy speaks to it, "the chair must become alive, quite as though his old boss were in it as he addresses him." Miller marveled that, "rather than being lit, the chair subtly seemed to begin emanating light" in the production. To achieve this effect, all of the surrounding lights on the stage had to be dimmed imperceptibly, rather than bringing up the spotlight on the chair, which would produce an effect too obvious to the audience.

This effect, and the attention that Mielziner and Kook gave to it, provide a good illustration of the designer's attitude toward the lighting of *Death of a Salesman*. Always a designer who made full artistic use of the scenic expression of lighting, Mielziner had decided that lighting was the key to *Salesman*'s time shifts. He decided to signify the passage of time on stage by creating two environments for the house through the lighting. When the set was first revealed, the audience saw the muslin backdrop lit from behind to show the oppressive apartment houses towering over the fragile house. When the scene shifted to the past, the lights behind the backdrop were dimmed out, and the buildings faded out as soft amber light and images of green leaves were projected onto the backdrop from a number of projection units that were carefully placed backstage, throughout the auditorium, and on the balcony. Mielziner felt that this visual symbol of the spring leaves, "liberating the house from the oppression of the surrounding structures and giving the stage a feeling of the free outdoors," was an "integral part of the Salesman's life story and had to be an easily recognized symbol of the springtime of that life." Combined with the music provided by Alex North, this lighting change would bring the audience effectively into the past along with Willy as each daydream began.

The painstaking work involved in the lighting of the original *Death of a Salesman* is almost inconceivable in these days of computerized stage lighting. Each of the 141 lighting units on the eight pipe battens above the stage had to be carefully hung and angled, and each light cue individually adjusted and marked up so that it could be re-created manually during each performance. It took three days for the hanging and angling, and another twenty-hour-day to set the approximately 150 light cues when the production was moved into the theater. In addition to the projection units, Mielziner had also persuaded Bloomgarden of the necessity of two special follow-spots, which could be manipulated to produce particular effects. Because their fine adjustments needed careful attention, each of these lights required a trained technician for its operation throughout the performance, a significant expense. Mielziner used the projection units to address spatial as well as temporal difficulties. He and Kazan had agreed early on that the most minimal of visual suggestions would suffice in creating the sets for the scenes to be played on the forestage — the Boston hotel room, the restaurant, and Howard's and Charley's offices. He created the hotel room by projecting a seedy wallpaper design from the theater balcony onto a section of the trellis at the side of the house. With the rest of the stage dimmed, this was enough to evoke the environment where Biff is disillusioned when he surprises Willy with The Woman.

This suggestiveness went along with the minimalism that Mielziner and Kazan had agreed on in the props. A few objects, such as the beds, the chairs, and the table, were required by the action on the stage. Most of the props, such as the refrigerator, the hot water heater, Willy's sample cases, the silk stockings, the rubber tubing, the hoe and seeds, and the gold fountain pen, served a necessary function but also took on a symbolic resonance. Kazan and Mielziner also agreed on several props which served primarily as material signifiers for the audience of some theme in the play, such as Biff's football trophy on a shelf over Willy's bed and a deflated football in the boys' room. The fact that props were kept to a minimum, with no attempt at realism, helped to foreground the few objects that did appear, encouraging the audience to perceive their symbolic significance.

Throughout the production process, the impulse was toward greater abstraction and symbolism, less realism. A good example is the Requiem scene, in which the original plan was to have a gravestone rise from a trick trapdoor in the forestage. Mielziner persuaded Kazan to use a simple bouquet of flowers to signify the grave instead, using a projection of autumn leaves to complete the symbolic statement of death in opposition to the life and hope suggested by the spring leaves in the daydream scenes. What made the production's style unique, however, was the juxtaposition of the abstract and poetic with the real and prosaic. The props that were introduced into the abstract suggestiveness of the set were authentic, battered objects that the Lomans might very well have owned. The kitchen table was covered with a cloth painted with an "oilcloth" design. The refrigerator was a careful reproduction of a typical model from the 1929 Sears Roebuck catalogue. It was vital to the production's aesthetic that these objects signify a specific time, place, class, and way of life in juxtaposition with the insistent visions in Willy's mind, and that they resonate with symbolic significance in the context of the play as a total experience.

Samuel Beckett

Samuel Beckett (1906–1989) was born in Dublin to an upper-middle-class Protestant family. After a privileged education at the Portora Royal School, he went to Trinity College, Dublin, where he studied French and Italian. He was an exceptionally good student and, in 1928 after graduation, taught English at the École Normale Supérieure in Paris.

Beckett early on straddled two literary cultures: Irish and Anglo-Irish. Most of the literary energy in Ireland in the 1920s and 1930s was split between the essentially conservative Anglo-Irish Protestants, such as William Butler Yeats and Lady Gregory, and the more avant-garde Catholics, such as James Joyce, with whom Beckett formed an enduring personal and literary friendship in Paris. Although much younger than Joyce, Beckett developed a close artistic sympathy with him. Beckett's first published work (1929) was one of the earliest critical essays on Joyce's most radical literary composition, the not-yet-published *Finnegans Wake*.

When he was first in France, Beckett's reading of French philosophers, especially Descartes, exerted a strong influence on his work. Beckett's earliest writings appeared in Eugene Jolas's avant-garde literary journal *transition*, which put him in the center of Parisian literary activity in the late 1920s. After 1930, his series of short stories published under the title *More Pricks Than Kicks* (1934) established him as an important writer. After settling in Paris in 1937, Beckett wrote the novel *Murphy* (1938), on a recognizably Irish theme of economic impoverishment, alienation, and inward meditation and spiritual complexity.

When World War II began in 1939, Beckett took up the cause of the French Resistance. After his activity caught the eye of the Gestapo, for two years he lay low in unoccupied France by working as a farmhand and also writing another novel, *Watt* (written in 1944 but published in 1953). After the war he took up residence again in Paris and began writing most of his work in French. His greatest novels were written in the five years after the war, and they are often referred to as his trilogy: *Molloy, Malone Dies,* and *The Unnamable*. These three novels are about men who have become disaffected with society and who have strange and compelling urgencies to be alone and to follow exacting and repetitive patterns of behavior. In a sense, they are archetypes of the kinds of protagonists that Beckett created in most of his work.

Beckett's first published play, *Waiting for Godot* (1952), was produced in Paris (1953), in London (1955), and in Miami (1956). From the first, its repetitive, whimsical, and sometimes nonsensical style established the play as a major postwar statement. In a barren setting, Vladimir and Estragon, two tramps who echo the comic vision of Charlie Chaplin, wait for Godot to come. They amuse themselves by doing vaudeville routines, but their loneliness and isolation are painfully apparent to the audience. Godot has promised to come, and as they wait, Vladimir and Estragon speculate on whether or not Godot will come.

The comic moments in the play, along with the enigma of Vladimir and Estragon's fruitless waiting, combined to capture the imagination of audiences and the press. They saw the play as a modern statement about the condition of humankind, although there was never any agreement on just what the statement was. Godot sends a boy to say that he will indeed come, but when the play ends, he has not arrived. The implication seems to be that he will never arrive. Most audiences saw Godot as a metaphor for God. Despite the critics' constant inquiries, Beckett never confirmed the view that Godot was God and kept Godot's identity open-ended.

The play itself was open-ended, as Beckett had hoped, and therefore could be interpreted in many ways. One was to see the play as a commentary on the futility of religion; another was to suggest that the play underscored the loneliness of humankind in an empty universe; yet a third implied that it was up to individuals, represented by the hapless Vladimir and Estragon, to shape the significance of their own lives, and their waiting represented that effort.

Many of the themes in *Waiting for Godot* are apparent in Beckett's later plays. The radio play *All That Fall* (1957) was followed by the very successful *Krapp's Last Tape* (1958). Also in 1957, *Endgame,* a play on the themes of the end of the world, was produced, followed in 1961 by *Happy Days.* Beckett experimented with minimalist approaches to drama, exemplified in *Act without Words I* and *Act without Words II,* both mime plays. Other plays experiment with minimalism in setting, props, and — in the mime plays — even words.

Beckett's plays reveal the deep influence of French postwar philosophers, such as Albert Camus and Jean-Paul Sartre, both existentialists. Their philosophy declares that people are not essentially good, bad, kind, or anything else but are what they make of themselves. Beckett's adaptation of existentialism sometimes borders on pessimism because his vision seems to negate many of the consolations of religious and secular philosophy. His style is antirealist, but the search for beliefs that are reasonable and plausible in a fundamentally absurd world, and the plight of individuals who must make their own meanings is central to most of his work.

Beckett's view of the world is not cheerful. But his vision is consistent, honest, and sympathetic to the persistence of his characters, who endure even in the face of apparent defeat. The significance of Beckett's achievements was recognized in 1969 when he was awarded the Nobel Prize for literature.

ENDGAME

The title of this play derives from the game of chess, which has three different strategies to mark the opening, the middle game, and the endgame. The strategy of the endgame is based on the protection of the king and depends on very few pieces being left on the board — the king and sometimes a rook and a pawn. The moves in the endgame are always restricted, often repetitive, and limited by the fact that the king, if it can move at all, cannot move more than one space at a time. In Beckett's *Endgame* Hamm is the king and the central character in the drama; however, he cannot move or even stand by himself. His parents, Nagg and Nell, stuck immobile in ashcans, resemble rooks, who protect the king by controlling spaces forward, backward, and side to side but have little reason themselves to move. Clov, who most closely resembles a pawn, cannot sit down and is the only character in the play who can move. He is also the only means by which Hamm can move. Beckett has described Hamm as "a king in the chess game lost from the start."

World politics in 1957, when the play was written, were dominated by the threat of nuclear war and the possible extinction of the human race. The circumstances of *Endgame* suggest that the play portrays a version of the end of the world. Clov's description of the world outside the window implies desolation and grief. At one point as Clov looks out the window, Hamm tells him to use his "glass," his telescope, and to report back to him. Clov says all is "Zero," and Hamm asks, "All is what?" "In a word?" says Clov. "Is that what you want to know?" And in a moment he reports his one word: "Corpsed."

Unlike Hamm and Clov, who seem rooted only in the present, Nagg and Nell have a past. They remember rowing on Lake Como on an April afternoon after they were engaged. It was a moment in which Nell remembers she was happy. But they also remember the day they crashed on their tandem bicycle and lost their legs. Nagg recalls it was in the Ardennes forest on the road to Sedan. Beckett is alluding to the French forest at Ardennes, site of the most appalling and murderous fighting in World War I, and to the French town of Sedan, the place where Napoleon III surrendered to the Germans in a battle during the Franco-Prussian war.

Ruby Cohn and other critics have noted that the characters' names echo associations with hammers and nails: Nell is a homophone for *nail*; Hamm is a shortened form of *hammer*; Nagg is from the German *nagel,* for *nail*; and Clov is from the French *clou,* also for *nail*. The characters thus seem to be equipped to rebuild their society, but they refuse to do so. By using English, French, and German versions of *nail,* Beckett involves the principal combatants of modern European wars.

Some critics have observed that Beckett's drama often focuses on elements of play. Plays are play; life is play. In chess an endgame is played. In Beckett's drama characters' actions seem to be performed as if they were part of a game. Clov exercises great precision, for example, in placing Hamm exactly where he wishes to be. When Clov has done the rounds and moved Hamm's chair back to its position, Hamm says, "I feel a little too far to the left. Now I feel a little too far to the right." In a game of chess it would matter if he were too far to the left or right. In an endgame the king might move to one square and then move back again and again. The movements of Hamm and Clov are repetitious and meaningful only within the "system" of the drama and its space, just as all moves in an endgame are meaningful only within the "system" of the game of chess. Clov continually enters and exits with his ladder and looks out the windows, only to find that nothing has changed. He picks up the lids of Nagg and Nell's ashcans and replaces them several times. He pushes Hamm's chair along the wall, making minute adjustments, for no apparent reason, when he returns the chair to the center of the room. His moves are part of an endgame, and *Endgame* is a play.

Beckett critic Ted Estess has said that "in Beckett's literature 'existence is play,'" implying a form of absurdity of the kind Martin Esslin talks about in his discussion of theater of the absurd. (See the commentary on p. 1266.) The absurd implies a nonmeaning, such as the meaningless movements of Hamm by Clov. The meaning of those moves is in the action itself, which strikes those in the audience as absurd. Beckett's use of the absurd helps him move away from the well-made play with its clearly marked beginning, middle, and end. In the process he pokes fun at that concept by embedding the end in the beginning of *Endgame*. As the lights go up and Clov removes the sheets from the ashcans and from Hamm in his chair, he intones to the audience: "Finished." The audience is meant to feel this irony. It is the endgame when the action — and the play — are expected to stop, but as Hamm says: "The end is in the beginning and yet you go on."

Endgame in Performance

Endgame was first produced in 1957. The year before, *Waiting for Godot* had been produced in Miami and New York, establishing Beckett as an important figure in modern absurdist drama. *Endgame,* his next major play, satisfied the critics but baffled the public. The first London production was in French, at the Royal Court Theatre, which was known for producing experimental plays. Roger Blin directed. The first Paris production began three weeks later, April 26, 1957, in the Studio des Champs-Élysées. The New York production, directed by Beckett's friend and interpreter Alan Schneider, opened on January 28, 1958. A number of important revivals of the play have attested to its continuing power. In 1964 *Endgame* was produced at The Royal Shakespeare Company's Aldwych Theatre. Beckett himself directed the play at the Schiller Theatre in Berlin in September 1967. In the 1970 Open Theater Production at the Loeb Theater in Cambridge, Massachusetts, Joseph Chaikin as Hamm created a richly nuanced performance:

> Joseph Chaikin as the chairbound Hamm throws an eerie light over the play. . . . He is sensual, domineering, crafty, and infinitely tender; he prattles and tells macabre stories and his dominion over the dwindling lives of his family is like the last hoarse gasp of King Lear over the strangled body of Cordelia.   (Samuel Hirsch, *Herald Traveler,* Boston, May 13, 1970)

Andre Gregory directed the play at the Manhattan Project in 1973. Clive Barnes noted the unusual staging of this production:

> Mr. Gregory has built himself a strange, bullring of a theater. It is hexagonal, and the audience is on two levels. The audience is placed in cubicles — each holding four chairs. Each cubicle is insulated from the stage and from the world by chicken wire. (*New York Times,* February 9, 1973)

The Royal Court played it in English during its Beckett Festival in 1976. Beckett directed the play again in London at the Young Vic in January 1980 and then in Chicago's Goodman Theater with the San Quentin Workshop in September 1980. In 1984 JoAnn Akalaitis staged a controversial *Endgame* at the American Repertory Theatre in Cambridge, Massachusetts. She set the play in a burned-out subway tunnel and commissioned an eerie musical score by minimalist composer Philip Glass. Grove Press, Beckett's representative, complained that the production disregarded "the playwright's sparse, rigorous scenic demands" and added uncalled-for music. As one critic noted, Akalaitis had "simply, vividly visualized and auralized *Endgame*'s nuclear-holocaustal implications, at the expense of its chess and theatrical imagery" (Carolyn Clay, *Boston Phoenix,* December 18, 1984). The production was allowed to continue after the American Repertory Theatre agreed to include a program insert, signed by Beckett, "decrying the interpretation."

Samuel Beckett (1906–1989)

ENDGAME

A PLAY IN ONE ACT

1957

The Characters

NAGG   HAMM
NELL   CLOV

(*Bare interior.*)
    (*Gray light.*)
    (*Left and right back, high up, two small windows, curtains drawn.*)
    (*Front right, a door. Hanging near door, its face to wall, a picture.*)
    (*Front left, touching each other, covered with an old sheet, two ashbins.°*)
    (*Center, in an armchair on casters, covered with an old sheet, Hamm.*)
    (*Motionless by the door, his eyes fixed on Hamm, Clov. Very red face.*)
    (*Brief tableau.*)

(*Clov goes and stands under window left. Stiff, staggering walk. He looks up at window left. He turns and looks at window right. He goes and stands under window right. He looks up at window right. He turns and looks at window left. He goes out, comes back immediately with a small stepladder, carries it over and sets it down under window left, gets up on it, draws back curtain. He gets down, takes six steps (for example) towards window right, goes back for ladder, carries it over and sets it down under window right, gets up on it, draws back curtain. He gets down, takes three steps towards window left, goes back for ladder, carries it over and sets it down under window left, gets up on it, looks out of window. Brief laugh. He gets down, takes one step towards window right, goes back for ladder, carries it over and sets it down under window right, gets*

ashbins: trash cans.

up *on it, looks out of window. Brief laugh. He gets down, goes with ladder towards ashbins, halts, turns, carries back ladder and sets it down under window right, goes to ashbins, removes sheet covering them, folds it over his arm. He raises one lid, stoops and looks into bin. Brief laugh. He closes lid. Same with other bin. He goes to Hamm, removes sheet covering him, folds it over his arm. In a dressing gown, a stiff toque° on his head, a large bloodstained handkerchief over his face, a whistle hanging from his neck, a rug over his knees, thick socks on his feet, Hamm seems to be asleep. Clov looks over him. Brief laugh. He goes to door, halts, turns towards auditorium.*)

CLOV (*fixed gaze, tonelessly*): Finished, it's finished, nearly finished, it must be nearly finished.

(*Pause.*)

Grain upon grain, one by one, and one day, suddenly, there's a heap, a little heap, the impossible heap.

(*Pause.*)

I can't be punished anymore.

(*Pause.*)

I'll go now to my kitchen, ten feet by ten feet by ten feet, and wait for him to whistle me.

(*Pause.*)

Nice dimensions, nice proportions, I'll lean on the table, and look at the wall, and wait for him to whistle me.

(*He remains a moment motionless, then goes out. He comes back immediately, goes to window right, takes up*

toque: A small, brimless, close-fitting hat.

the ladder and carries it out. Pause. Hamm stirs. He yawns under the handkerchief. He removes the handkerchief from his face. Very red face. Black glasses.)

HAMM: Me — (*he yawns*) — to play.

(*He holds the handkerchief spread out before him.*)

Old stancher!°

(*He takes off his glasses, wipes his eyes, his face, the glasses, puts them on again, folds the handkerchief and puts it back neatly in the breast pocket of his dressing gown. He clears his throat, joins the tips of his fingers.*)

Can there be misery — (*he yawns*) — loftier than mine? No doubt. Formerly. But now?

(*Pause.*)

My father?

(*Pause.*)

My mother?

(*Pause.*)

My . . . dog?

(*Pause.*)

Oh I am willing to believe they suffer as much as such creatures can suffer. But does that mean their sufferings equal mine? No doubt.

(*Pause.*)

No, all is a — (*he yawns*) — bsolute, (*proudly*) the bigger a man is the fuller he is.

(*Pause. Gloomily.*)

And the emptier.

(*He sniffs.*)

Clov!

(*Pause.*)

No, alone.

(*Pause.*)

What dreams! Those forests!

(*Pause.*)

Enough, it's time it ended, in the shelter too.

(*Pause.*)

And yet I hesitate, I hesitate to . . . to end. Yes there it is, it's time it ended and yet I hesitate to — (*he yawns*) — to end.

(*Yawns.*)

God, I'm tired, I'd be better off in bed.

(*He whistles. Enter Clov immediately. He halts beside the chair.*)

You pollute the air!

---

stancher: Item that stops, or stanches, the flow of blood.

(*Pause.*)

Get me ready, I'm going to bed.

CLOV: I've just got you up.

HAMM: And what of it?

CLOV: I can't be getting you up and putting you to bed every five minutes, I have things to do.

(*Pause.*)

HAMM: Did you ever see my eyes?

CLOV: No.

HAMM: Did you never have the curiosity, while I was sleeping, to take off my glasses and look at my eyes?

CLOV: Pulling back the lids?

(*Pause.*)

No.

HAMM: One of these days I'll show them to you.

(*Pause.*)

It seems they've gone all white.

(*Pause.*)

What time is it?

CLOV: The same as usual.

HAMM (*gesture towards window right*): Have you looked?

CLOV: Yes.

HAMM: Well?

CLOV: Zero.

HAMM: It'd need to rain.

CLOV: It won't rain.

(*Pause.*)

HAMM: Apart from that, how do you feel?

CLOV: I don't complain.

HAMM: You feel normal?

CLOV (*irritably*): I tell you I don't complain.

HAMM: I feel a little queer.

(*Pause.*)

Clov!

CLOV: Yes.

HAMM: Have you not had enough?

CLOV: Yes!

(*Pause.*)

Of what?

HAMM: Of this . . . this . . . thing.

CLOV: I always had.

(*Pause.*)

Not you?

HAMM (*gloomily*): Then there's no reason for it to change.

CLOV: It may end.

(*Pause.*)

All life long the same questions, the same answers.

HAMM: Get me ready.

(*Clov does not move.*)

Go and get the sheet.

(*Clov does not move.*)

Clov!

CLOV: Yes.

HAMM: I'll give you nothing more to eat.

CLOV: Then we'll die.

HAMM: I'll give you just enough to keep you from dying.
   You'll be hungry all the time.

CLOV: Then we won't die.

(*Pause.*)

I'll go and get the sheet.

(*He goes towards the door.*)

HAMM: No!

(*Clov halts.*)

I'll give you one biscuit per day.

(*Pause.*)

One and a half.

(*Pause.*)

Why do you stay with me?

CLOV: Why do you keep me?

HAMM: There's no one else.

CLOV: There's nowhere else.

(*Pause.*)

HAMM: You're leaving me all the same.

CLOV: I'm trying.

HAMM: You don't love me.

CLOV: No.

HAMM: You loved me once.

CLOV: Once!

HAMM: I've made you suffer too much.

(*Pause.*)

Haven't I?

CLOV: It's not that.

HAMM (*shocked*): I haven't made you suffer too much?

CLOV: Yes!

HAMM (*relieved*): Ah you gave me a fright!

(*Pause. Coldly.*)

Forgive me.

(*Pause. Louder.*)

I said, Forgive me.

CLOV: I heard you.

(*Pause.*)

Have you bled?

HAMM: Less.

(*Pause.*)

Is it not time for my painkiller?

CLOV: No.

(*Pause.*)

HAMM: How are your eyes?

CLOV: Bad.

HAMM: How are your legs?

CLOV: Bad.

HAMM: But you can move.

CLOV: Yes.

HAMM (*violently*): Then move!

(*Clov goes to back wall, leans against it with his forehead and hands.*)

Where are you?

CLOV: Here.

HAMM: Come back!

(*Clov returns to his place beside the chair.*)

Where are you?

CLOV: Here.

HAMM: Why don't you kill me?

CLOV: I don't know the combination of the cupboard.

(*Pause.*)

HAMM: Go and get two bicycle wheels.

CLOV: There are no more bicycle wheels.

HAMM: What have you done with your bicycle?

CLOV: I never had a bicycle.

HAMM: The thing is impossible.

CLOV: When there were still bicycles I wept to have one.
   I crawled at your feet. You told me to go to hell. Now
   there are none.

HAMM: And your rounds? When you inspected my paupers. Always on foot?

CLOV: Sometimes on horse.

(*The lid of one of the bins lifts and the hands of Nagg appear, gripping the rim. Then his head emerges. Nightcap. Very white face. Nagg yawns, then listens.*)

I'll leave you, I have things to do.

HAMM: In your kitchen?

CLOV: Yes.

HAMM: Outside of here it's death.

(*Pause.*)

All right, be off.

(*Exit Clov. Pause.*)

We're getting on.

NAGG: Me pap!

HAMM: Accursed progenitor!

NAGG: Me pap!

HAMM: The old folks at home! No decency left! Guzzle,
   guzzle, that's all they think of.

(*He whistles. Enter Clov. He halts beside the chair.*)

Well! I thought you were leaving me.

CLOV: Oh not just yet, not just yet.

NAGG: Me pap!
HAMM: Give him his pap.
CLOV: There's no more pap.
HAMM (*to Nagg*): Do you hear that? There's no more pap. You'll never get any more pap.
NAGG: I want me pap!
HAMM: Give him a biscuit.

(*Exit Clov.*)

   Accursed fornicator! How are your stumps?
NAGG: Never mind me stumps.

(*Enter Clov with biscuit.*)

CLOV: I'm back again, with the biscuit.

(*He gives biscuit to Nagg who fingers it, sniffs it.*)

NAGG (*plaintively*): What is it?
CLOV: Spratt's medium.
NAGG (*as before*): It's hard! I can't!
HAMM: Bottle him!

(*Clov pushes Nagg back into the bin, closes the lid.*)

CLOV (*returning to his place beside the chair*): If age but knew!
HAMM: Sit on him!
CLOV: I can't sit.
HAMM: True. And I can't stand.
CLOV: So it is.
HAMM: Every man his speciality.

(*Pause.*)

   No phone calls?

(*Pause.*)

   Don't we laugh?
CLOV (*after reflection*): I don't feel like it.
HAMM (*after reflection*): Nor I.

(*Pause.*)

   Clov!
CLOV: Yes.
HAMM: Nature has forgotten us.
CLOV: There's no more nature.
HAMM: No more nature! You exaggerate.
CLOV: In the vicinity.
HAMM: But we breathe, we change! We lose our hair, our teeth! Our bloom! Our ideals!
CLOV: Then she hasn't forgotten us.
HAMM: But you say there is none.
CLOV (*sadly*): No one that ever lived ever thought so crooked as we.
HAMM: We do what we can.
CLOV: We shouldn't.

(*Pause.*)

HAMM: You're a bit of all right, aren't you?
CLOV: A smithereen.

(*Pause.*)

HAMM: This is slow work.

(*Pause.*)

   Is it not time for my painkiller?
CLOV: No.

(*Pause.*)

   I'll leave you, I have things to do.
HAMM: In your kitchen?
CLOV: Yes.
HAMM: What, I'd like to know.
CLOV: I look at the wall.
HAMM: The wall! And what do you see on your wall? Mene, mene?° Naked bodies?
CLOV: I see my light dying.
HAMM: Your light dying! Listen to that! Well, it can die just as well here, *your* light. Take a look at me and then come back and tell me what you think of *your* light.

(*Pause.*)

CLOV: You shouldn't speak to me like that.

(*Pause.*)

HAMM (*coldly*): Forgive me.

(*Pause. Louder.*)

   I said, Forgive me.
CLOV: I heard you.

(*The lid of Nagg's bin lifts. His hands appear, gripping the rim. Then his head emerges. In his mouth the biscuit. He listens.*)

HAMM: Did your seeds come up?
CLOV: No.
HAMM: Did you scratch round them to see if they had sprouted?
CLOV: They haven't sprouted.
HAMM: Perhaps it's still too early.
CLOV: If they were going to sprout they would have sprouted.

(*Violently.*)

   They'll never sprout!

(*Pause. Nagg takes biscuit in his hand.*)

HAMM: This is not much fun.

(*Pause.*)

   But that's always the way at the end of the day, isn't it, Clov?
CLOV: Always.
HAMM: It's the end of the day like any other day, isn't it, Clov?
CLOV: Looks like it.

Mene, mene: The handwriting on the wall in Daniel 5:25 indicating the end of King Belshazzar's reign: "MENE, MENE, TEKEL, and PARSIN."

(*Pause.*)

HAMM (*anguished*): What's happening, what's happening?

CLOV: Something is taking its course.

(*Pause.*)

HAMM: All right, be off.

(*He leans back in his chair, remains motionless. Clov does not move, heaves a great groaning sigh. Hamm sits up.*)

I thought I told you to be off.

CLOV: I'm trying.

(*He goes to door, halts.*)

Ever since I was whelped.

(*Exit Clov.*)

HAMM: We're getting on.

(*He leans back in his chair, remains motionless. Nagg knocks on the lid of the other bin. Pause. He knocks harder. The lid lifts and the hands of Nell appear, gripping the rim. Then her head emerges. Lace cap. Very white face.*)

NELL: What is it, my pet?

(*Pause.*)

Time for love?

NAGG: Were you asleep?

NELL: Oh no!

NAGG: Kiss me.

NELL: We can't.

NAGG: Try.

(*Their heads strain towards each other, fail to meet, fall apart again.*)

NELL: Why this farce, day after day?

(*Pause.*)

NAGG: I've lost me tooth.

NELL: When?

NAGG: I had it yesterday.

NELL (*elegiac*): Ah yesterday!

(*They turn painfully towards each other.*)

NAGG: Can you see me?

NELL: Hardly. And you?

NAGG: What?

NELL: Can you see me?

NAGG: Hardly.

NELL: So much the better, so much the better.

NAGG: Don't say that.

(*Pause.*)

Our sight has failed.

NELL: Yes.

(*Pause. They turn away from each other.*)

NAGG: Can you hear me?

NELL: Yes. And you?

NAGG: Yes.

(*Pause.*)

Our hearing hasn't failed.

NELL: Our what?

NAGG: Our hearing.

NELL: No.

(*Pause.*)

Have you anything else to say to me?

NAGG: Do you remember —

NELL: No.

NAGG: When we crashed on our tandem and lost our shanks.

(*They laugh heartily.*)

NELL: It was in the Ardennes.

(*They laugh less heartily.*)

NAGG: On the road to Sedan.

(*They laugh still less heartily.*)

Are you cold?

NELL: Yes, perished. And you?

NAGG:

(*Pause.*)

I'm freezing.

(*Pause.*)

Do you want to go in?

NELL: Yes.

NAGG: Then go in.

(*Nell does not move.*)

Why don't you go in?

NELL: I don't know.

(*Pause.*)

NAGG: Has he changed your sawdust?

NELL: It isn't sawdust.

(*Pause. Wearily.*)

Can you not be a little accurate, Nagg?

NAGG: Your sand then. It's not important.

NELL: It is important.

(*Pause.*)

NAGG: It was sawdust once.

NELL: Once!

NAGG: And now it's sand.

(*Pause.*)

From the shore.

(*Pause. Impatiently.*)

Now it's sand he fetches from the shore.

NELL: Now it's sand.
NAGG: Has he changed yours?
NELL: No.
NAGG: Nor mine.

(*Pause.*)

I won't have it!

(*Pause. Holding up the biscuit.*)

Do you want a bit?
NELL: No.

(*Pause.*)

Of what?
NAGG: Biscuit. I've kept you half.

(*He looks at the biscuit. Proudly.*)

Three quarters. For you. Here.

(*He proffers the biscuit.*)

No?

(*Pause.*)

Do you not feel well?
HAMM (*wearily*): Quiet, quiet, you're keeping me awake.

(*Pause.*)

Talk softer.

(*Pause.*)

If I could sleep I might make love. I'd go into the woods. My eyes would see . . . the sky, the earth. I'd run, run, they wouldn't catch me.

(*Pause.*)

Nature!

(*Pause.*)

There's something dripping in my head.

(*Pause.*)

A heart, a heart in my head.

(*Pause.*)

NAGG (*soft*): Do you hear him? A heart in his head!

(*He chuckles cautiously.*)

NELL: One mustn't laugh at those things, Nagg. Why must you always laugh at them?
NAGG: Not so loud!
NELL (*without lowering her voice*): Nothing is funnier than unhappiness, I grant you that. But —
NAGG (*shocked*): Oh!
NELL: Yes, yes, it's the most comical thing in the world. And we laugh, we laugh, with a will, in the beginning. But it's always the same thing. Yes, it's like the funny story we have heard too often, we still find it funny, but we don't laugh anymore.

(*Pause.*)

Have you anything else to say to me?

NAGG: No.
NELL: Are you quite sure?

(*Pause.*)

Then I'll leave you.
NAGG: Do you not want your biscuit?

(*Pause.*)

I'll keep it for you.

(*Pause.*)

I thought you were going to leave me.
NELL: I am going to leave you.
NAGG: Could you give me a scratch before you go?
NELL: No.

(*Pause.*)

Where?
NAGG: In the back.
NELL: No.

(*Pause.*)

Rub yourself against the rim.
NAGG: It's lower down. In the hollow.
NELL: What hollow?
NAGG: The hollow!

(*Pause.*)

Could you not?

(*Pause.*)

Yesterday you scratched me there.
NELL (*elegiac*): Ah yesterday!
NAGG: Could you not?

(*Pause.*)

Would you like me to scratch you?

(*Pause.*)

Are you crying again?
NELL: I was trying.

(*Pause.*)

HAMM: Perhaps it's a little vein.

(*Pause.*)

NAGG: What was that he said?
NELL: Perhaps it's a little vein.
NAGG: What does that mean?

(*Pause.*)

That means nothing.

(*Pause.*)

Will I tell you the story of the tailor?
NELL: No.

(*Pause.*)

What for?

NAGG: To cheer you up.

NELL: It's not funny.

NAGG: It always made you laugh.

(*Pause.*)

The first time I thought you'd die.

NELL: It was on Lake Como.

(*Pause.*)

One April afternoon.

(*Pause.*)

Can you believe it?

NAGG: What?

NELL: That we once went out rowing on Lake Como.

(*Pause.*)

One April afternoon.

NAGG: We had got engaged the day before.

NELL: Engaged!

NAGG: You were in such fits that we capsized. By rights we should have been drowned.

NELL: It was because I felt happy.

NAGG (*indignant*): It was not, it was not, it was my story and nothing else. Happy! Don't you laugh at it still? Every time I tell it. Happy!

NELL: It was deep, deep. And you could see down to the bottom. So white. So clean.

NAGG: Let me tell it again.

(*Raconteur's voice.*)

An Englishman, needing a pair of striped trousers in a hurry for the New Year festivities, goes to his tailor who takes his measurements.

(*Tailor's voice.*)

"That's the lot, come back in four days, I'll have it ready." Good. Four days later.

(*Tailor's voice.*)

"So sorry, come back in a week, I've made a mess of the seat." Good, that's all right, a neat seat can be very ticklish. A week later.

(*Tailor's voice.*)

"Frightfully sorry, come back in ten days, I've made a hash of the crotch." Good, can't be helped, a snug crotch is always a teaser. Ten days later.

(*Tailor's voice.*)

"Dreadfully sorry, come back in a fortnight, I've made a balls of the fly." Good, at a pinch, a smart fly is a stiff proposition.

(*Pause. Normal voice.*)

I never told it worse.

(*Pause. Gloomy.*)

I tell this story worse and worse.

(*Pause. Raconteur's voice.*)

Well, to make it short, the bluebells are blowing and he ballockses the buttonholes.

(*Customer's voice.*)

"God damn you to hell, Sir, no, it's indecent, there are limits! In six days, do you hear me, six days, God made the world. Yes Sir, no less Sir, the WORLD! And you are not bloody well capable of making me a pair of trousers in three months!"

(*Tailor's voice, scandalized.*)

"But my dear Sir, my dear Sir, look — (*disdainful gesture, disgustedly*) — at the world — (*pause*) and look — (*loving gesture, proudly*) — at my TROUSERS!"

(*Pause. He looks at Nell who has remained impassive, her eyes unseeing, breaks into a high forced laugh, cuts it short, pokes his head towards Nell, launches his laugh again.*)

HAMM: Silence!

(*Nagg starts, cuts short his laugh.*)

NELL: You could see down to the bottom.

HAMM (*exasperated*): Have you not finished? Will you never finish?

(*With sudden fury.*)

Will this never finish?

(*Nagg disappears into his bin, closes the lid behind him. Nell does not move. Frenziedly.*)

My kingdom for a nightman!

(*He whistles. Enter Clov.*)

Clear away this muck! Chuck it in the sea!

(*Clov goes to bins, halts.*)

NELL: So white.

HAMM: What? What's she blathering about?

(*Clov stoops, takes Nell's hand, feels her pulse.*)

NELL (*to Clov*): Desert!

(*Clov lets go her hand, pushes her back in the bin, closes the lid.*)

CLOV (*returning to his place beside the chair*): She has no pulse.

HAMM: What was she driveling about?

CLOV: She told me to go away, into the desert.

HAMM: Damn busybody! Is that all?

CLOV: No.

HAMM: What else?

CLOV: I didn't understand.

HAMM: Have you bottled her?

CLOV: Yes.

HAMM: Are they both bottled?

CLOV: Yes.
HAMM: Screw down the lids.

(*Clov goes towards door.*)

Time enough.

(*Clov halts.*)

My anger subsides, I'd like to pee.
CLOV (*with alacrity*): I'll go and get the catheter.

(*He goes towards door.*)

HAMM: Time enough.

(*Clov halts.*)

Give me my painkiller.
CLOV: It's too soon.

(*Pause.*)

It's too soon on top of your tonic, it wouldn't act.
HAMM: In the morning they brace you up and in the evening they calm you down. Unless it's the other way round.

(*Pause.*)

That old doctor, he's dead naturally?
CLOV: He wasn't old.
HAMM: But he's dead?
CLOV: Naturally.

(*Pause.*)

You ask *me* that?

(*Pause.*)

HAMM: Take me for a little turn.

(*Clov goes behind the chair and pushes it forward.*)

Not too fast!

(*Clov pushes chair.*)

Right round the world!

(*Clov pushes chair.*)

Hug the walls, then back to the center again.

(*Clov pushes chair.*)

I was right in the center, wasn't I?
CLOV (*pushing*): Yes.
HAMM: We'd need a proper wheelchair. With big wheels. Bicycle wheels!

(*Pause.*)

Are you hugging?
CLOV (*pushing*): Yes.
HAMM (*groping for wall*): It's a lie! Why do you lie to me?
CLOV (*bearing closer to wall*): There! There!
HAMM: Stop!

(*Clov stops chair close to back wall. Hamm lays his hand against wall.*)

Old wall!

(*Pause.*)

Beyond is the . . . other hell.

(*Pause. Violently.*)

Closer! Closer! Up against!
CLOV: Take away your hand.

(*Hamm withdraws his hand. Clov rams chair against wall.*)

There!

(*Hamm leans towards wall, applies his ear to it.*)

HAMM: Do you hear?

(*He strikes the wall with his knuckles.*)

Do you hear? Hollow bricks!

(*He strikes again.*)

All that's hollow!

(*Pause. He straightens up. Violently.*)

That's enough. Back!
CLOV: We haven't done the round.
HAMM: Back to my place!

(*Clov pushes chair back to center.*)

Is that my place?
CLOV: Yes, that's your place.
HAMM: Am I right in the center?
CLOV: I'll measure it.
HAMM: More or less! More or less!
CLOV (*moving chair slightly*): There!
HAMM: I'm more or less in the center?
CLOV: I'd say so.
HAMM: You'd say so! Put me right in the center!
CLOV: I'll go and get the tape.
HAMM: Roughly! Roughly!

(*Clov moves chair slightly.*)

Bang in the center!
CLOV: There!

(*Pause.*)

HAMM: I feel a little too far to the left.

(*Clov moves chair slightly.*)

Now I feel a little too far to the right.

(*Clov moves chair slightly.*)

I feel a little too far forward.

(*Clov moves chair slightly.*)

Now I feel a little too far back.

(*Clov moves chair slightly.*)

Don't stay there (*i.e., behind the chair*), you give me the shivers.

(*Clov returns to his place beside the chair.*)

CLOV: If I could kill him I'd die happy.

(*Pause.*)

HAMM: What's the weather like?
CLOV: As usual.
HAMM: Look at the earth.
CLOV: I've looked.
HAMM: With the glass?
CLOV: No need of the glass.
HAMM: Look at it with the glass.
CLOV: I'll go and get the glass.

(*Exit Clov.*)

HAMM: No need of the glass!

(*Enter Clov with telescope.*)

CLOV: I'm back again, with the glass.

(*He goes to window right, looks up at it.*)

    I need the steps.
HAMM: Why? Have you shrunk?

(*Exit Clov with telescope.*)

    I don't like that, I don't like that.

(*Enter Clov with ladder, but without telescope.*)

CLOV: I'm back again, with the steps.

(*He sets down ladder under window right, gets up on it, realizes he has not the telescope, gets down.*)

    I need the glass.

(*He goes towards door.*)

HAMM (*violently*): But you have the glass!
CLOV (*halting, violently*): No, I haven't the glass!

(*Exit Clov.*)

HAMM: This is deadly.

(*Enter Clov with telescope. He goes towards ladder.*)

CLOV: Things are livening up.

(*He gets up on ladder, raises the telescope, lets it fall.*)

    I did it on purpose.

(*He gets down, picks up the telescope, turns it on auditorium.*)

    I see . . . a multitude . . . in transports . . . of joy.

(*Pause.*)

    That's what I call a magnifier.

(*He lowers the telescope, turns towards Hamm.*)

    Well? Don't we laugh?
HAMM (*after reflection*): I don't.
CLOV (*after reflection*): Nor I.

(*He gets up on ladder, turns the telescope on the without.*)

    Let's see.

(*He looks, moving the telescope.*)

    Zero . . . (*he looks*) . . . zero . . . (*he looks*) . . . and zero.
HAMM: Nothing stirs. All is —
CLOV: Zer —
HAMM (*violently*): Wait till you're spoken to!

(*Normal voice.*)

    All is . . . all is . . . all is what?

(*Violently.*)

    All is what?
CLOV: What all is? In a word? Is that what you want to know? Just a moment.

(*He turns the telescope on the without, looks, lowers the telescope, turns towards Hamm.*)

    Corpsed.

(*Pause.*)

    Well? Content?
HAMM: Look at the sea.
CLOV: It's the same.
HAMM: Look at the ocean!

(*Clov gets down, takes a few steps towards window left, goes back for ladder, carries it over and sets it down under window left, gets up on it, turns the telescope on the without, looks at length. He starts, lowers the telescope, examines it, turns it again on the without.*)

CLOV: Never seen anything like that!
HAMM (*anxious*): What? A sail? A fin? Smoke?
CLOV (*looking*): The light is sunk.
HAMM (*relieved*): Pah! We all knew that.
CLOV (*looking*): There was a bit left.
HAMM: The base.
CLOV (*looking*): Yes.
HAMM: And now?
CLOV (*looking*): All gone.
HAMM: No gulls?
CLOV (*looking*): Gulls!
HAMM: And the horizon? Nothing on the horizon?
CLOV (*lowering the telescope, turning towards Hamm, exasperated*): What in God's name could there be on the horizon?

(*Pause.*)

HAMM: The waves, how are the waves?
CLOV: The waves?

(*He turns the telescope on the waves.*)

    Lead.
HAMM: And the sun?
CLOV (*looking*): Zero.
HAMM: But it should be sinking. Look again.
CLOV (*looking*): Damn the sun.
HAMM: Is it night already then?
CLOV (*looking*): No.

HAMM: Then what is it?
CLOV (*looking*): Gray.

(*Lowering the telescope, turning towards Hamm, louder.*)

    Gray!

(*Pause. Still louder.*)

    GRRAY!

(*Pause. He gets down, approaches Hamm from behind, whispers in his ear.*)

HAMM (*starting*): Gray! Did I hear you say gray?
CLOV: Light black. From pole to pole.
HAMM: You exaggerate.

(*Pause.*)

    Don't stay there, you give me the shivers.

(*Clov returns to his place beside the chair.*)

CLOV: Why this farce, day after day?
HAMM: Routine. One never knows.

(*Pause.*)

    Last night I saw inside my breast. There was a big sore.
CLOV: Pah! You saw your heart.
HAMM: No, it was living.

(*Pause. Anguished.*)

    Clov!
CLOV: Yes.
HAMM: What's happening?
CLOV: Something is taking its course.

(*Pause.*)

HAMM: Clov!
CLOV (*impatiently*): What is it?
HAMM: We're not beginning to . . . to . . . mean something?

RIGHT: Hamm (Alvin Epstein), seated, and Clov (Peter Evans) in the 1984 Harold Clurman Theatre production of *Endgame*, directed by Alvin Epstein. FAR RIGHT: Nell (Alice Drummond), Nagg (James Greene), Hamm, and Clov.

CLOV: Mean something! You and I, mean something!

(*Brief laugh.*)

Ah that's a good one!

HAMM: I wonder.

(*Pause.*)

Imagine if a rational being came back to earth, wouldn't he be liable to get ideas into his head if he observed us long enough.

(*Voice of rational being.*)

Ah, good, now I see what it is, yes, now I understand what they're at!

(*Clov starts, drops the telescope and begins to scratch his belly with both hands. Normal voice.*)

And without going so far as that, we ourselves . . . (*with emotion*) . . . we ourselves . . . at certain moments . . .

(*Vehemently.*)

To think perhaps it won't all have been for nothing!

CLOV (*anguished, scratching himself*): I have a flea!

HAMM: A flea! Are there still fleas?

CLOV: On me there's one.

(*Scratching.*)

Unless it's a crablouse.

HAMM (*very perturbed*): But humanity might start from there all over again! Catch him, for the love of God!

CLOV: I'll go and get the powder.

(*Exit Clov.*)

HAMM: A flea! This is awful! What a day!

(*Enter Clov with a sprinkling tin.*)

CLOV: I'm back again, with the insecticide.

HAMM: Let him have it!

(*Clov loosens the top of his trousers, pulls it forward and shakes powder into the aperture. He stoops, looks, waits, starts, frenziedly shakes more powder, stoops, looks, waits.*)

CLOV: The bastard!

HAMM: Did you get him?

CLOV: Looks like it.

(*He drops the tin and adjusts his trousers.*)

Unless he's laying doggo.°
HAMM: Laying! Lying you mean. Unless he's *lying* doggo.
CLOV: Ah? One says lying? One doesn't say laying?
HAMM: Use your head, can't you. If he was laying we'd be bitched.
CLOV: Ah.

(*Pause.*)

What about that pee?
HAMM: I'm having it.
CLOV: Ah that's the spirit, that's the spirit!

(*Pause.*)

HAMM (*with ardor*): Let's go from here, the two of us! South! You can make a raft and the currents will carry us away, far away, to other . . . mammals!
CLOV: God forbid!
HAMM: Alone, I'll embark alone! Get working on that raft immediately. Tomorrow I'll be gone forever.
CLOV (*hastening towards door*): I'll start straight away.
HAMM: Wait!

(*Clov halts.*)

Will there be sharks, do you think?
CLOV: Sharks? I don't know. If there are there will be.

(*He goes towards door.*)

HAMM: Wait!

(*Clov halts.*)

Is it not yet time for my painkiller?
CLOV (*violently*): No!

(*He goes towards door.*)

HAMM: Wait!

(*Clov halts.*)

How are your eyes?
CLOV: Bad.
HAMM: But you can see.
CLOV: All I want.
HAMM: How are your legs
CLOV: Bad.
HAMM: But you can walk.
CLOV: I come . . . and go.
HAMM: In my house.

(*Pause. With prophetic relish.*)

One day you'll be blind, like me. You'll be sitting there, a speck in the void, in the dark, forever, like me.

(*Pause.*)

One day you'll say to yourself, I'm tired, I'll sit down,

doggo: In hiding.

and you'll go and sit down. Then you'll say, I'm hungry, I'll get up and get something to eat. But you won't get up. You'll say, I shouldn't have sat down, but since I have I'll sit on a little longer, then I'll get up and get something to eat. But you won't get up and you won't get anything to eat.

(*Pause.*)

You'll look at the wall a while, then you'll say, I'll close my eyes, perhaps have a little sleep, after that I'll feel better, and you'll close them. And when you open them again there'll be no wall anymore.

(*Pause.*)

Infinite emptiness will be all around you, all the resurrected dead of all the ages wouldn't fill it, and there you'll be like a little bit of grit in the middle of the steppe.

(*Pause.*)

Yes, one day you'll know what it is, you'll be like me, except that you won't have anyone with you, because you won't have had pity on anyone and because there won't be anyone left to have pity on.

(*Pause.*)

CLOV: It's not certain.

(*Pause.*)

And there's one thing you forget.
HAMM: Ah?
CLOV: I can't sit down.
HAMM (*impatiently*): Well you'll lie down then, what the hell! Or you'll come to a standstill, simply stop and stand still, the way you are now. One day you'll say, I'm tired, I'll stop. What does the attitude matter?

(*Pause.*)

CLOV: So you all want me to leave you.
HAMM: Naturally.
CLOV: Then I'll leave you.
HAMM: You can't leave us.
CLOV: Then I won't leave you.

(*Pause.*)

HAMM: Why don't you finish us?

(*Pause.*)

I'll tell you the combination of the cupboard if you promise to finish me.
CLOV: I couldn't finish you.
HAMM: Then you won't finish me.

(*Pause.*)

CLOV: I'll leave you, I have things to do.
HAMM: Do you remember when you came here?
CLOV: No. Too small, you told me.
HAMM: Do you remember your father?

CLOV (*wearily*): Same answer.

(*Pause.*)

    You've asked me these questions millions of times.
HAMM: I love the old questions.

(*With fervor.*)

    Ah the old questions, the old answers, there's nothing like them!

(*Pause.*)

    It was I was a father to you.
CLOV: Yes.

(*He looks at Hamm fixedly.*)

    You were that to me.
HAMM: My house a home for you.
CLOV: Yes.

(*He looks about him.*)

    This was that for me.
HAMM (*proudly*): But for me (*gesture towards himself*), no father. But for Hamm (*gesture towards surroundings*), no home.

(*Pause.*)

CLOV: I'll leave you.
HAMM: Did you ever think of one thmg?
CLOV: Never.
HAMM: That here we're down in a hole.

(*Pause.*)

    But beyond the hills? Eh? Perhaps it's still green. Eh?

(*Pause.*)

    Flora! Pomona!

(*Ecstatically.*)

    Ceres!°

(*Pause,*)

    Perhaps you won't need to go very far.
CLOV: I can't go very far.

(*Pause.*)

    I'll leave you.
HAMM: Is my dog ready?
CLOV: He lacks a leg.
HAMM: Is he silky?
CLOV: He's a kind of Pomeranian.
HAMM: Go and get him.
CLOV: He lacks a leg.
HAMM: Go and get him!

(*Exit Clov.*)

    We're getting on.

Flora . . . Ceres: Three Roman goddesses — Flora, of flowers; Pomona, of fruit; Ceres, of agriculture.

(*Enter Clov holding by one of its three legs a black toy dog.*)

CLOV: Your dogs are here.

(*He hands the dog to Hamm who feels it, fondles it.*)

HAMM: He's white, isn't he?
CLOV: Nearly.
HAMM: What do you mean, nearly? Is he white or isn't he?
CLOV: He isn't.

(*Pause.*)

HAMM: You've forgotten the sex.
CLOV (*vexed*): But he isn't finished. The sex goes on at the end.

(*Pause.*)

HAMM: You haven't put on his ribbon.
CLOV (*angrily*): But he isn't finished, I tell you! First you finish your dog and then you put on his ribbon!

(*Pause.*)

HAMM: Can he stand?
CLOV: I don't know.
HAMM: Try.

(*He hands the dog to Clov who places it on the ground.*)

    Well?
CLOV: Wait!

(*He squats down and tries to get the dog to stand on its three legs, fails, lets it go. The dog falls on its side.*)

HAMM (*impatiently*): Well?
CLOV: He's standing.
HAMM (*groping for the dog*): Where? Where is he?

(*Clov holds up the dog in a standing position.*)

CLOV: There.

(*He takes Hamm's hand and guides it towards the dog's head.*)

HAMM (*his hand on the dog's head*): Is he gazing at me?
CLOV: Yes.
HAMM (*proudly*): As if he were asking me to take him for a walk?
CLOV: If you like.
HAMM (*as before*): Or as if he were begging me for a bone.

(*He withdraws his hand.*)

    Leave him like that, standing there imploring me.

(*Clov straightens up. The dog falls on its side.*)

CLOV: I'll leave you.
HAMM: Have you had your visions?
CLOV: Less.
HAMM: Is Mother Pegg's light on?
CLOV: Light! How could anyone's light be on?
HAMM: Extinguished!

CLOV: Naturally it's extinguished. If it's not on it's extinguished.

HAMM: No, I mean Mother Pegg.

CLOV: But naturally she's extinguished!

(*Pause.*)

What's the matter with you today?

HAMM: I'm taking my course.

(*Pause.*)

Is she buried?

CLOV: Buried! Who would have buried her?

HAMM: You.

CLOV: Me! Haven't I enough to do without burying people?

HAMM: But you'll bury me.

CLOV: No I won't bury you.

(*Pause.*)

HAMM: She was bonny once, like a flower of the field.

(*With reminiscent leer.*)

And a great one for the men!

CLOV: We too were bonny — once. It's a rare thing not to have been bonny — once.

(*Pause.*)

HAMM: Go and get the gaff.

(*Clov goes to door, halts.*)

CLOV: Do this, do that, and I do it. I never refuse. Why?

HAMM: You're not able to.

CLOV: Soon I won't do it anymore.

HAMM: You won't be able to anymore.

(*Exit Clov.*)

Ah the creatures, the creatures, everything has to be explained to them.

(*Enter Clov with gaff.*)

CLOV: Here's your gaff. Stick it up.

(*He gives the gaff to Hamm who, wielding it like a punt-pole,° tries to move his chair.*)

HAMM: Did I move?

CLOV: No.

(*Hamm throws down the gaff.*)

HAMM: Go and get the oilcan.

CLOV: What for?

HAMM: To oil the casters.

CLOV: I oiled them yesterday.

HAMM: Yesterday! What does that mean? Yesterday!

CLOV (*violently*): That means that bloody awful day, long ago, before this bloody awful day. I use the

---

puntpole: A pole used to propel a punt, a flat-bottomed boat, through the water.

---

words you taught me. If they don't mean anything anymore, teach me others. Or let me be silent.

(*Pause.*)

HAMM: I once knew a madman who thought the end of the world had come. He was a painter — and engraver. I had a great fondness for him. I used to go and see him, in the asylum. I'd take him by the hand and drag him to the window. Look! There! All that rising corn! And there! Look! The sails of the herring fleet! All that loveliness!

(*Pause.*)

He'd snatch away his hand and go back into his corner. Appalled. All he had seen was ashes.

(*Pause.*)

He alone had been spared.

(*Pause.*)

Forgotten.

(*Pause.*)

It appears the case is . . . was not so . . . so unusual.

CLOV: A madman? When was that?

HAMM: Oh way back, way back, you weren't in the land of the living.

CLOV: God be with the days!

(*Pause. Hamm raises his toque.*)

HAMM: I had a great fondness for him.

(*Pause. He puts on his toque again.*)

He was a painter — and engraver.

CLOV: There are so many terrible things.

HAMM: No, no, there are not so many now.

(*Pause.*)

Clov!

CLOV: Yes.

HAMM: Do you not think this has gone on long enough?

CLOV: Yes!

(*Pause.*)

What?

HAMM: This . . . this . . . thing.

CLOV: I've always thought so.

(*Pause.*)

You not?

HAMM (*gloomily*): Then it's a day like any other day.

CLOV: As long as it lasts.

(*Pause.*)

All life long the same inanities.

HAMM: I can't leave you.

CLOV: I know. And you can't follow me.

(*Pause.*)

HAMM: If you leave me how shall I know?

CLOV (*briskly*): Well you simply whistle me and if I don't come running it means I've left you.

(*Pause.*)

HAMM: You won't come and kiss me good-bye?

CLOV: Oh I shouldn't think so.

(*Pause.*)

HAMM: But you might be merely dead in your kitchen.

CLOV: The result would be the same.

HAMM: Yes, but how would I know, if you were merely dead in your kitchen?

CLOV: Well . . . sooner or later I'd start to stink.

HAMM: You stink already. The whole place stinks of corpses.

CLOV: The whole universe.

HAMM (*angrily*): To hell with the universe.

(*Pause.*)

Think of something.

CLOV: What?

HAMM: An idea, have an idea.

(*Angrily.*)

A bright idea!

CLOV: Ah good.

(*He starts pacing to and fro, his eyes fixed on the ground, his hands behind his back. He halts.*)

The pains in my legs! It's unbelievable! Soon I won't be able to think anymore.

HAMM: You won't be able to leave me.

(*Clov resumes his pacing.*)

What are you doing?

CLOV: Having an idea.

(*He paces.*)

Ah!

(*He halts.*)

HAMM: What a brain!

(*Pause.*)

Well?

CLOV: Wait!

(*He meditates. Not very convinced.*)

Yes . . .

(*Pause. More convinced.*)

Yes!

(*He raises his head.*)

I have it! I set the alarm.

(*Pause.*)

HAMM: This is perhaps not one of my bright days, but frankly —

CLOV: You whistle me. I don't come. The alarm rings. I'm gone. It doesn't ring. I'm dead.

(*Pause.*)

HAMM: Is it working?

(*Pause. Impatiently.*)

The alarm, is it working?

CLOV: Why wouldn't it be working?

HAMM: Because it's worked too much.

CLOV: But it's hardly worked at all.

HAMM (*angrily*): Then because it's worked too little!

CLOV: I'll go and see.

(*Exit Clov. Brief ring of alarm off. Enter Clov with alarm clock. He holds it against Hamm's ear and releases alarm. They listen to it ringing to the end. Pause.*)

Fit to wake the dead! Did you hear it?

HAMM: Vaguely.

CLOV: The end is terrific!

HAMM: I prefer the middle.

(*Pause.*)

Is it not time for my painkiller?

CLOV: No!

(*He goes to door, turns.*)

I'll leave you.

HAMM: It's time for my story. Do you want to listen to my story?

CLOV: No.

HAMM: Ask my father if he wants to listen to my story.

(*Clov goes to bins, raises the lid of Nagg's, stoops, looks into it. Pause. He straightens up.*)

CLOV: He's asleep.

HAMM: Wake him.

(*Clov stoops, wakes Nagg with the alarm. Unintelligible words. Clov straightens up.*)

CLOV: He doesn't want to listen to your story.

HAMM: I'll give him a bonbon.

(*Clov stoops. As before.*)

CLOV: He wants a sugarplum.

HAMM: He'll get a sugarplum.

(*Clov stoops. As before.*)

CLOV: It's a deal.

(*He goes towards door. Nagg's hands appear, gripping the rim. Then the head emerges. Clov reaches door, turns.*)

Do you believe in the life to come?

HAMM: Mine was always that.

(*Exit Clov.*)

Got him that time!

NAGG: I'm listening.
HAMM: Scoundrel! Why did you engender me?
NAGG: I didn't know.
HAMM: What? What didn't you know?
NAGG: That it'd be you.

(*Pause.*)

You'll give me a sugarplum?
HAMM: After the audition.
NAGG: You swear?
HAMM: Yes.
NAGG: On what?
HAMM: My honor.

(*Pause. They laugh heartily.*)

NAGG: Two.
HAMM: One.
NAGG: One for me and one for —
HAMM: One! Silence!

(*Pause.*)

Where was I?

(*Pause. Gloomily.*)

It's finished, we're finished.

(*Pause.*)

Nearly finished.

(*Pause.*)

There'll be no more speech.

(*Pause.*)

Something dripping in my head, ever since the fontanelles.°

(*Stifled hilarity of Nagg.*)

Splash, splash, always on the same spot.

(*Pause.*)

Perhaps it's a little vein.

(*Pause.*)

A little artery.

(*Pause. More animated.*)

Enough of that, it's story time, where was I?

(*Pause. Narrative tone.*)

The man came crawling towards me, on his belly. Pale, wonderfully pale and thin, he seemed on the point of —

(*Pause. Normal tone.*)

No, I've done that bit.

(*Pause. Narrative tone.*)

since the fontanelles: Since soft membranes linked the incompletely developed skull bones in his infant head.

I calmly filled my pipe — the meerschaum, lit it with . . . let us say a vesta,° drew a few puffs. Aah!

(*Pause.*)

Well, what is it *you* want?

(*Pause.*)

It was an extraordinarily bitter day, I remember, zero by the thermometer. But considering it was Christmas Eve there was nothing . . . extraordinary about that. Seasonable weather, for once in a way.

(*Pause.*)

Well, what ill wind blows you my way? He raised his face to me, black with mingled dirt and tears.

(*Pause. Normal tone.*)

That should do it.

(*Narrative tone.*)

No no, don't look at me, don't look at me. He dropped his eyes and mumbled something, apologies I presume.

(*Pause.*)

I'm a busy man, you know, the final touches, before the festivities, you know what it is.

(*Pause. Forcibly.*)

Come on now, what is the object of this invasion?

(*Pause.*)

It was a glorious bright day, I remember, fifty by the heliometer,° but already the sun was sinking down into the . . . down among the dead.

(*Normal tone.*)

Nicely put, that.

(*Narrative tone.*)

Come on now, come on, present your petition and let me resume my labors.

(*Pause. Normal tone.*)

There's English for you. Ah well . . .

(*Narrative tone.*)

It was then he took the plunge. It's my little one, he said. Tsstss, a little one, that's bad. My little boy, he said, as if the sex mattered. Where did he come from? He named the hole. A good half-day, on horse. What are you insinuating? That the place is still inhabited? No, no, not a soul, except himself and the child — assuming he existed. Good. I inquired about the situation at Kov, beyond the gulf. Not a sinner. Good.

vesta: Wooden match.
heliometer: A telescope for measuring the apparent diameter of the sun.

And you expect me to believe you have left your little one back there, all alone, and alive into the bargain? Come now!

(*Pause.*)

It was a howling wild day, I remember, a hundred by the anemometer.° The wind was tearing up the dead pines and sweeping them . . . away.

(*Pause. Normal tone.*)

A bit feeble, that.

(*Narrative tone.*)

Come on, man, speak up, what is you want from me, I have to put up my holly.

(*Pause.*)

Well to make it short it finally transpired that what he wanted from me was . . . bread for his brat? Bread? But I have no bread, it doesn't agree with me. Good. Then perhaps a little corn?

(*Pause. Normal tone.*)

That should do it.

(*Narrative tone.*)

Corn, yes, I have corn, it's true, in my granaries. But use your head. I give you some corn, a pound, a pound and a half, you bring it back to your child and you make him — if he's still alive — a nice pot of porridge, (*Nagg reacts*) a nice pot and a half of porridge, full of nourishment. Good. The colors come back into his little cheeks — perhaps. And then?

(*Pause.*)

I lost patience.

(*Violently.*)

Use your head, can't you, use your head, you're on earth, there's no cure for that!

(*Pause.*)

It was an exceedingly dry day, I remember, zero by the hygrometer.° Ideal weather, for my lumbago.

(*Pause. Violently.*)

But what in God's name do you imagine? That the earth will awake in spring? That the rivers and seas will run with fish again? That there's manna in heaven still for imbeciles like you?

(*Pause.*)

Gradually I cooled down, sufficiently at least to ask him how long he had taken on the way. Three whole days. Good. In what condition he had left the child. Deep in sleep.

(*Forcibly.*)

But deep in what sleep, deep in what sleep already?

(*Pause.*)

Well to make it short I finally offered to take him into my service. He had touched a chord. And then I imagined already that I wasn't much longer for this world.

(*He laughs. Pause.*)

Well?

(*Pause.*)

Well? Here if you were careful you might die a nice natural death, in peace and comfort.

(*Pause.*)

Well?

(*Pause.*)

In the end he asked me would I consent to take in the child as well — if he were still alive.

(*Pause.*)

It was the moment I was waiting for.

(*Pause.*)

Would I consent to take in the child . . .

(*Pause.*)

I can see him still, down on his knees, his hands flat on the ground, glaring at me with his mad eyes, in defiance of my wishes.

(*Pause. Normal tone.*)

I'll soon have finished with this story.

(*Pause.*)

Unless I bring in other characters.

(*Pause.*)

But where would I find them?

(*Pause.*)

Where would I look for them?

(*Pause. He whistles. Enter Clov.*)

Let us pray to God.
NAGG: Me sugarplum!
CLOV: There's a rat in the kitchen!
HAMM: A rat! Are there still rats?
CLOV: In the kitchen there's one.
HAMM: And you haven't exterminated him?
CLOV: Half. You disturbed us.
HAMM: He can't get away?
CLOV: No.
HAMM: You'll finish him later. Let us pray to God.
CLOV: Again!
NAGG: Me sugarplum!

---

anemometer: An instrument for measuring wind speed.
hygrometer: Device for measuring humidity.

HAMM: God first!

(*Pause.*)

Are you right?

CLOV (*resigned*): Off we go.

HAMM (*to Nagg*): And you?

NAGG (*clasping his hands, closing his eyes, in a gabble*): Our Father which art —

HAMM: Silence! In silence! Where are your manners?

(*Pause.*)

Off we go.

(*Attitudes of prayer. Silence. Abandoning his attitude, discouraged.*)

Well?

CLOV (*abandoning his attitude*): What a hope! And you?

HAMM: Sweet damn all!

(*To Nagg.*)

And you?

NAGG: Wait!

(*Pause. Abandoning his attitude.*)

Nothing doing!

HAMM: The bastard! He doesn't exist!

CLOV: Not yet.

NAGG: Me sugarplum!

HAMM: There are no more sugarplums!

(*Pause.*)

NAGG: It's natural. After all I'm your father. It's true if it hadn't been me it would have been someone else. But that's no excuse.

(*Pause.*)

Turkish Delight,° for example, which no longer exists, we all know that, there is nothing in the world I love more. And one day I'll ask you for some, in return for a kindness, and you'll promise it to me. One must live with the times.

(*Pause.*)

Whom did you call when you were a tiny boy, and were frightened, in the dark? Your mother? No. Me. We let you cry. Then we moved you out of earshot, so that we might sleep in peace.

(*Pause.*)

I was asleep, as happy as a king, and you woke me up to have me listen to you. It wasn't indispensable, you didn't really need to have me listen to you.

(*Pause.*)

I hope the day will come when you'll really need to have me listen to you, and need to hear my voice, any voice.

Turkish Delight: Gummy candy.

(*Pause.*)

Yes, I hope I'll live till then, to hear you calling me like when you were a tiny boy, and were frightened, in the dark, and I was your only hope.

(*Pause. Nagg knocks on lid of Nell's bin. Pause.*)

Nell!

(*Pause. He knocks louder. Pause. Louder.*)

Nell!

(*Pause. Nagg sinks back into his bin, closes the lid behind him. Pause.*)

HAMM: Our revels now are ended.

(*He gropes for the dog.*)

The dog's gone.

CLOV: He's not a real dog, he can't go.

HAMM (*groping*): He's not there.

CLOV: He's lain down.

HAMM: Give him up to me.

(*Clov picks up the dog and gives it to Hamm. Hamm holds it in his arms. Pause. Hamm throws away the dog.*)

Dirty brute!

(*Clov begins to pick up the objects lying on the ground.*)

What are you doing?

CLOV: Putting things in order.

(*He straightens up. Fervently.*)

I'm going to clear everything away!

(*He starts picking up again.*)

HAMM: Order!

CLOV (*straightening up*): I love order. It's my dream. A world where all would be silent and still and each thing in its last place, under the last dust.

(*He starts picking up again.*)

HAMM (*exasperated*): What in God's name do you think you are doing?

CLOV (*straightening up*): I'm doing my best to create a little order.

HAMM: Drop it!

(*Clov drops the objects he has picked up.*)

CLOV: After all, there or elsewhere.

(*He goes towards door.*)

HAMM (*irritably*): What's wrong with your feet?

CLOV: My feet?

HAMM: Tramp! Tramp!

CLOV: I must have put on my boots.

HAMM: Your slippers were hurting you?

(*Pause.*)

CLOV: I'll leave you.

HAMM: No!

CLOV: What is there to keep me here?
HAMM: The dialogue.

(*Pause.*)

I've got on with my story.

(*Pause.*)

I've got on with it well.

(*Pause. Irritably.*)

Ask me where I've got to.
CLOV: Oh, by the way, your story?
HAMM (*surprised*): What story?
CLOV: The one you've been telling yourself all your days.
HAMM: Ah you mean my chronicle?
CLOV: That's the one.

(*Pause.*)

HAMM (*angrily*): Keep going, can't you, keep going!
CLOV: You've got on with it, I hope.
HAMM (*modestly*): Oh not very far, not very far.

(*He sighs.*)

There are days like that, one isn't inspired.

(*Pause.*)

Nothing you can do about it, just wait for it to come.

(*Pause.*)

No forcing, no forcing, it's fatal.

(*Pause.*)

I've got on with it a little all the same.

(*Pause.*)

Technique, you know.

(*Pause. Irritably.*)

I say I've got on with it a little all the same.
CLOV (*admiringly*): Well I never! In spite of everything you were able to get on with it!
HAMM (*modestly*): Oh not very far, you know, not very far, but nevertheless, better than nothing.
CLOV: Better than nothing! Is it possible?
HAMM: I'll tell you how it goes. He comes crawling on his belly —
CLOV: Who?
HAMM: What?
CLOV: Who do you mean, he?
HAMM: Who do I mean! Yet another.
CLOV: Ah him! I wasn't sure.
HAMM: Crawling on his belly, whining for bread for his brat. He's offered a job as gardener. Before —

(*Clov bursts out laughing.*)

What is there so funny about that?
CLOV: A job as gardener!
HAMM: Is that what tickles you?

CLOV: It must be that.
HAMM: It wouldn't be the bread?
CLOV: Or the brat.

(*Pause.*)

HAMM: The whole thing is comical, I grant you that. What about having a good guffaw the two of us together?
CLOV (*after reflection*): I couldn't guffaw again today.
HAMM (*after reflection*): Nor I.

(*Pause.*)

I continue then. Before accepting with gratitude he asks if he may have his little boy with him.
CLOV: What age?
HAMM: Oh tiny.
CLOV: He would have climbed the trees.
HAMM: All the little odd jobs.
CLOV: And then he would have grown up.
HAMM: Very likely.

(*Pause.*)

CLOV: Keep going, can't you, keep going!
HAMM: That's all. I stopped there.

(*Pause.*)

CLOV: Do you see how it goes on.
HAMM: More or less.
CLOV: Will it not soon be the end?
HAMM: I m afraid it will.
CLOV: Pah! You'll make up another.
HAMM: I don't know.

(*Pause.*)

I feel rather drained.

(*Pause.*)

The prolonged creative effort.

(*Pause.*)

If I could drag myself down to the sea! I'd make a pillow of sand for my head and the tide would come.
CLOV: There's no more tide.

(*Pause.*)

HAMM: Go and see is she dead.

(*Clov goes to bins, raises the lid of Nell's, stoops, looks into it. Pause.*)

CLOV: Looks like it.

(*He closes the lid, straightens up. Hamm raises his toque. Pause. He puts it on again.*)

HAMM (*with his hand to his toque*): And Nagg?

(*Clov raises lid of Nagg's bin, stoops, looks into it. Pause.*)

CLOV: Doesn't look like it.

(*He closes the lid, straightens up.*)

HAMM (*letting go his toque*): What's he doing?

(*Clov raises lid of Nagg's bin, stoops, looks into it. Pause.*)

CLOV: He's crying.

(*He closes lid, straightens up.*)

HAMM: Then he's living.

(*Pause.*)

Did you ever have an instant of happiness?
CLOV: Not to my knowledge.

(*Pause.*)

HAMM: Bring me under the window.

(*Clov goes towards chair.*)

I want to feel the light on my face.

(*Clov pushes chair.*)

Do you remember, in the beginning, when you took me for a turn? You used to hold the chair too high. At every step you nearly tipped me out.

(*With senile quaver.*)

Ah great fun, we had, the two of us, great fun.

(*Gloomily.*)

And then we got into the way of it.

(*Clov stops the chair under window right.*)

There already?

(*Pause. He tilts back his head.*)

Is it light?
CLOV: It isn't dark.
HAMM (*angrily*): I'm asking you is it light.
CLOV: Yes.

(*Pause.*)

HAMM: The curtain isn't closed?
CLOV: No.
HAMM: What window is it?
CLOV: The earth.
HAMM: I knew it!

(*Angrily.*)

But there's no light there! The other!

(*Clov pushes chair towards window left.*)

The earth!

(*Clov stops the chair under window left. Hamm tilts back his head.*)

That's what I call light!

(*Pause.*)

Feels like a ray of sunshine.

(*Pause.*)

No?
CLOV: No.
HAMM: It isn't a ray of sunshine I feel on my face?
CLOV: No.

(*Pause.*)

HAMM: Am I very white?

(*Pause. Angrily.*)

I'm asking you am I very white!
CLOV: Not more so than usual.

(*Pause.*)

HAMM: Open the window.
CLOV: What for?
HAMM: I want to hear the sea.
CLOV: You wouldn't hear it.
HAMM: Even if you opened the window?
CLOV: No.
HAMM: Then it's not worthwhile opening it?
CLOV: No.
HAMM (*violently*): Then open it!

(*Clov gets up on the ladder, opens the window. Pause.*)

Have you opened it?
CLOV: Yes.

(*Pause.*)

HAMM: You swear you've opened it?
CLOV: Yes.

(*Pause.*)

HAMM: Well . . . !

(*Pause.*)

It must be very calm.

(*Pause. Violently.*)

I'm asking you is it very calm!
CLOV: Yes.
HAMM: It's because there are no more navigators.

(*Pause.*)

You haven't much conversation all of a sudden. Do you not feel well?
CLOV: I'm cold.
HAMM: What month are we?

(*Pause.*)

Close the window, we're going back.

(*Clov closes the window, gets down, pushes the chair back to its place, remains standing behind it, head bowed.*)

Don't stay there, you give me the shivers!

(*Clov returns to his place beside the chair.*)

RIGHT: Clov (John Bottoms) and Hamm (Ben Halley, Jr.), seated, in the 1984 American Repertory Theatre production of *Endgame*, directed by JoAnne Akalaitis. BELOW: Hamm and Clov.

Father!

(*Pause. Louder.*)

Father!

(*Pause.*)

Go and see did he hear me.

(*Clov goes to Nagg's bin, raises the lid, stoops. Unintelligible words. Clov straightens up.*)

CLOV: Yes.
HAMM: Both times?

(*Clov stoops. As before.*)

CLOV: Once only.
HAMM: The first time or the second?

(*Clov stoops. As before.*)

CLOV: He doesn't know.
HAMM: It must have been the second.
CLOV: We'll never know.

(*He closes lid.*)

HAMM: Is he still crying?
CLOV: No.
HAMM: The dead go fast.

(*Pause.*)

What's he doing?
CLOV: Sucking his biscuit.
HAMM: Life goes on.

(*Clov returns to his place beside the chair.*)

Give me a rug,° I'm freezing.
CLOV: There are no more rugs.

(*Pause.*)

HAMM: Kiss me.

(*Pause.*)

Will you not kiss me?
CLOV: No.
HAMM: On the forehead.
CLOV: I won't kiss you anywhere.

(*Pause.*)

HAMM (*holding out his hand*): Give me your hand at least.

(*Pause.*)

Will you not give me your hand?
CLOV: I won't touch you.

(*Pause.*)

HAMM: Give me the dog.

(*Clov looks round for the dog.*)

rug: A small blanket to cover the lap, legs, and feet.

No!
CLOV: Do you not want your dog?
HAMM: No.
CLOV: Then I'll leave you.
HAMM (*head bowed, absently*): That's right.

(*Clov goes to door, turns.*)

CLOV: If I don't kill that rat he'll die.
HAMM (*as before*): That's right.

(*Exit Clov. Pause.*)

Me to play.

(*He takes out his handkerchief, unfolds it, holds it spread out before him.*)

We're getting on.

(*Pause.*)

You weep, and weep, for nothing, so as not to laugh, and little by little . . . you begin to grieve.

(*He folds the handkerchief, puts it back in his pocket, raises his head.*)

All those I might have helped.

(*Pause.*)

Helped!

(*Pause.*)

Saved.

(*Pause.*)

Saved!

(*Pause.*)

The place was crawling with them!

(*Pause. Violently.*)

Use your head, can't you, use your head, you're on earth, there's no cure for that!

(*Pause.*)

Get out of here and love one another! Lick your neighbor as yourself!

(*Pause. Calmer.*)

When it wasn't bread they wanted it was crumpets.

(*Pause. Violently.*)

Out of my sight and back to your petting parties!

(*Pause.*)

All that, all that!

(*Pause.*)

Not even a real dog!

(*Calmer.*)

The end is in the beginning and yet you go on.

(*Pause.*)

Perhaps I could go on with my story, end it and begin another.

(*Pause.*)

Perhaps I could throw myself out on the floor.

(*He pushes himself painfully off his seat, falls back again.*)

Dig my nails into the cracks and drag myself forward with my fingers.

(*Pause.*)

It will be the end and there I'll be, wondering what can have brought it on and wondering what can have . . . (*he hesitates*) . . . why it was so long coming.

(*Pause.*)

There I'll be, in the old shelter, alone against the silence and . . . (*he hesitates*) . . . the stillness. If I can hold my peace, and sit quiet, it will be all over with sound, and motion, all over and done with.

(*Pause.*)

I'll have called my father and I'll have called my . . . (*he hesitates*) . . . my son. And even twice, or three times, in case they shouldn't have heard me, the first time, or the second.

(*Pause.*)

I'll say to myself, He'll come back.

(*Pause.*)

And then?

(*Pause.*)

And then?

(*Pause.*)

He couldn't, he has gone too far.

(*Pause.*)

And then?

(*Pause. Very agitated.*)

All kinds of fantasies! That I'm being watched! A rat! Steps! Breath held and then . . .

(*He breathes out.*)

Then babble, babble, words, like the solitary child who turns himself into children, two, three, so as to be together, and whisper together, in the dark.

(*Pause.*)

Moment upon moment, pattering down, like the millet grains of . . . (*he hesitates*) . . . that old Greek, and all life long you wait for that to mount up to a life.

(*Pause. He opens his mouth to continue, renounces.*)

Ah let's get it over!

(*He whistles. Enter Clov with alarm clock. He halts beside the chair.*)

What? Neither gone nor dead?
CLOV: In spirit only.
HAMM: Which?
CLOV: Both.
HAMM: Gone from me you'd be dead.
CLOV: And vice versa.
HAMM: Outside of here it's death!

(*Pause.*)

And the rat?
CLOV: He's got away.
HAMM: He can't go far.

(*Pause. Anxious.*)

Eh?
CLOV: He doesn't need to go far.

(*Pause.*)

HAMM: Is it not time for my painkiller?
CLOV: Yes.
HAMM: Ah! At last! Give it to me! Quick!

(*Pause.*)

CLOV: There's no more painkiller.

(*Pause.*)

HAMM (*appalled*): Good . . . !

(*Pause.*)

No more painkiller!
CLOV: No more painkiller. You'll never get any more painkiller.

(*Pause.*)

HAMM: But the little round box. It was full!
CLOV: Yes. But now it's empty.

(*Pause. Clov starts to move about the room. He is looking for a place to put down the alarm clock.*)

HAMM (*soft*): What'll I do?

(*Pause. In a scream.*)

What'll I do?

(*Clov sees the picture, takes it down, stands it on the floor with its face to the wall, hangs up the alarm clock in its place.*)

What are you doing?
CLOV: Winding up.
HAMM: Look at the earth.
CLOV: Again!
HAMM: Since it's calling to you.
CLOV: Is your throat sore?

(*Pause.*)

Would you like a lozenge?

(*Pause.*)

No.

(*Pause.*)

Pity.

(*Clov goes, humming, towards window right, halts before it, looks up at it.*)

HAMM: Don't sing.
CLOV (*turning towards Hamm*): One hasn't the right to sing anymore?
HAMM: No.
CLOV: Then how can it end?
HAMM: You want it to end?
CLOV: I want to sing.
HAMM: I can't prevent you.

(*Pause. Clov turns towards window right.*)

CLOV: What did I do with that steps?

(*He looks around for ladder.*)

You didn't see that steps?

(*He sees it.*)

Ah, about time.

(*He goes towards window left.*)

Sometimes I wonder if I'm in my right mind. Then it passes over and I'm as lucid as before.

(*He gets up on ladder, looks out of window.*)

Christ, she's under water!

(*He looks.*)

How can that be?

(*He pokes forward his head, his hand above his eyes.*)

It hasn't rained.

(*He wipes the pane, looks. Pause.*)

Ah what a fool I am! I'm on the wrong side!

(*He gets down, takes a few steps towards window right.*)

Under water!

(*He goes back for ladder.*)

What a fool I am!

(*He carries ladder towards window right.*)

Sometimes I wonder if I'm in my right senses. Then it passes off and I'm as intelligent as ever.

(*He sets down ladder under window right, gets up on it, looks out of window. He turns towards Hamm.*)

Any particular sector you fancy? Or merely the whole thing?
HAMM: Whole thing.
CLOV: The general effect? Just a moment.

(*He looks out of window. Pause.*)

HAMM: Clov.
CLOV (*absorbed*): Mmm.
HAMM: Do you know what it is?
CLOV (*as before*): Mmm.
HAMM: I was never there.

(*Pause.*)

Clov!
CLOV (*turning towards Hamm, exasperated*): What is it?
HAMM: I was never there.
CLOV: Lucky for you.

(*He looks out of window.*)

HAMM: Absent, always. It all happened without me. I don't know what's happened.

(*Pause.*)

Do you know what's happened?

(*Pause.*)

Clov!
CLOV (*turning towards Hamm, exasperated*): Do you want me to look at this muckheap, yes or no?
HAMM: Answer me first.
CLOV: What?
HAMM: Do you know what's happened?
CLOV: When? Where?
HAMM (*violently*): When! What's happened? Use your head, can't you! What has happened?
CLOV: What for Christ's sake does it matter?

(*He looks out of window.*)

HAMM: I don't know.

(*Pause. Clov turns towards Hamm.*)

CLOV (*harshly*): When old Mother Pegg asked you for oil for her lamp and you told her to get out to hell, you knew what was happening then, no?

(*Pause.*)

You know what she died of, Mother Pegg? Of darkness.
HAMM (*feebly*): I hadn't any.
CLOV (*as before*): Yes, you had.

(*Pause.*)

HAMM: Have you the glass?
CLOV: No, it's clear enough as it is.
HAMM: Go and get it.

(*Pause. Clov casts up his eyes, brandishes his fists. He loses balance, clutches on to the ladder. He starts to get down, halts.*)

CLOV: There's one thing I'll never understand.

(*He gets down.*)

Why I always obey you. Can you explain that to me?
HAMM: No. . . . Perhaps it's compassion.

(*Pause.*)

A kind of great compassion.

(*Pause.*)

Oh you won't find it easy, you won't find it easy.

(*Pause. Clov begins to move about the room in search of the telescope.*)

CLOV: I'm tired of our goings on, very tired.

(*He searches.*)

You're not sitting on it?

(*He moves the chair, looks at the place where it stood, resumes his search.*)

HAMM (*anguished*): Don't leave me there!

(*Angrily Clov restores the chair to its place.*)

Am I right in the center?
CLOV: You'd need a microscope to find this —

(*He sees the telescope.*)

Ah, about time.

(*He picks up the telescope, gets up on the ladder, turns the telescope on the without.*)

HAMM: Give me the dog.
CLOV (*looking*): Quiet!
HAMM (*angrily*): Give me the dog!

(*Clov drops the telescope, clasps his hands to his head. Pause. He gets down precipitately, looks for the dog, sees it, picks it up, hastens towards Hamm and strikes him violently on the head with the dog.*)

CLOV: There's your dog for you!

(*The dog falls to the ground. Pause.*)

HAMM: He hit me!
CLOV: You drive me mad, I'm mad!
HAMM: If you must hit me, hit me with the axe.

(*Pause.*)

Or with the gaff, hit me with the gaff. Not with the dog. With the gaff. Or with the axe.

(*Clov picks up the dog and gives it to Hamm who takes it in his arms.*)

CLOV (*imploringly*): Let's stop playing!
HAMM: Never!

(*Pause.*)

Put me in my coffin.
CLOV: There are no more coffins.
HAMM: Then let it end!

(*Clov goes towards ladder.*)

With a bang!

(*Clov gets up on ladder, gets down again, looks for telescope, sees it, picks it up, gets up ladder, raises telescope.*)

Of darkness! And me? Did anyone ever have pity on me?
CLOV (*lowering the telescope, turning towards Hamm*): What?

(*Pause.*)

Is it me you're referring to?
HAMM (*angrily*): An aside, ape! Did you never hear an aside before?

(*Pause.*)

I'm warming up for my last soliloquy.
CLOV: I warn you. I'm going to look at this filth since it's an order. But it's the last time.

(*He turns the telescope on the without.*)

Let's see.

(*He moves the telescope.*)

Nothing . . . nothing . . . good . . . good . . . nothing . . . goo —

(*He starts, lowers the telescope, examines it, turns it again on the without. Pause.*)

Bad luck to it!
HAMM: More complications!

(*Clov gets down.*)

Not an underplot, I trust.

(*Clov moves ladder nearer window, gets up on it, turns telescope on the without.*)

CLOV (*dismayed*): Looks like a small boy!
HAMM (*sarcastic*): A small . . . boy!
CLOV: I'll go and see.

(*He gets down, drops the telescope, goes towards door, turns.*)

I'll take the gaff.

(*He looks for the gaff, sees it, picks it up, hastens towards door.*)

HAMM: No!

(*Clov halts.*)

CLOV: No? A potential procreator?
HAMM: If he exists he'll die there or he'll come here. And if he doesn't . . .

(*Pause.*)

CLOV: You don't believe me? You think I'm inventing?

(*Pause.*)

HAMM: It's the end, Clov, we've come to the end. I don't need you anymore.

(*Pause.*)

CLOV: Lucky for you.

(*He goes towards door.*)

HAMM: Leave me the gaff.

(*Clov gives him the gaff, goes towards door, halts, looks at alarm clock, takes it down, looks round for a better place to put it, goes to bins, puts it on lid of Nagg's bin. Pause.*)

CLOV: I'll leave you.

(*He goes towards door.*)

HAMM: Before you go . . .

(*Clov halts near door.*)

. . . say something.
CLOV: There is nothing to say.
HAMM: A few words . . . to ponder . . . in my heart.
CLOV: Your heart!
HAMM: Yes.

(*Pause. Forcibly.*)

Yes!

(*Pause.*)

With the rest, in the end, the shadows, the murmurs, all the trouble, to end up with.

(*Pause.*)

Clov. . . . He never spoke to me. Then, in the end, before he went, without my having asked him, he spoke to me. He said . . .
CLOV (*despairingly*): Ah . . . !
HAMM: Something . . . from your heart.
CLOV: My heart!
HAMM: A few words . . . from your heart.

(*Pause.*)

CLOV (*fixed gaze, tonelessly, towards auditorium*): They said to me, That's love, yes, yes, not a doubt, now you see how —
HAMM: Articulate!
CLOV (*as before*): How easy it is. They said to me, That's friendship, yes, yes, no question, you've found it. They said to me, Here's the place, stop, raise your head and look at all that beauty. That order! They said to me, Come now, you're not a brute beast, think upon these things and you'll see how all becomes clear. And simple! They said to me, What skilled attention they get, all these dying of their wounds.
HAMM: Enough!
CLOV (*as before*): I say to myself — sometimes, Clov, you must learn to suffer better than that if you want them to weary of punishing you — one day. I say to myself — sometimes, Clov, you must be there better than that if you want them to let you go — one day. But I feel too old, and too far, to form new habits. Good, it'll never end, I'll never go.

(*Pause.*)

Then one day, suddenly, it ends, it changes, I don't understand, it dies, or it's me, I don't understand, that either. I ask the words that remain — sleeping, waking, morning, evening. They have nothing to say.

(*Pause.*)

I open the door of the cell and go. I am so bowed I only see my feet, if I open my eyes, and between my legs a little trail of black dust. I say to myself that the earth is extinguished, though I never saw it lit.

(*Pause.*)

It's easy going.

(*Pause.*)

When I fall I'll weep for happiness.

(*Pause. He goes towards door.*)

HAMM: Clov!

(*Clov halts, without turning.*)

Nothing.

(*Clov moves on.*)

Clov!

(*Clov halts, without turning.*)

CLOV: This is what we call making an exit.
HAMM: I'm obliged to you, Clov. For your services.
CLOV (*turning, sharply*): Ah pardon, it's I am obliged to you.
HAMM: It's we are obliged to each other.

(*Pause. Clov goes towards door.*)

One thing more.

(*Clov halts.*)

A last favor.

(*Exit Clov.*)

Cover me with the sheet.

(*Long pause.*)

No? Good.

(*Pause.*)

Me to play.

(*Pause. Wearily.*)

Old endgame lost of old, play and lose and have done with losing.

(*Pause. More animated.*)

Let me see.

(*Pause.*)

Ah yes!

(*He tries to move the chair, using the gaff as before. Enter Clov, dressed for the road. Panama hat, tweed coat, raincoat over his arm, umbrella, bag. He halts by the door and stands there, impassive and motionless, his eyes fixed on Hamm, till the end. Hamm gives up.)*

Good.

(Pause.)

Discard.

(He throws away the gaff, makes to throw away the dog, thinks better of it.)

Take it easy.

(Pause.)

And now?

(Pause.)

Raise hat.

(He raises his toque.)

Peace to our . . . arses.

(Pause.)

And put on again.

(He puts on his toque.)

Deuce.

(Pause. He takes off his glasses.)

Wipe.

(He takes out his handkerchief and, without unfolding it, wipes his glasses.)

And put on again.

(He puts on his glasses, puts back the handkerchief in his pocket.)

We're coming. A few more squirms like that and I'll call.

(Pause.)

A little poetry.

(Pause.)

You prayed —

(Pause. He corrects himself.)

You CRIED for night; it comes —

(Pause. He corrects himself.)

It FALLS: now cry in darkness.

(He repeats, chanting.)

You cried for night; it falls: now cry in darkness.

(Pause.)

Nicely put, that.

(Pause.)

And now?

(Pause.)

Moments for nothing, now as always, time was never and time is over, reckoning closed and story ended.

(Pause. Narrative tone.)

If he could have his child with him. . . .

(Pause.)

It was the moment I was waiting for.

(Pause.)

You don't want to abandon him? You want him to bloom while you are withering? Be there to solace your last million last moments?

(Pause.)

He doesn't realize, all he knows is hunger, and cold, and death to crown it all. But you! You ought to know what the earth is like, nowadays. Oh I put him before his responsibilities!

(Pause. Normal tone.)

Well, there we are, there I am, that's enough.

(He raises the whistle to his lips, hesitates, drops it. Pause.)

Yes, truly!

(He whistles. Pause. Louder. Pause.)

Good.

(Pause.)

Father!

(Pause. Louder.)

Father!

(Pause.)

Good.

(Pause.)

We're coming.

(Pause.)

And to end up with?

(Pause.)

Discard.

(He throws away the dog. He tears the whistle from his neck.)

With my compliments.

(He throws whistle towards auditorium. Pause. He sniffs. Soft.)

Clov!

(Long pause.)

No? Good.

(*He takes out the handkerchief.*)

Since that's the way we're playing it . . . (*he unfolds handkerchief*) . . . let's play it that way . . . (*he unfolds*) . . . and speak no more about it . . . (*he finishes unfolding*) . . . speak no more.

(*He holds handkerchief spread out before him.*)

Old stancher!

(*Pause.*)

You . . . remain.

(*Pause. He covers his face with handkerchief, lowers his arms to armrests, remains motionless.*)

(*Brief tableau.*)

COMMENTARIES

Martin Esslin (*b. 1918*)
THE THEATER OF THE ABSURD   *1961*

Martin Esslin is a drama critic whose work has had wide currency. He was the first to write extensively about the theater of the absurd, a term that has come to describe the plays of Samuel Beckett and a number of other post–World War II playwrights such as Eugène Ionesco and Harold Pinter. The question of what use playwrights make of the absurd and why it is an appropriate term to reflect the achievement of Beckett is explored briefly in this excerpt.

The Theater of the Absurd shows the world as an incomprehensible place. The spectators see the happenings on the stage entirely from the outside, without ever understanding the full meaning of these strange patterns of events, as newly arrived visitors might watch life in a country of which they have not yet mastered the language. The confrontation of the audience with characters and happenings which they are not quite able to comprehend makes it impossible for them to share the aspirations and emotions depicted in the play. Brecht's famous *Verfremdungseffekt* (alienation effect), the inhibition of any identification between spectator and actor, which Brecht could never successfully achieve in his own highly rational theater, really comes into its own in the Theater of the Absurd. It is impossible to identify oneself with characters one does not understand or whose motives remain a closed book, and so the distance between the public and the happenings on the stage can be maintained. Emotional identification with the characters is replaced by a puzzled, critical attention. For while the happenings on the stage are absurd, they yet remain recognizable as somehow related to real life with *its* absurdity, so that eventually the spectators are brought face to face with the irrational side of their existence. Thus, the absurd and fantastic goings-on of the Theater of the Absurd will, in the end, be found to reveal the irrationality of the human condition and the illusion of what we thought was its apparent logical structure.

If the dialogue in these plays consists of meaningless clichés and the mechanical, circular repetition of stereotyped phrases — how many meaningless clichés and stereotyped phrases do we use in our day-to-day conversation? If the characters change their personality halfway through the action, how consistent and truly integrated are the people we meet in our real life? And if people in these plays appear as mere marionettes, helpless puppets without any will of their own, passively at the mercy of blind fate and meaningless circumstance, do we, in fact, in our overorganized world, still possess any genuine initiative or power to decide our own destiny? The spectators of the Theater of the Absurd are thus confronted with a grotesquely heightened picture of their own world: a world without faith, meaning, and genuine freedom of will. In this sense, the Theater of the Absurd is the true theater of our time.

The theater of most previous epochs reflected an accepted moral order, a world whose aims and objectives were clearly present to the minds of all its public, whether it was the audience of the medieval mystery plays with their solidly accepted faith in the Christian world order or the audience of the drama of Ibsen, Shaw, or Hauptmann with their unquestioned belief in evolution and progress. To such audiences, right and wrong were never in doubt, nor did they question the then accepted goals of human endeavor. Our own time, at least in the Western world, wholly lacks such a generally accepted and completely integrated world picture. The decline of religious faith, the destruction of the belief in automatic social and biological progress, the discovery of vast areas of irrational and unconscious forces within the human psyche, the loss of a sense of control over rational human development in an age of totalitarianism and weapons of mass destruction, have all contributed to the erosion of the basis for a dramatic convention in which the action proceeds within a fixed and self-evident framework of generally accepted values. Faced with the vacuum left by the destruction of a universally accepted and unified set of beliefs, most serious playwrights have felt the need to fit their work into the frame of values and objectives expressed in one of the contemporary ideologies: Marxism, psychoanalysis, aestheticism, or nature worship. But these, in the eyes of a writer like Adamov, are nothing but superficial rationalizations which try to hide the depth of man's predicament, his loneliness and his anxiety. Or, as Ionesco puts it:

> As far as I am concerned, I believe sincerely in the poverty of the poor, I deplore it; it is real; it can become a subject for the theatre; I also believe in the anxieties and serious troubles the rich may suffer from; but it is neither in the misery of the former nor in the melancholia of the latter, that I, for one, find my dramatic subject matter. Theatre is for me the outward projection onto the stage of an inner world; it is in my dreams, in my anxieties, in my obscure desires, in my internal contradictions that I, for one, reserve for myself the right of finding my dramatic subject matter. As I am not alone in the world, as each of us, in the depth of his being, is at the same time part and parcel of all others, my dreams, my desires, my anxieties, my obsessions do not belong to me alone. They form part of an ancestral heritage, a very ancient storehouse which is a portion of the common property of all mankind. It is this, which, transcending their outward diversity, reunites all human beings and constitutes our profound common patrimony, the universal language.[1]

In other words, the commonly acceptable framework of beliefs and values of former epochs which has now been shattered is to be replaced by the community of dreams and desires of a collective unconscious. And, to quote Ionesco again:

> . . . the new dramatist is one . . . who tries to link up with what is most ancient: new language and subject matter in a dramatic structure which aims at being clearer, more stripped of inessentials and more purely theatrical; the rejection of traditionalism to rediscover

[1]Eugène Ionesco, "L'Impromptu de l'Alma," *Théâtre* II (Paris, 1958).

tradition; a synthesis of knowledge and invention, of the real and imaginary, of the particular and the universal, or as they say now, of the individual and the collective. . . . By expressing my deepest obsessions, I express my deepest humanity. I become one with all others, spontaneously, over and above all the barriers of caste and different psychologies. I express my solitude and become one with all other solitudes.[2]

What is the tradition with which the Theater of the Absurd — at first sight the most revolutionary and radically new movement — is trying to link itself? It is in fact a very ancient and a very rich tradition, nourished from many and varied sources: the verbal exuberance and extravagant inventions of Rabelais, the age-old clowning of the Roman mimes and the Italian Commedia dell'Arte, the knock-about humor of circus clowns like Grock; the wild, archetypal symbolism of English nonsense verse, the baroque horror of Jacobean dramatists like Webster or Tourneur, the harsh, incisive, and often brutal tones of the German drama of Grabbe, Büchner, Kleist, and Wedekind with its delirious language and grotesque inventiveness; and the Nordic paranoia of the dreams and persecution fantasies of Strindberg.

[2]Ionesco, "The Avant-Garde Theatre," *World Theatre* 8.3 (Autumn 1959).

Sidney Homan (b. 1938)
THE ENDING OF *ENDGAME*   1984

Sidney Homan's book Beckett's Theaters: Interpretations for Performance *concentrates on the production of Beckett's plays. His discussion of* Endgame *focuses on the performance aspects of movement in the final moments of the play. The question of death is central to the question of* Endgame.

Despite its seeming chaos on the surface, Hamm's last speech, that string of short phrases and snatches of dialogue much like that of Winnie in *Happy Days*, provides the most sustained insight into his playwright's mentality. In the words of the Unnamable,° it is the "end of the joke," the aesthetic painkiller if you will, as handy as that literal painkiller in the cupboard was not. Unseen, except by us, Clov constitutes the onstage audience of one. The speech itself is surely meant to contrast with Hamm's opening dialogue: This time Hamm is not discovered but rather constitutes *all* the stage, at least as far as he knows, and the speech is about endings rather than beginnings. The proper verbal constructions, in terms of his opening lines, would be something akin to "Me to play having played." No fear of mere "reveling" here.

Hamm's speech seems to be madness without matter. As with the scattered fragments in the closing lines of Eliot's *The Waste Land,* however, there is here an order and a depth of reference below the surface. Clov is absent, though he stands impassive upstage. The sheet with which he "discovered" Hamm at the opening is now useless. In a larger sense, Hamm has been revealed, the play itself representing his disclosure as a symbol. The removal of the sheet itself is thereby the stimulus for an aesthetic revelation. He is now moving toward the purely symbolic, and the chess metaphor comes to the fore, chess itself a symbolic enactment of literal battles and

---

Unnamable: Narrator of *The Unnamable* (1958), third in a trilogy of novels by Beckett.

armies: "Me to play" and "Old endgame." Indeed, Hamm is moving toward the same sense of completeness found by Mr. Endon in *Murphy*. The King, the central piece, is now immobile at the center of the board, the word for both the theater and the field of chess pieces. Then "discard" the last life-support; the gaff is thrown away, though the dog, symbol of Hamm's artifice, is retained.

We see the artist now attempting to document the moment before human extinction. It is the process toward that movement, and not the actual event itself, defining the limits of our earthly inquiry.

Like Shakespeare, Beckett does not depict a hereafter. We may speculate on what will happen to Lear — can a pagan go to any sort of heaven? — but the Renaissance playwright, like the modern one, is content to show him approaching the end, promised or otherwise. There is a farewell here to the audience, obscene to be sure, and with that salute an identification with us as Hamm uses the plural possessive "our." The "You" who wants poetry, or the efficacy of prayer, or night to come is also the "you" that, in an absurdist or relative world, must cry in darkness. Again, we all die alone. Hamm's aesthetic consciousness, like that of the narrator in *Cascando,*° is now most acute: "Nicely put, that."

If relativity, both in terms of time itself and the mutability of all human things, relentlessly moves on, Hamm, now enveloped in his story, is about to make time run, to echo the Renaissance poet Marvell. The time is "over, reckoning closed and story ended." The wish for extinction, however, cannot hold as the life force, the final reference to the father and his starving son, is sounded. Hamm cannot shake off that memory. An invasion of his world, the story irritates the aesthetic fiber he has so closely woven. It is another world, with a past, with characters, and involving those issues of life and the sustenance of life that Hamm has otherwise so assiduously blocked out in his bomb shelter, in his circumscribed, lonely, inner world. The "Oh I put him before his responsibilities" sounds as much neurotic as convincing. Then with a *calm* — again, one of Beckett's favorite words — returning, Hamm reverses himself in the recognition that he is not alone, that he is part and parcel of all humanity, including us, including the fictive, or seemingly fictive father and his son: "Well, there we are, there I am, that's enough." This is something "truly," though the aesthetic inner world is itself in flux, only a momentary stay against reality, and yet Hamm will now be able to sustain this playwright-actor's posture at least until the end.

He approaches death with the same sense of "knowing" his story that several modern biblical scholars have attributed to Christ, an "actor" who plays the parts of a visitor to earth, prophet, crucified savior, and risen spirit. We approach now the closest thing to transcendence in Beckett, undercut, of course, by the fact that Hamm "*remains motionless*" as the curtain closes (he can no more leave his stage than Vladimir and Estragon can leave theirs). The dog is discarded, the last vestige of his creation; and then in a brilliant gesture he throws the whistle toward us, the audience — the "*auditorium.*" Though the isolation is illusory — again, Clov is backstage, visible to us if not to Hamm — for Hamm it is a convincing illusion. He is approaching the nonbeing sought by Nell in her vision of a silent, white ocean bottom, an empty world where nothingness is a fact, not a conceit, where we can cease to be like those talkative "political" artists who, in giving form to nothing,

Cascando: Beckett's radio play for voice and music (1962), first broadcast in English by the BBC in 1964.

are bound to fail. In essence, Hamm is trying to give up the last hold on life, even if that "life" be the illusory existence of the stage world.

The transcendence itself is aborted. However much he would later cut away at the time scheme or the plot or the place of his plays (witness *Breath*), Beckett cannot present us with nothing: "Nothing" itself can be spoken of but not enacted. A bare stage is only a bare stage and not a play. Here Beckett is like Emily Dickinson in "I heard a fly buzz when I died," as she tries poetically to cross the thin boundary line between life and death and is frustrated in that attempt when a fly intervenes between her eyes and the "light." Beckett is trying to go to the nonstate, if I may put it that way, of nonbeing. That is the way Hamm would "play it," so that he could "speak no more about it." I repeat his wish: "Speak no more." He seeks here not the failure of words, the very possibility that unnerves Winnie. Nor will he use words anymore to define nonbeing.

Now, without words and with the major character free of the tension in seeking physical life or death, we move to the level of mime. Our audience surrogate, the silent Clov, now sees Hamm hold the bloodied handkerchief before him and then cover his face. Two phrases act as glosses to the action. One is the descriptive "Old stancher," lest an audience member fail to identify properly the symbol, Hamm's Greek-like mask that is the physical correlative for his misery, for his suffering than which no one's is greater, as he reminds us early in the play. In effect, Hamm, like the figures in Greek myths, has passed through earthly existence and literally become a star. He has won his right to be a symbol, a symbol sustained by the play, a symbol that now wordlessly compresses all that he means, or has meant. This wretched piece of a costume, in effect, now equals the entire play. In Beckett, truly, the last shall be first. One also thinks of the handkerchief worn by Keaton in *Film*, and that used by Willie in *Happy Days*, though neither was so developed, nor so perfect a symbol of suffering.

The other phrase, a tantalizing one, is the closing "You . . . remain." Initially, it appears simply an appositive for "Old stancher," but I also take it as a reference to the audience. That is, Hamm has now *realized* his role; he has been elevated to a symbol. Our task has now just begun; we must leave the theater, refreshed by Beckett's mirror world, and must encounter the suffering anew. Outside of here it is hell, as the Beckett characters are fond of saying. We remain; we are the "mutes or audience" of the act to which Hamlet refers (V, ii, 338).

The play closes beyond words, as Hamm covers his face with the handkerchief and, like the Auditor in *Not I*, lowers his arms and in a mockery of mime and its movements stops on the stage direction to remain "*motionless*." Initiated by language, the play ends in silence, the "*Brief tableau*," like that called for by Beckett in *The Unnamable*. *Curtain*. It will also start again; as Winnie observes, even if the glass breaks, it will be there whole tomorrow. Tomorrow the handkerchief will revert to the old sheet covering Hamm, that, with the bloodstained handkerchief, will in turn be removed, discovering another potential tragic hero — or "figure," if "hero" sounds too affirmative for some readers. The uncovering will allow theatrical life to flow again, the act of artistic creation, the long creative process to which Hamm himself refers, the informing of a vision and the production of a symbol — a symbol that, at the end, will remain with us, only to be undone the next day, the next performance. Curtain.[. . .]

Lorraine Hansberry

Lorraine Hansberry (1930–1965), like John Millington Synge, died tragically young. Her loss to the American stage is incalculable; her successes were only beginning, and at her death she seemed on the verge of a remarkable career.

Hansberry grew up in a middle-class black family in Chicago. Her father, who was successful in real estate, founded one of the first banks for blacks in Chicago. However, he spent much of his life vainly trying to find a way to make a decent life for himself and his family in America. He eventually gave up on the United States, and, when he died in 1945, he was scouting for a place in Mexico where he could move his family to live comfortably.

Lorraine Hansberry went to college after her father died, and her first ambition was to become a visual artist. She attended the Art Institute of Chicago and numerous other schools before moving to New York. Once there, she became interested in some drama groups and soon married the playwright Howard Nemiroff. She began writing, sharing parts of her first play with friends in her own living room. They helped raise money to stage the play and, with black director Lloyd Richards and little-known Sidney Poitier as Walter Lee Younger, *A Raisin in the Sun* (1959) thrust her into the drama spotlight.

In 1959, only twenty-nine years old, Hansberry was the most promising woman writing for the American stage. She was also the first black American to win the New York Drama Critics' Circle Award for the best play of the year. She died of cancer the day her second produced play, *The Sign in Sidney Brustein's Window,* closed. She had finished a third play, *Les Blancs,* which was brought to Broadway by Nemiroff in 1970. Neither of her other plays was as popular as *Raisin,* but the two later plays demonstrate a deepening concern for and understanding of some of the key issues of racial and sexual politics that interested her throughout her career.

The Sign in Sidney Brustein's Window's hero is a Jewish intellectual in the 1950s in Greenwich Village. Feeling that all the radical struggle of the 1930s has been lost, he agitates for personal involvement, for emotional and intellectual action. This idealistic play anticipates the political agitation in the United States during the mid-1960s and early 1970s. *Les Blancs* takes as its central character a black African intellectual, Tshembe, and explores his relationship to both Europe and Africa. In his uneasiness with both cultures he discovers that he cannot live outside his own history. *Les Blancs* reveals some of Hansberry's deep interest in Pan-Africanism and the search for a personal heritage.

A posthumous work was put together by Howard Nemiroff from Hansberry's notes, letters, and early writings. Titled *To Be Young, Gifted, and Black* (1971), it has helped solidify her achievements. Although we will never know just how Hansberry's career would have developed had she lived, her gifts were so remarkable that we can only lament that she is not writing for the stage today.

A RAISIN IN THE SUN

When produced on Broadway in 1959, *A Raisin in the Sun* was somewhat prophetic. Lorraine Hansberry's themes of blacks pressing forward with legitimate demands and expressing interest in their African heritage were to become primary themes of black culture in the 1960s, 1970s, and, indeed, to this day. The title of her play is from a poem by Langston Hughes, one of the poets of the Harlem Renaissance. It warns of the social explosions that might occur if society permits blacks to remain unequal and unfree.

The work appeared at the beginning of renewed political activity on the part of African Americans; it reveals its historical position in the use of the word *Negro*, which black activists rejected in the 1960s as an enslaving euphemism. This play illustrates the American dream as it is felt not just by African Americans but by all Americans: if you work hard, save your money, are honorable, and hope, then you can one day buy your own home and have the kind of space and privacy that permit people to live with dignity. Yet this very theme has plagued the play from the beginning: its apparent emphasis on middle-class, bourgeois values. On the surface, it seems to celebrate a mild form of consumerism — the desire for the house in the suburbs with the TV set inside to anesthetize its occupants. Hansberry was shocked when such criticisms, from black critics as well as white, were leveled against the play. She had written it very carefully to explore just those issues but in a context that demonstrated that black families' needs paralleled white families' while also having a different dimension that most white families could not understand.

Hansberry was quick to admit that Walter Lee Younger was affected by the same craziness influencing all Americans who lusted after possessions and the power they might confer. Walter wants to take his father's insurance money to buy a liquor store in partnership with a con man. Lena Younger argues against her son's plan as a profanation of her husband's memory as well as an abuse of the American dream: she believes that the product of a liquor store will further poison the community. What she wants is not a consumer product but the emblem of identity and security that she feels her family deserves.

Hansberry is painfully honest in this play. Walter Lee's weaknesses are recognizable. His male chauvinistic behavior undoes him. He is caught up in the old, failing pattern of male dominance over women. But none of the women in his life will tolerate his behavior. Hansberry also admits the social distinctions among African Americans. George Murchison is a young man from a wealthy black family, and when Beneatha tells Lena that she will not marry George, she says, "The only people in the world who are more snobbish than rich white people are rich colored people." Beneatha's desire to be a doctor is obviously not rooted in consumerism any more than in the middle-class need to be comfortable and rich.

The confusion brought to the family by a native African, Asagai, is realistically portrayed. In the early days of the Pan-African movement in the 1960s, blacks were often bemused by the way Africans presented themselves. Interest in Africa on the part of the American blacks was distorted by Tarzan movies and *National Geographic* articles, none of which presented black Africans as role models. Therefore, the adjustment to black African pride — while made swiftly — was not without difficulties. The Youngers are presented as no more sophisticated about black Africans than the rest of black society would be.

The dignity of the Younger family finally triumphs. When Walter Lee stands up for himself, he is asserting not macho domination but black manhood — a manhood that needs no domination over women. He is expressing not a desire for a big house — as he had done when he reflected on the possessions of his rich employer — but a desire to demonstrate to members of the Clybourne Park Improvement Association that the Youngers are their social equals and that they have a right to live wherever they choose.

A Raisin in the Sun in Performance

Lloyd Richards directed the first production at the Ethel Barrymore Theater in New York on March 11, 1959. The play won major prizes, and Sidney Poitier as a passionate Walter Lee Younger was a signal success. *New York Times* critic Brooks Atkinson said, "Since the performance is also honest and since Sidney Poitier is a candid actor, *A Raisin in the Sun* has vigor as well as veracity and is likely to destroy the complacency of any one who sees it." Critics were astonished that a first play could have the sophistication and depth they saw onstage.

The Theater Guild staged the play in 1960 in Boston with a different cast but the production received similar reviews. The film version, with most of the New York cast, was directed by Daniel Petrie in 1961. A revival in Chicago in 1983 at the Art Institute of Chicago — Hansberry's alma mater — was not altogether successful, but critics felt the text held up well. The Chicago revival, like the 1985 Merrimack Repertory Theater revival in Lowell, Massachusetts, demonstrated only that the play needs strong actors to have the desired impact. A twenty-fifth anniversary production was directed by Lloyd Richards at the Yale Repertory Theatre in 1983. This production was taken to New York in 1986 and enjoyed a successful run. The setting was a realistic interior, emphasizing the play's realistic style. Critic Mel Gussow felt the revival demonstrated that the play is "an enduring work of contemporary theater." The production also revealed that Hansberry's language had not become dated, nor had the social issues of the play become any less critical and important for the lapse of twenty-five years. Like the proletarian plays of Sean O'Casey, who inspired Lorraine Hansberry, this play continues to move us because its problems are serious and still remain.

Lorraine Hansberry (1930–1965)

A Raisin in the Sun   1959

Harlem (A Dream Deferred)

What happens to a dream deferred?

   Does it dry up
   like a raisin in the sun?
   Or fester like a sore —
   And then run?
   Does it stink like rotten meat?

Or crust and sugar over —
like a syrupy sweet?

Maybe it just sags
like a heavy load.

Or does it explode?   — LANGSTON HUGHES

Characters

RUTH YOUNGER
TRAVIS YOUNGER
WALTER LEE YOUNGER (*brother*)
BENEATHA YOUNGER
LENA YOUNGER (*Mama*)
JOSEPH ASAGAI
GEORGE MURCHISON
MRS. JOHNSON
KARL LINDNER
BOBO
MOVING MEN

The action of the play is set in Chicago's Southside, sometime between World War II and the present.

Act I
Scene I: *Friday morning.*
Scene II: *The following morning.*

Act II
Scene I: *Later, the same day.*
Scene II: *Friday night, a few weeks later.*
Scene III: *Moving day, one week later.*

Act III
An hour later.

ACT I • Scene I

(*The Younger living room would be a comfortable and well-ordered room if it were not for a number of indestructible contradictions to this state of being. Its furnishings are typical and undistinguished and their primary feature now is that they have clearly had to accommodate the living of too many people for too many years — and they are tired. Still, we can see that at some time, a time probably no longer remembered by the family [except perhaps for Mama], the furnishings*

of this room were actually selected with care and love and even hope — and brought to this apartment and arranged with taste and pride.)

(*That was a long time ago. Now the once loved pattern of the couch upholstery has to fight to show itself from under acres of crocheted doilies and couch covers which have themselves finally come to be more important than the upholstery. And here a table or a chair has been moved to disguise the worn places in the carpet; but the carpet has fought back by showing its weariness, with depressing uniformity, elsewhere on its surface.*)

(*Weariness has, in fact, won in this room. Everything has been polished, washed, sat on, used, scrubbed too often. All pretenses but living itself have long since vanished from the very atmosphere of this room.*)

(*Moreover, a section of this room, for it is not really a room unto itself, though the landlord's lease would make it seem so, slopes backward to provide a small kitchen area, where the family prepares the meals that are eaten in the living room proper, which must also serve as dining room. The single window that has been provided for these "two" rooms is located in this kitchen area. The sole natural light the family may enjoy in the course of a day is only that which fights its way through this little window.*)

(*At left, a door leads to a bedroom which is shared by Mama and her daughter, Beneatha. At right, opposite, is a second room [which in the beginning of the life of this apartment was probably a breakfast room] which serves as a bedroom for Walter and his wife, Ruth.*)

(*Time: Sometime between World War II and the present.*)

(*Place: Chicago's Southside.*)

(*At rise: It is morning dark in the living room. Travis is asleep on the make-down bed at center. An alarm clock sounds from within the bedroom at right, and presently Ruth enters from that room and closes the door behind her. She crosses sleepily toward the window. As she passes her sleeping son she reaches down and shakes him a little. At the window she raises the shade and a dusky Southside morning light comes in feebly. She fills a pot with water and puts it on to boil. She calls to the boy, between yawns, in a slightly muffled voice.*)

(*Ruth is about thirty. We can see that she was a pretty girl, even exceptionally so, but now it is apparent that life has been little that she expected, and disappointment has already begun to hang in her face. In a few years, before thirty-five even, she will be known among her people as a "settled woman."*)

(*She crosses to her son and gives him a good, final, rousing shake.*)

RUTH: Come on now, boy, it's seven thirty! (*Her son sits up at last, in a stupor of sleepiness.*) I say hurry up, Travis! You ain't the only person in the world got to use a bathroom! (*The child, a sturdy, handsome little boy of ten or eleven, drags himself out of the bed and almost blindly takes his towels and "today's clothes" from drawers and a closet and goes out to the bathroom, which is in an outside hall and which is shared by another family or families on the same floor. Ruth crosses to the bedroom door at right and opens it and calls in to her husband.*) Walter Lee! . . . It's after seven thirty! Lemme see you do some waking up in there now! (*She waits.*) You better get up from there, man! It's after seven thirty I tell you. (*She waits again.*) All right, you just go ahead and lay there and next thing you know Travis be finished and Mr. Johnson'll be in there and you'll be fussing and cussing round here like a madman! And be late too! (*She waits, at the end of patience.*) Walter Lee — it's time for you to GET UP!

(*She waits another second and then starts to go into the bedroom, but is apparently satisfied that her husband has begun to get up. She stops, pulls the door to, and returns to the kitchen area. She wipes her face with a moist cloth and runs her fingers through her sleep-disheveled hair in a vain effort and ties an apron around her housecoat. The bedroom door at right opens and her husband stands in the doorway in his pajamas, which are rumpled and mismated. He is a lean, intense young man in his middle thirties, inclined to quick nervous movements and erratic speech habits — and always in his voice there is a quality of indictment.*)

WALTER: Is he out yet?
RUTH: What you mean *out*? He ain't hardly got in there good yet.
WALTER (*wandering in, still more oriented to sleep than to a new day*): Well, what was you doing all that yelling for if I can't even get in there yet? (*Stopping and thinking.*) Check coming today?
RUTH: They *said* Saturday and this is just Friday and I hopes to God you ain't going to get up here first thing this morning and start talking to me 'bout no money — 'cause I 'bout don't want to hear it.
WALTER: Something the matter with you this morning?
RUTH: No — I'm just sleepy as the devil. What kind of eggs you want?
WALTER: Not scrambled. (*Ruth starts to scramble eggs.*)

Paper come? (*Ruth points impatiently to the rolled up Tribune on the table, and he gets it and spreads it out and vaguely reads the front page.*) Set off another bomb yesterday.
RUTH (*maximum indifference*): Did they?
WALTER (*looking up*): What's the matter with you?
RUTH: Ain't nothing the matter with me. And don't keep asking me that this morning.
WALTER: Ain't nobody bothering you. (*Reading the news of the day absently again.*) Say Colonel McCormick is sick.
RUTH (*affecting tea-party interest*): Is he now? Poor thing.
WALTER (*sighing and looking at his watch*): Oh, me. (*He waits.*) Now what is that boy doing in that bathroom all this time? He just going to have to start getting up earlier. I can't be being late to work on account of him fooling around in there.
RUTH (*turning on him*): Oh, no he ain't going to be getting up no earlier no such thing! It ain't his fault that he can't get to bed no earlier nights 'cause he got a bunch of crazy good-for-nothing clowns sitting up running their mouths in what is supposed to be his bedroom after ten o'clock at night . . .
WALTER: That's what you mad about, ain't it? The things I want to talk about with my friends just couldn't be important in your mind, could they?

(*He rises and finds a cigarette in her handbag on the table and crosses to the little window and looks out, smoking and deeply enjoying this first one.*)

RUTH (*almost matter of factly, a complaint too automatic to deserve emphasis*): Why you always got to smoke before you eat in the morning?
WALTER (*at the window*): Just look at 'em down there . . . Running and racing to work . . . (*He turns and faces his wife and watches her a moment at the stove, and then, suddenly.*) You look young this morning, baby.
RUTH (*indifferently*): Yeah?
WALTER: Just for a second — stirring them eggs. Just for a second it was — you looked real young again. (*He reaches for her; she crosses away. Then, drily.*) It's gone now — you look like yourself again!
RUTH: Man, if you don't shut up and leave me alone.
WALTER (*looking out to the street again*): First thing a man ought to learn in life is not to make love to no colored woman first thing in the morning. You all some eeeevil people at eight o'clock in the morning.

(*Travis appears in the hall doorway, almost fully dressed and quite wide awake now, his towels and pajamas across his shoulders. He opens the door and signals for his father to make the bathroom in a hurry.*)

TRAVIS (*watching the bathroom*): Daddy, come on!

(*Walter gets his bathroom utensils and flies out to the bathroom.*)

RUTH: Sit down and have your breakfast, Travis.

TRAVIS: Mama, this is Friday. (*Gleefully.*) Check coming tomorrow, huh?

RUTH: You get your mind off money and eat your breakfast.

TRAVIS (*eating*): This is the morning we supposed to bring the fifty cents to school.

RUTH: Well, I ain't got no fifty cents this morning.

TRAVIS: Teacher say we have to.

RUTH: I don't care what teacher say. I ain't got it. Eat your breakfast, Travis.

TRAVIS: I *am* eating.

RUTH: Hush up now and just eat!

(*The boy gives her an exasperated look for her lack of understanding and eats grudgingly.*)

TRAVIS: You think Grandmama would have it?

RUTH: No! And I want you to stop asking your grandmother for money, you hear me?

TRAVIS (*outraged*): Gaaaleee! I don't ask her, she just gimme it sometimes!

RUTH: Travis Willard Younger — I got too much on me this morning to be —

TRAVIS: Maybe Daddy —

RUTH: *Travis!*

(*The boy hushes abruptly. They are both quiet and tense for several seconds.*)

TRAVIS (*presently*): Could I maybe go carry some groceries in front of the supermarket for a little while after school then?

RUTH: Just hush, I said. (*Travis jabs his spoon into his cereal bowl viciously and rests his head in anger upon his fists.*) If you through eating, you can get over there and make up your bed.

(*The boy obeys stiffly and crosses the room, almost mechanically, to the bed and more or less folds the bedding into a heap, then angrily gets his books and cap.*)

TRAVIS (*sulking and standing apart from her unnaturally*): I'm gone.

RUTH (*looking up from the stove to inspect him automatically*): Come here. (*He crosses to her and she studies his head.*) If you don't take this comb and fix this here head, you better! (*Travis puts down his books with a great sigh of oppression and crosses to the mirror. His mother mutters under her breath about his "slubbornness."*) 'Bout to march out of here with that head looking just like chickens slept in it! I just don't know where you get your slubborn ways . . . And get your jacket, too. Looks chilly out this morning.

TRAVIS (*with conspicuously brushed hair and jacket*): I'm gone.

RUTH: Get carfare and milk money — (*waving one finger*) — and not a single penny for no caps, you hear me?

TRAVIS (*with sullen politeness*): Yes'm.

(*He turns in outrage to leave. His mother watches after him as in his frustration he approaches the door almost*

comically. *When she speaks to him, her voice has become a very gentle tease.*)

RUTH (*mocking; as she thinks he would say it*): Oh, Mama makes me so mad sometimes, I don't know what to do! (*She waits and continues to his back as he stands stock-still in front of the door.*) I wouldn't kiss that woman good-bye for nothing in this world this morning! (*The boy finally turns around and rolls his eyes at her, knowing the mood has changed and he is vindicated; he does not, however, move toward her yet.*) Not for nothing in this world! (*She finally laughs aloud at him and holds out her arms to him and we see that it is a way between them, very old and practiced. He crosses to her and allows her to embrace him warmly but keeps his face fixed with masculine rigidity. She holds him back from her presently and looks at him and runs her fingers over the features of his face. With utter gentleness —*) Now — whose little old angry man are you?

TRAVIS (*the masculinity and gruffness start to fade at last*): Aw gaalee — Mama . . .

RUTH (*mimicking*): Aw — gaaaaalleeeee, Mama! (*She pushes him, with rough playfulness and finality, toward the door.*) Get on out of here or you going to be late.

TRAVIS (*in the face of love, new aggressiveness*): Mama, could I *please* go carry groceries?

RUTH: Honey, it's starting to get so cold evenings.

WALTER (*coming in from the bathroom and drawing a make-believe gun from a make-believe holster and shooting at his son*): What is it he wants to do?

RUTH: Go carry groceries after school at the supermarket.

WALTER: Well, let him go . . .

TRAVIS (*quickly, to the ally*): I *have* to — she won't gimme the fifty cents . . .

WALTER (*to his wife only*): Why not?

RUTH (*simply, and with flavor*): 'Cause we don't have it.

WALTER (*to Ruth only*): What you tell the boy things like that for? (*Reaching down into his pants with a rather important gesture.*) Here, son —

(*He hands the boy the coin, but his eyes are directed to his wife's. Travis takes the money happily.*)

TRAVIS: Thanks, Daddy.

(*He starts out. Ruth watches both of them with murder in her eyes. Walter stands and stares back at her with defiance and suddenly reaches into his pocket again on an afterthought.*)

WALTER (*without even looking at his son, still staring hard at his wife*): In fact, here's another fifty cents . . . Buy yourself some fruit today — or take a taxicab to school or something!

TRAVIS: Whoopee —

(*He leaps up and clasps his father around the middle with his legs, and they face each other in mutual appreciation; slowly Walter Lee peeks around the boy to catch the violent rays from his wife's eyes and draws his head back as if shot.*)

WALTER: You better get down now — and get to school, man.

TRAVIS (*at the door*): O.K. Good-bye.

(*He exits.*)

WALTER (*after him, pointing with pride*): That's my boy. (*She looks at him in disgust and turns back to her work.*) You know what I was thinking 'bout in the bathroom this morning?

RUTH: No.

WALTER: How come you always try to be so pleasant!

RUTH: What is there to be pleasant 'bout!

WALTER: You want to know what I was thinking 'bout in the bathroom or not!

RUTH: I know what you thinking 'bout.

WALTER (*ignoring her*): 'Bout what me and Willy Harris was talking about last night.

RUTH (*immediately — a refrain*): Willy Harris is a good-for-nothing loudmouth.

WALTER: Anybody who talks to me has got to be a good-for-nothing loudmouth, ain't he? And what you know about who is just a good-for-nothing loudmouth? Charlie Atkins was just a "good-for-nothing loudmouth" too, wasn't he! When he wanted me to go in the dry-cleaning business with him. And now — he's grossing a hundred thousand a year. A hundred thousand dollars a year! You still call *him* a loudmouth!

RUTH (*bitterly*): Oh, Walter Lee . . .

(*She folds her head on her arms over the table.*)

WALTER (*rising and coming to her and standing over her*): You tired, ain't you? Tired of everything. Me, the boy, the way we live — this beat-up hole — everything. Ain't you? (*She doesn't look up, doesn't answer.*) So tired — moaning and groaning all the time, but you wouldn't do nothing to help, would you? You couldn't be on my side that long for nothing, could you?

RUTH: Walter, please leave me alone.

WALTER: A man needs for a woman to back him up . . .

RUTH: Walter —

WALTER: Mama would listen to you. You know she listen to you more than she do me and Bennie. She think more of you. All you have to do is just sit down with her when you drinking your coffee one morning and talking 'bout things like you do and — (*He sits down beside her and demonstrates graphically what he thinks her methods and tone should be.*) — you just sip your coffee, see, and say easy like that you been thinking 'bout that deal Walter Lee is so interested in, 'bout the store and all, and sip some more coffee, like what you saying ain't really that important to you — And the next thing you know, she be listening good and asking you questions and when I come home — I can tell her the details. This ain't no fly-by-night proposition, baby. I mean we figured it out, me and Willy and Bobo.

RUTH (*with a frown*): Bobo?

WALTER: Yeah. You see, this little liquor store we got in mind cost seventy-five thousand and we figured the initial investment on the place be 'bout thirty thousand, see. That be ten thousand each. Course, there's a couple of hundred you got to pay so's you don't spend your life just waiting for them clowns to let your license get approved —

RUTH: You mean graft?

WALTER (*frowning impatiently*): Don't call it that. See there, that just goes to show you what women understand about the world. Baby, don't *nothing* happen for you in this world 'less you pay *somebody* off!

RUTH: Walter, leave me alone! (*She raises her head and stares at him vigorously — then says, more quietly.*) *Eat* your eggs, they gonna be cold.

WALTER (*straightening up from her and looking off*): That's it. There you are. Man say to his woman: I got me a dream. His woman say: Eat your eggs. (*Sadly, but gaining in power.*) Man say: I got to take hold of this here world, baby! And a woman will say: Eat your eggs and go to work. (*Passionately now.*) Man say: I got to change my life, I'm choking to death, baby! And his woman say — (*in utter anguish as he brings his fists down on his thighs*) — Your eggs is getting cold!

RUTH (*softly*): Walter, that ain't none of our money.

WALTER (*not listening at all or even looking at her*): This morning, I was lookin' in the mirror and thinking about it . . . I'm thirty-five years old; I been married eleven years and I got a boy who sleeps in the living room — (*very, very quietly*) — and all I got to give him is stories about how rich white people live . . .

RUTH: Eat your eggs, Walter.

WALTER (*slams the table and jumps up*): — DAMN MY EGGS — DAMN ALL THE EGGS THAT EVER WAS!

RUTH: Then go to work.

WALTER (*looking up at her*): See — I'm trying to talk to you 'bout myself — (*shaking his head with the repetition*) — and all you can say is eat them eggs and go to work.

RUTH (*wearily*): Honey, you never say nothing new. I listen to you every day, every night and every morning, and you never say nothing new. (*Shrugging.*) So you would rather *be* Mr. Arnold than be his chauffeur. So — I would *rather* be living in Buckingham Palace.

WALTER: That is just what is wrong with the colored woman in this world . . . Don't understand about building their men up and making 'em feel like they somebody. Like they can do something.

RUTH (*drily, but to hurt*): There *are* colored men who do things.

WALTER: No thanks to the colored woman.

RUTH: Well, being a colored woman, I guess I can't help myself none.

(*She rises and gets the ironing board and sets it up and attacks a huge pile of rough-dried clothes, sprinkling them in preparation for the ironing and then rolling them into tight fat balls.*)

WALTER (*mumbling*): We one group of men tied to a race of women with small minds!

(*His sister Beneatha enters. She is about twenty, as slim and intense as her brother. She is not as pretty as her sister-in-law, but her lean, almost intellectual face has a handsomeness of its own. She wears a bright red flannel nightie, and her thick hair stands wildly about her head. Her speech is a mixture of many things; it is different from the rest of the family's insofar as education has permeated her sense of English — and perhaps the Midwest rather than the South has finally — at last — won out in her inflection; but not altogether, because over all of it is a soft slurring and transformed use of vowels which is the decided influence of the Southside. She passes through the room without looking at either Ruth or Walter and goes to the outside door and looks, a little blindly, out to the bathroom. She sees that it has been lost to the Johnsons. She closes the door with a sleepy vengeance and crosses to the table and sits down a little defeated.*)

BENEATHA: I am going to start timing those people.

WALTER: You should get up earlier.

BENEATHA (*Her face in her hands. She is still fighting the urge to go back to bed.*): Really — would you suggest dawn? Where's the paper?

WALTER (*pushing the paper across the table to her as he studies her almost clinically, as though he has never seen her before*): You a horrible-looking chick at this hour.

BENEATHA (*drily*): Good morning, everybody.

WALTER (*senselessly*): How is school coming?

BENEATHA (*in the same spirit*): Lovely. Lovely. And you know, biology is the greatest. (*Looking up at him.*) I dissected something that looked just like you yesterday.

WALTER: I just wondered if you've made up your mind and everything.

BENEATHA (*gaining in sharpness and impatience*): And what did I answer yesterday morning — and the day before that?

RUTH (*from the ironing board, like someone disinterested and old*): Don't be so nasty, Bennie.

BENEATHA (*still to her brother*): And the day before that and the day before that!

WALTER (*defensively*): I'm interested in you. Something wrong with that? Ain't many girls who decide —

WALTER AND BENEATHA (*in unison*): — "to be a doctor."

(*Silence.*)

WALTER: Have we figured out yet just exactly how much medical school is going to cost?

RUTH: Walter Lee, why don't you leave that girl alone and get out of here to work?

BENEATHA (*exits to the bathroom and bangs on the door*): Come on out of there, please!

(*She comes back into the room.*)

WALTER (*looking at his sister intently*): You know the check is coming tomorrow.

BENEATHA (*turning on him with a sharpness all her own*): That money belongs to Mama, Walter, and it's for her to decide how she wants to use it. I don't care if she wants to buy a house or a rocketship or just nail it up somewhere and look at it. It's hers. Not ours — *hers.*

WALTER (*bitterly*): Now ain't that fine! You just got your mother's interest at heart, ain't you, girl? You such a nice girl — but if Mama got that money she can always take a few thousand and help you through school too — can't she?

BENEATHA: I have never asked anyone around here to do anything for me!

WALTER: No! And the line between asking and just accepting when the time comes is big and wide — ain't it!

BENEATHA (*with fury*): What do you want from me, Brother — that I quit school or just drop dead, which!

WALTER: I don't want nothing but for you to stop acting holy 'round here. Me and Ruth done made some sacrifices for you — why can't you do something for the family?

RUTH: Walter, don't be dragging me in it.

WALTER: You are in it — Don't you get up and go work in somebody's kitchen for the last three years to help put clothes on her back?

RUTH: Oh, Walter — that's not fair . . .

WALTER: It ain't that nobody expects you to get on your knees and say thank you, Brother; thank you, Ruth; thank you, Mama — and thank you, Travis, for wearing the same pair of shoes for two semesters —

BENEATHA (*dropping to her knees*): Well — I *do* — all right? — thank everybody! And forgive me for ever wanting to be anything at all! (*Pursuing him on her knees across the floor.*) FORGIVE ME, FORGIVE ME, FORGIVE ME!

RUTH: Please stop it! Your mama'll hear you.

WALTER: Who the hell told you you had to be a doctor? If you so crazy 'bout messing 'round with sick people — then go be a nurse like other women — or just get married and be quiet . . .

BENEATHA: Well — you finally got it said . . . It took you three years but you finally got it said. Walter, give up; leave me alone — it's Mama's money.

WALTER: *He was my father, too!*

BENEATHA: So what? He was mine, too — and Travis' grandfather — but the insurance money belongs to Mama. Picking on me is not going to make her give it to you to invest in any liquor stores — (*under breath, dropping into a chair*) — and I for one say, God bless Mama for that!

WALTER (*to Ruth*): See — did you hear? Did you hear!

RUTH: Honey, please go to work.

WALTER: Nobody in this house is ever going to understand me.

BENEATHA: Because you're a nut.

Ester Rolle as Lena Younger comforts her daughter-in-law Ruth in the Huntington Theatre Company's 1994 production of *A Raisin in the Sun.* Also in the scene are Marguerite Hannah as Ruth and B. W. Gonzalez as Beneatha.

WALTER: Who's a nut?

BENEATHA: You — you are a nut. Thee is mad, boy.

WALTER (*looking at his wife and his sister from the door, very sadly*): The world's most backward race of people, and that's a fact.

BENEATHA (*turning slowly in her chair*): And then there are all those prophets who would lead us out of the wilderness — (*Walter slams out of the house.*) — into the swamps!

RUTH: Bennie, why you always gotta be pickin' on your brother? Can't you be a little sweeter sometimes? (*Door opens. Walter walks in. He fumbles with his cap, starts to speak, clears throat, looks everywhere but at Ruth. Finally.*)

WALTER (*to Ruth*): I need some money for carfare.

RUTH (*looks at him, then warms; teasing, but tenderly*): Fifty cents? (*She goes to her bag and gets money.*) Here — take a taxi!

(*Walter exits. Mama enters. She is a woman in her early sixties, full-bodied and strong. She is one of those women of a certain grace and beauty who wear it so unobtrusively that it takes a while to notice. Her dark brown face is surrounded by the total whiteness of her hair, and, being a woman who has adjusted to many things in life and overcome many more, her face is full of strength. She has, we can see, wit and faith of a kind that keep her eyes lit and full of interest and expectancy. She is, in a word, a beautiful woman. Her bearing is perhaps most like the noble bearing of the women of the Hereros of Southwest Africa — rather as if she imagines that as she walks she still bears a basket or a vessel upon her head. Her speech, on the other hand, is as careless as her carriage is precise — she is inclined to slur everything — but her voice is perhaps not so much quiet as simply soft.)*

MAMA: Who that 'round here slamming doors at this hour?

(She crosses through the room, goes to the window, opens it, and brings in a feeble little plant growing doggedly in a small pot on the window sill. She feels the dirt and puts it back out.)

RUTH: That was Walter Lee. He and Bennie was at it again.

MAMA: My children and they tempers. Lord, if this little old plant don't get more sun than it's been getting it ain't never going to see spring again. (*She turns from the window.*) What's the matter with you this morning, Ruth? You looks right peaked. You aiming to iron all them things? Leave some for me. I'll get to 'em this afternoon. Bennie honey, it's too drafty for you to be sitting 'round half dressed. Where's your robe?

BENEATHA: In the cleaners.

MAMA: Well, go get mine and put it on.

BENEATHA: I'm not cold, Mama, honest.

MAMA: I know — but you so thin . . .

BENEATHA (*irritably*): Mama, I'm not cold.

MAMA (*seeing the make-down bed as Travis has left it*): Lord have mercy, look at that poor bed. Bless his heart — he tries, don't he?

(She moves to the bed Travis has sloppily made up.)

RUTH: No — he don't half try at all 'cause he knows you going to come along behind him and fix everything. That's just how come he don't know how to do nothing right now — you done spoiled that boy so.

MAMA (*folding bedding*): Well — he's a little boy. Ain't supposed to know 'bout housekeeping. My baby, that's what he is. What you fix for his breakfast this morning?

RUTH (*angrily*): I feed my son, Lena!

MAMA: I ain't meddling — (*Under breath; busybodyish.*) I just noticed all last week he had cold cereal, and when it starts getting this chilly in the fall a child ought to have some hot grits or something when he goes out in the cold —

RUTH (*furious*): I gave him hot oats — is that all right!

MAMA: I ain't meddling. (*Pause.*) Put a lot of nice butter on it? (*Ruth shoots her an angry look and does not reply.*) He likes lots of butter.

RUTH (*exasperated*): Lena —

MAMA (*To Beneatha. Mama is inclined to wander conversationally sometimes.*): What was you and your brother fussing 'bout this morning?

BENEATHA: It's not important, Mama.

(She gets up and goes to look out at the bathroom, which is apparently free, and she picks up her towels and rushes out.)

MAMA: What was they fighting about?

RUTH: Now you know as well as I do.

MAMA (*shaking her head*): Brother still worrying hisself sick about that money?

RUTH: You know he is.

MAMA: You had breakfast?

RUTH: Some coffee.

MAMA: Girl, you better start eating and looking after yourself better. You almost thin as Travis.

RUTH: Lena —

MAMA: Un-hunh?

RUTH: What are you going to do with it?

MAMA: Now don't you start, child. It's too early in the morning to be talking about money. It ain't Christian.

RUTH: It's just that he got his heart set on that store —

MAMA: You mean that liquor store that Willy Harris want him to invest in?

RUTH: Yes —

MAMA: We ain't no business people, Ruth. We just plain working folks.

RUTH: Ain't nobody business people till they go into business. Walter Lee say colored people ain't never going to start getting ahead till they start gambling on some different kinds of things in the world — investments and things.

MAMA: What done got into you, girl? Walter Lee done finally sold you on investing.

RUTH: No. Mama, something is happening between Walter and me. I don't know what it is — but he needs something — something I can't give him anymore. He needs this chance, Lena.

MAMA (*frowning deeply*): But liquor, honey —

RUTH: Well — like Walter say — I spec people going to always be drinking themselves some liquor.

MAMA: Well — whether they drinks it or not ain't none of my business. But whether I go into business selling it to 'em *is*, and I don't want that on my ledger this late in life. (*Stopping suddenly and studying her daughter-in-law.*) Ruth Younger, what's the matter with you today? You look like you could fall over right there.

RUTH: I'm tired.

MAMA: Then you better stay home from work today.

RUTH: I can't stay home. She'd be calling up the agency and screaming at them, "My girl didn't come in today — send me somebody! My girl didn't come in!" Oh, she just have a fit . . .

MAMA: Well, let her have it. I'll just call her up and say you got the flu —

RUTH (*laughing*): Why the flu?

MAMA: 'Cause it sounds respectable to 'em. Something white people get, too. They know 'bout the flu. Otherwise they think you been cut up or something when you tell 'em you sick.

RUTH: I got to go in. We need the money.

MAMA: Somebody would of thought my children done all but starved to death the way they talk about money here late. Child, we got a great big old check coming tomorrow.

RUTH (*sincerely, but also self-righteously*): Now that's your money. It ain't got nothing to do with me. We all feel like that — Walter and Bennie and me — even Travis.

MAMA (*thoughtfully, and suddenly very far away*): Ten thousand dollars —

RUTH: Sure is wonderful.

MAMA: Ten thousand dollars.

RUTH: You know what you should do, Miss Lena? You should take yourself a trip somewhere. To Europe or South America or someplace —

MAMA (*throwing up her hands at the thought*): Oh, child!

RUTH: I'm serious. Just pack up and leave! Go on away and enjoy yourself some. Forget about the family and have yourself a ball for once in your life —

MAMA (*drily*): You sound like I'm just about ready to die. Who'd go with me? What I look like wandering 'round Europe by myself?

RUTH: Shoot — these here rich white women do it all the time. They don't think nothing of packing up they suitcases and piling on one of them big steamships and — swoosh! — they gone, child.

MAMA: Something always told me I wasn't no rich white woman.

RUTH: Well — what are you going to do with it then?

MAMA: I ain't rightly decided. (*Thinking. She speaks now with emphasis.*) Some of it got to be put away for Beneatha and her schoolin' — and ain't nothing going to touch that part of it. Nothing. (*She waits several seconds, trying to make up her mind about something, and looks at Ruth a little tentatively before going on.*) Been thinking that we maybe could meet the notes on a little old two-story somewhere, with a yard where Travis could play in the summertime, if we use part of the insurance for a down payment and everybody kind of pitch in. I could maybe take on a little day work again, few days a week —

RUTH (*studying her mother-in-law furtively and concentrating on her ironing, anxious to encourage without seeming to*): Well, Lord knows, we've put enough rent into this here rat trap to pay for four houses by now . . .

MAMA (*looking up at the words "rat trap" and then looking around and leaning back and sighing — in a suddenly reflective mood —*): "Rat trap" — yes, that's all it is. (*Smiling.*) I remember just as well the day me and Big Walter moved in here. Hadn't been married but two weeks and wasn't planning on living here no more than a year. (*She shakes her head at the dissolved dream.*) We was going to set away, little by little, don't you know, and buy a little place out in Morgan Park. We had even picked out the house. (*Chuckling a little.*) Looks right dumpy today. But Lord, child, you should know, all the dreams I had 'bout buying that house and fixing it up and making me a little garden in the back — (*She waits and stops smiling.*) And didn't none of it happen.

(*Dropping her hands in a futile gesture.*)

RUTH (*keeps her head down, ironing*): Yes, life can be a barrel of disappointments, sometimes.

MAMA: Honey, Big Walter would come in here some nights back then and slump down on that couch there and just look at the rug, and look at me and look at the rug and then back at me — and I'd know he was down then . . . really down. (*After a second very long and thoughtful pause; she is seeing back to times that only she can see.*) And then, Lord, when I lost that baby — little Claude — I almost thought I was going to lose Big Walter too. Oh, that man grieved hisself! He was one man to love his children.

RUTH: Ain't nothin' can tear at you like losin' your baby.

MAMA: I guess that's how come that man finally worked hisself to death like he done. Like he was fighting his own war with this here world that took his baby from him.

RUTH: He sure was a fine man, all right. I always liked Mr. Younger.

MAMA: Crazy 'bout his children! God knows there was plenty wrong with Walter Younger — hard-headed, mean, kind of wild with women — plenty wrong with him. But he sure loved his children. Always wanted them to have something — be something. That's where Brother gets all these notions, I reckon. Big Walter used to say, he'd get right wet in the eyes sometimes, lean his head back with the water standing in his eyes and say, "Seem like God didn't see fit to give the black man nothing but dreams — but He did give us children to make them dreams seem worthwhile." (*She smiles.*) He could talk like that, don't you know.

RUTH: Yes, he sure could. He was a good man, Mr. Younger.

MAMA: Yes, a fine man — just couldn't never catch up with his dreams, that's all.

(*Beneatha comes in, brushing her hair and looking up to the ceiling, where the sound of a vacuum cleaner has started up.*)

BENEATHA: What could be so dirty on that woman's rugs that she has to vacuum them every single day?

RUTH: I wish certain young women 'round here who I could name would take inspiration about certain rugs in a certain apartment I could also mention.

BENEATHA (*shrugging*): How much cleaning can a house need, for Christ's sakes.

MAMA (*not liking the Lord's name used thus*): Bennie!

RUTH: Just listen to her — just listen!

BENEATHA: Oh, God!

MAMA: If you use the Lord's name just one more time —

BENEATHA (*a bit of a whine*): Oh, Mama —

RUTH: Fresh — just fresh as salt, this girl!

BENEATHA (*drily*): Well — if the salt loses its savor —

MAMA: Now that will do. I just ain't going to have you 'round here reciting the scriptures in vain — you hear me?

BENEATHA: How did I manage to get on everybody's wrong side by just walking into a room?

RUTH: If you weren't so fresh —

BENEATHA: Ruth, I'm twenty years old.

MAMA: What time you be home from school today?

BENEATHA: Kind of late. (*With enthusiasm.*) Madeline is going to start my guitar lessons today.

(*Mama and Ruth look up with the same expression.*)

MAMA: Your *what* kind of lessons?

BENEATHA: Guitar.

RUTH: Oh, Father!

MAMA: How come you done taken it in your mind to learn to play the guitar?

BENEATHA: I just want to, that's all.

MAMA (*smiling*): Lord, child, don't you know what to do with yourself? How long it going to be before you get tired of this now — like you got tired of that little play-acting group you joined last year? (*Looking at Ruth.*) And what was it the year before that?

RUTH: The horseback-riding club for which she bought that fifty-five-dollar riding habit that's been hanging in the closet ever since!

MAMA (*to Beneatha*): Why you got to flit so from one thing to another, baby?

BENEATHA (*sharply*): I just want to learn to play the guitar. Is there anything wrong with that?

MAMA: Ain't nobody trying to stop you. I just wonders sometimes why you has to flit so from one thing to another all the time. You ain't never done nothing with all that camera equipment you brought home —

BENEATHA: I don't flit! I — I experiment with different forms of expression —

RUTH: Like riding a horse?

BENEATHA: — People have to express themselves one way or another.

MAMA: What is it you want to express?

BENEATHA (*angrily*): Me! (*Mama and Ruth look at each other and burst into raucous laughter.*) Don't worry — I don't expect you to understand.

MAMA (*to change the subject*): Who you going out with tomorrow night?

BENEATHA (*with displeasure*): George Murchison again.

MAMA (*pleased*): Oh — you getting a little sweet on him?

RUTH: You ask me, this child ain't sweet on nobody but herself — (*Under breath.*) Express herself!

(*They laugh.*)

BENEATHA: Oh — I like George all right, Mama. I mean I like him enough to go out with him and stuff, but —

RUTH (*for devilment*): What does *and stuff* mean?

BENEATHA: Mind your own business.

MAMA: Stop picking at her now, Ruth. (*She chuckles — then a suspicious sudden look at her daughter as she turns in her chair for emphasis.*) What DOES it mean?

BENEATHA (*wearily*): Oh, I just mean I couldn't ever really be serious about George. He's — he's so shallow.

RUTH: Shallow — what do you mean he's shallow? He's *Rich!*

MAMA: Hush, Ruth.

BENEATHA: I know he's rich. He knows he's rich, too.

RUTH: Well — what other qualities a man got to have to satisfy you, little girl?

BENEATHA: You wouldn't even begin to understand. Anybody who married Walter could not possibly understand.

MAMA (*outraged*): What kind of way is that to talk about your brother?

BENEATHA: Brother is a flip — let's face it.

MAMA (*to Ruth, helplessly*): What's a flip?

RUTH (*glad to add kindling*): She's saying he's crazy.

BENEATHA: Not crazy. Brother isn't really crazy yet — he — he's an elaborate neurotic.

MAMA: Hush your mouth!

BENEATHA: As for George. Well. George looks good — he's got a beautiful car and he takes me to nice places and, as my sister-in-law says, he is probably the richest boy I will ever get to know and I even like him sometimes — but if the Youngers are sitting around waiting to see if their little Bennie is going to tie up the family with the Murchisons, they are wasting their time.

RUTH: You mean you wouldn't marry George Murchison if he asked you someday? That pretty, rich thing? Honey, I knew you was odd —

BENEATHA: No I would not marry him if all I felt for him was what I feel now. Besides, George's family wouldn't really like it.

MAMA: Why not?

BENEATHA: Oh, Mama — The Murchisons are honest-to-God-real-*live*-rich colored people, and the only people in the world who are more snobbish than rich white people are rich colored people. I thought everybody knew that. I've met Mrs. Murchison. She's a scene!

MAMA: You must not dislike people 'cause they well off, honey.

BENEATHA: Why not? It makes just as much sense as disliking people 'cause they are poor, and lots of people do that.

RUTH (*A wisdom-of-the-ages manner. To Mama.*): Well, she'll get over some of this —

BENEATHA: Get over it? What are you talking about, Ruth? Listen, I'm going to be a doctor. I'm not worried about who I'm going to marry yet — if I ever get married.

MAMA AND RUTH: *If!*

MAMA: Now, Bennie —

BENEATHA: Oh, I probably will . . . but first I'm going to be a doctor, and George, for one, still thinks that's pretty funny. I couldn't be bothered with that. I am going to be a doctor and everybody around here better understand that!

MAMA (*kindly*): 'Course you going to be a doctor, honey, God willing.

BENEATHA (*drily*): God hasn't got a thing to do with it.

MAMA: Beneatha — that just wasn't necessary.

BENEATHA: Well — neither is God. I get sick of hearing about God.

MAMA: Beneatha!

BENEATHA: I mean it! I'm just tired of hearing about God all the time. What has He got to do with anything? Does he pay tuition?

MAMA: You 'bout to get your fresh little jaw slapped!

RUTH: That's just what she needs, all right!

BENEATHA: Why? Why can't I say what I want to around here, like everybody else?

MAMA: It don't sound nice for a young girl to say things like that — you wasn't brought up that way. Me and your father went to trouble to get you and Brother to church every Sunday.

BENEATHA: Mama, you don't understand. It's all a matter of ideas, and God is just one idea I don't accept. It's not important. I am not going out and be immoral or commit crimes because I don't believe in God. I don't even think about it. It's just that I get tired of Him getting credit for all the things the human race achieves through its own stubborn effort. There simply is no blasted God — there is only man and it is *he* who makes miracles!

(*Mama absorbs this speech, studies her daughter and rises slowly and crosses to Beneatha and slaps her powerfully across the face. After, there is only silence and the daughter drops her eyes from her mother's face, and Mama is very tall before her.*)

MAMA: Now — you say after me, in my mother's house there is still God. (*There is a long pause and Beneatha stares at the floor wordlessly. Mama repeats the phrase with precision and cool emotion.*) In my mother's house there is still God.

BENEATHA: In my mother's house there is still God.

(*A long pause.*)

MAMA (*Walking away from Beneatha, too disturbed for triumphant posture. Stopping and turning back to her daughter.*): There are some ideas we ain't going to have in this house. Not long as I am at the head of this family.

BENEATHA: Yes, ma'am.

(*Mama walks out of the room.*)

RUTH (*almost gently, with profound understanding*): You think you a woman, Bennie — but you still a little girl. What you did was childish — so you got treated like a child.

BENEATHA: I see. (*Quietly.*) I also see that everybody thinks it's all right for Mama to be a tyrant. But all the tyranny in the world will never put a God in the heavens!

(*She picks up her books and goes out. Pause.*)

RUTH (*goes to Mama's door*): She said she was sorry.

MAMA (*coming out, going to her plant*): They frightens me, Ruth. My children.

RUTH: You got good children, Lena. They just a little off sometimes — but they're good.

MAMA: No — there's something come down between me and them that don't let us understand each other

and I don't know what it is. One done almost lost his mind thinking 'bout money all the time and the other done commence to talk about things I can't seem to understand in no form or fashion. What is it that's changing, Ruth.

RUTH (*soothingly, older than her years*): Now . . . you taking it all too seriously. You just got strong-willed children and it takes a strong woman like you to keep 'em in hand.

MAMA (*looking at her plant and sprinkling a little water on it*): They spirited all right, my children. Got to admit they got spirit — Bennie and Walter. Like this little old plant that ain't never had enough sunshine or nothing — and look at it . . .

(*She has her back to Ruth, who has had to stop ironing and lean against something and put the back of her hand to her forehead.*)

RUTH (*trying to keep Mama from noticing*): You . . . sure . . . loves that little old thing, don't you? . . .

MAMA: Well, I always wanted me a garden like I used to see sometimes at the back of the houses down home. This plant is close as I ever got to having one. (*She looks out of the window as she replaces the plant.*) Lord, ain't nothing as dreary as the view from this window on a dreary day, is there? Why ain't you singing this morning, Ruth? Sing that "No Ways Tired." That song always lifts me up so — (*She turns at last to see that Ruth has slipped quietly to the floor, in a state of semiconsciousness.*) Ruth! Ruth honey — what's the matter with you . . . Ruth!

Scene II

(*It is the following morning; a Saturday morning, and house cleaning is in progress at the Youngers'. Furniture has been shoved hither and yon and Mama is giving the kitchen-area walls a washing down. Beneatha, in dungarees, with a handkerchief tied around her face, is spraying insecticide into the cracks in the walls. As they work, the radio is on and a Southside disk jockey program is inappropriately filling the house with a rather exotic saxophone blues. Travis, the sole idle one, is leaning on his arms, looking out of the window.*)

TRAVIS: Grandmama, that stuff Bennie is using smells awful. Can I go downstairs, please?

MAMA: Did you get all them chores done already? I ain't seen you doing much.

TRAVIS: Yes'm — finished early. Where did Mama go this morning?

MAMA (*looking at Beneatha*): She had to go on a little errand.

(*The phone rings. Beneatha runs to answer it and reaches it before Walter, who has entered from bedroom.*)

TRAVIS: Where?

MAMA: To tend to her business.

BENEATHA: Haylo . . . (*Disappointed.*) Yes, he is. (*She tosses the phone to Walter, who barely catches it.*) It's Willie Harris again.

WALTER (*as privately as possible under Mama's gaze*): Hello, Willie. Did you get the papers from the lawyer? . . . No, not yet. I told you the mailman doesn't get here till ten-thirty . . . No, I'll come there . . . Yeah! Right away. (*He hangs up and goes for his coat.*)

BENEATHA: Brother, where did Ruth go?

WALTER (*as he exits*): How should I know!

TRAVIS: Aw come on, Grandma. Can I go outside?

MAMA: Oh, I guess so. You stay right in front of the house, though, and keep a good lookout for the postman.

TRAVIS: Yes'm. (*He darts into bedroom for stickball and bat, reenters, and sees Beneatha on her knees spraying under sofa with behind upraised. He edges closer to the target, takes aim, and lets her have it. She screams.*) Leave them poor little cockroaches alone, they ain't bothering you none! (*He runs as she swings the spraygun at him viciously and playfully.*) Grandma! Grandma!

MAMA: Look out there, girl, before you be spilling some of that stuff on that child!

TRAVIS (*safely behind the bastion of Mama*): That's right — look out, now! (*He exits.*)

BENEATHA (*drily*): I can't imagine that it would hurt him — it has never hurt the roaches.

MAMA: Well, little boys' hides ain't as tough as South-side roaches. You better get over there behind the bureau. I seen one marching out of there like Napoleon yesterday.

BENEATHA: There's really only one way to get rid of them, Mama —

MAMA: How?

BENEATHA: Set fire to this building! Mama, where did Ruth go?

MAMA (*looking at her with meaning*): To the doctor, I think.

BENEATHA: The doctor? What's the matter? (*They exchange glances.*) You don't think —

MAMA (*with her sense of drama*): Now I ain't saying what I think. But I ain't never been wrong 'bout a woman neither.

(*The phone rings.*)

BENEATHA (*at the phone*): Hay-lo . . . (*Pause, and a moment of recognition.*) Well — when did you get back! . . . And how was it? . . . Of course I've missed you — in my way . . . This morning? No . . . house cleaning and all that and Mama hates it if I let people come over when the house is like this . . . You *have*? Well, that's different . . . What is it — Oh, what the hell, come on over . . . Right, see you then. *Arrivederci.*

(*She hangs up.*)

MAMA (*who has listened vigorously, as is her habit*): Who is that you inviting over here with this house looking like this? You ain't got the pride you was born with!

BENEATHA: Asagai doesn't care how houses look, Mama — he's an intellectual.

MAMA: *Who?*

BENEATHA: Asagai — Joseph Asagai. He's an African boy I met on campus. He's been studying in Canada all summer.

MAMA: What's his name?

BENEATHA: Asagai, Joseph. Ah-sah-guy . . . He's from Nigeria.

MAMA: Oh, that's the little country that was founded by slaves way back . . .

BENEATHA: No, Mama — that's Liberia.

MAMA: I don't think I never met no African before.

BENEATHA: Well, do me a favor and don't ask him a whole lot of ignorant questions about Africans. I mean, do they wear clothes and all that —

MAMA: Well, now, I guess if you think we so ignorant 'round here maybe you shouldn't bring your friends here —

BENEATHA: It's just that people ask such crazy things. All anyone seems to know about when it comes to Africa is Tarzan —

MAMA (*indignantly*): Why should I know anything about Africa?

BENEATHA: Why do you give money at church for the missionary work?

MAMA: Well, that's to help save people.

BENEATHA: You mean save them from *heathenism* —

MAMA (*innocently*): Yes.

BENEATHA: I'm afraid they need more salvation from the British and the French.

(*Ruth comes in forlornly and pulls off her coat with dejection. They both turn to look at her.*)

RUTH (*dispiritedly*): Well, I guess from all the happy faces — everybody knows.

BENEATHA: You pregnant?

MAMA: Lord have mercy, I sure hope it's a little old girl. Travis ought to have a sister.

(*Beneatha and Ruth give her a hopeless look for this grandmotherly enthusiasm.*)

BENEATHA: How far along are you?

RUTH: Two months.

BENEATHA: Did you mean to? I mean did you plan it or was it an accident?

MAMA: What do you know about planning or not planning?

BENEATHA: Oh, Mama.

RUTH (*wearily*): She's twenty years old, Lena.

BENEATHA: Did you plan it, Ruth?

RUTH: Mind your own business.

BENEATHA: It is my business — where is he going to live, on the *roof*? (*There is silence following the remark as the three women react to the sense of it.*) Gee — I didn't mean that, Ruth, honest. Gee, I don't feel like that at all. I — I think it is wonderful.

RUTH (*dully*): Wonderful.

BENEATHA: Yes — really.

MAMA (*looking at Ruth, worried*): Doctor say everything going to be all right?

RUTH (*far away*): Yes — she says everything is going to be fine . . .

MAMA (*immediately suspicious*): "She" — What doctor you went to?

(*Ruth folds over, near hysteria.*)

MAMA (*worriedly hovering over Ruth*): Ruth honey — what's the matter with you — you sick?

(*Ruth has her fists clenched on her thighs and is fighting hard to suppress a scream that seems to be rising in her.*)

BENEATHA: What's the matter with her, Mama?

MAMA (*working her fingers in Ruth's shoulders to relax her*): She be all right. Women gets right depressed sometimes when they get her way. (*Speaking softly, expertly, rapidly.*) Now you just relax. That's right . . . just lean back, don't think 'bout nothing at all . . . nothing at all —

RUTH: I'm all right . . .

(*The glassy-eyed look melts and then she collapses into a fit of heavy sobbing. The bell rings.*)

BENEATHA: Oh, my God — that must be Asagai.

MAMA (*to Ruth*): Come on now, honey. You need to lie down and rest awhile . . . then have some nice hot food.

(*They exit, Ruth's weight on her mother-in-law. Beneatha, herself profoundly disturbed, opens the door to admit a rather dramatic-looking young man with a large package.*)

ASAGAI: Hello, Alaiyo —

BENEATHA (*holding the door open and regarding him with pleasure*): Hello . . . (*Long pause.*) Well — come in. And please excuse everything. My mother was very upset about my letting anyone come here with the place like this.

ASAGAI (*coming into the room*): You look disturbed too . . . Is something wrong?

BENEATHA (*still at the door, absently*): Yes . . . we've all got acute ghetto-itus. (*She smiles and comes toward him, finding a cigarette and sitting.*) So — sit down! No! Wait! (*She whips the spraygun off sofa where she had left it and puts the cushions back. At last perches on arm of sofa. He sits.*) So, how was Canada?

ASAGAI (*a sophisticate*): Canadian.

BENEATHA (*looking at him*): Asagai, I'm very glad you are back.

ASAGAI (*looking back at her in turn*): Are you really?

BENEATHA: Yes — very.

ASAGAI: Why? — you were quite glad when I went away. What happened?

BENEATHA: You went away.

ASAGAI: Ahhhhhhhh.

BENEATHA: Before — you wanted to be so serious before there was time.

ASAGAI: How much time must there be before one knows what one feels?

BENEATHA (*Stalling this particular conversation. Her hands pressed together, in a deliberately childish gesture.*): What did you bring me?

ASAGAI (*handing her the package*): Open it and see.

BENEATHA (*eagerly opening the package and drawing out some records and the colorful robes of a Nigerian woman*): Oh, Asagai! . . . You got them for me! . . . How beautiful . . . and the records too! (*She lifts out the robes and runs to the mirror with them and holds the drapery up in front of herself.*)

ASAGAI (*coming to her at the mirror*): I shall have to teach you how to drape it properly. (*He flings the material about her for the moment and stands back to look at her.*) Ah — Oh-pay-gay-day, oh-gbah-mushay. (*A Yoruba exclamation for admiration.*) You wear it well . . . very well . . . mutilated hair and all.

BENEATHA (*turning suddenly*): My hair — what's wrong with my hair?

ASAGAI (*shrugging*): Were you born with it like that?

BENEATHA (*reaching up to touch it*): No . . . of course not.

(*She looks back to the mirror, disturbed.*)

ASAGAI (*smiling*): How then?

BENEATHA: You know perfectly well how . . . as crinkly as yours . . . that's how.

ASAGAI: And it is ugly to you that way?

BENEATHA (*quickly*): Oh, no — not ugly . . . (*More slowly, apologetically.*) But it's so hard to manage when it's, well — raw.

ASAGAI: And so to accommodate that — you mutilate it every week?

BENEATHA: It's not mutilation!

ASAGAI (*laughing aloud at her seriousness*): Oh . . . please! I am only teasing you because you are so very serious about these things. (*He stands back from her and folds his arms across his chest as he watches her pulling at her hair and frowning in the mirror.*) Do you remember the first time you met me at school? . . . (*He laughs.*) You came up to me and you said — and I thought you were the most serious little thing I had ever seen — you said: (*He imitates her.*) "Mr. Asagai — I want very much to talk with you. About Africa. You see, Mr. Asagai, I am looking for my *identity!*"

(*He laughs.*)

BENEATHA (*turning to him, not laughing*): Yes —

(*Her face is quizzical, profoundly disturbed.*)

ASAGAI (*still teasing and reaching out and taking her face in his hands and turning her profile to him*): Well . . . it is true that this is not so much a profile of a Hollywood queen as perhaps a queen of the Nile — (*A mock dismissal of the importance of the question*.) But what does it matter? Assimilationism is so popular in your country.

BENEATHA (*wheeling, passionately, sharply*): I am not an assimilationist!

ASAGAI (*the protest hangs in the room for a moment and Asagai studies her, his laughter fading*): Such a serious one. (*There is a pause*.) So — you like the robes? You must take excellent care of them — they are from my sister's personal wardrobe.

BENEATHA (*with incredulity*): You — you sent all the way home — for me?

ASAGAI (*with charm*): For you — I would do much more . . . Well, that is what I came for. I must go.

BENEATHA: Will you call me Monday?

ASAGAI: Yes . . . We have a great deal to talk about. I mean about identity and time and all that.

BENEATHA: Time?

ASAGAI: Yes. About how much time one needs to know what one feels.

BENEATHA: You see! You never understood that there is more than one kind of feeling which can exist between a man and a woman — or, at least, there should be.

ASAGAI (*shaking his head negatively but gently*): No. Between a man and a woman there need be only one kind of feeling. I have that for you . . . Now even . . . right this moment . . .

BENEATHA: I know — and by itself — it won't do. I can find that anywhere.

ASAGAI: For a woman it should be enough.

BENEATHA: I know — because that's what it says in all the novels that men write. But it isn't. Go ahead and laugh — but I'm not interested in being someone's little episode in America or — (*with feminine vengeance*) — one of them! (*Asagai has burst into laughter again.*) That's funny as hell, huh!

ASAGAI: It's just that every American girl I have known has said that to me. White — black — in this you are all the same. And the same speech, too!

BENEATHA (*angrily*): Yuk, yuk, yuk!

ASAGAI: It's how you can be sure that the world's most liberated women are not liberated at all. You all talk about it too much!

(*Mama enters and is immediately all social charm because of the presence of a guest.*)

BENEATHA: Oh — Mama — this is Mr. Asagai.

MAMA: How do you do?

ASAGAI (*total politeness to an elder*): How do you do, Mrs. Younger. Please forgive me for coming at such an outrageous hour on a Saturday.

MAMA: Well, you are quite welcome. I just hope you understand that our house don't always look like this. (*Chatterish.*) You must come again. I would love to hear all about — (*not sure of the name*) — your country. I think it's so sad the way our American Negroes don't know nothing about Africa 'cept Tarzan and all that. And all that money they pour into these churches when they ought to be helping

you people over there drive out them French and Englishmen done taken away your land.

(*The mother flashes a slightly superior look at her daughter upon completion of the recitation.*)

ASAGAI (*taken aback by this sudden and acutely unrelated expression of sympathy*): Yes . . . yes . . .

MAMA (*smiling at him suddenly and relaxing and looking him over*): How many miles is it from here to where you come from?

ASAGAI: Many thousands.

MAMA (*looking at him as she would Walter*): I bet you don't half look after yourself, being away from your mama either. I spec you better come 'round here from time to time to get yourself some decent home-cooked meals . . .

ASAGAI (*moved*): Thank you. Thank you very much. (*They are all quiet, then —*) Well . . . I must go. I will call you Monday, Alaiyo.

MAMA: What's that he call you?

ASAGAI: Oh — "Alaiyo." I hope you don't mind. It is what you would call a nickname, I think. It is a Yoruba word. I am a Yoruba.

MAMA (*looking at Beneatha*): I — I thought he was from — (*Uncertain.*)

ASAGAI (*understanding*): Nigeria is my country. Yoruba is my tribal origin —

BENEATHA: You didn't tell us what Alaiyo means . . . for all I know, you might be calling me Little Idiot or something . . .

ASAGAI: Well . . . let me see . . . I do not know how just to explain it . . . The sense of a thing can be so different when it changes languages.

BENEATHA: You're evading.

ASAGAI: No — really it is difficult . . . (*Thinking.*) It means . . . it means One for Whom Bread — Food — Is Not Enough. (*He looks at her.*) Is that all right?

BENEATHA (*understanding, softly*): Thank you.

MAMA (*looking from one to the other and not understanding any of it*): Well . . . that's nice . . . You must come see us again — Mr. ——

ASAGAI: Ah-sah-guy . . .

MAMA: Yes . . . Do come again.

ASAGAI: Good-bye.

(*He exits.*)

MAMA (*after him*): Lord, that's a pretty thing just went out here! (*Insinuatingly, to her daughter.*) Yes, I guess I see why we done commence to get so interested in Africa 'round here. Missionaries my aunt Jenny!

(*She exits.*)

BENEATHA: Oh, Mama! . . .

(*She picks up the Nigerian dress and holds it up to her in front of the mirror again. She sets the headdress on haphazardly and then notices her hair again and clutches at it and then replaces the headdress and frowns at herself. Then she starts to wriggle in front of the mirror as she thinks a Nigerian woman might. Travis enters and stands regarding her.*)

TRAVIS: What's the matter, girl, you cracking up?
BENEATHA: Shut up.

(*She pulls the headdress off and looks at herself in the mirror and clutches at her hair again and squinches her eyes as if trying to imagine something. Then, suddenly, she gets her raincoat and kerchief and hurriedly prepares for going out.*)

MAMA (*coming back into the room*): She's resting now. Travis, baby, run next door and ask Miss Johnson to please let me have a little kitchen cleanser. This here can is empty as Jacob's kettle.
TRAVIS: I just came in.
MAMA: Do as you told. (*He exits and she looks at her daughter.*) Where you going?
BENEATHA (*halting at the door*): To become a queen of the Nile!

(*She exits in a breathless blaze of glory. Ruth appears in the bedroom doorway.*)

MAMA: Who told you to get up?
RUTH: Ain't nothing wrong with me to be lying in no bed for. Where did Bennie go?
MAMA (*drumming her fingers*): Far as I could make out — to Egypt. (*Ruth just looks at her.*) What time is it getting to?
RUTH: Ten twenty. And the mailman going to ring that bell this morning just like he done every morning for the last umpteen years.

(*Travis comes in with the cleanser can.*)

TRAVIS: She say to tell you that she don't have much.
MAMA (*angrily*): Lord, some people I could name sure is tight-fisted! (*Directing her grandson.*) Mark two cans of cleanser down on the list there. If she that hard up for kitchen cleanser, I sure don't want to forget to get her none!
RUTH: Lena — maybe the woman is just short on cleanser —
MAMA (*not listening*): — Much baking powder as she done borrowed from me all these years, she could of done gone into the baking business!

(*The bell sounds suddenly and sharply and all three are stunned — serious and silent — mid-speech. In spite of all the other conversations and distractions of the morning, this is what they have been waiting for, even Travis, who looks helplessly from his mother to his grandmother. Ruth is the first to come to life again.*)

RUTH (*to Travis*): Get down them steps, boy!

(*Travis snaps to life and flies out to get the mail.*)

MAMA (*her eyes wide, her hand to her breast*): You mean it done really come?
RUTH (*excited*): Oh, Miss Lena!
MAMA (*collecting herself*): Well . . . I don't know what

we all so excited about 'round here for. We known it was coming for months.
RUTH: That's a whole lot different from having it come and being able to hold it in your hands . . . a piece of paper worth ten thousand dollars . . . (*Travis bursts back into the room. He holds the envelope high above his head, like a little dancer, his face is radiant and he is breathless. He moves to his grandmother with sudden slow ceremony and puts the envelope into her hands. She accepts it, and then merely holds it and looks at it.*) Come on! Open it . . . Lord have mercy, I wish Walter Lee was here!
TRAVIS: Open it, Grandmama!
MAMA (*staring at it*): Now you all be quiet. It's just a check.
RUTH: Open it . . .
MAMA (*still staring at it*): Now don't act silly . . . We ain't never been no people to act silly 'bout no money —
RUTH (*swiftly*): We ain't never had none before — OPEN IT!

(*Mama finally makes a good strong tear and pulls out the thin blue slice of paper and inspects it closely. The boy and his mother study it raptly over Mama's shoulders.*)

MAMA: Travis! (*She is counting off with doubt.*) Is that the right number of zeros.
TRAVIS: Yes'm . . . ten thousand dollars. Gaalee, Grandmama, you rich.
MAMA (*She holds the check away from her, still looking at it. Slowly her face sobers into a mask of unhappiness.*): Ten thousand dollars. (*She hands it to Ruth.*) Put it away somewhere, Ruth. (*She does not look at Ruth; her eyes seem to be seeing something somewhere very far off.*) Ten thousand dollars they give you. Ten thousand dollars.
TRAVIS (*to his mother, sincerely*): What's the matter with Grandmama — don't she want to be rich?
RUTH (*distractedly*): You go on out and play now, baby. (*Travis exits. Mama starts wiping dishes absently, humming intently to herself. Ruth turns to her, with kind exasperation.*) You've gone and got yourself upset.
MAMA (*not looking at her*): I spec if it wasn't for you all . . . I would just put that money away or give it to the church or something.
RUTH: Now what kind of talk is that. Mr. Younger would just be plain mad if he could hear you talking foolish like that.
MAMA (*stopping and staring off*): Yes . . . he sure would. (*Sighing.*) We got enough to do with that money, all right. (*She halts then, and turns and looks at her daughter-in-law hard; Ruth avoids her eyes and Mama wipes her hands with finality and starts to speak firmly to Ruth.*) Where did you go today, girl?
RUTH: To the doctor.
MAMA (*impatiently*): Now, Ruth . . . you know better than that. Old Doctor Jones is strange enough in his

way but there ain't nothing 'bout him make somebody slip and call him "she" — like you done this
morning.

RUTH: Well, that's what happened — my tongue slipped.

MAMA: You went to see that woman, didn't you?

RUTH (*defensively, giving herself away*): What woman
you talking about?

MAMA (*angrily*): That woman who —

(*Walter enters in great excitement.*)

WALTER: Did it come?

MAMA (*quietly*): Can't you give people a Christian
greeting before you start asking about money?

WALTER (*to Ruth*): Did it come? (*Ruth unfolds the
check and lays it quietly before him, watching him
intently with thoughts of her own. Walter sits down
and grasps it close and counts off the zeros.*) Ten
thousand dollars — (*He turns suddenly, frantically
to his mother and draws some papers out of his
breast pocket.*) Mama — look. Old Willy Harris put
everything on paper —

MAMA: Son — I think you ought to talk to your wife . . .
I'll go on out and leave you alone if you want —

WALTER: I can talk to her later — Mama, look —

MAMA: Son —

WALTER: WILL SOMEBODY PLEASE LISTEN TO ME TODAY!

MAMA (*quietly*): I don't 'low no yellin' in this house,
Walter Lee, and you know it — (*Walter stares at them
in frustration and starts to speak several times.*) And
there ain't going to be no investing in no liquor stores.

WALTER: But, Mama, you ain't even looked at it.

MAMA: I don't aim to have to speak on that again.

(*A long pause.*)

WALTER: You ain't looked at it and you don't aim to
have to speak on that again? You ain't even looked at
it and *you* have decided — (*Crumpling his papers.*)
Well, *you* tell that to my boy tonight when you put
him to sleep on the living room couch . . . (*Turning
to Mama and speaking directly to her.*) Yeah — and
tell it to my wife, Mama, tomorrow when she has to
go out of here to look after somebody else's kids.
And tell it to *me*, Mama, every time we need a new
pair of curtains and I have to watch *you* go out and
work in somebody's kitchen. Yeah, you tell me then!

(*Walter starts out.*)

RUTH: Where you going?

WALTER: I'm going out!

RUTH: Where?

WALTER: Just out of this house somewhere —

RUTH (*getting her coat*): I'll come too.

WALTER: I don't want you to come!

RUTH: I got something to talk to you about, Walter.

WALTER: That's too bad.

MAMA (*still quietly*): Walter Lee — (*She waits and he
finally turns and looks at her.*) Sit down.

WALTER: I'm a grown man, Mama.

MAMA: Ain't nobody said you wasn't grown. But you

still in my house and my presence. And as long as you
are — you'll talk to your wife civil. Now sit down.

RUTH (*suddenly*): Oh, let him go on out and drink himself to death! He makes me sick to my stomach! (*She
flings her coat against him and exits to bedroom.*)

WALTER (*violently flinging the coat after her*): And you
turn mine too, baby! (*The door slams behind her.*)
That was my biggest mistake —

MAMA (*still quietly*): Walter, what is the matter with
you?

WALTER: Matter with me? Ain't nothing the matter with
me!

MAMA: Yes there is. Something eating you up like a
crazy man. Something more than me not giving you
this money. The past few years I been watching it
happen to you. You get all nervous acting and kind
of wild in the eyes — (*Walter jumps up impatiently
at her words.*) I said sit there now, I'm talking to you!

WALTER: Mama — I don't need no nagging at me today.

MAMA: Seem like you getting to a place where you
always tied up in some kind of knot about something. But if anybody ask you 'bout it you just yell at
'em and bust out the house and go out and drink
somewheres. Walter Lee, people can't live with that.
Ruth's a good, patient girl in her way — but you getting to be too much. Boy, don't make the mistake of
driving that girl away from you.

WALTER: Why — what she do for me?

MAMA: She loves you.

WALTER: Mama — I'm going out. I want to go off
somewhere and be by myself for a while.

MAMA: I'm sorry 'bout your liquor store, son. It just
wasn't the thing for us to do. That's what I want to
tell you about —

WALTER: I got to go out, Mama —

(*He rises.*)

MAMA: It's dangerous, son.

WALTER: What's dangerous?

MAMA: When a man goes outside his home to look for
peace.

WALTER (*beseechingly*): Then why can't there never be
no peace in this house then?

MAMA: You done found it in some other house?

WALTER: No — there ain't no woman! Why do women
always think there's a woman somewhere when a
man gets restless. (*Picks up the check.*) Do you know
what this money means to me? Do you know what
this money can do for us? (*Puts it back.*) Mama —
Mama — I want so many things . . .

MAMA: Yes, son —

WALTER: I want so many things that they are driving me
kind of crazy . . . Mama — look at me.

MAMA: I'm looking at you. You a good-looking boy.
You got a job, a nice wife, a fine boy and —

WALTER: A job. (*Looks at her.*) Mama, a job? I open and
close car doors all day long. I drive a man around in
his limousine and I say, "Yes, sir, no, sir; very good,
sir; shall I take the Drive, sir?" Mama, that ain't no

kind of job . . . that ain't nothing at all. (*Very quietly.*) Mama, I don't know if I can make you understand.

MAMA: Understand what, baby?

WALTER (*quietly*): Sometimes it's like I can see the future stretched out in front of me — just plain as day. The future, Mama. Hanging over there at the edge of my days. Just waiting for me — a big, looming blank space — full of *nothing*. Just waiting for *me*. But it don't have to be. (*Pause. Kneeling beside her chair.*) Mama — sometimes when I'm downtown and I pass them cool, quiet-looking restaurants where them white boys are sitting back and talking 'bout things . . . sitting there turning deals worth millions of dollars . . . sometimes I see guys don't look much older than me —

MAMA: Son — how come you talk so much 'bout money?

WALTER (*with immense passion*): Because it is life, Mama!

MAMA (*quietly*): Oh — (*Very quietly.*) So now it's life. Money is life. Once upon a time freedom used to be life — now it's money. I guess the world really do change . . .

WALTER: No — it was always money, Mama. We just didn't know about it.

MAMA: No . . . something has changed. (*She looks at him.*) You something new, boy. In my time we was worried about not being lynched and getting to the North if we could and how to stay alive and still have a pinch of dignity too . . . Now here come you and Beneatha — talking 'bout things we ain't never even thought about hardly, me and your daddy. You ain't satisfied or proud of nothing we done. I mean that you had a home, that we kept you out of trouble till you was grown, that you don't have to ride to work on the back of nobody's streetcar — You my children — but how different we done become.

WALTER (*A long beat. He pats her hand and gets up.*): You just don't understand, Mama, you just don't understand.

MAMA: Son — do you know your wife is expecting another baby? (*Walter stands, stunned, and absorbs what his mother has said.*) That's what she wanted to talk to you about. (*Walter sinks down into a chair.*) This ain't for me to be telling — but you ought to know. (*She waits.*) I think Ruth is thinking 'bout getting rid of that child.

WALTER (*slowly understanding*): — No — no — Ruth wouldn't do that.

MAMA: When the world gets ugly enough — a woman will do anything for her family. *The part that's already living.*

WALTER: You don't know Ruth, Mama, if you think she would do that.

(*Ruth opens the bedroom door and stands there a little limp.*)

RUTH (*beaten*): Yes I would too, Walter. (*Pause.*) I gave her a five-dollar down payment.

(*There is total silence as the man stares at his wife and the mother stares at her son.*)

MAMA (*presently*): Well — (*Tightly.*) Well — son, I'm waiting to hear you say something . . . (*She waits.*) I'm waiting to hear how you be your father's son. Be the man he was . . . (*Pause. The silence shouts.*) Your wife says she going to destroy your child. And I'm waiting to hear you talk like him and say we a people who give children life, not who destroys them — (*She rises.*) I'm waiting to see you stand up and look like your daddy and say we done give up one baby to poverty and that we ain't going to give up nary another one . . . I'm waiting.

WALTER: Ruth — (*He can say nothing.*)

MAMA: If you a son of mine, tell her! (*Walter picks up his keys and his coat and walks out. She continues, bitterly.*) You . . . you are a disgrace to your father's memory. Somebody get me my hat!

ACT II • Scene I

(*Time: Later the same day.*)

(*At rise: Ruth is ironing again. She has the radio going. Presently Beneatha's bedroom door opens and Ruth's mouth falls and she puts down the iron in fascination.*)

RUTH: What have we got on tonight!

BENEATHA (*emerging grandly from the doorway so that we can see her thoroughly robed in the costume Asagai brought*): You are looking at what a well-dressed Nigerian woman wears — (*She parades for Ruth, her hair completely hidden by the headdress; she is coquettishly fanning herself with an ornate oriental fan, mistakenly more like Butterfly° than any Nigerian that ever was.*) Isn't it beautiful? (*She promenades to the radio and, with an arrogant flourish, turns off the good loud blues that is playing.*) Enough of this assimilationist junk! (*Ruth follows her with her eyes as she goes to the phonograph and puts on a record and turns and waits ceremoniously for the music to come up. Then, with a shout —*) OCOMOGOSIAY!

(*Ruth jumps. The music comes up, a lovely Nigerian melody. Beneatha listens, enraptured, her eyes far away — "back to the past." She begins to dance. Ruth is dumfounded.*)

RUTH: What kind of dance is that?

BENEATHA: A folk dance.

RUTH (*Pearl Bailey*): What kind of folks do that, honey?

BENEATHA: It's from Nigeria. It's a dance of welcome.

RUTH: Who you welcoming?

BENEATHA: The men back to the village.

RUTH: Where they been?

BENEATHA: How should I know — out hunting or something. Anyway, they are coming back now . . .

Butterfly: Madame Butterfly, the title character in the opera by Puccini, set in Japan.

RUTH: Well, that's good.

BENEATHA (*with the record*): Alundi, alundi
Alundi alunya
Jop pu a jeepua
Ang gu soooooooooo

Ai yai yue . . .
Ayehaye — alundi . . .

(*Walter comes in during this performance; he has obviously been drinking. He leans against the door heavily and watches his sister, at first with distaste. Then his eyes look off — "back to the past" — as he lifts both his fists to the roof, screaming.*)

WALTER: YEAH . . . AND ETHIOPIA STRETCH FORTH HER HANDS AGAIN! . . .

RUTH (*drily, looking at him*): Yes — and Africa sure is claiming her own tonight. (*She gives them both up and starts ironing again.*)

WALTER (*all in a drunken, dramatic shout*): Shut up! . . . I'm digging them drums . . . them drums move me! . . . (*He makes his weaving way to his wife's face and leans in close to her.*) In my *heart of hearts* — (*he thumps his chest*) — I am much warrior!

RUTH (*without even looking up*): In your heart of hearts you are much drunkard.

WALTER (*coming away from her and starting to wander around the room, shouting*): Me and Jomo . . . (*Intently, in his sister's face. She has stopped dancing to watch him in this unknown mood.*) That's my man, Kenyatta. (*Shouting and thumping his chest.*) FLAMING SPEAR! HOT DAMN! (*He is suddenly in possession of an imaginary spear and actively spearing enemies all over the room.*) OCOMOGOSIAY . . .

BENEATHA (*to encourage Walter, thoroughly caught up with this side of him*): OCOMOGOSIAY, FLAMING SPEAR!

WALTER: THE LION IS WAKING . . . OWIMOWEH! (*He pulls his shirt open and leaps up on the table and gestures with his spear.*)

BENEATHA: OWIMOWEH!

WALTER (*On the table, very far gone, his eyes pure glass sheets. He sees what we cannot, that he is a leader of his people, a great chief, a descendant of Chaka, and that the hour to march has come.*): Listen, my black brothers —

BENEATHA: OCOMOGOSIAY!

WALTER: — Do you hear the waters rushing against the shores of the coastlands —

BENEATHA: OCOMOGOSIAY!

WALTER: — Do you hear the screeching of the cocks in yonder hills beyond where the chiefs meet in council for the coming of the mighty war —

BENEATHA: OCOMOGOSIAY!

(*And now the lighting shifts subtly to suggest the world of Walter's imagination, and the mood shifts from pure comedy. It is the inner Walter speaking: the Southside chauffeur has assumed an unexpected majesty.*)

WALTER: — Do you hear the beating of the wings of the birds flying low over the mountains and the low places of our land —

BENEATHA: OCOMOGOSIAY!

WALTER: — Do you hear the singing of the women singing the war songs of our fathers to the babies in the great houses? Singing the sweet war songs! (*The doorbell rings.*) OH, DO YOU HEAR, MY BLACK BROTHERS!

BENEATHA (*completely gone*): We hear you, Flaming Spear —

(*Ruth shuts off the phonograph and opens the door. George Murchison enters.*)

WALTER: Telling us to prepare for the GREATNESS OF THE TIME! (*Lights back to normal. He turns and sees George.*) Black Brother!

(*He extends his hand for the fraternal clasp.*)

GEORGE: Black Brother, hell!

RUTH (*having had enough, and embarrassed for the family*): Beneatha, you got company — what's the matter with you? Walter Lee Younger, get down off that table and stop acting like a fool . . .

(*Walter comes down off the table suddenly and makes a quick exit to the bathroom.*)

RUTH: He's had a little to drink . . . I don't know what her excuse is.

GEORGE (*to Beneatha*): Look honey, we're going *to* the theater — we're not going to be *in* it . . . so go change, huh?

(*Beneatha looks at him and slowly, ceremoniously, lifts her hands and pulls off the headdress. Her hair is close-cropped and unstraightened. George freezes mid-sentence and Ruth's eyes all but fall out of her head.*)

GEORGE: What in the name of —

RUTH (*touching Beneatha's hair*): Girl, you done lost your natural mind? Look at your head!

GEORGE: What have you done to your head — I mean your hair?

BENEATHA: Nothing — except cut it off.

RUTH: Now that's the truth — it's what ain't been done to it! You expect this boy to go out with you with your head all nappy like that?

BENEATHA (*looking at George*): That's up to George. If he's ashamed of his heritage —

GEORGE: Oh, don't be so proud of yourself, Bennie — just because you look eccentric.

BENEATHA: How can something that's natural be eccentric?

GEORGE: That's what being eccentric means — being natural. Get dressed.

BENEATHA: I don't like that, George.

RUTH: Why must you and your brother make an argument out of everything people say?

BENEATHA: Because I hate assimilationist Negroes!

RUTH: Will somebody please tell me what assimila-whoever means!

GEORGE: Oh, it's just a college girl's way of calling people Uncle Toms — but that isn't what it means at all.

RUTH: Well, what does it mean?

BENEATHA (*cutting George off and staring at him as she replies to Ruth*): It means someone who is willing to give up his own culture and submerge himself completely in the dominant, and in this case *oppressive* culture!

GEORGE: Oh, dear, dear, dear! Here we go! A lecture on the African past! On our Great West African Heritage! In one second we will hear all about the great Ashanti empires; the great Songhay civilizations; and the great sculpture of Bénin — and then some poetry in the Bantu — and the whole monologue will end with the word *heritage*! (*Nastily.*) Let's face it, baby, your heritage is nothing but a bunch of raggedy-assed spirituals and some grass huts!

BENEATHA: GRASS HUTS! (*Ruth crosses to her and forcibly pushes her toward the bedroom.*) See there . . . you are standing there in your splendid ignorance talking about people who were the first to smelt iron on the face of the earth! (*Ruth is pushing her through the door.*) The Ashanti were performing surgical operations when the English — (*Ruth pulls the door to, with Beneatha on the other side, and smiles graciously at George. Beneatha opens the door and shouts the end of the sentence defiantly at George*) — were still tatooing themselves with blue dragons! (*She goes back inside.*)

RUTH: Have a seat, George. (*They both sit. Ruth folds her hands rather primly on her lap, determined to demonstrate the civilization of the family.*) Warm, ain't it? I mean for September. (*Pause.*) Just like they always say about Chicago weather: If it's too hot or cold for you, just wait a minute and it'll change. (*She smiles happily at this cliché of clichés.*) Everybody say it's got to do with them bombs and things they keep setting off. (*Pause.*) Would you like a nice cold beer?

GEORGE: No, thank you. I don't care for beer. (*He looks at his watch.*) I hope she hurries up.

RUTH: What time is the show?

GEORGE: It's an eight-thirty curtain. That's just Chicago, though. In New York standard curtain time is eight forty.

(*He is rather proud of this knowledge.*)

RUTH (*properly appreciating it*): You get to New York a lot?

GEORGE (*offhand*): Few times a year.

RUTH: Oh — that's nice. I've never been to New York.

(*Walter enters. We feel he has relieved himself, but the edge of unreality is still with him.*)

WALTER: New York ain't got nothing Chicago ain't. Just a bunch of hustling people all squeezed up together — being "Eastern."

(*He turns his face into a screw of displeasure.*)

GEORGE: Oh — you've been?

WALTER: *Plenty* of times.

RUTH (*shocked at the lie*): Walter Lee Younger!

WALTER (*staring her down*): Plenty! (*Pause.*) What we got to drink in this house? Why don't you offer this man some refreshment. (*To George.*) They don't know how to entertain people in this house, man.

GEORGE: Thank you — I don't really care for anything.

WALTER (*feeling his head; sobriety coming*): Where's Mama?

RUTH: She ain't come back yet.

WALTER (*looking Murchison over from head to toe, scrutinizing his carefully casual tweed sports jacket over cashmere V-neck sweater over soft eyelet shirt and tie, and soft slacks, finished off with white buckskin shoes*): Why all you college boys wear them faggoty-looking white shoes?

RUTH: Walter Lee!

(*George Murchison ignores the remark.*)

WALTER (*to Ruth*): Well, they look crazy as hell — white shoes, cold as it is.

RUTH (*crushed*): You have to excuse him —

WALTER: No he don't! Excuse me for what? What you always excusing me for! I'll excuse myself when I needs to be excused! (*A pause.*) They look as funny as them black knee socks Beneatha wears out of here all the time.

RUTH: It's the college *style*, Walter.

WALTER: Style, hell. She looks like she got burnt legs or something!

RUTH: Oh, Walter —

WALTER (*an irritable mimic*): Oh, Walter! Oh, Walter! (*To Murchison.*) How's your old man making out? I understand you all going to buy that big hotel on the Drive? (*He finds a beer in the refrigerator, wanders over to Murchison, sipping and wiping his lips with the back of his hand, and straddling a chair backward to talk to the other man.*) Shrewd move. Your old man is all right, man. (*Tapping his head and half winking for emphasis.*) I mean he knows how to operate. I mean he thinks *big*, you know what I mean, I mean for a *home*, you know? But I think he's kind of running out of ideas now. I'd like to talk to him. Listen, man, I got some plans that could turn this city upside down. I mean think like he does. *Big.* Invest big, gamble big, hell, lose *big* if you have to, you know what I mean. It's hard to find a man on this whole Southside who understands my kind of thinking — you dig? (*He scrutinizes Murchison again, drinks his beer, squints his eyes, and leans in close, confidential, man to man.*) Me and you ought to sit down and talk sometimes, man. Man, I got me some ideas . . .

MURCHISON (*with boredom*): Yeah — sometimes we'll have to do that, Walter.

WALTER (*understanding the indifference, and offended*): Yeah — well, when you get the time, man. I know you a busy little boy.

RUTH: Walter, please —

WALTER (*bitterly, hurt*): I know ain't nothing in this world as busy as you colored college boys with your fraternity pins and white shoes . . .

RUTH (*covering her face with humiliation*): Oh, Walter Lee —

WALTER: I see you all all the time — with the books tucked under your arms — going to your (*British A — a mimic*) "clahsses." And for what! What the hell you learning over there? Filling up your heads — (*counting off on his fingers*) — with the sociology and the psychology — but they teaching you how to be a man? How to take over and run the world? They teaching you how to run a rubber plantation or a steel mill? Naw — just to talk proper and read books and wear them faggoty-looking white shoes . . .

GEORGE (*looking at him with distaste, a little above it all*): You're all wacked up with bitterness, man.

WALTER (*intently, almost quietly, between the teeth, glaring at the boy*): And you — ain't you bitter, man? Ain't you just about had it yet? Don't you see no stars gleaming that you can't reach out and grab? You happy? — You contented son-of-a-bitch — you happy? You got it made? Bitter? Man, I'm a volcano. Bitter? Here I am a giant — surrounded by ants! Ants who can't even understand what it is the giant is talking about.

RUTH (*passionately and suddenly*): Oh, Walter — ain't you with nobody!

WALTER (*violently*): No! 'Cause ain't nobody with me! Not even my own mother!

RUTH: Walter, that's a terrible thing to say!

(*Beneatha enters, dressed for the evening in a cocktail dress and earrings, hair natural.*)

GEORGE: Well — hey — (*Crosses to Beneatha; thoughtful, with emphasis, since this is a reversal.*) You look great!

WALTER (*seeing his sister's hair for the first time*): What's the matter with your head?

BENEATHA (*tired of the jokes now*): I cut it off, Brother.

WALTER (*coming close to inspect it and walking around her*): Well, I'll be damned. So that's what they mean by the African bush . . .

BENEATHA: Ha ha. Let's go, George.

GEORGE (*looking at her*): You know something? I like it. It's sharp. I mean it really is. (*Helps her into her wrap.*)

RUTH: Yes — I think so, too. (*She goes to the mirror and starts to clutch at her hair.*)

WALTER: Oh no! You leave yours alone, baby. You might turn out to have a pin-shaped head or something!

BENEATHA: See you all later.

RUTH: Have a nice time.

GEORGE: Thanks. Good night. (*Half out the door, he reopens it. To Walter.*) Good night, Prometheus!°

Prometheus: Defiantly inventive Titan who stole fire from the gods and gave it to humans.

(*Beneatha and George exit.*)

WALTER (*to Ruth*): Who is Prometheus?

RUTH: I don't know. Don't worry about it.

WALTER (*in fury, pointing after George*): See there — they get to a point where they can't insult you man to man — they got to go talk about something ain't nobody never heard of!

RUTH: How do you know it was an insult? (*To humor him.*) Maybe Prometheus is a nice fellow.

WALTER: Prometheus! I bet there ain't even no such thing! I bet that simple-minded clown —

RUTH: Walter —

(*She stops what she is doing and looks at him.*)

WALTER (*yelling*): Don't start!

RUTH: Start what?

WALTER: Your nagging! Where was I? Who was I with? How much money did I spend?

RUTH (*plaintively*): Walter Lee — why don't we just try to talk about it . . .

WALTER (*not listening*): I been out talking with people who understand me. People who care about the things I got on my mind.

RUTH (*wearily*): I guess that means people like Willy Harris.

WALTER: Yes, people like Willy Harris.

RUTH (*with a sudden flash of impatience*): Why don't you all just hurry up and go into the banking business and stop talking about it!

WALTER: Why? You want to know why? 'Cause we all tied up in a race of people that don't know how to do nothing but moan, pray, and have babies!

(*The line is too bitter even for him and he looks at her and sits down.*)

RUTH: Oh, Walter . . . (*Softly.*) Honey, why can't you stop fighting me?

WALTER (*without thinking*): Who's fighting you? Who even cares about you?

(*This line begins the retardation of his mood.*)

RUTH: Well — (*She waits a long time, and then with resignation starts to put away her things.*) I guess I might as well go on to bed . . . (*More or less to herself.*) I don't know where we lost it . . . but we have . . . (*Then, to him.*) I — I'm sorry about this new baby, Walter. I guess maybe I better go on and do what I started . . . I guess I just didn't realize how bad things was with us . . . I guess I just didn't really realize — (*She starts out to the bedroom and stops.*) You want some hot milk?

WALTER: Hot milk?

RUTH: Yes — hot milk.

WALTER: Why hot milk?

RUTH: 'Cause after all that liquor you come home with you ought to have something hot in your stomach.

WALTER: I don't want no milk.

RUTH: You want some coffee then?

WALTER: No, I don't want no coffee. I don't want nothing hot to drink. (*Almost plaintively.*) Why you always trying to give me something to eat?

RUTH (*standing and looking at him helplessly*): What else can I give you, Walter Lee Younger?

(*She stands and looks at him and presently turns to go out again. He lifts his head and watches her going away from him in a new mood which began to emerge when he asked her "Who cares about you?"*)

WALTER: It's been rough, ain't it, baby? (*She hears and stops but does not turn around and he continues to her back.*) I guess between two people there ain't never as much understood as folks generally thinks there is. I mean like between me and you — (*She turns to face him.*) How we gets to the place where we scared to talk softness to each other. (*He waits, thinking hard himself.*) Why you think it got to be like that? (*He is thoughtful, almost as a child would be.*) Ruth, what is it gets into people ought to be close?

RUTH: I don't know, honey. I think about it a lot.

WALTER: On account of you and me, you mean? The way things are with us. The way something done come down between us.

RUTH: There ain't so much between us, Walter . . . Not when you come to me and try to talk to me. Try to be with me . . . a little even.

WALTER (*total honesty*): Sometimes . . . sometimes . . . I don't even know how to try.

RUTH: Walter —

WALTER: Yes?

RUTH (*coming to him, gently and with misgiving, but coming to him*): Honey . . . life don't have to be like this. I mean sometimes people can do things so that things are better . . . You remember how we used to talk when Travis was born . . . about the way we were going to live . . . the kind of house . . . (*She is stroking his head.*) Well, it's all starting to slip away from us . . .

(*He turns her to him and they look at each other and kiss, tenderly and hungrily. The door opens and Mama enters — Walter breaks away and jumps up. A beat.*)

WALTER: Mama, where have you been?

MAMA: My — them steps is longer than they used to be. Whew! (*She sits down and ignores him.*) How you feeling this evening, Ruth?

(*Ruth shrugs, disturbed at having been interrupted and watching her husband knowingly.*)

WALTER: Mama, where have you been all day?

MAMA (*still ignoring him and leaning on the table and changing to more comfortable shoes*): Where's Travis?

RUTH: I let him go out earlier and he ain't come back yet. Boy, is he going to get it!

WALTER: Mama!

MAMA (*as if she has heard him for the first time*): Yes, son?

WALTER: Where did you go this afternoon?

MAMA: I went downtown to tend to some business that I had to tend to.

WALTER: What kind of business?

MAMA: You know better than to question me like a child, Brother.

WALTER (*rising and bending over the table*): Where were you, Mama? (*Bringing his fists down and shouting.*) Mama, you didn't go do something with that insurance money, something crazy?

(*The front door opens slowly, interrupting him, and Travis peeks his head in, less than hopefully.*)

TRAVIS (*to his mother*): Mama, I —

RUTH: "Mama I" nothing! You're going to get it, boy! Get on in that bedroom and get yourself ready!

TRAVIS: But I —

MAMA: Why don't you all never let the child explain himself.

RUTH: Keep out of it now, Lena.

(*Mama clamps her lips together, and Ruth advances toward her son menacingly.*)

RUTH: A thousand times I have told you not to go off like that —

MAMA (*holding out her arms to her grandson*): Well — at least let me tell him something. I want him to be the first one to hear . . . Come here, Travis. (*The boy obeys, gladly.*) Travis — (*she takes him by the shoulder and looks into his face*) — you know that money we got in the mail this morning?

TRAVIS: Yes'm —

MAMA: Well — what you think your grandmama gone and done with that money?

TRAVIS: I don't know, Grandmama.

MAMA (*putting her finger on his nose for emphasis*): She went out and she bought you a house! (*The explosion comes from Walter at the end of the revelation and he jumps up and turns away from all of them in a fury. Mama continues, to Travis.*) You glad about the house? It's going to be yours when you get to be a man.

TRAVIS: Yeah — I always wanted to live in a house.

MAMA: All right, gimme some sugar then — (*Travis puts his arms around her neck as she watches her son over the boy's shoulder. Then, to Travis, after the embrace.*) Now when you say your prayers tonight, you thank God and your grandfather — 'cause it was him who give you the house — in his way.

RUTH (*taking the boy from Mama and pushing him toward the bedroom*): Now you get out of here and get ready for your beating.

TRAVIS: Aw, Mama —

RUTH: Get on in there — (*Closing the door behind him and turning radiantly to her mother-in-law.*) So you went and did it!

MAMA (*quietly, looking at her son with pain*): Yes, I did.

RUTH (*raising both arms classically*): PRAISE GOD! (*Looks at Walter a moment, who says nothing. She crosses rapidly to her husband.*) Please, honey — let me be glad . . . you be glad too. (*She has laid her hands on his shoulders, but he shakes himself free of her roughly, without turning to face her.*) Oh, Walter . . . a home . . . *a home.* (*She comes back to Mama.*) Well — where is it? How big is it? How much it going to cost?

MAMA: Well —

RUTH: When we moving?

MAMA (*smiling at her*): First of the month.

RUTH (*throwing back her head with jubilance*): Praise God!

MAMA (*tentatively, still looking at her son's back turned against her and Ruth*): It's — it's a nice house too . . . (*She cannot help speaking directly to him. An imploring quality in her voice, her manner, makes her almost like a girl now.*) Three bedrooms — nice big one for you and Ruth . . . Me and Beneatha still have to share our room, but Travis have one of his own and (*with difficulty*) I figure if the — new baby — is a boy, we could get one of them double-decker outfits . . . And there's a yard with a little patch of dirt where I could maybe get to grow me a few flowers . . . And a nice big basement . . .

RUTH: Walter honey, be glad —

MAMA (*still to his back, fingering things on the table*): 'Course I don't want to make it sound fancier than it is . . . It's just a plain little old house — but it's made good and solid — and it will be *ours.* Walter Lee — it makes a difference in a man when he can walk on floors that belong to *him* . . .

RUTH: Where is it?

MAMA (*frightened at this telling*): Well — well — it's out there in Clybourne Park —

(*Ruth's radiance fades abruptly, and Walter finally turns slowly to face his mother with incredulity and hostility.*)

RUTH: Where?

MAMA (*matter-of-factly*): Four o six Clybourne Street, Clybourne Park.

RUTH: Clybourne Park? Mama, there ain't no colored people living in Clybourne Park.

MAMA (*almost idiotically*): Well, I guess there's going to be some now.

WALTER (*bitterly*): So that's the peace and comfort you went out and bought for us today!

MAMA (*raising her eyes to meet his finally*): Son — I just tried to find the nicest place for the least amount of money for my family.

RUTH (*trying to recover from the shock*): Well — well — 'course I ain't one never been 'fraid of no crackers,° mind you — but — well, wasn't there no other houses nowhere?

MAMA: Them houses they put up for colored in them areas way out all seem to cost twice as much as other houses. I did the best I could.

crackers: White people, often used to refer disparagingly to poor whites.

RUTH (*struck senseless with the news, in its various degrees of goodness and trouble, she sits a moment, her fists propping her chin in thought, and then she starts to rise, bringing her fists down with vigor, the radiance spreading from cheek to cheek again*): Well — well — All I can say is — if this is my time in life — MY TIME — to say good-bye — (*and she builds with momentum as she starts to circle the room with an exuberant, almost tearfully happy release*) — to these Goddamned cracking walls! — (*she pounds the walls*) — and these marching roaches! — (*she wipes at an imaginary army of marching roaches*) — and this cramped little closet which ain't now or never was no kitchen! . . . then I say it loud and good, HAL-LELUJAH! AND GOOD-BYE MISERY . . . I DON'T NEVER WANT TO SEE YOUR UGLY FACE AGAIN! (*She laughs joyously, having practically destroyed the apartment, and flings her arms up and lets them come down happily, slowly, reflectively, over her abdomen, aware for the first time perhaps that the life therein pulses with happiness and not despair.*) Lena?

MAMA (*moved, watching her happiness*): Yes, honey?

RUTH (*looking off*): Is there — is there a whole lot of sunlight?

MAMA (*understanding*): Yes, child, there's a whole lot of sunlight.

(*Long pause.*)

RUTH (*collecting herself and going to the door of the room Travis is in*): Well — I guess I better see 'bout Travis. (*To Mama.*) Lord, I sure don't feel like whipping nobody today!

(*She exits.*)

MAMA (*the mother and son are left alone now and the mother waits a long time, considering deeply, before she speaks*): Son — you — you understand what I done, don't you? (*Walter is silent and sullen.*) I — I just seen my family falling apart today . . . just falling to pieces in front of my eyes . . . We couldn't of gone on like we was today. We was going backwards 'stead of forwards — talking 'bout killing babies and wishing each other was dead . . . When it gets like that in life — you just got to do something different, push on out and do something bigger . . . (*She waits.*) I wish you say something, son . . . I wish you'd say how deep inside you you think I done the right thing —

WALTER (*crossing slowly to his bedroom door and finally turning there and speaking measuredly*): What you need me to say you done right for? *You* the head of this family. You run our lives like you want to. It was your money and you did what you wanted with it. So what you need for me to say it was all right for? (*Bitterly, to hurt her as deeply as he knows is possible.*) So you butchered up a dream of mine — you — who always talking 'bout your children's dreams . . .

MAMA: Walter Lee —

(*He just closes the door behind him. Mama sits alone, thinking heavily.*)

Scene II

(*Time: Friday night. A few weeks later.*)

(*At rise: Packing crates mark the intention of the family to move. Beneatha and George come in, presumably from an evening out again.*)

GEORGE: O.K. . . . O.K., whatever you say . . . (*They both sit on the couch. He tries to kiss her. She moves away.*) Look, we've had a nice evening; let's not spoil it, huh? . . .

(*He again turns her head and tries to nuzzle in and she turns away from him, not with distaste but with momentary lack of interest; in a mood to pursue what they were talking about.*)

BENEATHA: I'm *trying* to talk to you.

GEORGE: We always talk.

BENEATHA: Yes — and I love to talk.

GEORGE (*exasperated; rising*): I know it and I don't mind it sometimes . . . I want you to cut it out, see — The moody stuff, I mean. I don't like it. You're a nice-looking girl . . . all over. That's all you need, honey, forget the atmosphere. Guys aren't going to go for the atmosphere — they're going to go for what they see. Be glad for that. Drop the Garbo routine. It doesn't go with you. As for myself, I want a nice — (*groping*) — simple (*thoughtfully*) — sophisticated girl . . . not a poet — O.K.?

(*He starts to kiss her, she rebuffs him again, and he jumps up.*)

BENEATHA: Why are you angry, George?

GEORGE: Because this is stupid! I don't go out with you to discuss the nature of "quiet desperation" or to hear all about your thoughts — because the world will go on thinking what it thinks regardless —

BENEATHA: Then why read books? Why go to school?

GEORGE (*with artificial patience, counting on his fingers*): It's simple. You read books — to learn facts — to get grades — to pass the course — to get a degree. That's all — it has nothing to do with thoughts.

(*A long pause.*)

BENEATHA: I see. (*He starts to sit.*) Good night, George.

(*George looks at her a little oddly and starts to exit. He meets Mama coming in.*)

GEORGE: Oh — hello, Mrs. Younger.

MAMA: Hello, George, how you feeling?

GEORGE: Fine — fine, how are you?

MAMA: Oh, a little tired. You know them steps can get you after a day's work. You all have a nice time tonight?

GEORGE: Yes — a fine time. A fine time.

MAMA: Well, good night.

GEORGE: Good night. (*He exits. Mama closes the door behind her.*)

MAMA: Hello, honey. What you sitting like that for?

BENEATHA: I'm just sitting.

MAMA: Didn't you have a nice time?

BENEATHA: No.

MAMA: No? What's the matter?

BENEATHA: Mama, George is a fool — honest. (*She rises.*)

MAMA (*Hustling around unloading the packages she has entered with. She stops.*): Is he, baby?

BENEATHA: Yes.

(*Beneatha makes up Travis's bed as she talks.*)

MAMA: You sure?

BENEATHA: Yes.

MAMA: Well — I guess you better not waste your time with no fools.

(*Beneatha looks up at her mother, watching her put groceries in the refrigerator. Finally she gathers up her things and starts into the bedroom. At the door she stops and looks back at her mother.*)

BENEATHA: Mama —

MAMA: Yes, baby —

BENEATHA: Thank you.

MAMA: For what?

BENEATHA: For understanding me this time.

(*She exits quickly and the mother stands, smiling a little, looking at the place where Beneatha just stood. Ruth enters.*)

RUTH: Now don't you fool with any of this stuff, Lena —

MAMA: Oh, I just thought I'd sort a few things out. Is Brother here?

RUTH: Yes.

MAMA (*with concern*): Is he —

RUTH (*reading her eyes*): Yes.

(*Mama is silent and someone knocks on the door. Mama and Ruth exchange weary and knowing glances and Ruth opens it to admit the neighbor, Mrs. Johnson,° who is a rather squeaky wide-eyed lady of no particular age, with a newspaper under her arm.*)

MAMA (*changing her expression to acute delight and a ringing cheerful greeting*): Oh — hello there, Johnson.

JOHNSON (*this is a woman who decided long ago to be enthusiastic about EVERYTHING in life and she is inclined to wave her wrist vigorously at the height of her exclamatory comments*): Hello there, yourself! H'you this evening, Ruth?

RUTH (*not much of a deceptive type*): Fine, Mis' Johnson, h'you?

JOHNSON: Fine. (*Reaching out quickly, playfully, and patting Ruth's stomach.*) Ain't you starting to poke out none yet! (*She mugs with delight at the overfamiliar remark and her eyes dart around looking at the crates and packing preparation; Mama's face is a cold sheet of endurance.*) Oh, ain't we getting ready round here, though! Yessir! Lookathere! I'm telling

Mrs. Johnson: This character and the scene of her visit were cut from the original production and early editions of the play.

you the Youngers is really getting ready to "move on up a little higher!" — Bless God!

MAMA (*a little drily, doubting the total sincerity of the Blesser*): Bless God.

JOHNSON: He's good, ain't He?

MAMA: Oh yes, He's good.

JOHNSON: I mean sometimes He works in mysterious ways . . . but He works, don't He!

MAMA (*the same*): Yes, he does.

JOHNSON: I'm just soooooo happy for y'all. And this here child — (*about Ruth*) looks like she could just pop open with happiness, don't she. Where's all the rest of the family?

MAMA: Bennie's gone to bed —

JOHNSON: Ain't no . . . (*the implication is pregnancy*) sickness done hit you — I hope . . . ?

MAMA: No — she just tired. She was out this evening.

JOHNSON (*all is a coo, an emphatic coo*): Aw — ain't that lovely. She still going out with the little Murchison boy?

MAMA (*drily*): Ummmm huh.

JOHNSON: That's lovely. You sure got lovely children, Younger. Me and Isaiah talks all the time 'bout what fine children you was blessed with. We sure do.

MAMA: Ruth, give Mis' Johnson a piece of sweet potato pie and some milk.

JOHNSON: Oh honey, I can't stay hardly a minute — I just dropped in to see if there was anything I could do. (*Accepting the food easily.*) I guess y'all seen the news what's all over the colored paper this week . . .

MAMA: No — didn't get mine yet this week.

JOHNSON (*lifting her head and blinking with the spirit of catastrophe*): You mean you ain't read 'bout them colored people that was bombed out their place out there?

(*Ruth straightens with concern and takes the paper and reads it. Johnson notices her and feeds commentary.*)

JOHNSON: Ain't it something how bad these here white folks is getting here in Chicago! Lord, getting so you think you right down in Mississippi! (*With a tremendous and rather insincere sense of melodrama.*) 'Course I thinks it's wonderful how our folks keeps on pushing out. You hear some of these Negroes round here talking 'bout how they don't go where they ain't wanted and all that — but not me, honey! (*This is a lie.*) Wilhemenia Othella Johnson goes anywhere, any time she feels like it! (*With head movement for emphasis.*) Yes I do! Why if we left it up to these here crackers the poor niggers wouldn't have nothing — (*She clasps her hand over her mouth.*) Oh, I always forgets you don't 'low that word in your house.

MAMA (*quietly, looking at her*): No — I don't 'low it.

JOHNSON (*vigorously again*): Me neither! I was just telling Isaiah yesterday when he come using it in front of me — I said, "Isaiah, it's just like Mis' Younger says all the time —"

MAMA: Don't you want some more pie?

JOHNSON: No — no thank you; this was lovely. I got to get on over home and have my midnight coffee. I hear some people say it don't let them sleep but I finds I can't close my eyes right lessen I done had that laaaast cup of coffee . . . (*She waits. A beat. Undaunted.*) My Good-night coffee, I calls it!

MAMA (*with much eye-rolling and communication between herself and Ruth*): Ruth, why don't you give Mis' Johnson some coffee.

(*Ruth gives Mama an unpleasant look for her kindness.*)

JOHNSON (*accepting the coffee*): Where's Brother tonight?

MAMA: He's lying down.

JOHNSON: Mmmmmmm, he sure gets his beauty rest, don't he? Good-looking man. Sure is a good-looking man! (*Reaching out to pat Ruth's stomach again.*) I guess that's how come we keep on having babies around here. (*She winks at Mama.*) One thing 'bout Brother, he always know how to have a *good* time. And soooooo ambitious! I bet it was his idea y'all moving out to Clybourne Park. Lord — I bet this time next month y'all's names will have been in the papers plenty — (*Holding up her hands to mark off each word of the headline she can see in front of her.*) "NEGROS INVADE CLYBOURNE PARK — BOMBED!"

MAMA (*she and Ruth look at the woman in amazement*): We ain't exactly moving out there to get bombed.

JOHNSON: Oh, honey — you know I'm praying to God every day that don't nothing like that happen! But you have to think of life like it is — and these here Chicago peckerwoods is some baaaad peckerwoods.

MAMA (*wearily*): We done thought about all that Mis' Johnson.

(*Beneatha comes out of the bedroom in her robe and passes through to the bathroom. Mrs. Johnson turns.*)

JOHNSON: Hello there, Bennie!

BENEATHA (*crisply*): Hello, Mrs. Johnson.

JOHNSON: How is school?

BENEATHA (*crisply*): Fine, thank you. (*She goes out.*)

JOHNSON (*insulted*): Getting so she don't have much to say to nobody.

MAMA: The child was on her way to the bathroom.

JOHNSON: I know — but sometimes she act like ain't got time to pass the time of day with nobody ain't been to college. Oh — I ain't criticizing her none. It's just — you know how some of our young people gets when they get a little education. (*Mama and Ruth say nothing, just look at her.*) Yes — well. Well, I guess I better get on home. (*Unmoving.*) 'Course I can understand how she must be proud and everything — being the only one in the family to make something of herself. I know just being a chauffeur ain't never satisfied Brother none. He shouldn't feel like that, though. Ain't nothing wrong with being a chauffeur.

MAMA: There's plenty wrong with it.

JOHNSON: What?

MAMA: Plenty. My husband always said being any kind of a servant wasn't a fit thing for a man to have to be. He always said a man's hands was made to make things, or to turn the earth with — not to drive nobody's car for 'em — or — (*she looks at her own hands*) carry they slop jars. And my boy is just like him — he wasn't meant to wait on nobody.

JOHNSON (*rising, somewhat offended*): Mmmmmm-mmm. The Youngers is too much for me! (*She looks around.*) You sure one proud-acting bunch of colored folks. Well — I always thinks like Booker T. Washington said that time — "Education has spoiled many a good plow hand" —

MAMA: Is that what old Booker T. said?

JOHNSON: He sure did.

MAMA: Well, it sounds just like him. The fool.

JOHNSON (*indignantly*): Well — he was one of our great men.

MAMA: Who said so?

JOHNSON (*nonplussed*): You know, me and you ain't never agreed about some things, Lena Younger. I guess I better be going —

RUTH (*quickly*): Good night.

JOHNSON: Good night. Oh — (*Thrusting it at her.*) You can keep the paper! (*With a trill.*) 'Night.

MAMA: Good night, Mis' Johnson.

(*Mrs. Johnson exits.*)

RUTH: If ignorance was gold . . .

MAMA: Shush. Don't talk about folks behind their backs.

RUTH: You do.

MAMA: I'm old and corrupted. (*Beneatha enters.*) You was rude to Mis' Johnson, Beneatha, and I don't like it at all.

BENEATHA (*at her door*): Mama, if there are two things we, as a people, have got to overcome, one is the Klu Klux Klan — and the other is Mrs. Johnson. (*She exits.*)

MAMA: Smart aleck.

(*The phone rings.*)

RUTH: I'll get it.

MAMA: Lord, ain't this a popular place tonight.

RUTH (*at the phone*): Hello — Just a minute. (*Goes to door.*) Walter, it's Mrs. Arnold. (*Waits. Goes back to the phone. Tense.*) Hello. Yes, this is his wife speaking . . . He's lying down now. Yes . . . well, he'll be in tomorrow. He's been very sick. Yes — I know we should have called, but we were so sure he'd be able to come in today. Yes — yes, I'm very sorry. Yes . . . Thank you very much. (*She hangs up. Walter is standing in the doorway of the bedroom behind her.*) That was Mrs. Arnold.

WALTER (*indifferently*): Was it?

RUTH: She said if you don't come in tomorrow that they are getting a new man . . .

WALTER: Ain't that sad — ain't that crying sad.

RUTH: She said Mr. Arnold has had to take a cab for

three days . . . Walter, you ain't been to work for three days! (*This is a revelation to her.*) Where you been, Walter Lee Younger? (*Walter looks at her and starts to laugh.*) You're going to lose your job.

WALTER: That's right . . . (*He turns on the radio.*)

RUTH: Oh, Walter, and with your mother working like a dog every day —

(*A steamy, deep blues pours into the room.*)

WALTER: That's sad too — Everything is sad.

MAMA: What you been doing for these three days, son?

WALTER: Mama — you don't know all the things a man what got leisure can find to do in this city . . . What's this — Friday night? Well — Wednesday I borrowed Willy Harris's car and I went for a drive . . . just me and myself and I drove and drove . . . Way out . . . way past South Chicago, and I parked the car and I sat and looked at the steel mills all day long. I just sat in the car and looked at them big black chimneys for hours. Then I drove back and I went to the Green Hat. (*Pause.*) And Thursday — Thursday I borrowed the car again and I got in it and I pointed it the other way and I drove the other way — for hours — way, way up to Wisconsin, and I looked at the farms. I just drove and looked at the farms. Then I drove back and I went to the Green Hat. (*Pause.*) And today — today I didn't get the car. Today I just walked. All over the Southside. And I looked at the Negroes and they looked at me and finally I just sat down on the curb at Thirty-ninth and South Parkway and I just sat there and watched the Negroes go by. And then I went to the Green Hat. You all sad? You all depressed? And you know where I am going right now —

(*Ruth goes out quietly.*)

MAMA: Oh, Big Walter, is this the harvest of our days?

WALTER: You know what I like about the Green Hat? I like this little cat they got there who blows a sax . . . He blows. He talks to me. He ain't but 'bout five feet tall and he's got a conked head and his eyes is always closed and he's all music —

MAMA (*rising and getting some papers out of her handbag*): Walter —

WALTER: And there's this other guy who plays the piano . . . and they got a sound. I mean they can work on some music . . . They got the best little combo in the world in the Green Hat . . . You can just sit there and drink and listen to them three men play and you realize that don't nothing matter worth a damn, but just being there —

MAMA: I've helped do it to you, haven't I, son? Walter I been wrong.

WALTER: Naw — you ain't never been wrong about nothing, Mama.

MAMA: Listen to me, now. I say I been wrong, son. That I been doing to you what the rest of the world been doing to you. (*She turns off the radio.*) Walter — (*She stops and he looks up slowly at her and she meets his eyes pleadingly.*) What you ain't never understood is that I ain't got nothing, don't own nothing, ain't never really wanted nothing that wasn't for you. There ain't nothing as precious to me . . . There ain't nothing worth holding on to, money, dreams, nothing else — if it means — if it means it's going to destroy my boy. (*She takes an envelope out of her handbag and puts it in front of him and he watches her without speaking or moving.*) I paid the man thirty-five hundred dollars down on the house. That leaves sixty-five hundred dollars. Monday morning I want you to take this money and take three thousand dollars and put it in a savings account for Beneatha's medical schooling. The rest you put in a checking account — with your name on it. And from now on any penny that come out of it or that go in it is for you to look after. For you to decide. (*She drops her hands a little helplessly.*) It ain't much, but it's all I got in the world and I'm putting it in your hands. I'm telling you to be the head of this family from now on like you supposed to be.

WALTER (*stares at the money*): You trust me like that, Mama?

MAMA: I ain't never stop trusting you. Like I ain't never stop loving you.

(*She goes out, and Walter sits looking at the money on the table. Finally, in a decisive gesture, he gets up and, in mingled joy and desperation, picks up the money. At the same moment, Travis enters for bed.*)

TRAVIS: What's the matter, Daddy? You drunk?

WALTER (*sweetly, more sweetly than we have ever known him*): No, Daddy ain't drunk. Daddy ain't going to never be drunk again . . .

TRAVIS: Well, good night, Daddy.

(*The father has come from behind the couch and leans over, embracing his son.*)

WALTER: Son, I feel like talking to you tonight.

TRAVIS: About what?

WALTER: Oh, about a lot of things. About you and what kind of man you going to be when you grow up. . . . Son — son, what do you want to be when you grow up?

TRAVIS: A bus driver.

WALTER (*laughing a little*): A what? Man, that ain't nothing to want to be!

TRAVIS: Why not?

WALTER: 'Cause, man — it ain't big enough — you know what I mean.

TRAVIS: I don't know then. I can't make up my mind. Sometimes Mama asks me that too. And sometimes when I tell her I just want to be like you — she says she don't want me to be like that and sometimes she says she does. . . .

WALTER (*gathering him up in his arms*): You know what, Travis? In seven years you going to be seventeen years old. And things is going to be very different with us in seven years Travis. . . . One day when

you are seventeen I'll come home — home from my office downtown somewhere —

TRAVIS: You don't work in no office, Daddy.

WALTER: No — but after tonight. After what your daddy gonna do tonight, there's going to be offices — a whole lot of offices. . . .

TRAVIS: What you gonna do tonight, Daddy?

WALTER: You wouldn't understand yet, son, but your daddy's gonna make a transaction . . . a business transaction that's going to change our lives. . . . That's how come one day when you 'bout seventeen years old I'll come home and I'll be pretty tired, you know what I mean, after a day of conferences and secretaries getting things wrong the way they do . . . 'cause an executive's life is hell man — (*The more he talks the farther away he gets.*) And I'll pull the car up on the driveway . . . just a plain black Chrysler, I think, with white walls — no — black tires. More elegant. Rich people don't have to be flashy . . . though I'll have to get something a little sportier for Ruth — maybe a Cadillac convertible to do her shopping in. . . . And I'll come up the steps to the house and the gardener will be clipping away at the hedges and he'll say, "Good evening, Mr. Younger." And I'll say, "Hello, Jefferson, how are you this evening?" And I'll go inside and Ruth will come downstairs and meet me at the door and we'll kiss each other and she'll take my arm and we'll go up to your room to see you sitting on the floor with the catalogues of all the great schools in America around you. . . . All the great schools in the world! And — and I'll say, all right son — it's your seventeenth birthday, what is it you've decided? . . . Just tell me where you want to go to school and you'll *go*. Just tell me, what it is you want to be — and you'll *be* it. . . . Whatever you want to be — Yessir! (*He holds his arms open for Travis.*) You just name it, son . . . (*Travis leaps into them*) and I hand you the world!

(*Walter's voice has risen in pitch and hysterical promise and on the last line he lifts Travis high.*)

Scene III

(*Time: Saturday, moving day, one week later.*)

(*Before the curtain rises, Ruth's voice, a strident, dramatic church alto, cuts through the silence.*)

(*It is, in the darkness, a triumphant surge, a penetrating statement of expectation: "Oh, Lord, I don't feel no ways tired! Children, oh, glory hallelujah!"*)

(*As the curtain rises we see that Ruth is alone in the living room, finishing up the family's packing. It is moving day. She is nailing crates and tying cartons. Beneatha enters, carrying a guitar case, and watches her exuberant sister-in-law.*)

RUTH: Hey!

BENEATHA (*putting away the case*): Hi.

RUTH (*pointing at a package*): Honey — look in that

package there and see what I found on sale this morning at the South Center. (*Ruth gets up and moves to the package and draws out some curtains.*) Lookahere — hand-turned hems!

BENEATHA: How do you know the window size out there?

RUTH (*who hadn't thought of that*): Oh — Well, they bound to fit something in the whole house. Anyhow, they was too good a bargain to pass up. (*Ruth slaps her head, suddenly remembering something.*) Oh, Bennie — I meant to put a special note on that carton over there. That's your mama's good china and she wants 'em to be very careful with it.

BENEATHA: I'll do it.

(*Beneatha finds a piece of paper and starts to draw large letters on it.*)

RUTH: You know what I'm going to do soon as I get in that new house?

BENEATHA: What?

RUTH: Honey — I'm going to run me a tub of water up to here . . . (*With her fingers practically up to her nostrils.*) And I'm going to get in it — and I am going to sit . . . and sit . . . and sit in that hot water and the first person who knocks to tell *me* to hurry up and come out —

BENEATHA: Gets shot at sunrise.

RUTH (*laughing happily*): You said it, sister! (*Noticing how large Beneatha is absent-mindedly making the note.*) Honey, they ain't going to read that from no airplane.

BENEATHA (*laughing herself*): I guess I always think things have more emphasis if they are big, somehow.

RUTH (*looking up at her and smiling*): You and your brother seem to have that as a philosophy of life. Lord, that man — done changed so 'round here. You know — you know what we did last night? Me and Walter Lee?

BENEATHA: What?

RUTH (*smiling to herself*): We went to the movies. (*Looking at Beneatha to see if she understands.*) We went to the movies. You know the last time me and Walter went to the movies together?

BENEATHA: No.

RUTH: Me neither. That's how long it been. (*Smiling again.*) But we went last night. The picture wasn't much good, but that didn't seem to matter. We went — and we held hands.

BENEATHA: Oh, Lord!

RUTH: We held hands — and you know what?

BENEATHA: What?

RUTH: When we come out of the show it was late and dark and all the stores and things was closed up . . . and it was kind of chilly and there wasn't many people on the streets . . . and we was still holding hands, me and Walter.

BENEATHA: You're killing me.

(*Walter enters with a large package. His happiness is deep in him; he cannot keep still with his newfound exu-*berance. He is singing and wiggling and snapping his fingers. He puts his package in a corner and puts a phonograph record which he has brought in with him, on the record player. As the music, soulful and sensuous, comes up he dances over to Ruth and tries to get her to dance with him. She gives in at last to his raunchiness and in a fit of giggling allows herself to be drawn into his mood. They dip and she melts into his arms in a classic, body-melding "slow drag."*)

BENEATHA (*regarding them a long time as they dance, then drawing in her breath for a deeply exaggerated comment which she does not particularly mean*): Talk about — olddddddddddd — fashionedddddddd — Negroes!

WALTER (*stopping momentarily*): What kind of Negroes?

(*He says this in fun. He is not angry with her today, nor with anyone. He starts to dance with his wife again.*)

BENEATHA: Old-fashioned.

WALTER (*as he dances with Ruth*): You know, when these *New Negroes* have their convention — (*pointing at his sister*) — that is going to be the chairman of the Committee on Unending Agitation. (*He goes on dancing, then stops.*) Race, race, race! . . . Girl, I do believe you are the first person in the history of the entire human race to successfully brainwash yourself. (*Beneatha breaks up and he goes on dancing. He stops again, enjoying his tease.*) Damn, even the N double A C P takes a holiday sometimes! (*Beneatha and Ruth laugh. He dances with Ruth some more and starts to laugh and stops and pantomimes someone over an operating table.*) I can just see that chick someday looking down at some poor cat on an operating table and before she starts to slice him, she says . . . (*pulling his sleeves back maliciously*) "By the way, what are your views on civil rights down there? . . ."

(*He laughs at her again and starts to dance happily. The bell sounds.*)

BENEATHA: Sticks and stones may break my bones but . . . words will never hurt me!

(*Beneatha goes to the door and opens it as Walter and Ruth go on with the clowning. Beneatha is somewhat surprised to see a quiet-looking middle-aged white man in a business suit holding his hat and a briefcase in his hand and consulting a small piece of paper.*)

MAN: Uh — how do you do, miss. I am looking for a Mrs. — (*he looks at the slip of paper*) Mrs. Lena Younger? (*He stops short, struck dumb at the sight of the oblivious Walter and Ruth.*)

BENEATHA (*smoothing her hair with slight embarrassment*): Oh — yes, that's my mother. Excuse me. (*She closes the door and turns to quiet the other two.*) Ruth! Brother! (*Enunciating precisely but soundlessly: "There's a white man at the door!" They stop dancing, Ruth cuts off the phonograph, Beneatha opens the door. The man casts a curious quick glance at all of them.*) Uh — come in please.

MAN (*coming in*): Thank you.

BENEATHA: My mother isn't here just now. Is it business?

MAN: Yes . . . well, of a sort.

WALTER (*freely, the Man of the House*): Have a seat. I'm Mrs. Younger's son. I look after most of her business matters.

(*Ruth and Beneatha exchange amused glances.*)

MAN (*regarding Walter, and sitting*): Well — My name is Karl Lindner . . .

WALTER (*stretching out his hand*): Walter Younger. This is my wife — (*Ruth nods politely*) — and my sister.

LINDNER: How do you do.

WALTER (*amiably, as he sits himself easily on a chair, leaning forward on his knees with interest and looking expectantly into the newcomer's face*): What can we do for you, Mr. Lindner!

LINDNER (*some minor shuffling of the hat and briefcase on his knees*): Well — I am a representative of the Clybourne Park Improvement Association —

WALTER (*pointing*): Why don't you sit your things on the floor?

LINDNER: Oh — yes. Thank you. (*He slides the briefcase and hat under the chair.*) And as I was saying — I am from the Clybourne Park Improvement Association and we have had it brought to our attention at the last meeting that you people — or at least your mother — has bought a piece of residential property at — (*he digs for the slip of paper again*) — four o six Clybourne Street . . .

WALTER: That's right. Care for something to drink? Ruth, get Mr. Lindner a beer.

LINDNER (*upset for some reason*): Oh — no, really. I mean thank you very much, but no thank you.

RUTH: (*innocently*): Some coffee?

LINDNER: Thank you, nothing at all.

(*Beneatha is watching the man carefully.*)

LINDNER: Well, I don't know how much you folks know about our organization. (*He is a gentle man; thoughtful and somewhat labored in his manner.*) It is one of these community organizations set up to look after — oh, you know, things like block upkeep and special projects and we also have what we call our New Neighbors Orientation Committee . . .

BENEATHA (*drily*): Yes — and what do they do?

LINDNER (*turning a little to her and then returning the main force to Walter*): Well — it's what you might call a sort of welcoming committee, I guess. I mean they, we — I'm the chairman of the committee — go around and see the new people who move into the neighborhood and sort of give them the lowdown on the way we do things out in Clybourne Park.

BENEATHA (*with appreciation of the two meanings, which escape Ruth and Walter*): Un-huh.

LINDNER: And we also have the category of what the association calls — (*he looks elsewhere*) — uh — special community problems . . .

BENEATHA: Yes — and what are some of those?

WALTER: Girl, let the man talk.

LINDNER (*with understated relief*): Thank you. I would sort of like to explain this thing in my own way. I mean I want to explain to you in a certain way.

WALTER: Go ahead.

LINDNER: Yes. Well. I'm going to try to get right to the point. I'm sure we'll all appreciate that in the long run.

BENEATHA: Yes.

WALTER: Be still now!

LINDNER: Well —

RUTH (*still innocently*): Would you like another chair — you don't look comfortable.

LINDNER (*more frustrated than annoyed*): No, thank you very much. Please. Well — to get right to the point I — (*a great breath, and he is off at last*) I am sure you people must be aware of some of the incidents which have happened in various parts of the city when colored people have moved into certain areas — (*Beneatha exhales heavily and starts tossing a piece of fruit up and down in the air.*) Well — because we have what I think is going to be a unique type of organization in American community life — not only do we deplore that kind of thing — but we are trying to do something about it. (*Beneatha stops tossing and turns with a new and quizzical interest to the man.*) We feel — (*gaining confidence in his mission because of the interest in the faces of the people he is talking to*) — we feel that most of the trouble in this world, when you come right down to it — (*he hits his knee for emphasis*) — most of the trouble exists because people just don't sit down and talk to each other.

RUTH (*nodding as she might in church, pleased with the remark*): You can say that again, mister.

LINDNER (*more encouraged by such affirmation*): That we don't try hard enough in this world to understand the other fellow's problem. The other guy's point of view.

RUTH: Now that's right.

(*Beneatha and Walter merely watch and listen with genuine interest.*)

LINDNER: Yes — that's the way we feel out in Clybourne Park. And that's why I was elected to come here this afternoon and talk to you people. Friendly like, you know, the way people should talk to each other and see if we couldn't find some way to work this thing out. As I say, the whole business is a matter of *caring* about the other fellow. Anybody can see that you are a nice family of folks, hard-working and honest I'm sure. (*Beneatha frowns slightly, quizzically, her head tilted regarding him.*) Today everybody knows what it means to be on the outside of *something*. And of course, there is always somebody who is out to take advantage of people who don't always understand.

WALTER: What do you mean?

LINDNER: Well — you see our community is made up of people who've worked hard as the dickens for years to build up that little community. They're not rich and fancy people; just hard-working, honest people who don't really have much but those little homes and a dream of the kind of community they want to raise their children in. Now, I don't say we are perfect and there is a lot wrong in some of the things they want. But you've got to admit that a man, right or wrong, has the right to want to have the neighborhood he lives in a certain kind of way. And at the moment the overwhelming majority of our people out there feel that people get along better, take more of a common interest in the life of the community, when they share a common background. I want you to believe me when I tell you that race prejudice simply doesn't enter into it. It is a matter of the people of Clybourne Park believing, rightly or wrongly, as I say, that for the happiness of all concerned that our Negro families are happier when they live in their *own* communities.

BENEATHA (*with a grand and bitter gesture*): This, friends, is the Welcoming Committee!

WALTER (*dumfounded, looking at Lindner*): Is this what you came marching all the way over here to tell us?

LINDNER: Well, now we've been having a fine conversation. I hope you'll hear me all the way through.

WALTER (*tightly*): Go ahead, man.

LINDNER: You see — in the face of all the things I have said, we are prepared to make your family a very generous offer . . .

BENEATHA: Thirty pieces and not a coin less!

WALTER: Yeah!

LINDNER (*putting on his glasses and drawing a form out of the briefcase*): Our association is prepared, through the collective effort of our people, to buy the house from you at a financial gain to your family.

RUTH: Lord have mercy, ain't this the living gall!

WALTER: All right, you through?

LINDNER: Well, I want to give you the exact terms of the financial arrangement —

WALTER: We don't want to hear no exact terms of no arrangements. I want to know if you got any more to tell us 'bout getting together?

LINDNER (*taking off his glasses*): Well — I don't suppose that you feel . . .

WALTER: Never mind how I feel — you got any more to say 'bout how people ought to sit down and talk to each other? . . . Get out of my house, man.

(*He turns his back and walks to the door.*)

LINDNER (*looking around at the hostile faces and reaching and assembling his hat and briefcase*): Well — I don't understand why you people are reacting this way. What do you think you are going to gain by moving into a neighborhood where you just aren't wanted and where some elements — well — people can get awful worked up when they feel that their whole way of life and everything they've ever worked for is threatened.

WALTER: Get out.

LINDNER (*at the door, holding a small card*): Well — I'm sorry it went like this.

WALTER: Get out.

LINDNER (*almost sadly regarding Walter*): You just can't force people to change their hearts, son.

(*He turns and puts his card on a table and exits. Walter pushes the door to with stinging hatred, and stands looking at it. Ruth just sits and Beneatha just stands. They say nothing. Mama and Travis enter.*)

MAMA: Well — this all the packing got done since I left out of here this morning. I testify before God that my children got all the energy of the *dead*! What time the moving men due?

BENEATHA: Four o'clock. You had a caller, Mama.

(*She is smiling, teasingly.*)

MAMA: Sure enough — who?

BENEATHA (*her arms folded saucily*): The Welcoming Committee.

(*Walter and Ruth giggle.*)

MAMA (*innocently*): Who?

BENEATHA: The Welcoming Committee. They said they're sure going to be glad to see you when you get there.

WALTER (*devilishly*): Yeah, they said they can't hardly wait to see your face.

(*Laughter.*)

MAMA (*sensing their facetiousness*): What's the matter with you all?

WALTER: Ain't nothing the matter with us. We just telling you 'bout the gentleman who came to see you this afternoon. From the Clybourne Park Improvement Association.

MAMA: What he want?

RUTH (*in the same mood as Beneatha and Walter*): To welcome you, honey.

WALTER: He said they can't hardly wait. He said the one thing they don't have, that they just *dying* to have out there is a fine family of fine colored people! (*To Ruth and Beneatha.*) Ain't that right!

RUTH (*mockingly*): Yeah! He left his card —

BENEATHA (*handing card to Mama*): In case.

(*Mama reads and throws it on the floor — understanding and looking off as she draws her chair up to the table on which she has put her plant and some sticks and some cord.*)

MAMA: Father, give us strength. (*Knowingly — and without fun.*) Did he threaten us?

BENEATHA: Oh — Mama — they don't do it like that anymore. He talked Brotherhood. He said everybody ought to learn how to sit down and hate each other with good Christian fellowship.

(*She and Walter shake hands to ridicule the remark.*)

MAMA (*sadly*): Lord, protect us . . .

RUTH: You should hear the money those folks raised to buy the house from us. All we paid and then some.

BENEATHA: What they think we going to do — eat 'em?

RUTH: No, honey, marry 'em.

MAMA (*shaking her head*): Lord, Lord, Lord . . .

RUTH: Well — that's the way the crackers crumble. (*A beat.*) Joke.

BENEATHA (*laughingly noticing what her mother is doing*): Mama, what are you doing?

MAMA: Fixing my plant so it won't get hurt none on the way . . .

BENEATHA: Mama, you going to take *that* to the new house?

MAMA: Un-huh —

BENEATHA: That raggedy-looking old thing?

MAMA (*stopping and looking at her*): It expresses ME!

RUTH (*with delight, to Beneatha*): So there, Miss Thing!

(*Walter comes to Mama suddenly and bends down behind her and squeezes her in his arms with all his strength. She is overwhelmed by the suddenness of it and, though delighted, her manner is like that of Ruth and Travis.*)

MAMA: Look out now, boy! You make me mess up my thing here!

WALTER (*his face lit, he slips down on his knees beside her, his arms still about her*): Mama . . . you know what it means to climb up in the chariot?

MAMA (*gruffly, very happy*): Get on away from me now . . .

RUTH (*near the gift-wrapped package, trying to catch Walter's eye*): Psst —

WALTER: What the old song say, Mama . . .

RUTH: Walter — Now?

(*She is pointing at the package.*)

WALTER (*speaking the lines, sweetly, playfully, in his mother's face*): I got wings . . . you got wings . . .

All God's Children got wings . . .

MAMA: Boy — get out of my face and do some work . . .

WALTER: When I get to heaven gonna put on my wings, Gonna fly all over God's heaven . . .

BENEATHA (*teasingly, from across the room*): Everybody talking 'bout heaven ain't going there!

WALTER (*to Ruth, who is carrying the box across to them*): I don't know, you think we ought to give her that . . . Seems to me she ain't been very appreciative around here.

MAMA (*eyeing the box, which is obviously a gift*): What is that?

WALTER (*taking it from Ruth and putting it on the table in front of Mama*): Well — what you all think? Should we give it to her?

RUTH: Oh — she was pretty good today.

MAMA: I'll good you —

(*She turns her eyes to the box again.*)

BENEATHA: Open it, Mama.

(*She stands up, looks at it, turns, and looks at all of them, and then presses her hands together and does not open the package.*)

WALTER (*sweetly*): Open it, Mama. It's for you. (*Mama looks in his eyes. It is the first present in her life without its being Christmas. Slowly she opens her package and lifts out, one by one, a brand-new sparkling set of gardening tools. Walter continues, prodding.*) Ruth made up the note — read it . . .

MAMA (*picking up the card and adjusting her glasses*): "To our own Mrs. Miniver — Love from Brother, Ruth and Beneatha." Ain't that lovely . . .

TRAVIS (*tugging at his father's sleeve*): Daddy, can I give her mine now?

WALTER: All right, son. (*Travis flies to get his gift.*)

MAMA: Now I don't have to use my knives and forks no more . . .

WALTER: Travis didn't want to go in with the rest of us, Mama. He got his own. (*Somewhat amused.*) We don't know what it is . . .

TRAVIS (*racing back in the room with a large hatbox and putting it in front of his grandmother*): Here!

MAMA: Lord have mercy, baby. You done gone and bought your grandmother a hat?

TRAVIS (*very proud*): Open it!

(*She does and lifts out an elaborate, but very elaborate, wide gardening hat, and all the adults break up at the sight of it.*)

RUTH: Travis, honey, what is that?

TRAVIS (*who thinks it is beautiful and appropriate*): It's a gardening hat! Like the ladies always have on in the magazines when they work in their gardens.

BENEATHA (*giggling fiercely*): Travis — we were trying to make Mama Mrs. Miniver — not Scarlett O'Hara!

MAMA (*indignantly*): What's the matter with you all! This here is a beautiful hat! (*Absurdly.*) I always wanted me one just like it!

(*She pops it on her head to prove it to her grandson, and the hat is ludicrous and considerably oversized.*)

RUTH: Hot dog! Go, Mama!

WALTER (*doubled over with laughter*): I'm sorry, Mama — but you look like you ready to go out and chop you some cotton sure enough!

(*They all laugh except Mama, out of deference to Travis's feelings.*)

MAMA (*gathering the boy up to her*): Bless your heart — this is the prettiest hat I ever owned — (*Walter, Ruth, and Beneatha chime in — noisily, festively, and insincerely congratulating Travis on his gift.*) What are we all standing around here for? We ain't finished packin' yet. Bennie, you ain't packed one book.

(*The bell rings.*)

BENEATHA: That couldn't be the movers . . . it's not hardly two good yet —

(*Beneatha goes into her room. Mama starts for door.*)

WALTER (*turning, stiffening*): Wait — wait — I'll get it.

(*He stands and looks at the door.*)

MAMA: You expecting company, son?
WALTER (*just looking at the door*): Yeah — yeah . . .

(*Mama looks at Ruth, and they exchange innocent and unfrightened glances.*)

MAMA (*not understanding*): Well, let them in, son.
BENEATHA (*from her room*): We need some more string.
MAMA: Travis — you run to the hardware and get me some string cord.

(*Mama goes out and Walter turns and looks at Ruth. Travis goes to a dish for money.*)

RUTH: Why don't you answer the door, man?
WALTER (*suddenly bounding across the floor to embrace her*): 'Cause sometimes it hard to let the future begin! (*Stooping down in her face.*)
I got wings! You got wings!
All God's children got wings!
(*He crosses to the door and throws it open. Standing there is a very slight little man in a not too prosperous business suit and with haunted frightened eyes and a hat pulled down tightly, brim up, around his forehead. Travis passes between the men and exits. Walter leans deep in the man's face, still in his jubilance.*) When I get to heaven gonna put on my wings, Gonna fly all over God's heaven . . . (*The little man just stares at him.*) Heaven — (*Suddenly he stops and looks past the little man into the empty hallway.*) Where's Willy, man?
BOBO: He ain't with me.
WALTER (*not disturbed*): Oh — come on in. You know my wife.
BOBO (*dumbly, taking off his hat*): Yes — h'you, Miss Ruth.
RUTH (*quietly, a mood apart from her husband already, seeing Bobo*): Hello, Bobo.
WALTER: You right on time today . . . Right on time. That's the way! (*He slaps Bobo on his back.*) Sit down . . . lemme hear.

(*Ruth stands stiffly and quietly in back of them, as though somehow she senses death, her eyes fixed on her husband.*)

BOBO (*his frightened eyes on the floor, his hat in his hands*): Could I please get a drink of water, before I tell you about it, Walter Lee?

(*Walter does not take his eyes off the man. Ruth goes blindly to the tap and gets a glass of water and brings it to Bobo.*)

WALTER: There ain't nothing wrong, is there?
BOBO: Lemme tell you —
WALTER: Man — didn't nothing go wrong?
BOBO: Lemme tell you — Walter Lee. (*Looking at Ruth and talking to her more than to Walter.*) You know how it was. I got to tell you how it was. I mean first I got to tell you how it was all the way . . . I mean about the money I put in, Walter Lee . . .
WALTER (*with taut agitation now*): What about the money you put in?
BOBO: Well — it wasn't much as we told you — me and Willy — (*He stops.*) I'm sorry, Walter. I got a bad feeling about it. I got a real bad feeling about it . . .
WALTER: Man, what you telling me about all this for? . . . Tell me what happened in Springfield . . .
BOBO: Springfield.
RUTH (*like a dead woman*): What was supposed to happen in Springfield?
BOBO (*to her*): This deal that me and Walter went into with Willy — Me and Willy was going to go down to Springfield and spread some money 'round so's we wouldn't have to wait so long for the liquor license . . . That's what we were going to do. Everybody said that was the way you had to do, you understand, Miss Ruth?
WALTER: Man — what happened down there?
BOBO (*a pitiful man, near tears*): I'm trying to tell you, Walter.
WALTER (*screaming at him suddenly*): THEN TELL ME, GODDAMMIT . . . WHAT'S THE MATTER WITH YOU?
BOBO: Man . . . I didn't go to no Springfield, yesterday.
WALTER (*halted, life hanging in the moment*): Why not?
BOBO (*the long way, the hard way to tell*): 'Cause I didn't have no reasons to . . .
WALTER: Man, what are you talking about!
BOBO: I'm talking about the fact that when I got to the train station yesterday morning — eight o'clock like we planned . . . Man — *Willy didn't never show up.*
WALTER: Why . . . where was he . . . where is he?
BOBO: That's what I'm trying to tell you . . . I don't know . . . I waited six hours . . . I called his house . . . and I waited . . . six hours . . . I waited in that train station six hours . . . (*Breaking into tears.*) That was all the extra money I had in the world . . . (*Looking up at Walter with the tears running down his face.*) Man, *Willy is gone.*
WALTER: Gone, what you mean Willy is gone? Gone where? You mean he went by himself. You mean he went off to Springfield by himself — to take care of getting the license — (*Turns and looks anxiously at Ruth.*) You mean maybe he didn't want too many people in on the business down there? (*Looks to Ruth again, as before.*) You know Willy got his own ways. (*Looks back to Bobo.*) Maybe you was late

yesterday and he just went on down there without you. Maybe — maybe — he's been callin' you at home tryin' to tell you what happened or something. Maybe — maybe — he just got sick. He's somewhere — he's got to be somewhere. We just got to find him — me and you got to find him. (*Grabs Bobo senselessly by the collar and starts to shake him.*) We got to!

BOBO (*in sudden angry, frightened agony*): What's the matter· with you, Walter! *When a cat take off with your money he don't leave you no road maps!*

WALTER (*turning madly, as though he is looking for Willy in the very room*): Willy! . . . Willy . . . don't do it . . . Please don't do it . . . Man, not with that money . . . Man, please, not with that money . . . Oh, God . . . Don't let it be true . . . (*He is wandering around, crying out for Willy and looking for him or perhaps for help from God.*) Man . . . I trusted you . . . Man, I put my life in your hands . . . (*He starts to crumple down on the floor as Ruth just covers her face in horror. Mama opens the door and comes into the room, with Beneatha behind her.*) Man . . . (*He starts to pound the floor with his fists, sobbing wildly.*) THAT MONEY IS MADE OUT MY FATHER'S FLESH ——

BOBO (*standing over him helplessly*): I'm sorry, Walter . . . (*Only Walter's sobs reply. Bobo puts on his hat.*) I had my life staked on this deal, too . . .

(*He exits.*)

MAMA (*to Walter*): Son — (*She goes to him, bends down to him, talks to his bent head.*) Son . . . Is it gone? Son, I gave you sixty-five hundred dollars. Is it gone? All of it? Beneatha's money too?

WALTER (*lifting his head slowly*): Mama . . . I never . . . went to the bank at all . . .

MAMA (*not wanting to believe him*): You mean . . . your sister's school money . . . you used that too . . . Walter? . . .

WALTER: Yessss! All of it . . . It's all gone . . .

(*There is total silence. Ruth stands with her face covered with her hands; Beneatha leans forlornly against a wall, fingering a piece of red ribbon from the mother's gift. Mama stops and looks at her son without recognition and then, quite without thinking about it, starts to beat him senselessly in the face. Beneatha goes to them and stops it.*)

BENEATHA: Mama!

(*Mama stops and looks at both of her children and rises slowly and wanders vaguely, aimlessly away from them.*)

MAMA: I seen . . . him . . . night after night . . . come in . . . and look at that rug . . . and then look at me . . . the red showing in his eyes . . . the veins moving in his head . . . I seen him grow thin and old before he was forty . . . working and working and working like somebody's old horse . . . killing him-

self . . . and you — you give it all away in a day — (*She raises her arms to strike him again.*)

BENEATHA: Mama —

MAMA: Oh, God . . . (*She looks up to Him.*) Look down here — and show me the strength.

BENEATHA: Mama —

MAMA (*folding over*): Strength . . .

BENEATHA (*plaintively*): Mama . . .

MAMA: Strength!

ACT III

(*An hour later.*)

(*At curtain, there is a sullen light of gloom in the living room, gray light not unlike that which began the first scene of act I. At left we can see Walter within his room, alone with himself. He is stretched out on the bed, his shirt out and open, his arms under his head. He does not smoke, he does not cry out, he merely lies there, looking up at the ceiling, much as if he were alone in the world.*)

(*In the living room Beneatha sits at the table, still surrounded by the now almost ominous packing crates. She sits looking off. We feel that this is a mood struck perhaps an hour before, and it lingers now, full of the empty sound of profound disappointment. We see on a line from her brother's bedroom the sameness of their attitudes. Presently the bell rings and Beneatha rises without ambition or interest in answering. It is Asagai, smiling broadly, striding into the room with energy and happy expectation and conversation.*)

ASAGAI: I came over . . . I had some free time. I thought I might help with the packing. Ah, I like the look of packing crates! A household in preparation for a journey! It depresses some people . . . but for me . . . it is another feeling. Something full of the flow of life, do you understand? Movement, progress . . . It makes me think of Africa.

BENEATHA: Africa!

ASAGAI: What kind of a mood is this? Have I told you how deeply you move me?

BENEATHA: He gave away the money, Asagai . . .

ASAGAI: Who gave away what money?

BENEATHA: The insurance money. My brother gave it away.

ASAGAI: Gave it away?

BENEATHA: He made an investment! With a man even Travis wouldn't have trusted with his most worn-out marbles.

ASAGAI: And it's gone?

BENEATHA: Gone!

ASAGAI: I'm very sorry . . . And you, now?

BENEATHA: Me? . . . Me? . . . Me, I'm nothing . . . Me. When I was very small . . . we used to take our sleds out in the wintertime and the only hills we had were the ice-covered stone steps of some houses down the street. And we used to fill them in with snow and make them smooth and slide down them all day . . . and it was very dangerous, you know . . . far too steep . . . and sure enough one day a kid named Rufus came down too fast and hit the sidewalk and we saw his face just split open right there in front of us . . . And I remember standing there looking at his bloody open face thinking that was the end of Rufus. But the ambulance came and they took him to the hospital and they fixed the broken bones and they sewed it all up . . . and the next time I saw Rufus he just had a little line down the middle of his face . . . I never got over that . . .

ASAGAI: What?

BENEATHA: That that was what one person could do for another, fix him up — sew up the problem, make him all right again. That was the most marvelous thing in the world . . . I wanted to do that. I always thought it was the one concrete thing in the world that a human being could do. Fix up the sick, you know — and make them whole again. This was truly being God . . .

ASAGAI: You wanted to be God?

BENEATHA: No — I wanted to cure. It used to be so important to me. I wanted to cure. It used to matter. I used to care. I mean about people and how their bodies hurt . . .

ASAGAI: And you've stopped caring?

BENEATHA: Yes — I think so.

ASAGAI: Why?

BENEATHA (bitterly): Because it doesn't seem deep enough, close enough to what ails mankind! It was a child's way of seeing things — or an idealist's.

ASAGAI: Children see things very well sometimes — and idealists even better.

BENEATHA: I know that's what you think. Because you are still where I left off. You with all your talk and dreams about Africa! You still think you can patch up the world. Cure the Great Sore of Colonialism — (loftily, mocking it) with the Penicillin of Independence —!

ASAGAI: Yes!

BENEATHA: Independence and then what? What about all the crooks and thieves and just plain idiots who will come into power and steal and plunder the same as before — only now they will be black and do it in the name of the new Independence — WHAT ABOUT THEM?!

ASAGAI: That will be the problem for another time. First we must get there.

BENEATHA: And where does it end?

ASAGAI: End? Who even spoke of an end? To life? To living?

BENEATHA: An end to misery! To stupidity! Don't you see there isn't any real progress, Asagai, there is only one large circle that we march in, around and around, each of us with our own little picture in front of us — our own little mirage that we think is the future.

ASAGAI: That is the mistake.

BENEATHA: What?

ASAGAI: What you just said — about the circle. It isn't a circle — it is simply a long line — as in geometry, you know, one that reaches into infinity. And because we cannot see the end — we also cannot see how it changes. And it is very odd but those who see the changes — who dream, who will not give up — are called idealists . . . and those who see only the circle — we call them the "realists"!

BENEATHA: Asagai, while I was sleeping in that bed in there, people went out and took the future right out of my hands! And nobody asked me, nobody consulted me — they just went out and changed my life!

ASAGAI: Was it your money?

BENEATHA: What?

ASAGAI: Was it your money he gave away?

BENEATHA: It belonged to all of us.

ASAGAI: But did you earn it? Would you have had it at all if your father had not died?

BENEATHA: No.

ASAGAI: Then isn't there something wrong in a house — in a world — where all dreams, good or bad, must depend on the death of a man? I never thought to see you like this, Alaiyo. You! Your brother made a mistake and you are grateful to him so that now you can give up the ailing human race on account of it! You talk about what good is struggle, what good is anything! Where are we all going and why are we bothering!

BENEATHA: AND YOU CANNOT ANSWER IT!

ASAGAI (shouting over her): I LIVE THE ANSWER! (Pause.) In my village at home it is the exceptional man who can even read a newspaper . . . or who ever sees a book at all. I will go home and much of what I will have to say will seem strange to the people of my village. But I will teach and work and things will happen, slowly and swiftly. At times it will seem that nothing changes at all . . . and then again the sudden dramatic events which make history leap into the future. And then quiet again. Retrogression even. Guns, murder, revolution. And I even will have moments when I wonder if the quiet was not better than all that death and hatred. But I will look about my village at the illiteracy and disease and ignorance and I will not wonder long. And perhaps . . . perhaps I will be a great man . . . I mean perhaps I will hold on to the substance of truth and find my way always with the right course . . . and perhaps for it I will be butchered in my bed some night by the servants of empire . . .

BENEATHA: The martyr!

ASAGAI (he smiles): . . . or perhaps I shall live to be a very old man, respected and esteemed in my new nation . . . And perhaps I shall hold office and this is what I'm trying to tell you, Alaiyo: Perhaps the things I believe now for my country will be wrong and outmoded, and I will not understand and do terrible things to have things my way or merely to keep my power. Don't you see that there will be young men and women — not British soldiers then, but my own black countrymen — to step out of the shadows some evening and slit my then useless throat? Don't you see they have always been there . . . that they always will be. And that such a thing as my own death will be an advance? They who might kill me even . . . actually replenish all that I was.

BENEATHA: Oh, Asagai, I know all that.

ASAGAI: Good! Then stop moaning and groaning and tell me what you plan to do.

BENEATHA: Do?

ASAGAI: I have a bit of a suggestion.

BENEATHA: What?

ASAGAI (*rather quietly for him*): That when it is all over — that you come home with me —

BENEATHA (*staring at him and crossing away with exasperation*): Oh — Asagai — at this moment you decide to be romantic!

ASAGAI (*quickly understanding the misunderstanding*): My dear, young creature of the New World — I do not mean across the city — I mean across the ocean: home — to Africa.

BENEATHA (*slowly understanding and turning to him with murmured amazement*): To Africa?

ASAGAI: Yes! . . . (*Smiling and lifting his arms playfully.*) Three hundred years later the African Prince rose up out of the seas and swept the maiden back across the middle passage over which her ancestors had come —

BENEATHA (*unable to play*): To — to Nigeria?

ASAGAI: Nigeria. Home. (*Coming to her with genuine romantic flippancy.*) I will show you our mountains and our stars; and give you cool drinks from gourds and teach you the old songs and the ways of our people — and, in time, we will pretend that — (*very softly*) — you have only been away for a day. Say that you'll come — (*He swings her around and takes her full in his arms in a kiss which proceeds to passion.*)

BENEATHA (*pulling away suddenly*): You're getting me all mixed up —

ASAGAI: Why?

BENEATHA: Too many things — too many things have happened today. I must sit down and think. I don't know what I feel about anything right this minute.

(*She promptly sits down and props her chin on her fist.*)

ASAGAI (*charmed*): All right, I shall leave you. No — don't get up. (*Touching her, gently, sweetly.*) Just sit awhile and think . . . Never be afraid to sit awhile and think. (*He goes to door and looks at her.*) How often I have looked at you and said, "Ah — so this is what the New World hath finally wrought . . ."

(*He exits. Beneatha sits on alone. Presently Walter enters from his room and starts to rummage through things, feverishly looking for something. She looks up and turns in her seat.*)

BENEATHA (*hissingly*): Yes — just look at what the New World hath wrought! . . . Just look! (*She gestures with bitter disgust.*) There he is! *Monsieur le petit bourgeois noir°* — himself! There he is — Symbol of a Rising Class! Entrepreneur! Titan° of the system! (*Walter ignores her completely and continues frantically and destructively looking for something and hurling things to floor and tearing things out of their place in his search. Beneatha ignores the eccentricity of his actions and goes on with the monologue of insult.*) Did you dream of yachts on Lake Michigan, Brother? Did you see yourself on that Great Day sitting down at the Conference Table, surrounded by all the mighty bald-headed men in America? All halted, waiting, breathless, waiting for your pronouncements on industry? Waiting for you — Chairman of the Board! (*Walter finds what he is looking for — a small piece of white paper — and pushes it in his pocket and puts on his coat and rushes out without ever having looked at her. She shouts after him.*) I look at you and I see the final triumph of stupidity in the world!

(*The door slams and she returns to just sitting again. Ruth comes quickly out of Mama's room.*)

RUTH: Who was that?

BENEATHA: Your husband.

RUTH: Where did he go?

BENEATHA: Who knows — maybe he has an appointment at U.S. Steel.

RUTH (*anxiously, with frightened eyes*): You didn't say nothing bad to him, did you?

BENEATHA: Bad? Say anything bad to him? No — I told him he was a sweet boy and full of dreams and everything is strictly peachy keen, as the ofay° kids say!

(*Mama enters from her bedroom. She is lost, vague, trying to catch hold, to make some sense of her former command of the world, but it still eludes her. A sense of waste overwhelms her gait; a measure of apology rides on her shoulders. She goes to her plant, which has remained on the table, looks at it, picks it up and takes it to the window sill and sits it outside, and she stands and looks at it a long moment. Then she closes the window, straightens her body with effort, and turns around to her children.*)

MAMA: Well — ain't it a mess in here, though? (*A false cheerfulness, a beginning of something.*) I guess we all better stop moping around and get some work done. All this unpacking and everything we got to do. (*Ruth raises her head slowly in response to the sense of the line; and Beneatha in similar manner turns very slowly to look at her mother.*) One of you all better call the moving people and tell 'em not to come.

RUTH: Tell 'em not to come?

MAMA: Of course, baby. Ain't no need in 'em coming all the way here and having to go back. They charges for that too. (*She sits down, fingers to her brow, think-*

Monsieur . . . noir: Mr. Black Lower Middle Class.
Titan: Person of great power; originally, a god.
ofay: White person, usually used disparagingly.

ing.) Lord, ever since I was a little girl, I always remembers people saying, "Lena — Lena Eggleston, you aims too high all the time. You needs to slow down and see life a little more like it is. Just slow down some." That's what they always used to say down home — "Lord, that Lena Eggleston is a high-minded thing. She'll get her due one day!"

RUTH: No, Lena . . .

MAMA: Me and Big Walter just didn't never learn right.

RUTH: Lena, no! We gotta go. Bennie — tell her . . . (*She rises and crosses to Beneatha with her arms outstretched. Beneatha doesn't respond.*) Tell her we can still move . . . the notes ain't but a hundred and twenty-five a month. We got four grown people in this house — we can work . . .

MAMA (*to herself*): Just aimed too high all the time —

RUTH (*turning and going to Mama fast — the words pouring out with urgency and desperation*): Lena — I'll work . . . I'll work twenty hours a day in all the kitchens in Chicago . . . I'll strap my baby on my back if I have to and scrub all the floors in America and wash all the sheets in America if I have to — but we got to MOVE! We got to get OUT OF HERE!!

(*Mama reaches out absently and pats Ruth's hand.*)

MAMA: No — I sees things differently now. Been thinking 'bout some of the things we could do to fix this place up some. I seen a second-hand bureau over on Maxwell Street just the other day that could fit right there. (*She points to where the new furniture might go. Ruth wanders away from her.*) Would need some new handles on it and then a little varnish and it look like something brand-new. And — we can put up them new curtains in the kitchen . . . Why this place be looking fine. Cheer us all up so that we forget trouble ever come . . . (*To Ruth.*) And you could get some nice screens to put up in your room round the baby's bassinet . . . (*She looks at both of them, pleadingly.*) Sometimes you just got to know when to give up some things . . . and hold on to what you got. . . .

(*Walter enters from the outside, looking spent and leaning against the door, his coat hanging from him.*)

MAMA: Where you been, son?

WALTER (*breathing hard*): Made a call.

MAMA: To who, son?

WALTER: To The Man. (*He heads for his room.*) MAMA: What man, baby?

WALTER (*stops in the door*): The Man, Mama. Don't you know who The Man is?

RUTH: Walter Lee?

WALTER: *The Man.* Like the guys in the streets say — The Man. Captain Boss — Mistuh Charley . . . Old Cap'n Please Mr. Bossman:

BENEATHA (*suddenly*): Lindner!

WALTER: That's right! That's good. I told him to come right over.

BENEATHA (*fiercely, understanding*): For what? What do you want to see him for!

WALTER (*looking at his sister*): We going to do business with him.

MAMA: What you talking 'bout, son?

WALTER: Talking 'bout life, Mama. You all always telling me to see life like it is. Well — I laid in there on my back today . . . and I figured it out. Life just like it is. Who gets and who don't get. (*He sits down with his coat on and laughs.*) Mama, you know it's all divided up. Life is. Sure enough. Between the takers and the "tooken." (*He laughs.*) I've figured it out finally. (*He looks around at them.*) Yeah. Some of us always getting "tooken." (*He laughs.*) People like Willy Harris, they don't never get "tooken." And you know why the rest of us do? 'Cause we all mixed up. Mixed up bad. We get to looking 'round for the right and the wrong; and we worry about it and cry about it and stay up nights trying to figure out 'bout the wrong and the right of things all the time . . . And all the time, man, them takers is out there operating, just taking and taking. Willy Harris? Shoot — Willy Harris don't even count. He don't even count in the big scheme of things. But I'll say one thing for old Willy Harris . . . he's taught me something. He's taught me to keep my eye on what counts in this world. Yeah — (*Shouting out a little.*) Thanks, Willy!

RUTH: What did you call that man for, Walter Lee?

WALTER: Called him to tell him to come on over to the show. Gonna put on a show for the man. Just what he wants to see. You see, Mama, the man came here today and he told us that them people out there where you want us to move — well they so upset they willing to pay us *not* to move! (*He laughs again.*) And — and oh, Mama — you would of been proud of the way me and Ruth and Bennie acted. We told him to get out . . . Lord have mercy! We told the man to get out! Oh, we was some proud folks this afternoon, yeah. (*He lights a cigarette.*) We were still full of that old-time stuff . . .

RUTH (*coming toward him slowly*): You talking 'bout taking them people's money to keep us from moving in that house?

WALTER: I ain't just talking 'bout it, baby — I'm telling you that's what's going to happen!

BENEATHA: Oh, God! Where is the bottom! Where is the real honest-to-God bottom so he can't go any farther!

WALTER: See — that's the old stuff. You and that boy that was here today. You all want everybody to carry a flag and a spear and sing some marching songs, huh? You wanna spend your life looking into things and trying to find the right and the wrong part, huh? Yeah. You know what's going to happen to that boy someday — he'll find himself sitting in a dungeon, locked in forever — and the takers will have the key! Forget it, baby! There ain't no causes — there ain't nothing but taking in this world, and he who takes most is smartest — and it don't make a damn bit of difference *how.*

MAMA: You making something inside me cry, son. Some awful pain inside me.

WALTER: Don't cry, Mama. Understand. That white man is going to walk in that door able to write checks for more money than we ever had. It's important to him and I'm going to help him . . . I'm going to put on the show, Mama.

MAMA: Son — I come from five generations of people who was slaves and sharecroppers — but ain't nobody in my family never let nobody pay 'em no money that was a way of telling us we wasn't fit to walk the earth. We ain't never been that poor. (*Raising her eyes and looking at him.*) We ain't never been that — dead inside.

BENEATHA: Well — we are dead now. All the talk about dreams and sunlight that goes on in this house. It's all dead now.

WALTER: What's the matter with you all! I didn't make this world! It was give to me this way! Hell, yes, I want me some yachts someday! Yes, I want to hang some real pearls 'round my wife's neck. Ain't she supposed to wear no pearls? Somebody tell me — tell me, who decides which women is suppose to wear pearls in this world. I tell you I am a *man* — and I think my wife should wear some pearls in this world!

(*This last line hangs a good while and Walter begins to move about the room. The word "Man" has penetrated his consciousness; he mumbles it to himself repeatedly between strange agitated pauses as he moves about.*)

MAMA: Baby, how you going to feel on the inside?

WALTER: Fine! . . . Going to feel fine . . . a man . . .

MAMA: You won't have nothing left then, Walter Lee.

WALTER (*coming to her*): I'm going to feel fine, Mama. I'm going to look that son-of-a-bitch in the eyes and say — (*he falters*) — and say, "All right, Mr. Lindner — (*he falters even more*) — that's *your* neighborhood out there! You got the right to keep it like you want! You got the right to have it like you want! Just write the check and — the house is yours." And — and I am going to say — (*His voice almost breaks.*) "And you — you people just put the money in my hand and you won't have to live next to this bunch of stinking niggers! . . ." (*He straightens up and moves away from his mother, walking around the room.*) And maybe — maybe I'll just get down on my black knees . . . (*He does so; Ruth and Bennie and Mama watch him in frozen horror.*) "Captain, Mistuh, Bossman — (*Groveling and grinning and wringing his hands in profoundly anguished imitation of the slow-witted movie stereotype.*) A-hee-hee-hee! Oh, yassuh boss! Yasssssuh! Great white — (*voice breaking, he forces himself to go on*) — Father, just gi' ussen de money, fo' God's sake, and we's — we's ain't gwine come out deh and dirty up yo' white folks neighborhood . . ." (*He breaks down completely.*) And I'll feel fine! Fine! FINE! (*He gets up and goes into the bedroom.*)

BENEATHA: That is not a man. That is nothing but a toothless rat.

MAMA: Yes — death done come in this here house. (*She is nodding, slowly, reflectively.*) Done come walking in my house on the lips of my children. You what supposed to be my beginning again. You — what supposed to be my harvest. (*To Beneatha.*) You — you mourning your brother?

BENEATHA: He's no brother of mine.

MAMA: What you say?

BENEATHA: I said that that individual in that room is no brother of mine.

MAMA: That's what I thought you said. You feeling like you better than he is today? (*Beneatha does not answer.*) Yes? What you tell him a minute ago? That he wasn't a man? Yes? You give him up for me? You done wrote his epitaph too — like the rest of the world? Well, who give you the privilege?

BENEATHA: Be on my side for once! You saw what he just did, Mama! You saw him — down on his knees. Wasn't it you who taught me to despise any man who would do that? Do what he's going to do?

MAMA: Yes — I taught you that. Me and your daddy. But I thought I taught you something else too . . . I thought I taught you to love him.

BENEATHA: Love him? There is nothing left to love.

MAMA: There is *always* something left to love. And if you ain't learned that, you ain't learned nothing. (*Looking at her.*) Have you cried for that boy today? I don't mean for yourself and for the family 'cause we lost the money. I mean for him: what he been through and what it done to him. Child, when do you think is the time to love somebody the most? When they done good and made things easy for everybody? Well then, you ain't through learning — because that ain't the time at all. It's when he's at his lowest and can't believe in hisself 'cause the world done whipped him so! When you starts measuring somebody, measure him right, child, measure him right. Make sure you done taken into account what hills and valleys he come through before he got to wherever he is.

(*Travis bursts into the room at the end of the speech, leaving the door open.*)

TRAVIS: Grandmama — the moving men are downstairs! The truck just pulled up.

MAMA (*turning and looking at him*): Are they, baby? They downstairs?

(*She sighs and sits. Lindner appears in the doorway. He peers in and knocks lightly, to gain attention, and comes in. All turn to look at him.*)

LINDNER (*hat and briefcase in hand*): Uh — hello . . .

(*Ruth crosses mechanically to the bedroom door and opens it and lets it swing open freely and slowly as the lights come up on Walter within, still in his coat, sitting at the far corner of the room. He looks up and out through the room to Lindner.*)

RUTH: He's here.

(*A long minute passes and Walter slowly gets up.*)

LINDNER (*coming to the table with efficiency, putting his briefcase on the table and starting to unfold papers and unscrew fountain pens*): Well, I certainly was glad to hear from you people. (*Walter has begun the trek out of the room, slowly and awkwardly, rather like a small boy, passing the back of his sleeve across his mouth from time to time.*) Life can really be so much simpler than people let it be most of the time. Well — with whom do I negotiate? You, Mrs. Younger, or your son here? (*Mama sits with her hands folded on her lap and her eyes closed as Walter advances. Travis goes closer to Lindner and looks at the papers curiously.*) Just some official papers, sonny.

RUTH: Travis, you go downstairs —

MAMA (*opening her eyes and looking into Walter's*): No. Travis, you stay right here. And you make him understand what you doing, Walter Lee. You teach him good. Like Willy Harris taught you. You show where our five generations done come to. (*Walter looks from her to the boy, who grins at him innocently.*) Go ahead, son — (*She folds her hands and closes her eyes.*) Go ahead.

WALTER (*at last crosses to Lindner, who is reviewing the contract*): Well, Mr. Lindner. (*Beneatha turns away.*) We called you — (*there is a profound, simple groping quality in his speech*) — because, well, me and my family (*he looks around and shifts from one foot to the other*) Well — we are very plain people . . .

LINDNER: Yes —

WALTER: I mean — I have worked as a chauffeur most of my life — and my wife here, she does domestic work in people's kitchens. So does my mother. I mean — we are plain people . . .

LINDNER: Yes, Mr. Younger —

WALTER (*really like a small boy, looking down at his shoes and then up at the man*): And — uh — well, my father, well, he was a laborer most of his life. . . .

LINDNER (*absolutely confused*): Uh, yes — yes, I understand. (*He turns back to the contract.*)

WALTER (*a beat; staring at him*): And my father — (*With sudden intensity.*) My father almost *beat a man to death* once because this man called him a bad name or something, you know what I mean?

LINDNER (*looking up, frozen*): No, no, I'm afraid I don't —

WALTER (*A beat. The tension hangs; then Walter steps back from it.*): Yeah. Well — what I mean is that we come from people who had a lot of *pride*. I mean — we are very proud people. And that's my sister over there and she's going to be a doctor — and we are very proud —

LINDNER: Well — I am sure that is very nice, but —

WALTER: What I am telling you is that we called you over here to tell you that we are very proud and that this — (*Signaling to Travis.*) Travis, come here. (*Travis crosses and Walter draws him before him facing the man.*) This is my son, and he makes the sixth generation of our family in this country. And we have all thought about your offer —

LINDNER: Well, good . . . good —

WALTER: And we have decided to move into our house because my father — my father — he earned it for us brick by brick. (*Mama has her eyes closed and is rocking back and forth as though she were in church, with her head nodding the Amen yes.*) We don't want to make no trouble for nobody or fight no causes, and we will try to be good neighbors. And that's *all* we got to say about that. (*He looks the man absolutely in the eyes.*) We don't want your money. (*He turns and walks away.*)

LINDNER (*looking around at all of them*): I take it then — that you have decided to occupy . . .

BENEATHA: That's what the man said.

LINDNER (*to Mama in her reverie*): Then I would like to appeal to you, Mrs. Younger. You are older and wiser and understand things better I am sure . . .

MAMA: I am afraid you don't understand. My son said we was going to move and there ain't nothing left for me to say. (*Briskly.*) You know how these young folks is nowadays, mister. Can't do a thing with 'em! (*As he opens his mouth, she rises.*) Goodbye.

LINDNER (*folding up his materials*): Well — if you are that final about it . . . there is nothing left for me to say. (*He finishes, almost ignored by the family, who are concentrating on Walter Lee. At the door Lindner halts and looks around.*) I sure hope you people know what you're getting into.

(*He shakes his head and exits.*)

RUTH (*looking around and coming to life*): Well, for God's sake — if the moving men are here — LET'S GET THE HELL OUT OF HERE!

MAMA (*into action*): Ain't it the truth! Look at all this here mess. Ruth, put Travis's good jacket on him . . . Walter Lee, fix your tie and tuck your shirt in, you look like somebody's hoodlum! Lord have mercy, where is my plant? (*She flies to get it amid the general bustling of the family, who are deliberately trying to ignore the nobility of the past moment.*) You all start on down . . . Travis child, don't go empty-handed . . . Ruth, where did I put that box with my skillets in it? I want to be in charge of it myself . . . I'm going to make us the biggest dinner we ever ate tonight . . . Beneatha, what's the matter with them stockings? Pull them things up, girl . . .

(*The family starts to file out as two moving men appear and begin to carry out the heavier pieces of furniture, bumping into the family as they move about.*)

BENEATHA: Mama, Asagai asked me to marry him today and go to Africa —

MAMA (*in the middle of her getting-ready activity*): He did? You ain't old enough to marry nobody — (*Seeing the moving men lifting one of her chairs precariously.*) Darling, that ain't no bale of cotton, please handle it so we can sit in it again! I had that chair twenty-five years . . .

(*The movers sigh with exasperation and go on with their work.*)

BENEATHA (*girlishly and unreasonably trying to pursue the conversation*): To go to Africa, Mama — be a doctor in Africa . . .

MAMA (*distracted*): Yes, baby —

WALTER: *Africa!* What he want you to go to Africa for?

BENEATHA: To practice there . . .

WALTER: Girl, if you don't get all them silly ideas out your head! You better marry yourself a man with some loot . . .

BENEATHA (*angrily, precisely as in the first scene of the play*): What have you got to do with who I marry!

WALTER: Plenty. Now I think George Murchison —

BENEATHA: *George Murchison!* I wouldn't marry him if he was Adam and I was Eve!

(*Walter and Beneatha go out yelling at each other vigorously and the anger is loud and real till their voices diminish. Ruth stands at the door and turns to Mama and smiles knowingly.*)

MAMA (*fixing her hat at last*): Yeah — they something all right, my children . . .

RUTH: Yeah — they're something. Let's go, Lena.

MAMA (*stalling, starting to look around at the house*): Yes — I'm coming. Ruth —

RUTH: Yes?

MAMA (*quietly, woman to woman*): He finally come into his manhood today, didn't he? Kind of like a rainbow after the rain . . .

RUTH (*biting her lip lest her own pride explode in front of Mama*): Yes, Lena.

(*Walter's voice calls for them raucously.*)

WALTER (*offstage*): Y'all come on! These people charges by the hour you know!

MAMA (*waving Ruth out vaguely*): All right, honey — go on down. I be down directly.

(*Ruth hesitates, then exits. Mama stands, at last alone in the living room, her plant on the table before her as the lights start to come down. She looks around at all the walls and ceilings and suddenly, despite herself, while the children call below, a great heaving thing rises in her and she puts her fist to her mouth to stifle it, takes a final desperate look, pulls her coat about her, pats her hat, and goes out. The lights dim down. The door opens and she comes back in, grabs her plant, and goes out for the last time.*)

COMMENTARY

Brooks Atkinson (1894–1984)
REVIEW OF *A RAISIN IN THE SUN*   1959

It is clear from this review that Atkinson felt the "craftsmanship" of the play could have been more polished, but it is also clear that he was struck by the honesty of the entire enterprise. His praise for Sidney Poitier, who played Walter Lee Younger, and his praise for the director Lloyd Richards emphasize the eloquence and directness of their work.

In *A Raisin in the Sun,* which opened at the Ethel Barrymore last evening, Lorraine Hansberry touched on some serious problems. No doubt, her feelings about them are as strong as any one's.

But she has not tipped her play to prove one thing or another. The play is honest. She has told the inner as well as the outer truth about a Negro family in the southside of Chicago at the present time. Since the performance is also honest and since Sidney Poitier is a candid actor, *A Raisin in the Sun* has vigor as well as veracity and is likely to destroy the complacency of any one who sees it.

The family consists of a firm-minded widow, her daughter, her restless son and his wife and son. The mother has brought up her family in a tenement that is small, battered but personable. All the mother wants is that her children adhere to the code of honor and self-respect that she inherited from her parents.

The son is dreaming of success in a business deal. And the daughter, who is race-conscious, wants to become a physician and heal the wounds of her people. After a long delay the widow receives $10,000 as the premium on her husband's life insurance. The money projects the family into a series of situations that test their individual characters.

What the situations are does not matter at the moment. For *A Raisin in the Sun* is a play about human beings who want, on the one hand, to preserve their family pride and, on the other hand, to break out of the poverty that seems to be their fate. Not having any axe to grind, Miss Hansberry has a wide range of topics to write about — some of them hilarious, some of them painful in the extreme.

You might, in fact, regard *A Raisin in the Sun* as a Negro *The Cherry Orchard*. Although the social scale of the characters is different, the knowledge of how character is controlled by environment is much the same, and the alternation of humor and pathos is similar.

If there are occasional crudities in the craftsmanship, they are redeemed by the honesty of the writing. And also by the rousing honesty of the stage work. For Lloyd Richards has selected an admirable cast and directed a bold and stirring performance.

Mr. Poitier is a remarkable actor with enormous power that is always under control. Cast as the restless son, he vividly communicates the tumult of a high-strung young man. He is as eloquent when he has nothing to say as when he has a pungent line to speak. He can convey devious processes of thought as graphically as he can clown and dance.

As the matriarch, Claudia McNeil gives a heroic performance. Although the character is simple, Miss McNeil gives it nobility of spirit. Diana Sands's amusing portrait of the overintellectualized daughter; Ivan Dixon's quiet, sagacious student from Nigeria; Ruby Dee's young wife burdened with problems; Louis Gossett's supercilious suitor; John Fiedler's timid white man, who speaks sanctimonious platitudes — bring variety and excitement to a first-rate performance.

All the crises and comic sequences take place inside Ralph Alswang's set, which depicts both the poverty and the taste of the family. Like the play, it is honest. That is Miss Hansberry's personal contribution to an explosive situation in which simple honesty is the most difficult thing in the world. And also the most illuminating.

Wole Soyinka

Wole Soyinka (b. 1934) is one of Nigeria's several important writers to achieve international fame, winning the Nobel Prize for literature in 1986. His work includes novels, poems, and plays, but he admits that "there is no question at all that I think the Nobel Prize is for my drama."

Soyinka studied at University College, Ibadan, Nigeria, and began his literary career as an undergraduate, publishing poetry in the distinguished African literary magazine *Black Orpheus*. His work, especially his drama, has been an investigation of political, religious, and other forces in Nigerian culture. *The Swamp Dwellers* (1958) is a powerful play condemning African superstition. *The Lion and the Jewel* (1959) offers a comic view of Nigerian attitudes toward European values left over from the colonial period. Among his other plays are *The Trials of Brother Jero* (1960), about a corrupt evangelist, and *Kongi's Harvest* (1964). *A Dance of the Forests* (1960) was written to celebrate Nigerian independence, but it also alerted people to Nigeria's past violence and warned against its return.

Nigeria went through a bitter civil war in 1967, and Soyinka's political sympathies led to a term in prison, where he was placed in solitary confinement. He continued his writing, smuggling poems out of prison to give hope to his political allies. He even criticized his own tribe, the Yoruba, for murdering members of the Ibo during the war against Biafra.

Soyinka studied at the University of Leeds after his schooling in Ibadan. Most of his writing is in English, but he still writes some of his poetry in his tribal language, Yoruba. He has recommended Swahili as the national language of Nigeria. Soyinka has spoken out against cultural parochialism, including its manifestation in the negritude movement, which rejects Western culture as a form of pollution. He expressed his philosophy to another great African writer, Leopold Senghor: "A tiger is not forever shouting about his tigritude"; a duiker antelope does not have to "prove his duikertude; you will know him by his elegant leap."

Soyinka has been chair of the drama department at Ife University as well as of his own University College, Ibadan. He has also lectured in Cambridge, England, and in universities in North America. One of his most recent works, *A Play of Giants* (1984), is a scathing attack on abuse of power, indicting African tyrants such as Idi Amin, Jean-Bedel Bokassa, and others.

For all of his criticism of Nigerian politics, Soyinka has rooted his work in the religion and folklore of the Yoruba people. Ifa, the Yoruba religion, depends on a complex cosmology that sees experience as layered in interactive animal, mineral, and vegetable spheres. African critic Femi Osofisan has described Yoruba cosmology as holding "coeval the three historical, actual, and prospective planes of entity; . . . the animal and vegetable essences are correspondent; . . . the acknowledged deities are both anthropomorphic and symbiotic, each fusing in his personality a series of antinomies." Osofisan also notes "the comprehensive union of religious and secular intuition in the traditional Yoruba." Ifa plays a role in *The Strong Breed,* but the play is nonetheless understandable to those unfamiliar with the religion. Soyinka must be thought of as a traditional dramatist, writing in the tradition of his Yoruba people but reaching a worldwide audience.

THE STRONG BREED

The Strong Breed (1962), written at a time of political uncertainty in Nigeria, examines the interrelationship of ritual and community in African culture, describing one process by which a society renews itself. The "strong breed" are those men capable of the sacrifice needed annually to purify the community of its sins and to allow it to start over again. The community's sacrifice signals the beginning of a new year.

As the new year approaches, the elders of the community, Jaguna and Oroge, search for the appropriate "carrier" who can bear the burden of the community's guilt. The tradition in their community is to choose a stranger. Despite the elders' reluctance, Eman, one of the strong breed who has exiled himself from his own community, seems a logical choice until another outsider, the idiot Ifada, comes on the scene. Ifada seems heaven-sent to serve the community, but when he is chosen, he protests in terrified confusion. Eman explains to Jaguna and Oroge that no community should force a carrier to perform unwillingly. If he is unwilling, the guilt will not be carried away. Eman then offers himself as a willing sacrifice in Ifada's place.

The mythic pattern of sacrifice and renewal is basic to much Yoruba myth. Part of the tradition of Yoruba ritual drama is the reenactment of myths that resemble Eman's willing sacrifice. These are celebrated annually on the feast of Obatala, the god of creation. *The Strong Breed* has also been connected to ritual tragedies enacted in honor of Ogun, who suffers greatly for the good of the community.

The Strong Breed is informed by Soyinka's studies of Greek tragedy. Like Greek tragic figures, Soyinka's strong breed are genetically linked: they are fathers and sons who inherit their fathers' power. Soyinka's *The Bacchae of Euripides* (1973) deals with inspiration, intoxication, and mass hysteria. *Death and the King's Horseman* (1976), centering on death, also explores Greek themes of fate and inevitability. Soyinka demonstrates the universality of Greek themes in both European and African experience.

Certain patterns link Eman with Oedipus. Once Eman is identified by his father as one of the strong breed, he prepares himself for his mission by leaving his community. Like Oedipus, he unwittingly goes to another community where he ultimately must be sacrificed. Eman also resembles Christ: he is a teacher and healer; he refuses to exploit those around him; he lifts up the weak and has empathy for everyone, including the idiot Ifada. And, like Christ, those for whom he sacrifices himself do not hold him in high regard.

Despite its Greek and Christian overtones, the story is grounded in Yoruba tradition, with its initiation rites and concepts of heredity, community, and sacrifice. Soyinka's stagecraft includes traditional Yoruba music and dance as well as traditional Yoruba images, such as the effigy — the carrier doll — and the appearance of the human carrier in the form of Ifada. Soyinka demonstrates that everything in the past is part of the present by overlaying the ghosts of Omae, the woman Eman was to marry; his father (the Old Man); his tutor; and the priest. The past shapes the present just as his father's blood runs in his veins and shapes everything he does as a man.

The play leaves us wondering if Eman's sacrifice was wasteful or redeeming. Is the community led by Jaguna and Oroge worth dying for? Will Eman's death benefit Sunma, Ifada, and the Girl who betrayed him to his killers? Or does Eman die only because he is one of the strong breed, whose mission is to serve as the sacrifice for the community? Even the latter interpretation might imply a positive ending for the play, although it would be a different ending than suggesting that Eman has died *for* this village and thus has secured its renewal. Yoruba tradition implies that even if the community is unworthy, it shares in purification by the sacrifice of the willing. The subtlety of the issues in this play invites multiple interpretations.

The Strong Breed in Performance

In Ibadan in 1963, Soyinka created a twenty-five-minute version of *The Strong Breed* that omitted the flashbacks at the end of the play when Eman's past returns to him. This was done for Esso World Theatre and was included in the film *Culture in Transition*. The play was produced in its full-length version in 1964 at the Greenwich Mews Theatre in New York, and it has been performed by theater groups in several African nations. An African university theater group produced the play in its full-length version in Malawi in 1976 with Anthony Nazombe as Eman.

Wole Soyinka (b. 1934)
THE STRONG BREED

1962

Characters

EMAN, *a stranger*
SUNMA, *Jaguna's daughter*
IFADA, *an idiot*
A GIRL
JAGUNA
OROGE
ATTENDANT STALWARTS, *the villagers*

From Eman's past:
OLD MAN, *his father*
OMAE, *his betrothed*
TUTOR
PRIEST
ATTENDANTS, *the villagers*

The scenes are described briefly, but very often a darkened stage with lit areas will not only suffice but is necessary. Except for the one indicated place, there can be no break in the action. A distracting scene change would be ruinous.

(*A mud house, with space in front of it. Eman, in light buba and trousers stands at the window, looking out. Inside, Sunma is clearing the table of what looks like a modest clinic, putting the things away in a cupboard. Another rough table in the room is piled with exercise books, two or three worn textbooks, etc. Sunma appears agitated. Outside, just below the window crouches Ifada. He looks up with a shy smile from time to time, waiting for Eman to notice him.*)

SUNMA (*hesitant*): You will have to make up your mind soon, Eman. The lorry leaves very shortly.

(*As Eman does not answer, Sunma continues her work, more nervously. Two villagers, obvious travelers, pass hurriedly in front of the house, the man has a small raffia sack, the woman a cloth-covered basket, the man enters first, turns and urges the woman who is just emerging to hurry.*)

SUNMA (*seeing them, her tone is more intense*): Eman, are we going or aren't we? You will leave it till too late.
EMAN (*quietly*): There is still time — if you want to go.
SUNMA: If I want to go . . . and you?

(*Eman makes no reply.*)

SUNMA (*bitterly*): You don't really want to leave here. You never want to go away — even for a minute.

(*Ifada continues his antics. Eman eventually pats him on the head and the boy grins happily. Leaps up suddenly and returns with a basket of oranges which he offers to Eman.*)

EMAN: My gift for today's festival enh?

(*Ifada nods, grinning.*)

EMAN: They look ripe — that's a change.
SUNMA (*she has gone inside the room. Looks round the door*): Did you call me?
EMAN: No. (*She goes back.*) And what will you do tonight, Ifada? Will you take part in the dancing? Or perhaps you will mount your own masquerade?

(*Ifada shakes his head, regretfully.*)

EMAN: You won't? So you haven't any? But you would like to own one.

(*Ifada nods eagerly.*)

EMAN: Then why don't you make your own?

(*Ifada stares, puzzled by this idea.*)

EMAN: Sunma will let you have some cloth you know. And bits of wool . . .
SUNMA (*coming out*): Who are you talking to, Eman?
EMAN: Ifada. I am trying to persuade him to join the young maskers.
SUNMA (*losing control*): What does he want here? Why is he hanging round us?

EMAN (*amazed*): What . . . ? I said Ifada, Ifada.
SUNMA: Just tell him to go away. Let him go and play somewhere else!
EMAN: What is this? Hasn't he always played here?
SUNMA: I don't want him here. (*Rushes to the window.*) Get away, idiot. Don't bring your foolish face here anymore, do you hear? Go on, go away from here . . .
EMAN (*restraining her*): Control yourself, Sunma. What on earth has got into you?

(*Ifada, hurt and bewildered, backs slowly away.*)

SUNMA: He comes crawling round here like some horrible insect. I never want to lay my eyes on him again.
EMAN: I don't understand. It *is* Ifada you know. Ifada! The unfortunate one who runs errands for you and doesn't hurt a soul.
SUNMA: I cannot bear the sight of him.
EMAN: You can't do what? It can't be two days since he last fetched water for you.
SUNMA: What else can he do except that? He is useless. Just because we have been kind to him . . . Others would have put him in an asylum.
EMAN: You are not making sense. He is not a madman, he is just a little more unlucky than other children. (*Looks keenly at her.*) But what is the matter?
SUNMA: It's nothing. I only wish we had sent him off to one of those places for creatures like him.
EMAN: He is quite happy here. He doesn't bother anyone and he makes himself useful.
SUNMA: Useful! Is that one of any use to anybody? Boys of his age are already earning a living but all he can do is hang around and drool at the mouth.
EMAN: But he does work. You know he does a lot for you.
SUNMA: Does he? And what about the farm you started for him! Does he ever work on it? Or have you forgotten that it was really for Ifada you cleared that bush. Now you have to go and work it yourself. You spend all your time on it and you have no room for anything else.
EMAN: That wasn't his fault. I should first have asked him if he was fond of farming.
SUNMA: Oh, so he can choose? As if he shouldn't be thankful for being allowed to live.
EMAN: Sunma!
SUNMA: He does not like farming but he knows how to feast his dumb mouth on the fruits.
EMAN: But I want him to. I encourage him.
SUNMA: Well keep him. I don't want to see him anymore.
EMAN (*after some moments*): But why? You cannot be telling all the truth. What has he done?
SUNMA: The sight of him fills me with revulsion.
EMAN (*goes to her and holds her*): What really is it? (*Sunma avoids his eyes.*) It is almost as if you are forcing yourself to hate him. Why?
SUNMA: That is not true. Why should I?
EMAN: Then what is the secret? You've even played with him before.

SUNMA: I have always merely tolerated him. But I cannot anymore. Suddenly my disgust won't take him anymore. Perhaps . . . perhaps it is the new year. Yes, yes, it must be the new year.

EMAN: I don't believe that.

SUNMA: It must be. I am a woman, and these things matter. I don't want a misshape near me. Surely for one day in the year, I may demand some wholesomeness.

EMAN: I do not understand you. (*Sunma is silent.*) It was cruel of you. And to Ifada who is so helpless and alone. We are the only friends he has.

SUNMA: No, just you. I have told you, with me it has always been only an act of kindness. And now I haven't any pity left for him.

EMAN: No. He is not a wholesome being.

(*He turns back to looking through the window.*)

SUNMA (*half-pleading*): Ifada can rouse your pity. And yet if anything, I need more kindness from you. Every time my weakness betrays me, you close your mind against me . . . Eman . . . Eman . . .

(*A Girl comes in view, dragging an effigy° by a rope attached to one of its legs. She stands for a while gazing at Eman. Ifada, who has crept back shyly to his accustomed position, becomes somewhat excited when he sees the effigy. The Girl is unsmiling. She possesses in fact a kind of inscrutability which does not make her hard but is unsettling.*)

GIRL: Is the teacher in?

EMAN (*smiling*): No.

GIRL: Where is he gone?

EMAN: I don't really know. Shall I ask?

GIRL: Yes, do.

EMAN (*turning slightly*): Sunma, a girl outside wants to know . . .

(*Sunma turns away, goes into the inside room.*)

EMAN: Oh. (*Returns to the Girl, but his slight gaiety is lost.*) There is no one at home who can tell me.

GIRL: Why are you not in?

EMAN: I don't really know. Maybe I went somewhere.

GIRL: All right. I will wait until you get back.

(*She pulls the effigy to her, sits down.*)

EMAN (*slowly regaining his amusement*): So you are all ready for the new year.

GIRL (*without turning round*): I am not going to the festival.

EMAN: Then why have you got that?

GIRL: Do you mean my carrier? I am unwell you know. My mother says it will take away my sickness with the old year.

EMAN: Won't you share the carrier with your playmates?

GIRL: Oh, no. Don't you know I play alone? The other children won't come near me. Their mothers would beat them.

effigy: A figure or likeness in human shape.

EMAN: But I have never seen you here. Why don't you come to the clinic?

GIRL: My mother said No.

(*Gets up, begins to move off.*)

EMAN: You are not going away?

GIRL: I must not stay talking to you. If my mother caught me . . .

EMAN: All right, tell me what you want before you go.

GIRL (*stops. For some moments she remains silent*): I must have some clothes for my carrier.

EMAN: Is that all? You wait a moment.

(*Sunma comes out as he takes down a buba from the wall. She goes to the window and glares almost with hatred at the Girl. The Girl retreats hastily, still impassive.*)

By the way, Sunma, do you know who that girl is?

SUNMA: I hope you don't really mean to give her that.

EMAN: Why not? I hardly ever use it.

SUNMA: Just the same, don't give it to her. She is not a child. She is as evil as the rest of them.

EMAN: What has got into you today?

SUNMA: All right, all right. Do what you wish.

(*She withdraws. Baffled, Eman returns to the window.*)

EMAN: Here . . . will this do? Come and look at it.

GIRL: Throw it.

EMAN: What is the matter? I am not going to eat you.

GIRL: No one lets me come near them.

EMAN: But I am not afraid of catching your disease.

GIRL: Throw it.

(*Eman shrugs and tosses the buba. She takes it without a word and slips it on the effigy, completely absorbed in the task. Eman watches for a while, then joins Sunma in the inner room.*)

GIRL (*after a long, cool survey of Ifada*): You have a head like a spider's egg, and your mouth dribbles like a roof. But there is no one else. Would you like to play?

(*Ifada nods eagerly, quite excited.*)

GIRL: You will have to get a stick.

(*Ifada rushes around, finds a big stick, and whirls it aloft, bearing down on the carrier.*)

GIRL: Wait. I don't want you to spoil it. If it gets torn I shall drive you away. Now, let me see how you are going to beat it.

(*Ifada hits it gently.*)

GIRL: You may hit harder than that. As long as there is something left to hang at the end. (*She appraises him up and down.*) You are not very tall . . . will you be able to hang it from a tree?

(*Ifada nods, grinning happily.*)

GIRL: You will hang it up and I will set fire to it. (*Then, with surprising venom.*) But just because you are helping me, don't think it is going to cure you. I am the one who will get well at midnight, do you understand? It is my carrier and it is for me alone. (*She pulls at the rope to make sure that it is well attached to the leg.*) Well don't stand there drooling. Let's go.

(*She begins to walk off, dragging the effigy in the dust. Ifada remains where he is for some moments, seemingly puzzled. Then his face breaks into a large grin and he leaps after the procession, belaboring the effigy with all his strength. The stage remains empty for some moments. Then the horn of a lorry is sounded and Sunma rushes out. The hooting continues for some time with a rhythmic pattern. Eman comes out.*)

EMAN: I am going to the village . . . I shan't be back before nightfall.

SUNMA (*blankly*): Yes.

EMAN (*hesitates*): Well what do you want me to do?

SUNMA: The lorry was hooting just now.

EMAN: I didn't hear it.

SUNMA: It will leave in a few minutes. And you did promise we could go away.

EMAN: I promised nothing. Will you go home by yourself or shall I come back for you?

SUNMA: You don't even want me here?

EMAN: But you have to go home haven't you?

SUNMA: I had hoped we would watch the new year together — in some other place.

EMAN: Why do you continue to distress yourself?

SUNMA: Because you will not listen to me. Why do you continue to stay where nobody wants you?

EMAN: That is not true.

SUNMA: It is. You are wasting your life on people who really want you out of their way.

EMAN: You don't know what you are saying.

SUNMA: You think they love you? Do you think they care at all for what you — or I — do for them?

EMAN: *Them?* These are your own people. Sometimes you talk as if you were a stranger too.

SUNMA: I wonder if I really sprang from here. I know they are evil and I am not. From the oldest to the smallest child, they are nourished in evil and unwholesomeness in which I have no part.

EMAN: You knew this when you returned?

SUNMA: You reproach me then for trying at all?

EMAN: I reproach you with nothing? But you must leave me out of your plans. I can have no part in them.

SUNMA (*nearly pleading*): Once I could have run away. I would have gone and never looked back.

EMAN: I cannot listen when you talk like that.

SUNMA: I swear to you, I do not mind what happens afterwards. But you must help me tear myself away from here. I can no longer do it by myself . . . It is only a little thing. And we have worked so hard this past year . . . surely we can go away for a week . . . even a few days would be enough.

EMAN: I have told you, Sunma . . .

SUNMA (*desperately*): Two days, Eman. Only two days.

EMAN (*distressed*): But I tell you I have no wish to go.

SUNMA (*suddenly angry*): Are you so afraid then?

EMAN: Me? Afraid of what?

SUNMA: You think you will not want to come back.

EMAN (*pitying*): You cannot dare me that way.

SUNMA: Then why won't you leave here, even for an hour? If you are so sure that your life is settled here, why are you afraid to do this thing for me? What is so wrong that you will not go into the next town for a day or two?

EMAN: I don't want to. I do not have to persuade you or myself about anything. I simply have no desire to go away.

SUNMA (*his quiet confidence appears to incense her*): You are afraid. You accuse me of losing my sense of mission, but you are afraid to put yours to the test.

EMAN: You are wrong, Sunma. I have no sense of mission. But I have found peace here and I am content with that.

SUNMA: I haven't. For a while I thought that too, but I found there could be no peace in the midst of so much cruelty. Eman, tonight at least, the last night of the old year . . .

EMAN: No, Sunma. I find this too distressing; you should go home now.

SUNMA: It is the time for making changes in one's life, Eman. Let's breathe in the new year away from here.

EMAN: You are hurting yourself.

SUNMA: Tonight. Only tonight. We will come back tomorrow, as early as you like. But let us go away for this one night. Don't let another year break on me in this place . . . you don't know how important it is to me, but I will tell you, I will tell you on the way . . . but we must not be here today, Eman, do this one thing for me.

EMAN (*sadly*): I cannot.

SUNMA (*suddenly calm*): I was a fool to think it would be otherwise. The whole village may use you as they will but for me there is nothing. Sometimes I think you believe that doing anything for me makes you unfaithful to some part of your life. If it was a woman then I pity her for what she must have suffered.

(*Eman winces and hardens slowly. Sunma notices nothing.*)

Keeping faith with so much is slowly making you inhuman. (*Seeing the change in Eman.*) Eman. Eman. What is it?

(*As she goes toward him, Eman goes into the house.*)

SUNMA (*apprehensive, follows him*): What did I say? Eman, forgive me, forgive me please. (*Eman remains facing into the slow darkness of the room. Sunma, distressed, cannot decide what to do.*) I swear I didn't know . . . I would not have said it for all the world.

(*A lorry is heard taking off somewhere nearby. The sound comes up and slowly fades away into the distance. Sunma starts visibly, goes slowly to the window.*)

SUNMA (*as the sound dies off, to herself*): What happens now?

EMAN (*joining her at the window*): What did you say?

SUNMA: Nothing.

EMAN: Was that not the lorry going off?

SUNMA: It was.

EMAN: I am sorry I couldn't help you.

(*Sunma, about to speak, changes her mind.*)

EMAN: I think you ought to go home now.

SUNMA: No, don't send me away. It's the least you can do for me. Let me stay here until all the noise is over.

EMAN: But are you not needed at home? You have a part in the festival.

SUNMA: I have renounced it; I am Jaguna's eldest daughter only in name.

EMAN: Renouncing one's self is not so easy — surely you know that.

SUNMA: I don't want to talk about it. Will you at least let us be together tonight?

EMAN: But . . .

SUNMA: Unless you are afraid my father will accuse you of harboring me.

EMAN: All right, we will go out together.

SUNMA: Go out? I want us to stay here.

EMAN: When there is so much going on outside?

SUNMA: Someday you will wish that you went away when I tried to make you.

EMAN: Are we going back to that?

SUNMA: No. I promise you I will not recall it again. But you must know that it was also for your sake that I tried to get us away.

EMAN: For me? How?

SUNMA: By yourself you can do nothing here. Have you not noticed how tightly we shut out strangers? Even if you lived here for a lifetime, you would remain a stranger.

EMAN: Perhaps that is what I like. There is peace in being a stranger.

SUNMA: For a while perhaps. But they would reject you in the end. I tell you it is only I who stand between you and contempt. And because of this you have earned their hatred. I don't know why I say this now, except that somehow, I feel that it no longer matters. It is only I who have stood between you and much humiliation.

EMAN: Think carefully before you say any more. I am incapable of feeling indebted to you. This will make no difference at all.

SUNMA: I ask for nothing. But you must know it all the same. It is true I hadn't the strength to go by myself. And I must confess this now, if you had come with me, I would have done everything to keep you from returning.

EMAN: I know that.

SUNMA: You see, I bare myself to you. For days I had thought it over, this was to be a new beginning for us. And I placed my fate wholly in your hands. Now the thought will not leave me, I have a feeling which will not be shaken off, that in some way, you have tonight totally destroyed my life.

EMAN: You are depressed, you don't know what you are saying.

SUNMA: Don't think I am accusing you. I say all this only because I cannot help it.

EMAN: We must not remain shut up here. Let us go and be part of the living.

SUNMA: No. Leave them alone.

EMAN: Surely you don't want to stay indoors when the whole town is alive with rejoicing.

SUNMA: Rejoicing! Is that what it seems to you? No, let us remain here. Whatever happens I must not go out until all this is over.

(*There is silence. It has grown much darker.*)

EMAN: I shall light the lamp.

SUNMA (*eager to do something*): No, let me do it.

(*She goes into the inner room.*)

(*Eman paces the room, stops by a shelf and toys with the seeds in an "ayo" board, takes down the whole board and places it on a table, playing by himself.*)

(*The Girl is now seen coming back, still dragging her "carrier." Ifada brings up the rear as before. As he comes round the corner of the house two men emerge from the shadows. A sack is thrown over Ifada's head, the rope is pulled tight rendering him instantly helpless. The Girl has reached the front of the house before she turns round at the sound of scuffle. She is in time to see Ifada thrown over the shoulders and borne away. Her face betraying no emotion at all, the Girl backs slowly away, turns and flees, leaving the "carrier" behind. Sunma enters, carrying two kerosene lamps. She hangs one up from the wall.*)

EMAN: One is enough.

SUNMA: I want to leave one outside.

(*She goes out, hangs the lamp from a nail just above the door. As she turns she sees the effigy and gasps. Eman rushes out.*)

EMAN: What is it? Oh, is that what frightened you?

SUNMA: I thought . . . I didn't really see it properly.

(*Eman goes towards the object, stoops to pick it up.*)

EMAN: It must belong to that sick girl.

SUNMA: Don't touch it.

EMAN: Let's keep it for her.

SUNMA: Leave it alone. Don't touch it, Eman.

EMAN (*shrugs and goes back*): You are very nervous.

SUNMA: Let's go in.

EMAN: Wait. (*He detains her by the door, under the lamp.*) I know there is something more than you've told me. What are you afraid of tonight?

SUNMA: I was only scared by that thing. There is nothing else.

EMAN: I am not blind, Sunma. It is true I would not run away when you wanted me to, but that doesn't mean I do not feel things. What does tonight really mean that it makes you so helpless?

SUNMA: It is only a mood. And your indifference to me . . . let's go in.

(*Eman moves aside and she enters; he remains there for a moment and then follows.*)

(*She fiddles with the lamp, looks vaguely round the room, then goes and shuts the door, bolting it. When she turns, it is to meet Eman's eyes, questioning.*)

SUNMA: There is a cold wind coming in.

(*Eman keeps his gaze on her.*)

SUNMA: It *was* getting cold.

(*She moves guiltily to the table and stands by the "ayo" board, rearranging the seeds. Eman remains where he is a few moments, then brings a stool and sits opposite her. She sits down also and they begin to play in silence.*)

SUNMA: What brought you here at all, Eman? And what makes you stay?

(*There is another silence.*)

SUNMA: I am not trying to share your life. I know you too well by now. But at least we have worked together since you came. Is there nothing at all I deserve to know?

EMAN: Let me continue a stranger — especially to you. Those who have much to give fulfill themselves only in total loneliness.

SUNMA: Then there is no love in what you do.

EMAN: There is. Love comes to me more easily with strangers.

SUNMA: That is unnatural.

EMAN: Not for me. I know I find consummation only when I have spent myself for a total stranger.

SUNMA: It seems unnatural to me. But then I am a woman. I have a woman's longings and weaknesses. And the ties of blood are very strong in me.

EMAN (*smiling*): You think I have cut loose from all these — ties of blood.

SUNMA: Sometimes you are so inhuman.

EMAN: I don't know what that means. But I am very much my father's son.

(*They play in silence. Suddenly Eman pauses, listening.*)

EMAN: Did you hear that?

SUNMA (*quickly*): I heard nothing . . . it's your turn.

EMAN: Perhaps some of the mummers are coming this way.

(*Eman, about to play, leaps up suddenly.*)

SUNMA: What is it? Don't you want to play anymore?

(*Eman moves to the door.*)

SUNMA: No. Don't go out, Eman.

EMAN: If it's the dancers, I want to ask them to stay. At least we won't have to miss everything.

SUNMA: No, no. Don't open the door. Let us keep out everyone tonight.

(*A terrified and disordered figure bursts suddenly round the corner, past the window, and begins hammering at the door. It is Ifada. Desperate with terror, he pounds madly at the door, dumb-moaning all the while.*)

EMAN: Isn't that Ifada?

SUNMA: They are only fooling about. Don't pay any attention.

EMAN (*looks round the window*): That is Ifada. (*Begins to unbolt the door.*)

SUNMA (*pulling at his hands*): It is only a trick they are playing on you. Don't take any notice, Eman.

EMAN: What are you saying? The boy is out of his senses with fear.

SUNMA: No, no. Don't interfere, Eman. For God's sake, don't interfere.

EMAN: Do you know something of this then?

SUNMA: You are a stranger here, Eman. Just leave us alone and go your own way. There is nothing you can do.

EMAN (*he tries to push her out of the way but she clings fiercely to him*): Have you gone mad? I tell you the boy must come in.

SUNMA: Why won't you listen to me, Eman? I tell you it's none of your business. For your own sake, do as I say.

(*Eman pushes her off, unbolts the door. Ifada rushes in, clasps Eman round the knees, dumb-moaning against his legs.*)

EMAN (*manages to rebolt the door*): What is it, Ifada? What is the matter?

(*Shouts and voices are heard coming nearer the house.*)

SUNMA: Before it's too late, let him go. For once, Eman, believe what I tell you. Don't harbor him or you will regret it all your life.

(*Eman tries to calm Ifada who becomes more and more abject as the outside voices get nearer.*)

EMAN: What have they done to him? At least tell me that. What is going on, Sunma?

SUNMA (*with sudden venom*): Monster! Could you not take yourself somewhere else?

EMAN: Stop talking like that.

SUNMA: He could have run into the bush couldn't he? Toad! Why must he follow us with his own disasters!

VOICES OUTSIDE: It's here . . . Round the back . . . Spread, spread . . . this way . . . no, head him off . . . use the bush path and head him off . . . get some more lights . . .

(*Eman listens. Lifts Ifada bodily and carries him into the inner room. Returns at once, shutting the door behind him.*)

SUNMA (*slumps into a chair, resigned*): You always follow your own way.

JAGUNA (*comes round the corner followed by Oroge*

and three men, one bearing a torch): I knew he would come here.

OROGE: I hope our friend won't make trouble.

JAGUNA: He had better not. You, recall all the men and tell them to surround the house.

OROGE: But he may not be in the house after all.

JAGUNA: I know he is here . . . (*to the men*) . . . go on, do as I say. (*He bangs on the door.*) Teacher, open your door . . . you two, stay by the door. If I need you I will call you.

(*Eman opens the door.*)

JAGUNA (*speaks as he enters*): We know he is here.

EMAN: Who?

JAGUNA: Don't let us waste time. We are grown men, teacher. You understand me and I understand you. But we must take back the boy.

EMAN: This is my house.

JAGUNA: Daughter, you'd better tell your friend. I don't think he quite knows our ways. Tell him why he must give up the boy.

SUNMA: Father, I . . .

JAGUNA: Are you going to tell him or aren't you?

SUNMA: Father, I beg you, leave us alone tonight . . .

JAGUNA: I thought you might be a hindrance. Go home then if you will not use your sense.

SUNMA: But there are other ways . . .

JAGUNA (*turning to the men*): See that she gets home. I no longer trust her. If she gives trouble carry her. And see that the women stay with her until all this is over.

(*Sunma departs, accompanied by one of the men.*)

JAGUNA: Now, teacher . . .

OROGE (*restrains him*): You see, Mister Eman, it is like this. Right now, nobody knows that Ifada has taken refuge here. No one except us and our men — and they know how to keep their mouths shut. We don't want to have to burn down the house you see, but if the word gets around, we would have no choice.

JAGUNA: In fact, it may be too late already. A carrier should end up in the bush, not in a house. Anyone who doesn't guard his door when the carrier goes by has himself to blame. A contaminated house should be burnt down.

OROGE: But we are willing to let it pass. Only, you must bring him out quickly.

EMAN: All right. But at least you will let me ask you something.

JAGUNA: What is there to ask? Don't you understand what we have told you?

EMAN: Yes. But why did you pick on a helpless boy. Obviously he is not willing.

JAGUNA: What is the man talking about? Ifada is a godsend. Does he have to be willing?

EMAN: In my home, we believe that a man should be willing.

OROGE: Mister Eman, I don't think you quite understand. This is not a simple matter at all. I don't know what you do, but here, it is not a cheap task for any-body. No one in his senses would do such a job. Why do you think we give refuge to idiots like him? We don't know where he came from. One morning, he is simply there, just like that. From nowhere at all. You see, there is a purpose in that.

JAGUNA: We only waste time.

OROGE: Jaguna, be patient. After all, the man has been with us for some time now and deserves to know. The evil of the old year is no light thing to load on any man's head.

EMAN: I know something about that.

OROGE: You do? (*Turns to Jaguna who snorts impatiently.*) You see I told you so didn't I? From the moment you came I saw you were one of the knowing ones.

JAGUNA: Then let him behave like a man and give back the boy.

EMAN: It is you who are not behaving like men.

JAGUNA (*advances aggressively*): That is a quick mouth you have . . .

OROGE: Patience, Jaguna . . . if you want the new year to cushion the land there must be no deeds of anger. What did you mean, my friend?

EMAN: It is a simple thing. A village which cannot produce its own carrier contains no men.

JAGUNA: Enough. Let there be no more talk or this business will be ruined by some rashness. You . . . come inside. Bring the boy out, he must be in the room there.

EMAN: Wait.

(*The men hesitate.*)

JAGUNA (*hitting the nearer one and propelling him forward*): Go on. Have you changed masters now that you listen to what he says?

OROGE (*sadly*): I am sorry you would not understand, Mister Eman. But you ought to know that no carrier may return to the village. If he does, the people will stone him to death. It has happened before. Surely it is too much to ask a man to give up his own soil.

EMAN: I know others who have done more.

(*Ifada is brought out, abjectly dumb-moaning.*)

EMAN: You can see him with your own eyes. Does it really have meaning to use one as unwilling as that.

OROGE (*smiling*): He shall be willing. Not only willing but actually joyous. I am the one who prepares them all, and I have seen worse. This one escaped before I began to prepare him for the event. But you will see him later tonight, the most joyous creature in the festival. Then perhaps you will understand.

EMAN: Then it is only a deceit. Do you believe the spirit of a new year is so easily fooled?

JAGUNA: Take him out. (*The men carry out Ifada.*) You see, it is so easy to talk. You say there are no men in this village because they cannot provide a willing carrier. And yet I heard Oroge tell you we only use strangers. There is only one other stranger in the village, but I have not heard him offer himself (*spits*). It is so easy to talk is it not? (*He turns his back on him.*)

(*They go off, taking Ifada with them, limp and silent. The only sign of life is that he strains his neck to keep his eyes on Eman till the very moment that he disappears from sight. Eman remains where they left him, staring after the group.*)

(*A blackout lasting no more than a minute. The lights come up slowly and Ifada is seen returning to the house. He stops at the window and looks in. Seeing no one, he bangs on the sill. Appears surprised that there is no response. He slithers down on his favorite spot, then sees the effigy still lying where the Girl had dropped it in her flight. After some hesitation, he goes towards it, begins to strip it of the clothing. Just then the Girl comes in.*)

GIRL: Hey, leave that alone. You know it's mine.

(*Ifada pauses, then speeds up his action.*)

GIRL: I said it is mine. Leave it where you found it.

(*She rushes at him and begins to struggle for possession of the carrier.*)

GIRL: Thief! Thief! Let it go, it is mine. Let it go. You animal, just because I let you play with it. Idiot! Idiot!

(*The struggle becomes quite violent. The Girl is hanging to the effigy and Ifada lifts her with it, flinging her all about. The Girl hangs on grimly.*)

GIRL: You are spoiling it . . . why don't you get your own? Thief! Let it go, you thief!

(*Sunma comes in walking very fast, throwing apprehensive glances over her shoulder. Seeing the two children, she becomes immediately angry. Advances on them.*)

SUNMA: So you've made this place your playground. Get away, you untrained pigs. Get out of here.

(*Ifada flees at once, the Girl retreats also, retaining possession of the "carrier."*)

(*Sunma goes to the door. She has her hand on the door when the significance of Ifada's presence strikes her for the first time. She stands rooted to the spot, then turns slowly round.*)

SUNMA: Ifada! What are you doing here? (*Ifada is bewildered. Sunma turns suddenly and rushes into the house, flying into the inner room and out again.*) Eman! Eman! Eman! (*She rushes outside.*) Where did he go? Where did they take him? (*Ifada distressed, points. Sunma seizes him by the arm, drags him off.*) Take me there at once. God help you if we are too late. You loathsome thing, if you have let him suffer . . .

(*Her voice fades into other shouts, running footsteps, banged tins, bells, dogs, etc., rising in volume.*)

(*It is a narrow passageway between two mud houses. At the far end one man after another is seen running across the entry, the noise dying off gradually.*)

(*About halfway down the passage, Eman is crouching against the wall, tense with apprehension. As the noise dies off, he seems to relax, but the alert hunted look is still in his eyes, which are ringed in a reddish color. The rest of his body has been whitened with a floury substance. He is naked down to the waist, wears a baggy pair of trousers, calf-length, and around both feet are bangles.*)

EMAN: I will simply stay here till dawn. I have done enough.

(*A window is thrown open and a woman empties some slop from a pail. With a startled cry Eman leaps aside to avoid it and the woman puts out her head.*)

WOMAN: Oh, my head. What have I done! Forgive me, neighbor. . . . Eh, it's the carrier!

(*Very rapidly she clears her throat and spits on him, flings the pail at him, and runs off, shouting.*)

He's here. The carrier is hiding in the passage. Quickly, I have found the carrier!

(*The cry is taken up and Eman flees down the passage. Shortly afterwards his pursuers come pouring down the passage in full cry. After the last of them come Jaguna and Oroge.*)

OROGE: Wait, wait. I cannot go so fast.

JAGUNA: We will rest a little then. We can do nothing anyway.

OROGE: If only he had let me prepare him.

JAGUNA: They are the ones who break first, these fools who think they were born to carry suffering like a hat. What are we to do now?

OROGE: When they catch him I must prepare him.

JAGUNA: He? It will be impossible now. There can be no joy left in that one.

OROGE: Still, it took him by surprise. He was not expecting what he met.

JAGUNA: Why then did he refuse to listen? Did he think he was coming to sit down to a feast? He had not even gone through one compound before he bolted. Did he think he was taken round the people to be blessed? A woman, that is all he is.

OROGE: No, no. He took the beating well enough. I think he is the kind who would let himself be beaten from night till dawn and not utter a sound. He would let himself be stoned until he dropped dead.

JAGUNA: Then what made him run like a coward?

OROGE: I don't know. I don't really know. It is a night of curses, Jaguna. It is not many unprepared minds will remain unhinged under the load.

JAGUNA: We must find him. It is a poor beginning for a year when our own curses remain hovering over our homes because the carrier refused to take them.

(*They go. The scene changes. Eman is crouching beside some shrubs, torn and bleeding.*)

EMAN: They are even guarding my house . . . as if I would go there, but I need water . . . they could at least grant me that . . . I can be thirsty too . . . (*He pricks his ears.*) . . . there must be a stream nearby . . . (*As he looks round him, his eyes widen at a scene he encounters.*)

(*An Old Man, short and vigorous looking, is seated on a stool. He also is wearing calf-length baggy trousers, white. On his head, a white cap. An attendant is engaged in rubbing his body with oil. Round his eyes, two white rings have already been marked.*)

OLD MAN: Have they prepared the boat?
ATTENDANT: They are making the last sacrifice.
OLD MAN: Good. Did you send for my son?
ATTENDANT: He's on his way.
OLD MAN: I have never met the carrying of the boat with such a heavy heart. I hope nothing comes of it.
ATTENDANT: The gods will not desert us on that account.
OLD MAN: A man should be at his strongest when he takes the boat, my friend. To be weighed down inside and out is not a wise thing. I hope when the moment comes I shall have found my strength.

(*Enter Eman, a wrapper round his waist and a danski° over it.*)

OLD MAN: I meant to wait until after my journey to the river, but my mind is so burdened with my own grief and yours I could not delay it. You know I must have all my strength. But I sit here, feeling it all eaten slowly away by my unspoken grief. It helps to say it out. It even helps to cry sometimes.

(*He signals to the attendant to leave them.*)

Come nearer . . . we will never meet again, son. Not on this side of the flesh. What I do not know is whether you will return to take my place.
EMAN: I will never come back.
OLD MAN: Do you know what you are saying? Ours is a strong breed, my son. It is only a strong breed that can take this boat to the river year after year and wax stronger on it. I have taken down each year's evils for over twenty years. I hoped you would follow me.
EMAN: My life here died with Omae.
OLD MAN: Omae died giving birth to your child and you think the world is ended. Eman, my pain did not begin when Omae died. Since you sent her to stay with me, son, I lived with the burden of knowing that this child would die bearing your son.
EMAN: Father . . .
OLD MAN: Don't you know it was the same with you? And me? No woman survives the bearing of the strong ones. Son, it is not the mouth of the boaster that says he belongs to the strong breed. It is the tongue that is red with pain and black with sorrow. Twelve years you were away my son, and for those twelve years I knew the love of an old man for his daughter and the pain of a man helplessly awaiting his loss.

danski: A brief Yoruba garment.

EMAN: I wish I had stayed away. I wish I never came back to meet her.
OLD MAN: It had to be. But you know now what slowly ate away my strength. I awaited your return with love and fear. Forgive me then if I say that your grief is light. It will pass. This grief may drive you now from home. But you must return.
EMAN: You do not understand. It is not grief alone.
OLD MAN: What is it then? Tell me, I can still learn.
EMAN: I was away twelve years. I changed much in that time.
OLD MAN: I am listening.
EMAN: I am unfitted for your work, father. I wish to say no more. But I am totally unfitted for your call.
OLD MAN: It is only time you need, son. Stay longer and you will answer the urge of your blood.
EMAN: That I stayed at all was because of Omae. I did not expect to find her waiting. I would have taken her away, but hard as you claim to be, it would have killed you. And I was a tired man. I needed peace. Because Omae was peace, I stayed. Now nothing holds me here.
OLD MAN: Other men would rot and die doing this task year after year. It is strong medicine which only we can take. Our blood is strong like no other. Anything you do in life must be less than this, son.
EMAN: That is not true, father.
OLD MAN: I tell you it is true. Your own blood will betray you, son, because you cannot hold it back. If you make it do less than this, it will rush to your head and burst it open. I say what I know, my son.
EMAN: There are other tasks in life, father. This one is not for me. There are even greater things you know nothing of.
OLD MAN: I am very sad. You only go to give to others what rightly belongs to us. You will use your strength among thieves. They are thieves because they take what is ours, they have no claim of blood to it. They will even lack the knowledge to use it wisely. Truth is my companion at this moment, my son. I know everything I say will surely bring the sadness of truth.
EMAN: I am going, father.
OLD MAN: Call my attendant. And be with me in your strength for this last journey. A-ah, did you hear that? It came out without my knowing it; this is indeed my last journey. But I am not afraid.

(*Eman goes out. A few moments later, the attendant enters.*)

ATTENDANT: The boat is ready.
OLD MAN: So am I.

(*He sits perfectly still for several moments. Drumming begins somewhere in the distance, and the Old Man sways his head almost imperceptibly. Two men come in bearing a miniature boat, containing an indefinable mound. They rush it in and set it briskly down near the Old Man, and stand well back. The Old Man gets up slowly, the Attendant watching him keenly. He signs to the men, who lift the boat quickly onto the Old Man's head. As soon as it touches his head, he holds it down with both hands and runs off, the men give him a start, then follow at a trot.)*

(As the last man disappears Oroge limps in and comes face to face with Eman — as carrier — who is now seen still standing beside the shrubs, staring into the scene he has just witnessed. Oroge, struck by the look on Eman's face, looks anxiously behind him to see what has engaged Eman's attention. Eman notices him then, and the pair stare at each other. Jaguna enters, sees him and shouts, "Here he is," rushes at Eman who is whipped back to the immediate and flees, Jaguna in pursuit. Three or four others enter and follow them. Oroge remains where he is, thoughtful.)

JAGUNA (*reenters*): They have closed in on him now, we'll get him this time.

OROGE: It is nearly midnight.

JAGUNA: You were standing there looking at him as if he was some strange spirit. Why didn't you shout?

OROGE: You shouted didn't you? Did that catch him?

JAGUNA: Don't worry. We have him now. But things have taken a bad turn. It is no longer enough to drive him past every house. There is too much contamination about already.

OROGE (*not listening*): He saw something. Why may I not know what it was?

JAGUNA: What are you talking about?

OROGE: Hm. What is it?

JAGUNA: I said there is too much harm done already. The year will demand more from this carrier than we thought.

OROGE: What do you mean?

JAGUNA: Do we have to talk with the full mouth?

OROGE: S-sh . . . look!

(Jaguna turns just in time to see Sunma fly at him, clawing at his face like a crazed tigress.)

SUNMA: Murderer! What are you doing to him. Murderer! Murderer!

(Jaguna finds himself struggling really hard to keep off his daughter; he succeeds in pushing her off and striking her so hard on the face that she falls to her knees. He moves on her to hit her again.)

OROGE (*comes between*): Think what you are doing, Jaguna, she is your daughter.

JAGUNA: My daughter! Does this one look like my daughter? Let me cripple the harlot for life.

OROGE: That is a wicked thought, Jaguna.

JAGUNA: Don't come between me and her.

OROGE: Nothing in anger — do you forget what tonight is?

JAGUNA: Can you blame me for forgetting?

(Draws his hand across his cheek — it is covered with blood.)

OROGE: This is an unhappy night for us all. I fear what is to come of it.

JAGUNA: Let's go. I cannot restrain myself in this creature's presence. My own daughter . . . and for a stranger . . .

(They go off, Ifada, who came in with Sunma and had stood apart, horror-stricken, comes shyly forward. He helps Sunma up. They go off, he holding Sunma bent and sobbing.)

(Enter Eman — as carrier. He is physically present in the bounds of this next scene, a side of a round thatched hut. A young girl, about fourteen, runs in, stops beside the hut. She looks carefully to see that she is not observed, puts her mouth to a little hole in the wall.)

OMAE: Eman . . . Eman . . .

(Eman — as carrier — responds, as he does throughout the scene, but they are unaware of him.)

EMAN (*from inside*): Who is it?

OMAE: It is me, Omae.

EMAN: How dare you come here!

(Two hands appear at the hole and pushing outwards, create a much larger hole through which Eman puts out his head. It is Eman as a boy, the same age as the girl.)

Go away at once. Are you trying to get me into trouble!

OMAE: What is the matter?

EMAN: You. Go away.

OMAE: But I came to see you.

EMAN: Are you deaf? I say I don't want to see you. Now go before my tutor catches you.

OMAE: All right. Come out.

EMAN: Do what!

OMAE: Come out.

EMAN: You must be mad.

OMAE (*sits on the ground*): All right, if you don't come out I shall simply stay here until your tutor arrives.

EMAN (*about to explode, thinks better of it and the head disappears. A moment later he emerges from behind the hut*): What sort of a devil has got into you?

OMAE: None. I just wanted to see you.

EMAN (*his mimicry is nearly hysterical*): "None. I just wanted to see you." Do you think this place is the stream where you can go and molest innocent people?

OMAE (*coyly*): Aren't you glad to see me?

EMAN: I am not.

OMAE: Why?

EMAN: Why? Do you really ask me why? Because you are a woman and a most troublesome woman. Don't you know anything about this at all. We are not meant to see any woman. So go away before more harm's done.

OMAE (*flirtatious*): What is so secret about it anyway? What do they teach you?

EMAN: Nothing any woman can understand.

OMAE: Ha ha. You think we don't know eh? You've all come to be circumcised.

EMAN: Shut up. You don't know anything.

OMAE: Just think, all this time you haven't been circumcised, and you dared make eyes at us women.

EMAN: Thank you — woman. Now go.

OMAE: Do they give you enough to eat?

EMAN (*testily*): No. We are so hungry that when silly girls like you turn up, we eat them.

OMAE (*feigning tears*): Oh, oh, oh, he's abusing me. He's abusing me.

EMAN (*alarmed*): Don't try that here. Go quickly if you are going to cry.

OMAE: All right, I won't cry.

EMAN: Cry or no cry, go away and leave me alone. What do you think will happen if my tutor turns up now?

OMAE: He won't.

EMAN (*mimicking*): "He won't." I suppose you are his wife and he tells you where he goes. In fact this is just the time he comes round to our huts. He could be at the next hut this very moment.

OMAE: Ha-ha. You're lying. I left him by the stream, pinching the girls' bottoms. Is that the sort of thing he teaches you?

EMAN: Don't say anything against him or I shall beat you. Isn't it you loose girls who tease him, wiggling your bottoms under his nose?

OMAE (*going tearful again*): A-ah, so I am one of the loose girls eh?

EMAN: Now don't start accusing me of things I didn't say.

OMAE: But you said it. You said it.

EMAN: I didn't. Look, Omae, someone will hear you and I'll be in disgrace. Why don't you go before anything happens.

OMAE: It's all right. My friends have promised to hold your old rascal tutor till I get back.

EMAN: Then you go back right now. I have work to do. (*Going in.*)

OMAE (*runs after and tries to hold him. Eman leaps back, genuinely scared*): What is the matter? I was not going to bite you.

EMAN: Do you know what you nearly did? You almost touched me!

OMAE: Well?

EMAN: Well! Isn't it enough that you let me set my eyes on you? Must you now totally pollute me with your touch? Don't you understand anything?

OMAE: Oh, that.

EMAN (*nearly screaming*): It is not "oh that." Do you think this is only a joke or a little visit like spending the night with your grandmother? This is an important period of my life. Look, these huts, we built them with our own hands. Every boy builds his own. We learn things, do you understand? And we spend much time just thinking. At least, I do. It is the first time I have had nothing to do except think. Don't you see, I am becoming a man. For the first time, I understand that I have a life to fulfill. Has that thought ever worried you?

OMAE: You are frightening me.

EMAN: There. That is all you can say. And what use will

that be when a man finds himself alone — like that? (*Points to the hut.*) A man must go on his own, go where no one can help him, and test his strength. Because he may find himself one day sitting alone in a wall as round as that. In there, my mind could hold no other thought. I may never have such moments again to myself. Don't dare to come and steal any more of it.

OMAE (*this time, genuinely tearful*): Oh, I know you hate me. You only want to drive me away.

EMAN (*impatiently*): Yes, yes, I know I hate you — but go.

OMAE (*going, all tears. Wipes her eyes, suddenly all mischief*): Eman.

EMAN: What now?

OMAE: I only want to ask one thing . . . do you promise to tell me?

EMAN: Well, what is it?

OMAE (*gleefully*): Does it hurt?

(*She turns instantly and flees, landing straight into the arms of the returning tutor.*)

TUTOR: Te-he-he . . . what have we here? What little mouse leaps straight into the beak of the wise old owl eh?

(*Omae struggles to free herself, flies to the opposite side, grimacing with distaste.*)

TUTOR: I suppose you merely came to pick some fruits eh? You did not sneak here to see any of my children.

OMAE: Yes, I came to steal your fruits.

TUTOR: Te-he-he . . . I thought so. And that dutiful son of mine over there. He saw you and came to chase you off my fruit trees didn't he? Te-he-he . . . I'm sure he did, isn't that so, my young Eman?

EMAN: I was talking to her.

TUTOR: Indeed you were. Now be good enough to go into your hut until I decide your punishment. (*Eman withdraws.*) Te-he-he . . . now now, my little daughter, you need not be afraid of me.

OMAE (*spiritedly*): I am not.

TUTOR: Good. Very good. We ought to be friendly. (*His voice becomes leering.*) Now this is nothing to worry you, my daughter . . . a very small thing indeed. Although of course if I were to let it slip that your young Eman had broken a strong taboo, it might go hard on him you know. I am sure you would not like that to happen, would you?

OMAE: No.

TUTOR: Good. You are sensible, my girl. Can you wash clothes?

OMAE: Yes.

TUTOR: Good. If you will come with me now to my hut, I shall give you some clothes to wash, and then we will forget all about this matter eh? Well, come on.

OMAE: I shall wait here. You go and bring the clothes.

TUTOR: Eh? What is that? Now now, don't make me angry. You should know better than to talk back at your elders. Come now.

(*He takes her by the arm and tries to drag her off.*)

OMAE: No no, I won't come to your hut. Leave me. Leave me alone, you shameless old man.

TUTOR: If you don't come I shall disgrace the whole family of Eman, and yours too.

(*Eman reenters with a small bundle.*)

EMAN: Leave her alone. Let us go, Omae.

TUTOR: And where do you think you are going?

EMAN: Home.

TUTOR: Te-he-he . . . As easy as that eh? You think you can leave here any time you please? Get right back inside that hut!

(*Eman takes Omae by the arm and begins to walk off.*)

TUTOR: Come back at once.

(*He goes after him and raises his stick. Eman catches it, wrenches it from him, and throws it away.*)

OMAE (*hopping delightedly*): Kill him. Beat him to death.

TUTOR: Help! Help! He is killing me! Help!

(*Alarmed, Eman clamps his hand over his mouth.*)

EMAN: Old tutor, I don't mean you any harm, but you mustn't try to harm me either. (*He removes his hand.*)

TUTOR: You think you can get away with your crime. My report shall reach the elders before you ever get into town.

EMAN: You are afraid of what I will say about you? Don't worry. Only if you try to shame me, then I will speak. I am not going back to the village anyway. Just tell them I have gone, no more. If you say one word more than that I shall hear of it the same day and I shall come back.

TUTOR: You are telling me what to do? But don't think to come back next year because I will drive you away. Don't think to come back here even ten years from now. And don't send your children.

(*Goes off with threatening gestures.*)

EMAN: I won't come back.

OMAE: Smoked vulture! But Eman, he says you cannot return next year. What will you do?

EMAN: It is a small thing one can do in the big towns.

OMAE: I thought you were going to beat him that time. Why didn't you crack his dirty hide?

EMAN: Listen carefully, Omae . . . I am going on a journey.

OMAE: Come on. Tell me about it on the way.

EMAN: No, I go that way. I cannot return to the village.

OMAE: Because of that wretched man? Anyway you will first talk to your father.

EMAN: Go and see him for me. Tell him I have gone away for some time. I think he will know.

OMAE: But, Eman . . .

EMAN: I haven't finished. You will go and live with him till I get back. I have spoken to him about you. Look after him!

OMAE: But what is this journey? When will you come back?

EMAN: I don't know. But this is a good moment to go. Nothing ties me down.

OMAE: But, Eman, you want to leave me.

EMAN: Don't forget all I said. I don't know how long I will be. Stay in my father's house as long as you remember me. When you become tired of waiting, you must do as you please. You understand? You must do as you please.

OMAE: I cannot understand anything, Eman. I don't know where you are going or why. Suppose you never came back! Don't go, Eman. Don't leave me by myself.

EMAN: I must go. Now let me see you on your way.

OMAE: I shall come with you.

EMAN: Come with me! And who will look after you? Me? You will only be in my way, you know that! You will hold me back and I shall desert you in a strange place. Go home and do as I say. Take care of my father and let him take care of you.

(*He starts going but Omae clings to him.*)

OMAE: But, Eman, stay the night at least. You will only lose your way. Your father, Eman, what will he say? I won't remember what you said . . . come back to the village . . . I cannot return alone, Eman . . . come with me as far as the crossroads.

(*His face set, Eman strides off and Omae loses balance as he increases his pace. Falling, she quickly wraps her arms around his ankle, but Eman continues unchecked, dragging her along.*)

OMAE: Don't go, Eman . . . Eman, don't leave me, don't leave me . . . don't leave your Omae . . . don't go, Eman . . . don't leave your Omae . . .

(*Eman — as carrier — makes a nervous move as if he intends to go after the vanished pair. He stops but continues to stare at the point where he last saw them. There is stillness for a while. Then the Girl enters from the same place and remains looking at Eman. Startled, Eman looks apprehensively round him. The Girl goes nearer but keeps beyond arm's length.*)

GIRL: Are you the carrier?

EMAN: Yes. I am Eman.

GIRL: Why are you hiding?

EMAN: I really came for a drink of water . . . er . . . is there anyone in front of the house?

GIRL: No.

EMAN: But there might be people in the house. Did you hear voices?

GIRL: There is no one here.

EMAN: Good. Thank you. (*He is about to go, stops suddenly.*) Er . . . would you . . . you will find a cup on the table. Could you bring me the water out here? The water pot is in a corner.

(*The Girl goes. She enters the house, then, watching Eman carefully, slips out and runs off.*)

EMAN (*sitting*): Perhaps they have all gone home. It will be good to rest. (*He hears voices and listens hard.*) Too late. (*Moves cautiously nearer the house.*) Quickly, girl, I can hear people coming. Hurry up. (*Looks through the window.*) Where are you? Where is she? (*The truth dawns on him suddenly and he moves off, sadly.*)

(*Enter Jaguna and Oroge, led by the Girl.*)

GIRL (*pointing*): He was there.
JAGUNA: Ay, he's gone now. He is a sly one is your friend. But it won't save him forever.
OROGE: What was he doing when you saw him?
GIRL: He asked me for a drink of water.
JAGUNA: } Ah! (*They look at each other.*)
OROGE: }
OROGE: We should have thought of that.
JAGUNA: He is surely finished now. If only we had thought of it earlier.
OROGE: It is not too late. There is still an hour before midnight.
JAGUNA: We must call back all the men. Now we need only wait for him — in the right place.
OROGE: Everyone must be told. We don't want anyone heading him off again.
JAGUNA: And it works so well. This is surely the help of the gods themselves, Oroge. Don't you know at once what is on the path to the stream?
OROGE: The sacred trees.
JAGUNA: I tell you it is the very hand of the gods. Let us go.

(*An overgrown part of the village. Eman wanders in, aimlessly, seemingly uncaring of discovery. Beyond him, an area lights up, revealing a group of people clustered round a spot, all the heads are bowed. One figure stands away and separate from them. Even as Eman looks, the group breaks up and the people disperse, coming down and past him. Only three people are left, a man [Eman] whose back is turned, the village priest, and the isolated one. They stand on opposite sides of the grave, the man on the mound of earth. The Priest walks round to the man's side and lays a hand on his shoulder.*)

PRIEST: Come.
EMAN: I will. Give me a few moments here alone.
PRIEST: Be comforted.

(*They fall silent.*)

EMAN: I was gone twelve years but she waited. She whom I thought had too much of the laughing child in her. Twelve years I was a pilgrim, seeking the vain shrine of secret strength. And all the time, strange knowledge, this silent strength of my child-woman.
PRIEST: We all saw it. It was a lesson to us; we did not know that such goodness could be found among us.
EMAN: Then why? Why the wasted years if she had to perish giving birth to my child? (*They are both silent.*) I do not really know for what great meaning I

searched. When I returned, I could not be certain I had found it. Until I reached my home and I found her a full-grown woman, still a child at heart. When I grew to believe it, I thought, this, after all, is what I sought. It was here all the time. And I threw away my new-gained knowledge. I buried the part of me that was formed in strange places. I made a home in my birthplace.
PRIEST: That was as it should be.
EMAN: Any truth of that was killed in the cruelty of her brief happiness.
PRIEST (*looks up and sees the figure standing away from them, the child in his arms. He is totally still*): Your father — he is over there.
EMAN: I knew he would come. Has he my son with him?
PRIEST: Yes.
EMAN: He will let no one take the child. Go and comfort him, priest. He loved Omae like a daughter, and you all know how well she looked after him. You see how strong we really are. In his heart of hearts the old man's love really awaited a daughter. Go and comfort him. His grief is more than mine.

(*The Priest goes. The Old Man has stood well away from the burial group. His face is hard and his gaze unswerving from the grave. The Priest goes to him, pauses, but sees that he can make no dent in the man's grief. Bowed, he goes on his way.*)
    (*Eman, as carrier, walking towards the graveside, the other Eman having gone. His feet sink into the mound and he breaks slowly onto his knees, scooping up the sand in his hands and pouring it on his head. The scene blacks out slowly.*)

(*Enter Jaguna and Oroge.*)

OROGE: We have only a little time.
JAGUNA: He will come. All the wells are guarded. There is only the stream left him. The animal must come to drink.
OROGE: You are sure it will fail — the trap, I mean.
JAGUNA: When Jaguna sets the trap, even elephants pay homage — their trunks downwards and one leg up in the sky. When the carrier steps on the fallen twigs, it is up in the sacred trees with him.
OROGE: I shall breathe again when this long night is over.

(*They go out.*)
    (*Enter Eman — as carrier — from the same direction as the last two entered. In front of him is a still figure, the Old Man as he was, carrying the dwarf boat.*)

EMAN (*joyfully*): Father.

(*The figure does not turn round.*)

EMAN: It is your son, Eman. (*He moves nearer.*) Don't you want to look at me? It is I, Eman. (*He moves nearer still.*)
OLD MAN: You are coming too close. Don't you know what I carry on my head?

EMAN: But, Father, I am your son.

OLD MAN: Then go back. We cannot give the two of us.

EMAN: Tell me first where you are going.

OLD MAN: Do *you* ask that? Where else but to the river?

EMAN (*visibly relieved*): I only wanted to be sure. My throat is burning. I have been looking for the stream all night.

OLD MAN: It is the other way.

EMAN: But you said . . .

OLD MAN: I take the longer way, you know how I must do this. It is quicker if you take the other way. Go now.

EMAN: No, I will only get lost again. I shall go with you.

OLD MAN: Go back, my son. Go back.

EMAN: Why? Won't you even look at me?

OLD MAN: Listen to your father. Go back.

EMAN: But, father!

(*He makes to hold him. Instantly the old man breaks into a rapid trot. Eman hesitates, then follows, his strength nearly gone.*)

EMAN: Wait, father. I am coming with you . . . wait . . . wait for me, father . . .

(*There is a sound of twigs breaking, of a sudden trembling in the branches. Then silence.*)

(*The front of Eman's house. The effigy is hanging from the sheaves. Enter Sunma, still supported by Ifada, she stands transfixed as she sees the hanging figure. Ifada appears to go mad, rushes at the object, and tears it down. Sunma, her last bit of will gone, crumbles against the wall. Some distance away from them, partly hidden, stands the Girl, impassively watching. Ifada hugs the effigy to him, stands above Sunma. The Girl remains where she is, observing.*)

(*Almost at once, the villagers begin to return, subdued and guilty.*)

(*They walk across the front, skirting the house as widely as they can. No word is exchanged. Jaguna and Oroge eventually appear. Jaguna, who is leading, sees Sunma as soon as he comes in view. He stops at once, retreating slightly.*)

OROGE (*almost whispering*): What is it?

JAGUNA: The viper.

(*Oroge looks cautiously at the woman.*)

OROGE: I don't think she will even see you.

JAGUNA: Are you sure? I am in no frame of mind for another meeting with her.

OROGE: Let's go home.

JAGUNA: I am sick to the heart of the cowardice I have seen tonight.

OROGE: That is the nature of men.

JAGUNA: Then it is a sorry world to live in. We did it for them. It was all for their own common good. What did it benefit me whether the man lived or died. But did you see them? One and all they looked up at the man and words died in their throats.

OROGE: It was no common sight.

JAGUNA: Women could not have behaved so shamefully. One by one they crept off like sick dogs. Not one could raise a curse.

OROGE: It was not only him they fled. Do you see how unattended we are?

JAGUNA: There are those who will pay for this night's work!

OROGE: Ay, let us go home.

(*They go off. Sunma, Ifada, and the Girl remain as they are, the light fading slowly on them.*)

COMMENTARY

Lewis Nkosi (b. 1935)

INTERVIEW WITH WOLE SOYINKA   1962

    This early interview with Soyinka was taped in Lagos, Nigeria, in August 1962, while The Strong Breed *was very fresh in his mind. In fact, it had not yet had its first publication, which in Nigeria was in 1963. Nkosi in the interview highlights the impact of Bertolt Brecht's theater on Soyinka's writing.*

Nkosi: Well, Wole Soyinka, could you tell us what set you off on this road to writing?

Soyinka: I suppose that requires really going back a bit. I would say I began writing seriously, or rather taking myself seriously, taking my *writing* seriously about three, four years ago, but I can only presume that I have always been interested in writing. In school I wrote the usual little sketches for production, the occasional verse, you know, the short story, etc., and I think about 1951 I had the great excitement of having a short story of mine broadcast on the Nigerian Broadcasting Service and that was sort of my first public performance.

Nkosi: What schools did you attend?

Soyinka: I went to Government School, Ibadan; after that I spent a couple of years in the University College, Ibadan.

Nkosi: You have now published drama or rather you've had some plays produced?

Soyinka: Yes, "produced" is the correct word. I haven't had any plays published although some are in print right now and will come out shortly.

Nkosi: Could you tell us what those plays are?

Soyinka: There is *The Lion and the Jewel* which was the first play I wrote.

Nkosi: No, the second.

Soyinka: The first one I sent up, I suppose like most people do, is the *A Dance of Forests* which I wrote in 1960 and timed it for the Independence Celebrations; there is the *House of Banigeji* which has never been performed. And I have written about four one-acts including *The Trials of Brother Jero* which was done quite recently in Nigeria.

Nkosi: The *A Dance of the Forests* won you a prize, didn't it?

Soyinka: Yes, Nigerian Independence competition prize 1960.

Nkosi: Have you got any particular authors that have influenced you most?

Soyinka: This is a very difficult question for me because I am not aware of any conscious influence on my work, but I can say that if I wanted to aim at any particular kind of theater, I think, however subconsciously, I might aim at Brecht's kind of theater, which I admire tremendously, just his complete freedom with the medium of the theater.

Nkosi: In your last play, *A Dance of the Forests,* which caused a lot of people a tremendous amount of agony trying to figure out just exactly what it was trying to do — they felt that there were some hidden meanings contained in lots of symbolism which they couldn't gather. Now as you're the author, we are lucky to have you here, and we think that you probably might enlighten us about just what you were trying to say in that work of yours.

Soyinka: Well, let me say first of all that I think that my prime duty as a playwright is to provide excellent theater; in other words, I think that I have only one commitment to the public, and that is to my audience and that is to make sure they do not leave the theater bored. I don't believe that I have any obligation to enlighten, to instruct, to teach: I don't possess that sense of duty or didacticism — very much unlike Brecht for instance, for, you see, what I like in Brecht is his sort of theater, its liveliness and freedom, not so much his purpose or intentions. I believe my primary duty is just to see that I provide excellent theater for the audience. But inevitably, it is just common sense to say that one just cannot write about just nothing. In *A Dance of the Forests,* I was very much conscious of all the potentialities of existing theatrical idioms in Nigeria and I only know that there was one thing which motivated, maybe, guided the form and the shape of the play or the eventual fate of the characters. I use this word "motivated" quite cautiously because I do not think I consciously tried to preach or bring out, you know, a series of symbolisms at all, but the main thing was the realization that human beings are just destructive all over the world. I think this is it — I have thought about this again and again but during the production — I produced it myself — and in trying to see the play take shape on the stage, I find that the main thing is my own personal conviction or observation that human beings are simply cannibals all over the world so that their main preoccupation seems to be eating up one another. This I think is the main thing I would say was in the back of my mind when I wrote it.

Nkosi: Yes, that sounds very much like Tennessee Williams's idea of the world conscious of the evil.

Soyinka: Well, I don't sort of regard it so much as . . .

Nkosi: The ferocity of human beings.

Soyinka: Yes, the carnivorous nature of. . . .

Nkosi: Yes, I wonder whether now — have you pursued this theme in the other plays or are the other plays different?

Soyinka: . . . Fundamentally, I think they're different. I think that sort of semiconsciously the moment I realize I'm pursuing a theme again, it seems to ring a bell warning that I have preceded myself somewhere; I have such a feeling about this that I shirk from it but I would say there are traces of it in my other plays — in, for instance, my favorite one-act play which is *The Strong Breed*. I think this one is also very much mixed up with the whole element of sacrifice, so contrasting the idea of selfishness with willing self-sacrifice as opposed to the other general cannibalism of human beings.

Contemporary Drama

Experimentation

The experimentation in drama that flourished in the first half of the twentieth century has continued in contemporary drama. In fact, the achievements of Tennessee Williams, Arthur Miller, Samuel Beckett, and other midcentury playwrights encouraged later playwrights to experiment more daringly with mixing media such as film, video, opera, rock, and other music with live actors. Mixed-media approaches are still options for playwrights at the beginning of the twenty-first century, but most contemporary plays celebrated by critics and audiences have been relatively traditional. They build on the achievement of nineteenth-century realism and twentieth-century expressionism.

Harold Pinter's distinctive style, developed in the late 1950s and early 1960s, is connected with some of the absurdist experiments in drama. His dialogue is acerbic, repetitive, sometimes apparently aimless. However, he is able to produce intense emotional situations, such as that in *The Dumb Waiter* (1957), in which two "hit men" wait for instructions in a basement room. *The Caretaker* (1959) and *The Homecoming* (1965), his first commercial successes, established him as a major figure in modern theater. He has also been a screenwriter for such films as *The Quiller Memorandum* (1966), *The French Lieutenant's Woman* (1981), and *The Handmaid's Tale* (1990). His experiments with time and sequence in his full-length play *Betrayal* (1978), for which he also wrote the screenplay, have inspired other playwrights, such as Paula Vogel, to experiment with the backward movement of action.

Most of the interesting late twentieth-century experimental theater was done in groups such as Richard Schechner's Performance Group, which created what Schechner called ENVIRONMENTAL THEATER in New York City in the late 1960s, and Jerzy Grotowski's Polish Laboratory Theatre in Wroclaw, Poland, during the same period. Ensembles like the Bread and Puppet Theatre, San Francisco Mime Troupe, and Luis Valdez's El Teatro Campesino on the West Coast combined a radical political message with theatrical experimentation. The work of these groups is effective primarily at the level of performance; their texts are not representative of their impact on audiences.

Theater of Cruelty

The ensembles of the 1960s and 1970s were strongly influenced by the work of Antonin Artaud (1896–1948), French actor, director, and a theorist of theater. In creating what came to be known as the THEATER OF CRUELTY, he insisted on removing the comforting distance between actors and audience. Thus the audience was involved in a direct, virtually physical fashion with the dramatic action. Artaud designed theater to be a total experience — a sensational spectacle that did not depend on coherent plot or development. He concentrated on what he called a total theater that emphasized movement, gesture, music, sound, light, and other nonverbal elements to intensify the experience.

Artaud's manifestos collected in a work called *The Theater and Its Double* (1938) inspired some of the most important twentieth-century theater practitioners, including Peter Brook and Robert Wilson, among others. Artaud's notion of a "serious" theater is at the root of his influence:

> Our long habit of seeking diversion has made us forget the idea of a serious theater, which, overturning all our preconceptions, inspires us with the fiery magnetism of its images and acts upon us like a spiritual therapeutics whose touch can never be forgotten.
>
> Everything that acts is a cruelty. It is upon this idea of extreme action, pushed beyond all limits, that theater must be rebuilt.

Artaud compared the theater artist he envisioned to a victim "burnt at the stake, signaling through the flames."

Environmental Theater

Richard Schechner's most famous production, based on Euripides' *The Bacchae*, was *Dionysus in 69* (1968), in which Pentheus is torn to pieces in an impassioned frenzy. Part of the point of Schechner's production was to inspire the audience so much that they would take to the stage, becoming indistinguishable from the actors. *Dionysus in 69* was an effort to draw on the same spiritual energies tapped by Greek drama by connecting with the feasts of Dionysus, god of wine and ecstasy. The play was a spontaneous and partly improvised performance piece rather than a text meant to be read. At one point the audience and actors disrobed in a simulation of a Greek religious orgy and Schechner's goal of involving audience and actors in a pagan ritual was realized night after night during the run.

In a similar way Julian Beck and Judith Malina's Living Theatre maintained a special relationship with the audience. Beck's plays were designed to break down the absolutes of dramatic space and audience space by having the actors roam through the audience and interact apparently at random with audience members. *Paradise Now* (1968) is his best-known play. Like Schechner's *Dionysus in 69*, it was essentially a performance piece. Certain segments were improvised; therefore, as a reading text, it has relatively little power.

"Poor Theater"

Jerzy Grotowski called his work "poor theater" because it was meant to contrast with the "rich theater" of the commercial stage, with its expensive lighting, decorated stages, rich costumes, numerous props, and elaborate settings. Grotowski's Laboratory Theatre, begun in 1959, relied on preexisting texts but interpreted them broadly through a total reconception of their meaning. For example, Grotowski's *Akropolis* (1962; revised frequently from 1963 to 1975) adapted an older Polish drama by Stanislaw Wyspiański (1904) and reset it in modern times in Auschwitz with the actors, dressed in ragged sackcloth prison uniforms, looking wretched and starving. At the end of the play the prisoners follow a headless puppet-corpse, Christ, into an afterlife. They march in an eerie ritual procession offstage into the waiting prison camp ovens.

Grotowski's theater has been influential worldwide. When the Polish government clamped down on the Solidarity° movement in the late 1970s, Grotowski left Poland. After 1970 Grotowski shifted his focus from public performances to small, intense group workshops and to the ritual performances of cultures from all over the world. The first phase of his work with the Laboratory Theatre has remained the most influential. One of his actors, Richard Cieslak, traveled widely training people in Grotowski's methods.

Theater of Images

Robert Wilson experimented in the 1970s, 1980s, and 1990s with repetitive narratives that sometimes take eight hours to perform. His multimedia dramas involve huge casts and ordinarily cover an immense historic range (Figure 13). One of his most extraordinary successes was *Einstein on the Beach* (1976), an opera written in collaboration with composer Philip Glass. Eight hours long, it was originally produced in a conventional theater, but it uses dramatic techniques that involve extensive patterns of repetition, the creation of enigmatic and evocative images, and characters who are cartoonlike caricatures of historical people. The overall effect is hypnotic; one of the points of Wilson's work seems to be to induce a trancelike state in his audience. One of his multimedia productions, *CIVIL warS* (1983), continued to develop this concept of massive theater that transcends conventional dramatic boundaries. In 1994 Wilson produced a monologue version of *Hamlet* that received some acclaim.

Gay and Lesbian Theater and Other New Ensembles

Some of the most energetic theater of the late twentieth century came from groups that were excluded for long periods from representation in mainstream theater. Gay, lesbian, African American, Hispanic American, and Native American groups have been virtually ignored by commercial theater and as a result have formed their own collectives and groups.

One reason for the development of gay theater in the United States and Great Britain in the 1960s was the decriminalization of homosexuality beginning in 1967 in Boston. Depiction of homosexual love onstage waited even longer, until the Gay Workshop's plays in London beginning in 1976. The first openly gay play was Mart Crowley's *The Boys in the Band* (1968), a popular success produced just after the repeal of a New York law prohibiting homosexuality from being represented on stage.

The Ridiculous Theatrical Company, founded by Charles Ludlam (1940–1987) in 1969, produced a formidable body of work rooted in the experiences of the homosexual community of New York. Its influence spread to many parts of the world. One of Ludlam's catchphrases was "plays without the stink of art." His plays were often ridiculously funny. *Bluebeard* (1970), for example, focused on creating a third gender by inventing a third genital. *Camille* (1973), starring Ludlam himself in the title role, hilariously spoofed not only Dumas's play but most of the "Hallmark card" conventions about romantic love. A gifted female impersonator, Ludlam played Hedda Gabler at the American Ibsen Theatre in Pittsburgh. Under the direction of Ludlam's partner, Everett Quinton, the Ridiculous Theatrical Company continues to produce Ludlam's plays as well as new plays in his tradition.

Solidarity: A labor organizing movement in Communist Poland led by Lech Walesa.

Figure 13. Multimedia effects in Robert Wilson's *CIVIL warS.*

Many of the most-praised recent plays have addressed the issues of AIDS and its ravaging of the gay community. Harvey Fierstein's *Torch Song Trilogy* (1982) was named best play of the year and appeared several years later on television. *As Is* by William M. Hoffman (1985) has been described by Don Shewey as the "best gay play anyone has written on AIDS yet." Tony Kushner dazzled New York with *Angels in America Part One: Millennium Approaches* (1992) and *Part Two: Perestroika* (1992). This two-part drama approached the problems of gay life in America both on a personal and a public, political level. The plays are called a "fantasia" and use a free-form, nonrealistic style of presentation.

Lesbian theatrical groups have sprung up in the United States and Great Britain. They often merge with women's theater groups and address issues such as male violence, societal restrictions on women, and women's opportunities. A number of important collectives, such as the Rhode Island Women's Theater and At the Foot of the Mountain in Minneapolis, treated general women's issues in the 1970s. Groups such as Medusa's Revenge (founded 1976) and

Atlanta's Red Dyke Theater (1974) centered more on lesbian experience. These last two groups disbanded after a few years of successful productions. Megan Terry's Omaha Magic Theater, founded with Joanne Schmidman, has been a long-lasting theater focusing on women's issues. Other groups such as Spiderwoman, consisting of three Native American sisters, and the highly successful Split Britches consider Cafe WOW in New York's East Village to be the home of lesbian theater. Gay and lesbian theater groups have often been concerned with erasing stereotypes while also celebrating gay and lesbian lifestyles. Plays that once played only to gay and lesbian audiences — such as Martin Sherman's (b. 1938) *Bent* (1977) and Larry Kramer's (b. 1936) *The Normal Heart* (1985) — are now shown in theaters worldwide.

Other important women playwrights have made their mark in contemporary theater, with plays such as María Irene Fornés's *Fefu and Her Friends* (1977), a sprawling play featuring women in roles traditionally reserved for men. It has become a cult classic, with many productions in regional theaters. Her *The Conduct of Life* (1985) is a cruel parody of macho values in a Latin American dictatorship. It won an Obie Award for best play of the year. Caryl Churchill has been a dominant figure in British drama since the first production of *Cloud Nine* (1979), a drama that critiques colonialism and gender stereotyping. *Top Girls* (1982) is one of her most successful plays. It centers on an employment agency for women but has as its premise the introduction of famous women from the past of several cultures. It is a powerful feminist statement. *Fen* (1983), *Serious Money* (1987), and *The Skriker* (1994) have solidified her reputation as an experimental, powerful dramatist. Marsha Norman's *Getting Out* (1977), *'night Mother* (1982), and *The Secret Garden* (1991) have been produced to considerable acclaim. Norman has become an important presence in American drama. Emily Mann's *Execution of Justice* (1983) centers on the trial of Dan White, who murdered Harvey Milk, San Francisco's first openly gay mayor. Anne Devlin's *Ourselves Alone* (1986); Lynn Siefert's *Coyote Ugly* (1986); Tina Howe's *Painting Churches* (1982); and Suzan-Lori Parks's *The Death of the Last Black Man in the Whole Entire World* (1990), *The America Play* (1993), *Venus* (1996), and *In the Blood* (1999) have all added stature to the position of women in contemporary theater.

Through the 1970s, 1980s, and 1990s numerous black theatrical groups developed in many parts of the world. An important Afro-Caribbean theater group was formed in the Keskidee Center in North London, with Edgar White (b. 1947) as one of its directors. White's plays are often centered in Caribbean mystical experiences, including Rastafarianism. *The Nine Night* (1983), produced in London, focuses on a Jamaican funeral tradition designed to help the deceased enter the gates of heaven.

Experiments with Theater Space

Drama around the world has developed alternatives to the proscenium theater. Theater in the round, which seats audiences on all sides of the actors, has been exceptionally powerful for certain plays. Peter Weiss's *Persecution and Assassination of Jean-Paul Marat as Performed by the Inmates of the Asylum of Charenton under the Direction of the Marquis de Sade* (1964) was especially effective in this format. Other theatrical experiments explored the power of spaces one would not have thought appropriate for drama. For example, Wladimir Pereira Cardoso designed an elaborate welded-steel set for a production of Jean Genet's *The Balcony* in the Ruth Escobar Theater in São Paulo, Brazil. The set was a huge suspended cone in which people sat looking inward while the actors were suspended in the spherical space before them. The production was first staged in 1969 and was seen through 1971 and most of 1972 by many thousands of people. The set was constructed of eighty tons of iron assembled like a trellis and requiring 500,000 welds. The entire insides of the theater were torn out to accommodate the new set. The audience of 250 was seated on circular platforms and the actors moved through the space on ramps, on suspended cables, and on moving platforms. The same theater produced *The Voyage*, an adaptation of an epic poem, *The Lusiads*, about the origin of Portuguese people. That set used open welded platforms suggesting ships' decks. In Dubrovnik, Yugoslavia, a replica of Columbus's *Santa Maria* — built much larger than the original — was used to stage Miroslav Krleza's expressionist play *Christopher Columbus*, written in 1917. The ship was docked in Dubrovnik Harbor for the performances.

Richard Foreman's Ontological-Hysteric Theatre performs in a loft in New York City with all audience members facing in the same direction. This is not fundamentally different from the traditional proscenium theater, but the open loft space and the visible movements of actors offstage create a new relationship to the action. Foreman's work, such as *Sophia = (Wisdom)* (1970 and later), which has been performed in many parts, has none of the usually accepted narrative clues to its action. However, it aims to explore hitherto hidden aspects of experience, such as sexual taboos and unorthodox relationships. The relationship of the author to the performance is also experimental in his theater, since he directs his actors, often using a loud buzzer, as if they were extensions of his will. His work, begun in the 1960s, has continued to this day. He collaborated in the staging of Suzan-Lori Parks's *Venus* (1996).

Experimentation within the Tradition

Much of the powerful and lasting drama of the 1980s and 1990s has been achieved in a proscenium theater, using traditional methods of DRAMATURGY, the craft or techniques of dramatic composition. Contemporary dramatists are by no means shy of experimentation, but they are also sensitive to the continuing resources of the traditional stage as it was conceived by Chekhov and Ibsen and Miller. Marsha Norman, who wrote *'night, Mother,* has said that her plays are "wildly traditional. I'm a purist about structure. Plays are like plane rides. You [the audience] buy the ticket and you have to get where the ticket takes you. Or else you've been had."

Sam Shepard, one of the most prolific modern playwrights, experiments with his material, much of which premiered in small theaters in Greenwich Village, such as the La Mama Experimental Theater Club. But his most widely known plays, among them *Buried Child* (1978), are produced easily on conventional stages. Shepard's work is wide-ranging and challenging. His language is coarse, a representation of the way he has heard people speak, and the violence he portrays onstage is strong enough to alienate many in the audience. Shepard, important as he is, has not found a popular commercial audience for his plays. At root, his work is always experimental.

Athol Fugard, a South African, writes powerful plays that also work well on conventional proscenium stages. Like Shepard's, his subject matter is not the kind that permits an audience to sit back relaxed and appreciate the drama with a sense of detachment. Instead, the plays usually disturb audiences. His primary subject matter is the devastation — for blacks and whites — caused by apartheid in South Africa. Fugard's work with black actors in South Africa produced a vital experimental theater out of which his best early work grew.

Fugard's *The Blood Knot* (1961) and *Boesman and Lena* (1969), part of a trilogy on South Africa, are based on the theme of racial discrimination. But other plays, such as *A Lesson from Aloes* (1978) and *My Children! My Africa!* (1989), are involved with problems of individuals in relation to their political world. Fugard is in many ways a traditional playwright, except for his subject matter. His characters are thoroughly developed, but with great economy. In *"MASTER HAROLD"... and the boys,* for example, we are given a deep understanding of Hally and Sam, whose relationship, past, present, and future, is the center of the play. Fugard is not writing the well-made play, any more than the other contemporary playwrights in this collection are. There is nothing "mechanical" in Fugard's work but rather a sense of organic growth, of actions arising from perceptible conditions and historical circumstances. These contribute to the sense of integrity that his plays communicate.

Some of Caryl Churchill's plays, emphasizing themes of socialism, colonialism, and feminism, were developed in workshops and collaborations with actors and directors. When writing a play, she experiments early in the first stages by spending time in the environments her plays depict. When she worked on *Top Girls* (1982), she came up with the idea of setting the action in an employment agency after she had talked with many people whose lives are wrapped up in business. For *Serious Money* (1987), she and the group developing the play spent time at the London Stock Exchange, absorbing the atmosphere of frenetic buying and selling.

Though she claims to be a traditionalist, Marsha Norman has written experimental plays. Her first success, *Getting Out* (1977), portrays the same character at two periods in her life — as an adolescent and as an adult — on separate parts of the stage at the same time. The effect is startling, but the structure of the play is clear and simple: Arlene is trying to start life over after leaving prison, while Arlie, her younger, rebellious self, is still with her, commenting on what she is doing. The play ends with a reconciliation of the two parts of the character.

Norman's *'night, Mother* is another traditionally structured play. It respects the Aristotelian unities of time, place, and action, and it is confrontational. Thelma and her daughter, Jessie, are in a power struggle over Jessie's right to commit suicide. The technique is naturalistic, and the play's subject matter, as in the plays of Strindberg and Ibsen, is discomforting to its contemporary audiences.

August Wilson has been working on a series of ten plays on the subject of black life in modern America. So far he has written eight of those plays, and each of the first four won the New York Drama Critics' Circle Award for best play of the year. All of Wilson's plays have explored the way the heritage of blacks enables them to live intelligently in the present, with understanding and dignity. People in his plays have lost touch with the past and, for that reason, risk a loss of self-understanding. Wilson's plays also show the pain endured by blacks in an America that is supposed to be the land of opportunity. Like

Arthur Miller in *Death of a Salesman* and Lorraine Hansberry in *A Raisin in the Sun,* Wilson explores the nature and consequences of the American dream, especially for those effectively excluded from this dream. Blacks' frustration, exploitation, and suffering are presented in Wilson's powerful characters, such as Troy Maxson in *Fences* (1985). Troy is a garbage collector who was a star baseball player at a time when blacks could play only in their own leagues. (The major leagues were exclusively white until 1947, when Jackie Robinson joined the Brooklyn Dodgers and the game began to be integrated.) The play centers on Maxson's anger, his pride for his family, and his concerns for his son's growing up into a world in which he must empower himself to achieve what he most wants for himself. Cory, Troy's son, does not see the same kind of discrimination and has not felt the unfairness that was Troy's primary experience in growing up. Showing the world as Troy Maxson sees it is one of the functions of the play.

Wilson's plays have a naturalistic surface, but they also allude to the supernatural, as in *The Piano Lesson* (1990). Some of the roots of this tradition are in the black church and some in African religion, a source shared by Soyinka and Wilson, among others.

Among the current playwrights, David Henry Hwang has been active in writing for both stage and film. His work has often centered on Chinese Americans and the problems they encounter in their experiences in the United States. Hwang has sensitized audiences to subjects about which playwrights had hitherto been silent. His first success, *FOB* (1980), focused on how new immigrants were viewed by Chinese Americans who had already assimilated. The play's title is an acronym for "fresh off the boat." Hwang's most successful play, *M. Butterfly* (1987), is about a romance between a French diplomat and a transvestite Chinese opera singer.

David Mamet responds to a social situation in *Oleanna* (1992). The characters, a male college professor and a female student, at first adopt an ordinary teacher-student relationship; eventually, though, that relationship alters. Mamet explores questions of power and issues of sexual harassment. As the lines he draws shift back and forth, the audience never knows exactly how clear the lines are meant to be. The issues in the play are thus subject to a number of different interpretations.

Tony Kushner's two-part drama *Angels in America: Millennium Approaches* (1992) and *Perestroika* (1992) explores issues in modern American history, with an emphasis on religion, politics, and a variety of hysterias. The plays explore homophobia, red-baiting politics, and the impact of AIDS on contemporary society. The open, dynamic structure of the play is enormously powerful. The entire drama lasts six and a half hours and has been seen not only in San Francisco, where it opened, but also in New York, London, other European cities, and regional theaters throughout the United States.

In the late 1990s women and young men made important contributions to theater. José Rivera (b. 1955) presented two plays that drew on the tradition of magical realism that is prominent in Latin American fiction. *Marisol* (1992) and *Cloud Tectonics* (1995) are visually and emotionally impressive pieces that work counter to the Ibsenist tradition of realism. As especially theatrical pieces, they give the director a considerable degree of freedom in staging. Yasmina Reza (b. 1959) had major success in France, England, the United States, and many other nations with her award-winning comedy *"Art,"* which raises unexpected questions about taste and friendship. Martin McDonagh (b. 1970) startled the London theater scene with his Leenane trilogy: *The Beauty Queen of Leenane* (1996), *A Skull in Connemara* (1997), and *The Lonesome West* (1997). The three plays and his *The Cripple of Inishmaan* (1996) were produced at the same time in London, a record for a twenty-seven-year-old playwright. Paula Vogel (b. 1951) created a portrait of an adolescent girl, Li'l Bit, involved with an incestuous Uncle Peck in *How I Learned to Drive* (1997). The play won the Pulitzer Prize that year and established her as one of the most important American playwrights. The works of these playwrights demonstrate the vitality and energy that sustains drama in the first years of the twenty-first century.

Contemporary Drama Timeline

DATE	THEATER	POLITICAL	SOCIAL/CULTURAL
1950–present	**1951:** Anna Deavere Smith, African American playwright and actress, born. Among her works are *Fires in the Mirror* (1991) and *Twilight: Los Angeles, 1992* (1994).	**1950:** U.S. Senator Joseph McCarthy begins his war on Communism by investigating the alleged "un-American activities" of hundreds of U.S. citizens.	**1950:** Simone de Beauvoir (1908–1986), French author, publishes *The Second Sex.*
		1951: The USSR explodes its first atomic bomb.	
		1953: Joseph Stalin dies.	**1952:** Ralph Ellison (1914–1994), African American novelist, publishes *Invisible Man.*
	1954: Joseph Papp founds the New York Shakespeare festival.	**1954:** *Brown v. Board of Education* finds school segregation unconstitutional.	**1954:** Elvis Presley (1935–1977) makes his first recording at Sun Studios.
		1954: Senator Joseph McCarthy's witch hunt for Communist infiltration in the United States ends.	
	1956: John Osborne's *Look Back in Anger* is produced in London.	**1955:** Communist Eastern European allies sign the Warsaw Pact.	
	1956: Tony Kushner, American playwright, born. He is best known for the plays *Angels in America, Parts 1 and 2* (1992).	**1955:** Montgomery, Alabama, bus boycott	**1957:** Jack Kerouac (1922–1969) publishes *On the Road.*
	1959: Jerzy Grotowski establishes the Laboratory Theater in Poland. In 1968 he publishes *Towards a Poor Theatre.*	**1958:** Fidel Castro begins total war against Batista in Cuba; in 1959 he becomes premier.	
	1960s: Off-Off-Broadway flourishes with the formation of such groups as Café Cino (1958), La Mama ETC (1962), the Open Theatre (1963), and the Performance Group (1967).	**1958–1969:** Charles de Gaulle is president of France.	
		1960: The Belgian Congo is granted independence.	
	1961: Peter Schumann founds the Bread and Puppet Theatre, an influential political ensemble, in the United States.	**1961:** The Berlin Wall blocks immigration to and from East and West Germany.	
		1962: The cold war reaches one of its tensest moments when the United States confronts the USSR over Soviet nuclear missile bases in Cuba.	**1962:** James Watson and Francis Crick share the Nobel Prize for defining the 3-D molecular structure of DNA.
	1963: The National Theatre is established in London under the direction of Laurence Olivier.		**1962:** Cesar Chavez (1927–1993) organizes California migrant farm workers.
	1964: Ariane Mnouchkine forms the Théâtre du Soleil in France.	**1962:** The first U.S. combat troops are sent to fight in South Vietnam.	**1962:** Alexander Solzhenitsyn's *One Day in the Life of Ivan Denisovich* describes life in the Soviet gulag.
	1964: Peter Brook's production of Peter Weiss's *Marat/Sade* opens at the Royal Shakespeare Company.	**1963:** President John F. Kennedy is assassinated in Dallas.	**1964:** The Beatles appear on the *Ed Sullivan Show.*
		1965: Malcolm X is assassinated in New York.	**1965:** The National Endowment for the Arts is established by the U.S. government.

Contemporary Drama Timeline (continued)

DATE	THEATER	POLITICAL	SOCIAL/CULTURAL
1950–present (continued)	**1968:** The Negro Ensemble Company is established in the United States under the direction of Douglas Turner Ward.	**1967:** In the Six-Day War, Israel responds to Arab provocation by capturing territory from Egypt, Syria, and Jordan.	**1966:** The National Organization for Women (NOW) is established to end discrimination against women.
	1968: The Living Theatre produces its highly influential experimental work, *Paradise Now.*	**1967:** Thurgood Marshall (1908–1993) is the first African American appointed to the U.S. Supreme Court.	**1967:** Dr. Christiaan N. Barnard performs the world's first human heart transplant operation in South Africa.
	1968: Theatrical censorship, in place since the Licensing Act of 1737, is finally abolished in England.	**1968:** The American civil rights leader Martin Luther King Jr. is assassinated.	
	1968: *Hair!,* the first rock musical, hits Broadway; it is followed by *Jesus Christ Superstar* in 1971.	**1968:** Students demonstrate throughout France.	**1969:** U.S. astronaut Neil Armstrong walks on the moon.
	1968: The Performance Group produces *Dionysus in 69* under the direction of Richard Schechner.		**1969:** New York City police raid the Stonewall Inn, and the resulting three-day protest becomes a symbol for the emerging gay rights movement.
	1970: Peter Brook's acclaimed production of *A Midsummer Night's Dream* opens at the Royal Shakespeare Company.	**1970–1975:** Civil war is fought in Cambodia; Communist leader Pol Pot takes power in 1975 and begins genocidal campaign.	
		1972: U.S. President Richard Nixon and Soviet leader Leonid Breshnev sign the Strategic Arms Limitation Treaty (SALT).	
		1972: Philippine President Ferdinand Marcos declares martial law and assumes dictatorial powers.	
		1973: In *Roe v. Wade,* the U.S. Supreme Court legalizes abortion.	
		1973: U.S. troops are withdrawn from Vietnam.	
		1974: President Nixon resigns from office as a result of the Watergate scandal.	
	1975: Michael Bennett's musical *A Chorus Line* opens on Broadway and runs until 1990.	**1975:** The Spanish dictator Francisco Franco dies.	
		1976: The Chinese Communist leader Mao Zedong dies. Deng Xiaoping emerges as the new Chinese leader in 1978.	**1976:** The Episcopal Church approves the ordination of women to be priests and bishops.
		1976: Waves of violence against apartheid in Cape Town, Soweto, and Johannesburg, South Africa	

Contemporary Drama Timeline *(continued)*

DATE	THEATER	POLITICAL	SOCIAL/CULTURAL
1950–present (continued)	**1978:** Harold Pinter's *Betrayal* premiers at the National Theatre in London.		
	1979: Stephen Sondheim's *Sweeney Todd* opens on Broadway. Other musicals by the prolific composer include *Sunday in the Park with George* (1984), *Into the Woods* (1987), and *Passion* (1995).	**1979:** After the overthrow of Shah Mohammad Reza Pahlevi, the Ayatollah Khomeini establishes the Islamic Republic of Iran.	
	1980: Sam Shephard's *True West* premieres.	**1980:** The Iran-Iraq War begins when Iraq invades Iran; the war lasts for eight years.	
		1981: General Idi Amin begins his eight-year reign of terror in Uganda.	**1981:** Sandra Day O'Connor becomes the first woman appointed to the U.S. Supreme Court.
	1982: Athol Fugard's *"MASTER HAROLD"* . . . *and the boys* premieres at the Yale Repertory Theatre.	**1981:** Egyptian leader Anwar Sadat is assassinated by Muslim extremists.	**1981:** IBM markets its first personal computer.
	1982: Caryl Churchill's *Cloud Nine* premieres.		**1982:** Wisconsin becomes the first state to protect gays and lesbians under civil rights legislation.
	1983: Marsha Norman's *'night, Mother* opens at New York's Golden Theater and wins the Pulitzer Prize.		
	1985: August Wilson's *Fences* premieres at the Yale Repertory Theatre and wins the Pulitzer Prize in 1987.	**1985:** Mikhail Gorbachev becomes the leader of the Soviet Union and institutes a policy of *glasnost* (openness).	**1986:** In *Bowers v. Hardwick,* the U.S. Supreme Court upholds the constitutionality of the Georgia state law against sodomy.
	1987: The immensely popular Broadway adaptation of Victor Hugo's *Les Misérables* opens.	**1989:** A student demonstration in Beijing's Tiananmen Square results in bloodshed.	**1986:** The U.S. space shuttle *Challenger* explodes seconds after liftoff, killing all seven on board.
		1989: Communism crumbles in Eastern Europe, and the Berlin Wall is torn down.	
	1990s: In a proliferation of Shakespeare on film, new versions of *Hamlet, Henry V, Much Ado about Nothing, Othello,* and *Richard III* are released.	**1990:** Iraq invades Kuwait, which leads to the Gulf War in 1991.	**1990:** Octavio Paz, Mexican poet, receives the Nobel Prize for literature.
		1990: East and West Germany reunite after 45 years of separation.	**1990:** The National Endowment for the Arts is attacked when controversial awards are publicized.
		1990: The South African nationalist leader Nelson Mandela is released from prison.	

Contemporary Drama Timeline *(continued)*

DATE	THEATER	POLITICAL	SOCIAL/CULTURAL
1950–present (continued)		**1990–1991:** South Africa repeals its apartheid laws.	
		1991: The Soviet Union collapses. U.S. President Bush officially recognizes the twelve new countries created as a result.	
	1992: David Mamet's *Oleanna* premiers off-Broadway and runs for over 250 performances.	**1991:** Yugoslavia dissolves. Croatia, Slovenia, Bosnia-Herzegovina, and Macedonia declare independence, and bitter fighting ensues for several years.	**1993:** Toni Morrison (b. 1931), African American novelist, is awarded the Nobel Prize for literature.
		1994: Nelson Mandela (b. 1918) is elected the first black president of South Africa after that nation's first multiracial elections.	**mid-1990s:** *Internet* and *World Wide Web* become household words.
		1994: Chechnya declares independence from Russia; Russian troops invade the republic in 1994 and again in 1999.	
	1996: Jonathan Larson's *Rent,* a musical based on Puccini's *La Bohème,* wins the Pulitzer Prize.	**1995:** The Israeli leader Yitzhak Rabin is assassinated.	**1995:** Shannon Faulkner is the first woman to be admitted to the Citadel military academy.
	1997: Martin McDonagh, at age 27, has four plays running simultaneously in London.	**1997:** Hong Kong is returned to China after 156 years as a British colony.	**1995:** The National Endowment for the Arts budget is slashed by the newly elected Republican Congress. The Public Broadcasting Corporation and the National Endowment for the Humanities also come under fire.
	1998: Paula Vogel's play *How I Learned to Drive* wins the Pulitzer Prize.	**1998:** Asian nations face dramatic recession after economic booms of the 1980s and early 1990s.	
	1998: Yasmina Reza's *"Art"* wins a Tony Award for best play.	**1999:** Congress impeaches President Clinton for his improper conduct in the White House, but the president remains in office.	**1996:** In *Rome v. Evans,* the U.S. Supreme Court rules that the equal protection clause of the Constitution applies to lesbians and gay men.
		1999: U.N. troops keep a tentative peace between ethnic Albanians and Serbian Albanians in Kosovo.	**1997:** Scottish scientist Ian Wilmot clones a sheep.
		1999: The United States transfers Panama Canal to Panama.	
		1999: After East Timor votes for independence from Indonesia, the Indonesia militia occupy East Timor.	
		2000: Boris Yeltsin resigns as president of Russia.	

Luis Valdez

Luis Valdez, one of ten children, was born in 1940 in Delano, California, to *campesinos,* or farm workers. When he was six years old, he watched a teacher use part of a paper bag to make papier-mâché masks for a theater production. This experience transformed his world view and eventually led him to the theater. His experiences in the fields, however, lasted until he was eighteen, when he went to San Jose State College. Although he began college as a math and physics major, in deference to his parents, after less than a year at San Jose State he joined the theater and declared a major in English. He wrote and acted in plays at San Jose State, where his first full-length play, *The Shrunken Head of Pancho Villa* (1964) was produced.

After college he joined the famous San Francisco Mime Troupe. In 1965, still a member of Cesar Chavez's United Farm Workers Union, he founded El Teatro Campesino, or the Farm Workers Theater, for which he became artistic director and playwright. The theater, which has won a number of awards and is now part of the Mexican American Centro Campesino Cultural in Fresno, began as a theater for striking farm workers and their union, earning money for the union and spreading news about its activities. Eventually, Valdez began writing plays on a number of related subjects, such as the Vietnam War in *Dark Root of a Scream* (1967). He wrote several plays in a form he called *mito,* or myth. One of them, *Bernabé* (1970), introduced a figure who was a zoot suiter and focused on historical issues concerning Chicanos. Another of his important plays, *Los Vendidos (The Sellouts),* was written in 1967 and continues to be performed.

In 1978, Valdez produced *Zoot Suit,* his first major success, and went on to write *Bandido!* (1982), which he calls "an antimelodrama," about a Mexican bandit named Tiburcio Vásquez, who holds the unpleasant distinction of having been in 1875 the last man publicly executed by the law in San Jose, California. *I Don't Have to Show You No Stinking Badges!* (1986), set in California during Ronald Reagan's presidency, concerns Buddy Villa and his wife Connie, who have spent their working lives as extras in TV and films. Videotaped inserts and music make this play a multimedia experience.

In addition to his activities as a playwright, Luis Valdez also directs films and plays. He directed the film *Zoot Suit* (1981) and the film *La Bamba* (1987), the biography of the Mexican American rock 'n' roll singer Richie Valens, who died in a plane crash with Buddy Holly in 1959. Valdez also wrote the script for that film. In 1987, he produced a television version of his 1983 play, *Corridos! Tales of Passion and Revolution.* Performances of *Corridos!* filled a relatively large house in San Francisco for six months before moving to Los Angeles. Its subject is Mexican history, something many in his audience knew little about. Valdez is currently working on a film on the life of Cesar Chavez.

ZOOT SUIT

In some sense *Zoot Suit* is a musical drama, although it can be read as a straight drama as well. A zoot suit had baggy pleated trousers with narrow, pegged ankles and a jacket with wide lapels and long tails (drape), usually to the back of the knees. With it, a zoot suiter usually wore a gold watch chain that came down almost to the ankles and a hat with a long feather. In 1942 it was the epitome of "cool" in jazz circles and was a style favored by some Chicano youths in Los Angeles. Wartime rationing effectively banned the production of the suit, although demand continued to flout the regulations. El Pachuco in this play is the "spirit" of the zoot suiter, and Henry Reyna is the leader of the zoot suiters, a loosely formed gang.

The language of the play is a dialect that mixes English, Spanish, and Los Angeles Spanish slang. It is called Caló (for California/Los Angeles) or *pachuco*. Valdez makes no effort to translate for English-only speakers, but the sense of the language is generally clear to most audiences.

The play is partially based on the zoot-suit riots in Los Angeles in 1942 in which military personnel stripped the suits from zoot suiters who they felt were unpatriotic and during which a murder was committed. In the play, Henry Reyna is falsely accused and convicted of the murder and is imprisoned until an appeal can demonstrate that he was not involved in the crime. The play itself investigates the hopes and yearnings of Henry Reyna and his friends and family. The structure of the play takes us from a dance hall in Los Angeles, to a court for the trial, and then to San Quentin prison where Henry Reyna becomes close friends with Alice, a member of the press who buoys his hopes for justice.

Justice, however, seems less and less likely to be accorded to Henry, partly because the "system" needs a scapegoat, and Henry Reyna is available. But Henry has to make choices for himself, and in the process he changes some of his thinking. Though Henry eventually wins his appeal, the play ends without an ending. Instead of one ending, Valdez provides several possibilities, depending on who you think Henry Reyna is: a leader, victim, warrior, friend, or someone else. The audience decides.

***Zoot Suit*
in Performance**

Zoot Suit opened on July 30, 1978, in Los Angeles and played to full houses for almost a year. It then moved to a Broadway production in New York, where it ran for a month. It remains the first and only Chicano play to be performed on Broadway. Luis Valdez directed the film version of the play in 1981 with Daniel Valdez, his brother, in the role of Henry Reyna. Daniel Valdez also composed the music for the film.

Luis Valdez (b. 1940)
ZOOT SUIT   *1978*

Characters

EL PACHUCO°
HENRY REYNA

His Family:
ENRIQUE REYNA
DOLORES REYNA
LUPE REYNA
RUDY REYNA

His Friends:
GEORGE SHEARER
ALICE BLOOMFIELD

His Gang:
DELLA BARRIOS
SMILEY TORRES
JOEY CASTRO
TOMMY ROBERTS
ELENA TORRES
BERTHA VILLARREAL

The Downey Gang:
RAFAS
RAGMAN
HOBO
CHOLO
ZOOTER
GÜERA
HOBA
BLONDIE
LITTLE BLUE

Detectives:
LIEUTENANT EDWARDS
SERGEANT SMITH

The Press:
PRESS
CUB REPORTER
NEWSBOY

The Court:
JUDGE F. W. CHARLES
BAILIFF

The Prison:
GUARD

The Military:
BOSUN'S MATE
SAILORS
MARINE
SWABBIE
MANCHUKA
SHORE PATROLMAN

Others:
GIRLS
PIMP
CHOLO

Setting: *The giant facsimile of a newspaper front page serves as a drop curtain.*
    The huge masthead reads: LOS ANGELES HER-ALD EXPRESS Thursday, June 3, 1943.
    A headline cries out: ZOOT-SUITER HORDES IN-VADE LOS ANGELES. U.S. NAVY AND MARINES ARE CALLED IN.
    Behind this are black drapes creating a place of haunting shadows larger than life. The somber shapes and outlines of pachuco images hang subtly, black on black, against a background of heavy fabric evoking memories and feelings like an old suit hanging forgotten in the depths of a closet somewhere, sometime. . . . Below this is a sweeping, curving place of levels and rounded corners with the hard, ingrained brilliance of countless spit shines, like the memory of a dance hall.

ACT 1 • *Prologue*

(*A switchblade plunges through the newspaper. It slowly cuts a rip to the bottom of the drop. To the sounds of "Perdido" by Duke Ellington, El Pachuco*

El Pachuco: For some people the word *pachuco* indicates someone from El Paso. However, it also refers to a specific form of Chicano subculture that was prevalent in the 1940s in the Southwest. Considered gangsters by some, pachucos were characterized by their distinctive clothing, appearance, and language. Though not the only youth group to wear the zoot suit (an oversized suit), this was one of their cultural practices. They also developed particular versions of Spanish dialect. Some scholars call it Caló and trace it back to the language of gypsies in Spain; others see this language practice as innovation based on the encounter between two cultures, Mexican and American. In this account it is seen as a form of code switching and language adaptation. Regardless of their particular mannerisms, pachucos shared a general distrust of assimilation and insisted on forming their own identity outside of the U.S. mainstream, something that made them suspicious to both the U.S. legal system and Mexicans and Mexican Americans who were trying to assimilate.

*emerges from the slit. He adjusts his clothing, meticu-
lously fussing with his collar, suspenders, cuffs. He tends
to his hair, combing back every strand into a long luxurious ducktail, with infinite loving pains. Then he
reaches into the slit and pulls out his coat and hat. He
dons them. His fantastic costume is complete. It is a
zoot suit. He is transformed into the very image of the
pachuco myth, from his pork-pie hat to the tip of his
four-foot watch chain. Now he turns to the audience.
His three-soled shoes with metal taps click-clack as he
proudly, slovenly, defiantly makes his way downstage.
He stops and assumes a pachuco stance.*)

PACHUCO: ¿Que le watcha a mis trapos, ese?
    ¿Sabe qué, carnal?
    Estas garras me las planté porque
    Vamos a dejarnos caer un play, ¿sabe?

(*He crosses to center stage, models his clothes.*)

5   Watcha mi tacuche, ese. Aliviánese con mis calcos,
          tando,
       lisa, tramos, y carlango, ese.

(*Pause.*)

       Nel, sabe qué, usted está muy verdolaga. Como se
          me hace
       que es puro square.°

(*El Pachuco breaks character and addresses the audience in perfect English.*)

       Ladies and gentlemen
10   the play you are about to see
       is a construct of fact and fantasy.
       The Pachuco Style was an act in Life
       and his language a new creation.
       His will to be was an awesome force
15   eluding all documentation . . .
       A mythical, quizzical, frightening being
       precursor of revolution
       Or a piteous, hideous heroic joke
       deserving of absolution?
20   I speak as an actor on the stage.
       The Pachuco was existential
       for he was an Actor in the streets
       both profane and reverential.
       It was the secret fantasy of every bato
25   in or out of the Chicanada°
       to put on a Zoot Suit and play the Myth
       más chucote que la chingada.°

1, Prologue. 1–8. ¿Que le watcha . . . que es puro square:
You're looking at my clothes, man? / You know what, brother
(sense of soul brotherhood)? / I dressed up in these duds because / We are going to drop by a play, you know? Look at my
suit, man. It goes well with my shoes, hat, / shirt, pants, and
coat, dude. No, you know what, you are very inexperienced. It
seems to me / that you're a pure square.   **25. Chicanada:** Chicano world or community.   **27. más chucote que la chingada:**
More pachuco-like than hell.

(*Puts hat back on and turns.*)

    ¡Pos órale!°

(*Music. The newspaper drop flies. El Pachuco begins his
chuco stroll upstage, swinging his watch chain.*)

Scene 1. Zoot Suit

(*The scene is a barrio dance in the forties. Pachucos and
Pachucas in zoot suits and pompadours.
    They are members of the 38th Street Gang, led by
Henry Reyna, 21, dark, Indian-looking, older than his
years, and Della Barrios, 20, his girlfriend in miniskirt
and fingertip coat. A sailor called Swabbie dances with
his girlfriend Manchuka among the Couples. Movement. Animation. El Pachuco sings.*)

PACHUCO: PUT ON A ZOOT SUIT, MAKES YOU
        FEEL REAL ROOT
    LOOK LIKE A DIAMOND, SPARKLING,
        SHINING
    READY FOR DANCING
    READY FOR THE BOOGIE TONIGHT!

(*The Couples, dancing, join the Pachuco in exclaiming
the last term of each line in the next verse.*)

    THE HEPCATS UP IN HARLEM WEAR THAT
        DRAPE SHAPE   5
    COMO LOS PACHUCONES° DOWN IN L.A.
    WHERE HUISAS° IN THEIR POMPADOURS
        LOOK REAL KEEN
    ON THE DANCE FLOOR OF THE BALLROOMS
    DONDE BAILAN° SWING.

    YOU BETTER GET HEP TONIGHT   10
    AND PUT ON THAT ZOOT SUIT!

(*The Downey Gang, a rival group of pachucos enters
upstage left. Their quick dance step becomes a challenge
to 38th Street.*)

DOWNEY GANG: Downey . . . ¡Rifa!°
HENRY (*gesturing back*): ¡Toma!°

(*The music is hot. El Pachuco slides across the floor and
momentarily breaks the tension. Henry warns Rafas, the
leader of the Downey Gang, when he sees him push his
brother Rudy.*)

    ¡Rafas!
PACHUCO (*sings*): TRUCHA, ESE LOCO, VAMOS AL
        BORLO°   15
    WEAR THAT CARLANGO, TRAMOS Y TANDO

---

28. ¡Pos órale!: Well listen!   **1, 1. 6. COMO LOS PACHU-
CONES:** Like the pachucos.   **7. HUISAS:** Girls.   **9. DONDE
BAILAN:** Where they dance.   **12. ¡Rifa!:** The best. An equivalent expression might be "Rules!"   **13. ¡Toma!:** Take that (ref-
erencing the gesture).   **15. TRUCHA . . . AL BORLO:** Hey,
crazy man, we are going to party (dance).

DANCE WITH YOUR HUISA
DANCE TO THE BOOGIE TONIGHT!

'CAUSE THE ZOOT SUIT IS THE STYLE IN
CALIFORNIA
20   TAMBIÉN EN COLORADO Y ARIZONA°
THEY'RE WEARING THAT TACUCHE EN EL
PASO
Y EN TODOS LOS SALONES DE CHICAGO°

YOU BETTER GET HEP TONIGHT
AND PUT ON THAT ZOOT SUIT!

Scene 2. *The Mass Arrests*

(*We hear a siren, then another, and another. It sounds like gangbusters. The dance is interrupted. Couples pause on the dance floor.*)

PACHUCO: Trucha, la jura. ¡Pélenle!°

(*Pachucos start to run out, but Detectives leap onstage with drawn guns. A Cub Reporter takes flash pictures.*)

SGT. SMITH: Hold it right there, kids!
LT. EDWARDS: Everybody get your hands up!
RUDY: Watcha! This way! (*Rudy escapes with some others.*)
5   LT. EDWARDS: Stop or I'll shoot!

(*Edwards fires his revolver into the air. A number of pachucos and their girlfriends freeze. The cops round them up. Swabbie, an American sailor, and Manchuka, a Japanese-American dancer, are among them.*)

SGT. SMITH: ¡Ándale!° (*Sees Swabbie.*) You! Get out of here.
SWABBIE: What about my girl?
SGT. SMITH: Take her with you.

(*Swabbie and Manchuka exit.*)

10   HENRY: What about my girl?
LT. EDWARDS: No dice, Henry. Not this time. Back in line.
SGT. SMITH: Close it up!
LT. EDWARDS: Spread!

(*The Pachucos turn upstage in a line with their hands up. The sirens fade and give way to the sound of a teletype. The Pachucos turn and form a lineup, and the Press starts shooting pictures as he speaks.*)

15   PRESS: The City of the Angels, Monday, August 2, 1942. The *Los Angeles Examiner* Headline:
THE LINEUP (*in chorus*): Death Awakens Sleepy Lagoon (*Breath.*) L.A. Shaken by Lurid "Kid" Murder.

PRESS: The City of the Angels, Monday, August 2, 1942. The *Los Angeles Times* Headline: 20
THE LINEUP: One Killed, Ten Hurt in Boy Wars: (*Breath.*) Mexican Boy Gangs Operating Within City.
PRESS: The City of the Angels, August 2, 1942. *Los Angeles Herald Express* Headline: 25
THE LINEUP: Police Arrest Mexican Youths. Black Widow Girls° in Boy Gangs.
PRESS: The City of the Angels . . .
PACHUCO (*sharply*): El Pueblo de Nuestra Señora la Reina de los Ángeles de Porciúncula, pendejo.°   30
PRESS (*eyeing the Pachuco cautiously*): The *Los Angeles Daily News* Headline:
BOYS IN THE LINEUP: Police Nab 300 in Roundup.
GIRLS IN THE LINEUP: Mexican Girls Picked Up in Arrests.   35
LT. EDWARDS: Press Release, Los Angeles Police Department: A huge showup of nearly 300 boys and girls rounded up by the police and sheriff's deputies will be held tonight at eight o'clock in Central Jail at First and Hill Street. Victims of assault, robbery, purse   40 snatching, and similar crimes are asked to be present for the identification of suspects.
PRESS: Lieutenant . . . ?

(*Edwards poses as the Press snaps a picture.*)

LT. EDWARDS: Thank you.
PRESS: Thank you.   45

(*Smith gives a signal, and the lineup moves back, forming a straight line in the rear, leaving Henry up front by himself.*)

LT. EDWARDS: Move! Turn! Out!

(*As the rear line moves off to the left following Edwards, Smith takes Henry by the arm and pulls him downstage, shoving him to the floor.*)

Scene 3. *Pachuco Yo*

SGT. SMITH: Okay, kid you wait here till I get back. Think you can do that? Sure you can. You pachucos are regular tough guys.

(*Smith exits. Henry sits up on the floor. El Pachuco comes forward.*)

HENRY: Bastards. (*He gets up and paces nervously. Pause.*) ¿Ese? ¿Ese?°   5
PACHUCO (*behind him*): ¿Qué pues, nuez?°

---

20. TAMBIÉN . . . ARIZONA: Also in Colorado and Arizona.
21–22. TACUCHE . . . CHICAGO: Zoot suit in El Paso and in all of the dance halls of Chicago. **1, 2. 1. Trucha . . . ¡Pélenle!:** Watch out, the police. Get out of here (beat it)!
6. ¡Ándale!: Move it!

26–27. Black Widow Girls: Female gang whose members' distinctive dress included zoot jackets, short black skirts, and black fishnet stockings. **29–30. El Pueblo de . . . pendejo:** The city of Our Lady Queen of the Angels Portiuncula, idiot (the original Spanish name for Los Angeles). **1, 3. 5. ¿Ese? ¿Ese?:** Man? (Also dude or homeboy.) **6. ¿Qué pues, nuez:** Well what, nut?

HENRY (*turning*): Where the hell you been, ese?

PACHUCO: Checking out the barrio. Qué desmadre, ¿no?°

HENRY: What's going on, ese? This thing is big.

10 PACHUCO: The city's cracking down on pachucos, carnal.° Don't you read the newspapers? They're screaming for blood.

HENRY: All I know is they got nothing on me. I didn't do
anything.

15 PACHUCO: You're Henry Reyna, ese — Hank Reyna! The
snarling juvenile delinquent. The zootsuiter. The bitter young pachuco gang leader of 38th Street. That's
what they got on you.

HENRY: I don't like this, ese. (*Suddenly intense.*) I
20 DON'T LIKE BEING LOCKED UP!

PACHUCO: Calmantes montes, chicas patas.° Haven't I
taught you to survive? Play it cool.

HENRY: They're going to do it again, ese! They're going
to charge me with some phony rap and keep me until
25 they make something stick.

PACHUCO: So what's new?

HENRY (*pause*): I'm supposed to report for the Navy
tomorrow. (*The Pachuco looks at him with silent disdain.*) You don't want me to go, do you?

30 PACHUCO: Stupid move, carnal.

HENRY (*hurt and angered by Pachuco's disapproval*):
I've got to do something.

PACHUCO: Then hang tough. Nobody's forcing you to
do shit.

HENRY: I'm forcing me, ese — ME, you understand?

35 PACHUCO: Muy patriotic, eh?

HENRY: Yeah.

PACHUCO: Off to fight for your country.

HENRY: Why not?

PACHUCO: Because this ain't your country. Look what's
40 happening all around you. The Japs have sewed up
the Pacific. Rommel is kicking ass in Egypt but the
Mayor of L.A. has declared all-out war on Chicanos.
On you! ¿Te curas?°

HENRY: Órale.°

45 PACHUCO: Qué mamada, ¿no?° Is that what you want to
go out and die for? Wise up. These bastard paddy
cops have it in for you. You're a marked man. They
think you're the enemy.

HENRY (*refusing to accept it*): Screw them bastard cops!

50 PACHUCO: And as soon as the Navy finds out you're in
jail again, ya estuvo, carnal.° Unfit for military duty
because of your record. Think about it.

HENRY (*pause*): You got a frajo?

PACHUCO: Simón. (*He pulls out a cigarette, hands it to
Henry, lights it for him. Henry is pensive.*)

55 HENRY (*smokes, laughs ironically*): I was all set to come
back a hero, see? Me la rayo.° For the first time in

my life I really thought Hank Reyna was going someplace.

PACHUCO: Forget the war overseas, carnal. Your war is
on the homefront.   60

HENRY (*with new resolve*): What do you mean?

PACHUCO: The barrio needs you, carnal. Fight back!
Stand up to them with some style. Show the world a
Chicano has balls. Hang tough. You can take it.
Remember, Pachuco Yo!   65

HENRY (*assuming the style*): Con safos, carnal.°

Scene 4. The Interrogation

(*The Press enters, followed by Edwards and Smith.*)

PRESS (*to the audience*): Final Edition, the *Los Angeles
Daily News*. The police have arrested twenty-two
members of the 38th Street Gang, pending further
investigation of various charges.

LT. EDWARDS: Well, son, I was hoping I wouldn't see you   5
in here again.

HENRY: Then why did you arrest me?

LT. EDWARDS: Come on, Hank, you know why you're
here.

HENRY: Yeah. I'm a Mexican.   10

LT. EDWARDS: Don't give me that. How long have I
known you? Since '39?

HENRY: Yeah, when you got me for stealing a car, remember?

LT. EDWARDS: All right. That was a mistake. I didn't   15
know it was your father's car. I tried to make it up to
you. Didn't I help you set up the youth club?

SGT. SMITH: They turned it into a gang, Lieutenant.
Everything they touch turns to shit.

LT. EDWARDS: I remember a kid just a couple of years   20
back. Head boy at the Catholic Youth Center. His
idea of fun was going to the movies. What happened
to that nice kid, Henry?

PRESS: He's "Gone with the Wind," trying to look like
Clark Gable.   25

SGT. SMITH: Now he thinks he's Humphrey Bogart.

PACHUCO: So who are you, puto? Pat O'Brien?

LT. EDWARDS: This is the wrong time to be antisocial,
son. This country's at war, and we're under strict
orders to crack down on all malcontents.   30

SGT. SMITH: Starting with all pachucos and draft
dodgers.

HENRY: I ain't no draft dodger.

LT. EDWARDS: I know you're not. I heard you got accepted by the Navy. Congratulations. When do you   35
report?

HENRY: Tomorrow?

SGT. SMITH: Tough break!

LT. EDWARDS: It's still not too late, you know. I could
still release you in time to get sworn in.   40

---

8. **Qué desmadre, ¿no?:** What a mess.   **10–11. carnal:** Brother.
21. Calmantes . . . patas: Take it easy, Chicano.   **43. ¿Te
curas?:** Are you charged (excited)?   **44. Órale:** O.K.   **45. Qué
mamada, ¿no?:** What stupidity, right?   **51. ya estuvo, carnal:**
That's enough, brother.   **56. Me la rayo:** I would be in good
circumstances.

66. **Con safos, carnal:** Be safe, brother.

HENRY: If I do what?

LT. EDWARDS: Tell me, Henry, what do you know about a big gang fight last Saturday night, out at Sleepy Lagoon?

45 PACHUCO: Don't tell 'em shit.

HENRY: Which Sleepy Lagoon?

LT. EDWARDS: You mean there's more than one? Come on, Hank, I know you were out there. I've got a statement from your friends that says you were beaten up.

50 Is that true? Were you and your girl attacked?

HENRY: I don't know anything about it. Nobody's ever beat me up.

SGT. SMITH: That's a lie and you know it. Thanks to your squealer friends, we've got enough dope on you

55 to indict for murder right now.

HENRY: Murder?

SGT. SMITH: Yeah, murder. Another greaser named José Williams.

HENRY: I never heard of the bato.

60 SGT. SMITH: Yeah, sure.

LT. EDWARDS: I've been looking at your record, Hank. Petty theft, assault, burglary, and now murder. Is that what you want? The gas chamber? Play square with me. Give me a statement as to what happened at the

65 Lagoon, and I'll go to bat for you with the Navy. I promise you.

PACHUCO: If that ain't a line of gabacho bullshit, I don't know what is.

LT. EDWARDS: Well?

70 PACHUCO: Spit in his pinche face.

SGT. SMITH: Forget it, Lieutenant. You can't treat these animals like people.

LT. EDWARDS: Shut up! I'm thinking of your family, Hank. Your old man would be proud to see you in

75 the Navy. One last chance, son. What do you say?

HENRY: I ain't your son, cop.

LT. EDWARDS: All right, Reyna, have it your way.

(Edwards and Press exit.)

PACHUCO: You don't deserve it, ese, but you're going to get it anyway.

80 SGT. SMITH: All right, muchacho, it's just me and you now. I hear tell you pachucos wear these monkey suits as a kind of armor. Is that right? How's it work? This is what you zooters need — a little old-fashioned discipline.

85 HENRY: Screw you, flatfoot.

SGT. SMITH: You greasy son of a bitch. What happened at the Sleepy Lagoon? Talk! Talk! Talk!

(Smith beats Henry with a rubber sap. Henry passes out and falls to the floor, with his hands still handcuffed behind his back. Dolores his mother appears in a spot upstage, as he falls.)

DOLORES: Henry!

(Lights change. Four Pachuco Couples enter, dancing a 40s pasodoble (two-step) around Henry on the floor, as they swing in a clothesline of newspaper sheets. Music.)

PACHUCO: Get up and escape, Henry . . .
leave reality behind   90
with your buenas garras
muy chamberlain°
escape through the barrio streets of your mind
through a neighborhood of memories
all chuckhole lined   95
and the love
and the pain
as fine as wine . . .

(Henry sits up, seeing his mother Dolores folding newspaper sheets like clothes on a clothesline.)

DOLORES: Henry?

PACHUCO: It's a lifetime ago, last Saturday night . . . before Sleepy Lagoon and the big bad fight.   100

DOLORES: Henry!

PACHUCO: Tu mamá, carnal.°

(He recedes into the background.)

DOLORES *(at the clothesline)*: Henry, ¿hijo? Ven a cenar.°   105

HENRY *(gets up off the floor)*: Sorry, jefita,° I'm not hungry. Besides, I got to pick up Della. We're late for the dance.

DOLORES: Dance? In this heat? Don't you muchachos ever think of anything else? God knows I suffer la   110
pena negra° seeing you go out every night.

HENRY: This isn't just any night, jefa.° It's my last chance to use my tacuche.°

DOLORES: Tacuche? Pero tu padre . . .°

HENRY *(revealing a stubborn streak)*: I know what mi   115
'apá° said, 'amá. I'm going to wear it anyway.

DOLORES *(sighs, resigns herself)*: Mira, hijo.° I know you work hard for your clothes. And I know how much they mean to you. Pero por diosito santo,° I just don't know what you see en esa cochinada de   120
"soot zoot."°

HENRY *(smiling)*: Drapes, 'amá, we call them drapes.

DOLORES *(scolding playfully)*: Ay sí, drapes, muy funny, ¿verdad?° And what do the police call them, eh? They've put you in jail so many times. ¿Sabes qué?°   125
I'm going to send them all your clothes!

HENRY: A qué mi 'amá.° Don't worry. By this time next week, I'll be wearing my Navy blues. Okay?

1, 4. 91–92. **buenas . . . chamberlain:** Good threads, very high class (literally, good rags).   103. **Tu mamá, carnal:** Your mother, brother.   104–105. **Henry . . . cenar:** Henry, son? Come to dinner.   106. **jefita:** Mom (literally, little boss, an affectionate term for a parent).   110–111. **la pena negra:** Through hell (literally, the black pain).   112. **jefa:** Mom.   113. **tacuche:** Zoot suit.   114. **Pero tu padre:** But your father.   115–116. **mi 'apá:** My dad.   117. **Mira, hijo:** Look, son.   119. **Pero . . . santo:** But for God's sake.   120–121. **en esa . . . "soot zoot":** In that filthy thing, that "soot zoot" (mispronunciation indicating her generational distance from pachuco culture).   124. **¿verdad?:** Truthfully.   125. **¿Sabes qué?:** You know what?   127. **A qué mi 'amá:** That's my mom.

DOLORES: Bendito sea Dios.° I still can't believe you're
130   going off to war. I almost wish you were going back
    to jail.
HENRY: ¡Órale!°

(*Lupe Reyna, 16, enters dressed in a short skirt and
baggy coat. She is followed by Della Barrios, 17,
dressed more modestly. Lupe hides behind a newspaper
sheet on the line.*)

LUPE: Hank! Let's go, carnal. Della's here.
HENRY: Della . . . Órale, esa.° What are you doing here?
135   I told you I was going to pick you up at your house.
DELLA: You know how my father gets.
HENRY: What happened?
DELLA: I'll tell you later.
DOLORES: Della, hija, buenas noches.° How pretty you
140   look.
DELLA: Buenas noches.

(*Dolores hugs Della, then spots Lupe hiding behind the
clothesline.*)

DOLORES (*to Lupe*): ¿Oye y tú?° What's wrong with
    you? What are you doing back there.
LUPE: Nothing, 'amá.
145 DOLORES: Well, come out then.
LUPE: We're late, 'amá.
DOLORES: Come out, te digo.°

(*Lupe comes out exposing her extremely short skirt.
Dolores gasps.*)

    ¡Válgame Dios!° Guadalupe, are you crazy? Why
    bother to wear anything?
150 LUPE: Ay, 'amá, it's the style. Short skirt and fingertip
    coat. Huh, Hank?
HENRY: Uh, yeah, 'amá.
DOLORES: ¿Oh sí? And how come Della doesn't get to
    wear the same style?
155 HENRY: No . . . that's different. No, chale.°
ENRIQUE (*off*): ¡VIEJA!°
DOLORES: Ándale.° Go change before your father sees
    you.
ENRIQUE: I'm home. (*Coming into the scene.*) Buenas
160   noches, everybody. (*All respond. Enrique sees Lupe.*)
    ¡Ay, jijo!° Where's the skirt?!
LUPE: It's here.
ENRIQUE: Where's the rest of it?
DOLORES: She's going to the dance.
165 ENRIQUE: ¿Y a mí qué me importa?° Go and change
    those clothes. Ándale.
LUPE: Please, 'apá?

ENRIQUE: No, señorita.
LUPE: Chihuahua,° I don't want to look like a square.
ENRIQUE: ¡Te digo que no!° I will not have my daughter   170
    looking like a . . .
DOLORES: Like a puta° . . . I mean, a pachuca.
LUPE (*pleading for help*): Hank . . .
HENRY: Do what they say, sis.
LUPE: But you let Henry wear his drapes.   175
ENRIQUE: That's different. He's a man. Es hombre.
DOLORES: Sí, that's different. You men are all alike.
    From such a stick, such a splinter: De tal palo, tal
    astillota.
ENRIQUE: Natural, muy natural, and look how he came   180
    out. ¡Bien macho! Like his father. ¿Verdad, m'ijo?°
HENRY: If you say so, jefito.°
ENRIQUE (*to Della*): Buenas noches.
DELLA: Buenas noches.
HENRY: 'Apá, this is Della Barrios.   185
ENRIQUE: Mira, mira° . . . So this is your new girlfriend,
    eh? Muy bonita.° Quite a change from the last one.
DOLORES: Ay, señor.
ENRIQUE: It's true. What was her name?
DELLA: Bertha?   190
ENRIQUE: That's the one. The one with the tattoo.
DOLORES: Este hombre.° We have company.
ENRIQUE: That reminds me. I invited the compadres to
    the house mañana.°
DOLORES: ¿Que qué?°   195
ENRIQUE: I'm buying a big keg of cerveza° to go along
    with the menudo.°
DOLORES: Oye, ¿cuál menudo?°
ENRIQUE (*cutting him off*): ¡Qué caray, mujer!° It isn't
    every day a man's son goes off to fight for his   200
    country. I should know. Della, m'ija, when I was in
    the Mexican Revolution, I was not even as old as my
    son is.
DOLORES: N'ombre,° don't start with your revolution.
    We'll be here all night.   205
HENRY: Yeah, jefe, we've got to go.
LUPE (*comes forward. She has rolled down her skirt*):
    'Apá, is this better?
ENRIQUE: Bueno. And you leave it that way.
HENRY: Órale, pues.° It's getting late. Where's Rudy?
LUPE: He's still getting ready. Rudy!   210

(*Rudy Reyna, 19, comes downstage in an old suit made
into a tacuche.*)°

RUDY: Let's go everybody. I'm ready.

---

129. Bendito sea Dios: Blessed be God.   **132. ¡Órale!:** Come
on!   **134. Órale, esa:** Hey, girl.   **139. hija, buenas noches:**
Honey (literally, daughter), good evening.   **142. ¿Oye y tú?:**
Listen and you?   **147. te digo:** I told you.   **148. ¡Válgame
Dios!:** Goodness, gracious!   **155. No, chale:** No, no.
156. ¡Vieja!: Old woman (wife).   **157. Ándale:** That's it.
161. ¡Ay, jijo!: My goodness!   **165. ¿Y . . . importa?:** What
difference does that make to me?

169. Chihuahua: Expression of frustration.   **170. ¡Te digo que
no!:** I told you no!   **172. puta:** Whore.   **181. ¿Verdad, m'ijo?:**
Right, son?   **182. jefito:** Dad.   **186. Mira, mira:** Look, look.
187. Muy bonita: Very pretty.   **192. Este hombre:** This man.
194. mañana: Tomorrow.   **195. ¿Que qué?:** What's that?
196. cerveza: Beer.   **197. menudo:** Tripe soup, a dish eaten at
special occasions.   **198. Oye, ¿cuál menudo?:** Hey, what
menudo?   **199. ¡Qué caray, mujer!:** Damn it, woman!
204. N'ombre: No man.   **209. Órale, pues:** Come on, then.
210. tacuche: Zoot suit.

ENRIQUE: Oye, oye, ¿y tú?° What are you doing with my coat?

RUDY: It's my tacuche, 'apá.

215   ENRIQUE: ¡Me lleva la chingada!°

DOLORES: Enrique . . . ¡por el amor de Dios!°

ENRIQUE (to Henry): You see what you're doing? First that one and now this one. (To Rudy.) Hijo,° don't go out like that. Por favor. You look like an idiot,

220   pendejo.°

RUDY: Órale, Hank. Don't I look all right?

HENRY: Nel, ese,° you look fine. Watcha. Once I leave for the service, you can have my tacuche. Then you can really be in style. ¿Cómo la ves?°

225   RUDY: Chale.° Thanks, carnal, but if I don't join the service myself, I'm gonna get my own tacuche.

HENRY: You sure? I'm not going to need it where I'm going. ¿Tú sabes?°

RUDY: Are you serious?

230   HENRY: Simón.°

RUDY: I'll think about it.

HENRY: Pos, no hay pedo, ese.°

ENRIQUE: ¿Cómo que pedo? Nel, ¿Simón?° Since when did we stop speaking Spanish in this house? Have

235   you no respect?

DOLORES: Muchachos, muchachos, go to your dance.

(*Henry starts upstage.*)

HENRY: Buenas noches . . .

(*Enrique holds out his hand. Henry stops, looks, and then returns to kiss his father's hand. Then he moves to kiss his mother and Rudy in turn kisses Enrique's hand. Enrique says "Buenas Noches" to each of his sons.*)

HENRY: Órale, we'd better get going . . .

(*General "goodbyes" from everybody.*)

ENRIQUE (as Rudy goes past him): Henry! Don't let your

240   brother drink beer.

RUDY: Ay, 'apá. I can take care of myself.

DOLORES: I'll believe that when I see it. (*She kisses him on the nose.*)

LUPE: Ahí te watcho, 'amá.°

ENRIQUE: ¿Que qué?°

245   LUPE: I mean, I'll see you later.

(*Henry, Della, Lupe, and Rudy turn upstage. Music starts.*)

ENRIQUE: Mujer, why didn't you let me talk?

---

212. **Oye, oye, ¿y tú?:** Listen, listen, and you?   215. **¡Me lleva la chingada!:** I'm (vulgar term)!   216. **¡por el amor de Dios!:** For the love of God!   218. **Hijo:** Son.   220. **pendejo:** Idiot.   222. **Nel, ese:** No, man.   224. **¿Cómo la ves?:** How does that seem to you?   225. **Chale:** No.   228. **¿Tú sabes?:** You know?   230. **Simón:** Yes.   232. **Pos . . . ese:** Well, that's no lie, man.   233. **¿Cómo . . . Simón?:** What's this nonsense? No, Yes? (He is upset because his sons are speaking Chicano slang.)   243. **Ahí . . . 'amá:** See you later, mom.   244. **¿Que qué:** What's that?

DOLORES (*sighing*): Talk, señor, talk all you want. I'm listening.

(*Enrique and Dolores exit up right. Rudy and Lupe exit up left. Lights change. We hear hot dance music. Henry and Della dance at center stage. El Pachuco sings.*)

PACHUCO: CADA SÁBADO EN LA NOCHE
   YO ME VOY A BORLOTEAR   250
   CON MI LINDA PACHUCONA
   LAS CADERAS A MENEAR°

   ELLA LE HACE MUY DE AQUELLAS
   CUANDO EMPIEZA A GUARACHAR
   AL COMPÁS DE LOS TIMBALES   255
   YO ME SIENTO PETATEAR°

(*From upstage right, three pachucos now enter in a line, moving to the beat. They are Joey Castro, 17; Smiley Torres, 23; and Tommy Roberts, 19, Anglo. They all come downstage left in a diagonal.*)

   LOS CHUCOS SUAVES BAILAN RUMBA
   BAILAN LA RUMBA Y LE ZUMBAN
   BAILAN GUARACHA SABROSÓN
   EL BOTECITO Y EL DANZÓN!°   260

(*Chorus repeats, the music fades. Henry laughs and happily embraces Della.*)

Scene 5. The Press

(*Lights change. El Pachuco escorts Della off right. The Press appears at upstage center.*)

PRESS: *Los Angeles Times:* August 8, 1942.

(*A Newsboy enters, lugging in two more bundles of newspapers, hawking them as he goes. People of various walks of life enter at intervals and buy newspapers. They arrange themselves in the background reading.*)

NEWSBOY: EXTRA! EXTRAAA! READ ALL ABOUT IT. SPECIAL SESSION OF L.A. COUNTY GRAND JURY CONVENES. D.A. CHARGES CONSPIRACY IN SLEEPY LAGOON MURDER. EXTRAAA!   5

(*A Cub Reporter emerges and goes to the Press, as Lieutenant Edwards enters.*)

CUB REPORTER: Hey, here comes Edwards!

(*Edwards is beseiged by the Press, joined by Alice Bloomfield, 26, a woman reporter.*)

249–252. **CADA . . . MENEAR:** Every Saturday night / I go to party (dance) / With my beautiful pachuca / Shaking her hips.   253–256. **ELLA . . . PETATEAR:** She seems very fine / When she begins to dance / To the rhythm of the drums / I feel like I'm dying.   257–260. **LOS CHUCOS . . . DANZÓN!:** The fine pachucos dance the rumba / Dance the rumba and they get high / They dance the dance (similar to the flamenco) deliciously / The botecito (literally little jail or little boat; the name of a dance) / And the danzón (a Cuban dance)!

PRESS: How about it, Lieutenant? What's the real scoop on the Sleepy Lagoon? Sex, violence . . .

CUB REPORTER: Marijuana?

10 NEWSBOY: Read all about it! Mexican Crime Wave Engulfs L.A.

LT. EDWARDS: Slums breed crime, fellas. That's your story.

ALICE: Lieutenant. What exactly is the Sleepy Lagoon?

15 CUB REPORTER: A great tune by Harry James, doll. Wanna dance?

(*Alice ignores the Cub.*)

LT. EDWARDS: It's a reservoir. An old abandoned gravel pit, really. It's on a ranch between here and Long Beach. Serves as a swimming hole for the younger 20 Mexican kids.

ALICE: Because they're not allowed to swim in the public plunges?

PRESS: What paper are you with, lady? The *Daily Worker*?

25 LT. EDWARDS: It also doubles as a sort of lovers' lane at night — which is why the gangs fight over it. Now they've finally murdered somebody.

NEWSBOY: EXTRA! EXTRA! ZOOT-SUITED GOONS OF SLEEPY LAGOON!

30 LT. EDWARDS: But we're not going to mollycoddle these youngsters any more. And you can quote me on that.

PRESS: One final question, Lieutenant. What about the 38th Street Gang — weren't you the first to arrest Henry Reyna?

35 LT. EDWARDS: I was. And I noticed right away the kid had great leadership potential. However . . .

PRESS: Yes?

LT. EDWARDS: You can't change the spots on a leopard.

PRESS: Thank you, sir.

(*People with newspapers crush them and throw them down as they exit. Edwards turns and exits. Alice turns toward Henry for a moment.*)

40 NEWSBOY: EXTRA, EXTRA. READ ALL ABOUT THE MEXICAN BABY GANGSTERS. EXTRA, EXTRA.

(*The Press and Cub Reporter rush out happily to file their stories. The Newsboy leaves, hawking his papers. Alice exits, with determination. Far upstage, Enrique enters with a rolling garbage can. He is a street sweeper. During the next scene he silently sweeps up the newspapers, pausing at the last to read one of the news stories.*)

Scene 6. *The People's Lawyer*

JOEY: ¡Chale, ese, chale! Qué pinche agüite.°

SMILEY: Mexican Baby Gangsters?!

TOMMY: Zoot-suited goons! I knew it was coming. Every time the D.A. farts, they throw us in the can.

1, 6. 1. **¡Chale . . . agüite:** No, man no! What a damned nuisance.

SMILEY: Pos, qué chingados,° Hank. I can't believe this. 5 Are they really going to pin us with a murder rap? I've got a wife and kid, man!

JOEY: Well, there's one good thing anyway. I bet you know that we've made the headlines. Everybody knows we got the toughest gang in town. 10

TOMMY: Listen to this pip squeak. The biggest heist he ever pulled was a Tootsie Roll.

JOEY (*grabbing his privates*): Here's your Tootsie Roll, ese.

TOMMY: What, that? Get my microscope, Smiley. 15

JOEY: Why don't you come here and take a little bite, joto.

TOMMY: Joto? Who you calling a joto, maricón?°

JOEY: You, white boy. Did I ever tell you, you got the finest little duck ass in the world. 20

TOMMY: No, you didn't tell me that, culero.°

(*Joey and Tommy start sparring.*)

SMILEY (*furious*): Why don't you batos knock it off?

HENRY (*cool*): Cálmenla.°

SMILEY: ¡Pinches chavalos!° (*The batos stop.*)

JOEY: We're just cabuliando, ese. 25

TOMMY: Simón, ese. Horsing around. (*He gives Joey a final punch.*)

SMILEY (*with deep self-pity*): I'm getting too old for this pedo,° Hank. All this farting around con esos chavalillos.°

HENRY: Relax, carnal. No te agüites.° 30

SMILEY: You and me have been through a lot, Hank. Parties, chingazos,° jail. When you said let's join the pachucada,° I joined the pachucada. You and me started the 38th, bato. I followed you even after my kid was born, but what now, carnal? This pinche 35 pedo° is serious.

TOMMY: He's right, Hank. They indicted the whole gang.

JOEY: Yeah, you know the only one who ain't here is Rudy.

(*Henry turns sharply.*)

He was at the Sleepy Lagoon too, ese. Throwing 40 chingazos.°

HENRY: Yeah, but the cops don't know that, do they? Unless one of us turned stoolie.

JOEY: Hey, ese, don't look at me. They beat the shit out of me, but that's all they got. Shit. 45

TOMMY: That's all you got to give. (*Laughs.*)

HENRY: Okay! Let's keep it that way. I don't want my carnalillo° pulled into this. And if anybody asks

5. **Pos, qué chingados:** Anyhow, what (vulgar term).   18. **joto, maricón:** Homosexual (derogatory).   21. **culero:** (Vulgar term), son-of-a-bitch.   23. **Cálmenla:** Cool it.   24. **¡Pinches chavalos!:** Damned inexperienced boys.   28. **pedo:** Nonsense. 28–29. **con esos chavalillos:** With these little neophytes. 30. **No te agüites:** Don't let it get to you.   32. **chingazos:** Fights.   33. **pachucada:** World of the pachucos; pachuco population.   35–36. **pinche pedo:** Damned nonsense. 41. **chingazos:** Punches.   48. **carnalillo:** Little brother.

about him, you batos don't know nothing. You get
50   me?
       SMILEY: Simón.
       TOMMY: Crazy.
       JOEY (*throwing his palms out*): Say, Jackson, I'm cool.
          You know that.
55   HENRY: There's not a single paddy we can trust.
       TOMMY: Hey, ese, what about me?
       HENRY: You know what I mean.
       TOMMY: No, I don't know what you mean. I'm here
          with the rest of yous.
60   JOEY: Yeah, but you'll be the first one out, cabrón.°
       TOMMY: Gimme a break, maníaco. ¡Yo soy pachuco!°
       HENRY: Relax, ese. Nobody's getting personal with you.
          Don't I let you take out my carnala?° Well, don't I?
       TOMMY: Simón.
65   HENRY: That's because you respect my family. The rest
          of them paddies are after our ass.
       PACHUCO: Talk about paddies, ese, you got company.

(*George Shearer enters upstage right and comes down.
He is a middle-aged lawyer, strong and athletic, but with
the slightly frazzled look of a people's lawyer.*)

       GEORGE: Hi, boys.
       HENRY: Trucha!°
70   GEORGE: My name is George Shearer. I've been retained
          by your parents to handle your case. Can we sit and
          talk for a little bit?

(*Pause. The Boys eye George suspiciously. He slides a
newspaper bundle a few feet upstage.*)

       PACHUCO: Better check him out, ese. He looks like a
          cop.
75   HENRY (*to the Guys, sotto voce*): Pónganse al alba. Este
          me huele a chota.°
       GEORGE: What was that? Did you say I could sit down?
          Thank you. (*He pulls a bundle upstage. He sits.*)
          Okay, let me get your names straight first. Who's José
80   Castro?
       JOEY: Right here, ese. What do you want to know?
       GEORGE: We'll get to that. Ismael Torres?
       SMILEY (*deadpan*): That's me. But they call me Smiley.
       GEORGE (*a wide grin*): Smiley? I see. You must be
85   Thomas Roberts.
       TOMMY: I ain't Zoot Suit Yokum.
       GEORGE: Which means you must be Henry Reyna.
       HENRY: What if I am. Who are you?
       GEORGE: I already told you, my name's George Shearer.
90   Your parents asked me to come.
       HENRY: Oh yeah? Where did they get the money for a
          lawyer?
       GEORGE: I'm a people's lawyer, Henry.
       SMILEY: People's lawyer?
95   JOEY: Simón, we're people.

       TOMMY: At least they didn't send no animal's lawyer.
       HENRY: So what does that mean? You doing this for free
          or what?
       GEORGE (*surprise turning to amusement*): I try not to
          work for free, if I can help it, but I do sometimes. In   100
          this case, I expect to be paid for my services.
       HENRY: So who's paying you? For what? And how
          much?
       GEORGE: Hey, hey, hold on there. I'm supposed to ask
          the questions. You're the one going on trial, not me.   105
       PACHUCO: Don't let him throw you, ese.
       GEORGE: I sat in on part of the Grand Jury. It was quite
          a farce, wasn't it? Murder one indictment and all.
       SMILEY: You think we stand a chance?
       GEORGE: There's always a chance, Smiley. That's what   110
          trials are for.
       PACHUCO: He didn't answer your question, ese.
       HENRY: You still didn't answer my question, mister.
          Who's paying you? And how much?
       GEORGE (*getting slightly peeved*): Well, Henry, it's really   115
          none of your damned business.

(*The Boys react.*)

          But for whatever it's worth, I'll tell you a little story.
          The first murder case I ever tried, and won inciden-
          tally, was for a Filipino. I was paid exactly three dol-
          lars and fifty cents plus a pack of Lucky Strike   120
          cigarettes, and a note for a thousand dollars — never
          redeemed. Does that answer your question?
       HENRY: How do we know you're really a lawyer?
       GEORGE: How do I know you're Henry Reyna? What
          do you really mean, son? Do you think I'm a cop?   125
       HENRY: Maybe.
       GEORGE: What are you trying to hide from the cops?
          Murder?

(*The Boys react.*)

          All right! Aside from your parents, I've been called
          into this case by a citizens' committee that's forming   130
          in your behalf, Henry. In spite of evidence to the con-
          trary, there are some people out there who don't
          want to see you get the shaft.
       HENRY: ¿Sabes qué, mister?° Don't do us any favors.
       GEORGE (*starting to leave*): All right, you want another   135
          lawyer? I'll talk to the Public Defender's office.
       JOEY (*grabbing his briefcase*): Hey, wait a minute, ese.
          Where are you going?
       TOMMY: De cincho se le va a volar la tapa.°
       JOEY: Nel, este bolillo no sabe nada.°   140
       GEORGE (*exploding*): All right, kids, cut the crap!
       SMILEY (*grabs his briefcase and crosses to Henry*): Let's
          give him a break, Hank. (*Smiley hands the briefcase
          to George.*)

---

60. cabrón: Son-of-a-bitch. **61. maníaco . . . pachuco!:**
Maniac. I'm a pachuco! **63. carnala:** Sister. **69. Trucha!:**
Heads up! (Watch out!) **75–76. Pónganse . . . chota:** Put
yourselves on alert. I will uncover this cop.

134. ¿Sabes qué, mister?: You know what, mister? **139. De
cincho . . . tapa:** It's a cinch he's going to blow his top.
140. Nel . . . nada: No, this Anglo (derogatory) doesn't know a
thing.

GEORGE: Thank you. (*He starts to exit. Stops.*) You
145 know, you're making a big mistake. I wonder if you
know who your friends are? You boys are about to
get a mass trial. You know what that is? Well, it's a
new one on me too. The Grand Jury has indicted you
all on the same identical crime. Not just you four.
150 The whole so-called 38th Street Gang. And you
know who the main target is? You, Henry, because
they're saying you're the ringleader. (*Looks around
at the Guys.*) And I suppose you are. But you're leading your buddies here down a dead-end street. The
155 D.A.'s coming after you, son, and he's going to put
you and your whole gang right into the gas chamber.

(*George turns to leave. Smiley panics. Joey and Tommy
react with him.*)

SMILEY/JOEY/TOMMY (*all together*): Gas chamber! But
we didn't do nothing! We're innocent!
HENRY: ¡Cálmenla!°

(*The batos stop in their tracks.*)

160 Okay. Say we believe you're a lawyer, what does that
prove? The press has already tried and convicted us.
Think you can change that?
GEORGE: Probably not. But then, public opinion comes
and goes, Henry. What matters is our system of jus-
165 tice. I believe it works, however slowly the wheels
may grind. It could be a long uphill fight, fellas, but
we can make it. I know we can. I've promised your
parents the best defense I'm capable of. The question
is, Henry, will you trust me?
170 HENRY: Why should I? You're a gringo.
GEORGE (*calmly, deliberately*): ¿Cómo sabes?°
TOMMY (*shocked*): Hey, you speak Spanish?
GEORGE: Más o menos.°
JOEY: You mean you understood us a while ago?
175 GEORGE: More or less.
JOEY (*embarrassed*): ¡Híjole, qué gacho, ese!°
GEORGE: Don't worry. I'm not much on your pachuco
slang. The problem seems to be that I look like an
Anglo to you. What if I were to tell you that I had
180 Spanish blood in my veins? That my roots go back to
Spain, just like yours? What if I'm an Arab? What if
I'm a Jew? What difference does it make? The ques-
tion is, will you let me help you?

(*Pause. Henry glances at the Pachuco.*)

PACHUCO: ¡Chale!
185 HENRY (*pause*): Okay!
SMILEY: Me too!
JOEY: Same here!
TOMMY: ¡Órale!
GEORGE (*eagerly*): Okay! Let's go to work. I want to
190 know exactly what happened right from the begin-
ning. (*George sits down and opens his briefcase.*)

---

159. ¡Cálmenla!: Cool it.   171. ¿Cómo sabes?: How do you
know?   173. Más o menos: More or less.   176. ¡Híjole . . .
ese!: Heavens, how bad is that!

HENRY: Well, I think the pedo° really started at the
dance last Saturday night . . .

(*El Pachuco snaps his fingers and we hear dance music.
Lights change. George exits.*)

Scene 7. *The Saturday Night Dance*

(*Swabbie and Manchuka come running onstage as the
barrio dance begins to take shape. Henry and the batos
move upstage to join other Pachucos and Pachucas
coming in. Henry joins Della Barrios; Joey teams up
with Bertha Villarreal, Tommy picks up Lupe Reyna;
and Smiley escorts his wife Elena Torres. They represent
the 38th Street neighborhood. Also entering the dance
comes the Downey Gang, looking mean. Rudy stands
upstage, in the background, drinking a bottle of beer. El
Pachuco sings.*)

PACHUCO: CUANDO SALGO YO A BAILAR
YO ME PONGO MUY CATRÍN
LAS HUISITAS TODAS GRITAN, DADDY
VAMOS A BAILAR EL SWING!°

(*The Couples dance. A lively swing number. The music
comes to a natural break and shifts into a slow number.
Bertha approaches Henry and Della downstage on the
dance floor.*)

BERTHA: Ese, ¡surote!° How about a dance for old time's   5
sake? No te hagas gacho.°
HENRY (*slow dancing with Della*): Sorry, Bertha.
BERTHA: Is this your new huisa? This little fly chick?
DELLA: Listen, Bertha . . .
HENRY (*stops her*): Chale. She's just jealous. Beat it,   10
Bertha.
BERTHA: Beat it yourself. Mira. You got no hold on me,
cabrón. Not any more. I'm as free as a bird.
SMILEY (*coming up*): Ese, Hank, that's the Downey Gang
in the corner. You think they're looking for trouble?   15
HENRY: There's only a couple of them.
BERTHA: That's all we need.
SMILEY: Want me to alert the batos?
HENRY: Nel, be cool.
BERTHA: Be cool? Huy, yu, yui. Forget it, Smiley. Since   20
he joined the Navy, this bato forgot the difference
between being cool and being cool-O.

(*She laughs and turns but Henry grabs her angrily by the
arm. Bertha pulls free and walks away cool and tough.
The music changes and the beat picks up. El Pachuco
sings as the Couples dance.*)

PACHUCO: CUANDO VOY AL VACILÓN
Y ME METO YO A UN SALÓN

---

192. pedo: Nonsense.   **1, 7. 1–4. CUANDO . . . EL SWING!:**
When I go out dancing / I get dressed up very stylishly / The
girls all yell, Daddy / We're going to dance that swing!   **5. Ese,
¡surote!:** Hey dude, two-timer!   **6. No te hagas gacho:** Don't
become a bad man.

25   LAS CHAVALAS GRITAN, PAPI VENTE
       VAMOS A BAILAR DANSÓN!°

*(The dance turns Latin. The music comes to another
natural break and holds. Lupe approaches Henry on the
dance floor.)*

LUPE: Hank. Rudy's at it again. He's been drinking since
       we got here.
HENRY *(glancing over at Rudy)*: He's okay, sis, let the
30   carnal enjoy himself.
RUDY *(staggering over)*: ¡Ese, carnal!
HENRY: What you say, brother?
RUDY: I'm flying high, Jackson. Feeling good.
LUPE: Rudy, if you go home drunk again, mi 'apá's
35   going to use you for a punching bag.

(Rudy kisses her on the cheek and moves on.)

DELLA: How are you feeling?
HENRY: Okay.
DELLA: Still thinking about Bertha?
HENRY: Chale, ¿qué traes?° Listen, you want to go out
40   to the Sleepy Lagoon? I've got something to tell you.
DELLA: What?
HENRY: Later, later.
LUPE: You better tell Rudy to stop drinking.
HENRY: Relax, sis. If he gets too drunk, I'll carry him
45   home. *(Music picks up again. El Pachuco sings a
       third verse.)*
PACHUCO: TOCAN MAMBO SABROSÓN
         SE ALBOROTA EL CORAZÓN
         Y CON UNA CHAVALONA VAMOS
         VAMOS A BAILAR EL MAMBO°

*(The Couples do the mambo. In the background, Rudy
gets into an argument with Rafas, the leader of the
Downey Gang. A fight breaks out as the music comes
to a natural break. Rafas pushes Rudy, half drunk, onto
the floor.)*

50 RAFAS: ¡Y a ti qué te importa, puto!°
    RUDY *(he falls)*: ¡Cabrón!
    HENRY *(reacting immediately)*: Hey!

*(The whole dance crowd tenses up immediately, split-
ting into separate camps. Batos from 38th clearly out-
number the Guys from Downey.)*

RAFAS: He started it, ese. El comenzó a chingar conmigo.°
RUDY: You chicken shit, ese! Tú me haces la puñeta,
55   ¡pirujo!°

23–26. CUANDO . . . DANSÓN!: When I go to the fiesta /
And I get to the dancehall / The girls yell, Daddy come / We
are going to dance the dansón?   39. Chale, ¿qué traes?: No,
what's bothering you?   46–49. TOCAN . . . MAMBO: They
play mambo deliciously / The heart falls in love (gets excited) /
With a sweetheart we go / We go to dance the mambo.
50. ¡Y . . . puto!: And what does it matter to you, male prostitute?   53. El comenzó . . . conmigo: He started to fight with
me.   54–55. Tú me . . . ¡pirujo!: I'm better than you are,
homosexual (derogatory)!

RAFAS: Come over here and say that, puto!
HENRY *(pulling Rudy behind him)*: ¡Agüítala, carnal!°
       (Faces Rafas.) You're a little out of your territory,
       ¿que no Rafas?
RAFAS: It's a barrio dance, ese. We're from the barrio.   60
HENRY: You're from Downey.
RAFAS: Vale madre.° ¡Downey Rifa!
DOWNEY GANG: ¡SIMÓN!
RAFAS: What are you going to do about it?
HENRY: I'm going to kick your ass.   65

(The Two Sides start to attack each other.)

       ¡Cálmenla!

(All stop.)

RAFAS *(pulls out a switchblade)*: You and how many
       batos?
HENRY: Just me and you, cabrón. That's my carnalillo
       you started pushing around, see? And nobody chinga   70
       con mi familia° without answering to me, ese! Hank
       Reyna! *(He pulls out another switchblade.)*
BERTHA: ALL-RIGHT!
HENRY: Let's see if you can push me around like you did
       my little brother, ese. Come on . . . COME ON!   75

*(They knife fight. Henry moves in fast. Recoiling, Rafas
falls to the floor. Henry's blade is at his throat. El
Pachuco snaps his fingers. Everyone freezes.)*

PACHUCO: Qué mamada,° Hank. That's exactly what the
       play needs right now. Two more Mexicans killing
       each other. Watcha . . . Everybody's looking at you.
HENRY *(looks out at the audience)*: Don't give me that
       bullshit. Either I kill him or he kills me.   80
PACHUCO: That's exactly what they paid to see. Think
       about it.

(El Pachuco snaps again. Everybody unfreezes.)

HENRY *(kicks Rafas)*: Get out of here. ¡Píntate!°
BERTHA: What?
GÜERA *(Rafas's girlfriend runs forward)*: Rafas. ¡Vámo-   85
       nos!° *(She is stopped by other Downey batos.)*
RAFAS: Está suave.° I'll see you later.
HENRY: Whenever you want, cabrón.

*(The Downey Gang retreats, as the 38th razzes them all
the way out. Insults are exchanged. Bertha shouts
"¡Chinga tu madre!" and they are gone. The 38th
whoops in victory.)*

SMILEY: Órale, you did it, ese! ¡Se escamaron todos!°
TOMMY: We sure chased those jotos out of here.   90
BERTHA: I could have beat the shit out of those two
       rucas.°

57. ¡Agüítala, carnal!: Calm down, brother!   62. Vale madre:
That doesn't mean anything.   70–71. chinga con mi familia: (Vulgar term) with my family.   76. Qué mamada: What
stupidity.   83. ¡Píntate!: Scram!   85–86. ¡Vámonos!: Let's
go!   87. Está suave: That's cool.   89. ¡Se escamaron todos!:
They all got scared!   92. rucas: Homegirls.

JOEY: That pinche° Rafas is yellow without his gang, ese.

95 LUPE: So why didn't you jump out there?

JOEY: Chale, Rudy ain't my baby brother.

RUDY (*drunk*): Who you calling a baby, pendejo? I'll show you who's a baby!

JOEY: Be cool, ese.

100 TOMMY: Man, you're lucky your brother was here.

BERTHA: Why? He didn't do nothing. The old Hank would have slit Rafas' belly like a fat pig.

HENRY: Shut your mouth, Bertha!

RUDY: ¿Por qué, carnal?° You backed down, ese. I could

105 have taken that sucker on by myself.

HENRY: That's enough, Rudy. You're drunk.

DELLA: Hank, what if Rafas comes back with all his gang?

HENRY (*reclaiming his leadership*): We'll kill the sons of

110 bitches.

JOEY: ¡Órale! ¡La 38th rifa!°

(*Music. Everybody gets back with furious energy. El Pachuco sings.*)

PACHUCO: DE LOS BAILES QUE MENTÉ
Y EL BOLERO Y EL BEGUÍN
DE TODOS LOS BAILES JUNTOS

115 ME GUSTA BAILAR EL SWING! HEY!°

(*The dance ends with a group exclamation: HEY!*)

Scene 8. El Día de la Raza

(*The Press enters upstage level, pushing a small hand truck piled high with newspaper bundles. The batos and rucas on the dance floor freeze in their final dance positions. El Pachuco is the only one who relaxes and moves.*)

PRESS: October 12, 1942: Columbus Day. Four Hundred and Fiftieth Anniversary of the Discovery of America. Headlines!

(*In their places, the Couples now stand straight and recite a headline before exiting. As they do so, the Press moves the bundles of newspapers on the floor to outline the four corners of a jail cell.*)

SMILEY/ELENA: President Roosevelt Salutes Good Neigh-
5   bors In Latin America.

(*Smiley and Elena exit.*)

TOMMY/LUPE: British Begin Drive to Oust Rommel From North Africa.

---

93. pinche: Damned.   104. ¿Por qué, carnal?: Why, brother?
111. ¡Órale! ¡La 38th rifa!: Right on! The 38th (street gang)
rules!   112–15. DE LOS . . . HEY!: Of the dances that I mentioned / And the bolero and the beguin / Of all the dances
joined together / I like to dance swing! Hey!

(*Tommy and Lupe exit.*)

RUDY/CHOLO: Japs In Death Grip On Pacific Isles.

(*Rudy and Cholo exit. Press tosses another bundle.*)

ZOOTER/LITTLE BLUE: Web Of Zoot Crime Spreads.

(*Zooter and Little Blue exit.*)

MANCHUKA/SWABBIE: U.S. Marines Land Bridgehead 10
On Guadalcanal.

(*Manchuka and Swabbie exit.*)

JOEY/BERTHA: First Mexican Braceros Arrive in U.S.A.

(*Joey and Bertha exit.*)

DELLA: Sleepy Lagoon Murder Trial Opens Tomorrow.

(*Della and the Press exit. As they exit, George and Alice enter upstage left. Henry is center, in a "cell" outlined by four newspaper bundles left by the Press.*)

GEORGE: Henry? How you doing, son? Listen, I've brought somebody with me that wants very much to 15
meet you. I thought you wouldn't mind.

(*Alice crosses to Henry.*)

ALICE: Hello! My name is Alice Bloomfield and I'm a reporter from the *Daily People's World.*

GEORGE: And . . . And I might add, a red hot member of the ad hoc committee that's fighting for you guys. 20

ALICE: Oh, George! I'd hardly call it fighting, for Pete's sake. This struggle has just barely begun. But we're sure going to win it, aren't we, Henry?

HENRY: I doubt it.

GEORGE: Oh come on, Henry. How about it, son? You 25
all set for tomorrow? Anything you need, anything I can get for you?

HENRY: Yeah. What about the clean clothes you promised me? I can't go to court looking like this.

GEORGE: You mean they didn't give them to you? 30

HENRY: What?

GEORGE: Your mother dropped them off two days ago. Clean pants, shirt, socks, underwear, the works. I cleared it with the Sheriff last week.

HENRY: They haven't given me nothing. 35

GEORGE: I'm beginning to smell something around here.

HENRY: Look, George, I don't like being like this. I ain't dirty. Go do something, man!

GEORGE: Calm down. Take it easy, son. I'll check on it right now. Oh! Uh, Alice? 40

ALICE: I'll be okay, George.

GEORGE: I'll be right back.   (*He exits.*)

ALICE (*pulling out a pad and pencil*): Now that I have you all to myself, mind if I ask you a couple of questions? 45

HENRY: I got nothing to say.

ALICE: How do you know? I haven't asked you anything yet. Relax. I'm from the progressive press. Okay?

(*Henry stares at her, not knowing quite how to react. Alice sits on a bundle and crosses her goodlooking legs. Henry concentrates on that.*)

Now. The regular press is saying the Pachuco Crime
50   Wave is fascist inspired — any thoughts about that?
HENRY (*bluntly*): No.
ALICE: What about the American Japanese? Is it true
    they are directing the subversive activities of the
    pachucos from inside the relocation camps?

(*Henry turns to The Pachuco with a questioning look.*)

55 PACHUCO: This one's all yours, ese.
HENRY: Look, lady, I don't know what the hell you're
    talking about.
ALICE: I'm talking about you, Henry Reyna. And what
    the regular press has been saying. Are you aware
60   you're in here just because some bigshot up in San
    Simeon wants to sell more papers? It's true.
HENRY: So?
ALICE: So, he's the man who started this Mexican Crime
    Wave stuff. Then the police got into the act. Get the
65   picture? Somebody is using you as a patsy.
HENRY (*his machismo insulted*): Who you calling a patsy?
ALICE: I'm sorry, but it's true.
HENRY (*backing her up*): What makes you so god-
    damned smart?
ALICE (*starting to get scared and trying not to show it*):
70   I'm a reporter. It's my business to know.
PACHUCO: Puro pedo. She's just a dumb broad only
    good for you know what.
HENRY: Look, Miss Bloomfield, just leave me alone, all
    right?

(*Henry moves away. Alice takes a deep breath.*)

75 ALICE: Look, let's back up and start all over, okay?
    Hello. My name is Alice Bloomfield, and I'm not a
    reporter. I'm just somebody that wants very much to
    be your friend. (*Pause. With sincere feeling.*) Can you
    believe that?
80 HENRY: Why should I?
ALICE: Because I'm with you.
HENRY: Oh, yeah? Then how come you ain't in jail with
    me?
ALICE (*holding her head up*): We are all in jail, Henry.
85   Some of us just don't know it.
PACHUCO: Mmm, pues. No comment.

(*Pause. Henry stares at her, trying to figure her out.
Alice tries a softer approach.*)

ALICE: Believe it or not, I was born in Los Angeles just
    like you. But for some strange reason I grew up here,
    not knowing very much about Mexicans at all. I'm
90   just trying to learn.
HENRY (*intrigued, but cynical*): What?
ALICE: Little details. Like that tattooed cross on your
    hand. Is that the sign of the pachuco?

(*Henry covers his right hand with an automatic reflex,
then he realizes what he has done.*)

HENRY (*smiles to himself, embarrassed*): Órale.
95 ALICE: Did I embarrass you? I'm sorry. Your mother
    happened to mention it.
HENRY (*surprised*): My mother? You talked to my jefita?

ALICE (*with enthusiasm*): Yes! And your father and
    Lupe and Rudy. The whole family gave me a helluva
    interview. But your mother was sensational. I espe- 100
    cially liked her story about the midnight raid. How
    the police rushed into your house with drawn guns,
    looking for you on some trumped up charge, and
    how your father told them you were already in
    jail . . . God, I would have paid to have seen the 105
    cops' faces.
HENRY (*hiding his sentiment*): Don't believe anything
    my jefa tells you. (*Then quickly.*) There's a lot she
    doesn't know. I'm no angel.
ALICE: I'll just bet you're not. But you have been taken 110
    in for suspicion a dozen times, kept in jail for a few
    days, then released for lack of evidence. And it's all
    stayed on your juvenile record.
HENRY: Yeah, well I ain't no punk, see.
ALICE: I know. You're an excellent mechanic. And you 115
    fix all the guys' cars. Well, at least you're not one of
    the lumpen proletariat.
HENRY: The lumpen what?
ALICE: Skip it. Let's just say you're a classic social victim.
HENRY: Bullshit. 120
ALICE (*pause. A serious question*): Are you saying you're
    guilty?
HENRY: Of what?
ALICE: The Sleepy Lagoon Murder.
HENRY: What if I am? 125
ALICE: Are you?
HENRY (*pause, a serious answer*): Chale. I've pulled a
    lot of shit in my time, but I didn't do that.

(*George re-enters flushed and angry, trying to conceal
his frustration.*)

GEORGE: Henry, I'm sorry, but dammit, something's
    coming off here, and the clothes have been withheld. 130
    I'll have to bring it up in court.
HENRY: In court?
GEORGE: They've left me no choice.
ALICE: What's going on?
HENRY: It's a set up, George. Another lousy set up! 135
GEORGE: It's just the beginning, son. Nobody said this
    was going to be a fair fight. Well, if they're going to
    fight dirty, so am I. Legally, but dirty. Trust me.
ALICE (*passionately*): Henry, no matter what happens in
    the trial, I want you to know I believe you're inno- 140
    cent. Remember that when you look out, and it looks
    like some sort of lynch mob. Some of us . . . a lot of
    us . . . are right there with you.
GEORGE: Okay, Alice, let's scram. I've got a million
    things to do. Henry, see you tomorrow under the big 145
    top, son. Good luck, son.
ALICE: Thumbs up, Henry, we're going to beat this rap!

(*Alice and George exit. El Pachuco watches them go,
then turns to Henry.*)

PACHUCO: "Thumbs up, Henry, we're going to beat this
    rap." You really think you're going to beat this one,
    ese? 150

HENRY: I don't want to think about it.

PACHUCO: You've got to think about it, Hank. Everybody's playing you for a sucker. Wake up, carnal!

HENRY: Look, bato, what the hell do you expect me to
155   do?

PACHUCO: Hang tough. (*Grabs his scrotum.*) Stop going soft.

HENRY: Who's going soft?

PACHUCO (*incisively*): You're hoping for something that
160   isn't going to happen, ese. These paddies are leading you by the nose. Do you really believe you stand a chance?

HENRY (*stubborn all the more*): Yeah. I think I got a chance.

165 PACHUCO: Just because that white broad says so?

HENRY: Nel, ese, just because Hank Reyna says so.

PACHUCO: The classic social victim, eh?

HENRY (*furious but keeping his cool*): Mira, ese. Hank Reyna's no loser. I'm coming out of this on top. ¿Me
170   entiendes,° Mendez? (*He walks away with a pachuco gait.*)

PACHUCO (*forcefully*): Don't try to out-pachuco ME, ese! We'll see who comes out on top. (*He picks up a bundle of newspapers and throws it upstage center. It lands with a thud.*) Let's go to court!

Scene 9. *Opening of the Trial*

(*Music. The Judge's bench, made up of more newspaper bundles piled squarely on a four-wheeled hand truck is pushed in by the batos. The Press rides it in, holding the State and Federal Flags. A Bailiff puts it in place a hand cart: the Judge's throne. From the sides, spectators enter, including Henry's family and friends: Alice, Della, Bertha, Elena.*)

PRESS: The largest mass trial in the history of Los Angeles County opens this morning in the Superior Court at ten A.M. The infamous Sleepy Lagoon Murder case involves sixty-six charges against twenty-two
5   defendants with seven lawyers pleading for the defense, two for the prosecution. The District Attorney estimates that over a hundred witnesses will be called and has sworn — I quote —"to put an end to Mexican baby gangsterism." End quote.

10 BAILIFF (*bangs a gavel on the bench*): The Superior Court of the State of California. In and For the County of Los Angeles. Department forty-three. The honorable F. W. Charles, presiding. All rise!

(*Judge Charles enters. All rise. El Pachuco squats. The Judge is played by the same actor that portrays Edwards.*)

JUDGE: Please be seated.

1, 8. 169–170. **¿Me entiendes:** You understand me?

(*All sit. Pachuco stands.*)

Call this case, Bailiff.   15

BAILIFF (*reading from a sheet*): The people of the State of California Versus Henry Reyna, Ismael Torres, Thomas Roberts, Jose Castro and eighteen other . . . (*slight hesitation*) . . . pa-coo-cos.

JUDGE: Is Counsel for the Defense present?   20

GEORGE (*rises*): Yes, Your Honor.

JUDGE: Please proceed. (*Signals the Press.*)

PRESS: Your Honor . . .

GEORGE (*moving in immediately*): If the Court please, it was reported to me on Friday that the District Attor-   25 ney has absolutely forbidden the Sheriff's Office to permit these boys to have clean clothes or haircuts. Now, it's been three months since the boys were arrested . . .

PRESS (*jumping in*): Your Honor, there is testimony we   30 expect to develop that the 38th Street Gang are characterized by their style of haircuts . . .

GEORGE: Three months, Your Honor.

PRESS: . . . the thick heavy heads of hair, the ducktail comb, the pachuco pants . . .   35

GEORGE: Your Honor, I can only infer that the Prosecution . . . is trying to make these boys look disreputable, like mobsters.

PRESS: Their appearance is distinctive, Your Honor. Essential to the case.   40

GEORGE: You are trying to exploit the fact that these boys look foreign in appearance! Yet clothes like these are being worn by kids all over America.

PRESS: Your Honor . . .

JUDGE (*bangs the gavel*): I don't believe we will have any   45 difficulty if their clothing becomes dirty.

GEORGE: What about the haircuts, Your Honor?

JUDGE (*ruling*): The zoot haircuts will be retained throughout the trial for purposes of identification of defendants by witnesses.   50

PACHUCO: You hear that one, ese? Listen to it again.

(*Snaps. Judge repeats automatically.*)

JUDGE: The zoot haircuts will be retained throughout the trial for purposes of identification of defendants by witnesses.

PACHUCO: He wants to be sure we know who you are.   55

JUDGE: It has been brought to my attention the Jury is having trouble telling one boy from another, so I am going to rule the defendants stand each time their names are mentioned.

GEORGE: I object. If the Prosecution makes an accusa-   60 tion, it will mean self-incrimination.

JUDGE (*pause*): Not necessarily. (*To Press.*) Please proceed.

GEORGE (*still trying to set the stage*): Then if the Court please, might I request that my clients be allowed to   65 sit with me during the trial so that I might consult with them?

JUDGE: Request denied.

GEORGE: May I inquire of Your Honor, if the defendant
70   Thomas Robert might rise from his seat and walk
over to counsel table so as to consult with me during
the trial?
JUDGE: I certainly will not permit it.
GEORGE: You will not?
75   JUDGE: No. This is a small courtroom, Mr. Shearer. We
can't have twenty-two defendants all over the place.
GEORGE: Then I object. On the grounds that that is a
denial of the rights guaranteed all defendants by both
the federal and state constitutions.
80   JUDGE: Well, that is your opinion. (*Gavel.*) Call your
first witness.
PRESS: The prosecution calls Lieutenant Sam Edwards
of the Los Angeles Police Department.
PACHUCO (*snaps, does double take on Judge*): You know
85   what. We've already heard from that bato. Let's get
on with the defense.

(*Snaps. Press sits. George stands.*)

GEORGE: The defense calls Adela Barrios.
BAILIFF (*calling out*): Adeela Barreeos to the stand.

(*Della Barrios comes forth out of the spectators. Bertha
leans forward.*)

BERTHA (*among the spectators*): Don't tell 'em nothing.

(*The Bailiff swears in Della silently.*)

90   PACHUCO: Look at your gang. They do look like mobsters. Se watchan bien gachos.°

(*Henry looks at the batos, who are sprawled out in their
places.*)

HENRY (*under his breath*): Come on, Batos, sit up.
SMILEY: We're tired, Hank.
JOEY: My butt is sore.
95   TOMMY: Yeah, look at the soft chairs the jury's got.
HENRY: What did you expect? They're trying to make us
look bad. Come on! Straighten up.
SMILEY: Simón, batos, Hank is right.
JOEY: ¡Más alba nalga!°
100 TOMMY: Put some class on your ass.
HENRY: Sit up! (*They all sit up.*)
GEORGE: State your name please.
DELLA: Adela Barrios. (*She sits.*)
GEORGE: Miss Barrios, were you with Henry Reyna on
105   the night of August 1, 1942?
DELLA: Yes.
JUDGE (*to Henry*): Please stand.

(*Henry stands.*)

GEORGE: Please tell the court what transpired that night.
DELLA (*pause, takes a breath*): Well, after the dance that
110   Saturday night, Henry and I drove out to the Sleepy
Lagoon about eleven-thirty.

1, 9. 91. **Se watchan bien gachos:** They look like real bad guys.
99. **¡Más alba nalga!:** Sit up (literally, more alert rump)!

Scene 10. *Sleepy Lagoon*

(*Music: THE HARRY JAMES THEME. El Pachuco
creates the scene. The light changes. We see a shimmering pattern of light on the floor growing to the music. It
becomes the image of the Lagoon. As the music soars to
a trumpet solo, Henry reaches out to Della, and she
glides to her feet.*)

DELLA: There was a full moon that night, and as we
drove up to the Lagoon we noticed right away the
place was empty . . .

(*A pair of headlights silently pulls in from the black
background upstage center.*)

Henry parked the car on the bank of the reservoir
and we relaxed.   5

(*Headlights go off.*)

It was such a warm, beautiful night, and the sky was
so full of stars, we couldn't just sit in the car. So we
got out, and Henry took my hand . . .

(*Henry stands and takes Della's hand.*)

We went for a walk around the Lagoon. Neither of
us said anything at first, so the only sounds we could   10
hear were the crickets and the frogs . . .

(*Sounds of crickets and frogs, then music faintly in the
background.*)

When we got to the other side of the reservoir, we
began to hear music, so I asked Henry, what's that?
HENRY: Sounds like they're having a party.
DELLA: Where?   15
HENRY: Over at the Williams' Ranch. See the house
lights.
DELLA: Who lives there?
HENRY: A couple of families. Mexicanos. I think they
work on the ranch. You know, their name used to be   20
Gonzales, but they changed it to Williams.
DELLA: Why?
HENRY: I don't know. Maybe they think it gives 'em
more class.

(*We hear Mexican music.*)

Ay, jijo.° They're probably celebrating a wedding or   25
something.
DELLA: As soon as he said wedding, he stopped talking
and we both knew why. He had something on his
mind, something he was trying to tell me without
sounding like a square.   30
HENRY: Della . . . what are you going to do if I don't
come back from the war?
DELLA: That wasn't the question I was expecting, so I
answered something dumb, like I don't know, what's
going to keep you from coming back?   35

1, 10. 25. **Ay, jijo:** Heavens.

HENRY: Maybe wanting too much out of life, see? Ever since I was a kid, I've had this feeling like there's a big party going on someplace, and I'm invited, but I don't know how to get there. And I want to get there 40 so bad, I'll even risk my life to make it. Sounds crazy, huh?

(*Della and Henry kiss. They embrace and then Henry speaks haltingly.*)

If I get back from the war . . . will you marry me?
DELLA: Yes! (*She embraces him and almost causes them to topple over.*)
HENRY: ¡Órale! You'll knock us into the Lagoon. Listen, 45 what about your old man? He ain't going to like you marrying me.
DELLA: I know. But I don't care. I'll go to hell with you if you want me to.
HENRY: ¿Sabes qué?° I'm going to give you the biggest 50 pachuco wedding L.A. has ever seen.

(*Another pair of headlights comes in from the left. Della goes back to her narration.*)

DELLA: Just then another car pulled up to the Lagoon. It was Rafas and some drunk guys in a gang from Downey. They got out and started to bust the windows on Henry's car. Henry yelled at them, and they 55 started cussing at us. I told Henry not to say anything, but he cussed them back!
HENRY: You stay here, Della.
DELLA: Henry, no! Don't go down there! Please don't go down there!
60 HENRY: Can't you hear what they're doing to my car?
DELLA: There's too many of them. They'll kill you!
HENRY: ¡Chale!

(*Henry turns and runs upstage, where he stops in a freeze.*)

DELLA: Henry! Henry ran down the back of the Lagoon and attacked the gang by himself. Rafas had about 65 ten guys with him and they jumped on Henry like a pack of dogs. He fought them off as long as he could, then they threw him on the ground hard and kicked him until he passed out . . .

(*Headlights pull off.*)

After they left, I ran down to Henry and held him in 70 my arms until he came to. And I could tell he was hurt, but the first thing he said was . . .
PACHUCO: Let's go into town and get the guys.

(*Music: Glen Miller's "In the Mood." Henry turns to the batos and they stand. Smiley, Joey, and Tommy are joined by Rudy, Bertha, Lupe, and Elena, who enter from the side. They turn downstage in a body and freeze.*)

DELLA: It took us about an hour to go into town and come back. We got to the Lagoon with about eight cars, but the Downey gang wasn't there. 75
JOEY: Órale, ¿pos qué pasó?° Nobody here.
SMILEY: Then let's go to Downey.
THE BOYS (*ad lib*): Let's go!
HENRY: ¡Chale! ¡Chale!

(*Pause. They all stop.*)

Ya estuvo.° Everybody go home. 80

(*A collective groan from The Boys.*)

Go home!
DELLA: That's when we heard music coming from the Williams' Ranch again. We didn't know Rafas and his gang had been there too, causing trouble. So when Joey said . . . 85
JOEY: Hey, there's a party! Bertha, let's crash it.
DELLA: We all went there yelling and laughing.

(*The group of batos turns upstage in a mimetic freeze.*)

At the Williams' Ranch they saw us coming and thought we were the Downey Gang coming back again . . . They attacked us. 90

(*The group now mimes a series of tableaus showing the fight.*)

An old man ran out of the house with a kitchen knife and Henry had to hit him. Then a girl grabbed me by the hair and in a second everybody was fighting! People were grabbing sticks from the fence, bottles, anything! It all happened so fast, we didn't know 95 what hit us, but Henry said let's go!
HENRY: ¡Vámonos!° Let's get out of here.
DELLA: And we started to back off . . . Before we got to the cars, I saw something out of the corner of my eye . . . It was a guy. He was hitting a man on the 100 ground with a big stick.

(*El Pachuco mimes this action.*)

Henry called to him, but he wouldn't stop. He wouldn't stop . . . He wouldn't stop . . . He wouldn't stop . . .

(*Della in tears, holds Henry in her arms. The batos and rucas start moving back to their places, quietly.*)

Driving back in the car, everybody was quiet, like 105 nothing had happened. We didn't know José Williams had died at the party that night and that the guys would be arrested the next day for murder.

(*Henry separates from her and goes back to stand in his place. Della resumes the witness stand.*)

---

49. ¿Sabes qué?: You know what?

76. Órale, ¿pos qué pasó?: Hey man, well what happened?
80. Ya estuvo: That's enough.   **97. ¡Vámonos!:** Let's go!

Scene 11. The Conclusion of the Trial

(*Lights change back to courtroom, as Judge Charles bangs his gavel. Everyone is seated back in place.*)

GEORGE: Your witness.

PRESS (*springing to the attack*): You say Henry Reyna hit the man with his fist. (*Indicates Henry standing.*) Is this the Henry Reyna?

5 DELLA: Yes. I mean, no. He's Henry, but he didn't . . .

PRESS: Please be seated.

(*Henry sits.*)

Now, after Henry Reyna hit the old man with his closed fist, is that when he pulled the knife?

DELLA: The old man had the knife.

10 PRESS. So Henry pulled one out, too?

GEORGE (*rises*): Your Honor, I object to counsel leading the witness.

PRESS: I am not leading the witness.

GEORGE: You are.

15 PRESS: I certainly am not.

GEORGE: Yes, you are.

JUDGE: I would suggest, Mr. Shearer, that you look up during the noon hour just what a leading question is.

GEORGE: If the Court please, I am going to assign that
20 remark of Your Honor as misconduct.

JUDGE (*to Press*): Proceed.

(*George crosses back to his chair.*)

PRESS: Where was Smiley Torres during all this? Is it not true that Smiley Torres grabbed a woman by the hair and kicked her to the ground? Will Smiley Torres
25 please stand? (*Smiley stands.*) Is this the man?

DELLA: Yes, it's Smiley, but he . . .

PRESS: Please be seated.

(*Smiley sits. Press picks up a two-by-four.*)

Wasn't José Castro carrying a club of some kind?

GEORGE (*on his feet again*): Your Honor, I object! No
30 such club was ever found. The Prosecution is implying that this two-by-four is associated with my client
in some way.

PRESS: I'm not implying anything, Your Honor, I'm
merely using this stick as an illustration.

35 JUDGE: Objection overruled.

PRESS: Will José Castro please stand?

(*Joey stands.*)

Is this the man who was carrying a club?

(*Della refuses to answer.*)

Answer the question please.

DELLA: I refuse.

40 PRESS: You are under oath. You can't refuse.

JUDGE: Answer the question, young lady.

DELLA: I refuse.

PRESS: Is this the man you saw hitting another man with a two-by-four? Your Honor . . .

JUDGE: I order you to answer the question.   45

GEORGE: Your Honor, I object. The witness is obviously afraid her testimony will be manipulated by the
Prosecution.

PRESS: May I remind the court that we have a signed confession from one José Castro taken while in jail . . .   50

GEORGE: I object. Those were not confessions! Those are
statements. They are false and untrue, Your Honor,
obtained through beatings and coercion of the defendants by the police!

JUDGE: I believe the technical term is admissions, Mr.   55
Prosecutor. Objection sustained.

(*Applause from spectators.*)

At the next outburst, I will clear this courtroom. Go
on, Mr. Prosecutor.

PRESS: Sit down please.

(*Joey sits. George goes back to his seat.*)

Is Henry Reyna the leader of the 38th Street Gang?   60

(*Henry stands.*)

DELLA: Not in the sense that you mean.

PRESS: Did Henry Reyna, pachuco ringleader of the
38th Street Gang, willfully murder José Williams?

DELLA: No. They attacked us first.

PRESS: I didn't ask for your comment.   65

DELLA: But they did, they thought we were the Downey
gang.

PRESS: Just answer my questions.

DELLA: We were just defending ourselves so we could
get out of there.   70

PRESS: Your Honor, will you instruct the witness to be
cooperative.

JUDGE: I must caution you, young lady, answer the questions or I'll hold you in contempt.

PRESS: Was this the Henry Reyna who was carrying a   75
three-foot lead pipe?

GEORGE: I object!

JUDGE: Overruled.

DELLA: No.

PRESS: Was it a two-foot lead pipe?   80

GEORGE: Objection!

JUDGE: Overruled.

DELLA: No!

PRESS: Did he kick a woman to the ground?

DELLA: No, he was hurt from the beating.   85

PRESS: Sit down.

(*Henry sits.*)

Did Tommy Roberts rip stakes from a fence and hit a
man on the ground?

GEORGE: Objection!

JUDGE: Overruled.   90

DELLA: I never saw him do anything.

PRESS: Did Joey Castro have a gun?

GEORGE: Objection!

JUDGE: Overruled.

(*Joey stands.*)

95   PRESS: Sit down.

(*Joey sits.*)

Did Henry Reyna have a blackjack in his hand?

(*Henry stands.*)

DELLA: No.
PRESS: A switchblade knife?
DELLA: No.
100   PRESS: A two-by-four?
DELLA: No.
PRESS: Did he run over to José Williams, hit him on the head, and kill him?
DELLA: He could barely walk, how could he run to any
105   place?
PRESS (*moving in for the kill*): Did Smiley Torres?

(*The batos stand and sit as their names are mentioned.*)

Did Joey Castro? Did Tommy Roberts? Did Henry Reyna? Did Smiley Torres? Did Henry Reyna? Did Henry Reyna? Did Henry Reyna kill José Williams?!
110   DELLA: No, no, no!
GEORGE (*on his feet again*): Your Honor, I object! The Prosecution is pulling out objects from all over the place, none of which were found at Sleepy Lagoon, and none of which have been proven to be associated
115   with my clients in any way.
JUDGE: Overruled.
GEORGE: If Your Honor please, I wish to make an assignment of misconduct!
JUDGE: We have only had one this morning. We might as
120   well have another now.
GEORGE: You have it, Your Honor.
JUDGE: One more remark like that and I'll hold you in contempt. Quite frankly, Mr. Shearer, I am getting rather tired of your repeated useless objections.
125   GEORGE: I have not made useless objections.
JUDGE: I am sorry. Somebody is using ventriloquism. We have a Charlie McCarthy using Mr. Shearer's voice.
GEORGE: I am going to assign that remark of Your Honor as misconduct.
130   JUDGE: Fine. I would feel rather bad if you did not make an assignment of misconduct at least three times every session. (*Gavel.*) Witness is excused.

(*Della stands.*)

However, I am going to remand her to the custody of the Ventura State School for Girls for a period of one
135   year . . .
HENRY: What?
JUDGE: . . . to be held there as a juvenile ward of the State. Bailiff?
GEORGE: If the court please . . . If the court please . . .

(*Bailiff crosses to Della and takes her off left.*)

140   JUDGE: Court is in recess until tomorrow morning.

(*Judge retires. Press exits. Henry meets George halfway across center stage. The rest of the batos stand and stretch in the background.*)

GEORGE: Now, Henry, I want you to listen to me, please. You've got to remember he's the judge, Hank. And this is his courtroom.
HENRY: But he's making jokes, George, and we're getting screwed!   145
GEORGE: I know. I can't blame you for being bitter, but believe me, we'll get him.
HENRY: I thought you said we had a chance.
GEORGE (*passionately*): We do! This case is going to be won on appeal.   150
HENRY: Appeal? You mean you already know we're going to lose?
PACHUCO: So what's new?
GEORGE: Don't you see, Henry, Judge Charles is hanging himself as we go. I've cited over a hundred sepa-   155
rate cases of misconduct by the bench, and it's all gone into the record. Prejudicial error, denial of due process, inadmissible evidence, hearsay . . .
HENRY: ¿Sabes qué, George? Don't tell me any more.

(*Henry turns. Alice and Enrique approach him.*)

ALICE: Henry . . . ?   160
HENRY (*turns furiously*): I don't want to hear it, Alice!

(*Henry sees Enrique, but neither father nor son can think of anything to say. Henry goes back upstage.*)

ALICE: George, is there anything we can do?
GEORGE: No. He's bitter, and he has a right to be.

(*Judge Charles pounds his gavel. All go back to their places and sit.*)

JUDGE: We'll now hear the Prosecution's concluding statement.   165
PRESS: Your Honor, ladies and gentlemen of the jury. What you have before you is a dilemma of our times. The City of Los Angeles is caught in the midst of the biggest, most terrifying crime wave in its history. A crime wave that threatens to engulf the very founda-   170
tions of our civic well-being. We are not only dealing with the violent death of one José Williams in a drunken barrio brawl. We are dealing with a threat and danger to our children, our families, our homes. Set these pachucos free, and you shall unleash the   175
forces of anarchy and destruction in our society. Set these pachucos free and you will turn them into heroes. Others just like them must be watching us at this very moment. What nefarious schemes can they be hatching in their twisted minds? Rape, drugs,   180
assault, more violence? Who shall be their next inno-cent victim in some dark alley way, on some lonely street? You? You? Your loved ones? No! Henry Reyna and his Latin juvenile cohorts are not heroes. They are criminals, and they must be stopped. The   185
specific details of this murder are irrelevant before the overwhelming danger of the pachuco in our

midst. I ask you to find these zoot-suited gangsters guilty of murder and to put them in the gas chamber
190 where they belong.

(*The Press sits down. George rises and takes center stage.*)

GEORGE: Ladies and gentlemen of the jury, you have heard me object to the conduct of this trial. I have tried my best to defend what is most precious in our American society — a society now at war against the
195 forces of racial intolerance and totalitarian injustice. The prosecution has not provided one witness that actually saw, with his own eyes, who actually murdered José Williams. These boys are not the Downey gang, yet the evidence suggests that they were
200 attacked because the people at the ranch thought they were. Henry Reyna and Della Barrios were victims of the same bunch. Yes, they might have been spoiling for a revenge — who wouldn't under the circumstances — but not with the intent to conspire to
205 commit murder. So how did José Williams die? Was it an accident? Was it manslaughter? Was it murder? Perhaps we may never know. All the prosecution has been able to prove is that these boys wear long hair and zoot suits. And all the rest has been circumstan-
210 tial evidence, hearsay, and war hysteria. The prosecution has tried to lead you to believe that they are some kind of inhuman gangsters. Yet they are Americans. Find them guilty of anything more serious than a juvenile bout of fisticuffs, and you will condemn
215 all American youth. Find them guilty of murder, and you will murder the spirit of racial justice in America. (*George sits down.*)
JUDGE: The jury will retire to consider its verdict.

(*The Press stands and starts to exit with the Bailiff. El Pachuco snaps. All freeze.*)

PACHUCO: Chale. Let's have it.

(*Snaps again. The Press turns and comes back again.*)

220 JUDGE: Has the jury reached a verdict?
PRESS: We have, Your Honor.
JUDGE: How say you?
PRESS: We find the defendants guilty of murder in the first and second degrees.
225 JUDGE: The defendants will rise.

(*The batos come to their feet.*)

Henry Reyna, José Castro, Thomas Roberts, Ismael Torres, and so forth. You have been tried by a jury of your peers and found guilty of murder in the first and second degrees. The Law prescribes the capital pun-
230 ishment for this offense. However, in view of your youth and in consideration of your families, it is hereby the judgment of this court that you be sentenced to life imprisonment . . .
RUDY: No!
235 JUDGE: . . . and sent to the State Penitentiary at San Quentin. Court adjourned.

(*Gavel. Judge exits. Dolores, Enrique, and family go to Henry. Bertha crosses to Joey; Lupe goes to Tommy. Elena crosses to Smiley. George and Alice talk.*)

DOLORES: ¡Hijo mío! ¡Hijo de mi alma!°

(*Bailiff comes down with a pair of handcuffs.*)

BAILIFF: Okay, boys.

(*He puts the cuffs on Henry. Rudy comes up.*)

RUDY: ¿Carnal?

(*Henry looks at the Bailiff, who gives him a nod of permission to spend a moment with Rudy. Henry embraces him with the cuffs on. George and Alice approach.*)

GEORGE: Henry? I can't pretend to know how you feel, 240 son. I just want you to know that our fight has just begun.
ALICE: We may have lost this decision, but we're going to appeal immediately. We're going to stand behind you until your name is absolutely clear. I swear it! 245
PACHUCO: What the hell are they going to do, ese? They just sent you to prison for life. Once a Mexican goes in, he never comes out.
BAILIFF: Boys?

(*The Boys exit with the Bailiff. As they go Enrique calls after them.*)

ENRIQUE (*holding back tears*): Hijo. Be a man, hijo. 250 (*Then to his family.*) Vámonos . . . ¡Vámonos!

(*The family leaves and El Pachuco slowly walks to center stage.*)

Pachuco: We're going to take a short break right now, so you can all go out and take a leak, smoke a frajo. Ahí los watcho.

(*He exits up center and the newspaper backdrop comes down.*)

ACT 2 • *Prologue*

(*Lights up and El Pachuco emerges from the shadows. The newspaper drop is still down. Music.*)

PACHUCO: Watchamos pachucos
  los batos°
  the dudes
  street-corner warriors who fought and moved
  like unknown soldiers in wars of their own   5
  El Pueblo de Los was the battle zone
  from Sleepy Lagoon to the Zoot Suit wars
  when Marines and Sailors made their scores
  stomping like Nazis on East L.A. . . .

237. **¡Hijo mío! ¡Hijo de mi alma!:** My son! Son of my soul!
2, Prologue. 1–2. Watchamos . . . batos: We are watching pachucos, the dudes.

10   pero ¿saben qué?°
        That's later in the play. Let's pick it up in prison.
        We'll begin this scene
        inside the walls of San Quintín.

Scene 1. San Quentin

(*A bell rings as the drop rises. Henry, Joey, Smiley, and Tommy enter accompanied by a Guard.*)

GUARD: All right, people, lock up.

(*Boys move downstage in four directions. They step into "cells" simply marked by shadows of bars on the floor in their separate places. Newspaper handcarts rest on the floor as cots. Sound of cell doors closing. The Guard paces back and forth upstage level.*)

HENRY: San Quentin, California
        March 3, 1943
        Dear Family:
5   Coming in from the yard in the evening, we are quickly locked up in our cells. Then the clank and locking of the doors leaves one with a rather empty feeling. You are standing up to the iron door, waiting for the guard to come along and take the count, lis-
10   tening as his footsteps fade away in the distance. By this time there is a tense stillness that seems to crawl over the cellblock. You realize you are alone, so all alone.
PACHUCO: This all sounds rather tragic, doesn't it?
15   HENRY: But here comes the guard again, and he calls out your number in a loud voice . . .
GUARD (*calls numbers; Boys call name*): 24-545
HENRY: Reyna!
GUARD: 24-546
20   JOEY: Castro!
GUARD: 24-547
TOMMY: Roberts!
GUARD: 24-548
SMILEY: Torres!

(*Guard passes through dropping letters and exits up left.*)

25   HENRY: You jump to your feet, stooping to pick up the letter . . .
JOEY (*excited*): Or perhaps several letters . . .
TOMMY: You are really excited as you take the letters from the envelope.
30   SMILEY: The censor has already broken the seal when he reads it.
HENRY: You make a mental observation to see if you recognize the handwriting on the envelope.
SMILEY (*anxious*): It's always nice to hear from home . . .
35   JOEY: Or a close comrade . . .
TOMMY: Friends that you know on the outside . . .
HENRY: Or perhaps it's from a stranger.

2, 1. 10. pero ¿saben qué?: But what did they know?

(*Pause. Spotlight at upstage center. Alice walks in with casual clothes on. Her hair is in pigtails, and she wears a pair of drapes. She is cheerful.*)

Scene 2. The Letters

Dear Boys,
Announcing the publication (mimeograph) of the Appeal News, your very own newsletter, to be sent to you twice a month for the purpose of keeping you reliably informed of everything — the progress of the Sleeping   5
Lagoon Defense Committee (we have a name now) and, of course, the matter of your appeal.
Signed,
Your editor
Alice Bloomfield.   10

(*Music. "Perdido" by Duke Ellington. Alice steps down and sits on the lip of the upstage level. The Boys start swinging the bat, dribbling the basketball, shadow-boxing, and exercising. Alice mimes typing movements and we hear the sounds of a typewriter. Music fades. Alice rises.*)

ALICE: The Appeal News Volume I, Number I, April 7, 1943.
        Boys,
        You can, you must, and you will help us on the outside by what you do on the inside. Don't forget, what   15
        you do affects others. You have no control over that. When the time comes, let us be proud to show the record.
        Signed,
        Your editor.   20

(*Music up again. The Boys go through their activities. Alice moves downstage center and the music fades.*)

SMILEY (*stepping toward her*): April 10, 1943
        Dear Miss Bloomfield,
        I have discovered from my wife that you are conducting door-to-door fund-raising campaigns in Los Angeles. She doesn't want to tell you, but she feels   25
        bad about doing such a thing. It's not our custom to go around the neighborhoods asking for money.
ALICE (*turning toward Smiley*): Dear Smiley,
        Of course, I understand your feelings . . .
SMILEY (*adamant*): I don't want my wife going around   30
        begging.
ALICE: It isn't begging — it's fund-raising.
SMILEY: I don't care what you call it. If that's what it's going to take, count me out.
ALICE: All right. I won't bother your wife if she really   35
        doesn't want me to. Okay?

(*Smiley looks at her and turns back to his upstage position. Music. The batos move again. Tommy crosses to Alice. Another fade.*)

TOMMY: April 18, 1943
        Dear Alice,

Trying to find the words and expression to thank you
40 for your efforts in behalf of myself and the rest of the
batos makes me realize what a meager vocabulary I
possess . . .
ALICE: Dear Tommy,
Your vocabulary is just fine. Better than most.
45 TOMMY: Most what?
ALICE: People.
TOMMY (*glances at Henry*): Uh, listen, Alice. I don't
want to be treated any different than the rest of the
batos, see? And don't expect me to talk to you like
50 some square Anglo, some pinche gabacho.° You just
better find out what it means to be Chicano, and it
better be pretty damn quick.
ALICE: Look, Tommy, I didn't . . .
TOMMY: I know what you're trying to do for us and
55 that's reet, see? Shit. Most paddies would probably
like to see us locked up for good. I been in jail a
couple of times before, but never nothing this deep.
Strange, ain't it, the trial in Los? I don't really know
what happened or why. I don't give a shit what the
60 papers said. We didn't do half the things I read about.
I also know that I'm in here just because I hung
around with Mexicans . . . or pachucos. Well, just
remember this, Alicia . . . I grew up right alongside
most of these batos, and I'm pachuco too. Simón,
65 esa, you better believe it!

(*Music up. Movement. Tommy returns to his position.
Henry stands. Alice turns toward him, but he walks over
to The Pachuco, giving her his back.*)

JOEY (*stepping forward anxiously*): May 1, 1943
Dear Alice . . . Darling!
I can't help but spend my time thinking about you.
How about sending us your retra — that is, your
70 photograph? Even though Tommy would like one
of Rita Hayworth — he's always chasing Mexican
skirts (Ha! Ha!) — I'd prefer to see your sweet face
any day.
ALICE (*directly to him*): Dear Joey,
75 Thank you so much. I really appreciated receiving
your letter.
JOEY: That's all reet, Grandma! You mind if I call you
Grandma?
ALICE: Oh, no.
80 JOEY: Eres una ruca de aquellas.°
ALICE: I'm a what?
JOEY: Ruca. A fine chick.
ALICE (*pronounces the word*): Ruca?
JOEY: De aquellas. (*Makes a cool gesture, palms out at
hip level.*)
85 ALICE (*imitating him*): De aquellas.
JOEY: All reet! You got it. (*Pause.*) P.S. Did you forget
the photograph?
ALICE (*she hands it to him*): Dearest Joey,

2, 2. 50. **pinche gabacho:** Damned Anglo (derogatory).
80. **Eres . . . aquellas:** You are a fine chick.

Of course not. Here it is, attached to a copy of the
Appeal News. I'm afraid it's not exactly a pin-up.   90
JOEY (*kissing the photo*): Alice, honey, you're a doll!

(*Joey shows the photo to Tommy then Smiley, who is
curious enough to come into the circle. Alice looks at
Henry, but he continues to ignore her.*)

ALICE (*back at center*): The Appeal News, Volume I,
Number 3, May 5, 1943.
Dear Boys,
Feeling that el Cinco de Mayo is a very appropriate   95
day — the CIO radio program, "Our Daily Bread,"
is devoting the entire time this evening to a discussion
of discrimination against Mexicans in general and
against you guys in particular.

(*Music up. The repartee between Alice and the batos is
now friendly and warm. Even Smiley is smiling with
Alice. They check out her "drapes."*)

Scene 3. The Incorrigible Pachuco

(*Henry stands at downstage left, looks at the group,
then decides to speak.*)

HENRY: May 17, 1943
Dear Miss Bloomfield,
I understand you're coming up to Q this weekend,
and I would like to talk to you — in private. Can you
arrange it?   5

(*The batos turn away, taking a hint.*)

ALICE (*eagerly*): Yes, yes, I can. What can I do for you,
Henry?

(*Henry and Alice step forward toward each other. El
Pachuco moves in.*)

HENRY: For me? ¡Ni madre!°
ALICE (*puzzled*): I don't understand.
HENRY: I wanted you to be the first to know, Alice. I'm 10
dropping out of the appeal.
ALICE (*unbelieving*): You're what?
HENRY: I'm bailing out, esa. Dropping out of the case,
see?
ALICE: Henry, you can't!   15
HENRY: Why can't I?
ALICE: Because you'll destroy our whole case! If we
don't present a united front, how can we ask the pub-
lic to support us?
HENRY: That's your problem. I never asked for their   20
support. Just count me out.
ALICE (*getting nervous, anxious*): Henry, please, think
about what you're saying. If you drop out, the rest of
the boys will probably go with you. How can you
even think of dropping out of the appeal? What about 25
George and all the people that have contributed their

2, 3. 8. **¡Ni madre!:** It doesn't matter, or, it's not worth a damn.

time and money in the past few months? You just can't quit on them!

HENRY: Oh no? Just watch me.

30 ALICE: If you felt this way, why didn't you tell me before?

HENRY: Why didn't you ask me? You think you can just move in and defend anybody you feel like? When did I ever ask you to start a defense committee for me? Or a newspaper? Or a fundraising drive and all that

35 other shit? I don't need defending, esa. I can take care of myself.

ALICE: But what about the trial, the sentence. They gave you life imprisonment?

HENRY: It's my life!

40 ALICE: Henry, honestly — are you kidding me?

HENRY: You think so?

ALICE: But you've seen me coming and going. Writing to you, speaking for you, traveling up and down the state. You must have known I was doing it for you.

45 Nothing has come before my involvement, my attachment, my passion for this case. My boys have been everything to me.

HENRY: My boys? My boys! What the hell are we — your personal property? Well, let me set you straight,

50 lady, I ain't your boy.

ALICE: You know I never meant it that way.

HENRY: You think I haven't seen through your bullshit? Always so concerned. Come on, boys. Speak out, boys. Stand up for your people. Well, you leave my

55 people out of this! Can't you understand that?

ALICE: No, I can't understand that.

HENRY: You're just using Mexicans to play politics.

ALICE: Henry, that's the worst thing anyone has ever said to me.

60 HENRY: Who are you going to help next — the Colored People?

ALICE: No, as a matter of fact, I've already helped the Colored People. What are you going to do next — go to the gas chamber?

65 HENRY: What the hell do you care?

ALICE: I don't!

HENRY: Then get the hell out of here!

ALICE (*furiously*): You think you're the only one who doesn't want to be bothered? You ought to try work-

70 ing in the Sleepy Lagoon defense office for a few months. All the haggling, the petty arguments, the lack of cooperation. I've wanted to quit a thousand times. What the hell am I doing here? They're coming at me from all sides. You're too sentimental and emo-

75 tional about this, Alice. You're too cold hearted, Alice. You're collecting money and turning it over to the lawyers, while the families are going hungry. They're saying you can't be trusted because you're a Communist, because you're a Jew. Okay! If that's the

80 way they feel about me, then to hell with them! I hate them too. I hate their language, I hate their enchiladas, and I hate their goddamned mariachi music!

(*Pause. They look at each other. Henry smiles, then Alice — feeling foolish — and they both break out laughing.*)

HENRY: All right! Now you sound like you mean it.

ALICE: I do.

HENRY: Okay! Now we're talking straight.   85

ALICE: I guess I have been sounding like some square paddy chick. But, you haven't exactly been Mister Cool yourself . . . ese.

HENRY: So, let's say we're even Steven.

ALICE: Fair enough. What now?   90

HENRY: Why don't we bury the hatchet, you know what I mean?

ALICE: Can I tell George you'll go on with the appeal?

HENRY: Yeah. I know there's a lot of people out there who are willing and trying to help us. People who   95
feel that our conviction was an injustice. People like George . . . and you. Well, the next time you see them, tell them Hank Reyna sends his thanks.

ALICE: Why don't you tell them?

HENRY: You getting wise with me again?   100

ALICE: If you write an article — and I know you can — we'll publish it in the *People's World*. What do you say?

PACHUCO: Article! Pos who told you, you could write, ese?   105

HENRY (*laughs*): Chale.

ALICE: I'm serious. Why don't you give it a try?

HENRY: I'll think about it. (*Pause.*) Listen, you think you and I could write each other . . . outside the newsletter?   110

ALICE: Sure.

HENRY: Then it's a deal. (*They shake hands.*)

ALICE: I'm glad we're going to be communicating. I think we're going to be very good friends.

(*Alice lifts her hands to Henry's shoulder in a gesture of comradeship. Henry follows her hand, putting his on top of hers.*)

HENRY: You think so?   115

ALICE: I know so.

GUARD: Time, miss.

ALICE: I gotta go. Think about the article, okay? (*She turns to the Boys.*) I gotta go, boys.

JOEY: Goodbye, Grandma! Say hello to Bertha.   120

SMILEY: And to my wife!

TOMMY: Give my love to Lupe!

GUARD: Time!

ALICE: I've got to go. Goodbye, goodbye.

(*Alice exits, escorted by the Guard upstage left. As she goes, Joey calls after her.*)

JOEY: See you, Grandma.   125

TOMMY (*turning to Joey and Smiley*): She loves me.

PACHUCO: Have you forgotten what happened at the trial? You think the Appeals Court is any different? Some paddy judge sitting in the same fat-ass judgment of your fate.   130

HENRY: Come on, ese, give me a break!

PACHUCO: One break, coming up!

(*He snaps his fingers. The Guard blows his whistle.*)

GUARD: Rec time!

Jorge Galvan as El Pachuco in *Zoot Suit* at the San Diego Repertory Theatre, 1997.

Alice Bloomfield (Carla Harting) and Henry Reyna (David Barrear) talking in prison in *Zoot Suit* at the San Diego Repertory Theatre, 1997. El Pachuco stands in the background.

(*The batos move upstage to the upper level. Music. The Boys mime a game of handball against the backdrop. During the game, George enters at stage right and comes downstage carrying his briefcase. The Guard blows a whistle and stops the game.*)

GUARD: Reyna, Castro, Roberts, Torres! — You got a
135   visitor.

Scene 4. *Major George*

(*The Boys turn and see George. They come down enthusiastically.*)

JOEY: ¡Óra-leh! ¡Ese, Cheer!°
SMILEY: George!
GEORGE: Hi, guys!

(*The Boys shake his hand, pat him on the back. Henry comes to him last.*)

How are you all doing? You boys staying in shape?
5   JOEY: Ese, you're looking at the hero of the San Quentin athletic program. Right, batos? (*He shadowboxes a little.*)
TOMMY: Ten rounds with a busted ankle.
JOEY: ¡Simón! And I won the bout, too. I'm the terror of the flyweights, ese. The killer fly!
10   TOMMY: They got us doing everything, Cheer. Baseball, basketball.
SMILEY: Watch repairing.
GEORGE (*impressed*): Watch repairing?
SMILEY: I'm also learning to improve my English and
15   arithmetic.
GEORGE: Warden Duffy has quite a program. I hear he's a good man?
JOEY: Simón, he's a good man. We've learned our lesson . . . Well, anyway, I've learned my lesson, boy.
20   No more pachuquismo for me. Too many people depending on us to help out. The raza° here in Los. The whole Southwest. Mexico, South America! Like you and Grandma say, this is the people's world. If you get us out of here, I figure the only thing I could
25   do is become a union organizer. Or go into major league baseball.
GEORGE: Baseball?
JOEY: Simón, ese. You're looking at the first Mexican Babe Ruth. Or maybe, "Babe Root." Root! You get it?
30   TOMMY: How about "Baby Zoot"?
JOEY: Solid, Jackson.
GEORGE: Babe Zooter!
JOEY: Solid tudee, that's all reet, ese.
GEORGE: What about you, Henry? What have you been
35   doing?
HENRY: Time, George, I've been doing time.
TOMMY: Ain't it the truth?

2, 4. 1. ¡Ese, Cheer!: Hey it's Cheer! (nickname for George).
21. raza: The race, the people, Chicanos.

SMILEY: Yeah, George! When you going to spring us out of here, ese?
HENRY: How's the appeal coming?   40
GEORGE (*getting serious*): Not bad. There's been a development I have to talk to you about. But other than that . . .
HENRY: Other than what?
SMILEY (*pause*): Bad news?   45
GEORGE (*hedging*): It all depends on how you look at it, Smiley. It really doesn't change anything. Work on the brief is going on practically day and night. The thing is, even with several lawyers on the case now, it'll still be several months before we file. I want to be   50 honest about that.
HENRY (*suspiciously*): Is that the bad news?
GEORGE: Not exactly. Sit down, boys. (*Pause. He laughs to himself.*) I really don't mean to make such a big deal out of this thing. Fact is I'm still not quite used   55 to the idea myself. (*Pause.*) You see . . . I've been drafted.
JOEY: Drafted?
TOMMY: Into the Army?
SMILEY: You?   60
GEORGE: That's right. I'm off to war.
JOEY: But . . . you're old, Cheer.
HENRY (*a bitter edge*): Why you, George? Why did they pick on you?
GEORGE: Well, Henry, I wouldn't say they "picked" on   65 me. There's lots of men my age overseas. After all, it is war time and . . .
HENRY: And you're handling our appeal.
GEORGE (*pause*): We have other lawyers.
HENRY: But you're the one who knows the case!   70
GEORGE (*pause*): I knew you were going to take this hard. Believe me, Henry, my being drafted has nothing to do with your case. It's just a coincidence.
HENRY: Like our being in here for life is a coincidence?
GEORGE: No, that's another . . .   75
HENRY: Like our being hounded every goddam day of our life is a coincidence?
GEORGE: Henry . . .

(*Henry turns away furiously. There is a pause.*)

It's useless anger, son, believe me. Actually, I'm quite flattered by your concern, but I'm hardly indispens-   80 able.
HENRY (*deeply disturbed*): What the hell are you talking about, George?
GEORGE: I'm talking about all the people trying to get you out. Hundreds, perhaps thousands. Alice and I   85 aren't the only ones. We've got a heck of a fine team of lawyers working on the brief. With or without me, the appeal will be won. I promise you that.
HENRY: It's no use, George.
GEORGE: I realize all that sounds pretty unconvincing   90 under the circumstances, but it's true.
HENRY: Those bastard cops are never going to let us out of here. We're here for life and that's it.
GEORGE: You really believe that?

95 HENRY: What do you expect me to believe?
GEORGE: I wish I could answer that, son, but that's really for you to say.
GUARD: Time, Counselor.
GEORGE: Coming. (*Turns to the other Boys.*) Listen,
100 boys, I don't know where in the world I'll be the day your appeal is won — and it will be won — whether it's in the Pacific somewhere or in Europe or in a hole in the ground . . . Take care of yourselves.
TOMMY: See you around, George.
105 SMILEY: So long, George.
JOEY: 'Bye, Cheer.
GEORGE: Yeah. See you around. (*Pause.*) Goodbye, Henry. Good luck and God bless you.
HENRY: God bless you, too, George. Take care of your-
110 self.
TOMMY: Say, George, when you come back from the war, we're going to take you outa town and blast some weed.
JOEY: We'll get you a pair of buns you can hold in your
115 hands!
GEORGE: I may just take you up on that.

(*The Guard escorts George out, then turns back to the Boys.*)

GUARD: All right, new work assignments. Everybody report to the jute mill. Let's go.

(*Smiley, Joey, and Tommy start to exit. Henry hangs back.*)

What's the matter with you, Reyna? You got lead in
120 your pants? I said let's go.
HENRY: We're supposed to work in the mess hall.
GUARD: You got a new assignment.
HENRY: Since when?
GUARD: Since right now. Get going!
125 HENRY (*hanging back*): The warden know about this?
GUARD: What the hell do you care? You think you're something special? Come on, greaseball. Move!
HENRY: Make me, you bastard!
GUARD: Oh yeah.

(*The Guard pushes Henry. Henry pushes back. The batos react, as the Guard traps Henry with his club around the chest. The Boys move to Henry's defense.*)

130 Back!
HENRY (*to the batos*): Back off! BACK OFF! Don't be stupid.
GUARD: Okay, Reyna, you got solitary! Bastard, huh? Into the hole!

(*He pushes Henry onto center stage. Lights down. A single spot.*)

135 Line, greaseballs. Move out!

(*As they march.*)

Quickly, quickly. You're too slow. Move, move, move.

(*The Boys exit with the Guard.*)

Scene 5. *Solitary*

(*A lone saxophone sets the mood.*)

PACHUCO: Too bad, ese. He set you up again.
HENRY (*long pause. He looks around*): Solitary, ese . . . they gave me solitary. (*He sits down on the floor, a forlorn figure.*)
PACHUCO: Better get used to it, carnal. That's what this
5 stretch is going to be about, see? You're in here for life, bato.
HENRY: I can't accept it, ese.
PACHUCO: You've got to, Hank . . .
only this reality is real now,
10 only this place is real,
sitting in the lonely cell of your will . . .
HENRY: I can't see my hands.
PACHUCO: Then tell your eyes to forget the light, ese
Only the hard floor is there, carnal
15 Only the cold hard edge of this reality
and there is no time . . .
Each second is a raw drop of blood from your brain
that you must swallow
drop by drop
20 and don't even start counting
or you'll lose your mind . . .
HENRY: I've got to know why I'm here, ese! I've got to have a reason for being here.
PACHUCO: You're here, Hank, because you chose to
25 be — because you protected your brother and your family. And nobody knows the worth of that effort better than you, ese.
HENRY: I miss them, ese . . . my jefitos, my carnalillo, my sis . . . I miss Della.
PACHUCO (*a spot illuminates Henry's family standing up-stage; El Pachuco snaps it off*): Forget them!
30 Forget them all.
Forget your family and the barrio
beyond the wall.
HENRY: There's still a chance I'll get out.
PACHUCO: Fat chance.
35 HENRY: I'm talking about the appeal!
PACHUCO: And I'm talking about what's real! ¿Qué traes, Hank?° Haven't you learned yet?
HENRY: Learned what?
PACHUCO: Not to expect justice when it isn't there.
40 No court in the land's going to set you free.
Learn to protect your loves by binding them
in hate, ese! Stop hanging on to false hopes.
The moment those hopes come crashing down,
you'll find yourself on the ground foaming at
45 the mouth. ¡Como loco!°
HENRY (*turning on him furiously*): ¿Sabes qué? Don't tell me any more. I don't need you to tell me what to do. Fuck off! FUCK OFF!

2, 5. 37–38. **¿Qué traes, Hank?:** What's wrong, Hank?
46. ¡Como loco!: Like a lunatic!

(*Henry turns away from El Pachuco. Long pause. An anxious, intense moment. El Pachuco shifts gears and breaks the tension with a satirical twist. He throws his arms out and laughs.*)

50   PACHUCO: ¡Órale pues!°
     Don't take the pinche play so seriously, Jesús!
     Es puro vacilón!°
     Watcha.

(*He snaps his fingers. Lights change. We hear the sounds of the city.*)

     This is Los, carnal.
55   You want to see some justice for pachucos?
     Check out what's happening back home today.
     The Navy has landed, ese —
     on leave with full pay
     and war's breaking out in the streets of L.A.!

Scene 6. Zoot Suit Riots

(*We hear music: the bugle call from "Bugle Call Rag." Suddenly the stage is awash in colored lights. The city of Los Angeles appears in the background in a panoramic vista of lights tapering into the night horizon. Sailors and Girls jitterbug on the dance floor. It is the Avalon Ballroom. The music is hot, the dancing hotter. El Pachuco and Henry stand to the side.*

The scene is in dance and mostly pantomime. Occasionally words are heard over the music which is quite loud. On the floor are two Sailors [Swabbie is one] and a Marine dancing with the Girls. A Shore Patrolman speaks to the Cigarette Girl. A Pimp comes on and watches the action. Little Blue and Zooter are also on the floor. Rudy enters wearing Henry's zoot suit with Bertha and Lupe. Lupe takes their picture, then all three move up center to the rear of the ballroom. Cholo comes in down center, sees them and moves up stage. All four make an entrance onto the dance floor.

The Marine takes his girl aside after paying her. She passes the money to the Pimp. The Sailors try to pick up on Lupe and Bertha, and Cholo pushes one back. The Sailors complain to the Shore Patrol, who throws Cholo out the door down center. There is an argument that Rudy joins. The Sailors go back to Bertha and Lupe who resist. Cholo and Rudy go to their defense and a fight develops. Zooter and Little Blue split. Cholo takes the Girls out and Rudy pulls a knife. He is facing the three Sailors and the Marine, when The Pachuco freezes the action.)

PACHUCO (*forcefully*): Órale, that's enough!

(*El Pachuco takes Rudy's knife and with a tap sends him off-stage. Rudy exits with the Girls. El Pachuco is now facing the angry Servicemen. He snaps his fingers. The Press enters quickly to the beeping sound of a radio broadcast.*)

PRESS: Good evening, Mr. and Mrs. North and South America and all the ships at sea. Let's go to press. FLASH. Los Angeles, California, June 3, 1943. Serious rioting broke out here today as flying squadrons of Marines and soldiers joined the Navy in a new assault on zooter-infested districts. A fleet of twenty taxicabs carrying some two hundred servicemen pulled out of the Naval Armory in Chavez Ravine tonight and assembled a task force that invaded the eastside barrio.

(*Unfreeze. The following speeches happen simultaneously.*)

MATE: You got any balls in them funny pants, boy?
SAILOR: He thinks he's tough . . .
SWABBIE: How about it, lardhead? You a tough guy or just a draft dodger?
PRESS: The Zoot Suiters, those gamin' dandies . . .
PACHUCO (*cutting them off*): Why don't you tell them what I really am, ese, or how you've been forbidden to use the very word . . .
PRESS: We are complying in the interest of the war.
PACHUCO: How have you complied?
PRESS: We're using other terms.
PACHUCO: Like *pachuco* and *zoot suiter*?
PRESS: What's wrong with that? The Zoot Suit Crime Wave is even beginning to push the war news off the front page.
PACHUCO: The Press distorted the very meaning of the word "zoot suit."
     All it is for you guys is another way to say Mexican.
     But the ideal of the original chuco°
     was to look like a diamond
     to look sharp
     hip
     bonaroo°
     finding a style of urban survival
     in the rural skirts and outskirts
     of the brown metropolis of Los, cabrón.
PRESS: It's an afront to good taste.
PACHUCO: Like the Mexicans, Filipinos, and blacks who wear them.
PRESS: Yes!
PACHUCO: Even the white kids and the Wops and the Jews are putting on the drape shape.
PRESS: You are trying to outdo the white man in exaggerated white man's clothes!
PACHUCO: Because everybody knows
     that Mexicans, Filipinos, and blacks
     belong to the huarache°
     the straw hat and the dirty overall.

---

50. **¡Órale pues!:** Listen then!   52. **Es puro vacilón!:** It's pure fantasy!

2, 6. 29. **chuco:** Pachuco.   33. **bonaroo:** Wonderful.
47. **huarache:** Mexican sandal.

PRESS: You savages weren't even wearing clothes when
50   the white man pulled you out of the jungle.
MARINE: My parents are going without collars and cuffs
    so you can wear that shit.
PRESS: That's going too far, too goddamned far, and it's
55   got to be stopped!
PACHUCO: Why?
PRESS: Don't you know there's a war on? Don't you
    fucking well know you can't get away with that shit?
    What are we fighting for if not to annihilate the ene-
    mies of the American way of life?
60 MATE: Let's tear it off his back!
SAILORS/MARINE: Let's strip him! Get him! (Etc.)
PRESS: KILL THE PACHUCO BASTARD!!

(*Music: "American Patrol" by Glenn Miller. The Press
gets a searchlight from upstage center while the Four
Servicemen stalk El Pachuco.*)

SAILOR: Heh, zooter. Come on, zooter!
SWABBIE: You think you're more important than the
65   war, zooter?
MATE: Let's see if you got any balls in them funny pants,
    boy.
SWABBIE: Watch out for the knife.
SAILOR: That's a real chango monkey suit he's got on.
70 MATE: I bet he's half monkey — just like the Filipinos
    and niggers that wear them.
SWABBIE: You trying to outdo the white man in them
    glad rags, Mex?

(*They fight now to the finish. El Pachuco is overpowered and stripped as Henry watches helplessly from his
position. The Press and Servicemen exit with pieces of
El Pachuco's zoot suit. El Pachuco stands. The only item
of clothing on his body is a small loincloth. He turns
and looks at Henry, with mystic intensity. He opens his
arms as an Aztec conch blows, and he slowly exits backward with powerful calm into the shadows. Silence.
Henry comes downstage. He absorbs the impact of what
he has seen and falls to his knees at center stage, spent
and exhausted. Lights down.*)

Scene 7. *Alice*

(*The Guard and Alice enter from opposite sides of the
stage. The Guard carries a handful of letters and is reading one of them.*)

GUARD: July 2, 1943.
ALICE: Dear Henry,
    I hope this letter finds you in good health and good
    spirits — but I have to assume you've heard about
5   the riots in Los Angeles. It was a nightmare, and it
    lasted for a week. The city is still in a state of shock.
GUARD (*folds letter back into envelope, then opens
    another*): August 5, 1943.
ALICE: Dear Henry,
    The riots here in L.A. have touched off race riots
10   all over the country — Chicago, Detroit, even little

Beaumont, Texas, for Christ's sake. But the one in
Harlem was the worst. Millions of dollars worth of
property damage. 500 people were hospitalized, and
five Negroes were killed.
GUARD: Things are rough all over.   15
ALICE: Please write to me and tell me how you feel.
GUARD (*the Guard folds up the second letter, stuffs it
back into its envelope and opens a third*): August 20,
1943.
ALICE: Dear Henry,
    Although I am disappointed not to have heard from   20
    you, I thought I would send you some good news for
    a change. Did you know we had a gala fund-raiser at
    the Mocambo?
GUARD: The Mocambo . . . Hotcha!°
ALICE: . . . and Rita Hayworth lent your sister Lupe a   25
    ball gown for the occasion. She got dressed at Cecil B.
    DeMille's house, and she looked terrific. Her escort
    was Anthony Quinn, and Orson Welles said . . .
GUARD: Orson Welles! Well! Sounds like Louella Par-
    sons. (*He folds up the letter.*) September 1, 1943.   30
ALICE: Henry, why aren't you answering my letters?
GUARD: He's busy. (*He continues to stuff the envelope.*)
ALICE: Henry, if there's something I've said or done . . . ?

(*The Guard shuffles the envelopes.*)

    Henry . . .

(*Lights change. Guard crosses to center stage, where
Henry is still doubled up on the floor.*)

GUARD: Welcome back to the living, Reyna. It's been a   35
    long hot summer. Here's your mail.

(*The Guard tosses the letters to the floor directly in front
of Henry's head. Henry looks up slowly and grabs one
of the letters. He opens it, trying to focus. The Guard
exits.*)

ALICE: Henry, I just found out you did ninety days in
    solitary. I'm furious at the rest of the guys for keeping
    it from me. I talked to Warden Duffy, and he said you
    struck a guard. Did something happen I should know   40
    about? I wouldn't ask if it wasn't so important, but a
    clean record . . .

(*Henry rips up the letter he has been reading and scatters the others. Alarmed.*)

    Henry?

(*Henry pauses, his instant fury spent and under control.
He sounds almost weary, but the anger is still there.*)

HENRY: You still don't understand, Alice.
ALICE (*softly, compassionate*): But I do! I'm not accus-   45
    ing you of anything. I don't care what happened or
    why they sent you there. I'm sure you had your rea-
    sons. But you know the public is watching you.
HENRY (*frustrated, a deep question*): Why do you do
    this, Alice?   50

2, 7. 24. **Hotcha!:** Expression used as a song lyric or title.

ALICE: What?

HENRY: The appeal, the case, all the shit you do. You think the public gives a goddamn?

ALICE (*with conviction*): Yes! We are going to get you out of here, Henry Reyna. We are going to win!

HENRY (*probing*): What if we lose?

ALICE (*surprised but moving on*): We're not going to lose.

HENRY (*forcefully, insistent, meaning more than he is saying*): What if we do? What if we get another crooked judge, and he nixes the appeal?

ALICE: Then we'll appeal again. We'll take it to the Supreme Court. (*A forced laugh.*) Hell, we'll take it all the way to President Roosevelt!

HENRY (*backing her up — emotionally*): What if we still lose?

ALICE (*bracing herself against his aggression*): We can't.

HENRY: Why can't we?

ALICE (*giving a political response in spite of herself*): Because we've got too much support. You should see the kinds of people responding to us. Unions, Mexicans, Negroes, Oakies. It's fantastic.

HENRY (*driving harder*): Why can't we lose, Alice?

ALICE: I'm telling you.

HENRY: No, you're not.

ALICE (*starting to feel vulnerable*): I don't know what to tell you.

HENRY: Yes, you do!

ALICE (*frightened*): Henry . . . ?

HENRY: Tell me why we can't lose, Alice!

ALICE (*forced to fight back, with characteristic passion*): Stop it, Henry! Please stop it! I won't have you treat me this way. I never have been able to accept one person pushing another around . . . pushing me around! Can't you see that's why I'm here? Because I can't stand it happening to you. Because I'm a Jew, goddammit! I have been there . . . I have been there! If you lose, I lose.

(*Pause. The emotional tension is immense. Alice fights to hold back tears. She turns away.*)

HENRY: I'm sorry . . .

ALICE (*pause*): It's stupid for us to fight like this. I look forward to coming here for weeks. Just to talk to you, to be with you, to see your eyes.

HENRY (*pause*): I thought a lot about you when I was in the hole. Sometimes . . . sometimes I'd even see you walk in, in the dark, and talk to me. Just like you are right now. Same look, same smile, same perfume . . . (*He pauses.*) Only the other one never gave me so much lip. She just listened. She did say one thing. She said . . .

ALICE (*trying to make light of it, then more gently*): I can't say that to you, Henry. Not the way you want it.

HENRY: Why not?

ALICE (*she means it*): Because I can't allow myself to be used to fill in for all the love you've always felt and always received from all your women.

HENRY (*with no self-pity*): Give it a chance, Alice.

ALICE (*beside herself*): Give it a chance? You crazy idiot. If I thought making love to you would solve all your problems, I'd do it in a second. Don't you know that? But it won't. It'll only complicate things. I'm trying to help you, goddammit. And to do that, I have to be your friend, not your white woman.

HENRY (*getting angry*): What makes you think I want to go to bed with you. Because you're white? I've had more white pieces of ass than you can count, ¿sabes? Who do you think you are? God's gift to us brown animals.

ALICE (*slaps him and stops, horrified, a whirlpool of emotions*): Oh, Hank. All the love and hate it's taken to get us together in this lousy prison room. Do you realize only Hitler and the Second World War could have accomplished that? I don't know whether to laugh or cry.

(*Alice folds into her emotional spin, her body shaking. Suddenly she turns, whipping herself out of it with a cry, both laughing and weeping. They come to each other and embrace. Then they kiss — passionately. The Guard enters. He frowns.*)

GUARD: Time, Miss.

ALICE (*turning*): Already? Oh, my God, Henry, there's so many messages I was going to give you. Your mother and father send their love, of course. And Lupe and . . . Della. And . . . oh, yes. They want to know Rudy's in the Marines.

HENRY: The Marines.

ALICE: I'll write you all about it. Will you write me?

HENRY (*a glance at the Guard*): Yes.

GUARD (*his tone getting harsher*): Let's go, lady.

HENRY: Goodbye, Licha.

ALICE: I'll see you on the outside . . . Hank.

(*Alice gives Henry a thumb up gesture, and the Guard escorts her out. Henry turns downstage, full of thoughts. He addresses El Pachuco, who is nowhere to be seen.*)

HENRY: You were wrong, ese . . . There is something to hope for. I know now we're going to win the appeal. Do you hear me, ese? Ese! (*Pause.*) Are you even there any more?

(*The Guard re-enters at a clip.*)

GUARD: Okay, Reyna, come on.

HENRY: Where to?

GUARD: We're letting you go . . .

(*Henry looks at him incredulously. The Guard smiles.*)

. . . to Folsom Prison with all the rest of the hardcore cons. You really didn't expect to walk out of here a free man, did you? Listen, kid, your appeal stands about as much chance as the Japs and Krauts of winning the war. Personally, I don't see what that broad sees in you. I wouldn't give you the sweat off my balls. Come on!

(*Henry and the Guard turn upstage to leave. Lights change. El Pachuco appears halfway up the backdrop, fully dressed again and clearly visible. Henry stops with a jolt as he sees him. El Pachuco lifts his arms. Lights go down as we hear the high sound of a bomb falling to earth.*)

Scene 8. The Winning of the War

(*The aerial bomb explodes with a reverberating sound and a white flash that illuminates the form of pachuco images in the black backdrop. Other bombs fall and all hell breaks loose. Red flashes, artillery, gunfire, ack-ack. Henry and the Guard exit. The Four Servicemen enter as an honor guard. Music: Glen Miller's "Saint Louis Blues March." As the Servicemen march on we see Rudy down left in his marine uniform, belt undone. Enrique, Dolores, and Lupe join him. Dolores has his hat, Lupe her camera. Enrique fastens two buttons on the uniform as Rudy does up his belt. Dolores inspects his collar and gives him his hat. Rudy puts on his hat and all pose for Lupe. She snaps the picture and Rudy kisses them all and is off. He picks up the giant switchblade from behind a newspaper bundle and joins the Servicemen as they march down in drill formation. The family marches off, looking back sadly. The drill ends and Rudy and the Shore Patrol move to one side. As Rudy's interrogation goes on, People in the barrio come on with newspapers to mime daily tasks. The Press enters.*)

PRESS: The *Los Angeles Examiner*, July 1, 1943. Headline: WORLD WAR II REACHES TURNING POINT. If the late summer of 1942 was the low point, a year later the war for the Allies is pounding its way to certain victory.

SHORE PATROL: July 10!

RUDY: U.S., British, and Canadian troops invade Sicily, Sir!

SHORE PATROL: August 6!

RUDY: U.S. troops occupy Solomon Island, Sir!

SHORE PATROL: September 5!

RUDY: MacArthur's forces land on New Guinea, Sir!

SHORE PATROL: October 1!

RUDY: U.S. Fifth Army enters Naples, Sir!

PRESS: On and on it goes. From Corsica to Kiev, from Tarawa to Anzio. The relentless advance of the Allied armies cannot be checked.

(*One by one, Henry's family and friends enter, carrying newspapers. They tear the papers into small pieces.*)

The *Los Angeles Times*, June 6, 1944. Headline: Allied forces under General Eisenhower land in Normandy.

SHORE PATROL: August 19!

RUDY: American First Army reaches Germany, Sir!

SHORE PATROL: October 17!

RUDY: MacArthur returns to the Philippines, Sir!

PRESS: On the homefront, Americans go on with their daily lives with growing confidence and relief, as the war pushes on toward inevitable triumph. (*Pause.*) The *Los Angeles Daily News*, Wednesday, November 8, 1944. Headline: District Court of Appeals decides in Sleepy Lagoon murder case . . . boys in pachuco murder given . . .

PEOPLE: FREEDOM!!!

(*Music bursts forth as the joyous crowd tosses the shredded newspaper into the air like confetti. The Boys enter upstage center, and the crowd rushes to them, weeping and cheering. There are kisses and hugs and tears of joy. Henry is swept forward by the triumphal procession.*)

Scene 9. Return to the Barrio

(*The music builds and people start dancing. Others just embrace. The tune is "Soldado Razo" played to a lively corrido beat. It ends with joyous applause, laughter, and tears.*)

RUDY: ¡Ese carnal!

HENRY: Rudy!!

DOLORES: ¡Bendito sea Dios! Who would believe this day would ever come? Look at you — you're all home!

LUPE: I still can't believe it. We won! We won the appeal!

(*Cheers.*)

ENRIQUE: I haven't felt like this since Villa took Zacatecas. (*Laughter, cheers.*) ¡Pero mira!° Look who's here. Mis hijos. (*Puts his arm around Henry and Rudy.*) It isn't every day a man has two grown sons come home from so far away — one from the war, the other from . . . bueno, who cares? The Sleepy Lagoon is history, hombre. For a change, los Mexicanos have won!

(*Cheers.*)

GEORGE: Well, Henry. I don't want to say I told you so, but we sure taught Judge Charles a lesson in misconduct, didn't we? (*More cheers.*) Do you realize this is the greatest victory the Mexican-American community has ever had in the history of this whole blasted country?

DOLORES: Yes, but if it wasn't for the unselfish thoughtfulness of people like you and this beautiful lady — and all the people who helped out, Mexicanos, Negros, all Americanos — our boys would not be home today.

GEORGE: I only hope you boys realize how important you are now.

JOEY: Pos, I realize it, ese.

(*Laughter.*)

2, 9. 9. **¡Pero mira!:** But look!

30   RUDY: I came all the way from Hawaii just to get here, carnal. I only got a few days, but I'm going to get you drunk.

     HENRY: Pos, we'll see who gets who drunk, ese.

(Laughter and hoots. Henry spots El Pachuco entering from stage right.)

     DOLORES: Jorge, Licha, todos.° Let's go into the house,
35   eh? I've made a big pot of menudo, and it's for everybody.

     ENRIQUE: There's ice-cold beer too. Vénganse, vamos todos.°

     GEORGE *(to Alice)*: Alice . . . Menudo, that's Mexican
40   chicken soup?

(Everybody exits, leaving Henry behind with El Pachuco.)

     HENRY: It's good to see you again, ese. I thought I'd lost you.

     PACHUCO: H'm pues, it'd take more than the U.S. Navy to wipe me out.

45   HENRY: Where you been?

     PACHUCO: Pos, here in the barrio. Welcome back.

     HENRY: It's good to be home.

     PACHUCO: No hard feelings?

     HENRY: Chale — we won, didn't we?

50   PACHUCO: Simón.

     HENRY: Me and the batos have been in a lot of fights together, ese. But we won this one, because we learned to fight in a new way.

     PACHUCO: And that's the perfect way to end this play —
55   happy ending y todo. *(Pachuco makes a sweeping gesture. Lights come down. He looks up at the lights, realizing something is wrong. He flicks his wrist, and the lights go back up again.)*

     But life ain't that way, Hank.
     The barrio's still out there, waiting and wanting.
     The cops are still tracking us down like dogs.
     The gangs are still killing each other,
60   Families are barely surviving,
     And there in your own backyard . . . life goes on.

(Soft music. Della enters.)

     DELLA: Hank?

(Henry goes to her and they embrace.)

     HENRY: Where were you? Why didn't you come to the Hall of Justice to see us get out?

65   DELLA: I guess I was a little afraid things had changed. So much has happened to both of us.

     PACHUCO: Simón. She's living in your house.

     DELLA: After I got back from Ventura, my parents gave me a choice. Forget about you or get out.

70   HENRY: Why didn't you write to me?

---

34. **Jorge, Licha, todos:** George, Alice, everyone.   37–38. **Vénganse, vamos todos:** Come back, let's go everyone.

     DELLA: You had your own problems. Your jefitos took care of me. Hey, you know what, Hank, I think they expect us to get married.

     PACHUCO: How about it, ese? You still going to give her
     that big pachuco wedding you promised?   75

     HENRY: I have to think about it.

     ALICE *(off-stage)*: Henry?

     PACHUCO *(snaps fingers)*: Wish you had the time. But here comes Licha.

     ALICE *(entering)*: Henry, I've just come to say good night.   80

(Della freezes and Henry turns to Alice.)

     HENRY: Good night? Why are you leaving so soon?

     ALICE: Soon? I've been here all afternoon. There'll be other times, Henry. You're home now, with your family, that's what matters.

     HENRY: Don't patronize me, Alice.   85

     ALICE *(surprised)*: Patronize you?

     HENRY: Yeah. I learned a few words in the joint.

     ALICE: Yo también,° Hank. Te quiero.°

(Pachuco snaps. Alice freezes, and Rudy enters.)

     RUDY: Ese, carnal, congratulations, the jefita just told me about you and Della. That's great, ese. But if you   90
     want me to be best man, you better do it in the next three days.

     HENRY: Wait a minute, Rudy, don't push me.

     RUDY: Qué pues,° getting cold feet already?

(Henry is beginning to be surrounded by separate conversations.)

     DELLA: If you don't want me here, I can move out.   95

     RUDY: Watcha. I'll let you and Della have our room tonight, bato. I'll sleep on the couch.

     ALICE: You aren't expecting me to sleep here, are you?

     HENRY: I'm not asking you to.

     PACHUCO/ALICE/RUDY/DELLA: Why not?   100

     RUDY: The jefitos will never know, ese.

     ALICE: Be honest, Henry.

     DELLA: What do you want me to do?

     HENRY: Give me a chance to think about it. Give me a second!   105

     PACHUCO: One second!

(Pachuco snaps. Enrique enters.)

     ENRIQUE: Bueno, bueno, pues,° what are you doing out here, hijo? Aren't you coming in for menudo?

     HENRY: I'm just thinking, jefito.

     ENRIQUE: ¿De qué, hombre?° Didn't you do enough of   110
     that in prison? Andale, this is your house. Come in and live again.

     HENRY: 'Apá, did you tell Della I was going to marry her?

     ENRIQUE: Yes, but only after you did.

---

88. **Yo también:** Me too. **Te quiero:** I love you.   94. **Qué pues:** Well what.   107. **Bueno, bueno, pues:** Good, good, certainly.   110. **¿De qué, hombre?:** About what, man?

115　RUDY: ¿Qué traes, carnal?° Don't you care about Della anymore?

ALICE: If it was just me and you, Henry, it might be different. But you have to think of your family.

HENRY: I don't need you to tell me my responsibilities.

120　ALICE: I'm sorry.

RUDY: Sorry, carnal.

DELLA: I don't need anybody to feel sorry for me. I did what I did because I wanted to. All I want to know is what's going to happen now. If you still want me, órale, suave. If you don't, that's okay, too. But I'm not going to hang around like a pendeja all my life.

125

RUDY: Your huisa's looking finer than ever, carnal.

ALICE: You're acting as if nothing has happened.

ENRIQUE: You have your whole life ahead of you.

130　ALICE: You belong here, Henry. I'm the one that's out of place.

RUDY: If you don't pick up on her, I'm going to have to step in.

HENRY: That's bullshit. What about what we shared in prison? I've never been that close to anybody.

135

ALICE: That was in prison.

HENRY: What the hell do you think the barrio is?

RUDY: It's not bullshit!

HENRY: Shut up, carnalillo!

140　RUDY: Carnalillo? How can you still call me that? I'm not your pinche little brother no more.

GEORGE (entering): You guys have got to stop fighting, Henry, or the barrio will never change. Don't you realize you men represent the hope of your people?

145　ALICE: Della was in prison too. You know you had thousands of people clamoring for your release, but you were Della's only hope.

HENRY: Look, esa, I know you did a year in Ventura. I know you stood up for me when it counted. I wish I could make it up to you.

150

DELLA: Don't give me your bullshit, Henry. Give it to Alice.

ALICE: I think it's time for Alice Bloomfield to go home.

HENRY: Don't be jealous, esa.

155　DELLA: Jealous? Mira, cabrón, I know I'm not the only one you ever took to the Sleepy Lagoon.

RUDY: The Sleepy Lagoon ain't shit. I saw real lagoons in those islands, ese — killing Japs! I saw some pachucos go out there that are never coming back.

160　DELLA: But I was always there when you came back, wasn't I?

DOLORES (entering): Henry? Come back inside, hijo. Everybody's waiting for you.

RUDY: Why didn't you tell them I was there, carnal? I was at the Sleepy Lagoon. Throwing chingazos with everybody!

165

HENRY: Don't you understand, Rudy? I was trying to keep you from getting a record. Those bastard cops are never going to leave us alone.

GEORGE: You've got to forget what happened, Henry.　170

HENRY: What can I give you, Della? I'm an ex-con.

DELLA: So am I!

SMILEY (entering): Let's face it, Hank. There's no future for us in this town. I'm taking my wife and kid and moving to Arizona.　175

DOLORES (simultaneously): I know what you are feeling, hijo, it's home again. I know inside you are afraid that nothing has changed. That the police will never leave you in peace. Pero no le hace.° Everything is going to be fine now. Marry Della and fill this house with children. Just do one thing for me — forget the zoot suit clothes.

ENRIQUE: If there's one thing that will keep a man off the streets is his own familia.

GEORGE: Don't let this thing eat your heart out for the rest of your . . .　180

ALICE: Sometimes the best thing you can do for someone you love is walk away.　185

DELLA: What do you want, Hank?

RUDY: It cost me more than it did you.　190

SMILEY: We started the 38th and I'll never forget you, carnal. But I got to think about my family.　195

HENRY: Wait a minute! I don't know if I'll be back in prison tomorrow or not! I have nothing to give you, Della. Not even a piece of myself.

DELLA: I have my life to live, too, Hank. I love you. I would even die for you. Pero me chingan la madre° if I'm going to throw away my life for nothing.　200

HENRY: But I love you . . .

(Both Girls turn. Henry looks at Alice, then to the whole group upstage of him. Still turning, he looks at Della and goes to embrace her. The freeze ends and other people enter.)

LUPE: ¡Órale, Hank! Watcha Joey. The crazy bato went all the way to his house and put on his drapes.

JOEY: ¡Esos, batooooooosss! ¡Esas, huisaaaaaaass!°　205

TOMMY: Look at this cat! He looks all reet.

LUPE: Yeah, like a parakeet!

HENRY: ¿Y tú, ese?° How come you put on your tacuche? Where's the party?

JOEY: Pos, ain't the party here?　210

RUDY: Yeah, ese, but this ain't the Avalon Ballroom. The zoot suit died under fire here in Los. Don't you know that, cabrón?

ENRIQUE: Rudolfo!

LUPE: And he was supposed to get Henry drunk.　215

RUDY: Shut up, esa!

ENRIQUE: ¡Ya pues!° Didn't you have any menudo?

---

115. ¿Qué traes, carnal?: What's wrong, brother?

184. **Pero no le hace:** But it doesn't happen.　**200. Pero me chingan la madre:** But I'll be damned.　**205. ¡Esos . . . huisaaaaaaass!:** Hey dudes! Hey girls!　**208. ¿Y tú, ese?:** And you man?　**217. ¡Ya pues!:** Enough already!

Vieja,° fix him a great big bowl of menudo and put plenty of chile in it. We're going to sweat it out of him.

220 RUDY: I don't need no pinche menudo.

HENRY: Watch your language, carnal.

RUDY: And I don't need you! I'm a man. I can take care of myself!

JOEY: Muy marine el bato° . . .

225 ENRIQUE: Rudy, hijo. Are you going to walk into the kitchen or do I have to drag you?

RUDY: Whatever you say, jefito.

GEORGE: Well, Alice. This looks like the place where we came in. I think it's about time we left.

230 ALICE: Say the word, George, just say the word.

DOLORES: No, no. You can't leave so soon.

JOEY: Chale, chale, chale. You can't take our Grandma. ¿Qué se trae, carnal? Póngase más abusado, ese. No se haga tan square.°

235 GEORGE: Okay, square I got. What was the rest of it?

JOEY: Pos, le estoy hablando en chicas patas, ese. Es puro chicano.°

RUDY: ¿Qué chicano? Ni que madre, cabrón.° Why don't you grow up?

240 JOEY: Grow up, ese?

RUDY: Try walking downtown looking like that. See if the sailors don't skin your ass alive.

JOEY: So what? It's no skin off your ass. Come on, Bertha.

245 RUDY: She's staying with me.

JOEY: She's mine.

RUDY: Prove it, punk.

(*Rudy attacks Joey and they fight. The Batos and Rucas take out Joey. Henry pacifies Rudy, who bursts out crying. Enrique, Della, Dolores, Alice, Lupe, and George are the only ones left. Rudy in a flush of emotion.*)

Cabrones, se amontonaron.° They ganged up on me, carnal. You left me and they ganged up on me. You

250 shouldn't have done it, carnal. Why didn't you take me with you. For the jefitos? The jefitos lost me anyway.

HENRY: Come on in the house, Rudy . . .

RUDY: No! I joined the Marines. I didn't have to join,

255 but I went. ¿Sabes por qué? Because they got me, carnal. Me chingaron, ese.° (*Sobs.*) I went to the pinche show with Bertha, all chingón in your tacuche, ese. I was wearing your zoot suit, and they got me. Twenty sailors, Marines. We were up in the balcony. They

260 came down from behind. They grabbed me by the

neck and dragged me down the stairs, kicking and punching and pulling my greña.° They dragged me out into the streets . . . and all the people watched while they stripped me. (*Sobs.*) They stripped me, carnal. Bertha saw them strip me. Hijos de la chin-

265 gada,° they stripped me.

(*Henry goes to Rudy and embraces him with fierce love and desperation. Pause. Tommy comes running in.*)

TOMMY: ¡Órale! There's cops outside. They're trying to arrest Joey.

(*George crosses to Tommy.*)

GEORGE (*bursting out*): Joey?

TOMMY: They got him up against your car. They're try-

270 ing to say he stole it!

GEORGE: Oh, God. I'll take care of this.

ALICE: I'll go with you.

(*George, Tommy, and Alice exit.*)

HENRY: Those fucking bastards! (*He starts to exit.*)

DELLA: Henry, no! 275

HENRY: What the hell do you mean no? Don't you see what's going on outside?

DELLA: They'll get you again! That's what they want.

HENRY: Get out of my way! (*He pushes her out of the way, toward Dolores.*)

ENRIQUE (*stands up before Henry*): ¡Hijo! 280

HENRY: Get out of my way, jefe!°

ENRIQUE: You will stay here!

HENRY: Get out of my way!

(*Enrique powerfully pushes him back and throws Henry to the floor and holds.*)

ENRIQUE: ¡TE DIGO QUE NO!

(*Silent moment. Henry stands up and offers to strike Enrique. But something stops him. The realization that if he strikes back or even if he walks out the door, the family bond is irreparably broken. Henry tenses for a moment, then relaxes and embraces his father. Della goes to them and joins the embrace. Then Dolores, then Lupe, then Rudy. All embrace in a tight little group. Press enters right and comes down.*)

PRESS: Henry Reyna went back to prison in 1947 for 285

robbery and assault with a deadly weapon. While incarcerated, he killed another inmate and he wasn't released until 1955, when he got into hard drugs. He died of the trauma of his life in 1972.

PACHUCO: That's the way you see it, ese. But there's 290

other ways to end this story.

RUDY: Henry Reyna went to Korea in 1950. He was

---

218. Vieja: Old woman (wife).   **224. Muy marine el bato:** The dude's acting like a marine.   **233–234. ¿Qué . . . square:** What's wrong, brother? Smarten up, man. That doesn't seem very square.   **236–237. Pos . . . chicano:** Anyhow, I was speaking in Chicano, man. It's pure Chicano.   **238. ¿Qué . . . cabrón:** What Chicano? Nothing that matters (vulgar term).   **248. Cabrones, se amontonaron:** (Vulgar term) they ganged up on me.   **256. Me chingaron, ese:** They (vulgar term) me up, man.

262. greña: Hair.   **265–266. Hijos de la chingada:** (Vulgar term).   **281. jefe:** Dad.

shipped across in a destroyer and defended the 38th Parallel until he was killed at Inchon in 1952, being

295　posthumously awarded the Congressional Medal of Honor.

ALICE: Henry Reyna married Della in 1948 and they have five kids, three of them now going to the University, speaking calo and calling themselves Chi-

300　canos.

GEORGE: Henry Reyna, the born leader . . .

JUDGE: Henry Reyna, the social victim . . .

BERTHA: Henry Reyna, the street corner warrior . . .

SMILEY: Henry Reyna, el carnal de aquellas° . . .

JOEY: Henry Reyna, the zoot suiter . . .　　　　　　　305

TOMMY: Henry Reyna, my friend . . .

LUPE: Henry Reyna, my brother . . .

ENRIQUE: Henry Reyna . . .

DOLORES: Our son . . .

DELLA: Henry Reyna, my love . . .　　　　　　　　　310

PACHUCO: Henry Reyna . . . El Pachuco . . . The man . . . the myth . . . still lives. (*Lights down and fade out.*)

304. **el carnal de aquellas:** The outstanding brother.

Harold Pinter

Harold Pinter (b. 1930) has written plays for the commercial stage, radio, and television as well as film scripts produced by some of the best directors of his time. Pinter was born into relatively humble circumstances in East London, but his early schooling distinguished him, and he eventually enrolled in London's prestigious Royal Academy of Dramatic Arts to study acting. When he finished his studies, he joined a company, toured for several years, and began to write for the stage. His previous writing efforts had been in prose: short stories and a long novel, *The Dwarfs* (1956), purportedly autobiographical, but never finished and not published until 1990. Produced as a radio play in 1960, it expresses some of the themes of his best work: the disintegration of a mind and the cruelty of people to their fellow beings.

In 1957 Pinter wrote three important plays, the one-act *The Room* and *The Dumb Waiter* and the full-length *The Birthday Party* (finished in 1958). All were well received. They established his method in dialogue and to a large extent the style that has dominated his work. The critic Martin Esslin, who coined the term "theater of the absurd," saw in Pinter's work an absurdist strain, especially in the nihilism — the belief in nothing — that sometimes shows up in his work. Pinter's characters usually reveal no spiritual awareness and no longing for spiritual values.

Pinter's dialogue sometimes has qualities of aimlessness, at least on the surface. But always the dialogue penetrates the unconsciousness of the audience and reveals the nature of the characters and their situation. Even the repetitious dialogue makes the audience more aware of the limitations and the pain of the circumstances in which Pinter's people find themselves.

Early reaction to the plays sometimes saw the aimless dialogue and the absurdist qualities as shortcomings rather than as indictments of the social order from which the plays arose. Yet the brutality of his characters to one another, their lack of sympathy for one another, and their demands for dominance have all become hallmarks of late-twentieth-century life.

The first of Pinter's plays to catch the attention of the general theater public was the commercially produced *The Caretaker* (1960), a play about two brothers, one of whom, Aston, invites a bewildered and all but mentally destroyed tramp, Davies, to become a caretaker in his room. Davies hardly knows who he is. His identity is essentially reduced to nothing by his soul-destroying life, and he speaks in broken language, especially when he is trying to explain that he left his identity papers in his beloved Sidcup — some fifteen years before — and that if they could find those papers, he would know where he was born and who he was. At the end of the play the younger brother, Mick, torments Davies, demanding that he leave, twisting his arm, verbally abusing him, but then relenting. The play ends with the shards of a life, as Davies says: "Listen . . . if I . . . go down . . . if I was to . . . get my papers . . . would you . . . would you let . . . would you . . . if I got down . . . and got my . . . (*Long silence.*)"

Pinter's *The Homecoming* (1965) has a brutal, shocking quality. A professor returns to England from America with his wife, and it becomes clear that he plans to return to America but that his wife will stay on as a mistress to his father and his brothers. The matter-of-factness with which the situation is treated and the way the relationships are portrayed provide part of the play's shock value.

In 1968 his play *Landscape* was censored for the use of obscenities, but eventually it and another short play, *Silence*, were produced in London in 1969 and in New York in 1970. *Old Times* was produced in London and in New York in 1971. Throughout the 1970s Pinter directed many plays by other playwrights and acted in films and on stage. *The Hothouse*, which was revived in 1995, was first produced in Hampstead in 1980. He later directed it himself in Providence, Rhode Island. He wrote the screenplay for *Betrayal* in 1982, when he also wrote the screenplay for *The French Lieutenant's Woman*, which received an Academy Award nomination for best film. In 1992 he adapted Kazuo Ishiguro's novel *Remains of the Day* for the screen and also wrote the screenplay for Franz Kafka's *The Trial*.

Recent plays include the full-length *Moonlight* (1993) and the short play *Ashes to Ashes* (1996). His newest play, *Celebrations* (2000), is a short play and is expected to be paired with *The Room* (1957), his first play. Ordinarily, Pinter does not let his short plays be paired with other pieces. Even *Mountain Language* (1988), which lasted only twenty minutes, was produced alone by the Royal National Theatre in its Lyttelton Theatre. In addition to his playwriting, Pinter has also continued acting and appears in a major role as Sir Thomas Bertram in Patricia Rozema's film of Jane Austen's novel, *Mansfield Park* (1999).

BETRAYAL

Unlike many of Pinter's plays, in which people are specifically brutal toward one another, *Betrayal* shows people in an extraordinarily civil, although complex, relationship. The play concerns the betrayal of husbands and wives in adulterous relationships, but it also explores the power relations between the genders as well as the relationship between male friends. Jerry and Robert, best friends from college, are now business associates; Jerry, as literary agent, finds authors for Robert, who is a publisher. At first, the betrayal seems to have been committed by Jerry, the best man at Robert's marriage to Emma. As the play progresses, however, we see many levels of betrayal, including some appearing in the literature that Jerry promotes and Robert rejects, such as Spinks's novel, which Emma enjoys. Pinter examines the relationship of all three characters in great detail, revealing that Robert knew about Emma's affair with Jerry but never mentioned a word to Jerry. Indeed, Robert and Jerry continued to have civilized lunches, drink together at bars, and generally enjoy each other's company as if nothing had happened. All the while and unknown to Emma and Jerry, Robert was himself having affairs. Part of the cruel fun of the play is watching the reactions of characters as they discover that such behavior had been going on without their knowledge.

The structure of the play is unusual. At first, it seems to progress normally, with the date 1977 displayed prominently at the top of the stage during the first two scenes, which follow chronologically. After those scenes, however, the play moves backward in time. During the first production in London this effect was powerful, if only because it was so unexpected. Pinter puts the audience into a special relationship with the characters and their circumstances because the audience understands the implied ironies in much of the dialogue, as for example in Robert's going off to read Yeats on the island of Torcello. Not only had Robert and Jerry discussed Yeats as undergraduates, but Yeats, the Irish poet, had also been "betrayed" by the one he loved, Maud Gonne, and had "betrayed" her in turn. It is especially ironic for Robert to tell Jerry that his early morning hours alone on Torcello were the high point of his trip to Venice, since it was the evening before that he had first discovered Emma and Jerry's affair.

The dialogue is pure Pinter. The speeches are very short at first, the words simple, often only one syllable, and often questions or observations are repeated in what seems an almost needless fashion. Yet the dialogue accretes and the significance of things that seem casual and almost irrelevant grows until we catch the innuendo and understand the deeper implications. One useful experience is going back to the opening scene after reading through the play. The emotional coolness of that scene is a powerful counterpoint to the intense closing scene of the play.

Betrayal in Performance

Betrayal was produced first at the National Theatre in London in 1978, then in New York in 1979. In London Michael Gambon was Jerry, Penelope Wilton was Emma, and Daniel Massey was Robert. In New York Raul Julia played Jerry, Blythe Danner was Emma, and Roy Scheider was Robert. Both productions were highly successful. The staging for both was similar, with realistic sets for the opening scene in the restaurant and the following scenes in the flat. The film, which opened in February 1983, followed the structure of the play itself and stayed close to the original dialogue. Ben Kingsley was Robert; Jeremy Irons was Jerry; and a relative unknown, Patricia Hodge, played Emma. Of the film Vincent Canby said, "The writing is superb, and so quintessentially Pinter that it sometimes comes close to sounding like parody, though, in the screenplay, there's not one predictable line or gesture."

The play has been revived several times in London, first in 1983, then again at the Almeida Theater in 1991. The Royal National Theatre produced the play at the Lyttelton Theatre most recently in 1998. It has also been produced regionally in the United States as a popular work in repertory.

Harold Pinter (*b. 1930*)
BETRAYAL

Characters

EMMA
JERRY
ROBERT
A WAITER

In 1977 Emma is 38, Jerry and Robert are 40.

1977

Scene 1

Pub. 1977. Spring. *Noon.*
    Emma is sitting at a corner table. Jerry approaches with drinks, a pint of bitter for him, a glass of wine for her.
    He sits. They smile, toast each other silently, drink. He sits back and looks at her.

JERRY: Well . . .
EMMA: How are you?
JERRY: All right.
EMMA: You look well.
JERRY: Well, I'm not all that well, really.
EMMA: Why? What's the matter?
JERRY: Hangover.

(*He raises his glass.*)

    Cheers.

(*He drinks.*)

    How are you?
EMMA: I'm fine.

(*She looks round the bar, back at him.*)

    Just like old times.
JERRY: Mmn. It's been a long time.
EMMA: Yes.

(*Pause.*)

    I thought of you the other day.
JERRY: Good God. Why?

(*She laughs.*)

JERRY: Why?
EMMA: Well, it's nice, sometimes, to think back. Isn't it?
JERRY: Absolutely.

(*Pause.*)

    How's everything?

EMMA: Oh, not too bad.

(*Pause.*)

    Do you know how long it is since we met?
JERRY: Well I came to that private view, when was it — ?
EMMA: No, I don't mean that.
JERRY: Oh you mean alone?
EMMA: Yes.
JERRY: Uuh . . .
EMMA: Two years.
JERRY: Yes, I thought it must be. Mmnn.

(*Pause.*)

EMMA: Long time.
JERRY: Yes. It is.

(*Pause.*)

    How's it going? The Gallery?
EMMA: How do you think it's going?
JERRY: Well. Very well, I would say.
EMMA: I'm glad you think so. Well, it is, actually. I enjoy it.
JERRY: Funny lot, painters, aren't they?
EMMA: They're not at all funny.
JERRY: Aren't they? What a pity.

(*Pause.*)

    How's Robert?
EMMA: When did you last see him?
JERRY: I haven't seen him for months. Don't know why. Why?
EMMA: Why what?
JERRY: Why did you ask when I last saw him?
EMMA: I just wondered. How's Sam?
JERRY: You mean Judith.
EMMA: Do I?
JERRY: You remember the form. I ask about your husband, you ask about my wife.
EMMA: Yes, of course. How is your wife?
JERRY: All right.

(*Pause.*)

EMMA: Sam must be . . . tall.
JERRY: He is tall. Quite tall. Does a lot of running. He's a long distance runner. He wants to be a zoologist.
EMMA: No, really? Good. And Sarah?
JERRY: She's ten.
EMMA: God. I suppose she must be.
JERRY: Yes, she must be.

(*Pause.*)

    Ned's five, isn't he?

EMMA: You remember.
JERRY: Well, I would remember that.

(*Pause.*)

EMMA: Yes.

(*Pause.*)

   You're all right, though?
JERRY: Oh . . . yes, sure.

(*Pause.*)

EMMA: Ever think of me?
JERRY: I don't need to think of you.
EMMA: Oh?
JERRY: I don't need to *think* of you.

(*Pause.*)

   Anyway I'm all right. How are you?
EMMA: Fine, really. All right.
JERRY: You're looking very pretty.
EMMA: Really? Thank you. I'm glad to see you.
JERRY: So am I. I mean to see you.
EMMA: You think of me sometimes?
JERRY: I think of you sometimes.

(*Pause.*)

   I saw Charlotte the other day.
EMMA: No? Where? She didn't mention it.
JERRY: She didn't see me. In the street.
EMMA: But you haven't seen her for years.
JERRY: I recognised her.
EMMA: How could you? How could you know?
JERRY: I did.
EMMA: What did she look like?
JERRY: You.
EMMA: No, what did you think of her, really?
JERRY: I thought she was lovely.
EMMA: Yes. She's very . . . She's smashing. She's thirteen.

(*Pause.*)

   Do you remember that time . . . oh god it was . . . when you picked her up and threw her up and caught her?
JERRY: She was very light.
EMMA: She remembers that, you know.
JERRY: Really?
EMMA: Mmnn. Being thrown up.
JERRY: What a memory.

(*Pause.*)

   She doesn't know . . . about us, does she?
EMMA: Of course not. She just remembers you, as an old friend.
JERRY: That's right.

(*Pause.*)

   Yes, everyone was there that day, standing around, your husband, my wife, all the kids, I remember.
EMMA: What day?

JERRY: When I threw her up. It was in your kitchen.
EMMA: It was in your kitchen.

(*Silence.*)

JERRY: Darling.
EMMA: Don't say that.

(*Pause.*)

   It all . . .
JERRY: Seems such a long time ago.
EMMA: Does it?
JERRY: Same again?

(*He takes the glasses, goes to the bar. She sits still. He returns, with the drinks, sits.*)

EMMA: I thought of you the other day.

(*Pause.*)

   I was driving through Kilburn. Suddenly I saw where I was. I just stopped, and then I turned down Kinsale Drive and drove into Wessex Grove. I drove past the house and then stopped about fifty yards further on, like we used to do, do you remember?
JERRY: Yes.
EMMA: People were coming out of the house. They walked up the road.
JERRY: What sort of people?
EMMA: Oh . . . young people. Then I got out of the car and went up the steps. I looked at the bells, you know, the names on the bells. I looked for our name.

(*Pause.*)

JERRY: Green.

(*Pause.*)

   Couldn't see it, eh?
EMMA: No.
JERRY: That's because we're not there any more. We haven't been there for years.
EMMA: No we haven't.

(*Pause.*)

JERRY: I hear you're seeing a bit of Casey.
EMMA: What?
JERRY: Casey. I just heard you were . . . seeing a bit of him.
EMMA: Where did you hear that?
JERRY: Oh . . . people . . . talking.
EMMA: Christ.
JERRY: The funny thing was that the only thing I really felt was irritation, I mean irritation that nobody gossiped about us like that, in the old days. I nearly said, now look, she may be having the occasional drink with Casey, who cares, but she and I had an affair for seven years and none of you bastards had the faintest idea it was happening.

(*Pause.*)

EMMA: I wonder. I wonder if everyone knew, all the time.

JERRY: Don't be silly. We were brilliant. Nobody knew. Who ever went to Kilburn in those days? Just you and me.

(*Pause.*)

Anyway, what's all this about you and Casey?
EMMA: What do you mean?
JERRY: What's going on?
EMMA: We have the occasional drink.
JERRY: I thought you didn't admire his work.
EMMA: I've changed. Or his work has changed. Are you jealous?
JERRY: Of what?

(*Pause.*)

I couldn't be jealous of Casey. I'm his agent. I advised him about his divorce. I read all his first drafts. I persuaded your husband to publish his first novel. I escort him to Oxford to speak at the Union. He's my . . . he's my boy. I discovered him when he was a poet, and that's a bloody long time ago now.

(*Pause.*)

He's even taken me down to Southampton to meet his Mum and Dad. I couldn't be jealous of Casey. Anyway it's not as if we're having an affair now, is it? We haven't seen each other for years. Really, I'm very happy if you're happy.

(*Pause.*)

What about Robert?

(*Pause.*)

EMMA: Well . . . I think we're going to separate.
JERRY: Oh?
EMMA: We had a long talk . . . last night.
JERRY: Last night?
EMMA: You know what I found out . . . last night? He's betrayed me for years. He's had . . . other women for years.
JERRY: No? Good Lord.

(*Pause.*)

But we betrayed him for years.
EMMA: And he betrayed me for years.
JERRY: Well I never knew that.
EMMA: Nor did I.

(*Pause.*)

JERRY: Does Casey know about this?
EMMA: I wish you wouldn't keep calling him Casey. His name is Roger.
JERRY: Yes. Roger.
EMMA: I phoned *you*. I don't know why.
JERRY: What a funny thing. We were such close friends, weren't we? Robert and me, even though I haven't seen him for a few months, but through all those years, all the drinks, all the lunches . . . we had together, I never even gleaned . . . I never suspected . . .

that there was anyone else . . . in his life but you. Never. For example, when you're with a fellow in a pub, or a restaurant, for example, from time to time he pops out for a piss, you see, who doesn't, but what I mean is, if he's making a crafty telephone call, you can sort of sense it, you see, you can sense the pip pip pips. Well, I never did that with Robert. He never made any pip pip telephone calls in any pub I was ever with him in. The funny thing is that it was me who made the pip pip calls — to you, when I left him boozing at the bar. That's the funny thing.

(*Pause.*)

When did he tell you all this?
EMMA: Last night. I think we were up all night.

(*Pause.*)

JERRY: You talked all night?
EMMA: Yes. Oh yes.

(*Pause.*)

JERRY: I didn't come into it, did I?
EMMA: What?
JERRY: I just —
EMMA: I just phoned you this morning, you know, that's all, because I . . . because we're old friends . . . I've been up all night . . . the whole thing's finished . . . I suddenly felt I wanted to see you.
JERRY: Well, look, I'm happy to see you. I am. I'm sorry . . . about . . .
EMMA: Do you remember? I mean, you do remember?
JERRY: I remember.

(*Pause.*)

EMMA: You couldn't really afford Wessex Grove when we took it, could you?
JERRY: Oh, love finds a way.
EMMA: I bought the curtains.
JERRY: You found a way.
EMMA: Listen, I didn't want to see you for nostalgia, I mean what's the point? I just wanted to see how you were. Truly. How are you?
JERRY: Oh what does it matter?

(*Pause.*)

You didn't tell Robert about me last night, did you?
EMMA: I had to.

(*Pause.*)

He told me everything. I told him everything. We were up . . . all night. At one point Ned came down. I had to take him up to bed, had to put him back to bed. Then I went down again. I think it was the voices woke him up. You know . . .
JERRY: You told him everything?
EMMA: I had to.
JERRY: You told him everything . . . about us?
EMMA: I had to.

(*Pause.*)

JERRY: But he's my oldest friend. I mean, I picked his own daughter up in my own arms and threw her up and caught her, in my kitchen. He watched me do it.
EMMA: It doesn't matter. It's all gone.
JERRY: Is it? What has?
EMMA: It's all all over.

(*She drinks.*)

1977
LATER

Scene 2

Jerry's House. Study. 1977. Spring. *Jerry sitting. Robert standing, with glass.*

JERRY: It's good of you to come.
ROBERT: Not at all.
JERRY: Yes, yes, I know it was difficult . . . I know . . . the kids . . .
ROBERT: It's all right. It sounded urgent.
JERRY: Well . . . You found someone, did you?
ROBERT: What?
JERRY: For the kids.
ROBERT: Yes, yes. Honestly. Everything's in order. Anyway, Charlotte's not a baby.
JERRY: No.

(*Pause.*)

Are you going to sit down?
ROBERT: Well, I might, yes, in a minute.

(*Pause.*)

JERRY: Judith's at the hospital . . . on night duty. The kids are . . . here . . . upstairs.
ROBERT: Uh-huh.
JERRY: I must speak to you. It's important.
ROBERT: Speak.
JERRY: Yes.

(*Pause.*)

ROBERT: You look quite rough.

(*Pause.*)

What's the trouble?

(*Pause.*)

It's not about you and Emma, is it?

(*Pause.*)

I know all about that.
JERRY: Yes. So I've . . . been told.
ROBERT: Ah.

(*Pause.*)

Well, it's not very important, is it? Been over for years, hasn't it?

JERRY: It is important.
ROBERT: Really? Why?

(*Jerry stands, walks about.*)

JERRY: I thought I was going to go mad.
ROBERT: When?
JERRY: This evening. Just now. Wondering whether to phone you. I had to phone you. It took me . . . two hours to phone you. And then you were with the kids . . . I thought I wasn't going to be able to see you . . . I thought I'd go mad. I'm very grateful to you . . . for coming.
ROBERT: Oh for God's sake! Look, what exactly do you want to say?

(*Pause.*)
(*Jerry sits.*)

JERRY: I don't know why she told you. I don't know how she could tell you. I just don't understand. Listen, I know you've got . . . look, I saw her today . . . we had a drink . . . I haven't seen her for . . . she told me, you know, that you're in trouble, both of you . . . and so on. I know that. I mean I'm sorry.
ROBERT: Don't be sorry.
JERRY: Why not?

(*Pause.*)

The fact is I can't understand . . . why she thought it necessary . . . after all these years . . . to tell you . . . so suddenly . . . last night . . .
ROBERT: Last night?
JERRY: Without consulting me. Without even warning me. After all, you and me . . .
ROBERT: She didn't tell me last night.
JERRY: What do you mean?

(*Pause.*)

I know about last night. She told me about it. You were up all night, weren't you?
ROBERT: That's correct.
JERRY: And she told you . . . last night . . . about her and me. Did she not?
ROBERT: No, she didn't. She didn't tell me about you and her last night. She told me about you and her four years ago.

(*Pause.*)

So she didn't have to tell me again last night. Because I knew. And she knew I knew because she told me herself four years ago.

(*Silence.*)

JERRY: What?
ROBERT: I think I will sit down.

(*He sits.*)

I thought you knew.
JERRY: Knew what?
ROBERT: That I knew. That I've known for years. I thought you knew that.

JERRY: You thought I knew?
ROBERT: She said you didn't. But I didn't believe that.

(*Pause.*)

    Anyway I think I thought you knew. But you say you didn't?
JERRY: She told you . . . when?
ROBERT: Well, I found out. That's what happened. I told her I'd found out and then she . . . confirmed . . . the facts.
JERRY: When?
ROBERT: Oh, a long time ago, Jerry.

(*Pause.*)

JERRY: But we've seen each other . . . a great deal . . . over the last four years. We've had lunch.
ROBERT: Never played squash though.
JERRY: I was your best friend.
ROBERT: Well, yes, sure.

(*Jerry stares at him and then holds his head in his hands.*)

    Oh, don't get upset. There's no point.

(*Silence.*)
(*Jerry sits up.*)

JERRY: Why didn't she tell me?
ROBERT: Well, I'm not her, old boy.
JERRY: Why didn't you tell me?

(*Pause.*)

ROBERT: I thought you might know.
JERRY: But you didn't know for *certain*, did you? You didn't *know*!
ROBERT: No.
JERRY: Then why didn't you tell me?

(*Pause.*)

ROBERT: Tell you what?
JERRY: That you knew. You bastard.
ROBERT: Oh, don't call me a bastard, Jerry.

(*Pause.*)

JERRY: What are we going to do?
ROBERT: You and I are not going to do anything. My marriage is finished. I've just got to make proper arrangements, that's all. About the children.

(*Pause.*)

JERRY: You hadn't thought of telling Judith?
ROBERT: Telling Judith what? Oh, about you and Emma. You mean she never knew? Are you quite sure?

(*Pause.*)

    No, I hadn't thought of telling Judith, actually. You don't seem to understand. You don't seem to understand that I don't give a shit about any of this. It's true I've hit Emma once or twice. But that wasn't to defend a principle. I wasn't inspired to do it from any kind of moral standpoint. I just felt like giving her a good bashing. The old itch . . . you understand.

(*Pause.*)

JERRY: But you betrayed her for years, didn't you?
ROBERT: Oh yes.
JERRY: And she never knew about it. Did she?
ROBERT: Didn't she?

(*Pause.*)

JERRY: I didn't.
ROBERT: No, you didn't know very much about anything, really, did you?

(*Pause.*)

JERRY: No.
ROBERT: Yes you did.
JERRY: Yes I did. I lived with her.
ROBERT: Yes. In the afternoons.
JERRY: Sometimes very long ones. For seven years.
ROBERT: Yes, you certainly knew all there was to know about that. About the seven years of afternoons. I don't know anything about that.

(*Pause.*)

    I hope she looked after you all right.

(*Silence.*)

JERRY: We used to like each other.
ROBERT: We still do.

(*Pause.*)

    I bumped into old Casey the other day. I believe he's having an affair with my wife. We haven't played squash for years, Casey and me. We used to have a damn good game.
JERRY: He's put on weight.
ROBERT: Yes, I thought that.
JERRY: He's over the hill.
ROBERT: Is he?
JERRY: Don't you think so?
ROBERT: In what respect?
JERRY: His work. His books.
ROBERT: Oh his books. His art. Yes his art does seem to be falling away, doesn't it?
JERRY: Still sells.
ROBERT: Oh, sells very well. Sells very well indeed. Very good for us. For you and me.
JERRY: Yes.
ROBERT: Someone was telling me — who was it — must have been someone in the publicity department — the other day — that when Casey went up to York to sign his latest book, in a bookshop, you know, with Barbara Spring, you know, the populace queued for hours to get his signature on his book, while one old lady and a dog queued to get Barbara Spring's signature, on her book. I happen to think that Barbara Spring . . . is good, don't you?
JERRY: Yes.

(*Pause.*)

ROBERT: Still, we both do very well out of Casey, don't we?

JERRY: Very well.

(*Pause.*)

ROBERT: Have you read any good books lately?
JERRY: I've been reading Yeats.
ROBERT: Ah. Yeats. Yes.

(*Pause.*)

JERRY: You read Yeats on Torcello once.
ROBERT: On Torcello?
JERRY: Don't you remember? Years ago. You went over to Torcello in the dawn, alone. And read Yeats.
ROBERT: So I did. I told you that, yes.

(*Pause.*)

    Yes.

(*Pause.*)

    Where are you going this summer, you and the family?
JERRY: The Lake District.

1975

Scene 3

Flat. 1975. Winter. *Jerry and Emma. They are sitting.*

Silence.
JERRY: What do you want to do then?

(*Pause.*)

EMMA: I don't quite know what we're doing, any more, that's all.
JERRY: Mmnn.

(*Pause.*)

EMMA: I mean, this flat . . .
JERRY: Yes.
EMMA: Can you actually remember when we were last here?
JERRY: In the summer, was it?
EMMA: Well, was it?
JERRY: I know it seems —
EMMA: It was the beginning of September.
JERRY: Well, that's summer, isn't it?
EMMA: It was actually extremely cold. It was early autumn.
JERRY: It's pretty cold now.
EMMA: We were going to get another electric fire.
JERRY: Yes, I never got that.
EMMA: Not much point in getting it if we're never here.
JERRY: We're here now.
EMMA: Not really.

(*Silence.*)

JERRY: Well, things have changed. You've been so busy, your job, and everything.

EMMA: Well, I know. But I mean, I like it. I want to do it.
JERRY: No, it's great. It's marvellous for you. But you're not —
EMMA: If you're running a gallery you've got to run it, you've got to be there.
JERRY: But you're not free in the afternoons. Are you?
EMMA: No.
JERRY: So how can we meet?
EMMA: But look at the times you're out of the country. You're never here.
JERRY: But when I am here you're not free in the afternoons. So we can never meet.
EMMA: We can meet for lunch.
JERRY: We can meet for lunch but we can't come all the way out here for a quick lunch. I'm too old for that.
EMMA: I didn't suggest that.

(*Pause.*)

    You see, in the past . . . we were inventive, we were determined, it was . . . it seemed impossible to meet . . . impossible . . . and yet we did. We met here, we took this flat and we met in this flat because we wanted to.
JERRY: It would not matter how much we wanted to if you're not free in the afternoons and I'm in America.

(*Silence.*)

    Nights have always been out of the question and you know it. I have a family.
EMMA: I have a family too.
JERRY: I know that perfectly well. I might remind you that your husband is my oldest friend.
EMMA: What do you mean by that?
JERRY: I don't *mean* anything by it.
EMMA: But what are you trying to say by saying that?
JERRY: Jesus. I'm not *trying* to say anything. I've said precisely what I wanted to say.
EMMA: I see.

(*Pause.*)

    The fact is that in the old days we used our imagination and we'd take a night and make an arrangement and go to an hotel.
JERRY: Yes. We did.

(*Pause.*)

    But that was . . . in the main . . . before we got this flat.
EMMA: We haven't spent many nights . . . in this flat.
JERRY: No.

(*Pause.*)

    Not many nights anywhere, really.

(*Silence.*)

EMMA: Can you afford . . . to keep it going, month after month?
JERRY: Oh . . .
EMMA: It's a waste. Nobody comes here. I just can't bear

to think about it, actually. Just . . . empty. All day and night. Day after day and night after night. I mean the crockery and the curtains and the bedspread and everything. And the tablecloth I brought from Venice. (*Laughs.*) It's ridiculous.

(*Pause.*)

It's just . . . an empty home.
JERRY: It's not a home.

(*Pause.*)

I know . . . I know what you wanted . . . but it could never . . . actually be a home. You have a home. I have a home. With curtains, etcetera. And children. Two children in two homes. There are no children here, so it's not the same kind of home.
EMMA: It was never intended to be the same kind of home. Was it?

(*Pause.*)

You didn't ever see it as a home, in any sense, did you?
JERRY: No, I saw it as a flat . . . you know.
EMMA: For fucking.
JERRY: No, for loving.
EMMA: Well, there's not much of that left, is there?

(*Silence.*)

JERRY: I don't think we don't love each other.

(*Pause.*)

EMMA: Ah well.

(*Pause.*)

What will you do about all the . . . furniture?
JERRY: What?
EMMA: The contents.

(*Silence.*)

JERRY: You know we can do something very simple, if we want to do it.
EMMA: You mean sell it to Mrs. Banks for a small sum and . . . and she can let it as a furnished flat?
JERRY: That's right. Wasn't the bed here?
EMMA: What?
JERRY: Wasn't it?
EMMA: We bought the bed. We bought everything. We bought the bed together.
JERRY: Ah. Yes.

(*Emma stands.*)

EMMA: You'll make all the arrangements, then? With Mrs. Banks?

(*Pause.*)

I don't want anything. Nowhere I can put it, you see. I have a home, with tablecloths and all the rest of it.
JERRY: I'll go into it, with Mrs. Banks. There'll be a few quid, you know, so . . .

EMMA: No, I don't want any *cash*, thank you very much.

(*Silence. She puts coat on.*)

I'm going now.

(*He turns, looks at her.*)

Oh here's my key.

(*Takes out keyring, tries to take key from ring.*)

Oh Christ.

(*Struggles to take key from ring. Throws him the ring.*)

You take it off.

(*He catches it, looks at her.*)

Can you just do it please? I'm picking up Charlotte from school. I'm taking her shopping.

(*He takes key off.*)

Do you realise this is an afternoon? It's the Gallery's afternoon off. That's why I'm here. We close every Thursday afternoon. Can I have my keyring?

(*He gives it to her.*)

Thanks. Listen. I think we've made absolutely the right decision.

(*She goes.*)
(*He stands.*)

1974

Scene 4

Robert and Emma's House. Living room. 1974. Autumn.
Robert pouring a drink for Jerry. He goes to the door.

ROBERT: Emma! Jerry's here!
EMMA (*off*): Who?
ROBERT: Jerry.
EMMA: I'll be down.

(*Robert gives the drink to Jerry.*)

JERRY: Cheers.
ROBERT: Cheers. She's just putting Ned to bed. I should think he'll be off in a minute.
JERRY: Off where?
ROBERT: Dreamland.
JERRY: Ah. Yes, how is your sleep these days?
ROBERT: What?
JERRY: Do you still have bad nights? With Ned, I mean?
ROBERT: Oh, I see. Well, no. No, it's getting better. But you know what they say?
JERRY: What?
ROBERT: They say boys are worse than girls.
JERRY: Worse?
ROBERT: Babies. They say boy babies cry more than girl babies.

JERRY: Do they?

ROBERT: You didn't find that to be the case?

JERRY: Uh . . . yes, I think we did. Did you?

ROBERT: Yes. What do you make of it? Why do you think that is?

JERRY: Well, I suppose . . . boys are more anxious.

ROBERT: Boy babies?

JERRY: Yes.

ROBERT: What the hell are they anxious about . . . at their age? Do you think?

JERRY: Well . . . facing the world, I suppose, leaving the womb, all that.

ROBERT: But what about girl babies? They leave the womb too.

JERRY: That's true. It's also true that nobody talks much about girl babies leaving the womb. Do they?

ROBERT: I am prepared to do so.

JERRY: I see. Well, what have you got to say?

ROBERT: I was asking you a question.

JERRY: What was it?

ROBERT: Why do you assert that boy babies find leaving the womb more of a problem than girl babies?

JERRY: Have I made such an assertion?

ROBERT: You went on to make a further assertion, to the effect that boy babies are more anxious about facing the world than girl babies.

JERRY: Do you yourself believe that to be the case?

ROBERT: I do, yes.

(*Pause.*)

JERRY: Why do you think it is?

ROBERT: I have no answer.

(*Pause.*)

JERRY: Do you think it might have something to do with the difference between the sexes?

(*Pause.*)

ROBERT: Good God, you're right. That must be it.

(*Emma comes in.*)

EMMA: Hullo. Surprise.

JERRY: I was having tea with Casey.

EMMA: Where?

JERRY: Just around the corner.

EMMA: I thought he lived in . . . Hampstead or somewhere.

ROBERT: You're out of date.

EMMA: Am I?

JERRY: He's left Susannah. He's living alone round the corner.

EMMA: Oh.

ROBERT: Writing a novel about a man who leaves his wife and three children and goes to live alone on the other side of London to write a novel about a man who leaves his wife and three children —

EMMA: I hope it's better than the last one.

ROBERT: The last one? Ah, the last one. Wasn't that the one about the man who lived in a big house in

Hampstead with his wife and three children and is writing a novel about — ?

JERRY (*to Emma*): Why didn't you like it?

EMMA: I've told you actually.

JERRY: I think it's the best thing he's written.

EMMA: It may be the best thing he's *written* but it's still bloody dishonest.

JERRY: Dishonest? In what way dishonest?

EMMA: I've told you, actually.

JERRY: Have you?

ROBERT: Yes, she has. Once when we were all having dinner, I remember, you, me, Emma and Judith, where was it, Emma gave a dissertation over the pudding about dishonesty in Casey with reference to his last novel. *Drying Out.* It was most stimulating. Judith had to leave unfortunately in the middle of it for her night shift at the hospital. How is Judith, by the way?

JERRY: Very well.

(*Pause.*)

ROBERT: When are we going to play squash?

JERRY: You're too good.

ROBERT: Not at all. I'm not good at all. I'm just fitter than you.

JERRY: But why? Why are you fitter than me?

ROBERT: Because I play squash.

JERRY: Oh, you're playing? Regularly?

ROBERT: Mmnn.

JERRY: With whom?

ROBERT: Casey, actually.

JERRY: Casey? Good Lord. What's he like?

ROBERT: He's a brutally honest squash player. No, really, we haven't played for years. We must play. You were rather good.

JERRY: Yes, I was quite good. All right. I'll give you a ring.

ROBERT: Why don't you?

JERRY: We'll make a date.

ROBERT: Right.

JERRY: Yes. We must do that.

ROBERT: And then I'll take you to lunch.

JERRY: No, no. I'll take you to lunch.

ROBERT: The man who wins buys the lunch.

EMMA: Can I watch?

(*Pause.*)

ROBERT: What?

EMMA: Why can't I watch and then take you both to lunch?

ROBERT: Well, to be brutally honest, we wouldn't actually want a woman around, would we, Jerry? I mean a game of squash isn't simply a game of squash, it's rather more than that. You see, first there's the game. And then there's the shower. And then there's the pint. And then there's lunch. After all, you've been at it. You've had your battle. What you want is your pint and your lunch. You really don't want a woman buying you lunch. You don't actually want a woman within a mile of the place, any of the places, really. You don't want her in the squash court, you don't want her in the shower, or the pub, or the restaurant. You see, at lunch you want to talk about squash, or cricket, or books, or even women, with your friend, and be able to warm to your theme without fear of improper interruption. That's what it's all about. What do you think, Jerry?

JERRY: I haven't played squash for years.

(*Pause.*)

ROBERT: Well, let's play next week.

JERRY: I can't next week. I'm in New York.

EMMA: Are you?

JERRY: I'm going over with one of my more celebrated writers, actually.

EMMA: Who?

JERRY: Casey. Someone wants to film that novel of his you didn't like. We're going over to discuss it. It was a question of them coming over here or us going over there. Casey thought he deserved the trip.

EMMA: What about you?

JERRY: What?

EMMA: Do you deserve the trip?

ROBERT: Judith going?

JERRY: No. He can't go alone. We'll have that game of squash when I get back. A week, or at the most ten days.

ROBERT: Lovely.

JERRY (*to Emma*): Bye. Thanks for the drink.

EMMA: Bye.

(*Robert and Jerry leave. She remains still.*)

(*Robert returns. He kisses her. She responds. She breaks away, puts her head on his shoulder, cries quietly. He holds her.*)

1973

Scene 5

Hotel Room. Venice. 1973. Summer. *Emma on bed reading. Robert at window looking out. She looks up at him, then back at the book.*

EMMA: It's Torcello tomorrow, isn't it?

ROBERT: What?

EMMA: We're going to Torcello tomorrow, aren't we?

ROBERT: Yes. That's right.

EMMA: That'll be lovely.

ROBERT: Mmn.

EMMA: I can't wait.

(*Pause.*)

ROBERT: Book good?

EMMA: Mmn. Yes.

ROBERT: What is it?

EMMA: This new book. This man Spinks.

ROBERT: Oh that. Jerry was telling me about it.

EMMA: Jerry? Was he?

ROBERT: He was telling me about it at lunch last week.

EMMA: Really? Does he like it?

ROBERT: Spinks is his boy. He discovered him.

EMMA: Oh. I didn't know that.

ROBERT: Unsolicited manuscript.

(*Pause.*)

You think it's good, do you?

EMMA: Yes, I do. I'm enjoying it.

ROBERT: Jerry thinks it's good too. You should have lunch with us one day and chat about it.

EMMA: Is that absolutely necessary?

(*Pause.*)

It's not as good as all that.

ROBERT: You mean it's not good enough for you to have lunch with Jerry and me and chat about it?

EMMA: What the hell are you talking about?

ROBERT: I must read it again myself, now it's in hard covers.

EMMA: Again?

ROBERT: Jerry wanted us to publish it.

EMMA: Oh, really?

ROBERT: Well, naturally. Anyway, I turned it down.

EMMA: Why?

ROBERT: Oh . . . not much more to say on that subject, really, is there?

EMMA: What do you consider the subject to be?

ROBERT: Betrayal.

EMMA: No, it isn't.

ROBERT: Isn't it? What is it then?

EMMA: I haven't finished it yet. I'll let you know.

ROBERT: Well, do let me know.

(*Pause.*)

Of course, I could be thinking of the wrong book.

(*Silence.*)

By the way, I went into American Express yesterday.

(*She looks up.*)

EMMA: Oh?

ROBERT: Yes. I went to cash some travellers cheques. You get a much better rate there, you see, than you do in an hotel.

EMMA: Oh, do you?

ROBERT: Oh yes. Anyway, there was a letter there for you. They asked me if you were any relation and I said yes. So they asked me if I wanted to take it. I mean, they gave it to me. But I said no, I would leave it. Did you get it?

EMMA: Yes.

ROBERT: I suppose you popped in when you were out shopping yesterday evening?

EMMA: That's right.

ROBERT: Oh well, I'm glad you got it.

(*Pause.*)

To be honest, I was amazed that they suggested I take it. It could never happen in England. But these Italians . . . so free and easy. I mean, just because my name is Downs and your name is Downs doesn't mean that we're the Mr. and Mrs. Downs that they, in their laughing Mediterranean way, assume we are. We could be, and in fact are vastly more likely to be, total strangers. So let's say I, whom they laughingly assume to be your husband, had taken the letter, having declared myself to be your husband but in truth being a total stranger, and opened it, and read it, out of nothing more than idle curiosity, and then thrown it in a canal, you would never have received it and would have been deprived of your legal right to open your own mail, and all this because of Venetian *je m'en foutisme*.° I've a good mind to write to the Doge of Venice about it.

(*Pause.*)

That's what stopped me taking it, by the way, and bringing it to you, the thought that I could very easily be a total stranger.

(*Pause.*)

What they of course did not know, and had no way of knowing, was that I am your husband.
EMMA: Pretty inefficient bunch.
ROBERT: Only in a laughing Mediterranean way.

(*Pause.*)

EMMA: It was from Jerry.
ROBERT: Yes, I recognised the handwriting.

(*Pause.*)

How is he?
EMMA: Okay.
ROBERT: Good. And Judith?
EMMA: Fine.

(*Pause.*)

ROBERT: What about the kids?
EMMA: I don't think he mentioned them.
ROBERT: They're probably all right, then. If they were ill or something he'd have probably mentioned it.

(*Pause.*)

Any other news?
EMMA: No.

(*Silence.*)

ROBERT: Are you looking forward to Torcello?

(*Pause.*)

How many times have we been to Torcello? Twice. I remember how you loved it, the first time I took you

---

je m'en foutisme: Vulgar phrase indicating a lax attitude.

---

there. You fell in love with it. That was about ten years ago, wasn't it? About . . . six months after we were married. Yes. Do you remember? I wonder if you'll like it as much tomorrow.

(*Pause.*)

What do you think of Jerry as a letter writer?

(*She laughs shortly.*)

You're trembling. Are you cold?
EMMA: No.
ROBERT: He used to write to me at one time. Long letters about Ford Madox Ford. I used to write to him too, come to think of it. Long letters about . . . oh, W. B. Yeats, I suppose. That was the time when we were both editors of poetry magazines. Him at Cambridge, me at Oxford. Did you know that? We were bright young men. And close friends. Well, we still are close friends. All that was long before I met you. Long before he met you. I've been trying to remember when I introduced him to you. I simply can't remember. I take it I *did* introduce him to you? Yes. But when? Can you remember?
EMMA: No.
ROBERT: You can't?
EMMA: No.
ROBERT: How odd.

(*Pause.*)

He wasn't best man at our wedding, was he?
EMMA: You know he was.
ROBERT: Ah yes. Well, that's probably when I introduced him to you.

(*Pause.*)

Was there any message for me, in his letter?

(*Pause.*)

I mean in the line of business, to do with the world of publishing. Has he discovered any new and original talent? He's quite talented at uncovering talent, old Jerry.
EMMA: No message.
ROBERT: No message. Not even his love?

(*Silence.*)

EMMA: We're lovers.
ROBERT: Ah. Yes. I thought it might be something like that, something along those lines.
EMMA: When?
ROBERT: What?
EMMA: When did you think?
ROBERT: Yesterday. Only yesterday. When I saw his handwriting on the letter. Before yesterday I was quite ignorant.
EMMA: Ah.

(*Pause.*)

I'm sorry.

ABOVE: Imogen Stubbs as
Emma and Anthony Calf as
Robert in the Royal National
Theatre's production of
Betrayal at the Lyttelton
Theatre, London, 1998.
RIGHT: Douglas Hodge as
Jerry and Imogen Stubbs as
Emma in *Betrayal* at the Royal
National Theatre's production
at the Lyttelton Theatre,
London, 1998.

ROBERT: *Sorry?*

(*Silence.*)

Where does it . . . take place? Must be a bit awkward. I mean we've got two kids, he's got two kids, not to mention a wife . . .

EMMA: We have a flat.

ROBERT: Ah. I see.

(*Pause.*)

Nice?

(*Pause.*)

A flat. It's quite well established then, your . . . uh . . . affair?

EMMA: Yes.

ROBERT: How long?

EMMA: Some time.

ROBERT: Yes, but how long exactly?

EMMA: Five years.

ROBERT: *Five years?*

(*Pause.*)

Ned is one year old.

(*Pause.*)

Did you hear what I said?

EMMA: Yes. He's your son. Jerry was in America. For two months.

(*Silence.*)

ROBERT: Did he write to you from America?

EMMA: Of course. And I wrote to him.

ROBERT: Did you tell him that Ned had been conceived?

EMMA: Not by letter.

ROBERT: But when you did tell him, was he happy to know I was to be a father?

(*Pause.*)

I've always liked Jerry. To be honest, I've always liked him rather more than I've liked you. Maybe I should have had an affair with him myself.

(*Silence.*)

Tell me, are you looking forward to our trip to Torcello?

1973
LATER

Scene 6

Flat. 1973. Summer. *Emma and Jerry standing, kissing. She is holding a basket and a parcel.*

EMMA: Darling.

JERRY: Darling.

(*He continues to hold her. She laughs.*)

EMMA: I must put this down.

(*She puts basket on table.*)

JERRY: What's in it?

EMMA: Lunch.

JERRY: What?

EMMA: Things you like.

(*He pours wine.*)

How do I look?

JERRY: Beautiful.

EMMA: Do I look well?

JERRY: You do.

(*He gives her wine.*)

EMMA (*sipping*): Mmmnn.

JERRY: How was it?

EMMA: It was lovely.

JERRY: Did you go to Torcello?

EMMA: No.

JERRY: Why not?

EMMA: Oh, I don't know. The speedboats were on strike, or something.

JERRY: On strike?

EMMA: Yes. On the day we were going.

JERRY: Ah. What about the gondolas?

EMMA: You can't take a gondola to Torcello.

JERRY: Well, they used to in the old days, didn't they? Before they had speedboats. How do you think they got over there?

EMMA: It would take hours.

JERRY: Yes, I suppose so.

(*Pause.*)

I got your letter.

EMMA: Good.

JERRY: Get mine?

EMMA: Of course. Miss me?

JERRY: Yes. Actually, I haven't been well.

EMMA: What?

JERRY: Oh nothing. A bug.

(*She kisses him.*)

EMMA: I missed you.

(*She turns away, looks about.*)

You haven't been here . . . at all?

JERRY: No.

EMMA: Needs Hoovering.°

JERRY: Later.

(*Pause.*)

I spoke to Robert this morning.

EMMA: Oh?

Hoovering: Vacuuming.

JERRY: I'm taking him to lunch on Thursday.
EMMA: Thursday? Why?
JERRY: Well, it's my turn.
EMMA: No, I meant why are you taking him to lunch?
JERRY: Because it's my turn. Last time he took me to lunch.
EMMA: You know what I mean.
JERRY: No. What?
EMMA: What is the subject or point of your lunch?
JERRY: No subject or point. We've just been doing it for years. His turn, followed by my turn.
EMMA: You've misunderstood me.
JERRY: Have I? How?
EMMA: Well, quite simply, you often do meet, or have lunch, to discuss a particular writer or a particular book, don't you? So to those meetings, or lunches, there is a point or a subject.
JERRY: Well, there isn't to this one.

(*Pause.*)

EMMA: You haven't discovered any new writers, while I've been away?
JERRY: No. Sam fell off his bike.
EMMA: No.
JERRY: He was knocked out. He was out for about a minute.
EMMA: Were you with him?
JERRY: No. Judith. He's all right. And then I got this bug.
EMMA: Oh dear.
JERRY: So I've had time for nothing.
EMMA: Everything will be better, now I'm back.
JERRY: Yes.
EMMA: Oh, I read that Spinks, the book you gave me.
JERRY: What do you think?
EMMA: Excellent.
JERRY: Robert hated it. He wouldn't publish it.
EMMA: What's he like?
JERRY: Who?
EMMA: Spinks.
JERRY: Spinks? He's a very thin bloke. About fifty. Wears dark glasses day and night. He lives alone, in a furnished room. Quite like this one, actually. He's . . . unfussed.
EMMA: Furnished rooms suit him?
JERRY: Yes.
EMMA: They suit me too. And you? Do you still like it? Our home?
JERRY: It's marvellous not to have a telephone.
EMMA: And marvellous to have me?
JERRY: You're all right.
EMMA: I cook and slave for you.
JERRY: You do.
EMMA: I bought something in Venice — for the house.

(*She opens the parcel, takes out a tablecloth. Puts it on the table.*)

Do you like it?
JERRY: It's lovely.

(*Pause.*)

EMMA: Do you think we'll ever go to Venice together?

(*Pause.*)

No. Probably not.

(*Pause.*)

JERRY: You don't think I should see Robert for lunch on Thursday, or on Friday, for that matter?
EMMA: Why do you say that?
JERRY: You don't think I should see him at all?
EMMA: I didn't say that. How can you not see him? Don't be silly.

(*Pause.*)

JERRY: I had a terrible panic when you were away. I was sorting out a contract, in my office, with some lawyers. I suddenly couldn't remember what I'd done with your letter. I couldn't remember putting it in the safe. I said I had to look for something in the safe. I opened the safe. It wasn't there. I had to go on with the damn contract . . . I kept seeing it lying somewhere in the house, being picked up . . .
EMMA: Did you find it?
JERRY: It was in the pocket of a jacket — in my wardrobe — at home.
EMMA: God.
JERRY: Something else happened a few months ago — I didn't tell you. We had a drink one evening. Well, we had our drink, and I got home about eight, walked in the door, Judith said, hello, you're a bit late. Sorry, I said, I was having a drink with Spinks. Spinks? she said, how odd, he's just phoned, five minutes ago, wanted to speak to you, he didn't mention he'd just seen you. You know old Spinks, I said, not exactly forthcoming, is he? He'd probably remembered something he'd meant to say but hadn't. I'll ring him later. I went up to see the kids and then we all had dinner.

(*Pause.*)

Listen. Do you remember, when was it, a few years ago, we were all in your kitchen, must have been Christmas or something, do you remember, all the kids were running about and suddenly I picked Charlotte up and lifted her high up, high up, and then down and up. Do you remember how she laughed?
EMMA: Everyone laughed.
JERRY: She was so light. And there was your husband and my wife and all the kids, all standing and laughing in your kitchen. I can't get rid of it.
EMMA: It was your kitchen, actually.

(*He takes her hand. They stand. They go to the bed and lie down.*)

Why shouldn't you throw her up?

(*She caresses him. They embrace.*)

1973
LATER

Scene 7

Restaurant. 1973. Summer. *Robert at table drinking white wine. The waiter brings Jerry to the table. Jerry sits.*

JERRY: Hullo, Robert.
ROBERT: Hullo.
JERRY (*to the waiter*): I'd like a Scotch on the rocks.
WAITER: With water?
JERRY: What?
WAITER: You want it with water?
JERRY: No. No water. Just on the rocks.
WAITER: Certainly signore.
ROBERT: Scotch? You don't usually drink Scotch at lunchtime.
JERRY: I've had a bug, actually.
ROBERT: Ah.
JERRY: And the only thing to get rid of this bug was Scotch — at lunchtime as well as at night. So I'm still drinking Scotch at lunchtime in case it comes back.
ROBERT: Like an apple a day.
JERRY: Precisely.

(*Waiter brings Scotch on rocks.*)

    Cheers.
ROBERT: Cheers.
WAITER: The menus, signori.

(*He passes the menus, goes.*)

ROBERT: How are you? Apart from the bug?
JERRY: Fine.
ROBERT: Ready for some squash?
JERRY: When I've got rid of the bug, yes.
ROBERT: I thought you had got rid of it.
JERRY: Why do you think I'm still drinking Scotch at lunchtime?
ROBERT: Oh yes. We really must play. We haven't played for years.
JERRY: How old are you now, then?
ROBERT: Thirty six.
JERRY: That means I'm thirty six as well.
ROBERT: If you're a day.
JERRY: Bit violent, squash.
ROBERT: Ring me. We'll have a game.
JERRY: How was Venice?
WAITER: Ready to order, signori?
ROBERT: What'll you have?

(*Jerry looks at him, briefly, then back to the menu.*)

JERRY: I'll have melone. And Piccata al limone with a green salad.
WAITER: Insalata verde. Prosciutto e melone?
JERRY: No. Just melone. On the rocks.
ROBERT: I'll have prosciutto and melone. Fried scampi. And spinach.
WAITER: E spinaci. Grazie, signore.

ROBERT: And a bottle of Corvo Bianco straight away.
WAITER: Si, signore. Molte grazie.

(*He goes.*)

JERRY: Is he the one who's always been here or is it his son?
ROBERT: You mean has his son always been here?
JERRY: No, is *he* his son? I mean, is he the son of the one who's always been here?
ROBERT: No, he's his father.
JERRY: Ah. Is he?
ROBERT: He's the one who speaks wonderful Italian.
JERRY: Yes. Your Italian's pretty good, isn't it?
ROBERT: No. Not at all.
JERRY: Yes it is.
ROBERT: No, it's Emma's Italian which is very good. Emma's Italian is very good.
JERRY: Is it? I didn't know that.

(*Waiter with bottle.*)

WAITER: Corvo Bianco, signore.
ROBERT: Thank you.
JERRY: How was it, anyway? Venice.
WAITER: Venice, signore? Beautiful. A most beautiful place of Italy. You see that painting on the wall? Is Venice.
ROBERT: So it is.
WAITER: You know what is none of in Venice?
JERRY: What?
WAITER: Traffico.

(*He goes, smiling.*)

ROBERT: Cheers.
JERRY: Cheers.
ROBERT: When were you last there?
JERRY: Oh, years.
ROBERT: How's Judith?
JERRY: What? Oh, you know, okay. Busy.
ROBERT: And the kids?
JERRY: All right. Sam fell off —
ROBERT: What?
JERRY: No, no, nothing. So how was it?
ROBERT: You used to go there with Judith, didn't you?
JERRY: Yes, but we haven't been there for years.

(*Pause.*)

    How about Charlotte? Did she enjoy it?
ROBERT: I think she did.

(*Pause.*)

    I did.
JERRY: Good.
ROBERT: I went for a trip to Torcello.
JERRY: Oh, really? Lovely place.
ROBERT: Incredible day. I got up very early and — whoomp — right across the lagoon — to Torcello. Not a soul stirring.
JERRY: What's the "whoomp"?
ROBERT: Speedboat.

JERRY: Ah. I thought —

ROBERT: What?

JERRY: It's so long ago, I'm obviously wrong. I thought one went to Torcello by gondola.

ROBERT: It would take hours. No, no, — whoomp — across the lagoon in the dawn.

JERRY: Sounds good.

ROBERT: I was quite alone.

JERRY: Where was Emma?

ROBERT: I think asleep.

JERRY: Ah.

ROBERT: I was alone for hours, as a matter of fact, on the island. Highpoint, actually, of the whole trip.

JERRY: Was it? Well, it sounds marvellous.

ROBERT: Yes. I sat on the grass and read Yeats.

JERRY: Yeats on Torcello?

ROBERT: They went well together.

(*Waiter with food.*)

WAITER: One melone. One prosciutto e melone.

ROBERT: Prosciutto for me.

WAITER: Buon appetito.

ROBERT: Emma read that novel of that chum of yours — what's his name?

JERRY: I don't know. What?

ROBERT: Spinks.

JERRY: Oh Spinks. Yes. The one you didn't like.

ROBERT: The one I wouldn't publish.

JERRY: I remember. Did Emma like it?

ROBERT: She seemed to be madly in love with it.

JERRY: Good.

ROBERT: You like it yourself, do you?

JERRY: I do.

ROBERT: And it's very successful?

JERRY: It is.

ROBERT: Tell me, do you think that makes me a publisher of unique critical judgement or a foolish publisher?

JERRY: A foolish publisher.

ROBERT: I agree with you. I am a very foolish publisher.

JERRY: No you're not. What are you talking about? You're a good publisher. What are you talking about?

ROBERT: I'm a bad publisher because I hate books. Or to be more precise, prose. Or to be even more precise, modern prose, I mean modern novels, first novels and second novels, all that promise and sensibility it falls upon me to judge, to put the firm's money on, and then to push for the third novel, see it done, see the dust jacket done, see the dinner for the national literary editors done, see the signing in Hatchards done, see the lucky author cook himself to death, all in the name of literature. You know what you and Emma have in common? You love literature. I mean you love modern prose literature, I mean you love the new novel by the new Casey or Spinks. It gives you both a thrill.

JERRY: You must be pissed.

ROBERT: Really? You mean you don't think it gives Emma a thrill?

JERRY: How do I know? She's your wife.

(*Pause.*)

ROBERT: Yes. Yes. You're quite right. I shouldn't have to consult you. I shouldn't have to consult anyone.

JERRY: I'd like some more wine.

ROBERT: Yes, yes. Waiter! Another bottle of Corvo Bianco. And where's our lunch? This place is going to pot. Mind you, it's worse in Venice. They really don't give a fuck there. I'm not drunk. You can't get drunk on Corvo Bianco. Mind you . . . last night . . . I was up late . . . I hate brandy . . . it stinks of modern literature. No, look, I'm sorry . . .

(*Waiter with bottle.*)

WAITER: Corvo Bianco.

ROBERT: Same glass. Where's our lunch?

WAITER: It comes.

ROBERT: I'll pour.

(*Waiter goes, with melon plates.*)

No, look, I'm sorry, have another drink. I'll tell you what it is, it's just that I can't bear being back in London. I was happy, such a rare thing, not in Venice, I don't mean that, I mean on Torcello, when I walked about Torcello in the early morning, alone, I was happy, I wanted to stay there forever.

JERRY: We all . . .

ROBERT: Yes, we all . . . feel that sometimes. Oh you do yourself, do you?

(*Pause.*)

I mean there's nothing really wrong, you see. I've got the family. Emma and I are very good together. I think the world of her. And I actually consider Casey to be a first rate writer.

JERRY: Do you really?

ROBERT: First rate. I'm proud to publish him and you discovered him and that was very clever of you.

JERRY: Thanks.

ROBERT: You've got a good nose and you care and I respect that in you. So does Emma. We often talk about it.

JERRY: How is Emma?

ROBERT: Very well. You must come and have a drink sometime. She'd love to see you.

1971

Scene 8

Flat. 1971. Summer. *Flat empty. Kitchen door open. Table set; crockery, glasses, bottle of wine.*
Jerry comes in through front door, with key.

JERRY: Hullo.

(*Emma's voice from kitchen.*)

EMMA: Hullo.

(*Emma comes out of kitchen. She is wearing an apron.*)

I've only just got here. I meant to be here ages ago. I'm making this stew. It'll be hours.

(*He kisses her.*)

Are you starving?
JERRY: Yes.

(*He kisses her.*)

EMMA: No really. I'll never do it. You sit down. I'll get it on.
JERRY: What a lovely apron.
EMMA: Good.

(*She kisses him, goes into kitchen.*)
(*She calls. He pours wine.*)

EMMA: What have you been doing?
JERRY: Just walked through the park.
EMMA: What was it like?
JERRY: Beautiful. Empty. A slight mist.

(*Pause.*)

I sat down for a bit, under a tree. It was very quiet. I just looked at the Serpentine.

(*Pause.*)

EMMA: And then?
JERRY: Then I got a taxi to Wessex Grove. Number 31. And I climbed the steps and opened the front door and then climbed the stairs and opened this door and found you in a new apron cooking a stew.

(*Emma comes out of the kitchen.*)

EMMA: It's on.
JERRY: Which is now on.

(*Emma pours herself a vodka.*)

JERRY: Vodka? At lunchtime?
EMMA: Just feel like one.

(*She drinks.*)

I ran into Judith yesterday. Did she tell you?
JERRY: No, she didn't.

(*Pause.*)

Where?
EMMA: Lunch.
JERRY: Lunch?
EMMA: She didn't tell you?
JERRY: No.
EMMA: That's funny.
JERRY: What do you mean, lunch? Where?
EMMA: At Fortnum and Mason's.
JERRY: Fortnum and Mason's? What the hell was she doing at Fortnum and Mason's?
EMMA: She was lunching with a lady.
JERRY: A lady?
EMMA: Yes.

(*Pause.*)

JERRY: Fortnum and Mason's is a long way from the hospital.
EMMA: Of course it isn't.
JERRY: Well . . . I suppose not.

(*Pause.*)

And you?
EMMA: Me?
JERRY: What were you doing at Fortnum and Mason's?
EMMA: Lunching with my sister.
JERRY: Ah.

(*Pause.*)

EMMA: Judith . . . didn't tell you?
JERRY: I haven't really seen her. I was out late last night, with Casey. And she was out early this morning.

(*Pause.*)

EMMA: Do you think she knows?
JERRY: Knows?
EMMA: Does she know? About us?
JERRY: No.
EMMA: Are you sure?
JERRY: She's too busy. At the hospital. And then the kids. She doesn't go in for . . . speculation.
EMMA: But what about clues? Isn't she interested . . . to follow clues?
JERRY: What clues?
EMMA: Well, there must be some . . . available to her . . . to pick up.
JERRY: There are none . . . available to her.
EMMA: Oh. Well . . . good.

(*Pause.*)

JERRY: She has an admirer.
EMMA: Really?
JERRY: Another doctor. He takes her for drinks. It's . . . irritating. I mean, she says that's all there is to it. He likes her, she's fond of him, etcetera, etcetera . . . perhaps that's what I find irritating. I don't know exactly what's going on.
EMMA: Oh, why shouldn't she have an admirer? I have an admirer.
JERRY: Who?
EMMA: Uuh . . . you, I think.
JERRY: Ah. Yes.

(*He takes her hand.*)

I'm more than that.

(*Pause.*)

EMMA: Tell me . . . have you ever thought . . . of changing your life?
JERRY: Changing?
EMMA: Mmnn.

(*Pause.*)

JERRY: It's impossible.

(*Pause.*)

EMMA: Do you think she's being unfaithful to you?
JERRY: No. I don't know.
EMMA: When you were in America, just now, for instance?
JERRY: No.
EMMA: Have you ever been unfaithful?
JERRY: To whom?
EMMA: To me, of course.
JERRY: No.

(*Pause.*)

  Have you . . . to me?
EMMA: No.

(*Pause.*)

  If she was, what would you do?
JERRY: She isn't. She's busy. She's got lots to do. She's a very good doctor. She likes her life. She loves the kids.
EMMA: Ah.
JERRY: She loves me.

(*Pause.*)

EMMA: Ah.

(*Silence.*)

JERRY: All that means something.
EMMA: It certainly does.
JERRY: But I adore you.

(*Pause.*)

  I adore you.

(*Emma takes his hand.*)

EMMA: Yes.

(*Pause.*)

  Listen. There's something I have to tell you.
JERRY: What?
EMMA: I'm pregnant. It was when you were in America.

(*Pause.*)

  It wasn't anyone else. It was my husband.

(*Pause.*)

JERRY: Yes. Yes, of course.

(*Pause.*)

  I'm very happy for you.

1968

Scene 9

Robert and Emma's House. Bedroom. 1968. Winter.
The room is dimly lit. Jerry is sitting in the shadows. Faint music through the door.

  The door opens. Light. Music. Emma comes in, closes the door. She goes towards the mirror, sees Jerry.

EMMA: Good God.
JERRY: I've been waiting for you.
EMMA: What do you mean?
JERRY: I knew you'd come.

(*He drinks.*)

EMMA: I've just come in to comb my hair.

(*He stands.*)

JERRY: I knew you'd have to. I knew you'd have to comb your hair. I knew you'd have to get away from the party.

(*She goes to the mirror, combs her hair.*
He watches her.)

  You're a beautiful hostess.
EMMA: Aren't you enjoying the party?
JERRY: You're beautiful.

(*He goes to her.*)

  Listen. I've been watching you all night. I must tell you, I want to tell you, I have to tell you —
EMMA: Please —
JERRY: You're incredible.
EMMA: You're drunk.
JERRY: Nevertheless.

(*He holds her.*)

EMMA: Jerry.
JERRY: I was best man at your wedding. I saw you in white. I watched you glide by in white.
EMMA: I wasn't in white.
JERRY: You know what should have happened?
EMMA: What?
JERRY: I should have had you, in your white, before the wedding. I should have blackened you, in your white wedding dress, blackened you in your bridal dress, before ushering you into your wedding, as your best man.
EMMA: My husband's best man. Your best friend's best man.
JERRY: No. Your best man.
EMMA: I must get back.
JERRY: You're lovely. I'm crazy about you. All these words I'm using, don't you see, they've never been said before. Can't you see? I'm crazy about you. It's a whirlwind. Have you ever been to the Sahara Desert? Listen to me. It's true. Listen. You overwhelm me. You're so lovely.
EMMA: I'm not.
JERRY: You're so beautiful. Look at the way you look at me.
EMMA: I'm not . . . looking at you. Please.
JERRY: Look at the way you're looking at me. I can't wait for you, I'm bowled over, I'm totally knocked out, you dazzle me, you jewel, my jewel, I can't ever sleep again, no, listen, it's the truth, I won't walk, I'll be a cripple, I'll descend, I'll diminish, into total paralysis, my life is in your hands, that's what you're banishing

me to, a state of catatonia, do you know the state of catatonia? do you? do you? the state of . . . where the reigning prince is the prince of emptiness, the prince of absence, the prince of desolation. I love you.

EMMA: My husband is at the other side of that door.

JERRY: Everyone knows. The world knows. It knows. But they'll never know, they'll never know, they're in a different world. I adore you. I'm madly in love with you. I can't believe that what anyone is at this moment saying has ever happened has ever happened. Nothing has ever happened. Nothing. This is the only thing that has ever happened. Your eyes kill me. I'm lost. You're wonderful.

EMMA: No.

JERRY: Yes.

(*He kisses her.*
She breaks away.
He kisses her.)

(*Laughter off.*
She breaks away.
Door opens. Robert.)

EMMA: Your best friend is drunk.

JERRY: As you are my best and oldest friend and, in the present instance, my host, I decided to take this opportunity to tell your wife how beautiful she was.

ROBERT: Quite right.

JERRY: It is quite right, to . . . to face up to the facts . . . and to offer a token, without blush, a token of one's unalloyed appreciation, no holds barred.

ROBERT: Absolutely.

JERRY: And how wonderful for you that this is so, that this is the case, that her beauty is the case.

ROBERT: Quite right.

(*Jerry moves to Robert and takes hold of his elbow.*)

JERRY: I speak as your oldest friend. Your best man.

ROBERT: You are, actually.

(*He clasps Jerry's shoulder, briefly, turns, leaves the room.*)

(*Emma moves towards the door. Jerry grasps her arm. She stops still.*)

(*They stand still, looking at each other.*)

COMMENTARY

Katherine H. Burkman (b. 1934)

HAROLD PINTER'S *BETRAYAL:* LIFE BEFORE DEATH — AND AFTER   *1982*

Burkman's interest lies in the interplay of the characters and the dimensions of their betrayal of each other. She is concerned with Robert and Jerry's relationship and the role that Emma plays in their lives. The apparent simplicity of the play is belied by the complexities that lie beneath the surface, and Burkman's approach is to help reveal the play's depths.

In scene five of Harold Pinter's *Betrayal,* just before Robert learns from his wife Emma that she has betrayed him for five years with his best friend Jerry, they discuss the book she is reading. It is a book that her publisher husband has, he tells her, refused to publish himself, despite the urging of Jerry (the author's agent, Robert's friend, and Emma's lover) because there isn't "much more to say on that subject."[1] He considers the subject to be betrayal. Emma does not think the book is

---

[1] Harold Pinter, *Betrayal* (New York: Grove Press, Inc., 1978), p. 78. All subsequent quotations from the play are from this edition as reprinted in *The Bedford Introduction to Drama,* Fourth Edition, and are hereafter given parenthetically in the body of the essay.

about betrayal, but she hasn't finished reading it yet; she promises to let Robert know what it is about when she is done.

In this nicely self-reflexive moment, Pinter invites us to look beneath the cross currents of this play's love affairs for what remains the primary subject in all of his dramas — renewal. In *A Slight Ache* and *The Homecoming* Pinter's depiction of women disposing of their husbands and taking on new partners had all of the ritual connotations attendant on Sir James Frazer's fertility goddesses in *The Golden Bough*. The prototype of these goddesses is Diana in the Grove of Nemi, who must unite with the new god-king-priest of her grove when he defeats the old, just as spring must follow winter — if spring is to follow winter.[2] One may look in vain in *Betrayal* for the lush summer setting of *A Slight Ache* (1959) in which Flora assumes a new mate who will understand and nourish the garden with which her old mate could no longer connect, just as one may look in vain for the environmental alternatives that attend Ruth, whose disposal of her husband and assumption of his family in *The Homecoming* (1965) is a desperate choice of life in the English jungle over death in the American desert. Still, the battle in *Betrayal* (1978) is a desperate one, its issue is renewal, and its strategies may be detected and charted as they operate beneath the seemingly casual game of betrayal in which the characters are ostensibly engaged.

Betrayal does not end, as do *A Slight Ache* and *The Homecoming,* with the breakup of a marriage; we learn at the very beginning that Emma and Robert's marriage is over. Emma returns in scene one to her now ex-lover Jerry, ostensibly to tell him the news. Lest Jerry have any doubts, Robert confirms that the marriage is over in scene two. The rest of the play, with the exception of scenes five, six, and seven, moves backward in time, exploring the life of the now dead triangle and ending at the triangle's inception or birth; the final tableau reveals Robert's intrusion on the scene of Jerry's first "pass" at Emma.

This backward narrative or exploration of the triangle's life before death may seem at times like an autopsy on characters who have never been very fully alive. "Instead of suffering hell-fire and damnation," writes one critic, "the characters simply fall apart from each other; their personal relationships disintegrate."[3] For others the characters fail to arouse our "concern or compassion."[4] It seems to me, however, that Pinter continues in his best tradition here to give us a vision of "life honed to the injured bone."[5] Combining his surgical precision and black humor with a haunting compassion, Pinter probes not only into the triangle's life before death, but for its life in death, and after. Without some form of death, after all, there can be no renewal.

There is little doubt in the opening scenes of the play that the relationships in the triangle are coming to an end, yet there is a kind of life that still bristles in what is now supposedly dead. Why, for example, has Emma sought out Jerry at this point in time? Not apparently to rekindle their affair; it has been over for two years and she is involved with somebody else, Casey, a writer whom Jerry has discovered and

[2]Sir James George Frazer, *The Golden Bough,* abr. ed. in 1 vol. (New York: The Macmillan Co., 1951), p. 823.

[3]*Wall Street Journal,* 11 January 1980, quoted in *New York Theatre Critics' Review,* 41 (1980) 392.

[4]John Beaufort, *The Christian Science Monitor,* 11 January 1980, p. 19.

[5]Walter Kerr, "Play: Pinter's 'Betrayal,' Story of an Affair," *New York Times,* 7 January 1980, quoted in *New York Theatre Critics' Review,* 41 (1980) 390.

Robert has published. What Emma seems to need to share with Jerry is not even any great sense of loss over the end of her marriage. Rather, it is her sense of being betrayed.

> EMMA: You know what I found out . . . last night? He's betrayed me for years. He's had . . . other women for years.
> JERRY: No? Good Lord.
>
> (*Pause.*)
>
> But we betrayed him for years.
> EMMA: And he betrayed me for years.
> JERRY: Well I never knew that.
> EMMA: Nor did I.
>
> (*Pause.*)
>
> JERRY: Does Casey know about this?   [p. 1383]

Emma, it seems, is still involved enough with both husband and lover to care that she has been betrayed by the one and to share that sense of betrayal with the other. Jerry, in turn, is involved enough with Emma to be jealous of her current affair with his protégé, Casey, a jealousy which exudes from his flagrant denials. "I couldn't be jealous of Casey. I'm his agent. I advised him about his divorce. I read all his first drafts. I persuaded your husband to publish his first novel. I escort him to Oxford to speak at the Union. He's my . . . He's my boy. . . ." (p. 1383).

Jerry also cares enough about Robert to be deeply concerned that Emma has told her husband about their affair in the previous night's conversation during which they decided to terminate their marriage. He is even more deeply dismayed in the following scene when he discovers that Emma has not, as she implied, told Robert about their affair the previous night but had told him four years ago. And even worse, in Jerry's eyes, is Robert's betrayal of him by continuing to pretend not to know.

> JERRY: Then why didn't you tell me?
>
> (*Pause.*)
>
> ROBERT: Tell you what?
> JERRY: That you knew. You bastard.
> ROBERT: Oh, don't call me a bastard, Jerry.   [p. 1385]

Robert too, it appears, despite his constant disclaimers about caring, cares. "You don't seem to understand that I don't give a shit about any of this," Robert points out in unconvincing tones to Jerry. "It's true I've hit Emma once or twice. But that wasn't to defend a principle. I wasn't inspired to do it from any kind of moral standpoint. I just felt like giving her a good bashing. The old itch . . . you understand." (p. 1385).

At the end of the first scene, when Emma tells Jerry, "It doesn't matter. It's all gone," and he replies, "Is it? What has?" (p. 1384), we share Jerry's confusion. The relationships in the triangle may be terminating, but the members of the triangle are still very much caught up in the anguish and complexities of their mutual betrayals; there is life in their dying. As Pinter moves us backward in time, however, the confusion clears up and we discover not only further betrayals and betrayals within betrayals but more of the rules of the game, the nature of the players, and the stakes of the battle that the game conceals and reveals. As in so many of Pinter's plays, much remains unstated; the characters are "subtly inarticulate, almost to the point of code."[6] However, if one can detect what is being said "underneath what is said," filling in the pauses and the silences as well, one can crack the code and come to know almost too much.[7]

Major clues to the life principle of the triangle lie in Robert's reaction to Emma's fifth scene confession of the affair with Jerry. He has become suspicious when asked at American Express to deliver a letter to his wife and has recognized the handwriting as Jerry's. Pretending to be incensed at the Italians who in their "laughing Mediterranean way" may have given the letter to a stranger with the same name, he has declined to deliver the letter. "That's what stopped me taking it, by the way," he explains to Emma, "and bringing it to you, the thought that I could very easily be a total stranger." (p. 1390). That husband and wife have become strangers is clear to both of them, and Robert expresses his bitterness when speaking of their planned trip from Venice to Torcello: "How many times have we been to Torcello? Twice. I remember how you loved it, the first time I took you there. You fell in love with it. That was about ten years ago, wasn't it? About . . . six months after we were married. Yes. Do you remember? I wonder if you'll like it as much tomorrow." (p. 1390).

Robert continues turning the ironical knife, reminding Emma that Jerry was best man at their wedding as he pushes her to confession. When confession comes, however, Robert is not so much shocked at the fact, which we later find out he has probably guessed much earlier, but at the arrangements that have attended the betrayal and its time span — five years of meeting in a flat. He wonders too if Ned, their four-year-old, is his. When reassured that Jerry was away at the time, Robert drives home to Emma the doubleness of her betrayal.

> ROBERT: Did you tell him that Ned had been conceived?
> EMMA: Not by letter.
> ROBERT: But when you did tell him, was he happy to know I was to be a father?
>
> (*Pause.*)
>
> I've always liked Jerry. To be honest, I've always liked him rather more than I've liked you. Maybe I should have had an affair with him myself.
>
> (*Silence.*)
>
> Tell me, are you looking forward to our trip to Torcello?   [p. 1392]

One wonders why Robert even needs to hit Emma when he is capable of such verbal thrusts.[8] Understandably bitter over what he considers Emma's double role as whore — betraying him with Jerry but also betraying Jerry with him by having their child — Robert's "honest" admission that he has always liked Jerry better than Emma provides a key for her behavior and for his.

---

[6]Clive Barnes, "Pinter's Back with 'Betrayal,'" *New York Post*, quoted in *New York Theatre Critics' Review*, 41 (1980) 392.

[7]Harold Pinter, quoted in Katherine H. Burkman, *The Dramatic World of Harold Pinter: Its Basis in Ritual* (Ohio: Ohio State University Press, 1971), p. 9.

[8]Robert certainly knows how to fight back better than Teddy did in *The Homecoming*; Teddy weakly protests to Ruth as she leans toward taking on his family by reminding her that he has taken her to Venice.

In an interview with Mel Gussow, Pinter noted that, "the play is about a nine-year relationship between two men who are best friends."[9] The nature of that friendship would seem to be a classical example of what René Girard calls triangular desire, a situation in which two men, through the mechanism of imitative desire, wish to possess the same woman. Imitative desire, as defined by Girard, is universal in human relationships and need not necessarily involve homosexuality or latent homosexuality, though it may: "The impulse toward the object is ultimately an impulse toward the mediator . . ."[10] What occurs is that one man (Jerry, in this case) desires another woman (Robert's) because the other man desires her. Robert, in turn, not only becomes the internal mediator of Jerry's desire (internal rather than external because of the nearness and involvement of the men in each other's sphere of action), but offers a case of what Girard calls double mediation as he founds his own desire on that of his disciple/rival. "The person who is mediator without realizing it may himself be incapable of spontaneous desire. Thus he will be tempted to copy the copy of his own desire. . . . We now have a subject-mediator and a mediator-subject, a model-disciple and a disciple-model."[11] Because of the nearness of the mediators to each other, the object of desire, Emma, becomes less real; she becomes more and more a mere object to the men.[12]

Evidence in the play, other than Robert's stated preference for Jerry, suggests that Emma, who seems to be doing the most betraying, is actually the triangle's major victim, a prize or object for which the men vie mostly because of their interest in each other.[13] In scene four, for example, when Jerry drops in to see Robert and Emma, having just had tea with Casey around the corner, Emma is pointedly excluded by Robert when she offers to come and watch them play squash and treat them to lunch. "Well to be brutally honest," Robert informs his wife, "we wouldn't actually want a woman around, would we, Jerry?" (p. 1388). This is not only an exclusion of Emma from the battle they are engaged in, even though she may be the spoils of that battle, it is a triple put down of her. They have just discussed Casey's novel — which Emma has considered dishonest — hence the barb in Robert's, "Well to be brutally honest." Robert has also just told Jerry that Emma has given her reaction to Casey's work when the two couples had dinner together, at which ". . . Emma gave a dissertation over the pudding about dishonesty in Casey with reference to his last novel" (p. 1388). Robert excludes Emma from lunch, mocks her daring to call another dishonest, and clearly objects to a woman interrupting male talk about books and giving her own opinions on them.

One could excuse Robert's behavior on the ground that he has learned in the next scene (going backwards in time) of the extent of Emma's affair with Jerry and is obviously very angry. But there is an implication in the speech that Emma has

---

[9]Mel Gussow, "An Interview with Harold Pinter," *Sunday New York Times*, 30 December 1979, quoted in The Goodman Theatre of the Art Institute of Chicago program for their production of *Betrayal*, January 16–February 22, 1981, p. 17.

[10]René Girard, *Deceit, Desire, and the Novel: Self and Other in Literary Structure*, trans. Yvonne Freccero (Maryland: The Johns Hopkins University Press, 1965), pp. 9–10.

[11]Girard, p. 99.

[12]"The closer the mediator comes, the greater his role becomes and the smaller that of the object." Girard, p. 45.

[13]One is reminded of Pinter's play, *The Collection*, in which Stella tells her husband James that she has had a one night affair with a dress designer, apparently in an effort to get her husband's fuller attention. Her effort backfires as the husband becomes vindictively interested in his wife's alleged lover, who is a homosexual.

really been an interruption in his relationship with Jerry with whom he still intends to "play." His subtextual sparring with Jerry over playing squash is fraught with his knowledge of the affair, though neither Jerry nor the audience knows at this point that Robert knows. Robert challenges Jerry to the game, assures Jerry that he is not better than he, as Jerry fears, only fitter from practice with Casey; he then reminds Jerry that he used to be good, almost suggesting to him that he is no longer a worthy opponent in their current war, as Casey is. Jerry counters by putting off "playing" with Robert since he must accompany Casey to New York to talk about film rights to the novel Emma has called dishonest, a neat put-down of Robert (Casey is *his*) and of Emma, whose judgment must be faulty if Casey has become so successful.

Actually, despite his invitations to Jerry to play squash, part of Robert's game involves not playing squash with him. When Jerry expresses his dismay in scene two at the way their friendship has continued over the years despite Robert's knowledge of the affair, Robert remarks, "Never played squash though" (p. 1385). Later in the scene he also mentions bumping into Casey recently. "I believe he's having an affair with my wife. We haven't played squash for years, Casey and me. We used to have a damn good game" (p. 1385). Invitations to the contrary, apparently Robert draws the line at playing squash with his wife's lovers, but he is nostalgic over the loss of this strictly masculine activity.

While Jerry's war with Robert, like Robert's war with Jerry, seems to be of more interest to him than his love for Emma, the quality of that love is suspect from the beginning-ending and at the ending-beginning — as well as in the middle. As Emma tries to get some support from Jerry in the opening scene (doubtless the affairs Robert has confessed to are symbolic to her of what she must always have sensed, his lack of involvement with her), Jerry is really only concerned with her betrayal of him by telling Robert of their affair. "But he's my oldest friend," Jerry protests. "I mean, I picked his own daughter up in my arms and threw her up and caught her, in my kitchen. He watched me do it" (p. 1384). Later in the play, though earlier in time, when Jerry and Emma are breaking up their flat and their relationship, they speak of family obligations that have prevented them from meeting at night. "I might remind you," Jerry says testily to Emma, "that your husband is my oldest friend" (p. 1386), a remark that particularly offends her. Even when their affair is ostensibly at its height and Emma questions Jerry about his wife Judith's possible betrayal of him, Emma says to Jerry, "Oh, why shouldn't she have an admirer? I have an admirer" (p. 1396). When Jerry wants to know who that admirer is, Emma responds, "Uuh . . . you, I think" (p. 1396). Jerry's absentmindedness about Emma reveals her almost peripheral value for him in the drama of triangular desire and doubtless stems from the narcissistic quality of his initial attraction for her which we learn about when he first professes that love at the play's end. "You're so beautiful," Jerry says to her. "Look at the way you look at me" (p. 1397). Without her, he suggests, he will be "where the reigning prince is the prince of emptiness, the prince of absence, the prince of desolation" (p. 1398). With her, he is there too.

Betrayal is, in fact, a play in which the beginning is not only the ending, but the ending of the affair is suggested in its beginning at the play's end. Looking closely at the final conversation and movements among the three major characters at the end of the play, one gets a sense that at some level, despite the bitterness in his scene five discovery, Robert senses a good deal about the incipient affair before it really gets underway and that what the men are entering into is their own peculiar brand of squash, which they enjoy far more for sharing the sport than for Emma, the prize. In the concluding scene Emma assures Robert, as he enters and interrupts Jerry's lovemaking, that his "best friend is drunk," after which Jerry, admiring Emma's beauty, takes Robert by the elbow and assures him that he speaks "as your oldest friend. Your best man." When Robert replies, "You are, actually" (p. 1398), he leaves the room and leaves Emma to Jerry. The real passion here, restrained and understated, is between the two men, best friends become best enemies, both willing to sacrifice Emma for the fray — and in it. "Bit violent, squash," Jerry remarks of the game at one point in the play "Ring me. We'll have a game" (p. 1394) Robert replies.

If Jerry actually has any kind of passionate feelings for Emma, they are hostile feelings and relate back to Robert. Recalling how he was best man at her wedding at which he remembers her in white, a color which she denies having worn, he tells Emma of his fantasy: "I should have had you in your white, before the wedding. I should have blackened you in your white wedding dress, blackened you in your bridal dress, before ushering you into your wedding as your best man" (p. 1397). Jerry's dream is not one of possessing Emma — he doesn't even recall the color of her dress properly. It is a dream of desecrating her virginity, blackening her whiteness, and then, rather than keeping her for himself, delivering her to Robert as damaged goods.

In terms of her relationship with the men, Emma seems to be very much like her daughter Charlotte who was thrown up in the air as a child and caught by Jerry in the midst of both Emma's and Jerry's families. The image is a central one. Emma first brings up the incident in scene one after Jerry tells her he has seen Charlotte on the street and recognized her because she looks like Emma. Jerry recalls throwing Charlotte up in the air in Emma's kitchen, which Emma corrects — it was in his kitchen. At the end of scene one, then, when he is dismayed that Emma has told Robert of their now dead affair, he again recalls throwing Charlotte up in front of Robert, this time in his own kitchen. He is suggesting, I think, that Robert trusted him with his daughter, or given the earlier connection Jerry made between Charlotte and Emma, with his wife. The memory is brought up again in scene six with Jerry reverting (not exactly reverting since it is earlier in time) to the idea that he threw Charlotte up in Robert's kitchen and Emma correcting him when she has returned from Venice and the affair is still going forward. They have been discussing the possibility that Judith could easily have found them out (Robert, Emma knows and we know from scene five, has found out) but the memory is a pleasant one here, emphasizing the friendship of both families and Emma's trust of Jerry. "Why shouldn't you throw her up?" (p. 1393) Emma asks as they embrace. [. . .]

Caryl Churchill

Caryl Churchill (b. 1938) is in many ways a conventional middle-class citizen. She was born in London to a comfortable family: her father was a political cartoonist and her mother a model. During World War II, her family emigrated to Canada, and much of her growing up was done in Montreal. She returned to England for college, taking her degree in English literature at Oxford in Lady Margaret Hall.

Churchill says that through all these years she did all the right things. She was a proper intellectual, a proper student, a proper person. She began writing plays in Oxford, where they were produced by students. After college, she married David Harter, also from Oxford, who became a lawyer in London. She raised three sons and at the same time tried to keep alive her dream of being a writer. Most of her early work was written for radio, and many of the plays were short. With so many children in the house, she says, it was difficult to sustain a long project.

Churchill's social conscience has been a significant part of her playwriting and her life. She found herself sometimes depressed by the dullness of the middle-class life demanded of the wife of a barrister, and much of her early drama is satire directed at what many people thought was an enviable lifestyle.

In the early 1970s her husband left a very lucrative practice and has since devoted himself to helping the poor at a nearby legal aid center. She has become involved in theater groups, among them a group of women called Monstrous Regiment. She is closely aligned with the Royal Court Theatre in London, noted for producing satiric, biting, experimental drama with a punch.

Her first play staged at the Royal Court Theatre was a farcical but serious play called *Owners* (1972). It attacks the way that the concept of ownership destroys potential relationships. Churchill's basic socialist views are very apparent in the play, which is a critique of the values that most capitalists take for granted: being aggressive, getting ahead, doing well. Although this play is not explicitly feminist, Churchill combines socialism and feminism in most of her plays, thus producing an often unusual approach to her subject matter. *Owners* has been criticized for its Brechtian use of disconnected scenes and its loose plot, but when it was produced off Broadway in 1973 it marked Churchill as a serious playwright.

After a year as a playwright in residence at the Royal Court Theatre, Churchill produced *Objections to Sex and Violence* (1975). The play was not immensely successful, but it introduced themes of feminism into her work. Among other themes, the play examines in depth the domination of women by men and the relationship of violence to sex roles.

In 1976 Churchill produced *Vinegar Tom*, a play about witch hunts set in the seventeenth century. After researching witch trials, Churchill concluded that women were convenient scapegoats for men when times became difficult. A companion play also set in the seventeenth century is *Light Shining in*

Buckinghamshire, which studies revolutions. The play was developed by the Joint Stock Theatre Group and produced at the Royal Court Theatre to uniformly positive reviews.

Her first play to receive wide notice was *Cloud Nine* (1979). It treats several themes simultaneously, among them colonization. The first act is set in the Victorian era in a British colony of Africa. The play is broadly satirical, involving farcical moments in the relationships of colonialist and native, master and servant, and man and woman. Churchill cast certain parts of the play in a cross-gender fashion: a woman plays a sensitive schoolboy, a man plays an unfulfilled wife. The effect is both comic and instructive, since one of her most important purposes is to cast some light on gender distinctions. She said that she saw "parallels between the way colonizers treat the colonized and the way men tended to treat women in our own society." *Cloud Nine* was produced in the Lucille Lortel Theatre, where it ran for two years off Broadway and won an Obie award.

Top Girls (1982) played at the Royal Court Theatre in London and at the Public Theatre in New York, where the reviews were mixed. The play, essentially feminist in theme, was praised in England for being "the best British play ever from a woman dramatist." *Fen* (1983) was also warmly praised by critics and audiences alike. A study of the effects of poverty on women, the play was developed with the Joint Stock Theatre Group and researched in the area of England called the Fens, where women work the fields and most of the people are poor.

Churchill's *Serious Money* (1987) is a verse play (like her first Oxford play) about the London stock market. It ran on Broadway to exceptional acclaim, partly because it played just after the stock market crash of October 1987. The play is a satiric study of those for whom only greed and getting ahead matter.

Churchill has written a number of plays for radio and television, such as *Lovesick, Abortive, Not Not Not Not Not Enough Oxygen, Schreber's Nervous Illness, The Hospital at the Time of the Revolution,* and *The Judge's Wife.* These are gathered in a volume called *Shorts* (1990). *The Skriker* (1994) is an experiment in fantasy, with a spirit world that parallels the real world. Her most recent production, *Blue Heart* (1999), consists of two one-act plays: *Heart's Desire* and *Blue Kettle.* These are relatively realistic domestic dramas. *Heart's Desire* is a satire set in a sparkling kitchen where Alice and Brian wait, with Brian's sister Maisie, for the return of their daughter from Australia. Their peaceful setting is invaded by alcoholics and terrorists, among others, and yet the play has been described as "achingly, aggressively funny." *Blue Kettle* features a young man who searches for women who have given up children for adoption and then claims to be their lost son. It is a somber play and deals with the failure of language. Churchill has become one of the major dramatic voices of modern theater.

CLOUD NINE

Cloud Nine (1979) was commissioned by London's Joint Stock Theatre Group and developed with the help of director Max Stafford-Clark, who ran the Royal Court Theatre, one of London's most exciting experimental theaters. Many of Churchill's later plays were also developed at the Royal Court, and they helped establish it as one of the centers of new drama in England. The central subject of the play is sex, but the drama draws us into the worlds of politics, gender definition, and social mores.

The play is divided into two acts that are more disconnected than unified. The same characters appear in both acts, but the actors trade parts in act 2. Such a disjunction is so striking — especially to the first audiences who saw the play in 1979 — that we realize Churchill is telling us something radical about the continuity of psychological characters and thus about psychological realism. It is also true that the first act is set in British imperial Africa in the 1870s, while the second act is set in London in the 1970s, so it seems reasonable that different actors should play these characters in view of the time difference.

But there is more. The characters in act 1 play recognizable types. Clive is the patriarch of the Victorian family who rules his environment, sometimes with a whip. His wife Betty is played in both acts by a man, implying in the Victorian world of act 1 that the British woman was really a male ideal or in fact a male and was expected to act as one, while implying in the contemporary London of act 2 that gender liberation is within the realm of possibility. Act 1 is a study of the world of Victorian sexual repression and the system of gender expectations — the social construction of conventional gender behavior. Such expectations are spoofed by nine-year-old Edward, played by a grown woman, who holds his two-year-old sister's doll for safekeeping. He wants the doll for himself but tells his parents that he is "minding" his sister's doll, not playing with it. His merely holding the doll, however, unsettles his father, who insists that Edward do something more manly, such as riding with Harry Bagley, the mythic adventurer. Harry Bagley turns out to be bisexual and involved with the black servant, who is played by a white actor.

Part of the social comment of act 1 involves a critique of British colonial rule. Joshua, the servant, regards himself as inferior, while Clive, the representative of British authority, comports himself with no thought for the feelings of the "natives." British rule is intentionally oppressive. The sound of native drums implies a threatening "jungle" environment with the potential of an uprising. The situation is self-consciously developed as a cliché in a conventional romantic mode — typical of thrillers of the Victorian period.

But in addition to the play's commentary on the colonial ethos of the British is its critique of Victorian repression. Clive and others are sexually promiscuous. His relationship with Mrs. Saunders is conducted almost farcically. Other characters engage in homosexual relationships in secret. All sexuality is essentially relegated to secret hideaways while on the surface society maintains total conventionality. Churchill includes moments of comic relief, as when Ellen and

Betty are attracted to one another, and Betty instructs her son Edward to go and play with Uncle Harry, whom the audience knows is a pederast. That such sexual relationships occurred in 1870s England we now well know, but the image that survives of the period is one of absolute moral rectitude.

When act 2 introduces us to the sexual mores of 1970s London, it becomes clear that the period's usual reputation for sexual liberation is no more accurate than the official version we have of Victorian England. The portrait of two mothers, Victoria and Lin, introduces us to the modern world. Their children play with guns while Victoria remarks that in Sweden such toys are banned. Lin replies that she will give her daughter, Cathy, a rifle for Christmas with the suggestion that she shoot Victoria's son, Tommy. Victoria hardly hears when Lin says that she is a lesbian and has left her husband or notices her making sexual advances. At the end of the first scene Victoria and Lin may or may not have sex with each other.

Scene 2 reveals a casual sexual encounter between two men, Edward and Gerry, on the train from Victoria to Clapham (two coded destinations that imply the distance from Victorian England to the modern world). Sex is casual, and Martin tells Victoria and Betty that he's ready for almost anything: "Whatever you want to do, I'll be delighted." The comedy reaches an amusing moment at the end of scene 2 when Edward decides he is probably a lesbian because he thinks he likes women more than men.

Scene 3 looks further back into history at ancient cults, many of whose priestesses were interested in unusual sexual relationships. It is as if Churchill were suggesting that the more things change the more they remain the same. In the play the sexual liberation of the 1970s appears to be less radical and novel than it once seemed.

Cloud Nine in Performance

The first production of *Cloud Nine* was in the Dartington College of Arts in February 1979. It quickly went on tour and then to the Royal Court Theatre in London. The earliest versions of the play were revised based on contributions from the director and actors, and Churchill revised the text even after its first publication in 1979. The current version reflects changes made in performance and development until at least 1984.

Although much of the play is serious in tone, most productions have emphasized its burlesque elements. Some productions have approached the drama as if it were farce, creating a broad comic style and producing much laughter. Segments of act 1 have been compared with Monty Python sketches, some of whose purposes may have been similar to Churchill's.

The cross-casting — men playing women, women playing men, and adults playing children — was one of the striking elements of the earliest performances. The first act has been played with pith helmets and other emblems of the British empire. In one version a rhinoceros horn was positioned on the wall in such a way as to appear to be a phallic symbol. The 1979 production in the Royal Court Theatre established the play as a significant part of the modern English repertory.

Eighteen years later, after performances in many countries around the world, Peter Hall included it in a series of seven classic plays at the Old Vic in

London. He felt the play ranked with Shakespeare's *King Lear* and Chekhov's *The Seagull*. Not everyone agreed with him, but the Old Vic production in 1997 demonstrated that the play was still timely and potentially powerful. Theater critic Alastair Macaulay said of the second act: "It is shot through with mystery, it proceeds with dreamlike fluency, and, most beautifully, it allows each character, even while he or she grows more complex and more poignant, to remain an unanswered question."

Caryl Churchill (b. 1938)
CLOUD NINE

1979

Characters

(Act One)

CLIVE, *a colonial administrator*
BETTY, *his wife, played by a man*
JOSHUA, *his black servant, played by a white*
EDWARD, *his son, played by a woman*
VICTORIA, *his daughter, a dummy*
MAUD, *his mother-in-law*
ELLEN, *Edward's governess*
HARRY BAGLEY, *an explorer*
MRS. SAUNDERS, *a widow*

(Act Two)

BETTY
EDWARD, *her son*
VICTORIA, *her daughter*
MARTIN, *Victoria's husband*
LIN
CATHY, *Lin's daughter age 5, played by a man*
GERRY, *Edward's lover*

   (Except for Cathy, characters in Act Two are played by actors of their own sex.)
   (Act One takes place in a British colony in Africa in Victorian times.)
   (Act Two takes place in London in 1979. But for the characters it is twenty-five years later.)

ACT ONE • *Scene One*

(Low bright sun. Verandah. Flagpole with union jack. The Family — Clive, Betty, Edward, Victoria, Maud, Ellen, Joshua.)

ALL *(sing)*: Come gather, sons of England, come gather in your pride.
   Now meet the world united, now face it side by side;

Ye who the earth's wide corners, from veldt to prairie, roam.
   From bush and jungle muster all who call old England "home."
Then gather round for England,
Rally to the flag,
From North and South and East and West
Come one and all for England!
CLIVE: This is my family. Though far from home
   We serve the Queen wherever we may roam
   I am a father to the natives here,
   And father to my family so dear.

(He presents Betty. She is played by a man.)

   My wife is all I dreamt a wife should be,
   And everything she is she owes to me.
BETTY: I live for Clive. The whole aim of my life
   Is to be what he looks for in a wife.
   I am a man's creation as you see,
   And what men want is what I want to be.

(Clive presents Joshua. He is played by a white.)

CLIVE: My boy's a jewel. Really has the knack.
   You'd hardly notice that the fellow's black.
JOSHUA: My skin is black but oh my soul is white.
   I hate my tribe. My master is my light.
   I only live for him. As you can see,
   What white men want is what I want to be.

(Clive presents Edward. He is played by a woman.)

CLIVE: My son is young. I'm doing all I can
   To teach him to grow up to be a man.
EDWARD: What father wants I'd dearly like to be.
   I find it rather hard as you can see.

(Clive presents Victoria, who is a dummy, Maud, and Ellen.)

CLIVE: No need for any speeches by the rest.
   My daughter, mother-in-law, and governess.

ABOVE: The family from act One of Caryl Churchill's *Cloud Nine,* staged at the Old Vic Theatre in London, 1997.
RIGHT: Dominic West as Betty in *Cloud Nine* at the Old Vic Theatre in London, 1997.

ALL (*sing*): O'er countless numbers she, our Queen,
    Victoria reigns supreme;
    O'er Afric's sunny plains, and o'er
    Canadian frozen stream;
    The forge of war shall weld the chains of
       brotherhood secure;
    So to all time in ev'ry clime our Empire shall endure.

    Then gather round for England,
    Rally to the flag,
    From North and South and East and West
    Come one and all for England!

(*All go except Betty. Clive comes.*)

BETTY: Clive?
CLIVE: Betty. Joshua!

(*Joshua comes with a drink for Clive.*)

BETTY: I thought you would never come. The day's so long without you.
CLIVE: Long ride in the bush.
BETTY: Is anything wrong? I heard drums.
CLIVE: Nothing serious. Beauty is a damned good mare. I must get some new boots sent from home. These ones have never been right. I have a blister.

BETTY: My poor dear foot.

CLIVE: It's nothing.

BETTY: Oh but it's sore.

CLIVE: We are not in this country to enjoy ourselves. Must have ridden fifty miles. Spoke to three different headmen who would all gladly chop off each other's heads and wear them round their waists.

BETTY: Clive!

CLIVE: Don't be squeamish, Betty, let me have my joke. And what has my little dove done today?

BETTY: I've read a little.

CLIVE: Good. Is it good?

BETTY: It's poetry.

CLIVE: You're so delicate and sensitive.

BETTY: And I played the piano. Shall I send for the children?

CLIVE: Yes, in a minute. I've a piece of news for you.

BETTY: Good news?

CLIVE: You'll certainly think it's good. A visitor.

BETTY: From home?

CLIVE: No. Well of course originally from home.

BETTY: Man or woman?

CLIVE: Man.

BETTY: I can't imagine.

CLIVE: Something of an explorer. Bit of a poet. Odd chap but brave as a lion. And a great admirer of yours.

BETTY: What do you mean? Whoever can it be?

CLIVE: With an H and a B. And does conjuring tricks for little Edward.

BETTY: That sounds like Mr. Bagley.

CLIVE: Harry Bagley.

BETTY: He certainly doesn't admire me, Clive, what a thing to say. How could I possibly guess from that. He's hardly explored anything at all, he's just been up a river, he's done nothing at all compared to what you do. You should have said a heavy drinker and a bit of a bore.

CLIVE: But you like him well enough. You don't mind him coming?

BETTY: Anyone at all to break the monotony.

CLIVE: But you have your mother. You have Ellen.

BETTY: Ellen is a governess. My mother is my mother.

CLIVE: I hoped when she came to visit she would be company for you.

BETTY: I don't think mother is on a visit. I think she lives with us.

CLIVE: I think she does.

BETTY: Clive you are so good.

CLIVE: But are you bored my love?

BETTY: It's just that I miss you when you're away. We're not in this country to enjoy ourselves. If I lack society that is my form of service.

CLIVE: That's a brave girl. So today has been all right? No fainting? No hysteria?

BETTY: I have been very tranquil.

CLIVE: Ah what a haven of peace to come home to. The coolth, the calm, the beauty.

BETTY: There is one thing, Clive, if you don't mind.

CLIVE: What can I do for you, my dear?

BETTY: It's about Joshua.

CLIVE: I wouldn't leave you alone here with a quiet mind if it weren't for Joshua.

BETTY: Joshua doesn't like me.

CLIVE: Joshua has been my boy for eight years. He has saved my life. I have saved his life. He is devoted to me and to mine. I have said this before.

BETTY: He is rude to me. He doesn't do what I say. Speak to him.

CLIVE: Tell me what happened.

BETTY: He said something improper.

CLIVE: Well, what?

BETTY: I don't like to repeat it.

CLIVE: I must insist.

BETTY: I had left my book inside on the piano. I was in the hammock. I asked him to fetch it.

CLIVE: And did he not fetch it?

BETTY: Yes, he did eventually.

CLIVE: And what did he say?

BETTY: Clive —

CLIVE: Betty.

BETTY: He said Fetch it yourself. You've got legs under that dress.

CLIVE: Joshua!

(*Joshua comes.*)

Joshua, madam says you spoke impolitely to her this afternoon.

JOSHUA: Sir?

CLIVE: When she asked you to pass her book from the piano.

JOSHUA: She has the book, sir.

BETTY: I have the book now, but when I told you —

CLIVE: Betty, please, let me handle this. You didn't pass it at once?

JOSHUA: No sir, I made a joke first.

CLIVE: What was that?

JOSHUA: I said my legs were tired, sir. That was funny because the book was very near, it would not make my legs tired to get it.

BETTY: That's not true.

JOSHUA: Did madam hear me wrong?

CLIVE: She heard something else.

JOSHUA: What was that, madam?

BETTY: Never mind.

CLIVE: Now Joshua, it won't do you know. Madam doesn't like that kind of joke. You must do what madam says, just do what she says and don't answer back. You know your place, Joshua. I don't have to say any more.

JOSHUA: No sir.

BETTY: I expect an apology.

JOSHUA: I apologise, madam.

CLIVE: There now. It won't happen again, my dear. I'm very shocked Joshua, very shocked.

(*Clive winks at Joshua, unseen by Betty. Joshua goes.*)

CLIVE: I think another drink, and send for the children, and isn't that Harry riding down the hill? Wave,

wave. Just in time before dark. Cuts it fine, the blighter. Always a hothead, Harry.

BETTY: Can he see us?

CLIVE: Stand further forward. He'll see your white dress. There, he waved back.

BETTY: Do you think so? I wonder what he saw. Sometimes sunset is so terrifying I can't bear to look.

CLIVE: It makes me proud. Elsewhere in the empire the sun is rising.

BETTY: Harry looks so small on the hillside.

(*Ellen comes.*)

ELLEN: Shall I bring the children?

BETTY: Shall Ellen bring the children?

CLIVE: Delightful.

BETTY: Yes, Ellen, make sure they're warm. The night air is deceptive. Victoria was looking pale yesterday.

CLIVE: My love.

(*Maud comes from inside the house.*)

MAUD: Are you warm enough Betty?

BETTY: Perfectly.

MAUD: The night air is deceptive.

BETTY: I'm quite warm. I'm too warm.

MAUD: You're not getting a fever, I hope? She's not strong, you know, Clive. I don't know how long you'll keep her in this climate.

CLIVE: I look after Her Majesty's domains. I think you can trust me to look after my wife.

(*Ellen comes carrying Victoria, age 2. Edward, aged 9, lags behind.*)

BETTY: Victoria, my pet, say good evening to papa.

(*Clive takes Victoria on his knee.*)

CLIVE: There's my sweet little Vicky. What have we done today?

BETTY: She wore Ellen's hat.

CLIVE: Did she wear Ellen's big hat like a lady? What a pretty.

BETTY: And Joshua gave her a piggy back. Tell papa. Horsy with Joshy?

ELLEN: She's tired.

CLIVE: Nice Joshy played horsy. What a big strong Joshy. Did you have a gallop? Did you make him stop and go? Not very chatty tonight are we?

BETTY: Edward, say good evening to papa.

CLIVE: Edward my boy. Have you done your lessons well?

EDWARD: Yes papa.

CLIVE: Did you go riding?

EDWARD: Yes papa.

CLIVE: What's that you're holding?

BETTY: It's Victoria's doll. What are you doing with it, Edward?

EDWARD: Minding her.

BETTY: Well I should give it to Ellen quickly. You don't want papa to see you with a doll.

CLIVE: No, we had you with Victoria's doll once before, Edward.

ELLEN: He's minding it for Vicky. He's not playing with it.

BETTY: He's not playing with it, Clive. He's minding it for Vicky.

CLIVE: Ellen minds Victoria, let Ellen mind the doll.

ELLEN: Come, give it to me.

(*Ellen takes the doll.*)

EDWARD: Don't pull her about. Vicky's very fond of her. She likes me to have her.

BETTY: He's a very good brother.

CLIVE: Yes, it's manly of you Edward, to take care of your little sister. We'll say no more about it. Tomorrow I'll take you riding with me and Harry Bagley. Would you like that?

EDWARD: Is he here?

CLIVE: He's just arrived. There Betty, take Victoria now. I must go and welcome Harry.

(*Clive tosses Victoria to Betty, who gives her to Ellen.*)

EDWARD: Can I come, papa?

BETTY: Is he warm enough?

EDWARD: Am I warm enough?

CLIVE: Never mind the women, Ned. Come and meet Harry.

(*They go. The women are left. There is a silence.*)

MAUD: I daresay Mr. Bagley will be out all day and we'll see nothing of him.

BETTY: He plays the piano. Surely he will sometimes stay at home with us.

MAUD: We can't expect it. The men have their duties and we have ours.

BETTY: He won't have seen a piano for a year. He lives a very rough life.

ELLEN: Will it be exciting for you, Betty?

MAUD: Whatever do you mean, Ellen?

ELLEN: We don't have very much society.

BETTY: Clive is my society.

MAUD: It's time Victoria went to bed.

ELLEN: She'd like to stay up and see Mr. Bagley.

MAUD: Mr. Bagley can see her tomorrow.

(*Ellen goes.*)

MAUD: You let that girl forget her place, Betty.

BETTY: Mother, she is governess to my son. I know what her place is. I think my friendship does her good. She is not very happy.

MAUD: Young women are never happy.

BETTY: Mother, what a thing to say.

MAUD: Then when they're older they look back and see that comparatively speaking they were ecstatic.

BETTY: I'm perfectly happy.

MAUD: You are looking very pretty tonight. You were such a success as a young girl. You have made a most fortunate marriage. I'm sure you will be an excellent hostess to Mr. Bagley.

BETTY: I feel quite nervous at the thought of entertaining.

MAUD: I can always advise you if I'm asked.

BETTY: What a long time they're taking. I always seem to be waiting for the men.

MAUD: Betty you have to learn to be patient. I am patient. My mama was very patient.

(*Clive approaches, supporting Caroline Saunders.*)

CLIVE: It is a pleasure. It is an honor. It is positively your duty to seek my help. I would be hurt, I would be insulted by any show of independence. Your husband would have been one of my dearest friends if he had lived. Betty, look who has come, Mrs. Saunders. She has ridden here all alone, amazing spirit. What will you have? Tea or something stronger? Let her lie down, she is overcome. Betty, you will know what to do.

(*Mrs. Saunders lies down.*)

MAUD: I knew it. I heard drums. We'll be killed in our beds.

CLIVE: Now, please, calm yourself.

MAUD: I am perfectly calm. I am just outspoken. If it comes to being killed I shall take it as calmly as anyone.

CLIVE: There is no cause for alarm. Mrs. Saunders has been alone since her husband died last year, amazing spirit. Not surprisingly, the strain has told. She has come to us as her nearest neighbors.

MAUD: What happened to make her come?

CLIVE: This is not an easy country for a woman.

MAUD: Clive, I heard drums. We are not children.

CLIVE: Of course you heard drums. The tribes are constantly at war, if the term is not too grand to grace their squabbles. Not unnaturally Mrs. Saunders would like the company of white women. The piano. Poetry.

BETTY: We are not her nearest neighbors.

CLIVE: We are among her nearest neighbors and I was a dear friend of her late husband. She knows that she will find a welcome here. She will not be disappointed. She will be cared for.

MAUD: Of course we will care for her.

BETTY: Victoria is in bed. I must go and say goodnight. Mother, please, you look after Mrs. Saunders.

CLIVE: Harry will be here at once.

(*Betty goes.*)

MAUD: How rash to go out after dark without a shawl.

CLIVE: Amazing spirit. Drink this.

MRS. SAUNDERS: Where am I?

MAUD: You are quite safe.

MRS. SAUNDERS: Clive? Clive? Thank God. This is very kind. How do you do? I am sorry to be a nuisance. Charmed. Have you a gun? I have a gun.

CLIVE: There is no need for guns I hope. We are all friends here.

MRS. SAUNDERS: I think I will lie down again.

(*Harry Bagley and Edward have approached.*)

MAUD: Ah, here is Mr. Bagley.

EDWARD: I gave his horse some water.

CLIVE: You don't know Mrs. Saunders, do you Harry? She has at present collapsed, but she is recovering thanks to the good offices of my wife's mother who I

think you've met before. Betty will be along in a minute. Edward will go home to school shortly. He is quite a young man since you saw him.

HARRY: I hardly knew him.

MAUD: What news have you for us, Mr. Bagley?

CLIVE: Do you know Mrs. Saunders, Harry? Amazing spirit.

EDWARD: Did you hardly know me?

HARRY: Of course I knew you. I mean you have grown.

EDWARD: What do you expect?

HARRY: That's quite right, people don't get smaller.

MAUD: Edward. You should be in bed.

EDWARD: No, I'm not tired, I'm not tired am I Uncle Harry?

HARRY: I don't think he's tired.

CLIVE: He is overtired. It is past his bedtime. Say goodnight.

EDWARD: Goodnight, sir.

CLIVE: And to your grandmother.

EDWARD: Goodnight, grandmother.

(*Edward goes.*)

MAUD: Shall I help Mrs. Saunders indoors? I'm afraid she may get a chill.

CLIVE: Shall I give her an arm?

MAUD: How kind of you Clive. I think I am strong enough.

(*Maud helps Mrs. Saunders into the house.*)

CLIVE: Not a word to alarm the women.

HARRY: Absolutely.

CLIVE: I did some good today I think. Kept up some alliances. There's a lot of affection there.

HARRY: They're affectionate people. They can be very cruel of course.

CLIVE: Well they are savages.

HARRY: Very beautiful people many of them.

CLIVE: Joshua! (*To Harry.*) I think we should sleep with guns.

HARRY: I haven't slept in a house for six months. It seems extremely safe.

(*Joshua comes.*)

CLIVE: Joshua, you will have gathered there's a spot of bother. Rumors of this and that. You should be armed I think.

JOSHUA: There are many bad men, sir. I pray about it. Jesus will protect us.

CLIVE: He will indeed and I'll also get you a weapon. Betty, come and keep Harry company. Look in the barn, Joshua, every night.

(*Clive and Joshua go. Betty comes.*)

HARRY: I wondered where you were.

BETTY: I was singing lullabies.

HARRY: When I think of you I always think of you with Edward in your lap.

BETTY: Do you think of me sometimes then?

HARRY: You have been thought of where no white woman has ever been thought of before.

BETTY: It's one way of having adventures. I suppose I will never go in person.

HARRY: That's up to you.

BETTY: Of course it's not. I have duties.

HARRY: Are you happy, Betty?

BETTY: Where have you been?

HARRY: Built a raft and went up the river. Stayed with some people. The king is always very good to me. They have a lot of skulls around the place but not white men's I think. I made up a poem one night. If I should die in this forsaken spot, There is a loving heart without a blot, Where I will live — and so on.

BETTY: When I'm near you it's like going out into the jungle. It's like going up the river on a raft. It's like going out in the dark.

HARRY: And you are safety and light and peace and home.

BETTY: But I want to be dangerous.

HARRY: Clive is my friend.

BETTY: I am your friend.

HARRY: I don't like dangerous women.

BETTY: Is Mrs. Saunders dangerous?

HARRY: Not to me. She's a bit of an old boot.

(*Joshua comes, unobserved.*)

BETTY: Am I dangerous?

HARRY: You are rather.

BETTY: Please like me.

HARRY: I worship you.

BETTY: Please want me.

HARRY: I don't want to want you. Of course I want you.

BETTY: What are we going to do?

HARRY: I should have stayed on the river. The hell with it.

(*He goes to take her in his arms, she runs away into the house. Harry stays where he is. He becomes aware of Joshua.*)

HARRY: Who's there?

JOSHUA: Only me sir.

HARRY: Got a gun now have you?

JOSHUA: Yes sir.

HARRY: Where's Clive?

JOSHUA: Going round the boundaries sir.

HARRY: Have you checked there's nobody in the barns?

JOSHUA: Yes sir.

HARRY: Shall we go in a barn and fuck? It's not an order.

JOSHUA: That's all right, yes.

(*They go off.*)

Scene Two

(*An open space some distance from the house. Mrs. Saunders alone, breathless. She is carrying a riding crop. Clive arrives.*)

CLIVE: Why? Why?

MRS. SAUNDERS: Don't fuss, Clive, it makes you sweat.

CLIVE: Why ride off now? Sweat, you would sweat if you were in love with somebody as disgustingly capricious as you are. You will be shot with poisoned arrows. You will miss the picnic. Somebody will notice I came after you.

MRS. SAUNDERS: I didn't want you to come after me. I wanted to be alone.

CLIVE: You will be raped by cannibals.

MRS. SAUNDERS: I just wanted to get out of your house.

CLIVE: My God, what women put us through. Cruel, cruel. I think you are the sort of woman who would enjoy whipping somebody. I've never met one before.

MRS. SAUNDERS: Can I tell you something, Clive?

CLIVE: Let me tell you something first. Since you came to the house I have had an erection twenty-four hours a day except for ten minutes after the time we had intercourse.

MRS. SAUNDERS: I don't think that's physically possible.

CLIVE: You are causing me appalling physical suffering. Is this the way to treat a benefactor?

MRS. SAUNDERS: Clive, when I came to your house the other night I came because I was afraid. The cook was going to let his whole tribe in through the window.

CLIVE: I know that, my poor sweet. Amazing —

MRS. SAUNDERS: I came to you although you are not my nearest neighbor —

CLIVE: Rather than to the old major of seventy-two.

MRS. SAUNDERS: Because the last time he came to visit me I had to defend myself with a shotgun and I thought you would take no for an answer.

CLIVE: But you've already answered yes.

MRS. SAUNDERS: I answered yes once. Sometimes I want to say no.

CLIVE: Women, my God. Look the picnic will start, I have to go to the picnic. Please Caroline —

MRS. SAUNDERS: I think I will have to go back to my own house.

CLIVE: Caroline, if you were shot with poisoned arrows do you know what I'd do? I'd fuck your dead body and poison myself. Caroline, you smell amazing. You terrify me. You are dark like this continent. Mysterious. Treacherous. When you rode to me through the night. When you fainted in my arms. When I came to you in your bed, when I lifted the mosquito netting, when I said let me in, let me in. Oh don't shut me out, Caroline, let me in.

(*He has been caressing her feet and legs. He disappears completely under her skirt.*)

MRS. SAUNDERS: Please stop. I can't concentrate. I want to go home. I wish I didn't enjoy the sensation because I don't like you, Clive. I do like living in your house where there's plenty of guns. But I don't like you at all. But I do like the sensation. Well I'll have it then. I'll have it, I'll have it —

(*Voices are heard singing* The First Noël.)

Don't stop. Don't stop.

(*Clive comes out from under her skirt.*)

CLIVE: The Christmas picnic. I came.

MRS. SAUNDERS: I didn't.

CLIVE: I'm all sticky.

MRS. SAUNDERS: What about me? Wait.

CLIVE: All right, are you? Come on. We mustn't be found.

MRS. SAUNDERS: Don't go now.

CLIVE: Caroline, you are so voracious. Do let go. Tidy yourself up. There's a hair in my mouth.

(*Clive and Mrs. Saunders go off. Betty and Maud come, with Joshua carrying hamper.*)

MAUD: I never would have thought a guinea fowl could taste so like a turkey.

BETTY: I had to explain to the cook three times.

MAUD: You did very well dear.

(*Joshua sits apart with gun. Edward and Harry with Victoria on his shoulder, singing* The First Noël. *Maud and Betty are unpacking the hamper. Clive arrives separately.*)

MAUD: This tablecloth was one of my mama's.

BETTY: Uncle Harry playing horsy.

EDWARD: Crackers crackers.

BETTY: Not yet, Edward.

CLIVE: And now the moment we have all been waiting for.

(*Clive opens champagne. General acclaim.*)

CLIVE: Oh dear, stained my trousers, never mind.

EDWARD: Can I have some?

MAUD: Oh no Edward, not for you.

CLIVE: Give him half a glass.

MAUD: If your father says so.

CLIVE: All rise please. To Her Majesty Queen Victoria, God bless her, and her husband and all her dear children.

ALL: The Queen.

EDWARD: Crackers crackers.

(*General cracker pulling, hats. Clive and Harry discuss champagne.*)

HARRY: Excellent, Clive, wherever did you get it?

CLIVE: I know a chap in French Equatorial Africa.

EDWARD: I won, I won mama.

(*Ellen arrives.*)

BETTY: Give a hat to Joshua, he'd like it.

(*Edward takes hat to Joshua. Betty takes a ball from the hamper and plays catch with Ellen. Murmurs of surprise and congratulations from the men whenever they catch the ball.*)

EDWARD: Mama, don't play. You know you can't catch a ball.

BETTY: He's perfectly right. I can't throw either.

(*Betty sits down. Ellen has the ball.*)

EDWARD: Ellen, don't you play either. You're no good. You spoil it.

(*Edward takes Victoria from Harry and gives her to Ellen. He takes the ball and throws it to Harry. Harry, Clive, and Edward play ball.*)

BETTY: Ellen come and sit with me. We'll be spectators and clap.

(*Edward misses the ball.*)

CLIVE: Butterfingers.

EDWARD: I'm not.

HARRY: Throw straight now.

EDWARD: I did, I did.

CLIVE: Keep your eye on the ball.

EDWARD: You can't throw.

CLIVE: Don't be a baby.

EDWARD: I'm not, throw a hard one, throw a hard one —

CLIVE: Butterfingers. What will Uncle Harry think of you?

EDWARD: It's your fault. You can't throw. I hate you.

(*He throws the ball wildly in the direction of Joshua.*)

CLIVE: Now you've lost the ball. He's lost the ball.

EDWARD: It's Joshua's fault. Joshua's butterfingers.

CLIVE: I don't think I want to play any more. Joshua, find the ball will you?

EDWARD: Yes, please play. I'll find the ball. Please play.

CLIVE: You're so silly and you can't catch. You'll be no good at cricket.

MAUD: Why don't we play hide and seek?

EDWARD: Because it's a baby game.

BETTY: You've hurt Edward's feelings.

CLIVE: A boy has no business having feelings.

HARRY: Hide and seek. I'll be it. Everybody must hide. This is the base, you have to get home to base.

EDWARD: Hide and seek, hide and seek.

HARRY: Can we persuade the ladies to join us?

MAUD: I'm playing. I love games.

BETTY: I always get found straight away.

ELLEN: Come on, Betty, do. Vicky wants to play.

EDWARD: You won't find me ever.

(*They all go except Clive, Harry, Joshua.*)

HARRY: It is safe, I suppose?

CLIVE: They won't go far. This is very much my territory and it's broad daylight. Joshua will keep an open eye.

HARRY: Well I must give them a hundred. You don't know what this means to me, Clive. A chap can only go on so long alone. I can climb mountains and go down rivers, but what's it for? For Christmas and England and games and women singing. This is the empire, Clive. It's not me putting a flag in new lands. It's you. The empire is one big family. I'm one of its black sheep, Clive. And I know you think my life is rather dashing. But I want you to know I admire you. This is the empire, Clive, and I serve it. With all my heart.

CLIVE: I think that's about a hundred.

HARRY: Ready or not, here I come!

(*He goes.*)

CLIVE: Harry Bagley is a fine man, Joshua. You should be proud to know him. He will be in history books.

JOSHUA: Sir, while we are alone.

CLIVE: Joshua of course, what is it? You always have my ear. Any time.

JOSHUA: Sir, I have some information. The stable boys are not to be trusted. They whisper. They go out at night. They visit their people. Their people are not my people. I do not visit my people.

CLIVE: Thank you, Joshua. They certainly look after Beauty. I'll be sorry to have to replace them.

JOSHUA: They carry knives.

CLIVE: Thank you, Joshua.

JOSHUA: And, sir.

CLIVE: I appreciate this, Joshua, very much.

JOSHUA: Your wife.

CLIVE: Ah, yes?

JOSHUA: She also thinks Harry Bagley is a fine man.

CLIVE: Thank you, Joshua.

JOSHUA: Are you going to hide?

CLIVE: Yes, yes I am. Thank you. Keep your eyes open Joshua.

JOSHUA: I do, sir.

(*Clive goes. Joshua goes. Harry and Betty race back to base.*)

BETTY: I can't run, I can't run at all.

HARRY: There, I've caught you.

BETTY: Harry, what are we going to do?

HARRY: It's impossible, Betty.

BETTY: Shall we run away together?

(*Maud comes.*)

MAUD: I give up. Don't catch me. I have been stung.

HARRY: Nothing serious I hope.

MAUD: I have ointment in my bag. I always carry ointment. I shall just sit down and rest. I am too old for all this fun. Hadn't you better be seeking, Harry?

(*Harry goes. Maud and Betty are alone for some time. They don't speak. Harry and Edward race back.*)

EDWARD: I won, I won, you didn't catch me.

HARRY: Yes I did.

EDWARD: Mama, who was first?

BETTY: I wasn't watching. I think it was Harry.

EDWARD: It wasn't Harry. You're no good at judging. I won, didn't I grandma?

MAUD: I expect so, since it's Christmas.

EDWARD: I won, Uncle Harry. I'm better than you.

BETTY: Why don't you help Uncle Harry look for the others?

EDWARD: Shall I?

HARRY: Yes, of course.

BETTY: Run along then. He's just coming.

(*Edward goes.*)

Harry, I shall scream.

HARRY: Ready or not, here I come.

(*Harry runs off.*)

BETTY: Why don't you go back to the house, mother, and rest your insect-bite?

MAUD: Betty, my duty is here. I don't like what I see. Clive wouldn't like it, Betty. I am your mother.

BETTY: Clive gives you a home because you are my mother.

(*Harry comes back.*)

HARRY: I can't find anyone else. I'm getting quite hot.

BETTY: Sit down a minute.

HARRY: I can't do that. I'm he. How's your sting?

MAUD: It seems to be swelling up.

BETTY: Why don't you go home and rest? Joshua will go with you. Joshua!

HARRY: I could take you back.

MAUD: That would be charming.

BETTY: You can't go. You're he.

(*Joshua comes.*)

BETTY: Joshua, my mother wants to go back to the house. Will you go with her please.

JOSHUA: Sir told me I have to keep an eye.

BETTY: I am telling you to go back to the house. Then you can come back here and keep an eye.

MAUD: Thank you Betty. I know we have our little differences, but I always want what is best for you.

(*Joshua and Maud go.*)

HARRY: Don't give way. Keep calm.

BETTY: I shall kill myself.

HARRY: Betty, you are a star in my sky. Without you I would have no sense of direction. I need you, and I need you where you are, I need you to be Clive's wife. I need to go up rivers and know you are sitting here thinking of me.

BETTY: I want more than that. Is that wicked of me?

HARRY: Not wicked, Betty. Silly.

(*Edward calls in the distance.*)

EDWARD: Uncle Harry, where are you?

BETTY: Can't we ever be alone?

HARRY: You are a mother. And a daughter. And a wife.

BETTY: I think I shall go and hide again.

(*Betty goes. Harry goes. Clive chases Mrs. Saunders across the stage. Edward and Harry call in the distance.*)

EDWARD: Uncle Harry!

HARRY: Edward!

(*Edward comes.*)

EDWARD: Uncle Harry!

(*Harry comes.*)

There you are. I haven't found anyone have you?

HARRY: I wonder where they all are.

EDWARD: Perhaps they're lost forever. Perhaps they're dead. There's trouble going on isn't there, and nobody says because of not frightening the women and children.

HARRY: Yes, that's right.

EDWARD: Do you think we'll be killed in our beds?

HARRY: Not very likely.

EDWARD: I can't sleep at night. Can you?

HARRY: I'm not used to sleeping in a house.

EDWARD: If I'm awake at night can I come and see you? I won't wake you up. I'll only come in if you're awake.

HARRY: You should try to sleep.

EDWARD: I don't mind being awake because I make up adventures. Once we were on a raft going down to the rapids. We've lost the paddles because we used them to fight off the crocodiles. A crocodile comes at me and I stab it again and again and the blood is everywhere and it tips up the raft and it has you by the leg and it's biting your leg right off and I take my knife and stab it in the throat and rip open its stomach and it lets go of you but it bites my hand but it's dead. And I drag you onto the river bank and I'm almost fainting with pain and we lie there in each other's arms.

HARRY: Have I lost my leg?

EDWARD: I forgot about the leg by then.

HARRY: Hadn't we better look for the others?

EDWARD: Wait. I've got something for you. It was in mama's box but she never wears it.

(*Edward gives Harry a necklace.*)

You don't have to wear it either but you might like it to look at.

HARRY: It's beautiful. But you'll have to put it back.

EDWARD: I wanted to give it to you.

HARRY: You did. It can go back in the box. You still gave it to me. Come on now, we have to find the others.

EDWARD: Harry, I love you.

HARRY: Yes I know. I love you too.

EDWARD: You know what we did when you were here before. I want to do it again. I think about it all the time. I try to do it to myself but it's not as good. Don't you want to any more?

HARRY: I do, but it's a sin and a crime and it's also wrong.

EDWARD: But we'll do it anyway won't we?

HARRY: Yes of course.

EDWARD: I wish the others would all be killed. Take it out now and let me see it.

HARRY: No.

EDWARD: Is it big now?

HARRY: Yes.

EDWARD: Let me touch it.

HARRY: No.

EDWARD: Just hold me.

HARRY: When you can't sleep.

EDWARD: We'd better find the others then. Come on.

HARRY: Ready or not, here we come.

(*They go out with whoops and shouts. Betty and Ellen come.*)

BETTY: Ellen, I don't want to play any more.

ELLEN: Nor do I, Betty.

BETTY: Come and sit here with me. Oh Ellen, what will become of me?

ELLEN: Betty, are you crying? Are you laughing?

BETTY: Tell me what you think of Harry Bagley.

ELLEN: He's a very fine man.

BETTY: No, Ellen, what you really think.

ELLEN: I think you think he's very handsome.

BETTY: And don't you think he is? Oh Ellen, you're so good and I'm so wicked.

ELLEN: I'm not so good as you think.

(*Edward comes.*)

EDWARD: I've found you.

ELLEN: We're not hiding Edward.

EDWARD: But I found you.

ELLEN: We're not playing, Edward, now run along.

EDWARD: Come on, Ellen, do play. Come on, mama.

ELLEN: Edward, don't pull your mama like that.

BETTY: Edward, you must do what your governess says. Go and play with Uncle Harry.

EDWARD: Uncle Harry!

(*Edward goes.*)

BETTY: Ellen, can you keep a secret?

ELLEN: Oh yes, yes please.

BETTY: I love Harry Bagley. I want to go away with him. There, I've said it, it's true.

ELLEN: How do you know you love him?

BETTY: I kissed him.

ELLEN: Betty.

BETTY: He held my hand like this. Oh I want him to do it again. I want him to stroke my hair.

ELLEN: Your lovely hair. Like this, Betty?

BETTY: I want him to put his arm around my waist.

ELLEN: Like this, Betty?

BETTY: Yes, oh I want him to kiss me again.

ELLEN: Like this Betty?

(*Ellen kisses Betty.*)

BETTY: Ellen, whatever are you doing? It's not a joke.

ELLEN: I'm sorry, Betty. You're so pretty. Harry Bagley doesn't deserve you. You wouldn't really go away with him?

BETTY: Oh Ellen, you don't know what I suffer. You don't know what love is. Everyone will hate me, but it's worth it for Harry's love.

ELLEN: I don't hate you, Betty, I love you.

BETTY: Harry says we shouldn't go away. But he says he worships me.

ELLEN: I worship you Betty.

BETTY: Oh Ellen, you are my only friend.

(*They embrace. The others have all gathered together. Maud has rejoined the party, and Joshua.*)

CLIVE: Come along everyone, you mustn't miss Harry's conjuring trick.

(*Betty and Ellen go to join the others.*)

MAUD: I didn't want to spoil the fun by not being here.

HARRY: What is it that flies all over the world and is up my sleeve?

(*Harry produces a union jack from up his sleeve. General acclaim.*)

CLIVE: I think we should have some singing now. Ladies, I rely on you to lead the way.

ELLEN: We have a surprise for you. I have taught Joshua a Christmas carol. He has been singing it at the piano but I'm sure he can sing it unaccompanied, can't you, Joshua?

JOSHUA: In the deep midwinter
  Frosty wind made moan,
  Earth stood hard as iron,
  Water like a stone.
  Snow had fallen snow on snow
  Snow on snow,
  In the deep midwinter
  Long long ago.

  What can I give him
  Poor as I am?
  If I were a shepherd
  I would bring a lamb.
  If I were a wise man
  I would do my part
  What I can I give him,
  Give my heart.

Scene Three

(*Inside the house. Betty, Mrs. Saunders, Maud with Victoria. The blinds are down so the light isn't bright though it is day outside. Clive looks in.*)

CLIVE: Everything all right? Nothing to be frightened of.
                    (*Clive goes. Silence.*)

MAUD: Clap hands, daddy comes, with his pockets full of plums. All for Vicky.

(*Silence.*)

MRS. SAUNDERS: Who actually does the flogging?

MAUD: I don't think we want to imagine.

MRS. SAUNDERS: I imagine Joshua.

BETTY: Yes I think it would be Joshua. Or would Clive do it himself?

MRS. SAUNDERS: Well we can ask them afterwards.

MAUD: I don't like the way you speak of it, Mrs. Saunders.

MRS. SAUNDERS: How should I speak of it?

MAUD: The men will do it in the proper way, whatever it is. We have our own part to play.

MRS. SAUNDERS: Harry Bagley says they should just be sent away. I don't think he likes to see them beaten.

BETTY: Harry is so tender hearted. Perhaps he is right.

MAUD: Harry Bagley is not altogether — He has lived in this country a long time without any responsibilities. It is part of his charm but it hasn't improved his judg-

ment. If the boys were just sent away they would go back to the village and make more trouble.

MRS. SAUNDERS: And what will they say about us in the village if they've been flogged?

BETTY: Perhaps Clive should keep them here.

MRS. SAUNDERS: That is never wise.

BETTY: Whatever shall we do?

MAUD: I don't think it is up to us to wonder. The men don't tell us what is going on among the tribes, so how can we possibly make a judgment?

MRS. SAUNDERS: I know a little of what is going on.

BETTY: Tell me what you know. Clive tells me nothing.

MAUD: You would not want to be told about it, Betty. It is enough for you that Clive knows what is happening. Clive will know what to do. Your father always knew what to do.

BETTY: Are you saying you would do something different, Caroline?

MRS. SAUNDERS: I would do what I did at my own home. I left. I can't see any way out except to leave. I will leave here. I will keep leaving everywhere I suppose.

MAUD: Luckily this household has a head. I am squeamish myself. But luckily Clive is not.

BETTY: You are leaving here then, Caroline?

MRS. SAUNDERS: Not immediately. I'm sorry.

(*Silence.*)

MRS. SAUNDERS: I wonder if it's over.

(*Edward comes in.*)

BETTY: Shouldn't you be with the men, Edward?

EDWARD: I didn't want to see any more. They got what they deserved. Uncle Harry said I could come in.

MRS. SAUNDERS: I never allowed the servants to be beaten in my own house. I'm going to find out what's happening.

                    (*Mrs. Saunders goes out.*)

BETTY: Will she go and look?

MAUD: Let Mrs. Saunders be a warning to you, Betty. She is alone in the world. You are not, thank God. Since your father died, I know what it is to be unprotected. Vicky is such a pretty little girl. Clap hands, daddy comes, with his pockets full of plums. All for Vicky.

(*Edward, meanwhile, has found the doll and is playing clap hands with her.*)

BETTY: Edward, what have you got there?

EDWARD: I'm minding her.

BETTY: Edward, I've told you before, dolls are for girls.

MAUD: Where is Ellen? She should be looking after Edward. (*She goes to the door.*) Ellen! Betty, why do you let that girl mope about in her own room? That's not what she's come to Africa for.

BETTY: You must never let the boys at school know you like dolls. Never, never. No one will talk to you, you won't be on the cricket team, you won't grow up to be a man like your papa.

EDWARD: I don't want to be like papa. I hate papa.

MAUD: Edward! Edward!

BETTY: You're a horrid wicked boy and papa will beat you. Of course you don't hate him, you love him. Now give Victoria her doll at once.

EDWARD: She's not Victoria's doll, she's my doll. She doesn't love Victoria and Victoria doesn't love her. Victoria never even plays with her.

MAUD: Victoria will learn to play with her.

EDWARD: She's mine and she loves me and she won't be happy if you take her away, she'll cry, she'll cry, she'll cry.

(*Betty takes the doll away, slaps him, bursts into tears. Ellen comes in.*)

BETTY: Ellen, look what you've done. Edward's got the doll again. Now, Ellen, will you please do your job.

ELLEN: Edward, you are a wicked boy. I am going to lock you in the nursery until supper time. Now go upstairs this minute.

(*She slaps Edward, who bursts into tears and goes out.*)

I do try to do what you want. I'm so sorry.

(*Ellen bursts into tears and goes out.*)

MAUD: There now, Vicky's got her baby back. Where did Vicky's naughty baby go? Shall we smack her? Just a little smack. (*Maud smacks the doll hard.*) There, now she's a good baby. Clap hands, daddy comes, with his pockets full of plums. All for Vicky's baby. When I was a child we honored our parents. My mama was an angel.

(*Joshua comes in. He stands without speaking.*)

BETTY: Joshua?

JOSHUA: Madam?

BETTY: Did you want something?

JOSHUA: Sent to see the ladies are all right, madam.

(*Mrs. Saunders comes in.*)

MRS. SAUNDERS: We're very well thank you, Joshua, and how are you?

JOSHUA: Very well thank you, Mrs. Saunders.

MRS. SAUNDERS: And the stable boys?

JOSHUA: They have had justice, madam.

MRS. SAUNDERS: So I saw. And does your arm ache?

MAUD: This is not a proper conversation, Mrs. Saunders.

MRS. SAUNDERS: You don't mind beating your own people?

JOSHUA: Not my people, madam.

MRS. SAUNDERS: A different tribe?

JOSHUA: Bad people.

(*Harry and Clive come in.*)

CLIVE: Well this is all very gloomy and solemn. Can we have the shutters open? The heat of the day has gone, we could have some light, I think. And cool drinks on the verandah, Joshua. Have some lemonade yourself. It is most refreshing.

(*Sunlight floods in as the shutters are opened. Edward comes.*)

EDWARD: Papa, papa, Ellen tried to lock me in the nursery. Mama is going to tell you of me. I'd rather tell you myself. I was playing with Vicky's doll again and I know it's very bad of me. And I said I didn't want to be like you and I said I hated you. And it's not true and I'm sorry, I'm sorry and please beat me and forgive me.

CLIVE: Well there's a brave boy to own up. You should always respect and love me, Edward, not for myself, I may not deserve it, but as I respected and loved my own father, because he was my father. Through our father we love our Queen and our God, Edward. Do you understand? It is something men understand.

EDWARD: Yes papa.

CLIVE: Then I forgive you and shake you by the hand. You spend too much time with the women. You may spend more time with me and Uncle Harry, little man.

EDWARD: I don't like women. I don't like dolls. I love you, papa, and I love you, Uncle Harry.

CLIVE: There's a fine fellow. Let us go out onto the verandah.

(*They all start to go. Edward takes Harry's hand and goes with him. Clive draws Betty back. They embrace.*)

BETTY: Poor Clive.

CLIVE: It was my duty to have them flogged. For you and Edward and Victoria, to keep you safe.

BETTY: It is terrible to feel betrayed.

CLIVE: You can tame a wild animal only so far. They revert to their true nature and savage your hand. Sometimes I feel the natives are the enemy. I know that is wrong. I know I have a responsibility towards them, to care for them and bring them all to be like Joshua. But there is something dangerous. Implacable. This whole continent is my enemy. I am pitching my whole mind and will and reason and spirit against it to tame it, and I sometimes feel it will break over me and swallow me up.

BETTY: Clive, Clive, I am here. I have faith in you.

CLIVE: Yes, I can show you my moments of weakness, Betty, because you are my wife and because I trust you. I trust you, Betty, and it would break my heart if you did not deserve that trust. Harry Bagley is my friend. It would break my heart if he did not deserve my trust.

BETTY: I'm sorry, I'm sorry. Forgive me. It is not Harry's fault, it is all mine. Harry is noble. He has rejected me. It is my wickedness, I get bored, I get restless, I imagine things. There is something so wicked in me, Clive.

CLIVE: I have never thought of you having the weakness of your sex, only the good qualities.

BETTY: I am bad, bad, bad —

CLIVE: You are thoughtless, Betty, that's all. Women can be treacherous and evil. They are darker and more dangerous than men. The family protects us from that, you protect me from that. You are not that sort of woman. You are not unfaithful to me, Betty. I can't believe you are. It would hurt me so much to cast you off. That would be my duty.

BETTY: No, no, no.

CLIVE: Joshua has seen you kissing.

BETTY: Forgive me.

CLIVE: But I don't want to know about it. I don't want to know. I wonder of course, I wonder constantly. If Harry Bagley was not my friend I would shoot him. If I shot you every British man and woman would applaud me. But no. It was a moment of passion such as women are too weak to resist. But you must resist it, Betty, or it will destroy us. We must fight against it. We must resist this dark female lust, Betty, or it will swallow us up.

BETTY: I do, I do resist. Help me. Forgive me.

CLIVE: Yes I do forgive you. But I can't feel the same about you as I did. You are still my wife and we still have duties to the household.

(*They go out arm in arm. As soon as they have gone Edward sneaks back to get the doll, which has been dropped on the floor. He picks it up and comforts it. Joshua comes through with a tray of drinks.*)

JOSHUA: Baby. Sissy. Girly.

(*Joshua goes. Betty calls from off.*)

BETTY: Edward?

(*Betty comes in.*)

BETTY: There you are, my darling. Come, papa wants us all to be together. Uncle Harry is going to tell how he caught a crocodile. Mama's sorry she smacked you.

(*They embrace. Joshua comes in again, passing through.*)

BETTY: Joshua, fetch me some blue thread from my sewing box. It is on the piano.

JOSHUA: You've got legs under that skirt.

BETTY: Joshua.

JOSHUA: And more than legs.

BETTY: Edward, are you going to stand there and let a servant insult your mother?

EDWARD: Joshua, get my mother's thread.

JOSHUA: Oh little Eddy, playing at master. It's only a joke.

EDWARD: Don't speak to my mother like that again.

JOSHUA: Ladies have no sense of humor. You like a joke with Joshua.

EDWARD: You fetch her sewing at once, do you hear me? You move when I speak to you, boy.

JOSHUA: Yes sir, master Edward sir.

(*Joshua goes.*)

BETTY: Edward, you were wonderful.

(*She goes to embrace him but he moves away.*)

EDWARD: Don't touch me.

SONG ("*A Boy's Best Friend*"— ALL): While plodding on our way, the toilsome road of life,
How few the friends that daily there we meet.
Not many will stand in trouble and in strife,
With counsel and affection ever sweet.
But there is one whose smile will ever on us beam,
Whose love is dearer far than any other;
And wherever we may turn
This lesson we will learn
A boy's best friend is his mother.

Then cherish her with care
And smooth her silv'ry hair,
When gone you will never get another.
And wherever we may turn
This lesson we shall learn,
A boy's best friend is his mother.

Scene Four

The verandah as in Scene One. Early morning. Nobody there. Joshua comes out of the house slowly and stands for some time doing nothing. Edward comes out.

EDWARD: Tell me another bad story, Joshua. Nobody else is even awake yet.

JOSHUA: First there was nothing and then there was the great goddess. She was very large and she had golden eyes and she made the stars and the sun and the earth. But soon she was miserable and lonely and she cried like a great waterfall and her tears made all the rivers in the world. So the great spirit sent a terrible monster, a tree with hundreds of eyes and a long green tongue, and it came chasing after her and she jumped into a lake and the tree jumped in after her, and she jumped right up into the sky. And the tree couldn't follow, he was stuck in the mud. So he picked up a big handful of mud and he threw it at her, up among the stars, and hit her on the head. And she fell down onto the earth into his arms and the ball of mud is the moon in the sky. And then they had children which is all of us.

EDWARD: It's not true, though.

JOSHUA: Of course it's not true. It's a bad story. Adam and Eve is true. God made man white like him and gave him the bad woman who liked the snake and gave us all this trouble.

(*Clive and Harry come out.*)

CLIVE: Run along now, Edward. No, you may stay. You mustn't repeat anything you hear to your mother or your grandmother or Ellen.

EDWARD: Or Mrs. Saunders?

CLIVE: Mrs. Saunders is an unusual woman and does not require protection in the same way. Harry, there was trouble last night where we expected it. But it's all over now. Everything is under control but nobody should leave the house today I think.

HARRY: Casualties?

CLIVE: No, none of the soldiers hurt thank God. We did a certain amount of damage, set a village on fire and so forth.

HARRY: Was that necessary?

CLIVE: Obviously, it was necessary, Harry, or it wouldn't have happened. The army will come and visit, no doubt. You'll like that, eh, Joshua, to see the British army? And a treat for you, Edward, to see the soldiers. Would you like to be a soldier?

EDWARD: I'd rather be an explorer.

CLIVE: Ah, Harry, like you, you see. I didn't know an explorer at his age. Breakfast, I think, Joshua.

(*Clive and Joshua go in. Harry is following.*)

EDWARD: Uncle.

(*Harry stops.*)

EDWARD: Harry, why won't you talk to me?

HARRY: Of course I'll talk to you.

EDWARD: If you won't be nice to me I'll tell father.

HARRY: Edward, no, not a word, never, not to your mother, nobody, please. Edward, do you understand? Please.

EDWARD: I won't tell. I promise I'll never tell. I've cut my finger and sworn.

HARRY: There's no need to get so excited Edward. We can't be together all the time. I will have to leave soon anyway, and go back to the river.

EDWARD: You can't, you can't go. Take me with you.

ELLEN: Edward!

HARRY: I have my duty to the Empire.

(*Harry goes in. Ellen comes out.*)

ELLEN: Edward, breakfast time. Edward.

EDWARD: I'm not hungry.

ELLEN: Betty, please come and speak to Edward.

(*Betty comes.*)

BETTY: Why what's the matter?

ELLEN: He won't come in for breakfast.

BETTY: Edward, I shall call your father.

EDWARD: You can't make me eat.

(*He goes in. Betty is about to follow.*)

ELLEN: Betty.

(*Betty stops.*)

ELLEN: Betty, when Edward goes to school will I have to leave?

BETTY: Never mind, Ellen dear, you'll get another place. I'll give you an excellent reference.

ELLEN: I don't want another place, Betty. I want to stay with you forever.

BETTY: If you go back to England you might get married, Ellen. You're quite pretty, you shouldn't despair of getting a husband.

ELLEN: I don't want a husband. I want you.

BETTY: Children of your own, Ellen, think.

ELLEN: I don't want children, I don't like children. I just want to be alone with you, Betty, and sing for you and kiss you because I love you, Betty.

BETTY: I love you too, Ellen. But women have their duty as soldiers have. You must be a mother if you can.

ELLEN: Betty, Betty, I love you so much. I want to stay with you forever, my love for you is eternal, stronger than death. I'd rather die than leave you, Betty.

BETTY: No you wouldn't, Ellen, don't be silly. Come, don't cry. You don't feel what you think you do. It's the loneliness here and the climate is very confusing. Come and have breakfast, Ellen dear, and I'll forget all about it.

(*Ellen goes, Clive comes.*)

BETTY: Clive, please forgive me.

CLIVE: Will you leave me alone?

(*Betty goes back into the house. Harry comes.*)

CLIVE: Women, Harry. I envy you going into the jungle, a man's life.

HARRY: I envy you.

CLIVE: Harry, I know you do. I have spoken to Betty.

HARRY: I assure you, Clive —

CLIVE: Please say nothing about it.

HARRY: My friendship for you —

CLIVE: Absolutely. I know the friendship between us, Harry, is not something that could be spoiled by the weaker sex. Friendship between men is a fine thing. It is the noblest form of relationship.

HARRY: I agree with you.

CLIVE: There is the necessity of reproduction. The family is all important. And there is the pleasure. But what we put ourselves through to get that pleasure, Harry. When I heard about our fine fellows last night fighting those savages to protect us I thought yes, that is what I aspire to. I tell you Harry, in confidence, I suddenly got out of Mrs. Saunders' bed and came out here on the verandah and looked at the stars.

HARRY: I couldn't sleep last night either.

CLIVE: There is something dark about women, that threatens what is best in us. Between men that light burns brightly.

HARRY: I didn't know you felt like that.

CLIVE: Women are irrational, demanding, inconsistent, treacherous, lustful, and they smell different from us.

HARRY: Clive —

CLIVE: Think of the comradeship of men, Harry, sharing adventures, sharing danger, risking their lives together.

(*Harry takes hold of Clive.*)

CLIVE: What are you doing?

HARRY: Well, you said —

CLIVE: I said what?

HARRY: Between men.

(*Clive is speechless.*)

I'm sorry, I misunderstood, I would never have dreamt, I thought —

CLIVE: My God, Harry, how disgusting.

HARRY: You will not betray my confidence.

CLIVE: I feel contaminated.

HARRY: I struggle against it. You cannot imagine the shame. I have tried everything to save myself.

CLIVE: The most revolting perversion. Rome fell, Harry, and this sin can destroy an empire.

HARRY: It is not a sin, it is a disease.

CLIVE: A disease more dangerous than diphtheria. Effeminacy is contagious. How I have been deceived. Your face does not look degenerate. Oh Harry, how did you sink to this?

HARRY: Clive, help me, what am I to do?

CLIVE: You have been away from England too long.

HARRY: Where can I go except into the jungle to hide?

CLIVE: You don't do it with the natives, Harry? My God, what a betrayal of the Queen.

HARRY: Clive, I am like a man born crippled. Please help me.

CLIVE: You must repent.

HARRY: I have thought of killing myself.

CLIVE: That is a sin too.

HARRY: There is no way out. Clive, I beg of you, do not betray my confidence.

CLIVE: I cannot keep a secret like this. Rivers will be named after you, it's unthinkable. You must save yourself from depravity. You must get married. You are not unattractive to women. What a relief that you and Betty were not after all — good God, how disgusting. Now Mrs. Saunders. She's a woman of spirit, she could go with you on your expeditions.

HARRY: I suppose getting married wouldn't be any worse than killing myself.

CLIVE: Mrs. Saunders! Mrs. Saunders! Ask her now, Harry. Think of England.

(*Mrs. Saunders comes. Clive withdraws. Harry goes up to Mrs. Saunders.*)

HARRY: Mrs. Saunders, will you marry me?

MRS. SAUNDERS: Why?

HARRY: We are both alone.

MRS. SAUNDERS: I choose to be alone, Mr. Bagley. If I can look after myself, I'm sure you can. Clive, I have something important to tell you. I've just found Joshua putting earth on his head. He tells me his parents were killed last night by the British soldiers. I think you owe him an apology on behalf of the Queen.

CLIVE: Joshua! Joshua!

MRS. SAUNDERS: Mr. Bagley, I could never be a wife again. There is only one thing about marriage that I like.

(*Joshua comes.*)

CLIVE: Joshua, I am horrified to hear what has happened. Good God!

MRS. SAUNDERS: His father was shot. His mother died in the blaze.

(*Mrs. Saunders goes.*)

CLIVE: Joshua, do you want a day off? Do you want to go to your people?

JOSHUA: Not my people, sir.

CLIVE: But you want to go to your parents' funeral?

JOSHUA: No sir.

CLIVE: Yes, Joshua, yes, your father and mother. I'm sure they were loyal to the crown. I'm sure it was all a terrible mistake.

JOSHUA: My mother and father were bad people.

CLIVE: Joshua, no.

JOSHUA: You are my father and mother.

CLIVE: Well really. I don't know what to say. That's very decent of you. Are you sure there's nothing I can do? You can have the day off you know.

(*Betty comes out followed by Edward.*)

BETTY: What's the matter? What's happening?

CLIVE: Something terrible has happened. No, I mean some relatives of Joshua's met with an accident.

JOSHUA: May I go sir?

CLIVE: Yes, yes of course. Good God, what a terrible thing. Bring us a drink will you Joshua?

(*Joshua goes.*)

EDWARD: What? What?

BETTY: Edward, go and do your lessons.

EDWARD: What is it, Uncle Harry?

HARRY: Go and do your lessons.

ELLEN: Edward, come in here at once.

EDWARD: What's happened, Uncle Harry?

(*Harry has moved aside, Edward follows him. Ellen comes out.*)

HARRY: Go away. Go inside. Ellen!

ELLEN: Go inside, Edward. I shall tell your mother.

BETTY: Go inside, Edward at once. I shall tell your father.

CLIVE: Go inside, Edward. And Betty you go inside too.

(*Betty, Edward, and Ellen go. Maud comes out.*)

CLIVE: Go inside. And Ellen, you come outside.

(*Ellen comes out.*)

Mr. Bagley has something to say to you.

HARRY: Ellen. I don't suppose you would marry me?

ELLEN: What if I said yes?

CLIVE: Run along now, you two want to be alone.

(*Harry and Ellen go out. Joshua brings Clive a drink.*)

JOSHUA: The governess and your wife, sir.

CLIVE: What's that, Joshua?

JOSHUA: She talks of love to your wife, sir. I have seen them. Bad women.

CLIVE: Joshua, you go too far. Get out of my sight.

Scene Five

(*The verandah. A table with a white cloth. A wedding cake and a large knife. Bottles and glasses. Joshua is putting things on the table. Edward has the doll. Joshua sees him with it. He holds out his hand. Edward gives him the doll. Joshua takes the knife and cuts the doll open and shakes the sawdust out of it. Joshua throws the doll under the table.)*

MAUD: Come along Edward, this is such fun.

(Everyone enters, triumphal arch for Harry and Ellen.)

MAUD: Your mama's wedding was a splendid occasion, Edward. I cried and cried.

(Ellen and Betty go aside.)

ELLEN: Betty, what happens with a man? I don't know what to do.

BETTY: You just keep still.

ELLEN: And what does he do?

BETTY: Harry will know what to do.

ELLEN: And is it enjoyable?

BETTY: Ellen, you're not getting married to enjoy yourself.

ELLEN: Don't forget me, Betty.

(Ellen goes.)

BETTY: I think my necklace has been stolen Clive. I did so want to wear it at the wedding.

EDWARD: It was Joshua. Joshua took it.

CLIVE: Joshua?

EDWARD: He did, he did, I saw him with it.

HARRY: Edward, that's not true.

EDWARD: It is, it is.

HARRY: Edward, I'm afraid you took it yourself.

EDWARD: I did not.

HARRY: I have seen him with it.

CLIVE: Edward, is that true? Where is it? Did you take your mother's necklace? And to try and blame Joshua, good God.

(Edward runs off.)

BETTY: Edward, come back. Have you got my necklace?

HARRY: I should leave him alone. He'll bring it back.

BETTY: I wanted to wear it. I wanted to look my best at your wedding.

HARRY: You always look your best to me.

BETTY: I shall get drunk.

(Mrs. Saunders comes.)

MRS. SAUNDERS: The sale of my property is completed. I shall leave tomorrow.

CLIVE: That's just as well. Whose protection will you seek this time?

MRS. SAUNDERS: I shall go to England and buy a farm there. I shall introduce threshing machines.

CLIVE: Amazing spirit.

(He kisses her. Betty launches herself on Mrs. Saunders. They fall to the ground.)

CLIVE: Betty — Caroline — I don't deserve this — Harry, Harry.

(Harry and Clive separate them. Harry holding Mrs. Saunders, Clive Betty.)

CLIVE: Mrs. Saunders, how can you abuse my hospitality? How dare you touch my wife? You must leave here at once.

BETTY: Go away, go away. You are a wicked woman.

MAUD: Mrs. Saunders, I am shocked. This is your hostess.

CLIVE: Pack your bags and leave the house this instant.

MRS. SAUNDERS: I was leaving anyway. There's no place for me here. I have made arrangements to leave tomorrow, and tomorrow is when I will leave. I wish you joy, Mr. Bagley.

(Mrs. Saunders goes.)

CLIVE: No place for her anywhere I should think. Shocking behavior.

BETTY: Oh Clive, forgive me, and love me like you used to.

CLIVE: Were you jealous my dove? My own dear wife!

MAUD: Ah, Mr. Bagley, one flesh, you see.

(Edward comes back with the necklace.)

CLIVE: Good God, Edward, it's true.

EDWARD: I was minding it for mama because of the troubles.

CLIVE: Well done, Edward, that was very manly of you. See Betty? Edward was protecting his mama's jewels from the rebels. What a hysterical fuss over nothing. Well done, little man. It is quite safe now. The bad men are dead. Edward, you may do up the necklace for mama.

(Edward does up Betty's necklace, supervised by Clive, Joshua is drinking steadily. Ellen comes back.)

MAUD: Ah, here's the bride. Come along, Ellen, you don't cry at your own wedding, only at other people's.

CLIVE: Now, speeches, speeches. Who is going to make a speech? Harry, make a speech.

HARRY: I'm no speaker. You're the one for that.

ALL: Speech, speech.

HARRY: My dear friends — what can I say — the empire — the family — the married state to which I have always aspired — your shining example of domestic bliss — my great good fortune in winning Ellen's love — happiest day of my life.

(Applause.)

CLIVE: Cut the cake, cut the cake.

(Harry and Ellen take the knife to cut the cake. Harry steps on the doll under the table.)

HARRY: What's this?

ELLEN: Oh look.

BETTY: Edward.

EDWARD: It was Joshua. It was Joshua. I saw him.

CLIVE: Don't tell lies again.

(He hits Edward across the side of the head.)

Unaccustomed as I am to public speaking —

(Cheers.)

Harry, my friend. So brave and strong and supple.
Ellen, from neath her veil so shyly peeking.
I wish you joy. A toast — the happy couple.

Dangers are past. Our enemies are killed.
— Put your arm round her, Harry, have a kiss —
All murmuring of discontent is stilled.
Long may you live in peace and joy and bliss.

(*While he is speaking Joshua raises his gun to shoot Clive. Only Edward sees. He does nothing to warn the others. He put his hands over his ears.*)
(*Black.*)

ACT TWO • *Scene One*

(*Winter afternoon. Inside the hut of a one o'clock club, a children's playcenter in a park, Victoria and Lin, mothers. Cathy, Lin's daughter, age 5, played by a man, clinging to Lin. Victoria reading a book.*)

CATHY: Yum yum bubblegum.
  Stick it up your mother's bum.
  When it's brown
  Pull it down
  Yum yum bubblegum.
LIN: Like your shoes, Victoria.
CATHY: Jack be nimble, Jack be quick,
  Jack jump over the candlestick.
  Silly Jack, he should jump higher,
  Goodness gracious, great balls of fire.
LIN: Cathy, do stop. Do a painting.
CATHY: You do a painting.
LIN: You do a painting.
CATHY: What shall I paint?
LIN: Paint a house.
CATHY: No.
LIN: Princess.
CATHY: No.
LIN: Pirates.
CATHY: Already done that.
LIN: Spacemen.
CATHY: I never paint spacemen. You know I never.
LIN: Paint a car crash and blood everywhere.
CATHY: No, don't tell me. I know what to paint.
LIN: Go on then. You need an apron, where's an apron. Here.
CATHY: Don't want an apron.
LIN: Lift up your arms. There's a good girl.
CATHY: I don't want to paint.
LIN: Don't paint. Don't paint.
CATHY: What shall I do? You paint. What shall I do mum?
VICTORIA: There's nobody on the big bike, Cathy, quick.

(*Cathy goes out. Victoria is watching the children playing outside.*)

VICTORIA: Tommy, it's Jimmy's gun. Let him have it. What the hell.

(*She goes on reading. She reads while she talks.*)

LIN: I don't know how you can concentrate.
VICTORIA: You have to or you never do anything.

LIN: Yeh, well. It's really warm in here, that's one thing. It's better than standing out there. I got chilblains last winter.
VICTORIA: It is warm.
LIN: I suppose Tommy doesn't let you read much. I expect he talks to you while you're reading.
VICTORIA: Yes, he does.
LIN: I didn't get very far with that book you lent me.
VICTORIA: That's all right.
LIN: I was glad to have it, though. I sit with it on my lap while I'm watching telly. Well, Cathy's off. She's frightened I'm going to leave her. It's the babyminder didn't work out when she was two, she still remembers. You can't get them used to other people if you're by yourself. It's no good blaming me. She clings round my knees every morning up the nursery and they don't say anything but they make you feel you're making her do it. But I'm desperate for her to go to school. I did cry when I left her the first day. You wouldn't, you're too fucking sensible. You'll call the teacher by her first name. I really fancy you.
VICTORIA: What?
LIN: Put your book down will you for five minutes. You didn't hear a word I said.
VICTORIA: I don't get much time to myself.
LIN: Do you ever go to the movies?
VICTORIA: Tommy's very funny who he's left with. My mother babysits sometimes.
LIN: Your husband could babysit.
VICTORIA: But then we couldn't go to the movies.
LIN: You could go to the movies with me.
VICTORIA: Oh I see.
LIN: Couldn't you?
VICTORIA: Well yes, I could.
LIN: Friday night?
VICTORIA: What film are we talking about?
LIN: Does it matter what film?
VICTORIA: Of course it does.
LIN: You choose then. Friday night.

(*Cathy comes in with gun, shoots them saying Kiou kiou kiou, and runs off again.*)

Not in a foreign language, ok. You don't go in the movies to read.

(*Lin watches the children playing outside.*)

Don't hit him, Cathy, kill him. Point the gun, kiou, kiou, kiou. That's the way.
VICTORIA: They've just banned war toys in Sweden.
LIN: The kids'll just hit each other more.
VICTORIA: Well, psychologists do differ in their opinions as to whether or not aggression is innate.
LIN: Yeh?
VICTORIA: I'm afraid I do let Tommy play with guns and just hope he'll get it out of his system and not end up in the army.
LIN: I've got a brother in the army.
VICTORIA: Oh I'm sorry. Whereabouts is he stationed?
LIN: Belfast.

VICTORIA: Oh dear.

LIN: I've got a friend who's Irish and we went on a Troops Out march. Now my dad won't speak to me.

VICTORIA: I don't get on too well with my father either.

LIN: And your husband? How do you get on with him?

VICTORIA: Oh, fine. Up and down. You know. Very well. He helps with the washing up and everything.

LIN: I left mine two years ago. He let me keep Cathy and I'm grateful for that.

VICTORIA: You shouldn't be grateful.

LIN: I'm a lesbian.

VICTORIA: You still shouldn't be grateful.

LIN: I'm grateful he didn't hit me harder than he did.

VICTORIA: I suppose I'm very lucky with Martin.

LIN: Don't get at me about how I bring up Cathy, ok?

VICTORIA: I didn't.

LIN: Yes you did. War toys. I'll give her a rifle for Christmas and blast Tommy's pretty head off for a start.

(*Victoria goes back to her book.*)

LIN: I hate men.

VICTORIA: You have to look at it in a historical perspective in terms of learnt behavior since the industrial revolution.

LIN: I just hate the bastards.

VICTORIA: Well it's a point of view.

(*By now Cathy has come back in and started painting in many colors, without an apron. Edward comes in.*)

EDWARD: Victoria, mother's in the park. She's walking round all the paths very fast.

VICTORIA: By herself?

EDWARD: I told her you were here.

VICTORIA: Thanks.

EDWARD: Come on.

VICTORIA: Ten minutes talking to my mother and I have to spend two hours in a hot bath.

(*Victoria goes out.*)

LIN: Shit, Cathy, what about an apron. I don't mind you having paint on your frock but if it doesn't wash off just don't tell me you can't wear your frock with paint on, ok?

CATHY: Ok.

LIN: You're gay, aren't you?

EDWARD: I beg your pardon?

LIN: I really fancy your sister. I thought you'd understand. You do but you can go on pretending you don't, I don't mind. That's lovely Cathy, I like the green bit.

EDWARD: Don't go around saying that. I might lose my job.

LIN: The last gardener was ever so straight. He used to flash at all the little girls.

EDWARD: I wish you hadn't said that about me. It's not true.

LIN: It's not true and I never said it and I never thought it and I never will think it again.

EDWARD: Someone might have heard you.

LIN: Shut up about it then.

(*Betty and Victoria come up.*)

BETTY: It's quite a nasty bump.

VICTORIA: He's not even crying.

BETTY: I think that's very worrying. You and Edward always cried. Perhaps he's got concussion.

VICTORIA: Of course he hasn't mummy.

BETTY: That other little boy was very rough. Should you speak to somebody about him?

VICTORIA: Tommy was hitting him with a spade.

BETTY: Well he's a real little boy. And so brave not to cry. You must watch him for signs of drowsiness. And nausea. If he's sick in the night, phone an ambulance. Well, you're looking very well darling, a bit tired, a bit peaky. I think the fresh air agrees with Edward. He likes the open air life because of growing up in Africa. He misses the sunshine, don't you, darling? We'll soon have Edward back on his feet. What fun it is here.

VICTORIA: This is Lin. And Cathy.

BETTY: Oh Cathy what a lovely painting. What is it? Well I think it's a house on fire. I think all that red is a fire. Is that right? Or do I see legs, is it a horse? Can I have the lovely painting or is it for mummy? Children have such imagination, it makes them so exhausting. (*To Lin.*) I'm sure you're wonderful, just like Victoria. I had help with my children. One does need help. That was in Africa of course so there wasn't the servant problem. This is my son Edward. This is —

EDWARD: Lin.

BETTY: Lin, this is Lin. Edward is doing something such fun, he's working in the park as a gardener. He does look exactly like a gardener.

EDWARD: I am a gardener.

BETTY: He's certainly making a stab at it. Well it will be a story to tell. I expect he will write a novel about it, or perhaps a television series. Well what a pretty child Cathy is. Victoria was a pretty child just like a little doll — you can't be certain how they'll grow up. I think Victoria's very pretty but she doesn't make the most of herself, do you darling, it's not the fashion I'm told but there are still women who dress out of *Vogue*, well we hope that's not what Martin looks for, though in many ways I wish it was, I don't know what it is Martin looks for and nor does he I'm afraid poor Martin. Well I am rattling on. I like your skirt dear but your shoes won't do at all. Well do they have lady gardeners, Edward, because I'm going to leave your father and I think I might need to get a job, not a gardener really of course. I haven't got green fingers I'm afraid, everything I touch shrivels straight up. Vicky gave me a poinsettia last Christmas and the leaves all fell off on Boxing Day. Well good heavens, look what's happened to that lovely painting.

(*Cathy has slowly and carefully been going over the whole sheet with black paint. She has almost finished.*)

LIN: What you do that for silly? It was nice.

CATHY: I like your earrings.

VICTORIA: Did you say you're leaving Daddy?

BETTY: Do you darling? Shall I put them on you? My ears aren't pierced, I never wanted that, they just clip on the lobe.

LIN: She'll get paint on you, mind.

BETTY: There's a pretty girl. It doesn't hurt does it? Well you'll grow up to know you have to suffer a little bit for beauty.

CATHY: Look mum I'm pretty, I'm pretty, I'm pretty.

LIN: Stop showing off Cathy.

VICTORIA: It's time we went home. Tommy, time to go home. Last go then, all right.

EDWARD: Mum did I hear you right just now?

CATHY: I want my ears pierced.

BETTY: Ooh, not till you're big.

CATHY: I know a girl got her ears pierced and she's three. She's got real gold.

BETTY: I don't expect she's English, darling. Can I give her a sweety? I know they're not very good for the teeth, Vicky gets terribly cross with me. What does mummy say?

LIN: Just one, thank you very much.

CATHY: I like your beads.

BETTY: Yes they are pretty. Here you are.

(It is the necklace from Act One.)

CATHY: Look at me, look at me. Vicky, Vicky, Vicky look at me.

LIN: You look lovely, come on now.

CATHY: And your hat, and your hat.

LIN: No, that's enough.

BETTY: Of course she can have my hat.

CATHY: Yes, yes, hat, hat. Look look look.

LIN: That's enough, please, stop it now. Hat off, bye bye hat.

CATHY: Give me my hat.

LIN: Bye bye beads.

BETTY: It's just fun.

LIN: It's very nice of you.

CATHY: I want my beads.

LIN: Where's the other earring?

CATHY: I want my beads.

(Cathy has the other earring in her hand. Meanwhile Victoria and Edward look for it.)

EDWARD: Is it on the floor?

VICTORIA: Don't step on it.

EDWARD: Where?

CATHY: I want my beads. I want my beads.

LIN: You'll have a smack.

(Lin gets the earring from Cathy.)

CATHY: I want my beads.

BETTY: Oh dear oh dear. Have you got the earring? Thank you darling.

CATHY: I want my beads, you're horrid, I hate you, mum, you smell.

BETTY: This is the point you see where one had help.

Well it's been lovely seeing you dears and I'll be off again on my little walk.

VICTORIA: You're leaving him? Really?

BETTY: Yes you hear aright, Vicky, yes. I'm finding a little flat, that will be fun.

(Betty goes.)

Bye bye Tommy, granny's going now. Tommy don't hit that little girl, say goodbye to granny.

VICTORIA: Fucking hell.

EDWARD: Puking Jesus.

LIN: That was news was it, leaving your father?

EDWARD: They're going to want so much attention.

VICTORIA: Does everybody hate their mothers?

EDWARD: Mind you, I wouldn't live with him.

LIN: Stop snivelling, pigface. Where's your coat? Be quiet now and we'll have doughnuts for tea and if you keep on we'll have dogshit on toast.

(Cathy laughs so much she lies on the floor.)

VICTORIA: Tommy, you've had two last goes. Last last last last go.

LIN: Not that funny, come on, coat on.

EDWARD: Can I have your painting?

CATHY: What for?

EDWARD: For a friend of mine.

CATHY: What's his name?

EDWARD: Gerry.

CATHY: How old is he?

EDWARD: Thirty-two.

CATHY: You can if you like. I don't care. Kiou kiou kiou kiou.

(Cathy goes out. Edward takes the painting and goes out.)

LIN: Will you have sex with me?

VICTORIA: I don't know what Martin would say. Does it count as adultery with a woman?

LIN: You'd enjoy it.

Scene Two

(Spring. Swing, bench, pond nearby. Edward is gardening. Gerry sitting on a bench.)

EDWARD: I sometimes pretend we don't know each other. And you've come to the park to eat your sandwiches and look at me.

GERRY: That would be more interesting, yes. Come and sit down.

EDWARD: If the superintendent comes I'll be in trouble. It's not my dinner time yet. Where were you last night? I think you owe me an explanation. We always do tell each other everything.

GERRY: Is that a rule?

EDWARD: It's what we agreed.

GERRY: It's a habit we've got into. Look, I was drunk. I woke up at 4 o'clock on somebody's floor. I was sick. I hadn't any money for a cab. I went back to sleep.

EDWARD: You could have phoned.

GERRY: There wasn't a phone.

EDWARD: Sorry.

GERRY: There was a phone and I didn't phone you. Leave it alone, Eddy, I'm warning you.

EDWARD: What are you going to do to me, then?

GERRY: I'm going to the pub.

EDWARD: I'll join you in ten minutes.

GERRY: I didn't ask you to come. (*Edward goes.*) Two years I've been with Edward. You have to get away sometimes or you lose sight of yourself. The train from Victoria to Clapham still has those compartments without a corridor. As soon as I got on the platform I saw who I wanted. Slim hips, tense shoulders, trying not to look at anyone. I put my hand on my packet just long enough so that he couldn't miss it. The train came in. You don't want to get in too fast or some straight dumbo might get in with you. I sat by the window. I couldn't see where the fuck he'd got to. Then just as the whistle went he got in. Great. It's a six-minute journey so you can't start anything you can't finish. I stared at him and he unzipped his flies. Then he stopped. So I stood up and took my cock out. He took me in his mouth and shut his eyes tight. He was sort of mumbling it about as if he wasn't sure what to do, so I said, "A bit tighter son" and he said "Sorry" and then got on with it. He was jerking off with his left hand, and I could see he'd got a fairsized one. I wished he'd keep still so I could see his watch. I was getting really turned on. What if we pulled into Clapham Junction now. Of course by the time we sat down again the train was just slowing up. I felt wonderful. Then he started talking. It's better if nothing is said. Once you find he's a librarian in Walthamstow with a special interest in science fiction and lives with his aunt, then forget it. He said I hope you don't think I do this all the time. I said I hope you will from now on. He said he would if I was on the train, but why don't we go out for a meal? I opened the door before the train stopped. I told him I live with somebody, I don't want to know. He was jogging sideways to keep up. He said "What's your phone number, you're my ideal physical type, what sign of the zodiac are you? Where do you live? Where are you going now?" It's not fair, I saw him at Victoria a couple of months later and I went straight down to the end of the platform and I picked up somebody really great who never said a word, just smiled.

(*Cathy is on the swing.*)

CATHY: Batman and Robin
    Had a batmobile.
    Robin done a fart
    And paralyzed the wheel.
    The wheel couldn't take it,
    The engine fell apart,
    All because of Robin
    And his supersonic fart.

(*Cathy goes. Martin, Victoria and Betty walking slowly.*)

MARTIN: Tom!

BETTY: He'll fall in.

VICTORIA: No he won't.

MARTIN: Don't go too near the edge Tom. Throw the bread from there. The ducks can get it.

BETTY: I'll never be able to manage. If I can't even walk down the street by myself. Everything looks so fierce.

VICTORIA: Just watch Tommy feeding the ducks.

BETTY: He's going to fall in. Make Martin make him move back.

VICTORIA: He's not going to fall in.

BETTY: It's since I left your father.

VICTORIA: Mummy, it really was the right decision.

BETTY: Everything comes at me from all directions. Martin despises me.

VICTORIA: Of course he doesn't, mummy.

BETTY: Of course he does.

MARTIN: Throw the bread. That's the way. The duck can get it. Quack quack quack quack quack.

BETTY: I don't want to take pills. Lin says you can't trust doctors.

VICTORIA: You're not taking pills. You're doing very well.

BETTY: But I'm so frightened.

VICTORIA: What are you frightened of?

BETTY: Victoria, you always ask that as if there was suddenly going to be an answer.

VICTORIA: Are you all right sitting there?

BETTY: Yes, yes. Go and be with Martin.

(*Victoria joins Martin, Betty stays sitting on the bench.*)

MARTIN: You take the job, you go to Manchester. You turn it down, you stay in London. People are making decisions like this every day of the week. It needn't be for more than a year. You get long vacations. Our relationship might well stand the strain of that, and if it doesn't we're better out of it. I don't want to put any pressure on you. I'd just like to know so we can sell the house. I think we're moving into an entirely different way of life if you go to Manchester because it won't end there. We could keep the house as security for Tommy but he might as well get used to the fact that life nowadays is insecure. You should ask your mother what she thinks and then do the opposite. I could just take that room in Barbara's house, and then we could babysit for each other. You think that means I want to fuck Barbara. I don't. Well, I do, but I won't. And even if I did, what's a fuck between friends? What are we meant to do it with, strangers? Whatever you want to do, I'll be delighted. If you could just let me know what it is I'm to be delighted about. Don't cry again, Vicky, I'm not the sort of man who makes women cry.

(*Lin has come in and sat down with Betty, Cathy joins them. She is wearing a pink dress and carrying a rifle.*)

LIN: I've bought her three new frocks. She won't wear jeans to school any more because Tracy and Mandy called her a boy.

CATHY: Tracy's got a perm.

LIN: You should have shot them.

CATHY: They're coming to tea and we've got to have trifle. Not trifle you make, trifle out of a packet. And you've got to wear a skirt. And tights.

LIN: Tracy's mum wears jeans.

CATHY: She does not. She wears velvet.

BETTY: Well I think you look very pretty. And if that gun has caps in it please take it a long way away.

CATHY: It's got red caps. They're louder.

MARTIN: Do you think you're well enough to do this job? You don't have to do it. No one's going to think any the less of you if you stay here with me. There's no point being so liberated you make yourself cry all the time. You stay and we'll get everything sorted out. What it is about sex, when we talk while it's happening I get to feel it's like a driving lesson. Left, right, a little faster, carry on, slow down —

(*Cathy shoots Victoria.*)

CATHY: You're dead Vicky.

VICTORIA: Aaaargh.

CATHY: Fall over.

VICTORIA: I'm not falling over, the ground's wet.

CATHY: You're dead.

VICTORIA: Yes, I'm dead.

CATHY: The Dead Hand Gang fall over. They said I had to fall over in the mud or I can't play. That duck's a mandarin.

MARTIN: Which one? Look, Tommy.

CATHY: That's a diver. It's got a yellow eye and it dives. That's a goose. Tommy doesn't know it's a goose, he thinks it's a duck. The babies get eaten by weasels. Kiou kiou.

(*Cathy goes.*)

MARTIN: So I lost my erection last night not because I'm not prepared to talk, it's just that taking in technical information is a different part of the brain and also I don't like to feel that you do it better to yourself. I have read the Hite report. I do know that women have to learn to get their pleasure despite our clumsy attempts at expressing undying devotion and ecstasy, and that what we spent our adolescence thinking was an animal urge we had to suppress is in fact a fine art we have to acquire. I'm not like whatever percentage of American men have become impotent as a direct result of women's liberation, which I am totally in favor of, more I sometimes think than you are yourself. Nor am I one of your villains who sticks it in, bangs away, and falls asleep. My one aim is to give you pleasure. My one aim is to give you rolling orgasms like I do other women. So why the hell don't you have them? My analysis for what it's worth is that despite all my efforts you still feel dominated by me. I in fact think it's very sad that you don't feel able to take that job. It makes me feel very guilty. I don't want you to do it just because I encourage you to do it. But don't you think you'd feel better if you did take the job? You're the one who's talked about freedom.

You're the one who's experimenting with bisexuality, and I don't stop you, I think women have something to give each other. You seem to need the mutual support. You find me too overwhelming. So follow it through, go away, leave me and Tommy alone for a bit, we can manage perfectly well without you. I'm not putting any pressure on you but I don't think you're being a whole person. God knows I do everything I can to make you stand on your own two feet. Just be yourself. You don't seem to realize how insulting it is to me that you can't get yourself together.

(*Martin and Victoria go.*)

BETTY: You must be very lonely yourself with no husband. You don't miss him?

LIN: Not really, no.

BETTY: Maybe you like being on your own.

LIN: I'm seeing quite a lot of Vicky. I don't live alone. I live with Cathy.

BETTY: I would have been frightened when I was your age. I thought, the poor children, their mother all alone.

LIN: I've a lot of friends.

BETTY: I find when I'm making tea I put out two cups. It's strange not having a man in the house. You don't know who to do things for.

LIN: Yourself.

BETTY: Oh, that's very selfish.

LIN: Have you any women friends?

BETTY: I've never been so short of men's company that I've had to bother with women.

LIN: Don't you like women?

BETTY: They don't have such interesting conversations as men. There has never been a woman composer of genius. They don't have a sense of humor. They spoil things for themselves with their emotions. I can't say I do like women very much, no.

LIN: But you're a woman.

BETTY: There's nothing says you have to like yourself.

LIN: Do you like me?

BETTY: There's no need to take it personally, Lin.

(*Martin and Victoria come back.*)

MARTIN: Did you know if you put cocaine on your prick you can keep it up all night? The only thing is of course it goes numb so you don't feel anything. But you would, that's the main thing. I just want to make you happy.

BETTY: Vicky, I'd like to go home.

VICTORIA: Yes, mummy, of course.

BETTY: I'm sorry, dear.

VICTORIA: I think Tommy would like to stay out a bit longer.

LIN: Hello, Martin. We do keep out of each other's way.

MARTIN: I think that's the best thing to do.

BETTY: Perhaps you'd walk home with me, Martin. I do feel safer with a man. The park is so large the grass seems to tilt.

MARTIN: Yes, I'd like to go home and do some work. I'm writing a novel about women from the women's point of view.

(*Martin and Betty go. Lin and Victoria are alone. They embrace.*)

VICTORIA: Why the hell can't he just be a wife and come with me? Why does Martin make me tie myself in knots? No wonder we can't just have a simple fuck. No, not Martin, why do I make myself tie myself in knots. It's got to stop, Lin. I'm not like that with you. Would you love me if I went to Manchester?

LIN: Yes.

VICTORIA: Would you love me if I went on a climbing expedition in the Andes mountains?

LIN: Yes.

VICTORIA: Would you love me if my teeth fell out?

LIN: Yes.

VICTORIA: Would you love me if I loved ten other people?

LIN: And me?

VICTORIA: Yes.

LIN: Yes.

VICTORIA: And I feel apologetic for not being quite so subordinate as I was. I am more intelligent than him. I am brilliant.

LIN: Leave him Vic. Come and live with me.

VICTORIA: Don't be silly.

LIN: Silly, Christ, don't then. I'm not asking because I need to live with someone. I'd enjoy it, that's all, we'd both enjoy it. Fuck you. Cathy, for fuck's sake stop throwing stones at the ducks. The man's going to get you.

VICTORIA: What man? Do you need a man to frighten your child with?

LIN: My mother said it.

VICTORIA: You're so inconsistent, Lin.

LIN: I've changed who I sleep with, I can't change everything.

VICTORIA: Like when I had to stop you getting a job in a boutique and collaborating with sexist consumerism.

LIN: I should have got that job, Cathy would have liked it. Why shouldn't I have some decent clothes? I'm sick of dressing like a boy, why can't I look sexy, wouldn't you love me?

VICTORIA: Lin, you've no analysis.

LIN: No but I'm good at kissing aren't I? I give Cathy guns, my mum didn't give me guns. I dress her in jeans, she wants to wear dresses. I don't know. I can't work it out, I don't want to. You read too many books, you get at me all the time, you're worse to me than Martin is to you, you piss me off, my brother's been killed. I'm sorry to win the argument that way but there it is.

VICTORIA: What do you mean win the argument?

LIN: I mean be nice to me.

VICTORIA: In Belfast?

LIN: I heard this morning. Don't don't start. I've hardly seem him for two years. I rung my father. You'd think I'd shot him myself. He doesn't want me to go the funeral.

(*Cathy approaches.*)

VICTORIA: What will you do?

LIN: Go of course.

CATHY: What is it? Who's killed? What?

LIN: It's Bill. Your uncle. In the army. Bill that gave you the blue teddy.

CATHY: Can I have his gun?

LIN: It's time we went home. Time you went to bed.

CATHY: No it's not.

LIN: We go home and you have tea and you have a bath and you go to bed.

CATHY: Fuck off.

LIN: Cathy, shut up.

VICTORIA: It's only half past five, why don't we —

LIN: I'll tell you why she has to go to bed —

VICTORIA: She can come home with me.

LIN: Because I want her out of the fucking way.

VICTORIA: She can come home with me.

CATHY: I'm not going to bed.

LIN: I want her home with me not home with you, I want her in bed, I want today over.

CATHY: I'm not going to bed.

(*Lin hits Cathy, Cathy cries.*)

LIN: And shut up or I'll give you something to cry for.

CATHY: I'm not going to bed.

VICTORIA: Cathy —

LIN: You keep out of it.

VICTORIA: Lin for God's sake.

(*They are all shouting. Cathy runs off. Lin and Victoria are silent. Then they laugh and embrace.*)

LIN: Where's Tommy?

VICTORIA: What? Didn't he go with Martin?

LIN: Did he?

VICTORIA: God oh God.

LIN: Cathy! Cathy!

VICTORIA: I haven't thought about him. How could I not think about him? Tommy!

LIN: Cathy! Come on, quick, I want some help.

VICTORIA: Tommy! Tommy!

(*Cathy comes back.*)

LIN: Where's Tommy? Have you seen him? Did he go with Martin? Do you know where he is?

CATHY: I showed him the goose. We went in the bushes.

LIN: Then what?

CATHY: I came back on the swing.

VICTORIA: And Tommy? Where was Tommy?

CATHY: He fed the ducks.

LIN: No that was before.

CATHY: He did a pee in the bushes. I helped him with his trousers.

VICTORIA: And after that?

CATHY: He fed the ducks.

VICTORIA: No no.

CATHY: He liked the ducks. I expect he fell in.

LIN: Did you see him fall in?

VICTORIA: Tommy! Tommy!

LIN: What's the last time you saw him?

CATHY: He did a pee.
VICTORIA: Mummy said he would fall in. Oh God, Tommy!
LIN: We'll go round the pond. We'll go opposite ways round the pond.
ALL (*shout*): Tommy!

(*Victoria and Lin go off opposite sides. Cathy climbs the bench.*)

CATHY: Georgie Best, superstar
  Walks like a woman and wears a bra.
  There he is! I see him! Mum! Vicky! There he is! He's in the bushes.

(*Lin comes back.*)

LIN: Come on Cathy love, let's go home.
CATHY: Vicky's got him.
LIN: Come on.
CATHY: Is she cross?
LIN: No. Come on.
CATHY: I found him.
LIN: Yes. Come on.

(*Cathy gets off the bench. Cathy and Lin hug.*)

CATHY: I'm watching telly.
LIN: Ok.
CATHY: After the news.
LIN: Ok.
CATHY: I'm not going to bed.
LIN: Yes you are.
CATHY: I'm not going to bed now.
LIN: Not now but early.
CATHY: How early?
LIN: Not late.
CATHY: How not late?
LIN: Early.
CATHY: How early?
LIN: Not late.

(*They go off together. Gerry comes on. He waits. Edward comes.*)

EDWARD: I've got some fish for dinner. I thought I'd make a cheese sauce.
GERRY: I won't be in.
EDWARD: Where are you going?
GERRY: For a start I'm going to a sauna. Then I'll see.
EDWARD: All right. What time will you be back? We'll eat then.
GERRY: You're getting like a wife.
EDWARD: I don't mind that.
GERRY: Why don't I do the cooking sometime?
EDWARD: You can if you like. You're just not so good at it that's all. Do it tonight.
GERRY: I won't be in tonight.
EDWARD: Do it tomorrow. If we can't eat it we can always go to a restaurant.
GERRY: Stop it.
EDWARD: Stop what?
GERRY: Just be yourself.

EDWARD: I don't know what you mean. Everyone's always tried to stop me being feminine and now you are too.
GERRY: You're putting it on.
EDWARD: I like doing the cooking. I like being fucked. You do like me like this really.
GERRY: I'm bored, Eddy.
EDWARD: Go to the sauna.
GERRY: And you'll stay home and wait up for me.
EDWARD: No, I'll go to bed and read a book.
GERRY: Or knit. You could knit me a pair of socks.
EDWARD: I might knit. I like knitting.
GERRY: I don't mind if you knit. I don't want to be married.
EDWARD: I do.
GERRY: Well I'm divorcing you.
EDWARD: I wouldn't want to keep a man who wants his freedom.
GERRY: Eddy, do stop playing the injured wife, it's not funny.
EDWARD: I'm not playing. It's true.
GERRY: I'm not the husband so you can't be the wife.
EDWARD: I'll always be here, Gerry, if you want to come back. I know you men like to go off by yourselves. I don't think I could love deeply more than once. But I don't think I can face life on my own so don't leave it too long or it may be too late.
GERRY: What are you trying to turn me into?
EDWARD: A monster, darling, which is what you are.
GERRY: I'll collect my stuff from the flat in the morning.

(*Gerry goes. Edward sits on the bench. It gets darker. Victoria comes.*)

VICTORIA: Tommy dropped a toy car somewhere, you haven't seen it? It's red. He says it's his best one. Oh the hell with it. Martin's reading him a story. There, isn't it quiet?

(*They sit on the bench, holding hands.*)

EDWARD: I like women.
VICTORIA: That should please mother.
EDWARD: No listen Vicky. I'd rather be a woman. I wish I had breasts like that, I think they're beautiful. Can I touch them?
VICTORIA: What, pretending they're yours?
EDWARD: No, I know it's you.
VICTORIA: I think I should warn you I'm enjoying this.
EDWARD: I'm sick of men.
VICTORIA: I'm sick of men.
EDWARD: I think I'm a lesbian.

Scene Three

(*The park. Summer night. Victoria, Lin, and Edward drunk.*)

LIN: Where are you?
VICTORIA: Come on.

EDWARD: Do we sit in a circle?

VICTORIA: Sit in a triangle.

EDWARD: You're good at mathematics. She's good at mathematics.

VICTORIA: Give me your hand. We all hold hands.

EDWARD: Do you know what to do?

LIN: She's making it up.

VICTORIA: We start off by being quiet.

EDWARD: What?

LIN: Hush.

EDWARD: Will something appear?

VICTORIA: It was your idea.

EDWARD: It wasn't my idea. It was your book.

LIN: You said call up the goddess.

EDWARD: I don't remember saying that.

LIN: We could have called her on the telephone.

EDWARD: Don't be so silly, this is meant to be frightening.

LIN: Kiss me.

VICTORIA: Are we going to do it?

LIN: We're doing it.

VICTORIA: A ceremony.

LIN: It's very sexy, you said it is. You said the women were priests in the temples and fucked all the time. I'm just helping.

VICTORIA: As long as it's sacred.

LIN: It's very sacred.

VICTORIA: Innin, Innana, Nana, Nut, Anat, Anahita, Istar, Isis.

LIN: I can't remember all that.

VICTORIA: Lin! Innin, Innana, Nana, Nut, Anat, Anahita, Istar, Isis.

(*Lin and Edward join in and continue the chant under Victoria's speech.*)

Goddess of many names, oldest of the old, who walked in chaos and created life, hear us calling you back through time, before Jehovah, before Christ, before men drove you out and burnt your temples, hear us, Lady, give us back what we were, give us the history we haven't had, make us the women we can't be.

ALL: Innin, Innana, Nana, Nut, Anat, Anahita, Istar, Isis.

(*Chant continues under other speeches.*)

LIN: Come back, goddess.

VICTORIA: Goddess of the sun and the moon her brother, little goddess of Crete with snakes in your hands.

LIN: Goddess of breasts.

VICTORIA: Goddess of cunts.

LIN: Goddess of fat bellies and babies. And blood blood blood.

(*Chant continues.*)

I see her.

EDWARD: What?

(*They stop chanting.*)

LIN: I see her. Very tall. Snakes in her hands. Light light light — look out! Did I give you a fright?

EDWARD: I was terrified.

VICTORIA: Don't spoil it Lin.

LIN: It's all out of a book.

VICTORIA: Innin Innana — I can't do it now. I was really enjoying myself.

LIN: She won't appear with a man here.

VICTORIA: They had men, they had sons and lovers.

EDWARD: They had eunuchs.

LIN: Don't give us ideas.

VICTORIA: There's Attis and Tammuz, they're torn to pieces.

EDWARD: Tear me to pieces, Lin.

VICTORIA: The priestess chose a lover for a year and he was king because she chose him and then he was killed at the end of the year.

EDWARD: Hurray.

VICTORIA: And the women had the children and nobody knew it was done by fucking so they didn't know about fathers and nobody cared who the father was and the property was passed down through the maternal line —

LIN: Don't turn it into a lecture, Vicky, it's meant to be an orgy.

VICTORIA: It never hurts to understand the theoretical background. You can't separate fucking and economics.

LIN: Give us a kiss.

EDWARD: Shut up, listen.

LIN: What?

EDWARD: There's somebody there.

LIN: Where?

EDWARD: There.

VICTORIA: The priestesses used to make love to total strangers.

LIN: Go on then, I dare you.

EDWARD: Go on, Vicky.

VICTORIA: He won't know it's a sacred rite in honor of the goddess.

EDWARD: We'll know.

LIN: We can tell him.

EDWARD: It's not what he thinks, it's what we think.

LIN: Don't tell him till after, he'll run a mile.

VICTORIA: Hello. We're having an orgy. Do you want me to suck your cock?

(*The stranger approaches. It is Martin.*)

MARTIN: There you are. I've been looking everywhere. What the hell are you doing? Do you know what the time is? You're all pissed out of your minds.

(*They leap on Martin, pull him down and start to make love to him.*)

MARTIN: Well that's all right. If all we're talking about is having a lot of sex there's no problem. I was all for the sixties when liberation just meant fucking.

(*Another stranger approaches.*)

LIN: Hey you, come here. Come and have sex with us.

VICTORIA: Who is it?

(The stranger is a soldier.)

LIN: It's my brother.
EDWARD: Lin, don't.
LIN: It's my brother.
VICTORIA: It's her sense of humor, you get used to it.
LIN: Shut up Vicky, it's my brother. Isn't it? Bill?
SOLDIER: Yes it's me.
LIN: And you are dead.
SOLDIER: Fucking dead all right yeh.
LIN: Have you come back to tell us something?
SOLDIER: No I've come for a fuck. That was the worst thing in the fucking army. Never fucking let out. Can't fucking talk to Irish girls. Fucking bored out of my fucking head. That or shit scared. For five minutes I'd be glad I wasn't bored, then I was fucking scared. Then we'd come in and I'd be glad I wasn't scared and then I was fucking bored. Spent the day reading fucking porn and the fucking night wanking. Man's fucking life in the fucking army? No fun when the fucking kids hate you. I got so I fucking wanted to kill someone and I got fucking killed myself and I want a fuck.
LIN: I miss you. Bill. Bill.

(Lin collapses. Soldier goes. Victoria comforts Lin.)

EDWARD: Let's go home.
LIN: Victoria, come home with us. Victoria's coming to live with me and Edward.
MARTIN: Tell me about it in the morning.
LIN: It's true.
VICTORIA: It is true.
MARTIN: Tell me when you're sober.

(Edward, Lin, Victoria go off together. Martin goes off alone. Gerry comes on.)

GERRY: I come here sometimes at night and pick somebody up. Sometimes I come here at night and don't pick anybody up. I do also enjoy walking about at night. There's never any trouble finding someone. I can have sex any time. You might not find the type you most fancy every day of the week, but there's plenty of people about who just enjoy having a good time. I quite like living alone. If I live with someone I get annoyed with them. Edward always put on Capital radio when he got up. The silence gets wasted. I wake up at four o'clock sometimes. Birds. Silence. If I bring somebody home I never let them stay the night. Edward! Edward!

(Edward from Act One comes on.)

EDWARD: Gerry I love you.
GERRY: Yes, I know. I love you, too.
EDWARD: You know what we did? I want to do it again. I think about it all the time. Don't you want to any more?
GERRY: Yes, of course.
SONG (*"Cloud Nine"*— ALL):
It'll be fine when you reach Cloud Nine.

Mist was rising and the night was dark.
Me and my baby took a walk in the park.
He said Be mine and you're on Cloud Nine.

Better watch out when you're on Cloud Nine.

Smoked some dope on the playground swings
Higher and higher on true love's wings
He said Be mine and you're on Cloud Nine.

Twenty-five years on the same Cloud Nine.

Who did she meet on her first blind date?
The guys were no surprise but the lady was great
They were women in love, they were on Cloud Nine.

Two the same, they were on Cloud Nine.

The bride was sixty-five, the groom was seventeen,
They fucked in the back of the black limousine.
It was divine in their silver Cloud Nine.

Simply divine in their silver Cloud Nine.

The wife's lover's children and my lover's wife,
Cooking in my kitchen, confusing my life.
And it's upside down when you reach Cloud Nine.

Upside down when you reach Cloud Nine.

Scene Four

(The park. Afternoon in late summer. Martin, Cathy, Edward.)

CATHY: Under the bramble bushes,
  Under the sea boom boom boom,
  True love for you my darling,
  True love for me my darling,
  When we are married,
  We'll raise a family.
  Boy for you, girl for me,
  Boom tiddley oom boom
  SEXY.
EDWARD: You'll have Tommy and Cathy tonight then ok? Tommy's still on antibiotics, do make him finish the bottle, he takes it in Ribena. It's no good in orange, he spits it out. Remind me to give you Cathy's swimming things.
CATHY: I did six strokes, didn't I Martin? Did I do a width? How many strokes is a length? How many miles is a swimming pool? I'm going to take my bronze and silver and gold and diamond.
MARTIN: Is Tommy still wetting the bed?
EDWARD: Don't get angry with him about it.
MARTIN: I just need to go to the launderette so I've got a spare sheet. Of course I don't get fucking angry,

Eddy, for God's sake. I don't like to say he is my son but he is my son. I'm surprised I'm not wetting the bed myself.

CATHY: I don't wet the bed ever. Do you wet the bed Martin?

MARTIN: No.

CATHY: You said you did.

(*Betty comes.*)

BETTY: I do miss the sun living in England but today couldn't be more beautiful. You appreciate the weekend when you're working. Betty's been at work this week, Cathy. It's terrible tiring, Martin, I don't know how you've done it all these years. And the money, I feel like a child with the money, Clive always paid everything but I do understand it perfectly well. Look Cathy let me show you my money.

CATHY: I'll count it. Let me count it. What's that?

BETTY: Five pounds, Five and five is — ?

CATHY: One two three —

BETTY: Five and five is ten, and five —

CATHY: If I get it right can I have one?

EDWARD: No you can't.

(*Cathy goes on counting the money.*)

BETTY: I never like to say anything, Martin, or you'll think I'm being a mother-in-law.

EDWARD: Which you are.

BETTY: Thank you, Edward, I'm not talking to you. Martin, I think you're being wonderful. Vicky will come back. Just let her stay with Lin till she sorts herself out. It's very nice for a girl to have a friend; I had friends at school, that was very nice. But I'm sure Lin and Edward don't want her with them all the time. I'm not at all shocked that Lin and Edward aren't married and she already has a child, we all know first marriages don't always work out. But really Vicky must be in the way. And poor little Tommy. I hear he doesn't sleep properly and he's had a cough.

MARTIN: No, he's fine, Betty, thank you.

CATHY: My bed's horrible. I want to sleep in the big bed with Lin and Vicky and Eddy and I do get in if I've got a bad dream, and my bed's got a bump right in my back. I want to sleep in a tent.

BETTY: Well Tommy has got a nasty cough, Martin, whatever you say.

EDWARD: He's over that. He's got some medicine.

MARTIN: He takes it in Ribena.

BETTY: Well I'm glad to hear it. Look what a lot of money, Cathy, and I sit behind a desk of my own and I answer the telephone and keep the doctor's appointment book and it really is great fun.

CATHY: Can we go camping, Martin, in a tent? We could take the Dead Hand Gang.

BETTY: Not those big boys, Cathy? They're far too big and rough for you. They climb back into the park after dark. I'm sure mummy doesn't let you play with them, does she Edward? Well I don't know.

(*Ice cream bells.*)

CATHY: Ice cream. Martin you promised. I'll have a double ninety-nine. No I'll have a shandy lolly. Betty, you have a shandy lolly and I'll have a lick. No, you have a double ninety-nine and I'll have the chocolate.

(*Martin, Cathy, and Betty go, leaving Edward. Gerry comes.*)

GERRY: Hello, Eddy. Thought I might find you here.

EDWARD: Gerry.

GERRY: Not working today then?

EDWARD: I don't work here any more.

GERRY: Your mum got you into a dark suit?

EDWARD: No of course not. I'm on the dole. I am working, though, I do housework.

GERRY: Whose wife are you now then?

EDWARD: Nobody's. I don't think like that any more. I'm living with some women.

GERRY: What women?

EDWARD: It's my sister, Vic, and her lover. They go out to work and I look after the kids.

GERRY: I thought for a moment you said you were living with women.

EDWARD: We do sleep together, yes.

GERRY: I was passing the park anyway so I thought I'd look in. I was in the sauna the other night and I saw someone who looked like you but it wasn't. I had sex with him anyway.

EDWARD: I do go to the sauna sometimes.

(*Cathy comes, gives Edward an ice cream, goes.*)

GERRY: I don't think I'd like living with children. They make a lot of noise don't they?

EDWARD: I tell them to shut up and they shut up. I wouldn't want to leave them at the moment.

GERRY: Look why don't we go for a meal sometime?

EDWARD: Yes I'd like that. Where are you living now?

GERRY: Same place.

EDWARD: I'll come round for you tomorrow night about 7:30.

GERRY: Great.

(*Edward goes. Harry comes. Harry and Gerry pick each other up. They go off. Betty comes back.*)

BETTY: No, the ice cream was my treat, Martin. Off you go. I'm going to have a quiet sit in the sun.

(*Maud comes.*)

MAUD: Let Mrs. Saunders be a warning to you, Betty. I know what it is to be unprotected.

BETTY: But mother, I have a job. I earn money.

MAUD: I know we have our little differences but I always want what is best for you.

(*Ellen comes.*)

ELLEN: Betty, what happens with a man?

BETTY: You just keep still.

ELLEN: And is it enjoyable? Don't forget me, Betty.

(*Maud and Ellen go.*)

BETTY: I used to think Clive was the one who liked sex. But then I found I missed it. I used to touch myself when I was very little, I thought I'd invented something wonderful. I used to do it to go to sleep with or to cheer myself up, and one day it was raining and I was under the kitchen table, and my mother saw me with my hand under my dress rubbing away, and she dragged me out so quickly I hit my head and it bled and I was sick, and nothing was said, and I never did it again till this year. I thought if Clive wasn't looking at me there wasn't a person there. And one night in bed in my flat I was so frightened I started touching myself. I thought my hand might go through space. I touched my face, it was there, my arm, my breast, and my hand went down where I thought it shouldn't, and I thought well there is somebody there. It felt very sweet, it was a feeling from very long ago, it was very soft, just barely touching, and I felt myself gathering together more and more and I felt angry with Clive and angry with my mother and I went on and on defying them, and there was this vast feeling growing in me and all round me and they couldn't stop me and no one could stop me and I was there and coming and coming. Afterwards I thought I'd betrayed Clive. My mother would kill me. But I felt triumphant because I was a separate person from them. And I cried because I didn't want to be. But I don't cry about it any more. Sometimes I do it three times in one night and it really is great fun.

(*Victoria and Lin come in.*)

VICTORIA: So I said to the professor, I don't think this is an occasion for invoking the concept of structural causality — oh hello mummy.
BETTY: I'm going to ask you a question, both of you. I have a little money from your grandmother. And the three of you are living in that tiny flat with two children. I wonder if we could get a house and all live in it together? It would give you more room.
VICTORIA: But I'm going to Manchester anyway.
LIN: We'd have a garden, Vicky.
BETTY: You do seem to have such fun all of you.
VICTORIA: I don't want to.
BETTY: I didn't think you would.
LIN: Come on, Vicky, she knows we sleep together, and Eddy.
BETTY: I think I've known for quite a while but I'm not sure. I don't usually think about it, so I don't know if I know about it or not.
VICTORIA: I don't want to live with my mother.
LIN: Don't think of her as your mother, think of her as Betty.
VICTORIA: But she thinks of herself as my mother.
BETTY: I am your mother.
VICTORIA: But mummy we don't even like each other.
BETTY: We might begin to.

(*Cathy comes on howling with a nosebleed.*)

LIN: Oh Cathy what happened?
BETTY: She's been assaulted.
VICTORIA: It's a nosebleed.
CATHY: Took my ice cream.
LIN: Who did?
CATHY: Took my money.

(*Martin comes.*)

MARTIN: Is everything all right?
LIN: I thought you were looking after her.
CATHY: They hit me. I can't play. They said I'm a girl.
BETTY: Those dreadful boys, the gang, the Dead Hand.
MARTIN: What do you mean you thought I was looking after her?
LIN: Last I saw her she was with you getting an ice cream. It's your afternoon.
MARTIN: Then she went off to play. She goes off to play. You don't keep an eye on her every minute.
LIN: She doesn't get beaten up when I'm looking after her.
CATHY: Took my money.
MARTIN: Why the hell should I look after your child anyway? I just want Tommy. Why should he live with you and Vicky all week?
LIN: I don't mind if you don't want to look after her but don't say you will and then this happens.
VICTORIA: When I get to Manchester everything's going to be different anyway, Lin's staying here, and you're staying here, we're all going to have to sit down and talk it through.
MARTIN: I'd really enjoy that.
CATHY: Hit me on the face.
LIN: You were the one looking after her and look at her now, that's all.
MARTIN: I've had enough of you telling me.
LIN: Yes you know it all.
MARTIN: Now stop it. I work very hard at not being like this, I could do with some credit.
LIN: Ok you're quite nice, try and enjoy it. Don't make me sorry for you, Martin, it's hard for me too. We've better things to do than quarrel. I've got to go and sort those little bastards out for a start. Where are they, Cathy?
CATHY: Don't kill them, mum, hit them. Give them a nosebleed, mum.

(*Lin goes.*)

VICTORIA: Tommy's asleep in the pushchair. We'd better wake him up or he won't sleep tonight.
MARTIN: Sometimes I keep him up watching television till he falls asleep on the sofa so I can hold him. Come on, Cathy, we'll get another ice cream.
CATHY: Chocolate sauce and nuts.
VICTORIA: Betty, would you like an ice cream?
BETTY: No thank you, the cold hurts my teeth, but what a nice thought, Vicky, thank you.

(*Victoria goes. Betty alone. Gerry comes.*)

BETTY: I think you used to be Edward's flatmate.

GERRY: You're his mother. He's talked about you.

BETTY: Well never mind. Children are always wrong about their parents. It's a great problem knowing where to live and who to share with. I live by myself just now.

GERRY: Good, So do I. You can do what you like.

BETTY: I don't really know what I like.

GERRY: You'll soon find out.

BETTY: What do you like?

GERRY: Waking up at four in the morning.

BETTY: I like listening to music in bed and sometimes for supper I just have a big piece of bread and dip it in very hot lime pickle. So you don't get lonely by yourself? Perhaps you have a lot of visitors. I've been thinking I should have some visitors, I could give a little dinner party. Would you come? There wouldn't just be bread and lime pickle.

GERRY: Thank you very much.

BETTY: Or don't wait to be asked to dinner. Just drop in informally. I'll give you the address shall I? I don't usually give strange men my address but then you're not a strange man, you're a friend of Edward's. I suppose I seem a different generation to you but you are older than Edward. I was married for so many years it's quite hard to know how to get acquainted. But if there isn't a right way to do things you have to invent one. I always thought my mother was far too old to be attractive but when you get to an age yourself it feels quite different.

GERRY: I think you could be quite attractive.

BETTY: If what?

GERRY: If you stop worrying.

BETTY: I think when I do more about things I worry about them less. So perhaps you could help me do more.

GERRY: I might be going to live with Edward again.

BETTY: That's nice, but I'm rather surprised if he wants to share a flat. He's rather involved with a young woman he lives with, or two young women, I don't understand Edward but never mind.

GERRY: I'm very involved with him.

BETTY: I think Edward did try to tell me once but I didn't listen. So what I'm being told now is that Edward is "gay" is that right? And you are too. And I've been making rather a fool of myself. But Edward does also sleep with women.

GERRY: He does, yes, I don't.

BETTY: Well people always say it's the mother's fault but I don't intend to start blaming myself. He seems perfectly happy.

GERRY: I could still come and see you.

BETTY: So you could, yes. I'd like that. I've never tried to pick up a man before.

GERRY: Not everyone's gay.

BETTY: No, that's lucky isn't it.

(*Gerry goes. Clive comes.*)

CLIVE: You are not that sort of woman, Betty. I can't believe you are. I can't feel the same about you as I did. And Africa is to be communist I suppose. I used to be proud to be British. There was a high ideal. I came out onto the verandah and looked at the stars.

(*Clive goes. Betty from Act One comes. Betty and Betty embrace.*)

COMMENTARY

James Treadwell (b. 1942)
REVIEW OF THE OLD VIC PRODUCTION
OF *CLOUD NINE*   1997

London's Spectator *critic James Treadwell responds to the 1997 Old Vic production of* Cloud Nine *by commenting on its structure as a series of "difficult adjustments." In this production, the emphasis on the tension between private and public life helps give the play its peculiar "verve."*

This week, the Peter Hall Company delivers what will surely turn out to be the distinctive virtue of its nine-month residency at the Old Vic: a seamlessly cogent ensemble performance. Seven "classics" and five new plays will be presented before the year is out, but none will surpass Caryl Churchill's 1979 *Cloud Nine* for sheer theatrical verve. In this self-consciously experimental workshop drama, the Company gives a virtuoso display that turns out to be greater than the sum of its parts. There are individual strengths and weaknesses among the actors, but Churchill's polemical essay in sexual politics isn't about individuals: it's about relationships, communities, social rather than personal identity.

The characters are placed in two very different cultural milieux, each with its own shifting pressures and demands. Before the interval, we are in colonial Africa, witnessing a Victorian family's efforts to control its chaotic domestic politics with the official hierarchies of Empire. Clive (Tim McInnerny), the paterfamilias, stands for God, Queen, and country all at once, imposing what we would now call "family values" on his wife, children, servant, governess, and friend, who despite his efforts share an encyclopaedic variety of unpatriotic sexual proclivities. In the second half, the family has moved on 100 years to London in the seventies. Their problems are now entirely different: a permissive world offers bewildering freedom of sexual choice. Because the play explores the dialogue between desire and constraint in such an extreme way, the characters can't simply be themselves. Clive's wife Betty is played by a man, his son Edward by a woman, his black servant Joshua by a white actor: Dominic West, Janine Duvitski, and Stephen Noonan give mesmerizing performances.

In the second half, West becomes the grown-up son, Duvitski the middle-aged wife, and Noonan is a gay man who will forever change your conception of the Victoria-to-Clapham train journey. The patriarch Clive has no place in this brave new feminism, so McInnerny turns himself with astonishing conviction into a four-year-old girl. There's nothing remotely gimmicky about these metamorphoses. When the prepubescent Edward of the first half is being taught the ways of masculine imperialism — brutality, buggery, and cricket — his confusion over what the role requires is powerfully accentuated by his being played by a woman. Joshua looks like a stereotype of the domesticated African, were it not that we see him to be white. *Cloud Nine* wouldn't work if these confusions weren't convincing. The achievement of this production is that the audience can always see both sides of the characters: their private passions, and the public roles — dutiful wife, obedient child, gay man — in which society casts them.

It will be apparent from all this that *Cloud Nine*'s center of gravity is sex. The play isn't really about anything else. It dallies with colonialism and Northern Ireland, but even these issues are seen as extensions of gender politics. The relationships between the characters are conducted entirely and exclusively in sexual terms, from adultery all the way up to pederasty and incest. None of this is presented through the conventions of realist drama, which is why the play's explicitness is thought-provoking (and extremely funny) rather than merely shocking. On the night I was there, the younger sections of the audience were predictably delighted with Churchill's DIY° radicalism, but nearby pairs of elderly tourists were just as enthusiastic.

The strength of Churchill's feminism can be measured in part by the degree of sympathy she extends to those alienated from it. The two working-class gay characters in the second half are rather predictably well-adjusted, and Betty's gradual

---

DIY: "Do It Yourself."

liberation is genuinely moving (ending in the most lyrical description of masturbation you are ever likely to hear), but the straight male characters — both of them — are far from being mere ciphers. Like their more politically correct counterparts, they are trying to come to terms with their world: but in 1879 the world largely agrees with them, and in 1979 it doesn't. There are no heroes or villains, no triumphs or disasters; just a series of difficult adjustments being made at the most intimate, bodily level. Brilliant ensemble acting harmonizes these little private dramas into an absolutely compelling whole.

Sam Shepard

Samuel Shepard Rogers VII was born in Illinois in 1943, but his father was a career man in the army, and like most "army brats," Shepard found himself essentially uprooted, moving from base to base around the country. If he has roots as a writer, they are clearly in the American West, but not necessarily the West created by writers of westerns, comic books, and second-rate movies. Shepard's plays often have a surreal quality, as if they are set in a world of the imagination rather than in a real place like Paris, Texas.

Shepard is one of America's most important playwrights. He has won numerous awards, including ten Obie Awards (given to off-Broadway plays) between 1966 and 1979, an Obie Award for sustained achievement in 1980, the New York Drama Critics' Circle Award for *A Lie of the Mind* in 1985, and a Pulitzer Prize for *Buried Child* in 1979. His work has been produced primarily in the experimental theater of downtown New York in places such as La Mama and in regional theaters throughout the United States known for artistic integrity but not for reaching a broad spectrum of theatergoers. In his way Shepard has been an underground playwright who has won the respect of most theater people, including the best playwrights.

Shepard's love for, and frustrations with, music have found their way into a major theme of his work. He plays drums and guitar and has never realized an early desire for a career in rock music. But the subversive qualities of rock and jazz — their implicit critique of middle-class life — appear in his plays in his analyses of the middle-class family. His primary themes center on the family and its complications, the nature of the person alone, and the myth of the Old West. In each theme Shepard expresses a deep sense of longing and of loss, emotions that his audiences have found significant.

Because his father began to drink and family life became intolerable, Shepard left home after a year at college and toured with the Bishops Company Repertory Players. At nineteen he wound up in New York working in one of the best jazz clubs of the day, the Village Gate. During this time in Greenwich Village he began to write one-act plays with extraordinary energy. Like Jack Kerouac, he almost never revised his work. He wrote it in a burst of energy and then had it performed to audiences whose admiration grew.

In the 1970s Shepard began acting in major motion pictures. One of the ironies of his life is that he became a matinee idol after appearing in movies such as *The Right Stuff, Fool for Love, Country,* and *Crimes of the Heart.* The critic Harry Haun said of him, "He is the Recluse as Superstar, the man who has arrived on his own terms, carefully sculpting a special myth for himself."

His output for the stage has been prodigious, with dozens of one-act plays, and he has a central body of work that has gained him an enviable reputation. *Operation Sidewinder* (1970) was performed at the Vivian Beaumont Theater — a public theater at Lincoln Center in New York City — to mixed reviews. The play, set in the West, involves a giant mechanical snake designed to make contact with outer space travelers; it includes Hopi snake dances and military scenes. *The Tooth of Crime* (1972) is about turf wars between an aging rock star and an up-and-coming young star. Its brutality and directness make it intense, exciting, and revealing of the California rock 'n' roll scene in the early 1970s.

Curse of the Starving Class (1977) and *Buried Child* (1978) both helped solidify Shepard's reputation. *Suicide in B-Flat* (1976) and *True West* (1980) only made it clearer that his work was developing in a consistent vein of black humor and dark criticism of the sanctity of family life. *A Lie of the Mind* (1985), like *Buried Child,* is about disturbed family life. It is filled with secrets: incest, murder, and sin. *New York Times* critic Mel Gussow said that it explores "the damage that one does to filial, fraternal, and marital bonds." Incest — or potential incest — is also a theme in *Fool for Love* (1983), in which Shepard starred on film. The play is set in the West and contains all the themes for which his work is known.

Shepard began his work with a sense of the West drawn from popular literature, reshaped it, and produced it in a new form. If the American West has a reality that survived its mythicization in the dime novel and John Wayne's movies, then Shepard is partly responsible for the way we now see it.

TRUE WEST

True West (1980) portrays a family, or part of a family, shattered by unknown circumstances into individuals isolated in their inability to understand and express their feelings for one another. The past is a strange, silent land that no one seems to be able to discover. The image of the desert that lingers throughout the play — in contrast with the cricket-drenched suburban setting — is an image of a pure, strange, and liberating environment. In some plays it might represent a nostalgia for a happy past. Instead, in *True West* it seems to imply a place where a person, like the religious hermits of the early Christian church, can be alone and somehow commune with an inner self.

The theme of loneliness is woven in complex ways into the play. The father is in a desert somewhere drinking himself into oblivion. Mom goes vacationing alone to Alaska, a cold glacial desert that leaves her with a sense of longing not for people but for her plants. When the play opens, Austin, the screenwriter, has taken Mom's house while she is away so he can be alone and write in peace and quiet. Lee, the older, outsider brother, breaks in on his peace and quiet in the same manner that he breaks into houses in the neighborhood and steals TVs. But when he visits Mom's house and finds Austin, it is not a TV he ends up stealing: he steals Austin's livelihood and, in a fascinating way, his identity.

The struggle between Austin and Lee has a profound psychological quality that implies an almost unnatural terror. Lee and Austin are like two halves of the same person, but two halves that express totally antagonistic qualities. In their efforts to be one another, they are both trying to join the intellectual and violent sides of their nature. Early in the play Lee tells Austin "I always wondered what'd be like to be you." Austin's surprised response is to tell Lee that he has always pictured him somewhere — which is to say that he has felt much the same way.

In their aloneness Austin and Lee acknowledge a sense of incompleteness. Such an awareness is not expressed by Mom, nor is it implied about the father. In this sense, Lee and Austin are very different from their parents. Whether that difference represents a hopeful sign is an unanswered question. The play ends with a power struggle between the brothers, but a struggle not so much for ultimate control as for a successful merger of their identities. The outcome of the action is in every sense in doubt as the play ends.

The title of the play carries special irony. Saul, the producer, tells Austin that Lee's outline for a story has the ring of truth to it. Austin knows the Hollywood scene, the dishonesty that produces three hundred thousand dollar deals. Sam Shepard knows it, too. His commentary is on the Hollywood shams that pretend to be true pictures of the American West. Lee and Austin represent a portrait of the true West; and to an extent the loneliness of the Mojave Desert represents the true West. But paying attention to the truth is painful. The true West is not a B movie; it is not a piece of escapist claptrap. It is an almost schizoid disunity, a play of opposites and painful discords.

True West in Performance

True West premiered in 1980, directed by Shepard's friend Robert Woodruff at San Francisco's Magic Theater, with Shepard as playwright in residence. That production garnered considerable praise from reviewers. The acting, lighting, set, and directing all impressed audiences enough that the famed Joseph Papp readied the play for the Public Theater in New York, where Papp had produced *Curse of the Starving Class* in 1978.

Unfortunately, Papp and Shepard had a falling out. Woodruff went to New York to assist in the production but was so horrified by the heavy-handed way Papp handled the acting and staging that he resigned from the project. The play opened in December 1980 to mixed reviews. Shepard disclaimed the production and swore he would never let Papp have another of his plays.

The revival of *True West* at the Cherry Lane Theater off-Broadway in October 1982 with John Malkovich as Lee and Gary Sinise as Austin (also as the director) marked the beginning of the play as we now think of it. Malkovich and Sinise, of Chicago's Steppenwolf Theatre Company, made their New York debut in *True West* and created a sensation. The reviews agreed that Malkovich and Sinise had perfectly embodied the characters and perfectly interpreted the play. The Public Broadcasting System produced a televised version of the play in the summer of 1998, also with Malkovich and Sinise as the brothers.

In the most recent production of the play (March 2000), in New York's Circle in the Square, John C. Reilly and Philip Seymour Hoffman alternated in the roles of Lee and Austin. This was the first Broadway production of *True West*.

Sam Shepard *(b. 1943)*
TRUE WEST

1980

Characters

AUSTIN, *early thirties, light blue sports shirt, light tan cardigan sweater, clean blue jeans, white tennis shoes*

LEE, *his older brother, early forties, filthy white t-shirt, tattered brown overcoat covered with dust, dark blue baggy pants from the Salvation Army, pink suede belt, pointed black forties dress shoes scuffed up, holes in the soles, no socks, no hat, long pronounced sideburns, "Gene Vincent" hairdo, two days' growth of beard, bad teeth*

SAUL KIMMER, *late forties, Hollywood producer, pink and white flower print sports shirt, white sports coat with matching polyester slacks, black and white loafers*

MOM, *early sixties, mother of the brothers, small woman, conservative white skirt and matching jacket, red shoulder bag, two pieces of matching red luggage*

Scene: *All nine scenes take place on the same set; a kitchen and adjoining alcove of an older home in a Southern California suburb, about 40 miles east of Los Angeles. The kitchen takes up most of the playing area to stage left. The kitchen consists of a sink, upstage center, surrounded by counter space, a wall telephone, cupboards, and a small window just above it bordered by neat yellow curtains. Stage left of sink is a stove. Stage right, a refrigerator. The alcove adjoins the kitchen to stage right. There is no wall division or door to the alcove. It is open and easily accessible from the kitchen and defined only by the objects in it: a small round glass breakfast table mounted on white iron legs, two matching white iron chairs set across from each other. The two exterior walls of the alcove which prescribe a corner in the upstage right are composed of many small windows, beginning from a solid wall about three feet high and extending to the ceiling. The windows look out to bushes and citrus trees. The alcove is filled with all sorts of house plants in various pots, mostly Boston ferns hanging in planters at different levels. The floor of the alcove is composed of green synthetic grass.*

All entrances and exits are made stage left from the kitchen. There is no door. The actors simply go off and come onto the playing area.

Note on Set and Costume: *The set should be constructed realistically with no attempt to distort its dimensions, shapes, objects, or colors. No objects should be introduced which might draw special attention to themselves other than the props demanded by the script. If a stylistic "concept" is grafted onto the set design it will only serve to confuse the evolution of the characters' situation, which is the most important focus of the play.*

Likewise, the costumes should be exactly representative of who the characters are and not added on to for the sake of making a point to the audience.

Note on Sound: *The coyote of Southern California has a distinct yapping, doglike bark, similar to a hyena. This yapping grows more intense and maniacal as the pack grows in numbers, which is usually the case when they lure and kill pets from suburban yards. The sense of growing frenzy in the pack should be felt in the background, particularly in Scenes VII and VIII. In any case, these coyotes never make the long, mournful, solitary howl of the Hollywood stereotype.*

The sound of crickets can speak for itself.

These sounds should also be treated realistically even though they sometimes grow in volume and numbers.

ACT I • *Scene I*

(Night. Sound of crickets in dark. Candlelight appears in alcove, illuminating Austin, seated at glass table hunched over a writing notebook, pen in hand, cigarette burning in ashtray, cup of coffee, typewriter on table, stacks of paper, candle burning on table.)

(Soft moonlight fills kitchen illuminating Lee, beer in hand, six-pack on counter behind him. He's leaning against the sink, mildly drunk; takes a slug of beer.)

LEE: So, Mom took off for Alaska, huh?

AUSTIN: Yeah.

LEE: Sorta' left you in charge.

AUSTIN: Well, she knew I was coming down here so she offered me the place.

LEE: You keepin' the plants watered?

AUSTIN: Yeah.

LEE: Keepin' the sink clean? She don't like even a single tea leaf in the sink ya' know.

AUSTIN (*trying to concentrate on writing*): Yeah, I know.

(Pause.)

LEE: She gonna' be up there a long time?

AUSTIN: I don't know.

LEE: Kinda' nice for you, huh? Whole place to yourself.

AUSTIN: Yeah, it's great.

LEE: Ya' got crickets anyway. Tons a' crickets out there.
  (Looks around kitchen.) Ya' got groceries? Coffee?

AUSTIN (*looking up from writing*): What?

LEE: You got coffee?

AUSTIN: Yeah.

LEE: At's good. (*Short pause.*) Real coffee? From the bean?

AUSTIN: Yeah. You want some?

LEE: Naw. I brought some uh — (*Motions to beer.*)

AUSTIN: Help yourself to whatever's — (*Motions to refrigerator.*)

LEE: I will. Don't worry about me. I'm not the one to worry about. I mean I can uh — (*Pause.*) You always work by candlelight?

AUSTIN: No — uh — Not always.

LEE: Just sometimes?

AUSTIN (*puts pen down, rubs his eyes*): Yeah. Sometimes it's soothing.

LEE: Isn't that what the old guys did?

AUSTIN: What old guys?

LEE: The Forefathers. You know.

AUSTIN: Forefathers?

LEE: Isn't that what they did? Candlelight burning into the night? Cabins in the wilderness.

AUSTIN (*rubs hand through his hair*): I suppose.

LEE: I'm not botherin' you am I? I mean I don't wanna break into yer uh — concentration or nothin'.

AUSTIN: No, it's all right.

LEE: That's good. I mean I realize that yer line a' work demands a lota' concentration.

AUSTIN: It's okay.

LEE: You probably think that I'm not fully able to comprehend somethin' like that, huh?

AUSTIN: Like what?

LEE: That stuff yer doin'. That art. You know. Whatever you call it.

AUSTIN: It's just a little research.

LEE: You may not know it but I did a little art myself once.

AUSTIN: You did?

LEE: Yeah! I did some a' that. I fooled around with it. No future in it.

AUSTIN: What'd you do?

LEE: Never mind what I did! Just never mind about that. (*Pause.*) It was ahead of its time.

(*Pause.*)

AUSTIN: So, you went out to see the old man, huh?

LEE: Yeah, I seen him.

AUSTIN: How's he doing?

LEE: Same. He doin' just about the same.

AUSTIN: I was down there too, you know.

LEE: What d'ya' want, an award? You want some kinda' medal? You were down there. He told me all about you.

AUSTIN: What'd he say?

LEE: He told me. Don't worry.

(*Pause.*)

AUSTIN: Well —

LEE: You don't have to say nothin'.

AUSTIN: I wasn't.

LEE: Yeah, you were gonna' make somethin' up. Somethin' brilliant.

(*Pause.*)

AUSTIN: You going to be down here very long, Lee?

LEE: Might be. Depends on a few things.

AUSTIN: You got some friends down here?

LEE (*laughs*): I know a few people. Yeah.

AUSTIN: Well, you can stay here as long as I'm here.

LEE: I don't need your permission do I?

AUSTIN: No.

LEE: I mean she's my mother too, right?

AUSTIN: Right.

LEE: She might've just as easily asked me to take care of her place as you.

AUSTIN: That's right.

LEE: I mean I know how to water plants.

(*Long pause.*)

AUSTIN: So you don't know how long you'll be staying then?

LEE: Depends mostly on houses, ya' know.

AUSTIN: Houses?

LEE: Yeah. Houses. Electric devices. Stuff like that. I gotta' make a little tour first.

(*Short pause.*)

AUSTIN: Lee, why don't you just try another neighborhood, all right?

LEE (*laughs*): What'sa matter with this neighborhood? This is a great neighborhood. Lush. Good class a' people. Not many dogs.

AUSTIN: Well, our uh — Our mother just happens to live here. That's all.

LEE: Nobody's gonna' know. All they know is somethin's missing. That's all. She'll never even hear about it. Nobody's gonna' know.

AUSTIN: You're going to get picked up if you start walking around here at night.

LEE: Me? I'm gonna' git picked up? What about you? You stick out like a sore thumb. Look at you. You think yer regular lookin'?

AUSTIN: I've got too much to deal with here to be worrying about —

LEE: Yer not gonna' have to worry about me! I've been doin' all right without you. I haven't been anywhere near you for five years! Now isn't that true?

AUSTIN: Yeah.

LEE: So you don't have to worry about me. I'm a free agent.

AUSTIN: All right.

LEE: Now all I wanna' do is borrow yer car.

AUSTIN: No!

LEE: Just fer a day. One day.

AUSTIN: No!

LEE: I won't take it outside a twenty mile radius. I promise ya'. You can check the speedometer.

AUSTIN: You're not borrowing my car! That's all there is to it.

(*Pause.*)

LEE: Then I'll just take the damn thing.

AUSTIN: Lee, look — I don't want any trouble, all right?

LEE: That's a dumb line. That is a dumb fuckin' line. You git paid fer dreamin' up a line like that?

AUSTIN: Look, I can give you some money if you need money.

(*Lee suddenly lunges at Austin, grabs him violently by the shirt, and shakes him with tremendous power.*)

LEE: Don't you say that to me! Don't you ever say that to me! (*Just as suddenly he turns him loose, pushes him away, and backs off.*) You may be able to git away with that with the Old Man. Git him tanked up for a week! Buy him off with yer Hollywood blood money, but not me! I can git my own money my own way. Big money!

AUSTIN: I was just making an offer.

LEE: Yeah, well keep it to yourself!

(*Long pause.*)

Those are the most monotonous fuckin' crickets I ever heard in my life.

AUSTIN: I kinda' like the sound.

LEE: Yeah. Supposed to be able to tell the temperature by the number a' pulses. You believe that?

AUSTIN: The temperature?

LEE: Yeah. The air. How hot it is.

AUSTIN: How do you do that?

LEE: I don't know. Some woman told me that. She was a Botanist. So I believed her.

AUSTIN: Where'd you meet her?

LEE: What?

AUSTIN: The woman Botanist?

LEE: I met her on the desert. I been spendin' a lota' time on the desert.

AUSTIN: What were you doing out there?

LEE (*pause, stares in space*): I forgit. Had me a Pit Bull there for a while but I lost him.

AUSTIN: Pit Bull?

LEE: Fightin' dog. Damn I made some good money off that little dog. Real good money.

(*Pause.*)

AUSTIN: You could come up north with me, you know.

LEE: What's up there?

AUSTIN: My family.

LEE: Oh, that's right, you got the wife and kiddies now don't ya'. The house, the car, the whole slam. That's right.

AUSTIN: You could spend a couple of days. See how you like it. I've got an extra room.

LEE: Too cold up there.

(*Pause.*)

AUSTIN: You want to sleep for a while?

LEE (*pause, stares at Austin*): I don't sleep.

(*Lights to black.*)

Scene II

(*Morning. Austin is watering plants with a vaporizer, Lee sits at glass table in alcove drinking beer.*)

LEE: I never realized the old lady was so security-minded.

AUSTIN: How do you mean?

LEE: Made a little tour this morning. She's got locks on everything. Locks and double locks and chain locks and — What's she got that's so valuable?

AUSTIN: Antiques I guess. I don't know.

LEE: Antiques? Brought everything with her from the old place, huh. Just the same crap we always had around. Plates and spoons.

AUSTIN: I guess they have personal value to her.

LEE: Personal value. Yeah. Just a lota' junk. Most of it's phony anyway. Idaho decals. Now who in the hell wants to eat offa' plate with the State of Idaho starin' ya in the face. Every time ya' take a bite ya' get to see a little bit more.

AUSTIN: Well it must mean something to her or she wouldn't save it.

LEE: Yeah, well personally I don't wann' be invaded by Idaho when I'm eatin'. When I'm eatin' I'm home. Ya' know what I'm sayin'? I'm not driftin', I'm home. I don't need my thoughts swept off to Idaho. I don't need that!

(*Pause.*)

AUSTIN: Did you go out last night?

LEE: Why?

AUSTIN: I thought I heard you go out.

LEE: Yeah, I went out. What about it?

AUSTIN: Just wondered.

LEE: Damn coyotes kept me awake.

AUSTIN: Oh yeah, I heard them. They must've killed somebody's dog or something.

LEE: Yappin' their fool heads off. They don't yap like that on the desert. They howl. These are city coyotes here.

AUSTIN: Well, you don't sleep anyway do you?

(*Pause, Lee stares at him.*)

LEE: You're pretty smart aren't ya?

AUSTIN: How do you mean?

LEE: I mean you never had any more on the ball than I did. But here you are gettin' invited into prominent people's houses. Sittin' around talkin' like you know somethin'.

AUSTIN: They're not so prominent.

LEE: They're a helluva' lot more prominent than the houses I get invited into.

AUSTIN: Well you invite yourself.

LEE: That's right. I do. In fact I probably got a wider range a' choices than you do, come to think of it.

AUSTIN: I wouldn't doubt it.

LEE: In fact I been inside some pretty classy places in my time. And I never even went to an Ivy League school either.

John Malkovich as Lee in Steppenwolf Theatre Company's
Chicago production of *True West*. Gary Sinise, in the
background as Austin, directed the play in 1982.

AUSTIN: You want some breakfast or something?
LEE: Breakfast?
AUSTIN: Yeah. Don't you eat breakfast?
LEE: Look, don't worry about me pal. I can take care a'
   myself. You just go ahead as though I wasn't even
   here, all right?

(*Austin goes into kitchen, makes coffee.*)

AUSTIN: Where'd you walk to last night?

(*Pause.*)

LEE: I went up in the foothills there. Up in the San Ga-
   briels. Heat was drivin' me crazy.
AUSTIN: Well, wasn't it hot out on the desert?
LEE: Different kinda' heat. Out there it's clean. Cools off
   at night. There's a nice little breeze.
AUSTIN: Where were you, the Mojave?
LEE: Yeah. The Mojave. That's right.
AUSTIN: I haven't been out there in years.
LEE: Out past Needles there.
AUSTIN: Oh yeah.
LEE: Up here it's different. This country's real different.
AUSTIN: Well, it's been built up.
LEE: Built up? Wiped out is more like it. I don't even
   hardly recognize it.
AUSTIN: Yeah. Foothills are the same though, aren't they?
LEE: Pretty much. It's funny goin' up in there. The smells
   and everything. Used to catch snakes up there,
   remember?
AUSTIN: You caught snakes.
LEE: Yeah. And you'd pretend you were Geronimo or
   some damn thing. You used to go right out to lunch.
AUSTIN: I enjoyed my imagination.
LEE: That what you call it? Looks like yer still enjoyin' it.
AUSTIN: So you just wandered around up there, huh?
LEE: Yeah. With a purpose.
AUSTIN: See any houses?

(*Pause.*)

LEE: Couple. Couple a' real nice ones. One of 'em didn't
   even have a dog. Walked right up and stuck my head
   in the window. Not a peep. Just a sweet kinda' suburban silence.
AUSTIN: What kind of a place was it?
LEE: Like a paradise. Kinda' place that sorta' kills ya'
   inside. Warm yellow lights. Mexican tile all around.
   Copper pots hangin' over the stove. Ya' know like
   they got in the magazines. Blond people movin' in and
   outa' the rooms, talkin' to each other. (*Pause.*) Kinda'
   place you wish you sorta' grew up in, ya' know.
AUSTIN: That's the kind of place you wish you'd grown
   up in?
LEE: Yeah, why not?
AUSTIN: I thought you hated that kind of stuff.
LEE: Yeah, well you never knew too much about me did
   ya'?

(*Pause.*)

AUSTIN: Why'd you go out to the desert in the first place?
LEE: I was on my way to see the old man.
AUSTIN: You mean you just passed through there?
LEE: Yeah. That's right. Three months of passin' through.
AUSTIN: Three months?
LEE: Somethin' like that. Maybe more. Why?
AUSTIN: You lived on the Mojave for three months?
LEE: Yeah. What'sa matter with that?
AUSTIN: By yourself?
LEE: Mostly. Had a couple a' visitors. Had that dog for a
   while.

AUSTIN: Didn't you miss people?

LEE (*laughs*): People?

AUSTIN: Yeah. I mean I go crazy if I have to spend three nights in a motel by myself.

LEE: Yer not in a motel now.

AUSTIN: No, I know. But sometimes I have to stay in motels.

LEE: Well, they got people in motels don't they?

AUSTIN: Strangers.

LEE: Yer friendly aren't ya'? Aren't you the friendly type?

(*Pause.*)

AUSTIN: I'm going to have somebody coming by here later, Lee.

LEE: Ah! Lady friend?

AUSTIN: No, a producer.

LEE: Aha! What's he produce?

AUSTIN: Film. Movies. You know.

LEE: Oh, movies. Motion Pictures! A Big Wig Huh?

AUSTIN: Yeah.

LEE: What's he comin' by here for?

AUSTIN: We have to talk about a project.

LEE: Whadya' mean, "a project"? What's "a project"?

AUSTIN: A script.

LEE: Oh. That's what yer doin' with all these papers?

AUSTIN: Yeah.

LEE: Well, what's the project about?

AUSTIN: We're uh — it's a period piece.

LEE: What's "a period piece"?

AUSTIN: Look, it doesn't matter. The main thing is we need to discuss this alone. I mean —

LEE: Oh, I get it. You want me outa' the picture.

AUSTIN: Not exactly. I just need to be alone with him for a couple of hours. So we can talk.

LEE: Yer afraid I'll embarrass ya' huh?

AUSTIN: I'm not afraid you'll embarrass me!

LEE: Well, I tell ya' what — Why don't you just gimme the keys to yer car and I'll be back here around six o'clock or so. That give ya enough time?

AUSTIN: I'm not loaning you my car, Lee.

LEE: You want me to just git lost huh? Take a hike? Is that it? Pound the pavement for a few hours while you bullshit yer way into a million bucks.

AUSTIN: Look, it's going to be hard enough for me to face this character on my own without —

LEE: You don't know this guy?

AUSTIN: No I don't know — He's a producer. I mean I've been meeting with him for months but you never get to know a producer.

LEE: Yer tryin' to hustle him? Is that it?

AUSTIN: I'm not trying to hustle him! I'm trying to work out a deal! It's not easy.

LEE: What kinda' deal?

AUSTIN: Convince him it's a worthwhile story.

LEE: He's not convinced? How come he's comin' over here if he's not convinced? I'll convince him for ya'.

AUSTIN: You don't understand the way things work down here.

LEE: How do things work down here?

(*Pause.*)

AUSTIN: Look, if I loan you my car will you have it back here by six?

LEE: On the button. With a full tank a' gas.

AUSTIN (*digging in his pocket for keys*): Forget about the gas.

LEE: Hey, these days gas is gold, old buddy.

(*Austin hands the keys to Lee.*)

You remember that car I used to loan you?

AUSTIN: Yeah.

LEE: Forty Ford. Flathead.

AUSTIN: Yeah.

LEE: Sucker hauled ass didn't it?

AUSTIN: Lee, it's not that I don't want to loan you my car —

LEE: You are loanin' me yer car.

(*Lee gives Austin a pat on the shoulder, pause.*)

AUSTIN: I know. I just wish —

LEE: What? You wish what?

AUSTIN: I don't know. I wish I wasn't — I wish I didn't have to be doing business down here. I'd like to just spend some time with you.

LEE: I thought it was "Art" you were doin'.

(*Lee moves across the kitchen toward exit, tosses keys in his hand.*)

AUSTIN: Try to get back here by six, okay?

LEE: No sweat. Hey, ya' know, if that uh — story of yours doesn't go over with the guy — tell him I got a couple a' "projects" he might be interested in. Real commercial. Full a' suspense. True-to-life stuff.

(*Lee exits, Austin stares after Lee then turns, goes to papers at table, leafs through pages, lights fade to black.*)

Scene III

(*Afternoon. Alcove, Saul Kimmer and Austin seated across from each other at table.*)

SAUL: Well, to tell you the truth Austin, I have never felt so confident about a project in quite a long time.

AUSTIN: Well, that's good to hear, Saul.

SAUL: I am absolutely convinced we can get this thing off the ground. I mean we'll have to make a sale to television and that means getting a major star. Somebody bankable. But I think we can do it. I really do.

AUSTIN: Don't you think we need a first draft before we approach a star?

SAUL: No, no, not at all. I don't think it's necessary. Maybe a brief synopsis. I don't want you to touch the typewriter until we have some seed money.

AUSTIN: That's fine with me.

SAUL: I mean it's a great story. Just the story alone. You've really managed to capture something this time.

AUSTIN: I'm glad you like it, Saul.

(*Lee enters abruptly into kitchen carrying a stolen television set, short pause.*)

LEE: Aw shit, I'm sorry about that. I am really sorry Austin.

AUSTIN (*standing*): That's all right.

LEE (*moving toward them*): I mean I thought it was way past six already. You said to have it back here by six.

AUSTIN: We were just finishing up. (*To Saul.*) This is my, uh — brother, Lee.

SAUL (*standing*): Oh, I'm very happy to meet you.

(*Lee sets T.V. on sink counter, shakes hands with Saul.*)

LEE: I can't tell ya' how happy I am to meet you sir.

SAUL: Saul Kimmer.

LEE: Mr. Kipper.

SAUL: Kimmer.

AUSTIN: Lee's been living out on the desert and he just uh —

SAUL: Oh, that's terrific! (*To Lee.*) Palm Springs?

LEE: Yeah. Yeah, right. Right around in that area. Near uh — Bob Hope Drive there.

SAUL: Oh I love it out there. I just love it. The air is wonderful.

LEE: Yeah. Sure is. Healthy.

SAUL: And the golf. I don't know if you play golf, but the golf is just about the best.

LEE: I play a lota' golf.

SAUL: Is that right?

LEE: Yeah. In fact I was hoping I'd run into somebody out here who played a little golf. I've been lookin' for a partner.

SAUL: Well, I uh —

AUSTIN: Lee's just down for a visit while our mother's in Alaska.

SAUL: Oh, your mother's in Alaska?

AUSTIN: Yes. She went up there on a little vacation. This is her place.

SAUL: I see. Well isn't that something. Alaska.

LEE: What kinda' handicap do ya' have, Mr. Kimmer?

SAUL: Oh I'm just a Sunday duffer really. You know.

LEE: That's good 'cause I haven't swung a club in months.

SAUL: Well we ought to get together sometime and have a little game. Austin, do you play?

(*Saul mimes a Johnny Carson golf swing for Austin.*)

AUSTIN: No. I don't uh — I've watched it on T.V.

LEE (*to Saul*): How 'bout tomorrow morning? Bright and early. We could get out there and put in eighteen holes before breakfast.

SAUL: Well, I've got uh — I have several appointments —

LEE: No, I mean real early. Crack a' dawn. While the dew's still thick on the fairway.

SAUL: Sounds really great.

LEE: Austin could be our caddie.

SAUL: Now that's an idea. (*Laughs.*)

AUSTIN: I don't know the first thing about golf.

LEE: There's nothin' to it. Isn't that right, Saul? He'd pick it up in fifteen minutes.

SAUL: Sure. Doesn't take long. 'Course you have to play for years to find your true form. (*Chuckles.*)

LEE (*to Austin*): We'll give ya' a quick run-down on the club faces. The irons, the woods. Show ya' a couple pointers on the basic swing. Might even let ya' hit the ball a couple times. Whadya' think, Saul?

SAUL: Why not. I think it'd be great. I haven't had any exercise in weeks.

LEE: 'At's the spirit! We'll have a little orange juice right afterwards.

(*Pause.*)

SAUL: Orange juice?

LEE: Yea! Vitamin C! Nothin' like a shot a' orange juice after a round a' golf. Hot shower. Snappin' towels at each others' privates. Real sense a' fraternity.

SAUL (*smiles at Austin*): Well, you make it sound very inviting, I must say. It really does sound great.

LEE: Then it's a date.

SAUL: Well, I'll call the country club and see if I can arrange something.

LEE: Great! Boy, I sure am sorry that I busted in on ya' all in the middle of yer meeting.

SAUL: Oh that's quite all right. We were just about finished anyway.

LEE: I can wait out in the other room if you want.

SAUL: No really —

LEE: Just got Austin's color T.V. back from the shop. I can watch a little amateur boxing now.

(*Lee and Austin exchange looks.*)

SAUL: Oh — Yes.

LEE: You don't fool around in Television, do you Saul?

SAUL: Uh — I have in the past. Produced some T.V. Specials. Network stuff. But it's mainly features now.

LEE: That's where the big money is, huh?

SAUL: Yes. That's right.

AUSTIN: Why don't I call you tomorrow, Saul and we'll get together. We can have lunch or something.

SAUL: That'd be terrific.

LEE: Right after the golf.

(*Pause.*)

SAUL: What?

LEE: You can have lunch right after the golf.

SAUL: Oh, right.

LEE: Austin was tellin' me that yer interested in stories.

SAUL: Well, we develop certain projects that we feel have commercial potential.

LEE: What kinda' stuff do ya' go in for?

SAUL: Oh, the usual. You know. Good love interest. Lots of action. (*Chuckles at Austin.*)

LEE: Westerns?

SAUL: Sometimes.

AUSTIN: I'll give you a ring, Saul.

(*Austin tries to move Saul across the kitchen but Lee blocks their way.*)

LEE: I got a Western that'd knock yer lights out.

SAUL: Oh really?

LEE: Yeah. Contemporary Western. Based on a true story. 'Course I'm not a writer like my brother here. I'm not a man of the pen.

SAUL: Well —

LEE: I mean I can tell ya' a story off the tongue but I can't put it down on paper. That don't make any difference though does it?

SAUL: No, not really.

LEE: I mean plenty a' guys have stories don't they? True-life stories. Musta' been a lota' movies made from real life.

SAUL: Yes, I suppose so.

LEE: I haven't seen a good Western since *Lonely Are the Brave.* You remember that movie?

SAUL: No, I'm afraid I —

LEE: Kirk Douglas. Helluva' movie. You remember that movie, Austin?

AUSTIN: Yes.

LEE (*to Saul*): The man dies for the love of a horse.

SAUL: Is that right.

LEE: Yeah. Ya' hear the horse screamin' at the end of it. Rain's comin' down. Horse is screamin'. Then there's a shot. BLAM! Just a single shot like that. Then nothin' but the sound of rain. And Kirk Douglas is ridin' in the ambulance. Ridin' away from the scene of the accident. And when he hears that shot he knows that his horse has died. He knows. And you see his eyes. And his eyes die. Right inside his face. And then his eyes close. And you know that he's died too. You know that Kirk Douglas has died from the death of his horse.

SAUL (*eyes Austin nervously*): Well, it sounds like a great movie. I'm sorry I missed it.

LEE: Yeah, you shouldn't a' missed that one.

SAUL: I'll have to try to catch it some time. Arrange a screening or something. Well, Austin, I'll have to hit the freeway before rush hour.

AUSTIN (*ushers him toward exit*): It's good seeing you, Saul.

(*Austin and Saul shake hands.*)

LEE: So ya' think there's room for a real Western these days? A true-to-life Western?

SAUL: Well, I don't see why not. Why don't you uh — tell the story to Austin and have him write a little outline.

LEE: You'd take a look at it then?

SAUL: Yes. Sure. I'll give it a read-through. Always eager for new material. (*Smiles at Austin.*)

LEE: That's great! You'd really read it then huh?

SAUL: It would just be my opinion of course.

LEE: That's all I want. Just an opinion. I happen to think it has a lota' possibilities.

SAUL: Well, it was great meeting you and I'll —

(*Saul and Lee shake.*)

LEE: I'll call you tomorrow about the golf.

SAUL: Oh. Yes, right.

LEE: Austin's got your number, right?

SAUL: Yes.

LEE: So long Saul. (*Gives Saul a pat on the back.*)

(*Saul exits, Austin turns to Lee, looks at T.V. then back to Lee.*)

AUSTIN: Give me the keys.

(*Austin extends his hand toward Lee, Lee doesn't move, just stares at Austin, smiles, lights to black.*)

Scene IV

(*Night. Coyotes in distance, fade, sound of typewriter in dark, crickets, candlelight in alcove, dim light in kitchen, lights reveal Austin at glass table typing, Lee sits across from him, foot on table, drinking beer and whiskey, the T.V. is still on sink counter, Austin types for a while, then stops.*)

LEE: All right, now read it back to me.

AUSTIN: I'm not reading it back to you, Lee. You can read it when we're finished. I can't spend all night on this.

LEE: You got better things to do?

AUSTIN: Let's just go ahead. Now what happens when he leaves Texas?

LEE: Is he ready to leave Texas yet? I didn't know we were that far along. He's not ready to leave Texas.

AUSTIN: He's right at the border.

LEE (*sitting up*): No, see this is one a' the crucial parts. Right here. (*Taps paper with beer can.*) We can't rush through this. He's not right at the border. He's a good fifty miles from the border. A lot can happen in fifty miles.

AUSTIN: It's only an outline. We're not writing an entire script now.

LEE: Well ya' can't leave things out even if it is an outline. It's one a' the most important parts. Ya' can't go leavin' it out.

AUSTIN: Okay, okay. Let's just — get it done.

LEE: All right. Now. He's in the truck and he's got his horse trailer and his horse.

AUSTIN: We've already established that.

LEE: And he sees this other guy comin' up behind him in another truck. And that truck is pullin' a gooseneck.

AUSTIN: What's a gooseneck?

LEE: Cattle trailer. You know the kind with a gooseneck, goes right down in the bed a' the pick-up.

AUSTIN: Oh. All right. (*Types.*)

LEE: It's important.

AUSTIN: Okay. I got it.

LEE: All these details are important.

(*Austin types as they talk.*)

AUSTIN: I've got it.

LEE: And this other guy's got his horse all saddled up in the back a' the gooseneck.

AUSTIN: Right.

LEE: So both these guys have got their horses right along with 'em, see.

AUSTIN: I understand.

LEE: Then this first guy suddenly realizes two things.

AUSTIN: The guy in front?

LEE: Right. The guy in front realizes two things almost at the same time. Simultaneous.

AUSTIN: What were the two things?

LEE: Number one, he realizes that the guy behind him is the husband of the woman he's been —

(*Lee makes gesture of screwing by pumping his arm.*)

AUSTIN (*sees Lee's gesture*): Oh. Yeah.

LEE: And number two, he realizes he's in the middle of Tornado Country.

AUSTIN: What's "Tornado Country"?

LEE: Panhandle.

AUSTIN: Panhandle?

LEE: Sweetwater. Around in that area. Nothin'. No-where, and number three —

AUSTIN: I thought there was only two.

LEE: There's three. There's a third unforeseen realization.

AUSTIN: And what's that?

LEE: That he's runnin' outa' gas.

AUSTIN (*stops typing*): Come on, Lee.

(*Austin gets up, moves to kitchen, gets a glass of water.*)

LEE: Whadya' mean, "come on"? That's what it is. Write it down! He's runnin' outa' gas.

AUSTIN: It's too —

LEE: What? It's too what? It's too real! That's what ya' mean isn't it? It's too much like real life!

AUSTIN: It's not like real life! It's not enough like real life. Things don't happen like that.

LEE: What! Men don't fuck other men's women?

AUSTIN: Yes. But they don't end up chasing each other across the Panhandle. Through "Tornado Country."

LEE: They do in this movie!

AUSTIN: And they don't have horses conveniently along with them when they run out of gas! And they don't run out of gas either!

LEE: These guys run outa' gas! This is my story and one a' these guys runs outa' gas!

AUSTIN: It's just a dumb excuse to get them into a chase scene. It's contrived.

LEE: It is a chase scene! It's already a chase scene. They been chasin' each other fer days.

AUSTIN: So now they're supposed to abandon their trucks, climb on their horses, and chase each other into the mountains?

LEE (*standing suddenly*): There aren't any mountains in the Panhandle! It's flat!

(*Lee turns violently toward windows in alcove and throws beer can at them.*)

LEE: Goddamn those crickets! (*Yells at crickets.*) Shut up out there! (*Pause, turns back toward table.*) This place is like a fuckin' rest home here. How're you supposed to think!

AUSTIN: You wanna' take a break?

LEE: No, I don't wanna' take a break! I wanna' get this done! This is my last chance to get this done.

AUSTIN (*moves back into alcove*): All right. Take it easy.

LEE: I'm gonna be leavin' this area. I don't have time to mess around here.

AUSTIN: Where are you going?

LEE: Never mind where I'm goin'! That's got nothin' to do with you. I just gotta' get this done. I'm not like you. Hangin' around bein' a parasite offa' other fools. I gotta' do this thing and get out.

(*Pause.*)

AUSTIN: A parasite? Me?

LEE: Yeah, you!

AUSTIN: After you break into people's houses and take their televisions!

LEE: They don't need their televisions! I'm doin' them a service.

AUSTIN: Give me back my keys, Lee.

LEE: Not until you write this thing! You're gonna' write this outline thing for me or that car's gonna wind up in Arizona with a different paint job.

AUSTIN: You think you can force me to write this? I was doing you a favor.

LEE: Git off yer high horse will ya'! Favor! Big favor. Handin' down favors from the mountain top.

AUSTIN: Let's just write it, okay? Let's sit down and not get upset and see if we can get through this.

(*Austin sits at typewriter.*)
(*Long pause.*)

LEE: Yer not gonna' even show it to him, are ya'?

AUSTIN: What?

LEE: This outline. You got no intention of showin' it to him. Yer just doin' this 'cause yer afraid a' me.

AUSTIN: You can show it to him yourself.

LEE: I will, boy! I'm gonna' read it to him on the golf course.

AUSTIN: And I'm not afraid of you either.

LEE: Then how come yer doin' it?

AUSTIN (*pause*): So I can get my keys back.

(*Pause as Lee takes keys out of his pocket slowly and throws them on table, long pause. Austin stares at keys.*)

LEE: There. Now you got yer keys back.

(*Austin looks up at Lee but doesn't take keys.*)

LEE: Go ahead. There's yer keys.

(*Austin slowly takes keys off table and puts them back in his own pocket.*)

Now what're you gonna' do? Kick me out?

AUSTIN: I'm not going to kick you out, Lee.

LEE: You couldn't kick me out, boy.

AUSTIN: I know.

LEE: So you can't even consider that one. (*Pause.*) You could call the police. That'd be the obvious thing.

AUSTIN: You're my brother.

LEE: That don't mean a thing. You go down to the L.A. Police Department there and ask them what kinda' people kill each other the most. What do you think they'd say?

AUSTIN: Who said anything about killing?

LEE: Family people. Brothers. Brothers-in-law. Cousins. Real American-type people. They kill each other in the heat mostly. In the Smog-Alerts. In the Brush Fire Season. Right about this time a' year.

AUSTIN: This isn't the same.

LEE: Oh no? What makes it different?

AUSTIN: We're not insane. We're not driven to acts of violence like that. Not over a dumb movie script. Now sit down.

(*Long pause, Lee considers which way to go with it.*)

LEE: Maybe not. (*He sits back down at the table across from Austin.*) Maybe you're right. Maybe we're too intelligent, huh? (*Pause.*) We got our heads on our shoulders. One of us has even got a Ivy League diploma. Now that means somethin' don't it? Doesn't that mean somethin'?

AUSTIN: Look, I'll write this thing for you, Lee. I don't mind writing it. I just don't want to get all worked up about it. It's not worth it. Now, come on. Let's just get through it, okay?

LEE: Nah. I think there's easier money. Lotsa' places I could pick up thousands. Maybe millions. I don't need this shit. I could go up to Sacramento Valley and steal me a diesel. Ten thousand a week dismantling one a' those suckers. Ten thousand a week!

(*Lee opens another beer, puts his foot back up on table.*)

AUSTIN: No, really, look, I'll write it out for you. I think it's a great idea.

LEE: Nah, you got yer own work to do. I don't wanna' interfere with yer life.

AUSTIN: I mean it'd be really fantastic if you could sell this. Turn it into a movie. I mean it.

(*Pause.*)

LEE: Ya' think so huh?

AUSTIN: Absolutely. You could really turn your life around, you know. Change things.

LEE: I could get a house maybe.

AUSTIN: Sure you could get a house. You could get a whole ranch if you wanted to.

LEE (*laughs*): A ranch? I could get a ranch?

AUSTIN: 'Course you could. You know what a screenplay sells for these days?

LEE: No. What's it sell for?

AUSTIN: A lot. A whole lot of money.

LEE: Thousands?

AUSTIN: Yeah. Thousands.

LEE: Millions?

AUSTIN: Well —

LEE: We could get the old man outa' hock then.

AUSTIN: Maybe.

LEE: Maybe? Whadya' mean, maybe?

AUSTIN: I mean it might take more than money.

LEE: You were just tellin' me it'd change my whole life around. Why wouldn't it change his?

AUSTIN: He's different.

LEE: Oh, he's of a different ilk huh?

AUSTIN: He's not gonna' change. Let's leave the old man out of it.

LEE: That's right. He's not gonna' change but I will. I'll just turn myself right inside out. I could be just like you then, huh? Sittin' around dreamin' stuff up. Gettin' paid to dream. Ridin' back and forth on the freeway just dreamin' my fool head off.

AUSTIN: It's not all that easy.

LEE: It's not, huh?

AUSTIN: No. There's a lot of work involved.

LEE: What's the toughest part? Deciding whether to jog or play tennis?

(*Long pause.*)

AUSTIN: Well, look. You can stay here — do whatever you want to. Borrow the car. Come in and out. Doesn't matter to me. It's not my house. I'll help you write this thing or — not. Just let me know what you want. You tell me.

LEE: Oh. So now suddenly you're at my service. Is that it?

AUSTIN: What do you want to do Lee?

(*Long pause, Lee stares at him then turns and dreams at windows.*)

LEE: I tell ya' what I'd do if I still had that dog. Ya' wanna' know what I'd do?

AUSTIN: What?

LEE: Head out to Ventura. Cook up a little match. God that little dog could bear down. Lota' money in dog fightin'. Big money.

(*Pause.*)

AUSTIN: Why don't we try to see this through, Lee. Just for the hell of it. Maybe you've really got something here. What do you think?

(*Pause, Lee considers.*)

LEE: Maybe so. No harm in tryin' I guess. You think it's such a hot idea. Besides, I always wondered what'd be like to be you.

AUSTIN: You did?

LEE: Yeah, sure. I used to picture you walkin' around some campus with yer arms fulla' books. Blondes chasin' after ya'.

AUSTIN: Blondes? That's funny.

LEE: What's funny about it?

AUSTIN: Because I always used to picture you somewhere.

LEE: Where'd you picture me?

AUSTIN: Oh, I don't know. Different places. Adventures. You were always on some adventure.

LEE: Yeah.

AUSTIN: And I used to say to myself, "Lee's got the right

idea. He's out there in the world and here I am. What am I doing?"

LEE: Well you were settin' yourself up for somethin'.

AUSTIN: I guess.

LEE: We better get started on this thing then.

AUSTIN: Okay.

(*Austin sits up at typewriter, puts new paper in.*)

LEE: Oh. Can I get the keys back before I forget?

(*Austin hesitates.*)

You said I could borrow the car if I wanted, right? Isn't that what you said?

AUSTIN: Yeah. Right.

(*Austin takes keys out of his pocket, sets them on table, Lee takes keys slowly, plays with them in his hand.*)

LEE: I could get a ranch, huh?

AUSTIN: Yeah. We have to write it first though.

LEE: Okay. Let's write it.

(*Lights start dimming slowly to end of scene as Austin types, Lee speaks.*)

So they take off after each other straight into an endless black prairie. The sun is just comin' down and they can feel the night on their backs. What they don't know is that each one of 'em is afraid, see. Each one separately thinks that he's the only one that's afraid. And they keep ridin' like that straight into the night. Not knowing. And the one who's chasin' doesn't know where the other one is taking him. And the one who's being chased doesn't know where he's going.

(*Lights to black, typing stops in the dark, crickets fade.*)

ACT II • *Scene V*

(*Morning. Lee at the table in alcove with a set of golf clubs in a fancy leather bag, Austin at sink washing a few dishes.*)

AUSTIN: He really liked it, huh?

LEE: He wouldn't a' gave me these clubs if he didn't like it.

AUSTIN: He gave you the clubs?

LEE: Yeah. I told ya' he gave me the clubs. The bag too.

AUSTIN: I thought he just loaned them to you.

LEE: He said it was part a' the advance. A little gift like. Gesture of his good faith.

AUSTIN: He's giving you an advance?

LEE: Now what's so amazing about that? I told ya' it was a good story. You even said it was a good story.

AUSTIN: Well that is really incredible Lee. You know how many guys spend their whole lives down here trying to break into this business? Just trying to get in the door?

LEE (*pulling clubs out of bag, testing them*): I got no idea. How many?

(*Pause.*)

AUSTIN: How much of an advance is he giving you?

LEE: Plenty. We were talkin' big money out there. Ninth hole is where I sealed the deal.

AUSTIN: He made a firm commitment?

LEE: Absolutely.

AUSTIN: Well, I know Saul and he doesn't fool around when he says he likes something.

LEE: I thought you said you didn't know him.

AUSTIN: Well, I'm familiar with his tastes.

LEE: I let him get two up on me goin' into the back nine. He was sure he had me cold. You shoulda' seen his face when I pulled out the old pitching wedge and plopped it pin-high, two feet from the cup. He 'bout shit his pants. "Where'd a guy like you ever learn how to play golf like that?" he says.

(*Lee laughs, Austin stares at him.*)

AUSTIN: 'Course there's no contract yet. Nothing's final until it's on paper.

LEE: It's final, all right. There's no way he's gonna back out of it now. We gambled for it.

AUSTIN: Saul, gambled?

LEE: Yeah, sure. I mean he liked the outline already so he wasn't risking that much. I just guaranteed it with my short game.

(*Pause.*)

AUSTIN: Well, we should celebrate or something. I think Mom left a bottle of champagne in the refrigerator. We should have a little toast.

(*Austin gets glasses from cupboard, goes to refrigerator, pulls out bottle of champagne.*)

LEE: You shouldn't oughta' take her champagne, Austin. She's gonna' miss that.

AUSTIN: Oh, she's not going to mind. She'd be glad we put it to good use. I'll get her another bottle. Besides, it's perfect for the occasion.

(*Pause.*)

LEE: Yer gonna' get a nice fee for writin' the script a' course. Straight fee.

(*Austin stops, stares at Lee, puts glasses and bottle on table, pause.*)

AUSTIN: I'm writing the script?

LEE: That's what he said. Said we couldn't hire a better screenwriter in the whole town.

AUSTIN: But I'm already working on a script. I've got my own project. I don't have time to write two scripts.

AUSTIN: No, he said he was gonna' drop that other one.

(*Pause.*)

AUSTIN: What? You mean mine? He's going to drop mine and do yours instead?

LEE (*smiles*): Now look, Austin, it's jest beginner's luck ya' know. I mean I sank a fifty foot putt for this deal. No hard feelings.

(*Austin goes to phone on wall, grabs it, starts dialing.*)

He's not gonna' be in, Austin. Told me he wouldn't be in 'til late this afternoon.

AUSTIN (*stays on phone, dialing, listens*): I can't believe this. I just can't believe it. Are you sure he said that? Why would he drop mine?

LEE: That's what he told me.

AUSTIN: He can't do that without telling me first. Without talking to me at least. He wouldn't just make a decision like that without talking to me!

LEE: Well I was kinda' surprised myself. But he was real enthusiastic about my story.

(*Austin hangs up phone violently, paces.*)

AUSTIN: What'd he say! Tell me everything he said!

LEE: I been tellin' ya! He said he liked the story a whole lot. It was the first authentic Western to come along in a decade.

AUSTIN: He liked that story! Your story?

LEE: Yeah! What's so surprisin' about that?

AUSTIN: It's stupid! It's the dumbest story I ever heard in my life.

LEE: Hey, hold on! That's my story yer talkin' about!

AUSTIN: It's a bullshit story! It's idiotic. Two lamebrains chasing each other across Texas! Are you kidding? Who do you think's going to go see a film like that?

LEE: It's not a film! It's a movie. There's a big difference. That's somethin' Saul told me.

AUSTIN: Oh he did, huh?

LEE: Yeah, he said, "In this business we make movies, American movies. Leave the films to the French."

AUSTIN: So you got real intimate with old Saul huh? He started pouring forth his vast knowledge of Cinema.

LEE: I think he liked me a lot, to tell ya' the truth. I think he felt I was somebody he could confide in.

AUSTIN: What'd you do, beat him up or something?

LEE (*stands fast*): Hey, I've about had it with the insults buddy! You think yer the only one in the brain department here? Yer the only one that can sit around and cook things up? There's other people got ideas too, ya' know!

AUSTIN: You must've done something. Threatened him or something. Now what'd you do Lee?

LEE: I convinced him!

(*Lee makes sudden menacing lunge toward Austin, wielding golf club above his head, stops himself, frozen moment, long pause, Lee lowers club.*)

AUSTIN: Oh, Jesus. You didn't hurt him did you?

(*Long silence, Lee sits back down at table.*)

Lee! Did you hurt him?

LEE: I didn't do nothin' to him! He liked my story. Pure and simple. He said it was the best story he'd come across in a long, long time.

AUSTIN: That's what he told me about my story! That's the same thing he said to me.

LEE: Well, he musta' been lyin'. He musta' been lyin' to one of us anyway.

AUSTIN: You can't come into this town and start pushing people around. They're gonna put you away!

LEE: I never pushed anybody around! I beat him fair and square. (*Pause.*) They can't touch me anyway. They can't put a finger on me. I'm gone. I can come in through the window and go out through the door. They never knew what hit 'em. You, yer stuck. Yer the one that's stuck. Not me. So don't be warnin' me what to do in this town.

(*Pause, Austin crosses to table, sits at typewriter, rests.*)

AUSTIN: Lee, come on, level with me will you? It doesn't make any sense that suddenly he'd throw my idea out the window. I've been talking to him for months. I've got too much at stake. Everything's riding on this project.

LEE: What's yer idea?

AUSTIN: It's just a simple love story.

LEE: What kinda' love story?

AUSTIN (*stands, crosses into kitchen*): I'm not telling you!

LEE: Ha! 'Fraid I'll steal it huh? Competition's gettin' kinda' close to home isn't it?

AUSTIN: Where did Saul say he was going?

LEE: He was gonna' take my story to a couple studios.

AUSTIN: That's *my* outline you know! I wrote that outline! You've got no right to be peddling it around.

LEE: You weren't ready to take credit for it last night.

AUSTIN: Give me my keys!

LEE: What?

AUSTIN: The keys! I want my keys back!

LEE: Where you goin'?

AUSTIN: Just give me my keys! I gotta' take a drive. I gotta' get out of here for a while.

LEE: Where you gonna' go, Austin?

AUSTIN (*pause*): I might just drive out to the desert for a while. I gotta' think.

LEE: You can think here just as good. This is the perfect setup for thinkin'. We got some writin' to do here, boy. Now let's just have us a little toast. Relax. We're partners now.

(*Lee pops the cork of the champagne bottle, pours two drinks as the lights fade to black.*)

Scene VI

(*Afternoon. Lee and Saul in kitchen, Austin in alcove.*)

LEE: Now you tell him. You tell him, Mr. Kipper.

SAUL: Kimmer.

LEE: Kimmer. You tell him what you told me. He don't believe me.

AUSTIN: I don't want to hear it.

SAUL: It's really not a big issue, Austin. I was simply amazed by your brother's story and —

AUSTIN: Amazed? You lost a bet! You gambled with my material!

SAUL: That's really beside the point, Austin. I'm ready to

go all the way with your brother's story. I think it has a great deal of merit.

AUSTIN: I don't want to hear about it, okay? Go tell it to the executives! Tell it to somebody who's going to turn it into a package deal or something. A T.V. series. Don't tell it to me.

SAUL: But I want to continue with your project too, Austin. It's not as though we can't do both. We're big enough for that aren't we?

AUSTIN: "We"? *I* can't do both! I don't know about "we."

LEE (*to Saul*): See, what'd I tell ya'. He's totally unsympathetic.

SAUL: Austin, there's no point in our going to another screenwriter for this. It just doesn't make sense. You're brothers. You know each other. There's a familiarity with the material that just wouldn't be possible otherwise.

AUSTIN: There's no familiarity with the material! None! I don't know what "Tornado Country" is. I don't know what a "gooseneck" is. And I don't want to know! (*Pointing to Lee.*) He's a hustler! He's a bigger hustler than you are! If you can't see that, then —

LEE (*to Austin*): Hey, now hold on. I didn't have to bring this bone back to you, boy. I persuaded Saul here that you were the right man for the job. You don't have to go throwin' up favors in my face.

AUSTIN: Favors! I'm the one who wrote the fuckin' outline! You can't even spell.

SAUL (*to Austin*): Your brother told me about the situation with your father.

(*Pause.*)

AUSTIN: What? (*Looks at Lee.*)

SAUL: That's right. Now we have a clear-cut deal here, Austin. We have big studio money standing behind this thing. Just on the basis of your outline.

AUSTIN (*to Saul*): What'd he tell you about my father?

SAUL: Well — that he's destitute. He needs money.

LEE: That's right. He does.

(*Austin shakes his head, stares at them both.*)

AUSTIN (*to Lee*): And this little assignment is supposed to go toward the old man? A charity project? Is that what this is? Did you cook this up on the ninth green too?

SAUL: It's a big slice, Austin.

AUSTIN (*to Lee*): I gave him money! I already gave him money. You know that. He drank it all up!

LEE: This is a different deal here.

SAUL: We can set up a trust for your father. A large sum of money. It can be doled out to him in parcels so he can't misuse it.

AUSTIN: Yeah, and who's doing the doling?

SAUL: Your brother volunteered.

(*Austin laughs.*)

LEE: That's right. I'll make sure he uses it for groceries.

AUSTIN (*to Saul*): I'm not doing this script! I'm not writing this crap for you or anybody else. You can't blackmail me into it. You can't threaten me into it. There's no way I'm doing it. So just give it up. Both of you.

(*Long pause.*)

SAUL: Well, that's it then. I mean this is an easy three hundred grand. Just for a first draft. It's incredible, Austin. We've got three different studios all trying to cut each other's throats to get this material. In one morning. That's how hot it is.

AUSTIN: Yeah, well you can afford to give me a percentage on the outline then. And you better get the genius here an agent before he gets burned.

LEE: Saul's gonna' be my agent. Isn't that right, Saul?

SAUL: That's right. (*To Austin.*) Your brother has really got something, Austin. I've been around too long not to recognize it. Raw talent.

AUSTIN: He's got a lota' balls is what he's got. He's taking you right down the river.

SAUL: Three hundred thousand, Austin. Just for a first draft. Now you've never been offered that kind of money before.

AUSTIN: I'm not writing it.

(*Pause.*)

SAUL: I see. Well —

LEE: We'll just go to another writer then. Right, Saul? Just hire us somebody with some enthusiasm. Somebody who can recognize the value of a good story.

SAUL: I'm sorry about this, Austin.

AUSTIN: Yeah

SAUL: I mean I was hoping we could continue both things but now I don't see how it's possible.

AUSTIN: So you're dropping my idea altogether. Is that it? Just trade horses in midstream? After all these months of meetings.

SAUL: I wish there was another way.

AUSTIN: I've got everything riding on this, Saul. You know that. It's my only shot. If this falls through —

SAUL: I have to go with what my instincts tell me —

AUSTIN: Your instincts!

SAUL: My gut reaction.

AUSTIN: You lost! That's your gut reaction. You lost a gamble. Now you're trying to tell me you like his story? How could you possibly fall for that story? It's as phony as Hopalong Cassidy. What do you see in it? I'm curious.

SAUL: It has the ring of truth, Austin.

AUSTIN (*laughs*): Truth?

LEE: It is true.

SAUL: Something about the real West.

AUSTIN: Why? Because it's got horses? Because it's got grown men acting like little boys?

SAUL: Something about the land. Your brother is speaking from experience.

AUSTIN: So am I!

SAUL: But nobody's interested in love these days, Austin. Let's face it.

LEE: That's right.

AUSTIN (*to Saul*): He's been camped out on the desert for three months. Talking to cactus. What's he know about what people wanna' see on the screen? I drive on the freeway every day. I swallow the smog. I watch the news in color. I shop in the Safeway. I'm the one who's in touch! Not him!

SAUL: I have to go now, Austin.

(*Saul starts to leave.*)

AUSTIN: There's no such thing as the West anymore! It's a dead issue! It's dried up, Saul, and so are you.

(*Saul stops and turns to Austin.*)

SAUL: Maybe you're right. But I have to take the gamble, don't I?

AUSTIN: You're a fool to do this, Saul.

SAUL: I've always gone on my hunches. Always. And I've never been wrong. (*To Lee.*) I'll talk to you tomorrow, Lee.

LEE: All right, Mr. Kimmer.

SAUL: Maybe we could have some lunch.

LEE: Fine with me. (*Smiles at Austin.*)

SAUL: I'll give you a ring.

(*Saul exits, lights to black as brothers look at each other from a distance.*)

Scene VII

(*Night. Coyotes, crickets, sound of typewriter in dark, candlelight up on Lee at typewriter struggling to type with one finger system, Austin sits sprawled out on kitchen floor with whiskey bottle, drunk.*)

AUSTIN (*singing, from floor*): "Red sails in the sunset
   Way out on the blue
   Please carry my loved one
   Home safely to me

   Red sails in the sunset —"

LEE (*slams fist on table*): Hey! Knock it off will ya'! I'm tryin' to concentrate here.

AUSTIN (*laughs*): You're tryin' to concentrate?

LEE: Yeah. That's right.

AUSTIN: Now you're tryin' to concentrate.

LEE: Between you, the coyotes, and the crickets a thought don't have much of a chance.

AUSTIN: "Between me, the coyotes, and the crickets." What a great title.

LEE: I don't need a title! I need a thought.

AUSTIN (*laughs*): A thought! Here's a thought for ya'—

LEE: I'm not askin' fer yer thoughts! I got my own. I can do this thing on my own.

AUSTIN: You're going to write an entire script on your own?

LEE: That's right.

(*Pause.*)

AUSTIN: Here's a thought. Saul Kimmer —

LEE: Shut up will ya'!

AUSTIN: He thinks we're the same person.

LEE: Don't get cute.

AUSTIN: He does! He's lost his mind. Poor old Saul. (*Giggles.*) Thinks we're one and the same.

LEE: Why don't you ease up on that champagne.

AUSTIN (*holding up bottle*): This isn't champagne anymore. We went through the champagne a long time ago. This is serious stuff. The days of champagne are long gone.

LEE: Well, go outside and drink it.

AUSTIN: I'm enjoying your company, Lee. For the first time since your arrival I am finally enjoying your company. And now you want me to go outside and drink alone?

LEE: That's right.

(*Lee reads through paper in typewriter, makes an erasure.*)

AUSTIN: You think you'll make more progress if you're alone? You might drive yourself crazy.

LEE: I could have this thing done in a night if I had a little silence.

AUSTIN: Well you'd still have the crickets to contend with. The coyotes. The sounds of the Police Helicopters prowling above the neighborhood. Slashing their searchlights down through the streets. Hunting for the likes of you.

LEE: I'm a screenwriter now! I'm legitimate.

AUSTIN (*laughing*): A screenwriter!

LEE: That's right. I'm on salary. That's more'n I can say for you. I got an advance coming.

AUSTIN: This is true. This is very true. An advance. (*Pause.*) Well, maybe I oughta' go out and try my hand at your trade. Since you're doing so good at mine.

LEE: Ha!

(*Lee attempts to type some more but gets the ribbon tangled up, starts trying to rethread it as they continue talking.*)

AUSTIN: Well why not? You don't think I've got what it takes to sneak into people's houses and steal their T.V.s?

LEE: You couldn't steal a toaster without losin' yer lunch.

(*Austin stands with a struggle, supports himself by the sink.*)

AUSTIN: You don't think I could sneak into somebody's house and steal a toaster?

LEE: Go take a shower or somethin' will ya!

(*Lee gets more tangled up with the typewriter ribbon, pulling it out of the machine as though it was fishing line.*)

AUSTIN: You really don't think I could steal a crumby toaster? How much you wanna' bet I can't steal a toaster! How much? Go ahead! You're a gambler aren't you? Tell me how much yer willing to put on the line. Some part of your big advance? Oh, you haven't got that yet have you. I forgot.

LEE: All right. I'll bet you your car that you can't steal a toaster without gettin' busted.

AUSTIN: You already got my car!

LEE: Okay, your house then.

AUSTIN: What're you gonna' give me! I'm not talkin' about my house and my car, I'm talkin' about what are you gonna' give me. You don't have nothin' to give me.

LEE: I'll give you — shared screen credit. How 'bout that? I'll have it put in the contract that this was written by both of us.

AUSTIN: I don't want my name on that piece of shit! I want something of value. You got anything of value? You got any tidbits from the desert? Any Rattlesnake bones? I'm not a greedy man. Any little personal treasure will suffice.

LEE: I'm gonna' just kick yer ass out in a minute.

AUSTIN: Oh, so now you're gonna' kick me out! Now I'm the intruder. I'm the one who's invading your precious privacy.

LEE: I'm trying to do some screenwriting here!!

(*Lee stands, picks up typewriter, slams it down hard on table, pause, silence except for crickets.*)

AUSTIN: Well, you got everything you need. You got plenty a' coffee? Groceries. You got a car. A contract. (*Pause.*) Might need a new typewriter ribbon but other than that you're pretty well fixed. I'll just leave ya' alone for a while.

(*Austin tries to steady himself to leave, Lee makes a move toward him.*)

LEE: Where you goin'?

AUSTIN: Don't worry about me. I'm not the one to worry about.

(*Austin weaves toward exit, stops.*)

LEE: What're you gonna' do? Just go wander out into the night?

AUSTIN: I'm gonna' make a little tour.

LEE: Why don't ya' just go to bed for Christ's sake. Yer makin' me sick.

AUSTIN: I can take care a' myself. Don't worry about me.

(*Austin weaves badly in another attempt to exit, he crashes to the floor, Lee goes to him but remains standing.*)

LEE: You want me to call your wife for ya' or something?

AUSTIN (*from floor*): My wife?

LEE: Yeah. I mean maybe she can help ya' out. Talk to ya' or somethin'.

AUSTIN (*struggles to stand again*): She's five hundred miles away. North. North of here. Up in the North country where things are calm. I don't need any help. I'm gonna' go outside and I'm gonna' steal a toaster.

I'm gonna' steal some other stuff too. I might even commit bigger crimes. Bigger than you ever dreamed of. Crimes beyond the imagination!

(*Austin manages to get himself vertical, tries to head for exit again.*)

LEE: Just hang on a minute, Austin.

AUSTIN: Why? What for? You don't need my help, right? You got a handle on the project. Besides, I'm lookin' forward to the smell of the night. The bushes. Orange blossoms. Dust in the driveways. Rain bird sprinklers. Lights in people's houses. You're right about the lights, Lee. Everybody else is livin' the life. Indoors. Safe. This is a Paradise down here. You know that? We're livin' in a Paradise. We've forgotten about that.

LEE: You sound just like the old man now.

AUSTIN: Yeah, well we all sound alike when we're sloshed. We just sorta' echo each other.

LEE: Maybe if we could work on this together we could bring him back out here. Get him settled down someplace.

(*Austin turns violently toward Lee, takes a swing at him, misses, and crashes to the floor again. Lee stays standing.*)

AUSTIN: I don't want him out here! I've had it with him! I went all the way out there! I went out of my way. I gave him money and all he did was play Al Jolson records and spit at me! I gave him money!

(*Pause.*)

LEE: Just help me a little with the characters, all right? You know how to do it, Austin.

AUSTIN (*on floor, laughs*): The characters!

LEE: Yeah. You know. The way they talk and stuff. I can hear it in my head but I can't get it down on paper.

AUSTIN: What characters?

LEE: The guys. The guys in the story.

AUSTIN: Those aren't characters.

LEE: Whatever you call 'em then. I need to write somethin' out.

AUSTIN: Those are illusions of characters.

LEE: I don't give a damn what ya' call 'em! You know what I'm talkin' about!

AUSTIN: Those are fantasies of a long lost boyhood.

LEE: I gotta' write somethin' out on paper!!

(*Pause.*)

AUSTIN: What for? Saul's gonna' get you a fancy screenwriter isn't he?

LEE: I wanna' do it myself!

AUSTIN: Then do it! Yer on your own now, old buddy. You bulldogged yer way into contention. Now you gotta' carry it through.

LEE: I will but I need some advice. Just a couple a' things. Come on, Austin. Just help me get 'em talkin' right. It won't take much.

AUSTIN: Oh, now you're having a little doubt huh?

What happened? The pressure's on, boy. This is it. You gotta' come up with it now. You don't come up with a winner on your first time out they just cut your head off. They don't give you a second chance ya' know.

LEE: I got a good story! I know it's a good story. I just need a little help is all.

AUSTIN: Not from me. Not from yer little old brother. I'm retired.

LEE: You could save this thing for me, Austin. I'd give ya' half the money. I would. I only need half anyway. With this kinda' money I could be a long time down the road. I'd never bother ya' again. I promise. You'd never even see me again.

AUSTIN (*still on floor*): You'd disappear?

LEE: I would for sure.

AUSTIN: Where would you disappear to?

LEE: That don't matter. I got plenty a' places.

AUSTIN: Nobody can disappear. The old man tried that. Look where it got him. He lost his teeth.

LEE: He never had any money.

AUSTIN: I don't mean that. I mean his teeth! His real teeth. First he lost his real teeth, then he lost his false teeth. You never knew that did ya? He never confided in you.

LEE: Nah, I never knew that.

AUSTIN: You wanna' drink?

(*Austin offers bottle to Lee, Lee takes it, sits down on kitchen floor with Austin, they share the bottle.*)

Yeah, he lost his real teeth one at a time. Woke up every morning with another tooth lying on the mattress. Finally, he decides he's gotta' get 'em all pulled out but he doesn't have any money. Middle of Arizona with no money and no insurance and every morning another tooth is lying on the mattress. (*Takes a drink.*) So what does he do?

LEE: I dunno'. I never knew about that.

AUSTIN: He begs the government. G.I. Bill or some damn thing. Some pension plan he remembers in the back of his head. And they send him out the money.

LEE: They did?

(*They keep trading the bottle between them, taking drinks.*)

AUSTIN: Yeah. They send him the money but it's not enough money. Costs a lot to have all yer teeth yanked. They charge by the individual tooth, ya' know. I mean one tooth isn't equal to another tooth. Some are very expensive. Like the big ones in the back —

LEE: So what happened?

AUSTIN: So he locates a Mexican dentist in Juarez who'll do the whole thing for a song. And he takes off hitch-hiking to the border.

LEE: Hitchhiking?

AUSTIN: Yeah. So how long you think it takes him to get to the border? A man his age.

LEE: I dunno.

AUSTIN: Eight days it takes him. Eight days in the rain and the sun and every day he's droppin' teeth on the blacktop and nobody'll pick him up 'cause his mouth's full a' blood.

(*Pause, they drink.*)

So finally he stumbles into the dentist. Dentist takes all his money and all his teeth. And there he is, in Mexico, with his gums sewed up and his pockets empty.

(*Long silence, Austin drinks.*)

LEE: That's it?

AUSTIN: Then I go out to see him, see. I go out there and I take him out for a nice Chinese dinner. But he doesn't eat. All he wants to do is drink Martinis outa' plastic cups. And he takes his teeth out and lays 'em on the table 'cause he can't stand the feel of 'em. And we ask the waitress for one a' those doggie bags to take the Chop Suey home in. So he drops his teeth in the doggie bag along with the Chop Suey. And then we go out to hit all the bars up and down the highway. Says he wants to introduce me to all his buddies. And in one a' those bars, in one a' those bars up and down the highway, he left that doggie bag with his teeth laying in the Chop Suey.

LEE: You never found it?

AUSTIN: We went back but we never did find it. (*Pause.*) Now that's a true story. True to life.

(*They drink as lights fade to black.*)

Scene VIII

(*Very early morning, between night and day. No crickets, coyotes yapping feverishly in distance before light comes up, a small fire blazes up in the dark from alcove area, sound of Lee smashing typewriter with a golf club, lights coming up, Lee seen smashing typewriter methodically then dropping pages of his script into a burning bowl set on the floor of alcove, flames leap up, Austin has a whole bunch of stolen toasters lined up on the sink counter along with Lee's stolen T.V., the toasters are of a wide variety of models, mostly chrome, Austin goes up and down the line of toasters, breathing on them and polishing them with a dish towel, both men are drunk, empty whiskey bottles and beer cans litter floor of kitchen, they share a half empty bottle on one of the chairs in the alcove, Lee keeps periodically taking deliberate ax-chops at the typewriter using a nine-iron as Austin speaks, all of their mother's house plants are dead and drooping.*)

AUSTIN (*polishing toasters*): There's gonna' be a general lack of toast in the neighborhood this morning. Many, many unhappy, bewildered breakfast faces. I guess it's best not to even think of the victims. Not to even entertain it. Is that the right psychology?

LEE (*pauses*): What?

AUSTIN: Is that the correct criminal psychology? Not to think of the victims?

LEE: What victims?

(*Lee takes another swipe at typewriter with nine-iron, adds pages to the fire.*)

AUSTIN: The victims of crime. Of breaking and entering. I mean is it a prerequisite for a criminal not to have a conscience?

LEE: Ask a criminal.

(*Pause, Lee stares at Austin.*)

What're you gonna' do with all those toasters? That's the dumbest thing I ever saw in my life.

AUSTIN: I've got hundreds of dollars worth of household appliances here. You may not realize that.

LEE: Yeah, and how many hundreds of dollars did you walk right past?

AUSTIN: It was toasters you challenged me to. Only toasters. I ignored every other temptation.

LEE: I never challenged you! That's no challenge. Anybody can steal a toaster.

(*Lee smashes typewriter again.*)

AUSTIN: You don't have to take it out on my typewriter ya' know. It's not the machine's fault that you can't write. It's a sin to do that to a good machine.

LEE: A sin?

AUSTIN: When you consider all the writers who never even had a machine. Who would have given an eyeball for a good typewriter. Any typewriter.

(*Lee smashes typewriter again.*)

AUSTIN (*polishing toasters*): All the ones who wrote on matchbook covers. Paper bags. Toilet paper. Who had their writing destroyed by their jailers. Who persisted beyond all odds. Those writers would find it hard to understand your actions.

(*Lee comes down on typewriter with one final crushing blow of the nine-iron then collapses in one of the chairs, takes a drink from bottle, pause.*)

AUSTIN (*after pause*): Not to mention demolishing a perfectly good golf club. What about all the struggling golfers? What about Lee Trevino? What do you think he would've said when he was batting balls around with broomsticks at the age of nine. Impoverished.

(*Pause.*)

LEE: What time is it anyway?

AUSTIN: No idea. Time stands still when you're havin' fun.

LEE: Is it too late to call a woman? You know any women?

AUSTIN: I'm a married man.

LEE: I mean a local woman.

(*Austin looks out at light through window above sink.*)

AUSTIN: It's either too late or too early. You're the na-ture enthusiast. Can't you tell the time by the light in the sky? Orient yourself around the North Star or something?

LEE: I can't tell anything.

AUSTIN: Maybe you need a little breakfast. Some toast! How 'bout some toast?

(*Austin goes to cupboard, pulls out loaf of bread, and starts dropping slices into every toaster, Lee stays sitting, drinks, watches Austin.*)

LEE: I don't need toast. I need a woman.

AUSTIN: A woman isn't the answer. Never was.

LEE: I'm not talkin' about permanent. I'm talkin' about temporary.

AUSTIN (*putting toast in toasters*): We'll just test the merits of these little demons. See which brands have a tendency to burn. See which one can produce a perfectly golden piece of fluffy toast.

LEE: How much gas you got in yer car?

AUSTIN: I haven't driven my car for days now. So I haven't had an opportunity to look at the gas gauge.

LEE: Take a guess. You think there's enough to get me to Bakersfield?

AUSTIN: Bakersfield? What's in Bakersfield?

LEE: Just never mind what's in Bakersfield! You think there's enough goddamn gas in the car!

AUSTIN: Sure.

LEE: Sure. You could care less, right. Let me run outa' gas on the Grapevine. You could give a shit.

AUSTIN: I'd say there was enough gas to get you just about anywhere, Lee. With your determination and guts.

LEE: What the hell time is it anyway?

(*Lee pulls out his wallet, starts going through dozens of small pieces of paper with phone numbers written on them, drops some on the floor, drops others in the fire.*)

AUSTIN: Very early. This is the time of morning when the coyotes kill people's cocker spaniels. Did you hear them? That's what they were doing out there. Luring innocent pets away from their homes.

LEE (*searching through his papers*): What's the area code for Bakersfield? You know?

AUSTIN: You could always call the operator.

LEE: I can't stand that voice they give ya'.

AUSTIN: What voice?

LEE: That voice that warns you that if you'd only tried harder to find the number in the phone book you wouldn't have to be calling the operator to begin with.

(*Lee gets up, holding a slip of paper from his wallet, stumbles toward phone on wall, yanks receiver, starts dialing.*)

AUSTIN: Well I don't understand why you'd want to talk to anybody else anyway. I mean you can talk to me. I'm your brother.

LEE (*dialing*): I wanna' talk to a woman. I haven't heard a woman's voice in a long time.

AUSTIN: Not since the Botanist?

LEE: What?

AUSTIN: Nothing. (*Starts singing as he tends toast.*)
"Red sails in the sunset
Way out on the blue
Please carry my loved one.
Home safely to me."

LEE: Hey, knock it off will ya'! This is long distance here.

AUSTIN: Bakersfield?

LEE: Yeah, Bakersfield. It's Kern County.

AUSTIN: Well, what County are *we* in?

LEE: You better get yourself a 7-Up, boy.

AUSTIN: One County's as good as another.

(*Austin hums "Red Sails" softly as Lee talks on phone.*)

LEE (*to phone*): Yeah, operator look — first off I wanna' know the area code for Bakersfield. Right. Bakersfield! Okay. Good. Now I wanna' know if you can help me track somebody down. (*Pause.*) No, no I mean a phone number. Just a phone number. Okay. (*Holds a piece of paper up and reads it.*) Okay, the name is Melly Ferguson. Melly. (*Pause.*) I dunno'. Melly. Maybe. Yeah. Maybe Melanie. Yeah. Melanie Ferguson. Okay. (*Pause.*) What? I can't hear ya' so good. Sounds like yer under the ocean. (*Pause.*) You got ten Melanie Fergusons? How could that be? Ten Melanie Fergusons in Bakersfield? Well gimme all of 'em then. (*Pause.*) What d'ya mean? Gimme all ten Melanie Fergusons! That's right. Just a second. (*To Austin.*) Gimme a pen.

AUSTIN: I don't have a pen.

LEE: Gimme a pencil then!

AUSTIN: I don't have a pencil.

LEE (*to phone*): Just a second, operator. (*To Austin.*) Yer a writer and ya' don't have a pen or a pencil!

AUSTIN: I'm not a writer. You're a writer.

LEE: I'm on the phone here! Get me a pen or a pencil.

AUSTIN: I gotta' watch the toast.

LEE (*to phone*): Hang on a second, operator.

(*Lee lets the phone drop then starts pulling all the drawers in the kitchen out on the floor and dumping the contents, searching for a pencil, Austin watches him casually.*)

LEE (*crashing through drawers, throwing contents around kitchen*): This is the last time I try to live with people, boy! I can't believe it. Here I am! Here I am again in a desperate situation! This would never happen out on the desert. I would never be in this kinda' situation out on the desert. Isn't there a pen or a pencil in this house! Who lives in this house anyway!

AUSTIN: Our mother.

LEE: How come she don't have a pen or a pencil! She's a social person isn't she? Doesn't she have to make shopping lists? She's gotta' have a pencil. (*Finds a pencil.*) Aaha! (*He rushes back to phone, picks up receiver.*) All right operator. Operator? Hey! Operator! Goddamnit!

(*Lee rips the phone off the wall and throws it down, goes back to chair and falls into it, drinks, long pause.*)

AUSTIN: She hung up?

LEE: Yeah, she hung up. I knew she was gonna' hang up. I could hear it in her voice.

(*Lee starts going through his slips of paper again.*)

AUSTIN: Well, you're probably better off staying here with me anyway. I'll take care of you.

LEE: I don't need takin' care of! Not by you anyway.

AUSTIN: Toast is almost ready.

(*Austin starts buttering all the toast as it pops up.*)

LEE: I don't want any toast!

(*Long pause.*)

AUSTIN: You gotta' eat something. Can't just drink. How long have we been drinking anyway?

LEE (*looking through slips of paper*): Maybe it was Fresno. What's the area code for Fresno? How could I have lost that number! She was beautiful.

(*Pause.*)

AUSTIN: Why don't you just forget about that, Lee. Forget about the woman.

LEE: She had green eyes. You know what green eyes do to me?

AUSTIN: I know but you're not gonna' get it on with her now anyway. It's dawn already. She's in Bakersfield for Christ's sake.

(*Long pause, Lee considers the situation.*)

LEE: Yeah. (*Looks at windows.*) It's dawn?

AUSTIN: Let's just have some toast and —

LEE: What is this bullshit with the toast anyway! You make it sound like salvation or something. I don't want any goddamn toast! How many times I gotta' tell ya'! (*Lee gets up, crosses upstage to windows in alcove, looks out, Austin butters toast.*)

AUSTIN: Well it is like salvation sort of. I mean the smell. I love the smell of toast. And the sun's coming up. It makes me feel like anything's possible. Ya' know?

LEE (*back to Austin, facing windows upstage*): So go to church why don't ya'.

AUSTIN: Like a beginning. I love beginnings.

LEE: Oh yeah. I've always been kinda' partial to endings myself.

AUSTIN: What if I come with you, Lee?

LEE (*pause as Lee turns toward Austin*): What?

AUSTIN: What if I come with you out to the desert?

LEE: Are you kiddin'?

AUSTIN: No. I'd just like to see what it's like.

LEE: You wouldn't last a day out there pal.

AUSTIN: That's what you said about the toasters. You said I couldn't steal a toaster either.

LEE: A toaster's got nothin' to do with the desert.

AUSTIN: I could make it, Lee. I'm not that helpless. I can cook.

LEE: Cook?

AUSTIN: I can.

LEE: So what! You can cook. Toast.

AUSTIN: I can make fires. I know how to get fresh water from condensation.

(*Austin stacks buttered toast up in a tall stack on plate.*)
(*Lee slams table.*)

LEE: It's not somethin' you learn out of a Boy Scout handbook!

AUSTIN: Well how do you learn it then! How're you supposed to learn it!

(*Pause.*)

LEE: Ya' just learn it, that's all. Ya' learn it 'cause ya' have to learn it. You don't *have* to learn it.

AUSTIN: You could teach me.

LEE (*stands*): What're you, crazy or somethin'? You went to college. Here, you are down here, rollin' in bucks. Floatin' up and down in elevators. And you wanna' learn how to live on the desert!

AUSTIN: I do, Lee. I really do. There's nothin' down here for me. There never was. When we were kids here it was different. There was a life here then. But now — I keep comin' down here thinkin' it's the fifties or somethin'. I keep finding myself getting off the freeway at familiar landmarks that turn out to be unfamiliar. On the way to appointments. Wandering down streets I thought I recognized that turn out to be replicas of streets I remember. Streets I misremember. Streets I can't tell if I lived on or saw in a postcard. Fields that don't even exist anymore.

LEE: There's no point cryin' about that now.

AUSTIN: There's nothin' real down here, Lee! Least of all me!

LEE: Well I can't save you from that!

AUSTIN: You can let me come with you.

LEE: No dice, pal.

AUSTIN: You could let me come with you, Lee!

LEE: Hey, do you actually think I chose to live out in the middle a' nowhere? Do ya'? Ya' think it's some kinda' philosophical decision I took or somethin'? I'm livin' out there 'cause I can't make it here! And yer bitchin' to me about all yer success!

AUSTIN: I'd cash it all in in a second. That's the truth.

LEE (*pause, shakes his head*): I can't believe this.

AUSTIN: Let me go with you.

LEE: Stop sayin' that will ya'! Yer worse than a dog.

(*Austin offers out the plate of neatly stacked toast to Lee.*)

AUSTIN: You want some toast?

(*Lee suddenly explodes and knocks the plate out of Austin's hand, toast goes flying, long frozen moment where it appears Lee might go all the way this time when Austin breaks it by slowly lowering himself to his knees and begins gathering the scattered toast from the floor and stacking it back on the plate, Lee begins to circle Austin in a slow, predatory way, crushing pieces of*

toast in his wake, no words for a while, Austin keeps gathering toast, even the crushed pieces.)

LEE: Tell ya' what I'll do, little brother. I might just consider makin' you a deal. Little trade. (*Austin continues gathering toast as Lee circles him through this.*) You write me up this screenplay thing just like I tell ya'. I mean you can use all yer usual tricks and stuff. Yer fancy language. Yer artistic hocus pocus. But ya' gotta' write everything like I say. Every move. Every time they run outa' gas, they run outa' gas. Every time they wanna' jump on a horse, they do just that. If they wanna' stay in Texas, by God they'll stay in Texas! (*Keeps circling.*) And you finish the whole thing up for me. Top to bottom. And you put my name on it. And I own all the rights. And every dime goes in my pocket. You do that and I'll sure enough take ya' with me to the desert. (*Lee stops, pause, looks down at Austin.*) How's that sound?

(*Pause as Austin stands slowly holding plate of demolished toast, their faces are very close, pause.*)

AUSTIN: It's a deal.

(*Lee stares straight into Austin's eyes, then he slowly takes a piece of toast off the plate, raises it to his mouth, and takes a huge crushing bite never taking his eyes off Austin's, as Lee crunches into the toast the lights black out.*)

Scene IX

(*Midday. No sound, blazing heat, the stage is ravaged; bottles, toasters, smashed typewriter, ripped out telephone, etc. All the debris from previous scene is now starkly visible in intense yellow light, the effect should be like a desert junkyard at high noon, the coolness of the preceding scenes is totally obliterated. Austin is seated at table in alcove, shirt open, pouring with sweat, hunched over a writing notebook, scribbling notes desperately with a ballpoint pen. Lee with no shirt, beer in hand, sweat pouring down his chest, is walking a slow circle around the table, picking his way through the objects, sometimes kicking them aside.*)

LEE (*as he walks*): All right, read it back to me. Read it back to me!

AUSTIN (*scribbling at top speed*): Just a second.

LEE: Come on, come on! Just read what ya' got.

AUSTIN: I can't keep up! It's not the same as if I had a typewriter.

LEE: Just read what we got so far. Forget about the rest.

AUSTIN: All right. Let's see — okay — (*wipes sweat from his face, reads as Lee circles*) Luke says uh —

LEE: Luke?

AUSTIN: Yeah.

LEE: His name's Luke? All right, all right — we can change the names later. What's he say? Come on, come on.

AUSTIN: He says uh — (*reading*) "I told ya' you were a fool to follow me in here. I know this prairie like the back a' my hand."

LEE: No, no no! That's not what I said. I never said that.

AUSTIN: That's what I wrote.

LEE: It's not what I said. I never said "like the back a' my hand." That's stupid. That's one a' those — whadya' call it? Whadya' call that?

AUSTIN: What?

LEE: Whadya' call it when somethin's been said a thousand times before. Whadya' call that?

AUSTIN: Um — a cliché?

LEE: Yeah. That's right. Cliché. That's what that is. A cliché. "The back a' my hand." That's stupid.

AUSTIN: That's what you said.

LEE: I never said that! And even if I did, that's where yer supposed to come in. That's where yer supposed to change it to somethin' better.

AUSTIN: Well how am I supposed to do that and write down what you say at the same time?

LEE: Ya' just do, that's all! You hear a stupid line you change it. That's yer job.

AUSTIN: All right. (*Makes more notes.*)

LEE: What're you changin' it to?

AUSTIN: I'm not changing it. I'm just trying to catch up.

LEE: Well change it! We gotta' change that, we can't leave that in there like that. ". . . the back a' my hand." That's dumb.

AUSTIN (*stops writing, sits back*): All right.

LEE (*pacing*): So what'll we change it to?

AUSTIN: Um — How 'bout — "I'm on intimate terms with this prairie."

LEE (*to himself considering line as he walks*): "I'm on intimate terms with this prairie." Intimate terms, intimate terms. Intimate — that means like uh — sexual right?

AUSTIN: Well — yeah — or —

LEE: He's on sexual terms with the prairie? How dya' figure that?

AUSTIN: Well it doesn't necessarily have to mean sexual.

LEE: What's it mean then?

AUSTIN: It means uh — close — personal —

LEE: All right. How's it sound? Put it into the uh — the line there. Read it back. Let's see how it sounds. (*To himself.*) "Intimate terms."

AUSTIN (*scribbles in notebook*): Okay. It'd go something like this: (*reads*) "I told ya' you were a fool to follow me in here. I'm on intimate terms with this prairie."

LEE: That's good. I like that. That's real good.

AUSTIN: You do?

LEE: Yeah. Don't you?

AUSTIN: Sure.

LEE: Sounds original now. "Intimate terms." That's good. Okay. Now we're cookin! That has a real ring to it.

(*Austin makes more notes, Lee walks around, pours beer on his arms and rubs it over his chest feeling good about the new progress, as he does this Mom enters unobtrusively down left with her luggage, she stops and stares at the scene still holding luggage as the two men continue, unaware of her presence, Austin absorbed in his writing, Lee cooling himself off with beer.*)

LEE (*continues*): "He's on intimate terms with this prairie." Sounds real mysterious and kinda threatening at the same time.

AUSTIN (*writing rapidly*): Good.

LEE: Now — (*Lee turns and suddenly sees Mom, he stares at her for a while, she stares back, Austin keeps writing feverishly, not noticing, Lee walks slowly over to Mom and takes a closer look, long pause.*)

LEE: Mom?

(*Austin looks up suddenly from his writing, sees Mom, stands quickly, long pause, Mom surveys the damage.*)

AUSTIN: Mom. What're you doing back?

MOM: I'm back.

LEE: Here, lemme take those for ya'.

(*Lee sets beer on counter then takes both her bags but doesn't know where to set them down in the sea of junk so he just keeps holding them.*)

AUSTIN: I wasn't expecting you back so soon. I thought uh — How was Alaska?

MOM: Fine.

LEE: See any igloos?

MOM: No. Just glaciers.

AUSTIN: Cold huh?

MOM: What?

AUSTIN: It must've been cold up there?

MOM: Not really.

LEE: Musta' been colder than this here. I mean we're havin' a real scorcher here.

MOM: Oh? (*She looks at damage.*)

LEE: Yeah. Must be in the hundreds.

AUSTIN: You wanna' take your coat off, Mom?

MOM: No. (*Pause, she surveys space.*) What happened in here?

AUSTIN: Oh um — Me and Lee were just sort of celebrating and uh —

MOM: Celebrating?

AUSTIN: Yeah. Uh — Lee sold a screenplay. A story, I mean.

MOM: Lee did?

AUSTIN: Yeah.

MOM: Not you?

AUSTIN: No. Him.

MOM (*to Lee*): You sold a screenplay?

LEE: Yeah. That's right. We're sorta' finishing it up right now. That's what we're doing here.

AUSTIN: Me and Lee are going out to the desert to live.

MOM: You and Lee?

AUSTIN: Yeah. I'm taking off with Lee.

MOM (*she looks back and forth at each of them, pause*): You gonna go live with your father?

AUSTIN: No. We're going to a different desert Mom.

MOM: I see. Well, you'll probably wind up on the same desert sooner or later. What're all these toasters doing here?

AUSTIN: Well — we had kind of a contest.

MOM: Contest?

LEE: Yeah.

AUSTIN: Lee won.

MOM: Did you win a lot of money, Lee?

LEE: Well not yet. It's comin' in any day now.

MOM (*to Lee*): What happened to your shirt?

LEE: Oh. I was sweatin' like a pig and I took it off.

(*Austin grabs Lee's shirt off the table and tosses it to him, Lee sets down suitcases and puts his shirt on.*)

MOM: Well, it's one hell of a mess in here isn't it?

AUSTIN: Yeah, I'll clean it up for you, Mom. I just didn't know you were coming back so soon.

MOM: I didn't either.

AUSTIN: What happened?

MOM: Nothing. I just started missing all my plants.

(*She notices dead plants.*)

AUSTIN: Oh.

MOM: Oh, they're all dead aren't they. (*She crosses toward them, examines them closely.*) You didn't get a chance to water I guess.

AUSTIN: I was doing it and then Lee came and —

LEE: Yeah I just distracted him a whole lot here, Mom. It's not his fault.

(*Pause, as Mom stares at plants.*)

MOM: Oh well, one less thing to take care of I guess. (*Turns toward brothers.*) Oh, that reminds me — You boys will probably never guess who's in town. Try and guess.

(*Long pause, brothers stare at her.*)

AUSTIN: Whadya' mean, Mom?

MOM: Take a guess. Somebody very important has come to town. I read it, coming down on the Greyhound.

LEE: Somebody very important?

MOM: See if you can guess. You'll never guess.

AUSTIN: Mom — we're trying to uh — (*Points to writing pad.*)

MOM: Picasso. (*Pause.*) Picasso's in town. Isn't that incredible? Right now.

(*Pause.*)

AUSTIN: Picasso's dead, Mom.

MOM: No, he's not dead. He's visiting the museum. I read it on the bus. We have to go down there and see him.

AUSTIN: Mom —

MOM: This is the chance of a lifetime. Can you imagine? We could all go down and meet him. All three of us.

LEE: Uh — I don't think I'm really up for meetin' anybody right now. I'm uh — What's his name?

MOM: Picasso! Picasso! You've never heard of Picasso? Austin, you've heard of Picasso.

AUSTIN: Mom, we're not going to have time.

MOM: It won't take long. We'll just hop in the car and go down there. An opportunity like this doesn't come along every day.

AUSTIN: We're gonna' be leavin' here, Mom!

(*Pause.*)

MOM: Oh.

LEE: Yeah.

(*Pause.*)

MOM: You're both leaving?

LEE (*looks at Austin*): Well we were thinkin' about that before but now I —

AUSTIN: No, we are! We're both leaving. We've got it all planned.

MOM (*to Austin*): Well you can't leave. You have a family.

AUSTIN: I'm leaving. I'm getting out of here.

LEE (*to Mom*): I don't really think Austin's cut out for the desert do you?

MOM: No. He's not.

AUSTIN: I'm going with you, Lee!

MOM: He's too thin.

LEE: Yeah, he'd just burn up out there.

AUSTIN (*to Lee*): We just gotta finish this screenplay and then we're gonna' take off. That's the plan. That's what you said. Come on, let's get back to work, Lee.

LEE: I can't work under these conditions here. It's too hot.

AUSTIN: Then we'll do it on the desert.

LEE: Don't be tellin' me what we're gonna do!

MOM: Don't shout in the house.

LEE: We're just gonna' have to postpone the whole deal.

AUSTIN: I can't postpone it! It's gone past postponing! I'm doing everything you said. I'm writing down exactly what you tell me.

LEE: Yeah, but you were right all along see. It is a dumb story. "Two lamebrains chasin' each other across Texas." That's what you said, right?

AUSTIN: I never said that.

(*Lee sneers in Austin's face then turns to Mom.*)

LEE: I'm gonna' just borrow some a' your antiques, Mom. You don't mind do ya'? Just a few plates and things. Silverware.

(*Lee starts going through all the cupboards in kitchen pulling out plates and stacking them on counter as Mom and Austin watch.*)

MOM: You don't have any utensils on the desert?

LEE: Nah, I'm fresh out.

AUSTIN (*to Lee*): What're you doing?

MOM: Well some of those are very old. Bone China.

LEE: I'm tired of eatin' outa' my bare hands, ya' know. It's not civilized.

AUSTIN (*to Lee*): What're you doing? We made a deal!

MOM: Couldn't you borrow the plastic ones instead? I have plenty of plastic ones.

LEE (*as he stacks plates*): It's not the same. Plastic's not the same at all. What I need is somethin' authentic. Somethin' to keep me in touch. It's easy to get outa' touch out there. Don't worry I'll get 'em back to ya'.

(*Austin rushes up to Lee, grabs him by shoulders.*)

AUSTIN: You can't just drop the whole thing, Lee!

(*Lee turns, pushes Austin in the chest knocking him backward into the alcove, Mom watches numbly, Lee returns to collecting the plates, silverware, etc.*)

MOM: You boys shouldn't fight in the house. Go outside and fight.
LEE: I'm not fightin'. I'm leavin'.
MOM: There's been enough damage done already.
LEE (*his back to Austin and Mom, stacking dishes on counter*): I'm clearin' outa' here once and for all. All this town does is drive a man insane. Look what it's done to Austin there. I'm not lettin' that happen to me. Sell myself down the river. No sir. I'd rather be a hundred miles from nowhere than let that happen to me.

(*During this Austin has picked up the ripped-out phone from the floor and wrapped the cord tightly around his hands, he lunges at Lee whose back is still to him, wraps the cord around Lee's neck, plants a foot in Lee's back and pulls back on the cord, tightening it, Lee chokes desperately, can't speak and can't reach Austin with his arms, Austin keeps applying pressure on Lee's back with his foot, bending him into the sink, Mom watches.*)

AUSTIN (*tightening cord*): You're not goin' anywhere! You're not takin' anything with you. You're not takin' my car! You're not takin' the dishes! You're not takin' anything! You're stayin' right here!
MOM: You'll have to stop fighting in the house. There's plenty of room outside to fight. You've got the whole outdoors to fight in.

(*Lee tries to tear himself away, he crashes across the stage like an enraged bull dragging Austin with him, he snorts and bellows but Austin hangs on and manages to keep clear of Lee's attempts to grab him, they crash into the table, to the floor, Lee is face down thrashing wildly and choking, Austin pulls cord tighter, stands with one foot planted on Lee's back and the cord stretched taut.*)

AUSTIN (*holding cord*): Gimme back my keys, Lee! Take the keys out! Take 'em out!

(*Lee desperately tries to dig in his pockets, searching for the car keys, Mom moves closer.*)

MOM (*calmly to Austin*): You're not killing him are you?
AUSTIN: I don't know. I don't know if I'm killing him. I'm stopping him. That's all. I'm just stopping him.

(*Lee thrashes but Austin is relentless.*)

MOM: You oughta' let him breathe a little bit.
AUSTIN: Throw the keys out, Lee!

(*Lee finally gets keys out and throws them on floor but out of Austin's reach, Austin keeps pressure on cord, pulling Lee's neck back, Lee gets one hand to the cord but can't relieve the pressure.*)

Reach me those keys would ya', Mom.
MOM (*not moving*): Why are you doing this to him?
AUSTIN: Reach me the keys!
MOM: Not until you stop choking him.
AUSTIN: I can't stop choking him! He'll kill me if I stop choking him!
MOM: He won't kill you. He's your brother.
AUSTIN: Just get me the keys would ya'!

(*Pause. Mom picks keys up off floor, hands them to Austin.*)

AUSTIN (*to Mom*): Thanks.
MOM: Will you let him go now?
AUSTIN: I don't know. He's not gonna' let me get outa' here.
MOM: Well you can't kill him.
AUSTIN: I can kill him! I can easily kill him. Right now. Right here. All I gotta' do is just tighten up. See? (*He tightens cord, Lee thrashes wildly, Austin releases pressure a little, maintaining control.*) Ya' see that?
MOM: That's a savage thing to do.
AUSTIN: Yeah well don't tell me I can't kill him because I can. I can just twist. I can just keep twisting. (*Austin twists the cord tighter, Lee weakens, his breathing changes to a short rasp.*)
MOM: Austin!

(*Austin relieves pressure, Lee breathes easier but Austin keeps him under control.*)

AUSTIN (*eyes on Lee, holding cord*): I'm goin' to the desert. There's nothing stopping me. I'm going by myself to the desert.

(*Mom moving toward her luggage.*)

MOM: Well, I'm going to go check into a motel. I can't stand this anymore.
AUSTIN: Don't go yet!

(*Mom pauses.*)

MOM: I can't stay here. This is worse than being homeless.
AUSTIN: I'll get everything fixed up for you, Mom. I promise. Just stay for a while.
MOM (*picking up luggage*): You're going to the desert.
AUSTIN: Just wait!

(*Lee thrashes, Austin subdues him, Mom watches holding luggage, pause.*)

MOM: It was the worst feeling being up there. In Alaska. Staring out a window. I never felt so desperate before. That's why when I saw that article on Picasso I thought —
AUSTIN: Stay here, Mom. This is where you live.

(*She looks around the stage.*)

MOM: I don't recognize it at all.

(*She exits with luggage, Austin makes a move toward her but Lee starts to struggle and Austin subdues him again with cord, pause.*)

AUSTIN (*holding cord*): Lee? I'll make ya' a deal. You let me get outa' here. Just let me get to my car. All right, Lee? Gimme a little headstart and I'll turn you loose. Just gimme a little headstart. All right?

(*Lee makes no response, Austin slowly releases tension cord, still nothing from Lee.*)

AUSTIN: Lee?

(*Lee is motionless, Austin very slowly begins to stand, still keeping a tenuous hold on the cord and his eyes riv-eted to Lee for any sign of movement, Austin slowly drops the cord and stands, he stares down at Lee who appears to be dead.*)

AUSTIN (*whispers*): Lee?

(*Pause, Austin considers, looks toward exit, back to Lee, then makes a small movement as if to leave. Instantly Lee is on his feet and moves toward exit, blocking Austin's escape. They square off to each other, keeping a distance between them. Pause, a single coyote heard in distance, lights fade softly into moonlight, the figures of the brothers now appear to be caught in a vast desertlike landscape, they are very still but watchful for the next move, lights go slowly to black as the after-image of the brothers pulses in the dark, coyote fades.*)

Athol Fugard

Athol Fugard (b. 1932) was an actor before becoming a playwright. Fugard's wife, the actress Sheila Meiring, stimulated his interest in theater, and in 1956 he began working with a theater group called the Serpent Company in Cape Town, South Africa. The group included both black and white actors at a time when racial mixing was illegal and went on to make a notable contribution to world drama.

Fugard, who is white, met Zakes Mokae, a black musician and actor, in the early days of the Serpent players, and the two collaborated on several works. Mokae has said that the tradition in Africa was not so much for a solitary playwright to compose a work that others would act out as it was for people to develop a communal approach to drama, crafting a dramatic piece through their interaction. To some extent, Fugard in his early efforts did just that. He worked with actors, watched the developments among them, and then shaped the drama accordingly.

In 1960 he began to write a two-person play called *The Blood Knot* while he was in England trying to establish a theater group there. This play was part of a trilogy called *The Family*, with *Hello and Goodbye* (1965) and *Boesman and Lena* (1969). *The Blood Knot* was given its first performance in Dorkay House in Johannesburg late in 1961. As Fugard has said, the entire production, which starred Fugard and Mokae, was put together so quickly that the government never had time to stop it. The play is about two brothers, one black, the other light-skinned enough to pass for white. It is exceptionally powerful, and in the play's first performances in Johannesburg, it was a sensation. It toured South Africa and had a revival in New Haven and in New York in 1984 and 1985.

While they toured South Africa, Fugard and Mokae were victims of the country's apartheid policies. They could not travel in the same train car: Fugard went first class, and Mokae had to go in special cars for blacks. After *The Blood Knot*'s success the government passed laws making it all but impossible for black and white actors to work together on the stage, but that policy has now changed.

Fugard has had a considerable number of plays produced in New York and London in recent years. *Sizwe Banzi Is Dead* (1972), written with John Kani and Winston Ntshona, is about a man who exchanges identity with a corpse as a way of avoiding the racial laws of South Africa; it was well received. *The Island* (1975), also written with Kani and Ntshona, starred the latter two black actors, who have become associated with Fugard and his work. They portray prisoners who, while putting on *Antigone,* become immersed in the political themes of the play, seeing it as an example of the political repression they experience in their own lives.

His plays *A Lesson from Aloes* (1978) and *The Road to Mecca* (1984) were successful in their first American productions at the Yale Repertory Theatre and on Broadway. Fugard's works are not always concerned with racial problems, but they usually center on political issues and the stress that individuals feel in trying to be themselves in an intolerant society.

The situation in South Africa has improved since *"MASTER HAROLD" . . . and the boys* was first produced in 1982. Apartheid has been abolished, and the government is in the hands of the African National Congress. The shift has been more successful than white South Africans expected, although political tensions still exist. Fugard's attachment and commitment to South Africa remain deep and lifelong. He has been criticized by black writers for dealing with themes they feel belong to them, while also being criticized by whites for his sympathies toward blacks. In the new South Africa some of these problems have begun to sort themselves out. Fugard's latest play, *Valley Song* (1996), produced at London's Royal Court Theatre, explores the problems and the promise of the new South Africa.

"MASTER HAROLD" . . .
AND THE BOYS

Athol Fugard has said that *"MASTER HAROLD" . . . and the boys* (1982) is a very personal play in which he exorcises personal guilt (Fugard's entire name is Athol Harold Lannigan Fugard). As a white South African he has written numerous plays that represent the racial circumstances of life in that troubled nation. This play has won international distinction and has made a reputation for its stars, especially Zakes Mokae, with whom Fugard has worked for more than thirty years.

Hally reveals throughout the play (which is set in 1950) that he is more attached emotionally to Sam, the black waiter who has befriended him, than he is even to his own parents, owners of the restaurant. His attitude toward his father is complicated by his father's alcoholism and confinement. At that time in South Africa even such an alcoholic was considered automatically superior to a black man such as Sam, who is intelligent, quick, thoughtful, and generous. When Hally reveals his anxiety about his father, Sam warns him that it is dishonorable to treat one's father the way he does, but Sam's presumption in admonishing Hally triggers Hally's mean outburst toward him.

Zakes Mokae, who created the role of Sam in the first performance of the play at the Yale Repertory Theatre, has commented extensively about his role and the character of Sam. He has observed that some black audience members called out during a performance that he should beat Hally up the minute Hally demands that Sam call him Master Harold. But other black audience members spoke with him after the performance and agreed that, because Sam had never taken that kind of stand against Harold or his father, he was getting what he deserved. Mokae himself has pointed out that Sam is probably not living in

Port Elizabeth legally and that to have taken action, even if he wanted to, would have ended with his removal from the town into exile.

Zakes Mokae understands the character from his perspective as a black South African, and he realizes Sam's limits. But he has said that in his version of the play Sam would give Hally a beating and "suffer the consequences." He points out, however, that he is an urban South African, unlike Sam, and his attitude is quite different from anything that Sam would have understood. As an urban black, Mokae could not have been sent into exile, although he could certainly have been punished, for beating a white boy.

On the question of whether the play made a positive contribution to white-black relations in South Africa, Mokae feels that a play cannot change people's minds. Audiences were not likely to seek to change the government of South Africa simply because they had seen a play. But at the same time, he feels that it was productive to talk about the apartheid and racial distrust in South Africa.

Unfortunately, the government of South Africa decided that the play was too inflammatory for performance in its country, and it was banned briefly from performance in Johannesburg and other theatrical centers in South Africa. This suggests that while Zakes Mokae did not feel that one play would have much impact on injustices in South Africa, it is likely that the government feared otherwise.

In an important way, *"MASTER HAROLD" . . . and the boys* is a personal statement by Fugard that establishes the extent to which apartheid damages even a person sympathetic to black rights. It is astonishing in retrospect to think, as his interviewer, Heinrich von Staden, once said, that Hally could grow up to be Athol himself. If this is true, then it is also true that the play is hopeful.

One sign of hope is that the violence in the play is restrained. Sam does not beat Hally for humiliating him, although he probably would like to. And no one in the play makes a move to be physically threatening to Sam. However faint, these are signs of hope. And as Zakes Mokae has said about the situation in his homeland, "One is always optimistic. It can't go on forever." He was right. On June 5, 1991, Parliament abandoned apartheid, and South Africa had a new beginning.

"MASTER HAROLD" . . . and the boys in Performance

The world premiere of *"MASTER HAROLD" . . . and the boys* was at the Yale Repertory Theatre in March 1982. Fugard himself directed the play, with Zakes Mokae as Sam, Danny Glover as Willie, and Željko Ivanek as Hally. It was the first of his plays to premiere outside South Africa. Fugard chose New Haven in part because the play's setting was so personal that he feared it might disturb his brother and sister if it were produced first in South Africa. The setting was a bright tea room — a restaurant that serves light meals — interpreted to look like the tea room Fugard's mother actually ran in Port Elizabeth when he was a child. The space was open, the walls a whitish hue, everything simple and plain in decoration.

New York Times critic Frank Rich reviewed the premiere, saying, "'MASTER HAROLD' . . . and the boys is only an anecdote, really, and it's often as warm and musical as the men's dance. But somewhere along the way it rises up and breaks over the audience like a storm." Alan Stern of the *Boston Phoenix* linked the play with Greek tragedy:

> One reason for the play's potency is that, as in Greek tragedy, the events seem preordained — they're the by-product of social forces and human nature. Even as he spits in Sam's face, Hally realizes the magnitude of his action, that he is the one who will be harmed by it. And yet he can't help himself. Power corrupts, and in a society that sanctions the domination of one man — or set of men — over another, all relationships, even the promising ones, are poisoned.

Zakes Mokae and Danny Glover starred in the Broadway production in May 1982. After a brief period in which it was banned, the play was produced in Johannesburg, South Africa, in March 1983 with a South African cast. Joseph Lelyveld, in the *New York Times*, said of that production: "Athol Fugard's confessional drama about a white adolescent's initiation in the uses of racial power has come home to South Africa, and it left its multiracial audience . . . visibly shaken and stunned. . . . Many, blacks and whites, were crying."

The play was televised in 1984 with Matthew Broderick as Hally. It has had revivals in 1985 by the Trinity Repertory Company in Providence, in 1986 by the Boston Shakespeare Company in Boston, and in 1987 at the American Stage Festival in Milford, New Hampshire. These productions, although without Fugard's direction and without a "star" cast, had the same effect on their audiences as the major productions in New York and Johannesburg. Clifford Gallo in the *Boston Globe* called the American Stage production "a devastating look at the loss of racial innocence in a nation where political and social inequality are the norm."

Athol Fugard (b. 1932)

"MASTER HAROLD" . . . AND THE BOYS   1982

Characters

WILLIE
SAM
HALLY

(*The St. George's Park Tea Room on a wet and windy Port Elizabeth afternoon.*)

(*Tables and chairs have been cleared and are stacked on one side except for one which stands apart with a single chair. On this table a knife, fork, spoon and side plate in anticipation of a simple meal, together with a pile of comic books.*)

(*Other elements: a serving counter with a few stale cakes under glass and a not very impressive display of sweets, cigarettes and cool drinks, etc.; a few cardboard advertising handouts — Cadbury's Chocolate, Coca-Cola — and a blackboard on which an untrained hand has chalked up the prices of Tea, Coffee, Scones, Milkshakes — all flavors — and Cool Drinks; a few sad ferns in pots; a telephone; an old-style jukebox.*)

(*There is an entrance on one side and an exit into a kitchen on the other.*)

(*Leaning on the solitary table, his head cupped in one hand as he pages through one of the comic books, is Sam. A black man in his mid-forties. He wears the white coat of a waiter. Behind him on his knees, mopping down the floor with a bucket of water and a rag, is Willie. Also black and about the same age as Sam. He has his sleeves and trousers rolled up.*)

(*The year: 1950.*)

WILLIE (*singing as he works*): "She was scandalizin'
    my name,
    She took my money

She called me honey
But she was scandalizin' my name.
Called it love but was playin' a game. . . ."

(*He gets up and moves the bucket. Stands thinking for a moment, then, raising his arms to hold an imaginary partner, he launches into an intricate ballroom dance step. Although a mildly comic figure, he reveals a reasonable degree of accomplishment.*)

Hey, Sam.

(*Sam, absorbed in the comic book, does not respond.*)

Hey, Boet° Sam!

(*Sam looks up.*)

I'm getting it. The quickstep. Look now and tell me. (*He repeats the step.*) Well?

SAM (*encouragingly*): Show me again.

WILLIE: Okay, count for me.

SAM: Ready?

WILLIE: Ready.

SAM: Five, six, seven, eight. . . . (*Willie starts to dance.*) A-n-d one two three four . . . and one two three four. . . . (*Ad libbing as Willie dances.*) Your shoulders, Willie . . . your shoulders! Don't look down! Look happy, Willie! Relax, Willie!

WILLIE (*desperate but still dancing*): I am relax.

SAM: No, you're not.

WILLIE (*he falters*): Ag no man, Sam! Mustn't talk. You make me make mistakes.

SAM: But you're stiff.

WILLIE: Yesterday I'm not straight . . . today I'm too stiff!

SAM: Well, you are. You asked me and I'm telling you.

WILLIE: Where?

SAM: Everywhere. Try to glide through it.

WILLIE: Glide?

SAM: Ja, make it smooth. And give it more style. It must look like you're enjoying yourself.

WILLIE (*emphatically*): I wasn't.

SAM: Exactly.

WILLIE: How can I enjoy myself? Not straight, too stiff and now it's also glide, give it more style, make it smooth. . . . Haai! Is hard to remember all those things, Boet Sam.

SAM: That's your trouble. You're trying too hard.

WILLIE: I try hard because it *is* hard.

SAM: But don't let me see it. The secret is to make it look easy. Ballroom must look happy, Willie, not like hard work. It must . . . . Ja! . . . it must look like romance.

WILLIE: Now another one! What's romance?

SAM: Love story with happy ending. A handsome man in tails, and in his arms, smiling at him, a beautiful lady in evening dress!

WILLIE: Fred Astaire, Ginger Rogers.

SAM: You got it. Tapdance or ballroom, it's the same. Romance. In two weeks' time when the judges look

---

at you and Hilda, they must see a man and a woman who are dancing their way to a happy ending. What I saw was you holding her like you were frightened she was going to run away.

WILLIE: Ja! Because that is what she wants to do! I got no romance left for Hilda anymore, Boet Sam.

SAM: Then pretend. When you put your arms around Hilda, imagine she is Ginger Rogers.

WILLIE: With no teeth? You try.

SAM: Well, just remember, there's only two weeks left.

WILLIE: I know, I know! (*To the jukebox.*) I do it better with music. You got sixpence for Sarah Vaughan?

SAM: That's a slow foxtrot. You're practicing the quickstep.

WILLIE: I'll practice slow foxtrot.

SAM (*shaking his head*): It's your turn to put money in the jukebox.

WILLIE: I only got bus fare to go home. (*He returns disconsolately to his work.*) Love story and happy ending! She's doing it all right, Boet Sam, but is not me she's giving happy endings. Fuckin' whore! Three nights now she doesn't come practice. I wind up gramophone, I get record ready and I sit and wait. What happens? Nothing. Ten o'clock I start dancing with my pillow. You try and practice romance by yourself, Boet Sam. Struesgod, she doesn't come tonight I take back my dress and ballroom shoes and I find me new partner. Size twenty-six. Shoes size seven. And now she's also making trouble for me with the baby again. Reports me to Child Wellfed, that I'm not giving her money. She lies! Every week I am giving her money for milk. And how do I know is my baby? Only his hair looks like me. She's fucking around all the time I turn my back. Hilda Samuels is a bitch! (*Pause.*) Hey, Sam!

SAM: Ja.

WILLIE: You listening?

SAM: Ja.

WILLIE: So what you say?

SAM: About Hilda?

WILLIE: Ja.

SAM: When did you last give her a hiding?

WILLIE (*reluctantly*): Sunday night.

SAM: And today is Thursday.

WILLIE (*he knows what's coming*): Okay.

SAM: Hiding on Sunday night, then Monday, Tuesday, and Wednesday she doesn't come to practice . . . and you are asking me why?

WILLIE: I said okay, Boet Sam!

SAM: You hit her too much. One day she's going to leave you for good.

WILLIE: So? She makes me the hell-in too much.

SAM (*emphasizing his point*): *Too* much and *too* hard. You had the same trouble with Eunice.

WILLIE: Because she also make the hell-in, Boet Sam. She never got the steps right. Even the waltz.

SAM: Beating her up every time she makes a mistake in the waltz? (*Shaking his head.*) No, Willie! That takes the pleasure out of ballroom dancing.

Boet: Brother.

WILLIE: Hilda is not too bad with the waltz, Boet Sam. Is the quickstep where the trouble starts.

SAM (*teasing him gently*): How's your pillow with the quickstep?

WILLIE (*ignoring the tease*): Good! And why? Because it got no legs. That's her trouble. She can't move them quick enough, Boet Sam. I start the record and before halfway Count Basie is already winning. Only time we catch up with him is when gramophone runs down. (*Sam laughs.*) Haaikona, Boet Sam, is not funny.

SAM (*snapping his fingers*): I got it! Give her a handicap.

WILLIE: What's that?

SAM: Give her a ten-second start and then let Count Basie go. Then I put my money on her. Hot favorite in the Ballroom Stakes: Hilda Samuels ridden by Willie Malopo.

WILLIE (*turning away*): I'm not talking to you no more.

SAM (*relenting*): Sorry, Willie....

WILLIE: It's finish between us.

SAM: Okay, okay... I'll stop.

WILLIE: You can also fuck off.

SAM: Willie, listen! I want to help you!

WILLIE: No more jokes?

SAM: I promise.

WILLIE: Okay. Help me.

SAM (*his turn to hold an imaginary partner*): Look and learn. Feet together. Back straight. Body relaxed. Right hand placed gently in the small of her back and wait for the music. Don't start worrying about making mistakes or the judges or the other competitors. It's just you, Hilda and the music, and you're going to have a good time. What Count Basie do you play?

WILLIE: "You the cream in my coffee, you the salt in my stew."

SAM: Right. Give it to me in strict tempo.

WILLIE: Ready?

SAM: Ready.

WILLIE: A-n-d... (*Singing.*)
"You the cream in my coffee.
You the salt in my stew.
You will always be my necessity.
I'd be lost without you...." (*etc.*)

(*Sam launches into the quickstep. He is obviously a much more accomplished dancer than Willie. Hally enters. A seventeen-year-old white boy. Wet raincoat and school case. He stops and watches Sam. The demonstration comes to an end with a flourish. Applause from Hally and Willie.*)

HALLY: Bravo! No question about it. First place goes to Mr. Sam Semela.

WILLIE (*in total agreement*): You was gliding with style, Boet Sam.

HALLY (*cheerfully*): How's it, chaps?

SAM: Okay, Hally.

WILLIE (*springing to attention like a soldier and saluting*): At your service, Master Harold!

HALLY: Not long to the big event, hey!

SAM: Two weeks.

HALLY: You nervous?

SAM: No.

HALLY: Think you stand a chance?

SAM: Let's just say I'm ready to go out there and dance.

HALLY: It looked like it. What about you, Willie?

(*Willie groans.*)

What's the matter?

SAM: He's got leg trouble.

HALLY (*innocently*): Oh, sorry to hear that, Willie.

WILLIE: Boet Sam! You promised. (*Willie returns to his work.*)

(*Hally deposits his school case and takes off his raincoat. His clothes are a little neglected and untidy: black blazer with school badge, gray flannel trousers in need of an ironing, khaki shirt and tie, black shoes. Sam has fetched a towel for Hally to dry his hair.*)

HALLY: God, what a lousy bloody day. It's coming down cats and dogs out there. Bad for business, chaps.... (*Conspiratorial whisper.*)... but it also means we're in for a nice quiet afternoon.

SAM: You can speak loud. Your Mom's not here.

HALLY: Out shopping?

SAM: No. The hospital.

HALLY: But it's Thursday. There's no visiting on Thursday afternoons. Is my Dad okay?

SAM: Sounds like it. In fact, I think he's going home.

HALLY (*stopped short by Sam's remark*): What do you mean?

SAM: The hospital phoned.

HALLY: To say what?

SAM: I don't know. I just heard your Mom talking.

HALLY: So what makes you say he's going home?

SAM: It sounded as if they were telling her to come and fetch him.

(*Hally thinks about what Sam has said for a few seconds.*)

HALLY: When did she leave?

SAM: About an hour ago. She said she would phone you. Want to eat?

(*Hally doesn't respond.*)

Hally, want your lunch?

HALLY: I suppose so. (*His mood has changed.*) What's on the menu?... as if I don't know.

SAM: Soup, followed by meat pie and gravy.

HALLY: Today's?

SAM: No.

HALLY: And the soup?

SAM: Nourishing pea soup.

HALLY: Just the soup. (*The pile of comic books on the table.*) And these?

SAM: For your Dad. Mr. Kempston brought them.

HALLY: You haven't been reading them, have you?

SAM: Just looking.

HALLY (*examining the comics*): Jungle Jim... Batman

and *Robin . . . Tarzan . . .* God, what rubbish! Mental pollution. Take them away.

(*Sam exits waltzing into the kitchen. Hally turns to Willie.*)

HALLY: Did you hear my Mom talking on the telephone, Willie?

WILLIE: No, Master Hally. I was at the back.

HALLY: And she didn't say anything to you before she left?

WILLIE: She said I must clean the floors.

HALLY: I mean about my Dad.

WILLIE: She didn't say nothing to me about him, Master Hally.

HALLY (*with conviction*): No! It can't be. They said he needed at least another three weeks of treatment. Sam's definitely made a mistake. (*Rummages through his school case, finds a book and settles down at the table to read.*) So, Willie!

WILLIE: Yes, Master Hally! Schooling okay today?

HALLY: Yes, okay. . . . (*He thinks about it.*) . . . No, not really. Ag, what's the difference? I don't care. And Sam says you've got problems.

WILLIE: Big problems.

HALLY: Which leg is sore?

(*Willie groans.*)

Both legs.

WILLIE: There is nothing wrong with my legs. Sam is just making jokes.

HALLY: So then you *will* be in the competition.

WILLIE: Only if I can find a partner.

HALLY: But what about Hilda?

SAM (*returning with a bowl of soup*): She's the one who's got trouble with her legs.

HALLY: What sort of trouble, Willie?

SAM: From the way he describes it, I think the lady has gone a bit lame.

HALLY: Good God! Have you taken her to see a doctor?

SAM: I think a vet would be better.

HALLY: What do you mean?

SAM: What do you call it again when a racehorse goes very fast?

HALLY: Gallop?

SAM: That's it!

WILLIE: Boet Sam!

National Theatre of London's 1983 production of *"MASTER HAROLD" . . . and the boys* with (l. to r.) Ramolao Makene as Willie, Duart Sylwain as Hally, and John Kani as Sam.

HALLY: "A gallop down the homestretch to the winning post." But what's that got to do with Hilda?
SAM: Count Basie always gets there first.

(*Willie lets fly with his slop rag. It misses Sam and hits Hally.*)

HALLY (*furious*): For Christ's sake, Willie! What the hell do you think you're doing?
WILLIE: Sorry, Master Hally, but it's him. . . .
HALLY: Act your bloody age! (*Hurls the rag back at Willie.*) Cut out the nonsense now and get on with your work. And you too, Sam. Stop fooling around.

(*Sam moves away.*)

No. Hang on. I haven't finished! Tell me exactly what my Mom said.
SAM: I have. "When Hally comes, tell him I've gone to the hospital and I'll phone him."
HALLY: She didn't say anything about taking my Dad home?
SAM: No. It's just that when she was talking on the phone. . . .
HALLY (*interrupting him*): No, Sam. They can't be discharging him. She would have said so if they were. In any case, we saw him last night and he wasn't in good shape at all. Staff nurse even said there was talk about taking more X-rays. And now suddenly today he's better? If anything, it sounds more like a bad turn to me . . . which I sincerely hope it isn't. Hang on . . . how long ago did you say she left?
SAM: Just before two . . . (*His wrist watch.*) . . . hour and a half.
HALLY: I know how to settle it. (*Behind the counter to the telephone. Talking as he dials.*) Let's give her ten minutes to get to the hospital, ten minutes to load him up, another ten, at the most, to get home, and another ten to get him inside. Forty minutes. They should have been home for at least half an hour already. (*Pause — he waits with the receiver to his ear.*) No reply, chaps. And you know why? Because she's at his bedside in hospital helping him pull through a bad turn. You definitely heard wrong.
SAM: Okay.

(*As far as Hally is concerned, the matter is settled. He returns to his table, sits down, and divides his attention between the book and his soup. Sam is at his school case and picks up a textbook.*)

Modern Graded Mathematics for Standards Nine and Ten. (*Opens it at random and laughs at something he sees.*) Who is this supposed to be?
HALLY: Old fart-face Prentice.
SAM: Teacher?
HALLY: Thinks he is. And believe me, that is not a bad likeness.
SAM: Has he seen it?
HALLY: Yes.
SAM: What did he say?

HALLY: Tried to be clever, as usual. Said I was no Leonardo da Vinci and that bad art had to be punished. So, six of the best, and his are bloody good.
SAM: On your bum?
HALLY: Where else? The days when I got them on my hands are gone forever, Sam.
SAM: With your trousers down!
HALLY: No. He's not quite that barbaric.
SAM: That's the way they do it in jail.
HALLY (*flicker of morbid interest*): Really?
SAM: Ja. When the magistrate sentences you to "strokes with a light cane."
HALLY: Go on.
SAM: They make you lie down on a bench. One policeman pulls down your trousers and holds your ankles, another one pulls your shirt over your head and holds your arms. . . .
HALLY: Thank you! That's enough.
SAM: . . . and the one that gives you the strokes talks to you gently and for a long time between each one. (*He laughs.*)
HALLY: I've heard enough, Sam! Jesus! It's a bloody awful world when you come to think of it. People can be real bastards.
SAM: That's the way it is, Hally.
HALLY: It doesn't *have* to be that way. There is something called progress, you know. We don't exactly burn people at the stake anymore.
SAM: Like Joan of Arc.
HALLY: Correct. If she was captured today, she'd be given a fair trial.
SAM: And then the death sentence.
HALLY (*a world-weary sigh*): I know, I know! I oscillate between hope and despair for this world as well, Sam. But things will change, you wait and see. One day somebody is going to get up and give history a kick up the backside and get it going again.
SAM: Like who?
HALLY (*after thought*): They're called social reformers. Every age, Sam, has got its social reformer. My history book is full of them.
SAM: So where's ours?
HALLY: Good question. And I hate to say it, but the answer is: I don't know. Maybe he hasn't even been born yet. Or is still only a babe in arms at his mother's breast. God, what a thought.
SAM: So we just go on waiting.
HALLY: Ja, looks like it. (*Back to his soup and the book.*)
SAM (*reading from the textbook*): "Introduction: In some mathematical problems only the magnitude. . . ." (*He mispronounces the word "magnitude."*)
HALLY (*correcting him without looking up*): Magnitude.
SAM: What's it mean?
HALLY: How big it is. The size of the thing.
SAM (*reading*): ". . . magnitude of the quantities is of importance. In other problems we need to know whether these quantities are negative or positive. For example, whether there is a debit or credit bank balance . . ."

HALLY: Whether you're broke or not.

SAM: ". . . whether the temperature is above or below Zero. . . ."

HALLY: Naught degrees. Cheerful state of affairs! No cash and you're freezing to death. Mathematics won't get you out of that one.

SAM: "All these quantities are called . . ." (*spelling the word*) . . . s-c-a-l. . . .

HALLY: Scalars.

SAM: Scalars! (*Shaking his head with a laugh.*) You understand all that?

HALLY (*turning a page*): No. And I don't intend to try.

SAM: So what happens when the exams come?

HALLY: Failing a maths exam isn't the end of the world, Sam. How many times have I told you that examination results don't measure intelligence?

SAM: I would say about as many times as you've failed one of them.

HALLY (*mirthlessly*): Ha, ha, ha.

SAM (*simultaneously*): Ha, ha, ha.

HALLY: Just remember Winston Churchill didn't do particularly well at school.

SAM: You've also told me that one many times.

HALLY: Well, it just so happens to be the truth.

SAM (*enjoying the word*): Magnitude! Magnitude! Show me how to use it.

HALLY (*after thought*): An intrepid social reformer will not be daunted by the magnitude of the task he has undertaken.

SAM (*impressed*): Couple of jaw-breakers in there!

HALLY: I gave you three for the price of one. Intrepid, daunted, and magnitude. I did that once in an exam. Put five of the words I had to explain in one sentence. It was half a page long.

SAM: Well, I'll put my money on you in the English exam.

HALLY: Piece of cake. Eighty percent without even trying.

SAM (*another textbook from Hally's case*): And history?

HALLY: So-so. I'll scrape through. In the fifties if I'm lucky.

SAM: You didn't do too badly last year.

HALLY: Because we had World War One. That at least has some action. You try to find that in the South African Parliamentary system.

SAM (*reading from the history textbook*): "Napoleon and the principle of equality." Hey! This sounds interesting. "After concluding peace with Britain in 1802, Napoleon used a brief period of calm to insti-tute . . ."

HALLY: Introduce.

SAM: ". . . many reforms. Napoleon regarded all people as equal before the law and wanted them to have equal opportunities for advancement. All ves-ti-ges of the feu-dal sys-tem with its oppression of the poor were abol-ished." Vestiges, feudal system, and abolished. I'm all right on oppression.

HALLY: I'm thinking. He swept away . . . abol-ished . . . the last remains . . . vestiges . . . of the bad old days . . . feudal system.

SAM: Ha! There's the social reformer we're waiting for. He sounds like a man of some magnitude.

HALLY: I'm not so sure about that. It's a damn good title for a book, though. A man of magnitude!

SAM: He sounds pretty big to me, Hally.

HALLY: Don't confuse historical significance with greatness. But maybe I'm being a bit prejudiced. Have a look in there and you'll see he's two chapters long. And hell! . . . has he only got dates, Sam, all of which you've got to remember! This campaign and that campaign, and then, because of all the fighting, the next thing is we get Peace Treaties all over the place. And what's the end of the story? Battle of Waterloo, which he loses. Wasn't worth it. No, I don't know about him as a man of magnitude.

SAM: Then who would you say was?

HALLY: To answer that, we need a definition of greatness, and I suppose that would be somebody who . . . somebody who benefited all mankind.

SAM: Right. But like who?

HALLY (*he speaks with total conviction*): Charles Darwin. Remember him? That big book from the library. *The Origin of the Species.*

SAM: Him?

HALLY: Yes. For his Theory of Evolution.

SAM: You didn't finish it.

HALLY: I ran out of time. I didn't finish it because my two weeks was up. But I'm going to take it out again after I've digested what I read. It's safe. I've hidden it away in the Theology section. Nobody ever goes in there. And anyway who are you to talk? You hardly even looked at it.

SAM: I tried. I looked at the chapters in the beginning and I saw one called "The Struggle for an Existence." Ah ha, I thought. At last! But what did I get? Something called the mistiltoe which needs the apple tree and there's too many seeds and all are going to die except one . . . ! No, Hally.

HALLY (*intellectually outraged*): What do you mean, No! The poor man had to start somewhere. For God's sake, Sam, he revolutionized science. Now we know.

SAM: What?

HALLY: Where we come from and what it all means.

SAM: And that's a benefit to mankind? Anyway, I still don't believe it.

HALLY: God, you're impossible. I showed it to you in black and white.

SAM: Doesn't mean I got to believe it.

HALLY: It's the likes of you that kept the Inquisition in business. It's called bigotry. Anyway, that's my man of magnitude. Charles Darwin! Who's yours?

SAM (*without hesitation*): Abraham Lincoln.

HALLY: I might have guessed as much. Don't get sentimental, Sam. You've never been a slave, you know. And anyway we freed your ancestors here in South

Africa long before the Americans. But if you want to thank somebody on their behalf, do it to Mr. William Wilberforce.° Come on. Try again. I want a real genius.

(*Now enjoying himself, and so is Sam. Hally goes behind the counter and helps himself to a chocolate.*)

SAM: William Shakespeare.

HALLY (*no enthusiasm*): Oh. So you're also one of them, are you? You're basing that opinion on only one play, you know. You've only read my *Julius Caesar* and even I don't understand half of what they're talking about. They should do what they did with the old Bible: bring the language up to date.

SAM: That's all you've got. It's also the only one *you've* read.

HALLY: I know. I admit it. That's why I suggest we reserve our judgment until we've checked up on a few others. I've got a feeling, though, that by the end of this year one is going to be enough for me, and I can give you the names of twenty-nine other chaps in the Standard Nine class of the Port Elizabeth Technical College who feel the same. But if you want him, you can have him. My turn now. (*Pacing.*) This is a damned good exercise, you know! It started off looking like a simple question and here it's got us really probing into the intellectual heritage of our civilization.

SAM: So who is it going to be?

HALLY: My next man . . . and he gets the title on two scores: social reform and literary genius . . . is Leo Nikolaevich Tolstoy.

SAM: That Russian.

HALLY: Correct. Remember the picture of him I showed you?

SAM: With the long beard.

HALLY (*trying to look like Tolstoy*): And those burning, visionary eyes. My God, the face of a social prophet if ever I saw one! And remember my words when I showed it to you? Here's a *man*, Sam!

SAM: Those were words, Hally.

HALLY: Not many intellectuals are prepared to shovel manure with the peasants and then go home and write a "little book" called *War and Peace*. Incidentally, Sam, he was somebody else who, to quote, ". . . did not distinguish himself scholastically."

SAM: Meaning?

HALLY: He was also no good at school.

SAM: Like you and Winston Churchill.

HALLY (*mirthlessly*): Ha, ha, ha.

SAM (*simultaneously*): Ha, ha, ha.

HALLY: Don't get clever, Sam. That man freed his serfs of his own free will.

SAM: No argument. He was a somebody, all right. I accept him.

Mr. William Wilberforce: (1759–1833), British statesman who supported a bill outlawing the slave trade and suppressing slavery in the British Empire.

HALLY: I'm sure Count Tolstoy will be very pleased to hear that. Your turn. Shoot. (*Another chocolate from behind the counter.*) I'm waiting, Sam.

SAM: I've got him.

HALLY: Good. Submit your candidate for examination.

SAM: Jesus.

HALLY (*stopped dead in his tracks*): Who?

SAM: Jesus Christ.

HALLY: Oh, come on, Sam!

SAM: The Messiah.

HALLY: Ja, but still . . . No, Sam. Don't let's get started on religion. We'll just spend the whole afternoon arguing again. Suppose I turn around and say Mohammed?

SAM: All right.

HALLY: You can't have them both on the same list!

SAM: Why not? You like Mohammed, I like Jesus.

HALLY: I *don't* like Mohammed. I never have. I was merely being hypothetical. As far as I'm concerned, the Koran is as bad as the Bible. No. Religion is out! I'm not going to waste my time again arguing with you about the existence of God. You know perfectly well I'm an atheist . . . and I've got homework to do.

SAM: Okay, I take him back.

HALLY: You've got time for one more name.

SAM (*after thought*): I've got one I know we'll agree on. A simple straightforward great Man of Magnitude . . . and no arguments. And *he* really *did* benefit all mankind.

HALLY: I wonder. After your last contribution I'm beginning to doubt whether anything in the way of an intellectual agreement is possible between the two of us. Who is he?

SAM: Guess.

HALLY: Socrates? Alexandre Dumas? Karl Marx, Dostoevsky? Nietzsche?

(*Sam shakes his head after each name.*)

Give me a clue.

SAM: The letter *P* is important. . . .

HALLY: Plato!

SAM: . . . and his name begins with an *F.*

HALLY: I've got it. Freud and Psychology.

SAM: No. I didn't understand him.

HALLY: That makes two of us.

SAM: Think of moldy apricot jam.

HALLY (*after a delighted laugh*): Penicillin and Sir Alexander Fleming! And the title of the book: *The Microbe Hunters*. (*Delighted.*) Splendid, Sam! Splendid. For once we are in total agreement. The major breakthrough in medical science in the Twentieth Century. If it wasn't for him, we might have lost the Second World War. It's deeply gratifying, Sam, to know that I haven't been wasting my time in talking to you. (*Strutting around proudly.*) Tolstoy may have educated his peasants, but I've educated you.

SAM: Standard Four to Standard Nine.

HALLY: Have we been at it as long as that?

SAM: Yep. And my first lesson was geography.

HALLY (*intrigued*): Really? I don't remember.

SAM: My room there at the back of the old Jubilee Boarding House. I had just started working for your Mom. Little boy in short trousers walks in one afternoon and asks me seriously: "Sam, do you want to see South Africa?" Hey man! Sure I wanted to see South Africa!

HALLY: Was that me?

SAM: . . . So the next thing I'm looking at a map you had just done for homework. It was your first one and you were very proud of yourself.

HALLY: Go on.

SAM: Then came my first lesson. "Repeat after me, Sam: Gold in the Transvaal, mealies in the Free State, sugar in Natal, and grapes in the Cape." I still know it!

HALLY: Well, I'll be buggered. So that's how it all started.

SAM: And your next map was one with all the rivers and the mountains they came from. The Orange the Vaal, the Limpopo, the Zambezi. . . .

HALLY: You've got a phenomenal memory!

SAM: You should be grateful. That is why you started passing your exams. You tried to be better than me.

(*They laugh together. Willie is attracted by the laughter and joins them.*)

HALLY: The old Jubilee Boarding House. Sixteen rooms with board and lodging, rent in advance and one week's notice. I haven't thought about it for donkey's years . . . and I don't think that's an accident. God, was I glad when we sold it and moved out. Those years are not remembered as the happiest ones of an unhappy childhood.

WILLIE (*knocking on the table and trying to imitate a woman's voice*): "Hally, are you there?"

HALLY: Who's that supposed to be?

WILLIE: "What you doing in there, Hally? Come out at once!"

HALLY (*to Sam*): What's he talking about?

SAM: Don't you remember?

WILLIE: "Sam, Willie . . . is he in there with you boys?"

SAM: Hiding away in our room when your mother was looking for you.

HALLY (*another good laugh*): Of course! I used to crawl and hide under your bed! But finish the story, Willie. Then what used to happen? You chaps would give the game away by telling her I was in there with you. So much for friendship.

SAM: We couldn't lie to her. She knew.

HALLY: Which meant I got another rowing for hanging around the "servants' quarters." I think I spent more time in there with you chaps than anywhere else in that dump. And do you blame me? Nothing but bloody misery wherever you went. Somebody was always complaining about the food, or my mother was having a fight with Micky Nash because she'd caught her with a petty officer in her room. Maud Meiring was another one. Remember those two?

They were prostitutes, you know. Soldiers and sailors from the troopships. Bottom fell out of the business when the war ended. God, the flotsam and jetsam that life washed up on our shores! No joking, if it wasn't for your room, I would have been the first certified ten-year-old in medical history. Ja, the memories are coming back now. Walking home from school and thinking: "What can I do this afternoon?" Try out a few ideas, but sooner or later I'd end up in there with you fellows. I bet you I could still find my way to your room with my eyes closed. (*He does exactly that.*) Down the corridor . . . telephone on the right, which my Mom keeps locked because somebody is using it on the sly and not paying . . . past the kitchen and unappetizing cooking smells . . . around the corner into the backyard, hold my breath again because there are more smells coming when I pass your lavatory, then into that little passageway, first door on the right and into your room. How's that?

SAM: Good. But, as usual, you forgot to knock.

HALLY: Like that time I barged in and caught you and Cynthia . . . at it. Remember? God, was I embarrassed! I didn't know what was going on at first.

SAM: Ja, that taught you a lesson.

HALLY: And about a lot more than knocking on doors, I'll have you know, and I don't mean geography either. Hell, Sam, couldn't you have waited until it was dark?

SAM: No.

HALLY: Was it that urgent?

SAM: Yes, and if you don't believe me, wait until your time comes.

HALLY: No, thank you. I am not interested in girls. (*Back to his memories. . . . Using a few chairs he recreates the room as he lists the items.*) A gray little room with a cold cement floor. Your bed against that wall . . . and I now know why the mattress sags so much! . . . Willie's bed . . . it's propped up on bricks because one leg is broken . . . that wobbly little table with the washbasin and jug of water . . . Yes! . . . stuck to the wall above it are some pin-up pictures from magazines. Joe Louis. . . .

WILLIE: Brown Bomber. World Title. (*Boxing pose.*) Three rounds and knockout.

HALLY: Against who?

SAM: Max Schmeling.

HALLY: Correct. I can also remember Fred Astaire and Ginger Rogers, and Rita Hayworth in a bathing costume which always made me hot and bothered when I looked at it. Under Willie's bed is an old suitcase with all his clothes in a mess, which is why I never hide there. Your things are neat and tidy in a trunk next to your bed, and on it there is a picture of you and Cynthia in your ballroom clothes, your first silver cup for third place in a competition and an old radio which doesn't work anymore. Have I left out anything?

SAM: No.

HALLY: Right, so much for the stage directions. Now the characters. (*Sam and Willie move to their appropriate positions in the bedroom.*) Willie is in bed, under his blankets with his clothes on, complaining nonstop about something, but we can't make out a word of what he's saying because he's got his head under the blankets as well. You're on your bed trimming your toenails with a knife — not a very edifying sight — and as for me. . . . What am I doing?

SAM: You're sitting on the floor giving Willie a lecture about being a good loser while you get the checkerboard and pieces ready for a game. Then you go to Willie's bed, pull off the blankets and make him play with you first because you know you're going to win, and that gives you the second game with me.

HALLY: And you certainly were a bad loser, Willie!

WILLIE: Haai!

HALLY: Wasn't he, Sam? And so slow! A game with you almost took the whole afternoon. Thank God I gave up trying to teach you how to play chess.

WILLIE: You and Sam cheated.

HALLY: I never saw Sam cheat, and mine were mostly the mistakes of youth.

WILLIE: Then how is it you two was always winning?

HALLY: Have you ever considered the possibility, Willie, that it was because we were better than you?

WILLIE: Every time better?

HALLY: Not every time. There were occasions when we deliberately let you win a game so that you would stop sulking and go on playing with us. Sam used to wink at me when you weren't looking to show me it was time to let you win.

WILLIE: So then you two didn't play fair.

HALLY: It was for your benefit, Mr. Malopo, which is more than being fair. It was an act of self-sacrifice. (*To Sam.*) But you know what my best memory is, don't you?

SAM: No.

HALLY: Come on, guess. If your memory is so good, you must remember it as well.

SAM: We got up to a lot of tricks in there, Hally.

HALLY: This one was special, Sam.

SAM: I'm listening.

HALLY: It started off looking like another of those useless nothing-to-do afternoons. I'd already been down to Main Street looking for adventure, but nothing had happened. I didn't feel like climbing trees in the Donkin Park or pretending I was a private eye and following a stranger . . . so as usual: See what's cooking in Sam's room. This time it was you on the floor. You had two thin pieces of wood and you were smoothing them down with a knife. It didn't look particularly interesting, but when I asked you what you were doing, you just said, "Wait and see, Hally. Wait . . . and see". . . in that secret sort of way of yours, so I knew there was a surprise coming. You teased me, you bugger, by being deliberately slow and not answering my questions!

(*Sam laughs.*)

And whistling while you worked away! God, it was infuriating! I could have brained you! It was only when you tied them together in a cross and put that down on the brown paper that I realized what you were doing. "Sam is making a kite?" And when I asked you and you said, "Yes". . . ! (*Shaking his head with disbelief.*) The sheer audacity of it took my breath away. I mean, seriously, what the hell does a black man know about flying a kite? I'll be honest with you, Sam, I had no hopes for it. If you think I was excited and happy, you got another guess coming. In fact, I was shit-scared that we were going to make fools of ourselves. When we left the boarding house to go up onto the hill, I was praying quietly that there wouldn't be any other kids around to laugh at us.

SAM (*enjoying the memory as much as Hally*): Ja, I could see that.

HALLY: I made it obvious, did I?

SAM: Ja. You refused to carry it.

HALLY: Do you blame me? Can you remember what the poor thing looked like? Tomato-box wood and brown paper! Flour and water for glue! Two of my mother's old stockings for a tail, and then all those bits and pieces of string you made me tie together so that we could fly it! Hell, no, that was now only asking for a miracle to happen.

SAM: Then the big argument when I told you to hold the string and run with it when I let go.

HALLY: I was prepared to run, all right, but straight back to the boarding house.

SAM (*knowing what's coming*): So what happened?

HALLY: Come on, Sam, you remember as well as I do.

SAM: I want to hear it from you.

(*Hally pauses. He wants to be as accurate as possible.*)

HALLY: You went a little distance from me down the hill, you held it up ready to let it go. . . . "This is it," I thought. "Like everything else in my life, here comes another fiasco." Then you shouted, "Go, Hally!" and I started to run. (*Another pause.*) I don't know how to describe it, Sam. Ja! The miracle happened! I was running, waiting for it to crash to the ground, but instead suddenly there was something alive behind me at the end of the string, tugging at it as if it wanted to be free. I looked back . . . (*Shakes his head.*) . . . I still can't believe my eyes. It was flying! Looping around and trying to climb even higher into the sky. You shouted to me to let it have more string. I did, until there was none left and I was just holding that piece of wood we had tied it to. You came up and joined me. You were laughing.

SAM: So were you. And shouting, "It works, Sam! We've done it!"

HALLY: And we had! I was so proud of us! It was the most splendid thing I had ever seen. I wished there were hundreds of kids around to watch us. The part that scared me, though, was when you showed me how to make it dive down to the ground and then just when it was on the point of crashing, swoop up again!

SAM: You didn't want to try yourself.

HALLY: Of course not! I would have been suicidal if anything had happened to it. Watching you do it made me nervous enough. I was quite happy just to see it up there with its tail fluttering behind it. You left me after that, didn't you? You explained how to get it down, we tied it to the bench so that I could sit and watch it, and you went away. I wanted you to stay, you know. I was a little scared of having to look after it by myself.

SAM (*quietly*): I had work to do, Hally.

HALLY: It was sort of sad bringing it down, Sam. And it looked sad again when it was lying there on the ground. Like something that had lost its soul. Just tomato-box wood, brown paper and two of my mother's old stockings! But, hell, I'll never forget that first moment when I saw it up there. I had a stiff neck the next day from looking up so much.

(*Sam laughs. Hally turns to him with a question he never thought of asking before.*)

Why did you make that kite, Sam?

SAM (*evenly*): I can't remember.

HALLY: Truly?

SAM: Too long ago, Hally.

HALLY: Ja, I suppose it was. It's time for another one, you know.

SAM: Why do you say that?

HALLY: Because it feels like that. Wouldn't be a good day to fly it, though.

SAM: No. You can't fly kites on rainy days.

HALLY (*He studies Sam. Their memories have made him conscious of the man's presence in his life.*): How old are you, Sam?

SAM: Two score and five.

HALLY: Strange, isn't it?

SAM: What?

HALLY: Me and you.

SAM: What's strange about it?

HALLY: Little white boy in short trousers and a black man old enough to be his father flying a kite. It's not every day you see that.

SAM: But why strange? Because the one is white and the other black?

HALLY: I don't know. Would have been just as strange, I suppose, if it had been me and my Dad . . . cripple man and a little boy! Nope! There's no chance of me flying a kite without it being strange. (*Simple statement of fact — no self-pity.*) There's a nice little short story there. "The Kite-Flyers." But we'd have to find a twist in the ending.

SAM: Twist?

HALLY: Yes. Something unexpected. The way it ended with us was too straightforward . . . me on the bench and you going back to work. There's no drama in that.

WILLIE: And me?

HALLY: You?

WILLIE: Yes me.

HALLY: You want to get into the story as well, do you? I got it! Change the title: "Afternoons in Sam's Room". . . expand it and tell all the stories. It's on its way to being a novel. Our days in the old Jubilee. Sad in a way that they're over. I almost wish we were still in that little room.

SAM: We're still together.

HALLY: That's true. It's just that life felt the right size in there . . . not too big and not too small. Wasn't so hard to work up a bit of courage. It's got so bloody complicated since then.

(*The telephone rings. Sam answers it.*)

SAM: St. George's Park Tea Room . . . Hello, Madam . . . Yes, Madam, he's here. . . . Hally, it's your mother.

HALLY: Where is she phoning from?

SAM: Sounds like the hospital. It's a public telephone.

HALLY (*relieved*): You see! I told you. (*The telephone.*) Hello, Mom . . . Yes . . . Yes no fine. Everything's under control here. How's things with poor old Dad? . . . Has he had a bad turn? . . . What? . . . Oh, God! . . . Yes, Sam told me, but I was sure he'd made a mistake. But what's this all about, Mom? He didn't look at all good last night. How can he get better so quickly? . . . Then very obviously you must say no. Be firm with him. You're the boss. . . . You know what it's going to be like if he comes home. . . . Well then, don't blame me when I fail my exams at the end of the year. . . . Yes! How am I expected to be fresh for school when I spend half the night massaging his gammy leg? . . . So am I! . . . So tell him a white lie. Say Dr. Colley wants more X-rays of his stump. Or bribe him. We'll sneak in double tots of brandy in future. . . . What? . . . Order him to get back into bed at once! If he's going to behave like a child, treat him like one. . . . All right, Mom! I was just trying to . . . I'm sorry. . . . I said I'm sorry. . . . Quick, give me your number. I'll phone you back. (*He hangs up and waits a few seconds.*) Here we go again! (*He dials.*) I'm sorry, Mom. . . . Okay. . . . But now listen to me carefully. All it needs is for you to put your foot down. Don't take no for an answer. . . . Did you hear me? And whatever you do, don't discuss it with him. . . . Because I'm frightened you'll give in to him. . . . Yes, Sam gave me lunch. . . . I ate all of it! . . . No, Mom not a soul. It's still raining here. . . . Right, I'll tell them. I'll just do some homework and then lock up. . . . But remember now, Mom. Don't listen to anything he says. And phone me back and let me know what happens. . . . Okay. Bye, Mom. (*He hangs up. The men are staring at him.*) My Mom says that when you're finished with the floors you must do the windows. (*Pause.*) Don't misunderstand me, chaps. All I want is for him to get better. And if he was, I'd be the first person to say: "Bring him home." But he's not, and we can't give him the medical care and attention he needs at home. That's what hospitals are there for. (*Brusquely.*) So don't just stand there! Get on with it!

(*Sam clears Hally's table.*)

You heard right. My Dad wants to go home.

SAM: Is he better?

HALLY (*sharply*): No! How the hell can he be better when last night he was groaning with pain? This is not an age of miracles!

SAM: Then he should stay in hospital.

HALLY (*seething with irritation and frustration*): Tell me something I don't know, Sam. What the hell do you think I was saying to my Mom? All I can say is fuck-it-all.

SAM: I'm sure he'll listen to your Mom.

HALLY: You don't know what she's up against. He's already packed his shaving kit and pajamas and is sitting on his bed with his crutches, dressed and ready to go. I know him when he gets in that mood. If she tries to reason with him, we've had it. She's no match for him when it comes to a battle of words. He'll tie her up in knots. (*Trying to hide his true feelings.*)

SAM: I suppose it gets lonely for him in there.

HALLY: With all the patients and nurses around? Regular visits from the Salvation Army? Balls! It's ten times worse for him at home. I'm at school and my mother is here in the business all day.

SAM: He's at least got you at night.

HALLY (*before he can stop himself*): And we've got him! Please! I don't want to talk about it anymore. (*Unpacks his school case, slamming down books on the table.*) Life is just a plain bloody mess, that's all. And people are fools.

SAM: Come on, Hally.

HALLY: Yes, they are! They bloody well deserve what they get.

SAM: Then don't complain.

HALLY: Don't try to be clever, Sam. It doesn't suit you. Anybody who thinks there's nothing wrong with this world needs to have his head examined. Just when things are going along all right, without fail someone or something will come along and spoil everything. Somebody should write that down as a fundamental law of the Universe. The principle of perpetual disappointment. If there is a God who created this world, he should scrap it and try again.

SAM: All right, Hally, all right. What you got for homework?

HALLY: Bullshit, as usual. (*Opens an exercise book and reads.*) "Write five hundred words describing an annual event of cultural or historical significance."

SAM: That should be easy enough for you.

HALLY: And also plain bloody boring. You know what

he wants, don't you? One of their useless old ceremonies. The commemoration of the landing of the 1820 Settlers, or if it's going to be culture, Carols by Candlelight every Christmas.

SAM: It's an impressive sight. Make a good description, Hally. All those candles glowing in the dark and the people singing hymns.

HALLY: And it's called religious hysteria. (*Intense irritation.*) Please, Sam! Just leave me alone and let me get on with it. I'm not in the mood for games this afternoon. And remember my Mom's orders . . . you're to help Willie with the windows. Come on now, I don't want any more nonsense in here.

SAM: Okay, Hally, okay.

(*Hally settles down to his homework; determined preparations . . . pen, ruler, exercise book, dictionary, another cake . . . all of which will lead to nothing.*)

(*Sam waltzes over to Willie and starts to replace tables and chairs. He practices a ballroom step while doing so. Willie watches. When Sam is finished, Willie tries.*)

Good! But just a little bit quicker on the turn and only move in to her after she's crossed over. What about this one?

(*Another step. When Sam is finished, Willie again has a go.*)

Much better. See what happens when you just relax and enjoy yourself? Remember that in two weeks' time and you'll be all right.

WILLIE: But I haven't got partner, Boet Sam.

SAM: Maybe Hilda will turn up tonight.

WILLIE: No, Boet Sam. (*Reluctantly.*) I gave her a good hiding.

SAM: You mean a bad one.

WILLIE: Good bad one.

SAM: Then you mustn't complain either. Now you pay the price for losing your temper.

WILLIE: I also pay two pounds ten shilling entrance fee.

SAM: They'll refund you if you withdraw now.

WILLIE (*appalled*): You mean, don't dance?

SAM: Yes.

WILLIE: No! I wait too long and I practice too hard. If I find me new partner, you think I can be ready in two weeks? I ask Madam for my leave now and we practice every day.

SAM: Quickstep nonstop for two weeks. World record, Willie, but you'll be mad at the end.

WILLIE: No jokes, Boet Sam.

SAM: I'm not joking.

WILLIE: So then what?

SAM: Find Hilda. Say you're sorry and promise you won't beat her again.

WILLIE: No.

SAM: Then withdraw. Try again next year.

WILLIE: No.

SAM: Then I give up.

WILLIE: Haaikona, Boet Sam, you can't.

SAM: What do you mean, I can't? I'm telling you: I give up.

WILLIE (*adamant*): No! (*Accusingly.*) It was you who start me ballroom dancing.

SAM: So?

WILLIE: Before that I use to be happy. And is you and Miriam who bring me to Hilda and say here's partner for you.

SAM: What are you saying, Willie?

WILLIE: You!

SAM: But me what? To blame?

WILLIE: Yes.

SAM: Willie . . . ? (*Bursts into laughter.*)

WILLIE: And now all you do is make jokes at me. You wait. When Miriam leaves you is my turn to laugh. Ha! Ha! Ha!

SAM (*he can't take Willie seriously any longer*): She can leave me tonight! I know what to do. (*Bowing before an imaginary partner.*) May I have the pleasure? (*He dances and sings.*)
"Just a fellow with his pillow . . .
Dancin' like a willow . . .
In an autumn breeze. . . ."

WILLIE: There you go again!

(*Sam goes on dancing and singing.*)

Boet Sam!

SAM: There's the answer to your problem! Judges' announcement in two weeks' time: "Ladies and gentlemen, the winner in the open section . . . Mr. Willie Malopo and his pillow!"

(*This is too much for a now really angry Willie. He goes for Sam, but the latter is too quick for him and puts Hally's table between the two of them.*)

HALLY (*exploding*): For Christ's sake, you two!

WILLIE (*still trying to get at Sam*): I donner you, Sam! Struesgod!

SAM (*still laughing*): Sorry, Willie . . . Sorry. . . .

HALLY: Sam! Willie! (*Grabs his ruler and gives Willie a vicious whack on the bum.*) How the hell am I supposed to concentrate with the two of you behaving like bloody children!

WILLIE: Hit him too!

HALLY: Shut up, Willie.

WILLIE: He started jokes again.

HALLY: Get back to your work. You too, Sam. (*His ruler.*) Do you want another one, Willie?

(*Sam and Willie return to their work. Hally uses the opportunity to escape from his unsuccessful attempt at homework. He struts around like a little despot, ruler in hand, giving vent to his anger and frustration.*)

Suppose a customer had walked in then? Or the Park Superintendent. And seen the two of you behaving like a pair of hooligans. That would have been the end of my mother's license, you know. And your jobs? Well, this is the end of it. From now on there will be no more of your ballroom nonsense in here.

This is a business establishment, not a bloody New Brighton dancing school. I've been far too lenient with the two of you. (*Behind the counter for a green cool drink and a dollop of ice cream. He keeps up his tirade as he prepares it.*) But what really makes me bitter is that I allow you chaps a little freedom in here when business is bad and what do you do with it? The foxtrot! Specially you, Sam. There's more to life than trotting around a dance floor and I thought at least you knew it.

SAM: It's a harmless pleasure, Hally. It doesn't hurt anybody.

HALLY: It's also a rather simple one, you know.

SAM: You reckon so? Have you ever tried?

HALLY: Of course not.

SAM: Why don't you? Now.

HALLY: What do you mean? Me dance?

SAM: Yes. I'll show you a simple step — the waltz — then you try it.

HALLY: What will that prove?

SAM: That it might not be as easy as you think.

HALLY: I didn't say it was easy. I said it was simple — like in simple-minded, meaning mentally retarded. You can't exactly say it challenges the intellect.

SAM: It does other things.

HALLY: Such as?

SAM: Make people happy.

HALLY (*the glass in his hand*): So do American cream sodas with ice cream. For God's sake, Sam, you're not asking me to take ballroom dancing serious, are you?

SAM: Yes.

HALLY (*sigh of defeat*): Oh, well, so much for trying to give you a decent education. I've obviously achieved nothing.

SAM: You still haven't told me what's wrong with admiring something that's beautiful and then trying to do it yourself.

HALLY: Nothing. But we happen to be talking about a foxtrot, not a thing of beauty.

SAM: But that is just what I'm saying. If you were to see two champions doing, two masters of the art . . . !

HALLY: Oh God, I give up. So now it's also art!

HALLY: There's a limit, Sam. Don't confuse art and entertainment.

SAM: So then what is art?

HALLY: You want a definition?

SAM: Ja.

HALLY (*He realizes he has got to be careful. He gives the matter a lot of thought before answering.*): Philosophers have been trying to do that for centuries. What is Art? What is Life? But basically I suppose it's . . . the giving of meaning to matter.

SAM: Nothing to do with beautiful?

HALLY: It goes beyond that. It's the giving of form to the formless.

SAM: Ja, well, maybe it's not art, then. But I still say it's beautiful.

HALLY: I'm sure the word you mean to use is entertaining.

SAM (*adamant*): No. Beautiful. And if you want proof come along to the Centenary Hall in New Brighton in two weeks' time.

(*The mention of the Centenary Hall draws Willie over to them.*)

HALLY: What for? I've seen the two of you prancing around in here often enough.

SAM (*he laughs*): This isn't the real thing, Hally. We're just playing around in here.

HALLY: So? I can use my imagination.

SAM: And what do you get?

HALLY: A lot of people dancing around and having a so-called good time.

SAM: That all?

HALLY: Well, basically it is that, surely.

SAM: No, it isn't. Your imagination hasn't helped you at all. There's a lot more to it than that. We're getting ready for the championships, Hally, not just another dance. There's going to be a lot of people, all right, and they're going to have a good time, but they'll only be spectators, sitting around and watching. It's just the competitors out there on the dance floor. Party decorations and fancy lights all around the walls! The ladies in beautiful evening dresses!

HALLY: My mother's got one of those, Sam, and, quite frankly, it's an embarrassment every time she wears it.

SAM (*undeterred*): Your imagination left out the excitement.

(*Hally scoffs.*)

Oh, yes. The finalists are not going to be out there just to have a good time. One of those couples will be the 1950 Eastern Province Champions. And your imagination left out the music.

WILLIE: Mr. Elijah Gladman Guzana and his Orchestral Jazzonions.

SAM: The sound of the big band, Hally. Trombone, trumpet, tenor and alto sax. And then, finally, your imagination also left out the climax of the evening when the dancing is finished, the judges have stopped whispering among themselves and the Master of Ceremonies collects their scorecards and goes up onto the stage to announce the winners.

HALLY: All right. So you make it sound like a bit of a do. It's an occasion. Satisfied?

SAM (*victory*): So you admit that!

HALLY: Emotionally yes, intellectually no.

SAM: Well, I don't know what you mean by that, all I'm telling you is that it is going to be *the* event of the year in New Brighton. It's been sold out for two weeks already. There's only standing room left. We've got competitors coming from Kingwilliamstown, East London, Port Alfred.

(*Hally starts pacing thoughtfully.*)

HALLY: Tell me a bit more.

SAM: I thought you weren't interested . . . intellectually.

HALLY (*mysteriously*): I've got my reasons.

SAM: What do you want to know?

HALLY: It takes place every year?

SAM: Yes. But only every third year in New Brighton. It's East London's turn to have the championships next year.

HALLY: Which, I suppose, makes it an even more significant event.

SAM: Ah ha! We're getting somewhere. Our "occasion" is now a "significant event."

HALLY: I wonder.

SAM: What?

HALLY: I wonder if I would get away with it.

SAM: But what?

HALLY (*to the table and his exercise book*): "Write five hundred words describing an annual event of cultural or historical significance." Would I be stretching poetic license a little too far if I called your ballroom championships a cultural event?

SAM: You mean . . . ?

HALLY: You think we could get five hundred words out of it, Sam?

SAM: Victor Sylvester has written a whole book on ballroom dancing.

WILLIE: You going to write about it, Master Hally?

HALLY: Yes, gentlemen, that is precisely what I am considering doing. Old Doc Bromely — he's my English teacher — is going to argue with me, of course. He doesn't like natives. But I'll point out to him that in strict anthropological terms the culture of a primitive black society includes its dancing and singing. To put my thesis in a nutshell: The war-dance has been replaced by the waltz. But it still amounts to the same thing: the release of primitive emotions through movement. Shall we give it a go?

SAM: I'm ready.

WILLIE: Me also.

HALLY: Ha! This will teach the old bugger a lesson. (*Decision taken.*) Right. Let's get ourselves organized. (*This means another cake on the table. He sits.*) I think you've given me enough general atmosphere, Sam, but to build the tension and suspense I need facts. (*Pencil poised.*)

WILLIE: Give him facts, Boet Sam.

HALLY: What you called the climax . . . how many finalists?

SAM: Six couples.

HALLY (*making notes*): Go on. Give me the picture.

SAM: Spectators seated right around the hall. (*Willie becomes a spectator.*)

HALLY: . . . and it's a full house.

SAM: At one end, on the stage, Gladman and his Orchestral Jazzonions. At the other end is a long table with the three judges. The six finalists go onto the dance floor and take up their positions. When they are ready and the spectators have settled down, the Master of Ceremonies goes to the microphone. To start with, he makes some jokes to get people laughing. . . .

HALLY: Good touch. (*As he writes.*) ". . . creating a relaxed atmosphere which will change to one of tension and drama as the climax is approached."

SAM (*onto a chair to act out the M.C.*): "Ladies and gentlemen, we come now to the great moment you have all been waiting for this evening. . . . The finals of the 1950 Eastern Province Open Ballroom Dancing Championships. But first let me introduce the finalists! Mr. and Mrs. Welcome Tchabalala from Kingwilliamstown . . ."

WILLIE (*he applauds after every name*): Is when the people clap their hands and whistle and make a lot of noise, Master Hally.

SAM: "Mr. Mulligan Njikelane and Miss Nomhle Nkonyeni of Grahamstown; Mr. and Mrs. Norman Nchinga from Port Alfred; Mr. Fats Bokolane and Miss Dina Plaatjies from East London; Mr. Sipho Dugu and Mrs. Mable Magada from Peddie; and from New Brighton our very own Mr. Willie Malopo and Miss Hilda Samuels."

(*Willie can't believe his ears. He abandons his role as spectator and scrambles into position as a finalist.*)

WILLIE: Relaxed and ready to romance!

SAM: The applause dies down. When everybody is silent, Gladman lifts up his sax, nods at the Orchestral Jazzonions. . . .

WILLIE: Play the jukebox please, Boet Sam!

SAM: I also only got bus fare, Willie.

HALLY: Hold it, everybody. (*Heads for the cash register behind the counter.*) How much is in the till, Sam?

SAM: Three shillings. Hally . . . Your Mom counted it before she left.

(*Hally hesitates.*)

HALLY: Sorry, Willie. You know how she carried on the last time I did it. We'll just have to pool our combined imaginations and hope for the best. (*Returns to the table.*) Back to work. How are the points scored, Sam?

SAM: Maximum of ten points each for individual style, deportment, rhythm, and general appearance.

WILLIE: Must I start?

HALLY: Hold it for a second, Willie. And penalties?

SAM: For what?

HALLY: For doing something wrong. Say you stumble or bump into somebody . . . do they take off any points?

SAM (*aghast*): Hally . . . !

HALLY: When you're dancing. If you and your partner collide into another couple.

(*Hally can get no further. Sam has collapsed with laughter. He explains to Willie.*)

SAM: If me and Miriam bump into you and Hilda. . . .

(*Willie joins him in another good laugh.*)

Hally, Hally . . . !

HALLY (*perplexed*): Why? What did I say?

SAM: There's no collisions out there, Hally. Nobody trips or stumbles or bumps into anybody else. That's what that moment is all about. To be one of those finalists on that dance floor is like . . . like being in a dream about a world in which accidents don't happen.

HALLY (*genuinely moved by Sam's image*): Jesus, Sam! That's beautiful!

WILLIE (*can endure waiting no longer*): I'm starting!

(*Willie dances while Sam talks.*)

SAM: Of course it is. That's what I've been trying to say to you all afternoon. And it's beautiful because that is what we want life to be like. But instead, like you said, Hally, we're bumping into each other all the time. Look at the three of us this afternoon: I've bumped into Willie, the two of us have bumped into you, you've bumped into your mother, she bumping into your Dad. . . . None of us knows the steps and there's no music playing. And it doesn't stop with us. The whole world is doing it all the time. Open a newspaper and what do you read? America has bumped into Russia, England is bumping into India, rich man bumps into poor man. Those are big collisions, Hally. They make for a lot of bruises. People get hurt in all that bumping, and we're sick and tired of it now. It's been going on for too long. Are we never going to get it right? . . . Learn to dance life like champions instead of always being just a bunch of beginners at it?

HALLY (*deep and sincere admiration of the man*): You've got a vision, Sam!

SAM: Not just me. What I'm saying to you is that everybody's got it. That's why there's only standing room left for the Centenary Hall in two weeks' time. For as long as the music lasts, we are going to see six couples get it right, the way we want life to be.

HALLY: But is that the best we can do, Sam . . . watch six finalists dreaming about the way it should be?

SAM: I don't know. But it starts with that. Without the dream we won't know what we're going for. And anyway I reckon there are a few people who have got past just dreaming about it and are trying for something real. Remember that thing we read once in the paper about the Mahatma Gandhi? Going without food to stop those riots in India?

HALLY: You're right. He certainly was trying to teach people to get the steps right.

SAM: And the Pope.

HALLY: Yes, he's another one. Our old General Smuts° as well, you know. He's also out there dancing. You know, Sam, when you come to think of it, that's what the United Nations boils down to . . . a dancing school for politicians!

General Smuts: (1870–1950), South African statesman who fought the British in the Boer War in 1899, was instrumental in forming the Union of South Africa in 1910, and was active in the creation of the United Nations.

SAM: And let's hope they learn.

HALLY (*a little surge of hope*): You're right. We mustn't despair. Maybe there's some hope for mankind after all. Keep it up, Willie. (*Back to his table with determination.*) This is a lot bigger than I thought. So what have we got? Yes, our title: "A World Without Collisions."

SAM: That sounds good! "A World Without Collisions."

HALLY: Subtitle: "Global Politics on the Dance Floor." No. A bit too heavy, hey? What about "Ballroom Dancing as a Political Vision"?

(*The telephone rings. Sam answers it.*)

SAM: St. George's Park Tea Room ... Yes, Madam ... Hally, it's your Mom.

HALLY (*back to reality*): Oh, God, yes! I'd forgotten all about that. Shit! Remember my words, Sam? Just when you're enjoying yourself, someone or something will come along and wreck everything.

SAM: You haven't heard what she's got to say yet.

HALLY: Public telephone?

SAM: No.

HALLY: Does she sound happy or unhappy?

SAM: I couldn't tell. (*Pause.*) She's waiting, Hally.

HALLY (*to the telephone*): Hello, Mom ... No, everything is okay here. Just doing my homework. ... What's your news? ... You've what? ... (*Pause. He takes the receiver away from his ear for a few seconds. In the course of Hally's telephone conversation, Sam and Willie discreetly position the stacked tables and chairs. Hally places the receiver back to his ear.*) Yes, I'm still here. Oh, well, I give up now. Why did you do it, Mom? ... Well, I just hope you know what you've let us in for. ... (*Loudly.*) I said I hope you know what you've let us in for! It's the end of the peace and quiet we've been having. (*Softly.*) Where is he? (*Normal voice.*) He can't hear us from in there. But for God's sake, Mom, what happened? I told you to be firm with him. ... Then you and the nurses should have held him down, taken his crutches away. ... I know only too well he's my father! ... I'm not being disrespectful, but I'm sick and tired of emptying stinking chamber pots full of phlegm and piss. ... Yes, I do! When you're not there, he asks *me* to do it. ... If you really want to know the truth, that's why I've got no appetite for my food. ... Yes! There's a lot of things you don't know about. For your information, I still haven't got that science textbook I need. And you know why? He borrowed the money you gave me for it. ... Because I didn't want to start another fight between you two. ... He says that every time. ... All right, Mom! (*Viciously.*) Then just remember to start hiding your bag away again, because he'll be at your purse before long for money for booze. And when he's well enough to come down here, you better keep an eye on the till as well, because that is also going to develop a leak. ... Then don't complain to me when he starts his old tricks. ... Yes, you do. I get it from you on one side and from him on the other, and it makes life hell for me. I'm not going to be the peacemaker anymore. I'm warning you now: when the two of you start fighting again, I'm leaving home. ... Mom, if you start crying, I'm going to put down the receiver. ... Okay. ... (*Lowering his voice to a vicious whisper.*) Okay, Mom. I heard you. (*Desperate.*) No. ... Because I don't want to. I'll see him when I get home! Mom! ... (*Pause. When he speaks again, his tone changes completely. It is not simply pretense. We sense a genuine emotional conflict.*) Welcome home, chum! ... What's that? ... Don't be silly, Dad. You being home is just about the best news in the world. ... I bet you are. Bloody depressing there with everybody going on about their ailments, hey! ... How you feeling? ... Good. ... Here as well, pal. Coming down cats and dogs. ... That's right. Just the day for a kip° and a toss in your old Uncle Ned. ... Everything's just hunky-dory on my side, Dad. ... Well, to start with, there's a nice pile of comics for you on the counter. ... Yes, old Kemple brought them in. *Batman and Robin, Submariner* ... just your cup of tea. ... I will. ... Yes, we'll spin a few yarns tonight. ... Okay, chum, see you in a little while. ... No, I promise. I'll come straight home. ... (*Pause — his mother comes back on the phone.*) Mom? Okay. I'll lock up now. ... What? ... Oh, the brandy ... Yes, I'll remember! ... I'll put it in my suitcase now, for God's sake. I know well enough what will happen if he doesn't get it. ... (*Places a bottle of brandy on the counter.*) I *was* kind to him, Mom. I didn't say anything nasty! ... All right. Bye. (*End of telephone conversation. A desolate Hally doesn't move. A strained silence.*)

SAM (*quietly*): That sounded like a bad bump, Hally.

HALLY (*Having a hard time controlling his emotions. He speaks carefully.*): Mind your own business, Sam.

SAM: Sorry. I wasn't trying to interfere. Shall we carry on? Hally? (*He indicates the exercise book. No response from Hally.*)

WILLIE (*also trying*): Tell him about when they give out the cups, Boet Sam.

SAM: Ja! That's another big moment. The presentation of the cups after the winners have been announced. You've got to put that in.

(*Still no response from Hally.*)

WILLIE: A big silver one, Master Hally, called floating trophy for the champions.

SAM: We always invite some big-shot personality to hand them over. Guest of honor this year is going to be His Holiness Bishop Jabulani of the All African Free Zionist Church.

(*Hally gets up abruptly, goes to his table, and tears up the page he was writing on.*)

HALLY: So much for a bloody world without collisions.

kip: Nap.

SAM: Too bad. It was on its way to being a good composition.

HALLY: Let's stop bullshitting ourselves, Sam.

SAM: Have we been doing that?

HALLY: Yes! That's what all our talk about a decent world has been . . . just so much bullshit.

SAM: We did say it was still only a dream.

HALLY: And a bloody useless one at that. Life's a fuckup and it's never going to change.

SAM: Ja, maybe that's true.

HALLY: There's no maybe about it. It's a blunt and brutal fact. All we've done this afternoon is waste our time.

SAM: Not if we'd got your homework done.

HALLY: I don't give a shit about my homework, so, for Christ's sake, just shut up about it. (*Slamming books viciously into his school case.*) Hurry up now and finish your work. I want to lock up and get out of here. (*Pause.*) And then go where? Home-sweet-fucking-home. Jesus, I hate that word.

(*Hally goes to the counter to put the brandy bottle and comics in his school case. After a moment's hesitation, he smashes the bottle of brandy. He abandons all further attempts to hide his feelings. Sam and Willie work away as unobtrusively as possible.*)

Do you want to know what is really wrong with your lovely little dream, Sam? It's not just that we are all bad dancers. That does happen to be perfectly true, but there's more to it than just that. You left out the cripples.

SAM: Hally!

HALLY (*now totally reckless*): Ja! Can't leave them out, Sam. That's why we always end up on our backsides on the dance floor. They're also out there dancing . . . like a bunch of broken spiders trying to do the quickstep! (*An ugly attempt at laughter.*) When you come to think of it, it's a bloody comical sight. I mean, it's bad enough on two legs . . . but one and a pair of crutches! Hell, no, Sam. That's guaranteed to turn that dance floor into a shambles. Why you shaking your head? Picture it, man. For once this afternoon let's use our imaginations sensibly.

SAM: Be careful, Hally.

HALLY: Of what? The truth? I seem to be the only one around here who is prepared to face it. We've had the pretty dream, it's time now to wake up and have a good long look at the way things really are. Nobody knows the steps, there's no music, the cripples are also out there tripping up everybody and trying to get into the act, and it's all called the All-Comers-How-to-Make-a-Fuckup-of-Life Championships. (*Another ugly laugh.*) Hang on, Sam! The best bit is still coming. Do you know what the winner's trophy is? A beautiful big chamber pot with roses on the side, and it's full to the brim with piss. And guess who I think is going to be this year's winner.

SAM (*almost shouting*): Stop now!

HALLY (*suddenly appalled by how far he has gone*): Why?

SAM: Hally? It's your father you're talking about.

HALLY: So?

SAM: Do you know what you've been saying?

(*Hally can't answer. He is rigid with shame. Sam speaks to him sternly.*)

No, Hally, you mustn't do it. Take back those words and ask for forgiveness! It's a terrible sin for a son to mock his father with jokes like that. You'll be punished if you carry on. Your father is your father, even if he is a . . . cripple man.

WILLIE: Yes, Master Hally. Is true what Sam say.

SAM: I understand how you are feeling, Hally, but even so. . . .

HALLY: No, you don't!

SAM: I think I do.

HALLY: And I'm telling you you don't. Nobody does. (*Speaking carefully as his shame turns to rage at Sam.*) It's your turn to be careful, Sam. Very careful! You're treading on dangerous ground. Leave me and my father alone.

SAM: I'm not the one who's been saying things about him.

HALLY: What goes on between me and my Dad is none of your business!

SAM: Then don't tell me about it. If that's all you've got to say about him, I don't want to hear.

(*For a moment Hally is at loss for a response.*)

HALLY: Just get on with your bloody work and shut up.

SAM: Swearing at me won't help you.

HALLY: Yes, it does! Mind your own fucking business and shut up!

SAM: Okay. If that's the way you want it, I'll stop trying.

(*He turns away. This infuriates Hally even more.*)

HALLY: Good. Because what you've been trying to do is meddle in something you know nothing about. All that concerns you in here, Sam, is to try and do what you get paid for — keep the place clean and serve the customers. In plain words, just get on with your job. My mother is right. She's always warning me about allowing you to get too familiar. Well, this time you've gone too far. It's going to stop right now.

(*No response from Sam.*)

You're only a servant in here, and don't forget it.

(*Still no response. Hally is trying hard to get one.*)

And as far as my father is concerned, all you need to remember is that he is your boss.

SAM (*needled at last*): No, he isn't. I get paid by your mother.

HALLY: Don't argue with me, Sam!

SAM: Then don't say he's my boss.

HALLY: He's a white man and that's good enough for you.

SAM: I'll try to forget you said that.

HALLY: Don't! Because you won't be doing me a favor if you do. I'm telling you to remember it.

(*A pause. Sam pulls himself together and makes one last effort.*)

SAM: Hally, Hally . . . ! Come on now. Let's stop before it's too late. You're right. We *are* on dangerous ground. If we're not careful, somebody is going to get hurt.

HALLY: It won't be me.

SAM: Don't be so sure.

HALLY: I don't know what you're talking about, Sam.

SAM: Yes, you do.

HALLY (*furious*): Jesus, I wish you would stop trying to tell me what I do and what I don't know.

(*Sam gives up. He turns to Willie.*)

SAM: Let's finish up.

HALLY: Don't turn your back on me! I haven't finished talking.

(*He grabs Sam by the arm and tries to make him turn around. Sam reacts with a flash of anger.*)

SAM: Don't do that, Hally! (*Facing the boy.*) All right, I'm listening. Well? What do you want to say to me?

HALLY (*pause as Hally looks for something to say*): To begin with, why don't you also start calling me Master Harold, like Willie.

SAM: Do you mean that?

HALLY: Why the hell do you think I said it?

SAM: And if I don't?

HALLY: You might just lose your job.

SAM (*quietly and very carefully*): If you make me say it once, I'll never call you anything else again.

HALLY: So? (*The boy confronts the man.*) Is that meant to be a threat?

SAM: Just telling you what will happen if you make me do that. You must decide what it means to you.

HALLY: Well, I have. It's good news. Because that is exactly what Master Harold wants from now on. Think of it as a little lesson in respect, Sam, that's long overdue, and I hope you remember it as well as you do your geography. I can tell you now that somebody who will be glad to hear I've finally given it to you will be my Dad. Yes! He agrees with my Mom. He's always going on about it as well. "You must teach the boys to show you more respect, my son."

SAM: So now you can stop complaining about going home. Everybody is going to be happy tonight.

HALLY: That's perfectly correct. You see, you mustn't get the wrong idea about me and my Dad, Sam. We also have our good times together. Some bloody good laughs. He's got a marvelous sense of humor. Want to know what our favorite joke is? He gives out a big groan, you see, and says: "It's not fair, is it, Hally?" Then I have to ask: "What, chum?" And then he says: "A nigger's arse" . . . and we both have a good laugh.

(*The men stare at him with disbelief.*)

What's the matter, Willie? Don't you catch the joke? You always were a bit slow on the uptake. It's what is called a pun. You see, fair means both light in color and to be just and decent. (*He turns to Sam.*) I thought *you* would catch it, Sam.

SAM: Oh ja, I catch it all right.

HALLY: But it doesn't appeal to your sense of humor.

SAM: Do you really laugh?

HALLY: Of course.

SAM: To please him? Make him feel good?

HALLY: No, for heavens sake! I laugh because I think it's a bloody good joke.

SAM: You're really trying hard to be ugly, aren't you? And why drag poor old Willie into it? He's done nothing to you except show you the respect you want so badly. That's also not being fair, you know . . . and I mean just or decent.

WILLIE: It's all right, Sam. Leave it now.

SAM: It's me you're after. You should just have said "Sam's arse" . . . because that's the one you're trying to kick. Anyway, how do you know it's not fair? You've never seen it. Do you want to? (*He drops his trousers and underpants and presents his backside for Hally's inspection.*) Have a good look. A real Basuto arse . . . which is about as nigger as they can come. Satisfied? (*Trousers up.*) Now you can make your Dad even happier when you go home tonight. Tell him I showed you my arse and he is quite right. It's not fair. And if it will give him an even better laugh next time, I'll also let *him* have a look. Come, Willie, let's finish up and go.

(*Sam and Willie start to tidy up the tea room. Hally doesn't move. He waits for a moment when Sam passes him.*)

HALLY (*quietly*): Sam . . .

(*Sam stops and looks expectantly at the boy. Hally spits in his face. A long and heartfelt groan from Willie. For a few seconds Sam doesn't move.*)

SAM (*taking out a handkerchief and wiping his face*): It's all right, Willie.

(*To Hally.*)

Ja, well, you've done it . . . Master Harold. Yes, I'll start calling you that from now on. It won't be difficult anymore. You've hurt yourself, Master Harold. I saw it coming. I warned you, but you wouldn't listen. You've just hurt yourself *bad*. And you're a coward, Master Harold. The face you should be spitting in is your father's . . . but you used mine, because you think you're safe inside your fair skin . . . and this time I don't mean just or decent. (*Pause, then moving violently toward Hally.*) Should I hit him, Willie?

WILLIE (*stopping Sam*): No, Boet Sam.

SAM (*violently*): Why not?

WILLIE: It won't help, Boet Sam.

SAM: I don't want to help! I want to hurt him.

WILLIE: You also hurt yourself.

SAM: And if he had done it to you, Willie?

WILLIE: Me? Spit at me like I was a dog? (*A thought*

that had not occurred to him before. He looks at Hally.) Ja. Then I want to hit him. I want to hit him hard!

(*A dangerous few seconds as the men stand staring at the boy. Willie turns away, shaking his head.*)

But maybe all I do is go cry at the back. He's little boy, Boet Sam. Little *white* boy. Long trousers now, but he's still little boy.

SAM (*his violence ebbing away into defeat as quickly as it flooded*): You're right. So go on, then: groan again, Willie. You do it better than me. (*To Hally.*) You don't know all of what you've just done . . . Master Harold. It's not just that you've made me feel dirtier than I've ever been in my life . . . I mean, how do I wash off yours and your father's filth? . . . I've also failed. A long time ago I promised myself I was going to try and do something, but you've just shown me . . . Master Harold . . . that I've failed. (*Pause.*) I've also got a memory of a little white boy when he was still wearing short trousers and a black man, but they're not flying a kite. It was the old Jubilee days, after dinner one night. I was in my room. You came in and just stood against the wall, looking down at the ground, and only after I'd asked you what you wanted, what was wrong, I don't know how many times, did you speak and even then so softly I almost didn't hear you. "Sam, please help me to go and fetch my Dad." Remember? He was dead drunk on the floor of the Central Hotel Bar. They'd phoned for your Mom, but you were the only one at home. And do you remember how we did it? You went in first by yourself to ask permission for me to go into the bar. Then I loaded him onto my back like a baby and carried him back to the boarding house with you following behind carrying his crutches. (*Shaking his head as he remembers.*) A crowded Main Street with all the people watching a little white boy following his drunk father on a nigger's back! I felt for that little boy . . . Master Harold. I felt for him. After that we still had to clean him up, remember? He'd messed in his trousers, so we had to clean him up and get him into bed.

HALLY (*great pain*): I love him, Sam.

SAM: I know you do. That's why I tried to stop you from saying these things about him. It would have been so simple if you could have just despised him for being a weak man. But he's your father. You love him and you're ashamed of him. You're ashamed of so much! . . . And now that's going to include yourself. That was the promise I made to myself: to try and stop that happening. (*Pause.*) After we got him to bed you came back with me to my room and sat in a corner and carried on just looking down at the ground. And for days after that! You hadn't done anything wrong, but you went around as if you owed the world an apology for being alive. I didn't like seeing that! That's not the way a boy grows up to be a man! . . . But the one person who should have been

teaching you what that means was the cause of your shame. If you really want to know, that's why I made you that kite. I wanted you to look up, be proud of something, of yourself . . . (*bitter smile at the memory*) . . . and you certainly were that when I left you with it up there on the hill. Oh, ja . . . something else! . . . If you ever do write it as a short story, there *was* a twist in our ending. I couldn't sit down there and stay with you. It was a "Whites Only" bench. You were too young, too excited to notice then. But not anymore. If you're not careful . . . Master Harold . . . you're going to be sitting up there by yourself for a long time to come, and there won't be a kite in the sky. (*Sam has got nothing more to say. He exits into the kitchen, taking off his waiter's jacket.*)

WILLIE: Is bad. Is all bad in here now.

HALLY (*books into his school case, raincoat on*): Willie . . . (*It is difficult to speak.*) Will you lock up for me and look after the keys?

WILLIE: Okay.

(*Sam returns. Hally goes behind the counter and collects the few coins in the cash register. As he starts to leave. . . .*)

SAM: Don't forget the comic books.

(*Hally returns to the counter and puts them in his case. He starts to leave again.*)

SAM (*to the retreating back of the boy*): Stop . . . Hally. . . .

(*Hally stops, but doesn't turn to face him.*)

Hally . . . I've got no right to tell you what being a man means if I don't behave like one myself, and I'm not doing so well at that this afternoon. Should we try again, Hally?

HALLY: Try what?

SAM: Fly another kite, I suppose. It worked once, and this time I need it as much as you do.

HALLY: It's still raining, Sam. You can't fly kites on rainy days, remember.

SAM: So what do we do? Hope for better weather tomorrow?

HALLY (*helpless gesture*): I don't know. I don't know anything anymore.

SAM: You sure of that, Hally? Because it would be pretty hopeless if that was true. It would mean nothing has been learnt in here this afternoon, and there was a hell of a lot of teaching going on . . . one way or the other. But anyway, I don't believe you. I reckon there's one thing you know. You don't *have* to sit up there by yourself. You know what that bench means now, and you can leave it any time you choose. All you've got to do is stand up and walk away from it.

(*Hally leaves. Willie goes up quietly to Sam.*)

WILLIE: Is okay, Boet Sam. You see. Is . . . (*he can't find any better words*) . . . is going to be okay tomorrow. (*Changing his tone.*) Hey, Boet Sam! (*He is trying* hard.) You right. I think about it and you right. Tonight I find Hilda and say sorry. And make promise I won't beat her no more. You hear me, Boet Sam?

SAM: I hear you, Willie.

WILLIE: And when we practice I relax and romance with her from beginning to end. Nonstop! You watch! Two weeks' time: "First prize for promising newcomers: Mr. Willie Malopo and Miss Hilda Samuels." (*Sudden impulse.*) To hell with it! I walk home. (*He goes to the jukebox, puts in a coin and selects a record. The machine comes to life in the gray twilight, blushing its way through a spectrum of soft, romantic colors.*) How did you say it, Boet Sam? Let's dream. (*Willie sways with the music and gestures for Sam to dance.*)

(*Sarah Vaughan sings.*)

"Little man you're crying,
I know why you're blue,
Someone took your kiddy car away;
Better go to sleep now,
Little man you've had a busy day." (*etc., etc.*)
You lead. I follow.

(*The men dance together.*)

"Johnny won your marbles,
Tell you what we'll do;
Dad will get you new ones right away;
Better go to sleep now,
Little man you've had a busy day."

COMMENTARIES

Heinrich von Staden (b. 1939)
INTERVIEW WITH ATHOL FUGARD
1982

When "MASTER HAROLD" . . . and the boys was first produced at the Yale Repertory Theatre, Athol Fugard had the chance to respond to some questions about its significance to him. He revealed that the play was deeply personal and that through it he had been able to exorcise a demon that had haunted him for some time. In this interview Fugard details his involvement with South African drama and black actors in South Africa. He also comments on the extent to which censorship and other political pressures in South Africa made it difficult for his work to be produced in his own country.

von Staden: The bombs of fiction — Athol, aren't they more explosive than TNT?

Fugard: I'd like to believe that. You understand I've got to be careful about that one. I've got to be careful about flattering myself about the potency of the one area of activity which I've got, which is theater and being a writer.

von Staden: How often have there been productions of your plays for nonsegregated audiences in South Africa?

Fugard: I've had to change my tactics in terms of that over the years. At a period when the policy on segregated audiences in South Africa was rigid and very strictly enforced, I had to make a decision whether to take on an act of silence, just be silent because I couldn't go into a theater that was decent in my terms, or whether to take on the compromising circumstances of segregated audiences simply because I felt that if a play has got something to say, at least say it. And there were years when I decided to do the latter. I did perform before segregated audiences. In a sense I regret that decision now. I think I might possibly have looked after myself — and maybe the situation — better by not accepting that compromise. But I did.

von Staden: But do you think you had a genuine choice at that time?

Fugard: I had a choice between silence or being heard.

von Staden: Let me ask you along similar lines, when you are writing a play or a novel like *Tsotsi,* do you sense constraints on the way you are writing in view of the fact that certain things are anathema to the government, also in fiction?

Fugard: I would like to believe that I have operated at the table at which I sit and write, that I have operated totally without self-censorship. Maybe some awareness of what is possible and is not possible has operated subconsciously and is deciding choices I make in terms of what I favor. I think it may be pertinent to the conversation we are having, that *"MASTER HAROLD" . . . and the boys* is the first play of mine in twenty-four years of writing that will have its premiere outside of South Africa. And one of the reasons why I'm doing that this time is that there are elements in *"MASTER HAROLD" . . . and the boys* that might have run into censorship problems. [. . .]

von Staden: Here you are, a person who, critics say, has achieved exceptional insight into human nature, and you never obtained a university degree. What institutions, what processes do you think contributed most to the insights you have?

Fugard: Well, I think to be a South African is in a way to be at a university that teaches you about that. The South African experience is certainly one in which, if you're prepared to keep your eyes open and look, you're going to see a lot of suffering. But then, in terms of personal specifics, I suppose for me there was a very, very important relationship, a friendship, with a black man in what I suppose is any person's most formative and definitive years, the age between eleven, ten up until the age of twenty-one. It was a black man in Port Elizabeth, and my play *"MASTER HAROLD" . . . and the boys* reflects something of that friendship, tries to talk about it, look at it. I left South Africa, hitchhiked through the African continent, ended up as a sailor on a ship which, apart from the officers and engineers, had a totally nonwhite, had a totally black crew, and I was a sailor in a totally black crew. There was that, I think I can't nail down any one specific traumatic incident as being totally decisive. But I could be certain that *"MASTER HAROLD" . . . and the boys* deals with one specific moment which I'm trying to exorcise out of my soul.

von Staden: In all of your plays and in the novel you always have a South African setting. Yet your plays and your novels, though so rooted in the specifics of the South African situation, seem to have a tremendous appeal to audiences that are largely ignorant of the situation there. To what do you ascribe that?

Fugard: You take a chance. As a storyteller one year ago, I took a chance [. . .] I realized that it was finally time to deal with the story of a seventeen-year-old boy and his friendship with two black men. And it's a gamble. There's no formula. There is no way that you can make or decide or guarantee before the event that that story is going to resonate outside of its specific context. You just take a bloody chance.

Athol Fugard (*b. 1932*)
FROM *NOTEBOOKS 1960–1977*   *1983*

*Like most playwrights, Athol Fugard is a journal writer. In his notebooks he has
written scraps of memory that have special meaning to him. In one entry for March
1961, long before he began to write "MASTER HAROLD" . . . and the boys
(1982), he describes one of his childhood memories. It concerns the real-life Sam,
and it reveals — very painfully — exactly what the personal crime was that his
play deals with. His gesture of contempt for the man who was like a grandfather to
him became a demon that had to be exorcised.*

Sam Semela — Basuto — with the family fifteen years. Meeting him again when
he visited Mom set off string of memories.

The kite which he produced for me one day during those early years when Mom
ran the Jubilee Hotel and he was a waiter there. He had made it himself: brown
paper, its ribs fashioned from thin strips of tomato-box plank which he had
smoothed down, a paste of flour and water for glue. I was surprised and bewildered that he had made it for me.

I vaguely recall shyly "haunting" the servants' quarters in the well of the hotel —
cold, cement-gray world — the pungent mystery of the dark little rooms — a
world I didn't understand. Frightened to enter any of the rooms. Sam, broad-faced,
broader based — he smelled of woodsmoke. The "kaffir smell" of South Africa is
the smell of poverty — woodsmoke and sweat.

Later, when he worked for her at the Park café, Mom gave him the sack: ". . . he
became careless. He came late for work. His work went to hell. He didn't seem to
care no more." I was about thirteen and served behind the counter while he waited
on table.

Realize now he was the most significant — the only — friend of my boyhood
years. On terrible windy days when no one came to swim or walk in the park, we
would sit together and talk. Or I was reading — Introductions to Eastern Philosophy or Plato and Socrates — and when I had finished he would take the book back
to New Brighton.

Can't remember now what precipitated it, but one day there was a rare quarrel
between Sam and myself. In a truculent silence we closed the café, Sam set off home
to New Brighton on foot and I followed a few minutes later on my bike. I saw him
walking ahead of me and, coming out of a spasm of acute loneliness, as I rode up
behind him I called his name, he turned in mid-stride to look back and, as I cycled
past, I spat in his face. Don't suppose I will ever deal with the shame that overwhelmed me the second after I had done that.

Now he is thin. We had a long talk. He told about the old woman ("Ma")
whom he and his wife have taken in to look after their house while he goes to
work — he teaches ballroom dancing. "Ma" insists on behaving like a domestic —
making Sam feel guilty and embarrassed. She brings him an early morning cup of
coffee. Sam: "No, Ma, you mustn't, man." Ma: "I must." Sam: "Look, Ma, if I
want it, I can make it." Ma: "No, I must."

Occasionally, when she is doing something, Sam feels like a cup of tea but is too
embarrassed to ask her, and daren't make one for himself. Similarly, with his wash-

ing. After three days or a week away in other towns, giving dancing lessons, he comes back with underclothes that are very dirty. He is too shy to give them out to be washed so washes them himself. When Ma sees this she goes and complains to Sam's wife that he doesn't trust her, that it's all wrong for him to do the washing.

Of tsotsis,° he said: "They grab a old man, stick him with a knife, and ransack him. And so he must go to hospital and his kids is starving with hungry." Of others: "He's got some little moneys. So he is facing starvation for the weekend."

Of township snobs, he says there are the educational ones: "If you haven't been to the big school, like Fort Hare, what you say isn't true." And the money ones: "If you aren't selling shops or got a business or a big car, man, you're nothing."

Sam's incredible theory about the likeness of those "with the true seed of love." Starts with Plato and Socrates — they were round. "Man is being shrinking all the time. An Abe Lincoln, him too, taller, but that's because man is shrinking." Basically, those with the true seed of love look the same —"It's in the eyes."

He spoke admiringly of one man, a black lawyer in East London, an educated man — university background — who was utterly without snobbery, looking down on no one — any man, educated or ignorant, rich or poor, was another *man* to him, another human being, to be respected, taken seriously, to be talked to, listened to.

"They" won't allow Sam any longer to earn a living as a dancing teacher. "You must get a job!" One of his fellow teachers was forced to work at Fraser's Quarries.

---

tsotis: Gang members.

Marsha Norman

Marsha Norman was born in Louisville, Kentucky, in 1947. Because her mother was a deeply religious woman, she did not allow television in her house, and radios, though available, were never used. Movies were also forbidden. But Norman explains that her mother "did not know the dangers of books because she didn't read," so books were Marsha Norman's world for most of her childhood.

But they were not the only influence. Norman spent much of her youth playing the piano, and she enjoyed the children's productions of the Actors' Theatre of Louisville. The Actors' Theatre and its director, Jon Jory, later became influential on Norman's early career as a writer.

Norman has said many times that the best thing for a writer is to be able to see drama during childhood. She has intense memories of *The Glass Menagerie,* Peter Shaffer's *The Royal Hunt of the Sun,* which is about the last day of Montezuma's life, and Archibald MacLeish's *J.B.,* an adaptation of the Book of Job. The vigor and the violence of these plays were explicitly attractive to her. Some of the excitement of that kind of theatricality is present in her first play, *Getting Out* (1977), which had its first performance at the Actors' Theatre.

Norman was a philosophy major at Agnes Scott College in Georgia, but she spent a good deal of her energy in theater there. Yet when she left college she did not expect to do any writing. As she said, she was sure that she would have to work at something else for a living. But a combination of circumstances changed that.

Norman had worked with disturbed teenagers in a Kentucky state hospital and had met a thirteen-year-old girl who was violent, reckless, and frightening. Later when she was working in children's TV in Louisville, Jon Jory offered to commission her to write a play, but initially she was not interested. When she talked over her feelings, Jory advised her to reflect on a moment when she was truly frightened. It was then that she remembered the thirteen-year-old girl and thus began the gestation of *Getting Out.*

Her unusual approach in that play was to present two views of the same woman: Arlie as an imprisoned adolescent and Arlene as an adult trying to begin a reasonable life for herself in a shabby apartment. The two parts of the character share the stage simultaneously. The ultimate problem is how Arlene will learn to integrate the separate parts of her personality. It is a very effective work and ran for eight months off Broadway after a successful opening with the Actors' Theatre.

Norman also wrote some one-act plays for the Actors' Theatre — *The Laundromat* and *The Pool Hall* — and a full-length play, *Circus Valentine* (1979). She won the Pulitzer Prize for *'night, Mother* (1983), currently her most internationally successful play. *Traveler in the Dark* (1984) premiered at the American Repertory Theatre in Cambridge, Massachusetts, starring Sam

Waterston as a cancer surgeon suffering from the strain of guilt. She also wrote the script for *The Secret Garden* (1990), a prize-winning Broadway musical.

Norman has frequently talked about the structure of her plays, which follow a very traditional pattern. She has linked them often to a "ski lift. When you get in it, you must feel absolutely secure; you must know that this thing can hold you up." Her sense of the play as resembling a machine is based in part on her awareness of the audience's needs and expectations. She has said that a good play should follow several simple rules: "You must state the issue at the beginning of the play. The audience must know what is at stake; they must know when they will be able to go home."

Norman is deeply concerned with giving language to those who are inarticulate. The most important characters in her best plays have been women who would not have been able to express themselves clearly without someone like Marsha Norman to give them a voice. Such an ambition may owe something to her youthful desire "to save the world," the same desire that led her to work in the Kentucky hospital that provided the material for her first play.

'NIGHT, MOTHER

Marsha Norman's best-known and most successful play, *'night, Mother* (1983), has won numerous awards, including the Pulitzer Prize. Its subject — a middle-aged woman's determination to commit suicide and leave her mother behind — is not the uplifting fare usually offered to Broadway audiences. Such a play would seem to spell horror for a New York theater; while it ran for ten months after a shaky start, Norman had to accept a 50 percent reduction in her standard royalties to keep the play open.

Her strategy in the play was to face the issue of suicide squarely and directly. She chose not to have Jessie deal with her decision alone and merely leave a note, as had been done in many such plays in the past. Rather, she chose to make the play a dialogue, with Jessie having to confront the one person who loves her most and who most wants her to live and to give up her thoughts of killing herself.

Norman also made the play more difficult for popular audiences because she did not take the obvious path of giving Jessie a terminal disease, as some plays had done. She felt it was imperative that the issues of life and death, of personal choice and motive, be explored directly onstage, with the characters facing as squarely as possible the ramifications of their choices.

The ethical issues that suicide raises are naturally complex, and the play does not broach them directly. But such issues are always in the minds of the audience. In no sense does the play offer anyone reasons for committing suicide. Jessie's discussion with her mother is not equivalent to a debate: she has made up her mind based on her personal feelings about life, and she makes her decision seem inevitable.

Jessie is not a deep thinker, not a reflective person, and she does not concern herself with spiritual issues in making her decision. Her last evening's concerns are limited to the physical, material, and psychological comfort of her mother.

'night, Mother in Performance

'night, Mother opened on March 31, 1983, at New York's Golden Theater. Kathy Bates played the daughter, Jessie, and Anne Pitoniak played Thelma, her mother. Bates and Pitoniak were voted best actresses of the year by the Critics' Outer Circle, and the play was awarded the Pulitzer. The play ran for 388 performances.

Before its New York opening, the play premiered at the American Repertory Theatre under Robert Brustein's aegis in January 1983. Of that production Frank Rich, *New York Times* critic, said, "'night, Mother . . . is one of the most disturbing American plays of recent seasons. You can pick at it and argue with it, but you can't hide from its bruising impact." The fact that it premiered in Boston distinguished the play because it was the first time a playwright received a Pulitzer for a non–New York production. When the play moved to New York, Rich again reviewed it for the *Times*, praising "the superb actresses" and "the brilliant, unerring choreographic hand of the director Tom Moore."

In 1986 the film version appeared, with Tom Moore directing, Sissy Spacek as Jessie, and Anne Bancroft as Thelma. Some reviews complained of Moore's "busy-ness."

In a short time, the play had appeared in productions in thirty-six countries in Europe, South America, Scandinavia, and Africa. Marsha Norman has commented on the differences in the languages and the actresses in various national productions in her interview with David Savran on pages 1508–09. 'night, Mother has become a universal play, one that absorbs cultural differences and speaks to people everywhere.

Marsha Norman (b. 1947)

'NIGHT, MOTHER

1983

Characters

JESSIE CATES, *in her late thirties or early forties, is pale and vaguely unsteady physically. It is only in the last year that Jessie has gained control of her mind and body, and tonight she is determined to hold on to that control. She wears pants and a long black sweater with deep pockets, which contain scraps of paper, and there may be a pencil behind her ear or a pen clipped to one of the pockets of the sweater.*

As a rule, Jessie doesn't feel much like talking. Other people have rarely found her quirky sense of humor amusing. She has a peaceful energy on this night, *a sense of purpose, but is clearly aware of the time passing moment by moment. Oddly enough, Jessie has never been as communicative or as enjoyable as she is on this evening, but we must know she has not always been this way. There is a familiarity between these two women that comes from having lived together for a long time. There is a shorthand to the talk and a sense of routine comfort in the way they relate to each other physically. Naturally, there are also routine aggravations.*

THELMA CATES, MAMA, *is Jessie's mother, in her late fifties or early sixties. She has begun to feel her age and so takes it easy when she can, or when it serves her purpose to let someone help her. But she speaks quickly and enjoys talking. She believes that things are what she says they are. Her sturdiness is more a mental quality than a physical one, finally. She is chatty and nosy, and this is* her *house.*

(*The play takes place in a relatively new house built way out on a country road, with a living room and connecting kitchen, and a center hall that leads off to the bedrooms. A pull cord in the hall ceiling releases a ladder which leads to the attic. One of these bedrooms opens directly onto the hall, and its entry should be visible to everyone in the audience. It should be, in fact, the focal point of the entire set, and the lighting should make it disappear completely at times and draw the entire set into it at others. It is a point of both threat and promise. It is an ordinary door that opens onto absolute nothingness. That door is the point of all the action, and the utmost care should be given to its design and construction.*)

(*The living room is cluttered with magazines and needlework catalogues, ashtrays and candy dishes. Examples of Mama's needlework are everywhere — pillows, afghans, and quilts, doilies and rugs, and they are quite nice examples. The house is more comfortable than messy, but there is quite a lot to keep in place here. It is more personal than charming. It is not quaint. Under no circumstances should the set and its dressing make a judgment about the intelligence or taste of Jessie and Mama. It should simply indicate that they are very specific real people who happen to live in a particular part of the country. Heavy accents, which would further distance the audience from Jessie and Mama, are also wrong.*)

(*The time is the present, with the action beginning about 8:15. Clocks onstage in the kitchen and on a table in the living room should run throughout the performance and be visible to the audience.*)

(*Mama stretches to reach the cupcakes in a cabinet in the kitchen. She can't see them, but she can feel around for them, and she's eager to have one, so she's working pretty hard at it. This may be the most serious exercise Mama ever gets. She finds a cupcake, the coconut-covered, raspberry-and-marshmallow-filled kind known as a snowball, but sees that there's one missing from the package. She calls to Jessie, who is apparently somewhere else in the house.*)

MAMA (*unwrapping the cupcake*): Jessie, it's the last snowball, sugar. Put it on the list, O.K.? And we're out of Hershey bars, and where's that peanut brittle? I think maybe Dawson's been in it again. I ought to put a big mirror on the refrigerator door. That'll keep him out of my treats, won't it? You hear me, honey? (*Then more to herself.*) I hate it when the coconut falls off. Why does the coconut fall off?

(*Jessie enters from her bedroom, carrying a stack of newspapers.*)

JESSIE: We got any old towels?

MAMA: There you are!

JESSIE (*holding a towel that was on the stack of newspapers*): Towels you don't want anymore. (*Picking up Mama's snowball wrapper.*) How about this swimming towel Loretta gave us? Beach towel, that's the name of it. You want it? (*Mama shakes her head no.*)

MAMA: What have you been doing in there?

JESSIE: And a big piece of plastic like a rubber sheet or something. Garbage bags would do if there's enough.

MAMA: Don't go making a big mess, Jessie. It's eight o'clock already.

JESSIE: Maybe an old blanket or towels we got in a soap box sometime?

MAMA: I said don't make a mess. Your hair is black enough, hon.

JESSIE (*continuing to search the kitchen cabinets, finding two or three more towels to add to her stack*): It's not for my hair, Mama. What about some old pillows anywhere, or a foam cushion out of a yard chair would be real good.

MAMA: You haven't forgot what night it is, have you? (*Holding up her fingernails.*) They're all chipped, see? I've been waiting all week, Jess. It's Saturday night, sugar.

JESSIE: I know. I got it on the schedule.

MAMA (*crossing to the living room*): You want me to wash 'em now or are you making your mess first? (*Looking at the snowball.*) We're out of these. Did I say that already?

JESSIE: There's more coming tomorrow. I ordered you a whole case.

MAMA (*checking the TV Guide*): A whole case will go stale, Jessie.

JESSIE: They can go in the freezer till you're ready for them. Where's Daddy's gun?

MAMA: In the attic.

JESSIE: Where in the attic? I looked your whole nap and couldn't find it anywhere.

MAMA: One of his shoeboxes, I think.

JESSIE: Full of shoes. I looked already.

MAMA: Well, you didn't look good enough, then. There's that box from the ones he wore to the hospital. When he died, they told me I could have them back, but I never did like those shoes.

JESSIE (*pulling them out of her pocket*): I found the bullets. They were in an old milk can.

MAMA (*as Jessie starts for the hall*): Dawson took the shotgun, didn't he? Hand me that basket, hon.

JESSIE (*getting the basket for her*): Dawson better not've taken that pistol.

MAMA (*stopping her again*): Now my glasses, please. (*Jessie returns to get the glasses.*) I told him to take those rubber boots, too, but he said they were for fishing. I told him to take up fishing.

(*Jessie reaches for the cleaning spray and cleans Mama's glasses for her.*)

JESSIE: He's just too lazy to climb up there, Mama. Or

maybe he's just being smart. That floor's not very steady.

MAMA (*getting out a piece of knitting*): It's not a floor at all, hon, it's a board now and then. Measure this for me. I need six inches.

JESSIE (*as she measures*): Dawson could probably use some of those clothes up there. Somebody should have them. You ought to call the Salvation Army before the whole thing falls in on you. Six inches exactly.

MAMA: It's plenty safe! As long as you don't go up there.

JESSIE (*turning to go again*): I'm careful.

MAMA: What do you want the gun for, Jess?

JESSIE (*Not returning this time. Opening the ladder in the hall.*): Protection. (*She steadies the ladder as Mama talks.*)

MAMA: You take the TV way too serious, hon. I've never seen a criminal in my life. This is way too far to come for what's out here to steal. Never seen a one.

JESSIE (*taking her first step up*): Except for Ricky.

MAMA: Ricky is mixed up. That's not a crime.

JESSIE: Get your hands washed. I'll be right back. And get 'em real dry. You dry your hands till I get back or it's no go, all right?

MAMA: I thought Dawson told you not to go up those stairs.

JESSIE (*going up*): He did.

MAMA: I don't like the idea of a gun, Jess.

JESSIE (*calling down from the attic*): Which shoebox, do you remember?

MAMA: Black.

JESSIE: The box was black?

MAMA: The shoes were black.

JESSIE: That doesn't help much, Mother.

MAMA: I'm not trying to help, sugar. (*No answer.*) We don't have anything anybody'd want, Jessie. I mean, I don't even want what we got, Jessie.

JESSIE: Neither do I. Wash your hands. (*Mama gets up and crosses to stand under the ladder.*)

MAMA: You come down from there before you have a fit. I can't come up and get you, you know.

JESSIE: I know.

MAMA: We'll just hand it over to them when they come, how's that? Whatever they want, the criminals.

JESSIE: That's a good idea, Mama.

MAMA: Ricky will grow out of this and be a real fine boy, Jess. But I have to tell you, I wouldn't want Ricky to know we had a gun in the house.

JESSIE: Here it is. I found it.

MAMA: It's just something Ricky's going through. Maybe he's in with some bad people. He just needs some time, sugar. He'll get back in school or get a job or one day you'll get a call and he'll say he's sorry for all the trouble he's caused and invite you out for supper someplace dress-up.

JESSIE (*coming back down the steps*): Don't worry. It's not for him, it's for me.

MAMA: I didn't think you would shoot your own boy, Jessie. I know you've felt like it, well, we've all felt like shooting somebody, but we don't do it. I just don't think we need . . .

JESSIE (*interrupting*): Your hands aren't washed. Do you want a manicure or not?

MAMA: Yes, I do, but . . .

JESSIE (*crossing to the chair*): Then wash your hands and don't talk to me anymore about Ricky. Those two rings he took were the last valuable things I had, so now he's started in on other people, door to door. I hope they put him away sometime. I'd turn him in myself if I knew where he was.

MAMA: You don't mean that.

JESSIE: Every word. Wash your hands and that's the last time I'm telling you.

(*Jessie sits down with the gun and starts cleaning it, pushing the cylinder out, checking to see that the chambers and barrel are empty, then putting some oil on a small patch of cloth and pushing it through the barrel with the push rod that was in the box. Mama goes to the kitchen and washes her hands, as instructed, trying not to show her concern about the gun.*)

MAMA: I shoulda got you to bring down that milk can. Agnes Fletcher sold hers to somebody with a flea market for forty dollars apiece.

JESSIE: I'll go back and get it in a minute. There's a wagon wheel up there, too. There's even a churn. I'll get it all if you want.

MAMA (*coming over, now, taking over now*): What are you doing?

JESSIE: The barrel has to be clean, Mama. Old powder, dust gets in it . . .

MAMA: What for?

JESSIE: I told you.

MAMA (*reaching for the gun*): And I told you, we don't get criminals out here.

JESSIE (*quickly pulling it to her*): And I told you . . . (*Then trying to be calm.*) The gun is for me.

MAMA: Well, you can have it if you want. When I die, you'll get it all, anyway.

JESSIE: I'm going to kill myself, Mama.

MAMA (*returning to the sofa*): Very funny. Very funny.

JESSIE: I am.

MAMA: You are not! Don't even say such a thing, Jessie.

JESSIE: How would you know if I didn't say it? You want it to be a surprise? You're lying there in your bed or maybe you're just brushing your teeth and you hear this . . . noise down the hall?

MAMA: Kill yourself.

JESSIE: Shoot myself. In a couple of hours.

MAMA: It must be time for your medicine.

JESSIE: Took it already.

MAMA: What's the matter with you?

JESSIE: Not a thing. Feel fine.

MAMA: You feel fine. You're just going to kill yourself.

JESSIE: Waited until I felt good enough, in fact.

MAMA: Don't make jokes, Jessie. I'm too old for jokes.

JESSIE: It's not a joke, Mama.

(*Mama watches for a moment in silence.*)

MAMA: That gun's no good, you know. He broke it right before he died. He dropped it in the mud one day.

JESSIE: Seems O.K. (*She spins the chamber, cocks the pistol, and pulls the trigger. The gun is not yet loaded, so all we hear is the click, but it will definitely work. It's also obvious that Jessie knows her way around a gun. Mama cannot speak.*) I had Cecil's all ready in there, just in case I couldn't find this one, but I'd rather use Daddy's.

MAMA: Those bullets are at least fifteen years old.

JESSIE (*pulling out another box*): These are from last week.

MAMA: Where did you get those?

JESSIE: Feed store Dawson told me about.

MAMA: Dawson!

JESSIE: I told him I was worried about prowlers. He said he thought it was a good idea. He told me what kind to ask for.

MAMA: If he had any idea . . .

JESSIE: He took it as a compliment. He thought I might be taking an interest in things. He got through telling me all about the bullets and then he said we ought to talk like this more often.

MAMA: And where was I while this was going on?

JESSIE: On the phone with Agnes. About the milk can, I guess. Anyway, I asked Dawson if he thought they'd send me some bullets and he said he'd just call for me, because he knew they'd send them if he told them to. And he was absolutely right. Here they are.

MAMA: How could he do that?

JESSIE: Just trying to help, Mama.

MAMA: And then I told you where the gun was.

JESSIE (*smiling, enjoying this joke*): See? Everybody's doing what they can.

MAMA: You told me it was for protection!

JESSIE: It *is*! I'm still doing your nails, though. Want to try that new Chinaberry color?

MAMA: Well, I'm calling Dawson right now. We'll just see what he has to say about this little stunt.

JESSIE: Dawson doesn't have any more to do with this.

MAMA: He's your brother.

JESSIE: And that's all.

MAMA (*stands up, moves toward the phone*): Dawson will put a stop to this. Yes he will. He'll take the gun away.

JESSIE: If you call him, I'll just have to do it before he gets here. Soon as you hang up the phone, I'll just walk in the bedroom and lock the door. Dawson will get here just in time to help you clean up. Go ahead, call him. Then call the police. Then call the funeral home. Then call Loretta and see if *she'll* do your nails.

MAMA: You will not! This is crazy talk, Jessie!

(*Mama goes directly to the telephone and starts to dial, but Jessie is fast, coming up behind her and taking the receiver out of her hand, putting it back down.*)

JESSIE (*firm and quiet*): I said no. This is private. Dawson is not invited.

MAMA: Just me.

JESSIE: I don't want anybody else over here. Just you and me. If Dawson comes over, it'll make me feel stupid for not doing it ten years ago.

MAMA: I think we better call the doctor. Or how about the ambulance. You like that one driver, I know. What's his name, Timmy? Get you somebody to talk to.

JESSIE (*going back to her chair*): I'm through talking, Mama. You're it. No more.

MAMA: We're just going to sit around like every other night in the world and then you're going to kill yourself? (*Jessie doesn't answer.*) You'll miss. (*Again there is no response.*) You'll just wind up a vegetable. How would you like that? Shoot your ear off? You know what the doctor said about getting excited. You'll cock the pistol and have a fit.

JESSIE: I think I can kill myself, Mama.

MAMA: You're not going to kill yourself, Jessie. You're not even upset! (*Jessie smiles, or laughs quietly, and Mama tries a different approach.*) People don't really kill themselves, Jessie. No, mam, doesn't make sense, unless you're retarded or deranged, and you're as normal as they come, Jessie, for the most part. We're all *afraid* to die.

JESSIE: I'm not, Mama. I'm cold all the time, anyway.

MAMA: That's ridiculous.

JESSIE: It's exactly what I want. It's dark and quiet.

MAMA: So is the back yard, Jessie! Close your eyes. Stuff cotton in your ears. Take a nap! It's quiet in your room. I'll leave the TV off all night.

JESSIE: So quiet I don't know it's quiet. So nobody can get me.

MAMA: You don't know what dead is like. It might not be quiet at all. What if it's like an alarm clock and you can't wake up so you can't shut it off. Ever.

JESSIE: Dead is everybody and everything I ever knew, gone. Dead is dead quiet.

MAMA: It's a sin. You'll go to hell.

JESSIE: Uh-huh.

MAMA: You will!

JESSIE: Jesus was a suicide, if you ask me.

MAMA: You'll go to hell just for saying that. Jessie!

JESSIE (*with genuine surprise*): I didn't know I thought that.

MAMA: Jessie!

(*Jessie doesn't answer. She puts the now-loaded gun back in the box and crosses to the kitchen. But Mama is afraid she's headed for the bedroom.*)

MAMA (*in a panic*): You can't use my towels! They're my towels. I've had them for a long time. I like my towels.

JESSIE: I asked you if you wanted that swimming towel and you said you didn't.

MAMA: And you can't use your father's gun, either. It's mine now, too. And you can't do it in my house.

Kathy Bates and Anne Pitoniak in the American Repertory Theatre's 1983 production of 'night, Mother.

JESSIE: Oh, come on.

MAMA: No. You can't do it. I won't let you. The house is in my name.

JESSIE: I have to go in the bedroom and lock the door behind me so they won't arrest you for killing me. They'll probably test your hands for gunpowder, anyway, but you'll pass.

MAMA: Not in my house!

JESSIE: If I'd known you were going to act like this, I wouldn't have told you.

MAMA: How am I supposed to act? Tell you to go ahead? O.K. by me, sugar? Might try it myself. What took you so long?

JESSIE: There's just no point in fighting me over it, that's all. Want some coffee?

MAMA: Your birthday's coming up, Jessie. Don't you want to know what we got you?

JESSIE: You got me dusting powder, Loretta got me a new housecoat, pink probably, and Dawson got me new slippers, too small, but they go with the robe, he'll say. (*Mama cannot speak.*) Right? (*Apparently Jessie is right.*) Be back in a minute.

(*Jessie takes the gun box, puts it on top of the stack of towels and garbage bags, and takes them into her bedroom. Mama, alone for a moment, goes to the phone, picks up the receiver, looks toward the bedroom, starts to dial, and then replaces the receiver in its cradle as Jessie walks back into the room. Jessie wonders, silently. They have lived together for so long there is very rarely any reason for one to ask what the other was about to do.*)

MAMA: I started to, but I didn't. I didn't call him.

JESSIE: Good. Thank you.

MAMA (*starting over, a new approach*): What's this all about, Jessie?

JESSIE: About?

(*Jessie now begins the next task she had "on the schedule," which is refilling all the candy jars, taking the empty papers out of the boxes of chocolates, etc. Mama generally snitches when Jessie does this. Not tonight, though. Nevertheless, Jessie offers.*)

MAMA: What did I do?

JESSIE: Nothing. Want a caramel?

MAMA (*ignoring the candy*): You're mad at me.

JESSIE: Not a bit. I am worried about you, but I'm going to do what I can before I go. We're not just going to sit around tonight. I made a list of things.

MAMA: What things?

JESSIE: How the washer works. Things like that.

MAMA: I know how the washer works. You put the clothes in. You put the soap in. You turn it on. You wait.

JESSIE: You do something else. You don't just wait.

MAMA: Whatever else you find to do, you're still mainly waiting. The waiting's the worst part of it. The waiting's what you pay somebody else to do, if you can.

JESSIE (*nodding*): O.K. Where do we keep the soap?

MAMA: I could find it.

JESSIE: See?

MAMA: If you're mad about doing the wash, we can get Loretta to do it.

JESSIE: Oh now, that might be worth staying to see.

MAMA: She'd never in her life, would she?

JESSIE: Nope.

MAMA: What's the matter with her?

JESSIE: She thinks she's better than we are. She's not.

MAMA: Maybe if she didn't wear that yellow all the time.

JESSIE: The washer repair number is on a little card taped to the side of the machine.

MAMA: Loretta doesn't ever have to come over here again. Dawson can just leave her at home when he comes. And we don't ever have to see Dawson either if he bothers you. Does he bother you?

JESSIE: Sure he does. Be sure you clean out the lint tray every time you use the dryer. But don't ever put your house shoes in, it'll melt the soles.

MAMA: What does Dawson do, that bothers you?

JESSIE: He just calls me Jess like he knows who he's talking to. He's always wondering what I do all day. I mean, I wonder that myself, but it's my day, so it's mine to wonder about, not his.

MAMA: Family is just accident, Jessie. It's nothing personal, hon. They don't mean to get on your nerves. They don't even mean to be your family, they just are.

JESSIE: They know too much.

MAMA: About what?

JESSIE: They know things about you, and they learned it before you had a chance to say whether you wanted them to know it or not. They were there when it happened and it don't belong to them, it belongs to you, only they got it. Like my mail-order bra got delivered to their house.

MAMA: By accident!

JESSIE: All the same . . . they opened it. They saw the little rosebuds on it. (*Offering her another candy.*) Chewy mint?

MAMA (*shaking her head no*): What do they know about you? I'll tell them never to talk about it again. Is it Ricky or Cecil or your fits or your hair is falling out or you drink too much coffee or you never go out of the house or what?

JESSIE: I just don't like their talk. The account at the grocery is in Dawson's name when you call. The number's on a whole list of numbers on the back cover of the phone book.

MAMA: Well! Now we're getting somewhere. They're none of them ever setting foot in this house again.

JESSIE: It's not them, Mother. I wouldn't kill myself just to get away from them.

MAMA: You leave the room when they come over, anyway.

JESSIE: I stay as long as I can. Besides, it's you they come to see.

MAMA: That's because I stay in the room when they come.

JESSIE: It's not them.

MAMA: Then what is it?

JESSIE (*checking the list on her note pad*): The grocery won't deliver on Saturday anymore. And if you want your order the same day, you have to call before ten. And they won't deliver less than fifteen dollars' worth. What I do is tell them what we need and tell them to add on cigarettes until it gets to fifteen dollars.

MAMA: It's Ricky. You're trying to get through to him.

JESSIE: If I thought I could do that, I would stay.

MAMA: Make him sorry he hurt you, then. That's it, isn't it?

JESSIE: He's hurt me, I've hurt him. We're about even.

MAMA: You'll be telling him killing is O.K. with you, you know. Want him to start killing next? Nothing wrong with it. Mom did it.

JESSIE: Only a matter of time, anyway, Mama. When the call comes, you let Dawson handle it.

MAMA: Honey, nothing says those calls are always going to be some new trouble he's into. You could get one that he's got a job, that he's getting married, or how about he's joined the army, wouldn't that be nice?

JESSIE: If you call the Sweet Tooth before you call the grocery, that Susie will take your fudge next door to the grocery and it'll all come out together. Be sure you talk to Susie, though. She won't let them put it in the bottom of a sack like that one time, remember?

MAMA: Ricky could come over, you know. What if he calls us?

JESSIE: It's not Ricky, Mama.

MAMA: Or anybody could call us, Jessie.

JESSIE: Not on Saturday night, Mama.

MAMA: Then what is it? Are you sick? If your gums are swelling again, we can get you to the dentist in the morning.

JESSIE: No. Can you order your medicine or do you want Dawson to? I've got a note to him. I'll add that to it if you want.

MAMA: Your eyes don't look right. I thought so yesterday.

JESSIE: That was just the ragweed. I'm not sick.

MAMA: Epilepsy is sick, Jessie.

JESSIE: It won't kill me. (*A pause.*) If it would, I wouldn't have to.

MAMA: You don't *have* to.

JESSIE: No, I don't. That's what I like about it.

MAMA: Well, I won't let you!

JESSIE: It's not up to you.

MAMA: Jessie!

JESSIE: I want to hang a big sign around my neck, like Daddy's on the barn. GONE FISHING.

MAMA: You don't like it here.

JESSIE (*smiling*): Exactly.

MAMA: I meant here in my house.

JESSIE: I know you did.

MAMA: You never should have moved back in here with me. If you'd kept your little house or found another place when Cecil left you, you'd have made some new friends at least. Had a life to lead. Had your own things around you. Give Ricky a place to come see you. You never should've come here.

JESSIE: Maybe.

MAMA: But I didn't force you, did I?

JESSIE: If it was a mistake, we made it together. You took me in. I appreciate that.

MAMA: You didn't have any business being by yourself right then, but I can see how you might want a place of your own. A grown woman should . . .

JESSIE: Mama . . . I'm just not having a very good time and I don't have any reason to think it'll get anything but worse. I'm tired. I'm hurt. I'm sad. I feel used.

MAMA: Tired of what?

JESSIE: It all.

MAMA: What does that mean?

JESSIE: I can't say it any better.

MAMA: Well, you'll have to say it better because I'm not letting you alone till you do. What were those other things? Hurt . . . (*Before Jessie can answer.*) You had this all ready to say to me, didn't you? Did you write this down? How long have you been thinking about this?

JESSIE: Off and on, ten years. On all the time, since Christmas.

MAMA: What happened at Christmas?

JESSIE: Nothing.

MAMA: So why Christmas?

JESSIE: That's it. On the nose.

(*A pause. Mama knows exactly what Jessie means. She was there, too, after all.*)

JESSIE (*putting the candy sacks away*): See where all this is? Red hots up front, sour balls and horehound mixed together in this one sack. New packages of toffee and licorice right in back there.

MAMA: Go back to your list. You're hurt by what?

JESSIE (*Mama knows perfectly well*): Mama . . .

MAMA: O.K. Sad about what? There's nothing real sad going on right now. If it was after your divorce or something, that would make sense.

JESSIE (*looking at her list, then opening the drawer*): Now, this drawer has everything in it that there's no better place for. Extension cords, batteries for the radio, extra lighters, sandpaper, masking tape, El-

mer's glue, thumbtacks, that kind of stuff. The mousetraps are under the sink, but you call Dawson if you've got one and let him do it.

MAMA: Sad about what?

JESSIE: The way things are.

MAMA: Not good enough. What things?

JESSIE: Oh, everything from you and me to Red China.

MAMA: I think we can leave the Chinese out of this.

JESSIE (*crosses back into the living room*): There's extra light bulbs in a box in the hall closet. And we've got a couple of packages of fuses in the fuse box. There's candles and matches in the top of the broom closet, but if the lights go out, just call Dawson and sit tight. But don't open the refrigerator door. Things will stay cool in there as long as you keep the door shut.

MAMA: I asked you a question.

JESSIE: I read the paper. I don't like how things are. And they're not any better out there than they are in here.

MAMA: If you're doing this because of the newspapers, I can sure fix that!

JESSIE: There's just more of it on TV.

MAMA (*kicking the television set*): Take it out, then!

JESSIE: You wouldn't do that.

MAMA: Watch me.

JESSIE: What would you do all day?

MAMA (*desperately*): Sing. (*Jessie laughs.*) I would, too. You want to watch? I'll sing till morning to keep you alive, Jessie, please!

JESSIE: No. (*Then affectionately.*) It's a funny idea, though. What do you sing?

MAMA (*has no idea how to answer this*): We've got a good life here!

JESSIE (*going back into the kitchen*): I called this morning and canceled the papers, except for Sunday, for your puzzles; you'll still get that one.

MAMA: Let's get another dog, Jessie! You liked a big dog, now, didn't you? That King dog, didn't you?

JESSIE (*washing her hands*): I did like that King dog, yes.

MAMA: I'm so dumb. He's the one run under the tractor.

JESSIE: That makes him dumb, not you.

MAMA: For bringing it up.

JESSIE: It's O.K. Handi-Wipes and sponges under the sink.

MAMA: We could get a new dog and keep him in the house. Dogs are cheap!

JESSIE (*getting big pill jars out of the cabinet*): No.

MAMA: Something for you to take care of.

JESSIE: I've had you, Mama.

MAMA (*frantically starting to fill pill bottles*): You do too much for me. I can fill pill bottles all day Jessie, and change the shelf paper and wash the floor when I get through. You just watch me. You don't have to do another thing in this house if you don't want to. You don't have to take care of me, Jessie.

JESSIE: I know that. You've just been letting me do it so I'll have something to do, haven't you?

MAMA (*realizing this was a mistake*): I don't do it as well as you. I just meant if it tires you out or makes you feel used . . .

JESSIE: Mama, I know you used to ride the bus. Riding the bus and it's hot and bumpy and crowded and too noisy and more than anything in the world you want to get off and the only reason in the world you don't get off is it's still fifty blocks from where you're going? Well, I can get off right now if I want to, because even if I ride fifty more years and get off then, it's the same place when I step down to it. Whenever I feel like it, I can get off. As soon as I've had enough, it's my stop. I've had enough.

MAMA: You're feeling sorry for yourself!

JESSIE: The plumber's helper is under the sink, too.

MAMA: You're not having a good time! Whoever promised you a good time? Do you think I've had a good time?

JESSIE: I think you're pretty happy, yeah. You have things you like to do.

MAMA: Like what?

JESSIE: Like crochet.

MAMA: I'll teach you to crochet.

JESSIE: I can't do any of that nice work, Mama.

MAMA: Good time don't come looking for you, Jessie. You could work some puzzles or put in a garden or go to the store. Let's call a taxi and go to the A&P!

JESSIE: I shopped you up for about two weeks already. You're not going to need toilet paper till Thanksgiving.

MAMA (interrupting): You're acting like some little brat, Jessie. You're mad and everybody's boring and you don't have anything to do and you don't like me and you don't like going out and you don't like staying in and you never talk on the phone and you don't watch TV and you're miserable and it's your own sweet fault.

JESSIE: And it's time I did something about it.

MAMA: Not something like killing yourself. Something like . . . buying us all new dishes! I'd like that. Or maybe the doctor would let you get a driver's license now, or I know what let's do right this minute, let's rearrange the furniture.

JESSIE: I'll do that. If you want. I always thought if the TV was somewhere else, you wouldn't get such a glare on it during the day. I'll do whatever you want before I go.

MAMA (badly frightened by those words): You could get a job!

JESSIE: I took that telephone sales job and I didn't even make enough money to pay the phone bill, and I tried to work at the gift shop at the hospital and they said I made people real uncomfortable smiling at them the way I did.

MAMA: You could keep books. You kept your dad's books.

JESSIE: But nobody ever checked them.

MAMA: When he died, they checked them.

JESSIE: And that's when they took the books away from me.

MAMA: That's because without him there wasn't any business, Jessie!

JESSIE (putting the pill bottles away): You know I couldn't work. I can't do anything. I've never been around people my whole life except when I went to the hospital. I could have a seizure any time. What good would a job do? The kind of job I could get would make me feel worse.

MAMA: Jessie!

JESSIE: It's true!

MAMA: It's what you think is true!

JESSIE (struck by the clarity of that): That's right. It's what I think is true.

MAMA (hysterically): But I can't do anything about that!

JESSIE (quietly): No. You can't. (Mama slumps, if not physically, at least emotionally.) And I can't do anything either, about my life, to change it, make it better, make me feel better about it. Like it better, make it work. But I can stop it. Shut it down, turn it off like the radio when there's nothing on I want to listen to. It's all I really have that belongs to me and I'm going to say what happens to it. And it's going to stop. And I'm going to stop it. So. Let's just have a good time.

MAMA: Have a good time.

JESSIE: We can't go on fussing all night. I mean, I could ask you things I always wanted to know and you could make me some hot chocolate. The old way.

MAMA (in despair): It takes cocoa, Jessie.

JESSIE (gets it out of the cabinet): I bought cocoa, Mama. And I'd like to have a caramel apple and do your nails.

MAMA: You didn't eat a bite of supper.

JESSIE: Does that mean I can't have a caramel apple?

MAMA: Of course not. I mean . . . (Smiling a little.) Of course you can have a caramel apple.

JESSIE: I thought I could.

MAMA: I make the best caramel apples in the world.

JESSIE: I know you do.

MAMA: Or used to. And you don't get cocoa like mine anywhere anymore.

JESSIE: It takes time, I know, but . . .

MAMA: The salt is the trick.

JESSIE: Trouble and everything.

MAMA (backing away toward the stove): It's no trouble. What trouble? You put it in the pan and stir it up. All right. Fine. Caramel apples. Cocoa. O.K.

(Jessie walks to the counter to retrieve her cigarettes as Mama looks for the right pan. There are brief near-smiles, and maybe Mama clears her throat. We have a truce, for the moment. A genuine but nevertheless uneasy one. Jessie, who has been in constant motion since the beginning, now seems content to sit.)

(Mama starts looking for a pan to make the cocoa, getting out all the pans in the cabinets in the process. It looks like she's making a mess on purpose so Jessie will have to put them all away again. Mama is buying time, or trying to, and entertaining.)

JESSIE: You talk to Agnes today?

MAMA: She's calling me from a pay phone this week. God only knows why. She has a perfectly good Trimline at home.

JESSIE (*laughing*): Well, how is she?

MAMA: How is she every day, Jessie? Nuts.

JESSIE: Is she really crazy or just silly?

MAMA: No, she's really crazy. She was probably using the pay phone because she had another little fire problem at home.

JESSIE: Mother . . .

MAMA: I'm serious! Agnes Fletcher's burned down every house she ever lived in. Eight fires, and she's due for a new one any day now.

JESSIE (*laughing*): No!

MAMA: Wouldn't surprise me a bit.

JESSIE (*laughing*): Why didn't you tell me this before? Why isn't she locked up somewhere?

MAMA: 'Cause nobody ever got hurt, I guess. Agnes woke everybody up to watch the fires as soon as she set 'em. One time she set out porch chairs and served lemonade.

JESSIE (*shaking her head*): Real lemonade?

MAMA: The houses they lived in, you knew they were going to fall down anyway, so why wait for it, is all I could ever make out about it. Agnes likes a feeling of accomplishment.

JESSIE: Good for her.

MAMA (*finding the pan she wants*): Why are you asking about Agnes? One cup or two?

JESSIE: One. She's your friend. No marshmallows.

MAMA (*getting the milk, etc.*): You have to have marshmallows. That's the old way, Jess. Two or three? Three is better.

JESSIE: Three, then. Her whole house burns up? Her clothes and pillows and everything? I'm not sure I believe this.

MAMA: When she was a girl, Jess, not now. Long time ago. But she's still got it in her, I'm sure of it.

JESSIE: She wouldn't burn her house down now. Where would she go? She can't get Buster to build her a new one, he's dead. How could she burn it up?

MAMA: Be exciting, though, if she did. You never know.

JESSIE: You do too know, Mama. She wouldn't do it.

MAMA (*forced to admit, but reluctant*): I guess not.

JESSIE: What else? Why does she wear all those whistles around her neck?

MAMA: Why does she have a house full of birds?

JESSIE: I didn't know she had a house full of birds!

MAMA: Well, she does. And she says they just follow her home. Well, I know for a fact she's still paying on the last parrot she bought. You gotta keep your life filled up, she says. She says a lot of stupid things. (*Jessie laughs, Mama continues, convinced she's getting somewhere.*) It's all that okra she eats. You can't just willy-nilly eat okra two meals a day and expect to get away with it. Made her crazy.

JESSIE: She really eats okra twice a day? Where does she get it in the winter?

MAMA: Well, she eats it a lot. Maybe not two meals, but . . .

JESSIE: More than the average person.

MAMA (*beginning to get irritated*): I don't know how much okra the average person eats.

JESSIE: Do you know how much okra Agnes eats?

MAMA: No.

JESSIE: How many birds does she have?

MAMA: Two.

JESSIE: Then what are the whistles for?

MAMA: They're not real whistles. Just little plastic ones on a necklace she won playing Bingo, and I only told you about it because I thought I might get a laugh out of you for once even if it wasn't the truth, Jessie. Things don't have to be true to talk about 'em, you know.

JESSIE: Why won't she come over here?

(*Mama is suddenly quiet, but the cocoa and milk are in the pan now, so she lights the stove and starts stirring.*)

MAMA: Well now, what a good idea. We should've had more cocoa. Cocoa is perfect.

JESSIE: Except you don't like milk.

MAMA (*another attempt, but not as energetic*): I hate milk. Coats your throat as bad as okra. Something just downright disgusting about it.

JESSIE: It's because of me, isn't it?

MAMA: No, Jess.

JESSIE: Yes, Mama.

MAMA: O.K. Yes, then, but she's crazy. She's as crazy as they come. She's a lunatic.

JESSIE: What is it exactly? Did I say something, sometime? Or did she see me have a fit and's afraid I might have another one if she came over, or what?

MAMA: I guess.

JESSIE: You guess what? What's she ever said? She must've given you some reason.

MAMA: Your hands are cold.

JESSIE: What difference does that make?

MAMA: "Like a corpse," she says, "and I'm gonna be one soon enough as it is."

JESSIE: That's crazy.

MAMA: That's Agnes. "Jessie's shook the hand of death and I can't take the chance it's catching, Thelma, so I ain't comin' over, and you can understand or not, but I ain't comin'. I'll come up the driveway, but that's as far as I go."

JESSIE (*laughing, relieved*): I thought she didn't like me! She's scared of me! How about that! Scared of me.

MAMA: I could make her come over here, Jessie. I could call her up right now and she could bring the birds and come visit. I didn't know you ever thought about her at all. I'll tell her she just has to come and she'll come, all right. She owes me one.

JESSIE: No, that's all right. I just wondered about it. When I'm in the hospital, does she come over here?

MAMA: Her kitchen is just a tiny thing. When she comes over here, she feels like . . . (*Toning it down a little.*) Well, we all like a change of scene, don't we?

JESSIE (*playing along*): Sure we do. Plus there's no birds diving around.

MAMA: I hate those birds. She says I don't understand them. What's there to understand about birds?

JESSIE: Why Agnes likes them, for one thing. Why they stay with her when they could be outside with the other birds. What their singing means. How they fly. What they think Agnes is.

MAMA: Why do you have to know so much about things, Jessie? There's just not that much *to* things that I could ever see.

JESSIE: That you could ever *tell*, you mean. You didn't have to lie to me about Agnes.

MAMA: I didn't lie. You never asked before!

JESSIE: You lied about setting fire to all those houses and about how many birds she has and how much okra she eats and why she won't come over here. If I have to keep dragging the truth out of you, this is going to take all night.

MAMA: That's fine with me. I'm not a bit sleepy.

JESSIE: Mama . . .

MAMA: All right. Ask me whatever you want. Here.

(*They come to an awkward stop, as the cocoa is ready and Mama pours it into the cups Jessie has set on the table.*)

JESSIE (*as Mama takes her first sip*): Did you love Daddy?

MAMA: No.

JESSIE (*pleased that Mama understands the rules better now*): I didn't think so. Were you really fifteen when you married him?

MAMA: The way he told it? I'm sitting in the mud, he comes along, drags me in the kitchen, "She's been there ever since"?

JESSIE: Yes.

MAMA: No. It was a big fat lie, the whole thing. He just thought it was funnier that way. God, this milk in here.

JESSIE: The cocoa helps.

MAMA (*pleased that they agree on this, at least*): Not enough, though, does it? You can still taste it, can't you?

JESSIE: Yeah, it's pretty bad. I thought it was my memory that was bad, but it's not. It's the milk, all right.

MAMA: It's a real waste of chocolate. You don't have to finish it.

JESSIE (*putting her cup down*): Thanks, though.

MAMA: I should've known not to make it. I knew you wouldn't like it. You never did like it.

JESSIE: You didn't ever love him, or he did something and you stopped loving him, or what?

MAMA: He felt sorry for me. He wanted a plain country woman and that's what he married, and then he held it against me the rest of my life like I was supposed to change and surprise him somehow. Like I remember this one day he was standing on the porch and I told him to get a shirt on and he went in and got one and then he said, real peaceful, but to the point, "You're right, Thelma. If God had meant for people to go

around without any clothes on, they'd have been born that way."

JESSIE (*sees Mama's hurt*): He didn't mean anything by that, Mama.

MAMA: He never said a word he didn't have to, Jessie. That was probably all he'd said to me all day, Jessie. So if he said it, there was something to it, but I never did figure that one out. What did that mean?

JESSIE: I don't know. I liked him better than you did, but I didn't know him any better.

MAMA: How could I love him, Jessie. I didn't have a thing he wanted. (*Jessie doesn't answer.*) He got his share, though. You loved him enough for both of us. You followed him around like some . . . Jessie, all the man ever did was farm and sit . . . and try to think of somebody to sell the farm to.

JESSIE: Or make me a boyfriend out of pipe cleaners and sit back and smile like the stick man was about to dance and wasn't I going to get a kick out of that. Or sit up with a sick cow all night and leave me a chain of sleepy stick elephants on my bed in the morning.

MAMA: Or just sit.

JESSIE: I liked him sitting. Big old faded blue man in the chair. Quiet.

MAMA: Agnes gets more talk out of her birds than I got from the two of you. He could've had that GONE FISHING sign around his neck in that chair. I saw him stare off at the water. I saw him look at the weather rolling in. I got where I could practically see the boat myself. But you, you knew what he was thinking about and you're going to tell me.

JESSIE: I don't know, Mama! His life, I guess. His corn. His boots. Us. Things. You know.

MAMA: No, I don't know, Jessie! You had those quiet little conversations after supper every night. What were you whispering about?

JESSIE: We weren't whispering, you were just across the room.

MAMA: What did you talk about?

JESSIE: We talked about why black socks are warmer than blue socks. Is that something to go tell Mother? You were just jealous because I'd rather talk to him than wash the dishes with you.

MAMA: I was jealous because you'd rather talk to him than anything! (*Jessie reaches across the table for the small clock and starts to wind it.*) If I had died instead of him, he wouldn't have taken you in like I did.

JESSIE: I wouldn't have expected him to.

MAMA: Then what would you have done?

JESSIE: Come visit.

MAMA: Oh, I see. He died and left you stuck with me and you're mad about it.

JESSIE (*getting up from the table*): Not anymore. He didn't mean to. I didn't have to come here. We've been through this.

MAMA: He felt sorry for you, too, Jessie, don't kid yourself about that. He said you were a runt and he said it from the day you were born and he said you didn't have a chance.

JESSIE (*getting the canister of sugar and starting to refill the sugar bowl*): I know he loved me.

MAMA: What if he did? It didn't change anything.

JESSIE: It didn't have to. I miss him.

MAMA: He never really went fishing, you know. Never once. His tackle box was full of chewing tobacco and all he ever did was drive out to the lake and sit in his car. Dawson told me. And Bennie at the bait shop, he told Dawson. They all laughed about it. And he'd come back from fishing and all he'd have to show for it was . . . a whole pipe-cleaner *family* — chickens, pigs, a dog with a bad leg — it was creepy strange. It made me sick to look at them and I hid his pipe cleaners a couple of times but he always had more somewhere.

JESSIE: I thought it might be better for you after he died. You'd get interested in things. Breathe better. Change somehow.

MAMA: Into what? The Queen? A clerk in a shoe store? Why should I? Because he said to? Because you said to? (*Jessie shakes her head.*) Well I wasn't here for his entertainment and I'm not here for yours either, Jessie. I don't know what I'm here for, but then I don't think about it. (*Realizing what all this means.*) But I bet you wouldn't be killing yourself if he were still alive. That's a fine thing to figure out, isn't it?

JESSIE (*filling the honey jar now*): That's not true.

MAMA: Oh no? Then what were you asking about him for? Why did you want to know if I loved him?

JESSIE: I didn't think you did, that's all.

MAMA: Fine then. You were right. Do you feel better now?

JESSIE (*cleaning the honey jar carefully*): It feels good to be right about it.

MAMA: It didn't matter whether I loved him. It didn't matter to me and it didn't matter to him. And it didn't mean we didn't get along. It wasn't important. We didn't talk about it. (*Sweeping the pots off the cabinet.*) Take all these pots out to the porch!

JESSIE: What for?

MAMA: Just leave me this one pan. (*She jerks the silverware drawer open.*) Get me one knife, one fork, one big spoon, and the can opener, and put them out where I can get them. (*Starts throwing knives and forks in one of the pans.*)

JESSIE: Don't do that! I just straightened that drawer!

MAMA (*throwing the pan in the sink*): And throw out all the plates and cups. I'll use paper. Loretta can have what she wants and Dawson can sell the rest.

JESSIE (*calmly*): What are you doing?

MAMA: I'm not going to cook. I never liked it, anyway. I like candy. Wrapped in plastic or coming in sacks. And tuna. I like tuna. I'll eat tuna, thank you.

JESSIE (*taking the pan out of the sink*): What if you want to make apple butter? You can't make apple butter in that little pan. What if you leave carrots on cooking and burn up that pan?

MAMA: I don't like carrots.

JESSIE: What if the strawberries are good this year and you want to go picking with Agnes.

MAMA: I'll tell her to bring a pan. You said you would do whatever I wanted! I don't want a bunch of pans cluttering up my cabinets I can't get down to, anyway. Throw them out. Every last one.

JESSIE (*gathering up the pots*): I'm putting them all back in. I'm not taking them to the porch. If you want them, they'll be here. You'll bend down and get them, like you got the one for the cocoa. And if somebody else comes over here to cook, they'll have something to cook in, and that's the end of it!

MAMA: Who's going to come cook here?

JESSIE: Agnes.

MAMA: In my pots. Not on your life.

JESSIE: There's no reason why the two of you couldn't just live here together. Be cheaper for both of you and somebody to talk to. And if the birds bothered you, well, one day when Agnes is out getting her hair done, you could take them all for a walk!

MAMA (*as Jessie straightens the silverware*): So that's why you're pestering me about Agnes. You think you can rest easy if you get me a new babysitter? Well, I don't want to live with Agnes. I barely want to talk with Agnes. She's just around. We go back, that's all. I'm not letting Agnes near this place. You don't get off as easy as that, child.

JESSIE: O.K., then. It's just something to think about.

MAMA: I don't like things to think about. I like things to go on.

JESSIE (*closing the silverware drawer*): I want to know what Daddy said to you the night he died. You came storming out of his room and said I could wait it out with him if I wanted to, but you were going to watch *Gunsmoke*. What did he say to you?

MAMA: He didn't have *anything* to say to me, Jessie. That's why I left. He didn't say a thing. It was his last chance not to talk to me and he took full advantage of it.

JESSIE (*after a moment*): I'm sorry you didn't love him. Sorry for you, I mean. He seemed like a nice man.

MAMA (*as Jessie walks to the refrigerator*): Ready for your apple now?

JESSIE: Soon as I'm through here, Mama.

MAMA: You won't like the apple, either. It'll be just like the cocoa. You never liked eating at all, did you? Any of it! What have you been living on all these years, toothpaste?

JESSIE (*as she starts to clean out the refrigerator*): Now, you know the milkman comes on Wednesdays and Saturdays, and he leaves the order blank in an egg box, and you give the bills to Dawson once a month.

MAMA: Do they still make that orangeade?

JESSIE: It's not orangeade, it's just orange.

MAMA: I'm going to get some. I thought they stopped making it. You just stopped ordering it.

JESSIE: You should drink milk.

MAMA: Not anymore, I'm not. That hot chocolate was the last. Hooray.

JESSIE (*getting the garbage can from under the sink*): I told them to keep delivering a quart a week no matter what you said. I told them you'd run out of Cokes and you'd have to drink it. I told them I knew you wouldn't pour it on the ground . . .

MAMA (*finishing her sentence*): And you told them you weren't going to be ordering anymore?

JESSIE: I told them I was taking a little holiday and to look after you.

MAMA: And they didn't think something was funny about that? You who doesn't go to the front steps? You, who only sees the driveway looking down from a stretcher passed out cold?

JESSIE (*enjoying this, but not laughing*): They said it was about time, but why didn't I take you with me? And I said I didn't think you'd want to go and they said, "Yeah, everybody's got their own idea of vacation."

MAMA: I guess you think that's funny.

JESSIE (*pulling jars out of the refrigerator*): You know there never was any reason to call the ambulance for me. All they ever did for me in the emergency room was let me wake up. I could've done that here. Now, I'll just call them out and you say yes or no. I know you like pickles. Ketchup?

MAMA: Keep it.

JESSIE: We've had this since last Fourth of July.

MAMA: Keep the ketchup. Keep it all.

JESSIE: Are you going to drink ketchup from the bottle or what? How can you want your food and not want your pots to cook it in? This stuff will all spoil in here, Mother.

MAMA: Nothing I ever did was good enough for you and I want to know why.

JESSIE: That's not true.

MAMA: And I want to know why you've lived here this long feeling the way you do.

JESSIE: You have no earthly idea how I feel.

MAMA: Well, how could I? You're real far back there, Jessie.

JESSIE: Back where?

MAMA: What's it like over there, where you are? Do people always say the right thing or get whatever they want, or what?

JESSIE: What are you talking about?

MAMA: Why do you read the newspaper? Why don't you wear that sweater I made for you? Do you remember how I used to look, or am I just any old woman now? When you have a fit, do you see stars or what? How did you fall off the horse, really? Why did Cecil leave you? Where did you put my old glasses?

JESSIE (*stunned by Mama's intensity*): They're in the bottom drawer of your dresser in an old Milk of Magnesia box. Cecil left me because he made me choose between him and smoking.

MAMA: Jessie, I know he wasn't that dumb.

JESSIE: I never understood why he hated it so much when it's so good. Smoking is the only thing I know that's always just what you think it's going to be. Just like it was the last time, right there when you want it and real quiet.

MAMA: Your fits made him sick and you know it.

JESSIE: Say seizures, not fits. Seizures.

MAMA: It's the same thing. A seizure in the hospital is a fit at home.

JESSIE: They didn't bother him at all. Except he did feel responsible for it. It *was* his idea to go horseback riding that day. It was his idea I could do *anything* if I just made up my mind to. I fell off the horse because I didn't know how to hold on. Cecil left for pretty much the same reason.

MAMA: He had a girl, Jessie. I walked right in on them in the toolshed.

JESSIE (*after a moment*): O.K. That's fair. (*Lighting another cigarette.*) Was she very pretty?

MAMA: She was Agnes's girl, Carlene. Judge for yourself.

JESSIE (*as she walks to the living room*): I guess you and Agnes had a good talk about that, huh?

MAMA: I never thought he was good enough for you. They moved here from Tennessee, you know.

JESSIE: What are you talking about? You liked him better than I did. You flirted him out here to build your porch or I'd never even met him at all. You thought maybe he'd help you out around the place, come in and get some coffee and talk to you. God knows what you thought. All that curly hair.

MAMA: He's the best carpenter I ever saw. That little house of yours will still be standing at the end of the world, Jessie.

JESSIE: You didn't need a porch, Mama.

MAMA: All right! I wanted you to have a husband.

JESSIE: And I couldn't get one on my own, of course.

MAMA: How were you going to get a husband never opening your mouth to a living soul?

JESSIE: So I was quiet about it, so what?

MAMA: So I should have let you just sit here? Sit like your daddy? Sit here?

JESSIE: Maybe.

MAMA: Well, I didn't think so.

JESSIE: Well, what did you know?

MAMA: I never said I knew much. How was I supposed to learn anything living out here? I didn't know enough to do half the things I did in my life. Things happen. You do what you can about them and you see what happens next. I married you off to the wrong man, I admit that. So I took you in when he left. I'm sorry.

JESSIE: He wasn't the wrong man.

MAMA: He didn't love you, Jessie, or he wouldn't have left.

JESSIE: He wasn't the wrong man, Mama. I loved Cecil so much. And I tried to get more exercise and I tried to stay awake. I tried to learn to ride a horse. And I tried to stay outside with him, but he always knew I was trying, so it didn't work.

MAMA: He was a selfish man. He told me once he hated to see people move into his houses after he built them. He knew they'd mess them up.

JESSIE: I loved that bridge he built over the creek in back of the house. It didn't have to be anything special, a couple of boards would have been just fine, but he used that yellow pine and rubbed it so smooth . . .

MAMA: He had responsibilities here. He had a wife and son here and he failed you.

JESSIE: Or that baby bed he built for Ricky. I told him he didn't have to spend so much time on it, but he said it had to last, and the thing ended up weighing two hundred pounds and I couldn't move it. I said, "How long does a baby bed have to last, anyway?" But maybe he thought if it was strong enough, it might keep Ricky a baby.

MAMA: Ricky is too much like Cecil.

JESSIE: He is not. Ricky is as much like me as it's possible for any human to be. We even wear the same size pants. These are his, I think.

MAMA: That's just the same size. That's not you're the same person.

JESSIE: I see it on his face. I hear it when he talks. We look out at the world and we see the same thing: Not Fair. And the only difference between us is Ricky's out there trying to get even. And he knows not to trust anybody and he got it straight from me. And he knows not to try to get work, and guess where he got that. He walks around like there's loose boards in the floor, and you know who laid that floor, I did.

MAMA: Ricky isn't through yet. You don't know how he'll turn out!

JESSIE (going back to the kitchen): Yes I do and so did Cecil. Ricky is the two of us together for all time in too small a space. And we're tearing each other apart, like always, inside that boy, and if you don't see it, then you're just blind.

MAMA: Give him time, Jess.

JESSIE: Oh, he'll have plenty of that. Five years for forgery, ten years for armed assault . . .

MAMA (furious): Stop that! (Then pleading.) Jessie, Cecil might be ready to try it again, honey, that happens sometimes. Go downtown. Find him. Talk to him. He didn't know what he had in you. Maybe he sees things different now, but you're not going to know that till you go see him. Or call him up! Right now! He might be home.

JESSIE: And say what? Nothing's changed, Cecil, I'd just like to look at you, if you don't mind? No. He loved me, Mama. He just didn't know how things fall down around me like they do. I think he did the right thing. He gave himself another chance, that's all. But I did beg him to take me with him. I did tell him I would leave Ricky and you and everything I loved out here if only he would take me with him, but he couldn't and I understood that. (Pause.) I wrote that note I showed you. I wrote it. Not Cecil. I said "I'm sorry, Jessie, I can't fix it all for you." I said I'd always love me, not Cecil. But that's how he felt.

MAMA: Then he should've taken you with him!

JESSIE (picking up the garbage bag she has filled): Mama, you don't pack your garbage when you move.

MAMA: You will not call yourself garbage, Jessie.

JESSIE (taking the bag to the big garbage can near the back door): Just a way of saying it, Mama. Thinking about my list, that's all. (Opening the can, putting the garbage in, then securing the lid.) Well, a little more than that. I was trying to say it's all right that Cecil left. It was . . . a relief in a way. I never was what he wanted to see, so it was better when he wasn't looking at me all the time.

MAMA: I'll make your apple now.

JESSIE: No thanks. You get the manicure stuff and I'll be right there.

(Jessie ties up the big garbage bag in the can and replaces the small garbage bag under the sink, all the time trying desperately to regain her calm. Mama watches, from a distance, her hand reaching unconsciously for the phone. Then she has a better idea. Or rather she thinks of the only other thing left and is willing to try it. Maybe she is even convinced it will work.)

MAMA: Jessie, I think your daddy had little . . .

JESSIE (interrupting her): Garbage night is Tuesday. Put it out as late as you can. The Davises' dogs get in it if you don't. (Replacing the garbage bag in the can under the sink.) And keep ordering the heavy black bags. It doesn't pay to buy the cheap ones. And I've got all the ties here with the hammers and all. Take them out of the box as soon as you open a new one and put them in this drawer. They'll get lost if you don't, and rubber bands or something else won't work.

MAMA: I think your daddy had fits too. I think he sat in his chair and had little fits. I read this a long time ago in a magazine, how little fits go, just little blackouts where maybe their eyes don't even close and people just call them "thinking spells."

JESSIE (getting the slipcover out of the laundry basket): I don't think you want this manicure we've been looking forward to. I washed this cover for the sofa, but it'll take both of us to get it back on.

MAMA: I watched his eyes. I know that's what it was. The magazine said some people don't even know they've had one.

JESSIE: Daddy would've known if he'd had fits, Mama.

MAMA: The lady in this story had kept track of hers and she'd had eighty thousand of them in the last eleven years.

JESSIE: Next time you wash this cover, it'll dry better if you put it on wet.

MAMA: Jessie, listen to what I'm telling you. This lady had anywhere between five and five hundred fits a day and they lasted maybe fifteen seconds apiece, so that out of her life, she'd only lost about two weeks altogether, and she had a full-time secretary job and an IQ of 120.

JESSIE (amused by Mama's approach): You want to talk about fits, is that it?

MAMA: Yes. I do. I want to say . . .

JESSIE (interrupting): Most of the time I wouldn't even

know I'd had one, except I wake up with different clothes on, feeling like I've been run over. Sometimes I feel my head start to turn around or hear myself scream. And sometimes there *is* this dizzy stupid feeling a little before it, but if the TV's on, well, it's easy to miss.

(*As Jessie and Mama replace the slipcover on the sofa and the afghan on the chair, the physical struggle somehow mirrors the emotional one in the conversation.*)

MAMA: I can tell when you're about to have one. Your eyes get this big! But, Jessie, you haven't . . .

JESSIE (*taking charge of this*): What do they look like? The seizures.

MAMA (*reluctant*): Different each time, Jess.

JESSIE: O.K. Pick one, then. A good one. I think I want to know now.

MAMA: There's not much to tell. You just . . . crumple, in a heap, like a puppet and somebody cut the strings all at once, or like the firing squad in some Mexican movie, you just slide down the wall, you know. You don't know what happens? How can you not know what happens?

JESSIE: I'm busy.

MAMA: That's not funny.

JESSIE: I'm not laughing. My head turns around and I fall down and then what?

MAMA: Well, your chest squeezes in and out, and you sound like you're gagging, sucking air in and out like you can't breathe.

JESSIE: Do it for me. Make the sound for me.

MAMA: I will not. It's awful-sounding.

JESSIE: Yeah. It felt like it might be. What's next?

MAMA: Your mouth bites down and I have to get your tongue out of the way fast, so you don't bite yourself.

JESSIE: Or you. I bite you, too, don't I?

MAMA: You got me once real good. I had to get a tetanus! But I know what to watch for now. And then you turn blue and the jerks start up. Like I'm standing there poking you with a cattle prod or you're sticking your finger in a light socket as fast as you can . . .

JESSIE: Foaming like a mad dog the whole time.

MAMA: It's bubbling, Jess, not foam like the washer overflowed, for God's sake; it's bubbling like a baby spitting up. I go get a wet washcloth, that's all. And then the jerks slow down and you wet yourself and it's over. Two minutes tops.

JESSIE: How do I get to the bed?

MAMA: How do you think?

JESSIE: I'm too heavy for you now. How do you do it?

MAMA: I call Dawson. But I get you cleaned up before he gets here and I make him leave before you wake up.

JESSIE: You could just leave me on the floor.

MAMA: I want you to wake up someplace nice, O.K.? (*Then making a real effort.*) But, Jessie, and this is the reason I even brought this up! You haven't had a seizure for a solid year. A whole year, do you realize that?

JESSIE: Yeah, the phenobarb's about right now, I guess.

MAMA: You bet it is. You might never have another one, ever! You might be through with it for all time!

JESSIE: Could be.

MAMA: You are. I know you are!

JESSIE: I sure am feeling good. I really am. The double vision's gone and my gums aren't swelling. No rashes or anything. I'm feeling as good as I ever felt in my life. I'm even feeling like worrying or getting mad and I'm not afraid it will start a fit if I do, I just go ahead.

MAMA: Of course you do! You can even scream at me, if you want to. I can take it. You don't have to act like you're just visiting here, Jessie. This is your house, too.

JESSIE: The best part is, my memory's back.

MAMA: Your memory's always been good. When couldn't you remember things? You're always reminding me what . . .

JESSIE: Because I've made lists for everything. But now I remember what things mean on my lists. I see "dish towels," and I used to wonder whether I was supposed to wash them, buy them, or look for them because I wouldn't remember where I put them after I washed them, but now I know it means wrap them up, they're a present for Loretta's birthday.

MAMA (*finished with the sofa now*): You used to go looking for your lists, too, I've noticed that. You always know where they are now! (*Then suddenly worried.*) Loretta's birthday isn't coming up, is it?

JESSIE: I made a list of all the birthdays for you. I even put yours on it. (*A small smile.*) So you can call Loretta and remind her.

MAMA: Let's take Loretta to Howard Johnson's and have those fried clams. I *know* you love that clam roll.

JESSIE (*slight pause*): I won't be here, Mama.

MAMA: What have we just been talking about? You'll be here. You're well, Jessie. You're starting all over. You said it yourself. You're remembering things and . . .

JESSIE: I won't be here. If I'd ever had a year like this, to think straight and all, before now, I'd be gone already.

MAMA (*not pleading, commanding*): No, Jessie.

JESSIE (*folding the rest of the laundry*): Yes, Mama. Once I started remembering, I could see what it all added up to.

MAMA: The fits are over!

JESSIE: It's not the fits, Mama.

MAMA: Then it's me for giving them to you, but I didn't do it!

JESSIE: It's not the fits! You said it yourself, the medicine takes care of the fits.

MAMA (*interrupting*): Your daddy gave you those fits, Jessie. He passed it down to you like your green eyes and your straight hair. It's not my fault!

JESSIE: So what if he had little fits? It's not inherited. I fell off the horse. It was an accident.

MAMA: The horse wasn't the first time, Jessie. You had a fit when you were five years old.

JESSIE: I did not.

MAMA: You did! You were eating a popsicle and down you went. He gave it to you. It's *his* fault, not mine.

JESSIE: Well, you took your time telling me.

MAMA: How do you tell that to a five-year-old?

JESSIE: What did the doctor say?

MAMA: He said kids have them all the time. He said there wasn't anything to do but wait for another one.

JESSIE: But I didn't have another one.

(*Now there is a real silence.*)

JESSIE: You mean to tell me I had fits all the time as a kid and you just told me I fell down or something and it wasn't till I had the fit when Cecil was looking that anybody bothered to find out what was the matter with me?

MAMA: It wasn't *all the time,* Jessie. And they changed when you started to school. More like your daddy's. Oh, that was some swell time, sitting here with the two of you turning off and on like light bulbs some nights.

JESSIE: How many fits did I have?

MAMA: You never hurt yourself. I never let you out of my sight. I caught you every time.

JESSIE: But you didn't tell anybody.

MAMA: It was none of their business.

JESSIE: You were ashamed.

MAMA: I didn't want anybody to know. Least of all you.

JESSIE: Least of all me. Oh, right. That was mine to know, Mama, not yours. Did Daddy know?

MAMA: He thought you were . . . you fell down a lot. That's what he thought. You were careless. Or maybe he thought I beat you. I don't know what he thought. He didn't think about it.

JESSIE: Because you didn't tell him!

MAMA: If I told him about you, I'd have to tell him about him!

JESSIE: I don't like this. I don't like this one bit.

MAMA: I didn't think you'd like it. That's why I didn't tell you.

JESSIE: If I'd known I was an epileptic, Mama, I wouldn't have ridden any horses.

MAMA: Make you feel like a freak, is that what I should have done?

JESSIE: Just get the manicure tray and sit down!

MAMA (*throwing it to the floor*): I don't want a manicure!

JESSIE: Doesn't look like you do, no.

MAMA: Maybe I did drop you, you don't know.

JESSIE: If you say you didn't, you didn't.

MAMA (*beginning to break down*): Maybe I fed you the wrong thing. Maybe you had a fever sometime and I didn't know it soon enough. Maybe it's a punishment.

JESSIE: For what?

MAMA: I don't know. Because of how I felt about your father. Because I didn't want any more children. Because I smoked too much or didn't eat right when I was carrying you. It has to be something I did.

JESSIE: It does not. It's just a sickness, not a curse. Epilepsy doesn't mean anything. It just is.

MAMA: I'm not talking about the fits here, Jessie! I'm talking about this killing yourself. It has to be me that's the matter here. You wouldn't be doing this if it wasn't. I didn't tell you things or I married you off to the wrong man or I took you in and let your life get away from you or all of it put together. I don't know what I did, but I did it, I know. This is all my fault, Jessie, but I don't know what to do about it now!

JESSIE (*exasperated at having to say this again*): It doesn't have anything to do with you!

MAMA: Everything you do has to do with me, Jessie. You can't do *anything,* wash your face or cut your finger, without doing it to me. That's right! You might as well kill me as you, Jessie, it's the same thing. This has to do with me, Jessie.

JESSIE: Then what if it does! What if it has everything to do with you! What if you are all I have and you're not enough? What if I could take all the rest of it if only I didn't have you here? What if the only way I can get away from you for good is to kill myself? What if it is? I can *still* do it!

MAMA (*in desperate tears*): Don't leave me, Jessie! (*Jessie stands for a moment, then turns for the bedroom.*) No! (*She grabs Jessie's arm.*)

JESSIE (*carefully taking her arm away*): I have a box of things I want people to have. I'm just going to go get it for you. You . . . just rest a minute.

(*Jessie is gone. Mama heads for the telephone, but she can't even pick up the receiver this time and, instead, stoops to clean up the bottles that have spilled out of the manicure tray.*)

(*Jessie returns, carrying a box that groceries were delivered in. It probably says Hershey Kisses or Star-kist Tuna. Mama is still down on the floor cleaning up, hoping that maybe if she just makes it look nice enough, Jessie will stay.*)

MAMA: Jessie, how can I live here without you? I need you! You're supposed to tell me to stand up straight and say how nice I look in my pink dress, and drink my milk. You're supposed to go around and lock up so I know we're safe for the night, and when I wake up, you're supposed to be out there making the coffee and watching me get older every day, and you're supposed to help me die when the time comes. I can't do that by myself, Jessie. I'm not like you, Jessie. I hate the quiet and I don't want to die and I don't want you to go, Jessie. How can I . . . (*Has to stop a moment.*) How can I get up every day knowing you had to kill yourself to make it stop hurting and I was here all the time and I never even saw it. And then you gave me this chance to make it better, convince you to stay alive, and I couldn't do it. How can I live with myself after this, Jessie?

JESSIE: I only told you so I could explain it, so you wouldn't blame yourself, so you wouldn't feel bad. There wasn't anything you could say to change my mind. I didn't want you to save me. I just wanted you to know.

MAMA: Stay with me just a little longer. Just a few more years. I don't have that many more to go, Jessie. And as soon as I'm dead, you can do whatever you want. Maybe with me gone, you'll have all the quiet you want, right here in the house. And maybe one day you'll put in some begonias up the walk and get just the right rain for them all summer. And Ricky will be married by then and he'll bring your grandbabies over and you can sneak them a piece of candy when their daddy's not looking and then be real glad when they've gone home and left you to your quiet again.

JESSIE: Don't you see, Mama, everything I do winds up like this. How could I think you would understand? How could I think you would want a manicure? We could hold hands for an hour and then I could go shoot myself? I'm sorry about tonight, Mama, but it's exactly why I'm doing it.

MAMA: If you've got the guts to kill yourself, Jessie, you've got the guts to stay alive.

JESSIE: I know that. So it's really just a matter of where I'd rather be.

MAMA: Look, maybe I can't think of what you should do, but that doesn't mean there isn't something that would help. *You* find it. *You* think of it. You can keep trying. You can get brave and try some more. You don't have to give up!

JESSIE: I'm *not* giving up! This *is* the other thing I'm trying. And I'm sure there are some other things that might work, but *might* work isn't good enough anymore. I need something that *will* work. *This* will work. That's why I picked it.

MAMA: But something might happen. Something that could change everything. Who knows what it might be, but it might be worth waiting for! (*Jessie doesn't respond.*) Try it for two more weeks. We could have more talks like tonight.

JESSIE: No, Mama.

MAMA: I'll pay more attention to you. Tell the truth when you ask me. Let you have your say.

JESSIE: No, Mama! We wouldn't have more talks like tonight, because it's this next part that's made this last part so good, Mama. No, Mama. *This* is how I have my say. This is how I say what I thought about it *all* and I say no. To Dawson and Loretta and the Red Chinese and epilepsy and Ricky and Cecil and you. And me. And hope. I say no! (*Then going to Mama on the sofa.*) Just let me go easy, Mama.

MAMA: How can I let you go?

JESSIE: You can because you have to. It's what you've always done.

MAMA: You are my child!

JESSIE: I am what became of your child. (*Mama cannot answer.*) I found an old baby picture of me. And it was somebody else, not me. It was somebody pink and fat who never heard of sick or lonely, somebody who cried and got fed, and reached up and got held and kicked but didn't hurt anybody, and slept when-

ever she wanted to, just by closing her eyes. Somebody who mainly just laid there and laughed at the colors waving around over her head and chewed on a polka-dot whale and woke up knowing some new trick nearly every day, and rolled over and drooled on the sheet and felt your hand pulling my quilt back up over me. That's who I started out and this is who is left. (*There is no self-pity here.*) That's what this is about. It's somebody I lost, all right, it's my own self. Who I never was. Or who I tried to be and never got there. Somebody I waited for who never came. And never will. So, see, it doesn't much matter what else happens in the world or in this house, even. I'm what was worth waiting for and I didn't make it. Me . . . who might have made a difference to me . . . I'm not going to show up, so there's no reason to stay, except to keep you company, and that's . . . not reason enough because I'm not . . . very good company. (*Pause.*) Am I.

MAMA (*knowing she must tell the truth*): No. And neither am I.

JESSIE: I had this strange little thought, well, maybe it's not so strange. Anyway after Christmas, after I decided to do this, I would wonder, sometimes, what might keep me here, what might be worth staying for, and you know what it was? It was maybe if there was something I really liked, like maybe if I really liked rice pudding or cornflakes for breakfast or something, that might be enough.

MAMA: Rice pudding is good.

JESSIE: Not to me.

MAMA: And you're not afraid?

JESSIE: Afraid of what?

MAMA: I'm afraid of it, for me, I mean. When my time comes. I know it's coming, but . . .

JESSIE: You don't know when. Like in a scary movie.

MAMA: Yeah, sneaking up on me like some killer on the loose, hiding out in the back yard just waiting for me to have my hands full someday and how am I supposed to protect myself anyhow when I don't know what he looks like and I don't know how he sounds coming up behind me like that or if it will hurt or take very long or what I don't get done before it happens.

JESSIE: You've got plenty of time left.

MAMA: I forget what for, right now.

JESSIE: For whatever happens, I don't know. For the rest of your life. For Agnes burning down one more house or Dawson losing his hair or . . .

MAMA (*quickly*): Jessie, I can't just sit here and say O.K., kill yourself if you want to.

JESSIE: Sure you can. You just did. Say it again.

MAMA (*really startled*): Jessie! (*Quiet horror.*) How dare you! (*Furious.*) How dare you! You think you can just leave whenever you want, like you're watching television here? No, you can't, Jessie. You make me feel like a fool for being alive, child, and you are so wrong! I like it here, and I will stay here until they make me go, until they drag me screaming and I mean screeching into my grave, and you're real smart to get away before then because, I mean, honey, you've never heard noise like that in your life. (*Jessie turns away.*) Who am I talking to? You're gone already, aren't you? I'm looking right through you! I can't stop you because you're already gone! I guess you think they'll all have to talk about you now! I guess you think this will really confuse them. Oh yes, ever since Christmas you've been laughing to yourself and thinking, "Boy, are they all in for a surprise." Well, nobody's going to be a bit surprised, sweetheart. This is just like you. Do it the hard way, that's my girl, all right. (*Jessie gets up and goes into the kitchen, but Mama follows her.*) You know who they're going to feel sorry for? Me! How about that! Not you, me! They're going to be *ashamed* of you. Yes. *Ashamed!* If somebody asks Dawson about it, he'll change the subject as fast as he can. He'll talk about how much he has to pay to park his car these days.

JESSIE: Leave me alone.

MAMA: It's the truth!

JESSIE: I should've just left you a note!

MAMA (*screaming*): Yes! (*Then suddenly understanding what she has said, nearly paralyzed by the thought of it, she turns slowly to face Jessie, nearly whispering.*) No. No. I . . . might not have thought of all the things you've said.

JESSIE: It's O.K., Mama.

(*Mama is nearly unconscious from the emotional devastation of these last few moments. She sits down at the kitchen table, hurt and angry and desperately afraid. But she looks almost numb. She is so far beyond what is known as pain that she is virtually unreachable and Jessie knows this, and talks quietly, watching for signs of recovery.*)

JESSIE (*washes her hands in the sink*): I remember you liked that preacher who did Daddy's, so if you want to ask him to do the service, that's O.K. with me.

MAMA (*not an answer, just a word*): What.

JESSIE (*putting on hand lotion as she talks*): And pick some songs you like or let Agnes pick, she'll know exactly which ones. Oh, and I had your dress cleaned that you wore to Daddy's. You looked real good in that.

MAMA: I don't remember, hon.

JESSIE And it won't be so bad once your friends start coming to the funeral home. You'll probably see people you haven't seen for years, but I thought about what you should say to get you over that nervous part when they first come in.

MAMA (*simply repeating*): Come in.

JESSIE: Take them up to see their flowers, they'd like that. And when they say, "I'm so sorry, Thelma," you just say, "I appreciate your coming, Connie." And then ask how their garden was this summer or what they're doing for Thanksgiving or how their children . . .

MAMA: I don't think I should ask about their children. I'll talk about what they have on, that's always good. And I'll have some crochet work with me.

JESSIE: And Agnes will be there, so you might not have to talk at all.

MAMA: Maybe if Connie Richards does come, I can get her to tell me where she gets that Irish yarn, she calls it. I know it doesn't come from Ireland. I think it just comes with a green wrapper.

JESSIE: And be sure to invite enough people home afterward so you get enough food to feed them all and have some left for you. But don't let anybody take anything home, especially Loretta.

MAMA: Loretta will get all the food set up, honey. It's only fair to let her have some macaroni or something.

JESSIE: No, Mama. You have to be more selfish from now on. (*Sitting at the table with Mama.*) Now, somebody's bound to ask you why I did it and you just say you don't know. That you loved me and you know I loved you and we just sat around tonight like every other night of our lives, and then I came over and kissed you and said, "'Night, Mother," and you heard me close my bedroom door and the next thing you heard was the shot. And whatever reasons I had, well, you guess I just took them with me.

MAMA (*quietly*): It was something personal.

JESSIE: Good. That's good, Mama.

MAMA: That's what I'll say, then.

JESSIE: Personal. Yeah.

MAMA: Is that what I tell Dawson and Loretta, too? We sat around, you kissed me, "'Night, Mother"? They'll want to know more, Jessie. They won't believe it.

JESSIE: Well, then, tell them what we did. I filled up the candy jars. I cleaned out the refrigerator. We made some hot chocolate and put the cover back on the sofa. You had no idea. All right? I really think it's better that way. If they know we talked about it, they really won't understand how you let me go.

MAMA: I guess not.

JESSIE: It's private. Tonight is private, yours and mine, and I don't want anybody else to have any of it.

MAMA: O.K., then.

JESSIE (*standing behind Mama now, holding her shoulders*): Now, when you hear the shot, I don't want you to come in. First of all, you won't be able to get in by yourself, but I don't want you trying. Call Dawson, then call the police, and then call Agnes. And then you'll need something to do till somebody gets here, so wash the hot-chocolate pan. You wash that pan till you hear the doorbell ring and I don't care if it's an hour, you keep washing that pan.

MAMA: I'll make my calls and then I'll just sit. I won't need something to do. What will the police say?

JESSIE: They'll do that gunpowder test, I guess, and ask you what happened, and by that time, the ambulance will be here and they'll come in and get me and you know how that goes. You stay out here with Dawson and Loretta. You keep Dawson out here. I want the police in the room first, not Dawson, O.K.?

MAMA: What if Dawson and Loretta want me to go home with them?

JESSIE (*returning to the living room*): That's up to you.

MAMA: I think I'll stay here. All they've got is Sanka.

JESSIE: Maybe Agnes could come stay with you for a few days.

MAMA (*standing up, looking into the living room*): I'd rather be by myself, I think. (*Walking toward the box Jessie brought in earlier.*) You want me to give people those things?

JESSIE (*they sit down on the sofa, Jessie holding the box on her lap*): I want Loretta to have my little calculator. Dawson bought it for himself, you know, but then he saw one he liked better and he couldn't bring both of them home with Loretta counting every penny the way she does, so he gave the first one to me. Be funny for her to have it now, don't you think? And all my house slippers are in a sack for her in my closet. Tell her I know they'll fit and I've never worn any of them, and make sure Dawson hears you tell her that. I'm glad he loves Loretta so much, but I wish he knew not everybody has her size feet.

MAMA (*taking the calculator*): O.K.

JESSIE (*reaching into the box again*): This letter is for Dawson, but it's mostly about you, so read it if you want. There's a list of presents for you for at least twenty more Christmases and birthdays, so if you want anything special you better add it to this list before you give it to him. Or if you want to be surprised, just don't read that page. This Christmas, you're getting mostly stuff for the house, like a new rug in your bathroom and needlework, but next Christmas, you're really going to cost him next Christmas. I think you'll like it a lot and you'd never think of it.

MAMA: And you think he'll go for it?

JESSIE: I think he'll feel like a real jerk if he doesn't. Me telling him to, like this and all. Now, this number's where you call Cecil. I called it last week and he answered, so I know he still lives there.

MAMA: What do you want me to tell him?

JESSIE: Tell him we talked about him and I only had good things to say about him, but mainly tell him to find Ricky and tell him what I did, and tell Ricky you have something for him, out here, from me, and to come get it. (*Pulls a sack out of the box.*)

MAMA (*the sack feels empty*): What is it?

JESSIE (*taking it off*): My watch. (*Putting it in the sack and taking a ribbon out of the sack to tie around the top of it.*)

MAMA: He'll sell it!

JESSIE: That's the idea. I appreciate him not stealing it already. I'd like to buy him a good meal.

MAMA: He'll buy dope with it!

JESSIE: Well, then, I hope he gets some good dope with it, Mama. And the rest of this is for you. (*Handing Mama the box now. Mama picks up the things and looks at them.*)

MAMA (*surprised and pleased*): When did you do all this? During my naps, I guess.

JESSIE: I guess. I tried to be quiet about it. (*As Mama is puzzled by the presents.*) Those are just little presents. For whenever you need one. They're not bought presents, just things I thought you might like to look at, pictures or things you think you've lost. Things you didn't know you had, even. You'll see.

MAMA: I'm not sure I want them. They'll make me think of you.

JESSIE: No they won't. They're just things, like a free tube of toothpaste I found hanging on the door one day.

MAMA: Oh. All right, then.

JESSIE: Well, maybe there's one nice present in there somewhere. It's Granny's ring she gave me and I thought you might like to have it, but I didn't think you'd wear it if I gave it to you right now.

MAMA (*taking the box to a table nearby*): No. Probably not. (*Turning back to face her.*) I'm ready for my manicure, I guess. Want me to wash my hands again?

JESSIE (*standing up*): It's time for me to go, Mama.

MAMA (*starting for her*): No, Jessie, you've got all night!

JESSIE (*as Mama grabs her*): No, Mama.

MAMA: It's not even ten o'clock.

JESSIE (*very calm*): Let me go, Mama.

MAMA: I can't. You can't go. You can't do this. You didn't say it would be so soon, Jessie. I'm scared. I love you.

JESSIE (*takes her hands away*): Let go of me, Mama. I've said everything I had to say.

MAMA (*standing still a minute*): You said you wanted to do my nails.

JESSIE (*taking a small step backward*): I can't. It's too late.

MAMA: It's not too late!

JESSIE: I don't want you to wake Dawson and Loretta when you call. I want them to still be up and dressed so they can get right over.

MAMA (*as Jessie backs up, Mama moves in on her, but carefully*): They wake up fast, Jessie, if they have to. They don't matter here, Jessie. You do. I do. We're not through yet. We've got a lot of things to take care of here. I don't know where my prescriptions are and you didn't tell me what to tell Dr. Davis when he calls or how much you want me to tell Ricky or who I call to rake the leaves or . . .

JESSIE: Don't try and stop me, Mama, you can't do it.

MAMA (*grabbing her again, this time hard*): I can too! I'll stand in front of this hall and you can't get past me. (*They struggle.*) You'll have to knock me down to get away from me, Jessie. I'm not about to let you . . .

(*Mama struggles with Jessie at the door and in the struggle Jessie gets away from her and — *)

JESSIE (*almost a whisper*): 'Night, Mother. (*She vanishes into her bedroom and we hear the door lock just as Mama gets to it.*)

MAMA (*screams*): Jessie! (*Pounding on the door.*) Jessie,

you let me in there. Don't you do this, Jessie. I'm not going to stop screaming until you open this door, Jessie. Jessie! Jessie! What if I don't do any of the things you told me to do! I'll tell Cecil what a miserable man he was to make you feel the way he did and I'll give Ricky's watch to Dawson if I feel like it and the only way you can make sure I do what you want is you come out here and make me, Jessie! (*Pounding again.*) Jessie! Stop this! I didn't know! I was here with you all the time. How could I know you were so alone?

(*And Mama stops for a moment, breathless and frantic, putting her ear to the door, and when she doesn't hear anything, she stands up straight again and screams once more.*)

Jessie! Please!

(*And we hear the shot, and it sounds like an answer, it sounds like No.*)

(*Mama collapses against the door, tears streaming down her face, but not screaming anymore. In shock now.*)

Jessie, Jessie, child . . . Forgive me. (*Pause.*) I thought you were mine.

(*And she leaves the door and makes her way through the living room, around the furniture, as though she didn't know where it was, not knowing what to do. Finally, she goes to the stove in the kitchen and picks up the hot-chocolate pan and carries it with her to the telephone and holds on to it while she dials the number. She looks down at the pan, holding it tight like her life depended on it. She hears Loretta answer.*)

MAMA: Loretta, let me talk to Dawson, honey.

COMMENTARY

David Savran (b. 1950)
INTERVIEW WITH MARSHA NORMAN   1988

As Marsha Norman said during an interview, her dissatisfaction with other plays about suicide led her to be very direct in her own play and to confront the issue directly. Here she discusses how that decision changed her entire concept of the play and helped her shape the dramatic action.

Savran: How do you begin a play? With an outline, a character, a line of dialogue?

Norman: . . . With *'night, Mother* I knew I wanted to tell the story of this woman who kills herself, but I didn't have any idea how. At the time, in '81, there were a number of other plays on the subject. But I kept saying that these plays — particularly *Whose Life Is It Anyway?* — are tantrums. I wanted to put somebody in the room with this woman, somebody who cares deeply, wildly, madly, who will fight this person to the death to save her own life. This is a gladiator contest where the point is to keep the other person alive. And once I had that, I had all these parallels — gladiators and world heavyweight boxing championships — and I understood immediately how this has to work. You have to have a closed ring, nobody can get out or in, you can have only two people.

I knew going into *'night, Mother* that it was going to be the most treacherous act of my writing life. So I went to the world of music. I was in a mad Glenn Gould state at the time — I've spent my life at the piano. Okay, I thought, what if I do a little sonata form, a three-act play with no intermission? You can actually feel the moment when the orchestra stops and the conductor raises his hands and Jessie says, "You talked to Agnes today," and the second movement starts. The second movement ends when Jessie goes in to get the box of presents, Mama just having said, "Don't leave me, Jessie." The actors would come on stage knowing, "We don't have to go all the way to the end. We just have to get to the Agnes section." And then you start in on Agnes and think, "Great, I'll just get to 'Don't leave me, Jessie,' then I can take a breath"— this is from Mama's point of view —"and get down and wash the floor." And then all they have to do is go to the end. *'night, Mother* would be undoable if it weren't for that. People would fall out of it all the time. But they don't. So I think that if you don't have structure, you might as well not have anything to put in it. If you don't have the bookshelves, you don't have the books.

I have a great trick during that period of thinking about the play. I say, "I'm not writing until I absolutely have to, till I can no longer contain it." I build up the piece in a pressure cooker, as it were. All that time I'm writing myself notes in the form of questions. What did Daddy do? How long ago did he die? Where did he die? What did he ever do for Jessie? Those kinds of questions. Curiously enough, you'll find that just from asking the questions, you'll get all the answers during the next weeks. It's internal research into the lives of these people. From those questions will come lines of dialogue — you begin to hear the voicing, what they can talk about, what they think is funny. The first line of dialogue I wrote for *'night, Mother* was Jessie's line "We got any old towels?" As soon as I wrote it down, I understood that it was a ritual piece, that Jessie was coming in to celebrate this requiem mass, that she has these stacks of towels: here are the witnesses, the household objects. She comes in as though she is the altar boy.

I wait until I cannot avoid it anymore and by that time, I already know what the beginning is, because of all this scribbling down. Then it's really very easy. I keep two kinds of notebooks, one that has structure and information in it and the other that has my own thoughts —"Can we really have this? What about that? What would happen if this?" I have a wonderful piece of paper upstairs that says, "Have I written something that anybody will want to see? Have I written something that will last? Have I written something that will humiliate me?" This comes from a pretty grim moment in the writing of *'night, Mother.* I thought, "What is this that I've written?" Humiliation is easily a possibility.

Savran: What is the European reaction to *'night, Mother*?

Norman: *'night, Mother* is done all over the world. Any list that New Guinea is on is a long list. It's still running in Spain, four and a half years later, with all of the jokes taken out. Curiously enough, my work has always been popular in Eastern Europe. But this time I've caught the Mediterranean crowd. What strikes you as you watch it in a foreign country, in another language, is that the play seems to contain this other culture. In Italy you get enormous "Mama mia" Mamas, and the Jessies are always Ariels, little sprites. In Scandinavian countries it's quite the opposite. The mothers are really small, like the old woman who lived in the shoe, and the daughters are Valkyries, towering over these little Mamas. In the Latin American countries Mama and Jessie look like sisters.

August Wilson

August Wilson was born in Pittsburgh in 1945, the son of a white father who never lived with his family and a black mother who had come from North Carolina to a Pittsburgh slum, where she worked to keep her family together. Wilson's early childhood was spent in an environment very similar to that of his play *Fences,* and Troy Maxson seems to be patterned somewhat on Wilson's stepfather.

Wilson's writing is rooted to a large extent in music, specifically the blues. As a poet, writing over several years, Wilson found himself interested in the speech patterns and rhythms that were familiar to him from black neighborhoods, but the value of those patterns became clearer to him when he grew older and moved from Pittsburgh to Minneapolis. From a distance, he was able to see more clearly what had attracted him to the language and to begin to use the language more fully in his work.

In the 1960s and 1970s Wilson became involved in the civil rights movement and began to describe himself as a black nationalist, a term he has said he feels comfortable with. He began writing plays in the 1960s in Pittsburgh and then took a job in St. Paul writing dramatic skits for the Science Museum of Minnesota. He founded the Playwrights Center in Minneapolis and began writing a play, *Jitney,* about a gypsy cab station, which was first produced in 1982 and which was staged in New York in April 2000 in a revised version at the Second Stage Theater. *Fullerton Street,* about Pittsburgh, was another play written in this early period. Wilson's first commercial success, *Ma Rainey's Black Bottom,* eventually premiered at the Yale Repertory Theatre in 1984 and then went to Broadway, where it enjoyed 275 performances and won the New York Drama Critics' Circle Award.

Ma Rainey's Black Bottom was the first of a planned sequence of ten plays based on the black American experience. As Wilson said, "I think the black Americans have the most dramatic story of all mankind to tell." The concept of such a vast project echoes O'Neill's projected group of eleven plays based on the Irish-American experience. (Unfortunately, O'Neill destroyed all but *A Touch of the Poet* in his series.) Wilson's project, however, is ongoing and intense and so far has produced some of the most successful plays in the recent American theater.

Ma Rainey is about the legendary black blues singer who preceded Bessie Smith and Billie Holiday. The play is about the way in which she was exploited by white managers and recording executives and the way in which she knowingly dealt with her exploitation. In the cast of the play are several black musicians in the backup band. Levee, the trumpet player, has a dream of leading his own band and establishing himself as an important jazz musician. But he is haunted by memories of seeing his mother raped by a gang of white men when he was a boy. He wants to "improve" the session he's playing by making the old jazz tune "Black Bottom" swing in the new jazz style, but Ma Rainey keeps him in tow and demands that they play the tune in the old way. Levee finally cracks under the pressure, and the play ends painfully.

Fences opened at the Yale Repertory Theatre in 1985 and in New York in early 1987, where it won the Pulitzer Prize as well as the New York Drama Critics' Circle Award. This long-running success established Wilson firmly as an important writer. *Joe Turner's Come and Gone* opened at the Yale Repertory Theatre in late 1986 and moved to New York in early 1988, where it too has been hailed as an important play, winning its author the New York Drama Critics' Circle Award. Set in a rooming house in Pittsburgh in 1911, *Joe Turner* is a study of the children of former slaves. They have come north to find work, and some of them have been found by the legendary bounty hunter Joe Turner. As a study of a people in transition, the play is a quiet masterpiece. It incorporates a number of important African traditions, especially religious rituals of healing as performed by Bynum, the "bone man," a seer and a medicine man. In this play and others, Wilson makes a special effort to highlight the elements of African heritage that white society strips away from blacks.

The next play in Wilson's projected series, *The Piano Lesson,* which premiered at the Yale Repertory Theatre in 1987, also portrays the complexity of black attitudes toward the past and black heritage. The piano represents two kinds of culture: the white culture that produced the musical instrument and the black culture, in the form of Papa Boy Willie, who carved into it images from black Africa. The central question in the play is whether Boy Willie should sell the piano and use the money for a down payment on land and therefore on the future. Or should he follow his sister Berniece's advice and keep it because it is too precious to sell? The conflict is deep and the play ultimately focuses on a profound moment of spiritual exorcism. How one exorcises the past — how one lives with it or without it — is a central theme in Wilson's work.

The next play, *Two Trains Running,* is set in 1969, in the decade that saw the Vietnam War, racial and political riots, and the assassinations of John and Robert Kennedy, Malcolm X, and Martin Luther King Jr. The play premiered at the Yale Repertory Theatre in 1990 and opened on Broadway at the Walter Kerr Theater in April 1992, directed by Lloyd Richards. The characters remain in Memphis Lee's diner — scheduled for demolition — throughout the play. The two trains in the title are heading to Africa and to the old South, but the characters are immobile and seem indifferent to both of them. Wilson moved away from the careful structure of the well-made play in this work and produced an open-ended conclusion, leaving the racial and philosophical tensions unresolved.

Seven Guitars (1996) takes place in a backyard in Pittsburgh in 1948 on the eve of the landmark boxing match between Joe Louis and "Jersey" Joe Walcott. The play focuses on a blues musician, Floyd Barton, who hopes to regain his lost love, put his band back together, and move to Chicago to make his second recording. *Seven Guitars* emphasizes the blues, especially in its long first act, with Barton's friends gathered in his backyard to mourn his death and the loss of his talent. People did much the same when Joe Louis, the "Brown Bomber," lost his fight, a loss that punctuated the end of an era. The second act focuses on Hedley, a West Indian boarder, whom critic Margo Jefferson describes as "half madman and half prophet." Hedley recites a litany of racial injustices and gives voice to a torrent of wrongs. Hedley's voice is a counterpoint to the blues; he gives us a powerful range of responses to the condition of being black in Pittsburgh in the late 1940s.

Wilson's most recent play in the series is set in 1985. *King Hedley II* (1999) picks up some of the characters of *Seven Guitars,* including the character Hedley, and develops further the experience of living in the Hill District of Pittsburgh. Wilson describes *King Hedley II* as focusing on "the breakdown of the black community's extended-family structure." The sequence of the plays detailing the African American experience for each decade of the century needs only the first and last decades' coverage. Wilson now lives primarily in Seattle, but he returned to his hometown for the December 1999 premiere of *King Hedley II,* the first play produced in the new O'Reilly Theater by the Pittsburgh Public Theater. It moved in March 2000 to the Seattle Repertory Theater.

FENCES

Fences (1985), like most of August Wilson's recent plays, was directed by Lloyd Richards, who also directed the first production of Lorraine Hansberry's *A Raisin in the Sun.* Richards was, until 1991, the dean of the School of Drama at Yale University and ran the Yale Repertory Theatre, where he directed all of the plays Wilson has written in his projected ten-play cycle about black American life.

Fences presents a slice of life in a black tenement in Pittsburgh in the 1950s. Its main character, Troy Maxson, is a garbage collector who has taken great pride in keeping his family together and providing for them. When the play opens, he and his friend Bono are talking about Troy's challenge to the company and the union about blacks' ability to do the same "easy" work that whites do. Troy's rebellion and frustration set the tone of the entire play: he is looking for his rights, and, at age fifty-three, he has missed many opportunities to get what he deserves.

Troy's struggle for fairness becomes virtually mythic as he describes his wrestling with death during a bout with pneumonia in 1941. He describes a three-day struggle in which he eventually overcame his foe. Troy — a good baseball player who was relegated to the Negro leagues — sees death as nothing but a fastball, and he could always deal with a fastball. Both Bono and Troy's wife, Rose, show an intense admiration for him as he describes his ordeal.

The father-son relationship that begins to take a central role in the drama is complicated by strong feelings of pride and independence on both sides. Troy's son Cory wants to play football, and Troy wants him to work on the fence he's mending. Cory's youthful enthusiasm probably echoes Troy's own youthful innocence, but Troy resents it in Cory, seeing it as partly responsible for his own predicament. Cory cannot see his father's point of view and feels that he is exempt from the kind of prejudice his father suffered.

The agony of the father-son relationship, their misperceptions of each other, persist through the play. Rose's capacity to cope with the deepest of Troy's anxieties — his fear of death — is one of her most important achievements in the play. At the end of the play Rose demands that Cory give Troy the respect he deserves, although Cory's anger and inexperience make it all but impossible for him to see his father as anything other than an oppressor. Cory feels that he must say no to his father once, but Rose will not let him deny his father. When the play ends with Gabe's fantastic ritualistic dance, the audience feels a sense of closure, of spiritual finish.

Fences in Performance

Like many of America's best plays, *Fences* began in a workshop production. Its first version was performed in a reading without full production — no sets, no full lighting, actors working "on book" instead of fully memorizing the play — in the summer of 1983 at the Eugene O'Neill Center in Waterford, Connecticut. This early version was four hours long.

Once Wilson found the focus of his play, it premiered in 1985 at the Yale Repertory Theatre in New Haven. Lloyd Richards, then dean of Yale Drama School, directed this as well as the New York production. The New York opening on March 27, 1987, starred Mary Alice, James Earl Jones, and Ray Anranha, the cast from New Haven. Frank Rich in the *New York Times* praised James Earl Jones, congratulating him on finding "what may be the best role of his career." He also said, "*Fences* leaves no doubt that Mr. Wilson is a major writer, combining a poet's ear for vernacular with a robust sense of humor (political and sexual), a sure instinct for crackling dramatic incident and a passionate commitment to a great subject."

From the first, *Fences* was recognized as an important play. It won four Tony Awards: best play, best actor, best supporting actress, and best director. It also won the New York Drama Critics' Circle Award for best play. Before the New York production, it had traveled to Chicago, San Francisco, and Seattle. It has been performed numerous times since, with the 1990 Stage West production in Springfield, Massachusetts, among the most recent. A film version of the play is scheduled for release in 2000.

August Wilson (b. 1946)

FENCES

Characters

TROY MAXSON
JIM BONO, *Troy's friend*
ROSE, *Troy's wife*
LYONS, *Troy's oldest son by previous marriage*
GABRIEL, *Troy's brother*
CORY, *Troy and Rose's son*
RAYNELL, *Troy's daughter*

Setting: *The setting is the yard which fronts the only entrance to the Maxson household, an ancient two-story brick house set back off a small alley in a big-city neighborhood. The entrance to the house is gained by two or three steps leading to a wooden porch badly in need of paint.*

A relatively recent addition to the house and running its full width, the porch lacks congruence. It is a sturdy porch with a flat roof. One or two chairs of dubious value sit at one end where the kitchen window opens onto the porch. An old-fashioned icebox stands silent guard at the opposite end.

The yard is a small dirt yard, partially fenced, except for the last scene, with a wooden sawhorse, a pile of lumber, and other fence-building equipment set off to the side. Opposite is a tree from which hangs a ball made of rags. A baseball bat leans against the tree. Two oil drums serve as garbage receptacles and sit near the house at right to complete the setting.

The Play: *Near the turn of the century, the destitute of Europe sprang on the city with tenacious claws and an honest and solid dream. The city devoured them. They swelled its belly until it burst into a thousand furnaces and sewing machines, a thousand butcher shops and bakers' ovens, a thousand churches and hospitals and funeral parlors and money-lenders. The city grew. It nourished itself and offered each man a partnership limited only by his talent, his guile, and his willingness and capacity for hard work. For the immigrants of Europe, a dream dared and won true.*

The descendants of African slaves were offered no such welcome or participation. They came from places called the Carolinas and the Virginias, Georgia, Alabama, Mississippi, and Tennessee. They came strong, eager, searching. The city rejected them and they fled and settled along the riverbanks and under bridges in shallow, ramshackle houses made of sticks and tarpaper. They collected rags and wood. They sold the use of their muscles and their bodies. They cleaned houses and washed clothes, they shined shoes, and in quiet desperation and vengeful pride, they stole, and lived in pursuit of their own dream. That they could breathe free, finally, and stand to meet life with the force of dignity and whatever eloquence the heart could call upon.

By 1957, the hard-won victories of the European immigrants had solidified the industrial might of America. War had been confronted and won with new energies that used loyalty and patriotism as its fuel. Life was rich, full, and flourishing. The Milwaukee Braves won the World Series, and the hot winds of change that would make the sixties a turbulent, racing, dangerous, and provocative decade had not yet begun to blow full.

ACT I • *Scene I*

(It is 1957. Troy and Bono enter the yard, engaged in conversation. Troy is fifty-three years old, a large man with thick, heavy hands; it is this largeness that he strives to fill out and make an accommodation with. Together with his blackness, his largeness informs his sensibilities and the choices he has made in his life.)

(Of the two men, Bono is obviously the follower. His commitment to their friendship of thirty-odd years is rooted in his admiration of Troy's honesty, capacity for hard work, and his strength, which Bono seeks to emulate.)

(It is Friday night, payday, and the one night of the week the two men engage in a ritual of talk and drink. Troy is usually the most talkative and at times he can be crude and almost vulgar, though he is capable of rising to profound heights of expression. The men carry lunch buckets and wear or carry burlap aprons and are dressed in clothes suitable to their jobs as garbage collectors.)

BONO: Troy, you ought to stop that lying!
TROY: I ain't lying! The nigger had a watermelon this big.

(He indicates with his hands.)

Talking about . . ."What watermelon, Mr. Rand?" I liked to fell out! "What watermelon, Mr. Rand?". . . And it sitting there big as life.
BONO: What did Mr. Rand say?
TROY: Ain't said nothing. Figure if the nigger too dumb to know he carrying a watermelon, he wasn't gonna get much sense out of him. Trying to hide that great big old watermelon under his coat. Afraid to let the white man see him carry it home.

BONO: I'm like you . . . I ain't got no time for them kind of people.

TROY: Now what he look like getting mad cause he see the man from the union talking to Mr. Rand?

BONO: He come to me talking about . . ."Maxson gonna get us fired." I told him to get away from me with that. He walked away from me calling you a troublemaker. What Mr. Rand say?

TROY: Ain't said nothing. He told me to go down the Commissioner's office next Friday. They called me down there to see them.

BONO: Well, as long as you got your complaint filed, they can't fire you. That's what one of them white fellows tell me.

TROY: I ain't worried about them firing me. They gonna fire me cause I asked a question? That's all I did. I went to Mr. Rand and asked him, "Why? Why you got the white mens driving and the colored lifting?" Told him "what's the matter, don't I count? You think only white fellows got sense enough to drive a truck. That ain't no paper job! Hell, anybody can drive a truck. How come you got all whites driving and the colored lifting?" He told me "take it to the union." Well, hell, that's what I done! Now they wanna come up with this pack of lies.

BONO: I told Brownie if the man come and ask him any questions . . . just tell the truth! It ain't nothing but something they done trumped up on you cause you filed a complaint on them.

TROY: Brownie don't understand nothing. All I want them to do is change the job description. Give everybody a chance to drive the truck. Brownie can't see that. He ain't got that much sense.

BONO: How you figure he be making out with that gal be up at Taylors' all the time . . . that Alberta gal?

TROY: Same as you and me. Getting just as much as we is. Which is to say nothing.

BONO: It is, huh? I figure you doing a little better than me . . . and I ain't saying what I'm doing.

TROY: Aw, nigger, look here . . . I know you. If you had got anywhere near that gal, twenty minutes later you be looking to tell somebody. And the first one you gonna tell . . . that you gonna want to brag to . . . is gonna be me.

BONO: I ain't saying that. I see where you be eyeing her.

TROY: I eye all the women. I don't miss nothing. Don't never let nobody tell you Troy Maxson don't eye the women.

BONO: You been doing more than eyeing her. You done bought her a drink or two.

TROY: Hell yeah, I bought her a drink! What that mean? I bought you one, too. What that mean cause I buy her a drink? I'm just being polite.

BONO: It's all right to buy her one drink. That's what you call being polite. But when you wanna be buying two or three . . . that's what you call eyeing her.

TROY: Look here, as long as you known me . . . you ever known me to chase after women?

BONO: Hell yeah! Long as I done known you. You forgetting I knew you when.

TROY: Naw, I'm talking about since I been married to Rose?

BONO: Oh, not since you been married to Rose. Now, that's the truth, there. I can say that.

TROY: All right then! Case closed.

BONO: I see you be walking up around Alberta's house. You supposed to be at Taylors' and you be walking up around there.

TROY: What you watching where I'm walking for? I ain't watching after you.

BONO: I seen you walking around there more than once.

TROY: Hell, you liable to see me walking anywhere! That don't mean nothing cause you see me walking around there.

BONO: Where she come from anyway? She just kinda showed up one day.

TROY: Tallahassee. You can look at her and tell she one of them Florida gals. They got some big healthy women down there. Grow them right up out the ground. Got a little bit of Indian in her. Most of them niggers down in Florida got some Indian in them.

BONO: I don't know about that Indian part. But she damn sure big and healthy. Woman wear some big stockings. Got them great big old legs and hips as wide as the Mississippi River.

TROY: Legs don't mean nothing. You don't do nothing but push them out of the way. But them hips cushion the ride!

BONO: Troy, you ain't got no sense.

TROY: It's the truth! Like you riding on Goodyears!

(*Rose enters from the house. She is ten years younger than Troy, her devotion to him stems from her recognition of the possibilities of her life without him: a succession of abusive men and their babies, a life of partying and running the streets, the Church, or aloneness with its attendant pain and frustration. She recognizes Troy's spirit as a fine and illuminating one and she either ignores or forgives his faults, only some of which she recognizes. Though she doesn't drink, her presence is an integral part of the Friday night rituals. She alternates between the porch and the kitchen, where supper preparations are under way.*)

ROSE: What you all out here getting into?

TROY: What you worried about what we getting into for? This is men talk, woman.

ROSE: What I care what you all talking about? Bono, you gonna stay for supper?

BONO: No, I thank you, Rose. But Lucille say she cooking up a pot of pigfeet.

TROY: Pigfeet! Hell, I'm going home with you! Might even stay the night if you got some pigfeet. You got something in there to top them pigfeet, Rose?

ROSE: I'm cooking up some chicken. I got some chicken and collard greens.

TROY: Well, go on back in the house and let me and

Bono finish what we was talking about. This is men talk. I got some talk for you later. You know what kind of talk I mean. You go on and powder it up.

ROSE: Troy Maxson, don't you start that now!

TROY (*puts his arm around her*): Aw, woman . . . come here. Look here, Bono . . . when I met this woman . . . I got out that place, say, "Hitch up my pony, saddle up my mare . . . there's a woman out there for me somewhere. I looked here. Looked there. Saw Rose and latched on to her." I latched on to her and told her — I'm gonna tell you the truth — I told her, "Baby, I don't wanna marry, I just wanna be your man." Rose told me . . . tell him what you told me, Rose.

ROSE: I told him if he wasn't the marrying kind, then move out the way so the marrying kind could find me.

TROY: That's what she told me. "Nigger, you in my way. You blocking the view! Move out the way so I can find me a husband." I thought it over two or three days. Come back —

ROSE: Ain't no two or three days nothing. You was back the same night.

TROY: Come back, told her . . . "Okay, baby . . . but I'm gonna buy me a banty rooster and put him out there in the backyard . . . and when he see a stranger come, he'll flap his wings and crow . . ." Look here, Bono, I could watch the front door by myself . . . it was that back door I was worried about.

ROSE: Troy, you ought not talk like that. Troy ain't doing nothing but telling a lie.

TROY: Only thing is . . . when we first got married . . . forget the rooster . . . we ain't had no yard!

BONO: I hear you tell it. Me and Lucille was staying down there on Logan Street. Had two rooms with the outhouse in the back. I ain't mind the outhouse none. But when that goddamn wind blow through there in the winter . . . that's what I'm talking about! To this day I wonder why in the hell I ever stayed down there for six long years. But see, I didn't know I could do no better. I thought only white folks had inside toilets and things.

ROSE: There's a lot of people don't know they can do no better than they doing now. That's just something you got to learn. A lot of folks still shop at Bella's.

TROY: Ain't nothing wrong with shopping at Bella's. She got fresh food.

ROSE: I ain't said nothing about if she got fresh food. I'm talking about what she charge. She charge ten cents more than the A&P.

TROY: The A&P ain't never done nothing for me. I spends my money where I'm treated right. I go down to Bella, say, "I need a loaf of bread, I'll pay you Friday." She give it to me. What sense that make when I got money to go and spend it somewhere else and ignore the person who done right by me? That ain't in the Bible.

ROSE: We ain't talking about what's in the Bible. What sense it make to shop there when she overcharge?

TROY: You shop where you want to. I'll do my shopping where the people been good to me.

ROSE: Well, I don't think it's right for her to overcharge. That's all I was saying.

BONO: Look here . . . I got to get on. Lucille going be raising all kind of hell.

TROY: Where you going, nigger? We ain't finished this pint. Come here, finish this pint.

BONO: Well, hell, I am . . . if you ever turn the bottle loose.

TROY (*hands him the bottle*): The only thing I say about the A&P is I'm glad Cory got that job down there. Help him take care of his school clothes and things. Gabe done moved out and things getting tight around here. He got that job. . . . He can start to look out for himself.

ROSE: Cory done went and got recruited by a college football team.

TROY: I told that boy about that football stuff. The white man ain't gonna let him get nowhere with that football. I told him when he first come to me with it. Now you come telling me he done went and got more tied up in it. He ought to go and get recruited in how to fix cars or something where he can make a living.

ROSE: He ain't talking about making no living playing football. It's just something the boys in school do. They gonna send a recruiter by to talk to you. He'll tell you he ain't talking about making no living playing football. It's a honor to be recruited.

TROY: It ain't gonna get him nowhere. Bono'll tell you that.

BONO: If he be like you in the sports . . . he's gonna be all right. Ain't but two men ever played baseball as good as you. That's Babe Ruth and Josh Gibson.° Them's the only two men ever hit more home runs than you.

TROY: What it ever get me? Ain't got a pot to piss in or a window to throw it out of.

ROSE: Times have changed since you was playing baseball, Troy. That was before the war. Times have changed a lot since then.

TROY: How in hell they done changed?

ROSE: They got lots of colored boys playing ball now. Baseball and football.

BONO: You right about that, Rose. Times have changed, Troy. You just come along too early.

TROY: There ought not never have been no time called too early! Now you take that fellow . . . what's that fellow they had playing right field for the Yankees back then? You know who I'm talking about, Bono. Used to play right field for the Yankees.

ROSE: Selkirk?

TROY: Selkirk! That's it! Man batting .269, understand? .269. What kind of sense that make? I was hitting .432 with thirty-seven home runs! Man batting .269 and playing right field for the Yankees! I saw Josh Gibson's daughter yesterday. She walking around

Josh Gibson: (1911–1947), powerful black baseball player known in the 1930s as the Babe Ruth of the Negro leagues.

with raggedy shoes on her feet. Now I bet you Selkirk's daughter ain't walking around with raggedy shoes on her feet! I bet you that!

ROSE: They got a lot of colored baseball players now. Jackie Robinson was the first. Folks had to wait for Jackie Robinson.

TROY: I done seen a hundred niggers play baseball better than Jackie Robinson. Hell, I know some teams Jackie Robinson couldn't even make! What you talking about Jackie Robinson. Jackie Robinson wasn't nobody. I'm talking about if you could play ball then they ought to have let you play. Don't care what color you were. Come telling me I come along too early. If you could play . . . then they ought to have let you play.

(*Troy takes a long drink from the bottle.*)

ROSE: You gonna drink yourself to death. You don't need to be drinking like that.

TROY: Death ain't nothing. I done seen him. Done wrassled with him. You can't tell me nothing about death. Death ain't nothing but a fastball on the outside corner. And you know what I'll do to that! Lookee here, Bono . . . am I lying? You get one of them fastballs, about waist high, over the outside corner of the plate where you can get the meat of the bat on it . . . and good god! You can kiss it goodbye. Now, am I lying?

BONO: Naw, you telling the truth there. I seen you do it.

TROY: If I'm lying . . . that 450 feet worth of lying!

(*Pause.*)

That's all death is to me. A fastball on the outside corner.

ROSE: I don't know why you want to get on talking about death.

TROY: Ain't nothing wrong with talking about death. That's part of life. Everybody gonna die. You gonna die, I'm gonna die. Bono's gonna die. Hell, we all gonna die.

ROSE: But you ain't got to talk about it. I don't like to talk about it.

TROY: You the one brought it up. Me and Bono was talking about baseball . . . you tell me I'm gonna drink myself to death. Ain't that right, Bono? You know I don't drink this but one night out of the week. That's Friday night. I'm gonna drink just enough to where I can handle it. Then I cuts it loose. I leave it alone. So don't you worry about me drinking myself to death. 'Cause I ain't worried about Death. I done seen him. I done wrestled with him.

Look here, Bono . . . I looked up one day and Death was marching straight at me. Like Soldiers on Parade! The Army of Death was marching straight at me. The middle of July, 1941. It got real cold just like it be winter. It seem like Death himself reached out and touched me on the shoulder. He touch me just like I touch you. I got cold as ice and Death standing there grinning at me.

ROSE: Troy, why don't you hush that talk.

TROY: I say . . . What you want, Mr. Death? You be wanting me? You done brought your army to be getting me? I looked him dead in the eye. I wasn't fearing nothing. I was ready to tangle. Just like I'm ready to tangle now. The Bible say be ever vigilant. That's why I don't get but so drunk. I got to keep watch.

ROSE: Troy was right down there in Mercy Hospital. You remember he had pneumonia? Laying there with a fever talking plumb out of his head.

TROY: Death standing there staring at me . . . carrying that sickle in his hand. Finally he say, "You want bound over for another year?" See, just like that . . . "You want bound over for another year?" I told him, "Bound over hell! Let's settle this now!"

It seem like he kinda fell back when I said that, and all the cold went out of me. I reached down and grabbed that sickle and threw it just as far as I could throw it . . . and me and him commenced to wrestling.

We wrestled for three days and three nights. I can't say where I found the strength from. Every time it seemed like he was gonna get the best of me, I'd reach way down deep inside myself and find the strength to do him one better.

ROSE: Every time Troy tell that story he find different ways to tell it. Different things to make up about it.

TROY: I ain't making up nothing. I'm telling you the facts of what happened. I wrestled with Death for three days and three nights and I'm standing here to tell you about it.

(*Pause.*)

All right. At the end of the third night we done weakened each other to where we can't hardly move. Death stood up, throwed on his robe . . . had him a white robe with a hood on it. He throwed on that robe and went off to look for his sickle. Say, "I'll be back." Just like that. "I'll be back." I told him, say, "Yeah, but . . . you gonna have to find me!" I wasn't no fool. I wan't going looking for him. Death ain't nothing to play with. And I know he's gonna get me. I know I got to join his army . . . his camp followers. But as long as I keep my strength and see him coming . . . as long as I keep up my vigilance . . . he's gonna have to fight to get me. I ain't going easy.

BONO: Well, look here, since you got to keep up your vigilance . . . let me have the bottle.

TROY: Aw hell, I shouldn't have told you that part. I should have left out that part.

ROSE: Troy be talking that stuff and half the time don't even know what he be talking about.

TROY: Bono know me better than that.

BONO: That's right. I know you. I know you got some Uncle Remus° in your blood. You got more stories than the devil got sinners.

Uncle Remus: Black storyteller who recounts traditional African American tales in the book by Joel Chandler Harris.

TROY: Aw hell, I done seen him too! Done talked with the devil.

ROSE: Troy, don't nobody wanna be hearing all that stuff.

(*Lyons enters the yard from the street. Thirty-four years old, Troy's son by a previous marriage, he sports a neatly trimmed goatee, sport coat, white shirt, tieless and buttoned at the collar. Though he fancies himself a musician, he is more caught up in the rituals and "idea" of being a musician than in the actual practice of the music. He has come to borrow money from Troy, and while he knows he will be successful, he is uncertain as to what extent his lifestyle will be held up to scrutiny and ridicule.*)

LYONS: Hey, Pop.

TROY: What you come "Hey, Popping" me for?

LYONS: How you doing, Rose?

(*He kisses her.*)

Mr. Bono. How you doing?

BONO: Hey, Lyons . . . how you been?

TROY: He must have been doing all right. I ain't seen him around here last week.

ROSE: Troy, leave your boy alone. He come by to see you and you wanna start all that nonsense.

TROY: I ain't bothering Lyons.

(*Offers him the bottle.*)

Here . . . get you a drink. We got an understanding. I know why he come by to see me and he know I know.

LYONS: Come on, Pop . . . I just stopped by to say hi . . . see how you was doing.

TROY: You ain't stopped by yesterday.

ROSE You gonna stay for supper, Lyons? I got some chicken cooking in the oven.

LYONS: No, Rose . . . thanks. I was just in the neighborhood and thought I'd stop by for a minute.

TROY: You was in the neighborhood all right, nigger. You telling the truth there. You was in the neighborhood cause it's my payday.

LYONS: Well, hell, since you mentioned it . . . let me have ten dollars.

TROY: I'll be damned! I'll die and go to hell and play blackjack with the devil before I give you ten dollars.

BONO: That's what I wanna know about . . . that devil you done seen.

LYONS: What . . . Pop done seen the devil? You too much, Pops.

TROY: Yeah, I done seen him. Talked to him too!

ROSE: You ain't seen no devil. I done told you that man ain't had nothing to do with the devil. Anything you can't understand, you want to call it the devil.

TROY: Look here, Bono . . . I went down to see Hertzberger about some furniture. Got three rooms for two-ninety-eight. That what it say on the radio. "Three rooms . . . two-ninety-eight." Even made up a little song about it. Go down there . . . man tell me I can't get no credit. I'm working every day and can't get no credit. What to do? I got an empty house with some raggedy furniture in it. Cory ain't got no bed. He's sleeping on a pile of rags on the floor. Working every day and can't get no credit. Come back here — Rose'll tell you — madder than hell. Sit down . . . try to figure what I'm gonna do. Come a knock on the door. Ain't been living here but three days. Who know I'm here? Open the door . . . devil standing there bigger than life. White fellow . . . got on good clothes and everything. Standing there with a clipboard in his hand. I ain't had to say nothing. First words come out of his mouth was . . . "I understand you need some furniture and can't get no credit." I liked to fell over. He say, "I'll give you all the credit you want, but you got to pay the interest on it." I told him, "Give me three rooms worth and charge whatever you want." Next day a truck pulled up here and two men unloaded them three rooms. Man what drove the truck give me a book. Say send ten dollars, first of every month to the address in the book and everything will be all right. Say if I miss a payment the devil was coming back and it'll be hell to pay. That was fifteen years ago. To this day . . . the first of the month I send my ten dollars, Rose'll tell you.

ROSE: Troy lying.

TROY: I ain't never seen that man since. Now you tell me who else that could have been but the devil? I ain't sold my soul or nothing like that, you understand. Naw, I wouldn't have truck with the devil about nothing like that. I got my furniture and pays my ten dollars the first of the month just like clockwork.

BONO: How long you say you been paying this ten dollars a month?

TROY: Fifteen years!

BONO: Hell, ain't you finished paying for it yet? How much the man done charged you.

TROY: Ah hell, I done paid for it. I done paid for it ten times over! The fact is I'm scared to stop paying it.

ROSE: Troy lying. We got that furniture from Mr. Glickman. He ain't paying no ten dollars a month to nobody.

TROY: Aw hell, woman. Bono know I ain't that big a fool.

LYONS: I was just getting ready to say . . . I know where there's a bridge for sale.

TROY: Look here, I'll tell you this . . . it don't matter to me if he was the devil. It don't matter if the devil give credit. Somebody has got to give it.

ROSE: It ought to matter. You going around talking about having truck with the devil . . . God's the one you gonna have to answer to. He's the one gonna be at the Judgment.

LYONS: Yeah, well, look here, Pop . . . let me have that ten dollars. I'll give it back to you. Bonnie got a job working at the hospital.

TROY: What I tell you, Bono? The only time I see this nigger is when he wants something. That's the only time I see him.

LYONS: Come on, Pop, Mr. Bono don't want to hear all that. Let me have the ten dollars. I told you Bonnie working.

TROY: What that mean to me? "Bonnie working." I don't care if she working. Go ask her for the ten dollars if she working. Talking about "Bonnie working." Why ain't you working?

LYONS: Aw, Pop, you know I can't find no decent job. Where am I gonna get a job at? You know I can't get no job.

TROY: I told you I know some people down there. I can get you on the rubbish if you want to work. I told you that the last time you came by here asking me for something.

LYONS: Naw, Pop . . . thanks. That ain't for me. I don't wanna be carrying nobody's rubbish. I don't wanna be punching nobody's time clock.

TROY: What's the matter, you too good to carry people's rubbish? Where you think that ten dollars you talking about come from? I'm just supposed to haul people's rubbish and give my money to you cause you too lazy to work. You too lazy to work and wanna know why you ain't got what I got.

ROSE: What hospital Bonnie working at? Mercy?

LYONS: She's down at Passavant working in the laundry.

TROY: I ain't got nothing as it is. I give you that ten dollars and I got to eat beans the rest of the week. Naw . . . you ain't getting no ten dollars here.

LYONS: You ain't got to be eating no beans. I don't know why you wanna say that.

TROY: I ain't got no extra money. Gabe done moved over to Miss Pearl's paying her the rent and things done got tight around here. I can't afford to be giving you every payday.

LYONS: I ain't asked you to give me nothing. I asked you to loan me ten dollars. I know you got ten dollars.

TROY: Yeah, I got it. You know why I got it? Cause I don't throw my money away out there in the streets. You living the fast life . . . wanna be a musician . . . running around in them clubs and things . . . then, you learn to take care of yourself. You ain't gonna find me going and asking nobody for nothing. I done spent too many years without.

LYONS: You and me is two different people, Pop.

TROY: I done learned my mistake and learned to do what's right by it. You still trying to get something for nothing. Life don't owe you nothing. You owe it to yourself. Ask Bono. He'll tell you I'm right.

LYONS: You got your way of dealing with the world . . . I got mine. The only thing that matters to me is the music.

TROY: Yeah, I can see that! It don't matter how you gonna eat . . . where your next dollar is coming from. You telling the truth there.

LYONS: I know I got to eat. But I got to live too. I need something that gonna help me to get out of the bed in the morning. Make me feel like I belong in the world. I don't bother nobody. I just stay with my music cause that's the only way I can find to live in the world. Otherwise there ain't no telling what I might do. Now I don't come criticizing you and how you live. I just come by to ask you for ten dollars. I don't wanna hear all that about how I live.

TROY: Boy, your mamma did a hell of a job raising you.

LYONS: You can't change me, Pop. I'm thirty-four years old. If you wanted to change me, you should have been there when I was growing up. I come by to see you . . . ask for ten dollars and you want to talk about how I was raised. You don't know nothing about how I was raised.

ROSE: Let the boy have ten dollars, Troy.

TROY (*to Lyons*): What the hell you looking at me for? I ain't got no ten dollars. You know what I do with my money.

(*To Rose.*)

Give him ten dollars if you want him to have it.

ROSE: I will. Just as soon as you turn it loose.

TROY (*handing Rose the money*): There it is. Seventy-six dollars and forty-two cents. You see this, Bono? Now, I ain't gonna get but six of that back.

ROSE: You ought to stop telling that lie. Here, Lyons. (*She hands him the money.*)

LYONS: Thanks, Rose. Look . . . I got to run . . . I'll see you later.

TROY: Wait a minute. You gonna say, "thanks, Rose" and ain't gonna look to see where she got that ten dollars from? See how they do me, Bono?

LYONS: I know she got it from you, Pop. Thanks. I'll give it back to you.

TROY: There he go telling another lie. Time I see that ten dollars . . . he'll be owing me thirty more.

LYONS: See you, Mr. Bono.

BONO: Take care, Lyons!

LYONS: Thanks, Pop. I'll see you again.

(*Lyons exits the yard.*)

TROY: I don't know why he don't go and get him a decent job and take care of that woman he got.

BONO: He'll be all right, Troy. The boy is still young.

TROY: The *boy* is thirty-four years old.

ROSE: Let's not get off into all that.

BONO: Look here . . . I got to be going. I got to be getting on. Lucille gonna be waiting.

TROY (*puts his arm around Rose*): See this woman, Bono? I love this woman. I love this woman so much it hurts. I love her so much . . . I done run out of ways of loving her. So I got to go back to basics. Don't you come by my house Monday morning talking about time to go to work . . . 'cause I'm still gonna be stroking!

ROSE: Troy! Stop it now!

BONO: I ain't paying him no mind, Rose. That ain't nothing but gin-talk. Go on, Troy. I'll see you Monday.

TROY: Don't you come by my house, nigger! I done told you what I'm gonna be doing.

(*The lights go down to black.*)

Scene II

(*The lights come up on Rose hanging up clothes. She hums and sings softly to herself. It is the following morning.*)

ROSE (*sings*): Jesus, be a fence all around me every day
    Jesus, I want you to protect me as I travel on my
       way.
    Jesus, be a fence all around me every day.

(*Troy enters from the house.*)

    Jesus, I want you to protect me
    As I travel on my way.
    (*To Troy.*) 'Morning. You ready for breakfast? I can
fix it soon as I finish hanging up these clothes.
TROY: I got the coffee on. That'll be all right. I'll just
drink some of that this morning.
ROSE: That 651 hit yesterday. That's the second time
this month. Miss Pearl hit for a dollar . . . seem like
those that need the least always get lucky. Poor folks
can't get nothing.
TROY: Them numbers don't know nobody. I don't know
why you fool with them. You and Lyons both.
ROSE: It's something to do.
TROY: You ain't doing nothing but throwing your
money away.
ROSE: Troy, you know I don't play foolishly. I just play a
nickel here and a nickel there.
TROY: That's two nickels you done thrown away.
ROSE: Now I hit sometimes . . . that makes up for it. It
always comes in handy when I do hit. I don't hear
you complaining then.
TROY: I ain't complaining now. I just say it's foolish. Trying to guess out of six hundred ways which way the
number gonna come. If I had all the money niggers,
these Negroes, throw away on numbers for one
week — just one week — I'd be a rich man.
ROSE: Well, you wishing and calling it foolish ain't
gonna stop folks from playing numbers. That's one
thing for sure. Besides . . . some good things come
from playing numbers. Look where Pope done
bought him that restaurant off of numbers.
TROY: I can't stand niggers like that. Man ain't had two
dimes to rub together. He walking around with his
shoes all run over bumming money for cigarettes. All
right. Got lucky there and hit the numbers . . .
ROSE: Troy, I know all about it.
TROY: Had good sense, I'll say that for him. He ain't
throwed his money away. I seen niggers hit the
numbers and go through two thousand dollars in
four days. Man bought him that restaurant down
there . . . fixed it up real nice . . . and then didn't
want nobody to come in it! A Negro go in there and
can't get no kind of service. I seen a white fellow
come in there and order a bowl of stew. Pope picked
all the meat out the pot for him. Man ain't had nothing but a bowl of meat! Negro come behind him and
ain't got nothing but the potatoes and carrots. Talk-

ing about what numbers do for people, you picked a
wrong example. Ain't done nothing but make a
worser fool out of him than he was before.
ROSE: Troy, you ought to stop worrying about what
happened at work yesterday.
TROY: I ain't worried. Just told me to be down there at
the Commissioner's office on Friday. Everybody
think they gonna fire me. I ain't worried about them
firing me. You ain't got to worry about that.

(*Pause.*)

    Where's Cory? Cory in the house? (*Calls.*) Cory?
ROSE: He gone out.
TROY: Out, huh? He gone out 'cause he know I want
him to help me with this fence. I know how he is.
That boy scared of work.

(*Gabriel enters. He comes halfway down the alley and,
hearing Troy's voice, stops.*)

TROY (*continues*): He ain't done a lick of work in his life.
ROSE: He had to go to football practice. Coach wanted
them to get in a little extra practice before the season
start.
TROY: I got his practice . . . running out of here before
he get his chores done.
ROSE: Troy, what is wrong with you this morning?
Don't nothing set right with you. Go on back in there
and go to bed . . . get up on the other side.
TROY: Why something got to be wrong with me? I ain't
said nothing wrong with me.
ROSE: You got something to say about everything. First
it's the numbers . . . then it's the way the man runs
his restaurant . . . then you done got on Cory. What's
it gonna be next? Take a look up there and see if the
weather suits you . . . or is it gonna be how you
gonna put up the fence with the clothes hanging in
the yard.
TROY: You hit the nail on the head then.
ROSE: I know you like I know the back of my hand. Go
on in there and get you some coffee . . . see if that
straighten you up. 'Cause you ain't right this morning.

(*Troy starts into the house and sees Gabriel. Gabriel
starts singing. Troy's brother, he is seven years younger
than Troy. Injured in World War II, he has a metal plate
in his head. He carries an old trumpet tied around his
waist and believes with every fiber of his being that he is
the Archangel Gabriel. He carries a chipped basket with
an assortment of discarded fruits and vegetables he has
picked up in the strip district and which he attempts to
sell.*)

GABRIEL (*singing*): Yes, ma'am, I got plums
    You ask me how I sell them
    Oh ten cents apiece
    Three for a quarter
    Come and buy now
    'Cause I'm here today
    And tomorrow I'll be gone

(*Gabriel enters.*)

Hey, Rose!

ROSE: How you doing, Gabe?

GABRIEL: There's Troy . . . Hey, Troy!

TROY: Hey, Gabe.

(*Exit into kitchen.*)

ROSE (*to Gabriel*): What you got there?

GABRIEL: You know what I got, Rose. I got fruits and vegetables.

ROSE (*looking in basket*): Where's all these plums you talking about?

GABRIEL: I ain't got no plums today, Rose. I was just singing that. Have some tomorrow. Put me in a big order for plums. Have enough plums tomorrow for St. Peter and everybody.

(*Troy reenters from kitchen, crosses to steps.*)
(*To Rose.*)

Troy's mad at me.

TROY: I ain't mad at you. What I got to be mad at you about? You ain't done nothing to me.

GABRIEL: I just moved over to Miss Pearl's to keep out from in your way. I ain't mean no harm by it.

TROY: Who said anything about that? I ain't said anything about that.

GABRIEL: You ain't mad at me, is you?

TROY: Naw . . . I ain't mad at you, Gabe. If I was mad at you I'd tell you about it.

GABRIEL: Got me two rooms. In the basement. Got my own door too. Wanna see my key?

(*He holds up a key.*)

That's my own key! Ain't nobody else got a key like that. That's my key! My two rooms!

TROY: Well, that's good, Gabe. You got your own key . . . that's good.

ROSE: You hungry, Gabe? I was just fixing to cook Troy his breakfast.

GABRIEL: I'll take some biscuits. You got some biscuits? Did you know when I was in heaven . . . every morning me and St. Peter would sit down by the gate and eat some big fat biscuits? Oh, yeah! We had us a good time. We'd sit there and eat us them biscuits and then St. Peter would go off to sleep and tell me to wake him up when it's time to open the gates for the judgment.

ROSE: Well, come on . . . I'll make up a batch of biscuits.

(*Rose exits into the house.*)

GABRIEL: Troy . . . St. Peter got your name in the book. I seen it. It say . . . Troy Maxson. I say . . . I know him! He got the same name like what I got. That's my brother!

TROY: How many times you gonna tell me that, Gabe?

GABRIEL: Ain't got my name in the book. Don't have to have my name. I done died and went to heaven. He got your name though. One morning St. Peter was looking at his book . . . marking it up for the judgment . . . and he let me see your name. Got it in there under M. Got Rose's name . . . I ain't seen it like I seen yours . . . but I know it's in there. He got a great big book. Got everybody's name what was ever been born. That's what he told me. But I seen your name. Seen it with my own eyes.

TROY: Go on in the house there. Rose going to fix you something to eat.

GABRIEL: Oh, I ain't hungry. I done had breakfast with Aunt Jemimah. She come by and cooked me up a whole mess of flapjacks. Remember how we used to eat them flapjacks?

TROY: Go on in the house and get you something to eat now.

GABRIEL: I got to go sell my plums. I done sold some tomatoes. Got me two quarters. Wanna see?

(*He shows Troy his quarters.*)

I'm gonna save them and buy me a new horn so St. Peter can hear me when it's time to open the gates.

(*Gabriel stops suddenly. Listens.*)

Hear that? That's the hellhounds. I got to chase them out of here. Go on get out of here! Get out!

(*Gabriel exits singing.*)

Better get ready for the judgment
Better get ready for the judgment
My Lord is coming down

(*Rose enters from the house.*)

TROY: He gone off somewhere.

GABRIEL (*offstage*): Better get ready for the judgment
Better get ready for the judgment morning
Better get ready for the judgment
My God is coming down

ROSE: He ain't eating right. Miss Pearl say she can't get him to eat nothing.

TROY: What you want me to do about it, Rose? I done did everything I can for the man. I can't make him get well. Man got half his head blown away . . . what you expect?

ROSE: Seem like something ought to be done to help him.

TROY: Man don't bother nobody. He just mixed up from that metal plate he got in his head. Ain't no sense for him to go back into the hospital.

ROSE: Least he be eating right. They can help him take care of himself.

TROY: Don't nobody wanna be locked up, Rose. What you wanna lock him up for? Man go over there and fight the war . . . messin' around with them Japs, get half his head blown off . . . and they give him a lousy three thousand dollars. And I had to swoop down on that.

ROSE: Is you fixing to go into that again?

TROY: That's the only way I got a roof over my head . . . cause of that metal plate.

ROSE: Ain't no sense you blaming yourself for nothing. Gabe wasn't in no condition to manage that money. You done what was right by him. Can't nobody say you ain't done what was right by him. Look how long you took care of him . . . till he wanted to have his own place and moved over there with Miss Pearl.

TROY: That ain't what I'm saying, woman! I'm just stating the facts. If my brother didn't have that metal plate in his head . . . I wouldn't have a pot to piss in or a window to throw it out of. And I'm fifty-three years old. Now see if you can understand that!

(*Troy gets up from the porch and starts to exit the yard.*)

ROSE: Where you going off to? You been running out of here every Saturday for weeks. I thought you was gonna work on this fence?

TROY: I'm gonna walk down to Taylors'. Listen to the ball game. I'll be back in a bit. I'll work on it when I get back.

(*He exits the yard. The lights go to black.*)

Scene III

(*The lights come up on the yard. It is four hours later. Rose is taking down the clothes from the line. Cory enters carrying his football equipment.*)

ROSE: Your daddy like to had a fit with you running out of here this morning without doing your chores.

CORY: I told you I had to go to practice.

ROSE: He say you were supposed to help him with this fence.

CORY: He been saying that the last four or five Saturdays, and then he don't never do nothing but go down to Taylors'. Did you tell him about the recruiter?

ROSE: Yeah, I told him.

CORY: What he say?

ROSE: He ain't said nothing too much. You get in there and get started on your chores before he gets back. Go on and scrub down them steps before he gets back here hollering and carrying on.

CORY: I'm hungry. What you got to eat, Mama?

ROSE: Go on and get started on your chores. I got some meat loaf in there. Go on and make you a sandwich . . . and don't leave no mess in there.

(*Cory exits into the house. Rose continues to take down the clothes. Troy enters the yard and sneaks up and grabs her from behind.*)

Troy! Go on, now. You liked to scared me to death. What was the score of the game? Lucille had me on the phone and I couldn't keep up with it.

TROY: What I care about the game? Come here, woman. (*He tries to kiss her.*)

ROSE: I thought you went down Taylors' to listen to the game. Go on, Troy! You supposed to be putting up this fence.

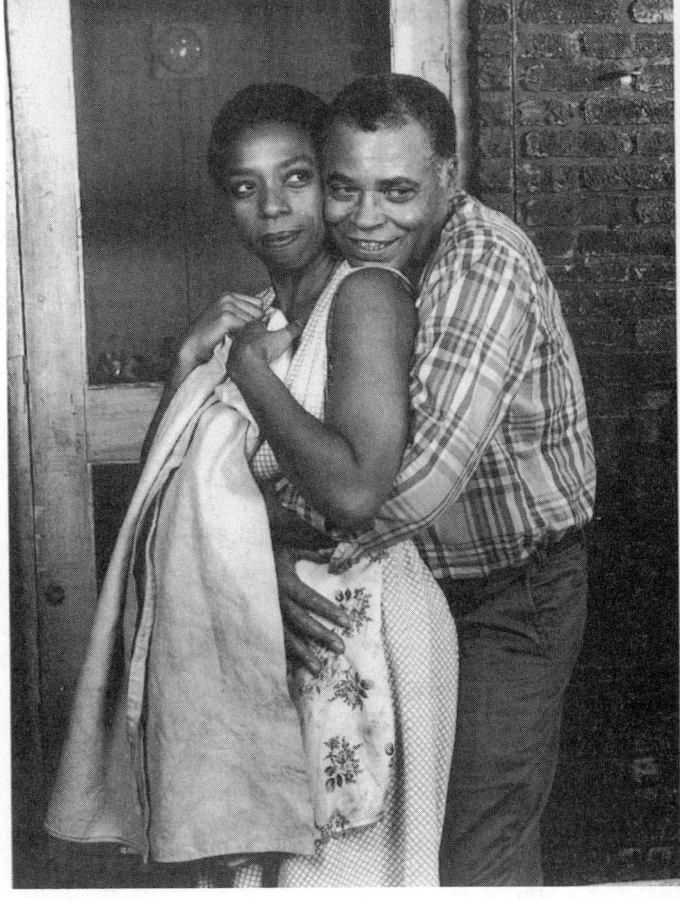

TROY (*attempting to kiss her again*): I'll put it up when I finish with what is at hand.

ROSE: Go on, Troy. I ain't studying you.

TROY (*chasing after her*): I'm studying you . . . fixing to do my homework!

ROSE: Troy, you better leave me alone.

TROY: Where's Cory? That boy brought his butt home yet?

ROSE: He's in the house doing his chores.

TROY (*calling*): Cory! Get your butt out here, boy!

(*Rose exits into the house with the laundry. Troy goes over to the pile of wood, picks up a board, and starts sawing. Cory enters from the house.*)

TROY: You just now coming in here from leaving this morning?

CORY: Yeah, I had to go to football practice.

TROY: Yeah, what?

CORY: Yessir.

TROY: I ain't but two seconds off you noway. The garbage sitting in there overflowing . . . you ain't done none of your chores . . . and you come in here talking about "Yeah."

CORY: I was just getting ready to do my chores now, Pop . . .

TROY: Your first chore is to help me with this fence on Saturday. Everything else come after that. Now get that saw and cut them boards.

(Cory takes the saw and begins cutting the boards. Troy continues working. There is a long pause.)

CORY: Hey, Pop . . . why don't you buy a TV?

TROY: What I want with a TV? What I want one of them for?

CORY: Everybody got one. Earl, Ba Bra . . . Jesse!

TROY: I ain't asked you who had one. I say what I want with one?

CORY: So you can watch it. They got lots of things on TV. Baseball games and everything. We could watch the World Series.

TROY: Yeah . . . and how much this TV cost?

CORY: I don't know. They got them on sale for around two hundred dollars.

TROY: Two hundred dollars, huh?

CORY: That ain't that much, Pop.

TROY: Naw, it's just two hundred dollars. See that roof you got over your head at night? Let me tell you something about that roof. It's been over ten years since that roof was last tarred. See now . . . the snow come this winter and sit up there on that roof like it is . . . and it's gonna seep inside. It's just gonna be a little bit . . . ain't gonna hardly notice it. Then the next thing you know, it's gonna be leaking all over the house. Then the wood rot from all that water and you gonna need a whole new roof. Now, how much you think it cost to get that roof tarred?

CORY: I don't know.

TROY: Two hundred and sixty-four dollars . . . cash money. While you thinking about a TV, I got to be thinking about the roof . . . and whatever else go

ABOVE LEFT: Lynn Thigpen and James Earl Jones in the 1987 production of *Fences.* ABOVE: James Earl Jones as Troy Maxson in *Fences.* RIGHT: Jones and Courtney Vance as his son Cory.

wrong around here. Now if you had two hundred dollars, what would you do . . . fix the roof or buy a TV?

CORY: I'd buy a TV. Then when the roof started to leak . . . when it needed fixing . . . I'd fix it.

TROY: Where you gonna get the money from? You done spent it for a TV. You gonna sit up and watch the water run all over your brand new TV.

CORY: Aw, Pop. You got money. I know you do.

TROY: Where I got it at, huh?

CORY: You got it in the bank.

TROY: You wanna see my bankbook? You wanna see that seventy-three dollars and twenty-two cents I got sitting up in there.

CORY: You ain't got to pay for it all at one time. You can put a down payment on it and carry it on home with you.

TROY: Not me. I ain't gonna owe nobody nothing if I can help it. Miss a payment and they come and snatch it right out your house. Then what you got? Now, soon as I get two hundred dollars clear, then I'll buy a TV. Right now, as soon as I get two hundred and sixty-four dollars, I'm gonna have this roof tarred.

CORY: Aw . . . Pop!

TROY: You go on and get you two hundred dollars and buy one if ya want it. I got better things to do with my money.

CORY: I can't get no two hundred dollars. I ain't never seen two hundred dollars.

TROY: I'll tell you what . . . you get you a hundred dollars and I'll put the other hundred with it.

CORY: All right, I'm gonna show you.

TROY: You gonna show me how you can cut them boards right now.

(*Cory begins to cut the boards. There is a long pause.*)

CORY: The Pirates won today. That makes five in a row.

TROY: I ain't thinking about the Pirates. Got an all-white team. Got that boy . . . that Puerto Rican boy . . . Clemente. Don't even half-play him. That boy could be something if they give him a chance. Play him one day and sit him on the bench the next.

CORY: He gets a lot of chances to play.

TROY: I'm talking about playing regular. Playing every day so you can get your timing. That's what I'm talking about.

CORY: They got some white guys on the team that don't play every day. You can't play everybody at the same time.

TROY: If they got a white fellow sitting on the bench . . . you can bet your last dollar he can't play! The colored guy got to be twice as good before he get on the team. That's why I don't want you to get all tied up in them sports. Man on the team and what it get him? They got colored on the team and don't use them. Same as not having them. All them teams the same.

CORY: The Braves got Hank Aaron and Wes Covington. Hank Aaron hit two home runs today. That makes forty-three.

TROY: Hank Aaron ain't nobody. That's what you supposed to do. That's how you supposed to play the game. Ain't nothing to it. It's just a matter of timing . . . getting the right follow-through. Hell, I can hit forty-three home runs right now!

CORY: Not off no major-league pitching, you couldn't.

TROY: We had better pitching in the Negro leagues. I hit seven home runs off of Satchel Paige.° You can't get no better than that!

CORY: Sandy Koufax. He's leading the league in strike-outs.

TROY: I ain't thinking of no Sandy Koufax.

CORY: You got Warren Spahn and Lew Burdette. I bet you couldn't hit no home runs off of Warren Spahn.

TROY: I'm through with it now. You go on and cut them boards.

(*Pause.*)

Your mama tell me you done got recruited by a college football team? Is that right?

CORY: Yeah. Coach Zellman say the recruiter gonna be coming by to talk to you. Get you to sign the permission papers.

TROY: I thought you supposed to be working down there at the A&P. Ain't you suppose to be working down there after school?

CORY: Mr. Stawicki say he gonna hold my job for me until after the football season. Say starting next week I can work weekends.

TROY: I thought we had an understanding about this football stuff? You suppose to keep up with your chores and hold that job down at the A&P. Ain't been around here all day on a Saturday. Ain't none of your chores done . . . and now you telling me you done quit your job.

CORY: I'm gonna be working weekends.

TROY: You damn right you are! And ain't no need for nobody coming around here to talk to me about signing nothing.

CORY: Hey, Pop . . . you can't do that. He's coming all the way from North Carolina.

TROY: I don't care where he coming from. The white man ain't gonna let you get nowhere with that football noway. You go on and get your book-learning so you can work yourself up in that A&P or learn how to fix cars or build houses or something, get you a trade. That way you have something can't nobody take away from you. You go on and learn how to put your hands to some good use. Besides hauling people's garbage.

CORY: I get good grades, Pop. That's why the recruiter wants to talk with you. You got to keep up your grades to get recruited. This way I'll be going to college. I'll get a chance . . .

TROY: First you gonna get your butt down there to the A&P and get your job back.

Satchel Paige: (1906–1982), legendary black pitcher in the Negro leagues.

CORY: Mr. Stawicki done already hired somebody else 'cause I told him I was playing football.

TROY: You a bigger fool than I thought . . . to let somebody take away your job so you can play some football. Where you gonna get your money to take out your girlfriend and whatnot? What kind of foolishness is that to let somebody take away your job?

CORY: I'm still gonna be working weekends.

TROY: Naw . . . naw. You getting your butt out of here and finding you another job.

CORY: Come on, Pop! I got to practice. I can't work after school and play football too. The team needs me. That's what Coach Zellman say . . .

TROY: I don't care what nobody else say. I'm the boss . . . you understand? I'm the boss around here. I do the only saying what counts.

CORY: Come on, Pop!

TROY: I asked you . . . did you understand?

CORY: Yeah . . .

TROY: What?!

CORY: Yessir.

TROY: You go on down there to that A&P and see if you can get your job back. If you can't do both . . . then you quit the football team. You've got to take the crookeds with the straights.

CORY: Yessir.

(*Pause.*)

Can I ask you a question?

TROY: What the hell you wanna ask me? Mr. Stawicki the one you got the questions for.

CORY: How come you ain't never liked me?

TROY: Liked you? Who the hell say I got to like you? What law is there say I got to like you? Wanna stand up in my face and ask a damn fool-ass question like that. Talking about liking somebody. Come here, boy, when I talk to you.

(*Cory comes over to where Troy is working. He stands slouched over and Troy shoves him on his shoulder.*)

Straighten up, goddammit! I asked you a question . . . what law is there say I got to like you?

CORY: None.

TROY: Well, all right then! Don't you eat every day?

(*Pause.*)

Answer me when I talk to you! Don't you eat every day?

CORY: Yeah.

TROY: Nigger, as long as you in my house, you put that sir on the end of it when you talk to me!

CORY: Yes . . . sir.

TROY: You eat every day.

CORY: Yessir!

TROY: Got a roof over your head.

CORY: Yessir!

TROY: Got clothes on your back.

CORY: Yessir.

TROY: Why you think that is?

CORY: Cause of you.

TROY: Ah, hell I know it's 'cause of me . . . but why do you think that is?

CORY (*hesitant*): Cause you like me.

TROY: Like you? I go out of here every morning . . . bust my butt . . . putting up with them crackers° every day . . . cause I like you? You about the biggest fool I ever saw.

(*Pause.*)

It's my job. It's my responsibility! You understand that? A man got to take care of his family. You live in my house . . . sleep you behind on my bedclothes . . . fill you belly up with my food . . . cause you my son. You my flesh and blood. Not 'cause I like you! Cause it's my duty to take care of you. I owe a responsibility to you! Let's get this straight right here . . . before it go along any further . . . I ain't got to like you. Mr. Rand don't give me my money come payday cause he likes me. He gives me cause he owe me. I done give you everything I had to give you. I gave you your life! Me and your mama worked that out between us. And liking your black ass wasn't part of the bargain. Don't you try and go through life worrying about if somebody like you or not. You best be making sure they doing right by you. You understand what I'm saying, boy?

CORY: Yessir.

TROY: Then get the hell out of my face, and get on down to that A&P.

(*Rose has been standing behind the screen door for much of the scene. She enters as Cory exits.*)

ROSE: Why don't you let the boy go ahead and play football, Troy? Ain't no harm in that. He's just trying to be like you with the sports.

TROY: I don't want him to be like me! I want him to move as far away from my life as he can get. You the only decent thing that ever happened to me. I wish him that. But I don't wish him a thing else from my life. I decided seventeen years ago that boy wasn't getting involved in no sports. Not after what they did to me in the sports.

ROSE: Troy, why don't you admit you was too old to play in the major leagues? For once . . . why don't you admit that?

TROY: What do you mean too old? Don't come telling me I was too old. I just wasn't the right color. Hell, I'm fifty-three years old and can do better than Selkirk's .269 right now!

ROSE: How's was you gonna play ball when you were over forty? Sometimes I can't get no sense out of you.

TROY: I got good sense, woman. I got sense enough not to let my boy get hurt over playing no sports. You been mothering that boy too much. Worried about if people like him.

crackers: White people (derogatory).

ROSE: Everything that boy do . . . he do for you. He wants you to say "Good job, son." That's all.

TROY: Rose, I ain't got time for that. He's alive. He's healthy. He's got to make his own way. I made mine. Ain't nobody gonna hold his hand when he get out there in that world.

ROSE: Times have changed from when you was young, Troy. People change. The world's changing around you and you can't even see it.

TROY (slow, methodical): Woman . . . I do the best I can do. I come in here every Friday. I carry a sack of potatoes and a bucket of lard. You all line up at the door with your hands out. I give you the lint from my pockets. I give you my sweat and my blood. I ain't got no tears. I done spent them. We go upstairs in that room at night . . . and I fall down on you and try to blast a hole into forever. I get up Monday morning . . . find my lunch on the table. I go out. Make my way. Find my strength to carry me through to the next Friday.

(Pause.)

That's all I got, Rose. That's all I got to give. I can't give nothing else.

(Troy exits into the house. The lights go down to black.)

Scene IV

(It is Friday. Two weeks later. Cory starts out of the house with his football equipment. The phone rings.)

CORY (calling): I got it!

(He answers the phone and stands in the screen door talking.)

Hello? Hey, Jesse. Naw . . . I was just getting ready to leave now.

ROSE (calling): Cory!

CORY: I told you, man, them spikes is all tore up. You can use them if you want, but they ain't no good. Earl got some spikes.

ROSE (calling): Cory!

CORY (calling to Rose): Mam? I'm talking to Jesse.

(Into phone.)

When she say that? (Pause.) Aw, you lying, man. I'm gonna tell her you said that.

ROSE (calling): Cory, don't you go nowhere!

CORY: I got to go to the game, Ma!

(Into the phone.)

Yeah, hey, look, I'll talk to you later. Yeah, I'll meet you over Earl's house. Later. Bye, Ma.

(Cory exits the house and starts out the yard.)

ROSE: Cory, where you going off to? You got that stuff all pulled out and thrown all over your room.

CORY (in the yard): I was looking for my spikes. Jesse wanted to borrow my spikes.

ROSE: Get up there and get that cleaned up before your daddy get back in here.

CORY: I got to go to the game! I'll clean it up when I get back.

(Cory exits.)

ROSE: That's all he need to do is see that room all messed up.

(Rose exits into the house. Troy and Bono enter the yard. Troy is dressed in clothes other than his work clothes.)

BONO: He told him the same thing he told you. Take it to the union.

TROY: Brownie ain't got that much sense. Man wasn't thinking about nothing. He wait until I confront them on it . . . then he wanna come crying seniority.

(Calls.)

Hey, Rose!

BONO: I wish I could have seen Mr. Rand's face when he told you.

TROY: He couldn't get it out of his mouth! Liked to bit his tongue! When they called me down there to the Commissioner's office . . . he thought they was gonna fire me. Like everybody else.

BONO: I didn't think they was gonna fire you. I thought they was gonna put you on the warning paper.

TROY: Hey, Rose!

(To Bono.)

Yeah, Mr. Rand like to bit his tongue.

(Troy breaks the seal on the bottle, takes a drink, and hands it to Bono.)

BONO: I see you run right down to Taylors' and told that Alberta gal.

TROY (calling): Hey, Rose! (To Bono.) I told everybody. Hey, Rose! I went down there to cash my check.

ROSE (entering from the house): Hush all that hollering, man! I know you out here. What they say down there at the Commissioner's office?

TROY: You supposed to come when I call you, woman. Bono'll tell you that.

(To Bono.)

Don't Lucille come when you call her?

ROSE: Man, hush your mouth. I ain't no dog . . . talk about "come when you call me."

TROY (puts his arm around Rose): You hear this Bono? I had me an old dog used to get uppity like that. You say, "C'mere, Blue!" . . . and he just lay there and look at you. End up getting a stick and chasing him away trying to make him come.

ROSE: I ain't studying you and your dog. I remember you used to sing that old song.

TROY (*he sings*): Hear it ring! Hear it ring! I had a dog his name was Blue.

ROSE: Don't nobody wanna hear you sing that old song.

TROY (*sings*): You know Blue was mighty true.

ROSE: Used to have Cory running around here singing that song.

BONO: Hell, I remember that song myself.

TROY (*sings*): You know Blue was a good old dog.
Blue treed a possum in a hollow log.
That was my daddy's song. My daddy made up that song.

ROSE: I don't care who made it up. Don't nobody wanna hear you sing it.

TROY (*makes a song like calling a dog*): Come here, woman.

ROSE: You come in here carrying on, I reckon they ain't fired you. What they say down there at the Commissioner's office?

TROY: Look here, Rose . . . Mr. Rand called me into his office today when I got back from talking to them people down there . . . it come from up top . . . he called me in and told me they was making me a driver.

ROSE: Troy, you kidding!

TROY: No I ain't. Ask Bono.

ROSE: Well, that's great, Troy. Now you don't have to hassle them people no more.

(*Lyons enters from the street.*)

TROY: Aw hell, I wasn't looking to see you today. I thought you was in jail. Got it all over the front page of the *Courier* about them raiding Sefus' place . . . where you be hanging out with all them thugs.

LYONS: Hey, Pop . . . that ain't got nothing to do with me. I don't go down there gambling. I go down there to sit in with the band. I ain't got nothing to do with the gambling part. They got some good music down there.

TROY: They got some rogues . . . is what they got.

LYONS: How you been, Mr. Bono? Hi, Rose.

BONO: I see where you playing down at the Crawford Grill tonight.

ROSE: How come you ain't brought Bonnie like I told you. You should have brought Bonnie with you, she ain't been over in a month of Sundays.

LYONS: I was just in the neighborhood . . . thought I'd stop by.

TROY: Here he come . . .

BONO: Your daddy got a promotion on the rubbish. He's gonna be the first colored driver. Ain't got to do nothing but sit up there and read the paper like them white fellows.

LYONS: Hey, Pop . . . if you knew how to read you'd be all right.

BONO: Naw . . . naw . . . you mean if the nigger knew how to *drive* he'd be all right. Been fighting with them people about driving and ain't even got a license. Mr. Rand know you ain't got no driver's license?

TROY: Driving ain't nothing. All you do is point the truck where you want it to go. Driving ain't nothing.

BONO: Do Mr. Rand know you ain't got no driver's license? That's what I'm talking about. I ain't asked if driving was easy. I asked if Mr. Rand know you ain't got no driver's license.

TROY: He ain't got to know. The man ain't got to know my business. Time he find out, I have two or three driver's licenses.

LYONS (*going into his pocket*): Say, look here, Pop . . .

TROY: I knew it was coming. Didn't I tell you, Bono? I know what kind of "Look here, Pop" that was. The nigger fixing to ask me for some money. It's Friday night. It's my payday. All them rogues down there on the avenue . . . the ones that ain't in jail . . . and Lyons is hopping in his shoes to get down there with them.

LYONS: See, Pop . . . if you give somebody else a chance to talk sometime, you'd see that I was fixing to pay you back your ten dollars like I told you. Here . . . I told you I'd pay you when Bonnie got paid.

TROY: Naw . . . you go ahead and keep that ten dollars. Put it in the bank. The next time you feel like you wanna come by here and ask me for something . . . you go on down there and get that.

LYONS: Here's your ten dollars, Pop. I told you I don't want you to give me nothing. I just wanted to borrow ten dollars.

TROY: Naw . . . you go on and keep that for the next time you want to ask me.

LYONS: Come on, Pop . . . here go your ten dollars.

ROSE: Why don't you go on and let the boy pay you back, Troy?

LYONS: Here you go, Rose. If you don't take it I'm gonna have to hear about it for the next six months.

(*He hands her the money.*)

ROSE: You can hand yours over here too, Troy.

TROY: You see this, Bono. You see how they do me.

BONO: Yeah, Lucille do me the same way.

(*Gabriel is heard singing offstage. He enters.*)

GABRIEL: Better get ready for the Judgment! Better get ready for . . . Hey! . . . Hey! . . . There's Troy's boy!

LYONS: How are you doing, Uncle Gabe?

GABRIEL: Lyons . . . The King of the Jungle! Rose . . . hey, Rose. Got a flower for you.

(*He takes a rose from his pocket.*)

Picked it myself. That's the same rose like you is!

ROSE: That's right nice of you, Gabe.

LYONS: What you been doing, Uncle Gabe?

GABRIEL: Oh, I been chasing hellhounds and waiting on the time to tell St. Peter to open the gates.

LYONS: You been chasing hellhounds, huh? Well . . . you doing the right thing, Uncle Gabe. Somebody got to chase them.

GABRIEL: Oh, yeah . . . I know it. The devil's strong.

The devil ain't no pushover. Hellhounds snipping at everybody's heels. But I got my trumpet waiting on the judgment time.

LYONS: Waiting on the Battle of Armageddon, huh?

GABRIEL: Ain't gonna be too much of a battle when God get to waving that Judgment sword. But the people's gonna have a hell of a time trying to get into heaven if them gates ain't open.

LYONS (*putting his arm around Gabriel*): You hear this, Pop. Uncle Gabe, you all right!

GABRIEL (*laughing with Lyons*): Lyons! King of the Jungle.

ROSE: You gonna stay for supper, Gabe. Want me to fix you a plate?

GABRIEL: I'll take a sandwich, Rose. Don't want no plate. Just wanna eat with my hands. I'll take a sandwich.

ROSE: How about you, Lyons? You staying? Got some short ribs cooking.

LYONS: Naw, I won't eat nothing till after we finished playing.

(*Pause.*)

You ought to come down and listen to me play, Pop.

TROY: I don't like that Chinese music. All that noise.

ROSE: Go on in the house and wash up, Gabe . . . I'll fix you a sandwich.

GABRIEL (*to Lyons, as he exits*): Troy's mad at me.

LYONS: What you mad at Uncle Gabe for, Pop.

ROSE: He thinks Troy's mad at him cause he moved over to Miss Pearl's.

TROY: I ain't mad at the man. He can live where he want to live at.

LYONS: What he move over there for? Miss Pearl don't like nobody.

ROSE: She don't mind him none. She treats him real nice. She just don't allow all that singing.

TROY: She don't mind that rent he be paying . . . that's what she don't mind.

ROSE: Troy, I ain't going through that with you no more. He's over there cause he want to have his own place. He can come and go as he please.

TROY: Hell, he could come and go as he please here. I wasn't stopping him. I ain't put no rules on him.

ROSE: It ain't the same thing, Troy. And you know it.

(*Gabriel comes to the door.*)

Now, that's the last I wanna hear about that. I don't wanna hear nothing else about Gabe and Miss Pearl. And next week . . .

GABRIEL: I'm ready for my sandwich, Rose.

ROSE: And next week . . . when that recruiter come from that school . . . I want you to sign that paper and go on and let Cory play football. Then that'll be the last I have to hear about that.

TROY (*to Rose as she exits into the house*): I ain't thinking about Cory nothing.

LYONS: What . . . Cory got recruited? What school he going to?

TROY: That boy walking around here smelling his piss . . . thinking he's grown. Thinking he's gonna do what he want, irrespective of what I say. Look here, Bono . . . I left the Commissioner's office and went down to the A&P . . . that boy ain't working down there. He lying to me. Telling me he got his job back . . . telling me he working weekends . . . telling me he working after school . . . Mr. Stawicki tell me he ain't working down there at all!

LYONS: Cory just growing up. He's just busting at the seams trying to fill out your shoes.

TROY: I don't care what he's doing. When he get to the point where he wanna disobey me . . . then it's time for him to move on. Bono'll tell you that. I bet he ain't never disobeyed his daddy without paying the consequences.

BONO: I ain't never had a chance. My daddy came on through . . . but I ain't never knew him to see him . . . or what he had on his mind or where he went. Just moving on through. Searching out the New Land. That's what the old folks used to call it. See a fellow moving around from place to place . . . woman to woman . . . called it searching out the New Land. I can't say if he ever found it. I come along, didn't want no kids. Didn't know if I was gonna be in one place long enough to fix on them right as their daddy. I figured I was going searching too. As it turned out I been hooked up with Lucille near about as long as your daddy been with Rose. Going on sixteen years.

TROY: Sometimes I wish I hadn't known my daddy. He ain't cared nothing about no kids. A kid to him wasn't nothing. All he wanted was for you to learn how to walk so he could start you to working. When it come time for eating . . . he ate first. If there was anything left over, that's what you got. Man would sit down and eat two chickens and give you the wing.

LYONS: You ought to stop that, Pop. Everybody feed their kids. No matter how hard times is . . . everybody care about their kids. Make sure they have something to eat.

TROY: The only thing my daddy cared about was getting them bales of cotton in to Mr. Lubin. That's the only thing that mattered to him. Sometimes I used to wonder why he was living. Wonder why the devil hadn't come and got him. "Get them bales of cotton in to Mr. Lubin" and find out he owe him money . . .

LYONS: He should have just went on and left when he saw he couldn't get nowhere. That's what I would have done.

TROY: How he gonna leave with eleven kids? And where he gonna go? He ain't knew how to do nothing but farm. No, he was trapped and I think he knew it. But I'll say this for him . . . he felt a responsibility toward us. Maybe he ain't treated us the way I felt he should have . . . but without that responsibility he could have walked off and left us . . . made his own way.

BONO: A lot of them did. Back in those days what you

talking about . . . they walk out their front door and just take on down one road or another and keep on walking.

LYONS: There you go! That's what I'm talking about.

BONO: Just keep on walking till you come to something else. Ain't you never heard of nobody having the walking blues? Well, that's what you call it when you just take off like that.

TROY: My daddy ain't had them walking blues! What you talking about? He stayed right there with his family. But he was just as evil as he could be. My mama couldn't stand him. Couldn't stand that evilness. She run off when I was about eight. She sneaked off one night after he had gone to sleep. Told me she was coming back for me. I ain't never seen her no more. All his women run off and left him. He wasn't good for nobody.

When my turn come to head out, I was fourteen and got to sniffing around Joe Canewell's daughter. Had us an old mule we called Greyboy. My daddy sent me out to do some plowing and I tied up Greyboy and went to fooling around with Joe Canewell's daughter. We done found us a nice little spot, got real cozy with each other. She about thirteen and we done figured we was grown anyway . . . so we down there enjoying ourselves . . . ain't thinking about nothing. We didn't know Greyboy had got loose and wandered back to the house and my daddy was looking for me. We down there by the creek enjoying ourselves when my daddy come up on us. Surprised us. He had them leather straps off the mule and commenced to whupping me like there was no tomorrow. I jumped up, mad and embarrassed. I was scared of my daddy. When he commenced to whupping on me . . . quite naturally I run to get out of the way.

(*Pause.*)

Now I thought he was mad cause I ain't done my work. But I see where he was chasing me off so he could have the gal for himself. When I see what the matter of it was, I lost all fear of my daddy. Right there is where I become a man . . . at fourteen years of age.

(*Pause.*)

Now it was my turn to run him off. I picked up them same reins that he had used on me. I picked up them reins and commenced to whupping on him. The gal jumped up and run off . . . and when my daddy turned to face me, I could see why the devil had never come to get him . . . cause he was the devil himself. I don't know what happened. When I woke up, I was laying right there by the creek, and Blue . . . this old dog we had . . . was licking my face. I thought I was blind. I couldn't see nothing. Both my eyes were swollen shut. I layed there and cried. I didn't know what I was gonna do. The only thing I knew was the time had come for me to leave my daddy's house.

And right there the world suddenly got big. And it was a long time before I could cut it down to where I could handle it.

Part of that cutting down was when I got to the place where I could feel him kicking in my blood and knew that the only thing that separated us was the matter of a few years.

(*Gabriel enters from the house with a sandwich.*)

LYONS: What you got there, Uncle Gabe?

GABRIEL: Got me a ham sandwich. Rose gave me a ham sandwich.

TROY: I don't know what happened to him. I done lost touch with everybody except Gabriel. But I hope he's dead. I hope he found some peace.

LYONS: That's a heavy story, Pop. I didn't know you left home when you was fourteen.

TROY: And didn't know nothing. The only part of the world I knew was the forty-two acres of Mr. Lubin's land. That's all I knew about life.

LYONS: Fourteen's kinda young to be out on your own. (*Phone rings.*) I don't even think I was ready to be out on my own at fourteen. I don't know what I would have done.

TROY: I got up from the creek and walked on down to Mobile. I was through with farming. Figured I could do better in the city. So I walked the two hundred miles to Mobile.

LYONS: Wait a minute . . . you ain't walked no two hundred miles, Pop. Ain't nobody gonna walk no two hundred miles. You talking about some walking there.

BONO: That's the only way you got anywhere back in them days.

LYONS: Shhh. Damn if I wouldn't have hitched a ride with somebody!

TROY: Who you gonna hitch it with? They ain't had no cars and things like they got now. We talking about 1918.

ROSE (*entering*): What you all out here getting into?

TROY (*to Rose*): I'm telling Lyons how good he got it. He don't know nothing about this I'm talking.

ROSE: Lyons, that was Bonnie on the phone. She say you supposed to pick her up.

LYONS: Yeah, okay, Rose.

TROY: I walked on down to Mobile and hitched up with some of them fellows that was heading this way. Got up here and found out . . . not only couldn't you get a job . . . you couldn't find no place to live. I thought I was in freedom. Shhh. Colored folks living down there on the riverbanks in whatever kind of shelter they could find for themselves. Right down there under the Brady Street Bridge. Living in shacks made of sticks and tarpaper. Messed around there and went from bad to worse. Started stealing. First it was food. Then I figured, hell, if I steal money I can buy me some food. Buy me some shoes too! One thing led to another. Met your mama. I was young and anxious to be a man. Met your mama and had you. What I do that for? Now I got to worry about feeding you and her. Got to steal three times as much. Went out one day looking for somebody to rob . . . that's what I was, a robber. I'll tell you the truth. I'm ashamed of it today. But it's the truth. Went to rob this fellow . . . pulled out my knife . . . and he pulled out a gun. Shot me in the chest. It felt just like somebody had taken a hot branding iron and laid it on me. When he shot me I jumped at him with my knife. They told me I killed him and they put me in the penitentiary and locked me up for fifteen years. That's where I met Bono. That's where I learned how to play baseball. Got out that place and your mama had taken you and went on to make life without me. Fifteen years was a long time for her to wait. But that fifteen years cured me of that robbing stuff. Rose'll tell you. She asked me when I met her if I had gotten all that foolishness out of my system. And I told her, "Baby, it's you and baseball all what count with me." You hear me, Bono? I meant it too. She say "Which one comes first?" I told her, "Baby, ain't no doubt it's baseball . . . but you stick and get old with me and we'll both outlive this baseball." Am I right, Rose? And it's true.

ROSE: Man, hush your mouth. You ain't said no such thing. Talking about, "Baby, you know you'll always be number one with me." That's what you was talking.

TROY: You hear that, Bono. That's why I love her.

BONO: Rose'll keep you straight. You get off the track, she'll straighten you up.

ROSE: Lyons, you better get on up and get Bonnie. She waiting on you.

LYONS (gets up to go): Hey, Pop, why don't you come on down to the Grill and hear me play?

TROY: I ain't going down there. I'm too old to be sitting around in them clubs.

BONO: You got to be good to play down at the Grill.

LYONS: Come on, Pop . . .

TROY: I got to get up in the morning.

LYONS: You ain't got to stay long.

TROY: Naw, I'm gonna get my supper and go on to bed.

LYONS: Well, I got to go. I'll see you again.

TROY: Don't you come around my house on my payday.

ROSE: Pick up the phone and let somebody know you coming. And bring Bonnie with you. You know I'm always glad to see her.

LYONS: Yeah, I'll do that, Rose. You take care now. See you, Pop. See you, Mr. Bono. See you, Uncle Gabe.

GABRIEL: Lyons! King of the Jungle!

(Lyons exits.)

TROY: Is supper ready, woman? Me and you got some business to take care of. I'm gonna tear it up too.

ROSE: Troy, I done told you now!

TROY (puts his arm around Bono): Aw hell, woman . . .

this is Bono. Bono like family. I done known this nigger since . . . how long I done know you?

BONO: It's been a long time.

TROY: I done known this nigger since Skippy was a pup. Me and him done been through some times.

BONO: You sure right about that.

TROY: Hell, I done know him longer than I known you. And we still standing shoulder to shoulder. Hey, look here, Bono . . . a man can't ask for no more than that.

(Drinks to him.)

I love you, nigger.

BONO: Hell, I love you too . . . but I got to get home see my woman. You got yours in hand. I got to go get mine.

(Bono starts to exit as Cory enters the yard, dressed in his football uniform. He gives Troy a hard, uncompromising look.)

CORY: What you do that for, Pop?

(He throws his helmet down in the direction of Troy.)

ROSE: What's the matter? Cory . . . what's the matter?

CORY: Papa done went up to the school and told Coach Zellman I can't play football no more. Wouldn't even let me play the game. Told him to tell the recruiter not to come.

ROSE: Troy . . .

TROY: What you Troying me for. Yeah, I did it. And the boy know why I did it.

CORY: Why you wanna do that to me? That was the one chance I had.

ROSE: Ain't nothing wrong with Cory playing football, Troy.

TROY: The boy lied to me. I told the nigger if he wanna play football . . . to keep up his chores and hold down that job at the A&P. That was the conditions. Stopped down there to see Mr. Stawicki . . .

CORY: I can't work after school during the football season, Pop! I tried to tell you that Mr. Stawicki's holding my job for me. You don't never want to listen to nobody. And then you wanna go and do this to me!

TROY: I ain't done nothing to you. You done it to yourself.

CORY: Just cause you didn't have a chance! You just scared I'm gonna be better than you, that's all.

TROY: Come here.

ROSE: Troy . . .

(Cory reluctantly crosses over to Troy.)

TROY: All right! See. You done made a mistake.

CORY: I didn't even do nothing!

TROY: I'm gonna tell you what your mistake was. See . . . you swung at the ball and didn't hit it. That's strike one. See, you in the batter's box now. You swung and you missed. That's strike one. Don't you strike out!

(Lights fade to black.)

ACT II • *Scene I*

(*The following morning. Cory is at the tree hitting the ball with the bat. He tries to mimic Troy, but his swing is awkward, less sure. Rose enters from the house.*)

ROSE: Cory, I want you to help me with this cupboard.

CORY: I ain't quitting the team. I don't care what Poppa say.

ROSE: I'll talk to him when he gets back. He had to go see about your Uncle Gabe. The police done arrested him. Say he was disturbing the peace. He'll be back directly. Come on in here and help me clean out the top of this cupboard.

(*Cory exits into the house. Rose sees Troy and Bono coming down the alley.*)

Troy . . . what they say down there?

TROY: Ain't said nothing. I give them fifty dollars and they let him go. I'll talk to you about it. Where's Cory.

ROSE: He's in there helping me clean out these cupboards.

TROY: Tell him to get his butt out here.

(*Troy and Bono go over to the pile of wood. Bono picks up the saw and begins sawing.*)

TROY (*to Bono*): All they want is the money. That makes six or seven times I done went down there and got him. See me coming they stick out their *hands*.

BONO: Yeah. I know what you mean. That's all they care about . . . that money. They don't care about what's right.

(*Pause.*)

Nigger, why you got to go and get some hard wood? You ain't doing nothing but building a little old fence. Get you some soft pine wood. That's all you need.

TROY: I know what I'm doing. This is outside wood. You put pine wood inside the house. Pine wood is inside wood. This here is outside wood. Now you tell me where the fence is gonna be?

BONO: You don't need this wood. You can put it up with pine wood and it'll stand as long as you gonna be here looking at it.

TROY: How you know how long I'm gonna be here, nigger? Hell, I might just live forever. Live longer than old man Horsely.

BONO: That's what Magee used to say.

TROY: Magee's a damn fool. Now you tell me who you ever heard of gonna pull their own teeth with a pair of rusty pliers.

BONO: The old folks . . . my granddaddy used to pull his teeth with pliers. They ain't had no dentists for the colored folks back then.

TROY: Get clean pliers! You understand? Clean pliers! Sterilize them! Besides we ain't living back then. All Magee had to do was walk over to Doc Goldblum's.

BONO: I see where you and that Tallahassee gal . . . that Alberta . . . I see where you all done got tight.

TROY: What you mean "got tight"?

BONO: I see where you be laughing and joking with her all the time.

TROY: I laughs and jokes with all of them, Bono. You know me.

BONO: That ain't the kind of laughing and joking I'm talking about.

(*Cory enters from the house.*)

CORY: How you doing, Mr. Bono?

TROY: Cory? Get that saw from Bono and cut some wood. He talking about the wood's too hard to cut. Stand back there, Jim, and let that young boy show you how it's done.

BONO: He's sure welcome to it.

(*Cory takes the saw and begins to cut the wood.*)

Whew-e-e! Look at that. Big old strong boy. Look like Joe Louis. Hell, must be getting old the way I'm watching that boy whip through that wood.

CORY: I don't see why Mama want a fence around the yard noways.

TROY: Damn if I know either. What the hell she keeping out with it? She ain't got nothing nobody want.

BONO: Some people build fences to keep people out . . . and other people build fences to keep people in. Rose wants to hold on to you all. She loves you.

TROY: Hell, nigger, I don't need nobody to tell me my wife loves me, Cory . . . go on in the house and see if you can find that other saw.

CORY: Where's it at?

TROY: I said find it! Look for it till you find it!

(*Cory exits into the house.*)

What's that supposed to mean? Wanna keep us in?

BONO: Troy . . . I done known you seem like damn near my whole life. You and Rose both. I done know both of you all for a long time. I remember when you met Rose. When you was hitting them baseball out the park. A lot of them old gals was after you then. You had the pick of the litter. When you picked Rose, I was happy for you. That was the first time I knew you had any sense. I said . . . My man Troy knows what he's doing . . . I'm gonna follow this nigger . . . he might take me somewhere. I been following you too. I done learned a whole heap of things about life watching you. I done learned how to tell where the shit lies. How to tell it from the alfalfa. You done learned me a lot of things. You showed me how to not make the same mistakes . . . to take life as it comes along and keep putting one foot in front of the other.

(*Pause.*)

Rose a good woman, Troy.

TROY: Hell, nigger, I know she a good woman. I been

married to her for eighteen years. What you got on your mind, Bono?

BONO: I just say she a good woman. Just like I say anything. I ain't got to have nothing on my mind.

TROY: You just gonna say she a good woman and leave it hanging out there like that? Why you telling me she a good woman?

BONO: She loves you, Troy. Rose loves you.

TROY: You saying I don't measure up. That's what you trying to say. I don't measure up cause I'm seeing this other gal. I know what you trying to say.

BONO: I know what Rose means to you, Troy. I'm just trying to say I don't want to see you mess up.

TROY: Yeah, I appreciate that, Bono. If you was messing around on Lucille I'd be telling you the same thing.

BONO: Well, that's all I got to say. I just say that because I love you both.

TROY: Hell, you know me . . . I wasn't out there looking for nothing. You can't find a better woman than Rose. I know that. But seems like this woman just stuck onto me where I can't shake her loose. I done wrestled with it, tried to throw her off me . . . but she just stuck on tighter. Now she's stuck on for good.

BONO: You's in control . . . that's what you tell me all the time. You responsible for what you do.

TROY: I ain't ducking the responsibility of it. As long as it sets right in my heart . . . then I'm okay. Cause that's all I listen to. It'll tell me right from wrong every time. And I ain't talking about doing Rose no bad turn. I love Rose. She done carried me a long ways and I love and respect her for that.

BONO: I know you do. That's why I don't want to see you hurt her. But what you gonna do when she find out? What you got then? If you try and juggle both of them . . . sooner or later you gonna drop one of them. That's common sense.

TROY: Yeah, I hear what you saying, Bono. I been trying to figure a way to work it out.

BONO: Work it out right, Troy. I don't want to be getting all up between you and Rose's business . . . but work it so it come out right.

TROY: Ah hell, I get all up between you and Lucille's business. When you gonna get that woman that refrigerator she been wanting? Don't tell me you ain't got no money now. I know who your banker is. Mellon don't need that money bad as Lucille want that refrigerator. I'll tell you that.

BONO: Tell you what I'll do . . . when you finish building this fence for Rose . . . I'll buy Lucille that refrigerator.

TROY: You done stuck your foot in your mouth now!

(*Troy grabs up a board and begins to saw. Bono starts to walk out the yard.*)

Hey, nigger . . . where you going?

BONO: I'm going home. I know you don't expect me to help you now. I'm protecting my money. I wanna see you put that fence up by yourself. That's what I want to see. You'll be here another six months without me.

TROY: Nigger, you ain't right.

BONO: When it comes to my money . . . I'm right as fireworks on the Fourth of July.

TROY: All right, we gonna see now. You better get out your bankbook.

(*Bono exits, and Troy continues to work. Rose enters from the house.*)

ROSE: What they say down there? What's happening with Gabe?

TROY: I went down there and got him out. Cost me fifty dollars. Say he was disturbing the peace. Judge set up a hearing for him in three weeks. Say to show cause why he shouldn't be recommitted.

ROSE: What was he doing that cause them to arrest him?

TROY: Some kids was teasing him and he run them off home. Say he was howling and carrying on. Some folks seen him and called the police. That's all it was.

ROSE: Well, what's you say? What'd you tell the judge?

TROY: Told him I'd look after him. It didn't make no sense to recommit the man. He stuck out his big greasy palm and told me to give him fifty dollars and take him on home.

ROSE: Where's he at now? Where'd he go off to?

TROY: He's gone on about his business. He don't need nobody to hold his hand.

ROSE: Well, I don't know. Seem like that would be the best place for him if they did put him into the hospital. I know what you're gonna say. But that's what I think would be best.

TROY: The man done had his life ruined fighting for what? And they wanna take and lock him up. Let him be free. He don't bother nobody.

ROSE: Well, everybody got their own way of looking at it I guess. Come on and get your lunch. I got a bowl of lima beans and some cornbread in the oven. Come on get something to eat. Ain't no sense you fretting over Gabe.

(*Rose turns to go into the house.*)

TROY: Rose . . . got something to tell you.

ROSE: Well, come on . . . wait till I get this food on the table.

TROY: Rose!

(*She stops and turns around.*)

I don't know how to say this.

(*Pause.*)

I can't explain it none. It just sort of grows on you till it gets out of hand. It starts out like a little bush . . . and the next thing you know it's a whole forest.

ROSE: Troy . . . what is you talking about?

TROY: I'm talking, woman, let me talk. I'm trying to find a way to tell you . . . I'm gonna be a daddy. I'm gonna be somebody's daddy.

ROSE: Troy . . . you're not telling me this? You're gonna be . . . what?

TROY: Rose . . . now . . . see . . .

ROSE: You telling me you gonna be somebody's daddy? You telling your *wife* this?

(*Gabriel enters from the street. He carries a rose in his hand.*)

GABRIEL: Hey, Troy! Hey, Rose!

ROSE: I have to wait eighteen years to hear something like this.

GABRIEL: Hey, Rose . . . I got a flower for you.

(*He hands it to her.*)

That's a rose. Same rose like you is.

ROSE: Thanks, Gabe.

GABRIEL: Troy, you ain't mad at me is you? Them bad mens come and put me away. You ain't mad at me is you?

TROY: Naw, Gabe, I ain't mad at you.

ROSE: Eighteen years and you wanna come with this.

GABRIEL (*takes a quarter out of his pocket*): See what I got? Got a brand new quarter.

TROY: Rose . . . it's just . . .

ROSE: Ain't nothing you can say, Troy. Ain't no way of explaining that.

GABRIEL: Fellow that give me this quarter had a whole mess of them. I'm gonna keep this quarter till it stop shining.

ROSE: Gabe, go on in the house there. I got some watermelon in the frigidaire. Go on and get you a piece.

GABRIEL: Say, Rose . . . you know I was chasing hellhounds and them bad mens come and get me and take me away. Troy helped me. He come down there and told them they better let me go before he beat them up. Yeah, he did!

ROSE: You go on and get you a piece of watermelon, Gabe. Them bad mens is gone now.

GABRIEL: Okay, Rose . . . gonna get me some watermelon. The kind with the stripes on it.

(*Gabriel exits into the house.*)

ROSE: Why, Troy? Why? After all these years to come dragging this in to me now. It don't make no sense at your age. I could have expected this ten or fifteen years ago, but not now.

TROY: Age ain't got nothing to do with it, Rose.

ROSE: I done tried to be everything a wife should be. Everything a wife could be. Been married eighteen years and I got to live to see the day you tell me you been seeing another woman and done fathered a child by her. And you know I ain't never wanted no half nothing in my family. My whole family is half. Everybody got different fathers and mothers . . . my two sisters and my brother. Can't hardly tell who's who. Can't never sit down and talk about Papa and Mama. It's your papa and your mama and my papa and my mama . . .

TROY: Rose . . . stop it now.

ROSE: I ain't never wanted that for none of my children. And now you wanna drag your behind in here and tell me something like this.

TROY: You ought to know. It's time for you to know.

ROSE: Well, I don't want to know, goddamn it!

TROY: I can't just make it go away. It's done now. I can't wish the circumstance of the thing away.

ROSE: And you don't want to either. Maybe you want to wish me and my boy away. Maybe that's what you want? Well, you can't wish us away. I've got eighteen years of my life invested in you. You ought to have stayed upstairs in my bed where you belong.

TROY: Rose . . . now listen to me . . . we can get a handle on this thing. We can talk this out . . . come to an understanding.

ROSE: All of a sudden it's "we." Where was "we" at when you was down there rolling around with some godforsaken woman? "We" should have come to an understanding before you started making a damn fool of yourself. You're a day late and a dollar short when it comes to an understanding with me.

TROY: It's just . . . She gives me a different idea . . . a different understanding about myself. I can step out of this house and get away from the pressures and problems . . . be a different man. I ain't got to wonder how I'm gonna pay the bills or get the roof fixed. I can just be a part of myself that I ain't never been.

ROSE: What I want to know . . . is do you plan to continue seeing her. That's all you can say to me.

TROY: I can sit up in her house and laugh. Do you understand what I'm saying. I can laugh out loud . . . and it feels good. It reaches all the way down to the bottom of my shoes.

(*Pause.*)

Rose, I can't give that up.

ROSE: Maybe you ought to go on and stay down there with her . . . if she's a better woman than me.

TROY: It ain't about nobody being a better woman or nothing. Rose, you ain't the blame. A man couldn't ask for no woman to be a better wife than you've been. I'm responsible for it. I done locked myself into a pattern trying to take care of you all that I forgot about myself.

ROSE: What the hell was I there for? That was my job, not somebody else's.

TROY: Rose, I done tried all my life to live decent . . . to live a clean . . . hard . . . useful life. I tried to be a good husband to you. In every way I knew how. Maybe I come into the world backwards, I don't know. But . . . you born with two strikes on you before you come to the plate. You got to guard it closely . . . always looking for the curve ball on the inside corner. You can't afford to let none get past you. You can't afford a call strike. If you going down . . . you going down swinging. Everything lined up against you. What you gonna do. I fooled them, Rose. I bunted. When I found you and Cory and a halfway decent job . . . I was safe. Couldn't nothing touch me. I wasn't gonna strike out no more. I wasn't going back to the penitentiary. I wasn't gonna lay in the streets with a bottle of wine. I was safe. I had me a family. A job. I wasn't gonna get that last strike. I was on first looking for one of them boys to knock me in. To get me home.

ROSE: You should have stayed in my bed, Troy.

TROY: Then when I saw that gal . . . she firmed up my backbone. And I got to thinking that if I tried . . . I just might be able to steal second. Do you understand after eighteen years I wanted to steal second.

ROSE: You should have held me tight. You should have grabbed me and held on.

TROY: I stood on first base for eighteen years and I thought . . . well, goddamn it . . . go on for it!

ROSE: We're not talking about baseball! We're talking about you going off to lay in bed with another woman . . . and then bring it home to me. That's what we're talking about. We ain't talking about no baseball.

TROY: Rose, you're not listening to me. I'm trying the best I can to explain it to you. It's not easy for me to admit that I been standing in the same place for eighteen years.

ROSE: I been standing with you! I been right here with you, Troy. I got a life too. I gave eighteen years of my life to stand in the same spot with you. Don't you think I ever wanted other things? Don't you think I had dreams and hopes? What about my life? What about me. Don't you think it ever crossed my mind to want to know other men? That I wanted to lay up somewhere and forget about my responsibilities? That I wanted someone to make me laugh so I could feel good? You not the only one who's got wants and needs. But I held on to you, Troy. I took all my feelings, my wants and needs, my dreams . . . and I buried them inside you. I planted a seed and watched and prayed over it. I planted myself inside you and waited to bloom. And it didn't take me no eighteen years to find out the soil was hard and rocky and it wasn't never gonna bloom.

But I held on to you, Troy. I held you tighter. You was my husband. I owed you everything I had. Every part of me I could find to give you. And upstairs in that room . . . with the darkness falling in on me . . . I gave everything I had to try and erase the doubt that you wasn't the finest man in the world. And wherever you was going . . . I wanted to be there with you. Cause you was my husband. Cause that's the only way I was gonna survive as your wife. You always talking about what you give . . . and what you don't have to give. But you take too. You take . . . and don't even know nobody's giving!

(*Rose turns to exit into the house; Troy grabs her arm.*)

TROY: You say I take and don't give!

ROSE: Troy! You're hurting me!

TROY: You say I take and don't give.

ROSE: Troy . . . you're hurting my arm! Let go!

TROY: I done give you everything I got. Don't you tell that lie on me.

ROSE: Troy!

TROY: Don't you tell that lie on me!

(*Cory enters from the house.*)

CORY: Mama!

ROSE: Troy. You're hurting me.

TROY: Don't you tell me about no taking and giving.

(*Cory comes up behind Troy and grabs him. Troy, surprised, is thrown off balance just as Cory throws a glancing blow that catches him on the chest and knocks him down. Troy is stunned, as is Cory.*)

ROSE: Troy. Troy. No!

(*Troy gets to his feet and starts at Cory.*)

Troy . . . no. Please! Troy!

(*Rose pulls on Troy to hold him back. Troy stops himself.*)

TROY (*to Cory*): All right. That's strike two. You stay away from around me, boy. Don't you strike out. You living with a full count. Don't you strike out.

(*Troy exits out the yard as the lights go down.*)

Scene II

(*It is six months later, early afternoon. Troy enters from the house and starts to exit the yard. Rose enters from the house.*)

ROSE: Troy, I want to talk to you.

TROY: All of a sudden, after all this time, you want to talk to me, huh? You ain't wanted to talk to me for months. You ain't wanted to talk to me last night. You ain't wanted no part of me then. What you wanna talk to me about now?

ROSE: Tomorrow's Friday.

TROY: I know what day tomorrow is. You think I don't know tomorrow's Friday? My whole life I ain't done nothing but look to see Friday coming and you got to tell me it's Friday.

ROSE: I want to know if you're coming home.

TROY: I always come home, Rose. You know that. There ain't never been a night I ain't come home.

ROSE: That ain't what I mean . . . and you know it. I want to know if you're coming straight home after work.

TROY: I figure I'd cash my check . . . hang out at Taylors' with the boys . . . maybe play a game of checkers . . .

ROSE: Troy, I can't live like this. I won't live like this. You livin' on borrowed time with me. It's been going on six months now you ain't been coming home.

TROY: I be here every night. Every night of the year. That's 365 days.

ROSE: I want you to come home tomorrow after work.

TROY: Rose . . . I don't mess up my pay. You know that now. I take my pay and I give it to you. I don't have no money but what you give me back. I just want to have a little time to myself . . . a little time to enjoy life.

ROSE: What about me? When's my time to enjoy life?

TROY: I don't know what to tell you, Rose. I'm doing the best I can.

ROSE: You ain't been home from work but time enough to change your clothes and run out . . . and you wanna call that the best you can do?

TROY: I'm going over to the hospital to see Alberta. She went into the hospital this afternoon. Look like she might have the baby early. I won't be gone long.

ROSE: Well, you ought to know. They went over to Miss Pearl's and got Gabe today. She said you told them to go ahead and lock him up.

TROY: I ain't said no such thing. Whoever told you that is telling a lie. Pearl ain't doing nothing but telling a big fat lie.

ROSE: She ain't had to tell me. I read it on the papers.

TROY: I ain't told them nothing of the kind.

ROSE: I saw it right there on the papers.

TROY: What it say, huh?

ROSE: It said you told them to take him.

TROY: Then they screwed that up, just the way they screw up everything. I ain't worried about what they got on the paper.

ROSE: Say the government send part of his check to the hospital and the other part to you.

TROY: I ain't got nothing to do with that if that's the way it works. I ain't made up the rules about how it work.

ROSE: You did Gabe just like you did Cory. You wouldn't sign the paper for Cory . . . but you signed for Gabe. You signed that paper.

(*The telephone is heard ringing inside the house.*)

TROY: I told you I ain't signed nothing, woman! The only thing I signed was the release form. Hell, I can't read, I don't know what they had on that paper! I ain't signed nothing about sending Gabe away.

ROSE: I said send him to the hospital . . . you said let him be free . . . now you done went down there and signed him to the hospital for half his money. You went back on yourself, Troy. You gonna have to answer for that.

TROY: See now . . . you been over there talking to Miss Pearl. She done got mad cause she ain't getting Gabe's rent money. That's all it is. She's liable to say anything.

ROSE: Troy, I seen where you signed the paper.

TROY: You ain't seen nothing I signed. What she doing got papers on my brother anyway? Miss Pearl telling a big fat lie. And I'm gonna tell her about it too! You ain't seen nothing I signed. Say . . . you ain't seen nothing I signed.

(*Rose exits into the house to answer the telephone. Presently she returns.*)

ROSE: Troy . . . that was the hospital. Alberta had the baby.

TROY: What she have? What is it?

ROSE: It's a girl.

TROY: I better get on down to the hospital to see her.

ROSE: Troy . . .

TROY: Rose . . . I got to go see her now. That's only right . . . what's the matter . . . the baby's all right, ain't it?

ROSE: Alberta died having the baby.

TROY: Died . . . you say she's dead? Alberta's dead?

ROSE: They said they done all they could. They couldn't do nothing for her.

TROY: The baby? How's the baby?

ROSE: They say it's healthy. I wonder who's gonna bury her.

TROY: She had family, Rose. She wasn't living in the world by herself.

ROSE: I know she wasn't living in the world by herself.

TROY: Next thing you gonna want to know if she had any insurance.

ROSE: Troy, you ain't got to talk like that.

TROY: That's the first thing that jumped out your mouth. "Who's gonna bury her?" Like I'm fixing to take on that task for myself.

ROSE: I am your wife. Don't push me away.

TROY: I ain't pushing nobody away. Just give me some space. That's all. Just give me some room to breathe.

(*Rose exits into the house. Troy walks about the yard.*)

TROY (*with a quiet rage that threatens to consume him*): All right . . . Mr. Death. See now . . . I'm gonna tell you what I'm gonna do. I'm gonna take and build me a fence around this yard. See? I'm gonna build me a fence around what belongs to me. And then I want you to stay on the other side. See? You stay over there until you're ready for me. Then you come on. Bring your army. Bring your sickle. Bring your wrestling clothes. I ain't gonna fall down on my vigilance this time. You ain't gonna sneak up on me no more. When you ready for me . . . when the top of your list say Troy Maxson . . . that's when you come around here. You come up and knock on the front door. Ain't nobody else got nothing to do with this. This is between you and me. Man to man. You stay on the other side of that fence until you ready for me. Then you come up and knock on the front door. Anytime you want. I'll be ready for you.

(*The lights go down to black.*)

Scene III

(*The lights come up on the porch. It is late evening three days later. Rose sits listening to the ball game waiting for Troy. The final out of the game is made and Rose switches off the radio. Troy enters the yard carrying an infant wrapped in blankets. He stands back from the house and calls.*)

(*Rose enters and stands on the porch. There is a long, awkward silence, the weight of which grows heavier with each passing second.*)

TROY: Rose . . . I'm standing here with my daughter in my arms. She ain't but a wee bittie little old thing. She don't know nothing about grownups' business. She innocent . . . and she ain't got no mama.

ROSE: What you telling me for, Troy?

(*She turns and exits into the house.*)

TROY: Well . . . I guess we'll just sit out here on the porch.

(*He sits down on the porch. There is an awkward indelicateness about the way he handles the baby. His largeness engulfs and seems to swallow it. He speaks loud enough for Rose to hear.*)

A man's got to do what's right for him. I ain't sorry for nothing I done. It felt right in my heart.

(*To the baby.*)

What you smiling at? Your daddy's a big man. Got these great big old hands. But sometimes he's scared. And right now your daddy's scared cause we sitting out here and ain't got no home. Oh, I been homeless before. I ain't had no little baby with me. But I been homeless. You just be out on the road by your lonesome and you see one of them trains coming and you just kinda go like this . . .

(*He sings as a lullaby.*)

Please, Mr. Engineer let a man ride the line
Please, Mr. Engineer let a man ride the line
I ain't got no ticket please let me ride the blinds

(*Rose enters from the house. Troy hearing her steps behind him, stands and faces her.*)

She's my daughter, Rose. My own flesh and blood. I can't deny her no more than I can deny them boys.

(*Pause.*)

You and them boys is my family. You and them and this child is all I got in the world. So I guess what I'm saying is . . . I'd appreciate it if you'd help me take care of her.

ROSE: Okay, Troy . . . you're right. I'll take care of your baby for you . . . cause . . . like you say . . . she's innocent . . . and you can't visit the sins of the father upon the child. A motherless child has got a hard time.

(*She takes the baby from him.*)

From right now . . . this child got a mother. But you a womanless man.

(*Rose turns and exits into the house with the baby. Lights go down to black.*)

Scene IV

(*It is two months later. Lyons enters from the street. He knocks on the door and calls.*)

LYONS: Hey, Rose! (*Pause.*) Rose!

ROSE (*from inside the house*): Stop that yelling. You gonna wake up Raynell. I just got her to sleep.

LYONS: I just stopped by to pay Papa this twenty dollars I owe him. Where's Papa at?

ROSE: He should be here in a minute. I'm getting ready to go down to the church. Sit down and wait on him.

LYONS: I got to go pick up Bonnie over her mother's house.

ROSE: Well, sit it down there on the table. He'll get it.

LYONS (*enters the house and sets the money on the table*): Tell Papa I said thanks. I'll see you again.

ROSE: All right, Lyons. We'll see you.

(*Lyons starts to exit as Cory enters.*)

CORY: Hey, Lyons.

LYONS: What's happening, Cory. Say man, I'm sorry I missed your graduation. You know I had a gig and couldn't get away. Otherwise, I would have been there, man. So what you doing?

CORY: I'm trying to find a job.

LYONS: Yeah I know how that go, man. It's rough out here. Jobs are scarce.

CORY: Yeah, I know.

LYONS: Look here, I got to run. Talk to Papa . . . he know some people. He'll be able to help get you a job. Talk to him . . . see what he say.

CORY: Yeah . . . all right, Lyons.

LYONS: You take care. I'll talk to you soon. We'll find some time to talk.

(*Lyons exits the yard. Cory wanders over to the tree, picks up the bat, and assumes a batting stance. He studies an imaginary pitcher and swings. Dissatisfied with the result, he tries again. Troy enters. They eye each other for a beat. Cory puts the bat down and exits the yard. Troy starts into the house as Rose exits with Raynell. She is carrying a cake.*)

TROY: I'm coming in and everybody's going out.

ROSE: I'm taking this cake down to the church for the bake sale. Lyons was by to see you. He stopped by to pay you your twenty dollars. It's laying in there on the table.

TROY (*going into his pocket*): Well . . . here go this money.

ROSE: Put it in there on the table, Troy. I'll get it.

TROY: What time you coming back?

ROSE: Ain't no use in you studying me. It don't matter what time I come back.

TROY: I just asked you a question, woman. What's the matter . . . can't I ask you a question?

ROSE: Troy, I don't want to go into it. Your dinner's in there on the stove. All you got to do is heat it up. And don't you be eating the rest of them cakes in there.

I'm coming back for them. We having a bake sale at the church tomorrow.

(*Rose exits the yard. Troy sits down on the steps, takes a pint bottle from his pocket, opens it, and drinks. He begins to sing.*)

TROY: Hear it ring! Hear it ring!
   Had an old dog his name was Blue
   You know Blue was mighty true
   You know Blue as a good old dog
   Blue trees a possum in a hollow log
   You know from that he was a good old dog

(*Bono enters the yard.*)

BONO: Hey, Troy.

TROY: Hey, what's happening, Bono?

BONO: I just thought I'd stop by to see you.

TROY: What you stop by and see me for? You ain't stopped by in a month of Sundays. Hell, I must owe you money or something.

BONO: Since you got your promotion I can't keep up with you. Used to see you every day. Now I don't even know what route you working.

TROY: They keep switching me around. Got me out in Greentree now . . . hauling white folks' garbage.

BONO: Greentree, huh? You lucky, at least you ain't got to be lifting them barrels. Damn if they ain't getting heavier. I'm gonna put in my two years and call it quits.

TROY: I'm thinking about retiring myself.

BONO: You got it easy. You can *drive* for another five years.

TROY: It ain't the same, Bono. It ain't like working the back of the truck. Ain't got nobody to talk to . . . feel like you working by yourself. Naw, I'm thinking about retiring. How's Lucille?

BONO: She all right. Her arthritis get to acting up on her sometime. Saw Rose on my way in. She going down to the church, huh?

TROY: Yeah, she took up going down there. All them preachers looking for somebody to fatten their pockets.

(*Pause.*)

   Got some gin here.

BONO: Naw, thanks. I just stopped by to say hello.

TROY: Hell, nigger . . . you can take a drink. I ain't never known you to say no to a drink. You ain't got to work tomorrow.

BONO: I just stopped by. I'm fixing to go over to Skinner's. We got us a domino game going over his house every Friday.

TROY: Nigger, you can't play no dominoes. I used to whup you four games out of five.

BONO: Well, that learned me. I'm getting better.

TROY: Yeah? Well, that's all right.

BONO: Look here . . . I got to be getting on. Stop by sometime, huh?

TROY: Yeah, I'll do that, Bono. Lucille told Rose you bought her a new refrigerator.

BONO: Yeah, Rose told Lucille you had finally built your fence . . . so I figured we'd call it even.

TROY: I knew you would.

BONO: Yeah . . . okay. I'll be talking to you.

TROY: Yeah, take care, Bono. Good to see you. I'm gonna stop over.

BONO: Yeah. Okay, Troy.

(*Bono exits. Troy drinks from the bottle.*)

TROY: Old Blue died and I dig his grave
   Let him down with a golden chain
   Every night when I hear old Blue bark
   I know Blue treed a possum in Noah's Ark.
   Hear it ring! Hear it ring!

(*Cory enters the yard. They eye each other for a beat. Troy is sitting in the middle of the steps. Cory walks over.*)

CORY: I got to get by.

TROY: Say what? What's you say?

CORY: You in my way. I got to get by.

TROY: You got to get by where? This is my house. Bought and paid for. In full. Took me fifteen years. And if you wanna go in my house and I'm sitting on the steps . . . you say excuse me. Like your mama taught you.

CORY: Come on, Pop . . . I got to get by.

(*Cory starts to maneuver his way past Troy. Troy grabs his leg and shoves him back.*)

TROY: You just gonna walk over top of me?

CORY: I live here too!

TROY (*advancing toward him*): You just gonna walk over top of me in my own house?

CORY: I ain't scared of you.

TROY: I ain't asked if you was scared of me. I asked you if you was fixing to walk over top of me in my own house? That's the question. You ain't gonna say excuse me? You just gonna walk over top of me?

CORY: If you wanna put it like that.

TROY: How else am I gonna put it?

CORY: I was walking by you to go into the house cause you sitting on the steps drunk, singing to yourself. You can put it like that.

TROY: Without saying excuse me???

(*Cory doesn't respond.*)

   I asked you a question. Without saying excuse me???

CORY: I ain't got to say excuse me to you. You don't count around here no more.

TROY: Oh, I see . . . I don't count around here no more. You ain't got to say excuse me to your daddy. All of a sudden you done got so grown that your daddy don't count around here no more . . . Around here in his own house and yard that he done paid for with the sweat of his brow. You done got so grown to where

you gonna take over. You gonna take over my house.
Is that right? You gonna wear my pants. You gonna
go in there and stretch out on my bed. You ain't got
to say excuse me cause I don't count around here no
more. Is that right?

CORY: That's right. You always talking this dumb stuff.
Now, why don't you just get out my way.

TROY: I guess you got someplace to sleep and something
to put in your belly. You got that, huh? You got that?
That's what you need. You got that, huh?

CORY: You don't know what I got. You ain't got to
worry about what I got.

TROY: You right! You one hundred percent right! I done
spent the last seventeen years worrying about what
you got. Now it's your turn, see? I'll tell you what to
do. You grown . . . we done established that. You a
man. Now, let's see you act like one. Turn your
behind around and walk out this yard. And when
you get out there in the alley . . . you can forget
about this house. See? 'Cause this is my house. You
go on and be a man and get your own house. You can
forget about this. 'Cause this is mine. You go on and
get yours 'cause I'm through with doing for you.

CORY: You talking about what you did for me . . .
what'd you ever give me?

TROY: Them feet and bones! That pumping heart, nigger! I give you more than anybody else is ever gonna
give you.

CORY: You ain't never gave me nothing! You ain't never
done nothing but hold me back. Afraid I was gonna
be better than you. All you ever did was try and make
me scared of you. I used to tremble every time you
called my name. Every time I heard your footsteps in
the house. Wondering all the time . . . what's Papa
gonna say if I do this? . . . What's he gonna say if I do
that? . . . What's Papa gonna say if I turn on the
radio? And Mama, too . . . she tries . . . but she's
scared of you.

TROY: You leave your mama out of this. She ain't got
nothing to do with this.

CORY: I don't know how she stand you . . . after what
you did to her.

TROY: I told you to leave your mama out of this!

(*He advances toward Cory.*)

CORY: What you gonna do . . . give me a whupping?
You can't whup me no more. You're too old. You just
an old man.

TROY (*shoves him on his shoulder*): Nigger! That's what
you are. You just another nigger on the street to me!

CORY: You crazy! You know that?

TROY: Go on now! You got the devil in you. Get on
away from me!

CORY: You just a crazy old man . . . talking about I got
the devil in me.

TROY: Yeah, I'm crazy! If you don't get on the other side
of that yard . . . I'm gonna show you how crazy I am!
Go on . . . get the hell out of my yard.

CORY: It ain't your yard. You took Uncle Gabe's money
he got from the army to buy this house and then you
put him out.

TROY (*Troy advances on Cory*): Get your black ass out
of my yard!

(*Troy's advance backs Cory up against the tree. Cory
grabs up the bat.*)

CORY: I ain't going nowhere! Come on . . . put me out! I
ain't scared of you.

TROY: That's my bat!

CORY: Come on!

TROY: Put my bat down!

CORY: Come on, put me out.

(*Cory swings at Troy, who backs across the yard.*)

What's the matter? You so bad . . . put me out!

(*Troy advances toward Cory.*)

CORY (*backing up*): Come on! Come on!

TROY: You're gonna have to use it! You wanna draw
that bat back on me . . . you're gonna have to use it.

CORY: Come on! . . . Come on!

(*Cory swings the bat at Troy a second time. He misses.
Troy continues to advance toward him.*)

TROY: You're gonna have to kill me! You wanna
draw that bat back on me. You're gonna have to
kill me.

(*Cory, backed up against the tree, can go no farther.
Troy taunts him. He sticks out his head and offers him a
target.*)

Come on! Come on!

(*Cory is unable to swing the bat. Troy grabs it.*)

TROY: Then I'll show you.

(*Cory and Troy struggle over the bat. The struggle is
fierce and fully engaged. Troy ultimately is the stronger
and takes the bat from Cory and stands over him ready
to swing. He stops himself.*)

Go on and get away from around my house.

(*Cory, stung by his defeat, picks himself up, walks
slowly out of the yard and up the alley.*)

CORY: Tell Mama I'll be back for my things.

TROY: They'll be on the other side of that fence.

(*Cory exits.*)

TROY: I can't taste nothing. Helluljah! I can't taste nothing no more. (*Troy assumes a batting posture and
begins to taunt Death, the fastball on the outside corner.*) Come on! It's between you and me now! Come
on! Anytime you want! Come on! I be ready for
you . . . but I ain't gonna be easy.

(*The lights go down on the scene.*)

Scene V

(*The time is 1965. The lights come up in the yard. It is the morning of Troy's funeral. A funeral plaque with a light hangs beside the door. There is a small garden plot off to the side. There is noise and activity in the house as Rose, Gabriel, and Bono have gathered. The door opens and Raynell, seven years old, enters dressed in a flannel nightgown. She crosses to the garden and pokes around with a stick. Rose calls from the house.*)

ROSE: Raynell!
RAYNELL: Mam?
ROSE: What you doing out there?
RAYNELL: Nothing.

(*Rose comes to the door.*)

ROSE: Girl, get in here and get dressed. What you doing?
RAYNELL: Seeing if my garden growed.
ROSE: I told you it ain't gonna grow overnight. You got to wait.
RAYNELL: It don't look like it never gonna grow. Dag!
ROSE: I told you a watched pot never boils. Get in here and get dressed.
RAYNELL: This ain't even no pot, Mama.
ROSE: You just have to give it a chance. It'll grow. Now you come on and do what I told you. We got to be getting ready. This ain't no morning to be playing around. You hear me?
RAYNELL: Yes, mam.

(*Rose exits into the house. Raynell continues to poke at her garden with a stick. Cory enters. He is dressed in a Marine corporal's uniform, and carries a duffel bag. His posture is that of a military man, and his speech has a clipped sternness.*)

CORY (*to Raynell*): Hi.

(*Pause.*)

I bet your name is Raynell.
RAYNELL: Uh huh.
CORY: Is your mama home?

(*Raynell runs up on the porch and calls through the screen door.*)

RAYNELL: Mama . . . there's some man out here. Mama?

(*Rose comes to the door.*)

ROSE: Cory? Lord have mercy! Look here, you all!

(*Rose and Cory embrace in a tearful reunion as Bono and Lyons enter from the house dressed in funeral clothes.*)

BONO: Aw, looka here . . .
ROSE: Done got all grown up!
CORY: Don't cry, Mama. What you crying about?
ROSE: I'm just so glad you made it.
CORY: Hey Lyons. How you doing, Mr. Bono.

(*Lyons goes to embrace Cory.*)

LYONS: Look at you, man. Look at you. Don't he look good, Rose. Got them Corporal stripes.
ROSE: What took you so long.
CORY: You know how the Marines are, Mama. They got to get all their paperwork straight before they let you do anything.
ROSE: Well, I'm sure glad you made it. They let Lyons come. Your Uncle Gabe's still in the hospital. They don't know if they gonna let him out or not. I just talked to them a little while ago.
LYONS: A Corporal in the United States Marines.
BONO: Your daddy knew you had it in you. He used to tell me all the time.
LYONS: Don't he look good, Mr. Bono?
BONO: Yeah, he remind me of Troy when I first met him.

(*Pause.*)

Say, Rose, Lucille's down at the church with the choir. I'm gonna go down and get the pallbearers lined up. I'll be back to get you all.
ROSE: Thanks, Jim.
CORY: See you, Mr. Bono.
LYONS (*with his arm around Raynell*): Cory . . . look at Raynell. Ain't she precious? She gonna break a whole lot of hearts.
ROSE: Raynell, come and say hello to your brother. This is your brother, Cory. You remember Cory.
RAYNELL: No, Mam.
CORY: She don't remember me, Mama.
ROSE: Well, we talk about you. She heard us talk about you. (*To Raynell.*) This is your brother, Cory. Come on and say hello.
RAYNELL: Hi.
CORY: Hi. So you're Raynell. Mama told me a lot about you.
ROSE: You all come on into the house and let me fix you some breakfast. Keep up your strength.
CORY: I ain't hungry, Mama.
LYONS: You can fix me something, Rose. I'll be in there in a minute.
ROSE: Cory, you sure you don't want nothing. I know they ain't feeding you right.
CORY: No, Mama . . . thanks. I don't feel like eating. I'll get something later.
ROSE: Raynell . . . get on upstairs and get that dress on like I told you.

(*Rose and Raynell exit into the house.*)

LYONS: So . . . I hear you thinking about getting married.
CORY: Yeah, I done found the right one, Lyons. It's about time.
LYONS: Me and Bonnie been split up about four years now. About the time Papa retired. I guess she just got tired of all them changes I was putting her through.

(*Pause.*)

I always knew you was gonna make something out yourself. Your head was always in the right direction. So . . . you gonna stay in . . . make it a career . . . put in your twenty years?

CORY: I don't know. I got six already, I think that's enough.

LYONS: Stick with Uncle Sam and retire early. Ain't nothing out here. I guess Rose told you what happened with me. They got me down the workhouse. I thought I was being slick cashing other people's checks.

CORY: How much time you doing?

LYONS: They give me three years. I got that beat now. I ain't got but nine more months. It ain't so bad. You learn to deal with it like anything else. You got to take the crookeds with the straights. That's what Papa used to say. He used to say that when he struck out. I seen him strike out three times in a row . . . and the next time up he hit the ball over the grandstand. Right out there in Homestead Field. He wasn't satisfied hitting in the seats . . . he want to hit it over everything! After the game he had two hundred people standing around waiting to shake his hand. You got to take the crookeds with the straights. Yeah, Papa was something else.

CORY: You still playing?

LYONS: Cory . . . you know I'm gonna do that. There's some fellows down there we got us a band . . . we gonna try and stay together when we get out . . . but yeah, I'm still playing. It still helps me to get out of bed in the morning. As long as it do that I'm gonna be right there playing and trying to make some sense out of it.

ROSE (calling): Lyons, I got these eggs in the pan.

LYONS: Let me go on and get these eggs, man. Get ready to go bury Papa.

(Pause.)

How you doing? You doing all right?

(Cory nods. Lyons touches him on the shoulder and they share a moment of silent grief. Lyons exits into the house. Cory wanders about the yard. Raynell enters.)

RAYNELL: Hi.

CORY: Hi.

RAYNELL: Did you used to sleep in my room?

CORY: Yeah . . . that used to be my room.

RAYNELL: That's what Papa call it. "Cory's room." It got your football in the closet.

(Rose comes to the door.)

ROSE: Raynell, get in there and get them good shoes on.

RAYNELL: Mama, can't I wear these. Them other one hurt my feet.

ROSE: Well, they just gonna have to hurt your feet for a while. You ain't said they hurt your feet when you went down to the store and got them.

RAYNELL: They didn't hurt then. My feet done got bigger.

ROSE: Don't you give me no backtalk now. You get in there and get them shoes on.

(Raynell exits into the house.)

Ain't too much changed. He still got that piece of rag tied to that tree. He was out here swinging that bat. I was just ready to go back in the house. He swung that bat and then he just fell over. Seem like he swung it and stood there with this grin on his face . . . and then he just fell over. They carried him on down to the hospital, but I knew there wasn't no need . . . why don't you come on in the house?

CORY: Mama . . . I got something to tell you. I don't know how to tell you this . . . but I've got to tell you . . . I'm not going to Papa's funeral.

ROSE: Boy, hush your mouth. That's your daddy you talking about. I don't want hear that kind of talk this morning. I done raised you to come to this? You standing there all healthy and grown talking about you ain't going to your daddy's funeral?

CORY: Mama . . . listen . . .

ROSE: I don't want to hear it, Cory. You just get that thought out of your head.

CORY: I can't drag Papa with me everywhere I go. I've got to say no to him. One time in my life I've got to say no.

ROSE: Don't nobody have to listen to nothing like that. I know you and your daddy ain't seen eye to eye, but I ain't got to listen to that kind of talk this morning. Whatever was between you and your daddy . . . the time has come to put it aside. Just take it and set it over there on the shelf and forget about it. Disrespecting your daddy ain't gonna make you a man, Cory. You got to find a way to come to that on your own. Not going to your daddy's funeral ain't gonna make you a man.

CORY: The whole time I was growing up . . . living in his house . . . Papa was like a shadow that followed you everywhere. It weighed on you and sunk into your flesh. It would wrap around you and lay there until you couldn't tell which one was you anymore. That shadow digging in your flesh. Trying to crawl in. Trying to live through you. Everywhere I looked, Troy Maxson was staring back at me . . . hiding under the bed . . . in the closet. I'm just saying I've got to find a way to get rid of that shadow, Mama.

ROSE: You just like him. You got him in you good.

CORY: Don't tell me that, Mama.

ROSE: You Troy Maxson all over again.

CORY: I don't want to be Troy Maxson. I want to be me.

ROSE: You can't be nobody but who you are, Cory. That shadow wasn't nothing but you growing into yourself. You either got to grow into it or cut it down to fit you. But that's all you got to make life with. That's all you got to measure yourself against that world out there. Your daddy wanted you to be everything he wasn't . . . and at the same time he tried to make you into everything he was. I don't know if he was right or wrong . . . but I do know he meant to do more good than he meant to do harm. He wasn't always right. Sometimes when he touched he bruised. And sometimes when he took me in his arms he cut.

When I first met your daddy I thought . . . Here is a man I can lay down with and make a baby. That's the first thing I thought when I seen him. I was thirty years old and had done seen my share of men. But when he walked up to me and said "I can dance a waltz that'll make you dizzy," I thought, Rose Lee, here is a man that you can open yourself up to and be filled to bursting. Here is a man that can fill all them empty spaces you been tipping around the edges of. One of them empty spaces was being somebody's mother.

I married your daddy and settled down to cooking his supper and keeping clean sheets on the bed. When your daddy walked through the house he was so big he filled it up. That was my first mistake. Not to make him leave some room for me. For my part in the matter. But at that time I wanted that. I wanted a house that I could sing in. And that's what your daddy gave me. I didn't know to keep up his strength I had to give up little pieces of mine. I did that. I took on his life as mine and mixed up the pieces so that you couldn't hardly tell which was which anymore. It was my choice. It was my life and I didn't have to live it like that. But that's what life offered me in the way of being a woman and I took it. I grabbed hold of it with both hands.

By the time Raynell came into the house, me and your daddy had done lost touch with one another. I didn't want to make my blessing off of nobody's misfortune . . . but I took on to Raynell like she was all them babies I had wanted and never had.

(*The phone rings.*)

Like I'd been blessed to relive a part of my life. And if the Lord see fit to keep up my strength . . . I'm gonna do her just like your daddy did you . . . I'm gonna give her the best of what's in me.

RAYNELL (*entering, still with her old shoes*): Mama . . . Reverend Tollivier on the phone.

(*Rose exits into the house.*)

RAYNELL: Hi.
CORY: Hi.
RAYNELL: You in the Army or the Marines?
CORY: Marines.
RAYNELL: Papa said it was the Army. Did you know Blue?
CORY: Blue? Who's Blue?
RAYNELL: Papa's dog what he sing about all the time.
CORY (*singing*): Hear it ring! Hear it ring!
    I had a dog his name was Blue
    You know Blue was mighty true
    You know Blue was a good old dog
    Blue treed a possum in a hollow log
    You know from that he was a good old dog.
    Hear it ring! Hear it ring!

(*Raynell joins in singing.*)

CORY AND RAYNELL: Blue treed a possum out on a
    limb
    Blue looked at me and I looked at him
    Grabbed that possum and put him in a sack
    Blue stayed there till I came back
    Old Blue's feets was big and round
    Never allowed a possum to touch the ground.

    Old Blue died and I dug his grave
    I dug his grave with a silver spade
    Let him down with a golden chain
    And every night I call his name
    Go on Blue, you good dog you
    Go on Blue, you good dog you

RAYNELL: Blue laid down and died like a man
    Blue laid down and died . . .
BOTH: Blue laid down and died like a man
    Now he's treeing possums in the Promised Land
    I'm gonna tell you this to let you know
    Blue's gone where the good dogs go
    When I hear old Blue bark
    When I hear old Blue bark
    Blue treed a possum in Noah's Ark
    Blue treed a possum in Noah's Ark.

(*Rose comes to the screen door.*)

ROSE: Cory, we gonna be ready to go in a minute.
CORY (*to Raynell*): You go on in the house and change them shoes like Mama told you so we can go to Papa's funeral.
RAYNELL: Okay, I'll be back.

(*Raynell exits into the house. Cory gets up and crosses over to the tree. Rose stands in the screen door watching him. Gabriel enters from the alley.*)

GABRIEL (*calling*): Hey, Rose!
ROSE: Gabe?
GABRIEL: I'm here, Rose. Hey Rose, I'm here!

(*Rose enters from the house.*)

ROSE: Lord . . . Look here, Lyons!
LYONS: See, I told you, Rose . . . I told you they'd let him come.
CORY: How you doing, Uncle Gabe?
LYONS: How you doing, Uncle Gabe?
GABRIEL: Hey, Rose. It's time. It's time to tell St. Peter to open the gates. Troy, you ready? You ready, Troy. I'm gonna tell St. Peter to open the gates. You get ready now.

(*Gabriel, with great fanfare, braces himself to blow. The trumpet is without a mouthpiece. He puts the end of it into his mouth and blows with great force, like a man who has been waiting some twenty-odd years for this single moment. No sound comes out of the trumpet. He braces himself and blows again with the same result. A third time he blows. There is a weight of impossible description that falls away and leaves him bare and exposed to a frightful realization. It is a trauma that a*) sane and normal mind would be unable to withstand. He begins to dance. A slow, strange dance, eerie and life-giving. A dance of atavistic signature and ritual. Lyons attempts to embrace him. Gabriel pushes Lyons away. He begins to howl in what is an attempt at song, or per-haps a song turning back into itself in an attempt at speech. He finishes his dance and the gates of heaven stand open as wide as God's closet.)

That's the way that go!

COMMENTARIES

David Savran (b. 1950)
INTERVIEW WITH AUGUST WILSON   *1987*

August Wilson is interested not only in the characters in his plays but also in their political circumstances. One of his primary efforts has been to help strip away the black male stereotypes so that his audiences can see his people as he sees them. In this interview he discusses the social conditions of African Americans and the relationship between Troy Maxson and his son Cory. Wilson's views about their relationship may be surprising, since he interprets it in a way that differs from many of the critics' interpretations.

Savran: In reading *Fences,* I came to view Troy more and more critically as the play progressed, sharing Rose's point of view. We see that Troy has been crippled by his father. That's being replayed in Troy's relationship with Cory. Do you think there's a way out of that cycle?

Wilson: Surely. First of all, we're all like our parents. The things we are taught early in life, how to respond to the world, our sense of morality — everything, we get from them. Now you can take that legacy and do with it anything you want to do. It's in your hands. Cory is Troy's son. How can he be Troy's son without shar-ing Troy's values? I was trying to get at why Troy made the choices he made, how they have influenced his values and how he attempts to pass those along to his son. Each generation gives the succeeding generation what they think they need. One question in the play is "Are the tools we are given sufficient to compete in a world that is different from the one our parents knew?" I think they are — it's just that we have to do different things with the tools. That's all Troy has to give. Troy's flaw is that he does not recognize that the world was changing. That's because he spent fifteen years in a penitentiary.

As African-Americans, we should demand to participate in society as Africans. That's the way out of the vicious cycle of poverty and neglect that exists in 1987 in America, where you have a huge percentage of blacks living in the equivalent of South African townships, in housing projects. No one is inviting these people to participate in society. Look at the poverty levels — $8,500 for a family of four, if you have $8,501 you're not counted. Those statistics would go up enormously if we had an honest assessment of the cost of living in America. I don't know how anybody can support a family of four on $8,500. What I'm saying is that 85 or 90 percent of blacks in America are living in abject poverty and, for the most part, are crowded into what amount to concentration camps. The situation for blacks in America is worse than it was forty years ago. Some sociologists will tell you about the tremendous progress we've made. They didn't put me out when I walked in the door. And you can always point to someone who works on Wall Street, or is a doctor. But they don't count in the larger scheme of things.

Savran: Do you have any idea how these political changes could take place?

Wilson: I'm not sure. I know that blacks must be allowed their cultural differences. I think the process of assimilation to white American society was a big mistake. We don't want to be like you. Blacks living in housing projects are isolated from the society, for the most part — living as they choose, as Africans. Only they don't realize the value in what they're doing because they have accepted their victimization. They've marked themselves as victims. Once they recognize that, they can begin to move through society in a different manner, from a stronger position, and claim what is theirs.

Savran: A project of yours is to point up what happens when oppression is internalized.

Wilson: Yes, transfer of aggression to the wrong target. I think it's interesting that the two roads open to blacks for "full participation" are entertainment and sports. *Ma Rainey* and *Fences,* and I didn't plan it that way. I don't think that they're the correct roads. I think Troy's right. Now with the benefit of historical perspective, I can say that the athletic scholarship was actually a way of exploiting. Now you've got two million kids who think they're going to play in the NBA. In the sixties the universities made a lot of money off of athletics. You had kids playing for free who, by and large, were not getting educated, were taking courses in basketweaving. Some of them could barely read.

Savran: Troy may be right about that issue, but it seems that he has passed on certain destructive traits in spite of himself. Take the hostility between father and son.

Wilson: I think every generation says to the previous generation: you're in my way, I've got to get by. The father-son conflict is actually a normal generational conflict that happens all the time.

Savran: So it's a healthy and a good thing?

Wilson: Oh, sure. Troy is seeing this boy walk around, smelling his piss. Two men cannot live in the same household. Troy would have been tremendously disappointed if Cory had not challenged him. Troy knows that this boy has to go out and do battle with that world: "So I had best prepare him because I know that's a harsh, cruel place out there. But that's going to be easy compared to what he's getting here. Ain't nobody gonna whip your ass like I'm gonna whip it." He has a tremendous love for the kid. But he's not going to say, "I love you," he's going to demonstrate it. He's carrying garbage for seventeen years just for the kid. The only world Troy knows is the one that he made. Cory's going to go on to find another one, he's going to arrive at the same place as Troy. I think one of the most important lines in the play is when Troy is talking about his father: "I got to the place where I could feel him kicking in my blood and knew that the only thing that separated us was the matter of a few years."

Hopefully, Cory will do things a bit differently with his son. For Troy, sports was not the way to go, the white man wouldn't let him get away with that. "Get you a job, with your hands, something that nobody can take away from you." The idea of school — he doesn't know what that is. That's for white folks. Very few blacks had paperwork jobs. But if you knew how to fix cars, you could always make some money. That's what Troy wants for Cory. There aren't many people who ever jumped up in Troy's face. So he's proud of the kid at the same time that he expresses a hurt that all men feel. You got to cut your kid loose at some point. There's that sense of loss and separation. You find out how Troy left his father's house and you see how Cory leaves his house. I suspect with Cory it will repeat with some differences and maybe, after five or six generations, they'll find a different way to do it.

Savran: Where Cory ends up is very ambiguous, as a marine in 1965.

Wilson: Yes. For the average black kid on the street, that was an alternative. You went into the army because you could learn how to do something. I can remember my parents talking about the son of some friends: "He's in the navy. He *did* something"— as opposed to standing on the street corner, shooting drugs, drinking wine, and robbing stores. Lyons says to Cory, "I always knew you were going to make something out of yourself." It really wounds me. He's a corporal in the marines. For blacks, that is a sense of accomplishment. Therein lies one of the tragedies of blacks in America. Cory says, "I don't know. I put in six years. That's enough." Anyone who goes into the army and makes a career out of it is a loser. They sit there and are nurtured by the army and they don't have to confront life. Then they get out of the army and find there's nothing to do. They didn't learn any skills. And if they did, they can't find a job. Four months later, they're shooting dope. In the sixties a whole bunch of blacks went over, fought and died in the Vietnam War. The survivors came back to the same street corners and found out nothing had changed. They still couldn't get a job.

At the end of *Fences* every person, with the exception of Raynell, is institutionalized. Rose is in a church. Lyons is in a penitentiary. Gabriel's in a mental hospital and Cory's in the marines. The only free person is the girl, Troy's daughter, the hope for the future. That was conscious on my part because in '57 that's what I saw. Blacks have relied on institutions which are really foreign — except for the black church, which has been our saving grace. I have some problems with it but I recognize it as a central social organization and sometimes an economic organization for the black community. I would like to see blacks develop their own institutions that respond to their needs.

Frank Rich (b. 1949)
REVIEW OF *FENCES*   1987

Frank Rich, the New York Times *critic, reviews* Fences *in context with August Wilson's other plays. Rich criticizes the old-fashioned structure of the plot, which he characterizes as "clunky," but he also admits that the play is "gripping," especially in the second act. Rich focuses on the struggle between father and son, which he sees as meaningful to "theatergoers from all kinds of families."*

To hear his wife tell it, Troy Maxson, the middle-aged Pittsburgh sanitation worker at the center of *Fences,* is "so big" that he fills up his tenement house just by walking through it. Needless to say, that description could also apply to James Earl Jones, the actor who has found what may be the best role of his career in August Wilson's new play, at the 46th Street Theater. But the remarkable stature of the character — and of the performance — is not a matter of sheer size. If Mr. Jones's Troy is a mountainous man prone to tyrannical eruptions of rage, he is also a digni-fied, delicate figure capable of cradling a tiny baby, of pleading gravely to his wife for understanding, of standing still to stare death unflinchingly in the eye. A black man, a free man, a descendant of slaves, a menial laborer, a father, a husband, a lover — Mr. Jones's Troy embraces all the contradictions of being black and male and American in his time.

That time is 1957 — three decades after the period of Mr. Wilson's previous and extraordinary *Ma Rainey's Black Bottom.* For blacks like Troy in the industrial North of *Fences,* social and economic equality is more a legal principle than a real-ity: the Maxson's slum neighborhood, a panorama of grimy brick and smokestack-blighted sky in James D. Sandefur's eloquent design, is a cauldron of busted promises, waiting to boil over. The conflagration is still a decade away — the streetlights burn like the first sparks of distant insurrection — so Mr. Wilson writes about the pain of an extended family lost in the wilderness of de facto segregation and barren hope.

It speaks of the power of the play — and of the cast assembled by the director, Lloyd Richards — that Mr. Jones's patriarch doesn't devour the rest of *Fences* so much as become the life force that at once nurtures and stunts the characters who share his blood. The strongest countervailing player is his wife, Rose, luminously acted by Mary Alice. Rose is a quiet woman who, as she says, "planted herself" in the "hard and rocky" soil of her husband. But she never bloomed: marriage brought frustration and betrayal in equal measure with affection.

Even so, Ms. Alice's performance emphasizes strength over self-pity, open anger over festering bitterness. The actress finds the spiritual quotient in the acceptance that accompanies Rose's love for a scarred, profoundly complicated man. It's rare to find a marriage of any sort presented on stage with such balance — let alone one in which the husband has fathered children by three different women. Mr. Wilson grants both partners the right to want to escape the responsibilities of their domes-tic drudgery while affirming their respective claims to forgiveness.

The other primary relationship of *Fences* is that of Troy to his son Cory (Court-ney B. Vance) — a promising 17-year-old football player being courted by a college recruiter. Troy himself was once a baseball player in the Negro Leagues — early enough to hit homers off Satchel Paige, too early to benefit from Jackie Robinson's breakthrough — and his bitter, long-ago disappointment leads him to decree a dif-ferent future for his son. But while Troy wants Cory to settle for a workhorse trade guaranteeing a weekly paycheck, the boy resists. The younger Maxson is somehow convinced that the dreams of his black generation need not end in the city's mean alleys with the carting of white men's garbage.

The struggle between father and son over conflicting visions of black identity, aspirations and values is the play's narrative fulcrum, and a paradigm of violent divisions that would later tear apart a society. As written, the conflict is also a didactic one, reminiscent of old-fashioned plays, black and white, about disputes between first-generation American parents and their rebellious children.

In *Ma Rainey* — set at a blues recording session — Mr. Wilson's characters were firecrackers exploding in a bottle, pursuing jagged theatrical riffs reflective of their music and of their intimacy with the Afro-American experience that gave birth to that music. The relative tameness of *Fences* — with its laboriously worked-out titular metaphor, its slow-fused Act I exposition — is as much an expression of its period as its predecessor was of the hotter 20s. Intentionally or not — and perhaps to the satisfaction of those who found the more esthetically daring *Ma Rainey* too "plotless"— Mr. Wilson invokes the clunkier dramaturgy of Odets, Miller and Hansberry on this occasion.

Such formulaic theatrical tidiness, while exasperating at times, proves a minor price for the gripping second act (strengthened since the play's Yale debut in 1985) and for the scattered virtuoso passages throughout. Like *Ma Rainey* and the latest Wilson work seen at Yale (*Joe Turner's Come and Gone,* also promised for New York), *Fences* leaves no doubt that Mr. Wilson is a major writer, combining a poet's ear for vernacular with a robust sense of humor (political and sexual), a sure instinct for crackling dramatic incident and a passionate commitment to a great subject.

Mr. Wilson continues to see history as fully as he sees his characters. In one scene, Troy and his oldest friend (played with brimming warmth by Ray Aranha) weave an autobiographical "talking blues" — a front-porch storytelling jaunt from the antebellum plantation through the pre-industrial urban South, jail and northward migration. *Fences* is pointedly bracketed by two disparate wars that swallowed up black manhood, and, as always with Mr. Wilson, is as keenly cognizant of its characters' bonds to Africa, however muted here, as their bondage to white America. One hears the cadences of a centuries-old heritage in Mr. Jones's efforts to shout down the devil. It is a frayed scrap of timeless blues singing, unpretty but unquenchable, that proves the over-powering cathartic link among the disparate branches of the Maxson family tree.

Under the exemplary guidance of Mr. Richards — whose staging falters only in the awkward scene transitions — the entire cast is impressive, including Frankie R. Faison in the problematic (but finally devastating) role of a brain-damaged, horn-playing uncle named Gabriel, and Charles Brown, as a Maxson son who falls into the sociological crack separating the play's two principal generations. As Cory, Courtney B. Vance is not only formidable in challenging Mr. Jones to a psychological (and sometimes physical) kill-or-be-killed battle for supremacy but also seems to grow into Troy's vocal timbre and visage by the final scene. Like most sons, Mr. Vance just can't elude "the shadow" of his father, no matter how hard he tries. Such is the long shadow Mr. Jones's father casts in *Fences* that theatergoers from all kinds of families may find him impossible to escape.

David Henry Hwang

Born in 1957, David Henry Hwang was raised in California's San Gabriel Valley by Asian-born parents. His father, a native of Shanghai, is a successful banker; his mother, born in the Philippines, is a professor of piano. As a child, Hwang was a proficient violinist, and today his sister makes a living as a cellist. Hwang plays jazz violin occasionally and has appeared on friends' albums. While art and music were influential as he grew, so too was his awareness of his ethnic roots; his interest in Asian-American experience developed out of personal observation. Up to now, much of his focus in drama has been on assimilation and on the power of Chinese culture, but he is also aware that he has other issues to explore in his writing.

Hwang's first play, *FOB* (1980), was written while an undergraduate at Stanford. The title of the play is an acronym standing for "Fresh Off the Boat," and the play examines the problems of immigrant assimilation. It is set in a restaurant in Chinatown with college-age characters who all reveal difficulties in fitting into the American way of life. Assimilated immigrants make fun of a young man who has just arrived from China. Hwang strips off the social pretensions of those who feel that getting ahead calls for abandoning their roots and humiliating others. The play, developed at the O'Neill Playwright's Conference, was then brought to the Public Theater in New York by Joseph Papp. It won a 1981 Obie Award for best play.

The Dance and the Railroad (1981) was developed in New York with the assurance that Joseph Papp would produce it. Hwang worked with actor John Lone, who had trained in Chinese opera in Hong Kong and who starred in the play. Hwang says that he tried to learn from Lone everything he could about the history and tradition of Chinese opera. This play demonstrates the need to understand and participate in the traditions of one's culture. The dance and operatic forms that Lone practices and values are at first rejected by Ma, the other central character in the play, but eventually win him over.

Hwang's other plays are *Family Devotions* (1981), *The House of Sleeping Beauties* (1983), *The Sound of a Voice* (1983), *Rich Relations* (1986), and *M. Butterfly* (1988), for which he is best known. *M. Butterfly* has been an international success, winning a Tony Award for best play in 1988. The story of a French diplomat's affair with a Chinese actress in the Peking Opera, it culminates in the astonishing discovery that the actress is a man. Further, their relationship, based on a true story of a more than two-decade affair, includes espionage and intrigue.

Hwang's activity since *M. Butterfly* has included more plays, films, and an opera libretto. He collaborated with Philip Glass on *1000 Airplanes on the Roof* (1988), a science fiction musical; and on *The Voyage* (1992), Glass's full-length opera. Hwang's *Bondage* (1992), a one-act play that premiered at the Humana Theatre Festival, explores the psychology of sadomasochism. Hwang's parody of *Miss Saigon*, called *Face Value* (1993), desentimentalizes the popular treatment of Vietnam. His film *Golden Gate* (1994) was based on a story he heard about Chinese immigrants arrested for sending money back to China. Hwang received an Obie Award for *Golden Child* (1997), a play loosely based on his own great-grandfather's break with Confucian tradition by his conversion to Christianity and the unbinding of his daughter's feet. Among the projects he has been working on recently are a screenplay based on Dostoevsky's *The Idiot* and a screenplay of A. S. Byatt's novel *Possession*.

M. BUTTERFLY

In his afterword to *M. Butterfly*, David Henry Hwang explains how he found the original material from which he built his play. A French diplomat had a twenty-year affair with an actor in the Peking Opera, during which time the Chinese actor was also a spy for Communist China. Eventually, the diplomat learned that the actor was not a woman, as he thought, but a man. To some extent, the drama is designed to begin answering the question of how the diplomat could have spent twenty years not knowing his lover was a man.

Hwang explains that he saw a connection between the story he read in the newspaper and the Puccini opera *Madame Butterfly* (1904), in which Pinkerton, an American naval officer, appears to marry a Japanese girl, Cio-Cio-San, but leaves for America without her. He eventually returns with his American wife, expecting to retrieve his child, and Cio-Cio-San, realizing that she has waited in vain to be reunited with her "husband," kills herself.

Hwang began the project without knowing details of the narrative of Puccini's opera and with a decision to do no research into the details of the original news article. This strategy left him free to explore his feelings about the opera and about the relationship of West to East.

At root, *M. Butterfly* examines both racist and sexist attitudes common to the Western male. As Song Liling, the actor who masquerades as a woman, tells us late in the play, "being an Oriental, I could never be completely a man." In explaining the role of stereotypes in the deception he also tells the judge: "The West thinks of itself as masculine — big guns, big industry, big money — so the East is feminine — weak, delicate, poor . . . but good at art, and full of inscrutable wisdom — the feminine mystique."

Hwang saw that all these qualities were prominent in Puccini's opera. The powerful American naval officer did exactly as he wished with his Madame Butterfly, with no understanding of her deepest feelings. The opening of *M. Butterfly* provides enough background on the opera for the audience to see the parallels to the story Gallimard tells us. But in Hwang's version, the Westerner is beguiled and imprisoned, and the "Oriental woman" is free. It is not by accident that this story is narrated primarily from Gallimard's dank prison cell and that the outcome of Hwang's narrative is exactly the reverse of Puccini's. The cell and reversal help explain what Hwang meant by his intention to deconstruct the story of *Madame Butterfly*.

The ingenious development of the dramatic line keeps us always aware that Gallimard behaves in a manner rooted in Puccini's opera. Like Pinkerton, he considers himself honorable in respecting Song Liling's "modesty" when "she" refuses to disrobe in light of what he thinks are normal Chinese customs. Gallimard is admittedly backward and reserved in relation to women. He expects women to be weaker, but he also expects that his passivity will be rewarded with ardor. Hwang places the explanation for the deception's success deep in the psychology of Gallimard. However, he explains a portion of that psychology in terms of what Song Liling describes as a "rape mentality."

Ironically, we learn at the end of the play that Gallimard's role in French intelligence is so hopeless that all his predictions — based on his superior "knowledge" of the Chinese — are completely false. In other words, French intelligence, or Western intelligence as represented by Gallimard, is false intelligence. The vaunted diplomat is essentially unintelligent when it comes to understanding the Chinese, just as he is unintelligent in understanding Song Liling. Hwang may have chosen the name Gallimard because it is also the name of a prominent French publisher whose books on the Orient attempt to explain the East.

M. Butterfly in Performance

The play premiered in Washington, D.C., in 1988 to generally good reviews. John Dexter was the director. In New York the play was received with enthusiasm and became a major success, winning a Tony Award for best play of the year. John Lithgow played Gallimard and B. D. Wong played Song Liling. The staging featured a rounded ascending ramp, designed by Eiko Ishioka, on which Song Liling dominates the space, while below, in a space resembling a prison cell, Gallimard can only look up as at a performance of an opera. The opening scenes of the production used Chinese red as a primary color both in the staging and the lighting, producing a rich sensuousness to contrast with the darkness of Gallimard's cell.

After its New York run, *M. Butterfly* toured across the United States and has enjoyed revivals in major cities here and abroad. It has proven to be a durable drama with a major appeal to a wide variety of audiences.

David Henry Hwang (b. 1957)

M. BUTTERFLY

1988

The Characters

RENE GALLIMARD
SONG LILING
MARC/MAN NO. 2/CONSUL SHARPLESS
RENEE/WOMAN AT PARTY/PINUP GIRL
COMRADE CHIN/SUZUKI/SHU-FANG
HELGA
TOULON/MAN NO. 1/JUDGE
DANCERS

Time and Place: *The action of the play takes place in a Paris prison in the present, and, in recall, during the decade 1960–1970 in Beijing, and from 1966 to the present in Paris.*

Playwright's Notes: *A former French diplomat and a Chinese opera singer have been sentenced to six years in jail for spying for China after a two-day trial that traced a story of clandestine love and mistaken sexual identity. . . .*

Mr. Boursicot was accused of passing information to China after he fell in love with Mr. Shi, whom he believed for twenty years to be a woman.
— THE NEW YORK TIMES, *May 11, 1986*

This play was suggested by international newspaper accounts of a recent espionage trial. For purposes of dramatization, names have been changed, characters created, and incidents devised or altered, and this play does not purport to be a factual record of real events or real people.

I could escape this feeling
With my China girl . . .   — DAVID BOWIE & IGGY POP

ACT I • Scene I

(*M. Gallimard's prison cell. Paris. 1988.*

Lights fade up to reveal Rene Gallimard, sixty-five, in a prison cell. He wears a comfortable bathrobe and looks old and tired. The sparsely furnished cell contains a wooden crate, upon which sits a hot plate with a kettle and a portable tape recorder. Gallimard sits on the crate staring at the recorder, a sad smile on his face.

Upstage Song, who appears as a beautiful woman in traditional Chinese garb, dances a traditional piece from the Peking Opera, surrounded by the percussive clatter of Chinese music.

Then, slowly, lights and sound cross-fade; the Chinese opera music dissolves into a Western opera, the "Love Duet" from Puccini's Madame Butterfly. *Song continues dancing, now to the Western accompaniment. Though her movements are the same, the difference in music now gives them a balletic quality.*

Gallimard rises, and turns upstage towards the figure of Song, who dances without acknowledging him.)

GALLIMARD: Butterfly, Butterfly . . .

(*He forces himself to turn away, as the image of Song fades out, and talks to us.*)

The limits of my cell are as such: four-and-a-half meters by five. There's one window against the far wall; a door, very strong, to protect me from autograph hounds. I'm responsible for the tape recorder, the hot plate, and this charming coffee table.

When I want to eat, I'm marched off to the dining room — hot, steaming slop appears on my plate. When I want to sleep, the light bulb turns itself off — the work of fairies. It's an enchanted space I occupy. The French — we know how to run a prison.

But, to be honest, I'm not treated like an ordinary prisoner. Why? Because I'm a celebrity. You see, I make people laugh.

I never dreamed this day would arrive. I've never been considered witty or clever. In fact, as a young boy, in an informal poll among my grammar school classmates, I was voted "least likely to be invited to a party." It's a title I managed to hold on to for many years. Despite some stiff competition.

But now, how the tables turn! Look at me: the life of every social function in Paris. Paris? Why be modest: My fame has spread to Amsterdam, London, New York. Listen to them! In the world's smartest parlors. I'm the one who lifts their spirits!

(*With a flourish, Gallimard directs our attention to another part of the stage.*)

Scene II

(*A party. 1988.*

Lights go up on a chic-looking parlor, where a well-dressed trio, two men and one woman, make conversation. Gallimard also remains lit; he observes them from his cell.)

WOMAN: And what of Gallimard?
MAN 1: Gallimard?
MAN 2: Gallimard!
GALLIMARD (*to us*): You see? They're all determined to say my name, as if it were some new dance.
WOMAN: He still claims not to believe the truth.
MAN 1: What? Still? Even since the trial?
WOMAN: Yes. Isn't it mad?
MAN 2 (*laughing*):   He says . . . it was dark . . . and she was very modest!

(*The trio break into laughter.*)

MAN 1: So — what? He never touched her with his hands?
MAN 2: Perhaps he did, and simply misidentified the equipment. A compelling case for sex education in the schools.
WOMAN: To protect the National Security — the Church can't argue with that.
MAN 1: That's impossible! How could he not know?
MAN 2: Simple ignorance.
MAN 1: For twenty years?
MAN 2: Time flies when you're being stupid.
WOMAN: Well, I thought the French were ladies' men.
MAN 2: It seems Monsieur Gallimard was overly anxious to live up to his national reputation.
WOMAN: Well, he's not very good-looking.
MAN 1: No, he's not.
MAN 2: Certainly not.
WOMAN: Actually, I feel sorry for him.
MAN 2: A toast! To Monsieur Gallimard!
WOMAN: Yes! To Gallimard!
MAN 1: To Gallimard!
MAN 2: *Vive la différence!*

(*They toast, laughing. Lights down on them.*)

Scene III

(*M. Gallimard's cell.*)

GALLIMARD (*smiling*): You see? They toast me. I've become a patron saint of the socially inept. Can they really be so foolish? Men like that — they should be scratching at my door, begging to learn my secrets! For I, Rene Gallimard, you see, I have known, and been loved by . . . the Perfect Woman.

> Alone in this cell, I sit night after night, watching our story play through my head, always searching for a new ending, one which redeems my honor, where she returns at last to my arms. And I imagine you — my ideal audience — who come to understand and even, perhaps just a little, to envy me.

(*He turns on his tape recorder. Over the house speakers, we hear the opening phrases of* Madame Butterfly.)

GALLIMARD: In order for you to understand what I did and why, I must introduce you to my favorite opera: *Madame Butterfly*. By Giacomo Puccini. First produced at La Scala, Milan, in 1904, it is now beloved throughout the Western world.

(*As Gallimard describes the opera, the tape segues in and out to sections he may be describing.*)

GALLIMARD: And why not? Its heroine, Cio-Cio-San, also known as Butterfly, is a feminine ideal, beautiful and brave. And its hero, the man for whom she gives up everything, is — (*He pulls out a naval officer's cap from under his crate, pops it on his head, and struts about.*) — not very good-looking, not too bright, and pretty much a wimp: Benjamin Franklin Pinkerton of the U.S. Navy. As the curtain rises, he's just closed on two great bargains: one on a house, the other on a woman — call it a package deal.

> Pinkerton purchased the rights to Butterfly for one hundred yen — in modern currency, equivalent to about . . . sixty-six cents. So, he's feeling pretty pleased with himself as Sharpless, the American consul, arrives to witness the marriage.

(*Marc, wearing an official cap to designate Sharpless, enters and plays the character.*)

SHARPLESS/MARC: Pinkerton!

PINKERTON/GALLIMARD: Sharpless! How's it hangin'? It's a great day, just great. Between my house, my wife, and the rickshaw ride in from town, I've saved nineteen cents just this morning.

SHARPLESS: Wonderful. I can see the inscription on your tombstone already: "I saved a dollar, here I lie." (*He looks around.*) Nice house.

PINKERTON: It's artistic. Artistic, don't you think? Like the way the shoji screens slide open to reveal the wet bar and disco mirror ball? Classy, huh? Great for impressing the chicks.

SHARPLESS: "Chicks"? Pinkerton, you're going to be a married man!

PINKERTON: Well, sort of.

SHARPLESS: What do you mean?

PINKERTON: This country — Sharpless, it is okay. You got all these geisha girls running around —

SHARPLESS: I know! I live here!

PINKERTON: Then, you know the marriage laws, right? I split for one month, it's annulled!

SHARPLESS: Leave it to you to read the fine print. Who's the lucky girl?

PINKERTON: Cio-Cio-San. Her friends call her Butterfly. Sharpless, she eats out of my hand!

SHARPLESS: She's probably very hungry.

PINKERTON: Not like American girls. It's true what they say about Oriental girls. They want to be treated bad!

SHARPLESS: Oh, please!

PINKERTON: It's true!

SHARPLESS: Are you serious about this girl?

PINKERTON: I'm marrying her, aren't I?

SHARPLESS: Yes — with generous trade-in terms.

PINKERTON: When I leave, she'll know what it's like to have loved a real man. And I'll even buy her a few nylons.

SHARPLESS: You aren't planning to take her with you?

PINKERTON: Huh? Where?

SHARPLESS: Home!

PINKERTON: You mean, America? Are you crazy? Can you see her trying to buy rice in St. Louis?

SHARPLESS: So, you're not serious.

(*Pause.*)

PINKERTON/GALLIMARD (*as Pinkerton*): Consul, I am a sailor in port. (*As Gallimard.*) They then proceed to sing the famous duet, "The Whole World Over."

(*The duet plays on the speakers. Gallimard, as Pinkerton, lip-syncs his lines from the opera.*)

GALLIMARD: To give a rough translation: "The whole world over, the Yankee travels, casting his anchor wherever he wants. Life's not worth living unless he can win the hearts of the fairest maidens, then hotfoot it off the premises ASAP." (*He turns towards Marc.*) In the preceding scene, I played Pinkerton, the womanizing cad, and my friend Marc from school . . . (*Marc bows grandly for our benefit.*) played Sharpless, the sensitive soul of reason. In life, however, our positions were usually — no, always — reversed.

Scene IV

(*École Nationale.° Aix-en-Provence. 1947.*)

GALLIMARD: No, Marc, I think I'd rather stay home.

MARC: Are you crazy?! We are going to Dad's condo in Marseilles! You know what happened last time?

GALLIMARD: Of course I do.

École Nationale: National School.

MARC: Of course you don't! You never know. . . . They stripped, Rene!

GALLIMARD: Who stripped?

MARC: The girls!

GALLIMARD: Girls? Who said anything about girls?

MARC: Rene, we're a buncha university guys goin' up to the woods. What are we gonna do — talk philosophy?

GALLIMARD: What girls? Where do you get them?

MARC: Who cares? The point is, they come. On trucks. Packed in like sardines. The back flips open, babes hop out, we're ready to roll.

GALLIMARD: You mean, they just — ?

MARC: Before you know it, every last one of them — they're stripped and splashing around my pool. There's no moon out, they can't see what's going on, their boobs are flapping, right? You close your eyes, reach out — it's grab bag, get it? Doesn't matter whose ass is between whose legs, whose teeth are sinking into who. You're just in there, going at it, eyes closed, on and on for as long as you can stand. (*Pause.*) Some fun, huh?

GALLIMARD: What happens in the morning?

MARC: In the morning, you're ready to talk some philosophy. (*Beat.*) So how 'bout it?

GALLIMARD: Marc, I can't . . . I'm afraid they'll say no — the girls. So I never ask.

MARC: You don't have to ask! That's the beauty — don't you see? They don't have to say yes. It's perfect for a guy like you, really.

GALLIMARD: You go ahead . . . I may come later.

MARC: Hey, Rene — it doesn't matter that you're clumsy and got zits — they're not looking!

GALLIMARD: Thank you very much.

MARC: Wimp.

(*Marc walks over to the other side of the stage, and starts waving and smiling at women in the audience.*)

GALLIMARD (*to us*): We now return to my version of *Madame Butterfly* and the events leading to my recent conviction for treason.

(*Gallimard notices Marc making lewd gestures.*)

GALLIMARD: Marc, what are you doing?

MARC: Huh? (*Sotto voce.*) Rene, there're a lotta great babes out there. They're probably lookin' at me and thinking, "What a dangerous guy."

GALLIMARD: Yes — how could they help but be impressed by your cool sophistication?

(*Gallimard pops the Sharpless cap on Marc's head, and points him offstage. Marc exits, leering.*)

Scene V

(*M. Gallimard's cell.*)

GALLIMARD: Next, Butterfly makes her entrance. We learn her age — fifteen . . . but very mature for her years.

(*Lights come up on the area where we saw Song dancing at the top of the play. She appears there again, now dressed as Madame Butterfly, moving to the "Love Duet." Gallimard turns upstage slightly to watch, transfixed.*)

GALLIMARD: But as she glides past him, beautiful, laughing softly behind her fan, don't we who are men sigh with hope? We, who are not handsome, nor brave, nor powerful, yet somehow believe, like Pinkerton, that we deserve a Butterfly. She arrives with all her possessions in the folds of her sleeves, lays them all out, for her man to do with as he pleases. Even her life itself — she bows her head as she whispers that she's not even worth the hundred yen he paid for her. He's already given too much, when we know he's really had to give nothing at all.

(*Music and lights on Song out. Gallimard sits at his crate.*)

GALLIMARD: In real life, women who put their total worth at less than sixty-six cents are quite hard to find. The closest we come is in the pages of these magazines. (*He reaches into his crate, pulls out a stack of girlie magazines, and begins flipping through them.*) Quite a necessity in prison. For three or four dollars, you get seven or eight women.

I first discovered these magazines at my uncle's house. One day, as a boy of twelve. The first time I saw them in his closet . . . all lined up — my body shook. Not with lust — no, with power. Here were women — a shelfful — who would do exactly as I wanted.

(*The "Love Duet" creeps in over the speakers. Special comes up, revealing, not Song this time, but a pinup girl in a sexy negligee, her back to us. Gallimard turns upstage and looks at her.*)

GIRL: I know you're watching me.

GALLIMARD: My throat . . . it's dry.

GIRL: I leave my blinds open every night before I go to bed.

GALLIMARD: I can't move.

GIRL: I leave my blinds open and the lights on.

GALLIMARD: I'm shaking. My skin is hot, but my penis is soft. Why?

GIRL: I stand in front of the window.

GALLIMARD: What is she going to do?

GIRL: I toss my hair, and I let my lips part . . . barely.

GALLIMARD: I shouldn't be seeing this. It's so dirty. I'm so bad.

GIRL: Then, slowly, I lift off my nightdress.

GALLIMARD: Oh, god. I can't believe it. I can't —

GIRL: I toss it to the ground.

GALLIMARD: Now, she's going to walk away. She's going to —

GIRL: I stand there, in the light, displaying myself.

GALLIMARD: No. She's — why is she naked?

GIRL: To you.
GALLIMARD: In front of a window? This is wrong. No —
GIRL: Without shame.
GALLIMARD: No, she must . . . like it.
GIRL: I like it.
GALLIMARD: She . . . she wants me to see.
GIRL: I want you to see.
GALLIMARD: I can't believe it! She's getting excited!
GIRL: I can't see you. You can do whatever you want.
GALLIMARD: I can't do a thing. Why?
GIRL: What would you like me to do . . . next?

(*Lights go down on her. Music off. Silence, as Gallimard puts away his magazines. Then he resumes talking to us.*)

GALLIMARD: Act Two begins with Butterfly staring at the ocean. Pinkerton's been called back to the U.S., and he's given his wife a detailed schedule of his plans. In the column marked "return date," he's written "when the robins nest." This failed to ignite her suspicions. Now, three years have passed without a peep from him. Which brings a response from her faithful servant, Suzuki.

(*Comrade Chin enters, playing Suzuki.*)

SUZUKI: Girl, he's a loser. What'd he ever give you? Nineteen cents and those ugly Day-Glo stockings? Look, it's finished! Kaput! Done! And you should be glad! I mean, the guy was a woofer! He tried before, you know — before he met you, he went down to geisha central and plunked down his spare change in front of the usual candidates — everyone else gagged! These are hungry prostitutes, and they were not interested, get the picture? Now, stop slathering when an American ship sails in, and let's make some bucks — I mean, yen! We are broke!

    Now, what about Yamadori? Hey, hey — don't look away — the man is a prince — figuratively, and, what's even better, literally. He's rich, he's handsome, he says he'll die if you don't marry him — and he's even willing to overlook the little fact that you've been deflowered all over the place by a foreign devil. What do you mean, "But he's Japanese"? What do you think you are? You think you've been touched by the whitey god? He was a sailor with dirty hands!

(*Suzuki stalks offstage.*)

GALLIMARD: She's also visited by Consul Sharpless, sent by Pinkerton on a minor errand.

(*Marc enters, as Sharpless.*)

SHARPLESS: I hate this job.
GALLIMARD: This Pinkerton — he doesn't show up personally to tell his wife he's abandoning her. No, he sends a government diplomat . . . at taxpayers' expense.
SHARPLESS: Butterfly? Butterfly? I have some bad — I'm going to be ill. Butterfly, I came to tell you —
GALLIMARD: Butterfly says she knows he'll return and if

he doesn't she'll kill herself rather than go back to her own people. (*Beat.*) This causes a lull in the conversation.
SHARPLESS: Let's put it this way . . .
GALLIMARD: Butterfly runs into the next room, and returns holding —

(*Sound cue: a baby crying. Sharpless, "seeing" this, backs away.*)

SHARPLESS: Well, good. Happy to see things going so well. I suppose I'll be going now. Ta ta. Ciao. (*He turns away. Sound cue out.*) I hate this job. (*He exits.*)
GALLIMARD: At that moment, Butterfly spots in the harbor an American ship — the *Abramo Lincoln!*

(*Music cue: "The Flower Duet." Song, still dressed as Butterfly, changes into a wedding kimono, moving to the music.*)

GALLIMARD: This is the moment that redeems her years of waiting. With Suzuki's help, they cover the room with flowers —

(*Chin, as Suzuki, trudges onstage and drops a lone flower without much enthusiasm.*)

GALLIMARD: — and she changes into her wedding dress to prepare for Pinkerton's arrival.

(*Suzuki helps Butterfly change. Helga enters, and helps Gallimard change into a tuxedo.*)

GALLIMARD: I married a woman older than myself — Helga.
HELGA: My father was ambassador to Australia. I grew up among criminals and kangaroos.
GALLIMARD: Hearing that brought me to the altar —

(*Helga exits.*)

GALLIMARD: — where I took a vow renouncing love. No fantasy woman would ever want me, so, yes, I would settle for a quick leap up the career ladder. Passion, I banish, and in its place — practicality!
    But my vows had long since lost their charm by the time we arrived in China. The sad truth is that all men want a beautiful woman, and the uglier the man, the greater the want.

(*Suzuki makes final adjustments of Butterfly's costume, as does Gallimard of his tuxedo.*)

GALLIMARD: I married late, at age thirty-one. I was faithful to my marriage for eight years. Until the day when, as a junior-level diplomat in puritanical Peking, in a parlor at the German ambassador's house, during the "Reign of a Hundred Flowers,"° I first saw her . . . singing the death scene from *Madame Butterfly.*

(*Suzuki runs offstage.*)

Reign of a Hundred Flowers: A brief period in 1957 when freedom of expression was allowed in China.

Scene VI

(*German ambassador's house. Beijing. 1960.*
The upstage special area now becomes a stage. Several chairs face upstage, representing seating for some twenty guests in the parlor. A few "diplomats"— Renee, Marc, Toulon — in formal dress enter and take seats.
Gallimard also sits down, but turns towards us and continues to talk. Orchestral accompaniment on the tape is now replaced by a simple piano. Song picks up the death scene from the point where Butterfly uncovers the hara-kiri knife.)

GALLIMARD: The ending is pitiful. Pinkerton, in an act of great courage, stays home and sends his American wife to pick up Butterfly's child. The truth, long deferred, has come up to her door.

(*Song, playing Butterfly, sings the lines from the opera in her own voice — which, though not classical, should be decent.*)

SONG: "Con onor muore / chi non puo serbar / vita con onore."

GALLIMARD (*simultaneously*): "Death with honor / Is better than life / Life with dishonor."

(*The stage is illuminated; we are now completely within an elegant diplomat's residence. Song proceeds to play out an abbreviated death scene. Everyone in the room applauds. Song, shyly, takes her bows. Others in the room rush to congratulate her. Gallimard remains with us.*)

GALLIMARD: They say in opera the voice is everything. That's probably why I'd never before enjoyed opera. Here . . . here was a Butterfly with little or no voice — but she had the grace, the delicacy . . . I believed this girl. I believed her suffering. I wanted to take her in my arms — so delicate, even I could protect her, take her home, pamper her until she smiled.

(*Over the course of the preceding speech, Song has broken from the upstage crowd and moved directly upstage of Gallimard.*)

SONG: Excuse me. Monsieur . . . ?

(*Gallimard turns upstage, shocked.*)

GALLIMARD: Oh! Gallimard. Mademoiselle . . . ? A beautiful . . .
SONG: Song Liling.
GALLIMARD: A beautiful performance.
SONG: Oh, please.
GALLIMARD: I usually —
SONG: You make me blush. I'm no opera singer at all.
GALLIMARD: I usually don't like *Butterfly*.
SONG: I can't blame you in the least.
GALLIMARD: I mean, the story —
SONG: Ridiculous.
GALLIMARD: I like the story, but . . . what?
SONG: Oh, you like it?

GALLIMARD: I . . . what I mean is, I've always seen it played by huge women in so much bad makeup.
SONG: Bad makeup is not unique to the West.
GALLIMARD: But, who can believe them?
SONG: And you believe me?
GALLIMARD: Absolutely. You were utterly convincing. It's the first time —
SONG: Convincing? As a Japanese woman? The Japanese used hundreds of our people for medical experiments during the war, you know. But I gather such an irony is lost on you.
GALLIMARD: No! I was about to say, it's the first time I've seen the beauty of the story.
SONG: Really?
GALLIMARD: Of her death. It's a . . . a pure sacrifice. He's unworthy, but what can she do? She loves him . . . so much. It's a very beautiful story.
SONG: Well, yes, to a Westerner.
GALLIMARD: Excuse me?
SONG: It's one of your favorite fantasies, isn't it? The submissive Oriental woman and the cruel white man.
GALLIMARD: Well, I didn't quite mean . . .
SONG: Consider it this way: what would you say if a blonde homecoming queen fell in love with a short Japanese businessman? He treats her cruelly, then goes home for three years, during which time she prays to his picture and turns down marriage from a young Kennedy. Then, when she learns he has remarried, she kills herself. Now, I believe you would consider this girl to be a deranged idiot, correct? But because it's an Oriental who kills herself for a Westerner — ah! — you find it beautiful.

(*Silence.*)

GALLIMARD: Yes . . . well . . . I see your point . . .
SONG: I will never do Butterfly again, Monsieur Gallimard. If you wish to see some real theater, come to the Peking Opera sometime. Expand your mind.

(*Song walks offstage. Other guests exit with her.*)

GALLIMARD (*to us*): So much for protecting her in my big Western arms.

Scene VII

(*M. Gallimard's apartment. Beijing. 1960.*
Gallimard changes from his tux into a casual suit. Helga enters.)

GALLIMARD: The Chinese are an incredibly arrogant people.
HELGA: They warned us about that in Paris, remember?
GALLIMARD: Even Parisians consider them arrogant. That's a switch.
HELGA: What is it that Madame Su says? "We are a very old civilization." I never know if she's talking about her country or herself.
GALLIMARD: I walk around here, all I hear every day,

everywhere is how *old* this culture is. The fact that "old" may be synonymous with "senile" doesn't occur to them.

HELGA: You're not going to change them. "East is east, west is west, and . . ." whatever that guy said.

GALLIMARD: It's just that — silly. I met . . . at Ambassador Koening's tonight — you should've been there.

HELGA: Koening? Oh god, no. Did he enchant you all again with the history of Bavaria?

GALLIMARD: No. I met, I suppose, the Chinese equivalent of a diva. She's a singer in the Chinese opera.

HELGA: They have an opera, too? Do they sing in Chinese? Or maybe — in Italian?

GALLIMARD: Tonight, she did sing in Italian.

HELGA: How'd she manage that?

GALLIMARD: She must've been educated in the West before the Revolution. Her French is very good also. Anyway, she sang the death scene from *Madame Butterfly*.

HELGA: *Madame Butterfly!* Then I should have come. (*She begins humming, floating around the room as if dragging long kimono sleeves.*) Did she have a nice costume? I think it's a classic piece of music.

GALLIMARD: That's what *I* thought, too. Don't let her hear you say that.

HELGA: What's wrong?

GALLIMARD: Evidently the Chinese hate it.

HELGA: She hated it, but she performed it anyway? Is she perverse?

GALLIMARD: They hate it because the white man gets the girl. Sour grapes if you ask me.

HELGA: Politics again? Why can't they just hear it as a piece of beautiful music? So, what's in their opera?

GALLIMARD: I don't know. But, whatever it is, I'm sure it must be *old*.

(*Helga exits.*)

Scene VIII

(*Chinese opera house and the streets of Beijing. 1960. The sound of gongs clanging fills the stage.*)

GALLIMARD: My wife's innocent question kept ringing in my ears. I asked around, but no one knew anything about the Chinese opera. It took four weeks, but my curiosity overcame my cowardice. This Chinese diva — this unwilling Butterfly — what did she do to make her so proud?

The room was hot, and full of smoke. Wrinkled faces, old women, teeth missing — a man with a growth on his neck, like a human toad. All smiling, pipes falling from their mouths, cracking nuts between their teeth, a live chicken pecking at my foot — all looking, screaming, gawking . . . at her.

(*The upstage area is suddenly hit with a harsh white light. It has become the stage for the Chinese opera performance. Two dancers enter, along with Song. Gallimard stands apart, watching. Song glides gracefully*

amidst the two dancers. Drums suddenly slam to a halt. Song strikes a pose, looking straight at Gallimard. Dancers exit. Light change. Pause, then Song walks right off the stage and straight up to Gallimard.)

SONG: Yes. You. White man. I'm looking straight at you.

GALLIMARD: Me?

SONG: You see any other white men? It was too easy to spot you. How often does a man in my audience come in a tie?

(*Song starts to remove her costume. Underneath, she wears simple baggy clothes. They are now backstage. The show is over.*)

SONG: So, you are an adventurous imperialist?

GALLIMARD: I . . . thought it would further my education.

SONG: It took you four weeks. Why?

GALLIMARD: I've been busy.

SONG: Well, education has always been undervalued in the West, hasn't it?

GALLIMARD (*laughing*): I don't think that's true.

SONG: No, you wouldn't. You're a Westerner. How can you objectively judge your own values?

GALLIMARD: I think it's possible to achieve some distance.

SONG: Do you? (*Pause.*) It stinks in here. Let's go.

GALLIMARD: These are the smells of your loyal fans.

SONG: I love them for being my fans, I hate the smell they leave behind. I too can distance myself from my people. (*She looks around, then whispers in his ear.*) "Art for the masses" is a shitty excuse to keep artists poor. (*She pops a cigarette in her mouth.*) Be a gentleman, will you? And light my cigarette.

(*Gallimard fumbles for a match.*)

GALLIMARD: I don't . . . smoke.

SONG (*lighting her own*): Your loss. Had you lit my cigarette, I might have blown a puff of smoke right between your eyes. Come.

(*They start to walk about the stage. It is a summer night on the Beijing streets. Sounds of the city play on the house speakers.*)

SONG: How I wish there were even a tiny café to sit in. With cappuccinos, and men in tuxedos, and bad expatriate jazz.

GALLIMARD: If my history serves me correctly, you weren't even allowed into the clubs in Shanghai before the Revolution.

SONG: Your history serves you poorly, Monsieur Gallimard. True, there were signs reading "No dogs and Chinamen." But a woman, especially a delicate Oriental woman — we always go where we please. Could you imagine it otherwise? Clubs in China filled with pasty, big-thighed white women, while thousands of slender lotus blossoms wait just outside the door? Never. The clubs would be empty. (*Beat.*) We have always held a certain fascination for you Caucasian men, have we not?

GALLIMARD: But . . . that fascination is imperialist, or so you tell me.

SONG: Do you believe everything I tell you? Yes. It is always imperialist. But sometimes . . . sometimes, it is also mutual. Oh — this is my flat.

GALLIMARD: I didn't even —

SONG: Thank you. Come another time and we will further expand your mind.

(*Song exits. Gallimard continues roaming the streets as he speaks to us.*)

GALLIMARD: What was that? What did she mean, "Sometimes . . . it is mutual"? Women do not flirt with me. And I normally can't talk to them. But tonight, I held up my end of the conversation.

Scene IX

(*Gallimard's bedroom. Beijing. 1960. Helga enters.*)

HELGA: You didn't tell me you'd be home late.

GALLIMARD: I didn't intend to. Something came up.

HELGA: Oh? Like what?

GALLIMARD: I went to the . . . to the Dutch ambassador's home.

HELGA: Again?

GALLIMARD: There was a reception for a visiting scholar. He's writing a six-volume treatise on the Chinese revolution. We all gathered that meant he'd have to live here long enough to actually write six volumes, and we all expressed our deepest sympathies.

HELGA: Well, I had a good night too. I went with the ladies to a martial arts demonstration. Some of those men — when they break those thick boards — (*she mimes fanning herself*) whoo-whoo!

(*Helga exits. Lights dim.*)

GALLIMARD: I lied to my wife. Why? I've never had any reason to lie before. But what reason did I have tonight? I didn't do anything wrong. That night, I had a dream. Other people, I've been told, have dreams when angels appear. Or dragons, or Sophia Loren in a towel. In my dream, Marc from school appeared.

(*Marc enters, in a nightshirt and cap.*)

MARC: Rene! You met a girl!

(*Gallimard and Marc stumble down the Beijing streets. Night sounds over the speakers.*)

GALLIMARD: It's not that amazing, thank you.

MARC: No! It's so monumental, I heard about it halfway around the world in my sleep!

GALLIMARD: I've met girls before, you know.

MARC: Name one. I've come across time and space to congratulate you. (*He hands Gallimard a bottle of wine.*)

GALLIMARD: Marc, this is expensive.

MARC: On those rare occasions when you become a formless spirit, why not steal the best?

(*Marc pops open the bottle, begins to share it with Gallimard.*)

GALLIMARD: You embarrass me. She . . . there's no reason to think she likes me.

MARC: "Sometimes, it is mutual"?

GALLIMARD: Oh.

MARC: "Mutual"? "Mutual"? What does that mean?

GALLIMARD: You heard?

MARC: It means the money is in the bank, you only have to write the check!

GALLIMARD: I am a married man!

MARC: And an excellent one too. I cheated after . . . six months. Then again and again, until now — three hundred girls in twelve years.

GALLIMARD: I don't think we should hold that up as a model.

MARC: Of course not! My life — it is disgusting! Phooey! Phooey! But, you — you are the model husband.

GALLIMARD: Anyway, it's impossible. I'm a foreigner.

MARC: Ah, yes. She cannot love you, it is taboo, but something deep inside her heart . . . she cannot help herself . . . she must surrender to you. It is her destiny.

GALLIMARD: How do you imagine all this?

MARC: The same way you do. It's an old story. It's in our blood. They fear us, Rene. Their women fear us. And their men — their men hate us. And, you know something? They are all correct.

(*They spot a light in a window.*)

MARC: There! There, Rene!

GALLIMARD: It's her window.

MARC: Late at night — it burns. The light — it burns for you.

GALLIMARD: I won't look. It's not respectful.

MARC: We don't have to be respectful. We're foreign devils.

(*Enter Song, in a sheer robe, her face completely swathed in black cloth. The "One Fine Day" aria creeps in over the speakers. With her back to us, Song mimes attending to her toilette. Her robe comes loose, revealing her white shoulders.*)

MARC: All your life you've waited for a beautiful girl who would lay down for you. All your life you've smiled like a saint when it's happened to every other man you know. And you see them in magazines and you see them in movies. And you wonder, what's wrong with me? Will anyone beautiful ever want me? As the years pass, your hair thins and you struggle to hold on to even your hopes. Stop struggling, Rene. The wait is over. (*He exits.*)

GALLIMARD: Marc? Marc?

(*At that moment, Song, her back still towards us, drops her robe. A second of her naked back, then a sound cue: a phone ringing, very loud. Blackout, followed in the next beat by a special up on the bedroom area, where a phone now sits. Gallimard stumbles across the stage and picks up the phone. Sound cue out. Over the course of his conversation, area lights fill in the vicinity of his bed. It is the following morning.*)

GALLIMARD: Yes? Hello?
SONG (*offstage*): Is it very early?
GALLIMARD: Why, yes.
SONG (*offstage*): How early?
GALLIMARD: It's . . . it's 5:30. Why are you — ?
SONG (*offstage*): But it's light outside. Already.
GALLIMARD: It is. The sun must be in confusion today.

(*Over the course of Song's next speech, her upstage special comes up again. She sits in a chair, legs crossed, in a robe, telephone to her ear.*)

SONG: I waited until I saw the sun. That was as much discipline as I could manage for one night. Do you forgive me?
GALLIMARD: Of course . . . for what?
SONG: Then I'll ask you quickly. Are you really interested in the opera?
GALLIMARD: Why, yes. Yes I am.
SONG: Then come again next Thursday. I am playing *The Drunken Beauty*. May I count on you?
GALLIMARD: Yes. You may.
SONG: Perfect. Well, I must be getting to bed. I'm exhausted. It's been a very long night for me.

(*Song hangs up; special on her goes off. Gallimard begins to dress for work.*)

Scene X

(*Song Liling's apartment. Beijing. 1960.*)

GALLIMARD: I returned to the opera that next week, and the week after that . . . she keeps our meetings so short — perhaps fifteen, twenty minutes at most. So I am left each week with a thirst which is intensified. In this way, fifteen weeks have gone by. I am starting to doubt the words of my friend Marc. But no, not really. In my heart, I know she has . . . an interest in me. I suspect this is her way. She is outwardly bold and outspoken, yet her heart is shy and afraid. It is the Oriental in her at war with her Western education.
SONG (*offstage*): I will be out in an instant. Ask the servant for anything you want.
GALLIMARD: Tonight, I have finally been invited to enter her apartment. Though the idea is almost beyond belief, I believe she is afraid of me.

(*Gallimard looks around the room. He picks up a picture in a frame, studies it. Without his noticing, Song enters, dressed elegantly in a black gown from the twenties. She stands in the doorway looking like Anna May Wong.°*)

Anna May Wong: (1905–1961), Chinese American actor known for her exotic beauty and most often cast as a villain.

SONG: That is my father.
GALLIMARD (*surprised*): Mademoiselle Song . . .

(*She glides up to him, snatches away the picture.*)

SONG: It is very good that he did not live to see the Revolution. They would, no doubt, have made him kneel on broken glass. Not that he didn't deserve such a punishment. But he is my father. I would've hated to see it happen.
GALLIMARD: I'm very honored that you've allowed me to visit your home.

(*Song curtseys.*)

SONG: Thank you. Oh! Haven't you been poured any tea?
GALLIMARD: I'm really not —
SONG (*to her offstage servant*): Shu-Fang! Cha! Kwailah! (*To Gallimard.*) I'm sorry. You want everything to be perfect —
GALLIMARD: Please.
SONG: — and before the evening even begins —
GALLIMARD: I'm really not thirsty.
SONG: — it's ruined.
GALLIMARD (*sharply*): Mademoiselle Song!

(*Song sits down.*)

SONG: I'm sorry.
GALLIMARD: What are you apologizing for now?

(*Pause; Song starts to giggle.*)

SONG: I don't know!

(*Gallimard laughs.*)

GALLIMARD: Exactly my point.
SONG: Oh, I am silly. Light-headed. I promise not to apologize for anything else tonight, do you hear me?
GALLIMARD: That's a good girl.

(*Shu-Fang, a servant girl, comes out with a tea tray and starts to pour.*)

SONG (*to Shu-Fang*): No! I'll pour myself for the gentleman!

(*Shu-Fang, staring at Gallimard, exits.*)

GALLIMARD: You have a beautiful home.
SONG: No, I . . . I don't even know why I invited you up.
GALLIMARD: Well, I'm glad you did.

(*Song looks around the room.*)

SONG: There is an element of danger to your presence.
GALLIMARD: Oh?
SONG: You must know.
GALLIMARD: It doesn't concern me. We both know why I'm here.
SONG: It doesn't concern me either. No . . . well perhaps . . .
GALLIMARD: What?
SONG: Perhaps I am slightly afraid of scandal.
GALLIMARD: What are we doing?
SONG: I'm entertaining you. In my parlor.
GALLIMARD: In France, that would hardly —
SONG: France. France is a country living in the modern era.

Perhaps even ahead of it. China is a nation whose soul is firmly rooted two thousand years in the past. What I do, even pouring the tea for you now . . . it has . . . implications. The walls and windows say so. Even my own heart, strapped inside this Western dress . . . even it says things — things I don't care to hear.

(*Song hands Gallimard a cup of tea. Gallimard puts his hand over both the teacup and Song's hand.*)

GALLIMARD: This is a beautiful dress.

SONG: Don't.

GALLIMARD: What?

SONG: I don't even know if it looks right on me.

GALLIMARD: Believe me —

SONG: You are from France. You see so many beautiful women.

GALLIMARD: France? Since when are the European women — ?

SONG: Oh! What am I trying to do, anyway?!

(*Song runs to the door, composes herself, then turns towards Gallimard.*)

SONG: Monsieur Gallimard, perhaps you should go.

GALLIMARD: But . . . why?

SONG: There's something wrong about this.

GALLIMARD: I don't see what.

SONG: I feel . . . I am not myself.

GALLIMARD: No. You're nervous.

SONG: Please. Hard as I try to be modern, to speak like a man, to hold a Western woman's strong face up to my own . . . in the end, I fail. A small, frightened heart beats too quickly and gives me away. Monsieur Gallimard, I'm a Chinese girl. I've never . . . never invited a man up to my flat before. The forwardness of my actions makes my skin burn.

GALLIMARD: What are you afraid of? Certainly not me, I hope.

SONG: I'm a modest girl.

GALLIMARD: I know. And very beautiful. (*He touches her hair.*)

SONG: Please — go now. The next time you see me, I shall again be myself.

GALLIMARD: I like you the way you are right now.

SONG: You are a cad.

GALLIMARD: What do you expect? I'm a foreign devil.

(*Gallimard walks downstage. Song exits.*)

GALLIMARD (*to us*): Did you hear the way she talked about Western women? Much differently than the first night. She does — she feels inferior to them — and to me.

Scene XI

(*The French embassy. Beijing. 1960.
Gallimard moves towards a desk.*)

GALLIMARD: I determined to try an experiment. In *Madame Butterfly,* Cio-Cio-San fears that the West-ern man who catches a butterfly will pierce its heart with a needle, then leave it to perish. I began to wonder: had I, too, caught a butterfly who would writhe on a needle?

(*Marc enters, dressed as a bureaucrat, holding a stack of papers. As Gallimard speaks, Marc hands papers to him. He peruses, then signs, stamps, or rejects them.*)

GALLIMARD: Over the next five weeks, I worked like a dynamo. I stopped going to the opera, I didn't phone or write her. I knew this little flower was waiting for me to call, and, as I wickedly refused to do so, I felt for the first time that rush of power — the absolute power of a man.

(*Marc continues acting as the bureaucrat, but he now speaks as himself.*)

MARC: Rene! It's me.

GALLIMARD: Marc — I hear your voice everywhere now. Even in the midst of work.

MARC: That's because I'm watching you — all the time.

GALLIMARD: You were always the most popular guy in school.

MARC: Well, there's no guarantee of failure in life like happiness in high school. Somehow I knew I'd end up in the suburbs working for Renault and you'd be in the Orient picking exotic women off the trees. And they say there's no justice.

GALLIMARD: That's why you were my friend?

MARC: I gave you a little of my life, so that now you can give me some of yours. (*Pause.*) Remember Isabelle?

GALLIMARD: Of course I remember! She was my first experience.

MARC: We all wanted to ball her. But she only wanted me.

GALLIMARD: I had her.

MARC: Right. You balled her.

GALLIMARD: You were the only one who ever believed me.

MARC: Well, there's a good reason for that. (*Beat.*) C'mon. You must've guessed.

GALLIMARD: You told me to wait in the bushes by the cafeteria that night. The next thing I knew, she was on me. Dress up in the air.

MARC: She never wore underwear.

GALLIMARD: My arms were pinned to the dirt.

MARC: She loved the superior position. A girl ahead of her time.

GALLIMARD: I looked up, and there was this woman . . . bouncing up and down on my loins.

MARC: Screaming, right?

GALLIMARD: Screaming, and breaking off the branches all around me, and pounding my butt up and down into the dirt.

MARC: Huffing and puffing like a locomotive.

GALLIMARD: And in the middle of all this, the leaves were getting into my mouth, my legs were losing circulation, I thought, "God. So this is *it?*"

MARC: You thought that?

GALLIMARD: Well, I was worried about my legs falling off.

MARC: You didn't have a good time?

GALLIMARD: No, that's not what I — I had a great time!

MARC: You're sure?

GALLIMARD: Yeah. Really.

MARC: 'Cuz I wanted you to have a good time.

GALLIMARD: I did.

(*Pause.*)

MARC: Shit. (*Pause.*) When all is said and done, she was kind of a lousy lay, wasn't she? I mean, there was a lot of energy there, but you never knew what she was doing with it. Like when she yelled "I'm coming!"— hell, it was so loud, you wanted to go, "Look, it's not that big a deal."

GALLIMARD: I got scared. I thought she meant someone was actually coming. (*Pause.*) But, Marc?

MARC: What?

GALLIMARD: Thanks.

MARC: Oh, don't mention it.

GALLIMARD: It was my first experience.

MARC: Yeah. You got her.

GALLIMARD: I got her.

MARC: Wait! Look at that letter again!

(*Gallimard picks up one of the papers he's been stamping, and rereads it.*)

GALLIMARD (*to us*): After six weeks, they began to arrive. The letters.

(*Upstage special on Song, as Madame Butterfly. The scene is underscored by the "Love Duet."*)

SONG: Did we fight? I do not know. Is the opera no longer of interest to you? Please come — my audiences miss the white devil in their midst.

(*Gallimard looks up from the letter, towards us.*)

GALLIMARD (*to us*): A concession, but much too dignified. (*Beat; he discards the letter.*) I skipped the opera again that week to complete a position paper on trade.

(*The bureaucrat hands him another letter.*)

SONG: Six weeks have passed since last we met. Is this your practice — to leave friends in the lurch? Sometimes I hate you, sometimes I hate myself, but always I miss you.

GALLIMARD (*to us*): Better, but I don't like the way she calls me "friend." When a woman calls a man her "friend," she's calling him a eunuch or a homosexual. (*Beat; he discards the letter.*) I was absent from the opera for the seventh week, feeling a sudden urge to clean out my files.

(*Bureaucrat hands him another letter.*)

SONG: Your rudeness is beyond belief. I don't deserve this cruelty. Don't bother to call. I'll have you turned away at the door.

GALLIMARD (*to us*): I didn't. (*He discards the letter;*

bureaucrat hands him another.) And then finally, the letter that concluded my experiment.

SONG: I am out of words. I can hide behind dignity no longer. What do you want? I have already given you my shame.

(*Gallimard gives the letter back to Marc, slowly. Special on Song fades out.*)

GALLIMARD (*to us*): Reading it, I became suddenly ashamed. Yes, my experiment had been a success. She was turning on my needle. But the victory seemed hollow.

MARC: Hollow?! Are you crazy?

GALLIMARD: Nothing, Marc. Please go away.

MARC (*exiting, with papers*): Haven't I taught you anything?

GALLIMARD: "I have already given you my shame." I had to attend a reception that evening. On the way, I felt sick. If there is a God, surely he would punish me now. I had finally gained power over a beautiful woman, only to abuse it cruelly. There must be justice in the world. I had the strange feeling that the ax would fall this very evening.

Scene XII

(*Ambassador Toulon's residence. Beijing. 1960.*
  Sound cue: party noises. Light change. We are now in a spacious residence. Toulon, the French ambassador, enters and taps Gallimard on the shoulder.)

TOULON: Gallimard? Can I have a word? Over here.

GALLIMARD (*to us*): Manuel Toulon. French ambassador to China. He likes to think of us all as his children. Rather like God.

TOULON: Look, Gallimard, there's not much to say. I've liked you. From the day you walked in. You were no leader, but you were tidy and efficient.

GALLIMARD: Thank you, sir.

TOULON: Don't jump the gun. Okay, our needs in China are changing. It's embarrassing that we lost Indochina. Someone just wasn't on the ball there. I don't mean you personally, of course.

GALLIMARD: Thank you, sir.

TOULON: We're going to be doing a lot more information-gathering in the future. The nature of our work here is changing. Some people are just going to have to go. It's nothing personal.

GALLIMARD: Oh.

TOULON: Want to know a secret? Vice-Consul LeBon is being transferred.

GALLIMARD (*to us*): My immediate superior!

TOULON: And most of his department.

GALLIMARD (*to us*): Just as I feared! God has seen my evil heart —

TOULON: But not you.

GALLIMARD (*to us*): — and he's taking her away just as . . . (*To Toulon.*) Excuse me, sir?

TOULON: Scare you? I think I did. Cheer up, Gallimard. I want you to replace LeBon as vice-consul.

GALLIMARD: You — ? Yes, well, thank you, sir.

TOULON: Anytime.

GALLIMARD: I . . . accept with great humility.

TOULON: Humility won't be part of the job. You're going to coordinate the revamped intelligence division. Want to know a secret? A year ago, you would've been out. But the past few months, I don't know how it happened, you've become this new aggressive confident . . . thing. And they also tell me you get along with the Chinese. So I think you're a lucky man, Gallimard. Congratulations.

(*They shake hands. Toulon exits. Party noises out. Gallimard stumbles across a darkened stage.*)

GALLIMARD: Vice-consul? Impossible! As I stumbled out of the party, I saw it written across the sky: There is no God. Or, no — say that there is a God. But that God . . . understands. Of course! God who creates Eve to serve Adam, who blesses Solomon with his harem but ties Jezebel to a burning bed° — that God is a man. And he understands! At age thirty-nine, I was suddenly initiated into the way of the world.

Scene XIII

(*Song Liling's apartment. Beijing. 1960.
Song enters, in a sheer dressing gown.*)

SONG: Are you crazy?

GALLIMARD: Mademoiselle Song —

SONG: To come here — at this hour? After . . . after eight weeks?

GALLIMARD: It's the most amazing —

SONG: You bang on my door? Scare my servants, scandalize the neighbors?

GALLIMARD: I've been promoted. To vice-consul.

(*Pause.*)

SONG: And what is that supposed to mean to me?

GALLIMARD: Are you my Butterfly?

SONG: What are you saying?

GALLIMARD: I've come tonight for an answer: are you my Butterfly?

SONG: Don't you know already?

GALLIMARD: I want you to say it.

SONG: I don't want to say it.

GALLIMARD: So, that is your answer?

SONG: You know how I feel about —

GALLIMARD: I do remember one thing.

SONG: What?

God who creates Eve . . . burning bed: Eve, Adam, Solomon, and Jezebel are biblical characters. See Gen. 2:18–25; I Kings 11:1–8; and II Kings 9:11–37.

GALLIMARD: In the letter I received today.

SONG: Don't.

GALLIMARD: "I have already given you my shame."

SONG: It's enough that I even wrote it.

GALLIMARD: Well, then —

SONG: I shouldn't have it splashed across my face.

GALLIMARD: — if that's all true —

SONG: Stop!

GALLIMARD: Then what is one more short answer?

SONG: I don't want to!

GALLIMARD: Are you my Butterfly? (*Silence; he crosses the room and begins to touch her hair.*) I want from you honesty. There should be nothing false between us. No false pride.

(*Pause.*)

SONG: Yes, I am. I am your Butterfly.

GALLIMARD: Then let me be honest with you. It is because of you that I was promoted tonight. You have changed my life forever. My little Butterfly, there should be no more secrets: I love you.

(*He starts to kiss her roughly. She resists slightly.*)

SONG: No . . . no . . . gently . . . please, I've never . . .

GALLIMARD: No?

SONG: I've tried to appear experienced, but . . . the truth is . . . no.

GALLIMARD: Are you cold?

SONG: Yes. Cold.

GALLIMARD: Then we will go very, very slowly.

(*He starts to caress her; her gown begins to open.*)

SONG: No . . . let me . . . keep my clothes . . .

GALLIMARD: But . . .

SONG: Please . . . it all frightens me. I'm a modest Chinese girl.

GALLIMARD: My poor little treasure.

SONG: I am your treasure. Though inexperienced, I am not . . . ignorant. They teach us things, our mothers, about pleasing a man.

GALLIMARD: Yes?

SONG: I'll do my best to make you happy. Turn off the lights.

(*Gallimard gets up and heads for a lamp. Song, propped up on one elbow, tosses her hair back and smiles.*)

SONG: Monsieur Gallimard?

GALLIMARD: Yes, Butterfly?

SONG: "*Vieni, vieni!*"

GALLIMARD: "Come, darling."

SONG: "*Ah! Dolce notte!*"

GALLIMARD: "Beautiful night."

SONG: "*Tutto estatico d'amor ride il ciel!*"

GALLIMARD: "All ecstatic with love, the heavens are filled with laughter."

(*He turns off the lamp. Blackout.*)

ACT II • *Scene I*

(*M. Gallimard's cell. Paris. 1988.*
Lights up on Gallimard. He sits in his cell, reading from a leaflet.)

GALLIMARD: This, from a contemporary critic's commentary on *Madame Butterfly:* "Pinkerton suffers from . . . being an obnoxious bounder whom every man in the audience itches to kick." Bully for us men in the audience! Then, in the same note: "Butterfly is the most irresistibly appealing of Puccini's 'Little Women.' Watching the succession of her humiliations is like watching a child under torture." (*He tosses the pamphlet over his shoulder.*) I suggest that, while we men may all want to kick Pinkerton, very few of us would pass up the opportunity to *be* Pinkerton.

(*Gallimard moves out of his cell.*)

Scene II

(*Gallimard and Butterfly's flat. Beijing. 1960.*
We are in a simple but well-decorated parlor. Gallimard moves to sit on a sofa, while Song, dressed in a cheongsam,° enters and curls up at his feet.)

GALLIMARD (*to us*): We secured a flat on the outskirts of Peking. Butterfly, as I was calling her now, decorated our "home" with Western furniture and Chinese antiques. And there, on a few stolen afternoons or evenings each week, Butterfly commenced her education.
SONG: The Chinese men — they keep us down.
GALLIMARD: Even in the "New Society"?
SONG: In the "New Society," we are all kept ignorant equally. That's one of the exciting things about loving a Western man. I know you are not threatened by a woman's education.
GALLIMARD: I'm no saint, Butterfly.
SONG: But you come from a progressive society.
GALLIMARD: We're not always reminding each other how "old" we are, if that's what you mean.
SONG: Exactly. We Chinese — once, I suppose, it is true, we ruled the world. But so what? How much more exciting to be part of the society ruling the world today. Tell me — what's happening in Vietnam?
GALLIMARD: Oh, Butterfly — you want me to bring my work home?
SONG: I want to know what you know. To be impressed by my man. It's not the particulars so much as the fact that you're making decisions which change the shape of the world.
GALLIMARD: Not the world. At best, a small corner.

(*Toulon enters, and sits at a desk upstage.*)

John Lithgow as Rene Gallimard and B. D. Wong as Song Liling in *M. Butterfly* at Broadway's Eugene O'Neill Theatre in 1988.

---

cheongsam: A fitted dress with a mandarin collar and side slits in the skirt.

Scene III

(*French embassy. Beijing. 1961.*
    Gallimard moves downstage, to Toulon's desk. Song remains upstage, watching.)

TOULON: And a more troublesome corner is hard to imagine.
GALLIMARD: So, the Americans plan to begin bombing?
TOULON: This is very secret, Gallimard: yes. The Americans don't have an embassy here. They're asking us to be their eyes and ears. Say Jack Kennedy signed an order to bomb North Vietnam, Laos. How would the Chinese react?
GALLIMARD: I think the Chinese will squawk —
TOULON: Uh-huh.
GALLIMARD: — but, in their hearts, they don't even like Ho Chi Minh.°

(*Pause.*)

TOULON: What a bunch of jerks. Vietnam was *our* colony. Not only didn't the Americans help us fight to keep them, but now, seven years later, they've come back to grab the territory for themselves. It's very irritating.
GALLIMARD: With all due respect, sir, why should the Americans have won our war for us back in fifty-four if we didn't have the will to win it ourselves?
TOULON: You're kidding, aren't you?

(*Pause.*)

GALLIMARD: The Orientals simply want to be associated with whoever shows the most strength and power. You live with the Chinese, sir. Do you think they like Communism?
TOULON: I live in China. Not with the Chinese.
GALLIMARD: Well, I —
TOULON: *You* live with the Chinese.
GALLIMARD: Excuse me?
TOULON: I can't keep a secret.
GALLIMARD: What are you saying?
TOULON: Only that I'm not immune to gossip. So, you're keeping a native mistress? Don't answer. It's none of my business. (*Pause.*) I'm sure she must be gorgeous.
GALLIMARD: Well . . .
TOULON: I'm impressed. You had the stamina to go out into the streets and hunt one down. Some of us have to be content with the wives of the expatriate community.
GALLIMARD: I do feel . . . fortunate.
TOULON: So, Gallimard, you've got the inside knowledge — what *do* the Chinese think?
GALLIMARD: Deep down, they miss the old days. You know, cappuccinos, men in tuxedos —
TOULON: So what do we tell the Americans about Vietnam?

Ho Chi Minh: (1890–1969), first president of North Vietnam (1945–1969).

GALLIMARD: Tell them there's a natural affinity between the West and the Orient.
TOULON: And that you speak from experience?
GALLIMARD: The Orientals are people too. They want the good things we can give them. If the Americans demonstrate the will to win, the Vietnamese will welcome them into a mutually beneficial union.
TOULON: I don't see how the Vietnamese can stand up to American firepower.
GALLIMARD: Orientals will always submit to a greater force.
TOULON: I'll note your opinions in my report. The Americans always love to hear how "welcome" they'll be. (*He starts to exit.*)
GALLIMARD: Sir?
TOULON: Mmmm?
GALLIMARD: This . . . rumor you've heard.
TOULON: Uh-huh?
GALLIMARD: How . . . widespread do you think it is?
TOULON: It's only widespread within this embassy. Where nobody talks because everybody is guilty. We were worried about you, Gallimard. We thought you were the only one here without a secret. Now you go and find a lotus blossom . . . and top us all. (*He exits.*)
GALLIMARD (*to us*): Toulon knows! And he approves! I was learning the benefits of being a man. We form our own clubs, sit behind thick doors, smoke — and celebrate the fact that we're still boys. (*He starts to move downstage, towards Song.*) So, over the —

(*Suddenly Comrade Chin enters. Gallimard backs away.*)

GALLIMARD (*to Song*): No! Why does she have to come in?
SONG: Rene, be sensible. How can they understand the story without her? Now, don't embarrass yourself.

(*Gallimard moves down center.*)

GALLIMARD (*to us*): Now, you will see why my story is so amusing to so many people. Why they snicker at parties in disbelief. Please — try to understand it from my point of view. We are all prisoners of our time and place. (*He exits.*)

Scene IV

(*Gallimard and Butterfly's flat. Beijing. 1961.*)

SONG (*to us*): 1961. The flat Monsieur Gallimard rented for us. An evening after he has gone.
CHIN: Okay, see if you can find out when the Americans plan to start bombing Vietnam. If you can find out what cities, even better.
SONG: I'll do my best, but I don't want to arouse his suspicions.
CHIN: Yeah, sure, of course. So, what else?
SONG: The Americans will increase troops in Vietnam to 170,000 soldiers with 120,000 militia and 11,000 American advisors.

CHIN (*writing*): Wait, wait, 120,000 militia and —
SONG: — 11,000 American —
CHIN: — American advisors. (*Beat.*) How do you remember so much?
SONG: I'm an actor.
CHIN: Yeah. (*Beat.*) Is that how come you dress like that?
SONG: Like what, Miss Chin?
CHIN: Like that dress! You're wearing a dress. And every time I come here, you're wearing a dress. Is that because you're an actor? Or what?
SONG: It's a . . . disguise, Miss Chin.
CHIN: Actors, I think they're all weirdos. My mother tells me actors are like gamblers or prostitutes or —
SONG: It helps me in my assignment.

(*Pause.*)

CHIN: You're not gathering information in any way that violates Communist Party principles, are you?
SONG: Why would I do that?
CHIN: Just checking. Remember: when working for the Great Proletarian State, you represent our Chairman Mao in every position you take.
SONG: I'll try to imagine the Chairman taking my positions.
CHIN: We all think of him this way. Good-bye, comrade. (*She starts to exit.*) Comrade?
SONG: Yes?
CHIN: Don't forget: there is no homosexuality in China!
SONG: Yes, I've heard.
CHIN: Just checking. (*She exits.*)
SONG (*to us*): What passes for a woman in modern China.

(*Gallimard sticks his head out from the wings.*)

GALLIMARD: Is she gone?
SONG: Yes, Rene. Please continue in your own fashion.

Scene V

(*Beijing. 1961–1963.*
   Gallimard moves to the couch where Song still sits. He lies down in her lap, and she strokes his forehead.)

GALLIMARD (*to us*): And so, over the years 1961, '62, '63, we settled into our routine, Butterfly and I. She would always have prepared a light snack and then, ever so delicately, and only if I agreed, she would start to pleasure me. With her hands, her mouth . . . too many ways to explain, and too sad, given my present situation. But mostly we would talk. About my life. Perhaps there is nothing more rare than to find a woman who passionately listens.

(*Song remains upstage, listening, as Helga enters and plays a scene downstage with Gallimard.*)

HELGA: Rene, I visited Dr. Bolleart this morning.
GALLIMARD: Why? Are you ill?
HELGA: No, no. You see, I wanted to ask him . . . that question we've been discussing.

GALLIMARD: And I told you, it's only a matter of time. Why did you bring a doctor into this? We just have to keep trying — like a crapshoot, actually.
HELGA: I went, I'm sorry. But listen: he says there's nothing wrong with me.
GALLIMARD: You see? Now, will you stop — ?
HELGA: Rene, he says he'd like you to go in and take some tests.
GALLIMARD: Why? So he can find there's nothing wrong with both of us?
HELGA: Rene, I don't ask for much. One trip! One visit! And then, whatever you want to do about it — you decide.
GALLIMARD: You're assuming he'll find something defective!
HELGA: No! Of course not! Whatever he finds — if he finds nothing, we decide what to do about nothing! But go!
GALLIMARD: If he finds nothing, we keep trying. Just like we do now.
HELGA: But at least we'll know! (*Pause.*) I'm sorry. (*She starts to exit.*)
GALLIMARD: Do you really want me to see Dr. Bolleart?
HELGA: Only if you want a child, Rene. We have to face the fact that time is running out. Only if you want a child. (*She exits.*)
GALLIMARD (*to Song*): I'm a modern man, Butterfly. And yet, I don't want to go. It's the same old voodoo. I feel like God himself is laughing at me if I can't produce a child.
SONG: You men of the West — you're obsessed by your odd desire for equality. Your wife can't give you a child, and *you're* going to the doctor?
GALLIMARD: Well, you see, she's already gone.
SONG: And because this incompetent can't find the defect, you now have to subject yourself to him? It's unnatural.
GALLIMARD: Well, what is the "natural" solution?
SONG: In Imperial China, when a man found that one wife was inadequate, he turned to another — to give him his son.
GALLIMARD: What do you — ? I can't . . . marry you, yet.
SONG: Please. I'm not asking you to be my husband. But I am already your wife.
GALLIMARD: Do you want to . . . have my child?
SONG: I thought you'd never ask.
GALLIMARD: But, your career . . . your —
SONG: Phooey on my career! That's your Western mind, twisting itself into strange shapes again. Of course I love my career. But what would I love most of all? To feel something inside me — day and night — something I know is yours. (*Pause.*) Promise me . . . you won't go to this doctor. Who is this Western quack to set himself as judge over the man I love? I know who is a man, and who is not. (*She exits.*)
GALLIMARD (*to us*): Dr. Bolleart? Of course I didn't go. What man would?

Scene VI

(*Beijing. 1963.*
  Party noises over the house speakers. Renee enters, wearing a revealing gown.)

GALLIMARD: 1963. A party at the Austrian embassy. None of us could remember the Austrian ambassador's name, which seemed somehow appropriate. (*To Renee.*) So, I tell the Americans, Diem° must go. The U.S. wants to be respected by the Vietnamese, and yet they're propping up this nobody seminarian as her president. A man whose claim to fame is his sister-in-law imposing fanatic "moral order" campaigns? Oriental women — when they're good, they're very good, but when they're bad, they're Christians.

RENEE: Yeah.

GALLIMARD: And what do you do?

RENEE: I'm a student. My father exports a lot of useless stuff to the Third World.

GALLIMARD: How useless?

RENEE: You know. Squirt guns, confectioner's sugar, Hula Hoops . . .

GALLIMARD: I'm sure they appreciate the sugar.

RENEE: I'm here for two years to study Chinese.

GALLIMARD: Two years!

RENEE: That's what everybody says.

GALLIMARD: When did you arrive?

RENEE: Three weeks ago.

GALLIMARD: And?

RENEE: I like it. It's primitive, but . . . well, this is the place to learn Chinese, so here I am.

GALLIMARD: Why Chinese?

RENEE: I think it'll be important someday.

GALLIMARD: You do?

RENEE: Don't ask me when, but . . . that's what I think.

GALLIMARD: Well, I agree with you. One hundred percent. That's very farsighted.

RENEE: Yeah. Well of course, my father thinks I'm a complete weirdo.

GALLIMARD: He'll thank you someday.

RENEE: Like when the Chinese start buying Hula Hoops?

GALLIMARD: There're a billion bellies out there.

RENEE: And if they end up taking over the world — well, then I'll be lucky to know Chinese too, right?

(*Pause.*)

GALLIMARD: At this point, I don't see how the Chinese can possibly take —

RENEE: You know what I *don't* like about China?

GALLIMARD: Excuse me? No — what?

RENEE: Nothing to do at night.

GALLIMARD: You come to parties at embassies like everyone else.

RENEE: Yeah, but they get out at ten. And then what?

GALLIMARD: I'm afraid the Chinese idea of a dance hall is a dirt floor and a man with a flute.

RENEE: Are you married?

GALLIMARD: Yes. Why?

RENEE: You wanna . . . fool around?

(*Pause.*)

GALLIMARD: Sure.

RENEE: I'll wait for you outside. What's your name?

GALLIMARD: Gallimard. Rene.

RENEE: Weird. I'm Renee too. (*She exits.*)

GALLIMARD (*to us*): And so, I embarked on my first extra-extramarital affair. Renee was picture perfect. With a body like those girls in the magazines. If I put a tissue paper over my eyes, I wouldn't have been able to tell the difference. And it was exciting to be with someone who wasn't afraid to be seen completely naked. But is it possible for a woman to be *too* uninhibited, *too* willing, so as to seem almost too . . . masculine?

(*Chuck Berry° blares from the house speakers, then comes down in volume as Renee enters, toweling her hair.*)

RENEE: You have a nice weenie.

GALLIMARD: What?

RENEE: Penis. You have a nice penis.

GALLIMARD: Oh. Well, thank you. That's very . . .

RENEE: What — can't take a compliment?

GALLIMARD: No, it's very . . . reassuring.

RENEE: But most girls don't come out and say it, huh?

GALLIMARD: And also . . . what did you call it?

RENEE: Oh. Most girls don't call it a "weenie," huh?

GALLIMARD: It sounds very —

RENEE: Small, I know.

GALLIMARD: I was going to say, "young."

RENEE: Yeah. Young, small, same thing. Most guys are pretty, uh, sensitive about that. Like, you know, I had a boyfriend back home in Denmark. I got mad at him once and called him a little weeniehead. He got so mad! He said at least I should call him a great big weeniehead.

GALLIMARD: I suppose I just say "penis."

RENEE: Yeah. That's pretty clinical. There's "cock," but that sounds like a chicken. And "prick" is painful, and "dick" is like you're talking about someone who's not in the room.

GALLIMARD: Yes. It's a . . . bigger problem than I imagined.

RENEE: I — I think maybe it's because I really don't know what to do with them — that's why I call them "weenies."

GALLIMARD: Well, you did quite well with . . . mine.

RENEE: Thanks, but I mean, really *do* with them. Like, okay, have you ever looked at one? I mean, really?

Diem: Ngo Dinh Diem (1901–1963), president of South Vietnam (1955–1963), assassinated in a coup d'état supported by the United States.

Chuck Berry: American musician (b. 1926) often called the father of rock 'n' roll music.

GALLIMARD: No, I suppose when it's part of you, you sort of take it for granted.

RENEE: I guess. But, like, it just hangs there. This little . . . flap of flesh. And there's so much fuss that we make about it. Like, I think the reason we fight wars is because we wear clothes. Because no one knows — between the men, I mean — who has the biggest . . . weenie. So, if I'm a guy with a small one, I'm going to build a really big building or take over a really big piece of land or write a really long book so the other men don't know, right? But, see, it never really works, that's the problem. I mean, you conquer the country, or whatever, but you're still wearing clothes, so there's no way to prove absolutely whose is bigger or smaller. And that's what we call a civilized society. The whole world run by a bunch of men with pricks the size of pins. (*She exits.*)

GALLIMARD (*to us*): This was simply not acceptable.

(*A high-pitched chime rings through the air. Song, dressed as Butterfly, appears in the upstage special. She is obviously distressed. Her body swoons as she attempts to clip the stems of flowers she's arranging in a vase.*)

GALLIMARD: But I kept up our affair, wildly, for several months. Why? I believe because of Butterfly. She knew the secret I was trying to hide. But, unlike a Western woman, she didn't confront me, threaten, even pout. I remembered the words of Puccini's *Butterfly:*

SONG: "*Noi siamo gente avvezza / alle piccole cose / umili e silenziose.*"

GALLIMARD: "I come from a people / Who are accustomed to little / Humble and silent." I saw Pinkerton and Butterfly, and what she would say if he were unfaithful . . . nothing. She would cry, alone, into those wildly soft sleeves, once full of possessions, now empty to collect her tears. It was her tears and her silence that excited me, every time I visited Renee.

TOULON (*offstage*): Gallimard!

(*Toulon enters. Gallimard turns towards him. During the next section, Song, up center, begins to dance with the flowers. It is a drunken, reckless dance, where she breaks small pieces off the stems.*)

TOULON: They're killing him.

GALLIMARD: Who? I'm sorry? What?

TOULON: Bother you to come over at this late hour?

GALLIMARD: No . . . of course not.

TOULON: Not after you hear my secret. Champagne?

GALLIMARD: Um . . . thank you.

TOULON: You're surprised. There's something that you've wanted, Gallimard. No, not a promotion. Next time. Something in the world. You're not aware of this, but there's an informal gossip circle among intelligence agents. And some of ours heard from some of the Americans —

GALLIMARD: Yes?

TOULON: That the U.S. will allow the Vietnamese generals to stage a coup . . . and assassinate President Diem.

(*The chime rings again. Toulon freezes. Gallimard turns upstage and looks at Butterfly, who slowly and deliberately clips a flower off its stem. Gallimard turns back towards Toulon.*)

GALLIMARD: I think . . . that's a very wise move!

(*Toulon unfreezes.*)

TOULON: It's what you've been advocating. A toast?

GALLIMARD: Sure. I consider this a vindication.

TOULON: Not exactly. "To the test. Let's hope you pass."

(*They drink. The chime rings again. Toulon freezes. Gallimard turns upstage, and Song clips another flower.*)

GALLIMARD (*to Toulon*): The test?

TOULON (*unfreezing*): It's a test of everything you've been saying. I personally think the generals probably will stop the Communists. And you'll be a hero. But if anything goes wrong, then your opinions won't be worth a pig's ear. I'm sure that won't happen. But sometimes it's easier when they don't listen to you.

GALLIMARD: They're your opinions too, aren't they?

TOULON: Personally, yes.

GALLIMARD: So we agree.

TOULON: But my opinions aren't on that report. Yours are. Cheers.

(*Toulon turns away from Gallimard and raises his glass. At that instant Song picks up the vase and hurls it to the ground. It shatters. Song sinks down amidst the shards of the vase, in a calm, childlike trance. She sings softly, as if reciting a child's nursery rhyme.*)

SONG (*repeat as necessary*): "The whole world over, the white man travels, setting anchor, wherever he likes. Life's not worth living, unless he finds, the finest maidens, of every land . . ."

(*Gallimard turns downstage towards us. Song continues singing.*)

GALLIMARD: I shook as I left his house. That coward! That worm! To put the burden for his decisions on my shoulders!

I started for Renee's. But no, that was all I needed. A schoolgirl who would question the role of the penis in modern society. What I wanted was revenge. A vessel to contain my humiliation. Though I hadn't seen her in several weeks, I headed for Butterfly's.

(*Gallimard enters Song's apartment.*)

SONG: Oh! Rene . . . I was dreaming!

GALLIMARD: You've been drinking?

SONG: If I can't sleep, then yes, I drink. But then, it gives me these dreams which — Rene, it's been almost three weeks since you visited me last.

GALLIMARD: I know. There's been a lot going on in the world.

SONG: Fortunately I am drunk. So I can speak freely. It's not the world, it's you and me. And an old problem. Even the softest skin becomes like leather to a man who's touched it too often. I confess I don't know how to stop it. I don't know how to become another woman.

GALLIMARD: I have a request.

SONG: Is this a solution? Or are you ready to give up the flat?

GALLIMARD: It may be a solution. But I'm sure you won't like it.

SONG: Oh well, that's very important. "Like it?" Do you think I "like" lying here alone, waiting, always waiting for your return? Please — don't worry about what I may not "like."

GALLIMARD: I want to see you . . . naked.

(Silence.)

SONG: I thought you understood my modesty. So you want me to — what — strip? Like a big cowboy girl? Shiny pasties on my breasts? Shall I fling my kimono over my head and yell "ya-hoo" in the process? I thought you respected my shame!

GALLIMARD: I believe you gave me your shame many years ago.

SONG: Yes — and it is just like a white devil to use it against me. I can't believe it. I thought myself so repulsed by the passive Oriental and the cruel white man. Now I see — we are always most revolted by the things hidden within us.

GALLIMARD: I just mean —

SONG: Yes?

GALLIMARD: — that it will remove the only barrier left between us.

SONG: No, Rene. Don't couch your request in sweet words. Be yourself — a cad — and know that my love is enough, that I submit — submit to the worst you can give me. (Pause.) Well, come. Strip me. Whatever happens, know that you have willed it. Our love, in your hands. I'm helpless before my man.

(Gallimard starts to cross the room.)

GALLIMARD: Did I not undress her because I knew, somewhere deep down, what I would find? Perhaps. Happiness is so rare that our mind can turn somersaults to protect it.

At the time, I only knew that I was seeing Pinkerton stalking towards his Butterfly, ready to reward her love with his lecherous hands. The image sickened me, pulled me to my knees, so I was crawling towards her like a worm. By the time I reached her, Pinkerton . . . had vanished from my heart. To be replaced by something new, something unnatural, that flew in the face of all I'd learned in the world — something very close to love.

(He grabs her around the waist; she strokes his hair.)

GALLIMARD: Butterfly, forgive me.

SONG: Rene . . .

GALLIMARD: For everything. From the start.

SONG: I'm . . .

GALLIMARD: I want to —

SONG: I'm pregnant. (Beat.) I'm pregnant. (Beat.) I'm pregnant.

(Beat.)

GALLIMARD: I want to marry you!

Scene VII

(*Gallimard and Butterfly's flat. Beijing. 1963.*
Downstage, Song paces as Comrade Chin reads from her notepad. Upstage, Gallimard is still kneeling. He remains on his knees throughout the scene, watching it.)

SONG: I need a baby.

CHIN (*from pad*): He's been spotted going to a dorm.

SONG: I need a baby.

CHIN: At the Foreign Language Institute.

SONG: I need a baby.

CHIN: The room of a Danish girl. . . . What do you mean, you need a baby?!

SONG: Tell Comrade Kang — last night, the entire mission, it could've ended.

CHIN: What do you mean?

SONG: Tell Kang — he told me to strip.

CHIN: Strip?!

SONG: Write!

CHIN: I tell you, I don't understand nothing about this case anymore. Nothing.

SONG: He told me to strip, and I took a chance. Oh, we Chinese, we know how to gamble.

CHIN (*writing*): ". . . told him to strip."

SONG: My palms were wet, I had to make a split-second decision.

CHIN: Hey! Can you slow down?!

(Pause.)

SONG: You write faster, I'm the artist here. Suddenly, it hit me —"All he wants is for her to submit. Once a woman submits, a man is always ready to become 'generous.'"

CHIN: You're just gonna end up with rough notes.

SONG: And it worked! He gave in! Now, if I can just present him with a baby. A Chinese baby with blond hair — he'll be mine for life!

CHIN: Kang will never agree! The trading of babies has to be a counterrevolutionary act!

SONG: Sometimes, a counterrevolutionary act is necessary to counter a counterrevolutionary act.

(Pause.)

CHIN: Wait.

SONG: I need one . . . in seven months. Make sure it's a boy.

CHIN: This doesn't sound like something the Chairman would do. Maybe you'd better talk to Comrade Kang yourself.

SONG: Good. I will.

(Chin gets up to leave.)

SONG: Miss Chin? Why, in the Peking Opera, are women's roles played by men?

CHIN: I don't know. Maybe, a reactionary remnant of male —

SONG: No. (*Beat.*) Because only a man knows how a woman is supposed to act.

(*Chin exits. Song turns upstage, towards Gallimard.*)

GALLIMARD (*calling after Chin*): Good riddance! (*To Song.*) I could forget all that betrayal in an instant, you know. If you'd just come back and become Butterfly again.

SONG: Fat chance. You're here in prison, rotting in a cell. And I'm on a plane, winging my way back to China. Your President pardoned me of our treason, you know.

GALLIMARD: Yes, I read about that.

SONG: Must make you feel . . . lower than shit.

GALLIMARD: But don't you, even a little bit, wish you were here with me?

SONG: I'm an artist, Rene. You were my greatest . . . acting challenge. (*She laughs.*) It doesn't matter how rotten I answer, does it? You still adore me. That's why I love you, Rene. (*She points to us.*) So — you were telling your audience about the night I announced I was pregnant.

(*Gallimard puts his arms around Song's waist. He and Song are in the positions they were in at the end of Scene VI.*)

Scene VIII

(*Same.*)

GALLIMARD: I'll divorce my wife. We'll live together here, and then later in France.

SONG: I feel so . . . ashamed.

GALLIMARD: Why?

SONG: I had begun to lose faith. And now, you shame me with your generosity.

GALLIMARD: Generosity? No, I'm proposing for very selfish reasons.

SONG: Your apologies only make me feel more ashamed. My outburst a moment ago!

GALLIMARD: Your outburst? What about my request?!

SONG: You've been very patient dealing with my . . . eccentricities. A Western man, used to women freer with their bodies —

GALLIMARD: It was sick! Don't make excuses for me.

SONG: I have to. You don't seem willing to make them for yourself.

(*Pause.*)

GALLIMARD: You're crazy.

SONG: I'm happy. Which often looks like crazy.

GALLIMARD: Then make me crazy. Marry me.

(*Pause.*)

SONG: No.

GALLIMARD: What?

SONG: Do I sound silly, a slave, if I say I'm not worthy?

GALLIMARD: Yes. In fact you do. No one has loved me like you.

SONG: Thank you. And no one ever will. I'll see to that.

GALLIMARD: So what is the problem?

SONG: Rene, we Chinese are realists. We understand rice, gold, and guns. You are a diplomat. Your career is skyrocketing. Now, what would happen if you divorced your wife to marry a Communist Chinese actress?

GALLIMARD: That's not being realistic. That's defeating yourself before you begin.

SONG: We conserve our strength for the battles we can win.

GALLIMARD: That sounds like a fortune cookie!

SONG: Where do you think fortune cookies come from!

GALLIMARD: I don't care.

SONG: You do. So do I. And we should. That is why I say I'm not worthy. I'm worthy to love and even to be loved by you. But I am not worthy to end the career of one of the West's most promising diplomats.

GALLIMARD: It's not that great a career! I made it sound like more than it is!

SONG: Modesty will get you nowhere. Flatter yourself, and you flatter me. I'm flattered to decline your offer. (*She exits.*)

GALLIMARD (*to us*): Butterfly and I argued all night. And, in the end, I left, knowing I would never be her husband. She went away for several months — to the countryside, like a small animal. Until the night I received her call.

(*A baby's cry from offstage. Song enters, carrying a child.*)

SONG: He looks like you.

GALLIMARD: Oh! (*Beat; he approaches the baby.*) Well, babies are never very attractive at birth.

SONG: Stop!

GALLIMARD: I'm sure he'll grow more beautiful with age. More like his mother.

SONG: "*Chi vide mai / a bimbo del Giappon . . .*"

GALLIMARD: "What baby, I wonder, was ever born in Japan"— or China, for that matter —

SONG: "*. . . occhi azzurrini?*"

GALLIMARD: "With azure eyes"— they're actually sort of brown, wouldn't you say?

SONG: "*E il labbro.*"

GALLIMARD: "And such lips!" (*He kisses Song.*) And such lips.

SONG: "*E i ricciolini d'oro schietto?*"

GALLIMARD: "And such a head of golden"— if slightly patchy —"curls?"

SONG: I'm going to call him "Peepee."

GALLIMARD: Darling, could you repeat that because I'm sure a rickshaw just flew by overhead.

SONG: You heard me.

GALLIMARD: "Song Peepee"? May I suggest Michael, or Stephan, or Adolph?

SONG: You may, but I won't listen.

GALLIMARD: You can't be serious. Can you imagine the time this child will have in school?

SONG: In the West, yes.

GALLIMARD: It's worse than naming him Ping Pong or Long Dong or —

SONG: But he's never going to live in the West, is he?

(*Pause.*)

GALLIMARD: That wasn't my choice.

SONG: It is mine. And this is my promise to you: I will raise him, he will be our child, but he will never burden you outside of China.

GALLIMARD: Why do you make these promises? I want to be burdened! I want a scandal to cover the papers!

SONG (*to us*): Prophetic.

GALLIMARD: I'm serious.

SONG: So am I. His name is as I registered it. And he will never live in the West.

(*Song exits with the child.*)

GALLIMARD (*to us*): Is it possible that her stubbornness only made me want her more? That drawing back at the moment of my capitulation was the most brilliant strategy she could have chosen? It is possible. But it is also possible that by this point she could have said, could have done . . . anything, and I would have adored her still.

Scene IX

(*Beijing. 1966.*
A driving rhythm of Chinese percussion fills the stage.)

GALLIMARD: And then, China began to change. Mao became very old, and his cult became very strong. And, like many old men, he entered his second childhood. So he handed over the reins of state to those with minds like his own. And children ruled the Middle Kingdom° with complete caprice. The doctrine of the Cultural Revolution° implied continuous anarchy. Contact between Chinese and foreigners became impossible. Our flat was confiscated. Her fame and my money now counted against us.

(*Two dancers in Mao suits and red-starred caps enter, and begin crudely mimicking revolutionary violence, in an agitprop fashion.*)

GALLIMARD: And somehow the American war went wrong too. Four hundred thousand dollars were being spent for every Viet Cong° killed; so General

---

Middle Kingdom: The royal domain of China during its feudal period.
Cultural Revolution: Reform campaign of 1965–1967 to purge counterrevolutionary thought in China that challenged Mao Zedong.
Viet Cong: Member of the National Liberation Front of South Vietnam, against which U.S. forces were fighting.

Westmoreland's° remark that the Oriental does not value life the way Americans do was oddly accurate. Why weren't the Vietnamese people giving in? Why were they content instead to die and die and die again?

(*Toulon enters. Percussion and dancers continue upstage.*)

TOULON: Congratulations, Gallimard.

GALLIMARD: Excuse me, sir?

TOULON: Not a promotion. That was last time. You're going home.

GALLIMARD: What?

TOULON: Don't say I didn't warn you.

GALLIMARD: I'm being transferred . . . because I was wrong about the American war?

TOULON: Of course not. We don't care about the Americans. We care about your mind. The quality of your analysis. In general, everything you've predicted here in the Orient . . . just hasn't happened.

GALLIMARD: I think that's premature.

TOULON: Don't force me to be blunt. Okay, you said China was ready to open to Western trade. The only thing they're trading out there are Western heads. And, yes, you said the Americans would succeed in Indochina. You were kidding, right?

GALLIMARD: I think the end is in sight.

TOULON: Don't be pathetic. And don't take this personally. You were wrong. It's not your fault.

GALLIMARD: But I'm going home.

TOULON: Right. Could I have the number of your mistress? (*Beat.*) Joke! Joke! Eat a croissant for me.

(*Toulon exits. Song, wearing a Mao suit, is dragged in from the wings as part of the upstage dance. They "beat" her, then lampoon the acrobatics of the Chinese opera, as she is made to kneel onstage.*)

GALLIMARD (*simultaneously*): I don't care to recall how Butterfly and I said our hurried farewell. Perhaps it was better to end our affair before it killed her.

(*Gallimard exits. Percussion rises in volume. The lampooning becomes faster, more frenetic. At its height, Comrade Chin walks across the stage with a banner reading: "The Actor Renounces His Decadent Profession!" She reaches the kneeling Song. At the moment Chin touches Song's chin, percussion stops with a thud. Dancers strike poses.*)

CHIN: Actor-oppressor, for years you have lived above the common people and looked down on their labor. While the farmer ate millet —

SONG: I ate pastries from France and sweetmeats from silver trays.

CHIN: And how did you come to live in such an exalted position?

General Westmoreland: William Westmoreland (b. 1914), commander of American troops in Vietnam from 1964 to 1968.

SONG: I was a plaything for the imperialists!

CHIN: What did you do?

SONG: I shamed China by allowing myself to be corrupted by a foreigner . . .

CHIN: What does this mean? The People demand a full confession!

SONG: I engaged in the lowest perversions with China's enemies!

CHIN: What perversions? Be more clear!

SONG: I let him put it up my ass!

(*Dancers look over, disgusted.*)

CHIN: Aaaa-ya! How can you use such sickening language?!

SONG: My language . . . is only as foul as the crimes I committed . . .

CHIN: Yeah. That's better. So — what do you want to do . . . now?

SONG: I want to serve the people!

(*Percussion starts up, with Chinese strings.*)

CHIN: What?

SONG: I want to serve the people!

(*Dancers regain their revolutionary smiles, and begin a dance of victory.*)

CHIN: What?!

SONG: I want to serve the people!!

(*Dancers unveil a banner: "The Actor Is Re-Habilitated!" Song remains kneeling before Chin, as the dancers bounce around them, then exit. Music out.*)

Scene X

(*A commune. Hunan Province. 1970.*)

CHIN: How you planning to do that?

SONG: I've already worked four years in the fields of Hunan, Comrade Chin.

CHIN: So? Farmers work all their lives. Let me see your hands.

(*Song holds them out for her inspection.*)

CHIN: Goddamn! Still so smooth! How long does it take to turn you actors into good anythings? Hunh. You've just spent too many years in luxury to be any good to the Revolution.

SONG: I served the Revolution.

CHIN: Serve the Revolution? Bullshit! You wore dresses! Don't tell me — I was there. I saw you! You and your white vice-consul! Stuck up there in your flat, living off the People's Treasury! Yeah, I knew what was going on! You two . . . homos! Homos! Homos! (*Pause; she composes herself.*) Ah! Well . . . you will serve the people, all right. But not with the Revolution's money. This time, you use your own money.

SONG: I have no money.

CHIN: Shut up! And you won't stink up China anymore

with your pervert stuff. You'll pollute the place where pollution begins — the West.

SONG: What do you mean?

CHIN: Shut up! You're going to France. Without a cent in your pocket. You find your consul's house, you make him pay your expenses —

SONG: No.

CHIN: And you give us weekly reports! Useful information!

SONG: That's crazy. It's been four years.

CHIN: Either that, or back to rehabilitation center!

SONG: Comrade Chin, he's not going to support me! Not in France! He's a white man! I was just his plaything —

CHIN: Oh yuck! Again with the sickening language? Where's my stick?

SONG: You don't understand the mind of a man.

(*Pause.*)

CHIN: Oh no? No I don't? Then how come I'm married, huh? How come I got a man? Five, six years ago, you always tell me those kind of things, I felt very bad. But not now! Because what does the Chairman say? He tells us *I'm* now the smart one, you're now the nincompoop! *You're* the blockhead, the harebrain, the nitwit! You think you're so smart? You understand "The Mind of a Man"? Good! Then *you* go to France and be a pervert for Chairman Mao!

(*Chin and Song exit in opposite directions.*)

Scene XI

(*Paris. 1968–1970.
Gallimard enters.*)

GALLIMARD: And what was waiting for me back in Paris? Well, better Chinese food than I'd eaten in China. Friends and relatives. A little accounting, regular schedule, keeping track of traffic violations in the suburbs. . . . And the indignity of students shouting the slogans of Chairman Mao at me — in French.

HELGA: Rene? Rene? (*She enters, soaking wet.*) I've had a . . . problem.

(*She sneezes.*)

GALLIMARD: You're wet.

HELGA: Yes, I . . . coming back from the grocer's. A group of students, waving red flags, they —

(*Gallimard fetches a towel.*)

HELGA: — they ran by, I was caught up along with them. Before I knew what was happening —

(*Gallimard gives her the towel.*)

HELGA: Thank you. The police started firing water cannons at us. I tried to shout, to tell them I was the wife of a diplomat, but — you know how it is . . .

(*Pause.*) Needless to say, I lost the groceries. Rene, what's happening to France?

GALLIMARD: What's — ? Well, nothing, really.

HELGA: Nothing?! The storefronts are in flames, there's glass in the streets, buildings are toppling — and I'm wet!

GALLIMARD: Nothing! . . . that I care to think about.

HELGA: And is that why you stay in this room?

GALLIMARD: Yes, in fact.

HELGA: With the incense burning? You know something? I hate incense. It smells so sickly sweet.

GALLIMARD: Well, I hate the French. Who just smell — period!

HELGA: And the Chinese were better?

GALLIMARD: Please — don't start.

HELGA: When we left, this exact same thing, the riots —

GALLIMARD: No, no . . .

HELGA: Students screaming slogans, smashing down doors —

GALLIMARD: Helga —

HELGA: It was all going on in China, too. Don't you remember?!

GALLIMARD: Helga! Please! (*Pause.*) You have never understood China, have you? You walk in here with these ridiculous ideas, that the West is falling apart, that China was spitting in our faces. You come in, dripping of the streets, and you leave water all over my floor. (*He grabs Helga's towel, begins mopping up the floor.*)

HELGA: But it's the truth!

GALLIMARD: Helga, I want a divorce.

(*Pause; Gallimard continues mopping the floor.*)

HELGA: I take it back. China is . . . beautiful. Incense, I like incense.

GALLIMARD: I've had a mistress.

HELGA: So?

GALLIMARD: For eight years.

HELGA: I knew you would. I knew you would the day I married you. And now what? You want to marry her?

GALLIMARD: I can't. She's in China.

HELGA: I see. You know that no one else is ever going to marry me, right?

GALLIMARD: I'm sorry.

HELGA: And you want to leave. For someone who's not here, is that right?

GALLIMARD: That's right.

HELGA: You can't live with her, but still you don't want to live with me.

GALLIMARD: That's right.

(*Pause.*)

HELGA: Shit. How terrible that I can figure that out. (*Pause.*) I never thought I'd say it. But, in China, I was happy. I knew, in my own way, I knew that you were not everything you pretended to be. But the pretense — going on your arm to the embassy ball, visiting your office and the guards saying, "Good morning, good morning, Madame Gallimard"— the

pretense . . . was very good indeed. (*Pause.*) I hope everyone is mean to you for the rest of your life. (*She exits.*)

GALLIMARD (*to us*): Prophetic.

(*Marc enters with two drinks.*)

GALLIMARD (*to Marc*): In China, I was different from all other men.

MARC: Sure. You were white. Here's your drink.

GALLIMARD: I felt . . . touched.

MARC: In the head? Rene, I don't want to hear about the Oriental love goddess. Okay? One night — can we just drink and throw up without a lot of conversation?

GALLIMARD: You still don't believe me, do you?

MARC: Sure I do. She was the most beautiful, et cetera, et cetera, blasé, blasé.

(*Pause.*)

GALLIMARD: My life in the West has been such a disappointment.

MARC: Life in the West is like that. You'll get used to it. Look, you're driving me away. I'm leaving. Happy, now? (*He exits, then returns.*) Look, I have a date tomorrow night. You wanna come? I can fix you up with —

GALLIMARD: Of course. I would love to come.

(*Pause.*)

MARC: Uh — on second thought, no. You'd better get ahold of yourself first.

(*He exits; Gallimard nurses his drink.*)

GALLIMARD (*to us*): This is the ultimate cruelty, isn't it? That I can talk and talk and to anyone listening, it's only air — too rich a diet to be swallowed by a mundane world. Why can't anyone understand? That in China, I once loved, and was loved by, very simply, the Perfect Woman.

(*Song enters, dressed as Butterfly in wedding dress.*)

GALLIMARD (*to Song*): Not again. My imagination is hell. Am I asleep this time? Or did I drink too much?

SONG: Rene!

GALLIMARD: God, it's too painful! That you speak?

SONG: What are you talking about? Rene — touch me.

GALLIMARD: Why?

SONG: I'm real. Take my hand.

GALLIMARD: Why? So you can disappear again and leave me clutching at the air? For the entertainment of my neighbors who — ?

(*Song touches Gallimard.*)

SONG: Rene?

(*Gallimard takes Song's hand. Silence.*)

GALLIMARD: Butterfly? I never doubted you'd return.

SONG: You hadn't . . . forgotten — ?

GALLIMARD: Yes, actually, I've forgotten everything. My mind, you see — there wasn't enough room in this hard head — not for the world *and* for you. No, there was only room for one. (*Beat.*) Come, look. See? Your bed has been waiting, with the Klimt° poster you like, and — see? The *xiang lu*° you gave me?

SONG: I . . . I don't know what to say.

GALLIMARD: There's nothing to say. Not at the end of a long trip. Can I make you some tea?

SONG: But where's your wife?

GALLIMARD: She's by my side. She's by my side at last.

(*Gallimard reaches to embrace Song. Song sidesteps, dodging him.*)

GALLIMARD: Why?!

SONG (*to us*): So I did return to Rene in Paris. Where I found —

GALLIMARD: Why do you run away? Can't we show them how we embraced that evening?

SONG: Please. I'm talking.

GALLIMARD: You have to do what I say! I'm conjuring you up in *my* mind!

SONG: Rene, I've never done what you've said. Why should it be any different in your mind? Now split — the story moves on, and I must change.

GALLIMARD: I welcomed you into my home! I didn't have to, you know! I could've left you penniless on the streets of Paris! But I took you in!

SONG: Thank you.

GALLIMARD: So . . . please . . . don't change.

SONG: You know I have to. You know I will. And anyway, what difference does it make? No matter what your eyes tell you, you can't ignore the truth. You already know too much.

(*Gallimard exits. Song turns to us.*)

SONG: The change I'm going to make requires about five minutes. So I thought you might want to take this opportunity to stretch your legs, enjoy a drink, or listen to the musicians. I'll be here, when you return, right where you left me.

(*Song goes to a mirror in front of which is a wash basin of water. She starts to remove her makeup as stagelights go to half and houselights come up.*)

ACT III • *Scene I*

(*A courthouse in Paris. 1986.*

As he promised, Song has completed the bulk of his transformation onstage by the time the houselights go down and the stagelights come up full. As he speaks to us, he removes his wig and kimono, leaving them on the floor. Underneath, he wears a well-cut suit.)

SONG: So I'd done my job better than I had a right to expect. Well, give him some credit, too. He's right — I was in a fix when I arrived in Paris. I walked from

---

Klimt: Gustav Klimt (1863–1918), Austrian painter in the art nouveau style, whose most famous painting is *The Kiss.* **xiang lu:** Incense burner.

---

the airport into town, then I located, by blind groping, the Chinatown district. Let me make one thing clear: whatever else may be said about the Chinese, they are stingy! I slept in doorways three days until I could find a tailor who would make me this kimono on credit. As it turns out, maybe I didn't even need it. Maybe he would've been happy to see me in a simple shift and mascara. But . . . better safe than sorry.

That was 1970, when I arrived in Paris. For the next fifteen years, yes, I lived a very comfy life. Some relief, believe me, after four years on a fucking commune in Nowheresville, China. Rene supported the boy and me, and I did some demonstrations around the country as part of my "cultural exchange" cover. And then there was the spying.

(*Song moves upstage, to a chair. Toulon enters as a judge, wearing the appropriate wig and robes. He sits near Song. It's 1986, and Song is testifying in a courtroom.*)

SONG: Not much at first. Rene had lost all his high-level contacts. Comrade Chin wasn't very interested in parking-ticket statistics. But finally, at my urging, Rene got a job as a courier, handling sensitive documents. He'd photograph them for me, and I'd pass them on to the Chinese embassy.

JUDGE: Did he understand the extent of his activity?

SONG: He didn't ask. He knew that I needed those documents, and that was enough.

JUDGE: But he must've known he was passing classified information.

SONG: I can't say.

JUDGE: He never asked what you were going to do with them?

SONG: Nope.

(*Pause.*)

JUDGE: There is one thing that the court — indeed, that all of France — would like to know.

SONG: Fire away.

JUDGE: Did Monsieur Gallimard know you were a man?

SONG: Well, he never saw me completely naked. Ever.

JUDGE: But surely, he must've . . . how can I put this?

SONG: Put it however you like. I'm not shy. He must've felt around?

JUDGE: Mmmmm.

SONG: Not really. I did all the work. He just laid back. Of course we did enjoy more . . . complete union, and I suppose he *might* have wondered why I was always on my stomach, but. . . . But what you're thinking is, "Of course a wrist must've brushed . . . a hand hit . . . over twenty years!" Yeah. Well, Your Honor, it was my job to make him think I was a woman. And chew on this: it wasn't all that hard. See, my mother was a prostitute along the Bundt before the Revolution. And, uh, I think it's fair to say she learned a few things about Western men. So I borrowed her knowledge. In service to my country.

JUDGE: Would you care to enlighten the court with this secret knowledge? I'm sure we're all very curious.

SONG: I'm sure you are. (*Pause.*) Okay, Rule One is: Men always believe what they want to hear. So a girl can tell the most obnoxious lies and the guys will believe them every time —"This is my first time"—"That's the biggest I've ever seen"— or *both,* which, if you really think about it, is not possible in a single lifetime. You've maybe heard those phrases a few times in your own life, yes, Your Honor?

JUDGE: It's not my life, Monsieur Song, which is on trial today.

SONG: Okay, okay, just trying to lighten up the proceedings. Tough room.

JUDGE: Go on.

SONG: Rule Two: As soon as a Western man comes into contact with the East — he's already confused. The West has sort of an international rape mentality towards the East. Do you know rape mentality?

JUDGE: Give us your definition, please.

SONG: Basically, "Her mouth says no, but her eyes say yes."
   The West thinks of itself as masculine — big guns, big industry, big money — so the East is feminine — weak, delicate, poor . . . but good at art, and full of inscrutable wisdom — the feminine mystique.
   Her mouth says no, but her eyes say yes. The West believes the East, deep down, *wants* to be dominated — because a woman can't think for herself.

JUDGE: What does this have to do with my question?

SONG: You expect Oriental countries to submit to your guns, and you expect Oriental women to be submissive to your men. That's why you say they make the best wives.

JUDGE: But why would that make it possible for you to fool Monsieur Gallimard? Please — get to the point.

SONG: One, because when he finally met his fantasy woman, he wanted more than anything to believe that she was, in fact, a woman. And second, I am an Oriental. And being an Oriental, I could never be completely a man.

(*Pause.*)

JUDGE: Your armchair political theory is tenuous, Monsieur Song.

SONG: You think so? That's why you'll lose in all your dealings with the East.

JUDGE: Just answer my question: did he know you were a man?

(*Pause.*)

SONG: You know, Your Honor, I never asked.

Scene II

(*Same.*
   Music from the "Death Scene" from Butterfly blares over the house speakers. It is the loudest thing we've heard in this play.
   Gallimard enters, crawling towards Song's wig and kimono.)

GALLIMARD: Butterfly? Butterfly?

(*Song remains a man, in the witness box, delivering a testimony we do not hear.*)

GALLIMARD (*to us*): In my moment of greatest shame, here, in this courtroom — with that . . . person up there, telling the world. . . . What strikes me especially is how shallow he is, how glib and obsequious . . . completely . . . without substance! The type that prowls around discos with a gold medallion stinking of garlic. So little like my Butterfly.
   Yet even in this moment my mind remains agile, flip-flopping like a man on a trampoline. Even now, my picture dissolves, and I see that . . . witness . . . talking to me.

(*Song suddenly stands straight up in his witness box, and looks at Gallimard.*)

SONG: Yes. You. White man.

(*Song steps out of the witness box, and moves downstage towards Gallimard. Light change.*)

GALLIMARD (*to Song*): Who? Me?

SONG: Do you see any other white men?

GALLIMARD: Yes. There're white men all around. This is a French courtroom.

SONG: So you are an adventurous imperialist. Tell me, why did it take you so long? To come back to this place?

GALLIMARD: What place?

SONG: This theater in China. Where we met many years ago.

GALLIMARD (*to us*): And once again, against my will, I am transported.

(*Chinese opera music comes up on the speakers. Song begins to do opera moves, as he did the night they met.*)

SONG: Do you remember? The night you gave your heart?

GALLIMARD: It was a long time ago.

SONG: Not long enough. A night that turned your world upside down.

GALLIMARD: Perhaps.

SONG: Oh, be honest with me. What's another bit of flattery when you've already given me twenty years' worth? It's a wonder my head hasn't swollen to the size of China.

GALLIMARD: Who's to say it hasn't?

SONG: Who's to say? And what's the shame? In pride? You think I could've pulled this off if I wasn't already full of pride when we met? No, not just pride. Arrogance. It takes arrogance, really — to believe you can will, with your eyes and your lips, the destiny of another. (*He dances.*) C'mon. Admit it. You still want me. Even in slacks and a button-down collar.

GALLIMARD: I don't see what the point of —

SONG: You don't? Well maybe, Rene, just maybe — I want you.

GALLIMARD: You do?

SONG: Then again, maybe I'm just playing with you. How can you tell? (*Reprising his feminine character, he sidles up to Gallimard.*) "How I wish there were even a small café to sit in. With men in tuxedos, and cappuccinos, and bad expatriate jazz." Now you want to kiss me, don't you?

GALLIMARD (*pulling away*): What makes you — ?

SONG: — so sure? See? I take the words from your mouth. Then I wait for you to come and retrieve them. (*He reclines on the floor.*)

GALLIMARD: Why?! Why do you treat me so cruelly?

SONG: Perhaps I *was* treating you cruelly. But now — I'm being nice. Come here, my little one.

GALLIMARD: I'm not your little one!

SONG: My mistake. It's I who am *your* little one, right?

GALLIMARD: Yes, I —

SONG: So come get your little one. If you like, I may even let you strip me.

GALLIMARD: I mean, you were! Before . . . but not like this!

SONG: I was? Then perhaps I still am. If you look hard enough. (*He starts to remove his clothes.*)

GALLIMARD: What — what are you doing?

SONG: Helping you to see through my act.

GALLIMARD: Stop that! I don't want to! I don't —

SONG: Oh, but you asked me to strip, remember?

GALLIMARD: What? That was years ago! And I took it back!

SONG: No. You postponed it. Postponed the inevitable. Today, the inevitable has come calling.

(*From the speakers, cacophony: Butterfly mixed in with Chinese gongs.*)

GALLIMARD: No! Stop! I don't want to see!

SONG: Then look away.

GALLIMARD: You're only in my mind! All this is in my mind! I order you! To stop!

SONG: To what? To strip? That's just what I'm —

GALLIMARD: No! Stop! I want you — !

SONG: You want me?

GALLIMARD: To stop!

SONG: You know something, Rene? Your mouth says no, but your eyes say yes. Turn them away. I dare you.

GALLIMARD: I don't have to! Every night, you say you're going to strip, but then I beg you and you stop!

SONG: I guess tonight is different.

GALLIMARD: Why? Why should that be?

SONG: Maybe I've become frustrated. Maybe I'm saying "Look at me, you fool!" Or maybe I'm just feeling . . . sexy. (*He is down to his briefs.*)

GALLIMARD: Please. This is unnecessary. I know what you are.

SONG: You do? What am I?

GALLIMARD: A — a man.

SONG: You don't really believe that.

GALLIMARD: Yes I do! I knew all the time somewhere that my happiness was temporary, my love a deception. But my mind kept the knowledge at bay. To make the wait bearable.

SONG: Monsieur Gallimard — the wait is over.

(*Song drops his briefs. He is naked. Sound cue out. Slowly, we and Song come to the realization that what*

we had thought to be Gallimard's sobbing is actually his laughter.)

GALLIMARD: Oh god! What an idiot! Of course!

SONG: Rene — what?

GALLIMARD: Look at you! You're a man! (*He bursts into laughter again.*)

SONG: I fail to see what's so funny!

GALLIMARD: "You fail to see — !" I mean, you never did have much of a sense of humor, did you? I just think it's ridiculously funny that I've wasted so much time on just a man!

SONG: Wait. I'm not "just a man."

GALLIMARD: No? Isn't that what you've been trying to convince me of?

SONG: Yes, but what I mean —

GALLIMARD: And now, I finally believe you, and you tell me it's not true? I think you must have some kind of identity problem.

SONG: Will you listen to me?

GALLIMARD: Why?! I've been listening to you for twenty years. Don't I deserve a vacation?

SONG: I'm not just any man!

GALLIMARD: Then, what exactly are you?

SONG: Rene, how can you ask — ? Okay, what about this?

(*He picks up Butterfly's robes, starts to dance around. No music.*)

GALLIMARD: Yes, that's very nice. I have to admit.

(*Song holds out his arm to Gallimard.*)

SONG: It's the same skin you've worshipped for years. Touch it.

GALLIMARD: Yes, it does feel the same.

SONG: Now — close your eyes.

(*Song covers Gallimard's eyes with one hand. With the other, Song draws Gallimard's hand up to his face. Gallimard, like a blind man, lets his hands run over Song's face.*)

GALLIMARD: This skin, I remember. The curve of her face, the softness of her cheek, her hair against the back of my hand . . .

SONG: I'm your Butterfly. Under the robes, beneath everything, it was always me. Now, open your eyes and admit it — you adore me. (*He removes his hand from Gallimard's eyes.*)

GALLIMARD: You, who knew every inch of my desires — how could you, of all people, have made such a mistake?

SONG: What?

GALLIMARD: You showed me your true self. When all I loved was the lie. A perfect lie, which you let fall to the ground — and now, it's old and soiled.

SONG: So — you never really loved me? Only when I was playing a part?

GALLIMARD: I'm a man who loved a woman created by a man. Everything else — simply falls short.

(*Pause.*)

SONG: What am I supposed to do now?

GALLIMARD: You were a fine spy, Monsieur Song, with an even finer accomplice. But now I believe you should go. Get out of my life!

SONG: Go where? Rene, you can't live without me. Not after twenty years.

GALLIMARD: I certainly can't live with you — not after twenty years of betrayal.

SONG: Don't be stubborn! Where will you go?

GALLIMARD: I have a date . . . with my Butterfly.

SONG: So, throw away your pride. And come . . .

GALLIMARD: Get away from me! Tonight, I've finally learned to tell fantasy from reality. And, knowing the difference, I choose fantasy.

SONG: *I'm* your fantasy!

GALLIMARD: You? You're as real as hamburger. Now get out! I have a date with my Butterfly and I don't want your body polluting the room! (*He tosses Song's suit at him.*) Look at these — you dress like a pimp.

SONG: Hey! These are Armani slacks and — ! (*He puts on his briefs and slacks.*) Let's just say . . . I'm disappointed in you, Rene. In the crush of your adoration, I thought you'd become something more. More like . . . a woman.

But no. Men. You're like the rest of them. It's all in the way we dress, and make up our faces, and bat our eyelashes. You really have so little imagination!

GALLIMARD: You, Monsieur Song? Accuse me of too little imagination? You, if anyone, should know — I am pure imagination. And in imagination I will remain. Now get out!

(*Gallimard bodily removes Song from the stage, taking his kimono.*)

SONG: Rene! I'll never put on those robes again! You'll be sorry!

GALLIMARD (*to Song*): I'm already sorry! (*Looking at the kimono in his hands.*) Exactly as sorry . . . as a Butterfly.

Scene III

(*M. Gallimard's prison cell. Paris. 1988.*)

GALLIMARD: I've played out the events of my life night after night, always searching for a new ending to my story, one where I leave this cell and return forever to my Butterfly's arms.

Tonight I realize my search is over. That I've looked all along in the wrong place. And now, to you, I will prove that my love was not in vain — by returning to the world of fantasy where I first met her.

(*He picks up the kimono; dancers enter.*)

GALLIMARD: There is a vision of the Orient that I have. Of slender women in cheongsams and kimonos who die for the love of unworthy foreign devils. Who are born and raised to be the perfect women. Who take whatever punishment we give them, and bounce back, strengthened by love, unconditionally. It is a vision that has become my life.

(*Dancers bring the washbasin to him and help him make up his face.*)

GALLIMARD: In public, I have continued to deny that Song Liling is a man. This brings me headlines, and is a source of great embarrassment to my French colleagues, who can now be sent into a coughing fit by the mere mention of Chinese food. But alone, in my cell, I have long since faced the truth.

And the truth demands a sacrifice. For mistakes made over the course of a lifetime. My mistakes were simple and absolute — the man I loved was a cad, a bounder. He deserved nothing but a kick in the behind, and instead I gave him . . . all my love.

Yes — love. Why not admit it all? That was my undoing, wasn't it? Love warped my judgment, blinded my eyes, rearranged the very lines on my face . . . until I could look in the mirror and see nothing but . . . a woman.

(*Dancers help him put on the Butterfly wig.*)

GALLIMARD: I have a vision. Of the Orient. That, deep within its almond eyes, there are still women. Women willing to sacrifice themselves for the love of a man. Even a man whose love is completely without worth.

(*Dancers assist Gallimard in donning the kimono. They hand him a knife.*)

GALLIMARD: Death with honor is better than life . . . life with dishonor. (*He sets himself center stage, in a seppuku position.*) The love of a Butterfly can withstand many things — unfaithfulness, loss, even abandonment. But how can it face the one sin that implies all others? The devastating knowledge that, underneath it all, the object of her love was nothing more, nothing less than . . . a man. (*He sets the tip of the knife against his body.*) It is 1988. And I have found her at last. In a prison on the outskirts of Paris. My name is Rene Gallimard — also known as Madame Butterfly.

(*Gallimard turns upstage and plunges the knife into his body, as music from the "Love Duet" blares over the speakers. He collapses into the arms of the dancers, who lay him reverently on the floor. The image holds for several beats. Then a tight special up on Song, who stands as a man, staring at the dead Gallimard. He smokes a cigarette; the smoke filters up through the lights. Two words leave his lips.*)

SONG: Butterfly? Butterfly?

(*Smoke rises as lights fade slowly to black.*)

COMMENTARIES

John Louis DiGaetani (b. 1943)

M. BUTTERFLY: AN INTERVIEW
WITH DAVID HENRY HWANG   *1989*

John Louis DiGaetani and David Henry Hwang discuss some of the more interesting aspects of the playwright's approach to writing M. Butterfly. *He explores the ideas that lay behind "orientalism" as Hwang worked with it in the play, and he comments on connections with Puccini's* Madame Butterfly.

David Henry Hwang's M. *Butterfly* went into rehearsal during the first week of January 1988 and into preview on February 6 at the National Theater in Washington, D.C. On February 10 the play opened and played to excellent reviews until the first week in March. On March 20, 1988, the play opened on Broadway at the Eugene O'Neill Theatre, where it has been successfully running ever since.

M. *Butterfly* takes place today in a Paris prison, and, in recall, the years 1960 to 1985 in Beijing and Paris. The events of the play were suggested by recent newspaper accounts of an actual international spy scandal. A French diplomat by the name of Bouriscot (Gallimard in the play) was stationed in Beijing, China, during the period of the American war in Vietnam. During Bouriscot's stay, he started a long-term affair with someone he thought was a female star of the Beijing Opera. When the lovers tried to enter France, they were both charged with espionage. Only then did the diplomat discover that his mistress was a spy for the Chinese government — and also a man. M. Bouriscot was tried, found guilty of espionage, and sentenced to prison. He was released from prison in 1988.

I spoke with Mr. Hwang in New York City in September 1988.

Hwang: I wrote M. *Butterfly* as an attempt to deal with some aspects of orientalism. I assumed that many in the audience would be coming to the theater because they hoped to see something exotic and mysterious, but what exactly is behind the desire to see the "exotic East"?

DiGaetani: One of the things I found interesting is that your play suggested the Western naivete about the East. Many Westerners tend to think of the East as a pretty little Madame Butterfly rather than seeing what is actually there in the orient. It's a kind of racism combined with sexism.

Hwang: Yes, that's true. The play has been taken as a commentary or a criticism of Western attitudes toward the East, and I think that's accurate. But I would like to think that the play is fairly even-handed in saying that the East also misperceives the West. The East is guilty or complicit in this dual form of cultural stereotyping. The West, having had the advantage of being the colonial power and of being the more powerful of the two over the past couple of hundred years, has an attitude of condescension toward the East. But the East has played up to that to its short-term advantage without thinking of the long-term ill effects that reinforcing those racial stereotypes causes. I think both parties are equally guilty.

In terms of Western misperceptions, there is Edward Said's term, "orientalism." I read Said's book after I wrote the play. John Dexter, the play's director, recommended it. It was one of the reasons he was interested in doing the play. This notion that the East is mysterious, inscrutable, and therefore ultimately inferior, is something that definitely is consistent with themes in Puccini's *Madame Butterfly*.

DiGaetani: Well, an aspect of the Puccini opera that I think is often overlooked is its attack on that Western view. Pinkerton is one of the great heels in all opera. Puccini presents the West as oafish and insensitive.

Hwang: Puccini presents that view at the same time that he presents a view of the East as helpless to resist. I think that the East has played into that stereotype by saying, "Oh, yes, we are helpless" and therefore trying to manipulate the situation to its own advantage.

DiGaetani: Naivete can be used as a ploy. One of the interesting things about the Puccini opera is that it presents the East as a place in the early stages of its victimization by an imperialist power. In other words, in the beginning people think that the changes are all wonderful and mean progress and the modern way. They don't realize that they are being used. Of course Madame Butterfly does eventually realize the horrible consequences of being colonized. Are you an opera fan?

Hwang: I was trained as a musician, so I'm a music fan in general. Opera is actually something that I've only become interested in during the past couple of years, and to some degree because of *M. Butterfly*. Ironically, when I decided I wanted to incorporate the plot of Puccini's *Madame Butterfly* into the play, I actually didn't know much about opera. So I started listening to a lot more of it, and particularly during the rehearsals for the play I started listening to the Puccini opera and I really learned to appreciate it. My play, which sets out to lampoon opera, has made me an opera buff.

DiGaetani: Your play brings up lots of interesting questions, one of which is: Can we love a person as a person if we are unsure of that person's gender?

Hwang: The play is to some degree about the nature of seduction — in the sense that we seduce ourselves. Sometimes when you have the desire to fall in love or you desire to have someone to be some kind of ideal, you can make that person ideal in your own mind whether or not the actual facts correspond to the reality. I think that it's often true in a smaller, less extreme sense that we get involved with people and decide to blind ourselves to their faults so that they can be the perfect love that we've always wanted. And on some level we're aware that that is not the case. But we prefer the fantasy over the reality. The play presents an obviously more extreme and less common situation, where the reality is so radically different from fantasy that at the core, even the simple, fundamental fact that it's a man instead of a woman is something that the person in love chooses to block out. But it's not actually that different qualitatively from everyday types of deceptions that people make in order to convince themselves they're in love.

DiGaetani: I remember when I first read the story in the newspaper. I thought, how could this have happened? What was your reaction?

Hwang: Of course, I had the same reactions as everybody else — how could it have happened? But then on some level it seemed natural to me that it should have happened, that given the degree of misperception generally between East and West and between men and women, it seemed inevitable that a mistake of this magnitude would one day take place. As a metaphor, the story made perfect sense in the context of the general misunderstanding that I have always perceived takes place between these different groups. In retrospect, it seems to me that that was what really piqued my imagination. I felt the impossibility of the situation and the inevitability of it, both at the same time.

DiGaetani: Men playing women is of course very much a part of Western theater. But one of the ways I interpret your play, and I'd like your comments about this, is that Gallimard was really a homosexual from day one. He was living in a much more homophobic period than today, and the thing about his affair with Song Liling, the thing about the mirage that he and Song Liling created, was that he never had to face his own homosexuality. In other words, he had an affair with a man and never told anyone, not even himself.

Hwang: The lines between gay and straight become very blurred in this play, but I think he knows he's having an affair with a man. Therefore, on some level he is gay. Our director John Dexter told me that he never found the situation to be that unbelievable because of an experience he once had. Dexter once shot a movie for Columbia called *Virgin Soldiers*. He hired macho Englishmen and brought them to Singapore where they went to Boogie Street, the transvestite street. A few of these men picked up these guys, I mean these women who were really men, and the next day Dexter overheard them talking and they said, "No, it was a girl. I know men and I know women, and that was a woman." If you want to believe it's a woman, that's fine. I mean, the fact is you're sleeping with a man, but if you choose to believe you're heterosexual, then that's your prerogative, to live in that fantasy. I think this would apply today to people in Chinese, Italian, Spanish, and some of the other Latin cultures. People in these cultures believe that if you have sex with a man and you do the screwing, you are not gay, but if you're screwed, you're gay. I mean, that sort of distinction has existed since time immemorial.

DiGaetani: Oh, the Chinese believe this is true?

Hwang: So what does gay mean at that point? I don't know.

DiGaetani: In what you're saying, gay means being a passive homosexual. If you're not passive, you're not gay.

Hwang: Correct. So, the situation in *M. Butterfly* is not so far-fetched. Gallimard chooses to believe he is heterosexual.

DiGaetani: Is Gallimard still in jail?

Hwang: The name of the real Gallimard is Bouriscot and he just got out of jail.

DiGaetani: Have you tried to contact him?

Hwang: No. I think we may want to have some kind of legal arrangement with him, but we'll see what happens.

DiGaetani: He might want a cut of the royalties.

Hwang: Probably.

DiGaetani: And he deserves it?

Hwang: I wouldn't mind giving him a little.

DiGaetani: Not a lot?

Hwang: No, since the play is not literally based on him. I don't know that it's his story. But on the other hand, I think the guy's been in jail, he's suffered a lot of indignity, so since it's him, why not?

DiGaetani: Have you tried to incorporate many elements of Oriental opera or theater into this play? Or was it primarily Dexter who wanted to do this?

Hwang: The main reason we ended up using Chinese opera was because it was relevant. In reality, Song Liling was a practitioner of Chinese opera. But I also wanted to explore why it is that in Asian theater and also in Shakespearean theater men play women's roles. It's just touched on briefly. Song Liling says, "Why are women's roles played by men?" And the answer is: "Because only a man knows how a woman should act." Let's look at that in kabuki terms because in kabuki it's expressed much more clearly. In kabuki they say that a woman can only be a woman whereas a man can be the idealization of a woman. This is obscene, and it's inherently sexist. What it's saying is that only a man can be a man's idealization of a woman.

DiGaetani: Not a woman's.

Hwang: Right. Song Liling is able to be such an effective fantasy for Gallimard because, as a man, she knows how a man wants to see women, and therefore can become a man's woman — which is why Gallimard says toward the end of the play: "I was a man in love with a woman created by a man, and now everything else simply falls short." I thought the play was a very interesting way to deal with the concept of the onnagata° in the context of a Western play.

DiGaetani: Another interesting conflict I saw in the play was between Japanese and Chinese cultures. They're really different.

Hwang: One of the things I wanted to do was to indicate both the differences between cultures as perceived by Asians and the similarities as perceived by Westerners. In other words, the West looks at the "East" as sort of a monolith. Whether we've been at war against Japan or Korea or Vietnam or in a cold war with China, it's all "Oriental." But of course the Asians see themselves as very different. I also have to say, again, that the reverse is true, that Asians tend to see the West as very monolithic. Perhaps from each point of view, it's a legitimate position to take because there are probably more similarities between the Asian cultures as opposed to the West than differences, and vice versa. But from the point of view of the West, America does not consider itself to be the same as France. And Japan does not consider itself to be China.

I think one of the more simple things the play's trying to say is that eventually one must look past all the cultural stereotyping we do of each other, West to East and East to West, and deal with each other just as humans if we're really to reach any point of true understanding.

---

onnagata: A male actor who plays a female role. In Chinese opera and Japanese kabuki drama, male actors study and perfect the art of female impersonation over the course of their careers.

John Gross (b. 1935)
REVIEW OF M. BUTTERFLY

1988

John Gross reviewed David Henry Hwang's play in the New York Times *in April 1988 and takes issue with a number of the details in the text. His review is not an attack, but it does examine some of the ideas that Hwang centers in the play and calls them into question in an interesting fashion.*

If you want to be taken seriously as a playwright, the quickest way is to set up as a thinker. Nothing is more calculated to make audiences assume a respectful expression than the suggestion that they are about to have some ideas dished out to them, and in a theater world that generally offers little in the way of intellectual nourishment, it is easy enough to see why.

But some ideas are better than others. It isn't enough, when a play raises large and far-reaching questions, to be grateful for the mere show of thinking; a certain amount of attention also needs to be paid to the quality of thought.

In *M. Butterfly*, which has recently opened at the Eugene O'Neill Theatre, David Henry Hwang has seized on a story that fairly bristles with opportunities for exploring social, cultural, and sexual themes. A true story that, as they say, nobody could have invented.

In 1966 a former French diplomat, Bernard Boursicot, and his Chinese lover, a former diva in the Beijing Opera called Shi Peipu, were both sentenced by a French court to six years in jail for spying for China. (Shi was subsequently deported.) They had begun their affair more than 20 years earlier, when Mr. Boursicot was stationed in Beijing; later Shi had followed him back to Paris with the child he was said to have fathered. It was only during the course of the trial that it was revealed, to Boursicot's consternation, that the singer was in fact a man.

There are a number of ways in which such a story could be tackled by a playwright — as a comedy of duplicity and gullibility, for instance, or as a chapter (a serious chapter, for all its outlandishness) in the annals of espionage. To Mr. Hwang, he tells us, it represents a chance to air some of his concerns about racism, sexism, and imperialism, all of them underlined by the analogies he draws with *Madama Butterfly*.

Puccini's opera (adapted from a turn-of-the-century play by an American, David Belasco) is a fable of submission, both female and Oriental, of a kind that no enlightened audience could comfortably endorse today. In Mr. Hwang's fictionalized version of the Boursicot story, the diplomat (for some reason he has been given the name of a celebrated French publisher, Gallimard) assumes that the singer (now known as Song Liling) is a modest, fluttering Butterfly, a delusion that Song skillfully abets. And although Gallimard himself is clumsy and inexperienced, he is soon preening himself on his supposed conquest. If he had a mustache, he'd be twirling it.

His new he-man confidence quickly spills over into his politics. With the conflict in Vietnam growing more intense (ominous roll of drums), he advises the French ambassador to Beijing to advise the Americans to hit the North Vietnamese hard; and when Ngo Dinh Diem's leadership in the South starts proving a liability, he recommends his assassination.

As an explanation of the Vietnam War, the play leaves something to be desired; but for the audience, the more immediate problem is that Gallimard's hawkishness seems utterly out of keeping with everything else about him. It isn't only that he is a dupe — he could, after all, have been a sinister or a belligerent dupe — but that he is generally so comic and pathetic and inept. (It may be just a chance physical resemblance, but watching John Lithgow in the part, I more than once found myself thinking of Basil Fawlty.)

Then what of the lesser and presumably more representative Western characters in the play, such as Gallimard's wife and his old friend Marc? They are almost all clumsy caricatures of the attitudes they are meant to represent — and, one might add, disconcertingly American-style caricatures. Marc, for example, may be a prime example of what French feminists call a phallocrate, a male chauvinist, but the particular brand of chauvinism he spouts was unmistakably born in the U.S.A.

Perhaps this doesn't matter very much in itself; perhaps it doesn't matter that Song is Chinese and that Madama Butterfly was Japanese (although at one point Westerners are upbraided for not understanding the difference, and for being unaware of Japanese atrocities in China in the 1930s and 40s). Both blurrings of the boundaries contribute, however, to a more pervasive sense of middle.

So do such episodes as the one featuring a sexy blonde, who makes a speech explaining the urge to make war in terms of masculine fears about sexual inadequacy. The sentiments seem to chime with Mr. Hwang's own, and with his presentation of Gallimard; but the blonde is another caricature of a Westerner, and the speech itself is a dreadful affair, with its leering talk. Where does it all leave us?

The most glaring discrepancy in the play is between its generalized view of the East as feminine victim and its rather more complex view of the actual regime in Beijing that Song serves. *Complexity* here is a strictly relative term: we don't learn all that much about the regime, either. But we are shown the Cultural Revolution working its ravages, with Song sentenced to hard labor in Hunan while a guard bawls at him through a loudspeaker and taunts him with cries of "homo!"

The only reasonable conclusion is that Song is far more victimized by the regime than he is by Gallimard (who is at least as much Song's victim, anyway). Toward the end of the play the original message is hammered home, rather desperately: the West is masculine, the East is feminine, and the West has a "rape mentality." But after everything that we have been shown, it doesn't really add up.

Yet if *M. Butterfly* is a mess, intellectually speaking, that doesn't mean that it isn't very well worth seeing. It can boast one truly outstanding performance in B. D. Wong's Song, and one very good one in John Lithgow's Gallimard; it has moments of undoubted theatrical power, especially the big transformation scenes and role reversals; and at its best it sweeps one up in a tense emotional drama.

That drama is almost wholly the story of two individuals, however. A strange story, certainly: whatever the truth of the relationship may have been in real life, it is hard to believe that, as presented on stage, it doesn't have strong homosexual undercurrents. But watching Gallimard and Song, one isn't inclined to fuss over such matters, or to dabble in amateur psychoanalysis. What we are left with is a tragedy of love, betrayal, and loss, and one that holds together on its own terms.

It would have been better, in fact, if Mr. Hwang hadn't been tempted to pile on the ideas; if he had kept them, at best, in second place, as implications and overtones. As it is, they clutter up the foreground of the play and seriously coarsen its texture. But luckily, despite these handicaps, the central action survives: bitter, affecting, and finally driven on by an anguish that even approaches — just a little — the passion of *Madama Butterfly*.

Brian Friel

Born in County Tyrone, Northern Ireland, in 1929, Brian Friel has become Ireland's major playwright. His distinction has grown in recent years with dramatic successes in Ireland, London, and New York. From 1950 to 1960 he was a schoolteacher, but since 1960 he has been a full-time writer. His first well-received play was *Philadelphia, Here I Come!* (1964), which tells the story of Gar O'Donnell, who is about to emigrate to the United States from his tiny hamlet of Ballybeg, County Donegal, the village Friel usually uses for his settings. Ballybeg is tiny, depressed, unable to offer work or dignity to its young men, and those with spirit find that their choices are circumscribed by the limitations of the economy. America offers the most hope, and that is where Gar decides to go. The play captured the imagination of many Irish Americans because of their response to the theme of emigration, but it transcends ethnic concerns. In many ways it has a universal theme — the story of all young men who grow up and realize they must break with their home and set out on their own.

The Loves of Cass McGuire (1966) was first broadcast as a radio play and then produced in New York, Belfast, and London. It tells the story of an old woman whose hopes in life have been dashed by circumstances, none of which improve during the play. Friel developed several strains in his work after demonstrating an interest in the pathos of individual lives such as those of Gar O'Donnell and Cass McGuire. He showed a satirical streak in the political play *The Mundy Scheme* (1969), which focuses on a crazy plan of Irish politicians to capitalize on the Irish specialty of holding wakes for the dead. Mundy's proposal is to convert Ireland into the graveyard of all Europe, thus turning much unarable land to good account. *Freedom of the City* was produced in Dublin, London, and Chicago in 1973 and in New York the following year. It tells the story of three very different people — Michael, twenty-two, and Skinner, twenty-one, both with differing social attitudes, and Lily, forty-three, mother of eleven — who occupy the mayor's office in the Guildhall (town hall) of Derry City during a student protest march. Eventually the three discover common political ground and through a series of unexpected incidents find themselves facing death at the hands of surrounding soldiers.

The Faith Healer (1979) ostensibly portrays a wandering man who heals people in a miraculous way. But the deep structure of the play is about art and the artist's responsibility for healing society. It played in New York and London to considerable acclaim. The most highly regarded of Friel's plays, until *Dancing at Lughnasa,* was *Translations* (1980). Produced in Derry, London, and New York to appreciative crowds, it is set in 1833 in Baile Beg (Ballybeg) and follows the efforts of English surveyors to rename Irish places while making survey maps. These maps translate Irish place names in high-handed, arbitrary fashion. For example, they choose Burnfoot for Bun na hAbbann, which in Irish means "mouth of the river," because Burnfoot is the closest they can get to the Irish word in English. Throughout the play Irish characters speak Irish — or at least we are to understand that they do — while the English speak English.

Much of Friel's work has concerned Irish political issues, but plays such as *Translations* are easy for non-Irish audiences to understand and appreciate. Despite its portraying the English as unconscious oppressors, audiences in London's National Theatre were wildly enthusiastic about it during its extensive 1981 run. *Making History* (1989), set in Elizabethan Ireland, again concerns English oppression and is part of a historical cycle of plays. Friel's *Dancing at Lughnasa* (1990) is a personal examination of a childhood in Ballybeg in the 1930s.

Brian Friel has never been an actor, but he brings to the stage a keen ear for language in the Irish tradition of William Congreve, Bernard Shaw, Oscar Wilde, Lady Gregory, John Millington Synge, Sean O'Casey, and Samuel Beckett. He makes his characters' speeches rich with the rhythms of everyday Irish country life and the color and metaphor of people whose joy in language is intense and satisfying. At the moment he is a member — along with critic Seamus Deane, poets Seamus Heaney and Tom Paulin, and actor Stephen Rea — of an Irish literary group called Field Day, which has its own press and publishes poetry, fiction, and drama and has recently (1991) produced an ambitious three-volume anthology of Irish literature. He has published *Selected Stories* (1979) and *The Diviner* (1983), a book of short stories. In addition to all this, he has also translated Chekhov's *Three Sisters* (1981) and adapted Turgenev's *Fathers and Sons* (1987) for the stage. He is a prodigious figure in contemporary literature.

DANCING AT LUGHNASA

Dancing at Lughnasa (1990) is a memory play told from the point of view of Michael, an older man who recalls the year 1936, when he was seven years old living in Ballybeg with his unwed mother and his aunts. Lughnasa "loo´-na-sa"— Gaelic for August — is the name of a festival on August 1 that has been celebrated in Ireland since pagan times. Lugh, a corn god, was expected to guarantee a good harvest. In modern times Lá Lughnasa was celebrated by a dance at the beginning of harvest in early August in which young men and women courted each other. The dances, like the other ritual aspects of the celebration, were held on hilltops throughout Ireland. The best dancing couple was chosen at each of the ceremonies. In Ganiamore in County Donegal — where the action of this play takes place — the reward for the best male dancer was his choice of a bride from all the eligible women at the celebration.

In addition to dancing, which is central to the celebration, people picked the dark blue bilberries that marked the harvest time. It was essential that everyone, including the old and the infirm, should eat the bilberries so as to participate in the reward of a rich harvest.

The play is a demonstration of the value of memory. Michael does not appear onstage as a child of seven, although his mother and aunts talk to an imaginary Michael as if he were there at that age. The setting is a typical Irish cottage — its walls cut away so we can peer inside — and the immediate areas outside its door. In the background is a stand of wheat, as high as one's waist, with a path cut through it to the town. Michael the man is present to our eyes, but the rest of the characters do not see him. He wanders among his mother, his father, his aunts, and his uncle and tenderly observes their efforts at regulating each other's lives.

His mother, Chris, has demonstrated an unusual spirit and independence in giving herself to a man, a ne'er-do-well who cannot afford to marry but who cuts a dashing figure and demonstrates, onstage, a remarkable skill as a dancer. Her sisters Agnes and the simple-minded Rose are not adventurous. They have made a life in the cottage occupation of knitting gloves to be sold elsewhere. They make very little money, and late in the play we discover that their little bit will be taken from them when the mill develops new machinery and hires only younger women. Kate, biting, strong, and critical, is a schoolteacher earning the living for all of them. Aunt Maggie acts as their housekeeper, using her wit and humor as well as her skills at keeping things tidy.

Among these women Gerry, Michael's father, is an exotic. He comes to visit, bringing excuses and promises — little more — but he has a charm that all the women except Kate respond to. Father Jack is one of Friel's most interesting characters. Friel usually includes a character who is an outsider to Ballybeg, and in this play Father Jack is that character. He was born in Ballybeg but has been in Africa in a leper colony for twenty-five years, where he has spoken little English. He becomes not just an outsider in the community, but an outsider whose language needs reconstruction — providing some of the humor of the play — and whose beliefs have been touched deeply, and much to Kate's horror, by his sympathies for African religion. We realize soon enough that this Irish Catholic priest will not be allowed to say Mass again, not because he is infirm and ill but because he has shifted his faith so far as to absorb the religious beliefs of the people he lived with for so many years. The ritual celebration of Lá Lughnasa is close in character to the celebrations Father Jack remembers in Uganda.

The spirit of the play is marked by a deep affection for all these characters. Friel is working from personal experience in the play: the Mundys, if not his own family, are very close to them. Donal Donnelly, the actor who has worked with Friel for thirty years and who played the part of Father Jack in the New York production, said, "Brian has not talked to me about this, but two of his aunts *did* die homeless in London. And, recently, two elderly nuns came to the theatre with a special request to meet 'Aunt Kate'— the actress — because they had both been taught by the real Aunt Kate."

Dancing at Lughnasa in Performance

The play premiered at the Abbey Theatre in Dublin on April 24, 1990. Barry McGovern created the role of Father Jack, and Alec McCowen took the role to London's National Theatre in October 1990, where the play enjoyed such a successful run that it transferred to a West End theater (the London equivalent of Broadway) and enjoyed a striking commercial success. Its run in New York, at the Plymouth Theater beginning in October 1991, enjoyed an equal success.

The actors and actresses in the New York production were mostly brought from the Abbey production, and consequently the American audience was given a strong and insightful performance whose language — including the sonority of English as it is spoken by the rural Irish — was authentic and powerful. The setting, emphasizing as it did the wheat field ready for harvest, was somewhat enigmatic, especially as the elaborately constructed path in the field was used only once. The style of the play mixes realism with ritual tableau — as at the beginning and end — and the imaginative observations of Michael as he watches his family. The overall effect is powerful.

A film version with Meryl Streep appeared in 1998.

Brian Friel (b. 1929)

DANCING AT LUGHNASA

1990

Characters

MICHAEL, *young man, narrator*
KATE, *forty, schoolteacher*
MAGGIE, *thirty-eight, housekeeper*
AGNES, *thirty-five, knitter*
ROSE, *thirty-two, knitter*
CHRIS, *twenty-six, Michael's mother*
GERRY, *thirty-three, Michael's father*
JACK, *fifty-three, missionary priest*

MICHAEL, who narrates the story, also speaks the lines of the boy, i.e., himself when he was seven.

Act 1: *A warm day in early August 1936.*

Act 2: *Three weeks later.*

The home of the Mundy family, two miles outside the village of Ballybeg, County Donegal, Ireland.

Set: *Slightly more than half the area of the stage is taken up by the kitchen on the right. (Left and right from the point of view of the audience.) The rest of the stage — i.e., the remaining area stage left — is the garden adjoining the house. The garden is neat but not cultivated.*

Upstage center is a garden seat.

The (unseen) boy has been making two kites in the garden and pieces of wood, paper, cord, etc., are lying on the ground close to the garden seat. One kite is almost complete.

There are two doors leading out of the kitchen. The front door leads to the garden and the front of the house. The second in the top right-hand corner leads to the bedrooms and to the area behind the house.

One kitchen window looks out front. A second window looks on to the garden.

There is a sycamore tree off right. One of its branches reaches over part of the house.

The room has the furnishings of the usual country kitchen of the thirties: a large iron range, large turf box beside it, table and chairs, dresser, oil lamp, buckets with water at the back door, etc., etc. But because this is the home of five women the austerity of the furnishings is relieved by some gracious touches — flowers, pretty curtains, an attractive dresser arrangement, etc.

Dress: *Kate, the teacher, is the only wage-earner. Agnes and Rose make a little money knitting gloves at home. Chris and Maggie have no income. So the clothes of all the sisters reflect their lean circumstances. Rose wears Wellingtons even though the day is warm. Maggie wears large boots with long, untied laces. Rose, Maggie, and Agnes all wear the drab, wraparound overalls/aprons of the time.*

In the opening tableau Father Jack is wearing the uniform of a British army officer chaplain — a magnificent and immaculate uniform of dazzling white; gold epaulettes and gold buttons, tropical hat, clerical collar, military cane. He stands stiffly to attention. As the text says, he is "resplendent," "magnificent." So resplendent that he looks almost comic opera.

In this tableau, too, Gerry is wearing a spotless white tricorn hat with splendid white plumage. (Soiled and shabby versions of Jack's uniform and Gerry's ceremonial hat are worn at the end of the play, i.e., in the final tableau.)

Rose is "simple." All her sisters are kind to her and protective of her. But Agnes has taken on the role of special protector.

ACT 1

(When the play opens Michael is standing downstage left in a pool of light. The rest of the stage is in darkness. Immediately Michael begins speaking, slowly bring up the lights on the rest of the stage.)

(Around the stage and at a distance from Michael the other characters stand motionless in formal tableau. Maggie is at the kitchen window (right). Chris is at the front door. Kate at extreme stage right. Rose and Gerry sit on the garden seat. Jack stands beside Rose. Agnes is upstage left. They hold these positions while Michael talks to the audience.)

MICHAEL: When I cast my mind back to that summer of 1936 different kinds of memories offer themselves to me. We got our first wireless set that summer — well, a sort of a set; and it obsessed us. And because it arrived as August was about to begin, my Aunt Maggie — she was the joker of the family — she suggested we give it a name. She wanted to call it Lugh after the old Celtic God of the Harvest. Because in the old days August the First was *Lá Lughnasa*, the feast day of the pagan god Lugh; and the days and weeks of harvesting that followed were called the Festival of Lughnasa. But Aunt Kate — she was a national schoolteacher and a very proper woman — she said it would be sinful to christen an inanimate object with any kind of name, not to talk of a pagan god. So we just called it Marconi because that was the name emblazoned on the set.

And about three weeks before we got that wireless, my mother's brother, my Uncle Jack, came home from Africa for the first time ever. For twenty-five years he had worked in a leper colony there, in a remote village called Ryanga in Uganda. The only time he ever left that village was for about six months during World War One when he was chaplain to the British army in East Africa. Then back to that grim hospice where he worked without a break for a further eighteen years. And now in his early fifties and in bad health he had come home to Ballybeg — as it turned out — to die.

And when I cast my mind back to that summer of 1936, these two memories — of our first wireless and of Father Jack's return — are always linked. So that

when I recall my first shock at Jack's appearance, shrunken and jaundiced with malaria, at the same time I remember my first delight, indeed my awe, at the sheer magic of that radio. And when I remember the kitchen throbbing with the beat of Irish dance music beamed to us all the way from Dublin, and my mother and her sisters suddenly catching hands and dancing a spontaneous stepdance and laughing — screaming! — like excited schoolgirls, at the same time I see that forlorn figure of Father Jack shuffling from room to room as if he were searching for something but couldn't remember what. And even though I was only a child of seven at the time I know I had a sense of unease, some awareness of a widening breach between what seemed to be and what was, of things changing too quickly before my eyes, of becoming what they ought not to be. That may have been because Uncle Jack hadn't turned out at all like the resplendent figure in my head. Or maybe because I had witnessed Marconi's voodoo derange those kind, sensible women and transform them into shrieking strangers. Or maybe it was because during those Lughnasa weeks of 1936 we were visited on two occasions by my father, Gerry Evans, and for the first time in my life I had a chance to observe him.

(The lighting changes. The kitchen and garden are now lit as for a warm summer afternoon.)

(Michael, Kate, Gerry, and Father Jack go off. The others busy themselves with their tasks. Maggie makes a mash for hens. Agnes knits gloves. Rose carries a basket of turf into the kitchen and empties it into the large box beside the range. Chris irons at the kitchen table. They all work in silence. Then Chris stops ironing, goes to the tiny mirror on the wall, and scrutinizes her face.)

CHRIS: When are we going to get a decent mirror to see ourselves in?

MAGGIE: You can see enough to do you.

CHRIS: I'm going to throw this aul cracked thing out.

MAGGIE: Indeed you're not, Chrissie. I'm the one that broke it and the only way to avoid seven years' bad luck is to keep on using it.

CHRIS: You can see nothing in it.

AGNES: Except more and more wrinkles.

CHRIS: D'you know what I think I might do? I think I just might start wearing lipstick.

AGNES: Do you hear this, Maggie?

MAGGIE: Steady on, girl. Today it's lipstick; tomorrow it's the gin bottle.

CHRIS: I think I just might.

AGNES: As long as Kate's not around. "Do you want to make a pagan of yourself?"

(Chris puts her face up close to the mirror and feels it.)

CHRIS: Far too pale. And the aul mousy hair. Need a bit of color.

AGNES: What for?

CHRIS: What indeed. *(She shrugs and goes back to her*

ironing. She holds up a surplice.°) Make a nice dress that, wouldn't it? . . . God forgive me . . .

(*Work continues. Nobody speaks. Then suddenly and unexpectedly Rose bursts into raucous song.*)

ROSE: "Will you come to Abyssinia, will you come?
  Bring your own cup and saucer and a bun . . ."

(*As she sings the next two lines she dances — a gauche, graceless shuffle that defies the rhythm of the song.*)

  "Mussolini will be there with his airplanes in the air,
  Will you come to Abyssinia, will you come?"
  Not bad, Maggie — eh?

(*Maggie is trying to light a very short cigarette butt.*)

MAGGIE: You should be on the stage, Rose.

(*Rose continues to shuffle and now holds up her apron skirt.*)

ROSE: And not a bad bit of leg, Maggie — eh?
MAGGIE: Rose Mundy! Where's your modesty!

(*Maggie now hitches her own skirt even higher than Rose's and does a similar shuffle.*)

  Is that not more like it?
ROSE: Good, Maggie — good — good! Look, Agnes, look!
AGNES: A right pair of pagans, the two of you.
ROSE: Turn on Marconi, Chrissie.
CHRIS: I've told you a dozen times: The battery's dead.
ROSE: It is not. It went for me a while ago.

(*She goes to the set and switches it on. There is a sudden, loud three-second blast of "The British Grenadiers."*)

  You see! Takes aul Rosie!

(*She is about to launch into a dance — and the music suddenly dies.*)

CHRIS: Told you.
ROSE: That aul set's useless.
AGNES: Kate'll have a new battery back with her.
CHRIS: If it's the battery that's wrong.
ROSE: Is Abyssinia in Africa, Aggie?
AGNES: Yes.
ROSE: Is there a war there?
AGNES: Yes. I've told you that.
ROSE: But that's not where Father Jack was, is it?
AGNES (*patiently*): Jack was in Uganda, Rosie. That's a different part of Africa. You know that.
ROSE (*unhappily*): Yes, I do . . . I do . . . I know that . . .

(*Maggie catches her hand and sings softly into her ear to the same melody as the "Abyssinia" song.*)

MAGGIE: "Will you vote for De Valera,° will you vote?
  If you don't, we'll be like Gandhi with his goat."

surplice: A loose-fitting, white garment worn by a priest over his black robe.
De Valera: Eamon De Valera (1882–1975) was from 1937 to 1948 the leader of the Irish government.

(*Rose and Maggie now sing the next two lines together.*)

  "Uncle Bill from Baltinglass has a wireless up his —"

(*They dance as they sing the final line of the song.*)

  "Will you vote for De Valera, will you vote?"
MAGGIE: I'll tell you something, Rosie: The pair of us should be on the stage.
ROSE: The pair of us should be on the stage, Aggie!

(*They return to their tasks. Agnes goes to the cupboard for wool. On her way back to her seat she looks out the window that looks on to the garden.*)

AGNES: What's that son of yours at out there?
CHRIS: God knows. As long as he's quiet.
AGNES: He's making something. Looks like a kite.

(*She taps on the window, calls "Michael!" and blows a kiss to the imaginary child.*)

  Oh, that was the wrong thing to do! He's going to have your hair, Chris.
CHRIS: Mine's like a whin-bush. Will you wash it for me tonight, Maggie?
MAGGIE: Are we all for a big dance somewhere?
CHRIS: After I've put Michael to bed. What about then?
MAGGIE: I'm your man.
AGNES (*at window*): Pity there aren't some boys about to play with.
MAGGIE: Now you're talking. Couldn't we all do with that?
AGNES (*leaving window*): Maggie!
MAGGIE: Wouldn't it be just great if we had a — (*Breaks off.*) Shhh.
CHRIS: What is it?
MAGGIE: Thought I heard Father Jack at the back door. I hope Kate remembers his quinine.
AGNES: She'll remember. Kate forgets nothing.

(*Pause.*)

ROSE: There's going to be pictures in the hall next Saturday, Aggie. I think maybe I'll go.
AGNES (*guarded*): Yes?
ROSE: I might be meeting somebody there.
AGNES: Who's that?
ROSE: I'm not saying.
CHRIS: Do we know him?
ROSE: I'm not saying.
AGNES: You'll enjoy that, Rosie. You loved the last picture we saw.
ROSE: And he wants to bring me up to the back hills next Sunday — up to Lough Anna. His father has a boat there. And I'm thinking maybe I'll bring a bottle of milk with me. And I've enough money saved to buy a packet of chocolate biscuits.
CHRIS: Danny Bradley is a scut, Rose.
ROSE: I never said it was Danny Bradley!
CHRIS: He's a married man with three young children.
ROSE: And that's just where you're wrong, missy — so there! (*To Agnes.*) She left him six months ago, Aggie, and went to England.

MAGGIE: Rose, love, we just want —

ROSE (*to Chris*): And who are you to talk, Christina Mundy! Don't you dare lecture me!

MAGGIE: Everybody in the town knows that Danny Bradley is —

ROSE (*to Maggie*): And you're jealous, too! That's what's wrong with the whole of you — you're jealous of me! (*To Agnes.*) He calls me his Rosebud. He waited for me outside the chapel gate last Christmas morning and he gave me this.

(*She opens the front of her apron. A charm and a medal are pinned to her jumper.*)

"That's for my Rosebud," he said.

AGNES: Is it a fish, Rosie?

ROSE: Isn't it lovely? It's made of pure silver. And it brings you good luck.

AGNES: It is lovely.

ROSE: I wear it all the time — besides my miraculous medal.° (*Pause.*) I love him, Aggie.

AGNES: I know.

CHRIS (*softly*): Bastard.

(*Rose closes the front of her apron. She is on the point of tears. Silence. Now Maggie lifts her hen bucket and using it as a dancing partner she does a very fast and very exaggerated tango across the kitchen floor as she sings in her parodic style the words from "The Isle of Capri."*)

MAGGIE: "Summer time was nearly over;
Blue Italian skies above.
I said, 'Mister, I'm a rover.
Can't you spare a sweet word of love?'"

(*And without pausing for breath she begins calling her hens as she exits by the back door.*)

Tchook-tchook-tchook-tchook-tchook-tchook-tchook-tchookeeeeeee . . .

(*Michael enters and stands stage left. Rose takes the lid off the range and throws turf into the fire.*)

CHRIS: For God's sake, I have an iron in there!

ROSE: How was I to know that?

CHRIS: Don't you see me ironing? (*Fishing with tongs.*) Now you've lost it. Get out of my road, will you!

AGNES: Rosie, love, would you give me a hand with this. (*Of wool.*) If we don't work a bit faster we'll never get two dozen pairs finished this week.

(*The convention must now be established that the [imaginary] Boy Michael is working at the kite materials lying on the ground. No dialogue with the Boy Michael must ever be addressed directly to adult Michael, the narrator. Here, for example, Maggie has her back to the narrator. Michael responds to Maggie in his ordinary narrator's voice. Maggie enters the garden from the back of the house.*)

miraculous medal: A religious medal depicting the Virgin Mary.

MAGGIE: What are these supposed to be?

BOY: Kites.

MAGGIE: Kites! God help your wit!

BOY: Watch where you're walking, Aunt Maggie — you're standing on a tail.

MAGGIE: Did it squeal? — haaaa! I'll make a deal with you, cub: I'll give you a penny if those things ever leave the ground. Right?

BOY: You're on.

(*She now squats down beside him.*)

MAGGIE: I've new riddles for you.

BOY: Give up.

MAGGIE: What goes round the house and round the house and sits in the corner? (*Pause.*) A broom! Why is a river like a watch?

BOY: You're pathetic.

MAGGIE: Because it never goes far without winding! Hairy out and hairy in, lift your foot and stab it in — what is it?

(*Pause.*)

BOY: Give up.

MAGGIE: Think!

BOY: Give up.

MAGGIE: Have you even one brain in your head?

BOY: Give up.

MAGGIE: A sock!

BOY: A what?

MAGGIE: A sock — a sock! You know — lift your foot and stab it —

(*She demonstrates. No response.*)

D'you know what your trouble is, cub? You-are-buck-stupid!

BOY: Look out — there's a rat!

(*She screams and leaps to her feet in terror.*)

MAGGIE: Where? — where? — where? — Jesus, Mary, and Joseph, where is it?

BOY: Caught you again, Aunt Maggie.

MAGGIE: You evil wee brat — God forgive you! I'll get you for that, Michael! Don't you worry — I won't forget that!

(*She picks up her bucket and moves off towards the back of the house. Stops.*)

And I had a barley sugar sweet for you.

BOY: Are there bits of cigarette tobacco stuck to it?

MAGGIE: Jesus Christ! Some day you're going to fill some woman's life full of happiness. (*Moving off.*) Tchook-tchook-tchook-tchook . . .

(*Again she stops and throws him a sweet.*)

There. I hope it chokes you. (*Exits.*) Tchook-tchook-tchook-tchook-tchookeeee . . .

MICHAEL: When I saw Uncle Jack for the first time the reason I was so shocked by his appearance was that I expected — well, I suppose, the hero from a schoolboy's book. Once I had seen a photograph of him radiant and splendid in his officer's uniform. It had fallen out of Aunt Kate's prayer book and she snatched it from me before I could study it in detail. It was a picture taken in 1917 when he was a chaplain to the British forces in East Africa and he looked — magnificent. But Aunt Kate had been involved locally in the War of Independence; so Father Jack's brief career in the British army was never referred to in that house. All the same the wonderful Father Jack of that photo was the image of him that lodged in my mind.

But if he was a hero to me, he was a hero and a saint to my mother and to my aunts. They pored over his occasional letters. They prayed every night for him and for his lepers and for the success of his mission. They scraped and saved for him — sixpence here, a shilling there — sacrifices they made willingly, joyously, so that they would have a little money to send to him at Christmas and for his birthday. And every so often when a story would appear in the *Donegal Enquirer* about "our own leper priest," as they called him — because Ballybeg was proud of him, the whole of Donegal was proud of him — it was only natural that our family would enjoy a small share of that fame — it gave us that little bit of status in the eyes of the parish. And it must have helped my aunts to bear the shame Mother brought on the household by having me — as it was called then — out of wedlock.

(*Kate enters left, laden with shopping bags. When she sees the Boy working at his kites her face lights up with pleasure. She watches him for a few seconds. Then she goes to him.*)

KATE: Well, that's what I call a busy man. Come here and give your Aunt Kate a big kiss.

(*She catches his head between her hands and kisses the crown of his head.*)

And what's all this? It's a kite, is it?

BOY: It's two kites.

KATE (*inspecting them*): It certainly is two kites. And they're the most wonderful kites I've ever seen. And what are these designs?

(*She studies the kite faces which the audience cannot see.*)

BOY: They're faces. I painted them.

KATE (*pretended horror*): Oh, good Lord, they put the heart across me! You did those? Oh, God bless us, those are scarifying! What are they? Devils? Ghosts? I wouldn't like to see those lads up in the sky looking down at me! Hold on now . . . (*She searches in her bags and produces a small, wooden spinning-top and whip.*) Do you know what this is? Of course you do — a spinning-top. Good boy. And this — this is the whip. You know how to use it? Indeed you do. What do you say?

BOY: Thanks.

KATE: Thank you, Aunt Kate. And do you know what I have in here? A new library book! With colored pictures! We'll begin reading it at bedtime.

(*Again she kisses the top of his head. She gets to her feet.*)

Call me the moment you're ready to fly them. I wouldn't miss that for all the world.

(*She goes into the kitchen.*)

D'you know what he's at out there? Did you see, Christina? Making two kites!

CHRIS: Some kites he'll make.

KATE: All by himself. No help from anybody.

AGNES: You always said he was talented, Kate.

KATE: No question about that. And very mature for his years.

CHRIS: Very cheeky for his years.

ROSE: I think he's beautiful, Chris. I wish he was mine.

CHRIS: Is that a spinning-top he has?

KATE: It's nothing.

(*Michael exits left.*)

CHRIS: Oh, Kate, you have him spoiled. Where did you get it?

KATE: Morgan's Arcade.

CHRIS: And I'm sure he didn't even thank you.

ROSE: I know why you went into Morgan's!

KATE: He did indeed. He's very mannerly.

ROSE: You wanted to see Austin Morgan!

KATE: Every field along the road — they're all out at the hay and the corn.

ROSE: Because you have a notion of that aul Austin Morgan!

KATE: Going to be a good harvest by the look of it.

ROSE: I know you have! She's blushing! Look! Isn't she blushing?

(*Chris holds up a skirt she is ironing.*)

CHRIS: You'd need to put a stitch in that hem, Rosie.

ROSE (*to Kate*): But what you don't know is that he's going with a wee young thing from Carrickfad.

KATE: Rose, what Austin Morgan does or doesn't do with —

ROSE: Why are you blushing then? She's blushing, isn't she? Why-why-why, Kate?

KATE (*sudden anger*): For God's sake, Rose, shut up, would you!

ROSE: Anyhow we all know you always had a —

AGNES: Rosie, pass me those steel needles — would you, please?

(*Pause.*)

CHRIS (*to Kate*): Are you tired?

(*Kate flops into a seat.*)

KATE: That road from the town gets longer every day. You can laugh if you want but I *am* going to get that old bike fixed up and I *am* going to learn to ride this winter.

AGNES: Many about Ballybeg?

KATE: Ballybeg's off its head. I'm telling you. Everywhere you go — everyone you meet — it's the one topic: Are you going to the harvest dance? Who are you going with? What are you wearing? This year's going to be the biggest ever and the best ever.

AGNES: All the same I remember some great harvest dances.

CHRIS: Don't we all.

KATE (*unpacking*): Another of those riveting Annie M. P. Smithson novels for you, Agnes.

AGNES: Ah. Thanks.

KATE: *The Marriage of Nurse Harding* — oh, dear! For you, Christina. One teaspoonful every morning before breakfast.

CHRIS: What's this?

KATE: Cod-liver oil. You're far too pale.

CHRIS: Thank you, Kate.

KATE: Because you take no exercise. Anyhow I'm in the chemist's shop and this young girl — a wee slip of a thing, can't even remember her name — her mother's the knitting agent that buys your gloves, Agnes —

AGNES: Vera McLaughlin.

KATE: Her daughter whatever you call her.

ROSE: Sophia.

KATE: Miss Sophia, who must be all of fifteen; she comes up to me and she says, "I hope you're not going to miss the harvest dance, Miss Mundy. It's going to be just *supreme* this year." And honest to God, if you'd seen the delight in her eyes, you'd think it was heaven she was talking about. I'm telling you — off its head — like a fever in the place. That's the quinine. The doctor says it won't cure the malaria but it might help to contain it. Is he in his room?

CHRIS: He's wandering about out the back somewhere.

KATE: I told the doctor you thought him very quiet, Agnes.

(*Agnes had stopped knitting and is looking abstractedly into the middle distance.*)

AGNES: Yes?

KATE: Well, didn't you? And the doctor says we must remember how strange everything here must be to him after so long. And on top of that Swahili has been his language for twenty-five years; so that it's not that his mind is confused — it's just that he has difficulty finding the English words for what he wants to say.

CHRIS: No matter what the doctor says, Kate, his mind is a bit confused. Sometimes he doesn't know the difference between us. I've heard him calling you Rose and he keeps calling me some strange name like —

KATE: Okawa.

CHRIS: That's it! Aggie, you've heard him, haven't you?

KATE: Okawa was his house boy. He was very attached to him. (*Taking off her shoe.*) I think I'm getting corns in this foot. I hope to God I don't end up crippled like poor mother, may she rest in peace.

AGNES: Wouldn't it be a good one if we all went?

CHRIS: Went where?

AGNES: To the harvest dance.

CHRIS: Aggie!

AGNES: Just like we used to. All dressed up. I think I'd go.

ROSE: I'd go, too, Aggie! I'd go with you!

KATE: For heaven's sake you're not serious, Agnes — are you?

AGNES: I think I am.

KATE: Hah! There's more than Ballybeg off its head.

AGNES: I think we should all go.

KATE: Have you any idea what it'll be like? — Crawling with cheeky young brats that I taught years ago.

AGNES: I'm game.

CHRIS: We couldn't, Aggie — could we?

KATE: And all the riff-raff of the countryside.

AGNES: I'm game.

CHRIS: Oh God, you know how I loved dancing, Aggie.

AGNES (*to Kate*): What do you say?

KATE (*to Chris*): You have a seven-year-old child — have you forgotten that?

AGNES (*to Chris*): You could wear that blue dress of mine — you have the figure for it and it brings out the color of your eyes.

CHRIS: Can I have it? God, Aggie, I could dance nonstop all night — all week — all month!

KATE: And who'd look after Father Jack?

AGNES (*to Kate*): And you look great in that cotton dress you got for confirmation last year. You're beautiful in it, Kate.

KATE: What sort of silly talk is —

AGNES (*to Kate*): And you can wear my brown shoes with the crossover straps.

KATE: This is silly talk. We can't, Agnes. How can we?

ROSE: Will Maggie go with us?

CHRIS: Will Maggie what! Try to stop her!

KATE: Oh God, Agnes, what do you think?

AGNES: We're going.

KATE: Are we?

ROSE: We're off! We're away!

KATE: Maybe we're mad — are we mad?

CHRIS: It costs four and six to get in.

AGNES: I've five pounds saved. I'll take you. I'll take us all.

KATE: Hold on now —

AGNES: How many years has it been since we were at the harvest dance? — at any dance? And I don't care how young they are, how drunk and dirty and sweaty they are. I want to dance, Kate. It's the Festival of Lughnasa. I'm only thirty-five. I want to dance.

KATE (*wretched*): I know, I know, Agnes, I know. All the same — oh my God — I don't know if it's —

AGNES: It's settled. We're going — the Mundy girls — all five of us together.

CHRIS: Like we used to.

AGNES: Like we used to.

ROSE: I love you, Aggie! I love you more than chocolate biscuits!

(*Rose kisses Agnes impetuously, flings her arms above her head, begins singing "Abyssinia," and does the first steps of a bizarre and abandoned dance. At this Kate panics.*)

KATE: No, no, no! We're going nowhere!

CHRIS: If we all want to go —

KATE: Look at yourselves, will you! Just look at yourselves! Dancing at our time of day? That's for young people with no duties and no responsibilities and nothing in their heads but pleasure.

AGNES: Kate, I think we —

KATE: Do you want the whole countryside to be laughing at us? — women of our years? — mature women, *dancing*? What's come over you all? And this is Father Jack's home — we must never forget that — ever. No, no, we're going to no harvest dance.

ROSE: But you just said —

KATE: And there'll be no more discussion about it. The matter's over. I don't want it mentioned again.

(*Silence. Maggie returns to the garden from the back of the house. She has the hen bucket on her arm and her hands are cupped as if she were holding something fragile between them. She goes to the kite materials.*)

MAGGIE: The fox is back.

BOY: Did you see him?

MAGGIE: He has a hole chewed in the henhouse door.

BOY: Did you get a look at him, Aunt Maggie?

MAGGIE: Wasn't I talking to him. He was asking for you.

BOY: Ha-ha. What's that you have in your hands?

MAGGIE: Something I found.

BOY: What?

MAGGIE: Sitting very still at the foot of the holly tree.

BOY: Show me.

MAGGIE: Say please three times.

BOY: Please-please-please.

MAGGIE: In Swahili.

BOY: Are you going to show it to me or are you not?

MAGGIE (*crouching down beside him*): Now, cub, put your ear over here. Listen. Shhh. D'you hear it?

BOY: I think so . . . yes.

MAGGIE: What do you hear?

BOY: Something.

MAGGIE: Are you sure?

BOY: Yes, I'm sure. Show me, Aunt Maggie.

MAGGIE: All right. Ready? Get back a bit. Bit further. Right?

BOY: Yes.

(*Suddenly she opens her hands and her eyes follow the rapid and imaginary flight of something up to the sky and out of sight. She continues staring after it. Pause.*)

What was it?

MAGGIE: Did you see it?

BOY: I think so . . . yes.

MAGGIE: Wasn't it wonderful?

BOY: Was it a bird?

MAGGIE: The colors are so beautiful. (*She gets to her feet.*) Trouble is — just one quick glimpse — that's all you ever get. And if you miss that . . .

(*She moves off towards the back door of the kitchen.*)

BOY: What was it, Aunt Maggie?

MAGGIE: Don't you know what it was? It was all in your mind. Now we're quits.

KATE (*unpacking*): Tea . . . soap . . . Indian meal . . . jelly . . .

MAGGIE: I'm sick of that white rooster of yours, Rosie. Some pet that. Look at the lump he took out of my arm.

ROSE: You don't speak to him right.

MAGGIE: I know the speaking he'll get from me — the weight of my boot. Would you put some turf on that fire, Chrissie; I'm going to make some soda bread.

(*Maggie washes her hands and begins baking.*)

ROSE (*privately*): Watch out. She's in one of her cranky moods.

KATE: Your ten Wild Woodbine, Maggie.

MAGGIE: Great. The tongue's out a mile.

ROSE (*privately*): You missed it all, Maggie.

MAGGIE: What did I miss this time?

ROSE: We were all going to go to the harvest dance — like the old days. And then Kate —

KATE: Your shoes, Rose. The shoemaker says, whatever kind of feet you have, only the insides of the soles wear down.

ROSE: Is that a bad thing?

KATE: That is neither a bad thing nor a good thing, Rose. It's just — distinctive, as might be expected.

(*Rose grimaces behind Kate's back.*)

Cornflour . . . salt . . . tapioca — it's gone up a penny for some reason . . . sugar for the bilberry jam — if we ever get the bilberries . . .

(*Agnes and Rose exchange looks.*)

MAGGIE (*privately to Rose*): Look at the packet of Wild Woodbine she got me.

ROSE: What's wrong with it?

MAGGIE: Only nine cigarettes in it. They're so wild one of them must have escaped on her.

(*They laugh secretly.*)

CHRIS: Doesn't Jack sometimes call you Okawa, too, Maggie?

MAGGIE: Yes. What does it mean?

CHRIS: Okawa was his house boy, Kate says.

MAGGIE: Dammit. I thought it was Swahili for gorgeous.

AGNES: Maggie!

MAGGIE: That's the very thing we could do with here — a house boy.

KATE: And the battery. The man in the shop says we

go through these things quicker than anyone in Ballybeg.

CHRIS: Good for us.

(*Chris takes the battery and leaves it beside Marconi.*)

KATE: I met the parish priest. I don't know what has happened to that man. But ever since Father Jack came home he can hardly look me in the eye.

MAGGIE: That's because you keep winking at him, Kate.

CHRIS: He was always moody, that man.

KATE: Maybe that's it . . . The paper . . . candles . . . matches . . . The word's not good on that young Sweeney boy from the back hills. He was anointed° last night.

MAGGIE: I didn't know he was dying?

KATE: Not an inch of his body that isn't burned.

AGNES: Does anybody know what happened?

KATE: Some silly prank up in the hills. He knows he's dying, the poor boy. Just lies there, moaning.

CHRIS: What sort of prank?

KATE: How would I know?

CHRIS: What are they saying in the town?

KATE: I know no more than I've told you, Christina.

(*Pause.*)

ROSE (*quietly, resolutely*): It was last Sunday week, the first night of the Festival of Lughnasa; and they were doing what they do every year up there in the back hills.

KATE: Festival of Lughnasa! What sort of —

ROSE: First they light a bonfire beside a spring well. Then they dance round it. Then they drive their cattle through the flames to banish the devil out of them.

KATE: Banish the — ! You don't know the first thing about what —

ROSE: And this year there was an extra big crowd of boys and girls. And they were off their heads with drink. And young Sweeney's trousers caught fire and he went up like a torch. That's what happened.

KATE: Who filled your head with that nonsense?

ROSE: They do it every Lughnasa. I'm telling you. That's what happened.

KATE (*very angry, almost shouting*): And they're savages! I know those people from the back hills! I've taught them! Savages — that's what they are! And what pagan practices they have are no concern of ours — none whatever! It's a sorry day to hear talk like that in a Christian home, a Catholic home! All I can say is that I'm shocked and disappointed to hear you repeating rubbish like that, Rose!

ROSE (*quietly, resolutely*): That's what happened. I'm telling you.

(*Pause.*)

MAGGIE: All the same it would be very handy in the wintertime to have a wee house boy to feed the hens:

---

anointed: Given the "last rites," a sacrament for the dying.

"Tchook-tchook-tchook-tchook-tchook-tchook-tchook-tchookeeee . . ."

(*Father Jack enters by the back door. He looks frail and older than his fifty-three years. Broad-brimmed black hat. Heavy gray top coat. Woolen trousers that stop well short of his ankles. Heavy black boots. Thick woolen socks. No clerical collar. He walks — shuffles quickly — with his hands behind his back. He seems uneasy, confused. Scarcely any trace of an Irish accent.*)

JACK: I beg your pardon . . . the wrong apartment . . . forgive me . . .

KATE: Come in and join us, Jack.

JACK: May I?

MAGGIE: You're looking well, Jack.

JACK: Yes? I expected to enter my bedroom through that . . . what I am missing — what I require . . . I had a handkerchief in my pocket and I think perhaps I —

CHRIS (*taking one from the ironing pile*): Here's a handkerchief.

JACK: I thank you. I am grateful. It is so strange: I don't remember the — the architecture? — the planning? — what's the word? — the layout! — I don't recollect the layout of this home . . . scarcely. That is strange, isn't it? I thought the front door was there. (*To Kate.*) You walked to the village to buy stores, Agnes?

KATE: It's Kate. And dozens of people were asking for you.

JACK: They remember me?

KATE: Of course they remember you! And when you're feeling stronger they're going to have a great public welcome for you — flags, bands, speeches, everything!

JACK: Why would they do this?

KATE: Because they're delighted you're back.

JACK: Yes?

KATE: Because they're delighted you're home.

JACK: I'm afraid I don't remember them. I couldn't name ten people in Ballybeg now.

CHRIS: It will all come back to you. Don't worry.

JACK: You think so?

AGNES: Yes, it will.

JACK: Perhaps . . . I feel the climate so cold . . . if you'll forgive me . . .

AGNES: Why don't you lie down for a while?

JACK: I may do that . . . thank you . . . you are most kind . . .

(*He shuffles off. Pause. A sense of unease, almost embarrassment.*)

KATE (*briskly*): It will be a slow process but he'll be fine. Apples . . . butter . . . margarine . . . flour . . . And wait till you hear! Who did I meet in the post office! Maggie, are you listening to me?

MAGGIE: Yes?

KATE: You'll never believe it — your old pal, Bernie O'Donnell! Home from London! First time back in twenty years!

MAGGIE: Bernie . . .

KATE: Absolutely gorgeous. The figure of a girl of eighteen. Dressed to kill from head to foot. And the hair! — as black and as curly as the day she left. I can't tell you — a film star!

MAGGIE: Bernie O'Donnell . . .

KATE: And beside her two of the most beautiful children you ever laid eyes on. Twins. They'll be fourteen next month. And to see the three of them together — like sisters, I'm telling you.

MAGGIE: Twin girls.

KATE: Identical.

MAGGIE: Identical.

KATE: Nora and Nina.

ROSE: Mother used to say twins are a double blessing.

MAGGIE: Bernie O'Donnell . . . oh my goodness . . .

KATE: And wait till you hear — they are pure blond! "Where in the name of God did the blond hair come from?" I asked her. "The father. Eric," she says. "He's from Stockholm."

AGNES: Stockholm!

ROSE: Where's Stockholm, Aggie?

KATE: So there you are. Bernie O'Donnell married to a Swede. I couldn't believe my eyes. But the same bubbly, laughing, happy Bernie. Asking about everybody by name.

(*Maggie goes to the window and looks out so that the others cannot see her face. She holds her hands, covered with flour, out from her body.*)

CHRIS: She remembered us all?

KATE: Knew all about Michael; had his age to the very month. Was Agnes still the quickest knitter in Ballybeg? Were none of us thinking of getting married? — and weren't we wise!

ROSE: Did she remember me?

KATE: "Rose had the sweetest smile I ever saw."

ROSE: There!

KATE: But asking specially for you, Maggie: how you were doing — what you were doing — how were you looking — were you as lighthearted as ever? Every time she thinks of you, she says, she has the memory of the two of you hiding behind the turf stack, passing a cigarette between you and falling about laughing about some boy called — what was it? — Curley somebody?

MAGGIE: Curley McDaid. An eejit of a fella. Bald as an egg at seventeen. Bernie O'Donnell . . . oh my goodness . . .

(*Pause.*)

AGNES: Will she be around for a while?

KATE: Leaving tomorrow.

AGNES: We won't see her so. That's a pity.

CHRIS: Nice names, aren't they? — Nina and Nora.

KATE: I like Nora. Nice name. Strong name.

AGNES: Not so sure about Nina. (*To Chris.*) Do you like Nina for a name?

CHRIS: Nina? No, not a lot.

KATE: Well, if there's a Saint Nina, I'm afraid she's not in my prayer book.

AGNES: Maybe she's a Swedish saint.

KATE: Saints in Sweden! What'll it be next!

ROSE: Mother used to say twins are a double blessing.

KATE (*sharply*): You've offered us that cheap wisdom already, Rose.

(*Pause.*)

CHRIS: You've got some flour on your nose, Maggie.

MAGGIE: When I was sixteen I remember slipping out one Sunday night — it was this time of year, the beginning of August — and Bernie and I met at the gate of the workhouse and the pair of us off to a dance in Ardstraw. I was being pestered by a fellow called Tim Carlin at the time but it was really Brian McGuinness that I was — that I was keen on. Remember Brian with the white hands and the longest eyelashes you ever saw? But of course he was crazy about Bernie. Anyhow the two boys took us on the bar of their bikes and off the four of us headed to Ardstraw, fifteen miles each way. If Daddy had known, may he rest in peace . . .

And at the end of the night there was a competition for the Best Military Two-step. And it was down to three couples: the local pair from Ardstraw; wee Timmy and myself — he was up to there on me; and Brian and Bernie . . .

And they were just so beautiful together, so stylish; you couldn't take your eyes off them. People just stopped dancing and gazed at them . . .

And when the judges announced the winners — they were probably blind drunk — naturally the local couple came first; and Timmy and myself came second; and Brian and Bernie came third.

Poor Bernie was stunned. She couldn't believe it. Couldn't talk. Wouldn't speak to any of us for the rest of the night. Wouldn't even cycle home with us. She was right, too: They should have won; they were just so beautiful together . . .

And that's the last time I saw Brian McGuinness — remember Brian with the . . . ? And the next thing I heard he had left for Australia . . .

She was right to be angry, Bernie. I know it wasn't fair — it wasn't fair at all. I mean they must have been blind drunk, those judges, whoever they were . . .

(*Maggie stands motionless, staring out of the window, seeing nothing. The others drift back to their tasks: Rose and Agnes knit; Kate puts the groceries away; Chris connects the battery. Pause.*)

KATE: Is it working now, Christina?

CHRIS: What's that?

KATE: Marconi.

CHRIS: Marconi? Yes, yes . . . should be . . .

(*She switches the set on and returns to her ironing. The music, at first scarcely audible, is Irish dance music — "The Mason's Apron," played by a ceili band. Very fast; very heavy beat; a raucous sound. At first we are aware of the beat only. Then, as the volume increases slowly, we hear the melody. For about ten seconds — until the sound has established itself — the women continue with their tasks. Then Maggie turns round. Her head is cocked to the beat, to the music. She is breathing deeply, rapidly. Now her features become animated by a look of defiance, of aggression; a crude mask of happiness. For a few seconds she stands still, listening, absorbing the rhythm, surveying her sisters with her defiant grimace. Now she spreads her fingers (which are covered with flour), pushes her hair back from her face, pulls her hands down her cheeks and patterns her face with an instant mask. At the same time she opens her mouth and emits a wild, raucous "Yaaaah!"— and immediately begins to dance, arms, legs, hair, long bootlaces flying. And as she dances she lilts — sings — shouts and calls, "Come on and join me! Come on! Come on!" For about ten seconds she dances alone — a white-faced, frantic dervish. Her sisters watch her.)*

(Then Rose's face lights up. Suddenly she flings away her knitting, leaps to her feet, shouts, grabs Maggie's hand. They dance and sing — shout together; Rose's Wellingtons pounding out their own erratic rhythm. Now after another five seconds Agnes looks around, leaps up, joins Maggie and Rose. Of all the sisters she moves most gracefully, most sensuously. Then after the same interval Chris, who has been folding Jack's surplice, tosses it quickly over her head and joins in the dance. The moment she tosses the vestment over her head Kate cries out in remonstration, "Oh, Christina — !" But her protest is drowned. Agnes and Rose, Chris and Maggie, are now all doing a dance that is almost recognizable. They meet — they retreat. They form a circle and wheel round and round. But the movements seem caricatured; and the sound is too loud; and the beat is too fast; and the almost recognizable dance is made grotesque because — for example — instead of holding hands, they have their arms tightly around one another's neck, one another's waist. Finally Kate, who has been watching the scene with unease, with alarm, suddenly leaps to her feet, flings her head back, and emits a loud "Yaaaah!")

(Kate dances alone, totally concentrated, totally private; a movement that is simultaneously controlled and frantic; a weave of complex steps that takes her quickly round the kitchen, past her sisters, out to the garden, round the summer seat, back to the kitchen; a pattern of action that is out of character and at the same time ominous of some deep and true emotion. Throughout the dance Rose, Agnes, Maggie, and Chris shout — call — sing to each other. Kate makes no sound.)

(With this too loud music, this pounding beat, this shouting — calling — singing, this parodic reel, there is a sense of order being consciously subverted, of the women consciously and crudely caricaturing themselves, indeed of near-hysteria being induced. The music stops abruptly in mid-phrase. But because of the noise they are making the sisters do not notice and continue dancing for a few seconds. Then Kate notices — and

stops. Then Agnes. Then Chris and Maggie. Now only Rose is dancing her graceless dance by herself. Then finally she, too, notices and stops. Silence. For some time they stand where they have stopped. There is no sound but their gasping for breath and short bursts of static from the radio. They look at each other obliquely, avoid looking at each other; half smile in embarrassment; feel and look slightly ashamed and slightly defiant. Chris moves first. She goes to the radio.)

CHRIS: It's away again, that aul thing. Sometimes you're good with it, Aggie.

AGNES: Feel the top. Is it warm?

CHRIS: Roasting.

AGNES: Turn it off till it cools down.

(Chris turns it off — and slaps it.)

CHRIS: Bloody useless set, that.

KATE: No need for corner-boy language, Christina.

AGNES: There must be some reason why it overheats.

CHRIS: Because it's a goddamn, bloody useless set — that's why.

ROSE: Goddamn bloody useless.

KATE: Are Wellingtons absolutely necessary on a day like this, Rose?

ROSE: I've only my Wellingtons and my Sunday shoes, Kate. And it's not Sunday, is it?

KATE: Oh, dear, we're suddenly very logical, aren't we?

MAGGIE *(lighting a cigarette)*: I'll tell you something, girls: This Ginger Rogers has seen better days.

KATE: It's those cigarettes are killing you.

MAGGIE *(exhaling)*: Wonderful Wild Woodbine. Next best thing to a wonderful, wild man. Want a drag, Kitty?

KATE: Go and wash your face, Maggie. And for goodness' sake tie those laces.

MAGGIE: Yes, miss. *(At window.)* Where's Michael, Chrissie?

CHRIS: Working at those kites, isn't he?

MAGGIE: He's not there. He's gone.

CHRIS: He won't go far.

MAGGIE: He was there ten minutes ago.

CHRIS: He'll be all right.

MAGGIE: But if he goes down to the old well —

CHRIS: Just leave him alone for once, will you, please?

(Maggie shrugs and goes out the back door. Pause.)

KATE: Who's making the tea this evening?

AGNES: Who makes the tea every evening?

CHRIS *(at radio)*: The connections seem to be all right.

KATE: Please take that surplice off, Christina.

CHRIS: Maybe a valve has gone — if I knew what a valve looked like.

KATE: Have you no sense of propriety?

CHRIS: If you ask me we should throw it out.

AGNES: I'd be all for that. It's junk, that set.

ROSE: Goddamn and bloody useless.

KATE *(to Agnes)*: And you'll buy a new one, will you?

AGNES: It was never any good.

KATE: You'll buy it out of your glove money, will you? I

thought what you and Rose earned knitting gloves was barely sufficient to clothe the pair of you.

AGNES: This isn't your classroom, Kate.

KATE: Because I certainly don't see any of it being offered for the upkeep of the house.

AGNES: Please, Kate —

KATE: But now it stretches to buying a new wireless. Wonderful!

AGNES: I make every meal you sit down to every day of the week —

KATE: Maybe I should start knitting gloves?

AGNES: I wash every stitch of clothes you wear. I polish your shoes. I make your bed. We both do — Rose and I. Paint the house. Sweep the chimney. Cut the grass. Save the turf. What you have here, Kate, are two unpaid servants.

ROSE: And d'you know what your nickname at school is? The Gander! Everybody calls you the Gander!

(*Maggie runs on and goes straight to the window.*)

MAGGIE: Come here till you see! Look who's coming up the lane!

AGNES: Who's coming?

MAGGIE: I only got a glimpse of him — but I'm almost certain it's —

AGNES: Who? Who is it?

MAGGIE (*to Chris*): It's Gerry Evans, Chrissie.

CHRIS: Christ Almighty.

MAGGIE: He's at the bend in the lane.

CHRIS: Oh, Jesus Christ Almighty.

(*The news throws the sisters into chaos. Only Chris stands absolutely still, too shocked to move. Agnes picks up her knitting and works with excessive concentration. Rose and Maggie change their footwear. Everybody dashes about in confusion — peering into the tiny mirror, bumping into one another, peeping out the window, combing hair. During all this hectic activity they talk over each other and weave around the immobile Chris. The lines overlap.*)

KATE: How dare Mr. Evans show his face here.

MAGGIE: He wants to see his son, doesn't he?

KATE: There's no welcome for that creature here.

ROSE: Who hid my Sunday shoes?

MAGGIE: We'll have to give him his tea.

KATE: I don't see why we should.

MAGGIE: And there's nothing in the house.

KATE: No business at all coming here and upsetting everybody.

ROSE: You're right, Kate. I hate him!

MAGGIE: Has anybody got spare shoelaces?

KATE: Look at the state of that floor.

MAGGIE: Maybe he just wants to meet Father Jack.

KATE: Father Jack may have something to say to Mr. Evans. (*Of the ironing.*) Agnes, put those clothes away.

(*Agnes does not hear her, so apparently engrossed is she in her knitting.*)

MAGGIE: My Woodbine! Where's my Woodbine?

ROSE: He won't stay the night, Kate, will he?

KATE: He most certainly won't stay the night in this house!

MAGGIE: Have you a piece of cord, Aggie? Anybody got a bit of twine?

KATE: Behave quite normally. Be very calm and very dignified. Stop peeping out, Rose!

ROSE (*at window*): There's nobody coming at all.

(*Silence. Then Agnes puts down her knitting, rushes to the window, pushes Rose aside, and looks out.*)

AGNES: Let me see.

ROSE: You imagined it, Maggie.

CHRIS: Oh God.

ROSE: He's not there at all.

AGNES (*softly*): Yes, he is. Maggie's right. There he is.

ROSE: Show me.

KATE: Has he a walking stick?

ROSE: Yes.

KATE: And a straw hat?

ROSE: Yes.

KATE: It's Mr. Evans all right.

AGNES: Yes. There he is.

CHRIS: Oh sweet God — look at the state of me — what'll I say to him? — how close is he?

ROSE: I couldn't look that man in the face. I just hate him — hate him!

KATE: That's a very unchristian thing to say, Rose. (*As Rose rushes off.*) There's no luck in talk like that!

CHRIS: Look at my hands, Kate — I'm shaking.

(*Kate catches her shoulders.*)

KATE: You are not shaking. You are perfectly calm and you are looking beautiful and what you are going to do is this. You'll meet him outside. You'll tell him his son is healthy and happy. And then you'll send him packing — yourself and Michael are managing quite well without him — as you always have.

(*Chris does not move. She is about to cry. Kate now takes her in her arms.*)

Of course ask him in. And give the creature his tea. And stay the night if he wants to. (*Firm again.*) But in the outside loft. And alone.

Now. I brought a newspaper home with me. Did anybody see where I left it?

(*Chris now rushes to the mirror and adroitly adjusts her hair and her clothes.*)

AGNES: Where is he, Maggie?

MAGGIE: In the garden.

KATE: Agnes, did you see where I left the paper?

MAGGIE: It's on the turf box, Kate.

(*Kate reads the paper — or pretends to. Agnes sits beside the radio and knits with total concentration. Maggie stands at the side of the garden window. Gerry*)

Evans enters left, his step jaunty, swinging his cane, his straw hat well back on his head. He knows he is being watched. Although he is very ill at ease the smile never leaves his face. Chris goes out to the garden where they meet. Gerry has an English accent.)

GERRY: How are you, Chrissie? Great to see you.

CHRIS: Hello, Gerry.

GERRY: And how have you been for the past six months?

CHRIS: Thirteen months.

GERRY: Thirteen? Never!

CHRIS: July last year; July the seventh.

GERRY: Wow-wow-wow-wow. Where does the time go? Thirteen months? Phew! A dozen times — two dozen times I planned a visit and then something turned up and I couldn't get away.

CHRIS: Well, you're here now.

GERRY: Certainly am. And that was a bit of good fortune. Last night in a bar in Sligo. Bump into this chappie with a brand new Morris Cowley who lets slip that he's heading for Ballybeg in the morning. Ballybeg? Something familiar about that name! So. Here I am. In the flesh. As a matter of interest. Bit of good luck that, wasn't it?

CHRIS: Yes.

GERRY: He just let it slip. And here I am. Oh, yes, wonderful luck.

CHRIS: Yes.

(*Pause.*)

MAGGIE: Looks terrified, the poor fella.

KATE: Terrified, my foot.

MAGGIE: Come here till you see him. Aggie.

AGNES: Not just now.

MAGGIE: I'm sure he could do with a good meal.

KATE: I'll give him three minutes. Then if she doesn't hunt him, I will.

GERRY: You're looking wonderful, Chrissie. Really great. Terrific.

CHRIS: My hair's like a whin-bush.

GERRY: Looks lovely to me.

CHRIS: Maggie's going to wash it tonight.

GERRY: And how's Maggie?

CHRIS: Fine.

GERRY: And Rose and Kate?

CHRIS: Grand.

GERRY: And Agnes?

CHRIS: Everybody's well, thanks.

GERRY: Tell her I was asking for her — Agnes.

CHRIS: I would ask you in but the place is —

GERRY: No, no, some other time; thanks all the same. The old schedule's a bit tight today. And the chappie who gave me the lift tells me Father Jack's home.

CHRIS: Just a few weeks ago.

GERRY: All the way from Africa.

CHRIS: Yes.

GERRY: Safe and sound.

CHRIS: Yes.

GERRY: Terrific.

CHRIS: Yes.

GERRY: Lucky man.

CHRIS: Yes.

(*Gerry uses the cane as a golf club and swings.*)

GERRY: Must take up some exercise. Putting on too much weight.

KATE: He's not still there, is he?

MAGGIE: Yes.

KATE: Doing what, in God's name?

MAGGIE: Talking.

KATE: Would someone please tell me what they have to say to each other?

MAGGIE: He's Michael's father, Kate.

KATE: That's a responsibility never burdened Mr. Evans.

CHRIS: A commercial traveler called into Kate's school last Easter. He had met you somewhere in Dublin. He had some stupid story about you giving dancing lessons up there.

GERRY: He was right.

CHRIS: He was not, Gerry!

GERRY: Cross the old ticker.

CHRIS: Real lessons?

GERRY: All last winter.

CHRIS: What sort of dancing?

GERRY: Strictly ballroom. You're the one should have been giving them — you were always far better than me. Don't you remember? (*He does a quick step and a pirouette.*) Oh, that was fun while it lasted. I enjoyed that.

CHRIS: And people came to you to be taught?

GERRY: Don't look so surprised! Everybody wants to dance. I had thousands of pupils — millions!

CHRIS: Gerry —

GERRY: Fifty-three. I'm a liar. Fifty-one. And when the good weather came, they all drifted away. Shame, really. Yes, I enjoyed that. But I've just started a completely new career, as a matter of interest. Never been busier. Gramophone salesman. Agent for the whole country, if you don't mind. "Minerva Gramophones — The Wise Buy."

CHRIS: Sounds good, Gerry.

GERRY: Fabulous. All I have to do is get the orders and pass them on to Dublin. A big enterprise, Chrissie; oh, one very big enterprise.

CHRIS: And it's going all right for you?

GERRY: Unbelievable. The wholesaler can't keep up with me. Do you see this country? This country is gramophone crazy. Give you an example. Day before yesterday; just west of Oughterard; spots this small house up on the side of a hill. Something seemed just right about it — you know? Off the bike, up the lane; knocks. Out comes this enormous chappie with red hair — what are you laughing at?

CHRIS: Gerry —

GERRY: I promise you. I show him the brochures; we talk about them for ten minutes; and just like that he takes four — one for himself and three for the married daughters.

CHRIS: He took four gramophones?

GERRY: Four brochures!

(*They both laugh.*)

But he'll buy. I promise you he'll buy. Tell you this, Chrissie: People thought gramophones would be a thing of the past when radios came in. But they were wrong. In my experience . . . Don't turn round; but he's watching us from behind that bush.

CHRIS: Michael?

GERRY: Pretend you don't notice. Just carry on. This all his stuff?

CHRIS: He's making kites if you don't mind.

GERRY: Unbelievable. Got a glimpse of him down at the foot of the lane. He is just enormous.

CHRIS: He's at school, you know.

GERRY: Never! Wow-wow-wow-wow. Since when?

CHRIS: Since Christmas. Kate got him in early.

GERRY: Fabulous. And he likes it?

CHRIS: He doesn't say much.

GERRY: He loves it. He adores it. They all love school nowadays. And he'll be brilliant at school. Actually I intended bringing him something small —

CHRIS: No, no; his aunts have him —

GERRY: Just a token, really. As a matter of interest I was looking at a bicycle in Kilkenny last Monday. But they only had it in blue and I thought black might be more — you know — manly. They took my name and all. Call next time I'm down there. Are you busy yourself?

CHRIS: Oh, the usual — housework — looking after his lordship.

GERRY: Wonderful.

CHRIS: Give Agnes and Rose a hand at their knitting. The odd bit of sewing. Pity you don't sell sewing machines.

GERRY: That's an idea! Do the two jobs together! Make an absolute fortune. You have the most unbelievable business head, Chrissie. Never met anything like it.

(*She laughs.*)

What are you laughing at?

MAGGIE: You should see the way she's looking at him — you'd think he was the biggest toff in the world.

KATE: Tinker, more likely! Loafer! Wastrel!

MAGGIE: She knows all that, too.

KATE: Too? That's all there is.

MAGGIE: Come over till you see them, Agnes.

AGNES: Not just now.

GERRY: You'd never guess what I met on the road out from the town. Talk about good luck! A cow with a single horn coming straight out of the middle of its forehead.

CHRIS: You never did!

GERRY: As God is my judge. Walking along by itself. Nobody near it.

CHRIS: Gerry —

GERRY: And just as I was passing it, it stopped and looked me straight in the eye.

CHRIS: That was no cow you met — that was a unicorn.

GERRY: Go ahead and mock. A unicorn has the body of a horse. This was a cow — a perfectly ordinary brown cow except that it had a single horn just here. Would I tell you a lie?

(*Chris laughs.*)

Go ahead. Laugh. But that's what I saw. Wasn't that a spot of good luck?

CHRIS: Was it?

GERRY: A cow with a single horn? Oh, yes, that must be a good omen. How many cows like that have you ever met?

CHRIS: Thousands. Millions.

GERRY: Stop that! I'm sure it's the only one in Ireland; maybe the only one in the world. And I met it on the road to Ballybeg. And it winked at me.

CHRIS: You never mentioned that.

GERRY: What?

CHRIS: That it winked at you.

GERRY: Unbelievable. That's what made it all so mysterious. Oh, yes, that must be a fabulous omen. Maybe this week I'm going to sell a gramophone or two after all.

CHRIS: But I thought you — ?

GERRY: Look! A single magpie! That's definitely a bad omen — one for sorrow. (*His stick as a gun.*) Bang! Missed. (*Mock serious.*) Where's my lucky cow? Come back, brown cow, come back!

(*They both laugh.*)

KATE: They're not *still* talking, are they?

MAGGIE: Laughing. She laughs all the time with him. D'you hear them, Aggie?

AGNES: Yes.

KATE: Laughing? Absolutely beyond my comprehension.

AGNES: Like so many things, Kate.

KATE: Two more minutes and Mr. Evans is going to talk to me. Laughing? Hah!

GERRY: Thinking of going away for a while, Chrissie.

CHRIS: Where to?

GERRY: But I'll come back to say good-bye first.

CHRIS: Are you going home to Wales?

GERRY: Wales isn't my home anymore. My home is here — well, Ireland. To Spain — as a matter of interest. Just for a short while.

CHRIS: To sell gramophones?

GERRY: Good God, no! (*Laughs.*) You'll never believe this — to do a spot of fighting. With the International Brigade. A company leaves in a few weeks. Bit ridiculous, isn't it? But you know old Gerry when the blood's up — bang-bang-bang! — missing everybody.

CHRIS: Are you serious?

GERRY: Bit surprised myself — as a matter of interest.

CHRIS: What do you know about Spain?

GERRY: Not a lot. A little. Enough, maybe. Yes, I know enough. And I thought I should try my hand at something worthy for a change. Give Evans a Big Cause and he won't let you down. It's only everyday stuff he's not so successful at. Anyhow I've still to enlist . . . He's still watching us. He thinks we don't see him. I wouldn't mind talking to him.

CHRIS: He's a bit shy.

GERRY: Naturally. And I'm a stranger to him practically . . . does he know my name?

CHRIS: Of course he knows your name.

GERRY: Good. Thanks. Well, maybe not so good. He's a very handsome child. With your eyes. Lucky boy.

(*"Dancing in the Dark" softly from the radio.*)

MAGGIE: Good for you, Aggie. What did you do to it?

AGNES: I didn't touch it.

KATE: Turn that thing off, Aggie, would you?

(*Agnes does not.*)

GERRY: You have a gramophone! I could have got it for you wholesale.

CHRIS: It's a wireless set.

GERRY: Oh, very posh.

CHRIS: It doesn't go half the time. Aggie says it's a heap of junk.

GERRY: I know nothing about radios but I'll take a look at it if you —

CHRIS: Some other time. When you come back.

(*Pause.*)

GERRY: And Agnes is well?

CHRIS: Fine — fine.

GERRY: Of all your sisters Agnes was the one that seemed to object least to me. Tell her I was asking for her.

CHRIS: I'll tell her.

(*They listen to the music.*)

GERRY: Good tune.

(*Suddenly he takes her in his arms and dances.*)

CHRIS: Gerry —

GERRY: Don't talk.

CHRIS: What are you at?

GERRY: Not a word.

CHRIS: Oh God, Gerry —

GERRY: Shhh.

CHRIS: They're watching us.

GERRY: Who is?

CHRIS: Maggie and Aggie. From the kitchen window.

GERRY: Hope so. And Kate.

CHRIS: And Father Jack.

GERRY: Better still! Terrific!

(*He suddenly swings her round and round and dances her lightly, elegantly across the garden. As he does he sings the song to her.*)

MAGGIE (*quietly*): They're dancing.

KATE: What!

MAGGIE: They're dancing together.

KATE: God forgive you!

MAGGIE: He has her in his arms.

KATE: He has not! The animal!

(*She flings the paper aside and joins Maggie at the window.*)

MAGGIE: They're dancing round the garden, Aggie.

KATE: Oh God, what sort of fool is she?

MAGGIE: He's a beautiful dancer, isn't he?

KATE: He's leading her astray again, Maggie.

MAGGIE: Look at her face — she's easy led. Come here till you see, Aggie.

AGNES: I'm busy! For God's sake can't you see I'm busy!

(*Maggie turns and looks at her in amazement.*)

KATE: That's the only thing that Evans creature could ever do well — was dance. (*Pause.*) And look at her, the fool. For God's sake, would you look at that fool of a woman? (*Pause.*) Her whole face alters when she's happy, doesn't it? (*Pause.*) They dance so well together. They're such a beautiful couple. (*Pause.*) She's as beautiful as Bernie O'Donnell any day, isn't she?

(*Maggie moves slowly away from the window and sits motionless.*)

GERRY: Do you know the words?

CHRIS: I never know any words.

GERRY: Neither do I. Doesn't matter. This is more important. (*Pause.*) Marry me, Chrissie. (*Pause.*) Are you listening to me?

CHRIS: I hear you.

GERRY: Will you marry me when I come back in two weeks?

CHRIS: I don't think so, Gerry.

GERRY: I'm mad about you. You know I am. I've always been mad about you.

CHRIS: When you're with me.

GERRY: Leave this house and come away with —

CHRIS: But you'd walk out on me again. You wouldn't intend to but that's what would happen because that's your nature and you can't help yourself.

GERRY: Not this time, Chrissie. This time it will be —

CHRIS: Don't talk anymore; no more words. Just dance me down the lane and then you'll leave.

GERRY: Believe me, Chrissie; this time the omens are terrific! The omens are unbelievable this time!

(*They dance off. After they have exited the music continues for a few seconds and then stops suddenly in mid-phrase. Maggie goes to the set, slaps it, turns it off. Kate moves away from the window.*)

KATE: They're away. Dancing.

MAGGIE: Whatever's wrong with it, that's all it seems to last — a few minutes at a time. Something to do with the way it heats up.

KATE: We probably won't see Mr. Evans for another year — until the humor suddenly takes him again.

AGNES: He has a Christian name.

KATE: And in the meantime it's Christina's heart that gets crushed again. That's what I mind. But what really infuriates me is that the creature has no sense of ordinary duty. Does he ever wonder how she clothes and feeds Michael? Does he ask her? Does he care?

(*Agnes rises and goes to the back door.*)

AGNES: Going out to get my head cleared. Bit of a headache all day.

KATE: Seems to me the beasts of the field have more concern for their young than that creature has.

AGNES: Do you ever listen to yourself, Kate? You are such a damned righteous bitch! And his name is Gerry! — Gerry! — Gerry!

(*Now on the point of tears, she runs off.*)

KATE: And what was that all about?

MAGGIE: Who's to say?

KATE: Don't I know his name is Gerry? What am I calling him? — St. Patrick?

MAGGIE: She's worried about Chris, too.

KATE: You see, that's what a creature like Mr. Evans does: appears out of nowhere and suddenly poisons the atmosphere in the whole house — God forgive him, the bastard! There! That's what I mean! God forgive me!

(*Maggie begins putting on her long-laced boots again. As she does she sings listlessly, almost inaudibly.*)

MAGGIE: "'Twas on the Isle of Capri that he found her
      Beneath the shade of an old walnut tree.
      Oh, I can still see the flowers blooming round her,
      Where they met on the Isle of Capri."

KATE: If you knew your prayers as well as you know the words of those aul pagan songs! . . . She's right: I am a righteous bitch, amn't I?

MAGGIE: "She was as sweet as a rose at the dawning
      But somehow fate hadn't meant it to be,
      And though he sailed with the tide in the morning,
      Still his heart's in the Isle of Capri."

(*Maggie now stands up and looks at her feet.*)

Now. Who's for a fox-trot?

KATE: You work hard at your job. You try to keep the home together. You perform your duties as best you can — because you believe in responsibilities and obligations and good order. And then suddenly, suddenly you realize that hair cracks are appearing everywhere; that control is slipping away; that the whole thing is so fragile it can't be held together much longer. It's all about to collapse, Maggie.

MAGGIE (*wearily*): Nothing's about to collapse, Kate.

KATE: That young Sweeney boy from the back hills — the boy who was anointed — his trousers didn't catch fire, as Rose said. They were doing some devilish thing with a goat — some sort of sacrifice for the Lughnasa Festival; and Sweeney was so drunk he

toppled over into the middle of the bonfire. Don't know why that came into my head . . .

MAGGIE: Kate . . .

(*Maggie goes to her and sits beside her.*)

KATE: And Mr. Evans is off again for another twelve months and next week or the week after Christina'll collapse into one of her depressions. Remember last winter? — all that sobbing and lamenting in the middle of the night. I don't think I could go through that again. And the doctor says he doesn't think Father Jack's mind is confused but that his superiors probably had no choice but send him home. Whatever he means by that, Maggie. And the parish priest did talk to me today. He said the numbers in the school are falling and that there may not be a job for me after the summer. But the numbers aren't falling, Maggie. Why is he telling me lies? Why does he want rid of me? And why has he never come out to visit Father Jack? (*She tries to laugh.*) If he gives me the push, all five of us will be at home together all day long — we can spend the day dancing to Marconi.

(*Now she cries. Maggie puts her arm around her. Michael enters left.*)

But what worries me most of all is Rose. If I died — if I lost my job — if this house were broken up — what would become of our Rosie?

MAGGIE: Shhh.

KATE: I must put my trust in God, Maggie, mustn't I? He'll look after her, won't he? You believe that, Maggie, don't you?

MAGGIE: Kate . . . Kate . . . Kate, love . . .

KATE: I believe that, too . . . I believe that . . . I do believe that . . .

(*Maggie holds her and rocks her.*)

(*Chris enters quickly left, hugging herself. She sees the Boy at his kites, goes to him, and gets down beside him. She speaks eagerly, excitedly, confidentially.*)

CHRIS: Well. Now you've had a good look at him. What do you think of him? Do you remember him?

BOY (*bored*): I never saw him before.

CHRIS: Shhh. Yes, you did; five or six times. You've forgotten. And he saw you at the foot of the lane. He thinks you've got very big. And he thinks you're handsome!

BOY: Aunt Kate got me a spinning-top that won't spin.

CHRIS: He's handsome. Isn't he handsome?

BOY: Give up.

CHRIS: I'll tell you a secret. The others aren't to know. He has got a great new job! And he's wonderful at it!

BOY: What does he do?

CHRIS: Shhh. And he has bought a bicycle for you — a black bike — a man's bike and he's going to bring it with him the next time he comes.

(*She suddenly embraces him and hugs him.*)

BOY: Is he coming back soon?

CHRIS (*eyes closed*): Maybe — maybe. Yes! Yes, he is!

BOY: How soon?

CHRIS: Next week — the week after — soon — soon — soon! Oh, yes, you have a handsome father. You are a lucky boy and I am a very, very lucky woman.

(*She gets to her feet, then bends down again and kisses him lightly.*)

And another bit of good news for you, lucky boy: You have your mother's eyes!

(*She laughs, pirouettes flirtatiously before him, and dances into the kitchen.*)

And what's the good news here?

MAGGIE: The good news here is . . . that's the most exciting turf we've ever burned!

KATE: Gerry's not gone, is he?

CHRIS: Just this minute.

(*Agnes enters through the back door. She is carrying some roses.*)

He says to thank you very much for the offer of the bed.

KATE: Next time he's back.

CHRIS: That'll be in a week or two — depending on his commitments.

KATE: Well, if the outside loft happens to be empty.

CHRIS: And he sends his love to you all. His special love to you, Aggie; and a big kiss.

AGNES: For me?

CHRIS: Yes! For you!

MAGGIE (*quickly*): Those are beautiful, Aggie. Would Jack like some in his room? Put them on his windowsill with a wee card —"ROSES"— so that the poor man's head won't be demented looking for the word. And now, girls, the daily dilemma: What's for the tea?

CHRIS: Let me make the tea, Maggie.

MAGGIE: We'll both make the tea. Perhaps something thrilling with tomatoes? We've got two, I think. Or if you're prepared to wait, I'll get that soda bread made.

AGNES: I'm making the tea, Maggie.

CHRIS: Let me, please. Just today.

AGNES (*almost aggressively*): I make the tea every evening, don't I? Why shouldn't I make it this evening as usual?

MAGGIE: No reason at all. Aggie's the chef. (*Sings raucously.*)

"Everybody's doing it, doing it, doing it.
Picking their noses and chewing it, chewing it, chewing it . . ."

KATE: Maggie, please!

MAGGIE: If she knew her prayers half as well as she knows the words of those aul pagan songs . . .
  (*Now at the radio.*) Marconi, my friend, you're not still asleep, are you?

(*Father Jack enters. He shuffles quickly across the kitchen floor, hands behind his back, eyes on the ground, as if he were intent on some engagement elsewhere. Now he becomes aware of the others.*)

JACK: If anybody is looking for me, I'll be down at the bank of the river for the rest of the . . . (*He tails off and looks around. Now he knows where he is. He smiles.*) I beg your pardon. My mind was . . . It's Kate.

KATE: It's Kate.

JACK: And Agnes. And Margaret.

MAGGIE: How are you, Jack?

JACK: And this is — ?

CHRIS: Chris — Christina.

JACK: Forgive me, Chris. You were only a baby when I went away. I remember Mother lifting you up as the train was pulling out of the station and catching your hand and waving it at me. You were so young you had scarcely any hair but she had managed to attach a tiny pink — a tiny pink — what's the word? — a bow! — a bow! — just about here; and as she waved your hand, the bow fell off. It's like a — a picture? — a camera picture — a photograph! — it's like a photograph in my mind.

CHRIS: The hair isn't much better even now, Jack.

JACK: And I remember you crying, Margaret.

MAGGIE: Was I?

JACK: Yes; your face was all blotchy with tears.

MAGGIE: You may be sure — beautiful as ever.

JACK (*to Agnes*): And you and Kate were on Mother's right and Rose was between you; you each had a hand. And Mother's face, I remember, showed nothing. I often wondered about that afterwards.

CHRIS: She knew she would never see you again in her lifetime.

JACK: I know that. But in the other life. Do you think perhaps Mother didn't believe in the ancestral spirits?

KATE: Ancestral — ! What are you blathering about, Jack? Mother was a saintly woman who knew she was going straight to heaven. And don't you forget to take your medicine again this evening. You're supposed to take it three times a day.

JACK: One of our priests took so much quinine that he became an addict and almost died. A German priest; Father Sharpeggi. He was rushed to hospital in Kampala but they could do nothing for him. So Okawa and I brought him to our local medicine man and Karl Sharpeggi lived until he was eighty-eight! There was a strange white bird on my windowsill when I woke up this morning.

AGNES: That's Rosie's pet rooster. Keep away from that thing.

MAGGIE: Look what it did to my arm, Jack. One of these days I'm going to wring its neck.

JACK: That's what we do in Ryanga when we want to please the spirits — or to appease them: We kill a rooster or a young goat. It's a very exciting exhibition — that's not the word, is it? — demonstration? — no — show? No, no; what's the word I'm looking for? Spectacle? That's not it. The word to describe a sacred and mysterious . . . ? (*Slowly, deliberately.*) You have a ritual killing. You offer up sacrifice. You have dancing and incantations. What is the name for that whole — for that — ? Gone. Lost it. My vocabulary has deserted me. Never mind. Doesn't matter . . . I think perhaps I should put on more clothes . . .

(*Pause.*)

MAGGIE: Did you speak Swahili all the time out there, Jack?

JACK: All the time. Yes. To the people. Swahili. When Europeans call, we speak English. Or if we have a — a visitor? — a visitation! — from the district commissioner. The present commissioner knows Swahili but he won't speak it. He's a stubborn man. He and I fight a lot but I like him. The Irish Outcast, he calls me. He is always inviting me to spend a weekend with him in Kampala — to keep me from "going native," as he calls it. Perhaps when I go back. If you cooperate with the English they give you lots of money for churches and schools and hospitals. And he gets so angry with me because I won't take his money. Reported me to my superiors in Head House last year; and they were very cross — oh, very cross. But I like him. When I was saying good-bye to him — he thought this was very funny! — he gave me a present of the last governor's ceremonial hat to take home with — Ceremony! That's the word! How could I have forgotten that? The offering, the ritual, the dancing — a ceremony! Such a simple word. What was I telling you?

AGNES: The district commissioner gave you this present.

JACK: Yes; a wonderful triangular hat with three enormous white ostrich plumes rising up out of the crown. I have it in one of my trunks. I'll show it to you later. Ceremony! I'm so glad I got that. Do you know what I found very strange? Coming back in the boat there were days when I couldn't remember even the simplest words. Not that anybody seemed to notice. And you can always point, Margaret, can't you?

MAGGIE: Or make signs.

JACK: Or make signs.

MAGGIE: Or dance.

KATE: What you must do is read a lot — books, papers, magazines, anything. I read every night with young Michael. It's great for his vocabulary.

JACK: I'm sure you're right, Kate. I'll do that. (*To Chris.*) I haven't seen young Michael today, Agnes.

KATE: Christina, Jack.

JACK: Sorry, I —

CHRIS: He's around there somewhere. Making kites, if you don't mind.

JACK: And I have still to meet your husband.

CHRIS: I'm not married.

JACK: Ah.

KATE: Michael's father was here a while ago . . . Gerry Evans . . . Mr. Evans is a Welshman . . . not that that's relevant to . . .

JACK: You were never married?

CHRIS: Never.

MAGGIE: We're all in the same boat, Jack. We're hoping that you'll hunt about and get men for all of us.

JACK (*to Chris*): So Michael is a love-child?

CHRIS: I — yes — I suppose so . . .

JACK: He's a fine boy.

CHRIS: He's not a bad boy.

JACK: You're lucky to have him.

AGNES: We're all lucky to have him.

JACK: In Ryanga women are eager to have love-children. The more love-children you have, the more fortunate your household is thought to be. Have you other love-children?

KATE: She certainly has not, Jack; and strange as it may seem to you, neither has Agnes nor Rose nor Maggie nor myself. No harm to Ryanga but you're home in Donegal now and much as we cherish love-children here they are not exactly the norm. And the doctor says if you don't take exercise your legs will seize up on you; so I'm going to walk you down to the main road and up again three times and then you'll get your tea and then you'll read the paper from front to back and then you'll take your medicine and then you'll go to bed. And we'll do the same thing tomorrow and the day after and the day after that until we have you back to what you were. You start off and I'll be with you in a second. Where's my cardigan?

(*Jack goes out to the garden. Kate gets her cardigan.*)

MICHAEL: Some of Aunt Kate's forebodings weren't all that inaccurate. Indeed some of them were fulfilled before the Festival of Lughnasa was over.

She was right about Uncle Jack. He had been sent home by his superiors, not because his mind was confused, but for reasons that became clearer as the summer drew to a close.

And she was right about losing her job in the local school. The parish priest didn't take her back when the new term began; although that had more to do with Father Jack than with falling numbers.

And she had good reason for being uneasy about Rose — and, had she known, about Agnes, too. But what she couldn't have foreseen was that the home would break up quite so quickly and that when she would wake up one morning in early September both Rose and Agnes would have left forever.

(*At this point in Michael's speech Jack picks up two pieces of wood, portions of the kites, and strikes them together. The sound they make pleases him. He does it again — and again — and again. Now he begins to beat out a structured beat whose rhythm gives him pleasure. And as Michael continues his speech, Jack begins to shuffle — dance in time to his tattoo — his body slightly bent over, his eyes on the ground, his feet moving rhythmically. And as he dances — shuffles, he mutters — sings — makes occasional sounds that are incomprehensible and almost inaudible. Kate comes out to the garden and stands still, watching him. Rose enters. Now Rose and Maggie and*

Meryl Streep as Kate, Brid Brennan as Agnes, and Sophie Thompson as Rose in the 1998 Sony
Pictures film version of *Dancing at Lughnasa.*

*Agnes are all watching him — some at the front door,
some through the window. Only Chris has her eyes
closed, her face raised, her mouth slightly open; remembering. Michael continues without stopping.*)

But she was wrong about my father. I suppose their
natures were so out of tune that she would always be
wrong about my father. Because he did come back in
a couple of weeks as he said he would. And although
my mother and he didn't go through a conventional
form of marriage, once more they danced together,
witnessed by the unseen sisters. And this time it was a
dance without music; just there, in ritual circles
round and round that square and then down the lane
and back up again; slowly, formally, with easy deliberation. My mother with her head thrown back, her
eyes closed, her mouth slightly open. My father holding her just that little distance away from him so that
he could regard her upturned face. No singing, no
melody, no words. Only the swish and whisper of
their feet across the grass.

I watched the ceremony from behind that bush.
But this time they were conscious only of themselves
and of their dancing. And when he went off to fight

with the International Brigade, my mother grieved as
any bride would grieve. But this time there was no
sobbing, no lamenting, no collapse into a depression.

(*Kate now goes to Jack and gently takes the sticks from
him. She places them on the ground.*)

KATE: We'll leave these back where we found them,
Jack. They aren't ours. They belong to the child.

(*She takes his arm and leads him off.*)

Now we'll go for our walk.

(*The others watch with expressionless faces.*)

ACT 2

(*Early September; three weeks later. Ink bottle and some
paper on the kitchen table. Two finished kites — their
artwork still unseen — lean against the garden seat.*)

(*Michael stands downstage left, listening to Maggie
as she approaches, singing. Now she enters left carrying
two zinc buckets of water. She is dressed as she was in
act 1. She sings in her usual parodic style.*)

MAGGIE: "Oh play to me, Gypsy;
    The moon's high above.
    Oh, play me your serenade,
    The song I love . . ."

(*She goes into the kitchen and from her zinc buckets she fills the kettle and the saucepan on the range. She looks over at the writing materials.*)

    Are you getting your books ready for school again?
BOY: School doesn't start for another ten days.
MAGGIE: God, I always hated school.

(*She hums the next line of the song. Then she remembers.*)

    You and I have a little financial matter to discuss. (*Pause.*) D'you hear me, cub?
BOY: I'm not listening.
MAGGIE: You owe me money.
BOY: I do not.
MAGGIE: Oh, yes, you do. Three weeks ago I bet you a penny those aul kites would never get off the ground. And they never did.
BOY: Because there was never enough wind; that's why.
MAGGIE: Enough wind! Would you listen to him. A hurricane wouldn't shift those things. Anyhow a debt is a debt. One penny please at your convenience. Or the equivalent in kind: one Wild Woodbine. (*Sings.*) "Beside your caravan
    The campfire's bright . . ."

(*She dances her exaggerated dance across to the table and tousles the Boy's hair.*)

BOY: Leave me alone, Aunt Maggie.
MAGGIE: "I'll be your vagabond
    Just for tonight . . ."
BOY: Now look at what you made me do! The page is all blotted!
MAGGIE: Your frank opinion, cub: Am I vagabond material?
BOY: Get out of my road, will you? I'm trying to write a letter.
MAGGIE: Who to? That's for me to know and you to find out. Whoever it is, he'd need to be smart to read that scrawl. (*She returns to her buckets.*)
BOY: It's to Santa Claus.
MAGGIE: In September? Nothing like getting in before the rush. What are you asking for?
BOY: A bell.
MAGGIE: A bell.
BOY: For my bicycle.
MAGGIE: For your bicycle.
BOY: The bike my daddy has bought me — stupid!
MAGGIE: Your daddy has bought you a bicycle?
BOY: He told me today. He bought it in Kilkenny. So there!

(*Her manner changes. She returns to the table.*)

MAGGIE (*softly*): Your daddy told you that?

BOY: Ask him yourself. It's coming next week. It's a black bike — a man's bike.
MAGGIE: Aren't you the lucky boy?
BOY: It's going to be delivered here to the house. He promised me.
MAGGIE: Well, if he promised you . . . (*Very brisk.*) Now! Who can we get to teach you to ride?
BOY: I know how to ride!
MAGGIE: You don't.
BOY: I learned at school last Easter. So there! But you can't ride.
MAGGIE: I can so.
BOY: I know you can't.
MAGGIE: Maybe not by myself. But put me on the bar, cub — magnificent!
BOY: You never sat on the bar of a bike in your life, Aunt Maggie!
MAGGIE: Oh yes, I did, Michael. Oh yes, indeed I did. (*She gathers up the papers.*) Now away and write to Santa some other time. On a day like this you should be out running about the fields like a young calf. Hold on — a new riddle for you.
BOY: Give up.
MAGGIE: A man goes to an apple tree with two apples on it. He doesn't take apples off it. He doesn't leave apples on it. How does he do that?
BOY: Give up.
MAGGIE: Think, will you!
BOY: Give up.
MAGGIE: Well, since you don't know, I will tell you. He takes one apple off! Get it? He doesn't take *apples* off! He doesn't leave *apples* on!
BOY: God!
MAGGIE: You might as well be talking to a turf stack.

(*Jack enters. He looks much stronger and is very sprightly and alert. He is not wearing the top coat or the hat but instead a garish-colored — probably a sister's — sweater. His dress looks now even more bizarre.*)

JACK: Did I hear the church bell ringing?
MAGGIE: A big posh wedding today.
JACK: Not one of my sisters?
MAGGIE: No such luck. A man called Austin Morgan and a girl from Carrickfad.
JACK: Austin Morgan — should I know that name?
MAGGIE: I don't think so. They own the Arcade in the town. And how are you today?
JACK: Cold as usual, Maggie. And complaining about it as usual.

(*Michael exits.*)

MAGGIE: Complain away — why wouldn't you? And it is getting colder. But you're looking stronger every day, Jack.
JACK: I feel stronger, too. Now! Off for my last walk of the day.
MAGGIE: Number three?
JACK: Number four! Down past the clothes line; across

the stream; round the old well; and up through the meadow. And when that's done Kate won't have to nag at me — nag? — nag? — sounds funny — something wrong with that — nag? — that's not a word, is it?

MAGGIE: Nag — yes; to keep on at somebody.

JACK: Yes? Nag. Good. So my English vocabulary is coming back, too. Great. Nag. Still sounds a bit strange.

(*Kate enters with an armful of clothes from the clothes line.*)

KATE: Time for another walk, Jack.

JACK: Just about to set out on number four, Kate. And thank you for keeping at me.

KATE: No sign of Rose and Agnes yet?

MAGGIE: They said they'd be back for tea. (*To Jack.*) They're away picking bilberries.

KATE (*to Jack*): You used to pick bilberries. Do you remember?

JACK: Down beside the old quarry?

MAGGIE: The very place.

JACK: Mother and myself; every Lughnasa; the annual ritual. Of course I remember. And then she'd make the most wonderful jam. And that's what you took to school with you every day all through the winter: a piece of soda bread and bilberry jam.

MAGGIE: But no butter.

JACK: Except on special occasions when you got scones and for some reason they were always buttered. I must walk down to that old quarry one of these days. "O ruddier than the cherry,
O sweeter than the berry,
O nymph more bright,
Than moonshine night,
Like kidlings blithe and merry."
(*Laughs.*) Where on earth did that come from? You see, Kate, it's all coming back to me.

KATE: So you'll soon begin saying Mass again?

JACK: Yes, indeed.

MAGGIE: Here in the house?

JACK: Why not? Perhaps I'll start next Monday. The neighbors would join us, wouldn't they?

KATE: They surely would. A lot of them have been asking me already.

JACK: How will we let them know?

MAGGIE: I wouldn't worry about that. Word gets about very quickly.

JACK: What Okawa does — you know Okawa, don't you?

MAGGIE: Your house boy?

JACK: My friend — my mentor — my counselor — and yes, my house boy as well; anyhow Okawa summons our people by striking a huge iron gong. Did you hear that wedding bell this morning, Kate?

KATE: Yes.

JACK: Well, Okawa's gong would carry four times as far as that. But if it's one of the bigger ceremonies, he'll spend a whole day going round all the neighboring villages, blowing on this enormous flute he made himself.

MAGGIE: And they all meet in your church?

JACK: When I had a church. Now we gather in the common in the middle of the village. If it's an important ceremony, you would have up to three or four hundred people.

KATE: All gathered together for Mass?

JACK: Maybe. Or maybe to offer sacrifice to Obi, our Great Goddess of the Earth, so that the crops will flourish. Or maybe to get in touch with our departed fathers for their advice and wisdom. Or maybe to thank the spirits of our tribe if they have been good to us; or to appease them if they're angry. I complain to Okawa that our calendar of ceremonies gets fuller every year. Now at this time of year over there — at the Ugandan harvest time — we have two very wonderful ceremonies: the Festival of the New Yam and the Festival of the Sweet Cassava; and they're both dedicated to our Great Goddess, Obi —

KATE: But these aren't Christian ceremonies, Jack, are they?

JACK: Oh, no. The Ryangans have always been faithful to their own beliefs — like these two festivals I'm telling you about; and they are very special, really magnificent ceremonies. I haven't described those two festivals to you before, have I?

KATE: Not to me.

JACK: Well, they begin very formally, very solemnly with the ritual sacrifice of a fowl or a goat or a calf down at the bank of the river. Then the ceremonial cutting and anointing of the first yams and the first cassava, and we pass these round in huge wooden bowls. Then the incantation — a chant, really — that expresses our gratitude and that also acts as a rhythm or percussion for the ritual dance. And then, when the thanksgiving is over, the dance continues. And the interesting thing is that it grows naturally into a secular celebration; so that almost imperceptibly the religious ceremony ends and the community celebration takes over. And that part of the ceremony is a real spectacle. We light fires round the periphery of the circle; and we paint our faces with colored powders; and we sing local songs; and we drink palm wine. And then we dance — and dance — and dance — children, men, women, most of them lepers, many of them with misshapen limbs, with missing limbs — dancing, believe it or not, for days on end! It is the most wonderful sight you have ever seen! (*Laughs.*) That palm wine! They dole it out in horns! You lose all sense of time . . . !

Oh, yes, the Ryangans are a remarkable people: There is no distinction between the religious and the secular in their culture. And of course their capacity for fun, for laughing, for practical jokes — they've such open hearts! In some respects they're not unlike us. You'd love them, Maggie. You should come back with me!

How did I get into all that? You must stop me telling these long stories. Exercise time! I'll be back in ten minutes; and only last week it took me half an hour to do number four. You've done a great job with me, Kate. So please do keep nagging at me.

(*He moves off — then stops.*)

It's not Gilbert and Sullivan, is it?
KATE: Sorry?
JACK: That quotation.
KATE: What's that, Jack?
JACK: "O ruddier than the cherry / O sweeter than the berry"— no, it's not Gilbert and Sullivan. But it'll come back to me, I promise you. It's all coming back.

(*Again he moves off.*)

KATE: Jack.
JACK: Yes?
KATE: You are going to start saying Mass again?
JACK: We've agreed on next Monday, haven't we? Haven't we, Maggie?
MAGGIE: Yes.
JACK: At first light. The moment Rose's white cock crows. A harvest ceremony. You'll have to find a big gong somewhere, Kate.

(*He leaves. Pause. Kate and Maggie stare at each other in concern, in alarm. They speak in hushed voices.*)

KATE: I told you — you wouldn't believe me — I told you.
MAGGIE: Shhh.
KATE: What do you think?
MAGGIE: He's not back a month yet.
KATE: Yesterday I heard about their medicine man who brought a woman back from death —
MAGGIE: He needs more time.
KATE: And this morning it was "the spirits of the tribe"! And when I mentioned Mass to him you saw how he dodged about.
MAGGIE: He said he'd say Mass next Monday, Kate.
KATE: No, he won't. You know he won't. He's changed, Maggie.
MAGGIE: In another month, he'll be —
KATE: Completely changed. He's not our Jack at all. And it's what he's changed into that frightens me.
MAGGIE: Doesn't frighten me.
KATE: If you saw your face . . . of course it does . . . Oh, dear God —

(*Maggie now drifts back to the range. Kate goes to the table and with excessive vigor wipes it with a damp cloth. Then she stops suddenly, slumps into a seat, and covers her face with her hands. Maggie watches her, then goes to her. She stands behind her and holds her shoulders with her hands. Kate grasps Maggie's hands in hers.*)

MAGGIE: All the same, Kitty, I don't think it's a sight I'd like to see.
KATE: What sight?
MAGGIE: A clatter of lepers trying to do the Military Two-step.

KATE: God forgive you, Maggie Mundy! The poor creatures are as entitled to —

(*She breaks off because Chris's laughter is heard off. Kate jumps to her feet.*)

This must be kept in the family, Maggie! Not a word of this must go outside these walls — d'you hear? — not a syllable!

(*Chris and Gerry enter left. He enters backways, pulling Chris who holds the end of his walking stick. Throughout the scene he keeps trying to embrace her. She keeps avoiding him.*)

GERRY: No false modesty. You know you're a great dancer, Chrissie.
CHRIS: No, I'm not.
GERRY: You should be a professional dancer.
CHRIS: You're talking rubbish.
GERRY: Let's dance round the garden again.
CHRIS: We've done that; and down the lane and up again — without music. And that's enough for one day. Tell me about signing up. Was it really in a church?
GERRY: I'm telling you — it was unbelievable.
CHRIS: It was a real church?
GERRY: A Catholic church as a matter of interest.
CHRIS: I don't believe a word of it.
GERRY: Would I tell you a lie? And up at the end — in the sanctuary? — there were three men, two of them with trench coats; and between them, behind this lectern and wearing a sort of military cap, this little chappie who spoke in an accent I could hardly understand. Naturally I thought he was Spanish. From Armagh, as it turned out.
CHRIS: I'm sure he couldn't understand you either.
GERRY: He described himself as the recruiting officer. "Take it from me, comrade, nobody joins the Brigade without my unanimity."

(*She laughs — and avoids his embrace.*)

CHRIS: It's a wonder he accepted you.
GERRY: "Do you offer your allegiance and your loyalty and your full endeavors to the Popular Front?"
CHRIS: What's the Popular Front?
GERRY: The Spanish government that I'm going to keep in power. "I take it you are a Syndicalist?" "No." "An Anarchist?" "No." "A Marxist?" "No." "A Republican, a Socialist, a Communist?" "No." "Do you speak Spanish?" "No." "Can you make explosives?" "No." "Can you ride a motorbike?" "Yes." "You're in. Sign here."
CHRIS: So you'll be a dispatch rider?

(*Gerry imitates riding a motorbike.*)

And you leave on Saturday?
GERRY: First tide.
CHRIS: How long will you be away?
GERRY: As long as it takes to sort the place out.
CHRIS: Seriously, Gerry.
GERRY: Maybe a couple of months. Everybody says it will be over by Christmas.

CHRIS: They always say it will be over by Christmas. I still don't know why you're going.

GERRY: Not so sure I know either. Who wants salesmen that can't sell? And there's bound to be *something* right about the cause, isn't there? And it's somewhere to go — isn't it? Maybe that's the important thing for a man: a *named* destination — democracy, Ballybeg, heaven. Women's illusions aren't so easily satisfied — they make better drifters. (*Laughs.*) Anyhow he held out a pen to sign on the dotted line and it was only when I was writing my name that I glanced over the lectern and saw the box.

CHRIS: What box?

GERRY: He was standing on a box. The chappie was a midget!

CHRIS: Gerry!

GERRY: No bigger than three feet.

CHRIS: Gerry, I —

GERRY: Promise you! And when we were having a drink afterwards he told me he was invaluable to the Brigade — because he was a master at disguising himself!

CHRIS: Gerry Evans, you are —

GERRY: Let's go down to the old well.

CHRIS: We're going nowhere. Come inside and take a look at this wireless. It stops and starts whenever it feels like it.

GERRY: I told you: I know nothing about radios.

CHRIS: I've said you're a genius at them.

GERRY: Chrissie, I don't even know how to —

CHRIS: You can try, can't you? Come on. Michael misses it badly.

(*She runs into the kitchen. He follows.*)

You should see Jack striding through the meadow. He looks like a new man.

KATE (*to Gerry*): Were you talking to him?

GERRY: He wants to do a swap with me: I'm to give him this hat and he's to give me some sort of a three-cornered hat with feathers that the district commissioner gave him. Sounds a fair exchange.

MAGGIE: Chrissie says you're great with radios, Gerry.

GERRY: I'll take a look at it — why not?

MAGGIE: All I can tell you is that it's not the battery. I got a new one yesterday.

GERRY: Let me check the aerial first. Very often that's where the trouble lies. Then I'll have a look at the ignition and sparking plugs. Leave it to Gerry.

(*He winks at Chris as he goes out the front door and off right.*)

MAGGIE: He sounds very knowledgeable.

CHRIS: It may be something he can't fix.

KATE: I know you're not responsible for Gerry's decisions, Christina. But it would be on my conscience if I didn't tell you how strongly I disapprove of this International Brigade caper. It's a sorry day for Ireland when we send young men off to Spain to fight for godless communism.

CHRIS: For democracy, Kate.

KATE: I'm not going to argue. I just want to clear my conscience.

CHRIS: That's the important thing, of course. And now you've cleared it.

(*Gerry runs on and calls through the window.*)

GERRY: Turn the radio on, Chrissie, would you?

MAGGIE: It's on.

GERRY: Right.

(*He runs off again.*)

CHRIS: Just as we were coming out of the town we met Vera McLaughlin, the knitting agent. (*Softly.*) Agnes and Rose aren't back yet?

MAGGIE: They'll be here soon.

CHRIS: She says she'll call in tomorrow and tell them herself. The poor woman was very distressed.

KATE: Tell them what?

CHRIS: She's not buying any more handmade gloves.

MAGGIE: Why not?

CHRIS: Too dear, she says.

KATE: Too dear! She pays them a pittance!

CHRIS: There's a new factory started up in Donegal Town. They make machine gloves more quickly there and far more cheaply. The people Vera used to supply buy their gloves direct from the factory now.

MAGGIE: That's awful news, Chrissie.

CHRIS: She says they're organizing buses to bring the workers to the factory and back every day. Most of the people who used to work at home have signed on. She tried to get a job there herself. They told her she was too old. She's forty-one. The poor woman could hardly speak.

MAGGIE: Oh God . . . poor Aggie . . . poor Rose . . . what'll they do?

(*Agnes enters the garden. Kate sees her.*)

KATE: Shhh. They're back. Let them have their tea in peace. Tell them later.

(*They busy themselves with their tasks. Agnes is carrying two small pails of blackberries which she leaves outside the door of the house. Just as she is about to enter the kitchen a voice off calls her.*)

GERRY (*off*): Who is that beautiful woman!

(*She looks around, puzzled.*)

AGNES: Gerry?

GERRY: Up here, Aggie!

AGNES: Where?

GERRY: On top of the sycamore.

(*Now she sees him. The audience does not see him.*)

AGNES: Mother of God!

GERRY: Come up and join me!

AGNES: What are you doing up there?

GERRY: You can see into the future from here, Aggie!

AGNES: The tree isn't safe, Gerry. Please come down.

GERRY: Come up and see what's going to happen to you!

AGNES: That branch is dead, Gerry. I'm telling you.

(*The branch begins to sway.*)

GERRY: Do you think I could get a job in a circus? Wow-wow-wow-wow-wow!

AGNES: Gerry — !

GERRY (*sings*): "He flies through the air with the greatest of ease —" Wheeeeeeeeee!

(*She covers her eyes in terror.*)

AGNES: Stop it, Gerry, stop it, stop it!

GERRY: "That daring young man on the flying trapeze . . ."

AGNES: You're going to fall! I'm not looking! I'm not watching!

(*She dashes into the house.*)

That clown of a man is up on top of the sycamore. Go out and tell him to come down, Chrissie.

MAGGIE: He's fixing the aerial.

AGNES: He's going to break his neck — I'm telling you!

MAGGIE: As long as he fixes the wireless first.

KATE: How are the bilberries, Agnes?

AGNES: Just that bit too ripe. We should have picked them a week ago.

CHRIS: Is that a purple stain on your gansey?

AGNES: I know. I'd only begun when I fell into a bush. And look at my hands — all scrabbed with briars. For all the sympathy I got from Rosie. Nearly died laughing at me. How is she now? (*Pause.*) Is she still in bed?

CHRIS: Bed?

AGNES: She wasn't feeling well. She left me and went home to lie down. (*Pause.*) She's here, isn't she?

(*Maggie rushes off to the bedroom.*)

KATE: I haven't seen her. (*To Chris.*) Have you?

CHRIS: No.

KATE: When did she leave you?

AGNES: Hours ago — I don't know — almost immediately after we got to the old quarry. She said she felt out of sorts.

CHRIS: And she went off by herself?

AGNES: Yes.

KATE: To come home?

AGNES: That's what she said.

(*Maggie enters.*)

MAGGIE: She's not in her bed.

AGNES: Oh God! Where could she —

KATE: Start at the beginning, Agnes. What exactly happened?

AGNES: Nothing "happened"— nothing at all. We left here together — when was it? — just after one o'clock —

CHRIS: That means she's missing for over three hours.

AGNES: We walked together to the quarry. She was chatting away as usual. I had my two buckets and she had —

KATE: Go on — go on!

AGNES: And just after we got there she said she wasn't feeling well. I told her not to bother about the bilberries — just to sit in the sun. And that's what she did.

KATE: For how long?,

AGNES: I don't know — five — ten minutes. And then I fell into the bush. And that was when she laughed. And then she said — she said — I've forgotten what she said — something about a headache and her stomach being sick and she'd go home and sleep for a while. (*To Maggie.*) You're sure she's not in her bed?

(*Maggie shakes her head.*)

KATE: Then what?

(*Agnes begins to cry.*)

AGNES: Where is she? What's happened to our Rosie?

KATE: What direction did she go when she left you?

AGNES: Direction?

KATE: Stop sniveling, Agnes! Did she go towards home?

AGNES: I think so . . . yes . . . I don't know . . . Maggie —

MAGGIE: She may have gone into the town.

CHRIS: She wouldn't have gone into town in her Wellingtons.

AGNES: She was wearing her good shoes.

KATE: Are you sure?

AGNES: Yes; and her blue cardigan and her good skirt. I said to her — I said, "You're some lady to go picking bilberries with." And she just laughed and said, "I'm some toff, Aggie, amn't I some toff?"

MAGGIE: Had she a bottle of milk with her?

AGNES: I think so — yes — in one of her cans.

MAGGIE: Had she any money with her?

AGNES: She had half-a-crown. That's all she has.

MAGGIE (*softly*): Danny Bradley.

KATE: What? — who?

MAGGIE: Danny Bradley . . . Lough Anna . . . up in the back hills.

CHRIS: Oh God, no.

KATE: What? — what's this? — what about the back hills?

CHRIS: She has some silly notion about that scamp, Bradley. She believes he's in love with her. He gave her a present last Christmas — she says.

KATE (*to Agnes*): What do you know about this Bradley business?

AGNES: I know no more than Chris has —

KATE: I've often seen you and Rose whispering together. What plot has been hatched between Rose and Mr. Bradley?

AGNES: No plot . . . please, Kate —

KATE: You're lying to me, Agnes! You're withholding! I want the truth!

AGNES: Honest to God, all I know is what Chris has just —

KATE: I want to know everything you know! Now! I want to —

MAGGIE: That'll do, Kate! Stop that at once! (*Calmly.*) She may be in the town. She may be on her way home now. She may have taken a weak turn on her way back from the quarry. We're going to find her. (*To Chris.*) You search the fields on the upper side of the lane. (*To Agnes.*) You take the lower side, down as far as the main road. (*To Kate.*) You go to the old well and search all around there. I'm going into the town to tell the police.

KATE: You're going to no police, Maggie. If she's mixed up with that Bradley creature, I'm not going to have it broadcast all over —

MAGGIE: I'm going to the police and you'll do what I told you to do.

CHRIS: There she is! Look — look! There she is!

(*She has seen Rose through the window and is about to rush out to greet her. Maggie catches her arm and restrains her. The four sisters watch Rose as she crosses the garden — Chris and Kate from the window, Maggie and Agnes from the door. Rose is unaware of their anxious scrutiny. She is dressed in the "good" clothes described by Agnes and they have changed her appearance. Indeed, had we not seen the Rose of act 1, we might not now be immediately aware of her disability. At first look this might be any youngish country woman, carefully dressed, not unattractive, returning from a long walk on a summer day. She walks slowly, lethargically, towards the house. From her right hand hangs a red poppy that she plucked casually along the road. Her face reveals nothing — but nothing is being deliberately concealed. She sees Agnes's cans of fruit. She stops beside them and looks at them. Then she puts her hand into one of the cans, takes a fistful of berries, and thrusts the fistful into her mouth. Then she wipes her mouth with her sleeve and the back of her hand. As she chews she looks at her stained fingers. She wipes them on her skirt. All of these movements — stopping, eating, wiping — are done not dreamily, abstractedly, but calmly, naturally. Now she moves towards the house. As she approaches the door Agnes rushes to meet her. Instead of hugging her, as she wants to, she catches her arm.*)

AGNES: Rosie, love, we were beginning to get worried about you.

ROSE: They're nice, Aggie. They're sweet. And you got two canfuls. Good for you.

(*Agnes leads her into the house.*)

AGNES: Is your stomach settled?

ROSE: My stomach?

AGNES: You weren't feeling well — remember? — when we were at the quarry?

ROSE: Oh, yes. Oh, I'm fine now, thanks.

AGNES: You left me there and you said you were coming home to lie down. D'you remember that?

ROSE: Yes.

CHRIS: But you didn't come home, Rosie.

ROSE: That's right.

AGNES: And we were very worried about you.

ROSE: Well . . . here I am.

CHRIS: Were you in the town?

AGNES: That's why you're all dressed up, isn't it?

CHRIS: You went into Ballybeg, didn't you?

(*Pause. Rose looks from one to the other.*)

MAGGIE (*briskly*): She's home safe and sound and that's all that matters. Now I don't know about you girls but I can tell you this chicken is weak with hunger. Let me tell you what's on the menu this evening. Our beverage is the usual hot, sweet tea. There is a choice between caraway-seed bread and soda bread, both fresh from the chef's oven. But now we come to the difficulty: There's only three eggs between the seven of us — I wish to God you'd persuade that white rooster of yours to lay eggs, Rosie.

CHRIS: There are eight of us, Maggie.

MAGGIE: How are there — ? Of course — the soldier up the sycamore! Not a great larder but a nice challenge to someone like myself. Right. My suggestion is . . . Eggs Ballybeg; in other words scrambled and served on lightly toasted caraway-seed bread. Followed — for those so inclined — by one magnificent Wild Woodbine. Everybody happy?

CHRIS: Excellent, Margaret!

MAGGIE: Settled.

(*Rose has taken off her shoe and is examining it carefully.*)

AGNES: We'll go and pick some more bilberries next Sunday, Rosie.

ROSE: All right.

AGNES: Remember the cans you had? You had your own two cans — remember? Did you take them with you?

ROSE: Where to, Aggie?

AGNES: Into the town . . . wherever you went . . .

ROSE: I hid them at the quarry behind a stone wall. They're safe there. I'll go back and pick them up later this evening. Does anybody know where my overall is?

MAGGIE: It's lying across your bed. And you'd need to bring some turf in, Rosie.

ROSE: I'll change first, Maggie.

MAGGIE: Be quick about it.

CHRIS: How many pieces of toast do you want?

MAGGIE: All that loaf. And go easy on the butter — that's all we have. Now. Parsley. And just a whiff of basil. I don't want you to be too optimistic, girls, but you should know I feel very creative this evening.

(*Rose moves towards the bedroom door. Just as she is about to exit.*)

KATE: I want to know where you have been, Rose.

(*Rose stops. Pause.*)

You have been gone for the entire afternoon. I want you to tell me where you've been.

AGNES: Later, Kate; after —

KATE: Where have you been for the past three hours?

ROSE (*inaudible*): Lough Anna.

KATE: I didn't hear what you said, Rose.

ROSE: Lough Anna.

CHRIS: Kate, just leave —

KATE: You walked from the quarry to Lough Anna?

ROSE: Yes.

KATE: Did you meet somebody there?

ROSE: Yes.

KATE: Had you arranged to meet somebody there?

ROSE: I had arranged to meet Danny Bradley there, Kate. He brought me out in his father's blue boat. (*To Maggie.*) I don't want anything to eat, Maggie. I brought a bottle of milk and a packet of chocolate biscuits with me and we had a picnic on the lake. (*To Agnes.*) Then the two of us went up through the back hills. He showed me what was left of the Lughnasa fires. A few of them are still burning away up there. (*To Kate.*) We passed young Sweeney's house — you know, the boy who got burned, the boy you said was dying. Well, he's on the mend, Danny says. His legs will be scarred but he'll be all right. (*To all.*) It's a very peaceful place up there. There was nobody there but Danny and me. (*To Agnes.*) He calls me his Rose-bud, Aggie. I told you that before, didn't I? (*To all.*) Then he walked me down as far as the workhouse gate and I came on home by myself. (*To Kate.*) And that's all I'm going to tell you. (*To all.*) That's all any of you are going to hear.

(*She exits, her shoes in one hand, the poppy in the other. Michael enters.*)

KATE: What has happened to this house? Mother of God, will we ever be able to lift our heads ever again . . . ?

(*Pause.*)

MICHAEL: The following night Vera McLaughlin arrived and explained to Agnes and Rose why she couldn't buy their hand-knitted gloves anymore. Most of her home knitters were already working in the new factory and she advised Agnes and Rose to apply immediately. The Industrial Revolution had finally caught up with Ballybeg.

They didn't apply, even though they had no other means of making a living, and they never discussed their situation with their sisters. Perhaps Agnes made the decision for both of them because she knew Rose wouldn't have got work there anyway. Or perhaps, as Kate believed, because Agnes was too notionate° to work in a factory. Or perhaps the two of them just wanted . . . away.

Anyhow, on my first day back at school, when we came into the kitchen for breakfast, there was a note propped up against the milk jug: "We are gone for good. This is best for all. Do not try to find us." It was written in Agnes's resolute hand.

Of course they did try to find them. So did the police. So did our neighbors who had a huge network of relatives all over England and America. But they had vanished without trace. And by the time I tracked them down — twenty-five years later, in London — Agnes was dead and Rose was dying in a hospice for the destitute in Southwark.

notionate: Strong-willed, stubborn.

The scraps of information I gathered about their lives during those missing years were too sparse to be coherent. They had moved about a lot. They had worked as cleaning women in public toilets, in factories, in the Underground. Then, when Rose could no longer get work, Agnes tried to support them both — but couldn't. From then on, I gathered, they gave up. They took to drink; slept in parks, in doorways, on the Thames Embankment. Then Agnes died of exposure. And two days after I found Rose in that grim hospice — she didn't recognize me, of course — she died in her sleep.

Father Jack's health improved quickly and he soon recovered his full vocabulary and all his old bounce and vigor. But he didn't say Mass that following Monday. In fact he never said Mass again. And the neighbors stopped inquiring about him. And his name never again appeared in the *Donegal Enquirer*. And of course there was never a civic reception with bands and flags and speeches.

But he never lost his determination to return to Uganda and he still talked passionately about his life with the lepers there. And each new anecdote contained more revelations. And each new revelation startled — shocked — stunned poor Aunt Kate. Until finally she hit on a phrase that appeased her: "his own distinctive spiritual search." "Leaping around a fire and offering a little hen to Uka or Ito or whoever is not religion as I was taught it and indeed know it," she would say with a defiant toss of her head. "But then Jack must make his own distinctive search." And when he died suddenly of a heart attack — within a year of his homecoming, on the very eve of the following Lá Lughnasa — my mother and Maggie mourned him sorely. But for months Kate was inconsolable.

My father sailed for Spain that Saturday. The last I saw of him was dancing down the lane in imitation of Fred Astaire, swinging his walking stick, Uncle Jack's ceremonial tricorn at a jaunty angle over his left eye. When he got to the main road he stopped and turned and with both hands blew a dozen theatrical kisses back to Mother and me.

He was wounded in Barcelona — he fell off his motorbike — so that for the rest of his life he walked with a limp. The limp wasn't disabling but it put an end to his dancing days; and that really distressed him. Even the role of maimed veteran, which he loved, could never compensate for that.

He still visited us occasionally, perhaps once a year. Each time he was on the brink of a new career. And each time he proposed to Mother and promised me a new bike. Then the war came in 1939; his visits became more infrequent; and finally he stopped coming altogether.

Sometime in the mid-fifties I got a letter from a tiny village in the south of Wales; a curt note from a young man of my own age and also called Michael Evans. He had found my name and address among the belongings of his father, Gerry Evans. He introduced himself as my half-brother and he wanted me to know that Gerry Evans, the father we shared, had died peacefully in the family home the previous week. Throughout his final illness he was nursed by his wife and his three grown children who all lived and worked in the village.

My mother never knew of that letter. I decided to tell her — decided not to — vacillated for years as my father would have done; and eventually, rightly or wrongly, kept the information to myself.

(*Maggie, Chris, Kate, and Agnes now resume their tasks.*)

CHRIS: Well, at least that's good news.

MAGGIE: What's that?

CHRIS: That the young Sweeney boy from the back hills is going to live.

MAGGIE: Good news indeed.

(*Chris goes to the door and calls.*)

CHRIS: Michael! Where are you? We need some turf brought in!

(*She now goes outside and calls up to Gerry. Michael exits.*)

Are you still up there?

GERRY (*off*): Don't stand there. I might fall on top of you.

CHRIS: Have you any idea what you're doing?

GERRY (*off*): Come on up here to me.

CHRIS: I'm sure I will.

GERRY (*off*): We never made love on top of a sycamore tree.

(*She looks quickly around: Did her sisters hear that?*)

CHRIS: If you fall and break your neck it'll be too good for you. (*She goes inside.*) Nobody can vanish quicker than that Michael fellow when you need him.

MAGGIE (*to Agnes*): I had a brilliant idea when I woke up this morning, Aggie. I thought to myself: What is it that Ballybeg badly needs and that Ballybeg hasn't got?

AGNES: A riddle. Give up.

MAGGIE: A dressmaker! So why doesn't Agnes Mundy who has such clever hands, why doesn't she dressmake?

AGNES: Clever hands!

(*Maggie looks around for her cigarettes.*)

MAGGIE: She'd get a pile of work. They'd come to her from far and wide. She'd make a fortune.

AGNES: Some fortune in Ballybeg.

MAGGIE: And not only would the work be interesting but she wouldn't be ruining her eyes staring at gray wool eight hours a day. Did you notice how Rosie squints at things now? It's the job for you, Aggie; I'm telling you. Ah, holy God, girls, don't tell me I'm out of fags! How could that have happened? (*Chris goes to the mantelpiece and produces a single cigarette.*)

Chrissie, you are one genius. Look, Kate. (*Scowls.*) Misery. (*Lights cigarette.*) Happiness! Want a drag?

KATE: What's keeping those wonderful Eggs Ballybeg?

MAGGIE: If I had to choose between one Wild Woodbine and a man of — say — fifty-two — widower — plump, what would I do, Kate? I'd take fatso, wouldn't I? God, I really am getting desperate.

(*Jack enters through the garden.*)

Maybe I should go to Ryanga with you, Jack.

JACK: I know you won't but I know you'd love it.

MAGGIE: Could you guarantee a man for each of us?

JACK: I couldn't promise four men but I should be able to get one husband for all of you.

MAGGIE: Would we settle for that?

CHRIS: One between the four of us?

JACK: That's our system and it works very well. One of you would be his principal wife and live with him in his largest hut —

MAGGIE: That'd be you, Kate.

KATE: Stop that, Maggie!

JACK: And the other three of you he'd keep in his enclosure. It would be like living on the same small farm.

MAGGIE: Snug enough, girls, isn't it? (*To Jack.*) And what would be — what sort of duties would we have?

JACK: Cooking, sewing, helping with the crops, washing — the usual housekeeping tasks.

MAGGIE: Sure that's what we do anyway.

JACK: And looking after his children.

MAGGIE: That he'd have by Kate.

KATE: Maggie!

JACK: By all four of you! And what's so efficient about that system is that the husband and his wives and his children make up a small commune where everybody helps everybody else and cares for them. I'm completely in favor of it.

KATE: It may be efficient and you may be in favor of it, Jack, but I don't think it's what Pope Pius XI considers to be the holy sacrament of matrimony. And it might be better for you if you paid just a bit more attention to our Holy Father and a bit less to the Great Goddess . . . Iggie.

(*Music of "Anything Goes" very softly on the radio.*)

CHRIS: Listen.

MAGGIE: And they have hens there, too, Jack?

JACK: We're overrun with hens.

MAGGIE: Don't dismiss it, girls. It has its points. Would you be game, Kate?

KATE: Would you give my head peace, Maggie.

CHRIS: Gerry has it going!

MAGGIE: Tell me this, Jack: What's the Swahili for "tchook-tchook-tchook-tchook-tchook"?

JACK: You'd love the climate, too, Kate.

KATE: I'm not listening to a word you're saying.

(*Gerry runs on.*)

GERRY: Well? Any good?

CHRIS: Listen.

GERRY: Aha. Leave it to the expert.

JACK: I have something for you, Gerry.

GERRY: What's that?

JACK: The plumed hat — the ceremonial hat — remember? We agreed to swap. With you in a second.

(*He goes to his bedroom.*)

MAGGIE: Good work, Gerry.

GERRY: Thought it might be the aerial. That's the end of your troubles. (*Listens. Sings a line of the song.*) Dance with me, Agnes.

AGNES: Have a bit of sense, Gerry Evans.

GERRY: Dance with me. Please. Come on.

MAGGIE: Dance with him, Aggie.

GERRY (*sings*): "In olden times a glimpse of stocking
Was looked on as something shocking —"
Give me your hand.

MAGGIE: Go on, Aggie.

AGNES: Who wants to dance at this time of —

(*Gerry pulls her to her feet and takes her in his arms.*)

GERRY (*sings*): ". . . anything goes.
Good authors, too, who once knew better words
Now only use four-letter words
Writing prose,
Anything goes . . ."

(*Bring up the sound. With style and with easy elegance they dance once around the kitchen and then out to the garden — Gerry singing the words directly to her face.*)

"If driving fast cars you like,
If low bars you like,
If old hymns you like,
If bare limbs you like,
If Mae West you like,
Or me undressed you like,
Why, nobody will oppose.
When ev'ry night, the set that's smart is intruding in nudist parties in
Studios,
Anything goes . . ."

(*They are now in the far corner of the garden.*)

You're a great dancer, Aggie.

AGNES: No, I'm not.

GERRY: You're a superb dancer.

AGNES: No, I'm not.

GERRY: You should be a professional dancer.

AGNES: Too late for that.

GERRY: You could teach dancing in Ballybeg.

AGNES: That's all they need.

GERRY: Maybe it is!

(*He bends down and kisses her on the forehead. All this is seen — but not heard — by Chris at the kitchen window. Immediately after this kiss Gerry bursts into song*

again, turns Agnes four or five times very rapidly, and dances her back to the kitchen.)

There you are. Safe and sound.

MAGGIE: I wish to God I could dance like you, Aggie.

AGNES: I haven't a breath.

GERRY: Doesn't she dance elegantly?

MAGGIE: Always did, our Aggie.

GERRY: Unbelievable. Now, Chrissie — you and I.

CHRIS (*sharply*): Not now. I wonder where Michael's got to?

GERRY: Come on, Chrissie. Once round the floor.

CHRIS: Not now, I said. Are you thick?

MAGGIE: I'll dance with you, Gerry! (*She kicks her Wellingtons off.*) Do you want to see real class?

GERRY: Certainly do, Maggie.

MAGGIE: Stand back there, girls. Shirley Temple needs a lot of space.

GERRY: Wow-wow-wow-wow!

MAGGIE: Hold me close, Gerry. The old legs aren't too reliable.

(*She and Gerry sing and dance.*)

"In olden times a glimpse of stocking
Was looked on as something shocking
But now —"

(*Chris suddenly turns the radio off.*)

CHRIS: Sick of that damned thing.

GERRY: What happened?

MAGGIE: What are you at there, Chrissie?

CHRIS: We're only wasting the battery and we won't get a new one until the weekend.

MAGGIE: It wasn't to be, Gerry. But there'll be another day.

GERRY: That's a promise, Maggie.

(*He goes to Chris at the radio.*)

Not a bad little set, that.

KATE: Peace, thanks be to God! D'you know what that thing has done? Killed all Christian conversation in this country.

CHRIS (*to Agnes, icily*): Vera McLaughlin's calling here tomorrow. She wants to talk to you and Rose.

AGNES: What about?

KATE (*quickly*): I didn't tell you, did I? — her daughter's got engaged!

MAGGIE: Which of them?

KATE: "The harvest dance is going to be just supreme this year, Miss Mundy"— that wee brat!

MAGGIE: Sophia. Is she not still at school?

KATE: Left last year. She's fifteen. And the lucky man is sixteen.

MAGGIE: Holy God. We may pack it in, girls.

KATE: It's indecent, I'm telling you. Fifteen and sixteen! Don't tell me that's not totally improper. It's the poor mother I feel sorry for.

AGNES: What does she want to talk to us about?

CHRIS (*relenting*): Something about wool. Didn't sound important. She probably won't call at all.

(*Chris turns the radio on again. No sound.*)

(*To Maggie.*) Go ahead and dance, you two.

MAGGIE: Artistes like Margaret Mundy can't perform on demand, Chrissie. We need to be in touch with other forces first, don't we, Gerry?

GERRY: Absolutely. Why is there no sound?

KATE: Maggie, are we never going to eat?

MAGGIE: Indeed we are — outside in the garden! Eggs Ballybeg *al fresco.*° Lughnasa's almost over, girls. There aren't going to be many warm evenings left.

KATE: Good idea, Maggie.

AGNES: I'll get the cups and plates.

GERRY (*with Chris at radio*): Are you all right?

CHRIS: It's not gone again, is it?

GERRY: Have I done something wrong?

CHRIS: I switched it on again — that's all I did.

MAGGIE: Take out those chairs, Gerry.

GERRY: What about the table?

MAGGIE: We'll just spread a cloth on the ground.

(*Maggie exits with the cloth which she spreads in the middle of the garden. Gerry kisses Chris lightly on the back of the neck.*)

GERRY: At least we know it's not the aerial.

CHRIS: According to you.

GERRY: And if it's not the aerial the next thing to check is the ignition.

CHRIS: Ignition! Listen to that bluffer!

GERRY: Bluffer? (*To Agnes as she passes.*) Did you hear what she called me? That's unfair, Agnes, isn't it?

(*Agnes smiles and shrugs.*)

Let's take the back off and see what's what.

(*Rose enters the garden from the back of the house. At first nobody notices her. She is dressed as in act 1. In her right hand she holds the dead rooster by the feet. Its feathers are ruffled and it is stained with blood. Rose is calm, almost matter-of-fact. Agnes sees her first and goes to her. Chris and Gerry join the others in the garden.*)

AGNES: Rosie, what is it, Rosie?

ROSE: My rooster's dead.

AGNES: Oh Rosie . . .

ROSE (*holding the dead bird up*): Look at him. He's dead.

AGNES: What happened to him?

ROSE: The fox must have got him.

AGNES: Oh, poor Rosie . . .

ROSE: Maggie warned me the fox was about again. (*To all.*) That's the end of my pet rooster. The fox must have got him. You were right, Maggie.

al fresco: In the open air.

(*She places it carefully on the tablecloth in the middle of the garden.*)

MAGGIE: Did he get at the hens?

ROSE: I don't think so.

MAGGIE: Was the door left open?

ROSE: They're all right. They're safe.

MAGGIE: That itself.

AGNES: We'll get another white rooster for you, Rosie.

ROSE: Doesn't matter.

MAGGIE: And I'll put manners on him early on.

ROSE: I don't want another.

MAGGIE (*quick hug*): Poor old Rosie. (*As she moves away.*) We can hardly expect him to lay for us now . . .

CHRIS: Where's that Michael fellow got to? Michael! He hears me rightly, you know. I'm sure he's jouking° about out there somewhere, watching us. Michael!

(*Rose sits on the garden seat.*)

MAGGIE: All right, girls, what's missing? Knives, forks, plates —

(*She sees Jack coming through the kitchen.*)

Jesus, Mary, and Joseph!

(*Jack is wearing a very soiled, very crumpled white uniform — a version of the uniform we saw him in at the very beginning of the play. One of the epaulettes is hanging by a thread and the gold buttons are tarnished. The uniform is so large that it looks as if it were made for a much larger man: His hands are lost in the sleeves and the trousers trail on the ground. On his head he wears a tricorn, ceremonial hat; once white like the uniform but now grubby, the plumage broken and tatty. He carries himself in military style, his army cane under his arm.*)

JACK: Gerry, my friend, where are you?

GERRY: Out here, Jack.

JACK: There you are. (*To all.*) I put on my ceremonial clothes for the formal exchange. There was a time when it fitted me — believe it or not. Wonderful uniform, isn't it?

GERRY: Unbelievable. I could do with that for Spain.

JACK: It was my uniform when I was chaplain to the British army during the Great War.

KATE: We know only too well what it is, Jack.

JACK: Isn't it splendid? Well, it was splendid. Needs a bit of a clean up. Okawa's always dressing up in it. I really must give it to him to keep.

KATE: It's not at all suitable for this climate, Jack.

JACK: You're right, Kate. Just for the ceremony — then I'll change back. Now, if I were at home, what we do when we swap or barter is this. I place my possession on the ground —

(*He and Gerry enact this ritual.*)

jouking: Hiding.

Go ahead. (*Of hat.*) Put it on the grass — anywhere — just at your feet. Now take three steps away from it — yes? — a symbolic distancing of yourself from what you once possessed. Good. Now turn round once — like this — yes, a complete circle — and that's the formal rejection of what you once had — you no longer lay claim to it. Now I cross over to where you stand — right? And you come over to the position I have left. So. Excellent. The exchange is now formally and irrevocably complete. This is my straw hat. And that is your tricorn hat. Put it on. Splendid! And it suits you! Doesn't it suit him?

CHRIS: His head's too big.

GERRY (*adjusting hat*): What about that? (*To Agnes.*) Is that better, Agnes?

AGNES: You're lovely.

(*Gerry does a Charlie Chaplin walk across the garden, his feet spread, his cane twirling. As he does he sings.*)

GERRY: "In olden times a glimpse of stocking
        Was looked on as something shocking . . ."

JACK (*adjusting his hat*): And what about this? Or like this? Or further back on my head?

MAGGIE: Would you look at them! Strutting about like a pair of peacocks! Now — teatime!

AGNES: I'll make the tea.

MAGGIE: You can start again tomorrow. Let me finish off Lughnasa. Chrissie, put on Marconi.

CHRIS: I think it's broken again.

AGNES: Gerry fixed it. Didn't you?

GERRY: Then Chrissie got at it again.

CHRIS: Possessed that thing, if you ask me.

KATE: I wish you wouldn't use words like that, Christina. There's still great heat in that sun.

MAGGIE: Great harvest weather.

KATE: I love September.

MAGGIE (*not moving*): Cooking time, girls.

KATE: Wait a while, Maggie. Enjoy the bit of heat that's left.

(*Agnes moves beside Rose.*)

AGNES: Next Sunday, then. Is that all right?

ROSE: What's next Sunday?

AGNES: We'll get some more bilberries.

ROSE: Yes. Yes. Whatever you say, Aggie.

(*Gerry examines the kites.*)

GERRY: Not bad for a kid of seven. Very neatly made.

KATE: Look at the artwork.

GERRY: Wow-wow-wow-wow! That is unbelievable!

KATE: I keep telling his mother — she has a very talented son.

CHRIS: So there, Mr. Evans.

GERRY: Have you all seen these?

MAGGIE: I hate them.

GERRY: I think they're just wonderful. Look, Jack.

(*For the first time we all see the images. On each kite is painted a crude, cruel, grinning face, primitively drawn, garishly painted.*)

I'll tell you something: This boy isn't going to end up selling gramophones.

CHRIS: Michael! He always vanishes when there's work to be done.

MAGGIE: I've a riddle for you. Why is a gramophone like a parrot?

KATE: Maggie!

MAGGIE: Because it . . . because it always . . . because a parrot . . . God, I've forgotten!

(*Maggie moves into the kitchen. Michael enters. The characters are now in positions similar to their positions at the beginning of the play — with some changes; Agnes and Gerry are on the garden seat. Jack stands stiffly to attention at Agnes's elbow. One kite, facing boldly out front, stands between Gerry and Agnes; the other between Agnes and Jack. Rose is upstage left. Maggie is at the kitchen window. Kate is downstage right. Chris is at the front door. During Michael's speech Kate cries quietly. As Michael begins to speak the stage is lit in a very soft, golden light so that the tableau we see is almost, but not quite, in a haze.*)

MICHAEL: As I said, Father Jack was dead within twelve months. And with him and Agnes and Rose all gone, the heart seemed to go out of the house.

 Maggie took on the tasks Rose and Agnes had done and pretended to believe that nothing had changed. My mother spent the rest of her life in the knitting factory — and hated every day of it. And after a few years doing nothing Kate got the job of tutoring the young family of Austin Morgan of the Arcade. But much of the spirit and fun had gone out of their lives; and when my time came to go away, in the selfish way of young men I was happy to escape.

(*Now fade in very softly, just audible, the music — "It is Time to Say Goodnight" [not from the radio speaker]. And as Michael continues everybody sways very slightly from side to side — even the grinning kites. The movement is so minimal that we cannot be quite certain if it is happening or if we imagine it.*)

And so, when I cast my mind back to that summer of 1936, different kinds of memories offer themselves to me.

 But there is one memory of that Lughnasa time that visits me most often, and what fascinates me about that memory is that it owes nothing to fact. In that memory atmosphere is more real than incident and everything is simultaneously actual and illusory. In that memory, too, the air is nostalgic with the music of the thirties. It drifts in from somewhere far away — a mirage of sound — a dream music that is both heard and imagined; that seems to be both itself and its own echo, a sound so alluring and so mesmeric that the afternoon is bewitched, maybe haunted, by it. And what is so strange about that memory is that everybody seems to be floating on those sweet sounds, moving rhythmically, languorously, in complete isolation; responding more to the mood of the music than to its beat. When I remember it, I think of it as dancing. Dancing with eyes half closed because to open them would break the spell. Dancing as if language had surrendered to movement — as if this ritual, this wordless cere- mony, was now the way to speak, to whisper private and sacred things, to be in touch with some other- ness. Dancing as if the very heart of life and all its hopes might be found in those assuaging notes and those hushed rhythms and in those silent and hyp- notic movements. Dancing as if language no longer existed because words were no longer necessary . . .

(*Slowly bring up the music. Slowly bring down the lights.*)

Suzan-Lori Parks

Suzan-Lori Parks (b. 1964) was named by Mel Gussow in the *New York Times* as the "year's most promising playwright" in 1989. She lives in New York City and teaches as writer-in-residence at the New School for Social Research. Her work has been supported by grants from numerous agencies, including the Rockefeller and Ford Foundations and the National Endowment for the Arts, from which she has received a playwriting fellowship twice. She also received a MacArthur Award in 1986. Her work has been seen primarily in off-Broadway theaters in New York as well as important regional theaters.

Parks was the child of an army officer and grew up in several different locations. She says, "I've heard horrible stories about twelve-step groups for army people. But I had a great childhood. My parents were really into experiencing the places we lived." She lived, for example, in a small town in Germany and attended German schools, studying in German. She went to Hampshire College, where she studied writing with James Baldwin. After that experience she went to London for a year to study acting. "It really made a difference in my writing. It dawned on me that a lot of people write with ideas in mind. . . . But I never really have ideas, per se. I have these movements, these gestures. Then I figure out how to put those gestures into words."

She is aware of being influenced by a number of important literary figures, among them Gertrude Stein, James Joyce, William Faulkner, and Samuel Beckett, but there are echoes of other writers such as Shakespeare and Richard Wright in *The Death of the Last Black Man in the Whole Entire World*. Parks's approach to language is partly vernacular as she attempts to reproduce speech both as it is spoken and as her audience assumes it may be spoken. But she is interested in the hypnotic and musical value of words, which accounts for much of the patterning of repetition that marks her work.

Her plays have been performed in the BACA (Brooklyn Arts Council Association) Downtown Theater, Manhattan Theater Club, and the Joseph Papp Public Theater in Manhattan. Her early short plays are *Betting on the Dust Commander, Fishes, The Sinners' Place*, and *The America Play*. Her full-length play *Imperceptible Mutabilities in the Third Kingdom*, directed by her long-time collaborator Liz Diamond, won the Obie Award for the best off-Broadway play of 1990. One section of *Mutabilities* takes place on Emancipation Day in 1865 and is played in whiteface by African American actors. Another section, "Greeks," makes reference to her own family, with a character called Mr. Sergeant Smith. Parts of the play have been described as "like a choral poem."

Parks has produced a film, *Anemone Me* (1990), that has been shown in New York. Her *Devotees in the Garden of Love* (1992) premiered at the Actors Theatre of Louisville, Kentucky. Her next play, *Venus* (1996), was a coproduction of the Joseph Papp Public Theater and Yale Repertory Theatre. It was directed by Richard Foreman, the founder of the Ontological-Hysteric Theater. The play focuses on the life of a black woman brought to England as the Venus Hottentot, a sideshow freak displaying "an intensely ugly figure, distorted beyond all European notions of beauty." The authorities put an end to the sideshow, and Parks explores this mysterious woman's life. Parks has also written *Girl 6* (1996), a film directed by Spike Lee.

Parks's newest play, *In the Blood* (1999), focuses on Hester, a welfare mother of five. She faces poverty, the welfare system's workfare, and sterilization. The play examines our attitudes toward poverty and responsibility. Parks is an energetic, carefully focused, and clearly directed playwright with a special interest in the language of speech and the language of gesture — in almost equal measure.

THE DEATH OF THE LAST BLACK MAN IN THE WHOLE ENTIRE WORLD

The Death of the Last Black Man in the Whole Entire World (1990) is not a straight-line narrative, nor is it situational in the manner of the Scribean well-made play. It consists of several sections:

Overture

Panel I: Thuh Holy Ghost

Panel II: First Chorus

Panel III: Thuh Lonesome 3some

Panel IV: Second Chorus

Panel V: In thuh Garden of HooDoo It

Final Chorus

The first production of the play, at the Brooklyn Arts Council Association (BACA) Downtown Theater, was directed by Liz Diamond in close collaboration with Suzan-Lori Parks. Although Parks's text provides no conventional stage directions, the BACA production created very powerful visual images in the staging and costuming. In Panels I, III, and IV the name of the panel was projected on the back of the stage, lighted brightly enough to be read, like the caption of a cartoon panel. The visual emblems that dominated the panels were powerful: an electric chair in "Thuh Holy Ghost," with Black Man, wearing only a pair of white jockey shorts, rising from a black catafalque to find himself seated in the chair with a metal helmet to facilitate the flow of electricity through his body. This emblem was duplicated: while one actor sat in the chair, another played his part downstage getting solace from Black Woman, who anointed him and washed his feet in the traditional Christian fashion.

In "Thuh Lonesome 3some" the emblem was three watermelons borne by Black Man with Watermelon, who struggles to understand the role these melons play in his life. The biblical references to melons in paradise ironically underpin this section. In "In thuh Garden of HooDoo It," another emblem of death, the lynched man, dangled over the action. Again, the Black Man was duplicated downstage with a noose around his neck and with a dead tree limb dragged onto the stage. In each instance the Black Man dies a different death, but he cannot die without the accompanying spirits telling their story.

Liz Diamond, the director, explained, "These are figures, not characters, and their function as figures must be understood." One of Diamond's greatest challenges was in bringing these figures onstage so the audience would understand that they are not "realistic" characters. They are epic types that Diamond calls spirits who will not let Black Man die before he hears them impart their wisdom. The figures come from many sources: And Bigger and Bigger and Bigger from Richard Wright's *Native Son*; Ham from the Bible; Black Man with Watermelon and Black Woman with Fried Drumstick from black folklore; Queen-then-Pharaoh Hatshepsut from history; Prunes and Prisms, an image of the black prom queen; and Voice on thuh Tee V, a contemporary image.

Each of these figures was costumed appropriately in the Diamond production. Hatshepsut wore the squared-off headdress found on the Sphinx with a gold pleated full-length dress. Black Man with Watermelon wore overalls; Black Woman wore a black matronly dress and later a black veil of mourning. Bigger wore a gold zoot suit; Voice on thuh Tee V wore a trench coat and carried a microphone. Ham, one of the most compelling figures, wore a multicolored shawl and headdress and carried a long staff. The inspiration for his character, as Parks and Diamond observed, was the "Times Square Prophet," a homeless wanderer who rants as if he were a holy man.

Ham's major section, Panel IV, is dominated by his biblical "voice." In the Bible, when Ham saw his father Noah's nakedness, he was condemned, and his progeny were forever black as a result. As Parks has said, "Ham doesn't get a chance to respond" in the Bible. But Parks provides Ham's response with a parody of the Bible's series of "begets." The figure Before Columbus was costumed like an African villager in an abbadan obie, an African tunic, and comments on the world when it was "flat." These figures are the stereotypes of blacks as created in the Western European imagination, beginning with the Bible.

Parks hears language as much as she sees it. Therefore in her text she spells words as she wants them to be heard and signifies meanings that sometimes transcend the limits of individual words. She adds the syllable *-ed* to a word such as *died*, and the result is a new word, in this case *dieded*. The effect is both ironic and rhythmically powerful and reinforcing. That kind of syllabic repetition also complements the repetition of important phrases, such as "You should write that down. You should write that down and hide it under uh rock." Much of history has been written down and hidden under rocks only to be discovered and deciphered by later generations. The point is to get it down in language somehow, to tell the story so that the future will know.

Music was used judiciously throughout the Yale performance, including a saxophone with a jazz riff, but no songs. A gong sounded to signal important moments like the string breaking in *The Cherry Orchard*. Subtle rhythmic effects are achieved with the repetition of words and phrases, and time becomes as plastic as space. The time of the play encompasses ancient Egypt, biblical Judea, the coming of Columbus, slavery in the American South, lynchings in the post–Civil War era, and contemporary electrocutions of blacks. *Last Black Man* is nothing if not inclusive.

The Death of the Last Black Man in the Whole Entire World in Performance

The Death of the Last Black Man in the Whole Entire World premiered in the BACA Downtown Theater in New York in September 1990. It was revived in a larger, full-scale production at the Yale Repertory Theatre Winterfest Program in early 1992. Audiences responded positively to a production that was more avant-garde than most drama being shown in regional theaters, and reviewers hailed Parks as an exciting new voice in theater.

Suzan-Lori Parks (b. 1964)

THE DEATH OF THE LAST BLACK MAN IN THE WHOLE ENTIRE WORLD   *1990*

When I die
I wont stay
Dead.   — BOB KAUFMAN

The Figures

BLACK MAN WITH WATERMELON
BLACK WOMAN WITH FRIED DRUMSTICK
LOTS OF GREASE AND LOTS OF PORK
YES AND GREENS BLACK-EYED PEAS CORNBREAD
QUEEN-THEN-PHARAOH HATSHEPSUT
BEFORE COLUMBUS
OLD MAN RIVER JORDAN
HAM
AND BIGGER AND BIGGER AND BIGGER
PRUNES AND PRISMS
VOICE ON THUH TEE V

The Sections

Overture
Panel I: *Thuh Holy Ghost*
Panel II: *First Chorus*
Panel III: *Thuh Lonesome 3some*
Panel IV: *Second Chorus*

Panel V: *In thuh Garden of HooDoo It*
Final Chorus

The action takes place in the present.

OVERTURE

BLACK MAN WITH WATERMELON: The black man moves his hands.

(*a bell sounds twice*)

LOTS OF GREASE AND LOTS OF PORK: Lots of grease and lots of pork.
QUEEN-THEN-PHARAOH HATSHEPSUT: Queen-then-Pharaoh Hatshepsut.
AND BIGGER AND BIGGER AND BIGGER: And Bigger and Bigger and Bigger.
PRUNES AND PRISMS: Prunes and Prisms.
HAM: Ham.
VOICE ON THUH TEE V: Voice on thuh Tee V.

OLD MAN RIVER JORDAN: Old Man River Jordan.

YES AND GREENS BLACK-EYED PEAS CORNBREAD: Yes and Greens Black-Eyed Peas Cornbread.

BEFORE COLUMBUS: Before Columbus.

(*a bell sounds once*)

BLACK MAN WITH WATERMELON: The black man moves his hands.

QUEEN-THEN-PHARAOH HATSHEPSUT: Not yet. Let Queen-then-Pharaoh Hatshepsut tell you when.

LOTS OF GREASE AND LOTS OF PORK: This is the death of the last black man in the whole entire world.

(*a bell sounds three times*)

BLACK WOMAN WITH FRIED DRUMSTICK: Yesterday today next summer tomorrow just uh moment uhgoh in 1317 dieded thuh last black man in thuh whole entire world. Uh! Oh. Don't be uhlarmed. Do not be afeared. It was painless. Uh painless passin. He falls twenty-three floors to his death. 23 floors from uh passin ship from space tuh splat on thuh pavement. He have uh head he been keepin under thuh Tee V. On his bottom pantry shelf. He have uh head that hurts. Don't fit right. Put it on tuh go tuh thuh store and it pinched him when he walks his thoughts don't got room. Why dieded he huh? Where he gonna go now that he done dieded? Where he gonna go tuh wash his hands?

YES AND GREENS BLACK-EYED PEAS CORNBREAD: You should write that down and you should hide it under a rock. This is the death of the last black man in the whole entire world.

LOTS OF GREASE AND LOTS OF PORK/PRUNES AND PRISMS: Not yet —

BLACK MAN WITH WATERMELON: The black man moves. His hands —

QUEEN-THEN-PHARAOH HATSHEPSUT: You are too young to move. Let me move it for you.

BLACK MAN WITH WATERMELON: The black man moves his hands. — He moves his hands round. Back. Back. Back tuh that.

LOTS OF GREASE AND LOTS OF PORK: (Not dat).

BLACK MAN WITH WATERMELON: When thuh worl usta be roun. Thuh worl usta be *roun.*

BLACK WOMAN WITH FRIED DRUMSTICK: Uh roun worl. Uh roun? Thuh worl? When was this.

QUEEN-THEN-PHARAOH HATSHEPSUT: Columbus. Before.

BEFORE COLUMBUS: Before. Columbus.

YES AND GREENS BLACK-EYED PEAS CORNBREAD: Before Columbus.

BLACK MAN WITH WATERMELON: HHH. HA!

QUEEN-THEN-PHARAOH HATSHEPSUT: Before Columbus thuh worl usta be *roun* they put uh /d/ on thuh end of roun makin round. Thusly they set in motion thuh end. Without that /d/ we coulda gone on spinnin for ever. Thuh /d/ thing ended things ended.

YES AND GREENS BLACK-EYED PEAS CORNBREAD: Before Columbus:

(*a bell sounds twice*)

BEFORE COLUMBUS: The popular thinking of the day back in them days was that the world was flat. They thought the world was flat. Back then when they thought the world was flat they were afeared and stayed at home. They wanted to go out back then when they thought the world was flat but the water had in it dragons of which meaning these dragons they were afeared back then when they thought the world was flat. They stayed at home. Them thinking the world was flat kept it roun. Them thinking the sun revolved around the earth kept them satellite-like. They figured out the truth and scurried out. Figuring out the truth put them in their place and they scurried out to put us in ours.

YES AND GREENS BLACK-EYED PEAS CORNBREAD: Mmmm. Yes. You should write this down. You should hide this under a rock.

LOTS OF GREASE AND LOTS OF PORK/PRUNES AND PRISMS: Not yet —

BLACK MAN WITH WATERMELON: The black man bursts into flames. The black man bursts into blames. Whose fault is it?

ALL: Ain't mines.

BLACK MAN WITH WATERMELON: Whose fault is it?

ALL: Ain't mines.

BLACK WOMAN WITH FRIED DRUMSTICK: I can't remember back that far.

QUEEN-THEN-PHARAOH HATSHEPSUT: And besides, I wasn't even there.

BLACK MAN WITH WATERMELON: Ha ha ha. The black man laughs out loud.

ALL (*except Ham*): HAM-BONE-HAM-BONE-WHERE-YOU-BEEN-ROUN-THUH-WORL-N-BACK-UH-*GAIN.*

YES AND GREENS BLACK-EYED PEAS CORNBREAD: Whatcha seen hambone girl?

BLACK WOMAN WITH FRIED DRUMSTICK: Didn't see you. I saw thuh worl.

QUEEN-THEN-PHARAOH HATSHEPSUT: I was there.

LOTS OF GREASE AND LOTS OF PORK: Didn't see you.

BLACK WOMAN WITH FRIED DRUMSTICK: I was there.

BLACK MAN WITH WATERMELON: Didn't see you. The black man moves his hands.

QUEEN-THEN-PHARAOH HATSHEPSUT: We are too young to see. Let them see it for you. We are too young to rule. Let them rule it for you. We are too young to have. Let them have it for you. You are too young to write. Let them — let them. Do it. Before you.

BLACK MAN WITH WATERMELON: The black man moves his hands.

YES AND GREENS BLACK-EYED PEAS CORNBREAD: You should write it down because if you dont write it down then they will come along and tell the future that we did not exist. You should write it down and you should hide it under a rock. You should write down the past and you should write down the present and in what in the future you should write it down. It will be of us but you should mention them from time to time so that in the future when they come along and know that they exist. You should hide it all under a rock so that in the future when they come along they will say that the rock did not exist.

BLACK WOMAN WITH FRIED DRUMSTICK: We getting somewheres. We getting down. Down down down down down down down down —

QUEEN-THEN-PHARAOH HATSHEPSUT: I saw Columbus comin. / I saw Columbus comin goin over tuh visit you. "To borrow a cup of sugar," so he said. I waved my hands in warnin. You waved back. I aint seen you since.

LOTS OF GREASE AND LOTS OF PORK: In the future when they came along I meeting them. On thuh coast. Uh! Thuh Coast! I — was — so — polite. But in thuh dirt, I wrote: "Ha. Ha. Ha."

ALL: Ha. Ha. Ha. Ha. Ha. Ha. Ha. Ha. Ha. Ha. Ha. Ha. Ha. Ha. Ha. Ha. HHHHHHHHHHHHHHHH.

BLACK MAN WITH WATERMELON: Thuh black man he move. He move he hans.

(*a bell sounds once*)

PANEL I: THUH HOLY GHOST

BLACK MAN WITH WATERMELON: Saint mines. Saint mines. Iduhnt it Nope: iduhnt. Saint mines cause everythin I calls mines got uh print uh me someway on it in it dont got uh print uh me someway on it so saint mines. Duhduhnt so saint: huh.

BLACK WOMAN WITH FRIED DRUMSTICK: Hen.

BLACK MAN WITH WATERMELON: Huh. Huh?

BLACK WOMAN WITH FRIED DRUMSTICK: Hen. Hen?

BLACK MAN WITH WATERMELON: Who gave birth tuh this I wonder. Who gave birth tuh this. I wonder.

BLACK WOMAN WITH FRIED DRUMSTICK: You comed back. Comin backs somethin in itself. You comed back.

BLACK MAN WITH WATERMELON: This does not belong tuh me. Somebody planted this on me. On me in my hands.

BLACK WOMAN WITH FRIED DRUMSTICK: Cold compress. Cold compress then some hen. Lean back. You comed back. Lean back.

BLACK MAN WITH WATERMELON: Who gave birth tuh this I wonder who.

BLACK WOMAN WITH FRIED DRUMSTICK: Comin for you. Came for you: that they done did. Comin for tuh take you. Told me tuh pack up your clothes. Told me tuh cut my bed in 2 from double tuh single. Cut off thuh bed-foot where your feets had rested. Told me tuh do that too. Burry your ring in his hidin spot under thuh porch! That they told me too to do. Didnt have uh ring so I didnt do diddly. They told and told

and told: proper instructions for thuh burial proper attire for thuh mournin. They told and told and told: I didnt do squat. Awe on that. You comed back. You got uhway. Knew you would. Hen?

BLACK MAN WITH WATERMELON: Who gave birth tuh this I wonder. Who? Not me. Saint mines.

BLACK WOMAN WITH FRIED DRUMSTICK: Killed every hen on thuh block. You comed back. Knew you would. Knew you would came back. Knew you will wanted uh good big hen dinner in waitin. Every hen on thuh block.

BLACK MAN WITH WATERMELON: Saint mines.

BLACK WOMAN WITH FRIED DRUMSTICK: Strutted down on up thuh road with my axe. By-myself-with-my-axe. Got tuh thuh street top 93 dyin hen din hand. Dropped thuh axe. Tooked tuh stranglin. 93 dyin hen din hand with no heads let em loose tuh run down tuh towards home infront of me. Flipped thuh necks of thuh next 23 more odd. Slinged um over my shoulders. Hens of thuh neighbors now in my pots. Feathers of thuh hens of thuh neighbors stucked in our mattress. They told and told and told. On me. Huh. Awe on that. Hen? You got uhway. Knew you would.

BLACK MAN WITH WATERMELON: Who gave birth tuh me I wonder.

BLACK WOMAN WITH FRIED DRUMSTICK: They dont speak tuh us no more. They pass by our porch but they dont nod. You been comed back goin on 9 years not even heard from thuh neighbors uh congratulation. Uh alienationed dum. Uh guess. Huh. Hen? *WE AINT GOT NO FRIENDS,* — sweetheart.

BLACK MAN WITH WATERMELON: *SWEET-HEART.*

BLACK WOMAN WITH FRIED DRUMSTICK: Hen!!

BLACK MAN WITH WATERMELON: Aint hungry.

BLACK WOMAN WITH FRIED DRUMSTICK: Hen.

BLACK MAN WITH WATERMELON: Aint eaten in years.

BLACK WOMAN WITH FRIED DRUMSTICK: Hen?

BLACK MAN WITH WATERMELON: Last meal I had was my last-mans-meal.

BLACK WOMAN WITH FRIED DRUMSTICK: You got uhway. Knew you would.

BLACK MAN WITH WATERMELON: This thing dont look like me!

BLACK WOMAN WITH FRIED DRUMSTICK: It dont. Do it. Should it? Hen: eat it.

BLACK MAN WITH WATERMELON: I kin tell whats mines by whets gots my looks. Ssmymethod. Try it by testin it and it turns out true. Every time. Fool proofly. Look down at my foot and wonder if its mine. Foot mine? I kin ask it and foot answers back with uh "yes Sir" — not like you and me say "yes Sir" but uh "yes Sir" peculiar tuh thuh foot. Foot mine? I kin ask it and through uh look that looks like my looks thuh foot gives me back uh "yes Sir." Ssmymethod. Try by thuh test tuh pass for true. Move on tuh thuh uther foot. Foot mine? And uh nother "yes Sir" so feets mine is understood. Got uh forearm thats up for question check myself out teeth by tooth. Melon mine? — . Dont look like me.

BLACK WOMAN WITH FRIED DRUMSTICK: Hen mine? Gobble it up and it will be. You got uhway. Fixed uh good big hen dinner for you. Get yourself uh mouthful afore it rots.

BLACK MAN WITH WATERMELON: Was we green and stripe-dly when we first comed out?

BLACK WOMAN WITH FRIED DRUMSTICK: Uh huhn. Thuh features comes later. Later comes after now.

BLACK MAN WITH WATERMELON: Oh. Later comes now: melon mine?

BLACK WOMAN WITH FRIED DRUMSTICK: They comed for you and tooked you. That was yesterday. Today you sit in your chair where you sat yesterday and thuh day afore yesterday afore they comed and tooked you. Things today is just as they are yesterday cept nothin is familiar cause it was such uh long time uhgoh.

BLACK MAN WITH WATERMELON: Later oughta be now by now huh?: melon mine?

BLACK WOMAN WITH FRIED DRUMSTICK: Thuh chair was portable. They take it from county tuh county. Only got one. Can only eliminate one at uh time. Woulda fried you right here on thuh front porch but we dont got enough electric. No onessgot enough electric. Not on our block. Dont believe in havin enough. Put thuh Chair in thuh middle of thuh City. Outdoors. In thuh square. Folks come tuh watch with picnic baskets. — Hen?

BLACK MAN WITH WATERMELON: Sweetheart?

BLACK WOMAN WITH FRIED DRUMSTICK: They juiced you some, huh?

BLACK MAN WITH WATERMELON: Just uh squirt. Sweetheart.

BLACK WOMAN WITH FRIED DRUMSTICK: Humpty Dumpty.

BLACK MAN WITH WATERMELON: Melon mines?

BLACK WOMAN WITH FRIED DRUMSTICK: Humpty damn Dumpty actin like thuh Holy Ghost. You got uhway. Thuh lights dimmed but you got uhway. Knew you would.

BLACK MAN WITH WATERMELON: They juiced me some.

BLACK WOMAN WITH FRIED DRUMSTICK: Just uh squirt.

BLACK MAN WITH WATERMELON: They had theirselves uh extender chord. Fry uh man in thuh town square needs uh extender tuh reach em thuh electric Hook up thuh chair tuh thuh power. Extender: 49 foot in length. Closer tuh thuh power I never been. Flip on up thuh go switch. Huh! Juice begins its course.

BLACK WOMAN WITH FRIED DRUMSTICK: Humpty damn Dumpty.

BLACK MAN WITH WATERMELON: Thuh straps they have on me are leathern. See thuh cord waggin full with uh jump-juice try me tuh wiggle from thuh waggin but belt leathern straps: width thickly. One round each forearm. Forearm mines? 2 cross thuh chest. Chest is mines: and it explodin. One for my left hand fingers left strapted too. Right was done thuh same. Jump-

juice meets me-mine juices I do uh slow soft shoe like on water. Town crier cries uh moan. Felt my nappy head go frizzly. Town follows thuh crier in uh sorta sing-uhlong-song.

BLACK WOMAN WITH FRIED DRUMSTICK: Then you got uhway. Got uhway in comed back.

BLACK MAN WITH WATERMELON: Uh extender chord 49 foot in length. Turned on thuh up switch in I started runnin. First 49 foot I was runnin they was still juicin.

BLACK WOMAN WITH FRIED DRUMSTICK: And they chase-ted you.

BLACK MAN WITH WATERMELON: — Melon mines?

BLACK WOMAN WITH FRIED DRUMSTICK: When you broked tuh seek your freedom they followed after, huh?

BLACK MAN WITH WATERMELON: Later oughta be now by now, huh?

BLACK WOMAN WITH FRIED DRUMSTICK: You comed back.

BLACK MAN WITH WATERMELON: — Not exactly.

BLACK WOMAN WITH FRIED DRUMSTICK: They comed for you tuh take you. Tooked you uhway: that they done did. You got uhway. Thuh lights dimmed. Had us uh brownout. You got past that. You comed back.

BLACK MAN WITH WATERMELON: Turned on thuh juice on me in me in I started runnin. First just runnin then runnin towards home. Couldnt find us. Think I got lost. Saw us on up uhhead but I flew over thuh yard. Couldnt stop. Think I overshot.

BLACK WOMAN WITH FRIED DRUMSTICK: Killed every hen on thuh block. Made you uh —

BLACK MAN WITH WATERMELON: Make me uh space 6 feet by 6 feet by 6. Make it big and mark it so as I wont miss it. If you would please, sweetness, uh mass grave-site. Theres company comin soonish. I would like tuh get up and go. I would like tuh move my hands.

BLACK WOMAN WITH FRIED DRUMSTICK: You comed back.

BLACK MAN WITH WATERMELON: Overshot. Overshot. I would like tuh move my hands.

BLACK WOMAN WITH FRIED DRUMSTICK: Cold compress?

BLACK MAN WITH WATERMELON: Sweetheart.

BLACK WOMAN WITH FRIED DRUMSTICK: How uhbout uh hen leg?

BLACK MAN WITH WATERMELON: Nothanks. Justate.

BLACK WOMAN WITH FRIED DRUMSTICK: Just ate?

BLACK MAN WITH WATERMELON: Justate. Thatsright. 6 by 6 by 6. Thatsright.

BLACK WOMAN WITH FRIED DRUMSTICK: Oh. — . They eat their own yuh know.

BLACK MAN WITH WATERMELON: HooDoo.

BLACK WOMAN WITH FRIED DRUMSTICK: Hen do. Saw it on thuh Tee V.

BLACK MAN WITH WATERMELON: Aint that nice.

(a bell sounds once)

PANEL II: FIRST CHORUS

BLACK MAN WITH WATERMELON: 6 by 6 by 6.

ALL: THATS RIGHT.

BLACK WOMAN WITH FRIED DRUMSTICK: Oh. They eat their own you know.

ALL: HOODOO.

BLACK WOMAN WITH FRIED DRUMSTICK: Hen do. Saw it on thuh Tee V.

ALL: Aint that nice.

AND BIGGER AND BIGGER AND BIGGER: WILL SOME-BODY TAKE THESE STRAPS OFF UH ME PLEASE? I WOULD LIKE TUH MOVE MY HANDS.

PRUNES AND PRISMS: Prunes and prisms will begin: prunes and prisms prunes and prisms prunes and prisms and prunes and prisms: 23.

VOICE ON THUH TEE V: Good evening. I'm Broad Caster. Headlining tonight: the news: is Gamble Major, the absolutely last living negro man in the whole entire known world — is dead. Major Gamble, born a slave, taught himself the rudiments of education to become a spearhead in the Civil Rights Movement. He was 38 years old. News of Major's death sparked controlled displays of jubilation in all corners of the world.

PRUNES AND PRISMS: Oh no no: world is roun.

AND BIGGER AND BIGGER AND BIGGER: WILL SOME-BODY TAKE THESE STRAPS OFF UH ME PLEASE? I WOULD LIKE TUH MOVE MY HANDS.

(*a bell sounds 4 times*)

LOTS OF GREASE AND LOTS OF PORK: This is the death of the last black man in the whole entire world.

PRUNES AND PRISMS: Not yet —

VOICE ON THUH TEE V: Good evening. Broad Caster. Head line tonight: Gamble Major, the absolutely last living negro man in the whole known entire world is dead. Gamble Major born a slave rose to become a spearhead in the Civil Rights Movement. He was 38 years old. The Civil Rights Movement. He was 38 years old.

AND BIGGER AND BIGGER AND BIGGER: WILL SOME-BODY TAKE THESE STRAPS OFF UH ME PLEASE? I WOULD LIKE TUH MOVE MY HANDS.

LOTS OF GREASE AND LOTS OF PORK: This is the death of the last black man in the whole entire world.

(*a bell sounds 3 times*)

PRUNES AND PRISMS: Prunes and prisms prunes and prisms prunes and prisms prunes and prisms.

QUEEN-THEN-PHARAOH HATSHEPSUT: Yesterday tuhday next summer tuhmorrow just uh moment uhgoh in 1317 dieded thuh last black man in thuh whole entire world. Uh! Oh. Dont be uhlarmed. Do not be afeared. It was painless. Uh painless passin. He falls 23 floors to his death.

PRUNES AND PRISMS: No.

QUEEN-THEN-PHARAOH HATSHEPSUT: 23 floors from uh passin ship from space tuh splat on thuh pavement.

PRUNES AND PRISMS: No.

QUEEN-THEN-PHARAOH HATSHEPSUT: He have uh head he been keepin under thuh Tee V. On his bottom pantry shelf.

PRUNES AND PRISMS: No.

QUEEN-THEN-PHARAOH HATSHEPSUT: He have uh head that hurts. Dont fit right. Put it on tuh go tuh thuh store in it pinched him when he walks his thoughts dont got room. Why dieded he huh?

PRUNES AND PRISMS: No.

QUEEN-THEN-PHARAOH HATSHEPSUT: Where he gonna go now that he done dieded?

PRUNES AND PRISMS: No.

BLACK WOMAN WITH FRIED DRUMSTICK: Where he gonna go tuh wash his hands?

CHORUS: You should write that down. You should write that down and you should hide it under uh rock.

VOICE ON THUH TEE V: Good evening. Broad Caster. Headlinin tonight: thuh news:

OLD MAN RIVER JORDAN: Tell you of uh news. Last news. Last news of thuh last man. Last man had last words say hearin it. He spoked uh speech spoked his-self uh chatter-tooth babble "ya-oh-may/chuh-naw" dribblin down his lips tuh puddle in his lap. Dribblin by droppletts. Drop by drop. Last news. News flashes then drops. Thuh last drop was uh all uhlone drop. Singular. Thuh last drop started it off it all. Started off with uh drop. Started off with uh jungle. Started sproutin in his spittle growin leaves off of his mines and thuh vines say drippin doin it. Last news leads tuh thuh first news. He is dead he crosses thuh river. He jumps in thuh puddle have his clothing: ON. On thuh other side thuh mountin yo he dripply wet with soppin. Do drop be dripted? I say "yes."

BLACK MAN WITH WATERMELON: Dont leave me hear. Dont leave me. Hear?

QUEEN-THEN-PHARAOH HATSHEPSUT: Where he gonna go tuh wash his dribblin hands?

PRUNES AND PRISMS: Where he gonna go tuh dry his dripplin clothes?

YES AND GREENS BLACK-EYED PEAS CORNBREAD: Did you write it down? On uh little slip uh paper stick thuh slip in thuh river afore you slip in that way you keep your clothes dry, man.

PRUNES AND PRISMS: Aintcha heard uh that trick?

BEFORE COLUMBUS: That tricks thuh method.

QUEEN-THEN-PHARAOH HATSHEPSUT: They used it on uhlong uhgoh still works every time.

OLD MAN RIVER JORDAN: He jumped in thuh water without uh word for partin come out drippley wet with soppin. Do drop be dripted? I say "do."

BLACK MAN WITH WATERMELON: In you all theres kin. You all kin. Kin gave thuh first permission kin be givin it now still. Some things is all thuh ways gonna be uh continuin sort of uh some thing. Some things go on and on till they dont stop. I am soppin wet. I

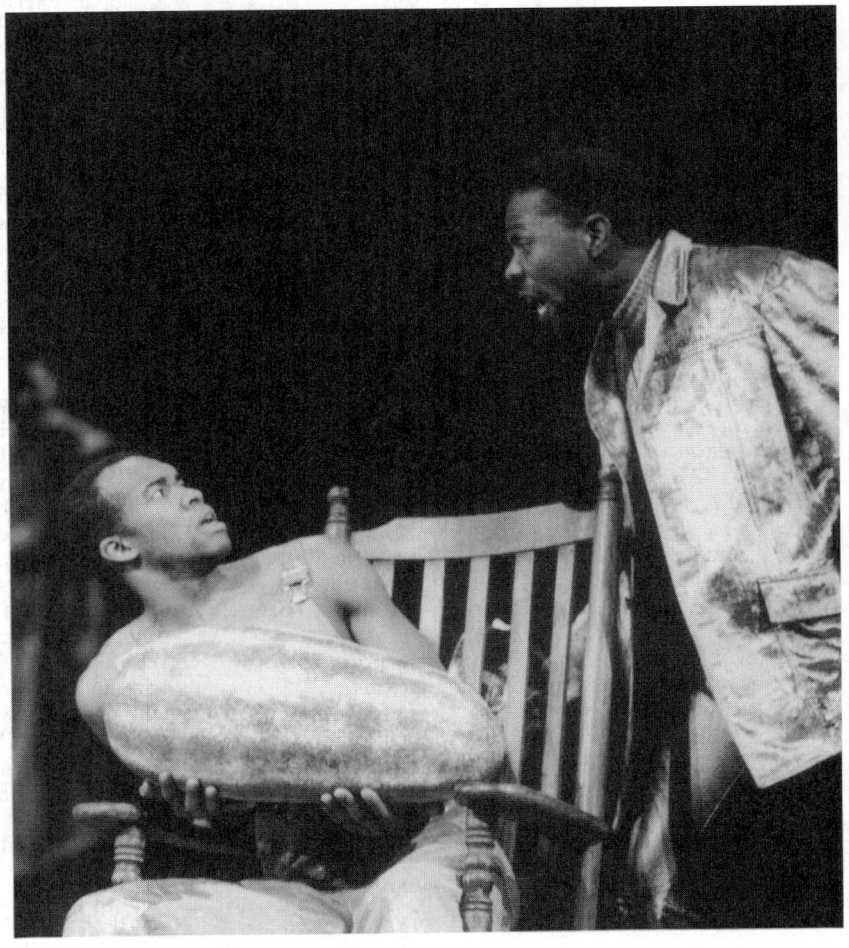

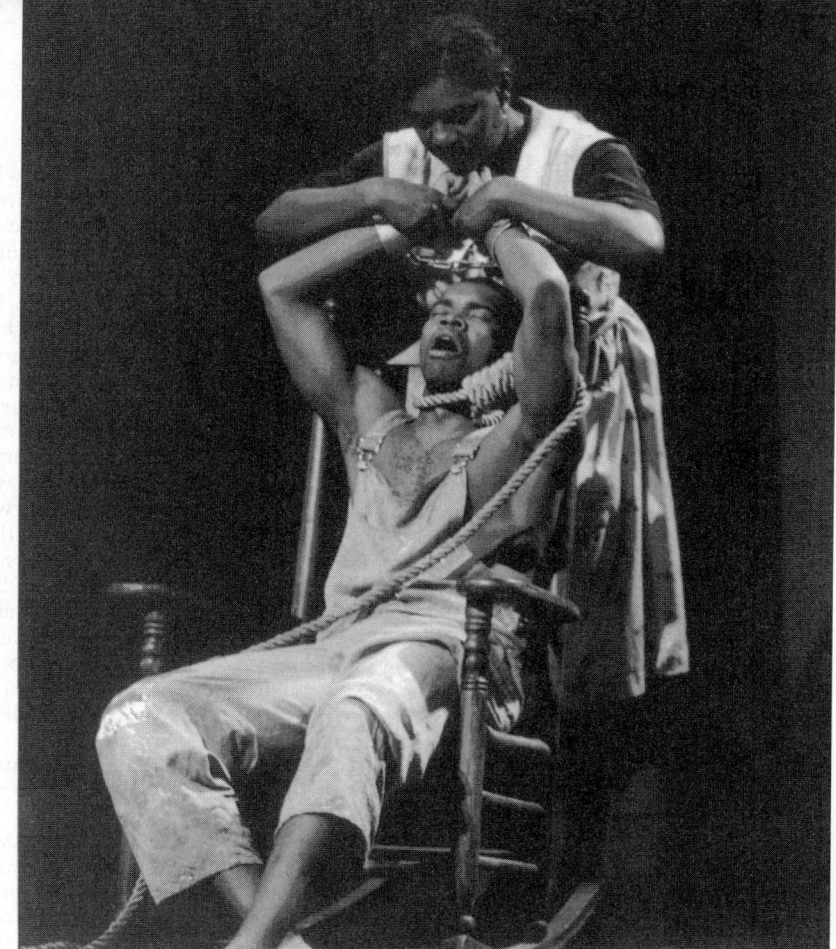

LEFT: Panel II: Prunes and Prisms (Karen A. Bishop), Black Woman with Fried Drumstick (Fanni Green), And Bigger and Bigger and Bigger (Michael Potts), Yes and Greens Black-Eyed Peas Cornbread (Melody J. Garrett), Old Man River Jordan (Ron Brice), and Black Man with Watermelon (Leon Addison Brown) in the 1992 Yale Repertory Theatre Winterfest production of *Last Black Man*. BELOW LEFT: Final Chorus: Black Man with Watermelon and And Bigger and Bigger and Bigger. RIGHT: Panel III: Black Man with Watermelon and Black Woman with Fried Drumstick.

left my scent behind in uh bundle of old clothing that was not thrown out. Left thuh scent in thuh clothin in thuh clothin on uh rooftop. Dogs surround my house and laugh. They are mockin thuh scent that I left behind. I jumped in thuh water without uh word. I jumped in thuh water without uh smell. I am in thuh river and in my skin is soppin wet. I would like tuh stay afloat now. I would like tuh move my hands.

AND BIGGER AND BIGGER AND BIGGER: Would somebody take these straps off uh me please? I would like tuh move my hands.

BLACK MAN WITH WATERMELON: Now kin kin I move my hands?

QUEEN-THEN-PHARAOH HATSHEPSUT: My black man my subject man my man uh all mens my my my no no not yes no not yes thuh hands. Let Queen-then-Pharaoh Hatshepsut tell you when. She is I am. An I am she passing by with her train. Pulling it behind her on uh plastic chain. Ooooh who! Ooooh who! Where you gonna go now, now that you done dieded?

CHORUS: Ha ha ha.

PRUNES AND PRISMS: Say "prunes and prisms" 40 times each day and you'll cure your big lips. Prunes and prisms prunes and prisms prunes and prisms: 19.

QUEEN-THEN-PHARAOH HATSHEPSUT: An I am Sheba-like she be me am passin on by she with her train. Pullin it behind / he on uh plastic chain. Ooch who! Ooch who! Come uhlong. Come uhlong.

BLACK WOMAN WITH FRIED DRUMSTICK: Say he was waitin on the right time.

AND BIGGER AND BIGGER AND BIGGER: Say he was waitin in thuh wrong line.

BLACK MAN WITH WATERMELON: I jumped in thuh river without a word. My kin are soppin wet.

QUEEN-THEN-PHARAOH HATSHEPSUT: Come uhlong. Come uhlong.

PRUNES AND PRISMS: Prunes and prisms prunes and prisms.

LOTS OF GREASE AND LOTS OF PORK: This is the death of the last black man in the whole entire world.

PRUNES AND PRISMS: Not yet.

LOTS OF GREASE AND LOTS OF PORK: Back tuh when thuh worl usta be roun.

QUEEN-THEN-PHARAOH HATSHEPSUT: Come uhlong come uhlong get on board come uhlong.

OLD MAN RIVER JORDAN: Back tuh that. Yes.

YES AND GREENS BLACK-EYED PEAS CORNBREAD: Back tuh then thuh worl usta be roun.

OLD MAN RIVER JORDAN: Uhcross thuh river in back tuh that. Yes. Do in diddly dip didded thuh drop. Out to thuh river uhlong to thuh sea. Long thuh long coast. Skirtin. Yes. Skirtin back tuh that. Come up back flip take uhway like thuh waves do. Far uhway. Uhway tuh where they dont speak thuh language and where they dont want tuh. Huh. Go on back tuh that.

YES AND GREENS BLACK-EYED PEAS CORNBREAD: Awe on uh interior before uh demarcation made it mapped. Awe on uh interior with out uh road-word called macadam. Awe onin uh interior that was uh whole was once. Awe on uh whole roun worl uh roun worl with uh river.

OLD MAN RIVER JORDAN: In thuh interior was uh river. Huh. Back tuh that.

CHORUS: The river was roun as thuh worl was. Roun.

OLD MAN RIVER JORDAN: He hacks his way through thuh tall grass. Tall grass scratch. Width: thickly. Grasses thickly comin from all angles at it. He runs along thuh path worn out by uh 9 million paddin bare footed feet. Uh path overgrown cause it aint as all as happened as of yet. Tuh be extracted from thuh jungle first he gotta go in hide.

BLACK MAN WITH WATERMELON: Chaseted me outa thuh trees now they tree me. Thuh dogs come out from their hidin spots under thuh porch and give me uhway. Thuh hidin spot was under thuh porch of uh house that werent there as of yet. Thuh dogs give me uhway by uh laugh aimed at my scent.

AND BIGGER AND BIGGER AND BIGGER: HA HA HA. Thats how thuh laugh sorta like be wentin.

PRUNES AND PRISMS: Where he gonna go now now that he done dieded?

QUEEN-THEN-PHARAOH HATSHEPSUT: Where he gonna go tuh move his hands?

BLACK MAN WITH WATERMELON: I. I. I would like tuh move my hands.

YES AND GREENS BLACK-EYED PEAS CORNBREAD: Back tuh when thuh worl usta be roun.

LOTS OF GREASE AND LOTS OF PORK: Uh roun. Thuh worl? Uh roun worl? When was this?

OLD MAN RIVER JORDAN: Columbus. Before.

PRUNES AND PRISMS: Before Columbus?

AND BIGGER AND BIGGER AND BIGGER: Ha!

QUEEN-THEN-PHARAOH HATSHEPSUT: Before Columbus thuh worl usta be roun. They put uh /d/ on thuh end of roun makin round. Thusly they set in motion thuh enduh. Without that /d/ we could uh gone on spinnin forever. Thuh /d/ thing endiduh things endiduh.

BEFORE COLUMBUS: Before Columbus.

(a bell sounds once)

BEFORE COLUMBUS: Thuh popular thinkin kin of thuh day back then in them days was that thuh worl was flat. They thought thuh worl was flat. Back then kin in them days when they thought thuh worl was flat they were afeared and stayed at home. They wanted tuh go out back then when they thought thuh worl was flat but thuh water had in it dragons.

AND BIGGER AND BIGGER AND BIGGER: Not lurkin in thuh sea but lurkin in thuh street, see? Sir name Tomus and Bigger be my christian name. Rise up out of uh made up story in grown Bigger and Bigger. Too big for my own name. Nostrils: flarin. Width: thickly. Breath: fire-laden and smellin badly.

BLACK WOMAN WITH FRIED DRUMSTICK: Huh. Whiffit.

BEFORE COLUMBUS: Dragons, of which meanin these dragons they were afeared back then. When they thought thuh worl was flat. They stayed at home. Them thinkin thuh worl was flat kept it roun. Them thinkin thuh sun revolved uhroun thuh earth kin kept them satellite-like. They figured out thuh truth and scurried out. Figurin out thuh truth kin put them in their place and they scurried out tuh put us in ours.

YES AND GREENS BLACK-EYED PEAS CORNBREAD: Mmmmm. Yes. You should write that down. You should write that down and you should hide it under uh rock.

BEFORE COLUMBUS: Thuh earthsgettin level with thuh land land HO and thuh lands gettin level with thuh sea.

PRUNES AND PRISMS: Not yet —

QUEEN-THEN-PHARAOH HATSHEPSUT: An I am Sheba she be me. Youll mutter thuh words and part thuh waves and come uhlong come uhlong.

AND BIGGER AND BIGGER AND BIGGER: I would like tuh fit in back in thuh storybook from which I camed.

BLACK MAN WITH WATERMELON: My text was writ in water. I would like tuh drink it down.

QUEEN-THEN-PHARAOH HATSHEPSUT: Down tuh float drown tuh float down. My son erased his mothers mark.

AND BIGGER AND BIGGER AND BIGGER: I am grown too big for thuh word thats me.

PRUNES AND PRISMS: Prunes and prisms prunes and prisms prunes and prisms: 14.

QUEEN-THEN-PHARAOH HATSHEPSUT: An I am Sheba me am (She be doo be wah waaaah doo wah). Come uhlong come on uhlong on.

BEFORE COLUMBUS: Before Columbus directs thuh traffic: left right left right.

PRUNES AND PRISMS: Prunes and prisms prunes and prisms.

QUEEN-THEN-PHARAOH HATSHEPSUT: I left my mark on all I made. My son erase his mothers mark.

BLACK WOMAN WITH FRIED DRUMSTICK: Where you gonna go now now that you done dieded.

AND BIGGER AND BIGGER AND BIGGER: Would somebody take these straps offuh me please? Gaw. I would like tuh drink in drown —

BEFORE COLUMBUS: There is uh tiny land mass just above my reach.

LOTS OF GREASE AND LOTS OF PORK: There is uh tiny land mass just outside of my vocabulary.

OLD MAN RIVER JORDAN: Do in dip diddly did-did thuh drop? Drop do it be dripted? Uh huh.

BEFORE COLUMBUS: Land:

AND BIGGER AND BIGGER AND BIGGER: HO!

QUEEN-THEN-PHARAOH HATSHEPSUT: I saw Columbus comin Before Columbus comin/goin over tuh meet you —

BEFORE COLUMBUS: Thuh first time I saw it. It was huge. Thuh green sea becomes uh hillside. Uh hillside populated with some peoples I will name. Thuh first time I saw it it was uh was-huge once one. Huh. It has been gettin smaller ever since.

QUEEN-THEN-PHARAOH HATSHEPSUT: Land:

BLACK MAN WITH WATERMELON: HO!

(a bell sounds once)

PANEL III: THUH LONESOME 3SOME

NOTE: * *indicates a glottal stop and choking sound)*

BLACK MAN WITH WATERMELON: It must have rained. Gaw.* Must-uh-rained-on-down-us-why. Aint that somethin. Must uh rained! Gaw. Our crops have prospered. Must uh rained why aint that somethin why aint that somethin-somethin gaw somethin: nice.

BLACK WOMAN WITH FRIED DRUMSTICK: Funny.

BLACK MAN WITH WATERMELON: Gaw. Callin on it spose we did: gaw — thuh uhrainin gaw huh? Gaw gaw. Lookie look-see gaw: where there were rivlets now there are some. Gaw. Cement tuh mudment accomplished with uh gaw uh flick of my wrist gaw. Huh. Look here now there is uh gaw uh wormlett. Came out tuhday. In my stools gaw gaw gaw gaw they all out tuhday. Come out tuh breathe gaw dontcha? Sure ya dontcha sure gaw ya dontcha sure ya dontcha do yell gaw. Gaw. Our one melon has given intuh 3. Callin what it gived birth callin it gaw. 3 August hams out uh my hands now surroundin me an is all of um mines? GAW. Uh huhn. Gaw gaw. Cant breathe.

BLACK WOMAN WITH FRIED DRUMSTICK: Funny how they break when I dropped em. Thought they was past that. Huh. 3 broke in uh row. Guess mmm on uh roll uh some sort, huh. Hell. Huh. Whiffit.

BLACK MAN WITH WATERMELON: Gaw. Gaw. Cant breathe.

BLACK WOMAN WITH FRIED DRUMSTICK: Some things still hold. Huh. Uh old rayed eggull break after droppin most likely. Huh. 4 in uh row. Awe on that.

BLACK MAN WITH WATERMELON: Gaw. Cant breathe you.

BLACK WOMAN WITH FRIED DRUMSTICK: You dont need to. No need for breathin for you no more, huh? 5. 6. Mm makin uh history. 7-hhh 8-hhh mm makin uh mess. Huh. Whiffit.

BLACK MAN WITH WATERMELON: Gaw. Gaw loosen my collar. No air in here.

BLACK WOMAN WITH FRIED DRUMSTICK: 7ssgot uh red dot. Awe on that.

BLACK MAN WITH WATERMELON: Sweetheart — . SWEETHEART?!

BLACK WOMAN WITH FRIED DRUMSTICK: 9. Chuh. Funny. Funny. Somethin still holdin on. Let me loosen your collar for you you comed home after uh hard days work. Your suit: tied. Days work was runnin from them we know aint chase-ted you. You comed back home after uh hard days work such uh hard days work that now you cant breathe, you. Now.

BLACK MAN WITH WATERMELON: Dont take it off just loosen it. Dont move thuh tree branch let thuh tree branch be.

BLACK WOMAN WITH FRIED DRUMSTICK: Your days work aint like any others day work: you bring your tree branch home. Let me loosen thuh tie let me loosen thuh neck-lace let me loosen up thuh noose that stringed him up let me leave thuh tree branch be. Let me rub your wrists.

BLACK MAN WITH WATERMELON: Gaw. Gaw.

BLACK WOMAN WITH FRIED DRUMSTICK: Some things still hold. Wrung thuh necks of them hens and they still give eggs. Huh: Like you. Still sproutin feathers even after they fried. Huh: like you too. 10. Chuh. Eggs still break. Thuh mess makes uh stain. Thuh stain makes uh mark. Whiffit. Whiffit.

BLACK MAN WITH WATERMELON: Put me on uh platform tuh wait for uh train. Uh who who uh who who uh where ya gonna go now — . Platform hitched with horses / steeds. Steeds runned off in left me there swingin. It had begun tuh rain. Hands behind my back. This time tied. I had heard of uh word called scaffold and thought that perhaps they just might build me one of um but uh uhn naw just outa my vocabulary but uh uhn new trees come cheaply.

BLACK WOMAN WITH FRIED DRUMSTICK: 8. 9. I aint hungry. 9. 10. You dont eat. Dont need to.

BLACK MAN WITH WATERMELON: Swingin from front tuh back uhgain. Back tuh — back tuh that was how I be wentin. Chin on my chest hangin down in restin eyes each on eyein my 2 feets. Left on thuh right one right one on thuh left. Crossed eyin. It was difficult tuh breathe. Toes uncrossin then crossin for luck. With my eyes. Gaw. It had begun tuh rain. Oh. Gaw. Ever so lightly. Blood came on up. you know: tough. Like riggamartins-stifly only — isolated. They some of em pointed they summoned uh laughed they some looked quick in an then they looked uhway. It had begun tuh rain. I hung on out tuh dry. They puttin uhway their picnic baskets. Ever so lightly gaw gaw it had begun tuh rain. They pullin out their umbrellas in hidedid up their eyes. Oh.

BLACK WOMAN WITH FRIED DRUMSTICK: I aint hungry you dont eat 12 13 and thuh floor will shine. Look: there we are. You in me. Reflectin. Hello! Dont move — .

BLACK MAN WITH WATERMELON: It had begun tuh rain. Now: huh. Sky flew open and thuh light went ZAP. Tree bowed over till thuh branch said BROKE. Uhround my necklace my neck uhround my neck my tree branch. In full bloom. It had begun tuh rain. Feet hit thuh ground in I started runnin. I was wet right through intuh through. I was uh wet that dont get dry. Draggin on my tree branch on back tuh home.

BLACK WOMAN WITH FRIED DRUMSTICK: On back tuh that.

BLACK MAN WITH WATERMELON: Gaw. What was that?

BLACK WOMAN WITH FRIED DRUMSTICK: "On back tuh that?" Huh. Somethin I figured. Huh. Chuh. Lord. Who! Whiffit.

BLACK MAN WITH WATERMELON: When I dieded they cut me down. Didnt have no need for me no more. They let me go.

BLACK WOMAN WITH FRIED DRUMSTICK: Thuh lights dimmed in thats what saved you. Lightnin comed down zappin trees from thuh sky. You got uhway.

BLACK MAN WITH WATERMELON: Not exactly.

BLACK WOMAN WITH FRIED DRUMSTICK: Oh. I see.

BLACK MAN WITH WATERMELON: They tired of me. Pulled me out of thuh trees then treed me then tired of me. Thats how it has gone. Thats how it be wentin.

BLACK WOMAN WITH FRIED DRUMSTICK: Oh. I see. Youve been dismissed. But-where-to? Must be somewhere else tuh go aside from just go gone. Huh. Whiffit: huh. You smell.

BLACK MAN WITH WATERMELON: Maybe I should bathe.

BLACK WOMAN WITH FRIED DRUMSTICK: I call those 3 thuh lonesome 3some. Maybe we should pray.

BLACK MAN WITH WATERMELON: Thuh lonesome 3some. Spose theyll do.

(*a bell sounds twice*)

PANEL IV: SECOND CHORUS

OLD MAN RIVER JORDAN: Come in look tuh looksee.

VOICE ON THUH TEE V: Good evening this is thuh news. A small sliver of uh tree branch has been found in *The Death of the Last Black Man*. Upon careful examination thuh small sliver of thuh treed branch what was found has been found tuh be uh fosilized bone fragment. With this finding authorities claim they are hot on his tail.

PRUNES AND PRISMS: Uh small sliver of uh treed branch growed from-tuh uh bone.

AND BIGGER AND BIGGER AND BIGGER: WILL SOMEBODY WILL THIS ROPE FROM ROUND MY NECK GOD DAMN I WOULD LIKE TUH TAKE MY BREATH BY RIGHTS GAW GAW.

LOTS OF GREASE AND LOTS OF PORK: This is the death of the last black man in the whole entire world.

(*a bell sounds slowly twice*)

BLACK MAN WITH WATERMELON: I had heard of uh word called scaffold and had hopes they just might maybe build me one by uh uh new gaw —

HAM: There was uh tree with your name on it.

BLACK MAN WITH WATERMELON: Jumpin out of uh tree they chase me tree me back tuh thuh tree. Thats where I be came from. Thats where I be wentin.

YES AND GREENS BLACK-EYED PEAS CORNBREAD: Someone ought tuh. Write that down.

LOTS OF GREASE AND LOTS OF PORK: There is a page dog eared at "Histree" hidin just outside my word hoard. Wheres he gonna come to now that he done gone from.

QUEEN-THEN-PHARAOH HATSHEPSUT: Wheres he gonna go come to now that he gonna go gone on?

OLD MAN RIVER JORDAN: For that you must ask Ham.

BLACK WOMAN WITH FRIED DRUMSTICK: Hen?

LOTS OF GREASE AND LOTS OF PORK: HAM.

QUEEN-THEN-PHARAOH HATSHEPSUT: Ham.

PRUNES AND PRISMS: Hmmmm.

(*a bell sounds twice*)

HAM: Ham's Begotten Tree (catchin up to um *in media res* that is we takin off from where we stopped up last time). Huh. NOW: She goned begotten One who in turn begotten Ours. Ours laughed one day uhloud in from thuh sound hittin thuh air smakity sprung up I, you, n He, She, It. They turned in engaged in simple multiplication thus tuh spawn of theirselves one We one You and one called They (They in certain conversation known as "Them" and in other certain conversation a.k.a. "Us"). Now very simply: Wassername she finally gave intuh It and tugether they broughted forth uh wildish one called simply Yo. Yo gone be wentin much too long without hisself uh comb in from thuh frizzly that resulted comed one called You (polite form). You (polite) birthed herself Mister, Miss Maam and Sir who in his later years with That brought forth Yuh Fathuh. Thuh fact that That was uh mother tuh Yuh Fathuh didnt stop them 2 relations from havin relations. Those strange relations between That thuh mother and Yuh Fathuh thuh son brought forth uh odd lot: called: Yes Massuh, Yes Missy, Yes Maam n Yes Suh Mistuh Suh which goes tuh show that relations with your relations produces complications. Thuh children of That and Yuh Fathuh aside from being plain peculiar was all cross-eyed. This defect enhanced their multiplicative possibilities, for example. Yes Suh Mistuh Suh breeded with hisself n gived us Wassername (thuh 2nd), and Wassernickname (2 twins in birth joindid at thuh lip). Thuh 2 twins lived next door tuh one called Uhnother bringin forth Themuhns, She (thuh 2nd) Auntie, Cousin, and Bro who makeshifted continuous compensations for his loud and odiforous bodily emissions by all thuh time saying excuse me n through his graciousness brought forth They (polite) who had mixed feelins with She (thuh 2nd) thus bringin forth Ussin who then went on tuh have MeMines.

YES AND GREENS BLACK-EYED PEAS CORNBREAD: Thuh list goes on in on.

HAM: MeMines gived out 2 offspring one she called Mines after herself thuh uther she called Them-uhns named after all them who comed before. Themuhns married outside thuh tribe joinin herself with uh man they called WhoDat. Themuhns n WhoDat brough forth only one child called WhoDatDere. Mines joined up with Wasshisname and from that union come AllYall.

BEFORE COLUMBUS: All us?

HAM: No. AllYall.

LOTS OF GREASE AND LOTS OF PORK: This list goes on in on.

HAM: Ah yes: Yo suddenly if by majic again became productive in after uh lapse of some great time came back intuh circulation to wiggled uhbout with Yes Missy (one of thuh cross-eyed daughters of That and Yuh Fathuh). Yo in Yes Missy begottin ThissunRightHere, Us, ThatOne, She (thuh 3rd) and one called Uncle (who from birth was gifted with great singin and dancin capabilities which helped him make his way in life but tended tuh bring shame on his family).

BEFORE COLUMBUS/BLACK MAN WITH WATERMELON: Shame on his family.

LOTS OF GREASE/BLACK MAN WITH WATERMELON: Shame on his family.

AND BIGGER AND BIGGER/BLACK MAN WITH WATERMELON: Shamed on his family gaw.

YES AND GREENS BLACK-EYED PEAS CORNBREAD: Write that down.

OLD MAN RIVER JORDAN: (Ham seed his daddy Noah neckked. From that seed, comed AllYall.)

(*a bell sounds twice*)

AND BIGGER AND BIGGER AND BIGGER: (Will somebody please will this rope —)

VOICE ON THUH TEE V: Good evening. This is thuh news: Whose fault is it?

BLACK MAN WITH WATERMELON: Saint mines.

VOICE ON THUH TEE V: Whose fault iszit??!

CHORUS: Saint mines!

OLD MAN RIVER JORDAN: I cant re-member back that far. (Ham can — but uh uh new gaw — Ham wuduhnt there, huh.)

CHORUS: HAM BONE HAM BONE WHERE YOU BEEN ROUN THUH WORL N BACK A-GAIN.

QUEEN-THEN-PHARAOH HATSHEPSUT: Whatcha seen. Hambone girl?

BLACK WOMAN WITH FRIED DRUMSTICK: Didnt see you. I saw thuh worl.

HAM: I was there.

PRUNES AND PRISMS: Didnt see you.

HAM: I WAS THERE.

VOICE ON THUH TEE V: Didnt see you.

BLACK MAN WITH WATERMELON / AND BIGGER: THUH BLACK MAN. HE MOOOVE.

CHORUS: HAM BONE HAM BONE WHATCHA DO? GOT UH CHANCE N FAIRLY FLEW.

BLACK WOMAN WITH FRIED DRUMSTICK: Over thuh front yard.

BLACK MAN WITH WATERMELON: Overshot.

CHORUS: 6 BY 6 BY 6.

BLACK MAN WITH WATERMELON: Thats right.

AND BIGGER AND BIGGER AND BIGGER: WILL SOMEBODY WILL THIS ROPE —

CHORUS: Good evening. This is the news.

VOICE ON THUH TEE V: Whose fault is it?

ALL: Saint mines!

VOICE ON THUH TEE V: Whose fault iszit?

HAM: SAINT MINES!

(*a bell rings twice*)

    — . Ham. Is. Not. Tuh. BLAME! WhoDatDere joinded with one called Sir 9th generation of thuh first Sir son of You (polite) thuh first daughter of You WhoDatDere with thuh 9th Sir begettin forth him —

BLACK MAN WITH WATERMELON: Ham?!

ALL (*except Ham*): HIM!

BLACK WOMAN WITH FRIED DRUMSTICK: sold.

HAM: SOLD! allyall[9] not tuh be confused w/allus[12] joinded w/allthem[3] in from that union comed forth wasshisname[21] SOLD wassername[19] still by thuh reputation uh thistree one uh thuh 2 twins loses her sight through fiddlin n falls w/ugly old yuhfathuh[4] given she[8] SOLD whodat[33] pairs w/you[23] (still polite) of which nothinmuch comes nothinmuch now nothinmuch[6] pairs with yessuhmistuhsuh[17] tuh drop one called yo now yo[9-0] still who gone be wentin now w/elle gived us el SOLD let us not forget ye[1-2-5] w/thee[3] givin us thou[9-2] who w/thuh they who switches their designation in certain conversation yes they[10] broughted forth onemore[2] at thuh same time in thuh same row right next door we have datone[12] w/ disone[14] droppin off duhutherone[2-2] SOLD let us not forget du and sie let us not forget yesssuhmassuhsuh[38] w/thou[8] who gived up memines[3-0] SOLD we are now rollin through thuh long division gimmie uh gimmie uh gimmie uh squared off route round it off round it off n round it out w/sistuh[4-3] who lives with one called saintmines[9] givin forth one uh year how it got there callin it jessgrew callin it saintmines callin it whatdat whatdat whatdat SOLD.

BLACK MAN WITH WATERMELON: Thuh list goes on and on. Dont it.

CHORUS: Ham Bone Ham Bone Ham Bone Ham Bone

BEFORE COLUMBUS: Left right left right.

QUEEN-THEN-PHARAOH HATSHEPSUT: Left left left whose left . . . ?

(*a bell sounds twice*)

LOTS OF GREASE AND LOTS OF PORK: This is the death of the last black man in the whole entire world.

---

[9]: The numbers in Ham's speech are chanted by several actors together as if they were auction prices or verses of the Bible.

PANEL V: IN THUH GARDEN OF HOODOO IT

BLACK WOMAN WITH FRIED DRUMSTICK: Somethins turnin. Huh. Whatizit. — Mercy. Mercy. Huh. Chew on this. Ssuh feather. Sswhatchashud be eatin now ya no. Ssuhfeather: stuffin. Chew on it. Huh. Feathers sprouted from thuh fried hens — dont ask me how. Somethins out uh whack. Somethins out uh rights. Your arms still on your elbows. I'm still here. Whensit gonna end. Soon. Huh. Mercy. Thuh Tree. Springtime. And harvest. Huh. Somethins turnin. So many melons. Huh. From one tuh 3 tuh many. Must be nature. Gnaw on this. Gnaw on this, huh? Gnaw on this awe on that.

BLACK MAN WITH WATERMELON: Aint eatable.

BLACK WOMAN WITH FRIED DRUMSTICK: I know.

BLACK MAN WITH WATERMELON: Aint eatable aint it. Nope. Nope.

BLACK WOMAN WITH FRIED DRUMSTICK: Somethins turnin. Huh. Whatizit.

BLACK MAN WITH WATERMELON: Aint eatable so I out in out ought not aint be eatin it aint that right. Yep. Nope. Yep. Uh huhn.

BLACK WOMAN WITH FRIED DRUMSTICK: Huh. Whatizit.

BLACK MAN WITH WATERMELON: I remember what I like. I remember what my likes tuh eat when I be in thuh eatin mode.

BLACK WOMAN WITH FRIED DRUMSTICK: Chew on this.

BLACK MAN WITH WATERMELON: When I be in thuh eatin mode.

BLACK WOMAN WITH FRIED DRUMSTICK: Swallow it down. I know. Gimmie your pit. Needs bathin.

BLACK MAN WITH WATERMELON: Choice between peas

and corns — my feets — . Choice: peas. Choice between peas and greens choice: greens. Choice between greens and potatoes choice: potatoes. Yams. Boiled or mashed choice: mashed. Aaah. Mmm. My likenesses.

BLACK WOMAN WITH FRIED DRUMSTICK: Mercy. Turns —

BLACK MAN WITH WATERMELON: My likenesses! My feets! Aaah! SWEET-HEART. Aaah! SPRINGTIME!

BLACK WOMAN WITH FRIED DRUMSTICK: Spring-time.

BLACK MAN WITH WATERMELON: SPRING-TIME!

BLACK WOMAN WITH FRIED DRUMSTICK: Mercy. Turns —

BLACK MAN WITH WATERMELON: I remembers what I likes. I remembers what I likes tuh eat when I bein in had been in thuh eatin mode. Bein in had been: now in then. I be eatin hen. Hen.

BLACK WOMAN WITH FRIED DRUMSTICK: Huh?

BLACK MAN WITH WATERMELON: HEN!

BLACK WOMAN WITH FRIED DRUMSTICK: Hen?

BLACK MAN WITH WATERMELON: Hen. Huh. My meals. Aaaah: my meals. *BRACH*-A-LEE.

BLACK WOMAN WITH FRIED DRUMSTICK: Whatizit. Huh. — GNAW ON THIS! Good. Uhther pit?

BLACK MAN WITH WATERMELON: We sittin on this porch right now aint we. Uh huhn. Aaah. Yes. Sittin right here right now on it in it ainthuh first time either iduhnt it. Yep. Nope. Once we was here once wuhduhnt we. Yep. Yep. Once we being here. Uh huhn. Huh. There is uh Now and there is uh Then. Ssall there is. (I bein in uh Now: uh Now bein in uh Then; I bein, in Now in Then, in I will be. I was be too but that uh Then thats past. That me that was be is uh me-has-been. Thuh Then that was be is uh has-been-Then too. Thuh me-has-been sits in thuh be-me: we sit on this porch. Same porch. Same me. Thuh Then that been somehow sits in thuh Then that will be: same Thens. I swing from uh tree. You cut me down and bring me back. Home. Here. I fly over thuh yard. I fly over thuh yard in all over. Them thens stays

fixed. Fixed Thens. Thuh Thems stays fixed too. Thuh Thems that come and take me and thuh Thems that greet me and then them Thems that send me back here. Home. Stays fixed. Them do.)

BLACK WOMAN WITH FRIED DRUMSTICK: Your feets.

BLACK MAN WITH WATERMELON: I: be. You: is. It: be. He, She: thats us. (Thats it.) We: thats he in she: you aroun me: us be here. You: still is. They: be. Melon. Melon. Melon: mines. I remember all my lookuh-likes. You. You. Remember me.

BLACK WOMAN WITH FRIED DRUMSTICK: Gnaw on this then swallow it down. Youll have your fill then we'll put you in your suit coat.

BLACK MAN WITH WATERMELON: Thuh suit coat I picked out? Thuh stripely one? HA! Peas. Choice: *BRACH*-A-LEE.

BLACK WOMAN WITH FRIED DRUMSTICK: Chew and swallow please.

BLACK MAN WITH WATERMELON: Thuh stripely one with thuh fancy patch pockets!

BLACK WOMAN WITH FRIED DRUMSTICK: Sweetheart.

BLACK MAN WITH WATERMELON: SPRING-TIME.

BLACK WOMAN WITH FRIED DRUMSTICK: Sweetheart.

BLACK MAN WITH WATERMELON: SPRING-TIME.

BLACK WOMAN WITH FRIED DRUMSTICK: This could go on forever.

BLACK MAN WITH WATERMELON: Lets. Hope. Not.

BLACK WOMAN WITH FRIED DRUMSTICK: — Sweetheart.

BLACK MAN WITH WATERMELON: SPRING-TIME.

BLACK WOMAN WITH FRIED DRUMSTICK: Sweetheart.

BLACK MAN WITH WATERMELON: SPRING-TIME.

BLACK WOMAN WITH FRIED DRUMSTICK: This could go on forever.

BLACK MAN WITH WATERMELON: Lets. Hope. Not.

BLACK WOMAN WITH FRIED DRUMSTICK: Must be somewhere else tuh go aside from just go gone.

BLACK MAN WITH WATERMELON: 6 by 6 by 6.

BLACK WOMAN WITH FRIED DRUMSTICK: Thats right.

BLACK MAN WITH WATERMELON: Rock reads "Hoo-Doo."

BLACK WOMAN WITH FRIED DRUMSTICK: Now you know. Know now dontcha. Somethins turnin — .

BLACK MAN WITH WATERMELON: Who do? Them do. Aint that nice. Huh. Miss me. Remember me. Miss-memissmewhatsmyname.

BLACK WOMAN WITH FRIED DRUMSTICK: Aaaaaah?

BLACK MAN WITH WATERMELON: Remember me. AAAH.

BLACK WOMAN WITH FRIED DRUMSTICK: Thats it. Open wide. Here it comes. Stuffin.

BLACK MAN WITH WATERMELON: Yeeeech.

BLACK WOMAN WITH FRIED DRUMSTICK: Eat uhnother. Hear. I eat one. You eat one more.

BLACK MAN WITH WATERMELON: Stuffed. Time tuh go.

BLACK WOMAN WITH FRIED DRUMSTICK: Not yet!

BLACK MAN WITH WATERMELON: I got uhway?

BLACK WOMAN WITH FRIED DRUMSTICK: Huh?

BLACK MAN WITH WATERMELON: I got uhway?

BLACK WOMAN WITH FRIED DRUMSTICK: Nope. Yep. Nope. Nope.

BLACK MAN WITH WATERMELON: Miss me.

BLACK WOMAN WITH FRIED DRUMSTICK: Miss me.

BLACK MAN WITH WATERMELON: Re-member me.

BLACK WOMAN WITH FRIED DRUMSTICK: Re-member me.

BLACK MAN WITH WATERMELON: My hands are on my wrists. Arms on elbows. Looks: old fashioned. Nothin fancy there. Toes curl up not down. My feets-now clean. Still got all my teeth. Re-member me.

BLACK WOMAN WITH FRIED DRUMSTICK: Re-member me.

BLACK MAN WITH WATERMELON: Call on me sometime.

BLACK WOMAN WITH FRIED DRUMSTICK: Call on me sometime. Hear? Hear? Thuh dirt itself turns itself. So many melons. From one tuh 3 tuh many. Look at um all. Ssuh garden. Awe on that. Winter processin back tuh back with spring-time. They roll on by us that way. Uh whole line gone roun. Chuh. Thuh worl he roun. Moves that way so they say. You comed back. Yep. Nope. Well. Well. Build uh well.

(*a bell sounds twice*)

FINAL CHORUS

ALL: "YES. OH, ME? CHUM, NO —"

VOICE ON THUH TEE V: Good morning. This is thuh news:

BLACK WOMAN WITH FRIED DRUMSTICK: Somethins turnin. Thuh page.

(*a bell sounds twice*)

LOTS OF GREASE AND LOTS OF PORK: This is the death of the last black man in the whole entire worl

PRUNES AND PRISMS: 19.

OLD MAN RIVER JORDAN: Uh blank page turnin with thuh sound of it. Thuh sound of movie hands.

BLACK WOMAN WITH FRIED DRUMSTICK: Yesterday today next summer tomorrow just uh moment uhgoh in 1317 dieded thuh last black man in thuh whole entire world. Uh! Oh. Dont be uhlarmed. Do not he afeared. It was painless. Uh painless passin. He falls twenty-three floors to his death.

CHORUS: yes.

BLACK WOMAN WITH FRIED DRUMSTICK: 23 floors from uh passin ship from space tuh splat on thuh pavement.

CHORUS: yes.

BLACK WOMAN WITH FRIED DRUMSTICK: He have uh head he been keepin under thuh Tee V.

CHORUS: yes.

BLACK WOMAN WITH FRIED DRUMSTICK: On his bottom pantry shelf.

CHORUS: yes.

BLACK WOMAN WITH FRIED DRUMSTICK: He have uh head that hurts. Dont fit right. Put it on tuh go tuh thuh store in it pinched him when he walks his thoughts dont got room. He diediduh he did, huh.

CHORUS: yes.

BLACK WOMAN WITH FRIED DRUMSTICK: Where he gonna go now now now now now that he done diediduh?

CHORUS: yes.

BLACK WOMAN WITH FRIED DRUMSTICK: Where he gonna go tuh. WASH.

PRUNES AND PRISMS: Somethins turnin. Thuh page.

AND BIGGER AND BIGGER AND BIGGER: Somethins burnin. Thuh tongue.

BLACK MAN WITH WATERMELON: Thuh tongue itself burns.

OLD MAN RIVER JORDAN: He jumps in thuh river. These words for partin.

YES AND GREENS BLACK-EYED PEAS CORNBREAD: And you will write them down.

(*a bell sounds 3 times*)

BEFORE COLUMBUS: All these boats passed by my coast.

PRUNES AND PRISMS: Somethins turnin. Thuh page.

QUEEN-THEN-PHARAOH HATSHEPSUT: I saw Columbus comin / I saw Columbus comin goin —

QUEEN-THEN-PHARAOH HATSHEPSUT/BEFORE COLUMBUS: Left left left whose left . . . ?

AND BIGGER AND BIGGER/BLACK MAN WITH WATERMELON: Somethins burnin. Thuh page.

BEFORE COLUMBUS: All those boats passed by me. My coast fell in-to-the-sea. All thuh boats. They stopped for me.

OLD MAN RIVER JORDAN: Land: HO!

QUEEN-THEN-PHARAOH HATSHEPSUT: I waved my hands in warnin. You waved back.

BLACK WOMAN WITH FRIED DRUMSTICK: Somethins burnin. Thuh page.

QUEEN-THEN-PHARAOH HATSHEPSUT: I have-not seen you since.

ALL: oh!

LOTS OF GREASE AND LOTS OF PORK: This is the death of the last black man in the whole entire worl

OLD MAN RIVER JORDAN: Do in diddley dip die-die thuh drop. Do drop he dripted? Why, of course.

AND BIGGER AND BIGGER AND BIGGER: Somethins burnin. Thuh tongue.

BLACK MAN WITH WATERMELON: The tongue itself hums itself.

HAM: . . . And from that seed comed All Us.

BLACK WOMAN WITH FRIED DRUMSTICK: Thuh page.

ALL: 6 BY 6 BY 6.

BLACK WOMAN WITH FRIED DRUMSTICK: Thats right.

(*a bell sounds twice*)

BEFORE COLUMBUS: LAND: HO!

YES AND GREENS BLACK-EYED PEAS CORNBREAD: You will write it down because if you dont write it down then we will come along and tell the future that we did not exist. You will write it down and you will carve it out of a rock.

(*pause*)

You will write down thuh past and you will write down thuh present and in what in thuh future. You will write it down.

(*pause*)

It will be of us but you will mention them from time to time so that in the future when they come along theyll know how they exist.

(*pause*)

It will be for us but you will mention them from time to time so that in the future when they come along theyll know why they exist.

(*pause*)

You will carve it all out of a rock so that in the future when they come along we will know that the rock did yes exist.

BLACK WOMAN WITH FRIED DRUMSTICK: Down down down down down down down down —

LOTS OF GREASE AND LOTS OF PORK: This is the death of the last black man in the whole entire worl

PRUNES AND PRISMS: Somethins turnin. Thuh page.

OLD MAN RIVER JORDAN: Thuh last news of thuh last man:

VOICE ON THUH TEE V: Good mornin. This is thuh last news:

BLACK MAN WITH WATERMELON: Miss me.

BLACK WOMAN WITH FRIED DRUMSTICK: Miss me.

BLACK MAN WITH WATERMELON: Re-member me.

BLACK WOMAN WITH FRIED DRUMSTICK: Re-member me. Call on me sometime. Call on me sometime. Hear? Hear?

HAM: In thuh future when they came along I meeting them. On thuh coast. Uuuuhh! My coast! I — was — so — po-lite! But. In thuh rock. I wrote: ha ha ha.

ALL: Ha. Ha. Ha. Ha. Ha. Ha. Ha. Ha. Ha. Ha. Ha. Ha. Ha. Ha. HHHHHHHHHHHH. HA!

BLACK WOMAN WITH FRIED DRUMSTICK: Thuh black man he move. He move. He hans.

(*a bell sounds once*)

ALL: Hold it. Hold it. Hold it. Hold it. Hold it. Hold it. Hold it.

COMMENTARIES

The following interviews with Suzan-Lori Parks and Liz Diamond resulted from a meeting following the Yale production of *The Last Black Man* in February 1992. After discussing the play in production, I asked the author and director to respond to a number of questions that would give them a chance to explore issues of interest to those who would read the play but probably not see it in production. I gave them the questions to consider at home, and they returned their responses. Both interviews give us insight into the issues of space and time and of theme and style in this play and into the opportunities available to playwright and director when approaching a fresh script in a style that is innovative and exciting.

Lee A. Jacobus (b. 1935)
INTERVIEW WITH SUZAN-LORI PARKS   1992

Jacobus: Your play takes a long view of history and in a way has a profound narrative scope. But the play also avoids the beginning-middle-end approach to storytelling. How would you describe your approach to narrative structure — particularly in relation to time — in *The Death of the Last Black Man in the Whole Entire World?*

Parks: I start with "knowns" and I get to thinking — not merely sitting at my desk and scratching my head — but I get to listening, I get to watching, hearing, seeing. If time is more curved than flat, then a plot line of a play can be more curved. Then we can refigure "plot." Things may happen over and over again with slight changes. Words may come back to us again and again. Jazz musicians have been doing this for years. They call it "repetition and revision."

Jacobus: You describe the sections of your play as "Panels" and "Choruses." What do these terms mean to you and what should they mean to your audience?

Parks: "Panels" and "Choruses" are two different words that I use to denote two different kinds of experience or attack. In a Panel there are only the two of them, the Black Man with Watermelon and the Black Woman with Fried Drumstick; during the Panels we see them at various points of confusion — which are the same points of confusion over and over again refigured with different variables. The idea of this comes partly from the Stations of the Cross — the tableaux of Christ which hang in churches. The Choruses are the spaces between those tableaux — if you've seen those Stations hanging in a church you know that between them hangs — nothing. A blank space. So the Choruses are figuring the blank space between. That's why the Choruses are so weird. They're coming out of that blank, unspoken, unfigured space and all eleven figures are onstage.

There are Greek choruses. There are choruses in pop songs. Unlike the choruses in most songs, however, my Choruses work differently. Think of a well-known song — "America the Beautiful" for example. The verses contain the information or meat, the choruses the fun, the fat, the gravy. The power of the chorus comes not from the presentation of new information but from its repeating. In *Last Black Man* this is what I'm exploring with certain speeches such as the "Yesterday today next summer tomorrow . . ." speech or the "You should write that down . . ." line. In terms of the Panels and Choruses, where you'd expect the Chorus to simply repeat, Liz [Diamond, the director] discovered early in rehearsal that it is in the Panels where actions are repeated (the Black Man comes back; he is dead; the Black Woman must manage; she is alive), and the Choruses were where the really new information is presented, where the action really happens. With *Last Black Man* I'm using elements of traditional song structure and inverting, subverting, converting those elements.

Jacobus: Your figures have some interesting names, such as Lots of Grease and Lots of Pork. Could you tell us how you visualized some of them onstage?

Parks: I saw them as human — I didn't imagine that Lots of Grease and Lots of Pork would go through the play dressed up as a pork chop — that *would* be avant-garde, wouldn't it? The most important thing about the figures is that they are *figures* and not *characters*. They are *signs* of something and not people just like people we know. *Figures* help to cue the shape of the play. This is epic theater. This is a play where one stands for a thousand. Epic is a state of existence which, I think, comes very naturally out of the day-to-day African American existence — we're a people who are often honored or damned because of the actions of one of our group. One of us stands for all of us. Those are epic stakes.

Also important is where these figures come from: Prunes and Prisms comes from a line in Joyce's *Ulysses*; And Bigger and Bigger and Bigger spins out of Wright's *Native Son*; Ham is the biblical Ham; Queen-then-Pharaoh Hatshepsut really was once.

So. The figures aren't real people but they're voices briefly embodied — embodied for the duration of the play. Part of Liz's preset [the stage setting before the play begins] was an audio track of the figures whispering their names. Those whispers helped create the feeling of *Last Black Man* as a visitation.

Jacobus: You've got a new play in production and you have been very productive in the last several years. What are the sources of your inspiration as a playwright? What directions do you feel yourself heading in?

Parks: What inspires? *Inspirare:* to breathe. What keeps me breathing? What keeps me going? I have good friends. Good friends who read my work and encourage me. Working with Liz Diamond is always a joy — we've done five shows together now and we both keep getting better. What else? I listen to music: Ornette Coleman, Sarah Vaughan, Bach, Wagner, Dionne Warwick. I do karate. Read read read all the time. I work hard. I play with words. Spelling casts a spell. I think the world is telling us. Telling us telling us something that is present but not written down. As a child I wanted to be a geologist. Writing is like digging. So in this play they write it down and they lower him down. Into the ground. I have often thought that I could read the shape of my whole life through this play. So where am I heading? Well. I've done about ten plays now. I finished writing this play in 1990. I've written three more since then. None of the new plays are like this one. So much for predictable trajectory. In all of my work I'm concerned with space and time and the phenomenon of moving through them. Hopefully I'll write more. Hopefully stay sharp. *Awake.* Looking at this play — it's such an extravaganza, such a pageant — you'd figure the writer's next work would be maybe an opera. Yep. She would either write an opera or move to Las Vegas.

Lee A. Jacobus (b. 1935)
INTERVIEW WITH LIZ DIAMOND   *1992*

Jacobus: Some people have commented on the fact that Suzan-Lori Parks provided no stage directions for *The Last Black Man in the Whole Entire World*. What were the problems — and the opportunities — that resulted from her decision?

Diamond: It is somewhat misleading to say that Suzan-Lori wrote no stage directions. In a conventional sense it is true that the director will not find acres of parenthetical notes describing the stage setting and stage action as envisioned by the playwright. Nevertheless, a close reading of the text reveals that Suzan-Lori has some very specific ideas about how the dramatic action of the text should be played. "In thuh Garden of HooDoo It," Panel V of the play, begins with a speech by Black Woman with Fried Drumstick, who observes:

> Somethins turnin. Huh. Whatizit. — Mercy. Mercy. Huh. Chew on this. Ssuh feather. Sswhatchashud be eatin now ya no. Ssuhfeather stuffin. Chew on it. Huh. Feathers sprouted from thuh fried hens — dont ask me how. Somethins out uh whack. Somethins out uh rights. Your arms still on your elbows. I'm still here. Whensit gonna end. Soon. Huh. Mercy. Thuh Tree. Springtime. And harvest. Huh. Somethins turnin. So many melons. Huh. From one tuh 3 tuh many. Must be nature. Gnaw on this. Gnaw on this, huh? Gnaw on this awe on that.

At the top of the speech Black Woman senses that something is different . . . the atmosphere, the emotional temperature of the play has changed. She senses it has something to do with mercy. Has it been bestowed? Does she sense a new atmosphere of forgiveness is in the air? She gives up trying to articulate what she senses for the moment with a "huh." And then moves on to the task at hand, which is, quite simply, to feed her beloved Black Man feathers which have mysteriously appeared. She must stuff him. Now, a director may or may not feel obliged to follow the stage direction that, I would argue, is quite explicitly embedded in the text. Nevertheless, it is there, and, I think, well worth exploring in rehearsal. In our production at the Yale Repertory Theatre, we did in fact have the Black Woman gently feed the Black Man feathers, then bathe him, in preparation for his final burial. These simple activities, in the context of the larger dramatic action of the text — to tell the Black Man's story and then to lay him to rest — achieved a metaphorical resonance that reinforced the text itself.

There is no doubt that I enjoyed and exercised a great deal of creative control over the visual and aural landscape of *The Death of the Last Black Man* by virtue of the fact that Suzan-Lori chose not to dictate details of set, costume, lighting, and sound. But the major design decisions I made — for example, to set the play in a highly ceremonial, ecclesiastical setting, a sort of surreal cathedral/burial ground, with a treelike pulpit and a huge black sarcophagus at the center that served as both coffin and altar, scaffold and auction block — all grew out of my reading of the play. I saw *Last Black Man* as a highly ritualized and presentational mourning and celebration of the death of the last black man in the whole entire world. Another director may well come along whose reading makes entirely different visual demands.

I do not believe that one reading is as good as another; a director's reading of the play not only must be internally coherent but must serve to open up the text to the spectator's understanding. The importance — or possibility — of honoring authorial intention in a stage production is a thorny issue better left to the critics. But a close reading of the text, a passionate hunt for every visual, aural clue the text has to offer — from its layout on the page, to punctuation (or lack of it), to scene titles, to spelling, to character names — all of this must be sharply observed for clues as to rhythm, tempo, and potential meaning.

Jacobus: One of your jobs as director was to help audiences see that the figures who appeared onstage to the Black Man and Black Woman were spirits. How did you solve the problem?

Diamond: Of course, one might first ask: Are those "figures," as they are called in the text, spirits? It doesn't explicitly state anywhere that Queen-then-Pharaoh Hatshepsut, Ham, etc. are any less real than the Black Man or Black Woman. But an offhand remark made by Suzan-Lori during one of our script conferences —"By the way, you could say that the only living human being onstage is the Black Woman. Everyone else is dead, some more than others, but dead"— suggested that something might be called for to help the audience discover that there is indeed a hierarchy of the dead in this play, moving in descending order from the biblical Ham, who "died" thousands of years ago, to the Voice on thuh Tee V, who perhaps died yesterday. But visually insisting on ghosts can get a bit silly in a play as stylistically unbound by the conventions of naturalism as is *The Death of the Last Black Man in the Whole Entire World*. So we decided (the costume designer, Caryn Neman, and myself) on "celestial" versions of each figure's own earthly dress. We put them all in what we called high church drag — the gold and glitter of the ultimate high mass, but kept each figure's costume pieces specific to the historic period or social role implied by their title. Thus Yes and Greens Black-Eyed Peas Cornbread wore the rags and pigtails of the pickaninny to be found in the racist cartoons and caricatures of the slave period but glowed with the gold and the glitter of the Promised Land. In contrast, the Black Woman wore a quite conventional black dress, the sort of garment any widow might wear to her husband's funeral.

Jacobus: Could you talk about your collaboration with Suzan-Lori in directing this play? Is it more or less difficult for the director when the playwright is in rehearsal?

Diamond: One of the many reasons Suzan-Lori and I love collaborating on a production is that we don't mess around in each other's business. She writes the play; I direct it. At the same time, we talk constantly. Before rehearsals begin, we read the play aloud together, with Suzan-Lori pointing out specific rhythmic requirements as they come up. She helps me decode the many and rich historic and fictional references woven into the text. She suggests books to read, artworks to examine, music to listen to. I try to avoid asking what a passage means, because I prefer to make those discoveries myself. I share with her my initial impressions, early hints as to where it all might take place, and obsessions begin to emerge as I read the play over and over. I listen carefully to her responses and to her elaborations on ideas I propose for setting, sound, action, etc. We cast the play together and I keep her abreast of the evolving design decisions. She attends the first read-through of the play. And then she does an amazing thing: She leaves us alone until the first run-through, which may be two or three weeks later. I consider the space she gives me and the actors — to make our own discoveries — an incredible gift, a little scary, and very smart. She understands our need to ask whatever comes into our heads, to try out all kinds of crazy solutions, and that it will be easier on everyone if the playwright is absent. By the time she comes back, of course, there is something reasonably coherent for her to respond to. She and I are likely to be in close touch by phone throughout the process, with me proposing textual changes as they come up in rehearsal, and with Suzan-Lori helping me untangle whatever staging knots I may be struggling with. It should be clear that what I am describing is an ongoing dialogue, one that thrives, I think, because we trust each other's judgment and taste, because we have so much fun tossing ideas back and forth and because we both get such a huge kick out of sitting in the back of the theater watching this *thing* we've created actually come to life.

Having a playwright come to rehearsal, in particular to that first run-through, is, of course, a terrifying moment for everyone. The writer is wondering: Will this play hold up? The director is wondering: Will this staging hold up? The actor is wondering: Am I about to be fired? But this atmosphere of near total paranoia is broken with the uttering of the first line of text, as private anxieties give way to this immense, collective rooting for the play to fly. The joy of working with Suzan-Lori is that when it's over, we collectively celebrate what works and collectively get to work on what doesn't. It is usually abundantly clear where the problems are, if not how to solve them, and very little ego gets in the way of just diving in and fixing them.

Alisa Solomon (b. 1956)
LANGUAGE IN *LAST BLACK MAN*   1990

> *Alisa Solomon focuses on Suzan-Lori Parks's use of language, particularly repetition, and on influences from jazz, which also depends on choruses, verses, and refrains of the kind Parks has written. The connection between American jazz and African ritual is one of Parks's most important inspirations.*

Parks's plays look like long, dialogic poems. There are no stage directions and little in the way of moorings for the unsuspecting director. But, Parks insists, movement is contained in the speech itself. Often leaving out punctuation that would delineate formal pauses, she lets words run together to find their own rhythms. And with a nod to Zora Neale Hurston's seamless welding of the "folkloric" and the "literary," Parks makes music of everyday usage. Even the way a word is spelled can imply stage action: "Thuh," she says, slumping, "makes the body do something very different"— and here she straightens up —"than 'The.' "

What's more, for African-Americans, the difference can mean the difference between work and unemployment, even between life and death. . . .

Parks goes even further in her experiments with language in her second major play, *The Death of the Last Black Man in the Whole Entire World*. If *Imperceptible Mutabilities* showed African-Americans in a perpetual state of middle passage, their identity hidden somewhere in the ocean-sized, centuries-old hyphen separating African from American, *Death of the Last Black Man*, with humor and pointedness, takes on the American side of the divide, confronting stereotypes and dismantling cultural myths.

Here, again, Parks addresses the themes of self-narration, the way language can confer autonomy, the gaps between image and reality, white America's denial of African-American history. But this play is even more complex in approach, more inventive in style, and, surprisingly — because its experiments are so formal — more passionate.

There's little that could be called plot here. Indeed, the idea of sequence is subverted again and again. Time itself is subverted, past and future conflated into the simultaneity of the theatrical present. When did the last black man die? "Yesterday tuhday next summer tuhmorrow just a moment ughoh in 1317."

Instead of relying on logical sequence, Parks creates a sense of progression through repetition. Her language gathers momentum through what Gertrude Stein called "the natural way to count . . . not that one and one make two but to go on counting by one and one. . . . One and one and one and one and one." Parks does not drive her plays with the mechanism of suspense: if there's any eagerness to find out what will happen next, it comes not from the hurtling forward of an event into its consequences, but from the variations she builds on established patterns.

Stein is one clear influence on this style; the other is jazz. Through listening to jazz, with its solos sculpted around revisions of a repeated theme, Parks says she's recently realized "how much this method is an integral part of the African and African-American literary and oral traditions."

In a note to other members of BACA's New Works Project — a workshop for writers and directors — Parks explains what intrigues her about this technique:

> Repetition — we accept it in poetry and call it incremental refrain. For the most part incremental refrain creates a weight and a rhythm. In dramatic writing it does the same — yes, but we want to get to the CLIMAX. Where does repetition fit? First, it's not just repetition, but repetition with *revision*. And in drama, change is the thing. Characters refigure their words. Secondly, a text based on the concept of repetition and revision is one which breaks from the text which we are told to write — the text which cleanly ARCS. Thirdly, Rep and Rev texts create a real challenge for the actor and director as they create a physical life appropriate to the text. In such pieces we are not moving from A–B but rather, for example, from A–A–A–B–A. Through such movement, we refigure A. And if we wish to continue to call this movement FORWARD PROGRESSION, which I think it is, then we refigure the concept of forward progression.

Subverting sequence changes the meaning of consequence. The teleological nature of naturalistic drama virtually requires some kind of huge event that brings on catastrophe — or at least consequences that the action of the play seeks to expose and explain. "If you stick to that kind of writing," Parks says, "then all you can write is plays about black men being killed by policemen, as if to indict society, you need a Big Event. But on stage, as in physics, an event doesn't have to be big to be a big deal. In the theater, someone can simply turn their hand palm up and that is an event."

In *Death of the Last Black Man,* history itself refuses to be linear or sequential. For Parks, history is round — or perhaps, roun'. "The worl usta be *roun,*" the Black Man with Watermelon says, "before Columbus." And then, Queen-then-Pharaoh Hatshepsut explains, "they put uh 'd' on thuh end of roun making round. Thusly they set in motion thuh end. Without that 'd' we coulda gone on spinnin for ever. The 'd' thing ended things ended." More than that, [Before Columbus] replies, "Them thinking the world was flat kept it roun. Them thinking the sun revolved around the earth kept them satellite-like. They figured out the truth and scurried out. Figuring out the truth put them in their place and they scurried out to put us in ours. [Yes and Greens Black-Eyed Peas Cornbread adds] Mmm. Yes. You should write this down. You should hide this under a rock."

The consequences Parks is concerned with are those that resulted from that "d" being appended to the roun worl. In one sequence, the Black Man appears with a noose around his neck, dragging a tree branch behind him. Over and over in the play this last black man *almost* dies: We hear of him falling from a ship, bursting into flames, being plucked from his homeland, being auctioned at the block. And in another extended sequence, he tells the Black Woman how he escaped from electrocution, even after "Jump-juice meets me-mine juices I do uh slow soft shoe like on water. Town crier cries uh moan. Felt my nappy head go frizzly." All these deaths — or near-deaths — are offset by a celebration of births, presented as a ritualized series of begets: "MeMines gived out 2 offspring one she called Mines after herself thuh uther she called Themuhns named after all them who comed before." But these generically named offspring are a dubious blessing; this resurgence is given theatrical extension by an onstage proliferation of watermelons.

Still, the play implies, the greatest death of the Black Man is his being written out of history. Over and over, speakers advise each other, "You should write it down because if you don't write it down then they will come along and tell the future that we did not exist." Gradually, it seems the characters learn this lesson. By the play's end, they have gathered into "uh multitude," recognizing the pull of their own "Nature, History, Gravity." In a triumphant finale, the chorus's "And we will lay us down" gives way to the Black Man and Black Woman's "And we will write us down."

This, of course, is precisely what Suzan-Lori Parks, young, gifted, and African-American, has been doing, capturing the contradictions and crises contained in her own project. As she is increasingly recognized, she too — as she well knows — will run the risk of seeing white institutions want to fix that flattening -d onto her roun writing. In the *New York Times*, Mel Gussow called Parks the most promising playwright of the year; *Imperceptible Mutabilities* won an Obie Award from *The Village Voice* last spring. . . . Meanwhile, the Women's Project has commissioned a play from Parks, and regional theaters are considering productions of *Imperceptible Mutabilities* — though, Parks quips, "If they decide to do it, it will have to be in February so people can have an explanation for it." She's referring, of course, to Black History Month.

David Mamet

The title of one of David Mamet's plays, *A Life in the Theatre* (1977), may have been autobiographically inspired. Mamet has spent his life — from high school onward — in the theater, as actor, director, playwright, and screenwriter. Born in Chicago in 1947, he graduated with an English major from Goddard College in Vermont, where he wrote several plays, including his undergraduate thesis, *Camel* (1968). *Sexual Perversity in Chicago* (1975), Mamet's first resounding commercial success, was first drafted when he was at Goddard. In the same year, *American Buffalo* premiered in the Goodman Theatre in Chicago, beginning a series of productions around the country. The Broadway production was not especially well received, but it was the first American play produced at London's new National Theatre in 1978. After a 1980 revival in New Haven's Long Wharf Theater with Al Pacino as Teach, it moved to Circle in the Square in New York in 1981 and then to Broadway in 1983. A study of petty thieves living a darkly comic underground life, *American Buffalo* has become one of Mamet's most highly regarded plays.

His much-acclaimed *Glengarry Glen Ross* (1983) premiered in London at the National Theatre, then moved to Broadway the following year, where it won the Pulitzer Prize and many other awards. This tale of scheming real estate salesmen derives in part from Mamet's experience working in a real estate office as a young man. The portrait of avarice and deceit is an indictment of one aspect of American business. *Glengarry Glen Ross* was eventually revised for film.

In the 1980s and 1990s Mamet wrote many stage plays, radio plays, and film scripts. He adapted Chekhov's *The Cherry Orchard* (1985), wrote *Goldberg Street* for radio performance, and wrote the screenplays for *The Untouchables* (1987), *House of Games* (1987, nominated for a Golden Globe Award), *Things Change* (1988), and *Homocide* (1991). *Speed The Plow* (1988) opened on Broadway with Madonna playing a secretary from a temp agency. It draws on Mamet's experience in the film industry and explores the insecurities and double-dealing of those who make decisions about producing movies. More recently, his play *The Cryptogram* (1994) was produced first in London in June 1994 and then in February 1995 at the American Repertory Theatre in Boston. The New York production was at the Westside Arts Theater in March 1995. *Boston Marriage* (1999) examines a blue-blood Victorian relationship between two women, a novel subject for Mamet and perhaps a new direction.

In the early 1970s Mamet was involved in Chicago's St. Nicholas Theatre Company, a group that gathered to produce a variety of plays, including some of his own. William H. Macy, Steven Schacter, and Patricia Cox were the principal actors, and others joined with them. Soon, however, Mamet's responsibilities as a writer and his occasional stints as a university professor at Goddard and elsewhere led him to leave Chicago and center himself in New York.

OLEANNA

The title of the play is ironic, referring to a folksong that yearns for a utopian community, Oleanna, in Wisconsin. There is nothing utopian about the play. It was first produced in a small off-Broadway theater in 1992, running for more than 250 performances and stirring an enormous amount of controversy. Shortly before the play was produced, the nation had been transfixed by Senate hearings on Anita Hill's accusation that Clarence Thomas, a U.S. Supreme Court nominee, sexually harassed her. Both held to stories that contradicted the other, and the nation took sides without knowing which was correct. *Oleanna* was not, according to Mamet, inspired by the hearings but, as many reviewers pointed out, certainly profited from them.

The play concerns a professor in his interchange with a female student who is having trouble in his course. When we first see him, John's tenure has been approved but not fully confirmed by the university. Carol, when we first meet her, is tentative, uncertain, and struggles with some of John's vocabulary. John is confident, swaggering, a bit condescending, generally enjoying being in a position of considerable power. Mamet explores the relationship as it begins to reverse itself. At the end of the play Carol, now heading an unnamed group of feminists, interprets the early events in such a way as to file charges of sexual harassment and rape against John and petitions to have his tenure denied.

All the while this grappling ensues, the telephone (critic Clive Barnes referred it to as the third actor onstage) rings incessantly with news from John's wife and real estate agent concerning the house they are trying to buy, now that they are confident that tenure will be awarded. The struggle of ideas between professor and student, the concerns for power, and the issues of patriarchy and sexual harassment become manifest in John's ultimate realization that the price for what he has done (if only he could understand what he has done) is the loss of his house and an ultimate threat to his family and his security.

The audience is in a privileged position because it has seen the events of the first two scenes of the play. John expresses a desire to help Carol and offers her an A if she will retake as a tutorial the course she failed. He reassures her when she says she cannot understand anything. He even good-naturedly criticizes the entire institution of education as a "warehousing of the young." He innocently embraces her in a show of confidence. But all these gestures, once Carol goes on the attack in act 2, are seen to have an entirely different significance than anything John seems to have intended. As Michael Feingold said in his review, "*Oleanna* is a tragedy built as a series of audience traps; the minute you get suckered into thinking it says one thing, you're likely to find it saying the exact opposite." The point is that from one position — that of power — a gesture will mean one thing; from another position — that of powerlessness — a gesture will take on another meaning. The audience, with good reason to distrust both John and Carol, given their obvious character flaws, is left to decide the meaning of events.

Oleanna in Performance

In production, whether in New York, New Haven, Croton Falls, or London, the play induced audiences to cry out in response to lines and to stand around afterward under marquees in forceful argument over the issues and outcome of the events. Whatever one may say about the flaws of the play — overreliance on the telephone, annoying stuttering dialogue, an unlikely reversal of Carol from a woman who misunderstood common words to a spokesperson for a coalition using complex language — it charged members of the audience. The feelings of frustration onstage seemed to find resonance in observers quick and ready to respond.

Mamet's treatment of women in his earlier plays has sometimes drawn fire. In discussing *Oleanna*, Otis Guernsey Jr. said that both Pinter and Mamet "seem to view women as ultimately unfathomable." Yet Guernsey felt that Mamet's direction of *Oleanna* "was a galvanizing theatrical experience." Not all critics agreed. Alisa Solomon in the *Village Voice* scorned it as a "twisted little play" in which the student is vilified and the professor made an object of sympathy. Jan Stuart in *New York Newsday* called it "scurrilous," and said, "*Oleanna* is loathsome and riveting in the way that only Mamet plays can be." Clive Barnes called it "a pretentious flop." Other critics saw it as powerful. David Sterritt in the *Christian Science Monitor* called it "a searing new play." David Patrick Stearns in *USA Today* said the play "gets under your skin and itches there for days."

The staging of the play depends on tightness of quarters. John's office is tight, small, uncluttered. The New Haven production used stark white surfaces and bright lighting, while the New York production seemed dingier, with an office that held obviously used furniture. The lighting was simple, even, and somewhat harsh. One reason given for choosing New York's small Orpheum Theatre was that it is itself somewhat small, virtually claustrophobic.

After its New York premiere the play was produced in London and regionally throughout the United States before being made into a film in 1994. A 1995 production in Croton Falls, New York, garnered exceptionally strong reviews, indicating that the play does not depend on star quality. As a curious note, the programs for the original production depicted a bull's-eye target, some with John's and some with Carol's face in the center. Mamet was clearly aware of the drama's potential for controversy.

David Mamet (b. 1947)

OLEANNA

1992

The want of fresh air does not seem much to affect the happiness of children in a London alley: the greater part of them sing and play as though they were on a moor in Scotland. So the absence of a genial mental atmosphere is not commonly recognized by children who have never known it. Young people have a marvelous faculty of either dying or adapting themselves to circumstances. Even if they are unhappy — very unhappy — it is astonishing how easily they can be prevented from finding it out, or at any rate from attributing it to any other cause than their own sinfulness.
— The Way of All Flesh
SAMUEL BUTLER

*"Oh, to be in Oleanna,
That's where I would rather be
Than be bound in Norway
And drag the chains of slavery."*
— FOLK SONG

Characters

CAROL, *a woman of twenty*
JOHN, *a man in his forties*

The play takes place in John's office.

ACT 1

(*John is talking on the phone. Carol is seated across the desk from him.*)

JOHN (*on phone*): And what about the land. (*Pause.*) The land. And what about the land? (*Pause.*) What about it? (*Pause.*) No. I don't understand. Well, yes, I'm I'm . . . no, I'm *sure* it's signif . . . I'm sure it's significant. (*Pause.*) Because it's significant to mmm-mmm . . . did you call Jerry? (*Pause.*) Because . . . no, no, no, no, no. What did they say . . . ? Did you speak to the *real* estate . . . where *is* she . . . ? Well, well, all right. Where are her notes? Where are the notes we took with her. (*Pause.*) I thought you were? No. No, I'm sorry, I didn't mean that, I just thought that I saw you, when we were there . . . what . . . ? I thought I saw you with a *pencil*. WHY NOW? is what I'm say . . . well, that's why I say "call Jerry." Well, I can't right now, be . . . no, I *didn't* schedule any . . . Grace: I *didn't* . . . I'm well aware . . . Look: Look. Did you call Jerry? Will you call Jerry . . . ? Because I can't now. I'll be there, I'm sure I'll be there in fifteen, in twenty. I intend to. No, we aren't *going* to lose the, we aren't *going* to lose the house. Look: Look, I'm not minimizing it. The "easement." Did she say "easement"? (*Pause.*) What did she *say*; is it a "term of art," are we *bound* by it . . . I'm sorry . . . (*Pause.*) are: we: yes. *Bound* by . . . Look: (*he checks his watch*) before the other side *goes home,* all right? "a term of art." Because: that's right (*Pause.*) The yard for the boy. Well, that's the whole . . . Look: I'm going to meet you there . . . (*He checks his watch.*) Is the realtor there? All right, tell her to show you the basement again. Look at the *this* because . . . Bec . . . I'm leaving in, I'm leaving in ten or fifteen . . . Yes. No, no, I'll meet you at the new . . . That's a good. If he thinks it's necc . . . you tell Jerry to meet . . . All right? We *aren't* going to lose the deposit. All right? I'm sure it's going to be . . . (*Pause.*) I hope so. (*Pause.*) I love you, too. (*Pause.*) I love you, too. As soon as . . . I will. (*He hangs up.*) (*He bends over the desk and makes a note.*) (*He looks up.*) (*To Carol*): I'm sorry . . .

CAROL (*pause*): What is a "term of art"?

JOHN (*pause*): I'm sorry . . . ?

CAROL (*pause*): What is a "term of art"?

JOHN: Is that what you want to talk about?

CAROL: . . . to talk about . . . ?

JOHN: Let's take the mysticism out of it, shall we? Carol? (*Pause.*) Don't you think? I'll tell you: when you have some "thing." Which must be broached. (*Pause.*) Don't you think . . . ? (*Pause.*)

CAROL: . . . don't I think . . . ?

JOHN: Mmm?

CAROL: . . . did I . . . ?

JOHN: . . . what?

CAROL: Did . . . did I . . . did I say something wr . . .

JOHN (*pause*): No. I'm sorry. No. You're right. I'm very sorry. I'm somewhat rushed. As you see. I'm sorry. You're right. (*Pause.*) What is a "term of art"? It seems to mean a *term,* which has come, through its use, to mean something *more specific* than the words would, to someone *not acquainted* with them . . . indicate. That, I believe, is what a "term of art," would mean. (*Pause.*)

CAROL: You don't know what it means . . . ?

JOHN: I'm not sure that I know what it means. It's one of those things, perhaps you've had them, that, you look them up, or have someone explain them to you, and you say "aha," and, you immediately *forget* what . . .

CAROL: You don't do that.

JOHN: . . . I . . . ?

CAROL: You don't do . . .

JOHN: . . . I don't, what . . . ?

CAROL: . . . for . . .

JOHN: . . . I don't for . . .

CAROL: . . . no . . .

JOHN: . . . forget things? Everybody does that.

CAROL: No, they don't.

JOHN: They don't . . .

CAROL: No.

JOHN (*pause*): No. Everybody does that.

CAROL: Why would they do that . . . ?

JOHN: Because. I don't know. Because it doesn't interest them.

CAROL: No.

JOHN: I think so, though. (*Pause.*) I'm sorry that I was distracted.

CAROL: You don't have to say that to me.

JOHN: You paid me the compliment, or the "obeisance"— all right — of coming in here . . . All right. *Carol*. I find that I am at a *standstill*. I find that I . . .

CAROL: . . . what . . .

JOHN: . . . one moment. In regard to your . . . to your . . .

CAROL: Oh, oh. You're buying a new house!

JOHN: No, let's get on with it.

CAROL: "get on"? (*Pause.*)

JOHN: I know how . . . *believe* me. I know how . . . potentially *humiliating* these . . . I have no desire to . . . I have no desire other than to help you. But (*he picks up some papers on his desk*) I won't even say "but." I'll say that as I go back over the . . .

CAROL: I'm just, I'm just trying to . . .

JOHN: . . . no, it will not do.

CAROL: . . . what? What will . . . ?

JOHN: No. I see, I see what you, it . . . (*He gestures to the papers.*) but your work . . .

CAROL: I'm just: I sit in class I . . . (*She holds up her notebook.*) I take notes . . .

JOHN (*simultaneously with* "notes"): Yes. I understand. What I am trying to *tell* you is that some, some basic . . .

CAROL: . . . I . . .

JOHN: . . . one moment: some basic missed communi . . .

CAROL: I'm doing what I'm told. I bought your book, I read your . . .

JOHN: No, I'm sure you . . .

CAROL: No, no, no. I'm doing what I'm told. It's *difficult* for me. It's *difficult* . . .

JOHN: . . . but . . .

CAROL: I don't . . . lots of the *language* . . .

JOHN: . . . please . . .

CAROL: The *language*, the "things" that you say . . .

JOHN: I'm sorry. No. I don't think that that's true.

CAROL: It *is* true. I . . .

JOHN: I think . . .

CAROL: It *is* true.

JOHN: . . . I . . .

CAROL: Why would I . . . ?

JOHN: I'll tell you why: you're an incredibly bright girl.

CAROL: . . . I . . .

JOHN: You're an incredibly . . . you have no problem with the . . . Who's kidding who?

CAROL: . . . I . . .

JOHN: No. No. I'll tell you why. I'll tell . . . I think you're *angry*, I . . .

CAROL: . . . why would I . . .

JOHN: . . . wait one moment. I . . .

CAROL: It is true. I have *problems* . . .

JOHN: . . . every . . .

CAROL: . . . I come from a different *social* . . .

JOHN: . . . ev . . .

CAROL: a different economic . . .

JOHN: . . . Look:

CAROL: No. I: when I *came* to this school:

JOHN: Yes. Quite . . . (*Pause.*)

CAROL: . . . does that mean nothing . . . ?

JOHN: . . . but look: look . . .

CAROL: . . . I . . .

JOHN (*picks up paper*): Here: Please: Sit down. (*Pause.*) Sit down. (*Reads from her paper.*) "I think that the ideas contained in this work express the author's feelings in a way that he intended, based on his results." What can that mean? Do you see? What . . .

CAROL: I, the best that I . . .

JOHN: I'm saying, that perhaps this course . . .

CAROL: No, no, no, you can't, you can't . . . I have to . . .

JOHN: . . . how . . .

CAROL: . . . I have to pass it . . .

JOHN: Carol, I:

CAROL: I *have* to pass this course, I . . .

JOHN: Well.

CAROL: . . . don't you . . .

JOHN: Either the . . .

CAROL: . . . I . . .

JOHN: . . . either the, I . . . either the *criteria* for judging progress in the class are . . .

CAROL: No, no, no, no, I have to pass it.

JOHN: Now, look: I'm a human being, I . . .

CAROL: I did what you told me. I did, I did everything that, I read your *book*, you told me to buy your book and read it. Everything you *say* I . . . (*She gestures to her notebook.*) (*The phone rings.*) I do. . . . Ev . . .

JOHN: . . . look:

CAROL: . . . everything I'm told . . .

JOHN: Look. Look. I'm not your *father*. (*Pause.*)

CAROL: What?

JOHN: I'm.

CAROL: Did I say you were my father?

JOHN: . . . no . . .

CAROL: Why did you say that . . . ?

JOHN: I . . .

CAROL: . . . why . . . ?

JOHN: . . . in class I . . . (*He picks up the phone.*) (*Into phone:*) Hello. I can't talk now. Jerry? Yes? I underst . . . I can't talk now. I know . . . I know . . . Jerry. I can't *talk* now. Yes, I. Call me back in . . . Thank you. (*He hangs up.*) (*To Carol.*) What do you want me to do? We are two people, all right? Both of whom have subscribed to . . .

CAROL: No, no . . .

JOHN: . . . certain arbitrary . . .

CAROL: No. You have to help me.

JOHN: Certain institutional . . . you tell me what you want me to do. . . . You tell me what you want me to . . .

CAROL: How can I go back and tell them the *grades* that I . . .

JOHN: . . . what can I do . . . ?

CAROL: *Teach* me. *Teach* me.

JOHN: . . . I'm trying to teach you.

CAROL: I read your book. I read it. I don't under . . .

JOHN: . . . you don't understand it.

CAROL: No.

JOHN: Well, perhaps it's not well *written* . . .

CAROL (*simultaneously with* "written"): No. No. No. I want to *understand* it.

JOHN: What don't you understand? (*Pause.*)

CAROL: *Any* of it. What you're trying to say. When you talk about . . .

JOHN: . . . yes . . . ? (*She consults her notes.*)

CAROL: "Virtual warehousing of the young" . . .

JOHN: "Virtual warehousing of the young." If we artificially prolong adolescence . . .

CAROL: . . . and about "The Curse of Modern Education."

JOHN: . . . well . . .

CAROL: I don't . . .

JOHN: Look. It's just a *course*, it's just a *book*, it's just a . . .

CAROL: No. No. There are *people* out there. People who came *here*. To know something they didn't *know*.

ABOVE AND BELOW: Mary McCann and William H. Macy in the 1993 New York production of *Oleanna*.

Who *came* here. To be *helped*. To be *helped*. So someone would *help* them. To *do* something. To *know* something. To get, what do they say? "To get on in the world." How can I do that if I don't, if I fail? But I don't *understand*. I don't *understand*. I don't understand what anything means . . . and I walk around. From morning 'til night: with this one thought in my head. I'm *stupid*.

JOHN: No one thinks you're stupid.

CAROL: No? What am I . . . ?

JOHN: I . . .

CAROL: . . . what am I, then?

JOHN: I think you're angry. Many people are. I have a *telephone* call that I have to make. And an *appointment,* which is rather *pressing*; though I sympathize with your concerns, and though I wish I had the time, this was not a previously scheduled meeting and I . . .

CAROL: . . . you think I'm nothing . . .

JOHN: . . . have an appointment with a *realtor,* and with my wife and . . .

CAROL: You think that I'm stupid.

JOHN: No. I certainly don't.

CAROL: You said it.

JOHN: No. I did not.

CAROL: You did.

JOHN: When?

CAROL: . . . you . . .

JOHN: No. I never did, or never would say that to a student, and . . .

CAROL: You said, "What can that mean?" (*Pause.*) "What can that mean?" . . . (*Pause.*)

JOHN: . . . and what did that mean to you . . . ?

CAROL: That meant I'm stupid. And I'll never learn. That's what that meant. And you're right.

JOHN: . . . I . . .

CAROL: But then. But then, what am I doing here . . . ?

JOHN: . . . if you thought that I . . .

CAROL: . . . when nobody wants me, and . . .

JOHN: . . . if you interpreted . . .

CAROL: Nobody *tells* me anything And I *sit* there . . . in the *corner.* In the *back.* And everybody's talking about "this" all the time. And "concepts," and "precepts" and, and, and, and, and, WHAT IN THE WORLD ARE YOU *TALKING* ABOUT? And I read your book. And they said, "Fine, go in that class." Because you talked about responsibility to the young. I DON'T KNOW WHAT IT MEANS AND I'M *FAILING* . . .

JOHN: May . . .

CAROL: No, you're right. "Oh, hell." I failed. Flunk me out of it. It's garbage. Everything I do. "The ideas contained in this work express the author's feelings." That's right. That's right. I know I'm stupid. I know what I am. (*Pause.*) I know what I am, Professor. You don't have to tell me. (*Pause.*) It's pathetic. Isn't it?

JOHN: . . . Aha . . . (*Pause.*) Sit down. Sit down. Please. (*Pause.*) Please sit down.

CAROL: Why?

JOHN: I want to talk to you.

CAROL: Why?

JOHN: Just sit down. (*Pause.*) Please. Sit down. Will you, please . . . ?

(*Pause. She does so.*)

Thank you.

CAROL: What?

JOHN: I want to tell you something.

CAROL (*pause*): What?

JOHN: Well, I know what you're talking about.

CAROL: No. You don't.

JOHN: I think I do. (*Pause.*)

CAROL: How can you?

JOHN: I'll tell you a story about myself. (*Pause.*) Do you mind? (*Pause.*) I was raised to think myself stupid. That's what I want to tell you. (*Pause.*)

CAROL: What do you mean?

JOHN: Just what I said. I was brought up, and my earliest, and most persistent memories are of being told that I was stupid. "You have such *intelligence.* Why must you behave so *stupidly*?" Or, "Can't you *understand*? Can't you *understand*?" And I could *not* understand. I could *not* understand.

CAROL: What?

JOHN: The simplest problem. Was beyond me. It was a mystery.

CAROL: What was a mystery?

JOHN: How people learn. How *I* could learn. Which is what I've been speaking of in class. And of *course* you can't hear it. Carol. Of *course* you can't. (*Pause.*) I used to speak of "real people," and wonder what the *real* people did. The *real* people. Who were they? *They* were the people other than myself. The *good* people. The *capable* people. The people who could do the things, *I* could not do: learn, study, retain . . . all that *garbage* — which is what I have been talking of in class, and that's *exactly* what I have been talking of — If you are told. . . . Listen to this. If the young child is told he cannot understand. Then he takes it as a *description* of himself. What am I? I am *that which can not understand.* And I saw you out there, when we were speaking of the concepts of . . .

CAROL: I can't understand any of them.

JOHN: Well, then, that's *my* fault. That's not your fault. And that is not verbiage. That's what I firmly hold to be the truth. And I am sorry, and I owe you an apology.

CAROL: Why?

JOHN: And I suppose that I have had some *things* on my mind. . . . We're buying a *house,* and . . .

CAROL: People said that you were stupid . . . ?

JOHN: Yes.

CAROL: When?

JOHN: I'll tell you when. Through my life. In my childhood; and, perhaps, they stopped. But I heard them continue.

CAROL: And what did they say?

JOHN: They said I was incompetent. Do you see? And when I'm tested the, the, the *feelings* of my youth about the *very subject of learning* come up. And I . . . I become, I feel "unworthy," and "unprepared." . . .

CAROL: . . . yes.

JOHN: . . . eh?

CAROL: . . . yes.

JOHN: And I feel that I must fail. (*Pause.*)

CAROL: . . . but then you *do* fail. (*Pause.*) You have to. (*Pause.*) Don't you?

JOHN: A *pilot.* Flying a plane. The pilot is flying the plane. He thinks: Oh, my *God,* my mind's been drifting! Oh, my God! What kind of a cursed imbecile am I, that I, with this so precious cargo of *Life* in my charge, would allow my attention to wander. Why was I born? How deluded are those who put their trust in me, . . . et cetera, so on, and he crashes the plane.

CAROL (*pause*): He could just . . .

JOHN: That's right.

CAROL: He could say:

JOHN: My attention *wandered* for a moment . . .

CAROL: . . . uh huh . . .

JOHN: I had a *thought* I did not like . . . but now:

CAROL: . . . but now it's . . .

JOHN: That's what I'm telling you. It's time to put my attention . . . see: it is not: this is what I learned. It is Not Magic. Yes. Yes. *You.* You are going to be frightened. When faced with what may or may not be but which you are going to perceive as a test. You will become frightened. And you will say: "I am incapable of . . ." and everything *in* you will think these two things. "I must. But I can't." And you will think: Why was I born to be the laughingstock of a world in which everyone is better than I? In which I am entitled to nothing. Where I can not learn. (*Pause.*)

CAROL: Is that . . . (*Pause.*) Is that what I have . . . ?

JOHN: Well. I don't know if I'd put it that way. Listen: I'm talking to you as I'd talk to my son. Because that's what I'd like him to have that I never had. I'm talking to you the way I wish that someone had talked to me. I don't know how to do it, other than to be *personal,* . . . but . . .

CAROL: Why would you want to be personal with me?

JOHN: Well, you see? That's what I'm saying. We can only interpret the behavior of others through the screen we . . . (*The phone rings.*) Through . . . (*To phone.*) Hello . . . ? (*To Carol.*) Through the screen we create. (*To phone.*) Hello. (*To Carol.*) Excuse me a moment. (*To phone.*) Hello? No, I can't talk nnn . . . I know I did. In a few . . . I'm . . . is he coming to the . . . yes. I talked to him. We'll meet you at the No, because I'm with a *student.* It's going to be fff . . . This is important, too. I'm with a *student,* Jerry's going to . . . Listen: the sooner I get off, the sooner I'll be down, all right. I love you. Listen, listen, I said "I love you," it's going to work *out* with the, because I feel that it is, I'll be right down. All right? Well, then it's going to take as long as it takes. (*He hangs up.*) (*To Carol.*) I'm sorry.

CAROL: What was that?

JOHN: There are some problems, as there usually are, about the final agreements for the new house.

CAROL: You're buying a new house.

JOHN: That's right.

CAROL: Because of your promotion.

JOHN: Well, I suppose that that's right.

CAROL: Why did you stay here with me?

JOHN: Stay here.

CAROL: Yes. When you should have gone.

JOHN: Because I like you.

CAROL: You like me.

JOHN: Yes.

CAROL: Why?

JOHN: Why? Well? Perhaps we're similar. (*Pause.*) Yes. (*Pause.*)

CAROL: You said "everyone has problems."

JOHN: Everyone has problems.

CAROL: Do they?

JOHN: Certainly.

CAROL: You do?

JOHN: Yes.

CAROL: What are they?

JOHN: Well. (*Pause.*) Well, you're perfectly right. (*Pause.*) If we're going to take off the Artificial *Stricture,* of "Teacher," and "Student," why should *my* problems be any more a mystery than your own? Of *course* I have problems. As you saw.

CAROL: . . . with what?

JOHN: With my *wife* . . . with *work* . . .

CAROL: With work?

JOHN: Yes. And, and, perhaps my problems are, do you see? *Similar* to yours.

CAROL: Would you tell me?

JOHN: All right. (*Pause.*) I came *late* to teaching. And I found it Artificial. The notion of "I know and you do not"; and I saw an *exploitation* in the education process. I told you. I hated school, I hated teachers. I hated everyone who was in the position of a "boss" because I *knew* — I didn't *think,* mind you, I *knew* I was going to fail. Because I was a fuckup. I was just no goddamned good. When I . . . late in life . . . (*Pause.*) When I *got out from under* . . . when I worked my way out of the need to fail. When I . . .

CAROL: How do you do that? (*Pause.*)

JOHN: You have to look at what you are, and what you feel, and how you act. And, finally, you have to look at how you act. And say: If that's what I *did,* that must be how I think of myself.

CAROL: I don't understand.

JOHN: If I fail all the time, it must be that I think of myself as a failure. If I do not want to think of myself as a failure, perhaps I should begin by *succeeding* now and again. Look. The tests, you see, which you encounter, in school, in college, in life, were designed, in the most part, for idiots. *By* idiots. There is no need to fail at them. They are not a test of your worth. They are a test of your ability to retain and spout back misinformation. Of *course* you fail them. They're *nonsense*. And I . . .

CAROL: . . . no . . .

JOHN: Yes. They're *garbage.* They're a *joke.* Look at me. Look at me. The Tenure Committee. The Tenure Committee. Come to judge me. The Bad Tenure Committee.

The "Test." Do you see? They put me to the test. Why, they had people voting on me I wouldn't employ to wax my car. And yet, I go before the Great Tenure Committee, and I have an urge, to *vomit,* to, to, to puke my *badness* on the table, to show them: "I'm no good. Why would you pick *me?*"

CAROL: They granted you tenure.

JOHN: Oh no, they announced it, but they haven't *signed.* Do you see? "At any moment . . ."

CAROL: . . . mmm . . .

JOHN: "They might not *sign*" . . . I might not . . . the *house* might not go through . . . Eh? Eh? They'll find out my "dark secret." (*Pause.*)

CAROL: . . . what is it . . . ?

JOHN: There *isn't* one. But *they* will find an index of my badness . . .

CAROL: Index?

JOHN: A ". . . pointer." A "Pointer." You see? Do you see? I *understand* you. I. Know. That. Feeling. Am I entitled to my job, and my nice *home,* and my *wife,* and my *family,* and so on. This is what I'm saying: That theory of education which, that *theory:*

CAROL: I . . . I . . . (*Pause.*)

JOHN: What?

CAROL: I . . .

JOHN: What?

CAROL: I want to know about my grade. (*Long pause.*)

JOHN: Of course you do.

CAROL: Is that bad?

JOHN: No.

CAROL: Is it bad that I asked you that?

JOHN: No.

CAROL: Did I upset you?

JOHN: No. And I apologize. Of *course* you want to know about your grade. And, of course, you can't concentrate on anyth . . . (*The telephone starts to ring.*) Wait a moment.

CAROL: I should go.

JOHN: I'll make you a deal.

CAROL: No, you have to . . .

JOHN: Let it ring. I'll make you a deal. You stay here. We'll start the whole course over. I'm going to say it was not you, it was I who was not paying attention. We'll start the whole course over. Your grade is an "A." Your final grade is an "A." (*The phone stops ringing.*)

CAROL: But the class is only half over . . .

JOHN (*simultaneously with* "over"): Your grade for the whole term is an "A." If you will come back and meet with me. A few more times. Your grade's an "A." Forget about the paper. You didn't like it, you

didn't like writing it. It's not important. What's important is that I awake your interest, if I can, and that I answer your questions. Let's start over. (*Pause.*)

CAROL: Over. With what?

JOHN: Say this is the beginning.

CAROL: The beginning.

JOHN: Yes.

CAROL: Of what?

JOHN: Of the class.

CAROL: But we can't start over.

JOHN: I say we can. (*Pause.*) I say we can.

CAROL: But I don't believe it.

JOHN: Yes, I know that. But it's true. What is The Class but you and me? (*Pause.*)

CAROL: There are rules.

JOHN: Well. We'll break them.

CAROL: How can we?

JOHN: We won't tell anybody.

CAROL: Is that all right?

JOHN: I say that it's fine.

CAROL: Why would you do this for me?

JOHN: I like you. Is that so difficult for you to . . .

CAROL: Um . . .

JOHN: There's no one here but you and me. (*Pause.*)

CAROL: All right. I did not understand. When you referred . . .

JOHN: All right, yes?

CAROL: When you referred to hazing.

JOHN: Hazing.

CAROL: You wrote, in your book. About the comparative . . . the comparative . . . (*She checks her notes.*)

JOHN: Are you checking your notes . . . ?

CAROL: Yes.

JOHN: Tell me in your own . . .

CAROL: I want to make sure that I have it right.

JOHN: No. Of course. You want to be exact.

CAROL: I want to know everything that went on.

JOHN: . . . that's good.

CAROL: . . . so I . . .

JOHN: That's very good. But I was suggesting, many times, that that which we wish to retain is retained oftentimes, I think, *better* with less expenditure of effort.

CAROL (*of notes*): Here it is: you wrote of *hazing.*

JOHN: . . . that's correct. Now: I said "hazing." It means ritualized annoyance. We shove this book at you, we say read it. Now, you say you've read it? I think that you're *lying.* I'll *grill* you, and when I find you've lied, you'll be disgraced, and your life will be ruined. It's a sick game. Why do we do it? Does it educate? In no sense. Well, then, what is higher education? It is something-other-than-useful.

CAROL: What is "something-other-than-useful"?

JOHN: It has become a ritual, it has become an article of faith. That all must be subjected to, or to put it differently, that all are entitled to Higher Education. And my point . . .

CAROL: You disagree with that?

JOHN: Well, let's address that. What do you think?

CAROL: I don't know.

JOHN: What do you think, though? (*Pause.*)

CAROL: I don't know.

JOHN: I spoke of it in class. Do you remember my example?

CAROL: Justice.

JOHN: Yes. Can you repeat it to me?

(*She looks down at her notebook.*)

Without your notes? I ask you as a favor to me, so that I can see if my idea was interesting.

CAROL: You said "justice" . . .

JOHN: Yes?

CAROL: . . . that all are entitled . . . (*Pause.*) I . . . I . . . I . . .

JOHN: Yes. To a speedy trial. To a fair trial. But they needn't be given a trial *at all* unless they stand accused. Eh? Justice is their right, should they choose to avail themselves of it, they should have a fair trial. It does not follow, of necessity, a person's life is incomplete without a trial in it. Do you see?

My point is a confusion between equity and *utility* arose. So we confound the *usefulness* of higher education with our, granted, right to equal access to the same. We, in effect, create a *prejudice* toward it, completely independent of . . .

CAROL: . . . that it is prejudice that we should go to school?

JOHN: Exactly. (*Pause.*)

CAROL: How can you say that? How . . .

JOHN: Good. Good. *Good.* That's right! Speak up! What is a prejudice? An unreasoned belief. We are all subject to it. None of us is not. When it is threatened, or opposed, we feel anger, and feel, do we not? As you do now. Do you not? Good.

CAROL: . . . but how can you . . .

JOHN: . . . let us examine. Good.

CAROL: How . . .

JOHN: Good. Good. When . . .

CAROL: I'M SPEAKING . . . (*Pause.*)

JOHN: I'm sorry.

CAROL: How can you . . .

JOHN: . . . I beg your pardon.

CAROL: That's all right.

JOHN: I beg your pardon.

CAROL: That's all right.

JOHN: I'm sorry I interrupted you.

CAROL: That's all right.

JOHN: You were saying?

CAROL: I was saying . . . I was saying . . . (*She checks her notes.*) How can you say in a class. Say in a college class, that college education is prejudice?

JOHN: I said that our predilection for it . . .

CAROL: Predilection . . .

JOHN: . . . you know what that means.

CAROL: Does it mean "liking"?

JOHN: Yes.

CAROL: But how can you say that? That College . . .

JOHN: . . . that's my *job,* don't you know.

CAROL: What is?

JOHN: To provoke you.

CAROL: No.

JOHN: Oh. Yes, though.

CAROL: To provoke me?

JOHN: That's right.

CAROL: To make me mad?

JOHN: That's right. To force you . . .

CAROL: . . . to make me mad is your job?

JOHN: To force you to . . . listen (*Pause.*) Ah. (*Pause.*) When I was young somebody told me, are you ready, the rich copulate less often than the poor. But when they do, they take more of their clothes off. Years. Years, mind you, I would compare experiences of my own to this dictum, saying, aha, this fits the norm, or ah, this is a variation from it. What did it mean? Nothing. It was some jerk thing, some school kid told me that took up room inside my head. (*Pause.*)

Somebody told *you,* and you hold it as an article of faith, that higher education is an unassailable good. This notion is so dear to you that when I question it you become angry. Good. Good, I say. Are not those the very things which we should question? I say college education, since the war, has become so a matter of course, and such a fashionable necessity, for those either of or aspiring *to* to the new vast middle class, that we *espouse* it, as a matter of right, and have ceased to ask, "What is it good for?" (*Pause.*)

What might be some reasons for pursuit of higher education?

One: A love of learning.

Two: The wish for mastery of a skill.

Three: For economic betterment.

(*Stops. Makes a note.*)

CAROL: I'm keeping you.

JOHN: One moment. I have to make a note . . .

CAROL: It's something that I said?

JOHN: No, we're buying a house.

CAROL: You're buying the new house.

JOHN: To go with the tenure. That's right. Nice *house,* close to the *private school* . . . (*He continues making his note.*) . . . We were talking of economic *betterment.* . . .

(*Carol writes in her notebook.*)

I was thinking of the School Tax. (*He continues writing.*) (*To himself.*) . . . *where is it written* that I have to send my child to public school. . . . Is it a law that I have to improve the City Schools at the expense of my own interest? And, is this not simply *The White Man's Burden?* Good. And (*looks up to Carol*) . . . does this interest you?

CAROL: No. I'm taking notes . . .

JOHN: You don't have to take notes, you know, you can just listen.

CAROL: I want to make sure I remember it. (*Pause.*)

JOHN: I'm not lecturing you, I'm just trying to tell you some things I think.

CAROL: What do you think?

JOHN: Should all kids go to college? *Why* . . .

CAROL (*pause*): To learn.

JOHN: But if he does not learn.

CAROL: If the child does not learn?

JOHN: Then why is he in college? Because he was told it was his "right"?

CAROL: Some might find college instructive.

JOHN: I would hope so.

CAROL: But how do they feel? Being told they are wasting their time?

JOHN: I don't think I'm telling them that.

CAROL: You said that education was "prolonged and systematic hazing."

JOHN: Yes. It can be so.

CAROL: . . . if education is so *bad,* why do you do it?

JOHN: I do it because I love it. (*Pause.*) Let's. . . . I suggest you look at the demographics, wage-earning capacity, college- and noncollege-educated men and women, 1855 to 1980, and let's see if we can wring some worth from the statistics. Eh? And . . .

CAROL: No.

JOHN: What?

CAROL: I can't understand them.

JOHN: . . . you . . . ?

CAROL: . . . the "charts." The *Concepts,* the . . .

JOHN: "Charts" are simply . . .

CAROL: When I leave here . . .

JOHN: Charts, do you see . . .

CAROL: No, I can't . . .

JOHN: You can, though.

CAROL: NO, NO — I DON'T UNDERSTAND. DO YOU SEE??? I DON'T *UNDERSTAND* . . .

JOHN: What?

CAROL: *Any* of it. *Any* of it. I'm *smiling* in class, I'm *smiling,* the whole time. What are you *talking* about? What is everyone *talking* about? I don't *understand.* I don't know what it *means.* I don't know what it means to *be* here . . . you tell me I'm intelligent, and then you tell me I should not be *here,* what do you *want* with me? What does it *mean?* Who should I *listen* to . . . I . . .

(*He goes over to her and puts his arm around her shoulder.*)

NO!

(*She walks away from him.*)

JOHN: Sshhhh.

CAROL: No, I don't under . . .

JOHN: Sshhhhh.

CAROL: I don't know what you're *saying* . . .

JOHN: Sshhhhh. It's all right.

CAROL: . . . I have no . . .

JOHN: Sshhhhh. Sshhhhh. Let it go a moment. (*Pause.*) Sshhhh . . . let it go. (*Pause.*) Just let it go. (*Pause.*) Just let it go. It's all right. (*Pause.*) Sshhhhh. (*Pause.*) I understand . . . (*Pause.*) What do you feel?

CAROL: I feel bad.

JOHN: I know. It's all right.

CAROL: I . . . (*Pause.*)

JOHN: What?

CAROL: I . . .

JOHN: What? Tell me.

CAROL: I don't understand you.

JOHN: I know. It's all right.

CAROL: I . . .

JOHN: What? (*Pause.*) What? *Tell* me.

CAROL: I can't tell you.

JOHN: No, you must.

CAROL: I can't.

JOHN: No. Tell me. (*Pause.*)

CAROL: I'm bad. (*Pause.*) Oh, God. (*Pause.*)

JOHN: It's all right.

CAROL: I'm . . .

JOHN: It's all right.

CAROL: I can't talk about this.

JOHN: It's all right. Tell me.

CAROL: Why do you want to know this?

JOHN: I don't want to know. I want to know whatever you . . .

CAROL: I always . . .

JOHN: . . . good . . .

CAROL: I always . . . all my life . . . I have never told anyone this . . .

JOHN: Yes. Go on. (*Pause.*) Go on.

CAROL: All of my life . . . (*The phone rings.*)

(*Pause. John goes to the phone and picks it up.*)

JOHN (*into phone*): I can't talk now. (*Pause.*) What? (*Pause.*) Hmm. (*Pause.*) All right, I . . . I. Can't. Talk. Now. No, no, no, I *Know* I did, but . . . What? Hello. What? She *what?* She *can't,* she said the agreement is void? How, how is the agreement *void?* That's *Our House.*

   I have the *paper;* when we come down, next week, with the payment, and the paper, that house is . . . wait, wait, wait, wait, wait, wait, wait: Did Jerry . . . is Jerry there? (*Pause.*) Is *she* there . . . ? Does she have a *lawyer* . . . ? How the *hell,* how the *Hell.* That is . . . it's a question, you said, of the *easement.* I don't underst . . . it's not the *whole agreement.* It's just the *easement,* why would she? Put, put, put, *Jerry* on. (*Pause.*) Jer, *Jerry:* What the *Hell* . . . that's my *house.* That's . . . Well, I'm, no, no, no, I'm *not* coming ddd . . . List, *Listen, screw* her. You *tell* her. You, listen: I want you to take *Grace,* you take Grace, and get out of that house. You *leave* her there. Her and her lawyer, and you *tell* them, we'll see them in court next . . . no. No. Leave her there, leave her to *stew* in it: You tell her, we're *getting* that house, and we are going to . . . No. I'm *not* coming down. I'll be damned if I'll sit in the same rrr . . . the next, you tell her the next time I *see* her is in court . . . I . . . (*Pause.*) What? (*Pause.*) What? I don't understand. (*Pause.*) Well, what about the house? (*Pause.*) There isn't any problem with the hhh . . . (*Pause.*) No, no, no, that's all right. All ri . . . All right . . . (*Pause.*) Of

course. Tha . . . Thank you. No, I will. Right away.
(*He hangs up.*) (*Pause*)

CAROL: What is it? (*Pause.*)

JOHN: It's a surprise party.

CAROL: It is.

JOHN: Yes.

CAROL: A party for you.

JOHN: Yes.

CAROL: Is it your birthday?

JOHN: No.

CAROL: What is it?

JOHN: The tenure announcement.

CAROL: The tenure announcement.

JOHN: They're throwing a party for us in our new house.

CAROL: Your new house.

JOHN: The house that we're buying.

CAROL: You have to go.

JOHN: It seems that I do.

CAROL (*pause*): They're proud of you.

JOHN: Well, there are those who would say it's a form of
aggression.

CAROL: What is?

JOHN: A surprise.

ACT 2

(*John and Carol seated across the desk from each other.*)

JOHN: You see, (*pause*) I love to teach. And flatter myself
I am *skilled* at it. And I love the, the aspect of *performance.* I think I must confess that.

When I found I loved to teach I swore that I
would not become that cold, rigid automaton of an
instructor which I had encountered as a child.

Now, I was not unconscious that it was given me
to err upon the other side. And, so, I asked and *ask*
myself if I engaged in heterodoxy, I will not say "gra-
tuitously" for I do not care to posit orthodoxy as a
given good — but, "to the detriment of, of my students." (*Pause.*)

As I said. When the possibility of tenure opened,
and, of course, I'd long pursued it, I was, of course
happy, and *covetous* of it.

I asked myself if I was wrong to covet it. And
thought about it long, and, I hope, truthfully, and
saw in myself several things in, I think, no particular
order. (*Pause.*)

That I *would* pursue it. That I *desired* it, that I
was not pure of longing for security, and that that,
perhaps, was not reprehensible in me. That I had
duties *beyond* the school, and that my duty to my
home, for instance, was, or should be, if it were not,
of an equal weight. That tenure, and security, and
yes, and *comfort,* were not, of themselves, to be
scorned; and were even worthy of honorable pursuit.
And that it was given me. Here, in this place, which I
enjoy, and in which I find comfort, to assure myself
of — as far as it rests in The Material — a continua-

tion of that joy and comfort. In exchange for what?
Teaching. Which I love.

What was the price of this security? To obtain
tenure. Which tenure the committee is in the process
of granting me. And on the basis of which I contracted to purchase a house. Now, as you don't have
your own family, at this point, you may not know
what that means. But to me it is important. A home.
A Good Home. To raise my family. Now: The Tenure
Committee will meet. This is the process, and a *good*
process. Under which the school has functioned for
quite a long time. They will meet, and hear your
complaint — which you have the right to make; and
they will dismiss it. They will *dismiss* your complaint; and, in the intervening period, I will lose my
house. I will not be able to close on my house. I will
lose my *deposit,* and the home I'd picked out for my
wife and son will go by the boards. Now: I see I have
angered you. I understand your anger at teachers. I
was angry with mine. I felt hurt and humiliated by
them. Which is one of the reasons that I went into
education.

CAROL: What do you want of me?

JOHN (*pause*): I was hurt. When I received the report. Of
the tenure committee. I was shocked. And I was hurt.
No, I don't mean to subject you to my weak sensibilities. All right. Finally, I didn't understand. Then I
thought: Is it not always at those points at which we
reckon ourselves unassailable that we are most vulnerable and . . . (*Pause.*) Yes. All right. You find me
pedantic. Yes. I am. By nature, by *birth,* by profession, I don't know . . . I'm always looking for a *paradigm* for . . .

CAROL: I don't know what a paradigm is.

JOHN: It's a model.

CAROL: Then why can't you use that word? (*Pause.*)

JOHN: If it is important to you. Yes, all right. I was looking for a model. To continue: I feel that one point . . .

CAROL: I . . .

JOHN: One second . . . upon which I am unassailable is
my unflinching concern for my students' dignity. I
asked you here to . . . in the spirit of *investigation,* to
ask you . . . to ask . . . (*Pause.*) What have I done to
you? (*Pause.*) And, and, I suppose, how I can make
amends. Can we not settle this now? It's pointless,
really, and I want to know.

CAROL: What you can do to force me to retract?

JOHN: That is not what I meant at all.

CAROL: To bribe me, to convince me . . .

JOHN: . . . No.

CAROL: To retract . . .

JOHN: That is not what I meant at all. I think that you
know it is not.

CAROL: That is not what I know. I *wish* I . . .

JOHN: I do not want to . . . you wish what?

CAROL: No, you said what amends can you make. To
force me to retract.

JOHN: That is not what I said.

CAROL: I have my notes.

JOHN: Look. Look. The Stoics say . . .

CAROL: The Stoics?

JOHN: The Stoical Philosophers say if you remove the phrase "I have been injured," you have removed the injury. Now: Think: I know that you're upset. Just tell me. Literally. Literally: what wrong have I done you?

CAROL: Whatever you have done to me — to the extent that you've done it to *me*, do you know, rather than to me as a *student,* and, so, to the student body, is contained in my report. To the tenure committee.

JOHN: Well, all right. (*Pause.*) Let's see. (*He reads.*) I find that I am sexist. That I am *elitist.* I'm not sure I know what that means, other than it's a derogatory word, meaning "bad." That I . . . That I insist on wasting time, in nonprescribed, in self-aggrandizing and theatrical *diversions* from the prescribed *text* . . . that these have taken both sexist and pornographic forms . . . here we find listed . . . (*Pause.*) Here we find listed . . . instances ". . . closeted with a student" . . . "Told a rambling, sexually explicit story, in which the frequency and attitudes of fornication of the poor and rich are, it would seem, the central point . . . moved to *embrace* said student and . . . all part of a pattern . . ." (*Pause.*)

(*He reads.*) That I used the phrase "The White Man's Burden" . . . that I told you how I'd asked you to my room because I quote like you. (*Pause.*)

(*He reads.*) "He said he 'liked' me. That he 'liked being with me.' He'd let me write my examination paper over, if I could come back oftener to see him in his office." (*Pause.*) (*To Carol.*) It's *ludicrous.* Don't you know that? It's not *necessary.* It's going to *humiliate* you, and it's going to cost me my *house,* and . . .

CAROL: It's *"ludicrous . . ."*?

(*John picks up the report and reads again.*)

JOHN: "He told me he had problems with his wife; and that he wanted to take off the artificial stricture of Teacher and Student. He put his arm around me . . ."

CAROL: Do you deny it? Can you deny it . . . ? Do you see? (*Pause.*) Don't you see? You don't see, do you?

JOHN: I don't see . . .

CAROL: You think, you think you can deny that these things happened; or, if they *did,* if they *did,* that they meant what you *said* they meant. Don't you see? You drag me in here, you drag us, to listen to you "go on"; and "go on" about this, or that, or we don't "express" ourselves very well. We don't say what we mean. Don't we? Don't we? We *do* say what we mean. And you say that "I don't understand you . . .": Then *you* . . . (*Points.*)

JOHN: "Consult the Report"?

CAROL: . . . that's right.

JOHN: You see. You see. Can't you. . . . You see what I'm saying? Can't you tell me in your own words?

CAROL: Those are my own words. (*Pause.*)

JOHN (*he reads*): "He told me that if I would stay alone with him in his office, he would change my grade to an A." (*To Carol.*) What have I done to you? Oh. My God, are you so hurt?

CAROL: What I "feel" is irrelevant. (*Pause.*)

JOHN: Do you know that I tried to help you?

CAROL: What I know I have reported.

JOHN: I would like to help you now. I would. Before this escalates.

CAROL (*simultaneously with* "escalates"): You see. I don't think that I need your help. I don't think I need anything you have.

JOHN: I feel . . .

CAROL: I don't *care* what you feel. Do you see? DO YOU SEE? You can't *do* that anymore. You. Do. Not. Have. The. Power. Did you misuse it? *Someone* did. Are you part of that group? *Yes. Yes.* You Are. You've *done* these things. And to say, and to say, "Oh. Let me help you with your problem . . ."

JOHN: Yes. I understand. I understand. You're *hurt.* You're *angry.* Yes. I think your *anger* is *betraying* you. Down a path which helps no one.

CAROL: I don't *care* what you think.

JOHN: You don't? (*Pause.*) But you talk of *rights.* Don't you see? *I* have rights too. Do you see? I have a *house* . . . part of the *real* world; and The Tenure Committee, Good Men and True . . .

CAROL: . . . Professor . . .

JOHN: . . . Please: *Also* part of that world: you understand? This is my *life.* I'm not a *bogeyman.* I don't "stand" for something, I . . .

CAROL: . . . Professor . . .

JOHN: . . . I . . .

CAROL: Professor. I came here as a *favor.* At your personal request. Perhaps I should not have done so. But I did. On my behalf, and on behalf of my group. And you speak of the tenure committee, one of whose members is a woman, as you know. And though you might call it Good Fun, or An Historical Phrase, or An Oversight, or, All of the Above, to refer to the committee as Good Men and True, it is a demeaning remark. It is a sexist remark, and to overlook it is to countenance continuation of that method of thought. It's a remark . . .

JOHN: OH COME ON. Come on. . . . Sufficient to deprive a family of . . .

CAROL: Sufficient? Sufficient? Sufficient? Yes. It is a *fact* . . . and that story, which I quote, is *vile* and *classist,* and *manipulative* and *pornographic.* It . . .

JOHN: . . . it's pornographic . . . ?

CAROL: What gives you the *right.* Yes. To speak to a *woman* in your private . . . Yes. Yes. I'm sorry. I'm sorry. You feel yourself empowered . . . you say so yourself. To *strut.* To *posture.* To "perform." To "Call me in here . . ." Eh? You say that higher education is a joke. And treat it as such, you *treat* it as such. And *confess* to a taste to play the *Patriarch* in your class. To grant *this.* To deny *that.* To embrace your students.

JOHN: How can you assert. How can you stand there and . . .

CAROL: How can you *deny* it. You did it to me. *Here.* You *did* . . . . You *confess.* You love the Power. To *deviate.* To *invent,* to transgress . . . to *transgress* whatever norms have been established for us. And you think it's charming to "question" in yourself this taste to mock and destroy. But you should question it. Professor. And you pick those things which you feel *advance* you: publication, *tenure,* and the steps to get them you call "harmless rituals." And you perform those steps. Although you say it is hypocrisy. But to the aspirations of your students. Of *hardworking students,* who come here, who *slave* to come here — you have no idea what it cost me to come to this school — you *mock* us. You call education "hazing," and from your so-protected, so-elitist seat you hold our confusion as a *joke,* and our hopes and efforts with it. Then you sit there and say "what have I done?" And ask me to understand that *you* have aspirations too. But I tell you. I tell you. That you are vile. And that you are exploitative. And if you possess one ounce of that inner honesty you describe in your book, you can look in yourself and see those things that I see. And you can find revulsion equal to my own. Good day. (*She prepares to leave the room.*)

JOHN: Wait a second, will you, just one moment. (*Pause.*) Nice day today.

CAROL: What?

JOHN: You said "Good day." I think that it is a nice day today.

CAROL: *Is* it?

JOHN: Yes, I think it is.

CAROL: And why is that important?

JOHN: Because it is the essence of all human communication. I say something conventional, you respond, and the information we exchange is not about the "weather," but that we both agree to converse. In effect, we agree that we are both human. (*Pause.*)

I'm not a . . . "exploiter," and you're not a . . . "deranged," what? *Revolutionary* . . . that we may, that we may have . . . positions, and that we may have . . . desires, which are in *conflict,* but that we're just human. (*Pause.*) That means that sometimes we're *imperfect.* (*Pause.*) Often we're in conflict . . . (*Pause.*) *Much* of what we do, you're right, in the name of "principles" is *self-serving* . . . much of what we do is *conventional.* (*Pause.*) You're right. (*Pause.*) You said you came in the class because you wanted to learn about *education.* I don't know that I can teach you about education. But I know that I can tell you what I *think* about education, and then *you* decide. And you don't have to fight with me. *I'm* not the subject. (*Pause.*) And where I'm *wrong* . . . perhaps it's not your job to "fix" me. I don't want to fix *you.* I would like to tell you what I *think,* because that *is* my job, conventional as it is, and flawed as I may be. And then, if you can show me some better *form,* then we can proceed from there. But, just like "nice day, isn't it . . . ?" I don't think we can proceed until we accept that each of us is human. (*Pause.*)

And we still can have difficulties. We *will* have them . . . that's all right too. (*Pause.*) Now:

CAROL: . . . wait . . .

JOHN: Yes. I want to hear it.

CAROL: . . . the . . .

JOHN: Yes. Tell me frankly.

CAROL: . . . my position . . .

JOHN: I want to hear it. In your own words. What you want. And what you feel.

CAROL: . . . I . . .

JOHN: . . . yes . . .

CAROL: My Group.

JOHN: Your "Group" . . . ? (*Pause.*)

CAROL: The people I've been talking to . . .

JOHN: There's no shame in that. Everybody needs advisers. Everyone needs to expose themselves. To various points of view. It's not wrong. It's essential. Good. Good. Now: You and I . . .

(*The phone rings.*)

You and I . . .

(*He hesitates for a moment, and then picks it up.*)

(*Into phone.*) Hello. (*Pause.*) Um . . . no, I know they do. (*Pause.*) I know she does. Tell her that I . . . can I call you back? . . . Then tell her that I think it's going to be fine. (*Pause.*) Tell her just, just hold on, I'll . . . can I get back to you? . . . Well . . . no, no, no, we're *taking* the house . . . we're . . . no, no, nn . . . no, she will nnn, it's not a *question* of refunding the dep . . . no . . . it's not a *question* of the deposit . . . will you call Jerry? Babe, baby, will you just call Jerry? Tell him, nnn . . . tell him they, well, they're to keep the deposit, because the deal, be . . . because the deal is going to go *through* . . . because I know . . . be . . . will you please? Just *trust* me. Be . . . well, I'm dealing with the complaint. Yes. Right *Now.* Which is why I . . . yes, no, no, it's really, I can't *talk* about it now. Call Jerry, and I can't talk now. Ff . . . fine. Gg . . . good-bye. (*Hangs up.*) (*Pause.*) I'm sorry we were interrupted.

CAROL: No . . .

JOHN: I . . . I was saying:

CAROL: You said that we should agree to talk about my complaint.

JOHN: That's correct.

CAROL: But we *are* talking about it.

JOHN: Well, that's correct too. You see? This is the *gist* of education.

CAROL: No, no. I mean, we're talking about it at the Tenure Committee Hearing. (*Pause.*)

JOHN: Yes, but I'm saying: we can talk about it *now,* as easily as . . .

CAROL: No. I think that we should stick to the process . . .

JOHN: . . . wait a . . .

CAROL: . . . the "conventional" process. As you said. (*She gets up.*) And you're right, I'm sorry if I was, um, if I was "discourteous" to you. You're right.

JOHN: Wait, wait a . . .

CAROL: I really should go.

JOHN: Now, look, granted. I have an interest. In the status quo. All right? Everyone does. But what I'm saying is that the *committee* . . .

CAROL: Professor, you're right. Just don't impinge on me. We'll take our differences, and . . .

JOHN: You're going to make a . . . look, look, look, you're going to . . .

CAROL: I shouldn't have come here. They told me . . .

JOHN: One moment. No. No. There are *norms,* here, and there's no reason. Look: I'm trying to *save* you . . .

CAROL: No one *asked* you to . . . you're trying to save *me?* Do me the courtesy to . . .

JOHN: I *am* doing you the courtesy. I'm talking *straight* to you. We can settle this *now.* And I want you to sit *down* and . . .

CAROL: You must excuse me . . . (*She starts to leave the room.*)

JOHN: Sit down, it seems we each have a . . . . Wait one moment. Wait one moment . . . just do me the courtesy to . . .

(*He restrains her from leaving.*)

CAROL: LET ME GO.

JOHN: I have no desire to *hold* you, I just want to *talk* to you . . .

CAROL: LET ME GO. LET ME GO. WOULD SOMEBODY *HELP* ME? WOULD SOMEBODY *HELP* ME PLEASE . . . ?

ACT 3

(*At rise, Carol and John are seated.*)

JOHN: I have asked you here. (*Pause.*) I have asked you here against, against my . . .

CAROL: I was most surprised you asked me.

JOHN: . . . against my better *judgment,* against . . .

CAROL: I was most surprised . . .

JOHN: . . . against the . . . yes. I'm sure.

CAROL: . . . If you would like me to leave, I'll leave. I'll go right now . . . (*She rises.*)

JOHN: Let us begin *correctly,* may we? I feel . . .

CAROL: That is what I wished to do. That's why I came here, but now . . .

JOHN: . . . I feel . . .

CAROL: But now perhaps you'd like me to leave . . .

JOHN: I don't want you to leave. I asked you to come . . .

CAROL: I didn't have to come here.

JOHN: No. (*Pause.*) Thank you.

CAROL: All right. (*Pause.*) (*She sits down.*)

JOHN: Although I feel that it *profits,* it would *profit* you something, to . . .

CAROL: . . . what I . . .

JOHN: If you would hear me out, if you would hear me out.

CAROL: I came here to, the court officers told me not to come.

JOHN: . . . the "court" officers . . . ?

CAROL: I was shocked that you asked.

JOHN: . . . wait . . .

CAROL: Yes. But I did *not* come here to hear what it "profits" me.

JOHN: The "court" officers . . .

CAROL: . . . no, no, perhaps I should leave . . . (*She gets up.*)

JOHN: Wait.

CAROL: No. I shouldn't have . . .

JOHN: . . . wait. Wait. Wait a moment.

CAROL: Yes? What is it you want? (*Pause.*) What is it you want?

JOHN: I'd like you to stay.

CAROL: You want me to stay.

JOHN: Yes.

CAROL: You do.

JOHN: Yes. (*Pause.*) Yes. I would like to have you hear me out. If you would. (*Pause.*) Would you please? If you would do that I would be in your debt. (*Pause.*) (*She sits.*) Thank You. (*Pause.*)

CAROL: What is it you wish to tell me?

JOHN: All right. I cannot . . . (*Pause.*) I cannot help but feel you are owed an apology. (*Pause.*) (*Of papers in his hands.*) I have read. (*Pause.*) And reread these accusations.

CAROL: What "accusations"?

JOHN: The, the tenure comm . . . what other accusations . . . ?

CAROL: The tenure committee . . . ?

JOHN: Yes.

CAROL: Excuse me, but those are not accusations. They have been *proved.* They are facts.

JOHN: . . . I . . .

CAROL: No. Those are not "accusations."

JOHN: . . . those?

CAROL: . . . the committee (*The phone starts to ring.*) the committee has . . .

JOHN: . . . All right . . .

CAROL: . . . those are not accusations. The Tenure Committee.

JOHN: ALL RIGHT. ALL RIGHT. ALL RIGHT. (*He picks up the phone.*) Hello. Yes. No. I'm here. Tell Mister . . . No, I can't talk to him now . . . I'm sure he has, but I'm fff . . . I know . . . No, I have no time t . . . tell Mister . . . tell Mist . . . tell Jerry that I'm *fine* and that I'll call him right aw . . . (*Pause.*) My wife . . . Yes. I'm sure she has. Yes, thank you. Yes, I'll call her too. I cannot talk to you now. (*He hangs up.*) (*Pause.*) All right. It was good of you to come. Thank you. I have studied. I have spent some time studying the indictment.

CAROL: You will have to explain that word to me.

JOHN: An "indictment" . . .

CAROL: Yes.

JOHN: Is a "bill of particulars." A . . .

CAROL: Ah right. Yes.

JOHN: In which is alleged . . .

CAROL: No. I cannot allow that. I cannot allow that. Nothing is alleged. Everything is proved . . .

JOHN: Please, wait a sec . . .

CAROL: I cannot *come* to allow . . .

JOHN: If I may . . . If I may, from whatever you feel is "established," by . . .

CAROL: The issue here is not what I "feel." It is not my "feelings," but the feelings of women. And men. Your superiors, who've been "polled," do you see? To whom *evidence* has been presented, who have *ruled*, do you see? Who have weighed the testimony and the evidence, and have *ruled*, do you see? That you are *negligent*. That you are *guilty*, that you are found *wanting*, and in *error*; and are *not*, for the reasons so-told, to be given tenure. That you are to be disciplined. For facts. For *facts*. Not "alleged," what is the word? But *proved*. Do you see? *By your own actions.*

That is what the tenure committee has said. That is what my lawyer said. For what you did in class. For what you did *in this office.*

JOHN: They're going to discharge me.

CAROL: As full well they should. You don't understand? You're angry? What has *led* you to this place? Not your sex. Not your race. Not your class. YOUR OWN ACTIONS. And you're *angry*. You *ask* me here. What *do* you want? You want to "charm" me. You want to "convince" me. You want me to recant. I will *not* recant. Why should I . . . ? What I say is right. You tell me, you are going to tell me that you have a wife and child. You are going to say that you have a career and that you've worked for twenty years for this. Do you know what you've *worked* for? *Power.* For *power*. Do you understand? And you sit there, and you tell me *stories*. About your *house*, about all the private *schools*, and about *privilege*, and how you are entitled. To *buy*, to *spend*, to *mock*, to *summon*. All your stories. All your silly weak *guilt*, it's all about *privilege*; and you won't know it. Don't you see? You worked twenty years for the right to *insult* me. And you feel entitled to be *paid* for it. Your Home. Your Wife . . . Your sweet "deposit" on your house . . .

JOHN: Don't you have feelings?

CAROL: That's my point. You see? Don't you have feelings? Your final argument. What is it that has no feelings. *Animals.* I don't take your side, you question if I'm Human.

JOHN: Don't you have feelings?

CAROL: I have a responsibility. I . . .

JOHN: . . . to . . . ?

CAROL: To? This institution. To the *students*. To my *group*.

JOHN: . . . your "group." . . .

CAROL: Because I speak, yes, not for myself. But for the group; for those who suffer what I suffer. On behalf of whom, even if I, were, inclined, to what, forgive? Forget? What? Overlook your . . .

JOHN: . . . my behavior?

CAROL: . . . it would be wrong.

JOHN: Even if you were inclined to "forgive" me.

CAROL: It would be wrong.

JOHN: And what would transpire.

CAROL: Transpire?

JOHN: Yes.

CAROL: "Happen?"

JOHN: Yes.

CAROL: Then *say* it. For Christ's sake. Who the *hell* do you think that you are? You want a post. You want unlimited power. To do and to say what you want. As it pleases you — Testing, Questioning, Flirting . . .

JOHN: I never . . .

CAROL: Excuse me, one moment, will you?

(*She reads from her notes.*)

The twelfth: "Have a good day, dear."

The fifteenth: "Now, don't *you* look fetching . . ."

April seventeenth: "If you girls would come over here . . ." I saw you. I saw you, Professor. For two semesters sit there, stand there and exploit our, as you thought, "paternal prerogative," and what is that but rape; I swear to God. You asked me in here to explain something to me, as a child, that I did not understand. But I came to explain something to you. You Are Not God. You ask me why I came? I came here to instruct you.

(*She produces his book.*)

And your book? You think you're going to show me some "light"? You "*maverick*." Outside of tradition. No, no, (*She reads from the book's liner notes.*) "*of* that fine tradition of *inquiry*. Of Polite *skepticism*" . . . and you say you believe in free intellectual discourse. YOU BELIEVE IN NOTHING. YOU BELIEVE IN NOTHING AT ALL.

JOHN: I believe in freedom of thought.

CAROL: Isn't that fine. *Do* you?

JOHN: Yes. I do.

CAROL: Then why do you question, for one moment, the committee's decision refusing your tenure? Why do you question your suspension? You believe in what *you call* freedom of thought. Then, fine. *You* believe in freedom-of-thought *and* a home, and, *and* prerogatives for your kid, *and* tenure. And I'm going to tell you. You believe *not* in "freedom of thought," but in an elitist, in, in a protected hierarchy which rewards you. And for whom you are the clown. And you mock and exploit the system which pays your rent. You're wrong. I'm not wrong. You're wrong. You think that I'm full of hatred. I know what you think I am.

JOHN: Do you?

CAROL: You think I'm a, of course I do. You think I am a frightened, repressed, confused, I don't know, abandoned young thing of some doubtful sexuality, who wants, power and revenge. (*Pause.*) *Don't* you? (*Pause.*)

JOHN: Yes. I do. (*Pause.*)

CAROL: Isn't that better? And I feel that that is the first

moment which you've treated me with respect. For you told me the truth. (*Pause.*) I did not come here, as you are assured, to gloat. Why would I want to gloat? I've profited nothing from your, your, as you say, your "misfortune." I came here, as you did me the honor to *ask* me here, I came here to *tell* you something. (*Pause.*)

That I think . . . that I think you've been wrong. That I think you've been terribly wrong. Do you hate me now? (*Pause.*)

JOHN: Yes.

CAROL: Why do you hate me? Because you think me wrong? No. Because I have, you think, *power* over you. Listen to me. Listen to me, Professor. (*Pause.*) It is the power that you hate. So deeply that, that any atmosphere of free discussion is impossible. It's not "unlikely." It's *impossible*. Isn't it?

JOHN: Yes.

CAROL: *Isn't* it . . . ?

JOHN: Yes. I suppose.

CAROL: Now. The thing which you find so cruel is the selfsame process of selection I, and my group, go through *every day of our lives*. In admittance to school. In our tests, in our class rankings. . . . Is it unfair? I can't tell you. But, if it is fair. Or even if it is "unfortunate but necessary" for us, then, by God, so must it be for you. (*Pause.*) You write of your "responsibility to the young." Treat us with respect, and that will *show* you your responsibility. You write that education is just hazing. (*Pause.*) But we worked to get to this school. (*Pause.*) And some of us. (*Pause.*) Overcame prejudices. Economic, sexual, you cannot begin to imagine. And endured humiliations I *pray* that you and those you love never will encounter. (*Pause.*) To gain admittance here. To pursue that same dream of security *you* pursue. We, who, who are, at any moment, in danger of being deprived of it. By . . .

JOHN: . . . by . . . ?

CAROL: By the administration. By the teachers. By *you*. By, say, one low grade, that keeps us out of graduate school; by one, say, one capricious or inventive answer on our parts, which, perhaps, you don't find amusing. Now you *know*, do you see? What it is to be subject to that power. (*Pause.*)

JOHN: I don't understand. (*Pause.*)

CAROL: My charges are not trivial. You see that in the haste, I think, with which they were accepted. A *joke* you have told, with a sexist tinge. The language you use, a verbal or physical caress, yes, yes, I know, you say that it is meaningless. I understand. I differ from you. To lay a hand on someone's shoulder.

JOHN: It was devoid of sexual content.

CAROL: I say it was not. I SAY IT WAS NOT. Don't you begin to *see* . . . ? Don't you begin to understand? IT'S NOT FOR YOU TO SAY.

JOHN: I take your point, and I see there is much good in what you refer to.

CAROL: . . . do you think so . . . ?

JOHN: . . . but, and this is not to say that I cannot change, in those things in which I am deficient . . . But, the . . .

CAROL: Do you hold yourself harmless from the charge of sexual exploitativeness . . . ? (*Pause.*)

JOHN: Well, I . . . I . . . I . . . You know I, as I said. I . . . think I am not too old to *learn,* and I *can* learn, I . . .

CAROL: Do you hold yourself innocent of the charge of . . .

JOHN: . . . wait, wait, wait . . . All right, let's go back to . . .

CAROL: YOU FOOL. Who do you think I am? To come here and be taken in by a *smile*. You little yapping fool. You think I want "revenge." I don't want revenge. I WANT UNDERSTANDING.

JOHN: . . . *do* you?

CAROL: I do. (*Pause.*)

JOHN: What's the use. It's over.

CAROL: Is it? What is?

JOHN: My job.

CAROL: Oh. Your job. That's what you want to talk about. (*Pause.*) (*She starts to leave the room. She steps and turns back to him.*) All right. (*Pause.*) What if it were possible that my Group withdraws its complaint. (*Pause.*)

JOHN: What?

CAROL: That's right. (*Pause.*)

JOHN: Why.

CAROL: Well, let's say as an act of friendship.

JOHN: An act of friendship.

CAROL: Yes. (*Pause.*)

JOHN: In exchange for what.

CAROL: Yes. But I don't think, "exchange." Not "in exchange." For what do we derive from it? (*Pause.*)

JOHN: "Derive."

CAROL: Yes.

JOHN (*pause*): Nothing. (*Pause.*)

CAROL: That's right. We derive nothing. (*Pause.*) Do you see that?

JOHN: Yes.

CAROL: That is a little word, Professor. "Yes." "I see that." But you will.

JOHN: And you might speak to the committee . . . ?

CAROL: To the committee?

JOHN: Yes.

CAROL: Well. Of course. That's on your mind. We might.

JOHN: "If" what?

CAROL: "Given" what. Perhaps. I think that that is more friendly.

JOHN: GIVEN WHAT?

CAROL: And, believe me, I understand your rage. It is not that I don't feel it. But I do not see that it is deserved, so I do not resent it. . . . All right. I have a list.

JOHN: . . . a list.

CAROL: Here is a list of books, which we . . .

JOHN: . . . a list of books . . . ?

CAROL: That's right. Which we find questionable.

JOHN: What?

CAROL: Is this so bizarre . . . ?

JOHN: I can't believe . . .

CAROL: It's not necessary you believe it.

JOHN: Academic freedom . . .

CAROL: Someone chooses the books. If you can choose them, others can. What are you, "God"?

JOHN: . . . no, no, the "dangerous." . . .

CAROL: You have an agenda, we have an agenda. I am not interested in your feelings or your motivation, but your actions. If you would like me to speak to the Tenure Committee, here is my list. You are a Free Person, you decide. (*Pause.*)

JOHN: Give me the list.

(*She does so. He reads.*)

CAROL: I think you'll find . . .

JOHN: I'm capable of reading it. Thank you.

CAROL: We have a number of *texts* we need re . . .

JOHN: I see that.

CAROL: We're amenable to . . .

JOHN: Aha. Well, let me look over the . . . (*He reads.*)

CAROL: I think that . . .

JOHN: LOOK. I'm reading your demands. All right?! (*He reads.*) (*Pause.*) You want to ban my book?

CAROL: We do not . . .

JOHN (*of list*): It says here . . .

CAROL: . . . We want it removed from inclusion as a representative example of the university.

JOHN: Get out of here.

CAROL: If you put aside the issues of personalities.

JOHN: Get the fuck out of my office.

CAROL: No, I think I would reconsider.

JOHN: . . . you think you can.

CAROL: We can and we *will*. Do you want our support? That is the only quest . . .

JOHN: . . . to ban my *book* . . . ?

CAROL: . . . that is correct . . .

JOHN: . . . this . . . this is a *university* . . . we . . .

CAROL: . . . and we have a statement . . . which we need you to . . . (*She hands him a sheet of paper.*)

JOHN: No, no. It's out of the question. I'm sorry. I don't know what I was thinking of. I want to tell you something. I'm a teacher. I am a teacher. Eh? It's my *name* on the door, and *I* teach the class, and that's what I do. I've got a book with my name on it. And my son will *see* that *book* someday. And I have a respon . . . No, I'm sorry I have a *responsibility* . . . to *myself*, to my *son*, to my *profession*. . . . I haven't been *home* for two days, do you know that? Thinking this out.

CAROL: . . . you haven't?

JOHN: I've been, no. If it's of interest to you. I've been in a *hotel*. *Thinking.* (*The phone starts ringing.*) *Thinking* . . .

CAROL: . . . you haven't been home?

JOHN: . . . *thinking*, do you see.

CAROL: Oh.

JOHN: And, and, I owe you a debt, I see that now. (*Pause.*) You're *dangerous*, you're *wrong* and it's my *job* . . . to say no to you. That's my job. You are absolutely right. You want to ban my book? Go to *hell*, and they can do whatever they want to me.

CAROL: . . . you haven't been home in two days . . .

JOHN: I think I told you that.

CAROL: . . . you'd better get that phone. (*Pause.*) I think that you should pick up the phone. (*Pause.*)

(*John picks up the phone.*)

JOHN (*on phone*): Yes. (*Pause.*) Yes. Wh . . . I. I. I had to be away. All ri . . . did they wor . . . did they worry ab . . . No. I'm all right, now, Jerry. I'm f . . . I got a little turned *around*, but I'm *sitting* here and . . . I've got it figured out. I'm fine. I'm fine don't worry about me. I got a little bit mixed up. But I am not sure that it's not a blessing. It cost me my job? Fine. Then the job was not worth having. Tell Grace that I'm coming home and everything is fff . . . (*Pause.*) What? (*Pause.*) *What*? (*Pause.*) What do you *mean*? WHAT? Jerry . . . Jerry. They . . . Who, who, what can they do . . . ? (*Pause.*) NO. (*Pause.*) NO. They can't do th . . . What do you mean? (*Pause.*) But how . . . (*Pause.*) She's, she's, she's *here* with me. To . . . Jerry. I don't underst . . . (*Pause.*) (*He hangs up.*) (*To Carol.*) What does this mean?

CAROL: I thought you knew.

JOHN: What. (*Pause.*) What does it mean. (*Pause.*)

CAROL: You tried to rape me. (*Pause.*) According to the law. (*Pause.*)

JOHN: . . . what . . . ?

CAROL: You tried to rape me. I was leaving this office, you "pressed" yourself into me. You "pressed" your body into me.

JOHN: . . . I . . .

CAROL: My Group has told your lawyer that we may pursue criminal charges.

JOHN: . . . no . . .

CAROL: . . . under the statute. I am told. It was battery.

JOHN: . . . no . . .

CAROL: Yes. And attempted rape. That's right. (*Pause.*)

JOHN: I think that you should go.

CAROL: Of course. I thought you knew.

JOHN: I have to talk to my lawyer.

CAROL: Yes. Perhaps you should.
(*The phone rings again.*) (*Pause.*)

JOHN (*picks up phone, into phone*): Hello? I . . . Hello . . . ? I . . . Yes, he just called. No . . . I. I can't talk to you now, Baby. (*To Carol.*) Get out.

CAROL: . . . your wife . . . ?

JOHN: . . . who it is is no concern of yours. Get out. (*To phone.*) No, no, it's going to be all right. I. I can't talk now, Baby. (*To Carol.*) Get out of here.

CAROL: I'm going.

JOHN: Good.

CAROL (*exiting*): . . . and don't call your wife "baby."

JOHN: What?

CAROL: Don't call your wife baby. You heard what I said.

(*Carol starts to leave the room. John grabs her and begins to beat her.*)

JOHN: You vicious little bitch. You think you can come in here with your political correctness and destroy my life?

(*He knocks her to the floor.*)

After how I treated you . . . ? You should be . . . *Rape you* . . . ? Are you kidding me . . . ?

(*He picks up a chair, raises it above his head, and advances on her.*)

I wouldn't touch you with a ten-foot pole. You little *cunt* . . .

(*She cowers on the floor below him. Pause. He looks down at her. He lowers the chair. He moves to his desk, and arranges the papers on it. Pause. He looks over at her.*)

. . . well . . .

(*Pause. She looks at him.*)

CAROL: Yes. That's right.

(*She looks away from him, and lowers her head. To herself:*) . . . yes. That's right.

Tony Kushner

Tony Kushner was born in 1956 in New York City, but his family soon moved to Louisiana, where his father ran the family lumberyard. His parents were classical musicians, and their home was filled with art. Kushner dates his interest in theater to early memories of seeing his mother onstage. He also recollects from childhood "fairly clear memories of being gay since I was six." He did not, however, "come out" until after he had tried psychotherapy to change his sexual orientation.

After finishing his undergraduate education at Columbia University, Kushner studied directing in graduate school at New York University, partly because he was not confident of his chances to become a playwright. Among his early plays are *Yes, Yes, No, No* (1985), a children's play produced in St. Louis; *Stella* (1987), an adaptation from Goethe produced in New York; *A Bright Room Called Day* (1987), produced in San Francisco; *The Illusion* (1988), adapted from Corneille, produced in New York, then in Hartford in 1990. He worked with Argentinian playwright Ariel Dorfman to adapt Dorfman's *Widows,* produced in Los Angeles in 1991. *A Bright Room Called Day,* about left-wing politics in Nazi Germany, was not well reviewed after its New York production in 1991. Frank Rich, for example, said that it was "an early front-runner for the most infuriating play of 1991." But some people saw in it the power that was to show up later in his work. The Eureka Theater in San Francisco commissioned him to write a play that ultimately turned out to be *Angels in America: A Gay Fantasia on National Themes* (1992), the play that catapulted him to international prominence.

Among Kushner's current projects is a series of three plays which he describes as having money as its subject — meaning, in part, the effects of economics, in the forms of both poverty and wealth, on individuals. The first of these plays, to be titled *Henry Box Brown,* centers on the true story of a black American who escaped slavery by being smuggled out of the South in a crate. Brown eventually made his way to England where he joined with a number of other former slaves in producing dramatic "panoramas" intended to discourage the English from buying slave-picked cotton, on which their textile industry largely relied. Kushner has said, "I've always been drawn to writing historical characters. . . . The best stories are the ones you find in history."

ANGELS IN AMERICA: MILLENNIUM APPROACHES

Kushner began work on the play shortly after Oskar Eustis of Eureka Theater commissioned a two-and-a-half hour play with songs. Once Kushner got a presentable version, he showed it to Eustis and realized that, even incomplete, it was already longer than a one-evening play. Eventually, *Millennium Approaches* and *Perestroika,* the second part of *Angels* (not included here), grew to be more than seven hours long. Although the two parts are thematically linked and contain many of the same characters, both parts of *Angels* stand on their own as complete plays. Kushner said that he never expected to see his play produced anywhere but in a small theater in San Francisco; certainly he never expected it to be a smash hit on Broadway. It won the 1993 Pulitzer Prize for drama, another surprise.

Angels in America has epic Brechtian proportions. Kushner has said that he set out to write a play on "AIDS, Mormons, and Roy Cohn." He chose AIDS because it is a scourge that has especially destroyed large numbers of the gay community. He chose Mormons because he saw in them a group that valued goodness and godliness but that could not tolerate gays. He chose Roy Cohn because when Cohn was an aid to Senator McCarthy during the anti-Communist hysteria of the 1950s, he persecuted gays although he was himself a closet homosexual. His homosexuality did not become public until he contracted AIDS and died in 1986. In Cohn, Kushner had found a villain whose rapacious individualism and unquenchable thirst for power helped symbolize the selfishness of the 1980s. In its New York production Ron Liebman was an overbearingly powerful Cohn, shouting orders, raising hypocrisy to an art form, with depths of contempt matching a profound love of power.

Kushner indicated that his play was a "fantasia on national themes," and it certainly lives up to its title. Kushner set his play in 1985, during the second presidential term of Ronald Reagan. He critiques the values of the Reagan years and politics in general. Jews, WASPs, and Mormons all suffer under his scrutiny. Moreover, he goes beyond national themes and introduces cosmological themes, notably with the introduction of an angel descending through the ceiling at the end of *Millennium Approaches.*

The play focuses as well on problems of individuals. Cohn's friend and protégé Joe Pitt works for the Reagan administration and struggles with his growing awareness that he is gay. A conservative Mormon, Joe faces honestly and painfully these complex, threatening feelings. Harper, Joe's wife, relies on pills, listens all day to talk shows, and has no job but thinks of herself as part of a traditional marriage and fights to hold on to it. Louis Ironson, a liberal but not profoundly political homosexual, is partnered with Prior Walter, dying from AIDS. Louis has hidden his sexuality from his family and finds it impossible to stay with Prior as his lover's illness worsens. Kushner makes sure that we see all these sets of people interrelated throughout the play, despite their distinctness and the unlikeliness of their ever knowing one another.

Though the scope of the play is enormous, its focus is essentially on politics. Kushner's own views contrast sharply with Cohn's conservative politics, and he is surprised that both conservatives and liberals found the play rewarding, since Kushner felt it to be a pointed attack on conservative values.

Angels in America: Millennium Approaches in Performance

The premiere of the play was in a workshop version in 1991 in the Eureka Theater in San Francisco. Its first full-scale production came in July 1992 at London's Royal National Theatre, where it was a sensation. Some reviewers speculated that in London the way was prepared for this play by the political theater of Caryl Churchill and other playwrights such as David Hare and David Edgar. The audiences were enormously enthusiastic, and the positive reviews the play received attracted attention in the United States. Despite Kushner's relatively unknown status, the two parts of the drama (over seven hours long) were staged in the Mark Taper Forum in Los Angeles in 1992, directed by Oskar Eustis. *Millennium Approaches* appeared on Broadway in April 1993 at the Walter Kerr Theater, directed by George C. Wolfe. Frank Rich gave it a strong, positive review and said, "When first seen a year or so ago, the play seemed defined by its anger at the reigning political establishment, which tended to reward the Roy Cohns and ignore the Prior Walters. Mr. Kushner has not revised the text since — a crony of Cohn's still boasts of a Republican lock on the White House until the year 2000 — but the shift in Washington has had the subliminal effect of making *Angels in America* seem more focused on what happens next than on the past."

The second part of the work, *Perestroika*, arrived on Broadway in November 1993. Frank Rich in the *New York Times* said it was "also a true millennial work of art, uplifting, hugely comic and pantheistically religious in a very American style." After its Broadway run, the play moved to regional theaters, touring throughout the United States. The staging of the drama includes moments that may be described as magical realism featuring ghosts, hallucinations, and other illusions. But Kushner has said, "The play benefits from a pared-down style of presentation, with minimal scenery and scene shifts done rapidly (no blackouts!), employing the cast as well as stagehands — which makes for an actor-driven event, as this must be." He said that it was not a problem if "wires showed," "but the magic should at the same time be thoroughly amazing."

Tony Kushner (b. 1956)

ANGELS IN AMERICA: MILLENNIUM APPROACHES   *1992*
A GAY FANTASIA ON NATIONAL THEMES

Characters

ROY M. COHN, *a successful New York lawyer and unofficial power broker*

JOSEPH PORTER PITT, *chief clerk for Justice Theodore Wilson of the Federal Court of Appeals, Second Circuit*

HARPER AMATY PITT, *Joe's wife, an agoraphobic with a mild Valium addiction*

LOUIS IRONSON, *a word processor working for the Second Circuit Court of Appeals*

PRIOR WALTER, *Louis's boyfriend. Occasionally works as a club designer or caterer, otherwise lives very modestly but with great style off a small trust fund.*

HANNAH PORTER PITT, *Joe's mother, currently residing in Salt Lake City, living off her deceased husband's army pension*

BELIZE, *a former drag queen and former lover of Prior's. A registered nurse. Belize's name was originally Norman Arriaga; Belize is a drag name that stuck.*

THE ANGEL, *four divine emanations, Fluor, Phosphor, Lumen and Candle; manifest in One: the Continental Principality of America. She has magnificent steel-gray wings.*

Other Characters in Part One

RABBI ISISOR CHEMELWITZ, *an orthodox Jewish rabbi, played by the actor playing Hannah*

MR. LIES, *Harper's imaginary friend, a travel agent, who in style of dress and speech suggests a jazz musician; he always wears a large lapel badge emblazoned "IOTA" (The International Order of Travel Agents). He is played by the actor playing Belize.*

THE MAN IN THE PARK, *played by the actor playing Prior*

THE VOICE, *the voice of The Angel*

HENRY, *Roy's doctor, played by the actor playing Hannah*

EMILY, *a nurse, played by the actor playing The Angel*

MARTIN HELLER, *a Reagan Administration Justice Department flackman, played by the actor playing Harper*

SISTER ELLA CHAPTER, *a Salt Lake City real-estate saleswoman, played by the actor playing the Angel*

PRIOR 1, *the ghost of a dead Prior Walter from the 13th century, played by the actor playing Joe. He is blunt, gloomy medieval farmer with a gutteral Yorkshire accent.*

PRIOR 2, *the ghost of a dead Prior Walter from the 17th century, played by the actor playing Roy. He is a Londoner, sophisticated, with a High British accent.*

THE ESKIMO, *played by the actor playing Joe*

THE WOMAN IN THE SOUTH BRONX, *played by the actor playing the Angel*

ETHEL ROSENBERG, *played by the actor playing Hannah*

Playwright's Notes

A Disclaimer: Roy M. Cohn, the character, is based on the late Roy M. Cohn (1927–1986), who was all too real; for the most part the acts attributed to the character Roy, such as his illegal conferences with Judge Kaufmann during the trial of Ethel Rosenberg, are to be found in the historical record. But this Roy is a work of dramatic fiction; his words are my invention, and liberties have been taken.

A Note about the Staging: The play benefits from a pared-down style of presentation, with minimal scenery and scene shifts done rapidly (no blackouts!), employing the cast as well as stagehands — which makes for an actor-driven event, as this must be. The moments of magic — the appearance and disappearance of Mr. Lies and the ghosts, the Book hallucination, and the ending — are to be fully realized, as bits of wonderful theatrical illusion — which means it's OK if the wires show, and maybe it's good that they do, but the magic should at the same time be thoroughly amazing.

> *In a murderous time*
> *the heart breaks and breaks*
> *and lives by breaking.*   — STANLEY KUNITZ
>   "THE TESTING-TREE"

ACT 1
BAD NEWS • *October–November 1985*

Scene 1

(*The last days of October. Rabbi Isidor Chemelwitz alone onstage with a small coffin. It is a rough pine box with two wooden pegs, one at the foot and one at the head, holding the lid in place. A prayer shawl embroidered with a Star of David is draped over the lid, and by the head a yarzheit candle is burning.*)

RABBI ISIDOR CHEMELWITZ (*he speaks sonorously, with a heavy Eastern European accent, unapologetically consulting a sheet of notes for the family names*): Hello and good morning. I am Rabbi Isidor

Chemelwitz of the Bronx Home for Aged Hebrews. We are here this morning to pay respects at the passing of Sarah Ironson, devoted wife of Benjamin Ironson, also deceased, loving and caring mother of her sons Morris, Abraham, and Samuel, and her daughters Esther and Rachel; beloved grandmother of Max, Mark, Louis, Lisa, Maria . . . uh . . . Lesley, Angela, Doris, Luke and Eric. (*Looks more closely at paper.*) Eric? This is a Jewish name? (*Shrugs.*) Eric. A large and loving family. We assemble that we may mourn collectively this good and righteous woman.

(*He looks at the coffin.*)

This woman. I did not know this woman. I cannot accurately describe her attributes, nor do justice to her dimensions. She was. . . . Well, in the Bronx Home of Aged Hebrews are many like this, the old, and to many I speak but not to be frank with this one. She preferred silence. So I do not know her and yet I know her. She was . . .

(*he touches the coffin*)

. . . not a person but a whole kind of person, the ones who crossed the ocean, who brought with us to America the villages of Russia and Lithuania — and how we struggled, and how we fought, for the family, for the Jewish home, so that you would not grow up *here*, in this strange place, in the melting pot where nothing melted. Descendants of this immigrant woman, you do not grow up in America, you and your children and their children with the goyische names. You do not live in America. No such place exists. Your clay is the clay of some Litvak shtetl, your air the air of the steppes — because she carried the old world on her back across the ocean, in a boat, and she put it down on Grand Concourse Avenue, or in Flatbush, and she worked that earth into your bones, and you pass it to your children, this ancient, ancient culture and home.

(*Little pause.*)

You can never make that crossing that she made, for such Great Voyages in this world do not any more exist. But every day of your lives the miles that voyage between that place and this one you cross. Every day. You understand me? In you that journey is.

So . . .

She was the last of the Mohicans, this one was. Pretty soon . . . all the old will be dead.

Scene 2

(*Same day. Roy and Joe in Roy's office. Roy at an impressive desk, bare except for a very elaborate phone system, rows and rows of flashing buttons which bleep and beep and whistle incessantly, making chaotic music underneath Roy's conversations. Joe is sitting, waiting. Roy conducts business with great energy, impatience and sensual abandon: gesticulating, shouting, cajoling, crooning, playing the phone, receiver and hold button with virtuosity and love.*)

ROY (*hitting a button*): Hold. (*To Joe.*) I wish I was an octopus, a fucking octopus. Eight loving arms and all those suckers. Know what I mean?

JOE: No, I . . .

ROY (*gesturing to a deli platter of little sandwiches on his desk*): You want lunch?

JOE: No, that's OK really I just . . .

ROY (*hitting a button*): Ailene? Roy Cohn. Now what kind of a greeting is. . . . I thought we were friends, Ai. . . . Look Mrs. Soffer you don't have to get. . . . You're upset. You're yelling. You'll aggravate your condition, you shouldn't yell, you'll pop little blood vessels in your face if you yell. . . . No that was a joke, Mrs. Soffer, I was joking. . . . I already apologized sixteen times for that, Mrs. Soffer, you . . . (*While she's fulminating, Roy covers the mouthpiece with his hand and talks to Joe.*) This'll take a minute, *eat* already, what is this tasty sandwich here it's — (*He takes a bite of a sandwich.*) Mmmmm, liver or some. . . . Here.

(*He pitches the sandwich to Joe, who catches it and returns it to the platter.*)

ROY (*back to Mrs. Soffer*): Uh huh, uh huh. . . . No, I already told you, it wasn't a vacation, it was business, Mrs. Soffer, I have clients in Haiti, Mrs. Soffer, I. . . . Listen, Ailene, YOU THINK I'M THE ONLY GODDAM LAWYER IN HISTORY EVER MISSED A COURT DATE? Don't make such a big fucking. . . . Hold. (*He hits the hold button.*) You HAG!

JOE: If this is a bad time . . .

ROY: *Bad* time? This is a *good* time! (*Button.*) Baby doll, get me. . . . Oh fuck, wait . . . (*Button, button.*) Hello? Yah. Sorry to keep you holding, Judge Hollins, I. . . . Oh *Mrs.* Hollins, sorry dear deep voice you got. Enjoying your visit? (*Hand over mouthpiece again, to Joe.*) She sounds like a truckdriver and he sounds like Kate Smith, very confusing. Nixon appointed him, all the geeks are Nixon appointees . . . (*To Mrs. Hollins.*) Yeah yeah right good so how many tickets dear? Seven. For what, *Cats, 42nd Street*, what? No you wouldn't like *La Cage*, trust me, I know. Oh for godsake. . . . Hold. (*Button, button.*) Baby doll, seven for *Cats* or something, anything hard to get, I don't give a fuck what and neither will they. (*Button; to Joe.*) You see *La Cage*?

JOE: No, I . . .

ROY: Fabulous. Best thing on Broadway. Maybe ever. (*Button.*) Who? Aw, Jesus H. Christ, Harry, *no*, Harry, Judge John Francis Grimes, Manhattan Family Court. Do I have to do every goddam thing myself? *Touch* the bastard, Harry, and don't call me on this line again, I told you not to . . .

JOE (*starting to get up*): Roy, uh, should I wait outside or . . .

ROY (*to Joe*): Oh sit. (*To Harry.*) You hold. I pay you to hold fuck you Harry you jerk. (*Button.*) Half-wit dick-brain. (*Instantly philosophical.*) I see the universe, Joe, as a kind of sandstorm in outer space with winds of mega-hurricane velocity, but instead of grains of sand it's shards and splinters of glass. You ever feel that way? Ever have one of those days?

JOE: I'm not sure I . . .

ROY: So how's life in Appeals? How's the Judge?

JOE: He sends his best.

ROY: He's a good man. Loyal. Not the brightest man on the bench, but he has manners. And a nice head of silver hair.

JOE: He gives me a lot of responsibility.

ROY: Yeah, like writing his decisions and signing his name.

JOE: Well . . .

ROY: He's a nice guy. And you cover admirably.

JOE: Well, thanks, Roy, I . . .

ROY (*button*): Yah? Who is *this*? Well who the fuck are *you*? Hold — (*button*) Harry? Eighty-seven grand, something like that. Fuck him. Eat me. New Jersey, chain of porno film stores in, uh, Weehawken. That's — Harry, that's the beauty of the law. (*Button.*) So, baby doll, what? *Cats*? Bleah. (*Button.*) *Cats!* It's about cats. Singing cats, you'll love it. Eight o'clock, the theatre's always at eight. (*Button.*) Fucking tourists. (*Button, then to Joe.*) Oh live a little, Joe, *eat* something for Christ sake —

JOE: Um, Roy, could you . . .

ROY: What? (*To Harry.*) Hold a minute. (*Button.*) Mrs. Soffer? Mrs. . . . . (*Button.*) God-fucking-dammit to hell, where is . . .

JOE (*overlapping*): Roy, I'd really appreciate it if . . .

ROY (*overlapping*): Well she was here a minute ago, baby doll, see if . . .

(*The phone starts making three different beeping sounds, all at once.*)

ROY (*smashing buttons*): Jesus fuck this goddam thing . . .

JOE (*overlapping*): I really wish you wouldn't . . .

ROY (*overlapping*): Baby doll? Ring the *Post* get me Suzy see if . . .

(*The phone starts whistling loudly.*)

ROY: CHRIST!

JOE: *Roy.*

ROY (*into receiver*): Hold. (*Button; to Joe.*) *What?*

JOE: Could you please not take the Lord's name in vain
    (*Pause.*)
    I'm sorry. But please. At least while I'm . . .

ROY (*laughs, then*): Right. Sorry. Fuck. Only in America. (*Punches a button.*) Baby doll, tell 'em all to fuck off. Tell'em I died. You handle Mrs. Soffer. Tell her it's on the way. Tell her I'm schtupping the judge. I'll call her back. I *will* call her. I *know* how much I borrowed. She's got four hundred times that stuffed up her. . . . Yeah, tell her I said that. (*Button. The phone is silent.*) So, Joe.

JOE: I'm sorry Roy, I just . . .

ROY: No no no no, principles count, I respect principles, I'm not religious but I like God and God likes me. Baptist, Catholic?

JOE: Mormon.

ROY: Mormon. Delectable. Absolutely. Only in America. So, Joe. Whattya think?

JOE: It's . . . well . . .

ROY: Crazy life.

JOE: Chaotic.

ROY: Well but God bless chaos. Right?

JOE: Ummm . . .

ROY: Huh. Mormons. I knew Mormons, in, um, Nevada.

JOE: Utah, mostly.

ROY: No, these Mormons were in Vegas.
    So. So, how'd you like to go to Washington and work for the Justice Department?

JOE: Sorry?

ROY: How'd you like to go to Washington and work for the Justice Department? All I gotta do is pick up the phone, talk to Ed, and you're in.

JOE: In . . . what, exactly?

ROY: Associate Assistant Something Big. Internal Affairs, heart of the woods, something nice with clout.

JOE: Ed . . . ?

ROY: Meese. The Attorney General.

JOE: Oh.

ROY: I just have to pick up the phone . . .

JOE: I have to think.

ROY: Of course.
    (*Pause.*)
    It's a great time to be in Washington, Joe.

JOE: Roy, it's incredibly exciting . . .

ROY: And it would mean something to me. You understand?

(*Little pause.*)

JOE: I . . . can't say how much I appreciate this Roy, I'm sort of . . . well, stunned, I mean. . . . Thanks, Roy. But I have to give it some thought. I have to ask my wife.

ROY: Your wife. Of course.

JOE: But I really appreciate . . .

ROY: Of course. Talk to your wife.

Scene 3

(*Later that day. Harper at home, alone. She is listening to the radio and talking to herself, as she often does. She speaks to the audience.*)

HARPER: People who are lonely, people left alone, sit talking nonsense to the air, imagining . . . beautiful systems dying, old fixed orders spiraling apart . . .
    When you look at the ozone layer, from outside, from a spaceship, it looks like a pale blue halo, a gentle, shimmering aureole encircling the atmosphere encircling the earth. Thirty miles above our heads, a thin layer of three-atom oxygen molecules, product of photosynthesis, which explains the fussy vegetable preference for visible light, its rejection of darker rays

and emanations. Danger from without. It's a kind of gift, from God, the crowning touch to the creation of the world: guardian angels, hands linked, make a spherical net, a blue-green nesting orb, a shell of safety for life itself. But everywhere, things are collapsing, lies surfacing, systems of defense giving way. . . . This is why, Joe, this is why I shouldn't be left alone.

(*Little pause.*)

I'd like to go traveling. Leave you behind to worry. I'll send postcards with strange stamps and tantalizing messages on the back. "Later maybe." "Nevermore . . ."

(*Mr. Lies, a travel agent, appears.*)

HARPER Oh! You startled me!

MR. LIES: Cash, check or credit card?

HARPER: I remember you. You're from Salt Lake. You sold us the plane tickets when we flew here. What are you doing in Brooklyn?

MR. LIES: You said you wanted to travel . . .

HARPER: And here you are. How thoughtful.

MR. LIES: Mr. Lies. Of the International Order of Travel Agents. We mobilize the globe, we set people adrift, we stir the populace and send nomads eddying across the planet. We are adepts of motion, acolytes of the flux. Cash, check or credit card. Name your destination.

HARPER: Antarctica, maybe. I want to see the hole in the ozone. I heard on the radio . . .

MR. LIES (*he has a computer terminal in his briefcase*): I can arrange a guided tour. Now?

HARPER: Soon. Maybe soon. I'm not safe here you see. Things aren't right with me. Weird stuff happens . . .

MR. LIES: Like?

HARPER: Well, like you, for instance. Just appearing. Or last week . . . well never mind.

People are like planets, you need a thick skin. Things get to me, Joe stays away and now. . . . Well look. My dreams are talking back to me.

MR. LIES: It's the price of rootlessness. Motion sickness. The only cure: to keep moving.

HARPER: I'm undecided. I feel . . . that something's going to give. It's 1985. Fifteen years till the third millennium. Maybe Christ will come again. Maybe seeds will be planted, maybe there'll be harvests then, maybe early figs to eat, maybe new life, maybe fresh blood, maybe companionship and love and protection, safety from what's outside, maybe the door will hold, or maybe . . . maybe the troubles will come, and the end will come, and the sky will collapse and there will be terrible rains and showers of poison light, or maybe my life is really fine, maybe Joe loves me and I'm only crazy thinking otherwise, or maybe not, maybe it's even worse than I know, maybe . . . I want to know, maybe I don't. The suspense, Mr. Lies, it's killing me.

MR. LIES: I suggest a vacation.

HARPER (*hearing something*): That was the elevator. Oh God, I should fix myself up, I. . . . You have to go, you shouldn't be here . . . you aren't even real.

MR. LIES: Call me when you decide . . .

HARPER: Go!

(*The Travel Agent vanishes as Joe enters.*)

JOE: Buddy?

Buddy? Sorry I'm late. I was just . . . out. Walking. Are you mad?

HARPER: I got a little anxious.

JOE: Buddy kiss.

(*They kiss.*)

JOE: Nothing to get anxious about.

So. So how'd you like to move to Washington?

Scene 4

(*Same day. Louis and Prior outside the funeral home, sitting on a bench, both dressed in funereal finery, talking. The funeral service for Sarah Ironson has just concluded and Louis is about to leave for the cemetery.*)

LOUIS: My grandmother actually saw Emma Goldman speak. In Yiddish. But all Grandma could remember was that she spoke well and wore a hat.

What a weird service. That rabbi . . .

PRIOR: A definite find. Get his number when you go to the graveyard. I want him to bury me.

LOUIS: Better head out there. Everyone gets to put dirt on the coffin once it's lowered in.

PRIOR: Oooh. Cemetery fun. Don't want to miss that.

LOUIS: It's an old Jewish custom to express love. Here, Grandma, have a shovelful. Latecomers run the risk of finding the grave completely filled.

She was pretty crazy. She was up there in that home for ten years, talking to herself. I never visited. She looked too much like my mother.

PRIOR (*hugs him*): Poor Louis. I'm sorry your grandma is dead.

LOUIS: Tiny little coffin, huh?

Sorry I didn't introduce you to. . . . I always get so closety at these family things.

PRIOR: Butch. You get butch. (*Imitating.*) "Hi Cousin Doris, you don't remember me I'm Lou, Rachel's boy." Lou, not Louis, because if you say Louis they'll hear the sibilant S.

LOUIS: I don't have a . . .

PRIOR: I don't blame you, hiding. Bloodlines. Jewish curses are the worst. I personally would dissolve if anyone ever looked me in the eye and said "Feh." Fortunately WASPs don't say "Feh." Oh and by the way, darling, cousin Doris is a dyke.

LOUIS: No.

Really?

PRIOR: You don't notice anything. If I hadn't spent the last four years fellating you I'd swear you were straight.

LOUIS: You're in a pissy mood. Cat still missing?

(*Little pause.*)

PRIOR: Not a furball in sight. It's your fault.

LOUIS: It is?

PRIOR: I warned you, Louis. Names are important. Call an animal "Little Sheba" and you can't expect it to stick around. Besides, it's a dog's name.

LOUIS: I wanted a dog in the first place, not a cat. He sprayed my books.

PRIOR: He was a female cat.

LOUIS: Cats are stupid, high-strung predators. Babylonians sealed them up in bricks. Dogs have brains.

PRIOR: Cats have intuition.

LOUIS: A sharp dog is as smart as a really dull two-year-old child.

PRIOR: Cats know when something's wrong.

LOUIS: Only if you stop feeding them.

PRIOR: They know. That's why Sheba left, because she knew.

LOUIS: Knew what?

(*Pause.*)

PRIOR: I did my best Shirley Booth this morning, floppy slippers, housecoat, curlers, can of Little Friskies; "Come back, Little Sheba, come back. . . ." To no avail. Le chat, elle ne reviendra jamais, jamais . . .°

(*He removes his jacket, rolls up his sleeve, shows Louis a dark-purple spot on the underside of his arm near the shoulder.*)

See.

LOUIS: That's just a burst blood vessel.

PRIOR: Not according to the best medical authorities.

LOUIS: What?

(*Pause.*)

Tell me.

PRIOR: K.S., baby. Lesion number one. Lookit. The wine-dark kiss of the angel of death.

LOUIS (*very softly, holding Prior's arm*): Oh please . . .

PRIOR: I'm a lesionnaire. The Foreign Lesion. The American Lesion. Lesionnaire's disease.

LOUIS: Stop.

PRIOR: My troubles are lesion.

LOUIS: Will you *stop.*

PRIOR: Don't you think I'm handling this well? I'm going to die.

LOUIS: Bullshit.

PRIOR: Let go of my arm.

LOUIS: No.

PRIOR: Let go.

LOUIS (*grabbing Prior, embracing him ferociously*): No.

PRIOR: I can't find a way to spare you baby. No wall like the wall of hard scientific fact. K.S. Wham. Bang your head on that.

LOUIS: Fuck you. (*Letting go.*) Fuck you fuck you fuck you.

PRIOR: Now that's what I like to hear. A mature reaction.

Le chat . . . jamais: The cat will never ever return.

Let's go see if the cat's come home.
Louis?

LOUIS: When did you find this?

PRIOR: I couldn't tell you.

LOUIS: Why?

PRIOR: I was scared, Lou.

LOUIS: Of what?

PRIOR: That you'll leave me.

LOUIS: Oh.

(*Little pause.*)

PRIOR: Bad timing, funeral and all, but I figured as long as we're on the subject of death . . .

LOUIS: I have to go bury my grandma.

PRIOR: Lou?

(*Pause.*)

Then you'll come home?

LOUIS: Then I'll come home.

Scene 5

(*Same day, later on. Split scene: Joe and Harper at home; Louis at the cemetery with Rabbi Isidor Chemelwitz and the little coffin.*)

HARPER: Washington?

JOE: It's an incredible honor, buddy, and . . .

HARPER: I have to think.

JOE: Of course.

HARPER: Say no.

JOE: You said you were going to think about it.

HARPER: I don't want to move to Washington.

JOE: Well I do.

HARPER: It's a giant cemetery, huge white graves and mausoleums everywhere.

JOE: We could live in Maryland. Or Georgetown.

HARPER: We're happy here.

JOE: That's not really true, buddy, we . . .

HARPER: Well happy enough! Pretend-happy. That's better than nothing.

JOE: It's time to make some changes, Harper.

HARPER: No changes. Why?

JOE: I've been chief clerk for four years. I make twenty-nine thousand dollars a year. That's ridiculous. I graduated fourth in my class and I make less than anyone I know. And I'm . . . I'm tired of being a clerk, I want to go where something good is happening.

HARPER: Nothing good happens in Washington. We'll forget church teachings and buy furniture at . . . at *Conran's* and become yuppies. I have too much to do here.

JOE: Like what?

HARPER: I *do* have things . . .

JOE: What things?

HARPER: I have to finish painting the bedroom.

JOE: You've been painting in there for over a year.

HARPER: I know, I. . . . It just isn't done because I never get time to finish it.

JOE: Oh that's . . . that doesn't make sense. You have all the time in the world. You could finish it when I'm at work.

HARPER: I'm afraid to go in there alone.

JOE: Afraid of what?

HARPER: I heard someone in there. Metal scraping on the wall. A man with a knife, maybe.

JOE: There's no one in the bedroom, Harper.

HARPER: Not now.

JOE: Not this morning either.

HARPER: How do you know? You were at work this morning. There's something creepy about this place. Remember *Rosemary's Baby*?

JOE: *Rosemary's Baby*?

HARPER: Our apartment looks like that one. Wasn't that apartment in Brooklyn?

JOE: No, it was . . .

HARPER: Well, it looked like this. It did.

JOE: Then let's move.

HARPER: Georgetown's worse. *The Exorcist* was in Georgetown.

JOE: The devil, everywhere you turn, huh, buddy.

HARPER: Yeah. Everywhere.

JOE: How many pills today, buddy?

HARPER: None. One. Three. Only three.

LOUIS (*pointing at the coffin*): Why are there just two little wooden pegs holding the lid down?

RABBI ISIDOR CHEMELWITZ: So she can get out easier if she wants to.

LOUIS: I hope she stays put.

I pretended for years that she was already dead. When they called to say she had died it was a surprise. I abandoned her.

RABBI ISIDOR CHEMELWITZ: "Sharfer vi di tson fun a shlang iz an umdankbar kind!"

LOUIS: I don't speak Yiddish.

RABBI ISIDOR CHEMELWITZ: Sharper than the serpent's tooth is the ingratitude of children. Shakespeare. *King Lear*.

LOUIS: Rabbi, what does the Holy Writ say about someone who abandons someone he loves at a time of great need?

RABBI ISIDOR CHEMELWITZ: Why would a person do such a thing?

LOUIS: Because he has to. Maybe because this person's sense of the world, that it will change for the better with struggle, maybe a person who has this neo-Hegelian positivist sense of constant historical progress towards happiness or perfection or something, who feels very powerful because he feels connected to these forces, moving uphill all the time . . . maybe that person can't, um, incorporate sickness into his sense of how things are supposed to go. Maybe vomit . . . and sores and disease . . . really frighten him, maybe . . . he isn't so good with death.

RABBI ISIDOR CHEMELWITZ: The Holy Scriptures have nothing to say about such a person.

LOUIS: Rabbi, I'm afraid of the crimes I may commit.

RABBI ISIDOR CHEMELWITZ: Please, mister. I'm a sick old rabbi facing a long drive home to the Bronx. You want to confess, better you should find a priest.

LOUIS: But I'm not a Catholic, I'm a Jew.

RABBI ISIDOR CHEMELWITZ: Worse luck for you, bubbulah. Catholics believe in forgiveness. Jews believe in Guilt. (*He pats the coffin tenderly.*)

LOUIS: You just make sure those pegs are in good and tight.

RABBI ISIDOR CHEMELWITZ: Don't worry, mister. The life she had, she'll stay put. She's better off.

JOE: Look, I know this is scary for you. But try to understand what it means to me. Will you try?

HARPER: Yes.

JOE: Good. Really try.

I think things are starting to change in the world.

HARPER: But I don't want . . .

JOE: Wait. For the good. Change for the good. America has rediscovered itself. Its sacred position among nations. And people aren't ashamed of that like they used to be. This is a great thing. The truth restored. Law restored. That's what President Reagan's done, Harper. He says "Truth exists and can be spoken proudly." And the country responds to him. We become better. More good. I need to be a part of that, I need something big to lift me up. I mean, six years ago the world seemed in decline, horrible, hopeless, full of unsolvable problems and crime and confusion and hunger and . . .

HARPER: But it still seems that way. More now than before. They say the ozone layer is . . .

JOE: Harper—

HARPER: And today out the window on Atlantic Avenue there was a schizophrenic traffic cop who was making these . . .

JOE: Stop it! I'm trying to make a point.

HARPER: So am I.

JOE: You aren't even making sense, you . . .

HARPER: My point is the world seems just as . . .

JOE: It only seems that way to you because you never go out in the world, Harper, and you have emotional problems.

HARPER: I do so get out in the world.

JOE: You don't. You stay in all day, fretting about imaginary . . .

HARPER: I get out. I do. You don't know what I do.

JOE: You don't stay in all day.

HARPER: No.

JOE: Well. . . . Yes you do.

HARPER: That's what you think.

JOE: Where do you go?

HARPER: Where do *you* go? When you walk.

(*Pause, then angrily.*) And I DO NOT have emotional problems.

JOE: I'm sorry.

HARPER: And if I do have emotional problems it's from living with you. Or . . .

JOE: I'm sorry buddy, I didn't mean to . . .

HARPER: Or if you do think I do then you should never have married me. You have all these secrets and lies.

JOE: I want to be married to you, Harper.

HARPER: You shouldn't. You never should.

(*Pause.*)

Hey buddy. Hey buddy.

JOE: Buddy kiss . . .

(*They kiss.*)

HARPER: I heard on the radio how to give a blowjob.

JOE: What?

HARPER: You want to try?

JOE: You really shouldn't listen to stuff like that.

HARPER: Mormons can give blowjobs.

JOE: *Harper.*

HARPER (*imitating his tone*): *Joe.*

It was a little Jewish lady with a German accent. This is a good time. For me to make a baby.

(*Little pause. Joe turns away.*)

HARPER: Then they went on to a program about holes in the ozone layer. Over Antarctica. Skin burns, birds go blind, icebergs melt. The world's coming to an end.

Scene 6

(*First week of November. In the men's room of the offices of the Brooklyn Federal Court of Appeals; Louis is crying over the sink; Joe enters.*)

JOE: Oh, um. . . . Morning.

LOUIS: Good morning, counselor.

JOE (*he watches Louis cry*): Sorry, I . . . I don't know your name.

LOUIS: Don't bother. Word processor. The lowest of the low.

JOE (*holding out hand*): Joe Pitt. I'm with Justice Wilson . . .

LOUIS: Oh, I know that. Counselor Pitt. Chief Clerk.

JOE: Were you . . . are you OK?

LOUIS: Oh, yeah. Thanks. What a nice man.

JOE: Not so nice.

LOUIS: What?

JOE: Not so nice. Nothing. You sure you're . . .

LOUIS: Life sucks shit. Life . . . just sucks shit.

JOE: What's wrong?

LOUIS: Run in my nylons.

JOE: Sorry . . . ?

LOUIS: Forget it. Look, thanks for asking.

JOE: Well . . .

LOUIS: I mean it really is nice of you.

(*He starts crying again.*)

Sorry, sorry, sick friend . . .

JOE: Oh, I'm sorry.

LOUIS: Yeah, yeah, well, that's sweet.

Three of your colleagues have preceded you to this baleful sight and you're the first one to ask. The others just opened the door, saw me, and fled. I hope they had to pee real bad.

JOE (*handing him a wad of toilet paper*): They just didn't want to intrude.

LOUIS: Hah. Reaganite heartless macho asshole lawyers.

JOE: Oh, that's unfair.

LOUIS: What is? Heartless? Macho? Reaganite? Lawyer?

JOE: I voted for Reagan.

LOUIS: You did?

JOE: Twice.

LOUIS: Twice? Well, oh boy. A Gay Republican.

JOE: Excuse me?

LOUIS: Nothing.

JOE: I'm not . . .

Forget it.

LOUIS: Republican? Not Republican? Or . . .

JOE: What?

LOUIS: What?

JOE: Not gay. I'm not gay.

LOUIS: Oh. Sorry.

(*Blows his nose loudly.*) It's just . . .

JOE: Yes?

LOUIS: Well, sometimes you can tell from the way a person sounds that . . . I mean you *sound* like a . . .

JOE: No I don't. Like what?

LOUIS: Like a Republican.

(*Little pause. Joe knows he's being teased; Louis knows he knows. Joe decides to be a little brave.*)

JOE (*making sure no one else is around*): Do I? Sound like a . . . ?

LOUIS: What? Like a . . . ? Republican, or . . . ? Do *I*?

JOE: Do you what?

LOUIS: Sound like a . . . ?

JOE: Like a . . . ?

I'm . . . confused.

LOUIS: Yes.

My name is Louis. But all my friends call me Louise. I work in Word Processing. Thanks for the toilet paper.

(*Louis offers Joe his hand, Joe reaches, Louis feints and pecks Joe on the cheek, then exits.*)

Scene 7

(*A week later. Mutual dream scene. Prior is at a fantastic makeup table, having a dream, applying the face. Harper is having a pill-induced hallucination. She has these from time to time. For some reason, Prior has appeared in this one. Or Harper has appeared in Prior's dream. It is bewildering.*)

PRIOR (*alone, putting on makeup, then examining the results in the mirror; to the audience*): "I'm ready for my closeup, Mr. DeMille."

One wants to move through life with elegance and grace, blossoming infrequently but with exquisite taste, and perfect timing, like a rare bloom, a zebra orchid. . . . One wants. . . . But one so seldom gets what one wants, does one? No. One does not. One gets fucked. Over. One . . . dies at thirty, robbed of . . . decades of majesty.

Fuck this shit. Fuck this shit.

(*He almost crumbles; he pulls himself together; he studies his handiwork in the mirror.*)

I look like a corpse. A corpsette. Oh my queen; you know you've hit rock-bottom when even drag is a drag.

(*Harper appears.*)

HARPER: Are you. . . . Who are you?

PRIOR: Who are you?

HARPER: What are you doing in my hallucination?

PRIOR: I'm not in your hallucination. You're in my dream.

HARPER: You're wearing makeup.

PRIOR: So are you.

HARPER: But you're a man.

PRIOR (*feigning dismay, shock, he mimes slashing his throat with his lipstick and dies, fabulously tragic. Then*): The hands and feet give it away.

HARPER: There must be some mistake here. I don't recognize you. You're not. . . . Are you my . . . some sort of imaginary friend?

PRIOR: No. Aren't you too old to have imaginary friends?

HARPER: I have emotional problems. I took too many pills. Why are you wearing makeup?

PRIOR: I was in the process of applying the face, trying to make myself feel better — I swiped the new fall colors at the Clinique counter at Macy's. (*Showing her.*)

HARPER: You stole these?

PRIOR: I was out of cash; it was an emotional emergency!

HARPER: Joe will be so angry. I promised him. No more pills.

PRIOR: These pills you keep alluding to?

HARPER: Valium. I take Valium. Lots of Valium.

PRIOR: And you're dancing as fast as you can.

HARPER: I'm not *addicted*. I don't believe in addiction, and I never . . . well, I *never* drink. And I *never* take drugs.

PRIOR: Well, smell *you*, Nancy Drew.

HARPER: Except Valium.

PRIOR: Except Valium; in wee fistfuls.

HARPER: It's terrible. Mormons are not supposed to be addicted to anything. I'm a Mormon.

PRIOR: I'm a homosexual.

HARPER: Oh! In my church we don't believe in homosexuals.

PRIOR: In my church we don't believe in Mormons.

HARPER: What church do . . . oh! (*She laughs.*) I get it.

I don't understand this. If I didn't ever see you before and I don't think I did then I don't think you should be here, in this hallucination, because in my experience the mind, which is where hallucinations come from, shouldn't be able to make up anything that wasn't there to start with, that didn't enter it from experience, from the real world. Imagination can't create anything new, can it? It only recycles bits and pieces from the world and reassembles them into visions. . . . Am I making sense right now?

PRIOR: Given the circumstances, yes.

HARPER: So when we think we've escaped the unbearable ordinariness and, well, untruthfulness of our lives, it's really only the same old ordinariness and falseness rearranged into the appearance of novelty and truth. Nothing unknown is knowable. Don't you think it's depressing?

PRIOR: The limitations of the imagination?

HARPER: Yes.

PRIOR: It's something you learn after your second theme party: It's All Been Done Before.

HARPER: The world. Finite. Terribly, terribly. . . . Well . . .

This is the most depressing hallucination I've ever had.

PRIOR: Apologies. I do try to be amusing.

HARPER: Oh, well, don't apologize, you. . . . I can't expect someone who's really sick to entertain me.

PRIOR: How on earth did you know . . .

HARPER: Oh that happens. This is the very threshhold of revelation sometimes. You can see things . . . how sick you are. Do you see anything about me?

PRIOR: Yes.

HARPER: What?

PRIOR: You are amazingly unhappy.

HARPER: Oh big deal. You meet a Valium addict and you figure out she's unhappy. That doesn't count. Of course I. . . . Something else. Something surprising.

PRIOR: Something surprising.

HARPER: Yes.

PRIOR: Your husband's a homo.

(*Pause.*)

HARPER: Oh, ridiculous.

(*Pause, then very quietly.*)

Really?

PRIOR (*shrugs*): Threshhold of revelation.

HARPER: Well I don't like your revelations. I don't think you intuit well at all. Joe's a very normal man, he . . .

Oh God. Oh God. He. . . . Do homos take, like, lots of long walks?

PRIOR: Yes. We do. In stretch pants with lavender coifs. I just looked at you, and there was . . .

HARPER: A sort of blue streak of recognition.

PRIOR: Yes.

HARPER: Like you knew me incredibly well.

PRIOR: Yes.

HARPER: Yes.

I have to go now, get back, something just . . . fell apart.

Oh God, I feel so sad . . .

PRIOR: I . . . I'm sorry. I usually say, "Fuck the truth," but mostly, the truth fucks you.

HARPER: I see something else about you . . .

PRIOR: Oh?

HARPER: Deep inside you, there's a part of you, the most inner part, entirely free of disease. I can see that.

PRIOR: Is that. . . . That isn't true.

HARPER: Threshold of revelation.

Home . . .

(*She vanishes.*)

PRIOR: People come and go so quickly here . . .

(*To himself in the mirror.*) I don't think there's any uninfected part of me. My heart is pumping polluted blood. I feel dirty.

(*He begins to wipe makeup off with his hands, smearing it around. A large gray feather falls from up above. Prior stops smearing the makeup and looks at the feather. He goes to it and picks it up.*)

A VOICE (*it is an incredibly beautiful voice*): Look up!

PRIOR (*looking up, not seeing anyone*): Hello?

A VOICE: Look up!

PRIOR: Who is that?

A VOICE: Prepare the way!

PRIOR: I don't see any . . .

(*There is a dramatic change in lighting, from above.*)

A VOICE: Look up, look up,
  prepare the way
  the infinite descent
  A breath in air
  floating down
  Glory to . . .

(*Silence.*)

PRIOR: Hello? Is that it? Helloooo!
  What the fuck . . . ? (*He holds himself.*)
  Poor me. Poor poor me. Why me? Why poor poor me? Oh I don't feel good right now. I really don't.

Scene 8

(*That night. Split scene: Harper and Joe at home; Prior and Louis in bed.*)

HARPER: Where were you?

JOE: Out.

HARPER: Where?

JOE: Just out. Thinking.

HARPER: It's late.

JOE: I had a lot to think about.

HARPER: I burned dinner.

JOE: Sorry.

HARPER: Not my dinner. My dinner was fine. Your dinner. I put it back in the oven and turned everything up as high as it could go and I watched till it burned black. It's still hot. Very hot. Want it?

JOE: You didn't have to do that.

HARPER: I know. It just seemed like the kind of thing a mentally deranged sex-starved pill-popping housewife would do.

JOE: Uh huh.

HARPER: So I did it. Who knows anymore what I have to do?

JOE: How many pills?

HARPER: A bunch. Don't change the subject.

JOE: I won't talk to you when you . . .

HARPER: No. No. Don't do that! I'm . . . I'm fine, pills are not the problem, not our problem, I WANT TO KNOW WHERE YOU'VE BEEN! I WANT TO KNOW WHAT'S GOING ON!

JOE: Going on with what? The job?

HARPER: Not the job.

JOE: I said I need more time.

HARPER: Not the job!

JOE: Mr. Cohn, I talked to him on the phone, he said I had to hurry . . .

HARPER: Not the . . .

JOE: But I can't get you to talk sensibly about anything so . . .

HARPER: SHUT UP!

JOE: Then what?

HARPER: Stick to the subject.

JOE: I don't know what that is. You have something you want to ask me? Ask me. Go.

HARPER: I . . . can't. I'm scared of you.

JOE: I'm tired, I'm going to bed.

HARPER: Tell me without making me ask. Please.

JOE: This is crazy, I'm not . . .

HARPER: When you come through the door at night your face is never exactly the way I remembered it. I get surprised by something . . . mean and hard about the way you look. Even the weight of you in the bed at night, the way you breathe in your sleep seems unfamiliar.
  You terrify me.

JOE (*cold*): I know who you are.

HARPER: Yes. I'm the enemy. That's easy. That doesn't change.
  You think you're the only one who hates sex; I do; I hate it with you; I do. I dream that you batter away at me till all my joints come apart, like wax, and I fall into pieces. It's like a punishment. It was wrong of me to marry you. I knew you . . . (*She stops herself.*) It's a sin, and it's killing us both.

JOE: I can always tell when you've taken pills because it makes you red-faced and sweaty and frankly that's very often why I don't want to . . .

HARPER: Because . . .

JOE: Well, you aren't pretty. Not like this.

HARPER: I have something to ask you.

JOE: Then ASK! ASK! What in hell are you . . .

HARPER: Are you a homo?
  (*Pause.*)
  Are you? If you try to walk out right now I'll put your dinner back in the oven and turn it up so high the whole building will fill with smoke and everyone in it will asphyxiate. So help me God I will.
  Now answer the question.

JOE: What if I . . .

(*Small pause.*)

HARPER: Then tell me, please. And we'll see.

JOE: No. I'm not.

I don't see what difference it makes.

LOUIS: Jews don't have any clear textual guide to the afterlife; even that it exists. I don't think much about it. I see it as a perpetual rainy Thursday afternoon in March. Dead leaves.

PRIOR: Eeeugh. Very Greco-Roman.

LOUIS: Well for us it's not the verdict that counts, it's the act of judgment. That's why I could never be a lawyer. In court all that matters is the verdict.

PRIOR: You could never be a lawyer because you are oversexed. You're too distracted.

LOUIS: Not distracted; *ab*stracted. I'm trying to make a point:

PRIOR: Namely:

LOUIS: It's the judge in his or her chambers, weighing, books open, pondering the evidence, ranging freely over categories: good, evil, innocent, guilty; the judge in the chamber of circumspection, not the judge on the bench with the gavel. The shaping of the law, not its execution.

PRIOR: The point, dear, the point . . .

LOUIS: That it should be the questions and shape of a life, its total complexity gathered, arranged and considered, which matters in the end, not some stamp of salvation or damnation which disperses all the complexity in some unsatisfying little decision — the balancing of the scales . . .

PRIOR: I like this; very zen; it's . . . reassuringly incomprehensible and useless. We who are about to die thank you.

LOUIS: You are not about to die.

PRIOR: It's not going well, really . . . two new lesions. My leg hurts. There's protein in my urine, the doctor says, but who knows what the fuck that portends. Anyway it shouldn't be there, the protein. My butt is chapped from diarrhea and yesterday I shat blood.

LOUIS: I really hate this. You don't tell me . . .

PRIOR: You get too upset, I wind up comforting you. It's easier . . .

LOUIS: Oh thanks.

PRIOR: If it's bad I'll tell you.

LOUIS: Shitting blood sounds bad to me.

PRIOR: And I'm telling you.

LOUIS: And I'm handling it.

PRIOR: Tell me some more about justice.

LOUIS: I *am* handling it.

PRIOR: Well Louis you win Trooper of the Month.

(*Louis starts to cry.*)

PRIOR: I take it back. You aren't Trooper of the Month.
This isn't working . . .
Tell me some more about justice.

LOUIS: You are not about to die.

PRIOR: Justice . . .

LOUIS: . . . is an immensity, a confusing vastness. Justice is God.
Prior?

PRIOR: Hmmm?

LOUIS: You love me.

PRIOR: Yes.

LOUIS: What if I walked out on this?
Would you hate me forever?

(*Prior kisses Louis on the forehead.*)

PRIOR: Yes.

JOE: I think we ought to pray. Ask God for help. Ask him together . . .

HARPER: God won't talk to me. I have to make up people to talk to me.

JOE: You have to keep asking.

HARPER: I forgot the question.
Oh yeah. God, is my husband a . . .

JOE (*scary*): Stop it. Stop it. I'm warning you.
Does it make any difference? That I might be one thing deep within, no matter how wrong or ugly that thing is, so long as I have fought, with everything I have, to kill it. What do you want from me? What do you want from me, Harper? More than that? For God's sake, there's nothing left, I'm a shell. There's nothing left to kill.
As long as my behavior is what I know it has to be. Decent. Correct. That alone in the eyes of God.

HARPER: No, no, not that, that's Utah talk, Mormon talk, I hate it, Joe, tell me, say it . . .

JOE: All I will say is that I am a very good man who has worked very hard to become good and you want to destroy that. You want to destroy me, but I am not going to let you do that.

(*Pause.*)

HARPER: I'm going to have a baby.

JOE: Liar.

HARPER: You liar.
A baby born addicted to pills. A baby who does not dream but who hallucinates, who stares up at us with big mirror eyes and who does not know who we are.

(*Pause.*)

JOE: Are you really . . .

HARPER: No. Yes. No. Yes. Get away from me.
Now we both have a secret.

PRIOR: One of my ancestors was a ship's captain who made money bringing whale oil to Europe and returning with immigrants — Irish mostly, packed in tight, so many dollars per head. The last ship he captained foundered off the coast of Nova Scotia in a winter tempest and sank to the bottom. He went down with the ship — la Grande Geste — but his crew took seventy women and kids in the ship's only longboat, this big, open rowboat, and when the weather got too rough, and they thought the boat was overcrowded, the crew started lifting people up and hurling them into the sea. Until they got the ballast right. They walked up and down the longboat, eyes to the waterline, and when the boat rode low in the water they'd grab the nearest passenger and throw them into the sea. The boat was leaky, see; seventy people; they arrived in Halifax with nine people on board.

LOUIS: Jesus.

PRIOR: I think about that story a lot now. People in a boat, waiting, terrified, while implacable, unsmiling men, irresistibly strong, seize . . . maybe the person next to you, maybe you, and with no warning at all, with time only for a quick intake of air you are pitched into freezing, turbulent water and salt and darkness to drown.

I like your cosmology, baby. While time is running out I find myself drawn to anything that's suspended, that lacks an ending — but it seems to me that it lets you off scot-free.

LOUIS: What do you mean?

PRIOR: No judgment, no guilt or responsibility.

LOUIS: For me.

PRIOR: For anyone. It was an editorial "you."

LOUIS: Please get better. Please.

Please don't get any sicker.

Scene 9

(*Third week in November. Roy and Henry, his doctor, in Henry's office.*)

HENRY: Nobody knows what causes it. And nobody knows how to cure it. The best theory is that we blame a retrovirus, the Human Immunodeficiency Virus. Its presence is made known to us by the useless antibodies which appear in reaction to its entrance into the bloodstream through a cut, or an orifice. The antibodies are powerless to protect the body against it. Why, we don't know. The body's immune system ceases to function. Sometimes the body even attacks itself. At any rate it's left open to a whole horror house of infections from microbes which it usually defends against.

Like Kaposi's sarcomas. These lesions. Or your throat problem. Or the glands.

We think it may also be able to slip past the blood-brain barrier into the brain. Which is of course very bad news.

And it's fatal in we don't know what percent of people with suppressed immune responses.

(*Pause.*)

ROY: This is very interesting, Mr. Wizard, but why the fuck are you telling me this?

(*Pause.*)

HENRY: Well, I have just removed one of three lesions which biopsy results will probably tell us is a Kaposi's sarcoma lesion. And you have a pronounced swelling of glands in your neck, groin, and armpits — lymphadenopathy is another sign. And you

have oral candidiasis and maybe a little more fungus under the fingernails of two digits on your right hand. So that's why . . .

ROY: This disease . . .

HENRY: Syndrome.

ROY: Whatever. It afflicts mostly homosexuals and drug addicts.

HENRY: Mostly. Hemophiliacs are also at risk.

ROY: Homosexuals and drug addicts. So why are you implying that I . . .

(*Pause.*)

What are you implying, Henry?

HENRY: I don't . . .

ROY: I'm not a drug addict.

HENRY: Oh come on Roy.

ROY: What, what, come on Roy what? Do you think I'm a junkie, Henry, do you see tracks?

HENRY: This is absurd.

ROY: Say it.

HENRY: Say what?

ROY: Say, "Roy Cohn, you are a . . ."

HENRY: Roy.

ROY: "You are a. . . ." Go on. Not "Roy Cohn you are a drug fiend." "Roy Marcus Cohn, you are a . . ."

Go on, Henry, it starts with an "H."

HENRY: Oh I'm not going to . . .

ROY: *With an "H,"* Henry, and it isn't "Hemophiliac." Come on . . .

HENRY: What are you doing, Roy?

ROY: No, say it. I mean it. Say: "Roy Cohn, you are a homosexual."

(*Pause.*)

And I will proceed, systematically, to destroy your reputation and your practice and your career in New York State, Henry. Which you know I can do.

(*Pause.*)

HENRY: Roy, you have been seeing me since 1958. Apart from the facelifts I have treated you for everything from syphilis . . .

ROY: From a whore in Dallas.

HENRY: From syphilis to venereal warts. In your rectum. Which you may have gotten from a whore in Dallas, but it wasn't a female whore.

(*Pause.*)

ROY: So say it.

HENRY: Roy Cohn, you are . . .

You have had sex with men, many many times, Roy, and one of them, or any number of them, has made you very sick. You have AIDS.

ROY: AIDS.

Your problem, Henry, is that you are hung up on words, on labels, that you believe they mean what they seem to mean. AIDS. Homosexual. Gay. Lesbian. You think these are names that tell you who someone sleeps with, but they don't tell you that.

HENRY: No?

ROY: No. Like all labels they tell you one thing and one

thing only: where does an individual so identified fit in the food chain, in the pecking order? Not ideology, or sexual taste, but something much simpler: clout. Not who I fuck or who fucks me, but who will pick up the phone when I call, who owes me favors. This is what a label refers to. Now to someone who does not understand this, homosexual is what I am because I have sex with men. But really this is wrong. Homosexuals are not men who sleep with other men. Homosexuals are men who in fifteen years of trying cannot get a pissant antidiscrimination bill through City Council. Homosexuals are men who know nobody and who nobody knows. Who have zero clout. Does this sound like me, Henry?

HENRY: No.

ROY: No. I have clout. A lot. I can pick up this phone, punch fifteen numbers, and you know who will be on the other end in under five minutes, Henry?

HENRY: The President.

ROY: Even better, Henry. His wife.

HENRY: I'm impressed.

ROY: I don't want you to be impressed. I want you to understand. This is not sophistry. And this is not hypocrisy. This is reality. I have sex with men. But unlike nearly every other man of whom this is true, I bring the guy I'm screwing to the White House and President Reagan smiles at us and shakes his hand. Because *what* I am is defined entirely by *who* I am. Roy Cohn is not a homosexual. Roy Cohn is a heterosexual man, Henry, who fucks around with guys.

HENRY: OK, Roy.

ROY: And what is my diagnosis, Henry?

HENRY: You have AIDS, Roy.

ROY: No, Henry, no. AIDS is what homosexuals have. I have liver cancer.

(*Pause.*)

HENRY: Well, whatever the fuck you have, Roy, it's very serious, and I haven't got a damn thing for you. The NIH in Bethesda has a new drug called AZT with a two-year waiting list that not even I can get you onto. So get on the phone, Roy, and dial the fifteen numbers, and tell the First Lady you need in on an experimental treatment for liver cancer, because you can call it any damn thing you want, Roy, but what it boils down to is very bad news.

ACT 2
IN VITRO • *December 1985–January 1986*

Scene 1

(*Night, the third week in December. Prior alone on the floor of his bedroom; he is much worse.*)

PRIOR: Louis, Louis, please wake up, oh God.

(*Louis runs in.*)

PRIOR: I think something horrible is wrong with me I can't breathe . . .

LOUIS (*starting to exit*): I'm calling the ambulance.

PRIOR: No, wait, I . . .

LOUIS: *Wait?* Are you fucking crazy? Oh God you're on fire, your head is on fire.

PRIOR: It hurts, it hurts . . .

LOUIS: I'm calling the ambulance.

PRIOR: I don't want to go to the hospital, I don't want to go to the hospital please let me lie here, just . . .

LOUIS: No, no, God, Prior, stand up . . .

PRIOR: DON'T TOUCH MY LEG!

LOUIS: We have to . . . oh God this is so crazy.

PRIOR: I'll be OK if I just lie here Lou, really, if I can only sleep a little . . .

(*Louis exits.*)

PRIOR: Louis?
     NO! NO! Don't call, you'll send me there and I won't come back, please, please Louis I'm begging, baby, please . . .
     (*Screams.*) LOUIS!!

LOUIS (*from off; hysterical*): WILL YOU SHUT THE FUCK UP!

PRIOR (*trying to stand*): Aaaah. I have . . . to go to the bathroom. Wait. Wait, just . . . oh. Oh God. (*He shits himself.*)

LOUIS (*entering*): Prior? They'll be here in . . .
     Oh my God.

PRIOR: I'm sorry, I'm sorry.

LOUIS: What did . . . ? What?

PRIOR: I had an accident.

(*Louis goes to him.*)

LOUIS: This is blood.

PRIOR: Maybe you shouldn't touch it . . . me. . . . I . . .
     (*He faints.*)

LOUIS (*quietly*): Oh help. Oh help. Oh God oh God oh God help me I can't I can't I can't.

Scene 2

(*Same night. Harper is sitting at home, all alone, with no lights on. We can barely see her. Joe enters, but he doesn't turn on the lights.*)

JOE: Why are you sitting in the dark? Turn on the light.

HARPER: No. I heard the sounds in the bedroom again. I know someone was in there.

JOE: No one was.

HARPER: Maybe actually in the bed, under the covers with a knife.
     Oh, boy. Joe. I, um, I'm thinking of going away. By which I mean: I think I'm going off again. You . . . you know what I mean?

JOE: Please don't. Stay. We can fix it. I pray for that. This is my fault, but I can correct it. You have to try too . . .

(*He turns on the light. She turns it off again.*)

HARPER: When you pray, what do you pray for?

JOE: I pray for God to crush me, break me up into little pieces and start all over again.

HARPER: Oh. Please. Don't pray for that.

JOE: I had a book of Bible stories when I was a kid. There was a picture I'd look at twenty times every day: Jacob wrestles with the angel. I don't really remember the story, or why the wrestling — just the picture. Jacob is young and very strong. The angel is . . . a beautiful man, with golden hair and wings, of course. I still dream about it. Many nights. I'm. . . . It's me. In that struggle. Fierce, and unfair. The angel is not human, and it holds nothing back, so how could anyone human win, what kind of a fight is that? It's not just. Losing means your soul thrown down in the dust, your heart torn out from God's. But you can't not lose.

HARPER: In the whole entire world, you are the only person, the only person I love or have ever loved. And I love you terribly. Terribly. That's what's so awfully, irreducibly real. I can make up anything but I can't dream that away.

JOE: Are you . . . are you really going to have a baby?

HARPER: It's my time, and there's no blood. I don't really know. I suppose it wouldn't be a great thing. Maybe I'm just not bleeding because I take too many pills. Maybe I'll give birth to a pill. That would give a new meaning to pill-popping, huh?

I think you should go to Washington. Alone. Change, like you said.

JOE: I'm not going to leave you, Harper.

HARPER: Well maybe not. But I'm going to leave you.

Scene 3

(*One AM, the next morning. Louis and a nurse, Emily, are sitting in Prior's room in the hospital.*)

EMILY: He'll be all right now.

LOUIS: No he won't.

EMILY: No. I guess not. I gave him something that makes him sleep.

LOUIS: Deep asleep?

EMILY: Orbiting the moons of Jupiter.

LOUIS: A good place to be.

EMILY: Anyplace better than here. You his . . . uh?

LOUIS: Yes. I'm his uh.

EMILY: This must be hell for you.

LOUIS: It is. Hell. The After Life. Which is not at all like a rainy afternoon in March, by the way, Prior. A lot more vivid than I'd expected. Dead leaves, but the crunchy kind. Sharp, dry air. The kind of long, luxurious dying feeling that breaks your heart.

EMILY: Yeah, well we all get to break our hearts on this one.

He seems like a nice guy. Cute.

LOUIS: Not like this.

Yes, he is. Was. Whatever.

EMILY: Weird name. Prior Walter. Like, "The Walter before this one."

LOUIS: Lots of Walters before this one. Prior is an old old family name in an old old family. The Walters go back to the Mayflower and beyond. Back to the Norman Conquest. He says there's a Prior Walter stitched into the Bayeux tapestry.

EMILY: Is that impressive?

LOUIS: Well, it's old. Very old. Which in some circles equals impressive.

EMILY: Not in my circle. What's the name of the tapestry?

LOUIS: The Bayeux tapestry. Embroidered by La Reine Mathilde.

EMILY: I'll tell my mother. She embroiders. Drives me nuts.

LOUIS: Manual therapy for anxious hands.

EMILY: Maybe you should try it.

LOUIS: Mathilde stitched while William the Conqueror was off to war. She was capable of . . . more than loyalty. Devotion.

She waited for him, she stitched for years. And if he had come back broken and defeated from war, she would have loved him even more. And if he had returned mutilated, ugly, full of infection and horror, she would still have loved him; fed by pity, by a sharing of pain, she would love him even more, and even more, and she would never, never have prayed to God, please let him die if he can't return to me whole and healthy and able to live a normal life. . . . If he had died, she would have buried her heart with him.

So what the fuck is the matter with me?

(*Little pause.*)

Will he sleep through the night?

EMILY: At least.

LOUIS: I'm going.

EMILY: Its one A.M. Where do you have to go at . . .

LOUIS: I know what time it is. A walk. Night air, good for the. . . . The park.

EMILY: Be careful.

LOUIS: Yeah. Danger.

Tell him, if he wakes up and you're still on, tell him goodbye, tell him I had to go.

Scene 4

(*An hour later. Split scene. Joe and Roy in a fancy [straight] bar; Louis and a Man in the Rambles in Central Park. Joe and Roy are sitting at the bar; the place is brightly lit. Joe has a plate of food in front of him but he isn't eating. Roy occasionally reaches over the table and forks small bites off Joe's plate. Roy is drinking heavily, Joe not at all. Louis and the Man are eyeing each other, each alternating interest and indifference.*)

JOE: The pills were something she started when she miscarried or . . . no, she took some before that. She had a really bad time at home, when she was a kid, her home was really bad. I think a lot of drinking and physical stuff. She doesn't talk about that, instead she talks about . . . the sky falling down, people with knives hiding under sofas. Monsters. Mormons. Everyone thinks Mormons don't come from homes like that, we aren't supposed to behave that way, but we do. It's not lying, or being two-faced. Everyone tries very hard to live up to God's strictures, which are very . . . um . . .

ROY: Strict.

JOE: I shouldn't be bothering you with this.

ROY: No, please. Heart to heart. Want another. . . . What is that, seltzer?

JOE: The failure to measure up hits people very hard. From such a strong desire to be good they feel very far from goodness when they fail.

What scares me is that maybe what I really love in her is the part of her that's farthest from the light, from God's love; maybe I was drawn to that in the first place. And I'm keeping it alive because I need it.

ROY: Why would you need it?

JOE: There are things. . . . I don't know how well we know ourselves. I mean, what if? I know I married her because she . . . because I loved it that she was always wrong, always doing something wrong, like one step out of step. In Salt Lake City that stands out. I never stood out, on the outside, but inside, it was hard for me. To pass.

ROY: Pass?

JOE: Yeah.

ROY: Pass as what?

JOE: Oh. Well. . . . As someone cheerful and strong. Those who love God with an open heart unclouded by secrets and struggles are cheerful; God's easy simple love for them shows in how strong and happy they are. The saints.

ROY: But you had secrets? Secret struggles . . .

JOE: I wanted to be one of the elect, one of the Blessed. You feel you ought to be, that the blemishes are yours by choice, which of course they aren't. Harper's sorrow, that really deep sorrow, she didn't choose that. But it's there.

ROY: You didn't put it there.

JOE: No.

ROY: You sound like you think you did.

JOE: I am responsible for her.

ROY: Because she's your wife.

JOE: That. And I do love her.

ROY: Whatever. She's your wife. And so there are obligations. To her. But also to yourself.

JOE: She'd fall apart in Washington.

ROY: Then let her stay here.

JOE: She'll fall apart if I leave her.

ROY: Then bring her to Washington.

JOE: I just can't, Roy. She needs me.

ROY: Listen, Joe. I'm the best divorce lawyer in the business.

(*Little pause.*)

JOE: Can't Washington wait?

ROY: You do what you need to do, Joe. What *you* need. *You.* Let her life go where it wants to go. You'll both be better for that. *Somebody* should get what they want.

MAN: What do you want?

LOUIS: I want you to fuck me, hurt me, make me bleed.

MAN: I want to.

LOUIS: Yeah?

MAN: I want to hurt you.

LOUIS: Fuck me.

MAN: Yeah?

LOUIS: Hard.

MAN: Yeah? You been a bad boy?

(*Pause. Louis laughs, softly.*)

LOUIS: Very bad. Very bad.

MAN: You need to be punished, boy?

LOUIS: Yes. I do.

MAN: Yes what?

(*Little pause.*)

LOUIS: Um, I . . .

MAN: Yes *what*, boy?

LOUIS: Oh. Yes sir.

MAN: I want you to take me to your place, boy.

LOUIS: No, I can't do that.

MAN: No *what*?

LOUIS: No sir, I can't, I . . .
    I don't live alone, sir.

MAN: Your lover know you're out with a man tonight, boy?

LOUIS: No sir, he . . .
    My lover doesn't know.

MAN: Your lover know you . . .

LOUIS: Let's change the subject, OK? Can we go to your place?

MAN: I live with my parents.

LOUIS: Oh.

ROY: Everyone who makes it in this world makes it because somebody older and more powerful takes an interest. The most precious asset in life, I think, is the ability to be a good son. You have that, Joe. Somebody who can be a good son to a father who pushes them farther than they would otherwise go. I've had many fathers, I owe my life to them, powerful, powerful men. Walter Winchell, Edgar Hoover. Joe McCarthy most of all. He valued me because I am a good lawyer, but he loved me because I was and am a good son. He was a very difficult man, very guarded and cagey; I brought out something tender in him. He would have died for me. And me for him. Does this embarrass you?

JOE: I had a hard time with my father.

ROY: Well sometimes that's the way. Then you have to find other fathers, substitutes, I don't know. The father-son relationship is central to life. Women are for birth, beginning, but the father is continuance.

The son offers the father his life as a vessel for carrying forth his father's dream. Your father's living?

JOE: Um, dead.

ROY: He was . . . what? A difficult man?

JOE: He was in the military. He could be very unfair. And cold.

ROY: But he loved you.

JOE: I don't know.

ROY: No, no, Joe, he did, I know this. Sometimes a father's love has to be very, very hard, unfair even, cold to make his son grow strong in a world like this. This isn't a good world.

MAN: Here, then.

LOUIS: I. . . . Do you have a rubber?

MAN: I don't use rubbers.

LOUIS: You should. (*He takes one from his coat pocket.*) Here.

MAN: I don't use them.

LOUIS: Forget it, then. (*He starts to leave.*)

MAN: No, wait.
  Put it on me. Boy.

LOUIS: Forget it, I have to get back. Home. I must be going crazy.

MAN: Oh come on please he won't find out.

LOUIS: It's cold. Too cold.

MAN: It's never too cold, let me warm you up. Please?

(*They begin to fuck.*)

MAN: Relax.

LOUIS (*a small laugh*): Not a chance.

MAN: It . . .

LOUIS: What?

MAN: I think it broke. The rubber. You want me to keep going? (*Little pause.*) Pull out? Should I . . .

LOUIS: Keep going.
  Infect me.
  I don't care. I don't care.

(*Pause. The Man pulls out.*)

MAN: I . . . um, look, I'm sorry, but I think I want to go.

LOUIS: Yeah.
  Give my best to mom and dad.

(*The Man slaps him.*)

LOUIS: Ow!

(*They stare at each other.*)

LOUIS: It was a joke.

(*The Man leaves.*)

ROY: How long have we known each other?

JOE: Since 1980.

ROY: Right. A long time. I feel close to you, Joe. Do I advise you well?

JOE: You've been an incredible friend, Roy, I . . .

ROY: I want to be family. Familia, as my Italian friends call it. La Familia. A lovely word. It's important for me to help you, like I was helped.

JOE: I owe practically everything to you, Roy.

ROY: I'm dying, Joe. Cancer.

JOE: Oh my God.

ROY: Please. Let me finish.
  Few people know this and I'm telling you this only because. . . . I'm not afraid of death. What can death bring that I haven't faced? I've lived; life is the worst. (*Gently mocking himself.*) Listen to me, I'm a philosopher.
  Joe. You must do this. You must must must. Love; that's a trap. Responsibility; that's a trap too. Like a father to a son I tell you this: Life is full of horror; nobody escapes, nobody; save yourself. Whatever pulls on you, whatever needs from you, threatens you. Don't be afraid; people are so afraid; don't be afraid to live in the raw wind, naked, alone. . . . Learn at least this: What you are capable of. Let nothing stand in your way.

Scene 5

(*Three days later. Prior and Belize in Prior's hospital room. Prior is very sick but improving. Belize has just arrived.*)

PRIOR: Miss Thing.

BELIZE: Ma cherie bichette.

PRIOR: Stella.

BELIZE: Stella for star. Let me see. (*Scrutinizing Prior.*) You look like shit, why yes indeed you do, comme la merde!°

PRIOR: Merci.

BELIZE (*taking little plastic bottles from his bag, handing them to Prior*): Not to despair, Belle Reeve. Lookie! Magic goop!

PRIOR (*opening a bottle, sniffing*): Pooh! What kinda crap is that?

BELIZE: Beats me. Let's rub it on your poor blistered body and see what it does.

PRIOR: This is not Western medicine, these bottles . . .

BELIZE: Voodoo cream. From the botanica° 'round the block.

PRIOR: And you a registered nurse.

BELIZE (*sniffing it*): Beeswax and cheap perfume. Cut with Jergen's Lotion. Full of good vibes and love from some little black Cubana witch in Miami.

PRIOR: Get that trash away from me, I am immune-suppressed.

BELIZE: I *am* a health professional. I *know* what I'm doing.

PRIOR: It stinks. Any word from Louis?

(*Pause. Belize starts giving Prior a gentle massage.*)

PRIOR: Gone.

comme la merde: Like shit.
botanica: Shop that sells magic charms and herbs.

BELIZE: He'll be back. I know the type. Likes to keep a girl on edge.

PRIOR: It's been . . .

(*Pause.*)

BELIZE (*trying to jog his memory*): How long?

PRIOR: I don't remember.

BELIZE: How long have you been here?

PRIOR (*getting suddenly upset*): I don't remember, I don't give a fuck. I want Louis. I want my fucking boyfriend, where the fuck is he? I'm dying, I'm dying, where's Louis?

BELIZE: Shhhh, shhh . . .

PRIOR: This is a very strange drug, this drug. Emotional lability, for starters.

BELIZE: Save a tab or two for me.

PRIOR: Oh no, not this drug, ce n'est pas pour la joyeux noël et la bonne année, this drug she is serious poisonous chemistry, ma pauvre bichette.°
   And not just disorienting. I hear things. Voices.

BELIZE: Voices.

PRIOR: A voice.

BELIZE: Saying what?

(*Pause.*)

PRIOR: I'm not supposed to tell.

BELIZE: You better tell the doctor. Or I will.

PRIOR: No no don't. Please. I want the voice; it's wonderful. It's all that's keeping me alive. I don't want to talk to some intern about it.
   You know what happens? When I hear it, I get hard.

BELIZE: Oh my.

PRIOR: Comme ça. (*He uses his arm to demonstrate.*) And you know I am slow to rise.

BELIZE: My jaw aches at the memory.

PRIOR: And would you deny me this little solace — betray my concupiscence to Florence Nightingale's storm troopers?

BELIZE: Perish the thought, ma bébé.°

PRIOR: They'd change the drug just to spoil the fun.

BELIZE: You and your boner can depend on me.

PRIOR: Je t'adore, ma belle nègre.°

BELIZE: All this girl-talk shit is politically incorrect, you know. We should have dropped it back when we gave up drag.

PRIOR: I'm sick, I get to be politically incorrect if it makes me feel better. You sound like Lou.

   (*Little pause.*)

   Well, at least I have the satisfaction of knowing he's in anguish somewhere. I loved his anguish. Watching him stick his head up his asshole and eat his guts out over some relatively minor moral conundrum — it was the best show in town. But Mother warned me: if they get overwhelmed by the little things . . .

BELIZE: They'll be belly-up bustville when something big comes along.

PRIOR: Mother warned me.

BELIZE: And they do come along.

PRIOR: But I didn't listen.

BELIZE: No. (*Doing Hepburn.*) Men are beasts.

PRIOR (*also Hepburn*): The absolute lowest.

BELIZE: I have to go. If I want to spend my whole lonely life looking after white people I can get underpaid to do it.

PRIOR: You're just a Christian martyr.

BELIZE: Whatever happens, baby, I will be here for you.

PRIOR: Je t'aime.°

BELIZE: Je t'aime. Don't go crazy on me, girlfriend, I already got enough crazy queens for one lifetime. For two. I can't be bothering with dementia.

PRIOR: I promise.

BELIZE (*touching him; softly*): Ouch.

PRIOR: Ouch. Indeed.

BELIZE: Why'd they have to pick on you?
   And eat more, girlfriend, you really do look like shit.

(*Belize leaves.*)

PRIOR (*after waiting a beat*): He's gone.
   Are you still . . .

VOICE: I can't stay. I will return.

PRIOR: Are you one of those "Follow me to the other side" voices?

VOICE: No. I am no nightbird. I am a messenger . . .

PRIOR: You have a beautiful voice, it sounds . . . like a viola, like a perfectly tuned, tight string, balanced, the truth. . . . Stay with me.

VOICE: Not now. Soon I will return, I will reveal myself to you; I am glorious, glorious; my heart, my countenance and my message. You must prepare.

PRIOR: For what? I don't want to . . .

VOICE: No death, no:
   A marvelous work and a wonder we undertake, an edifice awry we sink plumb and straighten, a great Lie we abolish, a great error correct, with the rule, sword and broom of Truth!

PRIOR: What are you talking about, I . . .

VOICE: I am on my way; when I am manifest, our Work begins:
   Prepare for the parting of the air,
   The breath, the ascent,
   Glory to . . .

Scene 6

(*The second week of January. Martin, Roy and Joe in a fancy Manhattan restaurant.*)

MARTIN: It's a revolution in Washington, Joe. We have a new agenda and finally a real leader. They got back

---

ce n'est pas . . . bichette: This drug isn't for a merry Christmas or a happy new year . . . my poor little bitch.
ma bébé: My baby.
Je t'adore . . . nègre: I adore you, my beautiful negro.

Je t'aime: I love you.

the Senate but we have the courts. By the nineties the Supreme Court will be block-solid Republican appointees, and the Federal bench — Republican judges like land mines, everywhere, everywhere they turn. Affirmative action? Take it to court. Boom! Land mine. And we'll get our way on just about everything: abortion, defense, Central America, family values, a live investment climate. We have the White House locked till the year 2000. And beyond. A permanent fix on the Oval Office? It's possible. By '92 we'll get the Senate back, and in ten years the South is going to give us the House. It's really the end of Liberalism. The end of New Deal Socialism. The end of ipso facto secular humanism. The dawning of a genuinely American political personality. Modeled on Ronald Wilson Reagan.

JOE: It sounds great, Mr. Heller.

MARTIN: Martin. And Justice is the hub. Especially since Ed Meese took over. He doesn't specialize in Fine Points of the Law. He's a flatfoot, a cop. He reminds me of Teddy Roosevelt.

JOE: I can't wait to meet him.

MARTIN: Too bad, Joe, he's been dead for sixty years!

(*There is a little awkwardness. Joe doesn't respond.*)

MARTIN: Teddy Roosevelt. You said you wanted to. . . . Little joke. It reminds me of the story about the . . .

ROY (*smiling, but nasty*): Aw shut the fuck up Martin.

(*To Joe.*) You see that? Mr. Heller here is one of the mighty, Joseph, in D.C. he sitteth on the right hand of the man who sitteth on the right hand of The Man. And yet I can say "shut the fuck up" and he will take no offense. Loyalty. He . . .

Martin?

MARTIN: Yes, Roy?

ROY: Rub my back.

MARTIN: Roy . . .

ROY: No no really, a sore spot, I get them all the time now, these. . . . Rub it for me darling, would you do that for me?

(*Martin rubs Roy's back. They both look at Joe.*)

ROY (*to Joe*): How do you think a handful of Bolsheviks turned St. Petersburg into Leningrad in one afternoon? *Comrades.* Who do for each other. Marx and Engels. Lenin and Trotsky. Josef Stalin and Franklin Delano Roosevelt.

(*Martin laughs.*)

ROY: *Comrades*, right Martin?

MARTIN: This man, Joe, is a Saint of the Right.

JOE: I know, Mr. Heller, I . . .

ROY: And you see what I mean, Martin? He's special, right?

MARTIN: Don't embarrass him, Roy.

ROY: Gravity, decency, smarts! His strength is as the strength of ten because his heart is pure! *And* he's a Royboy, one hundred percent.

MARTIN: We're on the move, Joe. On the move.

JOE: Mr. Heller, I . . .

MARTIN (*ending backrub*): We can't wait any longer for an answer.

(*Little pause.*)

JOE: Oh. Um, I . . .

ROY: Joe's a married man, Martin.

MARTIN: Aha.

ROY: With a wife. She doesn't care to go to D.C., and so Joe cannot go. And keeps us dangling. We've seen that kind of thing before, haven't we? These men and their wives.

MARTIN: Oh yes. Beware.

JOE: I really can't discuss this under . . .

MARTIN: Then *don't* discuss. Say yes, Joe.

ROY: Now.

MARTIN: Say yes I will.

ROY: Now.

Now. I'll hold my breath till you do, I'm turning blue waiting. . . . *Now*, goddammit!

MARTIN: Roy, calm down, it's not . . .

ROY: Aw, fuck it. (*He takes a letter from his jacket pocket, hands it to Joe.*)

Read. Came today.

(*Joe reads the first paragraph, then looks up.*)

JOE: Roy. This is . . . Roy, this is terrible.

ROY: You're telling me.

A letter from the New York State Bar Association, Martin.

They're gonna try and disbar me.

MARTIN: Oh my.

JOE: Why?

ROY: Why, Martin?

MARTIN: Revenge.

ROY: The whole Establishment. Their little rules. Because I know no rules. Because I don't see the Law as a dead and arbitrary collection of antiquated dictums, thou shall, thou shalt not, because, because I know the Law's a pliable, breathing, sweating . . . *organ*, because, because . . .

MARTIN: Because he borrowed half a million from one of his clients.

ROY: Yeah, well, there's that.

MARTIN: *And* he forgot to *return* it.

JOE: Roy, that's. . . . You borrowed money from a client?

ROY: I'm deeply ashamed.

(*Little pause.*)

JOE (*very sympathetic*): Roy, you know how much I admire you. Well I mean I know you have unorthodox ways, but I'm sure you only did what you thought at the time you needed to do. And I have faith that . . .

ROY: Not so damp, please. I'll deny it was a loan. She's got no paperwork. Can't prove a fucking thing.

(*Little pause. Martin studies the menu.*)

JOE (*handing back the letter, more official in tone*): Roy I really appreciate your telling me this, and I'll do whatever I can to help.

ROY (*holding up a hand, then, carefully*): I'll tell you what you can do.

I'm about to be tried, Joe, by a jury that is not a jury of my peers. The disbarment committee: genteel gentleman Brahmin lawyers, country-club men. I offend them, to these men . . . I'm what, Martin, some sort of filthy little Jewish troll?

MARTIN: Oh well, I wouldn't go so far as . . .

ROY: Oh well I would.

Very fancy lawyers, these disbarment committee lawyers, fancy lawyers with fancy corporate clients and complicated cases. Antitrust suits. Deregulation. Environmental control. Complex cases like these need Justice Department cooperation like flowers need the sun. Wouldn't you say that's an accurate assessment, Martin?

MARTIN: I'm not here, Roy. I'm not hearing any of this.

ROY: No. Of course not.

Without the light of the sun, Joe, these cases, and the fancy lawyers who represent them, will wither and die.

A well-placed friend, someone in the Justice Department, say, can turn off the sun. Cast a deep shadow on my behalf. Make them shiver in the cold. If they overstep. They would fear that.

(*Pause.*)

JOE: Roy. I don't understand.

ROY: You do.

(*Pause.*)

JOE: You're not asking me to . . .

ROY: Sssshhhh. Careful.

JOE (*a beat, then*): Even if I said yes to the job, it would be illegal to interfere. With the hearings. It's unethical. No. I can't.

ROY: Un-ethical.

Would you excuse us, Martin?

MARTIN: Excuse you?

ROY: Take a walk, Martin. For real.

(*Martin leaves.*)

ROY: Un-ethical. Are you trying to embarrass me in front of my friend?

JOE: Well it is unethical, I can't . . .

ROY: Boy, you are really something. What the fuck do you think this is, Sunday School?

JOE: No, but Roy this is . . .

ROY: This is . . . this is gastric juices churning, this is enzymes and acids, this is intestinal is what this is, bowel movement and blood-red meat — this stinks, this is *politics*, Joe, the game of being alive. And you think you're . . . What? Above that? Above alive is what? Dead! In the clouds! You're on earth, goddammit! Plant a foot, stay a while.

I'm sick. They smell I'm weak. They want blood this time. I must have eyes in Justice. In Justice you will protect me.

JOE: Why can't Mr. Heller . . .

ROY: Grow up, Joe. The administration can't get involved.

JOE: But I'd be part of the administration. The same as him.

ROY: Not the same. Martin's Ed's man. And Ed's Reagan's man. So Martin's Reagan's man.

And you're mine.

(*Little pause. He holds up the letter.*)

This will never be. Understand me?

(*He tears the letter up.*)

I'm gonna be a lawyer, Joe, I'm gonna be a lawyer, Joe, I'm gonna be a goddam motherfucking legally licensed member of the bar lawyer, just like my daddy was, till my last bitter day on earth, Joseph, until the day I die.

(*Martin returns.*)

ROY: Ah, Martin's back.

MARTIN: So are we agreed?

ROY: Joe?

(*Little pause.*)

JOE: I will think about it.

(*To Roy.*) I will.

ROY: Huh.

MARTIN: It's the fear of what comes after the doing that makes the doing hard to do.

ROY: Amen.

MARTIN: But you can almost always live with the consequences.

Scene 7

(*That afternoon. On the granite steps outside the Hall of Justice, Brooklyn. It is cold and sunny. A Sabrett wagon is selling hot dogs. Louis, in a shabby overcoat, is sitting on the steps contemplatively eating one. Joe enters with three hot dogs and a can of Coke.*)

JOE: Can I . . . ?

LOUIS: Oh sure. Sure. Crazy cold sun.

JOE (*sitting*): Have to make the best of it.

How's your friend?

LOUIS: My . . . ? Oh. He's worse. My friend is worse.

JOE: I'm sorry.

LOUIS: Yeah, well. Thanks for asking. It's nice. You're nice. I can't believe you voted for Reagan.

JOE: I hope he gets better.

LOUIS: Reagan?

JOE: Your friend.

LOUIS: He won't. Neither will Reagan.

JOE: Let's not talk politics, OK?

LOUIS (*pointing to Joe's lunch*): You're eating *three* of those?

JOE: Well . . . I'm . . . hungry.

LOUIS: They're really terrible for you. Full of rat-poo and beetle legs and wood shavings 'n' shit.

JOE: Huh.

LOUIS: And . . . um . . . irridium, I think. Something toxic.

JOE: You're eating one.

LOUIS: Yeah, well, the shape, I can't help myself, plus I'm *trying* to commit suicide, what's your excuse?

JOE: I don't have an excuse. I just have Pepto-Bismol.

(*Joe takes a bottle of Pepto-Bismol and chugs it. Louis shudders audibly.*)

JOE: Yeah I know but then I wash it down with Coke.

(*He does this. Louis mimes barfing in Joes lap. Joe pushes Louis's head away.*)

JOE: Are you *always* like this?

LOUIS: I've been worrying a lot about his kids.

JOE: Whose?

LOUIS: Reagan's. Maureen and Mike and little orphan Patti and Miss Ron Reagan Jr., the you-should-pardon-the-expression heterosexual.

JOE: Ron Reagan Jr. is *not.* . . . You shouldn't just make these assumptions about people. How do you know? About him? What he is? You don't know.

LOUIS (*doing Tallulah*): Well darling he never sucked *my* cock but . . .

JOE: Look, if you're going to get vulgar . . .

LOUIS: No no really I mean. . . . What's it like to be the child of the Zeitgeist? To have the American Animus as your dad? It's not really a *family,* the Reagans, I read *People,* there aren't any connections there, no love, they don't ever even speak to each other except through their agents. So what's it like to be Reagan's kid? Enquiring minds want to know.

JOE: You can't believe everything you . . .

LOUIS (*looking away*): But . . . I think we all know what that's like. Nowadays. No connections. No responsibilities. All of us . . . falling through the cracks that separate what we owe to our selves and . . . and what we owe to love.

JOE: You just. . . . Whatever you feel like saying or doing, you don't care, you just . . . do it.

LOUIS: Do what?

JOE: It. Whatever. Whatever it is you want to do.

LOUIS: Are you trying to tell me something?

(*Little pause, sexual. They stare at each other. Joe looks away.*)

JOE: No, I'm just observing that you . . .

LOUIS: Impulsive.

JOE: Yes, I mean it must be scary, you . . .

LOUIS (*shrugs*): Land of the free. Home of the brave. Call me irresponsible.

JOE: It's kind of terrifying.

LOUIS: Yeah, well, freedom is. Heartless, too.

JOE: Oh you're not heartless.

LOUIS: You don't know.
     Finish your weenie.

(*He pats Joe on the knee, starts to leave.*)

JOE: Um . . .

(*Louis turns, looks at him. Joe searches for something to say.*)

JOE: Yesterday was Sunday but I've been a little unfocused recently and I thought it was Monday. So I came here like I was going to work. And the whole place was empty. And at first I couldn't figure out why, and I had this moment of incredible . . . fear and also. . . . It just flashed through my mind: The whole Hall of Justice, it's empty, it's deserted, it's gone out of business. Forever. The people that make it run have up and abandoned it.

LOUIS (*looking at the building*): Creepy.

JOE: Well yes but. I felt that I was going to scream. Not because it was creepy, but because the emptiness felt so *fast.*
     And . . . well, good. A . . . happy scream.
     I just wondered what a thing it would be . . . if overnight everything you owe anything to, justice, or love, had really gone away. Free.
     It would be . . . heartless terror. Yes. Terrible, and . . .
     Very great. To shed your skin, every old skin, one by one and then walk away, unencumbered, into the morning.
     (*Little pause. He looks at the building.*)
     I can't go in there today.

LOUIS: Then don't.

JOE (*not really hearing Louis*): I can't go in, I need . . .
     (*He looks for what he needs. He takes a swig of Pepto-Bismol.*)
     I can't *be* this anymore. I need . . . a change, I should just . . .

LOUIS (*not a come-on, necessarily; he doesn't want to be alone*): Want some company? For whatever?

(*Pause. Joe looks at Louis and looks away, afraid. Louis shrugs.*)

LOUIS: Sometimes, even if it scares you to death, you have to be willing to break the law. Know what I mean?

(*Another little pause.*)

JOE: Yes.

(*Another little pause.*)

LOUIS: I moved out. I moved out on my . . .
     I haven't been sleeping well.

JOE: Me neither.

(*Louis goes up to Joe, licks his napkin and dabs at Joes mouth.*)

LOUIS: Antacid moustache.
     (*Points to the building.*) Maybe the court won't convene. Ever again. Maybe we are free. To do whatever.

Children of the new morning, criminal minds. Selfish and greedy and loveless and blind. Reagan's children.

You're scared. So am I. Everybody is in the land of the free. God help us all.

Scene 8

(*Late that night. Joe at a payphone phoning Hannah at home in Salt Lake City.*)

JOE: Mom?
HANNAH: Joe?
JOE: Hi.
HANNAH: You're calling from the street. It's . . . it must be four in the morning. What's happened?
JOE: Nothing, nothing, I . . .
HANNAH: It's Harper. Is Harper. . . . Joe? Joe?
JOE: Yeah, hi. No, Harper's fine. Well, no, she's . . . not fine. How are you, Mom?
HANNAH: What's happened?
JOE: I just wanted to talk to you. I, uh, wanted to try something out on you.
HANNAH: Joe, you haven't . . . have you been drinking, Joe?
JOE: Yes ma'am. I'm drunk.
HANNAH: That isn't like you.
JOE: No. I mean, who's to say?
HANNAH: Why are you out on the street at four A.M.? In that crazy city. It's dangerous.
JOE: Actually, Mom, I'm not on the street. I'm near the boathouse in the park.
HANNAH: What park?
JOE: Central Park.
HANNAH: CENTRAL PARK! Oh my Lord. What on earth are you doing in Central Park at this time of night? Are you . . .

Joe, I think you ought to go home right now. Call me from home.
(*Little pause.*)
Joe?
JOE: I come here to watch, Mom. Sometimes. Just to watch.
HANNAH: Watch what? What's there to watch at four in the . . .
JOE: Mom, did Dad love me?
HANNAH: What?
JOE: Did he?
HANNAH: You ought to go home and call from there.
JOE: Answer.
HANNAH: Oh now really. This is maudlin. I don't like this conversation.
JOE: Yeah, well, it gets worse from here on.

(*Pause.*)

HANNAH: Joe?
JOE: Mom. Momma. I'm a homosexual, Momma.
Boy, did that come out awkward.

(*Pause.*)
Hello? Hello?
I'm a homosexual.
(*Pause.*)
Please, Momma. Say something.
HANNAH: You're old enough to understand that your father didn't love you without being ridiculous about it.
JOE: What?
HANNAH: You're ridiculous. You're being ridiculous.
JOE: I'm . . .
What?
HANNAH: You really ought to go home now to your wife. I need to go to bed. This phone call. . . . We will just forget this phone call.
JOE: Mom.
HANNAH: No more talk. Tonight. This . . .
(*Suddenly very angry.*) Drinking is a sin! A sin! I raised you better than that. (*She hangs up.*)

Scene 9

(*The following morning, early. Split scene: Harper and Joe at home; Louis and Prior in Prior's hospital room. Joe and Louis have just entered. This should be fast and obviously furious; overlapping is fine; the proceedings may be a little confusing but not the final results.*)

HARPER: Oh God. Home. The moment of truth has arrived.
JOE: Harper.
LOUIS: I'm going to move out.
PRIOR: The fuck you are.
JOE: Harper. Please listen. I still love you very much. You're still my best buddy; I'm not going to leave you.
HARPER: No, I don't like the sound of this. I'm leaving.
LOUIS: I'm leaving.
I already have.
JOE: Please listen. Stay. This is really hard. We have to talk.
HARPER: We are talking. Aren't we. Now please shut up. OK?
PRIOR: Bastard. Sneaking off while I'm flat out here, that's low. If I could get up now I'd beat the holy shit out of you.
JOE: Did you take pills? How many?
HARPER: No pills. Bad for the . . . (*Pats stomach.*)
JOE: You aren't pregnant. I called your gynecologist.
HARPER: I'm seeing a new gynecologist.
PRIOR: You have no right to do this.
LOUIS: Oh, that's ridiculous.
PRIOR: No right. It's criminal.
JOE: Forget about that. Just listen. You want the truth. This is the truth.
I knew this when I married you. I've known this I guess for as long as I've known anything, but . . . I don't know, I thought maybe that with enough effort and will I could change myself . . . but I can't . . .

PRIOR: Criminal.

LOUIS: There oughta be a law.

PRIOR: There is a law. You'll see.

JOE: I'm losing ground here, I go walking, you want to know where I walk, I . . . go to the park, or up and down 53rd Street, or places where. . . . And I keep swearing I won't go walking again, but I just can't.

LOUIS: I need some privacy.

PRIOR: That's new.

LOUIS: Everything's new, Prior.

JOE: I try to tighten my heart into a knot, a snarl, I try to learn to live dead, just numb, but then I see someone I want, and it's like a nail, like a hot spike right through my chest, and I know I'm losing.

PRIOR: Apartment too small for three? Louis and Prior comfy but not Louis and Prior and Prior's disease?

LOUIS: Something like that.

I won't be judged by you. This isn't a crime, just — the inevitable consequence of people who run out of — whose limitations. . . .

PRIOR: Bang bang bang. The court will come to order.

LOUIS: I mean let's talk practicalities, schedules; I'll come over if you want, spend nights with you when I can, I can . . .

PRIOR: Has the jury reached a verdict?

LOUIS: I'm doing the best I can.

PRIOR: Pathetic. Who cares?

JOE: My whole life has conspired to bring me to this place, and I can't despise my whole life. I think I believed when I met you I could save you, you at least if not myself, but . . .

I don't have any sexual feelings for you, Harper. And I don't think I ever did.

(*Little pause.*)

HARPER: I think you should go.

JOE: Where?

HARPER: Washington. Doesn't matter.

JOE: What are you talking about?

HARPER: Without me, Joe. Isn't that what you want to hear?

(*Little pause.*)

JOE: Yes.

LOUIS: You can love someone and fail them. You can love someone and not be able to . . .

PRIOR: You *can*, theoretically, yes. A person can, maybe an editorial "you" can love, Louis, but not *you*, specifically you, I don't know, I think you are excluded from that general category.

HARPER: You were going to save me, but the whole time you were spinning a lie. I just don't understand that.

PRIOR: A person could theoretically love and maybe many do but we both know now you can't.

LOUIS: I do.

PRIOR: You can't even say it.

LOUIS: I love you, Prior.

PRIOR: I repeat. Who cares?

HARPER: This is so scary, I want this to stop, to go back . . .

PRIOR: We have reached a verdict, your honor. This man's heart is deficient. He loves, but his love is worth nothing.

JOE: Harper . . .

HARPER: Mr. Lies, I want to get away from here. Far away. Right now. Before he starts talking again. Please, please . . .

JOE: As long as I've known you Harper you've been afraid of . . . Of men hiding under the bed, men hiding under the sofa, men with knives.

PRIOR (*shattered; almost pleading; trying to reach him*): I'm dying! You stupid fuck! Do you know what that is! Love! Do you know what love means? We lived together four-and-a-half years, you animal, you idiot.

LOUIS: I have to find some way to save myself.

JOE: Who are these men? I never understood it. Now I know.

HARPER: What?

JOE: It's me.

HARPER: It is?

PRIOR: GET OUT OF MY ROOM!

JOE: I'm the man with the knives.

HARPER: You are?

PRIOR: If I could get up now I'd kill you. I would. Go away. Go away or I'll scream.

HARPER: Oh God . . .

JOE: I'm sorry . . .

HARPER: It is you.

LOUIS: Please don't scream.

PRIOR: Go.

HARPER: I recognize you now.

LOUIS: Please . . .

JOE: Oh. Wait, I. . . . Oh!

(*He covers his mouth with his hand, gags, and removes his hand, red with blood.*)

I'm bleeding.

(*Prior screams.*)

HARPER: Mr. Lies.

MR. LIES (*appearing, dressed in antarctic explorer's apparel*): Right here.

HARPER: I want to go away. I can't see him anymore.

MR. LIES: Where?

HARPER: Anywhere. Far away.

MR. LIES: Absolutamento.

(*Harper and Mr. Lies vanish. Joe looks up, sees that she's gone.*)

PRIOR (*closing his eyes*): When I open my eyes you'll be gone.

(*Louis leaves.*)

JOE: Harper?

PRIOR (*opening his eyes*): Huh. It worked.

JOE (*calling*): Harper?

PRIOR: I hurt all over. I wish I was dead.

Scene 10

(*The same day, sunset. Hannah and Sister Ella Chapter, a real-estate saleswoman, Hannah Pitt's closest friend, in front of Hannah's house in Salt Lake City.*)

SISTER ELLA CHAPTER: Look at that view! A view of heaven. Like the living city of heaven, isn't it, it just fairly glimmers in the sun.

HANNAH: Glimmers.

SISTER ELLA CHAPTER: Even the stone and brick it just glimmers and glitters like heaven in the sunshine. Such a nice view you get, perched up on a canyon rim. Some kind of beautiful place.

HANNAH: It's just Salt Lake, and you're selling the house *for* me, not *to* me.

SISTER ELLA CHAPTER: I like to work up an enthusiasm for my properties.

HANNAH: Just get me a good price.

SISTER ELLA CHAPTER: Well, the market's off.

HANNAH: At least fifty.

SISTER ELLA CHAPTER: Forty'd be more like it.

HANNAH: Fifty.

SISTER ELLA CHAPTER: Wish you'd wait a bit.

HANNAH: Well I can't.

SISTER ELLA CHAPTER: Wish you would. You're about the only friend I got.

HANNAH: Oh well now.

SISTER ELLA CHAPTER: Know why I decided to like you? I decided to like you 'cause you're the only unfriendly Mormon I ever met.

HANNAH: Your wig is crooked.

SISTER ELLA CHAPTER: Fix it.

(*Hannah straightens Sister Ella's wig.*)

SISTER ELLA CHAPTER: New York City. All they got there is tiny rooms.

I always thought: People ought to stay put. That's why I got my license to sell real estate. It's a way of saying: Have a house! Stay put! It's a way of saying traveling's no good. Plus I needed the cash. (*She takes a pack of cigarettes out of her purse, lights one, offers pack to Hannah.*)

HANNAH: Not out here, anyone could come by.

There's been days I've stood at this ledge and thought about stepping over.

It's a hard place, Salt Lake: baked dry. Abundant energy; not much intelligence. That's a combination that can wear a body out. No harm looking someplace else. I don't need much room.

My sister-in-law Libby thinks there's radon gas in the basement.

SISTER ELLA CHAPTER: Is there gas in the . . .

HANNAH: Of course not. Libby's a fool.

SISTER ELLA CHAPTER: 'Cause I'd have to include that in the description.

HANNAH: There's no gas, Ella. (*Little pause.*) Give a puff. (*She takes a furtive drag of Ella's cigarette.*) Put it away now.

SISTER ELLA CHAPTER: So I guess it's goodbye.

HANNAH: You'll be all right, Ella, I wasn't ever much of a friend.

SISTER ELLA CHAPTER: I'll say something but don't laugh, OK?

This is the home of saints, the godliest place on earth, they say, and I think they're right. That mean there's no evil here? No. Evil's everywhere. Sin's everywhere. But this . . . is the spring of sweet water in the desert, the desert flower. Every step a Believer takes away from here is a step fraught with peril. I fear for you, Hannah Pitt, because you are my friend. Stay put. This is the right home of saints.

HANNAH: Latter-day saints.

SISTER ELLA CHAPTER: Only kind left.

HANNAH: But still. Late in the day . . . for saints and everyone. That's all. That's all.

Fifty thousand dollars for the house, Sister Ella Chapter; don't undersell. It's an impressive view.

ACT 3
NOT-YET-CONSCIOUS, FORWARD DAWNING • *January 1986*

Scene 1

(*Late night, three days after the end of act 2. The stage is completely dark. Prior is in bed in his apartment, having a nightmare. He wakes up, sits up and switches on a nightlight. He looks at his clock. Seated by the table near the bed is a man dressed in the clothing of a 13th-century British squire.*)

PRIOR (*terrified*): Who are you?

PRIOR 1: My name is Prior Walter.

(*Pause.*)

PRIOR: My name is Prior Walter.

PRIOR 1: I know that.

PRIOR: Explain.

PRIOR 1: You're alive. I'm not. We have the same name. What do you want me to explain?

PRIOR: A ghost?

PRIOR 1: An ancestor.

PRIOR: Not *the* Prior Walter? The Bayeux tapestry Prior Walter?

PRIOR 1: His great-great grandson. The fifth of the name.

PRIOR: I'm the thirty-fourth, I think.

PRIOR 1: Actually the thirty-second.

PRIOR: Not according to Mother.

PRIOR 1: She's including the two bastards, then; I say leave them out. I say no room for bastards. The little things you swallow . . .

PRIOR: Pills.

PRIOR 1: Pills. For the pestilence. I too . . .

PRIOR: Pestilence. . . . You too what?

PRIOR 1: The pestilence in my time was much worse than now. Whole villages of empty houses. You could look outdoors and see Death walking in the morning, dew dampening the ragged hem of his black robe. Plain as I see you now.

PRIOR: You died of the plague.

PRIOR 1: The spotty monster. Like you, alone.

PRIOR: I'm not alone.

PRIOR 1: You have no wife, no children.

PRIOR: I'm gay.

PRIOR 1: So? Be gay, dance in your altogether for all I care, what's that to do with not having children?

PRIOR: Gay homosexual, not bonny, blithe and . . . never mind.

PRIOR 1: I had twelve. When I died.

(The second ghost appears, this one dressed in the clothing of an elegant 17th-century Londoner.)

PRIOR 1 *(pointing to Prior 2)*: And I was three years younger than him.

(Prior sees the new ghost, screams.)

PRIOR: Oh God another one.

PRIOR 2: Prior Walter. Prior to you by some seventeen others.

PRIOR 1: He's counting the bastards.

PRIOR: Are we having a convention?

PRIOR 2: We've been sent to declare her fabulous incipience. They love a well-paved entrance with lots of heralds, and . . .

PRIOR 1: The messenger come. Prepare the way. The infinite descent, a breath in air . . .

PRIOR 2: They chose us, I suspect, because of the mortal affinities. In a family as long-descended as the Walters there are bound to be a few carried off by plague.

PRIOR 1: The spotty monster.

PRIOR 2: Black Jack. Came from a water pump, half the city of London, can you imagine? His came from fleas. Yours, I understand, is the lamentable consequence of venery . . .

PRIOR 1: Fleas on rats, but who knew that?

PRIOR: Am I going to die?

PRIOR 2: We aren't allowed to discuss . . .

PRIOR 1: When you do, you don't get ancestors to help you through it. You may be surrounded by children but you die alone.

PRIOR: I'm afraid.

PRIOR 1: You should be. There aren't even torches, and the path's rocky, dark and steep.

PRIOR 2: Don't alarm him. There's good news before there's bad.

We two come to strew rose petal and palm leaf before the triumphal procession. Prophet. Seer. Revelator. It's a great honor for the family.

PRIOR 1: He hasn't got a family.

PRIOR 2: I meant for the Walters, for the family in the larger sense.

PRIOR *(singing)*: All I want is a room somewhere,
    Far away from the cold night air . . .

PRIOR 2 *(putting a hand on Prior's forehead)*: Calm, calm, this is no brain fever . . .

(Prior calms down, but keeps his eyes closed. The lights begin to change. Distant Glorious Music.)

PRIOR 1 *(low chant)*: Adonai, Adonai,
    Olam ha-yichud,
    Zefirot, Zazahot,
    Ha-adam, ha-gadol
    Daughter of Light,
    Daughter of Splendors,
    Fluor! Phosphor!
    Lumen! Candle!

PRIOR 2 *(simultaneously)*: Even now,
    From the mirror-bright halls of heaven,
    Across the cold and lifeless infinity of space,
    The Messenger comes
    Trailing orbs of light,
    Fabulous, incipient,
    Oh Prophet,
    To you . . .

PRIOR 1 AND PRIOR 2: Prepare, prepare,
    The Infinite Descent,
    A breath, a feather,
    Glory to . . .

(They vanish.)

Scene 2

(The next day. Split scene. Louis and Belize in a coffee shop. Prior is at the outpatient clinic at the hospital with Emily, the nurse; she has him on a pentamidine IV drip.)

LOUIS: Why has democracy succeeded in America? Of course by succeeded I mean comparatively, not literally, not in the present, but what makes for the prospect of some sort of radical democracy spreading outward and growing up? Why does the power that was once so carefully preserved at the top of the pyramid by the original framers of the Constitution seem drawn inexorably downward and outward in spite of the best effort of the Right to stop this? I mean it's the really hard thing about being Left in this country, the American Left can't help but trip over all these petrified little fetishes: freedom, that's the worst; you know, *Jeane Kirkpatrick°* for God's sake will go on and on about freedom and so what does that mean, the word freedom, when she talks about it, or human rights; you have Bush talking about human rights, and so what are these people talking about, they might as well be talking about the mating habits of Venusians, these people don't begin to know what, ontologically, freedom is or human

Jeane Kirkpatrick: Former U.S. ambassador to the United Nations. Kirkpatrick now teaches at Georgetown University and remains a member of the American Enterprise Institute for Public Policy and Research, a conservative think tank.

rights, like they see these bourgeois property-based Rights-of-Man-type rights but that's not enfranchisement, not democracy, not what's implicit, what's potential within the idea, not the idea with blood in it. That's just liberalism, the worst kind of liberalism, really, bourgeois tolerance, and what I think is that what AIDS shows us is the limits of tolerance, that it's not enough to be tolerated, because when the shit hits the fan you find out how much tolerance is worth. Nothing. And underneath all the tolerance is intense, passionate hatred.

BELIZE: Uh huh.

LOUIS: Well don't you think that's true?

BELIZE: Uh huh. It is.

LOUIS: *Power* is the object, not being tolerated. Fuck assimilation. But I mean in spite of all this the thing about America, I think, is that ultimately we're different from every other nation on earth, in that, with people here of every race, we can't. . . . Ultimately what defines us isn't race, but politics. Not like any European country where there's an insurmountable fact of a kind of racial, or ethnic, monopoly, or monolith, like all Dutchmen, I mean Dutch people, are well, Dutch, and the Jews of Europe were never Europeans, just a small problem. Facing the monolith. But here there are so many small problems, it's really just a collection of small problems, the monolith is missing. Oh, I mean, of course I suppose there's the monolith of White America. White Straight Male America.

BELIZE: Which is not unimpressive, even among monoliths.

LOUIS: Well, no, but when the race thing gets taken care of, and I don't mean to minimalize how major it is, I mean I know it is, this is a really, really incredibly racist country but it's like, well, the British. I mean, all these blue-eyed pink people. And it's just weird, you know, I mean I'm not all that Jewish-looking, or . . . well, maybe I am but, you know, in New York, everyone is . . . well, not everyone, but so many are but so but in England, in London I walk into bars and I feel like Sid the Yid, you know I mean like Woody Allen in *Annie Hall,* with the payess and the gabardine coat, like never, never anywhere so much — I mean, not actively despised, not like they're Germans, who I think are still terribly anti-Semitic, and racist too, I mean black-racist, they pretend otherwise but, anyway, in London, there's just . . . and at one point I met this black gay guy from Jamaica who talked with a lilt but he said his family'd been living in London since before the Civil War — the American one — and how the English never let him forget for a minute that he wasn't blue-eyed and pink and I said yeah, me too, these people are anti-Semites and he said yeah but the British Jews have the clothing business all sewed up and blacks there can't get a foothold. And it was an incredibly awkward moment of just. . . . I mean there we were, in this bar that was gay but it was a *pub,* you know,

the beams and the plaster and those horrible little, like, two-day-old fish and egg sandwiches — and just so British, so *old,* and I felt, well, there's no way out of this because both of us are, right now, too much immersed in this history, hope is dissolved in the sheer age of this place, where race is what counts and there's no real hope of change — it's the racial destiny of the Brits that matters to them, not their political destiny, whereas in America . . .

BELIZE: Here in America race doesn't count.

LOUIS: No, no, that's not. . . . I mean you *can't* be hearing that . . .

BELIZE: I . . .

LOUIS: It's — look, race, yes, but ultimately race here is a political question, right? Racists just try to use race here as a tool in a political struggle. It's not really about race. Like the spiritualists try to use that stuff, are you enlightened, are you centered, channeled, whatever, this reaching out for a spiritual past in a country where no indigenous spirits exist — only the Indians, I mean Native American spirits and we killed them off so now, there are no gods here, no ghosts and spirits in America, there are no angels in America, no spiritual past, no racial past, there's only the political, and the decoys and the ploys to maneuver around the inescapable battle of politics, the shifting downwards and outwards of political power to the people . . .

BELIZE: POWER to the People! AMEN! (*Looking at his watch.*) *OH MY GOODNESS!* Will you look at the time, I gotta . . .

LOUIS: Do you. . . . You think this is, what, racist or naive or something?

BELIZE: Well it's certainly *something.* Look, I just remembered I have an appointment . . .

LOUIS: What? I mean I really don't want to, like, speak from some position of privilege and . . .

BELIZE: I'm sitting here, thinking, eventually he's *got* to run out of steam, so I let you rattle on and on saying about maybe seven or eight things I find really offensive.

LOUIS: What?

BELIZE: But I know you, Louis, and I know the guilt fueling this peculiar tirade is obviously already swollen bigger than your hemorrhoids.

LOUIS: I don't have hemorrhoids.

BELIZE: I hear different. May I finish?

LOUIS: Yes, but I don't have hemorrhoids.

BELIZE: So finally, when I . . .

LOUIS: Prior told you, he's an asshole, he shouldn't have . . .

BELIZE: You promised, Louis. Prior is not a subject.

LOUIS: You brought him up.

BELIZE: I brought up hemorrhoids.

LOUIS: So it's indirect. Passive-aggressive.

BELIZE: Unlike, I suppose, banging me over the head with your theory that America doesn't have a race problem.

LOUIS: Oh be fair I never said that.

BELIZE: Not exactly, but . . .

LOUIS: I said . . .

BELIZE: . . . but it was close enough, because if it'd been that blunt I'd've just walked out and . . .

LOUIS: You deliberately misinterpreted! I . . .

BELIZE: Stop interrupting! I haven't been able to . . .

LOUIS: Just let me . . .

BELIZE: NO! What, *talk*? You've been running your mouth nonstop since I got here, yaddadda yaddadda blah blah blah, up the hill, down the hill, playing with your MONOLITH . . .

LOUIS (*overlapping*): Well, you could have joined in at any time instead of . . .

BELIZE (*continuing over Louis*): . . . and girlfriend it is truly an *awesome* spectacle but I got better things to do with my time than sit here listening to this racist bullshit just because I feel sorry for you that . . .

LOUIS: I am not a racist!

BELIZE: Oh come on . . .

LOUIS: So maybe I am a racist but . . .

BELIZE: Oh I really hate that! It's no fun picking on you Louis; you're so guilty, it's like throwing darts at a glob of jello, there's no satisfying hits, just quivering, the darts just blop in and vanish.

LOUIS: I just think when you are discussing lines of oppression it gets very complicated and . . .

BELIZE: Oh is that a fact? You know, we black drag queens have a rather intimate knowledge of the complexity of the lines of . . .

LOUIS: *Ex*-black drag queen.

BELIZE: Actually ex-ex.

LOUIS: You're doing drag again?

BELIZE: I don't. . . . Maybe. I don't have to tell you. Maybe.

LOUIS: I think it's sexist.

BELIZE: I didn't ask you.

LOUIS: Well it is. The gay community, I think, has to adopt the same attitude towards drag as black women have to take towards black women blues singers.

BELIZE: Oh my we *are* walking dangerous tonight.

LOUIS: Well, it's all internalized oppression, right, I mean the masochism, the stereotypes, the . . .

BELIZE: Louis, are you deliberately trying to make me hate you?

LOUIS: No, I . . .

BELIZE: I mean, are you deliberately transforming yourself into an arrogant, sexual-political Stalinist-slash-racist flag-waving thug for my benefit?

(*Pause.*)

LOUIS: You know what I think?

BELIZE: What?

LOUIS: You hate me because I'm a Jew.

BELIZE: I'm leaving.

LOUIS: It's true.

BELIZE: You have no basis except your . . .

Louis, it's good to know you haven't changed; you are still an honorary citizen of the Twilight

Zone, and after your pale, pale white polemics on behalf of racial insensitivity you have a flaming *fuck* of a lot of nerve calling me an anti-Semite. Now I really gotta go.

LOUIS: You called me Lou the Jew.

BELIZE: That was a joke.

LOUIS: I didn't think it was funny. It was hostile.

BELIZE: It was three years ago.

LOUIS: So?

BELIZE: You just called yourself Sid the Yid.

LOUIS: That's not the same thing.

BELIZE: Sid the Yid is different from Lou the Jew.

LOUIS: Yes.

BELIZE: Someday you'll have to explain that to me, but right now . . .

   You hate me because you hate black people.

LOUIS: I do not. But I do think most black people are anti-Semitic.

BELIZE: "Most black people." *That's* racist, Louis, and *I* think most Jews . . .

LOUIS: Louis Farrakhan.

BELIZE: Ed Koch.

LOUIS: Jesse Jackson.

BELIZE: Jackson. Oh really, Louis, this is . . .

LOUIS: Hymietown! Hymietown!

BELIZE: Louis, you voted for Jesse Jackson. You send checks to the Rainbow Coalition.

LOUIS: I'm ambivalent. The checks bounced.

BELIZE: All your checks bounce, Louis; you're ambivalent about everything.

LOUIS: What's that supposed to mean?

BELIZE: You may be dumber than shit but I refuse to believe you can't figure it out. Try.

LOUIS: I was never ambivalent about Prior. I love him. I do. I really do.

BELIZE: Nobody said different.

LOUIS: Love and ambivalence are. . . . Real love isn't ambivalent.

BELIZE: "Real love isn't ambivalent." I'd swear that's a line from my favorite bestselling paperback novel, *In Love with the Night Mysterious*, except I don't think you ever read it.

(*Pause.*)

LOUIS: I never read it, no.

BELIZE: You ought to. Instead of spending the rest of your life trying to get through *Democracy in America*. It's about this white woman whose Daddy owns a plantation in the Deep South in the years before the Civil War — the American one — and her name is Margaret, and she's in love with her Daddy's number-one slave, and his name is Thaddeus, and she's married but her white slave-owner husband has AIDS: Antebellum Insufficiently Developed Sex-organs. And there's a lot of hot stuff going down when Margaret and Thaddeus can catch a spare torrid ten under the cotton-picking moon, and then of course the Yankees come, and they set the slaves free, and the slaves string up old Daddy, and so on.

Historical fiction. Somewhere in there I recall Margaret and Thaddeus find the time to discuss the nature of love; her face is reflecting the flames of the burning plantation — you know, the way white people do — and his black face is dark in the night and she says to him, "Thaddeus, real love isn't ever ambivalent."

(*Little pause. Emily enters and turns off IV drip.*)

BELIZE: Thaddeus looks at her; he's contemplating her thesis; and he isn't sure he agrees.

EMILY (*removing IV drip from Prior's arm*): Treatment number . . . (*consulting chart*) four.

PRIOR: Pharmaceutical miracle. Lazarus breathes again.

LOUIS: Is he. . . . How bad is he?

BELIZE: You want the laundry list?

EMILY: Shirt off, let's check the . . .

(*Prior takes his shirt off. She examines his lesions.*)

BELIZE: There's the weight problem and the shit problem and the morale problem.

EMILY: Only six. That's good. Pants.

(*He drops his pants. He's naked. She examines.*)

BELIZE: And. He thinks he's going crazy.

EMILY: Looking good. What else?

PRIOR: Ankles sore and swollen, but the leg's better. The nausea's mostly gone with the little orange pills. BM's pure liquid but not bloody anymore, for now, my eye doctor says everything's OK, for now, my dentist says "Yuck!" when he sees my fuzzy tongue, and now he wears little condoms on his thumb and forefinger. And a mask. So what? My dermatologist is in Hawaii and my mother . . . well leave my mother out of it. Which is usually where my mother is, out of it. My glands are like walnuts, my weight's holding steady for week two, and a friend died two days ago of bird tuberculosis; bird tuberculosis; that scared me and I didn't go to the funeral today because he was an Irish Catholic and it's probably open casket and I'm afraid of . . . something, the bird TB or seeing him or. . . . So I guess I'm doing OK. Except for of course I'm going nuts.

EMILY: We ran the toxoplasmosis series and there's no indication . . .

PRIOR: I know, I know, but I feel like something terrifying is on its way, you know, like a missile from outer space, and it's plummeting down towards the earth, and I'm ground zero, and . . . I am generally known where I am known as one cool, collected queen. And I am ruffled.

EMILY: There's really nothing to worry about. I think that shochen bamromim hamtzeh menucho nechono al kanfey haschino.

PRIOR: What?

EMILY: Everything's fine. Bemaalos k'doshim ut'horim kezohar horokeea mazhirim . . .

PRIOR: Oh I don't understand what you're . . .

EMILY: Es nishmas Prior sheholoch leolomoh, baavur shenodvoo z'dokoh b'ad hazkoras nishmosoh.

PRIOR: Why are you doing that?! Stop it! Stop it!

EMILY: Stop what?

PRIOR: You were just . . . weren't you just speaking in Hebrew or something.

EMILY: *Hebrew?* (*Laughs.*) I'm basically Italian-American. No. I didn't speak in Hebrew.

PRIOR: Oh no, oh God please I really think I . . .

EMILY: Look, I'm sorry, I have a waiting room full of . . . I think you're one of the lucky ones, you'll live for years, probably — you're pretty healthy for someone with no immune system. Are you seeing someone? Loneliness is a danger. A therapist?

PRIOR: No, I don't need to see anyone, I just . . .

EMILY: Well think about it. You aren't going crazy. You're just under a lot of stress. No wonder . . . (*She starts to write in his chart.*)

(*Suddenly there is an astonishing blaze of light, a huge chord sounded by a gigantic choir, and a great book with steel pages mounted atop a molten-red pillar pops up from the stage floor. The book opens; there is a large Aleph inscribed on its pages, which bursts into flames. Immediately the book slams shut and disappears instantly under the floor as the lights become normal again. Emily notices none of this, writing. Prior is agog.*)

EMILY (*laughing, exiting*): Hebrew . . .

(*Prior flees.*)

LOUIS: Help me.

BELIZE: I beg your pardon?

LOUIS: You're a nurse, give me something, I . . . don't know what to do anymore, I. . . . Last week at work I screwed up the Xerox machine like permanently and so I . . . then I tripped on the subway steps and my glasses broke and I cut my forehead, here, see, and now I can't see much and my forehead . . . it's like the Mark of Cain,° stupid, right, but it won't heal and every morning I see it and I think, Biblical things, Mark of Cain, Judas Iscariot° and his silver and his noose, people who . . . in betraying what they love betray what's truest in themselves, I feel . . . nothing but cold for myself, just cold, and every night I miss him, I miss him so much but then . . . those sores, and the smell and . . . where I thought it was going. . . . I could be . . . I could be . . . sick too, maybe I'm sick too. I don't know.

  Belize. Tell him I love him. Can you do that?

BELIZE: I've thought about it for a very long time, and I still don't understand what love is. Justice is simple. Democracy is simple. Those things are unambivalent. But love is very hard. And it goes bad for you if you violate the hard law of love.

LOUIS: I'm dying.

BELIZE: He's dying. You just wish you were.

Mark of Cain: In Genesis Cain murdered his brother Abel and subsequently was marked on his forehead by God.
Judas Iscariot: An apostle who betrayed Jesus for thirty pieces of silver.

Oh cheer up, Louis. Look at that heavy sky out there.

LOUIS: Purple.

BELIZE: *Purple?* Boy, what kind of a homosexual are you, anyway? That's not purple, Mary, that color up there is (*very grand*) mauve.

All day today it's felt like Thanksgiving. Soon, this . . . ruination will be blanketed white. You can smell it — can you smell it?

LOUIS: Smell what?

BELIZE: Softness, compliance, forgiveness, grace.

LOUIS: No . . .

BELIZE: I can't help you learn that. I can't help you, Louis. You're not my business. (*He exits.*)

(*Louis puts his head in his hands, inadvertently touching his cut forehead.*)

LOUIS: Ow FUCK! (*He stands slowly, looks towards where Belize exited.*) Smell what?
(*He looks both ways to be sure no one is watching, then inhales deeply, and is surprised.*) Huh. Snow.

Scene 3

(*Same day. Harper in a very white, cold place, with a brilliant blue sky above; a delicate snowfall. She is dressed in a beautiful snowsuit. The sound of the sea, faint.*)

HARPER: Snow! Ice! Mountains of ice! Where am I? I . . .
I feel better, I do, I . . . feel better. There are ice crystals in my lungs, wonderful and sharp. And the snow smells like cold, crushed peaches. And there's something . . . some current of blood in the wind, how strange, it has that iron taste.

MR. LIES: Ozone.

HARPER: Ozone! Wow! Where am I?

MR. LIES: The Kingdom of Ice, the bottommost part of the world.

HARPER (*looking around, then realizing*): Antarctica. This is Antarctica!

MR. LIES: Cold shelter for the shattered. No sorrow here, tears freeze.

HARPER: Antarctica, Antarctica, oh boy oh boy, LOOK at this, I. . . . Wow, I must've really snapped the tether, huh?

MR. LIES: Apparently

HARPER: That's great. I want to stay here forever. Set up camp. Build things. Build a city, an enormous city made up of frontier forts, dark wood and green roofs and high gates made of pointed logs and bonfires burning on every street corner. I should build by a river. Where are the forests?

MR. LIES: No timber here. Too cold. Ice, no trees.

HARPER: Oh details! I'm sick of details! I'll plant them and grow them. I'll live off caribou fat, I'll melt it over the bonfires and drink it from long, curved goat-horn cups. It'll be great. I want to make a new world here. So that I never have to go home again.

MR. LIES: As long as it lasts. Ice has a way of melting . . .

HARPER: No. Forever. I can have anything I want here — maybe even companionship, someone who has . . . desire for me. You, maybe.

MR. LIES: It's against the by-laws of the International Order of Travel Agents to get involved with clients. Rules are rules. Anyway, I'm not the one you really want.

HARPER: There isn't anyone . . . maybe an Eskimo. Who could ice-fish for food. And help me build a nest for when the baby comes.

MR. LIES: There are no Eskimo in Antarctica. And you're not really pregnant. You made that up.

HARPER: Well all of this is made up. So if the snow feels cold I'm pregnant. Right? Here, I can be pregnant. And I can have any kind of a baby I want.

MR. LIES: This is a retreat, a vacuum, its virtue is that it lacks everything; deep-freeze for feelings. You can be numb and safe here, that's what you came for. Respect the delicate ecology of your delusions.

HARPER: You mean like no Eskimo in Antarctica.

MR. LIES: Correcto. Ice and snow, no Eskimo. Even hallucinations have laws.

HARPER: Well then who's that?

(*The Eskimo appears.*)

MR. LIES: An Eskimo.

HARPER: An antarctic Eskimo. A fisher of the polar deep.

MR. LIES: There's something wrong with this picture.

(*The Eskimo beckons.*)

HARPER: I'm going to like this place. It's my own National Geographic Special! Oh! Oh! (*She holds her stomach.*) I think . . . I think I felt her kicking. Maybe I'll give birth to a baby covered with thick white fur, and that way she won't be cold. My breasts will be full of hot cocoa so she doesn't get chilly. And if it gets really cold, she'll have a pouch I can crawl into. Like a marsupial. We'll mend together. That's what we'll do; we'll mend.

Scene 4

(*Same day. An abandoned lot in the South Bronx. A homeless Woman is standing near an oil drum in which a fire is burning. Snowfall. Trash around. Hannah enters dragging two heavy suitcases.*)

HANNAH: Excuse me? I said excuse me? Can you tell me where I am? Is this Brooklyn? Do you know a Pineapple Street? Is there some sort of bus or train or . . . ?
I'm lost, I just arrived from Salt Lake. City. Utah? I took the bus that I was told to take and I got off — well it was the very last stop, so I had to get off, and I

asked the driver was this Brooklyn, and he nodded yes but he was from one of those foreign countries where they think it's good manners to nod at everything even if you have no idea what it is you're nodding at, and in truth I think he spoke no English at all, which I think would make him ineligible for employment on public transportation. The public being English-speaking, mostly. Do you speak English?

(*The Woman nods.*)

HANNAH: I was supposed to be met at the airport by my son. He didn't show and I don't wait more than three and three-quarters hours for *anyone*. I should have been patient, I guess, I. . . . Is this . . .
WOMAN: Bronx.
HANNAH: Is that. . . . The *Bronx*? Well how in the name of Heaven did I get to the Bronx when the bus driver said . . .
WOMAN (*talking to herself*): Slurp slurp slurp will you STOP that disgusting slurping! YOU DISGUSTING SLURPING FEEDING ANIMAL! Feeding yourself, just feeding yourself, what would it matter, to you or to ANYONE, if you just stopped. Feeding. And DIED?

(*Pause.*)

HANNAH: Can you just tell me where I . . .
WOMAN: Why was the Kosciusko Bridge named after a Polack?
HANNAH: I don't know what you're . . .
WOMAN: That was a joke.
HANNAH: Well what's the punchline?
WOMAN: I don't know.
HANNAH (*looking around desperately*): Oh for pete's sake, is there anyone else who . . .
WOMAN (*again, to herself*): Stand further off you fat loathsome whore, you can't have any more of this soup, slurp slurp slurp you animal, and the — I know you'll just go pee it all away and where will you do that? Behind what bush? It's FUCKING COLD out here and I . . .
    Oh that's right, because it was supposed to have been a tunnel!
    That's not very funny.
    Have you read the prophecies of Nostradamus?
HANNAH: Who?
WOMAN: Some guy I went out with once somewhere, Nostradamus. Prophet, outcast, eyes like. . . . Scary shit, he . . .
HANNAH: Shut up. Please. Now I want you to stop jabbering for a minute and pull your wits together and tell me how to get to Brooklyn. Because you know! And you are going to tell me! Because there is no one else around to tell me and I am wet and cold and I am very angry! So I am sorry you're psychotic but just make the effort — take a deep breath — DO IT!

(*Hannah and the Woman breathe together.*)

HANNAH: That's good. Now exhale.

(*They do.*)

HANNAH: Good. Now how do I get to Brooklyn?
WOMAN: Don't know. Never been. Sorry. Want some soup?
HANNAH: Manhattan? Maybe you know . . . I don't suppose you know the location of the Mormon Visitor's . . .
WOMAN: 65th and Broadway.
HANNAH: How do you . . .
WOMAN: Go there all the time. Free movies. Boring, but you can stay all day.
HANNAH: Well. . . . So how do I.
WOMAN: Take the D Train. Next block make a right.
HANNAH: Thank you.
WOMAN: Oh yeah. In the new century I think we will all be insane.

Scene 5

(*Same day. Joe and Roy in the study of Roy's brownstone. Roy is wearing an elegant bathrobe. He has made a considerable effort to look well. He isn't well, and he hasn't succeeded much in looking it.*)

JOE: I can't. The answer's no. I'm sorry.
ROY: Oh, well, apologies . . .
    I can't see that there's anyone asking for apologies.

(*Pause.*)

JOE: I'm sorry, Roy.
ROY: Oh, well, apologies.
JOE: My wife is missing, Roy. My mother's coming from Salt Lake to . . . to help look, I guess. I'm supposed to be at the airport now, picking her up but. . . . I just spent two days in a hospital, Roy, with a bleeding ulcer, I was spitting up blood.
ROY: Blood, huh? Look, I'm very busy here and . . .
JOE: It's just a job.
ROY: A job? A *job*? *Washington*! Dumb Utah Mormon hick shit!
JOE: Roy . . .
ROY: *WASHINGTON*! When Washington called me I was younger than you, you think I said "Aw fuck no I can't go I got two fingers up my asshole and a little moral nosebleed to boot!" When Washington calls you my pretty young punk friend you go or you can go fuck yourself sideways 'cause the train has pulled out of the station, and you are *out*, nowhere, out in the cold. Fuck you, Mary Jane, get outta here.
JOE: Just let me . . .
ROY: Explain? Ephemera. You broke my heart. Explain that. Explain that.
JOE: I love you. Roy.
    There's so much that I want, to be . . . what you see in me, I want to be a participant in the world, in your world, Roy, I want to be capable of that, I've

tried, really I have but . . . I can't do this. Not because I don't believe in you, but because I believe in you so much, in what you stand for, at heart, the order, the decency. I would give anything to protect you, but. . . . There are laws I can't break. It's too ingrained. It's not me. There's enough damage I've already done.

Maybe you were right, maybe I'm dead.

ROY: You're not dead, boy, you're a sissy.

You love me; that's moving, I'm moved. It's nice to be loved. I warned you about her, didn't I, Joe? But you don't listen to me, why, because you say Roy is smart and Roy's a friend but Roy . . . well, he isn't nice, and you wanna be nice. Right? A nice, nice man!

(*Little pause.*)

You know what my greatest accomplishment was, Joe, in my life, what I am able to look back on and be proudest of? And I have helped make Presidents and unmake them and mayors and more goddam judges than anyone in NYC ever — AND several million dollars, tax-free — and what do you think means the most to me?

You ever hear of Ethel Rosenberg? Huh, Joe, huh?

JOE: Well, yeah, I guess I. . . . Yes.

ROY: Yes. Yes. You have heard of Ethel Rosenberg. Yes. Maybe you even read about her in the history books.

If it wasn't for me, Joe, Ethel Rosenberg would be alive today, writing some personal-advice column for *Ms.* magazine. She isn't. Because during the trial, Joe, I was on the phone every day, talking with the judge . . .

JOE: Roy . . .

ROY: Every day, doing what I do best, talking on the telephone, making sure that timid Yid nebbish on the bench did his duty to America, to history. That sweet unprepossessing woman, two kids, boo-hoo-hoo, reminded us all of our little Jewish mamas — she came this close to getting life; I pleaded till I wept to put her in the chair. Me. I did that. I would have fucking pulled the switch if they'd have let me. Why? Because I fucking hate traitors. Because I fucking hate communists. Was it legal? Fuck legal. Am I a nice man? Fuck nice. They say terrible things about me in the *Nation*. Fuck the *Nation*. You want to be Nice, or you want to be Effective? Make the law, or subject to it. Choose. Your wife chose. A week from today, she'll be back. SHE knows how to get what SHE wants. Maybe I ought to send *her* to Washington.

JOE: I don't believe you.

ROY: Gospel.

JOE: You can't possibly mean what you're saying.

Roy, you were the Assistant United States Attorney on the Rosenberg case, ex-parte communication with the judge during the trial would be . . . censurable, at least, probably conspiracy and . . . in a case that resulted in execution, it's . . .

ROY: What? Murder?

JOE: You're not well is all.

ROY: What do you mean, not well? Who's not well?

(*Pause.*)

JOE: You said . . .

ROY: No I didn't. I said what?

JOE: Roy, you have cancer.

ROY: No I don't.

(*Pause.*)

JOE: You told me you were dying.

ROY: What the fuck are you talking about, Joe? I never said that. I'm in perfect health. There's not a goddam thing wrong with me.

(*He smiles.*)

Shake?

(*Joe hesitates. He holds out his hand to Roy. Roy pulls Joe into a close, strong clinch.*)

ROY (*more to himself than to Joe*): It's OK that you hurt me because I love you, baby Joe. That's why I'm so rough on you.

(*Roy releases Joe. Joe backs away a step or two.*)

ROY: Prodigal son. The world will wipe its dirty hands all over you.

JOE: It already has, Roy.

ROY: Now go.

(*Roy shoves Joe, hard. Joe turns to leave. Roy stops him, turns him around.*)

ROY (*smoothing Joe's lapels, tenderly*): I'll always be here, waiting for you . . .

(*Then again, with sudden violence, he pulls Joe close, violently.*)

What did you want from me, what was all this, what do you want, treacherous ungrateful little . . .

(*Joe, very close to belting Roy, grabs him by the front of his robe, and propels him across the length of the room. He holds Roy at arm's length, the other arm ready to hit.*)

ROY (*laughing softly, almost pleading to be hit*): Transgress a little, Joseph.

(*Joe releases Roy.*)

ROY: There are so many laws; find one you can break.

(*Joe hesitates, then leaves, backing out. When Joe has gone, Roy doubles over in great pain, which he's been hiding throughout the scene with Joe.*)

ROY: Ah, Christ . . .
Andy! Andy! Get in here! Andy!

(*The door opens, but it isn't Andy. A small Jewish Woman dressed modestly in a fifties hat and coat stands in the doorway. The room darkens.*)

ROY: Who the fuck are you? The new nurse?

(*The figure in the doorway says nothing. She stares at Roy. A pause. Roy looks at her carefully, gets up, crosses to her. He crosses back to the chair, sits heavily.*)

ROY: Aw, fuck. Ethel.

ETHEL ROSENBERG (*her manner is friendly, her voice is ice-cold*): You don't look good, Roy.

ROY: Well, Ethel. I don't feel good.

ETHEL ROSENBERG: But you lost a lot of weight. That suits you. You were heavy back then. Zaftig, mit hips.

ROY: I haven't been that heavy since 1960. We were all heavier back then, before the body thing started. Now I look like a skeleton. They stare.

ETHEL ROSENBERG: The shit's really hit the fan, huh, Roy?

(*Little pause. Roy nods.*)

ETHEL ROSENBERG: Well the fun's just started.

ROY: What is this, Ethel, Halloween? You trying to scare me?

(*Ethel says nothing.*)

ROY: Well you're wasting your time! I'm scarier than you any day of the week! So beat it, Ethel! BOOO! BETTER DEAD THAN RED! Somebody trying to shake me up? HAH HAH! From the throne of God in heaven to the belly of hell, you can all fuck your-selves and then go jump in the lake because I'M NOT AFRAID OF YOU OR DEATH OR HELL OR ANYTHING!

ETHEL ROSENBERG: Be seeing you soon, Roy. Julius sends his regards.

ROY: Yeah, well send this to Julius!

(*He flips the bird in her direction, stands and moves towards her. Halfway across the room he slumps to the floor, breathing laboriously, in pain.*)

ETHEL ROSENBERG: You're a very sick man, Roy.

ROY: Oh God . . . ANDY!

ETHEL ROSENBERG: Hmmm. He doesn't hear you, I guess. We should call the ambulance.
　　(*She goes to the phone.*)
　　Hah! Buttons! Such things they got now.
　　What do I dial, Roy?

(*Pause. Roy looks at her, then:*)

ROY: 911.

ETHEL ROSENBERG (*dials the phone*): It sings!
　　(*Imitating dial tones.*) La la la . . .
　　Huh.
　　Yes, you should please send an ambulance to the home of Mister Roy Cohn, the famous lawyer.
　　What's the address, Roy?

ROY (*a beat, then*): 244 East 87th.

ETHEL ROSENBERG: 244 East 87th Street. No apartment number, he's got the whole building.
　　My name? (*A beat.*) Ethel Greenglass Rosenberg.
　　(*Small smile.*) Me? No I'm not related to Mr. Cohn. An old friend.
　　(*She hangs up.*)
　　They said a minute.

ROY: I have all the time in the world.

ETHEL ROSENBERG: You're immortal.

ROY: I'm immortal. Ethel. (*He forces himself to stand.*)
　　I have *forced* my way into history. I ain't never gonna die.

ETHEL ROSENBERG (*a little laugh, then*): History is about to crack wide open. Millennium approaches.

Scene 6

(*Late that night. Prior's bedroom. Prior 1 watching Prior in bed, who is staring back at him, terrified. Tonight Prior 1 is dressed in weird alchemical robes and hat over his historical clothing and he carries a long palm-leaf bundle.*)

PRIOR 1: Tonight's the night! Aren't you excited? Tonight she arrives! Right through the roof! Ha-adam, Ha-gadol . . .

PRIOR 2 (*appearing, similarly attired*): Lumen! Phosphor! Fluor! Candle! An unending billowing of scarlet and . . .

PRIOR: Look. Garlic. A mirror. Holy water. A crucifix. FUCK OFF! Get the fuck out of my room! GO!

PRIOR 1 (*to Prior 2*): Hard as a hickory knob, I'll bet.

PRIOR 2: We all tumesce when they approach. We wax full, like moons.

PRIOR 1: Dance.

PRIOR: Dance?

PRIOR 1: Stand up, dammit, give us your hands, dance!

PRIOR 2: Listen . . .

(*A lone oboe begins to play a little dance tune.*)

PRIOR 2: Delightful sound. Care to dance?

PRIOR: Please leave me alone, please just let me sleep . . .

PRIOR 2: Ah, he wants someone familiar. A partner who knows his steps. (*To Prior.*) Close your eyes. Imagine . . .

PRIOR: I don't . . .

PRIOR 2: Hush. Close your eyes.

(*Prior does.*)

PRIOR 2: Now open them.

(*Prior does. Louis appears. He looks gorgeous. The music builds gradually into a full-blooded, romantic dance tune.*)

PRIOR: Lou.

LOUIS: Dance with me.

PRIOR: I can't, my leg, it hurts at night . . .
    Are you . . . a ghost, Lou?

LOUIS: No. Just spectral. Lost to myself. Sitting all day on cold park benches. Wishing I could be with you. Dance with me, babe . . .

(*Prior stands up. The leg stops hurting. They begin to dance. The music is beautiful.*)

PRIOR 1 (*to Prior 2*): Hah. Now I see why he's got no children. He's a sodomite.
PRIOR 2: Oh be quiet, you medieval gnome, and let them dance.
PRIOR 1: I'm not interfering, I've done my bit. Hooray, hooray, the messenger's come, now I'm blowing off. I don't like it here.

(*Prior 1 vanishes.*)

PRIOR 2: The twentieth century. Oh dear, the world has gotten so terribly, terribly old.

(*Prior 2 vanishes. Louis and Prior waltz happily. Lights fade back to normal. Louis vanishes.*
Prior dances alone.
Then suddenly, the sound of wings fills the room.)

Scene 7

(*Split scene. Prior alone in his apartment; Louis alone in the park.*
Again, a sound of beating wings.)

PRIOR: Oh don't come in here don't come in . . . LOUIS!! No. My name is Prior Walter, I am . . . the scion of an ancient line, I am . . . abandoned I . . . no, my name is . . . is . . . Prior and I live . . . *here and now,* and . . . in the dark, in the dark, the Recording Angel opens its hundred eyes and snaps the spine of the Book of Life and . . . hush! Hush!
I'm talking nonsense, I . . .
No more mad scene, hush, hush.

(*Louis in the park on a bench. Joe approaches, stands at a distance. They stare at each other, then Louis turns away.*)

LOUIS: Do you know the story of Lazarus?
JOE: Lazarus?
LOUIS: Lazarus. I can't remember what happens, exactly.
JOE: I don't. . . . Well, he was dead, Lazarus, and Jesus breathed life into him. He brought him back from death.
LOUIS: Come here often?
JOE: No. Yes. Yes.
LOUIS: Back from the dead. You believe that really happened?
JOE: I don't know anymore what I believe.
LOUIS: This is quite a coincidence. Us meeting.
JOE: I followed you.
From work. I . . . followed you here.

(*Pause.*)

LOUIS: You followed me.
You probably saw me that day in the washroom and thought: there's a sweet guy, sensitive, cries for friends in trouble.
JOE: Yes.
LOUIS: You thought maybe I'll cry for you.
JOE: Yes.
LOUIS: Well I fooled you. Crocodile tears. Nothing . . .
(*He touches his heart, shrugs.*)

(*Joe reaches tentatively to touch Louis's face.*)

LOUIS (*pulling back*): What are you doing? Don't do that.
JOE (*withdrawing his hand*): Sorry. I'm sorry.
LOUIS: I'm . . . just not . . . I think, if you touch me, your hand might fall off or something. Worse things have happened to people who have touched me.
JOE: Please.
Oh, boy . . .
Can I . . .
I . . . want . . . to touch you. Can I please just touch you . . . um, here?
(*He puts his hand on one side of Louis's face. He holds it there.*)
I'm going to hell for doing this.
LOUIS: Big deal. You think it could be any worse than New York City?
(*He puts his hand on Joe's hand. He takes Joe's hand away from his face, holds it for a moment, then:*) Come on.
JOE: Where?
LOUIS: Home. With me.
JOE: This makes no sense. I mean I don't know you.
LOUIS: Likewise.
JOE: And what you do know about me you don't like.
LOUIS: The Republican stuff?
JOE: Yeah, well for starters.
LOUIS: I don't not like that. I *hate* that.
JOE: So why on earth should we . . .

(*Louis goes to Joe and kisses him.*)

LOUIS: Strange bedfellows. I don't know. I never made it with one of the damned before.
I would really rather not have to spend tonight alone.
JOE: I'm a pretty terrible person, Louis.
LOUIS: Lou.
JOE: No, I really really am. I don't think I deserve being loved.
LOUIS: There? See? We already have a lot in common.

(*Louis stands, begins to walk away. He turns, looks back at Joe. Joe follows. They exit.*)

(*Prior listens. At first no sound, then once again, the sound of beating wings, frighteningly near.*)

PRIOR: That sound, that sound, it. . . . What is that, like birds or something, like a *really* big bird, I'm frightened, I . . . no, no fear, find the anger, find the . . .

anger, my blood is clean, my brain is fine, I can handle pressure, I am a gay man and I am used to pressure, to trouble, I am tough and strong and. . . . Oh. Oh my goodness. I . . . (*He is washed over by an intense sexual feeling.*) Ooohhhh. . . . I'm hot, I'm . . . so . . . aw Jeez what is going on here I . . . must have a fever I . . .

(*The bedside lamp flickers wildly as the bed begins to roll forward and back. There is a deep bass creaking and groaning from the bedroom ceiling, like the timbers of a ship under immense stress, and from above a fine rain of plaster dust.*)

PRIOR: OH!
     PLEASE, OH PLEASE! Something's coming in here, I'm scared, I don't like this at all, something's approaching and I. . . . OH!

(*There is a great blaze of triumphal music, heralding. The light turns an extraordinary harsh, cold, pale blue, then a rich, brilliant warm golden color, then a hot, bil-ious green, and then finally a spectacular royal purple. Then silence.*)

PRIOR (*an awestruck whisper*): God almighty . . .
     Very Steven Spielberg.

(*A sound, like a plummeting meteor, tears down from very, very far above the earth, hurtling at an incredible velocity towards the bedroom; the light seems to be sucked out of the room as the projectile approaches; as the room reaches darkness, we hear a terrifying CRASH as something immense strikes earth; the whole building shudders and a part of the bedroom ceiling, lots of plaster and lathe and wiring, crashes to the floor. And then in a shower of unearthly white light, spreading great opalescent gray-silver wings, the Angel descends into the room and floats above the bed.*)

ANGEL: Greetings, Prophet;
     The Great Work begins:
     The Messenger has arrived.

(*Blackout.*)

COMMENTARY

Andrea Bernstein
INTERVIEW WITH TONY KUSHNER   *1995*

> *Andrea Bernstein, a freelance cultural critic, engaged Tony Kushner in a discussion of the politics in his plays. Kushner's responses to her questions establish his credentials as a left-thinking critic of contemporary political life. His discussion of his work is centered much more in political reality than it is in dramatic technique or concern for theater. Yet Kushner is able to zero in on the dramatic moment and present contemporary politics as a dialetical struggle.*

Tony Kushner, a gay Jewish socialist who was raised in Louisiana, won a Pulitzer Prize and two Tony Awards for his two-part, seven-hour Broadway production of *Angels in America: A Gay Fantasia on National Themes*. Other plays, *A Bright Room Called Day* (1985) and *Slavs!* (1994), are also concerned with the moral responsibilities of people in politically repressive times. Such concerns may be especially relevant in America today, where, as he observes: "What used to be called liberal is now called radical, what used to be called radical is now called insane, what used to be called reactionary is now called moderate, and what used to be called insane is now called solid conservative thinking."

Q: Angels in America opened on Broadway just months after the Clinton inauguration. It ends with a very hopeful speech about healing. Do you still feel that hope?

A: You have to have hope. It's irresponsible to give *false* hope, which I think a lot of playwrights are guilty of. But I also think it's irresponsible to simply be a nihilist, which quite a lot of playwrights, especially playwrights younger than me, have become guilty of. I don't believe you would bother to write a play if you really had no hope. That passage was one of the very first things I ever wrote when I was working on *Angels*. I read it to the woman who I was originally writing the part of the angel for, who died of breast cancer before the play was finished. In one of my last conversations with her, she told me that she thought about that image a lot and that she hoped I would include it in the play. I think I wouldn't have included it otherwise, but I'm glad I did now.

Q: Angels in America was a political play — and that's something Americans and critics frequently resist. How did you overcome that resistance?

A: What I found in the audience response is a huge hunger for political issues and political discussion. So I always wonder: Is it that Americans don't like politics, or is it that so much theater that is political isn't well-done? One of the things I learned in *Slavs!* is that it's much easier to talk about being gay than it is to talk about being a socialist. People are afraid of socialism, and plays that deal with economics are scarier to them. I'll learn more about that — my next three plays are all about money.

Also, *Angels* is very entertaining. It does things formally that are new, and people were excited by the size and the scope. It's a good play and that makes all the difference.

Thelma and Louise, for instance, is a really terrific movie, and genuinely left in its political sensibilities. It's well-made, so the fact that it is unquestionably coming from a feminist perspective didn't make it absolutely marginal the way you would expect such a film to be. It had guns — that probably helped.

Q: People loved *Forrest Gump,* too.

A: People shouldn't trust artists and they shouldn't trust art. Part of the fun of art is that it invites you to interpret it.

There's a very complicated relationship between form and content and between aesthetics and politics. Good politics will produce good aesthetics, really good politics will produce really good aesthetics, and really good aesthetics, if somebody's really asking the hard questions and answering them honestly, they'll probably produce truth, which is to say progressive politics.

Q: Is it hard to write characters that are not caricatures and to overcome the barrier that people have about listening to politics from a character on stage?

A: I think that a character's politics have to live in the same sort of relationship to the character's psyche that people's politics live in relationship to their own psyches. People are never consistent. People will always do surprising things, both good and bad, and the way that people surprise themselves and their audience are the most interesting moments of human behavior. The space between what we'd like to be and what we actually are is where you find out the most interesting things.

Q: Do you see your plays as part of a political movement?

A: I do. I would hate to write anything that wasn't. I would like my plays to be of use to progressive people. I think preaching to the converted is exactly what art ought to do.

I am happiest when people who are politically engaged in the world say, "Your play meant a lot to me; it helped me think about something, or made me feel like I wasn't the only person who felt this way."

It's the way you feel when you go to a demo, which is the only way to keep sane a lot of the time. You need to remind yourself there are many bodies who are as angry about something as you are.

When I teach writing, I always tell my students you should assume that the audience you're writing for is smarter than you. You can't write if you don't think they're on your side, because then you start to yell at them or preach down to them.

Q: The character Prelapsarianov — the "world's oldest living Bolshevik" — gives the same speech in both *Angels* and *Slavs!:* "How are we to proceed without theory? Is it enough to reject the past, is it wise to move forward in this blind fashion, without the cold brilliant light of theory to guide the way? . . . You who live in this sour little age cannot imagine the sheer grandeur of the prospect we gazed upon."

A: In both *Perestroika* [part two of *Angels*] and *Slavs!,* the whole play proceeds from the question: If you don't know where you're going, can you move? And do you even have a choice, or do you just dive in and work it out as you're going?

That speech came out of a fight I had with my friend Oskar Eustis about Gorbachev. Oskar's point, which became the basis of Prelapsarianov's speech, is that if you don't have a theory to start with — Gorbachev pretended to be about democratic socialism but actually sort of was and sort of wasn't; he was also sort of about preserving the Communist Party power elite — what do you do? It's one of those big conundrums.

Q: So what *do* you do?

A: You can't stay back. The fundamental question is: Are we made by history or do we make history — and the answer is yes. I was rereading Marx's *Eighteenth Brumaire of Louis Bonaparte* recently. The whole tradition in socialist struggle is looking to the past for an antecedent form upon which the present revolutionary response is to be modeled. We may need to stop doing that.

Q: Why does the play *Slavs!* end with the question: "What is to be done?"

A: I wanted someone to ask the question: What if this really is the end of history? What if there really is literally nothing to be done, and we're simply stuck with capitalism — although I don't really think it is a possibility.

I still believe in a dialectical ordering of the universe. There is a dynamic principle at work — it isn't always mechanically moving things toward the good, but there's always either some sort of progress or decay. And there's too much misery in the world. That is not something that can hold.

Q: What do you think is to be done?

A: I'm 38 now. One of the painful rites of passage that everyone on the left goes through is to realize it's a lifelong struggle. What we're dealing with from Nixon on as a counter-reaction to the '60s is a very widespread, long-term historical trend. It's going to take many years and probably a few decades to reverse. People need to be willing to take an issue that they feel passionately about, address themselves to it as extensively as they are capable of and build common cause between issue groups.

Everybody on the left needs to start talking about how to create, first on local levels and eventually on a national level, a third party or at least a party that could establish some kind of position in Congress. That's the eternal dream of the left.

Q: You think there's no hope for revitalizing the Democratic Party?

A: It's a waste of time at this point. There's a famous story about Paul Wellstone refusing to shake Jesse Helms' hand and being chastised by everyone in the Senate because he wouldn't do it — he was told this is a gentlemen's club where we're all colleagues. That's what's wrong.

Q: One of the characters in *A Bright Room Called Day* keeps saying — as Nazism progressively snatches power and the Weimar Republic falls — that each turn for the worse would be the essential spur for people to rise up and oppose fascism. That didn't happen. Do you see parallels today?

A: You don't want to be opportunistic about it and say, "Oh, goody, millions of people are going to be thrown out of their homes — now we'll really get things cooking." It's like people saying the AIDS epidemic helped organize the gay and lesbian community.

Q: Speaking of which, there's a lot of discussion now about the second wave of the AIDS epidemic, and about gay men not practicing safer sex. Where do you weigh in?

A: It's very difficult to ask people to abstain from pleasure indefinitely, especially sexual erotic pleasure, which is so incredibly important to human beings and the enjoyment of which among homosexuals is so much of a political battlefield. There is absolutely no question that safer sex is not as gratifying and that given all the despair and the unbelievably imponderable weight of loss that the community has had to deal with, self-destructive behaviors are going to be engaged in.

Q: Do you think the gay community should be discussing this publicly?

A: Of course it's going to be discussed publicly. But you have to be smart. When you make a public utterance you are responsible for being responsible. We're still an embattled community, and if you're stupid about it you'll give aid to the enemy.

Q: Do you have that conundrum as a playwright?

A: You have to say: What am I feeding into? I think you should ask yourself that question and then make the decision based on the answers you come up with. I regret having made the only black person in *Angels* a nurse; that was an inept thing to do.

I was very scared about writing a play where there's a couple, one has AIDS and the other walks out. I thought, this is transgressive and scary and am I going to become public enemy number one in the gay community for having written a character like Louis?

On the other hand, you have to be willing to scare the horses. You have to be interesting and you have to be daring and you have to be willing to write things that shock. Shock is part of art. Art that's polite is not much fun.

Yasmina Reza

Yasmina Reza (b. 1959) studied at Paris X University and later at the Jacques Lecoq Drama School. She began working as an actress in France and appeared in numerous plays by contemporary authors as well as plays by Molière, Marivaux, and Sacha Guitry. In 1987 she wrote *Conversations after a Burial* for performance in France and won the prestigious Molière Award for best author as well as many other awards. Following its performance in France, the play was produced in translation in Europe and South America.

Reza's French translation of Steven Berkoff's adaptation of Franz Kafka's novel *Metamorphosis* for performance by Roman Polanski was nominated for the 1988 Molière Award for translation. *Winter Crossing* (1990), her second play, won the 1990 Molière Award for best fringe production that year. *"Art"* premiered in Berlin and opened in Paris in 1994, where it won the Molière Award for best author, best play, and best production. It also won prizes in London for best comedy and in Germany for best foreign play. *The Unexpected Man* (1995) was produced in London, France, and several other European countries. It was revived in 1998 by the Royal Shakespeare Company at the Barbican in London. It has also played in New York.

In addition to playwriting, Yasmina Reza has also been engaged in screenwriting, with two recent films shown in Europe: *See You Tomorrow* and *Lulu Kreutz's Picnic*. Her novel, *Hammerklavier,* was published in 1997.

"ART"

"Art" is only partly about art. Essentially it is a play about three men who have been friends for fifteen years. Serge is a successful dermatologist who has bought an expensive painting by a painter named Antrios. It is a white painting with almost indistinguishable diagonal lines, and it cost two hundred thousand francs (close to fifty thousand dollars). Serge is a thoughtful man, knowledgeable about art and modernism. His friend Marc hates the painting. Marc is an aeronautical engineer who values his intellectual superiority and expects others to acknowledge it. Their friend Yvan is a man in therapy on the eve of a complicated but unavoidable marriage. Yvan is less sure of himself than Serge or Marc but has a touching emotional life that causes him to cry when stressed. He is not a successful man. He has been "in" textiles for years and recently began to work for his wife-to-be's uncle in stationery. The painting Serge has bought becomes a wedge that begins to pry apart the friendship.

"*Art*" is a study of close relationships and the dynamics that underlie them. Marc reveals at one point that he has always enjoyed playing mentor to Serge and pointing Serge in the direction of new interests and experiences. Marc's taste in painting is sharply realistic, as we learn from seeing his "Flemish"-style landscape of Carcasonne, and he resents Serge's independence as measured by his purchase of a nonrepresentative painting. Meanwhile, a third painting hangs on Yvan's wall and is described as a "daub," with no further details. For Marc, Yvan is something of a joker, and Yvan sees himself in the role of the joker. Yet Yvan is so deeply interested in learning about himself that he sees a therapist, Finkelzohn, who gives him some interesting advice: "If I'm who I am because I'm who I am and you're who you are because you're who you are, then I'm who I am and you're who you are. If, on the other hand, I'm who I am because you're who you are, and if you're who you are because I'm who I am, then I'm not who I am and you're not who you are." The implication is that people see each other as they wish to rather than as they really are. "*Art*" raises the question of what one knows about one's closest friends just as it raises the question of what one knows about art or values.

One important issue in the play concerns Serge's, Marc's, and Yvan's relationships with women. Yvan has the most interesting and lengthy speeches about the women in his life. Catherine, his wife-to-be, controls the wedding invitations. As a result, his detested stepmother's name will be on the invitations, and therefore his own mother wants her name removed. Serge has a wife from whom he is separated, and Marc's relationship with Paula has never really pleased Serge. In the course of the drama, the tensions aroused by these relationships begin to clarify the pressures on the men's relationships with each other.

"*Art*" is a comedy, and in performance it is often extremely funny. There is laughter in the play as well as tears. Audiences have found it moving, but most of all comic. A careful study of the play reveals much that is serious in the play, but it has some broadly humorous moments, and none are more amusing than the reactions of Marc and Yvan to Serge's painting.

"*Art*" in Performance

"*Art*" has been performed in more than twenty countries and almost as many languages. It has proved to be a durable comedy in whatever language it is played in. It premiered in Berlin, and in 1994 it opened in Paris. In 1996 it was produced in London's West End, the equivalent of New York's Broadway, and one newspaper declared it "the perfect West End play." It won the Evening Standard Award for best comedy in 1996 and the Laurence Olivier Award for best comedy in 1997. It was produced in Broadway's Royale Theatre and won the Tony Award for best play in 1998. The cast for the play in English varied throughout its run. In London Tom Courtenay, Ken Stott, and Albert Finney opened the play, and later Stacey Keach, George Wendt, and David Dukes continued. In New York, Alan Alda opened the play, and later Judd Hirsch, George Wendt, and Joe Morton took over. The cast was always important, but the play itself seems to have worked independently of the stars who have played in it.

The set and lighting were spare in the New York production. Before the lights came up the audience saw the back of the canvas, hung at the stage apron, facing into the stage space. Later, Serge holds up the painting for the audience and the actors to contemplate. The settings for Marc's and Yvan's apartments were essentially unchanged except for the substitution of Yvan's "daub" and Marc's landscape. The simplicity of the set and lighting and the effectiveness of the simple substitution of paintings helped to maintain a focus on the significance of the text and the action of the drama.

Yasmina Reza (b. 1959)

"ART"   *1994*

TRANSLATED BY CHRISTOPHER HAMPTON

Characters

MARC
SERGE
YVAN

Scene: *The main room of a flat.*
A single set. As stripped-down and neutral as possible. The scenes unfold, successively, at Serge's, Yvan's, and Marc's.
Nothing changes, except for the painting on the wall.

(*Marc, alone.*)

MARC: My friend Serge has bought a painting. It's a canvas about five foot by four: white. The background is white and if you screw up your eyes, you can make out some fine white diagonal lines.
  Serge is one of my oldest friends.
  He's done very well for himself, he's a dermatologist and he's keen on *art*.
  On Monday, I went to see the painting; Serge had actually got hold of it on the Saturday, but he'd been lusting after it for several months.
  This white painting with white lines.

(*At Serge's.*)
(*At floor level, a white canvas with fine white diagonal scars. Serge looks at his painting, thrilled. Marc looks at the painting. Serge looks at Marc looking at the painting.*)
(*Long silence: from both of them, a whole range of wordless emotions.*)

MARC: Expensive?
SERGE: Two hundred thousand.
MARC: Two hundred thousand?
SERGE: Huntingdon would take if off my hands for two hundred and twenty.
MARC: Who's that?
SERGE: Huntingdon?

MARC: Never heard of him.
SERGE: Huntingdon! The Huntingdon Gallery!
MARC: The Huntingdon Gallery would take it off your hands for two hundred and twenty?
SERGE: No, not the Gallery. Him. Huntingdon himself. For his own collection.
MARC: Then why didn't Huntingdon buy it?
SERGE: It's important for them to sell to private clients. That's how the market circulates.
MARC: Mm hm. . . .
SERGE: Well?
MARC: . . .
SERGE: You're not in the right place. Look at it from this angle.
  Can you see the lines?
MARC: What's the name of the . . . ?
SERGE: Painter. Antrios.
MARC: Well-known?
SERGE: Very. Very!

(*Pause.*)

MARC: Serge, you haven't bought this painting for two hundred thousand francs?
SERGE: You don't understand, that's what it costs. It's an Antrios.
MARC: You haven't bought this painting for two hundred thousand francs?
SERGE: I might have known you'd miss the point.
MARC: You paid two hundred thousand francs for this shit?

(*Serge, as if alone.*)

SERGE: My friend Marc's an intelligent enough fellow, I've always valued our relationship, he has a good job, he's an aeronautical engineer, but he's one of those new-style intellectuals, who are not only enemies of modernism, but seem to take some sort of incomprehensible pride in running it down. . . .

In recent years these nostalgia-merchants have become quite breathtakingly arrogant.

(*Same pair. Same place. Same painting.*)
    (*Pause.*)

SERGE: What do you mean, "this shit"?
MARC: Serge, where's your sense of humor? Why aren't you laughing? . . . It's fantastic, you buying this painting.

(*Marc laughs. Serge remains stony.*)

SERGE: I don't care how fantastic you think it is, I don't mind if you laugh, but I would like to know what you mean by "this shit."
MARC: You're taking the piss!°
SERGE: No, I'm not. By whose standards is it shit? If you call something shit, you need to have some criterion to judge it by.
MARC: Who are you talking to? Who do you think you're talking to? Hello! . . .
SERGE: You have no interest whatsoever in contemporary painting, you never have had. This is a field about which you know absolutely nothing, so how can you assert that any given object, which conforms to laws you don't understand, is shit?
MARC: Because it is. It's shit. I'm sorry.

(*Serge, alone.*)

SERGE: He doesn't like the painting.
        Fine. . . .
        But there was no warmth in the way he reacted.
        No attempt.
        No warmth when he dismissed it out of hand.
        Just that vile, pretentious laugh.
        A real know-all laugh.
        I hated that laugh.

(*Marc, alone.*)

MARC: It's a complete mystery to me, Serge buying this painting. It's unsettled me, it's filled me with some indefinable unease.
        When I left this place, I had to take three capsules of Gelsemium 9X which Paula recommended — Gelsemium or Ignatia,° she said, Gelsemium or Ignatia, which do you prefer, I mean, how the hell should I know? — because I couldn't begin to understand how Serge, my friend, could have bought that picture.
        Two hundred thousand francs!
        He's comfortably off, but he's hardly rolling in money.
        Comfortable, no more, just comfortable. And he spends two hundred grand on a white painting.
        I must go and see Yvan, he's a friend of ours, I have to discuss this with Yvan. Mind you, Yvan's a very tolerant bloke, which of course, when it comes to relationships, is the worst thing you can be.

taking the piss: You're getting irritated.
Gelsemium or Ignatia: Herbal remedies.

Yvan's very tolerant because he couldn't care less.
        If Yvan tolerates the fact that Serge has spent two hundred grand on some piece of white shit, it's because he couldn't care less about Serge.
        Obviously.

(*At Yvan's.*)
(*On the wall, some daub.*)
(*Yvan is on all fours with his back to us. He seems to be looking for something underneath a piece of furniture. As he does so, he turns to introduce himself.*)

YVAN: I'm Yvan.
        I'm a bit tense at the moment, because, having spent my life in textiles, I've just found a new job as a sales agent for a wholesale stationery business.
        People like me. My professional life has always been a failure and I'm getting married in a couple of weeks. She's a lovely intelligent girl from a good family.

(*Marc enters. Yvan has resumed his search and has his back to him.*)

MARC: What are you doing?
YVAN: I'm looking for the top of my pen.

(*Time passes.*)

MARC: All right, that's enough.
YVAN: I had it five minutes ago.
MARC: It doesn't matter.
YVAN: Yes, it does.

(*Marc gets down on his knees to help him look. Both of them spend some time looking. Marc straightens up.*)

MARC: Stop it. Buy another one.
YVAN: It's a felt-tip, they're special, they'll write on any surface. . . . It's just infuriating. Objects, I can't tell you how much they infuriate me. I had it in my hand five minutes ago.
MARC: Are you going to live here?
YVAN: Do you think it's suitable for a young couple?
MARC: Young couple! Ha, ha. . . .
YVAN: Try not to laugh like that in front of Catherine.
MARC: How's the stationery business?
YVAN: All right. I'm learning.
MARC: You've lost weight.
YVAN: A bit. I'm pissed off about that top. It'll all dry up. Sit down.
MARC: If you go on looking for that top, I'm leaving.
YVAN: OK, I'll stop. You want something to drink?
MARC: A Perrier, if you have one.
        Have you seen Serge lately?
YVAN: No. Have you?
MARC: Yesterday.
YVAN: Is he well?
MARC: Very.
        He's just bought a painting.
YVAN: Oh yes?
MARC: Mm.
YVAN: Nice?

MARC: White.

YVAN: White?

MARC: White.

Imagine a canvas about five foot by four . . . with a white background . . . completely white in fact . . . with fine white diagonal stripes . . . you know . . . and maybe another horizontal white line, towards the bottom. . . .

YVAN: How can you see them?

MARC: What?

YVAN: These white lines. If the background's white, how can you see the lines?

MARC: You just do. Because I suppose the lines are slightly grey, or vice versa, or anyway there are degrees of white! There's more than one kind of white!

YVAN: Don't get upset. Why are you getting upset?

MARC: You immediately start quibbling. Why can't you let me finish?

YVAN: All right. Go on.

MARC: Right. So, you have an idea of what the painting looks like.

YVAN: I think so, yes.

RIGHT: Alan Alda as Marc studying Serge's painting and Victor Garber as Serge admiring it in Yasmina Reza's *"Art"* at Broadway's Royale Theatre in 1998. BELOW: Yvan (Alfred Molina), Serge (Victor Garber), and Marc (Alan Alda) consider the painting in *"Art"* at Broadway's Royale Theatre in 1998.

MARC: Now you have to guess how much Serge paid for it.

YVAN: Who's the painter?

MARC: Antrios. Have you heard of him?

YVAN: No. Is he fashionable?

MARC: I knew you were going to ask me that!

YVAN: Well, it's logical. . . .

MARC: No, it isn't logical. . . .

YVAN: Of course it's logical, you ask me to guess the price, you know very well the price depends on how fashionable the painter might be. . . .

MARC: I'm not asking you to apply a whole set of critical standards, I'm not asking you for a professional valuation, I'm asking you what you, Yvan, would give for a white painting tarted up with a few off-white stripes.

YVAN: Bugger all.

MARC: Right. And what about Serge? Pick a figure at random.

YVAN: Ten thousand francs.

MARC: Ha!

YVAN: Fifty thousand.

MARC: Ha!

YVAN: A hundred thousand.

MARC: Keep going.

YVAN: A hundred and fifty? Two hundred?!

MARC: Two hundred. Two hundred grand.

YVAN: No!

MARC: Yes.

YVAN: Two hundred grand?

MARC: Two hundred grand.

YVAN: Has he gone crazy?

MARC: Looks like it.

(*Slight pause.*)

YVAN: All the same. . . .

MARC: What do you mean, all the same?

YVAN: If it makes him happy . . . he can afford it. . . .

MARC: So that's what you think, is it?

YVAN: Why? What do you think?

MARC: You don't understand the seriousness of this, do you?

YVAN: Er . . . no.

MARC: It's strange how you're missing the basic point of this story. All you can see is externals. You don't understand the seriousness of it.

YVAN: What is the seriousness of it?

MARC: Don't you understand what this means?

YVAN: Would you like a cashew nut?

MARC: Don't you see that suddenly, in some grotesque way, Serge fancies himself as a "collector."

YVAN: Well . . .

MARC: From now on, our friend Serge is one of the great connoisseurs.

YVAN: Bollocks.°

MARC: Well of course it's bollocks. You can't buy your way in that cheap. But that's what *he* thinks.

YVAN: Oh, I see.

Bollocks: Balls.

MARC: Doesn't that upset you?

YVAN: No. Not if it makes him happy.

MARC: If it makes him happy. What's that supposed to mean?

What sort of a philosophy is that, if it makes him happy?

YVAN: As long as it's not doing any harm to anyone else. . . .

MARC: But it is. It's doing harm to me! I'm disturbed, I'm disturbed, more than that, I'm hurt, yes, I am, I'm fond of Serge, and to see him let himself be ripped off and lose every ounce of discernment through sheer snobbery. . . .

YVAN: I don't know why you're so surprised. He's always haunted galleries in the most absurd way, he's always been an exhibition freak.

MARC: He's always been a freak, but a freak with a sense of humor. You see, basically, what really upsets me is that you can't have a laugh with him any more.

YVAN: I'm sure you can.

MARC: You can't!

YVAN: Have you tried?

MARC: Of course I've tried. I laughed. Heartily. What do you think I did? He didn't crack a smile.

Mind you, two hundred grand, I suppose it might be hard to see the funny side.

YVAN: Yes.

(*They laugh.*)

I'll make him laugh.

MARC: I'd be amazed. Any more nuts?

YVAN: He'll laugh, you just wait.

(*At Serge's.*)
(*Serge is with Yvan. The painting isn't there.*)

SERGE: . . . and you get on with the in-laws?

YVAN: Wonderfully. As far as they're concerned, I'm some berk tottering from one dodgy job to another and now I'm groping my way into the world of vellum. . . . This thing on my hand, what is it?

(*Serge examines it.*)

Is it serious?

SERGE: No.

YVAN: Oh, good. How are things?

SERGE: Nothing. Lot of work. Exhausted.

It's nice to see you. You never phone.

YVAN: I don't like to disturb you.

SERGE: You're joking. You just speak to my secretary and I'll call you back right away.

YVAN: I suppose so.

Your place gets more and more monastic. . . .

(*Serge laughs.*)

SERGE: Yes!

Seen Marc recently?

YVAN: Not recently, no.

Have you?

SERGE: Two or three days ago.

YVAN: Is he all right?

SERGE: Yes. More or less.

YVAN: Oh?

SERGE: No, he's all right.

YVAN: I talked to him on the phone last week, he seemed all right.

SERGE: Well, he is. He's all right.

YVAN: You seemed to be implying he wasn't all right.

SERGE: On the contrary, I said, he was all right.

YVAN: More or less, you said.

SERGE: Yes, more or less. More or less all right.

(*Long silence. Yvan wanders around the room.*)

YVAN: You been out? Seen anything?

SERGE: No. I can't afford to go out.

YVAN: Oh?

SERGE (*cheerfully*): I'm ruined.

YVAN: Oh?

SERGE: You want to see something special? Would you like to?

YVAN: Of course I would. Show me.

(*Serge exits and returns with the Antrios, which he turns round and sets down in front of Yvan.*

Yvan looks at the painting and, strangely enough, doesn't manage the hearty laugh he'd predicted.

A long pause, while Yvan studies the painting and Serge studies Yvan.)

Oh, yes. Yes, yes.

SERGE: Antrios.

YVAN: Yes, yes.

SERGE: It's a seventies Antrios. Worth mentioning. He's going through a similar phase now, but this one's from the seventies.

YVAN: Yes, yes.

Expensive?

SERGE: In absolute terms, yes. In fact, no.

You like it?

YVAN: Oh, yes, yes, yes.

SERGE: Plain.

YVAN: Plain, yes . . . Yes . . . And at the same time . . .

SERGE: Magnetic.

YVAN: Mm . . . yes . . .

SERGE: You don't really get the resonance just at the moment.

YVAN: Well, a bit . . .

SERGE: No, you don't. You have to come back in the middle of the day. That resonance you get from something monochromatic, it doesn't really happen under artificial light.

YVAN: Mm hm.

SERGE: Not that it is actually monochromatic.

YVAN: No! . . . How much was it?

SERGE: Two hundred thousand.

YVAN: Very reasonable.

SERGE: Very.

(*Silence. Suddenly Serge bursts out laughing, immediately followed by Yvan. Both of them roar with laughter.*)

Crazy, or what?

YVAN: Crazy!

SERGE: Two hundred grand!

(*Hearty laughter. They stop. They look at each other. They start again. Then stop.*

They've calmed down.)

SERGE: You know Marc's seen this painting.

YVAN: Oh?

SERGE: Devastated.

YVAN: Oh?

SERGE: He told me it was shit. A completely inappropriate description.

YVAN: Absolutely.

SERGE: You can't call this shit.

YVAN: No.

SERGE: You can say, I don't get it, I can't grasp it, you can't say "it's shit."

YVAN: You've seen his place.

SERGE: Nothing to see.

It's like yours, it's . . . what I mean is, you couldn't care less.

YVAN: His taste is classical, he likes things classical, what do you expect. . . .

SERGE: He started in with this sardonic laugh. . . . Not a trace of charm. . . . Not a trace of humor.

YVAN: You know Marc is moody, there's nothing new about that. . . .

SERGE: He has no sense of humor. With you, I can laugh. With him, I'm like a block of ice.

YVAN: It's true he's a bit gloomy at the moment.

SERGE: I don't blame him for not responding to this painting, he hasn't the training, there's a whole apprenticeship you have to go through, which he hasn't, either because he's never wanted to or because he has no particular instinct for it, none of that matters, no, what I blame him for is his tone of voice, his complacency, his tactlessness.

I blame him for his insensitivity. I don't blame him for not being interested in modern Art, I couldn't give a toss about that, I like him for other reasons. . . .

YVAN: And he likes you!

SERGE: No, no, no, no, I felt it the other day, a kind of . . . a kind of condescension . . . contempt with a really bitter edge. . . .

YVAN: No, surely not!

SERGE: Oh, yes! Don't keep trying to smooth things over. Where d'you get this urge to be the great reconciler of the human race? Why don't you admit that Marc is atrophying? If he hasn't already atrophied.

(*Silence.*)

(*At Marc's.*)

(*On the wall, a figurative painting: a landscape seen through a window.*)

YVAN: We had a laugh.

MARC: You had a laugh?

YVAN: We had a laugh. Both of us. We had a laugh. I promise you on Catherine's life, we had a good laugh, both of us, together.

MARC: You told him it was shit and you had a good laugh.

YVAN: No, I didn't tell him it was shit, we laughed spontaneously.

MARC: You arrived, you looked at the painting and you laughed. And then he laughed.

YVAN: Yes. If you like. We talked a bit, then it was more or less as you described.

MARC: A genuine laugh, was it?

YVAN: Perfectly genuine.

MARC: Well, then, I've made a mistake. Good. I'm really pleased to hear it.

YVAN: It was even better than you think. It was Serge who laughed first.

MARC: It was Serge who laughed first. . . .

YVAN: Yes.

MARC: He laughed first and you joined in.

YVAN: Yes.

MARC: But what made him laugh?

YVAN: He laughed because he sensed I was about to laugh. If you like, he laughed to put me at my ease.

MARC: It doesn't count if he laughed first.
If he laughed first, it was to defuse your laughter.
It means it wasn't a genuine laugh.

YVAN: It was a genuine laugh.

MARC: It may have been a genuine laugh, but it wasn't for the right reason.

YVAN: What is the right reason? I'm confused.

MARC: He wasn't laughing because his painting is ridiculous, you and he weren't laughing for the same reasons, you were laughing at the painting and he was laughing to ingratiate himself, to put himself on your wavelength, to show you that on top of being an aesthete who can spend more on a painting than you earn in a year, he's still your same old subversive mate who likes a good laugh.

YVAN: Mm hm . . .

(*A brief silence.*)

You know . . .

MARC: Yes. . . .

YVAN: This is going to amaze you. . . .

MARC: Go on. . . .

YVAN: I didn't like the painting . . . but I didn't actually hate it.

MARC: Well, of course. You can't hate what's invisible, you can't hate nothing.

YVAN: No, no, it has something. . . .

MARC: What do you mean?

YVAN: It has something. It's not nothing.

MARC: You're joking.

YVAN: I'm not as harsh as you. It's a work of art, there's a system behind it.

MARC: A system?

YVAN: A system.

MARC: What system?

YVAN: It's the completion of a journey. . . .

MARC: Ha, ha, ha!

YVAN: It wasn't painted by accident, it's a work of art which stakes its claim as part of a trajectory. . . .

MARC: Ha, ha, ha!

YVAN: All right, laugh.

MARC: You're parroting out all Serge's nonsense. From him, it's heart-breaking, from you it's just comical!

YVAN: You know, Marc, this complacency, you want to watch out for it. You're getting bitter, it's not very attractive.

MARC: Good. The older I get, the more offensive I hope to become.

YVAN: Great.

MARC: A system!

YVAN: You're impossible to talk to.

MARC: There's a system behind it! . . . You look at this piece of shit, but never mind, never mind, there's a system behind it! . . . You reckon there's a system behind this landscape? (*He indicates the painting on his wall.*) . . . No, uh? Too evocative. Too expressive. Everything's on the canvas! No scope for a system! . . .

YVAN: I'm glad you're enjoying yourself.

MARC: Yvan, look, speak for yourself. Describe your feelings to me.

YVAN: I felt a resonance.

MARC: You felt a resonance? . . .

YVAN: You're denying that I'm capable of appreciating this painting on my own account.

MARC: Of course I am.

YVAN: Well, why?

MARC: Because I know you. Because apart from your disastrous indulgence, you're quite sane.

YVAN: I wish I could say the same for you.

MARC: Yvan, look me in the eye.

YVAN: I'm looking at you.

MARC: Were you moved by Serge's painting?

YVAN: No.

MARC: Answer me this. You're getting married tomorrow and you and Catherine get this painting as a wedding present. Does it make you happy? . . .
Does it make you happy? . . .

(*Yvan, alone.*)

YVAN: Of course it doesn't make me happy.
It doesn't make me happy, but, generally speaking, I'm not the sort of person who can say I'm happy, just like that.
I'm trying to . . . I'm trying to think of an occasion when I could have said yes, I'm happy. . . . Are you happy to be getting married, my mother stupidly asked me one day, are you at least happy to be getting married? . . . Why wouldn't I be, mother?
What do you mean, why wouldn't I be? You're either happy or you're not happy, what's why wouldn't I be got to do with it? . . .

(*Serge, alone.*)

SERGE: As far as I'm concerned, it's not white.

When I say as far as I'm concerned, I mean objectively.

Objectively speaking, it's not white.

It has a white background, with a whole range of greys. . . .

There's even some red in it.

You could say it's very pale.

I wouldn't like it if it was white.

Marc thinks it's white . . . that's his limit. . . .

Marc thinks it's white because he's got hung up on the idea that it's white.

Unlike Yvan. Yvan can see it isn't white.

Marc can think what he likes, what do I care?

(Marc, alone.)

MARC: Obviously I should have taken the Ignatia.

Why do I have to be so categorical?

What possible difference can it make to me, if Serge lets himself be taken in by modern Art?

I mean, it is a serious matter. But I could have found some other way to put it to him.

I could have taken a less aggressive tone.

Even if it makes me physically ill that my best friend has bought a white painting, all the same I ought to avoid attacking him about it.

I ought to be nice to him.

From now on, I'm on my best behavior.

(At Serge's.)

SERGE: Feel like a laugh?
MARC: Go on.
SERGE: Yvan liked the Antrios.
MARC: Where is it? . . .
SERGE: You want another look?
MARC: Fetch it out.
SERGE: I knew you'd come round to it! . . .

(He exits and returns with the painting. A moment of contemplation.)

Yvan got the hang of it. Right away.
MARC: Mm.
SERGE: All right, listen, it's just a picture, we don't have to get bogged down with it, life's too short. . . . By the way, have you read this? *(He picks up De Vita Beata by Seneca° and throws it on to the low table just in front of Marc.)* Read it, it's a masterpiece.

(Marc picks up the book, opens it and leafs through it.)

Incredibly modern. Read that, you don't need to read anything else. What with the office, the hospital, Françoise, who's now decreed that I'm to see the children every weekend — which is something new for

---

De Vita Beata by Seneca: *On the Good Life,* a philosophical work by Lucius Seneca (4? B.C.–A.D. 65), a Roman philosopher, political leader, and author of tragedies. For Seneca, as for other Stoics, virtue and reason are the basis for a good life, which should be led simply and in accordance with nature.

Françoise, the notion that children need a father — I don't have time to read any more, I'm obliged to go straight for the essentials.
MARC: . . . As in the painting . . . Where you've ingeniously eliminated form and color. Those old chestnuts.
SERGE: Yes . . . Although I'm still capable of appreciating more figurative work. Like your Flemish job. Very restful.
MARC: What's Flemish about it? It's a view of Carcassonne.
SERGE: Yes, but I mean . . . it's slightly Flemish in style . . . the window, the view, the . . . in any case, it's very pretty.
MARC: It's not worth anything, you know that.
SERGE: What difference does that make? . . . Anyway, in a few years God knows if the Antrios will be worth anything! . . .
MARC: . . . You know, I've been thinking. I've been thinking and I've changed my mind. The other day, driving across Paris, I was thinking about you and I said to myself: isn't there, deep down, something really poetic about what Serge has done? . . . Isn't surrendering to this incoherent urge to buy in fact an authentically poetic impulse?
SERGE: You're very conciliatory today. Unrecognizable. What's this bland, submissive tone of voice? It doesn't suit you at all, by the way.
MARC: No, no, I'm trying to explain, I'm apologizing.
SERGE: Apologizing? What for?
MARC: I'm too thin-skinned, I'm too highly strung, I overreact. . . . You could say, I lack judgment.
SERGE: Read Seneca.
MARC: That's it. See, for instance, you say "read Seneca" and I could easily have got annoyed. I'm quite capable of being really annoyed by your saying to me, in the course of our conversation, "read Seneca." Which is absurd!
SERGE: No. It's not absurd.
MARC: Really?
SERGE: No, because you thought you could identify . . .
MARC: I didn't say I *was* annoyed. . . .
SERGE: You said you could easily . . .
MARC: Yes, yes. I could easily. . . .
SERGE: Get annoyed, and I understand that. Because when I said "read Seneca," you thought you could identify a kind of superiority. You tell me you lack judgment and my answer is "read Seneca," well, it's obnoxious!
MARC: It is, rather.
SERGE: Having said that, it's true you lack judgment, because I didn't say "read Seneca," I said "read Seneca!"
MARC: You're right. You're right.
SERGE: The fact of the matter is, you've quite simply lost your sense of humor.
MARC: Probably.
SERGE: You've lost your sense of humor, Marc. You really have lost your sense of humor, old chap. When I was talking to Yvan the other day, we agreed you'd

lost your sense of humor. Where the hell is he? He's incapable of being on time, it's infuriating! We'll miss the beginning!

MARC: . . . Yvan thinks I've lost my sense of humor? . . .

SERGE: Yvan agrees with me that recently you've somewhat lost your sense of humor.

MARC: The last time you saw each other, Yvan said he liked your painting very much and I'd lost my sense of humor. . . .

SERGE: Oh, yes, that, yes, the painting, really, very much. And he meant it. . . . What's that you're eating?

MARC: Ignatia.

SERGE: Oh, you believe in homeopathy now?

MARC: I don't believe in anything.

SERGE: Didn't you think Yvan had lost a lot of weight?

MARC: So's she.

SERGE: It's the wedding, eating away at them.

MARC: Yes.

(*They laugh.*)

SERGE: How's Paula?

MARC: All right. (*He indicates the Antrios.*) Where are you going to put it?

SERGE: Haven't decided. There. Or there? . . . Too ostentatious.

MARC: Are you going to have it framed?

(*Serge laughs discreetly.*)

SERGE: No! . . . No, no. . . .

MARC: Why not?

SERGE: It's not supposed to be framed.

MARC: Is that right?

SERGE: The artist doesn't want it to be. It mustn't be interrupted. It's already in its setting. (*He signals Marc over to examine the edge.*) Look . . . you see . . .

MARC: What is it, Elastoplast?

SERGE: No, it's a kind of Kraft paper. . . . Made up by the artist.

MARC: It's funny the way you say "the artist."

SERGE: What else am I supposed to say?

MARC: You say "the artist" when you could say "the painter" or . . . whatever his name is . . . Antrios. . . .

SERGE: So? . . .

MARC: But you say "the artist," as if he's a sort of . . . well, anyway, doesn't matter. What are we seeing? Let's try and see something with a bit of substance for once.

SERGE: It's eight o'clock. Everything will have started. I can't imagine how this man, who has nothing whatsoever to do — am I right? — manages to be late every single time. Where the fuck is he?

MARC: Let's just have dinner.

SERGE: All right. It's five past eight. We said we'd meet between seven and half-past. . . . What d'you mean, the way I say "the artist"?

MARC: Nothing. I was going to say something stupid.

SERGE: Well, go on.

MARC: You say "the artist" as if . . . as if he's some unattainable being. The artist . . . some sort of god. . . .

(*Serge laughs.*)

SERGE: Well, for me, he is a god! You don't think I'd have forked out a fortune for a mere mortal! . . .

MARC: I see.

SERGE: I went to the Pompidou on Monday, you know how many Antrioses they have at the Pompidou? . . . Three! Three Antrioses! . . . At the Pompidou!

MARC: Amazing.

SERGE: And mine's as good as any of them! If not better! . . .

Listen, I have a suggestion, let's give Yvan exactly three more minutes and then bugger off. I've found a very good new place. Lyonnaise.

MARC: Why are you so jumpy?

SERGE: I'm not jumpy.

MARC: Yes, you are jumpy.

SERGE: I am not jumpy, well, I am, I'm jumpy because this slackness is intolerable, this inability to practice any kind of self-discipline!

MARC: The fact is, I'm getting on your nerves and you're taking it out on poor Yvan.

SERGE: What do you mean, poor Yvan, are you taking the piss? You're not getting on my nerves, why should you be getting on my nerves?

SERGE: He is getting on my nerves. It's true.

He's getting on my nerves.

It's this ingratiating tone of voice. A little smile behind every word.

It's as if he's forcing himself to be pleasant.

Don't be pleasant, whatever you do, don't be pleasant!

Could it be buying the Antrios? . . . Could buying the Antrios have triggered off this feeling of constraint between us?

Buying something . . . without his backing? . . .

Well, bugger his backing! Bugger your backing, Marc!

MARC: Could it be the Antrios, buying the Antrios?

No —

It started some time ago. . . .

To be precise, it started on the day we were discussing some work of art and you uttered, quite seriously, the word *deconstruction*.

It wasn't so much the word *deconstruction* which upset me, it was the air of solemnity you imbued it with.

You said, humorlessly, unapologetically, without a trace of irony, the word *deconstruction*, you, my friend.

I wasn't sure how best to deal with the situation, so I made this throwaway remark, I said I think I must be getting intolerant in my old age, and you answered, who do you think you are? What makes you so high and mighty? . . .

What gives you the right to set yourself apart, Serge answered in the bloodiest possible way. And quite unexpectedly.

You're just Marc, what makes you think you're so special?

That day, I should have punched him in the mouth.

And when he was lying there on the ground, half-dead, I should have said to him, you're supposed to be my friend, what sort of a friend are you, Serge, if you don't think your friends are special?

(*At Serge's.*)
(*Marc and Serge, as we left them.*)

MARC: Lyonnaise, did you say? Bit heavy, isn't it? Bit fatty, all those sausages. . . . What do you think?

(*The doorbell rings.*)

SERGE: Twelve minutes past eight.

(*Serge goes to open the door to Yvan. Yvan walks into the room, already talking.*)

YVAN: So, a crisis, insoluble problem, major crisis, both stepmothers want their names on the wedding invitation. Catherine adores her stepmother, who more or less brought her up, she wants her name on the invitation, she wants it and her stepmother is not anticipating, which is understandable, since the mother is dead, not appearing next to Catherine's father, whereas my stepmother, whom I detest, it's out of the question her name should appear on the invitation, but my father won't have his name on it if hers isn't, unless Catherine's stepmother's is left off, which is completely unacceptable, I suggested none of the parents' names should be on it, after all we're not adolescents, we can announce our wedding and invite people ourselves, so Catherine screamed her head off, arguing that would be a slap in the face for her parents who were paying through the nose for the reception, and particularly for her stepmother, who's gone to so much trouble when she isn't even her daughter and I finally let myself be persuaded, totally against my better judgment, because she wore me down, I finally agreed that my stepmother, whom I detest, who's a complete bitch, will have her name on the invitation, so I telephoned my mother to warn her, mother, I said, I've done everything I can to avoid this, but we have absolutely no choice, Yvonne's name has to be on the invitation, she said, if Yvonne's name is on the invitation, take mine off it, mother, I said, please, I beg you, don't make things even more difficult, and she said, how dare you suggest my name is left to float around the card on its own, as if I was some abandoned woman, below Yvonne, who'll be clamped on to your father's surname, like a limpet, I said to her, mother, I have friends waiting for me, I'm going to hang up and we'll discuss all this tomorrow after a good night's sleep, she said, why is it I'm always an afterthought, what are you talking about, mother, you're not always an afterthought, of course I am and when you say don't make things even more difficult, what you mean is, everything's already been decided, everything's been organized without me, everything's been cooked up behind my back, good old Huguette, she'll agree to anything and all this, she said — to put the old tin lid on it — in aid of an event, the importance of which I'm having some trouble grasping, mother, I have friends waiting for me, that's right, there's always something better to do, anything's more important than I am, good-bye and she hung up, Catherine, who was next to me, but who hadn't heard her side of the conversation, said, what did she say, I said, she doesn't want her name on the invitation with Yvonne, which is understandable, I'm not talking about that, what was it she said about the wedding, nothing, you're lying, I'm not, Cathy, I promise you, she just doesn't want her name on the invitation with Yvonne, call her back and tell her when your son's getting married, you rise above your vanity, you could say the same thing to your stepmother, that's got nothing to do with it, Catherine shouted, it's me, I'm the one who's insisting her name's on it, it's not her, poor thing, she's tact personified, if she had any idea of the problem this is causing, she'd be down on her knees, begging for her name to be taken off the invitation, now call your mother, so I called her again, by now I'm in shreds, Catherine's listening on the extension, Yvan, my mother says, up to now you've conducted your affairs in the most chaotic way imaginable and just because, out of the blue, you've decided to embark on matrimony, I find myself obliged to spend all afternoon and evening with your father, a man I haven't seen for seventeen years and to whom I was not expecting to have to reveal my hip-size and my puffy cheeks, not to mention Yvonne who incidentally, I may tell you, according to Félix Perolari, has now taken up bridge — my mother also plays bridge — I can see none of this can be helped, but on the invitation, the one item everyone is going to receive and examine, I insist on making a solo appearance, Catherine, listening on the extension, shakes her head and screws up her face in disgust, mother, I say, why are you so selfish, I'm not selfish, I'm not selfish, Yvan, you're not going to start as well, you're not going to be like Mme Roméro this morning and tell me I have a heart of stone, that everybody in our family has a heart of stone, that's what Mme Roméro said this morning when I refused to raise her wages — she's gone completely mad, by the way — to sixty francs an hour tax-free, she had the gall to say everyone in the family had a heart of stone, when she knows very well about poor André's pacemaker, you haven't even bothered to drop him a line, yes, that's right, very funny, everything's a joke to you, it's not me who's the selfish one, Yvan, you've still got a lot to learn about life, off you go, my boy, go on, go on, go and see your precious friends. . . .

(*Silence.*)

SERGE: Then what? . . .

YVAN: Then nothing. Nothing's been resolved. I hung up. Minidrama with Catherine. Cut short, because I was late.

MARC: Why do you let yourself be buggered around by all these women?

YVAN: Why do I let myself be buggered around, I don't know! They're all insane.

SERGE: You've lost weight.

YVAN: Of course I have. Half a stone. Purely through stress.

MARC: Read Seneca. . . .

YVAN: *De Vita Beata,* Just what I need!
    What's he suggest?

MARC: It's a masterpiece.

YVAN: Oh?

SERGE: He hasn't read it.

YVAN: Oh.

MARC: No, but Serge just told me it was a masterpiece.

SERGE: I said it was a masterpiece because it is a masterpiece.

MARC: Quite.

SERGE: It is a masterpiece.

MARC: Why are you getting annoyed?

SERGE: You seem to be insinuating I use the word *masterpiece* at the slightest excuse.

MARC: Not at all. . . .

SERGE: You said the word in a kind of sarcastic way. . . .

MARC: Not at all!

SERGE: Yes, yes, the word *masterpiece* in a kind of . . .

MARC: Is he crazy? Not at all! . . . However, when you used the word, you qualified it by saying "incredibly modern."

SERGE: Yes. So?

MARC: You said "incredibly modern," as if modern was the highest compliment you could give. As if, when describing something, you couldn't think of anything more admirable, more profoundly admirable, than modern.

SERGE: So?

MARC: So nothing.
    And please note I made no mention of the word *incredibly.* . . . Incredibly modern!

SERGE: You're really needling me today.

MARC: No, I'm not . . .

YVAN: You're not going to quarrel all evening, that would just about finish me!

SERGE: You don't think it's extraordinary that a man who wrote nearly two thousand years ago should still be bang up to date?

MARC: No. Of course not. That's the definition of a classic.

SERGE: You're just playing with words.

YVAN: So, what are we going to do? I suppose the cinema's up the spout, sorry. Shall we eat?

MARC: Serge tells me you're very taken with his painting.

YVAN: Yes . . . I am quite . . . taken with it, yes. . . .
    You're not, I gather.

MARC: No.
    Let's go and eat. Serge knows a tasty spot. Lyonnaise.

SERGE: You think the food's too fatty.

MARC: I think the food's a bit on the fatty side, but I don't mind giving it a whirl.

SERGE: No, if you think the food's too fatty, we'll find somewhere else.

MARC: No, I don't mind giving it a whirl.

SERGE: We'll go to the restaurant if you think you'll like it. If not, we won't.
    (*To Yvan.*) You like Lyonnaise food?

YVAN: I'll do whatever you like.

MARC: He'll do whatever you like. Whatever you like, he'll always do.

YVAN: What's the matter with you? You're both behaving very strangely.

SERGE: He's right, you might once in a while have an opinion of your own.

YVAN: Listen, if you think you're going to use me as a coconut shy, I'm out of here! I've put up with enough today.

MARC: Where's your sense of humor, Yvan?

YVAN: What?

MARC: Where's your sense of humor, old chap?

YVAN: Where's my sense of humor? I don't see anything to laugh at. Where's my sense of humor, are you trying to be funny?

MARC: I think recently you've somewhat lost your sense of humor. You want to watch out, believe me!

YVAN: What's the matter with you?

MARC: Don't you think recently I've also somewhat lost my sense of humor?

YVAN: Oh, I see!

SERGE: All right, that's enough, let's make a decision. Tell you the truth, I'm not even hungry.

YVAN: You're both really sinister this evening.

SERGE: You want my opinion about your women problems?

YVAN: Go on.

SERGE: In my view, the most hysterical of them all is Catherine. By far.

MARC: No question.

SERGE: And if you're already letting yourself be buggered around by her, you're in for a hideous future.

YVAN: What can I do?

MARC: Cancel it.

YVAN: Cancel the wedding?

SERGE: He's right.

YVAN: But I can't, are you crazy?

MARC: Why not?

YVAN: Well, because I can't, that's all! It's all arranged. I've only been working at the stationery business for a month. . . .

MARC: What's that got to do with it?

YVAN: It's her uncle's stationery business, he had absolutely no need to take on anyone, least of all someone who's only ever worked in textiles.

SERGE: You must do what you like. I've told you what I think.

YVAN: I'm sorry, Serge, I don't mean to be rude, but you're not necessarily the person I'd come to for matrimonial advice. You can't claim to have been a great success in that field. . . .

SERGE: Precisely.

YVAN: I can't back out of the wedding. I know Catherine is hysterical but she has her good points. There are certain crucial qualities you need when you're marrying someone like me. . . . (*He indicates the Antrios.*) Where are you going to put it?

SERGE: I don't know yet.

YVAN: Why don't you put it there?

SERGE: Because there, it'd be wiped out by the sunlight.

YVAN: Oh, yes.
    I thought of you today at the shop, we ran off five hundred posters by this bloke who paints white flowers, totally white, on a white background.

SERGE: The Antrios is not white.

YVAN: No, of course not. I was just saying.

MARC: You think this painting is not white, Yvan?

YVAN: Not entirely, no. . . .

MARC: Ah. Then what color is it?

YVAN: Various colors. . . . There's yellow, there's grey, some slightly ochrish lines.

MARC: And you're moved by these colors?

YVAN: Yes . . . I'm moved by these colors.

MARC: You have no substance, Yvan. You're flabby, you're an amoeba.

SERGE: Why are you attacking Yvan like this?

MARC: Because he's a little arse-licker, he's obsequious, dazzled by money, dazzled by what he believes to be culture, and as you know culture is something I absolutely piss on.

(*Brief silence.*)

SERGE: . . . What's got into you?

MARC (*to Yvan*): How could you, Yvan? . . . And in front of me. In front of me, Yvan.

YVAN: What d'you mean, in front of you? . . . What d'you mean, in front of you?
    I find these colors touching. Yes. If it's all the same to you.
    Stop wanting to control everything.

MARC: How could you say, in front of me, that you find these colors touching?

YVAN: Because it's the truth.

MARC: The truth? You find these colors touching?

YVAN: Yes. I find these colors touching.

MARC: You find these colors touching, Yvan?!

SERGE: He finds these colors touching! He's perfectly entitled to!

MARC: No, he's not entitled to.

SERGE: What do you mean, he's not entitled to?

MARC: He's not entitled to.

YVAN: I'm not entitled to? . . .

MARC: No.

SERGE: Why is he not entitled to? I don't think you're very well, perhaps you ought to go and see someone.

MARC: He's not entitled to say he finds these colors touching, because he doesn't.

YVAN: I don't find these colors touching?

MARC: There are no colors. You can't see them. And you don't find them touching.

YVAN: Speak for yourself!

MARC: This is really demeaning, Yvan! . . .

SERGE: Who do you think you are, Marc? . . .
    Who are you to legislate? You don't like anything, you despise everyone. You take pride in not being a man of your time. . . .

MARC: What's that supposed to mean, a man of my time?

YVAN: Right. I'm off.

SERGE: Where are you going?

YVAN: I'm off. I don't see why I have to put up with your tantrums.

SERGE: Don't go! You're not going to start taking offense, are you? . . . If you go, you're giving in to him.

(*Yvan stands there, hesitating, caught between two possibilities.*)

A man of his time is a man who lives in his own time.

MARC: Balls. How can a man live in any other time but his own? Answer me that.

SERGE: A man of his time is someone of whom it can be said in twenty years' or in a hundred years' time, he was representative of his era.

MARC: Hm.
    To what end?

SERGE: What do you mean, to what end?

MARC: What use is it to me if one day somebody says, I was representative of my era?

SERGE: Listen, old fruit, we're not talking about you, if you can imagine such a thing! We don't give a fuck about you! A man of his time, I'm trying to explain to you, like most people you admire, is someone who makes some contribution to the human race. . . . A man of his time doesn't assume the history of Art has come to an end with a pseudo-Flemish view of Cavaillon. . . .

MARC: Carcassonne.

SERGE: Same thing. A man of his time plays his part in the fundamental dynamic of evolution. . . .

MARC: And that's a good thing, in your view.

SERGE: It's not good or bad, why do you always have to moralize, it's just the way things are.

MARC: And you, for example, you play your part in the fundamental dynamic of evolution.

SERGE: I do.

MARC: What about Yvan? . . .

YVAN: Surely not. What sort of part can an amoeba play?

SERGE: In his way, Yvan is a man of his time.

MARC: How can you tell? Not from that daub hanging over his mantelpiece!

YVAN: That is not a daub!

SERGE: It is a daub.

YVAN: It is not!

SERGE: What's the difference? Yvan represents a certain way of life, a way of thinking which is completely modern. And so do you. I'm sorry, but you're a typical man of your time. And in fact, the harder you try not to be, the more you are.

MARC: Well, that's all right then. So what's the problem?

SERGE: There's no problem, except for you, because you take pride in your desire to shut yourself off from humanity. And you'll never manage it. It's like you're in a quicksand, the more you struggle to get out of it, the deeper you sink. Now apologize to Yvan.

MARC: Yvan is a coward.

(*At this point, Yvan makes his decision, and exits in a rush.*)

(*Slight pause.*)

SERGE: Well done.

(*Silence.*)

MARC: It wasn't a good idea to meet this evening . . . was it? . . . I'd better go as well. . . .

SERGE: Maybe. . . .

MARC: Right.

SERGE: You're the coward . . . attacking someone who's incapable of defending himself . . . as you well know.

MARC: You're right . . . you're right and when you put it like that, it makes me feel even worse . . . the thing is, all of a sudden, I can't understand, I have no idea what Yvan and I have in common. . . . I have no idea what my relationship with him consists of.

SERGE: Yvan's always been as he is.

MARC: No. He used to be eccentric, kind of absurd . . . he was always unstable, but his eccentricity was disarming. . . .

SERGE: What about me?

MARC: What about you?

SERGE: Have you any idea what you and I have in common? . . .

MARC: That's a question that could take us down a very long road. . . .

SERGE: Lead on.

(*Short silence.*)

MARC: . . . I'm sorry I upset Yvan.

SERGE: Ah! At last you've said something approximately human. . . . What makes it worse is that the daub he has hanging over his mantelpiece was I'm afraid painted by his father.

MARC: Was it? Shit.

SERGE: Yes. . . .

MARC: But you said . . .

SERGE: Yes, yes, but I remembered as soon as I'd said it.

MARC: Oh, shit. . . .

SERGE: Mm. . . .

(*Slight pause.*)

(*The doorbell rings. Serge goes to answer it. Yvan enters immediately, talking as he arrives, as before.*)

YVAN: Yvan returns! The lift was full, I plunged off down the stairs, clattering all the way down thinking, a coward, an amoeba, no substance, I thought I'll come back with a gun and blow his head off, then he'll see how flabby and obsequious I am, I got to the ground floor and I said to myself, listen, mate, you haven't been in therapy for six years to finish up shooting your best friend and you haven't been in therapy for six years without learning that some deep malaise must lie behind his insane aggression, so I relaunch myself, telling myself as I mount the penitential stair, this is a cry for help. I have to help Marc if it's the last thing I do. . . . In fact the other day I discussed you both with Finkelzohn. . . .

SERGE: You discussed us with Finkelzohn?

YVAN: I discuss everything with Finkelzohn.

SERGE: And why exactly were you discussing us?

MARC: I forbid you to discuss me with that arsehole.

YVAN: You're in no position to forbid me anything.

SERGE: Why were you discussing us?

YVAN: I knew your relationship was under strain and I wanted Finkelzohn to explain. . . .

SERGE: And what did the bastard say?

YVAN: He said something rather amusing. . . .

MARC: They're allowed to give their opinions?

YVAN: No, they never give their opinions, but this time he did give his opinion, he even made a gesture and he never makes a gesture, he's always rigid, I sometimes say to him, for God's sake, move about a bit! . . .

SERGE: All right, what did he say?

MARC: Who gives a fuck what he said?

SERGE: What did he say?

MARC: What possible interest could we have in what he said?

SERGE: I want to know what the bastard said, all right? Shit!

(*Yvan reaches into his jacket pocket.*)

YVAN: You want to know? . . .

(*He fetches out a piece of folded paper.*)

MARC: You took notes?

YVAN (*unfolding it*): I wrote it down because it was complicated. . . . Shall I read it to you?

SERGE: Go on.

YVAN: . . . "If I'm who I am because I'm who I am and you're who you are because you're who you are, then I'm who I am and you're who you are. If, on the other hand, I'm who I am because you're who you are, and if you're who you are because I'm who I am, then I'm not who I am and you're not who you are. . . ."

You see why I had to write it down.

(*Short silence.*)

MARC: How much do you pay this man?

YVAN: Four hundred francs a session, twice a week.

MARC: Great.

SERGE: And in cash. I found something out, they don't allow you to pay by check. Freud said you have to feel the banknotes as they slip through your fingers.

MARC: What a lucky man you are, to be getting the benefit of this fellow's experience.

SERGE: Absolutely! . . . We'd really appreciate it if you'd copy that out for us.

MARC: Yes. It's bound to come in handy.

(*Yvan carefully refolds the piece of paper.*)

YVAN: You're wrong. It's very profound.

MARC: If it's because of him you've come back to turn the other cheek, you should be grateful to him. He's turned you into a pudding, but you're happy, that's all that counts.

YVAN (*to Serge*): And all this because he doesn't want to believe I like your Antrios.

SERGE: I don't give a fuck what you think of it. Either of you.

YVAN: The more I see it, the more I like it, honestly.

SERGE: Let's stop talking about the painting, shall we; once and for all. I have no interest in discussing it further.

MARC: Why are you so touchy?

SERGE: I am not touchy, Marc. You've told us what you think. Fine. The subject is closed.

MARC: You're getting upset.

SERGE: I am not getting upset. I'm exhausted.

MARC: See, if you're touchy about it, it means you're too caught up in other people's opinions.

SERGE: I'm exhausted, Marc. This is completely pointless. . . . To tell you the truth, I'm quite close to getting bored with the pair of you.

YVAN: Let's go and eat.

SERGE: You go, why don't you go off together?

YVAN: No! It's so rare the three of us are together.

SERGE: Just as well, by the look of it.

YVAN: I don't understand what's going on. Can't we just calm down? There's no reason to insult each other, especially over a painting.

SERGE: You realize all this "calm down" and behaving like the vicar is just adding fuel to the fire! Is this something new?

YVAN: I will not be undermined.

MARC: This is most impressive. Perhaps I should go to Finkelzohn! . . .

YVAN: You can't. There are no vacancies.
What's that you're eating?

MARC: Gelsemium.

YVAN: I've given in to the logic of events, marriage, children, death. Stationery. What can go wrong?

(*Moved by a sudden impulse, Serge picks up the Antrios and takes it back where he found it, in the next room. He returns immediately.*)

MARC: We're not worthy to look at it. . . .

SERGE: Exactly.

MARC: Or are you afraid, if it stays in my presence, you'll finish up looking at it through my eyes? . . .

SERGE: No. You know what Paul Valéry° says? And I'd go quite a bit further.

MARC: I don't give a fuck what Paul Valéry says.

SERGE: You've gone off Paul Valéry?

MARC: Don't quote Paul Valéry at me.

SERGE: But you used to love Paul Valéry.

MARC: I don't give a fuck what Paul Valéry says.

SERGE: But I discovered him through you. You're the one who put me on to Paul Valéry.

MARC: Don't quote Paul Valéry at me, I don't give a fuck what Paul Valéry says.

SERGE: What do you give a fuck about?

MARC: I give a fuck about you buying that painting.
I give a fuck about you spending two hundred grand on that piece of shit.

YVAN: Don't start again, Marc!

SERGE: I'm going to tell you what I give a fuck about — since everyone is coming clean — I give a fuck about your sniggering and insinuations, your suggestion that I also think this picture is a grotesque joke. You've denied that I could feel a genuine attachment to it. You've tried to set up some kind of loathsome complicity between us. And that's what's made me feel, Marc, to repeat your expression, that we have less and less in common recently, your perpetual display of suspicion.

MARC: It's true I can't imagine you genuinely loving that painting.

YVAN: But why?

MARC: Because I love Serge and I can't love the Serge who's capable of buying that painting.

SERGE: Why do you say, buying, why don't you say, loving?

MARC: Because I can't say loving, I can't believe loving.

SERGE: So why would I buy it, if I didn't love it?

MARC: That's the nub of the question.

SERGE (*to Yvan*): See how smug he is! All I'm doing is teasing him, and his answer is this serenely pompous heavy hint! . . . (*To Marc.*) And it never crossed your mind for a second, however improbable it might seem, that I might really love it and that your vicious, inflexible opinions and your disgusting assumption of complicity might be hurtful to me?

MARC: No.

SERGE: When you asked me what I thought of Paula — a girl who once spent an entire dinner party maintaining Elhers-Danlos syndrome° could be cured homeopathically — did I say I found her ugly, repellent, and charmless? I could have done.

MARC: Is that what you think of Paula?

SERGE: What's your theory?

Paul Valéry: (1871–1945), French poet, regarded by many as the greatest French writer of the twentieth century.
Elhers-Danlos syndrome: A group of connective-tissue disorders that cause fragile skin and unstable joints.

YVAN: No, of course he doesn't think that! You couldn't possibly think that of Paula!

MARC: Answer me.

SERGE: You see the effect you can have!

MARC: Do you think what you just said about Paula?

SERGE: Worse, actually.

YVAN: No!

MARC: Worse, Serge? Worse than repellent? Will you explain how someone can be worse than repellent?

SERGE: Aha! When it's something that concerns you personally, I see words can bite a little deeper! . . .

MARC: Serge, will you explain how someone can be worse than repellent. . . .

SERGE: No need to take that frosty tone. Perhaps it's — let me try and answer you — perhaps it's the way she waves away cigarette smoke.

MARC: The way she waves away cigarette smoke. . . .

SERGE: Yes. The way she waves away cigarette smoke. What appears to you a gesture of no significance, what you think of as a harmless gesture is in fact the opposite, and the way she waves away cigarette smoke sits right at the heart of her repellentness.

MARC: You're speaking to me of Paula, the woman who shares my life, in these intolerable terms, because you disapprove of her method of waving away cigarette smoke? . . .

SERGE: That's right. Her method of waving away cigarette smoke condemns her out of hand.

MARC: Serge, before I completely lose control, you'd better explain yourself. This is very serious, what you're doing.

SERGE: A normal woman would say, I'm sorry, I find the smoke a bit uncomfortable, would you mind moving your ashtray, but not her, she doesn't deign to speak, she describes her contempt in the air with this calculated gesture, wearily malicious, this hand movement she imagines is imperceptible, the implication of which is to say, go on, smoke, smoke, it's pathetic but what's the point of calling attention to it, which means you can't tell if it's you or your cigarette that's getting up her nose.

YVAN: You're exaggerating!

SERGE: You notice he doesn't say I'm wrong, he says I'm exaggerating, but he doesn't say I'm wrong. Her method of waving away cigarette smoke reveals a cold, condescending, and narrow-minded nature. Just what you're in the process of acquiring yourself. It's a shame, Marc, it's a real shame you've taken up with such a life-denying woman. . . .

YVAN: Paula is not life-denying! . . .

MARC: Take back everything you've just said, Serge.

SERGE: No.

YVAN: Yes, you must!

MARC: Take back what you've just said. . . .

YVAN: Take it back, take it back! This is ridiculous!

MARC: Serge, for the last time, I demand you take back what you've just said.

SERGE: In my view, the two of you are an aberration. A pair of fossils.

(*Marc throws himself at Serge. Yvan rushes forward to get between them.*)

MARC (*to Yvan*): Get off! . . .

SERGE (*to Yvan*): Mind your own business! . . .

(*A kind of bizarre struggle ensues, very short, which ends with a blow mistakenly landing on Yvan.*)

YVAN: Oh, shit! . . . Oh, shit! . . .

SERGE: Show me, show me. . . .

(*Yvan is groaning. More than is necessary, it would seem.*)

Come on, show me! . . . That's all right. . . . it's nothing. . . . Wait a minute. . . .

(*He goes out and comes back with a compress.*)

There you are, hold that on it for a while.

YVAN: . . . You're complete freaks, both of you. Two normal men gone completely insane!

SERGE: Don't get excited.

YVAN: That really hurt! . . . If I find out you've burst my eardrum! . . .

SERGE: Of course not.

YVAN: How do you know? You're not ear, nose, and throat! . . . Two old friends, educated people! . . .

SERGE: Go on, calm down.

YVAN: You can't demolish someone because you don't like her method of waving away cigarette smoke! . . .

SERGE: Yes, you can.

YVAN: But it doesn't make any sense!

SERGE: What do you know about sense?

YVAN: That's right, attack me, keep attacking me! . . . I could be hemorrhaging internally, I've just seen a mouse running past! . . .

SERGE: It's a rat.

YVAN: A rat?

SERGE: He comes and goes.

YVAN: You have a rat?!

SERGE: Don't take the compress away, leave it where it is.

YVAN: What's the matter with you? . . . What's happened between you? Something must have happened for you to go this demented.

SERGE: I've bought a work of art which makes Marc uncomfortable.

YVAN: You're starting again! . . . You're in a downward spiral, both of you, you can't stop yourselves. . . . It's like me and Yvonne. The most pathological relationship you can imagine!

SERGE: Who's Yvonne?

YVAN: My stepmother!

SERGE: It's a long time since you mentioned her.

(*Brief silence.*)

MARC: Why didn't you tell me right away what you thought about Paula?

SERGE: I didn't want to upset you.

MARC: No, no, no. . . .

SERGE: What do you mean, no, no, no? . . .

MARC: No.

When I asked you what you thought of Paula, what you said was: she's a perfect match for you.

SERGE: Yes. . . .

MARC: Which sounded quite positive, coming from you.

SERGE: Sure. . . .

MARC: Given the state you were in at the time.

SERGE: All right, what are you trying to prove?

MARC: But today, your assessment of Paula, or in other words me, is far harsher.

SERGE: . . . I don't understand.

MARC: Of course you understand.

SERGE: I don't.

MARC: Since I can no longer support you in your frenzied, though recent, craving for novelty, I've become "condescending," "narrow-minded,". . ."fossilized.". . .

YVAN: I'm in agony! It's like a corkscrew drilling through my brain!

SERGE: Have a drop of brandy.

YVAN: What do you think? . . . If something's shaken loose in my brain, don't you think alcohol's a bit of a risk?

SERGE: Would you like an aspirin?

YVAN: I'm not sure aspirin agrees with me. . . .

SERGE: Then what the hell do you want?

YVAN: Don't worry about me. Carry on with your preposterous conversation, don't pay any attention to me.

MARC: Easier said than done.

YVAN: You might squeeze out a drop of compassion. But no.

SERGE: I don't mind your spending time with Paula. I don't resent you being with Paula.

MARC: You've no reason to resent it.

SERGE: But you . . . you resent me . . . well, I was about to say, for being with the Antrios!

MARC: Yes!

SERGE: I'm missing something here.

MARC: I didn't replace you with Paula.

SERGE: Are you saying, I replaced you with the Antrios?

MARC: Yes.

SERGE: . . . I replaced you with the Antrios?

MARC: Yes. With the Antrios . . . and all it implies.

SERGE (to Yvan): Do you understand what he's talking about?

YVAN: I couldn't care less, you're both insane.

MARC: In my time, you'd never have bought that picture.

SERGE: What's that supposed to mean, in your time?

MARC: The time you made a distinction between me and other people, when you judged things by my standards.

SERGE: Was there such a time?

MARC: That's just cruel. And petty.

SERGE: No, I assure you, I'm staggered.

MARC: And if Yvan hadn't turned into such a sponge, he'd back me up.

YVAN: Go on, that's right, I've told you, it's water off a duck's back.

MARC (to Serge): There was a time you were proud to be my friend. . . . You congratulated yourself on my peculiarity, on my taste for standing apart. You enjoyed exhibiting me untamed to your circle, you, whose life was so normal. I was your alibi. But . . . eventually, I suppose, that sort of affection dries up. . . . Belatedly, you claim your independence.

SERGE: "Belatedly" is nice.

MARC: But I detest your independence. Its violence. You've abandoned me. I've been betrayed. As far as I'm concerned, you're a traitor.

(Silence.)

SERGE (to Yvan): . . . If I understand correctly, he was my mentor! . . .

(Yvan doesn't respond. Marc stares at him contemptuously. Slight pause.)

. . . And if I loved you as my mentor . . . what was the nature of your feelings?

MARC: You can guess.

SERGE: Yes, yes, but I want to hear you say it.

MARC: . . . I enjoyed your admiration. I was flattered. I was always grateful to you for thinking of me as a man apart. I even thought being a man apart was a somehow superior condition, until one day you pointed out to me that it wasn't.

SERGE: This is very alarming.

MARC: It's the truth.

SERGE: What a disaster . . . !

MARC: Yes, what a disaster!

SERGE: What a disaster!

MARC: Especially for me. . . . Whereas you've found a new family. Your penchant for idolatry has unearthed new objects of worship. The Artist! . . . *Deconstruction!*

(Short silence.)

YVAN: What is deconstruction? . . .

MARC: You don't know about deconstruction? . . . Ask Serge, he's very much on top of the subject. . . . (To Serge.) To convince me some ridiculous artwork is comprehensible, you pick a phrase from *Builders' Weekly.* . . . Oh, you're smiling! You see, when you smile like that, I think there's still some hope, like an idiot. . . .

YVAN: Why don't you make up? And let's spend an enjoyable evening, all this is ludicrous!

MARC: . . . It's my fault. We haven't seen much of one another recently. I've been away and you started mixing with the great and the good . . . the Ropses . . . the Desprez-Couderts . . . that dentist, Guy Hallié . . . he's the one who . . .

SERGE: No, no, no, no, not at all, he's from another world, he only likes conceptual Art. . . .

MARC: It's all the same thing.

SERGE: No, it's not all the same thing.

MARC: You see, more evidence of how I let you slip away . . . now when we talk we can't even make ourselves understood.

SERGE: I had no idea whatsoever — really, it's come as a complete surprise — the extent to which I was under your influence and in your control.

MARC: Not in my control, as it turns out. . . . You should never leave your friends unchaperoned. Your friends need to be chaperoned, otherwise they'll get away. . . .

Look at poor Yvan, whose chaotic behavior used to delight us, we've allowed him to become this timid stationer. . . . Practically married. . . . He brought us his originality and now he's making every effort to piss it away.

SERGE: Us! He brought us! Do you realize what you're saying? Everything has to revolve around you! Why can't you learn to love people for themselves, Marc?

MARC: What does that mean, for themselves?

SERGE: For what they are.

MARC: But what are they?! What are they?! . . .
Apart from my faith in them? . . .
I'm desperate to find a friend who has some kind of prior existence. So far, I've had no luck. I've had to mold you. . . . But you see, it never works. There comes a day when your creature has dinner with the Desprez-Couderts and, to confirm his new status, goes off and buys a white painting.

(*Silence.*)

SERGE: So here we are at the end of a fifteen-year friendship. . . .

MARC: Yes. . . .

YVAN: Pathetic. . . .

MARC: You see, if we'd only managed to have a normal discussion, that is, if I'd have been able to put my point of view without losing my temper. . . .

SERGE: Well? . . .

MARC: Nothing. . . .

SERGE: Yes. Go on. Why can't we exchange one single dispassionate word?

MARC: . . . I don't believe in the values which dominate contemporary Art. The rule of novelty. The rule of surprise.
Surprise is dead meat, Serge. No sooner conceived than dead.

SERGE: All right. So?

MARC: That's all.
Except that my appeal to you has always been my surprise value.

SERGE: What are you talking about?

MARC: A surprise which has lasted quite some time, I'll admit.

YVAN: Finkelzohn is a genius.
I told you he'd understood the whole thing!

MARC: I'd prefer it if you stopped refereeing, Yvan, and stopped imagining you're not fully implicated in this conversation.

YVAN: You want to implicate me, I refuse, what's it to do with me? I've already got a burst eardrum, you work things out for yourselves!

MARC: Perhaps he does have a burst eardrum. I hit him very hard.

(*Serge sniggers.*)

SERGE: Please, stop boasting.

MARC: See, Yvan, what I can't bear about you at the moment — quite apart from what I've already told you — is your urge to put Serge and me on the same level. You would like us to be equal. To indulge your cowardice. Talking on an equal footing, equal the way you thought of us when we were friends. But we never were equal, Yvan. You have to choose.

YVAN: I have chosen.

MARC: Excellent.

SERGE: I don't need a supporter.

MARC: You're not going to turn the poor boy down?

YVAN: Why do we see each other, if we hate each other? It's obvious we do hate each other! Or rather, I don't hate you, but you hate each other! And you hate me! So why do we see each other? . . . I was looking forward to a relaxing evening after a ridiculously fraught week, meeting my two best friends, going to the cinema, having a laugh, getting away from all these dramas. . . .

SERGE: Are you aware that you've talked about nothing but yourself?

YVAN: Well, who are you talking about? Everybody talks about themselves!

SERGE: You fuck up our evening, you . . .

YVAN: I fuck up your evening? . . .

SERGE: Yes.

YVAN: I fuck up your evening?! I?! I fuck up your evening?!

MARC: All right, don't get excited!

YVAN: You're saying it's me who's fucked up your evening?! . . .

SERGE: How many more times are you going to say it?

YVAN: Just answer the question, are you saying it's me who's fucked up your evening?! . . .

MARC: You arrive three-quarters of an hour late, you don't apologize, you deluge us with your domestic woes. . . .

SERGE: And your inertia, your sheer neutral spectator's inertia has lured Marc and me into the worst excesses.

YVAN: You as well! You're starting as well?

SERGE: Yes, because on this subject I'm entirely in agreement with him. You create the conditions of conflict.

MARC: You've been piping up with this finicky, subservient voice of reason ever since you arrived, it's intolerable.

YVAN: You know I could burst into tears. . . . I could start crying right now. . . . I'm very close to tears.

MARC: Cry.

SERGE: Cry.

YVAN: Cry! You're telling me to cry!

MARC: You've every reason to cry, you're marrying a gorgon, you're losing your two best friends. . . .

YVAN: That's it then, is it, it's all over!

MARC: You said it yourself, what's the point of seeing each other, if we hate each other?

YVAN: What about my wedding?! You're my witnesses, remember?
SERGE: Find someone else.
YVAN: I can't! You're on the invitation!
MARC: You can choose someone else at the last minute.
YVAN: You're not allowed to!
SERGE: Of course you are!
YVAN: You're not! . . .
MARC: Don't panic, we'll come.
SERGE: But what you ought to do is cancel the wedding.
MARC: He's right.
YVAN: Oh, shit! What have I ever done to you? Shit!

(*He bursts into tears.*)
 (*Time passes.*)

It's brutal what you're doing! You could have had your fight after the 12th, but no, you're determined to ruin my wedding, a wedding which is already a catastrophe, which has made me lose half a stone and now you're completely buggering it up! The only two people whose presence guaranteed some spark of satisfaction are determined to destroy one another, just my luck! . . . (*To Marc.*) You think I like packs of filofax paper or rolls of sellotape, you think any normal man wakes up one day desperate to sell expandable document wallets? . . . What am I supposed to do? I pissed around for forty years, I made you laugh, oh, yes, wonderful, I made all my friends laugh their heads off playing the fool, but come the evening, who was left solitary as a rat? Who crawled back into his hole every evening all on his own? This buffoon, dying of loneliness, who'd switch on anything that talks and who does he find on the answering machine? His mother. His mother. And his mother.

(*A short silence.*)

MARC: Don't get yourself in such a state.
YVAN: Don't get yourself in such a state! Who got me in this state in the first place? Look at me — I don't have your refined sensibilities. I'm a lightweight. I have no opinions.
MARC: Calm down. . . .
YVAN: Don't tell me to calm down! What possible reason do I have to calm down, are you trying to drive me demented, telling me to calm down? Calm down's the worst thing you can say to someone who's lost his calm! I'm not like you, I don't want to be an authority figure, I don't want to be a point of reference, I don't want to be self-sufficient, I just want to be your friend Yvan the joker! Yvan the joker!

(*Silence.*)

SERGE: Could we try to steer clear of pathos? . . .
YVAN: I've finished.
Haven't you got any nibbles? Anything, just to stop from passing out.
SERGE: I have some olives.
YVAN: Hand them over.

(*Serge reaches for a little bowl of olives and hands it to him.*)

SERGE (*to Marc*): Want some?

(*Marc nods. Yvan hands him the bowl. They eat olives.*)

YVAN: Is there somewhere to put the . . .
SERGE: Yes.

(*He fetches a saucer and puts it on the table. Pause.*)

YVAN (*still eating olives*): . . . To think we've reached these extremes. . . . Apocalypse because of a white square. . . .
SERGE: It is not white.
YVAN: A piece of white shit! . . .

(*He's seized by uncontrollable laughter.*)

That's what it is, a piece of white shit! . . . Let's face it, mate. . . . What you've bought is insane! . . .

(*Marc laughs, caught up by Yvan's extravagance. Serge leaves the room. He returns immediately with the Antrios.*)

SERGE: Do you have one of your famous felt-tips? . . .
YVAN: What for? . . . You're not going to draw on the painting.
SERGE: Do you or don't you?
YVAN: Just a minute. . . . (*He goes through the pockets of his jacket.*) Yes. . . . A blue one. . . .
SERGE: Give it to me.

(*Yvan hands the felt-tip to Serge.*)
 (*Serge takes the felt-tip, pulls the top off it, examines the tip for a moment, puts the top back on.*)
 (*He looks up at Marc and throws him the felt-tip. Marc catches it.*)
 (*Slight pause.*)

(*To Marc.*) Go on.

(*Silence.*)

Go on!

(*Marc approaches the painting. . . .
He looks at Serge. . . .
Then he takes the top off the felt-tip.*)

YVAN: You're not going to do it! . . .

(*Marc is looking at Serge.*)

SERGE: Come on.
YVAN: You're raving mad, both of you!

(*Marc leans towards the painting.
Under Yvan's horrified gaze, he draws the felt-tip along one of the diagonal scars. Serge remains impassive.
Then, carefully, on this slope, Marc draws a little skier with a woolly hat.
When he's finished, he straightens up and contemplates his work.*)
 (*Serge remains adamantine.*)
 (*Yvan is as if turned to stone.*)
 (*Silence.*)

SERGE: Well, I'm starving.
Shall we eat?

(*Marc tries a smile. He puts the top back on and play-fully throws the pen to Yvan, who catches it.*)

(*At Serge's.*)

(*At the back, hanging on the wall, the Antrios. Stand-ing in front of the canvas, Marc is holding a basin of water, into which Serge is dipping a little piece of cloth. Marc has rolled up his sleeves and Serge is wearing a little builder's apron which is too short for him. Round about are various cleaning products, bottles of white spirit and stain remover, rags and sponges. Moving very delicately, Serge puts the finishing touch to the cleaning of the painting.*)

(*The Antrios is as white as ever. Marc puts down the basin and looks at the painting. Serge turns to Yvan, who's sitting off to one side. Yvan nods approvingly. Serge steps back and contemplates the picture in his turn.*)

(*Silence.*)

YVAN (*as if alone, speaking in a slightly muffled voice*): . . . The day after the wedding, at the Mont-parnasse cemetery, Catherine put her wedding bou-quet and a little bag of sugared almonds on her mother's grave. I slipped away to cry behind a monument and in the evening, thinking again about this touching tribute, I started silently sobbing in my bed. I absolutely must speak to Finkelzohn about my tendency to cry, I cry all the time, it's not normal for someone my age. It started, or at least clearly revealed itself at Serge's, the evening of the white painting. After Serge, in an act of pure madness, had demonstrated to Marc that he cared more about him than he did about his painting, we went and had dinner, chez Emile. Over dinner, Serge and Marc took the decision to try to rebuild a relationship destroyed by word and deed. At a certain moment, one of them used the expression "trial period" and I burst into tears.
This expression, "trial period," applied to our

friendship, set off in me an uncontrollable and ridicu-lous convulsion.
In fact I can no longer bear any kind of rational argument, nothing formative in the world, nothing great or beautiful in the world has ever been born of rational argument.

(*Pause.*)

(*Serge dries his hands. He goes to empty the basin of water then puts away all the cleaning products, until there's no sign left of domestic activity. Once again he looks at his painting. Then he turns and advances towards the audience.*)

SERGE: When Marc and I succeeded in obliterating the skier, with the aid of Swiss soap with added ox gall, recommended by Paula, I looked at the Antrios and turned to Marc:
"Did you know ink from felt-tips was washable?"
"No," Marc said. . . ."No . . . did you?"
"No," I said, very fast, lying. I came within an inch of saying, yes, I did know. But how could I have launched our trial period with such a disappointing admission? . . . On the other hand, was it right to start with a lie? . . . A lie! Let's be reasonable. Why am I so absurdly virtuous? Why does my relationship with Marc have to be so complicated? . . .

(*Gradually, the light begins to narrow down on the Antrios. Marc approaches the painting.*)

MARC: Under the white clouds, the snow is falling.
You can't see the white clouds, or the snow.
Or the cold, or the white glow of the earth.
A solitary man glides downhill on his skis.
The snow is falling.
It falls until the man disappears back into the landscape.
My friend Serge, who's one of my oldest friends, has bought a painting.
It's a canvas about five foot by four.
It represents a man who moves across a space and disappears.

COMMENTARY

Louis Menand (b. 1952)

WHAT IS "ART"?   1998

Yasmina Reza's play is not really about art in the sense that Louis Menand considers in this discussion of the play and of modern avant-garde art. However, for those in the audience concerned about matters aesthetic and haunted by the issues that center on an abstract white-on-white painting, Menand's commentary is extremely useful. He examines the issues in the play in the context of modern art.

Yasmina Reza's one-act play *"Art,"* which opens here this winter, is about a white-on-white abstract painting that nearly ruins a friendship among three men. A character named Serge buys the painting for an extravagant sum; his friend Marc, invited to admire the new purchase, pronounces it "shit"; the third friend, Yvan, who has no aesthetic views (or is happy to see equal merit in both views), is made wretched by the subsequent bickering, to which most of the play's ninety minutes are devoted.

By far the most interesting thing about *"Art"* is its popularity. It premiered in Berlin and in 1994 opened in Paris, where it ran for eighteen months at the Comédie des Champs-Élysées and won the Molière Award for best play, best production, and best author. Sean Connery's wife, Micheline, saw the French production and persuaded her husband to bring the play to London, where, with Connery as coproducer, in a translation by Christopher Hampton, and starring Albert Finney and Tom Courtenay, it opened in 1996 and was a big hit all over again.

As the quotation marks in the title signal, the play basically sides with Marc, the character who thinks that his friend's notion of "art" is ridiculous. Still, it suggests, Marc is taking his outrage a shade too seriously, since, as phony as the painting probably is, there's no point in spoiling a friendship over it. This is evidently a view that suits the audience that has made *"Art"* an international success. When I saw the play in London last fall, the audience laughed earnestly at every one of Marc's rather blunt and obvious gibes but gasped in horror when, toward the end of the play, he defaced the painting with a felt-tip pen. They agreed that the canvas had no aesthetic merit, but they felt that its market value ought to be respected.

What's odd about the play is the notion that a white-on-white canvas represents the latest refinement in avant-garde pretension. White-on-white canvases were the latest refinement in avant-garde pretension forty years ago. And monochrome art didn't represent a sneer at aesthetic values. It represented the culmination of aestheticism, the final distillation of the idea of painting as painting. The fictional Serge has invested in one of the prime artifacts of an era that the real-life, present-day avant-garde is in boisterous reaction against. The tacky "representational" landscape that hangs in Marc's living room is a lot more plausibly postmodern than his friend's Greenbergian antique.

What does seem right about *"Art,"* though, is how inarticulate the characters become when they attempt to justify their reactions to Serge's painting ("shit" is perhaps not the critical *mot juste* for an all-white canvas) and how quickly the disagreement turns personal. This is, at bottom, what the audiences are probably responding to. They've been in these situations themselves, and, although the relationships in the play are not very convincing — it's hard to understand how these three guys ever got to be friends in the first place, so the damage to their friendship is somewhat lacking in poignancy — the spectacle of a disagreement about art devolving into a bitter spat about personalities carries a certain low-level shock of recognition.

The incoherence and inconclusiveness of the aesthetic arguments in *"Art"* strike a chord because people have lost any clear sense of what a coherent and conclusive aesthetic argument would look like. This is not the result of dumbing down; it's the result of smartening up. It derives from the view that aesthetic arguments are really only ex-post-facto justifications for art that people happen to like, and this seems to have become the advanced view on the subject.

Last fall when the *Times* asked seventeen "art-world participants and observers" the question "What is art?," all the experts gave the same answer. They said that the question has no answer. The art historians Thomas McEvilley ("It seems pretty clear by now that more or less anything can be designated as art") and Robert Rosenblum ("By now the idea of defining art is so remote I don't think anyone would dare to do it"), William Rubin, of the Museum of Modern Art ("There is no single definition of art"), Philippe de Montebello, of the Metropolitan Museum of Art ("There's no consensus about anything today"), Arthur Danto, a philosopher and the art critic of *The Nation* ("You can't say something's art or not art anymore. That's all finished"), and Peter Hoekstra, a Republican congressman from Michigan, who is a leading opponent of the National Endowment for the Arts ("Art is whatever people want to perceive it to be"), all agreed. There can be no definition of art because art is just whatever people say it is.

The triumph of the consensus of no consensus should be gratifying to Arthur Danto, who has been trying since 1984 to explain why it is no longer possible, by referring to the way it looks, to distinguish something that is a work of art from something that is not. His argument, eloquently summed up in his most recent book, *After the End of Art,* is that after Andy Warhol exhibited simulacra of Brillo boxes (actually of shipping cartons for Brillo boxes), in 1964, anything could be art. With *Brillo Box,* the history of art came to an end. There was no longer a master narrative dictating what form works of art should take next, since having a particular form no longer determined whether a thing was a work of art.

People in London who last fall walked from the theater where *"Art"* was playing across Piccadilly Circus to the Royal Academy of Arts could see realized, in an exhibition, from the Saatchi Collection, called "Sensation," the polymorphous vision that must have been dancing in Danto's head when he introduced his theory back in 1984: snapshots, videos, abstract paintings, figurative paintings, found objects, installations, and the dead animals of Damien Hirst. A characteristic piece — *Self,* by Marc Quinn — is listed in the catalogue as having been rendered in the following media: blood, stainless steel, Perspex, and refrigeration equipment. Chris Ofili's works on linen were executed in oil paint, polyester resin, map pins, and elephant dung. If Serge had a Lucite box containing the head of a cow crawling with maggots on display in his living room (which is the substance of a piece by Hirst entitled *A Thousand Years*), *"Art"* would seem a lot more up to date.

Danto still believes that art has essential qualities; he just doesn't think that those qualities reside in its appearance. But it's easy to slip from the recognition that anything could be art to the position that art is an arbitrary category: Danto calls his conception of posthistorical art "pluralist," meaning that all forms of expression are now permitted; and one reason so many of the people in the *Times* survey echo his view is that pluralism is the ascendant philosophy of the day. Nobody wants to get caught asserting that one type of art is inherently better than another — not even Congressman Hoekstra. Pluralist talk about tastes and values is everywhere. The belief that we should never fall into the grip of a single belief has us firmly in its grip.

Pluralism is an admirable point of view, but it wouldn't be much use if it prevented people from judging anything. The way to do the right pluralist thing today, therefore, seems to involve the following decorum: you do not criticize someone else's tastes or values by saying they are inferior, perverted, uncivilized, or "not art." That kind of talk is invidious, and suggests that you are applying standards you imagine to be impersonal. Instead, you say, "I don't happen to like it," and you are absolved of chauvinism. You are also absolved of attending to any reasons you should like it. When liking is all, disliking is enough.

If you are a pro-arts person, of course, you're supposed to keep your dislikes to yourself (which is why the audience for *"Art"* disapproves of Marc's antics, even though they sympathize with his exasperation). One of the pieces in the "Sensation" exhibition in London was a large clock — *A Bigger Clock,* by Darren Almond. Every sixty seconds, it emitted a tremendous reverberating noise, like the amplified sound of a prison door slamming shut. The piece was mounted in the lobby, where the tickets and the catalogues were sold. I bought my catalogue from a young guy who looked like the kind of fairly hip young guy you would expect to find selling catalogues in a gallery. I asked him if listening to this amplified sound of a prison door slamming shut every sixty seconds all day might possibly get a little — well, old. He gave me a look that said, "If I could get my hands on the guy who made that thing, I would personally strangle the bastard." But all he actually said was "A little."

In dispensing with a single definition of art, we are liberating ourselves less completely than we imagine. The regime of "no definition" is just as dictatorial as every previous regime. A pluralist consensus demands a pluralist art. When the official art-world position is that art can look like anything, you get the kind of art on display in the "Sensation" show — that is, art that looks the way art would look if art could look like anything. As long as "art" is a term that confers value on an object (and there's no reason to have the term at all if it doesn't), people will mean something by it, whether or not they are willing to say so to the *Times*. There is no exit from concepts.

For the artists themselves, philosophical definitions are usually secondary anyway. As easily persuaded of his own significance as he was, Warhol probably didn't think he was bringing the history of art to an end. He had a much more parochial ambition in mind: he wanted to succeed Jackson Pollock as the American art king. *POPism,* his brilliantly catty memoir of the demise of the genius-driven, Abstract Expressionist, macho New York art world of the fifties, has a story that's so close to the story of *"Art"* it's hard to believe Reza doesn't know it. One day around 1960, Warhol drops in on his friend Emile de Antonio, who owns one of Frank Stella's early black paintings, and finds him distraught. A neighbor had seen the Stella on the wall, de Antonio recounts, and asked what it was. When he told her it was a painting, she burst out laughing: *That* was a painting? And she walked over and poured a bottle of whiskey on it, completely ruining it. Just then, the phone rings and, coincidentally, it's Stella. De Antonio describes ruefully what has just happened to his painting. Stella tells him not to worry. He'll make him another one just like it.

Martin McDonagh

Martin McDonagh (b. 1970) is something of a marvel in contemporary theater. He left school at age sixteen and spent five years writing radio scripts and collecting rejection notices until two scripts were taken by stations in Australia. He spent eight days writing his first play, *The Beauty Queen of Leenane* (1996). By the time that play was first produced in London in 1997, McDonagh was twenty-seven and had four plays showing simultaneously in London. This is something few if any writers his age have accomplished. Moreover, while all his plays have been set in the west of Ireland, he has spent summers but never lived there. He and his brother were born in Camberwell, London, but his parents, who are from Galway, returned to Ireland and left Martin and his brother to live in the London flat.

McDonagh watched a great deal of television and watched a good many movies while he was beginning to write. He found himself essentially bored by theater in London — calling it "dull." His favorite play is said to be David Mamet's short excursion into the world of petty thieves called *American Buffalo*. After that, he claims to have been influenced by the films of David Lynch, Martin Scorsese, Terence Malick, and Quentin Tarentino.

Judging from the plays he has written, this training was exactly right for him. He does not claim much knowledge of classic English or Irish plays, although he has been frequently compared with John Millington Synge and Sean O'Casey, two of the most renowned Irish playwrights of the twentieth century. His use of language in *Beauty Queen* and related plays is very much in the same vein as the language that Synge created for *The Playboy of the Western World* and his other "peasant dramas." Like Synge, McDonagh did not live in the west but as a visitor listened to the daily speech of people remote from the city.

The Beauty Queen of Leenane is the first play in a trilogy of plays set in Leenane, a remote small town in Connemara, County Galway, north of the Aran Islands, where some of the people still speak Irish. The second play is *A Skull in Connemara* (1997), a dark play about Mick and his sidekick Mairtin, who have the contract from Father Welsh to dig up the graveyard to make room for new burials. Mick hesitates when he reaches the area in which his wife is buried, and Mairtin thinks the hesitation results from the fact that Mick killed his wife. Mick spent time in prison for his drinking and driving that caused the accident that killed his wife. It turns out the coffin is empty and Mairtin unknowingly reveals that he and a local policeman stole the corpse for the jewelry it wore. Mick tries to kill Mairtin but fails. The play is a brooding, dark play about death and guilt.

The last play in the trilogy, *The Lonesome West* (1997), also set in Leenane, examines the emotions between two brothers, Coleman and Valene. After Coleman kills their father with a shotgun, he convinces Valene to stand by him and claim that the shooting was an accident. In return, Valene demands everything they and their father owned. Father Welsh appears. He is an alcoholic but is able to bring a kind of peace between the two brothers, in part by helping them contemplate the power of forgiveness. Father Welsh, however, dies a suicide. Coleman and Valene manage to get along with one another because Welsh has told them he will go to hell if they hurt each other and to heaven if they refrain from fighting, but the play ends with the brothers violently threatening each other.

McDonagh has developed yet another trilogy, this time set on the Aran Islands. In the first play, *The Cripple of Inishmaan* (1996), Cripple Billy claims he has tuberculosis to meet Robert Flaherty, the filmmaker who is making the documentary film *Man of Aran* (1934). Cripple Billy goes to Hollywood but returns to Inishmaan because he cannot tolerate the stupid lines he is given to say in American films. At that point he learns he really does have tuberculosis and contemplates an early death. The other two plays in this trilogy are *The Lieutenant of Inishmore* and *The Banshees of Inisheer*. When asked whether he will always explore despair and violence in his plays, McDonagh has said that someday "I'll write a romantic comedy where hardly anyone gets murdered at all."

THE BEAUTY QUEEN OF LEENANE

The setting and situation of *The Beauty Queen of Leenane* (1996) harken back to a time when Irish country women held their children in an iron grip. Mag, the vindictive, grasping seventy-year-old mother of the play, will not let her forty-year-old daughter Maureen Folan from her grasp. They live in a damp, claustrophobic house with never-ending rain beating against the windows. There is no love lost between mother and daughter. Mag criticizes and complains, constantly demanding a cup of Complan, a warm drink. When Pato Dooley, a laborer back for a visit from London, tells Maureen that he thinks of her as the beauty queen of Leenane, Maureen begins to see an opportunity to leave Leenane with Pato. The tension that arises in the play from this situation is heightened by the fact that people do not talk directly to the subject, but discuss everyday things, gossip, and unrelated issues. Soon Maureen realizes that she must act if she is to make Pato understand her need, and in a remarkable scene of sexual tension, she invites his physical advances in such a way that he cannot misunderstand. Yet somehow he continues to be naive and unaware.

In a moment of dramatic crisis, Pato sends his brother Ray a letter to deliver to Maureen inviting her to come with him to Boston and put her mother in a home in Oughterard, not far from Leenane. The tension that surrounds the scene in which Ray visits with Mag, waiting for Maureen to return, is so great that some audiences have called out warnings to the actors much the way early moviegoers called out to screen heroes to beware of the villain sneaking up behind them.

The portrayal of character in the play dramatizes the darkest and most painful aspects of life in the west of Ireland, especially during the first decades of the twentieth century. Other writers, from George Moore (1852–1933) to John Millington Synge, have also portrayed the violence and despair of the west in similar ways. But the dramatic approach that McDonagh uses differs from that of Synge in that he employs some techniques of melodrama, such as letting the audience guess the action at crucial moments and delaying resolution of tension until audience members find it almost impossible not to cry out. Irish drama, especially of the late nineteenth century, has a considerable melodramatic tradition. McDonagh relies on it in this play more than others, to the extent that the level of audience involvement is unusual for serious modern drama.

The Beauty Queen of Leenane in Performance

The setting of the play is the interior of Mag Folan's cottage — simple, rustic, and inadequate. The rain outside the window virtually closets the inhabitants in a tiny space, and the sense of boundedness communicates itself to the audience. The costumes are country style — plain, worn, unattractive. The shadowy lighting also communicates a sense of darkness and depression associated with long winter nights. All this was developed for the earliest production by the Druid Theater Company in Galway, where the play premiered in the 400-seat theater in Town Hall in February 1996. Later that month the play moved to the Royal Court Theatre in London — first to its forty-seat stage and soon to its 586-seat main stage in July 1997. In September 1997, it moved to New York to the Atlantic Theater off-Broadway, and finally in April 1998 it opened on Broadway with its original Irish cast in the Walter Kerr Theatre. It won numerous prizes both in London and New York, including awards for best play.

Martin McDonagh (b. 1970)

THE BEAUTY QUEEN OF LEENANE

1996

Characters

MAUREEN FOLAN, *aged forty. Plain, slim.*
MAG FOLAN, *her mother, aged seventy. Stout, frail.*
PATO DOOLEY, *a good-looking local man, aged about forty.*
RAY DOOLEY, *his brother, aged twenty.*

Setting: *Leenane, a small town in Connemara, County Galway.*

SCENE ONE

(*The living-room/kitchen of a rural cottage in the west of Ireland. Front door stage left, a long black range along the back wall with a box of turf beside it and a rocking-chair on its right. On the kitchen side of the set is a door in the back wall leading off to an unseen hallway, and a newer oven, a sink, and some cupboards curving around the right wall. There is a window with an inner ledge above the sink in the right wall looking out onto fields, a dinner table with two chairs just right of center, a small TV down left, an electric kettle and a radio on one of the kitchen cupboards, a crucifix and a framed picture of John and Robert Kennedy on the wall above the range, a heavy black poker beside the range, and a touristy-looking embroidered tea-towel hanging further along the back wall, bearing the inscription "May you be half an hour in Heaven afore the Devil knows you're dead." As the play begins it is raining quite heavily. Mag Folan, a stoutish woman in her early seventies with short, tightly permed grey hair and a mouth that gapes slightly, is sitting in the rocking-chair, staring off into space. Her left hand is somewhat more shriveled and red than her right. The front door opens and her daughter, Maureen, a plain, slim woman of forty, enters carrying shopping and goes through to the kitchen.)*

MAG: Wet, Maureen?
MAUREEN: Of course wet.
MAG: Oh-h.

(Maureen takes her coat off, sighing, and starts putting the shopping away.)

MAG: I did take me Complan.°
MAUREEN: So you *can* get it yourself so.
MAG: I can. (*Pause.*) Although lumpy it was, Maureen.
MAUREEN: Well, can I help lumpy?
MAG: No.
MAUREEN: Write to the Complan people so, if it's lumpy.
MAG (*pause*): You do make me Complan nice and smooth. (*Pause.*) Not a lump at all, nor the comrade of a lump.
MAUREEN: You don't give it a good enough stir is what you don't do.
MAG: I gave it a good enough stir and there was still lumps.
MAUREEN: You probably pour the water in too fast so. What it says on the box, you're supposed to ease it in.
MAG: Mm.
MAUREEN: That's where you do go wrong. Have another go tonight for yourself and you'll see.
MAG: Mm. (*Pause.*) And the hot water too I do be scared of. Scared I may scould° meself.

(Maureen gives her a slight look.)

MAG: I *do* be scared, Maureen. I be scared what if me hand shook and I was to pour it over me hand. And with you at Mary Pender's, then where would I be?
MAUREEN: You're just a hypochondriac is what you are.
MAG: I'd be lying on the floor and I'm not a hypochondriac.
MAUREEN: You are too and everybody knows that you are. Full well.

Complan: A liquid, milk-based nutritional supplement.
scould: Scald.

MAG: Don't I have a urine infection if I'm such a hypochondriac?
MAUREEN: I can't see how a urine infection prevents you pouring a mug of Complan or tidying up the house a bit when I'm away. It wouldn't kill you.
MAG (*pause*): Me bad back.
MAUREEN: Your bad back.
MAG: And me bad hand. (*Mag holds up her shriveled hand for a second.*)
MAUREEN (*quietly*): Feck . . . (*Irritated.*) I'll get your Complan so if it's such a big job! From now and 'til doomsday! The one thing I ask you to do. Do you see Annette or Margo coming pouring your Complan or buying your oul cod in butter sauce for the week?
MAG: No.
MAUREEN: No is right, you don't. And carrying it up that hill. And still I'm not appreciated.
MAG: You *are* appreciated, Maureen.
MAUREEN: I'm not appreciated.
MAG: I'll give me Complan another go so, and give it a good stir for meself.
MAUREEN: Ah, forget your Complan. I'm expected to do everything else, I suppose that one on top of it won't hurt. Just a . . . just a blessed fecking skivvy is all I'm thought of!
MAG: You're not, Maureen.

(Maureen slams a couple of cupboard doors after finishing with the shopping and sits at the table, after dragging its chair back loudly. Pause.)

MAG: Me porridge, Maureen, I haven't had, will you be getting? No, in a minute, Maureen, have a rest for yourself. . . .

(But Maureen has already jumped up, stomped angrily back to the kitchen and started preparing the porridge as noisily as she can. Pause.)

MAG: Will we have the radio on for ourselves?

(Maureen bangs an angry finger at the radio's "on" switch. It takes a couple of swipes before it comes on loudly, through static — a nasally voice singing in Gaelic. Pause.)

MAG: The dedication Annette and Margo sent we still haven't heard. I wonder what's keeping it?
MAUREEN: If they sent a dedication at all. They only said they did. (*Maureen sniffs the sink a little, then turns to Mag.*) Is there a smell off this sink now, I'm wondering.
MAG (*defensively*): No.
MAUREEN: I hope there's not, now.
MAG: No smell at all is there, Maureen. I do promise, now.

(Maureen returns to the porridge. Pause.)

MAG: Is the radio a biteen loud there, Maureen?
MAUREEN: A biteen loud, is it?

(Maureen swipes angrily at the radio again, turning it off. Pause.)

MAG: Nothing on it, anyways. An oul fella singing nonsense.

MAUREEN: Isn't it you wanted it set for that oul station?

MAG: Only for Ceilidh Time and for whatyoucall.

MAUREEN: It's too late to go complaining now.

MAG: Not for nonsense did I want it set.

MAUREEN (*pause*): It isn't nonsense anyways. Isn't it Irish?

MAG: It sounds like nonsense to me. Why can't they just speak English like everybody?

MAUREEN: Why should they speak English?

MAG: To know what they're saying.

MAUREEN: What country are you living in?

MAG: Eh?

MAUREEN: What country are you living in?

MAG: Galway.

MAUREEN: Not what county!

MAG: Oh-h. . . .

MAUREEN: Ireland you're living in!

MAG: *Ireland.*

MAUREEN: So why should you be speaking English in Ireland?

MAG: I don't know why.

MAUREEN: It's Irish you should be speaking in Ireland.

MAG: It is.

MAUREEN: Eh?

MAG: Eh?

MAUREEN: "Speaking English in Ireland."

MAG (*pause*): Except where would Irish get you going for a job in England? Nowhere.

MAUREEN: If it wasn't for the English stealing our language, and our land, and our God-knows-what, wouldn't it be we wouldn't need to go over there begging for jobs and for handouts?

MAG: I suppose that's the crux of the matter.

MAUREEN: It *is* the crux of the matter.

MAG (*pause*): Except America, too.

MAUREEN: What except America too?

MAG: If it was to America you had to go begging for handouts, it isn't Irish would be any good to you. It would be English!

MAUREEN: Isn't that the same crux of the same matter?

MAG: I don't know if it is or it isn't.

MAUREEN: Bringing up kids to think all they'll ever be good for is begging handouts from the English and the Yanks. That's the selfsame crux.

MAG: I suppose.

MAUREEN: Of course you suppose, because it's true.

MAG (*pause*): If I had to go begging for handouts anywhere, I'd rather beg for them in America than in England, because in America it does be more sunny anyways. (*Pause.*) Or is that just something they say, that the weather is more sunny, Maureen? Or is that a lie, now?

(*Maureen slops the porridge out and hands it to Mag, speaking as she does so.*)

MAUREEN: You're oul and you're stupid and you don't know what you're talking about. Now shut up and eat your oul porridge.

(*Maureen goes back to wash the pan in the sink. Mag glances at the porridge, then turns back to her.*)

MAG: Me mug of tea you forgot!

(*Maureen clutches the edges of the sink and lowers her head, exasperated, then quietly, with visible self-control, fills the kettle to make her mother's tea. Pause. Mag speaks while slowly eating.*)

MAG: Did you meet anybody on your travels, Maureen? (*No response.*) Ah no, not on a day like today. (*Pause.*) Although you don't say hello to people is your trouble, Maureen. (*Pause.*) Although some people it would be better not to say hello to. The fella up and murdered the poor oul woman in Dublin and he didn't even know her. The news that story was on, did you hear of it? (*Pause.*) Strangled, and didn't even know her. That's a fella it would be better not to talk to. That's a fella it would be better to avoid outright.

(*Maureen brings Mag her tea, then sits at the table.*)

MAUREEN: Sure, that sounds exactly the type of fella I would *like* to meet, and then bring him home to meet you, if he likes murdering oul women.

MAG: That's not a nice thing to say, Maureen.

MAUREEN: Is it not, now?

MAG (*pause*): Sure why would he be coming all this way out from Dublin? He'd just be going out of his way.

MAUREEN: For the pleasure of me company he'd come. Killing you, it'd just be a bonus for him.

MAG: Killing *you* I bet he first would be.

MAUREEN: I could live with that so long as I was sure he'd be clobbering you soon after. If he clobbered you with a big axe or something and took your oul head off and spat in your neck, I wouldn't mind at all, going first. Oh no, I'd enjoy it, I would. No more oul Complan to get, and no more oul porridge to get, and no more. . . .

MAG (*interrupting, holding her tea out*): No sugar in this, Maureen, you forgot, go and get me some.

(*Maureen stares at her a moment, then takes the tea, brings it to the sink and pours it away, goes back to Mag, grabs her half-eaten porridge, returns to the kitchen, scrapes it out into the bin, leaves the bowl in the sink, and exits into the hallway, giving Mag a dirty look on the way and closing the door behind her. Mag stares grumpily out into space. Blackout.*)

SCENE TWO

(*Mag is sitting at the table, staring at her reflection in a hand-mirror. She pats her hair a couple of times. The TV is on, showing an old episode of The Sullivans. There is a knock at the front door, which startles her slightly.*)

MAG: Who. . . . ? Maureen. Oh-h. The door, Maureen.

(*Mag gets up and shuffles towards the kitchen window. There is another knock. She shuffles back to the door.*)

Who's at the door?

RAY (*off*): It's Ray Dooley, Mrs. From over the way.

MAG: Dooley?

RAY: Ray Dooley, aye. You know me.

MAG: Are you one of the Dooleys so?

RAY: I am. I'm Ray.

MAG: Oh-h.

RAY (*pause, irritated*): Well, will you let me in or am I going to talk to the door?

MAG: She's feeding the chickens. (*Pause.*) Have you gone?

RAY (*angrily*): Open the oul door, Mrs! Haven't I walked a mile out of me way just to get here?

MAG: Have you?

RAY: I have. "Have you?" she says.

(*Mag unlatches the door with some difficulty and Ray Dooley, a lad of about twenty, enters.*)

Thank you! An hour I thought you'd be keeping me waiting.

MAG: Oh, it's you, so it is.

RAY: Of course it's me. Who else?

MAG: You're the Dooley with the uncle.

RAY: It's only a million times you've seen me the past twenty year. Aye, I'm the Dooley with the uncle, and it's me uncle the message is.

(*Ray stops and watches the TV a moment.*)

MAG: Maureen's at the chickens.

RAY: You've said Maureen's at the chickens. What's on the telly?

MAG: I was waiting for the news.

RAY: You'll have a long wait.

MAG: I was combing me hair.

RAY: I think it's *The Sullivans*.

MAG: I don't know what it is.

RAY: You do get a good reception.

MAG: A middling reception.

RAY: Everything's Australian nowadays.

MAG: I don't know if it is or it isn't.

(*Mag sits in the rocking-chair.*)

At the chickens, Maureen is.

RAY: That's three times now you've told me Maureen's at the chickens. Are you going for the world's record in saying "Maureen's at the chickens"?

MAG (*pause, confused*): She's feeding them.

(*Ray stares at her a moment, then sighs and looks out through the kitchen window.*)

RAY: Well, I'm not wading through all that skitter just to tell her. I've done enough wading. Coming up that oul hill.

MAG: It's a big oul hill.

RAY: It *is* a big oul hill.

MAG: Steep.

RAY: Steep is right and if not steep then muddy.

MAG: Muddy and rocky.

RAY: Muddy and rocky is right. Uh-huh. How do ye two manage up it every day?

MAG: We do drive.

RAY: Of course. (*Pause.*) That's what I want to do is drive. I'll have to be getting driving lessons. And a car. (*Pause.*) Not a good one, like. A second-hand one, y'know?

MAG: A used one.

RAY: A used one, aye.

MAG: Off somebody.

RAY: Oul Father Welsh — Walsh — has a car he's selling, but I'd look a poof° buying a car off a priest.

MAG: I don't like Father Walsh — Welsh — at all.

RAY: He punched Mairtin Hanlon in the head once, and for no reason.

MAG: God love us!

RAY: Aye. Although, now, that was out of character for Father Welsh. Father Welsh seldom uses violence, same as most young priests. It's usually only the older priests go punching you in the head. I don't know why. I suppose it's the way they were brought up.

MAG: There was a priest in the news Wednesday had a babby with a Yank!

RAY: That's no news at all. That's everyday. It'd be hard to find a priest who hasn't had a babby with a Yank. If he'd punched that babby in the head, that'd be news. Aye. Anyways. Aye. What was I saying? Oh aye, so if I give you the message, Mrs., you'll be passing it on to Maureen, so you will, or will I be writing it down for you?

MAG: I'll be passing it on.

RAY: Good-oh. Me brother Pato said to invite yous to our uncle's going-away do. The Riordans' hall out in Carraroe.

MAG: Is your brother back so?

RAY: He is.

MAG: Back from England?

RAY: Back from England, aye. England's where he was, so that's where he would be back from. Our Yankee uncle's going home to Boston after his holiday and taking those two ugly duckling daughters back with him and that Dolores whatyoucall, Healey or Hooley, so there'll be a little to-do in the Riordans' as a goodbye or a *big* to-do knowing them show-off bastards and free food anyways, so me brother says ye're welcome to come or Maureen anyways, he knows you don't like getting out much. Isn't it you has the bad hip?

MAG: No.

RAY: Oh. Who is it has the bad hip so?

MAG: I don't know. I do have the urine infection.

RAY: Maybe that's what I was thinking of. And thanks for telling me.

MAG: Me urine.

---

poof: Homosexual (derogatory).

RAY: I know, your urine.

MAG: And me bad back. And me burned hand.

RAY: Aye, aye, aye. Anyways, you'll be passing the message on to that one.

MAG: Eh?

RAY: You'll be remembering the message to pass it on to that one?

MAG: Aye.

RAY: Say it back to me so.

MAG: Say it back to you?

RAY: Aye.

MAG (*long pause*): About me hip . . . ?

RAY (*angrily*): I should've fecking written it down in the first fecking place, I fecking knew! And save all this fecking time!

(*Ray grabs a pen and a piece of paper, sits at the table and writes the message out.*)

Talking with a loon!

MAG (*pause*): Do me a mug of tea while you're here, Pato. Em, Ray.

RAY: *Ray* my fecking name is! Pato's me fecking brother!

MAG: I do forget.

RAY: It's like talking to a . . . talking to a . . .

MAG: Brick wall.

RAY: Brick wall is right.

MAG (*pause*): Or some soup do me.

(*Ray finishes writing and gets up.*)

RAY: There. Forget about soup. The message is there. Point that one in the direction of it when she returns from beyond. The Riordans' hall out in Carraroe. Seven o'clock tomorrow night. Free food. Okay?

MAG: All right now, Ray. Are you still in the choir nowadays, Ray?

RAY: I am *not* in the choir nowadays. Isn't it ten years since I was in the choir?

MAG: Doesn't time be flying?

RAY: Not since I took an interest in girls have I been in the choir because you do get no girls in choirs, only fat girls and what use are they? No. I go to discos, me.

MAG: Good enough for yourself.

RAY: What am I doing standing around here conversing with you? I have left me message and now I am off.

MAG: Goodbye to you, Ray.

RAY: Goodbye to you, Mrs.

MAG: And pull the door.

RAY: I was going to pull the door anyways. . . .

(*Ray pulls the front door shut behind him as he exits.*)

(*Off.*) I don't need your advice!

(*As Ray's footsteps fade, Mag gets up, reads the message on the table, goes to the kitchen window and glances out, then finds a box of matches, comes back to the table, strikes a match, lights the message, goes to the range with it burning and drops it inside. Sound of footsteps approaching the front door. Mag shuffles back to her rocking-chair and sits in it just as Maureen enters.*)

MAG (*nervously*): Cold, Maureen?

MAUREEN: Of course cold.

MAG: Oh-h.

(*Mag stares at the TV as if engrossed. Maureen sniffs the air a little, then sits at the table, staring at Mag.*)

MAUREEN: What are you watching?

MAG: I don't know *what* I'm watching. Just waiting for the news I am.

MAUREEN: Oh aye. (*Pause.*) Nobody rang while I was out, I suppose? Ah no.

MAG: Ah no, Maureen. Nobody did ring.

MAUREEN: Ah no.

MAG: No. Who would be ringing?

MAUREEN: No, nobody I suppose. No. (*Pause.*) And nobody visited us either? Ah no.

MAG: Ah no, Maureen. Who would be visiting us?

MAUREEN: Nobody, I suppose. Ah no.

(*Mag glances at Maureen a second, then back at the TV. Pause. Maureen gets up, ambles over to the TV, lazily switches it off with the toe of her shoe, ambles back to the kitchen, staring at Mag as she passes, turns on the kettle, and leans against the cupboards, looking back in Mag's direction.*)

MAG (*nervously*): Em, apart from wee Ray Dooley who passed.

MAUREEN (*knowing*): Oh, did Ray Dooley pass, now?

MAG: He passed, aye, and said hello as he was passing.

MAUREEN: I thought just now you said there was no visitors.

MAG: There was no visitors, no, apart from Ray Dooley who passed.

MAUREEN: Oh, aye, aye, aye. Just to say hello he popped his head in.

MAG: Just to say hello and how is all. Aye. A nice wee lad he is.

MAUREEN: Aye. (*Pause.*) With no news?

MAG: With no news. Sure, what news would a gasur° have?

MAUREEN: None at all, I suppose. Ah, no.

MAG: Ah, no. (*Pause.*) Thinking of getting a car I think he said he was.

MAUREEN: Oh aye?

MAG: A second-hand one.

MAUREEN: Uh-huh?

MAG: To drive, y'know?

MAUREEN: To drive, aye.

MAG: Off Father Welsh — Walsh — Welsh.

MAUREEN: Welsh.

MAG: Welsh.

(*Maureen switches off the kettle, pours a sachet of Complan into a mug, and fills it up with water.*)

MAUREEN: I'll do you some of your Complan.

MAG: Have I not had me Complan already, Maureen? I have.

gasur: Young man.

MAUREEN: Sure, another one won't hurt.

MAG (*wary*): No, I suppose.

(*Maureen tops the drink up with tap water to cool it, stirs it just twice to keep it lumpy, takes the spoon out, hands the drink to Mag, then leans back against the table to watch her drink it. Mag looks at it in distaste.*)

MAG: A bit lumpy, Maureen.

MAUREEN: Never mind lumpy, Mam. The lumps will do you good. That's the best part of Complan is the lumps. Drink ahead.

MAG: A little spoon, do you have?

MAUREEN: No, I have no little spoon. There's no little spoons for liars in this house. No little spoons at all. Be drinking ahead.

(*Mag takes the smallest of sickly sips.*)

MAUREEN: The whole of it, now!

MAG: I do have a funny tummy, Maureen, and I do have no room.

MAUREEN: Drink ahead, I said! You had room enough to be spouting your lies about Ray Dooley had no message! Did I not meet him on the road beyond as he was going? The lies of you. The whole of that Complan you'll drink now, and suck the lumps down too, and whatever's left you haven't drank, it is over your head I will be emptying it, and you know well enough I mean it!

(*Mag slowly drinks the rest of the sickly brew.*)

MAUREEN: Arsing me around,° eh? Interfering with my life again? Isn't it enough I've had to be on beck and call for you every day for the past twenty years? Is it one evening out you begrudge me?

MAG: Young girls should not be out gallivanting with fellas . . . !

MAUREEN: Young girls! I'm forty years old, for feck's sake! Finish it!

(*Mag drinks again.*)

"Young girls"! That's the best yet. And how did Annette or Marge ever get married if it wasn't first out gallivanting that they were?

MAG: I don't know.

MAUREEN: Drink!

MAG: I don't like it, Maureen.

MAUREEN: Would you like it better over your head?

(*Mag drinks again.*)

MAUREEN: I'll tell you, eh? "Young girls out gallivanting." I've heard it all now. What have I ever done but *kissed* two men the past forty year?

MAG: Two men is plenty!

MAUREEN: Finish!

MAG: I've finished!

Arsing me around: Interfering with me.

(*Mag holds out the mug. Maureen washes it.*)

Two men is two men too much!

MAUREEN: To you, maybe. To you. Not to me.

MAG: Two men too much!

MAUREEN: Do you think I like being stuck up here with you? Eh? Like a dried up oul. . . .

MAG: Whore!

(*Maureen laughs.*)

MAUREEN: "Whore"? (*Pause.*) Do I not *wish*, now? Do I not wish? (*Pause.*) Sometimes I *dream*. . . .

MAG: Of being a . . . ?

MAUREEN: Of anything! (*Pause. Quietly.*) Of anything. Other than this.

MAG: Well an odd dream that is!

MAUREEN: It's not at all. Not at all is it an odd dream. (*Pause.*) And if it is it's not the only odd dream I do have. Do you want to be hearing another one?

MAG: I don't.

MAUREEN: I have a dream sometimes there of you, dressed all nice and white, in your coffin there, and me all in black looking in on you, and a fella beside me there, comforting me, the smell of aftershave off him, his arm round me waist. And the fella asks me then if I'll be going for a drink with him at his place after.

MAG: And what do you say?

MAUREEN: I say "Aye, what's stopping me now?"

MAG: You don't!

MAUREEN: I do!

MAG: At me funeral?

MAUREEN: At your bloody wake, sure! Is even sooner!

MAG: Well that's not a nice thing to be dreaming!

MAUREEN: I know it's not, sure, and it isn't a *dream*-dream at all. It's more of a day-dream. Y'know, something happy to be thinking of when I'm scraping the skitter out of them hens.

MAG: Not at all is that a nice dream. That's a mean dream.

MAUREEN: I don't know if it is or it isn't.

(*Pause. Maureen sits at the table with a pack of Kimberley biscuits.*)

I suppose now you'll never be dying. You'll be hanging on forever, just to spite me.

MAG: I *will* be hanging on forever!

MAUREEN: I know well you will!

MAG: Seventy you'll be at my wake, and then how many men'll there be round your waist with their aftershave?

MAUREEN: None at all, I suppose.

MAG: None at all is right!

MAUREEN: Oh aye. (*Pause.*) Do you want a Kimberley?

MAG (*pause*): Have we no shortbread fingers?

MAUREEN: No, you've ate all the shortbread fingers. Like a pig.

MAG: I'll have a Kimberley so, although I don't like

Kimberleys. I don't know why you get Kimberleys at all. Kimberleys are horrible.

MAUREEN: Me world doesn't revolve around your taste in biscuits.

(*Maureen gives Mag a biscuit. Mag eats.*)

MAG (*pause*): You'll be going to this do tomorrow so?

MAUREEN: I will. (*Pause.*) It'll be good to see Pato again anyways. I didn't even know he was home.

MAG: But it's all them oul Yanks'll be there tomorrow.

MAUREEN: So?

MAG: You said you couldn't stand the Yanks yesterday. The crux of the matter yesterday you said it was.

MAUREEN: Well, I suppose now, Mother, I will have to be changing me mind, but, sure, isn't that a woman's prerogative?

MAG (*quietly*): It's only prerogatives when it suits you.

MAUREEN: Don't go using big words you don't understand, now, Mam.

MAG (*sneers, pause*): This invitation was open to me too, if you'd like to know.

MAUREEN (*half-laughing*): Do you think you'll be coming?

MAG: I won't, I suppose.

MAUREEN: You suppose right enough. Lying the head off you, like the babby of a tinker.

MAG: I was only saying.

MAUREEN: Well, don't be saying. (*Pause.*) I think we might take a drive into Westport later, if it doesn't rain.

MAG (*brighter*): Will we take a drive?

MAUREEN: We could take a little drive for ourselves.

MAG: We could now. It's a while since we did take a nice drive. We could get some shortbread fingers.

MAUREEN: Later on, I'm saying.

MAG: Later on. Not just now.

MAUREEN: Not just now. Sure, you've only just had your Complan now.

(*Mag gives her a dirty look. Pause.*)

MAUREEN: Aye, Westport. Aye. And I think I might pick up a nice little dress for meself while I'm there. For the do tomorrow, y'know?

(*Maureen looks across at Mag, who looks back at her, irritated. Blackout.*)

SCENE THREE

(*Night. Set only just illuminated by the orange coals through the bars of the range. Radio has been left on low in the kitchen. Footsteps and voices of Maureen and Pato are heard outside, both slightly drunk.*)

PATO (*off. Singing*): "The Cadillac stood by the house . . ."

MAUREEN (*off*): Shh, Pato . . .

PATO (*off. Singing quietly*): "And the Yanks they were within." (*Speaking.*) What was it that oul fella used to say, now?

MAUREEN (*off*): What oul fella, now?

(*Maureen opens the door and the two of them enter, turning the lights on. Maureen is in a new black dress, cut quite short. Pato is a good-looking man of about the same age as her.*)

PATO: The oul fella who used to chase oul whatyoucall. Oul Bugs Bunny.

MAUREEN: Would you like a cup of tea, Pato?

PATO: I would.

(*Maureen switches the kettle on.*)

MAUREEN: Except keep your voice down, now.

PATO (*quietly*): I will, I will. (*Pause.*) I can't remember *what* he used to say. The oul fella used to chase Bugs Bunny. It was something, now.

MAUREEN: Look at this. The radio left on too, the daft oul bitch.

PATO: Sure, what harm? No, leave it on, now. It'll cover up the sounds.

MAUREEN: What sounds?

PATO: The smooching sounds.

(*He gently pulls her to him and they kiss a long while, then stop and look at each other. The kettle has boiled. Maureen gently breaks away, smiling, and starts making the tea.*)

MAUREEN: Will you have a biscuit with your tea?

PATO: I will. What biscuits do you have, now?

MAUREEN: Em, only Kimberleys.

PATO: I'll leave it so, Maureen. I do hate Kimberleys. In fact I think Kimberleys are the most horrible biscuits in the world.

MAUREEN: The same as that, I hate Kimberleys. I only get them to torment me mother.

PATO: I can't see why the Kimberley people go making them at all. Coleman Connor ate a whole pack of Kimberleys one time and he was sick for a week. (*Pause.*) Or was it Mikados? It was some kind of horrible biscuits.

MAUREEN: Is it true Coleman cut the ears off Valene's dog and keeps them in his room in a bag?

PATO: He showed me them ears one day.

MAUREEN: That's awful spiteful, cutting the ears off a dog.

PATO: It *is* awful spiteful.

MAUREEN: It would be spiteful enough to cut the ears off anybody's dog, let alone your own brother's dog.

PATO: And it had seemed a nice dog.

MAUREEN: Aye. (*Pause.*) Aye.

(*Awkward pause. Pato cuddles up behind her.*)

PATO: You feel nice to be giving a squeeze to.

MAUREEN: Do I?

PATO: Very nice.

(*Maureen continues making the tea as Pato holds her. A little embarrassed and awkward, he breaks away from her after a second and idles a few feet away.*)

MAUREEN: Be sitting down for yourself, now, Pato.

PATO: I will. (*Sits at table.*) I do do what I'm told, I do.

MAUREEN: Oh-ho, do you now? That's the first time tonight I did notice. Them stray oul hands of yours.

PATO: Sure, I have no control over me hands. They have a mind of their own. (*Pause.*) Except I didn't notice you complaining overmuch anyways, me stray oul hands. Not too many complaints at all!

MAUREEN: I had complaints when they were straying over that Yank girl earlier on in the evening.

PATO: Well, I hadn't noticed you there at that time, Maureen. How was I to know the beauty queen of Leenane was still yet to arrive?

MAUREEN: "The beauty queen of Leenane." Get away with ya!

PATO: Is true!

MAUREEN: Why so have no more than two words passed between us the past twenty year?

PATO: Sure, it's took me all this time to get up the courage.

MAUREEN (*smiling*): Ah, bollocks to ya!

(*Pato smiles. Maureen brings the tea over and sits down.*)

PATO: I don't know, Maureen. I don't know.

MAUREEN: Don't know what?

PATO: Why I never got around to really speaking to you or asking you out or the like. I don't know. Of course, hopping across to that bastarding oul place every couple of months couldn't've helped.

MAUREEN: England? Aye. Do you not like it there so?

PATO (*pause*): It's money. (*Pause.*) And it's Tuesday I'll be back there again.

MAUREEN: Tuesday? This Tuesday?

PATO: Aye. (*Pause.*) It was only to see the Yanks off I was over. To say hello and say goodbye. No time back at all.

MAUREEN: That's Ireland, anyways. There's always someone leaving.

PATO: It's always the way.

MAUREEN: Bad, too.

PATO: What can you do?

MAUREEN: Stay?

PATO (*pause*): I do ask meself, if there was good work in Leenane, would I stay in Leenane? I mean, there never will be good work, but hypothetically, I'm saying. Or even bad work. Any work. And when I'm over there in London and working in rain and it's more or less cattle I am, and the young fellas cursing over cards and drunk and sick, and the oul digs over there, all pee-stained mattresses and nothing to do but watch the clock . . . when it's there I am, it's here I wish I was, of course. Who wouldn't? But when it's here I am . . . it isn't *there* I want to be, of course not. But I know it isn't here I want to be either.

MAUREEN: And why, Pato?

PATO: I can't put my finger on why. (*Pause.*) Of course it's beautiful here, a fool can see. The mountains and the green, and people speak. But when everybody knows everybody else's business . . . I don't know. (*Pause.*) You can't kick a cow in Leenane without some bastard holding a grudge twenty year.

MAUREEN: It's true enough.

PATO: It is. In England they don't care if you live or die, and it's funny but that isn't altogether a bad thing. Ah, sometimes it is . . . ah, I don't know.

MAUREEN (*pause*): Do you think you'll ever settle down in the one place so, Pato? When you get married, I suppose.

PATO (*half-laughing*): "When I get married . . ."

MAUREEN: You will someday, I'll bet you, get married. Wouldn't you want to?

PATO: I can't say it's something I do worry me head over.

MAUREEN: Of course, the rake of women you have stashed all over, you wouldn't need to.

PATO (*smiling*): I have no rake of women.

MAUREEN: You have one or two, I bet.

PATO: I may have one or two. That I know to say hello to, now.

MAUREEN: Hello me . . . A-hole.

PATO: Is true. (*Pause.*) Sure, I'm no . . .

MAUREEN (*pause*): No what?

(*Pause. Pato shrugs and shakes his head, somewhat sadly. Pause. The song "The Spinning Wheel," sung by Delia Murphy, has just started on the radio.*)

MAUREEN (*continued*): Me mother does love this oul song. Oul Delia Murphy.

PATO: This is a creepy oul song.

MAUREEN: It *is* a creepy oul song.

PATO: She does have a creepy oul voice. Always scared me this song did when I was a lad. She's like a ghoul singing. (*Pause.*) Does the grandmother die at the end, now, or is she just sleeping?

MAUREEN: Just sleeping, I think she is.

PATO: Aye . . .

MAUREEN (*pause*): While the two go hand in hand through the fields.

PATO: Aye.

MAUREEN: Be moonlight.

PATO (*nods*): They don't write songs like that any more. Thank Christ.

(*Maureen laughs. Brighter.*)

Wasn't it a grand night though, Maureen, now?

MAUREEN: It was.

PATO: Didn't we send them on their way well?

MAUREEN: We did, we did.

PATO: Not a dry eye.

MAUREEN: Indeed.

PATO: Eh?

MAUREEN: Indeed.

PATO: Aye. That we did. That we did.

MAUREEN (*pause*): So who *was* the Yankee girl you did have your hands all over?

PATO (*laughing*): Oh, will you stop it with your "hands all over"?! Barely touched her, I did.

MAUREEN: Oh-ho!

PATO: A second cousin of me uncle, I think she is. Dolores somebody, Healey or Hooley. Boston, too, she lives.

MAUREEN: That was illegal so if it's your second cousin she is.

PATO: Illegal me arse, and it's not *my* second cousin she is anyway, and what's so illegal? Your second cousin's boobs aren't out of bounds, are they?

MAUREEN: They are!

PATO: I don't know about that. I'll have to consult with me lawyer on that one. I may get arrested the next time. And I have a defense anyways. She had dropped some Taytos on her blouse, there, I was just brushing them off for her.

MAUREEN: Taytos me areshole, Pato Dooley!

PATO: Is true! (*Lustful pause. Nervously.*) Like this is all it was . . .

(*Pato slowly reaches out and gently brushes at, then gradually fondles, Maureen's breasts. She caresses his hand as he's doing so, then slowly gets up and sits across his lap, fondling his head as he continues touching her.*)

MAUREEN: She was prettier than me.

PATO: You're pretty.

MAUREEN: She was prettier.

PATO: I like you.

MAUREEN: You have blue eyes.

PATO: I do.

MAUREEN: Stay with me tonight.

PATO: I don't know, now, Maureen.

MAUREEN: Stay. Just tonight.

PATO (*pause*): Is your mother asleep?

MAUREEN: I don't care if she is or she isn't. (*Pause.*) Go lower.

(*Pato begins easing his hands down her front.*)

MAUREEN: Go lower . . . Lower . . .

(*His hands reach her crotch. She tilts her head back slightly. The song on the radio ends. Blackout.*)

SCENE FOUR

(*Morning. Maureen's black dress is lying across the table. Mag enters from the hall carrying a potty of urine, which she pours out down the sink. She exits into the hall to put the potty away and returns a moment later, wiping her empty hands on the sides of her nightie. She spots the black dress and picks it up disdainfully.*)

MAG: Forty pounds just for that skimpy dress? That dress is just skimpy. And laying it around then?

(*She tosses the dress into a far corner, returns to the kitchen and switches the kettle on, speaking loudly to wake Maureen.*)

I suppose I'll have to be getting me own Complan too, the hour you dragged yourself in whatever time it was with your oul dress. (*Quietly.*) That dress just looks silly. (*Loudly.*) Go the whole hog and wear no dress would be nearer the mark! (*Quietly.*) Snoring the head off you all night. Making an oul woman get her Complan, not to mention her porridge. Well, I won't be getting me own porridge, I'll tell you that now. I'd be afeard. You won't catch me getting me own porridge. Oh no. You won't be catching me out so easily.

(*Pato has just entered from the hall, dressed in trousers and pulling on a shirt.*)

PATO: Good morning there, now, Missus.

(*Mag is startled, staring at Pato dumbfounded.*)

MAG: Good morning there, now.

PATO: Is it porridge you're after?

MAG: It is.

PATO: I'll be getting your porridge for you, so, if you like.

MAG: Oh-h.

PATO: Go ahead and rest yourself.

(*Mag sits in the rocking chair, keeping her eyes on Pato all the while as he prepares her porridge.*)

PATO: It's many the time I did get me brother his porridge of a school morning, so I'm well accustomed. (*Pause.*) You couldn't make it to the oul Yanks' do yesterday so?

MAG: No.

PATO: Your bad hip it was, Maureen was saying.

MAG (*still shocked*): Aye, me bad hip. (*Pause.*) Where's Maureen, now?

PATO: Em, having a lie-in a minute or two, she is. (*Pause.*) To tell you the truth, I was all for. . . . I was all for creeping out before ever you got yourself up, but Maureen said "Aren't we all adults, now? What harm?" I suppose we are, but . . . I don't know. It's still awkward, now, or something. D'you know what I mean? I don't know. (*Pause.*) The Yanks'll be touching down in Boston about now anyways. God willing anyways. Aye. (*Pause.*) A good oul send-off we gave them anyways, we did, to send them off. Aye. (*Pause.*) Not a dry eye. (*Pause.*) Aye. (*Pause.*) Was it a mug of Complan too you wanted?

MAG: It was.

(*Pato fixes her Complan and brings it over.*)

PATO: You like your Complan so.

MAG: I don't.

PATO: Do you not, now?

MAG: She makes me drink it when I don't like it and forces me.

PATO: But Complan's good for you anyways if you're old.

MAG: I suppose it's good for me.

PATO: It is. Isn't it chicken flavor?

Mag (Anna Manahan), Maureen (Marie Mullen), and Pato (Brian F. O'Byrne) in the 1998 New York production of *The Beauty Queen of Leenane*.

MAG: I don't know what flavor.

PATO (*checking box*): Aye, it's chicken flavor. That's the best flavor.

(*Pato returns to the porridge.*)

MAG (*quietly*): With all oul lumps you do make it, never minding flavor. *And* no spoon.

(*Pato gives Mag her porridge and sits at the table.*)

PATO: There you go, now. (*Pause.*) Whatever happened to your hand there, Missus? Red raw, it is.

MAG: Me hand, is it?

PATO: Was it a scould you did get?

MAG: It *was* a scould.

PATO: You have to be careful with scoulds at your age.

MAG: Careful, is it? Uh-huh. . . .

(*Maureen enters from the hall, wearing only a bra and slip, and goes over to Pato.*)

MAUREEN: Careful what? We was careful, weren't we, Pato?

(*Maureen sits across Pato's lap.*)

PATO (*embarrassed*): Maureen, now . . .

MAUREEN: Careful enough, 'cos we don't need any babies coming, do we? We do have enough babies in this house to be going on with.

(*Maureen kisses him at length. Mag watches in disgust.*)

PATO: Maureen, now . . .

MAUREEN: Just thanking you for a wonderful night, I am, Pato. Well worth the wait it was. *Well* worth the wait.

PATO (*embarrassed*): Good-oh.

MAG: Discussing me scoulded hand we was before you breezed in with no clothes!

MAUREEN: Ar, feck your scoulded hand. (*To Pato.*) You'll have to be putting that thing of yours in me again before too long is past, Pato. I do have a taste for it now, I do. . . .

PATO: Maureen . . .

(*She kisses him, gets off, and stares at Mag as she passes into the kitchen.*)

MAUREEN: A mighty oul taste. Uh-huh.

(*Pato gets up and idles around in embarrassment.*)

PATO: Em, I'll have to be off now in a minute anyways. I do have packing to do I do, and whatyoucall . . .

MAG (*pointing at Maureen, loudly*): She's the one that sclouded me hand! I'll tell you that, now! Let alone sitting on stray men! Held it down on the range she did! Poured chip-pan fat o'er it! Aye, and told the doctor it was me!

MAUREEN (*pause, nonplussed, to Pato*): Be having a mug of tea before you go, Pato, now.

PATO (*pause*): Maybe a quick one.

(*Maureen pours out the tea. Mag looks back and forth between the two of them.*)

MAG: Did you not hear what I said?!

MAUREEN: Do you think Pato listens to the smutterings of a senile oul hen?

MAG: Senile, is it? (*She holds up her left hand.*) Don't I have the evidence?

MAUREEN: Come over here a second, Pato. I want you to smell this sink for me.

MAG: Sinks have nothing to do with it!

MAUREEN: Come over here now, Pato.

PATO: Eh?

(*Pato goes into the kitchen.*)

MAUREEN: Smell that sink.

(*Pato leans into the sink, sniffs it, then pulls his head away in disgust.*)

MAG: Nothing to do with it, sinks have!

MAUREEN: Nothing to do with it, is it? Everything to do with it, *I* think it has. Serves as evidence to the character of me accuser, it does.

PATO: What is that, now? The drains?

MAUREEN: Not the drains at all. Not the drains at all. Doesn't she pour a potty of wee away down there every morning, though I tell her seven hundred times the lavvy to use, but oh no.

MAG: Me sclouded hand this conversation was, and not wee at all!

MAUREEN: And doesn't even rinse it either. Now is that hygienic? And she does have a urine infection too, is even less hygienic. I wash me praities° in there. Here's your tea now, Pato.

(*Pato takes his tea, sipping it squeamishly.*)

MAG: Put some clothes on you, going around the house half-naked! Would be more in your line!

MAUREEN: I do like going around the house half-naked. It does turn me on, it does.

MAG: I suppose it does, aye.

MAUREEN: It does.

MAG: And reminds you of Difford Hall in England, too, I'll bet it does. . . .

MAUREEN (*angrily*): Now you just shut your fecking. . . .

MAG: None of your own clothes they let you wear in there either, did they?

MAUREEN: Shut your oul gob, I said . . . !

MAG: Only long oul gowns and buckle-down jackets. . . .

praities: Potatoes.

(*Maureen approaches Mag, fists clenched. Pato catches her arm and steps between the two.*)

PATO: What's the matter with ye two at all, now . . . ?

MAG: Difford Hall! Difford Hall! Difford Hall . . . !

MAUREEN: Difford Hall, uh-huh. And I suppose . . .

MAG: Difford Hall! Difford Hall . . . !

MAUREEN: And I suppose that potty of wee was just a figment of me imagination?

MAG: Forget wee! Forget wee! D'you want to know what Difford Hall is, fella?

MAUREEN: Shut up, now!

MAG: It's a nut-house! An oul nut-house in England I did have to sign her out of and promise to keep her in me care. Would you want to be seeing the papers now?

(*Mag shuffles off to the hall.*)

As proof, like. Or to prove am I just a senile oul hen, like, or *who's* the loopy one? Heh! Pegging wee in me face, oh aye. . . .

(*Quiet pause. Maureen idles over to the table and sits. Pato pours his tea down the sink, rinses his mug, and washes his hands.*)

MAUREEN (*quietly*): It's true I was in a home there a while, now, after a bit of a breakdown I had. Years ago this is.

PATO: What harm a breakdown, sure? Lots of people do have breakdowns.

MAUREEN: A lot of doolally people, aye.

PATO: Not doolally people at all. A lot of well-educated people have breakdowns too. In fact, if you're well-educated it's even more likely. Poor Spike Milligan, isn't he forever having breakdowns? He hardly stops. I do have trouble with me nerves every now and then, too, I don't mind admitting. There's no shame at all in that. Only means you do think about things, and take them to heart.

MAUREEN: No shame in being put in a nut-house a month? Ah no.

PATO: No shame in thinking about things and worrying about things, I'm saying, and "nut-house" is a silly word to be using, and you know that well enough, now, Maureen.

MAUREEN: I do.

(*Pato goes over and sits across the table from her.*)

MAUREEN: In England I was, this happened. Cleaning work. When I was twenty-five. Me first time ever. Me only time ever. Me sister had just got married, me other sister just about to. Over in Leeds I was, cleaning offices. Bogs. A whole group of us, only them were all English. "Ya oul backward Paddy fecking. . . . The fecking pig's-backside face on ya." The first time out of Connemara this was I'd been. "Get back to that backward fecking pigsty of yours or whatever hole it was you drug yourself out of." Half of the swearing I didn't even understand. I had to have a black woman explain it to me. Trinidad she was from. They'd have a go at her too, but she'd just laugh. This big face she had, this big oul smile. And photos of Trinidad she'd show me, and "What the hell have you left there for?" I'd say. "To come to this place, cleaning shite?" And a calendar with a picture of Connemara on I showed her one day, and "What the hell have you left there for?" she said back to me. "To come to this place . . . " (*Pause.*) But she moved to London then, her husband was dying. And after that it all just got to me.

PATO (*pause*): That's all past and behind you now anyways, Maureen.

(*Pause. Maureen looks at him a while.*)

MAUREEN: Am I still a nut case you're saying, or you're wondering?

PATO: Not at all, now . . .

MAUREEN: Oh no . . . ?

(*Maureen gets up and wanders back to the kitchen.*)

PATO: Not at all. That's a long time in the past is all I'm saying. And nothing to be ashamed of. Put it behind you, you should.

MAUREEN: Put it behind me, aye, with that one hovering eyeing me every minute, like I'm some kind of . . . some kind of . . . (*Pause.*) And, no, I didn't scould her oul hand, no matter how doolally I ever was. Trying to cook chips on her own, she was. We'd argued, and I'd left her on her own an hour, and chips she up and decided she wanted. She must've tipped the pan over. God knows how, the eej. I just found her lying there. Only, because of Difford Hall, she thinks any accusation she throws at me I won't be any the wiser. I won't be able to tell the differ, what's true and what's not. Well, I *am* able to tell the differ. Well able, the smelly oul bitch.

PATO: You shouldn't let her get to you, Maureen.

MAUREEN: How can I help it, Pato? She's enough to drive anyone loopy, if they weren't loopy to begin with.

PATO (*smiling*): She is at that, I suppose.

MAUREEN (*smiling*): She is. It's surprised I am how sane I've turned out!

(*They both smile. Pause.*)

PATO: I *will* have to be off in a minute now, Maureen.

MAUREEN: Okay, Pato. Did you finish your tea, now?

PATO: I didn't. The talk of your mother's wee, it did put me off it.

MAUREEN: It would. It would anybody. Don't I have to live with it? (*Sadly.*) Don't I have to live with it? (*Looking straight at him.*) I suppose I do, now.

PATO (*pause*): Be putting on some clothes there, Maureen. You'll freeze with no fire down.

(*Pause. Maureen's mood has become somber again. She looks down at herself.*)

MAUREEN (*quietly*): "Be putting on some clothes"? Is it ugly you think I am now, so, "Be putting on some clothes. . . . "

PATO: No, Maureen, the cold, I'm saying. You can't go walking about. . . . You'll freeze, sure.

MAUREEN: It wasn't ugly you thought I was last night, or maybe it was, now.

PATO: No, Maureen, now. What . . . ?

MAUREEN: A beauty queen you thought I was last night, or you said I was. When it's "Cover yourself," now, "You do sicken me." . . .

PATO (*approaching her*): Maureen, no, now, what are you saying that for . . . ?

MAUREEN: Maybe that was the reason so.

PATO (*stops*): The reason what?

MAUREEN: Be off with you so, if I sicken you.

PATO: You don't sicken me.

MAUREEN (*almost crying*): Be off with you, I said.

PATO (*approaching again*): Maureen . . .

(*Mag enters, waving papers, stopping Pato's approach.*)

MAG: Eh? Here's the papers, now, Difford Hall, if I'm such a senile oul hen. Eh? Who wants an oul read, now? Eh? Proof this is, let alone pegging sinks at me! (*Pause.*) Eh?

PATO: Maureen . . .

MAUREEN (*composed, gently*): Be going now, Pato.

PATO (*pause*): I'll write to you from England. (*Pause. Sternly.*) Look at me! (*Pause. Softly.*) I'll write to you from England.

(*Pato puts on his jacket, turns for a last look at Maureen, then exits, closing the door behind him. Footsteps away. Pause.*)

MAG: He won't write at all. (*Pause.*) And I did throw your oul dress in that dirty corner too!

(*Pause. Maureen looks at her a moment, sad, despairing but not angry.*)

MAUREEN: Why? Why? Why do you . . . ?

(*Pause. Maureen goes over to where her dress is lying, crouches down beside it and picks it up, holding it to her chest. She lingers there a moment, then gets up and passes her mother.*)

Just look at yourself.

(*Maureen exits into hall.*)

MAG: Just look at *yourself* too, would be . . . would be . . .

(*Maureen shuts the hall door behind her.*)

. . . more in your line.

(*Mag is still holding up the papers rather dumbly. Pause. She lays the papers down, scratches herself, notices her uneaten porridge and sticks a finger in it. Quietly.*)

Me porridge is gone cold now. (*Loudly.*) Me porridge is gone cold now!

(*Mag stares out front, blankly.*)
(*Blackout.*)
(*Interval.*)

SCENE FIVE

(*Most of the stage is in darkness apart from a spot-light or some such on Pato sitting at the table as if in a bedsit in England, reciting a letter he has written to Maureen.*)

PATO: Dear Maureen, it is Pato Dooley and I'm writing from London, and I'm sorry it's taken so long to write to you but to be honest I didn't know whether you wanted me to one way or the other, so I have taken it upon myself to try and see. There are a lot of things I want to say but I am no letter-writer but I will try to say them if I can. Well, Maureen, there is no major news here, except a Wexford man on the site a day ago, a rake of bricks fell on him from the scaffold and forty stitches he did have in his head and was lucky to be alive at all, he was an old fella, or fifty-odd anyways, but apart from that there is no major news. I do go out for a pint of a Saturday or a Friday but I don't know nobody and don't speak to anyone. There is no one to speak to. The gangerman does pop his head in sometimes. I don't know if I've spelt it right, "gangerman," is it "e-r" or is it "a"? It is not a word we was taught in school. Well, Maureen, I am "beating around the bush" as they say, because it is you and me I do want to be talking about, if there is such a thing now as "you and me," I don't know the state of play. What I thought I thought we were getting on royally, at the goodbye to the Yanks and the part after when we did talk and went to yours. And I *did* think you were a beauty queen and I *do* think, and it wasn't anything to do with that at all or with you at all, I think you thought it was. All it was, it has happened to me a couple of times before when I've had a drink taken and was nothing to do with did I want to. I would have been honored to be the first one you chose, and flattered, and the thing that I'm saying, I was honored then and I am still honored, and just because it was not to be that night, does it mean it is not to be ever? I don't see why it should, and I don't see why you was so angry when you was so nice to me when it happened. I think you thought I looked at you differently when your breakdown business came up, when I didn't look at you differently at all, or the thing I said "Put on your clothes, it's cold," when you seemed to think I did not want to be looking at you in your bra and slip there, when nothing could be further from the truth, because if truth be told I could have looked at you in your bra and slip until the cows came home. I could never get my fill of looking at you in your bra and slip, and some day, God-willing, I will be looking at you in your bra and slip again. Which leads me on to my other thing, unless you still haven't forgiven me, in which case we should just forget about it and part as friends, but if you *have* forgiven me it leads me on to my other thing which I was lying to you before when I said I had no news because I do have

news. What the news is I have been in touch with me uncle in Boston and the incident with the Wexford man with the bricks was just the final straw. You'd be lucky to get away with your life the building sites in England, let alone the bad money and the "You oul Irish this-and-that," and I have been in touch with me uncle in Boston and a job he has offered me there, and I am going to take him up on it. Back in Leenane two weeks tomorrow I'll be, to collect up my stuff and I suppose a bit of a do they'll throw me, and the thing I want to say to you is do you want to come with me? Not straight away of course, I know, because you would have things to clear up, but after a month or two I'm saying, but maybe you haven't forgiven me at all and it's being a fool I'm being. Well, if you haven't forgiven me I suppose it'd be best if we just kept out of each other's way the few days I'm over and if I don't hear from you I will understand, but if you *have* forgiven me what's to keep you in Ireland? There's your sisters could take care of your mother and why should you have had the burden all these years, don't you deserve a life? And if they say no, isn't there the home in Oughterard isn't ideal but they do take good care of them, my mother before she passed, and don't they have bingo and what good to your mother does that big hill do? No good. (*Pause.*) Anyways, Maureen, I will leave it up to you. My address is up the top there and the number of the phone is in the hall, only let it ring a good while if you want to ring and you'll need the codes, and it would be grand to hear from you. If I don't hear from you, I will understand. Take good care of yourself, Maureen. And that night we shared, even if nothing happened, it still makes me happy just to think about it, being close to you, and even if I never hear from you again I'll always have a happy memory of that night, and that's all I wanted to say to you. Do think about it. Yours sincerely, Pato Dooley.

(*Spotlight cuts out, but while the stage is in darkness Pato continues with a letter to his brother.*)

Dear Raymond, how are you? I'm enclosing a bunch of letters I don't want different people snooping in on. Will you hand them out for me and don't be reading them, I know you won't be. The one to Mick Dowd you can wait till he comes out of hospital. Let me know how he is or have they arrested the lass who belted him. The one to poor Girleen you can give to her any time you see her, it is only to tell her to stop falling in love with priests. But the one to Maureen Folan I want you to go over there the day you get this and put it in her hand. This is important now, in her hand put it. Not much other news here. I'll fill you in on more of the America details nearer the time. Yes, it's a great thing. Good luck to you, Raymond, and P.S. Remember now, in Maureen's hand put it. Goodbye.

SCENE SIX

(*Afternoon. Ray is standing near the lit range, watching TV, somewhat engrossed, tapping a sealed envelope against his knee now and then. Mag watches him and the letter from the rocking-chair. Long pause before Ray speaks.*)

RAY: That Wayne's an oul bastard.
MAG: Is he?
RAY: He is. He never stops.
MAG: Oh-h.
RAY (*pause*): D'you see Patricia with the hair? Patricia's bad enough, but Wayne's a pure terror. (*Pause.*) I do like *Sons and Daughters*, I do.
MAG: Do ya?
RAY: Everybody's always killing each other and a lot of the girls do have swimsuits. That's the best kind of program.
MAG: I'm just waiting for the news to come on.
RAY (*pause*): You'll have a long wait.

(*The program ends. Ray stretches himself.*)

That's that then.
MAG: Is the news not next? Ah no.
RAY: No. For God's sake, *A Country Fecking Practice*'s on next. Isn't it Thursday?
MAG: Turn it off, so, if the news isn't on. That's all I do be waiting for.

(*Ray turns the TV off and idles around.*)

RAY: Six o'clock the news isn't on 'til. (*He glances at his watch. Quietly, irritated.*) Feck, feck, feck, feck, feck, feck, feck, feck, feck. (*Pause.*) You said she'd be home by now, didn't you?
MAG: I did. (*Pause.*) Maybe she got talking to somebody, although she doesn't usually get talking to somebody. She does keep herself to herself.
RAY: I know well she does keep herself to herself. (*Pause.*) Loopy that woman is, if you ask me. Didn't she keep the tennis ball that came off me and Mairtin Hanlon's swingball set and landed in yere fields and wouldn't give it back no matter how much we begged and that was ten years ago and I still haven't forgotten it?
MAG: I do have no comment, as they say.
RAY: Still haven't forgotten it and I never will forget it!
MAG: But wasn't it that you and Mairtin were pegging yere tennis ball at our chickens and clobbered one of them dead is why your ball was in our fields . . . ?
RAY: It was swingball we were playing, Missus!
MAG: Oh-h.
RAY: Not clobbering at all. Swingball it was. And never again able to play swingball were we. For the rest of our youth, now. For what use is a swingball set without a ball?
MAG: No use.
RAY: No use is right! No use at all. (*Pause.*) Bitch!

MAG (*pause*): Be off and give your letter to me so, Ray, now, and I'll make sure she gets it, and not have you waiting for a lass ruined your swingball set on you.

(*Ray thinks about it, tempted, but grudgingly decides against it.*)

RAY: I'm under strict instructions now, Missus.
MAG (*tuts*): Make me a mug of tea so.
RAY: I'm not making you a mug of tea. Under duress is all I'm here. I'm not skivvying about on top of it.
MAG (*pause*): Or another bit of turf on the fire pit. I'm cold.
RAY: Did I not just say?
MAG: Ah g'wan, Ray. You're a good boy, God bless you.

(*Sighing, Ray puts the letter — which Mag stares at throughout — on the table and uses the heavy black poker beside the range to pick some turf up and place it inside, stoking it afterwards.*)

RAY: Neverminding swingball, I saw her there on the road the other week and I said hello to her and what did she do? She outright ignored me. Didn't even look up.
MAG: Didn't she?
RAY: And what I thought of saying, I thought of saying, 'Up your oul hole, Missus', but I didn't say it, I just thought of saying it, but thinking back on it I should've gone ahead and said it and skitter on the bitch!
MAG: It would've been good enough for her to say it, up and ignoring you on the road, because you're a good gasur, Ray, fixing me fire for me. Ah, she's been in a foul oul mood lately.
RAY: She does wear horrible clothes. And everyone agrees. (*Finished at the range, poker still in hand, Ray looks over the tea-towel on the back wall.*) "May you be half an hour in Heaven afore the Devil knows you're dead."
MAG: Aye.
RAY (*funny voice*): "May you be half an hour in Heaven afore the Devil knows you're dead."
MAG (*embarrassed laugh*): Aye.

(*Ray idles around a little, wielding the poker.*)

RAY: This is a great oul poker, this is.
MAG: Is it?
RAY: Good and heavy.
MAG: Heavy and long.
RAY: Good and heavy and long. A half a dozen coppers you could take out with this poker and barely notice and have not a scratch on it and then clobber them again just for the fun of seeing the blood running out of them. (*Pause.*) Will you sell it to me?
MAG: I will not. To go battering the polis?
RAY: A fiver.
MAG: We do need it for the fire, sure.

(*Ray tuts and puts the poker back beside the range.*)

RAY: Sure, that poker's just going to waste in this house.

Mag (Anna Manahan) and Ray (Tom Murphy) in the 1998 New York production of *The Beauty Queen of Leenane.*

(*Ray idles into the kitchen. Her eye on the letter, Mag slowly gets out of her chair.*)

Ah, I could get a dozen pokers in town just as good if I wanted, and at half the price.

(*Just as Mag starts her approach to the letter, Ray returns, not noticing her, idles past and picks the letter back up on his way. Mag grimaces slightly and sits back down. Ray opens the front door, glances out to see if Maureen is coming, then closes it again, sighing.*)

A whole afternoon I'm wasting here. (*Pause.*) When I could be at home watching telly.

(*Ray sits at the table.*)

MAG: You never know, it might be evening before she's ever home.

RAY (*angrily*): You said three o'clock it was sure to be when I first came in!

MAG: Aye, three o'clock it usually is, oh aye. (*Pause.*) Just sometimes it does be evening. On occasion, like. (*Pause.*) Sometimes it does be *late* evening. (*Pause.*) Sometimes it does be *night.* (*Pause.*) *Morning* it was one time before she . . .

RAY (*interrupting angrily*): All right, all right! It's thumping you in a minute I'll be!

MAG (*pause*): I'm only saying now.

RAY: Well, stop saying! (*Sighs. Long pause.*) This house does smell of pee, this house does.

MAG (*pause, embarrassed*): Em, cats do get in.

RAY: Do cats get in?

MAG: They do. (*Pause.*) They do go to the sink.

RAY (*pause*): What do they go to the sink for?

MAG: To wee.

RAY: To wee? They go to the sink to wee? (*Piss-taking.*) Sure, that's might good of them. You do get a very considerate breed of cat up this way so.

MAG (*pause*): I don't know what breed they are.

(*Pause. Ray lets his head slump down onto the table with a bump, and slowly and rhythmically starts banging his fist down beside it.*)

RAY (*droning*): I don't want to be here, I don't want to be here, I don't want to be here, I don't want to be here. . . .

(*Ray lifts his head back up, stares at the letter, then starts slowly turning it around, end over end, sorely tempted.*)

MAG (*pause*): Do me a mug of tea, Ray. (*Pause.*) Or a mug of Complan do me, even. (*Pause.*) And give it a good stir to get rid of the oul lumps.

RAY: If it was getting rid of oul lumps I was to be, it wouldn't be with Complan I'd be starting. It would be much closer to home, boy. Oh aye, much closer. A big lump sitting in an oul fecking rocking-chair it would be. I'll tell you that!

MAG (*pause*): Or a Cup-a-Soup do me.

(*Ray grits his teeth and begins breathing in and out through them, almost crying.*)

RAY (*giving in sadly*): Pato, Pato, Pato. (*Pause.*) Ah what news could it be? (*Pause. Sternly.*) Were I to leave this letter here with you, Missus, it would be straight to that one you would be giving it, isn't that right?

MAG: It is. Oh, straight to Maureen I'd be giving it.

RAY (*pause*): And it isn't opening it you would be?

MAG: It is not. Sure, a letter is a private thing. If it isn't my name on it, what business would it be of mine?

RAY: And may God strike you dead if you do open it?

MAG: And may God strike me dead if I do open it, only He'll have no need to strike me dead because I won't be opening it.

RAY (*pause*): I'll leave it so.

(*Ray stands, places the letter up against a salt-cellar, thinks about it again for a moment, looks Mag over a second, looks back at the letter again, thinks once more, then waves a hand in a gesture of tired resignation, deciding to leave it.*)

I'll be seeing you then, Missus.

MAG: Be seeing you, Pato. *Ray*, I mean.

(*Ray grimaces at her again and exits through the front door, but leaves it slightly ajar, as he is still waiting outside. Mag places her hands on the sides of the rocking-chair, about to drag herself up, then warily remembers she hasn't heard Ray's footsteps away. She lets her hands rest back in her lap and sits back serenely. Pause. The front door bursts open and Ray sticks his head around it to look at her. She smiles at him innocently.*)

RAY: Good-oh.

(*Ray exits again, closing the door behind him fully this time. Mag listens to his footsteps fading away, then gets up, picks up the envelope and opens it, goes back to the range and lifts off the lid so that the flames are visible, and stands there reading the letter. She drops the first short page into the flames as she finishes it, then starts reading the second. Slow fade-out.*)

SCENE SEVEN

(*Night. Mag is in her rocking-chair, Maureen at the table, reading. The radio is on low, tuned to a request show. The reception is quite poor, wavering and crackling with static. Pause before Mag speaks.*)

MAG: A poor reception.

MAUREEN: Can I help it if it's a poor reception?

MAG (*pause*): Crackly. (*Pause.*) We can hardly hear the tunes. (*Pause.*) We can hardly hear what are the dedications or from what part of the country.

MAUREEN: I can hear well enough.

MAG: Can ya?

MAUREEN (*pause*): Maybe it's deaf it is you're going.

MAG: It's not deaf I'm going. Not nearly deaf.

MAUREEN: It's a home for deaf people I'll have to be putting you in soon. (*Pause.*) And it isn't cod in butter sauce you'll be getting in there. No. Not by a long chalk. Oul beans on toast or something is all you'll be getting in there. If you're lucky. And then if you don't eat it, they'll give you a good kick, or maybe a punch.

MAG (*pause*): I'd die before I'd let meself be put in a home.

MAUREEN: Hopefully, aye.

MAG (*pause*): That was a nice bit of cod in butter sauce, Maureen.

MAUREEN: I suppose it was.

MAG: Tasty.

MAUREEN: All I do is boil it in the bag and snip it with a scissor. I hardly need your compliments.

MAG (*pause*): Mean to me is all you ever are nowadays.

MAUREEN: If I am or if I'm not. (*Pause.*) Didn't I buy you a packet of wine gums last week if I'm so mean?

MAG (*pause*): All because of Pato Dooley you're mean, I suppose. (*Pause.*) Him not inviting you to his oul going-away do tonight.

MAUREEN: Pato Dooley has his own life to lead.

MAG: Only after one thing that man was.

MAUREEN: Maybe he was, now. Or maybe it was me who was only after one thing. We do have equality nowadays. Not like in your day.

MAG: There was nothing wrong in my day.

MAUREEN: Allowed to go on top of a man nowadays, we are. All we have to do is ask. And nice it is on top of a man, too.

MAG: Is it nice now, Maureen?

MAUREEN (*bemused that Mag isn't offended*): It is.

MAG: It does sound nice. Ah, good enough for yourself, now.

(*Maureen, still bemused, gets some shortbread fingers from the kitchen and eats a couple.*)

MAG: And not worried about having been put in the family way, are you?

MAUREEN: I'm not. We was careful.

MAG: Was ye careful?

MAUREEN: Aye. We was nice and careful. We was *lovely* and careful, if you must know.

MAG: I'll bet ye was lovely and careful, aye. Oh aye. Lovely and careful, I'll bet ye were.

MAUREEN (*pause*): You haven't been sniffing the paraffin lamps again?

MAG (*pause*): It's always the paraffin lamp business you do throw at me.

MAUREEN: It's a funny oul mood you're in so.

MAG: Is it a funny oul mood? No. Just a normal mood, now.

MAUREEN: It's a funny one. (*Pause.*) Aye, a great oul time me and Pato did have. I can see now what all the fuss did be about, but ah, there has to be more to a man than just being good in bed. Things in common too you do have to have, y'know, like what books do you be reading, or what are your politics and the like, so I did have to tell him it was no-go, no matter how good in bed he was.

MAG: When was this did you tell him?

MAUREEN: A while ago it was I did tell him. Back . . .

MAG (*interrupting*): And I suppose he was upset at that.

MAUREEN: He *was* upset at that but I assured him it was for the best and he did seem to accept it then.

MAG: I'll bet he accepted it.

MAUREEN (*pause*): But that's why I thought it would be unfair of me to go over to his do and wish him goodbye. I thought it would be awkward for him.

MAG: It would be awkward for him, aye, I suppose. Oh aye. (*Pause.*) So all it was was ye didn't have enough things in common was all that parted ye?

MAUREEN: Is all it was. And parted on amicable terms, and with no grudges on either side. (*Pause.*) No. No grudges at all. I did get what I did want out of Pato Dooley that night, and that was good enough for him, and that was good enough for me.

MAG: Oh aye, now. I'm sure. It was good enough for the both of ye. Oh aye.

(*Mag smiles and nods.*)

MAUREEN (*laughing*): It's a crazy oul mood you're in for yourself tonight!

(*Pause.*)

Pleased that tonight it is Pato's leaving and won't be coming pawing me again is what it is, I bet.

MAG: Maybe that's what it is. I *am* glad Pato's leaving.

MAUREEN (*smiling*): An interfering oul biddy is all you are. (*Pause.*) Do you want a shortbread finger?

MAG: I *do* want a shortbread finger.

MAUREEN: Please.

MAG: Please.

(*Maureen gives Mag a shortbread finger, after waving it phallically in the air a moment.*)

MAUREEN: Remind me of something,, shortbread fingers do.

MAG: I suppose they do, now.

MAUREEN: I suppose it's so long since you've seen what they remind me of, you do forget what they look like.

MAG: I suppose I do. And I suppose you're the expert.

MAUREEN: I am the expert.

MAG: Oh aye.

MAUREEN: I'm the king of the experts.

MAG: I suppose you are, now. Oh, I'm sure. I suppose you're the king of the experts.

MAUREEN (*pause, suspicious*): Why wouldn't you be sure?

MAG: With your Pato Dooley and your throwing it all in me face like an oul peahen, eh? When . . . (*Mag catches herself before revealing any more.*)

MAUREEN (*pause, smiling*): When what?

MAG: Not another word on the subject am I saying. I do have no comment, as they say. This is a nice shortbread finger.

MAUREEN (*with an edge*): When what, now?

MAG (*getting scared*): When nothing, Maureen.

MAUREEN (*forcefully*): No, when what, now? (*Pause.*) Have you been speaking to somebody?

MAG: Who would I be speaking to, Maureen?

MAUREEN (*trying to work it out*): You've been speaking to somebody. You've . . .

MAG: Nobody have I been speaking to, Maureen. You know well I don't be speaking to anybody. And, sure, who would Pato be telling about that . . . ?

(*Mag suddenly realizes what she's said. Maureen stares at her in dumb shock and hate, then walks to the kitchen, dazed, puts a chip-pan on the stove, turns it on high and pours a half-bottle of cooking oil into it, takes down the rubber gloves that are hanging on the back wall and puts them on. Mag puts her hands on the arms of the rocking-chair to drag herself up, but Maureen shoves a foot against her stomach and groin, ushering her back. Mag leans back into the chair, frightened, staring at Maureen, who sits at the table, waiting for the oil to boil. She speaks quietly, staring straight ahead.*)

MAUREEN: How do you know?

MAG: Nothing do I know, Maureen.

MAUREEN: Uh-huh?

MAG (*pause*): Or was it Ray did mention something? Aye, I think it was Ray. . . .

MAUREEN: Nothing to Ray would Pato've said about that subject.

MAG (*tearfully*): Just to stop you bragging like an oul peahen, was I saying, Maureen. Sure what does an oul woman like me know? Just guessing, I was.

MAUREEN: You know sure enough, and guessing me arse, and not on me face was it written. For the second time and for the last time I'll be asking, now. How do you know?

MAG: On your face it *was* written, Maureen. Sure that's the only way I knew. You still do have the look of a virgin about you you always have had. (*Without malice.*) You always will.

(*Pause. The oil has started boiling. Maureen rises, turns the radio up, stares at Mag as she passes her, takes the pan off the boil and turns the gas off, and returns to Mag with it.*)

MAG (*terrified*): A letter he did send you I read!

(*Maureen slowly and deliberately takes her mother's shriveled hand, holds it down on the burning range, and starts slowly pouring some of the hot oil over it, as Mag screams in pain and terror.*)

MAUREEN: Where is the letter?
MAG (*through screams*): I did burn it! I'm sorry, Maureen!
MAUREEN: What did the letter say?

(*Mag is screaming so much that she can't answer. Maureen stops pouring the oil and releases the hand, which Mag clutches to herself, doubled-up, still screaming, crying, and whimpering.*)

MAUREEN: What did the letter say?
MAG: Said he did have too much to drink, it did! Is why, and not your fault at all.
MAUREEN: And what else did it say?
MAG: He won't be putting me into no home!
MAUREEN: What are you talking about, no home? What else did it say?!
MAG: I can't remember, now, Maureen. I can't . . . !

(*Maureen grabs Mag's hand, holds it down again, and repeats the torture.*)

MAG: No . . . !
MAUREEN: What else did it say?! Eh?!
MAG (*through screams*): Asked you to go to America with him, it did!

(*Stunned, Maureen releases Mag's hand and stops pouring the oil. Mag clutches her hand to herself again, whimpering.*)

MAUREEN: What?
MAG: But how could you go with him? You do still have me to look after.
MAUREEN (*in a happy daze*): He asked me to go to America with him? Pato asked me to go to America with him?
MAG (*looking up at her*): But what about me, Maureen?

(*A slight pause before Maureen, in a single and almost lazy motion, throws the considerable remainder of the oil into Mag's midriff, some of it splashing up into her face. Mag doubles-up, screaming, falls to the floor, trying to pat the oil off her, and lies there convulsing, screaming, and whimpering. Maureen steps out of her way to avoid her fall, still in a daze, barely noticing her.*)

MAUREEN (*dreamily, to herself*): He asked me to go to America with him . . . ? (*Recovering herself.*) What

time is it? Oh feck, he'll be leaving! I've got to see him. Oh God . . . What will I wear? Uh . . . Me black dress! Me little black dress! It'll be a remembrance to him. . . .

(*Maureen darts off through the hall.*)

MAG (*quietly, sobbing*): Maureen . . . help me. . . .

(*Maureen returns a moment later, pulling her black dress on.*)

MAUREEN (*to herself*): How do I look? Ah, I'll have to do. What time is it? Oh God. . . .
MAG: Help me, Maureen. . . .
MAUREEN (*brushing her hair*): Help you, is it? After what you've done? Help you, she says. No, I won't help you, and I'll tell you another thing. If you've made me miss Pato before he goes, then you'll *really* be for it, so you will, and no messing this time. Out of me fecking way, now. . . .

(*Maureen steps over Mag, who is still shaking on the floor, and exits through the front door. Pause. Mag is still crawling around slightly. The front door bangs open and Mag looks up at Maureen as she breezes back in.*)

Me car keys I forgot. . . . (*Maureen grabs her keys from the table, goes to the door, turns back to the table and switches the radio off.*) Electricity.

(*Maureen exits again, slamming the door. Pause. Sound of her car starting and pulling off. Pause.*)

MAG (*quietly*): But who'll look after me, so?

(*Mag still shaking, looks down at her scalded hand. Blackout.*)

SCENE EIGHT

(*Same night. The only light in the room emanates from the orange coals through the grill of the range, just illuminating the dark shapes of Mag, sitting in her rocking-chair, which rocks back and forth of its own volition, her body unmoving, and Maureen, still in her black dress, who idles very slowly around the room, poker in hand.*)

MAUREEN: To Boston. To Boston I'll be going. Isn't that where them two were from, the Kennedys, or was that somewhere else, now? Robert Kennedy I did prefer over Jack Kennedy. He seemed to be nicer to women. Although I haven't read up on it. (*Pause.*) Boston. It does have a nice ring to it. Better than England it'll be, I'm sure. Although where wouldn't be better than England? No shite I'll be cleaning there, anyways, and no names called, and Pato'll be there to have a say-so anyways if there was to be names called, but I'm sure there won't be. The Yanks do love the Irish. (*Pause.*) Almost begged me, Pato did. Almost on his hands and knees, he was, near enough crying. At the station I caught him, not five minutes to spare, thanks to you. Thanks to your oul interfering. But too late to be interfering you are now. Oh aye. Be far too late, although you did give it a good go, I'll say that for you. Another five minutes and you'd have had it. Poor you. Poor selfish oul bitch, oul you. (*Pause.*) Kissed the face off me, he did, when he saw me there. Them blues eyes of his. Them muscles. Them arms wrapping me. "Why did you not answer me letter?" And all for coming over and giving you a good kick he was when I told him, but "Ah no," I said, "isn't she just a feeble-minded oul feck, not worth dirtying your boots on?" I was defending you there. (*Pause.*) "You will come to Boston with me so, me love, when you get up the money." "I will, Pato. Be it married or be it living in sin, what do I care? What do I care if tongues'd be wagging? Tongues have wagged about me before, let them wag again. Let them never stop wagging, so long as I'm with you, Pato, what do I care about tongues? So long as it's you and me, and the warmth of us cuddled up, and the skins of us asleep, is all I ever really wanted anyway." (*Pause.*) "Except we do still have a problem, what to do with your oul mam, there," he said. "Would an oul folks home be too harsh?" "It wouldn't be too harsh but it would be too expensive." "What about your sisters so?" "Me sisters wouldn't have the bitch. Not even a half-day at Christmas to be with her can them two stand. They clear forgot her birthday this year as well as that." "How do you stick her without going off your rocker?" they do say to me. Behind her back, like. (*Pause.*) "I'll leave it up to yourself so," Pato says. He was on the train be this time, we was kissing out the window, like they do in films. "I'll leave it up to yourself so, whatever you decide. If it takes a month, let it take a month. And if it's finally you decide you can't bear to be parted from her and have to stay behind, well, I can't say I would like it, but I'd understand. But if even a year it has to take for you to decide, it is a year I will be waiting, and won't be minding the wait." "It won't be a year it is you'll be waiting, Pato," I called out then, the train was pulling away. "It won't be a year nor yet nearly a year. It won't be a week!"

(*The rocking-chair has stopped its motions. Mag starts to slowly lean forward at the waist until she finally topples over and falls heavily to the floor, dead. A red chunk of skull hangs from a string of skin at the side of her head. Maureen looks down at her, somewhat bored, taps her on the side with the toe of her shoe, then steps onto her back and stands there in thoughtful contemplation.*)

'Twas over the stile she did trip. Aye. And down the hill she did fall. Aye. (*Pause.*) Aye.

(*Pause. Blackout.*)

SCENE NINE

(*A rainy afternoon. Front door opens and Maureen enters in funeral attire, takes her jacket off and idles around quietly, her mind elsewhere. She lights a fire in the range, turns the radio on low and sits down in the rocking-chair. After a moment she half-laughs, takes down the boxes of Complan and porridge from the kitchen shelf, goes back to the range and empties the contents of both on the fire. She exits into the hall and returns a moment later with an old suitcase which she lays on the table, brushing off a thick layer of dust. She opens it, considers for a second what she needs to pack, then returns to the hall. There is a knock at the door. Maureen returns, thinks a moment, takes the suitcase off the table and places it to one side, fixes her hair a little, then answers the door.*)

MAUREEN: Oh, hello there, Ray.
RAY (*off*): Hello there, Missus. . . .
MAUREEN: Come in ahead for yourself.
RAY: I did see you coming ahead up the road.

(*Ray enters, closing the door. Maureen idles to the kitchen and makes herself some tea.*)

I didn't think so early you would be back. Did you not want to go on to the reception or the whatyoucall they're having at Rory's so?
MAUREEN: No. I do have better things to do with me time.
RAY: Aye. Aye. Have your sisters gone on to it?
MAUREEN: They have, aye.
RAY: Of course. Coming back here after, will they be?
MAUREEN: Going straight home, I think they said they'd be.
RAY: Oh aye. Sure, it's a long oul drive for them. Or fairly long. (*Pause.*) It did all go off okay, then?
MAUREEN: It did.
RAY: Despite the rain.
MAUREEN: Despite the rain.
RAY: A poor oul day for a funeral.
MAUREEN: It was. When it could've been last month we buried her, and she could've got the last of the sun, if it wasn't for the hundred bastarding inquests, proved nothing.
RAY: You'll be glad that's all over and done with now, anyways.
MAUREEN: Very glad.
RAY: I suppose they do only have their jobs to do. (*Pause.*) Although no fan am I of the bastarding polis. Me two wee toes they went and broke on me for no reason, me arsehole drunk and disorderly.
MAUREEN: The polis broke your toes, did they?
RAY: They did.
MAUREEN: Oh. Tom Hanlon said what it was you kicked a door in just your socks.
RAY: Did he now? And I suppose you believe a policeman's word over mine. Oh aye. Isn't that how the Birmingham Six went down?

MAUREEN: Sure, you can't equate your toes with the Birmingham Six, now, Ray.

RAY: It's the selfsame differ. (*Pause.*) What was I saying, now?

MAUREEN: Some bull.

RAY: Some bull, is it? No. Asking about your mam's funeral, I was.

MAUREEN: That's what I'm saying.

RAY (*pause*): Was there a big turn-out at it?

MAUREEN: Me sisters and one of their husbands and nobody else but Maryjohnny Rafferty and oul Father Walsh — Welsh — saying the thing.

RAY: Father Welsh punched Mairtin Hanlon in the head once, for no reason. (*Pause.*) Are you not watching telly for yourself, no?

MAUREEN: I'm not. It's only Australian oul shite they do ever show on that thing.

RAY (*slightly bemused*): Sure, that's why I do like it. Who wants to see Ireland on telly?

MAUREEN: *I* do.

RAY: All you have to do is look out your window to see Ireland. And it's soon bored you'd be. "There goes a calf." (*Pause.*) I be bored anyway. I be continually bored. (*Pause.*) London I'm thinking of going to. Aye. Thinking of it, anyways. To work, y'know. One of these days. Or else Manchester. They have a lot more drugs in Manchester. Supposedly, anyways.

MAUREEN: Don't be getting messed up in drugs, now, Ray, for yourself. Drugs are terrible dangerous.

RAY: Terrible dangerous, are they? Drugs, now?

MAUREEN: You know full well they are.

RAY: Maybe they are, maybe they are. But there are plenty of other things just as dangerous, would kill you just as easy. Maybe even easier.

MAUREEN (*wary*): Things like what, now?

RAY (*pause, shrugging*): This bastarding town for one.

MAUREEN (*pause, sadly*): Is true enough.

RAY: Just that it takes seventy years. Well, it won't take me seventy years. I'll tell you that. No way, boy. (*Pause.*) How old was your mother, now, when she passed?

MAUREEN: Seventy, aye. Bang on.

RAY: She had a good innings, anyway. (*Pause.*) Or an innings, anyway. (*Sniffs the air.*) What's this you've been burning?

MAUREEN: Porridge and Complan I've been burning.

RAY: For why?

MAUREEN: Because I don't eat porridge or Complan. The remainders of me mother's, they were. I was having a good clear-out.

RAY: Only a waste that was.

MAUREEN: Do I need your say-so so?

RAY: I'd've been glad to take them off your hands, I'm saying.

MAUREEN (*quietly*): I don't need your say-so.

RAY: The porridge, anyway. I do like a bit of porridge. I'd've left the Complan. I don't drink Complan. Never had no call to.

MAUREEN: There's some Kimberleys left in the packet I was about to burn too, you can have, if it's such a big thing.

RAY: I *will* have them Kimberleys. I do love Kimberleys.

MAUREEN: I bet you do.

(*Ray eats a couple of Kimberleys.*)

RAY: Are they a bit stale, now? (*Chews.*) It does be hard to tell with Kimberleys. (*Pause.*) I think Kimberleys are me favorite biscuits out of any biscuits. Them or Jaffa Cakes. (*Pause.*) Or Wagon Wheels. (*Pause.*) Or would you classify Wagon Wheels as biscuits at all now. Aren't they more of a kind of a bar . . . ?

MAUREEN (*interrupting*): I've things to do now, Ray. Was it some reason you had to come over or was it just to discuss Wagon Wheels?

RAY: Oh aye, now. No, I did have a letter from Pato the other day and he did ask me to come up.

(*Maureen sits in the rocking-chair and listens with keen interest.*)

MAUREEN: He did? What did he have to say?

RAY: He said sorry to hear about your mother and all, and his condolences he sent.

MAUREEN: Aye, aye, aye, and anything else, now?

RAY: That was the main gist of it, the message he said to pass onto you.

MAUREEN: It had no times or details, now?

RAY: Times or details? No . . .

MAUREEN: I suppose . . .

RAY: Eh?

MAUREEN: Eh?

RAY: Eh? Oh, also he said he was sorry he didn't get to see you the night he left, there, he would've liked to've said goodbye. But if that was the way you wanted it, so be it. Although rude, too, I thought that was.

MAUREEN (*standing, confused*): I did see him the night he left. At the station, there.

RAY: What station? Be taxicab Pato left. What are you thinking of?

MAUREEN (*sitting*): I don't know now.

RAY: Be taxicab Pato left, and sad that he never got your goodbye, although why he wanted your goodbye I don't know. (*Pause.*) I'll tell you this, Maureen, not being harsh, but your house does smell an awful lot nicer now that your mother's dead. I'll say it does, now.

MAUREEN: Well, isn't that the best? With me thinking I did see him the night he left, there. The train that pulled away.

(*He looks at her as if she's mad.*)

RAY: Aye, aye. (*Mumbled, sarcastic.*) Have a rest for yourself. (*Pause.*) Oh, do you know a lass called, em. . . . Dolores Hooley, or Healey, now? She was over with the Yanks when they was over.

MAUREEN: I know the name, aye.

RAY: She was at me uncle's do they had there, dancing with me brother early on. You remember?

MAUREEN: Dancing with him, was it? Throwing herself at him would be nearer the mark. Like a cheap oul whore.

RAY: I don't know about that, now.

MAUREEN: Like a cheap oul whore. And where did it get her?

RAY: She did seem nice enough to me, there, now. Big brown eyes she had. And I do like brown eyes, me, I do. Oh aye. Like the lass used to be on *Bosco*. Or I *think* the lass used to be on *Bosco* had brown eyes. We had a black and white telly at that time. (*Pause.*) What was I talking about, now?

MAUREEN: Something about this Dolores Hooley or whoever she fecking is.

RAY: Oh aye. Herself and Pato did get engaged a week ago, now, he wrote and told me.

MAUREEN (*shocked*): Engaged to do what?

RAY: Engaged to get married. What do you usually get engaged for? "Engaged to do what?" Engaged to eat a bun!

(*Maureen is dumbstruck.*)

RAY: A bit young for him, I think, but good luck to him. A whirlwind oul whatyoucall. July next year, they're thinking of having it, but I'll have to write and tell him to move it either forward or back, else it'll coincide with the European Championships. I wonder if they'll have the European Championships on telly over there at all? Probably not, now, the Yankee bastards. They don't care about football at all. Ah well. (*Pause.*) It won't be much of a change for her anyways, from Hooley to Dooley. Only one letter. The "h". That'll be a good thing. (*Pause.*) Unless it's Healey that she is. I can't remember. (*Pause.*) If it's Healey, it'll be three letters. The "h", the "e" and the "a". (*Pause.*) Would you want me to be passing any message on, now, when I'm writing, Missus? I'm writing tomorrow.

MAUREEN: I get . . . I do get confused. Dolores Hooley . . . ?

RAY (*pause, irritated*): Would you want me to be passing on any message, now, I'm saying?

MAUREEN (*pause*): Dolores Hooley . . . ?

RAY (*sighing*): Fecking . . . The loons you do get in this house! Only repeating!

MAUREEN: Who's a loon?

RAY: Who's a loon, she says!

(*Ray scoffs and turns away, looking out the window. Maureen quietly picks up the poker from beside the range and, holding it low at her side, slowly approaches him from behind.*)

MAUREEN (*angrily*): Who's a loon?

(*Ray suddenly sees something hidden behind a couple of boxes on the inner window ledge.*)

RAY (*angrily*): Well, isn't that fecking just the fecking best yet . . . !

(*Ray picks up a faded tennis ball with a string sticking out of it from the ledge and spins around to confront Maureen with it, so angry that he doesn't even notice the poker. Maureen stops in her tracks.*)

Sitting on that fecking shelf all these fecking years you've had it, and what good did it do ya?! A tenner that swingball set did cost me poor ma and da and in 1979 that was, when a tenner was a lot money. The best fecking present I did ever get and only two oul months' play out of it I got before you went and confiscated it on me. What right did you have? What right at all? No right. And just left it sitting there then to fade to fecking skitter. I wouldn't've minded if you'd got some use out of it, if you'd taken the string out and played pat-ball or something agin a wall, but no. Just out of pure spite is the only reason you kept it, and right under me fecking nose. And then you go wondering who's a fucking loon? Who's a fecking loon, she says. I'll tell you who's a fecking loon, lady. *You're* a fecking loon!

(*Maureen lets the poker fall to the floor with a clatter and sits in the rocking-chair, dazed.*)

MAUREEN: I don't know why I did keep your swingball on you, Raymond. I can't remember at all, now. I think me head was in a funny oul way in them days.

RAY: "In them days," she says, as she pegs a good poker on the floor and talks about trains.

(*Ray picks the poker up and puts it in its place.*)

That's a good poker, that is. Don't be banging it against anything hard like that, now.

MAUREEN: I won't.

RAY: That's an awful good poker. (*Pause.*) To show there's no hard feelings over me swingball, will you sell me that poker, Missus? A fiver I'll give you.

MAUREEN: Ah, I don't want to be selling me poker now, Ray.

RAY: G'wan. Six!

MAUREEN: No. It does have sentimental value to me.

RAY: I don't forgive you, so!

MAUREEN: Ah, don't be like that, now, Ray. . . .

RAY: No, I don't forgive you at all. . . .

(*Ray goes to the front door and opens it.*)

MAUREEN: Ray! Are you writing to your brother, so?

RAY (*sighing*): I am. Why?

MAUREEN: Will you be passing a message on from me?

RAY (*sighs*): Messages, messages, messages, messages! What's the message, so? And make it a short one.

MAUREEN: Just say . . .

(*Maureen thinks about it a while.*)

RAY: This week, if you can!

MAUREEN: Just say . . . Just say, "The beauty queen of Leenane says hello." That's all.

RAY: "The beauty queen of Leenane says hello."

MAUREEN: Aye. No!

(*Ray sighs again.*)

MAUREEN: *Goodbye.* Goodbye. "The beauty queen of Leenane says *goodbye.*"

RAY: "The beauty queen of Leenane says goodbye." Whatever the feck that means, I'll pass it on. "The beauty queen of Leenane says goodbye," although after this fecking swingball business, I don't see why the feck I should. Goodbye to you so, Missus. . . .

MAUREEN: Will you turn the radio up a biteen too, before you go, there, Pato, now? *Ray*, I mean. . . .

RAY (*exasperated*): Feck . . .

(*Ray turns the radio up.*)

The exact fecking image of your mother you are, sitting there pegging orders and forgetting me name! Goodbye!

MAUREEN: And pull the door after you. . . .

RAY (*shouting angrily*): I was going to pull the fecking door after me!!

(*Ray slams the door behind him as he exits. Pause. Maureen starts rocking slightly in the chair, listening to the song by The Chieftains on the radio. The announcer's quiet, soothing voice is then heard.*)

ANNOUNCER: A lovely tune from The Chieftains there. This next one, now, goes out from Annette and Margo Folan to their mother Maggie, all the way out in the mountains of Leenane, a lovely part of the world there, on the occasion of her seventy-first birthday last month now. Well, we hope you had a happy one, Maggie, and we hope there'll be a good many of them to come on top of it. I'm sure there will. This one's for you, now.

(*"The Spinning Wheel" by Delia Murphy is played. Maureen gently rocks in the chair until about the middle of the fourth verse, when she quietly gets up, picks up the dusty suitcase, caresses it slightly, moves slowly to the hall door and looks back at the empty rocking-chair a while. It is still rocking gently. Slight pause, then Maureen exits into the hall, closing its door behind her as she goes. We listen to the song on the radio to the end, as the chair gradually stops rocking and the lights, very slowly, fade to black.*)

COMMENTARIES

Benedict Nightingale (b. 1939)
A NEW YOUNG PLAYWRIGHT
FULL OF OLD IRISH VOICES

1997

> *Benedict Nightingale, critic for the* London Times, *reviews the Royal Court production staged at the West End's Duke of York's Theatre where* The Beauty Queen of Leenane *ran in repertory with* A Skull in Connemara *and* The Lonesome West. *Nightingale makes some instructive comparisons with the work of John Millington Synge, especially his* The Playboy of the Western World.

Ninety years ago, the Abbey Theater in Dublin presented a play in which a young vagrant called Christy Mahon was feted as a hero by Irish villagers because they believed he had bashed in his father's brains with a hoe.

His hosts were more than satisfied with his explanation, which was simply that the old man was dirty and grumpy, "the way I couldn't put up with him at all." They were untroubled by their obligations to a church that regarded patricide as mortal sin. In fact, the local publican promptly hired Christy to guard his daughter, declaring "by the grace of God, herself will be safe this night, with a man killed his father holding danger from the door."

By such means did John Millington Synge's *Playboy of the Western World* reduce its first audience into a mad, screeching mob, enraged by what they regarded as a libel on the Irish peasantry and Ireland itself.

Martin McDonagh has yet to provoke riots, either in Ireland or among the London Irish. Indeed, the Galway-based Druid Theater Company has just brought his Leenane Trilogy to the West End after a highly successful run back home, and his *Cripple of Inishmaan* has just won a transfer from the tiny Cottesloe auditorium to the much larger Lyttelton at the National Theater.

Yet all these plays bring Synge's sting to the portrayal of Christy's descendants. Together, they have established Mr. McDonagh as the most wickedly funny, brilliantly abrasive young dramatist on either side of the Irish Sea.

Young? Actually, Mr. McDonagh is a mere twenty-seven, which is nine years younger than Synge when he wrote *Playboy* and an astonishing age at which to have four plays running simultaneously at upscale addresses in the British capital.

Mr. McDonagh is also a Londoner, though his parents come from Galway and he has often paid visits there. That helps to explain the mixture of sly detachment and rueful familiarity he is able to bring both to the Leenane Trilogy, which is set in Connemara today, and to *The Cripple of Inishmaan*, which occurs still farther west in 1934. Cumulatively, the plays leave you feeling that the unfolding twentieth century has brought only surface change to the Irish outback. Cumulatively, they suggest that religion and conventional morality play about as strong a part in ordinary rural lives as the Roman Catholic Catechism does among the cargo-cultists of New Guinea.

Throughout the Leenane Trilogy . . . a spotlighted crucifix teases the eye. It hangs behind and above the series of dingy, primitive rooms in which the characters gossip, drink moonshine, quarrel, and do what they can to banish boredom and forget the rain pelting down outside.

That's the way the director, Garry Hynes, and the designer, Francis O'Connor, emphasize the gulf between Christian claim and pagan reality in the village of the title. But they need not have bothered, for Leenane obsessively exposes its own endemic amorality. "It seems like God has no jurisdiction in this town, no jurisdiction at all," says the local priest, who has been driven to drink and despair by months spent hearing cozy confessions about "impure thoughts" from folk who would blithely break all Ten Commandments at once.

Leenane boasts two, maybe three murderers among what can only be a population of a few hundred. None of them gets caught, let alone convicted, which is perhaps why two representatives of order and decency drown themselves in the local lake in the course of the trilogy. Lesser acts of violence include plunging an old lady's hands into boiling fat, beating and half-strangling a man hurt in a car crash, and doing menacing things with deadly weapons. But virtually nobody, not even the victims, seems to regard such brutalities as particularly wrong or especially abnormal.

This is a community where the serious has become trivial, the trivial serious. It's kicking someone else's cow or cutting the ears off his dog that causes grudges and feuds lasting generations. "When I see them burned in hell I'll let bygones be bygones and not before," snarls an old woman in the trilogy's second play, *A Skull in Connemara*. And the offense of her three foes? Twenty-seven years earlier, when they were five years old, she caught them urinating in the church-yard, and, when she threatened to tell the priest, they called her "a fat oul biddy."

The first play, *The Beauty Queen of Leenane*, may come to New York in the fall — and with good reason. When the Royal Court staged its premiere last year, all the London critics admired Mr. McDonagh's precocious dramatic skills, as well as the punch he brought to his subject, the destructive symbiosis between a possessive mother and her frustrated and sometimes sadistic daughter. Once again, Marie Mullen plays pale, pinched Maureen, forlornly hoping her hopeless hopes, and once again, Anna Manahan's Mag waddles about like an old bunched toad, wheedling and whining and emptying her chamber pot into the kitchen sink. The acting is still superlative; but then Ms. Haynes, who stages the trilogy with admirable economy and lack of show, gets emotionally powerful yet funny performances from all her performers.

There are few lulls or pauses for breath in Mr. McDonagh's work. He loves to push both feeling and humor to extremes, sometimes at the same time. In *The Beauty Queen*, the emotion outmatches the fun, but in *A Skull in Connemara*, where the stakes are lower, it is the opposite. Though Mick Lally brings vulnerability as well as grit to the role, you don't feel so wrenched by the predicament of Mick Dowd, a gravedigger forced to exhume the wife that the local gossips suspect him of murdering. The mood becomes farcical, but with Mr. McDonagh, even farce is over the top and to the point. Maybe the wildest scene in the trilogy comes when a drunken Mick and his assistant pulverize old skulls with their mallets. It's part schoolboy prank, part Dionysiac catharsis, part symbolic revenge on the living ghouls and walking corpses of Leenane itself.

Two people stormed out of the theater at the play's London premiere, presumably sickened by the splintering bone. They weren't critics, but they might as well have been, for several reviewers have accused Mr. McDonagh of taking delight in the callousness and cruelty he purports to expose. Personally, I find this squeamish and would call in evidence the trilogy's closing play, *The Lonesome West*. This is as violent and funny as anything that has preceded it, but it adds a new gravity to the dramatic algebra.

Imagine Tweedledum and Tweedledee respectively armed with a shotgun and a huge carving knife or, in some weird biblical twist, a depraved Abel demanding Cain's property as the price of covering up the latter's murder of Adam. That's roughly the situation between Maeliosa Stafford's robust Coleman, who has just blown out his father's brains, and Brian F. O'Byrne's mincing, miserly Valene, who taunts his brother with his new possessions and won't give him as much as a potato chip to eat.

Then, suddenly but unsentimentally, the play acquires a moral center. Can the touchingly earnest if alcoholic appeals of David Ganly's Father Welsh change Leenane into Arcadia? With the brothers' initial apologies transmuting into accusations, and sibling rivalry again escalating toward fratricide, that seems a silly question. But at least Mr. McDonagh has the heart and soul to ask it.

Subtract the odd television set and Australian soap opera, and the ecology of *The Cripple of Inishmaan* is much the same. The setting this time is the Aran Islands, where Synge himself went to observe and write and, years later, Robert Flaherty shot a famous documentary. Indeed, it's the making of *Man of Aran* that gives Mr. McDonagh his plot.

Cripple Billy, as everyone derisively calls the title character, makes his way from the island of Inishmaan to its neighbor Inishmore, is taken to Hollywood for a screen test, but ends up back in his own parish, where his main leisure pursuit has been sitting and staring at cows.

If Irish drama often blends pain and laughter, it equally often deals with fantasies of escaping a dull, punishing environment. Here and in *The Beauty Queen of*

Leenane, whose protagonist yearns to escape to Boston with a likely man, Mr. McDonagh is indebted not only to Synge's *Playboy*, but to Sean O'Casey's *Juno and the Paycock*, Brian Friel's *Translations*, and even *Waiting for Godot*.

"Oh the dreaming, the dreaming!" cries a character in *John Bull's Other Island*, the only play Shaw set in his native Ireland, "the torturing, heart-scalding, never satisfying dreaming, dreaming, dreaming, dreaming!" Samuel Beckett's tramps would know what he means, and so would Ruaidhri Conroy's wispy, prematurely wizened Billy.

Nicholas Hytner's production at the National is more stylized and less immediate than Ms. Hynes's at the Duke of York's, but you cannot miss Mr. McDonagh's trademark fizz. It is a born storyteller who creates remarkably lively, original characters.

There is Aisling O'Sullivan's Slippy Helen, a ferocious tomboy, who ends a feud caused by a goose's attack on a cat by taking money from each owner to kill the other's creature. There is Ray McBride's Johnnypateenmike, who lives by cadging food in return for bringing people gossip, while he tries to kill his aged, sottish mother by supplying her with endless booze.

Like Leenane, Inishmaan is a drab, cut-off, enervating place. But again, like Leenane, Mr. McDonagh packs it with oddity and human resilience.

Nor have we heard the last of the island. *The Cripple of Inishmaan* may close at the National on Friday and finish with a tour to Norway, Cork, and Dublin. But it's only the first part of an Inishmaan trilogy that the prolific Mr. McDonagh is currently writing. The content of the next two plays is anybody's guess, but we can be pretty sure what their tone will be. At one point in *The Cripple of Inishmaan*, poor, twisted Billy tells a local boy he shouldn't laugh at other people's misfortunes. The answer is a genuinely astonished "why?" "I don't know why," answers Billy, "just you shouldn't is all." "But it's awful funny," says the boy, and Billy doesn't demur.

That, finally, is the contradiction that marks so much Irish drama and is at the heart of Mr. McDonagh's black comedies. When you can't change or leave a bleak, mean world, what better way is there of surviving it than laughing at the sheer frightfulness of things?

Alisa Solomon (b. 1956)

BEASTLY BEAUTY   *1998*

Not all critics loved The Beauty Queen of Leenane. *Alisa Solomon of the* Village Voice *saw the first New York production at the Atlantic Theater Company and complained that it was a play with an "attitude." She sees it as misanthropic and sentimental but also as a play that works. This is perhaps the most interesting aspect of it for her.*

By the time this review appears, the dailies will already have nominated Martin McDonagh for Beatitude. Never mind that the promotional interviews that preceded the twenty-eight-year-old Irish-British playwright's American premiere revealed him to be another smug and smarmy Angry Young Man. The play itself is being received as a masterpiece of sensitivity that skillfully lays bare the affecting yearnings of the lovelorn.

True, there's an adroit craftiness with which McDonagh repeatedly reverses seeming certainties of the plot. But the real genius of his writing is his ability to wring sentimentality out of a situation for which he evokes little true compassion. McDonagh can make you feel pity for his characters, stuck as they are in their stagnant rural world and their spiteful relationships. He can even make you hope, for a moment at least, that they will act with decency and be justly rewarded for doing so. But again and again McDonagh snatches away all reason for those perfectly plotted expectations of human kindness, generosity, or unselfish action. *The Beauty Queen of Leenane* is, at its core, a deeply misanthropic work.

The play unfolds in a dreary cottage in the western Ireland town of Leenane, where forty-year-old Maureen is enslaved to her shrewish seventy-year-old mother, Mag. It's not long into their squabbling over the lumps in Mag's Complan — a powdered hot drink — that a glimmer of escape presents itself to Maureen: their neighbor Ray invites them to a party. Maureen comes home from the party with Ray's older brother, Pato, who is visiting from London, and the two lonely hearts reach out for each other in an awkward, desperate heat. In the morning, Maureen flaunts the affair before her appalled mother. And in the next scene — a monologue soon to be repeated, no doubt, in countless acting school auditions — Pato writes Maureen a letter, asking her to be his wife and move to America with him. The action unwinds from there, with some disturbing surprises and some blatantly telegraphed twists.

The story has a simple line, but McDonagh's manipulation of our sympathies is snarled. First of all, because the more dismal the situation, the more comic he finds it: there's a running gag built on Mag dumping her pot of piss into the kitchen sink every morning; Ray is hilarious in his cocky aimlessness, complaining of boredom and dreaming of drugs and cop-bashing. But more so because McDonagh, unlike American playwrights who favor kitchen-sink realism, never lets his characters explain themselves. There's no psychobabble in Leenane. Just idiotic chitchat, bitter bickering, and terrible action.

And, in four full performances, a thoroughness and unselfconsciousness that one seldom encounters. Three of the four cast members performed in the original production in Galway and London. All of them create portraits of people with inner lives to which these characters just don't have access. As Mag, Anna Manahan lets out a grunt and expresses a lifetime's woe; as Maureen, Marie Mullen skips into girlish glee or slides into vindictive violence as though her actions were as inevitable as the Irish rain.

Beyond the gray panes of Maureen and Mag's hovel, rain streams down through much of the play. The technical trick that sends water gushing from the flies is the scenic equivalent of McDonagh's achievement: *The Beauty Queen of Leenane* is an extremely deft work. But it doesn't soak in anywhere.

Paula Vogel

Paula Vogel (b. 1951) came from a working-class family and knew she would have to make it on her own if she made it at all. For her, that knowledge was essentially the best inheritance she could have had. Her early years were marred by her parents' divorce and the loss of a father whom she came to know only in later years when her closest sibling, Carl, was dying of AIDS. Her earliest efforts in playwriting also met with rejection. After losing her scholarship to Bryn Mawr College and when she devoted herself to dramatic literature, she graduated from Catholic University in Washington and then was turned down by the Yale School of Drama. Her earliest plays were also turned down by the Eugene O'Neill National Playwright's Conference. In retrospect, she feels that these were good things because they made her learn her craft in a difficult — and original — way, which led eventually to her winning the Pulitzer Prize for *How I Learned to Drive.*

Vogel's earliest exposure to theater was in Washington, D.C. She talks about having "stumbled into drama class" when she was a sophomore in high school and beginning to find her way in theater. Her high school drama teacher was gay, and she feels he must have realized that she was herself a lesbian. She resisted taking acting roles — although she coached other students — and spent her years in high school as a stage manager. As a young playwright she found other friends who were trying to write, and they gathered together to read each other's work. They occasionally did exercises, some of which became useful teaching tools for Vogel at Brown University. For example, they wrote complete plays in forty-eight hours as a way of getting the essentials down as quickly as possible. Some of her earliest work had its origin in these experiments, including a version of *How I Learned to Drive.*

Some of her plays have startling images, such as a bizarre Groucho-Marx-like doctor treating a dying AIDS patient in *The Baltimore Waltz* (Obie Award for best play 1992), a play about the death of her beloved brother Carl, who had begun a professional career as an English professor but switched to being a librarian. He was gay, and homophobia, according to Vogel, hurt him more than the disease that killed him. Her plays are famous for scatological humor, jokes about the body, and extremely plain talk.

Among her early plays is one about lesbians who parent several little boys: *And Baby Makes Seven* (1984) — a daring excursion into territory that few playwrights have explored. Another early play, *The Oldest Profession* (1988), treats older prostitutes. *Hot 'n' Throbbing* (1994) examines the effect of theater on its characters. *The Mineola Twins* (1996) was written before *How I Learned to Drive* but was produced later, in 1999. Vogel thinks of this play as a comedy and something of a contrast to *How I Learned to Drive,* which is, if not a tragedy, certainly serious in nature. Yet it too has moments of genuine comedy.

Currently, Paula Vogel is preparing screenplays for two of her theater pieces: *The Oldest Profession* and *How I Learned to Drive.*

How I Learned to Drive

How I Learned to Drive was first produced in New York off-Broadway in 1997. It won not only the Pulitzer Prize but the New York Drama Critics' Circle, Drama Desk, and Obie awards for best play of the year. It is published in a volume with *The Mineola Twins* called *The Mammary Plays*. Vogel explains that large-busted women remained an emblem for her in the construction of both plays. As a feminist, Vogel is interested in our fetishization of women's bodies, and both these plays move toward revealing the way the culture, both men and women, regard women's bodies, even while praising their minds.

All the characters in Li'l Bit's family are named in an unusual way. Li'l Bit explains, "In my family, if we call someone 'Big Papa,' it's not because he's tall. In my family, folks tend to get nicknamed for their genitalia. Uncle Peck, for example. My mamma's adage was 'the titless wonder.' Even Li'l Bit was named after she was physically examined at birth. Uncle Peck, married to Li'l Bit's mother's sister Mary, is not a blood relation — a fact he constantly stresses to Li'l Bit — and he tells her he has loved her since she was small enough to hold in his hand. Even Big Papa chases Grandma around the house: it's an unusual and curious family.

The play is about sexual molestation — but about many other things, too. It is about families, about growing up, about becoming independent, and most of all about being a survivor. In a interview with Arthur Holmberg, Vogel has said, "My play dramatizes the gifts we receive from people who hurt us." When asked what gift Li'l Bit received, she responded, "She received the gift of how to survive." Vogel uses learning to drive as a complex metaphor for sexual initiation. At the same time, the metaphor examines what a man expects from a close relationship with a woman and what a woman expects from a close relationship with a man. Uncle Peck is careful never to hurt Li'l Bit and always reminds her that he doesn't want her to do anything she doesn't wish to do. But at the same time, Uncle Peck "has a way" with adolescent girls, as his wife tells us. He listens to Li'l Bit and becomes her confidante, patiently waiting for her to accept him on his own terms.

Although he is a predator, Uncle Peck is not necessarily a villain in the play. He takes advantage of Li'l Bit starting at age eleven and continues until she is eighteen and in college. For Vogel, part of the learning process for Li'l Bit is, as Vogel has said, becoming "an adult looking at and understanding her complicity." Then the next step is self-forgiveness. This step is essential to moving forward in her life.

How I Learned to Drive in Performance

The Vineyard Theatre in New York City produced the play in February 1997 and moved it to the large Century Theater in April. It was reviewed warmly and received positively by audiences, eventually winning Vogel the Pulitzer Prize for drama for 1997. The play relies on an interesting device, the Greek Chorus, a character who speaks in the voice of characters alluded to but not present, such as Li'l Bit's mother, grandmother, grandfather, and aunt. Vogel also wanted to have slides shown at critical moments, such as the scene in which Uncle Peck is taking photographs of Li'l Bit and in the scene in which Uncle Peck rhapsodizes over 1950s automobiles. Not all directors use the slides. For example, they were not used in the original New York production. Vogel's method of writing, like that of many playwrights, is to respond to the actors' interpretation of lines during rehearsal and rewriting. *How I Learned to Drive* benefited from that method.

In 1998 *How I Learned to Drive* had twenty-six regional productions and was the most produced play in America. More than thirty more productions are scheduled abroad.

Paula Vogel (*b. 1951*)
HOW I LEARNED TO DRIVE   *1997*

Characters

LI'L BIT, *A woman who ages forty-something to eleven years old.*

PECK, *Attractive man in his forties. Despite a few problems, he should be played by an actor one might cast in the role of Atticus in* To Kill A Mockingbird.

THE GREEK CHORUS, *If possible, these three members should be able to sing three-part harmony.*

> MALE GREEK CHORUS, *Plays Grandfather, Waiter, High School Boys. Thirties — forties.*
> FEMALE GREEK CHORUS, *Plays Mother, Aunt Mary, High School Girls. Thirty–fifty.*
> TEENAGE GREEK CHORUS, *Plays Grandmother, High School Girls, and the voice of eleven-year-old Li'l Bit. Note on the casting of this actor: I would strongly recommend casting a young woman who is "of legal age," that is, twenty-one to twenty-five years old, who can look as close to eleven as possible. The contrast with the other cast members will help. If the actor is too young, the audience may feel uncomfortable.*

(*As the house lights dim, a Voice announces:*)

Safety First — You and Driver Education.

(*Then the sound of a key turning the ignition of a car. Li'l Bit steps into a spotlight on the stage; "well-endowed," she is a softer-looking woman in the present time than she was at seventeen.*)

LI'L BIT: Sometimes to tell a secret, you first have to teach a lesson. We're going to start our lesson tonight on an early, warm summer evening.

In a parking lot overlooking the Beltsville Agricultural Farms in suburban Maryland.

Less than a mile away, the crumbling concrete of U.S. One wends its way past one-room revival churches, the porno drive-in, and boarded up motels with For Sale signs tumbling down.

Like I said, it's a warm summer evening.

Here on the land the Department of Agriculture owns, the smell of sleeping farm animal is thick on the air. The smells of clover and hay mix in with the smells of the leather dashboard. You can still imagine how Maryland used to be, before the malls took over. This countryside was once dotted with farmhouses — from their porches you could have witnessed the Civil War raging in the front fields.

Oh yes. There's a moon over Maryland tonight, that spills into the car where I sit beside a man old enough to be — did I mention how still the night is? Damp soil and tranquil air. It's the kind of night that makes a middle-aged man with a mortgage feel like a country boy again.

It's 1969. And I am very old, very cynical of the world, and I know it all. In short, I am seventeen years old, parking off a dark lane with a married man on an early summer night.

(*Lights up on two chairs facing front — or a Buick Riviera, if you will. Waiting patiently, with a smile on his face, Peck sits sniffing the night air. Li'l Bit climbs in beside him, seventeen years old and tense. Throughout the following, the two sit facing directly front. They do*) *not touch. Their bodies remain passive. Only their facial expressions emote.*)

PECK: Ummm. I love the smell of your hair.

LI'L BIT: Uh-huh.

PECK: Oh, Lord. Ummmm. (*Beat.*) A man could die happy like this.

LI'L BIT: Well, *don't.*

PECK: What shampoo is this?

LI'L BIT: Herbal Essence.

PECK: Herbal Essence. I'm gonna buy me some. Herbal Essence. And when I'm all alone in the house, I'm going to get into the bathtub, and uncap the bottle and —

LI'L BIT: — Be good.

PECK: What?

LI'L BIT: Stop being . . . bad.

PECK: What did you think I was going to say? What do you think I'm going to do with the shampoo?

LI'L BIT: I don't want to know. I don't want to hear it.

PECK: I'm going to wash my hair. That's all.

LI'L BIT: Oh.

PECK: What did you think I was going to do?

LI'L BIT: Nothing . . . I don't know. Something . . . nasty.

PECK: With shampoo? Lord, gal — your mind!

LI'L BIT: And whose fault is it?

PECK: Not mine. I've got the mind of a boy scout.

LI'L BIT: Right. A horny boy scout.

PECK: Boy scouts are always horny. What do you think the first Merit Badge is for?

LI'L BIT: There. You're going to be nasty again.

PECK: Oh, no. I'm good. Very good.

LI'L BIT: It's getting late.

PECK: Don't change the subject. I was talking about how good I am. (*Beat.*) Are you ever gonna let me show you how good I am?

LI'L BIT: Don't go over the line now.

PECK: I won't. I'm not gonna do anything you don't want me to do.

LI'L BIT: That's right.

PECK: And I've been good all week.

LI'L BIT: You have?

PECK: Yes. All week. Not a single drink.

LI'L BIT: Good boy.

PECK: Do I get a reward? For not drinking?

LI'L BIT: A small one. It's getting late.

PECK: Just let me undo you. I'll do you back up.

LI'L BIT: All right. But be quick about it.

(*Peck pantomimes undoing Li'l Bit's brassiere with one hand.*)

You know, that's amazing. The way you can undo the hooks through my blouse with one hand.

PECK: Years of practice.

LI'L BIT: You would make an incredible brain surgeon with that dexterity.

PECK: I'll bet Clyde — what's the name of the boy taking you to the prom?

LI'L BIT: Claude Souders.

PECK: Claude Souders. I'll bet it takes him two hands, lights on, and you helping him on to get to first base.

LI'L BIT: Maybe.

(*Beat.*)

PECK: Can I . . . kiss them? Please?

LI'L BIT: I don't know.

PECK: Don't make a grown man beg.

LI'L BIT: Just one kiss.

PECK: I'm going to lift your blouse.

LI'L BIT: It's a little cold.

(*Peck laughs gently.*)

PECK: That's not why you're shivering.

(*They sit, perfectly still, for a long moment of silence. Peck makes gentle, concentric circles with his thumbs in the air in front of him.*)

How does that feel?

(*Li'l Bit closes her eyes, carefully keeps her voice calm:*)

LI'L BIT: It's . . . okay.

(*Sacred music, organ music or a boy's choir swells beneath the following.*)

PECK: I tell you, you can keep all the cathedrals of Europe. Just give me a second with these — these celestial orbs —

(*Peck bows his head as if praying. But he is kissing her nipple. Li'l Bit, eyes still closed, rears back her head on the leather Buick car seat.*)

LI'L BIT: Uncle Peck — we've got to go. I've got graduation rehearsal at school tomorrow morning. And you should get on home to Aunt Mary —

PECK: — All right, Li'l Bit.

LI'L BIT: — *Don't* call me that no more. (*Calmer.*) Any more. I'm a big girl now, Uncle Peck. As you know.

(*Li'l Bit pantomimes refastening her bra behind her back.*)

PECK: That you are. Going on eighteen. Kittens will turn into cats. (*Sighs.*) I live all week long for these few minutes with you — you know that?

LI'L BIT: I'll drive.

(*A Voice cuts in with:*)

Idling in the Neutral Gear.

(*Sound of car revving cuts off the sacred music; Li'l Bit, now an adult, rises out of the car and comes to us.*)

LI'L BIT: In most families, relatives get names like "Junior," or "Brother," or "Bubba." In my family, if we call someone "Big Papa," it's not because he's tall. In my family, folks tend to get nicknamed for their genitalia. Uncle Peck, for example. My mama's adage was "the titless wonder," and my cousin Bobby got branded for life as "B.B."

(*In unison with Greek Chorus:*)

LI'L BIT: For blue balls.   GREEK CHORUS: For blue balls.

FEMALE GREEK CHORUS (*as Mother*): And of course, we were so excited to have a baby girl that when the nurse brought you in and said, "It's a girl! It's a baby girl!" I just had to see for myself. So we whipped your diapers down and parted your chubby little legs — and right between your legs there was —

(*Peck has come over during the above and chimes along:*)

PECK: Just a little bit.   GREEK CHORUS: Just a little bit.

FEMALE GREEK CHORUS (*as Mother*): And when you were born, you were so tiny that you fit in Uncle Peck's outstretched hand.

(*Peck stretches his hand out.*)

PECK: Now that's a fact. I held you, one day old, right in this hand.

(*A traffic signal is projected of a bicycle in a circle with a diagonal red slash.*)

LI'L BIT: Even with my family background, I was sixteen or so before I realized that pedophilia did not mean people who loved to bicycle . . . .

(*A Voice intrudes:*)

Driving in First Gear.

LI'L BIT: 1969. A typical family dinner.

FEMALE GREEK CHORUS (*as Mother*): Look, Grandma. Li'l Bit's getting to be as big in the bust as you are.

LI'L BIT: Mother! Could we please change the subject?

TEENAGE GREEK CHORUS (*as Grandmother*): Well, I hope you are buying her some decent bras. I never had a decent bra, growing up in the Depression, and now my shoulders are just crippled — crippled from the weight hanging on my shoulders — the dents from my bra straps are big enough to put your finger in. — Here, let me show you —

(*As Grandmother starts to open her blouse:*)

LI'L BIT: Grandma! Please don't undress at the dinner table.

PECK: I thought the entertainment came *after* the dinner.

LI'L BIT (*to the audience*): This is how it always starts. My grandfather, Big Papa, will chime in next with —

MALE GREEK CHORUS (*as Grandfather*): Yup. If Li'l Bit gets any bigger, we're gonna haveta buy her a wheelbarrow to carry in front of her —

LI'L BIT: — Damn it —

PECK: — How about those Redskins on Sunday, Big Papa?

LI'L BIT (*to the audience*): The only sport Big Papa followed was chasing Grandma around the house —

MALE GREEK CHORUS (*as Grandfather*): — Or we could write to Kate Smith. Ask her for somma her used brassieres she don't want anymore — she could maybe give to Li'l Bit here —

LI'L BIT: — I can't stand it. I can't.

PECK: Now, honey, that's just their way —

FEMALE GREEK CHORUS (*as Mother*): I tell you, Grandma, Li'l Bit's at that age. She's so sensitive, you can't say boo —

LI'L BIT: I'd like some privacy, that's all. Okay? Some goddamn privacy —

PECK: — Well, at least she didn't use the savior's name —

LI'L BIT (*to the audience*): And Big Papa wouldn't let a dead dog lie. No sirree.

MALE GREEK CHORUS (*as Grandfather*): Well, she'd better stop being so sensitive. 'Cause five minutes before Li'l Bit turns the corner, her tits turn first —

LI'L BIT (*starting to rise from the table*): — That's it. That's it.

PECK: Li'l Bit, you can't let him get to you. Then he wins.

LI'L BIT: I hate him. *Hate* him.

PECK: That's fine. But hate him and eat a good dinner at the same time.

(*Li'l Bit calms down and sits with perfect dignity.*)

LI'L BIT: The gumbo is really good, Grandma.

MALE GREEK CHORUS (*as Grandfather*): A'course, Li'l Bit's got a big surprise coming for her when she goes to that fancy college this fall —

PECK: Big Papa — let it go.

MALE GREEK CHORUS (*as Grandfather*): What does she need a college degree for? She's got all the credentials she'll need on her chest —

LI'L BIT: — Maybe I want to learn things. Read. Rise above my cracker° background —

PECK: — Whoa, now, Li'l Bit —

MALE GREEK CHORUS (*as Grandfather*): What kind of things do you want to read?

LI'L BIT: There's a whole semester course, for example, on Shakespeare —

(*Greek Chorus, as Grandfather, laughs until he weeps.*)

MALE GREEK CHORUS (*as Grandfather*): Shakespeare. That's a good one. Shakespeare is really going to help you in life.

PECK: I think it's wonderful. And on scholarship!

MALE GREEK CHORUS (*as Grandfather*): How is Shakespeare going to help her lie on her back in the dark?

(*Li'l Bit is on her feet.*)

LI'L BIT: You're getting old, Big Papa. You are going to die — very very soon. Maybe even *tonight*. And when you get to heaven, God's going to be a beautiful

---

cracker: A derogatory term for a poor, Southern, white person.

black woman in a long white robe. She's gonna look at your chart and say: Uh-oh. Fornication. Dog-ugly mean with blood relatives. Oh. Uh-oh. Voted for George Wallace. Well, one last chance: If you can name the play, all will be forgiven. And then she'll quote: "The quality of mercy is not strained." Your answer? Oh, too bad — *Merchant of Venice:* Act IV, Scene iii. And then she'll send your ass to fry in hell with all the other crackers. Excuse me, please.

(*To the audience.*) And as I left the house, I would always hear Big Papa say:

MALE GREEK CHORUS (*as Grandfather*): Lucy, your daughter's got a mouth on her. Well, no sense in wasting good gumbo. Pass me her plate, Mama.

LI'L BIT: And Aunt Mary would come up to Uncle Peck:

FEMALE GREEK CHORUS (*as Aunt Mary*): Peck, go after her, will you? You're the only one she'll listen to when she gets like this.

PECK: She just needs to cool off.

FEMALE GREEK CHORUS (*as Aunt Mary*): Please, honey — Grandma's been on her feet cooking all day.

PECK: All right.

LI'L BIT: And as he left the room, Aunt Mary would say:

FEMALE GREEK CHORUS (*as Aunt Mary*): Peck's so good with them when they get to be this age.

(*Li'l Bit has stormed to another part of the stage, her back turned, weeping with a teenage fury. Peck, cautiously, as if stalking a deer, comes to her. She turns away even more. He waits a bit.*)

PECK: I don't suppose you're talking to family. (*No response.*) Does it help that I'm in-law?

LI'L BIT: Don't you dare make fun of this.

PECK: I'm not. There's nothing funny about this. (*Beat.*) Although I'll bet when Big Papa is about to meet his maker, he'll remember *The Merchant of Venice.*

LI'L BIT: I've got to get away from here.

PECK: You're going away. Soon. Here, take this.

(*Peck hands her his folded handkerchief. Li'l Bit uses it, noisily. Hands it back. Without her seeing, he reverently puts it back.*)

LI'L BIT: I hate this family.

PECK: Your grandfather's ignorant. And you're right — he's going to die soon. But he's family. Family is . . . family.

LI'L BIT: Grown-ups are always saying that. Family.

PECK: Well, when you get a little older, you'll see what we're saying.

LI'L BIT: Uh-huh. So family is another acquired taste, like French kissing?

PECK: Come again?

LI'L BIT: You know, at first it really grosses you out, but in time you grow to like it?

PECK: Girl, you are . . . a handful.

LI'L BIT: Uncle Peck — you have the keys to your car?

PECK: Where do you want to go?

LI'L BIT: Just up the road.

PECK: I'll come with you.

LI'L BIT: No — please? I just need to . . . to drive for a little bit. Alone.

(*Peck tosses her the keys.*)

PECK: When can I see you alone again?

LI'L BIT: Tonight.

(*Li'l Bit crosses to center stage while the lights dim around her. A Voice directs:*)

Shifting Forward from First to Second Gear.

LI'L BIT: There were a lot of rumors about why I got kicked out of that fancy school in 1970. Some say I got caught with a man in my room. Some say as a kid on scholarship I fooled around with a rich man's daughter.

(*Li'l Bit smiles innocently at the audience.*) I'm not talking.

But the real truth was I had a constant companion in my dorm room — who was less than discreet. Canadian V.O. A fifth a day.

1970. A Nixon recession. I slept on the floors of friends who were out of work themselves. Took factory work when I could find it. A string of dead-end jobs that didn't last very long.

What I did, most nights, was cruise the Beltway and the back roads of Maryland, where there was still country, past the battlefields and farm houses. Racing in a 1965 Mustang — and as long as I had gasoline for my car and whiskey for me, the nights would pass. Full tanked, I would speed past the churches and the trees on the bend, thinking just one notch of the steering wheel would be all it would take, and yet some . . . reflex took over. My hands on the wheel in the nine and three o'clock position — I never so much as got a ticket. He taught me well.

(*A Voice announces:*)

You and the Reverse Gear.

LI'L BIT: Back up. 1968. On the Eastern Shore. A celebration dinner.

(*Li'l Bit joins Peck at a table in a restaurant.*)

PECK: Feeling better, missy?

LI'L BIT: The bathroom's really amazing here, Uncle Peck! They have these little soaps — instead of borax or something — and they're in the shape of shells.

PECK: I'll have to take a trip to the gentleman's room just to see.

LI'L BIT: How did you know about this place?

PECK: This inn is famous on the Eastern Shore — it's been open since the seventeenth century. And I know how you like history. . . .

(*Li'l Bit is shy and pleased.*)

LI'L BIT: It's great.

PECK: And you've just done your first, legal, long-distance drive. You must be hungry.

LI'L BIT: I'm starved.

PECK: I would suggest a dozen oysters to start, and the crab imperial. . . . (*Li'l Bit is genuinely agog.*) You might be interested to know the town history. When the British sailed up this very river in the dead of night — see outside where I'm pointing? — they were going to bombard the heck out of this town. But the town fathers were ready for them. They crept up all the trees with lanterns so that the British would think they saw the town lights and they aimed their cannons too high. And that's why the inn is still here for business today.

LI'L BIT: That's a great story.

PECK (*casually*): Would you like to start with a cocktail?

LI'L BIT: You're not . . . you're not going to start drinking, are you, Uncle Peck?

PECK: Not me. I told you, as long as you're with me, I'll never drink. I asked you if *you'd* like a cocktail before dinner. It's nice to have a little something with the oysters.

LI'L BIT: But . . . I'm not . . . legal. We could get arrested. Uncle Peck, they'll never believe I'm twenty-one!

PECK: So? Today we celebrate your driver's license — on the first try. This establishment reminds me a lot of places back home.

LI'L BIT: What does that mean?

PECK: In South Carolina, like here on the Eastern Shore, they're . . . (*Searches for the right euphemism.*) . . . "European." Not so puritanical. And very understanding if gentlemen wish to escort very attractive young ladies who might want a before-dinner cocktail. If you want one, I'll order one.

LI'L BIT: Well — sure. Just . . . one.

(*The Female Greek Chorus appears in a spot.*)

FEMALE GREEK CHORUS (*as Mother*): A Mother's Guide to Social Drinking:

A lady never gets sloppy — she may, however, get tipsy and a little gay.

Never drink on an empty stomach. Avail yourself of the bread basket and generous portions of butter. *Slather* the butter on your bread.

Sip your drink, slowly, let the beverage linger in your mouth — interspersed with interesting, fascinating conversation. Sip, never . . . slurp or gulp. Your glass should always be three-quarters full when his glass is empty.

Stay away from *ladies'* drinks: drinks like pink ladies, slow gin fizzes, piña coladas, mai tais, planters punch, white Russians, black Russians, red Russians, melon balls, blue balls, hummingbirds, hemorrhages, and hurricanes. In short, avoid anything with sugar, or anything with an umbrella. Get your vitamin C from *fruit*. Don't order anything with Voodoo or Vixen in the title or sexual positions in the name like Dead Man Screw or the Missionary. (*She sort of titters.*)

Believe me, they are lethal. . . . I think you were conceived after one of those.

Drink, instead, like a man: straight up or on the rocks, with plenty of water in between.

Oh, yes. And never mix your drinks. Stay with one all night long, like the man you came in with: bourbon, gin, or tequila till dawn, damn the torpedoes, full speed ahead!

(*As the Female Greek Chorus retreats, the Male Greek Chorus approaches the table as a Waiter.*)

MALE GREEK CHORUS (*as Waiter*): I hope you all are having a pleasant evening. Is there something I can bring you, sir, before you order?

(*Li'l Bit waits in anxious fear. Carefully, Uncle Peck says with command:*)

PECK: I'll have a plain iced tea. The lady would like a drink, I believe.

(*The Male Greek Chorus does a double take; there is a moment when Uncle Peck and he are in silent communication.*)

MALE GREEK CHORUS (*as Waiter*): Very good. What would the . . . lady like?

LI'L BIT (*a bit flushed*): Is there . . . is there any sugar in a martini?

PECK: None that I know of.

LI'L BIT: That's what I'd like then — a dry martini. And could we maybe have some bread?

PECK: A drink fit for a woman of the world. — Please bring the lady a dry martini, be generous with the olives, straight up.

(*The Male Greek Chorus anticipates a large tip.*)

MALE GREEK CHORUS (*as Waiter*): Right away. Very good, sir.

(*The Male Greek Chorus returns with an empty martini glass which he puts in front of Li'l Bit.*)

PECK: Your glass is empty. Another martini, madam?

LI'L BIT: Yes, thank you.

(*Peck signals the Male Greek Chorus, who nods.*)

So why did you leave South Carolina, Uncle Peck?

PECK: I was stationed in D.C. after the war, and decided to stay. Go North, Young Man, someone might have said.

LI'L BIT: What did you do in the service anyway?

PECK (*suddenly taciturn*): I . . . I did just this and that. Nothing heroic or spectacular.

LI'L BIT: But did you see fighting? Or go to Europe?

PECK: I served in the Pacific Theater. It's really nothing interesting to talk about.

LI'L BIT: It is to me. (*The Waiter has brought another*

empty glass.) Oh, goody. I love the color of the swizzle sticks. What were we talking about?

PECK: Swizzle sticks.

LI'L BIT: Do you ever think of going back?

PECK: To the Marines?

LI'L BIT: No — to South Carolina.

PECK: Well, we do go back. To visit.

LI'L BIT: No, I mean to live.

PECK: Not very likely. I think it's better if my mother doesn't have a daily reminder of her disappointment.

LI'L BIT: Are these floorboards slanted?

PECK: Yes, the floor is very slanted. I think this is the original floor.

LI'L BIT: Oh, good.

(*The Female Greek Chorus as Mother enters swaying a little, a little past tipsy.*)

FEMALE GREEK CHORUS (*as Mother*): Don't leave your drink unattended when you visit the ladies' room. There is such a thing as white slavery; the modus operandi is to spike an unsuspecting young girl's drink with a "mickey" when she's left the room to powder her nose.

But if you feel you have had more than your sufficiency in liquor, do go to the ladies' room — often. Pop your head out of doors for a refreshing breath of the night air. If you must, wet your face and head with tap water. Don't be afraid to dunk your head if necessary. A wet woman is still less conspicuous than a drunk woman.

(*The Female Greek Chorus stumbles a little; conspiratorially.*) When in the course of human events it becomes necessary, go to a corner stall and insert the index and middle finger down the throat almost to the epiglottis. Divulge your stomach contents by such persuasion, and then wait a few moments before rejoining your beau waiting for you at your table.

Oh, no. Don't be shy or embarrassed. In the very best of establishments, there's always one or two debutantes crouched in the corner stalls, their beaded purses tossed willy-nilly, sounding like cats in heat, heaving up the contents of their stomachs.

(*The Female Greek Chorus begins to wander off.*) I wonder what is it they do in the men's rooms. . . .

LI'L BIT: So why is your mother disappointed in you, Uncle Peck?

LI'L BIT: Every mother in Horry County has Great Expectations.

LI'L BIT: — Could I have another mar-ti-ni, please?

PECK: I think this is your last one.

(*Peck signals the Waiter. The Waiter looks at Li'l Bit and shakes his head no. Peck raises his eyebrow, raises his finger to indicate one more, and then rubs his fingers together. It looks like a secret code. The Waiter sighs, shakes his head sadly, and brings over another empty martini glass. He glares at Peck.*)

LI'L BIT: The name of the county where you grew up is "Horry?" (*Li'l Bit, plastered, begins to laugh. Then*

she stops.) I think your mother should be proud of you.

(*Peck signals for the check.*)

PECK: Well, missy, she wanted me to do — to *be* everything my father was not. She wanted me to amount to something.

LI'L BIT: But you have! You've amounted a lot. . . .

PECK: I'm just a very ordinary man.

(*The Waiter has brought the check and waits. Peck draws out a large bill and hands it to the Waiter. Li'l Bit is in the soppy stage.*)

LI'L BIT: I'll bet your mother loves you, Uncle Peck.

(*Peck freezes a bit. To Male Greek Chorus as Waiter:*)

PECK: Thank you. The service was exceptional. Please keep the change.

MALE GREEK CHORUS (*as Waiter, in a tone that could freeze*): Thank you, sir. Will you be needing any help?

PECK: I think we can manage, thank you.

(*Just then, the Female Greek Chorus as Mother lurches on stage; the Male Greek Chorus as Waiter escorts her off as she delivers:*)

FEMALE GREEK CHORUS (*as Mother*): Thanks to judicious planning and several trips to the ladies' loo, your mother once out-drank an entire regiment of British officers on a good-will visit to Washington! Every last man of them! Milquetoasts! How'd they ever kick Hitler's cahones, huh? No match for an American lady — I could drink every man in here under the table.

(*She delivers one last crucial hint before she is gently "bounced."*)

As a last resort, when going out for an evening on the town, be sure to wear a skin-tight girdle — so tight that only a surgical knife or acetylene torch can get it off you — so that if you do pass out in the arms of your escort, he'll end up with rubber burns on his fingers before he can steal your virtue —

(*A Voice punctures the interlude with:*)

Vehicle Failure.

Even with careful maintenance and preventive operation of your automobile, it is all too common for us to experience an unexpected breakdown. If you are driving at any speed when a breakdown occurs, you must slow down and guide the automobile to the side of the road.

(*Peck is slowly propping up Li'l Bit as they work their way to his car in the parking lot of the inn.*)

PECK: How are you doing, missy?

LI'L BIT: It's so far to the car, Uncle Peck. Like the lanterns in the trees the British fired on. . . .

(*Li'l Bit stumbles. Peck swoops her up in his arms.*)

PECK: Okay, I think we're going to take a more direct route.

(*Li'l Bit closes her eyes.*)

Dizzy?

(*She nods her head.*)

Don't look at the ground. Almost there — do you feel sick to your stomach?

(*Li'l Bit nods. They reach the "car." Peck gently deposits her on the front seat.*)

Just settle here a little while until things stop spinning.

(*Li'l Bit opens her eyes.*)

LI'L BIT: What are we doing?
PECK: We're just going to sit here until your tummy settles down.
LI'L BIT: It's such nice upholst'ry —
PECK: Think you can go for a ride, now?
LI'L BIT: Where are you taking me?
PECK: Home.
LI'L BIT: You're not taking me — upstairs? There's no room at the inn? (*Li'l Bit giggles.*)
PECK: Do you want to go upstairs?

(*Li'l Bit doesn't answer.*)

Or home?
LI'L BIT: — This isn't right, Uncle Peck.
PECK: What isn't right?
LI'L BIT: What we're doing. It's wrong. It's very wrong.
PECK: What are we doing?

(*Li'l Bit does not answer.*)

We're just going out to dinner.
LI'L BIT: You know. It's not nice to Aunt Mary.
PECK: You let me be the judge of what's nice and not nice to my wife.

(*Beat.*)

LI'L BIT: Now you're mad.
PECK: I'm not mad. It's just that I thought you . . . understood me, Li'l Bit. I think you're the only one who does.
LI'L BIT: Someone will get hurt.
PECK: Have I forced you to do anything?

(*There is a long pause as Li'l Bit tries to get sober enough to think this through.*)

LI'L BIT: . . . I guess not.
PECK: We are just enjoying each other's company. I've told you, nothing is going to happen between us until you want it to. Do you know that?
LI'L BIT: Yes.
PECK: Nothing is going to happen until you want it. (*A second more, with Peck staring ahead at the river*

while seated at the wheel of his car. Then, softly:) Do you want something to happen?

(*Peck reaches over and strokes her face, very gently. Li'l Bit softens, reaches for him, and buries her head in his neck. Then she kisses him. Then she moves away, dizzy again.*)

LI'L BIT: . . . I don't know.

(*Peck smiles; this has been good news for him — it hasn't been a "no."*)

PECK: Then I'll wait. I'm a very patient man. I've been waiting for a long time. I don't mind waiting.
LI'L BIT: Someone is going to get hurt.
PECK: No one is going to get hurt. (*Li'l Bit closes her eyes.*) Are you feeling sick?
LI'L BIT: Sleepy.

(*Carefully, Peck props Li'l Bit up on the seat.*)

PECK: Stay here a second.
LI'L BIT: Where're you going?
PECK: I'm getting something from the back seat.
LI'L BIT (*scared; too loud*): What? What are you going to do?

(*Peck reappears in the front seat with a lap rug.*)

PECK: Shhh. (*Peck covers Li'l Bit. She calms down.*) There. Think you can sleep?

(*Li'l Bit nods. She slides over to rest on his shoulder. With a look of happiness, Peck turns the ignition key. Beat. Peck leaves Li'l Bit sleeping in the car and strolls down to the audience. Wagner's* Flying Dutchman *comes up faintly.*) (*A Voice interjects:*)

Idling in the Neutral Gear.

TEENAGE GREEK CHORUS: Uncle Peck Teaches Cousin Bobby How to Fish.
PECK: I get back once or twice a year — supposedly to visit Mama and the family, but the real truth is to fish. I miss this the most of all. There's a smell in the Low Country — where the swamp and fresh inlet join the saltwater — a scent of sand and cypress, that I haven't found anywhere yet.

I don't say this very often up North because it will just play into the stereotype everyone has, but I will tell you: I didn't wear shoes in the summertime until I was sixteen. It's unnatural down here to pen up your feet in leather. Go ahead — take 'em off. Let yourself breathe — it really will make you feel better.

We're going to aim for some pompano today — and I have to tell you, they're a very shy, mercurial fish. Takes patience, and psychology. You have to believe it doesn't matter if you catch one or not.

Sky's pretty spectacular — there's some beer in the cooler next to the crab salad I packed, so help yourself if you get hungry. Are you hungry? Thirsty? Holler if you are.

Okay. You don't want to lean over the bridge like that — pompano feed in shallow water, and you don't want to get too close — they're frisky and shy little things — wait, check your line. Yep, something's been munching while we were talking.

Okay, look: We take the sand flea and you take the hook like this — right through his little sand flea rump. Sand fleas should always keep their backs to the wall. Okay. Cast it in, like I showed you. That's great! I can taste that pompano now, sautéed with some pecans and butter, a little bourbon — now — let it lie on the bottom — now, reel, jerk, reel, jerk —

Look — look at your line. There's something calling, all right. Okay, tip the rod up — not too sharp — hook it — all right, now easy, reel and then rest — let it play. And reel — play it out, that's right — really good! I can't believe it! It's a pompano. — Good work! Way to go! You are an official fisherman now. Pompano are hard to catch. We are going to have a delicious little —

What? Well, I don't know how much pain a fish feels — you can't think of that. Oh, no, don't cry, come on now, it's just a fish — the other guys are going to see you. — No, no, you're just real sensitive, and I think that's wonderful at your age — look, do you want me to cut it free? You do?

Okay, hand me those pliers — look — I'm cutting the hook — okay? And we're just going to drop it in — no I'm not mad. It's just for fun, okay? There — it's going to swim back to its lady friend and tell her what a terrible day it had and she's going to stroke him with her fins until he feels better, and then they'll do something alone together that will make them both feel good and sleepy. . . .

(*Peck bends down, very earnest.*) I don't want you to feel ashamed about crying. I'm not going to tell anyone, okay? I can keep secrets. You know, men cry all the time. They just don't tell anybody, and they don't let anybody catch them. There's nothing you could do that would make me feel ashamed of you. Do you know that? Okay. (*Peck straightens up, smiles.*)

Do you want to pack up and call it a day? I tell you what — I think I can still remember — there's a really neat tree house where I used to stay for days. I think it's still here — it was the last time I looked. But it's a secret place — you can't tell anybody we've gone there — least of all your mom or your sisters. — This is something special just between you and me. Sound good? We'll climb up there and have a beer and some crab salad — okay, B.B.? Bobby? Robert. . . .

(*Li'l Bit sits at a kitchen table with the two Female Greek Chorus members.*)

LI'L BIT (*to the audience*): Three women, three generations, sit at the kitchen table.
On Men, Sex, and Women: Part I:

FEMALE GREEK CHORUS (*as Mother*): Men only want one thing.

LI'L BIT (*wide-eyed*): But what? What is it they want?

FEMALE GREEK CHORUS (*as Mother*): And once they have it, they lose all interest. So Don't Give It to Them.

TEENAGE GREEK CHORUS (*as Grandmother*): I never had the luxury of the rhythm method. Your grandfather is just a big bull. A big bull. Every morning, every evening.

FEMALE GREEK CHORUS (*as Mother, whispers to Li'l Bit*): And he used to come home for lunch every day.

LI'L BIT: My god, Grandma!

TEENAGE GREEK CHORUS (*as Grandmother*): Your grandfather only cares that I do two things: have the table set and the bed turned down.

FEMALE GREEK CHORUS (*as Mother*): And in all that time, Mother, you never have experienced — ?

LI'L BIT (*to the audience*): — Now my grandmother believed in all the sacraments of the church, to the day she died. She believed in Santa Claus and the Easter Bunny until she was fifteen. But she didn't believe in —

TEENAGE GREEK CHORUS (*as Grandmother*): — Orgasm! That's just something you and Mary have made up! I don't believe you.

FEMALE GREEK CHORUS (*as Mother*): Mother, it happens to women all the time.

TEENAGE GREEK CHORUS (*as Grandmother*): — Oh, now you're going to tell me about the G force!

LI'L BIT: No, Grandma, I think that's astronauts —

FEMALE GREEK CHORUS (*as Mother*): Well, Mama, after all, you were a child bride when Big Papa came and got you — you were a married woman and you still believed in Santa Claus.

TEENAGE GREEK CHORUS (*as Grandmother*): It was legal, what Daddy and I did! I was fourteen and in those days, fourteen was a grown-up woman —

(*Big Papa shuffles in the kitchen for a cookie.*)

MALE GREEK CHORUS (*as Grandfather*): — Oh, now we're off on Grandma and the Rape of the Sa-bean Women!

TEENAGE GREEK CHORUS (*as Grandmother*): Well, you were the one in such a big hurry —

MALE GREEK CHORUS (*as Grandfather to Li'l Bit*): — I picked your grandmother out of that herd of sisters just like a lion chooses the gazelle — the plump, slow, flaky gazelle dawdling at the edge of the herd — your sisters were too smart and too fast and too scrawny —

LI'L BIT (*to the audience*): — The family story is that when Big Papa came for Grandma, my Aunt Lily was waiting for him with a broom — and she beat him over the head all the way down the stairs as he was carrying out Grandma's hope chest —

MALE GREEK CHORUS (*as Grandfather*): — And they were *mean*. 'Specially Lily.

FEMALE GREEK CHORUS (*as Mother*): Well, you were robbing the baby of the family!

TEENAGE GREEK CHORUS (*as Grandmother*): I still keep a broom handy in the kitchen! And I know how to use it! So get your hand out of the cookie jar and don't you spoil your appetite for dinner — out of the kitchen!

(*Male Greek Chorus as Grandfather leaves chuckling with a cookie.*)

FEMALE GREEK CHORUS (*as Mother*): Just one thing a married woman needs to know how to use — the rolling pin or the broom. I prefer a heavy, cast-iron fry pan — they're great on a man's head, no matter how thick the skull is.

TEENAGE GREEK CHORUS (*as Grandmother*): Yes, sir, your father is ruled by only two bosses! Mr. Gut and Mr. Peter! And sometimes, first thing in the morning, Mr. Sphincter Muscle!

FEMALE GREEK CHORUS (*as Mother*): It's true. Men are like children. Just like little boys.

TEENAGE GREEK CHORUS (*as Grandmother*): Men are bulls! Big bulls!

(*The Greek Chorus is getting aroused.*)

FEMALE GREEK CHORUS (*as Mother*): They'd still be crouched on their haunches over a fire in a cave if we hadn't cleaned them up!

TEENAGE GREEK CHORUS (*as Grandmother, flushed*): Coming in smelling of sweat —

FEMALE GREEK CHORUS (*as Mother*): — Looking at those naughty pictures like boys in a dime store with a dollar in their pockets!

TEENAGE GREEK CHORUS (*as Grandmother; raucous*): No matter to them what they smell like! They've got to have it, right then, on the spot, right there! Nasty! —

FEMALE GREEK CHORUS (*as Mother*): — Vulgar!

TEENAGE GREEK CHORUS (*as Grandmother*): Primitive! —

FEMALE GREEK CHORUS (*as Mother*): — Hot!

LI'L BIT: And just about then, Big Papa would shuffle in with —

MALE GREEK CHORUS (*as Grandfather*): — What are you all cackling about in here?

TEENAGE GREEK CHORUS (*as Grandmother*): Stay out of the kitchen! This is just for girls!

(*As Grandfather leaves:*)

MALE GREEK CHORUS (*as Grandfather*): Lucy, you'd better not be filling Mama's head with sex! Every time you and Mary come over and start in about sex, when I ask a simple question like, "What time is dinner going to be ready?," Mama snaps my head off!

TEENAGE GREEK CHORUS (*as Grandmother*): Dinner will be ready when I'm good and ready! Stay out of this kitchen!

(*Li'l Bit steps out.*)

(*A Voice directs:*)

When Making a Left Turn, You Must Downshift While Going Forward.

LI'L BIT: 1979. A long bus trip to Upstate New York. I settled in to read, when a young man sat beside me.

MALE GREEK CHORUS (*as Young Man; voice cracking*): "What are you reading?"

LI'L BIT: He asked. His voice broke into that miserable equivalent of vocal acne, not quite falsetto and not tenor, either. I glanced a side view. He was appealing in an odd way, huge ears at a defiant angle springing forward at ninety degrees. He must have been shaving, because his face, with a peach sheen, was speckled with nicks and styptic. "I have a class tomorrow," I told him.

MALE GREEK CHORUS (*as Young Man*): "You're taking a class?"

LI'L BIT: "I'm teaching a class." He concentrated on lowering his voice.

MALE GREEK CHORUS (*as Young Man*): "I'm a senior. Walt Whitman High."

LI'L BIT: The light was fading outside, so perhaps he was — with a very high voice.

I felt his "interest" quicken. Five steps ahead of the hopes in his head, I slowed down, waited, pretended surprise, acted at listening, all the while knowing we would get off the bus, he would just then seem to think to ask me to dinner, he would chivalrously insist on walking me home, he would continue to converse in the street until I would casually invite him up to my room — and — I was only into the second moment of conversation and I could see the whole evening before me.

And dramaturgically speaking, after the faltering and slightly comical "first act," there was the very briefest of intermissions, and an extremely capable and forceful and *sustained* second act. And after the second act climax and a gentle denouement — before the post-play discussion — I lay on my back in the dark and I thought about you, Uncle Peck. Oh. Oh — this is the allure. Being older. Being the first. Being the translator, the teacher, the epicure, the already jaded. This is how the giver gets taken.

(*Li'l Bit changes her tone.*) On Men, Sex, and Women: Part II:

(*Li'l Bit steps back into the scene as a fifteen-year-old, gawky and quiet, as the gazelle at the edge of the herd.*)

TEENAGE GREEK CHORUS (*as Grandmother, to Li'l Bit*): You're being mighty quiet, missy. Cat Got Your Tongue?

LI'L BIT: I'm just listening. Just thinking.

TEENAGE GREEK CHORUS (*as Grandmother*): Oh, yes, Little Miss Radar Ears? Soaking it all in? Little Miss Sponge? Penny for your thoughts?

(*Li'l Bit hesitates to ask but she really wants to know.*)

LI'L BIT: Does it — when you do it — you know, theoretically when I do it and I haven't done it before — I mean — does it hurt?

FEMALE GREEK CHORUS (*as Mother*): Does what hurt, honey?

LI'L BIT: When a . . . when a girl does it for the first time — with a man — does it hurt?

TEENAGE GREEK CHORUS (*as Grandmother; horrified*): *That's* what you're thinking about?

FEMALE GREEK CHORUS (*as Mother, calm*): Well, just a little bit. Like a pinch. And there's a little blood.

TEENAGE GREEK CHORUS (*as Grandmother*): Don't tell her that! She's too young to be thinking those things!

FEMALE GREEK CHORUS (*as Mother*): Well, if she doesn't find out from me, where is she going to find out? In the street?

TEENAGE GREEK CHORUS (*as Grandmother*): Tell her it hurts! It's agony! You think you're going to die! Especially if you do it before marriage!

FEMALE GREEK CHORUS (*as Mother*): Mama! I'm going to tell her the truth! Unlike you, you left me and Mary completely in the dark with fairy tales and told us to go to the priest! What does an eighty-year-old priest know about lovemaking with girls!

LI'L BIT (*getting upset*): It's not fair!

FEMALE GREEK CHORUS (*as Mother*): Now, see, she's getting upset — you're scaring her.

TEENAGE GREEK CHORUS (*as Grandmother*): Good! Let her be good and scared! It hurts! You bleed like a stuck pig! And you lay there and say, "Why, O Lord, have you forsaken me?!"

LI'L BIT: It's not fair! Why does everything have to hurt for girls? Why is there always blood?

FEMALE GREEK CHORUS (*as Mother*): It's not a lot of blood — and it feels wonderful after the pain subsides. . . .

TEENAGE GREEK CHORUS (*as Grandmother*): You're encouraging her to just go out and find out with the first drugstore joe who buys her a milkshake!

FEMALE GREEK CHORUS (*as Mother*): Don't be scared. It won't hurt you — if the man you go to bed with really loves you. It's important that he loves you.

TEENAGE GREEK CHORUS (*as Grandmother*): — Why don't you just go out and rent a motel room for her, Lucy?

FEMALE GREEK CHORUS (*as Mother*): I believe in telling my daughter the truth! We have a very close relationship! I want her to be able to ask me anything — I'm not scaring her with stories about Eve's sin and snakes crawling on their bellies for eternity and women bearing children in mortal pain —

Tim Crowe as Uncle Peck and Annie Sullivan as Li'l Bit in the Trinity Repertory Theater's production of *How I Learned to Drive.*

TEENAGE GREEK CHORUS (*as Grandmother*): — If she stops and thinks before she takes her knickers off, maybe someone in this family will finish high school!

(*Li'l Bit knows what is about to happen and starts to retreat from the scene at this point.*)

FEMALE GREEK CHORUS (*as Mother*): Mother! If you and Daddy had helped me — I wouldn't have had to marry that — that no-good-son-of-a —

TEENAGE GREEK CHORUS (*as Grandmother*): — He was good enough for you on a full moon! I hold you responsible!

FEMALE GREEK CHORUS (*as Mother*): — You could have helped me! You could have told me something about the facts of life!

TEENAGE GREEK CHORUS (*as Grandmother*): — I told you what my mother told me! A girl with her skirt up can outrun a man with his pants down!

(*The Male Greek Chorus enters the fray; Li'l Bit edges farther downstage.*)

FEMALE GREEK CHORUS (*as Mother*): And when I turned to you for a little help, all I got afterwards was —

MALE GREEK CHORUS (*as Grandfather*): You Made Your Bed; Now Lie On It!

(*The Greek Chorus freezes, mouths open, argumentatively.*)

LI'L BIT (*to the audience*): Oh, please! I still can't bear to listen to it, after all these years —

(*The Male Greek Chorus "unfreezes," but out of his open mouth, as if to his surprise, comes a bass refrain from a Motown song.*)

MALE GREEK CHORUS: "Do-Bee-Do-Wah!"

(*The Female Greek Chorus member is also surprised; but she, too, unfreezes.*)

FEMALE GREEK CHORUS: "Shoo-doo-be-doo-be-doo; shoo-doo-be-doo-be-doo."

(*The Male and Female Greek Chorus members continue with their harmony, until the Teenage member of the Chorus starts in with Motown lyrics such as "Dedicated to the One I Love," or "In the Still of the Night," or "Hold Me" — any Sam Cooke will do. The three modulate down into three-part harmony, softly, until they are submerged by the actual recording playing over the radio in the car in which Uncle Peck sits in the driver's seat, waiting. Li'l Bit sits in the passenger's seat.*)

LI'L BIT: Ahh. That's better.

(*Uncle Peck reaches over and turns the volume down; to Li'l Bit:*)

PECK: How can you hear yourself think?

(*Li'l Bit does not answer.*)

(*A Voice insinuates itself in the pause:*)

Before You Drive.
Always check under your car for obstructions — broken bottles, fallen tree branches, and the bodies of small children. Each year hundreds of children are crushed beneath the wheels of unwary drivers in their own driveways. Children depend on you *to watch them.*

(*Pause.*)

(*The Voice continues:*)

You and the Reverse Gear.

(*In the following section, it would be nice to have slides of erotic photographs of women and cars: women posed over the hood; women draped along the sideboards; women with water hoses spraying the car; and the actress playing Li'l Bit with a Bel Air or any 1950s car one can find for the finale.*)

LI'L BIT: 1967. In a parking lot of the Beltsville Agricultural Farms. The Initiation into a Boy's First Love.

PECK (*with a soft look on his face*): Of course, my favorite car will always be the '56 Bel Air Sports Coupe. Chevy sold more '55s, but the '56! — a V-8 with Corvette option, 225 horsepower; went from zero to sixty miles per hour in 8.9 seconds.

LI'L BIT (*to the audience*): Long after a mother's tits, but before a woman's breasts.

PECK: Super-Turbo-Fire! What a Power Pack — mechanical lifters, twin four-barrel carbs, lightweight valves, dual exhausts —

LI'L BIT (*to the audience*): After the milk but before the beer:

PECK: A specific intake manifold, higher-lift camshaft, and the tightest squeeze Chevy had ever made —

LI'L BIT (*to the audience*): Long after he's squeezed down the birth canal but before he's pushed his way back in: The boy falls in love with the thing that bears his weight with speed.

PECK: I want you to know your automobile inside and out. — Are you there? Li'l Bit?

(*Slides end here.*)

LI'L BIT: — What?

PECK: You're drifting. I need you to concentrate.

LI'L BIT: Sorry.

PECK: Okay. Get into the driver's seat. (*Li'l Bit does.*) Okay. Now. Show me what you're going to do before you start the car.

(*Li'l Bit sits, with her hands in her lap. She starts to giggle.*)

LI'L BIT: I don't know, Uncle Peck.

PECK: Now, come on. What's the first thing you're going to adjust?

LI'L BIT: My bra strap? —

PECK: — Li'l Bit. What's the most important thing to have control of on the inside of the car?

LI'L BIT: That's easy. The radio. I tune the radio from Mama's old fart tunes to —

(*Li'l Bit turns the radio up so we can hear a 1960s tune. With surprising firmness, Peck commands:*)

PECK: — Radio off. Right now. (*Li'l Bit turns the radio off.*) When you are driving your car, with your license, you can fiddle with the stations all you want. But when you are driving with a learner's permit in my car, I want all your attention to be on the road.

LI'L BIT: Yes, sir.

PECK: Okay. Now the seat — forward and up. (*Li'l Bit pushes it forward.*) Do you want a cushion?

LI'L BIT: No — I'm good.

PECK: You should be able to reach all the switches and controls. Your feet should be able to push the accelerator, brake and clutch all the way down. Can you do that?

LI'L BIT: Yes.

PECK: Okay, the side mirrors. You want to be able to see just a bit of the right side of the car in the right mirror — can you?

LI'L BIT: Turn it out more.

PECK: Okay. How's that?

LI'L BIT: A little more. . . . Okay, that's good.

PECK: Now the left — again, you want to be able to see behind you — but the left lane — adjust it until you feel comfortable. (*Li'l Bit does so.*) Next. I want you to check the rearview mirror. Angle it so you have a clear vision of the back. (*Li'l Bit does so.*) Okay. Lock your door. Make sure all the doors are locked.

LI'L BIT (*making a joke of it*): But then I'm locked in with you.

PECK: Don't fool.

LI'L BIT: All right. We're locked in.

PECK: We'll deal with the air vents and defroster later. I'm teaching you on a manual — once you learn manual, you can drive anything. I want you to be able to drive any car, any machine. Manual gives you *control*. In ice, if your brakes fail, if you need more power — okay? It's a little harder at first, but then it becomes like breathing. Now. Put your hands on the wheel. I never want to see you driving with one hand. Always two hands. (*Li'l Bit hesitates.*) What? What is it now?

LI'L BIT: If I put my hands on the wheel — how do I defend myself?

PECK (*softly*): Now listen. Listen up close. We're not going to fool around with this. This is serious business. I will never touch you when you are driving a car. Understand?

LI'L BIT: Okay.

PECK: Hands on the nine o'clock and three o'clock position gives you maximum control and turn.

(*Peck goes silent for a while. Li'l Bit waits for more instruction.*)

Okay. Just relax and listen to me, Li'l Bit, okay? I want you to lift your hands for a second and look at them.

(*Li'l Bit feels a bit silly, but does it.*)

Those are your two hands. When you are driving, your life is in your own two hands. Understand?

(*Li'l Bit nods.*)

I don't have any sons. You're the nearest to a son I'll ever have — and I want to give you something. Something that really matters to me.

There's something about driving — when you're in control of the car, just you and the machine and the road — that nobody can take from you. A power. I feel more myself in my car than anywhere else. And that's what I want to give to you.

There's a lot of assholes out there. Crazy men, arrogant idiots, drunks, angry kids, geezers who are blind — and you have to be ready for them. I want to teach you to drive like a man.

LI'L BIT: What does that mean?

PECK: Men are taught to drive with confidence — with aggression. The road belongs to them. They drive defensively — always looking out for the other guy. Women tend to be polite — to hesitate. And that can be fatal.

You're going to learn to think what the other guy is going to do before he does it. If there's an accident, and ten cars pile up, and people get killed, you're the one who's gonna steer through it, put your foot on the gas if you have to, and be the only one to walk away. I don't know how long you or I are going to live, but we're for damned sure not going to die in a car.

So if you're going to drive with me, I want you to take this very seriously.

LI'L BIT: I will, Uncle Peck. I want you to teach me to drive.

PECK: Good. You're going to pass your test on the first try. Perfect score. Before the next four weeks are over, you're going to know this baby inside and out. Treat her with respect.

LI'L BIT: Why is it a "she"?

PECK: Good question. It doesn't have to be a "she" — but when you close your eyes and think of someone who responds to your touch — someone who performs just for you and gives you what you ask for — I guess I always see a "she." You can call her what you like.

LI'L BIT (*to the audience*): I closed my eyes — and decided not to change the gender.

(*A Voice:*)

Defensive driving involves defending yourself from hazardous and sudden changes in your automotive environment. By thinking ahead, the defensive driver can adjust to weather, road conditions, and road kill. Good defensive driving involves mental and physical preparation. Are you prepared?

(Another Voice chimes in:)

You and the Reverse Gear.

Li'l Bit: 1966. The Anthropology of the Female Body in Ninth Grade — Or A Walk Down Mammary Lane.

(Throughout the following, there is occasional rhythmic beeping, like a transmitter signaling. Li'l Bit is aware of it, but can't figure out where it is coming from. No one else seems to hear it.)

Male Greek Chorus: In the hallway of Francis Scott Key Middle School.

(A bell rings; the Greek Chorus is changing classes and meets in the hall, conspiratorially.)

Teenage Greek Chorus: She's coming!

(Li'l Bit enters the scene; the Male Greek Chorus member has a sudden, violent sneezing and lethal allergy attack.)

Female Greek Chorus: Jerome? Jerome? Are you all right?
Male Greek Chorus: I — don't — know. I can't breathe — get Li'l Bit —
Teenage Greek Chorus: — He needs oxygen! —
Female Greek Chorus: — Can you help us here?
Li'l Bit: What's wrong? Do you want me to get the school nurse —

(The Male Greek Chorus member wheezes, grabs his throat and sniffs at Li'l Bit's chest, which is beeping away.)

Male Greek Chorus: No — it's okay — I only get this way when I'm around an allergy trigger —
Li'l Bit: Golly. What are you allergic to?
Male Greek Chorus *(with a sudden grab of her breast)*: Foam rubber.

(The Greek Chorus members break up with hilarity; Jerome leaps away from Li'l Bit's kicking rage with agility; as he retreats:)

Li'l Bit: Jerome! Creep! Cretin! Cro-Magnon!
Teenage Greek Chorus: Rage is not attractive in a girl.
Female Greek Chorus: Really. Get a Sense of Humor.

(A Voice echoes:)

Good defensive driving involves mental and physical preparation. Were You Prepared?

Female Greek Chorus: Gym Class: In the showers.

(The sudden sound of water; the Female Greek Chorus members and Li'l Bit, while fully clothed, drape towels across their fronts, miming nudity. They stand, hesitate, at an imaginary shower's edge.)

Li'l Bit: Water looks hot.
Female Greek Chorus: Yesss. . . .

(Female Greek Chorus members are not going to make the first move. One dips a tentative toe under the water, clutching the towel around her.)

Li'l Bit: Well, I guess we'd better shower and get out of here.
Female Greek Chorus: Yep. You go ahead. I'm still cooling off.
Li'l Bit: Okay. — Sally? Are you gonna shower?
Teenage Greek Chorus: After you —

(Li'l Bit takes a deep breath for courage, drops the towel and plunges in: The two Female Greek Chorus members look at Li'l Bit in the all together, laugh, gasp and high-five each other.)

Teenage Greek Chorus: Oh my god! Can you believe —
Female Greek Chorus: Told you! It's not foam rubber! I win! Jerome owes me fifty cents!

(A Voice editorializes:)

Were You Prepared?

(Li'l Bit tries to cover up; she is exposed, as suddenly 1960s Motown fills the room and we segue into:)

Female Greek Chorus: The Sock Hop.

(Li'l Bit stands up against the wall with her female classmates. Teenage Greek Chorus is mesmerized by the music and just sways alone, lip-synching the lyrics.)

Li'l Bit: I don't know. Maybe it's just me — but — do you ever feel like you're just a walking Mary Jane joke?
Female Greek Chorus: I don't know what you mean.
Li'l Bit: You haven't heard the Mary Jane jokes? *(Female Greek Chorus member shakes her head no.)* Okay. "Little Mary Jane is walking through the woods, when all of a sudden this man who was hiding behind a tree *jumps* out, *rips* open Mary Jane's blouse, and *plunges* his hands on her breasts. And Little Mary Jane just laughed and laughed because she knew her money was in her shoes."

(Li'l Bit laughs; the Female Greek Chorus does not.)

FEMALE GREEK CHORUS: You're weird.

(*In another space, in a strange light, Uncle Peck stands and stares at Li'l Bit's body. He is setting up a tripod, but he just stands, appreciative, watching her.*)

LI'L BIT: Well, don't you ever feel . . . self-conscious? Like you're being looked at all the time?

FEMALE GREEK CHORUS: That's not a problem for me. — Oh — look — Greg's coming over to ask you to dance.

(*Teenage Creek Chorus becomes attentive, flustered. Male Greek Chorus member, as Greg, bends slightly as a very short young man, whose head is at Li'l Bit's chest level. Ardent, sincere, and socially inept, Greg will become a successful gynecologist.*)

TEENAGE GREEK CHORUS (*softly*): Hi, Greg.

(*Greg does not hear. He is intent on only one thing.*)

MALE GREEK CHORUS (*as Greg, to Li'l Bit*): Good Evening. Would you care to dance?

LI'L BIT (*gently*): Thank you very much, Greg — but I'm going to sit this one out.

MALE GREEK CHORUS (*as Greg*): Oh. Okay. I'll try my luck later.

(*He disappears.*)

TEENAGE GREEK CHORUS: Oohhh.

(*Li'l Bit relaxes. Then she tenses, aware of Peck's gaze.*)

FEMALE GREEK CHORUS: Take pity on him. Someone should.

LI'L BIT: But he's so short.

TEENAGE GREEK CHORUS: He can't help it.

LI'L BIT: But his head comes up to (*Li'l Bit gestures*) here. And I think he asks me on the fast dances so he can watch me — you know — jiggle.

FEMALE GREEK CHORUS: I wish I had your problems.

(*The tune changes; Greg is across the room in a flash.*)

MALE GREEK CHORUS (*as Greg*): Evening again. May I ask you for the honor of a spin on the floor?

LI'L BIT: I'm . . . very complimented, Greg. But I . . . I just don't do fast dances.

MALE GREEK CHORUS (*as Greg*): Oh. No problem. That's okay.

(*He disappears. Teenage Greek Chorus watches him go.*)

TEENAGE GREEK CHORUS: That is just so — sad.

(*Li'l Bit becomes aware of Peck waiting.*)

FEMALE GREEK CHORUS: You know, you should take it as a compliment that the guys want to watch you jiggle. They're guys. That's what they're supposed to do.

LI'L BIT: I guess you're right. But sometimes I feel like these alien life forces, these two mounds of flesh have grafted themselves onto my chest, and they're using me until they can "propagate" and take over the world and they'll just keep growing, with a mind of their own until I collapse under their weight and they suck all the nourishment out of my body and I finally just waste away while they get bigger and bigger and — (*Li'l Bit's classmates are just staring at her in disbelief.*)

FEMALE GREEK CHORUS: — You are the strangest girl I have ever met.

(*Li'l Bit's trying to joke but feels on the verge of tears.*)

LI'L BIT: Or maybe someone's implanted radio transmitters in my chest at a frequency I can't hear, that girls can't detect, but they're sending out these signals to men who get mesmerized, like sirens, calling them to dash themselves on these "rocks" —

(*Just then, the music segues into a slow dance, perhaps a Beach Boys tune like "Little Surfer," but over the music there's a rhythmic, hypnotic beeping transmitted, which both Greg and Peck hear. Li'l Bit hears it too, and in horror she stares at her chest. She, too, is almost hypnotized. In a trance, Greg responds to the signals and is called to her side — actully, her front. Like a zombie, he stands in front of her, his eyes planted on her two orbs.*)

MALE GREEK CHORUS (*as Greg*): This one's a slow dance. I hope your dance card isn't . . . filled?

(*Li'l Bit is aware of Peck; but the signals are calling her to him. The signals are no longer transmitters, but an electromagnetic force, pulling Li'l Bit to his side, where he again waits for her to join him. She must get away from the dance floor.*)

LI'L BIT: Greg — you really are a nice boy. But I don't like to dance.

MALE GREEK CHORUS (*as Greg*): That's okay. We don't have to move or anything. I could just hold you and we could just *sway* a little —

LI'L BIT: — No! I'm sorry — but I think I have to leave; I hear someone calling me —

(*Li'l Bit starts across the dance floor, leaving Greg behind. The beeping stops. The lights change, although the music does not. As Li'l Bit talks to the audience, she continues to change and prepare for the coming session. She should be wearing a tight tank top or a sheer blouse and very tight pants. To the audience:*)

In every man's home some small room, some zone in his house, is set aside. It might be the attic, or the study, or a den. And there's an invisible sign as if from the old treehouse: Girls Keep Out. Here, away from female eyes, lace doilies and crochet, he keeps his manly toys: the Vargas pinups, the tackle. A scent of tobacco and WD-40. (*She inhales deeply.*) A dash of his Bay Rum. Ahhh . . . (*Li'l Bit savors it for just a moment more.*) Here he keeps his secrets: a violin or saxophone, drum set or darkroom, and the stacks of *Playboy*. (*In a whisper.*) Here, in my aunt's home, it was the basement. Uncle Peck's turf.

(*A Voice commands:*)

You and the Reverse Gear.

Li'l Bit: 1965. The Photo Shoot.

(*Li'l Bit steps into the scene as a nervous but curious thirteen-year-old. Music, from the previous scene, continues to play, changing into something like Roy Orbison later — something seductive with a beat. Peck fiddles, all business, with his camera. As in the driving lesson, he is all competency and concentration. Li'l Bit stands awkwardly. He looks through the Leica camera on the tripod, adjusts the back lighting, etc.*)

Peck: Are you cold? The lights should heat up some in a few minutes —
Li'l Bit: — Aunt Mary is?
Peck: At the National Theatre matinee. With your mother. We have time.
Li'l Bit: But — what if —
Peck: — And so what if they return? I told them you and I were going to be working with my camera. They won't come down.

(*Li'l Bit is quiet, apprehensive.*)

Look, are you sure you want to do this?
Li'l Bit: I said I'd do it. But —
Peck: — I know. You've drawn the line.
Li'l Bit (*reassured*): That's right. No frontal nudity.
Peck: Good heavens, girl, where did you pick that up?
Li'l Bit (*defensive*): I read.

(*Peck tries not to laugh.*)

Peck: And I read *Playboy* for the interviews. Okay. Let's try some different music.

(*Peck goes to an expensive reel-to-reel and forwards. Something like "Sweet Dreams" begins to play.*)

Li'l Bit: I didn't know you listened to this.
Peck: I'm not dead, you know, I try to keep up. Do you like this song?

(*Li'l Bit nods with pleasure.*)

Good. Now listen — at professional photo shoots, they always play music for the models. Okay? I want you to just enjoy the music. Listen to it with your body, and just — respond.
Li'l Bit: Respond to the music with my . . . body?
Peck: Right. Almost like dancing. Here — let's get you on the stool, first. (*Peck comes over and helps her up.*)
Li'l Bit: But nothing showing —

(*Peck firmly, with his large capable hands, brushes back her hair, angles her face. Li'l Bit turns to him like a plant to the sun.*)

Peck: Nothing showing. Just a peek.

(*He holds her by the shoulders, looking at her critically. Then he unbuttons her blouse to the midpoint, and runs his hands over the flesh of her exposed sternum, arranging the fabric, just touching her. Deliberately, calmly.*)

Asexually. Li'l Bit quiets, sits perfectly still, and closes her eyes.)

Okay?
Li'l Bit: Yes.

(*Peck goes back to his camera.*)

Peck: I'm going to keep talking to you. Listen without responding to what I'm saying; you want to *listen* to the music. Sway, move just your torso or your head — I've got to check the light meter.
Li'l Bit: But — you'll be watching.
Peck: No — I'm not here — just my voice. Pretend you're in your room all alone on a Friday night with your mirror — and the music feels good — just move for me, Li'l Bit —

(*Li'l Bit closes her eyes. At first self-conscious; then she gets more into the music and begins to sway. We hear the camera start to whir. Throughout the shoot, there can be a slide montage of actual shots of the actor playing Li'l Bit — interspersed with other models à la Playboy, Calvin Klein, and Victoriana/Lewis Carroll's Alice Liddell.*)

That's it. That looks great. Okay. Just keep doing that. Lift your head up a bit more, good, good, just keep moving, that a girl — you're a very beautiful young woman. Do you know that?

(*Li'l Bit looks up, blushes. Peck shoots the camera. The audience should see this shot on the screen.*)

Li'l Bit: No. I don't know that.
Peck: Listen to the music.

(*Li'l Bit closes her eyes again.*)

Well you are. For a thirteen-year-old, you have a body a twenty-year-old woman would die for.
Li'l Bit: The boys in school don't think so.
Peck: The boys in school are little Neanderthals in short pants. You're ten years ahead of them in maturity; it's gonna take a while for them to catch up.

(*Peck clicks another shot; we see a faint smile on Li'l Bit on the screen.*)

Girls turn into women long before boys turn into men.
Li'l Bit: Why is that?
Peck: I don't know, Li'l Bit. But it's a blessing for men.

(*Li'l Bit turns silent.*)

Keep moving. Try arching your back on the stool, hands behind you, and throw your head back.

(*The slide shows a* Playboy *model in this pose.*)

Oohh, great. That one was great. Turn your head away, same position. (*Whir.*) Beautiful.

(*Li'l Bit looks at him a bit defiantly.*)

Li'l Bit: I think Aunt Mary is beautiful.

(*Peck stands still.*)

PECK: My wife is a very beautiful woman. Her beauty doesn't cancel yours out. (*More casually; he returns to the camera.*) All the women in your family are beautiful. In fact, I think all women are. You're not listening to the music. (*Peck shoots some more film in silence.*) All right, turn your head to the left. Good. Now take the back of your right hand and put it on your right cheek — your elbow angled up — now slowly, slowly, stroke your cheek, draw back your hair with the back of your hand. (*Another classic* Playboy *or Vargas.*) Good. One hand above and behind your head; stretch your body; smile. (*Another pose.*) Li'l Bit. I want you to think of something that makes you laugh —

LI'L BIT: I can't think of anything.

PECK: Okay. Think of Big Papa chasing Grandma around the living room.

(*Li'l Bit lifts her head and laughs. Click. We should see this shot.*)

Good. Both hands behind your head. Great! Hold that. (*From behind his camera.*) You're doing great work. If we keep this up, in five years we'll have a really professional portfolio.

(*Li'l Bit stops.*)

LI'L BIT: What do you mean in five years?

PECK: You can't submit work to *Playboy* until you're eighteen. —

(*Peck continues to shoot; he knows he's made a mistake.*)

LI'L BIT: — Wait a minute. You're joking, aren't you, Uncle Peck?

PECK: Heck, no. You can't get into *Playboy* unless you're the very best. And you are the very best.

LI'L BIT: I would never do that!

(*Peck stops shooting. He turns off the music.*)

PECK: Why? There's nothing wrong with *Playboy* — it's a very classy maga —

LI'L BIT (*more upset*): But I thought you said I should go to college!

PECK: Wait — Li'l Bit — it's nothing like that. Very respectable women model for *Playboy* — actresses with major careers — women in college — there's an Ivy League issue every —

LI'L BIT: — I'm never doing anything like that! You'd show other people these — other *men* — what I'm doing. — Why would you do that?! Any *boy* around here could just pick up, just go into The Stop & Go and *buy* — Why would you ever want to — to share —

PECK: — Whoa, whoa. Just stop a second and listen to me. Li'l Bit. Listen. There's nothing wrong in what we're doing. I'm very proud of you. I think you have a wonderful body and an even more wonderful mind. And of course I want other people to *appreciate* it. It's not anything shameful.

LI'L BIT (*hurt*): But this is something — that I'm only doing for you. This is something — that you said was just between us.

PECK: It is. And if that's how you feel, five years from now, it will remain that way. Okay? I know you're not going to do anything you don't feel like doing. (*He walks back to the camera.*) Do you want to stop now? I've got just a few more shots on this roll —

LI'L BIT: I don't want anyone seeing this.

PECK: I swear to you. No one will. I'll treasure this — that you're doing this only for me.

(*Li'l Bit, still shaken, sits on the stool. She closes her eyes.*)

Li'l Bit? Open your eyes and look at me.

(*Li'l Bit shakes her head no.*)

Come on. Just open your eyes, honey.

LI'L BIT: If I look at you — if I look at the camera: You're gonna know what I'm thinking. You'll see right through me —

PECK: — No, I won't. I want you to look at me. All right, then. I just want you to listen. Li'l Bit.

(*She waits.*)

I love you.

(*Li'l Bit opens her eyes; she is startled. Peck captures the shot. On the screen we see right through her. Peck says softly.*)

Do you know that?

(*Li'l Bit nods her head yes.*)

I have loved you every day since the day you were born.

LI'L BIT: Yes.

(*Li'l Bit and Peck just look at each other. Beat. Beneath the shot of herself on the screen, Li'l Bit, still looking at her uncle, begins to unbutton her blouse.*
A neutral Voice cuts off the above scene with:)

Implied Consent.
As an individual operating a motor vehicle in the state of Maryland, you must abide by "Implied Consent." If you do not consent to take the blood alcohol content test, there may be severe penalties: a suspension of license, a fine, community service, and a possible jail sentence.

(*The Voice shifts tone:*)

Idling in the Neutral Gear.

MALE GREEK CHORUS (*announcing*): Aunt Mary on behalf of her husband.

(Female Greek Chorus checks her appearance, and with dignity comes to the front of the stage and sits down to talk to the audience.)

FEMALE GREEK CHORUS (*as Aunt Mary*): My husband was such a good man — is. Is such a good man. Every night, he does the dishes. The second he comes home, he's taking out the garbage, or doing yard work, lifting the heavy things I can't. Everyone in the neighborhood borrows Peck — it's true — women with husbands of their own, men who just don't have Peck's abilities — there's always a knock on our door for a jump start on cold mornings, when anyone needs a ride, or help shoveling the sidewalk — I look out, and there Peck is, without a coat, pitching in.

I know I'm lucky. The man works from dawn to dusk. And the overtime he does every year — my poor sister. She sits every Christmas when I come to dinner with a new stole, or diamonds, or with the tickets to Bermuda.

I know he has troubles. And we don't talk about them. I wonder, sometimes, what happened to him during the war. The men who fought World War II didn't have "rap sessions" to talk about their feelings. Men in his generation were expected to be quiet about it and get on with their lives. And sometimes I can feel him just fighting the trouble — whatever has burrowed deeper than the scar tissue — and we don't talk about it. I know he's having a bad spell because he comes looking for me in the house, and just hangs around me until it passes. And I keep my banter light — I discuss a new recipe, or sales, or gossip — because I think domesticity can be a balm for men when they're lost. We sit in the house and listen to the peace of the clock ticking in his well-ordered living room, until it passes.

(Sharply.) I'm not a fool. I know what's going on. I wish you could feel how hard Peck fights against it — he's swimming against the tide, and what he needs is to see me on the shore, believing in him, knowing he won't go under, he won't give up —

And I want to say this about my niece. She's a sly one, that one is. She knows exactly what she's doing; she's twisted Peck around her little finger and thinks it's all a big secret. Yet another one who's borrowing my husband until it doesn't suit her anymore.

Well. I'm counting the days until she goes away to school. And she manipulates someone else. And then he'll come back again, and sit in the kitchen while I bake, or beside me on the sofa when I sew in the evenings. I'm a very patient woman. But I'd like my husband back.

I am counting the days.

(A Voice repeats:)

You and the Reverse Gear.

MALE GREEK CHORUS: Li'l Bit's Thirteenth Christmas. Uncle Peck Does the Dishes. Christmas 1964.

(Peck stands in a dress shirt and tie, nice pants, with an apron. He is washing dishes. He's in a mood we haven't seen. Quiet, brooding. Li'l Bit watches him a moment before seeking him out.)

LI'L BIT: Uncle Peck?

(He does not answer. He continues to work on the pots.)

I didn't know where you'd gone to.

(He nods. She takes this as a sign to come in.)

Don't you want to sit with us for a while?
PECK: No. I'd rather do the dishes.

(Pause. Li'l Bit watches him.)

LI'L BIT: You're the only man I know who does dishes.

(Peck says nothing.)

I think it's really nice.
PECK: My wife has been on her feet all day. So's your grandmother and your mother.
LI'L BIT: I know. (*Beat.*) Do you want some help?
PECK: No. (*He softens a bit towards her.*) You can help by just talking to me.
LI'L BIT: Big Papa never does the dishes. I think it's nice.
PECK: I think men should be nice to women. Women are always working for us. There's nothing particularly manly in wolfing down food and then sitting around in a stupor while the women clean up.
LI'L BIT: That looks like a really neat camera that Aunt Mary got you.
PECK: It is. It's a very nice one.

(Pause, as Peck works on the dishes and some demon that Li'l Bit intuits.)

LI'L BIT: Did Big Papa hurt your feelings?
PECK (*tired*): What? Oh, no — it doesn't hurt me. Family is family. I'd rather have him picking on me than — I don't pay him any mind, Li'l Bit.
LI'L BIT: Are you angry with us?
PECK: No, Li'l Bit. I'm not angry.

(Another pause.)

LI'L BIT: We missed you at Thanksgiving. . . . I did. I missed you.
PECK: Well, there were . . . "things" going on. I didn't want to spoil anyone's Thanksgiving.
LI'L BIT: Uncle Peck? (*Very carefully.*) Please don't drink anymore tonight.
PECK: I'm not . . . overdoing it.
LI'L BIT: I know. (*Beat.*) Why do you drink so much?

(Peck stops and thinks, carefully.)

PECK: Well, Li'l Bit — let me explain it this way. There are some people who have a . . . a "fire" in the belly. I think they go to work on Wall Street or they run for office. And then there are people who have a "fire" in their heads — and they become writers or scientists or historians. (*He smiles a little at her.*) You. You've got a "fire" in the head. And then there are people like me.

LI'L BIT: Where do you have . . . a fire?

PECK: I have a fire in my heart. And sometimes the drinking helps.

LI'L BIT: There's got to be other things that can help.

PECK: I suppose there are.

LI'L BIT: Does it help — to talk to me?

PECK: Yes. It does. (*Quiet.*) I don't get to see you very much.

LI'L BIT: I know. (*Li'l Bit thinks.*) You could talk to me more.

PECK: Oh?

LI'L BIT: I could make a deal with you, Uncle Peck.

PECK: I'm listening.

LI'L BIT: We could meet and talk — once a week. You could just store up whatever's bothering you during the week — and then we could talk.

PECK: Would you like that?

LI'L BIT: As long as you don't drink. I'd meet you somewhere for lunch or for a walk — on the weekends — as long as you stop drinking. And we could talk about whatever you want.

PECK: You would do that for me?

LI'L BIT: I don't think I'd want Mom to know. Or Aunt Mary. I wouldn't want them to think —

PECK: — No. It would just be us talking.

LI'L BIT: I'll tell Mom I'm going to a girlfriend's. To study. Mom doesn't get home until six, so you can call me after school and tell me where to meet you.

PECK: You get home at four?

LI'L BIT: We can meet once a week. But only in public. You've got to let me — draw the line. And once it's drawn, you mustn't cross it.

PECK: Understood.

LI'L BIT: Would that help?

(*Peck is very moved.*)

PECK: Yes. Very much.

LI'L BIT: I'm going to join the others in the living room now. (*Li'l Bit turns to go.*)

PECK: Merry Christmas, Li'l Bit.

(*Li'l Bit bestows a very warm smile on him.*)

LI'L BIT: Merry Christmas, Uncle Peck.

(*A Voice dictates:*)

Shifting Forward from Second to Third Gear.

(*The Male and Female Greek Chorus members come forward.*)

MALE GREEK CHORUS: 1969. Days and Gifts: A Countdown:

FEMALE GREEK CHORUS: A note. "September 3, 1969. Li'l Bit: You've only been away two days and it feels like months. Hope your dorm room is cozy. I'm sending you this tape cassette — it's a new model — so you'll have some music in your room. Also that music you're reading about for class — *Carmina Burana*. Hope you enjoy. Only ninety days to go! — Peck."

MALE GREEK CHORUS: September 22. A bouquet of roses. A note: "Miss you like crazy. Sixty-nine days . . ."

TEENAGE GREEK CHORUS: September 25. A box of chocolates. A card: "Don't worry about the weight gain. You still look great. Got a post office box — write to me there. Sixty-six days. — Love, your candy man."

MALE GREEK CHORUS: October 16. A note: "Am trying to get through the Jane Austen you're reading — *Emma* — here's a book in return: *Liaisons Dangereuses*. Hope you're saving time for me." Scrawled in the margin the number: "47."

FEMALE GREEK CHORUS: November 16. "Sixteen days to go! — Hope you like the perfume. — Having a hard time reaching you on the dorm phone. You must be in the library a lot. Won't you think about me getting you your own phone so we can talk?"

TEENAGE GREEK CHORUS: November 18. "Li'l Bit — got a package returned to the P.O. Box. Have you changed dorms? Call me at work or write to the P.O. Am still on the wagon. Waiting to see you. Only two weeks more!"

MALE GREEK CHORUS: November 23. A letter. "Li'l Bit. So disappointed you couldn't come home for the turkey. Sending you some money for a nice dinner out — nine days and counting!"

GREEK CHORUS (*in unison*): November 25th. A letter:

LI'L BIT: "Dear Uncle Peck: I am sending this to you at work. Don't come up next weekend for my birthday. I will not be here —"

(*A Voice directs:*)

Shifting Forward from Third to Fourth Gear.

MALE GREEK CHORUS: December 10, 1969. A hotel room. Philadelphia. There is no moon tonight.

(*Peck sits on the side of the bed while Li'l Bit paces. He can't believe she's in his room, but there's a desperate edge to his happiness. Li'l Bit is furious, edgy. There is a bottle of champagne in an ice bucket in a very nice hotel room.*)

PECK: Why don't you sit?

LI'L BIT: I don't want to. — What's the champagne for?

PECK: I thought we might toast your birthday —

LI'L BIT: — I am so pissed off at you, Uncle Peck.

PECK: Why?

LI'L BIT: I mean, are you crazy?

PECK: What did I do?

LI'L BIT: You scared the holy crap out of me — sending me that stuff in the mail —

PECK: — They were gifts! I just wanted to give you some little perks your first semester —

LI'L BIT: — Well, what the hell were those numbers all about! Forty-four days to go — only two more weeks. — And then just numbers — 69 — 68 — 67 — like some serial killer!

PECK: Li'l Bit! Whoa! This is me you're talking to — I was just trying to pick up your spirits, trying to celebrate your birthday.

LI'L BIT: My *eighteenth* birthday. I'm not a child, Uncle Peck. You were counting down to my eighteenth birthday.

PECK: So?

LI'L BIT: So? So statutory rape is not in effect when a young woman turns eighteen. And you and I both know it.

(*Peck is walking on ice.*)

PECK: I think you misunderstand.

LI'L BIT: I think I understand all too well. I know what you want to do five steps ahead of you doing it. Defensive Driving 101.

PECK: Then why did you suggest we meet here instead of the restaurant?

LI'L BIT: I don't want to have this conversation in public.

PECK: Fine. Fine. We have a lot to talk about.

LI'L BIT: Yeah. We do.
(*Li'l Bit doesn't want to do what she has to do.*) Could I . . . have some of that champagne?

PECK: Of course, madam! (*Peck makes a big show of it.*) Let me do the honors. I wasn't sure which you might prefer — Taittingers or Veuve Clicquot — so I thought we'd start out with an old standard — Perrier Jouet. (*The bottle is popped.*)
Quick — Li'l Bit — your glass! (*Uncle Peck fills Li'l Bit's glass. He puts the bottle back in the ice and goes for a can of ginger ale.*) Let me get some of this ginger ale — my bubbly — and toast you.

(*He turns and sees that Li'l Bit has not waited for him.*)

LI'L BIT: Oh — sorry, Uncle Peck. Let me have another.

(*Peck fills her glass and reaches for his ginger ale; she stops him.*)

Uncle Peck — maybe you should join me in the champagne.

PECK: You want me — to drink?

LI'L BIT: It's not polite to let a lady drink alone.

PECK: Well, missy, if you insist. . . . (*Peck hesitates.*) — Just one. It's been a while. (*Peck fills another flute for himself.*) There. I'd like to propose a toast to you and your birthday! (*Peck sips it tentatively.*) I'm not used to this anymore.

LI'L BIT: You don't have anywhere to go tonight, do you?

(*Peck hopes this is a good sign.*)

PECK: I'm all yours. — God, it's good to see you! I've gotten so used to . . . to . . . talking to you in my head. I'm used to seeing you every week — there's so much — I don't quite know where to begin. How's school, Li'l Bit?

LI'L BIT: I — it's hard. Uncle Peck. Harder than I thought it would be. I'm in the middle of exams and papers and — I don't know.

PECK: You'll pull through. You always do.

LI'L BIT: Maybe. I . . . might be flunking out.

PECK: You always think the worst, Li'l Bit, but when the going gets tough —

(*Li'l Bit shrugs and pours herself another glass.*)

— Hey, honey, go easy on that stuff, okay?

LI'L BIT: Is it very expensive?

PECK: Only the best for you. But the cost doesn't matter — champagne should be "sipped."

(*Li'l Bit is quiet.*)

Look — if you're in trouble in school — you can always come back home for a while.

LI'L BIT: *No* — (*Li'l Bit tries not to be so harsh.*) — Thanks, Uncle Peck, but I'll figure some way out of this.

PECK: You're supposed to get in scrapes, your first year away from home.

LI'L BIT: Right. How's Aunt Mary?

PECK: She's fine. (*Pause.*) Well — how about the new car?

LI'L BIT: It's real nice. What is it, again?

PECK: It's a Cadillac El Dorado.

LI'L BIT: Oh. Well, I'm real happy for you, Uncle Peck.

PECK: I got it for you.

LI'L BIT: What?

PECK: I always wanted to get a Cadillac — but I thought, Peck, wait until Li'l Bit's old enough — and thought maybe you'd like to drive it, too.

LI'L BIT (*confused*): Why would I want to drive your car?

PECK: Just because it's the best — I want you to have the best.

(*They are running out of "gas"; small talk.*)

LI'L BIT: Listen, Uncle Peck, I don't know how to begin this, but —	PECK: I have been thinking of how to say this in my head, over and over —

PECK: Sorry.

LI'L BIT: You first.

PECK: Well, your going away — has just made me realize how much I miss you. Talking to you and being alone with you. I've really come to depend on you, Li'l Bit. And it's been so hard to get in touch with you lately — the distance and — and you're never in when I call — I guess you've been living in the library —

LI'L BIT: — No — the problem is, I haven't been in the library —

PECK: — Well, it doesn't matter — I hope you've been missing me as much.

LI'L BIT: Uncle Peck — I've been thinking a lot about this — and I came here tonight to tell you that — I'm not doing very well. I'm getting very confused — I can't concentrate on my work — and now that I'm away — I've been going over and over it in my mind — and I don't want us to "see" each other anymore. Other than with the rest of the family.

PECK (*quiet*): Are you seeing other men?

LI'L BIT (*getting agitated*): I — no, that's not the reason — I — well, yes, I am seeing other — listen, it's not really anybody's business!

PECK: Are you in love with anyone else?

LI'L BIT: That's not what this is about.

PECK: Li'l Bit — you're scared. Your mother and your grandparents have filled your head with all kinds of nonsense about men — I hear them working on you all the time — and you're scared. It won't hurt you — if the man you go to bed with really loves you. (*Li'l Bit is scared. She starts to tremble.*) And I have loved you since the day I held you in my hand. And I think everyone's just gotten you frightened to death about something that is just like breathing —

LI'L BIT: Oh, my god — (*She takes a breath.*) I can't see you anymore, Uncle Peck.

(*Peck downs the rest of his champagne.*)

PECK: Li'l Bit. Listen. Listen. Open your eyes and look at me. Come on. Just open your eyes, honey. (*Li'l Bit, eyes squeezed shut, refuses.*) All right then. I just want you to listen. Li'l Bit — I'm going to ask you just this once. Of your own free will. Just lie down on the bed with me — our clothes on — just lie down with me, a man and a woman . . . and let's . . . hold one another. Nothing else. Before you say anything else. I want the chance to . . . hold you. Because sometimes the body knows things that the mind isn't listening to . . . and after I've held you, then I want you to tell me what you feel.

LI'L BIT: You'll just . . . hold me?

PECK: Yes. And then you can tell me what you're feeling.

(*Li'l Bit — half wanting to run, half wanting to get it over with, half wanting to be held by him:*)

LI'L BIT: Yes. All right. Just hold. Nothing else.

(*Peck lies down on the bed and holds his arms out to her. Li'l Bit lies beside him, putting her head on his chest. He looks as if he's trying to soak her into his pores by osmosis. He strokes her hair, and she lies very still. The Male Greek Chorus member and the Female Greek Chorus member as Aunt Mary come into the room.*)

MALE GREEK CHORUS: Recipe for a Southern Boy:

FEMALE GREEK CHORUS (*as Aunt Mary*): A drawl of molasses in the way he speaks.

MALE GREEK CHORUS: A gumbo of red and brown mixed in the cream of his skin.

(*While Peck lies, his eyes closed, Li'l Bit rises in the bed and responds to her aunt.*)

LI'L BIT: Warm brown eyes —

FEMALE GREEK CHORUS (*as Aunt Mary*): Bedroom eyes —

MALE GREEK CHORUS: A dash of Southern Baptist Fire and Brimstone —

LI'L BIT: A curl of Elvis on his forehead —

FEMALE GREEK CHORUS (*as Aunt Mary*): A splash of Bay Rum —

MALE GREEK CHORUS: A closely shaven beard that he razors just for you —

FEMALE GREEK CHORUS (*as Aunt Mary*): Large hands — rough hands —

LI'L BIT: Warm hands —

MALE GREEK CHORUS: The steel of the military in his walk —

LI'L BIT: The slouch of the fishing skiff in his walk —

MALE GREEK CHORUS: Neatly pressed khakis —

FEMALE GREEK CHORUS (*as Aunt Mary*): And under the wide leather of the belt —

LI'L BIT: Sweat of cypress and sand —

MALE GREEK CHORUS: Neatly pressed khakis —

LI'L BIT: His heart beating Dixie —

FEMALE GREEK CHORUS (*as Aunt Mary*): The whisper of the zipper — you could reach out with your hand and —

LI'L BIT: His mouth —

FEMALE GREEK CHORUS (*as Aunt Mary*): You could just reach out and —

LI'L BIT: Hold him in your hand —

FEMALE GREEK CHORUS (*as Aunt Mary*): And his mouth —

(*Li'l Bit rises above her uncle and looks at his mouth; she starts to lower herself to kiss him — and wrenches herself free. She gets up from the bed.*)

LI'L BIT: — I've got to get back.

PECK: Wait — Li'l Bit. Did you . . . feel nothing?

LI'L BIT (*lying*): No. Nothing.

PECK: Do you — do you think of me?

(*The Greek Chorus whispers:*)

FEMALE GREEK CHORUS: Khakis —

MALE GREEK CHORUS: Bay Rum —

FEMALE GREEK CHORUS: The whisper of the —

LI'L BIT: — No.

(*Peck, in a rush, trembling, gets something out of his pocket.*)

PECK: I'm forty-five. That's not old for a man. And I haven't been able to do anything else but think of you. I can't concentrate on my work — Li'l Bit. You've got to — I want you to think about what I am about to ask you.

LI'L BIT: I'm listening.

(*Peck opens a small ring box.*)

PECK: I want you to be my wife.

LI'L BIT: This isn't happening.

PECK: I'll tell Mary I want a divorce. We're not blood-related. It would be legal —

LI'L BIT: — What have you been thinking! You are married to my aunt, Uncle Peck. She's my family. You

Mary-Louise Parker as Li'l Bit and David Morse as Uncle Peck in *How I Learned to Drive* in 1997 at the Vineyard Theatre, New York City.

have — you have gone way over the line. Family is family.

(*Quickly, Li'l Bit flies through the room, gets her coat.*) I'm leaving. Now. I am not seeing you. Again.

(*Peck lies down on the bed for a moment, trying to absorb the terrible news. For a moment, he almost curls into a fetal position.*)

I'm not coming home for Christmas. You should go home to Aunt Mary. Go home now, Uncle Peck.

(*Peck gets control, and sits, rigid.*)

Uncle Peck? — I'm sorry but I have to go.

(*Pause.*)

Are you all right?

(*With a discipline that comes from being told that boys don't cry, Peck stands upright.*)

PECK: I'm fine. I just think — I need a real drink.

(*The Male Greek Chorus has become a bartender. At a small counter, he is lining up shots for Peck. As Li'l Bit narrates, we see Peck sitting, carefully and calmly downing shot glasses.*)

LI'L BIT (*to the audience*): I never saw him again. I stayed away from Christmas and Thanksgiving for years after.

It took my uncle seven years to drink himself to

death. First he lost his job, then his wife, and finally his driver's license. He retreated to his house, and had his bottles delivered.

(*Peck stands, and puts his hands in front of him — almost like Superman flying.*)

One night he tried to go downstairs to the basement — and he flew down the steep basement stairs. My aunt came by weekly to put food on the porch, and she noticed the mail and the papers stacked up, uncollected.

They found him at the bottom of the stairs. Just steps away from his dark room.

Now that I'm old enough, there are some questions I would have liked to have asked him. Who did it to you, Uncle Peck? How old were you? Were you eleven?

(*Peck moves to the driver's seat of the car and waits.*)

Sometimes I think of my uncle as a kind of Flying Dutchman. In the opera, the Dutchman is doomed to wander the sea; but every seven years he can come ashore, and if he finds a maiden who will love him of her own free will — he will be released.

And I see Uncle Peck in my mind, in his Chevy '56, a spirit driving up and down the back roads of Carolina — looking for a young girl who, of her own free will, will love him. Release him.

(*A Voice states:*)

You and the Reverse Gear.

LI'L BIT: The summer of 1962. On Men, Sex, and Women: Part III:

(*Li'l Bit steps, as an eleven-year-old, into:*)

FEMALE GREEK CHORUS (*as Mother*): It is out of the question. End of Discussion.

LI'L BIT: But why?

FEMALE GREEK CHORUS (*as Mother*): Li'l Bit — we are not discussing this. I said no.

LI'L BIT: But I could spend an extra week at the beach! You're not telling me why!

FEMALE GREEK CHORUS (*as Mother*): Your uncle pays entirely too much attention to you.

LI'L BIT: He listens to me when I talk. And — and he talks to me. He teaches me about things. Mama — he knows an awful lot.

FEMALE GREEK CHORUS (*as Mother*): He's a small town hick who's learned how to mix drinks from Hugh Hefner.

LI'L BIT: Who's Hugh Hefner?

(*Beat.*)

FEMALE GREEK CHORUS (*as Mother*): I am not letting an eleven-year-old girl spend seven hours alone in the car with a man. . . . I don't like the way your uncle looks at you.

LI'L BIT: For god's sake, mother! Just because you've gone through a bad time with my father — you think every man is evil!

FEMALE GREEK CHORUS (*as Mother*): Oh no, Li'l Bit — not all men. . . . We . . . we just haven't been very lucky with the men in our family.

LI'L BIT: Just because you lost your husband — I still deserve a chance at having a father! Someone! A man who will look out for me! Don't I get a chance?

FEMALE GREEK CHORUS (*as Mother*): I will feel terrible if something happens.

LI'L BIT: Mother! It's in your head! Nothing will happen! I can take care of myself. And I can certainly handle Uncle Peck.

FEMALE GREEK CHORUS (*as Mother*): All right. But I'm warning you — if anything happens, I hold you responsible.

(*Li'l Bit moves out of this scene and toward the car.*)

LI'L BIT: 1962. On the Back Roads of Carolina: The First Driving Lesson.

(*The Teenage Greek Chorus member stands apart on stage. She will speak all of Li'l Bit's lines. Li'l Bit sits beside Peck in the front seat. She looks at him closely, remembering.*)

PECK: Li'l Bit? Are you getting tired?

TEENAGE GREEK CHORUS: A little.

PECK: It's a long drive. But we're making really good time. We can take the back road from here and see . . . a little scenery. Say — I've got an idea — (*Peck checks his rearview mirror.*)

TEENAGE GREEK CHORUS: Are we stopping, Uncle Peck?

PECK: There's no traffic here. Do you want to drive?

TEENAGE GREEK CHORUS: I can't drive.

PECK: It's easy. I'll show you how. I started driving when I was your age. Don't you want to? —

TEENAGE GREEK CHORUS: — But it's against the law at my age!

PECK: And that's why you can't tell anyone I'm letting you do this —

TEENAGE GREEK CHORUS: — But — I can't reach the pedals.

PECK: You can sit in my lap and steer. I'll push the pedals for you. Did your father ever let you drive his car?

TEENAGE GREEK CHORUS: No way.

PECK: Want to try?

TEENAGE GREEK CHORUS: Okay. (*Li'l Bit moves into Peck's lap. She leans against him, closing her eyes.*)

PECK: You're just a little thing, aren't you? Okay — now think of the wheel as a big clock — I want you to put your right hand on the clock where three o'clock would be; and your left hand on the nine —

(*Li'l Bit puts one hand to Peck's face, to stroke him. Then, she takes the wheel.*)

TEENAGE GREEK CHORUS: Am I doing it right?

PECK: That's right. Now, whatever you do, don't let go of the wheel. You tell me whether to go faster or slower —

TEENAGE GREEK CHORUS: Not so fast, Uncle Peck!

PECK: Li'l Bit — I need you to watch the road —

(*Peck puts his hands on Li'l Bit's breasts. She relaxes against him, silent, accepting his touch.*)

TEENAGE GREEK CHORUS: Uncle Peck — what are you doing?

PECK: Keep driving. (*He slips his hands under her blouse.*)

TEENAGE GREEK CHORUS: Uncle Peck — please don't do this —

PECK: — Just a moment longer . . . (*Peck tenses against Li'l Bit.*)

TEENAGE GREEK CHORUS (*trying not to cry*): This isn't happening.

(*Peck tenses more, sharply. He buries his face in Li'l Bit's neck, and moans softly. The Teenage Greek Chorus exits, and Li'l Bit steps out of the car. Peck, too, disappears.*)

(*A Voice reflects:*)

Driving in Today's World.

LI'L BIT: That day was the last day I lived in my body. I retreated above the neck, and I've lived inside the "fire" in my head ever since.

And now that seems like a long, long time ago. When we were both very young.

And before you know it, I'll be thirty-five. That's getting up there for a woman. And I find myself believing in things that a younger self vowed never to believe in. Things like family and forgiveness.

I know I'm lucky. Although I still have never known what it feels like to jog or dance. Any thing that . . . "jiggles." I do like to watch people on the dance floor, or out on the running paths, just jiggling away. And I say — good for them. (*Li'l Bit moves to the car with pleasure.*)

The nearest sensation I feel — of flight in the body — I guess I feel when I'm driving. On a day like today. It's five A.M. The radio says it's going to be clear and crisp. I've got five hundred miles of highway ahead of me — and some back roads too. I filled the tank last night, and had the oil checked. Checked the tires, too. You've got to treat her . . . with respect.

First thing I do is: Check under the car. To see if any two year olds or household cats have crawled beneath, and strategically placed their skulls behind my back tires. (*Li'l Bit crouches.*)

Nope. Then I get in the car. (*Li'l Bit does so.*)

I lock the doors. And turn the key. Then I adjust the most important control on the dashboard — the radio — (*Li'l Bit turns the radio on: We hear all of the Greek Chorus overlapping, and static:*)

FEMALE GREEK CHORUS (*overlapping*): — "You were so tiny you fit in his hand —"

MALE GREEK CHORUS (*overlapping*): — "How is Shakespeare gonna help her lie on her back in the —"

TEENAGE GREEK CHORUS (*overlapping*): — "Am I doing it right?"

(*Li'l Bit fine-tunes the radio station. A song like "Dedicated to the One I Love" or Orbison's "Sweet Dreams" comes on, and cuts off the Greek Chorus.*)

LI'L BIT: Ahh . . . (*Beat.*) I adjust my seat. Fasten my seat belt. Then I check the right side mirror — check the left side. (*She does.*) Finally, I adjust the rearview mirror.

(*As Li'l Bit adjusts the rearview mirror, a faint light strikes the spirit of Uncle Peck, who is sitting in the back seat of the car. She sees him in the mirror. She smiles at him, and he nods at her. They are happy to be going for a long ride together. Li'l Bit slips the car into first gear; to the audience:*)

And then — I floor it.

(*Sound of a car taking off. Blackout.*)

COMMENTARIES

Caridad Svich (b. 1963) *and Peter Franklin* (b. 1951)
COAST TO COAST WITH PAULA VOGEL   *1999*

> *Caridad Svich of the Dramatists Guild interviewed Paula Vogel in Los Angeles in 1999, and a few days later Vogel's literary agent, Peter Franklin, continued the interview in New York. The result is an intimate view of the way in which Paula Vogel works and how she developed into the playwright she has become.*

Los Angeles

Caridad Svich: My initial question is: how do you sustain your focus when you're working? *How I Learned to Drive* has had such extraordinary success, and well deserved, but you still have to write that next play. How do you keep yourself in line, on track?

Paula Vogel: I've been very lucky. I didn't come from a family with trust funds. I was lucky in that. I was also lucky that I wasn't accepted into Yale School of Drama. All along, I knew that there was not family money and that I knew no one in the arts. If I was to make it in this world, I would have to do the writing on top of at least forty hours a week or more of work. In my twenties and early thirties, when I was struggling in New York, I was working sixty hours a week and writing plays.

No one in my circle of friends was being produced, so we all got together as a group. There was Mac Wellman, Jeff Jones, Y York, and maybe Connie Congdon. We dared each other to write a play in forty-eight hours. Mac wrote this brilliant play called *Cleveland.* I wrote *Heirlooms,* which actually contains many of the seeds of *How I Learned to Drive,* and then I promptly put the play in a drawer and forgot about it. I became convinced that it was appropriate to do your first draft, if not in forty-eight hours, then in a week or two, because theater is a time-oriented form.

When I got my job at Brown University, I thought, "We're going to call it The Great American Play Bakeoff." Every year, we would do these bakeoffs at Brown, and something very interesting always happened. Because they had permission to play, the forty-eight-hour bakeoff plays actually contained the seeds of what would become major works.

The Mineola Twins is on its seventeenth draft, but I did the first draft in maybe three or four weeks. The first draft of *How I Learned to Drive* was written in two weeks. You can rewrite a play for the rest of your life, but for that first draft, you put the pedal to the metal. Yes, it may be underwritten, but that rush to get to the end gives the play energy.

So in terms of focus, the key is to give yourself the permission to play and the confinement of less time rather than more time to release your creativity. When we first started our bakeoffs, we thought, once upon a time, Racine and Corneille met over coffee and said to each other, "I dare you to do a Phèdre play." That sense of writing in community is very interesting to me. I don't think playwrights write in isolation. I think we're writing to our peer group. The more great art there is, the more we all can be great.

Svich: The idea of community is so important. In Los Angeles, it's hard to establish those communities, simply because of geography, but it can happen. I wonder how you view the work of other artists, particularly young artists.

Vogel: I think about this all the time. It's not a matter of needing new plays and new artists. We are blessed with a critical mass. We need new producers, new models of production. It's no longer "Let's write a play" but "Let's make a theater."

Of course, by the time you build a theater, it's already outmoded. By the time you raise the money, the next generation is writing something that's antithetical to that space. So it's important that institutions create opportunities for the next generation. The question is: can larger institutions accept the oedipal principle? That's something Molly Smith told me many years ago. When we were in our twenties, she formed Perseverance Theater, which is my favorite theater in the country. Molly was very frustrated, because she kept knocking on doors, and everyone said, "Go away, kid." She told me, "As we age as artists, we become the king. Then there come the king-slayers."

So the question is: how do we say, "Come through the door. Here's my breast, Oedipus. Come through the door. Your art is antithetical to everything I stand for, and isn't that wonderful? That's how it should be." Great artistic directors do this. Great institutional theaters do this. It's not just making plays. It's making new structures for collaborations among playwrights, directors, and actors.

Svich: I admire your continued excitement and passion for the younger voices. When I was in London, I heard you talk at Donmar Warehouse about decadent art and naïve art, which I found fascinating. I wonder if you could encapsulate some of those ideas for those who weren't there.

Vogel: That comes from Bert States, my mentor. He said, "Every art movement goes through three stages: naïve, sophisticated, and decadent." The naïve stage is the first time something is done. For example, at some point, someone said, "What if a guy steps out from the chorus? What if three people step out of the chorus?" Suddenly, it's a new game called "drama." After a while, you say, "Yeah, yeah, three guys and a chorus. I get it. So what?" Then you go into a sophisticated stage, where everyone has seen a drama. You become very refined in your devices, and you hide all the raw edges. Then, after you've seen two thousand dramas, you get to the decadent stage. You go to the theater and say, "This better be good. Tell me something I've never seen before. Surprise me." At that point, you are in the decadent stage, which is almost a return to the naïve stage. We again expose the devices. It's raw. We again play with the form, break down the walls, and dismantle the scenery. It's the difference among Aeschylus as naïve, Sophocles as sophisticated, and Euripedes as decadent. Let's go a step further.

In the first five minutes of a play, the audience is naïve. They don't know what the rules of the game are yet. By midway, they're sophisticated. They know the vocabulary. Then comes that great moment when you pull the rug out from under them. You deconstruct the play and expose the devices in a decadent mode. I know a play works when, while the audience runs through their computer brains of the two thousand plays they've seen and tries to calculate where the play is going, the emotion grabs them by the throat and they forget about all the other plays they've seen. I'm excited by younger artists, because they dismantle my assumptions. They dismantle the dramaturgy I've spent twenty years trying to formulate. It's a kick in the pants! [. . .]

New York

Peter Franklin: I'm very excited to be doing this. I've had many conversations with Paula Vogel but never one like this. I've been privileged to represent her work for a number of years now. Aside from being one of the most extraordinary writing talents in the world, she also happens to be one of the great people in the world, so this is a double pleasure for me. I want to begin with a question I've always wanted to ask you, Paula, but never have. If you see things going off-track in a production, how do you address them?

Paula Vogel: Very quickly. (*Laughter.*) On the first day of rehearsal, you usually get a sense if things are going in a different direction. I don't mean in a different direction from what you had visualized but in a direction that may be counterproductive to the play. On the first day, I often discover a difference of opinion that delights me, a different vision that's thrilling, but if something goes off-track, I talk to the director. However, I don't necessarily do it directly. I don't necessarily say, "This is what I want." I tell jokes. I have meals with them. I just spend a lot of time with the director. In the beginning, we talk about anything *but* the play, so the director gets a sense of my rhythm, my humor, and my take on the world. I don't want to threaten their autonomy or vision. It's not until much later in the process that we talk directly about the play. I believe in sending roses first.

Franklin: So it's an intuitive process?

Vogel: Yes. Anne Bogart was very crucial in teaching me how to talk to directors. I realize it's a mistake to answer questions directly. It's sometimes best to say, "I don't think I can answer that." If something is off-track, I'm comfortable saying, "That's a fascinating impulse. It will cause problems in act two, but if you want to go out on that limb now, that's great." However, it's not necessary to have a synthesis of ideas. On *Baltimore Waltz*, Anne called me and said, "We're at the hospital looking at lounge furniture." I said, "Anne, why are you at the hospital?" "We're looking at lounge furniture." "*Baltimore Waltz* takes place on this huge bed. I wrote it for this huge bed." "That's wonderful, but that's not the vision I have. I promise you won't miss the bed." At that point, a little voice in my head said, "Shut up, Vogel. You're talking to Anne Bogart!" (*Laughter.*) Anne said, "I promise I'll give you beds, but not *one* bed." The more she talked, the more I thought, "I'm not a smart director. I don't have that genius. Give it up."

Similarly, when Mark Brokaw and I talked about *How I Learned to Drive*, he said, "No slides." I had slides in my script, but he said, "I don't see slides." He told me why. He had a very clear vision. When you talk to directors and actors, you can see the passion in their face, hear it in their voice. I don't want to dampen that enthusiasm. So I told Mark, "Fine, no slides." I will give up an early battle, so that when there's something sacred in the script, I can keep it inviolable. The other reason is that I find words very cheap. Theater isn't all about words. It isn't about the text. Theater is created in the gaps between the text and the performers and the audience. I'm just the ghostwriter, not really the author. [. . .]

Q: I have a question about another subject, a nuts-and-bolts question. I read an interview with you in the *Dramatists Guild Quarterly*, where you mentioned that *How I Learned to Drive* has a circular structure. Could you talk a little more about that?

Vogel: Recently, I've been doing weeklong "boot camps" and one-day playwriting workshops. In a nutshell, I talk about plot, character, language, and plasticity. I break down the six basic plot forms. Of course, no play is purely written in one form. You play with the different forms.

Number one is the syllogistic plot. It's cause and effect — A causes B causes C causes D, then "Boom!" There's an explosion. For example, *Oedipus* or the middle plays of Ibsen. It's actually the hardest structure for me. *How I Learned to Drive* is actually written in reverse syllogistic plot — copied from Pinter's *Betrayal*. There is cause and effect, but you go backward. Number two is the epic or associative plot. There are many different names for it, but A makes B happen, then there's a song and dance, then F makes G happen, then there's a patter song, and then it all comes home. It's Shakespeare and Brecht. For example, in "The Scottish Play," after Duncan's assassination, you don't see the immediate aftermath. You see a drunken porter in the following scene. It's always moving forward, but there's no direct cause and effect from one scene to the next. I wrote *The Mineola Twins* in associative form.

Number three is the circular plot. For example, *Waiting for Godot*. You end and begin the play at the same instance. Number four is the pattern plot. In every scene, a pattern is repeated. For example, David Mamet's *Duck Variations*. There are two guys on a bench talking about ducks in just about every single scene. I wrote *Oldest Profession*, in which there are five prostitutes, then four, then three, then two. You begin to see a pattern. It's also *Same Time, Next Year* and *La Ronde*.

Number five is the conventional plot. We know the rules of the game before we go to the theater. It's the murder mystery, the Broadway musical, the detective story — even the wedding, as in *Tony 'n' Tina's Wedding*. Number six is what I call the "synthetic fragment" plot. My students [at Brown University] do it effortlessly, but it's very hard for me to do. For example, Heiner Mueller, the German playwright who wrote *Hamletmachine*. Time no longer goes forward. All time is onstage simultaneously.

In "boot camp" I ask people to take *Hamlet* and write six plot synopses in all six different forms. I've seen astonishing, amazing *Hamlet* plays. When you start to play with these things, with a syllogistic plot or a circular plot, you start to become aware of how to design your own plot structure, and it's fun. The greatest plot structure I've ever seen is in Tom Stoppard's *Artist Descending a Staircase*. It is sheer genius. I keep saying to myself, "One of these days, I don't know when, I'm going to do a playwriting book," but it would be an anti-playwriting playwriting book. Every time I read a playwriting book, I think, "That sounds good," but then I think, "Now, how do I break all the rules I just read?"

Franklin: Any other questions?

Q: What's your writing process like? Does it depend on the play?

Vogel: I've never been a morning writer or written in any regular block of time. I'm a binge writer. However, I think for a long, long time before I sit down and write. In the "boot camp" and at Brown, I make my students write a play in forty-eight hours. I don't write plays in forty-eight hours anymore, but I write in two or three weeks. I need that momentum. I push on to finish that first draft, even if I underwrite the play. I can always go back and fill in spots later.

As you know, we writers are always juggling a rewrite of one play with a first draft of another with a screenplay. I design a different soundtrack for every project, so I almost drool like a Pavlovian dog. When I hear "Dedicated to the One I Love" or Roy Orbison, I'm in the world of *How I Learned to Drive*. If I hear Teresa Brewer, I know I'm doing rewrites on *Mineola Twins*. Janet Jackson's "Nasty" is *Hot 'n' Throbbing*. It's very specific. Nobody can live with me when I'm writing, because I make tape loops that repeat and repeat. I'll shut myself away and listen to these tape loops for the two to three weeks. The other thing I do is use a specific font and format for each play. Screenwriting books tell us there's a standard format, but that's deadly. I take one look at the page, and I'm in the world of the play. It helps me program myself. I do rewrites in the blank hours between my chores, doing the dishes and all that. That gives me all the rewriting time I need. So that's my process.

Franklin: Is writing for the screen different for you than writing for the stage?

Vogel: With a screenplay, you have less control of the result, but you can envision things that you can't do on stage. It's extraordinary how you can play with images in film. It can be a superbly surrealistic medium, though only independents or Europeans really use it in a surrealistic way. Writing screenplays, I start to think, "Now, how would I do that on stage?" It increases my stage vocabulary. For example, *How I Learned to Drive* started with a screenplay image. I saw a woman driving someplace in the Arizona desert. She adjusts her rearview mirror, and a dead man materializes in the back seat.

There's a fabulous writer named John Jeserun. I saw something he did at La MaMa° about fifteen years ago. It began with a man lying on the floor, just watching the curling smoke from a cigarette standing upright on the floor in front of him. A woman's voice offstage said, "John, why are you lying on the floor?" There was a quick blackout. Then you saw the actor lying "on the floor," but standing upright gazing straight out at the audience. The woman's voice again said, "John, why are

---

La MaMa: La MaMa Experimental Theater Club, New York.

you lying on the floor?" The actor was lying against a Plexiglas sheet, which you couldn't see, with the cigarette pasted above his head as if the camera created the floor's POV. It created the most cinematic cut. It was mesmerizing and exciting. There's a whole host of writers that have a different kind of muscle and sinew, who are using a kind of cinematic vocabulary.

Q: When do you finish writing? If you see something that you're not happy with after a play is produced or published, will you change it?

Vogel: I see a couple of things that I'm not happy with, even now, in *How I Learned to Drive*. I don't think I've ever told you this, Peter. I wanted to put in a dance between Peck and Li'l Bit. I didn't, and I'm sorry about that. I miss it. I've actually told a couple of directors who've done it. It's not in the printed version, but I think, "Well, that's the way that goes."

Franklin: After the opening in London, I told Paula, "I'm hearing things in this play I don't even remember." She said, "Well, I put some things back in!" (*Laughter.*)

Vogel: It's true! I feel it's a mistake not to do rewrites during rehearsals of a first production. It's a mistake not to use those particular actors to full advantage. You should tailor a role for an actor who has your play for the first time. Though it may not have been your original intention, what she or he does is going to become "universal." In rehearsal for *How I Learned to Drive*, I'd be thinking, "Mary-Louise [Parker] doesn't need all those words. She doesn't need all those transitions." So I cut a lot. I'd be thinking, "We already know that. Skip over it." One or two times, she said, "I need a little more stage time here," and I put in lines. I really tailored it, so there was a logic and a rhythm in that first production. I'm not a perfectionist, but I do keep rewriting. This summer, I'm going back to *Hot 'n' Throbbing* and doing a major rewrite for a possible production. I literally haven't looked at the script for maybe four or five years. It was published, but I knew I messed up the ending. After I finished *How I Learned to Drive*, I realized how to fix it. That often happens. Your next play teaches you how to work on your previous play.

David Savran (b. 1950)
PAULA VOGEL   *1999*

David Savran, Paula Vogel's colleague in the English Department at Brown University, is well known for his series of interviews with contemporary playwrights. His interview with Paula Vogel appears in his book The Playwright's Voice (1999), *but this excerpt is his review of Vogel's career and precedes the interview itself. His observations describe in an economical fashion the special features of her work.*

In her playwriting classes, Paula Vogel always asks her students to write the impossible: a play with a dog as protagonist, a play that cannot be staged, a play that dramatizes the end of the world in five pages. And while these provocative exercises stretch students' imaginations in remarkable ways, they also inadvertently reveal much about Vogel's own playwriting. For all her plays endeavor to stage the impossible. They defy traditional theater logic, subtly calling conventions into question or, in some cases, pushing them well past their limits. What other playwright would dare memorialize her brother in a play filled with fart jokes and riotous sex, whose medical authority, a cross between Dr. Strangelove and Groucho Marx, ends up drinking his own piss? What other feminist would dare write so many jokes about tits?

For a Vogel play is never simply a politely dramatized fiction, it is always a meditation on the theater itself — on role-playing, on the socially sanctioned scripts from which characters diverge at their peril, and on a theatrical tradition that has punished women who don't remain quiet, passive and demure. Take, for example, *The Mineola Twins* (1996), which plays deliriously and chillingly with the age-old farcical convention of using one virtuosic actor (and a battery of wigs) to play two startlingly dissimilar identical twins. Or *Hot 'n' Throbbing* (1994), which transforms a theater into a living room and a living room into a theater in order to dramatize the fatal consequences of stage directions gone out of control. Or her Pulitzer Prize–winning *How I Learned to Drive* (1997), which does far more than explain the effects of sexual predation on a young girl; it literally splits her into two — a body and a voice — in order to represent the radical alienation from Self that results from having been molested.

In *How I Learned to Drive*, Vogel turns the theater itself into a vehicle for memory, using first gear to move forward in time and reverse to move backwards. By reenacting the driving lessons given her by her Uncle Peck, Li'l Bit remembers her strangely — and literally — intoxicating sexual initiation. For there is no question but that her uncle's seduction has caused her to retreat "above the neck." At the same time, Peck, that most charming of pedophiles and himself a victim of abuse, is the only member of her family who makes a real effort to understand, nurture, and help her grow up. For *How I Learned to Drive* is the story not only of Li'l Bit's molestation. It is also a slyly subversive dramatization of how a girl — perhaps any girl — becomes an adult.

At the beginning of the play, Li'l Bit remembers the suburban Maryland of her youth, completely absorbed in the touch, smell, and taste of a "warm summer evening." These sensory perceptions connect her to the past, to the land and to her own body as she renders herself miraculously whole again through the power of memory. But as Li'l Bit knows all too well — and any adult will tell you — this primordial wholeness cannot last, and the remainder of the play shows her being taken for a drive that will lead her into another realm, one dominated by the senses of sight and hearing. For if touch, smell, and taste are the tokens of intimacy and wholeness, then sight and hearing are undeniably the most objectifying of the senses; they introduce a radical separation between subject and object. This is perhaps why the very center of the play is a photo shoot, for it is in this scene that Li'l Bit most graphically becomes an object for Uncle Peck and, more ominously, for herself as well. Yet this sequence is so effective theatrically because it tacitly recognizes that sight and hearing are also the senses, by no mere coincidence, upon which theater depends. It demonstrates that the theater, like the photo shoot, will always produce figures who are subjected to the scrutiny of voyeuristic spectators (or lascivious uncles). Li'l Bit, in other words, suddenly discovers that she has become an actor in a drama that has been scripted for her by an exploitative, if well-meaning spectator who is, in turn, the product of a society that values women for their allure. Yet *How I Learned to Drive* is no more an indictment of theater than it is of eroticism. For it is precisely the theater that gives Li'l Bit the time and the place to remember, that is, to reconstruct herself, to put herself back together. In learning to drive, the play shows us, Li'l Bit learns how to desire, how to use the theater, and the act of self-presentation, to put herself quite literally in the driver's seat.

In *How I Learned to Drive*, Li'l Bit is literally haunted by the unquiet spirit of her Uncle Peck in the same way that Anna in *The Baltimore Waltz* (1992) — and Vogel herself — is haunted by the spirit of her dead brother, Carl. For in attempting to remember, Vogel's theater calls up ghosts, figures lighter than air yet heavy with the past. It is obsessed with commemorating what has been lost, while understanding that loss always pays a kind of dividend that is experienced both on a personal and cultural level. For Vogel's ghosts always materialize at the place where memory turns into history, the particular into the universal. Thus, *Baltimore Waltz* becomes an exhilarating tribute and love letter not only to Carl, but to everyone who has died of AIDS, in the same way that *Drive*, by staging Li'l Bit's singular journey, dramatizes the relentless process by which we are each being produced as the subjects and objects of our own dramas.

For all their precision in documenting the act of remembering, Vogel's plays are perhaps unique in the way that they locate memory in the body. For it is far more than her punning sensibility that inspires her to title her most recent collection *The Mammary Plays* (TCG, 1998). Summoning up the "full-figured gal" of TV-commercial fame, both *Drive* and *The Mineola Twins* simultaneously exploit and critique the cliché of this "stacked" femme fatale. Both tacitly acknowledge that female bodies are steeped in history, that "sometimes the body," as Uncle Peck puts it, "knows things that the mind isn't listening to." And like her other plays, they are intent on listening to and reclaiming that lost, forgotten history. For as a feminist writer, Vogel not only attends to the deeply contradictory representations of women in our culture, but also delineates female characters who are prepared to use their physical charms (if need be) to wrest control of their lives. From the sprightly geriatric prostitutes of *The Oldest Profession* (1988) who have seized the means of production; to Myra, Mineola's answer to Patricia Hearst and Patricia Ireland; to the lesbian parents of three imaginary little boys in *And Baby Makes Seven* (1984); Vogel's women are themselves playwrights who attempt to write their way out of difficult situations and script more creative, bountiful lives. Like Vogel herself, they are committed to redressing a history of oppression by rewriting the scenes they have been handed. By so turning her female characters (and her students!) into playwrights of no mean accomplishments, she suggests that although a triumphal feminist theater seems an impossibility in our time, one may nonetheless endeavor to stage that impossibility, along with the glittering promises it holds.

Jill Dolan (b. 1957)
REVIEW OF *HOW I LEARNED TO DRIVE*   *1997*

> *Jill Dolan reviewed the Vineyard Theatre production of* How I Learned to Drive *and examines the ways in which Paula Vogel establishes sympathy for Uncle Peck despite revealing him as a pedophile. Dolan sees sexuality as unstable and a matter of exploration in the drama, especially on Li'l Bit's part. In the process of commenting on the play Dolan gives us useful insights into the staging of the drama.*

Playwright Paula Vogel tends to select sensitive, difficult, fraught issues to theatricalize, and to spin them with a dramaturgy that's at once creative, highly imaginative, and brutally honest. In *How I Learned to Drive* — which won the 1997 Drama Desk Award for Best Play and several Obie Awards — Vogel's conceits remain personal, political, and highly theatrical. In a nonlinear narrative, Li'l Bit (Mary Louise Parker) tries to understand her relationship with her Uncle Peck (David Morse), whose driving lessons taught her as much about gender relations and her own sexuality as they did about the proper use of rearview mirrors, gearshifts, and turn signals.

Driving becomes the action that evokes Li'l Bit's memories; driving metaphors chart Li'l Bit's growth into automotive mastery and sexual mystery, punctuating the play's movement back and forth in time. Sitting in straight-backed chairs on a nearly bare set, Morse and Parker evoke the car rides that shape and intertwine their lives. Mark Brokaw's crisp, unsparing direction allows them to craft the scene with gesture and light, leaving the production unencumbered by more than minimal props and set pieces. The sparse set is framed by a map of Baltimore in the 1950s and 1960s, when the play's first memories occur. The geographical snippets, covered with interstates, route numbers, town names, and zip codes that move in and out of sight, remind spectators how difficult it is to truly map the territory of relationships, sexuality, and desire.

Vogel's choice to remember Li'l Bit and Peck's relationship nonchronologically illustrates its complexity, and allows the playwright to build sympathy for a man who might otherwise be despised and dismissed as a child molester. As played with affable gentility and gentleness by Morse, Peck is charming, kind, and sympathetic, a man driven toward children by his own demons but attentive to Li'l Bit's adolescent needs in ways that are never violent, paternalistic, or condescending. Peck takes the young woman seriously, and she takes great pleasure from believing that she helps him emotionally. Vogel paints their relationship as flirtatious and sexual, but also as a careful balance of power between Peck's adult desires and Li'l Bit's inchoate, exploratory impulses. Parker's lithe, erotic performance captures in subtle gestures and in postures weighted with ambivalence and desire the pleasure Li'l Bit takes in the power of saying no while her body urges her to say yes. The attraction between them becomes more urgent and mutual as the play progresses, along with Li'l Bit's knowledge that the relationship is not right. Li'l Bit's isolation in the face of strong emotions she can not understand is palpable; Parker's virtuosic performance illustrates the nuances of Li'l Bit's desire and loathing for a man who taught her so much and could finally give her so little.

Vogel builds the relationship in scenes sculpted with spare efficiency by Brokaw that crystallize moments of trust, disappointment, longing, and desire. When Peck's loneliness grips him, a very young Li'l Bit offers solace with weekly outings that are as much about companionship as they come to be about sex or driving lessons. Later, Peck photographs Li'l Bit in his basement studio, and although it's clear his motives are not pure, the experience instills in Li'l Bit a sense of her own allure, a glimpse of a budding sexuality that's powerful to her in a family life in which she is otherwise naive and powerless. Peck takes her to dinner at a sophisticated restaurant out of town when she passes her driving test. Under the disapproving eye of a sanctimonious waiter, Li'l Bit drinks martinis while one of the female chorus relates how to stay safe sexually while leaving the shores of sobriety in masculine company.

These interventions are delivered with wry and empathetic clarity directly to the audience by a three-actor chorus that shifts agilely through roles as family members and other commentators. The actors transform precisely and pointedly, with help from iconic costume pieces like glasses or scarves, into those who either deny or judge the relationship. Brokaw directs them on a nearly empty set, using chairs and the occasional table to evoke the car, the restaurant, the basement photo studio. The physical performances his actors achieve imaginatively flesh out the edges of this searing portrait.

How I Learned to Drive is only "about" incest after the scene of Li'l Bit's first molestation scene, when Li'l Bit asks the audience rhetorically, "How old were you when someone did this to you?" The moment is startling, because although the audience has witnessed Peck in an early scene prepare to molest a little boy (the boy is imagined and Morse elegantly, chillingly mimes the actions), the play has been about more than incest. Through Parker's and Morse's multilayered performances, power and danger are always present, but so are moments of understanding and mutuality.

Parker and Morse are empathetic and moving, and Johanna Day, Kerry O'Malley, and Michael Showalter, as the chorus, present tight economical sketches of Li'l Bit's family and the social characters with whom Bit and Peck interact. Vogel's wry, insightful humor captures the pain and awkward pleasure of growing into social awareness and understanding. Vogel's play is about forgiveness and family, about the instability of sexuality, about the unpredictable ways in which we learn who we are, how we desire, and how our growth is built on loss.

Writing about Drama

Why Write about Drama?

The act of writing involves making a commitment to ideas, and that commitment helps clarify your thinking. Your writing forces you to examine the details, the elements of a play that might otherwise pass unnoticed, and it helps you develop creative interpretations that enrich your appreciation of the plays you read. Besides deepening your own understanding, your writing can contribute to that of your peers and readers, as the commentaries in this book are meant to do.

Since every reader of plays has a unique experience and background, every reader can contribute something to the experience and awareness of others. You will see things that others do not. You will interpret things in a way that others will not. Naturally, every reader's aim is to respect the text, but it is not reasonable to think that there is only one way to interpret a text. Nor is it reasonable to think that only a few people can give "correct" interpretations. One of the most interesting aspects of writing about drama is that it is usually preceded by discussion, through which a range of possible interpretations begins to appear. When you start to write, you commit yourself to working with certain ideas, and you begin to deepen your thinking about those ideas as you write.

Conventions in Writing Criticism about Drama

Ordinarily, when you are asked to write about a play, you are expected to produce a critical and analytical study. A critical essay will go beyond any subjective experience and include a discussion of what the play achieves and how it does so. If you have a choice, you should choose a play that you admire and enjoy. If you have special background material on that play, such as a playbill or newspaper article, or if you have seen a production, these aids will be especially useful to you in writing.

For a critical study you will need to go far beyond retelling the events of the play. You may have to describe what you feel happens in a given scene or moment in a play, but simply rewriting the plot of the play in your own words does not constitute an interpretation. A critical reading of the play demands that you isolate evidence and comment on it. For example, you may want to quote passages of dialogue or stage direction to point out an idea that plays a key role in the drama. When you do so, quote in moderation. A critical essay that is merely a string of quotations linked together with a small amount of your commentary will not suffice. Further, make sure that the quotations you use are illustrations of your point; explain clearly their importance to your discussion.

Approaches to Criticism

Many critical approaches are available to the reader of drama. One approach might emphasize the response of audience members or readers, recognizing that the audience brings a great deal to the play even before the action begins. The audience's or reader's previous experience with drama influences expectations about what will happen on stage and about how the central characters will behave. Personal and cultural biases also influence how an audience member reacts to the unfolding drama. Reader response criticism pays close attention to these responses and to what causes them.

Another critical approach might treat the play as the coherent work of a playwright who intends the audience to perceive certain meanings in the play. This approach assumes that a careful analysis, or close reading, of the play will reveal the author's meanings. Either approach can lead to engaging essays on drama. In the pages that follow, you will find directions on how to pay attention to your responses as an audience member or reader and advice about how to read a play with close attention to dialogue, images, and patterns of action.

Reader Response Criticism

Response criticism depends on a full experience of the text — a good understanding of its meaning as well as of its conventions of staging and performance.

Your responses to various elements of the drama, whether to the characters, the setting, the theme, or the dialogue, may change and grow as you see a play or read it through. You might have a very different reaction to a play during a second reading or viewing of it. Keeping a careful record of your responses as you read is a first step in response criticism.

There is, however, a big difference between recording your responses and examining them. Douglas Atkins of the University of Kansas speaks not only of reader response in criticism but of reader responsibility, by which he means that readers have the responsibility to respond on more than a superficial level when they read drama. This book helps you reach deeper critical levels because you can read each play in light of the history of drama. The book also gives you important background material and commentary from the playwrights and from professional critics. Reading such criticism helps you understand what the critic's role is and what a critic can say about drama.

Reading drama in a historical perspective is important because it can highlight similarities between plays of different eras. Anyone who has read *Oedipus Rex* and *Antigone* will be better prepared to respond to *Hamlet*. In addition to the history and criticism of drama presented in this book, the variety of style, subject matter, and scope of the plays gives you the opportunity to read and respond to a broad range of drama. The more plays you read carefully, the better you will become at responding to drama and writing about it.

When you write response criticism, keep these guidelines in mind:

1. As you read, make note of the important effects the text has on you. Annotate in the margins moments that are especially effective. Do you find yourself alarmed, disturbed, sympathetic, or unsympathetic to a character? Do you sense suspense, or are you confused about what is happening? Do you feel personally involved with the action, or is it very distant? Do you find the situation funny? What overall response do you find yourself giving the play?

2. By analyzing the following two elements of your response, establish why the play had the effects you observe. Do you think it would have those effects on others? Have you observed that it does?

First, determine what it is about the play that causes you to have the response you do. Is it the structure of the play, the way the characters behave, their talk? Is it an unusual use of language, allusions to literature you know (or don't know)? Is the society portrayed especially familiar (or especially unfamiliar) to you? What does the author seem to expect the audience to know before the play begins?

Second, determine what it is about you, the reader, that causes you to respond as you do. Were you prepared for the dramatic conventions of the play, in terms of its genre as tragedy, comedy, tragicomedy or in terms of its place in the history of drama? How does your preparation affect your response? Did you have difficulty interpreting the language of the play because of unfamiliarity? Are you especially responsive to certain kinds of plays because of familiarity?

3. What do your responses to the play tell you about your own limitations, your own expertise, your own values, and your own attitudes toward social behavior, uses of language, and your sense of what is "normal"? Be sure to be willing to face your limitations as well as your strengths.[1]

Reader response criticism is flexible and useful in the way it allows you to explore possible interpretations of a text. Everyone is capable of responding to drama and everyone's response will differ depending on his or her preparation and background.

Close Reading

Analyzing a play by close reading means examining the text in detail, looking for patterns that might not be evident with a less attentive approach to the text. Annotation is the key to close reading, since the critic's job is to keep track of elements in the play that, innocent though they may seem alone, imply a greater significance when seen together.

Close reading implies rereading, since you do not know the first time through a text just what will be meaningful as the play unfolds, and you will want to read it again to confirm and deepen your impressions. You will usually make only a few discoveries the first time through. However, it is important to annotate the text even the first time you read it.

---

[1] Adapted from Kathleen McCormick, "Theory in the Reader: Bleich, Holland, and Beyond," *College English* 47 (1985): 838.

In annotating a play try following these guidelines:

1. Underline all the speeches and images you think are important. Look for dialogue that you think reveals the play's themes, the true nature of the characters, and the position of the playwright.

2. Watch for repetition of imagery (such as the garden and weed imagery in *Hamlet*) and keep track of it through annotation. Do the same for repeated ideas in the dialogue and for repeated comments on government or religion or psychology. Such repetitions will reveal their importance to the playwright.

3. Color-code or number-code various patterns in the text; then gather them either in photocopies or in lists for examination before you begin to plan your essay.

Criticism that uses the techniques of close reading pays very careful attention to the elements of drama — plot, characterization, setting, dialogue (use of language), movement, and theme — which were discussed earlier in relation to Lady Gregory's *The Rising of the Moon*. As you read a play, keep track of its chief elements because often they will give you useful ideas for your paper. You may find it helpful to refer to the earlier discussion of the elements in *The Rising of the Moon* since a short critical essay about that play is presented here (pp. 1789–91).

Annotating the special use of any of the elements will help you decide how important they are and whether a close study of them can contribute to an interesting interpretation of the play. You may not want to discuss all the elements in an essay, or if you do, only one may be truly dominant, but you should be aware of them in any play you write about.

From Prewriting to Final Draft: A Sample Essay on *The Rising of the Moon*

Most good writing results from good planning. When you write criticism about drama, consider these important stages:

1. When possible, choose a play that you enjoy.
2. Annotate the play very carefully.
3. Spend time prewriting.
4. Write a good first draft, then revise for content, organization, style, and mechanics.

The essay on Lady Gregory's *The Rising of the Moon* at the end of this section involved several stages of writing. First, the writer read and annotated the play. In the process of doing so, she noticed the unusual stage direction beginning the play, *Moonlight,* and noticed also that when the two policemen leave the Sergeant, they take the lantern, but the Sergeant reminds them that it is very lonely waiting there "with nothing but the moon." Second, she used the stage directions regarding moonlight to guide her in several important techniques of prewriting, including brainstorming, clustering, freewriting, drafting a trial thesis, and outlining.

The first stage, brainstorming, involved listing ideas, words, or phrases suggested by reading the play. The idea of moonlight and the moon recurred often. Then the writer practiced clustering: beginning with *moon,* a key term developed from brainstorming, then radiating from it all the associations that naturally suggested themselves.

Next the student chose the term *romance* because it had generated a number of responses, and she performed a freewriting exercise around that term. Freewriting is a technique in which a writer takes four or five minutes to write whatever comes to mind. The technique is designed to be done quickly so the conscious censor has to be turned off. Anything you write in freewriting may be useful because you may produce ideas you did not know you had.

The following passage is part of the freewriting exercise the student wrote using *romance* as a key term. The passage is also an example of invisible writing because the writing was done on a computer and the writer turned off the monitor so that she could not censor or erase what she was writing. The writer could only go forward, as fast as possible.

```
The setting of the play is completely romantic. In a lot of ways
the play wouldn't work in a different setting. When you think
about it the moon in the title is what makes all the action
possible. Moon associated with darkness, underworld, world of
fairies, so the moon is what makes all the action possible. Moon
makes Sergeant look at things differently. The moon is the rebel
moon--that's what title means. Rebel moon is rising, always
```

rising. So the world the policeman lives in--sun lights up
everything in practical and nonromantic way--is like lantern that
second policeman brings to dockside. It shows things in a harsh
light. Moon shows things in soft light. Without the moon there
would be a different play.

The freewriting gave the writer a new direction — discussing the setting of the play, especially the role of light. The clustering began with the moon, veered off to the concept of the romantic elements in the play, and then came back to the way the moon and the lantern function in the play. The writer was now ready to work up a trial thesis:

Lady Gregory uses light to create a romantic setting that helps us
understand the relationship between the rebel and the Sergeant and
the values that they each stand for.

Because the thesis is drafted before the essay is written, the thesis is like a trial balloon. It may work or it may not. At this point it gives the writer direction.

Next the student outlined the essay. Since the writer did not know the outcome of the essay yet, her outline was necessarily sketchy:

I.   Moonlight is associated with romance and rebellion; harsh
     light of lantern is associated with repressiveness of
     police.
     A. Rebel is associated with romance.
     B. Sergeant is associated with practicality and the
         law.
II. Without the lantern the Sergeant is under the influence
     of the romantic moon and the rebel.
     A. Sergeant feels resentment about his job.
     B. Rebel sings forbidden song and Sergeant reveals his
         former sympathies.
     C. Sergeant admits he was romantic when young.
III. Sergeant must choose between moon and lantern.
     A. Sergeant seems ready to arrest rebel.
     B. When police return with lantern the Sergeant sends
         them away.
     C. Rebel escapes and Sergeant remains in moonlight.

The prewriting strategies of brainstorming, clustering, freewriting, drafting a thesis, and outlining helped the student generate ideas and material for her first draft. After writing this draft, she revised it carefully for organization, clarity of ideas, expression, punctuation, and format. What follows is her final draft.

Andrea James

Professor Jacobus

English 233

19 October

The Use of Light in <u>The Rising of the Moon</u>

Lady Gregory uses light imagery in <u>The Rising of the Moon</u> to contrast rebellion and repressiveness. Her initial stage direction is basic: <u>Moonlight</u>. She suggests some of the values associated with moonlight, such as rebellion and romance, caution and secrecy, daring exploits, and even the underworld. All these are set against the policemen, who are governed not by the moon, which casts shadows and makes the world look magical, but by the lantern, which casts a harsh light that even the Sergeant eventually rejects.

The ballad singer, the rebel, is associated with romance from the start: "Dark hair--dark eyes, smooth face. . . . There isn't another man in Ireland would have broken jail the way he did" (27-28). He is dark, handsome, and recklessly brave. The Sergeant, by contrast, is a practical man, no romantic. He sees that he might have a chance to arrest the rebel and gain the reward for his capture if he stays right on the quay, a likely place for the rebel to escape from. But he unknowingly spoils his chances by refusing to keep the lantern the policemen offer. He tells the policemen, "You can take the lantern. Don't be too long now. It's very lonesome here with nothing but the moon" (28). What he does not realize is that with the lantern as his guiding light, he will behave like a proper Sergeant. But with the moon to guide him, he will side with the rebel.

It takes only a few minutes for the rebel to show up on the scene. At first, the Sergeant is very tough and abrupt with the rebel, who is disguised as "Jimmy Walsh, a ballad singer." The rebel tells the Sergeant that he is a traveler, that he is from Ennis, and that he has been to Cork. Unlike the Sergeant, who has stayed in one place and is a family man, the ballad singer appears to be a romantic figure, in the sense that he follows his mind to go where he wants to, sings what he wants to, and does what he wants to.

When the ballad singer begins singing, the Sergeant reacts badly, telling the singer, "Stop that noise" (28). Maybe he is

envious of the ballad singer's freedom. When the Sergeant tries
to make the rebel leave, the rebel instead begins telling stories
about the man the Sergeant is looking for. He reminds the Sergeant of deeds done that would frighten anyone. "It was after
the time of the attack on the police barrack at Kilmallock. . . .
Moonlight . . . just like this" (29). The moonlight of the tale
and the moonlight of the setting combine to add mystery and
suspense to the situation.

The effect of the rebel's talk--and of the moonlight--is to
make the Sergeant feel sorry for himself in a thankless job. "It's
little we get but abuse from the people, and no choice but to obey
our orders," he says bitterly while sitting on the barrel sharing
a pipe with the singer (29). When the rebel sings an illegal song,
the Sergeant corrects a few words, revealing his former sympathies
with the people. The rebel realizes this, telling the Sergeant,
"It was with the people you were, and not with the law you were,
when you were a young man" (30). The Sergeant admits that when he
was young he too was a romantic, but now that he is older he is
practical and law-abiding: "Well, if I was foolish then, that
time's gone. . . . I have my duties and I know them" (30).

Pulled by his past and his present, the Sergeant is suddenly
forced to choose when the ballad singer's signal to his friend
reveals the singer's identity to the Sergeant. He must decide
whether his heart is with the world of moonlight or the world of
the lantern. He seizes the rebel's hat and wig and seems about to
arrest him when the policemen, with their lantern, come back. The
Sergeant orders the policemen back to the station, and they offer
to leave the lantern with him. But the Sergeant refuses. We know
that he will not turn the rebel in. He has chosen the world of
moonlight, of the rebel.

Before they leave the policemen try to make the world of the
lantern seem the right choice. Policeman B says:

> Well, I thought it might be a comfort to you. I often
> think when I have it in my hand and can be flashing it
> about into every dark corner (doing so) that it's the
> same as being beside the fire at home, and the bits of
> bogwood blazing up now and again. (Flashes it about, now
> on the barrel, now on Sergeant.) (31)

The Sergeant reacts furiously and tells them to get out--"yourselves and your lantern!"

The play ends with the Sergeant giving the hat and wig back to
the rebel, obviously having chosen the side of the people. When
the rebel leaves, the Sergeant wonders if he himself was crazy for
losing his chance at the reward. But as the curtain goes down, the
Sergeant is still in the moonlight.

How to Write a Review

What Is the Purpose of a Review?

A review is more than a critical essay because it covers the actual performance of a play. As a reviewer you write after digesting an evening's entertainment and observing how actors and a director present a production for your enjoyment. Your responsibility is to respond both to the production and to the text of the play; thus, you will discuss the quality of the acting, the effectiveness of the setting, the interpretation of the text, and the power of the direction.

Reviews of plays ordinarily appear in daily newspapers or in weekly or semiweekly publications timely enough to help a prospective playgoer decide on whether to see the play. Considering the cost of tickets in contemporary theater, the best reviewers can perform a valuable service by letting readers know what they feel is most worth seeing. Regular reviewers, such as Frank Rich and Vincent Canby in the *New York Times,* John Simon in *Newsweek,* and John Lahr in *The New Yorker,* develop their own following because playgoers know from experience whether they can rely on these reviewers' judgments.

Another purpose of theater reviews is to set a standard to which producers aspire. Criticism can promote excellence because experienced and demanding critics force producers of drama to maintain high standards. The power of theater critics in major cities is legendary: more than a few plays have closed prematurely after savage reviews in London, New York, Chicago, and elsewhere. Knowing that they risk close examination by knowledgeable reviewers convinces writers, directors, actors, and producers to do their best.

What You Need to Write a Good Review

The best reviewers ordinarily bring three qualities to their work: experience in the theater, a knowledge of theatrical history, and a sensitivity to dramatic production. Some reviewers have had experience onstage as actors or as production assistants. They are familiar with the process of preparing a play for the stage and in some cases may actually have written for the stage. Reviewers without such experience have, instead, spent hours in the theater watching plays; their rich experience of seeing a variety of plays enables them to make useful comparisons.

Knowledge of the basics of theater history is fundamental equipment for a good reviewer. New plays that borrow from the traditions of the Greek chorus, or plays that emulate medieval pageants or nineteenth-century melodrama need reviewers who understand their sources. Suzan-Lori Parks, for example, admits responding to the influence of Bertolt Brecht and Samuel Beckett. While expecting her audience to recognize some of that influence, she knows that her reviewers will spot most or all of it. This book is structured around the history of drama so that readers will better understand drama's roots and evolution. In that sense this book is an aid in helping a theater enthusiast to become a competent reviewer.

Besides knowing the history of drama, the reviewer needs also to be extremely well read. Some reviewers, for example, have not had the opportunity to see all of Shakespeare's plays, but a good reviewer will have read most of them and can refer to them as necessary. The same will be true of the plays of Bernard Shaw, as many have not been produced in the last dozen years or so. In the case of contemporary playwrights, it is common for a reviewer to refer to the playwright's earlier work to put the current production in a useful context. A knowledgeable reviewer knows not only the history of theater but also the work of other playwrights that may be relevant to the play under review.

Most of us have enough sensitivity to dramatic productions to write adequate reviews. The most sensitive reviewers will pay close attention to the suitability of the acting almost as a matter of first importance, especially if the play is well known. Most contemporary reviews single out actors and comment on their performance in some detail. Reviewers usually know the work of the most busy actors, and in some cases they will make comparisons with earlier roles. They will also indicate whether the actor has developed further as an artist or has perhaps walked mechanically through the part. The reviewer's sensitivity to individual actors is developed in part from past experience and therefore from having a benchmark against which to match a performance. Curiosity about an actor's performance sometimes drives a review, as in John Lahr's examination of Ralph Fiennes's acting in *Hamlet* (p. 389), which was the main focus of his essay on the play.

Obviously, neither John Lahr nor any other reviewer is going to review *Hamlet* with an eye toward telling us that it is a good or bad play; the history of criticism has already done that. The reviewer of *Hamlet,* like the reviewer of any of Shakespeare's great plays, will aim to tell us about the quality of the acting or the effectiveness of the setting, as in Clive Barnes's review of *A Midsummer Night's Dream* (p. 322). Being sensitive to the effective use of lighting, props, costumes, and stage design is essential for any reviewer, but it is probably even more essential for a reviewer of classic theater.

Preparing to Review a Classic Play

If you have the opportunity to review a play that is well established — like most of the plays in this collection — you need special preparation. Besides having read the text before seeing the play, you need to imagine how the play should be staged. Once you understand what the play is about and what its implications may be, you then need to consult reviews or descriptions of early productions. You may do so by referring to the index of any major newspaper or to *New York Theatre Critics' Reviews,* which includes multiple reviews of important productions over the years. The point is simply to come to the experience of the drama as a fully informed viewer. Knowing how the play has been staged in the past will help you see the innovations and special interpretation of the current production.

Preparing to Review a New Play

Sometime you may have the opportunity to review a new play — one that playgoers, including the reviewers, have not had the chance to read in advance. In that case you need to pay special attention to the text, taking notes when necessary, to follow the development of the drama's ideas and issues. You are still responsible for commenting on the acting and the production, but in the case of a new play, your responsibility shifts to preparing the prospective audience to understand and respond to the play. They will need to know what the play is about, how it presents the primary issues in the drama, and what is at stake. You may need to tell something of the plot, but always with an eye toward not giving too much away, especially if the play involves suspense. Ask yourself how much the reader needs to know to decide whether to see the play.

Reviewers of new plays usually include a special commentary on a new or relatively unknown playwright. The most important information here would be any previous work of the playwright. The best reviewers will have seen that work and are prepared to relate it to the new play at hand. Reviewers of August Wilson, for example, spent time in the late 1980s establishing his credentials as a playwright. Now, when a new play of his is produced, reviewers usually attempt to describe how the new play fits into the growing body of his work. Since Wilson is in the process of writing a series of plays on African American life centering on specific decades of this century, the reviewer does the reader a service by explaining how a new play fits into his overall scheme.

Guidelines for Writing Reviews

Good reviewers approach the job of writing reviews from many different angles. Some of the reviews in this book begin with a generalization on the theme. Some begin with a personal observation about the play at hand or a personal experience in the theater. Others begin with a note on the background of the playwright, the actors, or the director. There is no one way to write a review, but the following suggestions can help you to structure your reaction.

1. If you are reviewing a professionally produced play, request a press kit from the theater. These kits usually include a great deal of information that could interest readers.

2. In your review provide any necessary background on a playwright who is contemporary or relatively unknown. The press kit should contain some information; if not, the program may do so. Check with the press representative or with the box office manager to see if the playwright is in the house and, before the play begins, ask to arrange an interview.

Sample Reviews

You can learn a great deal from some of the reviews in this book. Clive Barnes's review of *Hedda Gabler* (p. 742) is exemplary in many ways. First, Barnes clearly enjoyed the production and lets us know at the very start. He praises the director, Trevor Nunn, after praising the star, Glenda Jackson, who has been regarded as one of the most commanding Heddas in contemporary theater. In his first two paragraphs Barnes makes us aware that he regards the production as a landmark.

Barnes emphasizes the humor in the play, which he admits does not always come across. He goes so far as to describe Hedda's life as a "grotesque farce," and clarifies Ibsen's humor as satirical, ending with a "final stroke of tragic irony." His concern for the actors' interpretation of the text centers on "The production's bitter and emphatic insistence upon Ibsen's sardonic mockery of convention." The review focuses on Ibsen as a critic of "bourgeois parochialism."

Most important, perhaps, is the fact that Barnes attempts not only to describe the quality of this production but to analyze the play itself as he writes. You finish the review knowing that Barnes liked the play, the actors, and the production. He convinces us that even if we have seen *Hedda Gabler* before, this production is special enough for us to see it again because this is a fresh new interpretation.

Because August Wilson's *Fences* (1987) was completely unknown to his readers, Frank Rich had a different task in his review. He takes special care to discuss the details of the play's narrative and to comment on Wilson's other work, much of which may not be familiar to his audience. Rich carefully establishes the time period of the play, 1957, and the neighborhood in which it is set. He then goes on to examine the "mountainous" stature of Troy Maxson, played by James Earl Jones in what Rich feels may be one of his best roles. The struggle between Troy, the one-time player in the Negro baseball leagues, and his son, who is being courted by college football coaches, is central to the drama, and Rich helps us understand its import and its relevance to life in general, not just the play.

Rich reviews each of the main actors: James Earl Jones, Courtney Vance, Mary Alice, and Ray Aranha, clarifying the strength of their work. However, Rich also qualifies his praise of the play by suggesting that Wilson's earlier play, *Ma Rainey's Black Bottom,* is "more aesthetically daring." Yet that does not stop him from approving the power of Wilson's use of the "talking blues," and "Mr. Jones's efforts to shout down the devil." Rich ends with a useful comment on Lloyd Richards's direction and the dominant struggle, both psychological and physical, between father and son that ends the play. Rich leaves the reader with no question about the importance of going to see *Fences.*

Analysis of any of the other reviews in this book will show variations on the structure of Barnes and Rich. When you write your own review, be sure to set up a checklist based on the one that follows here:

Author and title of play

What the play is about

The play's main issues

Actors

Setting

Description of the action

Direction

Theater and dates of performance

Your recommendation

Take the list to the theater with you and keep your notes on it. When you begin writing your review look at some of the tips in this discussion and some of the reviews elsewhere in this book. Your review should provide your readers a valuable service.

Glossary of Dramatic Terms

Act. A major division in the action of a play. Most plays from the Elizabethan era until the nineteenth century were divided into five acts by the playwrights or by later editors. In the nineteenth century many writers began to write four-act plays. Today one-, two-, and three-act plays are most common.

Action. What happens in a play; the events that make up the **plot**.

Agon. The Greek word for "contest." In Greek tragedy the *agon* was often a formal debate in which the **chorus** divided and took the sides of the disputants.

Alienation effect. In his **epic theater**, Bertolt Brecht (1898–1956) tried to make the familiar unfamiliar (or to alienate it) to show the audience that familiar, seemingly "natural," and therefore unalterable social conditions could be changed. Different devices achieved the alienation effect by calling attention to the theater as theater — stage lights brought in front of the curtain, musicians put onstage instead of hidden in an orchestra pit, placards indicating scene changes and interrupting the linear flow of the action, actors distancing themselves from their characters to invite the audience to analyze and criticize the characters instead of empathizing with them. These alienating devices prevented the audience from losing itself in the illusion of reality. (See **epic theater**.)

Allegory. A literary work that is coherent on at least two levels simultaneously: a literal level consisting of recognizable characters and events and an allegorical level in which the literal characters and events represent moral, political, religious, or other ideas and meanings.

Anagnorisis. Greek term for a character's discovery or recognition of someone or something previously unknown. *Anagnorisis* often paves the way for a reversal of fortune (see *peripeteia*). An example in *Oedipus Rex* is Oedipus's discovery of his true identity.

Antagonist. A character or force in conflict with the **protagonist**. The antagonist is often another character but may also be an intangible force such as nature or society. The dramatic conflict can also take the form of a struggle with the protagonist's own character.

Anticlimax. See **plot**.

Antimasque. See **masque**.

Antistrophe. The second of the three parts of the verse ode sung by the **chorus** in Greek drama. While singing the **strophe** the chorus moves in a dance rhythm from right to left; during the antistrophe it moves from left to right back to its original position. The third part, the **epode,** was sung standing still.

Apron stage. The apron is the part of the stage extending in front of the **proscenium arch.** A stage is an apron stage if all or most of it is in front of any framing structures. The Elizabethan stage, which the audience surrounded on three sides, is an example of an apron stage.

Arena stage. A stage surrounded on all sides by the audience, actors make exits and entrances through the aisles. Usually used in **theater in the round.**

Arras. A curtain hung at the back of the Elizabethan playhouse to partition off an alcove or booth. The curtain could be pulled back to reveal a room or a cave.

Aside. A short speech made by a character to the audience which, by **convention**, the other characters onstage cannot hear.

Atellan farce. Broad and sometimes coarse popular humor indigenous to the town of Atella in Italy. By the third century B.C., the Romans had imported the Atellan farce, which they continued to modify and develop.

Blank verse. An unrhymed verse form often used in writing drama. Blank verse is composed of ten-syllable lines accented on the second, fourth, sixth eighth, and tenth syllables (**iambic pentameter**).

Bombast. A loud, pompous speech whose inflated diction is disproportionate to the subject matter it expresses.

Bourgeois drama. Drama that treats middle-class subject matter or characters rather than the lives of the rich and powerful.

Braggart soldier. A **stock character** in comedy who is usually cowardly, parasitical, pompous, and easily victimized by practical jokers. Sir John Falstaff in Shakespeare's *Henry IV* (parts 1, 2) is an example of this type.

Burla (plural, *burle*). Jests or practical jokes that were part of the comic **stage business** in the **commedia dell'arte.**

Buskin. A thick-soled boot possibly worn by Greek tragedians to increase their stature. Later called a *cothornus.*

Catastrophe. See **plot.**

Catharsis. The feeling of emotional purgation or release that, according to Aristotle, an audience should feel after watching a tragedy.

Ceremonial drama. Egyptian passion play about the god Osiris.

Character. Any person appearing in a drama or narrative.

Stock character. A stereotypical character type whose behavior, qualities, or beliefs conform to familiar dramatic **conventions,** such as the clever servant or the **braggart soldier.** (Also called *type character.*)

Chiton. Greek tunic worn by Roman actors.

Choregos. An influential citizen chosen to pay for the training and costuming of the **chorus** in Greek drama competitions. He probably also paid for the musicians and met other financial production demands not paid for by the state.

Chorus. A masked group that sang and danced in Greek tragedy. The chorus usually chanted in unison, offering advice and commentary on the action but rarely participating. See also **strophe, antistrophe,** and **epode.**

City Dionysia. See **Dionysus.**

Climax. See **plot.**

Closet drama. A drama, usually in verse, meant for reading rather than for performance. Hrosvitha's *Dulcitius,* Percy Bysshe Shelley's *Prometheus Unbound,* and John Milton's *Samson Agonistes* are examples.

Comedy. A type of drama intended to interest and amuse rather than to concern the audience deeply. Although characters experience various discomfitures, the audience feels confident that they will overcome their ill fortune and find happiness at the end.

Comedy of humors. Form of comedy developed by Ben Jonson in the seventeenth century in which characters' actions are determined by the preponderance in their systems of one of the four bodily fluids or humors — blood, phlegm, choler (yellow bile), and melancholy (black bile). Characters' dispositions are exaggerated and stereotyped; common types are the melancholic and the belligerent bully.

Comedy of manners. Realistic, often satiric comedy concerned with the manners and conventions of high society. Usually refers to the Restoration comedies of late seventeenth-century England, which feature witty dialogue or **repartee.** An example is William Congreve's *The Way of the World.*

Drawing room comedy. A type of comedy of manners concerned with life in polite society. The action generally takes place in a drawing room.

Farce. A short dramatic work that depends on exaggerated, improbable situations, incongruities, coarse wit, and horseplay for its comic effect.

High comedy. Comedy that appeals to the intellect, often focusing on the pretensions, foolishness, and incongruity of human behavior. **Comedy of manners** with its witty dialogue is a type of high comedy.

Low comedy. Comedy that lacks the intellectual appeal of **high comedy,** depending instead on boisterous buffoonery, "gags," and jokes for its comic effect.

Middle Comedy. This transitional Greek style of comedy extended from 375 to about 330 B.C. It marks a change, especially in language, which grew less formal and closer to the way people spoke. Little evidence of Middle Comedy exists, but from suriviving statuettes we can surmise that costumes on stage resembled what Athenians actually wore on the street.

New Comedy. Emerging between the fourth and third centuries B.C. in ancient Greece, New Comedy replaced the farcical **Old Comedy.** New Comedy, usually associated with Menander, is witty and intellectually engaging; it is often thought of as the first **high comedy.**

Old Comedy. Greek comedy of the fifth century B.C. that uses bawdy farce to attack satirically social, religious, and political institutions. Old Comedy is usually associated with Aristophanes.

Sentimental comedy. Comedy populated by stereotypical virtuous **protagonists** and villainous **antagonists** that resolves the domestic trials of middle-class people in a pat, happy ending.

Slapstick. **Low comedy** that involves little plot or character development but consists of physical horseplay or practical jokes.

Comic relief. The use of humorous characters, speeches, or scenes in an otherwise serious or tragic drama.

Commedia dell'arte. Italian **low comedy** dating from around the mid-sixteenth century in which professional actors playing **stock characters** improvised dialogue to fit a given **scenario.**

Complication. See **plot.**

Conflict. See **plot.**

Convention. Any feature of a literary work that has become standardized over time, such as the **aside** or the **stock character.** Often refers to an unrealistic device (such as Danish characters speaking English in *Hamlet*) that the audience tacitly agrees to accept.

Coryphaeus. See *koryphaios.*

Cosmic irony. See **irony.**

Cothurnes. See **buskin.**

Craft play. Medieval sacred drama based on Old and New Testament stories. Craft plays were performed outside the church by members of a particular trade guild, and their subject matter often reflected the guild's trade. The fisherman's guild, for example, might present the story of Noah and the flood.

Crisis. Same as **climax.** See **plot.**

Cycle. A group of medieval **mystery plays** written in the vernacular (the language in common use rather than Latin) for performance outside the church. Cycles, each of which treated biblical stories from creation through the last judgment, are named after the town in which they were produced. Most extant mystery plays are from the York, Chester, Wakefield (Towneley), and N-Town cycles.

Decorum. A quality that exists when the style of a work is appropriate to the speaker, the occasion, and the subject matter. Kings should speak in a "high style" and clowns in a "low style," according to many Renaissance authors. Decorum was a guiding critical principle in **neoclassicism.**

Defamiliarization effect (*Verfremdungseffkt*). See **alienation effect.**

Denouement. See **plot.**

Deus ex machina. Latin for "a god out of a machine." In Greek drama, a mechanical device called a *mechane* could lower "gods" onto the stage to solve the seemingly unsolvable problems of mortal characters. Also used to describe a playwright's use of a forced or improbable solution to plot complications — for example, the discovery of a lost will or inheritance that will pay off the evil landlord.

Dialogue. Spoken interchange or conversation between two or more characters. Also see **soliloquy.**

Diction. A playwright's choice of words or the match between language and subject matter. Also refers collectively to an actor's phrasing, enunciation, and manner of speaking.

Dionysus. Greek nature god of wine, mystic revelry, and irrational impulse. Greek tragedy probably sprang from dramatized ritual choral celebrations in his honor.

City Dionysia. (Also called Great or Greater Dionysia.) The most important of the four Athenian festivals in honor of Dionysus. This spring festival sponsored the first tragedy competitions; comedy was associated with the winter festival, the Lenaea.

Director. The person responsible for a play's interpretation and staging and for the guidance of the actors.

Disguising. Medieval entertainment featuring a masked procession of actors performing short plays in pantomime; probably the origin of the court **masque.**

Dithyramb. Ancient Greek choral hymn sung and danced to honor **Dionysus;** originally divided into an improvised story sung by a choral leader and a traditional refrain sung by the **chorus.** Believed by some to be the origin of Greek tragedy.

Domestic tragedy. A serious play usually focusing on the family and depicting the fall of a middle-class **protagonist** rather than of a powerful or noble hero. Also called *bourgeois tragedy.* An example is Arthur Miller's *Death of a Salesman,* which traces the emotional collapse and eventual suicide of Willy Loman, a traveling salesman.

Double plot. See **plot.**

Drama. A play written in prose or verse that tells a story through **dialogue** and actions performed by actors impersonating the characters of the story.

Dramatic illusion. The illusion of reality created by drama and accepted by the audience for the duration of the play.

Dramatic irony. See **irony.**

Dramatist. The author of a play; playwright.

Dramaturge. One who represents the playwright and guides the production. In some cases, the dramaturge researches different aspects of the production or earlier productions of the play.

Dramaturgy. The art of writing plays.

Drawing room comedy. See **comedy.**

Empathy. The sense of feeling *with* a character. (Distinct from sympathy, which is feeling *for* a character.)

Ensemble acting. Performance by a group of actors, usually members of a **repertory** company, in which the integrated acting of all members is emphasized over individual star performances. The famous nineteenth-century director Konstantin Stanislavsky promoted this type of acting in the Moscow Art Theatre.

Environmental theater. A term used by Richard Schechner, director of the Performance Group in the late 1960s and early 1970s, to describe his work and the work of other theater companies, including the Bread and Puppet Theatre, Open Theatre, and Living Theatre. He also used the term to describe the indigenous theater of Africa and Asia. Environmental theater occupies the whole of a performance space; it is not confined to a stage separated from the audience. Action can take place in and around the audience, and audience members are often encouraged to participate in the theater event.

Epic theater. A type of theater first associated with German director Erwin Piscator (1893–1966). Bertolt Brecht (1898–1956) used the term to distinguish his own theater from the "dramatic" theater that created the illusion of reality and invited the audience to identify and empathize with the characters. Brecht criticized the dramatic theater for encouraging the audience to believe that social conditions were "natural" and therefore unalterable. According to Brecht, the theater should show human beings as dependent on certain political and economic factors and at the same time as capable of altering them. "The spectator is given the chance to criticize human behavior from a social point of view, and the scene is played as a piece of history," he wrote. Epic theater calls attention to itself as theater, bringing the stage lights in front of the curtain and interrupting the linear flow of the action to help the audience analyze the action and characters onstage. (See **alienation effect.**)

Epilogue. A final speech added to the end of a play. An example is Puck's "If we shadows have offended . . ." speech that ends Shakespeare's *A Midsummer Night's Dream*.

Epitasis. Ancient term for the **rising action** of a **plot**. (See also **plot.**)

Epode. The third of three parts of the verse ode sung by the **chorus** in a Greek drama. The epode follows the **strophe** and **antistrophe.**

Exodos. The concluding scene, which includes the exit of all characters and the **chorus**, of a Greek drama.

Exposition. See **plot.**

Expressionism. Early twentieth-century literary movement in Germany that posited that art should represent powerful emotional states and moods. Expressionists abandon **realism** and **verisimilitude**, producing distorted, nightmarish images of the individual unconscious.

Falling action. See **plot.**

Farce. See **comedy.**

First Folio. The first collected edition of thirty-six of Shakespeare's plays, collected by two of his fellow actors and published posthumously in 1623.

Foil. A character who, through difference or similarity, brings out a particular aspect of another character. Laertes, reacting to the death of his father, acts as a foil for Hamlet.

Foreshadowing. Ominous hints of events to come that help to create an air of suspense in a drama.

Frons scaena. The elaborately decorated facade of the *scaena* or stage house used in presenting Roman drama. (Also called *scaena frons.*)

Hamartia. An error or wrong act through which the fortunes of the **protagonist** are reversed in a tragedy.

High comedy. See **comedy.**

History play. A drama set in a time other than that in which it was written. The term usually refers to Elizabethan drama, such as Shakespeare's Henry plays, that draws its plots from English historical materials such as Holinshed's *Chronicles*.

Hubris (or *hybris*). Excessive pride or ambition. In ancient Greek tragedy hubris often causes the **protagonist**'s fall.

Humor character. A stereotyped character in the **comedy of humors** (see **comedy**). Clever plots often play on the character's personality distortions (caused by an imbalance of humors), revealing his or her absurdity.

Iambic pentameter. A poetic meter that divides a line into five parts (or feet), each part containing an unaccented syllable followed by an accented syllable. The line "When I consider everything that grows" is an example of iambic pentameter verse.

Imitation. See *mimesis*.

Impressionism. A highly personal style of writing in which the author presents characters, scenes, or moods as they appear to him or her at a particular moment rather than striving for an objectively realistic description.

Interlude. A short play, usually either farcical or moralistic, performed between the courses of a feast or between the acts of a longer play. The interlude thrived during the late fifteenth and early sixteenth centuries in England.

Irony. The use of words to suggest a meaning that is the opposite of the literal meaning, as in "I can't wait to take the exam." Irony is present in a literary work that gives expression to contradictory attitudes or impulses to entertain ambiguity or to maintain detachment.

Cosmic irony. Irony present when destiny or the gods seem to be in favor of the **protagonist** but are actually engineering his or her downfall. (Same as *irony of fate.*)

Dramatic irony. Irony present when the outcome of an event or situation is the opposite of what a character expects.

Tragic irony. Irony that exists when a character's lack of complete knowledge or understanding (which the audience possesses) results in his or her fall or has tragic consequences for loved ones. An example from *Oedipus Rex* is Oedipus's declaration that he will stop at nothing to banish King Laios's murderer, whom the audience knows to be Oedipus himself.

Jongleur. Early medieval French musical entertainer who recited lyrics, ballads, and stories. Forerunner of the minstrel.

Koryphaios. The leader of the **chorus** in Greek drama.

Kothurnus. See **buskin.**

Lazzo (plural, *lazzi*). Comic routines or **stage business** associated with the stock situations and characters of the Italian **commedia dell'arte**. A scenario might, for example, call for the *lazzo* of fear.

Liturgical drama. Short dramatized sections of the medieval church service. Some scholars believe that these playlets evolved into the vernacular **mystery plays,** which were performed outside the church by lay people.

Low comedy. See **comedy.**

Mansion. Scenic structures used in medieval drama to indicate the locale or scene of the action. Mansions were areas inside the church used for performing liturgical drama; later more elaborate structures were built on pageant wagons to present **mystery plays** outside the church.

Mask. A covering used to disguise or ornament the face; used by actors in Greek drama and revived in the later **commedia dell'arte** and court **masque** to heighten dramatic effect.

Masque (also *mask*). A short but elaborately staged court drama, often mythological and allegorical, principally acted and danced by masked courtiers. (Professional actors often performed the major speaking and singing roles.) Popular in England during the late sixteenth and early seventeenth centuries, masques were often commissioned to honor a particular person or occasion. Ben Jonson was the most important masque writer; the genre's most elaborate sets and costumes were designed by Jonson's occasional partner Inigo Jones.

Antimasque. A parody of the court **masque** developed by Ben Jonson featuring broad humor, grotesque characters, and ludicrous actions.

Melodrama. A suspenseful play filled with situations that appeal to the audience's emotions. Justice triumphs in a happy ending: the good characters (completely virtuous) are rewarded and the bad characters (thoroughly villainous) are punished.

Method acting. A naturalistic technique of acting developed by the Russian director Konstantin Stanislavsky and adapted for American actors by Lee Strasberg, among others. The Method actor identifies with the **character** he or she portrays and experiences the emotions called for by the play in an effort to render the character with emotional **verisimilitude.**

Middle Comedy. See **comedy.**

Mimesis. The Greek word for "imitation." Aristotle used the term to define the role of art as an imitation of an action.

Miracle play. A type of medieval sacred drama that depicts the lives of saints, focusing especially on the miracles performed by saints.

Mise-en-scène. The stage setting of a play, including the use of scenery, props, and stage movement.

Moira. Greek word for "fate."

Morality play. Didactic late medieval drama (flourishing in England c. 1400–1550) that uses **allegory** to dramatize some aspects of the Christian moral life. Abstract qualities or entities such as Virtue, Vice, Good Deeds, Knowledge, and Death are cast as characters who discuss with the **protagonist** issues related to salvation and the afterlife. *Everyman* is an example.

Motivation. The reasons for a character's actions in a drama. For drama to be effective, the audience must believe that a character's actions are justified and plausible given what they know about him or her.

Mouth of hell. A stage prop in medieval drama suggesting the entrance to hell. Often in the shape of an open-mouthed monster's head, the mouth of hell was positioned over a smoke-and-fire-belching pit in the stage that appeared to swallow up sinners.

Mystery play. A sacred medieval play dramatizing biblical events such as the creation, the fall of Adam and Eve, and Christ's birth and resurrection. The genre probably evolved from **liturgical drama;** mystery plays were often incorporated into larger **cycles** of plays.

Naturalism. Literary philosophy popularized during the nineteenth century that casts art's role as the scientifically accurate reflection of a "slice of life." Naturalism is aligned with the belief that each person is a product of heredity and environment driven by internal and external forces beyond his or her control. August Strindberg's *Miss Julie,* with its focus on reality's sordidness and humankind's powerlessness, draws on naturalism.

Neoclassicism. A movement in sixteenth-century Italy and seventeenth-century France to revive and emulate classical attitudes toward art based on principles of order, harmony, unity, restrained wit, and **decorum.** The neoclassical movement in France gave rise to a corresponding movement in England during the late seventeenth and eighteenth centuries.

New Comedy. See **comedy.**

Ode. A dignified Greek three-part song sung by the **chorus** in Greek drama. The parts are the **strophe,** the **antistrophe,** and the **epode.**

Old Comedy. See **comedy.**

Orchestra. Literally the "dancing place"; the circular stage where the Greek **chorus** performed.

Pageant. A movable stage or wagon (often called a pageant wagon) on which a set was built for the performance of medieval drama. The term can also refer to the spectacle itself.

Pallium. Long white cloak or mantle worn by Greek actors or Romans in Greek-based plays.

Pantomime. Silent acting using facial expression, body movement, and gesture to convey the plot and the characters' feelings.

Parodos. The often stately entrance song of the **chorus** in Greek drama. The term also refers to the aisles (plural, *paradoi*) on either side of the orchestra by which the chorus entered the Greek theater.

Pastoral drama. A dramatic form glorifying shepherds and rural life in an idealized natural setting; usually implies a negative comparison to urban life.

Pathos. The quality of evoking pity.

Peripeteia. A reversal of fortune, for better or worse, for the **protagonist.** Used especially to describe the main character's fall in Greek tragedy.

Performance art. A mid-twentieth-century form that often mixes media: music, video, film, opera, dance, and spoken text. It was originally defined in terms of artists using a live production for dramatic effect. However, it has widened to include performances that cross defined dramatic "boundaries." Dancers Martha Clarke and Pina Bausch, musicians such as Laurie Anderson, and experimental directors such as Richard Foreman have been identified as performance artists.

Phallus. An appendage meant to suggest the penis added to the front of blatantly comic male characters' costumes in some Greek comedy; associated chiefly with the Greek **satyr play.**

Play. A literary genre whose plot is usually presented dramatically by actors portraying characters before an audience.

Play-within-the-play. A brief secondary drama presented to or by the characters of a play that reflects or comments on the larger work. An example is the Pyramus and Thisby episode in Shakespeare's *A Midsummer Night's Dream.*

Plot. The events of a play or narrative. The sequence and relative importance a **dramatist** assigns to these events.

    Anticlimax. An unexpectedly trivial or significant conclusion to a series of significant events; an unsatisfying resolution that often occurs in place of a conventional **climax.**

    Catastrophe. The outcome or conclusion of a play; usually applied specifically to tragedy. (**Denouement** is a parallel term applied to both comedy and tragedy.)

    Climax. The turning point in a drama's action, preceded by the **rising action** and followed by the **falling action.** Same as **crisis.**

    Complication. The part of the plot preceding the **climax** that establishes the entanglements to be untangled in the **denouement.** Part of the **rising action.**

    Conflict. The struggle between the **protagonist** and the **antagonist** that propels the **rising action** of the plot and is resolved in the **denouement.**

    Denouement. The "unknotting" of the plot's **complication;** the resolution of a drama's action. See **catastrophe.**

    Double plot. A dramatic structure in which two related plots function simultaneously.

    Exposition. The presentation of essential information, especially about events that have occurred prior to the first scene of a play. The exposition appears early in the play and initiates the **rising action.**

    Falling action. The events of the plot following the **climax** and ending in the **catastrophe** or resolution.

    Rising action. The events of the plot leading up to the **climax.**

    Subplot. A secondary plot intertwined with the main plot, often reflecting or commenting on the main plot.

    Underplot. Same as **subplot.**

Problem play. A drama that argues a point or presents a problem (usually a social problem). Ibsen is a notable writer of problem plays.

Prologos. In Greek drama, an introductory scene for actor or actors that precedes the entrance of the **chorus.** This **convention** has evolved into the modern dramatic introductory monologue or **prologue.**

Prologue. A preface or introduction preceding the play proper.

Proscaena. The space in front of the *scaena* in a Roman theater.

Proscenium arch. An arched structure over the front of the stage from which a curtain often hangs. The arch frames the action onstage and separates the audience from the action.

Proskenion. The playing space in front of the *skene* or scene house in Greek drama.

Protagonist. The main character in a drama. This character is usually the most interesting and sympathetic and is the person involved in the **conflict** driving the **plot.**

Protasis. Classical term for the introductory act or **exposition** of a drama.

Psychomachia. Psychological struggle; a war of souls.

Quem Quaeritis **trope.** A brief dramatized section of the medieval church's Easter liturgy. The oldest extant **trope** and the probable origin of liturgical drama, it enacts the visit of the three Marys to Christ's empty tomb (*quem quaeritis* means "whom do you seek?" in Latin).

Rising action. See **plot.**

Realism. The literary philosophy holding that art should accurately reproduce an image of life. Avoiding the use of dramatic **conventions** such as asides and soliloquies, it depicts ordinary people in ordinary situations. Ibsen's *A Doll House* is an example of realism in drama.

Recognition. See *anagnorisis.*

Repartee. Witty and pointed verbal exchanges usually found in the **comedy of manners.**

Repertory. A theater company or group of actors that presents a set of plays alternately throughout a season. The term also refers to the set of plays itself.

Restoration comedy. A type of **comedy of manners** that developed in England in the late seventeenth century. Often features **repartee** in the service of complex romantic plots. William Congreve's *The Way of the World* is an example.

Revenge tragedy. Sensational tragedy popularized during the Elizabethan age that is notable for bloody plots involving such elements as murder, ghosts, insanity, and crimes of lust.

Reversal. See *peripeteia.*

Riposte. A quick or sharp reply; similar to **repartee.**

Rising action. See **plot.**

Ritual. Repeated formalized or ceremonial practices, many of which have their roots in primitive cultures. Certain theorists hold that primitive ritual evolved into drama.

Satire. A work that makes fun of a social institution or human foible, often in an intellectually sophisticated way, to persuade the audience to share the author's views. Molière's *The Misanthrope* contains social satire.

Satyr play. A comic play performed after the tragic trilogy in Greek tragedy competitions. The satyr play provided **comic relief** and was usually a farcical, boisterous treatment of mythological material.

Scaena. The stage house in Roman drama; the facade of the *scaena* (called the *frons scaena*) was often elaborately ornamented.

Scenario. The plot outline around which professional actors of the **commedia dell'arte** improvised their plays. Most scenarios specified the action's sequence and the entrances of the main characters.

Scene. Division of an **act** in a drama. By traditional definition a scene has no major shift in place or time frame, and it is performed by a static group of actors onstage (in French drama, if an actor enters or exits, the group is altered and the scene, technically, should change). The term also refers to the physical surroundings or locale in which a play's action is set.

Scenery. The backdrop and set (furniture and so on) onstage that suggest to the audience the surroundings in which a play's **action** takes place.

Scenography. Painting of backdrops and hangings.

Senecan tragedy. Tragic drama modeled on plays written by Seneca. The genre usually has five acts and features a chorus; it is notable for its thematic concern with bloodshed, revenge, and unnatural crimes. (See also **revenge tragedy.**)

Sentimental. Refers to tender emotions in excess of what the situation calls for.

Setting. All details of time, location, and environment relating to a play.

Skene. The building or scene house in the Greek theater that probably began as a dressing room and eventually was incorporated into the action as part of the scenery.

Slapstick. See **comedy.**

Slice of life. See **naturalism.**

Social problem play. Same as **problem play.**

Sock. Derived from the Latin *soccus,* the term refers to a light slipper or sock worn by Roman comic actors.

Soliloquy. A speech in which an actor, usually alone onstage, utters his or her thoughts aloud, revealing personal feelings. Hamlet's "To be, or not to be" speech is an example.

Spectacle. In Aristotle's terms, the costumes and scenery in a drama — the elements that appeal to the eye.

Stage business. Minor physical action, including an actor's posture and facial expression, and the use of props, all of which make up a particular interpretation of a character.

Stichomythia. Dialogue in which two speakers engage in a verbal duel in alternating lines.

Stock character. See **character.**

Strophe. The first of three parts of the verse **ode** sung by the Greek **chorus.** While singing the strophe the chorus moves in a dancelike pattern from right to left. See also **antistrophe** and **epode.**

Subplot. See **plot.**

Subtext. A level of meaning implicit in or underlying the surface meaning of a text.

Surrealism. A literary movement flourishing in France during the early twentieth century that valued the unwilled expression of the unconscious (usually as revealed in dreams) over a rendering of "reality" structured by the conscious mind.

Suspense. The sense of tension aroused by an audience's uncertainty about the resolution of dramatic conflicts.

Suspension of disbelief. An audience's willingness to accept the world of the drama as reality during the course of a play.

Symbolism. A literary device in which an object, event, or action is used to suggest a meaning beyond its literal meaning. The guns in *Hedda Gabler* have a symbolic function.

Theater. The building in which a play is performed. Also used to refer to drama as an art form.

Theater in the round. The presentation of a play on an **arena stage** surrounded by the audience.

Theater of the absurd. A type of twentieth-century drama presenting the human condition as meaningless, absurd, and illogical. An example of the genre is Samuel Beckett's *Waiting for Godot.*

Theater of cruelty. A type of drama created by Antonin Artaud in the 1930s that uses shock techniques to expose the audience's primitive obsessions with cruelty and sexuality. The purpose was to overwhelm spectators' rational minds, leading them to understand and even participate in the cycle of cruelty and ritual purgation dramatized in the performance.

Three unities. Aristotle noted that a play's action usually occurs in one day or a little more and that the plot should reveal clearly ordered actions and incidents moving toward the plot's resolution. Later scholars and critics, especially those in the neoclassical tradition, interpreted Aristotle's ideas as rules (unity of time and unity of action) and added a third, unity of place (a play's action should occur in a single locale).

Thrust stage. A stage extending beyond the **proscenium arch,** usually surrounded on three sides by the audience.

Tiring house. From "attiring house," the backstage space in Elizabethan public theaters used for storage and as a dressing room. The term also refers to the changing space beneath the medieval pageant wagon.

Total theater. A concept of the theater as an experience synthesizing all the expressive arts including music, dance, lighting, and so on.

Tragedy. Serious drama in which a **protagonist,** traditionally of noble position, suffers a series of unhappy events culminating in a **catastrophe** such as death or spiritual breakdown. Shakespeare's *Hamlet,* which ends with the prince's death, is an example of Elizabethan tragedy.

Tragicomedy. A play that combines elements of tragedy and comedy. Chekhov's *The Cherry Orchard* is an example. Tragicomedies often include a serious plot in which the expected tragic **catastrophe** is replaced by a happy ending.

Trope. Interpolation into or expansion of an existing medieval liturgical text. These expansions, such as the *Quem Quaeritis* trope, gave rise to **liturgical drama.**

Type character. See **character.**

Underplot. See **plot.**

Unity. The sense that the events of a play and the actions of the characters follow one another naturally to form one complete action. Unity is present when characters' behavior seems **motivated** and the work is perceived to be a connected artistic whole. See also **three unities.**

Verfremdungseffkt. German term coined by Bertolt Brecht to mean "alienation." See also **alienation effect.**

Verisimilitude. The degree to which a dramatic representation approximates an appearance of reality.

Well-made play. Drama that relies for effect on the suspense generated by its logical, cleverly constructed plot rather than on characterization. Plots often involve a withheld secret, a battle of wits between hero and villain, and a resolution in which the secret is revealed and the **protagonist** saved. The plays of Eugène Scribe (1791–1861) have defined the type.

Selected Bibliography

Selected References for Periods of Drama

GREEK DRAMA

Aylen, Leo. *The Greek Theater.* Rutherford: Fairleigh Dickinson UP, 1985.

Bieber, Margaret. *The History of the Greek and Roman Theater.* 2nd ed. Princeton: Princeton UP, 1961.

Easterling, P. E., ed. *The Cambridge Companion to Greek Tragedy.* Cambridge: Cambridge UP, 1997.

Green, John R. *Theatre in Ancient Greek Society.* New York: Routledge, 1994.

Hamilton, Edith. *The Greek Way.* New York: Norton, 1983.

Hartigan, Karelisa V. *Greek Tragedy on the American Stage: Ancient Drama in the Commercial Theater 1882–1994.* New York: Greenwood, 1995.

Havelock, Eric. "The Double Vision of Greek Tragedy." Hudson Review 37 (1984): 244–70.

Kitto, H. D. F. *Form and Meaning in Drama: A Study of Six Greek Plays and of* Hamlet. 2nd ed. New York: Barnes, 1968.

———. *Greek Tragedy: A Literary Study.* 3rd ed. London: Methuen, 1966.

Knox, Bernard M. *Word and Action: Essays on the Ancient Theater.* Baltimore: Johns Hopkins UP, 1979.

Mills, Sophie. *Theseus, Tragedy, and the Athenian Empire.* Oxford: Oxford UP, 1997.

Pickard-Cambridge, Arthur W. *Dramatic Festivals of Athens.* 2nd ed. Revised by John Gould and D. M. Lewis. Oxford: Clarendon, 1962.

Silk, M. S., ed. *Tragedy and the Tragic: Greek Theatre and Beyond.* Oxford: Clarendon, 1996.

Steiner, George. *The Death of Tragedy.* New York: Knopf, 1961.

Taplin, Oliver. *Greek Tragedy in Action.* Berkeley: U of California P, 1978.

Taylor, David. *The Greek and Roman Stage.* Bristol: Bristol Classical, 1999.

Trendall, A. D., and T. B. L. Webster. *Illustrations of Greek Drama.* London: Phaidon, 1971.

Vickers, Brian. *Towards Greek Tragedy: Drama, Myth, Society.* London: Longman, 1973.

Walcot, Peter. *Greek Drama in Its Theatrical and Social Context.* Cardiff: U of Wales P, 1976.

Walton, Michael J. *Living Greek Theater: A Handbook of Classical Performance and Modern Production.* New York: Greenwood, 1987.

Webster, T. B. L. *Greek Theater Production.* 2nd ed. London: Methuen, 1970.

Winkler, John J., and Froma I. Zeitlin. *Nothing to Do with Dionysus? Athenian Drama in Its Social Context.* Princeton: Princeton UP, 1990.

Wise, Jennifer. *Dionysus Writes: The Invention of Theatre in Ancient Greece.* Ithaca: Cornell UP, 1998.

Zinman, Toby. "Still Dangerous after All These Years: Now's Your Chance to Get Reacquainted with Greek Tragedy's High-and-Mighty Heroines." *American Theatre* 16.3 (1999): 18–21, 62–63.

ROMAN DRAMA

Beare, William. *The Roman Stage.* 3rd ed. London: Methuen, 1969.

Bieber, Margaret. *The History of the Greek and Roman Theater.* 2nd ed. Princeton: Princeton UP, 1961.

Dodwell, Charles R. *Anglo-Saxon Gestures and the Roman Stage.* New York: Cambridge UP, 1999.

Duckworth, George E. *The Nature of Roman Comedy: A Study in Popular Entertainment.* Princeton: Princeton UP, 1952.

Grant, M. D. "Plautus and Seneca: Acting in Nero's Rome." *Greece and Rome* 46.1 (1999): 27–33.

Hunter, R. L. *The New Comedy of Greece and Rome.* New York: Cambridge UP, 1985.

Kenney, E. J., ed. *The Cambridge History of Classical Literature.* 2 vols. New York: Cambridge UP, 1982.

Konstan, David. *Roman Comedy.* Ithaca: Cornell UP, 1983.

Reinheimer, David A. "The Roman Actor, Censorship, and Dramatic Autonomy." *Studies in English Literature 1500–1900* 38.2 (1998): 317–32.

Segal, Erich. *Roman Laughter*. Cambridge: Harvard UP, 1968.

Wiles, David. *The Masks of Menander: Sign and Meaning in Greek and Roman Performances*. New York: Cambridge UP, 1991.

Wiseman, Timothy P. *Roman Drama and Roman History*. Exeter: University of Exeter Press, 1998.

MEDIEVAL DRAMA

Bevington, David, ed. *Medieval Drama*. Boston: Houghton, 1975.

Briscoe, Marianne G., and John C. Coldewey. *Contexts for Early English Drama*. Bloomington: Indiana UP, 1989.

Chambers, Edmund K. *English Literature at the Close of the Middle Ages*. Oxford: Clarendon, 1945.

———. *The Medieval Stage*. 2 vols. London: Oxford UP, 1967.

Cox, John D., and David S. Kastan, eds. *A New History of Early English Drama*. New York: Columbia UP, 1997.

Craig, Hardin. *English Religious Drama of the Middle Ages*. 2nd ed. Westport, CT: Greenwood, 1978.

Davidson, Clifford, et al., eds. *Drama in the Middle Ages*. New York: AMS, 1982.

———. *Material Culture and Medieval Drama*. Kalamazoo: Medieval Institute, 1999.

Dillon, Janette. *Language and Stage in Medieval and Renaissance England*. Cambridge: Cambridge UP, 1998.

Elliott, John R. *Playing God: Medieval Mysteries on the Modern Stage*. Toronto: U Toronto P, 1989.

Enders, Jody. *The Medieval Theater of Cruelty: Rhetoric, Memory, Violence*. Ithaca: Cornell UP, 1999.

Gassner, John, ed. *Medieval and Tudor Drama*. New York: Bantam, 1971.

Hardison, O. B., Jr. *Christian Rite and Christian Drama in the Middle Ages: Essays in the Origin and Early History of Modern Drama*. Baltimore: Johns Hopkins UP, 1965.

Spinrad, Phoebe. *The Summons of Death on the Medieval and Renaissance English Stage*. Columbus: Ohio State UP, 1987.

Vince, Ronald W. *Ancient and Medieval Theatre: A Historiographical Handbook*. Westport: Greenwood, 1984.

Wickham, Glynne. *The Medieval Theatre*. 3rd ed. New York: Cambridge UP, 1987.

Woolf, Rosemary. *The English Mystery Plays*. Berkeley: U of California P, 1972.

Wright, Stephen, K. "The Betrayer's Art: Translating Medieval Drama for Modern Readers." *Research Opportunities in Renaissance Drama* 35 (1996): 85–96.

RENAISSANCE DRAMA

Adams, John C. *The Globe Playhouse*. 2nd ed. New York: Barnes, 1961.

Altman, Joel B. *The Tudor Play of Mind: Rhetorical Inquiry and the Development of Elizabethan Drama*. Berkeley: U of California P, 1978.

Axton, Richard. *European Drama of the Early Middle Ages*. London: Hutchinson, 1974.

Bevington, David. *From Mankind to Marlowe: Growth of Structure in the Popular Drama of Tudor England*. Cambridge: Harvard UP, 1962.

Bradbrook, Muriel C. *The Growth and Structure of Elizabethan Comedy*. London: Chatto, 1955.

Braunmuller, A. R., and Michael Hathaway. *The Cambridge Companion to Renaissance Drama*. New York: Cambridge UP, 1990.

Bush, Douglas. *The Renaissance and English Humanism*. Toronto: U of Toronto P, 1939.

Bushnell, Rebecca W. *Tragedies of Tyrants: Political Thought and Theater in the English Renaissance*. Ithaca: Cornell UP, 1990.

Cairns, Christopher, ed. *The Renaissance Theatre: Texts, Performance, Design*. Aldershot, UK: Ashgate, 1999.

Cartwright, Kent. *Theatre and Humanism: English Drama in the Sixteenth Century*. Cambridge: Cambridge UP, 1999.

Cerasano, S. P., and Marion Wynne-Davies, eds. *Readings in Renaissance Women's Drama: Criticism, History, and Performance, 1594–1998*. London: Routledge, 1998.

Chambers, E. K. *The Elizabethan Stage*. 4 vols. Oxford: Clarendon, 1923.

Coyle, Martin. "*Hamlet*, Gertrude and the Ghost: The Punishment of Women in Renaissance Drama." *Q/W/E/R/T/Y* 6 (1996): 29–38.

Farnham, W. *The Medieval Heritage of Elizabethan Tragedy*. Berkeley: U of California P, 1936.

Findaly, Alison. *A Feminist Perspective on Renaissance Drama*. Oxford: Blackwell Publishers, 1999.

Fumerton, Patricia, and Simon Hunt, eds. *Renaissance Culture and the Everyday*. Philadelphia: U of Philadelphia P, 1999.

Happe, Peter. *English Drama Before Shakespeare*. London: Longman, 1999.

Hussey, Maurice. *The World of Shakespeare and His Contemporaries: A Visual Approach*. New York: Viking, 1972.

Kernodle, George. *From Art to Theatre: Form and Convention in the Renaissance*. Chicago: U of Chicago P, 1944.

Lea, Kathleen M. *Italian Popular Comedy: A Study of the Commedia dell'Arte, 1560–1620*. 2 vols. Oxford: Clarendon, 1934.

Leggatt, Alexander. *Introduction to English Renaissance Comedy*. Manchester: Manchester UP, 1999.

Leinwand, Theodore B. *Theatre, Finance, and Society in Early Modern England*. Cambridge: Cambridge UP, 1999.

Loomba, Ania. *Gender, Race, and Renaissance Drama.* New York: Manchester UP, 1989.

Marcus, Leah S. *Unediting the Renaissance: Shakespeare, Marlowe, Milton.* London: Routledge, 1996.

Masten, Jeffrey, and Wendy Wall. *Renaissance Drama.* Evanston: Northwestern UP, 1999.

McLuskie, Kathleen. *Renaissance Dramatists.* Atlantic Highlands: Humanities International, 1989.

Nicoll, Allardyce. *The World of Harlequin.* Cambridge: Cambridge UP, 1963.

Rose, Mary Beth. *The Expense of Spirit: Love and Sexuality in English Renaissance Drama.* Ithaca: Cornell UP, 1988.

Rose, Mary Beth, ed. *Renaissance Dramatic Culture.* Evanston: Northwestern UP, 1998.

Tetzell, Kurt von Rosador. "The Power of Magic: From Endimion to *The Tempest.*" Shakespeare Survey 43 (1991): 1–13.

Waith, Eugene M. *Patterns and Perspectives in English Renaissance Drama.* Newark: U of Delaware P, 1988.

Welsford, Enid. *The Court Masque.* Cambridge: Cambridge UP, 1927.

White, Martin. *Renaissance Drama in Action: An Introduction to Aspects of Theatre Practice and Performance.* London: Routledge, 1998.

Wind, Edgar. *Pagan Mysteries in the Renaissance.* New Haven: Yale UP, 1958.

Woodbridge, Linda. *Woman and the English Renaissance: Literature and the Nature of Womankind, 1540–1620.* Urbana: U of Illinois P, 1984.

Yates, Frances A. *Theatre of the World.* Chicago: U of Chicago P, 1969.

Late Seventeenth- and Eighteenth-Century Drama

Barber, Charles L. *The Idea of Honour in the English Drama, 1591–1700.* Stockholm: Göteborg, 1957.

Cox, Jeffrey N. *In the Shadows of Romance.* Athens: Ohio UP, 1987.

Grene, Nicholas. *Shakespeare, Jonson, Molière: The Comic Contract.* Totowa: Barnes, 1980.

Holland, Norman N. *The First Modern Comedies: The Significance of Etherege, Wycherley, and Congreve.* Cambridge: Harvard UP, 1959.

Hume, Robert. *The Rakish Stage: Studies in English Drama, 1660–1800.* Carbondale: Southern Illinois UP, 1983.

Kaplan, Deborah. "Representing the Nation: Restoration Comedies on the Early Twentieth-Century London Stage." *Theatre Survey* 36.2 (1995): 37–61.

Loftis, John, ed. *Restoration Drama.* New York: Oxford UP, 1966.

Lynch, Kathleen M. *The Social Mode of Restoration Comedy.* New York: Farrar, 1975.

Marshall, Geoffrey. *Restoration Serious Drama.* Norman: U of Oklahoma P, 1975.

McMillin, Scott, ed. *Restoration and Eighteenth-Century Comedy.* 2nd ed. New York: Norton, 1997.

Nicoll, Allardyce. *A History of Restoration Drama, 1600–1700.* New York: Cambridge UP, 1923.

Owen, Susan J. *Restoration Theatre and Crisis.* Oxford: Clarendon P, 1996.

Peters, Julie Stone. "'Things Govern'd by Words': Late Seventeenth-Century Comedy and the Reformers." *English Studies* 68 (1987): 142–53.

Powell, Jocelyn. *Restoration Theatre Production.* Boston: Routledge, 1984.

Price, Cecil. *Theatre in the Age of Garrick.* Oxford: Oxford UP, 1973.

Richards, K. R., ed. *Essays on the Eighteenth Century English Stage.* London: Methuen, 1972.

Rothstein, Eric. *The Designs of Carolean Comedy.* Carbondale: Southern Illinois UP, 1988.

Stynan, J. L. *Restoration Comedy in Performance.* New York: Cambridge UP, 1986.

Turnell, Martin. *The Classical Movement: Studies in Corneille, Molière, and Racine.* New York: New Directions, 1948.

Nineteenth-Century Drama through the Turn of the Century

Bank, Rosemarie K. *Theatre Culture in America, 1825–1860.* Cambridge Studies in American Theatre and Drama. Cambridge: Cambridge UP, 1997.

Bentley, Eric. *The Playwright as Thinker: A Study of Drama in Modern Times.* New York: Harcourt, 1967.

Bogard, Travis, ed. *Modern Drama: Essays in Criticism.* New York: Oxford UP, 1965.

Booth, Michael. *English Melodrama.* London: Jenkins, 1965.

Brustein, Robert. *The Theatre of Revolt.* Boston: Little, 1964.

Cole, Toby, ed. *Playwrights on Playwriting: The Meaning and Making of Modern Drama from Ibsen to Ionesco.* New York: Hill, 1960.

Detsi-Diamanti, Zoe. *Early American Women Dramatists, 1775–1860.* Garland Studies in American Popular History and Culture. New York: Garland, 1998.

Driver, Tom Faw. *Romantic Quest and Modern Query: A History of the Modern Theatre.* New York: Delacorte, 1970.

Finney, Gail. *Women in Modern Drama: Freud, Feminism, and European Theater at the Turn of the Century.* Ithaca: Cornell UP, 1989.

Fisher, Judith L., and Stephen Watt, eds. *When They Weren't Doing Shakespeare: Essays on Nineteenth-Century British and American Theatre.* Athens: U of Georgia P, 1989.

Gilman, Richard. *The Making of Modern Drama: A Study of Buchner, Ibsen, Strindberg, Chekhov, Pirandello, Brecht, Beckett, Handke.* New York: Farrar, 1974.

Jewett, William. *Fatal Autonomy: Romantic Drama and the Rhetoric of Agency.* Ithaca: Cornell UP, 1997.

Krasner, David. *Resistance, Parody, and Double*

Consciousness in African American Theatre, 1895–1910. Basingstoke: Macmillan, 1997.

Newey, Katharine. "Melodrama and Metatheatre: Theatricality in the Nineteenth Century Theatre." *Journal of Dramatic Theory and Criticism* 11.2 (1997): 85–100.

Marker, Fredrick J., and Christopher Innes, eds. *Modernism in European Drama: Ibsen, Strindberg, Pirandello, Beckett.* Toronto: U of Toronto P, 1998.

Quinsey, Katherine M., ed. *Broken Boundaries: Women and Feminism in Restoration Drama.* Lexington: U of Kentucky P, 1996.

Riis, Thomas. "Opera and the Operatic, Drama and the Melodramatic: What Was the State of Things in Nineteenth-Century America?" *Nineteenth Century Theatre* 23.1–2 (1995): 76–89.

Stynan, J. L. *Modern Drama in Theory and Practice.* 3 vols. New York: Cambridge UP, 1980.

Valency, Maurice Jacques. *The Flower and the Castle: An Introduction to Modern Drama.* New York: Schocken, 1982.

Whitaker, Thomas R. *Fields of Play in Modern Drama.* Princeton: Princeton UP, 1977.

Williams, Raymond. *Drama from Ibsen to Eliot.* New York: Oxford UP, 1953.

DRAMA IN THE EARLY AND MID-TWENTIETH CENTURY

Artaud, Antonin. *The Theatre and Its Double.* Trans. Mary C. Richards. New York: Grove, 1958.

Bentley, Eric. *The Theatre of Commitment and Other Essays on Drama in Our Society.* New York: Atheneum, 1967.

Blau, Herbert, *The Impossible Theatre: A Manifesto.* New York: Macmillan, 1964.

Bogard, Travis, and William I. Oliver, eds. *Modern Drama: Essays in Criticism.* New York: Oxford UP, 1965.

Booth, Michael R., and Joel H. Kaplan, eds. *The Edwardian Theatre: Essays on Performance and the Stage.* Cambridge: Cambridge UP, 1996.

Bordman, Gerald Martin. *American Theatre: A Chronicle of Comedy and Drama, 1930–1969.* New York: Oxford UP, 1996.

Brater, Enoch, and Ruby Cohn, eds. *Around the Absurd: Essays on Modern and Postmodern Drama.* Ann Arbor: U of Michigan P, 1990.

Brockett, Oscar G. *History of the Theatre.* 5th ed. Boston: Allyn, 1987.

Brook, Peter. *The Empty Space.* New York: Avon, 1968.

Cohn, Ruby. *From Desire to Godot: Pocket Theater of Postwar Paris.* Berkeley: U of California P, 1987.

Davidson, Clifford, C. J. Gianakaris, and John H. Stroupe, eds. *Drama in the Twentieth Century: Comparative and Critical Essays.* New York: AMS, 1984.

Demastes, William W., and Katherine E. Kelly. *British Playwrights, 1880–1956: A Research and Production Sourcebook.* Westport, CT: Greenwood, 1996.

Esslin, Martin. *The Theatre of the Absurd.* Woodstock, NY: Overlook, 1973.

Fearnow, Mark. *The American Stage and the Great Depression: A Cultural History of the Grotesque.* Cambridge Studies in American Theatre and Drama. Cambridge: Cambridge UP, 1997.

Gassner, John. *Theatre at the Crossroads.* New York: Holt, 1960.

Goldberg, RosaLee. *Performance: Live Art 1909 to the Present.* New York: Abrams, 1979.

Hebel, Udo J. "Early American Women Playwrights (1916–1930) and the Remapping of Twentieth-Century American Drama." *Arbeiten aus Anglistik und Amerikanistik* 21.2 (1996): 267–86.

Kernan, Alvin B., ed. *The Modern American Theater: A Collection of Critical Essays.* Englewood Cliffs: Prentice, 1967.

Kirby, Michael. *A Formalist Theatre.* Philadelphia: U of Pennsylvania P, 1987.

Mason, Jeffrey D., and Ellen Gainer, eds. *Performing America: Cultural Nationalism in American Theater.* Ann Arbor: U of Michigan P, 1999.

Miller, Jordan Yale. *American Drama between the Wars: A Critical History.* Twayne's Critical History of American Drama. Boston: Twayne, 1997.

Murray, Christopher. "Modern Drama from Ibsen to Fugard." *Moderna Sprak* 88.1 (1994): 98–100.

Orr, John. *Tragic Drama and Modern Society: Studies in Social and Literary Theory of Drama from 1870 to the Present.* New York: Macmillan, 1981.

Piscator, Erwin. *The Political Theatre: A History, 1914–1929.* Trans. Hugh Rorrison. London: Eyre Methuen, 1980.

Roose-Evans, James. *Experimental Theatre: From Stanislavsky to Today.* 2nd ed. London: Studio Vista, 1973.

Smith, Wendy. *Real Life Drama: The Group Theatre and America, 1931–1940.* New York: Knopf, 1990.

Szilassy, Zolt N. *American Theater of the 1960s.* Carbondale: U of Illinois P, 1986.

CONTEMPORARY DRAMA

Andreach, Robert J. *Creating Self in the Contemporary American Theatre.* Carbondale: Southern Illinois UP, 1998.

Betsko, Kathleen, and Rachel Koenig. *Interviews with Contemporary Women Playwrights.* New York: Beech Tree, 1987.

Bigsby, Christopher W. E. *Contemporary American Playwrights.* Cambridge: Cambridge UP, 1999.

Blau, Herbert. *Eye of Prey: Subversions of the Postmodern.* Bloomington: Indiana UP, 1987.

Blumenthal, Eileen. *Joseph Chaikin: Exploring at the Boundaries of Theatre.* New York: Cambridge UP, 1984.

Brecht, Stefan. *The Theatre of Visions: Robert Wilson.* Frankfurt am Main: Suhrkamp, 1978.

Carpenter, Charles A. *Modern Drama: Scholarship and*

Criticism, 1981–1990: An International Bibliography. Toronto: U of Toronto P, 1997.

Cheney, Sheldon. *New Movement in the Theatre.* Westport, CT: Greenwood, 1971.

Coen, Stephanie. "No Comparisons." *American Theatre* 11.6 (1994): 26.

DiGaetani, John L. "David Ives." *Interviews with Contemporary Playwrights.* Ed. John L. DiGaetani. New York: Greenwood, 1991. 183–90.

Dobrez, Livio A. C. *The Existential and Its Exits: Literary and Philosophical Perspectives on the Works of Beckett, Ionesco, Genet, and Pinter.* New York: St. Martin's, 1986.

Grotowski, Jerzy. *Towards a Poor Theatre.* New York: Simon, 1968.

Hart, Lynda, ed. *Making a Spectacle: Feminist Essays on Contemporary Women's Theatre.* Ann Arbor: U of Michigan P, 1989.

Hayman, Ronald. *Theatre and Anti-Theatre: New Movements since Beckett.* New York: Oxford UP, 1979.

Heilpern, John. *How Good Is David Mamet Anyway? Writings on Theatre and Why It Matters.* New York: Routledge, 1999.

Hill, Errol, ed. *The Theatre of Black Americans.* 2 vols. Englewood Cliffs: Prentice, 1980.

Inverso, MaryBeth. *The Gothic Impulse in Contemporary Drama.* Ann Arbor: U of Michigan P, 1990.

Marranca, Bonnie, ed. *The Theatre of Images.* New York: Drama Book Specialists, 1977.

McDonough, Carla J. *Staging Masculinity: Male Identity in Contemporary American Drama.* Jefferson, NC: McFarland, 1997.

Orr, John. *Tragicomedy and Contemporary Culture: Play and Performance from Beckett to Shepard.* Ann Arbor: U of Michigan P, 1990.

Parker, Dorothy. *Essays on Modern American Drama: Williams, Miller, Albee, and Shepard.* Toronto: U of Toronto P, 1987.

Peacock, D. Keith. *Thatcher's Theatre: British Theatre and Drama in the Eighties.* Contributions in Drama and Theatre Studies 88. Westport, CT: Greenwood, 1999.

Roudané, Matthew Charles. *American Drama since 1960: A Critical History.* New York: Twayne, 1997.

Savran, David. *In Their Own Words: Contemporary American Playwrights.* New York: Theatre Communications Group, 1988.

Schechner, Richard. *Environmental Theater.* New York: Hawthorn, 1973.

Sinfield, Alan. *Out on Stage: Lesbian and Gay Theatre in the Twentieth Century.* New Haven: Yale UP, 1999.

Smith, Iris. "Authors in America: Tony Kushner, Arthur Miller, and Anna Deveare Smith." *Centennial Review* 40.1 (1996): 125–42.

Watt, Stephen. *Postmodern Drama: Reading the Contemporary Stage.* Ann Arbor: U of Michigan P, 1998.

Wellworth, George E. *The Theater of Protest and Paradox.* New York: New York UP, 1971.

Selected References for Playwrights and Plays

AESCHYLUS

Brooks, Otis. *Cosmos and Tragedy: An Essay on the Meaning of Aeschylus.* Chapel Hill: U of North Carolina P, 1981.

Gannon, J. F. "Aeschylus's *Agamemnon.*" *Classical Quarterly* 39.1 (1989): 254–57.

Harrington, J. C. *Aeschylus.* New Haven: Yale UP, 1986.

Ireland, S. *Aeschylus, Greece and Rome.* 1947. Classical Association 18. Oxford: Clarendon, 1986.

Konishi, H. "Agamemnon's Reason for Yielding." *American Journal of Philology* 110 (1989): 210–22.

Podlecki, Anthony J. *The Political Background of Aeschylean Tragedy.* Ann Arbor: U of Michigan P, 1966.

Rosenmeyer, Thomas G. *The Art of Aeschylus.* Berkeley: U of California P, 1982.

Spatz, Lois. *Aeschylus.* Twayne's World Authors Series 675. Boston: Twayne, 1982.

Thalmann, W. G. "Aeschylus's Physiology of the Emotions." *American Journal of Philology* 107 (1986): 489–511.

Thomson, George Derwent. *Aeschylus and Athens: A Study in the Social Origins of Drama.* 2nd ed. London: Lawrence & Wishart, 1967.

Valentini, Valentina. "The '*Orestei*' of the Soìetas Raffaelo Sanzio." *Performance Research* 2.3 (1997): 58–64.

Winnington-Ingram, R. P. [Reginald Pepys]. *Studies in Aeschylus.* New York: Cambridge UP, 1983.

ARISTOPHANES

Colvin, Stephen. *Dialect in Aristophanes and the Politics of Language in Ancient Greek Literature.* Oxford: Clarendon, 1999.

Dane, Joseph A. *Parody: Critical Concepts versus Literary Practices, Aristophanes to Sterne.* Norman: U of Oklahoma P, 1988.

Deardon, C. W. *The Stage of Aristophanes.* London: Athlone, 1976.

Dover, K. J. *Aristophanic Comedy.* Berkeley: U of California P, 1972.

Forrest, W. G. "Aristophanes' *Lysistrata.*" *Classical Quarterly* 45.1 (1995): 240–41.

Harriott, Rosemary. *Aristophanes: Poet and Dramatist.* Baltimore: Johns Hopkins UP, 1986.

Henderson, Jeffrey. *Aristophanes' Lysistrata.* New York: Oxford UP, 1987.

Matz, D. "Ensuring That the Flea Wears Wax Slippers When Teaching Aristophanes and a One-Person Reenactment of a Choral Entry from *Lysistrata* in the Classroom." *Classical Journal* 87.1 (1991): 55–58.

McLeish, Kenneth. *The Theatre of Aristophanes.* New York: Taplinger, 1980.

Murray, Gilbert. *Aristophanes*. Oxford: Clarendon, 1933.

Reckford, Kenneth. *Aristophanes' Old-and-New Comedy*. Chapel Hill: U of North Carolina P, 1987.

Russo, Carlo Ferdinando. *Aristophanes: An Author for the Stage*. London: Routledge, 1997.

Segal, Erich, ed. *Oxford Readings in Aristophanes*. Oxford: Oxford UP, 1996.

Ussher, Robert Glenn. *Aristophanes*. New York: Oxford UP, 1979.

SAMUEL BECKETT

Andonian, Cathleen Culotta, ed. *The Critical Response to Samuel Beckett*. Westport, CT: Greenwood, 1998.

Astro, Alan. *Understanding Beckett*. Columbia: U of South Carolina P, 1990.

Athanason, Arthur N. Endgame: *The Ashbin Play*. New York: Twayne, 1993.

Begam, Richard. *Samuel Beckett and the End of Modernity*. Stanford: Stanford UP, 1996.

Beja, Morris, S. E. Gontarski, and Pierre Astier, eds. *Samuel Beckett: Humanistic Perspectives*. Columbus: Ohio State UP, 1983.

Ben-Zvi, Linda, ed. *Women in Beckett: Performance and Critical Perspectives*. Urbana: U of Illinois P, 1990.

Bloom, Harold. *Samuel Beckett's* Endgame. New York: Chelsea, 1988.

Brater, Enoch, ed. *Beckett at 80: Beckett in Context*. New York: Oxford UP, 1986.

———. *Why Beckett: With 122 Illustrations*. New York: Thames, 1989.

Bryden, Mary. "The Sacrificial Victim of Beckett's *Endgame*." *Literature and Theology* 4.2 (1990): 219–25.

Buning, Marius, and Lois Oppenheim, eds. *Beckett in the 1990s*. Amsterdam: Rodopi, 1993.

Burkman, Katherine. *Myth and Ritual in the Plays of Samuel Beckett*. Rutherford: Fairleigh Dickinson UP, 1987.

Butler, Lance S., and Robin J. Davis, eds. *Rethinking Beckett: A Collection of Critical Essays*. New York: St. Martin's, 1990.

Cohn, Ruby. *Just Play: Beckett's Theater*. Princeton: Princeton UP, 1980.

———, ed. *Samuel Beckett: A Collection of Criticism*. New York: McGraw, 1975.

Connor, Steven, ed. *Gender in Transition:* Waiting for Godot *and* Endgame. New York: St. Martin's, 1992.

Cronin, Anthony. *Samuel Beckett: The Last Modernist*. New York. Harper, 1997.

Dearlove, J. E. *Accommodating the Chaos: Samuel Beckett's Nonrelational Art*. Durham: Duke UP, 1982.

Doll, Mary Aswell. *Beckett and Myth: An Archetypal Approach*. Syracuse: Syracuse UP, 1988.

Esslin, Martin, ed. *Samuel Beckett: A Collection of Critical Essays*. Englewood Cliffs: Prentice, 1965.

Fletcher, Beryl S., et al. *A Student's Guide to the Plays of Samuel Beckett*. 2nd ed. Boston: Faber, 1985.

Fletcher, John. *Beckett: The Playwright*. New York: Hill, 1985.

Gidal, Peter. *Understanding Beckett*. New York: St. Martin's, 1986.

Gontarski, S. E. *On Beckett: Essays and Criticism*. New York: Grove, 1986.

Gordon, Lois G. *The World of Samuel Beckett*. New Haven: Yale UP, 1996.

Kenner, Hugh. *A Reader's Guide to Samuel Beckett*. New York: Farrar, 1973.

Knowlson, James. *Damned to Fame: The Life of Samuel Beckett*. London: Bloomsbury, 1997.

Kumar, K. Jeevan. "The Chess Metaphor in Samuel Beckett's *Endgame*." *Modern Drama* 40 (1997): 540–52.

Lawley, Paul. "Adoption in *Endgame*." *Modern Drama* 31 (1988): 529–35.

Lyons, Charles R. *Samuel Beckett*. New York: Grove, 1983.

Popovic, Poll. "Beckett's *Endgame* as a Bond of Dependency." *European Studies Journal* 11.1 (1994): 35–47.

Rosen, Steven J. *Samuel Beckett and the Pessimistic Tradition*. New Brunswick: Rutgers UP, 1976.

Smith, Joseph H., ed. *The World of Samuel Beckett*. Baltimore: Johns Hopkins UP, 1991.

Tassi, Marguerite. "Shakespeare and Beckett Revisited: A Phenomenology of Theatre." *Comparative Drama* 31 (1997): 248–76.

Uhlmann, Anthony. *Beckett and Poststructuralism*. Cambridge: Cambridge UP, 1999.

Worth, Katharine. *Samuel Beckett's Theatre: Life-Journeys*. Oxford: Clarendon, 1999.

APHRA BEHN

Armistid, J. M. *Four Restoration Playwrights: A Reference Guide to Thomas Shadwell, Aphra Behn, Nathaniel Lee, and Thomas Otway*. Boston: Hall, 1984.

Copeland, Nancy. "'Once a Whore and Ever'? Whore and Virgin in *The Rover* and Its Antecedents." *Early Women Writers: 1600–1720*. Ed. Anita Pacheco. London: Longman, 1998. 149–59.

DeRitter, Jones. "The Gypsy, The Rover, and the Wanderer: Aphra Behn's Revision of Thomas Killigrew." *Restoration: Studies in English Literary Culture, 1660–1700* 10.2 (1986): 82–92.

Diamond, Elin. "Gestus and Signature in Aphra Behn's *The Rover*." *Early Women Writers: 1600–1720*. Ed. Anita Pacheco. London: Longman, 1998. 160–82.

Gallagher, Catherine. "Who Was That Masked Woman? The Prostitute and the Playwright in the Comedies of Aphra Behn." *Last Laughs*. Ed. Gina Barreca. New York: Gordon, 1989. 23–42.

Jones, Jane. "New Light on the Background and Early Life of Aphra Behn." *Notes and Queries* 37 (1990): 288–93.

Link, Frederick M. *Aphra Behn*. Boston: Twayne, 1969.

Lussier, Mark. "'The Vile Mercandize of Fortune': Women, Economy, and Desire in Aphra Behn." *Women's Studies* 18.4 (1991): 379–93.

Mendelson, Sara Heller. *The Mental World of Stuart Women: Three Studies*. Amherst: U of Massachusetts P, 1987.

Munns, Jessica. "'I by a Double Right Thy Bounties Claim': Aphra Behn and Sexual Space." *Curtain Calls: British and American Women and the Theater, 1660–1820*. Ed. Mary Anne Schofield and Cecilia Macheski. Athens: Ohio UP, 1991.

Szilagyi, Stephen. "The Sexual Politics of Behn's *Rover* — After Patriarchy." *Studies in Philology* 95 (1998): 435–55.

Todd, Janet. *Aphra Behn*. New Casebooks. Basingstoke: Macmillan, 1999.

———. *Aphra Behn Studies*. Cambridge: Cambridge UP, 1996.

———. *The Critical Fortunes of Aphra Behn*. Columbia, SC: Camden House, 1998.

———. *The Secret Life of Aphra Behn*. London: Pandora, 1999.

Wiseman, S. J. *Aphra Behn*. Plymouth: Northcote House, 1996.

BERTOLT BRECHT

Bai, Ronnie. "Dances with Mei Lanfang: Brecht and the Alienation Effect." *Comparative Drama* 32 (1998): 389–433.

Bail, Henry, and Carol Martin, eds. *Bertolt Brecht: A Critical Anthology*. London: Routledge, 1999.

Beckley, Richard. "Brecht: The Reality and the Ideal." *Gestus* 2.1 (1986): 37–46.

Bodek, Richard. *Proletarian Performance in Weimar Berlin: Agitprop, Chorus, and Brecht*. Columbia: Camden House, 1997.

Brecht, Bertolt. *Brecht on Theatre: The Development of an Aesthetic*. Ed. and trans. John Willett. New York: Hill, 1964.

Brown, Russell E. *Intimacy and Intimidation: Three Essays on Bertolt Brecht*. Stuttgart: Steiner, 1990.

Bryant-Bertail, Sarah. "Women, Space, Ideology: Mutter Courage und Ihre Kinder." *The Brecht Yearbook* 12 (1983): 43–61.

Cima, Gay Gibson, Maarten Van Dijk, Liz Diamond, et al. "Brecht/'Brecht': A Symposium." *Theater* 25.2 (1994): 24–41.

Demetz, Peter, ed. *Brecht: A Collection of Critical Essays*. Englewood Cliffs: Prentice, 1962.

Docherty, Brian, ed. *Twentieth-Century European Drama*. New York: St. Martin's, 1994.

Eddershaw, Margaret. *Performing Brecht*. New York: Routledge, 1996.

Esslin, Martin. *Brecht: The Man and His Works*. Garden City: Doubleday, 1971.

Ewen, Frederick. *Bertolt Brecht: His Life, His Art and His Times*. New York: Citadel, 1967.

Fuegi, John. *Bertolt Brecht: Chaos, According to Plan*. New York: Cambridge UP, 1987.

———. *Brecht and Company: Sex, Politics, and the Making of Modern Drama*. New York: Grove, 1994.

Giles, Steve, and Rodney Livingstone, eds. *Bertolt Brecht: Centenary Essays*. Amsterdam: Rodopi, 1998.

Gleitman, Claire. "All in the Family: *Mother Courage* and the Ideology in the Gestus." *Comparative Drama* 25.2 (1991): 147–67.

Gray, Ronald. *Bertolt Brecht*. New York: Grove, 1967.

Harrington, R. "*Mother Courage and Her Children*." *Appalachian Journal* 24.2 (1997): 141–43.

Hill, Claude. *Bertolt Brecht*. New York: Twayne, 1975.

Jameson, Fredric. *Brecht and Method*. London: Verso, 1998.

Kleber, Pia, and Colin Visser, eds. *Re-Interpreting Brecht: His Influence on Contemporary Drama and Film*. Cambridge: Cambridge UP, 1990.

Mews, Siegfried, ed. *A Bertolt Brecht Reference Companion*. Westport, CT: Greenwood, 1997.

———, comp. *Critical Essays on Bertolt Brecht*. Boston: Hall, 1989.

Munk, Erika, ed. "On Brecht." *Theater* 25.2 (1994): 9–55.

Potter, Robert. "Writing *Mother Courage*." *The Brecht Yearbook* 24 (1999): 14–23.

Rouse, John. "Brecht and the Contradictory Actor." *Theatre Journal* 36.1 (1984): 25–41.

Schoeps, Karl Heinz. *Bertolt Brecht: Life, Work, and Criticism*. Fredericton: York, 1989.

Silberman, Marc. "A Postmodernized Brecht?" *Theatre Journal* 45.1 (1993): 1–19.

Spalter, Max. *Brecht's Tradition*. Baltimore: Johns Hopkins UP, 1967.

Speirs, Ronald. *Bertolt Brecht*. New York: St. Martin's, 1987.

Stern, Guy. "Enriching *Mother Courage*." *Communications from the International Brecht Society* 25.1 (1996): 60–68.

Thomson, Peter, and Glendyr Sachs, eds. *The Cambridge Companion to Brecht*. Cambridge: Cambridge UP, 1994.

Tian, Min. "Alienation-Effect for Whom? Brecht's (Mis)interpretation of the Classical Chinese Theatre." *Asian Theatre Journal* 14.2 (1997): 200–22.

Willet, John. *Brecht in Context: Comparative Approaches*. 2nd ed. London: Methuen, 1998.

———. *The Theatre of Bertolt Brecht*. New York, 1959.

Willits, Ross D. "The Through-line of Meaning in *Mother Courage* and Brecht." *Text and Presentation*. Ed. Karelisa Hartigan. Lanham, MD: UP of America, 1989.

PEDRO CALDERÓN DE LA BARCA

Cascardi, Anthony J. *The Limits of Illusion: A Critical Study of Calderón*. Cambridge, Cambridge UP, 1984.

De Armas, Frederick Alfred, David M. Gitlitz, and José A. Madrigal, eds. *Critical Perspectives on Calderón de la Barca.* Lincoln, NE: Society of Spanish and Spanish-American Studies, 1986.

Delgado, Manuel. *The Calderónian Stage: Body and Soul.* Lewisburg, PA: Bucknell UP, 1997.

Hesse, Everett W. *Calderón de la Barca.* New York: Twayne, 1967.

Honig, Edwin. *Calderón and the Seizures of Honor.* Cambridge: Harvard UP, 1972.

McGaha, Michael D., ed. *Approaches to the Theatre of Calderón.* Washington: UP of America, 1982.

Cascardi, Anthony J. *The Limits of Illusion: A Critical Study of Calderón.* Cambridge: Cambridge UP, 1984.

Greer, Margaret Rich. *The Play of Power: Mythological Court Dramas of Calderón de la Barca.* Princeton: Princeton UP, 1991.

Levin, Leslie. *Metaphors of Conversion in Seventeenth Century Spanish Drama.* Colección Tamesis. Serie A, Monografias 174. Woodbridge, UK: Tamesis, 1999.

Lund, Henry. *Pedro Calderón de la Barca: A Biography.* Edingburg, TX: Andres Noriega P, 1963.

O'Conner, Thomas Austin. *Myth and Mythology in the Theatre of Pedro Calderón de la Barca.* San Antonio: Trinity UP, 1988.

Parker, Alexander Augustine. *The Allegorical Drama of Calderón: An Introduction to the Autos Sacramentales.* Oxford: Dolphin, 1991.

———. *The Mind and Art of Calderón: Essays on the Comedias.* Cambridge: Cambridge UP, 1988.

Sloman, Albert E. *The Dramatic Craftsmanship of Calderón.* Oxford: Oxford UP, 1958.

Suscavage, Charlene E. *Calderón: The Imagery of Tragedy.* New York: Peter Lang, 1991.

Wardropper, Bruce W., ed. *Critical Essays in the Theatre of Calderón.* New York: New York UP, 1965.

ANTON CHEKHOV

Baldwin, James. "Chekhov, the Rediscovery of Realism: Michel Saint-Denis' Productions of *Three Sisters* and *The Cherry Orchard.*" *Theatre Notebook* 53.2 (1999): 96–115.

Barricelli, Jean-Pierre, ed. *Chekhov's Great Plays: A Critical Anthology.* New York: New York UP, 1981.

Clayton, J. Douglas, ed. *Chekhov Then and Now: The Reception of Chekhov in World Culture.* New York: Peter Lang, 1997.

Eekman, Thomas A. *Critical Essays on Anton Chekhov.* Boston: Hall, 1989.

Emeljanow, Victor. *Chekhov: The Critical Heritage.* Boston: Routledge, 1981.

Hingley, Ronald. *Chekhov: A Biographical and Critical Study.* New York: Barnes, 1966.

Jackson, Robert Louis. *Chekhov: A Collection of Critical Essays.* Englewood Cliffs: Prentice, 1967.

Karlinsky, Simon, and Michael Heim, eds. *Anton Chekhov's Life and Thought: Selected Letters and Commentary.* Berkeley: U of California P, 1975.

Magarshak, David. *Chekhov the Dramatist.* New York: Hill, 1960.

Meister, Charles. *Chekhov Criticism 1880 through 1986.* New York: McFarland, 1988.

Peace, Richard. *Chekhov: A Study of the Four Major Plays.* New Haven: Yale UP, 1983.

Rayfield, Donald. *Anton Chekhov: A Life.* London: Harper, 1997.

———. *Understanding Chekhov: A Critical Study of Chekhov's Prose and Drama.* Bristol: Bristol Classical, 1999.

Russell, Robert, and Andrew Barratt, eds. *Russian Theatre in the Age of Modernism.* New York: St. Martin's, 1990.

Senderovich, Savely. "*The Cherry Orchard*: Chekhov's Last Testament." *Russian Literature* 35 (1994): 223–42.

Senelick, Laurence. *The Chekhov Theatre: A Century of Plays in Performance.* Cambridge: Cambridge UP, 1999.

Stanislavsky, Konstantin. *My Life in Art.* New York: Routledge Chapman and Hall, 1924.

Stynan, J. L. *Chekhov in Performance.* Cambridge: Cambridge UP, 1971.

Toumanova, Princess Nina Andronikova. *Anton Chekhov: The Voice of Twilight Russia.* New York: Columbia UP, 1960.

Tulloch, John, Tom Burvill, and Andrew Hood. "Reinhabiting *The Cherry Orchard*: Class and History in Performing Chekhov." *New Theatre Quarterly* 13 (1997): 318–28.

Valency, Maurice. *The Breaking String: The Plays of Anton Chekhov.* New York: Oxford UP, 1966.

Welleck, Rene, and Nonna D. Welleck, eds. *Chekhov: New Perspectives.* Englewood Cliffs: Prentice, 1984.

Williams, Lee J. *Anton Chekhov, the Iconoclast.* Scranton: U of Scranton P, 1989.

CARYL CHURCHILL

Aston, Elaine. *Caryl Churchill. Writers and Their Work.* Plymouth, UK: Northcote House, 1997.

Brater, Enoch, and Ruby Cohn, eds. *Feminine Focus: The New Women Playwrights.* Oxford: Oxford UP, 1989.

Fitzsimmons, Linda. "'I Won't Turn Back for You or Anyone': Caryl Churchill's Socialist-Feminist Theatre." *Essays in Theatre* 6.1 (1987): 19–29.

Harding, James M. "Cloud Cover: (Re)dressing Desire and Comfortable Subversions in Caryl Churchill's *Cloud Nine.*" *PMLA* 113.2 (1998): 258–272.

Marohl, Joseph. "De-Realised Women: Performance and Identity in Churchill's *Top Girls*: Essays from Modern Drama." *Contemporary British Drama 1970–1990.* Ed. Hersh Zeifman and Cynthia Zimmerman. Toronto: U of Toronto P, 1993. 307–22.

Nischik, Reingard M. "Betrayal Psychohistorically: The Representation of Emotions in the British Drama of Manners." *Anglistentag* 1991 Dusseldorf. Ed. Wilhelm B. Busse. Tubingen: Niemeyer, 1992. 189–204.

Rabillard, Sheila Mary, ed. *Essays on Caryl Churchill: Contemporary Representations.* Winnipeg: Blizzard, 1998.

Randall, Phyllis R., ed. *Caryl Churchill: A Casebook.* New York: Garland, 1988.

Tonnies, Merle. "(Post)modernist Play with New Purposes: The Functioning of Language in Contemporary British Drama." *Zeitschrift für Anglistick und Amerikanistik* 46 (1998): 325–37.

Vanden-Heuvel, Michael. "Performing Gender(s)." *Contemporary Literature* 35.4 (1994): 804–13.

Waterman, David. "Caryl Churchill's *Cloud Nine*: The Fiction of Race and Gender in a System of Power." *Forum Modernes Theatre* 14.1 (1999): 86–92.

WILLIAM CONGREVE

Bartlett, Laurence. *William Congreve: An Annotated Bibliography, 1978–1994.* Lanham, MD: Scarecrow Press, 1996.

Dobree, Bonamy. *Congreve.* London: British Council, 1963.

Hodges, John C. *Congreve the Man: A Biography.* London: Oxford UP, 1941.

Kaplan, Deborah. "Learning to Speak the English Language: The Way of the World on the Twentieth-Century American Stage." *Theatre Journal* 49.3 (1997): 301–21.

Karman, E. "*The Way of the World.*" *TCI* 30.2 (1996): 14.

Love, Harold. *Congreve.* Oxford: Blackwell, 1974.

Lynch, Kathleen M. *The Social Mode of Restoration Comedy.* New York: Macmillan, 1926.

Markley, Robert. *Two-Edged Weapons: Style and Ideology in the Comedies of Etherege, Wycherley, and Congreve.* New York: Oxford UP, 1988.

Morris, Brian, ed. *Congreve: A Collection of Critical Studies.* London: Benn, 1972.

Mueschke, Paul, and Carol Mueschke. *A New View of Congreve's The Way of the World.* Ann Arbor: U of Michigan P, 1958.

Novak, Maximilian. *William Congreve.* Boston: Twayne, 1971.

Peters, Julie Stone. *Congreve: The Drama, and the Printed Word.* Stanford: Stanford UP, 1990.

Sieber, Anita. *Character Portrayal in Congreve's Comedies The Old Batchelour, Love for Love, and The Way of the World.* Lewiston: Mellen, 1996.

Van Voris, W. *The Cultivated Stance: The Designs of Congreve's Plays.* Dublin: Dolmen, 1965.

Williams, Aubrey Lake. *An Approach to Congreve.* New Haven: Yale UP, 1979.

EURIPIDES

Barlow, Shirley Anne. "Stereotype and Reversal in Euripides' *Medea.*" *Greece and Rome* 36 (1989): 158–71.

Burian, Peter, ed. *Directions in Euripidean Criticism.* Durham: Duke UP, 1985.

Collard, Christopher. *Euripides.* New York: Oxford UP, 1981.

Conacher, D. J. *Euripides and the Sophists: Some Dramatic Treatments of Philosophical Ideas.* London: Duckworth, 1998.

Foley, Helene P. "Medea's Divided Self." *Classical Antiquity* 8 (1989): 61–85.

———. *Ritual Irony: Poetry and Sacrifice in Euripides.* Ithaca: Cornell UP, 1985.

Halleran, Michael P. *Stagecraft in Euripides.* Totowa: Barnes, 1985.

Marks, Peter. "Theater Review: Anguish, Freeze-Dried and Served with Precision." *New York Times* 25 Sept. 1998: B1+.

Meagher, Robert E. *Mortal Vision: The Wisdom of Euripides.* New York: St. Martin's, 1989.

Michelini, Ann N. *Euripides and the Tragic Tradition.* Madison: U of Wisconsin P, 1987.

O'Connor, E. A. M. E. *Aspects of Human Sacrifice in the Tragedies of Euripides.* Amsterdam: Grüner, 1987.

Pucci, Pietro. *The Violence of Pity in Euripides' Medea.* Ithaca: Cornell UP, 1980.

Segal, Erich, ed. *Euripides: A Collection of Critical Essays.* Englewood Cliffs: Prentice, 1968.

Whitman, Cedric Hubbell. *Euripides and the Full Circle of Myth.* Cambridge: Harvard UP, 1974.

EVERYMAN

Bevington, David M. *From Mankind to Marlowe: Growth of Structure in the Popular Drama of Tudor England.* Cambridge: Harvard UP, 1962.

Cawley, A. C. *Everyman.* Manchester: Manchester UP, 1977.

———, ed. Everyman *and Medieval Miracle Plays.* New York: Dutton, 1977.

Cunningham, John. "Comedic and Liturgical Restoration in *Everyman.*" *Drama in the Middle Ages: Comparative and Critical Essays.* Second Series. Ed. Clifford Davidson and John H. Stroupe. New York: AMS, 1990.

Garner, Stanton B., Jr. "Theatricality in Mankind and *Everyman.*" *Studies in Philology* 84.3 (1987): 272–85.

Gilman, Donald, ed. Everyman *and Company: Essays on the Theme and Structure of the European Moral Play.* New York: AMS, 1989.

Pietropoli, Cecilia. "Towards a New *Everyman*: Medieval Drama as a Link between Classical and Renaissance Comedy." *International Conference on Aspects of European Medieval Drama.* 2 vols. Camerino: University degli Studi di Camerino, 1996.

Spinrad, Phoebe S. "The Last Temptation of *Everyman.*" *Philological Quarterly* 64.2 (1985): 185–94.

Staub, August W., and Michael J. Hussey. "Saints and Cyborgs: Mystical Performance Spaces (Re)visioned." *Journal of Dramatic Theory and Criticism* 13.1 (1998): 177–82.

Tanner, Ron. "Humor in *Everyman* and the Middle

English Morality Play." *Philological Quarterly* 70 (1991): 149–61.

White, D. Jerry. *Early English Drama: Everyman to 1580, A Reference Guide*. Boston: Hall, 1986.

BRIAN FRIEL

Delaney, Paul, ed. *Brian Friel in Conversation*. Ann Arbor: U Michigan P, 2000.

Friel, Brian. *Essays, Diaries, Interviews, 1964–1999*. Ed. Christopher Murray. London: Faber, 1999.

Kerwin, William, ed. *Brian Friel: A Casebook*. New York: Garland, 1997.

Krause, David. "The Failed Words of Brian Friel." *Modern Drama* 40.3 (1997): 359–73.

McGrath, Francis Charles. *Brian Friel's (Post) Colonial Drama: Language, Illusion, and Politics*. Syracuse: Syracuse UP, 1999.

McLullan, A. "'In Touch with Some Otherness': Gender Authority and the Body in *Dancing at Lughnasa*." *Irish University Review* 29.1 (1999): 90–100.

O'Brien, George. *Brian Friel: A Reference Guide, 1962–1992*. New York: Hall, 1995.

———. *The Diviner: The Art of Brian Friel*. Dublin: U College Dublin P, 1999.

———. "Meet Brian Friel." *Irish University Review* 29.1 (1999): 30–41.

Pine, Richard. *Brian Friel and Ireland's Drama*. London: Routledge, 1990.

ATHOL FUGARD

Barbera, Jack. "Athol Fugard Issue." *Twentieth-Century Literature* 39.4 (1993).

Benson, Mary. *Athol Fugard and Barney Simon: Bare Stage, A Few Props, Great Theatre*. Randburg, S. Africa: Ravan, 1997.

———. "Keeping an Appointment with the Future: The Theatre of Athol Fugard." *Theatre Quarterly* 7 (1977–78): 77–83.

Davmond, M. J., J. A. Jacobs, and Margaret Lenta, eds. *Momentum: On Recent South African Writing*. Pietermaritzburg: U of Natal P, 1984.

Durbach, Errol. "'MASTER HAROLD'. . . and the boys: Athol Fugard and the Psychopathology of Apartheid." *Modern Drama* 30.4 (1987): 505–13.

Fugard, Athol. "Fugard on Actors, Actors on Fugard." *Theatre Quarterly* 7 (1977–78): 83–7.

———. "Fugard on Fugard." *Yale Theatre* 1 (Winter 1973): 41–54.

———. "Letter from Athol Fugard." *Classic* 1 (1966): 78–80.

———. *Notebooks 1960–1977*. New York: Knopf, 1983.

Gray, Stephen, ed. *Athol Fugard*. Southern Africa Literature Series 1. Johannesburg: McGraw, 1982.

Heywood, Christopher. *Aspects of South African Literature*. London: Heinemann, 1976.

Hoegberg, David. E. "'Master Harold' and the Bard: Education and Succession in Fugard and Shakespeare." *Comparative Drama* 29.4 (1996): 415–35.

Jordan, John O. "Life in the Theatre: Politics and Romance in 'MASTER HAROLD' . . . and the boys." *Twentieth-Century Literature* 39.4 (1993): 461–72.

Kavanagh, Robert Mshengu. *Theatre and Cultural Struggle in South Africa*. London: Zed, 1985.

Post, Robert M. "Racism in Athol Fugard's 'MASTER HAROLD' . . . and the boys." *World Literature Written in English* 30.1 (1990): 97–102.

Seidenspinner, Margarete. *Exploring the Labyrinth: Athol Fugard's Approach to South African Drama*. Essen: Verlag Die Blaue Eule, 1986.

Sutton, Brian. "Fugard's 'Master Harold' . . . and the boys." *Explicator* 54.2 (1996): 120–23.

Vandenbrouke, Russell. *Truths the Hand Can Touch: The Theatre of Athol Fugard*. New York: Theatre Communications Group, 1985.

Walder, Dennis. *Athol Fugard*. New York: Grove, 1985.

Weales, Gerald. "Fugard Masters the Code." *Twentieth-Century Literature* 39.4 (1993): 503–16.

Wertheim, Albert. "Ballroom Dancing, Kites and Politics: Athol Fugard's 'MASTER HAROLD' . . . and the boys." *SPAN* 30 (1990): 141–55.

———. "Triangles of Race: Athol Fugard's *Master Harold . . . and the Boys* and Paul Slabolepszy's *Saturday Night at the Palace*." *Commonwealth Essays and Studies* 20.1 (1997): 86–95.

SUSAN GLASPELL

Ben-Zvi, Linda. "'Murder, She Wrote': The Genesis of Susan Glaspell's *Trifles*." *Theatre Journal* 44.2 (1992): 141–62.

———, ed. *Susan Glaspell: Essays on Her Theater and Fiction*. Ann Arbor: U of Michigan P, 1995.

———. "Susan Glaspell's Contributions to Contemporary Women Playwrights." *Feminine Focus: The New Women Playwrights*. Ed. Enoch Brater and Ruby Cohn. Oxford: Oxford UP, 1989.

Dymkowski, Christine. "On the Edge: The Plays of Susan Glaspell." *Modern Drama* 31.1 (1988): 91–105.

Kattwinkel, Susan. "Absence as a Site for Debate: Modern Feminism and Victorianism in the Plays of Susan Glaspell." *New England Theatre Journal* 7 (1996): 37–55.

Larabee, Ann E. "'Meeting the Outside Face to Face': Susan Glaspell, Djuna Barnes, and O'Neill's *The Emperor Jones*." *Modern American Drama: The Female Canon*. Ed. June Schlueter. Rutherford: Fairleigh Dickinson UP, 1990. 77–85.

Mael, Phyllis. "*Trifles*: The Path to Sisterhood." *Literature-Film Quarterly* 17.4 (1989): 281–84.

Makowsky, Veronica. *Susan Glaspell's Century of American Women: A Critical Interpretation of Her Work*. New York: Oxford UP, 1993.

Mustazza, Leonard. "Generic Translation and Thematic Shift in Susan Glaspell's *Trifles* and 'A Jury of Her Peers.'" *Studies in Short Fiction* 26.4 (1989): 489–96.

Noe, Marcia. "Region as Metaphor in the Plays of Susan Glaspell." *Western Illinois Regional Studies* 4.1 (1981): 77–85.

——. "Reconfiguring the Subject/Recuperating Realism: Susan Glaspell's Unseen Woman." *American Drama* 4.2 (1995): 36–54.

Oziebolo, Barbara. "Rebellion and Rejection: The Plays of Susan Glaspell." *Modern American Drama: The Female Canon.* Ed. June Schlueter. Rutherford: Fairleigh Dickinson UP, 1990.

Oziebol, Barbara. "Susan Glaspell." *American Drama.* Ed. Clive Bloom. New York: St. Martin's, 1995. 6–20.

Papke, Mary E. *Susan Glaspell: A Research and Production Sourcebook.* Westport, CT: Greenwood, 1993.

Russell, Judith K. "Glaspell's *Trifles.*" *Explicator* 55.2 (1997): 88–90.

LADY GREGORY (ISABELLA AUGUSTA GREGORY)

Adams, Hazard. *Lady Gregory.* Lewisburg: Bucknell UP, 1973.

Conlon, John J. "Shaw, Lady Gregory and the Abbey: A Correspondence and A Record." *English Literature in Transition 1880–1920.* 40.3 (1997): 345–47.

Coxhead, Elizabeth. *Lady Gregory: A Literary Portrait.* New York: Harcourt, 1961.

Gregory, Lady. *Lady Gregory's Diaries, 1892–1902.* New York: Oxford UP, 1996.

——. *Lady Gregory's Journals, 1910–1930.* New York: Oxford UP, 1978.

——. *Our Irish Theatre.* Gerrards Cross: Smythe, 1972.

Kiberg, Declan. *Inventing Ireland: The Literature of the Modern Nation.* London: Vintage, 1996.

Kohfeldt, Mary Lou. *Lady Gregory: The Woman Behind the Irish Renaissance.* New York: Atheneum, 1985.

Kopper, E. A., Jr. "Lady Gregory's *The Rising of the Moon.*" *Explicator* 47 (1989): 29–31.

Lenox-Conyngham, Melosina. *Diaries of Ireland: An Anthology, 1590–1987.* Dublin: Lilliput, 1998.

Maxwell, D. E. S. *A Critical History of Modern Irish Drama: 1891–1980.* New York: Cambridge UP, 1984.

O'Connor, Ulick. *All the Olympians.* New York: Atheneum, 1984.

Owens, C'il'n D., and Joan N. Radner. *Irish Drama: 1900–1980.* Washington: Catholic U of America P, 1990.

Saddlemyer, Ann. *In Defense of Lady Gregory, Playwright.* Dublin: Dolmen, 1966.

——. *Lady Gregory, Fifty Years After.* Totowa: Barnes, 1987.

LORRAINE HANSBERRY

Ashley, Leonard R. "Lorraine Hansberry and the Great Black Way." *Modern American Drama: The Female Canon.* Ed. June Schlueter. Rutherford: Fairleigh Dickinson UP, 1990. 151–60.

Carter, Steven R. *Hansberry's Drama: Commitment and Complexity.* Urbana: U of Illinois P, 1991.

Cheney, Anne. *Lorraine Hansberry.* Boston: Twayne, 1984.

Freedman, Morris. *American Drama in Social Context.* Carbondale: Southern Illinois UP, 1971.

Keyssar, Helene. "Rites and Responsibilities: The Drama of Black American Women." *The New Women Playwrights.* Ed. Enoch Brater and Ruby Cohn. Oxford: Oxford UP, 1989. 226–40.

Kodat, Catherine Gunther. "Confusion in a Dream Deferred: Context and Culture in Teaching *A Raisin in the Sun.*" *Studies in the Literary Imagination* 31.1 (1998): 149–64.

Leeson, Richard M. *Lorraine Hansberry: A Research and Production Sourcebook.* Westport, CT: Greenwood, 1997.

McKelly, James C. "Hymns of Sedition: Portraits of the Artist in Contemporary African-American Drama." *Arizona Quarterly* 48.1 (1992): 87–107.

Scheader, Catherine. *Lorraine Hansberry: Playwright and Voice of Justice.* Springfield, NJ: Enslow, 1998.

——. *They Found a Way: Lorraine Hansberry.* Chicago: Children's, 1978.

Schlueter, June, ed. *Modern American Drama: The Female Canon.* Rutherford: Fairleigh Dickinson UP, 1990.

Seaton, Sandra. "*A Raisin in the Sun*: A Study in Afro-American Culture." *Midwestern Miscellany* 20 (1992): 40–49.

Sinnott, Susan. *Lorraine Hansberry: Award-Winning Playwright and Civil Rights Activist.* Berkeley: Conari P, 1999.

Washington, J. Charles. "*A Raisin in the Sun* Revisited." *Black American Literature Forum* 22.1 (1988): 109–24.

Weales, Gerald. "Lorraine Hansberry." *Contemporary Dramatists.* Ed. D. L. Kirkpatrick. 4th ed. Chicago: St. James, 1988. 653–54.

Wilkerson, Margaret B. "Excavating Our History: The Importance of Biographies of Women of Color." *Black American Forum* 24.1 (1990): 73–84.

Williams, Mance. *Black Theatre in the 1960s and 1970s.* Westport: Greenwood, 1985.

HROSVITHA

Carlson, Marvin. "Impassive Bodies: Hrotsvit Stages Martyrdom." *Theatre Journal* 50.4 (1998): 473–87.

Schmitt, Miriam. "Hrotsvit: Medieval Playwright." *Medieval Women Monastics: Wisdom's Wellsprings.* Ed. Miriam Schmitt and Linda Kulzer. Collegeville, MN: Liturgical Press, 1996.

Wilson, Katharine M. *Hrotsvit of Gandersheim: The Ethics of Authorial Stance.* New York: Brill, 1988.

————. *Hrotsvit of Gandersheim: Rara Avis in Saxonia? A Collection of Essays.* Ann Arbor: MARC, 1987.

Zeydel, Edwin H. "Hrotsvit von Gandersheim and the Eternal Womanly." *Studies in the German Drama: A Festschrift in Honor of Walter Silz.* Chapel Hill: U of North Carolina P, 1974. 1–14.

DAVID HENRY HWANG

Cooperman, Robert. "Across the Boundaries of Cultural Identity: An Interview with David Henry Hwang." *Staging Difference: Cultural Pluralism in American Theatre and Drama.* Ed. Marc Maufort. New York: Peter Lang, 1995.

DiGaetani, John Louis. "*M. Butterfly:* An Interview with David Henry Hwang." *The Drama Review* 33.3 (Fall 1989): 141–53.

Frockt, Deborah. "David Henry Hwang." *The Playwright's Art: Conversations with Contemporary American Dramatists.* Ed. Jackson Bryer. New Brunswick, NJ: Rutgers UP, 1995. 123–46.

Hwang, David Henry. "Evolving a Multicultural Tradition." *MELUS* 16.3 (1989–90): 16–19.

Lyons, Bonnie. "'Making His Muscles Work for Himself': An Interview with David Henry Hwang." *The Literary Review* 42.2 (1999): 230–44.

Saal, Ilka. "Performance and Perception: Gender, Sexuality, and Culture in David Henry Hwang's *M. Butterfly.*" *American Studies* 43.4 (1998): 629–44.

Skloot, Robert. "Breaking the Butterfly: The Politics of David Henry Hwang." *Modern Drama* 33.1 (1990): 59–66.

Street, Douglas. *David Henry Hwang.* Western Writers Series no. 90. Boise: Boise State U, 1989.

Trudeau, Lawrence. *Asian American Literature: Reviews and Criticism of Works by American Writers of Asian Descent.* Detroit: Gale Research, 1999.

HENRIK IBSEN

List of Plays

Catiline, 1850
Grouse in Justedal, 1850
The Burial Mound, 1850
Norma, 1851
St. John's Eve, 1853
Lady Inger of Østraat, 1855
The Feast at Solhoug, 1856
Olaf Liljekrans, 1857
The Vikings at Helgeland, 1857
Love's Comedy, 1862
The Pretenders, 1864
Brand, 1866
Peer Gynt, 1867
The League of Youth, 1869

Emperor and Galilean, 1873
The Pillars of Society, 1877
A Doll House, 1879
Quicksands, 1880
Ghosts, 1881
The Child Wife, 1882
An Enemy of the People, 1882
The Wild Duck, 1884
Rosmersholm, 1886
The Lady from the Sea, 1888
Hedda Gabler, 1890
The Master Builder, 1892
Little Eyolf, 1894
John Gabriel Borkman, 1896
When We Dead Awaken, 1899

Ackerman, Gretchen P. *Ibsen and the English Stage, 1889–1903.* New York: Garland, 1987.

Chamberlain, John S. *Ibsen: The Open Vision.* London: Athlone, 1982.

Egan, Michael, ed. *Ibsen: The Critical Heritage.* London: Routledge, 1972.

Ferguson, Robert. *Henrik Ibsen: A New Biography.* London, R. Cohen, 1996.

Fjelde, Rolf, ed. *Ibsen: A Collection of Critical Essays.* Englewood Cliffs: Prentice, 1965.

Gaskell, Ronald. *Drama and Reality: The European Theatre since Ibsen.* London: Routledge, 1972.

Goldman, Michael. *Ibsen: The Dramaturgy of Fear.* New York: Columbia UP, 1999.

Lebowitz, Naomi. *Ibsen and the Great World.* Baton Rouge: Louisiana UP, 1990.

Marker, Frederick J. *Ibsen's Lively Art: A Performance Study of the Major Plays.* New York: Cambridge UP, 1989.

McFarlane, James, ed. *Discussions of Henrik Ibsen.* Boston: Heath, 1962.

Meyer, Michael, *Henrik Ibsen: A Biography.* 3 vols. Garden City: Doubleday, 1971.

Noreng, Harald, et al., eds. *Contemporary Approaches to Ibsen.* Oslo: Universitetsforlaget, 1977.

Northam, John. *Ibsen: A Critical Study.* Cambridge: Cambridge UP, 1973.

Shaw, Bernard. *The Quintessence of Ibsenism.* New York: Hill, 1957.

Shepherd-Barr, Kirsten. *Ibsen and Early Modernist Theatre, 1890–1900.* Westport, CT: Greenwood, 1997.

Theoharis, Theoharis Constantine. *Ibsen's Drama: Right Action and Tragic Joy.* New York: St. Martin's, 1996.

Thomas, David. *Henrik Ibsen.* New York: Grove, 1984.

A Doll House

Andreas-Salomé, Lou. *Ibsen's Heroines.* Ed. and trans. Siegfried Mandel. Austrian/German Culture Series. Redding Ridge, CT: Black Swan, 1985.

Bradbrook, M. C. "*A Doll's House* and the Unweaving of the Web." *Women and Literature, 1779–1982.* Vol. 2. Totowa: Barnes, 1982. 81–92. 2 vols.

Drake, David B. "Ibsen's *A Doll House.*" *Explicator* 53.1 (1994): 32–34.

Durbach, Errol. A Doll's House: *Ibsen's Myth of Transformation.* Boston: Twayne, 1991.

Ibsen, Henrik. "*Doll's House*" [Ibsen's notes on *A Doll House*]. *Playwrights on Playwriting.* Ed. Toby Cole. New York: Hill, 1960. 151–54.

Mitchell, Hayley R. *Readings on* A Doll's House. San Diego: Greenhaven, 1999.

Sprinchorn, E. M. "Ibsen and the Actors." *Ibsen and the Theatre.* Ed. Errol Durbach. New York: New York UP, 1980. 118–30.

Tornqvist, Egil. "Comparative Performance Semiotics: The End of Ibsen's *A Doll House.*" Theatre Research International 19.2 (1994): 156–164.

Hedda Gabler

Ackley, Katherine Anne. "A Rage to Live: The Violent Life and Death of Hedda Gabler." *Women and Violence in Literature: An Essay Collection.* Ed. Katherine Anne Ackley. New York: Garland, 1990. 163–73.

Braunmuller, A. R. "*Hedda Gabler* and the Sources of Symbolism." *Drama and Symbolism.* Ed. James Redmond. New York: Cambridge UP, 1982. 57–70.

Durbach, Erol. "Ibsenian Uterus, Strindbergian Seed: Ingmar Bergman's *Hedda Gabler.*" *Essays in Théâtre-Études Théâtrales* 12.1 (1993): 41–49.

Farfan, Penny. "From *Hedda Gabler* to *Votes for Women*: Elizabeth Robin's Early Feminist Critique of Ibsen." *Theatre Journal* 48.1 (1996): 59–78.

Fuchs, Elinor. "Mythic Structure in *Hedda Gabler*: The Mask behind the Face." *Comparative Drama* 19.3 (1985): 209–21.

Ibsen, Henrik. "*Hedda Gabler*" [Ibsen's notes on *Hedda Gabler*]. *Playwrights on Playwriting.* Ed. Toby Cole. New York: Hill, 1960. 156–70.

Low, Lisa Elaine. "In Defense of Hedda." *Massachusetts Studies in English* 8.3 (1982): 43–49.

Lyons, Charles R. Hedda Gabler: *Gender, Role, and World.* Boston: Twayne, 1991.

Norseng, Mary K. "Suicide and Ibsen's *Hedda Gabler*: The Seen and the Unseen, Sight and Site, in the Theater of the Mind." *Scandinavian Studies* 71.1 (1999): 1–40.

Olsen, Stein Haugom. "Why Does Hedda Gabler Marry Jorgen Tesman?" *Modern Drama* 28 (1985): 591–610.

Suzman, Janet. "*Hedda Gabler*: The Play in Performance." *Ibsen and the Theatre.* Ed. Errol Durbach. New York: New York UP, 1980. 83–104.

Watson, George J. "Ibsen and Miller: The Individual and Society." *Drama: An Introduction.* New York: St. Martin's, 1983. 112–31.

EUGÈNE IONESCO

Gaensbauer, Deborah B. *Eugène Ionesco Revisited.* New York: Twayne, 1996.

Jacquart, Emmanuel. "Ionesco and the Creative Drive." *Nottingham French Studies* 35.1 (1996): 74–86.

Kluback, William, and Michael Finkenthal. *The Clown in the Agora: Conversations about Eugène Ionesco.* Bern: Lang, 1998.

Lamont, Rosette C. *Ionesco: A Collection of Critical Essays.* Englewood Cliffs: Prentice, 1973.

———. *Ionesco's Imperatives: The Politics of Culture.* Ann Arbor: U of Michigan P, 1993.

———, Melvin Friedman, and Henri Peyre, eds. *The Two Faces of Ionesco.* Troy: Whitston, 1978.

Lane, Nancy. *Understanding Eugène Ionesco.* Columbia: U of South Carolina P, 1994.

McGuinness, Patrick. "Ionesco and Symbolist Theatre: Revolution and Restitution in the Avant-Garde." *Nottingham French Studies* 35.1 (1996): 108–19.

BEN JONSON

Butler, Martin, ed. *Re-presenting Ben Jonson: Text, History, Performance.* New York: St. Martin's, 1999.

Floyd-Wilson, Mary. "Temperature, Temperance, and Racial Difference in Ben Jonson's *The Masque of Blackness.*" *English Literary Renaissance* 28.2 (1998): 183–209.

Hirsh, James, ed. *New Perspectives on Ben Jonson.* Madison, NJ: Fairleigh Dickinson UP, 1997.

Orgel, Stephen. *Marginal Jonson.* Cambridge: Cambridge UP, 1998.

Sanders, Julie. *Ben Jonson's Theatrical Republics.* Basingstoke: Macmillan, 1998.

———, ed., with Kate Chedgzoy and Susan Wiseman. *Refashioning Ben Jonson: Gender, Politics, and the Jonsonian Canon.* New York: St. Martin's, 1998.

Summers, Claude J. *Ben Jonson Revised.* New York: Twayne, 1999.

Watson, Robert N. *Critical Essays on Ben Jonson.* New York: Hall, 1997.

TONY KUSHNER

Arons, Wendy. "'Preaching to the Converted?' 'You Couldn't Possibly Do Any Better!': An Interview with Tony Kushner. *Communications from the International Brecht Society* 23.2 (1994): 51–59.

Fisher, James. "'The Angels of Fructification': Tennessee Williams, Tony Kushner, and Images of Homosexuality on the American Stage." *Mississippi Quarterly* 49.1 (1995–96): 13–32.

Geis, Deborah R., and Steven F. Kuger, eds. *Approaching the Millennium: Essays on Angels in America.* Ann Arbor: U of Michigan P, 1997.

Kiefer, Daniel. "*Angels in America* and the Failure of Revelation." *American Drama* 4.1 (1994): 21–38.

Lowenthal, Michael. "On Art, Angels, and 'Postmodern Fascism.'" *Harvard Gay and Lesbian Review* 2.2 (1995): 10–12.

Posnock, Ross. "Roy Cohn in America." *Raritan* 13.3 (1994): 64–77.

Quinn, John R. "Corpus Juris Terium: Redemptive Jurisprudence in *Angels in America.*" *Theatre Journal* 48.1 (1996): 79–90.

Rogoff, Gordon. "*Angels in America*, Devils in the Wings." *Theater* 24.2 (1993): 21–29.

Savran, David. "Tony Kushner." *Speaking on Stage: Interviews with Contemporary American Playwrights.* Ed. Philip C. Kolin and Colby H. Kullman. Tuscaloosa: U of Alabama P, 1996. 291–313.

———. "Tony Kushner Considers the Longstanding Problems of Virtue and Happiness." *American Theatre* 11.8 (1994): 20–27+.

Steyn, Mark. "Communism Is Dead: Long Live the King." *New Criterion*: 13.6 (1995): 49–53.

Vorlicky, Robert, and Tony Kushner, eds. *Tony Kushner in Conversation.* Ann Arbor: U of Michigan P, 1998.

FEDERICO GARCÍA LORCA

Anderson, Andrew. "On Broadway, Off Broadway: García Lorca and the New York Theatre, 1929–1930." *Gestos* 8.16 (1993): 135–48.

Colecchia, Francesca. "A Selected Bibliography of Studies on Garcia Lorca's *La casa de Bernarda Alba.*" *Estreno-Cuadernos del Teatro Espa–ol Contemporaneo* 21.2 (1995): 39–41.

Dempsey, Andrew, ed. *A Life of Lorca: Drawings, Photographs, Words.* Norwich: U of East Anglia, 1997.

Duran, Manuel, and Francesca Colecchia, eds. *Lorca's Legacy: Essays on Lorca's Life, Poetry, and Theatre.* New York: Lang, 1991.

Fitzpatrick, Tim, and Sean Batten. "Watching the Watchers Watch: Some Implications of Audience Attention Patterns." *Gestos* 6.12 (1991): 11–31.

Gabriele, John P. "Of Mothers and Freedom: Adela's Struggle for Freedom in *La Casa de Bernardo Alba.*" *Symposium* 47.3 (1993): 188–99.

Handley, Sharon. "Garcia-Lorca: Poet of the Inmensa-Minora? Or Voice of the Andalusian Pueblo?" *Critica Hispanica* 18.2 (1996): 298–312.

Harvard, Robert, ed. *Lorca: Poet and Playwright.* Cardiff: U of Wales, 1992.

Hoeg, Jerry. "Steps to an Ecology of *La casa de Bernarda Alba.*" *Revista de Estudios Hispanicos* 30.1 (1996): 81–101.

Klein, Dennis A. *Blood Wedding, Yerma, and The House of Bernarda Alba: García Lorca's Tragic Trilogy.* Boston: Twayne, 1991.

Lanters, Jose. "The Theatre of Thomas Murphy and Federico García Lorca." *Modern Drama* 36.4 (1993): 481–89.

Parilla, Catherine Arturi. *A Theory for Reading Dramatic Texts: Selected Texts by Pirandello and García Lorca.* New York: Lang, 1995.

Podol, Peter L. "*La Casa de Bernarda Alba* in Performance: Three Productions in Three Media." *Estreno-Cuadernos del Teatro Español Contemporaneo* 21.2 (1995): 42–44.

Rees, Margaret A., ed. *Leeds Papers on Hispanic Drama.* Leeds: Trinity and All Saints College, 1991.

Soufas, C. Christopher. *Audience and Authority in the Modernist Theater of Federico Garcia Lorca.* Tuscaloosa: U of Alabama P, 1996.

———. "Dialectics of Vision: Pictorial vs. Photographic Representation in Lorca's *La Casa de Bernarda Alba.*" *Ojancano* 5 (1991): 52–66.

Wellington, Beth. *Reflections on Lorca's Private Mythology:* Once Five Years Pass *and the Rural Plays.* New York: Lang, 1993.

DAVID MAMET

Almansi, Guido. "David Mamet: A Virtuoso of Invective." *Critical Angles: European Views of Contemporary American Literature.* Ed. Marc Chenetier. Carbondale: Southern Illinois UP, 1986.

Blumberg, Marcia. "Eloquent Stammering in the Fog: O'Neill's Heritage in Mamet." *Perspectives on O'Neill: New Essays.* Ed. Shyamal Bagchee. Victoria: U of Victoria P, 1988. 97–111.

Dean, Anne. *David Mamet: Language as Dramatic Action.* Rutherford: Fairleigh Dickinson UP, 1990.

Esche, Edward J. "David Mamet." *American Drama.* Ed. Clive Bloom. New York: St. Martin's, 1995. 165–77.

Hubert, Liebler Pascale. "Dominance and Anguish: The Teacher-Student Relationship in the Plays of David Mamet." *Modern Drama* 31.4 (1988): 557–70.

Jacobs, Dorothy H. "Working Worlds in David Mamet's Dramas." *Midwestern Miscellany* 14 (1986): 47–57.

Kane, Leslie, ed. *David Mamet: A Casebook.* New York: Garland, 1991.

———. *Weasels and Wisemen: Ethics and Ethnicity in the Work of David Mamet.* Basingstoke: Macmillan, 1999.

Lundon, Edward. "Mamet and Mystery." *Publications of the Mississippi Philological Association* (1988): 106–14.

MacLeod, Christine. "The Politics of Gender, Language and Hierarchy in Mamet's *Oleanna.*" *Journal of American Studies* 29.2 (1995): 199–213.

Maufort, Marc. "Narrative Patterns in the Plays of David Mamet." *BELL* (1991): 112–19.

McDonough, Carla J. "Every Fear Hides a Wish: Unstable Masculinity in Mamet's Drama." *Theatre Journal* 44.2 (1992): 195–205.

———. *Staging Masculinity: Male Identity in Contemporary American Drama.* Jefferson, NC: McFarland, 1997.

Mufson, Daniel. "The Critical Eye: Sexual Perversity in *Viragos.*" *Theater* 24.1 (1993): 111–13.

Price, Steven. "AT&T: Anxiety, Telecommunications and the Theatre of David Mamet." *Cynos* 12.1 (1995): 59–67.

Roudané, Matthew. "David Mamet." *Speaking on Stage: Interviews with Contemporary American Playwrights.* Ed. Philip C. Kolin and Colby H. Kullman. Tuscaloosa: U of Alabama P, 1996.

———. "An Interview with David Mamet." *Studies in American Drama 1945–Present* 1 (1986): 73–81.

Walker, Craig Stewart. "Three Tutorial Plays: *The Lesson, The Prince of Naples* and *Oleana.*" *Modern Drama* 40.1 (1997): 149–62.

Zinman, Toby Silerman. "Jewish Aporia: The Rhythm of Talking in Mamet." *Theatre Journal* 44.2 (1992): 207–15.

CHRISTOPHER MARLOWE

Bartels, Emily C. "Authorizing Subversion: Strategies of Power in Marlowe's *Doctor Faustus.*" *Renaissance Papers* (1989): 65–74.

———, ed. *Critical Essays on Christopher Marlowe.* New York: Prentice, 1997.

Birrenger, Johannes. "Between Body and Language: 'Writing' *The Damnation of Faust.*" *Theatre Journal* 36.3 (1984): 301–20.

Bloom, Harold, ed. *Christopher Marlowe.* New York: Chelsea, 1986.

———. *Christopher Marlowe's* Doctor Faustus. New York: Chelsea, 1988.

Cole, Douglas. *Suffering and Evil in the Plays of Christopher Marlowe.* Princeton: Princeton UP, 1962.

Cox, John D. "Devils and Power in Marlowe and Shakespeare." *Yearbook of English Studies* 23 (1993): 46–64.

Cutts, John P. *The Left Hand of God.* Haddonfield, NJ: Haddonfield, 1973.

Ellis-Fermor, Una Mary. *Christopher Marlowe.* Hamden, CT: Anchor, 1967.

Farnham, Willard, comp. *Twentieth-Century Interpretation of Doctor Faustus: A Collection of Critical Essays.* Englewood Cliffs: Prentice, 1969.

Friedenreich, Kenneth, Roma Gill, and Constance Kuriyama, eds. *New Essays on Christopher Marlowe.* New York: AMS, 1988.

Godshalk, W. L. *The Marlovian World Picture.* The Hague: Mouton, 1974.

Golden, Kenneth. "Myth, Psychology and Marlowe's *Doctor Faustus.*" *College Literature* 12.3 (1985): 202–10.

Honigmann, Ernst. "Ten Problems in *Doctor Faustus.*" *The Arts of Performance in Elizabethan and Early Stuart Drama.* Ed. Murray Biggs et al. Edinburgh: Edinburgh UP, 1991. 173–191.

Jones, John Henry, ed. *The English Faust Book: A Critical Edition Based on the Text of 1592.* Cambridge: Cambridge UP, 1994.

Jones, Louise Conley. "A Textual Analysis of Marlow's *Doctor Faustus* with Director's Book: Stage Action as Metaphor." *Studies in Renaissance Literature* 12. Lewiston: Mellen, 1996.

Keefer, Michael H. "History and the Canon: The Case of *Doctor Faustus.*" *University of Toronto Quarterly* 56.4 (1987): 498–522.

Leech, Clifford, ed. *Marlowe: A Collection of Critical Essays.* Englewood Cliffs: Prentice, 1964.

Levin, Harry. *The Overreacher, A Study of Christopher Marlowe.* Boston: Beacon, 1964.

Marlowe, Christopher. *Complete Plays.* Ed., intro, and notes Irving Ribner. New York: Odyssey, 1963.

McAlindon, T. Doctor Faustus: *Divine in Show.* New York: Twayne, 1994.

Muir, Kenneth. "Three Marlowe Texts (*Doctor Faustus, The Jew of Malta* and *The Massacre at Paris*)." *Notes and Queries* 43.2 (1996): 142–44.

Ricks, Christopher. "*Doctor Faustus* and Hell on Earth." *Essays in Criticism* 35.2 (1985): 101–20.

Roberts, Peter, and Darryll Grantley, eds. *Christopher Marlowe and English Renaissance Culture.* Aldershot, UK: Ashgate, 1999.

Steane, J. B. *Marlowe: A Critical Study.* Cambridge: Cambridge UP, 1964.

Stover, David F. "The Individualism of *Doctor Faustus.*" *North Dakota Quarterly* 57.4 (1989): 146–61.

Wilson, Richard, ed. *Christopher Marlowe.* Longman Critical Readers. London: Longman, 1999.

ARTHUR MILLER

Anderson, M. C. "*Death of a Salesman*: A Consideration of Willy Loman's Role in Twentieth-Century Tragedy." *CRUX* 20.2 (1986): 25–29.

Babcock, Granger. "'What's the Secret?': Willy Loman as Desiring Machine." *American Drama* 2.1 (1992): 59–83.

Balakian, Jan. "Arthur Miller." *Speaking on Stage: Interviews with Contemporary American Playwrights.* Ed. Philip C. Kolin and Colby H. Kullman. Tuscaloosa: U of Alabama P, 1996. 40–57.

Bigsby, Christopher W. E. *Arthur Miller.* Cambridge Companions to Literature. Cambridge: Cambridge UP, 1997.

Bloom, Harold. *Arthur Miller.* Philadelphia: Chelsea, 1999.

———, ed. *Arthur Miller's* Death of a Salesman. New York: Chelsea, 1988.

———. *Willy Loman.* New York: Chelsea, 1990.

Brucher, Richard T. "Willy Loman and the Soul of a New Machine: Technology and the Common Man." *Journal of American Studies* 17.3 (1983): 325–36.

Carson, Neil. *Arthur Miller.* London: Macmillan; 1982.

Centola, Steven R. "Family Values in *Death of a Salesman.*" *College Language Association Journal* 37.1 (1993): 29–41.

Corrigan, Robert W., ed. *Arthur Miller: A Collection of Critical Essays.* Englewood Cliffs: Prentice, 1969.

Goldstein, Laurence, ed. "Aurthur Miller." *Michigan Quarterly Review* 37.4 [Special Issue] (1998).

Griffin, Alice. *Understanding Arthur Miller.* Columbia: U of South Carolina P, 1996.

Hadomi, Leah. "Fantasy and Reality: Dramatic Rhythm in *Death of a Salesman.*" *Modern Drama* 31.2 (1988): 157–74.

Harder, Harry. "*Death of a Salesman:* An American

Classic." *Censored Books: Critical Viewpoints.* Ed. Nicholas J. Karolides, Lee Burress, and John M. Kean. Metuchen, NJ: Scarecrow, 1993.

Hayman, Ronald. *Arthur Miller.* New York: Ungar, 1972.

Huftel, Sheila. *Arthur Miller: The Burning Glass.* New York: Citadel, 1965.

Jenckes, Norma, ed. "Arthur Miller." *American Drama* 6.1 [Special Issue] (1996).

Koon, Helene Wickham. Twentieth Century Interpretations of *Death of a Salesman.* Englewood Cliffs: Prentice, 1983.

Martin, Robert A., ed. *Arthur Miller: New Perspectives.* Englewood Cliffs: Prentice, 1982.

———. "The Nature of Tragedy in Arthur Miller's *Death of a Salesman.*" *South Atlantic Review* 61.4 (1996): 97–106.

Miller, Arthur. *Collected Plays.* New York: Viking, 1957.

———. *The Theater Essays of Arthur Miller.* Ed. and intro. Robert A. Martin. New York: Viking, 1978.

———. *Timebends: A Life.* New York: Grove, 1987.

Murphy, Brenda. "Arthur Miller: Revisioning Realism." *Realism and the American Dramatic Tradition.* Ed. William W. Demastes. Tuscaloosa: U of Alabama P, 1996. 189–202.

Roudane, Matthew C., ed. *Conversations with Arthur Miller.* Jackson: UP of Mississippi, 1987.

Schlueter, June, and James K. Flanagan. *Arthur Miller.* New York: Ungar, 1987.

Schockley, John S. "*Death of a Salesman* and American Leadership: Life Imitates Art." *Journal of American Culture* 17.2 (1994): 49–56.

Siebold, Thomas, ed. *Readings on Arthur Miller.* San Diego: Greenhaven, 1997.

———, ed. *Readings on Death of a Salesman.* San Diego: Greenhaven, 1999.

Stanton, Kay. "Women and the American Dream of *Death of a Salesman.*" *Feminist Rereadings of Modern American Drama.* Ed. June Schlueter. Rutherford: Fairleigh Dickinson UP, 1989.

MOLIÈRE (JEAN BAPTISTE POQUELIN)

Bermel, Albert. *Molière's Theatrical Bounty: A New View of the Plays.* Carbondale: Southern Illinois UP, 1990.

Edney, David. "Molière in North America: Problems of Translation and Adaptation." *Modern Drama* 41.1 (1998): 60–76.

Gaines, James F., and Michael S. Koppisch eds. *Approaches to Teaching Molière's Tartuffe and Other Plays.* New York: Modern Language Association of America, 1995.

———. *Molière's Theater.* Columbus: Ohio State UP, 1984.

Gaston Hall, H. "Molière's Roles Written for Himself." *Australian Journal of French Studies* 33 (1996): 414–27.

Gross, Nathan. *From Gesture to Idea: Esthetics and Ethics in Molière's Comedy.* New York: Columbia UP, 1982.

Guicharnaud, Jacques. *Molière: A Collection of Critical Essays.* Englewood Cliffs: Prentice, 1964.

Hall, H. Gaston. *Comedy in Context: Essays on Molière.* Jackson: UP of Mississippi, 1984.

Jagendorf, Zvi. *The Happy End of Comedy: Jonson, Molière, and Shakespeare.* Newark: U of Delaware P, 1984.

Knutson, Harold C. *The Triumph of Wit: Molière and Restoration Comedy.* Columbus: Ohio State UP, 1988.

Lalande, Roxanne Decker. *Intruders in the Play World: The Dynamics of Gender in Molière's Comedies.* Madison, NJ: Fairleigh Dickinson UP, 1996.

Molière. *Tartuffe: Comedy in Five Acts.* Trans. Richard Wilbur. New York: Harcourt, 1963.

Spingler, Michael, ed. *Molière Today.* Amsterdam: Harwood, 1997.

Walker, Hallam. *Molière.* Rev. ed. Boston: Twayne, 1990.

MARSHA NORMAN

Betsko, Kathleen, and Rachel Koenig. "Marsha Norman." *Interviews with Contemporary Women Playwrights.* New York: Beech Tree, 1987.

Browder, Sally. " 'I Thought You Were Mine': Marsha Norman's *'night, Mother.*" *Mother Puzzles: Daughters and Mothers in Contemporary American Literature.* Ed. Mickey Pearlman. Westport, CT: Greenwood, 1989.

Brown, Linda Ginter, ed. *Marsha Norman: A Casebook.* New York: Garland, 1996.

Brustein, Robert. "Robert Brustein on Theater." *New Republic* 2 May 1983: 25–26.

Burkman, Katherine H. "The Demeter Myth and Doubling in Marsha Norman's *'night, Mother.*" *Modern American Drama: The Female Canon.* Ed. June Schlueter. Rutherford: Fairleigh Dickinson UP, 1990. 254–63.

Demastes, William. "Jessie and Thelma Revisited: Conceptual Challenge in *'night, Mother.*" *Modern Drama* 36.1 (1993): 109–19.

Denby, David. "Stranger in a Strange Land." *Atlantic* Jan. 1985: 44–45.

DiGaetani, John L., ed. *A Search for a Postmodern Theater: Interviews with Contemporary Playwrights.* New York: Greenwood, 1991.

Forte, Jeanie. "Realism, Narrative and the Feminist Playwright: A Problem of Perception." *Modern Drama* 32.1 (1989): 115–27.

Greiff, Louis K. "Fathers, Daughters, and Spiritual Sisters: Marsha Norman's *'night, Mother* and Tennessee Williams's *The Glass Menagerie.*" *Text and Performance Quarterly* 9.3 (1989): 224–28.

Hart, Lynda. "Doing Time: Hunger for Power in Marsha Norman's Plays." *Southern Quarterly* 25.3 (1987): 67–69.

Kane, Leslie. "The Way Out, the Way In: Paths to Self in the Plays of Marsha Norman." *Feminine Focus: The New Women Playwrights*. Ed. Enoch Brater and Ruby Cohn. Oxford: Oxford UP, 1989. 255–74.

Porter, Laurin R. "Women Re-Conceived: Changing Perceptions of Women in Contemporary American Drama." *Conference of College Teachers of English Studies* 54 (1989): 53–59.

Sauvage, Leo. "Different Kinds of Kin." *New Leader* 18 April 1983: 21–22.

Savran, David. *In Their Own Words*. New York: Theater Communications Group, 1988.

Smith, Raynette Halvorsen. "' *'night, Mother'* and *'True West'*: Mirror Images of Violence and Gender." *Violence in Drama*. Ed. James Redmond. Cambridge: Cambridge UP, 1991.

Spencer, Jenny S. "Norman's *'night, Mother*: Psychodrama of Female Identity." *Modern Drama* 30.3 (1987): 364–75.

Stone, Elizabeth. "Playwright Marsha Norman: An Optimist Writes about Suicide, Confinement, and Despair." *Ms.* July 1983: 56–59.

Weales, Gerald. "Really 'Going On.'" *Commonweal* 17 June 1983: 370–71.

Wolfe, Irmgard H. "Marsha Norman: A Classified Bibliography." *Studies in American Drama, 1945–Present* 3 (1988): 148–75.

EUGENE O'NEILL

Ahuja, Chaman. *Tragedy, Modern Temper, and O'Neill*. Atlantic Highlands: Humanities, 1984.

Berlin, Normand. *Eugene O'Neill*. New York: Grove, 1987.

Black, Stephen A. *Eugene O'Neill: Beyond Mourning and Tragedy*. New Haven: Yale UP, 1999.

Bogard, Travis. *Contour in Time: The Plays of Eugene O'Neill*. New York: Oxford UP, 1988.

Cargill, Oscar, N. Bryllion Fagan, and William J. Fisher, eds. *O'Neill and His Plays: Four Decades of Criticism*. New York: New York UP, 1961.

Cunningham, Frank R. "Eugene O'Neill and Reality in America." *Realism and the American Dramatic Tradition*. Ed. William W. Demastes. Tuscaloosa: U of Alabama P, 1996.

Fleche, Anne. *Mimetic Disillusion: Eugene O'Neill, Tennessee Williams, and U.S. Dramatic Realism*. Tuscaloosa: U of Alabama P, 1997.

Floyd, Virginia. *The Plays of Eugene O'Neill: A New Assessment*. New York: Ungar, 1985.

Frenz, Horst, and Susan Tuck, eds. *Eugene O'Neill's Critics: Voices from Abroad*. Boulder: netLibrary, 1999.

Gallup, Donald. *Eugene O'Neill and His Eleven-Play Cycle: "A Tale of Possessors Self-Possessed."* New Haven: Yale UP, 1998.

Gassner, John, ed. *O'Neill: A Collection of Critical Essays*. Englewood Cliffs: Prentice, 1964.

Leech, Clifford. *Eugene O'Neill*. New York: Grove, 1963.

Manheim, Michael, ed. *Eugene O'Neill*. Cambridge Companions to Literature. Cambridge: Cambridge UP, 1998.

Maufort, Marc, ed. *Eugene O'Neill and the Emergence of American Drama*. Atlanta: Rodopi, 1989.

Miller, Jordan Yale. *Eugene O'Neill and American Criticism: A Bibliographical Checklist*. 2nd ed. Hamden: Anchor, 1973.

Moorton, Richard F., Jr. *Eugene O'Neill's Century: Centennial Views on America's Foremost Critic*. New York: Greenwood, 1991.

Mottram, Eric. "Eugene O'Neill." *American Drama*. Ed. Clive Bloom. New York: St. Martin's, 1995. 21–45.

O'Neill, Eugene. *Long Day's Journey into Night*. New Haven: Yale UP, 1956.

———. *The Plays of Eugene O'Neill*. 3 vols. New York: Modern Library, 1982.

Pacheco, Gilda. "The Female Image in Eugene O'Neill's *Desire under the Elms* and *A Moon for the Misbegotten*." *Revista de Filologia y Linguistica de la Universidad de Costa Rica* 21.1 (1995): 55–63.

Pfister, Joel. *Staging Depth: Eugene O'Neill and the Politics of Psychological Discourse*. Boulder: netLibrary, 1999.

Porter, Laurin. *The Banished Prince: Time, Memory, and Ritual in the Late Plays of Eugene O'Neill*. Ann Arbor: UMI Research, 1988.

Ranald, Margaret Loftus. *The Eugene O'Neill Companion*. Westport, CT: Greenwood, 1984.

Siebold, Thomas. *Readings on Eugene O'Neill*. San Diego: Greenhaven, 1998.

Wainscott, Ronald Harold. *Staging O'Neill: The Experimental Years, 1920–1934*. New Haven: Yale UP, 1988.

SUZAN-LORI PARKS

Bernard, Louise. "The Musicality of Language: Redefining History in Suzan-Lori Parks's *The Death of the Last Black Man in the Whole Entire World*." *African American Review* 31 (1997): 687–97.

Carr, C. "Review of Imperceptible Mutabilities in the Third Kingdom." *Artforum* November 1989: 154.

Gussow, Mel. Review of *The Death of the Last Black Man in the Whole Entire World*. *New York Times* 25 Sept. 1990: C15.

———. Review of Imperceptible Mutabilities in the Third Kingdom. *New York Times* 20 Sept. 1989: C24.

Holden, Stephen. Review of Betting on the Dust Commander. *New York Times* 26 June 1991: C12.

Jiggetts, Shelby. "Interviews with Suzan-Lori Parks." *Callaloo*. 19.2 (1996): 309–17.

Rayner, Alice, and Harry J. Elam, Jr. "Unfinished Business: Reconfiguring History in Suzan-Lori Parks's

The Death of the Last Black Man in the Whole Entire World." *Theatre Journal* 46 (1994): 447–61.

HAROLD PINTER

Aragay, Mireia. "Writing, Politics, and Ashes to Ashes: An Interview with Harold Pinter." *Pinter Review: Annual Essays* (1996).

Barnett, Claudia. "The Metadramatic Prison of *Betrayal.*" *The Pinter Review: Annual Essays* (1992–93):69–72.

Behera, Charan. *Reality and Illusion in the Plays of Harold Pinter.* New Delhi: Atlantic, 1998.

Billington, Michael. *The Life and Work of Harold Pinter.* London: Faber and Faber, 1996.

Bloom, Harold, ed. *Harold Pinter.* New York: Chelsea, 1987.

Bold, Alan, ed. *Harold Pinter: You Never Heard Such Silence.* Critical Studies Series. Totowa: Barnes, 1985.

Burkman, Katherine H. *The Dramatic World of Harold Pinter.* Columbia: Ohio State UP, 1971.

Chevallier, Genevieve, ed. "Harold Pinter." *Cycnos* 14.1 [Special Issue] (1997).

Conklin, Robert. "*Old Times* and *Betrayal* as Rorschach Test." *Pinter Review* (1992–93): 69–72.

Deer, Harriet. "Melodramatic Problematics in Pinter's Film of *Betrayal.*" *Pinter Review* (1990): 61–70.

Diamond, Elin. *Pinter's Comic Play.* Lewisburg: Bucknell UP, 1985.

Dukore, Bernard F. *Harold Pinter.* 2nd ed. New York: Macmillan, 1988.

Esslin, Martin. *Pinter: The Playwright.* New York: Methuen, 1984.

Gale, Steven H., ed. *Critical Essays on Harold Pinter.* Boston: Hall, 1990.

———. "Harold Pinter." *British Playwrights, 1956–1995: A Research and Production Sourcebook.* Ed. William W. Demastes. Westport, CT: Greenwood, 1996. 301–25.

———. *Harold Pinter: Critical Approaches.* Rutherford: Fairleigh Dickinson UP, 1986.

Ganz, Arthur F., ed. *Pinter: A Collection of Critical Essays.* Englewood Cliffs: Prentice, 1979.

Gordon, Lois, ed. *Harold Pinter: A Casebook.* New York: Garland, 1990.

Hayman, Ronald. *Harold Pinter.* New York: Ungar, 1973.

Hinchliffe, Arnold P. *Harold Pinter.* Boston: Twayne, 1981.

Jalote, S. R. *The Plays of Harold Pinter: A Study in Neurotic Anxiety.* New Delhi: Harman House, 1996.

Kerr, Walter. *Harold Pinter.* New York: Columbia UP, 1967.

Knowles, Ronald. *Understanding Harold Pinter.* Columbia: U of South Carolina P, 1995.

Mayberry, Bob. *Theatre of Discord: Dissonance in Beckett, Albee, and Pinter.* Rutherford: Fairleigh Dickinson UP, 1989.

Peacock, D. Keith. *Harold Pinter and the New British Theatre.* Westport, CT: Greenwood, 1997.

Pearce, Howard. "The Doll House in Harold Pinter's *Betrayal.*" *Text and Presentation* 17 (1996): 46–52.

Pinter, Harold. *Complete Works.* 3 vols. New York: Grove, 1977–78.

Quigley, Austin E. *The Pinter Problem.* Princeton: Princeton UP, 1975.

Strunk, Volker. *Harold Pinter: Towards a Poetics of His Plays.* New York: Lang, 1989.

Sykes, Arlene. *Harold Pinter.* New York: Humanities, 1970.

Woodroffe, Graham. "From Kinsale Drive to Wessex Grove: A Psychoanalytical Study of Harold Pinter's *Betrayal.*" *Literature and Psychology* 35.3 (1989): 43–63.

Zeifman, Hersh, and Cynthia Zimmerman, eds. *Contemporary British Drama 1970–90.* Toronto: U of Toronto P, 1993.

LUIGI PIRANDELLO

Bassabesem, Fiora A. *Understanding Luigi Pirandello.* Columbia: U of South Carolina P, 1997.

Bassnett, Susan. *File on Pirandello.* London: Methuen, 1989.

Bassnett-McGuire, Susan. *Luigi Pirandello.* New York: Grove, 1983.

Bentley, Eric. *The Pirandello Commentaries.* Evanston: Northwestern UP, 1986.

Biasin, Gian-Paolo, and Manuela Giere, eds. *Luigi Pirandello: Contemporary Perspectives.* Toronto: U of Toronto P, 1999.

Bloom, Harold. *Luigi Pirandello.* New York: Chelsea, 1989.

Büdel, Oscar. *Pirandello.* New York: Hillary, 1969.

Caesar, Ann. *Characters and Authors in Luigi Pirandello.* Oxford: Clarendon, 1998.

Cambon, Glauco, ed. *Pirandello: A Collection of Critical Essays.* Englewood Cliffs: Prentice, 1967.

Caputi, Anthony. *Pirandello and the Crisis of Modern Consciousness.* Urbana: U of Illinois P, 1988.

Dashwood, Julie R. *Luigi Pirandello: The Theatre of Paradox.* Lewiston: Mellen, 1996.

Guidice, Gaspare. *Pirandello: A Biography.* Trans. Alastair Hamilton. New York: Oxford UP, 1975.

Hornby, Richard. "Three Modern Playwrights (Pirandello, Strindberg, Chekhov)." *Seewanee Review* 105 (1997): 595–99.

Mariani, Umberto. "The 'Pirandellian' Character." *Canadian Journal of Italian Studies* 12.38–39 (1989): 1–9.

Mazzaro, Jerome. "Pirandello's *Sei Personaggi* and Expressive Form." *Comparative Drama* 30 (1996–97): 503–24.

Oliver, Roger W. *Dreams of Passion: The Theater of Luigi Pirandello.* New York: New York UP, 1979.

Paolucci, Anne. *Pirandello's Theater.* Carbondale: Southern Illinois UP, 1974.

Pirandello, Luigi. *Naked Masks, Five Plays*. Ed. Eric Bentley. New York: Dutton, 1952.

———. *Short Stories*. Ed. and trans. Frederick May. New York: Oxford UP, 1965.

Ragusa, Olga. "Comparative Perspectives on Pirandello." *Atenea* 8.1 (1988): 19–36.

Starkie, Walter. *Luigi Pirandello, 1867–1936*. 3rd ed. Berkeley: U of California P, 1965.

Stone, Jennifer. *Pirandello's Naked Prompt: The Structure of Repetition in Modernism*. Ravenna: Longo Editore, 1989.

PLAUTUS

Anderson, William Scovil. *Barbarian Play: Plautus' Roman Comedy*. Toronto: University of Toronto Press, 1996.

Moore, Timothy J. *The Theater of Plautus: Playing to the Audience*. Austin: U of Texas P, 1999.

Segal, Erich. *Roman Laughter: The Comedy of Plautus*. New York: Oxford UP, 1987.

Slater, Niall W. *Plautus in Performance: The Theater of the Mind*. Princeton: Princeton UP, 1985.

YASMINA REZA

Danto, Arthur C. "'*Art*,' from France to the U.S." *Nation* 29 June 1998: 28–31.

SENECA

Fairweather, Janet. *Seneca the Elder*. New York: Cambridge UP, 1981.

Stewart, J. "Challenging Prescriptions for Discourse: Seneca's Use of Paradox and Psymoron." *Mosaic* 30.1 (1997): 1–17.

Tarrant, R. J. *Seneca's* Thyestes. Atlanta: Scholars, 1985.

WILLIAM SHAKESPEARE

List of Plays

Comedies
The Comedy of Errors, 1592–94
The Taming of the Shrew, 1593–94
The Two Gentlemen of Verona, 1594
Love's Labor's Lost, 1594–95
A Midsummer Night's Dream, 1595–96
The Merchant of Venice, 1596–97
The Merry Wives of Windsor, 1597
Much Ado about Nothing, 1598–99
As You Like It, 1599
Twelfth Night, or What You Will, 1601–02
All's Well That Ends Well, 1602–03
Measure for Measure, 1604

Histories
Henry the Sixth, Part One, 1589–90
Henry the Sixth, Part Two, 1590–91

Henry the Sixth, Part Three, 1590–91
Richard the Third, 1592–93
King John, 1594–96
Richard the Second, 1595
Henry the Fourth, Part One, 1596–97
Henry the Fourth, Part Two, 1598
Henry the Fifth, 1599
Henry the Eighth, 1612–13

Tragedies
The Tragedy of Titus Andronicus, 1593
The Tragedy of Romeo and Juliet, 1595–96
The Tragedy of Julius Caesar, 1599
The Tragedy of Hamlet, 1600–01
The History of Troilus and Cressida, 1601–02
The Tragedy of Othello, the Moor of Venice, 1604
The Tragedy of King Lear, 1605
The Tragedy of Macbeth, 1606
The Tragedy of Antony and Cleopatra, 1606
The Tragedy of Coriolanus, 1607
The Life of Timon of Athens, 1607

Romances
Pericles, Prince of Tyre, 1607–08
Cymbeline, 1609–10
The Winter's Tale, 1610–11
The Tempest, 1611
Two Noble Kinsmen, 1613

Bamber, Linda. *Comic Women, Tragic Men: A Study of Gender and Genre in Shakespeare*. Stanford: Stanford UP, 1982.

Barber, C. L. *Shakespeare's Festive Comedy*. Princeton: Princeton UP, 1968.

Bloom, Harold. *Shakespeare: The Invention of the Human*. London: Fourth Estate, 1999.

Bradley, A. C. *Shakespearean Tragedy*. New York: Meridian, 1955.

Bullough, Geoffrey, ed. *Narrative and Dramatic Sources of Shakespeare*. 8 vols. New York: Columbia UP, 1957–75.

Chute, Marchette. *Shakespeare of London*. New York: Dutton, 1949.

Doran, Madeleine. *Shakespeare's Dramatic Language*. Madison: U of Wisconsin P, 1976.

Drakakis, John, ed. *Alternative Shakespeares*. New York: Methuen, 1985.

Dusinberre, Juliet. *Shakespeare and the Nature of Women*. 2nd. ed. New York: St. Martin's, 1996.

Dutton, Richard. *Shakespeare: A Literary Life*. New York: St. Martin's, 1989.

Eagleton, Terry. *William Shakespeare*. New York: Blackwell, 1986.

Erikson, Peter. *Rewriting Shakespeare, Rewriting Ourselves*. Berkeley: U of California P, 1991.

Frye, Northrop. *On Shakespeare*. New Haven: Yale UP, 1986.

Goddard, Harold C. *The Meaning of Shakespeare*. Chicago: U of Chicago P, 1951.

Grady, Hugh. *The Modernist Shakespeare: Critical Texts in a Material World.* New York: Oxford UP, 1991.

Granville-Barker, H. *Prefaces to Shakespeare.* Princeton: Princeton UP, 1946.

Greene, G., et al., eds. *The Women's Part: Feminist Criticism of Shakespeare.* Urbana: U of Illinois P, 1980.

Honan, Park. *Shakespeare: A Life.* Oxford: Oxford UP, 2000.

Hyland, Peter. *An Introduction to Shakespeare: The Dramatist in His Context.* Houndmills, UK: Macmillan, 1996.

Ioppolo, Grace. *Revising Shakespeare.* Cambridge: Harvard UP, 1991.

Jacobus, Lee. *Shakespeare and the Dialectic of Certainty.* New York: St. Martin's Press, 1992.

Jardine, Lisa. *Still Harping on Daughters: Women and Drama in the Age of Shakespeare.* Totowa: Barnes, 1983.

Kermode, Frank, ed. *Four Centuries of Shakespearean Criticism.* New York: Avon, 1974.

Kiernan, Pauline. *Shakespeare's Theory of Drama.* Cambridge: Cambridge UP, 1998.

Kiernan, Ryan, ed. *Shakespeare: Texts and Contexts.* New York: St. Martin's, 1999.

Kott, Jan. *Shakespeare Our Contemporary.* New York: Norton, 1974.

McDonald, Russ. *The Bedford Companion to Shakespeare: An Introduction with Documents.* Boston: Bedford, 1996.

Meagher, John C. *Shakespeare's Shakespeare: How the Plays Were Made.* New York: Continuum, 1997.

Orgel, Stephen and Sean Keilen. *Shakespeare in the Theatre.* Shakespeare: The Critical Complex 8. New York: Garland, 1999.

Righter, Anne. *Shakespeare and the Idea of the Play.* London: Chatto, 1962.

Schoenbaum, Samuel. *William Shakespeare: A Documentary Life.* New York: Oxford UP, 1975.

Schwartz, Murray M., and Coppelia Kahn, eds. *Representing Shakespeare: New Psychoanalytic Essays.* Baltimore: Johns Hopkins UP, 1981.

Scott, Michael. *Shakespeare and the Modern Dramatist.* New York: St. Martin's, 1989.

Shakespeare Quarterly. Annual Bibliography.

Shakespeare Survey 9.

Shellard, Dominic. *William Shakespeare.* The British Library Writers' Lives. New York: Oxford UP, 1998.

Wells, Stanley W., ed. *Shakespeare and Language.* Cambridge: Cambridge UP, 1997.

———, ed. *Shakespeare in the Theatre: An Anthology of Criticism.* Oxford: Clarendon, 1997.

———. *Shakespeare: The Poet and His Plays.* London: Methuen, 1997.

Hamlet

Berkoff, Steven. *I Am Hamlet.* New York: Grove, 1990.

Bloom, Harold, ed. *William Shakespeare's* Hamlet. New York: Chelsea, 1986.

Calderwood, James. *To Be and Not to Be: Negation and Metadrama in* Hamlet. New York: Columbia UP, 1983.

Cantor, Paul A. *Shakespeare,* Hamlet. New York: Cambridge UP, 1989.

Charney, Maurice. Hamlet*'s Fictions.* New York: Routledge, 1988.

Cohen, Michael. Hamlet *in My Mind's Eye.* Athens: U of Georgia P, 1989.

Duffy, Kevin Thomas. *The Elsinor Appeal: People vs.* Hamlet. New York: St. Martin's, 1996.

Frye, Northrop. *Fools of Time: Studies in Shakespearean Tragedy.* Buffalo: U of Toronto P, 1973.

Farley-Hills, David, ed. "Critical Responses to *Hamlet,* 1600–1900." *The Hamlet Collection* 3. New York: AMS, 1999.

Gay, Jean de. "Playing (with) Shakespeare." *New Theatre Quarterly* 14 (1998): 125–38.

Jones, Ernest. *Hamlet and Oedipus.* New York: Norton, 1976.

Lacan, Jacques. "Desire and the Interpretation of Desire in *Hamlet.*" *Literature and Psychoanalysis: The Question of Reading Otherwise.* Ed. Shoshana Felman. Baltimore: Johns Hopkins UP, 1982.

Levin, Harry. *The Question of Hamlet.* New York: Oxford UP, 1959.

Mills, John A. Hamlet *on Stage: The Great Tradition.* Westport, CT: Greenwood, 1985.

Prosser, Eleanor. Hamlet *and Revenge.* Stanford: Stanford UP, 1967.

Ribner, Irving. *Patterns in Shakespearean Tragedy.* New York: Barnes, 1960.

Showalter, Elaine. "Representing Ophelia: Women, Madness, and the Responsibilities of Feminist Criticism." *Shakespeare and the Question of Theory.* Ed. Patricia Parker and Geoffrey Hartman. New York: Methuen, 1985.

Trewin, J. C. *Five and Eighty Hamlets.* New York: New Amsterdam, 1987.

Wilson, John Dover. *What Happens in* Hamlet. Cambridge: Cambridge UP, 1967.

A Midsummer Night's Dream

Bloom, Harold, ed. *William Shakespeare's* A Midsummer Night's Dream. New York: Chelsea, 1987.

Brown, John Russell. *Shakespeare and His Comedies.* London: Methuen, 1968.

Fleissner, Robert F. "Shakespeare's *A Midsummer Night's Dream.*" *Explicator* 55.2 (1997): 72–73.

Garber, Marjorie. *Dream in Shakespeare: From Metaphor to Metamorphosis.* New Haven: Yale UP, 1974.

Girard, Rene. "Myth and Ritual in Shakespeare: *A Midsummer Night's Dream.*" *Textual Strategies: Perspectives in Post-Structuralist Criticism.* Ithaca: Cornell UP, 1979.

Griffiths, Trevor R., ed. *A Midsummer Night's Dream.* Shakespeare in Production. Cambridge: Cambridge UP, 1996.

Hawkes, Terrence. *A Midsummer Night's Dream*. New Casebooks. New York: St. Martin's, 1996.

Hendricks, Margo. "Obscured by Dreams, Race, Empire, and Shakespeare's *A Midsummer Night's Dream*." *Shakespeare Quarterly* 47.1 (1996): 37–60.

Kehler, Dorothea, ed. A Midsummer Night's Dream: *Critical Essays*. New York: Garland, 1998.

Latham, Minor White. *The Elizabethan Fairies: The Fairies of Folklore and the Fairies of Shakespeare*. New York: Columbia UP, 1930.

Legatt, Alexander. A Midsummer Night's Dream: *Shakespeare's Comedy of Love*. London: Methuen, 1974.

Montrose, Louis Adrian. "'Shaping Fantasies': Figurations of Gender and Power in Elizabethan Culture." *Representations* 1.2 (1983): 61–94.

Paster, Gail Kern and Skiles Howard, eds. A Midsummer Night's Dream: *Texts and Contexts*. Boston: Bedford, 1999.

Shelbourne, David. *The Making of* A Midsummer Night's Dream. London: Methuen, 1982.

Wiles, David. "The Carnivalesque in *A Midsummer Night's Dream*." *Shakespeare and Carnival: After Bakhtin*. Ed. Ronald Knowles. New York: St. Martin's, 1998. 61–82.

Young. David P. *Something of Great Constancy: The Art of* A Midsummmer Night's Dream. New Haven: Yale UP, 1966.

Othello

Bernard, J. "Theatricality and Textuality: The Example of *Othello*." *New Literary History* 26 (1995): 931–49.

Ghazoul, Ferial J. The Arabization of *Othello*." *Comparative Literature* 50.1 (1998): 1–31.

Hadfield, Andrew. "Race in *Othello*: The 'History and Description of Africa' and the Black Legend." *Notes and Queries* 45 (1998): 336–38.

Hogan, Patrick C. "*Othello*, Racism, and Despair." *College Language Association Journal* 41 (1998): 431–51.

Honigmann, E. A. J. *The Texts of* Othello *and Shakespearean Revision*. London: Routledge, 1996.

Pechter, Edward. Othello *and Interpretive Traditions*. Iowa City: U of Iowa P, 1999.

Widmayer, M. "Brabantio and Othello." *English Studies* 77.2 (1996): 113–26.

Xiaojing, Zhou. "Othello's Color in Shakespeare's Tragedy." *College Language Association Journal* 41 (1998): 335–48.

BERNARD SHAW

Bentley, Eric. *Bernard Shaw*. 2nd ed. London: Methuen, 1967.

Berst, Charles A. *Bernard Shaw and the Art of Drama*. Urbana: U of Illinois P, 1973.

Bloom, Harold, ed. *George Bernard Shaw*. New York: Chelsea, 1987.

Bloomfield, Zachary. "America's Response to George Bernard Shaw: A Study of Professional Productions." *Theatre Studies* 36 (1991): 5–17.

Bosha, Francis J. "William James's Unpublished Correspondence with Bernard Shaw." *Notes and Queries* 37 (1990): 432–33.

Brown, John Ivor. *Shaw in His Time*. London: Nelson, 1965.

Evans, T. F. *Shaw: The Critical Heritage*. Boston: Routledge, 1976.

Fisher, James. "Edy Craig and the Pioneer Players' Production of *Mrs. Warren's Profession*." *Shaw: The Annual of Bernard Shaw Studies* 15 (1995): 37–56.

Gainor, J. Ellen. "G. B. S. and the New Woman." *New England Theatre Journal* 1.1 (1990): 1–17.

———. *Shaw's Daughters: Dramatic and Narrative Constructions of Gender*. Ann Arbor: U of Michigan P, 1991.

Ganz, Arthur F. *George Bernard Shaw*. New York: Grove, 1983.

Gibbs, A. M. *The Art and Mind of Shaw: Essays in Criticism*. New York: St. Martin's, 1983.

———, ed. *Shaw: Interviews and Recollections*. Iowa City: U of Iowa P, 1990.

Gordon, David J. *Bernard Shaw and the Comic Sublime*. New York: St. Martin's, 1990.

Grecco, Stephen. "Vivie Warren's Profession: A New Look at *Mrs. Warren's Profession*." *Shaw: The Annual of Bernard Shaw Studies* 10 (1967): 93–99.

Greene, Nicholas. *Bernard Shaw: A Critical View*. New York: St. Martin's, 1984.

Hugo, Leon. *Edwardian Shaw: The Writer and His Age*. Basingstoke: Macmillan, 1999.

Innes, Christopher D., ed. *George Bernard Shaw*. Cambridge Companions to Literature. Cambridge: Cambridge UP, 1998.

Kauffmann, Stanley. "The Late Beginner: Bernard Shaw Becoming a Dramatist." *South Atlantic Quarterly* 91.2 (1992): 289–301.

Kaufman, R. J., ed. *G. B. Shaw: A Collection of Critical Essays*. Englewood Cliffs: Prentice, 1965.

Larson, Gale K. *Shaw and History*. University Park: Pennsylvania State UP, 1999.

May, Keith M. *Ibsen and Shaw*. New York: St. Martin's, 1985.

Mudford, Peter. "*Mrs. Warren's Profession*." *The Shavian: The Journal of Bernard Shaw* 6.5 (1987): 4–10.

Peters, Sally. *Bernard Shaw: The Ascent of the Superman*. New Haven: Yale UP, 1996.

Shaw, Bernard. *An Autobiography*. Ed. Stanley Weintraub. 2 vols. New York: Weybright, 1969.

———. *Collected Letters*. Ed. Dan H. Laurence. New York: Dodd, 1972.

———. *Complete Plays with Prefaces*. New York: Dodd, 1962.

———. *Plays and Players: Essays on the Theatre*. Ed. A. C. Ward. New York: Oxford UP, 1963.

———. *Shaw on Shakespeare: An Anthology of Bernard Shaw's Writings on the Plays and Production* of Shakespeare. Ed. Edwin Wilson. New York: Dutton, 1961.

Silver, Arnold. *Bernard Shaw: The Darker Side.* Stanford: Stanford UP, 1982.

Skidelsky, R. "Doing Good and Being Good: The Conflicting Ideals of Bernard Shaw and John Maynard Keynes." *Times Literary Supplement* 26 March 1999: 12–14.

Sterner, Mark H. "The Changing Status of Women in Late Victorian Drama." *Within the Dramatic Spectrum.* Lanham, MD: UP of America, 1986. 199–212.

Turner, Tramble T. *George Bernard Shaw.* Westport: Greenwood, 1997.

Valency, Maurice. *The Cart and the Trumpet: The Plays of George Bernard Shaw.* New York: Schocken, 1983.

Weintraub, Stanley. *The Unexpected Shaw: Biographical Approaches to G.B.S. and His Work.* New York: Ungar, 1982.

Wiley, Catherine. "The Matter with Manners: The New Woman and the Problem Play." *Women in Theatre.* Ed. James Redmond. Cambridge: Cambridge UP, 1989. 109–27.

Wisenthal, J.L. "Wilde, Shaw and the Play of Conversation." *Modern Drama* 37.1 (1994): 206–19.

Yae, Young-soo. "Individual Will and Social Environment in G. B. Shaw's *Mrs. Warren's Profession.*" *Journal of English Language and Literature* 37.1 (1991): 213–32.

Yorks, Samuel A. *The Evolution of Bernard Shaw.* Washington: UP of America, 1981.

SAM SHEPARD

Auerbach, Doris. *Sam Shepard, Arthur Kopit, and the Off-Broadway Theatre.* Twayne's United States Author Series 432. Boston: Twayne, 1982.

Bottoms, Stephen J. *The Theatre of Sam Shepard: States of Crisis.* Cambridge: Cambridge UP, 1998.

Callens, Johan, ed. *Sam Shepard: Between the Margin and the Center.* 2 vols. Contemporary Theatre Review 8, 3–4. Chur, Switz.: Harwood, 1998.

Cohn, Ruby. *New American Dramatists: 1960–1980.* New York: Grove, 1982.

Cott, Jonathan. "The Rolling Stone Interview: Sam Shepard." *Rolling Stone* 18 Dec. 1986–1 Jan. 1987: 166–72+.

Falk, Florence. "The Role of Performance in Sam Shepard's Plays." *Theatre Journal* May 1981: 182–98.

Gilman, Richard. Introduction. *Sam Shepard: Seven Plays.* New York: Bantam, 1981. ix–xiv.

Hart, Lynda. *Sam Shepard's Metaphorical Stages.* Westport, CT: Greenwood, 1987.

King, Kimball, ed. *Sam Shepard: A Casebook.* New York: Garland, 1988.

Lanier, Gregory W. "*True West?* Sam Shepard's Mythic Misdirection." *Text and Presentation* 12 (1992): 49–54.

March, Christie. "The Real and Illusory in Sam Shepard's *True West.*" *The Image of the American West in Literature, the Media, and Society.* Ed. Will Wright and Stephen Kaplan. Pueblo, CO: U of Southern Colorado, 1996. 251–54.

Mottram, Ron. *Inner Landscapes: The Theater of Sam Shepard.* Columbia: U of Missouri P, 1984.

Orbison, Tucker. "Mythic Levels in Sam Shepard's *True West.*" *Modern Drama* 27 (Dec. 1984): 506–19.

Oumano, Ellen. *Sam Shepard: The Life and Work of an American Dreamer.* New York: St. Martin's, 1986.

Sessums, Kevin. "Geography of a Horse Dreamer: Playwright, Actor, and Movie Director Sam Shepard." *Interview* Sept. 1988: 70–78.

Shewey, Don. *Sam Shepard.* 2nd ed. New York: Da Capo, 1997.

St. Pierre, Ronald. " 'True-to-Life-Stuff': Versions of the West in Shepard's *True West.*" *Shoin Literary Review* 29 (1996): 37–50.

Wade, Leslie A. *Sam Shepard and the American Theatre.* Westport, CT: Praeger, 1997.

Williams, Megan. "Nowhere Man and the Twentieth-Century Cowboy: Images of Identity and American History in Sam Shepard's *True West.*" *Modern Drama* 40 (1997): 57–73.

Wilson, Ann. "Fool of Desire: The Spectator to the Plays of Sam Shepard." *Modern Drama* 30.1 (1987): 46–57.

———, ed. *Rereading Shepard: Contemporary Critical Essays on the Plays of Sam Shepard.* New York: St. Martin's, 1993.

SOPHOCLES

List of Plays

(Sophocles wrote in the fifth century B.C. The exact dates for his plays are unknown.)

Oedipus Rex
Antigone
Oedipus at Colonus
Philoctetes
Ajax
Trachiniae
Elektra
Ichneutai
Aleadae

Bloom, Harold, ed. *Sophocles.* New York: Chelsea, 1990.

———, ed. *Sophocles' Oedipus Plays:* Oedipus the King, Oedipus at Colonus, *and* Antigone. Bloom's Notes. Broomhall, PA: Chelsea, 1999.

Bowra, Sir Maurice. *Sophoclean Tragedy.* Oxford: Clarendon, 1944.

Burton, Reginald William Boteler. *The Chorus in Sophocles' Tragedies.* New York: Oxford UP, 1980.

Bushnell, Rebecca. *Prophesying Tragedy: Sign and Voice in Sophocles' Theban Plays.* Ithaca: Cornell UP, 1988.

Buxton, R. G. A. *Sophocles.* New York: Clarendon, 1984.

Gardiner, Cynthia P. *The Sophoclean Chorus: A Study of Character and Function*. Iowa City: U of Iowa P, 1987.

Hogan, James C. *A Commentary on the Plays of Sophocles*. Boulder: netLibrary, 1999.

Kitto, H. D. F. *Sophocles: Dramatist and Philosopher*. London: Oxford UP, 1958.

Knox, Bernard M. *Sophocles at Thebes: Sophocles' Tragic Hero and His Time*. New York: Norton, 1971.

Reinhardt, Karl. *Sophokles*. Trans. D. Harvey and H. Harvey. New York: Barnes, 1978.

Scodel, Ruth. *Sophocles*. Boston: Twayne, 1984.

Segal, Charles. *Tragedy and Civilization: An Interpretation of Sophocles*. Cambridge: Harvard UP, 1981.

Waldock, A. J. A. *Sophocles the Dramatist*. Cambridge: Cambridge UP, 1951.

Wiles, David. *The Masks of Menander: Sign and Meaning in Greek and Roman Performances*. Cambridge: Cambridge UP, 1991.

Winnington-Ingram, R. P. *Sophocles: An Interpretation*. New York: Cambridge UP, 1980.

Woodard, T. M, ed. *Sophocles: A Collection of Critical Essays*. Englewood Cliffs: Prentice, 1966.

Antigone

Brown, Andrew. *A New Companion to Greek Tragedy*. Totowa: Barnes, 1983.

Chanter, Tina. "Tragic Discolations: Antigone's Modern Theatrics." *Differences: A Journal of Feminist Cultural Studies* 10.1 (1998): 75–97.

Goheen, R. F. *The Imagery of Sophocles'* Antigone: *A Study of Poetic Language and Structure*. Princeton: Princeton UP, 1951.

Linforth, I. M. *Antigone and Creon*. Berkeley: U of California P, 1961.

"Review: *Antigone*." *Theatre Record* 18.6 (1998): 320–21.

Steiner, George. *Antigones*. New York: Clarendon, 1984.

Oedipus Rex

Bloom, Harold. *Sophocles'* Oedipus Rex. New York: Chelsea, 1988.

Cameron, Alister. *The Identity of Oedipus the King: Five Essays on the "Oedipus Tyrannus."* New York: New York UP, 1968.

Edmonds, Lowell. *Oedipus: The Ancient Legend and Its Later Analogues*. Baltimore: Johns Hopkins UP, 1985.

Fergusson, Francis. *The Idea of a Theater*. Princeton: Princeton UP, 1949.

———. "*Oedipus Rex*: The Tragic Rhythm of Action." *Ritual and Myth: Robertson Smith, Farzer, Hooke, and Harrison*. Ed. Robert A. Segal. New York: Garland, 1996. 67–95.

O'Brien, M. J., ed. *Twentieth Century Interpretations of Oedipus Rex*. Englewood Cliffs: Prentice, 1968.

Rudnytsky, Peter L. *Freud and Oedipus*. New York: Columbia UP, 1987.

Tonelli, Franco. "Sophocles' *Oedipus* and the Tale of the Theatre." *Speculum Artium Series* 12. Ravenna: Longo Editore, 1983.

Verhoeff, Han, and Harly Sonne. "Does Oedipus Have His Complex?" *Style* 18.3 (1984): 261–83.

WOLE SOYINKA

Byam, Dale. "Art, Exile and Resistance." *American Theatre* 14.1 (1997): 26–29.

Euba, Femi. "Wole Soyinka (1934)." *Postcolonial African Writers: A Bio-Bibliographical Critical Source Book*. Ed. Naidu Parekh et al. Westport, CT: Greenwood, 1998. 438–54.

Gibbs, James. "The BBC Became a Glutton for Punishment: Wole Soyinka's Dealings with the BBC (1953–1959)." *Crisis and Creativity in the New Literatures in English: Cross/Cultures*. Ed. Geoffrey Davis and Hena Maes-Jelinek. Amsterdam: Rodopi, 1990. 205–17.

———. *Critical Perspectives on Wole Soyinka*. Washington: Three Continents, 1980.

———. "'Marrying Earth to Heaven': A Nobel Laureate at the End of the Eighties." *International Literature in English: Essays on the Major Writers*. Ed. Robert L. Ross. New York: Garland, 1991.

———. *Wole Soyinka*. New York: Grove, 1986.

Hepburn, Joan. "Mediators of Ritual Closure." *Black American Literature Forum* 22.3 (1988): 576–614.

Jones, Eldred D. *The Writing of Wole Soyinka*. Portsmouth: Heinemann, 1988.

Katrak, Ketu H. *Wole Soyinka and Modern Tragedy: A Study of Dramatic Theory and Practice*. Westport, CT: Greenwood, 1986.

King, Bruce, ed. *Post-Colonial English Drama: Commonwealth Drama since 1960*. New York: St. Martin's, 1992.

Larsen, Stephan. *A Writer and His Gods: A Study of the Importance of Yoruba Myths and Religious Ideas to the Writing of Wole Soyinka*. Stockholm: U of Stockholm P, 1983.

Lindfors, Bernth. "Beating the White Man at His Own Game: Nigerian Reactions to the Nobel Prize in Literature." *Literary Criterion* 25.1 (1990): 43–59.

Maduakor, Obi. *Wole Soyinka: An Introduction to His Writings*. New York: Garland, 1987.

Maja-Pearce, Adewale. *Who's Afraid of Wole Soyinka? Essays on Censorship*. London: Heinemann, 1991.

———, ed. *Wole Soyinka: An Appraisal*. Oxford: Heinemann, 1994.

Moody, David. "The Prodigal Father: Discursive Rupture in the Plays of Wole Soyinka." *ARIEL* 23.1 (1992): 25–38.

Ndiava, Marieme. "Female Stereotypes in Wole Soyinka's *The Strong Breed* and *The Lion and the Jewel*." *Bridges* 5 (1993): 19–24.

Ogbaa, Kalu, ed. *The Gong and the Flute: African Literary Development and Celebration*. Westport, CT: Greenwood, 1994.

Ojewuyi, Olesegun. "Wole Soyinka: The Hunter, the Hunt." *Theater* 28.1 (1998): 58–59.

———, and Shawn-Marie Garrett. "A World of Amusement and Pity." *Theater* 28.1 (1998): 61–68.

Okome, Onookome. *Ogun's Children: The Literature and Politics of Wole Soyinka Since the Nobel Prize.* Trenton: Africa World P, 1999.

Soyinka, Wole. *Ake: The Years of Childhood.* New York: Random, 1981.

———. *Isara: A Voyage Round Essay.* New York: Random, 1989.

———. *The Man Died: The Prison Notes of Wole Soyinka.* London: Collings, 1972.

———. "Twice Bitten: The Fate of Africa's Culture Producers." *PMLA* 105.1 (1990): 110–120.

Wright, Derek. "Ritual and Revolution: Soyinka's Dramatic Theory." *ARIEL* 23.1 (1992): 39–53.

———. "Wole Soyinka as Yoruba Theatre Historian." *Post-Colonial Stages: Critical and Creative Views on Drama, Theatre and Performance.* Ed. Helen Gilbert. London: Dangaroo, 1999. 161–73.

———. *Wole Soyinka: Life, Work and Criticism.* Fredericton, NB: York, 1996.

———. *Wole Soyinka Revisited.* New York: Twayne, 1993.

AUGUST STRINDBERG

Carlson, Harry Gilbert. *Out of Inferno: Strindberg's Reawakening as an Artist.* Seattle: U of Washington P, 1996.

———. *Strindberg and the Poetry of Myth.* Berkeley: U of California P, 1982.

Chaudhuri, U. "Private Part: Sex, Class, and Stage Space in *Miss Julie.*" *Theatre Journal* 45.3 (1993): 317–32.

Franchuk, E. S. "Symbolism in *Miss Julie.*" *Theatre Research International* 18 (1993): 11–15.

Lally, M. L. K. "Strindberg's *Miss Julie.*" *Explicator* 48.3 (1990): 196–98.

Lucas, F. L. *The Drama of Ibsen and Strindberg.* London: Cassell, 1962.

Meidal, Bjorn. "A Strindberg Forgery: Carl Ohman's August Strindberg and the Origin of Scenic Expressionism." *Scandinavica* 34.1 (1995): 61–69.

Parker, Brian. "Strindberg's *Miss Julie* and the Legend of Salome." *Modern Drama* 32 (1989): 469–84.

Reinert, Otto, ed. *Strindberg: A Collection of Critical Essays.* Englewood Cliffs: Prentice, 1971.

Robinson, Michael. "August Strindberg: His True Life?" *Scandinavica* 28.2 (1989): 185–91.

———. *Studies in Strindberg.* Norwich, Eng.: Norvik, 1998.

Shideler, Ross. "The Absent Authority: From Darwin to Nora and Julie." *Space and Boundaries in Literature.* Proceedings of the Twelfth Congress of the International Comparative Literature Association. Ed. Roger Bauer and Donwe Fokkema. Munich: Iudicium, 1990.

Sprinchorn, Evert. *Strindberg as Dramatist.* New Haven: Yale UP, 1982.

Steene, Birgitta. *The Greatest Fire: A Study of August Strindberg.* Carbondale: Southern Illinois UP, 1973.

Stockenstrom, Goran, ed. *Strindberg's Dramaturgy.* Minneapolis: U of Minnesota P, 1988.

Tornqvist, Egil. Strindberg's *"Miss Julie"*: A Play and Its Transpositions. Norwich, Eng.: Norvik, 1988.

JOHN MILLINGTON SYNGE

Benson, Eugene. *J. M. Synge.* New York: Grove, 1983.

Casey, Daniel J., ed. *Critical Essays on John Millington Synge.* New York: Hall, 1994.

Castle, Gregory. "Staging Ethnography: *Playboy of the Western World* and the Problem of Cultural Translation." *Theatre Journal* 49.3 (1997): 265–86.

Corkery, Daniel. *Synge and Anglo-Irish Literature.* Cork: Cork UP, 1955.

Devlin, Joseph. "J. M. Synge's *Playboy of the Western World* and the Culture of Western Ireland under Late Colonial Rule." *Modern Drama* 41.3 (1998): 371–85.

———. "The Source of Synge's *Playboy of the Western World.*" *Notes on Modern Irish Literature* 7.2 (1995): 5–9.

Doggett, R. "The Three Fathers of the Past: A Sociological Reading of *The Playboy of the Western World* and the *Playboy* Riots." *Colby Quarterly* 33.4 (1997): 281–94.

Gerstenberger, Donna Lorine. *John Millington Synge.* 2nd ed. Boston: Twayne, 1990.

Gonzales, Alexander G. *Assessing the Achievement of J. M. Synge.* Westport, CT: Greenwood, 1996.

Greene, David H., and Edward M. Stephens. *John Millington Synge, 1871–1909.* 2nd ed. New York: New York UP, 1989.

Kiberd, Declan. *Synge and the Irish Language.* London: Macmillan, 1979.

King, Mary C. *The Drama of J. M. Synge.* Syracuse: Syracuse UP, 1985.

Kopper, Edward A. *A John Millington Synge Literary Companion.* New York: Greenwood, 1988.

Price, Alan. *Synge and Anglo-Irish Drama.* London: Methuen, 1961.

Roche, A. "Friel and Synge: Towards a Theatrical Language." *Irish University Review* 29.1 (1999): 145–61.

Skelton, Robin. *J. M. Synge and His World.* New York: Viking, 1971.

———. *The Writings of J. M. Synge.* London: Thames, 1971.

Solomont, Susan. *The Comic Effect of* Playboy of the Western World *by John Millington Synge.* Bangor, ME: Signalman, 1962.

Whitaker, Thomas R., comp. *Twentieth Century Interpretations of* The Playboy of the Western World: *A Collection of Critical Essays.* Englewood Cliffs: Prentice, 1969.

TERENCE

Forehand, Walter. *Terence*. Boston: Twayne, 1985.

Goldberg, Sander M. *Understanding Terence*. Princeton: Princeton UP, 1986.

LUIS VALDEZ

Elam, Harry Justin. *Taking it to the Streets: The Social Protest Theatre of Luis Valdez and Amiri Baraka*. Ann Arbor: U of Michigan P, 1997.

Morton, Carlos. *Critical Response to Zoot Suit and Corridos*. El Paso: U of Texas at El Paso, 1984.

Valdez, Luis. *Luis Valdez—Early Works*: Actors, Bernabé, *and* Pensamiento serpentino. Houston: Arte Publico, 1990.

Pizzato, M. "Brechtian and Aztec Violence in Valdez' *Zoot Suit*." *Journal of Popular Film and Television* 26.2 (1998): 52–61.

PAULA VOGEL

Parker, Mary-Louise. "Paula Vogel." *Bomb* 61 (1997): 44–49.

Sova, Kathy. "Time to Laugh." *American Theatre* 14.2 (1997): 24.

OSCAR WILDE

Beckson, Karl E. *The Oscar Wilde Encyclopedia*. New York: AMS, 1998.

Bloom, Harold. *Oscar Wilde's* The Importance of Being Earnest. New York: Chelsea, 1988.

Byrne, Patrick. *The Wildes of Merrion Square: The Family of Oscar Wilde*. New York: Staples, 1953.

Calloway, Stephen. *Oscar Wilde: An Exquisite Life*. London: Orion Media, 1999.

Cohen, Ed. "Writing Gone Wild: Homoerotic Desire in the Closet of Representation." *PMLA* 102 (1987): 801–13.

Cohen, Philip K. *The Moral Vision of Oscar Wilde*. Rutherford: Fairleigh Dickinson UP, 1978.

Danson, Lawrence. *Wilde's Intentions. The Artist in His Criticism*. Oxford: Clarendon, 1997.

Ellmann, Richard. *Oscar Wilde*. New York: Knopf, 1988.

———. *Oscar Wilde: A Collection of Critical Essays*. Englewood Cliffs: Prentice, 1969.

Eltis, Sos. *Revisiting Wilde: Society and Subversion in the Plays of Oscar Wilde*. Oxford: Clarendon, 1996.

Erikson, Donald. *Oscar Wilde*. Boston: Twayne, 1977.

Gagnier, Regenia. *Idylls of the Marketplace: Oscar Wilde and the Victorian Public*. Stanford: Stanford UP, 1986.

Haley, Bruce. "Wilde's 'Decadence' and the Positivist Tradition." *Victorian Studies* 28 (1985): 215–29.

Hart-Davis, Rupert, ed. *Letters of Oscar Wilde*. New York: Harcourt, 1962.

———. *More Letters of Oscar Wilde*. New York: Vanguard, 1985.

Hodge, James H. *Famous Trials*. Baltimore: Penguin, 1963.

Mackie, W. Craven. "Bunburry Pure and Simple." *Modern Drama* 41.2 (1998): 327–30.

McCormack, Jerusha Hull, ed. *Wilde the Irishman*. New Haven: Yale UP, 1998.

Mikhail, E. H. *Oscar Wilde: Interviews and Recollections*. New York: Barnes, 1979.

Miller, Robert Keith. *Oscar Wilde*. New York: Ungar, 1982.

Poznar, Walter. "Life and Play in Wilde's *The Importance of Being Earnest*." *Midwest Quarterly* 30.4 (1989): 515–28.

Raby, Peter, ed. *The Cambridge Companion to Oscar Wilde*. Cambridge: Cambridge UP, 1997.

———. "The Origins of *The Importance of Being Earnest*." *Modern Drama* 37.1 (1994): 139–47.

San Juan, Epifanio. *The Art of Oscar Wilde*. Princeton: Princeton UP, 1963.

Smith, Philip E., and Michael S. Heffland, eds. *Oscar Wilde's Oxford Notebooks*. New York: Oxford UP, 1989.

Sullivan, Kevin. *Oscar Wilde*. Columbia Essays on Modern Writers 64. New York: Columbia UP, 1972.

Varty, Anne. *A Preface to Oscar Wilde*. Preface Books. London: Longman, 1998.

Weintraub, Stanley. *The Literary Criticism of Oscar Wilde*. Lincoln: U of Nebraska P, 1968.

Wilde, Oscar. *The Complete Works*. New York: Doubleday, 1923.

———. *The Plays of Oscar Wilde*. New York: Random, 1980.

TENNESSEE WILLIAMS

List of Plays

American Blues, 1939 (published 1948)
Battle of Angels, 1940 (published 1945)
The Glass Menagerie, 1944
A Streetcar Named Desire, 1947
Summer and Smoke, 1947
The Rose Tatoo, 1950
Camino Real, 1953
Cat on a Hot Tin Roof, 1955
Orpheus Descending, 1957
Suddenly Last Summer, 1958
Sweet Bird of Youth, 1959
Period of Adjustment, 1960
The Night of the Iguana, 1962
The Milk Train Doesn't Stop Here Anymore, 1963
The Eccentricities of a Nightingale, 1965
The Seven Descents of Myrtle, 1968
In the Bar of a Tokyo Hotel, 1969
Small Craft Warnings, 1972
A Lovely Sunday for Creve Coeur, 1979
Clothes for a Summer Hotel, 1980

Aisbong, Emmanuel B. *Tennessee Williams: The Tragic Tension*. Elms Court: Stockwell, 1978.

Boxill, Roger. *Tennessee Williams*. New York: St. Martin's, 1987.

Bruhm, Steven. "Blackmailed by Sex: Tennessee Williams and the Economics of Desire." *Modern Drama* 34.4 (1991): 528–37.

Cranell, George W., ed. *The Critical Response to Tennessee Williams*. Westport, CT: Greenwood, 1996.

Devlin, Albert J., ed. *Conversations with Tennessee Williams*. Jackson: UP of Mississippi, 1986.

Donahue, Francis. *The Dramatic World of Tennessee Williams*. New York: Ungar, 1964.

Falk, Signi Lenea. *Tennessee Williams*. 2nd ed. Boston: Twayne, 1978.

Griffin, Alice. *Understanding Tennessee Williams*. Columbia: U of South Carolina P, 1995.

Hayman, Ronald. *Tennessee Williams: Everyone Else Is an Audience*. New Haven: Yale UP, 1993.

Koprince, Susan. "Tennessee Williams's Unseen Characters." *Southern Quarterly* 33.1 (1994): 87–95.

Leavitt, Richard Freeman, ed. *The World of Tennessee Williams*. New York: Putnam's, 1978.

Leverich, Lyle. *Tom: The Unknown Tennessee Williams*. London: Scepter, 1996.

Martin, Robert A., ed. *Critical Essays on Tennessee Williams*. New York: Hall, 1997.

Parker, R. B., ed. The Glass Menagerie: *A Collection of Critical Essays*. Englewood Cliffs: Prentice, 1983.

Roudané, Matthew Charles, ed. *The Cambridge Companion to Tennessee Williams*. Cambridge: Cambridge UP, 1997.

Sarotte, Georges-Michel. "Fluidity and Differentiation in Three Plays by Tennessee Williams: *The Glass Menagerie, A Streetcar Named Desire*, and *Cat on a Hot Tin Roof*." *Staging Difference: Cultural Pluralism in American Theatre and Drama*. Ed. Marc Maufort. New York: Peter Lang, 1995. 141–56.

Savran, David. " 'By coming suddenly into a room that I thought was empty': Mapping the Closet with Tennessee Williams." *Studies in the Literary Imagination* 24.2 (1991): 57–74.

———. *Communists, Cowboys and Queers: The Politics of Masculinity in the Work of Arthur Miller and Tennessee Williams*. Minneapolis: U of Minnesota P, 1992.

Spoto, Donald. *The Kindness of Strangers: The Life of Tennessee Williams*. Boston: Little, 1985.

Stanton, Stephen, ed. *Tennessee Williams: A Collection of Critical Essays*. Englewood Cliffs: Prentice, 1977.

Thompson, Judith. *Tennessee Williams' Plays: Memory, Myth, and Symbol*. New York: Lang, 1987.

Wilhelmi, Nancy O. "The Language of Power and Powerlessness: Verbal Combat in the Plays of Tennessee Williams." *The Text and Beyond: Essays in Literary Linguistics*. Ed. Cynthia Goldin-Bernstein. Tuscaloosa: U of Alabama P, 1994.

Williams, Dakin, with Shepherd Mead. *Tennessee Williams: An Intimate Biography*. New York: Arbor, 1983.

Williams, Tennessee. *Memoirs*. Garden City: Doubleday, 1975

Cat on a Hot Tin Roof

Atkinson, Brooks. "Williams' 'Tin Roof.' " *New York Times* 3 Apr. 1955: B1.

Huzzard, Jere. "Williams' *Cat on a Hot Tin Roof*." *Explicator* 43.2 (1985):46–47.

Inge, Thomas M. "The South, Tragedy and Comedy in Tennessee Williams's *Cat on a Hot Tin Roof*." *The United States South: Regionalism and Identity*. Ed. Tjebbe Westendorp. Rome: Bulzone, 1991.

Kalem, T. E. "Fate Strikes the Delta." *Time* 6 Dec. 1976: 97–98.

"London Sees Cat; Opinion Is Divided." *New York Times* 31 Jan. 1958: 24.

Mayberry, Susan Nela. "A Study of Illusion and the Grotesque in Tennessee Williams' *Cat on a Hot Tin Roof*." *Southern Studies* 22.4 (1983): 359–65.

Rev. of *Cat on a Hot Tin Roof*. *New York Theatre Critics' Reviews* 20 Mar. 1955: 342–43.

Rev. of *Cat on a Hot Tin Roof*. *New York Theatre Critics' Reviews* 25 Sept. 1974: 242–46.

The Glass Menagerie

Bloom, Harold. *Tennessee Williams's* The Glass Menagerie. New York: Chelsea, 1988.

Cardullo, Bert. "The Blue Rose of St. Louis: Laura, Romanticism, and *The Glass Menagerie*." *Tennessee Williams Annual Review* (1998).

Greiff, Louis K. "Fathers, Daughters, and Spiritual Sisters: Marsha Norman's *'night, Mother* and Tennessee Williams's *The Glass Menagerie*." *Text and Performance Quarterly* 9.3 (1989): 224–28.

Jones, John H. "The Missing Link: The Father in *The Glass Menagerie*." *Notes on Mississippi Writers* 20.1 (1988): 29–38.

Kolin, Philip C. "The Black and Multi-Racial Productions of Tennessee Williams's *The Glass Menagerie*." *Journal of Dramatic Theory and Criticism* 9.2 (1995): 96–128.

Levy, Eric P. "Through Soundproof Glass: The Prison of Self-Consciousness in *The Glass Menagerie*." *Modern Drama* 36.4 (1993): 529–37.

Parker, R. B. "The Circle Closed: A Psychological Reading of *The Glass Menagerie* and the Two Character Play." *Modern Drama* 28 (1985): 517–34.

Presley, Delma Eugene. The Glass Menagerie: *An American Memory*. Boston: Twayne, 1990.

Reynolds, James. "The Failure of Technology in *The Glass Menagerie*." *Modern Drama* 34.4 (1991): 522–27.

Siebold, Thomas., ed. *Readings on* The Glass Menagerie. San Diego: Greenhaven, 1998.

Smith, William Jay. "Tom: The Making of *The Glass Menagerie*." *The New Criterion* 14 (1996): 72–77.

Thierfelder, William R. "Williams's *The Glass Menagerie*." *Explicator* 48.4 (1990): 284–85.

Usui, Masami. "'A World of Her Own' in Tennessee Williams's *The Glass Menagerie.*" *Studies in Culture and the Humanities* 1 (1992): 21–37.

AUGUST WILSON

Arthur, Thomas H. "Looking for My Relatives: The Political Implications of 'Family' in Selected Works of Athol Fugard and August Wilson." *South African Theatre Journal* 6.2 (1992): 5–16.

Bogumil, Mary L. *Understanding August Wilson.* Columbia: U of South Carolina P, 1999.

DiGaetani, John L. *A Search for a Postmodern Theater: Interviews with Contemporary Playwrights.* New York: Greenwood, 1991.

Freedman, Samuel G. "A Voice from the Streets." *New York Times Magazine* 15 Mar. 1987: 33+.

———. "Wilson's New *Fences* Nurtures a Partnership." *New York Times* 5 May 1985, sec. I: 80.

Gerard, Jeremy. "Waterford to Broadway: Well-Traveled *Fences.*" *New York Times* 9 April 1987, sec. 3: 21.

Henderson, Heather. "Building Fences: An Interview with Mary Alice and James Earl Jones." *Yale Theater* 12 (Summer/Fall 1985): 67–70.

Herrington, Joan. *I Ain't Sorry for Nothin' I Done: August Wilson's Process of Playwrighting.* New York: Limelight, 1998.

Kelley, Kevin. "August Wilson an Heir to O'Neill." *Boston Globe* 24 Jan. 1988: A1+.

Lyons, B. "An Interview with August Wilson." *Contemporary Literature* 40.1 (1999): 1–21.

Nadel, Alan, ed. *May All Your Fences Have Gates: Essays on the Drama of August Wilson.* Iowa City: U of Iowa P, 1994.

Pereira, Kim. *August Wilson and the African American Odyssey.* Urbana: U of Illinois P, 1995.

Plum, Jay. "Blues, History and the Dramaturgy of August Wilson." *African American Review* 27.4 (1993): 561–67.

Rich, Frank. "Theater: Family Ties in Wilson's *Fences.*" *New York Times* 27 Mar. 1987, sec. II: 1.

Shannon, Sandra, "Blues, History, and Dramaturgy: An Interview with August Wilson." *African American Review* 27.4 (1993): 539–59.

———. "Conversing with the Past: Joe Turner's Come and Gone and *The Piano Lesson.*" *CEA Magazine* 4.1 (1991): 33–42.

Sterling, E. "Protecting Home: Patriarchal Authority in August Wilson's *Fences.*" *Essays in Theatre-Etudes Theatrales* 17.1 (1996): 53–62.

Wang, Qun. *An In-Depth Study of the Major Plays of African American Playwright August Wilson: Vernacularizing the Blues on Stage.* Lewiston: Mellen, 1999.

Wessling, J. H. "Wilson's *Fences.*" *Explicator* 57.2 (1999): 123–27.

Selected List of Film, Video, and Audiocassette Resources

The following list of audiovisual resources supplements the teaching of plays in *The Bedford Introduction to Drama*. The resources are listed alphabetically by playwright.

The films and videos marked with an asterisk (*) are available for rental from member institutions of the Consortium of College and University Media Centers. For further information, consult Media Sources: Consortium of College and University Media Centers, 1st ed. on CD-ROM.

Many of the videos are available for rental from local video outlets. Others are available through a distributor. Check the Directory of Distributors following this list for information.

AESCHYLUS

Aeschylus, *The Oresteia*. 230 minutes, 1985. VHS, Beta, 3/4″ U-matic cassette. Directed by Peter Hall. The National Theatre of Great Britain performs Aeschylus's classic dramas, each available separately. Distributed by Films for the Humanities and Sciences.

Aeschylus and the Death of Tragedy. 80 minutes, 1963. Audiocassette. Walter Kaufmann. Kaufmann argues that although Aeschylus is generally considered the creator of tragedy, his world-view contains central elements that are usually associated with the death of tragedy in our time. The *Oresteia* trilogy is examined. Distributed by Audio-Forum.

ANONYMOUS

Anonymous, *Everyman*. 25 minutes, color, 1971. 16 mm film. Abridged by H. Frances Clark. Distributed by Coronet/MTI Film & Video.

Anonymous, *Everyman*. 53 minutes, color, 1991. VHS. Produced in conjunction with medieval literature scholar Holward Schless of Columbia University. Authentically staged in period costume. Distributed by Insight Media.

ARISTOPHANES

Aristophanes, *Lysistrata*. 97 minutes, color, 1987. VHS, Beta. A contemporary adaptation, shot on location at the Acropolis. In Greek with English subtitles. Distributed by New York Film Annex.

SAMUEL BECKETT

Samuel Beckett, *Endgame*. 92 minutes, color, 1989. Part of the "Literature in the Modern World" series. Starring Norman Beaton, Stephen Rea, and Kate Binchy. Distributed by the Roland Collection.

Samuel Beckett, *Endgame*. 96 minutes, color, 1992. Starring Bud Thorpe, Rick Cluchey, and Teresita Garcia Suro. Distributed by Smithsonian Institution Press.

Samuel Beckett, *Endgame*. 96 minutes, color, 1992. VHS. Samuel Beckett's work as presented by the University of Maryland in Collaboration with PBS. Distributed by Insight Media.

Samuel Beckett. 80 minutes, color, 1989. Beta, VHS, 3/4″ U-matic cassette. An autobiographical portrait of Beckett's artistic life through his work. Distributed by Films for the Humanities and Sciences.

BERTOLT BRECHT

Bertolt Brecht. 55 minutes, color, 1989. VHS, 3/4″ U-matic cassette. A biographical portrait of Brecht through his works. Distributed by Films for the Humanities and Sciences.

Gisela May: Reflections on the Theater of Brecht. 30 minutes, color, 1979. Beta, VHS, 1/2″ open reel (EIAJ), 3/4″ U-matic cassette, 2″ quadraplex open reel. Gisela May of the Berliner Ensemble performs excerpts from Brecht's plays. Distributed by Camera Three Productions Inc. and Creative Arts Television Archive.

ANTON CHEKHOV

Anton Chekhov. 30 minutes, color and b/w, 1996. VHS. A documentary filmed where Chekhov lived and worked. Part of the Great Authors series. Distributed by Kultur.

Anton Chekhov, *The Cherry Orchard.* 3 audiocassettes. Translated by Leonid Kipnis and performed by Jessica Tandy and Hume Cronyn. Distributed by Caedmon/Harper Audio.

Anton Chekhov, *The Cherry Orchard, Part I: Chekhov, Innovator of Modern Drama.* 21 minutes, color and b/w, 1968. Beta, VHS, 3/4″ U-matic cassette, 16-mm film. Important scenes with discussion led by Norris Houghton. Distributed by Encyclopaedia Britannica Educational Corp.

Anton Chekhov, *The Cherry Orchard, Part II: Comedy or Tragedy?* 21 minutes, color and b/w, 1967. Beta, VHS, 3/4″ U-matic cassette, 16-mm film. Important scenes with discussion led by Norris Houghton. Covers Chekhov's technique of dramatization of interior actions and examines the notion of subtext. Distributed by Encyclopaedia Britannica Educational Corp.

Anton Chekhov: A Writer's Life.. 37 minutes, b/w, 1974. VHS, 3/4″ U-matic cassette. A biographical portrait of the playwright. Distributed by Films for the Humanities and Sciences.

Chekhov. 1080 minutes, 1989. 12 audiocassettes. By Henri Troyat, read by Wolfram Kandinsky. A biography of the writer. Distributed by Books on Tape, Inc.

Chekhov: Humanity's Advocate. 46 minutes, 1968. Audiocassette. By Ernest J. Simmons. Explores various facets of Chekhov's works and his artistic principals. Classics of Russian Literature Series. Distributed by Audio-Forum.

WILLIAM CONGREVE

William Congreve, *The Way of the World.* 60 minutes, color, 1978. Beta, VHS, 3/4″ U-matic cassette. Hosted by Jose Ferrer and Anna Russell. Focuses on main characters and eliminates some subplots. Distributed by Public Media/Home Vision.

EURIPIDES

Euripides, *Medea.* 107 minutes, b/w, 1959. VHS. With Judith Anderson and Colleen Dewhurst. Directed by Jose Quintero. Distributed by Ivy Video.

Euripides, *Medea.* 118 minutes, color, 1970. Beta, VHS. With Maria Callas, Guiseppe Gentile, and Laurent Tarzieff. Directed by Pier Paolo Passolini. In Italian with English subtitles. Distributed by Video Artists International.

Euripides, *Medea.* 70 minutes, color, 1979. VHS. With Marina Goderdzishvili and Vladimir Julukhadze. A free adaptation for ballet. Distributed by Kultur.

Euripides, *Medea.* 90 minutes, color, 1982. VHS, 3/4″ U-matic cassette. With Zoe Caldwell and Judith Anderson. A Kennedy Center production based on the poet Robinsons Jeffers's version. Distributed by Films for the Humanities and Sciences.

Euripides, *Medea.* 2 audiocassettes. Translated by Rex Warner. Performed by Judith Anderson and Anthony Quayle. Distributed by Caedmon/Harper Audio.

BRIAN FRIEL

Brian Friel, *Dancing at Lughnasa.* 94 minutes, color, 1998. VHS, DVD. Starring Meryl Streep and Michael Gambon. Directed by Pat O'Connor. Distributed by Columbia Tristar.

ATHOL FUGARD

Athol Fugard, *"MASTER HAROLD" . . . and the boys.* 90 minutes, color, 1984. Beta, VHS. With Matthew Broderick. Directed by Michael Lindsay-Hogg. A made-for-cable production. Distributed by Warner Home Video, Inc.

LORRAINE HANSBERRY

Lorraine Hansberry: The Black Experience in the Creation of Drama. 35 minutes, color, 1975. Beta, VHS, 3/4″ U-matic cassette. With Sidney Poitier, Ruby Dee, and Al Freeman, Jr. Narrated by Claudia McNeil. A profile of the playwright's life and work. Distributed by Films for the Humanities and Sciences.

Lorraine Hansberry Speaks Out: Art and the Black Revolution. Audiocassette. By Lorraine Hansberry, edited by Robert Nemiroff. Distributed by Caedmon/HarperAudio.

A Raisin in the Sun. 128 minutes, b/w, 1961. Beta, VHS. With Sidney Poitier, Claudia McNeil and Ruby Dee. Directed by Daniel Petrie. Distributed by Columbia Tristar.

A Raisin in the Sun. 171 minutes, color, 1989. Beta, VHS. With Danny Glover, Esther Rolle, and Starletta DuPois. Directed by Bill Duke. An American Playhouse made-for-television production. Distributed by Chuck Fries Productions.

A Raisin in the Sun. 141 minutes. 2 audiocassettes. Dramatization performed by Ossie Davis and Ruby Dee. Distributed by Caedmon/Harper Audio.

To Be Young, Gifted, and Black. 90 minutes, color, 1981. Beta, VHS, 1/2″ open reel (EIAJ), 3/4″ U-matic cassette, 16-mm film. With Ruby Dee, Al Freeman, Jr., Claudia McNeil, Barbara Barrie, Lauren Jones, Roy Scheider, and Blythe Danner. A play about the life of Lorraine Hansberry. Distributed by Monterey Home Video.

DAVID HENRY HWANG

David Henry Hwang, *M. Butterfly*. 101 minutes, color, 1994. VHS. With Jeremy Irons, Ian Richardson, and Barbara Sukowa. Distributed by Warner Home Video.

David Henry Hwang, *M. Butterfly*. 2 audiocassettes. Directed by Steve Albrezzi. With John Lithgow, Margaret Cho, and B.D. Wong. Distributed by the L.A. Theater Works.

HENRIK IBSEN

A Doll's House. 180 minutes, 1993. 3 audiocassettes. Read by Flo Gibson. Distributed by Audio Book Contractors.

A Doll's House, Part I: The Distinction of Illusion. 34 minutes, color, 1968. Beta, VHS, 3/4" U-matic cassette, 16-mm film. Norris Houghton discusses the subsurface tensions in the play. Distributed by Encyclopaedia Britannica Educational Corp.

A Doll's House, Part II: Ibsen's Themes. 29 minutes, color, 1968. Beta, VHS, 3/4" U-matic cassette, 16-mm film. Norris Houghton examines the case of characters and the themes in the play. Distributed by Encyclopaedia Britannica Educational Corp.

Henrik Ibsen, *A Doll's House*. 89 minutes, b/w, 1959. Beta, VHS, 3/4" U-matic cassette. With Julie Harris, Christopher Plummer, Jason Robards, Hume Cronyn, Eileen Heckart, and Richard Thomas. An original television production. Distributed by MGM/UA Entertainment.

Henrik Ibsen, *A Doll's House*. 98 minutes, color, 1973. VHS, 16-mm film. With Jane Fonda, Edward Fox, and Trevor Howard. Screenplay by Christopher Hampton. Distributed by Prism Entertainment.

Henrik Ibsen, *A Doll's House*. 39 minutes, color, 1977. VHS. With Claire Bloom, Anthony Hopkins, and Ralph Richardson. Distributed by AIMS Media.

Henrik Ibsen, *Hedda*. 102 minutes, color, 1975. Beta, VHS. With Glenda Jackson, Peter Eyre, and Timothy West. Directed by Trevor Nunn. Distributed by Fox Video.

Henrik Ibsen, *Hedda Gabler*. 78 minutes, color, 1994. Directed by David Cunliffe. Starring Diana Rigg, John Osborne, and Denis Lill. Distributed by Films for the Humanities and Sciences.

Henrik Ibsen, *Hedda Gabler*. 124 minutes. 3 audiocassettes. Directed by Howard Sackler. Starring Joan Plowright. Distributed by Caedmon.

Ibsen's Life and Times, Part I: Youth and Self-Imposed Exile. 28 minutes, color. VHS. The conflict between individual and society is illustratd in scenes from *Ghosts*, featuring Beatrice Straight as Mrs. Alving. Includes a biographical segment on the playwright. Distributed by Insight Media.

Ibsen's Life and Times, Part II: The Later Years. 24 minutes, color. VHS. Includes scenes from *The Master Builder* and *Lady from the Sea*, emphasizing the realism in Ibsen's plays. A biographical segment includes on-location footage. Distributed by Insight Media.

EUGÈNE IONESCO

Eugène Ionesco: Voices, Silences. 61 minutes, color, VHS, 3/4" U-matic cassette, 16-mm film. Directed by Thierry Zeno. Narrated by Eugène Ionesco. Ionesco comments on several of his plays. Distributed by the Roland Collection.

FEDERICO GARCÍA LORCA

Federico García Lorca: El Balcon Abierto. 90 minutes, color. VHS, 3/4" U-matic cassette. In Spanish. An examination of García Lorca's work, life, and violent death. Distributed by Films for the Humanities and Sciences.

Lorca: A Murder in Granada. 55 minutes, 1983. VHS, 3/4" U-matic cassette. In Spanish and English. The authoritative film biography of García Lorca. Distributed by Films for the Humanities and Sciences.

DAVID MAMET

David Mamet, *Oleanna*. 90 minutes, 1994. VHS. With William H. Macy and Debra Eisenstadt. Directed by David Mamet. Distributed by Hallmark Home Entertainment.

CHRISTOPHER MARLOWE

Christopher Marlowe, *Doctor Faustus*. 93 minutes, 1968. VHS, Beta. Adaptation of Marlowe's classic. With Richard Burton and Elizabeth Taylor. Directed by Richard Burton and Neville Coghill. Distributed by Columbia Tristar Home Video.

ARTHUR MILLER

Death of a Salesman. 135 minutes, color, 1985. Beta, VHS. With Dustin Hoffman, John Malkovich, Charles Durning, and Stephen Lang. Directed by Volker Schlondorff. A made-for-television adaptation of the play. Distributed by Facets Multimedia and Warner Home Video.

Arthur Miller, *Death of a Salesman*. 2 audiocassettes. Performed by Lee J. Cobb and Mildred Dunnock. Distributed by Caedmon/Harper Audio.

Arthur Miller, *Death of a Salesman*. 44 minutes, 1986. Audiocassette. Dramatization performed by Paul Douglas. Distributed by Sounddeluxe Audio Publishing.

Private Conversations on the Set of Death of a Salesman. 82 minutes, color, 1985. Beta, VHS. With Arthur Miller, Dustin Hoffman, Volker Schlondorff, and John Malkovich. This PBS documentary presents heated discussion between actor, director, and playwright. Various interpretations of the play emerge and viewers gain insight into how each part contributed to the final production. Distributed by Video Learning Library.

MOLIÈRE

Molière, *Le Misanthrope.* 52 minutes, color, 1975. VHS. With Cyril Ritchard, Edward Petherbridge, and Neil Stacy. Distributed by Films for the Humanities and Sciences.

Molière, *Le Misanthrope.* 140 minutes, color, 1986. VHS, 3/4″ U-matic cassette. In French with English subtitles. Distributed by Films for the Humanities and Sciences.

Molière, *Le Misanthrope.* 89 minutes. 2 audiocassettes. With Richard Easton. Distributed by Caedmon.

Molière, *Le Misanthrope.* 104 minutes. 2 audiocassettes. Recorded live as part of L.A. Theater Works' The Play's the Thing series of performance productions. Distributed by L.A. Theater Works.

MARSHA NORMAN

Marsha Norman. 60 minutes, color, 1995. Playwright Marsha Norman reflects on her early years growing up in Kentucky and discusses her work. Distributed by Annenberg/CPB.

Marsha Norman, *'night, Mother.* 97 minutes, color, 1986. Beta, VHS, laser optical videodisc. With Sissy Spacek and Anne Bancroft. Directed by Tom Moore. Distributed by Universal Studios Home Video.

Marsha Norman, *'night, Mother.* 67 minutes. Audiocassette. Part of the L.A. Theater Works' audio-theater series The Play's the Thing, a series of live performance productions. Features the voices of Sharon Gless and Katherine Helmond. Distributed by L.A. Theater Works.

EUGENE O'NEILL

Eugene O'Neill. 30 minutes, b/w and color, 1996. VHS. A commentary on the author's life. Part of the Famous Authors series. Distributed by Kultur.

Eugene O'Neill, *Desire under the Elms.* 111 minutes, b/w, 1958. Beta, VHS, LaserDisc. Starring Anthony Perkins, Burl Ives, and Sophia Loren. Directed by Delbert Mann. Distributed by Paramount Home Video.

HAROLD PINTER

Harold Pinter, *Betrayal.* 95 minutes, color, 1983. VHS. With Ben Kingsley, Patricia Hodge, and Jeremy Irons. Directed by David Jones. Distributed by CBS/Fox Video.

Harold Pinter with Benedict Nightingale. 55 minutes, 1989. VHS. Interview with Pinter. Distributed by Insight Media.

LUIGI PIRANDELLO

Luigi Pirandello, *Six Characters in Search of an Author.* 52 minutes, color, 1976. VHS, 3/4″ U-matic cassette. Joseph Heller discusses the boundaries between reality and fiction. Distributed by Films for the Humanities and Sciences.

Luigi Pirandello, *Six Characters in Search of an Author.* 60 minutes, color, 1978. VHS, 3/4″ U-matic cassette. Hosted by Jose Ferrer. As an accompaniment to the play, Ossie Davis discusses Pirandello's work in the theater. Distributed by RMI Media Production, Inc.

Luigi Pirandello, *Six Characters in Search of an Author.* 96 minutes, b/w, 1998. A BBC Production featuring John Hurt, Brian Cox, and Tara Fitzgerald. Distributed by Films for the Humanities and Sciences.

WILLIAM SHAKESPEARE

Hamlet

Hamlet: The Age of Elizabeth, I. 30 minutes, color, 1979. Beta, VHS, 3/4″ U-matic cassette, 16-mm film. An introduction to Elizabethan theater. Distributed by Encyclopaedia Britannica Educational Corp.

Hamlet: The Poisoned Kingdom, III. 30 minutes, color, 1959. Beta, VHS, 3/4″ U-matic cassette, 16-mm film. Observes that poisoning in the play is both literal and figurative and affects all the characters. Distributed by Encyclopaedia Britannica Educational Corp.

Hamlet: The Readiness Is All, IV. 30 minutes, color, 1959. Beta, VHS, 3/4″ U-matic cassette, 16-mm film. *Hamlet* is presented as a coming-of-age story. Distributed by Encyclopaedia Britannica Educational Corp.

Hamlet: The Trouble with Hamlet. 23 minutes, color, 1969. 16-mm film. Emphasizes Hamlet's existentialist dilemma. Distributed by the National Broadcasting Company.

Hamlet: What Happens in Hamlet, II. 30 minutes, color and b/w, 1959. Beta, VHS, 3/4″ U-matic cassette, 16-mm film. Analyzes the play as a ghost story, a detective story, and a revenge story. Uses scenes from Acts I, III, and V to introduce the principal characters and present the structure of each substory. Distributed by Encyclopaedia Britannica Educational Films.

Shakespeare and His Stage: Approaches to Hamlet. 45 minutes, color, 1979. VHS. Includes footage of the four greatest Hamlets of this century: John Barrymore, Laurence Olivier, John Gielgud, and Nicol Williamson. Shows a young actor learning the role. Narrated by Gielgud. Distributed by Films for the Humanities and Sciences.

William Shakespeare, *Hamlet.* 153 minutes, b/w, 1948. VHS, beta, and laser disc. With Laurence Olivier, Basil Sydney, Felix Aylmer, Jean Simmons, Stanley Holloway, Peter Cushing, and Christopher Lee. Voice of John Gielgud. Directed by Olivier. Photographed in Denmark. Cut scenes include all of Rosencrantz and Guildenstern. Emphasizes Oedipal implications in the play. Distributed by Paramount Home Video.

William Shakespeare, *Hamlet*. 115 minutes, color, 1969. With Nicol Williamson and Anthony Hopkins. Directed by Tony Richardson. Distributed by Filmic Archives.

William Shakespeare, *Hamlet*. 222 minutes, color, 1979. VHS, other formats by arrangement. Directed by Derek Jacobi. Distributed by Filmic Archives.

William Shakespeare, *Hamlet*. 135 minutes, color, 1990. VHS. With Mel Gibson, Glenn Close, Alan Bates, Paul Scofield, Iam Holm, and Helena Bonham-Carter. Directed by Franco Zeffirelli. Distributed by Critics' Choice.

William Shakespeare, *Hamlet*. 242 minutes, color, 1996. Laser, DDS, VHS. With Kenneth Branagh, Kate Winslet, Julie Christie, and Charlton Heston. Directed by Kenneth Branagh. Distributed by Columbia Tristar Home Video.

William Shakespeare, *Hamlet*. 3 audiocassettes. Performed by Paul Scofield and Diana Wynyard. Distributed by Caedmon/Harper Audio.

The Tragedie of Hamlet: Prince of Denmark. 22 minutes, color, 1988. VHS. Actors depict Shakespeare and his contemporary, Richard Burbage, rehearsing the play. "Shakespeare" gives a line-by-line analysis of scenes from the play along with insight into plot and character. Part of the Shakespeare in Rehearsal Series. Distributed by Coronet/MTI Film & Video.

A Midsummer Night's Dream

A Midsummer Night's Dream. 120 minutes. 2 audiocassettes. Performed by Robert Helpmann and Moira Shearer. An Old Vic production. Distributed by Durkin Hayes Publishing.

William Shakespeare, *A Midsummer Night's Dream*. 118 minutes, b/w, 1935. VHS. With James Cagney, Mickey Rooney, Olivia DeHaviland, and Dick Powell. Distributed by Critics' Choice.

William Shakespeare, *A Midsummer Night's Dream*. 111 minutes, b/w, 1963. Beta, VHS, 3/4″ U-matic cassette. With Patrick Allen, Eira Heath, Cyril Luckham, Tony Bateman, and Jill Bennett. A live BBC-TV performance, with Mendelsohn's incidental music. Distributed by Video Yesteryear.

William Shakespeare, *A Midsummer Night's Dream*. 120 minutes, 1968. VHS. With Diana Rigg and David Warner. Directed by Peter Hall. A Royal Shakespeare Company performance. Distributed by Critics' Choice.

William Shakespeare, *A Midsummer Night's Dream*. 120 minutes, color, 1982. Beta, VHS. With Helen Mirren, Peter McEnery, and Brian Glover. Distributed by Filmic Archives.

William Shakespeare, *A Midsummer Night's Dream*. 165 minutes, color, 1983. Beta, VHS, 3/4″ U-matic cassette. With William Hurt and Michelle Shay. A

lively interpretation by Joseph Papp. Distributed by Films for the Humanities and Sciences.

William Shakespeare, *A Midsummer Night's Dream*. 194 minutes, color, 1987. VHS. With Ileana Cotrubas, James Bowman, and Curt Appelgren. Directed by Peter Hall. A performance of the Benjamin Britten opera, taped at the Glyndebourne Festival Opera. Distributed by Critics' Choice.

William Shakespeare, *A Midsummer Night's Dream*. 115 minutes, color, 1999. VHS, DVD. Starring Kevin Kline, Michelle Pfeiffer, Calista Flockhart, and Stanley Tucci. Distributed by Twentieth Century Fox.

William Shakespeare, *A Midsummer Night's Dream*. 2 audio compact discs. Dramatization performed by Paul Scofield and Joy Parker. With an introductory essay by scholar Harold Bloom. Distributed by Caedmon/Harper Audio.

Othello

Otello. 146 minutes, color, 1997. VHS. With Placido Domingo, Kiri Te Kanawa, and Sergei Leiferkus. Opera by Giuseppe Verdi. Conducted by Georg Solti. Production at the Royal Opera House, Covent Garden, London. Distributed by Public Media/Home Vision.

William Shakespeare, *Othello*. 92 minutes, b/w, 1952. VHS, laser disc. Directed by Orson Welles. The original version as it appeared in the 1952 Cannes Film Festival. Distributed by Voyager.

William Shakespeare, *Othello*. 208 minutes, color, 1982. VHS. With Bob Hoskins and Anthony Hopkins. Distributed by Ambrose Video Publishing, Inc.

William Shakespeare, *Othello*. 90 minutes, color, 1993. Various actors perform key scenes as scholars provide commentary. Distributed by the Video Catalog.

William Shakespeare, *Othello*. 124 minutes, color, 1995, VHS. With Laurence Fishburne, Kenneth Branagh, and Irene Jacob. Distributed by Castle Rock Entertainment.

William Shakespeare, *Othello*. 2 audiocassettes. Performed by Cyril Cusack and Alan Bates. Distributed by Caedmon/Harper Audio.

General

The Life and Times of William Shakespeare 1: The Historical Setting. 25 minutes, color, 1978. VHS. An overview of Elizabethan England. Distributed by the University of Wyoming Audio-Visual Services.

The Life and Times of William Shakespeare 2: English Drama. 20 minutes, color, 1978. VHS. History of drama from the Greeks to that of Shakespeare's time. Distributed by the University of Wyoming Audio-Visual Services.

The Life and Times of William Shakespeare 3: Stratford Years. 18 minutes, color, 1978. VHS. Deals with Shakespeare's early life. Distributed by the University of Wyoming Audio-Visual Services.

The Life and Times of William Shakespeare 4: London Years. 33 minutes, color, 1978. VHS. A history of the center of the English-speaking world. Distributed by the University of Wyoming Audio-Visual Services.

Shakespeare and the Globe. 31 minutes, color, 1985. VHS, 3/4″ U-matic cassette. A survey of Shakespeare's life, work, and cultural milieu. Distributed by Films for the Humanities and Sciences.

Shakespeare and His Stage. 47 minutes, color, 1975. VHS, 16-mm film. Provides a montage of Shakespearean background, including scenes from Hamlet and the preparation of various actors for the role. Distributed by Films for the Humanities and Sciences.

Shakespeare's Heritage. 29 minutes, color, 1988. 16-mm film. Narrated by Anthony Quayle. Explores Stratford and the life of the playwright. Distributed by Encyclopaedia Britannica Educational Corp.

Shakespeare's Theater. 13 minutes, color, 1946. 16-mm film. Re-creates the experience of going to a play at the Globe Theatre in Shakespeare's time. Distributed by the Indiana University Instructional Support Services.

Shakespeare's Theater: The Globe Playhouse. 18 minutes, b/w, 1953. VHS. Provides a model of the Globe Theater and a discussion of the original staging of some of Shakespeare's plays. Distributed by the University of California Extension Media Center.

The Two Traditions. 50 minutes, color, 1983. VHS. Deals with the problem of overcoming barriers of time and culture to make Shakespeare relevant today. Examples from *Hamlet, Coriolanus, The Merchant of Venice,* and *Othello.* Part of the Playing Shakespeare Series. Distributed by Films for the Humanities and Sciences.

Understanding Shakespeare: His Sources. 20 minutes, color, 1972. Beta, VHS, 3/4″ U-matic cassette, 16-mm film, other formats by special arrangement. Examines how Shakespeare's plays grew out of sources available to him, and how he enhanced the material with his own imagination. Distributed by Coronet/MTI Film & Video.

GEORGE BERNARD SHAW

George Bernard Shaw. 30 minutes, b/w and color, 1996. VHS. An examination of the social and political forces relevant to Shaw's work. Part of the Famous Authors series. Distributed by Kultur.

George Bernard Shaw, *Mrs. Warren's Profession.* 115 minutes, color, 1976. VHS. Directed by Herbert Wise. With Coral Browne, Penelope Wilton, and James Grout. Distributed by Time-Life Multimedia.

George Bernard Shaw, *Mrs. Warren's Profession.* 1 audiocassette. Directed by Nicholas Rudall. With Paul Gutrecht, Kaitlin Hopkins, and Shirley Knight. Recorded live as part of L.A. Theater Works' The Play's the Thing, a series of recorded performances. Distributed by L.A. Theater Works.

SAM SHEPARD

Sam Shepard, *True West.* 110 minutes, color, 1983. Directed by Gary Sinise. With John Malkovich and Gary Sinise. Distributed by Academy Home Entertainments.

SOPHOCLES

Antigone

Antigone: Rites of Passion. 85 minutes, color, 1992. VHS. With Amy Greenfield, Bertram Ross, and Janet Eilber. Director by Amy Greenfield. A retelling of Sophocles' tragedy through action, dance, and rock music. Distributed by Mystic Fire Video.

Antigone. 2 audiocassettes. Dramatization of the Fitts and Fitzgerald translation. Performed by Dorothy Tutin and Max Adrian. Distributed by Caedmon/Harper Audio.

Sophocles, *Antigone.* 88 minutes, b/w, 1962. VHS. With Irene Papas. Directed by George Tzavellas. In Greek with English subtitles. Distributed by Ivy Video.

Sophocles, *Antigone.* 120 minutes, 1987. VHS, 3/4″ U-matic cassette. With Juliet Stevenson, John Shrapnel, and John Gielgud. Staged version. Distributed by Films for the Humanities and Sciences.

Sophocles, *Antigone.* 58 minutes, color, 1994. VHS. With Seymour Simon. Distributed by RMI Media Productions.

Oedipus

Oedipus Rex: Age of Sophocles, I. 31 minutes, color and b/w, 1959. Beta, VHS, 3/4″ U-matic cassette, 16-mm film. Discusses Greek civilization, the classic Greek theater, and the theme of man's fundamental nature. Distributed by Encyclopaedia Britannica Educational Corp.

Oedipus Rex: The Character of Oedipus, II. 31 minutes, color and b/w, 1959. Beta, VHS, 3/4″ U-matic cassette, 16-mm film. Debates whether Oedipus's trouble is a result of character flaws or of fate. Distributed by Encyclopaedia Britannica Educational Corp.

Oedipus Rex: Man and God, III. 30 minutes, color and b/w, 1959. Beta, VHS, 3/4″ U-matic cassette, 16-mm film. Deals with the idea that Oedipus, although a worldly ruler, cannot overcome the gods and his destiny. Distributed by Encyclopaedia Britannica Educational Corp.

Oedipus Rex: Recovery of Oedipus, IV. 30 minutes, color and b/w, 1959. Beta, VHS, 3/4″ U-matic cassette, 16-mm film. Deals with man's existence in between God and beast. Distributed by Encyclopaedia Britannica Educational Corp.

Sophocles, *Oedipus Rex.* 20 minutes, color, 1957. Beta, VHS, 3/4″ U-matic cassette. Sophocles' play, presented in a signed version for the deaf. Distributed by Gallaudet University Library.

Sophocles, *Oedipus Rex.* 87 minutes, color, 1957. VHS, 16-mm film. With Douglas Campbell, Douglas Rain, Eric House, and Eleanor Stuart. Based on William Yeats's translation. Directed by Tyrone Guthrie. Contained and highly structured rendering by the Stratford (Ontario) Festival Players. Distributed by Water Bearer Films.

Sophocles, *Oedipus the King.* 97 minutes, color, 1967. VHS. With Donald Sutherland, Christopher Plummer, Lilli Palmer, Orson Welles, Cyril Cusack, Richard Johnson, and Roger Livesey. Directed by Philip Saville. Simplified film version of the play, filmed in Greece using an old amphitheater to serve as the background for much of the action. Distributed by Crossroads Video.

Sophocles, *Oedipus the King.* 45 minutes, color, 1975. Beta, VHS, 3/4″ U-matic cassette, 16-mm film. With Anthony Quayle, James Mason, Claire Bloom, and Ian Richardson. A production by the Athens Classical Theatre Company, with an English soundtrack. Distributed by Films for the Humanities and Sciences.

Sophocles, *Oedipus the King.* 120 minutes, color, 1987. VHS. With John Gielgud, Michael Pennington, and Claire Bloom. Distributed by Films for the Humanities and Sciences.

Sophocles, *Oedipus Rex.* 2 audiocassettes. Translated by William Butler Yeats. Performed by Douglas Campbell and Eric House. Dramatization. Distributed by Caedmon/Harper Audio.

Sophocles, *Oedipus at Colonus.* 120 minutes, color, 1987. Beta, VHS, 3/4″ U-matic cassette. With Anthony Quayle, Juliet Stevenson, and Kenneth Haigh. Staged version. Distributed by Films for the Humanities and Sciences.

Sophocles: The Theban Plays. 360 minutes, color, 1986. 3 videocassettes, VHS, 3/4″ U-matic cassette. Distributed by Films for the Humanities and Sciences.

WOLE SOYINKA

Wole Soyinka. 50 minutes, color, 1985. VHS, 3/4″ U-matic cassette. An interview with the playwright, who discusses political and cultural life in Africa and the United States and what it means to be an artist. Distributed by The Roland Collection.

Wole Soyinka. 50 minutes, 1989. VHS. From the Writers in Conversation Series. Soyinka lectures on creative traditions and the "climate of terror" in which they are born. Also discusses the growth of contemporary African self-awareness. Distributed by the Roland Collection.

AUGUST STRINDBERG

August Strindberg, *Miss Julie.* 90 minutes, b/w, 1950. VHS. Starring Anita Bjork and Ulf Palme. Directed by Alf Sjoberg. Distributed by Public Media/Home Vision.

August Strindberg, *Miss Julie.* 105 minutes, color, 1972. VHS. With Helen Mirren. A production of the Royal Shakespeare Company. Distributed by MasterVision.

August Strindberg, *Miss Julie.* 60 minutes, color, 1978. Beta, VHS, 3/4″ U-matic cassette. Ancillary materials available. With Patrick Stewart and Lisa Harrow. Hosted by Jose Ferrer. Opens with the rehearsal of a crucial scene and closes with a full-dress production of the play. In between, the actors show different ways of interpreting a scene. Distributed by Films, Inc.

August Strindberg, *Miss Julie.* 100 minutes, color, 1997. VHS. Directed by Michael Simpson. Distributed by Films for the Humanities and Sciences.

JOHN MILLINGTON SYNGE

John Millington Synge, *Playboy of the Western World.* 96 minutes, color, 1963. VHS. Starring Siobhan McKenna and Gary Raymond. Directed by Brian Desmond Hurst. Distributed by HBO Video, Inc.

John Millington Synge, *Playboy of the Western World.* 140 minutes, color, 1985. VHS, U-matic cassette. Distributed by Films for the Humanities and Sciences.

John Millington Synge, *Playboy of the Western World.* 2 audiocassettes. Starring Cyril Cusack and Siobhan McKenna. Distributed by Caedmon.

LUIS VALDEZ

Luis Valdez, *Zoot Suit.* 92 minutes, b/w, 1981. VHS. The film adaptation of Valdez's play. Distributed by Universal Pictures.

OSCAR WILDE

Oscar Wilde, *The Importance of Being Earnest.* 95 minutes, color, 1952. Beta, VHS. With Michael Redgrave, Edith Evans, Margaret Rutherford, Michael Dennison, and Joan Greenwood. Directed by Anthony Asquith. Staged version. Distributed by Paramount Home Video.

Oscar Wilde, *The Importance of Being Earnest.* 2 audiocassettes. Performed by Lynn Redgrave and Gladys Cooper. Distributed by Caedmon/Harper Audio.

Oscar Wilde: Spendthrift of Genius. 60 minutes, color, 1989. VHS. A portrait of this multitalented author. Distributed by Films for the Humanities and Sciences.

TENNESSEE WILLIAMS

Cat on a Hot Tin Roof

Tennessee Williams, *Cat on a Hot Tin Roof.* 108 minutes, color, 1958. With Paul Newman, Burl Ives, Elizabeth Taylor, and Jack Carson. Directed by Richard Brooks. Distributed by MGM/UA Home Video.

Tennessee Williams, *Cat on a Hot Tin Roof.* 148 minutes, color, 194. With Jessica Lange, Tommy Lee

Jones, and Rip Torn. Directed by Jack Hofsiss. Distributed by MGM/UA Home Video.

The Glass Menagerie

The Glass Menagerie. 134 minutes, color, 1987. Beta, VHS. With Joanne Woodward, Karen Allen, John Malkovich, and James Naughton. Directed by Paul Newman. See local retailer.

Tennessee Williams, *The Glass Menagerie.* 2 audiocassettes. Performed by Montgomery Clift and Julie Harris. Distributed by Caedmon/Harper Audio.

Tennessee Williams, *Tennessee Williams Reads "The Glass Menagerie" and Others.* Audiocassette. Read by Tennessee Williams. Includes *The Glass Menagerie* (opening monologue and closing scene); "Cried the Fox"; "The Eyes"; "The Summer Belvedere"; "Some Poems Meant for Music"; "Little Horse"; "Which Is My Little Boy"; "Little One"; "Gold-Tooth Blues"; "Kitchen-Door Blues"; "Heavenly Grass"; and "The Yellow Bird." Distributed by Caedmon/Harper Audio.

The Glass Menagerie. Audiocassette. Read by Tennessee Williams. Includes "The Yellow Bird" (short story) and poems. Distributed by the American Audio Prose Library.

General

In the Country of Tennessee Williams. 30 minutes, color, 1977. Beta, VHS, 1/2" reel, 3/4" U-matic cassette, 2" Quad. A one-act play about how Williams developed as a writer. Distributed by the New York State Education Department.

General Resources

Black Theatre: The Making of a Movement. 113 minutes, color, VHS, 1978. A look at black theater born from the Civil Rights movement of the 1950s, 1960s, and 1970s. Recollections from Ossie Davis, James Earl Jones, Amiri Baraka, and Ntozake Shange. Distributed by California Newsreel.

A Day at the Globe. 30 minutes, color. VHS. Starts with a brief overview of early drama and of seventeenth-century England, then discusses the Globe Theater, using still images. Explains how actors, artisans, and other company members prepared for performances and presents dramatic readings, period costumes, music, and sound effects in order to help students envision how Shakespearean drama actually looked. Distributed by Insight Media.

Drama Comes of Age. 30 minutes, b/w, 1957. 16-mm film. Discusses the Shakespearean theater and neoclassic drama. Demonstrates early realism with a scene from *Hedda Gabler.* Distributed by the Indiana University Instructional Support Services.

Drama: How It Began. 30 minutes, b/w, 1957. 16-mm film. Discusses the early beginnings of the theater.

Explains the techniques of the Greek theater and how playwriting developed. Illustrates the chorus technique with a scene from *Oedipus the King.* Distributed by the Indiana University Instructional Support Services.

The Elizabethan Age. 30 minutes, color. VHS. A discussion of the resurgence of enthusiasm for the arts and letters that swept seventeenth-century England. Uses original sources. Distributed by Insight Media.

Greek Tragedy. Audiocassette. Works of Euripides and Sophocles, Performed by Katina Paxinou and Alexis Minotis. Distributed by Caedmon/Harper Audio.

The Theatre in Ancient Greece. 26 minutes, color, 1989. Beta, VHS, 3/4" U-matic cassette. Program explores ancient theatre design, the origins or tragedy, the audience, the comparative roles of the writer/director and actors, and the use of landscape in many plays. Examines the theaters of Herodus, Atticus, Epidauros, Corinth, and numerous others. Distributed by Films for the Humanities and Sciences.

Directory of Distributors

AIMS Multimedia, 9710 DeSoto Avenue, Chatsworth, CA 91311-4409, (818) 773-4300, (800) 367-2467

Ambrose Video Publishing Inc., 28 West 44th Street, New York, NY 10036, (212) 768-7373, (800) 526-4663

American Audio Prose Library, PO Box 842, Crestland Avenue, Columbia, MO 65205, (573) 443-0361, (800) 447-2275

Annenberg/CPB, 901 E Street NW, Washington, DC 20004, (202) 879-9600

Applause Productions, 85-A Fernwood Lane, Roslyn, NY 11576, (516) 365-1259, (800) 253-5351

Audio Book Contractors, PO Box 40115, Washington, DC 20016, (202) 363-3429.

Audio-Forum, Jeffrey Norton Publishers, 96 Broad Street, Guilford, CT 06437, (203) 453-9794, (800) 243-1234

Books on Tape, Inc., PO Box 7900, Newport Beach, CA 92658, (800) 626-3333

Caedmon/Harper Audio, PO Box 588, Dunmore, PA 18512, (717) 343-4761, (800) 242-7737, (800) 982-4377 (in Pennsylvania)

California Newsreel, 149 Ninth Street, Suite 420, San Francisco, CA 94103, (415) 621-6196, (800) 621-6196

Camera Three Productions and Creative Arts Television Archive, Box 739, Kent, CT 06757, (860) 868-1771

Castle Rock Entertainment. See local retailers.

CBS/FOX Video. See local retailers.

Chuck Fries Productions, 6922 Hollywood Boulevard, Los Angeles, CA 90028, (323) 466-2266

Columbia Tristar Home Video. See local retailers.

Coronet/MTI Film & Video, 2349 Chaffee Drive, St. Louis, MO 63146, (314) 569-0211, (800) 221-1274

Crossroads Video, 15 Buckminster Lane, Manhasset, NY 11030, (516) 365-3715, (800) 548-5757

Durkin Hayes Publishing, 2221 Niagara Falls Boulevard, Niagara Falls, NY 14304, (716) 731-9177, (800) 962-5200

Encyclopaedia Britannica Educational Corporation, 310 South Michigan Avenue, Chicago, IL 60604, (312) 347-7900, (800) 621-3900

Facets Multimedia Inc., 1517 West Fullerton Avenue, Chicago, IL 60614, (773) 281-9075 (800) 331-6197

Filmic Archives, The Cinema Center, Botsford, CT 06404 (203) 261-1920

Films for the Humanities and Sciences, PO Box 2053, Princeton, NJ 08543-2053, (609) 275-1400, (800) 257-5126

Gallaudet University Library, Gallaudet Media Distribution, 800 Florida Avenue NE, Washington, DC 20002, (202) 651-5579, (202) 651-5440

Hallmark Home Entertainment. See local retailers.

Image Entertainment, 9333 Oso Avenue, Chatsworth, CA 91311

Indiana University Instructional Support Services, Franklin Hall, Room 0001, Bloomington, IN 47405-5901, (812) 855-2853

Insight Media, 2162 Broadway, New York, NY 10024, (212) 721-6316

Ivy Video, PO Box 18376, Asheville, NC 28814, (828) 285-9995, (800) 669-4057

Kultur, 195 Highway #36, West Long Branch, NJ 07764, (732) 229-0066, (800) 4-KULTUR

MasterVision, 969 Park Avenue, New York, NY 10028, (212) 879-0448

MGM/UA. See local retailers.

Monterey Home Video, 566 St. Charles Drive, Thousand Oaks, CA 91360, (805) 494-7199, (800) 424-2593

Mystic Fire Video, PO Box 422, Prince Street Station, New York, NY 10012, (212) 941-0999

National Broadcasting Company, 30 Rockefeller Plaza, New York, NY 10112, (212) 664-4444

National Public Radio, Audience Services, 635 Massachusetts Avenue NW, Washington, DC 20001, (202) 414-3232

New York Film Annex, 1618 West 4th Street, Brooklyn, NY 11223, (718) 382-8868

New York State Education Department, Media Distribution Network, Room 7-C-CEC, Empire State Plaza, Albany, NY 12230, (518) 474-3168

Paramount Home Video. See local retailers.

PBS Video, 1320 Braddock Place, Alexandria, VA 22314, (800) 344-3337

Prism Entertainment, 1888 Century Park East, Suite 350, Los Angeles, CA 90067, (310) 277-3270

Public Media/Home Vision, 4411 North Ravenswood Avenue, Chicago, IL 60640, (773) 878-2600, (800) 826-3456

RMI Media Productions, Inc., 1365 Winchester, Olathe, KS, 66061, (913) 768-1696, (800) 745-5480

The Roland Collection, 22D Hollywood Avenue, Hohokus, NJ 07423, (201) 251-8200, (800) 59-ROLAND

Smithsonian Institution Press, 470 L'Enfante Plaza, Suite 7100, Washington, DC 20650, (202) 287-3738

Sounddeluxe, Box H, Novato City, CA 94949, (800) 227-2020

Time-Life Video and Television, 1450 East Parham Road, Richmond, VA 23280, (800) 621-7026

Twentieth Century Fox Film Corporation. See local retailers.

Universal Studios Home Video. See local retailers.

University of California Extension Media Center, 2000 Center Street, Suite 400, Berkeley, CA 94704, (510) 642-0460

University of Wyoming Audio-Visual Services, Box 3273, Laramie, WY 82071, (307) 766-3184

Video Artists International, 109 Wheeler Avenue, Pleasantville, NY 10570, (914) 769-3691, (800) 477-7146

The Video Catalog Company, Inc., 561 Broadway, New York, NY 10012, (212) 334-0340

Video Learning Library, 15838 North 62 Street, Suite 101, Scottsdale, AZ 85254, (602) 596-9970, (800) 383-8811

Video Yesteryear, Box C, Sandy Hook, CT 06482, (800) 243-0987

Voyager, 424 35 Avenue, Seattle, WA 98122, (206) 323-1112

Warner Home Video. See local retailers.

Water Bearer Films, 48 West 21st Street, Suite 301, New York, NY 10010, (212) 242-8686, (800) 551-8304

Acknowledgments
(continued from p. iv)

Agamemnon from *The Oresteia by Aeschylus: A New Translation for the State* by David Grene and Wendy Doniger O'Flaherty. Copyright © 1989 by The University of Chicago. Reprinted by permission of The University of Chicago Press. Photo: © Richard Feldman (p. 55).

"Orestes and the Gods" by Albrecht Dihle, excerpt from *A History of Greek Literature,* translated by Clare Krojzl (Routledge). Reprinted by permission of International Thomson Publishing Services.

"*Oresteia*: Trilogy Preserved" from *Aeschylus* by Lois S. Spatz. Copyright © 1982 by G. K. Hall & Co. Reprinted by permission of The Gale Group.

Photo: A sculptural bust of Sophocles in marble. Museo Capitolino, Rome, Italy. Photo: CORBIS/Gianni Dagli Orti (p. 69).

Oedipus Rex from *Sophocles: The Oedipus Cycle, An English Version* by Dudley Fitts and Robert Fitzgerald, copyright 1949 by Harcourt, Inc. and renewed 1977 by Cornelia Fitts and Robert Fitzgerald. Reprinted by permission of the publisher. Photos: Henry S. Kranzler, all rights reserved (pp. 76–77); Museum for Gesaltung Zurich (p. 77); © Dr. Jaromir Svoboda (p. 79); Act One, Ltd./Michael Paul (p. 88).

"Poetics: Comedy and Epic and Tragedy" by Aristotle, from *Poetics,* translated by Gerald F. Else (1967). Reprinted by permission of The University of Michigan Press.

Excerpt from "The Structural Study of Myth" by Claude Levi-Strauss. Reprinted from *The Bibliographical and Special Series* of the American Folklore Society, Vol. 5 (1955).

Antigone from *Sophocles: The Oedipus Cycle, An English Version* by Dudley Fitts and Robert Fitzgerald, copyright 1939 by Harcourt, Inc. and renewed 1967 by Dudley Fitts and Robert Fitzgerald. Reprinted by permission of the publisher. CAUTION: All rights, including professional, amateur, motion picture, recitation, lecturing, performance, public reading, radio broadcasting, and television, are strictly reserved. Inquiries on all rights should be addressed to Harcourt Brace and Company, Permissions Department, Orlando, FL 32887-6777. Photos: © Martha Swope (pp. 110–11, 115–16).

"Emotion and Meaning in Greek Tragedy," excerpt from *Greek Tragedy in Action* by Oliver Taplin (Routledge). Reprinted by permission of International Thomson Publishing Services.

Excerpt from *Antigone* by Jean Anouilh, adapted and translated by Lewis Galantière. Copyright 1946 by Random House, Inc. and renewed 1974 by Lewis Galantière. Reprinted by permission of Random House, Inc.

Medea is reprinted from *Three Plays of Euripedes: Alcestis, Medea, The Bacchae,* translated by Paul Roche, with the permission of W. W. Norton & Company, Inc. Copyright © 1974 by Paul Roche. Photos: © Donald Cooper/PHOTOSTAGE (p. 150); © Joan Marcus (p. 156).

Review of *Medea* by John Simon from "Murder, She Wrought" by John Simon. Copyright © 1994 K-III Magazine Corporation. All rights reserved. Reprinted by permission of *New York Magazine.*

Lysistrata: An English Version from *Aristophanes: Four Comedies* by Dudley Fitts, copyright 1954 by Harcourt, Inc. and renewed 1982 by Cornelia Fitts, Daniel H. Fitts, and Deborah W. Fitts. Reprinted by permission of the publisher. CAUTION: Professionals and amateurs are hereby warned that all titles included in this volume, being fully protected under the copyright laws of the United States of America, Canada, the British Empire, and all other countries which are signatories to the Universal Copyright Convention and the International Copyright Union, are subject to royalty. All rights, including professional, amateur, motion picture, recitation, lecturing, public reading, radio broadcasting, television and the rights of translation into foreign languages, are strictly reserved. Inquiries on professional rights should be addressed to Lucy Kroll Agency, 390 West End Avenue, New York, NY 10024. Inquiries on all other rights should be addressed to Harcourt Brace and Company, Permissions Department, Orlando, Florida 32887-6777. Photo: © Donald Cooper/PHOTOSTAGE (p. 179).

Review of *Lysistrata* by Brooks Atkinson. Copyright © 1930 by The New York Times Company. Reprinted by permission.

Roman Drama

Figure 3. The ancient Theater of Sabratha, in Sabratha, Libya. CORBIS/Roger Wood.

Figure 4. Theater of Marcellus from *The History of Greek and Roman Theater* by Margarete Bieber. Copyright 1939, 1961 by Princeton University Press. Fig. 641 after Peruzzi; redrawn by Mrs. Wadhams. Reprinted by permission of Princeton University Press.

Excerpt from *The Twin Menaechmi* from *Six Plays of Plautus* by Plautus, translated by Lionel Casson. Translation copyright © 1963 by Lionel Casson. Reprinted by permission of Doubleday, a division of Random House, Inc.

Excerpt from *The Brothers* from *The Mother-In-Law* by Terence from *Comedies of Terence,* translated by Robert Graves. Reprinted by permission of A. P. Watt Ltd. on behalf of The Trustees of the Robert Graves Copyright Trust.

Excerpt from *Theyestes* by Seneca from *The Complete Roman Drama* by George E. Duckworth. Copyright 1942 and renewed 1970 by Random House, Inc. Reprinted by permission of Random House, Inc.

Medieval Drama

Figure 5. Pageant wagon from *Early English Stages 1300 to 1660* by Glynne William Gladstone Wickham. Reprinted by permission of Columbia University Press and Routledge & Kegan Paul Ltd.

Dulcitius by Hrotsvitha copyright © 1989. From *The Plays of Hrosvit of Gandersheim,* Vol. 51, Series B, translated by Kathrina M. Wilson. Reproduced by permission of Taylor & Francis/Garland Publishing, http://www.taylorandfrancis.com.

"Reading Hrosvit's Tormented Bodies" excerpted from "Impassive Bodies: Hrotsvit Stages Martyrdom" by Marla Carlson. *Theatre Journal* 50 (December 1998). © The Johns Hopkins University Press. Reprinted by permission.

"Re-viewing Hrotsvit" excerpted from "Re-viewing Hrotsvit" by Sue Ellen Case. *Theatre Journal* 35 (December 1983). © The Johns Hopkins University Press. Reprinted by permission.

Everyman edited by A. C. Cawley reprinted from the *Everyman's Library* edition, 1974, with footnotes by A. C. Cawley, by permission of David Campbell Publishers Ltd. Photo: Act One, Ltd./Michael Paul (p. 233).

Renaissance Drama

Figure 6. Teatro Olimpico in Vicenza, Italy, Alinari/Art Resource New York.

Figure 7. Perspective setting designed by Peruzzi, Scala/Art Resource New York.

Figure 8. C. Walter Hodges, diagram of the Globe Theatre from *The Globe Restored,* published by Oxford University Press. © 1968 by C. Walter Hodges. Reprinted by permission of Oxford University Press.

Doctor Faustus by Christopher Marlowe from *Doctor Faustus: Text and Major Criticism,* edited with notes by Irving Ribner. Copyright © 1985. Reprinted by permission of Prentice-Hall, Inc., Upper Saddle River, NJ. Photo: Donald Cooper/PHOTOSTAGE (p. 261).

Excerpt from Ernst Honigmann's "Ten Problems in Dr. Faustus" in *The Arts of Performance in Elizabethan and Early Stuart Drama,* edited by Murray Biggs et al. (Edinburgh, 1991), reprinted by permission of Edinburgh University Press.

Photo: Image of William Shakespeare included on the First Folio. Reprinted by permission of The Folger Shakespeare Library (p. 281).

A Midsummer Night's Dream and *Hamlet* by William Shakespeare from *The Complete Works of Shakespeare,* 4th edition, by David Bevington. Copyright © 1997 by Addison-Wesley Educational Publishers, Inc. Reprinted by permission. Photos: Richard M. Feldman (pp. 294–95, pp. 344–45); Mario Tursi © 1999 Twentieth Century Fox Film Corporation. Monarchy Enterprises B.V. and Regency Entertainment (USA), Inc. (p. 295); © Martha Swope (pp. 304–05); Osterreichisches Theatermuseum (p. 309); © Donald Cooper/PHOTOSTAGE (pp. 358–59); Rolf Konow © Castle Rock Entertainment (p. 358).

"Masque Elements in *A Midsummer Night's Dream*" by Enid Welsford from *The Court Masque* by Enid Welsford. Cambridge: Cambridge University Press; New York: The Macmillan Company, 1927. Reprinted by permission of Cambridge University Press.

"On *A Midsummer Night's Dream*" by Linda Bamber. Reprinted from *Comic Women, Tragic Men: A Study of Gender and Genre in*

Shakespeare by Linda Bamber with the permission of the publishers, Stanford University Press. Copyright © 1982 by the Board of Trustees of the Leland Stanford Junior University.

"The Play Is the Message . . . " by Peter Brook from *The Shifting Point* by Peter Brook. Copyright © 1987 by Peter Brook. Reprinted by permission of HarperCollins Publishers, Inc.

Review of *A Midsummer Night's Dream* by Clive Barnes. Copyright © 1970 by The New York Times Company. Reprinted by permission.

"Hamlet and His Problems" from "Hamlet" in *Selected Essays* by T. S. Eliot, copyright 1950 by Harcourt Brace and Company, renewed 1978 by Esme Valerie Eliot. Reprinted by permission of Harcourt Brace and Company and Faber and Faber Ltd.

Review of Hamlet from "Matinee Idolatry" in *Light Fantastic* by John Lahr. Copyright © 1996 by John Lahr. Reprinted by permission of The Dial Press/Dell Publishing, a division of Random House, Inc.

Othello by William Shakespeare, text and notes by Gerald Eades Bentley (Penguin Books, revised edition, 1970). © Penguin Books, Inc. 1958, 1970. Reprinted by permission of Penguin Books Ltd. Photos: Harvard Theatre Collection (p. 406); T. Charles Erickson Photography (p. 406); Rolf Konow © Castle Rock Entertainment (p. 416); Special Collections and University Archives, Rutgers University Libraries (p. 425).

Casebook Photos: Portrait of Abdul El-Ouahed Ben Messasud. Oil on panel. Artist unknown. University of Birmingham Collections (p. 450); The Shakespeare Theatre's 1997–98 production of *Othello*. Photo: Carol Rosegg (p. 466).

"Macready's Othello" from *Othello: A Contextual History* by Virginia Mason Vaughan. Copyright © 1994. Reprinted by permission of Cambridge University Press.

"Going It Alone: A Review of Olivier's Othello" by John Holstrom from Plays and Players (June 1964). *Theater Magazine*. Reprinted by permission of Duke University Press.

Excerpt from *Mandeville's Travels* by Sir John Mandeville, 1357. Edited by M.C. Seymour. Copyright © 1968. Reprinted by permission of Oxford University Press.

Excerpt from "*Othello* and Colour Prejudice" by G. K. Hunter from *Dramatic Identities and Cultural Tradition: Studies in Shakespeare and His Contemporaries* by G. K. Hunter, © 1978. Reprinted by permission of Rowman & Littlefield Publishers, Inc.

Review of Patrick Stewart's Othello by Peter Marks. Copyright © 1997 by The New York Times Company. Reprinted by permission.

The Masque of Blackness by Ben Jonson, from *Ben Jonson: The Complete Masques*, edited by Stephen Orgel. Copyright © 1969 by Yale University. Reprinted by permission of Yale University Press. Photo: Devonshire Collection, Chatsworth (p. 472).

"Africa in English Masque and Pageantry" by Eldred Jones from *Othello's Countrymen* by Eldred Jones. Copyright © 1965. Reprinted by permission of Oxford University Press.

Life Is a Dream by Pedro Calderón de la Barca, translated by Roy Campbell from *Life Is a Dream and Other Spanish Classics*, edited by Eric Bentley and translated by Roy Campbell. Copyright © 1959, 1958 by Eric Bentley. Reprinted by permission of Applause Theatre Book Publishers. Photos: T. Charles Erickson Photography (pp. 488–89); Douglas Robertson (p. 489).

Review of the 1998 Edinburgh Festival Production of *Life Is a Dream*, by Michael Billington from the *Guardian*, August 20, 1998. Reprinted by permission.

Review of José Rivera's Production of *Sueño* from *American Theatre* 15:5 (May/June 1998). Reprinted by permission of Theatre Communications Group.

"The *Hamlet* of Spain, in a Fevered Setting" by Matt Wolf. Copyright © 1999 by The New York Times Company. Reprinted by permission.

Late Seventeenth- and Eighteenth-Century Drama

Figure 9. Early Restoration Theater, illustration by Peter Kahn. From *The Frohlicks; or, The Lawyer Cheated* by Elizabeth Polwhele, edited by Judith Milhous and Robert D. Hume, Cornell University Press, 1977. Used by permission of the publisher, Cornell University Press.

The Misanthrope by Molière, translated by Richard Wilbur, copyright © 1955 and renewed 1983 by Richard Wilbur, reprinted by permission of Harcourt Brace & Company. CAUTION: Professionals and amateurs are hereby warned that this translation, being fully protected under the copyright laws of the United States, the British Commonwealth, the Dominion of Canada, and all other countries which are signatories to the Universal Copyright Convention, is subject to royalty. All rights, including professional, amateur, motion picture, recitation, lecturing, public reading, radio broadcasting, and television, are strictly reserved. Particular emphasis is laid on the question of readings, permission for which must be secured from the author's agent in writing. Inquiries on professional rights should be addressed to Mr. Gilbert Parker, William Morris Agency, 1350 Avenue of the Americas, New York, NY 10019. Inquiries on all other rights should be addressed to Harcourt Brace and Company, Permissions Department, Orlando, FL 32887-6777. The amateur acting rights of *The Misanthrope* are controlled exclusively by the Dramatists Play Service, Inc., 440 Park Avenue South, New York, NY 10016. No amateur performance of the play may be given without obtaining in advance the written permission of the Dramatists Play Service, Inc. and paying the requisite fee. Photo: Courtesy of the Williamstown Theatre Festival. Photo by Michael C. Durling (p. 538).

"Alceste's Love for Célimène," excerpt from *Men and Masks: A Study of Molière* by Lionel Gossman. Reprinted by permission of Johns Hopkins University Press. Copyright © 1963.

The Rover; or, The Banished Cavaliers. Photo: Courtesy of the Williamstown Theatre Festival. Photo by Nina Krieger (p. 565).

"On Aphra Behn," excerpt from *A Room of One's Own* by Virginia Woolf. Copyright © 1929 by Harcourt Brace and Company and renewed 1957 by Leonard Woolf. Reprinted by permission of the publisher.

"Courtship and Marriage in *The Rover*," excerpt from *Virtue of Necessity English Women's Writing* by Elaine Hobby. Copyright © 1988 by Elaine Hobby. Reprinted by permission of the University of Michigan Press.

The Way of the World. Photos: © Richard Feldman (p. 608); Spingold Theatre, Brandeis University (p. 617).

Review of *The Way of the World* by Howard Taubman. Copyright © 1965 by The New York Times Company. Reprinted by permission.

Excerpt from *Amendments of Mr. Collier's False and Imperfect Citations, etc.* by William Congreve, from *Dramatic Theory and Criticism* edited by Bernard F. Dukore. Copyright © 1974. Reprinted by permission of Holt, Rhinehart, and Winston.

"Comedy, Manners, and Brickbats" by Arnold Aronson. Copyright © 1991 by The New York Times Company. Used by permission.

Nineteenth-Century Drama to the Turn of the Century

Figure 10. Auditorium, Chicago, 1889. Photo: Henrich Blessing. Courtesy of the Auditorium Theatre Council.

Figure 11. Realistic setting in Anton Chekhov's *The Cherry Orchard*, Harvard Theatre Collection.

Photos: Henrik Ibsen (c. 1896), CORBIS/Bettmann (p. 654); Realistic stage setting of Ibsen's *The Wild Duck*, Bibliothèque de l'Arsenal, Paris (p. 656); Edvard Munch's stage design for Ibsen's *Ghosts*, Munch Museum, Oslo Photo: Munch Museum (p. 657).

A Doll House and *Hedda Gabler* from *The Complete Major Prose Plays of Henrik Ibsen* by Henrik Ibsen, translated by Rolf Fjelde, Translation copyright © 1965, 1970, 1978, by Rolf Fjelde. Used by permission of Dutton Signet, a division of Penguin Putnam Inc. Photos: © 1992 Martha Swope (pp. 668–69); Donald Cooper/PHOTOSTAGE (pp. 676–77, 710, 714–15); Sara Krulwich/NYT Pictures (p. 687); © T. Charles Erickson Photography (pp. 722–23).

"*A Doll's House*: Ibsen the Moralist" by Muriel C. Bradbrook from *Ibsen the Norwegian* by Muriel C. Bradbrook. Reprinted by permission of Random Century.

"Notes for *Hedda Gabler*," selection from Ibsen's "Notes on *Hedda Gabler*" translated by Evert Sprinchorn, from *Playwrights on Playwriting*, edited by Toby Cole. Copyright © 1960 and renewal copyright © 1988 by Toby Cole. Reprinted by permission of Hill and Wang, a division of Farrar, Straus and Giroux, Inc.

Review of *Hedda Gabler* by Clive Barnes. Copyright © 1970 by The New York Times Company. Reprinted by permission.

"Thematic Symbols in *Hedda Gabler*" by Caroline Mayerson. Reprinted by permission of the author.

"On *Hedda Gabler*," excerpt from "Ibsen Read Anew" by Jan Kott from *The Theatre of Essence and Other Essays* by Jan Kott. Copyright © 1984 by Jan Kott. Reprinted by permission of the author.

Miss Julie by August Strindberg, and excerpt from the Preface to *Miss Julie* from *Strindberg: Five Plays*, Harry Carlson, editor and translator. Copyright © 1983 The Regents of the University of California. Reprinted by permission of the University of California Press. Photo: © Donald Cooper/PHOTOSTAGE (p. 754).

The Importance of Being Earnest. Photos: © Richard Feldman (p. 775); Carol Rosegg (p. 787).

"An Unpublished Letter from Oscar Wilde on *The Importance of Being Earnest*" from "The Making of *The Importance of Being Earnest*" by Peter Raby. *Times Literary Supplement* No. 4629, December 1991. Reprinted by permission of Peter Raby. Oscar Wilde's letter to George Alexander is reprinted by permission of Merlin Holland.

The Cherry Orchard by Anton Chekhov from *The Major Plays of Anton Chekhov* by Anton Chekhov, translated by Ann Dunnigan. Translation copyright © 1964 by Ann Dunnigan. Used by permission of New American Library, a division of Penguin Books USA Inc. Photos: © Richard Feldman (p. 811).

"From Chekhov's Letters," two letters from *Letters of Anton Chekhov* translated by Michael Henry Heim with Simon Karlinsky. Copyright © 1973 by Harper & Row Publishers, Inc. Reprinted by permission of HarperCollins Publishers, Inc.

Excerpt from "Recollections" by Maxim Gorky from *Reminiscences of Tolstoy, Chekhov and Andreyev* by Maxim Gorky. Reprinted by permission of Random Century.

Review of *The Cherry Orchard* by John Corbin. Copyright © 1923 by The New York Times Company. Reprinted by permission.

"On Chekhov" by Peter Brook from *The Shifting Point* by Peter Brook. Copyright © 1987 by Peter Brook. Reprinted by permission of HarperCollins Publishers, Inc.

Mrs. Warren's Profession. Photos: T. Charles Erickson Photography (p. 847).

Casebook Photos: Scene from a brothel from *National Police Gazette*, July 26, 1879, © Collection of the New York Historical Society (p. 882); directory of brothels from *The Gentleman's Directory, Temples of Love, Address Listings*, 1870, © Collection of the New York Historical Society (p. 886).

"The Woman Question: Women's Rights" from the Preface to *Getting Married*, Part I, by August Strindberg. Translated from the Swedish by Mary Sandbach. Viking Press, New York. © 1972 translation copyright by Sandbach Cheetham. Reprinted by permission of Victor Gollancz Ltd.

"A Nineteenth-Century Husband's Letter to His Wife, 1844," translated by Hans Panofsky. Original German text in the Archive of the Leo Baeck Institute, New York. Reprinted by permission of the Leo Baeck Institute and Margaret A. Panofsky.

Drama in the Early and Mid-Twentieth Century

Figure 12. Expressionistic setting in Arthur Miller's *Death of a Salesman*, the Billy Rose Theatre Collection of New York Public Library for the Performing Arts/Astor, Lenox, and Tilden Foundations.

The Playboy of the Western World. Photos: SPRINGER/CORBIS-BETTMAN (p. 906); T. Charles Erickson Photography (p. 908).

"Producing the *Playboy*" and "Community Drama" from *The Fays of the Abbey Theatre* by W. G. Fay and Catherine Carswell. Copyright 1935. Reprinted by permission of Harcourt, Inc.

Casebook Photos: The Abbey Theatre, Dublin, The Raymond Mander & Joe Mitchenson Theatre Collection (p. 929); Lady Gregory, The National Library of Ireland (p. 933); Maud Gonne, The National Library of Ireland (p. 935); Maud Gonne in *Cathleen Ni Houlihan*, 1902, The Raymond Mander & Joe Mitchenson Theatre Collection (p. 941); W. B. Yeats, The National Library of Ireland (p. 949).

"The Abbey Theatre" from *The Story of the Abbey Theatre: From Its Origins in 1899 to the Present* by Peter Kavanagh. The Devin-Adair Company. Copyright 1950.

"Journal Entries on the *Playboy* Riots" from *Joseph Holloway's Abbey Theatre: A Selection from His Unpublished Journal, Impressions of a Dublin Playgoer*, by Joseph Holloway. Edited by Robert Hogan and Michael J. O'Neill. Copyright 1967. Reprinted by permission of Southern Illinois University Press.

"On the Edge: The Plays of Susan Glaspell" by Christine Dymkowski

from *Modern Drama* 31 (March 1988). Reprinted by permission of the University of Toronto Press.

Six Characters in Search of an Author copyright 1922 by E. P. Dutton. Renewed 1950 in the names of Stefano, Fausto, and Lietta Pirandello from *Naked Masks: Five Plays by Luigi Pirandello*, edited by Eric Bentley. Translation copyright 1922, 1952 by E. P. Dutton. Renewed 1950 in the names of Stefano, Fausto, and Lietta Pirandello. Introduction copyright 1952, © renewed 1980 by Eric Bentley. Used by permission of Dutton Signet, a division of Penguin Books USA Inc. Photo: © Richard Feldman (p. 973).

Desire under the Elms by Eugene O'Neill. Copyright 1924 and renewed 1952 by Eugene O'Neill. Reprinted from *The Plays of Eugene O'Neill* by Eugene O'Neill by permission of Random House, Inc. Photo: T. Charles Erickson Photography (p. 1006).

Review of *Desire under the Elms* by Stark Young. Copyright © 1924 by The New York Times Company. Reprinted by permission.

The House of Bernarda Alba by Frederico García Lorca from *Three Tragedies*. Copyright © 1947 by New Directions Publishing Corp. Reprinted by permission of New Directions Publishing Corp. Photo: © Carol Rosegg (p. 1028).

"Religion in *The House of Bernarda Alba*" by John Gilmour in "The Cross of Pain and Death: Religion in the Rural Tragedies" from *Lorca: Poet and Playwright*, edited by Robert Harvard. Copyright © 1992. Reprinted by permission of St. Martin's Press, Inc.

The Lesson by Eugène Ionesco, translated by Donald Allen. Copyright © 1958 by Grove Press, Inc. Reprinted by permission of Grove Atlantic. Photo: Rachel Hogancamp (p. 1054).

Mother Courage and Her Children by Bertolt Brecht. Copyright © 1940 by Arvid Englind Teaterforlag, a.b., renewed June 1967 by Stefan S. Brecht; copyright © 1949 by Suhrkamp Verlag, Frankfurt am Main. Translation copyright © 1980 Stefan S. Brecht. Reprinted from *Mother Courage and Her Children* by Bertolt Brecht, published by Arcade Publishing Inc., New York, New York. Photo: Photofest (p. 1065).

"The Alienation Effect" by Bertolt Brecht, translated by John Willett from *Brecht on Theatre*, edited and translated by John Willett. Copyright © 1964. Hill and Wang. Reprinted by permission of Farrar, Straus and Giroux.

"Notes for *Mother Courage*" by Bertolt Brecht from *Directors on Directing*, edited by Toby Cole and Helen Krich Chinoy. Copyright © 1963. Reprinted by permission of Prentice-Hall, Inc.

Photo: Tennessee Williams on the set of *Night of the Iguana* at the Savoy Theatre in 1965. CORBUS/Hulton Deutsch Collection.

The Glass Menagerie by Tennessee Williams Copyright 1945 by Tennessee Williams and Edwina D. Williams and renewed 1973 by Tennessee Williams. Reprinted by permission of Random House, Inc. Photos: The Billy Rose Theatre Collection of the New York Public Library for the Performing Arts/Astor, Lenox, and Tilden Foundations (pp. 1108–09); Estate of Jo Mielziner, used by permission of Jo Mielziner (p. 1109); Joan Marcus/Arena Stage (p. 1116–17).

Review of *The Glass Menagerie* by Lewis Nichols. Copyright © 1945 by The New York Times Company. Reprinted by permission.

"Laurette Taylor in *The Glass Menagerie*," excerpt from *The Kindness of Strangers: The Life of Tennessee Williams* by Donald Spoto. Copyright © 1985 by Donald Spoto. Reprinted by permission of Little, Brown and Company.

"Problems in *The Glass Menagerie*" by Benjamin Nelson. Excerpt from *Tennessee Williams: The Man and His Work* by Benjamin Nelson (New York: 1961). Reprinted by permission of the author.

Cat on a Hot Tin Roof by Tennessee Williams. Copyright © 1954, 1955, 1971, 1975 by Tennessee Williams. Reprinted by permission of New Directions Publishing Corporation. Photos: © 1992 Martha Swope (p. 1139); © Michael Tighe/Visages 1992 (p. 1148); Fred Fehl/the Billy Rose Theatre Collection of the New York Public Library for the Performing Arts/Astor, Lenox, and Tilden Foundations (p. 1158).

"Memoirs," excerpt from *Tennessee Williams: Memoirs* by Tennessee Williams. Copyright © 1972, 1975 by Tennessee Williams. Reprinted by permission of Doubleday, a division of Random House, Inc.

"Tennessee Williams and Elia Kazan Collaborate on *Cat*," excerpt from *Tennessee Williams and Elia Kazan: A Collaboration in the Theatre* by Brenda Murphy. Copyright © 1991 by Cambridge University Press. Reprinted by permission of Cambridge University Press.

Death of a Salesman by Arthur Miller. Copyright 1949, renewed © 1977 by Arthur Miller. All rights reserved. Used by permission of Viking Penguin, a division of Penguin Putnam Inc. Photos of the Goodman Theatre production of *Death of a Salesman* by Eric Y. Exit (pp. 1191, 1221); Photofest (p. 1219).

"In Memoriam" by Arthur Miller is reprinted by permission of the author and International Creative Management, Inc. Copyright © 1995 by Arthur Miller. First appeared in *The New Yorker.*

"Tragedy and the Common Man," excerpt from *The Theatre Essays of Arthur Miller* by Arthur Miller, edited by Robert A. Martin. Copyright 1949, renewed © 1977 by Arthur Miller. Used by permission of Viking Penguin, a division of Penguin Putnam Inc.

"A Salesman Who Transcends Time" by Michiko Kakutani. Copyright © 1999 by The New York Times Company. Reprinted by permission.

"*Death of a Salesman*: The Design Process" from *Miller: Death of a Salesman* by Brenda Murphy. Copyright © 1995. Reprinted by permission of Cambridge University Press.

Endgame by Samuel Beckett. Copyright © 1958 by Grove Press, Inc.; copyright renewed © 1986 by Samuel Beckett. Used by permission of Grove Press, Inc. Photos: © 1992 Martha Swope (pp. 1248–49); Richard M. Feldman (p. 1259).

Excerpt from *The Theatre of the Absurd* by Martin Esslin. Reprinted by permission of the author.

"The Ending of *Endgame*," excerpt from *Beckett's Theaters: Interpretations for Performance* by Sidney Homan (Bucknell University Press). Reprinted by permission of Associated University Presses.

A Raisin in the Sun by Lorraine Hansberry. Copyright © 1958 by Robert Nemiroff, as an unpublished work. Copyright © 1959, 1966, 1984 by Robert Nemiroff. Reprinted by permission of Random House, Inc.

"Dream Deferred" ("Harlem") by Langston Hughes from *The Panther and the Lash* by Langston Hughes. Copyright 1951 by Langston Hughes. Reprinted by permission of Alfred A. Knopf, Inc.

Review of *A Raisin in the Sun* by Brooks Atkinson. Copyright © 1959 by The New York Times Company. Reprinted by permission. Photo: © Richard Feldman (p. 1279).

The Strong Breed by Wole Soyinka. Copyright © Oxford University Press 1964. Reprinted from *Wole Soyinka: Collected Plays* 1 (1973) by permission of Oxford University Press.

"Interview with Wole Soyinka," excerpt from *African Writers Talking: A Collection of Radio Interviews*, edited by Cosmo Pieterse and Dennis Duerden (New York: Holmes & Meier, 1972). Copyright © 1972 by Cosmo Pieterse and Dennis Duerden. Reprinted by permission of the publisher.

Contemporary Drama

Figure 13. Multimedia effects in Robert Wilson's *CIVIL warS*, Richard M. Feldman.

Zoot Suit by Luis Valdez is reprinted with permission from the publisher of *Zoot Suit and Other Plays* (Houston: Arte Publico Press, University of Houston, 1992). Photos: Ken Jacques (p. 1367).

Betrayal by Harold Pinter copyright © 1978 by H. Pinter Ltd. Reprinted by permission of Grove/Atlantic, Inc. and Faber and Faber Ltd. Photos: © Donald Cooper/PHOTOSTAGE (p. 1391).

"Harold Pinter's *Betrayal*: Life Before Death—and After" from *Theatre Journal* (December 1982). Reprinted by permission of Johns Hopkins University Press.

Cloud Nine by Caryl Churchill is reprinted by arrangement with Nick Hern Books, 14 Larden Road, London W3 7ST, UK. *Cloud Nine* is published in the USA by Theatre Communications Group, 355 Lexington Ave, New York, NY 10017-6603. *Cloud Nine* © 1979, 1980, 1983, 1984, 1985 by Caryl Churchill. Photos: © Donald Cooper/PHOTOSTAGE (p. 1410).

Review of the Old Vic production of *Cloud Nine* by James Treadwell from *The Spectator*, March 29, 1977. Reprinted by permission of the publisher.

True West by Sam Shepard, copyright © 1981 by Sam Shepard, from *Seven Plays* by Sam Shepard. Used by permission of Bantam Books, a division of Random House, Inc. Photo: Michael Brosilow (p. 1444).

"*Master Harold*" . . . *and the Boys* by Athol Fugard. Copyright © 1982 by Athol Fugard. Reprinted by permission of Alfred A. Knopf, Inc. Photo: © Donald Cooper/PHOTOSTAGE (p. 1469).

"Interview with Athol Fugard" by Heinrich von Staden from *Theater* (Yale), Vol. 14, No. 1, Winter 1982. Reprinted by permission of the author.

Excerpt from *Notebooks 1960–1977* by Athol Fugard. Copyright © 1983 by Athol Fugard. Reprinted by permission of Alfred A. Knopf, Inc.

'night, Mother by Marsha Norman. Copyright © 1983 by Marsha Norman. Reprinted by permission of Hill and Wang, a division of Farrar, Straus and Giroux, Inc. CAUTION: Professionals and amateurs are hereby warned that *'night, Mother*, being fully protected under the copyright laws of the United States of America and all other countries of the Berne and Universal Copyright Conventions, is subject to a royalty. All rights including, but not limited to, professional, amateur, recording, motion picture, recitation, lecturing, public reading, radio and television broadcasting, and the rights of translation into foreign languages, are expressly reserved. All inquiries concerning rights should be addressed to the author's agent, The Tantleff Office, 375 Greenwich Street, Suite 700, New York, NY 10013, Attn: Charmaine Ferenczi. No performance of the play may be given without obtaining in advance the written permission of the agent and paying the requisite fee. Photo: © Richard Feldman (p. 1494).

"Interview with Marsha Norman," "Interview with Maria Irene Fornes," and "Interview with August Wilson" by David Savran from *In Their Own Voices* by David Savran. Reprinted by permission of Theatre Communications Group.

Fences by August Wilson. Copyright © 1986 August Wilson. Used by permission of Dutton Signet, a division of Penguin Putnam Inc. Photos: © Photofest (pp. 1522–23).

Excerpt from an interview with August Wilson by David Savran from *In Their Own Words*. Reprinted by permission of Theatre Communications Group.

Review of *Fences* by Frank Rich ("Theatre: Family Ties in Wilson's '*Fences*'"). Copyright © 1987 by The New York Times Company. Reprinted by permission.

M. Butterfly by David Henry Hwang, copyright © 1986, 1987, 1988 by David Henry Hwang. Reprinted by permission of Dutton Signet, a division of Penguin Putnam Inc. Photo: Joan Marcus (p. 1561).

"*M. Butterfly*: An Interview with David Henry Hwang" by John Louis DiGaetani from *The Drama Review* 33 (Fall 1989). Reprinted by permission.

Review of *M. Butterfly* by John Gross. Copyright © 1988 by The New York Times Company. Reprinted by permission.

Dancing at Lughnasa by Brian Friel. Copyright © 1990 by Brian Friel. Reprinted by permission of Faber & Faber Ltd. and Farrar, Straus & Giroux, Inc. Photo: Jonathan Hession (p. 1601).

The Death of the Last Black Man in the Whole Entire World by Suzan-Lori Parks copyright © 1990 by Suzan-Lori Parks. All rights reserved. Reprinted by permission of George Lane at the William Morris Agency. CAUTION: Professionals and amateurs are hereby warned that *The Death of the Last Black Man in the Whole Entire World* is subject to a royalty. It is fully protected under the copyright laws of the United States of America, and of all countries covered by the International Copyright Union (including the Dominion of Canada and the rest of the British Commonwealth), and of all countries covered by the Pan-American Copyright Convention and the Universal Copyright Convention, and of all countries with which the United States has reciprocal copyright relations. All rights, including professional, amateur, motion picture, recitation, lecturing, public reading, radio broadcasting, television, video or sound recording, all other forms of mechanical or electronic reproduction, such as information storage and retrieval systems and photocopying, and the rights of translation into foreign languages, are strictly reserved. Particular emphasis is laid upon the matter of readings, permission for which must be secured from the author's agent in writing. Inquiries concerning rights should be addressed to William Morris Agency, Inc., 1325 Avenue of the Americas, New York, NY 10019, Attn: George Lane. Photos: © 1992 Gerry Goodstein (pp. 1622–23, 1628–29).

"Interview with Suzan-Lori Parks" by Lee A. Jacobus. Reprinted by permission of the William Morris Agency.

"Interview with Liz Diamond" by Lee A. Jacobus. Reprinted by permission of Liz Diamond.

"Language in *Last Black Man,*" excerpt from "Signifying on the Signi-fyin" by Alisa Solomon, *Theater* Vol. 21, No. 3, 1990, pp. 76, 79–80. Reprinted by permission of Duke University Press.

Oleanna by David Mamet. Copyright © 1992 by David Mamet. Reprinted by permission of Vintage Books, a Division of Random House, Inc. Photos: © Gerry Goodstein (p. 1644).

Angels in America, Part One: Millennium Approaches by Tony Kushner. Copyright © 1993 by Tony Kushner. Reprinted by permission of Theatre Communications Group, Inc. Photos: © Joan Marcus (pp. 1690–91).

"Interview with Tony Kushner" by Andrea Bernstein reprinted with permission from *Mother Jones* magazine, © 1995, Foundation for National Progress.

"*Art*" by Yasmina Reza, translated by Christopher Hampton. Copyright © 1994 by Yasmina Reza. Translation copyright © Yasmina Reza and Christopher Hampton, 1996. First published in 1996 by Faber & Faber Ltd. Reprinted by permission of the publisher. Photos: © Joan Marcus (p. 1701).

"What Is '*Art*'?" by Louis Menand from *The New Yorker* 73 (February 9, 1998). Reprinted by permission of the author.

The Beauty Queen of Leenane by Martin McDonagh. Copyright © 1996 by Martin McDonagh. Reprinted by permission of Vintage Books, a Division of Random House, Inc. Photos: Carol Rosegg (pp. 1732, 1737).

Review of *The Beauty Queen of Leenane* ("A New Young Playwright Full of Old Irish Voices"). Copyright © 1997 by The New York Times Company. Reprinted by permission.

"Beastly *Beauty*" by Alisa Solomon from the *Village Voice* 43 (March 10, 1998). Reprinted by permission of the publisher.

How I Learned to Drive by Paula Vogel from *The Mammary Plays* © 1998 by Paula Vogel. Reprinted by permission of Theatre Communications Group, Inc. Photos: T. Charles Erickson Photography (p. 1760).

"Coast to Coast with Paula Vogel" by Caridad Svich and Peter Franklin from *The Dramatist* (July/August 1999). Reprinted by permission of the Dramatists Guild Inc.

"Paula Vogel" by David Savran from *The Playwright's Voice: American Dramatists on Memory, Writing and the Politics of Culture* by David Savran. Copyright © 1999 by David Savran. Reprinted by permission of Theatre Communications Group, Inc.

Review of *How I Learned to Drive* by Jill Dolan from *Theatre Journal* 50 (March 1998). Copyright © The Johns Hopkins University Press. Reprinted by permission.